EPISCOPAL CLERICAL DIRECTORY 2017

Revised every two years

Church Publishing
NEW YORK

Please note: The contents of the biographical entries reported herein are drawn from the Church Pension Group's databases and by information provided by the biographees themselves.

To purchase additional copies of the *Episcopal Clerical Directory*, please access Church Publishing's website at **www.churchpublishing.org**.

To submit changes to the Directory, the cleric may make updates through the **Clergy Update Questionnaire**. While most changes will not appear in print until the 2019 directory, changes to public contact information will appear in Clergy QuickFind.

Foreword

The 2017 *Episcopal Clerical Directory* represents further progress toward our goal of providing The Episcopal Church with the most comprehensive and reliable data possible about the clergy who serve this Church. This forty-seventh edition of the ECD includes biographical information on 19,038 clergy in good standing as of the date indicated on page 2.

Because of our constant concern to protect clergy privacy and prevent identity theft, the 2017 edition of the *Directory* continues the policy started in 2015 that limits the kinds of data that are displayed in a cleric's biographical entry:

- The address that the cleric designated as his or her "published address" during the 2017 *Episcopal Clerical Directory* Clergy Information Update process is displayed. If the cleric did not specify a published address, no address is displayed.
- Only the cleric's year of birth is displayed; the month and date of birth are no longer displayed.
- Only the first names of the cleric's parents are displayed. We ceased publishing the cleric's mother's name at birth in the late 1990s because that information is often used as a security question for online and financial transactions. Now, as an additional safeguard against identity theft, we will no longer publish the parents' surnames in the cleric's biographical entry.
- An email address is displayed only if the cleric identified an "office" email when updating her or his information during the update process. If the cleric did not enter any data into the "office" field, no email address will display.

Further, as we began to do with the 2005 edition of the *Directory* and in response to requests from an increasing number of clergy, we no longer publish information on previous marriages, even those that resulted in children. The number of children, if any, from a cleric's previous marriage will continue to be displayed.

For over 10 years, the affiliate companies of the Church Pension Group have collaborated on the development of the Common Reference Database, a significant undertaking that enables all of the affiliates of the Pension Group to "read off the same page" about clergy and institutions and to serve them with an even greater degree of efficiency. Thus, for example, a cleric's ministry history—the chronological list of congregations in which s/he has served—is supplied by referencing the Pension Fund database. As ever, we count on our clergy to inform us when incorrect information appears.

Clergy who completed the 2017 Clergy Information Update questionnaire are identified in boldface type in the book. Because we receive updates from clergy and institutions nearly every day, new contact information and current position information submitted after the production deadline for this edition will be available online at the ECDPlus website: **www.ecdplus.org**.

Again in this edition, multiple current positions, including non-parochial ministry-related positions such as health care, school, and military chaplaincies, are shown. All current positions are listed near the beginning of each biography to help the reader discern at a glance each cleric's present ministry. These positions appear with the cleric's current employment position first, followed by the most recent appointed or voluntary positions on Episcopal Church-related bodies such as General Convention commissions, committees, agencies, and boards; diocesan councils; standing committees; or boards of church-related nonprofit organizations.

Clergy who died since the 2015 edition of the *Directory* was released, but whose death was reported prior to the date indicated on page 2, have their date of death noted in their biographical entries in place of their current ecclesiastical employment position.

Ordination data and changes in canonical residence are noted by the Recorder of Ordinations after written confirmation from the diocese has been submitted to the Recorder. Biographies of clergy who have transferred into The Episcopal Church from another province of the Anglican Communion, or who have been received from the Roman Catholic Church or another church in full communion with The Episcopal Church, do not include the dates of their ordinations to the diaconate and priesthood, nor the names of the non-Episcopal Church bishops who ordained them. Instead, the name of the Episcopal Church bishop who accepted their transfer or received them is listed, along with the date on which that transfer or reception took effect.

Faithfully,

Matthew J. Price
Editor

To purchase additional copies of the *Episcopal Clerical Directory*, visit Church Publishing's website at **www.churchpublishing.com**.

To submit changes to the Directory, the cleric may make updates through the **Clergy Update Questionnaire**. While most changes will not appear in print until the 2019 directory, changes to public contact information will appear in Clergy QuickFind.

Abbreviations Used in This Text

AA	Alcoholics Anonymous
AAM	Association of Anglican Musicians
AAMFC	American Association of Marriage and Family Counselors
AAPC	American Association of Pastoral Counselors
AAR	American Academy of Religion
AAUP	American Association of University Professors
AAUW	American Association of University Women
ABA	American Bar Association
ABS	American Bible Society
Acad	Academic, Academy
ACC	Association for Creative Change
Acct	Accountant
Acctg	Accounting
ACLU	American Civil Liberties Union
ACPE	Association for Clinical Pastoral Education
Actg	Acting
ACU	American Church Union
Adj	Adjacent, Adjunct
ADLMC	Association of Diocesan Liturgy and Music Commissions
Admin	Administration, Administrative, Administrator
Admssns	Admissions
Adopt	Adopted
Adv	Advent
Advert	Advertiser, Advertising
Advncd	Advanced
Advoc	Advocate
Advsr	Adviser, Advisor
Advsry	Advisory
AEC	Association of Episcopal Colleges
AEHC	Assembly of Episcopal Hospitals and Chaplains
AF	Air Force
AFB	Air Force Base
Affrs	Affairs
AFP	Anglican Fellowship of Prayer
Afr	Africa, African
Agcy	Agency
AGO	American Guild of Organists
Agt	Agent
Aid	Aidan
AIM	Adventures in Ministry
Alb	Alban
Alco	Alcohol
Alcosm	Alcoholism
Allctns	Allocations
Allnce	Alliance
Alt	Alternate
AltGld	Altar Guild
Alum	Alumna, Alumnae, Alumni, Alumnus
AMA	American Medical Association
Ambr	Ambrose
Amer	America, American
AmL	American Legion
Andr	Andrew
Ang	Angel(s)
Angl	Anglican
Anniv	Anniversary
Annunc	Annunciation
Anth	Anthony
AP	Associated Parishes for Liturgy and Mission
APA	American Psychological Association
Apos	Apostle(s)
Apportnmt	Apportionment
A-RC	Anglican-Roman Catholic Consultation/Dialogue
Archbp	Archbishop
Archd	Archdeacon
Archdnry	Archdeaconry
Archeol	Archaeological, Archaeologist, Archaeology
Archit	Architecture, Architect, Architectural
Archv	Archival, Archives, Archivist
ArmdF	Armed Forces
arts	articles
Ascen	Ascension
ASOR	American School of Oriental Research
Assn	Association
Assoc	Associate(s)
ASSP	All Saints' Sisters of the Poor
Asst	Assistant
Asstg	Assisting
Athan	Athanasius
Atone	Atonement
ATR	Anglican Theological Review
Atty	Attorney
Aug	Augustine
Auth	Author
Aux	Auxiliary
Av	Avenue
A/V	Audiovisual
Awd	Award(ed)
b	born
BACAM	Bishop's Advisory Commission of Aspirants to the Ministry
BACOM	Bishop's Advisory Commission on Ordained Ministry
Bapt	Baptist
Barn	Barnabas
Barth	Bartholomew
Bch	Beach
BCP	The Book of Common Prayer
Bd	Board, Board of
Bdgt	Budget
BEC	Board of Examining Chaplains
Ben	Benedict
Bern	Bernard
BEST	Bishops' Executive Secretaries Together
Beth	Bethesda
Biblic	Biblical
Bk	Book
Bklet	Booklet
Bldg	Building
Blvd	Boulevard
Bon	Boniface
Bp	Bishop

Bro	Brother, Brotherhood	Cmncatn	Communication(s)
BroSA	Brotherhood of St. Andrew	Cmnctr	Communicator(s)
BSA	Boy Scouts of America	Cmnty	Community
BSG	Brotherhood of St. Gregory	Cmpgn	Campaign
Bus	Business	Cmsn	Commission
Busmn	Businessman, Businessmen, Businesswoman, Businesswomen	Cmssnr	Commissioner
		Cn	Canon(s)
		Cncl	Canonical
		Cnfrmtn	Confirmation
c	number of children	Cntr	Center, Centre
C-14	Coalition 14	Cntrl	Central
CABp	Council of Advice, House of Bishops	Cnty	County
CAC	The Church Agency Corporation	Cnvnr	Convener
CALC	Clergy and Laity Concerned	Cnvnt	Convent
Calv	Calvary	Co	Company
CAM	Coalition for the Apostolic Ministry	Coadj	Coadjutor
C&C	Camp and Conference Center(s)	COCU	Consultation on Church Union
Can	Canada, Canadian	CODE	Conference of Diocesan Executives
CAP	Civil Air Patrol	Coll	College
Cath	Catholic	Collgt	Collegiate
Cathd	Cathedral	COLM	Committee on Lay Ministry
Cathr	Catherine	Com	Committee
Cbnt	Cabinet	COM	Commission on Ministry, Commission on Ordained Ministry
CBS	Confraternity of the Blessed Sacrament		
Cbury	Canterbury	Comf	Comforter
CCM	College of Church Musicians	Comm	Communion
CCU	Catholic Clerical Union	Comp	Companion(s), Companionship
CDO	Church Deployment Office(r)	Compstn	Compensation
CE	Christian Education	Compsr	Composer
CEEP	Consortium of Endowed Episcopal Parishes	Con	Consecrated
CERN	Christian Education Resources Network	Concep	Conception
Cert	Certificate, Certified	Conf	Conference, Confraternity
CFC	The Church Finance Corporation	Confrat	Confraternity
Ch	Church(es)	Cong	Congregation
Chal Br	Chalice Bearer(s)	Congr	Congress
Chap	Chapel	Congrl	Congregational, Congregationalist
Chapl	Chaplain(s), Chaplaincy	Const	Constitution, Constitutional
Chapt	Chapter	Consult	Consultant, Consultation, Consult
Chars	Charities	Cont	Continued, Continuing
Chart	Charter, Chartered	Contrib	Contributor
Chas	Charles	Contrllr	Comptroller, Controller
Chem	Chemical, Chemist, Chemistry	Conv	Convention
Chf	Chief	Convoc	Convocation, Convocational
Chld	Child, Children	Coop	Cooperation, Cooperative
ChmbrCom	Chamber of Commerce	Coordntng	Coordinating
Chncllr	Chancellor	Coordntr	Coordinator
Chr	Christ, Christian	COP	Company of the Paraclete
Chris	Christopher	Corn	Cornelius
Chrmstr	Choirmaster	Corp	Corporate, Corporation
Chrsmtc	Charismatic	Coun	Council, Councilor
Chrsnty	Christianity	Counslg	Counseling
Chrys	Chrysostom	Counslr	counselor
CHS	Community of the Holy Spirit	Cov	Covenant
CIC	The Church Insurance Company	CP	Community of the Paraclete
Cir	Circle	CPA	Certified Public Accountant
cl	cum laude	CPC	Church Periodical Club
Clem	Clement	CPE	Clinical Pastoral Education
Cler	Clergy, Clerical, Clericus	CPF	The Church Pension Fund
CLIC	The Church Life Insurance Company	CPF & Affil	The Church Pension Fund and Affiliates
Clincl	Clinical	CPG	Church Pension Group
Clnc	Clinic	CPI	Church Publishing Incorporated
Cltn	Coalition	Cred	Credential(s)
Cmdr	Commander	Cres	Crescent

Crisp	Crispin	EAM	Episcopal Appalachian Ministries
Crspndg	Corresponding	EBA	Episcopal Booksellers Association
Crt	Court	ECA	Episcopal Church Army
Crucif	Crucifixion	ECBF	Episcopal Church Building Fund
CSB	Confraternity of St. Benedict	Eccl	Ecclesiastical
CSF	Community of St. Francis	ECDEC	Episcopal Conference of the Deaf of the Episcopal Church in the USA
CSJ	Community of Servants of Jesus		
CSJB	Community of St. John the Baptist	ECEC	Executive Council of the Episcopal Church
CSM	Community of St. Mary	ECF	Episcopal Church Foundation
CSR	Christian Social Relation	ECharF	Episcopal Charismatic Fellowship
CT	Community of the Transfiguration	ECM	Evangelical and Catholic Mission
Cur	Curate	ECom	Episcopal Communicators
Curric	Curricula, Curricular, Curriculum	Econ	Economic, Economics, Economist, Economy
Curs	Cursillo	Ecum	Ecumenical, Ecumenism
Cuth	Cuthbert	ECW	Episcopal Church Women
CWM	Council for Women's Ministry	Ed	Editing, Edition, Editor, Editorial
CWU	Church Women United	EDEO	Episcopal Diocesan Ecumenical Officers
Cyp	Cyprian	Edm	Edmund
		Educ	Education
		Eductr	Educator
d	daughter of	Edw	Edward
D	Deacon	EEE	Episcopal Engaged Encounter
DAR	Daughters of the American Revolution	EFM	Education for Ministry
Dav	David	EGB	Episcopal Guild for the Blind
DCE	Director of Christian Education	Elctns	Elections
DD	Doctor of Divinity	Elem	Elementary
(dec)	deceased	Elis	Elisabeth
Del	Delegate, Delegation	Eliz	Elizabeth
Dep	Deputy	EME	Episcopal Marriage Encounter
Deploy	Deployment	Emer	Emeritus
Dept	Department	Emm	Emmanuel
Deptl	Departmental	Endwmt	Endowment
Diac	Diaconal, Diaconate	Engl	England, English
Dig	Digest	Engr	Engineering, Engineer(s)
D-in-c	Deacon-in-charge	Environ	Environment(al)
Dio	Diocese(of)	EPF	Episcopal Peace Fellowship
Dioc	Diocesan	Epiph	Epiphany
Dir	Director(s), Directress	Epis	Episcopal, Episcopalian
Disabil	Disabilities, Disability	ERM	Episcopal Renewal Ministries
dist	distinction	ESA	Episcopal Synod of America
Dist	District	ESCRU	Episcopal Society for Cultural and Racial Unity
Distr	Distributor	ESMA	Episcopal Society for Ministry to the Aging
(div)	divorced	ESMHE	Episcopal Society for Ministry in Higher Education
Div	Divine, Divinity, Division	ESRC	Episcopal Social Relations Conferences
Dn	Dean	Estrn	Eastern
Dnry	Deanery	ETN	Episcopal Training Network
DOK	Daughters of the King	EUC	Episcopal Urban Caucus
Dom	Domestic	Euch	Eucharist
Dplma	Diploma, Diplomat	Evaltn	Evaluation
Dplymt	Deployment	Evang	Evangelical, Evangelism, Evangelist
DRE	Director of Religious Education	EvangES	Evangelical Education Society
DS	Divinity School	EWC	Episcopal Women's Caucus
DSA	Distinguished Service Award	EWHP	Episcopal Women's History Project
DSC	Distinguished Service Cross	Exam	Examiner, Examining
DSM	Distinguished Service Medal	Exch	Exchange
Dss	Deaconess(es)	Exec	Executive
Dunst	Dunstan	Ext	Extension
Dvlp	Develop, Developer	EYC	Episcopal Youth Commission
Dvlpmt	Development		
		FA	Faith Alive
E	East	Fac	Faculty, Facilitator
EAAM	Episcopal Asiamerica Ministries	Fam	Family

Fed	Federation, Federated, Federal	Hsng	Housing
Fell	Fellow	Hstgr	Historiographer
Fest	Festival		
Fin	Finance, Financial		
Fllshp	Fellowship	IACCA	International Association of Conference Center Administrators
FMP	Forward Movement Publications		
Fndr	Founder	Ign	Ignatius
Fndt	Foundation	Imm	Immanuel
Form	Former, Formerly	Immac	Immaculate
Forw	Forward	Incarn	Incarnation
Fr	Father	Indep	Independent
Fran	Francis	Indn	Indian
Frgn	Foreign	Indstrl	Industrial
Ft	Fort	Info	Information
		Innoc	Innocents
		Ins	Insurance
Gabr	Gabriel	Inspctn	Inspection
GAS	Guild of All Souls	Inspctr	Inspector
GBEC	General Board of Examining Chaplains	Inst	Institute, Institution
GC	General Convention	Instnl	Institutional
Gd	Good	Instr	Instructor
Gdnc	Guidance	Instrn	Instruction
Geo	George	Int	Interim
Geth	Gethsemane	Integ	Integrity, Inc.
GFS	Girls Friendly Society	Interp	Interpretation
Gk	Greek	Intl	International
Gld	Guild	Intrnshp	Internship
Gnrl	General	Intro	Introduction
Govt	Government	Intsn	Intercession
Gr	Grace	Invstmt	Investment
Grad	Graduate	IPC	Interparish Council
Greg	Gregory		
Grp	Group		
Grtr	Greater	Jas	James
GSA	Girl Scouts of America	JCCMA	Joint Commission on the Church in Metropolitan Areas
GTF	Graduate Theological Foundation		
Gvnr	Governor(s)	JCP	Joint Commission on Peace
Gvrng	Governing	Jct	Junction
		Jn	John
		Jos	Joseph
H	Holy	Journ	Journal(s)
HabHum	Habitat for Humanity	JPIC	Justice, Peace, and the Integrity of Creation
Happ	Happening		
Hd	Head	Jr	Junior
Heav	Heavenly	Jrnlst	Journalist
Hebr	Hebrew	JSCN	Joint Standing Committee on Nominations
HEW	Health, Education, and Welfare	JSCPBF	Joint Standing Committee on Program, Budget, and Finance
Hisp	Hispanic		
Hist	Historian, Historical, History	Jub	Jubilee Ministries
Hlth	Health	Juris	Jurisdiction
Hm	Home(s)	Jvnl	Juvenile
HOB	House of Bishops		
HOD	House of Deputies		
Homil	Homiletic(s)	Kath	Katherine
Hmnts	Humanities	KEEP	Kiyosato Education Experiment Project
hon	honor(s)		
Hon	Honorary		
Hosp	Hospital, Hospitality	Lang	Language
Hq	Headquarters	Lawr	Lawrence
HR	Human Resources	LayR	Lay Reader
HS	High School	Ldr	Leader
Hse	House	Ldrshp	Leadership
		Lectr	Lecturer
HSEC	Historical Society of the Episcopal Church	Legis	Legislation, Legislator, Legislative

LEM	Lay Eucharistic Minister/Ministry	Mssnr	Missioner
Lg	Large	Mssy	Missionary
Lgr	Larger	Mstr	Master
Libr	Library, Librarian	Mt	Mount
Lic	License(d), Licentiate	Mths	Matthias
Lit	Literature	Mtn	Mountain
Liturg	Liturgical, liturgics, Liturgist, Liturgy	Mtyr	Martyr
LivCh	The Living Church	Mus	Music, Musical, Musician
Lk	Luke	Mvmt	Movement
LMFT	Licensed Marriage and Family Therapist		
LMN	Lay Ministry Network	NAACP	National Association for the Advancement of Colored People
Ln	Lane	NAAD	North American Association for the Diaconate
Loc	Local	NACA	National Association of Church Administrators
LocTen	Locum Tenens	NAECED	National Association of Episcopal Christian Education Directors
Long-R	Long-range	NACMB	National Association of Church Business Managers
LP	Lay Pastor	NAES	National Association of Episcopal Schools
Lrng	Learning	NAMMA	North American Maritime Ministries Association
Luc	Lucian	Narc	Narcotic(s)
Luth	Lutheran	NASSAM	National Association for the Self-Supporting Active Ministry
Lv	Leave	NASW	National Association of Social Workers
		Nath	Nathaniel
m	married	Nativ	Nativity
mag	magazine(s)	Natl	National
Magd	Magdalene	NCA	National Cathedral Association
Mar	Marriage	NCCC	National Council of the Churches of Christ in the USA
Marg	Margaret	NCD	National Center for the Diaconate
Mart	Martin	NCEH	National Conference of Episcopal Historians
Matt	Matthew	NCHM	National Commission for Hispanic Ministries
mcl	magna cum laude	NE	Northeast, Northeastern
Med	Medical, Medicine	NEA	National Education Association
Medtr	Mediator	NEAC	National Episcopal AIDS Coalition
Mem	Member, Membership	NECAD	National Episcopal Coalition on Alcohol and Drugs
Memi	Memorial	NG	National Guard
Merc	Merciful	Nbrhd	Neighborhood
Meth	United Methodist	Nich	Nicholas
Metropltn	Metropolitan	Nilt	National Institute of Lay Training
Mex	Mexican, Mexico	NMHA	National Mental Health Association
MFCC	Marriage, Family and Child Counselor	NNECA	National Network of Episcopal Clergy Associations
Mfg	Manufacturing	NNLP	National Network of Lay Professionals
Mgr	Manager	No	North
Mgmt	Management	NOEL	National Organization of Episcopalians for Life
MHA	Mental Health Association	Nomin	Nominated, Nominating, Nominations
MHE	Ministry in Higher Education	Non-par	Non-parochial
Mich	Michael	Non-stip	Non-stipendary
Min	Minister, Ministerium	Novc	Novice
M-in-c	Minister-in-charge	Nrsng	Nursing
Mk	Mark	Nrsry	Nursery
Mltry	Military	NRTA	National Retired Teacher's Association
Mng	Managing	NT	New Testament
Mnstrl	Ministerial	Nthrn	Northern
Mnstrs	Ministries	Ntwk	Network
Mnstry	Ministry	NW	Northwest, Northwestern
Mntl	Mental	Nwsltr	Newsletter
Mo	Mother	Nwspr	Newspaper
Mod	Modern		
Monstry	Monastery		
MRI	Mutual Responsibility and Interdependence in the Body of Christ		
Mrkt	Market		
Mssh	Messiah		
Mssn	Mission		
Mssngr	Messenger		

OAR	Order of Agape and Reconciliation
OA	Order of the Ascension
OCSA	Oblate Congregation of St. Augustine
Off	Office(r)(s)
Offcl	Official(s)
OGS	Oratory of the Good Shepherd
OHC	Order of the Holy Cross
OHF	Order of the Holy Family
OI	Order of the Incarnation
Oprtns	Operations
Optr	Operator
opt mer	optimum meritum
Ord	Ordained, Ordination, Order(s)
Ordnry	Ordinary
Org	Organist
Org/Choir	Organist/Choir Director
Orgnztn	Organizational, Organization(s)
Orth	Orthodox
OSA	Order of St. Anne
OSB	Order of St. Benedict
OSF	Order of St. Francis
OSH	Order of St. Helena
OSL	Order of St. Luke
OT	Old Testament
OTCG	Order of the Teachers of the Children of God
Ovrs	Overseas
P	Priest
Par	Parish, Parochial
Partnr	Partner(s)
Pat	Patrick
PB	Prayer Book
PBFWR	Presiding Bishop's Fund for World Relief
PBS	Bible and Common Prayer Book Society of the Episcopal Church
PECUSA	Protestant Episcopal Church in the USA
Penit	Penitentiary
PerpD	Perpetual Deacon
Personl	Personnel
Phil	Philip, Phillip
Philos	Philosopher, Philosophical, Philosophy
PHS	Public Health Service
Physcn	Physician
PI	Philippine Islands
P-in-c	Priest-in-charge
P-in-res	Priest-in-residence
Pk	Park
Pkwy	Parkway
Plcy	Policy
Plnng	Planning
Post	Postulancy, Postulant
PPF	Planned Parenthood Federation
Pract	Practice
Prchr	Preacher
Pres	President
Presb	Presbyter, Presbyterian, Presbytery
PBp	Presiding Bishop
Priv	Private
Prlmntrn	Parliamentarian
Prncpl	Principal
Prod	Production
Prof	Professor

Profsnl	Professional
Prog	Program(s), Programmer
Proj	Project
Prom	Promotion
Prot	Protestant
Prov	Province, Provincial
Provsnl	Provisional
Pryr	Prayer
Pstr	Pastor, Pastoral
Psych	Psychiatric, Psychiatrist, Psychiatry, Psychotherapist, Psychotherapy
Psychol	Psychology, Psychologist, Psychological
P-t	Part-time
Ptr	Peter
Pub	Publication(s), Published, Publisher(s), Publishing
Publ	Public, Publicity
Pvrty	Poverty
R	Rector
RACA	Recovered Alcoholic Clergy Association
RC	Roman Catholic
Rcrdng	Recording
Rcreatn	Recreation
Rdr	Reader
Rec	Received, Recipient
Recon	Reconciliation
Redeem	Redeemer
Redemp	Redemption
Reg	Region, Regional
Rehab	Rehabilitation
Rel	Religion(s), Religious
Relatns	Relations, Relationship
Renwl	Renewal
Rep	Representative
Res	Residence, Resident, Residentiary
Reserv	Reservation
Resolutns	Resolutions
Resrch	Research(er)
Resurr	Resurrection
Ret	Retired, Retirement
Revs	Review(s), Revision
Rgnts	Regents
Rgstr	Registrar, Registered
RSCM	Royal School of Church Music
Rt	Right
Rtrdtn	Retardation
Rts	Rights
RurD	Rural Dean
RWF	Rural Workers Fellowship
s	son of
S	Saint
SACEM	Society for Advancement of Continuing Education for Ministry
Sacr	Sacrament, Sacred
Samar	Samaritan
SAMS	South American Missionary Society
Sanat	Sanatorium
Sav	Savior, Saviour
SBL	Society of Biblical Literature

SCAIPWJ	Standing Commission on Anglican and International Peace with Justice
SCCC	Standing Commission on Constitutions and Canons
SCCM	Standing Commission on Church Music
SCCSC	Standing Commission on the Church in Small Communities
SCDFMS	Standing Commission on Domestic and Foreign Missionary Society of PECUSA
SCDME	Standing Commission on Domestic Mission and Evangelism on Ministry
SCER	Standing Commission on Ecumenical Relations
SCF/A	ECEC Standing Committee on Finance/Administration
Sch	School
SCHAH	Standing Commission on Human Affairs and Health
SCHC	Society of the Companions of the Holy Cross
Schlr	Scholar
Schlrshp	Scholarship
Sci	Science, Scientist, Scientific
SCI	Seamen's Church Institute
scl	summa cum laude
SCLM	Standing Commission on Liturgy and Music
SCMD	Standing Commission on Ministry Development
SCNC	Standing Commission on National Concerns
SCNMCS	Standing Commission on National Mission in Church and Society
SComC	ECEC Standing Committee on Communications
SCP	Standing Committee on Peace
SCSC	Standing Commission on the Structure of the Church
SCSD	Standing Commission on Stewardship and Development
SCWM	Standing Commission on World Mission
SCWMCS	Standing Commission on World Mission in Church and Society
SE	Southeast, Southeastern
Sec	Secretariat
Sectn	Section
Secy	Secretary
Sem	Seminarian, Seminary
Serv	Served, Service(s), Server
Servnt	Servant(s)
sev	several
Sfty	Safety
Shltr	Shelter
SHN	Sisterhood of the Holy Nativity
Shpd	Shepherd
Sis	Sister(s), Sisterhood
SLC	Standing Liturgical Commission
Slsmn	Salesman, Salesmen, Saleswoman, Saleswomen
Sm	Small
So	South
Soc	Social, Society
Sociol	Sociological, Sociologist, Sociology
SocMary	Society of Mary
SocOLW	Society of Our Lady of Walsingham
SOMA	Sharing of Ministries Abroad
SPBCP	Society for the Preservation of the Book of Common Prayer
SPCK	Society for the Promotion of Christian Knowledge
Spec	Special, Specialist, Specialized
Spkng	Speaking

Spnsr	Sponsor
Spprt	Support
Sprg	Spring(s)
Sprt	Spirit
Sprtl	Spiritual
Sprtlty	Spirituality
Sq	Square
Sr	Senior
SS	Saints(')
SSAP	Society of St. Anna the Prophet
SSB	Society of St. Barnabas
SSC	Society of the Holy Cross
SSF	Society of St. Francis
SSJE	Society of St. John the Evangelist
SSM	Society of St. Margaret
SSP	Society of St. Paul
St	State, Street
Sta	Station
Stds	Studies
Stdt	Student
Steph	Stephen
Stff	Staff, Staffing
Sthrn	Southern
Stndg	Standing
Strng	Steering
Strtgy	Strategy
Stwdshp	Stewardship
Suffr	Suffragan
Sum	Summer
Supt	Superintendent
Supvsr	Supervisor
SW	Southwest, Southwestern
Sxlty	Sexuality
Syn	Synod
Tchg	Teaching
Tchr	Teacher
Tech	Technical, Technician, Technological, Technologist, Technology
TEE	Theological Education by Extension: Education for Ministry
T/F	Task Force
Thad	Thaddeus
Theo	Theodore
Theol	Theologian, Theological, Theology
Ther	Therapist, Therapy
Thos	Thomas
Tim	Timothy
Tit	Titus
TMN	Total Ministry Network
Trans	Transferred
Transltr	Translator
Treas	Treasurer
Trien	Triennial
Trin	Trinity
Trng	Training
Trnr	Trainer
Trsfg	Transfiguration
Trst	Trustee(s)
TS	School of Theology, Theological Seminary, Theological School
TSSF	Tertiary of the Society of St. Francis

U	University
UBE	Union of Black Episcopalians
Un	Union
Untd	United
USA	United States of America
US-A	United States Army
USAF	United States Air Force
USAFR	United States Air Force Reserve
US-AR	United States Army Reserve
USCG	United States Coast Guard
USIA	United States Information Agency
USMC	United States Marine Corps
USMCR	United States Marine Corps Reserve
USN	United States Navy
USNR	United States Navy Reserve
USO	United Service Organization
UTO	United Thank Offering
Var	Various
VetA	Veterans Administration
VFW	Veterans of Foreign Wars
Vic	Vicar
Vill	Village
VIM	Venture in Mission
Vinc	Vincent
VISTA	Volunteers in Service to America
Vlly	Valley
Vol	Volunteer(s), Voluntary

VP	Vice President
Vrgn	Virgin
Vstng	Visiting
Vstry	Vestry
w	with
W	West
WBHS	Worker Brothers of the Holy Spirit
WCC	World Council of Churches
Welf	Welfare
Wit	The Witness
Wk	Work
Wlfd	Wilfred
Wm	William
Wmn	Woman, Women('s)
Wrdn	Warden
Wrld	World
Wrshp	Worship
WSHS	Workers Sisters of the Holy Spirit
Wstrn	Western
WTF	Women's Task Force
YA	Young Adult(s)
YP	Young People
YPF	Young People's Fellowship
Yth	Youth

Dioceses and Missionary Districts

AFFM	Armed Forces and Federal Ministries
AFFM	Office Of Bsh For Armed Forces
AFMicr	Armed Forces and Micronesia
Ak	Alaska
Ala	Alabama
Alb	Albany
Ark	Arkansas
At	Atlanta
Az	Arizona
Be	Bethlehem
Cal	California
CFla	Central Florida
CGC	Central Gulf Coast
Chi	Chicago
CNY	Central New York
Colo	Colorado
Colom	Colombia
Colom	Iglesia Episcopal En Colombia
CPa	Central Pennsylvania
CR	Costa Rica
Ct	Connecticut
Dal	Dallas
Del	Delaware
DomRep	Iglesia Episcopal De Dominicana
DomRep	Iglesia Episcopal Dominicana
DR	Dominican Republic
Eas	Easton
Eau	Eau Claire
EC	East Carolina
ECR	El Camino Real
EcuC	Central Ecuador
EcuC	Iglesia Episcopal Del Ecuador
Ecu	Ecuador
EcuL	Litoral Ecuador
EMich	Eastern Michigan
EO	Eastern Oregon
EpisSanJ	Episcopal San Joaquin
ES	El Salvador
ETenn	East Tennessee
Eur	Convocation of American Churches in Europe
Eur	Convocation of Episcopal Churches in Europe
FdL	Fond du Lac
Fla	Florida
Frgn	Foreign
FtW	Fort Worth
Ga	Georgia
Gua	Guatemala

Hai	Haiti
Haw	Hawaii
HB	Secretary House of Bishops
Hond	Honduras
Ia	Iowa
Ida	Idaho
Ind	Indianapolis
Kan	Kansas
Ky	Kentucky
La	Louisiana
Lex	Lexington
Lib	Liberia
LI	Long Island
Los	Los Angeles
Mass	Massachusetts
Md	Maryland
Me	Maine
Mex	Mexico
MexSE	Southeastern Mexico
Mich	Michigan
Micr	Micronesia
Mil	Milwaukee
Minn	Minnesota
Miss	Mississippi
Mo	Missouri
Mont	Montana
NAM	Navajoland Area Mission
NAM	Navajoland Council
NCal	Northern California
NC	North Carolina
NcPh	North Central Philippines
ND	North Dakota
Neb	Nebraska
Nev	Nevada
NH	New Hampshire
Nic	Nicaragua
NI	Northern Indiana
NJ	New Jersey
NLuz	Northern Luzon
NMich	Northern Michigan
NonD	Non-Diocesan
NPh	Northern Philippines
Nwk	Newark
NwPa	Northwestern Pennsylvania
NwT	Northwest Texas
NY	New York
Oki	Okinawa

Okla	Oklahoma		
Oly	Olympia		
O	Ohio	Tai	Taiwan
Ore	Oregon	Tenn	Tennessee
		Tex	Texas
Pa	Pennsylvania		
Pgh	Pittsburgh	USC	Upper South Carolina
PR	Puerto Rico	U	Utah
Q	Quincy	Va	Virginia
		Ve	Venezuela
		VI	Virgin Islands
RG	Rio Grande	Vt	Vermont
RI	Rhode Island		
Roch	Rochester		
RP	Panama	WA	Washington
		WDC	Washington, DC
		WK	Western Kansas
SanD	San Diego	WLa	Western Louisiana
SC	South Carolina	WMass	Western Massachusetts
SD	South Dakota	WMich	Western Michigan
SeFla	Southeast Florida	WMo	West Missouri
SJ	San Joaquin	WNC	Western North Carolina
SO	Southern Ohio	WNY	Western New York
SPh	Southern Philippines	WTenn	West Tennessee
Spok	Spokane	WTex	West Texas
Spr	Springfield	WVa	West Virginia
SVa	Southern Virginia	Wyo	Wyoming
SwFla	Southwest Florida		
SwVa	Southwestern Virginia		

Colleges, Universities, Seminaries

Adel	Adelphi University		Harv	Harvard University
Alleg	Allegheny College		Hav	Haverford College
Amh	Amherst College		Hob	Hobart College
ATC	Anglican Theological College of British Columbia		How	Howard University
			Hur	Huron College
Berk	Berkeley Divinity School			
Bex	Bexley Hall		IL Wesl	Illinois Wesleyan University
Bos	Boston University			
Bow	Bowdoin College			
Bps	Bishop's University, Canada		JCU	John Carroll University
Br	Brown University		JHU	Johns Hopkins University
Bryn	Bryn Mawr College			
Buc	Bucknell University			
			Ken	Kenyon College
			K SU	Kansas State University
Camb	Cambridge University			
Carl	Carlton College			
CDSP	Church Divinity School of the Pacific		L&C	Lewis and Clark College
Cit	The Citadel		Laf	Lafayette College
Col	Columbia University		Lawr	Lawrence University
Colg	Colgate University		Leh	Lehigh University
Cor	Cornell University		Linc	Lincoln University
CRDS	Colgate-Rochester Divinity School		LIU	Long Island University
CUA	Catholic University of America		LMU	Lincoln Memorial University
CUNY	City University of New York		Lon	University of London
			LSU	Louisiana State University
Dart	Dartmouth College			
Duke	Duke University		Man	Manchester University
Dur	Durham University		Mar	Marietta College
			Marq	Marquette University
			Merc	Mercer University
EDS	Episcopal Divinity School		Mia	Miami University
Emml	Emmanuel College		Mid	Middlebury College
Ers	Erksine College		MI SU	Michigan State University
ETS	Episcopal Theological School		MIT	Massachusetts Institute of Technology
ETSBH	Episcopal Theological School Claremont Bloy House		MWC	Mary Washington College
ETSC	Episcopal Theological Seminary of the Caribbean			
ETSKy	Episcopal Theological Seminary of Kentucky		Nash	Nashotah House
ETSSw	The Episcopal Theological Seminary of the Southwest		NEU	Northeastern University
			NWU	Northwestern University
			NYTS	New York Theological Seminary
			NYU	New York University
FD	Fairleigh Dickinson University			
F&M	Franklin and Marshall College			
Ford	Fordham University		Ob	Oberlin College
			Occ	Occidental College
			OH SU	Ohio State University
Gall	Gallaudet College		OR SU	Oregon State University
Gan	Gannon College		Oxf	Oxford University
Ge	Gettysburg College			
Geo	Georgetown University			
Gri	Grinnell College		PDS	Philadelphia Divinity School
GTS	General Theological Seminary		Penn	Pennsylvania State University
GW	George Washington University		Pr	Princeton University
			PrTS	Princeton Theological Seminary
			PSR	Pacific School of Religion
Ham	Hamilton College		Pur	Purdue University

Rad	Radcliffe College
Rice	Rice Institute
Roa	Roanoke College
Rol	Rollins College
RPI	Rensselaer Polytechnic Institute
Rut	Rutgers - The State University
SATS	St. Andrews Theological Seminary, Philippines
Sea	Seabury Divinity School
SFTS	San Francisco Theological Seminary
S Jn Ca	St. John's College, Canada
Smith	Smith College
SMU	Southern Methodist University
Stan	Stanford University
STUSo	School of Theology, University of the South
SUNY	State University of New York
SWTS	Seabury-Western Theological Seminary
Syr	Syracuse University
Tab	Tabor College
TCU	Texas Christian University
Tem	Temple University
TESM	Trinity Episcopal School for Ministry
Trin	Trinity College
Tufts	Tufts College
Tul	Tulane University
U CA	University of California
U CB	University of California - Berkeley
U Chi	University of Chicago
U Cinc	University of Cincinnati
UCLA	University of California at Los Angeles
U CO	University of Colorado
U Denv	University of Denver
U GA	University of Georgia
U IL	University of Illinois
U MI	University of Michigan
U MN	University of Minnesota

U NC	University of North Carolina
U NoC	University of Northern California
U Pac	University of the Pacific
U Pgh	University of Pittsburgh
Ups	Upsala College
U Rich	University of Richmond
U Roch	University of Rochester
U Sask	University of Saskatchewan
USC	University of Southern California
USMA	United States Military Academy
USMMA	United States Merchant Marine Academy
USNA	United States Naval Academy
U So	University of the South
U Tor	University of Toronto
UTS	Union Theological Seminary
Van	Vanderbilt University
Vas	Vassar College
VMI	Virginia Military Institute
VPI	Virginia Polytechnic Institute
VTS	Virginia Theological Seminary
Wag	Wagner College
WA SU	Washington State University
Wayne	Wayne State University
Wesl	Wesleyan University
Witt	Wittenberg University
W&J	Washington and Jefferson College
W&L	Washington and Lee University
W&M	College of William and Mary
Wms	Williams College
Wood	Woodstock College
WPC	William Paterson College
Wyc	Wycliffe College, Canada
Ya	Yale University
Ya Berk	Berkeley Divinity School at Yale

The Episcopal Clerical Directory
2017
Edition

The name of any biographee not printed in boldface type
indicates that no reply to our information update mailing was received
prior to the submission deadline.

A

AALAN, Joshua Canon (Pa) 2013 Appletree St, Philadelphia PA 19103 B 1964 D 12/16/2000 P 7/23/2001 Bp Russell Edward Jacobus. R Ch Of The Incarn Morrisville PA 2003-2009; Cur S Clements Ch Philadelphia PA 2002-2003. joshua_aalan@outlook.com

AARON, Stephen Craig (Wyo) 618 Saunders Cir, Evanston WY 82930 B Evanston WY 1950 s William & Clara. D 4/2/2003 P 10/29/2003 Bp Bruce Caldwell. m 5/28/1988 Sharlyn April Aaron c 3. saaron@vcn.com

AARON LUDWIG, Stephanie (Wyo) D 6/25/2016 Bp John Smylie.

ABBOTT, Barbara Leigh (Pa) 110 Llanfair Rd, Ardmore PA 19003 **Ch Of The H Apos Wynnewood PA 2016-** B Detroit MI 1954 D 6/19/2004 P 12/18/2004 Bp Charles Ellsworth Bennison Jr. m 12/29/1988 James B Abbott c 5. S Fran-In-The-Fields Malvern PA 2015-2016; Trin Ch Buckingham PA 2013-2015; S Jas Ch Collegeville PA 2011-2013; The Epis Ch Of The Adv Kennet Sq PA 2010-2011; S Jn's Ch Huntingdon Vlly PA 2007-2009; Assoc R Ch Of The Redeem Bryn Mawr PA 2004-2007.

ABBOTT, Gail Eoline (Mil) B Cherry Point NC 1948 d Ralph & Florence. AS Miami-Dade Cmnty Coll 1974; BS Florida Intl U 1991; MS U of Miami 1993; MDiv GTS 2003. D 6/21/2003 P 12/20/2003 Bp Leo Frade. c 2. R S Paul's Epis Ch Beloit WI 2004-2014; COM Dio Milwaukee Milwaukee WI 2005-2012.

ABBOTT SR, Gary Louis (Ga) 92 Camden Way, Hawkinsville GA 31036 B Millen GA 1947 s Albert & Viola. Post Grad Study TS, Sewanee; BA Merc 1969; MDiv SW Bapt TS 1972; DMin New Orleans Bapt TS 1978. D 8/3/2002 P 2/10/2003 Bp Henry Irving Louttit. m 7/26/1969 Billie Avalie Uselton c 2. S Lk's Epis Hawkinsville GA 2004-2015; Dio Georgia Savannah GA 2002-2003.

ABBOTT, Grant H (Minn) 2163 Carter Ave, Saint Paul MN 55108 B Seattle WA 1945 s James & Geraldine. BS U of Washington 1968; MDiv PrTS 1971; CAS EDS 1974. D 10/23/1974 P 10/25/1975 Bp Ivol I Curtis. m 7/28/1974 Elaine Elizabeth Tarone c 2. Epis Cmnty Serv Inc Minneapolis MN 2012, Exec Dir 2012; Exec Dir St Paul Area Coun Of Ch S Paul MN 2003-2011; St. Paul Area Coun of Ch 2003-2011; R S Matt's Ch S Paul MN 1981-1998; P Assoicate Cathd Ch Of S Mk Minneapolis MN 1980-1981; Int P All SS Ch Northfield MN 1979-1980; P Assoc S Mk's Cathd Seattle WA 1978-1979; WA & BC FOR 1976-1978; Cur S Jas Epis Ch Kent WA 1974-1976; Ecum and Interfaith Off Dio Minnesota Minneapolis MN 1997-2003, GC Dep 1996-2003, Pres, Cler Assn 1993-1995, Stndg Com 1991-1997, Pres, Exam Chapl 1989-1991, Exam Chapl 1985-1991, Reg 7 Dn 1983-1985.

ABBOTT, James Michael (Tex) 6507 Allentown Dr, Spring TX 77389 **R H Comf Epis Ch Sprg TX 2012-** B Pasadena CA 1985 s William & Christine. BA U of Texas 2006; MDiv VTS 2010. D 6/19/2010 P 12/19/2010 Bp C Andrew Doyle. m 6/12/2010 Margaret Chisholm Abbott c 1. Cur S Alb's Epis Ch Waco TX 2010-2012.

ABBOTT, Richard (VI) Po Box 686, Frederiksted VI 00841 B Saint Thomas VI 1940 s James & Sarah. BA Inter Amer U of Puerto Rico 1960; STB ETSC 1963; MA Col 1968. D 6/15/1963 P 5/23/1964 Bp Cedric Earl Mills. m 2/2/1993 Mary V Abbott. Iglesia San Francisco Epis Frederiksted St Croix VI 1998-2000; S Jn's Ch Christiansted St Croix VI 1998-2000; Epis Ch of the H Cross Kingshill St Croix VI 1978-1987, Vic 1964-1966; Dio Vrgn Islands Charlotte Amalie St Thom VI 1977; Non-par 1967-1977.

ABBOTT, Samuel Bassett (Alb) 1 Church St, Cooperstown NY 13326 B East Orange NJ 1942 s Frederic & Frances. BA Harv 1963; JD U CA 1969; LLM Ya 1972. D 6/7/1980 Bp Morris Fairchild Arnold P 6/11/1981 Bp John Bowen Coburn. m 7/5/1968 Edith Abbott c 2. R Chr Ch Cooperstown NY 2004-2009; R Epiph Par Walpole MA 2000-2004; Int Trin Ch Tariffville CT 1999; R Gr Epis Ch New York NY 1992-2000; R S Jas' Epis Ch Cambridge MA 1983-1992; Asst All SS Par Brookline MA 1981-1982, D 1980.

ABBOTT, Sefton Frank James (WNC) 27 Hildebrand St, Asheville NC 28801 **Ret 2011-** B Baltimore MD 1941 s Sefton & Jean. AB Duke 1963; BA Duke 1963; MDiv VTS 1966. D 6/29/1966 P 6/24/1967 Bp Thomas Augustus Fraser Jr. m 8/22/1964 Diane McKay Abbott c 2. P-in-c Ch Of S Mths Asheville NC 1999-2011; R S Martins-In-The-Field Columbia SC 1982-1997; R S Thos Epis Ch Reidsville NC 1978-1982; Dio No Carolina Raleigh NC 1971-1978; Asst S Fran Ch Greensboro NC 1968-1971; M-in-c S Paul's Epis Ch Thomasville NC 1966-1968. Bk, "Unfinished Journey: A Brief Racial Hist of the Dio WNC," Dio WNC, Cmsn to Dismantle Racism, 2011.

ABDELNOUR, Mark Anthony (USC) St. Simon & St. Jude Epis Church, 1110 Kinley Rd., Irmo SC 29063 **R Epis Ch Of S Simon And S Jude Irmo SC 2008-** B Jacksonville FL 1955 s Nassif & Elizabeth. BA The U So 1977; MDiv GTS 2007. D 5/26/2007 P 2/2/2008 Bp Dorsey Henderson. m 9/4/1977 Clarinda Abdelnour c 2. Asst S Barth's Ch No Augusta SC 2007-2008.

ABDY, Anne (Ore) **Rehab Ther Oregon St Psych Hosp 2016-** B Cape Town - South Africa 1966 AA Cottey Coll; BS Missouri St U; M.Ed. The U GA; M.Div. Sewanee: The U So, TS 2016. D 7/8/2016 P 1/28/2017 Bp Michael Hanley.

ABELL, Jesse W (WMass) 3 John Street, Westborough MA 01581 **R S Steph's Ch Westborough MA 2011-; Dioc BEC Dio Wstrn Massachusetts Springfield 2012-** B Columbus IN 1982 s Gary & Donna. BS Indiana Wesl 2004; MPhil U of Cambridge 2005; MDiv Sewanee: The U So, TS 2007. D 12/21/2006 P 9/9/2007 Bp Edward Stuart Little II. m 6/12/2010 Allison J Abell. Stff Chapl Bellevue Med Cntr Bellevue NE 2010-2011; Assoc R S Fran In The Fields Zionsville IN 2007-2010; Ecum and Interfaith Off Dio Indianapolis Indianapolis IN 2009-2010. Contributing Auth, "Interpretative processes [in exegesis]," *Jesus and Psychol*, Darton, Longman, & Todd, 2008; Co-Auth, "Cyberporn use in the context of religiosity," *Journ of Psychol and Theol*, Biola U, 2006. Epis Ch Ntwk for Sci, Tech, and Faith 2007; Epis Ntwk for Animal Welf 2007; Soc of Cath Priests 2008. rector@ststeph.com

ABER, Jack Albert 522 Portsmouth Ct, Doylestown PA 18901 B Buffalo NY 1954 s Richard & Kathleen. AA Hilbert Coll Hamburg NY 1974; BS SUNY 1976; MDiv CDSP 1989; MDiv GTS 1991. D 6/1/1993 Bp Edward Harding MacBurney P 8/30/1994 Bp James Winchester Montgomery. Int Ch Of The Annuniciation Philadelphia PA 2003-2004; S Mk's Ch Philadelphia PA 2001-2002; Asst S Paul's Ch Doylestown PA 1998-2001; Asst S Paul's Par Washington DC 1995-1998; Non-par 1993-1995. Philadelphia CCU; SocMary; SSC.

ABERNATHEY, James Milton (Tex) 1903 E. Bayshore Dr., Palacios TX 77465 B Atchison KS 1935 s Hugh & Marguerite. BS U of Texas 1958; BD Epis TS of the SW 1970. D 6/19/1970 Bp Scott Field Bailey P 5/31/1971 Bp James Milton Richardson. c 6. Int S Jn's Epis Ch Sealy TX 2007-2010; Int S Mk's Ch Bay City TX 2005-2006; Int S Fran Epis Ch Victoria TX 2004-2005; Int S Ptr's Epis Ch Rockport TX 2003-2004; R Chr The King Epis Ch Humble TX 1989-2001; The Great Cmsn Fndt Houston TX 1982-1998; S Jn's Epis Ch Silsbee TX 1982-1988; R S Paul's Epis Ch Freeport TX 1974-1982; Chr Ch Matagorda TX 1970-1974; Vic S Jn's Epis Ch Palacios TX 1970-1974.

ABERNATHY, Paul (WA) 1050 Willis Rd, Spartanburg SC 29301 B Saint Louis MO 1952 s William & Clara. MDiv The GTS; BA Westminster Coll 1974; MDiv GTS 1977. D 7/30/1977 P 4/15/1978 Bp William Augustus Jones Jr. m 4/3/1988 Pontheolla Mack-Abernathy c 1. R S Mk's Ch Washington DC 1998-2015; R Trin Ch Washington DC 1988-1998; R Calv Ch Charleston SC 1982-1988; R Mssh-S Barth Epis Ch Chicago IL 1979-1982; Cur Calv Ch Columbia MO 1977-1979. Auth, "For The Living Of These Days," Inifnity Pub, 2013.

ABERNATHY JR, W Harry (NY) 50 Bedford Rd, Armonk NY 10504 B Charlotte NC 1948 s William & Pearl. BA U NC 1970; SMU 1984; MDiv GTS 1986. D 5/31/1986 Bp Richard Frank Grein P 12/6/1986 Bp Robert Campbell Witcher Sr. m 2/16/1974 Penelope Anne Muse c 2. Int Sandhills Cluster Carthage NC 2011-2013; Int Trin Ch Fuquay Varina NC 2010-2011; Stndg Com Dio New York New York NY 1997-2001, Stndg Com 1997-2001, Conf Of Deans 1993-1996; R S Steph's Ch Armonk NY 1989-2008; Cur Trin-St Jn's Ch Hewlett NY 1986-1989. OHC. Phi Beta Kappa U Of Nc 1970.

ABERNETHY-DEPPE, David Edward (Cal) 19938 Josh Pl, Castro Valley CA 94546 **Epis Sch For Deacons Berkeley CA 2007-** B St Paul Minnesota 1940 s Edward & Earlene. BA Concordia Sr Coll 1961; DMin Chr Sem-Seminex 1983; PhD S Louis U 1991; MDiv Concordia Sem S Louis 2007. Rec 6/2/2007 Bp Marc Handley Andrus. m 7/29/2008 Jonathan Abernethy c 4. S Jas Ch Fremont CA 2008-2009; Dio California San Francisco CA 2007, Stwdshp Off 2005-2008; Prog Dir Horizon Mntl Hlth 2003-2005; Consult Horizon Mntl Hlth 1994-2002; Fac Sch For Deacons.

ABERNETHY-DEPPE, Jonathan (Cal) 2322 Oakcrest Dr, Palm Springs CA 92264 B Grand Rapids MI 1947 s Raymond & Rosalie. BMus Pacific Luth U 1969; MDiv Evang Luth TS 1973; MSM Witt 1978. Rec 6/14/2008 Bp Marc Handley Andrus. m 7/29/2008 David Edward Abernethy-Deppe. Asst S Paul In The Desert Palm Sprg CA 2011-2012; Dio California San Francisco CA 2008, Sr Stff Exec Asst 2002-2008.

ABEYARATNE, K Anoma (Mass) 4 Greenough Cir, Brookline MA 02445 B London UK 1955 d Ponniah & Mangayakarasi. BS MI SU 1985; MDiv EDS 2001; BCC Assn of Profsnl Chapl 2005. D 6/2/2001 Bp Barbara Clementine Harris P 6/8/2002 Bp M(Arvil) Thomas Shaw. m 6/18/1977 Rohan Chandra Abeyaratne. P Assoc S Paul's Ch Brookline MA 2011-2012; P Chapl Chld's Hosp. Longwood Av Boston MA 2005-2009; Cox Fell The Cathd Ch Of S Paul Boston MA 2004-2005; Cox Fell Dio Massachusetts Boston MA 2002-2003.

ABIDARI, Mehrdad (Cal) Cathedral School for Boys, 1257 Sacramento St, San Francisco CA 94108 **Cathd Sch For Boys San Francisco CA 2005-; Chapl Cathd Sch for Boys San Francisco CA 2005-** B Abadan IR 1953 s Aziz & Soraya. BSFS Geo 1975; MDiv GTS 1983. D 6/11/1983 Bp John Thomas Walker P 5/1/1984 Bp William Benjamin Spofford. m 12/28/1976 Jennifer Abidari. S Matt's Epis Ch San Mateo CA 2001-2005; S Jas Ch Fremont CA 2000-2001; Assoc S Fran Ch Houston TX 1999; R S Geo's Epis Ch Texas City TX 1997-1999; The Great Cmsn Fndt Houston TX 1990-1996; Chapl Rice U 1990-1995; Cur Gr Ch Cathd Charleston SC 1985-1990; Chapl Med U Of Sc Charleston 1985-1989; Asst Epis Ch of the Gd Shpd Summerville SC 1983-1985; Dir S Bede Epis Ch Houston TX 1990-1995. Auth, "Var arts & Revs". COM, Multicultural Cmsn.

ABRAHAM, Billie Patterson (Miss) P.O. Box 921, Vicksburg MS 39181 **S Alb's Epis Ch Vicksburg MS 2008-** B Memphis TN 1947 d William & Elizabeth. BA U of Mississippi 1969; MDiv Wesley TS 2006; Cert Ang Stud Sewanee: The U So, TS 2007. D 6/2/2007 P 9/21/2008 Bp Duncan Montgomery Gray III. c 3.

ABRAHAM, John Laurence (Az) 9138 North Palm Brook Dr., Tucson AZ 85743 **Dio Arizona Phoenix AZ 1985-** B Newark NJ 1947 s Maurice & F Joan. Dplma Peddie Sch Hightstown NJ 1965; BA Colg 1969; MDiv VTS 1973. D 5/19/1973 Bp William Henry Mead P 6/1/1974 Bp Thomas Augustus Fraser Jr. c 2. Pstr Whispering Hills Ch 2006-2009; Assoc S Phil's In The Hills Tucson AZ 1992-1994; R S Chris's Ch Milwaukee WI 1990-1992; R Ch Of S Matt Tucson AZ 1985-1990; S Ptr's By-The-Lake Ch Montague MI 1985; Gr Ch Grand Rapids MI 1983-1985; S Elis's Epis Ch Memphis TN 1980-1982; R Gr Epis Ch Pike Road AL 1977-1980; Asst S Jn's Ch Georgetown Par Washington DC 1974-1977; D S Mary's Epis Ch High Point NC 1973-1974. "Foreward," *I Died Laughing*, Upper Access, Inc., 2001; "The Cler and the Disnefranchised," *Disnefranchised Greif*, Lexington Books, 1989; Auth, "Jest Death Column," *Journ Forum Death Educ*, ADEC, 1985; "Death--The Gift of Life," *Thanatos*, Thanatos, 1982. Compassion and Choices 2003; Final Exit Ntwk / Hemlock Soc 1980. Certification as Fell in Thanatology Assn for Death Educ & Counslg 2008; Certification as Fell in Thanatology Assn for Death Educ &

Counslg 2005; Certification as Thanatologist Assn for Death Educ & Counslg 2003.

ABRAHAMSON, Wendy Kay (Ia) St. John's Episcopal Church, 120 First St. NE, Mason City IA 50401 **R S Paul's Epis Ch Grinnell IA 2013-** B Saint Paul MN 1960 d Ellis & Edythe. BFA U MN 1988; MFA Pratt Inst 1991; MS Pratt Inst 1993; MDiv VTS 2002. D 6/15/2002 P 12/16/2002 Bp Peter J Lee. m 8/8/2009 Stephen Paul Carroll. R S Jn's Ch Mason City IA 2004-2013; Asst Trin Ch Fredericksbrg VA 2002-2004. wendystpaulsgrinnell@gmail.com

ABRAMS, Mary Elizabeth (Ky) 4100 Southern Pkwy, Louisville KY 40214 B Louisville KY 1946 d Claude & Esther. BA Estrn Kentucky U 1969; MA Estrn Kentucky U 1973; PhD Spalding U 1986. D 4/17/2010 Bp Ted Gulick Jr. m 7/1/1983 Jan Abrams c 1.

ABRAMS, Ronald George (EC) 3309 Upton Ct, Wilmington NC 28409 **Bd Episcoapl Framworkser Mnstry 2010-; Bd Gd Shpd Fndt 2010-; Mem Hse of Dep Comm on St of Ch 2006-; R S Jas Par Wilmington NC 1999-; Trst Epis Ch Cntr New York NY 2006-, Pres Stndg Comm 2002-2005** B Hempstead NY 1957 s Jack & Rita. BA LIU 1979; MDiv VTS 1982. D 6/7/1982 P 12/18/1982 Bp Robert Campbell Witcher Sr. m 6/8/1985 Kathleen F Abrams c 2. Dep GC Dio E Carolina Kinston NC 2000-2006; R H Trin Epis Ch Fayetteville NC 1991-1999; R S Ann's Epis Ch Bridgehampton NY 1984-1991; Chapl Southampton (NY) Coll 1984-1991; Asst S Mk's Ch Westhampton Bch NY 1982-1984. Auth, *A Look Beyond Our Dio Walls*, 1994; Auth, *One Hundred Years of Nations Hallowed Ground*, 1993.

ABSHIER, Patsy Ann (Kan) Po Box 1175, Wichita KS 67201 B San Antonio TX 1934 d Newton & Anna. BS U of Kansas 1957. D 10/6/1999 Bp William Edward Smalley. D S Jn's Ch Wichita KS 2008; D S Jas Ch Wichita KS 1999-2006.

ABSHIRE, Lupton P (Colo) Saint Luke's Episcopal Church, 2000 Stover St, Fort Collins CO 80525 **R S Lk's Epis Ch Ft Collins CO 2013-** B Washington DC 1958 s David & Carolyn. BS Bos 1981; MDiv Bos TS 1989; STM GTS 1993; MA California Inst of Integral Stds 2004. D 6/27/1992 P 1/16/1993 Bp Douglas Edwin Theuner. m 10/28/1995 Diane Hawley Abshire c 4. P Gr Mssn Ch Tallahassee FL 2011-2012; R S Jn's Epis Ch Tallahassee FL 2008-2010; R Emm Ch Middleburg VA 2004-2008; Assoc Chr Ch Georgetown Washington DC 1992-2001. rector@stlukesfc.org

ABSTEIN II, W(Illiam) Robert (Tenn) 9210 Sawyer Brown Rd, Nashville TN 37221 B Jacksonville FL 1940 s William & Edith. BA Florida St U 1962; MDiv Sewanee: The U So, TS 1965; DMin Sewanee: The U So, TS 1978. D 6/24/1965 P 3/25/1966 Bp Edward Hamilton West. m 7/1/1966 Roberta Joy Abstein c 2. Int R Ch of the Resurr Franklin TN 2013-2015; Int S Jn's Ch Tallahassee FL 2010; Bd Mem Nets for Life 2007-2011; Int S Ann's Ch Nashville TN 2006-2008; Vice Chair Epis Relief & Dvlpmt 2002-2007; R S Geo's Ch Nashville TN 1994-2004; R S Jn's Epis Ch Tallahassee FL 1984-1994; R S Jude's Ch Marietta GA 1970-1984; P-in-c S Cyp's Epis Ch Pensacola FL 1965-1967; S Monica's Cantonment FL 1965-1967; Ch Pension Com Dio Tennessee Nashville TN 2007-2015, COM 1995-1998; Evang Com Dio Florida Jacksonville 1985-1991. Auth, "Stndg in the Breach," *Bk of Poetry*, Preservation Fndt, Nashville Tennessee, 2014; Auth, "Dating the Last Supper," *S Lk Journ*, 1982. Red Ribbon Soc 1964. Faithful Alum Awd U So 1983.

ABT, Audra (NC) 2105 W Market St, Greensboro NC 27403 **JBduPont Grant Mgr Dio No Carolina Raleigh NC 2013-, 2010-2011, COM for the Diac 2012-** B Wooster OH 1979 d John & Belicia. BA Ob 2001; SWTS 2007; MDiv Bex Sem 2010. D 6/5/2010 Bp Mark Hollingsworth Jr. Asst S Andr's Ch Greensboro NC 2011-2015.

ABUCHAR CURY, Rafael (Colom) **Iglesia Epis En Colombia Bogota 2003-** B Cartagena 1954 s Enrique & Hortencia. Rec 11/1/1999. m 1/27/1996 Nicolasa Maria Sierra Molina c 3.

ACCIME, Max (Hai) C/O Lynx Air, PO Box 407139, Fort Lauderdale FL 33340 **P-in-c S Basil the Great Gonaives HI 2003-; Serving Dio Haiti Port-au-Prince HT 1994-, 1992-** B Port-au-Prince HT 1964 s Marc & Andrea. Haiti TS 1992. D 12/6/1992 Bp Luc Anatole Jacques Garnier P 9/21/1993 Bp Jean Zache Duracin. m 12/15/1994 Anne Marie Andre c 4. Prist in charge S Andr Ch Hinche HI 1994-2003; Asst S Mk's Ch Honolulu HI 1992-1994. Soc of S Marg 1989.

ACEVEDO, Miriam (NH) 92 Nashua Rd, Pelham NH 03076 B New York NY 1951 d Tomas & Carmen. BFA Pratt Inst 1975; MDiv GTS 1983; DMin EDS 1998. D 6/4/1983 Bp Paul Moore Jr P 6/8/1984 Bp Lyman Cunningham Ogilby. Vic S Chris's Ch Hampstead NH 2000-2017; R Chr Ch Hyde Pk MA 1997-2000; Dio Massachusetts Boston MA 1996-2000; Chapl Tufts U Medford MA 1995-2000; Int Ch Of Our Sav Arlington MA 1995-1997; Int S Andr's Ch Framingham MA 1995; S Mary's Epis Ch Philadelphia PA 1987-1994; Asst Chr Ch Philadelphia Philadelphia PA 1983-1987.

ACEVEDO, Sheila Devine (SeFla) St. Andrew's Episcopal Church, 100 N Palmway, Lake Worth FL 33460 B Kearney NE 1948 d Arthur & Lorraine. Cert of Completion Dioc Sch of the Dio SE Florida; Theol Educ by Ext Sewanee: The U So, TS; BA U of Cntrl Florida 1972; MEd U of Cntrl Florida 1977; ABD

Florida St U 1980; Doctoral Coursework Nova SE U 2004; Diac Dioc Sch of SE Florida 2014. D 11/19/2016 Bp Peter David Eaton. c 2.

ACKAAH, Vincent Abisi (NY) PO Box 950A, Bronx NY 10451 B Sefwi Subiri Ghana 1949 s Kwaku & Susuana. Dplma Trin 1977; MA St Jn's U 1995; MSEd St Jn's U 2004; Cert Rel Stds Wadham Coll 2007. Trans 12/1/2014 as Priest Bp Andrew Marion Lenow Dietsche. m 1/15/2004 Lydia Ackaah Abisi c 3. Other Lay Position S Simeon's Ch Bronx NY 2014-2016. saintsimeonchurch@verizon.net

ACKER, Patricia Small (CFla) PO Box 290245, Pt Orange FL 32129 B Malden MA 1947 d Francis & Catherine. BA U of Massachusetts Boston 1974; MSW Barry U 1992. D 12/10/2011 Bp John Wadsworth Howe. c 2.

ACKERMAN, Chase Dumont (SwFla) **St Johns Epis Ch Tampa FL 2016-** B Mississippi 1982 s Peter & Barbara. M.Div. Sewanee: The U So, TS; B.S. USNA 2005. D 12/5/2015 P 6/18/2016 Bp Dabney Tyler Smith. m 11/6/2010 Jeanne Marie Zimmerman c 1. cackerman@stjohnstampa.org

ACKERMAN, Patricia Elizabeth (NY) 86 Piermont Ave, Nyack NY 10960 **Assoc S Mary's Manhattanville Epis Ch New York NY 2007-** B Hackensack NJ 1958 d Charles & Carolyn. BA New Sch U 1991; MDiv UTS 1994. D 6/14/1997 P 12/1/1997 Bp Richard Frank Grein. The Fllshp Of Recon Nyack NY 2003; Assoc S Paul's Ch Sprg Vlly NY 2002; Asst Gr Epis Ch Nyack NY 2000-2002; Dio New York New York NY 1998-2000; D Chr Ch Patterson NY 1997-2000; The Ch of S Clem Alexandria VA 1997. Amer Soc For Grp Psych 1994-2011. Riverkeeper Awd Riverkeeper 2008; Julius T Hansen Memi Awd UTS 1994; Living w Aids Volunteerism Awd People w Aids Cltn 1991.

ACKERMAN, Peter (Va) 101 N. Quaker Ln, Alexandria VA 22304 **R S Chris's Ch Springfield VA 2011-** B 1962 s Harry & Elinor. AA Los Angeles Vlly Coll 1983; BA California St U 2004; MDiv VTS 2007. D 5/19/2007 P 12/17/2007 Bp Joseph Jon Bruno. m 9/26/1987 Marie Ackerman c 2. VTS Alexandria VA 2014, 2013, 2012; Assoc R Imm Ch-On-The-Hill Alexandria VA 2007-2011.

ACKERMAN, Thomas Dieden (Mil) 4875 Easy St, Unit # 12, Hartland WI 53029 B Milwaukee WI 1938 s Lloyd & Dorothy. BS U of Wisconsin 1961; MSW U CA 1963; MDiv Nash 1973. D 4/28/1973 Bp Donald H V Hallock P 11/3/1973 Bp Charles Thomas Gaskell. Assoc Chr Ch Par La Crosse WI 2004-2007; Fam Ther, PT Mar & Fam Hlth Serv Eau Claire WI 2004-2007; Foster Care Supvsr Fam Works Madison WI & Black River Falls 2000-2005; Supvsr Fam & Childrens' Cntr LaCrosse WI 1997-2000; Supvsr Quakerdale New Providence IA 1991-1997; Prog Dir Anchorage Hse Beverly MA 1988-1991; SW Supvsr Vermont Achievement Cntr Rutland VT 1987-1988; Res Dir S Fran Acad Lake Placid NY 1983-1987; S Fran Cmnty Serv Inc. Salina KS 1983-1987; R S Ptr's Ch Milwaukee WI 1975-1983; Cur S Lk's Ch Racine WI 1973-1974.

ACKERMANN, John Frederick (Oly) B Centralia WA 1938 AA Lower Columbia Coll. D 6/29/2003 Bp Sanford Zangwill Kaye Hampton. m 6/23/1962 Sharon Katherine Ackermann c 2.

ACKERSON, Charles Garrett (LI) Po Box 113, Mastic Beach NY 11951 **Adj Prof of Philos St Jn's U Queens NY 2007-** B New York NY 1946 s Charles & Viola. BA CUNY Hunter Coll 1967; MDiv PDS 1970; MS SUNY-Albany 1971; PhD SUNY-Albany 1988; MA SUNY-Stony Brook 1991. D 6/13/1970 P 12/19/1970 Bp Jonathan Goodhue Sherman. Vstng Lectr VTS 1999; VTS Alexandria VA 1999; Prof of CE Mercer TS Garden City NJ 1990-2000; R All SS Ch Baldwin NY 1987-2013; Assoc S Mary's Ch Ronkonkoma NY 1986-1987; R S Paul's Ch Patchogue NY 1982-1987; Chapl Salem Cnty Jail Salem NJ 1979-1982; R S Geo's Ch Pennsville NJ 1976-1982; Chapl S Glens Falls Fire Dept S. Glens Falls NY 1974-1976; Vic S Tim Glens Falls NY 1974-1976; Actg Prncpl St Johns Day Sch Troy NY 1971-1972; Asst S Jn's Epis Ch Troy NY 1970-1972; Mem of Cathd Chapt Cathd Of The Incarn Garden City NY 2006-2013; Adj Prof of Psychol Dowling Coll Oakdale NY 1987-2016; Mem of Cathdral Chapt Trin Cathd Trenton NJ 1980-1982; Mem, Dept of Pstr Care Salem Country Memi Hosptial Salem NJ 1976-1982; Adj Prof of Philos Wilmington Coll New Castle DE 1976-1982; Secy, Com of CE Dio Albany Greenwich NY 1974-1976; Conservation Advsry Coun Moreau NY 1974-1976; Adj Prof of Psychol Schenectady Cnty Cmnty Coll Schenectady NY 1972-1976. APA; Amer Psychol Soc; Rel Resrch Assn; Soc for the Sci Study of Rel. Hon Cn Cathd of the Incarn, Garden City, NY 2011.

ACKLAND III, Lauren Dreeland (Nwk) 321 N Wyoming Ave Apt 1b, South Orange NJ 07079 B Buffalo NY 1944 d William & Edith. BA Rad 1967; MDiv GTS 1984. D 6/9/1984 Bp James Stuart Wetmore P 12/11/1984 Bp Walter Decoster Dennis Jr. m 6/12/1982 George Robert Hayman. R Gr Ch Madison NJ 1996-2016; Vic S Alb's Ch Oakland NJ 1987-1996; The GTS New York NY 1987-1996; Cur Ch Of The Ascen New York NY 1984-1987.

ACKLEY, Susan M (NH) 28 River St, Ashland NH 03217 B Syracuse NY 1944 d Benjamin & Frances. BA Manhattanville Coll 1966; MA Col 1973; MA Col 1975; MDiv EDS 1999. D 6/12/1999 P 12/21/1999 Bp Douglas Edwin Theuner. m 6/11/1977 William D Cabell c 1. R Ch Of The H Sprt Plymouth NH 2001-2010; Assoc Old No Chr Ch Boston MA 1999-2001. Untd Rel Initiative.

ACOSTA, Juan Maria (SanD) 3552 Hatteras Ave, San Diego CA 92117 **Died 8/18/2016** B Morelos Sonora MX 1942 s Juan & Carmen. BA Instituto de Filosofia Juan Duns Scotto Franciscan Theol Sem 1969; MDiv Instituto Nacional de Estudios Ecclesiasticos Mex City MX 1973; BA S Marys U San Antonio TX 1975; S Marys U San Antonio TX 1977; Epis TS of the SW 1978. D 6/5/1978 P 12/19/1978 Bp Scott Field Bailey. c 4. Ret 2009-2016; S Mary's/Santa Maria Virgen Imperial Bch CA 2006-2008; Vic / P In-charge S Mary's/Santa Maria Imperial Bch California CA 2005-2008; S Jn's Ch Indio CA 1999-2009; Vic Mssnr Santa Rosa Del Mar Desert Shores Califonira CA 1997-2003; P-in-c S Matt's Ch Natl City CA 1984-1996, Dir of Hisp Mnstry 1980-1984; Dio San Diego San Diego CA 1980-2005; Asst Santa Fe Epis Mssn San Antonio TX 1978-1980.

ACOSTA RODRIGUEZ, Richard (Colom) **Iglesia Epis En Colombia Bogota 2017-** B Cali Valle Colombia 1973 s Luis & Martha. D 12/8/2016 Bp Francisco Jose Duque-Gomez. m 7/9/2011 Jenny Carolina Gil Triana c 1.

ACREE, Nancy Pickering (Ga) 207 High Pt, Saint Simons Island GA 31522 B Laurel MS 1935 d Willis & Evie. Cert Sewanee: The U So, TS; Sewanee: The U So, TS; BA Eckerd Coll 1997. D 9/18/1994 Bp Robert Gould Tharp P 2/19/2000 Bp Charles Glenn VonRosenberg. Assoc Chr Ch Frederica St Simons Is GA 2002-2010; Asst Ch Of The Ascen Knoxville TN 2000, D 1996-1999.

ADAIR, Maryly S (NCal) **R S Ptr's Epis Ch Red Bluff CA 2010-, 2004-2005** B Berkeley CA 1946 d David & Eunice. BA California St U 1969; MS California St U 1983; MDiv CDSP 2002. D 6/20/2003 P 3/12/2004 Bp Jerry Alban Lamb. m 12/28/1980 Michael F Adair c 2. The Epis Dio Nthrn California Sacramento CA 2006-2009; Non-stip D/Assoc. P Trin Epis Cathd Sacramento CA 2003-2004.

ADAM, Barbara Ann (Kan) 10500 W 140th Ter, Overland Park KS 66221 **D Chr Ch Overland Pk KS 1993-** B Kansas City KS 1935 d James & Helen. U of Kansas; BS U of Dayton 1958. D 3/25/1993 Bp William Edward Smalley. m 12/18/1956 Paul James Adam c 2.

ADAM, Betty Conrad (Tex) 3501 Chevy Chase Dr, Houston TX 77019 B Houston TX 1939 d George & Grace. Baylor U 1958; BA U of Texas 1961; MA U CA 1973; MA Rice U 1981; PhD Rice U 1983; MDiv Houston Grad TS 1989; CTh Epis TS of the SW 1990. D 9/2/1990 Bp Anselmo Carral-Solar P 3/1/1991 Bp Maurice Manuel Benitez. m 5/12/1973 William Adam c 2. Cn Chr Ch Cathd Houston TX 1993-2008; S Jn The Div Houston TX 1991-1992.

ADAM, John Todd (Neb) 2621 CR 59, Alliance NE 69301 **D S Matt's Ch Allnce NE 1999-** B Hyannis NE 1944 s George & Marcella. BA Chadron St Coll 1967. D 12/10/1999 Bp James Edward Krotz. m 10/31/1970 Anne Catherine Adam c 2. NAAD.

ADAMIK, George F (NC) 221 Union St, Cary NC 27511 **R S Paul's Epis Ch Cary NC 1999-** B Yonkers NY 1953 s George & Margaret. BA Cathd Coll of the Immac Concep 1975; MDiv S Josephs Sem Yonkers 1979; MS Ford 1985. Rec 6/24/1990 as Priest Bp Harold Barrett Robinson. m 10/4/1986 Mary Adamik c 2. Stndg Com Dio No Carolina Raleigh NC 2008-2011, Dioc Trst 2010-, 2004-2009; R S Steph's Ch Pearl River NY 1991-1999; Serv RC Ch 1978-1986; Rdr for GOE Retakes Dio New York New York NY 1997-1998, Co-Chair of Cler Wellness Com 1996-1999, COM 1995-1998, Congrl Spprt Plan Com 1994-1997, Dn of Cler 1993-1997.

ADAMS, Chris (RG) 231 Amberleigh Dr Apt 102, Wilmington NC 28411 **Trin On The Hill Epis Ch Los Alamos NM 2015-** B Galveston TX 1985 s Kenneth & Kristi. BA E Carolina U 2006; MDiv Duke DS 2010; MDiv Duke DS 2010; Post Grad Dplma in Angl Stds VTS 2013. D 6/1/2013 P 12/14/2013 Bp Peter J Lee. m 5/2/2009 Karen M Proctor c 1. Cur S Andr's On The Sound Ch Wilmington NC 2013-2015.

ADAMS, David Robert (NJ) B Atlantic City NJ 1939 s Richard & Grace. BA Ya 1961; BD Yale DS 1965; PhD Ya 1979; GTS 1987. D 6/11/1988 P 2/25/1989 Bp George Phelps Mellick Belshaw. m 8/25/1962 Ann Macdonald c 2. Asst The Ch Of S Lk In The Fields New York NY 2000-2009; Prof VTS Alexandria VA 1991-1994; Int Chr Ch New Brunswick NJ 1990-1991; Int Gr St Pauls Ch Trenton NJ 1989-1990; Asst Prof of NT PrTS Princeton NJ 1976-1986; Vstng Instr Yale DS New Haven CT 1975-1976; Instr in Rel Dart Hanover NH 1970-1975.

ADAMS, Deanna Sue (U) 603 W 2350 S, Perry UT 84302 B Chattanooga TN 1942 d William & Mamie. Dplma Jn Hopkins Hosp 1963; BS Athens St U 1980; MEd Alabama A&M U 1982; BSN Weber St U 1995. D 6/10/2006 Bp Carolyn Tanner Irish. m 5/26/1989 Ivan Adams c 2.

ADAMS, Debra Jeanne (Ida) **Assoc S Fran Of The Tetons Alta WY 2014-** D 6/22/2014 P 12/21/2014 Bp Brian James Thom.

ADAMS, Eloise Ellen (Ct) 495 Laurel Hill Rd Apt 4B, Norwich CT 06360 B Norwich CT 1947 d Charles & Eloise. BS Seattle Pacific U 1969. D 12/12/1998 Bp Clarence Nicholas Coleridge. c 3. D S Dav's Ch Gales Ferry CT 1998-2004.

ADAMS, Frank George (NJ) 107 Devon Dr, Chestertown MD 21620 **P-in-c Chr Ch Worton MD 2011-; Vol Chapl, Pstr Care Chester River Hosp Cntr Chestertown MD 2005-; Chapl BroSA Chestertown MD 2004-** B New York NY 1925 s Hans & Andree. BS Rutgers The St U of New Jersey 1953; MS Drexel U 1969; Coll of Preachers 1971; AA Nash 1972; MA Villanova U 1978; MBA Monmouth U 1985. D 4/11/1970 P 10/24/1970 Bp Alfred L Banyard. m 9/9/1950 Lisbeth Ann Yates. Assoc Emm Epis Ch Chestertown MD

1993-2003; Vic Trin Ch Riverside NJ 1977-1993; Cur S Mary's Ch Burlington NJ 1970-1977; Chairman, Archit Commision Dio New Jersey Trenton NJ 1976-1993; Trst The Evergreens Moorestown NJ 1972-1992. SSC 1972. Natl Bus Admin hon Soc Monmouth U 1985; Natl Mechanical Engr hon Soc Rutgers U 1952; Natl Engr hon Soc Rutgers U 1952.

ADAMS, F Richard Richard

ADAMS, Gary Jay (ECR) 3002 Hauser Ct, Carson City NV 89701 **Ret 1993-** B Tonopah NV 1930 s Albert & Amy. BA U of Nevada at Reno 1951; MDiv CDSP 1964; DMin Claremont TS 1981. D 6/19/1964 P 1/6/1965 Bp William G Wright. m 6/5/1949 Marguerite Adams. R S Mk's Epis Ch Santa Clara CA 1987-1993; S Jn's Epis Ch Marysville CA 1980-1987; Ch Of The Mssh Santa Ana CA 1973-1980; Rur D Dio Los Angeles Los Angeles CA 1969-1973; R S Edm's Par San Marino CA 1966-1969; P-in-c Ch Of The H Innoc San Francisco CA 1965-1966; S Jn's In The Wilderness Ch Glenbrook NV 1964-1965; Vic S Pat's Ch Incline Vlg NV 1964-1965. Auth, "The Operation Of Salvation In Par & Person: Soteriological Praxis In Sacramental Context". Alb Inst. Mdiv w dist CDSP 1964.

✠ **ADAMS III, The Rt Rev Gladstone Bailey** (CNY) The Episcopal Church in South Carolina, PO Box 20485, Charleston SC 29413 **Provsnl Bp So Carolina 2016-** B Baltimore MD 1952 s Gladstone & Evelyn. BS Towson U 1976; MDiv VTS 1980. D 4/26/1980 P 11/8/1980 Bp David Keller Leighton Sr Con 10/27/2001 for CNY. m 8/26/1978 Bonnie J Adams c 3. Bp of Cntrl New York Dio Cntrl New York Liverpool NY 2001-2016; R S Jas Ch Skaneateles NY 1994-2001; R S Thos Epis Ch Chesapeake VA 1985-1994; S Mk's Ch Groveton NH 1982-1985; Vic S Paul's Ch Lancaster NH 1982-1985; Cur S Ptr's Epis Ch Ellicott City MD 1980-1982. Cristosal Bd Trst 2001; OHC 1980. DD VTS 2002. bpadams@episcopalchurchsc.org

ADAMS, Helen Kandl (CFla) 103 Shady Branch Trl, Ormond Beach FL 32174 B Norwalk CT 1953 d Albert & Helen. U of Cntrl Florida; AS Daytona Bch Cmnty Coll 1975; Inst for Chr Stuides 1997. D 6/6/1998 Bp John Wadsworth Howe. m 11/21/1981 Omar Adams.

ADAMS JR, Holmes S (Miss) All Saints' Church, 608 W Jefferson St, Tupelo MS 38804 **The Ch of the Gd Shpd Austin TX 2017-** B Flowood MS 1977 s Holmes & Gayle. AB Pr 2000; JD U of Texas Austin 2003; MDiv Sewanee: The U So, TS 2012; MDiv U So TS 2012. D 6/2/2012 P 12/19/2012 Bp John Bauerschmidt. m 6/21/2001 Lucy Duncan Adams c 3. All SS' Epis Ch Tupelo MS 2012-2014.

ADAMS, James Harold (Roch) 517 Castle St, Geneva NY 14456 **Lake Delaware Boys Camp Delhi NY 2008-; R S Ptr's Meml Geneva NY 1981-** B Staten Island NY 1952 s Kenneth & Gertrude. BA Wag 1975; MDiv Nash 1978. D 6/10/1978 P 1/6/1979 Bp Wilbur Emory Hogg Jr. m 9/21/1974 Suzanne J Adams c 4. Dio Rochester Henrietta 2012-2014, Dn 2011-, D Ne Dist 1993, Stndg Com 1987-1991, COM 1986-1991, Pres Stndg Com 1991, Dep Gc 1987-1989, Chair Yth Commision 1981-1984; S Paul's Ch Plymouth WI 1982-1986; Cur Chr Ch Cooperstown NY 1978-1981; Chair Yth Commision Dio Albany Greenwich NY 1979-1981. jimandsueadams@gmail.com

✠ **ADAMS JR, The Rt Rev James Marshall** (CFla) 428 W Cobblestone Loop, Hernando FL 34442 B El Paso TX 1948 s James & Mary. BA of Texas El Paso 1971; MDiv GTS 1979; DD GTS 2003. D 8/6/1979 P 5/9/1980 Bp Richard Mitchell Trelease Jr Con 3/16/2002 for WK. m 8/21/1971 Stacey B Brookman c 1. R Shpd Of The Hills Epis Ch Lecanto FL 2010-2013; Bp Dio Wstrn Kansas Hutchinson KS 2002-2010; R Trin Ch Milwaukee WI 1998-2002; Advsry Bd Dio Milwaukee Milwaukee WI 1998-2001; Instr Sch for Deacons Dio Kansas Topeka KS 1995-1998; CE Cmsn Prov VII 1995-1998; R Trin Epis Ch El Dorado KS 1993-1998; T/F on CE Prov V 1990-1993; Dir Diac Sch Dio Fond du Lac Green Bay WI 1987-1993; R Dio Fond du Lac Green Bay WI 1987-1993; R Chr Ch Green Bay WI 1987-1992; Dio Fond du Lac Appleton WI 1982-1986, Chair Liturg Cmsn 1982-1992, CE Cmsn 1982-1992; Vic S Paul's Ch Plymouth WI 1982-1986; Asst R Ch of the H Faith Santa Fe NM 1980-1982; Chapl New Mex Girl's Hm 1979-1980; Cur S Mich And All Ang Ch Albuquerque NM 1979-1980. DD GTS 2003.

ADAMS, James Patrick (NC) 120 East Edenton Street, Raleigh NC 27601 **R Chr Epis Ch Raleigh NC 2010-** B New London CT 1965 s Francis & Carol. MDiv VTS 1997. D 5/31/1997 P 12/5/1997 Bp Douglas Edwin Theuner. m 1/1/2011 Allene Cooley Adams c 6. S Alb's Ch Cape Eliz ME 2001-2010; Asst R S Thos Ch Hanover NH 1997-2000. jadams@christchurchraleigh.org

ADAMS, Jennifer Lin (WMich) 536 College Ave, Holland MI 49423 **R Gr Ch Holland MI 1994-** B Royal Oak MI 1968 d Marshall & Linda. BA Kalamazoo Coll 1990; MDiv CDSP 1994. D 6/11/1994 P 12/17/1994 Bp Edward Lewis Lee Jr. m 3/16/2012 Elizabeth A Trembley.

ADAMS JR, Jesse Roland (La) 6306 Prytania St, New Orleans LA 70118 B Bruce MS 1941 s Jesse & Eulalie. BA U of Mississippi 1963; JD U of Mississippi 1967. D 1/25/2004 P 8/6/2004 Bp Charles Edward Jenkins III. m 1/25/2003 Nancy Blum Adams. Asst Trin Ch New Orleans LA 2004-2015.

ADAMS, John (Neb) 450 Bordeaux St., Chadron NE 69337 **R Gr Epis Ch Chadron NE 2017-; Cur Dio Nebraska Omaha NE 2014-** B Fairfax VA 1985

BA W&M 2007; MDiv VTS 2014. D 4/27/2014 P 11/14/2014 Bp Scott Scott Barker.

ADAMS JR, John Davry (Va) 1731 Cloister Dr, Richmond VA 23238 B Troy NY 1928 s John & Ella. BBA Emory U 1950; MDiv VTS 1961. D 7/6/1961 P 6/14/1962 Bp Noble C Powell. m 6/26/1982 Suzanne P Adams c 4. Ch Of Our Sav Montpelier VA 1990-1998; P Ch Of S Jas The Less Ashland VA 1988-1989; Cbury Bk Shop Richmond VA 1985-1998; P Chr Ch Waverly VA 1985-1986; P-in-c Varina Epis Ch Henrico VA 1983-1984; R S Thos' Ch Richmond VA 1967-1981; R Chr Epis Ch Gordonsville VA 1964-1967; Cur S Anne's Par Annapolis MD 1961-1964; Chair Stewardships Dept Dio Virginia Richmond VA 1970-1977, Exec Coun 1965-1969.

ADAMS, John Stockton (ECR) 24745 Summit Field Road, Carmel CA 93923 B Towaco NJ 1944 s Ernestus & Anna. BA U of Virginia 1966; BTh GTS 1969; MA Antioch U 1986; PrTS 1986. D 6/4/1969 Bp Leland Stark P 12/14/1969 Bp George E Rath. m 6/25/1983 Tracey Adams c 2. All SS Ch Carmel CA 1995-1999; Chapl York Sch Monterey CA 1992-1995; P-in-c S Barn' Par Pasadena CA 1991-1992; P-in-c S Bede's Epis Ch Los Angeles CA 1989-1990; P-in-c Ch Of The Ascen Tujunga CA 1987-1989; Chapl Harvard Sch CA 1979-1986; Chapl Harvard-Westlake Sch Studio City CA 1979-1986; Chapl Hoosac Sch Hoosac NY 1977-1979; Chapl Hoosac Sch Hoosick NY 1977-1979; R S Andr's Ch Millinocket ME 1972-1976; Cur Ch Of The Atone Tenafly NJ 1969-1972.

ADAMS, John Torbet (Alb) 262 Center Rd, Lyndeborough NH 03082 B Muncie IN 1945 s William & Julia. BS Ashland U 1968; MDiv VTS 1971; Andover Newton TS 1991. D 6/11/1971 P 12/28/1971 Bp John P Craine. S Paul's Ch Salem NY 2000-2003; Chr Ch Coxsackie NY 1993-1995; P-in-c Calv Epis Ch Cairo NY 1989-1997; Gloria Dei Epis Ch Palenville NY 1989-1990; S Jn In-The-Wilderness Copake Falls NY 1987-1988; Ch Of Our Sav Boston MA 1985-1986; Ch Of Our Sav Hartville WY 1985; Int Dio Massachusetts Boston MA 1981-1987; S Jas Epis Ch Arlington VT 1975-1979.

ADAMS, Jonathan Vaughn (Tex) B Jacksonville FL 1974 s Robert & Linda. Study Samford U 1996; BS Liberty U 1998; MDiv SE TS 2001. Trans 3/29/2017 as Priest Bp C Andrew Doyle. m 7/17/1998 Jana Martin Adams c 3.

ADAMS, Lesley (Roch) 6200 Mount Rd, Trumansburg NY 14886 **Chr Epis Ch Willard NY 2015-; S Jn's Chap Geneva NY 1995-** B Washington DC 1958 d James & Virginia. AB Smith 1980; MDiv Harvard DS 1986. D 6/13/1987 Bp Ronald Hayward Haines P 3/30/1988 Bp William George Burrill. m 8/14/2003 David Newman c 2. Chapl Hobart And Wm Smith Colleges Geneva NY 1995-2015; P-in-c S Ptr's Epis Ch Bloomfield NY 1988-1989, D 1987-1989; Dn of Students, Rgstr, Dir FA Colgate Rochester/Bex Rochester NY 1987-1994. DD Hobart and Wm Smith 2015. ladams@hws.edu

ADAMS, Margaret Louise (Tenn) 411 Annex Ave Apt F-1, Nashville TN 37209 B Chillicothe MO 1949 d Charles & Margaret. BD IL Wesl 1971; MS U of Tennessee 1975; MDiv Sewanee: The U So, TS 1998. D 5/24/1998 P 4/25/1999 Bp Bertram Nelson Herlong. Ch Of Our Sav Gallatin TN 2006-2008; S Geo's Ch Nashville TN 2000-2005; Asst S Phil's Ch Nashville TN 1998-1999.

ADAMS, Marilyn Mccord (Los) Po Box 208306, New Haven CT 06520 **Died 3/22/2017** B Oak Park IL 1943 d William & Wilmah. BA IL U 1964; PhD Cor 1967; MTh PrTS 1984; ThM PrTS 1985. D 6/20/1987 Bp Oliver Bailey Garver Jr P 12/1/1987 Bp John Mc Gill Krumm. m 6/10/1987 Robert Merrihew Adams. Assoc Trin Cathd Trenton NJ 2013-2017; Asst S Thos's Ch New Haven CT 1999-2002, Asst 1994-1998; Asst Chr Ch New Haven CT 1997-1999, Asst 1993-1996; St Mary in Palms Los Angeles CA 1993-2007; Asst S Aug By-The-Sea Par Santa Monica CA 1990-1992; Asst All SS Par Beverly Hills CA 1988-1989; Adj Chapl U Of Ca Los Angeles Los Angeles CA 1987-1993; Asst Trin Epis Par Los Angeles CA 1985-1988. Auth, "Horrendous Evils & Goodness Of God," 1999; Auth, "Wm Ockham," 1987. Aar 2000; Amer Philos Assn 1967; Soc For Med & Renaissance Philos 1978; Soc Of Chr Philosophers 1978. Henry Luce Iii Fllshp 2002; Gifford Lectr 1999; Guggenheim Fllshp 1988.

ADAMS, Mary Lynn (FdL) **D S Anne's Epis Ch De Pere WI 2013-** B Milwaukee 1949 BS U of Wisconsin 1971; BS U of Wisconsin 1987. D 12/3/2005 Bp Russell Edward Jacobus.

ADAMS, Michael K (Tex) 209 W 27th St, Austin TX 78705 **R All SS Epis Ch Austin TX 2004-** B Seoul KR 1963 s William & Gloria. BS LSU 1985; MDiv SWTS 1989. D 6/10/1989 P 12/9/1989 Bp Willis Ryan Henton. m 8/2/2014 Michele D Adams c 4. R S Barn Epis Ch Lafayette LA 1998-2004; R The Epis Ch Of The Epiph New Iberia LA 1993-1998; Asst R Ch Of The Ascen Lafayette LA 1990-1993; D S Jas Epis Ch Shreveport LA 1989. mike@allsaints-austin.org

ADAMS, Patricia Wessels (Ak) 3506 Cherokee Dr S, Salem OR 97302 **Nonpar 1988-** B Lakota IA 1935 d Herman & Mable. RN Methodist-Kahler Sch of Nrsng 1956; U of Washington 1958; BS Oklahoma City U 1978; MDiv SMU Perkins 1984; Claremont Coll 1992. D 3/14/1987 P 1/1/1989 Bp Gerald Nicholas Mcallister. m 9/27/1958 Ralph Edwin Adams c 3. Asst P S Mary's Ch Anchorage AK 1995-2000; D-Transitional S Paul's Cathd Oklahoma City OK 1987-1988; Dio Oklahoma Oklahoma City OK 1987, Jubilee Off 1986-1988;

Chapl/Dir of Urban Mnstry Gld of St. Geo Oklahoma City OK 1985-1987. cl Perkins TS 1984.

ADAMS, Richard Carl (Oly) Po Box 336, Hinesburg VT 05461 **1976-** B South Bend IN 1925 s Ralph & Myrtle. BS NWU 1947; MDiv SWTS 1952; STM GTS 1958; GTS 1961. D 3/10/1952 P 10/5/1952 Bp James Reginald Mallett. Res P S Andr's Ch Northford CT 1971-1976; Asst Chr Ch Ansonia CT 1967-1971; Asst Trin Ch Branford CT 1964-1966; Asst Gr Ch Madison NJ 1962-1964; Chapl S Mary Hosp Bayside NY 1961-1962; Asst Ch Of The Medtr Bronx NY 1957-1961; Asst Chr Ch Tacoma WA 1956-1957; Tutor/Instr Hellenistic Gk Bexley Seabury Fed Chicago IL 1953-1955; Asst The Cathd Ch Of S Jas So Bend IN 1952-1953; Tutor/Fell The GTS New York NY 1958-1960. Co-Auth, "Through the Years Celebrating...," 2008; Auth, *Meditation and Celebration [CD ROM]*, Quinnipiac Coll, 1999; Auth, *The Sprt of Sport*, Wyndham Hall; Bristol, IN, 1987. Cntr for Theol and Natural Sci; Berkeley, CA 1996; Temple of Understanding 1983. Advsry Bd Temple of Understanding.

ADAMS, Samuel Bowman (Tenn) 4715 Harding Pike, Nashville TN 37205 **Assoc S Geo's Ch Nashville TN 2014-** B Orange TX 1983 s William & Sharon. BS Texas A&M U 2007; MDiv Wycliffe Coll 2014; MDiv Wycliffe Coll Toronto CA 2014. D 5/31/2014 Bp John Tarrant P 12/11/2014 Bp John Bauerschmidt.

ADAMS JR, Thomas Edwin (Mass) PO Box 522, Falmouth MA 02541 **Asst The Ch Of The Adv Boston MA 2005-** B Palm Beach FL 1944 s Thomas & Caroline. BA U of Pennsylvania 1966; EDS 1969; Oxf GB 1972. D 6/28/1969 Bp William Foreman Creighton P 1/1/1970 Bp The Bishop Of Tokyo. m 7/19/2011 Candace Roosevelt. R S Mk's Epis Ch Fall River MA 1997-1999, P-in-c 1990-1994; Serv Ch in the Prov of the W Indies 1994-1996; S Barn Ch Falmouth MA 1988; Asst Ch Of The Mssh Woods Hole MA 1979-1981; Sevier Hse Georgetown U Washington DC 1976-1978; Hoosac Sch Hoosick NY 1974-1976; S Agnes' Sch Alexandria VA 1973-1974; Asst S Alb's Ch Tokyo Japan 1969-1971; S Paul's Ch Rikkyo Tokyo 1969-1971.

ADAMS, William J (NCal) 95 Malaga Ct, Ukiah CA 95482 B Los Angeles CA 1952 s James & Virginia. Dplma Coll of California Med Affiliates 1977; BA California St U 1981; MDiv CDSP 1985. D 6/16/1985 P 12/18/1985 Bp John Lester Thompson III. m 8/26/1972 Kathlyne Ann Adams c 2. P-in-c H Trin Epis Ch Ukiah CA 2011-2013; R Trin Ch Sutter Creek CA 1986-2008; Asst S Mich's Epis Ch Carmichael CA 1985-1986; COM The Epis Dio Nthrn California Sacramento CA 1998-2007, Ecum Off 1986-1997.

ADAMS, William Rian (WNC) 6329 Frederica Rd, St Simons Island GA 31522 **Calv Epis Ch Fletcher NC 2016-** B Marianna FL 1982 s William & Brenda. BA Intl Bible Coll 2004; MDiv Wesley Sem 2008; MDiv Wesley TS 2008. D 12/10/2014 Bp Joseph Jon Bruno. m 6/3/2000 Amber Leah Adams c 1. Chr Ch Frederica St Simons Is GA 2015-2016.

ADAMS, William Seth (Oly) 2707 Silver Crest Court, Langley WA 98260 B Fort Smith AR 1940 s William Seth & Hortense. BS Washington U 1964; BD Bex Sem 1967; MA Pr 1971; PhD Pr 1973. D 6/24/1967 P 1/21/1968 Bp George Leslie Cadigan. m 6/3/1995 Amy Donohue-Adams c 2. Int S Jas Ch Austin TX 1998-2001; Prof Luth Sem Prog in the SW 1982-2007; Prof Epis TS Of The SW Austin TX 1982-2005; Prof/Chapl Vancouver TS Vancouver BC 1975-1982; Assoc Calv Ch Columbia MO 1973-1975; Assoc All SS Ch Princeton NJ 1969-1973; M-in-c S Paul's Ch Palmyra MO 1967-1969. Auth, "Moving the Furniture: Liturg Theory, Pract and Environmental Theory," Ch Pub, 1999; Auth, "Shaped by Images: One Who Presides," Ch Hymnal, 1995; Co-Ed, "Our Heritage and Common Life," U Press of Amer, 1994. No Amer Acad of Liturg 1977-2009; Societas Liturgica 1980-1991.

ADAMS-HARRIS, Anne Jane (Wyo) Po Box 4086, Santa Barbara CA 93140 **Chapl Trin Epis Hse 2000-** B London UK 1932 d John & Doreen. EFM Sewanee: The U So, TS. D 10/18/1998 Bp Onell Asiselo Soto. m 3/12/1960 Harry Clark Harris c 1. D S Mk's Ch Cheyenne WY 2006-2011. DOK; Sis Of The H Nativ.

ADAMS-MASSMANN, Jennifer Helen (Eur) Sebastian-Rinz-Str 22, Frankfurt Germany Germany **Asstg P The Angl/Epis Ch Of Chr The King Frankfurt am Main 60323 2007-, D 2006-2007** B Norwood MA 1974 d Clifford & Rebecca. BA U NC 1996; MDiv Duke DS 2003. D 5/27/2006 P 5/5/2007 Bp Pierre W Whalon. m 12/29/2004 Alexander Massmann.

ADAMSON, Thomas I (NI) 909 S Darling St, Angola IN 46703 **H Fam Ch Angola IN 2017-** B Lafayette IN 1978 s William & Laura. BA Indiana Wesl 2011; MDiv STUSo 2017. D 12/23/2016 P 6/24/2017 Bp Doug Sparks. m 6/19/1999 Elizabeth A Adamson c 8.

ADAMS-RILEY, Daniel W (Va) 815 E Grace St, Richmond VA 23219 **R S Paul's Ch Richmond VA 2008-** B Columbia SC 1971 s Weston & Elizabeth. BA U So 1993; MDiv VTS 2001. D 6/16/2001 P 5/1/2002 Bp Dorsey Henderson. m 7/7/2001 Gena D Adams-Riley c 2. Vic S Jn's Cathd Jacksonville FL 2006-2008; Cler Res Chr Epis Ch Pensacola FL 2003-2006; Asst/Cler Res Chr Ch Alexandria VA 2001-2003.

ADAMS-RILEY, Gena D (Fla) 815 E Grace St, Richmond VA 23219 B VT 1971 d Winston & Mary. BS U of Utah 1996; MDiv VTS 2002. D 7/11/2002 P 2/8/2003 Bp Carolyn Tanner Irish. m 7/7/2001 Daniel W Adams-Riley c 1.

Cn S Jn's Cathd Jacksonville FL 2006-2008; Assoc for Pstr Care Chr Epis Ch Pensacola FL 2003-2006; Asst to the R Ch Of The Ascen Silver Sprg MD 2002-2003.

ADAMS-SHEPHERD, Kathleen E (Ct) Christ Church Cathedral, 1210 Locust St, Saint Louis MO 63103 **Chr Ch Cathd S Louis MO 2017-** B Boston MA 1955 d Raymond & Patricia. BS Bridgewater Coll 1977; MDiv UTS 1981. D 6/5/1982 Bp John Bowen Coburn P 6/25/1983 Bp O'Kelley Whitaker. m 2/28/1981 Richard A Shepherd c 1. R Trin Ch Newtown CT 1996-2016; R Chr Ch Clayton NY 1987-1996; St Jn's Ch Cape Vinc NY 1987-1996; Ch Of The Resurr Oswego NY 1982-1987; Stndg Com Dio Cntrl New York Liverpool NY 1987-1996. kas@christchurchcathedral.us

ADDIEGO, Jeffrey Clark (Nev) 1429 Bronco Rd, Boulder City NV 89005 **Dn-SE Dio Nevada Las Vegas 2011-** B San Francisco CA 1952 s Alfred & Doris. BS U Pac 1975. D 5/29/2001 P 2/7/2002 Bp Katharine Jefferts Schori. P S Matt's Ch Las Vegas NV 2002-2013.

ADDISON, Orlando J (CFla) 6990 S US Highway 1, Port St Lucie FL 34952 **Vic H Faith Epis Ch Port St Lucie FL 2013-** B Tela HN 1961 s Charles & Rosa. BA Universidad De Honduras San Pedro Sula Hn 1988; MDiv VTS 2000. D 5/1/2000 Bp Leo Frade P 2/24/2001 Bp Wendell Nathaniel Gibbs Jr. m 10/14/2016 Martha J Fernandez c 2. S Jas-In-The-Hills Epis Ch Hollywood FL 2006-2013; Cn Cathd Ch Of S Paul Detroit MI 2001-2006; Asst S Jn's Ch Royal Oak MI 2000-2001. Auth, "Afro-Latin Song," *Afro-Latin Son / Canto Afrolatino*, Createspace, 2016; Auth, "Ernesto Gamboa," *Ernesto Gamboa Engl Ed*, Createspace, 2016; Auth, "Night Was Afraid to Fall," *Night Was Afraid to Fall / La Noche Tuvo Miedo*, Alexandria Libr, 2015; Auth, "Ernesto Gamboa Spanish Ed," *Ernesto Gamboa Spanish Ed*, Createspace, 2014.

ADE, Daniel Gerard George (Los) 242 E Alvarado St, Pomona CA 91767 **Vice Dn St Johns Pro-Cathd Los Angeles CA 2006-** B New York NY 1958 s Raymond & Maureen. BA S Johns U 1980; MDiv GTS 1992. D 6/13/1992 P 12/12/1992 Bp Richard Frank Grein. m 3/1/1992 Walter T Killmer. S Paul's Pomona Pomona CA 2003-2006; The Ch Of S Lk In The Fields New York NY 1996-2003; Chapl St Ptr Cmnty Outreach Cntr Inc Dio New York New York NY 1995-1996; S Ptr's Epis Ch Peekskill NY 1995; Asst S Thos Ch New York NY 1992-1994.

ADEBONOJO, Mary Bunton (Pa) 50 Bagdad Rd, Durham NH 03824 B Chicago IL 1936 d Ansel & Mildred. BA Rad 1957; MA U CA Berkeley 1967; PDS 1974; Luth TS 1976. D 4/13/1977 P 4/1/1980 Bp Lyman Cunningham Ogilby. m 2/17/2001 Wayne Douglas Shirley c 3. Dio New York New York NY 1998-2001; Chap Of S Jn The Div Tomkins Cove NY 1997-2002; Chr Epis Ch Sparkill NY 1997-2002; S Paul's Ch Sprg Vlly NY 1997-2002; Assoc Trin Epis Ch Garnerville NY 1997-2002; Chapl (Hosp/Hospice) Taylor Hosp Taylor Hospice Ridley Pk 1985-1997; Int P Ch Of S Lk And Epiph Philadelphia PA 1984-1985; Chapl Presb Hosp Ridley Pk 1984-1985; Int S Mths Ch Philadelphia PA 1981-1984; Yth Min Dio Pennsylvania Philadelphia PA 1979-1981; Consult Stdg Ctte On Rel Ed Epis Ch Exec Coun 1973-1977. Auth, "Free To Choose," Judson Press, 1980. Oblate, Cmnty of St. Jn Bapt.

ADELIA, Laura A (Az) 100 W Roosevelt St, Phoenix AZ 85003 **Wing Chapl 129th Air Rescue Wing California Air NG CA 2011-; Fac - Rel Stds Mesa Cmnty Coll Mesa AZ 2001-** B Chicago IL 1961 d Michael & Alice. BA Arizona St U 1987; MDiv Other 1999; MDiv Other 1999; MDiv PSR 1999; MDiv PSR, Berkeley, CA 1999; Cert Arizona St U 2007. D 12/11/2010 P 7/2/2011 Bp Kirk Stevan Smith. P in Charge S Ptr's Ch Casa Grande AZ 2013-2015; Chapl Res VA Hosp Palo Alto CA 2011-2012; Prot Chapl McMurdo Sta Antarctica NSF / USAF 2010; Wing Chapl 136th Airlift Wing Texas Air NG TX 2009-2011; Wing Chapl 380 Expeditioanry Wing USAF Deploy 2009; Asst Min Shadow Rock Congrl Ch Phoenix AZ 2007-2009; Wing Chapl 944 Fighter Wing USAF Lk AFB 2004-2009; Chapl 56 Fighter Wing Lk AFB 2001-2004; Asst Min Scottsdale Congrl Ch (UCC) AZ 1999-2000; Chapl 158 Corps Spprt Battalion AZ ARNG 1998-2001.

ADER, Thomas Edmund (At) 3596 Liberty Ln, Marietta GA 30062 B Dayton KY 1949 s John & Avenell. U Cinc; BA Mia 1971. D 10/18/1998 Bp Onell Asiselo Soto. m 7/2/1983 Barbara Francis Ader c 2. The Epis Ch Of S Ptr And S Paul Marietta GA 2006-2009. Bro Of S Andr.

ADERS, Magdalena Mary (NJ) 18 Ryers Ln, Matawan NJ 07747 B Red Bank NJ 1958 d Otto & Louise. D 5/9/2015 Bp William H Stokes. c 1.

ADESSA, Denise Mcgovern (Ct) 311 Broad St, Windsor CT 06095 **D Gr Epis Ch Windsor CT 2014-** B Hartford CT 1957 d Robert & Carol. BFA U of Connecticut 1982. D 9/10/2011 Bp Laura Ahrens. m 5/9/1992 Richard F Adessa c 1. D S Jn's Ch Pine Meadow CT 2011-2014. deacondenise@gracewindsor.org

ADINOLFI OJN, Debora (Az) 901 W. Eire St, Chandler AZ 85225 **Asst S Matt's Ch Chandler AZ 2015-** B Castro Valley CA 1958 d Richard & Doreen. BTh Camb 2012; Westcott Hse Theol Coll 2012. D 6/7/2014 P 2/14/2015 Bp Kirk Stevan Smith. dadinolfi@saintmatthewschurch.org

ADINOLFI JR, Jerry Domenick (Kan) 131 Country Estates Rd, Greenville NY 12083 **Chapl AmL Post 291 Greenville NY 2014-2018** B Brooklyn NY 1941 s Jerry & Rose. BS USAF Acad 1963; MS USAF Inst of Tech 1969; Cert GW 1990; MDiv Untd TS Dayton OH 1996; Cert VTS 1996. D 6/29/1996

Bp Herbert Thompson Jr P 4/5/1997 Bp Kenneth Lester Price. m 8/25/2012 Isabella Marjorie Croote c 2. Chapl Coffeyville Reg Med Ctr Coffeyville KS 2000-2011; R S Paul's Epis Ch Coffeyville KS 1998-2011; Cur S Matt's Epis Ch Westerville OH 1996-1997; Reg Dn SE Convoc Dio Kansas 2003-2011; Dio Kansas Topeka KS 2002-2011. AF Assn 1993; Intl Ord of S Lk the Physcn, Chapl 1996. Bp's Cross Dio Kansas 2011. jerryadinolfi@mhcable.com

ADKINS, Edna Fishburne (Ga) Po Box 1601, Tybee Island GA 31328 **D All SS Ch Tybee Island GA 1997-** B Charleston SC 1933 d Francis & Edna. BS Winthrop U 1955; MEd Georgia Sthrn U 1974; EdS U GA 1982. D 1/11/1997 Bp Henry Irving Louttit. m 6/30/1956 Robert Adkins c 2. NAAD.

ADKINS JR, Robert Frederick (CNY) 956 Graylea Cir, Elmira NY 14905 **P Emm Ch Elmira NY 2004-; Ret 1995-** B Detroit MI 1933 s Robert & Mildred. BA U of Massachusetts 1959; MDiv EDS 1963. D 6/22/1963 Bp Anson Phelps Stokes Jr P 5/16/1964 Bp John Melville Burgess. m 12/5/1998 Dagmar Adkins. Vic S Paul's Ch Utica NY 1997-1998; Dist Dn Dio Cntrl New York Liverpool NY 1985-1991; R S Matt's Epis Ch Horseheads NY 1980-1995; R All SS Ch Utica NY 1975-1980; P-in-c S Geo's Epis Ch Chadwicks NY 1971-1975; Cmnty Min Calv Ch Utica NY 1970-1971; P-in-c Ch of the Gd Shpd Oriskany Fls NY 1968-1970; R Gr Epis Ch Waterville NY 1966-1970; Cur Epis Ch Of S Thos Taunton MA 1963-1966. Soc Of S Marg.

ADLER, John Stuart (SwFla) 1406 S. Larkwood Square, Fort Myers FL 33919 **P-in-c S Raphael's Ch Ft Myers Bch FL 2015-** B Harvey IL 1942 s Gordon & Catherine. BS U IL 1970; JD IIT-Chicago-Kent Coll of Law 1973; MDiv SWTS 1989; DMin SWTS 1999. D 6/16/1989 Bp Frank Tracy Griswold III P 12/16/1989 Bp Rogers Sanders Harris. m 8/11/1962 Wanda L Billings c 2. R Iona Hope Epis Ch Ft Myers FL 1998-2014; Vic S Monica's Epis Ch Naples FL 1992-1998; Asst S Bon Ch Sarasota FL 1989-1991; Cn Mssner Ft Myers Dio SW Florida Parrish FL 1993-2000. *Rt START: A NOTEBOOK FOR Ch PLANTING (CO-Auth)*, Seabury Resources, 2001; *A LETTER TO CHRIS: THE FIRST SEVEN YEARS OF A NEW PLANT Cong*, Doctoral Dissertation/SWTS, 1999. johnadler@comcast.net

ADLER, Paul (Pa) 6769 Ridge Ave, Philadelphia PA 19128 **S Alb's Ch Roxborough Philadelphia PA 2015-** B Hackensack NJ 1986 s Carlton & Susan. BA St Olaf Coll 2009; MDiv PrTS 2012; Angl Stds Luth Sem 2013. D 6/8/2013 Bp George Edward Councell P 12/14/2013 Bp William H Stokes. m 10/22/2011 Lindsay Barrett c 1. Gr Ch Madison NJ 2013-2015. padler@churchofstalban.com

ADOLPHSON, Donald Richard (Cal) 552 Old Orchard Dr, Danville CA 94526 **D S Paul's Epis Ch Walnut Creek CA 1993-** B Rockford IL 1930 s Axel & Alida. BS Illinois Inst of Tech 1953; MS U IL 1957; Cert California Sch for Deacons 1983. D 6/25/1983 Bp William Edwin Swing. m 8/18/1956 Nancy Ann Adolphson c 3. D S Mths Epis Ch San Ramon CA 1992-1993, D 1983-1991; unknown 1990-1992.

ADORNO ANDINO, Hector Luis (PR) Iglesia Episcopal Puertorriquena, PO Box 902, Saint Just PR 00978 Puerto Rico **Dio Puerto Rico Trujillo Alto PR 2012-** B Carolina PR 1952 s Ernesto & Maria. BA Universidad Interamericana de PR 1976; MDiv Seminario San Pedro y San Pablo 2009; MA Seminario Evangelico de PR 2012. D 11/22/2009 P 6/27/2010 Bp David Andres Alvarez-Velazquez. m 2/28/1991 Kathryn Iacono Morillo.

ADU-ANDOH, Samuel (Pa) 1121 Serrill Ave, Yeadon PA 19050 **Ch Of S Andr And S Monica Philadelphia PA 1999-** B Sefwi Bodi GH 1948 s Samson & Susana. LTh U of Ghana Legon Gh 1974; DIT TESM 1975; MDiv Sewanee: The U So, TS 1980; STM Sewanee: The U So, TS 1981; PhD Pr 1986. Trans 7/13/1999 Bp Charles Ellsworth Bennison Jr. m 4/20/1974 Margaret Adu-Andoh c 3. Asst S Paul's Ch Doylestown PA 1983-1984.

ADWELL, Lynn (Minn) 334 E Fremont Dr, Tempe AZ 85282 **D Ch Of The Epiph Tempe AZ 2013-** B Des Moines IA 1951 d Dennis & Beverly. D 6/28/2007 Bp James Louis Jelinek. m 8/10/2007 Jerry M Adwell c 2. D Chr Ch Austin MN 2007-2012; Tchr/ Counslr Pacell HS 1998-2006.

ADZIMA, Melissa Lian (Colo) 2015 Glenarm Pl, Denver CO 80205 **S Andr's Ch Denver CO 2014-** B Franklin PA 1986 d Kelly & Edie. BA Gannon U 2008; MDiv VTS 2011. D 12/4/2010 P 6/4/2011 Bp Sean Walter Rowe. m 8/28/2010 Alan Adzima. S Mk's Ch Erie PA 2011-2014.

AFANADOR-KAFURI, Hernan (Ala) 176 Ridgewood Dr., Remlap AL 35133 **Hisp Mssnr Epis Dio Alabama Birmingham AL 2004-; R/P in charge Iglesia de la Gracia Cmnty 2004-** B Dagua CO 1954 s Primitivo & Saide. BA Sem of Cali Cali CO 1977; MA Sem of Manizales CO 1982; U of San Buenaventura of Bogota Colombia 1986; PhD GTF of Indiana 2008. Rec 3/21/2002 as Priest Bp John Wadsworth Howe. m 2/22/2001 Patricia Afanador c 2. Chapl Dio Alabama Birmingham 2004-2014; H Faith Epis Ch Port St Lucie FL 2004; Ch of Our Sav Okeechobee FL 2002-2004. hernan.afanador54@gmail.com

AFFER, Licia (At) 3098 Saint Annes Ln NW, Atlanta GA 30327 **S Anne's Epis Ch Atlanta GA 2014-** B Milan ITALY 1969 MA Universita degli Studi Milan Italy 2001; MDiv GTS 2008. D 10/20/2007 P 5/31/2008 Bp Kirk Stevan Smith. m 9/18/1999 Maurizio Affer c 1. Assoc R All SS Ch Phoenix AZ 2010-2014; Dioc Coordntr Epis Relief and Dvlpmt 2009-2011; Asst to Cathd Dn Dio Arizona Phoenix AZ 2008-2010.

AGAR JR, Ralph Wesley (Neb) 2315 Georgetown Pl, Bellevue NE 68123 **D S Mart Of Tours Ch Omaha NE 2008-; D S Martha's Epis Ch Papillion NE 2006-; Dioc Sfty Off Dio Nebraska Omaha NE 2011-** B Newton IA 1950 s Ralph & Wilma. AA Des Moines Area Cmnty Coll 1970; BS Bellevue U 1998. D 12/23/2006 Bp Joe Goodwin Burnett. m 12/21/1974 Elizabeth Kay Agar c 4.

AGBAJE, John Olasoji (SO) 1 Paddle Ct, Portsmouth VA 23703 B NG 1956 s Joseph & Esther. Med Inst of MN MN 1979; BA U MN 1982; MA U MN 1984; MDiv VTS 1995. D 6/28/1995 P 1/11/1996 Bp James Louis Jelinek. m 10/8/1984 Olubunmi O Agbaje c 3. R S Jas Epis Ch Portsmouth VA 2001-2013; S Edm's Epis Ch Chicago IL 1997-2001; Dio Minnesota Minneapolis MN 1995-1997; S Paul's Ch Brainerd MN 1995.

AGBO, Godwin (Ct) 61 Grove St, Putnam CT 06260 B Udi Nigeria 1965 s Kenneth & Felicia. Trans 7/1/2004 Bp Andrew Donnan Smith. m 11/16/1996 Gladys Agbo c 4. P-in-c S Phil's Epis Ch Putnam CT 2004-2007.

AGGELER, Harold Griffith (Ida) B Ada County ID 1936 s Harold & Margaret. Idaho Diac. Rec 6/1/1998 as Priest Bp John Stuart Thornton. m 7/27/1996 Marilyn Eola Raymer. D S Dav's Epis Ch Caldwell ID 1998-2002.

AGIM, Emeka Ngozi (Tex) 16203 Dryberry Ct, Houston TX 77083 B Kaduna Nigeria 1963 s George & Alice. Dplma in Rel Stds U of Ibadan Nigeria 1996; Dplma in Theol Imm Coll of Theol Ibadan Nigeria 1997; B.A U of Ibadan Nigeria 2002; Mstr in Div Houston Grad TS 2012; Mstr in Div Other 2012. Trans 3/8/2005 Bp Don Adger Wimberly. m 4/17/1999 Julia N Agim c 5. Bp's Fell/Chapl St. Lk's Epis Hosp Houston 2009-2011; Dio Texas Houston TX 2005-2009; The Great Cmsn Fndt Houston TX 2005-2009.

AGNER, Georgia Ellen (Eau) 17823 57th Ave, Chippewa Falls WI 54729 B Thomasville GA 1942 d Garland & Ruth. BD U of Missouri 1965. D 6/9/1991 Bp Roger John White. m 2/4/1967 Hugh Raymond Agner c 2. D S Jn The Div Epis Ch Burlington WI 1991-2004.

AGNEW, Christopher Mack (Va) **Chair, Faith and Ord Cmsn Virginia Coun of Ch Richmond VA 2002-; Ecum Off Dio Virginia Richmond VA 2009-, Assoc Ecum Off 2002-2009; Exec Bd EDEO Ft Myers FL 2008-** B Santa Barbara CA 1944 s Jack & Agnes. BA Buc 1967; MA U of Delaware 1975; PhD U of Delaware 1980; STM GTS 1991. D 6/8/1991 P 6/13/1992 Bp Cabell Tennis. m 4/25/1998 Elizabeth Lewis Agnew. Natl Chair Natl Workshop on Chr Unity 2008-2009; Vic S Paul's Epis Ch Montross VA 2002-2012; P-in-c Vauters Ch Loretto VA 2002-2009; P-in-c S Paul's Owens King Geo VA 2000-2002; S Ptr's Ch In The Great Vlly Malvern PA 1997-1999; Int Ch Of The Ascen Norfolk VA 1997; Int S Mich's Ch Litchfield CT 1995-1997; Int All Hallows Ch Wyncote PA 1995; S Mart's Ch Maywood NJ 1995; Assoc All Ang' Ch New York NY 1992-1995; P-in-c S Mk's Ch Teaneck NJ 1992; D S Thos's Par Newark DE 1991-1992; Assoc Ecum Epis Ch Cntr New York NY 1989-1995; Angl RC Consult USA 1989-1994; SCER Stff GC 1989-1994; Rgstr Dio Delaware Wilmington 1985-1989; Mem Faith and Ord Cmsn Natl Coun Of Ch New York NY 1991-1995, Interfaith Working Grp/Relatns Cmsn 1990-1999, Chr-Jewish Relatns Com 1989-1999. Compiler, "Families of St. Paul's Epis Ch, King Geo Cnty," *Tidewater Virginia Families: A mag of Hist and Genealogy*, 2004; Auth, "Angl Statements on Ecclesiology," *The Riverdale Report*, Forw Mvmt, 1994; Auth, "The Reverend Chas Wharton, Bp Wm White & The Proposed Bk Of Common Pryr," *Angl and Epis Hist*, 1989; Ed, "Var," *The Ecum Bulletin*, The Ecum Off of the Epis Ch, 1989; Auth, "God w Us: Cont Presence," Imm Ch, New Castle, Delaware, 1987; Auth, "An Introductory Hist Of Danville Vt," *Danville Town Report*, Town of Danville, Vermont, 1987; Auth, "The Dio Delaware: A Bicentennial Yearbook," The Dio Deleware, 1985. HSEC 1980; Natl Epis Historians and Archivists 1984; No Amer Acad Of Ecumenists 1990; No Amer Gld Of Change Ringers 1984-1994. Cn Jn W. Davis Awd Natl Epis Historians and Archivists 2014; Faith in Action Awd Virginia Coun of Ch 2013.

AGNEW JR, ML (WLa) 113 Whispering Pines Dr, Bullard TX 75757 **P-in-c S Jn The Bapt Ch Tyler TX 2010-; Ret 2007-** B Meridian MS 1942 s Martin & Josephine. BA U So 1964; MDiv VTS 1967. D 6/24/1967 P 5/23/1968 Bp John Maury Allin. m 8/28/1965 Patricia S Agnew c 2. Int S Cyp's Ch Lufkin TX 2008-2009; S Ann's Ch Kennebunkport ME 1996-1999; Mem Epis Ch Exec Coun 1994-2000; Dn S Mk's Cathd Shreveport LA 1990-2007; R Chr Epis Ch Tyler TX 1981-1990; R Trin Ch Natchez MS 1975-1981; Cn Pstr S Andr's Cathd Jackson MS 1972-1975; Chapl Sewanee Acad Sewanee TN 1970-1972; Cur Chr Ch Bay S Louis MS 1968-1970; Vic Ch Of The Nativ Greenwood MS 1967-1968; Mem Bd of Trst The CPG New York NY 1997-2007; Stndg Com on Admin & Fin Epis Ch Cntr New York NY 1994-2000. mla@embarqmail.com

AGUILAR, Norman (Hond) **Dio Honduras San Pedro Sula 1998-** B 1961 m 4/24/1991 Nimia Enriquez Menjivar c 2.

AGUILAR, Richard (Az) 15650 Miami Lakeway N, Miami Lakes FL 33014 **Vic S Jn's Epis Ch Bisbee AZ 2015-; Vic S Steph's Epis Ch Douglas AZ 2015-** B San Antonio TX 1956 s Raphael & Fela. BA U So 1979; MDiv Epis TS of the SW 1986. D 6/22/1986 Bp Scott Field Bailey P 1/10/1987 Bp John Herbert MacNaughton. m 12/22/1984 Janet F Aguilar c 1. Dio Arizona Phoenix AZ 2013-2015; St Margarets and San Francisco de Asis Epis Ch Hialeah FL

2009-2012; Ch Of The Adv Brownsville TX 2004-2009, 1991-1993; Dio Sthrn Ohio Cincinnati OH 2002-2004; R S Andr's Epis Ch Seguin TX 1996-2002; Asst S Mk's Epis Ch San Antonio TX 1993-1996; Asst S Paul's Epis Ch Brownsville TX 1991-1993, P-in-c 1988-1990; Int Ch Of The Redeem Eagle Pass TX 1987-1988, Asst 1986-1987.

AGUILAR DE RAMIREZ, Ana Roselia (Hond) **Dio Honduras San Pedro Sula 2006-; Iglesia Epis Hondurena San Pedro Sula 2006-; Maestra Educacion Cristiana Iglesia Epis 1991-** B Puerto Cortes 1959 d Enrique & Julia. DIT Catolica Romana; Nuestra Senora De La Paz; DIT Programa Diocena Educaion Teologica. D 10/28/2005 Bp Lloyd Emmanuel Allen. m 12/18/1992 Jorge Ramirez Lara c 4.

AGUSTIN, Miguel (SPh) **Died 4/11/2016** B 1951 c 1. Dio Sthrn Philippines 1976-1988.

AHLENIUS, Robert Orson (Dal) 2541 Pinebluff Drive, Dallas TX 75228 **Ret 1998-** B Chicago IL 1938 s William & Kathryn. BA IL Wesl 1960; MDiv Nash 1963; MA NWU 1970. D 6/1/1963 Bp Albert A Chambers P 12/31/1963 Bp Donald H V Hallock. m 8/13/1960 Barbara B Ahlenius c 4. S Justin's Canton TX 1997-1998; Long-term Supply S Jas' Epis Ch Kemp TX 1996-2003; R St Mk's Epis Ch Mt Pleasant TX 1992-1995; Area Min, Purchase Area Dio Kentucky Louisville KY 1987-1992; Purchase Area Reg Coun Paducah KY 1987-1992; Dio Kansas Topeka KS 1986-1987; R Gr Ch Chanute KS 1975-1987; R Ch of the H Trin Columbus NE 1970-1975; Gr Ch Par -Epis Columbus NE 1970-1975; Cur S Mich And All Ang Ch Mssn KS 1966-1969; Mssnr to Deaf Dio Milwaukee Milwaukee WI 1963-1966. LAND 1984-1987; RWF, Inc 1986-2002.

AHLVIN, Judith L (ECR) 18325 Crystal Dr, Morgan Hill CA 95037 **D Ch Of The H Sprt Campbell CA 2002-, D 1999-2001** B Santa Monica CA 1947 d Lloyd & Lois. BA San Jose St U 1984; BA Sch for Deacons 1998. D 6/24/1998 Bp Richard Lester Shimpfky. m 8/23/1969 Bruce R Ahlvin. S Jn The Div Epis Ch Morgan Hill CA 2002-2003; D S Mk's Epis Ch Santa Clara CA 2000-2002.

AHN, Matthew Y (Los) 10555 Bel Air Dr, Cherry Valley CA 92223 B Taegu KR 1936 s Theodore & Anna. BTh Yonsei U 1964; MA McCormick TS 1970. P 11/1/1975 Bp Robert Claflin Rusack. m 8/22/1967 Grace H Ahn. NCCC 1990-1992; Vic S Nich Korean Mssn Los Angeles CA 1978-1990; St. Nichols Ch Los Angeles CA 1977-1989; Dio Los Angeles Los Angeles CA 1975-1976; Vic S Mary's Ch Chicago IL 1971-1976; Serv Ch In Korea 1966-1969.

AHN, Paul C (Chi) 5801 N Pulaski Rd #348, Chicago IL 60646 B 1938 s Eun & Cha. BD Hankook TS 1965; St Mich Angl Sem 1967. D 8/4/1967 P 9/8/1967 Bp James Winchester Montgomery. m 11/15/1967 Clara Ahn c 2. Vic S Mary's Ch Chicago IL 1980-1985.

✠ AHRENS, The Rt Rev Laura (Ct) 2 Cannondale Dr, Danbury CT 06810 **Bp Suffr of Connecticut Dio Connecticut Meriden CT 2004-** B Wilmington DE 1962 d Herbert & Joan. BA Pr 1984; MDiv Ya Berk 1991; DMin Hartford Sem 2000. D 6/1/1991 Bp David Elliot Johnson P 6/17/1992 Bp Vincent Waydell Warner Con 6/30/2007 for Ct. R S Jas Epis Ch Danbury CT 2000-2007; Assoc R S Lk's Par Darien CT 1995-2000; Assoc R Trin Ch Concord MA 1993-1995; Cur S Ptr's Ch Osterville MA 1991-1993. Soc Of S Jn The Evang.

AHRON, Linda W (Los) 31641 La Novia Ave, San Juan Capistrano CA 92675 **Chapl/Asst P S Marg Of Scotland Par San Juan Capo CA 2014-** B Billings MT 1959 d Thomas & Lorna. BSBA U of Missouri 1981; MDiv GTS 2012; MDiv The GTS 2012. D 6/2/2013 Bp Joseph Jon Bruno P 1/11/2014 Bp Diane Jardine Bruce. m 6/13/2015 Richard Ahron c 2. lracen@smes.org

AIDNIK, Aileen Marie (NCal) 988 Collier Dr, San Leandro CA 94577 **D S Fran Epis Ch Fair Oaks CA 2006-** B Red Bluff CA 1945 d William & Lillian. AA Chabot Coll 1974; BD H Name U 1982; BA Sch for Deacons 1990. D 12/5/1992 Bp William Edwin Swing. m 4/4/1964 Joseph C Aidnik. D S Cuth's Epis Ch Oakland CA 1992-2000. NAAD.

AIKEN JR, Charles Duval (Va) 4210 Hanover Ave, Richmond VA 23221 B Richmond VA 1937 s Charles & Roberta. BS W&L 1960; BD VTS 1963. D 6/15/1963 P 6/5/1964 Bp Robert Fisher Gibson Jr. m 12/30/1967 Barbara G Garnett c 1. S Mk's Ch Richmond VA 1995-2006; Non-par 1975-1989; P-in-c S Dav's Ch Aylett VA 1966-1975; Asst Chr Ch Lancaster VA 1963-1966.

AIKEN, Richard Lloyd (Ct) P.O. Box 1130, Truro MA 02666 B New York NY 1929 s Frank & Margaret. BA Trin 1953; BD VTS 1956; EdM Harv 1967; Tninity Coll 1973. D 6/1/1956 Bp Frederick D Goodwin P 12/1/1956 Bp Harry Sherbourne Kennedy. c 2. Chapl S Mich's Chap So Kent CT 1976-1981, Assoc R 1970-1975; Chapl So Kent Sch So Kent CT 1976-1981; Hd of Sch The Choate Sch Wallingford CT 1971-1976; Chapl, Hd of Sch Choate Sch Wallingford CT 1970-1971; Chair Dept Of Sacr Stds S Paul Sch Concord NH 1965-1970; Mstr Sacr Stds, Chapl, Sch Counslr S Paul Sch Concord NH 1960-1965; Assoc R Of The H Nativ Honolulu HI 1958-1960. Auth, "The Tchg Of Rel," *Findings*; Auth, "The Tchg Of Rel," *So Kent Quarterly*.

AIKEN JR, Warwick (NC) 700 Riverside Dr, Eden NC 27288 **Died 2/1/2016** B Memphis TN 1920 s Warwick & Jean. BA LSU 1942; MTh Dallas TS 1946; PDS 1950. D 7/27/1950 P 7/27/1951 Bp Duncan Montgomery Gray. m 9/7/1946 Marianne S Aiken c 2. R S Lk's Ch Eden NC 1973-1983, R 1955-1967; S Mary's Ch Eden NC 1973-1983, Vic 1958-1967; R Epis Ch of the Gd Shpd

Charleston SC 1970-1973; R Ch Of The Mssh Rockingham NC 1967-1970; M-in-c Ch Of The Epiph Tunica MS 1950-1955. Auth, "Var arts," *Greensboro NC News and Record*, 2000; Auth, *Know the Chr*, Rockingham, NC, 1969; Auth, *The Easter Night Bible Class*, Rockingham, NC, 1968.

AIN, Judith Pattison (ECR) 286 Thompson Rd Rear, Watsonville CA 95076 **Co-Ldr Watsoville Lyme Educ Grp 2011-; Pilgrim Mnstry of Presence among persons living w Tick Borne Di 2004-; Pilgrim Mnstry Of Presence Among Survivors Of Cler Sexual Abuse 1993-; Pilgrim for Justice, Peace, and Healing Emmaus Road Mnstry Watsonville CA 1986-; Pilgrim for Justice, Peace, and Healing Emmaus Road Mnstry Watsonville CA 1986-** B Hollywood CA 1953 d Robert & Diantha. BS Stan 1976; MDiv CDSP 1984. D 6/29/1984 Bp Charles Shannon Mallory. Chapl Global Walk for a Livable Wrld 1990; D All SS Epis Ch Watsonville CA 1988-2000; Chapl Amer/Soviet Peace Walks 1987-1988; Chapl Great Peace March for Global Nuclear Disarmament 1986; Dio El Camino Real Salinas CA 1985; Assoc Calv Epis Ch Santa Cruz CA 1984-1985; Chapl U Ca Santa Cruz 1984-1985. Auth, "Responsive Reading," *A Recon and Healing Serv between the victims of Cler abuse and the RC Dio Oakland*, 2000. EPF 1986; Magd Sacr Ord Of Fools 1984; SNAP 1993. Phi Beta Kappa Stan 1976.

AINSLEY, Matthew Brian (CFla) **Epis Ch Of The Ascen Orlando FL 2015-** D 3/10/2015 P 9/16/2015 Bp Gregory Orrin Brewer.

AINSWORTH, Mark J (Pa) 262 Bent Road, Wyncote PA 19095 **R All Hallows Ch Wyncote PA 1999-; Crspndg Secy Bp White PB Soc 2003-** B London UK 1964 s John & Christine. CTh Oxf GB 1989; MTh Lon GB 1992. Trans 8/1/1997 as Priest Bp Allen Lyman Bartlett Jr. m 5/18/1991 Claudia L Ainsworth. Assoc R Ch Of S Mart-In-The-Fields Philadelphia PA 1997-1999; Asst R Washington Memi Chap Vlly Forge PA 1993-1995; Serv Ch of Engl 1989-1993; COM Dio Pennsylvania Philadelphia PA 2006-2011; Crspndg Secy Soc for the Advancement of Chrsnty in Pennsylvania 2001-2010. MTh w dist Lon 1992.

AIRD, Isabel May (WVa) 1209 1/2 Williams St, Parkersburg WV 26101 **Died 6/20/2017** B Osaka JP 1927 d Hubert & Amy. BA Barnard Coll of Col 1947; MA Syr 1967; BA Med Coll of Virginia 1979. D 6/10/1995 Bp John Henry Smith. m 3/1/1953 Alanson Aird c 1. D The Memi Ch Of The Gd Shpd Parkersburg WV 1995-2002.

AIS, Jean Nesly (Hai) c/o Diocese of Haiti, Boite Postale 1309, Port au Prince Haiti B 1972 D 1/25/2006 P 2/18/2007 Bp Jean Zache Duracin. m 7/17/2008 Marie Christelle O Ais c 1.

AITON JR, Alexander Anthony (Ia) 717 10th St, Ames IA 50010 **R Epis Par of Ames Ames IA 1991-** B Newark NJ 1949 s Alexander & Marie. BBA S Johns U 1972; MDiv GTS 1977; DMin Drew U 1990. D 6/11/1977 P 12/17/1977 Bp George E Rath. c 3. Cn Planned Giving & Ch Dvlpmt Dio Cntrl Pennsylvania Harrisburg PA 1988-1991; R S Jn's Ch Salem NJ 1984-1988; P-in-c H Trin Ch Pennsauken NJ 1982-1984; R Chr Ch Palmyra NJ 1981-1984; Chapl Riverview Hospice Red Bank NJ 1980-1981; Cur S Geo's-By-The-River Rumson NJ 1977-1981; Chapl Monmouth Coll W Long Branch NJ 1977-1979. Hon Cn S Steph Cathd 1991. fralaiton@stjohns-ames.org

AJAX, Kesner (Hai) C/O Agape Flights Acc. #2519, 100 Airport Avenue, Venice FL 34285 **Bp Tharp Inst Les Cayes 2013-; R Ascen Beraud Torbeck 2011-; Dn Bus and Tech Inst Cayes Haiti 2006-; Chapl Dioc Sem Haiti Port au Prince 1996-; Dio Haiti Port-au-Prince HT 1991-, Dioc Stndg Com, Pres 2015-, Dioc Jubilee Off 2007-, Dioc Stndg Com, Secy 2002-2015, Examination Chapl Com, Pres 2002-2015, COM, Secy 1998-2015, Cler Conf, Secy 1998-2013, Dioc Exec Coun, Secy 1998-, Comp Dioc, Pres 1994-, Scouts Assn Dio Haiti, Pres 1991-2000** B Port-au-Prince HT 1961 s Lanier & Elodie. BA Cntr Pilote de Formation Profesional Port-au-Prince HT 1986; BA Haiti TS 1989; MA Boston Coll 1997; DMin U So Sewanee 2008. D 7/22/1990 P 3/14/1991 Bp Luc Anatole Jacques Garnier. m 7/29/1993 Jardine Hyppolite Ajax c 1. R Epiph Port au Prince Haiti 2004-2006; Dir H Trin Trade Sch Port au Prince Haiti 2003-2006; R St. Mart of Tours Port au Prince Haiti 1998-2003; R Annunc Par Darbonne 1993-1998; R St Peters Par Mirebalais Haiti 1991-1993. Auth, "A Pstr Response to Haitian Voudou: A nightmare for Rel leaders seeking true converts to Chrsnty," Lambert Acad Pub, 2013. EPF 1989; Soc S Margareth 1985; Soc of S Jn the Evang 1987. kesnerajax@hotmail.com

AKAMATSU, Mary Catherine (Ala) St Matthew's Episcopal Church, 786 Hughes Rd, Madison AL 35758 B Tampa FL 1966 d Robert & Mary Ann. BS U of No Alabama 1988; MDiv Sewanee: The U So, TS 2012; MDiv U So TS 2012. D 5/17/2012 P 12/1/2012 Bp John Mckee Sloan Sr. m 6/14/2003 Jeffrey Clyde Akamatsu c 2. St Thos Epis Ch Huntsville AL 2015-2016; Chr Epis Ch Albertville AL 2013-2014; St. Matt's Epis Ch Madison AL 2012-2013.

AKER, Edwina Sievers (Mont) 32413 Skidoo Ln, Polson MT 59860 B Albuquerque NM 1938 d Edwin & Dorothy. BA U of Montana 1959. D 10/30/1982 P 11/17/1984 Bp David Bell Birney IV. m 10/18/1959 Charles Aker c 2. Int R Chr Epis Ch Kalispell MT 2008-2009; Int S Andr's Epis Ch Polson MT 2006-2007, 1996-2004; Stndg Com Dio Montana Helena MT 1997-2000; Vic Ch Of H Nativ Meridian ID 1992-1993; Vic S Jas Ch Mtn Hm ID 1988-1992; COM Dio Idaho Boise ID 1985-1991; Chapl S Alphonsus RC Hosp Boise

ID 1984-1988; D S Steph's Boise ID 1982-1984; Chapl S Lk Hosp Boise ID 1982-1983.

AKES, Amanda Ann (WA) Grace Church, 1607 Grace Church Rd, Silver Spring MD 20910 **Asst Gr Epis Ch Silver Sprg MD 2013-** B Slidell LA 1984 d Robert & Patricia. BA St Edw's U 2006; MDiv EDS 2010; MDiv EDS 2010. D 3/5/2011 P 9/10/2011 Bp Mark Sean Sisk. S Jas Ch Glastonbury CT 2011-2013.

AKIN, Mary Anne (Ala) 3525 Great Oak Lk Ln, Birmingham AL 35223 B Nashville TN 1950 d Earl & Mary. BA Webster Coll 1972; MDiv Candler TS Emory U 1975; Cert Amer Assn of Profsnl Chapl 1992. D 9/9/1977 Bp Bennett Jones Sims P 7/27/1978 Bp Furman Charles Stough. Chapl S Martins-In-The-Pines Ret Comm Birmingham AL 2012-2015, 1995-1997; Assoc Ch Of The Nativ Epis Huntsville AL 2007-2012; Assoc S Steph's Ch Richmond VA 2006-2007; Chapl S Thos Hosp Nashville TN 2002-2005; Assoc R Ch Of The H Comf Vienna VA 1999-2002; R Chr Ch Milford DE 1998; Dir Pstr Serv S Mart's Ret Cmnty Birmingham AL 1995-1998; Cn Pstr S Jn's Epis Cathd Knoxville TN 1994-1995; Dir Pstr Care Childrens Hosp Knoxville TN 1988-1994; R S Jas The Less Madison TN 1986-1987; Pstr TS Sewanee U So TS Sewanee TN 1985-1986; Assoc S Andrews's Epis Ch Birmingham AL 1982-1984; Dir Pstr Care So Highlands Hosp Birmingham AL 1979-1984; S Alb's Ch Hoover AL 1979-1982; Chapl Bapt Montclair Hosp Birmingham AL 1977-1978. Auth, "Listening to the Elder Voices, Chapl Today," *Vol. 18 #1,* 2002; Auth, "Saturday Night," *Wmn Uncommon Prayers,* Morehouse, 2000; Auth, "Mudsong," *Journ of Pstr Care,* 1993. AEHC Natl Secretar 1992; Bd Cert Chapl, Amer Assn of Profsnl. MDiv mcl Emory U 1975; BA cl Webster Coll 1972.

AKIN, Mary Barbara (NwPa) 201 Hillcrest Cir, Grove City PA 16127 B Chicago IL 1932 d Richard & Margaret. BA S Xavier U Chicago 1962; MA U Chi 1965; PhD U Chi 1970; Cert SWTS 1978. D 6/16/1979 P 10/5/1985 Bp Donald James Davis. Mem Ch Of The Epiph Grove City PA 1985-2008; Dio NW Pennsylvania Erie PA 1985-1988; D Ch Of The Redeem Hermitage PA 1979-1983; Epis Ch Cntr New York NY 1985-1991. "An Intro to Hist Resrch," Copley Pub Grp, 1991.

AKINA, Eleanore Mayo (Haw) 1237 Mokulua Dr, Kailua HI 96734 **Died 3/29/2016** B Philadelphia PA 1921 d Leroy & Charlotte. BA Swarthmore Coll 1942; MD U of Pennsylvania 1945. D 11/11/1983 Bp Edmond Lee Browning. Ret 1999-2016; D Emm Epis Ch Kailua HI 1983-1999.

AKINKUGBE, Felix Olagboye (FtW) 2995 Celian Dr, Grand Prairie TX 75052 B Ondo NG 1944 s Emmanuel & Simisola. BA Bowie St U 1972; MA U Pgh 1974; Emml of Theol Ibadan Ng 1993. Trans 2/6/2001 Bp Jack Leo Iker. m 8/30/1971 Margaret Akinkugbe c 3. Vic Dio Ft Worth Ft Worth TX 2000-2006; S Phil The Apos Arlington TX 2000-2006; Cur S Jas's Epis Ch Grand Prairie TX 1999; Asst P S Lk's In The Meadow Epis Ch Ft Worth TX 1998-1999; Serv Ch Of Nigeria 1989-1998. Auth, "The Living Faith," Ibadan U Press, 1997; Auth, "Living w God In Pryr Fasting And Faith," Ibadan U Press, 1997. Bro Of S Andrews 1999; Full Gospel Busmn Fllshp Intl 1990; Rotary Club Intl 1993. DD Nash 2012; Cn of the Cathd Ondo Dio Ch of Nigeria Angl 1997.

AKINS, Keith Edward (Kan) 900 Sw 31st St Apt 219, Topeka KS 66611 **D Dio Kansas Topeka KS 1993-** B Salina KS 1926 s Murphy & Bertha. BS Emporia St U 1950; MA U MI 1957. D 12/11/1993 Bp William Edward Smalley. m 9/3/1948 Reeta DeAun Akins c 6. Gr Cathd Topeka KS 1993-2009. Hall of Fame Awd Kansas St HS Activities Assn.

AKIYAMA, Diana D (Haw) 2745 Glendower Ave, Los Angeles CA 90027 **Kohala Epis Mssn Kapaau HI 2015-; Dir, Rel and Sprtl Life Occ Los Angeles CA 2003-** B Wheeler OR 1958 d Saburo & Betty. BS U of Oregon 1981; MDiv CDSP 1988; PhD USC 2001. D 6/19/1988 P 4/25/1989 Bp Rustin Ray Kimsey. m 4/13/1991 Michael J Jackson. Vic S Jas Epis Ch Kamuela HI 2015; All SS Ch Pasadena CA 1997; Assoc Dn Stanford Memi Ch Stanford CA 1988-1995.

AKRIDGE, Alan M (Ga) 108 Worthing Rd, St Simons Island GA 31522 **R S Mk's Ch Brunswick GA 2009-** B Mobile AL 1967 s David & Ann. MA VTS 1998; MDiv Wake Forest U 2003. D 5/29/2004 Bp Bob Johnson P 12/4/2004 Bp Porter Taylor. m 9/26/1998 Kathleen L Akridge c 2. Assoc R S Alb's Ch Hickory NC 2004-2009.

ALAGNA, Frank J (NY) Po Box 1, Rhinecliff NY 12574 B Brooklyn NY 1945 s Anthony & Marie. MDiv Maryknoll TS 1970; ThM Maryknoll TS 1971; MA U of Connecticut 1977; PhD U of Connecticut 1978. Rec 12/19/1982 as Priest Bp Paul Moore Jr. m 4/20/2015 John Francis Meehan c 1. P-in-c Ch Of The H Cross Kingston NY 2011-2017, P-in-c 2011-; Int S Andr's Ch Beacon NY 2008-2010; Vic Dio New York New York NY 1999-2014; S Marg's Ch Staatsburg NY 1999-2006; Serv RC 1970-1979.

ALAN, Stacy (Chi) 5540 S Woodlawn Ave, Chicago IL 60637 **S Helena's Ch Burr Ridge IL 2016-; Chapl Brent Hse (U Of Chicago) Chicago IL 2005-; Prov Coordntr Prov V Higher Educ Mnstrs 2014-** B Lafayette IN 1964 d Franklin & Eliene. BA Seattle U 1985; MDiv UTS 1992; GTS 1997. D 6/13/1998 P 12/19/1998 Bp Richard Frank Grein. c 2. Asst to R S Lk's Par Kalamazoo MI 1999-2004; Coordntr of Hlth Prog Casa de Amistad So Bend IN 1998-1999; Coordntr of Vol Prog Ch Of The H Apos New York NY 1992-1998;

Cathd Chapt Cathd Of S Jas Chicago IL 2010-2012. Alpha Sigma Nu 1983; Soc of Campus Ministers 2014.

ALAVA VILLAREAL, Geronimo (EcuL) Casilla 0901-5250, Guayaquil Ecuador **Litoral Dio Ecuador Guayaquil 2004-** B Guayquil ECUADOR 1968 s Geronimo & Lillian. Litoral Sem Guayaquil Ec 2001. D 7/14/2002 P 10/12/2004 Bp Terencio Alfredo Morante-Espana. m 7/23/1988 Cecilia Garcia c 4.

ALBANO, Randolph Nolasco (Haw) St. Paul's Episcopal Church, 229 Queen Emma Square, Honolulu HI 96813 **S Pauls Ch Honolulu HI 1999-; Vic S Pauls Ch Honolulu HI 1999-; Cn for Filipino Mnstry The Epis Ch in Hawaii Honolulu HI 2009-, Mem, Cathd Chapt 2009-, Stndg Com 2009-, COM 2005-2006, Dioc Coun Mem 2003-2006, 2000-2008** B Bacarra Ilocos Norte PH 1955 s Alejo & Florencia. AA Trin of Quezon City PH 1975; BTh S Andrews TS Manila PH 1980; MDiv S Andrews TS Manila PH 1988. Rec 6/10/2000 as Priest Bp Richard Sui On Chang. m 1/2/1989 Minina Santiago Albano c 2. Serv Philippine Indep Ch 1980-1990; Chapl, Intl Seafarers' Cntr Dio Texas Houston TX 1991-1999; Chapl, Seamen Ch Inst NY/NJ Dio Newark Newark NJ 1990-1991. Soc of the Gd Shpd Phillipines 2000.

ALBERCA MERINO, Francisco Venito (Eur) Via Napoli, 58, Roma, Italy 00184 Italy B Loja Ecuador 1966 s Tomas & Carmen. Bachillerato en Filosofia Seminario Mayor Reina de El Cisne; Laurea in Filosofia The Pontifical Gregorian Universi; PhD Università Cattolica del Sacro Cuore. Rec 5/29/2014 as Priest Bp Pierre W Whalon. m 8/3/2005 Paula Luca c 2.

ALBERGATE, Scott P (Pa) 249 N. Belfield Ave, Havertown PA 19083 **Hisp Mnstry T/F S Jn's Ch Norristown PA 2012-; Counsel for Incorporation Dio Pennsylvania Philadelphia PA 2014-, 2012-** B Glen Rock NJ 1955 s Alfred & Evelyn. BA Seton Hall U 1977; JD New York Law Sch 1986; MDiv Nash 2000; DMin SWTS 2007; MFT Coun for Relationships 2015. D 12/18/1999 P 6/17/2000 Bp Jack Leo Iker. m 9/15/2001 Katherine K Albergate. R S Paul's Ch New Orleans LA 2009-2012; Cn Dio Louisiana New Orleans LA 2007-2009, Cler Dep to GC 2011-2012, COM 2009-2012; R The Epis Ch Of The Ascen Middletown OH 2006-2007; R S Jn's Ch Gap PA 2003-2005; R S Lk's Ch Eastchester NY 2001-2003; Asst R S Mart In The Fields Ch Keller TX 2000-2001. "Sermon, Dreamers," *Preaching As Prophetic Calling: Sermons That Wk XII,* Morehouse Pub, 2004; Auth, "Var arts," *Living Ch.* Amer Assn of Mar and Fam Therapists 2013; The Angl Soc 1998. Polly Bond Awd ECom 2001; MDiv cl Nash 2000.

ALBERS, Barbara Ann (RG) 8540 S Southpoint Rd, Empire MI 49630 B Salina KS 1943 d George & Christine. Wstrn Michigan U; Whitaker TS 1991. D 6/21/1991 Bp Henry Irving Mayson. m 5/5/2013 Arlo Dean Albers c 2. Bound Together Inc Auburn Hills MI 2000-2005; All SS Epis Ch Pontiac MI 1995; Nativ Cmnty Epis Ch Holly MI 1993-1995; D S Mary's-In-The-Hills Ch Lake Orion MI 1991-1993. Auth, "Homelessness," *Meditations on Homelessness,* 1992. "Vill Warrior" Awd for express Mnstry to Afro-Amer c Pontiac Cmnty 2000; Cy Green Awd for Wk in Afr Amer Cmnty 1999; Cy Green Awd for Wk in Afr Amer Cmnty 1999; Dioc Jubilee Off Dio Michigan 1996.

ALBERT II, Edwin Edward (SO) 1924 Timberidge Dr., Loveland OH 45140 B Bangor ME 1957 BA S Jos Sem Coll 1981; MDiv Notre Dame Sem Grad TS 1985; MBA U Cinc 1992. Rec 6/3/2001 as Priest Bp Herbert Thompson Jr. m 8/20/1988 Susan Gibson c 3. S Barn Epis Ch Cincinnati OH 2005-2011.

ALBERT, Hilario A (NY) 535 King St, Port Chester NY 10573 **P-in-c Dio New York New York NY 2015-; P-in-c S Ptr's Ch Port Chester NY 2004-** B La Romana DO 1947 s Huntley & Susan. MDiv NYTS; BA RUM Mayaguez PR 1974. D 3/8/2003 P 9/20/2003 Bp Mark Sean Sisk. m 4/1/1995 Sandra Gonzalez Albert c 3. Asst P St. Matt & St. Tim New York NY 2003-2004; D Ch Of The H Trin New York NY 2003. stpeterspc@gmail.com

ALBERT III, Jules Gilmore (La) 6249 Canal Blvd, New Orleans LA 70124 B New Orleans LA 1953 s Jules & Nancy. D 12/4/2010 Bp Morris King Thompson Jr. m 6/5/1976 Margaret Albert c 2. D S Paul's Ch New Orleans LA 2010-2013.

ALBINGER JR, William Joseph (Haw) B 1945 B.A. Yale Coll 1967; J.D. U of Pennsylvania 1972; M.Div. Drew U 2002. D 9/13/2003 Bp John Palmer Croneberger P 4/17/2004 Bp Martin Gough Townsend. m 4/10/2005 Mark Stephen Ledoux. R H Innoc' Epis Ch Lahaina HI 2005-2014; Int S Geo's Ch Lee MA 2004-2005; Cur S Jn's Epis Ch Boonton NJ 2003-2004.

ALBRECHT, John Herman (Mich) 293 Scottsdale Dr, Troy MI 48084 B Detroit MI 1928 s Herman & Esther. BA Amh 1954; MDiv VTS 1959. D 6/13/1959 Bp Robert McConnell Hatch P 5/1/1961 Bp Robert Lionne DeWitt. m 11/7/1986 Christa Tews Albrecht c 5. Long-Term Supply S Dav's Ch Southfield MI 2007-2008; Asst Chr Ch Detroit MI 2004-2007; Long-Term Supply S Columba Ch Detroit MI 1998-2004; R Trin Ch St Clair Shrs MI 1996-1998; R S Mary's-In-The-Hills Ch Lake Orion MI 1973-1981; R S Jn's Ch Royal Oak MI 1969-1973; R S Kath's Ch Williamston MI 1965-1969; Asst Min Chr Ch Cranbrook Bloomfield Hills MI 1961-1965, Marquis Fllshp 1959-1960; Cathd Chapt Dio Michigan Detroit MI 1968-1970, Dn, Capital Convoc 1968-1969, MRI Cmsn 1964-1965. Auth, "Two Sermons," *Seabury Press,* Seabury Press, 1970. Bd Dir Cranbrook Sch Alum Coun 2013; Mem Michigan St Bd Mar Counselors

1977; Fell Coll of Preachers, Washington, D.C. 1969; Opening Pryr U.S. Hse of Representatives 1968.

ALBRETHSEN, Karen Anne (Nev) 777 Sage St, Elko NV 89801 **P S Paul's Epis Ch Elko NV 2008-** B Jerome ID 1954 d Holger & Anne Jeanette. BA Adams St Coll 1976; MLIS U CB 1991. D 10/24/2008 P 5/9/2009 Bp Dan Thomas Edwards. m 6/27/1987 Frederick B Lee c 7.

ALBRIGHT, John Taylor (WMass) 525 Suffield St, Agawam MA 01001 **Southwick Cmnty Epis Ch Southwick MA 1998-** B Norfolk VA 1957 s John & Catharine. S Marys Sem and U; BA U of Maryland 1979; MDiv Gordon-Conwell TS 1988. D 6/20/1998 P 12/19/1998 Bp Gordon Scruton. m 6/21/1986 Katharine F Albright c 2. Assoc S Mk's Epis Ch E Longmeadow MA 2000-2006, Cur 1998-1999. glor2god@aol.com

ALBRIGHT, Meredyth L (FdL) **R S Aug's Epis Ch Rhinelander WI 2016-** B Ripon WI 1957 d Donald & Grace. MDiv Nash 2011. D 12/17/2011 P 6/30/2012 Bp Russell Edward Jacobus. S Paul's Ch Marinette WI 2015-2016; Ch of the Nativ-St Steph Newport PA 2013-2015; Int Trin Epis Ch Oshkosh WI 2012-2013.

ALBRIGHT, Timothy Scott (Be) 383 N Hunter Hwy, Drums PA 18222 **Supply P-in-c No Par Epis Ch St. Clair PA 2012-** B Pottstown PA 1959 s Clarence & Barbara. BS Leh 1981; Dio Bethlehem 2008; Dplma GTS 2009. D 2/2/2009 Bp John Palmer Croneberger P 9/29/2009 Bp Paul Victor Marshall. m 6/18/1983 Sharon L Albright c 2. Supply P-in-c S Jas Ch Shuykl Haven PA 2012-2014; Cur S Ptr's Epis Ch Hazleton PA 2009-2012.

ALBURY, Ronald Graham (NJ) 28 Maine Trl, Medford NJ 08055 **Pstr Assoc S Ptr's Ch Medford NJ 2003-; Ret 1995-** B Cranford NJ 1930 s Charles & Mabelle. BA Ripon Coll Ripon WI 1951; BD SWTS 1954; STM Tem 1958; EdD NYU 1976. D 5/8/1954 Bp Wallace J Gardner P 11/20/1954 Bp Alfred L Banyard. m 5/27/2000 Daryl R Albury c 7. Chapl for Ret Cler Dio New Jersey Trenton NJ 1995-2000; R H Cross Epis Ch Plainfield NJ 1970-1995; R Chr Ch Epis Shrewsbury NJ 1964-1970; R Chr Ch So Amboy NJ 1957-1964; Cur Gr Ch Merchantville NJ 1954-1957. Auth, "arts," *Living Ch*, Vintage Voice, 2006. Cmnty of S Jn the Bapt 1994. Baha'i Race Unity Day Awd 1985; Hon Cn Trin Cathd 1979.

ALCORN, Jim (Tex) 906 Sugar Mountain Ct, Sugar Land TX 77478 **Died 3/11/2017** B Washington DC 1942 s James & Frances. Geo 1962; BS Trin U San Antonio 1965; MDiv Sewanee: The U So, TS 1971. D 6/8/1971 Bp Richard Earl Dicus P 12/19/1971 Bp Harold Cornelius Gosnell. c 2. Dir Pstr Care Cullen Mem Chap Houston TX 1986-2005; Chapl/Dir Pstr Care and Educ S Lk's Epis Hosp Houston TX 1986-2005; Dir Pstr Care S Lk's Epis Hosp Houston TX 1986-2005; R Ch Of The Epiph Houston TX 1982-1986; R Ch Of The Epiph Kingsville TX 1977-1982; S Lk's Epis Ch San Antonio TX 1975-1977; Chapl/Dir Texas Mltry Inst San Antonio TX 1974-1977; Chapl Texas Mltry Inst TX 1974-1977; Assoc Chr Epis Ch San Antonio TX 1971-1974. Auth, *AIDS: One Life to Give*; Contrib, *Essays on Human Relatns*.

ALDANA ROJAS, Javier (Colom) **Iglesia Epis En Colombia Bogota 2016-** B 1966 s Juan & Alicia. Rec 2/2/2006 as Priest Bp Francisco Jose Duque-Gomez. m 11/24/2006 Claudia del Pilar Campus Figuitiva c 1.

ALDAY, Kristen Nowell (CFla) 1017 E. Robinson Street, Orlando FL 32801 **Archd Dio Cntrl Florida Orlando FL 2010-** B Dalton GA 1962 d David & Hazel. BA Rol 1985; MA Asbury TS 2010. D 12/18/2004 Bp John Wadsworth Howe. m 3/26/1983 Thomas G Alday. D Epis Ch Of The H Sprt Apopka FL 2005-2007. Co-Auth, "30 Days Towards Healing Your Grief," *30 Days Towards Healing Your Grief*, Ch Pub, 2017. kalday@cfdiocese.org

ALDER, Steve (U) 2215 Molino Ave Apt A, Signal Hill CA 90755 **D The Par Ch Of S Lk Long Bch CA 2014-** B Albuquerque NM 1956 s John & Marilyn. BA Pepperdine U 1977. D 6/10/2006 Bp Carolyn Tanner Irish. m 10/3/2008 Richard John Grennon. Assn for Epis Deacons 2004.

ALDRICH, Dawn Marie (NMich) 1310 Ashmun St, Sault Sainte Marie MI 49783 **D S Jas Ch Of Sault S Marie Sault Sainte Marie MI 2006-** B Grand Rapids MI 1938 d Myron & Dawn. D 5/28/2006 Bp James Arthur Kelsey. m 7/27/1991 Robert Paul Aldrich c 3.

ALDRICH JR, Kenneth Davis (NJ) 400 4th St., Huntingdon PA 16652 B Philadelphia PA 1941 s Kenneth & Janice. U of Paris-Sorbonne FR 1962; BA Trin Hartford CT 1963; MDiv PDS 1966; PrTS 1968; STM PDS 1973; DMin GTF 1997. D 4/23/1966 P 10/29/1966 Bp Alfred L Banyard. m 5/4/1974 Sharon C Aldrich c 3. Dn Monmouth Convoc Dio New Jersey Trenton NJ 1999-2002, Dioc Coun 1989-1998; Pres Grtr Red Bank Min Red Bank NJ 1990-1996; R Trin Epis Ch Red Bank NJ 1980-2005; Chapt Major Trin Cathd Trenton NJ 1978-1980; Chapl Rowan St Coll Glassboro NJ 1971-1974; R S Lk's Ch Westville NJ 1970-1979; Vic S Jn The Evang Ch Blackwood NJ 1968-1970; Cur H Trin Ch Collingswood NJ 1966-1968. Auth, *Television Dialogue*, WPVI-TV, 1973; Auth, "Serv rendered in Rite I Lang," *The Cranmer Gld*; Auth, "arts," *LivCh*. Mercersburg Soc 1994.

ALDRICH, Robert Paul (NMich) **P S Jas Ch Of Sault S Marie Sault Sainte Marie MI 1986-** B Sault Ste Marie MI 1943 s Paul & Virginia. BA Cntrl Michigan U 1965; MA Cntrl Michigan U 1967. D 11/28/2005 P 5/28/2006 Bp James Arthur Kelsey. m 7/27/1991 Dawn Marie Aldrich.

ALEXANDER, Bruce Ames (Me) 292 Alexander Rd, Dresden ME 04342 **Vic 1995-** B Rockland ME 1930 s Leonard & Nettie. D 5/28/1983 Bp Frederick Barton Wolf P 7/5/1998 Bp Chilton Richardson Knudsen. m 9/9/1953 Marjorie Alexander c 4. St Mths Epis Ch Brunswick ME 1995-2005; R's Vic Chr Ch Gardiner ME 1983-2000.

ALEXANDER, Conor Matthew (SVa) **P-in-c S Fran Ch Virginia Bch VA 2010-; Ecum Off Dio Sthrn Virginia Newport News VA 2014-, Disciplinary Bd 2013-, Liturg Cmsn 2013-** B Syracuse NY 1978 s Larry & Sandra. BS Cor 2001; MDiv VTS 2007. D 6/9/2007 Bp Gladstone Bailey Adams III P 12/10/2007 Bp John Clark Buchanan. m 5/20/2006 Samantha Ann Vincent-Alexander. Asst Chr and S Lk's Epis Ch Norfolk VA 2007-2010; Temporary Worker Don Richard Assoc 2007; Pres of the Bd Chanco on the Jas Surry VA 2011-2013. Epis Dioc Ecum and Interreligious Off 2015.

ALEXANDER II, George Wilson (At) 3468 Summerford Ct, Marietta GA 30062 B Louisville KY 1936 s Jesse & Reella. BA Cntrl St U 1958; BD Sthrn Bapt TS 1962; MA Col 1971; DMin Pittsburgh TS 1984; MPA Georgia St U 1990. D 10/23/1993 P 1/1/1994 Bp Frank Kellogg Allan. m 5/22/1965 Norma J Alexander. All SS Epis Ch Atlanta GA 1993-2001; Serv Bapt Ch 1962-1986.

ALEXANDER, Gerald G (Fla) 4311 Ortega Forest Dr, Jacksonville FL 32210 B Jacksonville FL 1948 s John & Claudia. BA Wofford Coll 1970; JD Stetson U 1973; MDiv GTS 1981. D 6/7/1981 Bp Frank S Cerveny P 1/24/1982 Bp Paul Moore Jr. Assoc All SS Epis Ch Jacksonville FL 2008-2013; R Ch of S Jude Wantagh NY 1996-1998; Int Trin Epis Ch Roslyn NY 1995-1996; S Paul's Ch Glen Cove NY 1994-1996; Asst St. Barth Ch New York NY 1993-1995; Asst Ch Of The Gd Shpd New York NY 1989-1992; Vic Calv and St Geo New York NY 1981-1989.

ALEXANDER, Jane Biggs (WLa) 2015 East Northside Dr., Jackson MS 39211 B Jackson MS 1939 d Thomas & Louise. Tul 1959; CAS Ya Berk 1990; MDiv Yale DS 1990; BD Millsaps Coll 1997. D 5/31/1990 Bp Duncan Montgomery Gray Jr P 1/19/1991 Bp Arthur Edward Walmsley. m 8/8/1959 John Davidson Alexander c 3. Cn Pstr S Mk's Cathd Shreveport LA 1994-2006; Asst S Jas's Ch W Hartford CT 1991-1993; St Jas Epis Ch Hartford CT 1991-1993; Ya Berk New Haven CT 1990-1991; S Alb's Epis Ch St Petersburg FL 1990-1991; Exec Asst to Dn S Paul And S Jas New Haven CT 1990-1991; Exam Chapl Dio Wstrn Louisiana Alexandria LA 1998-2006; COM Dio Connecticut Meriden CT 1992-1994. Hicks Prize Ya Berk 1990.

ALEXANDER, Jason L (Ark) The Episcopal Diocese of Arkansas, P.O. Box 164668, Little Rock AR 72216 **Cn Dio Arkansas Little Rock AR 2009-** B Hot Springs AR 1978 s Drew & Twylla. BA Hendrix Coll 2000; MDiv CDSP 2007. D 12/4/2006 Bp Mark Lawrence Macdonald P 6/7/2007 Bp Marc Handley Andrus. m 7/30/2005 Kathryn Bellm c 3. Cur Trin Cathd Little Rock AR 2007-2009. jalexander@episcopalarkansas.org

⊕ **ALEXANDER, The Rt Rev J Neil** (At) 335 Tennessee Avenue, Sewanee TN 37383 **Dn, Prof of Liturg, Quintard Prof of Theol Sewanee U So TS Sewanee TN 2012-, 1997-2001** B Winston-Salem NC 1954 s Jasper & Jeannette. BA Moravian TS 1976; M.Mus. U of So Carolina 1979; MDiv Luth Theol Sthrn Sem 1980; ThD GTS 1993; DD GTS 2001; DD Sewanee: The U So, TS 2002. D 6/11/1988 P 11/18/1988 Bp George Phelps Mellick Belshaw Con 7/7/2001 for At. c 3. Bp of Atlanta Dio Atlanta Atlanta GA 2001-2012; Adj Prof Of Liturg Stds Drew U Madison NJ 1999-2009; Trin Ch Prof Of Liturg & Preaching The GTS New York NY 1995-1997, Trin Ch Assoc Prof Of Liturg & Preaching 1989-1995; Vstng Prof Berkeley Divnity Sch at Yale 1987-1988; Prof Waterloo Luth Sem Can 1984-1987. Auth, "Celebrating Liturg Time: Days, Weeks, and Seasons," Ch Pub, 2014; Auth, "This Far By Gr: A Bp's Journey w Questions about Homosexuality," Cowley, 2003; Auth, "w Ever Joyful Hearts," Ch Pub Inc, 1999; Auth, "Waiting For The Coming," Pstr Press, 1993; Auth, "Time & Cmnty," Pstr Press, 1990; Auth, "Luther's Reform Of The Daily Off," *Wrshp*, 1983. Acad Of Homil 1984; Liturg Conf 1978; No Amer Acad Of Liturg 1982; Societas Liturgica 1982. Hon Cn Theol Dio Bethlehem 1986. jnalexan@sewanee.edu

ALEXANDER, John David (RI) 974 Pine St, Seekonk MA 02771 **R S Steph's Ch Providence RI 2000-; Dioc BEC Dio Rhode Island Providence RI 2017-, COM 2008-2014, Cmsn on Congrl Dvlpmt 2001-2004; Mem of Coun GAS Amer Branch 2003-; P Assoc Cmnty of S Mary's Estrn Prov Greenwich NY 1999-** B Belfast Northern Ireland 1958 s Harold & Joyce. PhD Bos; BA JHU 1979; MA JHU 1980; MDiv VTS 1992; STM Nash 2004. D 6/13/1992 P 6/5/1993 Bp Allen Lyman Bartlett Jr. m 5/21/1988 Elizabeth Mary Alexander c 2. R Ch Of The Ascen Staten Island NY 1994-2000; Cur S Mary's Ch Wayne PA 1992-1994; Superior SocMary Amer Reg 2011-2013; Mem of Coun SocMary Amer Reg 2010-2011; Mem of Bd Gvnr Staten Island Coun of Ch Staten Island New York 1997-2000. Auth, "Springtime of the Sprt," Forw Mvmt, 2016; Auth, "Dawn from on High," Forw Mvmt, 2014; Auth, "Environ Sin and Recon in the BCP 1979," *Ambassadors for God: Envisioning Recon Rites for the 21st Century [Liturg Stds Five]*, Ch Pub, 2010. CBS USA 2012; GAS, Amer Branch 2003; Soc of King Chas the Mtyr, Amer Reg 2009; SocMary, Amer Reg 1998; SSC 1994. Ord of Laud Soc of King Chas the Mtyr, Amer Reg 2013; Phi Beta Kappa JHU 1979. rector@sstephens.necoxmail.com

ALEXANDER, Jonna Ruth (Ore) 2220 Cedar St, Berkeley CA 94709 B La Jolla CA 1952 d Roderick & Ruth. BS Portland St U 1983; Doctor of Naturopathic Med Natl Coll of Naturopathic Med 1987; Cert Angl Stds CDSP 2013; MDiv CDSP 2015. D 6/21/2014 P 6/13/2015 Bp Michael Hanley.

ALEXANDER, Kathryn Bellm (Ark) CHRIST CHURCH, 509 SCOTT ST, LITTLE ROCK AR 72201 **Assoc R Chr Epis Ch Little Rock AR 2007-; Pres, Stndg Com Dio Arkansas Little Rock AR 2013-** B Long Beach CA 1972 s James & Claire. BA Mills Coll 1995; MA Harvard DS 1998; PhD Grad Theol Un 2012. D 6/4/2005 P 12/3/2005 Bp William Edwin Swing. m 7/30/2005 Jason L Alexander c 3. Bk, "Saving Beauty: A Theol Aesthetics of Nature," Fortress Press, 2014. AAR 2013. Fell ECF 2002.

ALEXANDER, Patricia Phaneuf (WA) 8804 Postoak Rd, Potomac MD 20854 **Prof VTS Alexandria VA 2017-; P Assoc Imm Ch-On-The-Hill Alexandria VA 2013-; Middle and Upper Sch Chapl S Andr's Epis Sch Potomac MD 2011-** B Boston MA 1966 d Edgar & Dorothy. BA Ya 1988; MA Mid 1994; MDiv VTS 2001. D 3/10/2001 Bp Richard Frank Grein P 9/16/2001 Bp Mark Sean Sisk. m 8/22/1998 Randy Alexander c 1. P Assoc Par of Chr the Redeem Pelham NY 2011-2013; Vic Gr Ch Bronx NY 2004-2011; Asst Min S Matt's Ch Bedford NY 2001-2005; Personal Resrch Asst to the Archbp of Cbury Ch of Engl London Engl 1999-2000. MDiv cl VTS 2001; BA mcl Ya 1988. palexander@saes.org

ALEXANDER JR, Randy (Va) 3606 Seminary Rd, Alexandria VA 22304 **Prof VTS Alexandria VA 2016-; R Imm Ch-On-The-Hill Alexandria VA 2013-** B Marion VA 1966 s Joseph & Mildred. BA U of Virginia 1988; MDiv GTS 1994. D 6/9/1994 Bp A(rthur) Heath Light P 12/10/1994 Bp Craig Barry Anderson. m 8/22/1998 Patricia Phaneuf c 3. R Par of Chr the Redeem Pelham NY 2000-2013; Serv Ch Of Engl 1999-2000; Asst R S Paul's Par Baltimore MD 1997-1999; Cur S Jn's Ch Larchmont NY 1994-1997. Omicron Delta Kappa. Mdiv cl GTS 1994.

ALEXANDER, Sharon Ann (La) 3552 Morning Glory Ave, Baton Rouge LA 70808 **R Trin Epis Ch Baton Rouge LA 2014-; T/F on the Episcopacy GC-Epis Ch Cntr New York NY 2016-, Stndg Cmsn on Structure, Governance, Const & Cn 2015-2016, Legis Com on Governance and Governance 2015; Dep to GC (Chair 2015; First Alt 2018) Dio Louisiana New Orleans LA 2015-, Dioc Conv Plnng/Dispatch Chair 2013-2016, Exec Bd 2012-2015, Partnr in Mssn Com 2012-2014; Bd Trst (ex officio) Epis HS Baton Rouge Baton Rouge LA 2014-** B Edinburg TX 1959 d Ralph & LuAnn. BA U of Texas 1981; MBA U of Texas 1985; JD SMU 1990; MDiv SMU Perkins 2010. D 2/2/2011 P 8/6/2011 Bp Morris King Thompson Jr. P-in-c S Mich's Epis Ch Mandeville LA 2011-2014; Bd Dir Epis Cmnty Serv of Louisiana New Orleans LA 2012-2016. Contrib, "The CEB Wmn Bible," Chr Resources Dvlpmt Corp, 2016. sharon@trinitybr.org

ALEXANDER, Stephen Gray (Lex) 5300 Hamilton Ave Apt 906, Cincinnati OH 45224 **Ret 1996-** B Jacksonville FL 1940 s George & Mary. BA Ken 1962; MDiv VTS 1965. D 6/29/1965 Bp John Vander Horst P 4/18/1966 Bp William Evan Sanders. c 2. Secy of Bd APSO 1984-1991; S Paul's Ch Newport KY 1981-1996; Dio Lexington Lexington 1981-1990, CE Chairman 1985-1993; R H Trin Epis Ch Fayetteville NC 1977-1979; CE Co-Chair Dio Upper So carolina 1975-1977; Asst S Martins-In-The-Field Columbia SC 1973-1977; R S Lk's Epis Ch Jacksonville FL 1968-1972; P-in-c Ch Of The Redeem Shelbyville TN 1966-1968; D S Ptr's Ch Columbia TN 1965-1966.

ALEXANDER, William David (Okla) **Pstr Care Dir Claremore Reg Hosp Claremore OK 1995-; D NE Reg Dio Oklahoma 1995-; Pres Mnstrl Allnce 1995-** B Chicago IL 1953 s Lulius & Helen. ThD Carolina U; ThM SWTS; BS Missouri Vlly Coll 1975; MDiv SWTS 1993. D 12/26/1987 Bp Frank Tracy Griswold III P 9/1/1993 Bp Robert Manning Moody. m 11/4/1978 Connie Alexander. R S Paul's Ch Claremore OK 1993-2000; D S Jn's Epis Ch Naperville IL 1993; Non-par 1987-1992.

ALEXANDRE, Hickman (LI) 260 Beaver Dam Road, Brookhaven NY 11719 **Dio Long Island Garden City NY 2017-, Dep to GC 2012-, Trst to the Estate 2009-2012, Bd Managers Epis Hlth Serv 2004-2007, COM 2002-2011, Dioc Coun 2002-2007; Vic S Jas Ch Brookhaven NY 2002-** B Brooklyn NY 1973 s Mathieu & Marie. BS CUNY 1995; MDiv SWTS 2000. D 6/29/2000 Bp Rodney Rae Michel P 1/20/2001 Bp Orris George Walker Jr. m 7/28/2001 Pierrette Jean-Mary Alexandre c 2. P-in-c S Mk's Epis Ch Medford NY 2011-2012; S Andr's Ch Mastic Bch NY 2002-2007; Asst R and Chapl S Ptr's by-the-Sea Epis Ch Bay Shore NY 2000-2002.

ALEXANDRE, Soner (Hai) B 1970 D. m 4/29/2004 Yolande F Alexandre c 3. Dio Haiti Port-au-Prince HT 2002-2015.

ALEXIS, Alicia (NC) PO Box 20427, Greensboro NC 27420 **Ch Of The Redeem Greensboro NC 2008-** B Trinidad WI 1955 d George & Cynthia. MS U of Maryland 1986; MA of Maryland 2003; MDiv Bex Sem 2005; MDiv Bex Sem 2005. D 6/24/2006 P 3/25/2008 Bp John L Rabb. c 1. S Jn's Ch Hvre De Gr MD 2008-2009; H Cross Ch St MD 2008; S Phil's Ch Annapolis MD 2006.

ALEXIS, Judith (Ct) 628 Main St, Stamford CT 06901 B New York NY 1970 d Jean. CUNY; ALA Broward Cmnty Coll 2003; DST Epis TS of the SW 2006. D 7/22/2006 Bp James Hamilton Ottley P 4/13/2007 Bp Mark Hollingsworth Jr.

Dio Connecticut Meriden CT 2009-2014; Trin Cathd Cleveland OH 2006-2009; Apartment Mgr 2003-2006.

ALFORD, Billy J (Ga) 3041 Hummingbird Ln, Augusta GA 30906 **S Alb's Epis Ch Augusta GA 1992-** B Sylvester GA 1953 s M H & Johnnie. BA Albany St U 1976; AA Darton Coll 1976; MDiv VTS 1992. D 6/11/1992 P 3/25/1993 Bp Harry Woolston Shipps. m 8/16/1975 Patricia Ann Randall c 2.

ALFORD JR, Harold Bennett (Ala) 680 Calder St, Beaumont TX 77701 B Albertville AL 1948 s Harold & Eunice. BS U So 1970; MDiv SWTS 1987. D 6/15/1987 Bp William Hopkins Folwell P 1/4/1988 Bp James Barrow Brown. m 4/1/1972 Lynn Alford c 1. R Trin Ch Wetumpka AL 2006-2011; S Mk's Ch Beaumont TX 2003-2006; R S Geo's Epis Ch New Orleans LA 1991-2003, Asst To R 1987-1991; S Paul's Ch New Orleans LA 1987-1991.

ALFORD, Joseph Stanley Trowbridge (Kan) 2618 W 24th Terrace, Lawrence KS 66047 **P-in-c S Mart-In-The-Fields Edwardsville KS 2012-; Souljourners Incorporated 1997-** B Memphis TN 1945 s Joseph & Georgia. BA Rhodes Coll 1967; MA U of Memphis 1974; MDiv GTS 1978. D 6/29/1978 Bp William F Gates Jr P 4/18/1979 Bp William Evan Sanders. m 5/11/1976 Julie Trowbridge-Alford c 2. R Imm Ch Ripley TN 2006-2008; Strng Ctte Dio Kansas 1993-1994; Cnvnr - Commision On Sprtl Dvlpmt Cbury At Kansas U Lawr KS 1992-2005; Dio Kansas Topeka KS 1992-2005; Assoc Calv Ch Memphis TN 1986-1991; Cmncatn Off Dio Tennessee Nashville TN 1982-1986; Vic S Fran' Ch Norris TN 1979-1982; D S Jn's Epis Cathd Knoxville TN 1978-1979. ESMHE. Awd For Merit Associated Ch Presses. stmartinepiscopal@gmail.com

ALFORD, William T (CPa) 302 S Liberty St, Centreville MD 21617 B Coronado CA 1949 s William & Frances. BS Pk U 1987; MDiv Epis TS of the SW 1995. D 1/25/1995 P 8/1/1995 Bp Larry Maze. m 3/19/2005 Kate Harrigan. St Andr's in the Vlly Epis Ch Harrisburg PA 2009-2015; S Jas Ch Lancaster PA 2008; Dio Cntrl Pennsylvania Harrisburg PA 2003-2008; R S Paul's Ch Centreville MD 1999-2003; Dio Arkansas Little Rock AR 1998-1999; Vic S Matt's Epis Ch Benton AR 1997-1998, Cur Intern 1995-1997. S Andr'S Soc Of The Estrn Shore Of Maryland 2001.

ALFORD-HARKEY, April L (Ct) D 1/28/2017 Bp Laura Ahrens.

ALFRIEND, John Daingerfield (WVa) 224 Muirfield Ct, Charles Town WV 25414 **Ret 1995-** B Weston WV 1927 s John & Fannie. BA Hampden-Sydney Coll 1950; BD VTS 1959. D 12/16/1959 Bp David Shepherd Rose P 12/17/1960 Bp George P Gunn. m 2/16/1974 Nancy Alfriend c 4. P-in-c Gr Epis Ch Kearneysville WV 2008-2010; P-in-c S Paul's Ch Sharpsburg MD 1998-2006; Mssnr Nelson Cluster Of Epis Ch 1991-1994; Nelson Cluster Of Epis Ch Rippon WV 1991-1994; R Zion Epis Ch Chas Town WV 1989-1990; R Ch Of The Epiph Norfolk VA 1978-1987; Non-par 1971-1978; Dio Sthrn Virginia Newport News VA 1966, 1963-1965, Dept Of CSR 1962; R Gr Ch Yorktown Yorktown VA 1964-1971; Chr Ch Boydton VA 1959-1964; P-in-c S Jas Ch Boydton VA 1959-1964; S Tim's Epis Ch Clarksville VA 1959-1964. Bd Dir ESMA 1991-1993.

ALGERNON, Marcel Glenford (SwFla) 2055 Woodsong Way, Fountain CO 80817 **Vic S Anselm Epis Ch Lehigh Acres FL 2005-** B New Amsterdam GY 1962 s Heyligar & Miriam. BA U of The W Indies 1986; MA CUNY 1992; MEd CUNY 1994. Trans 4/20/1993 Bp Orris George Walker Jr. m 12/30/2016 Delirys Cruz. Off Of Bsh For ArmdF New York NY 1996-2004; Ch Of The H Apos Brooklyn NY 1993-1995; S Andr's Ch Oceanside NY 1993, Supply P 1989-1993; Asst Ch Of S Thos Brooklyn NY 1988-1989.

ALIMOLE, Chisara Rose (NY) 1415 Pelhamdale Ave, Pelham NY 10803 B Umunumo 1962 d Isaac & Philomena. MS Touro Coll; BA Touro Coll 2000; EFM EFM 2008. D 5/13/2017 Bp Andrew Marion Lenow Dietsche. m 4/4/1983 Ozichi Alimole c 4.

ALLAGREE, The Rev. Harry R. (NCal) 361 Lincoln Avenue, Cotati CA 94931 B Dayton OH 1937 s Robert & Grace. S Josephs Coll Rensselaer IN 1957; BA U of Dayton 1960; S Chas Sem Carthagena OH 1964. Rec 6/2/1982 as Priest Bp John Lester Thompson III. c 2. Reg Mssnr St. Fran in the Redwoods Epis Ch Willits CA 2006-2007; Reg Mssnr H Trin Epis Ch Ukiah CA 1996-2007; The Epis Dio Nthrn California Sacramento CA 1996-2007, Chapl for Ret Cler & Spouses 2008-2009; R S Jn The Evang Ch Chico CA 1986-1996; Vic Gd Shpd Epis Ch Susanville CA 1983-1986; Vic H Sprt Mssn Lake Almanor CA 1983-1986; Asst S Matt's Epis Ch Sacramento CA 1982-1983; Serv RC Ch 1964-1969. Ord of Julian of Norwich, Oblate 1997. Hon Alum CDSP 1993.

ALLAIN, Thomas A (Miss) 615 18th St S, Birmingham AL 35233 **Trin Ch Hattiesburg MS 2016-; Other Lay Position Dio Mississippi Jackson MS 2012-** B Natchez MS 1986 s Henry & Melissa. Rel Stds Millsaps Coll 2009; MDiv VTS 2015. D 6/13/2015 P 1/16/2016 Bp Brian Seage.

✠ ALLAN, The Rt Rev Frank Kellogg (At) 1231 Briarcliff Rd Ne, Atlanta GA 30306 B Hammond IN 1935 s Bryan & Julia. BA Emory U 1956; MDiv Sewanee: The U So, TS 1959; STM Sewanee: The U So, TS 1970; Coll of Preachers 1972; DMin Candler TS Emory U 1977. D 6/16/1959 P 12/1/1959 Bp Randolph R Claiborne Con 2/7/1987 for At. m 6/11/1957 Elizabeth Ansley c 4. Fac, Angl Stds Prog Candler TS Emory U Atlanta GA 2000-2005; The Wk of Our Hands Atlanta GA 2000-2003; Bp of Atlanta Dio Atlanta Atlanta GA 1989-2000, Bp Coadj of Atlanta 1987-1988; R S Anne's Epis Ch Atlanta GA 1977-1987; R S

Paul's Ch Macon GA 1968-1977; R S Ptr's Ch Columbia TN 1967-1968; R S Mk's Ch Dalton GA 1959-1967. DD (Hon) STUSo 1988.

ALLARD, Bradley Richard (WMich) 114 Union Ave Ne # 1, Grand Rapids MI 49503 **D H Trin Epis Ch Wyoming MI 2009-** B Muskegon MI 1949 s Raymond & Lila. D 11/19/2005 Bp Robert R Gepert.

ALLEE, Roger G (SeFla) 2212 S Cypress Bend Dr Apt 107, Pompano Beach FL 33069 B Port Jervis NY 1946 s Hager & Lillian. Mercer Cnty Cmnty Coll; BS Trenton St Coll 1972; MS Nova SE U 1981. D 1/26/1996 Bp John Lewis Said P 11/3/2002 Bp Leo Frade. m 6/25/2011 Robert Midolo c 3. P-in-c Ch Of The Intsn Ft Lauderdale FL 2008-2010; Assoc All SS Prot Epis Ch Ft Lauderdale FL 2002-2010; S Benedicts Ch Ft Lauderdale FL 1998-2002.

ALLEMAN, Timothy Lee (Be) 20B Buckingham Street, Luzerne PA 18709 **R H Cross Epis Ch Wilkes Barre PA 2011-; Stff Chapl Geisinger Wyoming Vlly Med Cntr Wilkes-Barre PA 2010-** B Warren, PA 1977 s Leland & Phyllis. BA Thiel Coll 1999; MDiv Luth TS 2003. Rec 7/22/2010 as Priest Bp Paul Victor Marshall. m 5/21/2011 Karie Alleman c 1.

ALLEMEIER, James Elmer (Chi) 4306 34th Avenue Pl, Moline IL 61265 **Asst All SS Epis Ch Moline IL 2008-; Ret 2001-** B Perrysburg OH 1936 s Elmer & Myrtle. BA Ohio Wesl 1958; MDiv SWTS 1968. D 6/22/1968 Bp Russell S Hubbard P 12/22/1968 Bp John Joseph Meakin Harte. m 7/18/1964 Marguerite W Allemeier. R Chr Ch Moline IL 1972-2001; Cur S Andr's Ch Downers Grove IL 1970-1972; Chapl All SS Ch Phoenix AZ 1969-1970; Epis Par Of S Mich And All Ang Tucson AZ 1968-1970; P-in-c Epis Par of S Mich and All Ang Paradise VA 1968-1970; Vic S Eliz Phoenix AZ 1968-1970. MDiv scl SWTS 1968.

ALLEN, Abraham Claude (Mass) 17 Winthrop St, Marlborough MA 01752 B McRae GA 1949 s Abe & Lola. BA Shawnee St U 1973; MDiv PrTS 1989; MA EDS 1991. D 6/4/1994 P 12/1/1994 Bp David Elliot Johnson. m 8/30/1981 Frankie Maureen Allen. Trin Ch Concord MA 1996-1998.

ALLEN, Barbara (WA) 6919 Strathmore St Apt C, Bethesda MD 20815 B Kilgore TX 1937 d Robert & Carrie. AA Pasadena City Coll 1957; Pasadena City Coll Sch of Nrsng 1958; BA Geo 1989; MDiv Sthrn Bapt TS 1990; GTS 1999. D 6/24/2000 P 5/13/2001 Bp Charles Ellsworth Bennison Jr. c 2. Vic S Barn' Epis Ch Of The Deaf Chevy Chase MD 2002-2011; Dio Washington Washington DC 2002-2009; Asst Calv Ch Conshohocken PA 2001-2002, D 2000-2001; Dio Pennsylvania Philadelphia PA 2000-2002. Epis Conf of the Deaf 1993.

ALLEN, Charles William (Ind) 4118 Byram Ave, Indianapolis IN 46208 **Chapl Dio Indianapolis Indianapolis IN 2004-; Sch For Mnstry Indianapolis IN 2004-** B Fayetteville AR 1953 BA U of Arkansas; BA U of Arkansas 1976; MDiv Sthrn Bapt TS 1980; PhD U Chi 1987. D 6/28/2003 P 2/14/2004 Bp Cate Waynick. c 2. Trin Ch Indianapolis IN 2014; Coordntr Chr Theol 2003-2004; Affiliate Chr Theol 1993-2004.

ALLEN, Curtis Tilley (WTenn) 133 Jefferson Sq, Nashville TN 37215 **Ret 1992-** B Durham NC 1930 s Lyle & Min. BS U NC 1953; BD Epis TS of the SW 1959. D 9/18/1959 P 3/1/1960 Bp Richard Henry Baker. R Chr Ch Memphis TN 1979-1992; R S Phil's Ch Nashville TN 1971-1979; Vic S Anne's Ch Millington TN 1966-1971; Vic S Mary's Epis Ch Middlesboro KY 1961-1966; Asst R S Mich's Ch Tarboro NC 1960-1961; Vic Gr Ch Lawr NC 1959-1961; Vic St Marys Epis Ch Speed NC 1959-1961.

ALLEN SSJE, David Eastman (Mass) 980 Memorial Dr, Cambridge MA 02138 **Bursar SSJE Monstry of S Mary and S Jn Cambridge 2004-; Life Professed SSJE Monstry of S Mary and S Jn Cambridge MA 1961-** B Spokane WA 1929 s Clyde & Harriet. BA WA SU 1952; MDiv CDSP 1958. D 6/17/1958 Bp Edward Makin Cross P 12/21/1958 Bp Spence Burton. Sacristan SSJE Monstry of S Mary and S Jn Cambridge MA 2002-2006; SSJE Monstry of S Mary and S Jn Cambridge MA 1998-2002; Sacristan SSJE Monstry of S Mary and S Jn Cambridge MA 1997-1998; Guest Mstr Emery Hse W Newbury MA 1994-1997; Guest Hse Stff SSJE Monstry of S Mary and S Jn Cambridge MA 1988-1994; Sacristan SSJE Monstry of S Mary and S Jn Cambridge MA 1978-1988; Emery Hse W Newberry MA 1976-1978; Stff/ Prov Superior SSJE Monstry of S Mich Oyama Japan 1965-1975; S Jn's Hse Tokyo Japan 1962-1965; Monk Soc-St Jn The Evang Cambridge MA 1958-1995; Post & Novc SSJE Monstry of S Mary and S Jn Cambridge MA 1958-1961. Auth, "Var arts," *Mitsukai, Cowley*, SSJE, 1961. Epis Asiamerica Mnstry 1978; EPF 1965.

ALLEN, David Edward (Mass) PO Box 1052, Barnstable MA 02630 B Swampscott MA 1937 s Edward & Blanche. BS Bos 1962; MDiv Ya Berk 1965. D 6/26/1965 P 5/31/1966 Bp John Melville Burgess. m 6/27/1965 Ruthanne Allen. R S Mary's Epis Ch Barnstable MA 1979-2002; Commun Ctte Dio Massachusetts Boston MA 1972-1991; R Ch Of Our Sav Middleboro MA 1968-1979; Cur Par Of Chr Ch Andover MA 1965-1968. Auth, "Pstr Care Handbook," *same*, EDS, 1995.

ALLEN, Donald Frederick (Ct) 34 Ashlar Vlg, Wallingford CT 06492 B New Haven CT 1926 s Frederick & Mildred. Cert U of New Haven 1955; BS U of New Haven 1974. D 6/8/1996 Bp Clarence Nicholas Coleridge. m 11/20/1948 Augusta Hazel Allen c 2. D S Jn's Ch No Haven CT 2002-2009; D S Paul's Epis Ch Shelton CT 1996-2002; Chapl Ashlar Vill Wallingford CT. Alpha Sigma Lambda; OHC.

ALLEN, E(arl) Michael (Nwk) 55 George St, Allendale NJ 07401 **R Trin Epis Ch of Bergen Cnty Allendale NJ 2007-; Ch Of The Resurr New York NY 2005-** B San Francisco CA 1948 s Earl & Joyce. BS The Coll of Idaho 1989; MDiv GTS 1991. D 6/8/1991 Bp Earl Nicholas Mc Arthur Jr P 12/20/1991 Bp Harold Barrett Robinson. m 10/1/2004 Penelope Braun c 2. Dio Newark Newark NJ 2013; R Chr Ch New Brighton Staten Island NY 1997-2004; Asst The Ch of S Matt And S Tim New York NY 1994-1997; Asst S Mk's Ch Mt Kisco NY 1992-1994; Asst S Thos Ch New York NY 1991-1992. GAS 2000; SocMary 1999.

ALLEN, Edward Powell (Los) 49 Captains Row, Mashpee MA 02649 **Died 7/9/2016** B Shanghai CN 1928 s Arthur & Edith. BA Pomona Coll 1949; BD CDSP 1956. D 6/25/1956 Bp Francis E I Bloy P 2/11/1957 Bp Donald J Campbell. m 6/15/1956 Alice Jean Pierce c 3. Asst S Mary's Epis Ch Barnstable MA 1994-2000; Ret 1991-2016; Ret 1990-2016; Epis Ch Of S Andr And S Chas Granada Hills CA 1976-1990; Dio Los Angeles Los Angeles CA 1966-1976; Vic S Mich And All Ang Par Corona Dl Mar CA 1960-1966; Cur The Par Ch Of S Lk Long Bch CA 1956-1959.

ALLEN II, George Curwood (SO) 988 Duxbury Ct, Cincinnati OH 45255 B Parkersburg WV 1950 s George & Betty. Cert (MA equivalent) USAF Air War Coll; AB W Liberty St Coll 1972; MDiv EDS 1977. D 6/8/1977 P 5/20/1978 Bp Robert Poland Atkinson. m 8/26/1972 Judith Lyn Irby c 2. Assoc Forw Mvmt of the Epis Ch Cincinnati OH 1999-2009; Asst to Chf, USAF Chapl Serv US AF 1999-2004; R Dio Newark Newark NJ 1982-1986; R The Ch Of The Annunc Oradell NJ 1980-1999; Chapl US AF 1979-2004; Chapl, Brigadier Gnrl US AF 1979-2004; Assoc R Dio W Virginia Charleston WV 1977-1980; Trin Epis Ch Martinsburg WV 1977-1980. Auth, "S Nich," *S Nich*, Forw Mvmt, 2007. Meritorious Serv Medallion Bp Suffr for Chaplaincies, The Epis Ch 2006; Legion of Merit U S AF 2004.

ALLEN, Gordon Richard (NH) 237 Emerys Bridge Rd, South Berwick ME 03908 **Died 12/7/2016** B Liverpool UK 1929 s Richard & Katherine. BA S Johns Coll Durham GB 1954; DIT S Johns Coll Durham GB 1955; U of Durham GB 1955; MA S Johns Coll Durham GB 1958. Trans 5/1/1973 Bp Philip Alan Smith. Ret 1995-2016; R S Jn's Ch Portsmouth NH 1975-1995; R The Epis Ch Of S Jn The Bapt Sanbornville NH 1971-1975; Chapl Virginia Epis Sch Lynchburg Virginia 1968-1971; Serv Ch of Engl 1964-1968; Serv Ch of the Prov of Uganda 1958-1963.

ALLEN JR, John Gwin (Ky) 1512 Valley Brook Rd, Louisville KY 40222 **Asst Chapl S Lk's Chap Louisville KY 2009-; Pstr Mssh Trin Ch Louisville KY 2005-** B Baton Rouge LA 1942 s John & Jonetta. BA LSU 1964; STB Ya Berk 1967. D 7/8/1967 Bp Girault M Jones P 5/11/1968 Bp Iveson Batchelor Noland. m 7/2/1966 Cynthia R Allen c 3. R S Thos Epis Ch Louisville KY 1992-1999; Asst to Bp Dio Kentucky Louisville KY 1989-1997; Cn For Mnstry Dio Lexington Lexington 1987-1989, Curs Com 1982-1986, Pres Stndg Com 1980-1981, 1979-1982, 1979, Ctte On Mutual Respon/Interdependent Body of Chr 1982-1986, Curs Com 1982-1986; Dir of Stds Epis TS Lexington KY 1986-1989; R Emm Epis Ch Winchester KY 1982-1986; R Ch Of The Cross Columbia SC 1978-1982; Vic S Marg's Epis Ch Baton Rouge LA 1974-1978; R S Fran Ch Denham Spgs LA 1969-1977; Asst R S Paul's Ch New Orleans LA 1967-1969; Bd Dir Global Teams Forest City NC 1984-1986; Sprtl Dir Curs Dio Louisiana New Orleans LA 1976-1978.

ALLEN, John M (Oly) 4415 Colebrooke Lane SE, Lacey WA 98513 B Philadelphia PA 1945 s John & Dorothy. BA Rutgers The St U of New Jersey 1971; MBA U of Pennsylvania 1974; MDiv CDSP 2002. D 6/29/2002 Bp Vincent Waydell Warner P 12/7/2002 Bp William Edwin Swing. m 6/1/1974 Georgene Allen c 2. R S Jn's Epis Ch Olympia WA 2010-2015; R S Lk's Epis Ch Vancouver WA 2005-2010; Int All SS Epis Ch Palo Alto CA 2004-2005; Assoc Pstr Gr Cathd San Francisco CA 2002-2003.

ALLEN, John Shepley (NH) 229 Shore Dr, Laconia NH 03246 **Ret 2000-** B Glen Ridge NJ 1938 s Frank & Margaret. BA Carleton Coll 1961; BD VTS 1963; MDiv VTS 1965. D 6/12/1965 P 12/1/1965 Bp Leland Stark. m 6/18/1965 Ursula Walch. S Steph's Ch Pittsfield NH 1992-1999; P-in-c Ch Of The Mssh No Woodstock NH 1990-1991; S Jas Epis Ch Laconia NH 1975-1987; R H Trin Epis Ch Hillsdale NJ 1969-1975; Cur S Geo's Epis Ch Maplewood NJ 1965-1969. AAPC.

ALLEN, John Tait (Mil) 515 Oak St., South Milwaukee WI 53172 B Lost Angeles CA 1945 s M William & Margarette. AA Fullerton Coll 1964; BA Fullerton Coll 1967; MDiv Wartburg TS 1972; DMin GTF 1988. Rec 4/27/2005 Bp Steven Andrew Miller. m 10/21/1972 Marilyn Jodell Allen c 3. S Mk's Ch S Milwaukee WI 2005-2013; Chapl Froedtert Luth Hosp Milwaukee WI 1996-2002; Chapl Saini Samar Hosp Milwaukee WI 1995-1996; Par Pstr Unity Luth Ch Milwaukee WI 1992-1995; Par Pstr Elim Luth Ch Marshalltown IA 1982-1992; Assoc. Pstr Zion Luth Ch Waterloo IA 1980-1982; Mssy Evang Luth Of Kenya (Evang. Luth Of Tanzania) 1976-1980; Par Pstr Salem Luth Ch Wooster OH 1973-1976; Par Pstr Mart Luther Luth Ch Mobile AL 1971-1973.

ALLEN, Larry J (WMo) 3212 S. Jeffrey Cir., Independence MO 64055 B Jackson MO 1942 BD Calv Bible Coll 1965. D 2/7/2004 Bp Barry Howe. m 8/

14/1971 Mary Elizabeth Darroch c 3. D S Mich's Epis Ch Independence MO 2004-2006, D 2004-.

ALLEN, Leland Eugene (Kan) 811 E Wood St, Clearwater KS 67026 **D S Chris's Epis Ch Wichita KS 1998-** B Hutchinson KS 1921 s Mary & Flora. D 10/30/1987 Bp Richard Frank Grein. m 12/17/1966 Roberta Cynthia Allen c 2. D S Andrews Ch Derby KS 1991-2015; D S Jude's Ch Wellington KS 1987-2007.

✠ ALLEN, The Rt Rev Lloyd Emmanuel (Hond) Diocese of Honduras, PO Box 523900, Miami FL 33152 **Bp Suffr of Texas Dio Honduras San Pedro Sula 2012-, Bp of Honduras 2001-2012** B Tela Atlantida HN 1956 s Franklyn & Lusia. MA Epis TS of the SW; MA Sewanee: The U So, TS; Universidad Autonoma; BA Triunfo De La Cruz 1977. D 1/6/1989 P 1/1/1991 Bp Leo Frade Con 10/20/2001 for Hond. m 2/26/1983 Rose Allen.

ALLEN, Mark Frederick (NCal) 5872 Oliver Rd, Paradise CA 95969 **R Ch Of S Mart Davis CA 2004-** B Prairie City OR 1951 s Albert & Helen. BS Willamette U 1973; MEd L&C 1977; CTh Oxf GB 1985; MDiv CDSP 1986. D 6/11/1986 P 2/14/1987 Bp Robert Louis Ladehoff. m 5/19/1973 Nancy A Allen c 5. R Ch Of S Nich Paradise CA 1990-2004; Asst S Barth's Ch Beaverton OR 1986-1990. Ord Of S Lk.

ALLEN, Mary Louise (Del) 3 Thornberry Dr, Ocean View DE 19770 **R S Martha's Epis Ch Bethany Bch DE 2011-** B Prairie City OR 1955 d Albert & Helen. BS Willamette U 1977; MDiv CDSP 1986. D 6/10/1986 P 2/2/1987 Bp Robert Louis Ladehoff. S Phil Ch Marysville WA 2004-2011; R Gr Epis Ch St Geo UT 2000-2004, Vic 1995-2000; Dio Utah Salt Lake City UT 1995-2004; Assoc Ch Of The Gd Shpd Ogden UT 1991-1995; Asst S Steph's Epis Ch Longview WA 1989-1991; Asst R S Jas Epis Ch Portland OR 1986-1989. Auth, "A Stwdshp Plan," *The Vineyard*, 1989.

ALLEN, Morgan S (Tex) 3201 Windsor Rd, Austin TX 78703 **R The Ch of the Gd Shpd Austin TX 2009-** B Monroe LA 1975 s Hubert & Mary. BA LSU 1997; BA LSU 1997; MDiv Epis TS of the SW 2003. D 6/7/2003 P 2/23/2004 Bp D Avid Bruce Macpherson. m 5/16/1998 Susan Melissa Allen c 2. R S Barn Epis Ch Lafayette LA 2005-2009; Cur S Mths Epis Ch Shreveport LA 2003-2005; Lay Asst to the Dn & Cathd Sch Chapl S Dav's Ch Austin TX 2000-2003; S Mk's Cathd Shreveport LA 2000-2003; Yth Dir Trin Epis Ch Baton Rouge LA 1994-1998.

ALLEN, Patrick Scott 886 Seafarer Way, Charleston SC 29412 B Lakeland FL 1968 s James & Elizabeth. BA Hampden-Sydney Coll 1990; MDiv Cov TS S Louis 1996; DAS Sewanee: The U So, TS 2000. D 7/23/2000 P 1/24/2001 Bp Edward Lloyd Salmon Jr. m 5/3/2003 Ashley Ann Duckett c 1. Ch Of The H Comm Charleston SC 2007-2012; S Jos Of Arimathaea Ch Hendersonvlle TN 2006-2007; R S Matt's Ch (Ft Motte) St Matthews SC 2000-2003.

ALLEN JR, Radford Bonnie (FtW) 1804 Dakar Rd W, Fort Worth TX 76116 **Ret 1990-** B Lufkin TX 1925 s Radford & Clara. BS Louisiana Tech U 1951; Lic Sacr Theol Angl TS 1979; U of Durham GB 1981. D 6/25/1978 Bp Robert Elwin Terwilliger P 5/20/1979 Bp Archibald Donald Davies. m 9/6/1950 Lina Lusk Allen c 1. Mssn Com Dio Ft Worth Ft Worth TX 1987-1989; R S Jn's Epis Ch Brownwood TX 1986-1990, Int 1985-1986; Chapl (LtCol) CAP 1983-1993; Cur All SS' Epis Ch Ft Worth TX 1982-1986; Vic S Mart In The Fields Ch Keller TX 1979-1982; Cur Chr The King Epis Ch Ft Worth TX 1978-1979. CBS 1971; GAS 1971. Chapl of Year CAP, TX Wing 1985.

ALLEN, Robert Edward (Ark) 1101 Glenwood Dr, El Dorado AR 71730 **Stated Supply P S Mk's Ch Crossett AR 2008-** B Stuttgart AR 1941 s Robert & Margaret. BA Hendrix Coll 1963; BD SMU 1966; STM SMU 1968; MA U of Dallas 1970; Cert U So 1974. D 5/18/1974 Bp Girault M Jones P 9/21/1974 Bp Christoph Keller Jr. c 1. Stated Supply P Dio Arkansas Little Rock AR 2008-2013, Chair Liturg Cmsn 1978-1979; R S Mary's Epis Ch El Dorado AR 1991-2007; Cn Dio W Tennessee Memphis 1984-1991, Liturg Cmsn 1983-1991; Cn S Mary's Cathd Memphis TN 1984-1991; R Ch of the H Apos Collierville TN 1981-1984, Vic 1979-1981; Vic Calv Epis Ch Osceola AR 1974-1979; Chapl Trsfg Day Sch Dallas TX. Ed, *Ch News*, WTenn, 1991; Auth, "H Places," *Liturg Perkins Journ*; Contrib, *S Lukes Journ*.

ALLEN, Roger D (At) St. James Episcopal Church, 161 Church St NE, Marietta GA 30060 **R S Jas Epis Ch Marietta GA 2011-** B Thomasville GA 1954 s Washington & Mavelene. ABJ U GA 1976; JD Tul 1980; MDiv Sewanee: The U So, TS 2005. D 12/29/2004 P 7/1/2005 Bp Charles Edward Jenkins III. m 5/14/1994 Elisabeth F Allen. R S Jas' Epis Ch Alexander City AL 2007-2011; Chapl Chap Of The H Comf New Orleans LA 2005-2007; Dio Louisiana New Orleans LA 2005-2007; Chair COM Dio Atlanta Atlanta GA 2015-2017, Co-Chair COM 2014-2015. roger.allen@stjamesmarietta.com

ALLEN, Russell Harvey (Ct) 28 Seaward Ln, Harwich MA 02645 B Hartford CT 1943 s Samuel & Lillian. BA Bard Coll 1965; MDiv GTS 1968; MA Nthrn Michigan U 1990. D 6/11/1968 Bp Walter H Gray P 5/24/1969 Bp John Henry Esquirol. m 6/1/1968 Louisa M Allen c 2. Assoc S Ptr's Ch Osterville MA 2006-2015; R Ch Of The H Adv Clinton CT 1999-2006; Exec PA Comm UMHE Harrisburg PA 1991-1999; Pennsylvania Cmsn Harrisburg PA 1991-1998; S Mths Ch Coventry RI 1990-1991; Dio Connecticut Meriden CT 1986-1989; Vic All SS Ch Wolcott CT 1981-1989; Dio Milwaukee Milwaukee

WI 1979-1981; Chapl Dio Milwaukee Milwaukee WI 1979-1981; Chapl Notthrrn MI U Marquette Marquette MI 1973-1979; Untd Mnstrs In Higher Educ Marquette MI 1973-1979; Dio W Virginia Charleston WV 1972-1973; Emm Ch Keyser WV 1972-1973; Emm Ch Moorefield WV 1972-1973; Chapl Potomac St Coll Keyser WV 1972-1973; Asst S Mary's Epis Ch Manchester CT 1969-1972; Cur S Paul's Epis Ch Willimantic CT 1968-1969. Auth, *Hist: A Revs of New Books*.

ALLEN, Stephanie Perry (NC) Church of the Nativity, 8849 Ray Road, Raleigh NC 27613 **R Ch Of The Nativ Raleigh NC 2011-** B Asheville NC 1975 d Daniel & Marcia. BA U So 1997; MDiv GTS 2008. D 3/15/2008 P 9/20/2008 Bp Mark Sean Sisk. m 8/5/2000 Michael C Allen c 2. Asst Ch Of The Gd Shpd Rocky Mt NC 2008-2011; St. Barth Ch New York NY 1998-2003. sa@nativityonline.org

ALLEN, Susan Van Leunen (ECR) PO Box 173, King City CA 93930 **Assoc S Matt's Ch San Ardo CA 2007-; S Matt's Ch San Ardo CA 2000-, P-in-c 1997-1999** B Cincinnati OH 1944 d Paul & Helen. BS Mia 1966; MA CDSP 1988. D 11/26/1996 P 6/24/1997 Bp Richard Lester Shimpfky. c 2. Vic S Mk's Ch King City CA 1998-2004, Asst 1995-1997. "Masters Thesis," Grad Theol Un Libr, Burkeley CA, 1988.

ALLEN, Thomas Scott (Be) 713 Cherokee St, Bethlehem PA 18015 **R S Andr's Epis Ch Allentown PA 2007-** B Heidelburg Germany 1956 s Billy & Rebecca. BS W Virginia U 1979; MDiv Ya Berk 1983. D 6/1/1983 P 4/7/1984 Bp Robert Poland Atkinson. S Eliz's Ch Schnecksville PA 2001-2006; R S Barth's Ch Pittsboro NC 1995-1999; Assoc R S Matt's Ch Wheeling WV 1985-1989; Int Trin Ch Parkersburg WV 1984, Asst R 1983-1984; GC Dep Dio Bethlehem Bethlehem PA 2010-2013, GC Dep 2008-2010, Stndg Com 2006-2015, Soc Mssnr 1989-2006. Auth, "Article," *Wit*, 1981. EPF 1983; EUC 1994; Grad Soc-Ya Berk 1983; Integrity 1999.

ALLEN, Thomas Wynn (Md) 1 St. Mary's Church Rd., Abingdon MD 21009 **R S Mary's Ch Abingdon MD 2011-** B Fort Campbell KY 1969 s John & Mary Ann. BA Montreat Coll 1997; MDiv TESM 2003. Rec 8/1/2007 Bp Edward Lloyd Salmon Jr. m 10/10/2014 Heather Sue Allen c 4. R H Cross Stateburg Sumter SC 2007-2011; Vic Angl Prov Of Anerica 2004-2007. st.marys1928@gmail.com

ALLEN, Walter Drew (Colo) Po Box 5958, Vail CO 81658 **Asst S Jas Epis Ch Taos NM 2007-** B Hearne TX 1933 s Drew & Dorthea. D 1/6/2003 P 7/19/2003 Bp William Jerry Winterrowd.

ALLEN, W Frank (Pa) 763 Valley Forge Rd, Wayne PA 19087 **R S Dav's Ch Wayne PA 1997-; Stndg Committee Dio Pennsylvania Philadelphia PA 2009-, Dio Com on Fin & Property Mem 2006-2010, Dn's Coun 2003-2006, Ch Fndt Bd Mem 1999-2010** B Dallas TX 1958 s James & Laura. BA Duke 1981; MDiv VTS 1995. D 6/10/1995 Bp Allen Lyman Bartlett Jr P 6/11/1996 Bp A(rthur) Heath Light. m 7/9/1983 Amy J Allen c 3. COM Dio SW Virginia Roanoke VA 1996-1997; Asst S Jn's Ch Roanoke VA 1995-1997. Auth, *Epis Ch Curric for Jr High*.

ALLEN-FAIELLA, Wilifred Sophia Nelly (SeFla) 16745 Southwest 74th Avenue, Miami FL 33157 **Dio SE Florida Miami 2006-; R S Steph's Ch Coconut Grove Miami FL 2001-; Dio Pennsylvania Philadelphia 2000-** B Paris FR 1951 d George & Jelisaveta. BA Bryn 1973; MA Schiller Coll Berlin 1974; MDiv VTS 1978. D 6/13/1987 P 3/24/1988 Bp Peter J Lee. m 6/22/1980 Christopher James Faiella c 2. Stndg Com Dio Pennsylvania Philadelphia PA 1997-2001, 1997-2000; Trin Ch Gulph Mills Kng Of Prussia PA 1991-2001; VTS Alexandria VA 1989-1991; Asst Imm Ch-On-The-Hill Alexandria VA 1987-1991. Finalist Best Sermon Competition 1991; MDiv cl VTS 1987.

ALLEN-HERRON, Dawn (Ak) 3886 S Tongass Hwy, Ketchikan AK 99901 **R S Andr's Epis Ch Petersburg AK 2003-** B Corpus Christi TX 1959 d Charles & Mary. BA Baylor U 1982; MDiv Austin Presb TS 1989. D 9/14/2002 P 3/25/2003 Bp Mark Lawrence Macdonald. m 5/16/1981 Norman C Herron.

ALLEY, Ann Leonard (Spr) 913 W Washington St, Champaign IL 61821 **Assisting D St. Chris Epis Ch 2003-** B Fayetteville AR 1948 D 6/29/2004 Bp Peter Hess Beckwith. m 11/24/1978 Clarenece Alley c 4.

ALLEY, Charles Dickson (Va) 1101 Forest Ave, Richmond VA 23229 B Hackensack NJ 1949 s Charles & Helen. BS W&M 1971; MA W&M 1972; PhD Med Coll of Virginia 1977; MDiv VTS 1991. D 5/29/1991 Bp Robert Oran Miller P 1/22/1992 Bp Peter J Lee. m 2/8/1975 Nancye SN Alley c 3. R S Matt's Ch Richmond VA 1994-2017; Asst Truro Epis Ch Fairfax VA 1991-1994. "A Tale Of Two Sinners," *LivCh*, 2001.

ALLEY, Marguerite Cole (SVa) 1917 Indian Run Rd, Virginia Beach VA 23454 **Title IV Intake Off Dio Sthrn Virginia Newport News VA 2011-** B Petersburg VA 1960 d Lofton & Mary. BA Jas Madison U 1982; MA Loyola U 1990; MEd W&M 1996; D. Min GTF 2013; D. Min Other 2013. D 6/13/1998 Bp Frank Harris Vest Jr. D Emm Ch Virginia Bch VA 2011-2015, D 2001-2015; D Ch Of The Ascen Norfolk VA 1998-2001. Assn of Epis Deacons 1998.

ALLEYNE, Edmund Torrence (LI) 972 E 93rd St, Brooklyn NY 11236 **R S Gabr's Ch Brooklyn NY 2007-** B Barbados 1961 s Keith & Inez. Cert U of The W Indies; BA Codrington Coll 1988. Trans 12/19/2002 as Priest Bp Orris

George Walker Jr. m 12/29/2001 Kay Smith-Alleyne c 3. P-in-c Ch Of The H Apos Brooklyn NY 2003-2006; Ch Of The Nativ Brooklyn NY 2003-2006.

ALLICK, Paul Delain (Cal) 162 Hickory St, San Francisco CA 94102 **Ch Of The Adv Of Chr The King San Francisco CA 2016-** B Great Falls MT 1968 s Paul & Dolores. BA U MN 1993; MDiv SWTS 1996. D 6/7/1996 P 12/7/1996 Bp James Louis Jelinek. m 2/14/2014 Keith H Schaumann. P-in-c St Geo's Epis Ch Minneapolis MN 2008-2016; Int S Edw The Confessor Wayzata MN 2007-2008; U Epis Cntr Minneapolis MN 2006-2007, Int 2005-2006; P-in-c S Thos Ch Minneapolis MN 2004-2006, 1999-2003; Dio Minnesota Minneapolis MN 1999-2001; P-in-c Ch Of The H Apos S Paul MN 1997-1998; Assoc S Chris's Epis Ch S Paul MN 1996-1997. rector@advent-sf.org

ALLIN, Hailey Wile (Miss) PO Box 1366, Jackson MS 39215 **S Andr's Cathd Jackson MS 2015-** B Meridian MS 1979 d Frederick & Sarah. ThD Emory U-Candler TS; B.S Van 2001; MDiv GTS 2005. D 6/13/2015 P 1/16/2016 Bp Brian Seage. m 8/4/2001 John Maury Allin c 2.

ALLING, Frederic Augustus (Nwk) 3 Mariners Ln, Marblehead MA 01945 B Newark NJ 1930 s Frederic & Helen. BA Pr 1952; STB GTS 1955; MD Col 1961. D 6/11/1955 P 12/17/1955 Bp Benjamin M Washburn. m 12/29/1956 Martha Alling c 3. Ret P Dio Massachusetts Boston MA 1999-2011; Non-par Dio Newark Newark 1958-1961; Dio Newark Newark NJ 1957-1961; Chapl, Chicago Med Cntr Anderson Hse Chicago IL 1956-1957; Cur Chr Ch Teaneck NJ 1955-1956. "Brief Flights," *Bk*, iUniverse, 2008; "Listening for God w the Third Ear," *Journ of Rel and Hlth*, Journ of Rel and Hlth, 2000.

ALLING JR, Roger (Ct) 125 N 28th St, Camp Hill PA 17011 B Pawtucket RI 1933 s Roger & Mary. BA Ken 1956; Oxf GB 1959; BLitt Oxf GB 1963. D 6/28/1959 Bp The Bishop Of Oxford P 4/25/1960 Bp Dudley S Stark. m 1/30/1982 Dian Alling c 4. S Fran Acad Inc. Salina KS 1993; Dir Epis Preaching Excellence Prog 1988-2005; Pres Epis Preaching Fndt Inc 1988-2005; Stwdshp and Planned Giving Off Dio Connecticut Meriden CT 1988-1992; R S Mary's Epis Ch Reading PA 1981-1987; R Chr Epis Ch Williamsport PA 1970-1981; Asst Calv and St Geo New York NY 1969; Consult, Stwdshp and Evang Dept Dio Newark Newark NJ 1965-1969; Vic S Andr's Epis Ch Lincoln Pk NJ 1961-1965; P-in-c Gr Ch Amherst MA 1960-1961, Cur 1959-1960; Asst Chapl Amh Amherst MA 1959-1961. Auth, "What Do Your Hands Want to Say?," *Sermons That Wk Volume I - XIV*, Morehouse Pub, 2005; Auth, "Methods of Evang," *ART*. Assoc, Soc of St. Jn the Bapt 1967; Soc of the Descendants of the Colonial Cler 1959. DD CDSP 2006.

✠ **ALLISON, The Rt Rev Christopher FitzSimons** (SC) 1081 Indigo Ave, Georgetown SC 29440 B Columbia SC 1927 s James & Susan. BA U So 1949; MDiv VTS 1952; PhD Oxf GB 1956. D 6/11/1952 P 5/1/1953 Bp John J Gravatt Con 9/25/1980 for SC. m 6/10/1950 Martha Allison c 4. Ret Bp of SC Carolina Charleston SC 1990-2012, Bp 1982-1990, Bp Coadj 1980-1982; R Gr Epis Ch New York NY 1975-1980; Prof VTS Alexandria VA 1967-1975; Assoc Sewanee U So TS Sewanee TN 1956-1967; Asst Trin Cathd Columbia SC 1952-1954; Chapl U of So Carolina at Columbia 1952-1954. Auth, "Fear, Love & Wrshp," Regent Coll Pub; Auth, "Guilt, Anger & God," Regent Coll Pub; Auth, "The Rise of Moralism," Regent Coll Pub; Auth, "The Cruelty of Heresy," Morehouse. DD VTS 1980; DD U So TS 1978; DD Epis TS in Kentucky 1977.

ALLISON II, C Roy (SwFla) St. Mark's Episcopal Church, 13312 Cain Rd, Tampa FL 33625 **R S Mk's Epis Ch Of Tampa Tampa FL 2014-; Dioc Disciplinary Bd - Mem Dio SW Florida Parrish FL 2012-** B St Petersburg FL 1969 s Charles & Patricia. BA Eckerd Coll 2003; MDiv Nash 2012. D 12/10/2011 P 6/16/2012 Bp Dabney Tyler Smith. m 4/8/1995 Marcia Arlene Allison c 1. Assoc S Mary's Epis Ch Bonita Sprg FL 2012-2014. revcroya2@gmail.com

ALLISON, John Leroy (Me) D 6/11/2016 P 2/2/2017 Bp Stephen Taylor Lane.

ALLISON, Judith Anne (SanD) **P Assoc S Tim's Ch San Diego CA 2015-** B Canada 1937 d John & Rosena. BS U Tor 1959; MA Roosevelt U 1975; PhD US Intl U 1986; MDiv Ya Berk 2005. D 6/11/2005 P 12/18/2005 Bp Jim Mathes. c 2. Assoc R for Pstr Care S Barth's Epis Ch Poway CA 2009-2015, Assoc R 2007-2009; Pstr Care Assoc The Epis Ch Of S Andr Encinitas CA 2005-2006.

ALLISON, Marianne Stirling (Ore) **Dio Oregon Portland OR 2016-** D 6/29/2016 P 1/18/2017 Bp Michael Hanley.

ALLISON, Nancy Jean (NC) 3110 Belvin Dr, Raleigh NC 27609 B Allentown PA 1943 d John & Mildred. BA Elmhurst Coll 1965; BA Elmhurst Coll 1965; MDiv UTS 1968; MDiv UTS 1968; Cert GTS 1987; Cert GTS 1987. D 1/6/1988 Bp William Arthur Beckham P 9/14/1988 Bp Rogers Sanders Harris. Asst Ch Of The Nativ Raleigh NC 2010; Assoc Chr Epis Ch Raleigh NC 1994-2009; R All SS Epis Ch Clinton SC 1991-1994; Asst S Mich And All Ang' Columbia SC 1988-1991; D S Chris's Ch Spartanburg SC 1988.

ALLISON-HATCH, Mary Susan (RG) 1625 Escalante Ave SW, Albuquerque NM 87104 **Asstg Cler S Mich And All Ang Ch Albuquerque NM 2010-; Chapl St. Mart's Hosp Cntr 2010-** B St Paul MN 1948 d John & Jane. BA U MN 1970; MA Stan 1990; MDiv CDSP 2003. D 6/28/2003 P 1/3/2004 Bp Richard Lester Shimpfky. m 7/11/1981 Timothy Allison-Hatch. R Trin Ch Sonoma CA 2007-2009; S Paul's Ch Oakland CA 2004-2007; Assoc S Paul's

Day Sch Of Oakland Oakland CA 2004-2007; Pstr Assoc All SS Epis Ch Palo Alto CA 2003-2004.

ALLMAN, Denny Paul (Miss) 8008 Bluebonnet Blvd Apt 13-2, Baton Rouge LA 70810 **Supply S Mary's Ch Vicksburg MS 2009-; Ret 1998-** B Perry OK 1932 s Cecil & Billie. U of New Mex 1954; LTh Sewanee: The U So, TS 1984. D 5/18/1984 P 12/4/1984 Bp Duncan Montgomery Gray Jr. m 4/29/1952 Norma Allman c 3. St. Mary's Epis Ch Vicksburg MS 2004-2014; Supply All SS Ch Inverness MS 1999-2004, Vic 1984-1988; SpirDirCllo Dio Mississippi Jackson MS 1995-1997; R Chr Epis Ch Vicksburg MS 1988-1998; S Thos Ch Belzoni MS 1984-1988. Auth, "Bk Revs," *Epis Life*, 1999; Auth, "Benediction," *Living Ch*, 1984. Cath Fllshp Epis Ch 1993; Cmnty of S Mary 1985.

ALLMAN, Mary Katherine (SanD) 7946 Calle De La Plata, La Jolla CA 92037 **Chapl The Bp's Sch La Jolla CA 2000-** B Monterey CA 1951 d John & Elizabeth. BA Texas St U San Marcos 1973; MEd Texas St U San Marcos 1976; MDiv Epis TS of the SW 1990; DMin EDS 2000. D 6/15/1990 Bp Earl Nicholas Mc Arthur Jr P 12/20/1990 Bp John Herbert MacNaughton. The Bp's Sch La Jolla CA 2000-2011; S Mary's Epis Sch Memphis TN 1992-1998; Asst To The R S Mk's Ch Crp Christi TX 1990-1992.

ALLMAN, Susan G (U) 1016 E. High Cedar Highlands Dr., Cedar City UT 84720 B Richmond VA 1945 d John & Marjorie. AB Randolph-Macon Wmn's Coll 1967; MA U CA -- Santa Barbarb 1975. D 1/18/2001 P 8/4/2001 Bp Carolyn Tanner Irish. c 1. Dio Utah Salt Lake City UT 2007-2014, 2005-2006, 2005-, 2004-2005, Dep to GC 2011-2012, Dep to GC 2008-2009, Pres of Stndg Com 2006-2008, Dep to GC 2005-2006, Mem of Stndg Com 2005-2006, Mem of Dioc Coun 2004-2005, Mem of Stndg Com 2002-2004; P-in-c Sprt of the Desert Ivins UT 2007-2008; Assoc R Gr Epis Ch St Geo UT 2001-2006, P-in-c 2001-2006; Mem of Bd Cedar Area Interfaith Allnce 2010-2011; Pres Cedar Area Interfaith Allnce - Cedar City UT 2009-2010.

ALLPORT II, William H (Nwk) 113 Engle St, Englewood NJ 07631 **S Paul's Ch Englewood NJ 2014-** B Baltimore MD 1976 s George & Connie. BA Dickinson Coll 1998; MDiv VTS 2002. D 6/8/2002 P 2/1/2003 Bp Michael Whittington Creighton. m 7/6/2002 Mary Carolyn M Allport c 2. R S Helena's Epis Ch Boerne TX 2010-2012; R S Ptr's Ch Honolulu HI 2004-2010; Mem, Dioc Coun The Epis Ch in Hawaii Honolulu HI 2004-2010; Assoc R S Thos Ch Lancaster PA 2002-2004; Chair, Yth Cmsn Dio Cntrl Pennsylvania Harrisburg PA 1998-2004. revballport@stpaulsenglewood.org

ALLRED, Jennifer Allison (Minn) D 6/27/2017 Bp Brian N Prior.

ALLTOP, Bob (Mich) Cathedral Church of St Paul, 4800 Woodward Ave, Detroit MI 48201 **Cn Res Cathd Ch Of S Paul Detroit MI 2012-** B Phoenix AZ 1964 s James & Margaret. BA U of Arizona 1986; M. Div. Bos 1989; MBA U Roch 1994; Cert Angl Stds SWTS 2011. D 6/9/2012 P 12/8/2012 Bp Wendell Nathaniel Gibbs Jr. m 6/18/1994 Elizabeth Townsend c 3. balltop@detroitcathedral.org

ALMENDAREZ BAUTISTA, Javier E (NC) **Assoc S Paul's Epis Ch Cary NC 2016-; Other Lay Position S Phil's Ch Durham NC 2013-** B 1987 M.Div. Duke DS 2013; Angl Stds Dplma VTS 2016. D 6/11/2016 P 12/17/2016 Bp Anne Hodges-Copple. javier@stpaulscary.org

ALMODIEL JR, Arsolin Diones (Nev) Dioces of Nevada, 9480 S Eastern Ave, Las Vegas NV 89123 B Philippines 1964 s Arsolin & Sotera. BA S Andr TS 1991. Rec 11/16/2013 as Priest Bp Dan Thomas Edwards. m 8/5/2000 Bernadette N Yalung-Almodiel c 1. Dio Nevada Las Vegas 2012.

ALMON JR, Austin Albert (RI) 116 Daggett Ave, Pawtucket RI 02861 **D Gr Ch N Attleboro MA 2006-** B Pawtucket RI 1943 s Austin & Jeanie. BS Johnson & Wales U 1976; MBA Wstrn New Engl Coll 1983; Rhode Island Sch For Deacons 1985. D 7/13/1985 Bp George Nelson Hunt III. m 2/10/1968 Jacqueline Louise Tonge c 2. D S Paul's Ch Portsmouth RI 1993-2006; Serv Gr Ch In Providence Providence RI 1991-1993, D 1985-1990; D Ch Of The Epiph Providence RI 1990-1991; St Mich & Gr Ch Rumford RI 1985-1993. Fllshp Way Cross.

ALMONO ROQUE, Joel Antonio (Mass) 1524 Summit Ave, Saint Paul MN 55105 **Gr Epis Ch Lawr MA 2006-** B San Francisco de Macoris DO 1959 s Ramon & Adriana. U of Santo Domingo Do; Methodist TS 1982; U Third Age Law 1994. D 4/2/1995 P 9/24/1996 Bp Julio Cesar Holguin-Khoury. m 4/3/1993 Susan Seaquist c 5. La Mision El Santo Nino Jesus S Paul MN 2004-2006, 1998-2004, Sub-D 1994-1998; Dio Minnesota Minneapolis MN 1998-2004; Hd Of Evang Dio The Dominican Republic (Iglesia Epis Dominicana) Gazcue Santo Domingo 1996-1998, Hd Of Evang 1993-; Serv Methodist Ch 1982-1988. Auth, "Cantos Apocalipticos," *El Nuevo Diario*, 1996; Auth, "Dolor Del Tiempo".

ALMONTE, Salvador (DR) Calle Santiago #114 Gazcue, Santo Domingo Dominican Republic **Dio The Dominican Republic (Iglesia Epis Dominicana) Gazcue Santo Domingo 1995-** B Gaspar Hernandez 1952 s Salvador & Gregoria. Rec 7/1/1995 as Priest Bp Julio Cesar Holguin-Khoury. m 8/31/1991 Ana Lidia Toribio. Serv RC Ch 1984-1991.

ALMOS, Richard Wayne (La) 996 Marina Dr, Slidell LA 70458 **D Chr Ch Slidell LA 2005-** B La Crosse WI 1938 s Willard & Beatrice. D 10/23/2005 Bp Charles Edward Jenkins III. m 6/28/1980 Jean Evelyn Almos c 2.

ALMQUIST SSJE, Curtis Gustav (Mass) Society of St. John the Evangelist, 980 Memorial Drive, Cambridge MA 02138 **Monk Soc of S Jn the Evang Cambridge MA 1987-** B Moline IL 1952 s Donald & Beatrice. BA Wheaton Coll 1974; MA MI SU 1978; MDiv Nash 1984; DD Ya Berk 2004. D 6/16/1984 Bp Quintin Ebenezer Primo Jr P 12/15/1984 Bp James Winchester Montgomery. Superior Soc of S Jn the Evang Cambridge MA 2001-2010; Pub Cowley Pub Cambridge MA 2001-2005; Asst Superior Soc of S Jn the Evang Cambridge MA 1997-2000; Guardian of Novices Soc of S Jn the Evang Cambridge MA 1994-1999; Chapl HOB 1994-1998; Sr Bro Emery Hse 1992-1994; Bro S Jn's Chap Cambridge MA 1987-2014; Soc-St Jn The Evang Cambridge MA 1987-2014; Cur S Simons Ch Arlington Hts IL 1984-1987. "The Twelve Days of Christmas," Cowley, 2006; "God's Conditional Love," *I Have Called You Friends*, Cowley, 2006.

ALONGE-COONS, Katherine Grace (Alb) Grace Church, 34 3rd St, Waterford NY 12188 **Gr Ch Waterford NY 2007-, D 2005-2006; Asst Gr Ch Waterford NY 2006-** B Hudson NY 1959 d Charles & Judith. BA Siena Coll 1980; MS SUNY 1985; MDiv S Bernards TS and Mnstry 2006. D 6/11/2005 Bp Daniel William Herzog P 1/7/2006 Bp David John Bena. m 6/12/1982 Earl Alfred Coons c 2.

ALONSO MARINA, Jesus Daniel (EcuC) Ava Y Maldonado, Guayaquil Ecuador B Burgos ES 1948 s Daniel & Carmen. San Jeronimo Sem Mayor; Inst Espanol De Misiones Extranjeras 1969; Inst Espanol De Misiones Extranjeras 1975. Rec 12/31/1990 as Priest Bp Luis Caisapanta. m 6/27/1988 Miriam Alexandra Aguayo Bailon. Litoral Dio Ecuador Guayaquil 1991-1996, P 1990-.

ALONZO, Mary Parsons (Roch) 541 Linden St, Rochester NY 14620 B South Orange NJ 1937 d Joseph & Mary. Cert U CO; BA Vas 1959; MDiv Bex Sem 1991. D 4/30/1992 Bp William George Burrill. m 12/26/1994 Daniel Arthur Alonzo.

ALONZO MARTINEZ, Gerardo Antonio (Hond) **Dio Honduras San Pedro Sula 2006-; Dn Iglesia Epis Hondurena San Pedro Sula 2006-** B Ojojona, F.M 1965 s Daniel & Adela. DIT Programa Diocesana De Ecuc Teologica 2003; Dip.en Other 2004; Dip.en Universidad Biblica Latino Americana 2004. D 10/29/2005 Bp Lloyd Emmanuel Allen. m 12/16/1989 Iris Yolanda Godoy Ordonez c 3. Dir Casa Alianza De Honduras 1988-1996.

ALSAY, Joseph Caldwell (Okla) 14700 N MAY AVE, OKLAHOMA CITY OK 73134 **R S Aug Of Cbury Oklahoma City OK 2010-** B Chicago IL 1973 s Glenzia & Beatrice. Phillips TS; BA Oklahoma Bapt U 1996; MDiv Luth TS at Chicago 2004. Rec 1/15/2011 Bp Edward Joseph Konieczny. m 8/6/2005 Cecelia Alsay-Gray c 4.

ALTENBACH, Julie Kay (CFla) **D Ch Of The Mssh Winter Garden FL 2015-** D 9/12/2015 Bp Gregory Orrin Brewer.

ALTIZER, Aimee Marie (U) D 12/10/2015 P 9/13/2016 Bp Scott Byron Hayashi.

ALTIZER, Caryl Jean (WTenn) 1830 S 336th St Apt C-202, Federal Way WA 98003 B Huntington WV 1945 d Emmett & Susan. U So; BS Bethel U 1967; MA OH SU 1969; MDiv Candler TS Emory U 1984. D 5/22/1984 P 12/18/1984 Bp Furman Charles Stough. The Epis Counslg Cntr Memphis TN 1986-1988; Int S Mich's Epis Ch Birmingham AL 1985-1986; Asst H H Cross Trussville AL 1984-1986.

ALTON, Frank (Los) 840 Echo Park Ave, Los Angeles CA 90026 **Dio Los Angeles Los Angeles CA 2012-** B Santa Monica CA 1952 s John & Merle. BA Pomona Coll 1973; MDiv Fuller TS 1977; DMin Fuller TS 1985. D 4/26/2012 Bp Mary Douglas Glasspool P 10/27/2012 Bp Joseph Jon Bruno. m 9/6/2014 Saul Renterin c 3. falton@ladiocese.org

ALTON, Richard (Pa) St. Clement's Church, 2013 Appletree Street, Philadelphia PA 19103 **R S Clements Ch Philadelphia PA 2014-** B Manchester CT 1955 s Richard & Elizabeth. BA Boston Coll 1978; MAR Yale DS 1980; Cert Ang Stud GTS 1988. D 6/11/1988 Bp Arthur Edward Walmsley P 2/25/1989 Bp Clarence Nicholas Coleridge. m 10/20/1979 Barbara B Alton c 1. R The Ch Of The Gd Shpd Rosemont PA 2012-2014; P-in-c S Andr's Ch Stamford CT 2007-2012; R S Mk's Ch Philadelphia PA 1997-2007; Cur S Thos Ch New York NY 1994-1997; Cur Trin Epis Ch Southport CT 1990-1994; Cur S Mary's Epis Ch Manchester CT 1988-1990. The Most Venerable Ord of the Hosp of St. Jn of Jerusalem 1995.

ALTOPP, Whitney F (Ct) Saint Stephen's Church, 351 Main St, Ridgefield CT 06877 **S Steph's Ch Ridgefield CT 2012-** B Champaign IL 1972 d Lawrence & Deborah. BA Greenville Coll 1994; MDiv GTS 2002. D 6/15/2002 P 1/6/2003 Bp Gladstone Bailey Adams III. m 3/21/1992 Michael P Altopp c 4. Assoc S Thos' Ch Whitemarsh Ft Washington PA 2007-2012; Asst S Jas Ch Montclair NJ 2002-2007; Intern S Mich's Ch New York NY 2000-2001; Yth Dir S Jas Ch Skaneateles NY 1994-1997.

ALVARADO FIGUEROA, Luis A (PR) **Dio Puerto Rico Trujillo Alto PR 2004-** B 1959

ALVARADO-PALADA, Carlos (Hond) **Dio Honduras San Pedro Sula 1998-** B 1957 m 12/24/1994 Mayra Suyapa Velasquez.

ALVAREZ-ADORNO, Aida-Luz (PR) **Dio Puerto Rico Trujillo Alto PR 2007-** B 1955 d Juan & Carmen. San Pedro Y San Pablo; MA Universidad Cntrl; BA Caribbean U 1980. D 8/27/2006 P 2/11/2007 Bp David Andres Alvarez-Velazquez. c 3.

ALVAREZ-ESTRADA, Miguel (WNC) 5383 E Owens Ave, Las Vegas NV 89110 **Cn Dio Wstrn No Carolina Asheville NC 2015-** B 1960 s Andres & Gertrudis. Rec 11/16/2013 as Priest Bp Dan Thomas Edwards. m 12/19/1999 Rosario Ricardez Alvarez c 1. Dio Nevada Las Vegas 2015.

✠ ALVAREZ-VELAZQUEZ, The Rt Rev David Andres (PR) 4735 Ave. Isla Verde, Cond. Villas del Mar Oeste, Apt. 3-E, Carolina PR 00979 B Ponce Puerto Rico 1941 s Lorenzo & Paula. MDiv. Seminario Epis del Caribe 1965; Psy. D. Centro Caribeno Estudios- Graduados 1987. D 5/22/1965 P 11/27/1965 Bp Francisco Reus-Froylan Con 11/28/1987 for PR. m 12/10/1981 Maryleen Rose Mullert c 3. Bp of Puerto Rico Dio Puerto Rico Trujillo Alto PR 1987-2013, Bp of Puerto Rico 1965-1987. obispoalvarez@gmail.com

ALVES, David Alan (NCal) 13840 Tulsa Ct, Magalia CA 95954 **D Ch Of S Nich Paradise CA 1999-** B Dartmouth MA 1935 s Albert & Olive. New Bedford Inst of Tech; Sch for Deacons. D 8/31/1980 Bp Charles Shannon Mallory. m 2/17/1963 Marianne Alves c 2. D Gd Samar Epis Ch San Jose CA 1991-1999, D 1980-1990; D Ch Of S Jos Milpitas CA 1982-1991.

ALVES, Robert (EC) St John's Episcopal Church, 302 Green St, Fayetteville NC 28301 **R S Jn's Epis Ch Fayetteville NC 2010-, Asst 1989-1993; Dep GC 2015, 2018 Dio E Carolina Kinston NC 2015-, Trst of the Dio E Carolina 2015-, Stndg Com, Pres 2014-2015 2012-2015, Historic Properties Com 2012-, Tri-Dioc Hist Com 2011-, Trst U So 2011-, Yth Cmsn (Chair 1991-1993 1990-1993, Liturg Cmsn 1989-1992** B Philadelphia PA 1958 s James & Louella. BA U So 1981; MDiv VTS 1989. D 6/10/1989 Bp John Thomas Walker P 1/13/1990 Bp Ronald Hayward Haines. m 11/26/1983 Polly B Alves c 2. R S Barn Epis Ch Greenwich CT 2004-2010; Secy of the Dio Dio No Carolina Raleigh NC 2003-2004, Alt Dep Gc 2003, Dioc Coun 1996-1999, GC 1st Alt Dep 2003-2004, GC Dep 2000-2002, Stndg Com 1999-2002, Transition Com, Chair 1999-2001, St of the Ch Com, Chair (1992-1993) 1993-1996; R All SS Ch Roanoke Rapids NC 1993-2004; Cathd Chapt Dio Connecticut Meriden CT 2009-2010, Transition Com 2009-2010, Prog and Bdgt Com 2008-2010; Strng Com: Darkness into Day: Restoring Hope after Kartina ECF Inc New York NY 2006-2009; Stwdshp Cmsn Dio Washington Washington DC 1982-1986. Ord of St. Jn 2009.

ALVEY JR, John Thomas (Ala) 110 W Hawthorne Rd, Birmingham AL 35209 **S Paul's Ch Selma AL 2014-; Stndg Com Dio Alabama Birmingham 2011-** B Birmingham AL 1984 s John & Heidi. BS U of Alabama 2006; MDiv VTS 2009. D 5/27/2009 P 12/18/2009 Bp Henry Nutt Parsley Jr. m 5/30/2009 Jamie Bryars Alvey c 1. Assoc R All SS Epis Ch Birmingham AL 2009-2014. jackalvey@gmail.com

ALWINE, David W (Tex) 527 Shem Butler Ct., Charleston SC 29414 B Biloxi MS 1953 s Wayne & Janie. BA Belhaven Coll 1975; MDiv Reformed TS 1978; MS U of Sthrn Mississippi 1981; STM Sewanee: The U So, TS 1983. D 12/21/1985 P 1/6/1987 Bp Donis Dean Patterson. m 6/30/1979 Margaret T Alwine c 2. R Chr Epis Ch Temple TX 2000-2014; R Gr Epis Ch Paris TN 1993-1999; R Ch Of The Ascen (Hagood) Rembert SC 1990-1993; Assc. R S Mich's Epis Ch Charleston SC 1987-1990; Ch Of The Epiph Richardson TX 1985-1987.

AMADIO, Carol M (FdL) Po Box 51, Washington Island WI 54246 **Assoc Prof Loyola U Sch Of Soc Wk Chicago IL 1988-** B Austin TX 1945 d William & Carol. BA U CO 1968; MS Loyola U 1971; JD Loyola U 1975; MDiv McCormick TS 1980; LLM Illinois Inst of Tech 1982; LLM Kent St U 1982. D 6/11/1980 Bp James Winchester Montgomery P 2/24/1981 Bp Quintin Ebenezer Primo Jr. m 9/16/1968 Anselm Henry Amadio. Asst S Simons Ch Arlington Hts IL 2000-2002; Non-par 1994-2000; Int S Bede's Epis Ch Bensenville IL 1992-1993; Vice-Chncllr Dio Chicago Chicago IL 1989-1997; Int Gr Ch Chicago IL 1989-1991; Int Ch Of S Paul And The Redeem Chicago IL 1988-1989; Asst/P-in-c S Mk's Ch Evanston IL 1982-1988; D Ch Of Our Sav Chicago IL 1980-1982.

AMAYA, Adrian A (CNY) 1612 W Genesee St, Syracuse NY 13219 **P S Mk The Evang Syracuse NY 2008-** B Alice TX 1966 s Alex & Mary. BA U of Texas 1992; MDiv Sewanee: The U So, TS 1999. D 6/16/1999 Bp Robert Boyd Hibbs P 1/13/2000 Bp James Edward Folts. m 11/13/1993 Anna Amaya c 2. R S Phil's Ch Beeville TX 2002-2008; S Barth's Ch Corpus Christi TX 1999-2002.

AMBELANG, John Edward (Eau) 506 Fairway Dr, Sheboygan WI 53081 **Ret 2000-** B Saint Louis MO 1944 s Charles & Audry. BA U of Wisconsin 1966; MDiv Nash 1969. D 3/1/1969 Bp Donald H V Hallock P 9/13/1969 Bp William W Horstick. m 9/11/1965 Karen Ruth Ambelang. R S Mary's Epis Ch Tomah WI 2002-2010; R S Jn's Epis Ch Mauston WI 2000-2012; R Fran Ch Menomonee Falls WI 1997-2002; R S Mich's Epis Ch Racine WI 1981-1997; R S Mk's Ch Beaver Dam WI 1976-1981; Vic S Steph's Shell Lake WI 1973-1976; Cur Chr Ch Cathd Eau Claire WI 1972-1973; S Alb's Ch Spooner WI 1969-1976; St Stephens Ch Spooner WI 1969-1976.

AMBLER V, John Jaquelin (SwVa) 507 Sunset Dr, Amherst VA 24521 **Ret 1997-** B Dante VA 1931 s John & Cynthia. BA S Johns Coll 1953; MDiv VTS 1959. D 6/12/1959 P 6/1/1960 Bp Frederick D Goodwin. m 8/24/1958 Mirosanda Ambler c 4. P-in-c S Paul's Mssn Bear Mtn VA 1971-1978; Vic S Steph's

Ch Romney WV 1963-1969; Asst S Paul's Ch Richmond VA 1959-1963. Auth, "Syllabus For Tchg The Abacus".

AMBLER JR, Michael Nash (Me) 912 Middle St, Bath ME 04530 **Dio Maine Portland ME 2014-, 2000-2002** B New York NY 1964 BA Pr 1985; JD U MI 1989; MDiv EDS 2000. D 6/3/2000 P 12/16/2000 Bp Chilton Richardson Knudsen. m 7/13/1985 Deborah S Ambler c 3. R Gr Epis Ch Bath ME 2002-2014; Asst S Dav's Epis Ch Kennebunk ME 2000-2002.

AMBROISE, Rospignac (Mass) Box 1309, Port-Au-Prince Haiti **S Jn's S Jas Epis Ch Boston MA 2013-; Vic Gr Ch Everett MA 2012-; P-in-c Resirr Gros-Morn 1994-** B Mirebabais HT 1963 s Anne. Haiti TS 1992. D 12/6/1992 Bp Luc Anatole Jacques Garnier P 9/1/1993 Bp Jean Zache Duracin. m 12/29/1994 Junie Ambroise c 3. Dio Haiti Port-au-Prince HT 1992-2006, Asst P 1992-1993. Soc Of S Marg. pignacambro@yahoo.com

AMBROSE, Barbara (Va) 236 S Laurel St, Richmond VA 23220 **D S Andr's Ch Richmond VA 2011-** B Ft Stewart GA 1957 d Jacob & Sarah. BA Randolph-Macon Coll 1979; MA UTS and Presb Sch of Ed 2003; MSW Virginia Commonwealth U 2003; Diac Formation Inst 2010. D 2/5/2011 Bp Shannon Sherwood Johnston. m 10/7/1995 John Ambrose. Transition Com for Bp Suffr Dio Virginia Richmond VA 2011-2012. Assn of Epis Deacons 2011.

AMBROSE, Colin Moore (Tenn) 116 N. Academy St., Murfreesboro TN 37130 **Assoc S Paul's Epis Ch Murfreesboro TN 2013-, 2009-2013; Fndt Bd Mem Middle Tennessee Med Cntr 2012-** B Knoxville TN 1978 s Paul & Kathleen. BA U NC 2000; MDiv Nash 2009. D 10/23/2008 P 5/16/2009 Bp Keith Lynn Ackerman. m 10/7/2001 Trisha Ambrose c 3. Bp and Coun Dio Tennessee Nashville TN 2012-2014, Disciplinary Revs Bd 2011-2012, Eccl Crt 2010-2012. Auth, "Desiring to be Justified: An Examination of the Parable of the Gd Samar in Lk 10:25-37," *Sewanee Theol Revs*, Sewanee Theol Revs, 2010.

AMBROSE, Theodore (Va) 2609 N Glebe Rd # P, Arlington VA 22207 **Ware Epis Ch Gloucester VA 2014-** B Washington NC 1979 s Theodore & Bonnie. BA No Carolina Wesleyan Coll 2001; MDiv VTS 2011. D 6/11/2011 Bp Clifton Daniel III. m 11/14/2013 Martha R Ambrose. Asst S Mary's Epis Ch Arlington VA 2011-2014.

AMBROSE, Valerie Twomey (WMich) 6308 Greenway Drive SE, Grand Rapids MI 49546 B North Hollywood CA 1947 d Lawrence & Celine. BA TCU 1967; MRE Wstrn TS 1996. D 4/26/1997 P 1/17/1998 Bp Edward Lewis Lee Jr. m 9/15/2014 Virginia Catherine Searls c 3. P-in-c S Jn's Ch Fremont MI 2011-2012; Exec Dir Legal Assistance Cntr Grand Rapids MI 2007-2011; Assoc S Andr's Ch Grand Rapids MI 2007-2010; Int S Mk's Ch Grand Rapids MI 2003-2007; Int Epis Par Of S Jn The Bapt Portland OR 2000-2002; Int S Jas Epis Ch Portland OR 2000-2001; Int S Tim Ch Richland MI 1999; Assoc S Mart Of Tours Epis Ch Kalamazoo MI 1998-1999; VP Holland Cmnty Hosp Holland MI 1995-1998; Exec Dir Evergreen Commons Sr Cntr Holland MI 1985-1995. Auth, "Developing a Seasonal Wrshp Template," *Open*, 2001. Associated Parishes Coun 1994-2004; Attending Cler Assn Holland Hosp 1997-1999; Epis Sr Living Serv (Pres.) 2000-2002. Dioc Designee Natl Wmn Hist Proj ECW 1994.

AMBURGEY, Cristina Goubaud (Oly) 3213 17th Street Pl Se, Puyallup WA 98374 B Guatamala City GT 1947 d Antonio & Frances. BS Arizona St U 1985. D 6/23/2001 Bp Sanford Zangwill Kaye Hampton. m 6/13/1981 Robert M Amburgey c 4. Dio Olympia Olympia WA 2006-2007; Dio Olympia Olympia WA 2003-2007; D S Andr's Epis Ch Tacoma WA 2001-2006. NAAD 1996-2006; Sis of S Jos of Peace - Assoc 1995.

AMEND, Albert Edward (LI) 13821 Willow Bridge Dr, North Fort Myers FL 33903 **Died 6/25/2017** B Columbus OH 1930 s Albert & Marie. BA Iona Coll 1957; MA CUNY 1961; Cert Mercer TS 1971. D 6/13/1970 P 6/12/1971 Bp Jonathan Goodhue Sherman. m 6/28/1958 Virginia D Amend c 2. S Lk's Ch Ft Myers FL 1994-2003; Ret 1993-2017; R Epis Ch of The Resurr Williston Pk NY 1976-1992; P-in-c Ch Of S Jn The Bapt Ctr Moriches NY 1972-1976; Dio Long Island Garden City NY 1971-1976; Asst S Paul's Ch Patchogue NY 1970-1971. CCU 1980-1993; Comp & Area Chapl for FL FODC 1993; ESA 1979-1993; SSC 1990.

AMEND, Russell Jay (WNY) 25 Caspian Ct, Amherst NY 14228 B New York NY 1933 s Russell & Marion. BA CUNY Queens Coll 1955; MDiv Ya Berk 1958. D 4/12/1958 P 10/25/1958 Bp James Pernette DeWolfe. m 6/30/1956 Joan Katherine Amend c 2. Dioc Coun Dio Wstrn New York Tonawanda NY 1968-1972; P-in-c H Apos Epis Ch Tonawanda NY 1965-1998; P & R St. Barth's Ch Tonawanda N.Y. 1965-1998; P-in-c Ch Of The Redeem Niagara Falls NY 1960-1965; Cur Epis Ch of The Resurr Williston Pk NY 1958-1960. Bd Dir: Bible Soc of Wstrn New York 1967-1992. P of the Year Dio Wstrn New York, Bp Dav C. Bowman 1995.

AMERMAN, Lucy S.L. (Pa) PO Box 57, Buckingham PA 18912 B Sewickley PA 1950 d Lockhart & Louise. BA Goucher Coll 1972; JD Widener U 1976; MDiv PrTS 2002; Dplma Oxf GB 2006. D 6/28/2003 Bp David Bruce Joslin P 1/5/2004 Bp George Edward Councell. m 8/8/2010 Norman J Haas c 4. Dio Pennsylvania Philadelphia PA 2013-2016; R Trin Ch Buckingham PA 2006-2013; Asst R S Ptr's Epis Ch Arlington VA 2003-2006. lucya@diopa.org

AMES, David A (RI) 130 Slater Ave, Providence RI 02906 **P-in-c All SS' Memi Ch Providence RI 2010-; Bd Dir Cntr for Recon Dio pf RI 2015-** B Glendale OH 1938 s Malcolm & Jane. BA Mia 1960; MDiv EDS 1966; Fell Coll of Preachers 1974; DMin EDS 1984; Exec Serv Corps of New Engl 2004; Int Mnstry Prog 2005. D 6/25/1966 P 1/6/1967 Bp Roger W Blanchard. m 1/30/1982 Carol Landau c 2. Cmnty & Congrl Relatns Global AIDS Interfaith Allnce San Francisco CA 2008-2009; Adj Prof of Philos Rhode Island Coll Providence RI 2006-2015; P-in-c S Mk's Epis Ch Riverside RI 2006-2008; R Gr Ch New Bedford MA 2005; R S Mart's Ch Providence RI 2004-2005, 2002-2003; P-in-c St. Mart's Ch Providence RI 2003-2005; Exec Dir Assoc For Rel & Intellectual Life New Rochelle NY 1989-1993; Epis Chapl RISD / Brown Provdence RI 1974-2003; Chapl Dio Rhode Island Providence RI 1972-2003; Ecum Chapl, Rhode Island Coll Rhode Island St Coun of Ch Providence RI 1971-1974; Asst Gr Ch In Providence Providence RI 1969-1971; P Ch Of S Edw Columbus OH 1966-1969; Cler Advsry Bd PPF of Amer 2010-2017. Ames, D.A., "A Pstr Perspective on Death and Those Who Survive," *Med and Hlth/Rhode Island*, Rhode Island Med Assn, 2005; Ames, Dav A., "The Role of the Ch in the New Genetics," *A Chr Response to the New Genetics*, Rowman & Littlefiled, 2003; Ames, D.A., "Cultural Ambiguity and Moral Ldrshp," *Plumbline*, Plumbline, 1995. ESMHE 1973-2003. Appreciation for Strategic Plnng Holocaust Educ and Resource Cntr of Rhode Island 2006; Fac Serv Awd Brown Med Sch 2004; DSA PPF of Amer 2003; Years of Serv Awd Br 2000; Cert of Recognition Brown Med Sch 1999; Gilman Angier Awd Planned Parenthood of Rhode Island 1995.

AMES, Richard Kenneth (SeFla) 4917 Ravenswood Dr Apt 1709, San Antonio TX 78227 **Chapl Hollywood FL Police Hollywood FL 1991-** B Tappan NY 1935 s Donald & Virginia. BS WA SU 1965; MPA Auburn U 1973; Grad U.S. Indstrl Coll of the Armed Forced 1975; MDiv Nash 1983. D 7/28/1982 Bp Edward Mason Turner P 6/1/1983 Bp William Cockburn Russell Sheridan. m 10/5/1956 Dolores Natalie Ames c 3. S Mk's Ch Palm Bch Garden FL 1994; R S Jn's Ch Hollywood FL 1986-1994; R S Anne's Epis Ch Warsaw IN 1983-1986. Bro Awd Hollywood Interfaith 1990.

AMMONS JR, B Wiley (Fla) 7500 Southside Blvd, Jacksonville FL 32256 **R The Epis Ch of The Redeem Jacksonville FL 2016-** B Jacksonville FL 1980 s Benjamin & Janice. BS U of Florida 2002; MDiv VTS 2011. D 12/5/2010 P 6/19/2011 Bp Samuel Johnson Howard. m 12/15/2001 Laura C Chiles c 1. Ch Of The Gd Shpd Jacksonville FL 2014-2016; Cn, Yth Mnstry Dio Florida Jacksonville 2011-2014. wiley@redeemerjax.org

AMPAH OSH, Rosina A (NY) 3042 Eagle Dr, Augusta GA 30906 B Tarkwa GH 1941 d Samuel & Christina. BA Coll of New Rochelle 1990; MDiv NYTS 1993. D 6/12/1993 P 12/11/1993 Bp Richard Frank Grein. St Jn the Evang Epis Ch Lynbrook NY 1993-1995; Asst S Jn's Of Lattingtown Locust Vlly NY 1993-1994. Ord of S Helena.

AMPARO TAPIA, Milton Mauricio (DR) Juan Luis Franco Bido #21, Santo Domingo Dominican Republic B Castillo Provincia Duarte 1966 s Carlos & Virginia. MS The London Sch of Econ and Political Sci; BA Intec 1992; BA Instituto Santo Inacio 1998. Rec 8/15/1998 Bp Julio Cesar Holguin-Khoury. m 7/2/2005 Kattia Severino de Amparo. Dio The Dominican Republic (Iglesia Epis Dominicana) Gazcue Santo Domingo 2007-2015.

AMSDEN, Helen Prince (Neb) 9459 Jones Cir, Omaha NE 68114 **D 1985-** B Grand Island NE 1928 d Harold & Mary. Smith; BA U of Nebraska 1949. D 11/8/1985 Bp James Daniel Warner. m 2/5/1955 Don Bruce Amsden c 3.

AMUZIE, Charles C (WA) 3601 Alabama Ave SE, Washington DC 20020 B NG 1956 s Nathan & Edna. DMiss Asbury TS; BS U of Nigeria 1982; DIT Imm Coll of Theol Ibadan NG 1986; MDiv Epis TS of the SW 1989; ThM Fuller TS 1992; PhD U of Kentucky 2004. Trans 11/28/1995 Bp Henry Irving Louttit. m 11/26/1983 Nena Amuzie c 4. R S Tim's Epis Ch Washington DC 2009-2012; R S Athan Ch Brunswick GA 1995-2008; Vic S Andr's Ch Lexington KY 1992-1995; Assoc. P S Jas Ch Austin TX 1986-1989; Yth Min S Lk's Of The Mountains La Crescenta CA 1991-1992.

ANCHAN, Israel D (Chi) 298 S. Harrison Ave., Kankakee IL 60901 **R/Cn All SS Ch Stoneham MA 2013-; Dir/Hd Pstr care Epis Hospitals/St. Andrews Hse Chicago 2013-; R S Paul's Ch Kankakee IL 2009-** B 1955 s Benony & Leelavathi. BD Serampore U 1983; STM UTS 2001; ThM Luth TS 2003; DMin Luth TS 2008. Trans 12/15/2008 Bp Jeff Lee. m 5/26/1985 Ruth J Anchan c 2.

ANDERHEGGEN, George Curtis (Ct) 6 Rosewood Cir, Monroe CT 06468 **Ret 1994-** B Portland OR 1928 s William & Josephine. BS U of Connecticut 1958; MDiv Ya Berk 1966; PhD Columbia Pacific U 1988. D 6/11/1966 P 3/1/1967 Bp Walter H Gray. m 9/27/1980 Jean Zalkind Anderheggen c 5. Non-par 1971-1994; Asst S Jn's Ch Bridgeport CT 1967-1971; Cur S Jn's Ch E Hartford CT 1966-1967. Auth, "A Wish For Your Christmas," *Elem Fun*; Auth, "Willy The Weenie Whiner," *Elem Fun*; Auth, "For Better, For Worse, Struggles," *Pilgrimage*. Amer Assn Of Behavioral Therapists; Amer Assn Of Mar & Fam Therapists; Amer Assn Of Sex Educators, Counselors, & Therapists; Natl Gld Of Hypnotists. Williams Curtis Awd For Rel Natl Gld Of Hypnotists 2002.

ANDERS, Florence Kay Houghton (RG) Holy Family Episcopal Church, 10 A Bisbee Court, Santa fe NM 87508 **Vic Epis Ch Of The H Fam Santa Fe NM**

A

2008- B Stockton CA 1947 d Paul & Elizabeth. BA U of Nthrn Colorado 1969; MA U of New Mex 1972; BS U of New Mex 1989; MDiv TESM 2008. D 11/10/2007 P 6/3/2008 Bp William Carl Frey. m 5/9/1998 Peter Anders.

ANDERSEN, Francis Ian (Cal) 5 Epsom Court, Donvale Victoria VI 3111 Australia **Chapl New Coll 1989-** B Warwick WA AU 1925 s Rasmus & Hilda. BS U of Queensland Brisbane Qld Au 1947; BA U of Melbourne 1951; MS U of Melbourne 1956; BD Lon GB 1957; MA JHU 1959; PhD JHU 1960. Trans 9/1/1990 Bp William Edwin Swing. m 12/5/1952 Lois Clarissa Andersen. Prof Of The OT Fuller TS Pasadena CA 1994-1997; Prof Of Rel Stds U Of Queensland 1980-1989; Prof CDSP Berkeley CA 1963-1972; Vice Prncpl Ridley Coll Melbourne Australia 1958-1962. Auth, "Var Books".

ANDERSEN, John Day (CNY) 2702 W Old State Road 34, Lizton IN 46149 **Vic Ch Of S Lawr Alexandria Bay NY 2005-; 1972-; Ret Vic 1991-** B Auburn NY 1933 s Robert & Arlene. BA Hobart and Wm Smith Colleges 1960; MDiv Ya Berk 1963. D 6/11/1963 Bp Walter H Gray P 12/14/1963 Bp John Henry Esquirol. m 1/30/1993 Janet Lewis Andersen. Epis Camps & Conf Centers Inc. Live Oak 1999-2006; Roslyn Managers Corp Richmond VA 1972-1992; Roslyn Conf Cntr Richmond VA 1972-1991; Asst S Mk's Ch New Canaan CT 1969-1972; Vic S Jn Greenwich CT 1963-1969. Ed, "ECCC Update," *Epis Camps and Conf Centers*, 1985; Ed, "The Journ," *Intl Assn*, Conf Cntr Admin, 1978. ECCC 1998; IACCA 1972. Washburn Awd for Disting Serv to Conf Ctr Ldrshp IACCA; Fouding Exec and Life Mem Natl Asociation of Epis Camps and Conf Centers; Staub Awd for Cmnty Serv Thousand Island Pk, New York.

ANDERSEN, Judith Ann (NMich) 500 Ogden Ave, Escanaba MI 49829 B Detroit MI 1941 d Raymond & Helen. D 12/7/2014 Bp Rayford J Ray. m 10/21/1961 Larry Ray Andersen c 3.

ANDERSEN, Paul John (Va) **R Chr Ch Par-Epis Christchurch VA 2006-; R Chr Epis Ch Christchurch VA 2006-** B Worcester MA 1949 s Albert & Anna. BA U of Alabama 1971; MDiv VTS 1977. D 5/26/1977 Bp Furman Charles Stough. m 5/22/1986 Lilith Peklic c 2. Dio Wstrn Massachusetts Springfield 2002-2005; R Trin Epis Ch Milford MA 2002-2005; Calv Ch Washington DC 1977.

ANDERSEN, Raynor Wade (Ct) 199 Eastgate Dr, Cheshire CT 06410 **Interpreter Amer Sign Lang 1973-; Mssy S Paul's Mssn of the Deaf 1972-** B New York NY 1944 s Haakon & Olive. BA Col 1966; STD PDS 1970. D 6/5/1970 P 12/1/1970 Bp Horace W B Donegan. m 8/7/1981 Karla Mary Scholz c 2. Bd Connecticut Cmsn on the Deaf 1973-1978; St Pauls Mssn of the Deaf W Hartford CT 1972-2004; Prog/Bdgt Com Dio Connecticut Meriden CT 1972-2003; Asst Gr Ch Merchantville NJ 1971-1972; Asst S Ann's Ch For The Deaf New York NY 1970-1971. Cranmer Cup, Victorius Chair 2000-2002; Epis Conf of the Deaf 1972; Oblate, Mulligan Soc 1975; Porter Cup 1996.

ANDERSEN, Richard Belden (Nwk) 275 E Franklin Tpke, Ho Ho Kus NJ 07423 **Ret 1992-** B Bakersfield CA 1926 s Richard & Marion. BA U of Redlands 1950; BD Colgate Rochester Crozer DS 1953; BD CRDS 1953; GTS 1967; MA FD 1974; MS FD 1974. D 1/8/1967 Bp George E Rath P 5/1/1967 Bp Dudley S Stark. Int S Jn's Memi Ch Ramsey NJ 2000-2002; R S Eliz's Ch Ridgewood NJ 1972-1991; Assoc Chr Ch Short Hills NJ 1971-1972, Asst 1967-1971; Serv Bapt Ch 1953-1966.

ANDERSEN, Steven C (U) 75 South 200 East, P.O. Box 3090, Salt Lake City UT 84110 **Bd Dir INN Between SLC UT 2017-; Chf Fin Off Dio Utah Salt Lake City UT 2009-; Advsr, Admin Trust II 2009-; Bd Dir Epis Mgmt Corp 2005-; Bd Trst/Treas Mt. Olivet Cemetary 2005-** B Jerome ID 1956 s Keith & LaVerne. BSBA U of Phoenix 1991. D 6/19/2003 P 2/21/2004 Bp Carolyn Tanner Irish. c 1. All SS Ch Salt Lake City UT 2014. sandersen@episcopal-ut.org

ANDERSON, Alissa Goudswaard (Ind) 802 Broadway, New York NY 10003 **S Jn's Ch Larchmont NY 2017-** B East Grand Rapids MI 1988 d Arie & Grace. D 1/28/2017 Bp Cate Waynick. m 8/17/2014 Joshua M Anderson. Gr Epis Ch New York NY 2017.

ANDERSON, Angela Mary (Nev) D 5/6/2017 Bp Dan Thomas Edwards.

ANDERSON, Ann Johnston (ND) 2405 W Country Club Dr S, Fargo ND 58103 B Bismarck ND 1955 d James & Joyce. AA No Dakota St U 1977. D 5/10/2002 P 5/9/2003 Bp Andrew Fairfield. m 11/24/1984 David Frederick Anderson. D Geth Cathd Fargo ND 2002-2003.

ANDERSON, Anthony (Neb) **Cur Dio Nebraska Omaha NE 2017-** D 1/19/2017 Bp Scott Scott Barker.

ANDERSON, Augusta (WNC) 2 Cedarcliff Road, Asheville NC 28803 **Cn Dio Wstrn No Carolina Asheville NC 2017-** B San Rafael CA 1969 d Richard & Katherine. BA Hobart and Wm Smith Colleges 1991; MDiv VTS 1999. D 6/12/1999 Bp Ronald Hayward Haines P 12/11/1999 Bp Bob Johnson. m 7/21/2001 James Stephen Anderson c 3. Ch Of The Trsfg Saluda NC 2014-2017; S Jas Ch Black Mtn NC 2010-2013; R S Thos Epis Ch Burnsville NC 2004-2007; Cn The Cathd Of All Souls Asheville NC 1999-2003. canonaugusta@diocesewnc.org

ANDERSON JR, Bert A (Los) 612 Chestnut St, Ashland OR 97520 **Asstg P Trin Epis Ch Ashland Ashland OR 2002-; Non-par 1967-** B Los Angeles CA 1929 s Bert & Alma. BA California St U 1956; MDiv CDSP 1959; PhD

Sierra U Costa Mesa CA 1988. D 6/22/1959 P 2/1/1960 Bp Francis E I Bloy. m 12/2/1973 Nancy Anderson c 3. Trin Epis Ch Redlands CA 1986-1988; Vic Ch Of The H Sprt Bullhead City AZ 1980-1982; Bd Epis Cmnty Serv San Diego CA 1966-1967; R S Andr's By The Sea Epis Par San Diego CA 1960-1967; Chapl to Jvnl Institutions Epis Cmnty Serv San Diego CA 1959-1960; Chair Cmsn On Stwdshp Educ Dio Los Angeles Los Angeles CA 1965-1966. Authur, "Curious: A Life Sacr and Secular," Create Space, 2017; Auth, "TRaNZ," *Play*, Self-Pub, 2012; Auth, "Mr. Brightside and the Bonfire Nights," *Play*, Self-Pub, 2010; Auth, "BONE: Dying Into Life," *Play*, Self-Pub, 2008; Auth, "Dyspnea During Panic Attacks," *Behavior Modification*, Behavior Modification, 2001; Auth, "Healing Panic Recovery Prog," Self-Pub, 1998. Amer Assn Of Psychophysiology And Biofeedback 1985-2001; California Assn Of Fam Therapists 1985-1998; Int Soc For The Advancement Of Respiratory Psychophysiology 1999-2004.

ANDERSON, Betsy (Los) 315 Lorraine Blvd, Los Angeles CA 90020 B Los Angeles CA 1948 d James & Jeanne. BA Stan 1970; MDiv Ya Berk 1997. D 6/21/1997 P 1/17/1998 Bp Frederick Houk Borsch. m 6/17/1972 Carl T Anderson c 2. Assoc The Par Of S Matt Pacific Plsds CA 1997-2014.

ANDERSON, Bettina Galer (Colo) 822 Fox Hollow Ln, Golden CO 80401 B Seattle WA 1943 d Frederick & Vera. BS Colorado St U 1965; MS Colorado St U 1967; PhD Colorado St U 1971; MDiv Pontifical Coll Josephinum 1985. D 6/8/1985 P 12/1/1985 Bp William Grant Black. m 10/4/1973 Wesley D Anderson. R Ch Of S Jn Chrys Golden CO 1995-2000; R S Ptr's Epis Ch Delaware OH 1987-1995; Asst R S Jas Epis Ch Columbus OH 1985-1987, D-in-Trng 1985.

ANDERSON, Bill (At) 2510 Two Oaks Dr, Charleston SC 29414 B Aiken SC 1944 s Marcus & Thelma. MA Roosevelt U; BA U GA 1966. D 11/4/1999 Bp Edward Lloyd Salmon Jr. m 11/12/1965 Jane Ellen Anderson. S Chris's At-The-Crossroads Epis Perry GA 2003-2008. cindy.davis10@charter.net

ANDERSON, Carmen Marie (Kan) 375 Lake Shore Drive, Alma KS 66401 B Wichita KS 1940 d Harold & Mildred. BS K SU 1963. D 6/20/1987 Bp Richard Frank Grein. c 3. Gd Shpd Epis Ch Wichita KS 1990-1992.

ANDERSON, Carol (NY) 115 E 87th St Apt 6B, New York NY 10128 B Easton PA 1945 d William & Doris. BA Lycoming Coll 1967; MDiv EDS 1970. D 11/13/1971 P 1/3/1977 Bp Horace W B Donegan. R All SS Par Beverly Hills CA 1989-2010; Inst for Cler Renwl Fairfax VA 1986-1989; R All Ang' Ch New York NY 1979-1986; Asst S Jas Ch New York NY 1972-1979; Exec Asst Epis Mssn Soc Epis Ch Cntr New York NY 1971-1972. Auth, *Knowing Jesus in Your Life*, Morehouse Pub, 1993. DD GTS 2013; DD Ya Berk 1992.

ANDERSON, Carolyn Kinsey (Ga) 4221 Blue Heron Ln, Evans GA 30809 **Died 6/29/2017** B Harvey IL 1939 Sthrn Illinois U. D 7/10/2002 Bp Henry Irving Louttit. c 3.

ANDERSON, Christian S (Los) St Marys Episcopal Church, 623 Se Ocean Blvd, Stuart FL 34994 **S Mary's Epis Ch Stuart FL 2016-** B 1977 s Burr & Lila. MDiv (1 Year of Study) Fuller TS; MDiv VTS 2016. D 6/4/2016 Bp Joseph Jon Bruno P 12/17/2016 Bp Peter David Eaton. Angl Comm Prize VTS 2016; cl VTS 2016. christian@stmarys-stuart.org

ANDERSON JR, C Newell (At) 1884 Rugby Ave, College Park GA 30337 B Columbia SC 1937 s Claude & Kathleen. BA Georgia Inst of Tech; MDiv Sewanee: The U So, TS. D 6/24/1972 Bp Milton Legrand Wood P 4/1/1973 Bp Bennett Jones Sims. m 12/30/1983 Curtissa Anderson. P-in-c S Simon's Epis Ch Conyers GA 1999-2003; The Epis Ch Of S Ptr And S Paul Marietta GA 1998-1999; S Cathr's Epis Ch Marietta GA 1997-1998; S Jos's On-The-Mtn Mentone AL 1993; Cur S Jn's Atlanta GA 1982-1992; Cn Cathd Of S Phil Atlanta GA 1981-1982, Cn 1974-1976; Cmncatn Off Dio Atlanta Atlanta GA 1976-1978. Auth, "Dio".

✠ ANDERSON, The Rt Rev Craig Barry (SD) PO Box 1316, Ranchos de Taos NM 87557 B Glendale CA 1942 s Alvin & Glenn. BA Valparaiso U 1963; MDiv Sewanee: The U So, TS 1975; MDiv Sewanee: The U So, TS 1975; MA Van 1981; PhD Van 1986; DD Sewanee: The U So, TS 1987; Sewanee: The U So, TS 1987; OH SU 1993; DHL Valparaiso U 1993; Uppsala U 1998. D 12/21/1974 Bp William Carl Frey P 6/29/1975 Bp Girault M Jones Con 7/27/1984 for SD. m 8/2/1970 Lizbeth Anderson c 3. R Orcas Island Eastsound WA 2007-2013; Int R and Asstg Bp in Olympia Emm Ch Orcas Island Eastsound WA 2007-2013; Int R and Asstg Bp in Idaho S Thos Epis Ch Sun Vlly ID 2006-2007; Educ Com HOB 2000-2005; Int Bp Dio Vermont Burlington VT 2000-2001; Headmaster S Paul's Sch Concord NH 1997-2005; Pres Natl Coun of Ch USA 1995-1997; Co-Chair Ctte On Contin'G Dialogue On Human Sxlty GC 1994-1997; Asst Bp Dio New York New York NY 1993-1997; Dn, Pres and Prof of Theol The GTS New York NY 1993-1997; Dio So Dakota Pierre SD 1993, Bp 1984-1993; Asst Bp Dio Sthrn Ohio Cincinnati OH 1992-1993; Stndg Com On Prog GC 1987-1991; Theol Com HOB 1985-1999; Chair JSCN GC 1985-1989; Bd Mem ECBF 1985-1988; P-in-c Chr Ch Alto Decherd TN 1978-1984; Prof Of Pstr Theol Sewanee U So TS Sewanee TN 1978-1984; Chapl (Col) US-A Reserves 1975-1997; Chapl S Andr's Chap S Andrews TN 1973-1975; Cmncatn Com HOB; Plnng Com HOB. Auth, "Two Realms And Their Relationships," *Sci mag*, 1999; Auth, "Fragmentation Of Knowledge," *U Of Tulsa Bell Lecture Series*, 1999; Auth, "Theol Method And Epis Vocation," *ATR*, 1995. Chapl Dok 1991-1994; Cmnty Of S Mary, Assoc

1975; Vstng Bp Ord Of S Helena 1993-1997. Fjellstedt Fell (Post-Doctoral) 1997; Mershon Fell (Post-Doctoral) OH SU 1992; Great Sioux Nation Peace Medal 1991; Gvnr'S Awd For Recon 1991; Woods Ldrshp Awd U So 1973.

ANDERSON, David R (Ct) Saint Luke's Parish, 1864 Post Rd, Darien CT 06820 **R S Lk's Par Darien CT 2003-, Assoc R 1989-1992** B Yankton SD 1956 s Gerald & Aldoris. BA Bob Jones U 1978; MA U Chi 1980; MDiv Ya Berk 1989. D 6/17/1989 Bp Frank Tracy Griswold III P 1/27/1990 Bp Clarence Nicholas Coleridge. m 6/3/1978 Pamela Anderson c 2. R Trin Ch Solebury PA 1992-2003. Dav Robert Anderson, "Losing Your Faith, Finding Your Soul," Convergent Books, 2013; Auth, "Breakfast Epiphanies," Beacon Press, 2002.

ANDERSON, Douglas Evan (Dal) 413 Olive St, Texarkana TX 75501 **R S Jas Epis Ch Texarkana TX 2004-; Chapl St Jas' Day Sch 2004-; Chapl St. Jas' Sch Texarkana TX 2004-** B Orillia CA 1968 s Harry & Margaret. BA Trin, U Tor 1991; BA U Tor CA 1991; MDiv Nash 1994. D 6/10/1994 P 12/15/1994 Bp Russell Edward Jacobus. m 6/24/1995 Traci L Eldridge-Anderson c 3. R Chr Ch In Woodbury Woodbury NJ 1997-2004; Cur Ch Of S Mths Dallas TX 1994-1996. Auth, *Var arts.* Associated Parishes for Liturg & Mssn 2012; P Assoc of the H Hse of the Shrine of Our Lady of Walsingham 2005; Rel Cmncatn Assn 2012. MDiv cl Nash 1994; BA cl Trin, U Toronto 1991.

ANDERSON, Douglas Reid (Mont) 408 Westview Dr, Missoula MT 59803 **D Ch Of The H Sprt Missoula MT 2003-, D 1995-2002** B Moscow ID 1940 s Carl & Etheta. BS U of Idaho 1965. D 7/8/1995 Bp Charles I Jones III. m 8/26/1961 Judith Kay Finney Anderson c 2. holyspiritparish@qwestsoffice.net

ANDERSON JR, E Bernard (Md) 3800 Rodman St NW Apt 304, Washington DC 20016 B Miami FL 1958 s Emmett & Louise. MS U of the DC; B.A Morehouse Coll 2007; MDiv VTS 2015. D 1/10/2015 P 7/9/2015 Bp Eugene Taylor Sutton. m 7/7/2015 Lawrence Bernard Campbell. Par P St. Mary's Epis Ch Washington DC 2016-2017; Mnstry Res S Jn's Ch Ellicott City MD 2015-2016. Soc of Cath Priests 2013-2017. banderson@stmarysfoggybottom.org

ANDERSON, Eldon Wayne (SJ) P O Box 146, 18232 Smoke St, Jamestown CA 95327 B Broken Bow NE 1944 s Oscar & Olive. BSEd Chadron St Coll 1973; MDiv CDSP 2011; MDiv CDSP 2011. D 3/10/2012 P 10/6/2012 Bp Chester Lovelle Talton. m 2/13/1969 Karen Lynn Anderson c 2. P-in-c St Jas Epis Ch Sonora CA 2013-2014. eldonanderson@sbsglobal.net

ANDERSON III, Elenor Lucius 'Andy' (Ala) 447 McClung Ave SE, Huntsville AL 35801 **R Ch Of The Nativ Epis Huntsville AL 2003-; Dioc Cler Trst to U So Dio Alabama Birmingham 2017-, Dioc Cler Trst to the U So 2013-2016, Trst for the Dioc Funds 2009-2011, Dept of Fin 2007-2011, GC 1st Alt Dep 2005-2018; Dio Alabama Trst The U So Sewanee TN 2017-** B Statesboro GA 1955 s Elenor & Wudie. BA U GA 1977; MBA Georgia St U 1986; MDiv Sewanee: The U So, TS 1994; DMin Sewanee: The U So, TS 2006. D 6/4/1994 P 12/10/1994 Bp Frank Kellogg Allan. m 10/17/1981 Tippen H Harvey c 2. R Gr Epis Ch Anderson SC 1999-2003; Cn Eductr for Chld, Yth and Families Cathd Of S Phil Atlanta GA 1994-1999; Dio Alabama Trst The U So Sewanee TN 2013-2016; VP for Ch Relatns The U So Sewanee TN 2005-2011; Class Agt Sewanee U So TS Sewanee TN 2002-2010, Alum Coun 1996-2002; Trst for the Associated Alum The U So Sewanee TN 2000-2002; Diocsesn Coun Dio Atlanta Atlanta GA 1995-1998, Fin Com 1994-1998. "Forming Communities of Recon: The Nativ Cntr for Pilgrimage and Recon," *U So*, U So, 2006. MDiv mcl STUSo 1994.

ANDERSON, Elizabeth May (Chi) 141 Main St Unit 323, Racine WI 60046 B Waukegan IL 1954 d Eric & Madge. BA Lake Forest Coll 1976; MTS Nash 1979; MDiv SWTS 1994. D 6/18/1994 P 12/17/1994 Bp Frank Tracy Griswold III. P-in-c Ch Of The H Fam Lake Villa IL 2003-2009; R Ch Of The Annunc Bridgeview IL 1997-2002; Asst S Lawr Epis Ch Libertyville IL 1994-1997; On-Call Chapl (nights) NW Memi Hosp Arlington Heights IL 1994-1996; Waukegan Dnry Del, Suffr Bp Search Com Dio Chicago Chicago IL 1988-1989. Ed-in-Chf, "Let Us Keep the Feast," *Daughters of Sarah*, Daughters of Sarah, Inc., 1996; Ed-in-Chf, "Always Acceptable in Thy Sight," *Daughters of Sarah*, Daughters of Sarah, Inc., 1995; Ed-in-Chf, "The Redemp of Power and Eros," *Daughters of Sarah*, Daughters of Sarah, Inc., 1995; Ed-in-Chf, "On Sprtl Motherhood," *Daughters of Sarah*, Daughters of Sarah, Inc., 1995; Ed-in-Chf, "Contemplative Life and Wrshp," *Daughters of Sarah*, Daughters of Sarah, Inc., 1995.

ANDERSON, Eric A (WMo) 2001 Windsor Dr, Newton KS 67114 B Salina KS 1964 s Donald & Edwina. BS California St U 1986; MDiv Wartburg TS 1992; Cert Epis TS of the SW 2004. D 6/26/2004 P 1/26/2005 Bp Dean E Wolfe. St Lk's Chap Kansas City MO 2012-2014; R S Matt's Epis Ch Newton KS 2008-2010; Asst Gr Epis Ch Silver Sprg MD 2005-2008; Chapl Gr Epis Day Sch Silver Sprg MD 2005-2008.

ANDERSON, Evangeline H (RI) 719 Hope St Apt 1, Bristol RI 02809 B Baltimore MD 1947 d Thomas & Anna. BA Br 1971; BA Rhode Island Coll 1986; MDiv GTS 1994. D 6/18/1994 P 12/18/1994 Bp George Nelson Hunt III. c 2. R S Alb's Ch N Providence RI 1997-2011; Int Calv Ch Pascoag RI 1996-1997; Assoc R S Columba's Chap Middletown RI 1995-1996; Asst R S Barn Ch Warwick RI 1994-1995.

ANDERSON, Forrest E (USC) 3333 Oakwell Ct Apt 529, San Antonio TX 78218 B Harrison AR 1939 s Don & Louise. Christus Santa Rosa Hosp, San Antonio, Tx; BD U of Cntrl Arkansas 1962; MDiv VTS 1977. D 6/11/1977 P 3/16/1978 Bp Christoph Keller Jr. m 8/20/1966 Patricia B Bill. Chapl McKenna Memi Hosp New Braunfels TX 2000-2002; Chapl Christus Santa Rosa Hosp San Antonio TX 1997-1999; Vic S Geo Ch Anderson SC 1990-1994; Vic H Trin Epis Ch In Countryside Clearwater FL 1987-1989; R S Paul's Ch Kilgore TX 1982-1987; R S Jn's Ch Camden AR 1978-1982; Cur S Lk's Ch Hot Sprg AR 1977-1978.

ANDERSON, Gene Ray (SwVa) 5631 Warwood Dr, Roanoke VA 24018 **Part Time Supply S Paul's Ch Martinsville VA 2008-** B Independence MO 1934 s Lewis & Naomi. BS U of Cntrl Missouri 1956; MDiv Epis TS of the SW 1964. D 6/27/1964 P 1/1/1965 Bp Paul Moore Jr. m 3/1/1975 Suzan L Anderson c 3. Int S Mk's Ch Fincastle VA 2007-2008, Int 1997-2007; Int Chr Ch Martinsville VA 2002-2003, Int 1999-2000; Dioc Transition Off Dio SW Virginia Roanoke VA 1998-2013; Int Gr Ch Radford VA 1995-1996; Vic Ch Of The Epiph Trumansburg NY 1993-1995; Personl Cmsn Dio Cntrl New York Liverpool NY 1986-1988; R S Jn's Ch Marcellus NY 1978-1993; S Anne's Par Annapolis MD 1977-1978; Vic S Lk's Ch Annapolis MD 1976-1978; Yth Conf Ldr Dio Maryland Baltimore MD 1972-1977; R S Mk's Ch Highland MD 1968-1974; R All SS Ch Oakley Av MD 1965-1968; D S Andr's Ch Leonardtown California MD 1964-1965. Bp's Cross Diocee of SW Virginia 2012; Outstanding Adult Eductr Elmira Coll, Elmira NY 1991.

ANDERSON, George Michael (CFla) Grace Episcopal Church, 503 SE Broadway St, Ocala FL 34471 **Died 1/8/2016** B Columbus OH 1954 s Robert & Ann. D 12/8/2012 Bp Gregory Orrin Brewer. m 10/24/1987 Susan Finger Anderson c 3.

ANDERSON, Gordon James (Ind) 2522 E Elm St, New Albany IN 47150 **D S Paul's Epis Ch New Albany IN 1997-** B New Albany IN 1948 s George & Marjorie. SOE Indiana U. D 6/24/1997 Bp Edward Witker Jones. m 6/24/1995 Christy T Chanley.

ANDERSON, Hannah Pedersen (NH) 54 Dunklee St, Concord NH 03301 **Cn to the Ordnry Dio New Hampshire Concord NH 2013-** B Norristown PA 1953 d Christian & Susan. BA U of Washington 1976; MDiv Sewanee: The U So, TS 1994; DMin SWTS 2007. D 6/10/1994 P 6/3/1995 Bp Charlie Fuller Mcnutt Jr. m 4/20/1996 Robert G Anderson c 2. R S Steph's Ch Pittsfield MA 2005-2012; Cn Ch Of The H Comm Mahopac NY 2002-2005; Dio New York New York NY 2002-2005; R All SS' Epis Ch Briarcliff NY 1999-2002; R Gr Epis Ch Allentown PA 1996-1999; Mt Calv Camp Hill PA 1995-1996; Hosp Chapl Hershey Med Cntr Hershey PA 1994-1995; St Andrews in the City Epis Ch Harrisburg PA 1994-1995. CHS 2000-2004. Jonathan Daniels Fllshp Awd EDS 1993. handerson@nhepiscopal.org

ANDERSON, Howard Rae (Los) PO Box 37, Pacific Palisades CA 90272 B Sioux City IA 1948 s Carleton & Ethel. BA Hamline U 1970; MA U of Hawaii 1972; PhD U of Hawaii 1976; Cert Theol Stud S Johns Coll Winnipeg MN CA 1988. D 4/12/1993 Bp Robert Marshall Anderson P 11/28/1993 Bp James Louis Jelinek. m 12/27/1969 Linda Le Anderson c 2. The Par Of S Matt Pacific Plsds CA 2008-2013; Wrdn of Cathd Coll Cathd of St Ptr & St Paul Washington DC 2004-2008; R The Par of St Paul's Epis Ch Duluth MN 1994-2004; Dio Minnesota Minneapolis MN 1993-1994, Exec Dir Cmsn for Indn Wk 1982-1988, GC Dep 1985-2004; Prog Off Dio No Dakota Fargo ND 1984-1989; The Native Amer Theol Assn (now I.T.T.I) 1977-1982. Auth, *Winter Count: Stories of Native Amer Stwdshp*, Epis Ch Cntr, 1989; Auth, *Recalling, Reliving, Reviewing: Creation Theol in Native Amer & Chr and Jewish Tradition*, NATA Press, 1980; Auth, *The Sprtl Formation of Native Amer Yth*, NATA Press, 1980. Mn Epis Cler Assn 1993; Washington Cler Assn 2004. The Bp Whipple Cross Dio Minnesota 1990. lindaleeanderson@gmail.com

ANDERSON, James Arthur (Mil) 10041 Beckford St, Pickerington OH 43147 B Chicago IL 1952 s Vernon & Elizabeth. U IL 1973; BA NE Illinois U 1975; MDiv Sewanee: The U So, TS 1989. D 6/17/1989 Bp Frank Tracy Griswold III P 12/18/1989 Bp James Barrow Brown. m 10/24/1981 Bernadine Anderson. R S Jn The Div Epis Ch Burlington WI 1991-1994; Cur S Lk's Ch Baton Rouge LA 1989-1991. Soc For Promoting Chr Knowledge.

ANDERSON, James Desmond (WA) 9556 Chantilly Farm Ln, Chestertown MD 21620 B Christiansburg VA 1933 s Walter & Sarah. BA NWU 1955; BD VTS 1961; VTS 1997. D 6/24/1961 Bp Charles L Street P 12/1/1961 Bp Donald H V Hallock. m 6/14/1955 Winifred G Anderson. The Cathd Coll Washington DC 1981-1993; Bd Pres Alb Inst 1974-1976; Mssn Dvlpmt Advsry Com Dio Washington Washington DC 1973-1980, Preceptor Consult Intermet 1973-1976, Assn For Mnstry 1971-1981, Asst To Bp 1971-1978, Bd Metropltn Ecum Trng Cntr 1971-1976, Bd Atlantic Trng Com 1971-1975, Com 1970-1980, 1967-1981; Advsry Bd Proj Test Pattern 1972-1974; Dir CE Dio Virginia Richmond VA 1967-1971; Dept Of CE 1966-1967; P-in-c S Jn's Ch Neosho MO 1965-1967; Dir CE The Epis Ch Of Beth-By-The-Sea Palm Bch FL 1963-1965; Assoc S Matt's Ch Kenosha WI 1961-1963; Educ Revs Bd Acad Of Mgmt. Auth, "To Come Alive".

ANDERSON, James Russell (WA) 3111 Ritchie Rd, Forestville MD 20747 **Vic H Redeem Mitchellville MD 1993-; Hon Asst S Paul's Par Washington DC 2001-** B Lynchburg VA 1943 s John & Rosalind. BA U of Maryland 1970; MDiv GTS 1974. D 6/22/1974 Bp William Foreman Creighton P 3/1/1975 Bp John Thomas Walker. S Fran Ch Virginia Bch VA 2003-2010; Ch Of The Epiph Washington DC 2000-2003; H Redeem Mssn Capitol Hgts MD 1993-1999; Int S Mk's Ch Cheyenne WY 1992-1993; Off Of Bsh For ArmdF New York NY 1976-1991; Chapl (Ltc) USAF 1976-1991; Dio Washington Washington DC 1974-1976; Urban Mssnr S Phil's Epis Ch Laurel MD 1974-1976.

ANDERSON, Jami (Wyo) PO Box 847, Pinedale WY 82941 **R St Jn the Bapt Epis Ch Big Piney WY 2010-** B Havre MT 1954 d Donald & Marilyn. BA U of Nthrn Colorado 1977; MEd U of Wyoming 1981; MDiv SWTS 2005. D 6/20/2005 P 12/20/2005 Bp Joe Goodwin Burnett. m 6/11/1976 John Leonard Anderson c 4. Ch Of S Andr's In The Pines Pinedale WY 2010-2017; R S Eliz's Ch Holdrege NE 2005-2010; R S Pauls Epis Ch Arapahoe NE 2005-2010.

ANDERSON, Jennie (Vt) PO Box 265, Norwich VT 05055 **P-in-Partnership S Barn Ch Norwich VT 2016-** B Boston MA 1964 d John & Elizabeth. AA Cape Cod Cmnty Coll 1984; BS U of Massachusetts 1987; MDiv Epis TS of the SW 2007. D 6/2/2007 P 1/12/2008 Bp M(Arvil) Thomas Shaw. c 1. Supt Bldg and Ground St Jas Sch Philadelphia PA 2014-2016; R Ch Of The Epiph Royersford PA 2009-2014.

ANDERSON, Jerry (Los) 339 West Avenue 45, Los Angeles CA 90065 **Dir of Pstr Care Gd Samar Hosp Los Angeles CA 2003-** B Herrin IL 1942 s Everett & Reva. BA Sthrn Illinois U 1965; STB GTS 1968; CPE Rush Presb-St Lukes Med Cntr 1973. D 6/8/1968 Bp Albert A Chambers P 12/20/1968 Bp James Winchester Montgomery. Gd Samar Hosp Los Angeles CA 2003-2014; Pstr Int S Paul's Pomona Pomona CA 2002-2003; Dir/Chapl Epis AIDS Mnstry Epis Aids Mnstry Miami FL 1996-2001; Trin Cathd Miami FL 1996-2001; Chapl Epis Caring Response to AIDS Dio Washington Washington DC 1987-1995; Epis Caring Response To Aids Washington DC 1987-1995; S Monica's Epis Ch Washington DC 1987; S Pat's Ch Washington DC 1981-1986; Chapl Bp Anderson Hse IL Med Cntr Chicago IL 1974-1977; Navajoland Area Mssn Farmington NM 1974-1976; P-in-c Gr Epis Ch Menominee MI 1973; Asst S Aug's Epis Ch Wilmette IL 1968-1973.

ANDERSON JR, Jesse Fosset (Pa) 4848 Carrington Cir, Sarasota FL 34243 **Died 4/4/2017** B New York NY 1937 s Jesse & Elizabeth. BA Linc 1958; MDiv GTS 1961. D 6/10/1961 Bp Andrew Y Tsu P 12/16/1961 Bp Joseph Gillespie Armstrong. m 10/12/2002 Constance Drew Anderson c 6. R The Afr Epis Ch Of S Thos Philadelphia PA 1991-2001; R S Monica's Ch Hartford CT 1985-1990; S Phil The Evang Washington DC 1979-1985; Dio Washington Washington DC 1973-1979, Exec Coun 1969-1972; Pres UBE Natl 1971-1973; Del Prov III Syn 1968-1982; Chapl& Adj Prof SE U Washington DC 1967-1984; Urban Mssnr and Assoc S Pat's Ch Washington DC 1966-1973; R Hse Of Pryr Philadelphia PA 1963-1966; Cur Geo W So Ch of Advoc Philadelphia PA 1961-1963. Kappa Alpha Psi 1955; UBE 1978.

ANDERSON, Joan Wilkinson (ECR) 425 Carmel Ave, Marina CA 93933 B San Francisco CA 1937 d Harry & Gloria. AA Mt San Antonio Coll 1958; BA San Jose St U 1977; Diac Stds Epis Sch For Deacons 2006. D 2/7/2009 Bp Mary Gray-Reeves. c 2.

ANDERSON, Jon R (ETenn) 663 Douglas Street, Chattanooga TN 37403 **Founding Parson Wrshp in the Wilderness 2007-** B Dallas TX 1961 s Robert & Beverly. BS U of Tennessee 1984; MBA U of Kansas 1986; MDiv CDSP 2002. D 6/2/2002 Bp Chester Lovelle Talton P 12/14/2002 Bp Joseph Jon Bruno. m 1/2/1988 Anne-Drue M Anderson c 1. P-in-c Under Spec Circumstances Chr Ch - Epis Chattanooga TN 2011-2014; Asst S Bede's Epis Ch Santa Fe NM 2007-2011; R S Andr's Epis Ch Ojai CA 2005-2007; Cur/Assoc R Ch of the H Faith Santa Fe NM 2002-2005.

ANDERSON, Judith Kay Finney (Mont) 408 Westview Dr, Missoula MT 59803 **D Ch Of The H Sprt Missoula MT 2005-** B Denver CO 1940 d Charles & Mildred. BS U of Idaho 1963; Mnstry Formation Prog 2000. D 10/14/2000 Bp Charles I Jones III. m 8/26/1961 Douglas Reid Anderson c 2.

ANDERSON, Juliana Collins (Mass) 1770 Massachusetts Ave, Cambridge MA 02140 B Pittsburgh PA 1945 d James & Dorothea. BA Carnegie Mellon U 1967; MDiv EDS 1978. D 6/25/1981 Bp Morris Fairchild Arnold P 5/1/1982 Bp Roger W Blanchard. m 3/22/1969 Will C Anderson. S Jn's Ch Barrington RI 2005; Trin Ch Concord MA 2003-2004; S Mk's Ch Foxborough MA 1997-2000; Ch Of S Jn The Evang Boston MA 1995-1996; Chr Ch Hyde Pk MA 1985-1993; Int The Ch Of The Gd Shpd Acton MA 1982-1983, Asst 1981-1982.

ANDERSON, Karen Sue (Neb) 1517 Broadway Ste 104, Scottsbluff NE 69361 **P S Fran Epis Ch Scottsbluff NE 2009-** B Deadwood SD 1953 d Earle & Maxine. Exec Secretarial Watertown Bus U 1972. D 4/18/2006 P 5/12/2007 Bp Joe Goodwin Burnett. c 4.

ANDERSON, Kenneth Edwin (RG) 258 Riverside Dr, El Paso TX 79915 B ND 1929 s Edwin & Minnie. D 7/28/2001 Bp Terence Kelshaw. m 2/24/1951 Jessie Anderson.

ANDERSON III, Lennel Vincent (Pgh) 2081 Husband Rd, Somerset PA 15501 **D S Fran In The Fields Somerset PA 2010-** B Youngstorm, OH 1973 s Lennel & Deborah. BA Westminster Coll 1995; MDiv Gordon-Conwell TS 2000; Virginia TS 2008. D 2/20/2010 P 9/25/2010 Bp Bud Shand. m 3/28/2000 Kelly Jennifer Anderson. Old Wye Ch Wye Mills MD 2006-2009.

ANDERSON, Louise Thomas (NC) 901 N Main St, Tarboro NC 27886 **D S Lk's Ch Tarboro NC 2013-; D Ch Of The Gd Shpd Rocky Mt NC 2005-** B Raleigh NC 1962 d Erwin & Anne. D 11/9/2005 Bp Michael B Curry. m 6/2/1984 Samuel Anderson c 1.

ANDERSON, Marilyn Lea (Ct) 180 Cross Highway, Redding CT 06896 **Mentor, Fresh Start Prog Dio Connecticut Meriden CT 2013-, Transition Com chairperson 2008-2009, Consult, P-in-c Prog 2013-; R Chr Ch Redding CT 2005-** B Pittsburgh PA 1953 d John & Alice. BA W&M 1975; MS U IL 1983; Dip Ang Stud Ya Berk 1998; MDiv Yale DS 1998; STM GTS 2000. D 6/8/2002 Bp Andrew Donnan Smith P 1/4/2003 Bp James Elliot Curry. m 8/16/1975 Barry Michael Anderson c 2. Mentor, Annand Sprtlty Prog Ya Berk New Haven CT 2006-2007; Asst R S Andr's Ch Madison CT 2002-2005. Designated mcl Yale DS 1998.

ANDERSON, Mark S (Fla) **Cur S Mk's Epis Ch Jacksonville FL 2016-** D 12/6/2015 P 7/10/2016 Bp Samuel Johnson Howard.

ANDERSON, Martha O (SanD) P. O. Box 334, Del Mar CA 92014 **S Ptr's Epis Ch Del Mar CA 2014-; Exec Coun Dio San Diego San Diego CA 2012-** B Portsmouth VA 1956 d Curtis & Martha Ann. BA Converse Coll 1978; JD U of San Diego 1984; MDiv ETSBH 2011. D 4/9/2011 Bp Jim Mathes. c 2. P-in-c All Souls' Epis Ch San Diego CA 2011-2014.

ANDERSON, Mary Petty (Oly) 10450 NE Yaquina Ave, Bainbridge Island WA 98110 **Assoc Gr Ch Bainbridge Island WA 2008-** B Centreville MS 1948 d Fred & Polly. BA LSU 1970; MA Mississippi Coll 1991; MDiv Epis TS of the SW 1998. D 6/7/1999 P 12/1/1999 Bp Robert Jefferson Hargrove Jr. c 2. Emm Epis Ch Mercer Island WA 2006, Asst 2004-2006; Asst St.Hilda - St. Pat's Epis Ch 2003-2004; S Pat's Epis Ch W Monroe LA 2000-2001; Int Chr Ch Bastrop LA 2000; Int S Andr's Epis Ch Mer Rouge LA 1999.

ANDERSON, Mary Sterrett (O) 2581 Norfolk Rd, Cleveland Heights OH 44106 B Dayton OH 1945 d William & Marion. BA Colorado Coll 1967; MDiv EDS 1974. D 11/16/1974 Bp John Maury Allin P 1/4/1977 Bp John Harris Burt. m 9/8/1973 Philip Alden Anderson c 2. S Thos' Epis Ch Port Clinton OH 2000-2002; Asst Chr Ch Epis Hudson OH 2000-2001; P-in-c S Hubert's Epis Ch Mentor OH 1996-1997; Int Ch Of The Gd Shpd Lyndhurst OH 1992-1993; Asst S Chris's By-The River Gates Mills OH 1988-1991; Chapl Dio Ohio Cleveland 1983-2006; Chapl Pediatric Intensive Care Unit U Hosp Cleveland OH 1982-2006; Asst Chr Ch Shaker Heights OH 1977-1978; Chapl Cleveland Clnc Cleveland OH 1974-1976; D Intern Emm Ch Cleveland OH 1974-1975.

ANDERSON, Megan Elizabeth (NCal) Trinity Cathedral, 2620 Capitol Ave, Sacramento CA 95816 **P Trin Epis Cathd Sacramento CA 2013-** B Sacramento CA 1987 d Robert & Cathryn. BA U CA 2009; MDiv Ya Berk 2013. D 6/29/2013 P 2/8/2014 Bp Barry Leigh Beisner. megan@trinitycathedral.org

ANDERSON, Michael Eddie (Chi) 1225 Asbury Ave, Evanston IL 60202 B Milwaukee WI 1948 s Gerald & Aldoris. ABS Wheaton Coll 1975; MDiv Nash 1984. D 6/16/1984 Bp Quintin Ebenezer Primo Jr P 12/1/1984 Bp James Winchester Montgomery. m 8/17/1972 Katharine Anderson c 3. Ch Of The H Nativ Chicago IL 1986-1998; Ch Of The H Nativ Clarendon Hls IL 1986-1998; R The Ch of the H Nativ Clarendon Hills IL 1986-1998; Assoc R S Greg's Epis Ch Deerfield IL 1984-1986. Auth, "Chapt," *Evangelicals on the Cbury Trail*, Morehouse Pub, 1989.

ANDERSON JR, Otto Harold (Okla) 40024 Harveston Dr Apt 318, Temecula CA 92591 B Galveston TX 1924 s Otto & Angeline. Coll of Preachers; Sewanee: U So; BA Phillips U 1948; BD Brite DS 1952; Fell Coll of Preachers 1969. D 10/25/1954 P 4/25/1955 Bp Chilton R Powell. Asst St Mary in Palms Los Angeles CA 2011-2016; Asst S Mk's Par Glendale CA 2003-2011; Asst S Thos The Apos Hollywood Los Angeles CA 1994-2001; Asst The Par Of S Matt Pacific Plsds CA 1984-1994; R S Jn's Ch Norman OK 1963-1969; Chapl U of OK Norman OK 1959-1963; R S Lk's Epis Ch Ada OK 1955-1959, D 1954-1955; Dep GC- Epis Ch Cntr New York NY 1969, Dep 1967; Dioc Coun Dio Oklahoma Oklahoma City OK 1964-1969.

ANDERSON, Otto Suen (SO) 409 E High St, Springfield OH 45505 **D Chr Epis Ch Of Springfield Springfield OH 2013-** B Sidney, NY 1957 s Carl & Dorothy. BS Clarkson Coll 1979; BS USAF Inst of Tech 1982; MS Cntrl Michigan 1989. D 6/13/2009 Bp Thomas Edward Breidenthal. m 11/2/2002 Jamie Anderson c 2. D S Paul's Epis Ch Dayton OH 2009-2012.

ANDERSON III, Paul Kemper (At) 302 West Avenue, P.O. Box 85, Cedartown GA 30125 **S Jas Ch Cedartown GA 2015-** B Miami FL 1959 s Paul & Mary. BS Kennesaw St Coll 1993; MPA Kennesaw St U 1999; MDiv Sewanee: The U So, TS 2015. D 12/20/2014 P 6/20/2015 Bp Robert Christopher Wright. m 12/5/1992 Philippa Jane Buhayar c 3. fatherkemper@gmail.com

ANDERSON, Philip Alden (O) 2581 Norfolk Rd, Cleveland Heights OH 44106 **Credo Inst Inc. Memphis TN 2014-; Fac Credo Inst Inc Memphis TN US 1999-; D S Paul's Epis Ch Cleveland OH 1995-** B Cambridge MA 1948 s

David & Madeleine. AB Harv 1970; MDiv EDS 1973; MD Case Wstrn Reserve U 1978. D 1/10/1976 Bp John Harris Burt. m 9/8/1973 Mary Sterrett c 3. MD alpha omega alpha Med Sch Case Wstrn Reserve U 1978.

ANDERSON, Polly Chambers (WLa) 4037 Highway 15, Calhoun LA 71225 **Mssy/Ambassador Mustard Seed Babies Hm Hoima Uganda 2004-** B New Orleans LA 1945 d Fred & Marion. BS MSU 1973. D 6/4/2005 Bp D Avid Bruce Macpherson. c 2. S Pat's Epis Ch W Monroe LA 2005-2007; Fndr Refuge of Hope (through St. Alb's Epis Ch) Monroe 1998-2001.

ANDERSON JR, Ralph W (WMass) 114 Lake St, Shrewsbury MA 01545 B Worcester MA 1937 s Ralph & Virginia. BBA Clark U 1959; MA Anna Maria Coll 1994. D 6/20/1981 Bp Alexander D Stewart. m 6/5/1965 Marcia K Anderson c 2. 1992-2008; D All SS Ch Worcester MA 1989-1992; 1986-1989; Chapl Doctors' Hosp Worcester MA 1984-1986; Asst Trin Epis Ch Shrewsbury MA 1981-1986. The Intl Thos Merton Soc 2004.

ANDERSON, Richard John (NY) 2635 2nd Ave Apt 203, San Diego CA 92103 **Ret St. Mk's Mt. Kisko NY 1994-** B Iowa City IA 1934 s Bernard & Helene. BA San Diego St U 1958; BD CDSP 1961; STM Dubuque TS 1969. D 6/16/1961 P 12/21/1961 Bp Gordon V Smith. c 3. R S Mk's Ch Mt Kisco NY 1987-1994; ECBF New York NY 1986-1987; Exec for Cmncatn Epis Ch Cntr New York NY 1980-1986, Exec Asst to PBp 1975-1980; Asst to the PBp Epis Chruch Cntr New York New York NY 1975-1980; Cn to the Ordnry Dio Wstrn New York Buffalo NY 1971-1975; R S Jn's Gr Ch Buffalo NY 1969-1971; R S Jn's Epis Ch Dubuque IA 1965-1969; Vic S Paul's Ch Durant IA 1961-1965; Exec Coun Dio New York New York NY 1990-1994; Exec Coun Dio Iowa Des Moines IA 1965-1969. Auth, "There Shall Be A GC of This Ch," 1973.

ANDERSON, Richard Rupert (EMich) 221 Purdy Dr, Alma MI 48801 **P-in-c S Jn's Ch St. Jn's MI 2005-** B Florence CO 1924 s Lyman & Fleda. BA Wayne 1950; MDiv Bex Sem 1953; MDiv Ken 1953; Coll of Preachers 1968; Emergency Med Tech 1976; DMin Drew U 1994. D 7/5/1953 P 1/23/1954 Bp Richard Stanley Merrill Emrich. m 6/19/1948 Carolyn Bertha Anderson c 6. Dn Saginaw Vlly Convoc Dio Estrn Michigan Saginaw MI 1992-1995; Instr NT Whitaker TS Dio Michigan 1954-1995; R S Jn's Epis Ch Alma MI 1954-1991; Vic S Jn's Ch Chesaning MI 1953-1954.

ANDERSON, Robert Jay (WVa) 1006 Frostwood St, Huntsville TX 77340 B Bloomington IN 1953 s Arvin & Norma. MDiv EDS 1994. D 6/10/1994 P 6/1/1995 Bp John Henry Smith. m 4/25/1980 Diana Lynn Anderson. The Sthrn Cluster Northfork WV 1994-1995.

ANDERSON, Robert Melville (CFla) 350 Lake Talmadge Rd., Deland FL 32724 B Orlando FL 1938 s Robert & Gertrude. BA Parsons Coll 1962; MDiv Nash 1982. D 6/16/1982 P 3/1/1983 Bp William Hopkins Folwell. m 11/11/1989 Rebecca Anderson c 4. R The Ch Of The H Presence Deland FL 1995-2003; R H Trin Epis Ch Bartow FL 1993-1995; Vic S Ptr's Epis Ch Lake Mary FL 1985-1989; Asst H Cross Epis Ch Sanford FL 1982-1984. frander@earthlink.net

ANDERSON, Rosemarie (ECR) 355 Redwood Dr, Boulder Creek CA 95006 **Prof of Sprtlty Inst of Transpersonal Psychol 1992-** B Englewood NJ 1947 d Roy & Miriam. BA Cntrl Coll 1969; MA U of Nebraska 1971; PhD U of Nebraska 1973; MDiv PSR 1983. D 12/6/1986 P 12/5/1987 Bp William Edwin Swing. Calv Epis Ch Santa Cruz CA 1993-1995; Chapl Cbury Fndt Santa Cruz CA 1991-1993; Santa Cruz Cbury Fndt Santa Cruz CA 1991-1992; All Souls' Epis Ch San Diego CA 1988-1990; Acad Dn European Div U of Maryland 1983-1987; Ovrs Lectr Asian Div U of Maryland 1977-1979. Auth, *Celtic Oracles*, Random Hse, 1998; Auth, *Transpersonal Resrch Methods for Soc Sci*, Sage Pubs, 1998. AAR; APA; Assn for Transpersonal Psychol; Inst of Noetic Sci; Westar Inst.

ANDERSON, Scott Crawford (USC) Episcopal Church Of The Redeemer, 120 Mauldin Rd, Greenville SC 29605 **R Epis Ch Of The Redeem Greenville SC 2012-** B Aurora IL 1954 BA Babson Coll; MDIV TS 2003; MDIV Sewanee: The U So, TS 2003. D 6/14/2003 P 12/13/2003 Bp William Jerry Winterrowd. m 8/20/1988 Jane K Anderson c 3. R S Jas Epis Ch Wheat Ridge CO 2006-2012; Assoc S Lk's Epis Ch Ft Collins CO 2003-2006.

ANDERSON JR, Theodore Lester (NJ) 47 S Ensign Dr, Little Egg Harbor NJ 08087 **St Mary's Hosp W Palm Bch FL 1992-** B Perth Amboy NJ 1958 s Theodore & Loretta. BA Rutgers The St U of New Jersey 1980; MDiv Nash 1984. D 6/2/1984 Bp George Phelps Mellick Belshaw P 2/2/1985 Bp Vincent King Pettit. c 1. R S Mths Ch Hamilton NJ 1995-2010; Palm Bch Reg Hosp Lake Worth FL 1993-2003; Chapl S Mary's Hosp W Palm Bch FL 1992-1993; H Trin Epis Ch W Palm Bch FL 1987-1993; Cur Ch Of The Gd Shpd Jacksonville FL 1985-1986; Cur S Simeon's By The Sea Wildwood NJ 1984-1985.

ANDERSON, Tim (Neb) P.O. Box 64, Ashland NE 68003 B Kearney NE 1949 s Joyce & Ardis. BS U of Nebraska 1981; MDiv Nash 1986. D 2/25/1987 P 9/11/1987 Bp James Daniel Warner. m 3/11/1973 Carla Anderson c 2. Epis Tri-Faith Fndt Omaha NE 2011-2014; Cn Dio Nebraska Omaha NE 2004-2011, Bp & Trst 2004-2011; R S Steph's Ch Grand Island NE 1991-2004; R S Mary's Epis Ch Blair NE 1987-1991; Fin For Mssn Com Exec Coun Appointees New York NY 2009-2012, Strategic Plnng Com 2008-2012, Exec Coun Mem 2006-2012.

ANDERSON, William C (Md) 415 Helmsman Way, Severna Park MD 21146 **P-in-c S Mary's Epis Ch Woodlawn Gwynn Oak MD 2012-** B Princeton IL 1941 s Clarence & Ruth. BS Nthrn Illinois U 1962; MS U IL 1966; Wstrn Washington U 1967; PhD Florida St U 1976; MDiv VTS 2002. D 6/14/1997 Bp Charles Lindsay Longest P 2/2/2003 Bp Peter Hess Beckwith. m 3/20/1971 Jane Farley Anderson c 2. Assoc Epis Ch Of Chr The King Baltimore MD 2007-2008; P-in-c S Andr's Ch Pasadena MD 2005-2006; R S Paul's Epis Ch Pekin IL 2003-2005; D S Steph's Ch Severn Par Crownsville MD 1999-2000; D S Barth's Ch Baltimore MD 1997-1999.

ANDERSON III, William Marcellus (NY) B 1935 BD Ya Berk 1960; MBA Cor 1966. D 6/20/1960 P 6/24/1961 Bp John Joseph Meakin Harte. Cur S Jn's Ch Ithaca NY 1961-1964; Cur S Mich And All Ang Ch Dallas TX 1960-1961.

ANDERSON-KRENGEL, William Erich (Ct) 191 Margarite Rd, Middletown CT 06457 B Nürnburg DE 1961 s Walter & Carol. D 6/9/2001 Bp Andrew Donnan Smith P 2/16/2002 Bp James Elliot Curry. m 6/9/1984 Sarah Jennings Anderson-Krengel. P Dio Connecticut Meriden CT 2001-2012.

ANDERSON-SMITH, Susan (Az) Third Floor, 232 E 11th St, New York NY 10003 B Vicksburg MS 1957 d Bertram & Edna. BA U of Mississippi 1979; MDiv EDS 1997. D 6/12/1999 P 4/26/2000 Bp Ronald Hayward Haines. m 12/22/2015 Anne M Sawyer. Chapl Imago Dei Middle Sch Tucson AZ 2007-2017; Assoc S Phil's In The Hills Tucson AZ 2000-2007; Coordntr Dioc Conv Dio Massachusetts Boston MA 1999-2000; COM Dio Arizona Phoenix AZ 2010-2017, Arizona Epis Schools Fndt 2008-2011, Stndg Com 2008-2009, Epis Fndt Bd for Campus Mnstry 2001-2008. Auth, "Accident or Imperative? Rel Pluralism and Epis Schools," *Reasons for Being*, NAES, 2010. Bp Atwood of Arizona Awd EDS 1997; BA cl U of MS 1979.

ANDONIAN, Kathryn Ann (Pa) 942 Masters Way, Harleysville PA 19438 **Vic Ch Of The H Sprt Harleysville PA 2004-; Mem, Bd Dir Keystone Opportunity Cntr Souderton PA 2015-; Secy, Stndg Com Dio Pennsylvania Philadelphia PA 2014-, Del to GC 2013-, COM 2012-, Stndg Com 2011-, Vice Chairperson, Dioc Coun 2009-2011, Chairperson, Liturg Cmsn 2007-2010, Dioc Coun 2006-2011, Fresh Start Fac 2005-, Resolutns Com 2004-2007** B Billings MT 1959 d George & Phyllis. BA U CO 1981; MDiv Luth TS 2002; CAS VTS 2003. D 6/21/2003 P 5/29/2004 Bp Charles Ellsworth Bennison Jr. m 1/5/1985 Marc Hansen Andonian c 1. Cathd Ch of Our Sav Philadelphia PA 2003-2004. Deaconness Fund 2010-2013; Philadelphia Theol Inst 2007. revkathy@churchoftheholyspirit.us

ANDRE, Wildaine (Hai) **Dio Haiti Port-au-Prince HT 2012-** B 1982 s Andius & Eugenie. Lic Seminaire de Theologie 2011; BA École de Droit et des Sciences Économiques des Gonaïves 2014. D 7/29/2012 P 3/13/2014 Bp Jean Zache Duracin.

ANDRES, Anthony Francis (Ind) 795 Elk Mountain Rd, Afton VA 22920 **Vic H Cross Ch Afton VA 2001-** B Youngstown OH 1938 s Anton & Frances. BA DePauw U 1960; MDiv VTS 1964; JD Jn Marshall Law Sch 1977. D 6/13/1964 P 12/20/1964 Bp Nelson Marigold Burroughs. m 7/19/1986 Emily Lewis c 1. P S Chris's Epis Ch Carmel IN 1977-2000; R S Lk's Ch Cleveland OH 1967-1977; Asst Ch Of The Epiph Euclid OH 1964-1967.

ANDRES, Justo Rambac (SJ) 115 E Miner Ave, Stockton CA 95202 **Epis Ch Of S Anne Stockton CA 1998-** B Bacarra PH 1929 s Ciriaco & Juliana. BTh S Andrews TS Manila PH 1955; Far Estrn U PI Ph 1962; Garrett-Evang TS 1968. Rec 4/1/1955 as Priest Bp The Bishop Of Manila. c 1. H Cross Epis Mssn Stockton CA 1984-1995; Epis Dio San Joaquin Modesto CA 1983, Jubilee Off 1992-; The Par Of Gd Shpd Epis Ch Wailuku HI 1976-1983; Chapl US-A 1961-1965; Serv Prot Epis Ch 1955-1961; Transltr Bk Of Common Pryr; Chapl Police. Ang Mnstry; Cntrl Mnstrl Assn; Mnstry To Seamen. Citation Gvnr Of Hi.

ANDREW OSH, Carol (Ga) 3042 Eagle Dr, Augusta GA 30906 **OSH 1972-** B Hamilton BM 1948 d David & Patricia. BA DePauw U 1969; Ya 1972; GTS 1991; GTS 1993. D 6/12/1993 Bp Richard Frank Grein P 3/18/1994 Bp Craig Barry Anderson. Ord Of S Helena 1972.

ANDREW SR, Robert Nelson (O) 3800 W 33rd St, Cleveland OH 44109 **Chapl S Barn Ch Bay Vill OH 1999-** B Waterbury CT 1933 s Walter & Ruby. Carroll Coll; New Haven St Teachers Coll; U of Connecticut; Ch Army Trng Coll 1959; JCU 1979. D 5/12/1980 P 11/29/1980 Bp John Harris Burt. m 10/17/1959 Eleanor Ann Andrew c 4. S Agnes Ch Cleveland OH 1980-2000; Ch Of S Phil The Apos Cleveland OH 1980-1998; Ch Army Captain-in-charge S Steph's Mssn Vermilion OH 1967-1974; Ch Army Captain-in-charge Zion Ch Monroeville OH 1961-1967; Ch Army Captain-in-charge Gr Epis Ch Sandusky OH 1960-1961; Ch Army Captain-in-charge S Paul Epis Ch Conneaut OH 1958-1959. Ch Army Captain 1959; Ord of S Lk Chapl 2001.

ANDREW-MACONAUGHEY, Debra Elaine (SeFla) 111 W Indies Dr, Ramrod Key FL 33042 **S Columba Epis Ch Marathon FL 2007-** B Denison TX 1957 d Thomas & Ruth. BA Tem 1979; MFA NYU 1984; MA VTS 2004. D 1/6/2007 P 6/6/2007 Bp Leo Frade. m 5/11/2001 Kirk Maconaughey c 2. Prog Mgr Big Bro/Big Sis 2004-2006; S Paul's Epis Ch Alexandria VA 1996-2003. downtime@hotmail.com

ANDREWS, Alfred John (Neb) PO Box 141, Sidney NE 69162 B Townsville 1930 Moore Theol Coll. Trans 11/7/2003 Bp Joe Goodwin Burnett. c 2. P Chr Ch Sidney NE 2003-2013.

ANDREWS, Arthur Edward (Ore) 1704 Se 22nd Ave, Portland OR 97214 B Portland OR 1948 s Edgar & Irma. BA Gri 1970; ETSBH 1974; MA Fuller TS 1974; CDSP 1975. D 7/22/1975 P 12/15/1976 Bp Matthew Paul Bigliardi. m 11/22/2003 Sharon S Flegal c 2. Chapl Legacy Gd Samar Hosp Portland OR 1998-2010, Chapl 1975-1998; Supvsr Res Epis Hlth Serv Uniondale NY 1997-1998; Asst S Ptr's by-the-Sea Epis Ch Bay Shore NY 1997-1998; P-in-c Ch Of The Gd Shpd Sandy OR 1994-1996; Asst S Aid's Epis Ch Portland OR 1984-1988; Chapl St Judes Hm Inc Sandy OR 1983; Vic H Cross Epis Ch Boring OR 1980-1983. AEHC 1988-1992; Assn of Profsnl Chapl 1991-2010.

ANDREWS, Carl Machin (Colo) The Diocese of Colorado, 1300 Washington Street, Denver CO 80203 B Wright-Patterson Air Force Base OH 1948 s Thomas & Kathleen. BS Colorado St U 1970; MDiv Nash 1977. D 12/21/1976 P 6/1/1977 Bp William Carl Frey. m 10/7/1973 Lynne J Andrews c 2. Cn to the Ordnry Dio Colorado Denver CO 2010-2016, Cn to the Ordnry 2010-; Wing Chapl (Colonel) 37 Trng Wing San Antonio TX 2007-2010; Command Chapl (Chapl, Colonel) Untd States Air Forces in Europe Ramstein Germany 2004-2007; Wing Chapl (Colonel) US AF Spangdahlem AFB Germany Germany 2002-2004; Chf of Plans and Readiness; Chapl (Lt Col) Pentagon Washington DC 1998-2002; Chf of Plans and Prog Chapl (Lt Col) US AF Scott Base O'Fallon IL 1995-1998; Sr Prot Chapl (Major) Edwards AFB USAF Lancaster CA 1992-1995; Sr Prot Chapl (Major) Us AF Elmendorf AFB Anchorage AK 1989-1992; Chapl (Major) Us AF Woomera Air Sta Australia Australia 1987-1989; USAF Chapl Off Of Bsh For ArmdF New York NY 1984-2010; Chapl (Captain) Us AF Malmstrom AFB Great Falls MT 1984-1987; Vic S Mk's Ch Craig CO 1979-1984; Cur S Tim's Epis Ch Littleton CO 1977-1979. Auth, "The Role of the Chapl," *USAF Chapl Pub*, USAF, 2006; Auth, "Var parts of DVDs on Chapl Corp Readiness," *USAF DVD Chapl Corp*, USAF, 2000. Associated Parishes, Tertiary Of The Soc Of S Fran 1977. Mltry Awards USAF 2010.

ANDREWS JR, David Tallmadge (Del) 732 Nottingham Rd, Wilmington DE 19805 **R Ch of St Andrews & St Matthews Wilmington DE 2010-** B Bronxville NY 1957 s David & Kathryn. BA Muskingum Coll 1980; MDiv EDS 1985; MS Marywood U 1996. D 12/15/1990 P 9/11/1991 Bp William George Burrill. m 8/11/1984 Emily Stearns Gibson. R Trin Ch Castine ME 2006-2010; Vic Trin Ch Camden NY 1998-2001; Vic S Paul's Ch Chittenango NY 1997-2006; Vic Ch Of The Gd Shpd Nedrow NY 1992-1994. dandrews@ssam.org

ANDREWS, David Thomas (WA) 500 Merton Woods Way, Millersville MD 21108 B Salem NJ 1940 s Gilbert & Mary. BA Campbell U 1966; PDS 1966. D 4/23/1966 P 10/29/1966 Bp Alfred L Banyard. m 6/11/1966 Kathleen M Andrews c 2. R H Trin Epis Ch Bowie MD 1974-2006; Stff S Paul's Epis Ch Westfield NJ 1968-1974; Cur H Cross Epis Ch Plainfield NJ 1966-1968; Dioc Ecum Off Dio Washington Washington DC 1996-2002. Assoc OHC; Washington Epis Cler Assn.

ANDREWS, Dianne P (Oly) 1613 California Ave SW #301, Seattle WA 98116 **S Paul's Epis Ch Port Townsend WA 2013-** B Sacramento CA 1955 d Glenn & Margaret. BS U CA 1978; MDiv Starr King Sch for the Mnstry 1992; CAS CDSP 1994. D 11/9/1996 P 11/9/1997 Bp Michael Whittington Creighton. c 1. Komo Kulshan Cluster Mt Vernon WA 2012-2013; Gr Epis Ch Hulmeville PA 2002-2010; Asst to R S Jn's Epis Ch Lancaster PA 1998-2002; Mt Calv Camp Hill PA 1997, 1996-1997; Chapl Res Milton S. Hershey Med Cntr 1995-1996.

ANDREWS II, George Edward (SeFla) 20 Vine St, Marion MA 02738 **Headmaster S Andr's Sch 1989-** B Saginaw MI 1942 s Edward & Mary. BA Trin 1966; MDiv VTS 1971. D 6/26/1971 Bp John Melville Burgess P 4/15/1972 Bp Dean Theodore Stevenson. m 6/24/1966 Lillian Coe Andrews. Chapl U Liggett Sch Grosse Pointe Farms MI 1974-1984.

ANDREWS II, George Strafford (Chi) 102 Starling Ln, Longwood FL 32779 **1989-** B New York NY 1929 s George & Mary. BA Harv 1952; MBA NWU 1959; MDiv Sewanee: The U So, TS 1970. D 6/13/1970 Bp James Winchester Montgomery P 12/19/1970 Bp Gerald Francis Burrill. m 6/12/1953 Anne Andrews c 3. Adj Fac Bexley Seabury Fed Chicago IL 1984-1989; R S Elis's Ch Glencoe IL 1978-1989; Dioc Coun Dio Chicago Chicago IL 1975-1978, Secy Dioc Conv 1976-1980; Vic Ch Of The H Apos Wauconda IL 1974-1978; Assoc Gr Epis Ch Hinsdale IL 1970-1974. St. Andrews Soc, Cntrl Fl. Chapt, Chapl 1995.

ANDREWS, John Anthony (NY) PO Box 547, Lima NY 14485 **P-in-c Chr Epis Ch Hornell NY 2011-; Supply P Dio Rochester Henrietta 2006-; Dio Washington Washington DC 2006-; Ret Rochester NY 2000-** B Ottawa Ontario CA 1942 s Clifford & Elizabeth. BS Ed SUNY 1964; BS SUNY 1964; STM GTS 1967. D 6/3/1967 Bp Allen Webster Brown P 12/9/1967 Bp Charles Bowen Persell Jr. c 4. Int Ch Of The Atone Washington DC 2004-2005; Ch Of The Incarn Uppr Marlboro MD 2002; Adj P S Marg's Ch Washington DC 2002; Int S Mich And All Ang Hyattsville MD 2002; Chr Ch Of Ramapo Suffern NY 1980-2002, Cur 1969-1973; Vic S Aug Of Cbury Ch Edinboro PA

1977-1980; S Ptr's Ch Waterford PA 1977-1980; S Jos's Ch Port Allegan PA 1973-1977; S Matt's Epis Ch Eldred PA 1973-1977; Asst S Andr's Ch Brewster NY 1969-1973. Auth, "Healing," *Sharing mag.* Ord of S Lk 1980.

ANDREWS, John Joseph (Colo) 5968 S Zenobia Ct, Littleton CO 80123 B Denver CO 1943 s C & Helen. BA U CO 1966; MDiv Nash 1987. D 6/6/1987 P 12/12/1987 Bp William Carl Frey. m 6/5/1965 Carol Andrews c 2. Asst Ch Of The Epiph Tempe AZ 2012-2015; Asst S Mich's Ch Coolidge AZ 2011; Assoc R Ch Of The Trsfg Evergreen CO 2001-2003; Chapl Vlly Hope Drug and Alco Treatment Cntr Parker CO 2000-2001; Int S Mart In The Fields Aurora CO 1997-1998; Treas Colorado Coun of Ch Denver CO 1996-1997; Epis Rep Colorado Coun of Ch Denver CO 1993-1997; R St Gabr the Archangel Epis Ch Englewood CO 1991-1997; Dn Mtn Dnry Dio Colorado Denver CO 1988-1991, COM 1996-1998, Eccl Crt 1994-1998, Ecum Off 1993-1997, Budet and Fin Com 1988-1992, COM 1988-1990, LARC (Luth Angl RC Dialogue 1988-1990; Epis Ch Of S Jn The Bapt Granby CO 1987-1991; Vic Trin Ch Kremmling CO 1987-1991; Chapl Masonic Nrsng Hm Dousman WI 1985-1986.

ANDREWS, Lyde Coley (Ga) St Philips Episcopal Church, 302 E General Stewart Way, Hinesville GA 31313 B Florence SC 1968 s Coley & Rhonda. BS Cit 1993; MDiv Emory U 2005; MDiv Emory U 2005; DMin Erskine Sem 2012. D 6/30/2012 P 1/4/2013 Bp Scott Anson Benhase. m 4/7/2006 Nitsa Calas-Andrews.

ANDREWS, Pati Mary (Va) 8217 Roxborough Loop, Gainesville VA 20155 **R S Steph's Epis Ch Catlett VA 2007-** B Washington DC 1948 d Carl & Margaret. BA Geo Mason U 1994; MDiv VTS 2000. D 6/24/2000 P 2/6/2001 Bp Peter J Lee. R S Steph's Ch Catlett VA 2006-2015; P-in-c S Steph's Epis Ch Catlett VA 2005-2006; Vic Ch Of The Gd Shpd Greer SC 2003-2005; Assoc H Innoc Epis Ch Valrico FL 2000-2002. Ord of S Lk 2002; Sursum Corda, Sprtl Dir 2003.

ANDREWS, Robert Forrest (Colo) 30 Hutton Ln, Colorado Springs CO 80906 **Ret 1993-** B DeKalb IL 1931 s Forrest & Grace. BS VMI 1953; MDiv Nash 1963. D 6/15/1963 Bp James Winchester Montgomery P 12/21/1963 Bp Joseph Summerville Minnis. m 4/9/1983 Jane Andrews c 3. R S Jas Epis Ch Wheat Ridge CO 1984-1992; P-in-c S Jn's Ch Moorhead MN 1982-1984; P-in-c Trin Lisbon ND 1982-1984; R S Steph's Ch Fargo ND 1981-1984; R S Jas Ch Grosse Ile MI 1980-1981; R S Paul's Epis Ch St Jos MI 1968-1980; R All SS Epis Ch Denver CO 1966-1968; Vic Intsn Epis Ch Denver CO 1963-1966.

ANDREWS, Shirley May (Mass) 2 Palmer St, Barrington RI 02806 B Fall River MA 1936 d Thomas & Mary. BA Stratford Coll Danville VA 1970; MEd U of Virginia 1974; MDiv GTS 1990. D 6/1/1990 Bp Walter Cameron Righter P 1/19/1991 Bp Charlie Fuller Mcnutt Jr. m 7/17/1954 Ronald Andrews c 2. R Ch Of The Ascen Fall River MA 2002-2005; Assoc S Jn's Ch Barrington RI 1992-2001, Asst 1991-1992; Cur Dio Cntrl Pennsylvania Harrisburg PA 1990-1991; S Andr's Ch St Coll PA 1990-1991.

ANDREWS III, William E (WTenn) St Mary's Cathedral, 692 Poplar Ave, Memphis TN 38105 **S Mary's Cathd Memphis TN 2007-** B Greenville MS 1967 s William & Mary. BBA U of Mississippi 1989; MDiv Epis TS of the SW 1996. D 11/3/1996 P 4/1/1997 Bp James Barrow Brown. m 5/20/2000 Anne F Andrews c 3. S Timothys Epis Ch Southaven MS 2004-2007; Cn S Andr's Cathd Jackson MS 1998-2003; S Jas Epis Ch Baton Rouge LA 1996-1998.

ANDREWS-WECKERLY, Jennifer N. (SVa) 8300 Richmond Rd, Toano VA 23168 **Hickory Neck Ch Toano VA 2016-** B Atlanta GA 1976 d Harry & Felicia. AB Duke 1999; MDiv VTS 2009. D 6/24/2009 P 1/9/2010 Bp Wayne Wright. m 8/4/2001 Scott J Weckerly c 2. R S Marg's Ch Plainview NY 2011-2016; Cur Chr Ch Christiana Hundred Wilmington DE 2009-2011.

ANDRUS, Archie Leslie (HB) 2701 Bellefontaine St, Houston TX 77025 **Non-par 1970-** B 1935 BA U of SW Louisiana 1957; STB GTS 1963. D 6/25/1963 Bp Girault M Jones P 5/1/1964 Bp Iveson Batchelor Noland. m 4/15/1966 Diana Lee Cutler. Assoc R S Paul's Epis Ch San Antonio TX 1966-1970; Ch Of The Redeem Oak Ridge LA 1965-1966; Vic S Andr's Epis Ch Mer Rouge LA 1965-1966.

✠ ANDRUS, The Rt Rev Marc Handley (Cal) Episcopal Diocese Of California, 1055 Taylor St, San Francisco CA 94108 **Bp of California Dio California San Francisco CA 2006-** B Oak Ridge TN 1956 s Francis & Mary. BS U of Tennessee 1979; MA Virginia Tech U 1984; MDiv VTS 1987. D 6/20/1987 P 4/1/1988 Bp Claude Charles Vache Con 2/7/2002 for Ala. m 9/1/1979 Sheila M Andrus c 1. Bp Suffr Dio Alabama Birmingham 2002-2006; R Emm Ch Middleburg VA 1997-2001; Chapl Epis HS 1990-1997; Epis HS Alexandria VA 1990-1997; Asst Ch Of The Redeem Bryn Mawr PA 1987-1990. bishopmarc@diocal.org

ANDUJAR, Alexander (SwFla) **S Vinc's Epis Ch St Petersburg FL 2016-** D 12/7/2013 P 6/29/2014 Bp Dabney Tyler Smith.

ANEI, Abraham Muong (WMich) **D Sudanese Gr Epis Ch 2006-** B Sudan 1981 s Aivei & Adhet. Koyper Coll Grand Rapids MI; Trin Sem. D 12/9/2006 Bp Robert R Gepert. m 1/1/2003 Uyai Ajak. Factory Worker Abc Grp.

ANGELICA, David M (Mass) 15 Colonial Club Dr Apt 300, Boynton Beach FL 33435 B Hartford CT 1947 s Joseph & Josephine. BA Trin Hartford CT 1970; MDiv GTS 1973; PhD NYU 1976; Cert U of Connecticut 1978. D 6/9/1973 P

12/28/1973 Bp Joseph Warren Hutchens. R The Ch Of The H Sprt Orleans MA 1999-2008; Asst S Mary's Epis Ch Barnstable MA 1995-1998; R S Andr's Ch Milford CT 1980-1994; Cur S Andr's Ch Stamford CT 1977-1980; Asst S Lk's Par Darien CT 1974-1976; Assoc Epis Ch of Gr and Resurr E Elmhurst NY 1973-1974. dmangelica@comcast.net

ANGELL, Debra Lanning (Colo) 13866 W 2nd Ave, Golden CO 80401 B Denver CO 1952 d Wayland & Elizabeth. BA Colorado Coll 1974; BMus U Denv 1981; MDiv Iliff TS 1998. D 6/6/1998 P 12/13/1998 Bp William Jerry Winterrowd. m 6/1/1974 Richard Lee Angell c 3. Assoc R S Barn Epis Ch Denver CO 2002-2017; Asst St Gabr the Archangel Epis Ch Englewood CO 1999-2002; Pstr Asst/Cur Epiph Epis Ch Denver CO 1998. Bm mcl U Denv 1981; Ba cl Colorado Coll 1974.

ANGELL, Michael R (Mo) 7401 Delmar Blvd, Saint Louis MO 63130 **Ch Of The H Comm S Louis MO 2015-** B Denver CO 1982 s Richard & Debra. BA U of San Diego 2005; MDiv VTS 2011. D 4/9/2011 P 10/8/2011 Bp Jim Mathes. m 8/15/2013 Ellis B Anderson. Epis Ch Cntr New York NY 2014-2015; S Jn's Ch Lafayette Sq Washington DC 2011-2014; Dio San Diego San Diego CA 2006-2008. mangell@holycommunion.net

ANGELO, Patrice Lonnette (Los) 1818 Monterey Blvd, Hermosa Beach CA 90254 B Pasadena CA 1955 d John & Genevieve. Rel Stds California St U 2010; MDiv Claremont TS 2016; Cert of Angl Stds The ETS at Claremont 2017. D 2/12/2017 Bp Joseph Jon Bruno. m 4/26/1980 Christopher Edmond Angelo c 1.

ANGERER JR, John David (La) 112 Hazel Drive, River Ridge LA 70123 **S Mart's Epis Sch Metairie LA 2016-; R All SS Epis Ch New Orleans LA 2009-** B Hockessin DE 1970 s John & Mary. B.A. Virginia Commonwealth U 1993; MDiv SWTS 2002. D 6/8/2002 P 12/21/2002 Bp Wayne Wright. m 4/19/1997 Lisa G Angerer c 2. Vic Gd Shpd Epis Ch Wilmington DE 2005-2009; Epis Campus Min/ Asst S Thos's Par Newark DE 2002-2004.

ANGLE, Nancy Scott (Colo) 150 Sipprelle Dr, Battlement Mesa CO 81635 **D All SS Epis Ch Battlement Mesa CO 2009-** B Houston TX 1937 d William & Ruth Mildred. BA U CO 1958; MBS U CO 1974. D 11/14/2009 Bp Robert John O'Neill. m 8/10/1974 Marshall Alan Martin c 4.

ANGULO ZAMORA, Gina Mayra (EcuL) Iglesia Episcopal del Ecuador Diocese Litoral, Amarilis Fuente 603, Avenida 09015250, Guayaquil Ecuador Ecuador **D Litoral Dio Ecuador Guayaquil 2008-** B Ricaurte 1979 d Zenon & Ninfa. D 4/13/2008 Bp Terencio Alfredo Morante-Espana.

ANGUS, Caroline Helen (O) 2716 Colchester Rd, Cleveland Heights OH 44106 **Ret 1998-** B Grand Rapids MI 1936 d Donald & Loraine. SWTS; BA MI SU 1958; MA U MI 1959; SWTS 1981. D 1/22/1983 P 9/1/1983 Bp John Harris Burt. m 6/25/1960 John Angus c 2. S Lk's Ch Cleveland OH 1983-1998; DCE Emm Cleveland OH 1963-1980.

ANGUS, David E (WMo) Grace Cathedral, 415 W 13th St, Kansas City MO 64105 B Riverside AFB CA 1967 s William & Carol. BA Hope Coll 1988; MDiv Iliff TS 1994; MSW Sch of Soc Welf, The U of Kansas 1997. D 6/2/2012 P 12/1/2012 Bp Martin Scott Field. S Aug's Ch Kansas City MO 2014-2016. ANGUS_D@WMHCI.ORG

ANGUS, Joslyn Lloyd (Ga) 88 Oakwood Dr., Hardeeville SC 29927 B Saint Catherine JM 1939 s Lorenzo & Verena. Dip Mico U (Trng) Coll 1963; BD Lon GB 1969; MA McCormick TS 1973; Cert SWTS 1976; DMin McCormick TS 1980; PhD GTF 1998. D 5/2/1976 P 9/1/1976 Bp Quintin Ebenezer Primo Jr. m 8/30/1967 Rita S Angus c 3. R S Matt's Ch Savannah GA 1997-2005; R S Phil's Epis Ch Jacksonville FL 1981-1997; Vic Ch Of The H Cross Chicago IL 1976-1980. Auth, "Dynamic Chrsnty: The Impact Of Pan-Afr Immigrants On The Chr Churh In The USA," Auth Hse, 2006; Auth, "Vitalization Process Of An Urban Black Epis Cong".

ANKUDOWICH, Stephen (SwFla) 197 Corsica St, Tampa FL 33606 **Died 11/28/2016** B Northampton MA 1948 s Kostanty & Mary. BA Trin 1970; MDiv EDS 1974; DMin EDS 1991. D 6/14/1974 P 12/1/1974 Bp Alexander D Stewart. m 2/12/1972 Denise Ankudowich c 3. P-in-c S Anne Of Gr Epis Ch Seminole FL 2014-2016, 2004; R S Andr's Epis Ch Tampa FL 1990-2003; R Ch Of The Gd Shpd Wareham MA 1984-1989; Asst R S Mk's Ch New Canaan CT 1976-1978; Dio Wstrn Massachusetts Springfield 1974-1976; Asst R S Mich's-On-The-Heights Worcester MA 1974-1976. stevankstand@aol.com

ANSCHUTZ, Mark Semmes (Mass) 162 Pleasant Street, South Yarmouth MA 02664 B Carthage MO 1944 s John & Madeleine. BA Drury U 1966; STM Ya Berk 1969; DMin Andover Newton TS 1976. D 5/28/1969 P 1/25/1970 Bp William Foreman Creighton. m 6/25/1970 Margaret C Anschutz c 2. R S Mich And All Ang Ch Dallas TX 1995-2006; R S Jas Ch New York NY 1992-1995; R Chr Ch Alexandria VA 1977-1992; R S Lk's Ch Worcester MA 1971-1977; Assoc And Coll Chapl S Jn's Ch Northampton MA 1969-1971; Trst Ya Berk New Haven CT 1983-1987. Auth, "From the R," Full Crt Press, 2002; Auth, "Grant Them Wisdom". Omecron Delta Kappa 1965. DD STUSo 1997.

ANSCHUTZ, Maryetta Madeleine (Los) P.O. Box 691404, Los Angeles CA 90069 **Hd of Sch The Epis Sch of Los Angeles Los Angeles CA 2010-** B Worcester MA 1974 d Mark & Margaret. BA U So 1997; MDiv Ya Berk 2001. D 11/17/2001 Bp Peter J Lee P 6/6/2002 Bp James Elliot Curry. Assoc All SS Par Beverly Hills CA 2006-2010; Assoc Dn Ya Berk New Haven CT 2004-2006; Asst Chr And H Trin Ch Westport CT 2001-2004. Contributing Auth, "Sermons," *Feasting on the Word*, Knox, 2010. Monk Preaching Prize Ya Berk 2001.

ANTHONY, Benjamin J (At) **Trin Ch Indianapolis IN 2017-; Sewanee U So TS Sewanee TN 2015-** B Mansfield OH 1978 BA Wabash Coll 2000; MDiv Candler TS Emory U 2003. D 6/18/2005 P 7/14/2006 Bp Cate Waynick. m 4/6/2004 Rebecca Ann Trimm c 1. Dio Atlanta Atlanta GA 2007-2009; Young And YA Coordntr S Lk's Epis Ch Atlanta GA 2005-2007.

ANTHONY, Carol R (Pa) 627 Kenilworth St, Philadelphia PA 19147 **Dio Pennsylvania Philadelphia PA 2014-, 2001-2004** B Jackson MS 1957 d Willie & Maudie. BS Mississippi U For Wmn 1979; MRE SW Bapt TS 1985; CAS GTS 1995; STM GTS 1996. D 6/22/1996 P 4/5/1997 Bp Alfred Marble Jr. c 1. S Gabr's Epis Ch Philadelphia PA 2014; Ch Of S Lk And Epiph Philadelphia PA 2011-2014; S Ptr's Ch Philadelphia PA 2010-2011; Chr Ch Philadelphia Philadelphia PA 2005-2009, 2000-2003; P-in-c Ch Of S Jn The Evang Philadelphia PA 2003-2004; Epis Cmnty Serv Philadelphia PA 1998-2001; Cur S Andr's Cathd Jackson MS 1996-1998.

ANTHONY II, Henry F (RI) 727 Hampton Woods Ln SW, Vero Beach FL 32962 **Ret 1994-; Ret 1994-** B Providence RI 1933 s Ralph & Mary. BA Amh 1956; MDiv Sewanee: The U So, TS 1987. D 6/27/1987 P 1/1/1988 Bp George Nelson Hunt III. Assoc Ch Of The Gd Shpd Lookout Mtn TN 1992-1994; S Mart's Ch Providence RI 1991-1992; S Ptr's By The Sea Narragansett RI 1989-1991; Vic S Ptr's by-the-Sea Narragansett RI 1989-1991; Assoc R Trin Ch Newport RI 1987-1989.

ANTHONY, Joan (Oly) 1549 MW 57th St., Seattle WA 98107 **Gr Ch Bainbridge Island WA 2016-** B Seattle WA 1948 d John & Anne. BA WA SU 1970; MDiv SWTS 1991; MA Seattle U 1991. D 5/14/1991 P 11/1/1991 Bp Vincent Waydell Warner. Cn for Congrl Dvlpmt Dio Olympia Olympia WA 2005-2008; Cn to the Ordnry Dio Olympia Seattle 2003-2014; Mssnr Dio Olympia Olympia WA 2003-2005; Vic S Ben Epis Ch Lacey WA 1996-2003; Asst R Epis Ch Of S Fran-In-The-Vlly Green Vlly AZ 1994-1996; Asst R S Jn's Epis Ch Olympia WA 1991-1994. janthonypl@yahoo.com

ANTHONY JR, Joseph Daniel (At) 389 Dorsey Cir Sw, Lilburn GA 30047 **Nonpar 1985-** B Atlanta GA 1933 s Joseph & Lucy. BS USNA 1956; BD VTS 1964. D 6/29/1964 P 9/1/1965 Bp Gray Temple. c 3. Vic S Barn Ch Trion GA 1983-1985; Asst Par Ch of St. Helena Beaufort SC 1969; Chr Ch Denmark SC 1965-1969; P-in-c S Alb's Ch Blackville SC 1965-1969; D H Sprt No Charleston SC 1964-1965.

ANTHONY, Lloyd Lincoln (LI) 9910 217th Ln, Queens Village NY 11429 **Prot Chapl Coler-Goldwater Specialty Hosp and Nrsng Facility Roos 2000-** B BZ 1950 s Thomas & Delcy. Belize Teachers Coll 1972; BA Untd Theol Coll of the W Indies 1977; STM NYTS 1983. Trans 10/21/1982 as Priest Bp Robert Campbell Witcher Sr. m 7/14/1999 Wilma G Anthony c 3. Sheltering Arms Chld and Fam Serv Inc New York NY 2003-2012; R S Jos's Ch Queens Vlg NY 1987-2012; P-in-c Ch Of The H Sprt Brooklyn NY 1983-1984; S Johns Epis Hosp Far Rockaway NY 1981-1986; Chapl S Jn's Hosp and Hm for the Aged and Blind Brookl 1981-1986; Assoc Ch Of S Thos Brooklyn NY 1980-1983; R Angl Ch in Jamaica Jamaica W Indies 1978-1980; Ch Of S Jas The Less Jamaica NY 1978-1979; Prncl Tchr Prncl Tchr Belixe Cntrl Amer 1972-1973. Cn Dio Wiawso, Ghana 2009.

ANTHONY, Robert Williams (RI) 104 Old Stage Rd, Centerville MA 02632 B Port Chester NY 1940 s Robert & Gladys. BA Amh 1962; STB GTS 1965; MDiv GTS 1972. D 6/19/1965 P 2/1/1966 Bp John S Higgins. m 9/12/1964 Mary Ann Anthony c 2. R Chr Ch Westerly RI 1988-2006; The GTS New York NY 1987-1993; Dn Hampden Dnry Dio Wstrn Massachusetts 1985-1988; Dept of Soc Serv Dio Wstrn Massachusetts Springfield 1980-1983, Dioc Coun 1979-1985, 1976-1988; R Ch Of The Atone Westfield MA 1976-1988; Chapl U of New Haven New Haven CT 1972-1976; Chapl Veteran's Admin Hosp 1971-1976; R Ch of the H Sprt W Haven CT 1968-1976; Cur S Barn Ch Warwick RI 1965-1968; Chapl Westerly Fire Dept; Stndg Com Pres Dio Rhode Island Providence RI 2006-2007, Fin & Missions Cmsn 1994-2006, Dn Narragansett Dnry 1990-1993.

ANTHONY, Thomas Murray (PR) B 1935 STM GTS 1961.

ANTHONY-CHARLES, Ana Graciela (Ve) **Dio Venezuela Caracas 2004-** B 1949 D 1/18/1999 P 5/17/2002 Bp Orlando Jesus Guerrero.

ANTOCI, Peter M (WA) 3117 Perry St, Mount Rainier MD 20712 **Adj Cler S Marg's Ch Washington DC 2016-; Evening TS VTS Alexandria VA 2016-** B New York NY 1963 s Santo & Helen. BA GW 1985; MA CUA 1989; PhD CUA 1995; Cert Natl Institutes of Hlth 2000; CAS VTS 2000. D 6/9/2001 Bp Jane Hart Holmes Dixon P 5/26/2002 Bp Allen Lyman Bartlett Jr. m 2/25/2011 Donald Davis. Assoc R for Adult Formation S Columba's Ch Washington DC 2012-2016; Actg Int All Souls Memi Epis Ch Washington DC 2007; Prof of Rel Stds U of Maryland 2004-2012; U Chapl Dio Washington Washington DC 2003-2012, Mem: Com For the Diac 2015-, Chair: Campus Mnstry Advsry Grp 2014-2016, Mem of Stndg Com 2012-2014, Dep to GC 2009-2012, Mem of Dioc Coun 2005-2012, Mem of Dioc Coun 2003-2009; Chairman Epis Fndt U of Maryland 2003-2012; Adj Prof Rel Stds Prog U of Maryland 2003-2012; Adj Cler S Andr's Epis Ch Coll Pk MD 2003-2012; Cur Gr Epis Ch Silver Sprg MD 2001-2004; Chapl Gr Epis Day Sch Kensington MD 2001-2004; Dir: Sergeant Shriver Peaceworker Fllshp Prog The Shriver Cntr U of Maryland 1998-2003; Exec Dir Jubilee Hsng Washington DC 1990-1997; Adj Prof Rel Stds Dept CUA 1988-1998; Bp's Trst S Andr's Epis Sch Potomac MD 2014-2017; Coordntr of Higher Educ Mnstrs Prov III Baltimore MD 2009-2013; Dir: The Sargent Shriver Peaceworker Prog Shriver Cntr U of Maryland Baltimore 1998-2003; Exec Dir Jubilee Hsng Washington DC 1990-1997. Auth, "Link By Link: Creating An Online Par Resource Cntr," *Key Resources: Cntr For the Mnstry of Tchg*, VTS, 2014; Auth, "Angl Ecclesiological Musings: Called Out For What? Sent Forth For Whom?," *(Monograph)*, St. Columba's Epis Ch, DC, 2013; Auth, "Reflections On the Sprtlty of Campus Mnstry: A Play In Four Acts," *(Bk)*, Emeth Press, 2012; Auth, "An Epis Ecclesiology of Apostolocity, ATR," *ATR: Vol. 84 #2*, The ATR, 2002; Auth, "Serv & Mutuality," *From Cloister To Common: Concepts & Models for Serv-Lrng in Rel Stds*, Amer Assn For Higher Educ, 2002; Auth, "Scandal and Marginality in the Vitae of H Fools, Chrsnty and Lit," *Chrsnty & Lit: Vol. 44 # 3-4*, The Conf On Chrsnty & Lit, 1996. AAR 1989; HSEC 2010; Ldrshp Washington 1998; Prov III Epis Chapl 2003; Washington Epis Cler Assn 2001. Portaro Awd For Creative Expression & Intellectual Inquiry Off for YA & Campus Mnstry, TEC 2012; Dioc Coun, Mem 2006-2009 Epis Dio Washington 2006; Trst 1995-1997 Jubilee Hsng, Inc. 1995; Tchg and Resrch Fellowships 1988-1995 Cath U 1988.

ANTOLINI, Holly Lyman (Mass) 11 Quincy St, Arlington MA 02476 **R S Jas' Epis Ch Cambridge MA 2008-; Dn Dio Massachusetts Boston MA 2010-** B Philadelphia PA 1952 d Richard & Elizabeth. BA Ya 1974; MDiv CDSP 1991. D 12/8/1990 P 12/9/1991 Bp William Edwin Swing. c 2. Assoc S Paul's Ch Richmond VA 2003-2007; Dio Maine Portland ME 2002-2003, Stndg Com Mem 1999-2003, Stndg Com Mem 1998-2003, Dep to GC 1997-2003, Dep to GC 1996-2003; P-in-c S Eliz Of Hungary Portland ME 2002-2003; Int S Ptr's Ch Rockland ME 2002, Cur 1992; Int S Mk's Ch Waterville ME 1999-2001; Vic S Brendan's Epis Ch Deer Isle ME 1993-1999; D S Bede's Epis Ch Menlo Pk CA 1990-1991; Dn Dio Virginia Richmond VA 2006-2008; Prov Rep Epis Prov Of New Engl Portland ME 1994-1999. Auth, "A Letter to the Nigerian Ch from an Epis P," *Do Justice!: Unofficial Angl Pages*, Dr. Louie Crew, 2005; Auth, "The Da Vinci Code: Vehicle of Gr?," *bellsouthpwp2.net*, 2004; Auth, "Going Loc In Midcoast Maine," *Wit*, 2002; Auth, "Naming Our Demons," *Wit*, 1999; Auth, "Of Pryr And Compost," *Wit*, 1999; Auth, "Mnstry w Teenagers Who are Allergic to Organized Rel," *Progressive Chrsnty.org*, 1998; Auth, "An Environ Stations of the Cross," *Earthministry.org*, 1993. Masters of Div w hon CDSP 1991; BA w hon in Hist Ya 1974.

ANTTONEN, Jennifer Parker (Ida) 288 E Kite Dr, Eagle ID 83616 **Chapl to the Ret Dio Idaho Boise ID 2010-** B Dayton OH 1949 d Robert & Nancy. BS WA SU 1994; MDiv CDSP 1998. D 6/7/1998 Bp Frank Jeffrey Terry P 12/19/1998 Bp Harry Brown Bainbridge III. m 11/13/1971 John Helmer Anttonen c 2. R S Dav's Epis Ch Caldwell ID 2005-2006; Vic Emm Ch Hailey ID 1998-2003. Bp's Outstanding Cong Recognition Dio Idaho 2002; Make a Difference Day $10,000 Natl Awd USA Weekend mag 2002; Friends of Educ Awd Blaine Cnty Educ Assn 2000; BS cl WA SU 1994.

ANUSZKIEWICZ, Sarah Elisabeth (WNY) St Paul's Episcopal Church, 4275 Harris Hill Rd, Williamsville NY 14221 **P-in-c Trin Ch Warsaw NY 2014-; Creative Dir No-Exceptions.org Proj 2012-; Asst Dir Pirate Gnome Proj 2012-; Consult Soc Media Consult & Digital Mssnr 2012-; Consult Par Redeveloper 2011-; Writer Auth Blogger Reviewer 2010-; Sprtl Dir Retreat Ldr & Sprtl Dir 2010-** B Clearwater FL 1978 d Robert & Donna. BA SUNY 2001; MSW SUNY 2003; MDiv VTS 2006. D 12/26/2005 P 12/1/2006 Bp Michael Garrison. m 7/12/2012 Michael Anuszkiewicz. P-in-c H Apos Epis Ch Tonawanda NY 2009; Asst R Trin Epis Ch Buffalo NY 2006-2009.

APOLDO, Deborah D (USC) **Assoc Ch Of The Adv Spartanburg SC 2015-** B Philadelphia PA 1955 BS Ithaca Coll 1977; MDiv VTS 2003. D 6/14/2003 Bp Peter J Lee P 12/13/2003 Bp Ted Gulick Jr. c 3. Assoc for Evang & Discipleship S Fran In The Fields Harrods Creek KY 2003-2014; The Falls Ch Epis Falls Ch VA 1994-2000.

APPELBERG, Helen Marie Waller (Tex) 301 University Blvd, Galveston TX 77555 B Blooming Grove TX 1930 d Charles & Johnnie. AA Tyler Jr Coll 1949; BA U of No Texas 1951; MEd U of Virginia 1955; MEd Oklahoma City U 1977; MA Epis TS of the SW 1990; DMin Austin Presb TS 1995. D 6/16/1990 Bp Maurice Manuel Benitez P 1/1/1991 Bp William Elwood Sterling. c 1. S Lk's Epis Hosp Houston TX 1990-2002; S Mart's Epis Ch Houston TX 1990-2001. "Cmnty Of Hope," 14 Module Curric, 1996; "S Lk'S Epis," Hosp Med Cntr Houston Tx. Dok 1986; Ord Of S Ben 1996; Ord Of S Lk 1985; Wrld Cmnty Chr Meditation 1996.

APPLEGATE, Stephen Holmes (SO) 360 E Sharon Rd, Glendale OH 45246 **R S Lk's Ch Granville OH 2003-** B Nashville TN 1952 s Arthur & Betty. BA Ham 1974; MDiv GTS 1980. D 5/15/1980 P 11/1/1980 Bp Harold Barrett Robinson. c 1. S Andr's Epis Ch Cincinnati OH 2002-2003; Chr Ch - Glendale Cincinnati OH 1985-1990; Stndg Com Dio Albany Greenwich NY 1984-1985, BEC

1981-1987; S Paul's Cathd Buffalo NY 1981-1985; S Ptr's Ch Albany NY 1981-1985; Asst S Jas' Ch Batavia NY 1980-1981; Stndg Com Dio Sthrn Ohio Cincinnati OH 1988. Auth, "Hist mag Pec". Buffalo Area Metropltn Ministers Soc Of S Jn The Evang. Mdiv cl GTS 1980.

APPLEQUIST, Alice Mae (Minn) 17221 Highway 30 SE, Chatfield MN 55923 **P S Matt's Epis Ch Chatfield MN 1997-** B Rochester MN 1959 d Donald & Elizabeth. AA Rochester Cmnty Coll 1979; BS Winona St U 1982. D 7/28/1996 P 2/14/1998 Bp James Louis Jelinek. 4 Day 24/7 Pryr Grp 1997; Cancer Victors Pryr Grp 1997; Chatfield Mnstrl 1995; Chatfield Prayers for Healing Soc 1996.

APPLETON, Mary Ellen (CFla) 200 Saint Andrews Blvd Apt 1406, Winter Park FL 32792 B Brighton MI 1939 d Lawrence & Helen. Wheaton Coll 1960; BS Estrn Michigan U 1964; MEd Kent St U 1969. D 10/15/1988 Bp William Hopkins Folwell. D All SS Ch Of Winter Pk Winter Pk FL 1996-2002; D S Sebastian's By The Sea Melbourne Bch FL 1991-1995; D Ch of Our Sav Palm Bay FL 1988-1991. Chapl Ord Of S Lk.

APPLEYARD, Dan (Mo) 9 S Bompart Ave, Webster Groves MO 63119 B Greenwich CT 1954 s Robert & Katharine. BA Webster U 1976; MDiv Ya Berk 1983. D 6/23/1983 P 3/1/1984 Bp William Augustus Jones Jr. m 11/20/1989 Elizabeth Appleyard c 2. R Emm Epis Ch S Louis MO 2009-2016; R Chr Ch Dearborn MI 1993-2009; R S Lk's Epis Ch Shawnee KS 1986-1993; Cur Gr Ch S Louis MO 1983-1986; Cmncatn Com Dio Kansas Topeka KS 1986-1993.

APPLEYARD, Jonathan Briggs (Me) 26 Montsweag Road, Woolwich ME 04579 B Watertown CT 1949 s Robert & Katharine. BA Wms 1972; MDiv GTS 1976. D 5/29/1976 P 1/8/1977 Bp Robert Bracewell Appleyard. m 7/13/1996 Ruth B Wiggins c 3. Pstr Counslr Coll of the Atlantic 2008-2010; R S Sav's Par Bar Harbor ME 2002-2011; Exec Dir of Yth & Camp Mnstry Dio Massachusetts Boston MA 2000-2002; Dir of Dvlpmt Camp Dudley Ymca Inc Westport NY 1997-2000; Camp Chapl Camp Dudley YMCA Westport NY 1996-1999; R S Paul's Ch Brunswick ME 1988-1996; Dir of Educ Trin Par New York NY 1984-1988; Asst Dn of Stdt Affrs The GTS New York NY 1978-1984; Dio Pittsburgh Pittsburgh PA 1976-1978; Carnegie Mellon Univ The Ch Of The Redeem Pittsburgh PA 1976-1978; U of Vermont Dio Vermont Burlington VT 1974-1975; Mem at Lg Solid Waste Com Woolwich Maine 2013-2015; Treas of the Bd Healthy Acadia Bar Har Harbor Maine 2004-2010; Cler Day Com Dio Maine Portland ME 2001-2012, Com on H Ord 1990-2001; Founding Mem and Chair Consortium of Camps Westport New York 1997-1999; Cmsn of Total Mnstrs Exec Coun Appointees New York NY 1992-1995; Bd Mem Tedford Homeless Shltr Brunswick Maine 1989-1994; Mem, Co-Chair, Chair of the Racism T/F Dio New York New York NY 1980-1987. Soc of S Jn the Evang 1975. Cler Renwl Awd Lilly Endwmt Inc. 2008; MDiv w hon GTS 1976; BA mcl Wms 1972.

APPLEYARD JR, Robert Bracewell (Mass) 2036 Acton Ridge Rd, Acton ME 04001 B New York NY 1947 s Robert & Katharine. BA Alleg 1969; MDiv VTS 1972. D 6/10/1972 P 12/9/1972 Bp Robert Bracewell Appleyard. m 8/22/1970 Deborah W Appleyard c 1. Dn Cape Cod & The Islands MA 1996-2007; S Barn Ch Falmouth MA 1992-2007; R S Mich's Ch Milton MA 1977-1992; Asst R Fox Chap Epis Ch Pittsburgh PA 1972-1977; Exam Chapl Dio Massachusetts Boston MA 1987-1993. 1920 Club 1977-1992; Massachusetts Cler Assn 1977.

APPLING, Elizabeth Faragher (Oly) St. Paul's Episcopal Church, P.O. Box 753, Port Townsend WA 98368 B San Mateo CA 1945 d Richard & Kathleen. BA Occ 1967; MA Stan 1970; MDiv CDSP 1995. D 6/3/1995 P 6/1/1996 Bp William Edwin Swing. m 5/9/2015 Karen A Eaton. R S Paul's Epis Ch Port Townsend WA 2006-2013; Dio Olympia Seattle 2004; Dioc Coun Mem/Pres Dio California San Francisco CA 1998-2002, Dioc Stwdshp Cmsn 1996-2002; S Tim's Ch Danville CA 1995-2002.

APPOLLONI, Sharyn L (Nev) 1965 Golden Gate Dr, Reno NV 89511 B Wausau WI 1953 d Albert & Leone. BA Gonzaga U 1984; MA Gonzaga U 1986; EdD U of Nevada at Reno 1993. D 3/15/1997 Bp Stewart Clark Zabriskie. m 9/20/1980 Rodney Ross Petzak. D S Jn's In The Wilderness Ch Glenbrook NV 1997-2003.

ARACK, Mara (NCal) St Francis Episcopal Church, 568 16th St, Fortuna CA 95540 **S Fran Ch Fortuna CA 2016-** B Mount Kisco NY 1950 d Henry & Eleanor. BA Humboldt St U 1984; MA Humboldt St U 1987; BDS Epis Sch For Deacons 2015. D 8/13/2016 Bp Barry Leigh Beisner. m 4/11/2015 George Arack c 5.

ARAICA, Alvaro (Chi) 4609 Main St, Skokie IL 60076 **Dio Chicago Chicago IL 2012-, 1995-1996; Cristo Rey Chicago IL 1996-** B Jinotega NI 1960 s Ernesto & Maura. BEd Natl U of Nicaragua 1984; MDiv SWTS 1995; DMIn Congrl Stds SWTS 2009. D 10/17/1987 P 7/1/1989 Bp Sturdie Wyman Downs. m 5/10/1982 Marta Araica c 3. Iglesia Epis Santa Teresa De Avila Chicago IL 1995-1996.

ARAMBULO, Arnulfo (NY) 231 City View Ter, Kingston NY 12401 **Chr Ch Poughkeepsie NY 2000-** B CO 1943 s Sinforoso & Agripina. PH Natl Sem 1971; San Buenaventura U 1975. Rec 12/31/1994 Bp Joe Doss. m 11/27/1986 Maria Arambulo c 2. Ch Of The H Cross Kingston NY 2007-2009, Latina Mssnr 2000; Dio New York New York NY 2000-2009; Vic/Hisp Mssnr Ch Of The Gd Shpd Newburgh NY 2000; Gr Epis Ch Eliz NJ 1997-1999.

ARAQUE GALVIS, Alirio (PR) Iglesia Episcopal Puertorriquena, PO Box 902, Saint Just PR 00978 Puerto Rico **Dio Puerto Rico Trujillo Alto PR 2009-** B San Gil Colombia 1960 s Maria. BA Seminario Mayor Bucaramanga; BA Universita Septentrional - Milan; MA Universitat Innsbruck. Rec 6/28/2009 as Priest Bp David Andres Alvarez-Velazquez. m 8/26/2007 Emma Margarita Rios Benitez c 5.

ARASE-BARHAM, Michael Preston (Cal) PO Box 555, Half Moon Bay CA 94019 **Ch Of The H Fam Fresno CA 2013-; Gd Shpd Epis Ch Belmont CA 2013-** B Orlando FL 1975 s Robert & Janet. BA Millsaps Coll 1999; MDiv Duke DS 2003; CAS CDSP 2008; DMin CDSP 2012. D 6/13/2008 P 12/6/2008 Bp Marc Handley Andrus. m 5/21/2013 Jiro Arase. Assoc R Par of St Clem Honolulu HI 2008-2013. vicar@holyfamilyhmb.org

ARBOGAST, Stephen Kirkpatrick (WA) St. Mark's School of Texas, 10600 Preston Rd, Dallas TX 75230 **S Marks Sch Of Texas Dallas TX 2015-; Sr Chapl & Chair of the Rel Stds Dept Natl Cathd Sch 2012-; Affiliated P Gr Epis Ch New York NY 2007-; Chair: Rel, Philos, & Ethics Dept Trin Sch New York NY 2004-** B Dallas TX 1956 s Edward & Barbara. Dplma Ya Berk 2003; MDiv Yale DS 2003; ThM Harvard DS 2005; D.Min. Candidate VTS 2014. D 6/4/2005 P 1/7/2006 Bp M(Arvil) Thomas Shaw. Cathd of St Ptr & St Paul Washington DC 2012-2015; Assoc Trin Par New York NY 2006-2007; Chair; Rel, Philos, & Ethics Dept Trin Sch New York NY 2004-2012. arbogast@smtexas.org

ARBOLEDA, Guillermo Alejandro (Ga) B Levittown NY 1991 s Guillermo & Evelyn. B.A. Mssh Coll 2012; M.Div. Duke DS 2015. D 11/14/2015 P 5/21/2016 Bp Scott Anson Benhase. m 5/3/2014 Kelly Ann Steele. Legis Aide GC-Epis Ch Cntr New York NY 2015. HSEC 2014. frgaa@stmattsav.org

ARBUCKLE, Jacquelyn Fenelon (Vt) 54 Morse Pl, Burlington VT 05401 B Lynn MA 1942 d Eugene & Margaret. RN New Engl Bapt Hosp 1963; MEd Antioch U New Engl 1983. D 7/30/1991 Bp Daniel Lee Swenson. m 11/7/1964 Allan Rainsbury Arbuckle c 2. D S Jn's In The Mountains Stowe VT 2007-2009; D All SS' Epis Ch S Burlington VT 1991-2007. NAAD.

ARCHER, Arthur William (Del) 650 Willow Valley Sq # K-401, Lancaster PA 17602 **Ret 1994-; Chapl AFAM of DE DE 1989-** B Sewickley PA 1932 s Harry & Hazel. BA Ken 1954; STB Ya Berk 1957; STM SEWANEE 1966. D 6/29/1957 Bp William S Thomas P 12/21/1957 Bp Austin Pardue. m 9/8/1956 Carolyn Archer c 3. Chapl AFAM of DE DE 1982-1983; R S Jas Epis Ch Newport Newport DE 1980-1994; R Trin Ch New Phila OH 1971-1980; Cur S Mk's Epis Ch Toledo OH 1965-1971; R S Paul's Ch Monongahela PA 1960-1964; Asst S Steph's Epis Ch Mckeesport PA 1957-1960.

ARCHER, Carolyn (Ct) B Milford CT 1955 D 9/15/2007 Bp Andrew Donnan Smith.

ARCHER, John Richard (Cal) 80 Harmon St, Hamden CT 06517 **Non-par 1992-** B Buffalo NY 1945 s John & Gertrude. Colg 1964; BA SUNY 1967; Canisius Coll 1970; MDiv GTS 1974; PhD Gnrl Theol Un Berkeley CA 1984. D 5/22/1974 Bp Harold Barrett Robinson P 11/1/1974 Bp George E Rath. m 11/7/1998 Susan Abel. R All Souls Par In Berkeley Berkeley CA 1989-1992; Cathd of St Ptr & St Paul Washington DC 1986-1989; Dir Acad Affrs CP Washington DC 1986-1989; Lectr Ch Hist And Liturg CDSP Berkeley CA 1986, Lectr Ch Hist And Liturg 1981-1983; Int Ch Of The Resurr Pleasant Hil CA 1984-1986; Fac Dio California San Francisco CA 1980-1986; Vic S Edm's Epis Ch Pacifica CA 1978-1984; R Ch Of The Trsfg Ironwood MI 1975-1978; Cur Gr Ch Nutley NJ 1974-1975. Auth, "The Preaching Of Phil Repindon Bp Of Lincoln".

ARCHER, Jonathan Gurth Adam (SeFla) 3481 Hibiscus St, Miami FL 33133 **Chr Epis Ch Miami FL 2013-** B Nassau Bahamas 1976 s Gurth & Angela. AA Coll of the Bahamas 1997; BA Codrington Coll (UWI) 2001; BA Codrington TS (Barbados) 2001; BA Codrington TS/UWI (Barbados) 2001; Dplma Coll of the Bahamas 2003. Trans 8/1/2013 as Priest Bp Leo Frade. m 11/12/2011 Nicola Marva Archer.

ARCHER, Melinda (Az) 5265 NE 3rd Court, Lincoln City OR 97367 **Dio Arizona AZ 2006-** B Dallas TX 1946 d Horace & Irene. BA SMU 1967; MA SMU 1970; MDiv SMU Perkins 1991. D 9/11/1999 P 8/26/2000 Bp Julio Cesar Holguin-Khoury. c 2. P-in-c S Jas Ch Lincoln City OR 2011-2014; R S Andr's Ch Glendale AZ 2005-2010; Assoc S Barn Ch Garland TX 2002-2005; Vic Iglesia Epis San Juan El Bautista Bonao 2000-2001; Dio The Dominican Republic (Iglesia Epis Dominicana) Gazcue Santo Domingo 1999-2001.

ARCHER, Michael (Los) 18631 Chapel Ln, Huntington Beach CA 92646 **P-in-c S Wilfrid Of York Epis Ch Huntington Bch CA 2008-** B Oklahoma City OK 1960 s Ronald & Mary Eva. D 4/16/2008 P 10/18/2008 Bp Joseph Jon Bruno. m 12/2/2011 Cindy L Archer c 4. michael@stwilfridschurch.org

ARCHER, Nell B (LI) 199 Carroll St, Brooklyn NY 11231 **P-in-c Dio Long Island Garden City NY 2015-, Asst 2009-2010** B Memphis TN 1961 d Arthur & Louise. BA Duke 1983; MDiv GTS 2009. D 6/22/2009 Bp James Hamilton Ottley P 1/16/2010 Bp Lawrence C Provenzano. m 1/21/2015 Nancy Patricia Webster c 3. S Phil's Ch Brooklyn NY 2012-2013; Asst S Paul's Ch Brooklyn NY 2010-2015; S Ann And The H Trin Brooklyn NY 2010-2012.

ARCHIBALD, David Jost (Del) 32216 Bixler Rd, Selbyville DE 19975 **P S Mk's Ch Millsboro DE 2015-, R 2002-2014** B East Orange NJ 1943 s William & Marjorie. Washington and Jefferson U 1963; W Virginia U 1966; BA Thos Edison St Coll 1985; MDiv Sewanee: The U So, TS 1989. D 7/14/1990 P 1/19/1991 Bp George Lazenby Reynolds Jr. m 6/24/1972 Susan M Archibald c 2. S Martins-In-The-Fields Wilmington DE 2003; Dio Delaware Wilmington 2002-2014; Chr Epis Ch Tracy City TN 1998-2002; Dio Tennessee Nashville TN 1991-2003; Vic Chr Ch Decherd TN 1990-2002; Chr Ch Alto Decherd TN 1990-1994; St Jas Epis Ch Sewanee TN 1990-1991.

ARCHIBALD, David Roberts (WTex) 6110 NW Loop 410, San Antonio TX 78238 **S Andr's Epis Ch San Antonio TX 2007-** B Dayton OH 1960 s Rennie & Mary. BS Jas Madison U 1984; MDiv VTS 1991. D 6/8/1991 Bp Don Adger Wimberly P 12/18/1991 Bp Joseph Thomas Heistand. m 6/18/2016 Kimberly Ann Winter c 1. S Steph's Epis Ch Houston TX 2002-2006; S Fran Ch Heber Sprg AR 1998-2002; Asst All SS Epis Ch Corpus Christi TX 1994-1998; Chapl Memi Med Cntr Corpus Christi TX 1993-1994; Asst Ch Of The Gd Shpd Corpus Christi TX 1991-1993.

ARCHIE, Andrew John (Mo) 6345 Wydown Blvd, Saint Louis MO 63105 **R S Mich & S Geo S Louis MO 2000-** B Highland Park IL 1957 s Robert & Carol. BA W&L 1979; MDiv VTS 1986. D 6/14/1986 Bp James Winchester Montgomery P 1/1/1987 Bp Claude Charles Vache. m 6/25/1983 Margaretta Archie c 3. R S Ptr's Epis Ch Purcellville VA 1987-2000; Manakin Epis Ch Midlothian VA 1986-1987; S Lk's Ch Powhatan VA 1986-1987. Ord of St. Jn of Jerusalem 2012.

ARCINIEGA, Roberto (Ore) 2065 Se 44th Ave Apt 248, Hillsboro OR 97123 **Dio Oregon Portland OR 2006-** B Jocotitlan MX 1956 s Juan & Oliva. BA Sem Conculiar de Toluca MX 1975; BA Inst Superior De Estudies Eclesasticol 1980. Rec 5/1/1991 Bp John Lester Thompson III. m 5/26/2006 Kelly Arciniega c 2. P-in-c S Mich's/San Miguel Newberg OR 2006-2017, 1996-1997; Dio El Camino Real Salinas CA 1995; Mssnr The Epis Dio Nthrn California Sacramento CA 1991-1995; Serv RC Ch 1980-1983.

ARD, Eddie Jackson (At) 3880 Glenhurst Dr Se, Smyrna GA 30080 B Manchester GA 1956 s Sylvester & Lovie. BA Presb Coll 1977; MDiv VTS 1983. D 6/11/1983 P 5/6/1984 Bp Charles Judson Child Jr. m 12/20/1986 Jo Ann Ard c 1. R S Anne's Epis Ch Atlanta GA 1999-2013; R Emm Epis Ch Athens GA 1995-1999; R Gr Ch Anniston AL 1989-1994; Asst R H Innoc Ch Atlanta GA 1983-1989.

ARD JR, Robert F (Mo) 6518 Michigan Ave, St. Louis MO 63111 **R Ch Of The H Cross Tryon NC 2016-** B Bronxville NY 1972 s Robert & Kathryn. MTh Aquinas Inst of Theol 2002; MDiv Eden TS 2008; STM Sewanee: The U So, TS 2010. D 5/22/2010 P 12/21/2010 Bp George Wayne Smith. m 9/16/2006 Sharol Warner Ard c 1. S Paul's Ch S Louis MO 2010-2016. robert@holycrosstryon.org

ARD, Roger Hoyt (At) 104 Sequoia Dr SE, Rome GA 30161 B Manchester GA 1952 s Sylvester & Lovie. BA Presb Coll 1973; MDiv Candler TS Emory U 1976; Emory U 1982. D 6/14/1980 Bp Bennett Jones Sims P 4/1/1981 Bp Charles Judson Child Jr. m 11/20/2004 Elizabeth O Orr c 2. R S Ptr's Ch Rome GA 2002-2011; Int R Epis Ch Of The H Sprt Cumming GA 1999-2001; Int R S Steph's Ch Milledgeville GA 1999; Int Dn Cathd Of S Phil Atlanta GA 1997-1998; R S Paul's Epis Ch Westfield NJ 1993-1997; Int R S Lk's Epis Ch Atlanta GA 1991-1992; Assoc R S Anne's Epis Ch Atlanta GA 1989-1991, P-in-c 1987-1988; R S Mths Epis Ch Toccoa GA 1980-1984. Consult Ldr, "Involuntary Termination of Cler Within the Epis Ch," *Involuntary Termination of Cler Within the Epis Ch*, ECF, 1996; Auth, "Six Stages of Faith Dvlpmt," *Natl Cath Reporter*, 1979.

ARDLEY, Evan Lloyd (NCal) 435 43rd Ave, #301, San Francisco CA 94121 **Died 9/4/2016** B Motueka NZ 1947 s Frank & Nita. LTh Chr Ch TS Chr Ch NZ 1969; STh Joint Bd TS Auckland NZ 1975; Lic Trin of Mus London UK 1975; MTh CDSP 1976; DMin Grad Theol Un 1980; PhD GTF 2000. Trans 9/1/1976 as Priest Bp Clarence Rupert Haden Jr. m 5/25/1973 Diana Ardley c 2. Mgr Mgr Sprtl Serv Hospice By the Bay 2006-2016; Mgr Mgr of Sprtl Serv Sutter VNA&Hospice 2001-2005; R Ch Of The Incarn Santa Rosa CA 1988-2000; R St Johns Epis Ch Lafayette IN 1983-1988; Assoc All SS Ch San Diego CA 1980-1983; Headmaster All SS Sch San Diego CA 1980-1983; Vic S Tim's Ch Gridley CA 1976-1979; Serv Angl Ch in New Zealand 1969-1975. Auth, "Martyrs of Uganda Hymn," *Ch of Uganda*; Auth, "AIDS Hymn," *Dio Los Angeles*. Assoc of Amer Hospice and Palliative Med 2005; Natl Hospice and Palliative Care Orgnztn 2000. LTh w hon Chr Ch TS 1969; R Hd Mem Awd Outstanding Min to PWAs.

ARDREY-GRAVES, Sara (NC) St Paul Episc Church, 520 Summit St, Winston Salem NC 27101 **Assoc S Paul's Epis Ch Winston Salem NC 2015-** B Yukon OK 1980 d Thomas & Peggy. BS Appalachian St U 2002; MDiv Duke DS 2005; MDiv Duke DS 2005; Dip Ang Stud Sewanee: The U So, TS 2010. D 5/23/2010 P 1/8/2011 Bp Porter Taylor. m 5/21/2005 Mark W Ardrey-Graves. Assoc Emm Ch Harrisonburg VA 2010-2015; Chapl Res Spartanburg Reg Hosp 2008-2009; Vol Coordntr HabHum of Spartanburg SC 2007-2008; Yth Dir Ch Of The Gd Shpd Raleigh NC 2005-2010.

ARELLANO, Donna (NCal) D 6/10/2017 Bp Barry Leigh Beisner.

ARENAS TORO, William Henry (Colom) B 1961 s Mauro & Teresita. Sacerdote Seminario Carmelitano 2000. Rec 11/11/2011 as Priest Bp Francisco Jose Duque-Gomez. m 12/24/2007 Constanza Munoz Munoz Silva c 1.

ARENTS, Gina (Md) 1511 Long Quarter Ct, Lutherville MD 21093 B New York NY 1944 d George & Jane. BA Goucher Coll 1975; PhD JHU 1987; MTh Ecum Inst at St Marys Sem 2007; MDiv VTS 2009. D 6/2/2001 Bp Robert Wilkes Ihloff P 12/18/2010 Bp John L Rabb. Asst Chr Ch Columbia MD 2010-2011; D S Ptr's Epis Ch Ellicott City MD 2004-2010; D All SS Epis Ch Reisterstown MD 2001-2004.

ARGUE, Douglas (SO) 22 Glencoe Rd, Columbus OH 43214 B Detroit MI 1966 s Daniel & Carla. BA U of Evansville 1988; MSW Indiana U 1992. D 6/14/2008 Bp Thomas Edward Breidenthal. m 2/20/2015 Russell Miller. douglas.argue@cohhio.org

ARIS-PAUL, Maria Marta (NY) 1 Merlot Dr, Unit 138, Highland NY 12528 **Died 10/7/2015** B Guatemala City GT 1933 d Enrique & Marta. BA Smith 1976; MDiv UTS 1981. D 11/29/1982 Bp Paul Moore Jr P 6/25/1983 Bp Walter Decoster Dennis Jr. c 7. Pstr Gr Ch White Plains NY 1992-1994; Exec Dir Instituto Pstr Hispano New York NY 1990-1994; Pstr Mision San Juan Bautista Bronx NY 1988-1991; Exec Dir Insituto Pstr Hispano New York City New York NY 1986-1994; P-in-c S Andr's Epis Ch New Paltz NY 1984-1986; Sr Chapl Wallkill Correctional Facility Wallkill NY 1983-1986. Auth, "Latin Amer and Caribbean Immigrants in the USA: The Invisible and Forgotten," *Revolution of Sprt Ecum Theol in Global Context*, W Erdmansn, 1998; Auth, "A Question: The Ch and the Hisp Cmnty," *ATR*, 1994; Auth, "Lrng Together," *Mnstry Dvlpmt Journ*, 1988. AB cl Smith 1976.

ARLEDGE JR, Thomas Lafayette (At) 909 Massee Ln, Perry GA 31069 B Chattano GA 1938 s Thomas & Louise. BS U of Tennessee 1961; MS U of Tennessee 1963; BD Sewanee: The U So, TS 1970. D 6/28/1970 P 2/1/1971 Bp R aymond Stewart Wood Jr. m 10/5/1963 Lora Lee Arledge. P-in-c S Lk's Epis Hawkinsville GA 1996-1998; S Paul's Ch Macon GA 1995; S Steph's Ch Griffin GA 1994-1995; Dio Atlanta Atlanta GA 1970-1994; S Chris's At-The-Crossroads Epis Perry GA 1970-1993; S Mary's Epis Ch Montezuma GA 1970-1993.

ARLIN, Charles Noss (Nwk) 1078B Long Beach Blvd, Long Beach Twp. NJ 08008 **Assoc The Ch Of The H Innoc Bch Haven NJ 2014-** B Cuba NY 1938 s Aubrey & Edith. BA Hobart and Wm Smith Colleges 1961; STB GTS 1964. D 6/1/1964 Bp Ned Cole P 6/10/1965 Bp Walter M Higley. m 10/10/1964 Jane M Arlin c 4. Int S Jn's Ch New City NY 2011-2015; Int Ch Of The H Cross Kingston NY 2009-2011; Chapl Fire Dept Midland Pk NJ 2003-2009; R Ch Of The Gd Shpd Midland Pk NJ 2002-2009; P-in-c All SS Ch Bergenfield NJ 1997-2002; Int Epis Ch On W Kaua'i Eleele HI 1989; Vic H Cross Perth Amboy NJ 1977-1997; Chapl US Army 1970-1991; Fac Gr Sch NY 1968-1977; Asst S Lk the Evang Roselle NJ 1968-1976; Asst S Jn's Ch New York NY 1966-1968; Mssy S Ambr Groton NY 1964-1966.

ARMENTROUT, Katharine Jacobs (At) 202 Griffith Rd, Jasper GA 30143 B Montclair NJ 1941 d Jay & Phyllis. BA Br 1963; JD U of Maryland 1983. D 6/5/2004 Bp Robert Wilkes Ihloff. m 8/21/1965 Walter Scott Armentrout c 2.

ARMER, Mary Carolyn (WMo) 8170 Halsey St, Lenexa KS 66215 **Stff Chapl S Lk's Hosp Dio W Missouri MO 2004-** B Phoenix AZ 1943 d John & Mary. MA Arizona St U; BS Nthrn Arizona U 1964; Cert Grand Canyon U 1976; MDiv Epis TS of the SW 1991. Trans 1/1/2004 as Priest Bp Harry Brown Bainbridge III. c 1. St Lk's Chap Kansas City MO 2004-2011; St Lk's So Chap Overland Pk KS 2004-2010; Stff Chapl S Lk's Hosp Boise ID 1995-2004; S Steph's Boise ID 1995; Emm Ch Hailey ID 1994-1995; D/Asst Cathd Ch Of S Mk Salt Lake City UT 1993-1994; Chapl Res Dio Utah Salt Lake City UT 1991-1993. Assn Profsnl Chapl 1995.

ARMER, Susan Charlee (Oly) 10064 E Durham Rd, Dewey AZ 86327 B Phoenix AZ 1949 d Charles & Lillian. BA U of Arizona 1982; MDiv Bex Sem 1988. D 6/2/1988 P 12/8/1988 Bp Joseph Thomas Heistand. c 1. R S Matthews Auburn WA 2001-2014; Cn Pstr Cathd Ch Of S Mk Salt Lake City UT 1991-2001; Assoc R Chr Epis Ch Dayton OH 1988-1991.

ARMINGTON, Shawn Aaron (NJ) 118 Jefferson Rd, Princeton NJ 08540 **Assoc Trin Cathd Trenton NJ 2011-** B Portsmouth NH 1958 s Allan & Frances. BA Cor 1980; MA Ya Berk 1983; MDiv GTS 1986; ThM PrTS 1994; PhD PrTS 2000. D 6/7/1986 Bp David Standish Ball P 12/21/1986 Bp Vincent King Pettit. m 5/1/1982 Karen Louise Armington. Vic Trin Ch Rocky Hill NJ 1997-2002; Vic S Jn's Epis Ch Maple Shade NJ 1987-1994; Chr Ch So Amboy NJ 1986-1987. Auth, "Koinonia". SBL. Ba mcl Cornell 1980; Green Fllshp OT Phd Stds.

ARMSTEAD, Delaney Wendell (Nev) 2552 Orangeglory Dr, Henderson NV 89052 **Died 5/14/2016** B Youngstown OH 1928 s Abram & Dorothy. BA California Sch for Deacons 1988. D 12/7/1996 Bp William Edwin Swing. m 8/17/1996 Joann Shirley Roberts. D S Aug's Ch Oakland CA 1996-2000; S Chris's Ch San Lorenzo CA 1996-2000. Bro Of S Andr; CBS; OHC, Berkeley, Ca 1997.

ARMSTRONG, Barbara Keegan (NC) 509 Sleepy Valley Rd, Apex NC 27523 B Brooklyn NY 1939 d Milton & Rita. Geo; BA Meredith Coll 1983; MRE Duke DS 1986. D 10/4/1987 Bp Robert Whitridge Estill. m 1/2/1959 Robert Armstrong c 3. Dir D Formation Dio No Carolina Raleigh NC 2001-2006; D Ch Of The H Fam Chap Hill NC 1991-2008.

ARMSTRONG, Elizabeth (NCal) 1008 Linier Ct., Roseville CA 95678 **Vic S Aug Of Cbury Rocklin CA 2011-** B Poughkeepsie NY 1954 d Richard & Elizabeth. BA California St U 1981; MA California St U 1983; MDiv CDSP 2001. D 6/9/2001 P 1/12/2002 Bp Jerry Alban Lamb. c 2. Asst R Faith Epis Ch Carmeron Pk CA 2001-2011.

ARMSTRONG, Geoffrey Macgregor (NY) 10 Lanes End, Mervin Village NH 03850 **Ret 1995-** B Detroit MI 1936 s Charles & Beatrice. BA Bow 1958; STB GTS 1961; MA Wstrn Connecticut St U 1972; JD Pace U 1981. D 6/10/1961 P 12/1/1961 Bp Horace W B Donegan. m 6/21/1958 Beverly Julie Armstrong. Cur S Thos Ch Mamaroneck NY 1962-1964; Cur S Paul's Ch Winter Haven FL 1961-1962.

ARMSTRONG, Michael N (Fla) 2349 SW Bascom Norris Dr, Lake City FL 32025 **P-in-c S Cathr's Ch Jacksonville FL 2015-** B Athens AL 1944 d Robert & Mary. BD Jacksonville U 1995; MDiv Sewanee: The U So, TS 1999. D 6/13/1999 Bp Stephen Hays Jecko P 12/18/1999 Bp Roger John White. Emm Ch Orlando FL 2002; Assoc Gr Ch Madison WI 1999-2001.

ARMSTRONG, Phyllis (SO) 2841 Urwiler Ave, Cincinnati OH 45211 B Cincinnati OH 1943 d Henry & Margaret. BD U Cinc 1991; Diac Stds Sch For Deaconal Mnstry 2005. D 6/4/2005 Bp Herbert Thompson Jr. m 10/13/2001 James M Armstrong c 2. Rn Cinti Chld's Hosp 1987-2004.

ARMSTRONG, Richard Sweet (Mass) 35 Old Fields Way, Castine ME 04421 **1974-** B Attleboro MA 1944 s Paul & Marian. BS MIT 1965; MS MIT 1966; BD EDS 1969. D 6/21/1969 Bp Anson Phelps Stokes Jr P 4/1/1970 Bp Donald J Campbell. m 9/2/2011 Carol Adams c 2. Trin Ch Castine ME 2014-2016, Assoc 2011-; Assoc of Div Cherwick Cntr Boston MA 1978-1980; Ch Fin Serv Boston MA 1972-1974; Dio Massachusetts Boston MA 1972-1974; Harv Cambridge MA 1970-1972; Cur S Andr's Ch Framingham MA 1969-1970. Auth, *Proj Metran*; Auth, *Underused Ch Property: A Search for Solutions*.

ARMSTRONG, Robert Hancock (SVa) 4600 Bruce Rd, Chester VA 23831 B Richmond VA 1932 s Thomas & Julia. BA U Rich 1954; MDiv VTS 1963. D 6/21/1963 P 6/1/1964 Bp Robert Fisher Gibson Jr. c 4. R S Jn's Ch Chester VA 1968-2003; Asst St Jas Ch Richmond VA 1963-1968; Exec Bd Dio Sthrn Virginia Newport News VA 1993-1996.

ARMSTRONG, Susan J (NCal) 1765 Virginia Way, Arcata CA 95521 **P-in-c Chr Ch Eureka CA 2013-; Assoc Chr Ch Epis Eureka CA 2007-** B Minneapolis 1941 d Daniel & Shirley. BA Bryn 1963; PhD Bryn 1976; Cert Ang Stud CDSP 2006. D 6/3/2006 P 12/16/2006 Bp Jerry Alban Lamb. c 4. P Assoc (Vol) S Alb's Ch Arcata CA 2006-2012. Sis of the Trsfg (Assoc) 1993. ccpriest@att.net

ARMSTRONG, William H (WVa) 320 Old Bluefield Rd, Princeton WV 24740 **Vic Ch Of The Heav Rest Princeton WV 2011-** B Pensacola FL 1946 s William. BA Un Coll Barbourville KY 1968; MDiv Duke DS 1972. D 6/12/1999 Bp John Henry Smith P 6/10/2000 Bp Claude Charles Vache. m 6/6/1986 Shirley Ann Armstrong c 1.

ARMSTRONG, Zenetta M (Mass) 58 Crawford St Apt 2, Dorchester MA 02121 **R Ch Of The H Sprt Mattapan MA 2000-, Co-R 1992-2000, Assoc 1990-1991, 1988-1990** B All Saints AG 1951 d Hubert & Enid. CUNY; EDS; GW. D 6/11/1988 P 6/1/1989 Bp Don Edward Johnson.

ARMY, Virginia (Ct) The Rectory School, Pomfret CT 06258 **P-in-c S Jn's Epis Ch Vernon Rock Vernon Rockville CT 2008-; Cler-In-Res Chr Ch Pomfret CT 1992-; Chapl S Andr's Chap Pomfret CT 1991-** B Groton MA 1957 d Paul & Priscilla. BA Wesl 1979; MDiv Ya Berk 1982. D 12/18/1992 P 6/1/1993 Bp Arthur Edward Walmsley. m 6/14/1980 Thomas F Army Jr c 4.

ARNASON, Tryggvi Gudmundur (WNC) 130 39th Avenue Pl NW, Hickory NC 28601 **R S Alb's Ch Hickory NC 2011-** B Reykdavik IS 1964 s Árni & Bjarney. BA U of W Florida 1992; MDiv Candler TS Emory U 1997. D 7/14/2005 P 2/26/2006 Bp J Neil Alexander. m 6/12/2004 Lee Ann G Arnason c 2. Asst H Innoc Ch Atlanta GA 2005-2011; Chapl H Innoc' Epis Sch Atlanta GA 2005-2007.

ARNEY, Carol Mary (Haw) 1840 University Ave W, Apt. 104, Saint Paul MN 55104 B Bremerton WA 1945 d Vernon & Margaret. BA U of Hawaii 1969; MDiv Sewanee: The U So, TS 1995. D 6/24/1995 P 2/1/1996 Bp George Nelson Hunt III. The Epis Ch in Hawaii Honolulu HI 2011-2014; Gd Samar Epis Ch Honolulu HI 2008-2011; Chr Ch Kealakekua HI 1997-2008; Assoc R S Mich And All Ang Ch Lihue HI 1995-1997.

ARNHART, James Rhyne (Tenn) 1710 Riverview Dr, Murfreesboro TN 37129 **Supply P Dio Tennessee Nashville TN 1985-** B Ashville NC 1924 s James & Eula. BS Maryville Coll 1951; MS Washington U 1953; JD Nashville Sch of Law 1971. D 7/25/1979 P 6/1/1980 Bp William Evan Sanders. m 1/1/1952 Bobbye Lynn. Vic S Mk's Ch Antioch TN 1983-1985; Asst S Paul's Epis Ch Murfreesboro TN 1979-1982.

ARNOLD, Beth Kelly (Los) 1231 E. Chapman Ave., Fullerton CA 92831 **R S Andr's Par Fullerton CA 2011-** B Caldwell ID 1958 BA The Coll of Idaho 1979; MDiv CDSP 1987; DMin CDSP 2013. D 12/5/1987 P 12/7/1988 Bp

William Edwin Swing. Sr Assoc R The Epis Ch Of S Mary The Vrgn San Francisco CA 1999-2011; Ch Of Our Sav Mill Vlly CA 1996-2000; Chr Ch Sausalito CA 1993-1999; 1991-1992; Asst R S Paul's Epis Ch Burlingame CA 1988-1991. saintandrewsrector@gmail.com

ARNOLD, Christopher John (FdL) St Andrew's, 828 Commercial Street, Emporia KS 66801 **Trin Epis Ch Oshkosh WI 2016-** B Newcastle, UK 1974 s Geoffrey & Meredith. BA U CA Santa Cruz 1995; MDiv CDSP 2008; MA Grad Theol Un 2010. D 6/12/2010 Bp Barry Leigh Beisner P 12/20/2010 Bp Stacy F Sauls. m 12/28/2004 Celeste R Williams. P-in-c S Andr's Epis Ch Emporia KS 2013-2015; Cler-in-Charge S Mary's Epis Ch Middlesboro KY 2010-2013; Stndg Com Dio Lexington Lexington 2011-2013. GAS 2009; Soc of Cath Priests 2010; SocMary 2009.

ARNOLD, Donna J (Alb) 4 Pine Ledge Ter, Gansevoort NY 12831 B Troy NY 1946 d Henry & Elizabeth. BA SUNY 1969; JD Wstrn New Engl Coll 1984; MA S Bernards TS and Mnstry 2004; MA St Bernards Sch of Mnstry and Theol 2004. D 6/11/2005 Bp Daniel William Herzog P 1/14/2006 Bp David John Bena. m 12/21/1969 Alan Daniel Arnold c 2. Vic Trin Ch Whitehall NY 2008-2014; Asst Chr Epis Ch Ballston Spa NY 2005-2007. Sr. Mem of Law Revs, "Legis-Implied Consent Legis In Drunk Driving Cases: The Case for Repeal," *Wstrn New Engl Law Revs, Vol. 6, Issue 2, 1983*, Wstrn New Engl Coll Sch of Law, 1983. Ret Plaque Saratoga Cnty Bar Assn 2003.

ARNOLD, Duane Wade-Hampton (NY) 5815 Lawrence Dr., Indianapolis IN 46226 B Fort Wayne IN 1953 s Herman & Louise. BA SUNY 1979; MA Concordia TS 1981; Dur 1984; STh Lambeth Coll 1984; Dplma U of Cambridge 1984; PhD Dur 1989; Coll of Preachers 1992. D 6/27/1987 P 11/1/1987 Bp H Coleman Mcgehee Jr. m 10/1/1980 Janet Lee Drew. Prncpl St. Chad's Coll Durham UK 1994-1998; Cur S Thos Ch New York NY 1991-1994; Precentor Cathd Ch Of S Paul Detroit MI 1988-1990; Epis/Luth Chapl at Wayne Grosse Pointe MI 1987-1991; Chapl Wayne S U Detroit MI 1987-1991; Ecum Cmsn Dio New York New York NY 1991-1994; Ecum Cmsn Dio Michigan Detroit MI 1987-1991. Auth, "Mas Alla de la Fe," Vida, 2004; Auth, "Fieis ate o Fim," Vida, 2003; Auth, "Beyond Belief," Zondervan, 2002; Auth/Ed, "De Doctrina Christiana," U of Notre Dame Press, 1995; Auth, "Praying w Donne & Herbert," SPCK, 1992; Auth, "Prayers Of The Martyrs," Harper Row, 1991; Auth, "Athan Of Alexandria," U. of Notre Dame Press, 1991; Auth, "Fran, A Call to Conversion," Zondervan, 1988; Auth, "In Dire Straits," U. of Detroit, 1987; Auth, "The Way, The Truth, The Life," Baker, 1982. Chapl Ord Of S Jn Of Jerusalem 1989; Soc Of The Anchor 1994.

ARNOLD, Kimball Clark (Az) 3150 Spence Springs Rd, Prescott AZ 86305 **D S Lk's Ch Prescott AZ 2000-** B Chicago IL 1950 d Donald & Helen. Nthrn Arizona U 1970. D 10/14/2000 Bp Robert Reed Shahan. m 4/8/1972 Thomas Eads Arnold c 2. ChinoPaulden Mnstrl Assn 2000; NAAD 2000.

ARNOLD, Margaret L (Mass) 149 High St Apt 1, Wareham MA 02571 **P Gr Epis Ch Medford MA 2014-** B 1973 d John & Kathryn. BFA Nova Scotia Coll of Art and Design 1995; MFA U of the Arts 1997; MDiv Bos TS 2008. D 6/6/2009 Bp M(Arvil) Thomas Shaw. m 8/23/1997 Elias Rouston c 1.

ARNOLD, Robert D (WNY) 29 University Park, Fredonia NY 14063 B Buffalo NY 1951 s Dale & Lois. Utica Coll 1971; BA Scarritt Coll 1973; MDiv Candler TS Emory U 1976; Cert SWTS 1992. D 6/7/1992 P 12/1/1992 Bp David Charles Bowman. m 4/18/1982 Patricia I Dahl. R Trin Epis Ch Fredonia NY 2006-2017; Vic Ch Of The H Comm Lake View NY 2001-2006; P-in-c S Mich's Epis Ch Oakfield NY 1995-2001; R S Jn's Ch Medina NY 1992-2001; Pstr Meth Ch 1975-1991.

ARNOLD, Robyn Elizabeth (Ala) 2146 Santa Clara Ave Apt 1, Alamed CA 94501 **Gr Ch Birmingham AL 2012-** B Mt Vernon KY 1963 d James & Hilda. BS Cumberland Coll 1986; MS Mississippi St U 1997; PhD U of Alabama Birmingham 2002; MDiv CDSP 2008. D 5/31/2008 P 12/16/2008 Bp Henry Nutt Parsley Jr. Dio California San Francisco CA 2008-2011.

ARNOLD, Scott A (Ala) 1204 Valridge N, Prattville AL 36066 **R S Mk's Ch Prattville AL 2005-** B Memphis TN 1960 s David & Betty. BS Middle Tennessee St U 1982; MDiv Sewanee: The U So, TS 1987; MS Alabama A&M U 1996. D 7/5/1987 P 2/1/1988 Bp George Lazenby Reynolds Jr. m 9/9/1995 Diane Arnold c 4. All SS Epis Ch Birmingham AL 1997-2000; R S Paul's Epis Ch Corinth MS 1992-1995; Int S Andr's Ch Burke VA 1991-1992; Stff S Ptr's Epis Ch Arlington VA 1989-1991; R The Epis Ch Of The Mssh Pulaski TN 1988-1989; Dio Tennessee Nashville TN 1987-1988; Vic S Matt's Epis Ch Mcminnville TN 1987-1988. Auth, "Cler And Divorce," *Alb Inst Action Info*, 1994; Auth, "Paying The Pstr," *The Disciple*, 1990; Auth, "Silent Racism And The Kkk," *Wit*, 1988. APA 1996.

ARNOLD, Susan Louise (ECR) Church Divinity School Of The Pacific, Morro Bay CA 93442 B Riverside CA 1955 d William & Barbara. Cert Sch for Deacons 2015. D 6/6/2015 Bp Mary Gray-Reeves. m 5/1/2010 James Moore Arnold c 2.

ARNOLD, William Bruce (SwFla) 114 Fairway Ct, Greenwood SC 29649 B Owensboro KY 1931 s Charles & Martha. BS U of No Dakota 1954; MEd Florida Atlantic U 1966; PhD Florida St U 1969. D 9/30/1974 Bp William Hopkins Folwell. m 6/15/1954 Marloue Arnold c 3. D S Jn's Epis Ch Clearwater FL 1988-2003; D S Dunst's Epis Ch Largo FL 1974-1988.

ARNOLD JR, William Stevenson Maclaren (Nev) 1855 Baring Blvd Apt 301, Sparks NV 89434 **Asst S Paul's Epis Ch Sparks NV 2003-** B Monterey CA 1953 s William & Mary. U of Hawaii; U of Nevada at Reno. D 7/7/2002 P 1/25/2003 Bp Katharine Jefferts Schori. m 11/7/1987 Evelyn Pieter.

ARNOLD-BOYD, Annette Ruth (Oly) 12420 SW Tremont St, Portland OR 97225 B Portland OR 1946 d Charles & Doris. BS Wstrn Oregon U 1968; MA Cntrl Washington U 1971; MDiv SWTS 1976. D 9/25/1977 Bp Matthew Paul Bigliardi P 11/20/1978 Bp H Coleman Mcgehee Jr. m 6/14/1981 Scott W Boyd c 1. Assoc S Lk's Epis Ch Vancouver WA 1993-2011; Assoc S Steph's Epis Par Portland OR 1985-1986. Chapl CAP - Washington Cnty, OR 1999-2010; Intl Assn of Wmn Ministers 1976.

ARPEE, Stephen T(Rowbridge) (WA) 3810 39th St NW Apt A-121, Washington DC 20016 B Evanston IL 1934 s Edward & Katherine. BA Coll of Wooster 1957; MDiv GTS 1965. D 6/12/1965 Bp Leland Stark P 9/4/1966 Bp The Bishop Of Iran. m 6/12/1961 Janet M Arpee c 2. R Chr Ch S Jn's Par Accokeek MD 2002-2007; P-in-c S Paul's Epis Par Pt Of Rocks MD 1997-1999; P-in-c All SS' Epis Ch Chevy Chase MD 1997; P-in-c Ch Without Walls Washington DC 1986-1997; R S Marg's Ch Washington DC 1979-1986; Serv The Epis Dio Iran Tehran 1965-1979. stephen.arpee@gmail.com

ARQUES, Rafael (PR) B 1932 s Jose & Rosario. D P. m 5/2/1982 Hilda Margarita Reyes-Rey. Dio Puerto Rico Trujillo Alto PR 1984-1997.

ARRINGTON, Sandra Clark (Roch) 20 Trumbull Lane, Pittsford NY 14534 B Ticonderoga NY 1944 d Raymond & Harriet. SUNY 1963; BA SUNY 1966; MDiv S Bernards TS and Mnstry 1991; Bex Sem 1992. D 1/29/1994 P 8/6/1994 Bp William George Burrill. c 3. Int Assoc. R S Thos Epis Ch Rochester NY 2005-2006; Int S Mk's Epis Ch Le Roy NY 2004-2005; Int S Lk's Ch Fairport NY 2003-2004; Int Zion Ch Avon NY 2002-2003; Assoc S Paul's Ch Rochester NY 1995-2002; Asst Ch Of The Ascen Rochester NY 1994-1995. MDiv w dist S Bern's Inst 1991.

ARROYO, Jose Del Carmen (Chi) 25291 W Lehmann Blvd, Lake Villa IL 60046 **Vic Ch Of The H Fam Lake Villa IL 2010-** B Dominican Republic 1961 s Jose & Juana. Rec 6/27/2009 as Priest Bp Victor Alfonso Scantlebury. m 10/21/2001 Licelot Ramirez c 1.

ARROYO, Margarita Eguia (WTex) 721 S Missouri Ave, Weslaco TX 78596 B Laredo TX 1966 d Daniel & Elisa. BSW Texas St U San Marcos 1989; MS Our Lady of the Lake U 1993; MDiv Epis TS of the SW 2000. D 8/31/2000 P 3/14/2001 Bp James Edward Folts. m 6/15/1996 Eric C Arroyo c 1. Asst S Jas Ch Austin TX 2004-2010; R Gr Ch Weslaco TX 2002-2004; Asst Ch Of The Gd Shpd Corpus Christi TX 2000-2002.

ARROYO-SANCHEZ, Jose (PR) B 1924

ARRUNATEGUI, Herbert (CFla) 3468 Capland Ave, Clermont FL 34711 **Ret 1999-** B Panama City PA 1934 s Joaquin & Aura. Lic U of Panama PA 1958; STB UTS 1961; MTh Drew U 1972; DMin Drew U 1985. D 5/8/1965 P 11/1/1965 Bp Reginald Heber Gooden. m 12/28/1960 Geny Arrunategui. Off Hisp Mnstrs Epis Ch Cntr New York NY 1978-2000; San Jose Epis Ch Eliz NJ 1977; Dio New Jersey Trenton NJ 1974-1999; S Paul's Epis Ch Westfield NJ 1969-1977; P-in-c S Stephan Puerto Armuelles 1965-1969; P-in-c Mssn Boquette Rp. Hon Cn El Redentor Cathd 1986.

ARTHUR, Anne Tilley (NCal) 2620 Capitol Ave, Sacramento CA 95816 B Ann Arbor MI 1948 d Thomas & Elizabeth. BA U MI 1972; MBA San Francisco St U 1979; CLAD Natl U 2001; MDiv CDSP 2013; MDiv CDSP 2013. D 6/29/2013 P 2/8/2014 Bp Barry Leigh Beisner. c 1. S Matt's Epis Ch Sacramento CA 2014.

ARTMAN, Melinda M (Be) 201 S Wilbur Ave, Sayre PA 18840 **P-in-c Ch Of The Redeem Sayre PA 2017-** B Batavia NY 1957 d Charles & Jill. BA SUNY - Albany NY 1979; MCRP Rutgers U 1981; MDiv VTS 2014. D 12/7/2013 P 6/14/2014 Bp Mariann Edgar Budde. m 8/28/2004 Nina D Seebeck. The Ch Of The Ascen Lexingtn Pk MD 2015-2017; S Jn's Ch Ellicott City MD 2014-2015.

ARTRESS, Lauren (Cal) 309 Coleridge St, San Francisco CA 94110 **Fndr Veriditas Inc. San Francisco 1996-** B Cleveland OH 1945 d Gordon & Olive. BS OH SU 1967; MA PrTS 1969; Cert in Pstr Counslg Inst for Rel and Hlth 1974; DMin Andover Newton TS 1986; Hon Doctorate California Inst of Integral Stds 1999. D 6/14/1975 Bp Paul Moore Jr P 11/13/1982 Bp Walter Decoster Dennis Jr. Cn Pstr Gr Cathd San Francisco CA 1986-1995; Adj Prof The GTS New York NY 1979-1986; Pstr Counslr Counslg & Human Dvlpmt S Jas Cntr New York NY 1978-1986. Auth, "The Sacr Path Comp," Riverhead/Putnam Penguin, 2006; Auth, "The Labyrinth Seed Kit," Tuttle Pub, 1996; Auth, "Walking A Sacr Path: Rediscovering The Labyrinth As A Sprtl Tool," Riverhead/Putnam Penguin, 1995. AAMFT, Clincl Mem 1979; Dplma AAPC 1978. Hon Cn of Gr Cathd Gr Cathd 2004; Ghandi/King/Ikeda Peace Awd Morehouse Coll 2002; Hon Ph. D California Inst for Integral Stds 1999.

ASBURY, Eldridge Eugene (Miss) 742 Mcneece St, Tupelo MS 38804 **Died 11/16/2015** B Elberton GA 1929 s James & Ruth. Emory U 1947; BA U GA 1950; MDiv Sewanee: The U So, TS 1987. D 5/16/1987 P 11/29/1987 Bp Duncan Montgomery Gray Jr. m 11/29/1963 Karen Maria Ellington c 2. Assoc All SS'

Epis Ch Tupelo MS 1999-2007; R Par Of The Medtr-Redeem Mccomb MS 1994-1999; Vic Epis Ch Of The Incarn W Point MS 1987-1994.

ASEL, John Kenneth (Wyo) 407 F Street Suite 104, North Wilkesboro NC 28659 **S Jn's Epis Ch Jackson WY 2003-** B Dallas TX 1949 s Kenneth & Evelyn. BA Van 1970; MDiv SWTS 1973; MRE Notre Dame Sem Grad TS 1976; DMin GTF 1986. D 4/28/1973 by James Winchester Montgomery P 11/1/1973 Bp Iveson Batchelor Noland. m 2/15/1992 Janice D M Morrison c 2. Int Ch Of The Gd Shpd Knoxville TN 2015-2016; R Ch Of The Trsfg Jackson WY 2003-2015; R S Paul's Ch Wilkesboro NC 1992-2003; R Emm Ch Farmville NC 1991-1992; CDO Dio E Carolina Kinston NC 1991; Assoc/Admin S Lk's Epis Ch San Antonio TX 1987-1991; R S Dav's Ch Denton TX 1986-1987; R St Mich's Epis Ch Pineville LA 1979-1986; Educ Consult Dio Louisiana New Orleans LA 1976-1979; Asst to Dn Chr Ch Cathd New Orleans LA 1973-1979. Auth, "video," *Verna Dozier Looks Lk*, 1988; Auth, "video," *What Episcopalians Believe*, 1984; Auth, "article," *Making Sense of Things*, 1981.

ASGILL, Edmondson Omotayo (CFla) 381 N Lincoln St, Daytona Beach FL 32114 B Sierra Leone 1946 s Nicholas & Violet. MA Inst of Afr Stds, U of Ghana 1975; PhD U of So Florida 1988. D 9/27/2014 Bp Gregory Orrin Brewer. c 3.

ASH JR, Evan Arnold (Kan) 1114 E Northview St, Olathe KS 66061 **P-in-c St. Mary Magd Belton MO 2016-** B Saint Louis MO 1944 s Evan & Ada. Kansas Bar Assn; BA U of Nebraska 1970; MDiv SWTS 1973; MS U of Nebraska 1979; Advncd CPE 1981. D 2/14/1974 Bp Robert Patrick Varley P 4/13/1977 Bp James Daniel Warner. m 2/14/1965 Rosalie Ash c 2. LocTen Trin Atchiosn KS 2014-2015; Vic S Aid's Ch Olathe KS 1996-2001; Medtr Kansas Tenth Judicial Dist Olathe KS 1995-2014; P-in-c Trin Ch Arkansas City KS 1994; R S Matt's Epis Ch Newton KS 1992-1993; Chapl Legacy Gd Samar Hosp Portland OR 1989-1992; Chapl Chld's Meml Hosp Omaha NE 1985-1989; Assoc Chapl Bp Clarkson Hosp (Epis) Omaha NE 1983-1985; Chapl Nebraska Hlth System Omaha NE 1983-1985; Rel Tchr Boys Town HS Omaha NE 1981-1983; P-n-charge Al SS Mssn Winnebago NE 1979-1980; R S Mart Of Tours Ch Omaha NE 1977-1980; R S Lk's Ch Plattsmouth NE 1976-1978; D Trin Cathd Omaha NE 1975-1976; D Ch Of The H Sprt Bellevue NE 1974; Mediation Clincl Supvsr Kansas 10th Judicial Dist 1996-2014. Auth, "The Need for Personal Reflection in the Midst of Diversity," *Fam Mediation News*, Assn for Conflct Resolution, 2003; Auth, "The Chapl's Role in Ethical Triage," *Nwsltr of the Soc For Bioethics Consult*, Soc For Bioethics Consult, 1992; Auth, "The Promise of Sorrow: The Gift of Personal Growth that Accompanies G," *The Care Giver Journ*, Coll of Chapl, 1990; Auth, "Blessing Our Anger," *Bereavement Revs*, King's Coll, London, Ontario, 1989; Auth, "Var," *mediation*, www.mediate.com. Assn for Conflict Resolution 1998-2012; Fell, Coll Of Chapl 1985-1993; Ord Of S Ben 1971. Awd of Excellence Heartland Mediators Assn 2014; Acorn Awd Heartland Mediators Assn 2011. priest@marymag.com

ASH, Gerald Arnold (Md) 10450 Lottsford Rd Apt 1101, Mitchellville MD 20721 **Ret 2004-** B Danbury CT 1941 s George & Kathleen. BSME Un Coll 1964; BS Un Coll 1964; MDiv GTS 1973. D 6/10/1973 P 6/24/1974 Bp Robert Rae Spears Jr. c 4. Dir Of Pstr Care Specialty Hosp U Of Maryland Baltimore 1996-2004; Chapl Res Presb Hosp Philadelphia PA 1994-1995; R Trin Ch Oxford Philadelphia PA 1992-1995; Assoc R S Marg's Ch Annapolis MD 1985-1991; R Ch Of The Gd Samar Amelia OH 1983-1985; R S Jn's Epis Ch Oneida NY 1979-1982; Cn St Paul's Syracuse Syracuse NY 1976-1979; Vic Chr Ch Sackets Hbr NY 1973-1976; Cur Trin Epis Ch Watertown NY 1973-1976. Assn of Profsnl Chapl, BCC 2001.

ASH, Linda D (EMich) 111 S Shiawassee St, Corunna MI 48817 B Owosso MI 1945 d John & Laura. D 2/23/2008 Bp Steven Todd Ousley. m 12/15/1973 Edward H Ash c 2.

ASHBY, Alice Kay Neel (O) 344 Shepard Rd, Mansfield OH 44907 **Extended Supply S Matt's Ch Ashland OH 2007-** B Winter Haven FL 1956 d Earl & Alice. BA U of Arkansas 1979; MA Epis TS of the SW 1982; MDiv Lexington TS 1988. D 6/23/1990 P 2/1/1991 Bp Herbert Alcorn Donovan Jr. m 3/22/1981 Joe Lyn Ashby c 1. Dio Wstrn Michigan MI 2002-2004; R S Alb's Mssn N. Muskegon MI 1999-2006; Dio Arkansas Little Rock AR 1996-1999, Exec Coun 1996-1998, Pres Stndg Com 1996-1998, Stndg Com 1995-1998; Gr Ch Siloam Sprg AR 1994-1996; Chapl S Jas Ch Eureka Spgs AR 1991-1999; S Thos Ch Springdale AR 1991-1993; Chapl S Vinc Med Cntr Little Rock AR 1988-1991.

ASHBY, Joe Lyn (O) 402 Channel Rd, N Muskegon MI 49445 **Gr Epis Ch Mansfield OH 2006-** B Evansville IN 1955 s Lindy & Elizabeth. BA Transylvania U 1976; MDiv Epis TS of the SW 1982. D 6/13/1982 P 6/1/1983 Bp David Reed. m 3/22/1981 Alice Kay Neel Ashby c 1. S Paul's Ch Muskegon MI 1999-2006; Chapl St Fran Hse Madison WI 1992-1999, Bd Dir 1988-1991; S Thos Ch Springdale AR 1991-1999; Chair Dio Arkansas Little Rock AR 1990, Day Sch Cmsn 1988-1990, CE Cmsn 1987-1991; Assoc S Lk's Epis Ch N Little Rock AR 1987-1991; S Raphael's Ch Lexington KY 1985-1987; Ch S Mich The Archangel Lexington KY 1983-1985; D-In-Res Gr Ch Hopkinsville KY 1982-1983; Exec Coun Dio Wstrn Michigan Kalamazoo MI 1997-2002.

ASHBY, Julia Sizemore (SVa) 4205 Cheswick Ln, Virginia Beach VA 23455 **Ch Of The Epiph Norfolk VA 2014-** B Cherry Point NC 1954 d Nearous & Joan. BA Longwood U 1976; MDiv SWTS 1997. D 6/14/1997 Bp Frank Harris Vest Jr P 1/1/1998 Bp David Conner Bane Jr. m 5/17/1975 Charles Chandler Ashby c 2. Sr. Assoc R Estrn Shore Chap Virginia Bch VA 1997-2012.

ASHBY, Lucinda Beth (Ida) 1858 Judith Ln, Boise ID 83705 **Cn Dio Idaho Boise ID 2011-** B Kirkwood MO 1959 d Malcolm & Patricia. BA Ob 1982; MDiv CDSP 2004. D 1/9/2004 P 7/24/2004 Bp Jerry Alban Lamb. m 7/22/1995 Robert McEvilly c 2. R S Matt's Epis Ch Sacramento CA 2005-2011; P Ch Of S Mart Davis CA 2004-2005. lashby@idahodiocese.org

ASHCROFT, Ernie (Minn) 4015 Sunnyside Road, Edina MN 55424 B Saint Helens Lancashire UK 1945 s Fredrick & Elizabeth. BS U of Leeds Gb 1967; PhD U of Leeds Gb 1970; DIT U of Nottingham GB 1973. Trans 2/1/1983 Bp Robert Marshall Anderson. m 7/9/2005 Elizabeth S Ashcroft c 3. P Chr Ch S Paul MN 2006-2015; Int Chr Ch Red Wing MN 2005-2006; R S Steph The Mtyr Ch Minneapolis MN 1992-2004; Chair of Bd Epis Wrld Mssn 1987-1991; Bd Trst Epis Renwl Mssn 1986-1989; R Mssh Epis Ch S Paul MN 1983-1992. kritter@visi.com

ASHCROFT, Mary Ellen (Minn) PO Box 1093, Grand Marais MN 55604 **Vic Sprt of the Wilderness Grand Marais MN 2011-; Ldr WindCradle Retreat 2008-** B Salem OR 1952 d Leslie & Grace. Cert S Johns Coll Nottingham 1974; BA S Cathr U 1987; PhD U MN 1992; Cert U of Cambridge 2000. D 12/20/2001 P 6/20/2002 Bp James Louis Jelinek. c 3. Chapl, Prof of Engl Kalamazoo Coll Kalamazoo MI 2005-2008; Trin Ch Excelsior MN 2004, 2002-2003; Prof Of Engl Bethel Coll St. Paul MN 1990-2004. Auth, ,*Dogspell*, Seabury-Ch Pub, 2008; Auth, ,*Spirited Wmn*, Augsburg Fortress, 2004; Auth, ,*The Magd Gospel*, Augsburg Fortress, 2002.

ASHER, Charles William (Los) B 1942 BS U of Wisconsin 1964; M.Div UTS 1967; M.A New Sch for Soc Resrch 1969; DMin Andover Newton TS 1973. D 6/9/2005 Bp Chester Lovelle Talton P 1/14/2006 Bp Frank Tracy Griswold III. m 8/12/1989 Susan Cole.

ASHFORD, Raphiell (Miss) **Admin S Mk's Ch Jackson MS 2003-; Mem of the Racial Recon T/F Dio Mississippi Jackson MS 2010-** D 6/10/2017 Bp Brian Seage.

ASHLEY, Danae M (Oly) 4805 NE 45th Street, Seattle WA 98105 **S Steph's Epis Ch Seattle WA 2014-** B Spokane WA 1976 d Alan & Jamie. MA Adler Grad Sch; U of Aberdeen Scotland 1998; BA Whitworth U 1998; Gonzaga U Spokane Washington 2006; MDiv Sewanee: The U So, TS 2008. D 6/7/2008 Bp James E Waggoner Jr P 12/21/2008 Bp Porter Taylor. m 10/2/2010 Henry Lebedinsky. P-in-c S Edw The Confessor Wayzata MN 2011-2014; Tri-Par Mnstry Hornell NY 2011; Assoc R Epis Ch Of S Ptr's By The Lake Denver NC 2008-2010. Contributing Auth, "Still a Mo: Journeys through Perinatal Bereavement," Judson Press, 2016.

ASHMORE, Christopher Lee (Spr) 17 Forest Park W, Jacksonville IL 62650 B Pittsfield IL 1950 s Jesse & Harriet. Nash; BS U of Maryland 1972; MDiv SW Bapt TS 1976; PrTS 1977; Epis TS of the SW 1978. D 6/19/1978 P 1/7/1979 Bp Scott Field Bailey. m 6/15/1974 Kathryn Louella Ashmore c 2. R Trin Ch Jacksonville IL 1998-2016; R Ch Of The H Sprt San Antonio TX 1996-1998; Asst Ch Of Recon San Antonio TX 1980-1983; Cur Ch Of The Adv Brownsville TX 1978-1980.

ASHMORE JR, Robert Michael (WNC) PO Box 956, Mars Hill NC 28754 B Greenville SC 1958 s Robert & Eleanor. BA Chapman U 2002. D 1/10/2015 Bp Porter Taylor.

ASIS, Debra (Az) 12111 N La Cholla Blve, Oro Valley AZ 85755 **Vic Ch Of The Apos Oro Vlly AZ 2013-** B East Orange NJ 1950 d Kenneth & Ruth. BA U of Rhode Island 1976; MA U of Rhode Island 1979; MDiv CDSP 2010. D 6/6/2009 P 12/18/2010 Bp Kirk Stevan Smith. c 1. P S Barn On The Desert Scottsdale AZ 2011-2013, Asst 2006-2007. dasis@ovapostles.org

ASKEW, Angela Victoria (NY) 659 E 17th St, Brooklyn NY 11230 B Peterborough UK 1943 d B Julyan & Peggy. BA Lon GB 1966; MDiv EDS 1978; MA UTS 1982. D 5/7/1978 Bp John Maury Allin P 9/1/1980 Bp John Mc Gill Krumm. P-in-c S Ann And The H Trin Brooklyn NY 2003-2010; Asst Min S Jn's Ch Brooklyn NY 1992-2000; Prof NYTS 1986-1995; Ch Of The Intsn New York NY 1985-1988; P-in-c S Mary's Manhattanville Epis Ch New York NY 1983-1985, Assoc 1982-1983. Grad Fell ECF 1978.

ASKEW, Jerry Wayne (ETenn) 600 S Chestnut St, Knoxville TN 37914 B Ahoskie NC 1954 s Jerome & Daphne. D Trng Prog; BA The U NC 1976; BA U NC 1976; MS Memphis St U 1979; MS Memphis St U 1979; MS The U of Memphis 1979; MS The U of Memphis 1979; PhD 1982; PhD The OH SU 1982. D 2/6/2016 Bp George Young III. m 3/25/1986 Robyn Jarvis Askew c 2.

ASKEW, Patricia Tanzer (Wyo) D 6/25/2016 P 6/2/2017 Bp John Smylie.

ASKEW, Stephen (Wyo) 104 S 4th St, Laramie WY 82070 **S Matt's Epis Cathd Laramie WY 2013-; Cn to the Ordnry Dio E Tennessee Knoxville TN 2005-** B Tuscaloosa AL 1952 s William & Laura. BS U of Alabama 1974; MEd U of Alabama 1976; MDiv Nash 1982; DMin Sewanee: The U So, TS 2007. D 6/13/1982 P 12/16/1982 Bp Furman Charles Stough. m 9/25/1999 Patricia Tanzer c 2. Cn to the Ordnry/Dioc Deploy Off Dio E Tennessee Knoxville

TN 2005-2013, Stndg Com 2003-2005; Asst S Paul's Epis Ch Chattanooga TN 1997-2005; R S Thos Epis Ch Knoxville TN 1988-1997; R S Tim's Epis Ch Athens AL 1984-1988; Cur Ch Of The Ascen Montgomery AL 1982-1984. Ord of S Lk. MDiv cl Nash 1982. stmattsdean@gmail.com

ASKREN, Robert Darling (Fla) 11366 Tacito Creek Dr. South, Jacksonville FL 32223 B Springfield OH 1941 s Joseph & Beulah. BA U of Florida 1963; MDiv VTS 1966; Cert Assn of Profsnl Chapl 1995; PhD Middleham UniversityEngland 2000; MEd Stamford Hill U Engl 2004. D 6/29/1966 Bp Henry I Louttit P 12/29/1966 Bp James Loughlin Duncan. m 4/9/1994 Ann Askren c 3. Cn for Adult Educ (P/T) St.Jn's Cathd Jacksonville Fl. 2006-2012; Int Trin Ch Ft Wayne IN 2004-2006; Int Trin Epis Ch St Aug FL 2002-2004; Assoc R Ch Of Our Sav Jacksonville FL 1996-2002; R S Pat's Ch Ocala FL 1978-1996; R S Agnes Ch Sebring FL 1969-1977; Asst & Headmaster Chr The King Epis Ch Orlando FL 1968-1969; Asst & Headmaster S Thos Miami FL 1966-1968. Ed, "Readings In Philos Volumes 1-5," So Florida Cmnty Coll, 1975. Bd Cert Assn Prof Chapl 1995; Curs Mnstry 1979-2008; EFM Mentor 1998-2013; Kairos Prison Mnstry 1981-1996; OHC Assoc 1984. Dn of Ocala Dnry Dio Cntrl Florida 1996; Trst U So Dio Cntrl Florida 1988; Fndr of Ocala Hospice Marion Cnty Hospice 1982.

ASMAN, Mark Elliott (Los) 1500 State St, Santa Barbara CA 93101 **R Trin Epis Ch Santa Barbara CA 1996-, Vic 1994-1995** B Oakland CA 1950 s Cecil & Mary. BA Willamette U 1972; MDiv GTS 1975. D 6/28/1975 Bp George Richard Millard P 1/11/1976 Bp Chauncie Kilmer Myers. m 8/11/2013 William Jay Wood. Serv S Thos The Apos Hollywood Los Angeles CA 1992-1994; Serv Ch Of The Adv Of Chr The King San Francisco CA 1984-1990; R S Paul's Epis Ch Oroville CA 1978-1982; Cur Calv Epis Ch Santa Cruz CA 1975-1978.

ASONYE, Collins Enyindah (Va) **R Meade Memi Epis Ch Alexandria VA 2008-** B Nigeria 1961 s Walter & Evelyn. Dip Trin Un Theogical Coll 1989; MA U of Port Harcourt 1997; MTh Franciscan U of Steubenville 2000. Trans 7/24/2003 Bp J Clark Grew II. m 9/29/1984 Peace E Asonye c 2. Epis Shared Mnstry Of NW Ohio Sherwood OH 2003-2008; R Gr Ch Defiance OH 2003-2008; Campus Min S Andr's Epis Ch Toledo OH 2001-2003; S Michaels In The Hills Toledo OH 2001-2003; S Steph's Epis Ch Steubenville OH 1998-2001. Non. Dn of W Deanary Dio Ohio 2005; Cn Niger Delta Dio 1994.

ASSON, Marla Lynn (Nev) Holy Cross/ St Christopher, 3740 Meridian St N, Huntsville AL 35811 B Florence AL 1963 d Lonnie & Betty. BS Auburn U 1985; MBA Columbia Sthrn U 2010. D 10/1/2011 Bp John Mckee Sloan Sr. m 9/19/2004 Arthur Russell Asson c 2.

ASTARITA, Susan Gallagher (WA) PO Box 816, Del Mar CA 92014 **Long-Term Supply S Lk's Ch San Diego CA 2013-; P Res Cathd Ch Of S Paul San Diego CA 2007-; Sprtl Dir/Pstr Counslr San Diego Pstr Counslg Cntr San Diego CA 2007-; I. R Ascen Sligo 2004-** B Wilmington DE 1941 d Hugh & Alice. AB Randolph-Macon Coll 1963; MA Geo 1973; MDiv ETSBH 1992; STM Ya Berk 1993. D 6/27/1992 P 12/1/1992 Bp Gethin Benwil Hughes. c 1. Ch Of The Ascen Silver Sprg MD 2004-2006; Mem, Bd Trst Collington Epis Lifecare Cmnty Mitchellville MD 2003-2006; Asst S Geo's Ch Glenn Dale MD 2003-2004; Chr Ch Prince Geo's Par Rockville MD 2000-2003; Mem, Bd Washington Epis Cler Assn 1996-2000; Dio Washington Washington DC 1994-2000, Mem, Hisp Mnstrs Com 2003-2006, Mem, Fin Com 1998-2000, Mem, Stwdshp Com 1996-1998, Dioc Coun 1995-1998, Mem, Angus Dun Com 1994-1998; Vic/Chapl U Of Maryland Mssn Coll Pk MD 1994-2000; D Gr And S Ptr's Epis Ch Hamden CT 1992-1993.

ASTLEFORD, Elise Linder (Oly) 2515 NE 80th St, Vancouver WA 98665 **Ret 2003-** B Mansfield OH 1941 d Albert & Louise. BA w hon Denison U 1963; MRE Andover Newton TS 1965; Westcott Hse Cambridge 1985; Westcott Hse Cambridge, Engl 1985. D 5/4/1976 Bp Matthew Paul Bigliardi P 9/27/1985 Bp David Rea Cochran. m 2/11/1996 Joseph Fee Astleford c 2. Int S Lk's Epis Ch Gresham OR 2006-2008; Yth Dir S Lk's Epis Ch Vancouver WA 1990-1992; Vic Ch Of The H Sprt Episco Battle Ground WA 1987-2003; Chapl Oregon Epis Sch Portland OR 1985-1987; Chapl Oregon Epis Sch Portland OR 1985-1987; Asst Chapl Gd Samar Hosp Portland OR 1977-1980; S Barth's Ch Beaverton OR 1976-1984; Chapl Legacy Gd Samar Hosp Portland OR 1976-1979. Auth, "Sharing," 1988. NNECA 1993.

ASTON, Geraldine Patricia (Ala) 544 S Forest Dr, Homewood AL 35209 B Newark NJ 1942 d Lawrence & Helen. BS Rutgers The St U of New Jersey 1964; MS U of Alabama 1971. D 10/30/2004 Bp Henry Nutt Parsley Jr.

ATAMIAN, Thomas Michael (Chi) 272 Presidential Ln, Elgin IL 60123 **Asst S Dav's Ch Glenview IL 2010-, Assoc 1986-1992** B Chicago IL 1953 s John & Higo. BA U of So Alabama 1975; MDiv VTS 1979. D 6/9/1979 Bp Quintin Ebenezer Primo Jr P 12/8/1979 Bp James Winchester Montgomery. m 10/14/1978 Marilyn Atamian c 1. R S Hugh Of Lincoln Epis Ch Elgin IL 1992-2010; R S Mich's Ch Grand Rapids MI 1984-1986; Assoc S Jn's Epis Ch Sharon PA 1981-1984; Cur Ch Of The H Nativ Clarendon Hls IL 1979-1981.

ATCHESON, Charles (Oly) 8529 Caroline Ave N, Seattle WA 98103 **Ret 1998-** B Elmhurst IL 1938 s Frederick & Annie. Dplma Roosevelt HS Seattle WA 1957; BA Stan 1961; MDiv EDS 1964. D 6/29/1964 Bp William F Lewis P 3/1/1965 Bp Ivol I Curtis. m 8/28/1976 Barbara A Atcheson. Int S Clem's Ch

Woodlake CA 2002-2003; R All SS Epis Ch Braine-l'Alleud 1991-1998; All SS Rectory Waterloo 1991-1998; R S Barn Ch Arroyo Grande CA 1988-1991; Vic Ch Of The H Cross Redmond WA 1979-1988; Dio Olympia Seattle 1976-1979, Stwdshp Off 1970-1977; Campus Mnstry U Of Washington Seattle WA 1976-1979; Cn S Mk's Cathd Seattle WA 1973-1975; S Jn's Epis Ch Gig Harbor WA 1968-1973; Vic St Bede Epis Ch Port Orchard WA 1968-1973; Vic S Pat Everett WA 1966-1968; Cur Trin Epis Ch Everett WA 1964-1965. Hon Cn Amer Cathd In Paris 1998.

ATCHLEY, Joyce Eileen (Ore) D 11/4/2016 Bp Michael Hanley.

ATCITTY, Janice Nacke (Ida) Po Box 388, Fort Hall ID 83203 B Pocatello ID 1955 d Louis & Charlene. Ft Lewis Coll; Idaho St U. D 1/29/1994 Bp John Stuart Thornton. c 2.

ATEEK, Sari N (WA) 6701 Wisconsin Ave, Chevy Chase MD 20815 **S Jn's Ch Chevy Chase MD 2010-** B Haifa Israel 1977 s Naim & Maha. BS Birmingham-Sthrn Coll 2000; MDiv Fuller TS 2006; Cert VTS 2006. D 6/3/2006 P 1/6/2007 Bp Joseph Jon Bruno. m 7/14/2001 Tanory R Ateek c 2. Assoc S Jas' Par So Pasadena CA 2006-2010.

ATEM, Garang G (U) **All SS Ch Salt Lake City UT 2016-** D 12/5/2015 P 10/1/2016 Bp Scott Byron Hayashi.

ATHEY JR, Kenneth F (Del) PO Box 88, 10719 Grove St, Delmar DE 19940 **P-in-c All SS Epis Ch Delmar DE 2011-; Cler Mem Dioc Coun Inc Wilmington DE 2012-** B Winchester VA 1948 s Kenneth & Estella. Shpd Coll 1971; MTS VTS 2007. D 6/18/2011 P 1/21/2012 Bp Wayne Wright. m 7/27/1969 Marjorie Athey c 2.

ATKINS, Hannah E (Tex) Trinity Episcopal Church, 1015 Holman St, Houston TX 77004 **Trin Ch Houston TX 2007-** B Indianapolis IN 1968 d Henry & Lucy. BA Rutgers The St U of New Jersey 1990; MDiv GTS 1996. D 1/27/1996 Bp Joe Doss P 9/6/1996 Bp Martin De Jesus Barahona-Pascacio. m 7/15/2000 Elmer Chavarra c 2. S Jn's Ch Lafayette Sq Washington DC 1999-2007; Dio El Salvador Ambato Tu 1998-1999; Serv Ch In El Salvador 1996-2000; Exec Coun Appointees New York NY 1996-1998. Auth, "Dale Color A La Vida," *For Iglesa Epis De El Salvador*; Auth, "Conoce Tu Iglesia," *For Iglesa Epis De El Salvador*. Ord Of S Helena.

ATKINS JR, Henry (NJ) 3210 Louisiana St, Apt 1413, Houston TX 77006 B Hickory NC 1939 s Henry & Edith. BA Randolph-Macon Coll 1961; MDiv VTS 1964; Oxf GB 1981; DMin GTF 1992. D 6/13/1964 Bp Robert Fisher Gibson Jr P 6/5/1965 Bp Samuel B Chilton. m 2/20/1965 Lucy D Atkins c 3. Int S Mths' Par Whittier CA 2011; Int S Mich and All Ang Epis Ch Studio City CA 2008-2010; Int S Thos Ch Hanover NH 2003-2007; The Epis Campus Mnstry at Rutgers New Brunswick NJ 1984-2003; Epis Chapl The Wm Alexander Procter Fndt Trenton NJ 1984-2003; Dio No Carolina Raleigh NC 1979-1984; Epis Chapl U NC Greensboro NC 1979-1984; Dir Experimental Mnstrs Cathd of St Ptr & St Paul Washington DC 1976-1979; Dio Washington Washington DC 1976-1979; Bp's Stff Dio Rochester Henrietta 1972-1976, Exec Chr Soc Relatns 1972-1976; Serv Ch In Dominican Republic 1969-1972; R Dio The Dominican Republic (Iglesia Epis Dominicana) Gazcue Santo Domingo 1969-1972; Asst All SS Ch Indianapolis IN 1965-1969; Cur St Jas Ch Richmond VA 1964-1965. Auth, "A Ti Juventud (Intro)"; Auth, "arts," *Plumbline*; Auth, "arts," *Sojourners*; Auth, "arts," *Witness*. Epis Ntwk for Econ Justice; EUC; Ord Of S Helena; S Greg Abbey. Geo Cabot Ward Prize GTS 2012; Hugh White Awd ENEJ 2010; Hon Cn Ch In Costa Rica 1984.

ATKINS, John Merritt (SO) 33 W Dixon Ave, Dayton OH 45419 **S Paul's Epis Ch Dayton OH 2017-; Gr Ch And The Incarn King of Prussia PA 2014-** B Kansas City MO 1958 s John & Barbara. BA Wm Jewell Coll 1981; MDiv PrTS 1985; CAS GTS 1987; MSW Rutgers The St U of New Jersey 1994. D 6/11/1988 Bp George Phelps Mellick Belshaw P 6/24/1989 Bp Vincent King Pettit. m 9/11/2016 Theodore John Brown. R Ch Of The H Nativ Wrightstown PA 2008-2014; R S Pat's Ch Brunswick OH 2001-2008; Ch Planter Dio Ohio Cleveland 1999-2000; Vic All SS Crescentville Philadelphia PA 1994-1999; P-in-c Ch Of The Crucif Philadelphia PA 1993-1994; Vic Ch Of The H Sprt Tuckerton NJ 1989-1992; D S Lk's Epis Ch Atlanta GA 1988-1989. "And All Will Be Well: Planting a New Ch," *Ch Life, Vol. 107, # 1*, The Dio Ohio, 2003; "H and Passionate God," *Race and Pryr*, Morehouse Pub,, 2003; "The Tale of a Ch Planter," *LivCh, Vol. 226, # 12*, LivCh Fndt, 2003. frjohn@stpauls-dayton.org

ATKINSON, Andrew James (EC) 321 Pettigrew Dr, Wilmington NC 28412 **D H Cross Epis Ch 2005-** B Columbia SC 1947 s Aubrey & Wyarian. BS E Carolina U 1969. D 2/11/1988 Bp Brice Sidney Sanders. m 5/20/1972 Ada Katherine Atkinson c 2.

ATKINSON, Herschel Robert (At) 509 Rhodes Dr, Elberton GA 30635 **Ret 1997-; Secy Dio Atlanta 1989-** B Lebanon OH 1925 s Ernest & Mary. none OH SU 1944; non Georgia St U 1967; LTh Sewanee: The U So, TS 1970; none OH SU 2044. D 6/27/1970 Bp Randolph R Claiborne P 2/27/1971 Bp Milton Legrand Wood. Alt GC 2006-2009; Alt Dep GC 2006-2009; Crt of Revs Mem Prov IV 2006-2009; SCCC Secy GC 1991-1997; Dep GC 1988-2000; Alt GC 1985-1988; Dep GC 1982-1985; Alt GC 1976-1982; R S Alb's Ch Elberton GA 1970-1997; S Andr's Ch Hartwell GA 1970-1997. Hist Soc of TEC 1995.

ATKINSON JR, Joel Walter (Be) 321 Wyandotte St, Bethlehem PA 18015 B Ocala FL 1938 s Joel & Helen. BA Florida St U 1961; U of Florida 1969; MDiv SWTS 1985. D 6/16/1985 Bp Frank S Cerveny P 12/1/1985 Bp Robert Shaw Kerr. m 3/9/1985 Josette B Myers-Atkinson. Cn Cathd Ch Of The Nativ Bethlehem PA 1999-2005; R S Lk's Ch Blackstone VA 1991-1999; R Chr Epis Ch Harlan KY 1989-1991; R S Jn's Ch S Cloud MN 1987-1989; Cur Imm Ch Bellows Falls VT 1985-1987.

ATKINSON, Kate Bigwood (NH) **R S Paul's Ch Concord NH 2009-; Chapl to the Hse of Representatives New Hampshire Hse of Representatives 2015-; Strng Com Kids4Peace New Hampshire 2014-; Soc Chapl SCHC 2014-** B New Rochelle NY 1956 d Guy & Jane. BA Smith 1979; Cert Theol Stud U of Durham GB 1996. Trans 9/7/2003 Bp Katharine Jefferts Schori. m 4/25/1997 Michael G Atkinson c 1. Int S Andr's Ch Saratoga CA 2007-2009; Int S Paul's Epis Ch Sparks NV 2005-2007; P-in-c S Pat's Ch Incline Vlg NV 2003-2005; Dep to GC Dio New Hampshire Concord NH 2014-2015, Title IV Conciliator 2012-, Bp Search Com 2011-2012, Dioc Coun 2010-, Mem of Cergy Dvlpmt Com 2010-; Chapl to the Senate New Hampshire Senate 2013-2014; Mem of Bp's Com Dio Nevada Las Vegas 2006-2007, Dioc Fresh Start Fac 2005-2007. rector@stpaulsconcord.org

ATKINSON, Mark W (Fla) 7801 Lone Star Rd, Jacksonville FL 32211 **R S Andr's Ch Jacksonville FL 2008-** B Kansas City MO 1952 s Warren & Edith. BBA SMU Dallas TX 1978; MBA Jacksonville U 1991; MDiv Sewanee: The U So, TS 2006. D 6/4/2006 P 12/10/2006 Bp Samuel Johnson Howard. m 3/14/1986 Dallas S Atkinson c 2. Assoc R Ch Of Our Sav Jacksonville FL 2006-2008. fathermark@standrewsjax.com

ATKINSON, William Harold (Vt) 40 Water St, Meredith NH 03253 **Ret 1984-** B Lawrence MA 1926 s Harold & Sarah. BS Springfield Coll 1950; MEd Springfield Coll 1960. D 6/11/1964 Bp Walter H Gray P 12/1/1971 Bp Harvey D Butterfield. c 2. S Eliz's Epis Ch Zephyrhills FL 1991-1998; S Mart's Epis Ch Fairlee VT 1972-1984; Asst Calv Ch Suffield CT 1964-1969.

ATON JR, James Keyes (Ga) 3321 Wheeler Rd, Augusta GA 30909 **D S Aug Of Cbury Ch Augusta GA 1987-** B Saint Petersburg FL 1933 s James & May. U of Florida 1952; BA Emory U 1954; MD U of Maryland 1958. D 12/13/1987 Bp Harry Woolston Shipps. m 11/21/1946 Margaret Joan Aton c 4.

ATTEBURY, Rich Earl (EO) Po Box 123, Lostine OR 97857 **P S Pat's Epis Ch Enterprise OR 1998-** B Pendleton OR 1942 s Raymond & Joye. BS U of Oregon 1964; MA U of Oregon 1970; Cert High Desert Chr Coll 1989. D 6/10/1998 P 12/17/1998 Bp Rustin Ray Kimsey. m 8/19/1978 Nancy Lee Garhan.

ATWELL, John Joseph (Az) 6043 E Ellis St, Mesa AZ 85205 **Died 2/7/2016** B Shady Side MD 1917 s William & Effie. U of Maryland 1948; Washington DC U 1948; VTS 1950. D 6/23/1950 P 5/1/1951 Bp Noble C Powell. c 2. Ret 1990-2016; Epis Ch Of The Trsfg Mesa AZ 1976-1988, Vic 1963-1973; Vic Chr Ch Florence AZ 1971-1984, Vic 1957-1970; Dio Arizona Phoenix AZ 1967-1976; Chapl Williams AFB Chandler AZ 1958-1962; S Matt's Ch Chandler AZ 1957-1963; R S Matt's Par Oakland MD 1955-1957; P-in-c Missions Garrett Cnty MD 1954-1957; Vic Missions Garrett Cnty MD 1950-1954; Corporal US-A 1942-1945; Captain Army 1939-1966.

ATWOOD, Mary Hill (Los) 546 Bradford Ct, Claremont CA 91711 B Washington DC 1944 d Robert & Lois. BA Wilson Coll 1966; MDiv CDSP 1980. D 6/28/1980 P 5/31/1981 Bp William Edwin Swing. c 1. Int S Ambr Par Claremont CA 2005-2006; Ch Of The Incarn San Francisco CA 1999-2002; True Sunshine Par San Francisco CA 1998-1999; Chr Epis Ch Sei Ko Kai San Francisco CA 1995-1997; Ch Of The Gd Samar San Francisco CA 1983-1985; Vic Iglesia Epis Del Buen Samaritano San Francisco CA 1983-1985; St Johns Pro-Cathd Los Angeles CA 1980-1983. Int Mnstry Ntwk.

ATWOOD JR, Theodore Oertel (Ga) 6785 El Banquero Pl, San Diego CA 92119 B Augusta GA 1936 s Theodore & Frances. BA U GA 1960; MDiv CDSP 1963. D 6/15/1963 P 4/25/1964 Bp Albert R Stuart. c 2. Assoc H Cross Epis Ch Carlsbad CA 2006-2010; Int S Mich's Ch Waynesboro GA 2003-2005; R Chr Ch Augusta GA 1994-2003; Asst S Alb's Epis Ch El Cajon CA 1993-1994; Asst S Dunst's Epis Ch San Diego CA 1989-1993; Chapl Off Of Bsh For ArmdF New York NY 1969-1989; Captain, Chapl Corps US Navy 1969-1989; Yth Advsr Dio Georgia Savannah GA 1966-1969; R S Jn's Epis Ch Bainbridge GA 1964-1969; Chapl US Naval Reserve Tallahassee FL 1963-1969; Cur Chr Ch Frederica St Simons Is GA 1963-1964. Legion of Merit USN 1989.

AUBERT, Keri T (Ct) 830 Whitney Ave, New Haven CT 06511 **S Thos's Ch New Haven CT 2015-** B Baton Rouge 1962 d Joseph & Virginia. BS LSU 1984; MS U of Alaska 1990; MDiv CDSP 2006. D 12/18/2005 P 12/2/2006 Bp Thomas C Ely. m 12/6/2009 Jakki Renee Flanagan. S Jas Ch Glastonbury CT 2013-2015; CDSP Berkeley CA 2010-2012; Int S Dunst's Epis Mssn Waitsfield VT 2010; Int All SS' Epis Ch S Burlington VT 2008-2009; Prog Dir Joint Urban Mnstry Proj Burlington VT 2007-2010; Assoc Cathd Ch Of S Paul Burlington VT 2006-2008; Dio Vermont Burlington VT 2006. k.aubert@stthomasnewhaven.org

AUBREY, Norman Edward (WMass) 5 College View Hts, South Hadley MA 01075 **D All SS' 1982-** B Stamford CT 1927 s Gwilym & Marion. BS Ya 1950;

PhD Ya 1954. D 10/9/1982 Bp Alexander D Stewart. m 7/3/1965 Barbara Ann Higgins. Soc Of S Jn The Evang.

AUCHINCLOSS, R Anne (NY) 250 W 94th St # 4F, New York NY 10025 **per-diem Chapl New York Presb / Weill Cornell NY NY 2010-; D The Ch Of The Epiph New York NY 2010-** B Syracuse NY 1937 d Anthony & Julia. BA Syr 1968; D Formation Prog 2002. D 5/18/2002 Bp Mark Sean Sisk. c 2. D Ch Of The Ascen New York NY 2007-2010; D S Jn's Ch New York NY 2002-2007.

AUCHINCLOSS, Susan Carpenter (NY) 2342 Glasco Tpk., Woodstock NY 12498 **Dio New York New York NY 2011-, Ecum and Interfaith Cmsn 2011-** B Monroe MI 1938 d Malcolm & Aileen. BA Stan 1962; MDiv CDSP 1982. D 6/8/1985 P 6/1/1986 Bp William Edwin Swing. m 9/2/1972 Stuart Auchincloss c 2. R S Jn's Ch New City NY 1996-2004; Ch Of The Gd Shpd Granite Spgs NY 1995-1996; The Melrose Sch Brewster NY 1994-1995; Lower Sch Chapl Natl Cathd Sch Washington DC 1989-1990; S Paul's Epis Ch Burlingame CA 1985-1988. Susan Auchincloss, "Var sermonns," *Pulpit Dig.* Mdiv w dist CDSP 1982.

AUELUA, Royston Toto'A Stene (NCal) 6963 Riata Dr, Redding CA 96002 B Birmingham UK 1944 s Toto'A & Gladys. BA San Jose St U. D 6/29/1974 Bp Chauncie Kilmer Myers P 5/1/1975 Bp George Richard Millard. m 1/6/1968 Judith Auelua c 1. R S Mich's Ch Anderson CA 2008-2016, R 2001-2008, 2001; The Epis Dio Nthrn California Sacramento CA 2002-2003; Vic Ch Of The Gd Shpd Orland CA 1999-2003; Gd Shpd Epis Ch Belmont CA 1976-1999; Assoc S Edw Los Gatos CA 1974-1976.

AUER, Dorothy Kogler (NJ) 320 Glenburney Dr Apt 106, Fayetteville NC 28303 B Syracuse NY 1933 d Charles & Dorothy. BS Syr 1955; MA Syr 1963; Rutgers The St U of New Jersey 1977. D 6/9/1990 Bp George Phelps Mellick Belshaw P 11/23/1999 Bp Herbert Alcorn Donovan Jr. Mem, Dioc Coun S Barn Ch Burlington NJ 2001-2005; D in Charge S Mich's Ch Trenton NJ 1995-1997; Chapl Architects Hsng Trenton NJ 1992-2000; Chapl Trenton St Coll 1989-1995; Dio New Jersey Trenton NJ 1992-2004, Mem, Dioc Coun 1992-1995; Bd Mem The Evergreens Moorestown NJ 1992-1994. Outstanding Adj Prof Of Engl Bucks Cnty Cmnty Coll 1988.

AUER, Nancy Ann (NMich) D 10/6/2015 P 4/10/2016 Bp Rayford J Ray.

AUGHENBAUGH, Kelly Anne (O) 18001 Detroit Ave, Lakewood OH 44107 **S Ptr's Epis Ch Lakewood OH 2016-** B Santa Maria CA 1988 d Richard & Laila. BA The Coll of Wooster 2010; MDiv CDSP 2016. D 5/28/2016 Bp Mark Hollingsworth Jr.

AUGUSTE, Pierre (Hai) B 1966 D. m 10/4/2001 Nancie Saint-Louis Auguste c 2. Dio Haiti Port-au-Prince HT 1999-2016.

AUGUSTE, Roldano (Hai) **Dio Haiti Port-au-Prince HT 2014-** B Haiti 1972 s Lucien & Margerite. STM Luth TS 2005. Rec 1/29/2014 Bp Jean Zache Duracin. m 10/10/2002 Beline P Auguste c 2.

AUGUSTIN, Dale Lee (Nev) 422 Red Canvas Pl, Las Vegas NV 89144 **P-in-c Gr in the Desert Summerlin NV 2007-** B East Saint Louis IL 1942 s LaVerne & Eileen. Nthrn Montana Coll 1963; U of Nevada at Las Vegas 1969. D 12/9/1982 P 6/12/1983 Bp Wesley Frensdorff. m 5/15/1965 Maureen Augustin c 2. P-in-c Gr In The Desert Epis Ch Las Vegas NV 2007-2012; Chr Ch Las Vegas NV 2001-2006; P Dio Nevada Las Vegas 1982-2000. Lambda Chi Alpha (hon); Sis of Charity. Lambda Chi Alpha.

AUGUSTINE, Patrick Parvez (Eau) 427 14th St S, La Crosse WI 54601 **R Chr Ch Par La Crosse WI 2003-** B Gojra Punjab PK 1950 s Barkat & Shiela. Dplma M. B. HS, Gojra, Pakistan 1965; BA U of Punjab Pakistan 1972; Dip. Theol Lahore DS, Lahore 1976; MDiv Gujrawala TS 1982; Cert Coll of Preachers Washington DC 1993; D.Min. VTS 2008; D.D. Nash 2013. Trans 4/11/1986 as Priest Bp James Winchester Montgomery. m 10/24/1977 Myra S Augustine c 3. S Jn's Epis Ch Waynesboro VA 1996-2003; Asst/Assoc R Ch Of The H Comf Vienna VA 1990-1996; Asst S Greg's Epis Ch Deerfield IL 1987-1988; Asst S Mich's Ch Barrington IL 1984-1986; Mssnr To So Asians S Phil's Epis Palatine IL 1983-1989; Army Chapl Gnrl Hq of Army of Pakistan 1979-1982; Cur and Vic The Ch Of Pakistan (Untd) 1977-1982; Cn and Commissary to the Archbp of Sudan Epis Ch of Sudan 2000-2008. Auth, "From Conflict To Road Of Peace- Bleeding In Kashmir And Human Rts Crisis In The Sub-Continent," Aug Desktop Pub, 2000; Auth, "Hear My People's Cry," Aug Desktop Pub, 1998; Auth, "3 Lessons On The Forgiveness Of Intl Debt," *Lambeth Conf 1998;* Auth, "Var arts," *Var Ch And Secular Periodicals.* DD Nash TS 2013; Cross of St. Aug Awd Archbp of Cbury 2012; DD GTS 2010; Montgomery Prize for Highest GPA in a Jr the GTS 2003; Shield For Peace And Recon Wk Prime Min Of Azad, Kashmir 2000.

AUGUSTINE, Peter John (Eau) 111 9th St N, La Crosse WI 54601 **S Jn's Epis Ch Sparta WI 2015-; Chapl Jail and Restorative Justice Mnstry Monroe Cnty WI 2006-; Asstg P Chr Ch Par La Crosse WI 2005-; Chapl mayo Clnc Hlth System Franciscan Hlth Care 2005-; Chapl mayo Clnc Hlth System Franciscan Hlth Care 2005-** B Pakistan 1952 s Barkat & Begum. Trans 4/6/2008 Bp Keith Whitmore. m 8/26/1983 Lily Augustine c 3.

AULENBACH JR, William Hamilton (Haw) The Groves 59, 5200 Irvine Blvd, Irvine CA 92620 B Detroit MI 1932 s W Hamilton & Pearl. BA Ken 1954;

MDiv CDSP 1960; MS U of Hawaii 1972; PhD Glendale U 2007. D 6/11/1960 Bp Oliver J Hart P 12/9/1960 Bp Harry Sherbourne Kennedy. m 6/17/1961 Anne A Lowry c 3. Pstr Asst S Mary's Par Laguna Bch CA 2000-2003; Non-par People Helpers Inc. 1985-2000; Worker P S Paul 1978-1985; P-in-c S Chris La Mirada CA 1976-1978; P-in-c Ascen Ch In Marshall Islands La Mirada CA 1973-1975; Dir Prog & Oprtns The Epis Ch in Hawaii Honolulu HI 1969-1975; Chapl US Marine Corps Camp Maui Honolulu HI 1965-1967; R Archd Of Maui Gd Shpd Wailuku HI 1964-1967; Yth Min Ch Of The H Nativ Honolulu HI 1967-1969, Yth Min 1960-1966. Auth, "Cramming for the Finals," *Bk*, Summit Run Press, 2017; Auth, "What's Love Got to w?...Everything Says Jesus," *Bk*, Self, 2008; Auth, "How To Get To Heaven Without Going To Ch," *Bk*, Self, 1997; Auth, "Let Us Pray," *Bk*, Self, 1985.

AULETTA, Kimberlee (NY) **Dio Long Island Garden City NY 2017-** B New York City 1970 d Richard & Mary. BA Hartford Coll 1992; MDiv UTS 2008; Angl Dplma Gnrl Sem 2012. D 3/2/2013 P 9/7/2013 Bp Andrew Marion Lenow Dietsche. m 7/19/2008 Eric Landau c 2. P-in-c Ch Of The Nativ Brooklyn NY 2013-2016.

AURAND, Benjamin Kyte (Tex) 2421 Gate 11 Rd, Two Harbors MN 55616 B Minneapolis MN 1941 s Calvin & Eleanor. BA Amh 1963; MEd Harv 1964; MBA U Chi 1971; MDiv Sewanee: The U So, TS 1982. D 6/19/1982 Bp Quintin Ebenezer Primo Jr P 2/1/1983 Bp Maurice Manuel Benitez. m 8/24/1965 Nancy Aurand c 3. U So Sewanee TN 1990-1993; Ch Of The Epiph Calvert TX 1988-2004; Vic S Thos Epis Ch Coll Sta TX 1988-2004; Cur S Matt's Ch Austin TX 1982-1988.

AUSAS-COMBES, Jose (PR) B 1932 Dio The Dominican Republic (Iglesia Epis Dominicana) Gazcue Santo Domingo 1980; Dio Puerto Rico Trujillo Alto PR 1971-1978.

AUSTIN, Dorothy Ann (Nwk) Harvard Yard, Cambridge MA 02138 B Fall River MA 1943 d Donald & Bessie. BD Andover Newton TS 1969; ThD Harv 1981; MSW Bos 2008. D 11/18/1997 Bp Jack Marston Mckelvey P 5/16/1998 Bp John Shelby Spong. m 7/4/2004 Diana Eck.

AUSTIN, Evette Eliene (Alb) 9 E Main St, Canton NY 13617 B Barbados West Indies 1952 d Jeffrey & Evette. BS Sacr Heart U 2002; MDiv GTS 2005. D 6/11/2005 Bp Andrew Donnan Smith P 1/22/2006 Bp David John Bena. m 7/11/1981 Clarence Austin. Gr Epis Ch Canton NY 2005-2014.

AUSTIN, Henry Whipple (Neb) 4509 Anderson Cir, Papillion NE 68133 B New Brunswick NJ 1938 D 7/5/2002 Bp James Edward Krotz. m 6/23/1962 Charlotte Small Howard c 4.

AUSTIN, Jean E (Vt) 545 Shore Road, Digby NS B0V 1A0 Canada B Wooster OH 1947 d Horace & Martha. BA Coll of Wooster 1968; MDiv EDS 1998. D 5/23/1998 Bp Mary Adelia Rosamond Mcleod P 12/19/1998 Bp M(Arvil) Thomas Shaw. m 5/23/2013 Elizabeth Kennedy c 2. Int S Lk's Ch S Albans VT 2007-2009; Int Dio Wstrn Massachusetts Springfield 2005-2007; P-in-c S Andr's Ch Winthrop ME 2003-2005; Int S Phil's Ch Wiscasset ME 2001-2003; Int S Paul's Epis Ch White Riv Jct VT 1999-2001; Asst S Ptr's Ch Beverly MA 1998-1999.

AUSTIN, Margaret Sutton (Colo) 2526 Gates Cir, Apt. 2611, Baton Rouge LA 70809 B New Orleans LA 1946 d Edward & Marie. BA SE Louisiana U 1968; Cert SE Louisiana U 1975; MDiv Epis TS of the SW 1994. D 6/11/1994 P 1/20/1995 Bp James Barrow Brown. Vic S Ptr's Ch Basalt CO 2009-2013; R S Steph's Ch Lubbock TX 2003-2009; Assoc R S Steph's Ch Richmond VA 1997-2003; Assoc Calv Ch Pittsburgh PA 1995-1997; Sewanee U So TS Sewanee TN 1994-1995.

AUSTIN JR, Vernon Arthur (Pa) 4397 Buttercup Cir, Collegeville PA 19426 B Trenton NJ 1934 s Vernon & Elizabeth. BA Hampden-Sydney Coll 1956; MDiv GTS 1959. D 5/9/1959 Bp Oliver J Hart P 11/14/1959 Bp Andrew Y Tsu. m 6/6/1964 Judith H Austin c 2. R S Jn's Ch Norristown PA 1976-1996; R Emer S Jn's Ch Norristown PA 1976-1996; R Trin Ch Gloversville NY 1967-1976; Chr Ch Herkimer NY 1964-1967; Cur S Geo's Epis Ch Schenectady NY 1961-1964; Cur Trin Epis Ch Ambler PA 1959-1961; Alt Dep GC Dio Pennsylvania Philadelphia PA 1982-1989, Dn Vlly Forge Dnry 1977-1981; Alt Dep GC Dio Albany Greenwich NY 1964-1976. SSC 1984. BA cl Hampden-Sydney Coll 1956.

AUSTIN, Victor Lee (NY) 3966 Mckinney Ave, Dallas TX 75204 **Theol-in-Res Dio Dallas Dallas TX 2016-; Prog Dir Cntr for Cath and Evang Theol Northfield Minn 2015-** B Oklahoma City OK 1956 s Marshall & Dorothy. BA S Johns Coll Santa Fe NM 1978; MA U of New Mex 1982; MDiv GTS 1985; PhD Ford 2002. D 6/26/1985 Bp Richard Mitchell Trelease Jr P 2/8/1986 Bp James Stuart Wetmore. c 2. Theol-in-Res S Thos Ch New York NY 2005-2016; P-in-res H Trin Epis Ch Hollidaysburg PA 2004; Asst Prof of Theol, Philos, and Rel Stds Mt Aloysius Coll Cresson PA 2003-2004; Chapl Melrose Sch Brewster NY 1994-1995; Tutor The GTS New York NY 1994; R Ch Of The Resurr Hopewell Jct NY 1989-2003; Cur Zion Epis Ch Wappingers Falls NY 1985-1989; Angl-RC Dialogue USA Dom And Frgn Mssy Soc- Epis Ch Cntr New York NY 2012-2015; Natl Coun of Ch T/F on Ecclesiology 1993-1998; Angl-RC Dialogue NY, Co-Chair Dio New York New York NY 2008-2016, Luth-Epis Dialogue 1989-1995. Auth, "Losing Susan: Brain Disease, the P's

Wife, and the God Who Gives and Takes Away," Brazos Press, 2016; Auth, "Chr Ethics: A Guide for the Perplexed," T & T Clark / Bloomsbury, 2012; Auth, "Up w Authority: Why We Need Authority to Flourish as Human Beings," Continuum / T & T Clark, 2010; Auth, "P in New York: Ch, St, and Theol," S Thos Ch, 2010; Auth, "Jn Paul II's Ironic Legacy in Political Theol," *Pro Ecclesia*, 2007; Auth, "A P's Journ," Ch Publishing, 2001; Auth, "Method In Oliver O'Donovan Desire Of The Nations," *ATR*; Auth, "Ecclesiology Of The Proposed Luth- Epis Concordat Of Agreement," *Mid-Stream*; Auth, "Is There An Angl Method In Theol? Hints From The Lux Mundi Era," *Sewanee Theol Revs*. AAR 2016; Angl Soc, Ed of The Angl 1996-2004; Soc for the Study of Chr Ethics (UK) 2003; Soc of Chr Ethics 2003. vaustin@edod.org

AUSTIN, Wilborne Adolphus (Ct) 18 Richard Rd, East Hartford CT 06108 **Vic S Steph's Epis Ch Bloomfield CT 2004-** B BB 1937 s Norman & Enid. Andover Newton TS; Cert Hartford Sem 1986; BD TESM 2002. D 6/12/1993 Bp Arthur Edward Walmsley P 1/22/1994 Bp Clarence Nicholas Coleridge. m 4/17/1965 Mary Austin. Asst/Cn Chr Ch Cathd Hartford CT 1994-2004; D S Monica's Ch Hartford CT 1993. Ord Of S Lk.

AUSTIN, William Bouldin (CFla) 3508 Lakeshore Dr SW, Smyrna GA 30082 **Assoc S Jude's Ch Marietta GA 2011-; P Assoc St. Jude's Ch Smyrna GA 2011-** B Abilene TX 1949 s William & Johnnie. BA U So 1971; MDiv SWTS 1975. P 4/4/1976 Bp Anselmo Carral-Solar. c 1. Chapl S Jos Hosp 1991-1998; Cathd Of S Phil Atlanta GA 1990-1991; R The Epis Ch Of The Redeem Avon Pk FL 1981-1987; Serv The Ch In The Prov Of The W Indies 1975-1981; Dio Arizona Phoenix AZ 1975-1976. Fell Coll Of Chap; OHC.

AUSTIN, William Paul (WNC) 112 Trotter Pl, Asheville NC 28806 **P Assoc S Mary's Ch Asheville NC 2000-** B Boston MA 1930 s Mansfield & Grace. MDiv Ya Berk; BA Trin Hartford CT 1951; Br 1956; Yonsei U 1962; GTS 1966; S Vladimirs Orth TS 1966; Cidoc Cuernavaca Mx 1971; Cbury Coll 1972; U of Rome Rome IT 1973; Orth Acad Crete 1983. D 6/20/1959 Bp Anson Phelps Stokes Jr P 2/4/1960 Bp Joseph Summerville Minnis. St Georges Epis Ch Asheville NC 1987-1990; Dio SW Virginia Roanoke VA 1987; Untd Campus Chap Radford VA 1986-1987; Hilo Campus Min The Epis Ch in Hawaii Honolulu HI 1979-1986; Hilo Campus Mnstry Hilo HI 1979-1984; Dio Wstrn No Carolina Asheville NC 1976-1979; Trin Ch Kings Mtn NC 1975-1976; Dn Shelby Dnry 1972-1978; Ch Of The Gd Shpd Tryon NC 1970-1973; P-in-c S Gabr's Ch Rutherfordton NC 1968-1978; Asst P S Andr's Ch Stamford CT 1966-1968; Serv The Angl Ch Of Korea 1961-1964; Cur S Mary Denver CO 1959-1961. Auth, "Chr In Prison Today-New Verses For Old Hymns," 2000; Auth, "New Hope". Alcuin Club; Ecumenissts; No Amer Acad; No Amer Acad Of Liturg; Soc Liturgica.

AVCIN, Janet Elaine (CPa) 228 Charles St, Harrisburg PA 17102 B Pittsburgh PA 1954 d Matthew & Janet. BA S Fran Coll Loretto PA 1986; MDiv Lancaster TS 1989. D 6/14/1991 Bp Charlie Fuller Mcnutt Jr P 2/1/1996 Bp Michael Whittington Creighton. m 8/20/1988 Mark Randolph Salter. Ch Of The Trsfg Blue Ridge Summit PA 1997; Cathd Ch Of S Steph Harrisburg PA 1992-1997.

AVENI JR, James Vincent (NwT) Po Box 1064, Clarendon TX 79226 B Washington DC 1952 s James & Patricia. AA Amarillo Coll 1976; BS W Texas A&M U 1978; MS Our Lady of the Lake U 1980. D 11/13/1999 P 10/20/2001 Bp C Wallis Ohl. m 4/4/1975 Rhonda Redding. Ministral Allnce.

AVERY, Daniel Thomas (SVa) 118 Nina Lane, Williamsburg VA 23188 B Bainbridge GA 1948 s Andrew & Alva. MDiv Sthrn Bapt TS 1974; EdD W&M 1984. D 6/15/2002 P 1/30/2003 Bp David Conner Bane Jr. m 1/13/1973 Patricia Jo Kinman Avery c 2. Asstg P Bruton Par Williamsburg VA 2003-2014.

AVERY, Gail (NH) Seafarer's Friend, 77 Broadway, Chelsea MA 02150 **Int S Thos Ch Dover NH 2014-; Hon Maritime Chapl Mssn To Seafarers 2012-; Angl/Epis representative for Can, US, & Caribbean No Amer Maritime Mnstry Assn 2010-; Port Chapl Seafarer's Friend Chelsea MA 2007-; Dioc Coun Mem Dio New Hampshire Concord NH 2011-, Dioc Outreach Cmsn, Ondjiva Angola Sch Proj Com Chair 2010-, Cler Dvlpmt Com 2009-, Prov One Syn Cler Rep 2007-, MDG Com Mem 2006-** B Boston MA 1954 d Shailer & Rebecca. BS U of New Hampshire 1976; MDiv EDS 2006. D 8/28/2007 P 6/11/2008 Bp Vicky Gene Robinson. m 12/21/1985 Kirk A Trachy c 4. Sch Chapl Heron Field Hampton Falls NH 2009-2011; Asst S Chris's Ch Hampstead NH 2008-2014; D S Andr's-In-The-Vlly Tamworth NH 2007-2008. Intl Chr Maritime Assn 2007; No Amer Maritime Mnstry Assn 2007. Excellence in Internation Mssn and Ecum Engagement Boston Theol Inst 2006.

AVERY III, Gilbert Stiles (Pa) 65 W 30th Ave Apt 3527, Eugene OR 97405 **Died 8/10/2015** B Mason City IA 1931 s Gilbert & Susan. BBA SMU 1952; STM EDS 1955. D 6/23/1955 P 12/23/1955 Bp Everett H Jones. m 12/21/1956 Laura Graves c 2. Ret 1991-2015; Exec Dir Epis Cmnty Serv Philadelphia PA 1981-1991; Epis Cmnty Serv Philadelphia PA 1981-1991; Epis City Mssn Boston MA 1966-1981; Epis City Mssn Boston MA 1966-1981; R S Jn's S Jas Epis Ch Boston MA 1960-1966; Cur S Aug's Ch New York NY 1957-1960; Cur S Mk's Epis Ch San Antonio TX 1955-1957; Dep to GC Dio Massachusetts Boston MA 1969-1973.

AVERY, Harold Dennison (CNY) 112 Arbordale Pl, Syracuse NY 13219 B Syracuse NY 1928 s Harold & Anne. BA Syr 1949; BD EDS 1952. D 6/11/

1952 Bp Malcolm E Peabody P 6/21/1953 Bp Dudley S Stark. m 5/25/1985 Jeanne Marie Garrison c 3. Syracuse Urban Cluster Syracuse NY 1985-1994; R Trin Syracuse NY 1970-1994; Trin Ch Syracuse NY 1970-1984; R S Jn's Ch Canandaigua NY 1959-1970; P-in-c S Jn's Ch Mt Morris NY 1955-1959; Chapl S Mary Hosp Rochester NY 1954-1955; Cur S Thos Epis Ch Rochester NY 1953-1955; Cur Trin Epis Ch Watertown NY 1952-1953.

AVERY, Joyce Marie (Oly) 1022 Monte Elma Rd, Elma WA 98541 **D S Mk's Epis Ch Montesano WA 1999-** B Aberdeen WA 1930 d John & Jean. Graduated No River HS 2047. D 3/15/1999 Bp Sanford Zangwill Kaye Hampton. m 5/3/1980 Lee Arnold Avery. Altar Soc 1970.

AVERY, Richard Norman (Los) 1026 Goldenrod St, Placentia CA 92870 B Yuma AZ 1934 s Charles & Lois. BA San Diego St U 1955; BD SMU 1958; SWTS 1963; California St Polytechnic U 1976. D 9/5/1963 P 3/12/1964 Bp Francis E I Bloy. m 6/21/1953 Marjorie W Avery c 3. Asst The Epis Ch Of The Blessed Sacr Placentia CA 1994-2013; S Ambr Par Claremont CA 1989-1994; 1977-1980; S Jn's Mssn La Verne CA 1969-1976; Vic Mt Olive Sylmar CA 1966-1969; Cur Cathd Ch Of S Paul San Diego CA 1963-1966. ESA; SSC.

AVERY, Steven Walter (Ore) PO Box 2617, Florence OR 97439 B Hollywood CA 1945 s Arthur & Kathryn. AA SW Coll Winfield KS 1968; BA California St U 1970; MA Untd States Intl U 1971; PhD Untd States Intl U 1976; Cert Paths to Serv 1996. D 12/11/1993 Bp Steven Charleston. m 8/8/1971 Margaret Boggs c 2. Dio Oregon Portland OR 2008-2009; S Andr's Epis Ch Florence OR 2008-2009; D S Jas The Fisherman Kodiak AK 1993-2000.

AVILA, Ricardo (Cal) 600 Colorado Ave, Palo Alto CA 94306 **The Par Ch Of S Lk Long Bch CA 2014-; Asst P S Mk's Epis Ch Palo Alto CA 2012-** B Chicago IL 1966 s Jose & Maria. BA U of Wisconsin 1989; MDiv CDSP 2010. D 6/5/2010 P 12/4/2010 Bp Marc Handley Andrus. m 10/18/2008 William Bonnell. Asst P S Mary's Epis Ch Boston MA 2011-2012; Asst P S Lk's Ch San Francisco CA 2010-2011. office@stlukeslb.org

AVILA-NATIVI, Rigoberto (NY) PO Box 3786, Poughkeepsie NY 12603 B Honduras 1956 s Vergilio & Maria. BA SUNY 2005; MDiv GTS 2006. D 3/11/2006 P 9/23/2006 Bp Mark Sean Sisk. m 4/29/1990 Jacqueline K Reed c 3. Dio New York New York NY 2010-2012, 2009.

AVRIL, Wilky (Hai) **Dio Haiti Port-au-Prince HT 2012-** B 1979 s Marie. D 7/29/2012 P 3/13/2014 Bp Jean Zache Duracin. m 5/1/2014 Dorothie A Avril.

AWAN, Abraham Kuol (Chi) 7100 N Ashland Blvd, Chicago IL 60626 B South Sudan 1979 s Awan & Athiek. Trans 6/27/2013 Bp Jeff Lee. m 1/6/2008 Elizabeth Nyanwut Ajak c 1.

AXBERG, Keith (Mont) Trinity Church Jeffers, PO Box 336, Ennis MT 59729 B Seattle WA 1951 s Oscar & Eileen. BS WA SU 1974; MDiv Vancouver TS CA 1984. D 9/13/1984 P 7/13/1985 Bp Leigh Allen Wallace Jr. m 5/12/1979 Barbara J Axberg c 2. R Trin Ch Ennis MT 2012-2017; Ch Of The H Fam Fresno CA 2003-2009; R S Paul's Epis Ch Benicia CA 2001-2003; S Mich And All Ang Epis Ch Lincoln Pk MI 1990-2001; Epis Ch Of The Redeem Republic WA 1984-1990; S Jn's Epis Ch Colville WA 1984-1990. Columnist, "THIS OUR Vlly," *Madera Tribune Nwspr*, Madera Tribune, 2009. trinity@3rivers.net

AYALA TORRES, Carlos Anibal (EcuC) Bogota S/N Jose Vicente Trujillo, Guayaquil Ecuador B Tumbabiro-Ibarra EC 1935 s Jukio & Rosa Victoria. Coll Tecnico Daniel Geyes Reval; BTh Facultad Limena De Sagraduatea Teologia 1967. P 4/27/1985 Bp Adrian Delio Caceres-Villavicencio. m 9/7/1973 Nancy Carabajo Vera. Litoral Dio Ecuador Guayaquil 1986-1994; Iglesia Epis Del Ecuador Quito 1985.

AYBAR-MARTE, Pantaleon (PR) B Monte Plata, D.R. 1956 s Ramon & Terminia. LIC St. Thos Aquinas Pontifical Sem 1984. Rec 7/11/1993 as Priest Bp David Andres Alvarez-Velazquez. m 4/28/1996 Porfidia Colon Torres. Dio Puerto Rico Trujillo Alto PR 2004-2016. Chapl at Hosp Epis San Lucas for 7.5 years Dio Puerto Rico, S Just, PR 2014. pbropanta@yahoo.com

AYCOCK, David Haskell (CFla) 759 Phoenix Ln, Oviedo FL 32765 **D Ch of the Incarn 2007-** B Spartanburg SC 1937 BA Florida Chr U 2001. D 12/15/2003 Bp John Wadsworth Howe. m 7/3/1963 Jill Ann Aycock c 3.

AYCOCK JR, Marvin Brady (NC) 669 N. 6th St., Albemarle NC 28001 B Greenville SC 1932 s Marvin & Arminda. Clemson U 1953; BA Furman U 1958; MDiv SE Bapt TS 1962; GTS 1994. D 10/2/1988 Bp Robert Whitridge Estill P 6/1/1995 Bp Robert Carroll Johnson Jr. m 8/15/1959 Sally Rheta Thompson c 3. Vic S Paul's Epis Ch Thomasville NC 2006-2008; Vic S Matt Ch Salisbury NC 2001-2004; Yadkin Vlly Cluster Salisbury NC 2001-2003; Emm Ch Warrenton NC 1996-2004; Vic All SS Ch Warrenton NC 1996-2001; Warrenton Epis Ch Cluster Warrenton NC 1996-2001; Asst to R S Andr's Epis Ch Charlotte NC 1995-1996; D S Paul's Ch Salisbury NC 1993-2004; D Chr Ch Albemarle NC 1988-1993; Serv Bapt Ch 1961-1970.

AYER, Kelly Lane (Roch) 10 Park Pl, Avon NY 14414 **Zion Ch Avon NY 2010-** B Mecklenburg NC 1973 d Charles & Helen. BS Wingate U 1999; MDiv Van 2004; MDiv Van 2004; STM GTS 2010. D 12/4/2010 Bp Michael B Curry P 7/16/2011 Bp Prince Grenville Singh. m 4/18/2015 Margaret M Ayer. S Jn's Ch Mt Morris NY 2011-2012. kayer@gts.edu

AYERBE, Reynaldo (SwFla) 4012 Penhurst Park, Sarasota FL 34235 B CO 1928 s Julio & Adeliaida. PhD NYU; BA Vincentian Sem Bogota CO. Trans 2/9/2002 Bp John Bailey Lipscomb. m 8/12/1961 Elin Ayerbe.

AYERS, Barbara (Alb) D 12/9/2012 Bp William Howard Love.

AYERS, John Cameron (Cal) 13601 Saratoga Ave, Saratoga CA 95070 **Assoc Ch Of The H Innoc San Francisco CA 2011-; Chapl S Andr's Sch Saratoga CA 2011-** B Los Angeles CA 1956 s John & Nancy. BA Loyola Marymount U 1978; MA Gonzaga 1981; MDiv Weston Jesuit TS 1986. Rec 7/27/2011 as Priest Bp Marc Handley Andrus. m 9/19/2015 Charles Edward Prescott. R Ch Of The Nativ San Rafael CA 2014.

AYERS, Margaret (WLa) St James Episcopal Church, PO Box 494, Port Gibson MS 39150 B Billings, MT 1958 d David & Helen. BS Montana St U 1981; MDiv Epis TS of the SW 2007. D 6/18/2007 Bp Charles Franklin Brookhart Jr P 2/1/2008 Bp Duncan Montgomery Gray III. S Jas Epis Ch Port Gibson MS 2007-2016.

AYERS, Mary Louise (Spok) 7315 N Wall St, Spokane WA 99208 **S Dav's Ch Spokane WA 2016-** B Spokane 1974 d Herbert & Phyllis. BA Whitman Coll 1997; MA Gonzaga U 2008. D 10/18/2015 P 6/18/2016 Bp James E Waggoner Jr.

AYERS, Phillip Wallace (Ore) 3232 NE 12th Ave, Portland OR 97212 **Assoc Trin Epis Cathd Portland OR 2014-; Asst SS Ptr & Paul Par Portland OR 2006-** B Newton KS 1941 s Leo & Aloha. BME Wichita St U 1965; MDiv Ya Berk 1970; Cert Ya 1984; Cert Abbott NW Hosp Minneapolis MN 1992. D 6/17/1970 P 12/16/1970 Bp Edward Clark Turner. m 7/31/1965 La Vera M Goering c 2. Assoc S Ptr And Paul Epis Ch Portland OR 2006-2014; Assoc S Steph's Epis Par Portland OR 2004-2005; R Ascen Par Portland OR 1999-2004; R Trin Epis Ch Marshall MI 1993-1998; Long Term Supply Ch Of The H Cross Dundas MN 1993; Counslr Hammer Residences Inc. Wayzata 1992-1993; Assoc S Clem's Ch S Paul MN 1991-1993; Chapl Abbott NW Hosp Minneapolis MN 1991-1992; R S Paul's On-The-Hill Epis Ch Minneapolis MN 1988-1991; Cmnty Chapl Yale New Haven Hosp New Haven CT 1985-1987; Par Fieldwork Supvsr Ya Berk New Haven CT 1975-1988; R S Jn's Ch No Haven CT 1974-1988; Asst/Mus Dir S Dav's Epis Ch Topeka KS 1971-1974; Cur S Paul's Epis Ch Visalia CA 1971-1972; Ch Of The Epiph Sedan KS 1970-1971; R S Matt's Ch Cedar Vale KS 1970-1971; Fresh Start Fac Dio Oregon Portland OR 2009-2013. Auth, "Bk Revs," *ATR*, 2016; Compiler, "Plain Prayers for a Vstry," H Cross Monstry, 1995; Auth, "Bk Revs," *Angl and Epis Hist*, Hist Soc of Epis Ch; Auth, "Bk Revs," *Angl and Epis Hist*, Hist Soc of Epis Ch; Auth, "Revs and arts," *The Hstgr*. Iona Cmnty-Assoc 1985; Natl Epis Historians & Archivists 2002; OHC-Assoc 1961.

AYERS, Robert Curtis (CNY) 6010 E. Lake Rd., Cazenovia NY 13035 **Ret 1998-** B Roanoke VA 1927 s Walter & Lena. BA Roa 1947; MDiv Luth TS 1950; Coll of Preachers 1963; U of Munich 1966; PhD Syr 1981. D 9/29/1953 P 4/4/1954 Bp Malcolm E Peabody. m 9/4/1950 Vivian E Harper. R Epis Ch Of SS Ptr And Jn Auburn NY 1991-1998, Vic 1988-1990; Int Emm Ch Norwich NY 1988; Vic Trin Ch Camden NY 1983-1988; Epis Chapl Syr Syracuse NY 1958-1980; Chapl US Navy Reserve 1956-1970; P-in-c Emm Ch Adams NY 1954-1958; Zion Ch Pierrepont Manor NY 1954-1958; Dio Cntrl New York Liverpool NY 1953-1980; Serv Luth Ch 1950-1952. "Der Mann heisst Grannan...," *Festschrift f. Christoph Weber*, Verlag Ptr Lang, 2008; "From Tavern to Temple," Cloudbank Creations, 2005; "Baroness of the Ripetta," Cloudbank Creations, 2004.

AYERS, Russell C (Mass) 3737 Seminary Rd, Alexandria VA 22304 B Salisbury MD 1938 s Roger & Edna. Moody Bible Inst 1961; BA Gordon Coll 1965; MDiv VTS 1970. D 6/20/1970 P 3/18/1971 Bp John Melville Burgess. Sthrn Afr Info Access Dio Washington Washington DC 1993-1997, 1987-1997, Dir Life/Wk Plnng Cntr 1987-1993; Ch Of The Ascen Silver Sprg MD 1988-1991; Team Ldr Nyanga Zimbabwe Mssn Proj Dio Massachusetts Boston MA 1986, Team Ldr Nyanga Zimbabwe Mssn Proj 1986, Zimbabwe Com 1985-1987; R S Mk's Ch Foxborough MA 1973-1987; Cur S Paul's Ch Newburyport MA 1970-1973. Auth, Alb Inst, WDC, 1990. Admin, Friends Of Zimbabwe 1989-1999; Comp In Wrld Mssn, Washington Dc 1990-1998; Convenor, Afr Round Table, St. Alb's WDC 2002-2010; Convenor, Epis Partnership For Global Mssn 1999-2000; Dir, Computers for Afr Angl Theol Educ 1999-2006; Dir, Life Wk Plnng Cntr,WDC 1988-2005; Pres, Angl Afr Internet Info Soc 1992-2013; Pres, Sthrn Afr Internet Access 1989-1999.

AYMERICH, Ramon Ignacio (Mass) **R Chr Ch Teaneck NJ 2004-** B Havana CU 1948 s Ramon & Josefina. BA S Johns Vianney Sem 1971; STB Pontifical Gregorian U Rome IT 1974; GTS 1984. Rec 11/1/1983 Bp Harold Barrett Robinson. m 1/6/1984 Darlene Joy Rodgers c 2. S Anne's Ch Lowell MA 2004-2008; R S Jas-In-The-Hills Epis Ch Hollywood FL 1999-2003; R Ch Of The H Comf Miami FL 1987-1998; Hisp Mssn Iglesia De Santa Maria Reading PA 1984-1987; Vic S Mary's Epis Ch Reading PA 1984-1987; Serv RC Ch 1975-1982. Cleric Of Year 1976; Af Humanitarian Serv Awd.

AYRES, Stephen T (Mass) 193 Salem St, Boston MA 02113 **Old No Fndt Of Boston Inc. Boston MA 2013-; Vic Old No Chr Ch Boston MA 1997-** B Media PA 1954 s Russell & Rebecca. BA Ham 1976; MDiv EDS 1980; MA

Tufts U 1988. D 6/11/1980 Bp William Grant Black P 12/14/1980 Bp Arthur Anton Vogel. m 10/26/1996 Lisa R Ayres c 1. R Emm Epis Ch Wakefield MA 1991-1997; S Jn's Ch Charlestown (Boston) Charlestown MA 1990-1991; Int Ch Of Our Sav Roslindale MA 1986-1987; Ch Of Our Sav Boston MA 1986-1987; Int S Jas Ch Amesbury MA 1985-1986; Assoc S Jas Ch Oneonta NY 1982-1985; Chr Epis Ch Springfield MO 1980-1982; Stndg Com, Pres 2010-2011 Dio Massachusetts Boston MA 2007-2011, Trst of Donations, Chair SRI Com 1992-.

AZAR, Antoinette Joann (Lex) 201 Providence Hill, Ashland KY 41101 **Calv Epis Ch Ashland KY 2012-** B Washington DC 1957 d Anthony & Eleanor. AB Ohio U 1979; MA Ohio U 1983; MDiv Bex Sem 2009. D 6/13/2009 P 6/19/2010 Bp Thomas Edward Breidenthal. m 7/28/2011 George C Ayres c 2. Asst R S Anne Epis Ch W Chester OH 2009-2012. Assoc, CHS 2004. tj.azar@hotmail.com

AZARIAH, Khushnud M (Los) 6563 East Ave, Etiwanda CA 91739 **S Geo's Ch Riverside CA 2012-** B Pakistan 1949 d JS & Florence. MEd Punjab Coll 1971; BD Trin Theol Coll 1974; PhD Claremont TS 2005. Trans 3/4/2010 Bp Joseph Jon Bruno. m 7/14/1978 Samuel R Azariah c 3. Ch Of Our Sav Par San Gabr CA 2010-2012. kazariah123@gmail.com

B

BAAR, David Josef (Haw) B San Francisco CA 1937 s Josef & Erla. BA U CA 1959; BD CDSP 1962. D 6/24/1962 P 3/2/1963 Bp James Albert Pike. m 10/20/1979 Geraldine H Aughton c 2. S Jn's Epis Ch Kula HI 1999-2004, Assoc 1981-1991; Non-par 1992-1998; Non-par 1967-1980; Chapl To Bp/Chancery Clerk Dio California San Francisco CA 1965-1967; Cur S Andr's Ch Saratoga CA 1962-1965. Bd w dist CDSP 1962.

BABB, Trevor R (SO) 401 Newfield Ave, Bridgeport CT 06607 B BB 1955 s Stanley & Gladys. Barbados Inst of Mgmt and Productivity 1989; Codrington Coll 1989; BA U of The W Indies 1989. Trans 12/31/1992 Bp Andrew Frederick Wissemann. m 7/30/1983 Marcella Y Babb c 2. R S Simon Of Cyrene Epis Ch Cincinnati OH 2005-2016; R S Mk's Ch Bridgeport CT 1994-2005; Dio Wstrn Massachusetts Springfield 1993-1994; Int S Mary's Epis Ch Thorndike MA 1992-1994; Serv Ch Of Barbados 1989-1992. Chapl Grtr Bridgeport UBE; Cleric Vol Goodwill Industries 1995; Med Detox Unit 96-. Ba w hon U Of The W Indies 1989.

BABCOCK, Harold Ross Manly (NH) Old Rossier Farm, 238 Rossier Rd., Montgomery Center VT 05471 **Non-par 1983-** B Johnson VT 1938 s William & Geraldine. BA Estrn Nazarene Coll 1960; STB ETSBH 1965; Harv 1972. D 6/26/1965 Bp John Melville Burgess P 5/21/1966 Bp Frederic Cunningham Lawrence. m 5/31/1985 Carolyn Sue Hesterberg. R S Mk's Ch Groveton NH 1975-1981; S Paul's Ch Lancaster NH 1975-1981; R Portland Par (Actg) Ch In The W Indies 1973-1974; R Trin Epis Ch Weymouth MA 1968-1972; Asst R Chr Ch Waltham MA 1965-1968.

BABCOCK, Jessica A (CGC) St Marks Episcopal Church, 4129 Oxford Ave, Jacksonville FL 32210 **P Chr Epis Ch Pensacola FL 2015-** B Anniston AL 1965 d Albert & Terry. BA Cntr Coll of Kentucky 1988; MSEd Georgia St U 1995; MDiv Sewanee: The U So, TS 2013; MDiv The TS at The U So 2013. D 12/9/2012 Bp Samuel Johnson Howard P 6/8/2013 Bp Philip Menzie Duncan II. m 8/1/1992 Dwight C Babcock c 2. S Chris's Ch Pensacola FL 2013-2015.

BABCOCK, Linda Mae (WMo) Saint Anne'S Church, Lebanon MO 65536 B Nampa ID 1941 d William & Ethel. S Thos Sem; AA Riverside City Coll 1961; BS California St Polytechnic U 1963. D 10/24/1992 Bp William Jerry Winterrowd. S Steph's Epis Ch Aurora CO 1993; Consult CE S Paul's Epis Ch Lakewood CO 1992.

BABCOCK, Lori Hale (Md) 1700 South Rd, Baltimore MD 21209 B York, PA 1967 BA Goucher Coll 1989; MDiv GTS 2007. D 6/2/2007 P 12/12/2007 Bp Bud Shand. m 7/11/1987 John Babcock c 4. R S Jn's Ch Mt Washington Baltimore MD 2009-2016; Trin Cathd Easton MD 2007-2009.

BABCOCK, Margaret Anderson (Wyo) 4230 S Oak St, Casper WY 82601 **Dir Comp Way Consulting Serv 2010-** B Waterloo IA 1953 d Karl & Margaret. BA S Olaf Coll 1974; MS Minnesota St U Mankato 1978; MDiv SWTS 1980; DMin SWTS 1998. D 6/14/1980 Bp Walter Cameron Righter P 2/14/1981 Bp Joseph Thomas Heistand. m 6/12/1976 Charles Babcock c 2. Cn for Mnstry and Congrl Dvlpmt Dio Wyoming Casper 2006-2010; Cn for Congrl Dvlpmt Dio Idaho Boise ID 2001-2006; R Ch Of S Matt Tucson AZ 1991-2000; Dio Arizona Phoenix AZ 1987-1991; Vic St Johns Epis-Luth Ch Williams AZ 1985-1989; Asst S Alb's Epis Ch Tucson AZ 1980-1985. Auth, "New Growth in God's Garden," LeaderResources, 2012; Auth, "Rooted in God," LeaderResources, 1992.

BABCOCK, Mary Kathleen (Kan) 400 E. Maple St, Independence KS 67301 B Independecne KS 1944 d Gerald & Mary. BA Emporia St U 1965; MPhil U of Kansas 1972; JD U of Kansas 1976; MDiv VTS 2010. D 6/6/2009 P 6/5/2010 Bp Dean E Wolfe.

BABCOCK, Ted (Pgh) The Episcopal Diocese of Pittsburgh, 325 Oliver Ave, Pittsburgh PA 15222 B Bronxville NY 1950 s Henry & Mary. BA U MI 1973; MA U of Virginia 1974; MBA Harv 1982; MDiv GTS 2001; ThD GTF/Oxf 2009. D 6/9/2001 P 1/19/2002 Bp Andrew Donnan Smith. m 7/2/1988 Lyn C Ackerman c 3. S Brendan's Epis Ch Franklin Pk PA 2016-2017; Cn to the Ordnry Dio Cntrl Pennsylvania Harrisburg PA 2010-2013; R S Andr's Epis Ch Shippensburg PA 2005-2010; Asst to the R Chr Ch Greenwich CT 2001-2005; Intern S Dav's Ch Bronx NY 1998-2001. tbabcock@episcopalpgh.org

BABENKO-LONGHI, Julie P (Chi) 1850 Landre Ct, Burlington WI 53105 B 1954 d James & Patricia. BS Nthrn Illinois U 1978; Sch for Deacons 1997. D 2/7/1998 Bp Herbert Alcorn Donovan Jr. m 5/7/2011 Anthony Peter Longhi c 1. Cler Rep, Human Relatns Cmsn City of McHenry IL McHenry 2000-2002; S Paul's Ch Mchenry IL 1998-2002; Asst. Admin. of D Sch for Mnstry Dio Chicago Chicago IL 1997-2002; Deacons Coun Mem Dio Chicago Chicago IL 1997-2003, Dioc AIDS T/F Mem 1997-2000.

BABIN, Alexander Raymond (Mich) 69440 Brookhill Dr, Romeo MI 48065 **Int Ch Of The H Cross Novi MI 2008-** B Detroit MI 1934 s Anthony & Margaret. BBA U MI 1957; MBA U MI 1963; Cert Whittaker TS 1974; DMin Ecum TS 1994. D 2/12/1972 Bp Archie H Crowley P 5/4/1974 Bp H Coleman Mcgehee Jr. m 7/9/1984 Linda M Babin c 3. Dep Gc Dio Michigan Detroit MI 1988-1994, Hod Ctte - Stew & Dev 1988-1994, Mnstry w The Poor Com 1987-1991, Exec Coun 1987-1990, Dep Gc 1979-1996, Int Mnstry 2002-, Sprtl Dir Curs 1990-2001, Convoc Dn 1984-1989, Exec Coun 1980-1983, 1979, Chair COM 1976-1978, COM 1974-1975; St Paul's Epis Romeo MI 1977-2000; Asst S Columba Ch Detroit MI 1972-1976. Auth, "Toward Sprtl Wholeness Sprtlty, Recovery & The Ch (Not Pub," *(Dissertation)*, 2003. OHC Assoc 1994.

BABIN, Alice Elizabeth Duffy (Md) 65 Verde Valley School Rd Apt C-13, Sedona AZ 86351 B New Orleans LO 1937 d John & Alice. AA Stephens Coll 1957; LTh SWTS 1975. D 6/6/1975 Bp James Winchester Montgomery P 3/1/1977 Bp Quintin Ebenezer Primo Jr. R S Geo's Epis Ch Mt Savage MD 1996-1998; S Andr's Priory Sch Honolulu HI 1995-1996; Chapl S Andr's Priory Sch Honolulu HI 1994-1996; Chapl/Supvsr Duke Med Cntr Durham NC 1989-1991; 1986-1989; R Chr Ch Kealakekua HI 1980-1986; 1978-1980; S Lawr Epis Ch Libertyville IL 1977-1978; Dio Chicago Chicago IL 1975-1976; Cur Gr Epis Ch Freeport IL 1975-1976.

BABIN, Kyle James (WA) D 11/12/2016 P 6/17/2017 Bp Mariann Edgar Budde.

BABLER, Emmett John (Minn) 9411 E Parkside Dr, Sun Lakes AZ 85248 B Saint Paul MN 1948 s John & Margaret. AA Lakewood 1975; BA Metropltn St U 1976; MA Uop 1989. D 8/28/1976 Bp Philip Frederick McNairy. m 3/9/1968 Joan Burnette Stevens c 3. D S Steph's Ch Sierra Vista AZ 1982-1984; D S Mich & All Ang Ch Monticello MN 1978-1982; Asst Ch Of The H Apos S Paul MN 1977-1978.

BABNEW JR, Rodger Allan (Az) D 6/10/2017 Bp Kirk Stevan Smith.

BABNIS, Mariann C (WA) 33203 W Batten St, Lewes DE 19958 **Chr Ch Port Republic MD 2016-** B Sharon PA 1957 d Frank & Catherine. BA Clarion U of Pennsylvania 1979; MA Ohio U Athens OH 1980; MDiv VTS 2004. D 6/12/2004 P 1/22/2005 Bp John Bryson Chane. Chr Ch Chaptico MD 2014-2015; Int S Martha's Epis Ch Bethany Bch DE 2013; Int S Paul's Ch Georgetown DE 2010-2011; Int S Mary's Epis Ch Pocomoke City MD 2009-2010; Assoc H Trin Epis Ch Bowie MD 2005-2008.

BABSON, Katharine E (Me) 149 Pennellville Rd, Brunswick ME 04011 **VTS Alexandria VA 2017-, 2013; Adj Fac, Mssn & Wrld Rel VTS 2001-; Mssy to Myanmar/Burma The Epis Ch 1994-** B Boston MA 1950 d Roger & Edith. Vas 1970; Ba Wms 1972; MDiv VTS 1992; DMin Wesley TS 2009. D 6/13/1992 Bp Roland Poland Atkinson P 12/1/1992 Bp Peter J Lee. m 8/5/1972 Bradley Ogden Babson c 2. P-in-c St Mths Epis Ch Brunswick ME 2010-2012; Epis Ch Of S Mary The Vrgn Falmouth ME 2005; S Ptr's Epis Ch Arlington VA 1997-2000; Founded The Intl Ch of Hanoi Vietnam 1993-1999; Serv The Intl Ch of Bangkok Thailand 1993-1994; S Geo's Epis Ch Arlington VA 1992. Auth, "The Prov of Myanmar (Burma)," *The Oxford Guide to BCP*, Oxf Press, 2006; Auth, "Preaching and the Film Jesus of Montreal," *The Evang Outlook Vol 29 #4*, EvangES, 1992. EPGM 2001-2011; SCWM 2003-2009.

BACAGAN, Magdaleno K (Los) 225 W Linfield St, Glendora CA 91740 **Ret 1999-** B La Union PH 1932 s Pedro & Benita. Jerusalem St Georges Sum Sch; ThB S Andrews TS Manila PH 1958; BA U of The Philippines 1959; VTS 1972; Cbury Sum Sch Engl 1983; S Georges Coll Jerusalem 1985; MDiv S Andrews TS 1987. D 8/10/1958 Bp Lyman Cunningham Ogilby P 8/1/1959 Bp Benito C Cabanban. Ch Of The H Comm Gardena CA 1983-1998; Vic Dio California San Francisco CA 1983-1998; Vic Dio Los Angeles Los Angeles CA 1983-1998; Asst 1979-1982; Cmssnr Epis Asian- Amer Mnstry Cmsn 1982-1985; Convenor Filipino Convoc 1980-1985; Ch Of The Atone Washington DC 1972-1978; Assoc Dio Washington Washington DC 1972-1978; Serv The Epis Ch In The Philippines 1959-1973.

BACHMANN, Douglas P (Cal) 419 Orchard View Ave, Martinez CA 94553 B New Brunswick NJ 1949 s Nicholas & Muriel. BA Amer U 1971; W&M 1972; PDS 1974; MDiv GTS 1975; GTS 1985; MA Jn F Kennedy U 2001. D 4/26/

1975 Bp Albert Wiencke Van Duzer P 1/31/1976 Bp Gray Temple. m 1/3/1976 Dawn Bachmann. Assoc R Ch Of The Resurr Pleasant Hil CA 2001-2007; R S Jn's Epis Ch Mankato MN 1995-1997; R Chr Ch Austin MN 1990-1995; Int Chr Ch Red Wing MN 1988-1989; Int Ch Of The H Apos S Paul MN 1987-1988; R S Jas On The Pkwy Minneapolis MN 1985-1986; P S Anne's By The Fields Ankeny IA 1979-1984; Serv Ch Of Engl 1977-1979; Asst R Trin Ch Myrtle Bch SC 1975-1977.

BACHSCHMID, Edward Karl (RG) 9024 N Congress St, New Market VA 22844 **D Emm Ch Harrisonburg VA 2006-** B Washington DC 1940 D 6/19/2004 Bp John Herbert MacNaughton. m 8/22/1964 Judith K Bachschmid c 2. D S Jas' Epis Ch Las Cruces NM 2004-2006.

BACIGALUPO, Joseph Andrew (ECR) 1343 Wylie Way, San Jose CA 95130 B Jersey City NJ 1931 D 9/27/1972 Bp George Richard Millard P 7/1/1981 Bp Charles Shannon Mallory. m 4/22/1954 Willemke Zuydendorp.

BACK, George (Okla) 2520 NW 59 St, Oklahoma City OK 73112 **Asst S Jn's Ch Oklahoma City OK 2014-** B New York NY 1942 s George & Grace. BA Bard Coll 1964; STB GTS 1967. D 6/17/1967 P 12/23/1967 Bp Jonathan Goodhue Sherman. m 9/30/1967 Margaret Andrews c 3. Dn S Paul's Cathd Oklahoma City OK 1982-2010; Cn Cathd Ch Of S Lk Orlando FL 1979-1982; R Chr Memi Ch No Brookfield MA 1971-1979; Cur S Jn's Ch Portsmouth NH 1967-1971. Auth, "Christmas Joy: Let Heaven & Nature Sing," *Bk*, Sprt & Intelligence Press, 2007; Bk Revs, "Uncertainty: The Life & Sci of Werner Heisenberg," *CTNS Bulletin*, Cntr for Theol & the Natural Sciences, 1993. Bp's Awd Dio Oklahoma 2006.

BACK, Heather Back (Ky) 744 Sherwood Dr, Bowling Green KY 42103 **Calv Ch Louisville KY 2015-; Asst R The Ch of St. Mich and St. Geo St. Louis MO 2001-** B Portsmouth NH 1969 d George & Margaret. BA U of Oklahoma 1990; MDiv VTS 1996. D 6/29/1996 P 12/21/1996 Bp Robert Manning Moody. c 2. Chr Epis Ch Bowling Green KY 2013-2014, 2011-2012; S Mich & S Geo S Louis MO 2001-2008; The Great Cmsn Fndt Houston TX 2001; Assoc R All SS Epis Ch Austin TX 1999-2001; Assoc The Epis Ch Of S Thos The Apos Dallas TX 1997-2002; S Thos The Apos Epis Ch Houston TX 1997-1999; Dio Oklahoma Oklahoma City OK 1996-1997; Cur Gr Ch Muskogee OK 1996-1997.

BACK, Luke (NwT) 602 Meander St, Abilene TX 79602 **R Ch of the Heav Rest Abilene Abilene TX 2010-** B Ware MA 1972 s George & Margaret. BA U of Oklahoma 1995; MEd U of Oklahoma 1999; MDiv VTS 2002. D 6/29/2002 P 1/11/2003 Bp Robert Manning Moody. m 6/1/2002 Meredith B Bishop c 3. S Paul's Cathd Oklahoma City OK 2002-2010.

BACKER, Karri Anne (Los) 1231 E. Chapman Ave., Fullerton CA 92832 **Bloy Hse Claremont CA 2017-; Claremont TS Wichita KS 2015-** B Longview WA 1970 d Larry & Bonnie. BA U CA Los Angeles 2000; MA Antioch U Los Angeles 2005; MDiv Claremont TS Bloy Hse 2011; MDiv ETSBH 2011. D 6/11/2011 P 1/7/2012 Bp Diane Jardine Bruce. m 4/9/1997 David Nicholas Gordon Main c 1. S Andr's Par Fullerton CA 2012-2015; Luth Epis Campus Mnstry CSULB Long Bch CA 2012. karri.backer@gmail.com

BACKHAUS, Oliver Keith (SwFla) St Mark's Episcopal Church, 513 Nassau St S, Venice FL 34285 **D S Mk's Epis Ch Venice FL 2012-** B Washington MO 1947 s Oliver & Ruby. D 10/21/2011 Bp Dabney Tyler Smith. m 8/31/1968 Pamela D Backhaus.

BACKLUND, Michael Anders (SJ) 10449 Oak Valley Rd, Angels Camp CA 95222 **S Clare of Assisi Epis Ch Avery CA 2016-; Assoc S Paul's Epis Ch Sacramento CA 2005-** B San Bernardino CA 1951 s James & Dorothy. BA U of San Diego 1973; MS U of San Diego 1975; MDiv S Patricks Sem 1979; PhD Palo Alto U 1990. Rec 6/1/1981 as Deacon Bp William Arthur Dimmick. m 7/5/2008 Daniel T Brower. Assoc Trin Ch San Francisco CA 1992-2003; Assoc Gr Cathd San Francisco CA 1987-1990; Asst S Phil's Ch San Jose CA 1985-1986; Asst All SS Epis Ch Palo Alto CA 1982-1984; Vic Chr Ch Calumet Larium MI 1981-1982; Dio Nthrn Michigan Marquette MI 1981-1982; Transitional D Serv RC Ch 1979-1981. Auth, "Faith & AIDS: Life Crisis as a Stimulus to Faith Stage Transition," *Dissertation Abstracts*, 1990. Fell ECF 1984.

BACKSTRAND, Brian E (Mil) 804 E Juneau Ave, Milwaukee WI 53202 **Vic Dio Milwaukee Milwaukee WI 2008-** B Tacoma WA 1945 s Samuel & Esther. BA Carleton Coll 1967; MDiv No Pk TS 1971; MA U of Wisconsin 1973; DS SWTS 2008. D 6/26/2008 P 1/3/2009 Bp Steven Andrew Miller. m 6/21/1969 Marilee Backstrand c 3. Trin Epis Ch Mineral Point WI 2015-2017; Trin Epis Ch Platteville WI 2015-2017; S Andr's Epis Ch Monroe WI 2008-2015.

BACKUS, Brett Paul (ETenn) The Episcopal Church of the Ascension, 800 S. Northshore Drive, Knoxville TN 37919 **Assoc R Ch Of The Ascen Knoxville TN 2008-** B Knoxville TN 1981 s Paul & Ann. BA U of Tennessee 2004; MDiv VTS 2008. D 5/31/2008 P 1/17/2009 Bp Charles Glenn VonRosenberg. m 7/2/2005 Carla Backus c 2.

BACKUS, Howard G (NC) 600 South Central Avenue, Laurel DE 19956 **R S Phil's Ch Laurel DE 2008-** B Richwood WV 1947 s Arthur & Marilee. BA W Virginia Wesleyan Coll 1969; Duke DS 1971; MDiv VTS 1973; DMin VTS 1999; CE Cntr for Congrl Hlth 2007. D 6/5/1972 P 2/16/1973 Bp Wilburn Camrock Campbell. m 6/1/1968 Sue Ann H Backus c 3. Int S Thos Epis Ch Reidsville NC 2007-2008; R S Tim's Epis Ch Winston Salem NC 1990-2007;

S Steph's Epis Ch Beckley WV 1978-1990; Chapl Clemson U Clemson SC 1975-1978; Asst H Trin Par Epis Clemson SC 1975-1978; Vic Ascen Epis Ch Hinton WV 1973-1975. Laurel Mnstrl Assn 2008; YCORE Partnership for Int Mnstry 2007. Doctor Of Mnstry VTS 1999.

BACKUS, Timothy Warren (CGC) PO Box 12683, Pensacola FL 32591 **S Fran Of Assisi Gulf Breeze FL 2015-** B Beckley WVA 1981 s Howard & Sue Ann. BMus Appalachian St U; BS Appalachian St U 2005; MDiv VTS 2009. D 6/13/2009 Bp Michael B Curry P 1/29/2011 Bp Duncan Montgomery Gray III. Assoc Chr Epis Ch Pensacola FL 2009-2015. revbackus@stfrancisgulfbreeze.org

BACON JR, James Edwin (Ala) 3239 Heathrow Downs, Hoover AL 35226 B Jesup GA 1948 s James & Nancy. BA Merc 1969; MA Candler TS Emory U 1979. D 6/12/1982 P 5/19/1983 Bp Bennett Jones Sims. m 2/14/1971 Hope Hendricks Bacon c 2. R All SS Ch Pasadena CA 1995-2016; Dn S Andr's Cathd Jackson MS 1989-1995; R S Mk's Ch Dalton GA 1984-1989; S Lk's Epis Ch Atlanta GA 1982-1984; Dio Atlanta Atlanta GA 1982-1983. Soc Of S Jn The Evang. Cler Ldrshp Proj 1992.

BACON, Lynne Lazier (Neb) 719 Crestridge Rd, Omaha NE 68154 **D All SS Epis Ch Omaha NE 1993-** B Denver CO 1946 d Harry & Genevieve. BA Colorado Coll 1968; MS U of Nebraska 1982. D 9/25/1993 Bp James Edward Krotz. m 8/9/1968 Walter Meredith Bacon.

BACON JR, Robert (Mass) 51 Ledgelawn Ave, Lexington MA 02420 **R S Paul's Ch Lynnfield MA 2015-; Chapl Seafarers Friend 2011-** B Boston MA 1959 s Robert & Katharine. Mar 1978; BA U of Oklahoma 1983; MDiv Andover Newton TS 1997. D 6/5/1999 P 6/3/2000 Bp M(Arvil) Thomas Shaw. m 4/16/1988 Sonia E Demarta c 3. Chapl MWRA (Robert Bacon) Lexington MA 2012-2015; Dir of Veterans Mnstrs Dio Massachusetts Boston MA 2008-2009, Dir of Yth Ministres 2002-2008; Assoc for Families & Yth Trin Ch Epis Boston MA 1999-2002; Yth Min Trin Boston 1993-2002. rbacon@stpaulslynnfield.org

BADDERS JR, John David (WTex) 11 Saint Lukes Ln, San Antonio TX 78209 **S Lk's Epis Ch San Antonio TX 2010-** B San Antonio TX 1950 s John & Ruby. BBA Texas Tech U 1973; MDiv Sewanee: The U So, TS 1996. D 6/18/1996 Bp Robert Boyd Hibbs P 2/14/1997 Bp James Edward Folts. m 6/4/2011 Christine Welsh c 2. R S Jn's Ch McAllen TX 2000-2010; R S Fran By The Lake Canyon Lake TX 1996-2000.

BADE, James Robert (Az) 6300 N Central Ave, Phoenix AZ 85012 **D All SS Ch Phoenix AZ 2012-** B Chicago IL 1943 s Robert & Florence. BS U of Phoenix 2005. D 5/5/2012 Bp Kirk Stevan Smith. m 5/14/2007 Jennie Lu Bade c 3.

BADER-SAYE, Demery Letisha (Be) 334 Knapp Rd, Clarks Summit PA 18411 B Albuquerque NM 1971 BA U of Nthrn Colorado. D 4/20/2004 P 10/31/2004 Bp Paul Victor Marshall. m 12/22/1996 Scott C Bader-Saye c 2. Dio Bethlehem Bethlehem PA 2004-2009.

BADGETT, Benjamin R (WTenn) **Ch Of The H Comm Memphis TN 2015-** B Marietta OH 1980 s Karl & Janice. BA Wstrn Kentucky U 2004; MDiv VTS 2012. D 11/11/2011 P 6/13/2012 Bp Terry Allen White. m 6/18/2005 Kendall M Terrett c 3. Asst R and Coll Chapl Chr Epis Ch Bowling Green KY 2012-2015. bbadgett@holycommunion.org

BAER, Kirsten Herndon (Okla) 13316 SW 3rd St, Yukon OK 73099 **Vic Gr Ch Epis Yukon OK 2013-** B Oklahoma City OK 1983 d Christopher & Karen. BA U of Oklahoma 2006; MEd U of Oklahoma 2008; MDiv VTS 2011. D 1/22/2011 P 7/23/2011 Bp Edward Joseph Konieczny. m 8/11/2007 Timothy Christopher Baer c 1. Dio Oklahoma Oklahoma City OK 2013-2014; Cur Pat's Epis Ch Broken Arrow OK 2011-2013.

BAER, Timothy Christopher (Okla) 13316 SW 3rd St, Yukon OK 73099 **Vic Gr Ch Epis Yukon OK 2013-** B Waterbury CT 1985 s Henry & Heather. BA U of Oklahoma 2007; MDiv VTS 2011. D 1/22/2011 P 7/23/2011 Bp Edward Joseph Konieczny. m 8/11/2007 Kirsten Herndon Baer c 2. Dio Oklahoma Oklahoma City OK 2013-2014; S Jn's Epis Ch Tulsa OK 2011-2013. tbaer07@gmail.com

BAER, Walter Jacob (Eur) Convocation of Episcopal Churches in Europe, 23 avenue George V, Paris AS 75008 France **Archd Convoc of Epis Ch in Europe Paris 2017-** B Monroe WI 1954 s Walter & Helen. U of Karlsruhe DE 1975; BS U of Wisconsin 1979; MDiv Nash 1985; DMin Columbia TS 2011. D 3/30/1985 P 10/28/1985 Bp Roger John White. m 12/27/2012 Peter Thomas Neusser c 2. Team Mnstry Old Cath Ch of Austria 2016-2017; P-in-c S Mich's Epis Ch Mandeville LA 2014-2015; Pstr Deutscher Gottesdienst New Orleans LA 2013-2015; P-in-c The Ch Of The Annunc New Orleans LA 2012-2014; Int Headmaster S Mart's Epis Sch Metairie LA 2010-2012, Chapl 2008-2014; P-in-c Chap Of The H Comf New Orleans LA 2009-2012; P-in-c All SS Epis Ch New Orleans LA 2008-2009; R Gr Ch New Orleans LA 2003-2008; Hd of Dioc Sch for Mnstry Dio Wstrn Louisiana Alexandria LA 1996-2003, Cn to the Ordnry 1990-1995, GC Alt Dep 2003, GC Dep 2000, GC Dep 1994, GC Alt Dep 1991, COM 1989-2002, Ecum Cmsn 1987-2003; R S Thos' Ch Monroe LA 1996-2003; S Mk's Cathd Shreveport LA 1985-1990; Chapl S Mk's Cathd Day Sch Shreveport LA 1985-1987; D S Andr's Ch Milwaukee WI 1985; Int Pstr Old Cath Ch Vienna Austria 2016-2017; Jubilee Off Dio Louisiana New Orleans LA 2005-2015, Ecum Cmsn 2004-2015, Cmsn on Missions 2003-2008; Mayor's Human Relatns Cmsn City of New Orleans Louisiana 2004-2009.

ADLMC 1989-1996; CODE 1990-1996; Fllshp of St. Jn the Evang 2005; Soc of Cath Priests 2012. MDiv cl Nash 1985. archdeacon@tec-europe.org

BAETZ III, Bertrand Oliver (Tex) 7307 Quiet Glen Dr, Sugar Land TX 77479 **R S Mk's Epis Ch Richmond TX 2011-; Trst of the Camp Allen Bd Dio Texas Houston TX 2012-, Mem of the Liturg Cmsn 2010-2013, Mem and Chair of the Resolutns Com 2009-2013** B San Antonio TX 1979 s Bertrand & Marie Elizabeth. BA U of Texas 2001; MDiv Duke DS 2005; MDiv Duke DS 2005; Dip Theol Stud Epis TS of the SW 2008. D 6/28/2008 P 2/10/2009 Bp Don Adger Wimberly. m 12/22/2007 Sarah Bass Baetz c 2. Assoc R S Mk's Ch Austin TX 2008-2011; Chapl/Tchr S Andrews Epis Sch 2005-2008. Gathering of Leaders 2009.

BAGAY, Martin (At) all saints episcopal church, 1708 Watson boulevard, warner robins GA 31093 **Gr Epis Ch Pike Road AL 2016-** B Donora PA 1950 s Andrew & Anne. BA Duquesne U 1972; Pittsburgh TS 1974; MDiv EDS 1978; VTS 1986; Appreciative Inquiry Clergyleadership 2015. D 6/3/1978 Bp Robert Bracewell Appleyard P 12/4/1978 Bp John Harris Burt. m 4/13/1991 Katherine Elder c 3. Int R S Fran Indn Sprg Alabama 2015; Int R Gr Monroe Louisiana 2013-2015; R All SS Ch Warner Robins GA 2007-2012; Chr Ch Charlotte NC 2005-2006; R S Mk's Epis Ch Huntersville NC 2002-2005; R S Mary's Ch Sparta NJ 1998-2002; Off Of Bsh For ArmdF New York NY 1987-1990; Assoc Gr Epis Ch Sandusky OH 1982-1984; Chair Stds Min Assn Ch Living New Philadelphia 1981-1982; R Trin Ch New Phila OH 1980-1982; Assoc S Mart's Ch Chagrin Fall OH 1978-1980.

BAGBY, Durwood Ray (Tex) PO Box 510, Cameron TX 76520 **Vic All SS Ch Cameron TX 2009-** B Richmond VA 1941 s Thomas & Mary. BS USMA 1963; MBA U of So Carolina 1981; PhD U of So Carolina 1983. D 6/20/2009 Bp C Andrew Doyle P 1/22/2010 Bp Dena Arnall Harrison. m 7/16/1985 Janet Bagby c 1.

BAGBY, John Blythe (Ala) 3516 Country Club Road, Birmingham, AL 35213 **P-in-c Ch Of The Mssh Heflin AL 2010-, R 2010-** B Birmingham AL 1949 s Arthur & Anna. BA U of Alabama 1973; MDiv VTS 1990. D 6/14/1990 P 12/1/1990 Bp Robert Oran Miller. m 8/19/1972 Nancy Bagby c 2. Int H Comf Ch Gadsden AL 2008-2009; S Simon Ptr Ch Pell City AL 2005-2007; P-in-c St. Simon Ptr Pell City Al. 2005-2007; S Mk's Ch Prattville AL 2004-2005; Int St. Mk's Prattville Alabama 2004-2005; S Mths Epis Ch Tuscaloosa AL 2003-2004; Int St. Mths Tuscaloosa Alabama 2003-2004; Ch Of The Nativ Epis Huntsville AL 2002-2003; Int Asst Nativ Huntsville Alabama 2002-2003; R All SS Epis Ch Birmingham AL 1999-2002; R S Paul's Ch Selma AL 1994-1999; R Gr Ch Cullman AL 1991-1994; Asst St Thos Epis Ch Huntsville AL 1990-1991.

BAGGETT, Heather Kathleen (ND) 601 N 4th St, Bismarck ND 58501 B Winter Park FL 1985 d David & Sarah. BA Geo 2007; MDiv Brite DS 2011; MDiv Brite DS 2011; Dplma of Angl Stds Sem of the SW 2012. D 4/21/2012 P 10/27/2012 Bp C Wallis Ohl. m 4/13/2013 David Shaddix Baggett.

BAGLEY, Robert Chambers (Mil) 4701 Erie St, Racine WI 53402 B Washington DC 1943 s Francis & Betty. BS U of Maryland 1968; MS Stritch U 1983. D 6/5/2010 Bp Steven Andrew Miller. m 2/14/1993 Judith Bagley c 3.

BAGUER II, Miguel A (SeFla) 300 Sunrise Dr Apt 1b, Key Biscayne FL 33149 **D S Chris's By-The-Sea Epis Ch Key Biscayne FL 2004-** B Havana Cuba 1934 s Miguel & Gertrudis. BA U of Havana Cu 1955. D 11/6/2004 Bp Leo Frade. Trin Cathd Miami FL 2004-2008.

BAGUYOS, Avelino T (Kan) PO Box 40222, Overland Park KS 66204 B Rosario La Union PH 1938 s Gabriel & Rosenda. U of The Philippines 1964; BTh S Andrews TS Manila PH 1965; BA U of The Philippines 1972; MDiv S Andrews TS Manila PH 1973; ACPE S Lukes Hosp Houston TX 1980. D 10/19/1965 P 4/25/1966 Bp Benito C Cabanban. m 10/5/1967 Erlinda C Baguyos c 2. R S Chris's Epis Ch Wichita KS 2002-2006, Vic-R 1996-2000; LocTens 1993-1995; CPE Supvsr Veterans Affrs Med Cntr Dayton OH 2000-2001; Chf Chapl Serv/CPE Coordntr Veterans' Affrs/Reg Off Cntr Wichita KS 1993-2000; CPE Supvsr Veterans Affrs Med Cntr Atlants GA 1988-1993; Assoc Chapl/CPE Supvsr St Lk's Chap Kansas City MO 1978-1988; Asst S Barth's Ch Corpus Christi TX 1978; Stff Chapl/CPE Supvsr Memi Med Cntr Corpus Christi TX 1976-1978; P-in-c Dio Cntrl Philippines Queson City 1965-1977; Serv The Epis Ch In The Philippines 1965-1974. Assn of CPE 1976; Coll of Chapl 1985-1995; Comp Worker Sis of H Sprt 1978-1989.

BAGWELL BSG, Robert Randall McDonald (Mass) 401 E 60th St, Savannah GA 31405 **Assoc The Collgt Ch of St Paul the Apos Savannah GA 2010-** B Greenville SC 1958 s Robert & Carolyn. BA Furman U 1982; MDiv Duke DS 1985; Cert Nash 1987. D 8/14/1987 Bp William Louis Stevens P 10/18/1988 Bp William George Burrill. R Trin Epis Ch Stoughton MA 1998-2009; R S Anne of Gr Epis Ch Seminole FL 1993-1998; Int Gd Samar Epis Ch Clearwater FL 1992-1993; Cur All SS Ch Tarpon Spgs FL 1988-1992; All SS' Epis Ch Chevy Chase MD 1987-1988; Asst H Cross Faith Memi Epis Ch Pawleys Island SC 1987; S Cyp's Epis Ch Georgetown SC 1987. Assn Shrine Of Our Lady Of Walsingham 1995; Bro Of S Greg 2001; Conf Of Blessed Sacr 2010; Ord S Vinc 1998; Soc of S Jn The Evang, SocMary 1986.

BAHLOW, Harold (ETenn) 4026 Starview Lane, Evans GA 30809 B Windsor Ontario CA 1935 s Norman & Olive. BA Sacr Heart Sem 1958; STM S Johns Prov Sem 1962; MS Nova SE U 1983. Rec 2/5/1995 Bp Calvin Onderdonk Schofield Jr. m 10/15/1988 Arnetta Bahlow. R S Barth's Ch Mtn City TN 2000-2010; S Barth's Ch Nashville TN 2000-2010; S Columba's Epis Ch Bristol TN 2000-2010; S Mary Magd Ch Fayetteville TN 2000-2010; P-in-c S Mary the Vrgn Erwin TN 2000-2010; P S Thos Ch Elizabethton TN 2000-2010; Dio E Tennessee Knoxville TN 2000-2007; R S Jn's Epis Ch S Johns MI 1998-2000; Sunday Supply P Dio Cntrl Gulf Coast Pensacola FL 1997-1998; Serv RC Ch 1961-1972.

BAILEY, Abbott Abbott (Va) 423 1/2 S Laurel St., Richmond VA 23220 **R S Andr's Ch Richmond VA 2008-** B Clarksburg, WV 1969 d Gary & Martha. BA Eckerd Coll 1992; MPA GW 2000; MDiv Ya Berk 2006. D 6/18/2005 P 12/19/2005 Bp Peter J Lee. Assoc S Steph's Ch Richmond VA 2006-2008; D Par of St Paul's Ch Norwalk Norwalk CT 2005.

BAILEY, Anne Cox (Cal) 750 Adella Ave, Coronado CA 92118 **Trnr Positive Approach to Care Walnut Creek CA 2014-** B Glendale GA 1953 d Arthur & Elizabeth. BA Jn F Kennedy U 1997; MDiv CDSP 2001. D 6/3/2001 P 12/1/2001 Bp William Edwin Swing. m 8/31/1985 Henry Mayberry Bailey c 1. R S Lk's Ch Walnut Creek CA 2007-2017; Int R S Aug's Ch Oakland CA 2004-2005; Pstr Care Bd Mem Jn Muir Hosp Walnut Creek CA 2014-2017. Contributing Auth, "The Great Dance Of Life," *Mod Profiles Of An Ancient Faith*, Dio Of. California, 2001.

BAILEY, Audrey Veronica (NY) 777 E 222nd St, Bronx NY 10467 **S Fran Assisi And S Martha White Plains NY 2015-** B Jamaica 1957 Dip Min Stud The Untd Theol Coll in the W Indies 1993; BA U of the W Indies 1993. Trans 11/10/2010 as Priest Bp Mark Sean Sisk. Int Dio New York New York NY 2015-2016, 2014-2015; S Lk's Epis Ch Bronx NY 2010-2012.

BAILEY, B(Ertram) Cass (Va) 1118 Preston Ave, Charlottesville VA 22903 **Vic Trin Epis Ch Charlottesvlle VA 2010-** B New York NY 1960 s James & Lena. BA Amh 1982; Cert Ya Berk 1995; MDiv Yale DS 1995. D 6/3/1995 Bp Barbara Clementine Harris P 6/9/1996 Bp Alexander D Stewart. m 5/6/1995 Patricia V Polgar Bailey c 2. R S Chris's Ch Kailua HI 1998-2010; Asst Dio Wstrn Massachusetts Springfield 1997-1998; Asst R S Paul And S Jas New Haven CT 1996-1998; Dir Yth Theater Proj Trin Epis Ch Hartford CT 1995-1998.

BAILEY, Charles James (Lex) B 1926 D 6/14/1956 P 12/27/1956 Bp William R Moody.

BAILEY, Charles Leroy (Alb) 15 Richards Ave, Oneonta NY 13820 B Oneonta NY 1950 D 6/12/2004 Bp Daniel William Herzog. m 7/3/1976 Pauline Rose York c 2.

BAILEY, David Bruce (SO) 9097 Cascara Dr, West Chester OH 45069 B Cincinnati OH 1951 s Samuel & Virginia. BS Mia 1973; PhD U of So Carolina 1980; MDiv Untd TS Dayton OH 2001. D 6/24/2000 P 1/6/2001 Bp Herbert Thompson Jr. m 8/16/1986 Mary S Bailey c 2. R S Steph's Epis Ch Cincinnati OH 2003-2015; The Epis Ch Of The Ascen Middletown OH 2000-2002. Amer Chem Soc 1973; Soc of Ord Scientists 2010.

☖ BAILEY, The Rt Rev David Earle (NAM) PO Box 720, Farmington NM 87499 **Bp of Navajoland Area Mssn Farmington NM 2010-** B Canton OH 1940 s Frank & Evelyn. Glendale Cmnty Coll; DST Epis TS of the SW 1979; MDiv Epis TS of the SW 1991; BA Ottawa U 1991; DMin U of Creation Sprtlty Oakland CA 2001. D 6/24/1979 P 2/10/1980 Bp Joseph Thomas Heistand Con 8/7/2010 for NAM. m 5/20/1963 Anne Bailey c 3. Dio Utah Salt Lake City UT 2002-2006, GC Dep 2000-2009, Cn Mssnr/Deploy Off 1998-2001; P-in-c Gd Samar Scottsdale AZ 1989-1994; Chair Native Amer Mnstrs Com Dio Arizona Phoenix AZ 1988-1993, Co-Chair Camp/Conf Cntr 1988-1991, Cmsn On Campus Mnstry 1988-1990, T/F On Human Sxlty 1986-1989, Chair Action Com 1985-1991, Pres Epis Cmnty Serv 1985-1990, Fin Com 1984-1991, Exec Coun 1983-1991, Bd Trst Epis Cmnty Serv 1981-1990, Dn Jr High Camp 1979-1992, Bp's Dep to C-14 1989-1993, Bp's Dep to C-14 1986-1988, 1984-1985, Sprtl Dir Curs 1981-1983, Chair Cmsn On Alcosm & Drug Abuse 1979-1980; Vic Resurr Mssn Scottsdale AZ 1981-1983; S Steph's Ch Phoenix AZ 1979-1998. ecndbailey@gmail.com

BAILEY III, Douglass Moxley (NC) B Clarksburg WV 1938 BA Wake Forest U. D 6/11/1964 P 12/1/1964 Bp Wilburn Camrock Campbell. m 1/18/1961 Carolyn Bailey. Calv Ch Lombard IL 2000-2003; Calv Ch Memphis TN 1978-2002; S Jn's Par Hagerstown MD 1972-1978. Auth, "Little Scraps Of Wonder"; Auth, "From Ashes To Alleluia". DD VTS.

BAILEY, Edwin Pearson (NC) Po Box 2001, Southern Pines NC 28388 **Died 10/4/2016** B Aldie VA 1928 s William & Mary. BA U of Virginia 1950; MDiv VTS 1955; Fell VTS 1977; Coll of Preachers 1979; Tchr Skills Inst 1982; Sm Ch Ldrshp Conf 1999. D 6/3/1955 Bp Frederick D Goodwin P 6/16/1956 Bp Robert Fisher Gibson Jr. c 3. Ch Of The Ascen At Fork Advance NC 1988-2000; Vic Ch Of The Gd Shpd Cooleemee NC 1988-2000; CFS The Sch At Ch Farm Exton PA 1986-1988; Chapl Ch Farm Sch Paoli PA 1986-1988; R S Jn's Ch Winnsboro SC 1984-1986; R S Paul's Epis Ch Smithfield NC 1980-1983; Vic Great Falls Epis Ch Great Falls VA 1975-1980; S Fran Epis Ch Great Falls VA 1975-1980; Asst S Jn's Epis Ch Mc Lean VA 1975-1980; R S

Geo's Ch Newport RI 1965-1975; Chapl Virginians NYC 1961-1966; Chr Ch Greenwich CT 1959-1965; Asst Min S Barn Epis Ch Greenwich CT 1959-1965; R St Johns Ch W Hartford CT 1956-1959; S Jn's Ch Warsaw VA 1956-1957; D-in-c S Jn's Ch Warsaw VA 1955-1956; Cmsn on Evang Dio Rhode Island Providence RI 1972-1975. No Carolina Epis Cler Assn 1980-1983; No Carolina Epis Cler Assn 1988.

BAILEY, Frank Hudson (Md) 7474 Washington Blvd, Elkridge MD 21075 B Winchester KY 1944 s Frank & Gladys. BA U of Kentucky Coll of Arts & Sci 1966; JD U of Kentucky Coll of Law 1968. D 9/10/2015 Bp Eugene Taylor Sutton. m 9/12/1992 Denise Ann Vesuvio c 1.

BAILEY, Gregory Bruce (Alb) Trinity Episcopal Church, 30 Park St, Gouverneur NY 13642 **D Vic Trin Ch Gouverneur NY 2007-** B Gouverneur NY 1952 s Bruce & Verda. D 6/10/2006 Bp Daniel William Herzog. m 3/22/1974 Trudy Jean Bailey c 2.

BAILEY, Jefferson Moore (Az) PO Box 492, Tucson AZ 85702 **D S Andr's Epis Ch Tucson AZ 2006-** B Schenectady NY 1944 s Claude & Martha. BA U of So Carolina 1967. D 10/14/2006 Bp Kirk Stevan Smith. m 5/2/2007 Richard Steen c 1.

BAILEY, Lydia Collins (O) 21000 Lake Shore Blvd, Euclid OH 44123 B Erie PA 1956 d William & Constance. BA Reed Coll 1979; graduated Sch for Diac Formation 2013. D 6/1/2013 Bp Mark Hollingsworth Jr. m 7/2/1989 Thomas Bailey c 2.

BAILEY, Marjean (NH) 21 Kings Ln, Kennebunkport ME 04046 B Pittsburgh PA 1929 d Peter & Emily. Cert Perceptual Lrng Consult; Cert Psychosynthesis Ther; BA Alleg 1951; MDiv UTS 1954. D 5/9/1981 P 5/1/1982 Bp H Coleman Mcgehee Jr. m 5/22/1954 John Amadee Bailey. Dioc Coun Dio New Hampshire Concord NH 1989-1993, Chair Educ Com 1986-1990, COM 1989-2000, 1986-1993; Vic S Ptr's Epis Ch Londonderry NH 1987-2001; Assoc Par Of Chr Ch Andover MA 1982-1986; S Andr's Epis Ch Flint MI 1982, Cur 1981-1982. Cert Perceptual Lrng Consult; Cert Psychosynthesis Ther. Cert Psychosynthesis Ther.

BAILEY, Max (Colo) 1303 S Bross Ln, Longmont CO 80501 **R S Steph's Ch Longmont CO 1990-** B Bakersfield CA 1953 s Ralph & Minnie. BA U CO 1981; MDiv SWTS 1984. D 6/16/1984 Bp William Carl Frey P 12/21/1984 Bp William Harvey Wolfrum. m 5/29/2010 Anne Kranidas c 4. Asst Ch Of S Mich The Archangel Colorado Spg CO 1987-1990; Dioc Counc Epis Ch Of The Trsfg Vail CO 1986-1987; Vic Gr Ch Buena Vista CO 1984-1986; Vic S Geo Epis Mssn Leadville CO 1984-1986; Dio Colorado Denver CO 1986-1993. Fell AAPC 1989. rector@ststephenslongmont.org

BAILEY, Noel (RI) St Luke's Episcopal Church, 99 Pierce St, East Greenwich RI 02818 **Asst S Lk's Epis Ch E Greenwich RI 2013-; Mem, Dioc Coun Dio Rhode Island Providence RI 2015-; Mem, Bd Dir, Epis Chars Dio Rhode Island 2015-** B Providence RI 1941 d Sumner & Elizabeth. Rhode Island Sch of Design 1963; MDiv EDS 1986; Cert Ldrshp Acad for New Directions 1995; Berkshire Cmnty Coll 2004; Cler Ldrshp Inst; Appreciative Inquiry 2008; Cler Ldrshp Inst; Mng Change 2008. D 6/11/1988 Bp David Elliot Johnson P 5/26/1989 Bp George Nelson Hunt III. c 2. Vic Ch Of The Epiph Lisbon Lisbon NH 2011-2012; Int All SS Epis Ch Littleton NH 2007-2008; P-in-c The Chap Of All SS Leominster MA 2005-2007; Int S Paul's Ch Lancaster NH 2000-2013; R S Geo's Ch Lee MA 1997-2007; Chapl Hospice Care 1996-1997; P-in-c Trin And S Michaels Ch Middleville NY 1991-1997; Asst S Mich's Ch Bristol RI 1988-1990; Mem, Conv Bus Com Dio New Hampshire Concord NH 2011-2012, Mem, Dioc Advance Fund 2010-2011, Mem, Cler Dvlpmt Comittee 2009-2011; Mem, Stndg Com Dio Wstrn Massachusetts Springfield 2001-2007, Mem, Cathd Chapt 2000-2003, Mem, Sprtl Formation Team 1998-2004; Mem, Dioc Coun Dio Albany Greenwich NY 1993-1997. FVC 1991.

BAILEY, Patricia Ann (RI) 1357 Wampanoag Trl, Apt 130, Riverside RI 02915 **Died 7/21/2016** B Cleveland OH 1929 d William & Thelma. OH SU; BA Case Wstrn Reserve U 1951; MLS U of Rhode Island 1972. D 6/24/1995 Bp J Clark Grew II. c 2. S Alb's Ch N Providence RI 2002-2016; D S Thos Ch Greenville RI 1999-2001; D Ch Of The Mssh Providence RI 1995-1999.

BAILEY, Pauline Rose (Alb) 15 Richards Ave, Oneonta NY 13820 B Oneonta NY 1955 D 6/12/2004 Bp Daniel William Herzog. m 7/3/1976 Charles Leroy Bailey c 2.

BAILEY, Paul Milton (La) Po Box 1086, Hammond LA 70404 **R Gr Memi Hammond LA 1999-** B Fort Worth TX 1954 s George & Stella. Cert Wine Profsnl Cert Culinary Inst of Amer; BFA SW U Georgetown TX 1975; MA U of Kansas 1976; U of Texas 1983; MDiv Epis TS of the SW 1985; Cert Shalem Inst of Sprtl Formation Washington DC 1990; Cert Shalem Inst of Sprtl Formation Washington DC 2001. D 6/13/1993 P 12/12/1993 Bp James Barrow Brown. m 9/2/1990 Laura Bailey. R St. Matt's Epis Ch Madison AL 1995-1999; Chr Ch Covington LA 1993-1995; Chapl Chr Epis Sch Covington LA 1991-1995. AAPC; Soc of S Jn the Evang, Fllshp 1986; Sprtl Dir Intl . BFA mcl SW U 1975.

BAILEY, Ricardo Z (At) 2744 Peachtree Rd NW, Atlanta GA 30305 **H Innoc' Epis Sch Atlanta GA 2016-; Vic Dio Atlanta Atlanta GA 2015-** B Atlanta GA 1973 s Harrision & Elizabeth. BA Xavier U of Louisiana 1997; STB

and MDiv S Mary's Sem and U 2003. Rec 11/7/2013 Bp Robert Christopher Wright. m 9/10/2011 Marica Bailey. Cathd Of S Phil Atlanta GA 2013-2015. rbailey@stphilipscathedral.org

BAILEY SR, Robert Jerome (RG) 1505 Knudsen Ave, Farmington NM 87401 **Died 5/31/2017** B Portland OR 1931 s Clayton & Naomi. BD Colegio Franco Espanol 1948; MD Universidad Nacion/Autonoma de Mex 1958; Dip Dioc Sch for Mnstry 2005. D 10/21/2006 P 10/21/2007 Bp Jeffrey Neil Steenson. m 7/15/1977 Rhonda Bailey c 3. Assoc St Johns Epis Ch Farmington NM 2007-2017; PHS Indn Hlth Serv 1994-2002; Captain, Med Corps US Navy US Navy 1964-1994. St Lk's Soc 2002.

BAILEY, Sarah E (WVa) 401 S Washington St, Berkeley Springs WV 25411 B Pittsburgh PA 1942 d John & Phyllis. RN S Marg Hosp Sch of Nrsng Pittsburgh PA 1963; BA Antioch Coll 1989; Untd TS Dayton OH 1992; MDiv SWTS 1993. D 6/26/1993 P 5/14/1994 Bp Herbert Thompson Jr. c 2. R S Mk's Epis Ch Berkeley Spg WV 2000-2003; Assoc Calv Ch Columbia MO 1995-2000; Chapl Cbury Crt Ret Facility W Carrollton OH 1993-1995; Chr Epis Ch Dayton OH 1993-1995. Cler Ldrshp Proj Viii; ECW; Natl Epis Aids Cltn; Natl Ntwk Epis Cler Assn.

BAILEY III, Theodore Harbour (SVa) 133 Leon Dr, Williamsburg VA 23188 **Ret 1989-** B Baltimore MD 1922 s Theodore & Florence. BA W&M 1947; MDiv Ya Berk 1958; VTS 1977; DMin UTS Richmond 1985. D 6/17/1958 P 12/23/1958 Bp Noble C Powell. c 2. Int Chr Epis Ch Smithfield VA 2000-2002; Int S Jn's Ch Portsmouth VA 1998-1999; Int S Barn Epis Ch No Chesterfield VA 1995-1997; Int S Thos Epis Ch Chesapeake VA 1994-1995; Int S Jn's Ch Hopewell VA 1993; Int Ch Of The Gd Shpd Norfolk VA 1992-1993; Int S Mk's Ch Hampton VA 1991-1992; Int S Anne's Ch Appomattox VA 1990-1991; R S Jn's Epis Ch Richmond VA 1975-1988; Asst Cathd Of The Incarn Baltimore MD 1973-1975; R S Jn's Ch Mt Washington Baltimore MD 1966-1973; S Ptr's Epis Ch Ellicott City MD 1958-1966; Vic St. Ptr's Ch Middleham Chap Solomons 1958-1966. ASSP.

BAILEY FISCHER, Valerie Dianne (Nwk) 283 Herrick Avenue, Teaneck NJ 07666 **Dio New York New York NY 2016-** B Philadelphia, PA 1965 d John & Doretha. BA Penn 1988; MDiv UTS 2004; STM Bos 2009. D 6/2/2007 P 1/12/2008 Bp M(Arvil) Thomas Shaw. m 4/1/2000 Robert P Fischer c 1. Hse Of Pryr Epis Ch Newark NJ 2014-2015; R S Mk's Ch Teaneck NJ 2011-2014; Asst S Eliz's Ch Sudbury MA 2009-2011; All SS Par Brookline MA 2008-2009; YA Min All SS Brookline MA 2008; Asst Ch Of The H Sprt Wayland MA 2007-2008; Chapl Framingham St The Dio Massachusetts 2007-2008.

BAILLARGEON JR, Henri Albert (SVa) 4604 Sewaha St, Tampa FL 33617 B Fall River MA 1952 AS Lake City Cmnty Coll 1978; Florida Sthrn Coll 1988; BA U of So Florida 1991; MDiv VTS 1994. D 6/25/1994 P 1/14/1995 Bp Rogers Sanders Harris. c 2. R Gd Samar Epis Ch Virginia Bch VA 2000-2007; P S Paul's Ch Vanceboro NC 1998-1999; S Christophers Ch Elizabethtown NC 1994-1996.

BAIN, Robert Walker (WMass) 1673 Huasna Dr, San Luis Obispo CA 93405 **Ret 1996-** B Framingham MA 1924 s George & Estelle. Coll of Pathology; MD Bos 1952; Mallory Inst of Pathology 1968. D 6/23/1962 Bp Walter H Gray P 5/1/1977 Bp Alexander D Stewart. m 8/18/1955 Beverly Jean Wright. Assoc S Matt's Ch Worcester MA 1988-1996; Vic S Andr's Ch No Grafton MA 1986-1988; S Steph's Ch Westborough MA 1970-1986. CBS; Fvc; GAS; OHC 1962.

BAIRD, Carolyn Mroczkowski (Cal) 1026 Springhouse Dr, Ambler PA 19002 B Raleigh NC 1953 d Charles & Zita. AAS Brookdale Cmnty Coll 1985; BS W Chester U of Pennsylvania 1990; MDiv CDSP 1997. D 11/20/1999 P 6/3/2000 Bp William Edwin Swing. m 8/21/1976 Robert Charlton Baird c 1. Pstr Care S Greg Of Nyssa Ch San Francisco CA 1999-2006.

BAIRD, Gary Clifton (Ark) 617 Tahleguah, Siloan Springs AR 72761 B McLeansboro IL 1950 s James & Helen. D 10/28/2000 Bp Larry Maze. m 5/27/1972 Sally Ann Smith c 2. D Gr Ch Siloam Sprg AR 2000-2005.

BAIRD, Joseph Paul (Pgh) St. Peter's Episcopal Church, 36 W Campbell St, Blairsville PA 15717 B Pittsburgh PA 1950 s John & Margaret. BS Alfred U. D 6/4/2016 P 1/22/2017 Bp Dorsey McConnell. m 5/9/2009 Kathleen Anne Perras c 3.

BAIRD, Kathryn Jo Anne (Az) 4442 E Bermuda St, Tucson AZ 85712 B Cedar Rapids IA 1957 d Robert & Mavis. MS San Diego St U 1987; PhD U of Arizona 2005; MDiv CDSP 2010. D 6/6/2009 P 12/4/2010 Bp Kirk Stevan Smith. Assoc Gr St Pauls Epis Ch Tucson AZ 2011, Assoc 2011-.

BAIRD, Stephen Earl (Colo) PO Box 1000, Vail CO 81658 B Richmond IN 1943 s Robert & Dorothy. D 11/20/2010 Bp Robert John O'Neill. m 1/2/1965 Karen Baird c 3.

BAKAL, Pamela (Nwk) 200 Highfield Ln, Nutley NJ 07110 **R Gr Ch Nutley NJ 1997-** B Philadelphia PA 1951 d Donald & Louise. Bennington Coll 1971; BA CUNY 1973; UTS 1990; MDiv GTS 1992. D 6/13/1992 P 3/1/1993 Bp Orris George Walker Jr. m 2/8/1981 Stuart Bakal c 3. Gr Ch Brooklyn NY 1992-1997.

BAKELY, Catherine Mae (SVa) P.O. Box 186, Oak Hall VA 23416 B Baltimore MD 1939 d Albert & Ruth. Dioc Sch for Mnstry 2008. D 11/16/2008 Bp John Clark Buchanan. m 9/23/1961 Ronald Herbert Bakely c 3.

BAKER, Andrea (NCal) 2620 Capitol Ave, Sacramento CA 95816 B Ft Belvoir VA 1962 d Eugene & Claire. BS USMA 1984; MA U of Hawaii 1996; MDiv CDSP 2010. D 6/12/2010 P 12/18/2010 Bp Barry Leigh Beisner. m 5/24/1984 Brian Neal Baker c 2. Asst Faith Epis Ch Carmeron Pk CA 2015-2016, 2013-2014; Epiph Epis Ch Vacaville CA 2011-2012; Assoc P Trin Epis Cathd Sacramento CA 2010-2012; S Thos Epis Ch Sun Vlly ID 2000-2006. andrea@faithec.org

BAKER, Brian Neal (NCal) 1160 Los Molinos Way, Sacramento CA 95864 **Dn Trin Epis Cathd Sacramento CA 2006-** B Del Rio TX 1961 s George & Ruth. BS USMA 1983; MDiv VTS 1991; DMin SWTS 1999. D 6/29/1991 P 12/28/1991 Bp Donald Purple Hart. m 5/24/1984 Andrea Allen c 2. R S Thos Epis Ch Sun Vlly ID 1998-2006; Cn Pstr S Mich's Cathd Boise ID 1994-1998; Cur Ch Of The H Nativ Honolulu HI 1991-1994; Chapl H Nativ Sch Honolulu HI 1991-1994. tvrbaker@trinitycathedral.org

BAKER, Brock (Alb) PO Box 1374, Lake Placid NY 12946 B New York NY 1947 s Alfred & Priscilla. AB Harv 1970; BTh Wycliffe Hall 2008. D 5/31/2008 P 12/13/2008 Bp William Howard Love. m 9/26/1987 Elizabeth H Baker c 2. R S Eustace Ch Lake Placid NY 2008-2011.

BAKER, Bruce D'Aubert (Be) St Mary's Episcopal Church, 100 W Windsor St, Reading PA 19601 **P-in-c S Mary's Epis Ch Reading PA 2012-** B New Orleans LA 1941 s William & Suzanne. B.A. Baylor U 1963; BA Baylor U 1963; M.A. Loyola Marymount U 1975; MA Loyola Marymount U 1975; M.A.P.S. Washington Theol Un 1999; MA Washington Theol Un 1999. Rec 6/10/2008 Bp Paul Victor Marshall. m 8/18/2007 Susan Bowers Baker c 8. Regular Supply P No Par 2010-2012; Assoc P S Alb's Epis Ch Reading PA 2008-2012; Chapl Dir Berks Heim Nrsng & Rehab Hosp Leesport PA 2008-2011. Auth, "Praying to Hear From You in Your Word," *Share The Word*, Paulist Natl Cath Evangelization Assn, 2004.

BAKER, Carenda D (CPa) 206 E Burd St, Shippensburg PA 17257 **Trin Epis Ch Chambersburg PA 2015-** B Carlisle PA 1959 d Theodore & Darlene. B.A Sci Elizabethtown Coll 1982; M.A Div The TS of Drew U 1989; M.A Soc Wk U Pgh 1994; DAS Sewanee: The U So, TS 2014; DAS The TS-Sewanee 2014; DAS The TS at The U So 2014. D 8/23/2014 P 7/11/2015 Bp Robert R Gepert. rector.trinitychambersburg@gmail.com

BAKER JR, Charles Mulford (Ct) PO Box 296, Gales Ferry CT 06335 B Wilmington DE 1944 s Charles & Lillian. BA U of Delaware 1970; MDiv VTS 1987. D 6/11/1987 Bp George Edward Haynsworth P 6/19/1988 Bp Christopher FitzSimons Allison. c 2. R S Dav's Ch Gales Ferry CT 2000-2010; P-in-c S Marys Epis Ch Goose Creek SC 1988-2000; Epis Ch of the Gd Shpd Charleston SC 1987-1988.

BAKER, Clarence Dawson (Ark) 692 Poplar Ave, Memphis TN 38105 **R S Lk's Ch Hot Sprg AR 2006-** B San Diego CA 1945 s Calvin & Pauline. BD U of Memphis 1988; MS U of Memphis 1990; MDiv VTS 1994. D 6/22/1994 Bp Alex Dockery Dickson P 1/26/1995 Bp James Malone Coleman. m 7/29/2007 Mary Baker c 4. S Mary's Cathd Memphis TN 1994-2006. Ord Of H Cross.

BAKER, Douglas Macintyre (NJ) B 1958 Trans 1/31/1994 Bp George Phelps Mellick Belshaw. m 6/20/1987 Joan Burke. Epis Ch Of The Epiph Ventnor City NJ 1994-1996.

BAKER, Frank Danforth (Mass) 7 Sturtevant St, Waterville ME 04901 **Died 4/5/2017** B Woburn MA 1922 s John & May. UTS; AA Bos 1948; BS Bos 1950. D 6/13/1959 P 6/24/1960 Bp Robert McConnell Hatch. c 9. Ret 1988-2017; R Emm Ch Boston MA 1966-1987; Emm Ch W Roxbury MA 1966-1987; R S Lk's Ch Hudson MA 1961-1966; Asst S Mich's-On-The-Heights Worcester MA 1959-1961.

BAKER, J Jeffrey (O) 160 Keagler Dr, Steubenville OH 43953 **R Chr Epis Ch Warren OH 2011-; ECS Chairman Dio Ohio Cleveland 2009-, Cmsn on Global and Dom Mssn 2008-** B Bloomington IN 1965 s James & Lyn. Van 1985; BA Baldwin-Wallace Coll 1988; MDiv Bex Sem 2007. D 6/9/2007 Bp Mark Hollingsworth Jr P 12/15/2007 Bp David Charles Bowman. m 7/14/1990 Kristin M Baker c 2. S Steph's Epis Ch Steubenville OH 2007-2011; Sexton Gr Epis Ch 2003-2006.

BAKER, Johanna M (NwPa) 62 Pickering St., Brookville PA 15825 **All SS Ch Phoenix AZ 2016-** B Brookville PA 1980 d Dennis & Nancy. BA Thiel Coll 2003; Dip Ang Stud Ya Berk 2008; MDiv Yale DS 2008. D 11/1/2008 P 5/30/2009 Bp Sean Walter Rowe. m 1/3/2004 Shawn Baker c 1. Assoc Trin Epis Ch New Castle PA 2011-2014; D Ch Of The H Trin Brookville PA 2008-2011.

BAKER, John (Va) 8531 Riverside Rd, Alexandria VA 22308 **R S Aid's Ch Alexandria VA 1999-** B San Diego CA 1953 s Samuel & Marjorie. BA U of Memphis 1992; MDiv VTS 1995. D 6/3/1995 P 6/1/1996 Bp James Malone Coleman. m 10/24/1980 Mary F Baker c 1. Gr - S Lk's Ch Memphis TN 1995-1999.

BAKER JR, John Thurlow (Cal) 2055 Northshore Rd, Bellingham WA 98226 B Kauai HI 1941 s John & Jane. BA Willamette U 1963; MDiv VTS 1966; MS San Francisco St U 1971; EdD Nova SE U 1980. D 6/29/1966 P 6/1/1967 Bp Clarence Rupert Haden Jr. m 2/5/1966 Victoria Coralee DeMarco c 3. Assoc S Steph's Ch Gilroy CA 2003-2006; Assoc S Eliz's Epis Ch San Diego CA 1995-2001; Non-par 1990-1995; Assoc S Jas Ch Fremont CA 1969-1990; Asst S Paul's Epis Ch Burlingame CA 1968-1969; Cur S Jn's Epis Ch Marysville CA 1966-1968; VP, Stdt Serv Ciitrus Coll Glendora California 2011-2012; VP, Stdt Serv El Camino Coll Torrence California 2007-2008; VP, Stdt Serv Gavilan Coll Gilroy California 2001-2004; VP, Stdt Serv San Diego Mesa Coll San Diego California 1997-2001; VP, Stdt Serv Alameda Coll Alameda California 1991-1994; Counslg Fac Ohlone Coll Fremont California 1971-1991; VP, Stdt Serv Diablo Vlly Coll Pleasant Hill Calfiornia 1920-2011.

BAKER, Josephine Louise Redenius (Pa) Po Box 429, Wayne PA 19087 B Oceanville NJ 1920 d Jacob & Josephine. BA Amer U 1962; MA Amer U 1963; Indstrl Coll of The ArmdF 1964; LHD Tem 1964; MS S Chas Borromeo 1981; MDiv Estrn Bapt TS 1984; DMin ETSBH 1990. D 11/27/1987 Bp Calvin Onderdonk Schofield Jr. m Milton Grafly Baker. D All SS Ch Norristown PA 1993-1997; Bd On Morals And Ethics Miami Heart Inst 1991-1993; Chapl Miami Heart Inst 1988-1993; D All Souls' Epis Ch Miami Bch FL 1987-1993; Pres/D S Corn The Centurion Chap Vlly Forge PA 1976; Comp Dio Com Dio SE Florida Miami 1991-1993. Auth, "Mltry Security In Relation To Freedom Of Press"; Auth, "Permanent Diac Serving The Aging In The Dio SE Florida". Dok; Soc Of S Fran. Distinguished Alum Amer U 1969; Legion Of Merit 1967.

BAKER, Joseph Scott (SVa) St. Stephen's Episcopal Church, 372 Hiden Blvd., Newport News VA 23606 **R S Steph's Ch Newport News VA 2005-** B Greensboro NC 1967 s James & Carolyn. BS Wstrn Carolina U 1990; MDiv Sewanee: The U So, TS 2000. D 9/23/2000 P 5/18/2001 Bp Dorsey Henderson. m 1/25/1992 Sheryl W Baker c 1. S Andr's Ch Ayer MA 2002-2005; D Gr Epis Ch Anderson SC 2000-2002.

BAKER, Joseph Stannard (Vt) 2 Cherry St., Burlington VT 05401 **D Cathd Ch Of S Paul Burlington VT 2010-** B Manhattan KS 1946 s Clarence & Hermione. BA Swarthmore Coll 1968; MA Lesley U 1988. D 1/6/2009 Bp Thomas C Ely. m 8/13/2000 Peter Harrigan.

BAKER, K. Drew (SwVa) 2411 Shiraz Lane, Charleston SC 29414 **Ch Of The Epiph Danville VA 2013-** B Falls Church VA 1965 s K D & Mary. BS Hampden-Sydney Coll 1986; MD Med Coll of Virginia 1990; MDiv Candler TS Emory U 2001. D 5/31/2003 P 12/13/2003 Bp Bob Johnson. Asst S Steph's Epis Ch Charleston SC 2008-2012; The Tazewell Cnty Cluster Of Epis Parishes Tazewell VA 2006-2008; S Matt's Epis Ch Spartanburg SC 2004-2006; Gr Ch Morganton NC 2003-2004.

BAKER, Kim Turner (WA) St. Peter and St. Paul, Mt. St. Albans, Washington DC 20016 B Des Moines IA 1956 d Edward & Billye. BA U MI 1978; JD Case Wstrn Reserve U 1983; MDiv Epis TS of the SW 2002. D 6/26/2002 Bp Robert Boyd Hibbs P 2/28/2003 Bp James Edward Folts. m 8/20/1979 Jeffrey Jay Baker c 3. S Jn's Par Hagerstown MD 2015-2016; Cn Pstr Cathd of St Ptr & St Paul Washington DC 2013-2015; Washington Epis Sch Beth MD 2008-2013; R S Ptr's Ch Westfield NY 2004-2008; S Thos Epis Ch And Sch San Antonio TX 2002-2003.

BAKER, Mark James (At) 126 wild horse cove circle, cleveland GA 30528 B Alexandria VA 1947 s Harry & Jane. BA New Engl Conservatory of Mus 1969; MDiv EDS 1979. D 6/9/1979 Bp John Bowen Coburn P 12/1/1979 Bp Morris Fairchild Arnold. m 6/9/2007 Jennifer Ruth Inglis c 2. Int Ch Of The Gd Shpd New York NY 2003-2004; Dio Atlanta Atlanta GA 2003; Vic Ch Of The H Comf Atlanta GA 1995-2002; S Lk's Epis Ch Atlanta GA 1994-1995, 1993-1994; Non-par 1984-1992; Assoc Gr Epis Ch Lawr MA 1979-1982.

BAKER, Mathew Scott (Alb) PO Box 183, Greenwich NY 12834 B Glens Falls NY 1965 s Ronald & Avril. AA Hudson Vlly 1989; BS SUNY - Cortland 1991; MM Nash 2013. D 6/1/2013 P 12/7/2013 Bp William Howard Love. m 12/14/1994 Brandii A Baker c 3. Dio Albany Greenwich NY 2013-2016, 1993-2000.

BAKER, M Clark (Tenn) 780 Laurel Branch Trl, Sewanee TN 37375 B Macon GA 1933 s Emmett & Martha. BS U So 1955; LTh GTS 1958. D 6/22/1958 Bp John Vander Horst P 6/25/1959 Bp Theodore N Barth. m 5/29/1982 Rowan Elaine Elrod. P S Matt's Epis Ch Mcminnville TN 2008-2010, Stated Supply 2008-2010; Ch Of The H Comf Monteagle TN 1998-2002, Vic 1995-2002, P-in-c 1961-1963; Dir Mid-Cumberland Mtn Mnstry 1995-2002; S Bern's Ch Sewanee TN 1995-2002, Vic 1995-2002; Vic S Bede's Epis Ch Manchester TN 1989-1994; Vic S Andr's Epis Ch New Johnsonville TN 1983-1987; P Gr Epis Ch Sprg Hill TN 1980-1983; P-in-c S Mary Magd Ch Fayetteville TN 1978-1979; S Phil Ch Memphis TN 1977-1978; P Bp Otey Memi Ch Memphis TN 1977; P-in-c Emm Ch Memphis TN 1972-1977; P-in-c S Paul's Ch Mason TN 1970-1971; P-in-c Trin Ch Mason TN 1968-1971; P-in-c Chr Ch Brownsville TN 1967-1968; Cur Chr Ch Memphis TN 1966; R Thankful Memi Ch Chattanooga TN 1963-1966; P-in-c St Jas Epis Ch Sewanee TN 1961-1963; S Jas Epis Ch Un City TN 1958-1961; P-in-c S Jn's Ch Mart TN 1958-1961; Stndg Committe Mem Dio Tennessee Nashville TN 1989-1993.

BAKER, Milledge Leonard (CGC) 699 S Hwy 95A, Cantonment FL 32533 B Walnut Hill FL 1942 s Marion & Ruby. DMin Logos Grad Sch 2002. D 11/23/2008 P 6/20/2009 Bp Philip Menzie Duncan II. m 9/23/1970 Barbara Baker c 1. P-in-c S Monica's Cantonment FL 2010-2012.

BAKER, Patricia Thomas (Oly) PO Box 369, Snoqualmie WA 98065 **Vic S Clare of Assisi Epis Ch Snoqualmie WA 2004-; Dioc Disaster Coordntr Epis Relief & Dvlpmt 2014-** B Eugene OR 1954 d Donn & Mary. BS OR SU 1976; MDiv Seattle U 1999. D 6/28/2003 Bp Vincent Waydell Warner P 1/17/2004 Bp Sanford Zangwill Kaye Hampton. m 7/10/1976 Loren A Baker c 2. D S Steph's Epis Ch Seattle WA 2003-2004; Dioc Rep. Cathd Vstry S Mk's Cathd Seattle WA 2009-2011. revpattyb@stclares.church

BAKER, Paul Edgar (Alb) 4 St Lukes Pl, Cambridge NY 12816 B Tarrytown NY 1936 s Francis & Grace. AAS SUNY 1957; BA SUNY 1960; MA SUNY 1961; MDiv GTS 1982. D 6/19/1982 P 12/1/1982 Bp Wilbur Emory Hogg Jr. c 3. R S Lk's Ch Cambridge NY 1982-2006.

BAKER, Powell E (Dal) 14500 Marsh Lane, Apt. 176, Addison TX 75001 B Harlingen TX 1934 s Powell & Velma. BA SW U Georgetown TX 1956; MDiv Epis TS of the SW 1959; MSSW U of Texas 1973. Trans 5/2/1966 Bp Scott Field Bailey. c 1. Psych Crosspoint Counslg Cntr 1986-1998; Psych. Soc Worker Terrell St Hosp Terrell TX 1976-1986; Mar And Fam Counslr Fam Clnc Garland TX 1973-1976; Crisis Counsellor Epis Cmnty Serv Dallas TX 1969-1971; Asst S Lk's Epis Ch Dallas TX 1969-1971; Chapl S Jude Hse Dallas TX 1968-1973; Asst Chr Epis Ch Dallas TX 1965-1969; Vic H Trin Carrizo Sprg TX 1959-1962; S Tim's Ch Cotulla TX 1959-1962. Acad Cert Soc Workers 1973; C. G. Jung Soc of No Texas 1977.

BAKER, Rhonda (Va) Po Box 59, Goochland VA 23063 B Lynchburg VA 1950 d Mervyn & Rhoda. BD U IL 1987; MDiv SWTS 1995. D 6/17/1995 P 12/1/1995 Bp Frank Tracy Griswold III. m 6/29/1972 Robert S Baker. R Gr Epis Ch Goochland VA 2001-2016; Ch Of The H Comm Maywood IL 1996-2001; Assoc One In Chr Ch Prospect Heights IL 1995-1997. Tertiary Of The Soc Of S Fran.

BAKER, Richard Henry (Mo) 3139 Barrett Station Rd, Saint Louis MO 63122 **Non-par 1993-** B Detroit MI 1937 s Henry & Josephine. BA Carleton Coll 1959; MA U of Missouri 1961; MDiv EDS 1964; PhD S Louis U 1980. D 6/21/1964 P 12/1/1964 Bp George Leslie Cadigan. m 8/5/1961 Sandra Kaye Baker c 3. Ch Of The Gd Shpd S Louis MO 2005-2006, LocTen 1978-2004; LocTen Ch Of The H Comm S Louis MO 2001-2002; LocTen S Mart's Ch Ellisville MO 1999-2000; LocTen Ch Of The Trsfg Lake S Louis MO 1995-1996; Cn/Subdean Chr Ch Cathd S Louis MO 1988-1992, LocTen 1986-1987; Spnsr Yth Grp 1967-1985; LocTen S Steph's Ch S Louis MO 1985; LocTen S Matt's Epis Ch Warson Woods Kirkwood MO 1984; LocTen S Ptr's Epis Ch S Louis MO 1980-1983; Int S Mich & S Geo S Louis MO 1977-1978; LocTen S Lk's Epis Ch Manchester MO 1975-1977; R S Augustines Ch S Louis MO 1968-1971; S Judes Ch Monroe City MO 1964-1967; R S Paul's Ch Palmyra MO 1964-1967.

BAKER, Robert (SwFla) 906 S Orleans Ave, Tampa FL 33606 **Cur St Johns Epis Ch Tampa FL 2014-** B Tuscola FL 1962 s Richard & Nancy. Angl Stds Nash; ThM PrTS 2002; ThM PrTS 2002; PhD Baylor U 2004; PhD Baylor U 2004; Angl Stds Nash 2014. D 6/29/2014 P 1/4/2015 Bp Dabney Tyler Smith. m 9/5/2008 Evelyn D Baker c 4.

BAKER, Ruth Louise (Mont) 52120 Lake Mary Ronan Rd, Proctor MT 59929 **R S Pat's Epis Ch Bigfork MT 2012-** B Saint Albans NY 1946 d Claude & Ruth. U of Redlands 1965; BA U of Montana 1968; MDiv VTS 1998. D 6/13/1998 P 12/13/1998 Bp John Bailey Lipscomb. m 9/1/1967 James A Baker c 2. Assoc Gr Epis Ch Liberty MO 2010-2012, P Assoc 2010-; R Ch Of The Redeem Kansas City MO 2005-2009; R S Matt's Ch St Petersburg FL 1999-2005; Assoc S Thos' Epis Ch St Petersburg FL 1998-1999; Chair COM Dio W Missouri Kansas City MO 2008-2009, Mem Chr Formation Com 2006-2008; Mem Congrl Dvlpmt Dio SW Florida Parrish FL 2002-2005. Ord of S Lk 1993. MDiv cl VTS 1998.

BAKER, Shireen R (Chi) 116 E Church St, Elmhurst IL 60126 **Ch Of Our Sav Elmhurst IL 2016-** B Tehran Iran 1977 d Robert & Rhonda. BA U CA, Los Angeles 2009; MDiv VTS 2013. D 6/8/2013 Bp Joseph Jon Bruno P 1/11/2014 Bp Mary Douglas Glasspool. Asst S Clem's-By-The-Sea Par San Clemente CA 2013-2015. revshireen@scbythesea.org

BAKER, Ursula Paula (Az) D 6/10/2017 Bp Kirk Stevan Smith.

BAKER-BORJESON, Susan C (Alb) 3425 South Atlantic Avenue, #1006, Daytona Beach Shores FL 32118 **Co-Fndr Jubilate Deo Mnstrs Inc 2008-; Dio Albany 2005-; Alpha Reg Advsr Dio Albany 2004-; Cmsn on Alco Concerns Dio Massachusetts Boston MA 1992-, 1990-2009; Dn, Hudson Vlly Dnry Dio Albany Greenwich NY 2007-** B Garden City NY 1942 d Allan & Muriel. BA Ohio Wesl 1964; Cert U of Paris-Sorbonne FR 1965; MDiv VTS 1979. D 6/25/1979 Bp Robert Marshall Anderson P 1/18/1980 Bp John Brooke Mosley. m 1/9/1988 Ralph William Borjeson c 1. R Chr Ch Coxsackie NY 2004-2008; R S Ptr's Ch Dartmouth MA 1994-2004, Int 1992-1994; Clinician/Coordntr Fam/Wmn Grp Ther - Highpoint Ther Cntr 1990-1992; Assoc R Ch Of S Jn The Evang Duxbury MA 1989-1991, Int 1986-1988; Assoc Chapl Groton Sch Groton MA 1981-1986; Asst R S Ptr's Ch Glenside PA 1979-1981. DOK 2006. jubilatedeoministries@gmail.com

BAKER-WRIGHT, Michelle (Los) 1325 Monterey Rd, South Pasadena CA 91030 **Assoc S Jas' Par So Pasadena CA 2011-** B San Jose CA 1973 d Robert & Charlene. Fuller TS; BMus USC 1995; MDiv Fuller TS 2006. D 6/12/2010 P 1/8/2011 Bp Mary Douglas Glasspool. m 8/30/2003 Mark Baker-Wright.

BAKKER, Cheryl Anne (CFla) 7416 W Seven Rivers Dr, Crystal River FL 34429 **D S Anne's Ch Crystal River FL 2001-** B Elyria OH 1948 d Eric & Marguerite. BS OH SU 1972. D 12/8/2001 Bp John Wadsworth Howe. m 5/25/1984 Bert Bakker. bbakker1@tampabay.rr.com

BAKKER, Gregory Kendall (SJ) 41 Station Road, Sholing, Southampton SO19 8FN Great Britain (UK) **Serv Ch of Engl 2000-** B Modesto CA 1966 s Harry & Donna. AA Modesto Jr Coll 1987; BA California St U 1989; MDiv TESM 1992; Trin Bristol Gb 2000. D 6/6/1992 P 5/30/1993 Bp David Mercer Schofield. m 2/17/2001 Jane Judith Bakker c 1. Serv Angl Ch In Tanzania 1996-1999; Asst Trin Ch Tariffville CT 1992-1996.

BAKKUM, Carleton Benjamin (SVa) PO Box 123, Yorktown VA 23690 **R Gr Ch Yorktown Yorktown VA 1989-** B Dalton GA 1953 s Peter & Johnnie. BA Eckerd Coll 1976; MDiv PrTS 1982; CAS GTS 1984. D 6/8/1985 P 12/14/1985 Bp John Thomas Walker. m 9/28/1985 Elsa Bakkum c 3. Asst Trin Ch Upperville VA 1985-1989.

BALCOM, John Murray (Mass) 2 Autumn Ln, Amherst MA 01002 **Died 1/3/2017** B Boston MA 1918 s Rubric & Grace. BA U of Massachusetts 1939; BD EDS 1942; STM Harvard DS 1955. D 6/3/1942 P 12/9/1942 Bp Henry Knox Sherrill. m 6/14/1946 Jeanne Balcom c 3. Ret 1982-2017; Chapl U of Massachussetts Boston MA 1965-1975; Epis Chapl Bos Boston MA 1962-1965; R Par Of S Paul Newton Highlands MA 1953-1981; R All SS Ch Chelmsford MA 1948-1953; R S Jn's Epis Ch Holbrook MA 1947; Mssnr Dist of Alaska 1944-1947; R Epiph Par Walpole MA 1943-1944; Cur Gr Ch Norwood MA 1942-1943. Cler Club of Boston (Pres) 1943-1981.

BALDERSON, Scott (NC) 304 E Franklin St, Chapel Hill NC 27514 B Virginia Beach VA 1966 s Gene & Shelby. BS Nova SE U 1998. D 1/28/2017 Bp Anne Hodges-Copple. m 5/2/1992 Christina Karseras c 2.

BALDRIDGE SR, Kempton Dunn (Eur) 605 Woodland Drive, Paducah KY 42001 **Chapl for the Ohio River Reg Seamens Ch Inst New York NY 2010-** B Cincinnati OH 1955 s Dickson & Edith. BA Cit 1978; MDiv Ya Berk 1988; MDiv Yale DS 1988. D 6/23/1988 Bp Christopher FitzSimons Allison P 6/1/1989 Bp George Edward Haynsworth. m 9/22/1984 Isabel Baldridge c 2. R All SS Epis Ch Braine-l'Alleud 1999-2010; U Vic S Thos's Par Newark DE 1993-1999; US Navy Chapl Off Of Bsh For ArmdF New York NY 1990-1993; Chapl Us Navy 1989-1993; Yth Min S Lk's Epis Ch Hilton Hd Island SC 1989-1990; Asst R Ch Of The Redeem Orangeburg SC 1988-1989; Chair, COMB Convoc of Epis Ch in Europe Paris 2005-2010, Cler Dep, GC 2003-2009, Cmsn on the Mnstry of the Baptized 1999-2010. Auth, "Sir Wm DeLancey: an Amer at Waterloo," *The Hstgr*, HSEC, 2009. Gospel Mus Assn 1994-2001.

BALDWIN, Allan (WMass) **Died 1/13/2017** B Whitinsville MA 1932 s Leonard & Ida. AS Becker Jr Coll 1954; BS TCU 1961; MDiv Epis TS of the SW 1965. D 6/24/1965 P 12/26/1965 Bp Robert McConnell Hatch. m 7/9/2009 Bertha Aldonna Kulish c 2. P-in-c S Mary's Epis Ch Thorndike MA 1997-2006, 1996; Ret 1996-2017; Ret 1996-2017; Cn Dio Wstrn Massachusetts Springfield 1987-1996, Chair-Cmsn on Aging 1982-1986, Cmsn on Aging 1974-1996, Hosp Chapl 1971-1996; Chapl Ring Nrsng Hm 1976-1996; Res Cn Chr Ch Cathd Springfield MA 1975-1988; Asst S Lk's Ch Springfield MA 1966-1971; Gr Ch Chicopee MA 1966-1968; Chapl/Intern Rusk Inst New York NY 1965-1966.

BALDWIN, Frederick Stephen (NJ) 1710 Restoration Court, Charleston SC 29414 **Chapl Luth Hospice Mt Pleasant SC 2017-** B Syracuse NY 1946 s Robert & Elizabeth. BA Geo 1968; MDiv EDS 1976. D 6/16/1976 P 5/4/1977 Bp Ned Cole. m 9/8/2011 Derrick Carr c 1. Chapl Moffitt Cancer Cntr Tampa FL 2009-2011; R S Bern's Ch Bernardsville NJ 1984-2005; Assoc S Jas Epis Ch New York NY 1981-1984; Dir, PR and Dvlpmt Assn of Episcopal Colleges NY NY 1979-1981; Ch Of The H Trin New York NY 1976-1979. Chapl for the UN Ch Cntr 1976; Epis Chapl for the Holland Lodge 1979; Ord of S Jn the Bapt 1985; Pres for S Mart's Hse 1984-2006.

BALDWIN, Gary (CGC) 188 Grindstone Creek Dr, Clarkesville GA 30523 B Bucyrus OH 1949 s Elsworth & Florence. BA Sthrn Nazarene U 1972; MA Sthrn Nazarene U 1976; MEd Georgia St U 1977; MDiv Sewanee: The U So, TS 1988; DMin Winebrenner TS 2012. D 6/1/1988 P 12/14/1988 Bp Robert Oran Miller. m 7/30/1989 Kathleen M Baldwin c 2. P-in-c Trin On The Hill Epis Ch Los Alamos NM 2013-2015; Int R S Dav's Ch Glenview IL 2012-2013; Int Emm Epis Ch Shawnee OK 2011-2012; R S Steph's Ch Brewton AL 2003-2011; R The Epis Ch Of The Mssh Pulaski TN 1991-2003; R S Mary's Epis Ch Childersburg AL 1988-1990.

BALDWIN, Gayle R (Wyo) ????, Greybull WY 82426 **Non-par 1990-** B Orangeburg SC 1946 d Willie & Elizabeth. BM S Andrews Presb Coll 1969; BA S Andrews Presb Coll 1969; MA U of No Amer 1972; MA U of the Americas 1972; BS Appalachian St U 1975; MDiv Epis TS of the SW 1979; PhD Marq 1993. D 6/30/1979 P 1/1/1980 Bp William Gillette Weinhauer P 1/1/1980 Bp Bob Gordon Jones. m 6/23/2011 Kathleen Tiemann. S Andr's Ch Basin WY 1998; S Andr's Ch Meeteetse WY 1998, 1979-1983; R S Mary's Epis Ch Summit WI 1987-1989; Asst Ch Of The H Trin So Bend IN 1986-1987; Non-par 1983-1985. AAR; Cat.

BALDWIN, Jerome M (SO) 9477 N Maura Ln., Brown Deer WI 53223 **Non-par 1977-** B Seattle WA 1934 s Maynard & Eleanor. BA Mia 1956; BD Oberlin TS 1963; MS U of Wisconsin 1986. D 3/1/1964 P 12/1/1964 Bp Roger W Blanchard. m 6/24/1967 Johanna Baldwin. Chair Cmsn Of Instnl Ministers Ohio Coun Of Ch 1970-1972; R Our Sav Ch Mechanicsburg OH 1967-1977; Cur Chr Epis Ch Of Springfield Springfield OH 1964-1966; Asst Chapl Ohio St Penit 1963-1964.

BALDWIN, John Anson (SVa) 5181 Singleton Way, Virginia Beach VA 23462 B Washington DC 1950 s Langford & Margaret. BA Ob 1973; MDiv EDS 1978. D 6/17/1978 Bp Alexander D Stewart P 12/21/1978 Bp Charles Bennison Sr. m 8/19/1978 Ann Scherm c 2. Pres NNECA 2000-2002; R Emm Ch Virginia Bch VA 1997-2014; R St Geo's Epis Ch Minneapolis MN 1987-1997; R St Johns Broad Creek Ft Washington MD 1981-1987; Cur Gr Ch Grand Rapids MI 1978-1981; Dep for GC Dio Sthrn Virginia Newport News VA 2003-2013, Congrl Dvlpmt Cmsn 1999-2011; Dioc Coun Dio Minnesota Minneapolis MN 1995-1997, Stndg Com 1988-1994; Dioc Coun Dio Washington Washington DC 1983-1985; Chair Hunger T/F Dio Wstrn Michigan Kalamazoo MI 1980-1981. Auth, "Geocaching for Chr," *Jamestown Cross*. Soc of the Cinncinnati.

BALDWIN, Judith Anne (Nwk) 119 Main St, Millburn NJ 07041 B Utica NY 1949 d Mervin & Mary. BA Syr 1971; MA U CA 1976; MDiv EDS 1986. D 6/21/1986 Bp O'Kelley Whitaker P 4/1/1987 Bp Douglas Edwin Theuner. m 2/1/1987 Cornelius Tarplee c 1. Hse Of Pryr Epis Ch Newark NJ 2004-2006; S Steph's Ch Millburn NJ 2000-2001; Asst Ch Of The Gd Shpd Nashua NH 1986-1992.

BALDWIN, Marilyn E (Minn) 12336 Eagle Cir NW, Coon Rapids MN 55448 **Assoc P for Pstr Care Ch Of The Ascen Stillwater MN 2013-** B St. Paul MN 1948 d Martin & Sally. BA Metropltn St U; MS Cardinal Stritch U 1990; CATS SWTS 2006; MDiv Untd TS of the Twin Cities 2006. D 6/8/2006 P 12/21/2006 Bp James Louis Jelinek. m 7/16/1976 Thomas Edward Carroll. S Jn In The Wilderness S Paul MN 2006-2012; S Paul's On-The-Hill Epis Ch Minneapolis MN 2006-2007; Mgr, Intl Ord Serv The Toro Co 1978-2003. m.baldwin@aechurch.org

BALDWIN, Rob (Kan) 1011 Vermont St, Lawrence KS 66044 **R Trin Ch Lawr KS 2010-** B Lakeland FL 1971 s Dennis & Janice. BA Trin Hartford CT 1993; MDiv Trin Luth Sem 2002. D 10/20/2001 P 6/1/2002 Bp Herbert Thompson Jr. m 1/25/1997 Valerie I McCord c 2. P S Jas Ch Piqua OH 2002-2010; S Jn's Ch Worthington OH 1998-2001. office@trinitylawrence.org

BALDWIN, Victoria Evelyn (Ct) 27 Babcock Ave, Plainfield CT 06374 **Int S Paul's Ch Plainfield CT 2012-** B Glen Cove NY 1954 d Roland & Kathryn. BA Mid 1976; MLS Pratt Inst 1984; MDiv Ya Berk 2005. D 6/12/2010 P 1/8/2011 Bp Ian Theodore Douglas. Asst S Paul And S Jas New Haven CT 2010-2012.

BALDWIN-MCGINNIS, Carissa E. (Los) 1220 Omar St, Houston TX 77008 **St Andrews Epis Ch Houston TX 2016-** B Austin TX 1972 d Randall & Elizabeth. BA Wellesley Coll 1994; MDiv Epis TS of the SW 2007. D 6/23/2007 P 1/26/2008 Bp Don Adger Wimberly. m 11/1/2013 Pamela Jean McGinnis. All SS Ch Pasadena CA 2010-2012; Asst S Steph's Epis Ch Houston TX 2007-2010.

BALDYGA, Andrea (Be) 69 Pleasant St, Sayre PA 18840 B Boston MA 1955 d Anthony & Genevieve. BA Bos 1977; MD Bos 1980; MDiv EDS 1998. D 6/20/1998 Bp J Clark Grew II P 2/27/1999 Bp Arthur Williams Jr. P-in-c Ch Of The Redeem Sayre PA 2008-2012; Assoc Trin Ch Easton PA 2007-2008; Int S Lk's Ch Phillipsburg NJ 2004-2007; R S Thos Ch Alexandria Pittstown NJ 2001-2004; Epis W Side Shared Mnstry Cleveland OH 1998-2001; Assoc Westside Shared Min 1998-2001. Auth, "Ethical Dilemmas Postoperative Icu"; Auth, "Hemodialysis Octogenarians".

BALES, Janice Stebing (RG) 3112 La Mancha Pl Nw, Albuquerque NM 87104 B Auburn IN 1943 d Walter & Virginia. Dioc Sch for Mnstry; BA Indiana U 1965. D 10/27/1982 Bp Richard Mitchell Trelease Jr. m 8/28/1965 Frederick Bales c 2. S Mich And All Ang Ch Albuquerque NM 2005-2009; The Storehouse Albuquerque NM 1986-1989; Ret.

BALES, Joshua Morris (CFla) 130 N Magnolia Ave, Orlando FL 32801 **Cn Cathd Ch Of S Lk Orlando FL 2015-** B Chattanooga TN 1981 s Ronald & Janet. Angl Cert Nash; BA Bryan Coll 2013; MA Reformed TS 2014; MA Reformed TS 2014; MA Reformed TS Oviedo FL 2014; MDiv Reformed TS 2016; MDiv Reformed TS 2016; MDiv Reformed TS Oviedo FL 2016. D 5/23/2015 P 12/13/2015 Bp Gregory Orrin Brewer. m 8/21/2010 Miranda Michelle Bales c 1.

BALES, William Oliver (SO) 29405 Blosser Rd, Logan OH 43138 **Nativ Epis Ch Bloomfield Township MI 2002-; S Mk's Ch Seminole OK 2002-; D/ Pstr Trin Ch and McArthur Presb McArthur OH 2002-** B Detroit MI 1936 s William & Muriel. D 10/28/1995 Bp Herbert Thompson Jr. m 5/17/1958 Kathryn Edith Bales. Trin Ch Mc Arthur OH 2002-2011.

BALFE, Martin Kevin (Minn) 315 State St W, Cannon Falls MN 55009 **D Ch Of The Mssh Prairie Island Welch MN 2005-** B Faribault MN 1945 s Kevin & Evelyn. D 10/29/2005 Bp James Louis Jelinek. m 9/20/1986 Loretta J Balfe c 7.

BALICKI, John (Me) 104 Echo Rd, Brunswick ME 04011 **R S Mk's Ch Waterville ME 2011-; Chair, Conv Plnng Com Dio Maine Portland ME 2010-** B Detroit MI 1949 s Eugene & Eugenia. BS Wayne 1972; MRP Penn 1976; MDiv CUA 1983. P. m 8/4/1990 Karen Balicki c 2. Assoc R S Alb's Ch Cape Eliz ME 2005-2011.

BALIIRA, Nelson Kuule (CPa) **St Andr's in the Vlly Epis Ch Harrisburg PA 2016-** Trans 5/10/2016 as Priest Bp Audrey Scanlan.

BALK, Roger Allen (O) 5828 Avenue De L'Esplanade, Montreal QC H2T 3A3 Canada **Died 10/10/2015** B Toledo OH 1930 s Earl & Luella. BA Harv 1952; UTS 1953; U of St Andrews 1956; PhD Concordia U 1989. D 12/6/1957 Bp Nelson Marigold Burroughs P 6/1/1958 Bp Beverley D Tucker. m 5/22/1953 Patricia Ann Raymond. Non-par 1986-2015; Angl Chapl Mcgill U Montreal Pq Can 1972-1985; Prof Dawson Coll Montreal Pq Can 1970-1985; Lectr Sir Geo Williams U Montreal Pq Can 1966-1970; Mc Gill U Montreal QC 1961-1984; Actg Chapl Ken Gambier OH 1959-1960; R Harcourt Par Gambier OH 1958-1961. Hon Asst Chr Ch Cathd.

BALKE JR, Steven M 4090 Delaware St, Beaumont TX 77706 **S Steph's Ch Beaumont TX 2017-; S Paul's Ch Waco TX 2015-** B Ann Arbor MI 1982 s Steven & Micheal. B.S Indiana Wesl 2012; MDiv VTS 2015. D 1/24/2015 Bp Cate Waynick P 9/1/2015 Bp Dena Arnall Harrison. m 10/1/2011 Katherine MacDougall c 2. Transitional D S Pat's Ch Washington DC 2015. sbalke@ststephensbmt.org

✠ BALL, The Rt Rev David Standish (Alb) 3 Park Hill Dr Apt 5, Albany NY 12204 **Died 4/18/2017** B Albany NY 1926 s Percival & Hazelton. BA Colg 1950; STB GTS 1953; GTS 1984. D 6/14/1953 P 12/21/1953 Bp Frederick Lehrle Barry Con 2/20/1984 for Alb. Ret Bp of Albany Dio Albany Greenwich NY 1998-2017, Bp of Albany 1984-1998; Bp Cathd Of All SS Albany NY 1998, Dn 1960-1983, Cn Precentor 1958-1960, Cn Sacrist 1956-1958; Cur Ch Of Beth Saratoga Spg NY 1953-1956.

BALL, Edwin (CFla) 3740 Pinebrook Cir, Bradenton FL 34209 **Ret 1979-** B Newark NJ 1914 s Robert & Miriam. Pur 1933; AA Lake-Sumter Cmnty Coll 1985; BA U of So Florida 1992. D 2/28/1959 Bp Dudley S Stark. m 1/31/1940 Priscilla Marsten Ball c 3. Asst S Edw The Confessor Mt Dora FL 1976-1979; Asst S Paul's Epis Ch Pittsburgh PA 1975-1976; Non-par 1972-1974; Asst S Mk's Ch Basking Ridge NJ 1965-1971; Asst The Ch Of The Sav Denville NJ 1963-1964; Asst All SS Ch Millington NJ 1960-1971; Asst Gr Ch Madison NJ 1959-1960; S Paul's Epis Ch Chatham NJ 1959.

BALL, John Arthur (WA) 46455 Hyatt Ct, Drayden MD 20630 **Hospice Chapl Hospice of St. Mary's Cnty 2009-; R S Mary's Chap Ridge Ridge MD 1994-; R St Marys Par St Marys City MD 1994-** B Ilion NY 1950 s William & Anne. Cntrl Virginia Cmnty Coll Lynchburg VA 1972; AA GW 1974; BS Geo Mason U 1977; MDiv VTS 1991. D 5/31/1991 P 12/18/1991 Bp A(rthur) Heath Light. m 8/31/1974 Linda Sue Ball c 2. VTS Alexandria VA 2012, 2011; Adj Instr Liturg VirginiaTheological Sem 2011; Asst Gr Epis Ch Silver Sprg MD 1991-1994; Stff Chapl H Cross RC Hosp Silver Sprg MD 1991-1994. Auth, "Fest Of Amer Folklife-A Handbook For Teachers," 1978. Alpha Chi Natl Scholastic Soc 1978; Alpha Chi Natl Scholastic Soc 1978.

BALL JR, John Coming (SC) 1 Bishop Gadsden Way, Apt 155, Charleston SC 29412 **Ret 1987-** B Summerville SC 1923 s John & Annie-Arden. MDiv Sewanee: The U So, TS; BS U So 1947; BD Sewanee: The U So, TS 1958. D 6/12/1958 P 5/16/1959 Bp Thomas N Carruthers. c 4. Cathd Of S Lk And S Paul Charleston SC 1987-1988, Cn Pstr 1987-; S Phil's Ch Charleston SC 1986-1988, P 1985-1987; So Carolina Charleston SC 1982-1986, Dioc Coun 1982-1986; Vic Chr Ch Denmark SC 1979-1986, 1958-1986, Vic 1958-1961; Ch Of The H Apos Barnwell SC 1979-1986, Vic 1979-1986; S Alb's Ch Blackville SC 1979-1986, Vic 1979-1986, 1958-1978, Vic 1958-1961; S Mk's Epis Ch San Antonio TX 1976-1979, Asst 1976-1979; Dio Atlanta Atlanta GA 1968-1970, Exec Coun 1968-1970; Sewanee U So TS Sewanee TN 1966-1968, Trst 1966-1968; S Anne's Epis Ch Atlanta GA 1961-1976, R 1961-1976.

BALL, Raymond Carl (Dal) 5421 Victor St, Dallas TX 75214 B Lubbock TX 1952 s Raymond & Anita. BS Baylor U 1974; BD Chr Congrl Ministrial Trng 1975; STL Angl TS 1988; DMin Trin Evang DS 1994; DMin Trin Evang DS 1994. D 6/18/1988 P 6/10/1989 Bp Donis Dean Patterson. m 9/10/1994 Bridgette C Ball. R All SS Epis Ch Dallas TX 1992-2011, Cur 1988-1992; Prof, Ch Hist Angl TS Dallas Texas 1989-2005. Auth, "One Lord, One Faith, One Baptism," Berean Bible Coll, 1978; Auth, "Primer In Prot Mysticism," Berean Bible Coll, 1977. Intl Ord Of S Lk the Physcn 1982; Soc of Cath Priests (SCP) 2009; SocMary 1992; Tertiary Of The Soc Of S Fran 1989. none 1988.

BALLANTINE, Lucia (NY) 402 Route 22, North Salem NY 10560 B Princeton NJ 1951 d John & Lucia. BA Kirkland Coll 1973; MDiv Ya Berk 1976. D 6/2/1979 Bp Albert Wiencke Van Duzer P 12/1/1979 Bp George Phelps Mellick Belshaw. m 11/20/2005 Elizabeth B Walden c 1. S Jas' Ch No Salem NY 2001-2015; S Mk's Ch Mt Kisco NY 1999-2000; Assoc S Ptr's Epis Ch Arlington VA 1994-1995; Assoc All SS Epis Par Hoboken NJ 1992-1993; Assoc Ch

55

Of The Incarn New York NY 1987-1992; Assoc The Ch Of S Lk In The Fields New York NY 1979-1987; Chapl S Jas Epis Ch Farmington CT 1976-1978. CHS.

BALLARD, Chris Christopher (LI) St Lukes and St Matthew's Episcopal Church, 520 Clinton Ave, Brooklyn NY 11238 **P Trin-St Jn's Ch Hewlett NY 2015-; Trst Estate of the Dio Long Island Garden City NY 2013-** B Omaha NE 1965 s John & Pamela. BS Iowa St U 1991; MA Iowa St U 1993; MDiv GTS 2012; MDiv The GTS 2012. D 6/2/2012 P 12/8/2012 Bp Lawrence C Provenzano. m 7/19/2012 Seale Harris Ballenger. Property Dvlpmt Proj Mgr Dio Long Island Garden City NY 2012-2014; Cur The Ch Of S Lk and S Matt Brooklyn NY 2012-2014.

BALLARD, James David (Vt) 139 Sanderson Rd, Milton VT 05468 **D S Lk's Ch S Albans VT 2004-** B Burlington VT 1953 s Eugene & Elizabeth. BA Johnson St Coll 1976. D 6/5/2004 Bp Thomas C Ely. m 6/11/1977 Linda Jill Ballard c 2.

BALLARD JR, Joseph Howard (Tenn) 17525 Shady Elm Ave, Baton Rouge LA 70816 B Louisville KY 1951 s Joseph & Mary. BS U of Tennessee 1973; MBA U of Tennessee 1980; Bossey Ecum Inst 1992; MDiv Sewanee: The U So, TS 1992. D 6/13/1992 P 1/9/1993 Bp Robert Gould Tharp. m 9/4/1971 Barbara F Freeman c 2. R Otey Memi Par Ch Sewanee TN 2008-2013; Pres Dio E Tennessee Knoxville TN 1998-2001, Coordntr Soc Prog 1994-2001; Bd Mem Vol Mnstry Cntr 1997-1999; R St Jas Epis Ch at Knoxville TN 1996-2008; Asst S Lk's Ch Cleveland TN 1992-1996.

BALLARD, Kathleen Miller (Nwk) **D Hse Of Pryr Epis Ch Newark NJ 2004-** B Newark NJ 1925 d Kenneth & Florence. BA U CA 1965; MA Seton Hall Universtiy 1975; Cert Newark TS 2005. D 5/21/2005 Bp John Palmer Croneberger. c 2.

BALL-DAMBERG, Sarah (NC) 1014 Monmouth Ave, Durham NC 27701 **Asst Ch Of The H Fam Chap Hill NC 2012-** B Manchester TN 1963 d Milner & June. BA Mid 1984; MA U MI 1990; MDiv Duke DS 2005. D 12/17/2005 P 6/24/2006 Bp Michael B Curry. m 5/21/1988 Richard C Damberg c 2. St Elizabeths Epis Ch Apex NC 2009-2012; Dio No Carolina Raleigh NC 2006-2008; S Phil's Ch Durham NC 2005-2006.

BALLENTINE JR, George Young (SVa) 305 Park Blvd N, Venice FL 34285 **Ret 1982-; Dio SW Florida St. Petersburg FL 1982-; Chapl Intern Gnrl Hosp WDC 1959-** B Newport News VA 1929 s George & Adele. BA U So 1952; MDiv VTS 1955; MA Oklahoma St U 1970. D 6/24/1955 P 6/30/1956 Bp George P Gunn. m 11/10/1973 Emma Jean Ballentine c 2. Dio SW Florida Parrish FL 1982-1994; Asst S Mk's Epis Ch Venice FL 1979-1981; Dio SW Virginia Roanoke VA 1966-1979; Dio Sthrn Virginia Norfolk VA 1966-1979; Asst S Andr's Ch Norfolk VA 1964-1966; Assoc All Souls Memi Epis Ch Washington DC 1962-1964; Chr The Redeem Manassas VA 1959-1962; P-in-c Chr Chantilly VA 1959-1962; S Jn's Ch Centreville VA 1959-1962; Cur Chr and S Lk's Epis Ch Norfolk VA 1956-1959; All SS Ch Richmond VA 1955-1956; P-in-c All SS Ch Toano VA 1955-1956. BA om U So 1952.

BALLENTINE, Jabriel Simmonds (CFla) 1000 Bethune Dr, Orlando FL 32805 B Detroit MI 1980 s Krim & Rosalie. BS U of Maryland 2007; MDiv VTS 2012. D 3/3/2012 Bp Edward Gumbs P 12/21/2012 Bp Leo Frade. m 3/12/2013 Sonya R Scott c 2. The Epis Ch Of S Jn The Bapt Orlando FL 2013-2016; S Thos Epis Par Miami FL 2012-2013. jballentine@gmail.com

BALLERT JR, Irving Frank (Alb) 25 Sharon St, Sidney NY 13838 **Ret 1991-** B Cohoes NY 1926 s Irving & Elizabeth. BME RPI 1950; BS RPI 1954; MS SUNY 1972. D 6/16/1962 P 12/16/1962 Bp Allen Webster Brown. m 6/19/1949 Dorothy Grace Bridge Ballert c 3. Chapl to Ret Cler Dio Albany 2002-2007; Supply P S Tim's Ch Westford NY 2001-2008; Supply P Var Parishes NY 1991-2001; AIDS Advsry Coun, Sidney NY 1988-1991; Dio Albany Greenwich NY 1986-1989, Dioc Yth Cmsn 1986-1987, Weekend Team Sprtl Advsr - Curs 1982-1986, Chair T/Fs Renew 1982-1985, Chair., Renwl Evang., Stew. & Lay Mnstrs 1982-1985, Consult Par Vancancy 1982-1985, Sprtl Dir - Curs 1982-1984, Dn-Dnry of the Susquehanna 1981-1983, COM 1975-1981, Chair Div of Yth 1966-1975, Yth Advsr Troy Dnry 1963-1965; Supply P S Matt's Ch Unadilla NY 1982-1983; DE Communit5y Serv Bd Sidney NY 1981-1983; Dep Coord. Tri-Town Cmnty. Refugee Prog. Com. Sidney NY 1979-1983; Dir, Tri-Town Chap. ARC Sidney NY 1974-1977; Supt. Curric. Advsry Coun. Sidney Cntrl Sch Dist. Sidney NY 1969-1971; R S Paul's Ch Sidney NY 1965-1991; Cur S Jn's Epis Ch Troy NY 1962-1965; Design, Sales, etc. Var Engr Employment 1950-1962; Infantry U.S. Army 1944-1946. Franciscan Cmnty of the H Cross 2006.

BALLEW, Thelma Johanna (NH) 1 Park Ct, Durham NH 03824 B Baltimore MD 1953 d John & Thelma. Mstr of Arts (Theol Stds) Andover Newton TS; BS Wstrn Maryland Coll/MacDaniel Coll 1975. D 1/14/2012 Bp Donald Purple Hart. m 7/14/1977 Phillip Leon Ballew.

BALLING, Valerie L (NJ) 142 Sand Hill Road, Monmouth Junction NJ 08852 **R S Barn Epis Ch Monmouth Jct NJ 2011-; Stndg Com Dio New Jersey Trenton NJ 2015-, Dep to GC 2010-, Dioc Coun 2009-2011, Bp's Advsry Com on Liturg 2007-, Dioc Conv Arrangmnts 2006-2008, Stndg Cmsn on Cler Compstn 2006-** B Livingston NJ 1973 d Peter & Lynn. BA MI SU 1995;

MDiv GTS 2005; MA Villanova U 2011. D 6/11/2005 P 12/17/2005 Bp George Edward Councell. Vic S Steph's Ch Mullica Hill NJ 2005-2011; Transition Com Dio New Jersey 2012-2013. revballing@stbarnabas-sbnj.org

BALLINGER, Carolyn Tucker (WK) **Dio Wstrn Kansas Hutchinson KS 2016-** B Wichita KS 1946 d Carrol & Lois. BS,Ed U of Kansas 1968; BS,Ed U of Kansas 1968; MEd U of Washington 1973; MEd U of Washington 1973; PhD U of Washington 1982; PhD U of Washington 1982; Completion Bp Kemper Sch for Mnstry 2014. D 5/25/2013 P 5/31/2014 Bp Mike Milliken. c 2. D Gr Ch Anth KS 2013-2014. adventuresofapioneerwoman@gnail.com

BALLINGER, Kathryn Elisabeth (Oly) 9210 Ne 123rd St, Kirkland WA 98034 **D S Thos Epis Ch Medina WA 2004-** B Seattle WA 1942 d Gunnar & Hazel. RN Sacr Heart Sch of Nrsng Spokane WA 1966; BSN Gonzaga U 1981; MA Whitworth U 1985; Cert Dio Spokane TS 2000. D 7/22/2000 Bp John Stuart Thornton. m 6/29/1991 Philip Albert Ballinger c 3. D W Cntrl Epis Mssn Spokane WA 2001-2003; S Steph's Epis Ch Spokane WA 2000-2001.

BALLOU, Diedre Schuler (NwT) 6304 Roadrunner Ct, Amarillo TX 79119 **VP For Fin + Contrllr Cal Farley's Boys Ranch 2004-** B Lubbock TX 1961 d Ted & Shirley. BBA Texas Tech U 1983. D 10/29/2006 Bp C Wallis Ohl. m 8/31/2002 William David Ballou.

BALMER, Randall (Ct) 720 Pattrell Road, Norwich VT 05055 **Chair, Dept of Rel Dart Hanover NH 2012-; Mem Epis Ch - Meth Dialogue 2015-** B Chicago IL 1954 s Clarence & Nancy. BA Trin Deerfield IL 1976; MA Trin DS 1981; AM Pr 1982; PhD Pr 1985; MDiv UTS 2001. D 5/20/2006 P 12/7/2006 Bp Jeffrey Neil Steenson. m 1/23/1998 Catharine Louise Randall c 3. R Chr Epis Ch Middle Haddam CT 2010-2012; R S Jn's Ch Washington CT 2008-2009; Prof of Amer Rel Hist Barnard Coll New York NY 1990-2012; Prof of Amer Rel Hist Col New York NY 1985-1989. Auth, "Redeem: The Life of Jimmy Carter," Basic Books, 2014; Auth, "The Making of Evangelicalism: From Revivalism to Politics and Beyond," Baylor U Press, 2010; Auth, "God in the White Hse: How Faith Shaped the Presidency from Jn F. Kennedy to Geo W. Bush," HarperOne, 2008; Auth, "Thy Kingdom Come: How the Rel Rt Distorts the Faith and Threatens Amer," Basic Books, 2006; Auth, "Growing Pains: Lrng to Love My Fr's Faith," Brazos Press, 2001; Auth, "Blessed Assurance: A Hist of Evangelicalism in Amer," Beacon Press, 1999; Auth, "Grant Us Courage: Travels along the Mainline of Amer Protestantism," Oxf Press, 1996; Auth, "The Presbyterians," Greenwood Press, 1993; Auth, "Perfect Babel of Confusion: Dutch Rel and Engl Culture in the Middle Colonies," Oxf Press, 1989; Auth, "Mine Eyes Have Seen the Glory: A Jourrney into the Evang Subculture in Amer," Oxf Press, 1989. AAR; Amer Soc of Ch Hist. Doctor of Humane Letters Estrn U 2008.

BALMER, William John (NJ) 380 Sycamore Ave, Shrewsbury NJ 07702 **Chr Ch Epis Shrewsbury NJ 2015-** B Long Branch NJ 1950 s John & Anne. BA York Coll of Pennsylvania 1975. D 5/9/2015 Bp William H Stokes. m 8/7/1969 Jane E Evans c 2.

BALTUS, Donald Barrington (NY) 123 E 15th St # 1504, New York NY 10003 B Columbia SC 1947 s Donald & Ida. BA Coll of Charleston 1969; NYU 1973; GTS 1974. D 3/8/1975 Bp Charles Waldo MacLean P 12/1/1975 Bp Jonathan Goodhue Sherman. Dio New York New York NY 2001-2005; P-in-c S Andr's Epis Ch Staten Island NY 2000-2006; S Gabr's Ch Brooklyn NY 1999-2000; Hse Chapl Seamens Ch Inst New York NY 1996-2000; Assoc Ch Of The Resurr New York NY 1995-1999; Cluster Covenor Dio W Tennessee Memphis 1994-1995, Alco And Drugs Com 1994, Coll Wk Com 1989-1995, Chair Aids T/F 1988-1995, T/F On Abortion 1987-1995, A-RC 1983-1995; R The Ch Of The Gd Shpd (Epis) Memphis TN 1983-1995; Epis-Luth Dialogue Dio Long Island Garden City NY 1982-1983, Missions 1980-1982, Exec Com Queens Archdeanery 1980-1983; R S Ptr's Ch Rosedale NY 1976-1983; Cur S Andr's Ch Oceanside NY 1975-1976. CBS 1964; Ord Of Julian Of Norwich 1998; SSC 1989.

BALTZ, Ann Marie Halpin (Ida) 8947 Springhurst Dr, Boise ID 83704 B New Orleans LA 1935 d William & Evelyn. BS Spalding U 1963. D 6/19/1998 Bp John Stuart Thornton. m 7/22/1971 Stephen Matthew Baltz.

BALTZ, Francis Burkhardt (At) 369 Merrydale Dr SW, Marietta GA 30064 **Tchg Assoc ACTS 29 Mnstrs Marietta GA 2007-; Stwdshp Cmsn Mem Dio Atlanta Atlanta GA 2013-** B Irvington NJ 1944 s Francis & Hilda. AA Palm Bch Jr Coll 1964; BA Florida St U 1966; MDiv Nash 1969; STM Nash 1979. D 6/29/1969 P 1/4/1970 Bp Albert Ervine Swift. m 6/25/1966 Virginia Baltz c 3. R S Jude's Ch Marietta GA 1985-2007; R S Jn's Epis Ch Of Kissimme Kissimmee FL 1972-1985; Cur S Jas Epis Ch Ormond Bch FL 1969-1972. Auth, "Anges Sanford: A Creative Intercessor," *Unpublished STM Thesis, Nash*, 1979.

BAMBERGER, Michael Andrew (Los) 241 Ramona Ave, Sierra Madre CA 91024 **Partnr in Response Epis Relief and Dvlpmt 2012-; R The Ch Of The Ascen Sierra Madre CA 1985-; Partnr in Response Epis Relief and Dvlpmt New York NY 2015-; Dioc Disaster Coordntr, ER&D Dio Los Angeles Los Angeles CA 2011-, Dn, Dnry V 2009-, Co-chair of the COM 2003-, Lead Trnr, Misconduct Prevention 2001-** B Riverside CA 1955 s Jack & Patricia. BA U CA 1977; MDiv Nash 1981. D 6/20/1981 P 12/20/1981 Bp Robert Claflin

Rusack. m 8/25/1979 Debra Jean Owen Bamberger c 2. Battalion Chf Sierra Madre Fire Dept 1989-2011; Vic S Jn The Evang Mssn Needles CA 1981-1985. Hon Cn Cathd Cntr of St. Paul 2004.

BAMBRICK, Barbara Nichols (SeFla) 1802 Pine St, Perry IA 50220 B Minneapolis MN 1930 d Chester & Dell. BA U MN 1952; Sch of Mnstry in SE Florida 1972; MS Marywood U 1977. D 7/12/1992 Bp Calvin Onderdonk Schofield Jr. m 5/26/1984 Andrew Bambrick c 3. D S Bern De Clairvaux N Miami Bch FL 1992-1997.

BAMFORD, Marilyn Halverson (Minn) PO Box 3247, Duluth MN 55803 B Marquette MI 1944 d Lynn & Mary. Kalamazoo Coll 1964; BA U MI 1965; D Formation Prog 1989; MS U of Wisconsin 1992. D 7/19/1989 Bp Sanford Zangwill Kaye Hampton. m 12/22/1965 Joel Thomas Bamford c 2. D S Edw's Ch Duluth MN 2002-2006; D Duluth Area 1996-2006; H Apos Ch Duluth MN 1989-1995. NAAD.

BAMFORTH, Richard Anderson (Me) Po Box 5068, Augusta ME 04332 **Died 1/6/2017** B Lynn MA 1930 s Charles & Dorothy. BA Bow 1951; MDiv Ya Berk 1958; EdM Bos 1982. D 6/21/1958 Bp Frederic Cunningham Lawrence P 12/20/1958 Bp Arthur C Lichtenberger. m 10/24/1959 Patricia P Bamforth c 2. Int S Mk's Ch Augusta ME 1993-1994; Ret 1992-2017; R S Mary's Epis Ch Rockport MA 1966-1992; R H Cross Epis Ch Poplar Bluff MO 1960-1966; Cur Gr Ch S Louis MO 1958-1960. Ed, "Iron Jaw," Dorrance, 2002.

BANAKIS, Kathryn Loretta (Chi) 939 Hinman Ave, Evanston IL 60202 B Evanston IL 1980 d Christopher & Gayle. BA Ya 2003; MDiv Ya Berk 2009. D 6/11/2011 Bp Laura Ahrens P 3/10/2012 Bp James Elliot Curry. P and Cmnty Connector S Lk's Ch Evanston IL 2011-2015. Auth, "Bubble Girl: An Irreverent Journey of Faith," *Bubble Girl: An Irreverent Journey of Faith*, Chalice Press, 2013; Contributing Auth, "Politeuomai," *Split Ticket: Indep Faith in a Time of Partisan Politics*, Chalice Press, 2010; Contributing Auth, "Var," *Lifting Wmn Voices: Prayers to Change the Wrld*, Ch Pub, 2009. Beatitudes Soc 2009. Awd for Excellence Associated Ch Press 2001; Best Original Cartoon Natl Nwspr Assn 1971.

BANCROFT, John Galloway (At) 1865 Highway 20 W, Mcdonough GA 30253 B Houston TX 1948 s John & Myrah. BA Texas A&M U 1970; MDiv VTS 1978. D 6/16/1978 Bp Roger Howard Cilley P 6/7/1979 Bp James Milton Richardson. m 6/25/1983 Mary S Bancroft c 2. R S Jos's Epis Ch Mcdonough GA 2000-2012; R S Mary's Epis Ch Reading PA 1988-2000; Chr Epis Ch Mexia Mexia TX 1978-1988; The Great Cmsn Fndt Houston TX 1978-1988; St Mths Ch Waco TX 1978-1984.

BANCROFT, Stephen Haltom (Mich) 27310 Wellington Rd, Franklin MI 48025 **Assoc Sprt of Gr Luth Epis Ch W Bloomfield MI 2012-; Ret 2007-** B Kansas City MO 1946 s John & Myrah. BA Texas A&M U 1969; MDiv VTS 1972. D 6/28/1972 Bp Frederick P Goddard P 6/5/1973 Bp James Milton Richardson. m 12/28/1971 Margaret K Bancroft c 3. Dn Cathd Ch Of S Paul Detroit MI 1995-2007; R Trin Ch Houston TX 1987-1995; R S Cyp's Ch Lufkin TX 1978-1986; Asst S Jn The Div Houston TX 1975-1978; Asst Chr Ch Nacogdoches TX 1972-1975; Chapl Steph F Austin St U Nacogdoches TX 1972-1975.

BANDY, Talmage Gwaltney (NC) 22 Bogie Dr, Whispering Pines NC 28327 B Norfolk VA 1933 d Talmage & Elizabeth. AA Virginia Intermont Coll 1952. D 6/24/1999 Bp Robert Carroll Johnson Jr. m 11/28/1953 Wilton Claude Bandy c 2.

✠ BANE JR, The Rt Rev David Conner (SVa) 163 Pelican Pointe Dr, Elizabeth City NC 27909 B Morgantown WV 1942 s David & Barbara. BA Bethany Coll 1964; MBA W Virginia U 1970; MDiv VTS 1985; LHD S Pauls Coll Lawrenceville 1998; LHD S Pauls Coll Lawrenceville 1998; D.Div VTS 1998. D 6/5/1985 P 12/7/1985 Bp Robert Poland Atkinson Con 9/6/1997 for SVa. m 2/6/1965 Alice Bane c 4. Dio Sthrn Virginia Newport News VA 2006-2007, Bp 1997-2006, 1997-1998; R Chr Epis Ch Dayton OH 1991-1997; Dio New Hampshire Concord NH 1988-1990, Chair Ch Dvlpmt Cmsn 1989-1991, Dnry Convenor 1987-1988; R Par Of S Jas Ch Keene NH 1987-1991; R S Jn Wheeling WV 1985-1987. Doctor of Humane Letters St. Paul's Coll 1997; Hon DD VTS 1997.

BANE, Jack Donald (NY) 210 Old North Rd, St Paul's Episcopal Church, Camden DE 19934 B Beaumont TX 1935 s Jack & Lois. BA Rice U 1958; STB GTS 1962; Cert Fndt For Rel & Mntl Hlth 1972; MS Iona Coll 1973; ACPE 1979. D 6/22/1962 P 6/1/1963 Bp Frederick P Goddard. m 6/23/1984 Arline Bane. P-in-c Ch Of S Nich On The Hudson New Hamburg NY 1998-2003; Dio New York New York NY 1998-2002; Chr Epis Ch Tarrytown NY 1998; S Aug's Epis Ch Croton Hdsn NY 1995; Chr Ch Bronxville NY 1994, Cur 1966-1969; Trin Epis Ch Ossining NY 1992-1993; Int S Ptr's Epis Ch Peekskill NY 1987-1988; Int S Phil's Ch Garrison NY 1986-1987; Non-par 1972-1987; S Barn Ch Irvington NY 1969-1972; Asst S Mk's Ch Beaumont TX 1964-1966; Hon Cn Chr Ch San Aug TX 1962-1964; S Jn's Epis Ch Cntr TX 1962-1964; Chr Ch Cathd Houston TX 1962-1964. Auth, "Death & Mnstry: Pstr Care Of The Dying & The Bereaved"; Auth, "Pstr Psychol & Pulpit Dig". AAPC 1974; Chairman Profsnl Concerns Com Estrn Reg 1988-1992; Clincl Mem ACPE; Diplomate 1979.

BANKOWSKI, Thomas (CFla) D 9/27/2014 Bp Gregory Orrin Brewer.

BANKS, Cynthia Kay Rauh (WNC) 272 Maple Ridge Dr, Boone NC 28607 **R S Lk's Ch Boone NC 2004-** B Louisville KY 1965 d Stephen & Virginia. BS U of Louisville 1988; MDiv GTS 1994. D 6/25/1994 P 1/6/1995 Bp Ted Gulick Jr. m 2/5/2000 James Douglas Banks c 2. Assoc Chr Ch Cathd Louisville KY 2000-2004; Dio Kentucky Louisville KY 1998-1999; S Thos Ch Campbellsvlle KY 1998-1999; Chapl Wstrn Kentucky U 1995-1998; Asst R Chr Epis Ch Bowling Green KY 1994-1998. Auth, "Uncommon Witness: Luth-Epis Mnstrs Bring Concordat To Life," *Journ Of Wmn Mnstrs (Sum)*, 1998. BS/BA Valedictorian U Of Louisville 1988.

BANKS JR, Frederick David (Ky) 2541 Southview Dr, Lexington KY 40503 **Non-par 1975-** B Louisville KY 1945 s Fred & Patricia. BS U of Louisiana 1968; MDiv UTS 1971; AS U of Louisiana 1973; JD U of Louisiana 1980. D 6/21/1971 P 3/1/1973 Bp Charles Gresham Marmion. m 5/17/1969 Laverne Thorpe. Chr Ch Cathd Louisville KY 1975-1978; Dio Kentucky Louisville KY 1974-1975, 1973-1974, Dir CALC 1971-1972. Hon Cn Chr Cathd 1975.

BANKS JR, Ralph Alton (SeFla) 940 Eucalyptus Rd, North Palm Beach FL 33408 B Savannah GA 1931 s Ralph & Lucille. BA U So 1954; STB GTS 1959; MEd Florida Atlantic U 1979. D 6/16/1957 P 2/1/1958 Bp Albert R Stuart. R S Jn The Apos Ch Belle Glade FL 1995-2000; H Nativ Pahokee FL 1993-2000; 1972-1977; Asst Trin Ch Vero Bch FL 1969-1971; Asst S Phil's Ch Coral Gables FL 1966-1969; R S Mich's Ch Mobile AL 1965; Vic S Matt's Epis Ch Fitzgerald GA 1959-1963; Cur S Paul's Ch Augusta GA 1957-1958.

BANKS, Richard Allan (La) 1444 Cabrini Ct, New Orleans LA 70122 B Warren OH 1951 s Paul & Florence. Untd Theol Coll of The W Indies Kingston Jm; BA U of The W Indies 1993. Trans 6/6/2003 Bp Charles Edward Jenkins III. m 2/28/1986 Barbara Ann Banks c 2. Ch Of The H Fam San Pedro Garza Nuevo Leon 2008-2009; H Fam Epis Ch Midland MI 2008-2009; Chap Of The H Comf New Orleans LA 2007-2008; R S Lk's Ch New Orleans LA 2003-2005; Int Trin Ch Arlington VA 2001-2002.

BANKSTON, Van A (Be) 509 W Pine St, Hattiesburg MS 39401 **Ch Of The Gd Shpd And S Jn Milford PA 2014-** B Greenwood MS 1954 s Arthur & Mildred. BLA Mississippi St U 1976; MAT Mississippi Vlly St U 2004; MDiv GTS 2011. D 6/4/2011 P 6/2/2012 Bp Duncan Montgomery Gray III. Trin Ch Hattiesburg MS 2011-2014.

BANNER, Daniel Lee (Chi) 2431 Bradmoor Dr, Quincy IL 62301 **Ret 1992-** B Bloomington IL 1928 s Francis & Margaret. BA Millikin U 1950; BD SWTS 1953; MDiv SWTS 1954. D 3/25/1953 P 9/29/1953 Bp Charles A Clough. R S Paul's By The Lake Chicago IL 1970-1992; R S Jos's Ch Chicago IL 1959-1970; St Johns Ch Quincy IL 1959-1970; Cur S Lk's Ch Evanston IL 1956-1959; S Jn's Ch Centralia IL 1953-1956; S Thos Ch Salem IL 1953-1956; Cur S Paul's and Trin Chap Alton IL 1953. SSC 1974.

BANNER, Shelly Ann (CNY) 41 Highmore Dr, Oswego NY 13126 **Eductr Trin Cath Sch 1996-** B Oneida NY 1949 d Harold & Isabel. Loc Formation Prog By Bexley And Dio Cntrl NY. D 11/19/2005 Bp Gladstone Bailey Adams III. m 8/6/1994 Leon F Carapetyan.

BANSE JR, Robert Lee (Va) 221 Orr Rd, Pittsburgh PA 15241 **R Trin Ch Upperville VA 2007-** B Brooklyn NY 1957 s Robert & Gertrude. Drew U; BA Geo 1980; MDiv VTS 1985. D 5/7/1986 Bp Frederick Warren Putnam P 1/1/1987 Bp Donald Purple Hart. m 12/31/1985 Jane Clark Banse c 3. S Steph's Epis Ch Pittsburgh PA 2006-2007; R S Paul's Epis Ch Pittsburgh PA 1998-2005; R S Jn's Epis Ch Wilmington NC 1994-1998; Cn Pstr S Mich's Cathd Boise ID 1990-1993; Ch Of The Resurr (Chap) So Cle Elum WA 1987-1990; R Gr Ch Ellensburg WA 1987-1990; Pstr Asst S Andr's Cathd Honolulu HI 1986-1987; Coun Dio Spokane Spokane WA 1988-1990.

BAPTISTE-WILLIAMS, Barbara Jeanne (SeFla) 6041 Sw 63rd Ct, Miami FL 33143 B Miami FL 1941 d Edwin & Elaine. BS Tuskegee Inst 1962; MA U of Nthrn Colorado 1974; MDiv VTS 1996. D 11/23/1996 Bp Calvin Onderdonk Schofield Jr P 5/1/1997 Bp John Lewis Said. m 6/29/1974 Clinton Williams c 1. R Ch Of The Trsfg Opa Locka FL 1997-2007. First Black Wmn R Dio SE Florida 1997.

BARBARA, Beam Jean Wedow (WMo) 6336 SE Hamilton Rd, Lathrop MO 64465 **P All SS Epis Ch Kansas City MO 2008-; Ret 2006-** B Kansas City MO 1941 d Robert & Jean. BA Avila Coll 1964; Dioc W Missouri Sch For Mnstry 1994; Dioc Sc Trng Prog For Sprtl Dir 1996. D 2/4/1995 P 3/25/1999 Bp John Clark Buchanan. c 2. P-in-c S Jn's Ch Neosho MO 2004-2006; Dioc Coun Dio W Missouri Kansas City MO 2000-2004, BEC 1995-2000; Vic S Nich Ch Noel MO 1998-2006; D S Mary's Epis Ch Kansas City MO 1995-1998. Conf S Greg Abbey.

BARBARITO, Melanie Repko (FtW) 5005 Dexter Ave, Fort Worth TX 76107 **Pstr Assoc All SS' Epis Ch Ft Worth TX 2009-** B Battle Creek MI 1953 d Joseph & Irene. SUNY 1974; BS NY St Rgnts Coll 1988; MDiv Bex Sem 1996. D 6/15/1996 Bp William George Burrill P 1/6/1997 Bp Herbert Thompson Jr. c 2. Vic S Fran Epis Ch Eureka MO 2001-2009; Cur The Ch of the Redeem Cincinnati OH 1996-2001.

BARBER, Barbara Jean (Kan) 5518 Sw 17th Ter, Topeka KS 66604 B Plainfield NJ 1926 d Robert & Edith. BA Tem 1949; MLS Emporia St U 1995; GTS 1995.

D 2/2/1997 Bp William Edward Smalley. m 9/25/1949 Robert Barber. D Gr Cathd Topeka KS 1997-2009. NAAD.

BARBER, Elaine Elizabeth Rybak Clyborne (Minn) 4830 Acorn Ridge Rd, Minnetonka MN 55345 **supply P Dio Minnesota Minneapolis MN 2003-** B New Praque NM 1937 d Matthew & Mary. Marq; BS U MN 1959; MEd U MN 1976; Cert SWTS 2003; MDiv Untd TS 2003. D 11/14/1992 Bp Sanford Zangwill Kaye Hampton P 6/12/2003 Bp James Louis Jelinek. m 6/2/1994 Richard Barber c 4. Rel Eductr Breck Sch Minneapolis MN 1983-2000; Chapl Dio Minnesota Minneapolis MN 1983-2000; D Dio Minnesota 1983-2000.

BARBER, Grant Woodward (Mass) 102 Branch St., Scituate MA 02066 **R S Lk's Epis Ch Scituate MA 2005-** B San Francisco CA 1957 s Robert & Lois. BA Baylor U 1980; MDiv Ya Berk 1987. D 6/13/1987 Bp Arthur Edward Walmsley P 1/1/1988 Bp Jeffery William Rowthorn. m 5/22/1982 Denise Fox c 1. R H Trin Epis Ch Oxford OH 1998-2005; Epis Ch At Yale New Haven CT 1990-1998; Chapl Epis Ch Yale New Haven CT 1990-1997; Cur S Paul's Epis Ch Willimantic CT 1987-1990.

BARBER, Grethe Ann (Oly) 690 N Shepherd Rd, Washougal WA 98671 **Hosp Chapl SW WA Med Cntr Vancouver WA 2008-** B Rochester MN 1942 d Olav & Mildred. MA Marylhurst U 1994; MDiv Ya Berk 2000. D 1/20/2002 Bp Vincent Waydell Warner P 8/24/2002 Bp Sanford Zangwill Kaye Hampton. c 4. Ch Of The Gd Shpd Vancouver WA 2002-2009; Chapl Providence Med Cntr Portland OR 2000-2007. Assn of Profsnl Chapl 2001.

BARBER, James Frederick (FtW) 3217 Chaparral Ln, Fort Worth TX 76109 **Int The Epis Ch Of The Trsfg Dallas TX 2013-; Bd Mem Bd Texas Conf of Ch 2013-** B Portsmouth VA 1944 s James & Cora. BA Barton Coll 1966; MDiv Van 1970; DMin Van 1971; Air Command & Stff USAF 1997; Air War Coll USAF 2003. D 7/6/1975 P 11/8/1975 Bp Robert Bruce Hall. m 8/20/1967 Judith S Barber c 2. Dir Field Educ TCU Brite DS Ft Worth 2011-2012; Dir Dir of Epis Stds Brite Div Ft Worth 2010-2013; Del GC Del 2009 2009-2013; Theol Reflection Grp Ldr TCU Brite DS Ft Worth 2004-2013; R Trin Epis Ch Ft Worth TX 1999-2010; Hosp Hlth Ins T/F Dio Wstrn New York Tonawanda NY 1994-1996, Pres Stndg Com 1989-1993; R Ch Of The Adv Buffalo NY 1989-1999; Colonel US AF Reserve 1983-2004; R Chr Ch Lockport NY 1980-1989; R S Mary's Ch Colonial Bch VA 1977-1980; Cur Chr Epis Ch Luray VA 1975-1977; Del to GC Dio Ft Worth Ft Worth TX 2009-2011, Pres Stndg Com 2009, Ecum Off 2000-2013. Auth, "Guidelines For Epis/RC Marriages"; Auth, "Operation Desert Storm-Homefront". Operation Desert Storm - Homefront Red Cross; Meritorius Serv Medal (3 Oak Leaf Cluster) Us AF.

BARBER, James S (Mo) 313 W Hardy St, Saint James MO 65559 **Died 4/19/2016** B Springfield MO 1952 s Fred & Aileen. D 12/20/2006 P 7/7/2007 Bp George Wayne Smith. m 10/5/1986 Glenda Barber. D Trin Ch S Jas MO 2007-2016.

BARBER JR, Vernon H (Eau) 502 County Road Ff, Hudson WI 54016 **Died 4/14/2016** B W Palm Beach FL 1936 s Vernon & Lois. BBA Georgia St U; Dplma Gordon Mltry; MA Nash. D 5/30/2009 P 12/12/2009 Bp Russell Edward Jacobus. m 7/3/1997 Leslie Johnson c 2. Asstg P S Paul's Ch Hudson WI 2009-2010.

BARBERIA, Kristin Neily (Los) c/o St. Matthew's Parish School, 1031 Bienveneda Avenue, Pacific Palisades CA 90272 **Sch Chapl The Par Of S Matt Pacific Plsds CA 2007-, Assoc R 1995-2000; Mem, Cmsn on Schools Dio Los Angeles Los Angeles CA 2013-** B San Jose CA 1964 d Robert & Nancy. BA Kalamazoo Coll 1987; Dplma Ya Berk 1990; Cert Inst of Sacr Mus 1990; MDiv Yale DS 1990. D 6/23/1990 P 1/23/1991 Bp R aymond Stewart Wood Jr. m 7/3/1993 Frank C Barberia c 2. Assoc for Formation and Inclusion S Jas Par Los Angeles CA 2006-2007; All SS Ch Pasadena CA 2002-2003, Chld & Yth 2002-2003, Yth Mnstry 1990-1995; Bd Trsts Ya Berk New Haven CT 1992-1995; Sum Week Chapl Camp Steven's Julian CA 1991-2005. Berkeley Grad Soc. Rel and Arts Prize Berk 1990.

BARBOUR OHC, Grady Frederic Waddell (Ala) 565 12th Ct, Pleasant Grove AL 35127 B Columbia SC 1946 s William & Gwendolyn. BA U of Miami 1967; MDiv VTS 1973; ACPE ACPE 1981; Cert Int Pstr - Int Consult 1986; Coll of Pstr Supervision and Psych 1992. D 6/7/1973 P 2/1/1974 Bp Wilburn Camrock Campbell. m 7/24/1982 Martha Elise Barbour c 1. R S Mich's Epis Ch Birmingham AL 2004-2009; P-in-c S Jn's Ch Birmingham AL 2001-2004; R So Talladega Cnty Epis Mnstry Sylacauga AL 1995-1997; R So Talladega Cnty Mnstry AL 1994-1997; Int S Mths Epis Ch Tuscaloosa AL 1992-1994; Chapl Chld's Hosp Birmingham AL 1991-1992; Int R/Consult Int R/Int Consult 1986-1992; Cn The Cathd Ch Of The Adv Birmingham AL 1986-1988; Chapl JHU Med Cntr Baltimore MD 1982-1987; Supvsr CPE JHU Med Cntr Baltimore MD 1982-1987; Baltimore City Hospitals/Fran Scott Key Med Inst Dio Maryland Baltimore MD 1981-1986, Baltimore City Hospitals/Fran Scott Key Med Inst 1981-1986, Johns Hopkins Med Institutions, Chapl 1981-1986; Chapl Sprg Grove Hosp Catonsville MD 1980-1982; Chapl Res U Of Virginia Charlottesville VA 1979-1980; Vic Epis Ch of the Trsfg Buckhannon WV 1973-1979. Auth, "Co-Creators w God," *EARTH Letter*, Earth Mnstry, 2011. Appalacian Inst 1974; ACPE 1986; Coll Pstr Supervision & Psych 1992. Archontes Soc U of Miami 1965.

BARBUTO, Judith Steele (U) 11146 S Heather Grove Ln, South Jordan UT 84095 B Saint Louis MO 1950 d Joseph & Virginia. BS U of Utah 1976; JD U of Utah 1981; ETSBH 1996. D 3/25/1998 P 1/23/1999 Bp Carolyn Tanner Irish. c 2. Epis Cmnty Serv Inc Salt Lake City UT 1998-2001; All SS Ch Salt Lake City UT 1998; Dio Utah Salt Lake City UT 1994-1998. ACPE; Assn Profsnl Chapl; Delta Soc; Intermountain Ther Animals; Ut Assn Pstr Care. Wm H. Leary Schlr U of Utah Coll of Law 1978; Phi Beta Kappa U of Utah 1976; Bs mcl U Of Utah 1976. judithbarbuto@hotmail.com

BARDEN III, Albert A (Ct) 254 Father Rasle Rd, Norridgewock ME 04957 **Non-par 1976-** B Fort Jackson SC 1945 s Albert & Elizabeth. BA Br 1967; MDiv Ya Berk 1970; Cert Ya Berk 1971. D 6/12/1971 Bp Joseph Warren Hutchens P 1/1/1972 Bp Morgan Porteus. m 6/15/1968 Carolyn Pilkinton c 1. Cur Chr And H Trin Ch Westport CT 1971-1976. Auth, "Finnish Fireplace Construction Manual"; Auth, "Finnish Fireplaces/Heart Of The Hm"; Auth, "Albiecore Construction Manual".

BARDOS, Gordon A (Vt) 9449 N 110th Ave, Sun City AZ 85351 **Associated P St Mary's Phoenix AZ 2010-2025** B Gary IN 1939 s Alex & Helen. BA Franklin Coll 1965; Texas Tech U 1967; MDiv SWTS 1982; DMin GTF 1995. D 5/29/1982 P 12/4/1982 Bp Robert Shaw Kerr. c 2. Rdr GOE 2003-2006; Dep GC 2000-2006; Gr Epis Ch Brandon VT 1986-2006; R S Thos' Epis Ch Brandon VT 1986-2006; Vic S Mk's-S Lk's Epis Mssn Fair Haven VT 1982-1986; Brookhaven Hm Dio Vermont Burlington VT 1984-1994. Angl Soc 1986; Assoc, SSJE 1995; Associated Parishes 1986; CBS 1969.

BARDSLEY, Nancy Louise (Ida) 1154 Camps Canyon Rd, Troy ID 83871 B Ripon WI 1938 d Nelson & Winifred. BA Ripon Coll 1977; MSW Estrn Washington U 1990. D 5/14/1994 Bp John Stuart Thornton. c 4.

BARDUSCH JR, Richard Evans (Mass) PO Box 149, Taunton MA 02780 **R Epis Ch Of S Thos Taunton MA 2010-** B Hampton VA 1964 s Richard & Doris. BA Emory and Henry Coll 1987; MDiv Duke DS 1992; Cert EDS 1995; Cert EDS 1995; DMin Drew U 2006. D 6/5/1995 Bp Robert Carroll Johnson Jr P 4/20/1996 Bp Frank Harris Vest Jr. Assoc R Gr Ch In Providence Providence RI 2006-2009; Ch Of The Mssh Providence RI 2005-2006; Dio Rhode Island Providence RI 2004-2007; Cn for Congrl Dvlpmt & Mssn Dio Rhode Island Providence RI 2003-2006; R Ch of the Mssh Providence RI 2002-2006; Open Door Reg Mnstry Providence RI 2002-2004; R S Ptr's And S Andr's Epis Providence RI 2002-2003; Dir Yth Mnstrs Dio Newark Newark NJ 1997-2002; Cur S Jn's Ch Hampton VA 1996-1997; Gr Ch Yorktown Yorktown VA 1995. "Sneakers," *Sage Advice*, Abingdon Press, 2003; "Mo Cooper," *Sage Advice*, Abingdon Press, 2003; "They Went Thataway," *Sage Advice*, Abingdon Press, 2003; "Keep Paddling," *Sage Advice*, Abingdon Press, 2003.

BAREBO, Charles Vincent (Be) 333 Wyandotte St, Bethlehem PA 18015 B Vincennes IN 1958 s Charles & Theresa. BS U of Utah 1981; Advncd Mgt U of Pennsylvania 2000. D 4/19/2015 Bp Sean Walter Rowe. m 9/19/1992 Lorraine F Barebo c 2.

BARFIELD, David S (Ala) 4908 Masters Rd, Pell City AL 35128 **Cmsn on Mssn and Outreach Dio Alabama Birmingham 2012-** B Columbus GA 1944 s James & Mary Elizabeth. MEd Columbus St U; PhD Auburn U 1981. D 10/1/2011 Bp John Mckee Sloan Sr. m 9/18/1993 Gemma J Barfield c 5. D S Mich and All Ang Aniston AL 2014-2016; D H Comf Ch Gadsden AL 2011-2014.

BARFIELD, DeOla Edwina (Ct) 744 Lakeside Dr, Bridgeport CT 06606 B Winston-Salem NC 1942 d Edwin & Mildred. BA No Carolina Cntrl U 1964; MS U of Bridgeport 1972; Fairfield U 1987. D 12/9/2000 Bp Andrew Donnan Smith. m 8/13/1983 William Earl Barfield. NAAD (No Amer Assoc. for the Diac) 2000.

BARFIELD, Karen C (NC) 501 E Poplar Ave, Carrboro NC 27510 **S Jos's Ch Durham NC 2011-** B Memphis 1966 d James & Caroline. BA Rice U 1988; MS U of Memphis 1990; MDiv Candler TS Emory U 1994. D 11/22/2003 P 5/29/2004 Bp Don Edward Johnson. m 5/26/1990 Raymond Carlton Barfield c 2. Ch Of The Advoc Chap Hill NC 2010-2011; Chapl Dio No Carolina Raleigh NC 2009-2010; Int Duke Epis Cntr Durham NC 2009-2010; Assoc R Gr - S Lk's Ch Memphis TN 2007-2008; Cn for Cmnty Mnstrs S Mary's Cathd Memphis TN 2005-2007; Int R S Elis's Epis Ch Memphis TN 2003-2005; COM Dio W Tennessee Memphis 2006-2008, Dn of Cler 2005-2006. Theta Phi hon Soc in Rel 1994.

BARFIELD, William G (Ind) PO Box 141, Danville IN 46122 **R S Aug's Epis Ch Danville IN 2012-** B Jackson MS 1964 M Div SWTS 2004. D 6/18/2004 P 2/2/2005 Bp Duncan Montgomery Gray III. m 9/6/2003 Susan A Barfield. R S Mk's Epis Ch St Albans WV 2008-2012; Chapl Ch Of The Ascen Hattiesburg MS 2004-2008.

BARFORD, Lee Alton (ECR) 561 Keystone Ave #434, Reno NV 89503 **Assoc to the Dn for Latino Mnstry Trin Cathd San Jose CA 2012-, D 2005-; Pres Shires Cntr San Jose CA US 2005-** B Cheltenham PA 1961 s Robert & Frances. BA Tem 1982; MS Cor 1985; PhD Cor 1987; BTh Sch for Deacons 2005; MTh U of Wales Trin S Dav 2014. D 6/17/2005 Bp Sylvestre Donato Romero. m 1/27/1996 Kirsten A Nelson c 1. Auth, "Thos Nagel: Mind and Cosmos: Why the Materialist Neo-Darwinian Concep of Nature Is Almost Certainly False," *ATR*, 2014; Auth, "Chr Eberhart: The Sacrifice of Jesus: Understanding the Atone Biblically," *ATR*, 2012. Inst of Electrical and Electronics Engr (IEEE) 1983; Soc of Ord Scientists 2017. lee.barford@trinitysj.org

BARGETZI, David Michael (O) 1417 Larchmont Ave, Lakewood OH 44107 **S Lk's Ch Cleveland OH 2014-** B Endicott NY 1957 s Robert & Helen. BA Tul 1979; U of Paris Fr 1979; MDiv Nash 1987. D 5/30/1987 P 12/1/1987 Bp Furman Charles Stough. m 8/1/2008 Robert Stephen Gracey. Epis W Side Shared Mnstry Cleveland OH 1999-2013; P-in-c S Jn's Ch Cleveland OH 1997-1998; R Cbury Chap and Coll Cntr Tuscaloosa AL 1995-1997; Chapl S Dunst's: The Epis Ch at Auburn U Auburn AL 1989-1995; Cur Chr Ch Tuscaloosa AL 1987-1989. Phi Beta Kappa Tul 1979.

BARGIEL, Mary Victoria (Ind) 3243 N Meridian St, Indianapolis IN 46208 B Port Huron MI 1968 d Edward & Sylvia. BM U MI 1990; MM The U of Akron 1993; MDiv Bex 2010; MDiv Bex Sem 2010. D 1/24/2015 Bp Cate Waynick P 4/29/2016 Bp George Young III. c 2.

BARHAM, Patsy Griffin (Tex) St Matthew's Episcopal Church, 214 College Ave, Henderson TX 75654 **P-in-c S Matt's Ch Henderson TX 2007-** B Mesa AZ 1948 d B V & Bettie. BA Steph F Austin St U 1971; MEd Steph F Austin St U 1981; MDiv Iona Sch for Mnstry 2007. D 6/23/2007 Bp Don Adger Wimberly P 1/11/2008 Bp Rayford Baines High Jr. m 8/31/1968 George Stephen Barham c 3.

BARKER, Ann Biddle (Va) 6231 Kilmer Ct, Falls Church VA 22044 **R S Jn's Epis Ch Arlington VA 2001-** B Charleston WV 1956 BA U NC 1978; MA Indiana U 1980; MDiv Candler TS Emory U 1996; Cert Sewanee: The U So, TS 1999. D 6/5/1999 Bp Onell Asiselo Soto P 1/29/2000 Bp Herbert Thompson Jr. c 1. Asst R S Pat's Epis Ch Dublin OH 2000-2001; Asst R S Jn's Ch Worthington OH 1999-2000. MDiv mcl Candler TS 1996; BA w hon U NC/Chap Hill, NC 1978.

BARKER, Christie Dalton (NC) 981 Valiant Dr., Statesville NC 28677 B Charlotte NC 1966 d Jerry & Judy. BA Arizona St U 2006; MDiv Wake Forest U 2011. D 10/5/2002 Bp Robert Reed Shahan. m 12/31/1994 Jesse Russell Barker. Trin Epis Ch Statesville NC 2003-2011. DOK, St. Clare Chapt 2004. Jerry M. Crainshaw Preaching Awd Wake Forest U Sch of Div 2011.

BARKER, Christopher Haskins (Pgh) 1062 Old Orchard Dr, Gibsonia PA 15044 B Jacksonville FL 1943 s Robinson & Mary. BA MacMurray Coll 1967; BD VTS 1970; MA Duquesne U 1987; PhD Duquesne U 1995. D 6/6/1970 Bp William S Thomas P 12/19/1970 Bp Robert Bracewell Appleyard. m 8/31/1968 Mary Eleanor Barker c 2. S Chris's Epis Ch Mars PA 1978-1999; R S Lk's Epis Ch Smethport PA 1975-1978; Asst Trin By The Cove Naples FL 1971-1975; Cn Trin Cathd Pittsburgh PA 1970-1971. Auth, "Crosses Or Blessings," *Envoy: Journ Of Formative Reading 13:5*, 1986. Natl Dn's List.

BARKER, Daniel W (CNY) 324 Harding Ave, Vestal NY 13850 B Painesville OH 1943 s Kenneth & Grace. BA U of Massachusetts 1971; MDiv Westminster TS 1980. D 9/28/1981 P 3/28/1982 Bp Alexander D Stewart. m 12/19/1970 Margaret G Barker c 4. Vic S Ann's-By-The-Sea Block Island RI 2008; R The Ch Of The H Innoc Henderson NC 2000-2003; S Ptr's Ch Great Falls SC 1997-1999; Chapl Epis Ch Hm at York Place Inc Columbia SC 1996-2000; Dio Cntrl New York Liverpool NY 1993-2008; R S Andr's Ch Vestal NY 1987-1996; S Dav's Ch Feeding Hills MA 1983-2008; R S Thos Epis Ch Auburn MA 1983-1987; Cur/Asst Ch Of The Atone Westfield MA 1981-1983. danielbarker@hotmail.com

BARKER, Gary Joseph (Va) 111 S Church St, Smithfield VA 23430 **Kingston Par Epis Ch Mathews VA 2013-** B Glendale CA 1956 s Joseph & Jeanne. BA Tul 1980; MA U of Virginia 1983; MDiv VTS 1990; Cert GTS 1998. D 6/2/1990 Bp Peter J Lee P 2/14/1991 Bp Robert Poland Atkinson. m 7/28/1984 Gail B Barker c 4. R Chr Epis Ch Smithfield VA 2002-2012; Vic Gr Ch Stanardsville VA 1994-2002; Asst R Emm Ch Harrisonburg VA 1990-1994; Chapl Jas Madison U Harrisonburg VA 1990-1994. Mdiv cl VTS 1990.

BARKER, Herbert James (SanD) 11727 Mesa Verde Dr, Valley Center CA 92082 B Marlow GA 1942 s Lawrence & Ole. EdD U of San Diego 1957; BA Berry Coll 1965; MDiv Duke DS 1968; STM Dubuque TS 1971. D 3/11/1997 P 9/1/1997 Bp Gethin Benwil Hughes. m 11/5/2004 Li Hua Han. Exec Coun Appointees New York NY 2010-2014; Pstr S Mary's In The Vlly Ch Ramona CA 2008-2010.

BARKER, Jane Daugherty (Tex) **D S Jn's Epis Ch Cntr TX 2016-** B Washington, D.C. 1945 Dplma in Theol IONA Sch for Mnstry; M.A. St. Leo U 2007. D 6/25/2016 Bp C Andrew Doyle.

BARKER, Jo Ann D (Del) 241 Louisiana Circl, Sewanee TN 37375 **Mentor Trnr EFM Sewanee TN 37375 2012-** B LaPorte IN 1948 d Rudolph & Helen. AA Ancilla Coll 1969; BS S Fran U Ft Wayne IN 1971; Memphis TS 1991; MDiv Sewanee: The U So, TS 1994; DMin SWTS 2006. D 7/9/1994 P 1/14/1995 Bp Larry Maze. m 7/13/1974 Charles Lawrence Barker c 3. R St Annes Epis Ch Middletown DE 2009-2011; R S Mk's Epis Ch Jonesboro AR 2004-2009, Cur 1994-1996; R S Jn's Ch Harrison AR 1996-2004.

BARKER, Kenneth Lee (CGC) 9409 E 65th St, Tulsa OK 74133 B Shattuck OK 1952 s Alvin & Anna. BA Oral Roberts U 1975; MDiv Epis TS of the SW 1978; MA U of No Florida 1990; DMin Reformed TS 2000. D 6/17/1978 Bp Gerald Nicholas Mcallister P 6/25/1979 Bp James Milton Richardson. m 7/3/1986 Ellen Knowles Barker. R Gr Epis Ch Panama City Bch FL 1996-2000; Ch Of Our Sav Jacksonville FL 1992-1996; Non-par 1984-1992; Dio Oklahoma Oklahoma City OK 1980-1984; Vic S Marg's Ch Lawton OK 1980-1984; Asst S Jn The Div Houston TX 1978-1980. Auth, "The Effects Of Ther/Client Value Similarity On"; Auth, "Self-Disclosure In Counslg"; Auth, "Mobilizing Ch Members For Meaningful Mnstry"; Auth, "Orgnztn Culture," *Cmd Revs*. Soc-Mary.

BARKER, Lynn Kay (Miss) 29 Melody Ln, Purvis MS 39475 B Staunton VA 1955 d Nolan & Helen. BA U of Virginia 1976; MA U NC 1978; PhD U NC 1988; MDiv Sewanee: The U So, TS 2002. D 5/25/2002 P 12/7/2002 Bp Duncan Montgomery Gray III. All SS Epis Ch Grenada MS 2004-2010; Trin Ch Hattiesburg MS 2002-2004.

BARKER, Patrick Morgan (Ark) 1521 Mcarthur Dr, Jacksonville AR 72076 B Little Rock AR 1949 s Ernest & Virginia. BA U of Arkansas 1980; MDiv Epis TS of the SW 1983; PhD ETSBH 1993. D 5/12/1984 P 12/1/1984 Bp Herbert Alcorn Donovan Jr. m 5/12/1979 Neva R Barker c 3. Trin Par Ch Epis Searcy AR 2006-2016; Dio So Dakota Pierre SD 2004-2006; S Ptr's Par Rialto CA 1998-2004; P-in-c S Mths' Par Whittier CA 1996-1998; S Mk's Epis Sch Upland CA 1996-1997; S Mk's Epis Ch Upland CA 1995-1996; P-in-c S Alb's Epis Ch Yucaipa CA 1990; S Raphaels Ch San Rafael CA 1988-1990; Vic S Ptr's Ch Conway AR 1984-1989; S Alb's Ch Stuttgart AR 1984-1988; St Ptr's Epis Ch Devalls Bluff AR 1984-1988.

BARKER, Paula Suzanne (Md) St Alban's Church, 105 1st Ave SW, Glen Burnie MD 21061 B Ann Arbor MI 1952 d Joseph & Doris. BA U MI 1974; MDiv Yale DS 1977; PhD U Chi 1990. D 4/21/1993 Bp Frank Tracy Griswold III P 10/20/1993 Bp William Walter Wiedrich. c 2. S Alb's Epis Ch Glen Burnie MD 2013-2017; S Thos' Ch Garrison Forest Owings Mills MD 2011-2013; Bexley Seabury Fed Chicago IL 1993-2010. Auth, "Caritas Pirckheimer: A Female Humanist Confronts the Reformation," *16th Century Journ*, 1995; Auth, "Lord Teach us Pray: Hist & Theol Prespectives on Expanding Liturgal Lang," *How Shall We Pray*, 1994; Auth, "The Motherhood of God in Julian of Norwich's Theol," *The Downside Revs*, 1982. BM w dist U MI 1974. stalbans.church@verizon.net

✠ **BARKER, The Rt Rev Scott Scott** (Neb) 109 N 18th St, Omaha NE 68102 **Bp Dio Nebraska Omaha NE 2011-** B Omaha NE 1963 s Joseph & Susan. BA Ya 1985; MDiv Ya Berk 1992. D 6/24/1992 P 12/21/1992 Bp James Edward Krotz Con 10/8/2011 for Neb. m 10/1/1988 Anne E Barker c 2. R Chr Ch Warwick NY 2002-2011; R Ch Of The Resurr Omaha NE 1997-2002; Cn Trin Cathd Omaha NE 1992-1997. Auth, "I Want My Ch to Grow," Forw Mvmt, 2007; Auth, "Future of Our Generation in Ch," *Gathering the Next Generation*, Morehouse Pub, 2000; Auth, "A Tale Too Big To Get Your Arms Around," *Sermons That Wk IX*, Morehouse Pub, 2000; Auth, "Easter Terror," *Sermons That Wk VI-II*, 1999. Mersick Prize- Exceptional Promise for Pstr Mnstry Ya Berk 1992; Tweedy Prize- Excellence in Preaching Ya Berk 1992. sbarker@episcopal-ne.org

BARLEY, Linda Elizabeth (SwFla) 10922 106th Ave, Largo FL 33778 B Russleville AL 1948 S Vincents Sch of Nrsng Birmingham AL. D 1/18/2003 Bp John Bailey Lipscomb. c 2.

BARLOWE, Michael (Cal) 815 Second Avenue, New York City NY 10017 **Dom And Frgn Mssy Soc- Epis Ch Cntr New York NY 2013-; Epis Ch Cntr New York NY 2013-; Hon Cn The Cathd Ch Of S Paul Des Moines IA 2000-, Dn 1991-2001; Secy of the HOD Exec & Secy Off New York NY 2015-, Secy of the HOD 2013-2015; Secy of Exec Coun Exec Coun Appointees New York NY 2013-, Secy of the Dom and Frgn Mssy Soc 2013-; Exec Off GC- Epis Ch Cntr New York NY 2013-** B North Carolina 1955 s Ercel & Pearl. Bachelor of Arts cl Harvard Coll 1977; Mstr of Div cl GTS 1983; Doctor of Mnstry CDSP 2006. D 6/4/1983 Bp Paul Moore Jr P 12/14/1983 Bp George Phelps Mellick Belshaw. m 7/11/2008 Paul Anthony Burrows. Cn to the Ordnry Dio California San Francisco CA 2002-2013; R Dio Iowa Des Moines IA 1991-2000; R Gr Epis Ch Plainfield NJ 1986-1991; Cur S Paul's Epis Ch Westfield NJ 1983-1986. DD CDSP 2017. mbarlowe@episcopalchurch.org

BARNARD, Nancy Alexandra Sandra (ECR) 1267 Black Sage Cir, Nipomo CA 93444 B Whittier CA 1929 d Thomas & Irene. AA Stephens Coll 1949; BS U NC 1951; MDiv Fuller TS 1982. D 12/19/1987 P 6/27/1988 Bp Charles Shannon Mallory. m 8/16/1952 Roger Barnard c 4. Assoc S Barn Ch Arroyo Grande CA 1994-2013; Asst S Mk's-In-The-Vlly Epis Los Olivos CA 1991-1992; Asst S Lk's Ch Atascadero CA 1987-1990. Chapl Ord Of S Lk 1991.

BARNES JR, Bennett Herbert (SwFla) 7 Fiddlehead Fern TRL, Brunswick ME 04011 **Ret 1999-** B Waterbury CT 1933 s Bennett & Mildred. BA Colg 1955; STB Ya Berk 1958; U of Durham GB 1963; STM Ya Berk 1967; EdM Harv 1972; DMin Bos 1993; Ya Berk 1994. D 6/11/1958 Bp Walter H Gray P 12/27/1958 Bp John Henry Esquirol. m 7/14/1962 Beth L Barnes c 2. Assoc S Ptr's Ch Portland ME 2012-2016; Trin Epis Ch Lewiston ME 2006-2008; Int S Matt's Ch S Petersburg FL 2005-2006; Int S Barth's Ch S Petersburg FL 2004-2005; Int Annunc Ch Anna Maria FL 2003-2004; S Geo's Epis Ch Bradenton FL 2000-2004; Cn Dio SW Florida 1999-2000; Dn Manasota Dnry Dio SW Florida Parrish FL 1995-1999; All Ang By The Sea Longboat Key

FL 1992-1999; Headmaster S Steph's Sch Bradenton FL 1976-1986; Chapl & Chair Dept Rel Casady Sch Oklahoma City OK 1963-1976; Vic S Edw Chap Oklahoma City OK 1963-1976; Serv Ch of Engl 1961-1963; Vic S Jn's Ch Stamford CT 1958-1961. Cn Pstr Dio SW Florida 2000.

BARNES, Brian J (Cal) Church Of The Holy Innocents, 455 Fair Oaks St, San Francisco CA 94110 **Died 9/5/2015** B Philadelphia PA 1964 s John & Andrea. BA Sch for Deacons; U of San Francisco; BA U of Texas. D 12/14/2006 Bp Marc Handley Andrus. Archd Dio California San Francisco CA 2011-2015; Ch Of The H Innoc San Francisco CA 2007-2008; Ther Myofascial Release 1997-2015.

BARNES, Chuck (EO) Po Box 317, Hermiston OR 97838 **D S Jn's Ch Hermiston OR 1996-** B Boise ID 1947 s Demas & Arlene. BTh NW Chr Coll Eugene OR 1971; Cert Oregon Cntr For The Diac Eugene OR 1977; MBA Portland St U 1991. D 3/23/1996 Bp Rustin Ray Kimsey. m 6/14/1970 Robin Lynn Turbyne. NAAD. chuckb@eotnet.net

BARNES, Jeffry Parker (SD) 21285 E Highway 20 Apt 127, Bend OR 97701 B Saint Paul MN 1941 s Russell & Margaret. BA U MN 1963; MA U MN 1967; Harvard DS 1973; MDiv Nash 1976. D 6/29/1976 P 3/25/1978 Bp Philip Frederick McNairy. m 7/14/1962 Shirley Ann Barnes c 3. Int Vic Ch Of The H Apos Sioux Falls SD 2008-2010; P-in-c Cheyenne River Epis Mssn 1998-2006; Cheyenne River Epis Mssn Dio So Dakota Pierre SD 1998-2006; R S Jas Epis Ch Zanesville OH 1989-1998; R S Mart's Epis Ch Fairmont MN 1982-1989; Breck Memi Mssn Ponsford MN 1980-1982; Vic S Columba White Earth MN 1980-1982; P in Charge Chr Ch Duluth MN 1977-1980; R S Andr's Ch Cloquet MN 1977-1980; Dio Minnesota Minneapolis MN 1976-1982. Mdiv cl Nash 1976; Ba mcl U MN 1963.

BARNES, John David (Ala) 401 N Main Ave, Demopolis AL 36732 **R Trin Ch Demopolis AL 2008-** B Gadsden AL 1973 BS U of Alabama 1995; MDiv Epis TS of the SW 2006. D 6/1/2006 P 12/12/2006 Bp Henry Nutt Parsley Jr. m 8/3/1996 Amanda Carroll Barnes c 2. Assoc R St Thos Epis Ch Huntsville AL 2006-2008. barnes8@gmail.com

BARNES, Rebecca A (Be) 20 Cumming St, New York NY 10034 **S Lk's Ch Scranton PA 2015-; Vic H Trin Epis Ch Inwood New York NY 2013-** B Kingston PA 1963 d Willis & Barbara. BA Hartwick Coll 1986; MM Manhattan Sch of Mus 1993; MDiv GTS 2012. D 3/3/2012 P 9/29/2012 Bp Mark Sean Sisk. m 10/25/2011 Elizabeth Grohowski. Vic Dio New York New York NY 2013-2015; The Ch of S Ign of Antioch New York NY 2012-2013. r_barnes36@hotmail.com

BARNES, Susan Johnston (Minn) St John The Baptist Episc Ch, 4201 Sheridan Ave S, Minneapolis MN 55410 **R S Jn The Bapt Epis Ch Minneapolis MN 2012-; Personl Com Dio Minnesota Minneapolis MN 2014-** B Houston Texas 1948 d Charles & Marguerite. BA Rice U 1970; MA NYU 1980; PhD NYU 1986; MDiv Epis TS of the SW 2001. D 6/16/2001 P 6/19/2002 Bp Claude Edward Payne. m 12/12/2012 Claudia Ruth Helt. Chr Ch Cathd Houston TX 2012; Assoc R S Matt's Ch Austin TX 2001-2012; Bd Trst Epis TS Of The SW Austin TX 2011-2013; Stndg Com; Chair of Mssn Subcommittee Dio Texas Houston TX 2007-2010, Chair, Wrld Mssn 2005-2010, COM 2004-2007, Exam Chapl 2004-2007. Co-Auth, "Van Dyck: A complete Catalogue," Ya Press, 2004; Co-Auth, "Van Dyck a Genova," Electa, 1997; Co-Auth, "Anth Van Dyck," Natl Gallery of Art, 1990; Auth, "The Rothko Chap, An Act of Faith," U of Texas, 1989. Medal Comune di Genova 1997; Fell Amer Ldrshp Forum 1996; Fell Philos Soc of Texas 1994; Fell Amer Acad in Rome 1981; Dav E. Finley Fell Natl Gallery of Art 1981. sbarnes@stjohns-mpls.org

BARNETT, Andrew K (WA) Washington National Cathedral, 3101 Wisconsin Ave NW, Washington DC 20016 **Cathd of St Ptr & St Paul Washington DC 2016-; Affiliated P All SS Par Beverly Hills CA 2015-; Assoc for Mus and Wrshp, Washington Natl Cathd Dio Washington Washington DC 2016-** B Minneapolis MN 1984 s Edward & Diane. BA Ob; BMus Oberlin Conservatory; MDiv Ya Berk 2012; Mstr of Environ Mgmt Yale Environ Sch 2012. D 6/30/2011 P 6/28/2012 Bp Brian N Prior. Campbell Hall Vlly Vlg CA 2014-2016; S Paul And S Jas New Haven CT 2011-2012; Bp's Chair for Environ Stds The Bp of the Prot Epis Ch in the Dio Los Angeles Los Angeles CA 2014-2016. Band Ldr, "Theodicy Jazz Collective," Cbury Jazz Mass, Self Pub Rcrdng, 2015; Band Ldr, "Theodicy Jazz Collective," Jazz Vespers, Self Pub Rcrdng, 2015.

BARNETT, Becca Fleming (Cal) 435 Euclid Ave Apt 1, San Francisco CA 94118 **Mem Akido IN 1995-** B Parkersburg WV 1952 d Frederick & Ida. BA Alfred U 1978; MS U Roch 1982; MDiv CDSP 1986; MA California Sch of Profsnl Psychol 1991; PhD California Sch of Profsnl Psychol 2003. D 6/3/1989 P 12/1/1990 Bp William Edwin Swing. Nonstipendiary P S Aid's Ch San Francisco CA 2000-2002; Int Ch Of The H Innoc San Francisco CA 1999-2000; Int S Andr's Epis Ch San Bruno CA 1998-1999; Int S Amber Foster City CA 1996-1998; Int S Ambr Epis Ch Foster City CA 1996-1997; St Johns Epis Ch Ross CA 1995-1996; Assoc S Greg Of Nyssa Ch San Francisco CA 1992-1995; Assoc Gr Cathd San Francisco CA 1989-1992; P Dio California San Francisco CA 1989-1991. Oblate S Ben Camaldolese.

BARNETT, Edwin Wilson (FtW) 808 Voltamp Dr., Fort Worth TX 76108 **Catechist S Chris's Ch And Sch Ft Worth TX 2010-; P-in-c St Andr Epis Ch Ft Worth TX 2010-** B Tyler TX 1954 s Edwin & Carolyn. BS Lamar U 1982; MS U of Arkansas 1984; MS SMU 1994; MDiv Nash 1997. D 6/21/1997 P 12/20/1997 Bp Jack Leo Iker. m 5/25/1991 Leigh Ann Barnett c 2. Dio Fort Worth Ft Worth TX 2010-2014; Asst, Catechist All SS' Epis Ch Ft Worth TX 2009-2010; R S Paul's Ch Doylestown PA 2005-2009; Asst R S Paul's Par Washington DC 1999-2005; Cur S Mk's Ch Arlington TX 1997-1999.

BARNETT, Maxine Maria Veronica (LI) Church of Saint Jude, 3606 Lufberry Ave, Wantagh NY 11793 **Cur Ch of S Jude Wantagh NY 2015-** B St Andrew Jamaica 1956 d Lwyd & Marjorie. BA Brooklyn Coll 1981; MS NYU 1982; MDiv VTS 2015. D 1/31/2015 P 9/12/2015 Bp Lawrence C Provenzano.

BARNETT, Thomas (EC) 1219 Forest Hills Dr., Wilmington NC 28403 **R S Jn's Epis Ch Wilmington NC 2008-; Trst Epis Dio E Carolina 2012-; Mem, Epis Fndt of E Carolina Epis Dio E Carolina 2011-** B Palo Alto CA 1952 s Charles & Mildred. BA California St U 1976; MDiv Fuller TS 1979; DMin Sewanee: The U So, TS 1990; PhD S Louis U 1998. D 3/30/1980 P 4/5/1981 Bp Victor Manuel Rivera. m 8/2/1980 Lynann M Barnett c 3. Int St Mths Epis Ch Waukesha WI 2005-2008; Int Chr Ch Springfield IL 2002-2005; Int S Mich & S Geo S Louis MO 1999-2001; Chapl Off Of Bsh For ArmdF New York NY 1986-2006; Chapl U.S. AF--active duty St. Louis & Pacific Air Forces 1986-2006; R S Matt's Epis Ch Warson Woods Kirkwood MO 1986-1997; Vic S Andr's Ch Taft CA 1983-1986; Cur S Paul's Ch Bakersfield CA 1980-1982; Chair Evang Com Dio Missouri S Louis MO 1989-1993. Auth, "Who's Afraid of Evang ?: Identifying Pstr Concerns Hindering Evang in the Par," S Lk Journ Theol; Contrib, Selected Sermons. AAR (AAR) 1995; OHC 1982; SBL 1995; Soc of Ch Hist 1995.

BARNEY, David Marshall (Mass) 310 Hayward Mill Rd, Concord MA 01742 B Richmond VA 1940 s Marshall & Mary. BA U of Virginia 1962; BD Sewanee: The U So, TS 1965; MLitt U of Cambridge 1975; DMin Sewanee: The U So, TS 1996. D 6/21/1965 P 6/18/1966 Bp Gray Temple. m 8/29/1964 Beverly G Barney c 1. R Trin Ch Concord MA 1981-2001; Dep GC Dio Cntrl Gulf Coast Pensacola FL 1979-1982; S Paul's Epis Ch Daphne AL 1972-1981; 1969-1971; Int Trin Epis Ch Pinopolis SC 1968; Asst to Dn Cathd Of S Lk And S Paul Charleston SC 1965-1968.

BARNEY, Roger Alexander (ECR) 19040 Portos Dr, Saratoga CA 95070 **Asst S Andr's Ch Saratoga CA 1998-, Asst 1982-1997** B Martinsburg WV 1939 s James & Odetta. BA Shpd U 1961; Cert Sch for Deacons 1980. D 3/25/1982 P 3/19/1984 Bp Charles Shannon Mallory. m 8/1/1970 Jeannette Keit. Asst S Tim's Epis Ch Mtn View CA 1994-1998.

BARNHILL JR, James W (USC) Grace Episcopal Church And Kindergarten, 1315 Lyttleton St, Camden SC 29020 **P-in-c S Ptr's Ch Jacksonville FL 2017-** B Durham NC 1956 s James & Gladys. BMus The U of So Carolina 1977; MBA The Amer U of Washington DC 1985; MDiv TESM 2008. D 1/10/2009 P 7/6/2009 Bp Mark Joseph Lawrence. m 12/5/1998 Donna West-Barnhill. Gr Epis Ch Camden SC 2012-2016; R S Paul's Ch Bennettsville SC 2009-2012.

BARNHOUSE, David H (Los) 6844 Penham Pl, Pittsburgh PA 15208 **Pstr Asst Ch Of The Ascen Pittsburgh PA 1993-, D 1986-1993** B Philadelphia PA 1929 s Donald & Ruth. BA Harv 1949; MD Col 1954. D 6/7/1986 P 8/20/1993 Bp Alden Moinet Hathaway. m 5/31/1952 Mary Alice Young. AMA; Amer Urologic Assn. Ba cl Harv 1949.

BARNICLE, Brendan John (Ore) Dio Oregon Portland OR 2017- D 6/10/2017 Bp Michael Hanley.

BARNS, George Stewart (Mass) PO Box 381164, Cambridge MA 02238 **Chapl Emer Harv Cambridge MA 2005-; Chapl Harv Cambridge MA 1978-** B Grand Rapids MI 1945 s George & Margaret. PhD Bos; BA Trin Hartford CT 1967; BD EDS 1970; MTh Harvard DS 1978. D 6/20/1970 P 5/9/1971 Bp John Melville Burgess. Consult Harvard Hlth Serv Harv Cambridge MA 1986-2005; Epis Chapl At Harvard & Radcliffe Cambridge MA 1978-2004; Prot Chapl New Engl Med Cntr Boston MA 1976-1978; The Cathd Ch Of S Paul Boston MA 1976-1978; Ch Of The H Sprt Mattapan MA 1976; Asst Trin Ch Epis Boston MA 1970-1975; Dir Interfaith YA Mnstrs Of Boston Boston MA 1970-1972. Auth, "The Way Of The Cross"; Auth, "The Emerging Spiritulity Of Young Adulthood"; Auth, "Counslg & Referrals When Rel Issues Are Significant Factors".

BARNUM, Barbara Coxe (Los) 11359 Perris Blvd, Moreno Valley CA 92557 **D Gr Mssn Moreno Vlly CA 2010-** B Wilmington DE 1924 d Louis & Irene. BA U of Delaware 1944; MA ETSBH 1987; MDiv Claremont TS 2008. D 12/10/2011 Bp Joseph Jon Bruno. m 11/25/1944 Ferdinand Barnum c 2.

BARNUM, Elena (Ct) 112 Bentwood Dr, Stamford CT 06903 B Cambridge MA 1943 d Edwin & Sylvia. Sch of The Museum of Fine Arts 1963; BS Rhode Island Sch of Design 1965; Cert New York Psychoanalytic Soc and Inst 1989. D 12/7/1991 Bp Arthur Edward Walmsley. m 7/30/1994 Malcolm McGregor Barnum. NAAD.

BARNUM, Malcolm McGregor (Ct) 112 Bentwood Dr, Stamford CT 06903 **Dio Connecticut Meriden CT 2011-, Archd 1991-2005** B Detroit MI 1927 s Richard & Jessie. BA U MI 1949; PMG Stan 1968; Dio Southwark London

UK 1975; Dio Connecticut 1986. D 12/6/1986 Bp Arthur Edward Walmsley. m 7/30/1994 Elena Barnum c 3. Par of St Paul's Ch Norwalk Norwalk CT 2005-2010; D S Paul's Ch Riverside CT 1998-2007; D Epis Ch of Chr the Healer Stamford CT 1991-1997; D Chr Ch Greenwich CT 1986-1991. Servnt Soc.

BARNWELL, William (La) 1917 Audubon St, New Orleans LA 70118 **Artist-in-Res VTS Alexandria VA 2007-; Dir and Auth Disciples of Chr in Cmnty--adult study Prog 2002-** B Charleston SC 1938 s William & Mary. BA U So 1960; BD VTS 1967; MA Tul 1976. D 6/24/1967 P 6/18/1968 Bp Gray Temple. m 8/17/1976 Corinne Freeman Barnwell c 3. P S Lk's Ch New Orleans LA 2012-2014; P Assoc Trin Ch New Orleans LA 2008-2011, Assoc R 1983-1996; Cn Mssnr Cathd of St Ptr & St Paul Washington DC 2008; Cn Washington Natl Cathd Washington DC 2005-2008; Engl Instr U of New Orleans N.O. Louisiana 2002-2004; Assoc R Trin Ch Epis Boston MA 1996-2002; Engl Instr U of New Orleans N.O. Louisiana 1978-1983; Chapl Tul New Orleans LA 1970-1983; Chapl Ch Of The H Sprt New Orleans LA 1970-1978; Asst R S Martins-In-The-Field Columbia SC 1968-1970; Vic St Anne's Epis Ch Conway SC 1967-1969; The Epis Ch Of The Resurr Myrtle Bch SC 1967-1969; Chair, Racial Recon Com Dio Louisiana New Orleans LA 2008-2011; Dn, Boston Harbor Dnry Dio Massachusetts Boston MA 1997-2002. Auth, "Called to Heal the Brokenhearted:," *Stories from the Kairos Prison Mnstry Intl at the Louisiana St Penit at Angola & Beyond*, U Press of Mississippi, 2016; Auth, "In Richard's Wrld: The Battle of Charleston 1966," *Sthrn Classics Series*, Univ. of So Carolina Press, 2013; Auth, "Lead Me On, Let Me Stand:," *A Clergyman's Story in White and Black*, Andover, 2012; Auth, *Reflections: A Thematic Rdr (w Julia P. Thigpen)*, Houghton-Mifflin Co, 1983; Auth, *Writing for a Reason: A Basic Writing Course*, Houghton-Mifflin Co, 1983; Auth, *Our Story According to S Mk*, HarperOne, 1982; Auth, *The Resourceful Writer: A Basic Writing Course*, Houghton-Mifflin Co, 1978; Auth, *In Richard's Wrld*, Houghton-Mifflin Co, 1968. Com of Seventy 2007; Dn, Boston Harbor Dnry 1997-2002; Louisiana Epis Cler Assn 1970-1996; Massachusettes Epis Cler Assn 1996-2002. BD cl VTS 1967.

BARON, Christian John (WMich) 555 Michigan Ave, Holland MI 49423 **S Phil's Ch Beulah MI 2016-** B Grand Rapids MI 1976 s Edward & Nancy. BS Kuyper Coll 2005; MDiv Epis TS Of The SW 2014; MDiv Epis TS of the SW 2014. D 6/14/2014 P 12/20/2014 Bp Whayne Miller Hougland Jr. m 8/26/2000 Jodi Lynn Baron c 3. P Gr Ch Holland MI 2014-2016.

BARON, Jodi Lynn (WMich) 555 Michigan Ave, Holland MI 49423 **S Phil's Ch Beulah MI 2016-** B Kalamazoo MI 1977 d James & Joan. BA Grand Vlly St U 1999; MDiv Epis TS Of The SW 2014; MDiv Epis TS of the SW 2014. D 6/14/2014 P 12/20/2014 Bp Whayne Miller Hougland Jr. m 8/26/2000 Christian John Baron c 3. Asst Gr Ch Holland MI 2014-2016.

BAROODY, Roger Anis (NY) 218 Luke Mountain Rd, Covington VA 24426 B Beirut LB 1941 s Anis & Agnes. BA U of Virginia 1964; MDiv UTS 1991. D 6/13/1992 P 12/1/1992 Bp Richard Frank Grein. Dio New York New York NY 1997-2009; Trin Epis Ch Garnerville NY 1997-2009; Int Epis Shared Mnstry Of Rockland.

BARR, David Lee (Fla) 8227 Bateau Rd S, Jacksonville FL 32216 B San Antonio TX 1942 s Bernice & Doris. BS Texas A&M U 1968; MDiv Epis TS of the SW 1977. D 6/21/1977 P 1/1/1978 Bp Scott Field Bailey. m 6/5/1965 Patsy A Martyn c 2. Asst San Jose Epis Ch Jacksonville FL 2004-2005; R S Eliz's Epis Ch Jacksonville FL 1999-2003; Cn For Stwdshp Dio Florida Jacksonville 1996-1999, Chapl, DOK 1996-1999; Dir Of Dvlpmt Nash Nashotah WI 1993-1996; Chapl Texas Mltry Inst San Antonio TX 1983-1988; Dn of Fac, Hd of Rel Dept Texas Mltry Inst San Antonio TX 1983-1988; Asst S Barth's Ch Corpus Christi TX 1981-1983; R S Paul's Ch Brady TX 1979-1981; Assoc Ch Of Recon San Antonio TX 1977-1979. DOK Chapl 2006-2008; DOK Chapl 1996-1999.

BARR, Donna Faulconer (Lex) 2140 Woodmont Dr, Lexington KY 40502 B Lexington KY 1947 d James & Anna. BEd U of Kentucky 1969; CPE U of Kentucky 1989; EFM Sewanee: The U So, TS 1991; CPE U of Kentucky 1991. D 12/21/1994 Bp Don Adger Wimberly. m 6/9/1967 Garland Hale Barr c 1. Hosp Chapl.

BARR, Gillian Rachel (RI) 275 N Main St, Providence RI 02903 **Dio Rhode Island Providence RI 2014-** B Annapolis MD 1968 d Richard & Eleanor. BA W&M 1990; MDiv PrTS 1995; Dip Ang Stud VTS 2010. D 9/9/2010 P 4/9/2011 Bp Jim Mathes. P Assoc Chr and S Lk's Epis Ch Norfolk VA 2013-2014; Epis Chapl, Old Dominion U Cbury Epis Campus Mnstry Norfolk VA 2011-2014; P Assoc Ch Of The Gd Shpd Norfolk VA 2011-2013; P Assoc Ch Of The Gd Samar San Diego CA 2010-2011; Campus Mssnr, UC San Diego Dio San Diego San Diego CA 2010-2011; ECom 2016; Forma (Form Natl Assn for Epis CE Dir) 2000; Soc of Cath Priests 2013. gillian@episcopalri.org

BARR, Jane Wallace (Va) 209 Macarthur Rd, Alexandria VA 22305 **Chr Epis Ch Gordonsville VA 2017-** B Columbia MS 1945 d Sardis & Ethel. BA Mississippi Coll 1967; MA GW 1975; MDiv VTS 1992. D 6/20/1992 Bp Duncan Montgomery Gray Jr P 3/23/1993 Bp Peter J Lee. m 10/2/1981 Hubert B Barr c 1. P Goodwin Hse Baileys Crossroads Falls Ch VA 2011-2015; S Jas Ch Woodstock VT 2010-2011; Int All SS Ch Harrison NY 2008-2009; Int S Thos Epis

Ch Mclean VA 2005-2007; Ch Of The H Cross Dunn Loring VA 2004-2005; Gr Ch Stanardsville VA 2003-2004; S Jn's Epis Ch Carlisle PA 2000-2003; Ch Of Our Redeem Aldie VA 1996-2000; Chr Ch Alexandria VA 1993-1995; Asst S Tim's Ch Herndon VA 1992-1993.

BARR, Norma Margaret (Chi) **Stff Chapl Aurora Hlth Care Milwaukee WI 2005-** B Dunfermline Scotland 1941 d Norman & Noreen. BA Trin Theol Coll Bristol Uk 1999. Trans 7/6/2003 Bp Bill Persell. c 2. P-in-c Gr Ch Pontiac IL 2003-2005.

BARRAGAN, Juan (Los) 9046 Gallatin Rd., Pico Rivera CA 90660 **Vic S Barth's Mssn Pico Rivera CA 2003-** B Mexico City 1953 s Hector & Maria. Cert Escuela Sup Ventas 1978; Cert Theol Stud ETSBH 1998. D 6/6/1998 P 1/9/1999 Bp Frederick Houk Borsch. m 1/16/1993 Petra Santillana c 3. Vic Epis Chap Of S Fran Los Angeles CA 2001-2002; Asst S Mich's Mssn Anaheim CA 1999-2001; Asst All SS Par Los Angeles CA 1998-1999.

BARRAZA, Rene (Los) St Athanasius and St Paul's, 840 Echo Park Ave, Los Angeles CA 90026 B Olocuilta El Salvador 1943 s Rosaura. D 7/29/2007 P 2/23/2008 Bp Joseph Jon Bruno. m 8/19/1967 Maria A Barraza c 4. Dio Los Angeles Los Angeles CA 2007-2012; Cathd Cong Los Angeles CA 2007; Sexton Cathd Cntr of St Paul 1994-2007.

BARRE, James Lyman (Vt) 1009 Robert E. Lee Drive, Wilmington NC 28412 **1972-** B Brattleboro VT 1935 s Ernest & Gladys. BA U of Vermont 1964; STB GTS 1967. D 6/10/1967 P 12/16/1967 Bp Harvey D Butterfield. m 4/28/1973 Carol Ann Barre c 3. Chapl Cathd Ch Of S Paul Burlington VT 1971-1972; P-in-c Chr Ch Island Pond VT 1969-1970; R S Mk's Epis Ch Newport VT 1967-1970.

BARRERA FLORES, Olga I (Hond) IMS SAP Dept 215. PO BOX 523900, Miami FL 33152 Honduras **Dio Honduras San Pedro Sula 2011-** B 1969 d Domingo & Maria Isabel. D 3/11/2007 P 2/5/2011 Bp Lloyd Emmanuel Allen. c 3.

BARRETT, Constance Yvonne (Mil) 3560 N Summit Ave, Shorewood WI 53211 **Non-par 1990-** B Pittsburgh PA 1943 BA U Pgh 1972; MDiv Pittsburgh TS 1975. D 12/12/1981 Bp Robert Bracewell Appleyard P 5/29/1986 Bp Alden Moinet Hathaway. m 1/27/1980 G Richard Meadows. S Chris's Ch Milwaukee WI 1986-1990; Non-par 1984-1986; S Paul's Ch Milwaukee WI 1982-1983; Dir Pstr Care Dept Passavant Hosp Pittsburgh PA 1975-1978; Asst Calv Ch Pittsburgh PA 1971-1978.

BARRETT, Gina (CPa) **S Jn's Ch Marietta PA 2016-; Alt Cler Dep to GC Dio Cntrl Pennsylvania Harrisburg PA 2015-2018, Dn of the Lancaster Convoc 2015-, Yth Com 2013-, Lay Dep to GC--Serv on Mnstry Com 2012-2015, Lay Dep to GC 2009-2012** B Columbus OH 1960 d Humberto & Carol. Bachelor of Mus U MI 1982; Grad Performance Dplma Peabody Conservatory 1992; MDiv Lancaster TS 2012; Post Grad Dplma VTS 2013. D 6/2/2013 P 3/1/2014 Bp Nathan Dwight Baxter. m 12/22/1999 Patrick A Barrett. S Thos Ch Lancaster PA 2013-2015.

BARRETT, Johanna Elizabeth Langley (Mass) Trinity Church, 124 River Road, Topsfield MA 01983 **R Trin Ch Topsfield MA 2005-** B Utica NY 1955 d Edwin & Edith. BA Mt Holyoke Coll 1977; MS Amer U 1984; MDiv VTS 1994. D 6/11/1994 P 12/14/1994 Bp Peter J Lee. Assoc R S Thos Epis Ch Rochester NY 1998-2005; Asst R Chr Ch Corning NY 1995-1998; Asst To Int Ch Of The Resurr Alexandria VA 1994-1995; Asst To Chapl Epis HS Alexandria VA 1994-1995. Auth, "Vstry Resource Guide," 1997.

BARRETT, John Hammond (WTex) 3527 Vancouver Dr, Dallas TX 75229 B Paris TX 1960 s Henry & Joan. BA U So 1982; MA Ford 1991; MEd Ford 1996; MDiv TESM 2002. D 6/8/2002 P 3/1/2003 Bp James Monte Stanton. m 5/27/1995 Barbara B Barrett c 4. Trin Sch Of Midland Inc. Midland TX 2012-2016; Chr Epis Ch San Antonio TX 2005-2012; Gd Shpd Epis Sch Dallas TX 2004-2005; Cur S Lk's Epis Ch Dallas TX 2002-2004.

BARRETT JR, John Henry (CNY) 41 S Woody Hill Rd, Westerly RI 02891 **P Assoc Chr Ch Westerly RI 2002-** B Westerly RI 1937 s John & Mildred. BA U of Rhode Island 1959; MDiv Ya Berk 1963; St Georges Coll Jerusalem 1989. D 6/22/1963 P 5/9/1964 Bp John S Higgins. m 8/25/1962 Carol Wells c 3. R All SS Epis Ch Johnson City NY 1996-2002; R The Ch Of The H Name Swampscott MA 1970-1996; Asst Trin Ch Concord MA 1967-1970; Cur Chr And H Trin Ch Westport CT 1964-1967; Mssnr Cathd Of S Jn Providence RI 1963-1964; Dioc Coun Dio Massachusetts Boston MA 1985-1988, Com on election of a Bp 1975-1984. Silver Beaver Awd for Serv to Yth BSA 1988.

BARRETT, John Richard (Tex) St Martin's Episcopal Church, 1602 S Fm 116, Copperas Cove TX 76522 B Dallas TX 1949 s Frank & Helen. BS LSU 1971; MD SW Med Sch 1975; Iona Sch for Mnstry 2007. D 6/23/2007 Bp Don Adger Wimberly P 1/12/2008 Bp Dena Arnall Harrison. m 6/22/1974 Margaret B Barrett c 3. Vic S Mart's Epis Ch Copperas Cove TX 2008-2013, D in Charge 2007-2008. Auth, "Renal Sodium Wastin," *Salt Wasting Nephropathy*, Texas Med, 1979. Amer Coll of Physicians 1978. Bd Dir Cranbrook Sch Alum Coun 2013; Fell, ACP Amer Coll of Physicians 2012; Hood 'Hero' for Indiv Quality Ft Hood 2012; D.D. EDS 1997.

BARRETT BSJE, Patricia Callan (Mass) **MECA Bd Dio Massachusetts 2010-; Chapl Falmouth Fire Dept 2009-** B Brooklyn NY 1949 d Peter & Evelyn. BA Mt Holyoke Coll 1971; MA Amer Intl Coll 1975; MDiv EDS 1998. D

6/10/2000 Bp Gordon Scruton P 12/10/2000 Bp Barbara Clementine Harris. m 1/23/1971 William F Barrett c 2. R S Barn Ch Falmouth MA 2009-2016; Stndg Com Dio El Camino Real Salinas CA 2007-2009, Stndg Com 2005-2008, Mem Ord Com 2005-2006; Com. On Mnstry Dio El Camino Real 2005-2008; R Epis Ch Of The Gd Shpd Salinas CA 2004-2009; Int S Lk's Epis Ch Scituate MA 2003-2004; Asst S Paul's Ch In Nantucket Nantucket MA 2000-2002; Mem Dioc Coun Dio Massachusetts Boston MA 2001-2004. "Sacr Garden," Morehouse, 2000; "Too Busy To Clean," Storey Pub, 1994. Soc of ST Jn The Evang Assoc 2004.

BARRETT, Rilla Diane (Oly) 670 Rainbow Dr, Sedro-Woolley WA 98284 **St Steph's Epis Ch Oak Harbor WA 2013-** B Seattle WA 1947 d Edwin & Dorothy. BA Wstrn Washington U 1969; MEd Seattle Pacific U 1989; MDiv Vancouver TS CA 2009. D 4/17/2009 Bp Gregory Harold Rickel P 11/19/2009 Bp Bavi Edna Rivera. m 8/8/1991 Michael Stephen Barrett c 3. P in Charge Ch Of Our Sav Monroe WA 2011-2013; Cur Komo Kulshan Cluster Mt Vernon WA 2010-2011.

BARRETT, Robin Carter (EO) 9310 Parakeet Dr, Bonanza OR 97623 B Pasadena CA 1925 s I Carter & Elizabeth. D 8/16/1992 P 7/1/1993 Bp Rustin Ray Kimsey. m 8/16/1952 Marvel Mae Ikenberry Wilson. P S Barn Par Portland OR 1993-2007, D 1992.

BARRETT OSB, Sr Helena (Nwk) **Assoc Trin Ch Easton PA 2012-** B Lawrence KS 1946 d Linton & Marie. BA Albertus Magnus Coll 1970; MA NYU 1972; MDiv GTS 1975; PhD NYU 1986. D 12/15/1975 P 1/10/1977 Bp Paul Moore Jr. m 7/18/2013 Alison Joy Whybrow. Life Professed Sis OSB Comp of St. Lk OSB 2008-2013; Int S Jn's Ch Un City NJ 2008-2011; Novc Sis Cmnty of St Mary the Vrgn Wantage Engl 2005-2007; Adj Drew U TS Madison NJ 2004-2005; Int S Jas Ch Montclair NJ 2004-2005; Dio New York New York NY 2004, 1981-1983; Int Ch Of The Medtr Bronx NY 2003; Int S Andr And H Comm Ch So Orange NJ 2000-2002; R Bergen Epis Area Mnstry Maywood NJ 1997-2000; Assoc The Ch of S Ign of Antioch New York NY 1995-1996; Lectr UTS 1994-2002; Asst S Jn's Ch New York NY 1988-1992; Assoc The Ch Of S Lk In The Fields New York NY 1980-1988; Assoc S Mk's Par Berkeley CA 1977-1980, D 1975-1977. Auth, "Var arts". Chapl Ord Colonial Lords Of Manors Amer 1991-2000; Eccl Hist Soc (Britain) 1985-2000; Fllshp Of S Jn The Evang 1988-2001. Mdiv cl GTS 1975.

BARRETT, Timothy Lewis (Nwk) 10 Crestmont Rd, Montclair NJ 07042 B Dallas TX 1945 D 6/13/2002 P 12/15/2002 Bp John Palmer Croneberger. m 5/31/1969 Mary Elizabeth Barrett c 1.

BARRIE, David Paul (NY) 2109 Broadway # 1241, New York NY 10023 **Ret 1995-** B Toledo OH 1933 s John & Rose. BA U of Toledo 1956; MFA CUA 1968; MDiv NYTS 1990. D 6/8/1991 P 12/14/1991 Bp Richard Frank Grein. Chapl DeWitt Nrsng and Rehab Cntr 1992-2011. Amer Soc On Aging; Coll Of Chapl.

BARRINGTON, Dominic M J (Chi) 65 E Huron St, Chicago IL 60611 **Dn Cathd Of S Jas Chicago IL 2015-** B London UK 1962 s Donald & Dawn. BA Dur 1984; MSC Dur 1985; MA Oxf 1994; MTS CDSP, 1995. Trans 8/24/2015 as Priest Bp Jeff Lee. m 9/7/1991 Katherine Alison Barrington c 2. dean@saintjamescathedral.org

BARRINGTON JR, E Tom (Mass) 27 6th Ave, North Chelmsford MA 01863 **Bristol Trin Epis Ch No Easton MA 2016-; Direct Care Supvsr Lowell Transition Living Cntr 2013-** B Boston MA 1956 s Evan & Helene. BA Muhlenberg Coll 1979; MDiv EDS 1988. D 6/11/1988 Bp David Elliot Johnson P 6/17/1989 Bp O'Kelley Whitaker. m 6/7/1980 Linda A Barrington c 2. S Anne's Ch Lowell MA 2012; Dn Merrimack Vlly Dnry 2001-2009; R All SS Ch Chelmsford MA 1999-2012; Chapl Elmchrest Chld's Cntr Syracuse NY 1998-2000; Vic Ch Of The Gd Shpd Nedrow NY 1994-1999; Vic Emm Ch E Syracuse NY 1992-1999; Cn St Paul's Syracuse Syracuse NY 1988-1992. tbarrington4@gmail.com

BARRIOS, Luis (NY) 295 Saint Anns Ave, Bronx NY 10454 B Rio Piechas PR 1952 s Esteban & Maria. BA Wrld U 1978; PhD Caribbean Cntr for Advncd Stds 1983; MDiv NYTS 1991. D 6/8/1991 P 12/1/1991 Bp Richard Frank Grein. m 7/28/1990 Minerva Barrios. S Ann's Ch Of Morrisania Bronx NY 1992-1993, D 1991; D S Mary's Manhattanville Epis Ch New York NY 1991-2000. Ord Of Ascen.

BARRIOS, Maria Trevino (Dal) 534 W 10th St, Dallas TX 75208 **S Barn Ch Garland TX 2017-** B Mexico 1957 d Miguel & Tomaja. D 11/10/2007 Bp James Monte Stanton. m 1/6/1979 M Armando Barrios c 2. S Matt's Cathd Dallas TX 2012-2016.

BARRON JR, Caldwell Alexander (SC) 168 Club Cir, Pawleys Island SC 29585 **Ret 2006-** B Charleston SC 1945 s Caldwell & Helen. BA Cit 1967; MDiv Sewanee: The U So, TS 1970. D 6/29/1970 P 5/9/1971 Bp John Adams Pinckney. m 8/24/1968 Margaret H Barron. Assoc H Cross Faith Memi Epis Ch Pawleys Island SC 2009-2011; Assoc Ch Of The Ascen Knoxville TN 1999-2005; Trin Ch Myrtle Bch SC 1994-1999; S Agnes Epis Ch Franklin NC 1993; Ch Of The Gd Shpd Cashiers NC 1991-1994; R S Mk's Ch Marco Island FL 1984-1991; Chapl Cit Charleston SC 1982-1984; So Carolina Charleston SC 1982-1984; Chapl (Cmdr) USNR 1980-2000; R Epis Ch of the Gd Shpd Charleston SC

1979-1984; Assoc Gr Epis Ch Anderson SC 1977-1979; P-in-c Calv Ch Pauline SC 1977; R Ch Of The Nativ Un SC 1974-1977; Asst Gr Epis Ch Hinsdale IL 1972-1974; Cur Ch Of The Adv Spartanburg SC 1970-1972.

BARRON, Carol Dunn (SeFla) 3954 SE Fairway E, Stuart FL 34997 **Co-R St. Lk's Epis Ch Port Salerno FL 2005-; Assoc S Lk's Epis Ch Stuart FL 2001-** B Oklahoma City OK 1948 d Gene & Dorothy. BS Palm Bch Atlantic U 1973; JD Shepard Broad Cntr For Study of Law Ft Lauderdale FL 1981; MDiv Sewanee: The U So, TS 2001. D 6/16/2001 P 4/26/2002 Bp Leo Frade. m 3/22/2005 Richard John Barron.

BARRON, Scott William (Chi) 1148 N Douglas Ave, Arlington Heights IL 60004 B Chicago Heights IL 1952 s William & Ann. BA Sthrn Illinois U 1976; MA U Chi 1978; DMin Meadville Lombard TS 1980. D 6/15/2002 P 12/21/2002 Bp Bill Persell. m 9/6/1980 Mary McCarthy c 3. R S Jn's Epis Ch Mt Prospect IL 2003-2014. SocMary 2005.

BARRON, Thomas Lemuel (Ga) **Other Lay Position S Andr's Ch Darien GA 2013-** D 5/27/2017 Bp Scott Anson Benhase.

BARROW, Alan Lester (Okla) 5635 E. 71st St., Tulsa OK 74136 **Dir Sprtl Direction 2011-; D S Dunst's Ch Tulsa OK 2004-; Fac Oklahoma Dept. of Corrections Vol MRT Provider 1998-** B Bethesda MD 1952 s Vernie & Betty. AA Tulsa Cmnty Coll 1991; Certification Sprtl Direction SMU 2013. D 6/21/2003 Bp Robert Manning Moody. m 5/3/1975 Libby Barrow c 3. Chair Cmsn on Prison Mnstry Dio Oklahoma Oklahoma City OK 2006-2010.

BARROW, Colin Vere (SO) 8592 Roswell Rd Apt.218, Sandy Springs GA 30350 B Saint George BB 1928 s Clyde & Verna. DIT Codrington Coll 1954; BA Lon GB 1964; STM NYTS 1979; ThD Intl Bible Inst & TS 1983. Trans 10/1/1975 as Priest Bp Paul Moore Jr. m 1/4/1976 Winsome E Barrow c 4. Int S Paul's Epis Ch Greenville OH 2000-2002; Dn W Dayton Dnry Dio Sthrn Ohio Cincinnati OH 1992-1999; R S Marg's Ch Dayton OH 1985-1999; S Lk's Ch Ft Vlly GA 1980-1985; Dio Atlanta Atlanta GA 1980-1981; P-in-c S Lk's Cnvnt Av New York NY 1977-1980; S Mart's Ch New York NY 1975-1980; Serv Ch of Barbados & British Guiana 1955-1974; Chapl Ft Vlly St Coll. Bro of S Andr 1975; USPG 1955.

BARROW, John Condict Hurst (Ind) 8920 Washington Blvd West Dr, Indianapolis IN 46240 **Vol AIDS T/F 1984-** B Chicago IL 1956 s Gordon-Hurst & Josephine. BA Col 1979; MDiv Ya Berk 1984; STM Ya Berk 1985; Sthrn Bapt TS 1989. D 12/18/1985 Bp Gerald Nicholas Mcallister P 6/1/1986 Bp Frank S Cerveny. m 3/17/1985 Frances Stallings Hale. S Paul's Epis Ch Gas City IN 1999; S Steph's Elwood IN 1998-1999; Epis Ch Of The Gd Shpd Lake Chas LA 1993-1994; Asst Ch Of The Adv Louisville KY 1989-1993; Asst S Tim's Epis Ch Winston Salem NC 1987-1989; Chapl Alco & Rehab Cntr Tallahassee FL 1985-1987; Asst S Jn's Epis Ch Tallahassee FL 1985-1987; Chapl S Raphael's Hosp New Haven CT 1984-1985. fringelids@me.com

BARROW, John Thomas (SJ) Po Box 3231, Mammoth Lakes CA 93546 B Wilmington DE 1940 s Ernest & Helen. BS California St U 1989; MDiv TESM 1993. D 7/10/1993 P 3/1/1994 Bp David Mercer Schofield. m 3/23/1991 Margaret Aird Barrow. S Andr's Ch Taft CA 1996-2000; S Thos Of Cbury Mammoth Lakes CA 1993-1996.

BARROW, Suzanne (Ky) B LaGrange KY 1949 BA U of Louisiana. D 3/22/2003 P 9/28/2003 Bp Ted Gulick Jr. All SS Epis Cntr Leitchfield KY 2013-2014; Dio Kentucky Louisville KY 2006-2017, 2003; S Andr's Ch Glasgow KY 2004-2016.

BARROWCLOUGH, Lisa Shirley (SeFla) St. Mark's Episcopal Church and School, 3395 Burns Road, Palm Beach Gardens FL 33410 **Chapl The Ch Of The Gd Shpd Augusta GA 2012-; Trnr Safeguarding God's Chld 2004-** B Burlington Ontario CA 1974 d David & Shirley. BA U of Wstrn Ontario CA 1996; MDiv Queens Coll 1999; DMin VTS 2009. Trans 6/12/2004 as Priest Bp John Bailey Lipscomb. Sch Chapl S Mk's Ch Palm Bch Garden FL 2006-2012; Ch Of The Gd Shpd Punta Gorda FL 2004-2006; Mem And Educ Subcommittee Chair Dio SW Florida 2004-2006; Gd Shpd Chld Care Cntr Charleston WV 2004-2006; Camp Chapl Dio Sw Florida 2004-2005; Chr Formation Cmsn Sw Florida 2003-2006; Day Sch Chapl Gd Shpd Day Sch Punta Gorda FL 2003-2006; R St. Columbas Peers Alberta 1999-2002; Yth Mnstry Fac And Camp Chapl Dio Edmonton 1999-2001.

BARROWS, Jennifer Eve (NY) 1585 Route 9 West, West Park NY 12493 B Vellore IN 1944 d James & Eva. BA Hope Coll 1966; MDiv UTS 1992; STM GTS 2001. D 3/10/2001 Bp Richard Frank Grein P 9/16/2001 Bp Mark Sean Sisk. c 2. P-in-c Ch Of The Ascen And H Trin W Pk NY 2013-2016, P-in-c 2001-, D 2000-2001; Dio New York New York NY 2001-2016. revbarrows@hvc.rr.com

BARRUS, Donald Sidney (Fla) 516 Balmora Dr, St Augustine FL 32092 **Died 4/15/2016** B Springfield MA 1924 s Donald & Agnes. BS U of Massachusetts 1949; BD VTS 1955; MEd Florida Atlantic U 1971. D 6/11/1952 Bp William A Lawrence P 12/1/1952 Bp Duncan Montgomery Gray. m 9/1/1951 Mary Jaudon c 4. Ret 1985-2016; R S Andr's Ch Jacksonville FL 1980-1985; R S Jn's Ch Hollywood FL 1977-1980; Assoc S Greg's Ch Boca Raton FL 1975-1977; Chapl Atlantic U Boca Raton FL 1968-1974; Dn Palm Bch Dnry Dio SE Florida Miami 1961-1968; H Trin Epis Ch W Palm Bch FL 1960-1968; R S Dav's Epis Ch Lakeland FL 1955-1960; Asst S Jn's Epis Par Waterbury CT 1952-1955.

BARRY, Brian Clark (LI) St Ann's Episcopal Church, 262 Middle Rd, Sayville NY 11782 B Glencove NY 1980 s Brian & Theresa. D 1/30/2016 Bp Lawrence C Provenzano. m 6/4/2016 Holly Cooper.

BARRY, Eugenia Clare Mackenzie (WNC) 11 Lone Pine Rd, Asheville NC 28803 B Washington DC 1952 d Foster & Eugenia. BA U of New Hampshire 1975; MALS Dart 1994; MSW U NC 2000; DMin GTF 2006. D 11/23/2002 Bp Bob Johnson. Epis Ch Of The H Sprt Mars Hill NC 2004-2008; D Gr Ch Asheville NC 2002-2003.

BARRY, Peggy Sue (Ark) 400 Hill St, Forrest City AR 72335 B Yell County AR 1935 d Sam & Virginia. BSE U of Cntrl Arkansas 1958; MA Arkansas St U 1993. D 8/17/2010 P 3/11/2011 Bp Larry Benfield. m 3/10/1959 David Barry c 2.

BARRY-MARQUESS, Richard Livingston (SeFla) 19540 Nw 8th Ave, Miami FL 33169 B Miami FL 1940 s Albert & Olive. BA S Augustines Coll Raleigh NC 1962; Amer U 1963; MDiv VTS 1968; Candler TS Emory U 1974; Emory U Candler Sem 1974; Fell U of Munich 1978; Oxf GB 2005. D 6/22/1968 Bp James Loughlin Duncan P 12/22/1968 Bp William Loftin Hargrave. m 8/18/1962 Virla Barry c 1. R S Agnes Ch Miami FL 1977-2010; Vic Ch Of S Simon The Cyrenian Ft Pierce FL 1968-1977; P-in-c S Monica's Ch Stuart FL 1968-1975. Phi Beta Sigma, AAPC. Invested Hon Cn Trin Cathd, Miami 2000; Invested Hon Cn Afr Orth Ch 1995; DD Virginia Sem 1989.

BARTA, Heather Marie (EMich) 156 Guanonocque St, Auburn Hills MI 48326 **Dio Chicago Chicago IL 2017-; Ch Of The Resurr Clarkston MI 2016-; Chapl Cbury NW 2004-** B Lakeside AZ 1973 d Marvin & Garyle. MDiv SWTS 2004. D 12/18/2003 P 8/21/2004 Bp Robert R Gepert. m 8/11/2006 Henry Barta. P-in-c S Jude's Epis Ch Fenton MI 2015-2016; P-in-c Trin Epis Ch Flushing MI 2013-2014; S Paul's Epis Ch Flint MI 2009-2011; Chr Epis Ch Owosso MI 2006-2008; Cbury NW Evanston IL 2004-2006.

BARTELS, Judith Tallman (Oly) none----moved from there, lacey WA 98117 B Nyack NY 1936 d Frank & Eileen. BA Pomona Coll 1957; Oregon Cntr for the Diac 1992; Cert Marylhurst U 1996. D 6/24/1992 Bp Robert Louis Ladehoff. m 8/17/1957 Ronald Earl Bartels c 3. D S Steph's Epis Ch Seattle WA 1997-1999; D S Paul's Ch Seattle WA 1995-1996; D Epis Par Of S Jn The Bapt Portland OR 1992-1994. Sprtl Dir Intl 1996. BA w hon Pomona Coll 1957.

BARTH, Barbara L (Me) 42 Tailwind Ct Apt 78 D, Auburn ME 04210 **Gender Equity Coordntr Cntrl Maine Cmnty Coll Auburn ME 2011-; Supply P Dio Maine Portland ME 2009-, Com Wk, etc. 1998-2009; Adj Fac Cntrl Maine Cmnty Coll Auburn ME 2007-** B Niagara Falls NY 1957 BS Niagara U 1980; MA U of Connecticut 1982; MDiv Chr Sem -Seminex/LSTC Chicago IL 1986; Cert Epis TS of the SW 1998. D 6/20/1998 Bp Claude Edward Payne P 6/23/1999 Bp Leopoldo Jesus Alard. Com Wk, etc. The Par of S Mich's Auburn ME 2000-2009; Vic S Paul's Epis Ch Woodville TX 1998-1999; Adj Fac Galveston Coll Galveston TX 1994-1997; Pstr Evang Luth Ch in Can 1986-1993; Adj Fac Forest Pk Cmnty Coll St. Louis MO 1982-1983. Adj Fac Mem/Year Cntrl Maine Cmnty Coll 2012; Exceptional Serv Awd Galveston Coll 1997; Delta Epsilon Sigma Niagara U 1980; BA mcl Niagara U 1980.

BARTHELEMY, Paul Berge (Ore) 4524 Trillium Woods, Lake Oswego OR 97035 **Int R All SS Epis Ch Hillsboro OR 2015-** B Saint Paul MN 1942 s Carl & Juliet. BA U IL 1964; MFA Pr 1967; MDiv Nash 1975. D 6/28/1975 P 5/15/1976 Bp Chauncie Kilmer Myers. m 5/22/1980 Mary Barthelemy c 3. Int R St Jas Epis Ch Tigard OR 2012-2013; Vic S Cathr Of Alexandria Epis Ch Nehalem OR 2002-2010; Exec Dir Portland Yth Philharmonic Portland OR 1994-2003; Chapl Hawaii Preparatory Acad Kamuela HI 1990-1994; Headmaster S Mich Day Sch CA 1989-1990; Headmaster S Marg Sch Tappannock VA 1984-1989; Assoc Epis Par Of S Jn The Bapt Portland OR 1977-1984; Chapl Ore Epis Sch Portland OR 1977-1984; Chapl Oregon Epis Sch Portland OR 1977-1984; Asst Chr Epis Ch Los Altos CA 1975-1977.

BARTHOLOMEW, Adam Gilbert Leinbach (NY) 802 Broadway, New York NY 10003 B Pottstown PA 1943 s Gilbert & Emma. BA U Pgh 1965; BD Lancaster TS 1968; PhD UTS 1974. D 10/20/2001 P 6/1/2002 Bp Herbert Thompson Jr. m 10/16/1999 Linda Milavec Bartholomew c 1. Int Ch Of The Ascen Mt Vernon NY 2008-2012; Int The Ch Of The Ascen Rockville Ct NY 2006-2008; Int Chr Ch Poughkeepsie NY 2005-2006; Dio Sthrn Ohio Cincinnati OH 2001-2005; Indn Hill Ch Cincinnati OH 2001-2005; Assoc To The Dn Angl Acad Columbus OH 2000-2005; Serv Parishes in Untd Ch of Chr 1971-1997. Co-Auth, "Preaching Verse by Verse," WJK, 2000; Auth, "Pass it on," *Telling and Hearing Stories from Jn*, Untd Ch of Chr, 1992. Ntwk of Biblic Storytellers 1985.

BARTHOLOMEW, Linda Milavec (Spok) Church Of The Resurrection, 15319 E 8th Ave, Spokane Valley WA 99037 **P-in-c Ch Of The Resurr Veradale WA 2012-** B Pasco WA 1951 d Donald & Roberta. BD U of Dayton/Marian Coll 1975; MDiv S Fran Sem 1983; DMin McCormick TS 1991; Cert SWTS 1995. D 6/21/1997 P 2/21/1998 Bp Herbert Thompson Jr. m 10/16/1999 Adam Gilbert Leinbach Bartholomew c 1. Gr Epis Ch New York NY 2004-2012; Cn Chr Ch Cathd Cincinnati OH 1998-2004; S Jas Epis Ch Cincinnati OH 1997-1998; Pstr Assoc/Intern S Geo's Epis Ch Dayton OH 1996-1997. Ntwk Of Biblic Storytellers 1990-2000. Honorable Mention, Best Thesis Mccormick TS 1991; Maranatha Awd S Fran Sem 1983.

BARTLE, Edward Bartholomew (CFla) 330 Hickory Ave, Orange City FL 32763 **Assoc R S Geo Epis Ch The Villages FL 2015-; Loc Chapt, Dioc Co-ordntr The Bro Of S Andr Inc. Ambridge PA 2015-; Mem Curs 1984-** B Cass City MI 1943 s Leonard & Enola. D 12/18/2004 P 5/30/2009 Bp John Wadsworth Howe. m 12/23/1983 Phyllis Ann Cooper c 5. R S Edw The Confessor Mt Dora FL 2009-2015; S Jude's Ch Orange City FL 2009.

BARTLE, John Dixon (Alb) Po Box E, Richfield Springs NY 13439 **R Ch of the Gd Shephard Warren NY 1990-** B Bryn Mawr PA 1945 s Harvey & Dorothy. BS U of Pennsylvania 1967; JD Penn St Dickinson Sch of Law 1970; MDiv EDS 1985. D 6/21/1986 Bp Lyman Cunningham Ogilby P 5/1/1987 Bp Allen Lyman Bartlett Jr. m 8/27/2016 Lynn Bush c 2. R S Jn's Ch Richfld Spgs NY 1990-2016; Asst S Mary's Ch Portsmouth RI 1989-1990; Asst S Jn's Ch Barrington RI 1987-1989; Int Geo W So Ch of Advoc Philadelphia PA 1987; Cur Nevil Memi Ch Of S Geo Ardmore PA 1986-1987.

BARTLE, Leonard William (CFla) 3520 Curtis Dr, Apopka FL 32703 **D Epis Ch Of The H Sprt Apopka FL 1979-** B Cass City MI 1923 s John & Alice. D 11/20/1979 Bp William Hopkins Folwell. m 10/8/1982 Mary Heidl c 3.

BARTLE, Phyllis Ann (CFla) 330 Hickory Ave, Orange City FL 32763 **R S Jude's Ch Orange City FL 2006-** B Coldwater MI 1953 d Harry & Donna. Valencia Cmnty Coll; BS Rol 1990; MDiv TESM 2006. D 5/27/2006 P 12/10/2006 Bp John Wadsworth Howe. m 12/23/1983 Edward Bartholomew Bartle c 2. Dir of Yth Mnstrs St. Barn Epis 2001-2005.

✠ BARTLETT JR, The Rt Rev Allen Lyman (Pa) 600 E. Cathedral Rd., Apt. L-209, Philadelphia PA 19128 **Ret Bp of Pennsylvania Dio Pennsylvania Philadelphia PA 1998-, Bp of Pennsylvania 1987-1998, Bp Coadj of Pennsylvania 1986-1987** B Birmingham AL 1929 s Allen & Edith. BA U So 1951; MDiv VTS 1958; DMin VTS 1980; DD VTS 1986; DD U So 1988. D 7/2/1958 Bp George Mosley Murray P 6/16/1959 Bp Charles C J Carpenter Con 2/15/1986 for Pa. m 12/28/1957 Jerriette K Kohlmeier c 3. Asstg Bp Dio Washington Washington DC 2001-2004; Mem, Justice w Peace Cmsn The Epis Ch 1994-1997; Chair Metro Ch Coun of Philadelphia Philadelphia PA 1993-1997; Mem, Exec Coun The Epis Ch 1979-1985; Dn Chr Ch Cathd Louisville KY 1970-1986; Trst VTS Alexandria VA 1964-1969; R Zion Epis Ch Chas Town WV 1961-1970; Trst U So TS Sewanee TN 1960-1963; Vic S Barn Epis Ch Roanoke AL 1958-1961; Vic S Jas' Epis Ch Alexander City AL 1958-1961. Un League of Philadelphia 1995. DD U So 1988; DD VTS 1986; Phi Beta Kappa U So 1950.

BARTLETT, Anne Kristin (Ore) 281 Talent Ave, Talent OR 97540 **P Trin Epis Ch Ashland Ashland OR 2013-, R 2001-2010, 2000-2001** B Saint Louis MO 1946 d Thomas & Anita. BA Washington U 1967; MA Washington U 1969; MDiv Eden TS 1984; Cert Care and Counslg Cntr of St Louis 1985; Cert SWTS 1987. D 5/16/1987 P 11/1/1987 Bp William Augustus Jones Jr. m 4/16/1983 William E Bartlett c 2. Assoc Epis Par Of S Jn The Bapt Portland OR 1995-2000; Assoc S Mk's Epis Par Medford OR 1992-1995; P Gr Ch S Louis MO 1990-1992; P Ch Of The Adv S Louis MO 1987-1989; Stndg Com Dio Oregon Portland OR 2005-2009, Bd Trst 1997-2005. "Taking Our Places at the Table," *Sermons that Wk XI*, Morehouse, 2003; "Consider How You Have Fared," *Sermons that Wk VII*, Morehouse, 1998; "But Who Do You Say That I Am?," *Sermons that Wk VI*, Morehouse, 1997.

BARTLETT, Basil A (VI) PO Box 7386, St Thomas VI 00801 B Anguilla B.W.I 1937 s Oguise & Hilda. D 6/28/2008 Bp Edward Gumbs. m 8/18/1965 Emeline Bartlett c 4.

BARTLETT, Harwood (At) 4345 Erskine Rd, Clarkston GA 30021 **Ret 1999-** B New York NY 1934 s George & Thelma. BS Georgia Inst of Tech 1956; MDiv VTS 1962. D 6/30/1962 P 5/1/1963 Bp Randolph R Claiborne. m 5/27/1983 Carol P Bartlett c 3. Prog Dir Corp for Supportive Hsng Atlanta GA 1994-1999; Dio Atlanta Atlanta GA 1982-1994; Dir, Epis Chars Fndt Dio Atlanta Atlanta GA 1982-1994; R S Barth's Epis Ch Atlanta GA 1972-1982; Bd Mem Appleton Ch Hm (Epis) Atlanta GA 1967-1972; Vic S Fran Ch Macon GA 1967-1972; Chapl All SS Epis Ch Atlanta GA 1962-1967; Fndr, Chair of the Bd Georgia Interfaith Power & Light 2003-2010; Fndr, Chair of Bd Transition Hse Atlanta Georgia 1985-1995; Dep GC 1973-1982. Auth, "Living By Surprise: A Chr Response to the Environ Crisis," Paulist Press, 2003; Auth, "A Chr Discovers the Environ Crisis," *Journ of the Med Assn of Georgia*, 1999. Ch and City Conf 1982-1994. Individual Achievement in Affordable Hsng Progressive Redevelopment Inc. 2000; Outstanding Personal Mnstry Chr Coun of Metro Atlanta 1988; Ldrshp Atlanta 1975; Young Man of the Year in Rel Atlanta Jaycees 1967.

BARTLETT, Laurie Lee (Alb) Calvary Church, PO Box 41, Burnt Hills NY 12027 B Hartford CT 1957 d Francis & Lena. Manchester Cmnty Coll 1976; Hartford Coll for Wmn 1980. D 6/2/2012 Bp William Howard Love. m 5/15/1976 Michael S Bartlett c 4.

BARTLETT, Lois Sherburne (Be) 2716 Tennyson Ave, Sinking Spring PA 19608 B Potsdam NY 1936 d Frank & Dorothy. BS SUNY 1958; MDiv GTS 1991. D 6/8/1991 P 12/22/1991 Bp James Michael Mark Dyer. c 3. Chr Ch Reading PA 2001-2007; R S Geo's Epis Ch Hellertown PA 1998-2001; Int S Mich's Epis Ch Birdsboro PA 1996-1998; S Mich's Epis Ch Birdsboro PA

1996-1997; No Par Epis Ch St. Clair PA 1993-1996; P-in-c No Par Epis Ch Ashland PA 1991-1996; Dio Bethlehem Bethlehem PA 1991-1992. Gnrl Soc of Mayflower Decendents, Commonwealth of Pennsylvania 2010; Gnrl Soc of Mayflower Descendents 2010.

BARTLETT, Stephen I Ves (WMich) 8975 Shawbacoung Trail, Shelby MI 49455 **Ret Ret 2012-** B Hartford CT 1947 s Richard & Janice. AB Bow 1969; MDiv SWTS 1981; DMin Ecum TS 1993. D 6/13/1981 Bp H Coleman Mcgehee Jr P 6/28/1982 Bp Harold Barrett Robinson. m 10/6/1984 Martha McR McRoberts. R S Mk's Ch Coldwater MI 1999-2012; R Ch Of The Mssh Detroit MI 1997-1999; Int S Jn's Ch Royal Oak MI 1996-1997; R S Martha's Ch Detroit MI 1985-1994; Asst S Jas' Ch Batavia NY 1982-1985; Asst S Tim's Ch Detroit MI 1981-1982. OHC, Assoc 1979.

BARTLETT, Susan Mansfield (Mo) 906 Mallard Sq, Rolla MO 65401 B Lexington KY 1945 d Paul & Mildred. D 11/18/2005 Bp George Wayne Smith. c 2. D Chr Ch Rolla MO 2005-2013.

BARTLETT, Thomas Albert (Mass) 25 Monmouth St, Brookline MA 02446 B Summit NJ 1958 s Ralph & Natalie. BS Leh 1980; MBA Rutgers U 1981. D 6/4/2016 Bp Alan Gates. m 10/23/1982 Francesca Sturiale c 2. thomas.bartlett@ americantower.com

BARTOLOMEO, Michael Edward (LI) 124 Balaton Ave, Lake Ronkonkoma NY 11779 **R Trin Ch Northport NY 2011-, R 2011-** B Port Jefferson NY 1965 s Michael & Helen. BA SUNY 1988; MDiv SWTS 1993. D 6/23/1995 P 3/25/1996 Bp Orris George Walker Jr. m 7/8/2000 Joanne Bartolomeo c 1. S Paul's Ch Roosevelt NY 2008-2009; Dioc Coun Dio Long Island Garden City NY 2002-2005; R S Jas Epis Ch S Jas NY 1999-2004; Cur S Mk's Ch Islip NY 1995-1998. Dio Long Island 2003; Dio Long Island 2002; Dio Long Island 2000; Geo Mercer TS,Garden City Ny 1997-2000.

BARTON, Alexander Doyle (O) D 6/1/2017 Bp Mark Hollingsworth Jr.

BARTON, Anne (Spok) 5205 Sycamore Dr, Yakima WA 98901 **R S Tim's Epis Ch Yakima WA 2010-** B Minneapolis MN 1963 d James & Patricia. BA U of New Hampshire 1985; MDiv CDSP 1998. D 9/2/1998 Bp Chilton Richardson Knudsen P 6/26/1999 Bp Creighton Leland Robertson. S Paul's Epis Mssn Kennewick WA 2005-2010; Dio Olympia Seattle 2004-2005; Vic Gd Samar Epis Ch Sammamish WA 2002-2004; Cur Emm Epis Par Rapid City SD 1998-2002.

BARTON III, Bill (Tenn) Trinity Episcopal Church, 213 1st Ave NW, Winchester TN 37398 **Vic Epiphony Ch Sherwood Tennessee 2010-; P-in-c Trin Ch Winchester TN 2010-; Vic SE Tennessee Epis Mnstry (STEM) 2009-** B Pensacola FL 1949 s William & Barbara. MDiv Sewanee: The U So, TS 2009. D 6/6/2009 P 12/5/2009 Bp John Bauerschmidt. m 9/13/1997 Sara D Barton c 2. P-in-c S Paul's Ch Franklin TN 2015-2017; Dio Tennessee Nashville TN 2009-2015. bill@stpaulsfranklin.com

BARTON, Charles Denis Hampden (Mass) 3602 Stembridge Ct, Wilmington NC 28409 **R S Jn's Epis Ch Wilmington NC 2009-** B Wellington NSW AU 1933 s Denis & Mary. ThL Moore Theol Coll Sydney 1962; BD London U 1963; Moore Theol Coll Sydney 1964; STM Bos 1972; PhD Bos 1982. D 2/24/1964 P 2/24/1965 Bp David Reed. m 8/21/1963 Margaret Evelyn Barton c 4. Gr Epis Ch Lawr MA 2000; S Paul's Ch Newburyport MA 1994; S Jas Ch Groveland Groveland MA 1982-2002; Asst S Jn's Ch Arlington MA 1968-1970; D and P Angl Ch of Australia 1964-1968.

BARTON, Charlie (Md) 3101 Monkton Rd, Monkton MD 21111 **R S Jas Ch Monkton MD 2004-, P-in-c 1998-, Cur 1995-1998** B Honolulu HI 1953 s Charles & Mary. Catonsville Cmnty Coll; Gri; JHU; MDiv Sewanee: The U So, TS 1995. D 6/10/1995 Bp Charles Lindsay Longest P 5/18/1996 Bp Robert Wilkes Ihloff. m 3/5/1976 Debra Donnelly Barton c 2.

BARTON JR, John Clib (Ark) 1024 Stanford Dr Ne, Albuquerque NM 87106 B Fort Smith AR 1936 s John & Wilma. BA SMU 1958; MDiv SMU Perkins 1961. D 1/18/1965 P 7/21/1965 Bp Robert Raymond Brown. m 5/29/1992 Sandra Jan Wayland c 3. Pstr S Jn The Bapt Epis Ch Milton DE 2006-2014; Gr Ch Siloam Sprg AR 1999-2003; S Paul's Ch Mc Gehee AR 1993-2000; Ch Of The Gd Shpd Little Rock AR 1993-1999; Dio Arkansas Little Rock AR 1993-1999; Mssnr Chapl Emm Ch Lake Vill AR 1993-1999; S Mary's Epis Ch Monticello AR 1993-1999; S Mich's Epis Ch Little Rock AR 1987-1989; Vic S Mk's Ch Hope AR 1983-1991; S Jas Ch Magnolia AR 1981-1985; Vic S Alb's Ch Stuttgart AR 1977-1979; R S Lk's Ch Hot Sprg AR 1969-1975; Vic/R Gr Ch Pine Bluff AR 1965-1969; All SS Epis Ch Russellville AR 1964-1965; Vic Trin Ch Van Buren AR 1964-1965. ACPE 1993.

BARTON JR, Lane Wickham (Cal) 12616 Se 11th St, Vancouver WA 98683 **Ret 1994-** B Shelby OH 1925 s Lane & Mary. BA Harv 1950; MA Oxf GB 1958; BD CDSP 1959. D 6/19/1959 P 12/1/1959 Bp Lane W Barton. Non-par 1967-1994; Chapl Stan Stanford CA 1965-1967; Vic S Barn Ch San Francisco CA 1959-1965.

BARTUSCH, Robert Frederic (WTenn) 2851 Neeley St # 113, Batesville AR 72501 **D Calv Ch Memphis TN 1969-** B Memphis TN 1925 s Arno & Olga. BBA Tul 1946. D 9/21/1969 Bp John Vander Horst. m 11/26/1952 Nancy Brown c 2.

BARTZ, James Perkins (Wyo) St John's Church, 170 N Glenwood St, Jackson WY 83001 **S Jn's Epis Ch Jackson WY 2016-; R Thad's Santa Monica CA**

2006- B Houston TX 1970 s Tasso & Sylvia. BA U of Texas 1994; MDiv VTS 1999. D 6/19/1999 P 6/23/2000 Bp Claude Edward Payne. m 6/3/1995 Cynthia N Nentwich c 2. R Thads Santa Monica CA 2006-2016; Assoc All SS Par Beverly Hills CA 2002-2006; The Great Cmsn Fndt Houston TX 1999-2002; Chapl U Of Texas Austin TX 1999-2002.

BARWICK III, Frederick Ernest (NC) 5941 Leasburg Rd., Roxboro NC 27574 B Charlotte NC 1936 s Frederick & Virginia. BA U NC 1962. D 6/10/2001 Bp Michael B Curry. m 1/3/2015 Phyllis Gay Bridgeman c 3. D S Mk's Epis Ch Roxboro NC 2002-2014.

BARWICK, Mark (Eur) avenue du Préau 16, Brussels 01040 Belgium **Cur All SS Epis Ch Braine-l'Alleud 2009-** B Cheverly MD 1956 s Gerald & Mary. BA Washington Coll 1978; MDiv Wesley TS 1989. D 11/1/2009 P 6/5/2010 Bp Pierre W Whalon. m 6/29/2010 Corinna Kreutz c 4. S Jas Ch Charleston SC 1999-2002.

BASCOM, Cathleen (Ia) Cathedral Church of St. Paul, 815 High Street, Des Moines IA 50309 **Trin Ch Emmetsburg IA 2016-; Provost Cathd Ch of S Paul Des Moines IA 2007-** B Denver CO 1962 d Bruce & Marilyn. BA U of Kansas 1984; MDiv SWTS 1990; MA U of Exeter 1991; DMin 2005. D 6/9/1990 Bp William Edward Smalley P 12/1/1990 Bp Frank Tracy Griswold III. m 11/27/1987 Timothy P Bascom c 2. Dn The Cathd Ch Of S Paul Des Moines IA 2007-2014; R S Steph's Ch Newton IA 2001-2007; Dio Kansas Topeka KS 1993-2001; Chapl S Fran Of Cbury Manhattan KS 1993-2001; Asst R S Greg's Epis Ch Deerfield IL 1990-1993. "Rel Experience in the Chronicles of Narnia," *The Chronicles of Narnia Study Guide*, St. Mk's, 1999; "Campus Mnstry and a Hungry Heart," *Disorganized Rel: the Evangelsim of Yth and YA*, Cowley, 1998. cathleen.bascom@waldorf.edu

BASCOM, Joshua L (Va) D 6/10/2017 Bp Shannon Sherwood Johnston.

BASDEN, Michael Paul (SwFla) 495 Galleon Dr, Naples FL 34102 B Orlando FL 1959 s Richard & Lavelle. BA U of Cntrl Florida 1981; MDiv Nash 1985. D 6/15/1985 P 1/6/1986 Bp William Hopkins Folwell. m 8/14/1981 Jill R Basden c 2. R Trin By The Cove Naples FL 1999-2015; R S Anne's Epis Ch Warsaw IN 1987-1999; Cur S Mk's Ch Cocoa FL 1985-1987.

BASINGER JR, Elvin David (Ala) 21526 Silver Oaks Circle, Athens AL 35613 **P-in-c S Barn' Epis Ch Hartselle AL 2012-** B Woodland CA 1946 s Elvin & Verna. AA Sacramento City Coll 1967; U of Albuquerque 1977; MDiv Sewanee: The U So, TS 1996. D 6/13/1996 P 12/14/1996 Bp Henry Irving Louttit. m 6/30/1968 Lynda Basinger. R S Tim's Epis Ch Athens AL 2008-2011; Chapl Dio Louisiana New Orleans LA 2006-2008; R S Fran Ch Denham Spgs LA 2002-2006; Asst S Augustines Ch Metairie LA 1999-2002; Vic S Matt's Epis Ch Fitzgerald GA 1997-1999; D S Thos Aquinas Mssn Baxley GA 1996-1999; Gr Ch Waycross GA 1996.

✠ BASKERVILLE-BURROWS, The Rt Rev Jennifer (Ind) **Dio Indianapolis Indianapolis IN 2017-; Chapl Hendricks Chap Syr NY 2004-** B Staten Island NY 1966 d Harry & Brenda. BA Smith 1988; MA Cor 1994; MDiv CDSP 1997. D 6/11/1997 P 2/7/1998 Bp David Bruce Joslin Con 4/29/2017 for Ind. m 3/22/2003 Harrison Burrows c 1. Dio Cntrl New York Liverpool NY 2004-2012; Gr Epis Ch Syracuse NY 2004-2012; Dio Chicago Chicago IL 2003-2017; Pstr Assoc All SS' Ch San Francisco CA 2002-2007; Dir Of Alum/Ae And Ch Relatns CDSP Berkeley CA 2002-2004; Assoc S Ptr's Ch Morristown NJ 1999-2002; Asst R S Paul's Ch Endicott NY 1997-1999. Auth, "To Be Young, Priested And Black: Raising Up The Next Generation Of Black Cler," *Gathering The Next Generation*, Morehouse Pub, 2000. Fllshp Soc Of S Jn The Evang. Bishop@ indydio.org

BASKIN, Cynthia Oppen (WA) 10924 Citreon Ct, N Potomac MD 20878 **Int Pstr New Jerusalem Luth Ch 2016-** B Minneapolis MN 1946 d Eldar & Georgia. BA S Olaf Coll 1968; MAT U of St Thos 1971; MDiv VTS 1995. D 5/24/1995 Bp Stephen Hays Jecko P 12/1/1995 Bp Frank Harris Vest Jr. m 6/4/1988 Robert Marion Baskin. R S Jas Ch Potomac MD 1999-2015; Assoc Ch Of The Redeem Midlothian VA 1995-1999; Prog Dir H Trin Epis Ch Gainesville FL 1981-1992.

BASS-CHOATE, Yamily (NY) 4 Gateway Rd, Unit 1-D, Yonkers NY 10703 **Advsry Bd The Epis New Yorker 2010-; Dio New York New York NY 2005-; Mem Hisp Mnstry New York NY 2005-** B Bogota CO 1957 d Antonio & Ilva. MDiv GTS 1999. D 7/31/1999 P 3/4/2000 Bp Alfred Marble Jr. m 11/12/1988 Horace Choate c 2. Vic San Andres Ch Yonkers NY 2005-2013; Cn For Hisp Mnstry Dio Mississippi Jackson MS 2001-2005; Dioc S Andr's Cathd Jackson MS 2001-2005; Dir Of Educ The Epis Ch Of The Medtr Meridian MS 1999-2001. ybass-choate@diocesenv.org

BASSUENER, Barbara A. (Eas) 20 3rd St, Pocomoke City MD 21851 **S Lk's Ch Denver CO 2016-** B Sheboygan WI 1946 d Oliver & Helen. BA W&M 1968; JD Marshall-Wythe Sch of Law 1971; MDiv VTS 2010. D 6/5/2010 Bp Shannon Sherwood Johnston P 2/5/2011 Bp Bud Shand. Int Ch Of S Paul's By The Sea Ocean City MD 2015-2016; S Mary's Epis Ch Pocomoke City MD 2010-2015. revbarbara@verizon.net

BAST, Robert Lee (Eas) 201 Crosstown Dr Apt 3013, Peachtree City GA 30269 **Ret 1989-** B Baltimore MD 1923 s Charles & Beulah. BA Laf 1944; BD VTS 1947; Roa 1974. D 10/26/1946 P 5/1/1947 Bp William McClelland. m 7/2/1955

Frances Bast c 2. Ch Of The H Trin Oxford MD 1986-1989; R S Paul's Epis Ch Jacksonville FL 1982-1986; R S Tim's Ch Fairfield CT 1973-1982; Stndg Com Dio Kansas Topeka KS 1970-1973, BEC 1966-1973; Chr Ch Overland Pk KS 1964-1973; R S Matt's Epis Ch Newton KS 1961-1964; R S Jn's Ch Mt Washington MD 1949-1961; P-in-c Dorchester Cnty Missions Taylors Island MD 1947-1948; P-in-c Old Trin Ch Ch Creek MD 1947-1948; S Andr's Hurlock MD 1947-1948; S Paul's Ch Vienna MD 1947-1948; S Steph's Epis Ch E New Mrkt MD 1947-1948.

BASTIAN, Martin James (Tex) 5714 Jackwood St, Houston TX 77096 **S Mart's Epis Ch Houston TX 2007-, 2006, 2005, Asst 1996-1999** B Milwaukee WI 1963 s James & Rita. BA U of Kansas 1986; MDiv VTS 1996. D 6/15/1996 Bp Peter J Lee P 2/1/1997 Bp Claude Edward Payne. Epis HS Bellaire TX 2001-2008. SAMS.

BATARSEH, Peter Bahjat (Tenn) 312 Battle Avenue, Franklin TN 37064 **Vic/P Ch of the Gd Samar Franklin TN 2006-** B Adjloun Jordan 1967 s Bahjat & Martha. Elim Bible Inst 1985; Sewanee: The U So, TS 2005; TESM 2005. D 6/5/2005 P 4/22/2006 Bp Bertram Nelson Herlong. m 6/12/2009 Diana Batarseh c 3. Ch of the Gd Samar Franklin TN 2008; Dio Tennessee Nashville TN 2005-2007; S Phil's Ch Nashville TN 2005-2006.

BATCHELDER JR, Kelsey Chase (NY) B 1932 D 6/20/1959 P 12/21/1959 Bp Hamilton Hyde Kellogg. m 6/26/1965 Marla Shilton.

BATEMAN, David (CPa) 3312 Brisban St, Harrisburg PA 17111 B Chicago IL 1954 s Philip & Roberta. BA Ken 1976; MDiv Nash 1987. D 6/13/1987 P 4/14/1988 Bp Peter J Lee. m 5/6/2017 Diane Elizabeth Johnson c 2. S Jn's Epis Ch Carlisle PA 2015-2017; S Paul's Ch Bloomsburg PA 2012-2014; Mt Calv Camp Hill PA 2009-2011; Thankful Memi Ch Chattanooga TN 2008-2009; R S Thaddaeus' Epis Ch Chattanooga TN 1995-2007; Dio Upper So Carolina Columbia SC 1989-1995; Asst H Trin Par Epis Clemson SC 1989-1995; Asst Abingdon Epis Ch White Marsh VA 1987-1989. Auth, "Come & Wrshp: A Chld's Liturg of the Word," Ldr Resources, 2002.

BATES, Allen Layfield (Ark) 1902 W Magnolia St, Rogers AR 72758 B Little Rock AR 1950 s William & Viola. BA U of Arkansas 1973; MDiv Sewanee: The U So, TS 1978. D 6/10/1978 P 6/1/1979 Bp Christoph Keller Jr. m 5/22/1974 Melinda Leah Bates c 2. R S Andr's Ch Rogers AR 1983-2008; Vic S Alb's Ch Stuttgart AR 1980-1983; Int S Steph's Epis Ch Jacksonville AR 1980; S Lk's Epis Ch N Little Rock AR 1979-1980; S Paul's Ch Fayetteville AR 1978-1979; Chair CE Dio Arkansas Little Rock AR 1979-1984. Frederick Denison Maurice Soc.

BATES, Charlotte McKnight (Chi) 15136 S. Dillman, Plainfield IL 60544 **S Thos Ch Morris IL 2004-** B Detroit MI 1944 d Robert & Dorothy. Alma Coll. D 1/30/1999 Bp Herbert Alcorn Donovan Jr. m 1/23/1971 John Kenneth Bates c 1. D S Edw The Mtyr and Chr Epis Ch Joliet IL 1999-2004. dnchereb@comcast.net

BATES, James Brent (Nwk) 31 Woodland Ave, Summit NJ 07901 **R Gr Ch Newark NJ 2011-** B Garland TX 1976 s James & Malda. BA Harding U 1998; MDiv Abilene Chr U 2001; PhD Drew U 2008; Dip Ang Stud GTS 2008. D 6/7/2008 Bp George Edward Councell P 12/13/2008 Bp Mark M Beckwith. m 12/18/1999 Jennifer J Thweatt-Bates c 2. Asst Calv Epis Ch Summit NJ 2008-2011.

BATES, J Barrington (Nwk) 15 Warren St Unit 117, Jersey City NJ 07302 **S Lk's Epis Ch Montclair NJ 2017-; Adj Untd Luth Sem Philadelphia 2017-; Bd Mem Corp for the Relief of Widows New Jersey 2013-; Bd Mem GBEC 2012-; Ch Revs Ed HSEC 2011-; Bd Mem Corp for the Relief of Widows Widowers and Chld 2013-; Rdr, Gnrl Ord Examination Epis Ch Cntr New York NY 2012-** B Philadelphia PA 1955 s James & Lauralou. BA Bos 1979; MDiv CDSP 1997; MA Grad Theol Un 1997; STM GTS 2004; MPhil Drew U 2006; PhD Drew U 2009. D 12/5/1998 P 6/5/1999 Bp William Edwin Swing. m 11/12/2005 James D MacKenzie c 1. Adj Luth TS at Philadelphia 2017; The Ch Of The Epiph New York NY 2017; S Ptr's Ch Essex Fells NJ 2015-2016; Instr Diakonia Trng Prog New York 2015; Zion Luth Ch Staten Island NY 2014-2015; Int S Jn's Epis Ch Montclair NJ 2013-2014; Gr Ch Van Vorst Jersey City NJ 2012-2013; Adj Prof GTS 2012; Dioc Coun Dio Newark 2010-2013; Admin Dir Gd Shpd Cmnty Serv Inc. 2010-2011; Chair HR 2007-2014; R The Ch Of The Annunc Oradell NJ 2007-2011; Mem Liturg Cmsn Dio New York New York NY 2005-2007; Exec Dir Ascen Outreach Inc. 2004-2007; Bd Mem Epis Response to AIDS 2002-2010; Cur Ch Of The Ascen New York NY 2002-2007; Instr Mercer TS Garden City NY 2002-2005; P Asst S Aug's Epis Ch Croton Hdsn NY 2001-2002; Vic The Ch of S Ign of Antioch New York NY 2001-2002; Asst P Ch Of S Mary The Vrgn New York NY 2000-2002; P Asst S Mich's Ch New York NY 1999-2000; Asst S Fran' Epis Ch San Francisco CA 1998-1999; Agcy Advsry Bd Food Bank for New York City 2004-2007. Auth, "On the Search for the Authentic Liturg of the Apos: The Diversity of the Early Ch as Normative for Anglicans," *Journ of Angl Stds*, 2013; Auth, "Expressing What Christians Believe: Angl Principles for Liturg Revs," *ATR*, 2010; Auth, "Giving What Is Sacr to Dogs? Welcoming All to the Eucharistic Feast," *Journ of Angl Stds*, 2005; Auth, "Reflections on Liturg at Ground Zero," *Journ of Pstr Care and Counslg*, 2005; Auth, "Am

I Blue? Some Hist Evidence for Liturg colors," *Studia Liturgica*, 2003; Auth, "The Problem of Cler Misconduct: Preaching Liberation from Bondage to Sin in an Age of Moral Freedom," *Journ for Preachers*, 2002; Auth, "Meetings And Accomplishments," *Preaching Through The Year Of Lk: Sermons That Wk Ix*, 2000. AAR 2007; EPF 1999; Hymn Soc of Amer 1999; Integrity 1992; Intl Angl Liturg Consult 2011; No Amer Acad of Liturg 2003; OHC (Assoc) 1995; Screen Actors Gld 2002; Societas Liturgica 2007; Soc of Cath Priests 2011; Sons of the Amer Revolution 2017. Who's Who among Students in Amer Universities and Colleges Who's Who 2008. revdocbates@gmail.com

BATES, Percy Quin (La) **S Mk's Epis Ch Harvey LA 2004-** B New Orleans LA 1944 s Henry & Mildred. D 10/23/2005 Bp Charles Edward Jenkins III. m 2/9/1968 Lauranel Quin Bates c 2. Off Mgr Witco Corp - Mgr 1968-2000.

BATES, Robert Seaton (Chi) 121 W Macomb St, Belvidere IL 61008 **Non-par 1992-** B Colorado Springs CO 1948 s Ralph & Margaret. BMus U CO 1970; MDiv Nash 1973. D 4/28/1973 P 11/1/1973 Bp Donald H V Hallock. R S Ptr's Epis Ch Sycamore IL 1989-1992; R Chr Ch Streator IL 1983-1989; The Epis Ch Of The H Trin Belvidere IL 1980; R Ch Of The H Comm Lake Geneva WI 1979-1980; R S Jn The Bapt Portage WI 1975-1979; Cn Precentor All SS' Cathd Milwaukee WI 1973-1975.

BATES, Steven Byron (CGC) 508 S Market St, Scottsboro AL 35768 **R H Nativ Epis Ch Panama City FL 2006-** B Oak Ridge TN 1957 s John & Lena. BS U of Alabama 1979; MBA Samford U 1983; MDiv Sewanee: The U So, TS 2002. D 5/16/2002 P 12/3/2003 Bp Henry Nutt Parsley Jr. m 7/12/1986 Lori Lebere Bates c 2. D S Lk's Ch Scottsboro AL 2002-2005.

BATES, Stuart Alan (Tex) 345 Piney Point Rd, Houston TX 77024 **R S Fran Ch Houston TX 2007-** B Saint Louis MO 1961 s Fred & Anne. BA U of Texas 1984; MA Dallas TS 1991; MDiv Epis TS of the SW 1996. D 6/22/1996 Bp Claude Edward Payne P 1/23/1997 Bp Leopoldo Jesus Alard. m 3/10/2012 Lisa Meng R Bates c 3. S Mart's Epis Ch Houston TX 1996-2006.

BATES, Thomas Justin (RG) **Ch Of The Gd Shpd Silver City NM 2001-; BroSA Coordntr Dio The Rio Grande Albuquerque 2001-, BroSA Coordntr 2001-** B Wolf Point MT 1940 s Earl & Helen. MPS Wstrn Kentucky U 1976; MA Wstrn Kentucky U 1977; TESM 2001. D 7/28/2001 Bp Terence Kelshaw. m 4/21/1962 Jane Spencer Bates c 2. BroSA 1994.

BATES, Toppie (CNY) 5623 Mack Rd, Skaneateles NY 13152 **Chair of Dioc Discernment Team Dio Cntrl New York Liverpool NY 2011-, COM 2008-** B Binghamton NY 1943 d Victor & Katherine. BS SUNY 1964; MDiv Bex Sem 2005. D 11/13/2004 P 9/17/2005 Bp Gladstone Bailey Adams III. m 8/20/1966 C David Bates c 2. Assoc R S Jas Ch Skaneateles NY 2005-2015; D Gr Ch Baldwinsville NY 2004. toppiebates@verizon.net

BATIZ MEJIA, Jose David (Hond) IMS SAP Dept 215, PO BOX 523900, Miami FL 33152 Honduras B Honduras 1966 s Simeona. Rec 3/11/2007 Bp Lloyd Emmanuel Allen. m 12/1/2009 Elizabeth Lopez Santos c 1.

BATKIN, Jeff (Fla) 395 Winfield Cove Rd., Saluda NC 28773 **Died 6/6/2017** B Mount Vernon NY 1947 s Abraham & Marilyn. BA Emory U 1969; MDiv Sewanee: The U So, TS 1972; DMin Luth Theol Sthrn Sem 1990. D 6/24/1972 Bp Milton Legrand Wood P 4/15/1973 Bp Bennett Jones Sims. m 8/30/1969 Marguerite Batkin c 2. Sm Ch Mnstrs Dio Wstrn No Carolina Asheville NC 2010-2013; Int Ch Of The H Fam Mills River NC 2007-2009; Chapl Police Dept Hendersonville NC 2004-2011; Int R Ch Of The Adv Spartanburg SC 2004-2006; R Trin Epis Ch St Aug FL 1998-2003; Dio Upper So Carolina Columbia SC 1992-1993, Dio Upper So Carolina, Curs Coun 1991, 1984-1990, Dio Upper So Carolina, Chair Dept of Constit 1981-1983, Alt Del, GC 1997-2017, Pres of the Stndg Com 1992-1994, Stndg Com Mem 1991-1994; R Gr Epis Ch Anderson SC 1990-1998; Cn S Jn's Cathd Jacksonville FL 1986-1990; Vic S Fran of Assisi Chapin SC 1980-1986; Asst Ch Of Our Sav Rock Hill SC 1978-1980; Vic S Chris's Epis Ch Garner NC 1975-1978; Cur S Barth's Epis Ch Atlanta GA 1972-1975. Allin Fllshp The Epis Ch 1988.

BATSON, Lloyd Samuel (Nwk) 160 W South Orange Ave, South Orange NJ 07079 B 1960 s Lloyd & Mavis. D 5/2/2009 Bp Mark M Beckwith. m 12/26/1988 Donnetta Batson c 3.

BATSON, Sara Chapman (Pa) 6102 Treyburn Point Dr, Durham NC 27712 B Clarksville TN 1941 d William & Evelyn. BSN U of Evansville 1985; MDiv PrTS 1995; Cert GTS 1997. D 10/25/1997 P 4/25/1998 Bp Joe Doss. m 10/21/2006 James Brunnquell c 1. R Chr Ch Media PA 1998-2007; Assoc Ch Of The Redeem Bryn Mawr PA 1997-1998. Chld's Crisis Treatment Cntr Of Philadelphia 1998-2007; Cler Advsry Bd-Epis Cmnty Serv 1998-2007; Comp To OGS 1997-2007; Natl Epis Cler Assn Mem 1997; Philadelphia Theol Inst 1998-2007.

BATSON III, Stephen Radford (NY) 3721 Wares Ferry Rd Apt 500, Montgomery AL 36109 B Columbia SC 1943 s Stephen & Orleans. BA U of Virginia 1968; MDiv EDS 1974. D 6/8/1974 P 10/1/1976 Bp Paul Moore Jr. S Mk's Epis Ch Charleston SC 1981-1982; Asst Ch Of S Mary The Vrgn New York NY 1979-1980; Asst The Ch of S Matt And S Tim New York NY 1977-1979; Asst S Steph's Epis Ch Boston MA 1976-1977; Asst The Ch Of The Adv Boston MA 1975-1976; Asst All SS Par Brookline MA 1974-1975. SocMary 2003.

BATTLE, Michael Jesse (NC) 1611 East Millbrook Rd, Raleigh NC 27609 **The GTS New York NY 2015-; Six Prchr Cbury Engl Ch Of Engl London**

2011-; Sprtl Fac Credo Inst Inc. Memphis TN 1998- B New Orleans LA 1963 s Lorenzo & Sadie. U of Notre Dame; BA Duke 1986; MDiv PrTS 1989; STM Ya Berk 1990; Cert Shalem Inst 1993; PhD Duke 1995. D 2/10/1993 Bp Huntington Williams Jr P 12/12/1995 Bp Desmond Mpilo Tutu. m 7/18/1996 Rachael Leslie c 3. EDS Cambridge MA 2014-2015; S Tit Epis Ch Durham NC 2013-2014; R Ch Of Our Sav Par San Gabr CA 2008-2013; Provost & Cn Theol Cath Ctr of St Paul Dio Los Angeles Los Angeles CA 2007; Advsry Com to Bonnie Anderson VTS Alexandria VA 2005-2007; R S Ambroses Ch Raleigh NC 2001-2004; Asst P Ch Of The H Fam Chap Hill NC 2000-2001; Asst Duke Epis Cntr Durham NC 1999-2004; Asst Prof Of Sprtlty And Moral Theol Sewanee U So TS Sewanee TN 1995-1999; Non-par 1993-2000; Serv Ch Of The Prov Of Sthrn Afr 1993-1994; Sprtl Formation and Curric Epis Ch Cntr New York NY 2011-2013, Anglical RC Dialogue 2003-2006, Chapl to the HOB 2000-2006, Theol Com 2000-; Exec Coun Appointees New York NY 2005-2009. Auth, "Black Battle, White Knight," Seabury, 2011; Auth, "Ubuntu," Seabury, 2009; Auth, "The Black Ch in Amer: An Afr Amer Sprtlty," Blackwell, 2006; Auth, "Practicing Recon in a Violent Wrld," Morehouse, 2005; Auth, "The Ch Enslaved: A Sprtlty of Racial Recon," Fortress, 2005; Ed, "The Quest for Recon and Liberation," Westminster Jn Knox, 2004; Auth, "Blessed Are the Peacemakers," Merc, 2003; Auth, "The Wisdom Of Desmond Tutu," Westminster Jn Knox, 1998; Auth, "Recon: The Ubuntu Theol Of Desmond Tutu," Pilgrim Press, 1997.

BATTON JR, Robert Nolton (RG) 4304 Carlisle Blvd NE, Albuquerque NM 87107 B New Orleans LA 1939 s Robert & Alice. BA U of Louisiana at Lafayette 1960; Cert of Theol Study The Prchr Lewis Sch 1985. D 4/9/1987 Bp Richard Mitchell Trelease Jr P 2/29/1988 Bp William Davidson. m 12/16/1967 Gretchen Frances Batton c 4.

BAUER, Audrey T (NMich) 6837 Lahti Ln, Pellston MI 49769 D Trsfg Epis Ch Indn River MI 2010-, D 2008- B Toronto ON CA 1936 d George & Christina. Border Hosp Coll of Nrsng Scotland; RN Peel Hosp Sch of Nrsng Galashiels GB 1961. D 6/22/1997 Bp Thomas Kreider Ray. c 2. D Ch Of The Gd Shpd S Ignace MI 2008-2011; D S Mk's Ch Crystal Falls MI 1997-2008.

BAUER, Charles (SVa) **Hickory Neck Ch Toano VA 2016-** B Milwaukee 1985 s Bruce & Catherine. BA The W&M 2008; MDiv GTS 2016. D 6/11/2016 P 12/17/2016 Bp Herman Hollerith IV. m 8/7/2010 Kelly Lorraine McEvoy c 1. cbauer@hickoryneck.org

BAUER, Charles David (Eau) B Noblesville IN 1952 s Donald & Betty. AB Marion Coll 1974; MDiv Asbury TS 1977. D 11/15/2014 P 5/14/2015 Bp William Jay Lambert III. m 6/7/1975 Elizabeth Lou Quesenbery c 1.

BAUER, Kathryn Ann (WMo) Po Box 996, Kremmling CO 80459 B Dodge City KS 1943 d Ernest & Wilma. BA 1966; MA 1972; MS 1984. D 11/20/1993 Bp John Clark Buchanan P 6/1/1998 Bp William Jerry Winterrowd. m 3/28/1981 William Eugene Bauerstep. Vic Trin Ch Kremmling CO 2000-2004, Cleric 1998-2000; D Dio W Missouri Kansas City MO 1993-1998. NAAD. Psi Chi.

BAUER, Ronald Coleman (Los) 27292 Via Callejon Unit B, San Juan Capistrano CA 92675 B Saint Louis MO 1935 s Herman & Charlotte. BA U of Oklahoma 1963; BD Nash 1965. D 6/20/1965 P 12/1/1965 Bp Chilton R Powell. m 6/27/1993 Dianne L Bauer c 2. R S Marg Of Scotland Par San Juan Capo CA 1990-1998, R Emiritus 1998-; R St Dav's Epis Ch Minnetonka MN 1973-1990; R No Convoc Palmyra MO 1970-1973; Assoc S Paul's Ch Manhattan KS 1969-1970; Assoc Trin Epis Ch Ft Worth TX 1967-1969; Vic S Steph's Ch Guymon OK 1965-1967.

BAUER, Thomas William (Md) 3148 Gracefield Rd Apt CL412, Silver Spring MD 20904 B Pittsburgh PA 1936 s Frank & Wilhelmina. BA Ya 1958; MDiv GTS 1961; STM Yale DS 1965; MA Ya 1965; EdD Harv 1986; Cert. Advncd Study Loyola U 2006. D 7/6/1961 Bp Noble C Powell P 6/20/1962 Bp Harry Lee Doll. c 2. Chapl S Geo's Ch Ft Meade MD 2007-2014; Serv Angl Ch of Bermuda St. Dav's Chap 2002-2004; Int S Andr's Ch Pasadena MD 2000-2001; Int All SS Ch So Hadley MA 1999-2000; R S Paul's Ch Petersburg VA 1994-1999; R Westover Epis Ch Chas City VA 1991-1994; Int Chr Ch Chaptico MD 1990-1991; Headmaster Gr And S Ptr Sch Baltimore MD 1987-1990; Assoc Gr And S Ptr's Ch Baltimore MD 1987-1990, Cur 1961-1962; R Par Of S Paul Newton Highlands MA 1983-1987; Int Trin Ch Canton MA 1982-1983; Int Emm Epis Ch Delaplane Delaplane VA 1982; Cathd of St Ptr & St Paul Washington DC 1980-1982; Chapl S Albans Sch Washington DC 1980-1982; Ascen Epis Ch Amherst VA 1979-1980; Int S Mk's Ch Amherst VA 1979-1980; Chapl Virginia Epis Sch Lynchburg VA 1977-1980; R Ch Of The Gd Shpd New York NY 1971-1977; Int Ch Of Chr The King E Meadow NY 1969-1971; Int S Steph's Epis Ch Woodlaw Bronx NY 1967-1969; P-in-c Gr Ch (W Farms) Bronx NY 1965-1967, Vic 1965-1967; P-in-c Bp Seabury Ch Groton CT 1964-1965; Asst S Jn's Epis Par Waterbury CT 1963-1964, Asst 1962-1964; Cur S Mich And All Ang Ch Baltimore MD 1962; Sch Bd Mem (also Govnr's Sch) Petersburg VA 1994-1998. Auth, "Illustrated Bible"; Auth, "Moral Climate & The Cmnty Of Faith". Soc of King Chas the Mtyr 1957. mcl Ya 1958.

✠ BAUERSCHMIDT, The Rt Rev John (Tenn) 50 Vantage Way Ste 107, Nashville TN 37228 **Bp of Tennessee Dio Tennessee Nashville TN 2007-** B Portsmouth VA 1959 s Alan & Conally. BA Ken 1981; MDiv GTS 1984; DPhil Oxf GB 1996. D 6/9/1984 P 6/1/1985 Bp William Arthur Beckham Con 1/27/2007 for Tenn. m 1/4/1986 Caroline Barnard Bauerschmidt c 3. R Chr Ch Covington LA 1997-2006; R Chr Ch Albemarle NC 1992-1997; Serv Ch Of Engl 1987-1991; Cur All SS Ch Worcester MA 1984-1987; GC Dep Dio Louisiana New Orleans LA 2006-2007, Stndg Com 2001-2005; Ecum Off Dio No Carolina Raleigh NC 1994-1997. Soc of S Jn The Evang 1985. bishop@edtn.org

BAUGHMAN, David Lee (Chi) 804 James Court, Wheaton IL 60189 **D S Mk's Ch Geneva IL 2004-** B Columbus OH 1939 s Harold & Florence. AA Morton Coll 1959; BS Illinois St U 1961; MS Illinois Inst of Tech 1966; EdD Nthrn Illinois U 1981. D 2/15/1997 Bp Frank Tracy Griswold III. m 4/13/1963 Marilyn Ann Ostby c 1. D Trin Epis Ch Wheaton IL 1997-2004; Dir, Dioc Sch for Diac Dio Chicago Chicago IL 1998-2001. BroSA 1991-1994. Fell Natl Sci Fndt 1964.

BAUKNIGHT JR, Mack Miller (SwFla) 2440 26th Ave S, Saint Petersburg FL 33712 B Augusta GA 1951 s Mack & Ocie. Paine Coll 1970; Aiken Tech Coll Aiken SC 1975. D 6/25/1994 Bp Rogers Sanders Harris. m 1/1/2001 Lafaye Bauknight c 1.

BAUM, Denis Blaine (CGC) 532 Skyline Drive, N Little Rock AR 72116 **Int H Nativ 2004-; Int Co-R S Jude's Epis Ch Niceville FL 2002-** B Toledo OH 1937 s James & Freda. BA Bowling Green St U 1959; BD EDS 1963; MA GW 1974. D 6/15/1963 P 12/1/1963 Bp Nelson Marigold Burroughs. m 6/26/1988 Judith W Baum. H Sprt Epis Ch Gulf Shores AL 1992-1999; R S Thos Ch Greenville AL 1984-1992; Off Of Bsh For ArmdF New York NY 1976-1984; Cur S Jas Ch Painesville OH 1963-1965. 4 Meritorius Serv Medals USAF.

BAUM, George R (O) 13415 Ardoon Ave, Cleveland OH 44120 **S Tim's Epis Ch Massillon OH 2016-** B Niagara Falls NY 1963 s William & Carol. BA Concordia Coll 1990; MDiv GTS 2009. D 6/13/2009 P 12/19/2009 Bp Mark Hollingsworth Jr. m 9/15/1990 Christin L Baum c 2. P-in-c S Pat's Ch Brunswick OH 2009-2012.

BAUM, Nancy Louise (Mich) 411 Walnut St # 3371, Green Cove Springs FL 32043 B Guelph ON CA 1949 d George & Alva. BA U of Guelph Guelph ON CA 1986; MDiv U of Wstrn Ontario CA 1993. Trans 1/6/1999 Bp R aymond Stewart Wood Jr. m 6/22/1996 John Leo Rowland. Dio Michigan Detroit MI 2003; Int S Chris-S Paul Epis Ch Detroit MI 2000-2002; S Andr's Ch Ann Arbor MI 1999-2000; S Geo's Epis Ch Warren MI 1996-1998; Supply R S Pat's Epis Ch Madison Hts MI 1996-1998.

BAUMAN, Dwayne Ray (Ark) 176 State Road YY, Tunas MO 65764 B Colorado Springs CO 1964 s Donald & Carolyn. BS Emmaus Bible Coll Dubuque IA 1988; MA Denver Sem 1997; MDiv Epis TS of the SW 2000. D 6/24/2000 P 12/19/2000 Bp Larry Maze. m 5/1/2008 Julia Zimmerman Bauman c 2. R S Alb's Epis Ch Arlington TX 2004-2005, R 2002-2005, P-in-c 2002-; S Alb's Ch Stuttgart AR 2000-2002, Vic 2000-2002; St Ptr's Epis Ch Devalls Bluff AR 2000-2002, Vic 2000-2002.

BAUMAN, Ward J (Minn) 1111 Upton Ave N, Minneapolis MN 55411 **Dir Hse of Pryr Collegeville MN 2004-** B Los Angeles CA 1945 s Clifford & Joann. BA Biola U 1968; MDiv CDSP 1989. D 6/18/1989 P 12/1/1989 Bp John Lester Thompson III. m 11/27/2000 David Harris c 1. Dio Minnesota Minneapolis MN 2002-2003; Vic S Edm's Epis Ch Pacifica CA 1991-2002; Asst S Lk's Ch San Francisco CA 1989-1991. Auth, "Sacr Food for Soulful Living," Lilja Press, 2010; Co-Auth, "The Luminous Gospels," Praxis Pub, 2008.

BAUMANN, David Michael (Spr) PO Box 303, Salem IL 62881 B Glendale CA 1948 s Billy & Nancy. BA U CA Los Angeles 1970; ATC 1972; MDiv Vancouver TS CA 1973; MDiv Vancouver TS Can 1973. D 9/15/1973 P 3/16/1974 Bp Robert Claflin Rusack. m 12/9/2013 Elizabeth Ward c 2. R The Epis Ch Of The Blessed Sacr Placentia CA 1978-2012; P-in-c S Anselm Of Cbury Par Garden Grove CA 1978, Cur 1975-1977; Cur S Clem's-By-The-Sea Par San Clemente CA 1973-1974. Auth, "The Starman Saga (10 volumes)," Americana Pub, 2011; Auth, "Love Stronger Than Death," Lulu, 2006; Auth, "Sprtl Life for the Overbusy," Forw Mvmt Press, 1987. Forw in Faith 1989; Gld of the Living Rosary 1972; SocMary 1980; SSC 1990. starbrow730@gmail.com

BAUMGARTEN, Betsy (Miss) 14294 John Lee Road, Biloxi MS 39532 **Camp Mitchell Epis Ch Morrilton AR 2016-; Chapl Coast Epis Schools Inc Long Bch MS 2011-** B Duluth MN 1980 d William & Julie. BA S Olaf Coll 2003; MDiv VTS 2008. D 7/26/2007 P 7/8/2008 Bp James Louis Jelinek. m 4/19/2008 Robert W Wetherington. P-in-c S Patricks Epis Ch Long Bch MS 2013-2016; Delta Mssnr Dio Mississippi Jackson MS 2011-2013, 2009-2011; Asst S Thos Epis Ch Mclean VA 2008-2009; Yth Min The Par of St Paul's Epis Ch Duluth MN 2003-2005.

BAUMGARTEN, Jonathan David (Chi) 41 E. 8th St. Apt. 2001, Chicago IL 60605 **D Gr Ch Oak Pk IL 2004-** B Praire du Sac WI 1960 BA St Johns Coll Annapolis MD 1982. D 2/7/2004 Bp Victor Alfonso Scantlebury. m 8/14/1982 Marion Tucker Betor c 2.

BAUMGARTEN, William Paul (Mont) 845 2nd Ave E, Kalispell MT 59901 B Seattle WA 1944 s Otto & Virginia. BA Villanova U 1967; MA Augustinian Coll 1971; MA CUA 1971. Rec 12/21/1979 as Priest Bp Robert Munro Wolterstorff. m 6/22/1977 Barbara Baumgarten c 3. Int S Paul's Ch Hamilton MT

2014-2015; Int S Steph's Epis Ch Stevensville MT 2014-2015; P-in-c Chr Epis Ch Kalispell MT 2000-2009; Dio Montana Helena MT 2000-2009; S Paul's Epis Ch Santa Paula CA 1989-2000; R S Jn The Div Epis Ch Morgan Hill CA 1983-1989; Asst All SS Ch San Diego CA 1979-1982; Chapl Santa Paula Fire Dept.

BAUSCHARD, Michael Robert Thomas (NwPa) 5 Cottage Pl, Warren PA 16365 **D Epis Ch Of The Trsfg Mesa AZ 2010-** B 1945 s Robert & Joan. Diac Sch of Mnstry 1998. D 6/13/1998 Bp Robert Deane Rowley Jr. D S Fran Of Assisi Epis Ch Youngsville PA 2002-2010; D Trin Memi Ch Warren PA 1998-2002.

BAUSTIAN, Donald Edward (Ark) 1801 20th St Unit K-15, Ames IA 50010 **Ret 1997-** B Iowa City IA 1932 s Adolph & Jennie. BA Augustana Coll 1954; STB GTS 1957. D 6/8/1957 P 12/21/1957 Bp Gordon V Smith. m 6/15/1957 Beverly Ann Kaiser Baustian c 3. Vic S Jas Ch Magnolia AR 1994-1997; Vic S Jn's Ch Camden AR 1991-1997; S Mk's Ch Hope AR 1991-1994; Exec Coun Appointees New York NY 1988-1991; Fac TS of the Epis Ch in Haiti Haiti 1988-1991; Dio Arkansas Little Rock AR 1982-1997; R Chr Epis Ch Little Rock AR 1981-1988; R S Jn's Ch Keokuk IA 1967-1981; Secy Prov VI of the Epis Ch 1965-1981; S Peters Ch Fairfield IA 1964-1967; Ch Of S Thos Algona IA 1957-1964; Vic Trin Ch Emmetsburg IA 1957-1964; BEC, Mem Dio Iowa Des Moines IA 1964-1970, Dep't of CE, Mem, then chairman 1964-1968, Exec Coun, Mem 1964-1968.

BAUTISTA, Simon (Tex) Christ Church Cathedral, 1117 Texas St, Houston TX 77002 **P Chr Ch Cathd Houston TX 2014-; Latino Mssnr Dio Washington Washington DC 2006-, 2005-2014; Ch Of The Cross Columbia SC 2005-** B Dominican Republic 1958 Rec 1/10/2004 as Priest Bp John Bryson Chane. m 3/20/1995 Amarilis Vargas-Bautista c 4. Ch Of The Ascen Gaithersburg MD 2004. sbautista@christchurchcathedral.org

BAVARO, Carolyn Margaret (Chi) P.O. Box 30247, Chicago IL 60630 B Chicago IL 1952 BS Elmhurst Coll 1982; MDiv SWTS 2003. D 6/21/2003 P 12/20/2003 Bp Bill Persell. m 7/29/1975 Louis Rodriguez. Gr Ch Pontiac IL 2006-2011; R S Jn's Epis Ch Chicago IL 2005; La Iglesia De Nuestra Senora De Las Americas Chicago IL 2004-2006; Cur Ch Of The Adv Chicago IL 2003-2004; Assoc P Nuestra Senora de las Americas - Chicago IL 2003-2004.

BAXLEY, Todd Lee (NwT) 1601 S Georgia St, Amarillo TX 79102 B Tucumcari NM 1965 s Michael & Paula. D 9/11/2009 Bp James Scott Mayer. D S Andr's Epis Ch Amarillo TX 2009-2016.

BAXTER, Barbara (WNY) 16 N Phetteplace St, Falconer NY 14733 **P Assoc S Lk's Epis Ch Jamestown NY 2008-** B Buffalo NY 1950 d Edward & Betty. BA Hiram Coll 1972; MMus TCU 1985; MDiv Bex Sem 1991. D 6/8/1991 P 1/1/1992 Bp David Charles Bowman. m 5/27/2006 Gordon De La Vars. P S Barn Ch Franklinville NY 2014-2016; Assoc R Calv Epis Ch Williamsville NY 2004-2005; Hse Supvsr Canaan Mnstrs 2002-2004; R St Johns Epis Youngstown NY 1993-2000; P-in-c S Aid's Ch Alden NY 1992-1993; Pstr Assoc S Ptr's Ch Westfield NY 1991-1992; Pstr Assoc Trin Epis Ch Hamburg NY 1991-1992; BEC Dio Wstrn New York Tonawanda NY 1994-2009, Mus Cmsn 1994-2007. AAM 1997; Hymn Soc Amer And Can 1984.

BAXTER JR, Donald Leslie (NwPa) 300 Hilltop Rd, Erie PA 16509 **Gr Ch Lake City PA 2002-** B Pensicola FL 1955 D 4/19/2002 P 11/17/2002 Bp Robert Deane Rowley Jr. m 5/13/1978 Susan Rose Paradise c 2.

BAXTER, Jane Ann (CNY) 151 Hawkins Rd, Ferrisburgh VT 05456 B Flint MI 1955 d Russell & Anita. Cert Champlain Coll 1978; U of Sthrn Maine 2002. D 3/23/2002 Bp Chilton Richardson Knudsen. c 3. Chapl Van Duyn Cntr for Rehab and Nrsng 2005-2015; Dio Cntrl New York Liverpool NY 2005-2006; St Paul's Syracuse Syracuse NY 2004-2013; Epis Ch Of S Mary The Vrgn Falmouth ME 2002-2003; Chapl Van Duyn Hm & Hosp Syracuse NY.

BAXTER, Lisette Dyer (Vt) 112 Lakewood Pkwy, Burlington VT 05408 **R S Andr's Epis Ch Colchester VT 1996-** B Montreal QC CA 1946 d Romeo & Carmelle. BTh McGill U; BA U of Montreal 1967; BS Westminster Coll 1977; MDiv Montreal TS CA 1992. D 6/1/1977 Bp Otis Charles P 6/24/1992 Bp Daniel Lee Swenson. m 7/28/1979 Larry J Baxter c 2. Trin Ch Shelburne VT 1992-1996; D Cathd Ch Of S Paul Burlington VT 1979-1990; D S Jas Epis Ch Midvale UT 1977-1979. CCN 1981; Soc of S Jn the Evang 1993.

BAXTER SSAP, Nancy Julia (At) 1223 Clifton Rd NE, Atlanta GA 30307 **Superior SSAP Atlanta GA 2005-** B Atlanta GA 1945 d Harry & Edith. BA Mt Holyoke Coll 1967; MDiv scl Candler TS Emory U 1981. D 6/13/1981 Bp Charles Judson Child Jr P 5/1/1982 Bp Bennett Jones Sims. c 2. Assoc S Barth's Epis Ch Atlanta GA 1995-2007; Dio Atlanta Atlanta GA 1982-2007; Chapl Emory Epis Campus Mnstry Atlanta GA 1982-2007; D Cathd Of S Phil Atlanta GA 1981-1982. Fell Coll of Preachers 1991.

✠ BAXTER, The Rt Rev Nathan Dwight (CPa) 115 N Duke St, Lancaster PA 17602 B Coatesville PA 1948 s Belgium & Augusta. Coll of Preachers; Harrisburg Cmnty Coll 1972; MDiv Lancaster TS 1976; DMin Lancaster TS 1984; Grad Theol Un 1985; STD Dickinson Coll 1990; Harv 1998. D 6/10/1977 P 12/16/1977 Bp Dean Theodore Stevenson Con 10/21/2006 for CPa. m 5/10/1969 Mary Ellen Baxter c 2. Bp of Cntrl Pennsylvania Dio Cntrl Pennsylvania Harrisburg PA 2006-2014, 1977-1978; R S Jas Ch Lancaster PA 2003-2006; Dn

Cathd of St Ptr & St Paul Washington DC 1992-2003; Assoc Prof EDS Cambridge MA 1990-1992; Lancaster TS Lancaster PA 1986-1990; Dn And Assoc Prof TS Lancaster PA 1986-1990; S Paul's Coll Lawrenceville VA 1984-1986; Chapl And Prof S Paul's Coll Lawrenceville VA 1984-1986; Reg Educ Coordntr Prov III 1979-1982; R S Cyp's Epis Ch Hampton VA 1978-1984; Bp of Cntrl Pennsylvania S Jn's Epis Ch Carlisle PA 1977-1978. Auth, "Pub Sermons," *Cases & Essays.* OHC; UBE.

BAXTER, Philip Roland (Va) 612 South Ingraham Avenue, Lakeland FL 33801 **Died 6/14/2016** B Weyauwega WI 1922 s Perry & Florence. BA Carroll Coll 1948; MDiv McCormick TS 1951; GTS 1956; MS U of Wisconsin 1987. D 10/18/1956 Bp Horace W B Donegan P 4/25/1957 Bp Donald H V Hallock. m 7/4/1984 Dorothea F James c 3. Ret Assoc S Paul's Ch Winter Haven FL 1999-2012; Supply P S Dav's Epis Ch Lakeland FL 1995-1996; Counslr Personal & Fam Counslr Cath Soc Serv 1990-1995; Assoc All SS Epis Ch Lakeland FL 1990-1994; Ret 1988-2016; Asst H Trin Epis Ch Bowie MD 1986-1988, R 1958-1985; Trin Epis Ch Oshkosh WI 1986-1988; Asst S Jn's Epis Ch Mc Lean VA 1982-1984; 1970-1982; Vic S Barn Ch Noberly MO 1968-1969; S Barn Ch Moberly MO 1967-1969. Auth, "Comments on Counslg," *The Wisconsin Counslr*, 1992. AFP 1965; Fllshp Contemplative Pryr 1961. Phi Mu Alpha; Kappa Sigma Phi.

BAXTER, Rae Lee (Mich) 430 Nicolet St, Walled Lake MI 48390 **P S Anne's Epis Ch Walled Lake MI 2011-** B Pontiac MI 1958 d Howard & Blanche. D 11/3/2010 P 6/21/2011 Bp Wendell Nathaniel Gibbs Jr. c 1.

BAYACA, Greg G(uerrero) (Los) B Caba La Union Philippines 1936 S Andrews Epis TS Quezon Ph. Trans 1/1/2003 Bp Joseph Jon Bruno. c 1. Dio Los Angeles Los Angeles CA 2002-2003; S Jn's And H Chld Wilmington CA 1995-2008. grbaya@aol.com

BAYANG, Martin Eugenio (RG) 1406 S Cliff Dr, Gallup NM 87301 B Sagada PH 1935 s Eugenio & Agustina. BA U of The Philippines 1960; BTh S Andrews TS Manila PH 1961; EDS 1965; STM Bos 1966; PhD Bos 1974. D 5/30/1961 P 2/14/1962 Bp Lyman Cunningham Ogilby. m 6/10/1965 Veronica Ag-a Bayang c 5. Vic All SS Ch Milan NM 1976-2004; Epis Asiamerican Strtgy Epis Ch Cntr New York NY 1974-1975; Asst S Lk's And S Marg's Ch Allston MA 1973-1974; Asst Stndg Rock Mssn ND 1969-1970; Serv Epis Ch in the Philippines 1966-1969; Serv Epis Ch in the Philippines 1961-1964. BTh cl S Andr's TS 1961.

BAYFIELD, Ralph Wesley (Va) 300 Westminster Canterbury Dr Apt 405, Apt 405, Winchester VA 22603 **Vic Ch Of The Gd Shpd Bluemont VA 2011-** B Philadelphia PA 1934 s Ralph & Caroline. Penn 1953; BA Wesl 1956; MDiv VTS 1959; STM Luth TS at Mt Airy-Philadelphia 1966; Camb 1988; DMin VTS 1997. D 5/9/1959 Bp William P Roberts P 11/24/1959 Bp Nelson Marigold Burroughs. m 8/20/2005 Maeva Hair Harris-Bayfield c 2. Int Vic S Peters-In-The-Woods Epis Ch Fairfax Sta VA 2008-2009; Trin Epis Ch St Aug FL 2000-2004; R S Thos' Ch Richmond VA 1991-2000; R S Tim's Ch Herndon VA 1974-1991; Chapl Hopistal Commonwealth Senate PA 1973-1974; Dn Dio Pennsylvania Philadelphia PA 1970-1974; R S Jas Ch Collegeville PA 1968-1974; Asst. Football Coach/ Chapl Ursinus Coll Collegeville PA 1968-1974; Chapl Eugene DuPont Memi Convalescent Hosp Wilmington DE 1963-1968; Assoc Chr Ch Christiana Hundred Wilmington DE 1960-1968; Asst S Paul's Epis Ch Cleveland OH 1959-1960; Evang Cmsn Dio Virginia Richmond VA 1986-1999. Auth, "Self-Differentiated Ldrshp through Pstr Vision," VTS, 1997; Auth, "Early Evansburg," Nace, 1974; Auth, "Selma Diary," Chr Ch Christians Hundred, 1966. Secy, EvangES 1990-1992.

BAYLES, Joseph Austin (Kan) 1341 N River Blvd, Wichita KS 67203 **Ret 2003-; Ret 1996-** B Wichita KS 1934 s Milan & Lura. BS K SU 1956; MDiv Andover Newton TS 1960. D 7/23/1967 P 11/30/1967 Bp William Davidson. c 3. R S Barth's Ch Wichita KS 1996-2003; S Jas Ch Wichita KS 1987-1988; Asst S Stephens Epis Churchrch Wichita KS 1982-1984; Vic Chr Ch Kingman KS 1971-1977; Chapl Hutchinson Correctional Facility Hutchinson KS 1969-1996; Vic S Anne's Ch Mcpherson KS 1969-1971; Cur Gr Epis Ch Hutchinson KS 1968-1969; Chapl Hutchinson Correctional Facility 1962-1968; Serv Bapt Ch 1958-1962. Amer Correctional Assn 1980-1996; Kansas Assn of Chapl 1962; Kansas Assn of Chapl, Exec Dir 2002-2003; Kansas Correctional Assn 1975-1996. Chapl of the Year Kansas Assn of Chapl 1993.

BAYLES, Richard Allen (Oly) Po Box 1115, South Bend WA 98586 B Ottawa KS 1939 s Milan & Lura. BA K SU 1961; Andover Newton TS 1963; MDiv EDS 1971; Non-degree Stds Cntrl Washington U 1975. D 7/13/1971 P 5/1/1972 Bp John Raymond Wyatt. m 1/7/1983 Sharon Kulish c 2. P-in-c S Ptr's Ch Seaview WA 2008-2009; Vic S Matt Ch Castle Rock WA 1995-2002; Vic S Jn's Ch Yakima WA 1973-1983; Yth Dir S Tim's Epis Ch Yakima WA 1971-1973. Phi Kappa Phi Phi Kappa Phi Acad Hon 1961. rickb98685@aol.com

BAYNE, Bruce George Cuthbert (Cal) 2875 Idledwild Dr, #108, Reno NV 89505 **Ret NV 2008-** B Seattle WA 1948 s Stephen & Lucie. BA Amh 1970; MDiv EDS 1975. D 6/14/1975 Bp Paul Moore Jr P 10/23/1976 Bp Harold Louis Wright. c 2. P-in-c Chap Of S Jas The Fisherman Wellfleet MA 2004-2011;

R S Lk's Ch San Francisco CA 1993-2008; Dir Of Ch And Alum Relatns EDS Cambridge MA 1989-1993; R Trin Ch Canton MA 1983-1989; Assoc R S Paul's Epis Ch Indianapolis IN 1979-1983; R S Ptr's By-The-Sea Sitka AK 1977-1979; Asst Chr Epis Ch Tarrytown NY 1975-1976.

BAYNES, Leopold Cornelius (LI) 2306 98th St, East Elmhurst NY 11369 B Georgetown VC 1943 s Donald & Venola. Codrington Coll 1973; Blanton-Peale Grad Inst 1997. Trans 5/5/1999 Bp Orris George Walker Jr. m 9/12/1985 Miranda Baynes c 2. Int Epis Ch of Gr and Resurr E Elmhurst NY 2013-2015; R Gr Ch Corona NY 1999-2015; Assoc S Mk's Ch Brooklyn NY 1995-1999; R S Andr's Ch Brooklyn NY 1978-1997.

BAYS, Terri (NI) 84 Broadway, New Haven CT 06511 **Cn Dio Nthrn Indiana So Bend IN 2016-** B Dallas TX 1968 d Martin & Almeta. BA NWU 1989; PhD UCLA 2000; MDiv Ya Berk 2012. D 12/21/2011 P 7/24/2012 Bp Edward Stuart Little II. m 9/17/1989 Timothy James Bays c 2. The Cathd Ch Of S Jas So Bend IN 2012-2016. missioner.bays@ednin.org

BAZIN, Jean Jacques Emmanuel Fritz (SeFla) 525 NE 15 Street, Miami FL 33132 **Non-par 1969-** B St. Marc HT 1941 s Antoine & Lucienne. BA Coll of S Pierre HT 1963. D 12/3/1966 P 6/4/1967 Bp Charles Alfred Voegeli. m 6/4/1983 Pamela H Bazin c 1. Jackson Memi Hosp Miami FL 2002; Dio SE Florida Miami 1998-2005, Archd for Immigration & Soc Justice 2006-; St Paul et Les Martyrs D'Haiti Miami FL 1993-1998, 1992, 1981-1986.

BEACH, Deborah Elizabeth (Alb) 132 Duanesburg - Churches Road, Duanesburg NY 12056 **Hlth Min Chr Epis Ch Duanesburg NY 2012-; D Chr's Ch Duanesburg NY 2011-** B Schenectady NY 1959 d Robert & Marie. AAS Maria Coll Albany NY 1979; BS Russell Sage Coll 1991. D 5/30/2009 Bp William Howard Love. D Calv Epis Ch Burnt Hills NY 2009-2011.

BEACH, Diana Lee (Nwk) 88 Main Street, Thomaston ME 04861 **Pstr Psych and Sprtl Direction Priv Pract Thomaston ME 2007-** B Calgary AB CA 1946 d Hugh & Lucille. BA Smith 1968; MDiv Ya Berk 1971; CG Jung Inst 1977; DMin NYTS 1980. D 6/3/1978 P 12/17/1978 Bp Paul Moore Jr. Co-Coordntr Greenfire Wmn Retreat Cntr Tenants Harbor ME 2006-2007; Assoc Chr Ch Short Hills NJ 1996-2000; P-in-c S Matt's Ch Jersey City NJ 1995-1996; Gr Ch Van Vorst Jersey City NJ 1984; Ch Of The H Innoc W Orange NJ 1980-1983; Assoc Ch of the H Innoc Hoboken NJ 1980-1983; Pstr Psych Priv Pract New York NY 1977-2006; Dn of Pstr Stds NYTS New York NY 1975-1983; Chapl Taft Sch Watertown CT 1971-1972. Auth, "Approaching Merlin's Cave: Ret and Soulwork," 2005; Auth, *In Search of the Goddess,* Ruach, 1992; Auth, *Womansoul Descending: Reflections on Feminine Sprtly,* D.Min. thesis, 1980; Auth, "But the Queen Doesn't Believe in God," 1977; Auth, *Sex Role Stereotyping in Ch Sch Curric,* Jn Knox Press, 1973. Cmnty of St. Jn Bapt, Assoc 2004; Kilin, Dio NY 1981-1999; Schlr's Grp, Dio Newark 1981-1984. Alum Awd Ya Berk 1988; MDiv cl, first in class Ya Berk 1971.

BEACH, John Tappan (Mass) 39, Route De Malagnou, Geneva 01208 Switzerland **S Paul's Ch In Nantucket Nantucket MA 2015-** B New Haven CT 1957 s Prescott & Marjorie. BA McGill U 1980; BTh McGill U 1982; MDiv McGill U 1983. Trans 2/1/2006 Bp Pierre W Whalon. m 8/21/1982 Denise M Beneteau c 2. Emm Epis Ch Geneva 1201 2006-2015; Chapl, Trin Angl Ch of Can 2001-2006; Dio Florida Jacksonville 1995-2001; Chapl Epis U Cntr Tallahassee FL 1995-2001; Serv Angl Ch Of Can 1983-1995.

BEACH, Joseph Lawrence (ETenn) 4768 Edens View Rd, Kingsport TN 37664 B Richmond VA 1936 s Joseph & Mary. BS U of Tennessee 1958; MS U of Tennessee 1960. D 1/27/1985 Bp William Evan Sanders. m 10/14/1961 Emily Faye Beach c 3. Serv S Tim's Epis Ch Kingsport TN 1985-1996.

BEACH, Kay Joan (Ia) 201 E Church St, Marshalltown IA 50158 **D S Paul's Ch Marshalltown IA 2014-** B Riverton NE 1941 d Frank & Elsie. BA Sterling Coll 1962; MA Geo Peabody Coll for Teachers 1963; MA Geo Peebody Coll for Teachers 1963. D 7/5/2014 Bp Alan Scarfe. c 2.

BEACHAM III, Albert Burton (U) 1420 N 3000 W, Vernal UT 84078 B Powell WY 1938 s Albert & Thelma. D 12/26/1985 Bp Otis Charles P 8/1/1987 Bp George Edmonds Bates. m 6/27/1981 Merilyn Beacham. Dio Utah Salt Lake City UT 2003-2004; S Paul's Epis Ch Vernal UT 1987-2003.

BEACHY, William Nicholas (WMo) 431 W 60th Ter, Kansas City MO 64113 **Ret 1987-** B Idaho Falls ID 1923 s William & Gwendolyn. MD LSU 1949; STB Ya Berk 1956. D 6/21/1956 P 12/21/1956 Bp Edward Randolph Welles II. m 6/15/1949 Catherine Ditchburn Beachy c 3. Chapl St Lk's Chap Kansas City MO 1960-1986; Chapl St. Lk's Hosp Kansas City MO 1960-1986; Vic S Steph's Ch Monett MO 1956-1960. Auth, "My Secret of Healing," *Sharing mag,* OSL the Physcn, 2000. Chapl Worker Sis of the H Sprt 1979; Intl OSL The Physcn 1958; The Schools of Pstr Care 1958-1990.

BEAL, Jennifer D (Los) 1745 Wedgewood Cmn, Concord MA 01742 **Chr Ch Needham Hgts MA 2016-; Assoc The Ch Of The Ascen Sierra Madre CA 2008-, Assoc 2004-2008** B Boston MA 1961 d Thomas & Barbara. BA Ob 1983; MDiv Ya Berk 1988. D 6/2/1990 P 6/15/1991 Bp David Elliot Johnson. m 8/26/2011 Julian Cole c 1. S Dunstans Epis Ch Dover MA 2016; Chapl VITAS Hospice Inc. Covina CA 2007-2008; Choir Dir Presb Ch USA 2002-2004; Dioc Coun Mem Dio Los Angeles Los Angeles CA 2001-2002; Int Trin Par Fillmore CA 2000-2002; Assoc Ch Of The Ang Pasadena CA 2000; R Emm

Ch Braintree MA 1998-1999; Asst S Steph's Ch Cohasset MA 1996-1998; Assoc S Steph's Epis Ch Boston MA 1993-1996; Asst S Paul's Ch Brookline MA 1992-1993; Cox Fell Dio Massachusetts Boston MA 1990-1992. jennifer.beal@mindspring.com

BEAL, Madeleine Elizabeth (Me) 35 Beal Rd, Chesterville ME 04938 **D AMIA Maine Fllshp 2003-** B San Diego CA 1959 d William & Madeleine. RN Framingham St Coll 1979; BS U of Maine 1986; Maine Diac Formation Prog 1991. D 4/8/1991 Bp Edward Cole Chalfant. m 6/2/1979 Douglas Foster Beal c 2. D S Lk's Ch Farmington ME 2000-2003, D 1991-1999; Yth Mssnr Dio Maine Portland ME 1996-1998; D S Matt's Epis Ch Lisbon Falls ME 1993-2000. NAAD 1991.

BEAL, Stephen Thomas (NCal) 2301 Polk St, Apt 3, San Francisco CA 94109 B Santa Rosa CA 1948 s Donald & Patricia. BA U of Arizona 1978; CTh Oxf GB 1980; MDiv CDSP 1981. D 10/28/1981 P 6/1/1982 Bp John Lester Thompson III. Spprt Serv Mgr Epis Cmnty Serv San Francisco CA 2001-2003; R S Lk's Ch Woodland CA 1989-1995; R Ch Of S Nich Paradise CA 1981-1989.

BEALE, Mary I (NH) 45 Derryfield Ct, Manchester NH 03104 **Non-par 1995-** B Geneva NY 1948 d George & Margaret. BFA Washington U 1970; MDiv Andover Newton TS 1973; MEd Bos 1975. D 6/17/1973 P 5/1/1977 Bp William Crittenden. m 8/1/2010 Susanne Marie Fortier. Vic Gr Epis Ch Concord NH 1982-1994; Asst S Geo's Ch Durham NH 1981-1982; S Paul's Sch Concord NH 1977-1980; Tchr Of Rel S Paul's Sch Concord NH 1977-1980; Non-par 1973-1976; Trin Memi Ch Warren PA 1973-1974.

BEALE, Norman Victor (Mass) 141 W. Oak St., Ramsey NJ 07446 **Chaplian Dept Mltry and Veterans Affrs 2011-** B Jacksonville FL 1952 s Warren & Louise. BA Furman U 1976; MS CUNY Hunter Coll 1983; MA Fuller TS 1983; MA TESM 1996; Tribhuvan U Kathmandu 2000. D 11/22/1995 P 5/1/1996 Bp Keith Lynn Ackerman. m 12/20/1980 Elizabeth Anne Beale c 2. R S Mk's Ch Westford MA 2003-2008; Assoc Gr Epis Ch Orange Pk FL 2001-2003; Dn, Anglcan Ch in Nepal Ch of the Prov of So E Asia Singapore 1999-2009; Mssy Angl Frontier Missions Richmond VA 1996-1999, Appointed Mssy 1994-2001; Mssy Angl Frontier Missions Richmond VA 1994-2001; Mssy Cmnty Dvlpmt Untd Mssn to Nepal 1988-1994; Mssy Mssn To Unreached Peoples Seattle WA 1987-1994; Tchr Gr Ch Sch (Epis) NY NY 1978-1983. Angl Frontier Mssn; Cerid Resrch Affiliate; Cntrl Asia Fllshp; Himalayan Mnstry Ntwk; Tamang Literacy Proj; Tamang Mnstry Ntwk.

BEALES, Rosemary Elizabeth (Va) St Stephen's & St Agnes School, 400 Fontaine St, Alexandria VA 22302 **Assoc S Paul's Epis Ch Alexandria VA 2008-; Lower Sch Chapl St. Steph's And St. Agnes Sch Alexandria VA 2008-; Trnr Godly Play Fndt 2000-; Godly Play Trnr Godly Play Fndt Sewanee TN 2000-** B Washington DC 1949 d Charles & Rosemary. Cont Educ VTS; BS U of Maryland 1972; MDiv VTS 2005; DMin VTS 2012. D 6/11/2005 Bp Robert Wilkes Ihloff P 12/17/2005 Bp John L Rabb. c 3. Assoc R S Jn's Ch Ellicott City MD 2005-2008. Auth, "Nurturing the Nurturers: Equipping Parents as Their Chld's Primary Sprtl Guides," *DMin thesis,* VTS, 2012. Mid Atlantic Epis Schools Assn (Bd Mem) 2012-2015. Fac Excellence Awd St. Steph's & St. Agnes Sch 2011.

BEALL, Nathan Andrew (WA) PO Box 207, St Marys City VA 20686 **Dio Washington Washington DC 2015-; St Marys Par St Marys City MD 2015-** B Alexandria VA 1988 s Stanley & Diana. BA St Mary's Coll 2011; MDiv Berk 2014; MDiv Ya Berk 2014. D 2/28/2015 P 11/21/2015 Bp Mariann Edgar Budde.

BEAM, Marcia Mckay (SeFla) 805 SW 6th Ave, Delray Beach FL 33444 **P-in-c S Matt's Epis Ch Delray Bch FL 2005-** B Delray Beach FL 1947 d George & Marguerette. BA S Augustines Coll Raleigh NC 1968; MDiv Bex Sem 2003. D 2/16/2004 P 12/20/2004 Bp Michael B Curry. m 12/31/1970 Ronnie Deleon Beam c 2. D Ch Of The H Fam Chap Hill NC 2004. stmattdb@bellsouth.net

BEAMER, Charles Wesley (O) 3920 Spokane Ave, Cleveland OH 44109 B Cumberland MD 1939 s Charles & Loretta. BA Frostburg St U 1969; MDiv PDS 1971. D 6/22/1971 Bp Harry Lee Doll P 4/1/1974 Bp David Keller Leighton Sr. m 1/5/1974 Yvonne Marie Beamer. Ch Of The Trsfg Cleveland OH 2000-2004; S Andr's Ch Cleveland OH 1998-2000; R Gr Ch OH 1988-1995; Gr Epis Ch Willoughby OH 1988-1995; Par Of The H Apos Mt Airy MD 1982-1988; Vic S Jas Epis Ch Mt Airy MD 1982-1985; All Souls Ch Halethorpe MD 1974-1982; Vic All Souls Baltimore MD 1974-1982; Asst Ch Of The H Cross Cumberland MD 1972-1973. EUC.

BEAN, Kevin D (WMass) All Saints Church, 10 Irving St., Worcester MA 01609 B Salonika GR 1954 s Harry & Marilyn. Ohio Wesl 1974; BD U of Edinburgh Scotland UK 1977; ETS Edinburgh Scotland UK 1978; EDS 1980; Harvard DS 1980. D 12/5/1981 P 6/24/1982 Bp Arthur Edward Walmsley. m 7/14/1978 Megan H Bean c 3. R All SS Ch Worcester MA 2008-2013; Vic St. Barth Ch New York NY 2005-2008; R Wyman Memi Ch of St Andr Marblehead MA 1997-2005; Trin Epis Old Swedes Ch Swedesboro NJ 1992-1997; Assoc Trin Epis Old Swedes Ch Wilmington DE 1992-1997; Trin Par Wilmington DE 1992-1997; Asst Old S Paul's Edinburgh Untd Kingdom 1988-1989; Old St Paul's Ch Edinburgh 1988-1989; P-in-c S Marg's Edinburgh Untd Kingdom 1988-1989; Assoc S Lk's Par Darien CT 1983-1988; Peace Cmsn Dio

Connecticut Meriden CT 1982-1985, Coordntr EUC 1980-1981; Cur S Andr's Ch Meriden CT 1981-1983; Dioc Mssn Strtgy Com Dio Massachusetts Boston MA 2000-2005. Auth, "arts," *Bulletin of the Atomic Scientists*; Auth, "arts," *Commonweal*; Auth, "arts," *Cross Currents*; Auth, "arts," *Soc Sci Journ*; Auth, "arts," *Sojourners*; Auth, "arts," *The New York Times*. Wm Sloane Coffin / Joan Bates Forsberg Fell Yale DS / Berk 1995.

BEAN, Rebecca Anne (EC) PO Box 1333, Goldsboro NC 27533 B New Jersey 1975 d William & Ruth. BS Van 1997; MS Florida Intl U 2004. D 6/20/2015 Bp Robert Stuart Skirving. m 7/8/2006 Cory Duane Bean c 1.

BEANE, Emmetri Monica (Va) PO Box 367, Rixeyville VA 22737 **D Little Fork Epis Ch Rixeyville VA 2014-** B Bronx NY 1966 d Emmett & Susie. Cert Diac Formation Inst (Dio Virginia); BA U of Virginia 1987; JD Geo Mason U Sch of Law 1991; MS Geo Mason U 1999. D 2/23/2013 Bp Shannon Sherwood Johnston. c 2. D S Gabr's Epis Ch Leesburg VA 2013-2014; D S Steph's Epis Ch Culpeper VA 2013. DOK 2014.

BEAR, Susan Dowler (Miss) 3600 Arlington Loop, Hattiesburg MS 39402 **R Ch Of The Ascen Hattiesburg MS 2004-; Dn, Sowashee Convoc Dio Mississippi Jackson MS 2006-** B Trenton NJ 1947 d Thomas & Evelyn. BA Wilson Coll 1969; MEd Auburn U 1980; MDiv Sewanee: The U So, TS 1994; DMin Sewanee: The U So, TS 2007. D 6/25/1994 P 11/4/1995 Bp James Monte Stanton. m 12/21/1974 John E Bear c 2. R Gr Epis Ch Houston TX 2001-2004; R Chap Of The Cross Rolling Fork MS 1996-2001; Cur All SS Ch Jackson MS 1995. coa@megagate.com

BEARD, Bryan Benjamin (Okla) 9309 N 129th East Ave, Owasso OK 74055 B Midwest City OK 1974 s John & Donna. BS Oklahoma St U 1997; Grad Iona Sch of Formation 2015. D 8/1/2015 P 3/2/2016 Bp Edward Joseph Konieczny. m 9/21/2003 Julie Ann Poston c 2.

BEARDEN, Jane Bostick (Mass) 77 Westchester Dr, Haverhill MA 01830 **P-in-c Trin Epis Ch Haverhill MA 2009-** B Winnsboro LA 1948 d John & Alice. BS Centenary Coll 1970; MT Memi Hosp Houston TX 1972; MS Mississippi St U 1985; MA EDS 2006. D 10/6/2001 P 6/3/2006 Bp M(Arvil) Thomas Shaw. c 3. P-in-c Dio Massachusetts Boston MA 2007-2009; Assoc to the R The Epis Ch Of The Redeem Biloxi MS 2007-2009; S Andr's Ch Methuen MA 2006-2007; D S Steph's Memi Ch Lynn MA 2001-2006.

BEASLEY, Battle Alexander (Tenn) 1613 Fatherland St, Nashville TN 37206 **R S Mk's Ch Antioch TN 2001-** B Bolahoon LR 1952 s William & Marion. Georgetown Coll; BA U of Kentucky 1978; MDiv Sewanee: The U So, TS 1986. D 6/5/1986 P 6/1/1987 Bp Alex Dockery Dickson. m 9/27/1997 Amy Dawn Harwell c 2. S Ann's Ch Nashville TN 1999-2001; R Ch Of The Redeem Shelbyville TN 1994-1998; Int Chr Ch Memphis TN 1992-1994; Assoc Gr - S Lk's Ch Memphis TN 1989-1992; Dio W Tennessee Memphis 1986-1989; Cur S Paul's Ch Memphis TN 1986-1989. Sthrn buddhist sunday Sch Assn all day meeting and 1985; the labyrinth Soc 1998-2001.

BEASLEY, Carl H (Eas) 720 NE 4th Ave Apt 506, Fort Lauderdale FL 33304 **Assoc P All SS Prot Epis Ch Ft Lauderdale FL 2015-** B York PA 1946 s Carl & Frances. BA Ken 1968; MTS VTS 1976; MA Washington Coll 1988; Cert Wilson Coll 1990. D 2/2/1977 P 11/29/1978 Bp Dean Theodore Stevenson. c 1. Tchr & Chapl W Nottingham Acad Colora MD 2000-2014; Tchr & Chapl Carson Long Mltry Inst New Bloomfield PA 1996-2000; Tchr & Chapl Phelps Sch Malvern PA 1994-1996; R S Jn's Ch Marietta PA 1989-1991; R S Mary's Epis Ch Waynesboro PA 1979-1986; Cur The Epis Ch Of S Jn The Bapt York PA 1977-1979. Assoc, Epis Carmel 2011. Who's Who Among Amer's Teachers 2001.

BEASLEY, Christopher Ryan (Ind) **S Ptr's Ch Lebanon IN 2014-** B Princeton IN 1976 s Wesley & Patricia. BGS Ball St U 1998; MA Ball St U 2001; MDiv Bexley-Seabury 2014. D 3/8/2014 P 9/6/2014 Bp Cate Waynick. c 1. P-in-c Dio Indianapolis Indianapolis IN 2014-2015.

BEASLEY, Helen Roberts (SwVa) Po Box 1266, Galax VA 24333 B Knoxville TN 1944 d Richard & Carrie. BA Hobart and Wm Smith Colleges 1966; MDiv UTS 1990. D 6/11/1993 P 12/21/1993 Bp Richard Frank Grein. c 2. S Jn's Ch Roanoke VA 2006-2007; Trin Epis Ch Rocky Mt VA 1999-2005; S Andr's Epis Ch Hartsdale NY 1996-1999; Wstrn Dutchess Mnstry Wappingers Falls NY 1995-1996; Assoc Chr Ch Bronxville NY 1994-1996; Assoc Trin S Paul's Epis New Rochelle NY 1993-1996; Dir Proj Hope S Ptr's Epis Ch Peekskill NY 1992-1993; Chapl Cabrini Med Cntr In New York City 1988-1990. Ord Of S Lk; SCHC.

BEASLEY, Nicholas (USC) 126 Blyth Avenue, Greenwood SC 29649 **R Ch Of The Resurr Greenwood SC 2007-** B Memphis TN 1975 s Robert & Joy. BA U So 1997; MDiv Ya Berk 2000; PhD Van 2006. D 9/23/2000 P 3/25/2001 Bp Dorsey Henderson. m 8/17/2002 Elizabeth Irwin Beasley c 2. Postdoctoral Fell Candler TS Atlanta GA 2006-2007; P Assoc H Trin Par Decatur GA 2006-2007; P Assoc S Geo's Ch Nashville TN 2003-2006; Asst R Chr Ch Greenville SC 2000-2002. Auth, "Chr Ritual and the Creation of British Slave Societies, 1650-1780," U GA Press, 2009; Auth, "Dom Rituals: Mar and Baptism in the British Plantation Colonies, 1650-1780," *Angl and Epis Hist*, HSEC, 2007; Auth, "Ritual Time in British Plantation Colonies, 1650-1780," *Ch Hist*, Amer Soc of Ch Hist, 2007; Auth, "Wars of Rel in the Circum-Caribbean: Engl

Iconoclasm in Spanish Amer, 1580-1702," *SS and their Cults in the Atlantic Wrld*, U of So Carolina Press, 2006. HSEC 2005. Asst, Emeritaus Prince of Peace Epis Ch, Woodland Hills, CA 2012; Nelson Burr Prize HSEC 2008; ECF Felllow ECF 2003; Phi Beta Kappa Phi Beta Kappa 1996.

BEASLEY, Robert (ETenn) 121 E. Harper Avenue, Maryville TN 37804 B Somerset KY 1949 s Ray & Grapel. BA U of Memphis 1971; MDiv SWTS 1974. D 6/26/1974 Bp John Vander Horst P 5/24/1975 Bp William F Gates Jr. m 10/12/1985 Martha Lee Beasley. Int S Andr's Ch Maryville TN 2007-2009; S Phil's Epis Ch Laurel MD 2005-2007; R S Jn's Ch Roanoke VA 2002-2005; R S Phil's Ch Southport NC 1991-2002; Asst R Chr Ch New Bern NC 1988-1991; 1984-1988; Asst Ch Of The Ascen Knoxville TN 1980-1984; Asst S Paul's Ch Augusta GA 1979-1980; Dio Tennessee Nashville TN 1975-1978; Vic S Mary Magd Ch Fayetteville TN 1975-1978; D-in-Trng S Geo's Ch Germantown TN 1974-1975. Auth, "The R Painted His Nails," *A Tapestry of Voices*, Knoxville Writers Gld, 2011; Auth, "The Paved Road," *The Storyteller*, 2008; Auth, "What 'Gd News' is Gd," *Witness*, 1990; Auth, "Experiencing the Way of Tea," *Honolulu*, 1987; Auth, "Necessary Number Racket," *Your Ch*, 1984.

BEASLEY JR, Thomas Edward (Fla) 6003 Brookridge Rd, Jacksonville FL 32210 B Nashville TN 1945 s Thomas & Martha. BS Florida St U 1970; VTS 1972; Cert Angl Inst Live Oak FL 2004. D 11/9/2004 P 5/26/2005 Bp Samuel Johnson Howard. m 5/26/1995 Pixianne Carlton Beasley c 2. Mntl Hlth Overly Spec River Reg Human Serv Jacksonville FL 1996-2000; Loc P Baker Correctional Inst. & Un Correctional Inst. FL.

BEASON, Kenneth G (ECR) 438 N 5th St, Cheney WA 99004 **Died 10/11/2016** B Columbus OH 1942 s Carl & Helen. BD U of Nebraska 1969; MDiv SWTS 1972. D 6/4/1972 P 12/1/1972 Bp Robert Patrick Varley. m 12/8/2000 Laurel A Beason. R S Jas Ch Paso Robles CA 2000-2007; Cathd Of S Jn The Evang Spokane WA 1996-2000; Off Of Bsh For ArmdF New York NY 1974-1996; R SS Jn & Jas Boston MA 1973-1974; Urban Vic Dio Nebraska Omaha NE 1972-1973. Auth, "Pstr Care & USAF Chapl". UBE.

BEATTIE, Richard Edward (Ct) 438 Old Tavern Rd, Orange CT 06477 B New Haven CT 1943 s Edward & Ethel. BCC ACPE & APC - CPE 1996; MA Sacr Heart U 1996; BS U of New Haven 1966. D 12/6/1986 Bp Arthur Edward Walmsley P 1/12/2002 Bp Wilfrido Ramos-Orench. m 6/19/1965 Marilyn Jane Beattie c 3. Chr Ch Ansonia CT 2012-2015; Assoc Ch of the H Sprt W Haven CT 2010-2012; P-in-c Chr And Epiph Ch E Haven CT 2007-2009; D S Ptr's Epis Ch Milford CT 2001; Chapl Yale-New Haven Hosp New Haven CT 1994-2009.

BEATTIE, Richard Sherman (Ct) 25 Stuart Dr, Old Greenwich CT 06870 **Died 4/2/2017** B Paris FR 1928 s Ernest & Dorothy. BA Trin Hartford CT 1949; MDiv GTS 1952. D 6/17/1952 P 12/19/1952 Bp Walter H Gray. m 6/28/1958 Joan M Beattie c 1. P-in-c S Andr's Ch Stamford CT 2000-2007; Chr Ch Greenwich CT 1982-1983; Round Hill Cmnty Ch Inc Greenwich CT 1978-1979; Nonpar 1971-2000; R S Paul's Ch Columbus IN 1967-1971; Chapl And Exec Dir Dept Of Coll Wk SUNY Buffalo NY 1961-1966; Assoc Ch Of The Heav Rest New York NY 1957-1960; Asst Cathd Ch Of S Paul Burlington VT 1953-1957; Chapl U Of Vermont 1953-1957; Chr Ch Bethany CT 1952-1953; Vic Ch Of The Gd Shpd Orange CT 1952-1953. Phi Delta Kappa.

BEATTY, Anne M (NCal) 1515 Shasta Dr Apt 1335, Davis CA 95616 **Assoc Ch Of S Mart Davis CA 2013-, Asst 1993-1999** B Lafayette IN 1949 d Earl & Margaret. BA Pomona Coll 1971; MDiv Fuller TS 1985; CDSP 1992. D 1/6/1993 P 7/27/1993 Bp Jerry Alban Lamb. c 2. R Trin Epis Ch Pocatello ID 2002-2010; Int Ascen Epis Ch Vallejo CA 2001-2002; Int S Paul's Epis Ch Benicia CA 1999-2001; OC Dep Dio Idaho Boise ID 2006.

BEATTY, Steve (Va) 10267 Lakeridge Square CT, Apt B, Ashland VA 23005 **P-in-c Emm Epis Ch Powhatan VA 2013-** B Clarksburg WV 1955 s Calvin & Margaret. BA W Virginia Wesleyan Coll 1977; W Virginia U 1979; Grad Sch of Rel Pk Coll Parkville MO 1988; Rockhurst Jesuit Coll 1988; MDiv Ya Berk 1994. D 9/21/1989 P 6/5/1994 Bp John Clark Buchanan. m 6/29/1985 Angela Marie Beatty c 1. Vic Ch Of Our Sav Montpelier VA 2008-2010; R Chr Ch Somers Point NJ 2000-2007; R Chr Ch Warrensburg MO 1994-2000; D S Mk's Ch New Canaan CT 1992-1994; D S Mary's Epis Ch Kansas City MO 1990-1991; D Trin Ch Independence MO 1989-1990; Non-par Untd States Postal Serv Kansas City MO 1979-1991. Auth, "Sermon for Lent 4," *Sermons That Wk*, Epis Ch, 2000; Auth, "A Statistical Abstract Of W Virginia Reg Vii," Appalachian Reg Plnng Cmsn, 1977. Omicron Delta Kappa. stephanbeatty@embarqmail.com

BEATY, Maureen Kay (Colo) St Mary Magdalene, 4775 Cambridge St, Boulder CO 80301 B Denver CO 1961 d James & Ruth. BS Colorado St U 1984. D 11/17/2007 Bp Robert John O'Neill. c 2.

BEAUCHAMP, Robert William (SwVa) PO Box 227, Norton VA 24273 **H Trin Epis Ch Hertford NC 2017-; S Mk's Ch S Paul VA 2008-** B Washington DC 1962 s Irving & Carol. BA Emory and Henry Coll 1989; MDiv Sewanee: The U So, TS 1999. D 6/20/1999 P 12/17/1999 Bp Neff Powell. m 5/14/1989 Laura Sherry Beauchamp c 2. All SS Epis Ch Norton VA 2008-2016; S Andr's Ch Pasadena MD 2002-2005; Asst R Gr Ch Kilmarnock VA 2000-2002; R Chr Epis Ch Marion VA 1999-2000.

B

BEAUHARNOIS, Patricia Ann (Alb) 18 Butternut St, Champlain NY 12919 B Massena NY 1966 d Albert & Judith Ann. BA SUNY 1990. D 6/2/2012 Bp William Howard Love. m 10/10/1996 Steffen Eric Beauharnois c 1.

BEAULAC, David Armand (Alb) St Mary's Church, PO Box 211, Lake Luzerne NY 12846 **R S Mary's Ch Lake Luzerne NY 2012-; Dn Sthrn Adirondack Dnry 2014-** B Putnam CT 1952 s Armand & Lorraine. BA U of Connecticut 1974; MA Fairfield U 1976; MA Nash 2012. D 6/2/2012 P 12/8/2012 Bp William Howard Love. m 6/25/1977 Barbara Waldron Beaulac c 2. admin@stmarysluzerne.org

BEAULIEU, Cynthia Rae (Me) 650 Main St, Caribou ME 04736 **D Aroostook Epis Cluster Caribou ME 2008-** B Presque Isle ME 1949 d Jack & Capitola. D 8/9/2008 Bp Chilton Richardson Knudsen. m 11/8/1997 Gerald Beaulieu c 3.

BEAULIEU, Delores Joyce (Minn) Rr 2 Box 246, Bagley MN 56621 B Bagley MN 1934 d George & Emily. D 10/29/2005 Bp James Louis Jelinek. c 2.

BEAULIEU, Joyce (Chi) 223 W Royal Dr, Dekalb IL 60115 **Gr Epis Ch Galesburg IL 2016-; Assoc S Paul's Ch Dekalb IL 2013-; Chair, Total Mnstry T/F Dio Chicago Chicago IL 2013-, Dn, Rockford Dnry 2011-2012; Spirital Dir, Retreat Ldr Soul Source DeKalb IL 2012-** B Burlington IA 1952 d Gail & Betty. AB IL Wesl 1974; MPH U Roch 1976; PhD U MI 1985; MDiv SWTS 2006. D 6/10/2006 P 3/24/2007 Bp Stacy F Sauls. m 8/12/2011 Mary Lovelock. S Bride's Epis Ch Oregon IL 2014-2015; R The Epis Ch Of The H Trin Belvidere IL 2008-2012; P Epis Ch of Our Sav Richmond KY 2008; P-in-c Dio Lexington Lexington 2007-2008; Campus Mssnr Dio Lexington Lexington KY 2007-2008; Asst Chapl Cbury NW Evanston IL 2006-2007. Gr Place Campus Mnstry Bd Dir 2012; Natl Epis Hlth Mnstrs Bd Dir 2011; Soc of Comp of the H Cross 1997; Wmn Caucus 2006. Stevenson Awd for Practical Theol Seabury Sem 2006; Wmn Bd Awd to Outstanding Sr Wmn Seabury Wmn Bd 2006.

BEAUMONT, Jerrold Foster (CFla) 8494 Ridgewood Ave Apt 4201, Cape Canaveral FL 32920 B Highland Park MI 1926 s Francis & Clara. Dioc TS; Lawr Tech U; Sacr Heart Sem 1975; MTh Int Mnstry Prog 1985; Int Mnstry Prog 1986. D 5/12/1973 Bp Richard Stanley Merrill Emrich P 6/1/1975 Bp H Coleman Mcgehee Jr. m 6/2/1951 Marjorie Doris Hesman. Vic S Barn' Ch Chelsea MI 1975-2001. Auth, "Success Begins w Me"; Auth, "Reformation-The Ch In Process". Min Assn Faith In Action, Engl Soc Detroit; Ord S Paul. Chapl Of The Year USAF / CAP 1992.

BEAUMONT, Katharine Jenetta (Az) B 1943 d Robert & Netta. BA Whitman Coll 1965; MA U of Idaho 1968. D 1/26/2008 Bp Kirk Stevan Smith. m 6/18/1966 Randolph Beaumont c 3.

BEAUVOIR, Jonas (Hai) c/o Diocese of Haiti, Boite Postale 1309, Port au Prince Haiti Haiti **Dio Haiti Port-au-Prince HT 2008-** B 1971 s Joseph & Claircile. D 1/25/2006 P 2/18/2007 Bp Jean Zache Duracin. m 12/29/2007 Luvernia Mevoicy M Beauvoir.

✠ BEAUVOIR, The Rt Rev Oge (Hai) 76 Avenue Christophe, Port-Au-Prince Haiti **Dn TS 2005-** B Gros-Morne HT 1956 s Joseph & Claircine. BTh U of Montreal 1988; Montreal TS CA 1989; MA U of Montreal 1993. Trans 3/31/2000 Bp Richard Frank Grein Con 5/22/2012 for Hai. m 7/16/1983 Serette Beauvoir c 2. Bp Suffr of Haiti Dio Haiti Port-au-Prince HT 2012-2015; Mssnr to Haiti Exec Coun Appointees New York NY 2005-2012; Vol For Mssn New York NY 2004-2012; Prog Assoc Trin Par New York NY 1999-2005; Serv Angl Ch Of Can 1989-1999. Pres Exec Coun Of Franophone Angl Ch 2000.

BEAVEN, John Clinton (Me) 22 Willow Grove Rd, Brunswick ME 04011 **Ret 1989-** B New York NY 1927 s Walter & Florence. BA Col 1949; MA Col 1951; MDiv GTS 1956. D 6/3/1956 Bp Horace W B Donegan P 12/21/1956 Bp Chandler W Sterling. m 5/5/1951 Margaret Mackinnon c 3. Trst The GTS New York NY 1987-1992; Dn Cathd Ch Of S Lk Portland ME 1982-1989; Cathd Of St Jn The Div New York NY 1975-1978; R Gr Ch Millbrook NY 1969-1982; Chapl Kent Sch Kent CT 1964-1969; P-in-c Ch Of The Ascen Forsyth MT 1959-1964; Emm Ch Miles City MT 1959-1964; P-in-c S Paul's Ch Ft Benton MT 1956-1959; Chair COM Dio Maine Portland ME 1986-1988; Dioc Coun Dio New York New York NY 1975-1979; Exec Coun Dio Montana Helena MT 1960-1963.

BEAZLEY, Robert W (Fla) PO Box 409, Sewanee TN 37375 B Tallahassee FL 1990 s Jon & Evelyn. AA Tallahassee Cmnty Coll 2010; BS Florida St U 2012; MDiv The TS at The U So 2016. D 12/6/2015 Bp Samuel Johnson Howard. m 5/18/2017 Liz Embler.

BEBB JR, Ernest Leo (U) 6452 South 1650 East, Murray UT 84121 **Assoc All SS Ch Salt Lake City UT 1988-** B Scottsbluff NE 1932 s Ernest & Nellie. BS U of Nebraska 1954; MA MI SU 1963. D 1/22/1988 P 11/1/1988 Bp George Edmonds Bates. m 7/11/1959 Jane Woollam. Dir, U Un U of Utah Salt Lake City Utah 1968-1995.

BEBBER, Gerald King 1821 Mcgougan Rd, Fayetteville NC 28303 **Off Of Bsh For ArmdF New York NY 1985-** B Moline IL 1947 s Donald & Ruth. Command and Gnrl Stff Coll; BA U NC 1971; MDiv VTS 1979; US-A Airborne Sch Ft Benning GA 1986; Cert US-A Ft Monmouth NJ 1991; US-A Ft Bragg NC 1993. Trans 9/20/1981 Bp Donald James Parsons. m 8/2/1975 Irene Rachel Bebber c 1. Vic S Jas Epis Ch Lewistown IL 1981-1985; Serv Angl Ch Of Can

1978-1981. CBS, Archconference Of The H Agony, ESA, Skcm; SSC. Mstr Parachutist Us-Army 1995; The Soldier'S Medal Us-Army.

BECHERER, Carl John (Minn) Rec 4/25/1975.

BECHTEL, A(Lpha) Gillett (Los) 36176 Golden Gate Dr, Yucaipa CA 92399 **Died 9/9/2016** B Venice CA 1921 s Alpha & Ruth. BS U CA 1944; MDiv Garrett-Evang TS 1947; MA San Diego St U 1966; Claremont Coll 1973. D 2/24/1953 P 10/29/1953 Bp Donald J Campbell. c 4. Ret 1987-2016; Assoc Shpd by the Sea Epis/Luth Mssn Gualala CA 1987-2012; Bloy Hse Claremont CA 1974-1985; S Fran Of Assisi Par Sn Bernrdno CA 1974-1985; Asst S Ambr Par Claremont CA 1969-1973; Chapl Claremont Coll Claremont CA 1968-1969; Chapl San Diego St Coll San Diego CA 1956-1968; Vic Redeem Los Angeles 1953-1956. Auth, "The Mex Epis Ch," *A Century Of Reform & Revolution*, 1966.

BECHTOLD, Bryant Coffin (FtW) 3290 Lackland Rd, Fort Worth TX 76116 B Orlando FL 1951 s Kenneth & Fern. BD Georgia Inst of Tech 1973; MA Georgia Inst of Tech 1975; PhD U of Utah 1978; MDiv Sewanee: The U So, TS 1986. D 6/7/1986 P 5/9/1987 Bp William Arthur Beckham. m 5/7/1994 Susan R Bechtold c 2. Chr The King Epis Ch Ft Worth TX 1997-2006; Ascen S Matt's Ch Price UT 1990-1997; Vic Ch Of The H Trin E Carbon UT 1990-1997; Dio Utah Salt Lake City UT 1990-1997; Asst All SS Epis Ch Deltona FL 1987-1989; Dio Upper So Carolina Columbia SC 1986-1987; D S Lk's Epis Ch Atlanta GA 1986-1987.

BECK, Brien Patrick (FdL) 347 Libal St, De Pere WI 54115 **D Ch of the Blessed Sacr Green Bay WI 2012-** B Milwaukee WI 1966 s James & Patricia. D 5/7/2011 Bp Russell Edward Jacobus. m 5/12/1986 Jean Beck c 2.

BECK, Jacob David (WA) 13 Victor Dr, Thurmont MD 21788 **Died 4/5/2017** B Philadelphia PA 1933 s Jacob & Anna. BS U of Pennsylvania 1955; MDiv PDS 1958. D 5/10/1958 P 11/29/1958 Bp Oliver J Hart. m 11/24/1962 Carla Beck c 3. Ret 1996-2017; Fin Cmsn Dio Maryland Baltimore MD 1994-1996, Dioc Coun 1993-1995; Int Harriet Chap Catoctin Epis Par Thurmont MD 1991-1996; Int S Andr's Ch Pasadena MD 1990-1991; Int S Barn Epis Ch Temple Hills MD 1989-1990; Int Gr Ch Elkridge MD 1988-1989; Int S Dunst's Ch Mc Lean VA 1986-1988; Int S Phil's Epis Ch Laurel MD 1985-1986; Chr Ch Prince Geo's Par Rockville MD 1981-1985; Cmsn on Angl-RC Relatns Dio Montana Helena MT 1975-1981, Cmsn on the Ch and Soc 1975-1981, Eccl Crt 1973-1981, Exec Coun 1969-1979; S Paul's Ch Ft Benton MT 1965-1981; R S Fran Epis Ch Great Falls MT 1964-1981; Cur Ch Of The H Sprt Missoula MT 1959-1962; Cur Ch Of Our Sav Jenkintown PA 1958-1959; Peace Cmsn Dio Washington Washington DC 1989-1996, Mssy Dvlpmt Advsry Com 1985-1988. "The Evangel," Ed Dioc Nwspr Dio Montana, 1965. Fllshp of St. Jn, Ret Cler of Assoc. of Dio 1996; Int Ntwk 1982; Natl Epis Cler Assn 1985; Silver Eagles Ret Cler Assn 1985; Washington Epis Cler Assn 1982. Human Rts Awd Educational Assn 1976.

BECK, Judith Taw (Pa) 3300 W Penn St, Philadelphia PA 19129 B Cleveland OH 1942 d Dudley & Louise. Keuka Coll 1961; BSN U of Pennsylvania 1964; MDiv Luth TS at Philadelphia 1989. D 6/11/1988 P 6/17/1989 Bp Allen Lyman Bartlett Jr. c 3. Assoc R S Ptr's Ch Philadelphia PA 2000-2004; S Ptr's Ch Germantown Philadelphia PA 1992-1999; Chapl Swarthmore Coll Swarthmore PA 1990-1992; Asst S Chris's Ch Gladwyne PA 1990, D 1988-1989. Soc Of S Marg.

BECK, Laura E (Colo) **S Mths Epis Ch Monument CO 2017-** B Bartlesville OK 1963 d Terry & Minnie. BSN U of Pennsylvania 1985; MSN U of Texas Hlth Sci Cntr 1987; MDiv Sewanee: The U So, TS 2013; MDiv The TS at The U So 2013. D 12/29/2012 P 7/6/2013 Bp Edward Joseph Konieczny. Cur S Pat's Epis Ch Broken Arrow OK 2013-2015.

BECK, Randall Alan (NwPa) St John's Episcopal Church, 226 W State St, Sharon PA 16146 **D S Jn's Epis Ch Sharon PA 2012-** B Belview PA 1963 s Robert & June. BS Grove City Coll 1985. D 5/20/2012 Bp Sean Walter Rowe. m 11/1/1986 Jacque Carey Beck c 2.

BECK, Sue Ann (Los) St. John The Divine, 183 E. Bay St., Costa Mesa CA 92627 **D S Jn The Div Epis Ch Costa Mesa CA 2009-** B Carroll IA 1948 d Herbert & Shirley. BS U of Nthrn Colorado 1971; MA Antioch Coll 1979; PhD California Grad Inst 1989; MDiv Claremont TS 2005. D 11/15/2007 Bp Chester Lovelle Talton. m 5/8/1982 Robert Beck.

BECK, Tanya (Ind) 5810 Kingsley Dr., Indianapolis IN 46220 **All SS Ch Indianapolis IN 2000-** B Anderson IN 1932 d Robert & Margaret. Chr TS; BA DePauw U 1954; MA Ball St U 1955. D 9/28/1974 Bp John P Craine P 1/8/1976 Bp John Mc Gill Krumm. c 4. Transition P S Mk's Ch Plainfield IN 2008-2010; Int Dn Chr Ch Cathd Indianapolis IN 2005-2008; Int S Matt's Ch Indianapolis IN 2003-2005; Int Gr Ch Muncie IN 2002-2009; Ch Of The H Sprt Sfty Harbor FL 2000-2001; Min Of Sprtl Growth S Jn; Dir The Pilgrimage. Outstanding Wmn In Rel 90; Sagamore Of The Wabash Gvnr'S Awd; Outstanding Alum Awd 90 Depauw U.

BECK, Thomas Francis (Ct) 4 Willow Ct, Cromwell CT 06416 B Newark NJ 1933 s William & Helen. BA Ups 1955; BD VTS 1963; MEd Iona Coll 1976. D 6/8/1963 P 12/1/1963 Bp Dudley S Stark. m 3/21/2015 Gail E Beck. Gr Ch Stafford Sprg CT 1994-1998; Middlesex Area Cluster Mnstry Higganum

CT 1992-1994; Gr Epis Ch Yantic CT 1979-1983; Epis Soc Serv Ansonia CT 1977-1986; R S Jas' Ch New Haven CT 1967-1975; Cur S Ptr Caldwell NJ 1965-1967; Cur S Jas Ch Montclair NJ 1963-1965. Auth, "Hope When I Despair". AAPC.

BECKER, Arthur Paul (Minn) 2901 Pearson Pkwy, Brooklyn Park MN 55444 **P Assoc S Mk's Cathd 2003-; Ret 1995-** B Stevens Pt WI 1928 s George & Irene. BA Lawr 1952; MDiv GTS 1956; Coll of Preachers 1960; U of Iowa 1969; MA U of So Dakota 1972. D 6/14/1956 P 12/19/1956 Bp William Hampton Brady. m 8/23/1958 Lois Maxine Becker c 3. Prof Theol Mt St Clare Coll Clinton IA 1993-1994; Dio Iowa Des Moines IA 1991-1996, Reg Coordntr Prov 6 of ECAEvangelism 1983-1990; Prof of Theol Mt S Clare Coll 1990-1999; Dio Iowa 1990-1996; R S Jn's Ch Clinton IA 1988-1995; R S Jn's Ch Clinton IA 1988-1994; COM Dio Iowa 1979-1988; CDO Dio Iowa 1976-1988; Mssn and Educ Dio Iowa 1974-1988; Archd Individual Accounts Des Moines IA 1974-1988; Chapl Law Enforcement Acad 1974-1988. ACES 1999; APGA 1999; OHC 1953.

BECKER, CS Honey (Haw) PO Box 819, Kailua HI 96734 **D S Matt's Epis Ch Waimanalo HI 2008-** B New Orleans LA 1946 LSU; Tulane; U of Hawaii. D 7/15/2001 Bp Richard Sui On Chang. c 3. St. Geo's Coll Mssnr Dio Jerusalem 2012-2016; D S Jn's By The Sea Kaneohe HI 2010-2011; D S Andr's Cathd Honolulu HI 2001-2010.

BECKER, Kim (WNC) PO Box 177, Glendale Springs NC 28629 **Par Of The H Comm Glendale Sprg NC 2015-; P Assoc Ch Of The Ascen Gaithersburg MD 2011-** B Augusta GA 1965 d Hoyt & Geneva. BA U NC 1987; MA U NC 1989; MDiv VTS 2000. D 6/24/2000 Bp Clifton Daniel III P 12/13/2000 Bp Jane Hart Holmes Dixon. c 1. Asst R S Jn's Ch Olney MD 2004-2005; Asst R Chr Ch Par Kensington MD 2000-2003. Auth, "Words Facing E," WordTech Editions, 2011.

BECKER, Mary Clovis (Kan) D 6/11/2016 Bp Dean E Wolfe.

BECKER, Mary Elizabeth (Ind) 2076 E County Rd 375 S, Winslow IN 47598 **Ret S Jas Ch Vincennes IN 2010-** B Baltimore MD 1941 d Adrian & Mary. BS Towson U 1963; MEd Towson U 1982; MA S Marys Sem & U Ecum Inst 2000. D 6/14/1997 Bp Charles Lindsay Longest. m 8/21/1965 Paul Frederick Becker c 2. D S Andr's Ch Baltimore MD 2002-2007; D S Andr's Epis Ch Glenwood MD 1996-2002; Epis Chapl Towson U Towson MD 1984-2002.

BECKER, Nora Anne (Eas) **Chr Ch Clarksburg WV 2016-** D 6/4/2016 Bp Henry Nutt Parsley Jr P 1/28/2017 Bp William Michie Klusmeyer.

BECKER, Robert Andrew (Va) 1124 Handlebar Rd, Reston VA 20191 **Ch Of The H Cross Dunn Loring VA 2008-** B Long Branch NJ 1940 s Andrew & Marjorie. BA GW 1963; MDiv VTS 1997. D 6/24/2006 P 2/3/2007 Bp Peter J Lee. m 1/25/1964 Carolyn D Becker c 2. Ch Of The Resurr Alexandria VA 2006-2007.

BECKER, Stephen David (Va) 13 Braxton Dr, Sterling VA 20165 **Vic Chr Epis Ch Lucketts Leesburg VA 2013-; Chapl Capital Caring Hospice Leesburg VA 2010-** B Washington DC 1951 s Francis & Mary. AS Anderson Coll Anderson SC 1973; BTh Amer Chrisitan TS 1976; MDiv TESM 1992. D 7/12/1992 P 4/4/1993 Bp Andrew Fairfield. m 9/17/1977 Ellen Joy Becker c 3. Int Emm Epis Ch Delaplane Delaplane VA 2009-2012; R S Paul's Ch New Orleans LA 2003-2005; R S Geo's Epis Ch Summerville SC 1999-2003; Cn Cathd Ch Of S Ptr St. Petersburg FL 1996-1999; Asst Ch Of The Adv Tallahassee FL 1994-1996; D/P Trin Ch Wahpeton ND 1992-1994.

BECKETT, Kimberly Youngblood (Ala) 113 Brown Ave, Rainbow City AL 35906 **Exec Dir Anniston Soup Bowl 2011-** B Anniston AL 1957 d Horace & Eleanor. D 10/1/2011 Bp John Mckee Sloan Sr. m 3/23/1980 Scott Wilkins Beckett c 1. S Mich And All Ang Anniston AL 1992-2010.

BECKETT JR, Norman James (Los) 3157 E Avenue, #B-4, Lancaster LA 93535 Costa Rica **Non-par 1976-** B Medford MA 1943 s Norman & Leontine. BA Trin 1965; STB EDS 1968; PhD California Sch of Profsnl Psychol 1974. D 6/11/1968 Bp Walter H Gray P 3/8/1969 Bp Francis E I Bloy. Epis Ch Of S Andr And S Chas Granada Hills CA 1971-1976; Dio Los Angeles Los Angeles CA 1971-1973; Cur S Thos Of Cbury Par Long Bch CA 1969-1971; Cur S Mich and All Ang Epis Ch Studio City CA 1968-1969.

BECKHAM JR, M Edwin (At) 3172 Legion Dr SE, Covington GA 30014 **R Ch Of The Gd Shpd Covington GA 2015-, P-in-c 2013-2015; Convoc Cler Rep. Dioc Exec Bd Dio Atlanta Atlanta GA 2015-, Mem, Global Missions Cmsn 2011-, Chair, YA Mnstry Cmsn 2010-2013, Mem, Liturg Cmsn 2009-2012** B Greenville SC 1968 s Maurice & Martha. N/A The U GA; N/A The U of Maryland; BA Furman U 1990; MDiv Epis TS of the SW 2008. D 12/21/2007 P 6/29/2008 Bp J Neil Alexander. m 4/6/1991 Laura McHugh c 2. Assoc R Emm Epis Ch Athens GA 2008-2013. The HSEC 2017; The Soc of Cath Priests 2009. ebeckham.cgse.cov@gmail.com

BECKLES, William Anthony (NY) Po Box 1067, Mount Vernon NY 10551 B BB 1942 s John & Caris. BA U of The W Indies 1966; MA McMaster U 1967; PhD U Ab 1971; MEd U Tor 1977. Trans 10/26/1992 Bp John Palmer Croneberger. S Paul's Ch Mt Vernon OH 1998-2014; Dio New York New York NY 1998-2011; Gr Ch Corona NY 1997-1998; S Paul's Ch-In-The-Vill Brooklyn NY 1994-1996; S Andr's Ch Newark NJ 1991-1993; Trin Ch Irvington NJ

1991-1993; Serv Ch In The Prov Of The W Indies - Jamaica 1980-1991. Amer Assn Chr Counslr, Associated Parishes, Amer Acad Mnstry.

✠ BECKWITH, The Rt Rev Mark M (Nwk) Episcopal Diocese of Newark, 312 Mulberry St, Newark NJ 07102 **Bp of Newark Dio Newark Newark NJ 2006-, Co-Chair Dioc T/F 1991-1992; co-convenor Bishops Untd against Gun Violence 2013-** B Milwaukee WI 1951 s Andrew & Heiden. BA Amh 1973; MDiv Ya Berk 1978; Ya Berk 2008; GTS 2010. D 6/9/1979 P 2/9/1980 Bp Morgan Porteus Con 1/27/2007 for Nwk. m 5/15/1982 Marilyn C Olson c 2. R All SS Ch Worcester MA 1993-2006; R Chr Ch Hackensack NJ 1985-1993; Assoc S Ptr's Ch Morristown NJ 1982-1985; Chapl Hartford Hosp Hartford CT 1981-1982; Trin Epis Ch Hartford CT 1981-1982; Asst S Jas Epis Ch Farmington CT 1979-1981. Auth, "From Scarcity To Abundance," Tens, 2001. Fell, SSJE 2001-2011. Bergen Cnty Cmnty Action Prog Serv Awd 1987. mbeckwith@dioceseofnewark.org

✠ BECKWITH, The Rt Rev Peter Hess (Spr) 7451 E Bacon Rd, Hillsdale MI 49242 B Battle Creek MI 1939 s Robert & Florence. BA Hillsdale Coll 1961; MDiv Sewanee: The U So, TS 1964; STM Nash 1974; ThD Hillsdale Coll 1988; LHD Nash 1992; DD Sewanee: The U So, TS 1999. D 6/29/1964 Bp Richard Stanley Merrill Emrich P 1/6/1965 Bp Archie H Crowley Con 2/29/1992 for Spr. m 7/10/1965 Melinda Jo Foulke c 2. Chapl Hillsdale Coll Hillsdale MI 2010-2016; Bp of Springfield Dio Springfield Springfield IL 1992-2010; R S Jn's Ch Worthington OH 1978-1992; Chapl Untd States Naval Reserve 1972-1999; R S Matt's Epis Ch Saginaw MI 1970-1978; Asst R S Paul's Epis Ch Jackson MI 1966-1970; Chapl Sthrn Michigan St Prison Jackson MI 1966-1970; Cur S Jn's Ch Plymouth MI 1964-1966; Const And Cn Com Dio Sthrn Ohio Cincinnati OH 1979-1981, Cler Compstn Com 1978. Auth, "Premarital Counslg: Its Place & Purpose," *STM Thesis*, Nash, 1974; Auth, "What Else in Viet Nam?," *LivCh*, LivCh, 1968. Assn Cnvnt Trsfg 1982; Assn of Naval Aviation 1984; Assn of the USN 2006; Marine Corps Reserve Assn 1980; Mltry Chapl Assn 1974; Mltry Off Assn of Amer 2006; Naval Reserve Assn 1974; Navy League 1976; Reserve Off Assn 1975; Ret Off Assn 1999; Sons of the Amer Revolution 1958; The AmL 1985. Chapl Emer Hillsdale Coll 2016; Athletic Hall of Fame Hillsdale Coll 2001; Alumnini Achievement Awd Hillsdale Coll 1984.

BEDARD, Caren Marie (Minn) 408 N 7th St, Brainerd MN 56401 B St Paul MN 1946 d John & Helen. BA U of Iowa 1969; BA U of iowa 1969; BA Coll of S Scholastica 1989. D 6/20/2015 Bp Brian N Prior. c 3.

BEDDINGFIELD, John Floyd (NY) 316 E 88th St, New York NY 10128 **Ch Of The H Trin New York NY 2015-** B Raleigh NC 1964 s Clarence & Virginia. DMin VTS; BA U NC 1987; MDiv PrTS 1991; STM GTS 1999. D 3/8/2003 P 9/20/2003 Bp Mark Sean Sisk. m 4/5/2010 Erwin S DeLeon. R All Souls Memi Epis Ch Washington DC 2007-2015; Cur Ch Of S Mary The Vrgn New York NY 2003-2007. jfbeddingfield@holytrinity-nyc.org

BEDELL, Bryan Douglas (Roch) 28 Village Trl, Honeoye Falls NY 14472 B Ludington MI 1943 s Glen & Gertrude. BA MI SU 1968; MS Rochester Inst of Tech 1977; MDiv Bex Sem 2007. D 6/30/2007 P 2/21/2008 Bp Jack Marston Mckelvey. m 10/26/2003 Marion Overslaugh c 4. P S Ptr's Epis Ch Bloomfield NY 2010-2012, 2009; S Geo's Ch Hilton NY 2007-2009; Trin Ch Rochester NY 2007-2009; Mgr Strategic Plnng Xerox Corp 1972-2002.

BEDFORD, Michael John (Mich) 25831 Lexington Dr Unit 1, South Lyon MI 48178 **S Jn's Ch Detroit MI 2001-, 1997-2000; Ret 1994-** B Louisville NY 1929 s Sanders & Muriel. Michigan TS 1980. D 6/26/1976 Bp H Coleman Mcgehee Jr P 7/24/1982 Bp Henry Irving Mayson. c 7. S Eliz's Ch Redford Chart Township MI 1983-1994, D-in-c 1981-1982; Asst S Jn's Ch Plymouth MI 1976-1981. SSC 1990.

BEDINGFIELD, John Davis (WLa) 400 Camellia Blvd, Lafayette LA 70503 **R S Barn Epis Ch Lafayette LA 2011-; Title IV Intake Off Dio Wstrn Louisiana Alexandria LA 2014-, Dn, Acadiana Convoc 2012-2016, Chair, COM 2012-, Pres, Stndg Com 2012-** B Dallas TX 1956 s Billy & Phyllis. BA U of Texas Dallas 1984; JD U of Texas 1988; MDiv Epis TS of the SW 2005. D 6/11/2005 Bp Don Adger Wimberly P 12/13/2005 Bp Rayford Baines High Jr. m 4/22/1978 Donna J Jarvis c 3. R S Jn's Epis Ch Silsbee TX 2007-2011; Assoc R H Sprt Epis Ch Houston TX 2005-2007; Dn, SE Convoc Dio Texas Houston TX 2009-2011. rector@saintbarnabas.us

BEDROSIAN, Magar (Ct) 6283 Darien Way, Spring Hill FL 34606 **Died 1/18/2017** B Milford MA 1927 s Tanal & Nevart. BA U of Massachusetts 1955; MDiv Ya Berk 1958. D 6/15/1958 Bp Robert McConnell Hatch P 12/20/1958 Bp John Henry Esquirol. Assoc S Andr's Epis Ch Sprg Hill FL 1996-2005; Ret 1994-2017; R Ch of the H Sprt W Haven CT 1983-1993; Dio Rhode Island Providence RI 1978-1983; S Eliz's Ch Hope Vlly RI 1970-1983; Vic S Eliz Canonchet RI 1964-1983; Vic S Thos' Alton Wood River Jct RI 1964-1983; Vic Trin Ch N Scituate RI 1959-1964; Cur S Jn's Ch E Hartford CT 1958-1959.

BEE, Robert D (Neb) 5109 N Jefferson St, Gladstone MO 64118 B Washington DC 1938 s Max & Florence. BA Omaha U 1965; MDiv GTS 1968; Cert Assn of Profsnl Chapl 1985. D 6/13/1968 P 12/15/1968 Bp Russell T Rauscher. m 9/3/1966 Diana M Parker c 3. Mnstry Dev Asst Dio Nebraska Omaha NE 2001-2008; Assoc Ch Of The H Sprt Bellevue NE 2000-2006; Adj Fac Clarkson Coll Omaha NE 2000-2001; Mgr, Pstr Care Nebraska Hlth System Omaha NE 1979-1999; Chapl Clarkson Hosp Omaha NE 1979-1997; R S Mary's Epis Ch Blair NE 1970-1979; Cur All SS Epis Ch Omaha NE 1968-1970. Assembly of Epis Healthcare Chapl Pres 1993-1994; Assn of Profsnl Chapl 1985-2015; Bd Cert Chapl 1985-2015.

BEEBE, Christine Fair (WNC) 395 N Main St, Rutherfordton NC 28139 **R S Fran' Epis Ch Rutherfordton NC 2011-; Co-Chair Congrl Vitality Mnstry Dio Wstrn No Carolina Asheville NC 2013-** B Memphis TN 1951 d Burrell & Celia. MDiv Sewanee: The U So, TS 2008. D 3/15/2008 P 9/21/2008 Bp Larry Benfield. c 1. Dn of Convoc Dio Arkansas Little Rock AR 2009-2011; Vic All SS Epis Ch Paragould AR 2008-2011. rector@stfrancisrutherfordton.org

BEEBE SR, Fred H (Fla) 124 Peninsular Dr, Crescent City FL 32112 B Newark NJ 1943 s Donald & Dorothy. AS Brookdale Cmnty Coll 1976. D 10/31/1998 Bp Joe Doss P 10/12/2010 Bp Charles Lovett Keyser. m 6/27/1998 Genevieve Ann Tullo. Vic Ch Of The H Comf Cres City FL 2010-2016, Vic 2010-, D 2000-2010; Emm Ch Welaka FL 2010-2016; D All SS Memi Ch Navesink NJ 1998-2000.

BEEBE, James Russell (Nev) 205 Mackinaw Ave, Akron OH 44333 B Neenah WI 1949 s Robert & Mary. BA Denison U 1971; MA Oklahoma St U 1978; MDiv SE Bapt TS 1982. D 12/5/1992 Bp Brice Sidney Sanders P 6/12/1993 Bp Arthur Williams Jr. m 3/22/1969 Deborah Beebe c 2. S Pat's Ch Incline Vlg NV 2005-2012; Assoc S Paul's Ch Akron OH 1992-2005.

BEEBE, Jane Alice (WMass) B Asheville NC 1955 d David & Joan. M.Div. Andover Newton TS; BA Coll of Wooster; MSLS U NC Chap Hill; MM U of Tennessee Knoxville. D 12/10/2016 P 6/24/2017 Bp Doug Fisher.

BEEBE SR, Jeffrey (SeFla) 151 S County Rd, Palm Beach FL 33480 B Hinsdale IL 1954 AB U IL 1977; MDiv Berk of Yale 2002. D 6/16/2002 P 12/21/2002 Bp Leo Frade. m 12/30/1995 Susan Rafter Beebe c 2. Other Lay Position Meadow Pk Ch Coral Sprg FL. jbeebe@st-gregorys.com

BEEBE, Susan Rafter (SeFla) 151 S County Rd, Palm Beach FL 33480 B Clewiston FL 1972 d Jack & Mary. BA Asbury U 1992; MAR Ya Berk 2002. D 6/22/2011 Bp Leo Frade P 1/8/2012 Bp Michael Garrison. m 12/30/1995 Jeffrey Beebe c 2. Other Lay Position The Epis Ch Of Beth-By-The-Sea Palm Bch FL 1997-2000.

BEEBE-BOVE, Polly (Vt) 3 Cathedral Sq Apt 2G, Burlington VT 05401 B East Charlotte VT 1922 d Forrest & Mary. RN Mary Fletcher Hosp Sch of Nrsng 1943; Cert Dioc Study Prog 1988; BA Trin 1995. D 6/14/1989 Bp Daniel Lee Swenson. c 1. D S Jas Epis Ch Essex Jct VT 1993-1997; D Cathd Ch Of S Paul Burlington VT 1989-1993; Ret. NAAD; Ord of S Fran.

BEECHAM, Troy (Ia) 815 High St, Des Moines IA 50309 **Dn The Cathd Ch Of S Paul Des Moines IA 2015-** B Houston TX 1968 Jerusalem U Coll Jerusalem IL 1991; BA Webc Baton Rouge LA 1991; MA Wheaton Coll 1994; STM GTS 2002. D 2/8/2003 P 9/4/2003 Bp Henry Irving Louttit. Soc-St Jn The Evang Cambridge MA 2013-2014; R S Jn's Atlanta GA 2008-2013; R Ch Of The Gd Shpd Granite Spgs NY 2005-2008; Int Chr Ch Augusta GA 2003-2004. dean@cathedralchurchofstpaul.org

BEECHER, Jo (Oly) 7134 Steelhead Ln, Burlington WA 98233 **Bd Mem Skagit Cmnty Action 2013-; Bd Mem Skagit Immigrant Rts Coun 2005-** B Seattle WA 1952 d Henry & Doris. BA Antioch U 1998; MDiv Seattle U 2002. D 11/9/2002 Bp Vincent Waydell Warner P 5/30/2003 Bp Martin De Jesus Barahona-Pascacio. m 8/1/2006 Mary McConnaughey c 1. Hisp Mssnr Komo Kulshan Cluster Mt Vernon WA 2008-2012; Vic La Iglesia Epis de la Resurreccion Mt Vernon WA 2003-2012; Pres of Stndg Com Dio Olympia Seattle 2010-2011, Bp Suffr Search Com 2004-2010, Indo-Hisp Mnstry Com 1995-2012. Ruby Awd Mt Vernon Soroptimists 2013; Racial Justice Awd YWCA 2012; Distinguished Alum Antioch U Seattle 2006; Ecumenist of the Year Ecum Mnstrs of Oregon 2006.

BEELEY, Christopher Alfred (Tex) 1527 Sunnymede Ave, South Bend IN 46615 B Houston TX 1968 s Robert & Susan. U of Notre Dame; BA W&L 1990; MDiv Ya Berk 1994. D 6/25/1994 Bp Maurice Manuel Benitez P 1/1/1995 Bp Claude Edward Payne. m 4/6/1991 Shannon Betsy Beeley. Chr And H Trin Ch Westport CT 2014-2015; S Jn's Ch New Haven CT 2012-2013; S Mich And All Ang Ch So Bend IN 1998-1999; Asst S Dav's Ch Austin TX 1994-1996. Fllshp S Alb & S Sergius. Presidential Fllshp U Notre Dame.

BEEM, Charles Lee (Be) 9 Plymouth Pl, Wyomissing PA 19610 **Assoc S Alb's Epis Ch Reading PA 1977-** B Richland WA 1947 s Charles & Anna. BS Baker U 1969; MDiv VTS 1972; MA U of Missouri 1976. D 8/12/1972 P 8/11/1973 Bp William Davidson. m 6/2/1973 Jacqueline M Beem. Counsellor Caron Fndt Wenersville PA 1976-1994; Vic S Alb's Epis Ch Fulton MO 1975-1976; Vic Trin Epis Ch Norton KS 1974-1975. Auth, "8 Pub".

BEEMAN, Patricia Houston (O) 220 Pennswood Rd, Bryn Mawr PA 19010 **Died 1/26/2017** B Cleveland OH 1946 d Egon & Barbara. Skidmore Coll 1967; Ursuline Coll 1993. D 11/8/1996 Bp J Clark Grew II. m 3/3/2017 Richard Ernest Beeman. D Ch Of The Trsfg Cleveland OH 1996-2000.

BEER, David Frank (Tex) 6810 Thistle Hill Way, Austin TX 78754 B Dorking Surrey UK 1939 s Frank & Eva. BA U of Arizona 1963; MA Arizona St U 1965; PhD U of New Mex 1972; MA Epis TS of the SW 1979. D 8/6/1979 Bp Richard Mitchell Trelease Jr P 4/9/1980 Bp Scott Field Bailey. m 9/24/1971 Ruth Elaine Beer c 1. Asstg Cler S Jn's Epis Ch Austin TX 2003-2013; Asst The Ch of the Gd Shpd Austin TX 1992-2000; Non-Stipendiary Supply P 1982-1990; Int S Fran By The Lake Canyon Lake TX 1981-1982; Int S Steph's Epis Ch Wimberley TX 1980-1981; Chapl Austin St Hosp Austin TX 1979-1980; Asst Ch Of The Annunc Luling TX 1979-1980. Auth, "Guide to Writing as an Engr, 4th ed.," Wiley, 2009; Auth, "Writing & Spkng In The Tech Professions," IEEE, 1992. IEEE 1985-2001; Wrld War 1 Hist Assn 2005. Excellence in Engr Tchg Coll of Engr, U of Texas at Austin 1989; Fulbright Awd 1977.

BEERS, William Rogers (Chi) 120 1st St, Lodi WI 53555 **Food for the Poor Coconut Creek FL 1997-** B Boston MA 1948 s Roland & Helen. BA Ge 1967; MDiv EDS 1975; PhD U Chi 1989. D 6/15/1985 Bp Frank Tracy Griswold III P 2/22/1986 Bp Arthur Edward Walmsley. m 10/15/2007 Joann Crowley Beers. Dir of Pstr Care S Clare Hosp 1997-2007; Dir of Chapl Serv Rockville Gnrl Hosp 1985-1995; Chapl U Chi Med Cntr Chicago IL 1984-1985. Auth, "Fantast and Mourning," *Journ of Pstr Care*, 2006; Auth, *Wmn & Sacrifice*, Wayne Press, 1992; Auth, "Anxiety & Creation in the CPE Context," *Journ of Pstr Care*, 1990; Auth, "The Confessions of Aug," *Amer Imago*, 1988.

BEERY, Bill (NY) 905 Osprey Ct, New Bern NC 28560 B Brooklyn NY 1947 s Edwin & Evelyn. BA Colg 1969; MDiv Ya Berk 1972; MDiv Ya Berk 1972; MDiv Ya Berk 1972; PhD NYU 1983. D 6/17/1972 P 12/23/1972 Bp Jonathan Goodhue Sherman. m 2/28/1981 Ellen Beery c 4. Sr Assoc R S Lk's Par Darien CT 2003-2007; Worker P S Lk's Par Darien CT 1984-2003; Var Parishes - Int and Supply Dio New York New York NY 1973-2011; Asst S Thos Ch Mamaroneck NY 1972-1973. Auth, *Multi-Occidental Prot Cler: A Test of Hollands Theory*, 1983. Who's Who Among Human Serv Professionals Marquis Who's Who 1983; Who's Who in Amer Marquis Who's Who 1972; Watson Fllshp Ya 1972.

BEERY, Susan Beem (U) 228 S Pitt St, Alexandria VA 22314 B La Grande OR 1957 d Charles & Fern. BS OR SU 1980; MDiv EDS 1984. D 8/11/1984 P 8/13/1985 Bp Rustin Ray Kimsey. m 8/1/1991 John M Beery c 2. Dio Utah Salt Lake City UT 2004-2009; S Paul's Epis Ch Alexandria VA 1998-2001; Asst Ch Of The Epiph San Carlos CA 1995-1996; Epis Mnstry To The Oh St U Columbus OH 1990; S Steph's Epis Ch And U Columbus OH 1986-1989; Asst S Ptr's Ch La Grande OR 1985-1986.

BEESLEY, Kevin D (SO) **S Andr's Ch Pickerington OH 2016-** D 6/11/2016 P 6/10/2017 Bp Thomas Edward Breidenthal.

BEHEN, Ralph Joseph (WMo) **Cler Ch Of The Redeem Kansas City MO 2011-, Cler 2011-** B 1964 MDiv Epis TS of the SW 2007. D 6/2/2007 P 12/1/2007 Bp Barry Howe. m 8/24/2004 Karen Elizabeth Behen c 2. Cler Gr And H Trin Cathd Kansas City MO 2007-2011.

BEHM, Nancy Anne (FdL) 1703 Doemel St, Oshkosh WI 54901 **D Trin Epis Ch Oshkosh WI 2003-** B Chicago IL 1949 D 11/29/2003 Bp Russell Edward Jacobus.

BEHNKE, Cathleen Ann (Mich) 4800 Woodward Ave, Detroit MI 48201 B Detroit MI 1961 d Robert & Margaret. BA U MI 1983; MA U MI 1984; MBA U MI 1992. D 6/22/2013 Bp Wendell Nathaniel Gibbs Jr. m 10/7/1989 Curtis Joseph Behnke c 2.

BEHNSTEDT, Patrice Faith (CFla) 500 W Floral Ave, Bartow FL 33830 **D H Trin Epis Ch Bartow FL 2015-** B Chattanooga TN 1954 d Everett & Barbara. BA Mt Holyoke Coll 2000; JD U of Miami, Sch of Law 2003; MA U of So Florida 2010. D 9/12/2015 Bp Gregory Orrin Brewer. m 5/29/2004 Richard Lawrence Doyen.

BEHRENS, Marilyn Jean (Oly) 7417 Hill Ave Apt 2, Gig Harbor WA 98335 **D S Jn's Epis Ch Gig Harbor WA 2013-** B San Francisco CA 1947 d Silvio & Lorraine. San Francisco St U; AA Coll of San Mateo 1968; BA Sch for Deacons 1997. D 6/20/1997 Bp Richard Lester Shimpfky. D S Ben's Par Los Osos CA 1997-2012.

BEIKIRCH, Paula Marie (CFla) 4915 Deter Rd, Lakeland FL 33813 **Exec Dir/ Nurse Practitioner Talbot Hse Mnstrs 1997-** B Olean NY 1945 d Carlyle & Marjorie. BS Florida Sthrn Coll 1990; MS U of So Florida 1993. D 12/9/2006 Bp John Wadsworth Howe. c 2.

BEILSTEIN, Joan Elizabeth (WA) 400 Hinsdale Ct, Silver Spring MD 20901 **R Ch Of The Ascen Silver Sprg MD 2007-** B Washington DC 1960 d Frederick & Anna. BA U of Maryland 1983; MDiv GTS 1993; DMin VTS 2007. D 6/12/1993 P 1/1/1994 Bp Ronald Hayward Haines. m 12/14/2010 Elizabeth Mary Griffin. Int All Souls Memi Epis Ch Washington DC 2005-2007; Nativ Epis Ch Temple Hills MD 1999-2005, 1997-1998; Chapl S Eliz Hosp Wdc 1993-1999. Ch and Soc Awd The GTS 1993.

BEIMDIEK, Jill (EC) St. Stephen's Episcopal Church, 200 North James St, Goldsboro NC 27530 **S Mary's Ch Columbia SC 2016-** B Portland OR 1956 BA Whitman Coll 1978; MA Duke 1991; DAS Ya Berk 2004; MDiv Yale DS 2004. D 6/19/2004 Bp Michael B Curry P 12/18/2004 Bp Charles Ellsworth Bennison Jr. m 10/8/2010 Charles C Faulkner. S Steph's Ch Goldsboro NC 2014-2016; S Paul's Epis Ch Greenville NC 2011-2013; Assoc R H Trin Epis

Ch Fayetteville NC 2007-2011; S Steph's Epis Ch Norwood PA 2004-2007. SSM 2003.

BEIMES, Phyllis Mahilani (Haw) St Matthew's Episcopal Church, Po Box 70, Waimanalo HI 96795 B Kahaluu, Oahu HI 1948 d Harry & Dolores. BA Chaminade U 1996; Cert in Theol Stds Waiolaihui'ia 2015; Cert in Theol Stds Waiolaihuia'ia 2015; Cert in Theol Stds Waiolaihuia'ia 2015. D 10/23/2015 P 6/25/2016 Bp Robert Leroy Fitzpatrick. m 7/20/1971 William Henry Beimes c 4.

☩ BEISNER, The Rt Rev Barry Leigh (NCal) Episcopal Diocese Of Northern California, 350 University Ave Ste 280, Sacramento CA 95825 **Bp of Nthrn California The Epis Dio Nthrn California Sacramento CA 2006-, Cn 2002-2006, Bp of Nthrn California 2002-** B Dayton OH 1951 s Max & Dolores. BA U CA 1973; MDiv CDSP 1978; STM GTS 1994; DD GTS 2006. D 6/24/1978 Bp William Foreman Creighton P 5/19/1979 Bp Daniel Corrigan Con 9/30/2006 for The Episcopal NCal. m 5/2/1998 L Ann Hallisey c 3. R Ch Of S Mart Davis CA 1989-2002; R Ch Of The Incarn San Francisco CA 1983-1989; Asst S Mk's Epis Ch Columbus OH 1980-1983; Campus Min California Polytechnic St U San Luis Obispo CA 1978-1980; S Paul's Ch Cambria CA 1978-1980; Asst S Steph's Epis Ch Sn Luis Obispo CA 1978-1979. DD GTS 2007. barry@norcalepiscopal.org

BEITZEL, Wallace Dickens (U) 9475 Brookside Ave, Ben Lomond CA 95005 **Assoc St Phil the Aostle Scotts Vlly CA 2008-** B Olympia WA 1944 s Stuart & Gordon. BA California St U 1966; MA California St U 1972. D 4/8/1981 P 1/8/1982 Bp Otis Charles. m 9/10/1965 Mary Elizabeth Beitzel c 2. Chr Ch Par Redondo Bch CA 2006-2007; Asst S Ptr's Ch Clearfield UT 1981-1983. Auth, "Math Applied to Electronics," Prentice Hall, 1980; Auth, "Practical Math for Electronics," The Educ Press, 1970.

BEIZER, Lance Kurt (ECR) P.O. Box 1047 (9 Blackberry Way), Canaan CT 06018 **Assoc S Jn's Ch Salisbury CT 2009-; Cn-Vic Trin Cathd San Jose CA 2006-; VP Housatonic Yth Serv Bureau Falls Vill CT 2011-; Bd Gvnr The Hotchkiss Sch Lakeville CT 2009-** B Hartford CT 1938 s Lawrence & Victoria. BA Brandeis U 1960; MA San Jose St U 1967; JD U of San Diego 1975; MDiv CDSP 2005. D 12/18/2004 P 9/10/2005 Bp Sylvestre Donato Romero. m 7/27/2007 Ann Beizer. Asst Ch Of The H Sprt Campbell CA 2005-2006; Pres Salisbury Rotary 2013-2014; Dioc Coun Dio El Camino Real Salinas CA 2007-2008, Eccl Trial Crt 2007-2008; VP Chld Abuse Coun Santa Clara Cnty CA 2006-2008; Bd Mem Santa Clara Cnty Coun of Ch CA 2006-2008; Bd Managers (Chair 1992-3) SW YMCA Saratoga CA 1988-2008. OSL (Chapl) 2005.

BEK, Susan (Los) 3290 Loma Vista Rd, Ventura CA 93003 **R S Paul's Epis Ch Ventura CA 2013-** B Van Nuys CA 1963 d Odell & Marjorie. BA Pacific Wstrn U 1996; MDiv Claremont TS 2010; Cert Theol Stud ETSBH 2010. D 7/9/2010 P 2/12/2011 Bp Joseph Jon Bruno. m 2/12/1983 Jon L Bek c 4. Assoc S Steph's Epis Ch Valencia CA 2012-2013, P-in-c 2011-2013, Cur 2010-2011, Sch Chapl 2004-2013, Dir of Yth & Chld's Mnstrs 1995-2010; Coordntr of Chld's Prog at GC 2009 Dio Los Angeles Los Angeles CA 2006-2009, 2006-. Natl Assn of CE Dir 2008. Highest Acad Achievement ETS, Claremont/Bloy Hse 2010; Fac Awd for Excellence in the Study of H Scripture ETS, Claremont/Bloy Hse 2007. revsusanbek@gmail.com

BELA, Robert Joseph (Mass) 475 Breeding Loop, Breeding KY 42715 B Philadelphia PA 1939 s Joseph & Helen. BA La Salle U 1967; MA Chr TS 1978; MDiv EDS 1980; MA Univversity of Massachusetts - Boston 2010. D 6/24/1980 P 3/1/1981 Bp Edward Witker Jones. c 3. Pstr St Helenas Chap Lenox MA 2001-2005; Int Pstr Trin Par Lenox MA 1997-1998; R Gr Ch 1993-1997; Pstr Gr Epis Ch Medford MA 1992-1997; Int Pstr S Paul's Epis Ch Bedford MA 1991-1992; Int Pstr Emm Epis Ch Wakefield MA 1989-1991; Int Pstr All SS Ch Chelmsford MA 1986-1988; Int S Jas' Epis Ch Cambridge MA 1986-1988; Assoc R Chr Ch S Hamilton MA 1984-1986; Int S Jn's Epis Ch Gloucester MA 1983-1984; The Cathd Ch Of S Paul Boston MA 1983; Cur S Paul's Epis Ch Evansville IN 1980-1981.

BELANGER, Fanny Sohet (Eur) B St Martin D'Heres France 1976 d Sohet & Borel. MDiv VTS 2013. D 3/16/2013 P 2/1/2014 Bp Pierre W Whalon. m 4/28/2007 Xavier Belanger. S Dunst's Ch Mc Lean VA 2015-2017.

BELASCO, Elizabeth Anne (LI) 612 Forest Ave, Massapequa NY 11758 **Died 8/3/2016** B Jamaica NY 1930 d William & Lucile. BS CUNY 1950; MA NYU 1952; PhD NYU 1956; CTh Mercer TS 1985; Cert GTS 1996. D 12/21/1984 Bp Robert Campbell Witcher Sr. Ret Gr Epis Ch Massapequa NY 2010-2013; D S Steph's Ch Prt Washington NY 2005-2010; Chapl Chf Med Exam's Off New York NY 2002-2016; D S Ptr's by-the-Sea Epis Ch Bay Shore NY 2002-2005; D Ch Of The Redeem Astoria NY 2001-2002; Chapl Ground Zero New York NY 2001-2002; Ch Of S Fran Of Assisi Levittown NY 2000-2001; D Epis Ch of The Resurr Williston Pk NY 2000-2001; Dio Long Island Garden City NY 1999-2002, Dioc Coun 1986-1998; D The Ch Of The Ascen Rockville Ct NY 1998-2000; Geo Mercer TS Garden City NY 1994-2000. NAAD 1984. Tchr Of The Year The Wheatley Sch 1984.

BELCHER, Nancy Spencer (Mo) PO Box 6065, Fulton MO 65251 B Richmond KY 1950 d Charles & Mary. MS Estrn Kentucky U 1977; BS Estrn Kentucky

U 1980; MLS Rutgers U 1986; Epis Sch for Mnstry 2013. D 11/21/2014 Bp George Wayne Smith. m 6/6/1970 Dennis Wayne Belcher.

BELCHER, Sandra Alves (Ct) 165 Grassy Hill Rd, Woodbury CT 06798 **Chapl Yale-New Haven Hosp 2012-** B Mount Holly NJ 1948 d Joseph & Mary. BA Mt Holyoke Coll 1969; MA Van 1972; MDiv Ya Berk 1985. D 6/1/1985 P 9/1/1986 Bp John Bowen Coburn. m 5/28/1972 Robert P Belcher c 1. Chapl The Hosp of St Raphael 1997-2012; Chapl Yale-New Haven Hosp 1996-1997; Chapl Bridgeport Hosp 1995-1996; S Steph's Ch Ridgefield CT 1987-1994. Assembly of Epis Healthcare Chapl 2001; Assn of Profsnl Chapl 1999.

BELKNAP, Charles (Los) 1386 Beddis Road, Salt Spring Island BC V8K 2C9 Canada **P-in-c Angl Ch of Can 2010-** B Pittsburgh PA 1948 s Charles & Rosalie. Trin Hartford CT 1971; BA Hampshire Coll 1972; MDiv VTS 1976. D 6/5/1976 Bp George E Rath P 1/14/1977 Bp Robert Claflin Rusack. m 4/19/1997 Sarah Koelling Belknap c 2. Asst S Ptr's Par San Pedro CA 2005-2009; Assoc S Aid's Epis Ch Malibu CA 2002-2004; Assoc St Cross Epis Ch Hermosa Bch CA 1995-2002; Int H Trin Alhambra CA 1994-1995; Int S Jn's Mssn La Verne CA 1993-1994; Int S Jos's Par Buena Pk CA 1991-1992; Dir of Cmnty Dvlpmt Natl Mntl Hlth Assoc. of Grtr Los Angeles 1988-2009; MHA Long Bch CA 1988-2007; Vic Incarn Norwalk CA 1984-1989; S Fran Mssn Norwalk CA 1981-1989; P-in-c H Fam Mssn N Hollywood CA 1980-1984; Assoc St Johns Pro-Cathd Los Angeles CA 1976-1980.

BELKNAP, Sarah Koelling (Los) 2066 Empress Ave, South Pasadena CA 91030 B Chicago IL 1948 d Robert & Margaret. BA Rhodes Coll 1970; MSW U of Tennessee 1974; MDiv ETSBH 1986. D 6/25/1988 P 1/21/1989 Bp Frederick Houk Borsch. m 4/19/1997 Charles Belknap. R S Ptr's Par San Pedro CA 2003-2009; Assoc Ch Of Our Sav Par San Gabr CA 1999-2003; Assoc S Paul's Epis Ch Tustin CA 1996-1999; Chapl Cbury Irvine Irvine CA 1991-1996; S Wilfrid Of York Epis Ch Huntington Bch CA 1991-1995; Asst/Int Gr Epis Ch Glendora CA 1988-1991. ESMHE 1991-1996. BA cl SW at Memphis 1970.

BELL, Beth Ann (Okla) 13112 N Rockwell Ave, Oklahoma City OK 73142 **D Epis Ch Of The Resurr Oklahoma City OK 1999-** B Chicago IL 1952 d Richard & Doris. AA Amarillo Coll 1973; BS Sthrn Nazarene U 2003; MDiv Phillips TS 2011. D 6/19/1999 Bp Robert Manning Moody. m 12/31/1972 Robert Rex Bell c 2.

BELL, Daniel Peter (Mass) **Other Lay Position Life Together Cmnty Brookline MA 2014-** B Port Jefferson NY 1986 s William & Cynthia. BA Gordon Coll 2008; MAR Yale DS 2010; MDiv Berk 2013. D 6/3/2017 Bp Gayle Harris.

BELL, David Allen (Ind) 8320 E 10th St, Indianapolis IN 46219 **Died 9/26/2016** B Anderson IN 1958 s Donald & Patricia. BA Indiana U 1983; MDiv Sewanee: The U So, TS 1988. D 6/24/1988 P 3/17/1989 Bp Edward Witker Jones. m 11/28/1981 Marion Zella Rosene c 3. R S Matt's Ch Indianapolis IN 2000-2003; Asst R S Chris's Ch Pensacola FL 1989-1992; Cur S Alb's Ch Indianapolis IN 1988-1989.

BELL, Emily Susan Richardson (Los) 190 Avenida Aragon, San Clemente CA 92672 **P-in-c Faith Epis Ch Laguna Niguel CA 2002-** B New York NY 1940 d Wallace & Ruthella. Cushing Acad Ashburnham MA 1957; BA New Sch U 1967. D 12/6/1985 P 6/8/1986 Bp William Benjamin Spofford. m 11/17/1990 Leonard Miller. P-in-c S Mk's Epis Ch Upland CA 2000-2001; Int S Clem's-By-The-Sea Par San Clemente CA 1998-2000; P H Trin Epis Ch Fallon NV 1986-1989.

BELL, G erald Michael (Miss) 602 Riverview Dr, Florence AL 35630 **Ret 2003-** B Jackson MS 1942 s Gerald & Thelma. BS U of Sthrn Mississippi 1964; MDiv SWTS 1967. D 6/9/1967 P 5/23/1968 Bp John Maury Allin. m 8/22/1964 Sandra Jean Dunn c 1. Off Of Bsh For ArmdF New York NY 1977-2003; Chapl USAF 1977-2003; R The Epis Ch Of The Medtr Meridian MS 1973-1977; Asst R Gr - S Lk's Ch Memphis TN 1972-1973; Vic Ch Of The Ascen Hattiesburg MS 1971-1972; Chapl U Of Sthrn Mississippi 1971-1972; Vic Gr Ch Carrollton MS 1968-1971; Vic Immanel Ch Winona MS 1968-1971; S Mary's Ch Lexington MS 1968-1971; Cur Ch Of The Nativ Greenwood MS 1967-1968.

BELL JR, Hugh Oliver (Tex) 919 S John Redditt Dr, Lufkin TX 75904 **Ret Asstg Ch Of The Ascen Clearwater FL 2011-** B Tampa FL 1941 s Hugh & Frances. BA U of Mississippi 1965; MDiv Sewanee: The U So, TS 1977. D 6/24/1977 Bp Robert Elwin Terwilliger P 1/10/1978 Bp Archibald Donald Davies. m 8/25/1968 Florence G Bell. S Jn's Epis Ch Clearwater FL 2014, Ret Asstg 2006-2011; Int R S Mk's Ch Palm Bch Garden FL 2004-2005; R S Cyp's Ch Lufkin TX 1998-2004; Asst R S Simon's On The Sound Ft Walton Bch FL 1989-1998; Vic S Fran Ch Edmond OK 1984-1989; Chapl Army Chapl NG and Reserves Var States 1980-1994; Dio Oklahoma Oklahoma City OK 1979-1989; S Lk's Ch Chickasha OK 1979-1984; Vic S Mich And All Ang Ch Lindsay OK 1979-1982; Cur S Jn's Epis Ch Corsicana TX 1977-1979. Ord Of S Lk 1985.

BELL, Jocelyn (ETenn) 643 Westview Rd, Chattanooga TN 37415 B Salisbury MD 1941 d Henry & Rosemary. BA Mt Holyoke Coll 1963; MA Yale DS 1965; MDiv SWTS 1993. D 6/19/1993 Bp R aymond Stewart Wood Jr P 4/20/1994 Bp William Walter Wiedrich. c 2. R Chr Ch - Epis Chattanooga TN 1999-2010; Vic Trin Epis Ch Kirksville MO 1994-1999; CE Coordntr S Chris's Epis Ch Oak Pk IL 1993-1994; S Alb's Ch Simsbury CT 1968-1969; S Jas Epis Ch

Farmington CT 1966-1968; St Johns Ch W Hartford CT 1965-1966. EPF 2002; EUC 2002. BA mcl Mt Holyoke Coll 1963.

BELL, John Michael (WMich) 406 2nd St, Manistee MI 49660 B Murphysboro IL 1945 s Howard & Virginia. MA Sthrn Illinois U 1971; MDiv EDS 2003. D 6/19/2005 P 12/17/2005 Bp Edwin Max Leidel Jr. m 11/17/1990 Helen Ann Bell c 1. R H Trin Epis Ch Manistee MI 2009-2015; Calv Epis Ch Hillman MI 2005-2009; R Gr Epis Ch Lachine MI 2004-2009.

BELL JR, John Robinson (Oly) 2454 E Palm Canyon Dr # 4d, Palm Springs CA 92264 **Ret 1996-** B Monroe GA 1932 s John & Clara. BA Emory U 1954; MDiv Sewanee: The U So, TS 1960. D 6/22/1960 P 12/22/1960 Bp Randolph R Claiborne. Int P S Anth Of The Desert Desert Hot Sprg CA 2003-2007; S Jn's Epis Ch Snohomish WA 1989-1996; Non-par 1988-1992; All SS Epis Ch Seattle WA 1988; Int S Mk's Cathd Seattle WA 1988-1988; R S Ptr's Ch Jacksonville FL 1964-1986; Vic S Paul's Epis Ch Newnan GA 1960-1964. Auth, "The H Sprt Among Episcopalians"; Contrib, "The Journey". ACC.

BELL, Karl Edwin (Eur) Po Box 171, Fifty Lakes MN 56448 **Died 4/27/2017** B Saint Paul MN 1933 s Clifford & Louise. BA U MN 1956; MDiv SWTS 1961; Ya 1965; Oxf GB 1971. D 6/24/1961 Bp Hamilton Hyde Kellogg P 6/1/1962 Bp Philip Frederick McNairy. P-in-c Chr Ch Clermont-Ferrand France Royat 63130 2002-2004; R Ch of S Aug of Cbury 65189 Wiesbaden 1992-1993; R Chr Ch Par La Crosse WI 1979-1992; R Chr Ch Albert Lea MN 1976-1978; Serv Ch In Venezuela 1971-1976; Vic S Paul's Ch Naples FL 1967-1970; Trin By The Cove Naples FL 1967-1968; Chapl And Instr Of Rel Shattuck Sch Faribault MN 1965-1967; Asst Min The Epis Cathd Of Our Merc Sav Faribault MN 1961-1965; Stndg Com Dio Eau Claire Eau Claire WI 1990-1991, Epis Asiamerican Mnstry 1989. Auth, "What Price Man?".

BELL, Mary Cynthia (Mass) 22 Hathaway Pond Circle, Rochester MA 02770 **Chapl Hospice 2009-; Ret 2007-** B Flushing NY 1932 d Edward & Mary. AAS Endicott Coll Prides Crossing MA 1952; BA Coll of New Rochelle 1976; MA GTS 1991; Cert Ang Stud GTS 1995. D 6/3/1995 P 12/9/1995 Bp Richard Frank Grein. m 12/20/1952 Stanley Parsons Bell c 2. Assoc S Gabr's Ch Marion MA 2001-2007; S Gabr's Epis Ch Marion MA 2001-2007; P-in-c S Jas' Ch No Salem NY 1997-2001; Assoc P S Jn's Ch Larchmont NY 1995-1997. SCHC 2011.

BELL, Michael S (Los) 5801 Crestridge Rd, Rancho Palos Verdes CA 90275 **Gd Samar Hosp Los Angeles CA 2016-** B TX 1969 s Martin & Shurley. BA Texas A&M at Commerce 1992; EdM Harvard Grad Sch of Educ 1996; MTS Harvard DS 1997; CDSP 2009; ETS at Claremont 2009. D 6/12/2010 Bp Mary Douglas Glasspool P 1/8/2011 Bp Dean E Wolfe. Chapl at The Cbury Epis Communities & Serv Pasadena CA 2013-2016; Campus Mnstry Ntwk Coordntr Prov VII Fairfax VA 2012-2013; Campus Mssnr Dio Kansas Topeka KS 2010-2013, Com on Nomin and Elctns 2011-2013; Sem in-Res S Aug By-The-Sea Par Santa Monica CA 2009-2010; Off Admin P-t St Jn's Pro-Cathd Los Angeles 2009-2010; Proj Mgr / Mtg Planner Integrity USA 2009; Campus Mnstry Ntwk Cooridnator Prov VII of the Epis Ch 2012-2013; Co-Chair, Coordntng Team for Consecrations of new Bishops Suffr Dio Los Angeles Los Angeles CA 2010. Thos Cranmer Schlrshp ETS at Claremont 2009.

✠ BELL, The Rt Rev Patrick W (EO) 501 E Wallace Ave, Coeur D Alene ID 83814 B Spokane WA 1952 s William & Beverly. BA Whitworth U 1974; MA Fuller TS 1977; CTh Epis TS of the SW 1989; SWTS 1999. D 6/12/1989 Bp Leigh Allen Wallace Jr P 12/15/1989 Bp Rustin Ray Kimsey Con 4/16/2016 for EO. m 3/16/2002 Tina M Bell c 3. Sprtl Dircetor Curs Of Spokane 2004-2006; R S Lk's Ch Coeur D Alene ID 2002-2016; Deploy Off Dio Estrn Oregon Cove OR 1996-2001, Secy Of Dioc Conv 1996-2000, Dioc Coun 1992-2000; R S Matt's Epis Ch Ontario OR 1989-2001; Chair Of Stwdshp Dept Dio Spokane Spokane WA 1986-1988. Dom Mssy Partnership 1994-2003; RWF 1989-1992. pbell@episdioeo.org

BELL OSB, Roger C (Pgh) 56500 Abbey Rd, Three Rivers MI 49093 **Monk Ord of S Ben Three Rivers MI 1971-** B Otwell IN 1928 s William & Edna. BA Indiana U 1949; MDiv Nash 1960. D 12/22/1956 Bp Donald H V Hallock P 6/29/1957 Bp William W Horstick. R The Ch Of The Adv Jeannette PA 1963-1971; Chr Ch Chippewa Fls WI 1958-1963; Vic S Simeon's Ch Chippewa Falls WI 1958-1963.

BELL, Susan Endicott Wright (WLa) 403 East Flournoy Lucas Road, 04/01/0158, Shreveport LA 71115 **Died 2/15/2017** B New Haven CT 1932 d William & Marian. BA U of Texas 1954; MEd U of Louisiana 1982; Cert Theol Stud Epis TS of the SW 2001. D 6/23/2001 P 1/5/2002 Bp Robert Jefferson Hargrove Jr. c 3. Asst St Jas Epis Ch 2005-2007; Serv Coordntr Ch Of The H Cross Shreveport LA 2002-2017.

BELL JR, William R (Md) 2901 Boston St Apt 601, Baltimore MD 21224 B Durham NC 1952 s William & Nell. BA Rice U 1974; MD Duke 1978; Duke U Med Cntr 1982; MDiv Ya Berk 2007. D 6/2/2007 P 5/10/2008 Bp Philip Menzie Duncan II. m 5/29/2012 Jo Marie Leslie c 3. Asst S Anne's Par Annapolis MD 2011-2017; Epis Chapl to Johns Hopkins Hospitals Dio Maryland Baltimore MD 2009-2011; Cur H Nativ Epis Ch Panama City FL 2007-2009; Middle Sch Chapl and Tchr of Rel/Ethics H Nativ Epis Sch Panama City FL

2007-2009. Assn of Profsnl Chapl 2010. Bd Cert Chapl Bd Certifying Chapl, Inc 2011.

BELL, Winston Alonzo (LI) 2263 Sedgemont Dr, Winston Salem NC 27103 **Non-par 1994-** B Winchester KY 1930 s Edward & Margaret. BA Fisk U 1951; MA U MI 1955; EdD U MI 1963; STB GTS 1964. D 6/20/1964 P 12/21/1964 Bp James Pernette DeWolfe. R Ch S Jas The Less Jamaica NY 1967-1974; Cur S Aug's Ch New York NY 1964-1966.

BELLAIMEY, John Edward (Minn) 4233 Linden Hills Blvd, Minneapolis MN 55410 B Detroit MI 1955 s Henry & Mary. BA Harv 1976; MDiv Harvard DS 1989. D 6/24/1989 Bp H Coleman Mcgehee Jr P 1/9/1990 Bp Robert Marshall Anderson. m 10/13/1984 Lynnell Mickelsen. Auth, "Wrld Rel: A Journey For Teachers & Their Students," Naes, 1992; Auth, "The Wheel Of The Year"; Auth, "The Five Senses & H Objects".

BELLAIS, William Frank (WMo) 440 Dickinson St, Chillicothe MO 64601 B Colon PA 1934 s Charles & Dorothy. BA New Mex St U 1960; MA New Mex St U 1980; Cert Prchr Lewis Sch of Mnstry 1983; EdD New Mex St U 1988. D 11/14/1983 Bp Richard Mitchell Trelease Jr P 6/22/1991 Bp John Clark Buchanan. m 10/22/1960 Eleanoar Bellais c 2. Chapl Hedrick Med Cntr St. Lk's System Chillicothe 2004-2010; Gr Epis Ch Chillicothe MO 1993-2006; Chr Ch Epis Boonville MO 1992; Dio W Missouri Kansas City MO 1991; Vic S Mary's Ch Fayette MO 1990-1992; Chapl Kemper Mltry Sch & Coll Boonville MO 1988-1990; D S Andr's Epis Ch Las Cruces NM 1983-1988; Chapl Vlly View Hosp Las Cruces NM 1983-1988. Auth, "An Owl Among the Ruins," Vantage Press, 2008. Phi Delta Kappa 1982; Phi Kappa Phi 1980. Bronze Star Medal U.S. Army 1969.

BELLIS, Elaine (Chi) 1747 E 93rd St, Chicago IL 60617 **Archd Dio Chicago Chicago IL 2001-; D-in-c The Ch of the H Cross 2015-** B East Grand Rapids MI 1943 d George & Henrietta. Art Inst of Chicago; Roosevelt U; D Sch of Dio Chicago 1995; Other 1999. D 1/30/1999 Bp Herbert Alcorn Donovan Jr. c 1. D Mssh-S Barth Epis Ch Chicago IL 1999-2001.

BELLISS, Richard Guy (Los) 25454 Via Heraldo, Santa Clarita CA 91355 B Pittsfield MA 1932 s Francis & Vaughan. BA Whittier Coll 1953; MDiv CDSP 1956. D 6/25/1956 P 2/19/1957 Bp Francis E I Bloy. c 2. Asst S Steph's Epis Ch Valencia CA 1994; R All SS Epis Ch Riverside CA 1969-1994; R S Anselm Of Cbury Par Garden Grove CA 1958-1969; Cur St Cross Epis Ch Hermosa Bch CA 1956-1958.

BELLNER, Elisabeth Ann (Md) B 1945 AS Valencia Cmnty Coll 1985; AA Valencia Cmnty Coll 1993. D 12/10/2005 Bp John Wadsworth Howe. m 12/14/1991 Joseph Ann Bellner c 2. Montage Banking Apf Lenders Inc. 2005-2006.

BELLOWS, Carol Hartley (WMass) 33 Fernald Street, Wilton ME 04294 B Plainfield NJ 1934 d John & Jessie. U of Massachusetts 1953; BS Westfield St Coll 1971; Hartford Sem 1980; Dio Wstrn Mass 1982. D 10/9/1982 Bp Alexander D Stewart. m 6/6/1953 Richard S Bellows c 4. D Fawncrest Meadows Farm & Retreat Lyman ME 1998-2009; D S Paul's Epis Ch Stockbridge MA 1988-1991; D S Paul's Ch Kinderhook NY 1986-1988; D T/F Mt Kilimangaro Dio Wstrn Massachusetts 1984-1991; T/F on Mt. Kilimanjaro Mssn Ch Of The Atone Westfield MA 1982-1986; D Grey Logs Retreat Middlefield MA 1982-1986; Cmsn on Wrld Mssn Dio Wstrn Massachusetts Springfield 1982-1991; DWM Epis Rep-Secy Interfaith Coun of Wstrn Massachusetts 1982-1987; Dioc Rep AFP 1982-1986. Auth, "Benjamin Monkey," *(Books for Middle Age Students)*, Authorhouse, 2010; Auth, "The Whack of The Closing Stanchions-Far From Papa's Hill in Vietnam 1967," *(For All Ages)*, Authorhouse, 2010; Auth, "Icabog Bear and Icey," *(Books for Young Chld)*, Authorhouse, 2009; Auth, "Fall - A Performance of Peace," *Kittery to the Kennebunks*, Pilot Press, 1999. Wk in Elem Educ Outstanding Teachers of Amer 1972; 50 year recognition Fndr Dir Tchr Ch of The Atone Weekday Nrsry Sch 1959.

BELLOWS, Richard Sears (WMass) 21 Briarcliff Dr, Westfield MA 01085 B 1959 s Richard & Carol. AB Dart 1981; MDiv SWTS 1992. D 6/13/1992 Bp David Standish Ball P 12/19/1992 Bp Orris George Walker Jr. m 8/6/1988 Danielle Moeske Bellows c 2. R Ch Of The Atone Westfield MA 1998-2007; R Chemung Vlly Cluster Elmira NY 1994-1998; Cur S Ptr's by-the-Sea Epis Ch Bay Shore NY 1992-1994. Tertiary Of The Soc Of S Fran 1997.

BELLOWS, Scott P (Md) Saint Davids Church, 4700 Roland Ave, Baltimore MD 21210 **R S Dav's Ch Baltimore MD 2008-** B Tupper Lake NY 1960 s G & Eva. BA Ob 1987; MBA SUNY-Binghamton 1992; MDiv GTS 1996. D 6/1/1996 P 12/7/1996 Bp Richard Frank Grein. R S Jn's Par Hagerstown MD 2001-2008; Asst All SS Ch Frederick MD 1996-2001; Deputation Chair, 77th GC Dio Maryland Baltimore MD 2011-2014, Mem, Prov III Coun 2011-2014, Co-Chair, Bp Claggett Cntr Capital Cmpgn 2011-2013, Dep, 76th GC 2008-2011, Stndg Com (Pres, 2007-2010) 2006-2010, Dep Alt, 75th GC 2005-2008, Chair, Dioc Conv Liturg Plnng Team 2005-2007, Mem, Dioc Coun 2003-2004, Mem, Bp Sufragan Search Com 1997-1998.

BELL-WOLSKI, Dedra Ann (Ga) 32464 Willow Parke Circle, Fernandina Beach FL 32034 **Int Chr Ch S Marys GA 2012-** B Joliet IL 1958 d Robert & Donna. BA Florida Sthrn Coll 1980; MDiv GTS 1983; Certification Grief Recovery Inst 2004. D 6/11/1984 Bp Calvin Onderdonk Schofield Jr P 1/18/1985 Bp John Shelby Spong. m 7/26/1997 Vincent Neale Wolski c 2. Chapl Off

Of Bsh For ArmdF New York NY 1992-2011; Non-par 1988-1991; Cn Chr Ch Cathd Indianapolis IN 1987-1988; Int Trin Cathd Miami FL 1986-1987; Pstr Lincoln Cathd Ch Of Engl Lincoln Engl 1985-1986; S Paul's Epis Ch Paterson NJ 1984-1985. retnavychaps@comcast.net

BELMONT JR, John C (NJ) 300 S Main St, Pennington NJ 08534 B Trenton NJ 1946 s John & Hannah. BA Rider U 1968; MDiv PDS 1971; STM NYTS 1982. D 4/24/1971 P 10/1/1971 Bp Alfred L Banyard. m 6/10/1989 Sandra Y Belmont c 2. Epis Election Com 1992-1993; Dioc Fndt Dio New Jersey Trenton NJ 1988-1991, Chair Of Loan Com 1983-1987, Dioc Fndt 1982-1984, Chair Of COM 1999-2003, Stndg Com 1984-1998; R S Matt's Ch Pennington NJ 1976-2013; Asst S Lk's Ch Gladstone NJ 1973-1976; R Ch Of S Andr The Apos Camden NJ 1971-1973; Cathd Chapt Trin Cathd Trenton NJ 1981-1983.

BELMONTES, Mervyn Lancelot (LI) 812 Nebraska Ave, Bay Shore NY 11706 B 1939 s Leo & Eastlyl. Codrington Coll 1974; Queens Coll 1979; Lehman Coll 1984. Trans 11/27/1985 as Priest Bp The Bishop Of Trinidad. m 8/9/1975 Carol P Belmontes c 3. R S Gabr's Ch Brooklyn NY 2000-2006; R S Steph's Epis Ch Jamaica NY 1992-2000; Vic Ch Of The Mssh Cntrl Islip NY 1985-1992; Asst S Lk's Epis Ch Bronx NY 1980-1984; Cur Ch In The Prov Of The W Indies 1974-1979; Chair-Com of Miscellaneous Bus Dio Long Island Garden City NY 2001-2006, Dioc Coun 1997-2006, Cmsn on Mnstrs 1995-2001.

BELMORE JR, Buck (Nev) 4626 Grand Dr Unit 2, Las Vegas NV 89169 **Chapl Clark Cnty Detention Cntr 2011-** B Macon GA 1952 s Kent & Frances. BA U NC at Asheville 1974; MDiv GTS 1982. D 6/7/1982 Bp Robert Campbell Witcher Sr P 12/1/1982 Bp William Gillette Weinhauer. m 8/22/1981 Constance Stroupe c 2. R Chr Ch Las Vegas NV 2007-2011; R All SS Epis Ch Mobile AL 2004-2007; Dio Atlanta Atlanta GA 1995, 1994, 1993-1994; R Ch Of The H Cross Decatur GA 1988-2004; Ch Of The H Comm Charleston SC 1985-1988; Cur Gr Ch Cathd Charleston SC 1983-1985; Cur S Ptr's by-the-Sea Epis Ch Bay Shore NY 1982-1983. Cumberland Soc.

BELMORE, Constance (Nev) 4626 Grand Drive #2, Las Vegas NV 89169 **Stff Chapl St. Rose San Mart Hosp Las Vegas NV 2009-** B Charlotte NC 1955 d Thomas & Patricia. BA U NC 1978; MDiv GTS 1983. D 6/25/1983 Bp Brice Sidney Sanders P 4/25/1984 Bp William Moultrie Moore Jr. m 8/22/1981 Buck Belmore c 2. CPE Chapl Banner Hlth Phoenix AZ 2008-2009; Mssn P S Anna's Ch Atmore AL 2005-2007; Cn for Cmnty Mnstrs Dio Atlanta Atlanta GA 1994-2004, Assoc Dir Of Cmnty Mnstrs 1989-1994; Assoc Ch Of The H Cross Decatur GA 1988-2004; Chapl Gr Ch Cathd Charleston SC 1983-1988. Assn of Profsnl Chapl 2009. Wmn Of The Year So Carolina Bus And Profsnl Wmn 1986.

BELNAP, Ronald Victor (U) 8952 Golden Field Way, Sandy UT 84094 **Asst All SS Ch Salt Lake City UT 2005-; Ret 1997-** B Salt Lake City UT 1932 s Orsen & Mary. BS U of Utah 1960; MSW U of Utah 1962; MDiv CDSP 1992. D 6/2/1991 P 12/5/1991 Bp George Edmonds Bates. m 5/24/1974 Nancy Smith Belnap c 3. Prison Mnstry Cedar City UT 1992-2003; P-in-c S Jude's Ch Cedar City UT 1992-1997; Dio Utah Salt Lake City UT 1991-1997.

BELSER, Jo J (Va) 2280 N Beauregard St, Alexandria VA 22311 **R Ch Of The Resurr Alexandria VA 2015-, P-in-c 2013-2015** B Potsdam NY 1956 d Bernard & Norma. BS Houghton Coll 1977; CPL Geo 1991; MIS The GW 1996; MDiv VTS 2012. D 6/2/2012 Bp Ted Gulick Jr P 12/15/2012 Bp Shannon Sherwood Johnston. m 8/29/2011 Lenore Marie Funkhouser. Pres Dio Virginia Richmond VA 2017. priest@welcometoresurrection.org

✠ BELSHAW, The Rt Rev George Phelps Mellick (NJ) 15 Boudinot St, Princeton NJ 08540 **BD ATR 1993-; Bd Dir Amer Teilhard de Chardin Assn 1976-** B Plainfield NJ 1928 s Harold & Edith. BA Other 1951; BA Sewanee, U So 1951; STB GTS 1954; STM GTS 1959; Coll of Preachers 1968; Hon DD Ham 2003. D 6/19/1954 Bp Norman B Nash P 12/18/1954 Bp Harry Sherbourne Kennedy Con 2/3/1975 for NJ. c 3. Cltn for Peace Action Princeton NJ 1999-2003; Actg Dn & Pres The GTS New York NY 1997-1998, Chair, Bd Trst 1992-2000, Lectr 1968-1991; Epis Ch Cntr New York NY 1993-1996; VP Prov II 1993-1996; PBp's Coun of Advice Dio New Jersey Trenton NJ 1993-1994; Bp 1983-1992, Bp Suffr 1975-1982, Ret Bp of New Jersey 1995-; Econ Justice Implementation Com 1988-1995; Pres EUC 1986-1989; JCP 1979-1985; Westminster Choir Coll 1976-1982; R S Geo's-By-The-River Rumson NJ 1965-1975; R Chr Ch Dover DE 1959-1965; Vic S Matt's Epis Ch Waimanalo HI 1954-1957. "The Rel of the Incarn," *ATR*, 1994; "The issue of Chr Sprtlty," *ATR*, 1967; *Lent w Wm Temple*, Morehouse Barlow, 1966; *Lent w Evelyn Underhill*, Morehouse Barlow, 1964; "Theol Definition and Explanation," *ATR*, 1963. DD U So 1994; DD GTS 1975; Fell Coll of Preachers 1968; Fell GTS 1957.

BELSHAW, Richard W (NH) 18 Highland Street, Ashland NH 03217 **Chr Ch No Conway NH 2016-** B Honolulu HI 1957 s George & Elizabeth. BA Connecticut Coll 1979; MDiv EDS 2008. D 12/3/2011 P 7/24/2012 Bp Vicky Gene Robinson. m 12/14/1991 Julia G Belshaw c 2. Vic S Mk's Ch Ashland NH 2014-2016; P-in-c Ch Of S Jn The Evang Dunbarton NH 2011-2013.

BELSKY, Emil Eugene (U) 2714 Sierra Vista Road, Grand Junction CO 81503 B Omaha NE 1948 s Emil & Louise. BA U of St Thos 1970; MA S Thos Sem 1974. Rec 4/7/1993 Bp James Edward Krotz. m 6/29/1990 Cynthia Louise Belsky c 2. R S Paul's Ch Salt Lake City UT 2006-2013; Asst to R All SS Epis Ch

Omaha NE 1993-2006; Serv Archdiocese of Omaha RC Ch 1974-1985; Epis Transition Team Dio Utah Salt Lake City UT 2010, Dioc Coun 2007-2010, Cncl Revs T/F 2007-2008. Assoc, OHC 1996.

BELT, Michel (Ct) 119 Huntington St, New London CT 06320 **Gr Ch Madison NJ 2016-; Hon Cn St. Andr's Cathd Aberdeen Scotland UK 2014-; Bd Secy New London Rotary Fndt New London CT 2014-; Bd Mem-Secy Vstng Nurses Assn of SECT Waterford CT 2012-; Title IV Conciliator Dio Connecticut Meriden CT 2011-; Bd Mem-Treas New London Homeless Hosp Cntr New London CT 2006-; Bd Mem Cov Shltr New London CT 2002-** B Wichita KS 1948 s Harold & Alice. BME Wichita St U 1970; MBA U of Miami 1983; MDiv EDS 1997. D 5/31/1997 Bp Jack Marston Mckelvey P 12/6/1997 Bp John Shelby Spong. R S Jas Ch New London CT 2002-2015; Vic S Greg's Epis Ch Parsippany NJ 1997-2002. OHC, Assoc.

BELTON, Allan Edgar (O) 3490 E Prescott Cir, Cuyahoga Falls OH 44223 **R S Mk's Epis Ch Wadsworth OH 2011-** B Akron OH 1941 s Edgar & Freda. BA U of Akron 1963; BD Bex Sem 1966; MA Cleveland St U 1971. D 6/12/1966 P 12/18/1966 Bp Nelson Marigold Burroughs. m 2/12/2000 Ruth Anne McGavack c 2. Int S Jn's Epis Ch Cuyahoga Fls OH 2004-2006; Assoc Chr Ch Epis Hudson OH 2001-2004, Cur 1968-1970; R Chr Ch Albemarle NC 1999-2001; Int S Martins-In-The-Field Columbia SC 1998-1999; Int Gr Epis Ch Willoughby OH 1995-1996; Int New Life Epis Ch Uniontown OH 1993-1998; Int Chr Epis Ch Kent OH 1992-1995; Int S Paul's Epis Ch Of E Cleveland Cleveland OH 1990-1992; Int Dio Ohio Cleveland 1987-1998; P-in-c Ch Of The Incarn Cleveland OH 1987-1990; P-in-c Incarn Cleveland OH 1987-1990; Vic S Tim's Ch Macedonia OH 1976-1979; Non-par 1971-1986; Cur S Andr Epis Ch Mentor OH 1966-1968. Bdiv cl Bex 1966.

BELTON, Colin Charles (Alb) 18 Trinity Pl., Plattsburgh NY 12901 **Ch Of S Sacrement Bolton Landing NY 2015-** B 1950 s John & Margaret. Trans 6/15/2009 Bp William Howard Love. m 7/29/1989 Penelope A Tucker c 2. R Trin Ch Plattsburgh NY 2008-2015.

BELTON, Randy Samuel (Wyo) Church Of Saint Andrew's In The Pines, Po Box 847, Pinedale WY 82941 B Loiriet France 1957 s Hardin & Ida. D 6/25/2016 P 2/28/2017 Bp John Smylie. m 7/9/1988 Julie Ann Belton c 4.

BELZER, John Alfred (Okla) 13 Lake Ln, Shawnee OK 74804 **D Emm Epis Ch Shawnee OK 2005-** B Washington DC 1944 s John & Clara. BA Oklahoma St U 1967; MEd U of Cntrl Oklahoma 1974; PhD U of Oklahoma 1988. D 6/18/2005 Bp Robert Manning Moody. m 2/27/1990 Alma Lee Belzer c 2.

BEMIS, Harlan Arnold (WNC) 30 Hidden Meadow Dr, Candler NC 28715 **Died 11/14/2016** B Providence RI 1939 s Harlan & Margaret. BS Worcester Polytechnic Inst 1959; GTS 1962; CG Jung Inst 1968. D 11/12/1972 Bp Paul Moore Jr P 6/3/1973 Bp Roger W Blanchard. m 12/23/1998 Joan M Bemis. Assoc S Andr's Epis Ch Canton NC 2004-2016; Ch of the Ascen Merrill WI 1999-2005; P S Aelred Cluster Antigo WI 1999-2005; Vic S Barn Epis Ch Tomahawk WI 1999-2005; St Ambr Epis Ch Antigo WI 1999-2005; Int Dio Estrn Michigan Saginaw MI 1998-1999; Int Thumb Epis Area Mnstry Deford MI 1997-1999; Int S Mk's Ch Warren RI 1995-1997; Int Ch Of The Mssh Foster RI 1989-1995; Int Galilee Mssn To Fisherman Narragansett RI 1984-1986; Int Dio Rhode Island Providence RI 1983-1997; Int Emm Epis Ch Cumberland RI 1983-1984; Int Epis Sr Communities Lafayette CA 1979; Int Epis Seamens Serv San Francisco CA 1977-1981; Int S Cyp's Ch San Francisco CA 1976-1977; Chapl Epis Seaman's Serv San Francisco CA 1975-1980; Asst P S Jn's Ch New York NY 1974-1991; Int Dio California San Francisco CA 1973-1980.

BENAVIDES, Laurie Pauline (RG) 112 Goldenrod Ln, Alto NM 88312 **D Epis Ch In Lincoln Cnty Ruidoso NM 2012-, D 2006-2009; D Dio the Rio Grande Lincoln Cnty NM 2006-** B San Antonio TX 1954 d Richard & LeMoyne. BS Texas St U San Marcos 1976; MEd Texas St U San Marcos 1980. D 10/29/2006 Bp C Wallis Ohl. m 12/18/1983 Roy Benavides c 3. D Gr Epis Ch Georgetown TX 2009-2012. Assn of Epis Deacons 2007; The Ord of the DOK 1996. lpbenavides@gmail.com

BENBROOK, James Gordon (WLa) 125 Woodstone Dr., Ruston LA 71270 B Herber Springs AR 1948 s Maurice & Bonnie. AA Essex Coll Essex MD 1972; BS Towson U 1976; MDiv Sewanee: The U So, TS 2005. D 6/4/2005 P 9/2/2006 Bp D Avid Bruce Macpherson. m 4/22/1988 Rebecca June Benbrook c 3. S Paul's Ch Abbeville LA 2013-2014; Epis Ch Of The Gd Shpd Lake Chas LA 2012-2013; H Trin Epis Ch Sulphur LA 2012-2013; R Ch Of The Redeem Ruston LA 2009-2012; D The Epis Ch Of The Gd Shpd Vidalia LA 2005-2008.

BENCKEN, Cathi Head (Ia) 211 Walnut St., Muscatine IA 52761 **R Trin Ch Muscatine IA 2008-** B Harlan IA 1951 d Robert & Phyllis. BSN U of Iowa Coll of Nrsng 1973; Spanish Centro Intercultural de Documacion 1974; Spanish Centro Intercultural de Documenacion 1974; MDiv Bex Sem 2007; Cert WINGS Sprtl Direction 2013. D 4/13/2007 P 12/8/2007 Bp Michael Garrison. m 12/27/1997 Charles F Bencken c 5. Supply P Dio Mississippi 2008; Assoc S Paul's Epis Ch Lewiston NY 2007-2008; Supply P Dio Mississippi 2007. Sprtl Dir Intl 2013. trinity@machlink.com

BENCKEN, Charles F (WNY) 2461 Longhurst Ct., Muscatine IA 52761 **S Alb's Ch Davenport IA 2015-** B Chico CA 1938 s George & Anna. MA; EdD U of San Francisco; BA S Josephs Minor Sem Mtn View CA 1958; S Patricks Coll/

Major Sem Menlo Pk CA 1964; MA TS U of San Francisco 1969; EdS U of Iowa 1972; JD U Pac McGeorge Sch of Law 1989. Rec 5/16/1999 as Priest Bp Stewart Clark Zabriskie. m 12/27/1997 Cathi Head c 5. Int S Thos' Epis Ch Sioux City IA 2008-2009; R Chr Ch Albion NY 2005; Vic Ch Of The Epiph Niagara Falls NY 2001-2004; Ch Of The Redeem Niagara Falls NY 2001-2004; S Ptr's Ch Niagara Falls NY 2001-2004; Dio Nevada Las Vegas 1999-2001.

BENDALL, Douglas (Nwk) 26 Howard Court, Newark NJ 07103 **Fndr and Pres The Newark TS Newark NJ 1997-; Founding Bd Mem CLBSJ Cntr & Libr for Bible and Soc Justice 2011-** B Baltimore MD 1939 s Robert & Lillian. BA S Johns Coll 1961; MDiv Epis TS of the SW 1968; U CA/Berkeley 1971; U of Tubingen Germany 1972; PhD Grad Theol Un 1977. D 7/25/1968 Bp Everett H Jones P 1/26/1969 Bp Harold Cornelius Gosnell. c 2. Vic S Andr's Ch Newark NJ 1995-2005; Vic H Sprt Mssn Lake Almanor CA 1987-1994; Lectr U of Nevada Reno 1985-1990; Lectr Georgia St U Atlanta 1981-1984; Lectr U of Laverne 1981-1984; Lectr U of San Francisco 1979-1981; Asst S Paul's Epis Ch San Antonio TX 1968-1969. Auth, "PhD Dissertation," *The Naturalization of Whitehead's God*, Dissertation Abstracts Ann Arbor Mich., 1977.

BENDER, David Randa (NY) 104 Fairview Avenue, Poughkeepsie NY 12601 **D S Jas Ch Hyde Pk NY 1999-** B Long Branch NJ 1947 D 12/11/1982 Bp Addison Hosea. m 12/6/1969 Carol Lynn.

BENDER, Jane (Be) 557 W 3rd St Apt K, Bethlehem PA 18015 B Greenville SC 1951 d John & Jane. BA Furman U 1973; MDiv Moravian TS 1997; DAS GTS 1998. D 9/19/1998 P 5/29/1999 Bp Paul Victor Marshall. c 1. P-in-c All SS Epis Ch Lehighton PA 2006-2016; S Anne's Epis Ch Trexlertown PA 2001-2005, D 1998-1999; Int Cathd Ch Of The Nativ Bethlehem PA 1999-2000. Soc For Promoting Chr Knowledge, EPF. Mdiv cl Moravian TS 1997.

BENDER, John Charles (Tenn) Our Saviour Episcopal Church, 704 Hartsville Pike, Gallatin TN 37066 **Int R St. Mk's Epis Ch Cocoa FL 2016-** B Marietta OH 1949 s Samuel & Caroline. BA Marshall U 1971; Dip Ang Stud Sewanee: The U So, TS 2007. D 2/23/2008 P 12/20/2008 Bp John Bauerschmidt. m 7/23/1974 Lynda G Bender c 2. R Ch Of Our Sav Gallatin TN 2008-2015; D Dio Tennessee Nashville TN 2008.

BENDER, Richard E (ECR) P.O. Box 2400, Saratoga CA 95070 **D S Fran Epis Ch San Jose CA 2013-; COM Dio El Camino Real Salinas CA 2011-; Bd Dir Epis Chapl at Stanford Hosp & Clinics San Francisco CA 2011-** B San Jose CA 1974 s Glenus & Brenda. BTS Epis Sch for Deacons 2011; BTS Other 2011. D 10/22/2011 Bp Mary Gray-Reeves. m 9/18/1999 Sharon B Bender c 2. D S Andr's Ch Saratoga CA 2011-2013.

BENDER, William Dexter (Ala) 402 S Scott St, Scottsboro AL 35768 **S Phil's Ch Ft Payne AL 2015-** B Gainesville FL 1946 s William & Leona. BA Shpd U 1969; MDiv VTS 1994. D 6/25/1994 P 1/6/1995 Bp Rogers Sanders Harris. m 4/30/1977 Heidi C Chiappini c 6. R S Lk's Ch Scottsboro AL 2009-2015; Int St Thos Epis Ch Huntsville AL 2008-2009; Int Ch Of The Gd Shpd Lookout Mtn TN 2006-2008; Assoc R Chr Ch Bradenton FL 2000-2006; R S Chris's Ch Tampa FL 1996-2000; Asst S Andr's Epis Ch Tampa FL 1994-1996.

BENDER-BRECK, Barbara (Cal) 3226 Adeline St, Oakland CA 94608 B Dallas TX 1949 d Robert & Eleanor. BA Notre Dame Coll 1971; JD U of San Francisco 1975; MDiv CDSP 1993. D 6/4/1993 P 6/1/1994 Bp William Edwin Swing. c 2. S Barth's Ch Beaverton OR 2009-2011; Int S Lk's Ch San Francisco CA 2008-2009; S Anne's Ch Fremont CA 2006-2007; Ch Of The H Trin Richmond CA 2004-2005; Ch Of Our Sav Mill Vlly CA 2003-2004; S Mich And All Ang Concord CA 2002-2003; Assoc Gr Cathd San Francisco CA 1999-2002; Ch Of The Redeem San Rafael CA 1996-1999; S Paul's Epis Ch San Rafael CA 1994-1996. Tertiary Of The Soc of S Fran.

BENEDICT, Richard Alan Davis (NJ) 1625 SE 10th Ave Apt 602, Fort Lauderdale FL 33316 **Assoc P Trin Cathd Miami FL 2008-** B Toledo OH 1948 s Edward & Adell. BA U of Toledo 1973; MA U of Toledo 1974; MDiv SWTS 1977. D 6/25/1977 Bp John Harris Burt P 1/28/1978 Bp David Keller Leighton Sr. R Chr Ch Bordentown NJ 1985-2008; Asst to R All SS Ch Frederick MD 1977-1984. CCU.

BENES, Sandra S (Mich) 122 White Lake Dr, Brooklyn MI 49230 B Adrian MI 1943 d Michael & Martha. Siena Heights U; U of Toledo; Whitaker TS. D 7/2/1980 Bp William Jones Gordon Jr P 5/22/1984 Bp H Coleman Mcgehee Jr. m 8/25/1962 E Michael Benes c 4. Dn of Lyster Area Dio Michigan Detroit MI 2008-2010, Dn of Lyster Area Coun 1994-2008, Dn of SW Convoc 1988-1993, Co-Dn of Lyster Dnry 2007-; R S Mich And All Ang Brooklyn MI 1982-2005.

BENESH, Jimi Brown (NCal) 334 D St, Redwood City CA 94063 B FJ 1944 s Lewis & Esita. D 12/7/2002 P 12/6/2003 Bp William Edwin Swing. m 12/7/1964 Violet Koi. D S Ptr's Epis Ch Redwood City CA 2002-2008.

✠ **BENFIELD, The Rt Rev Larry** (Ark) Episcopal Diocese of Arkansas, 310 W 17th St, Little Rock AR 72206 **Bp of Arkansas Dio Arkansas Little Rock AR 2007-, Cn Admin 1998-2000; Chair, Gnrl Bd Exam Chapl Dom And Frgn Mssy Soc- Epis Ch Cntr New York NY 2015-, Coll for Bishops, Bd 2014-, Mem, HOB Theol Com 2010-, Mem, PB Coun of Advice 2008-** B Johnson City TN 1955 s Clyde & Madge. BS U of Tennessee 1977; MBA U of Pennsylvania 1979; MDiv VTS 1990. D 6/16/1990 Bp Maurice Manuel Benitez P 1/31/1991 Bp Anselmo Carral-Solar Con 1/6/2007 for Ark. R Chr Epis Ch Little

Rock AR 2001-2006; Int S Lk's Ch Hot Sprg AR 1996-1997; S Mk's Epis Ch Little Rock AR 1992-1996; Chapl of the Epis Stdt Cntr The Great Cmsn Fndt Houston TX 1990-1992. DD VTS 2008; DD U So 2007. lbenfield@episcoar. org

BENHAM, David D (Ark) 2701 Old Greenwood Rd, Fort Smith AR 72903 **S Andr's Ch Rogers AR 2011-** B Fayetteville AR 1942 s Hoyt & Ida. BSEd U of Arkansas 1965; MRE SW Bapt Theol 1969; DMin Golden Gate Bapt TS 1985. D 10/16/2010 P 5/7/2011 Bp Larry Benfield. m 6/15/1962 Jessie A Evans-Benham c 3.

✠ BENHASE, The Rt Rev Scott Anson (Ga) 611 E Bay St, Savannah GA 31401 **Bp of Georgia Dio Georgia Savannah GA 2010-** B Lancaster OH 1957 s Carl & Annaree. BA DePauw U 1979; MDiv VTS 1983; MS Cleveland St U 1990; DMin VTS 2009. D 6/23/1983 P 3/17/1984 Bp Edward Witker Jones Con 1/23/2010 for Ga. m 5/12/1984 Kelly J Benhase c 3. R S Alb's Par Washington DC 2006-2009; R S Phil's Ch Durham NC 1995-2006; Vic Trin Epis Ch Charlottesvlle VA 1990-1995; R S Paul's Epis Ch Of E Cleveland Cleveland OH 1986-1990; Cur Trin Ch Indianapolis IN 1983-1986. OA 1988. DD Sewanee: The U So, TS 2011; Who's Who in Amer 2010. bishop@gaepiscopal.org

BENISTE, Jean C (SeFla) 2430 K St NW, Washington DC 20037 **Ch Of The H Redeem Lake Worth FL 2015-** B Haiti 1970 s Marc & Celidia. BA Grand Seminaire Notre Dame D'Haiti; MDiv VTS 2014. D 11/23/2013 P 5/31/2014 Bp Leo Frade. m 2/15/2001 Monica Beniste c 2. S Paul's Par Washington DC 2014-2015. jeanbeniste@gmail.com

BENITEZ, Wilfredo (LI) St George's Church, 13532 38th Ave, Flushing NY 11354 **S Geo's Par Flushing NY 2012-** B Bronx NY 1956 s Julio & Angelina. BA Universidad Interamericana De Puerto Rico Mercedita PR 1979; MEd Bank St Coll of Educ 1982; MDiv GTS 1991. D 6/8/1991 P 12/1/1991 Bp Richard Frank Grein. m 6/7/2014 Rose Deats. S Anselm Of Cbury Par Garden Grove CA 1993-2012; S Clem's-By-The-Sea Par San Clemente CA 1993; Asst For Latino Mnstrs Chr Ch Poughkeepsie NY 1991-1993.

BENJAMIN, Judith Ellen (Cal) 1400 Loma Drive, Ojai CA 93023 B Salem MA 1948 d Richard & Lois. BS U CA 1971; BA Sch for Deacons 2000. D 6/2/2001 Bp William Edwin Swing. m 1/22/1989 Ian Hall c 2. S Bede's Epis Ch Menlo Pk CA 2001-2010.

BENKO, Andrew G (FtW) 908 Rutherford St, Shreveport LA 71104 B Metairie LA 1980 s Ronald & Dean. BA Coll of Santa Fe 2002; MDiv SWTS 2005. D 12/29/2004 Bp Charles Edward Jenkins III P 6/29/2006 Bp George Wayne Smith. m 9/17/2005 Hope T Benko c 1. S Chris's Ch And Sch Ft Worth TX 2014-2016; Trin Epis Ch Ft Worth TX 2011-2013; Dio Wstrn Louisiana Alexandria LA 2010-2011; S Mk's Cathd Shreveport LA 2009-2011; Dio Missouri S Louis MO 2007-2009.

BENKO, Hope T (FtW) 9700 Saints Cir, Fort Worth TX 76108 **Epis TS Of The SW Austin TX 2016-; All SS' Epis Sch Of Ft Worth Ft Worth TX 2011-** B Alexandria LA 1981 d Richard & Mary. BS Stephens Coll 2003; MDiv SWTS 2006. D 12/21/2005 P 6/29/2006 Bp George Wayne Smith. m 9/17/2005 Andrew G Benko c 3. S Mk's Cathd Shreveport LA 2009-2011; Asst R Emm Epis Ch S Louis MO 2006-2009.

BENNER, Stephen Thomas (Ind) 636 W Grace St Apt 2w, Chicago IL 60613 B Streator IL 1968 s Lawrence & Evelyn. BA Illinois St U 1990; Johann-Wolfgang-Goethe Universität Frankfurt am Main Germa 1991; MA The OH SU Columbus OH 1993; Rheinische-Friedrich Wilhelms Universitat Bonn Germany 1996; PhD The OH SU Columbus OH 2000; MDiv Bex Sem 2007; Indiana Wesl Marion IN 2012. D 6/23/2007 Bp Cate Waynick P 2/2/2008 Bp Kenneth Lester Price. m 5/31/1988 David K Worley. Confrater, Ord of S Ben (St. Greg' Abbey, Three R 1987. Fulbright Schlr German-Amer Fulbright Cmsn 1990.

BENNETT, Richard Wilson (FdL) 7220 Newell Road, Hazelhurst WI 54531 B San Francisco CA 1928 s Richard & Helen. BA Colg 1951; MEd U of Vermont 1968; PhD U CO 1971; MDiv Nash 1988. D 3/19/1991 P 9/19/1991 Bp Charles I Jones III. m 2/4/1996 Joellen Bennet. Ret Dio Fond du Lac Appleton WI 1997; R Ch Of S Jn The Bapt Wausau WI 1994-1997; Dio Montana Helena MT 1993-1994; Ch Of The Trsfg Billings MT 1992-1993; Assoc Yellowstone Cluster Mnstry 1991-1994.

BENNETT III, Arthur Lasure (WVa) 16 Ashwood Dr, Vienna WV 26105 **Cn Theol Dio W Virginia Charleston WV 2008-, Archd for the No 1994-2002** B Clarksburg WV 1943 s Arthur & Betty. BA W Virginia Wesleyan Coll 1966; MDiv Bex Sem 1969; ThD Columbia Pacific U 1988. D 6/11/1969 P 12/1/1969 Bp Wilburn Camrock Campbell. m 8/20/1966 Linda Bennett c 2. R The Memi Ch Of The Gd Shpd Parkersburg WV 1984-2009; R St Chris Epis Ch Charleston WV 1973-1984; R S Paul's Ch Wheeling WV 1970-1973; Cur S Steph's Epis Ch Beckley WV 1969-1970.

BENNETT JR, Bertram George (NY) 384 E 160th St, Bronx NY 10451 **P-in-c Dio New York New York NY 1997-** B New York NY 1951 s Bertram & Marjorie. BA Shaw U 1973; MDiv GTS 1977. D 6/11/1977 Bp Paul Moore Jr P 6/1/1978 Bp James Stuart Wetmore. m 4/12/1982 Ledda Del Rosario Bennett c 3. S Dav's Ch Bronx NY 1980-1996; Cur The Ch of S Matt And S Tim New York NY 1979-1980; S Marg's Ch Bronx NY 1977-1979. st.david@verizon.net

BENNETT, Betsy Blake (Neb) 325 W. 11th St., Hastings NE 68901 **Stndg Com Mem Dio Nebraska Omaha NE 2016-, Archd 2012-2016, Exec Cmsn Mem 2011-2016** B Akron OH 1951 d Bruce & Jeannette. BA Earlham Coll 1973; MA OH SU 1975. D 6/21/2004 Bp Joe Goodwin Burnett. m 3/22/1975 Gary Lee Bennett c 2. D S Steph's Ch Grand Island NE 2007-2013; D S Mk's Epis Pro-Cathd Hastings NE 2004-2007.

BENNETT, Christine Aikens (Me) 30 Turtle Cove Rd, Raymond ME 04071 B Cambridge MA 1946 d Keith & Catherine. U of Maine; U of Sthrn Maine. D 10/17/1998 Bp Chilton Richardson Knudsen. m 6/7/1969 Lawrence Bennett c 3. D S Ann's Epis Ch Windham Windham ME 1998-2007. admin@smary.org

BENNETT, Debra Q (O) 1933 Kingsley Ave, Akron OH 44313 **R Ch Of Our Sav Akron OH 2014-, P-in-c 2012-2014** B New York, NY 1958 d Gerald & Clara. BA Wag 1980; MDiv Bex Sem 2009. D 6/22/2009 Bp James Hamilton Ottley P 1/16/2010 Bp Lawrence C Provenzano. revdebcoos@episcopalakron.org

BENNETT, Denise Harper (Roch) 2882 Country Road 13, Clifton Springs NY 14432 B New Rochelle NY 1946 d James & Barbara. BA Cedar Crest Coll 1968; CSD GTS 1998; MDiv Drew U 2003. D 6/7/2003 P 12/6/2003 Bp John Palmer Croneberger. m 11/16/1968 Thomas M Bennett c 2. R S Jn's Ch Clifton Spgs NY 2007-2014; Assoc R Dir of Mnstry Dvlpmt S Mk's Ch Teaneck NJ 2004-2007; Asst Ch Of The Redeem Morristown NJ 2003-2004.

BENNETT, E Gene (Miss) 981 S Church St, Brookhaven MS 39601 **Died 1/11/2016** B Chattanooga TN 1941 s Ernest & Sarah. BS U So 1963; MDiv Sewanee: The U So, TS 1967; Van 1970. D 7/2/1967 Bp William F Gates Jr P 4/1/1968 Bp John Vander Horst. m 11/27/1986 Carole Petro c 1. R Ch Of The Redeem Brookhaven MS 2001-2009; Int Trin Ch Hattiesburg MS 2000-2001; Writer/Ed Self Employed - San Francisco California 1994-2000; R S Geo's Par La Can CA 1991-1994; R S Barn On The Desert Scottsdale AZ 1988-1991; R S Lk's Ch Brandon MS 1974-1988; Vic Ch Of Our Sav Gallatin TN 1968-1971; D Ch Of The Ascen Knoxville TN 1967-1968; S Jas Ch Jackson MS 1871-1973. Auth, "S Lk Journ Of Theol"; Auth, "Dance Of The Pilgrim"; Auth, "The Secular Chr"; Auth, "Image Of Man In Mod Lit". AAMFT 1971.

BENNETT, Ernest L (CFla) Diocese of Central Florida, 1017 E Robinson St, Orlando FL 32801 **R S Jas Epis Ch Ormond Bch FL 2014-** B Norfolk VA 1943 s Ernest & Edith. BA U of Florida 1965; MDiv VTS 1968. D 6/24/1968 Bp Henry I Louttit P 12/28/1968 Bp James Loughlin Duncan. m 5/25/1968 Roslyn Bennett c 2. Cn to the Ordnry Dio Cntrl Florida Orlando FL 1993-2014; R S Andr's Epis Ch Ft Pierce FL 1985-1993; R S Andr's Epis Ch Sprg Hill FL 1973-1985; Asst Trin By The Cove Naples FL 1968-1971. erniebennett43@gmail.com

BENNETT JR, Franklin Pierce (EMich) 1051 Virginia Ave, Marysville MI 48040 **Ret 1998-** B Syracuse NY 1935 s Franklin & Florence. BA Harv 1957; Emory U 1960; BD EDS 1961; SeAtlantic / Rockefeller U 1973; Dio Missouri 1990; Fell PrTS 1990. D 6/29/1961 Bp Richard Stanley Merrill Emrich P 2/1/1962 Bp Archie H Crowley. m 2/5/1983 Marsha Ann Bennett c 1. Asst Gr Epis Ch Port Huron MI 2001-2006; Supply P Dio Estrn Michigan Saginaw MI 1998-2006; Long-term Supply P S Jn's Epis Ch Dryden MI 1997; P-in-c Gr Ch Detroit MI 1992-1995; R S Paul's Epis Ch Grand Forks MI 1988-1990; R S Paul's Epis Ch S Clair MI 1969-1988; Assoc Chr Ch Grosse Pointe Grosse Pointe Farms MI 1963-1969; Asst Chr Ch Dearborn MI 1961-1963. Allin Fllshp Dio Missouri 1990; Par Mnstry Fllshp Sealantic /Rockefeller 1973; Danforth Sem Intrnshp Danforth Fndt 1959.

BENNETT, Gail Louise (NJ) 803 Prospect Ave, Spring Lake NJ 07762 **D Trin Ch Asbury Pk NJ 2004-** B 1938 d Frank & Norma. D 4/13/1985 Bp George Phelps Mellick Belshaw. c 2. D/Asst S Jas Ch Bradley Bch NJ 1985-2013.

BENNETT, Gerald L (SwFla) 5134 Wedge Ct E, Bradenton FL 34203 B Detroit MI 1934 s William & Hattie. BS Wayne 1962; MEd Wayne 1965; EdD Estrn Michigan U 1971; TS Harvard DS 1985. D 7/9/1977 Bp William Jones Gordon Jr P 10/4/1985 Bp Henry Irving Mayson. c 1. Assoc Ch of the Nativ Sarasota FL 1996-2001; R S Geo's Epis Ch Bradenton FL 1990-1995; Int Ch Of The H Sprt Osprey FL 1989-1990; Int S Barth's Ch St Petersburg FL 1988; Asst Vic Ch Of The H Cross Novi MI 1979-1988; S Anne's Epis Ch Walled Lake MI 1979-1988.

BENNETT, JoAnne (Ore) PO Box 1791, Roseburg OR 97470 B South Hampton NY 1955 d David & Joan. BA U CA 1978; MDiv CDSP 2001. D 12/1/2001 P 6/1/2002 Bp William Edwin Swing. Dio Oregon Portland OR 2015-2016; R S Geo's Epis Ch Roseburg OR 2009-2015; Vic S Chris's Ch San Lorenzo CA 2001-2008.

BENNETT, Kyle Vernon (SwFla) St. Mark's Episcopal Church, 1101 N. Collier Blvd, Marco Island FL 34145 **Dir Camp Able 2006-; R S Mk's Ch Marco Island FL 2005-** B Sandusky OH 1963 s Michael & Kristen. MA U of Mississippi; BA U So 1985; MDiv Epis TS of the SW 1994; DMin Sewanee: The U So, TS 2009. D 6/4/1994 P 4/2/1995 Bp Alfred Marble Jr. m 3/15/1986 Dody Louise Bennett c 2. Assoc St Thos Epis Ch Huntsville AL 2003-2005; Chapl Coast Epis Sch 1997-2003; R S Patricks Epis Ch Long Bch MS 1997-2003; S Ptr's Ch Oxford MS 1996-1997; Chapl U Of Mississippi 1994-1997; Dio Mis-

sissippi Jackson MS 1994-1995; Yth Min S Thos Epis Ch Diamondhead MS 1987-1989. Sprt of Marco Island winner Rotary 2007.

BENNETT, Marionette Elvena (Colo) 15625 E Atlantic Cir, Aurora CO 80013 **D S Steph's Epis Ch Aurora CO 1996-** B Charleston SC 1949 d John & Rosena. BS Paine Coll 1970. D 11/2/1996 Bp William Jerry Winterrowd. NAAD.

BENNETT, Pattiann Benner (Mont) 324 Terning Dr W, Eureka MT 59917 **R S Mich And All Ang Eureka MT 2004-, 2002-2003** B Skowhegan ME 1951 d Roy & Joanne. Mnstry Formation Prog 2000. D 10/9/2001 P 9/20/2002 Bp Charles Lovett Keyser. m 6/30/1979 Bruce Bennett c 2. H Trin Epis Ch Troy MT 2009-2013; S Lk's Ch Libby MT 2009-2013.

BENNETT, Phillip (Pa) 2001 Hamilton St Apt 303, Philadelphia PA 19130 **Adj P Cathd Ch of Our Sav Philadelphia PA 2013-; Fresh Start Stff Dio Pennsylvania Philadelphia PA 2006-, Dir of Sprtl Formation, Sch for the Diac 1990-1995, Chair, Sprtl Growth Com 1984-1988, 1982-2005** B Pasadena CA 1952 s Charles & May. BA Beloit Coll 1975; MDiv SWTS 1979; STM UTS 1992; PhD Un U 1994. D 6/9/1979 Bp Quintin Ebenezer Primo Jr P 6/13/1980 Bp James Winchester Montgomery. m 8/20/2004 Joseph G Schaller. Asstg P Ch Of S Mart-In-The-Fields Philadelphia PA 2008-2013; Asstg P S Ptr's Ch Philadelphia PA 1992-2000; P-in-c S Ptr's Ch Germantown Philadelphia PA 1990-1992; Assoc S Mk's Ch Philadelphia PA 1982-1990; Assoc S Mk's Epis Ch Glen Ellyn IL 1980-1982; Asst to the Bp Dio Colorado Denver CO 1979-1980; Dioc Coun Dio Chicago Chicago IL 1980-1982. Auth, "Let Yourself Be Loved," Paulist Press, 1997. AAPC 1989; APA 1990; Shalem Inst Sprtl Direction Assoc 1994. Phi Beta Kappa Beloit Coll 1975.

BENNETT, Rachel Marybelle (ECR) 201 Glenwood Cir Apt 19e, Monterey CA 93940 **Decaon La Iglesia De San Pablo Seaside CA 1999-** B Carmel CA 1954 d Norman & Mary. AA Monterey Peninsula Coll 1974; BA Sonoma St U 1976; Cert Sonoma St U 1977; BA Sch for Deacons 1996. D 12/2/1996 Bp Richard Lester Shimpfky. NAAD.

BENNETT, R Dudley (Nwk) 16 Warwick Way, Jackson NJ 08527 **Non-par 1976-** B Grand Rapids MI 1928 s Roscoe & Laura. BA Calvin Coll 1950; Army Gnrl Sch 1953; STB Ya Berk 1956; Inst of Advance Pstr Stds 1962; Coll of Preachers 1963; Rutgers The St U of New Jersey 1968. D 6/23/1956 Bp Dudley B McNeil P 1/16/1957 Bp Archie H Crowley. m 5/24/2007 Marcia Bennett c 3. Ch Of The Trsfg Towaco NJ 1976-1977; Dir Corp Secy City Natl Bank Of New Jersey 1973-1988; Headmaster The Orchard Sch W Caldwell NJ 1965-2003; Chapl Rutgers U Newark NJ 1963-1967; P-in-c H Trin Highland NY 1959-1963; P-in-c S Andr's Epis Ch New Paltz NY 1959-1963; Chapl SUNY At New Paltz New Paltz NY 1959-1963; Vic S Paul's Ch Greenville MI 1956-1959. Auth, "Const Of Planet Earth," Authorhouse, 2011; Auth, "Rebirthing The Amer Dream," Authorhouse, 2009; Auth, "Pedagogy of Silence," Authorhouse, 2008; Auth, "Successful Team Bldg," Amacom, 1980; Auth, "Transactional Analysis And The Mgr," Amacom, 1976. Amer Natl Trng 1970-2010. Humanitarian Awd Municipal Cnty City Of Newark 1990.

BENNETT, Robert Avon (Mass) Po Box 380367, Cambridge MA 02238 B Baltimore MD 1933 s Robert & Irene. BA Ken 1954; U of Copenhagen Copenhagen DK 1954; STB GTS 1958; JHU 1963; STM GTS 1966; PhD Harv 1974. D 6/17/1958 P 2/21/1959 Bp Harry Lee Doll. m 8/15/1982 Marceline Malica Donaldson c 3. Int S Barth's Epis Ch Cambridge MA 1986-1988; Chair Inclusive Lang Ctte Epis Ch GC 1982-1985; Int S Cyp's Ch Boston MA 1976-1978; EDS Cambridge MA 1968-1993; Asst S Anne's In The Fields Epis Ch Lincoln MA 1965-1968; Tutor The GTS New York NY 1963-1965; Chapl Morgan St Coll Baltimore MD 1959-1963; Asst S Jas' Epis Ch Baltimore MD 1958-1963. Auth, "The Bk of Zephaniah," *The New Interpreter's Bible Volume VII*, Abingdon Press, 1996; Auth, "Afr," *Oxford Comp to the Bible*, Oxford Press, 1993; Auth, "Black Experience and the Bible," *Afr Amer Rel Stds*, Duke Press, 1989; Auth, "Zephaniah," *The Books of the Bible Volume I*, Scribner's, 1989; Auth, "The Power of Lang in Wrshp," *Theol Today*, 1987; Auth, *An Inclusive Lang Lectionary: Readings For Year C/ Year B/ Year A*, Westminster, 1985; Auth, "Black Episcopalians and the Dio Massachusetts," *The Epis Dio Massachusetts*, Epis Dio Massachusetts, 1984; Auth, "Howard Thurman and the Bible," *God and Human Freedom: A Festschrift in hon of Howard Thurman*, Friends Untd Press, 1983; Auth, "Episcopalians," *Encyclopedia of Black Amer*, McGraw Hill, 1981; Auth, *The Bible for Today's Ch*, Seabury Press, 1979; Auth, "Symposium on Biblic Criticism," *Theol Today*, 1977; Auth, *God's Wk of Liberation: A Journey Through the OT w the Liberation Heroes of Israel*, Morehouse-Barlow, 1976; Auth, "Biblic Theol and Black Theol," *Journ of the Interdenominational Theol*, 1976; Auth, "Freedom Motifs in Psalm 14:53," *Bulletin of the Amer Schools of Oriental Resrch*, 1975; Auth, "Black Episcopalians: A Hist From the Colonial Period to the Present," *The Hist mag of the Prot Epis Ch*, 1974; Auth, "Afr and the Biblic Period," *Harvard Theol Revs*, 1971. Fulbright Awd Danish Govt 1954; AB mcl Ken 1954; Phi Beta Kappa Ken 1953.

BENNETT, Sarah Galloway (Tex) 7002 Rusty Fig Dr, Austin TX 78750 B Shreveport LA 1963 d Edgar & Julia. BA U of Houston 1996; MDiv Epis TS of the SW 1998. D 6/20/1998 Bp Claude Edward Payne P 6/29/1999 Bp Leopoldo Jesus Alard. m 1/12/1985 Gregg P Bennett c 2. Vic S Mart's Epis Ch Copperas

Cove TX 2002-2004; The Great Cmsn Fndt Houston TX 2002-2004; S Paul's Ch Waco TX 1998-2002.

BENNETT, Susan P (Ind) 610 Perry St, Vincennes IN 47591 B Orangeburg SC 1952 d Marion & Mattie. BA U NC 1974; MDiv Sewanee: The U So, TS 2011. D 12/18/2010 P 1/26/2012 Bp J Neil Alexander. c 3. R Dio Indianapolis Indianapolis IN 2013-2016; S Jas Ch Vincennes IN 2012-2013.

BENNETT, Thad (Vt) 17 Lane Dr, Newfane VT 05345 **Consult ECF Inc New York NY 2011-, NDNV Coordntr 2010-2012; Epis Election Consult Epis Ch 2010-; Epis Election Consult Epis Ch 2010-; Fac Credo Inst Inc. Memphis TN 1997-** B New York NY 1952 s Earl & Betty. BA Dart 1976; MDiv GTS 1980. D 6/14/1980 P 1/24/1981 Bp Morgan Porteus. m 5/28/2004 George T Connell. S Lk's Ch Chester VT 2014; Cn Dio Vermont Burlington VT 2013-2014, 2001-2005; Consult SCLM 2010-2012; NDNV Coordntr The ECF Champaign IL 2010-2012, Consult NDNV 2000-2012; R St Mary's In The Mountains Epis Wilmington VT 2001-2010; Cn Dio Los Angeles Los Angeles CA 1995-2001; Int S Mk's Par Altadena CA 1994-1995; Prov VIII San Diego CA 1993-1997; Prog Dir/Exec Dir Prov of the Pacific Los Angeles 1993-1997; Int S Mk's Par Berkeley CA 1992-1993; Joint Cmsn on AIDS367045 Epis Ch GC 1991-1994; Fndr and Pres NEAC 1988-1991; Exec Dir of AIDS Mnstrs Dio Connecticut Meriden CT 1987-1992; P Ch Of The Gd Shpd Hartford CT 1980-1987. Auth, *Fresh Start: A Resource for Cong and Cler in Transition*, DFMS, 2000; Auth, *Being Chr in Age of AIDS*, DFMS, 1995; Auth, *Epis Guide To TAP (Teens for AIDS Prevention)*, DFMS, 1994; Auth, *The Poor Pay More: Food Shopping in Hartford*, 1986.

BENNETT, Virginia Lee (Spr) 1404 Gettysburg Lndg, Saint Charles MO 63303 **Assoc Gr Ch S Louis MO 2015-, 2013-2014** B Des Moines IA 1946 d Clifton & Dorothy. DC Cleveland Chiropractic Coll 1972; AA Missouri Bapt Med Cntr Sch of Nrsng 1981; M.Div./MA systematic Theol Aquinas Inst of Theol 1988; DMin SWTS 1993. D 6/4/1989 P 1/25/1990 Bp William Augustus Jones Jr. c 2. Instr Springfield Sch For Mnstry 2000-2002; R S Andr's Epis Ch Edwardsville IL 1996-2013; Assoc S Mich And All Ang Ch Mssn KS 1994-1995; R All SS Ch Florence SC 1993-1994; Int S Fran Epis Ch Eureka MO 1992-1993; Assoc S Mich & S Geo S Louis MO 1990-1992, D 1989-1990; Cur Ch Of The Gd Shpd S Louis MO 1989-1990; Co-Chair Of BEC Dio Springfield Springfield IL 1997-2002. Auth, "(3 Homilies) Homilies For The Chr People," *Homilies for The Chr People*, Pueblo Pub Co, 1989. M.Div./M.A. (systematic Theol) Aquinas Inst Of Theol 1988. virginia.bennett@gracekirkwood.org

BENNETT, Vivian Rose Kerr (Pa) 934 Overfield RD, Meshoppen PA 18630 B Mount Ephraim NJ 1937 d Hugh & Alice. BA Glassboro St U 1964; Cert Widener U 1977; Cert Trng & Formation for Deacons Dio Pennsylvania 1992. D 2/20/1993 Bp Franklin Delton Turner P 3/25/2001 Bp Paul Victor Marshall. m 3/30/1957 Normand Joseph Bennett c 3. P-in-c S Ptr's Epis Ch Tunkhannock PA 2009, P-in-c 2006-2010, D 1998-2002; P-in-c Prince Of Peace Epis Ch Dallas PA 2002-2005; D Chr Ch Media PA 1995-1998; D S Mary's Epis Ch Philadelphia PA 1993-1995; D Ch Of S Jn The Evang Philadelphia PA 1990-1993. NAAD 1990-2001.

BENNETT, William (Tex) 3711 Hidden Holw, Austin TX 78731 B Birmingham AL 1945 s Clyde & Mildred. BS Portland St U 1975; MDiv CDSP 1982; DD Epis TS of the SW 1997. D 6/27/1992 P 2/1/1993 Bp Maurice Manuel Benitez. m 11/1/1969 Molly Bennett c 1. R S Mk's Ch Austin TX 1997-2007; Provost Epis TS Of The SW Austin TX 1992-1996; VP TS San Anselmo CA 1983-1985; VP CDSP Berkeley CA 1976-1982. Ch Hist Soc Of The Dio Texas 1997.

BENNETT JR, William Doub (NC) Po Box 28024, Raleigh NC 27611 **Assoc R Ch Of The Gd Shpd Raleigh NC 1999-** B Greenville NC 1955 s William & Ruby. BA E Carolina U 1978; MDiv Sewanee: The U So, TS 1994. D 6/24/ 1994 Bp Huntington Williams Jr P 12/1/1994 Bp Harry Woolston Shipps. m 9/8/2001 Jessica Nicole Whaley Kozma. Vic Trin Ch Cochran GA 1996-1999; Vic Chr Epis Ch Cordele GA 1994-1999; S Matt's Epis Ch Fitzgerald GA 1994. Alb Inst; Associated Parishes; Cath Fllshp Of The Epis Ch; Liturg Conf.

✠ BENNISON JR, The Rt Rev Charles Ellsworth (Pa) 279 S 4th St, Philadelphia PA 19106 **Ret Bp of Pennsylvania Dio Pennsylvania Philadelphia PA 2013-, Bp of Pennsylvania 1997-2012** B Minneapolis MN 1943 s Charles & Marjorie. BA Lawr 1965; SWTS SWTS 1966; BD Harvard DS 1968; ThM Harvard DS 1970; MA Claremont TS 1977; Coll of Preachers 1979; STM UTS 1992; EDS 1997. D 9/13/1968 P 7/13/1969 Bp Charles Bennison Sr Con 2/22/1997 for Pa. m 6/17/1967 Joan R Bennison c 2. Dir of Congrl Stds EDS Cambridge MA 1992-1997; Strng Com Cornerstone Proj 1990-1995; Basic Issues Com ATS 1990-1994; R S Lk's Epis Ch Atlanta GA 1988-1992; Fndr/P-in-c S Clare Of Assisi Rancho Cucamonga CA 1986-1988; Pres Dioc Corp 1985-1988; Fndr/P-in-c S Eliz's Chino CA 1984-1986; Bd Trst VIM 1982-1984; Lectr in Homil Claremont TS 1976-1979; R S Mk's Epis Ch Upland CA 1971-1988; Fndr S Mk Sch. Auth, *In Praise of Congregations*, Cowley Press, 1999; Auth, "arts & Revs," *ATR*. mcl Warner U 2012; D.D. EDS 1997. cebennison@verizon.net

BENO, Brian Martin (FdL) 17 Yorkshire Dr, Fond du Lac WI 54935 B Milwaukee WI 1949 s Emil & Hedwig. BA S Fran Sem Coll Milwaukee WI 1971; MDiv S Fran Sem 1976; CAS SWTS 2001. Rec 3/22/2005 Bp Russell Edward

Jacobus. m 2/6/2005 Theresa L Hansen. Dn St Paul's Epis Cathd Fond Du Lac WI 2008-2016; R S Mk's Ch Waupaca WI 2005-2008; R Roman Archdiocese of Milwaukee WI 1976-2004.

BENOIT JOSEPH, Arlette Dierdre (At) 294 Peyton Rd SW, Atlanta GA 30311 **Asst S Paul's Epis Ch Atlanta GA 2013-** B Trinidad and Tobago 1982 d Arthur & Caroline. BSC Claflin U 2006; MDiv GTS 2013; MDiv The GTS 2013. D 12/15/2012 P 6/22/2013 Bp Robert Christopher Wright. m 12/31/2016 Junior Joseph. Epis Ch Cntr New York NY 2013-2015.

BENSHOFF, Bruce L (Mass) 11 Meadowlark Dr, Middleboro MA 02346 B Ravenna OH 1943 s Robert & Eleanor. BA Kent St U 1966; MDiv Andover Newton TS 1971. D 6/26/1971 Bp John Harris Burt P 6/8/1972 Bp Charles Francis Hall. m 4/12/1965 Joanne R Benshoff c 2. Asst S Jn's Ch Sandwich MA 2004-2013; Co-Mssnr Bristol Cluster No Easton MA 2003-2012; R Ch Of Our Sav Middleboro MA 1981-2003; Vic S Dav's Ch Feeding Hills MA 1975-1981; Asst R S Alb's Epis Ch Annandale VA 1974-1975; Cur S Jn's Ch Portsmouth NH 1971-1974; Dioc Counsel Dio Massachusetts Boston MA 1984-1985; Ecum Cmsn Dio Wstrn Massachusetts Springfield 1977-1981. Hon Citizen Awd Town Of Agawam.

BENSON, David Howard (Mo) 6309 Burnham Cir Apt 323, Inver Grove Heights MN 55076 **Ret 1994-** B New Haven CT 1928 s John & Lillie. Augustana Coll 1948; U Tor 1950; BA U MN 1952; MDiv SWTS 1957. D 6/24/1957 P 2/8/1958 Bp Hamilton Hyde Kellogg. c 3. Asst-Non stipendary Emm Epis Ch S Louis MO 1982-2003; 1982-1984; R S Ptr's Epis Ch S Louis MO 1965-1981; Assoc S Jn The Evang S Paul MN 1961-1965; CE Dept Dio Minnesota Minneapolis MN 1958-1963; Vic Ch Of The Gd Samar Sauk Cntr MN 1957-1961; S Steph's Epis Ch Paynesville MN 1957-1961; Chair of the Epis City Mssn Dio Missouri S Louis MO 1976-1980, Long-R Plnng Com 1972-1975. Auth, "A Field Study of End User Computing," *MIS Quarterly*, 1983. MDiv mcl SWTS 1957; BA mcl U MN 1952.

BENSON, E Heather (CNY) 60 Elm St, Ilion NY 13357 **Long-term Supply P St Dav's Epis Ch Barneveld NY USA 2017-** B Camp LeJeune NC 1944 d Alexander & Claire. BA Washington Coll 1965; MDiv EDS 1976; ThM Trin /U Tor 1987. D 6/12/1976 P 4/25/1978 Bp Lyman Cunningham Ogilby. R Trin Epis Ch Canastota NY 2004-2012; P in Charge S Paul's Ch Utica NY 1999-2004; Vic S Mk's Ch Clark Mills NY 1995-1998; Chapl S Lk Hosp Utica NY 1994-1999; R S Geo's Ch Utica NY 1990-2000; Vic S Ptr's Ch Oriskany NY 1990-1998; Int Paris Cluster Chadwicks NY 1988-1989; Trin Ch Lowville NY 1985-1987; Vic Ch Of The H Comm Lake View NY 1983-1984; Dio Toronto Toronto ON 1980-1982; Serv Angl Ch of Can 1976-1982; COM Dio Cntrl New York Liverpool NY 1993-1995, Int R 1985-1992. SBL 1976. MDiv w dist EDS 1976.

BENSON, George Andrew (Neb) 8800 Holdrege St, Lincoln NE 68505 B Cincinnati OH 1952 s George & Ann. BA S Louis U 1973; MDiv GTS 1976; STM UTS 1977; MBA W Texas A&M U 1982. D 8/22/1976 Bp William Augustus Jones Jr P 2/20/1977 Bp George Leslie Cadigan. m 12/29/1974 Katherine Benson c 1. S Dav Of Wales Epis Ch Lincoln NE 2006-2011; New Life Epis Cluster Seward NE 2003-2005; S Mk's Epis Ch Aberdeen SD 1998-2003; Cmsn On Recon Dio So Dakota Pierre SD 1996-2003, Pres Of Stndg Com 1996-2003, 1995-1998; S Matt's Epis Ch Rapid City SD 1994; S Steph's Ch Blytheville AR 1994, Vic 1986-1994; Calv Epis Ch Osceola AR 1983-1994; Cmsn On Mssn And Mnstry Dio NW Texas Lubbock TX 1980-1983, 1979-1983, Instr In Bible Dept 1979-1982; Vic Epis Ch Of S Geo Canyon TX 1979-1982; Asst S Nich' Epis Ch Midland TX 1978-1979; Cur The Ch Of The Epiph New York NY 1976-1978. Auth, "Will The Byte From The Apple Be More Than We Can Swallow?"; Auth, "Computing & Ethics: Where To Next?". Outstanding Young Men Of Amer.

BENSON, H William (NY) 1 Tongore Kill Rd, Olivebridge NY 12461 **Died 3/26/2017** B Mount Vernon NY 1939 s Harold & Jean. BA CUNY 1961; STB GTS 1965; MLS Pratt Inst 1971. D 6/12/1965 P 12/1/1968 Bp Horace W B Donegan. S Greg's Epis Ch Woodstock NY 2002-2017; Ret 1976-2017; Assoc Ch Of The Ascen New York NY 1967-1976; Cur S Ptr's Epis Ch Peekskill NY 1965-1967.

BENSON, J(ohn) Bradley (Roch) 110 Robie St, Bath NY 14810 **R S Thos' Ch Bath NY 2005-** B 1953 s Gilbert & Gwendolyn. BA U of Wyoming 1975; MFA Syr 1981; MDiv Bex Sem 2001. D 6/1/2002 P 3/1/2003 Bp Jack Marston Mckelvey. m 5/28/2010 Carl Johengen. Asst for Cmncatn and Congrl Dvlpmt Dio Rochester Henrietta 2012-2014, Dist Dn 2012-2014, GC Dep 2010-, Pres Stndg Com 2009-2010, Co-chair Transition Com 2008-2009, Stndg Com 2008-, Stndg Com 2007-, COM 2005-2008; Vic Ch Of The Gd Shpd Savona NY 2010-2013; Cur The Ch Of The Epiph Gates NY 2002-2005.

BENSON, Kathleen (Del) 4830 Kennett Pike Apt 2537, Wilmington DE 19807 **P-in-c Imm Ch Highlands Wilmington DE 2004-** B ChattanoogaTN 1929 d Henry & Kathleen. VTS; BA Van 1951; MEd U of Delaware 1972; MDiv Lancaster TS 1985. D 6/15/1985 Bp William Hawley Clark P 4/1/1986 Bp Quintin Ebenezer Primo Jr. m 4/24/2004 Robert Benson c 3. Int S Lk's Epis Ch Seaford DE 1994-1995; Dio Delaware Wilmington 1986-1988, Stndg Com 1992-1996;

Assoc S Jas Epis Ch Newport Newport DE 1986-1988; Vic S Nich' Epis Ch Newark DE 1985-1993. Delaware Epis Cleric Assoc, EWC.

BENSON, Ricky Lynn (Tex) 1616 Driftwood Ln, Galveston TX 77551 B San Diego CA 1948 s Jack & Bette. BA U of the Incarnate Word 1976; MDiv Sewanee: The U So, TS 1983. D 6/29/1983 Bp Stanley Fillmore Hauser P 1/6/1984 Bp Scott Field Bailey. m 5/6/2006 Susan Walker c 4. S Mk's Epis Ch Richmond TX 2003-2009; S Lk's Epis Hosp Houston TX 2002-2003; Stff Chapl S Lk's Epis Hosp Houston TX 2002-2003; R Gr Ch Galveston TX 1990-2002; Chapl Lamar U Beaumont TX 1988-1990; Assoc R S Steph's Ch Beaumont TX 1988-1990; Dio W Texas San Antonio TX 1985-1988; Chapl San Antonio Coll San Antonio TX 1985-1988; Vic H Comm Epis Ch Yoakum TX 1983-1984; Vic S Jas Ch Hallettsville TX 1983-1984.

BENSON, Thomas (Me) 21 Boyd St. Apt. 1406, Bangor ME 04401 **Died 11/13/2016** B Winthrop MA 1924 s John & Beatrice. D 6/3/1978 Bp Frederick Barton Wolf. m 6/5/1948 Marteile Butler c 2. D S Jn's Ch Bangor ME 1978-2010.

BENSON, Virginia (Los) 1432 Engracia Ave, Torrance CA 90501 **All SS Ch Vista CA 2014-** B Orange CA 1951 d James & Lillian. BS U CA 1974; MS California St U 1979; ETSBH 1991; MDiv Ya Berk 1993. D 6/12/1993 Bp Chester Lovelle Talton P 1/15/1994 Bp Frederick Houk Borsch. S Jn's Ch Fallbrook CA 2013-2014; Epis Communities & Serv Pasadena CA 2012-2013; S Andr's Par Torrance CA 2007-2012; Asst S Anselm Of Cbury Par Garden Grove CA 2005-2007; Asst S Wilfrid Of York Epis Ch Huntington Bch CA 2004-2005; P-in-c St Andr Epis Ch Irvine CA 2000-2004; Int Chr Ch Par Redondo Bch CA 1999-2000; Assoc R St Cross Epis Ch Hermosa Bch CA 1994-1999; The Par Ch Of S Lk Long Bch CA 1993-1994.

BENTER JR, Harry William (SwFla) 1010 American Eagle Blvd, Apt 348, Sun City Center FL 33573 B Duluth MN 1935 s Harry & Leona. BS Bradley U 1961; MS GW 1971; MDiv EDS 1989. D 6/10/1989 P 1/13/1990 Bp Edward Cole Chalfant. m 1/17/2004 Jacqualine H Hodous c 4. Asst S Jn The Div Epis Ch Sun City Cntr FL 2006-2011, Asst 1996-2005; Asst R St Johns Epis Ch Tampa FL 2000-2002; Assoc Trin-St Jn's Ch Hewlett NY 1989-1996.

BENTLEY JR, John R (Tex) 15410 Misty Forest Ct., Houston TX 77068 B Houston TX 1942 s John & Elizabeth. U So 1966; BA U of No Texas 1972; MDiv VTS 1975. D 6/16/1975 Bp Scott Field Bailey P 6/15/1976 Bp John Elbridge Hines. m 12/11/1982 Pamela Bentley c 3. P Assoc for Pstr Care S Mart's Epis Ch Houston TX 2008-2012, Dir of Pstr Care 2004-2008, 1975-1977; R S Dunst's Epis Ch Houston TX 1984-2004; Dn of the Cntrl Convoc Dio Texas Houston TX 1980-1984; R S Ptr's Epis Ch Brenham TX 1977-1984.

BENTLEY, Stephen Richard (SJ) 316 N El Dorado St, Stockton CA 95202 B Los Angeles, CA 1954 s Nicholas & Dolores. AA Pasadena 1975; AA Pasadena City Coll 1975; Cert. of completion The Sch for Deacons 2011. D 7/20/2013 Bp Chester Lovelle Talton. c 1.

BENTLEY, Susan Bliss Emmons (SwVa) 4515 Delray St Nw, Roanoke VA 24012 **R S Jas Ch Roanoke VA 2000-** B Chicago IL 1953 d Olin & Mary. BA Hollins U 1975; MDiv SWTS 1990. D 6/25/1990 P 4/10/1991 Bp A(rthur) Heath Light. m 8/10/1985 Michael L Bentley c 3. Gr Ch Radford VA 1999-2000, P-in-c 1999-2000, D 1990-1991; P-in-c S Thos Epis Christiansbrg VA 1998-1999; P-in-c S Ptr's Epis Ch Callaway VA 1997-1998; Assoc S Lk's Ch Evanston IL 1991-1996. DOK 2002.

BENTLEY-SHELTON, Elizabeth Michael (Wyo) 2511 Coffeen Ave, Sheridan WY 82801 **D S Ptr's Epis Ch Sheridan WY 2003-** B Long Beach CA 1935 d James & Fanny. BA Carleton Coll 1957. D 10/8/2003 Bp Bruce Caldwell. m 5/26/1959 Richard Lee Shelton c 3.

BENTRUP, Alan Dale (Tex) **S Mary's Epis Ch Cypress TX 2016-** B Fort Worth - Texas 1979 s Dale & Margaret. Bachelor of Arts U Texas at Arlington 2003; Mstr in Div VTS 2016. D 6/25/2016 Bp C Andrew Doyle. m 6/18/2005 Elizabeth C Crawford c 2. revdalan@stmaryscypress.org

BENVENUTI, Anne Cecilia (Chi) 4945 S Dorchester Ave, Chicago IL 60615 B Fullerton CA 1953 d Benjamin & Corinne. PhD U CA Los Angeles 1992. D 4/26/2009 Bp Jeff Lee P 11/22/2009 Bp Victor Alfonso Scantlebury. m 6/22/2008 Elizabeth Jayne Louise Hill. Ch Of S Paul And The Redeem Chicago IL 2010.

BENZ, Charles Frederick (NC) 4118 Pin Oak Dr, Durham NC 27707 **1981-** B Chicago IL 1948 s Ralph & Charlotte. BA U of Arizona 1971; BA U Trin Bristol UK 1977; MDiv CDSP 1978. D 9/7/1978 Bp Robert Bracewell Appleyard P 7/1/1979 Bp Robert Hume Cochrane. m 9/9/1974 Mary Hays c 1. P-in-c S Alb's Ch Littleton NC 1993-2001; P-in-c S Anna's Ch Littleton NC 1993-2001; Dio San Diego San Diego CA 1987-1988; Asst Emm Epis Ch Mercer Island WA 1978-1981. Aafrc 1980; CFCE 2010; Nahd 1996; Npga 1987; Nsfre 1988; Sopgrt. Cert Profsnl Coach Intl Coach Acad 2010; Cert Planned Giving Exec 1988; Cert Fund Raising Exec 1987.

BERARD, Jeffrey Jerome (Mil) 1622 Quincy Ave, Racine WI 53405 **Horizon Yth Mnstry Racine WI 1991-** B Racine WI 1956 s Francis & Vera. Cert Nash 1990. D 4/13/1991 Bp Roger John White. m 5/31/1986 Lynda Kay Berard c 2. D S Mich's Epis Ch Racine WI 1991-2002; Chapl S Lk's Hosp Racine WI 1989-2001.

BERBERICH, Gloria Carroll Kennedy (Va) 673 Evergreen Ave, Charlottesville VA 22902 **Ret 2000-** B Fredericksburg VA 1928 d Carroll & Eula. BS Geo Mason U 1973; MDiv VTS 1976. D 5/22/1976 Bp John Alfred Baden P 5/21/1977 Bp Robert Bruce Hall. m 12/15/1951 John Valentine Berberich. Asst Chr Epis Ch Charlottesvlle VA 1985-2000; Vic S Lk's Simeon Charlottesville VA 1982-2000; Chapl USI Windam Crozet VA 1981-1982.

BERCOVICI, Hillary Rea (NY) 8 Sound Shore Dr Ste 130, Greenwich CT 06830 **Sr Fell Trin Inst 2004-** B New York NY 1954 s Ralph & Genevieve. BA Trin 1977; MDiv TESM 1983; PhD Un Grad Sch Cincinnati OH 1986. D 6/2/1984 P 12/18/1984 Bp Alden Moinet Hathaway. m 6/16/1979 Priscilla Williams Willams c 2. Sr Fell Trin Inst Greenwich CT 2004-2016; R S Mary's Ch Of Scarborough Briarcliff NY 1989-2004; R S Mary's Epis Ch Pocomoke City MD 1986-1989; Asst Ch Of The Sav Ambridge AL 1984-1985.

BERDAHL, Peder (Ind) 5 Oak Brook Club Dr. Apr P2S, Oak Brook IL 60523 B Fresno CA 1943 s Arthur & Mildred. BA S Olaf Coll 1965; MDiv SWTS 1973. D 6/17/1973 P 12/16/1973 Bp Edward Clark Turner. m 12/8/1981 Betty Berdahl c 2. Cn to the Ordnry Dio Indianapolis Indianapolis IN 2005-2008, Dn of the SE Deanry 1994-1998; R S Paul's Ch Columbus IN 1988-2005; R S Andrews Ch Derby KS 1983-1988; Vic S Lk's Ch Wamego KS 1980-1983; S Mk's Ch Blue Rapids KS 1980-1983; 1979-1980; Assoc S Mk's Epis Ch Glen Ellyn IL 1975-1979; Vic Calv Ch Yates Cntr KS 1973-1975; S Tim's Ch Iola KS 1973-1975; Pres of Stndg Com Dio Kansas Topeka KS 1984-1987.

BERENDS, April L (ETenn) St. Mark's Episcopal Church, 2618 N. Hackett Ave., Milwaukee WI 53211 **Chr Ch - Epis Chattanooga TN 2016-** B 1976 DAS Ya Berk; MDiv Ya Berk 2002. D 12/22/2004 Bp James Hamilton Ottley P 7/22/2005 Bp Leo Frade. m 6/8/2002 Michael Andrew Bunting c 2. S Mk's Ch Milwaukee WI 2008-2014; Cathd of St Ptr & St Paul Washington DC 2005-2008; Mem, Stndg Com Dio Milwaukee Milwaukee WI 2010-2014, Mem, COM 2009-2012. aprilberends@yahoo.com

BERESFORD, David Charles (Pa) 145 W Springfield Rd, Springfield PA 19064 **Ch Of The Redeem Springfield PA 2016-** B Auckland New Zealand 1956 s Charles & June. Trans 10/1/2016 as Priest Bp Daniel Gutierrez. m 1/16/2016 Ruth Lawson c 2.

BERESFORD, Ruth Lawson (Del) P. O. Box 3510, Greenville, 507 East Buck Road, Wilmington DE 19807 **R Chr Ch Christiana Hundred Wilmington DE 2007-; Dep, 79th GC Dio Delaware Wilmington 2016-, Dep, 78th GC 2014-2016, Pres of Stndg Com 2013-2015, Mem, Stndg Com 2015, Dep, 77th GC 2011-2014** B Newark NJ 1961 d Peter & Mary. BA Indiana U 1983; MDiv VTS 1989. D 6/23/1989 P 5/1/1990 Bp Edward Witker Jones. m 1/16/2016 David Charles Beresford c 2. R S Ptr's Ch Glenside PA 1993-2007; Asst S Paul's Ch Philadelphia PA 1989-1993; Secy Joint Nom. Co. for Election of the PB 2012-2015; Dep, GC Dio Pennsylvania Philadelphia PA 2004-2006, Dn, Montgomery Dnry 2000-2006. Contrib, "Meditations," *Walking w God Day by Day*, FMP, 2011; Contrib, "Meditations," *Wisdom found: Stories of Wmn Transfigured by Faith*, FMP, 2011. rberesford@christchurchde.org

BERG, Dustin David (O) Saint Mark's Church, 515 48th St NW, Canton OH 44709 **P-in-c S Mk's Ch Canton OH 2011-** B Bemidji MN 1980 s Palmer & Constance. BA Concordia Coll 2002; Dip Ya Berk 2007; MDiv Yale DS 2007. D 12/11/2006 P 6/29/2007 Bp Michael Smith. m 1/30/2010 Heather L Hill c 2. Supply Ch Of S Thos Berea OH 2010; Supply Gr Epis Ch Willoughby OH 2009-2010; Campus Chapl S Aid's Epis Ch Boulder CO 2007-2009.

BERG, James Christopher (Mich) 642 Woodcreek Dr, Waterford MI 48327 B Brooklyn NY 1948 s James & Margaret. BA Knox Coll 1970; MDiv GTS 1975; DMin GTF 1998; MA U of Detroit Mercy 2004. D 6/5/1976 Bp Jonathan Goodhue Sherman P 12/7/1976 Bp William Arthur Dimmick. m 5/24/1980 Elizabeth Berg c 1. Dn of Oakland Convoc Dio Michigan Detroit MI 1990-1994; R S Andr's Ch Waterford MI 1987-2008; Emm Ch Detroit MI 1980-1985; Chr Ch Calumet Larium MI 1976-1980; Dio Nthrn Michigan Marquette MI 1976-1980. Outstanding Adj Fac for 2007 Oakland Cmnty Coll 2007; Allen S Whitney Educ Awd U MI 1985; Phi Beta Kappa Knox Coll 1970.

BERGE JR SSF, William Clark (Oly) P.O. Box 399, Mount Sinai NY 11766 **Franciscans San Francisco CA 2015-; Min Gnrl SSF 2007-** B 1958 s William & Eleanor. BA Whitman Coll 1980; MDiv GTS 1984. D 6/30/1984 Bp Robert Hume Cochrane P 9/1/1985 Bp The Bishop Of Polynesia. Chapl Stony Brook U 2000-2005; Clnc Dir Cmnty Fam Plnng Coun 1992-1995; Chapl Annie Wright Sch 1985-1989; Asst Chr Ch Tacoma WA 1985-1989; D Ch Of S Mary The Vrgn New York NY 1984-1985.

BERGEN, Franklyn Joseph (Az) 4076 N Hidden Cove Pl, Tucson AZ 85749 **Assoc Ch Of S Matt Tucson AZ 2010-; Dio Arizona Phoenix AZ 2006-; Assoc St Andr's Epis Ch 2005-; Epis Cmnty Serv Bd Dio Arizona Phoenix AZ 2006-** B Waterbury CT 1935 s Franklyn & Doris. Fairfield U 1955; BA Boston Coll 1959; MA Boston Coll 1960; MDiv Weston Jesuit TS 1967; MA U CA 1970. Rec 12/8/1994 as Priest Bp Chester Lovelle Talton. m 9/2/1989 Patricia Ann Chase. All SS Epis Ch Las Vegas NV 2002-2004; Int Ch Of The H Apos Hilo HI 2000-2001; Assoc Ch Of The Apos Oro Vlly AZ 1999-2005; Int S Steph's Ch Sierra Vista AZ 1998-1999; Chapl Handmaker Hospice 1997-1999; Assoc Gr St Pauls Epis Ch Tucson AZ 1995-1998; Asst S Mk's Par Altadena CA 1994-1995; Serv RC Ch 1966-1972.

BERGER, Fred (Ia) 25111 Valley Drive, Pleasant Valley IA 52767 B Davenport IA 1934 s Fred & Alice. JD U of Iowa 1957. D 11/16/1996 Bp Chris Christopher Epting. m 12/19/1956 Shirley Ann Vollmer. D Trin Cathd Davenport IA 1996-2009.

BERGER, Jere Schindel (Alb) Montvert Road #1125, Middletown Springs VT 05757 **Supply P All SS Ch N Granville NY 1995-** B Philadelphia PA 1931 s Carl & Mary. BA Ob 1953; MDiv EDS 1956; STM UTS 1965; MFA Carnegie Mellon U 1969; PhD Carnegie Mellon U 1973. D 6/30/1956 Bp Joseph Gillespie Armstrong P 1/19/1957 Bp Oliver J Hart. m 8/28/1954 Josephine N Berger c 5. S Paul's Ch Salem NY 1989-1996; R S Paul's Ch Salem NY 1988-1995; Trin Ch Rutland VT 1987; P-in-c S Thos' Epis Ch Brandon VT 1986-1987; P-in-c Zion Ch Manchestr Ctr VT 1985-1986; Vic Gr Ch Mt Washington PA 1967-1969; Vic S Tim's Ch Mc Kees Rock PA 1967-1969; P-in-c Trin Ch Swarthmore PA 1966-1967; 1964-1966; Assoc Gr Ch Amherst MA 1959-1964; Chapl U of Massachusetts 1959-1964; Vic Ch Of The H Sprt Plymouth NH 1957-1959; Cur S Ptr's Ch Glenside PA 1956-1957. Auth, "The Wheelbarrow (play produced at Martinique Theatre, NY," *NY)*, 1968; Auth, "selected poems," *The Massachusetts Revs*, 1964; Auth, "selected poems," *The U of Massachusetts Literary mag*, 1962. Dorset Players 1996; Green Mtn Gld 1976-1990; Middletown Sprg Hist Soc 1986; Vermont Symphony Orchestra Chorus 1997. Danforth Fllshp Danforth Fndt 1965; Hon Mention Jennie Tane Awd for poetry 1964.

BERGER, Martha Branson (Mil) 1616 Martha Washington Dr, Wauwatosa WI 53213 **P-in-c S Fran Ch Menomonee Falls WI 2011-** B Beatrice NE 1953 d Vernon & Jessie. BA U of Kansas 1975; BSN U of Kansas 1977; MN U of Kansas 1983; MDiv Nash 1996. D 5/18/1996 P 11/23/1996 Bp Roger John White. m 7/16/1983 William Langston Berger c 2. Int S Lk's Ch Racine WI 2006-2009; P-in-c S Anskar's Epis Ch Hartland WI 2004-2006; Int S Dav Of Wales Ch New Berlin WI 2002-2003; Int S Mart's Ch Milwaukee WI 2001-2002; Int S Jas Ch W Bend WI 1999-2001; Int S Jn In The Wilderness Elkhorn WI 1998-1999; Int S Thos Of Cbury Ch Greendale WI 1997-1998.

BERGERON, Mary Lee (ETenn) 6823 Sheffield Dr, Knoxville TN 37909 B Huntsville TX 1940 d Lawrence & Verna. BS Louisiana Coll 1963; MS Case Wstrn Reserve U 1965; Sewanee: The U So, TS 2004. D 6/28/1998 Bp Robert Gould Tharp P 6/12/2004 Bp Charles Glenn VonRosenberg. m 9/7/1968 Paul H Bergeron c 3. P Assoc Ch Of The Ascen Knoxville TN 2008-2012; Cn S Jn's Epis Cathd Knoxville TN 2004-2007, D 1999-2004. Ord of S Lk.

BERGH JR, Palmer A (Ida) 180 kings court, mountain home ID 83647 B Watertown SD 1934 s Palmer & Bertina. BS So Dakota St U 1957. D 1/29/1994 P 10/1/1994 Bp John Stuart Thornton. m 8/5/1955 Roberta J Hunter c 4. Cn S Jas Ch Mtn Hm ID 1994-2006.

BERGIE, Patricia Ann (Wyo) Po Box 903, Fort Washakie WY 82514 **D Our Fr's Hse Lander WY 1996-** B WY 1946 d Enos & Barbara. Cert Cntrl Bus Coll 1965. D 7/21/1996 Bp Bob Gordon Jones. m 8/27/1969 Frank Bergie c 1.

BERGIN, Joseph Alphonsus (CNY) 6312 N Manlius Rd, Kirkville NY 13082 **P Chr Epis Ch Jordan NY 2010-** B Dublin IE 1935 s Patrick & Mary. Cert Dominican Hse of Stds 1961; BA U Coll Cork Cork Ie 1964. Rec 10/15/1991 as Priest Bp William Louis Stevens. m 6/9/1990 Loreen M Bergin. S Mk The Evang Syracuse NY 1996-2007; Serv Angl Ch Of Can 1992-1996; Serv RC Ch 1960-1987.

BERGMANN, J(ohn) Stephen (O) 577 Wetherby Terrace Dr, Ballwin MO 63021 **Died 11/7/2015** B Saint Louis MO 1942 s John & Dorthea. BA Drury U 1964; BD Bex Sem 1968; U of Indianapolis and Chr Theol Seminar 1990. D 6/22/1968 Bp George Leslie Cadigan P 12/22/1968 Bp Roger W Blanchard. m 2/24/1990 Nancy Ellen Bergmann c 2. Asst S Mart's Ch Ellisville MO 2012-2014; Asst S Ptr's Epis Ch S Louis MO 2006-2012; Int S Matt's Par Of Jamestown Jamestown RI 2004-2006; Int S Mary's Ch Portsmouth RI 2003-2004; Int S Chris's By-The River Gates Mills OH 2001-2003; R S Paul's Epis Ch Medina OH 1995-2001; R Calv Epis Ch Sedalia MO 1991-1995; Int S Jn's Ch Washington IN 1991; R S Tim's Ch Indianapolis IN 1986-1990; R Chr Ch Cape Girardeau MO 1970-1986; Cur S Alb's Epis Ch Of Bexley Columbus OH 1968-1970; Trst Bex Sem Columbus OH 2002-2015; Trst Bex Sem 2000-2015; Stwdshp Consult Dio Ohio Cleveland 1996-2002; Dioc Coun Dio W Missouri Kansas City MO 1992-1995, Chair Camp Bd 1991-1995; Stndg Com Dio Missouri S Louis MO 1977-1980.

BERGMANN, William Carl (WMass) 85 E Main St, Ayer MA 01432 **R Ch Of The Gd Shpd 2005-; BEC Dio Wstrn Massachusetts Springfield 2002-, 1994-2003; P-in-c The Chap Of All SS Leominster MA 2002-; Ch Of The Gd Shpd Clinton MA 1994-** B Syracuse NY 1952 s Donald & Isabel. BS Loyola U 1974; MDiv Nash 1979; MA Sem of The Immac Concep Huntington NY 1991; ThD Bos 2001. D 6/9/1979 Bp Quintin Ebenezer Primo Jr P 12/8/1979 Bp James Winchester Montgomery. m 10/10/1998 Maria M Bergmann c 5. Assoc S Mich's-On-The-Heights Worcester MA 2000-2002; Int Chr Ch Fitchburg MA 1999-2000; Trin Epis Ch Ware MA 1996-1998; S Mk's Ch Leominster MA 1994-1996; R Trin Ch Northport NY 1988-1992; R S Ann's Ch Woodstock IL 1982-1988; Epis Chapl Niu 1979-1982; Cur S Paul's Ch Dekalb IL

1979-1982; Cmsn On Higher Educ Dio Chicago Chicago IL 1983-1988. AAR, SBL 1993-2000; Napts 1994; Soc Of S Jn The Evang 1977. Mdiv cl Nash 1979.

BERGMANS, Susan Estelle (Cal) 1320 Addison St Apt C130, Berkeley CA 94702 **Chapl Hlth Mnstry 1997-** B Berkeley CA 1944 d Hubert & Lois. RN Highland Sch of Nrsng Oakland CA 1967; BS H Names Coll 1970; MDiv CD-SP 1975. D 6/28/1975 Bp George Richard Millard P 1/5/1977 Bp Chauncie Kilmer Myers. Exec Dir The Parsonage San Francisco CA 1991-1992; Chapl Wmn's Mnstry 1986-1997; Int The Epis Ch Of The Gd Shpd Berkeley CA 1984-1985, Asst 1979-1983; Dep Vic S Clare's Epis Ch Pleasanton CA 1976-1977; Assoc S Anselm's Epis Ch Lafayette CA 1975-1976. Integrity 1977.

BERGNER, Mario J (Spr) 149 Asbury St, South Hamilton MA 01982 **Assoc Chr Ch of Hamilton and Wenham So Hamilton MA 2006-** B Thet Ford Mines QC CA 1958 s Richard & Jinette. BFA U of Wisconsin 1985; MDiv TESM 1995. D 2/15/2001 P 2/17/2001 Bp Keith Lynn Ackerman. m 5/11/1996 Nancy Pearce c 5. Assoc R Chr Ch S Hamilton MA 2006-2009; D S Andr's Ch Peoria IL 2001-2006. "Setting Love In Ord," *Bk*, Baker Bk Hse, 1995.

BERGNER, Robert Allen (Ct) 200 Seabury Dr, Bloomfield CT 06002 **Seabury Ret Cmnty Bloomfield CT 2014-, 2014-** B France 1961 s Lawrence & Marilyn. BA Mid 1995; BTh McGill U 2007; MDiv Montreal Dioc Theol Coll 2008. Trans 11/25/2014 Bp Ian Theodore Douglas. m 12/12/1992 Pamela Newell.

BERGSTROM, Carl Edwin (Mass) 2914 109 Street ST NW APPT 1211, Edmonton T6J 7E8 Canada **Died 6/3/2016** B Medford MA 1929 s Carl & Ellen. BA Butler U 1952; MDiv VTS 1958. D 5/31/1958 Bp William A Lawrence P 12/16/1958 Bp Robert McConnell Hatch. m 9/17/1988 Patricia Marjorie Bergstrom c 7. Serv Angl Ch of Can Edmonton AB 1999-2016; Supply P S Lk's Epis Ch Malden MA 1994-1997; Ret 1993-2016; Chf of Chapl Serv Veterans' Admin Med Cntr Boston MA 1981-1993; Chapl Veterans' Admin Med Cntr Boston MA 1964-1993; Vic Gr Ch Oxford MA 1963-1964; Chapl S Vinc's Hosp Worcester MA 1960-1964; Vic S Thos Epis Ch Auburn MA 1959-1964; Chapl Chld's Cntr Laurel MD 1958-2016.

BERGSTROM, Fiona Mabel (NC) 11 Fleet St, Umina Beach NSW NC 02257 Australia B Letchworth Hertfordshire UK 1942 d Robert & Agnes. BA Coll of New Jersey 1992; MDiv Duke DS 1995; CAS Sewanee: The U So, TS 1995. D 3/28/1987 Bp Roger John White P 12/21/1995 Bp Robert Carroll Johnson Jr. m 6/9/1965 Lars Anders Bergstrom c 2. S Cyp's Ch Oxford NC 2000-2006; Vic S Steph's Ch Oxford NC 2000-2006; The Epis Ch of Oxford Oxford NC 2000-2006; Asst R All SS' Epis Ch Concord NC 1996-2000; S Mk's Epis Ch Raleigh NC 1995-1996; Admin for COM Dio New Jersey Trenton NJ 1990-1991; Chapl Mercer Cnty Cmnty Coll Trenton NJ 1989-1991; D S Matt's Ch Pennington NJ 1988-1992; D S Ptr's Ch Milwaukee WI 1987-1988; Rel Cmnty Liaison Sojourner Truth Hse Milwaukee WI 1986-1988. EWC 1990-2006; Ord of S Lk 1998-2000.

BERGSTROM, Jeremy W (Dal) St John's Church, 1 W Macon St, Savannah GA 31401 B Mt Clemens MI 1977 s William & Pamela. Angl Study Cert Nash Theo Sem; MTh S Vladimir's Sem 2008; PhD U of Durham 2012. D 8/31/2013 P 3/18/2014 Bp Edward Stuart Little II. m 6/9/2001 Jacqueline L Maik c 3. S Jn's Ch Savannah GA 2013-2015.

BERITELA, Gerry (CNY) 360 S Collingwood Ave, Syracuse NY 13206 **Vic Ch Of The Sav Syracuse NY 2002-; Vic Emm Ch E Syracuse NY 2002-; Adj Asst. Prof Le Moyne Coll Syracuse NY 1994-; Liturg & Mus Cmsn Mem Dio Cntrl New York Liverpool NY 2007-, Mnstry Grant Com 2004-2008, Jubilee Grant Com, Chair 2001-2004, Prog Com, Chair 1999-2003** B Rochester NY 1954 s Frederick & Clara. BA S Jn Fisher Coll 1977; MDiv Nash 1983; MPhil Syr 2001; PhD Syr 2009. D 7/22/1983 Bp William Harvey Wolfrum P 1/28/1984 Bp Addison Hosea. Assoc St Paul's Syracuse Syracuse NY 2000-2001; Vic Gr Ch Mex NY 1994-2000; Int Emm Ch Adams NY 1993-1994; Zion Ch Pierrepont Manor NY 1993-1994; Int S Matt's Epis Ch Liverpool NY 1992-1993; Supply Dio Montana Helena MT 1988-1991; Vic S Paul's Ch Hamilton MT 1988; S Steph's Epis Ch Stevensville MT 1988; Asst Majestic Mountains Mnstry Sheridan MT 1986-1988; Int S Steph's Epis Ch Aurora CO 1985-1986; Asst Calv Epis Ch Ashland KY 1983-1985. Auth, "Supergirls and Mild-Mannered Men: Gender Trouble in Metropolis," *The Amazing Transforming Superhero! Essays on the Revs of Characters in Comic Books, Film and Television.*, McFarland, 2007. Ba scl S Jn Fisher Coll 1977.

BERK, Dennis Bryan Alban (Be) 27 Grace Avenue, Schuylkill Haven PA 17972 B Akron OH 1965 s Clarence & Olga. BA Wheaton Coll 1986; MDiv U Tor CA 1990; DMin Lancaster TS 1998. Trans 11/1/1995 Bp James Michael Mark Dyer. c 1. Int R Gr Epis Ch Kingston PA 2008-2009; Int Chr Memi Epis Ch Danville PA 2007-2008; Int S Andr's Epis Ch Lewisburg PA 2006-2007; Exec Coun Appointees New York NY 2003-2006; S Jn's Epis Ch Lancaster PA 2001-2003; R S Alb's Epis Ch Reading PA 1996-2001; Hon. Assoc. S Mary's Epis Ch Reading PA 1994-1996. Auth, "Martyrs, SS and Sinners," Morris Pub, 2009; Auth, "Sprtl Sightseeing," Morris Pub, 2007; Auth, "Zambian Journ," Morris Pub, 2007; Auth, "Embracing Inclusion," Morris Pub, 1999; Auth, "Comprehensiveness in Anglicanism," UMI Press, 1998. Fraternity of Friends of St. Albans Abbey 2007.

BERKHOUSE, Casey Stephen (WTex) 343 N Getty St, Uvalde TX 78801 **S Jn's Epis Ch Sonora TX 2017-** B Tyler TX 1964 s Richard & Nancy. BS Texas St U 1987; MS Texas St U 1991; MDiv The TS 2015. D 12/28/2014 Bp Gary Richard Lillibridge P 7/7/2015 Bp David Mitchell Reed. m 7/5/1986 Kelli Michelle Price c 2. S Phil's Ch Uvalde TX 2015-2017.

BERKLEY, John Clayton Ashton (NI) 26824 County Road 4, Elkhart IN 46514 B Elkhart IN 1964 s Arthur & Elizabeth. Computer Sci/Sophomore Indiana U So Bend; Dioc Loc Formation Prog Nthrn Indiana TS. D 4/4/2014 Bp Edward Stuart Little II. m 7/31/1993 Sheryl JoAnn Berkley.

BERKOWE, Kathleen Hawkins (Ct) 16 Truesdale Dr, Croton On Hudson NY 10520 **P-in-c S Mk's Ch New Britain CT 2016-** B Milwaukee WI 1951 d Robert. AB Harv 1973; JD Bos Sch of Law 1976; MDiv GTS 2010. D 3/13/2010 P 9/25/2010 Bp Mark Sean Sisk. c 2. Asst to the R S Jn's Ch Stamford CT 2010-2016.

BERKTOLD, Brenda Clare (Ore) 170 Brookside Dr, Eugene OR 97405 B Birmingham Warwickshire UK 1935 d John & Clara. BS Minnesota St U Moorhead 1979; STB Universite de Leuven Leuven Belgium 1981. D 12/27/1982 Bp Matthew Paul Bigliardi. m 7/20/1974 Ted Berktold c 3. Chapl Serenity Ln Treatment Cntr 1990-2009; Dn - Cntr for the Diac Dio Oregon Portland OR 1990-2000; Asst to the Par S Mary's Epis Ch Eugene OR 1990-2000. ESMA 1988-2004; NAAD 1982-2009.

BERKTOLD, Ted (Ore) 170 Brookside Dr, Eugene OR 97405 B Lake City MN 1946 s Engelbert & Margaret. BA S Marys U MN 1967; BD EDS 1971; STM UTS 1972. D 6/30/1971 P 6/7/1972 Bp Philip Frederick McNairy. m 7/20/1974 Brenda Clare Berktold c 3. S Mary's Epis Ch Eugene OR 2001-2010, R 1982-2000; Asst Cn H Trin Cathd Brussels - Dio Europe Belgium 1979-1981; The Amer Cathd of the H Trin Paris 75008 1979-1981; S Jn's Ch Moorhead MN 1974-1979; R S Lk's Ch Detroit Lakes MN 1974-1979; Dio Minnesota Minneapolis MN 1972-1979. ESMHE, 1982-2009; Ord of S Lk 1982-2009.

BERLENBACH, Betty Lorraine (Vt) 1961 Plains Rd., Perkinsville VT 05151 B Huntington NY 1944 d Joseph & Elizabeth. BA Binghamton U 1966; MDiv PrTS 1983. D 6/11/1988 Bp George Phelps Mellick Belshaw P 4/15/1989 Bp Vincent King Pettit. m 8/27/1966 John Berlenbach c 2. Geth Ch Proctorsville VT 1995-2004; The Epis Ch Of The H Comm Fair Haven NJ 1990-1995; Gr Ch Pemberton NJ 1988-1989; Asst S Dav's Ch Cranbury NJ 1982-1987. Auth, "Sharing Our Vision & Story," *Designs For CE.*

BERLENBACH, Kirk Thomas (Pa) 6429 Sherwood Rd, Philadelphia PA 19151 **R S Tim's Ch Roxborough Philadelphia PA 2003-** B Philadelphia PA 1969 s Thomas & Prudence. BA Ham 1991; MDiv PrTS 1994; MSW Rutgers The St U of New Jersey 1995. D 5/9/1998 P 1/19/1999 Bp Joe Doss. m 12/12/1992 Rebekah Ariaantje Sassi c 2. Asst S Alb's Ch Newtown Sq PA 1999-2003; Chapl Vitas Hospice 1998-1999; Stndg Com Dio Pennsylvania Philadelphia PA 2016-2017, Stndg Com 2013-2015, Bdgt Com, Chair 2012-2015, Fin Com, Chair 2012-, Com on Fin and Property, Chair 2010-2012, Fin Revs Com 2010-2012, Dep to GC 2010-, Prog Bdgt Com, Chair 2008-2010, Dioc Coun 2004-2010.

BERLIN II, George Albert (Colo) 3155 Kendall St, Wheat Ridge CO 80214 B Denver CO 1948 s George & Avis. BA U of Nthrn Colorado 1970; LTh Epis TS in Kentucky 1973. Trans 1/15/1979 Bp William Carl Frey. m 6/3/2000 Sarah Aline Berlin c 3. R Ch Of S Phil And S Jas Denver CO 2000-2017; S Thos Epis Ch Denver CO 1995-1997; Assoc Chr Epis Ch Denver CO 1988-1992; Chr Epis Ch Denver CO 1987-1990; All SS' Epis Sch Vicksburg MS 1986-1987; Epis Ch Of S Jn The Bapt Breckenridge CO 1984-1986; 1979-1982; Chapl Colorado Sch Mines 1977-1978; Cur Epiph Epis Ch Denver CO 1976-1977; R S Paul's Ft Chipewyan Alta CO 1973-1976.

BERLIN, Sarah Aline (Colo) 3155 Kendall St, Wheat Ridge CO 80214 **S Phil and S Jas hurch Denver CO 2002-** B Denver CO 1948 d Leon & Hester. BA Coll of the Rockies 1973; MA Regis 1987. D 7/26/1987 Bp Paul Victor Marshall P 5/25/1994 Bp William Jerry Winterrowd. m 6/3/2000 George Albert Berlin c 2. S Jos's Ch Lakewood CO 2007-2008; Ch Of S Phil And S Jas Denver CO 2006; R Ch Of S Jn Chrys Golden CO 2002-2005; S Jn's Cathd Denver CO 1990-2002. Auth, "Contemplative Compassion," *Renovare,* Renovare, 2009; Auth, "Lectio Divina as a Tool For Discernment," *Sewanee Theol Revs,* Sewanee Theol Revs, 2000; Auth, "Caring Mnstry: A Contemplative Approach to Pstr Care," *Continuum,* Continuum, 1999; Auth, "Pstr Care & Centering Pryr," *Sewanee Theol Revs,* Sewanee Theol Revs, 1996. AIDS Interfaith Ntwk 1990-1994.

BERMAN, **Elizabeth Sievert** (Mass) 6 Heritage Dr, Lexington MA 02420 **Cn for Congregations Dio Massachusetts Boston MA 2011-** B Huron SD 1964 d Richard & Ruth. BA Harv 1986; MEd Harv 1992; MDiv EDS 1998. D 6/2/2001 Bp Barbara Clementine Harris P 6/8/2002 Bp M(Arvil) Thomas Shaw. m 8/18/1991 Mark Elliot Berman c 2. -- -- 2011-2004; -- -- 2011-2000; P-in-c Ch Of The Adv Medfield MA 2008-2011; Int Emm Epis Ch Wakefield MA 2006-2008; Actg Chapl Harvard DS Cambridge MA 2004-2005; Asst S Eliz's Ch Sudbury MA 2001-2003; Dir of Admssns and Fin Aid EDS Cambridge MA 1998-2000.

BERNACCHI, Jacqueline A (Minn) 1730 Clifton Pl Ste 201, Minneapolis MN 55403 **Dio Minnesota Minneapolis MN 2013-** B 1951 D 2/9/2001 P 9/7/2001 Bp Andrew Fairfield. Trin Epis Ch Watertown SD 2011-2013; Dio No Dakota Fargo ND 2001-2009; R All SS Ch Minot ND 2001-2007.

BERNACKI, James Bernard (NC) P.O. Box 657, Albemarle NC 28002 **R Chr Ch Albemarle NC 2003-** B Buffalo NY 1950 s John & Lottie. BA Canisius Coll 1975; EdM SUNY 1977; MDiv Chr the King Sem 1987; Cert SWTS 1990; DMin SWTS 2002. Rec 6/29/1990 Bp David Charles Bowman. m 9/9/1988 Sandra L Bernacki c 2. Vic Gr Ch Ravenswood WV 1997-2003; Mssnr River Bend Cluster Ravenswood WV 1997-2003; S Jn's Ripley WV 1997-2003; R Chr Ch Point Pleasat WV 1994-2003; R S Matt's Ch Buffalo NY 1991-1994; Serv RC Ch 1978-1988.

BERNAL, Jose Juan (RG) 635 N Story Rd, Irving TX 75061 **S Chris's Epis Ch El Paso TX 2015-** B MX 1961 s Ernesto & Florentina. MDiv S Josephs Sem MX 1989; MA FST Gtu Berkeley CA 1995; CAS CDSP 2003. D 6/5/2004 P 6/4/2005 Bp William Edwin Swing. m 5/22/1993 Rosario Hernandez c 3. R S Mary's Epis Ch And Sch Irving TX 2008-2015; S Lk's Epis Ch Dallas TX 2007-2008; Dio California San Francisco CA 2005-2007.

BERNARD, Michael Allen (Kan) 305 Old Colony Ct, North Newton KS 67117 **Asst S Matt's Epis Ch Newton KS 2003-; Asst H Trin 1981-** B Winslow AZ 1945 s Bennett & Emma. D 11/8/1981 P 5/1/1982 Bp Richard Mitchell Trelease Jr. m 6/1/1968 Patricia Austin.

BERNARDEZ JR, Teogenes Kalaw (Nev) 832 N Eastern Ave, Las Vegas NV 89101 B Philippines 1969 s Teogenes & Catherine. Trans 7/3/2008 Bp Dan Thomas Edwards. m 11/20/2004 Clarice Kawi c 2. R S Lk's Epis Ch Las Vegas NV 2009.

BERNARDI, Frank Alan (SJ) 1815 S Teddy St, Visalia CA 93277 **Serving the Dio Egypt/No Afr 2001-** B Merced CA 1970 BA California St U. D 8/18/2001 P 5/24/2003 Bp David Mercer Schofield. m 12/29/1995 Anne Elizabeth Douglas c 3.

BERNHARD, Margaret (Ore) 1180 NW Country Ct, Corvallis OR 97330 **Chapl Samar Vill Corvallis Or 2013-** B Orange NJ 1942 d William & Lorraine. BA Cor 1964; MEd W&M 1982. D 7/10/1990 Bp Robert Louis Ladehoff. m 6/27/1964 Robert Bernhard c 2. Dio Oregon Portland OR 2006-2008, Cmsn on Litugy and Mus 2011-, Chapl, Diac Cntr 1994-2008; The Epis Ch Of The Gd Samar Corvallis OR 2002-2006. CHS 1994. First Place in Sermon Competition Epis Evang Fndt,Inc. 1994.

BERNIER, Daniel L (Mass) PO Box 719, Wareham MA 02571 **R Ch Of The Gd Shpd Wareham MA 2010-** B Sanford ME 1963 s Ronald & Rachel. BA Wadhams Hall Sem Coll 1989; MDiv S Marys Sem and U 1993. Rec 4/9/2005 Bp Vicky Gene Robinson. m 6/1/2001 Leslie A Bernier c 1. Vic Chr Ch Portsmouth NH 2005-2010.

BERNIER, Noe (Hai) **Dio Haiti Port-au-Prince HT 1998-** B 1970 D. m 7/26/2001 Rose Sherly Michel Bernier c 5.

BERNTHAL, Gail Elizabeth (SJ) 519 N Douty St, Hanford CA 93230 B New Rochelle NY 1955 d Joseph & Barbara. MSPA U of Washington 1978; AuD Arizona Sch of Hlth Sciences 2006; Cert of Angl Stds CDSP 2015. D 8/15/2015 P 4/23/2016 Bp David C Rice. m 9/11/1976 Craig Allan Bernthal c 2. ecosoffice1@gmail.com

BERRA, Robert M (Az) St Augustine's Episcopal Church, 1735 S College Ave, Tempe AZ 85281 **ASU Incarn Campus Mnstry Mesa AZ 2015-** B Mobile AL 1983 s Christopher & Karen. BS U of So Alabama 2007; MA Arizona St U 2010; MDiv Ya Berk 2013. D 5/5/2012 P 6/15/2013 Bp Kirk Stevan Smith. m 6/21/2008 Laura C Berra. Dio Arizona Phoenix AZ 2013-2015.

BERRY, Beverly (Pa) 212 W Lancaster Ave, Paoli PA 19301 **Cler Assoc Ch Of The Gd Samar Paoli PA 2006-** B Cadillac MI 1951 d Wilfred & Ella. BS Florida St U 1972; JD Florida St U 1985; MDiv TESM 2006. D 6/4/2006 P 12/10/2006 Bp Samuel Johnson Howard. m 8/21/1971 Michael L Berry.

BERRY JR, Charles (WTex) 1100 Grand Blvd Apt 223, Boerne TX 78006 **Ret 1991-** B Rochester MN 1927 s Charles & Edith. BA Macalester Coll 1951; MDiv Bex Sem 1954; S Georges Coll Jerusalem IL 1977. D 2/21/1954 Bp Stephen E Keeler P 8/8/1954 Bp Hamilton Hyde Kellogg. m 12/27/1950 Zona Berry c 2. Dn of Cntrl Convoc Dio W Texas San Antonio TX 1983-1986, Prov Del 1971-1982; R S Steph's Epis Ch San Antonio TX 1971-1991; Asst S Lk's Epis Ch San Antonio TX 1965-1971; Asst R S Barn On The Desert Scottsdale AZ 1964-1965; Dio Olympia Seattle 1961-1964; Vic S Lk's Ch Sequim WA 1959-1964; S Paul's Epis Ch Port Townsend WA 1959-1964; Chr Epis Ch Grand Rapids MN 1955-1959; The Par of St Paul's Epis Ch Duluth MN 1955-1959; Bp's Coun Dio Minnesota Minneapolis MN 1958-1959.

BERRY JR, Graham Gardner (Chi) 1021 S Orange Grove Blvd, Unit 107, Pasadena CA 91105 **Asst St Mk's Altadena CA 2006-; Asst S Mk's Par Altadena CA 2005-; 1998-** B Riverside CA 1944 s Graham & Cynthia. BS K SU 1979; MS K SU 1980; MDiv SWTS 1983. D 6/10/1983 Bp Arthur Anton Vogel P 1/12/1985 Bp James Winchester Montgomery. m 11/28/1987 Virginia Berry c 2. Vic S Bon Ch Tinley Pk IL 1992-1997; P-in-c Gr Epis Ch New Lenox IL 1991-1992; Vic Ch of the H Name Dolton IL 1987-1991; Trin Epis Ch Lansing

IL 1987-1991; Chr Ch Waukegan IL 1985-1987; D Ch Of The H Apos Wauconda IL 1983-1984.

BERRY, John Emerson (NMich) B Parkersburg WVA 1954 s Myron & Betty. BA Ripon Coll 1976; JD Thos M Cooley Law Sch 1981. D 8/17/2005 P 2/26/2006 Bp James Arthur Kelsey. m 8/19/1978 Scarlet Berry c 4.

BERRY, Mary Helen (Miss) D 6/13/1999 Bp Stephen Hays Jecko P 3/4/2000 Bp Alfred Marble Jr.

BERRYMAN II, Jerome Woods (Colo) 5455 Landmark PL Unit 807, Greenwood Village CO 80111 B Ashland KS 1937 s Jerome & Marjorie. BA U of Kansas 1959; MDiv PrTS 1962; JD U of Tulsa 1969; DMin PrTS 1996. D 7/28/1985 Bp Maurice Manuel Benitez P 12/10/1985 Bp Gordon Taliaferro Charlton. m 6/3/1961 Dorothea Grace Berryman c 2. Dir Cntr For The Theol Of Childhood Houston TX 1994-2007; H Sprt Epis Ch Houston TX 1994-1995; Chr Ch Cathd Houston TX 1985-1994. Auth, "The Sprtl Gdnc of Chld: The Montessori Tradition and Godly Play," Morehouse, 2013; Auth, "The Complete Guide To Godly Play, Volume 8," Morehouse Educ Resources, 2012; Auth, "Tchg Godly Play: How to Mentor the Sprtl Dvlpmt of Chld," Morehouse Educ Resources, 2009; Auth, "Chld and the Theologians," Morehouse, 2009; Auth, "Godly Play: A Way of Rel Educ," HarperSanFrancisco, 1991. ABA (Fam Law); Amer Montessori Soc; Assn Of Professors & Researchers In Rel Educ; Intl Seminar For Rel Educ & Values. D.D. VTS 2010; D.D. The GTS 2009; Nomin Com Natl Philanthropy Day 2007; Kilgore Creati e Mnstry Awd Claremont TS 1997; Vol and Chapl of the Year City of Moses Lake, WA 1992; MA Humanitarian Soc Actionj Awd Intl Christians for Unity and Soc Action 1987.

BERSIN, Ruth Ann Hargrave (Ct) 4 Holmes Rd, Boxford MA 01921 **Ther New Engl Pstr Inst 2005-; Refugee Immigration Mnstry Boston MA 1998-** B LaPorte IN 1939 d Jacob & Rowena. BS Indiana U 1962; MA Colgate Rochester Crozer DS 1965; MA CRDS 1965; MDiv Ya Berk 1982; DMin GTF 1994; PhD GTF 2008. D 6/11/1983 Bp Arthur Edward Walmsley P 5/2/1984 Bp Clarence Nicholas Coleridge. m 7/25/1976 Richard Bersin c 2. Assoc Trin Ch Topsfield MA 2011; Refugee Immigration Mnstry Malden MA 1998-2011; Ther Grtr Lowell Pstr Counslg Cntr 1997-2005; Assoc Gr Epis Ch Lawr MA 1996-1999; Phoenix Cmnty Serv Burke VA 1995-1997; Ch Of The Gd Shpd Burke VA 1994; Interfaith Conf Of Metropltn Wash Dc Washington DC 1992-1993; Tell 1989-1992; Exec Dir Tokyo Engl Life Line 1989-1992; Ascen Ch New Haven CT 1989; Epis Soc Serv Ansonia CT 1983-1989; Coordntr of Refugee Serv Div Epis Soc Serv 1982-1990; Dir Of Cmnty Serv Div Epis Soc Serv 1982-1990; Ecum Cmsn Dio Washington Washington DC 1995-1996; Ecum Cmsn Dio Connecticut Meriden CT 1984-2005. Auth, *Healing Traumatic Memories: A Sprtl Journey (Libr for the 21st Century)*, Peterson, Rodney, Eerdmans, 2002; Auth, *Basic Reading Skills*, 1983; Auth, *Let's Begin*, 1974; Auth, *Engl Through Folk Songs*, 1973. AAWW; AAPC 1992-2007; AEHC 1994-2003; Assn Fundraising Profsnl 1987-2003; IATSC 1994-2003; ISTSS 1995-1998; NSFRF. Humanitarian Awd Boston Theol Inst 2007.

BERTOLOZZI, Michael Alan (Nev) 3625 Marlborough Ave, Las Vegas NV 89110 B Valdosta GA 1953 s Kenneth & Florence. D 9/29/2000 Bp George Nelson Hunt III. m 12/1/1974 C Belinda Bertolozzi.

BERTRAND, Michael Elmore (WTex) 2310 N Stewart Rd, Mission TX 78574 B Homestead AFB FL 1977 s Richard & Charlene. BA U So 2000; MDiv Nash 2005. D 12/29/2004 P 8/7/2005 Bp Charles Edward Jenkins III. m 8/20/2005 Lydia Bertrand c 3. S Jn's Ch McAllen TX 2016; Vic St Ptr & St Paul Ch Mssn TX 2011-2016; Cur St Jas Epis Ch and Sch Alexandria LA 2008-2011; Vic S Eliz's Mssn Collins MS 2006-2008; S Steph's Ch Columbia MS 2006-2008; Cur S Paul's Ch New Orleans LA 2005; Dioc Coun Dio Wstrn Louisiana Alexandria LA 2009-2011.

BESCHTA, Gerald Thomas (WNC) 175 Mimosa Way, Hendersonville NC 28739 **COM Dio Wstrn No Carolina Asheville NC 2007-** B Los Angeles CA 1940 s George & Edith. BS USC 1963. D 11/23/2002 Bp Bob Johnson. m 5/2/1987 Joyce Marie Beschta c 2.

BESCHTA, Joyce Marie (WNC) 65 Mimosa Way, Hendersonville NC 28739 **D Ch Of S Jn In The Wilderness Flat Rock NC 2006-; D S Jn in the Wilderness Flat Rock NC 2006-** B Roanoke VA 1945 d Edgar & Cora. GW; BS MWC 1984. D 1/28/2006 Bp Porter Taylor. m 5/2/1987 Gerald Thomas Beschta c 2.

BESENBRUCH, Peter Ray (Haw) 1679 California Ave, Wahiawa HI 96786 B New York NY 1956 s Max & Elizabeth. BA Carleton Coll 1979; MDiv SWTS 1982; U of Hawaii 1987. D 6/24/1982 P 1/1/1983 Bp Robert Marshall Anderson. m 6/10/1979 Valarie Lynn Naughton. The Epis Ch in Hawaii Honolulu HI 2012-2016; Supply Cler S Matt's Epis Ch Waimanalo HI 2008-2012; H Cross Kahuku HI 2001-2003; S Lk's Epis Ch Honolulu HI 2001; S Nich Epis Ch Aiea HI 1999-2000; S Geo's Epis Ch Honolulu HI 1997-1998; S Steph's Ch Wahiawa HI 1990-1993, P-in-c 1985-1990; Ch Of The Epiph Honolulu HI 1986; Cur S Greg's Epis Ch Deerfield IL 1982-1984.

BESHEARS, Earl D (SwFla) 331 56th Ave S, St Petersburg FL 33705 B portsmouth, va 1946 s Howard & Lela. BS No Carolina St U 1972; MS No Carolina St U 1974; MDiv VTS 2001. D 5/19/2001 Bp Martin Gough Townsend P 11/17/2001 Bp Charles Lindsay Longest. m 1/13/1968 Lydia Jean Beshears c 1.

Assoc S Mk's Epis Ch Venice FL 2010-2012; R S Paul's Ch Georgetown DE 2002-2010; Chr Ch St Michaels Par S Mich MD 2001-2002; Ch Of The Resurr Alexandria VA 1999-2001.

BESHEER, Kimbrough Allan (Oly) 600 1st Ave Ste 632, Seattle WA 98104 B Kansas City MO 1951 s Norman & Patricia. BA U of Missouri 1978; MDiv EDS 1981; Dip CG Jung Inst 1991. D 6/20/1981 P 5/16/1982 Bp George Nelson Hunt III. c 2. Int Ch Of The H Sprt Vashon WA 2009-2010; Int S Fran Epis Ch Bothell WA 1997-1999; P-in-c Gr Ch Duvall WA 1996-1997; Int S Columba's Epis Ch Kent WA 1995-1996; Emm Epis Ch Mercer Island WA 1994-1995; P-in-c S Geo Epis Ch Maple Vlly WA 1994-1995; Asst Chapl St Andr's Angl Zurich Switzerland 1987-1990; Assoc S Steph's Epis Ch Longview WA 1983-1986; Asst S Aug's Ch Kingston RI 1981-1983; Chapl U of Rhode Island at Kingston Kingston RI 1981-1983. Intl Assn for Analytical Psychol 1991.

BESIER, Bettine Elisabeth (RI) 30 Scotch Cap Rd, Quaker Hill CT 06375 **Vic S Thos' Alton Wood River Jct RI 1997-** B Denver CO 1957 d Rudolph & Ruth. BS U of Connecticut 1979; MA SUNY 1981; MDiv Ya Berk 1988. D 6/10/1989 Bp Arthur Edward Walmsley P 12/15/1989 Bp Clarence Nicholas Coleridge. m 6/7/1986 James Albert Nuttall c 4. DRE Calv Ch Stonington CT 1995-1996; DRE S Jn's Epis Ch Niantic CT 1993-1995; Cur S Mk's Ch Mystic CT 1989-1993.

BESS JR, Walter (Cal) 118 Tamalpais Rd, Fairfax CA 94930 **Dir IHS Mnstrs Fairfax CA 1988-** B Dade County FL 1948 s Walter & Edna. BA New Coll of California 1974; MDiv Nash 1981. D 6/19/1982 P 12/1/1983 Bp William Edwin Swing. m 9/26/1982 Rebecca A Bess. Asst S Columba's Ch Inverness CA 1983-1987; Cur S Lk's Of The Mountains La Crescenta CA 1982-1983.

BESSE, Alden (Mass) 86 Weaver Ln # 4069, Vineyard Haven MA 02568 B Syracuse NY 1924 s Arthur & Eleanor. BA Harv 1948; MDiv VTS 1951. D 6/8/1951 Bp Frederick D Goodwin P 12/11/1951 Bp Noble C Powell. m 10/12/1957 Barbara Besse c 3. Gr Ch Vineyard Haven MA 1990-2003; Dn of Estrn and Sthrn Worcester Deaneries Dio Wstrn Massachusetts Springfield 1985-1988, 1980-1989; R Trin Epis Ch Whitinsville MA 1980-1990; Dn of Estrn Bay Deanry Dio Rhode Island Providence RI 1978-1980, Chair of Com on Extra-Dioc Missions 1975-1980; Ch of the Epiph Rumford RI 1963-1980; St Mich & Gr Ch Rumford RI 1963-1980; Cathd Ch Of S Steph Harrisburg PA 1957-1963; R S Lk's Epis Ch Altoona PA 1957-1963; M-in-c S Lk's Ch Annapolis MD 1951-1957; S Anne's Par Annapolis MD 1951-1956. Auth, "Gd News for You," *Forw Day by Day*, FMP. FWC 1969. Hon Cn of St. Steph's Cathd Epis Dio Cntrl Pennsylvania 1960.

BESSLER, Jeffrey Lee (Ind) B Milwaukee WI 1950 BA Luther Coll. D 6/29/2002 P 7/13/2003 Bp Cate Waynick. m Barry Barry Cramer. S Jas Ch Piqua OH 2014-2016, 2011-2012; Chr Ch Cathd Indianapolis IN 2014, 2014, 2013, 2013, 2006-2007; S Ptr's Ch Lebanon IN 2003-2006.

BESSON JR, Michael Wallace (Tex) 9610 Roarks Psge, Missouri City TX 77459 **Vic St. Cathr Of Sienna Missouri City TX 2010-** B Beaumont TX 1965 s Michael & Carol. BS Lamar U 1990; MDiv Sewanee: The U So, TS 2004. D 6/12/2004 Bp Don Adger Wimberly P 12/15/2004 Bp Rayford Baines High Jr. m 10/26/1991 Eleanor A Besson c 1. R S Jn's Ch La Porte TX 2006-2010; Asst. To R Ch Of The Gd Shpd Tomball TX 2004-2006. Urban T. Holmes Excellence In Preaching U So 2004.

BEST, Steve (Oly) 17421 Ne 139th Pl, Redmond WA 98052 **P/Assoc For Couples And Fam Life S Thos Epis Ch Medina WA 2002-** B Seattle WA 1957 s Irvin & Patricia. BA U of Washington 1980; MDiv PrTS 1984; MS Seattle Pacific U 1987. D 6/28/1997 P 1/13/2007 Bp Vincent Waydell Warner. m 10/28/1989 M Janine Best c 1. D Ch Of The H Cross Redmond WA 1997-2001; Dir/Stff Ther Epis Counslg Serv 1988-1994; COM Dio Olympia Seattle 2005-2008. Tertiary Of The Soc Of S Fran.

BETANCES, Ramon Antonio (At) 925 Whitlock Ave Apt 1308, Marietta GA 30064 **Hisp Mssnr Dio Atlanta Atlanta GA 2007-; Gd Shpd Epis Ch Austell GA 2007-** B Dominican Republic 1961 s Antonio & Andreita. St Thos Santo Domingo. Rec 12/3/2006 Bp J Neil Alexander. m 11/15/2003 Gregoria Betances c 2. S Jude's Ch Marietta GA 2006-2011.

BETANCUR ORTIZ, Ricardo Antonio (Colom) c/o Diocese of Colombia, Cra 6 No. 49-85 Piso 2, Bogota, BDC Colombia **Iglesia Epis En Colombia Bogota 2017-** B 1972 s Ricardo & Ligia. Especialistas en Derecho Administrativo Universidad Militar Nueva Granada; Universidad Nacional De Colombia 2002; Abogado Universidad Nacional De Colombia 2002; Universidad Militar Nueva Granada 2012; Licenciado Estudios Teologicos MINTS 2014; Licenciado Estudios Teologicos Miami Intl Sem 2014. D 7/25/2015 Bp Francisco Jose Duque-Gomez.

BETE, Vincent Songaben (Ia) 204 E. 5th St., Ottumwa IA 52501 **S Anne's By The Fields Ankeny IA 2017-** B Baguio City Philippines 1970 s Robert & Francisca. Trans 6/18/2007 Bp Alan Scarfe. m 6/9/1995 Isabelle Bete c 3. Vic Trin Ch Ottumwa IA 2009-2016; Serv Epis Ch in the Philippines 1993-2007. padi_vincent@hotmail.com

BETENBAUGH, Helen R (CGC) B Morristown, NJ 1943 d Paul & Norma. BMus Westminster Choir Coll 1964; MM Peabody Conservatory of Mus 1967; MDiv SMU Perkins 1993; 2nd Degree Usui Reiki 1996; DMin SMU Perkins

1997; 3rd Degree Usui Reiki 1998; Lic Veriditas 2000; Lic Veriditas 2000. D 6/29/1996 P 6/17/1997 Bp James Monte Stanton. c 2. R S Lk's Ch Marianna FL 2004-2006; R S Alb's Epis Ch Wichita KS 1999-2003; Assoc Epis Ch Of The Ascen Dallas TX 1998-1999; Cur Ch Of The Gd Shpd Dallas TX 1997; DCE The Epis Ch Of The Trsfg Dallas TX 1990-1996. Auth, "My Journey to H Ord," *Spkng Out*, UMAMD, 2012; Auth, "Journeys In Bldg The Ch Of Today," *Ruach*, EWC, 2001; Auth, "Disabil: A Lived Theolgy," *Theol Today*, PrTS, 2000; Co-Auth, "Prayers of Truth and Transformation," *Ch Mus Workshop*, Abingdon Press, 1998; Co-Auth, "Disabling The Lie: Prayers Of Truth And Transformation," *Human Disabil & The Serv Of God*, Abingdon Press, 1997; Auth, "ADA and the Ch: The Moral Case," *A Look Back: The Birth of the Americans w Disabil Act*, The Haworth Press, 1996; Auth, "ADA and the Ch: The Moral Case," *Journ of Rel in Disabil & Rehab*, Haworth Pstr Press, 1996; Auth, "The Ch and Disabil: A Trin of Issues," *Disabil Stds Quarterly*, Brandeis Univ. Press, 1995; Auth, "Not Frederick," *Re-Imagining*, Re-Imagining Cmnty, 1995; Auth, "A Vessel Full Of Hist," *Re-Membering & Re-Imagining*, Re-Imagining Cmnty, 1995; Auth, "Disabil In The Wrld Of The Hebr Scriptures," *Catechist*, Ptr Li, Inc., 1994; Ed, "Prog Bk (232 pgs)," *Natl Conv Guide 1994*, AGO, 1994; Auth, "Transforming The M.D.eity," *A Journ Of Wmn Mnstrs*, ECUSA, 1993; Auth, "A Letter from Leah," *A Letter from Leah*, EWC, Dio Dallas, 1992; Auth, "22 arts 1968-1988," *Var Ch Mus Journ & AGO*, Var, 1968. AGO 1962; AAM 1991; EWC 1991; Integrity 1996; Mensa 1979; No Amer Acad Of Liturg 1999; The Labyrinth Soc 1999. Biographee Who's Who - Madison 2006; Biographee Dictionary of Intl Biography 2004; Biographee Who's Who in the Wrld 2004; Biographee Who's Who in Amer 2003; Biographee Intl Who's Who of Bus and Profsnl Wmn 2000; Biographee Who's Who of Amer Wmn 1997; Graduation Awd in Soc Ethics B'Nai B'rith, Dallas at Perkins, SMU 1993; W. D. Jernett Awd in Homil Perkins, SMU 1993; Who's Who in Mus Intl Who's Who in Mus 1992; Handicapped Profsnl Wmn of the Year Pilot Club & Sears 1988.

BETHANCOURT JR, A Robert (Los) 1145 W Valencia Mesa Dr, Fullerton CA 92833 **R Emm Par Fullerton CA 1983-** B Phoenix AZ 1952 s Arthur & Martha. USAF Acad 1971; BA Arizona St U 1974; MDiv CDSP 1978. D 12/2/1978 P 2/9/1980 Bp John Lester Thompson III. m 8/9/1973 Cynthia H Bethancourt c 2. Assoc St Johns Epis Ch Petaluma CA 1980-1983; S Jn The Evang Ch Chico CA 1979-1980. Auth, "Let the Chld Come," *Mus for Chld's Chap*, Barking Dog Productions, 2001; Auth, "He is the Light," *Praise and Wrshp*, Homecourt Productions, 1993; Auth, "Mr. Noah's Fabulous Floating Zoo," *Chld's Mus*, Homecourt Productions, 1990; Auth, "Emm: God w Us," *Rite II Eucharistic Mus*, Homecourt Productions, 1990. rbethancou@aol.com

BETHEA, Mary (Los) 31641 La Novia Ave, San Juan Capistrano CA 92675 **S Marg's Epis Sch San Juan Capo CA 2010-** B Charleston SC 1982 d James & Linda. BA Pepperdine U 2004; MDiv Fuller CA 2009; NCC Fuller TS 2010. D 6/12/2010 P 1/8/2011 Bp Mary Douglas Glasspool. S Marg Of Scotland Par San Juan Capo CA 2010-2013.

BETHEA, Robert (Oly) 1549 NW 57th St., Seattle WA 98107 **Died 10/30/2015** B Augusta GA 1940 s Robert & Anne. BA Presb Coll 1982; MDiv SWTS 1982. D 8/3/1982 P 8/1/1983 Bp Robert Hume Cochrane. c 4. P-in-c St. Antony of Egypt Silverdale WA 2007-2008; Ch Of The Resurr Bellevue WA 1996-2003; P-in-c S Fran Epis Ch Bothell WA 1984-1996; Asst S Mich And All Ang Ch Issaquah WA 1982-1984.

BETHELL, John Christian (USC) Holy Trinity, 193 Old Greenville Hwy, Clemson SC 29631 B New York NY 1981 s John & Zyhra. BA Excelsior Coll 2013; MDiv GTS 2013; MDiv The GTS 2013. D 6/1/2013 P 2/1/2014 Bp W illiam Andrew Waldo. D H Trin Par Epis Clemson SC 2013-2015; Dio Upper So Carolina Columbia SC 2013-2014; Bp Gravatt Cntr Aiken SC 2013. jbethell@holytrinityclemson.org

BETHELL, Talbot James (Tex) 290 Fall Creek Dr., Oceanside OR 97134 **Ret 2002-** B Redlands CA 1942 s James & Elizabeth. BA U of Redlands 1964; BD CDSP 1967; DD CDSP 2000. D 6/21/1967 P 4/5/1968 Bp George Henry Quarterman. m 10/14/1967 Anne Maxwell Bethell. Int Ch Of The Gd Shpd Vancouver WA 2006-2008; Int S Mich And All Ang Ch Lihue HI 2004-2006; R S Dav's Ch Austin TX 1981-2002; R S Dav's Epis Ch Topeka KS 1974-1981; Chapl W Texas St U Canyon TX 1970-1974; Vic S Jn's Epis Ch Odessa TX 1967-1970; S Mths Ch Andrews TX 1967-1970. Associated Parishes 1974-1990; Downtown Epis Cler Of The New So 1991-2002; Urban-Surban Cler Conference 1997-2002.

BETIT, John D (LI) 5 Pleasant St, Sutton MA 01590 **Chr And H Trin Ch Westport CT 2017-** B Pittsfield MA 1967 Rec 8/11/2002 Bp Gordon Scruton. m 1/20/2002 Dianna L Betit c 3. Cn to the Ordnry Dio Long Island Garden City NY 2010-2016; S Jn's Epis Ch Sutton MA 2002-2010. johndbetit@gmail.com

BETSINGER, Vicki Lynn (Oly) 280 E Wheelright St, Allyn WA 98524 B Key West FL 1946 d Charles & Lucille. AA Olympic Coll 1966; MGMT Cert U of Washington 1997; AA Dioc - Sanctioned Loc Curric Prog 2015. D 4/10/2015 P 10/13/2015 Bp Gregory Harold Rickel. m 9/23/1995 Barry Alan Betsinger c 1.

BETTACCHI, Karen (Mass) 6 Garfield St, Lexington MA 02421 **Died 3/22/2017** B Washington DC 1943 d Howard & Alice. BA Greenville Coll 1965; MS Loyola Coll 1977; MDiv EDS 1992. D 5/30/1992 P 5/30/1993 Bp David Elliot Johnson. m 4/4/1970 Robert John Bettacchi c 2. S Mich's Epis Ch Holliston MA 2004; R S Lk's And S Marg's Ch Allston MA 1996-2001; Asst R The Ch Of Our Redeem Lexington MA 1993-1996; D S Mary's Epis Ch Boston MA 1992-1993. Massachusetts Epis Cleric Assn 1997.

BETTINGER, Robert Louis (Cal) 3940 Park Blvd Apt 911, San Diego CA 92103 **Ret 1988-** B Springfield MA 1928 s Jesse & Florence. BA Hobart and Wm Smith Colleges 1952; Ya Berk 1955; MS Sthrn Connecticut St U 1970; PhD Saybrook U San Francisco CA 1975. D 6/11/1955 Bp William A Lawrence P 12/21/1955 Bp Henry Hean Daniels. c 4. Int St Paul's/San Pablo Epis Ch Salinas CA 1988; P Epis Ch of St Jn the Bapt Aptos Aptos CA 1984-1987; P S Mths Epis Ch San Ramon CA 1982-1984; P S Barth's Epis Ch Livermore CA 1982; Asstg P S Aid's Ch San Francisco CA 1975-1982; Chapl Campus Mnstry Bridgeport CT 1965-1969; P S Andr's Ch Madison WI 1962-1965; Cur Chr Ch Westerly RI 1961-1962; Chapl Beloit Coll 1960; R H Trin Epis Ch Sulphur LA 1957-1959; P in charge Geth Ch Manhattan MT 1956-1957; S Jas Ch Bozeman MT 1956-1957.

BETTS III, A(Lbert) Raymond (SO) 5810 Mccray Ct, Cincinnati OH 45224 **Died 1/13/2016** B Cincinnati OH 1925 s Albert & Lucille. BA Ya 1948; EDS 1955; MA U Cinc 1972. D 6/15/1955 P 12/1/1955 Bp Henry W Hobson. m 5/11/1985 Mary McClain c 3. Non-par 1991-1992; S Dav Vandalia OH 1989-1990; S Andr's Epis Ch Elyria OH 1988; The Par Of Gd Shpd Epis Ch Wailuku HI 1987-1988; S Andr's Ch Dayton OH 1986-1987; S Alb Epis Ch Cleveland OH 1985-1986; Chr Ch - Glendale Cincinnati OH 1984-1985; S Lk's Epis Ch Idaho Falls ID 1983-1984; R Gr Ch Cincinnati OH 1966-1983; R S Paul's Ch Chillicothe OH 1960-1966; R Chr Ch Xenia OH 1955-1960.

BETTS, Ian Randolph (NY) 6515 Palisade Ave Apt 201, West New York NJ 07093 **D Ch Of The Trsfg New York NY 2010-** B Brockville ON CA 1960 s John & Annie. NY D Formation Prog 1998; BS Concordia Coll Bronxville NY 2008. D 5/16/1998 Bp Richard Frank Grein. Assoc Account Spec, Med Trust The CPG New York NY 2007-2013; D Cathd Of St Jn The Div New York NY 2002-2010; Asst to Congrl Dvlpmt Grp Dio New York New York NY 2002-2007, Conv Plnng Com 2017-, Commisson on Mnstry 2002-; D Ch Of The Gd Shpd New York NY 1998-2002.

BETTS, Robert Hamilton (Pa) 1126 Foulkeways, Gwynedd PA 19436 B Kansas City MO 1938 s Lindley & Alice. PrTS; BA U of Missouri 1960; MDiv EDS 1965; PrTS 1973; MA Washington U 1977; MSW Washington U 1980. D 6/19/1965 P 1/12/1966 Bp George Leslie Cadigan. m 7/12/1975 Susan B Betts c 4. Int All SS Ch Norristown PA 2009-2010; Exec Dir Epis Cmnty Serv Dio Pennsylvania Philadelphia PA 1991-2003; Int S Jn's Ch No Haven CT 1988-1989; Int Gr Ch Old Saybrook CT 1987-1988; Exec Dir Epis Soc Serv Dio Connecticut Meriden CT 1980-1987; S Matt's Epis Ch Warson Woods Kirkwood MO 1977-1979; Asst S Tim's Epis Ch S Louis MO 1975-1977; Vic S Barn Ch Moberly MO 1974-1975; Ex. Dir. Ecum Team MHE U of Missour at Columbia Columbia MO 1974-1975; Chapl/Instr Lindenwood Coll S Chas MO 1968-1974; R Trin Ch S Chas MO 1968-1974; Cur Gr Ch Salem MA 1966-1968; Cur S Mich & S Geo S Louis MO 1965-1966. Epis Cmnty Serv, USA 2000; Urban Cacsus 1980-1999.

BETTY, Claude William (NwT) 2200 S Jefferson St, Perryton TX 79070 **Died 5/19/2017** B Alva OK 1938 s Gerald & Mary. BA Texas Tech U 1960; MD U of Texas SW Med Cntr 1964. D 6/8/2013 P 12/17/2013 Bp James Scott Mayer. m 1/9/1965 Mary Dale Betty c 4.

BETZ, David Emanuel (NwPa) D 5/7/2017 Bp Sean Walter Rowe.

BETZ, Nancy Elizabeth (CNY) 412 Hugunin St, Clayton NY 13624 **P-in-c S Lk's Ch Remington VA 2011-** B Amsterdam NY 1944 d James & Sylvia. AAS Big Bend Cmnty Coll 1976; BS SUNY 1987; MDiv Bex Sem 1994. D 6/18/1994 P Bp William George Burrill P 12/21/1994 Bp Arthur Williams Jr. c 3. P Chr Epis Ch Brandy Sta VA 2011-2012; Chr Ch Clayton NY 1997-2010; R St Jn's Ch Cape Vinc NY 1997-2010; R S Paul's Epis Ch Put In Bay OH 1994-1997.

BETZ-SHANK, Erin L (NwPa) **Vic Trin Epis Ch New Castle PA 2016-** D 6/7/2014 P 1/31/2015 Bp Sean Walter Rowe.

BEUKMAN, Christian Arnold (Mass) 12 Quincy Ave, Quincy MA 02169 **D Epiph Par Walpole MA 2012-; Pstr Mnstrs Mgr Linden Ponds HIngham Mass 2004-** B 1956 s Cornelis & Adriana. MDiv Harvard DS 1983; DMin Andover Newton TS 1996. D 6/6/2009 Bp M(Arvil) Thomas Shaw. m 10/17/1982 Lucy Joan Sollogub c 2. D Chr Ch Quincy MA 2009-2012.

BEVANS, Bruce Sinclair (WVa) PO Box P, Moundsville WV 26041 **P-in-c Trin Ch Moundsville WV 2011-; Chapl/Bd Dir Reynolds Memi Hosp Glen Dale WV 2011-** B Cambridge MA 1953 s William & Natalie. BA Geo Mason U 1989; MDiv VTS 1996; Cert Chesterfield Cnty Police Acad VA 2006. D 6/15/1996 P 1/17/1997 Bp Peter J Lee. m 12/18/1999 Marjorie Salling Bevans c 3. P-in-c S Jn's Ch Petersburg VA 2007-2011; Police Off Hopewell Police Dept 2003-2013; R S Jn's Ch Hopewell VA 2003-2007; R Manakin Epis Ch Midlothian VA 2000-2003; R Calv Ch Bath Par Mc Kenney VA 1998-2000; Ch of the Gd Shpd Mc Kenney VA 1998-2000; Asst S Andr's Ch Burke VA 1996-1998. Meritorious Serv Medal Us AF 1993; Outstanding Achievement In Philos Geo Mason U 1989; Ba w dist Geo Mason U 1989.

BEVANS, Marjorie Salling (WVa) 903 Charles St, Parkersburg WV 26101 **R The Memi Ch Of The Gd Shpd Parkersburg WV 2010-** B Nassawadox VA 1960 d Everett & Ruthann. BA U of Virginia 1987; MDiv Nash 2000. D 6/3/2000 P 1/28/2001 Bp Donald Purple Hart. m 12/18/1999 Bruce Sinclair Bevans. S Andr's Epis Ch Lawrenceville VA 2010; Dn Dio Sthrn Virginia Newport News VA 2006-2009, Exec Bd 2005-2008; Int S Paul's Ch Petersburg VA 2005-2009; Int S Mk's Ch Richmond VA 2004-2005; Asst S Mich's Ch Richmond VA 2001-2004; Asst R Merchants Hope Epis Ch Prince Geo No Prince Geo VA 2000-2001; S Jn's Ch Chester VA 2000-2001.

BEVENS, Myrna Eloise (Colo) 46 N Albion St, Colorado Springs CO 80911 B Colorado Springs CO 1942 d Edger & Evelyn. S Thos Sem; TESM; BA Wstrn St Coll of Colorado 1964; MDiv Chr Gospel Intl 1971. D 10/18/1985 P 6/13/1990 Bp William Harvey Wolfrum. S Andr's Ch Manitou Sprg CO 1989-2007; Dio Colorado Denver CO 1987-2007; Ch Of Our Sav Colorado Sprg CO 1986-1988.

BEVERIDGE, Robert Hanna (CNY) 1416 34th Ave, Seattle WA 98122 **Died 9/2/2016** B Richmond VA 1932 s George & Charlotte. S Lawr Canton NY; Whitworth U; BA Emory U 1956; MDiv CDSP 1969. D 7/3/1969 Bp Edward McNair P 2/5/1970 Bp Clarence Rupert Haden Jr. m 8/29/1959 Alberta Anne Beveridge c 4. Ret 1995-2016; R Trin Epis Ch Fayetteville NY 1987-1994; Assoc S Geo's Epis Ch Arlington VA 1982-1987; S Barth's Ch Beaverton OR 1980-1981; Chapl USAFR 1972-1988; R S Mk's Epis Ch Moscow ID 1971-1980; Cur Trin Epis Cathd Sacramento CA 1969-1971. EPF 1993; EUC 1983; Fllshp of Recon 1997; Natl Ntwk of Epis Cler Assn 1971.

BEVERIDGE, Robin Lorraine (NY) **D The Epis Ch Of Chr The King Stone Ridge NY 2009-** B Washington DC 1956 BFA SUNY at New Paltz 1978; AAS Dutchess Cmnty Coll 1984. D 5/14/2005 Bp Mark Sean Sisk. m 7/9/1988 William Beveridge c 3. D S Jn's Ch Cornwall NY 2005-2008.

BEYER, Jeanie Tillotson (Fla) 2872 N. Hannon Hill Dr., Tallahassee FL 32309 **Archd COM Dio Florida 2010-; Archd Dio Florida Jacksonville 2010-; D Gr Mssn Ch Tallahassee FL 2008-; D Gr Mssn Tallahassee FL 2008-; Bd Natl Epis Recovery Bd 2006-** B Kansas City MO 1948 d John & Shirley. BA U of Missouri 1971; W Missouri Sch of Mnstry 1977; MA S Paul TS 2002. D 2/14/1998 Bp John Clark Buchanan. m 1/15/1972 Philip Beyer c 2. D Ch Of The Redeem Kansas City MO 2006-2007; D St. Lk's Epis Hosp Kansas City MO 2005-2006; Dioc Yth Coun 2002-2004; D COM Dio W. Mo. 2000-2006; D All SS Epis Ch Kansas City MO 1998-2005. Assn of Profsnl Chapl 2006; COM 2000-2006; Dioc Yth Coun 2002-2004; Haitian Epis Lrng Proj 1995-2006; NAAD, Gd Samariatn Ca.

BEZILLA, Gregory (NJ) 134 Mercer Street, Princeton NJ 08540 **R H Trin Ch So River NJ 2015-** B Chitose JP 1962 s Robert & Elaine. BA JHU 1984; MA Col 1985; MA Col 1989; MDiv Candler TS Emory U 1998. D 6/2/2001 P 1/19/2002 Bp David Bruce Joslin. m 8/6/1994 Jacqueline E Lapsley c 2. Epis Ch Cntr New York NY 2011; Chapl The Epis Campus Mnstry at Rutgers New Brunswick NJ 2004-2014; Cur S Geo's-By-The-River Rumson NJ 2001-2004; Chapl Capital Hlth System Trenton NJ 1998-2001. therector@holytrinitysr.org

BEZY, Bernard Anthony (Lex) 1407 Gemstone Blvd, Hanahan SC 29410 **Off Of Bsh For ArmdF New York NY 1998-; Chapl US Navy 1998-** B New Albany IN 1959 s Gustave & Esther. BS Indiana U 1983; MDiv Asbury TS 1990. D 12/30/1995 P 6/1/1997 Bp Don Adger Wimberly. m 8/2/1986 Jennifer Lynn Bigler c 3. Asst to R Ch Of The Resurr Nicholasville KY 1996-2000; Ch Of The Ascen Frankfort KY 1996; Chapl Hospice Of Bluegrass Frankfort KY 1994-1998.

BIANCHI, Mary Elizabeth (Nev) 1674 Harper Drive, Carson City NV 89701 **D S Barth's Ch Ely NV 2000-** B Bradley FL 1932 d Benjamin & Retha. RN Orange Memi Sch of Nrsng Orlando FL 1953. D 4/2/2000 Bp John Stuart Thornton. m 9/29/1956 Valentino A Bianchi c 3.

BIBENS, Robert Lee (Okla) 4642 E 57th Pl, Tulsa OK 74135 **All SS Chap Tulsa OK 1993-; D Holland Hall Sch Tulsa OK 1993-** B Kansas City MO 1956 s Robert & Evelyn. BS U of Oklahoma 1978; MA Cntrl St U 1982. D 6/27/1987 Bp Gerald Nicholas Mcallister. m 6/1/1985 Susan Eleanor Bibens c 3. Trin Ch Tulsa OK 1990-1993. Auth, "Yth Mnstry: Simplified (audio)," Indep, 1986; Contributing Auth, "Passion For Tchg".

BICE, Michael Kenneth (Chi) 1244 N Astor St, Chicago IL 60610 **Asst Epis Ch Of The Atone Chicago IL 2011-** B Australia 1938 s Kenneth & Winifred. MD U of Sydney 1963; MDiv GTS 1967. D 5/20/1967 Bp Harvey D Butterfield P 12/16/1967 Bp Horace W B Donegan. Bp Anderson Hse Chicago IL 1975-1977; Asst Navajoland Area Mssn Farmington NM 1975-1977; Chapl, Med Schools Angl Chapl Lon Engl 1972-1975. Fulbright Schlr USA 1964.

BICKERTON, Frances Catherine Baur (NJ) 164 Buttonwood Dr, Fair Haven NJ 07704 **Dir of CPE Overlook Med Cntr 2007-; Assoc Chr Ch Middletown NJ 1984-** B Philadelphia PA 1949 d Robert & Frances. BA Vas 1971; MDiv Pittsburgh TS 1974; DMin Drew U 2006. D 1/18/1975 Bp Robert Bracewell Appleyard P 2/5/1977 Bp Lyman Cunningham Ogilby. m 8/31/1974 Michael W Bickerton c 3. Dir of Pstr Care/CPE Supvsr Cmnty Med Cntr 1992-2003; CPE Supvsr Robert Wood Johnson U Hosp 1985-1991; Asst S Mary's Epis Ch Ardmore PA 1979-1984, Asst 1975-1979; Asst S Elis's Ch Philadelphia PA 1977-1979. "Theodicy and CPE: Exploring the Problem of Suffering through

the Stories of Holocaust Survivors," ProQuest, 2006. ACPE, Inc., Decatur, GA 1982; Assn of Profsnl Chapl 1993-2007. DMin w dist Drew U 2006; MDiv mcl Pittsburgh TS 1974.

BICKFORD, Wayne Elva (HB) 8212 Kelsey Whiteface Rd, Cotton MN 55724 **Non-par 1981-** B Grand Rapids MI 1941 s Hp & Jenny. MDiv. D 6/29/1973 P 4/1/1974 Bp Philip Frederick McNairy. m 1/28/1961 Sandra Bickford. R S Tim's Epis Ch Henderson NV 1979-1981; S Jn's Ch Eveleth MN 1975-1979; R S Paul's Ch Virginia MN 1975-1979; Dio Minnesota Minneapolis MN 1973-1975.

BICKING, David (WVa) 813 Bowling Green Rd, Front Royal VA 22630 B West Chester PA 1942 s Frank & Kathryn. BS Penn 1965; MDiv VTS 1975. D 5/24/1975 Bp Robert Poland Atkinson P 12/1/1975 Bp Wilburn Camrock Campbell. m 8/25/1990 Sara Bicking. P-in-c Mt Zion Epis Ch Hedgesville WV 1990-2003; Vic S Phil's Ch Chas Town WV 1979-1988; Asst R S Jn's Epis Ch Charleston WV 1977-1979; R S Lk's Ch Wheeling WV 1975-1977. westbury106@comcast.net

BICKLEY, Robert James (Mich) Oakwood Common, 16351 Rotunda Dr #311, Grosse Pointe Park MI 48120 **Died 10/23/2016** B Wyandotte MI 1928 s Joseph & Maude. BA U MI 1950; BD EDS 1954; MS Wayne 1980. D 7/10/1954 P 1/1/1955 Bp Richard Stanley Merrill Emrich. c 3. Asst S Andr's Ch Ann Arbor MI 2008-2016; All SS Ch Detroit MI 1991-1993; 1981-2016; S Columba Ch Detroit MI 1962-1981; R S Columba Ch Detroit MI 1961-1981; All SS Ch Brooklyn MI 1957-1960; R Calv and St Geo New York NY 1957-1959; Vic S Geo's Ch Milford MI 1952-1957; Int All SS Detroit MI 2016; Int Gr Ch Detroit MI 2016; Int S Clements Inkster MI 2016; Int S Steph's Wyamdotte MI 2016; Int Trin Ch Farmington Hills MI 2016.

BIDDLE, Blair Charles (Alb) Po Box 1029, Plattsburgh NY 12901 **D S Paul's Ch Keesville NY 1998-** B Philadelphia PA 1943 s C Ralph & Eva. AAS USAF Cmnty Coll; BS SUNY 2001. D 11/18/1995 Bp David Standish Ball. m 10/19/1982 Joella Claire Biddle. D Trin Ch Plattsburgh NY 1995-1998. Diakoneo.

BIDDLE III, Craig (Va) 364 Friar Trl, Annapolis MD 21401 **Ret 1996-** B Philadelphia PA 1931 s Craig & Alice. BA Wms 1953; MDiv VTS 1964; MTh PrTS 1970. D 6/13/1964 P 12/1/1964 Bp Leland Stark. m 4/3/2006 Jane Grissmer c 7. Int Ch Of The Resurr Alexandria VA 1993-1996; Int Trin Ch Upperville VA 1991-1993; S Columba's Ch Washington DC 1987-1995; Impact Inc- Epis Ch Cntr New York NY 1984-1987; Impact-Washington Washington DC 1984-1987; 1983-1990; R S Paul's Ch Richmond VA 1977-1983; R Trin Ch On The Green New Haven CT 1970-1977; R The Ch Of The Annunc Oradell NJ 1966-1970; Cur S Ptr's Ch Morristown NJ 1964-1966. Auth, *Contrib Var Books & mag.*

BIDDY, Eric (Chi) 545 S East Ave, Oak Park IL 60304 **S Chris's Epis Ch Oak Pk IL 2014-** B Marietta GA 1982 s Dana & Judy. BA Lee U 2004; MTS Candler TS 2006; MTS Candler TS Emory U 2006. D 6/28/2014 Bp John Clark Buchanan P 1/13/2015 Bp Jeff Lee. m 7/17/2009 Jacqueline Christina Pingel c 1. ericbiddy@gmail.com

BIDWELL, Mary Almy (NH) 1145 Jerusalem Rd, Bristol VT 05443 **R Jerusalem Gathering E Middlebury VT 1994-** B Bronxville NY 1943 d John & Anne. BA Hollins U 1965; MDiv EDS 1969. D 6/29/1972 Bp Charles Francis Hall P 1/18/1977 Bp Philip Alan Smith. m 7/19/1969 Charles Radley. S Paul's Epis Ch Wells VT 1994-2000; Chapl / Tchr S Paul's Sch Concord NH 1988-1994; Chapl Phil Exeter Acadamy 1985-1988; Chapl Bryant Coll Smithfield RI 1984-1985; Chapl White Mtn Sch Littleton NH 1983-1984; Chapl / Tchr S Paul's Sch Concord NH 1973-1978.

BIDWELL-WAITE, Davidson (Cal) 3641 20th St., San Francisco CA 94110 **D Mssnr to Haiti Dio California 2015-** B Santa Ana CA 1948 s David & Dorothy. BA U CA 1970; MPA U CA 1972; JD Armstrong Colloge Sch of Law 1980; Diac Stds The Sch for Deacons 2006. D 12/1/2007 Bp Marc Handley Andrus. D Trsfg Epis Ch San Mateo CA 2007-2015.

BIEDENHARN III, James P (WTenn) 3245 Central Ave, Memphis TN 38111 **Chr Ch Greenville SC 2017-; Asst S Jn's Epis Ch Memphis TN 2012-** B New Orleans LA 1983 s James & Clare. BA Millsaps Coll 2005; MDiv Candler TS 2008; MDiv Candler TS Emory U 2008. D 6/2/2012 P 1/12/2013 Bp Don Edward Johnson. m 5/24/2008 Louise Chandler Biedenharn c 2. jay@stjohnsmemphis.org

BIEGA, Richard A (WNC) 426 English Rd, Spruce Pine NC 28777 **R Trin Ch Spruce Pine NC 2013-** B Perth Amboy NJ 1947 s Andrew & Helen. BA S Mary Orchard Lake 1968; MDiv SS Cyril and Methodius Sem 1977; Wake Forest U 1982; Cert Epis TS of the SW 1989. Rec 4/29/1989 as Priest Bp John Herbert MacNaughton. m 11/23/1996 Elizabeth A Biega c 5. R H Trin Epis Ch Hot Sprg AR 2007-2013; Int All Souls' Mssn Columbia SC 2006-2007; Dio Upper So Carolina Columbia SC 2006-2007, 1991-1996; S Mich And All Ang' Columbia SC 2004-2006; R All SS Ch Cayce SC 1996-2004; Chapl U of So Carolina at Columbia 1991-1996; S Eliz's Epis Ch Buda TX 1990-1991; R Emm Epis Ch Lockhart TX 1989-1991; Serv RC Ch 1974-1985.

BIEGLER, James Cameron (Dal) 1632 Jensen Dr, Ellison Bay WI 54210 B Elmhurst IL 1950 s John & Jeannette. BA U Chi 1972; MDiv Nash 1975. D 6/14/1975 Bp Quintin Ebenezer Primo Jr P 1/1/1976 Bp James Winchester Montgomery. m 8/7/2004 Linda N Nelson. Fndt Exec S Paul's Par Riverside IL 2010-2012; R The Epis Ch Of The H Nativ Plano TX 1994-2003; Dio Cntrl Florida Orlando FL 1988-1991; R S Paul's Epis Ch New Smyrna Bch FL 1983-1994; Vic S Pat's Epis Ch W Monroe LA 1979-1983; Cur St Jas Epis Ch and Sch Alexandria LA 1977-1979; Cur The Ch Of S Uriel The Archangel Sea Girt NJ 1976-1977.

BIELSKI, Diane Irene (Colo) P O Box 1558, Fraser CO 80442 **D Epis Ch Of S Jn The Bapt Granby CO 2008-** B Passaic NJ 1953 D 11/6/1999 Bp William Jerry Winterrowd. m 1/1/2001 Daniel Bielski.

BIEVER, Robert Ray (Oly) 3310 N Bennett St, Tacoma WA 98407 B Fargo ND 1952 s Milo & Dorothy. BA Minnesota St U Moorhead 1974; MDiv Nash 1979. D 6/24/1979 Bp George T Masuda P 3/24/1980 Bp Emerson Paul Haynes. Vic All SS Ch Tacoma WA 1992-2017; Asst P S Jn's Epis Ch Olympia WA 1986-1987; Vic St Chris's Ch - A Fed Cong Olympia WA 1984-1992; Asst Chr Ch Tacoma WA 1984-1985; Chapl Annie Wright Sch Tacoma WA 1981-1984; Cur S Hilary's Ch Ft Myers FL 1979-1981.

BIFFLE, Robin Lee (Spok) 111 S. Jefferson St., Moscow ID 83843 **R S Mk's Epis Ch Moscow ID 2008-** B Pueblo CO 1951 d Robert & Mary. BA Whitman Coll 1974; MDiv Sewanee: The U So, TS 2008. D 6/1/2008 Bp Charles Franklin Brookhart Jr P 12/13/2008 Bp James E Waggoner Jr. c 1.

BIGELOW, Thomas Seymour (Oly) Box 20489, Seattle WA 98102 **Assoc S Clem's Epis Ch Seattle WA 2007-** B Milwaukee WI 1933 s Chester & Marion. BS USC 1955; MDiv CDSP 1963. D 6/23/1963 P 5/16/1964 Bp C J Kinsolving III. R S Lk's Epis Ch Renton WA 1994-2004; Assoc S Lk's Epis Ch Seattle WA 1968-1970; Vic S Steph's Ch Lubbock TX 1966-1968; Vic S Mk's Epis Ch Pecos TX 1964-1966; S Steph's Epis Ch Ft Stockton TX 1964-1966; Cur Pro Cathd Epis Ch Of S Clem El Paso TX 1963-1964. OSH 1994; OHC 1994.

BIGFORD, Jack Norman (Oly) 520 Scenic Way, Kent WA 98030 **Ret 1987-** B Seattle WA 1922 s Everett & Esther. MS U of Massachusetts; Bp Huston TS 1968. D 10/5/1968 Bp Ivol I Curtis. D /Asst S Jas Epis Ch Kent WA 1968-1987.

BIGGADIKE, Maylin Teresa (Nwk) 398 Shelbourne Ter, Ridgewood NJ 07450 **Chapl Angl Wmn Empowerment New York NY 2008-; Assoc S Eliz's Ch Ridgewood NJ 2000-** B 1948 d Emilio & Graciela. BA U of Massachusetts 1974; MA Boston Coll 1976; MA GTS 1994; MA GTS 1994; PhD UTS 2006. D 5/30/1998 P 10/30/1999 Bp John Shelby Spong. m 8/16/1970 Ernest Biggadike c 3. D's Asst All SS' Epis Ch Glen Rock NJ 1998-2000. "A Chr Soc Ethical Response to Pvrty," *Econ Dvlpmt Through the Eyes of Poor Wmn in Developing Countries*, 2006.

BIGGERS, Helen Hammond (Spok) 4803 W Shawnee Ave, Spokane WA 99208 B Ventura CA 1928 d Stephen & Hattie. AA Huntington Memi Sch of Nrsng 1950. D 12/21/2002 Bp James E Waggoner Jr. m 12/16/1949 Walter David Biggers c 5.

BIGGERS, Jackson Cunningham (Miss) 10100 Hillview Dr Apt 537, Pensacola FL 32514 **Bp Emer Prov Of Cntrl Afr - Dio Nthrn Malawi 2002-; Ret 2001-; Prov Of Cntrl Afr - Dio Nthrn Malawi 1983-** B Corinth MS 1937 s Neal & Sarah. BA U of Mississippi 1960; BD Sewanee: The U So, TS 1963; Sewanee: The U So, TS 2000. D 6/24/1963 Bp John Maury Allin P 4/1/1964 Bp Duncan Montgomery Gray. Bp Prov Of Cntrl Afr - Dio Nthrn Malawi 1995-2001; Dio Mississippi Jackson MS 1995-1997; R The Epis Ch Of The Redeem Biloxi MS 1977-1995, Cur 1970-1971; Ch in the Prov Of The W Indies New York NY 1975-1977; Serv Prov Of The W Indies - Dio Of Nassau And The Bahamas 1975-1977; Chapl To The PBp Epis Ch Cntr New York NY 1974-1975; Serv Prov Of Cntrl Afr - Dio Nthrn Malawi 1972-1974; R S Steph's Epis Ch Indianola MS 1971-1972; Serv Prov Of Cntrl Afr - Dio Nthrn Malawi 1965-1969; Cur S Jas Ch Jackson MS 1963-1965. Cmnty Of S Mary (Assoc); SSC. Bp Emer Dioc Syn, No Malawi 2002; Hon Cn Likoma Cathd Dio Lake Malawi Cntrl Afr 1983.

BIGGS, Carolyn (CFla) 6071 Sabal Hammock Cir, Port Orange FL 32128 **Chr The King Ch Lakeland FL 2015-; R St. Matt's Epis Ch St. Petersburg FL 2006-** B Kansas City KS 1957 d William & Juanita. U of Cntrl Florida 1999; SWTS 2002. D 6/8/2002 P 12/7/2002 Bp John Wadsworth Howe. m 5/10/2005 David L Biggs c 2. S Matt's Ch St Petersburg FL 2006-2010; Asst R Gr Epis Ch Inc Port Orange FL 2002-2006.

BIGGS, John (WMo) 2632 S Wallis Smith Blvd, Springfield MO 65804 B Danville IL 1937 s Harold & Alwilda. BA U of Missouri Kansas City 1959; MDiv Nash 1962. D 4/24/1962 P 11/8/1962 Bp Edward Randolph Welles II. m 8/18/1962 Marcia C Biggs c 3. Dio Fond du Lac Appleton WI 1996-1999; R S Aug's Epis Ch Rhinelander WI 1988-2001; Dioc Coun Dio W Missouri Kansas City MO 1984-1986; R S Jas' Ch Springfield MO 1983-1988; Gr Ch Carthage MO 1978-1983; R S Lk's Ch Ft Madison IA 1973-1978; R The Epis Ch Of The H Trin Belvidere IL 1968-1973; S Jn's Epis Ch Mauston WI 1964-1968; S Mary's Epis Ch Tomah WI 1964-1968. Fllshp of St. Jn; Life Mem Conf Of The Bless Sacr. Bp'S Cross Dio Fond Du Lac 2001; Bp'S Shield Dio W Missouri 1985; Eagle Scout BSA.

BIGLEY, Mark Charles (WTex) Church of the Annunciation, PO Box 106, Luling TX 78648 **Ch Of The Annunc Luling TX 2016-** B Toledo OH 1951 s Charles & Yvonne. BA Bowling Green St U 1973; MDiv VTS 1977; MA Ash-

land TS 1983; MSW Wayne 2005. D 6/25/1977 Bp John Harris Burt P 2/24/1978 Bp Scott Field Bailey. m 3/17/2006 Kathleen J McGinnis c 2. R S Alb's Epis Ch Hixson TN 2011-2016; P-in-c S Paul's Ch Oregon OH 2006-2009; Int All SS Epis Ch Toledo OH 2004-2006; Asst S Alb's Epis Ch Arlington TX 1998-2001; R S Raphael Epis Ch Colorado Sprg CO 1995-1998; Assoc Trin Ch Victoria TX 1993-1995; Vic Calv Ch Menard TX 1992-1993; Trin Ch Jct TX 1992-1993; R Trin Ch Lander WY 1990-1992; Assoc R Ch Of Recon San Antonio TX 1983-1990; R S Thos' Epis Ch Port Clinton OH 1979-1983; Asst S Barth's Ch Corpus Christi TX 1977-1979. Chapl, "Death: The Crumbling Of Our Assumptive Words And Sprtl Growth," *In Intouch Ohio Hospice And Palliative Care Orgnztn*, In Intouch Ohio Hospice And Palliative Care Orgnztn, 2003. Confrater S Greg Abbey.

BILBY, Gary Eugene (NwT) 1501 S Grinnell St, Perryton TX 79070 B 1939 s Carl & Shirley. D 10/29/1999 Bp C Wallis Ohl.

BILLER, Larry Ray (NI) 9064 E Koher Rd S, Syracuse IN 46567 B Goshen IN 1942 s Lowell & Bette. D 6/9/2006 Bp Edward Stuart Little II. m 8/24/1963 Gertrude Biller c 3. P-in-c S Jas' Epis Ch Goshen IN 2008-2014; D All SS Ch Syracuse IN 2006-2014.

BILLINGSLEA, Wendy Ward (Fla) 400 San Juan Dr, Ponte Vedra Beach FL 32082 B Corpus Christi TX 1955 d John & Joy. BA Wells Coll 1978; MDiv Epis TS of the SW 1996. D 6/8/1996 Bp R aymond Stewart Wood Jr P 1/18/1997 Bp Calvin Onderdonk Schofield Jr. m 5/26/1979 Arthur C Billingslea c 3. Chr Epis Ch Ponte Vedra FL 2009-2013; R S Andr's Ch Greensboro NC 2001-2009; Asst S Thos Epis Par Miami FL 1996-2001.

BILLINGSLEY, Michael (Mass) Saint Paul's Episcopal Church, 61 Wood St., Hopkinton MA 01748 **R S Paul's Epis Ch Hopkinton MA 2009-, P-in-res 2005-2013** B Holyoke MA 1947 s George & Georgia. BS USCG Acad 1969; MS Pur 1977; MDiv VTS 1992. D 6/6/1992 P 12/12/1992 Bp Frank Kellogg Allan. m 6/7/1969 Judith Ann Billingsley c 2. R Chr Ch Medway MA 2009-2015, P-in-c 2007-2009; R S Teresa Acworth GA 1996-2005; Asst S Cathr's Epis Ch Marietta GA 1992-1996. Bro Of S Andr 1996-2005; Phillips Brooks Cler 2005.

BILLINGTON, James Hadley (Cal) 1 S El Camino Real, San Mateo CA 94401 B Philadelphia PA 1961 s James & Marjorie. BA Harv 1983; MBA Harv 1987; MDiv EDS 1996. D 6/24/1996 P 2/1/1997 Bp Edward Witker Jones. m 8/29/1992 Julia Ann Billington c 2. S Matt's Epis Ch San Mateo CA 1999-2006; Matt's Ch Bedford NY 1996-1999.

BILLMAN, Daniel Robert (Ind) 8165 Gwinnett Pl., Indianapolis IN 46250 **Affiliate All SS Ch Indianapolis IN 2007-; Ret 2002-; P-in-c S Mths Ch Rushville IN 1987-** B Indianapolis IN 1936 s Vernon & Lena. BS U Cinc 1959. D 6/24/1986 P 5/1/1987 Bp Edward Witker Jones. m 2/21/1959 Muriel Jane Billman.

BILLMAN, Sharon Lynn (Kan) 1738 24000 Rd, Parsons KS 67357 **Vic S Jn's Ch Parsons KS 2005-, D 2002-2003; P-in-c S Jn's Ch Parsons KS 2004-** B Erie KS 1946 d Edward & Irene. AA Labette Cmnty Coll 1986; BA Pittsburg St U 1989; MS Pittsburg St U 1989; Kansas Sch of Mnstry 2001. D 12/21/2002 P 6/22/2003 Bp William Edward Smalley. m 6/4/1966 David Billman c 1.

BILLOW JR, William Pierce (WA) PO Box 242, Barboursville VA 22923 **Chapl S Alb Sch Washington DC 1991-; Trst Epis Chapl At Harvard & Radcliffe Cambridge MA 2013-; Trst Prot Epis Cathd Fndt Washington DC 2011-; Trst Bp Jn T Walker Sch Washington DC 2010-** B Elgin IL 1953 s William & Nancy. BA U of Washington 1976; MDiv VTS 1979. D 6/9/1979 Bp Quintin Ebenezer Primo Jr P 12/1/1979 Bp James Winchester Montgomery. Cathd of St Ptr & St Paul Washington DC 1985-2010; Assoc Chapl S Alb Sch Washington DC 1985-1991; Asst R S Columba's Ch Washington DC 1981-1985; Cur S Mk's Barrington IL 1979-1981. Wm Pierce Billow Jr Chair in Chapl St Albans Sch 2010; Wm Pierce Billow Chair in Chapl St Albans Sch 2010; Wm Pierce Billow Jr Chair in Chapl St Albans Sch 2010.

BILLUPS, Beatrice Moore (Md) 1514 Gordon Cove Dr, Annapolis MD 21403 B Jacksonville FL 1940 d Charles & Beatrice. Villanova U 1989; MDiv GTS 1992. D 6/13/1992 P 5/1/1993 Bp Allen Lyman Bartlett Jr. m 11/30/1963 Frederick H Billups. S Andr The Fisherman Epis Mayo MD 1997-1998; Chr Ch Par Kent Island Stevensville MD 1992-1997; Dioc Com Dio Easton Easton MD 1994-1999.

BIMBI, Jim (Del) 4828 Hogan Dr, Wilmington DE 19808 **R S Jas Ch Wilmington DE 2002-; Stndg Com Dio Delaware Wilmington 2010-, Dioc Coun 2003-2004** B Newark NJ 1951 s Louis & Alice. Monmouth Coll 1971; MDiv Nash 1992. D 6/20/1992 P 12/19/1992 Bp William Jerry Winterrowd. m 1/16/1999 Cynthia A Bimbi c 5. R Ch Of S Ptr The Apos Pueblo CO 1994-2002; Asst R Trin Ch Greeley CO 1992-1994; Cmsn on HIV/AIDS Dio Colorado Denver CO 1994-1996.

BINDER, Donald Drew (Va) 9301 Richmond Hwy, Lorton VA 22079 **Field Educ Advsr VTS 2002-; R Pohick Epis Ch Lorton VA 2001-** B Allentown PA 1962 s Donald & Joy. BS Penn 1984; Cert of Stds S Georges Coll Jerusalem IL 1988; MDiv VTS 1989; Fell ECF 1997; ECF 1997; PhD SMU 1997; Fell VTS 1997; Post-Grad Resrch Fell Tantur Ecum Inst 2013. D 6/12/1989 P 12/16/1989 Bp Calvin Onderdonk Schofield Jr. m 7/6/1985 Christine T Trevorrow c 3.

Prof Dio Dallas Dallas TX 1998-2001; Adj Prof SMU 1996-2000; Asst P S Jn's Epis Ch Dallas TX 1994-2001; Prof Dio SE Florida Miami 1990-1993; Asst to Dn Trin Cathd Miami FL 1989-1993; Mem, Epis Transition Com Dio Virginia Richmond VA 2011-2012, Dn, Reg VI 2007-2011, Chair, Cmsn on Liturg & Mus 2003-2007. Auth, "Ostia," *Encyclopedia of Second Temple Judaism*, T & T Clark, 2017; Auth, "Tabernacle/Temple/Synagogue," *Oxford Encyclopedia of Bible and Theol*, Oxf Press, 2015; Co-Ed, "A City Set on a Hill: Essays in hon of Jas F. Strange," *A City Set on a Hill: Essays in hon of Jas F. Strange*, Border-Stone, 2014; Auth, "The Mystery of the Magdala Stone," *A City Set on a Hill: Essays in hon of Jas F. Strange*, BorderStone, 2014; Auth, "The Synagogue and the Gentiles," *Attitudes to Gentiles in Ancient Judaism and Early Chrsnty*, T & T Clark, 2013; Co-Auth, "The Ancient Synagogue from Its Origins to 200 CE," *The Ancient Synagogue from Its Origins to 200 CE*, Brill, 2008; Auth, "The Origins of the Synagogue: An Evaltn," *The Ancient Synagogue*, Coniectanea Biblica, 2003; Auth, "Into The Temple Courts," *Into The Temple Courts*, SBL, 1999. Assn of Angl Biblic Scholars 1995. ECF Fell ECF 1996; Bell-Woolfall Fllshp VTS 1994; MDiv cl VTS 1989.

BINDER, Thomas Francis (Mil) **D Chr Ch Milwaukee WI 2001-** B Milwaukee WI 1938 s Frank & Elizabeth. D 1/20/2001 Bp Roger John White. m 7/9/1988 Christine Ann Vajoa Fluegel. D S Aid's 2004-2005.

BINFORD, John Edward (Tex) 909 Texas St Unit 1314, Houston TX 77002 **Died 10/4/2015** B Houston TX 1937 s Thomas & Mildred. BS U of Houston 1959; MEd U of Houston 1964; MDiv Epis TS of the SW 1972. D 6/28/1972 Bp Scott Field Bailey P 6/1/1973 Bp James Milton Richardson. m 6/10/1957 Clara Bing Binford. Int S Lk The Evang Houston TX 2008-2015; S Paul's Epis Ch Chattanooga TN 1991-1999; R St Andrews Epis Ch Houston TX 1978-1999; R S Barth's Ch Hempstead TX 1976-1978; Asst S Chris's Ch Houston TX 1974-1976; Asst S Dav's Ch Austin TX 1972-1974.

BINGHAM, Elizabeth Jane (Mich) D 6/10/2017 Bp Wendell Nathaniel Gibbs Jr.

BINGHAM, John Pratt (NCal) 17538 Caminito Balata, San Diego CA 92128 B Los Angeles CA 1945 s Edwin & Anne. BA Willamette U 1967; MDiv VTS 1971; MA Antioch Coll 1979; CG Jung Inst 1980. D 9/11/1971 P 3/18/1972 Bp Francis E I Bloy. m 7/23/1989 Barbara Lynn Dunn c 3. Consult The Epis Dio Nthrn California Sacramento CA 2009-2013; Exec Dir Samar Counslg Cntr of Grtr Sacramento 1994-2001; R S Lk's Epis Ch Monrovia CA 1975-1978; Asst Cathd Ch Of S Paul San Diego CA 1971-1975. Auth, "Hangtown," Bingham Books, 2015; Auth, "God and Dreams," Resource Pub, 2010; Auth, "Inner Treasure," *Reflections on Teachings of Jesus*, Dove Pub, 1989. Authors Gld of Amer 1984. Emer Mem California Assn of Mar and Fam Therapists 2014; Heath Hodgson Awd Heroes in Healthcare 1999.

BINGHAM, Patricia M (Cal) 1 Key Capri 713 East, Treasure Island FL 33706 B Ottawa KS 1941 d John & Dorothy. BA U of Kansas 1963; MDiv CDSP 1985; Appalachian Sch of Law 2001. D 6/8/1985 P 6/7/1986 Bp William Edwin Swing. m 12/21/1961 David A Bingham c 2. Asst P S Lk's Epis Ch Merritt Island FL 1992-1993; Coordntr & Pstr Cbury Retreat And Conf Cntr 1991-1992; Assoc R S Jas Ch Oakland CA 1989-1991; Org And Chrmstr 1979-1988; Vic S Lk's Ch Detroit Lakes MN 1986-1989; Cur S Steph's Epis Ch Orinda CA 1985-1986. Spanish Campo Schlrshp Prov 3/Dio Ca 1990; Provencial Del: Prov VI Dio Minnesota 1988; Preaching Schlrshp Knights Templar Soc 1984.

BINGHAM, Sally Grover (Cal) 7 Laurel St, San Francisco CA 94118 **for the Environ Dio California San Francisco CA 2008-, Cn for the Envioronment 2008-; Pres The Regeneration Proj/Interfaith Power & Light 1995-; Fndr and Pres The Regeneration Proj San Francisco CA 1994-** B San Francisco CA 1941 d Lafayette & Esther. BA U of San Francisco 1989; MDiv CDSP 1994. D 6/7/1997 P 12/6/1997 Bp William Edwin Swing. c 3. Environ Mnstry S Lk's Ch San Francisco CA 1997-1999. Auth, "Love God Heal Earth," *21 Essays*, St. Lynn's Press, 2009; Auth, "Comm w Life," *essay, H Ground*, Sierra Club, 2008; Auth, "Epis Power & Light," *Earth Light mag*, 2002; Auth, "Almighty Power," *Time*, 2001; Auth, "Epis Power & Light," *Yes mag (Winter Ed)*, 2000. Hon Doctorate Ch DS of Pacific 2010; Hon Doctorate H Cross 2010; Hon Doctorate U of So, Sewanee 2008; Climate Protection Awd US Environ Protection Agcy 2007; Energy Globe Awd Energiesparverband 2002; Green Power Ldrshp Awd Dept Of Energy / Cntr For Resource Solutions 2001; Cert Of hon: Sacr Gift To The Planet Wrld Wildlife Fund / Allnce For Rel & Conservation 2000; Ba mcl U Of San Francisco 1989.

BIORNSTAD, Nathan Allan (Los) 122 S California Ave, Monrovia CA 91016 **S Lk's Epis Ch Monrovia CA 2016-; Ch Of The Trsfg Arcadia CA 2015-** B Portland OR 1978 s Greg & Mary. AA Mt Hood Cmnty Coll 1998; BS Portland St U 2001; MDiv Fuller TS 2005. D 6/6/2015 Bp Diane Jardine Bruce P 1/16/2016 Bp Joseph Jon Bruno.

BIPPUS JR, William Lloyd (FdL) 917 Church St, Marinette WI 54143 B Hartford CT 1948 s William & Shirley. BA Br 1971; MA Trin Hartford 1981; MDiv SWTS 1984. D 6/16/1984 Bp William Jackson Cox P 3/30/1985 Bp Gerald Nicholas Mcallister. m 6/15/2017 Robert Edgar Wallace. R S Paul's Ch Marinette WI 1986-2014; Cur S Mich's Epis Ch Norman OK 1984-1986; Pres. COM Dio Fond du Lac Appleton WI 2001-2010, Pres, Stndg Com 1994-1995. SHN, Conf of the Blessed S.

BIRCH, Lucene Kirkland (Fla) 6812 Mapperton Drive, Windermere FL 34786 B Webb AL 1926 d Arthur & Rossie. BA Florida St U 1955; MA Emory U 1958. D 9/13/1998 Bp Stephen Hays Jecko. m 11/21/1992 Donald Birch. D H Comf Epis Ch Tallahassee FL 1998-2010.

BIRCHER, Victor Malcolm (Miss) 102 Edie St, Columbia MS 39429 **Ret 1997-** B Salem MO 1938 s Victor & Ruth. BA Cntrl Methodist U 1960; LTh Sewanee: The U So, TS 1963. D 6/15/1963 Bp George Leslie Cadigan P 12/16/1963 Bp Charles Gresham Marmion. c 2. Vic S Steph's Ch Columbia MS 1980-1997; S Alb's Epis Ch Vicksburg MS 1970-1980; R S Matt's Ch Covington TN 1968-1970; Vic S Paul's Epis Ch Corinth MS 1965-1968; Cur Gr Ch Paducah KY 1963-1965.

BIRD, David John (ECR) 81 North 2 Street, San Jose CA 95113 **Dn Trin Cathd San Jose CA 2003-** B Solihull Warwickshire UK 1946 s John & Winifred. BA S Davids Coll Lampeter Wales 1970; STM GTS 1974; PhD Duquesne U 1987. Trans 9/1/1978 as Priest Bp Alexander D Stewart. m 6/9/1979 Diane Elizabeth Bird c 2. R Gr Ch Washington DC 1989-2003; Cn Theol Dio Pittsburgh Pittsburgh PA 1988-1989; R S Andr's Epis Ch New Kensington PA 1979-1989; Vic Chr Ch Rochdale MA 1978-1979; Assoc Chr And S Steph's Ch New York NY 1977-1978; Chapl and Hd of Dept of Rel Trin Sch New York NY 1973-1978; Serv Ch of Engl 1970-1972. Auth, *Serving Unity*, EDEO-NADEO, 2000; Auth, *Toward a Gd Chr Death*, Morehouse, 1999; Auth, *Assisted Suicide and Euthanasia*, Morehouse, 1997; Auth, *Before You Need Them*, Forw Mvmt, 1995; Auth, *Receiving the Vision*, Liturg Press, 1995. Rotary 1979-1987; Rotary 2012.

BIRD, Edith (Mo) 1325 Margaret St, Cape Girardeau MO 63701 **Chr Ch Cape Girardeau MO 2014-** B Bethesda MD 1961 d John & Mary. BA Harv 1983; Cert Epis TS of the SW 1989; MDiv Weston Jesuit TS 1989. D 6/17/1989 P 5/1/1990 Bp Robert Manning Moody. m 8/10/2016 Steven Essner c 2. Dio W Missouri Kansas City MO 2012-2014; Int S Andr's Ch Rogers AR 2009-2010; S Jas Ch Eureka Spgs AR 2000-2008; S Mart's U Cntr Fayetteville AR 2000-2002; S Paul's Ch Fayetteville AR 1999; P-in-c St Mart of Tours Epis Ch Pryor OK 1998; 1996-1998; Vic S Aid's Epis Ch Tulsa OK 1991-1993; Dio Oklahoma Oklahoma City OK 1989-1993; Cur And Hosp Chapl S Dunst's Ch Tulsa OK 1989-1991. Auth, "Our Disregard For The Earth Is Killing Us," *Epis Life*, 2002; Auth, "Setting Thos Merton On Fire," *Epis New Yorker*, 2000; Auth, "On Either Side Of Forgiveness," *Sojourners*, 1999. edie.bird@att.net

BIRD IV, Edward T (Chi) 306 S Prospect Ave, Park Ridge IL 60068 **S Paul's Dekalb IL 2017-** B Pittsburgh PA 1969 s Edward & Louise. BLS U of Memphis 1994; MSW SUNY - Albany 1998; MDiv McCormick TS 2012; Dplma Seabury Wstrn 2012. D 2/4/2012 P 8/25/2012 Bp Jeff Lee. m 4/21/2012 Elizabeth Anne Lee. S Andr's Ch Chicago IL 2015-2017; S Mary's Ch Pk Ridge IL 2012-2015. ebirdiv@comcast.net

BIRD, Frederick L (WVa) 1009 S Henry Ave, Elkins WV 26241 **The No Cntrl Cluster Buckhannon WV 2003-; Epis Ch of the Trsfg Buckhannon WV 1999-; Stff Gr Epis Ch Elkins WV 1999-; S Mths Grafton WV 1999-; D No Cntrl Cluster In Buckhannon WV 1998-** B Montgomery WV 1946 s Wilford & Wava. BA W Virginia U 1969; MS U of Tennessee 1973. D 6/13/1998 P 6/12/1999 Bp John Henry Smith. m 10/23/1993 Donetta Elizabeth Bird c 3. NASW, Acsw.

BIRD JR, John Edwin (NJ) 304 S Girard St, Woodbury NJ 08096 **Ret Ret 1998-** B Pittsburgh PA 1940 s John & Esther. BA Monmouth U 1966; MDiv PDS 1969; DMin VTS 1993. D 4/19/1969 P 10/25/1969 Bp Alfred L Banyard. m 5/20/1961 Mary Beth Kiel c 2. R The Ch Of S Uriel The Archangel Sea Girt NJ 1988-1999; R Ch Of The Gd Shpd Jacksonville FL 1983-1988; R Ch Of S Lk And Epiph Philadelphia PA 1975-1983; Cur Chr Ch In Woodbury Woodbury NJ 1969-1975. Ma w hon PDS 1969; Ba cl Monmouth U 1966.

BIRD, Julie Childs (SC) B Baltimore MD 1936 MDiv Harvard DS 1997. D 9/14/2002 Bp Edward Lloyd Salmon Jr. m 5/22/1998 Edward Dennis Bird. D S Augustines In-The-Woods Epis Par Freeland WA 2004-2013; D Gr Ch Cathd Charleston SC 2002-2004.

BIRD, Michael Andrew (NY) 7 Library Ln, Bronxville NY 10708 **R Chr Ch Bronxville NY 2004-** B Philadelphia PA 1967 s John & Mary. BA Swarthmore Coll 1989; MDiv GTS 1997. D 5/3/1997 Bp Joe Doss P 11/1/1997 Bp Herbert Alcorn Donovan Jr. m 7/22/1989 Catherine Murray Bird c 2. S Mk's Ch New Canaan CT 1997-2004.

BIRD, Patricia A (Del) 30851 Crepe Myrtle Dr Unit 60, Millsboro DE 19966 B Baltimore MD 1942 d Clifford & Lena. BA Philadelphia Mus Acad 1964; MDiv Bex Sem 1977; MA Mundelein Coll 1983. D 6/4/1977 P 4/1/1978 Bp Harold Barrett Robinson. Int Trin Par Wilmington DE 2006-2008; Int S Paul's Par Kent Chestertown MD 2005-2006; Int S Ptr's Ch Lewes DE 2004-2005; Int S Annes Epis Ch Middletown DE 2002-2003; Int S Christophers Epis Ch Oxford PA 2000-2002; P-in-res S Jn's Ch Bala Cynwyd PA 1997-2000; Assoc to R S Ptr's Ch Phoenixville PA 1993-1996; 1985-1993; S Matt's Ch Evanston IL 1983-1985; Asst S Matt's Wilmette IL 1983-1985; Vic S Jn's Ch Wilson NY 1978-1982; Serv Presb Ch 1977-1978; Asst S Paul's Cathd Buffalo NY 1977-1978; COM Dio Delaware Wilmington 2006-2008. Auth, "More Than All Rt," iUniverse, 2010; Auth, "Vocalise-Rachmaninoff," E.C. Schirmer,

1968; Auth, "Pavane-Faure," E.C. Schirmer, 1968; Auth, "Prelude on Picardy," Galaxy, 1964.

BIRD, Peter Robert (FdL) 315 E. Jefferson St., Waupun WI 53963 **P-in-c H Trin Waupun WI 1999-** B Kansas City MO 1943 s Robert & Nellie. BA Ripon Coll Ripon WI 1966; JD SMU 1972; MDiv Nash 1977. D 6/18/2000 P 12/21/2000 Bp Russell Edward Jacobus. m 6/3/2000 Lila L Roberts-Bird c 2. H Trin Epis Ch Waupun WI 2000-2012.

BIRD, Robert Dale (Mich) 824 W Maple Ave, Adrian MI 49221 B Ridgeway MI 1935 s Walter & Jennie. Whitaker TS 1987. D 9/10/1987 Bp H Coleman Mcgehee Jr. m 5/11/1957 Eunice Jane Bird c 3. D Chr Ch Adrian MI 1987-2005. NAAD 1987.

BIRD, Virginia Lee (SD) Po Box 9412, Rapid City SD 57709 **Mem BEC/Theol Educ Dio o 2001-** B Holloman Air Force Base NM 1950 d Walter & Virginia. California St Polytechnic U 1970; BS Loma Linda U 1972; MA TCU 1982. D 9/14/1987 Bp Craig Barry Anderson. Chapl Dio So Dakota Pierre SD 2007-2009; Dep GC Dep Dio So Dakota SD 1997-2006; Mem COM Dio So Dakota SD 1996-2011; Mem Cmsn on Liturg Mus & Allied Arts 1989-2011; D S Andr's Epis Ch Rapid City SD 1987-2013. Recognition of Diac Mnstry in the tradition of St. Stephe NAAD (NAAD) 2007.

BIRDSALL, James Andrew (Ct) PO Box 2252, Orleans MA 02653 **Ret 1995-** B Toledo OH 1932 s Russell & Beatrice. Adel 1954; MDiv Ya Berk 1957; Harv 1986. D 4/27/1957 Bp James Pernette DeWolfe P 11/23/1957 Bp Jonathan Goodhue Sherman. m 8/25/1956 Marcia A Birdsall c 4. Chapl Rectory Sch CT 1976-1986; Chapl Pomfret Sch CT 1974-1986; Chr Ch Pomfret CT 1973-1994; Vic S Ptr's Ch So Windsor CT 1962-1972; Vic Gr Ch Broad Brook CT 1961-1965; Cur All SS Ch Great Neck NY 1957-1961. Rotary Racine Awd For Cmnty Serv 1994; Lions Club Man of the Year 1970; BA mcl Adel 1954.

BIRDSALL, John Burton (Eas) 419a Evans St Apt 2, Williamsville NY 14221 **Ret 1989-** B Highland Park MI 1925 s Otis & Dorothy. BA Ken 1949; LTh GTS 1952; STB GTS 1960. D 6/9/1952 P 2/12/1953 Bp Lauriston L Scaife. c 2. Assoc S Paul's Epis Ch Harris Hill Buffalo NY 1994-2008; R S Steph's Ch Earleville MD 1981-1988; Hon Cn S Paul's Cathd Buffalo NY 1979-1989; R S Ptr's Epis Ch Buffalo NY 1967-1980; Asst Calv Epis Ch Williamsville NY 1962-1967; Serv Angl Comm in Japan 1954-1962; Cur The Epis Ch Of The Gd Shpd Buffalo NY 1952-1954. Epis Curs 1982.

BIRDSEY, Robert B (EC) 2206 Rosewood Ave, Richmond VA 23220 B Macon GA 1947 s Herbert & Cynthia. BA Van 1970; MDiv Candler TS Emory U 1977. D 6/11/1977 P 3/9/1978 Bp Bennett Jones Sims. m 1/30/1971 Brenda H Hicks c 2. Int Ch Of The H Comf Richmond VA 2006-2008; Int S Jas' Epis Ch Dexter MI 2004-2006; Int S Ptr's By-The-Sea Swansboro NC 2004; R S Paul's Ch Beaufort NC 2001-2003; Assoc S Phil's Ch Brevard NC 1998-2001; R The Epis Ch Of The Medtr Allentown PA 1986-1998; R Epis Ch Of The H Sprt Cumming GA 1981-1986; Asst S Jude's Ch Marietta GA 1977-1981; Ed, Dioc Nwspr Dio Atlanta 1981-1986.

BIRDSONG, Jerre Eugene (Mo) 4714 Clifton Ave, Saint Louis MO 63109 **D S Mk's Ch S Louis MO 2014-; Dioc Disaster Coordntr Dio Missouri S Louis MO 2016-, Pres, Stndg Com 2014-2016** B Pulaski TN 1954 s Thomas & Margaret. Grad Cert U of Missouri - St. Louis; BA Rhodes Coll 1976; MS Pur 1977; Cert Epis Sch for Mnstry 2004. D 11/21/2014 Bp George Wayne Smith. c 1. Phi Beta Kappa 1975.

BIRKBY, Charles H (CNY) 1505 Pershing Pl Apt A, Rolla MO 65401 **Ret Dio Cntrl New York Liverpool NY 2004-** B Washington DC 1942 s Fred & Estella. BA Auburn U 1964; PDS 1966; Coll of Preachers 1980; SUNY 1988. D 4/20/1968 P 10/26/1968 Bp Alfred L Banyard. m 8/17/1968 Dorothy F Lutz c 3. 1986-2004; R Emm Ch E Syracuse NY 1981-1986; P Assoc Dio New Jersey Trenton NJ 1981; Trin Cathd Trenton NJ 1981; Assoc R S Ptr's Ch Medford NJ 1978-1980; Vic The Ch Of The Gd Shpd Berlin NJ 1973-1978; Sem in Charge/ Vic Ch Of The H Sprt Tuckerton NJ 1966-1973. Auth, ""Invisible Prisoners,"" *Living Ch.* GAS 1981. fchbsr@gmail.com

BIRKENHEAD, Harold George (Mass) 8 Nevin Rd, South Weymouth MA 02190 **Ch Of The H Nativ S Weymouth MA 2006-** B Boston MA 1948 s William & Mary. AA Massasoit Cmnty Coll 1986; BS Bridgewater Coll 1988; MDiv VTS 1992. D 5/30/1992 P 5/15/1993 Bp David Elliot Johnson. m 3/23/2006 Charlene Birkenhead c 4. S Ptr's Ch Portland ME 1995-2006; Asst to R Epis Ch Of S Thos Taunton MA 1992-1995. Auth, "Investigating Cromwell," *Investigating Cromwell*, Ex-l-ence Pub, 2015; Auth, "God Is w Us In Our Pain & Suffering," Dow Pub, 1997. Portland Chapl Awd City of Portland, Maine 2005; Mateer Life Saving Awd St of Massachusetts 1980. office@ holynativityweymouth.org

BIRNBAUM, Rachelle Eskenaizi (Va) 942A Heritage Vlg, Southbury CT 06488 B Bronx NY 1948 d Leo & Sarina. BA Drew U 1972; MDiv Ya Berk 1977. D 12/21/1977 P 11/1/1978 Bp Paul Moore Jr. R All SS Ch Alexandria VA 1998-2013; Assoc Mssnr S Marg's Epis Ch Little Rock AR 1995-1998; Assoc Trin Ch Epis Boston MA 1990-1994; Dn of Students CDSP Berkeley CA 1984-1990; Assoc for Ovrs Ldrshp Trng Epis Ch Cntr New York NY 1981-1984; Asst Par Of The Epiph Winchester MA 1980-1981; P Assoc Chr

And S Steph's Ch New York NY 1978-1984; Chapl to the Bp Dio New York New York NY 1977-1980.

BIRNEY, Edith Hazard (Me) 11 Perkins St, Topsham ME 04086 B Louisville KY 1947 d Charles & Edith. Hollins U 1967; Katharine Gibbs Sch 1967; BA Bow 1985. D 6/12/1999 Bp Chilton Richardson Knudsen. m 11/27/2004 James Gillespie Birney c 4. S Paul's Ch Brunswick ME 2001-2002. Auth, *Singing for Your Supper*, Algonquin, 1996; Auth, *Rising to the Occasion*, Algonquin, 1993.

BIRNEY III, James Gillespie (Me) 1110 North Rd, North Yarmouth ME 04097 B Hanover NH 1950 s James & Marion. BA Wms 1972; MDiv VTS 1979. D 7/14/1979 P 2/6/1980 Bp Harold Barrett Robinson. m 11/27/2004 Edith Hazard Birney c 2. S Nich Epis Ch Scarborough ME 1991-2000; Vic S Nich' Epis Ch Scarborough ME 1991-2000; R S Barth's Epis Ch Yarmouth ME 1983-1990; S Barth's Epis Ch Yarmouth ME 1983-1989; S Paul's Sch Concord NH 1980-1983; Chapl Hoosac Sch Hoosick NY 1979-1980. EPF.

BIRTCH, John Edward McKay (SwFla) 1001 Carpenters Way Apt H108, Lakeland FL 33809 **Asst P All SS Epis Ch Lakeland FL 1999-; Ret 1994-** B Woodstock Ontario Canada 1929 s John & Evelyn. BA U of Wstrn Ontario CA 1951; LTh Hur CA 1952; DIT S Augustines Coll Cbury Gb 1955; BD Hur CA 1961; DMin VTS 2001. Rec 8/1/1971 as Priest Bp The Bishop Of Huron. m 8/19/1953 Patricia Joanne Birtch. R Calv Ch Indn Rk Bc FL 1978-1994; R S Barth's Ch St Petersburg FL 1971-1978; Serv Angl Ch Of Can 1952-1971. "Pryr Workshop 101 Proj Thesis," Virginia Sem, 2001. AFP, Trst; Ord Of S Lk, Bro Of S Andr. Hon Cn Trin Cathd 1971; R Emer Calv Epis Indn Rocks Bch Fl.

BISHOP, Barbara Elaine (Chi) 827 Canterbury Dr, Crystal Lake IL 60014 **D Pstr Assisant S Mary Epis Ch Crystal Lake IL 1991-** B DeKalb IL 1942 d Charles & Marian. BA Alderson-Broaddus Coll 1964; MRE Nthrn Bapt TS 1966; Cert Dio Chicago Sch for Deacons 1991. D 12/7/1991 Bp Frank Tracy Griswold III. Admin COM Dio Chicago Chicago IL 1999-2009; Chapl Nurses Spprt Grp Gd Shpd Hosp Barrington IL 1992-1995; On-Call Chapl Gd Shpd Hosp Barrington IL 1989-1995; Admin D's Sch For Mnstry And Formation Chicago IL 1994-1999. Contrib, "Many Servnt," *Many Servnt: An Intro to Deacons*, Cowley, 2004. Bd Mem NAAD 1999-2011; Dio Chicago Deacons' Coun 1992-2002; No Amer Assn for Diac 1990; Pres NAAD 2007-2009; Vice Pres/ Pres Elect NAAD 2005-2007.

BISHOP, Christopher (Pa) **P-in-c S Mart's Ch Wayne PA 2011-; Liturg Plnng Cmsn Dio Pennsylvania Philadelphia PA 2011-** B Cincinnati OH 1960 s John & Joann. BA S Lawr Canton NY 1983; MFA Col Nyc 1988; MDiv Luth TS 2007. D 6/9/2007 Bp Charles Ellsworth Bennison Jr P 12/15/2007 Bp Franklin Delton Turner. m 8/3/2012 Amanda B Eiman. All SS Epis Day Sch Hoboken NJ 2007-2009; Chapl All SS Epis Par Hoboken NJ 2007-2008; Adj Prof Film Stds 1998-1999; Film Maker Self-Employed 1988-2004.

BISHOP, Edwin (Ore) 1900 Lauderdale Dr Apt D115, Henrico VA 23238 **Ret 1995-** B Seattle WA 1930 s Edwin & Velma. BA U of Washington 1952; STB GTS 1955; MEd Virginia Commonwealth U 1977; MA Presb Sch of CE Richmond VA 1978. D 6/29/1955 P 2/6/1956 Bp Stephen F Bayne Jr. m 8/11/1956 Joan Gail Avery c 3. Int All SS' Ch Sthrn Shores NC 2002-2003; Int Hickory Neck Ch Toano VA 2000-2001; Int Ch Of The Gd Shpd Raleigh NC 1994-1995; Int All SS' Epis Ch Ft Worth TX 1992-1994; Int S Jn's Par Hagerstown MD 1991-1992; Int Pac Cure Par Cartersville VA 1989-1990; Int Chr And Gr Ch Petersburg VA 1988-1989; Int H Innoc' Epis Ch Lahaina HI 1987-1988; Int Ch Of The Creator Mechanicsvlle VA 1987; Int Ch Of The H Comf Richmond VA 1986-1987; Int S Andr's Ch Richmond VA 1985; Int S Cyp's Epis Ch Hampton VA 1984-1985; Intrim Spec Dio Sthrn Virginia Newport News VA 1984; Int S Mich's Ch Colonial Heights VA 1982-1983; Int S Andr's Ch Norfolk VA 1982; Int Gr Epis Ch Goochland VA 1981; Int Emm Ch At Brook Hill Richmond VA 1979; Int S Mths Epis Ch Midlothian VA 1978-1979; Int Spec Dio No Carolina Raleigh NC 1977-1995; Int Spec Dio Virginia Richmond VA 1977-1995; Int S Paul's Ch Petersburg VA 1977-1978; Chapl Untd States Naval Reserve 1973-1990; Chapl U.S. Naval Reserve 1972-1990; Chapl S Marg's Sch Tappahannock VA 1972-1976; Chapl S Marg's Sch Tappahannock VA 1972-1976; Chapl USN 1968-1973; Chapl U.S. Navy 1967-1972; Chapl Dagwell Hall Sch Portland OR 1966-1967; R All SS Ch Hillsboro OR 1960-1966; Yth Mnstrs S Mk's Ch Tonopah NV 1958-1960; Vic S Anne's Epis Ch Washougal WA 1955-1958; Cur S Lk's Epis Ch Vancouver WA 1955-1957; Dio Nevada Las Vegas 1958-1960; Dept of Missions Dio Olympia Seattle 1957-1958. Auth, *Occasional Mnstrs*, U.S. Navy, 1984; Auth, *Love in Deed*. Int Mnstry Ntwk 1980; Mltry & Hospitaler Ord S Jn Jerusalem 1986; OHC 1947.

BISHOP, Genevieve R (NJ) D 12/14/2016 Bp William H Stokes.

BISHOP JR, Harold Ellsworth (Md) Box 128, Cottage 505-B, Quincy PA 17247 **Ret 1994-** B Cumberland MD 1928 s Harold & Minnie. BS W Virginia U 1950; MS Frostburg St U 1971. D 6/2/1982 P 6/1/1983 Bp Robert Poland Atkinson. m 1/19/1951 Norma Virginia Crump. Assoc S Mary's Epis Ch Waynesboro PA 1994-2014; R S Geo's Epis Ch Mt Savage MD 1986-1994; Emm Ch Keyser WV 1982-1984; Cur Emm Ch Moorefield WV 1982-1984.

BISHOP, Kathleen Gayle (NJ) St Mary's by-the-sea, 804 Bay Ave, Point Pleasant Beach NJ 08742 B S. Hampton NY 1954 d Howard & Shirley. BA Florida St U 1976; MDiv Drew TS 1994; MDiv Drew U 1994; PhD Drew Grad Sch 2002. D 6/18/2011 P 12/16/2011 Bp George Edward Councell. m 6/3/2006 James Jones c 2.

BISHOP, Nila Ruth (WMo) 1433 NW R D Mize Rd, Blue Springs MO 64015 B Linn Co. MO 1944 d Ora & Emma Ruth. Geo Herbert Inst of Pstr Stds. D 6/4/2011 P 12/3/2011 Bp Martin Scott Field. c 2.

BISSELL-THOMPSON, Geraldine Vina (Alb) 225 Back West Creek Rd, Newark Valley NY 13811 B Eugene OR 1942 d Clare & Vina. BA U of Oregon 1969; MA U of Oregon 1970; PhD U of Oregon 1974; LTh McGill U 1985. D 6/8/1985 P 10/26/1986 Bp O'Kelley Whitaker. m 2/2/1963 Howard Dale Thompson c 6. Gr Epis Ch Canton NY 1999-2004; S Barn Ch Warwick RI 1997-1999; P-in-c Trin Chap Morley Canton NY 1988-2002; Trin Ch Lowville NY 1988-1997; P Emm Ch E Syracuse NY 1986-1988; D Chr Ch Morristown NY 1985-1986.

BISSOONDIAL, Dinesh (CFla) St Peter's Episcopal Church, 700 Rinehart Rd, Lake Mary FL 32746 B San Fernando, Trinidad 1966 s Ramnath & Baby. BSc. Transformational Chr Mnstry Warner U 2012. D 12/8/2012 Bp Gregory Orrin Brewer. m 2/21/2009 Heidi Bissoondial c 2. D S Ptr's Epis Ch Lake Mary FL 2012-2013. Omicron Psi Gold Natl hon Soc 2012; Theta Alpha Kappa Natl hon Soc 2012. S Stephens Awd AED 2013; mcl Warner U 2012.

BITSBERGER, Donald Edward (Va) 4970 Sentinel Dr Apt 505, Bethesda MD 20816 **Died 7/5/2017** B Fort Wayne IN 1928 s William & Nellie. BA Ya 1950; MDiv EDS 1953. D 6/13/1953 P 5/1/1954 Bp William A Lawrence. c 2. Asst Ch Of Our Sav Silver Sprg MD 1998-2004; Vice Chair The CPG New York NY 1994-1997; Ret Beth MD 1993-2017; Int (Locum Teneus) S Pat's Ch Washington DC 1993-1994; Chr Ch Alexandria VA 1990-1991; Assoc Fac Coll of Preachers 1989-2008; Epis EvangES Arlington VA 1987-1993; EDS Cambridge MA 1984-1985, 1978-1983; GBEC Epis Ch GC 1976-1985; R Ch Of The Redeem Chestnut Hill MA 1968-1987; Dep GC Dio Massachusetts Boston MA 1982-1985. Auth, "Forw Day By Day," 1985. Polly Bond Awd for Excellence, Theol Reflection 2011; Yale Medal DSA Ya 1950.

BITTNER, Merrill (Me) 118 Lone Pine Rd, Newry ME 04261 **Ret 2007-** B Pasadena CA 1946 d John & Ethel. BA Lake Erie Coll 1969; MDiv Bex Sem 1972; MS U of Sthrn Maine 1996. D 1/6/1973 Bp Robert Rae Spears Jr P 7/29/1974 Bp Daniel Corrigan. m 4/3/2013 Nancy A Noppa. S Barn Ch Rumford ME 2001-2006; Hospice Chapl Androscoggin Hm Care & Hospice Lewiston ME 2001-2004; 1975-1998; Dio Rochester Henrietta 1973-1976; Assoc Ch Of The Gd Shpd Webster NY 1973-1975.

BJORNBERG JR, Philip John (Ct) Trinity Episcopal Church, 345 Main St, Portland CT 06480 **Trin Ch Portland CT 2016-** B Norfolk VA 1956 s Philip & Frances. BS Albertus Magnus Coll; MATM Fuller TS 2014. D 6/14/2016 P 12/21/2016 Bp Ian Theodore Douglas. m 6/25/1977 Susan L Bjornberg c 2.

BLACK, Cynthia (Nwk) 36 South St, Morristown NJ 07960 **R Ch Of The Redeem Morristown NJ 2011-** B Newton MA 1959 d William & Barbara. BA Hobart and Wm Smith Colleges 1981; MDiv CDSP 1985; D.D. CDSP 2006. D 7/6/1985 Bp William George Burrill P 1/18/1986 Bp John Shelby Spong. m 9/2/2011 Rebecca Walker. Int Ch Of The Epiph Epis Minneapolis MN 2010-2011; Dn Cathd Par Of Chr The King Portage MI 1991-2010; Int S Ptr's Ch Essex Fells NJ 1990-1991, Assoc 1985-1989; Exec Coun Com on the Status of Wmn Epis Ch Cntr New York NY 2006-2012, Exec Coun 2000-2006. Dir and Producer, "Voices of Witness Afr," 2009; Auth, "Var arts," *Ruach*. Polly Bond Awd ECom 2007; Lifetime Mem EWC 2000.

BLACK, George Donald (At) 215 N Edenfield Ridge Dr, Rome GA 30161 B Swainsboro GA 1935 s George & Runelle. BA U Rich 1962; MDiv Sewanee: The U So, TS 1963; Fllshp Sewanee: The U So, TS 1972; DMin Sewanee: The U So, TS 1990; The Cbury Course Cbury Cathd 1996. D 6/27/1963 Bp David Shepherd Rose P 6/11/1964 Bp George P Gunn. m 6/29/1963 Suzanne D Black c 2. Int Ch of the Trsfg 2011-2012; Vic S Jas Ch Cedartown GA 2002-2009; R S Ptr's Ch Rome GA 1986-2000; R Chr Ch Blacksburg VA 1978-1986; R S Mths Epis Ch Midlothian VA 1969-1978; R S Geo's Ch Pungoteague Pungoteague VA 1965-1968; S Jas' Ch Accomac VA 1965-1968; Cur Ch Of The Ascen Norfolk VA 1963-1965. Contrib, "Walking w Wounded Feet," *Simul Iustus et Peccator*, The TS, Sewanee, 2003; Auth, "Lord of All Hopefulness," *St. Lk's Journ*, The TS, Sewanee, 1982. The DuBose Awd for Serv The TS, Sewanee 2005.

BLACK, Katharine C (Mass) 13 Louisburg Sq, Boston MA 02108 **P-in-c Ch Of S Jn The Evang Boston MA 2006-; Cathd Chapt Dio Massachusetts Boston MA 2007-, Eccl Trial Crt 2001-2007; GBEC Dom And Frgn Mssy Soc- Epis Ch Cntr New York NY 2000-** B Boston MA 1945 d Mandel & Winifred. BA Rad 1962; PhD CUA 1985; MDiv EDS 1986. D 6/11/1988 P 5/11/1989 Bp David Elliot Johnson. m 6/15/1967 Peter McLaren Black c 5. The Cathd Ch Of S Paul Boston MA 2013-2016; Chr Ch Needham Hgts MA 2002; Trin Par Melrose MA 1999-2001; S Eliz's Ch Sudbury MA 1997-1998; S Mk's Ch Westford MA 1995-1996; S Paul's Ch In Nantucket Nantucket MA 1992-1993; Par Of The Epiph Winchester MA 1990-1991; Asst 1989-1990; Asst S Mich's Ch Marblehead MA 1989-1990, Cur 1987-1988.

BLACK JR, Milton England (WTex) 149 Cordula St, Corpus Christi TX 78411 **R Ch Of The Gd Shpd Corpus Christi TX 2008-** B Houston TX 1962 s Milton & Bess. BA U of Texas 1986; MBA U of Texas 1994; MDiv VTS 2000. D 6/17/2000 Bp Claude Edward Payne P 6/29/2001 Bp Don Adger Wimberly. m 10/7/1989 Elizabeth Black c 2. Archd Dio W Texas San Antonio TX 2007-2008; R S Jn's Epis Ch Sonora TX 2004-2007; R Trin Ch Longview TX 2002-2003, Cur 2000-2002. mblack@cotgs.org

BLACK, Rebecca Lynn (Mass) 128 Village St, Millis MA 02054 B Millington TN 1960 d William & Marcia. Marist Coll; BA Estrn Connecticut St U 1984; MDiv EDS 2000. D 5/22/2000 Bp M(Arvil) Thomas Shaw P 5/23/2001 Bp Barbara Clementine Harris. c 1. P-in-c Chr Ch Medway MA 2014-2017; S Paul's Epis Ch Hopkinton MA 2014; Chr Ch Swansea MA 2013-2014; Epiph Par Walpole MA 2011-2013, Assoc 2010-; R S Paul's Ch Millis MA 2005-2010; Asst S Andr's Ch Framingham MA 2000-2004. rebecblack@gmail.com

BLACK, Robert E. (Ct) 21Jerimoth Dr., Bradford CT 06405 B Lima OH 1922 s Hezekiah & Dessie. BA Wayne 1946; MA U MN 1948; Schlr 1956; MDiv Bex Sem 1959; STM NYTS 1969. D 6/15/1957 P 12/1/1957 Bp Arthur C Lichtenberger. m 11/30/1984 Patricia Dondero c 1. Vic S Jn The Evang Yalesville CT 1966-1972; R Ch Of The Gd Shpd Houlton ME 1959-1966; Vic S Matt's Epis Ch Warson Woods Kirkwood MO 1957-1959. Auth, "Var arts". Soc Of S Jn The Evang 1962-1967. Firestone Schlr 1955.

BLACK JR, Robert William (NC) 131 West Council Street, Salisbury NC 28144 **R S Lk's Ch Salisbury NC 2014-; Stndg Com Dio No Carolina Raleigh NC 2016-, Dioc Coun 2012-2014, Galilee Comission 2012-2014** B Hollywood FL 1984 s Robert & Patricia. DMin Sewanee: The U So, TS; BA Wake Forest U 2006; MDiv VTS 2009. D 6/13/2009 Bp Michael B Curry P 1/16/2010 Bp John Bryson Chane. m 5/27/2008 Tyler Brynn Chapman c 2. Asst R S Fran Ch Greensboro NC 2010-2014; Asst R S Jn's Ch Lafayette Sq Washington DC 2009-2010. rblack@stlukessalisbury.net

BLACK, Ruth Buck Wallace (Miss) 1704 Poplar Blvd, Jackson MS 39202 **Chapl U Of Mississippi Med Cntr 1984-** B Nashville TN 1939 d John & Ruth. BA Belhaven Coll 1960; Harv 1971; Harv 1971; PhD Harv 1979; CPE Jackson St U 1981; EFM Sewanee: The U So, TS 1985. D 5/31/1986 P 2/1/1987 Bp Duncan Montgomery Gray Jr. m 6/6/1970 Dewitt Carlisle Black c 1. Dio Mississippi Jackson MS 1997-2011, 1988-1992; Cur S Phil's Ch Jackson MS 1986-1988. Auth, "Scraps From An Organic Quilt"; Auth, "The Gospel Imperative In The Midst Of Aids". Comp H Cross Soc, ACPE. Ndea Fell & Harvard Schlr Harv 1968.

BLACK, Sherry Leonard (Spr) 12806 Mallard Dr., Whittington IL 62897 **P-in-c S Mk's Ch W Frankfort IL 2013-; Sprtl Care Mgr Herrin Hosp Herrin IL 2011-; Sprtl Care Mgr/Chapl Herrin Hosp Herrin IL 2011-** B Farmington NM 1959 d John & Audrey. BS Greenville Coll 2004; MDiv TESM 2008. D 2/2/2008 P 11/1/2008 Bp Peter Hess Beckwith. c 1. P-in-c S Jas Chap Marion Marion IL 2011-2013; Asst Hale Dnry Team Mnstry Eldorado IL 2008-2011; Chair, Dept. Soc Concerns Dio Springfield Springfield IL 2008-2011.

BLACK, Timothy H (At) 4393 Garmon Rd NW, Atlanta GA 30327 **Yth Dir All SS Epis Ch Atlanta GA 2012-; Asst H Innoc Ch Atlanta GA 2010-** B Marietta GA 1966 s Reuben & Marjorie. BA Furman U 1988; MDiv Candler TS Emory U 2010. D 12/19/2009 Bp J Neil Alexander. m 10/12/1991 Patricia Babuka Black c 3. Ch Of The Incarn Atlanta GA 2012; H Innoc' Epis Sch Atlanta GA 2010-2011.

BLACK, Vicki Kay (Me) 73 Bristol Rd, Damariscotta ME 04543 B Cordell OK 1961 d William & Nancy. BA SMU 1983; MDiv Nash 1987. D 3/28/1987 Bp Roger John White. D S Andr's Ch Newcastle ME 2006-2013; D S Dav's Epis Mssn Pepperell MA 1992-2002; Dekoven Fndt for Ch Wk Racine WI 1990-1991; S Mk's Ch Milwaukee WI 1990-1991; COM Dio Milwaukee Milwaukee WI 1988-1991, 1987-1989, Admin Of Catechumenate 1987-1988; D Trin Ch Milwaukee WI 1987-1988. "Welcome To BCP," Morehouse Pub, 2005; "And A Little Chld Shall Lead Them," Atr, 2004; "Welcome To The Ch Year," Morehouse Pub, 2004. NAAD. Phi Beta Kappa SMU 1983.

BLACK, Vincent E (O) 2230 Euclid Ave, Cleveland OH 44115 **Cn for Chr Formation Dio Ohio Cleveland 2009-** B Cleveland OH 1969 s Dennis & Eleanor. BA JCU 1992; MDiv Bex Sem 2009. D 6/13/2009 P 4/10/2010 Bp Mark Hollingsworth Jr. m 11/25/2011 Roger E Barnhard. vblack@dohio.org

BLACKBURN, Elliot Hillman (Spr) 603 South Grant, Mason City IA 50401 **S Matt's-By-The-Bridge Epis Ch Iowa Falls IA 2007-** B Springfield MA 1936 s George & Vera. BA Drew U 1958; MDiv Ya Berk 1962. D 6/16/1962 P 12/21/1962 Bp Robert McConnell Hatch. m 6/6/1959 Helen C Blackburn c 3. R S Geo's Ch Belleville IL 1984-2000; R S Jn's Ch Mason City IA 1970-1984; Vic Epis Par of Ames Ames IA 1965-1970; Cur Ch Of The Atone Westfield MA 1962-1965. Hon Cn Cathd Ch of St. Paul, Springfield, IL 2002.

BLACKBURN, Gerald Jackson (EC) 4212 Stratton Village Ln, Wilmington NC 28409 B West Point GA 1944 s Marvin & Lila. BA Samford U 1968; MDiv Sthrn Bapt TS 1973; CE VTS 1998. D 9/30/1994 P 9/1/1995 Bp Brice Sidney Sanders. m 6/1/1968 Marilyn Blackburn c 2. Dir Of Mltry Mnstrs Epis Ch Cntr New York NY 2001-2010; Off Of Bsh For ArmdF New York NY

1994-2001; D-In-Trng S Ptr's By-The-Sea Swansboro NC 1994-1995; Chapl USN 1979-2001.

BLACKBURN, Gregory Benjamin (SeFla) 1121 Andalusia Ave, Coral Gables FL 33134 **S Phil's Epis Sch Coral Gables FL 2011-** B Clarksville AR 1954 s Dillon & Deloris Patricia. PhD U of Mississippi 1986. D 11/23/2013 Bp Leo Frade. m 8/16/1980 Cathy J Blackburn c 1. gblackburn@saintphilips.net

BLACKBURN, James Clark (Md) 105 Tunbridge Rd, Baltimore MD 21212 **Died 5/21/2016** B Cleveland OH 1934 s Paul & Sylvia. BA Amh 1956; BD VTS 1959; MA U of Pennsylvania 1969. D 5/31/1959 Bp Joseph Gillespie Armstrong P 12/19/1959 Bp Oliver J Hart. m 6/14/1986 Judith Stewart c 3. Ret 1999-2016; Int All Hallows Par So River Edgewater MD 1996-1999; Int Epis Ch Of Chr The King Baltimore MD 1995-1996; Int Chr Ch St Michaels Par S Mich MD 1994-1995; Int All SS Epis Par Sunderland MD 1992-1993; Int S Geo's Ch Perryman MD 1990-1992; Int S Jn's Ch Georgetown Par Washington DC 1989-1990; Int Dio Maryland Baltimore MD 1988-1989; Int S Mich And All Ang Ch Baltimore MD 1987-1988; Int S Marg's Ch Washington DC 1985-1987; Assoc The Ch Of The Redeem Baltimore MD 1981-1985; Archd for Prog Dio Newark Newark NJ 1978-1981; Glascow Ecum Mnstry Middletown DE 1976-1978; Founding Pstr Glasgow Ecummenical Mnstry Middletown DE 1974-1978; Coordntr Recon Prog Dio Pennsylvania Philadelphia PA 1970-1973; Assoc S Mart's Ch Wayne PA 1967-1970; R S Paul's Ch Philadelphia PA 1963-1967; St Pauls Epis Ch Oaks PA 1963-1967; Archd Dio Wstrn Kansas Hutchinson KS 1962-1963; Cur S Paul's Ch Philadelphia PA 1959-1962. "Ed," *Var arts*, Leaven NNECA, 1976; *Var arts*, Leaven NNECA, 1963. Phi Beta Kappa Amh 1956; BA mcl Amh 1956.

BLACKBURN, Terry Gene (NJ) 35-50 85th Street 5J, Jackson Heights NY 11372 **R St Jn the Bapt Epis Ch Linden NJ 2001-** B Warren OH 1946 s Harry & Leonna. BA MI SU 1967; AMLS U MI 1968; MDiv GTS 1988. D 6/11/1988 P 12/11/1988 Bp Paul Moore Jr. R S Lk the Evang Roselle NJ 1992-2007; Cur Par of Chr the Redeem Pelham NY 1988-1992. Auth, "Send Us Now Into the Wrld," *Liturg*, 1987.

BLACKERBY JR, William (Ala) 4307 Clairmont Ave S, Birmingham AL 35222 **Int R Ch of the H Sprt Alabaster AL 2017-** B Birmingham AL 1953 s William & Annie. BA Birmingham-Sthrn Coll 1975; MA U of Alabama at Birmingham 1984; MDiv SWTS 1987. D 6/6/1987 P 12/1/1987 Bp Furman Charles Stough. m 7/30/1983 Margaret Anne Blackerby c 2. St. Cathr's Epis Ch Chelsea AL 2015-2016; Int Gr Ch Cullman AL 2014-2015; S Jn's Ch Birmingham AL 1996-1999, Int P-in-c 1994-1995; Chapl Dio Alabama Birmingham 1993-2014; Cur S Mary's-On-The-Highlands Epis Ch Birmingham AL 1988-1993; Cur S Mich's Ch Barrington IL 1987-1988.

BLACKHAM, Todd Patten (Los) 1325 Monterey Rd, South Pasadena CA 91030 **Dir of Yth Mnstrs S Jas' Par So Pasadena CA 2011-** B Aurora CO 1981 s Craig & Laurinda. BA U Denv 2003; MTS Harvard DS 2005. D 6/7/2014 P 1/17/2015 Bp Joseph Jon Bruno.

BLACKLOCK, Martha Grace (NJ) POBox 2973, Silver City NM 88062 B Saint Louis MO 1940 d Carl & Maurine. BA Baldwin-Wallace Coll 1962; MFA U of Montana 1971; MDiv GTS 1976; DMin EDS 1996. D 6/5/1976 Bp George E Rath P 1/18/1977 Bp John Shelby Spong. m 7/15/2010 Twana Sparks. S Mary's Ch Keyport NJ 1999-2004; Vic S Mk's Epis Ch Keansburg NJ 1999-2001; Vic S Clem's Ch New York NY 1980-1984; P Newark Epis Coop For Min & Miss Newark NJ 1979-1980; P No Porch Wmn & Infants Centers Newark NJ 1979-1980; R S Barn Ch Newark NJ 1978-1980; Dio Newark Newark NJ 1977-1978; Archd Voice Dioc Paper Newark NJ 1977-1978; Bp and Resource Cntr Newark NJ 1977; Min Mo Thunder Mssn 1976-1982.

BLACKMER, Stephen D (NH) Kairos Earth, 107 Hackleboro Road, Canterbury NH 03224 **P Assoc S Steph's Ch Pittsfield NH 2015-; Chapl Ch of the Woods 2014-; Exec Dir Kairos Earth 2014-** B Boston MA 1955 s Donald & Joan. MAR Ya Berk; AB Dart; AB Dart 1979; MF Ya 1983. D 2/2/2013 P 9/7/2013 Bp A Robert Hirschfeld. m 3/15/2007 Kelly M Short c 2. Assoc S Paul's Ch Concord NH 2013. sdblackmer@kairosearth.org

BLACKMON, Andrew Thomas (La) 120 S New Hampshire St, Covington LA 70433 B Jacksonville FL 1947 s Warren & Della. Davidson Coll 1966; BA U of Florida 1969; MDiv EDS 1975. D 5/18/1975 P 3/1/1976 Bp James Loughlin Duncan. m 2/1/1992 Mary M Steele c 2. R Chr Ch Covington LA 2008-2013; Assoc Ch Of The Incarn Dallas TX 1999-2008; Dir of Prog Godly Play Fndt 1999-2005; Sr Assoc S Mich And All Ang Ch Dallas TX 1984-1999; Assoc S Alb's Par Washington DC 1977-1984; Cur H Trin Epis Ch W Palm Bch FL 1975-1977; R and Trst Chr Epis Sch 2008-2015; Trst Christwood Ret Cmnty 2008-2015; Trst The CPG New York NY 2000-2012; Trst St. Phlip's Sch & Cmnty Cntr 1991-2003; Directotr / Ed NNECA / Leaven 1984-1998. Auth, "A Matter Of Faith"; Auth, "Leaven". Ch & CityCity Conf 1981-1986; Consortium of Endowed Parishes 1997-2013; Cornerstone Proj Ch 1988-1996; EvangES 1980-1990; Natl Assn of Epis CE Direct 1997-2013; Natl Ntwk Of Epis Cler Ass'ns 1979-2002. Kentucky Colonel Gvnr of the Commonwealth of Kentucky 2009; Nancy Dillard Lyons Awd St. Phil's Sch 1998.

BLACKWELL, Norma Lee (WA) 10754 Main St Apt 202, Fairfax VA 22030 **Chapl Fairfax Nrsng Cntr 1996-** B Metropolis IL 1942 d Phinis & Minnie.

BA Sthrn Illinois U 1964; MA Sthrn Illinois U 1966; MDiv VTS 1982. D 6/12/1982 P 1/1/1983 Bp John Thomas Walker. Dio Washington Washington DC 1991-1994; Int Chapl How Washington DC 1991-1994; Asst R Calv Ch Washington DC 1988-1991; Asst S Andr's Ch Burke VA 1985-1987; Ch Liaison One Mnstry Inner City Washington DC 1984-1985; Cathd of St Ptr & St Paul Washington DC 1982-1984; Asst Chapl Natl Cathd Sch Washington DC 1982-1984. Ord Of S Lk.

BLACKWELL, Robert Hunter (Ala) 1016 Broadway Ave SW, Cullman AL 35055 B Decatur AL 1956 s Paul & Sarah. BA Auburn U 1978; MDiv Nash 1984. D 5/29/1984 P 12/18/1984 Bp Furman Charles Stough. m 5/13/1978 Mary Katherine Blackwell c 2. R Gr Ch Cullman AL 2007-2014; Exec Coun Appointees New York NY 2005-2006; R S Ptr's Epis Ch Talladega AL 1988-2005; R S Jos's On-The-Mtn Mentone AL 1984-1988.

BLACKWOOD, Deb (NC) 14103 Wilford Ct, Charlotte NC 28277 B Charleston WV 1943 d Edward & Betty. BA W Virginia U 1965; MA W Virginia U 1967; PhD Ohio U 1974; Duke DS 2009. D 6/12/1999 Bp John Bailey Lipscomb. c 1. Coord Pstr Care Ch Of The H Comf Charlotte NC 2009-2015; Dir of Cmncatn/Tech S Jn's Epis Ch Charlotte NC 2009-2010; Chapl, Tech Catalyst Trin Epis Sch Charlotte NC 2005-2009; Chapl; Tech Catalyst Trin Epis Sch Charlotte NC 2005-2009; Dio SW Florida Parrish FL 2001-2004; Dn Dio SWFL: Sch For Mnstry Sarasota FL 2001-2004. deb.blackwood@episdionc.org

BLADON, Doyle Gene (Az) 310 W Union Ave, Monticello AR 71655 **Ret 1984-** B Clearfield IA 1926 s Vernon & Vera. BA U of Iowa 1956; DDS U of Iowa 1959. D 3/1/1977 Bp Joseph Thomas Heistand. m 5/24/1952 Helen Troy Martin c 2. D S Mich's And All Ang' 1977-1984.

BLAESS, Kristine Amend (Tenn) 4715 Harding Pike, Nashville TN 37205 **S Geo's Ch Nashville TN 2016-** B Bozeman MT 1973 d John & Joann. BA St Olaf 1994; MDiv Luther NW TS 1999; MDiv LutherNorthwestern TS 1999; MDiv LutherNorthwestern TS 1999; DMin Louiville Presb 2012. Rec 1/20/2016 as Priest Bp John Bauerschmidt. m 1/1/1997 Michael Blaess c 2.

BLAESS, Michael (Tenn) **S Geo's Ch Nashville TN 2016-** B Edina, Minnesota 1973 s Paul & Sharon. Bachelor of Arts U MN 1995; Mstr of Div Luther Sem 1999. Rec 1/20/2016 as Priest Bp John Bauerschmidt. m 1/1/1997 Kristine Amend Kristine Anne Amend c 2. michael.blaiss@stgeorgesnashville.org

BLAGG, James Raymond (Okla) 117 Sandpiper Cir, Durant OK 74701 **R S Jn's Ch Durant OK 1988-** B Brownwood TX 1953 s Richard & Rosemary. BA Angelo St U 1974; MDiv Brite DS 1977; U So 1979; MS SE Oklahoma St U 1995. D 6/16/1979 P 6/1/1980 Bp Willis Ryan Henton. m 8/21/1976 Caroline Kinloch Terrell c 2. Counslr HCI of Denison TX 2005-2009; Assoc R Ch of the Heav Rest Abilene TX 1987-1988; Vic S Jas Ch Monahans TX 1980-1987; S Ptr's Ch Kermit TX 1980-1985; Chapl St Hosp Big Sprg TX 1979-1980; Cur The Epis Ch Of S Mary The Vrgn Big Sprg TX 1979-1980.

BLAIES-DIAMOND, Sarah (NC) 3430 Old US 70 PO BOX 37, Cleveland NC 27013 **P-in-c Chr Epis Ch Cleveland NC 2012-, 2011** B New Hampshire 1961 d Donald & Joan. BS Carroll Coll; MDiv GTS 2009. D 2/19/2009 Bp Keith Whitmore P 1/16/2011 Bp Michael B Curry. m 9/3/2005 Daryl Edward Diamond c 3. Asst P S Pat's Epis Ch Mooresville NC 2010-2011. momjbe@aol.com

BLAINE, Carol McGown (Tex) 307 Palm Dr, Marlin TX 76661 B Houston TX 1940 d Thomas & Charlotte. BA U of Texas 1963; MDiv Epis TS of the SW 2002. D 6/22/2002 Bp Claude Edward Payne P 7/19/2003 Bp Don Adger Wimberly. c 3. Ch Of The Gd Shpd Friendswood TX 2011-2012; R Gr Epis Ch Houston TX 2005-2011; P-in-c S Jn's Epis Ch Marlin TX 2002-2005.

BLAINE, Patti (Roch) 3825 E Henrietta Rd Ste 100, Henrietta NY 14467 B Endicott NY 1959 d Keith & Lois. SUNY at Buffalo; BS Roberts Wesleyan Coll 1981; Cert in Sch for Chr Ldrshp Colgate Rochester Crozer DS 2013. D 1/28/2017 Bp Prince Grenville Singh. m 5/13/1983 Bruce Evan Blaine c 1.

BLAINE-WALLACE, William Edwards (Me) 161 Wood Street, Lewiston ME 04240 **All SS Epis Ch Skowhegan ME 2013-; Coll Chapl Bates Coll Lewiston ME 2006-** B Salisbury NC 1951 s William & Lucy. BA Lenoir-Rhyne Coll 1975; MDiv Luth Theol Sthrn Sem 1980; PhD Caholic Univerity of Brabant the Netherlands 2009. D 9/26/1992 P 4/1/1993 Bp Don Edward Johnson. m 7/7/2001 Victoria Blaine-Wallace c 3. Ch Of Our Sav 2005-2006; Ch Of Our Sav Arlington MA 2005-2006; R Emm Ch Boston MA 1993-2005. Auth of Chapt in Bk, "The Politics of Tears," *Inustice and the Care of Souls*, Fortress, 2009; Auth, "Water In The Wastelands," Cowley, 2003.

BLAIR, Alexander (Cal) 1801 Marin Ave, Berkeley CA 94707 B Greensboro NC 1925 s Alexander & Dorothy. BS Georgia Inst of Tech 1946; MA Harv 1950; MDiv CDSP 1957; CDSP 1982; PhD Grad Theol Un 1984. D 8/25/1957 P 12/1/1958 Bp C J Kinsolving III. m 6/30/1956 Joan Blair. Assoc All Souls Par In Berkeley Berkeley CA 1993, Assoc 1978-1992; S Alb's Epis Ch Brentwood CA 1988-1993; Ch Of The Nativ San Rafael CA 1986; Instr in Sch for Deacons Dio California San Francisco CA 1982-2006, Dioc Coun 1991-1993; CDSP Berkeley CA 1980-1982; The Cbury Cntr Albuquerque NM 1971-1978; Chair Cbury Cntr NMSU Dio The Rio Grande Albuquerque 1971-1977, COM 1975-1977, Dioc Coun 1969-1974; R S Jn's Epis Ch Alamogordo NM 1964-1970; Vic S Anne El Paso TX 1958-1964; Asst San Juan Mssn Farmington NM 1957-1958.

BLAIR, Rebecca H (RI) 40 Hoppin Hill Avenue, North Attleboro MA 02760 **Ch Of The Gd Shpd Fairhaven MA 2015-; R S Andr's Ch New Bedford MA 2003-** B New Delhi IN 1958 d Henry & Martha. BA Pomona Coll 1984; MDiv Harvard DS 1986. D 6/11/1988 Bp David Elliot Johnson P 6/28/1989 Bp Brice Sidney Sanders. m 7/25/1987 James A Blair c 3. R Emm Epis Ch Cumberland RI 1995-2003; Asst All SS Ch Worcester MA 1994-1995; Dio Wstrn Massachusetts Springfield 1994-1995; Int S Lk's Ch Worcester MA 1993-1994; Int S Jas' Epis Ch Mt Vernon VA 1993; Asst Trin Ch Manassas VA 1990-1992; Asst Emm Ch Farmville NC 1988-1989; Asst S Steph's Ch Goldsboro NC 1988-1989.

BLAIR JR, Thom Williamson (Va) Po Box 1059, Kilmarnock VA 22482 B Key West FL 1944 s Thom. BA Davison 1966; BD VTS 1970; PhD Duke 1977. D 6/25/1970 Bp Thomas Augustus Fraser Jr P 11/1/1973 Bp James Winchester Montgomery. m 6/6/1969 Mary Louisa Blair. S Steph's Ch Richmond VA 1994-2005, 1977-1979; Gr Ch Kilmarnock VA 1984-1994; R S Matt's Epis Ch Warson Woods Kirkwood MO 1979-1984; Cur S Mk's Barrington IL 1974-1977.

BLAIR-HUBERT, Paige Michele (SanD) PO Box 336, Del Mar CA 92014 **R S Ptr's Epis Ch Del Mar CA 2009-; DOK, co-Chapl Dio San Diego San Diego CA 2010-** B March Air Force Base CA 1970 d Michael & Letitia. BA Bos 1992; MDiv Bos TS 1995; CAGS EDS 1996. D 5/1/1996 P 2/1/1997 Bp Donald Purple Hart. m 10/4/2015 Daniel J Hubert c 1. R S Geo's Epis Ch York ME 2000-2009; Assoc R S Jn's Ch Beverly MA 1997-2000; Bos Epis Chap Brookline MA 1996-1997; S Lk's And S Marg's Ch Allston MA 1996-1997; D and Chapl to the ARK Proj S Andr's Ch Edgartown MA 1996; Prot Chapl Assoc Bos Boston MA 1992-1995; Strategic Plnng Com Exec Coun Appointees New York NY 2009-2010; Com on H Ord, co-chair Dio Maine Portland ME 2002-2009; GC Alt 2002-2005, Com on H Ord, Mem 2001-2002; Mus and Liturg Com Dio Massachusetts Boston MA 1999-2000, Micah Proj Bd Dir 1998-2000, Coll Wk Com 1996-2000. Contrib, "U2charist," *Ancient Faith Future Mssn: Fresh Expressions in the Sacramental Tradition*, Cbury Press and Ch Pub, Inc, 2009; Auth, "Finding God in a Single's Bar & Other Watering Holes," *ABF Bulletin*, 1993. Phi Beta Kappa Bos 1992; BA scl Bos 1992.

BLAIR-LOY, Mary Frances (SanD) 747 W University Ave, San Diego CA 92103 **Non-par 1990-** B El Paso TX 1962 d Alexander & Joan. BA U Chi 1983; MDiv Harvard DS 1987; PhD U Chi 1997. D 12/6/1987 P 12/1/1988 Bp William Edwin Swing. m 9/8/1990 John David Blair-Loy. Dio San Diego San Diego CA 2005-2006; Asst To R S Fran Of Assisi Ch Novato CA 1987-1990. Auth, "Amer Sociol Revs"; Auth, "Amer Journ Sociol".

BLAIS, Heather Jeanette (WMass) 73 Federal St, Wiscasset ME 04578 **P-in-c S Jas' Ch Greenfield MA 2013-** B Portsmouth VA 1984 d Richard & Rebecca. Mstr of Div Bangor TS; Bachelor of Arts S Anselm Coll. D 6/25/2011 P 12/17/2011 Bp Stephen Taylor Lane. m 8/19/2006 Jason J Blais c 2. Dio Maine Portland ME 2011-2013; S Phil's Ch Wiscasset ME 2011-2013. heather.blais@gmail.com

BLAKE, Sandra Jean (Colo) **Designed Stained Glass Windows The Windows of S Martins in the Desert Epi. Ch NV 2012-** B Phillips County KS 1943 d Dean & Dorothy. BFA U CO 1964; MDiv Iliff TS 2004. D 6/11/2005 P 12/17/2005 Bp Robert John O'Neill. m 1/29/1965 Peter Blake c 2. Vic S Eliz's Epis Ch Brighton CO 2011-2014; S Tim's Epis Ch Littleton CO 2008-2011; Part Time Assoc S Steph's Epis Ch Aurora CO 2005-2007. Auth, "Disguised as a Poem," *ATR*, 2002.

BLAKE, Sidney Spivey (NY) 204 W 134th St, New York NY 10030 **Died 6/22/2017** B Mount Vernon NY 1940 s Joseph & Lylace. BA CUNY Hunter Coll 1972. D 5/2/2009 Bp Mark Sean Sisk. m 7/5/1986 Philip Spivey. D S Phil's Ch New York NY 2009-2017.

BLAKE, Susan Lynn (CFla) 460 N Grandview St, Mount Dora FL 32757 B St Louis MO 1955 d Thomas & Nancy. BS Framingham St Coll 1979; MS Marywood U 1985; MDiv Nash 2010. D 12/10/2011 Bp John Wadsworth Howe P 10/22/2014 Bp Gregory Orrin Brewer. Transitional D S Edw The Confessor Mt Dora FL 2010-2012.

BLAKE JR, Thomas William (Ind) B Wilmington NC 1972 s Thomas & Permelia. BA Duke 1994; MDiv VTS 2000. D 6/24/2000 Bp Clifton Daniel III P 6/8/2001 Bp Robert Wilkes Ihloff. m 9/25/2015 Chad Robert Adamik. R Gr Ch Muncie IN 2004-2017; Asst to R Middleham & S Ptr's Par Lusby MD 2001-2004; Asst To R S Mk's Ch Highland MD 2000-2001. tblakeabc@gmail.com

BLAKELOCK, Douglas Paul (Alb) 295 Main St, Unadilla NY 13849 B Rotterdam NY 1928 s Douglas & Harriet. AAS Paul Smiths Coll 1951; U of Maine 1953. D 1/12/2002 Bp David John Bena. m 9/19/1953 Sally Ann Lyons c 5. D S Zion Ch Morris NY 2005-2010; D S Matt's Ch Unadilla NY 2002-2005.

BLAKELY, Wayne Allen (Kan) 2805 Woodmont Dr, Louisville KY 40220 **Ret 1997-; Supply P New Harmony Epis Ch New Yarmony Ind 1997-** B Lyons KS 1930 s Ansel & Ella. BA Ashbury Coll 1953; BD Candler TS Emory U 1957; MA Emory U 1958; PhD Emory U 1964. D 8/24/1989 Bp John Forsythe Ashby P 2/1/1990 Bp William Edward Smalley. c 2. MidWeek Serv S Mk's Ch Washington DC 2011; Supply P All SS Epis Ch Jacksonville FL 1997-2006;

Barren River Area Coun Russellville KY 1996-1997; Chr Ch Columbia MD 1993-1997; S Andr's Ch Glasgow KY 1993-1997; Gr Epis Ch Winfield KS 1992-1994; R Epis Ch Of The Redeem Oklahoma City OK 1990-1992; S Barth's Ch Wichita KS 1990; Asst S Jas Ch Wichita KS 1990; Serv Meth Ch 1953-1984.

BLAKEMORE, Barbara Keller (Va) 8499 Anderson Ct, Mechanicsville VA 23116 B Roanoke VA 1938 d Peyton & Mary. BA Randolph-Macon Coll 1960; BA Randolph-Macon Wmn's Coll 1960; MDiv VTS 1990. D 5/26/1990 Bp Claude Charles Vache P 2/23/1991 Bp Frank Harris Vest Jr. m 7/23/1960 William A Blakemore c 3. R S Paul's Ch Hanover VA 1996-2003; S Thos Epis Ch Chesapeake VA 1990-1996.

BLAKLEY, Dave Edward (NwT) B Sherman, Tx 1950 s Marshall & Louella. BBA W Texas St U 1972. D 1/23/2016 Bp James Scott Mayer. c 2.

BLAKLEY, J. Ted (WK) 402 N Topeka St, Wichita KS 67202 **Gr Epis Ch Hutchinson KS 2015-** B Woodward OK 1969 s Ray & Wanda. BA;BA; Friends U 1993; BA Friends U 1993; BA Friends U 1993; MDiv Fuller TS 2001; PhD U of St Andrews 2008; PhD U of St Andrews 2008. D 8/24/2013 Bp Dean E Wolfe. m 5/21/1994 Rebekah Blakley c 4. S Jn's Ch Wichita KS 2013-2015. Auth, "A Lector's Guide and Commentary to the Revised Common Lectionary," *Year B*, St. Mk's Press, 2011; Auth, "A Lector's Guide and Commentary to the Revised Common Lectionary," *Year A*, St. Mk's Press, 2010; Auth, "A Lector's Guide and Commentary to the Revised Common Lectionary," *Year C*, St. Mk's Press, 2009. frted.grace@gmail.com

BLAKLEY, Raymond Leonard (WTenn) 761 Spaulding Dr, Roseville CA 95678 **Asst Iona Hope Epis Ch 2004-** B Christchurch NZ 1926 s Vernon & Edith. MS New Zealand U Nz 1947; PhD New Zealand U Nz 1951; DSC The Australian Natl U 1965. Trans 5/1/1972 Bp Walter Cameron Righter. m 5/12/1949 Beryl Elizabeth Blakley c 1. Asst P S Hilary's Ch Ft Myers FL 1999-2001; Non-par 1978-1998; P-in-c S Fran Cmnty 1974-1978; Non-par 1971-1974; Serv Angl Ch Of Australia 1957-1969.

BLAKSLEE, John Charles (NI) 15606 W 103rd Lane, Dyer IN 46311 **P-in-c S Steph's Epis Ch Hobart IN 1997-** B Canton IL 1934 s Claude & Barbara. BS U IL 1959; JD U IL 1962; MDiv Nash 1972. D 6/19/1971 Bp Gerald Francis Burrill P 12/18/1971 Bp James Winchester Montgomery. m 4/17/1982 Helen Elizabeth Blakslee c 3. Dir Of Dioc Fndt Dio Nthrn Indiana So Bend IN 1998-2000, Dir Of Dioc Fndt 1991-1997, Pres Of Stndg Com 1988-1990; S Paul's Epis Ch Munster IN 1975-1996; Vic S Tim's Ch Griffith IN 1975-1977; R S Paul's Ch Milwaukee WI 1972-1975; Dvlpmt Off Nash Nashotah WI 1970-1975. Auth, "Intro to Today's Lessons," *Pub for congregaton members*, Self, 2015; Auth, "arts Legal Ethics," *Journ Of The ABA*, ABA, 1966; Auth, "The H Euch From A Biblic Perspective," Self Pub through donors; Auth, "Brf Journey Through The Word-Romans," Bible Reading Fllshp.

BLANCH, Paul F (NCal) 2150 Benton Dr, Redding CA 96003 **Educ Prog Bd Mem Capital Reg Theol Cntr 2012-** B Durham England 1956 s Frederick & Doreen. Cert Theol Stud Chichester Theol Coll 1986; BA Dur 1997. Trans 10/16/2009 as Priest Bp William Howard Love. m 3/8/1997 Margaret Blanch c 2. R All SS Epis Ch Redding CA 2014-2017; The Reverend S Geo's Epis Ch Schenectady NY 2009-2014. P Assoc of the H Hse of Our Lady of Walsingham 1986. asecrector@gmail.com

BLANCHARD, Louise Browner (Va) St. Mary's Episcopal Church, 12291 River Road, Richmond VA 23238 **P S Mary's Epis Ch Richmond VA 2015-** B Charlottesville VA 1957 d George & Sara. BA U of Virginia 1979; JD W&L 1985; MDiv UTS Richmond 2007; VTS 2007. D 6/16/2007 P 12/18/2007 Bp Peter J Lee. m 11/30/1985 Charles A Blanchard c 4. Vic S Steph's Ch Richmond VA 2012-2015, Assoc R 2007-2014, Dir Of Childrens Mnstrs 2002-2004. wblanchard@stmarysgoochland.org

BLANCHARD, Louise Sharon (Colo) 6774 Tabor St, Arvada CO 80004 B Boulder CO 1949 d E George & Gloria. BS Colorado St U 1971; MDiv Iliff TS 1989; Cert S Thos Sem 1991. D 6/15/1991 P 12/7/1991 Bp William Jerry Winterrowd. m 8/22/1971 Frank Blanchard c 2. Dio Colorado Denver CO 2001-2016, Cn 2005-, Exec Coun 1992-1995; R 1996-2005; The Ch Of Chr The King (Epis) Arvada CO 1996-2005; Assoc R S Lk's Epis Ch Ft Collins CO 1995-1996; S Ambr Epis Ch Boulder CO 1991-1996. Auth, *Living The Gd News Adult Curric*, 1991. lblanchard@coloradodiocese.org

BLANCHARD, Margaret (WVa) D 1/6/2017 Bp William Michie Klusmeyer.

BLANCHARD, Mary (ETenn) 100 Steven Ln., Harriman TN 37748 **Non-par 2003-** B Chattanooga TN 1949 d Ettore & Edna. BA Kennesaw St U 1985; MDiv Sewanee: The U So, TS 1991. D 6/8/1991 P 12/21/1991 Bp Robert Oran Miller. S Lk's Ch Boone NC 2002; S Jas Epis Ch of Greeneville Greeneville TN 2000-2002; Vic S Mk's Ch Copperhill TN 1995-2000; Dio E Tennessee Knoxville TN 1995-1999; Assoc S Eliz's Epis Ch Knoxville TN 1993-1994; Cur S Paul's Ch Selma AL 1991-1993. Cath Fllshp Of Epis Ch. Outstanding Alum Kennesaw Coll 1992.

BLANCHARD, Sudie Mixter (Me) St. George's Episcopal Church, PO Box 364, York Harbor ME 03911 **D S Geo's Epis Ch York ME 2006-** B Boston MA 1947 d James & Phebe. BA Vas 1970; MLS U MI 1972. D 6/24/2006 Bp Chilton Richardson Knudsen. m 4/14/1973 Peter Blanchard c 2. Chapl York

Hosp York ME 2011-2016. Assn of Profsnl Chapl 2011-2016; NAAD 2004. sblanchard@stgeorgesyorkharbor.org

BLANCHETT, David Harvey (Haw) 1100 Pullman Dr, Wasilla AK 99654 B Vallejo CA 1945 s Powertan & Sarajane. BA U of Alaska 1975; Cert AMEZ AK Conf Theol Anchorage AK 1982. D 6/6/2004 P 12/7/2004 Bp Mark Lawrence Macdonald. m 8/7/1982 Martha N Blanchett c 7. The Epis Ch in Hawaii Honolulu HI 2012; Bp's Stff Off Dio Alaska Fairbanks AK 2008-2011, Bp's Stff Off 2007-2008, 2005, 20/20 And Ecum Off 2005-.

BLANCK, Charles Kenneth (WNC) 977 Collins Rd, Sparta NC 28675 B Rockford IL 1931 s Edward & Ione. BA Duke 1952; BD Epis TS of the SW 1964; STM Luth Theol Sthrn Sem 1970. D 6/27/1964 P 6/29/1965 Bp John Adams Pinckney. c 3. Chr Epis Ch Sparta NC 2003-2009; Vic/R S Lk's Ch Boone NC 1975-1996; R/D-in-Res S Tim's Ch Columbia SC 1964-1966; Chr Ch Greenville SC 1960-1975.

BLANCO-MONTERROSO, Leonel (Okla) 5500 S Western Ave., Oklahoma City OK 73109 B 1945 s Julio & Adela. Escuela de Bellas Artes; Instituto Teologico Epis. D 11/12/1974 P 11/1/1975 Bp Anselmo Carral-Solar. m 5/14/1967 Clara Blanco. Mssnr Santa Maria Virgen Epis Oklahoma City OK 2004-2013; Dio Honduras San Pedro Sula 1988-2003; Dio Guatemala New York NY 1974-1988; Serv Iglesia Anglicana de la Reg Cntrl de Amer -Guatemala.

BLAND, John Dilkes (Minn) 1431 Cherry Hill Rd, Mendota Heights MN 55118 **Ret 1987-** B Jersey City NJ 1923 s Percival & Mildred. Drew U; BS U MN 1949. D 6/24/1968 Bp Hamilton Hyde Kellogg. m 6/30/1945 Betty Lois Burley c 3. Pstr Care Dept Untd Hosp St Paul MN 1982-1987; Asst Mssh Epis Ch S Paul MN 1978-1986; Asst S Mary's Ch S Paul MN 1968-1978. Epis Conf of the Deaf of the Epis Ch in the.

BLAND, Leslie Rasmussen (NC) D 1/24/2015 Bp Anne Hodges-Copple.

BLAND SR, Thomas James (NC) 4608 Pine Cove Rd, Greensboro NC 27410 B Philadelphia PA 1942 NYU. D 1/18/1997 Bp James Gary Gloster. Dir Of Food Pantry S Andr's Ch Greensboro NC 1997-1998; D S Matt's Epis Ch Kernersville NC 2004.

BLASCO, Natalie (SeFla) 1801 Ludlam Dr, Miami Springs FL 33166 **S Chris's By-The-Sea Epis Ch Key Biscayne FL 2015-** B San Juan PR 1972 d Raul & Carmen. AA Broward Coll 2008; BA Florida Intl U 2012; MDiv Berk 2015; MDiv Ya Berk 2015. D 12/12/2014 P 12/5/2015 Bp Leo Frade. m 2/4/1997 Antonio Christopher Buehler. nblasco@stchriskb.org

BLASDELL, Machrina Loris (Cal) 804 Cottonwood Dr., Lansing KS 66043 B Phoenix AZ 1953 d James & Machrina. BA Colorado St U 1975; MA Arizona St U 1980; MDiv CDSP 1984. D 5/31/1984 Bp Joseph Thomas Heistand P 6/1/1985 Bp William Edwin Swing. m 8/20/1983 Michael Munro c 2. Affiliated S Paul's Ch Leavenworth KS 2000-2004, Asst 2000-; Serv as Exec Dir Coun of Ch/Interfaith Coun of Contra Costa Count 1989-2000; Asst S Jas' Epis Ch Warrenton VA 1986-1987, Asst 1986-1987; Ch Of The Gd Shpd Burke VA 1985-1987; Asst Trin Par Menlo Pk CA 1984-1985, Asst 1984-1985. Interfaith Coun, Contra Costa Cnty 1988; Soc Of S Fran, Third Ord Amer Prov; Tertiary Of The Soc Of S Fran 1979-2006.

BLATZ, Edward Nils (LI) 79 Zophar Mills Road, Wading River NY 11792 **Int Ch Of The Redeem Mattituck NY 2002-; Prov II 1993-** B Oceanside NY 1940 s Irving & Elizabeth. BA Bow 1962; STB GTS 1965. D 6/19/1965 P 12/21/1965 Bp Jonathan Goodhue Sherman. m 8/25/1962 Leslie D Blatz c 4. R Gr Ch Brooklyn NY 1994-2002; Dio Long Island Garden City NY 1982-2002, Chair of Chr Fndt 1973-1981, 1972, 1966-1971; Instr in Psychol and Rel Friends Acad Locust Vlly NY 1979-1994; Dn No Nassau Dnry 1979-1980; R Trin Epis Ch Roslyn NY 1972-1994, Cur 1965-1967; S Dav's Ch Wayne PA 1967-1972. OHC - Assoc 1990-1994.

BLAUSER, Dennis Alan (NwPa) 215 Dermond Rd, Hermitage PA 16148 B Oil City PA 1947 s Norman & Mary. BA Thiel Coll 1974; MDiv SWTS 1979. D 6/16/1979 P 12/21/1979 Bp Donald James Davis. m 12/18/1965 Nancy Lee Irvine c 5. Vic Trin Epis Ch New Castle PA 2011-2015; R Trin Ch New Castle PA 2004-2010; Archd Dio NW Pennsylvania Erie PA 1991-2004, GC Dep 1988-2016, Stndg Com 1984-2016; R Ch Of The Redeem Hermitage PA 1984-1991; Chapl Gd Shpd Clarion PA 1982-1983; Vic Chr Ch Punxsutawney PA 1979-1984; Ch Of The H Trin Brookville PA 1979-1984.

BLAUVELT II, Charles (NH) 162 Sagamore St., Manchester NH 03104 B Morristown NJ 1952 s Charles & Margel. BA Susquahanna U 1974; MDiv GTS 1983. D 6/10/1983 P 12/17/1983 Bp Charlie Fuller Mcnutt Jr. c 2. R Gr Ch Manchester NH 2002-2010; R S Tim's Ch Roxborough Philadelphia PA 1993-2002; R S Mary's Epis Par Northfield VT 1988-1993; S Paul's Epis Ch Harrisburg PA 1983-1988.

BLAUVELT, Jeremy David (USC) 125 Church Ave, Pass Christian MS 39571 B 1976 s James & Joyce. BA Iowa St U 2000; MDiv TESM 2005. D 2/17/2008 Bp Robert William Duncan P 8/17/2008 Bp Duncan Montgomery Gray III. m 12/29/2004 Jessica L Blauvelt c 1. R S Jn's Epis Ch Congaree Hopkins SC 2010-2012; Yth & Fam Pstr Trin Ch Epis Pass Chr MS 2008-2010; Off Asst The Bro Of S Andr Ambridge PA 2003-2005.

BLAVIER JR, Donald Charles (WTex) 404 Salisbury Ln, Victoria TX 77904 **Ret 1997-** B Chester PA 1933 s Donald & Marguerite. BFA U of Houston 1954;

Epis TS of the SW 1961; MA U of Houston at Victoria Victoria TX 1990; PhD Texas Tech U 1993. D 6/2/1961 P 5/1/1962 Bp Frederick P Goddard. m 8/4/1974 Betsy Benton Blavier. 1993-1997; P-in-c S Lk's Epis Ch Levelland TX 1990-1993; P-in-c Gr Ch Falfurrias TX 1988-1990; S Jas Epis Ch Hebbronville TX 1988-1990; Gr Ch Port Lavaca TX 1988; R Trin Ch Victoria TX 1974-1988; R Chr Epis Ch Temple TX 1966-1970; Vic All SS Epis Ch San Benito TX 1964-1966; S Andr's Ch Port Isabel TX 1964-1966; R Chr Ch Jefferson TX 1963-1964, M-in-c 1961-1962. Auth, "Internalized Shame and Perceptions of Marital Equity, Intimacy," *Amer Journ of Marital Ther*, 1993. AAMFT.

BLAYER, Brian David (LI) 15117 14 Rd, Whitestone NY 11357 B New York NY 1970 s Norman & Christine. BA Queens Coll 1992; MDiv GTS 2006. D 4/25/2006 P 10/28/2006 Bp Orris George Walker Jr. m 7/12/1998 Susan D Blayer c 1. R Gr Epis Ch Whitestone NY 2010-2017; Asst S Ann's Ch Sayville NY 2008-2010; S Anselm's Ch Shoreham NY 2006-2008; Cur S Mk's Epis Ch Medford NY 2006-2008.

BLAYLOCK, Joy Harrell (CGC) 7125 Hitt Rd, Mobile AL 36695 **The Ch Of The Redeem Mobile AL 2017-** B Mobile AL 1971 d Kelly & Jessica. MA Sprg Hill Coll 1996; PhD The CUA 2004. Rec 5/1/2017 as Priest Bp Russell Kendrick. m 2/18/2002 Roy Lee Blaylock c 1.

BLAZEK, Laura Sue (Okla) 1601 W Imhoff Rd, Norman OK 73072 B Midwest City OK 1966 d Gerald & Helen. DVM Oklahoma St U 1991; Cert in Theol Stds Iona Sch of Formation - Dio Oklahoma 2015. D 8/1/2015 Bp Edward Joseph Konieczny. m 5/18/1991 Eric Martin Blazek c 2.

BLEDSOE, Alwen Grace (Colo) D 6/13/2015 P 6/18/2016 Bp Robert John O'Neill.

BLEDSOE OSH, Faith E (WTex) St. Francis Episcopal Church, 3002 Miori Lane, Victoria TX 77901 B Chickasha OK 1960 d Charles & Katherine. BS K SU 1983; MA K SU 1985; MDiv Epis TS of the SW 2002. D 6/18/2002 Bp Robert Louis Ladehoff P 2/28/2003 Bp James Edward Folts. R S Fran Epis Ch Victoria TX 2005-2011; Assoc R All SS Epis Ch Corpus Christi TX 2002-2005.

BLEDSOE, Sharon Calloway (SVa) 116 Victorian Lane, Jupiter FL 33458 B Saskatoon SK CA 1945 d Charles & Aline. BA U Sask CA 1967; MA Pur 1972; MDiv GTS 1997. D 6/14/1997 Bp Frank Harris Vest Jr P 4/18/1998 Bp Rodney Rae Michel. m 7/11/1997 Richard L Cosnotti c 2. Cur St Jn's Ch Cold Sprg Harbor NY 1997-2001. Auth, "Mary Magdalen: The Lost Diary," Fair Havens Press, Inc., 2011. Cmdr Ord of S Jn of Jerusalem 2010; Sub-Chapl Ord Of S Jn Of Jerusalem 1998; BA cl U Sask 1967.

BLEND, Jennifer Davis (Colo) 4775 Cambridge St, Boulder CO 80301 B Paterson NJ 1943 d William & Elizabeth. BTh The Coll of Emm and S Chad CA 1993. Trans 2/1/1996 Bp William Jerry Winterrowd. Serv Angl Ch Of Can 1993-1994. Auth, "Dream Kitchen," *Kitchen Talk*. SBL.

BLESSING, Kamila Abrahamova (Pgh) 6211 Wrightsville Ave. Unit 147, Wilington NC 28403 **Non-par Blessing Taxes 2010-; Non-par Blessing Transitions Mediation and Consulting 2004-; Dioc Life Com Mem Dio Pittsburgh Pittsburgh PA 2011-, Campus Mnstry Cmsn Mem 1979-2011** B Pittsburgh PA 1948 d Karel & Lillian. BS Carnegie Mellon U 1971; MS U Pgh 1976; PhD U Pgh 1977; MA Other 1984; MA Pittsburgh TS 1984; PhD Duke 1996; Cert Int Mnstry Ntwk 2004; Certificates Lombard Mennonite Pewace Cntr 2004; Certificates Lombard Mennonite Peace Cntr 2005; Cert IRS 2013. D 10/15/1983 P 5/16/1984 Bp Alden Moinet Hathaway. P in charge S Barn Ch Brackenridge PA 2011-2013, P-in-c 2011-; Int S Paul's Epis Ch Pittsburgh PA 2005-2006; Int S Lk's Epis Ch Montclair NJ 2004; Int S Mary's Ch Sparta NJ 2002-2004; Int Emm Epis Ch S Louis MO 2001-2002; VP/CE Chr Bd Pub S Louis MO 2000-2001; P-in-c Ch Of The Adv Enfield NC 1996-1998; P-in-c S Jn's Ch Battleboro NC 1996-1998; P-in-c Chr Ch Rocky Mt NC 1993-1998; Int S Paul's Epis Ch Kittanning PA 1989-1990; Vic S Ptr's Epis Ch Brentwood Pittsburgh PA 1987-1989; R S Andr Rome NY (cluster w St. Jas above) 1985-1986; S Jas' Ch Clinton NY 1985-1986; R St Andrews Epis Ch Rome NY 1985-1986; Pstr Min Ch Of The Ascen Pittsburgh PA 1983-1985; CE Cmsn Mem Dio Missouri S Louis MO 2000-2001; Campus Min Carnegie Mellon U 1978-1983. Auth, "For Those who Are Alone: 52 Meditations," *(Bk)*, Sacr Winds Press, 2012; Auth, "Speak Ye First the Kingdom: A Mainline Pstr's Journey into Abundance," *(Bk)*, Ecum Stwdshp Fndt, 2011; Auth, "Families of the Bible: A New Perspective," *(Bk)*, Praeger, 2010; Auth, "Commentary on Jn," *IVP Wmn Bible Commentary*, IVP, 2000; Auth, "Murray Bowen'S Fam Systems Theory As Bible Hermeneutic Using The Fam Of The Prodigal, Lk 15:11-32," *Journ Of Psychol And Chrsnty*, 2000; Auth, "It Was a Miracle: Stories of Ordnry People and Extraordinary Healing," *(Bk)*, Augsburg Fortress, 1999; Auth, "Many Journ arts on systems theory as hermeneutic; and healing.," 1990. CHS 1981; Int Mnstry Ntwk 2002; Ord Of S Lk 1987; SBL 1990.

BLESSING, Pastor Mary (ECR) 5271 Scotts Valley Dr, Scotts Valley CA 95066 **Bd Trst Dio El Camino Real Salinas CA 2010-, T/F on Pvrty 2011-, Chair T/F Plcy Protect Chld 2005-; R S Phil The Apos Scotts Vlly CA 2006-; R St. Phil the Apos Epis Ch Scotts Vlly CA 2006-** B Oakland CA 1954 d John & Ruth. Ob 1972; BA Mills Coll 1976; MDiv CDSP 1992. D 6/1/1996 P 6/7/1997 Bp William Edwin Swing. m 4/2/1977 James Edward Blessing c 2. Assoc R Ch Of S Jude The Apos Cupertino CA 2000-2006; Asst R S Tim's Epis Ch Mtn

91

View CA 1998-2000; Pstr Assoc S Mich And All Ang Concord CA 1996-1997; Coordntr Gr Cathd San Francisco CA 1992-1994; Asst Chapl Epis Sanctuary San Francisco San Francisco CA 1990-1991. Chair, Dioc Bdgt Com 2001-2002; Chair, ECR Peace and Justice Cmsn 2004-2006; Dept of Missions 2008-2011; ECR Dioc Coun 2000-2002; El Camino Cler Orgnztn, Bd Mem 1994; NNECA 1994.

BLESSING, Robert Alan (SanD) 12539 Sundance Ave, San Diego CA 92129 **R S Andr's Ch La Mesa CA 2011-, P 2006-2013** B Eugene OR 1958 s William & Norma. Fuller TS; BA U of Washington 1980; MDiv CDSP 1984. Trans 1/15/2004 Bp Don Adger Wimberly. m 12/12/1987 Anne Christine Blessing c 2. Chapl Spec Mobilization Spprt Plan Washington DC 2010-2011; Assoc P Ch Of The Gd Samar San Diego CA 2003-2006; Chapl Pension Fund Mltry New York NY 2002-2003; R S Mich And All Ang' Epis Ch Longview TX 2000-2002; Chapl US-A 1995-2000; Chapl Off Of Bsh For ArmdF New York NY 1994-2000; Vic Gr Ch Kent WA 1992-1995; Gr Epis Ch Kent WA 1992-1994; Vic S Dav Emm Epis Ch Shoreline WA 1992-1993; Serv Angl Ch of Korea 1987-1992; Asst S Lk's Epis Ch Seattle WA 1985-1986. NOVAC 2013.

BLESSING, Wren Tyler (Mont) Diocese Of Montana, PO Box 2020, Helena MT 59624 **Cn Dio Montana Helena MT 2013-** B Newport News VA 1983 d William & Carol Anne. BA Wheaton Coll 2005; MDiv Duke DS 2009; MDiv Duke DS 2009; Angl Stds SWTS 2011. D 6/16/2012 P 3/3/2013 Bp Michael B Curry. c 2. CE Dir Ch Of The H Fam Chap Hill NC 2012-2013, 2011-2012. christianformation@diomontana.com

BLEVINS, Isaac (ETenn) D 2/11/2017 Bp George Young III.

BLEYLE, Douglas Karl (RG) 318 Silver Ave SW, Albuquerque NM 87102 **S Steph's Epis Ch Espanola NM 2014-** B Denver CO 1967 s Donald & Mary. BA Metropltn St Coll 2003; MDiv Iliff TS 2006; ThM Candler TS Emory U 2008. D 1/6/2012 P 5/25/2013 Bp Michael Vono. m 9/1/1996 Jennifer Lynn Bleyle c 1. Dio The Rio Grande Albuquerque 2012-2014.

BLINMAN, Clifford Louis (Ore) 2092 E. Bighorn Mountain Dr, Oro Valley AZ 85755 **Vol Assoc S Phil's In The Hills Tucson AZ 2000-** B Sacramento CA 1936 s Foster & Edna. Penn 1969; Cert CDSP 1981; BA Sch for Deacons 1985. D 9/18/1978 Bp Chauncie Kilmer Myers P 7/22/1981 Bp William Edwin Swing. m 2/27/2010 Mary Sue Blinman c 3. R Trin Epis Ch Ashland Ashland OR 1993-1999; S Anne's Ch Fremont CA 1988-1993; S Tim's Ch Danville CA 1987-1988; Asst S Paul's Epis Ch Walnut Creek CA 1978-1988.

BLISS, John Derek Clegg (Cal) 4 Edgewater Hillside, Westport CT 06880 B Wisbech Cambridgeshire UK 1940 s Clarence & Cicely. Salisbury TS Gb; U of Durham GB. Trans 2/17/1981 Bp Victor Manuel Rivera. Asst S Steph's Ch Coconut Grove Miami FL 2001; Non-par 1989-1992; R H Trin Epis Ch Madera CA 1980-1989; Serv Ch Of Engl 1968-1980. Human Outreach Agnecy, Hayward Ca 1992-1996.

BLISS, Robert Francis (Tex) 881 North Main Street, PO Box 797, Salado TX 76571 **Vic S Lk's Epis Ch Salado TX 2013-, R 2011-2013; Vic St Jos's Epis Ch Salado TX 2013-** B Houston TX 1948 s Cecil & Mary. BS Texas A&M U 1976; Iona Sch for Mnstry 2010; Iona Sch for Mnstry 2010; Other 2010. D 6/19/2010 Bp C Andrew Doyle P 1/8/2011 Bp Dena Arnall Harrison. m 11/17/1989 Melanie Bliss c 3.

BLISS, Vernon Powell (CNY) 86 E Taylor Hill Rd, Montague MA 01351 B Cincinnati OH 1934 s Vernon & Hilma. BA Ken 1957; MDiv GTS 1960; PhD Un Inst 1975. D 6/29/1960 P 1/1/1961 Bp Roger W Blanchard. m 10/15/2005 Sarah Bliss c 2. Mssy S Geo's Epis Ch Chadwicks NY 1961-1967; Cur Ch Of The Adv Cincinnati OH 1960-1961.

BLIZZARD, Charles Fortunate-Eagle (Okla) 1301 Andover Ct, Oklahoma City OK 73120 **Casady Sch Oklahoma City OK 2006-; Vic/Chapl S Edw Chap Oklahoma City OK 2006-** B Alpine TX 1981 s Franklin & Susan. BS Sul Ross St U 2003; MDiv TESM 2006. D 5/20/2006 Bp Jeffrey Neil Steenson P 7/14/2007 Bp Robert Manning Moody. m 7/2/2004 Nicolette Fortunate-Eagle Blizzard.

BLOOM, Barry Moffett (Mass) 3030 Union St, Oakland CA 94608 **Non-par 1975-** B Newton MA 1937 s Galen & Elizabeth. BA Wesl 1960; BD CDSP 1963. D 6/23/1963 Bp James Albert Pike P 5/1/1964 Bp George Richard Millard. m 9/5/1958 Linda Lindergreen c 3.

BLOOM, Carl Richard (Spr) 1989 East Gleneagle Drive, Chandler AZ 85249 **Ret Dio Springfield 1995-** B Chicago IL 1928 s Carl & Helga. BA Augustana Coll 1951; BD SWTS 1954; MDiv SWTS 1971. D 1/9/1954 P 7/17/1954 Bp Charles L Street. c 5. Asst S Mk's Epis Ch Mesa AZ 1998-2007; Dio Springfield Springfield IL 1988-1995; S Jas Chap Marion Marion IL 1988-1995; S Mk's Ch W Frankfort IL 1988-1995; Lead P - Team Mnstry S Steph's Ch Harrisburg IL 1988-1995; R Calv Ch Lombard IL 1968-1977; R The Epis Ch Of The H Trin Belvidere IL 1960-1968; Vic Chr The King Epis Ch Huntington IN 1956-1960; Gr Epis Ch Galena IL 1954-1956; Exec Coun Dio Chicago Chicago IL 1965-1968, Chapl to Shimer Coll 1954-1964. Chapl Ord of S Lk 1972; OHC 1956.

BLOOMER, Nancy Hester (NY) 4 Grant St, Essex Junction VT 05452 **1997-** B Binghamton NY 1939 d Ronald & Ruth. BA SUNY 1969; MA SUNY 1970;

PhD SUNY 1976; MDiv GTS 1986. D 6/13/1987 Bp Paul Moore Jr P 12/18/1987 Bp Daniel Lee Swenson. c 2. S Paul's And Trin Par Tivoli NY 1995-1998; Int Zion Ch Manchestr Ctr VT 1994-1995; Int S Mary's Epis Par Northfield VT 1993-1994; Assoc S Jn's In The Mountains Stowe VT 1991-1992; S Ann's Ch Burlington VT 1990-1991; S Matt's Ch Enosburg Fls VT 1987-1990; Chair of Environ Mnstry Team Dio Vermont Burlington VT 2002-2005, Dioc Coun 1989-2001. "Var arts," *The Living Pulpit*, 2007; Auth, "Greed," *The Living Pulpit*, 2003; Auth, "Preaching to Heal thePreaching to Heal the Earth," *The Living Pulpit*, 2000; Auth, "Sabbath Time," *The Living Pulpit*, 1998. Ord of S Helena, Assoc; OHC, Assoc.

BLOSSOM JR, John Dickson (Chi) 125 Sw Jefferson Ave, Peoria IL 61602 **Bread of Life Angl Fllshp Peoria IL 2013-; Cn for Strategic Plnng Dio Quincy Peoria IL 2005-, Cn 1998-2004** B Peuria IL 1940 s John & Jane. U CO 1962; MBA GTF 1972. D 6/6/1973 Bp Francis W Lickfield P 6/1/1974 Bp Donald James Parsons. m 5/15/1987 Linda Blossom c 2. Cn St Paul's Epis Ch Peoria IL 1992-2006; P-in-c All SS Ch Quincy IL 1987-1992; Asst P S Andr's Ch Peoria IL 1986-1987; P-in-c S Steph's Ch 1974-1986. Mem of Amer Soc of Pension Actuaries 1971. Outstanding Young Man of 1974 Jr ChmbrCom 1974; Mem Amer Soc Pension Actuaries. johnb@oldsailorshome.com

BLOTTNER, William Eugene (Chi) 510 First Ave, Farmville VA 23901 **Ret 1994-** B Richmond VA 1929 s Herman & Gwynn. BS VPI 1951; MDiv VTS 1956; MA Cleveland St U 1980; DMin GTF 1994. D 6/1/1956 P 7/13/1957 Bp Frederick D Goodwin. c 3. EfM Mentor Johns Memi Epis Ch Farmville VA 2009-2014, Coll Chapl 1996-2008; Int R Ch of the Gd Shpd Mc Kenney VA 1997-1998; Int Dio Sthrn Virginia Newport News VA 1996-2004; Int R S Andr's Epis Ch Lawrenceville VA 1996-1997, 1957-1958; Int R S Anne's Ch Appomattox VA 1995-1996; Int R S Fran Epis Ch Chicago IL 1989-1994; Int Ch Of The Redeem Lorain OH 1988-1989; Int R S Andr Epis Ch Mentor OH 1986-1988; Int R S Ptr's Ch Akron OH 1985-1986; Int R All SS Ch Cleveland OH 1984-1985; Int R S Paul Epis Ch Norwalk OH 1982-1983; Int R S Paul's Epis Ch Of E Cleveland Cleveland OH 1981-1982; Vic S Steph Vermillion OH 1977-1979; Part Time Vic St Stephens Ch Vermilion OH 1977-1979; Int P S Andr's Ch Cleveland OH 1968-1969; P-in-c S Agnes Ch Cleveland OH 1967-1970; Vic S Matt & S Lk Cleveland OH 1966-1968; Asst S Mich's Ch Richmond VA 1960-1965, Asst to R 1958-1959; Asst to R S Tim's Ch Catonsville MD 1958-1960; D-in-c Epis Ch Of Leeds Par Markham VA 1956-1957. Sociol Hon Soc Alpha Kappa Delta 1978.

BLUBAUGH, Susan Jo (NI) 1305 S 2nd St, Lafayette IN 47905 B Elkhart IN 1953 d Frederick & Barbara. BS Ball St U 1976; MA Ball St U 1980; Cert Theol Stud SWTS 1991; Cert Pur 1999. D 12/20/1991 P 7/8/1992 Bp Francis Campbell Gray. m 6/26/1976 Robert Daniel Blubaugh c 3. Sch Counslr/ Tchr Lowell HS (Tri-Creek Sch Corp) 1999-2012; P S Mary's Fllshp Monticello IN 1994-2007; Chld Advoc and Counslr N. C. Indiana Crisis Cntr (battered Wmn Shltr) 1994-1997; P S Ptr's Ch Rensselaer IN 1992; Tchr (middle Sch) Rensselaer Cntrl Sch Corp 1986-1991; Tchr (HS) No White Sch Corp 1979-1984; COM Dio Nthrn Indiana So Bend IN 2000-2005.

BLUE, Eddie Michael (Md) 7 Park Ave Apt 1, Westminster MD 21157 B Indianapolis IN 1950 s Houston & Johnnie. Mstr of Div Bex; BA Indiana U 1972; MDiv Bex Sem 1979. D 5/31/1979 Bp Edward Witker Jones P 6/24/1980 Bp Lyman Cunningham Ogilby. m 5/8/1982 Lucy Brady c 3. Dep Gc Dio Maryland Baltimore MD 1994-2009; R Ch Of The H Trin Baltimore MD 1984-2017; Non-par 1982-1984; Dio Pennsylvania Philadelphia PA 1979-1982; Asst S Mary Epis Ch Chester PA 1979-1981. Auth, "Living in Hope," *Sermons That Wk*, Ch Pub, 2001. Maryland Clerics Assn.

BLUE, Gordon K (Ak) 2902 Sawmill Creek Rd, Sitka AK 99835 **The Ch Of The H Trin Juneau AK 2013-** B Seattle WA 1951 s Harold & Virginia. MDiv Vancouver TS CA 2006. D 11/1/2004 P 4/9/2005 Bp Mark Lawrence Macdonald. m 7/11/1998 Sarah Lynn Blue c 3. S Jas The Fisherman Kodiak AK 2011-2013; Sitka Counslg & Prevention Serv Inc Sitka AK 2007-2011; Asst S Ptr's By-The-Sea Sitka AK 2005-2011. frblue@trinityjuneau.org

BLUE, Susan Neff (WA) 270 El Diente Dr., Durango CO 81301 B Kalamazoo MI 1942 d Richard & Wilma. Duke 1962; BS NYU 1965; MDiv GTS 1986; ThM New Brunswick TS 1989. D 6/14/1986 P 1/17/1987 Bp George Phelps Mellick Belshaw. c 2. Mem Past Grp Addressing GC Resolution CO56 2009-2011; VTS Alexandria VA 2006, 2004, 2003; Dep Alt GC 2003-2004; Adj Cler The Cathd Coll Washington DC 2002-2009; Adj Cler VTS Alexandria VA 2002-2008; Exec Committee Coun--1998-2003 Dio Washington Washington DC 1998-2005; R S Marg's Ch Washington DC 1997-2010; Initial Cnvnr Cnvnr Const & Cn Conv 1995; Initial Convenor Convenor Const ; Cn Conv 1995; Gnrl Dep Dio NJ Coun 1994-1997; Mem Dio NJ Coun 1993-1996; R Trin Ch Matawan NJ 1991-1997; Cur S Lk's Epis Ch Metuchen NJ 1986-1991; Anti-racism Com Dio Washington Washington DC 2007-2010; Fin Com Dio New Jersey Trenton NJ 1993-1997.

BLUME, Andrew C (NY) 160 West 95th Street, Apt. 8B, New York NY 10025 **R The Ch of S Ign of Antioch New York NY 2007-; BEC Dio New York New York NY 2013-, Com on Campus Mnstry 2010-, COM 2009-, Com on Deacons 2009-, Angl-RC Dialogue in New York 2008-2010, Ecum Cmsn**

2008-2010 B Bethesda MD 1967 s Ralph & Nancy. BA Trin Hartford CT 1989; PhD Harv 1995; MDiv EDS 2005. D 6/4/2005 Bp M(Arvil) Thomas Shaw P 1/7/2006 Bp Roy Frederick Cederholm Jr. m 10/3/1993 Jacalyn Ruth Blume c 1. Asst The Ch Of The Adv Boston MA 2006-2007; Asst S Andr's Ch Framingham MA 2005-2006; Var Tchg and Admin Positions Harv Cambridge Mass 1992-2002; Com on Liturg and Mus Dio Massachusetts Boston MA 2004-2007. "Numerous arts in Acad Journ". Pilgrims of the Untd States 2012. Faith in Action Awd Virginia Coun of Ch 2013; M.St.J. Ord of S Jn of Jerusalem 2010.

BLUMENSTOCK, Robert (NCal) 732 Shoreside Dr, Sacramento CA 95831 B Bakersfield CA 1944 s Warren & Benda. AA Bakersfield Cmnty Coll 1966; BA San Francisco St U 1969; MDiv VTS 1988. D 6/3/1989 Bp William Edwin Swing P 1/25/1990 Bp Charles Farmer Duvall. m 8/23/1975 Doni Blumenstock c 3. Trin Ch Sutter Creek CA 2008-2009, 2008-2009; St Marys Ch Elk Grove Sacramento CA 2004-2007; Int R St.Mary's Ch 2004-2007; S Lk's Ch Galt CA 1997-2003, Vic 1997-2003; Ch Of Our Sav Somerset MA 1995-1997, Int R 1995-1997; R S Andr's Ch New Bedford MA 1991-1995, 1991-1994; Trin Epis Ch Mobile AL 1989-1991, Cur 1989-1991. EvangES, Cath Fell Epis Ch.

BLUMER, Gary R (Be) Po Box 623, Portland PA 18351 B Minneapolis MN 1935 s Charles & Erna. BA U MN 1957; MDiv Nash 1960; STM GTS 1979. D 2/4/1960 Bp Albert Ervine Swift P 8/1/1960 Bp William W Horstick. S Jn's Ch Norristown PA 1994-1996; S Jn's Epis Ch Hamlin PA 1994-1996; Trin Epis Ch Williamsport PA 1994-1996; Chr Ch Forest City PA 1992-1993; Trin Epis Ch Carbondale PA 1992-1993; Par Of The H Fam Pen Argyl PA 1991-1992; Int S Jos's Ch Pen Argyl PA 1990-1992; Int Chr Ch Media PA 1989-1990; S Mary's Ch Keyport NJ 1987-1988; Dio New Jersey Trenton NJ 1987; Asst Chr Ch New Brunswick NJ 1980-1986; Non-par 1975-1980; R Chr Ch Chippewa Fls WI 1967-1975; S Simeon's Ch Chippewa Falls WI 1967-1975; Vic Our Sav Luggerville WI 1962-1967; Vic S Marg's Epis Ch Pk Falls WI 1962-1967; Cur Chr Ch Par La Crosse WI 1960-1962.

BLUNDELL, Gayle Ann (ECR) 2100 Emmons Rd, Cambria CA 93428 B Saint Louis MO 1936 d Gale & Clara. BA Syr 1957; MA Fuller TS 1989. D 6/22/1999 Bp Richard Lester Shimpfky. m 10/19/1957 William Edward Blundell. D S Lk's Ch Atascadero CA 1998-2004; Dir S Geo's Par La Can CA 1978-1983.

BLUNT, Elizabeth E (Az) Christ Church of the Ascension, 4015 E Lincoln Dr, Paradise Valley AZ 85253 **Trin Par New York NY 2016-** B Kalamazoo MI 1974 d William & Diane. AB Bow 1996; MDiv Yale DS 2014. D 6/22/2013 P 5/31/2014 Bp Kirk Stevan Smith. Chr Ch Of The Ascen Paradise Vlly AZ 2014-2016.

BLUNT JR, Howard Elton (LI) 125 Eastern Parkway #5D, Brooklyn NY 11238 **S Ptr's Ch Bronx NY 2003-; Assoc Trin Ch Of Morrisania Bronx NY 2003-; Chapl/Assoc Dir Of Rel Serv S Lk-Roosevelt Hosp New York NY 1998-** B Providence RI 1941 s Howard & L'Marie. BA Leh 1964; STB GTS 1967; Dio New York New York NY 1999. D 6/17/1967 P 3/1/1968 Bp John S Higgins. m 10/13/2009 Donald George Beckman c 2. Int S Phil's Ch 1996-1998; Dio New York New York NY 1989-2001, 1976-1981; Epis Mssn Soc New York NY 1987-1989; Assoc Chapl Goldwater Meml Hosp Brooklyn NY 1987-1989; The GTS New York NY 1986-1987; P-in-c S Phil's Ch New York NY 1985; Asst Ch Of S Simon The Cyrenian New Rochelle NY 1982-1985; S Lk's-Roosevelt Hosp Cntr New York NY 1973-2001; Assoc Chapl S Lk-Roosevelt Hosp New York NY 1973-1981; Asst S Aug's Ch New York NY 1969-1973; Cur S Mart's Ch Providence RI 1967-1969. Cler, Manhattan No Bd S Margeret Cntr; Epis Black Caucus New York.

BOARD, John Curtis (Mont) 2704 Gold Rush Ave, Helena MT 59601 **Cathd Ch Of The Nativ Bethlehem PA 2005-** B Onarga IL 1936 s Victor & Georgia. BA Ball St Teachers Coll 1958; MA U of Wyoming 1964; MLS U of Oregon 1972; Montana Mnstry Formation Prog 2005. D 9/18/2005 Bp Charles Franklin Brookhart Jr. m 6/15/1965 Mait Birgitt Erickson Board c 2. "Great Teachers Are Not Solo Performers," *Educ Week*, Educ Week, 1992; "A Spec Relatns: Our Teachers and How We Learned (B00K)," *A Spec Relatns: Our Teachers and How We Learned(Bk)*, Pushcart Press, 1991; "Passion is the shared trait among great teachers," *The Middletown Press*, The Middletown Press (Connecticut), 1991; "Jeannette Rankin: The Lady from Montana," *Montana, The mag of Wstrn Hist*, Montana Hist Soc, 1967.

BOARD III, John Paul (O) 313 E Wayne St, Maumee OH 43537 **R S Paul's Ch Maumee OH 1997-** B Wertzburg DE 1964 s John & Ruth. BA U So 1989; MDiv VTS 1995; DMin SWTS 2007. D 6/24/1995 Bp R aymond Stewart Wood Jr P 2/12/1996 Bp J Clark Grew II. m 7/17/1993 Lori A Board c 3. Asst R Chr Epis Ch Warren OH 1995-1997.

BOASE, David John (Spr) 4902 Blu Fountain Dr, Godfrey IL 62035 B Millom UK 1949 s Donald & Jean. BA U of Durham GB 1971; PGCE Oxf UK 1973; Cert Theol Stud Ripon Coll Cuddesdon GB 1973. Trans 11/1/2004 Bp Peter Hess Beckwith. c 2. R S Paul's and Trin Chap Alton IL 2004-2014.

BOATRIGHT-SPENCER, Angela (NY) 801 Willow St, Wadesboro NC 28170 B Newark NJ 1951 d John & Laura. BA Cor 1973; MS Col 1975; MDiv UTS 1988; Dplma GTS 1991; Cert So Piedmont Comm Coll 2008. D 6/15/1991 Bp Orris George Walker Jr P 1/25/1992 Bp Frank Kellogg Allan. m 6/30/2007 Richard Lewis Spencer c 3. Permanent Supply Chap Of Chr The King Charlotte NC 2010-2014; Longterm Supply Ch Of The Mssh Rockingham NC 2008; Dio New York New York NY 2002-2007; S Paul's Ch Sprg Vlly NY 2002-2007; Assoc Trin Epis Ch Garnerville NY 2002-2007; Chapl S Mary's Cntr New York NY 1997-2001; Asst S Mary's Manhattanville Epis Ch New York NY 1997-2001; Chapl St. Mary's Cntr Inc. New York NY 1996-2001; Vic S Tim's Decatur GA 1994-1996; P-in-c S Steph's Ch Griffin GA 1991-1994. Auth, "Recon, Redemp & Gr," *Wisdom Found (edited by Lindsay Hardin Freeman)*, Forw Mvmt, 2010; Co-Auth, "The Heir," XLibris, 2008; Auth, "Spec Delivery , Thanksgiving Pryr," *Race and Pryr (edited by M. Boyd and C.Talton)*, Morehouse, 2003; Auth, "In The Time Of Trouble," Ldr Resources, 2002. Ord Of S Helena 1982-1984. Wmn of dist Awd Alpha Phi Alpha 2007; Cert of Merit NY St Senate 2006; Cert of Merit NY St Assembly 2005; DSA Rockland Cnty Legislature 2004; Humanitarian Awd NAACP 2003.

BOATWRIGHT, William (NJ) 1901 N. DuPont Highway, New Castle DE 19720 **P-in-c S Geo's Ch Pennsville NJ 2013-; Chapl Delaware Psych Cntr 2006-** B Avon Park FL 1953 s Manuel & Thelma. BA Stetson U 1977; Chandler TS 1979; MDiv Andover Newton TS 1982; Cert Ang Stud Nash 1986; STM GTS 1989. D 10/19/1987 Bp Henry Boyd Hucles III P 12/1/1988 Bp Orris George Walker Jr. m 4/17/2003 Kahlil Boatright c 1. Asst Cathd Ch Of S Jn Wilmington DE 2005-2006; Int S Andr's Ch New York NY 2000-2001, Int 1997-1998; Int Chr Ch-Epis Prt Jefferson NY 2000; Chapl St Marys Cnvnt Greenwich NY 1999-2000; Assoc S Jas Epis Ch Fordham Bronx NY 1998-2000, P-in-c 1998-2000; Dio New York New York NY 1998-1999; Chapl Dio Atlanta Atlanta GA 1991-1996; Asst S Mk's Ch Brooklyn NY 1990-1998, Asst 1990-1998; Cur S Phil's Epis Ch 1989-2001; S Phil's Ch Brooklyn NY 1989-1990; Asst S Phil's 1989-1990; Asst Dio Long Island Garden City NY 1987-1989.

BOBBITT, Kathleen Morrisette (SVa) 1005 Windsor Rd, Virginia Beach VA 23451 **Int Galilee Epis Ch Virginia Bch VA 2008-** B Norfolk VA 1942 d William & Myra. BS U of Maryland European Div Heidelberg Germa 1988; MDiv VTS 1993. D 6/5/1993 Bp Jack Marston Mckelvey P 1/15/1994 Bp John Shelby Spong. m 12/16/1967 Joseph Rosser Bobbitt c 3. Emm Ch Virginia Bch VA 2014-2015; P-in-c Trin Ch Portsmouth VA 2012-2014; Int S Thos Epis Ch Chesapeake VA 2011-2012; Int S Geo's Epis Ch Newport News VA 2010; Dn Dio Sthrn Virginia Newport News VA 2006-2010; Assoc Estrn Shore Chap Epis Ch Virginia Bch VA 2005-2008; Assoc Estrn Shore Chap Virginia Bch VA 2005-2008; Dir Of Chapl Serv Goodwin Hse Inc. Alexandria VA 2000-2005; Chapl Goodwin Hse Incorporated Alexandria VA 2000-2005; Assoc R For Pstr Care S Jn's Epis Ch Mc Lean VA 1995-2000; Cur Trin Ch Arlington VA 1993-1995. Assn Of Friends Of The Warterloo Com 1996; Colonial Dames 2002; Jr League 1972-1987.

BOBO, Melinda (Wyo) P.O. Box 1177, Dubois WY 82513 **S Thos Ch Dubois WY 2014-** B Washington DC 1964 d Charles & Annie. BA Pur 1984; MA Pur 1986; U of Wyoming 1998; MDiv SWTS 2001. D 6/20/2001 P 12/20/2001 Bp Bruce Caldwell. Mnstry Dvlp Dio Wyoming Casper 2010-2013; Supply P Dio Wyoming WY 2006-2010; Vic S Mk's Ch Craig CO 2004-2005; Asst R S Mart's By The Lake Epis Minnetonka Bch MN 2001-2004.

BOCCHINO, Jim (RI) 589 Smithfield Rd, North Providence RI 02904 B Pawtucket RI 1950 s John & Josephine. BS Wag 1972; MDiv EDS 1984. D 6/23/1984 P 3/2/1985 Bp George Nelson Hunt III. m 11/30/2002 Barbara Elizabeth Fox. Dio Maine Portland ME 2013-2017; P-in-c S Barn Ch Warwick RI 2013-2017; Int S Ptr's Ch Rockland ME 2013; Int Chr Ch Westerly RI 2010-2013; Int S Jn's Ch Barrington RI 2008-2010; Chapl S Mary's Hm for Chld No ProvidenceRI 1989-1993; R All SS' Meml Ch Providence RI 1987-2008; Asst S Mary's Ch Portsmouth RI 1984-1987. frjim@stbarnabaswarwick.org

BOCCINO, Kenneth Robert (Nwk) 550 Ridgewood Rd, Maplewood NJ 07040 B Teaneck NJ 1962 s Robert & Carol. BS Case Wstrn Reserve U 1984; MS Pace U 1991; Cert in Diac Stds Newark TS 2015. D 5/16/2015 Bp Mark M Beckwith. m 4/16/1994 Nerissa C Teekasingh c 2.

BOCK, Susan Kay (Mich) 529 E Kirby St, Detroit MI 48202 B Pontiac MI 1948 d William & Patricia. Sch of Nrsng Henry Ford U Hosp 1970; Epis TS of the SW 1984. D 6/30/1984 Bp Henry Irving Mayson P 10/1/1985 Bp H Coleman Mcgehee Jr. m 1/6/2008 James Brown c 2. P Gr Ch Mt Clemens MI 2010-2017; R S Gabr's Epis Ch Eastpointe MI 2001-2012; Cn S Andr's Cathd Jackson MS 1998-2001; R S Aid's Ch Ann Arbor MI 1997-1998; S Clare Of Assisi Epis Ch Ann Arbor MI 1989-1997; Assoc S Clare of Assisi Ann Arbor MI 1989-1997; Asst P S Mich's Ch Grosse Pointe MI 1986-1989; Asst P S Dav's Ch Southfield MI 1985-1988. Auth, "Liturg for the Whole Ch: Multigenerational Resources for Wrshp," Ch Pub, 2008.

BOCKUS, Ian Lawrence (Me) 496 N Searsport Rd, Prospect ME 04981 **Assoc Trin Ch Castine ME 2011-** B Cowansville QC CA 1933 s Elton & Carrie. BA Bishops U QC CA 1954; BD McGill U 1957; LTh Montreal Dioc Coll 1957. Trans 7/1/1961 Bp Oliver L Loring. m 9/3/2011 Brian A Macfarland c 2. Cn Cathd Ch Of S Lk Portland ME 1997-2000; R S Pat's Ch Brewer ME 1984-1998; S Paul's Epis Ch Vermillion SD 1982-1984; R H Apos Epis Ch Trenton NJ 1970-1982; R S Andr Plainfield NJ 1966-1970; Asst Chr Ch Par

Kensington MD 1964-1966; R S Lk's Ch Caribou ME 1961-1964; Serv Angl Ch of Can 1956-1961. Hon Cn S Lk's Cathd 1997.

BODIE, Park McDermit (NY) 235 W 56th St Apt 11m, New York NY 10019 B South Charleston WV 1950 s George & Jean. BA W Virginia St U 1981; MDiv Sewanee: The U So, TS 1986. D 6/29/1986 P 4/21/1987 Bp William Evan Sanders. m 11/20/1981 Suzanne Bodie c 2. Supply P Chr Ch Garden City NY 2009-2010; Int S Barn Ch Irvington NY 2008-2009; Int S Eliz's Ch Eliz NJ 2007-2008; Consult Trin Par New York NY 2006; Precentor S Thos Ch New York NY 1997-2005; Vic S Columba's Epis Ch Bristol TN 1988-1997; Bp's Coun Dio E Tennessee Knoxville TN 1988-1992, Cler Spprt and Dvlpmt Com 1988-1992; Cur S Tim's Ch Signal Mtn TN 1986-1988.

BOEGER, Daniel Edward (NCal) D.

BOEGER, Mary Rose Steen (NCal) D 10/18/2014 Bp Barry Leigh Beisner.

BOELTER, Phillip R (Minn) Gethsemane Episcopal Church, 905 4th Avenue South, Minneapolis MN 55404 B Dallas TX 1956 s Melvin & Elizabeth. BA Baylor U 1979; MDiv Luther NW Theo Sem 1990; MA U of Notre Dame 1998. D 12/19/2013 P 6/26/2014 Bp Brian N Prior. m 2/24/2016 Mark A Bray c 2. Geth Ch Minneapolis MN 2015-2017; S Matt's Ch S Paul MN 2013-2015. phil@amindtowork.org

BOELTER, Sarah (Cal) 41485 S. I-94 Service Drive, Belleville MI 48111 B Detroit MI 1947 d Albert & Lilah. BA Cntrl Michigan U 1969; MLS Estrn Michigan U 1986; MDiv Ecum TS 1995; MDiv SWTS 1995. D 6/24/1995 P 4/1/1996 Bp R aymond Stewart Wood Jr. m 6/21/1969 Richard Boelter c 2. Assoc R S Paul's Epis Ch Burlingame CA 2007-2011; GC, Del Alt Dio Lexington 2005-2006; R S Raphael's Ch Lexington KY 2002-2007; Trin Ch Belleville MI 1995-2002. Blue Ribbon Awd.

BOESCHENSTEIN, Kathryn C (Colo) B Brooklyn NY 1944 BA CUNY 1966; MA CUNY Hunter Coll 1973; MDiv GTS 2003. D 6/14/2003 Bp William Jerry Winterrowd P 12/20/2003 Bp Robert John O'Neill. c 2. Vic S Lk's Ch Westcliffe CO 2007-2012; R S Andr's Epis Ch Polson MT 2005-2007; St Gabr the Archangel Epis Ch Englewood CO 2003-2005.

BOESSER, Mark Alan (Ak) 17585 Point Lena Loop Rd, Juneau AK 99801 **Ret 1991-** B Winston-Salem NC 1926 s Christian & Sara. BS U of Texas 1946; BD VTS 1951; DMin Andover Newton TS 1974. D 6/2/1951 P 5/1/1952 Bp Edwin A Penick. P-in-c/R S Dav's Epis Ch Wasilla AK 1977-1991; Dio Alaska Fairbanks AK 1973-1991; R The Ch Of The H Trin Juneau AK 1959-1973; P-in-c S Chris's Ch League City TX 1955-1959; Chapl U Of Tx At Galveston Med Branch Galveston TX 1955-1959; Galloway Meml Chap Elkin NC 1951-1955; M-in-c Trin Ch Mt Airy NC 1951-1955. Soc Of S Simeon & S Anna.

BOEVE, Phillip Dale (Spr) 303 Merchants Avenue, Fort Atkinson WI 53538 B Holland MI 1953 s Dale & Patricia. BA No Cntrl Michigan U 1977; BA Hope Coll 1981; MDiv VTS 1984. D 7/25/1984 Bp Charles Ellsworth Bennison Jr P 6/1/1985 Bp Howard Samuel Meeks. c 4. S Barn Ch Havana IL 2010-2015; R S Peters Epis Ch Ft Atkinson WI 1993-2009; Chapl Jefferson Cnty Jail Mnstry 1993-1998; Chapl Untd States Naval Reserve 1988-1999; R S Mary's Epis Ch Cadillac MI 1986-1993; Cur S Thos Epis Ch Battle Creek MI 1984-1986. ERM; Epis Untd; EvangES, Associated Parishes.

BOGAL-ALLBRITTEN, Rose (Ky) 1504 Kirkwood Dr, Murray KY 42071 **Archd Dio Kentucky Louisville KY 2014-; Dir, Dioc Sch of Mnstry Dio Kentucky Louisville KY 2007-; D S Jn's Ch Murray KY 2004-** B Chicago IL 1951 d Edward & Mary. BA Loyola U 1972; MS Loyola U 1974; PhD Loyola U 1977. D 5/2/2004 Bp Ted Gulick Jr. m 3/6/1982 William Allbritten c 1. Assn for Epis Deacons 2003.

BOGAN III, Leslie Eugene (CGC) 1336 Greenvista Ln, Gulf Breeze FL 32563 B Houston TX 1936 s Leslie & Margarita. BA Van 1958; BD Epis TS of the SW 1961; STM Epis TS of the SW 1964. D 7/18/1961 Bp Everett H Jones P 2/6/1962 Bp Richard Earl Dicus. m 3/3/1982 Eleanor Bogan c 3. Asst to R S Fran Of Assisi Gulf Breeze FL 1993-2002; Non-par 1967-1993; Asst The Epis Ch Of The Medtr Allentown PA 1965-1967; R Ch Of The H Sprt Graham TX 1963-1965; Vic Gr Ch Llano TX 1961-1963. Auth, "(Var Columns) 1967-1970," *Bethlehem Globe Times*; Auth, "News Stories 1970-1976," *Pensacola News Journ.*

BOGEL, Marianne (Oly) 11844 Bandera Rd #148, HELOTES TX 78023 B Oklahoma City OK 1945 d Amos & Erile. RN Barnes Hosp Sch of Nrsng 1966; GTS 1976. D 6/4/1976 P 1/1/1977 Bp Furman Charles Stough. S Hilda's - S Pat's Epis Ch Edmonds WA 1982-1987; Vic Mssh Dexter ME 1979-1981; Ch Of The Mssh Dexter ME 1979-1980; Non-par 1977-1979; Chapl S Vinc's Hosp Birmingham AL 1976-1977. Soc Of S Marg.

BOGERT-WINKLER, Hilary Megan (WMass) 14 Boltwood Ave., Amherst MA 01002 **P Assoc Dio Wstrn Massachusetts Springfield 2009-** B Louisville KY 1983 d Christopher & Ronnah. PhD U of Connecticut; BA Wstrn Kentucky U 2005; MTS Harvard DS 2007; Cert Ang Stud Ya Berk 2009; MAR Yale DS 2009. D 6/19/2009 P 1/16/2010 Bp Ted Gulick Jr. m 7/25/2009 Richard Winkler.

BOGGS, Timothy A (Me) 12 Oakhurst Road, Cape Elizabeth ME 04107 **R S Alb's Ch Cape Eliz ME 2011-** B Wisconsin 1950 s Russell & Valarie. Geo; BA U of Wisconsin; MDiv GTS 2007. D 6/9/2007 P 1/19/2008 Bp John Bryson

Chane. Cathd of St Ptr & St Paul Washington DC 2010; Assoc S Alb's Par Washington DC 2007-2010. Auth, "Through the Gates Into the City," GTS, 2007.

BOGHETICH, Barbara Ann (Hond) IMC-SAP 564, PO Box 52-3900, Miami FL 33152 B Milwaukee WS 1937 d Erwin & Dorothy. Epis TS of the SW; BBA Adel 1960; MDiv Houston Grad TS 1996. D 10/28/2005 P 1/12/2008 Bp Lloyd Emmanuel Allen. SAMS Ambridge PA 2005-2009, 1997-2005.

BOHLER JR, Lewis Penrose (Los) PO Box 16216, Augusta GA 30919 **Ret 1999-; Ret 1996-** B Augusta GA 1927 s Lewis & Margie. BA W Virginia St U 1951; MDiv Ob 1954; MDiv Bex Sem 1955. D 6/18/1955 P 6/23/1956 Bp Nelson Marigold Burroughs. c 2. Chr Ch Augusta GA 2002-2004; S Mary's Ch Augusta GA 1996-1999; R Epis Ch Of The Adv Los Angeles CA 1961-1996; M-in-c S Aug's Epis Ch Youngstown OH 1955-1961. Auth, "The Mt Vernon Plan".

BOHNER, Charles Russell (Del) 1309 Grinnell Rd # N33, Wilmington DE 19803 **R St Annes Epis Ch Middletown DE 2014-** B Wilmington DE 1965 s Charles & Mary. BA U of Delaware 1989; MDiv SWTS 2003. D 1/18/2003 P 10/16/2003 Bp Wayne Wright. m 11/6/2004 Diane Bohner c 2. Asst Chr Ch Christiana Hundred Wilmington DE 2008-2014; Asst S Barn Ch Wilmington DE 2003-2008. rector@st-annes-church.com

BOIVIN, Barbara Ann (Nev) B Harrisburg IL 1937 d Hiram & Geneva. D 10/15/2005 Bp Katharine Jefferts Schori. m 3/23/2000 Jean Roland Boivin c 3. N.A.A.D. 2006.

BOJARSKI, Mitchell T (Ky) 116 S. Columbia St., Campbellsville KY 42718 **The Ch Of Chr The King Alpine CA 2013-** B Buffalo NY 1978 s Alan & Martha. BA Roberts Wesleyan Coll 2000; MDiv VTS 2008. D 5/24/2008 Bp Peter J Lee P 1/11/2009 Bp Ted Gulick Jr. m 4/21/2001 Beth M Frary c 1. All SS Epis Ch Brawley CA 2013; S Thos Ch Campbellsvlle KY 2010-2012; Assoc R Chr Epis Ch Bowling Green KY 2008-2010. Rosary Soc 2005. fr.mitch. bojarski@gmail.com

BOLAND, Geoffrey Allan (CFla) 1861 Peninsular Dr, Haines City FL 33844 B Jamaica NY 1946 s Arthur & Shirley. BA SUNY 1969; MDiv Nash 1974. D 12/22/1973 Bp Allen Webster Brown P 11/30/1974 Bp Charles Bowen Persell Jr. m 8/30/1969 Alayne Noyes Boland c 1. St Nich Ch Haines City FL 2007-2008; S Mk's Epis Ch Haines City FL 1999-2007; Environ Cmsn Dio Wstrn New York Tonawanda NY 1991-1999, Dn Of Cattaraugus Dnry 1989-1999, Yth Conf Stff 1981-1995, CE Cmsn 1981-1990, Dioc Coun 1989-1992, Dioc Coun 1981-1988; R S Mary's Ch Salamanca NY 1981-1999; Chr Ch Coxsackie NY 1980-1981; Trin Ch Coxsackie NY 1976-1981; R Trin Athens NY 1976-1981; Dio Albany Greenwich NY 1976-1979; Cur S Jas Ch Oneonta NY 1974-1976.

BOLDINE, Charles Stanley (RG) 6009 Costa Brava Ave NW, Albuquerque NM 87114 **Ret 2006-** B Ely MN 1950 s Stanley & Justine. Tchr Cert UTEP; AA Vermillion St Jr Coll 1971; BS S Cloud St U 1973; MDiv SWTS 1987. D 8/5/1987 Bp Richard Mitchell Trelease Jr P 4/1/1988 Bp William Davidson. m 2/25/2006 Mary Boldine c 3. R Ch Of The H Cross Edgewood NM 1998-2006; Int H Sprt Epis Ch El Paso TX 1995-1996; R St Lk's Epis Ch Anth NM 1989-1993; Pstr S Mary's Ch Lovington NM 1987-1989.

BOLI, Judith Davis (EMich) 4444 State St Apt F-318, Saginaw MI 48603 **R S Paul's Epis Ch Saginaw MI 1999-, 1995-1996, Assoc 1976-1993** B Detroit MI 1938 d Calvin & Elma. BS Wayne 1959; Cert Whitaker TS 1978; MA MI SU 1984. D 6/29/1976 Bp H Coleman Mcgehee Jr P 1/1/1978 Bp Henry Irving Mayson. c 2. Phi Kappa Phi.

BOLIN, William Eugene (Md) 244 Braeburn Cir, Walkersville MD 21793 B Baltimore MD 1940 s Carroll & Helen. BA U of Washington 1965; MDiv UTS 1984; DAS VTS 1992. D 11/14/1992 Bp Ronald Hayward Haines P 5/1/1993 Bp Jane Hart Holmes Dixon. m 12/31/2010 Marion Northern c 1. The Gathering: A Fam Of Faith Epis Ch Walkersville MD 2004-2006; Dio Maryland Baltimore MD 1997-2003, Ch Planter 1994-2006; P-in-c S Anne's Ch Damascus MD 1993-1997; Dio Washington Washington DC 1992-1993; Chapl U Of Maryland At Coll Pk Coll Pk MD 1992-1993; Serv Bapt Ch 1980-1991. Auth, "Chr Witness On Campus," Broadman Press; Auth, "Growing Up Caring," McGraw-Hill. SBL, EPF, Nat.

BOLLE, Stephen M (NY) 1 Chipping Ct, Greenville SC 29607 B Oconomowoc WI 1940 s Victor & Lucille. BA Mia 1963; STB Ya Berk 1967; S Georges Coll Jerusalem IL 1988. D 4/1/1967 P 10/28/1967 Bp Donald H V Hallock. m 7/27/1974 Margaret Ann Muncie c 2. Int R S Andr's Epis Ch Greenville SC 2013-2016; Int Dn Trin Cathd Columbia SC 2010-2012; P in charge Ch Of The Adv Spartanburg SC 2008-2009; Int R Chr Ch Greenville SC 2008; Int R S Mk's Ch Mt Kisco NY 2007-2008; Assoc R S Mich's Ch New York NY 2000-2007; Cn to the Dn Chr Ch Cathd Cincinnati OH 1995-2000; Int R S Thos Epis Ch Terrace Pk OH 1994-1995, Assoc 1990-1995; P/T Asst S Barn Epis Ch Greenwich CT 1989-1990; R St Lk's Ch Katonah NY 1972-1989; Asst S Mk's Ch Islip NY 1967-1972. Epis Cmnty Serv, Dio Sthrn Ohio 1996-2000. rector@ standrewsgreenvill.com

BOLLE, Winnie Mckenzie Hoilette (SeFla) 6055 Verde Trl S Apt H316, Boca Raton FL 33433 **Asst Chap Of S Andr Boca Raton FL 1997-; Ret 1992-** B JM 1924 d Luther & Rosa. BS Lon GB 1959; MA U CA 1968; MDiv CDSP

1969. P 6/5/1982 Bp Calvin Onderdonk Schofield Jr. Dio SE Florida Miami 1982-1991; Assoc Trin Cathd Miami FL 1980-1997. Fell Coll Of Chapl. Hon Cn Trin Cathd 1996.

BOLLES-BEAVEN, Anne Elizabeth (Nwk) 32 Yale St, Maplewood NJ 07040 **Ch Of The H Innoc W Orange NJ 2014-; Assoc S Andr And H Comm Ch So Orange NJ 2004-; Bd Trst No Porch Wmn & Infants Centers Newark NJ 2000-** B Indianapolis IN 1959 d Herbert & Elizabeth. BA Barnard Coll of Col 1981; MDiv GTS 1988. D 10/22/1988 P 3/3/1990 Bp George Nelson Hunt III. m 1/2/1982 Paul William Bolles-Beaven c 2. S Jn's Epis Ch Montclair NJ 2010; S Geo's Epis Ch Maplewood NJ 2009, Assoc 1994-1998; Int S Ptr's Ch Essex Fells NJ 2002-2004; Int S Mk's Ch W Orange NJ 2000-2002; Int Ch Of The H Sprt Verona NJ 1999-2000; S Ann And The H Trin Brooklyn NY 1989-1993; CE Cmsn Dio Newark Newark NJ 2001-2003. Auth, "Monthly Column," *Rhode Island Epis News*, 1997; Auth, "Books In Revs," *Epis Life*, 1994; Auth, "Naming Wmn Priests Reveals Dilemma About God," *Epis Life*, 1992; Auth, "The Eye Of The Needle (Poem)," *LivCh*, 1988. COM, Dio Newark 2006; No Porch Bd 2001; Wmn Cmsn, Dio Newark 2000-2005. Wmn of Influence Brooklyn YWCA 1990.

BOLLINGER II, David Glenn (CNY) 206 John St, Binghamton NY 13905 B Mount Vernon OH 1954 s Charles & Frances. Eisenhower Coll Rit 1979; MDiv EDS 1983; Oxf GB 1991; Oxf GB 1998; SUNY 2003. D 6/11/1983 Bp Ned Cole P 5/9/1984 Bp O'Kelley Whitaker. m 8/13/1977 Kelly Adair Bollinger c 3. Dio Cntrl New York Liverpool NY 2005, COM 1990-1993; R S Paul's Ch Owego NY 1986-2005; Asst S Mary's Epis Ch Barnstable MA 1984-1986; Asst S Lk's Ch Gladstone NJ 1983-1984. Consortium Endowed Epis Parishes; Fllshp Of The Soc Of S Jn The Evang.

BOLLINGER, Matthew D (NJ) 514 W Adams Blvd, Los Angeles CA 90007 B Sioux Falls SD 1984 d Craig & Marilyn. MDiv PrTS 2010; Cert Ang Stud Berk 2011; Cert Ang Stud Ya Berk 2011; STM Yale DS 2011; STM Yale DS 2011. D 6/18/2011 Bp George Edward Councell P 1/7/2012 Bp Mary Douglas Glasspool. St Johns Pro-Cathd Los Angeles CA 2011-2012.

BOLMAN DWIGHT, Robert Bolman (SO) 115 W Monument Ave, #1201, Dayton OH 45402 **Chr Epis Ch Dayton OH 1971-** B Visalia CA 1935 s Herbert & Marian. BA Stan 1958; BD 1962; MS U of Oregon 1969; PhD U of Oregon 1971. D 6/13/1962 P 12/19/1962 Bp James Walmsley Frederic Carman. m 12/29/1962 Rose Dwight c 3. Int Trin Epis Ch Troy OH 2002-2003, Int 1986-2002; Non-par 1981-1986; P-in-c S Dav Vandalia OH 1978-1981; Non-par 1968-1978; R Ch Of The Resurr Eugene OR 1966-1968; Cur S Mary's Epis Ch Eugene OR 1962-1966.

BOLT, Michelle Warriner (ETenn) 413 Cumberland Ave, Knoxville TN 37902 **Tyson Hse Stdt Fndt Knoxville TN 2006-** B Atlanta GA 1975 d John & Joan. BA U of Tennessee 1997; MA Harvard DS 2000; MDiv SWTS 2006. D 5/27/2006 P 9/29/2007 Bp Charles Glenn VonRosenberg. m 5/26/2001 Patrick McClure Bolt c 1. Dio E Tennessee Knoxville TN 2007-2009; Asst S Paul's Epis Ch Burlingame CA 2006-2007.

BOLTON, Carolyn Marie (Cal) 1125 Brush St, Oakland CA 94607 **D S Paul's Ch Oakland CA 2011-** B Oakland CA 1948 d Adam & Nathalie. AA Laney Jr Coll 2003; BA Sch for Deacons 2005. D 12/3/2005 Bp William Edwin Swing. m 4/26/1980 Howard Bolton c 3. Archd Dio California San Francisco CA 2012-2016. NAAD 2010; Soroptimist Intl of Oakland 1994; St. Mary's Cntr Bd - Oakland 2005; UBE 2000.

BOLTON, John Donald (At) 16245 Birmingham Hwy, Milton GA 30004 **Cn Chapl Dio Atlanta Atlanta GA 2014-** B Cullercoats Northumberland UK 1940 s John & Dorothy. Lic St of Georgia; Lic St of Virginia; U So 1964; Exch Stdt U So TS 1964; M.Div Theol Coll of Edinburgh UK 1965; TS of Edinburgh Gb 1965; MS Virginia Commonwealth U 1980; MS Virginia Commonwealth U 1980; Lic. Profsnl Counslr St of Virginia 1981; Lic Profsnl Counslr St of Georgia 1983. Trans 7/1/1973 as Priest Bp David Shepherd Rose. m 7/5/2002 Linda A Sparks c 4. The Ch Of Our Sav Atlanta GA 2006-2010, 1991-1997; R Ch of the Resurr Sautee Nacoochee GA 2002-2006; S Anth's Epis Ch Winder GA 2001-2002; Int Chr Epis Ch Kennesaw GA 2000-2001; S Tim's Epis Ch Of The H Fam Jasper GA 1990-1991; S Tim's Epis Ch Calhoun GA 1990-1991; Int The Epis Ch Of S Ptr And S Paul Marietta GA 1989-1990; Gr Epis Ch Goochland VA 1982-1983; Ch Of The Gd Shpd Richmond VA 1975-1979; Asst Chr And Gr Ch Petersburg VA 1973-1975; Serv Ch Of Scotland 1965-1973.

BOMAN, Ruth Kay (Okla) 424 E St Nw, Miami OK 74354 **All SS Epis Ch Miami OK 1996-** B Wichita KS 1953 d William & Alice. BA Oklahoma St U 1975; MS Pittsburg St U 1980. D 6/22/1996 Bp Robert Manning Moody.

BOMAN, Samuel Ratliff (Neb) 262 Parkside Ln, Lincoln NE 68521 **Ret 1991-; Ret 1990-** B Pierceville KS 1927 s Samuel & Artemecia. BA SW Coll Winfield KS 1948; SWTS 1950. D 11/7/1950 P 9/21/1951 Bp Goodrich R Fenner. m 6/2/1947 Mary Ann Boman c 4. Ch Of The H Trin Lincoln NE 1993-1995; S Dav Of Wales Epis Ch Lincoln NE 1976-1990; P-in-c S Steph's Ashland NE 1976-1977; P-in-c All SS' Eclipse NE 1963-1967; R Ch Of Our Sav No Platte NE 1960-1976; Ch of Our Sav No Platte NE 1960-1976; R Chr Ch Epis Beatrice NE 1954-1959; S Mk's Ch Blue Rapids KS 1952-1953; P-in-c S Paul's Ch Marysville KS 1952-1953; Asst S Lk's Ch Wamego KS 1950-1951; S Paul's Ch Manhattan KS 1950-1951.

BON, Brin Carol (Tex) 1500 N Capital Of Texas Hwy, Austin TX 78746 **S Mich's Ch Austin TX 2015-** B Denver CO 1980 d Roger & Cynthia. BA U of Utah 2008; MDiv Ya Berk 2013. D 6/29/2013 P 2/28/2014 Bp Scott Byron Hayashi. m 10/31/2000 Jenkyn E Powell c 3. S Matt's Ch Austin TX 2014-2015; Trin Epis Sch Of Austin W Lake Hills TX 2013-2015. brin@st-michaels.org

BONADIE, LeRoy Rowland (Md) 609 Wellington Ln, Cumberland ND 21502 B St Vincent, West Indies 1939 s Vincent & Muriel. D 10/21/2000 Bp David Bruce Joslin P 1/6/2007 Bp John L Rabb. m 10/9/1994 Barbara English c 4.

BOND, Barbara Lynn (O) 455 Santa Clara St Nw, Canton OH 44709 B Washington DC 1945 d Francis & Althea. BA Carleton Coll 1967; MA Steph F Austin St U 1974; MFA Hochschule der Kunste Berlin DE 1979; MDiv SWTS 1993; DMin SWTS 2005. D 1/6/1996 P 7/29/1996 Bp John Stuart Thornton. m 4/20/2002 Henry Norman Van Cleve. R S Paul's Ch Canton OH 2006-2016; R S Paul's Ch Lock Haven PA 2000-2006; Vic Ch Of H Nativ Meridian ID 1996-2000; Chapl S Alphonsus Reg Med Cntr Boise ID 1995-2000. Assn Profsnl Chapl 1998-2009.

BOND, Eric B (Pa) 2122 Washington Ln, Huntingdon Valley PA 19006 **P-in-c Ch Of Our Sav Jenkintown PA 2011-; S Jn's Ch Huntingdon Vlly PA 2009-** B Des Plaines IL 1976 s David & Catherine. BA Penn 1998; MA U Chi 2002; MDiv EDS 2006. D 6/10/2006 P 12/16/2006 Bp Charles Ellsworth Bennison Jr. m 6/26/1999 Carolyn B Bond c 5. CFS The Sch At Ch Farm Exton PA 2006-2009.

BOND, Jeremy William (CPa) 676 N 12th Street Unit 25, Grover Beach CA 93433 **Sunday Supply Wk El Camino Real Dio CA 2004-; Ret P S Barn Ch Arroyo Grande CA 2004-** B Detroit MI 1938 s Julian & Eleanor. BA Ken 1959; MDiv GTS 1962. D 6/9/1962 P 12/22/1962 Bp Horace W B Donegan. m 9/29/1962 Kathleen R B Bond c 3. Cn Cathd Ch Of S Steph Harrisburg PA 1993-2003, Cn 1964-1992; S Mk's Epis Ch Northumberlnd PA 1989-1994; R S Matt's Epis Ch Sunbury PA 1979-2003; R S Paul's Epis Ch Harrisburg PA 1968-1979; Asst Min Cathd Of St Jn The Div New York NY 1962-1964. Ord of Ascen 1992. Hon Cn Cathd Ch of St. Steph, Harrisburg, PA 1993.

BOND, Leonard Wayne (Oly) 5810 Fleming St Unit 66, Everett WA 98203 B Elmhurst IL 1930 s Leland & Cleo. BA Florida Sthrn Coll 1953; MDiv Garrett-Evang TS 1956; BA U of Oregon 1968; BS Cntrl Washington U 1981. D 12/12/1961 P 6/21/1962 Bp Russell S Hubbard. m 8/17/1951 Marie Jean Bond. Asst Trin Epis Ch Everett WA 1977-1997; Ch Of Our Sav Monroe WA 1976-1977; Serv S Phil Ch Marysville WA 1973-1974; Serv S Jn's Epis Ch Snohomish WA 1969-1972; DCE S Thos' Epis Ch Eugene OR 1968-1969; Vic S Chris's Ch Port Orford OR 1962-1966; S Jn-By-The-Sea Epis Ch Bandon OR 1962-1966.

BOND, Michael David (Chi) PO Box 438, Cedar Lake IN 46303 **D Brent Hse (U Of Chicago) Chicago IL 2011-, Pstr Assoc 2011-** B Bryn Mawr PA 1948 s Richard & Mary. D 2/5/2000 Bp Bill Persell. m 8/11/1990 Mary Jean Lenski. Bldg and Prod Mgr Dio Chicago Chicago IL 2000-2011; D Chr The King Ch Lansing IL 2000-2007. aBSG 2000; aOHC 2001.

BOND, Michele (Eas) 19524 Meadowbrook Rd, Hagerstown MD 21742 B Baltimore MD 1944 d Edward & Audrey. BA Pepperdine U 1966; MDiv VTS 1989. D 6/17/1989 Bp Albert Theodore Eastman P 5/7/1990 Bp Charles Lindsay Longest. m 6/29/1969 Ronald Bond c 3. R S Paul's Ch Trappe MD 2007-2009; Dir of Fam Mnstrs Trin Evang Luth Ch Hagerstown MD 2002-2007; Dir of Fam Mnstrs Cathd Of The Incarn Baltimore MD 1996-2000; Assoc S Jas Ch Monkton MD 1989-1995.

BOND JR, Walter Douglas (Mass) 10 Dana St Apt 212, Cambridge MA 02138 **Affiliated Min The Memi Ch at Harv 2010-** B Evanston IL 1944 s Walter & Mary. BA Cor 1967; MDiv EDS 1972; CSS Harv 1993. D 6/9/1973 Bp Paul Moore Jr P 6/10/1975 Bp Ned Cole. Asst All SS Par Brookline MA 1983-1984; R S Geo's Ch Maynard MA 1977-2004; Int Chr Ch Medway MA 1976-1977; Assoc Chr Ch Waltham MA 1974-1976. Soc of King Chas the Mtyr.

BONDURANT, Stephen Bryce (SO) 785 Ludlow Ave, Cincinnati OH 45220 B Saint Louis MO 1945 s Bryce & Helen. BA Drury U 1967; MEd S Louis U 1970; MDiv Eden TS 1972; U of Edinburgh GB 1974; EdD U Cinc 1977. D 12/22/1985 P 5/1/1986 Bp Don Adger Wimberly. m 5/17/1980 Rachelle M Bruno. Gr Ch Cincinnati OH 2003-2006, Int 1996-1997; R S Alb's Ch Indianapolis IN 1994-1995; S Mary's Epis Ch Hillsboro OH 1992-1993; Asst to R S Andr's Ch Ft Thos KY 1986-1990; Serv Presb Ch 1978-1985. Auth, "This Monday Morning I Have a Confession," *Monday Morning mag*, 1978; Auth, *Collection of Poems*, Catacomb Poets, 1973. AAR; APA 1978; Assn CT 1995; No Amer Paul Tillich Soc 1990. Phi Delta Kappa U Cinc 1977.

BONE, Patrick Joseph (ETenn) Po Box 129, Church Hill TN 37642 **Hisp Mnstry Dio E Tennessee Knoxville TN 2003-** B San Antonio TX 1942 s Patrick & Anne. MEd Assumption Sem 1970; DMin VTS 2006. Rec 5/11/2003 Bp Charles Glenn VonRosenberg. m 6/1/1992 Ina Katherine Sifferd. "Aliens Of Transylvania Cnty," Silver Dagger Mysteries, 2002; "Amelungeon Winter," Silver Dagger Mysteries, 2001; "Blood Mary: The Mystery Of Amanda'S Magic Mirror," The Overmountain Press, 1999.

BONEBRAKE, Aletha Green (EO) 2347 Campbell St, Baker City OR 97814 **Vic S Steph's Baker City OR 2010-** B Seattle WA 1941 d Philip & Charlotte. AA GW 1961; BA U of Wisconsin 1982; MLS U of Wisconsin 1983; GOE Dio Estrn Oregon Sup Prog 2006. D 11/22/2006 Bp William O Gregg P 12/13/2007 Bp James E Waggoner Jr. c 3. Libr Dir Baker Co. Libr Dist 1985-2007.

BONELL, John Winston (NH) 3 Bodfish Av, Wareham MA 02571 B Pasadena CA 1951 s William & Blanche. BA U CA 1976; MDiv CDSP 1980. D 6/20/1981 Bp Robert Claflin Rusack P 1/1/1982 Bp Arthur Anton Vogel. m 2/9/2002 Nancy Bonell c 2. P-in-c S Ptr's Ch On The Canal Buzzards Bay MA 2005-2007; S Andr's Ch Methuen MA 2002-2003; Int S Sav's Epis Ch Old Greenwich CT 2000-2002; R Ch Of The Trsfg Derry NH 1990-2000; Asst R, Coll Chapl All SS Epis Ch Atlanta GA 1985-1990; Chapl Of Par Day Sch S Paul's Ch Kansas City MO 1981-1985. ESMHE 1983-1989.

BONES JR, William Lyle (Mich) 3865 Lincoln Rd, Bloomfield Hills MI 48301 **Died 10/22/2015** B Detroit MI 1928 s William & Charlotte. BS Pur 1952; Whitaker TS 1994. D 6/11/1994 Bp R aymond Stewart Wood Jr. m 10/26/1966 Martha Katherine Bones. D S Jas Epis Ch Birmingham MI 1994-2000.

BONEY, Samuel Ashford (Miss) 10100 Hillview Dr. Apt 433, Pensacola FL 32514 **Ret 1991-** B Athens GA 1927 s Sam & Kathryn. BA U So 1955; MDiv Sewanee: The U So, TS 1958. D 6/22/1958 Bp Theodore N Barth P 3/14/1959 Bp John Vander Horst. m 8/6/1955 Marcia Lois Kline c 3. Cn Pstr S Andr's Cathd Jackson MS 1984-1991; Asst S Paul's Epis Ch Chattanooga TN 1981-1984; R S Mary's Epis Ch Dyersburg TN 1960-1980; Chr Ch Brownsville TN 1958-1960; P-in-c Imm Ch Ripley TN 1958-1960.

BONIN, Raymond Thomas (NH) 1 Hood Rd, Derry NH 03038 **P-in-c Ch Of The Trsfg Derry NH 2012-** B Byfield MA 1954 s Honore & Claire. BA Marq 1976; MDiv Washington Theol Un 1982. Rec 2/5/2012 as Priest Bp Vicky Gene Robinson.

BONNER, Bruce (Tex) 3520 W. Whitestone Blvd., Cedar Park TX 78613 **S Cuth's Epis Ch Houston TX 2014-** B Corpus Christi TX 1957 s Robert & Donna. BS Pk U 1993; MDiv Epis TS of the SW 1999. D 6/19/1999 P 6/22/2000 Bp Claude Edward Payne. m 8/26/1989 Kathryn Bonner c 2. Chr Epis Ch Cedar Pk TX 2005-2014; R S Mk's Ch Bay City TX 2002-2005; Ch Of The Epiph Houston TX 1999-2002. revbruce@thecectx.org

BONNER, George Llewellyn (LI) 783 E 35th St, Brooklyn NY 11210 **S Alb's Ch Brooklyn NY 1987-** B BZ 1947 s Wilfred & Lessie. DIT Codrington Coll 1977; BA U of The W Indies 1977; MS CUNY 1990. Trans 2/11/1987 as Priest Bp Robert Campbell Witcher Sr. m 8/26/2000 Marjorie Bonner c 2. R St.Clem's & Swithin Barbados W.I 1978-1984; D ,St.Mary's Ch - Dio of Belize-C P W I Belize City Belize 1977-1978.

BONNER III, John Hare (ETenn) Holy Trinity Episcopal Church, 207 S Church St, Hertford NC 27944 **Int R S Ptr's Ch Chattanooga TN 2016-** B Lumberton NC 1947 s John & Henrietta. Int Trng Dio E Tennessee; BS U of Tennessee 1976; MDiv VTS 1987. D 6/28/1987 P 5/1/1988 Bp William Evan Sanders. m 6/5/1971 Deborah R Bonner c 3. R H Trin Epis Ch Hertford NC 2006-2015; R S Jas' Epis Ch Alexander City AL 2003-2006; R Chr Ch Epis S Pittsburg TN 1988-2003; D-In-Trng Ch Of The Ascen Knoxville TN 1987-1988; Mem of Stndg Com Dio E Carolina Kinston NC 2014-2015, Dn of Albemarle Dnry 2012-2015, Mem of Exec Coun 2010-2014; Dn Albemarle Dnry Albemarle NC 2010-2015.

BONNER-STEWART, Ann (NC) St Mary's Chapel, 900 Hillsborough St, Raleigh NC 27603 **Chapl S Mary's Chap Sch Raleigh NC 2009-; S Mary's Sch Raleigh NC 2009-** B Greenville SC 1979 d William & Myra. AB Duke 2001; MDiv Ya Berk 2006. D 6/3/2006 Bp M(Arvil) Thomas Shaw P 12/9/2006 Bp Clifton Daniel III. m 7/19/2003 Jeffrey Franklin Bonner-Stewart c 2. Assoc R S Paul's Epis Ch Greenville NC 2006-2009. R. Lansing Hicks Prize Ya Berk 2006; Thos Philips Memi Reward Ya Berk 2006; Eleanor Lee McGee Prize Ya Berk 2004.

BONNEVILLE, Jerome (Spok) D 10/18/2015 P 6/26/2016 Bp James E Waggoner Jr.

BONNEY, Isaac Kojo Nyame (WA) Saint Mark's Church, 12621 Old Columbia Pike, Silver Spring MD 20904 **S Mk's Ch Fairland Silver Sprg MD 2013-; Asst. R The Afr Epis Ch of St. Thos Philadelphia PA 2005-** B Adjabeng Accra Ghana 1977 s Frank & Elizabeth. BA Wabash Coll 2000; MDiv Candler TS Emory U 2004. Trans 8/31/2006 as Priest Bp Charles Ellsworth Bennison Jr. m 9/12/2009 Doreen D Bonney c 1. The Afr Epis Ch Of S Thos Philadelphia PA 2006-2013.

BONNINGTON, Robert Lester (NwT) 2820 Goddard Pl, Midland TX 79705 **Died 2/28/2017** B Brooklyn NY 1932 s Lester & Ethel. PhD U of Iowa 1968; MDiv Epis TS of the SW 1982. D 6/6/1982 P 1/6/1983 Bp Sam Byron Hulsey. m 7/21/1972 Hazel Joanne Bonnington. S Ptr's Ch Kermit TX 1998-2017; Ret 1995-2017; R S Paul's Epis Ch Sikeston MO 1992-1995; The Epis Ch Of S Mary The Vrgn Big Sprg TX 1982-1992. Auth, "Mod Bus: A Systems Approach".

BONNYMAN, Anne Berry (Mass) 50 Sonnet Lane, Asheville NC 28804 B Knoxville TN 1949 d Gordon & Isabel. BA U of Tennessee 1971; MA Villanova U 1976; MDiv VTS 1982. D 6/30/1982 Bp William F Gates Jr P 5/12/1983

Bp William Evan Sanders. c 3. R Trin Ch Epis Boston MA 2006-2012; R Trin Par Wilmington DE 1995-2006; Int Ch Of The Ascen Knoxville TN 1994-1995, Asst 1982-1984; Ch Of The Gd Samar Knoxville TN 1988-1994; Vic S Eliz's Epis Ch Knoxville TN 1985-1988; Dio E Tennessee Knoxville TN 1985-1987.

BONOAN, Raynald Sales (SwFla) 18612 Chemille Dr, Lutz FL 33558 **R Ch Of The H Sprt Sfty Harbor FL 2001-** B Bacarra I Locos Norte PH 1954 s Emerson & Alicia. AA Trin U of Asia Phil 1975; BTh S Andrews TS Ph 1979; MDiv S Andrews TS Manila PH 1989. Rec 6/13/1998 Bp John Bailey Lipscomb. m 3/31/1979 Unidad R Reyes c 3. Dio SW Florida Parrish FL 1999-2001; Cn S Andr's Epis Ch Tampa FL 1999-2001; Vic S Lk's Ch Land O Lakes FL 1998-1999; St Lukes Ch Ellenton FL 1998. Auth, "Gentle Yoke, Light Burden Pstr'S Corner," *The Laker*, 1994; Auth, "To Believe Is To Know Pstr'S Corner," *The Laker*, 1994.

BONSEY, Steven Charles (Mass) 138 Tremont St, Boston MA 02111 B Molokai HI 1956 s W(Illiam) & Kathryn. AB Harv 1978; MDiv Ya Berk 1984; STM Ya Berk 1987. D 12/7/1986 P 11/1/1987 Bp Christoph Keller Jr. m 8/28/1982 Elisabeth Wilson Keller c 4. Epis City Mssn Boston MA 2014-2017; Cn The Cathd Ch Of S Paul Boston MA 2005-2014; Int Ch Of The Redeem Chestnut Hill MA 2003-2004; Chr Ch Somerville MA 2000-2003; Epis Chapl At Tufts Medford MA 2000-2003; Epis Chapl Tufts Medford MA 2000-2003; Par of St Clem Honolulu HI 1995-2000; S Jas' Epis Ch Cambridge MA 1992-1993; Gr Epis Ch Medford MA 1991-1995; Epis Chapl Tufts Medford MA 1991-1995; Assoc S Paul's Memi Charlottesvlle VA 1987-1990. "A Reluctant Giver's Guide to the Pract of Stwdshp," Dio Massachusetts, 2006; "A Shy Person's Guide To The Pract Of Evang," Dio Massachusetts, 2004. ESMHE 1988-1996; Fllshp of S Jn 1998.

BONSEY, W(Illiam) Edwin (Haw) 401 SAnta Clara Av e Apt 309, Oakland CA 94610 **Ret 1992-** B Greeley CO 1929 s William & Hannah. BA Ob 1951; MDiv CDSP 1954. D 6/19/1954 Bp Henry H Shires P 12/17/1954 Bp Harry Sherbourne Kennedy. m 6/17/1952 Kathryn B Bonsey c 4. Camp Mokule'Ia Waialua HI 1988-1992; R Ch Of The H Apos Hilo HI 1974-1988; R S Eliz's Ch Honolulu HI 1963-1974; Vic S Steph's Ch Wahiawa HI 1957-1963; Vic Gr Ch Hoolehua HI 1954-1957.

BONSTEEL, Susan Layh (NY) 94 Clifton Ave, Kingston NY 12401 **Mid-Hudson D for Jail and Prison Mnstry S Jn's Epis Ch Kingston NY 2008-, D 1998-2003** B Staten Island NY 1948 d Joseph & Marilyn. BS Keuka Coll 1970. D 5/16/1998 Bp Richard Frank Grein. m 7/25/1970 Roger Edward Bonsteel c 2. D S Paul's Ch Poughkeepsie NY 2007-2008; Mem D Com NY 2003-2011; D The Epis Ch Of Chr The King Stone Ridge NY 2003-2007; Mem COM NY 2003-2006; Reg Coordntr PBp's Fund NY 1999-2003.

BONWITT, Martha (WA) 14303 Old Marlboro Pike, Upper Marlboro MD 20772 **R Trin Ch Uppr Marlboro MD 2000-** B Kearny NJ 1950 d George & Elinore. BA Montclair St U 1991; MDiv UTS 1996. D 6/1/1996 Bp John Shelby Spong P 12/7/1996 Bp Jack Marston Mckelvey. m 3/17/1996 William Bonwitt c 1. Dio New York New York NY 1997-2000; S Andr's So Fallsburg So Fallsburg NY 1997-2000; P-in-c S Jas Ch Callicoon NY 1997-2000; Gr Ch Nutley NJ 1997. Interfaith Outreach Untd 1997-2000.

BOODT, Mary Ione (Ind) 100 Oakview Dr, Mooresville IN 46158 B Kokomo IN 1938 d Malcolm & Mary. BA Marian Coll 1971; MS Pur 1973; PhD Indiana U 1979; MA SWTS 1992; Cert SWTS 1993. D 6/24/1993 P 2/26/1994 Bp Edward Witker Jones. Vic S Mary's Epis Ch Martinsville IN 1997-2003; Int S Jn's Epis Ch Crawfordsvlle IN 1995-1997; S Mk's Ch Plainfield IN 1995, Assoc R 1994-1995; Chapl Gd Shpd Hosp Barrington IL 1993-1994; Pstr Asst S Lk's Ch Evanston IL 1993-1994. OHC.

BOOHER, David Lewis (SVa) 724 West H St., Elizabethton TN 37643 **The Sav Epis Ch Newland NC 2011-; Retiree Ret Elizabethton TN 2007-** B Wheeling WV 1946 s Samuel & Helen. BA U of Mississippi 1969; MDiv Sewanee: The U So, TS 1975. D 5/28/1975 P 5/4/1976 Bp Duncan Montgomery Gray Jr. m 12/21/1968 Leslie W Williams c 3. Int S Mary's Epis Ch Middlesboro KY 2008-2009; R Emm Ch Halifax VA 2000-2007; R S Jn's Epis Ch Halifax VA 2000-2007; R S Steph's Epis Ch New Harmony IN 1990-2000; R S Alb's Epis Ch Vicksburg MS 1983-1990; All SS Ch Inverness MS 1978-1983; Vic S Thos Ch Belzoni MS 1978-1983; Asst S Paul's Ch Columbus MS 1975-1978. Assoc, Cmnty of S Mary 1994; Oblate, OSB, Archabbey of St. Meinrad 1997.

BOOK, Robert TM (At) 170 Trinity Ave SW, Atlanta GA 30303 B Detroit MI 1949 s Robert & Mina. BA Hillsdale Coll 1972; BEd Dalhousie U 1977; MDiv Waterloo Luth Sem CA 1989. D 3/28/2008 Bp J Neil Alexander P 10/15/2008 Bp Keith Whitmore. m 7/28/1973 Holly M Book c 3. Assoc The Ch of the Common Ground Atlanta GA 2014-2015, 2009-2017.

BOOKER JR, James Howard (Az) 700 E Georgia Ave, Deland FL 32724 B Beaumont TX 1957 s James & Eleanor. U of Exeter Exeter Engl; Cert Ocean Corp 1983; MDiv Edinburgh Theol Coll Edinburgh Scotland 1989; MTh Sheffield U GB 2002; BTh Aberdeen U Aberdeen Scotland 2003. Trans 2/14/2006 Bp Kirk Stevan Smith. m 5/29/2003 Christine Herbert c 2. H Cross Epis Ch Sanford FL 2015-2016; Vic S Thos Of The Vlly Epis Clarkdale AZ 2006-2010, Vic 2005-2010, Supply 2004; Peterhead Scottish Epis Ch Edinburgh 1990-1992, Longside, Old Deer & Strichen (w Peterhead) 1989-1990.

Thesis, "Escape to Zoar," *2002*, Sheffield U Press, 2002. Profsnl Assn of Dive Instructors 2002. 2nd Class hon U of Aberdeen, Scotland 2003.

BOOKER, Vaughan P L (WA) 5537 Holmes Run Pkwy, Alexandria VA 22304 B Philadelphia PA 1942 s Lorenzo & Mary. AGE Northampton Cnty Cmnty Coll 1975; BA Villanova U 1978; MDiv VTS 1992. D 3/1/1975 Bp Lyman Cunningham Ogilby P 6/1/1992 Bp George Phelps Mellick Belshaw. m 6/30/1979 Portia Booker c 2. Dio Washington Washington DC 2006-2007; Calv Ch Washington DC 2003-2006; Dio Sthrn Ohio Cincinnati OH 1998-2000; R Meade Memi Epis Ch Alexandria VA 1993-1998; Non-par 1989-1993; D S Alb's Epis Ch New Brunswick NJ 1984-1989; Epis Cmnty Serv Philadelphia PA 1975-1979. Alpha Sigma Lambda 1977; Natl Hon Soc.

BOOKSTEIN, Nancey Johnson (Colo) 110 Johnson St, Frederick CO 80530 B Syracuse NY 1946 d Stanley & Shirley. MS Med Coll of Virginia 1978; EdD U of Nthrn Colorado 1998. D 6/13/2015 Bp Robert John O'Neill. m 9/17/2011 Joan A Johnson.

BOOMGAARD, Michelle C (Pgh) **Assoc S Paul's Epis Ch Pittsburgh PA 2012-; Mem Com on Const and Cn 2015-; Secy Pittsburgh Epis Cler Assn 2015-; Bd Mem Pittsburgh Epis Cler Assn 2013-; Cathd Chapt Mem Trin Cathd Pittsburgh PA 2013-** B Wilkinsburg PA 1971 d Dirk & Charita. BA Brandeis U 1992; PhD Cath U 2002; MDiv Ya Berk 2011. D 6/29/2011 Bp Thomas Edward Breidenthal P 1/25/2012 Bp Kenneth Lester Price. The Ch Of The Redeem Pittsburgh PA 2012; D S Ptr's Epis Ch Brentwood Pittsburgh PA 2011.

BOONE, Arthur Robinson (Vt) 1616 Harmon St, Berkeley CA 94703 **Non-par 1972-** B Yonkers NY 1938 s Frank & Gladys. BA Pr 1960; MA Br 1962; BD UTS 1965. D 6/12/1965 P 12/21/1965 Bp Horace W B Donegan. c 4. Int S Aug's Ch Oakland CA 2005-2006, Int 1995-1996, 1982-1983; Serv Dio Vermont Burlington VT 1971-1972; Asst Trin Ch Rutland VT 1968-1971; Cur Ch Of The Trsfg Providence RI 1967-1968; Asst Ch Of The Mssh Providence RI 1965-1967. "Intro to Recycling," *Total Recycling Assoc*, 2006; Auth, "Eeo Trng Resources," 1982; Auth, "Investigating Charges Of Employment Discrimination," 1980. Hitchcock Prize In Ch Hist UTS 1965.

BOONE, Connie Louise (EO) 42893 Pocahontas Rd, Baker City OR 97814 B Hardin MT 1945 d Hugh & Lena. D 1/6/2002 Bp William O Gregg. m 5/7/1966 Douglas Roy Boone c 2. D S Steph's Baker City OR 2002-2013. Cert Alco and Drug Counslr ACCBO 1996.

BOONE JR, Robert Augustus (WNC) 41 Cobblers Way Apt 333, Asheville NC 28804 B Birmingham AL 1946 s Robert & Rosemond. BS U of Mobile 1968; MA U of So Alabama 1972; MDiv Sewanee: The U So, TS 1980. D 6/14/1980 Bp George Mosley Murray P 5/1/1981 Bp Charles Farmer Duvall. m 10/29/2006 Sharon C Boone c 2. Cn Dio Wstrn No Carolina Asheville NC 2005-2009, Cn for Lifelong Chr Formation 2005-2009; R Ch Of The Ascen Hickory NC 1999-2005; R S Jas Epis Ch Greenville SC 1988-1999; S Chris's Ch Pensacola FL 1980-1988. Auth, "Receiving Chld Into the Cong," *The Rel Educ of Preschool Chld*, Sheed and Ward, 1989. swannaboone@charter.net

BOOTH, Errol Kent (WA) 2811 Deep Landing Rd, Huntingtown MD 20639 B JM 1945 s Azariah & Viola. MDiv VTS 1984. D 6/9/1984 P 1/5/1985 Bp John Thomas Walker. m 1/3/1970 Olga Booth c 3. R Chr Epis Ch Clinton MD 2001-2009; Ch Of Our Sav Washington DC 1999-2001; Int Our Sav Washington DC 1999-2001; P-in-c S Phil's Chap Baden Brandywine MD 1990-1999; R S Agnes And S Paul's Ch E Orange NJ 1986-1989; St Agnes Ch E Orange NJ 1986-1989; Int S Phil The Evang Washington DC 1985-1986; Cur S Geo's Ch Washington DC 1984-1985.

BOOTH, James Alexander (ECR) 48 Miramoute Rd., Carmel Valley CA 93924 **Dio El Camino Real Salinas CA 1993-** B Fort Smith AK 1950 s Kenneth & Miriam. BS U of So California 1972; BA Sch for Deacons 1992. D 6/6/1992 Bp Richard Lester Shimpfky. m 12/16/2000 Bridget Booth c 2. Archd All SS Ch Carmel CA 2007-2013; S Dunst's Epis Ch Carmel CA 2000-2009; Archd Ch of S Mary's by the Sea Pacific Grove CA 1995-2000. NAAD.

BOOTH, Karen Workman (Fla) 7423 San Jose Blvd, Jacksonville FL 32217 **S Raphael's Ch Lexington KY 2016-** B Lexington KY 1968 d Herschel & Brenda. BA Estrn Kentucky U 1991; MDiv Sewanee: The U So, TS 2011. D 6/5/2011 Bp Stacy F Sauls P 12/18/2011 Bp Samuel Johnson Howard. m 6/22/2001 Robert H Booth. Assoc Ch Of Our Sav Jacksonville FL 2014-2016; San Jose Epis Ch Jacksonville FL 2011-2013. straphaelepch@worldnet.att.net

BOOTH, Stephen P (WMass) B Oldham, Lancashire, UK 1943 s Enoch & Mabel. B.A. Amh 1965; M.Div Epis TS of the SW 1971; Grad Dplma U of Guelph 2002. Trans 12/14/2004 Bp Gordon Scruton. m 10/5/1984 Gillian Booth c 2. R Trin Par Lenox MA 2003-2011; P Dio Toronto Angl Ch of Can 1971-2002; Hon Can Dio Wstrn Massachusetts Springfield 2008-2011, Mem U Chapl Com 2006-2011, Reg Dn 2006-2009; Vice-Pres Housatonic Vlly Assn 2006-2011. Auth, "Essays and Revs," *Journ of the Epis Ch Hist Soc*, Epis Ch, 1970.

BOOZER, Alcena Elaine Caldwell (Ore) 5256 NE 48th Ave, Portland OR 97218 B Portland OR 1938 d Lawrence & Marcelene. BS OR SU 1970; MS Portland St U 1974; Cert CDSP 1984. D 8/24/1979 Bp Matthew Paul Bigliardi P 6/29/1984 Bp David Rea Cochran. c 2. Dio Oregon Portland OR 2000-2010; S Phil

The D Epis Ch Portland OR 2000-2010, 1998-2000, Par Asst 1979-1984; Asst S Steph's 1987-1993; Vic S Aug's Clatskanie 1985-1987.

BORBON, Samuel (Ore) 1704 NE 43rd Ave, Portland OR 97213 **Dom And Frgn Mssy Soc- Epis Ch Cntr New York NY 2017-; S Mary's Ch Woodburn OR 2015-; Other Lay Position S Mich And All Ang Ch Portland OR 2013-** B Mexico 1978 s Hector & Guadalupe. BA Centro Cultural; MDiv Seminario Dio de Tijuana. Rec 5/21/2014 as Priest Bp Michael Hanley. m 1/2/2011 Blanca E Lopez c 4. P Dio Oregon Portland OR 2013-2017.

BORDADOR, Noel Estrella (NY) **Epis Ch Of Our Sav New York NY 2013-** B 1964 D 3/10/2001 Bp Richard Frank Grein P 9/16/2001 Bp Mark Sean Sisk. St. Mary's Cntr Inc. New York NY 2002. sacerdotium2004@yahoo.com

BORDELON, Joseph Ardell (WLa) 5704 Monroe Hwy, Ball LA 71405 **H Comf Ch Lecompte LA 1992-; Vic Trin Epis Ch Cheneyville LA 1992-** B Pineville LA 1933 s Pierre & Mary. D 9/16/1989 Bp Willis Ryan Henton P 9/11/1993 Bp Robert Jefferson Hargrove Jr. m 3/8/1954 Grace Leona Bordelon c 5. Int S Tim's Ch Alexandria LA 1997-1998; P-in-c Chap of the H Fam Pollock LA 1993-1996; Hardtner C&C Pollock LA 1992-1997; Dio Wstrn Louisiana Alexandria LA 1990-1992, 1981-1989; Non-par 1989-1997. No Amer Assn Of Diac 1989-1993; Rfw 1980.

BORDELON, Michael Joseph (WLa) **Gr Epis Ch Monroe LA 2016-** B Alexandria VA 1984 s Kevin & Judy. BS Louisiana Coll 2006. D 12/27/2014 P 8/1/2015 Bp Jacob W Owensby. m 6/1/2013 Lauren Ashley Guillory. St Jas Epis Ch and Sch Alexandria LA 2015.

BORDEN, Robert Bruce (Vt) P0 Box 554, East Middlebury VT 05740 B Boston MA 1933 s Milton & Elizabeth. BA Ya 1954; MA Bos 1974. D 10/22/2000 Bp Mary Adelia Rosamond Mcleod P 7/14/2001 Bp Thomas C Ely. m 12/17/2012 Catherine Palmer Nichols. P Chr Ch Bethel VT 2000-2013.

BORDEN, Theorphlis Marzetta (SO) St Simon Of Cyrene, 810 Matthews Dr, Cincinnati OH 45215 **D S Simon Of Cyrene Epis Ch Cincinnati OH 2010-** B Bessemer AL 1934 d Israel & Fanella. Attended Mia 1951; Attended Mia 1953; Attended Indiana U 1954; Lic in Servnt Mnstry Epis TS in Kentucky 1991. D 5/4/1991 Bp William Grant Black. c 3. Assoc - CT 2005; SCHC 2011.

BORDENKIRCHER, Amanda Jane (CFla) 942 Cobbler Ct, Longwood FL 32750 **Corpus Christi Epis Ch Okahumpka FL 2010-** B 1959 d Ronald & Joyce. BA Regis U 2001; MDiv Asbury TS 2008. D 5/30/2009 P 12/12/2009 Bp John Wadsworth Howe. m 6/21/2014 Daniel William Bordenkircher c 4.

BORDERS, Calvin Leroy (Oly) 602 24th Ave, Longview WA 98632 **R S Matt's Epis Ch 2004-** B Rushville NE 1931 BA Nebraska Wesl 1954; LLB U of Washington 1959. D 2/28/2004 Bp Sanford Zangwill Kaye Hampton P 11/13/2004 Bp Vincent Waydell Warner. m 1/1/2001 Donna Borders.

BORDIN, Richard F (CFla) 832 Summeroaks Rd, Winter Garden FL 34787 **H Cross Ch Winter Haven FL 2008-** B Reno NV 1947 s Willard & Rosaline. BA U of No Florida 1975; DMin Drew U 1990; Cert Ang Stud Sewanee 2006; Cert Ang Stud Sewanee 2006. D 5/27/2006 P 12/23/2006 Bp John Wadsworth Howe. m 12/31/1999 Shannon M Bordin c 2. Ch Of The Mssh Winter Garden FL 2006-2008; Dist Mgr Jr Achievement 1999-2003.

BORDNER, Ken (Roch) 3471 Cerrillos Rd Trlr 78, Santa Fe NM 87507 B Canton OH 1941 s Edward & Evelyn. ABD Univ. of California, Berkeley; BA Pr 1963; MA U of Massachusetts 1965; MFA U of Massachusetts 1966; MDiv VTS 1996. D 6/8/1996 Bp William Jerry Winterrowd P 1/1/1997 Bp Peter J Lee. m 7/13/1963 Elizabeth C Bordner c 3. R S Steph's Ch Rochester NY 1999-2007; Assoc S Anne's Epis Ch Reston VA 1996-1999.

BORG, Manuel (Chi) 1072 Ridge Ave, Elk Grove Village IL 60007 **P-in-c S Nich w the H Innoc Ch Elk Grove Vlg IL 2009-** B Detroit MI 1958 s Charles & Martha. Rec 7/29/2009 as Priest Bp Jeff Lee. m 12/27/2013 Douglas Allen Vanhouten.

BORG, Marianne (Ore) 1133 Nw 11th Ave Apt 403, Portland OR 97209 B Dhahran SA 1951 d Ralph & Margaret. U of Oregon; BA OR SU 1986; MDiv CDSP 1991. D 6/11/1991 P 12/11/1991 Bp Robert Louis Ladehoff. c 2. Trin Epis Cathd Portland OR 1993-2011; Asst S Barth's Ch Beaverton OR 1991-1993.

BORGEN, Linda Suzanne Cecelia (CGC) **The Epis Ch Of The Nativ Dothan AL 2015-** D 11/22/2014 P 5/26/2015 Bp Philip Menzie Duncan II.

BORGES, Maria Cristina (SanD) 521 E 8th St, National City CA 91950 **S Matt's Ch Natl City CA 2015-** B Cuba 1963 d Raul & Gloria. Licenciada en Educacion Espanol-Ingles Jose Marti Coll of Educ 1988; MDiv Seminario Evangelico de Teologia 2004. Trans 1/27/2015 as Priest Bp Jim Mathes. m 1/21/1997 Carlos Eduardo Exposito Irarragorri c 2.

BORGESON, Josephine (NCal) 458 Occidental Cir, Santa Rosa CA 95401 B Duxbury MA 1946 d John & Harriet. AB Rad 1968; BA Rad 1968; MDiv CDSP 1974. D 6/22/1974 Bp Wesley Frensdorff. D Trin Ch Sonoma CA 2011-2014; Mnstry Dvlp The Epis Dio Nthrn California Sacramento CA 2007-2010; H Fam Epis Ch Rohnert Pk CA 2005-2006; Faith Ntwk Coordntr Natl Cntr for Sci Educ 2001-2004; S Lk's Mssn Calistoga CA 2001-2004; D S Barn' Epis Ch Los Angeles CA 1991-2000; CE Mssnr Dio Los Angeles Los Angeles CA 1990-1995; Mnstry Dvlp Dio Nevada Las Vegas 1975-1989. Auth,

"Reshaping Mnstry," *Reshaping Mnstry*, Jethro Pub, 1990. Soc of Ord Scientists 2012. DD CDSP 2008; MDiv w hon CDSP 1974; AB cl Rad 1968.

BORGMAN, Dean Wylie (Mass) 5 Heritage Dr, Rockport MA 01966 **Asstg Chr Ch S Hamilton MA 1997-, Assoc 1982-1996; Fndr/Ed Cntr for Yth Stds 1985-; Prof. Yth Ministires Gordon-Conwell TS 1973-** B Bridgeport CT 1928 s Arnold & Winifred. BA Wheaton Coll 1950; MA Fairfield U 1954; CAGS NEU 1975. D 6/7/1980 Bp Morris Fairchild Arnold P 6/1/1981 Bp John Bowen Coburn. m 12/28/1973 Gail Renee Borgman. Auth, "Hear My Story: Understanding the Cries of Troubled Yth," Hendrickson Pub, 2003; Auth, "When Kumbaya Is Not Enough: a Practical Theol for Yth Mnstry," Hendrickson Pub. Assn of Yth Ministy Educators 1998; Intl Assn for the Study of Yth Mnstry 1995. Distinguished Serv & Achievement Assn of Yth Mnstry Educators 2006.

BORMES, Richard Joseph (Minn) 4350 Brookside Ct Apt 117, Edina MN 55436 **Died 7/1/2017** B Saint Paul MN 1937 s Louis & Ruth. S Thos Coll St Paul MN 1957; AMS U MN 1959; MDiv SWTS 1989. D 6/22/1989 Bp Robert Marshall Anderson P 12/16/1989 Bp Frank Tracy Griswold III. c 3. P H Trin Epis Ch Elk River MN 2006-2010; S Jn's Ch S Cloud MN 2004-2006; Dio Minnesota Minneapolis MN 1999-2003; Cn to the Ordnry Dio Missouri S Louis MO 1993-1999; Vic S Matthews Epis Ch Mex MO 1990-1993; Assoc S Chas Ch St. Chas IL 1989-1990. Bd, S Andr Fndt; Cathd Mssn Soc; Epis Cmnty Serv.

BORREGO, John Edward (Okla) 422 E Noble Ave, Guthrie OK 73044 B Bogota CO 1951 s Edward & Mary. BA Ya 1973; MDiv VTS 1978; U of Oklahoma 1994. D 6/17/1978 Bp Gerald Nicholas Mcallister P 6/1/1979 Bp Thomas Augustus Fraser Jr. m 6/17/1977 Lynn Griffith c 1. R Trin Ch Guthrie OK 2007-2014; Epis Ch Of The Resurr Oklahoma City OK 1997-1999; Dio Oklahoma Oklahoma City OK 1994-1996; S Andr's Epis Ch Lawton OK 1987-1993; S Andr's Epis Ch Charlotte NC 1980-1987; S Fran Ch Greensboro NC 1978-1980. Auth, "Angl & Epis Hist".

BORREGO, Lynn Griffith (Okla) 422 E Noble Ave, Guthrie OK 73044 **Vic S Mk's Ch Seminole OK 2002-, 1999; P-in-c S Paul's Ch Clinton OK 1997-** B San Francisco CA 1951 d Reese & Rosalind. AA W Vlly Cmnty Coll 1972; BA San Jose St U 1974; MDiv VTS 1978. D 6/13/1992 P 12/12/1992 Bp Robert Manning Moody. m 6/17/1977 John Edward Borrego c 2. Part Time/ Int Vic S Aug Of Cbury Oklahoma City OK 2008-2010; Vic S Paul's Epis Ch Holdenville OK 1999-2008; Dio Oklahoma Oklahoma City OK 1997-2007; Chapl Fam Hospice 1995-1997; Cur S Mary's Ch Edmond OK 1993-1995.

✠ BORSCH, The Rt Rev Frederick Houk (Los) 2930 Corda Ln, Los Angeles CA 90049 **Died 4/11/2017** B Chicago IL 1935 s Reuben & Pearl. BA Pr 1957; BA Oxf GB 1959; STB GTS 1960; PhD U of Birmingham 1966; DD SWTS 1978; STD CDSP 1981; STD Ya Berk 1985; DD GTS 1988. D 6/18/1960 Bp Gerald Francis Burrill P 12/17/1960 Bp Charles L Street Con 6/18/1988 for Los. m 6/25/1960 Barbara Edgeley Borsch c 3. Chair- Angl Stds Luth TS Philadelphia Philadelphia 2003-2009; Int Dn Ya Berk New Haven CT 2002-2003; Bp Of Los Angeles Dio Los Angeles Los Angeles CA 1988-2002; Chair Of Com On Theol HOB 1988-2000; Rep Angl Consultive Coun 1984-1988; Epis Ch Exec Coun GC 1981-1988; Dn of Chap, Prof of Rel Pr Princeton NJ 1981-1988; Pres CDSP Berkeley CA 1972-1980; Prof The GTS New York NY 1971-1972; Assoc Prof Of NT Bexley Seabury Fed Chicago IL 1966-1969; Tutor Queen's Coll Birmingham Uk 1963-1966; Cur Gr Ch Oak Pk IL 1960-1963. Auth, "My Life for Yours," CreateSpace, 2014; Auth, "Keeping Faith at Princeton: a Brief Hist of Rel Pluralism at Princeton and Other Universities," Princeton Uniersity Press, 2012; Auth, "Parade: Poems of Light and Dark Alike," Cathd Cntr Press, 2010; Auth, "Our First Atom An All-Americn Story," IUniverse, 2009; Auth, "Introducing the Lessons Of The Ch Year: A Guide For Lay Readers And Congregations," Seabury Press/Trin Int'L, 2009; Auth, "Day by Day: Loving the Lord More Nearly," Morehouse/Ch Pub, 2009; Auth, "The Sprt Searches Everythin: Keeping Life's Questions," Cowley, 2005; Auth, "The Magic Word: Stirrings and Stories of Faith and Mnistry," Cathd Cntr Press, 2001; Auth, "Outrage And Hope: A Bp'S Reflections In Times Of Change And Challenge," Trin Press Intl , 1996; Auth, "Chr Discipleship And Sxlty," Forw Mvmt Press, 1993; Ed, Trin Press Intl , 1993; Auth, "Many Things In Parables: Extravagant Stories Of New Cmnty," Fortress Press, 1988; Auth, "Jesus: The Human Life Of God," Forw Mvmt Press, 1987; Auth, "Anglicanism And The Bible," Morehouse-Barlow, 1984; Auth, "Power In Weakness: New Hearing For Gospel Stories Of Healing And Discipleship," Fortress Press, 1983; Auth, "Coming Together In The Sprt," Forw Mvmt Press, 1980; Auth, "God's Parable," SCM/Westminster, 1976; Auth, "Introducing The Lessons Of The Ch Year: A Guide For Lay Readers And Congregations," Seabury Press/Trin Int'L, 1976; Auth, "The Chr And Gnostic s Man," Scm Press, 1970; Auth, "The s Man In Myth And Hist," Scm/Westminster, 1967. AAR 1966; Soc Of Arts, Rel And Contemporary Culture 1986; SBL 1966; Studiorum Novi Testamentum Societas 1964. Frederick Houk Borsch Chair of Angl Stds Luth TS at Philadelphia 2014; Humanitarian Awd Natl Conf For Cmnty And Justice 2000; DD GTS 1988; STD Ya Berk 1985; STD CDSP 1981; DD Seabury-Wstrn Theoloigcal Sem 1978; Stb cl GTS 1960; Ab w First Class Honours Oxf 1959; Phi Beta Kappa Pr 1957; Ab scl Pr 1957; Keasby Schlr The Keasby Fndt 1957.

BORSCH, Kathleen Ann (Ore) **Sr Bus Asst Texas Tech Univ Hlth Sciences Ctr 2001-** B 1955 d Harry & Barbara. D Formation Prog Dio NW Texas; California St U 1974; Cert So Plains Coll 1986. D 10/29/2006 Bp C Wallis Ohl. c 3.

BORZUMATO, Judith Alice (NY) 500 State Rte 299 Apt 24C, Highland NY 12528 **D The Epis Ch Of Chr The King Stone Ridge NY 1992-** B Woonsocket RI 1936 d Frederic & Sibyl. Emerson Coll 1955; AAS Ulster Cnty Cmnty Coll 1980. D 5/30/1992 Bp Richard Frank Grein. m 6/15/1957 Lawrence Paul Borzumato c 1. OHC 1978.

BOSBYSHELL, William Allen (SwFla) 106 21st Ave Ne, Saint Petersburg FL 33704 **Asst S Bede's Ch St. Petersburg FL 2009-; Ret S Bede's Epis Ch St. Petersburg FL 1999-** B Philadelphia PA 1933 s John & Lilla. BA Swarthmore Coll 1955; STB GTS 1958; MEd U of Florida 1967; PhD U of Florida 1970. D 5/11/1958 Bp William P Roberts P 11/29/1958 Bp Oliver J Hart. m 5/31/1958 Caroline Bosbyshell c 3. Cn Cathd Ch Of S Ptr St. Petersburg FL 1990-1998; Asst S Jn's Epis Ch Clearwater FL 1977-1990; Dir of Samar Cntr Dio SW Florida Parrish FL 1976-1990; Asst Ch Of The Ascen Clearwater FL 1972-1976; The Samar Cntr Clearwater FL 1970-1990; LocTen S Barth's Ch High Sprg FL 1967-1969; LocTen S Jn Newberry FL 1967-1969; R S Jn's Ch Melbourne FL 1962-1966; Cathd Ch Of S Lk Orlando FL 1959-1962; Cur Gr Ch Mt. Airy Philadelphia PA 1958-1959. AAPC, Fell 1972; Mem, APA 1972; Mem, Assn for Psychol Type 1972-1999.

BOSLER, Sarah Mather (Be) 1188 Ben Franklin Hwy E, Douglassville PA 19518 **D S Gabr's Ch Douglassville PA 2007-** B Baltimore MD 1948 d Frank & Caroline. BA Buc 1970. D 9/29/2007 Bp Paul Victor Marshall. m 7/19/1969 Thomas Bosler c 3.

BOSS, Bruce William (Ind) 133 Belvedere Dr, Georgetown KY 40324 B Louisville KY 1949 s Edward & Mary. BA U of Kentucky 1971; MDiv VTS 1974; DMin SWTS 2003. D 6/1/1974 P 12/6/1974 Bp Addison Hosea. m 5/24/1970 Virginia C Cooper c 1. R Ch Of The Nativ Indianapolis IN 2002-2014; R Ch Of The Adv Louisville KY 1993-2002; Vic Ch Of The Resurr Nicholasville KY 1986-1992; Vic St Gabriels Ch Lexington KY 1977-1985; Vic S Jas Epis Ch Prestonsburg KY 1974-1977; Dep to GC Dio Indianapolis Indianapolis IN 2009-2013, Stndg Com 2009-2012, Dep to GC 2007-2010, Dep to GC 2004-2007, COM 2003-2009; COM Dio Kentucky Louisville KY 1995-2001, Trst & Coun 1994-1997; Dep to GC Dio Lexington Lexington 1989-1992, Dep to GC 1986-1989, Exec Coun 1986-1989, Eccl Crt 1985-1986, Dep to GC 1983-1986, Stndg Com 1982-1985, Exec Coun 1979-1981. Phi Beta Kappa U Of Kentucky 1971.

BOSSCHER, Molly Boscher (Va) 251 E Lake Brantley Dr, Longwood FL 32779 **S Paul's Ch Richmond VA 2015-; Asstg P Epis Ch of the Resurr 2008-** B Lansing Michigan 1975 d David & Mary. BA U of Virginia 2003; MDiv Sewanee: The U So, TS 2008. D 5/24/2008 Bp Peter J Lee P 12/10/2008 Bp John Wadsworth Howe. c 2. Assoc Epis Ch Of The Resurr Longwood FL 2010-2015; Chapl Sweetwater Epis Acad Longwood FL 2008-2015.

BOSS WOLLNER, Ernesto Sieghard (Colom) Cra 86 # 46-38 Apto 202, Medellin ANTIOQUIA Colombia **Iglesia Epis En Colombia Bogota 2012-** B Bogota Colombia 1951 s Arno Joaquin & Eva. Universidad Eafit 1975; BA Centro de Estudios Teologicos 2005. D 10/14/2006 P 6/16/2007 Bp Francisco Jose Duque-Gomez. m 6/16/1976 Luz Helena Agudelo Hoyos c 2.

BOST, Emily Catherine (Ark) 217 N East Ave, Fayetteville AR 72701 **Advoc CASA NWA Springdale AR 2012-; D S Paul's Ch Fayetteville AR 2007-; COM Dio Arkansas Little Rock AR 2010-** B Heber Springs AR 1943 d Rockie & Marise. RN St Vinc Sch of Nrsng 1964; RN St Vinc Sch of Nrsng 1969; Chinese Watercolor & Calligraphy Zhejiang Acad of Fine Arts 1988; Visual Arts San Antonio Art Inst 1990; Cert Vol Mgmt Vol Mgmt 2005; Ord D Formation Prog Dio Arkansas 2006. D 12/16/2006 Bp Larry Maze. m 7/2/1976 James Bost c 3. Wrshp Coordntr NWACCC Fayetteville AR 2009-2012; Dir Bright Light Tutoring Fayetteville AR 2007-2012. emily@stpaulsfay.org

BOSTIAN, Nathan Louis (WTex) 20955 W Tejas Trl, San Antonio TX 78257 **Texas Mltry Inst San Antonio TX 2010-** B North Little Rock AR 1974 s Rondall & Peggy. BA Texas A&M U 1996; MDiv SMU Perkins 2008. D 12/13/2008 P 11/21/2009 Bp James Monte Stanton. m 1/9/1999 Kimberly Kristen Bostian c 3. Dir of Coll & YA S Mich And All Ang Ch Dallas TX 2009-2010; Campus Mnstry Dio Dallas Dallas TX 2008-2009, Campus Mnstrs 2000-2008.

BOSTON, Dane E (USC) Trinity Cathedral, 1100 Sumter St, Columbia SC 29201 **Chr Ch Cooperstown NY 2016-; Trin Cathd Columbia SC 2014-** B Dunedin FL 1986 s Ethan & Denise. BA W&L 2008; MDiv Ya Berk 2011. D 11/30/2011 P 6/5/2012 Bp Neff Powell. m 8/1/2009 Deborah Newell Boston c 2. Cur Chr Ch Greenwich CT 2011-2014.

BOSTON, James Terrell (Ore) 518 NE Dean Dr, Grants Pass OR 97526 **Chapl, Ethics Comm Three Rivers Cmnty Hosp 2009-; P-in-c S Mths Epis Ch Cave Jct OR 2000-; Bd; Ed of FACETS Global Epis Mssn Ntwk 1997-; Chair, Mem Jos. Cnty Substance Abuse Cmnty Action Team 1995-; Stndg Com, Yth Com, Fin Dept, Global Mssn Comm Dio Oregon chaired: 1980-; Chapl Vol Rogue Vlly Yth Correctional Facility 2000-** B Patuxent River MD 1947 s Leadore & Mary. BA Amer U 1968; MDiv CDSP 1976; Cert Oxf GB 1977; Ldrshp Acad for New Directions 1986; DMin VTS 2002. D 11/30/

1976 Bp The Bishop Of Oxford P 1/24/1978 Bp Matthew Paul Bigliardi. m 11/12/1995 Pamela Boston. Strng Comm. Epis Partnership for Global Mssn 2010-2012; City Coun City of Grants Pas OR 2009-2010; S Lk's Ch Grants Pass OR 2003-2009, R 1987-2003; Vice chair Jo Cnty Comm for Chld & Families 1999-2001; Treas NNECA 1996-2008; Pres Friends of the Symphony 1987-2000; Dio.Coun, Jubilee Off, Covn.Dn Dio Oregon 1985-2008; Chapl Untd States Naval Reserve 1985-1999; Pres Lincoln Shltr and Serv 1983-1986; Vic S Jas Ch Lincoln City OR 1980-1986; Pres Lincoln Cnty Food Share 1980-1984; Vic Ch Of Chr The King On The Santiam Stayton OR 1978-1980; Assoc S Paul's Epis Ch Salem OR 1978-1980; City Coun City of Grants Pas OR 2009-2010; Dioc Coun, Mssn Chair Dio Oregon Portland OR 2006-2009, Dioc Coun, Agenda Chair 1992-2005, Convoc Dn, Jubilee Off 1990-2001, R 1987-1991, Gen Conv Dep (2) , 1st Alt (3), Alt (3) 1982-2011, Chair: Yth Ctte, Fin Dept, Bdgt Revs, Comp Dio Ctte 1980-; Trst Oregon Epis Sch Portland OR 1978-1980. Ord of H Cross, Assoc 1976.

BOSWELL JR, Frederick Philip (Colo) 9200 W 10th Ave, Lakewood CO 80215 B Saint Louis MO 1944 s Frederick & Caroline. BA Laf 1967; BD VTS 1970. D 6/13/1970 Bp George Leslie Cadigan P 12/1/1970 Bp Christoph Keller Jr. c 2. R S Paul's Epis Ch Lakewood CO 1997-2006; Int Chr Ch Cn City CO 1996-1997; Int Gd Shpd Epis Ch Centennial CO 1995-1996; Chapl Montclair St Montclair NJ 1987-1993; S Jas Ch Montclair NJ 1986-1993; R S Steph's Ch Fairview PA 1981-1986; Trin Ch Hannibal MO 1978-1981; River Parishes Reg Mnstry Hannibal MO 1974-1977; Calv Epis Ch Osceola AR 1971-1974; P-in-c S Steph's Ch Blytheville AR 1971-1974; DCE Chr Epis Ch Little Rock AR 1970-1971. Bp'S Outstanding Serv Awd 1992.

BOSWELL, Kathryn Mary (Alb) 21 Cherry St., Potsdam NY 13676 **Exec Bd Mem Helping Hands Compassionate Mnstrs of NNY 2011-; R S Phil's Ch Norwood NY 2010-** B Springfield, MA 1956 d John & Francine. BA SUNY Potsdam 2006; MA Nash 2010. D 6/5/2010 Bp William Howard Love. m 6/2/1973 Carroll Boswell c 10.

BOTH, M Blair (EC) 305 S 5th Ave, Wilmington NC 28401 B Roanoke VA 1943 d Richard & Blair. BA Sweet Briar Coll 1965; MDiv TESM 1987. D 7/22/1987 Bp Robert Whitridge Estill P 9/24/1988 Bp Frank Harris Vest Jr. m 5/21/2016 Inza Bell Watson. Int Ch Of The Servnt Wilmington NC 2006-2008; Assoc Ch Of The H Comm Memphis TN 2003-2004; Int S Tim's Ch Wilson NC 2000-2002; R S Mart's Epis Ch Charlotte NC 1995-1998; Asst S Mich's Ch Raleigh NC 1987-1995; Chair of Stwdshp Cmsn Dio No Carolina Raleigh NC 1991-1995.

BOTT, Harold Ray (At) 3750 Peachtree Rd NE Apt 905, Atlanta GA 30319 **Died 3/29/2016** B Shreveport LA 1928 s Whewell & Clara. BS Louisiana Tech U 1950; STB Ya Berk 1954. D 6/2/1954 Bp Girault M Jones P 5/1/1955 Bp Iveson Batchelor Noland. c 2. Ret 1990-2016; R S Jn's Atlanta GA 1965-1990; Vic S Mich And All Ang Lake Chas LA 1954-1958.

BOTTOM, Jacob Alan (Dal) Saint David's Episcopal Church, 623 Ector St, Denton TX 76201 B Lexington KY 1981 s Timothy & Rosemary. MA Dallas TS; MDiv Nash; BA U of Kentucky. D 4/30/2016 Bp Paul Emil Lambert P 11/30/2016 Bp George Robinson Sumner Jr. m 9/28/2013 Gina Fortune Gina Rene Fortune. jacobbottom@stdavidsdenton.org

BOTTONE, Doreen Ann (Ct) 68 Main St, Berlin CT 06037 B New Britain CT 1949 d Stanley & Ann. BA U of Connecticut 1971; MA S Jos Coll 1985; MA Hartford Sem 1990. D 9/15/2007 Bp Andrew Donnan Smith. m 4/3/1971 Timothy Bottone c 2.

BOUCHER, Edward Charles (RI) 341 Seaview Ave, Swansea MA 02777 B Central Falls RI 1945 s Reginald & Pauline. BA Providence Coll 1967; MA U of Virginia 1968; MDiv Ya Berk 1978. D 6/17/1978 P 12/20/1978 Bp Frederick Hesley Belden. m 6/2/1989 Janice Boucher c 3. P-in-c Ch Of The Gd Shpd Pawtucket RI 2004-2009; Int All SS Par Whitman MA 2002-2003; R Chr Ch Swansea MA 1981-2003; Cur Ch Of The Trsfg Providence RI 1978-1981.

BOUCHER, John (SVa) 600 Farnham Ct, North Chesterfield VA 23236 B Detroit MI 1948 s Joseph & Zay. BA CUA 1970; MDiv Candler TS Emory U 1976; DMin Sewanee: The U So, TS 1988. D 6/12/1976 P 6/3/1977 Bp Bennett Jones Sims. m 1/6/1973 Laura Scott Sims c 2. R S Mths Epis Ch Midlothian VA 2000-2013; Cn to the Ordnry Dio Easton Easton MD 1998-2000; R S Thos Epis Ch Columbus GA 1996-1997; Dio Michigan Detroit MI 1994-1995; Gr Epis Ch Port Huron MI 1988-1995; S Phil's Ch Nashville TN 1983-1988; Assoc Chr Ch Cathd Nashville TN 1981-1983; R S Marg's Ch Carrollton GA 1977-1981; Asst S Pat's Epis Ch Atlanta GA 1976-1977. Auth, "Stress on the Episcopate," *Living Ch*, 2000; Auth, "Does a Call End?," *Living Ch*, 1988; Auth, *Ret as a Rite of Passage*, 1988; Auth, "Re-ing Cler Need a Rite of Passage," *Episcopate*, 1985. HSEC 1993-1996.

BOULTER, Matthew Rutherford (Tex) 118 S. Bois d'Arc, Tyler TX 77702 **P Chr Epis Ch Tyler TX 2010-** B Lubbock TX 1972 s Eldon & Rosemary. BA U of Texas 1996; MDiv Westminster TS 2000; Dip Ang Stud Epis TS of the SW 2009. D 11/22/2009 Bp C Andrew Doyle P 5/25/2010 Bp Dena Arnall Harrison. m 8/30/1997 Bouquet Boulter c 2. Asst S Richard's Of Round Rock Round Rock TX 2009-2010. mboulter@christchurchtyler.org

BOULTER OHC, Richard Ottmuller (Mich) 11575 Belleville Rd, Belleville MI 48111 **D Trin Ch Belleville MI 2009-; Risk Mgr Dioc Risk Mgr Cl-V 2003-; Bp's Advsry Com on the Diac Dio Michigan Detroit MI 2010-** B Louisville Twp NY 1939 s Thomas & Jennie. AA Trenton Jr Coll 1960; BS Trenton St Coll 1969; Cert The Whitaker TS 2008. D 6/13/2009 Bp Wendell Nathaniel Gibbs Jr. m 2/3/1962 Judith M Moore c 3. Cler Mem COM 2010-2014. Assoc of the Ord of H Cross 1997.

BOULTER, Robert J (Md) Cathedral of the Incarnation, 4 E University Pkwy, Baltimore MD 21218 **Cathd Of The Incarn Baltimore MD 2014-** B Watertown NY 1963 s John & Elizabeth. BMus Ithaca Coll 1985; Cert Ang Stud Ya Berk 2006; MDiv Yale DS 2006. D 6/10/2006 P 12/16/2006 Bp Andrew Donnan Smith. m 9/19/1987 Sally G Boulter c 2. Assoc S Columba's Ch Washington DC 2008-2014; Assoc Cathd of St Ptr & St Paul Washington DC 2006-2008; VP, Tech Serv Profsnl Testing Corp 1987-2003. rboulter@incarnationbaltimore.org

BOURDEAU, Mary Ellen (Md) 2 Saint Peters Pl, Lonaconing MD 21539 B Allentown PA 1940 d Arthur & Ellen. BA Syr 1962. D 9/7/2008 Bp John L Rabb. c 2. stpeters.lonaconing@mail.com

BOURGEAULT OSB, Cynthia Warren (Colo) HC 2 Box 16, Sunset ME 04683 **Principles Tchr The Contemplative Soc 1998-; Tchr In Res The Contemplative Soc 1998-** B Philadelphia PA 1947 d Warren & Mary. BA OH SU 1967; PhD U of Pennsylvania 1972; EDS 1975. D 12/19/1975 P 8/1/1979 Bp Lyman Cunningham Ogilby. c 2. Chr Epis Ch Aspen CO 2004-2013, Asst 1994-2003; Aspen Chap Aspen CO 2004-2012; Downeast Epis Cluster Swans Island ME 1991-1992, 1990-1991; P-in-c S Brendan Navigator Stonington ME 1989-1992; Non-par 1981-1988; Asst Nevil Memi Ch Of S Geo Ardmore PA 1978-1980; Dir Aspen Wisdom Sch Aspen CO 1975-1977. "The Wisdom Jesus," Shambhala, 2008; "Chanting the Psalms," Shambhala, 2006; Auth, "Centering Pryr and Inner Awakening," Cowley, 2004; "The Wisdom Way of Knowing," Wiley, 2003; Auth, "Mystical Hope," Cowley, 2001; Auth, "Love is Stronger than Death," Bell Tower Praxis, 1998; Ed, "Intimacy w God," 1993; Ed/Co-Auth, "Medieval Mus Drama," Oxf Press, 1980. Oblate Ord Of S Ben.

BOURHILL, John William (NY) 26 Huron Rd, Yonkers NY 10710 B Bronxville NY 1935 s James & Elenor. D 5/19/2001 Bp Richard Frank Grein. m 6/2/2002 Susan Summitt-Bourhill c 2.

✠ BOURLAKAS, The Rt Rev Dr Mark (SwVa) 421 S 2nd St, Louisville KY 40202 **Bp Dio SW Virginia Roanoke VA 2013-** B Vincennes IN 1963 s Luke & Judy. BA U So 1985; MDiv SWTS 1997. D 5/24/1997 P 12/6/1997 Bp Robert Gould Tharp Con 7/20/2013 for SwVa. m 5/6/1989 Martha Elizabeth Bourlakas c 3. Dn Chr Ch Cathd Louisville KY 2007-2013; R S Alb's Ch Davidson NC 2003-2007; R S Fran of Assisi Chapin SC 2000-2003; Asst Chr Ch Greenville SC 1998-2000; Cur S Lk's Ch Cleveland TN 1997-1998. bishopmark@dioswva.org

BOURNE, Nathaniel Francis (WNC) D 12/17/2016 Bp Jose Antonio McLoughlin.

BOURNE-RAISWELL, Margaret Lafayette (ECR) 20025 Glen Brae Dr, Saratoga CA 95070 B Fresno CA 1950 d Robert & Margaret. BA U Pac 1972; MS California St U 1975; MDiv CDSP 1991. D 5/29/1991 P 6/3/1992 Bp Richard Lester Shimpfky. m 5/29/1976 Dwight Goodwin. S Andrews Epis Ch Port Angeles WA 2007-2008; Ch Of The H Sprt Campbell CA 1999-2001; Assoc S Andr's Ch Saratoga CA 1993-1999; Ch Of S Jude The Apos Cupertino CA 1991-1992; Chair Of Cmsn For Deaf And Hearing-Impaired Dio El Camino Real Salinas CA 1991-1993. Bd Managers Ymca 1991; Chair Dio Cmsn For The Deaf & Hearing Impaired 1991-1993; Dio Cmsn On Stwdshp 1999.

BOURQUE, Mary Elizabeth (Me) 20 Union St., Hallowell ME 04347 B Camden ME 1943 d Clarence & Elvira. BS U of Maine Orono 1965; BS U of Maine Farmington 1997. D 6/20/2009 Bp Stephen Taylor Lane. m 10/15/1966 Peter Bourque c 3. D S Matt's Epis Ch Hallowell ME 2009-2010.

BOURQUIN, Eugene Alphonse (NY) 296 9th Ave, New York NY 10001 B Queens NY 1952 s Eugene & Hughetta. BS CUNY Baccalaureate Baruch Coll; MA NYU; Doctorate Heath Admin Sch of Advncd Stds at U of Phoenix; Cert in Ascetical Theol The Gnrl Theol 2014. D 5/13/2017 Bp Andrew Marion Lenow Dietsche.

BOUSFIELD, Nigel J (FdL) 1432 Foxfire Ct, Waupaca WI 54981 **R S Mk's Ch Waupaca WI 2008-** B Kent UK 1957 s Maurice & Enid. AA Scottsdale Cmnty Coll 2000; MDiv Nash 2003. D 12/14/2002 P 6/29/2003 Bp Keith Lynn Ackerman. Chr Ch Babylon NY 2006-2008; S Jn's Ch Huntington NY 2003-2006.

BOUSQUET, Michael (Mass) PO Box 395, Barnstable MA 02630 B Norfolk VA 1983 s Joseph & Susan. AB Dart 2005; MDiv Harvard DS 2009; Cert in Advncd Angl Stds EDS 2013. D 6/6/2015 P 1/6/2016 Bp Gayle Harris. m 3/27/2015 David King Lee. Asst S Mary's Epis Ch Barnstable MA 2015-2017. associate@stmarys-church.org

BOWDEN, George Edward (Mo) 624 Saffron Ct, Myrtle Beach SC 29579 B Paterson NJ 1943 s George & Jean. BA Leh 1965; MDiv GTS 1969. D 6/14/1969 P 12/13/1969 Bp Dudley S Stark. m 5/27/1967 Helen Frances Bowden c 2. R H Cross Epis Ch Poplar Bluff MO 1999-2009; Int S Andr's Ch Dayton OH 1998-1999; R S Andr's Epis Ch Wshngtn Ct Hs OH 1992-1998; R All

SS Epis Ch Lakewood NJ 1979-1990; R St Jn the Bapt Epis Ch Linden NJ 1971-1975; Cur S Ptr's Epis Ch Livingston NJ 1969-1971; Dioc Coun Dio Missouri S Louis MO 2005-2007; Cler Cont Educ Com Dio Sthrn Ohio Cincinnati OH 1994-1996.

BOWDEN JR, Talmadge Arton (Ga) 3409 Wheeler Rd, Augusta GA 30909 **Asst Ch Of The H Comf 2005-; Asst The Ch Of The Gd Shpd Augusta GA 2002-** B Coral Gables FL 1940 s Talmadge & Nellie. MD Med Coll of Georgia 1966; DMin Cert U So 2000. D 9/18/2001 P 3/21/2002 Bp Henry Irving Louttit. m 12/11/1993 Cecilia Murphy c 2.

BOWDEN, Teresa Thomas (Haw) 2573 California Ave, Wahiawa HI 96786 **Asst S Steph's Ch Wahiawa HI 2005-; Dio Hawaii 2004-** B Jacksonville FL 1936 BS U GA 1977; MDiv Epis TS of the SW 2001. D 6/17/2001 P 4/14/2002 Bp Richard Sui On Chang. m 2/28/1959 William Eugene Bowden c 2. Int/Supply H Cross Malaekuhana HI 2004-2005; Assoc S Tim's Ch Aiea HI 2002-2004.

BOWDISH, Lynn Eastman (Cal) 172 Northgate Ave, Daly City CA 94015 **Assoc H Chld At S Mart Epis Ch Daly City CA 2010-** B Eureka CA 1937 d Philip & Hally. BA U Pac 1959; MDiv CDSP 1978; DMin VTS 1991. D 6/24/1978 Bp William Foreman Creighton P 6/16/1979 Bp George West Barrett. c 2. Dio California San Francisco CA 2000-2009; Vic S Eliz's Epis Ch S San Fran CA 1981-2009; S Andr's Epis Ch San Bruno CA 1980-1981. Tertiary Of The Soc Of S Fran. Grant Rec Lilly Fndt 2000.

BOWEN, Anthony DeLisle (LI) 180 Kane St, Brooklyn NY 11231 **D Chr Ch Cobble Hill Brooklyn NY 2009-** B 1948 s Harcourt & Ena. Cert Geo Mercer Jr Memi TS; AA Borough of Manhattan Cmnty Coll 1978. D 6/1/2009 Bp Richard Lester Shimpfky. m 6/17/2011 Marilyn Bowen c 1.

BOWEN, Carol Staley (Cal) 2019 Monroe Ave, Belmont CA 94002 B Columbus OH 1946 d Charles & Florence. BA New Coll of California 1988; MA Coll of Notre Dame 1994; MA Coll of Notre Dame 1996; BA Sch for Deacons 1997. D 12/5/1998 Bp William Edwin Swing. m 3/2/1984 Mike Bowen. S Mk's Epis Ch Palo Alto CA 2000-2004. Amer Art Ther Assn; Caamft; D Coun Dio Ca; NAAD.

BOWEN, Elizabeth Anne (Mo) Trinity Episcopal Church, 318 S Duchesne Dr, Saint Charles MO 63301 B Kingston Jamaica 1939 d Arthur & Hyacinth. Epis Sch of Mnstry 2007. D 10/23/2007 Bp George Wayne Smith. m 8/24/1962 David Bowen c 3. D Trin Ch S Chas MO 2007-2014.

BOWEN, George Harry (Nwk) 308 River Oaks Dr, Rutherford NJ 07070 **Cn Trin And S Phil's Cathd Newark NJ 1993-** B East Rutherford NJ 1932 s Charles & Mary. BA Trin Hartford CT 1954; GTS 1957. D 6/15/1957 P 12/21/1957 Bp Benjamin M Washburn. Gr Ch Newark NJ 1976-1994, Cur 1957-1961; Admin Epis Cntr Delaware NJ 1974-1976; Pres of Hackensack Convoc Dio Newark NJ 1972-1974; R Trin Ch Cliffside Pk NJ 1961-1974. Hon Cn, Trin and S Phil's Cathd 1993.

BOWEN, Pauline Mason (WNY) 138 Castle Hill Rd, East Aurora NY 14052 **BEC Dio Wstrn New York Tonawanda NY 2011-, BEC 2000-2011, Diac Formation 1994-1999, Educ Cmsn 1988-1993, Dioc Coordntr, EFM 1988-; D S Mths Epis Ch E Aurora NY 2001-** B State College PA 1936 d David & Leda. AAS Trocaire Coll 1973; BS Medaille Coll 1988; MA Chr the King Sem 1991; MDiv Chr the King Sem 1999. D 6/11/1988 Bp David Charles Bowman. m 5/14/1955 Charles Daniel Bowen c 3. Auth, "Prog," *Letting Go*, 1992; Auth, "Prog," *Journeying Hm*, 1991; Auth, *arts & Poetry*. Ord of S Lk 1981-1989. hon - Scripture Chr the King Sem 1999.

BOWEN, Paul Roger (Tex) 324 Sherwood Ave, Staunton VA 24401 B Mobile AL 1944 s Paul & Helen. BA Cit 1965; MDiv VTS 1968. D 6/11/1968 P 12/18/1968 Bp Wilburn Camrock Campbell. m 11/28/1969 Martha Kennon Bowen c 2. S Steph's Epis Sch Austin TX 2002-2007; York Sch Monterey CA 1994-2002; Dir S Steph's & S Agnes Upper Sch Alexandria VA 1991-1994; St. Steph's And St. Agnes Sch Alexandria VA 1991-1994; Dio Virginia Richmond VA 1986-1988; Chair Dept of Rel S Albans Sch Washington DC 1982-1991; Chapl S Alb's Sch Washington DC 1982-1991; CFS The Sch At Ch Farm Exton PA 1979-1982; Chapl Ch Farm Sch Paoli PA 1979-1982; Serv Angl Ch in Tonga SoPac Washington 1977-1979; Assoc Chapl S Alb's Sch Washington DC 1974-1977; Cathd of St Ptr & St Paul Washington DC 1973-1991; Serv Angl Ch in Polynesia 1970-1972; R Peace Corps - Tonga Washington 1970-1972; Asst S Matt's Ch Wheeling WV 1968-1970. Auth, "Opportunities for Mnstry in Epis Schools," *NAES Reasons for Being*, 1997; Auth, "Challenge," *The Cathd Age*, 1986. Outstanding Tchr Washingtonian mag.

BOWEN, Peter Scott (Me) 20 Sky Harbor Dr, Biddeford ME 04005 **Chapl Maine Veterans' Hm Scarborough 2006-** B Hartford CT 1944 s Harvey & Anita. BA S Michaels Coll 1967; MA Nasson Coll 1986; MDiv Bangor TS 2006. D 6/24/2006 Bp Chilton Richardson Knudsen. m 11/23/2002 Shirley Williams c 2. Chapl St. Andres Healthcare Biddeford Maine 2010-2015; D Chr Ch Biddeford ME 2006-2012; Chapl Maine Med Cntr Portland 2006-2009.

BOWEN, Shirley Williams (Me) 20 Sky Harbor Drive, Biddeford ME 04005 **Seeds of Hope Jubilee Cntr Portland ME 2013-; R Chr Ch Biddeford ME 2007-; Campus Mssnr Dio Maine Portland ME 2005-, Mssnr for Campus Mnstry/Epis Chapl @ USM 2005-** B Marietta OH 1959 d Merrill & Kathleen. BA Glenville St Coll 1981; MEd W Virginia U 1985; MDiv EDS 2004. D 6/11/

2005 P 12/10/2005 Bp Chilton Richardson Knudsen. m 11/23/2002 Peter Scott Bowen.

BOWER, Alice W (Oly) 2400 NW 9th Ave, Battle Ground WA 98604 B Corvallis OR 1949 d Harry & Henrianne. BA U CA; C.P.K Lon; MA Ch DS of Pacific 1997. D 12/12/2015 P 6/21/2016 Bp Gregory Harold Rickel. m 8/24/1974 John S Bower c 3.

BOWER, Bruce E (WMo) 6401 Wornall Ter, Kansas City MO 64113 **Archd Dio Connecticut Meriden CT 2016-** B Mt Clemens MI 1950 s Allan & Eleanor. Bp Kemper Sch for Mnstry; BS MI SU 1972; MS MI SU 1973. D 11/7/2014 Bp Martin Scott Field. m 7/21/1979 Joy M Kaufman c 3.

BOWER, Jeffrey L (Ind) 4160 Broadway St, Indianapolis IN 46205 **S Paul's Epis Ch Indianapolis IN 2017-; Vic/P-in-c S Jn's Epis Ch Indianapolis IL 2007-** B Greensburg IN 1961 s Ora & Frances. BA Wabash Coll 1983; MA Chr TS 1997; MDiv Chr TS 1999; CTh SWTS 2004. D 6/24/2006 P 2/10/2007 Bp Cate Waynick. m 8/15/2012 David Blake Duncan c 2. S Johns Ch Indianapolis IN 2007-2017. Assn of Profsnl Chapl 2003. Presidential Schlr Chr TS 1998.

BOWER, John Allen (SO) 418 Sugar Maple Ln, Springdale OH 45246 **Ret 1998-** B Parkersburg WV 1937 s Joanne. U IL - Chicago 1958; BA Nthrn Illinois U 1960; MDiv Nash 1963. D 6/15/1963 Bp James Winchester Montgomery P 12/21/1963 Bp Gerald Francis Burrill. m 8/10/1963 Louise Annette Emenheiser c 3. Gr Ch Cincinnati OH 2001-2006; Int St. Simon of Cyrene Lincoln Heights OH 2001-2005; Int S Mary's Ch Waynesville OH 2000-2001; R Zion Epis Ch Chas Town WV 1991-1998; The Soc of the Trsfg Cincinnati OH 1980-1991; R Chr Epis Ch Ottawa IL 1971-1979; Vic S Pat Franklin Pk IL 1965-1971; Cur Chr Ch Waukegan IL 1963-1965; Procter Conf. Cntr Bd Dio Sthrn Ohio Cincinnati OH 2007-2009, Evang Com 2005-2010, Conf Cntr Bd 2002-2009, Evang Cmsn 2000-2007, Bp Nomin Com 1997-1998, Evang and Renwl Cmsn 1986-1997, Dioc Coun 1984-1985; Peterkin Com Dio W Virginia Charleston WV 1992-1997. CT Assoc 1980.

BOWER, Richard Allen (CNY) 681 N Hill Cross Rd, Ludlow VT 05149 **Ret 2000-** B Santa Ana CA 1940 s Gerald & Mary. BA USC 1965; MDiv Fuller TS 1968; ThM PrTS 1969; Cert EDS 1970; EDS 1990. D 4/11/1970 P 10/24/1970 Bp Alfred L Banyard. m 8/8/1964 Stephanie D Dardenne-Ankringa c 3. Pstr Min L'Arche USA 2009-2013; Exec Dir Fundacion Cristosal San Salvador El Salvador 1999-2011; Dn and R St Paul's Syracuse Syracuse NY 1991-2000; Int Chr Ch Ridgewood NJ 1990-1991; Proctor Fell EDS Cambridge MA 1989-1990; Rep of Panama Exec Coun Appointees New York NY 1986-1990; Dn Catedral San Lucas Cuidad Panama 1986-1989; Assoc R Trin Ch Princeton NJ 1979-1986; R Ch Of S Mary's By The Sea Pt Pleas Bch NJ 1973-1979; Cur S Lk's Epis Ch Metuchen NJ 1970-1973; Fndr and Exec Dir Cristosal Fndt 2001-2014; Pstr Min L'Arche USA 1995-2013. Auth, "Cuentos Panamenos," *Cuentos Panamenos:Stories of Struggle & Faith in Rural Panama*, Friendship Press, 1993; Auth, "Liturg as Lang," *Chld in the Euch*, Epis Ch Cntr, 1990; Auth, "Par Priesthood: Expectations and Reality," *ATR*, 1984; Auth, "Unity, Constancy & Peace: Liturg & Simplicity, Liturg & Simplicity," *Seabury Press NYC*, 1984; Auth, "Daring to Learn," *Making Sense of Things*, Seabury, 1981; Auth, "Meaning of Epituchano in Epistles of S Ign of Antoich, Vigiliae Christianae Vol. 28," *Vigiliae Christianae*, No Holland Publ. Co, Amsterdam, 1974. OHC 1970; Pstr Min, L'Arche Zone USA 1995-2013; l'Arche Intl 1994. Elected Dn Emer St Paul's Cathd, Syracuse NY 2000; Cert of Recognition for Wk in Human Rts St Assembly, NY St 1999. rabvt@tds.net

BOWER, Roger Andrew (NI) 505 Bullseye Lake Rd, Valparaiso IN 46383 **R S Andr's Epis Ch Valparaiso IN 2010-** B Concord MA 1961 s Leroy & Roberta. BA U of St Thos 1985; MDiv S Thos Univ Sch of Theo St Paul 1989. Rec 10/24/2000 as Priest Bp Daniel William Herzog. m 2/14/1996 Barbara Douglas Bower c 2. Dio Colorado Denver CO 2009; R H Apos Epis Ch Englewood CO 2004-2009; Assoc S Marg's Epis Ch Palm Desert CA 2003; R S Lk's Ch Mechanicville NY 2000-2003.

BOWERFIND, Ellis Tucker (Va) 8727 Bluedale St, Alexandria VA 22308 **R S Lk's Ch Alexandria VA 2003-** B Cleveland OH 1958 s Edgar & Maria. BA S Johns Coll 1984; MDiv Ya Berk 1991; MA Ursuline Coll 1999. Trans 10/9/2003 Bp (Arvil) Thomas Shaw. m 10/3/1992 Delea Free Bowerfind c 4. Assoc R S Mary's Epis Ch Barnstable MA 1999-2003; Assoc R S Paul's Epis Ch Cleveland OH 1991-1999; Tchr U Sch Shaker Heights Ohio 1991-1999.

BOWERS, Albert Wayne (Alb) 17 Woodbridge Ave, Sewaren NJ 07077 B Macon GA 1942 s Louie & Mattie. BA Estrn Nazarene Coll 1976; MDiv GTS 1986. D 6/14/1986 Bp William Gillette Weinhauer P 12/20/1986 Bp Vincent King Pettit. c 1. Zion Ch Hudson Falls NY 2000-2009; Cn Mssnr S Mk's-S Lk's Epis Mssn Fair Haven VT 1998-2000; Slate Vlly Mnstry Poultney VT 1998-2000; Vic S Lk And All SS' Ch Un NJ 1991-1998; S Jn's Ch Sewaren NJ 1991-1997; Cur Trin Ch Woodbridge NJ 1986-1991. Auth, "A Cognitive Model Of Original Sin Arise & Shine".

BOWERS, David Douglas (SwFla) 513 Nassau St S, Venice FL 34285 B Thomasville GA 1963 s George & Elizabeth Ann. BA U So 1985; MDiv Nash 1989. D 5/14/1989 P 4/1/1990 Bp Harry Woolston Shipps. S Mk's Epis Ch Venice FL 1991-1995; The Ch Of The Gd Shpd Augusta GA 1990-1991;

Chapl Georgia Sthrn Coll Statesboro GA 1989-1991; Trin Ch Statesboro GA 1989-1990.

BOWERS, George Franklin (Ga) Po Box 2408, Darien GA 31305 **Died 8/20/ 2015** B Berwick Nova Scotia 1935 D 2/3/2001 P 11/26/2002 Bp Henry Irving Louttit. m 10/5/1985 Patricia Bowers c 1.

BOWERS, John Edward (SO) 1276 Coonpath Rd Nw, Lancaster OH 43130 **Ret 1998-** B Cincinnati OH 1936 s Harry & Mary. BA Ken 1958; MDiv Bex Sem 1965. D 6/26/1965 P 1/1/1966 Bp Roger W Blanchard. m 6/21/1986 Nancy Bowers. Int S Pat's Epis Ch Dublin OH 2002-2003; E Cntrl Ohio Area Mnstry Bridgeport OH 1997-1998; S Jn's Epis Ch Cambridge OH 1979-1996; Chapl Cincinnati Correctional Instititute Cincinnati OH 1978-1979; P-in-c S Phil's Ch Cincinnati OH 1974-1979; P-in-c H Sprt Epis Ch Cincinnati OH 1967-1970; Cur S Jas Epis Ch Cincinnati OH 1965-1966.

BOWERS, Marvin Nelson (NCal) 202 Tucker St, Healdsburg CA 95448 B Sapulpa OK 1944 s Marvin & Cecil. BA U CA Santa Barbara 1966; MDiv GTS 1969. D 7/1/1969 Bp Edward McNair P 1/31/1970 Bp Clarence Rupert Haden Jr. m 6/25/1966 Bonnie Bowers c 5. S Paul's Ch Healdsburg CA 1972-2006; Vic S Lk's Mssn Calistoga CA 1969-1972; RurD The Epis Dio Nthrn California Sacramento CA 1995-1999, RurD 1976-1994.

BOWERS, Terry L. (Chi) 1900 Etton Dr, Fort Collins CO 80526 **Lic to officiate Dio Colorado 2009-** B Rockford IL 1953 d Bernard & B Dawn. BS Colorado St U 1975; MDiv SWTS 2003. D 1/31/2007 Bp Victor Alfonso Scantlebury P 9/11/2007 Bp Bill Persell. m 9/14/2014 Sharon Louise Hamman c 3.

BOWERS, Thomas Dix (NY) 304 Lord Granville Dr, Morehead City NC 28557 **Ret 1994-** B Norfolk VA 1928 s George & Nellie. BS VMI 1949; BA U So 1953; MDiv VTS 1956; Hon DDiv Nash 1983; Nash 1983; Hon DDiv VTS 1983; VTS 1983; Hon DDiv Sewanee: The U So, TS 1984; Sewanee: The U So, TS 1984. D 6/13/1956 Bp William A Brown 6/17/1957 Bp George P Gunn. m 12/26/2003 Palmer Bowers c 4. Int S Dav's Ch Austin TX 2002-2003; Int S Jn's Ch Lafayette Sq Washington DC 1993-1994; R St. Barth Ch New York NY 1978-1993; R S Lk's Epis Ch Atlanta GA 1971-1978; R S Pat's Ch Washington DC 1961-1971; Assoc S Alb's Par Washington DC 1959-1961; S Geo's Ch Pungoteague Pungoteague VA 1956-1959; R S Jas' Ch Accomac VA 1956-1959. Auth, "Come To The Table," *Come to the Table*. DEACONS 1973-1993; The Club 1979-1993. Thos Dix Bowers Preaching Fndt Est. 2008 VTS 2008; Tom Bowers's Day Atlanta Est. 1978 Mayor Maynard Jackson 1978; Human Relatns Awd Mart Luther King Cntr Soc Change 1977. pubowers@yahoo.com

BOWERSOX, Ned Ford (WTex) 8607 Tomah Dr, Austin TX 78717 B Midland MI 1942 s Ford & Mildred. AA Florida St U 1965; BS Florida St U 1969; MDiv VTS 1973. D 5/18/1973 P 12/5/1973 Bp William Hopkins Folwell. m 6/22/ 1968 Phyllis A Bowersox c 2. Int St Stephens 2012; Int S Mk's Ch San Marcos TX 2010-2012; Int S Helena's Epis Ch Boerne TX 2000-2010; R Ch Of The Gd Shpd Corpus Christi TX 1995-2007; R S Jn's Ch Melbourne FL 1979-1994; S Chris's Ch Orlando FL 1976-1979; Vic Ch Of The New Cov Winter Spgs FL 1975-1979; Dio Cntrl Florida Orlando FL 1975-1976; Asst Gr Epis Ch Of Ocala Ocala FL 1973-1975.

BOWERSOX, Sally Ann (Colo) 620 S Alton Way Apt 4d, Denver CO 80247 **Exec Dir St Ben Hlth and Healing Mnstry Boulder CO 2007-; Exec Dir St. Ben Hlth and Healing Mnstry Boulder CO 2005-** B Lakewood OH 1954 d Robert & Beatrice. AS Lansing Cmnty Coll 1975; MA Naropa U 1987; MDiv Iliff TS 2002; CSD Vincentian Cntr for Sprtlty at Wk Denver CO 2005; Rgstr Yoga Tchr 200 Core Power Yoga 2012. D 6/8/2002 P 12/21/2002 Bp William Jerry Winterrowd. c 1. Adj Cler S Ambr Epis Ch Boulder CO 2005-2007; Asst P Our Merc Sav Epis Ch Denver CO 2002-2005; Our Merc Sav Mnstrs Denver CO 2002-2005; Mem of the Dioc Com on Spritual Direction Dio Colorado Denver CO 2004-2009, Chapl to ECW in Dio Colorado 2002-2007. ECW 2002-2008; Natl Jubilee Mnstry 2005; Publ Plcy Advsry Bd, Dio Colorado 2008-2013; Sprtl Dir Intl 2005. sally@sbhhm.org

BOWES, Bruce (NY) 254 Bloomer Rd, Lagrangeville NY 12540 B Mount Vernon NY 1941 s Nelson & Naomi. BA Washington and Jefferson U 1964; MDiv Nash 1967. D 6/3/1967 P 12/1/1967 Bp Horace W B Donegan. m 6/29/1968 Adele Evelyn Bowes. Ch Of The Resurr Hopewell Jct NY 1974-1988; Asst R Gr Epis Ch Nyack NY 1967-1969.

BOWHAY, Christopher A (Tenn) St. Peter's Episcopal Church, 311 W 7th St, Columbia TN 38401 **S Ptr's Ch Columbia TN 2015-** B Santa Ana CA 1968 BA U CA Berkeley 1991; B.A. Sacr Theol St Jos of Arimathea Angl Theol Coll 1992; MA Stan 2000. D 6/12/2004 P 1/6/2005 Bp Don Adger Wimberly. m 10/4/1997 Sally B Brooks c 2. Assoc S Geo's Ch Nashville TN 2012-2015; Rectory S Thos Ch Houston TX 2006-2012; Dir, Fam, Yth, and Outreach Mnstrs S Mart's Epis Ch Houston TX 2004-2006; Vic St. Thos' Ch San Francisco 1995-1998; Assoc Par of Chr the King Washington DC 1992-1995.

BOWLIN BSG, Howard B (ETenn) PO Box 6259, Maryville TN 37802 **P-in-c S Thos Epis Ch Knoxville TN 2010-** B East Saint Louis IL 1946 s Howard & Helen. BA U IL 1972; U CO 1973; MDiv VTS 1992. D 6/13/1992 P 1/16/1993 Bp Ronald Hayward Haines. m 5/15/1976 Gail Anne Bowlin c 1. Int S Fran Of Assisi Epis Ch Ooltewah TN 2008-2009; R S Matt's Epis Ch Bloomington IL

1998-2007; R Chr Ch Lockport NY 1993-1998; Asst R S Alb's Epis Ch Annandale VA 1992-1993. BSG 2000.

BOWMAN, Andrea C (Spok) 104 E 17th Ave, Ellensburg WA 98926 B Everett WA 1946 D 8/20/2000 Bp John Stuart Thornton P 6/2/2001 Bp James E Waggoner Jr. Ch Of The Resurr (Chap) So Cle Elum WA 2009-2011, 2004-2008.

BOWMAN, Lani Louise (Haw) D 7/2/2016 Bp Robert Leroy Fitzpatrick.

BOWMAN, Sallie W (Ore) Department Of Spiritual Care, 1015 NW 22nd Ave, Portland OR 97210 **Dir, Dept of Sprtl Care Legacy Gd Samar Hosp Portland OR 2004-; Assoc S Mich And All Ang Ch Portland OR 2003-** B Richmond VA 1957 d Charles & Sallie. BA W&M 1979; MDiv CDSP 2003. D 4/ 30/2003 Bp Robert Louis Ladehoff P 11/15/2003 Bp Johncy Itty. m 7/30/2005 Kathleen Tytus Buhl c 1. Int Dir, Dept of Sprtl Care Legacy Gd Samar Med Cntr Portland OR 2011-2012; Chapl Legacy Gd Samar Med Cntr Portland OR 2003-2011.

BOWMAN, Susan Blount (Alb) 16 Mansion Blvd, Apt B, Delmar NY 12054 **Pstr Serv Meth Ch 2005-** B Richmond VA 1947 d Howard & Belle. BA W&M 1969; MDiv Sewanee: The U So, TS 1984. D 2/23/1985 P 1/25/1986 Bp Claude Charles Vache. c 1. Jermain Meth Ch 2006-2007; Vic S Mk's Ch Hoosick Falls NY 2001-2005; Non-par 2000-2001; S Mich's Albany NY 1991-2001; Vic All SS Ch So Hill VA 1987-1991; Jackson Field Hm Jarratt VA 1986-1987; Chapl Jackson-Field Epis Hm Jarratt 1985-1987; Pres Of Stndg Com Dio Albany Greenwich NY 1995-1996. Auth, "Bk," *Lady Fr*, Aberdeen Bay, 9011; Auth, "Bk," *Lady Fr*, Aberdeen Bay, 2011.

BOWRON, Josh (At) 1623 Carmel Rd, Charlotte NC 28226 **P S Mart's Epis Ch Charlotte NC 2014-** B Detroit MI 1975 s Brian & Sue. BA Merc 2000; MDiv Sewanee: The U So, TS 2011. D 12/18/2010 P 6/18/2011 Bp J Neil Alexander. m 3/16/2002 Brittany Stewart Bowron c 3. Asst S Jn's Epis Ch Charlotte NC 2011-2014.

BOWYER, Charles Lester (NwT) 5806 Emory St, Lubbock TX 79416 **Oblate Benedictine Oblate Our Lady of Guadalupe Abbey 2015-** B Richwood WV 1939 s Charles & Delores. BA Berea Coll 1961; MDiv Epis TS in Kentucky 1964; DMin GTF 1991; PhD La Salle U 1995. D 5/30/1964 Bp William R Moody P 5/8/1965 Bp George Henry Quarterman. ER Chapl/Ethics/Crisis Intervention Hosp Chapl 1986-2005; Stff Chapl ST.Mary/Cov Hosp System 1986-2005; Assoc S Paul's On The Plains Epis Ch Lubbock TX 1975-1984; Vic S Jn's Ch Snyder TX 1966-1975; Cur The Epis Ch Of S Mary The Vrgn Big Sprg TX 1964-1966.

BOYCE, Ryan Antonio (NJ) 1709 Arctic Ave, Atlantic City NJ 08401 B Barbados 1980 s Erma. Trans 7/27/2016 Bp William H Stokes. c 1. rev.rboyce@aol. com

BOYD, Catherine Tyndall (Tex) 104 Cove Point Ln, Williamsburg VA 23185 **S Mart's Epis Ch Williamsburg VA 2017-** B Columbia MO 1958 d Brent & Constance. BA U of Missouri 1980; Lexington TS 2003; MDiv Epis TS of the SW 2006. D 6/24/2006 P 1/13/2007 Bp Don Adger Wimberly. m 5/9/1981 David Boyd c 2. Assoc R Trin Epis Ch Marble Falls TX 2013-2017; S Dav's Ch Austin TX 2012; Trin Epis Sch Of Austin W Lake Hills TX 2007-2013; Asst R S Jn's Epis Ch Austin TX 2006-2007; Exec Dir, S Agnes Hse Epis Dio Lexington Lexington KY 2001-2003; Yth Dir Ch S Mich The Archangel Lexington KY 1998-2000; Cmncatn Ofcr Epis Dio Milwaukee 1991-1997; Cmncatn Dir Epis Dio Milwaukee 1990-1996; Marketing Dir St. Barn Cntr Epis Dio Milwaukee 1988-1991; Cmncatn Dir St. Barn Cntr Rogers Memi Hosp Oconomowoc WI 1988-1989. ECom 1987-1992; Fllshp of SSJE 1997. ctyndallboyd@gmail.com

BOYD, David (Tex) 104 Cove Point Ln, Williamsburg VA 23185 B Janesville WI 1955 s Ronald & Sidney. BS Sthrn Illinois U 1977; MDiv Nash 1984. D 4/7/ 1984 P 10/27/1984 Bp Charles Thomas Gaskell. m 5/9/1981 Catherine Tyndall c 2. Dom And Frgn Mssy Soc- Epis Ch Cntr New York NY 2015-2016; Epis Ch Cntr New York NY 2015-2016; R S Dav's Ch Austin TX 2003-2015; R Ch S Mich The Archangel Lexington KY 1996-2003; S Andr's Ch Milwaukee WI 1990-1996; Urban Mssnr S Jn Ch/Mision San Juan Milwaukee WI 1990-1994; R S Jn The Div Epis Ch Burlington WI 1986-1990; Asst Gr Ch Madison WI 1984-1986; Mem, Stndg Com Dio Texas Houston TX 2007-2010; Mem, Stndg Com Dio Lexington Lexington 2000-2003, Mem, Exec Coun 1998-2000; Mem, Stndg Com Dio Milwaukee Milwaukee WI 1989-1994. Cler Ldrshp Proj 1992-1995; Fllshp of SSJE 2000. dboydfly@gmail.com

BOYD, James Richard (WTenn) 6367 Shadowood Ln, Memphis TN 38119 B Providence RI 1947 s John & Lucile. BA Van 1969; MDiv Inter/Met Sem 1977. D 12/17/1976 P 6/25/1977 Bp William Hopkins Folwell. m 11/28/1970 Martha Boyd c 3. Pres Bridges Inc Memphis TN 1995-2011; Non-par Bridges Memphis 1995-2011; R S Paul's Epis Ch Salem OR 1990-1995; R H Trin Epis Ch Fayetteville NC 1984-1990; Cn Evang Dio W Tennessee Memphis 1983-1984; Exec Dir Epis Metropltn Mnstry Of Memphis Memphis TN 1980-1982; Cn Cathd Ch Of S Lk Orlando FL 1977-1980; Asst Min S Mk's Ch Washington DC 1976-1977.

BOYD, Jeffrey Howard (Mass) 57 Bethany Woods Rd, Bethany CT 06524 **Non-par 1970-** B Morristown NJ 1943 s Francis & Ruth. BA Br 1965; BD Harvard DS 1968; MD Case Wstrn Reserve U 1976; MA Ya 1981. D 6/22/1968 Bp Anson Phelps Stokes Jr P 1/1/1969 Bp John Melville Burgess. m 6/29/1968 Patricia Ann Boyd. "Being Sick Well: Joyful Living Despite Chronic Illness," Baker Books, 2005.

BOYD, Julia Woolfolk (NC) Po Box 6124, Charlotte NC 28207 B Bloominton IN 1969 d William & Margaret. BA Davidson Coll 1991; MDiv Yale DS 1995. D 10/9/1999 Bp James Gary Gloster P 10/28/2000 Bp Michael B Curry. S Paul's Epis Ch Winston Salem NC 2005-2008; Asst Chr Ch Charlotte NC 1999-2005; S Ptr's Epis Ch Charlotte NC 1996-1998.

BOYD, Lawrence Robert (Neb) 2325 S 24th St, Lincoln NE 68502 B Kansas City KS 1941 s Robert & Helen. BA Wichita St U 1965; BD SWTS 1968. D 6/1/1968 P 12/18/1968 Bp Edward Clark Turner. c 4. R S Matt's Ch Lincoln NE 1999-2006; R S Ptr's Ch Litchfield Pk AZ 1993-1999; R Gr Epis Ch Lk Havasu City AZ 1992-1993; 1988-1990; Dn Chr Ch Cathd Eau Claire WI 1983-1987; R Gr Epis Ch Ponca City OK 1978-1982; R Ch of St Jn the Evang Wisconsin Rapids WI 1973-1978; Asst Trin Epis Ch Oshkosh WI 1971-1973; Cur S Dav's Epis Ch Topeka KS 1968-1971.

BOYD, Linda Koerber (Md) D 6/11/2016 Bp Eugene Taylor Sutton.

BOYD, Sally Ann (Wyo) 436 Sundance Circle, Wright WY 82732 **Cn S Fran On The Prairie Ch Wright WY 1998-** B Brighton CO 1951 d Theodore & Ella. BA Wstrn St Coll of Colorado 1977. D 4/14/1998 P 5/19/1999 Bp Bruce Caldwell. m 2/25/1979 Timothy Boyd. Dio Wyoming Casper 2012-2016, 2012.

BOYD, Samuel L (Tex) Po Box 1884, Chandler TX 75758 B Tyler TX 1946 s Robert & Margaret. AA Tyler Jr Coll 1967; BBA Baylor U 1970; MDiv Sewanee: The U So, TS 1999. D 6/22/2002 Bp Claude Edward Payne. m 6/3/1967 Jan Jordan Boyd. S Phil's Epis Ch Palestine TX 2004-2009; Vic Trin Ch Jacksonville TX 1999-2004.

BOYD, Sandra Hughes (Colo) 8251 E Phillips Pl, Englewood CO 80112 **Adj Fac Iliff TS Denver 2006-; GOE Rdr GBEC 2003-; Adj Fac Regis (Jesuit) U 1993-** B Council Bluffs IA 1938 d Floyd & Jane. BA Colorado Coll 1961; MA U MN 1966; MDiv EDS 1978; ABD Iliff TS/U Denv 2003. D 6/17/1978 Bp William Jones Gordon Jr P 4/21/1979 Bp H Coleman Mcgehee Jr. c 2. Pres Colorado Coun of Ch 2006-2008; Int S Barn Epis Ch Denver CO 2006-2007; Ch Of The Trsfg Evergreen CO 2006; Int St Gabr the Archangel Epis Ch Englewood CO 2004-2005; The Ch Of Chr The King (Epis) Arvada CO 2003; Int S Raphael Epis Ch Colorado Sprg CO 1998-2000; Exec Coun Colorado Coun of Ch 1997-2009; Ecum Off Dio Colorado Denver CO 1997-2009, Exam Chapl 1995-, Ecum Off 1997-2009, Com On Sprtl Direction 1995-2000, BEC 1995-; Int S Paul's Epis Ch Lakewood CO 1997; Int Ch Of S Jn Chrys Golden CO 1994-2002; The Ch Of The Ascen Denver CO 1994; Asst Gd Shpd Epis Ch Centennial CO 1992-1993; Int S Jn's Ch Charlestown (Boston) Charlestown MA 1983-1984; Assoc Chr Ch Cambridge Cambridge MA 1981-1986; Alum/ae Exec Coun EDS Cambridge MA 2006-2013, Adj 1978-2006. Auth, "Epis Wmn: Gender," *Sprtlty & Commitment*, 1992; Auth, "Wmn In Amer Rel Hist: A Bibliography & Guide To Sources," 1985; Auth, "Cultivating Our Roots: Guide To Womens Hist For Ch Wmn"; Auth, "Wmn P In The 80'S:An Autobiographical Essay". Whitely Awd For Excellence In Sociol 1996.

BOYD, Virginia Ann (Md) 10901 Farrier Rd, Frederick MD 21701 B Shreveport LA 1944 d Fletcher & Bess. PhD LSU 1971; MA S Marys Sem and U 2003; Cert EDS 2004. D 7/29/2004 Bp John L Rabb P 2/20/2005 Bp Robert Wilkes Ihloff. m 2/15/2017 Virginia Francene Stanford c 1. R S Jn's Par Hagerstown MD 2010-2015, Asst R 2004-2005; R S Paul's Epis Ch Mt Airy MD 2005-2010. Ann Boyd and M. Najati, "Hlth Care in a Democracy," *Eubios Journ of Asian and Intl Bioethics*, 19:98-103, 2009; Ann Boyd, "Moral Theol and Ethics Meet at the Bedside of the Dying," *Moral Theol*, U Press of the So, 2009; L Gravey and A Boyd, "Global Hlth Concerns and Publ Hlth for the Common Gd," *Eubios Journ of Asian and Intl Bioethics*, 18:40-45, 2008; Ann Boyd, "HIV/AIDS Exposes Gender Injustice," *Eubios Journ of Asian and Intl Bioethics*, 17:144-149, 2007; Ann Boyd, "HIV/AIDS Exposes Gender Injustice," *Eubios Journ of Asian and Intl Bioethics*, 0149-04-01, 2007; A.L. Boyd, "Anagogy of Autonomy," *Eubios Journ of Asian and Internatinoal Bioethics*, 10:113-119, 2000; A.L. Boyd, "Anagogy of Autonomy," *Eubios Journ of Asian and International Bioethics*, 0119-03-01, 2000. Amer Soc of Microbiology 1971; Intl AIDS Soc 1990; Intl Assn for Educ in Ethics 2010; Phi Kappa Phi 1971; Sigma Xi 1971. Grad Sch Outstanding Tchr Awd Hood Coll 2007; Jas Arthur Muller Prize in Hist EDS 2004; Deans Awd for Ethics and Moral Theol Ecum Inst of Theol 2003; Wm Fenn Lectr Unit5ed Bd CE 1996; Amer Acad of Microbiology Fell ASM 1994; Tchg excellence Awd Hood Coll 1991.

BOYD, William Marvin (Fla) 338 River Rd, Carrabelle FL 32322 B Memphis TN 1948 s Roger & Ruby. BA U of Sthrn Colorado 1981; BA U of Sthrn Colorado 1981; MDiv Nash 1986. D 6/14/1986 P 12/1/1986 Bp William Carl Frey. m 9/6/1968 Deborah Christine Ratliff c 4. S Eliz's Epis Ch Jacksonville FL 1998-1999; S Jas' Epis Ch Lake City FL 1995-1998; Chapl S Anne's Denver CO 1989-1995; S Anne's Epis Sch Denver CO 1989-1991; Dio Colorado Denver CO 1987-1993; Gr Ch Buena Vista CO 1986-1987. wmbfcsx@gmail.com

BOYD, William Orgill (At) 210 E Robert Toombs Ave, Washington GA 30673 **Ret 1984-; Chapl US-AR 1955-** B Brownsville TN 1924 s Graham & Florence. BA U So 1949; VTS 1952. D 6/24/1952 Bp Edmund P Dandridge P 6/23/1953

Bp Theodore N Barth. m 9/26/1953 Betty Boyd c 2. Dio Atlanta Atlanta GA 1977-1981; Vic Ch Of The Medtr Washington GA 1972-1990; Ch Of The Redeem Greensboro GA 1972-1983; Vic S Jas Ch Cedartown GA 1966-1972; P-in-c All SS' Epis Ch Morristown TN 1953-1966; Asst Trin Ch Clarksville TN 1952-1953.

BOYD-ELLIS, Sue (WNY) 1439 Schoellkopf Rd, Lake View NY 14085 B Jamestown NY 1945 d Frederick & Helen. BA SUNY 1985. D 6/13/1987 Bp Harold Barrett Robinson. D Trin Epis Ch Hamburg NY 1997-2003; D Campus Mnstry Suny At Fredonia Fredonia NY 1987-1997.

BOYDEN-EDMONDS, Marjorie Jennifer (LI) 10017 32nd Ave, East Elmhurst NY 11369 B Jamaica WI 1948 d Linton & Madge. MDiv Mercer TS 1996; Mercer TS 1996; Cert Mercer TS 1996. D 1/31/2015 Bp Lawrence C Provenzano. m 5/20/1995 Victor Calvin Edmonds c 2.

BOYER JR, Ernest Leroy (ECR) PO Box 360832, Milpitas CA 95036 B Orlando FL 1951 s Ernest & Kathryn. BA Earlham Coll 1973; MLS SUNY Albany 1976; MDiv Harvard DS 1984; MDiv Harvard DS 1984; ThD Harvard DS 2002; Cert Ang Stud CDSP 2008; Cert Ang Stud CDSP 2008. D 6/6/2009 P 12/12/2009 Bp Mary Gray-Reeves. m 5/26/2002 Sondra Allphin c 3. Ch Of S Jos Milpitas CA 2010-2017; D S Lk's Ch Los Gatos CA 2009.

BOYER, Geoffrey Thomas (Mich) 2600 Milscott Dr Apt 1335, Decatur GA 30033 B Youngstown OH 1947 s Thomas & Martha. BME Florida St U 1969; MA Florida St U 1971; MDiv SWTS 1990; DMin SWTS 2003. D 6/30/1990 Bp John Wadsworth Howe P 6/11/1991 Bp John Henry Smith. m 6/19/1971 Susan Jo Hawkins c 1. SPE Fell Ecum TS Detroit (MI) 2007-2010; R S Phil's Epis Ch Rochester MI 2003-2013; R S Mich's Epis Ch Lansing MI 1996-2003; Dn Dioc Study Prog in W Virginia 1993-1996; Vic S Mths Grafton WV 1993-1996; Vic S Barn Bridgeport WV 1992-1996; The No Cntrl Cluster Buckhannon WV 1992-1996; Chapl Marshall U Huntington (WV) 1991-1992; Cur Trin Ch Huntington WV 1990-1992; COM Dio Michigan Detroit MI 2004-2009, Ldrshp Trng Prog 2004-2007, Ldrshp Prog for Par Musicians 2003-2006, Eccl Crt 2002-2005, Dioc Coun & Exec Com 2001-2002, RurD, Capital Area Coun 1997-2000; Dioc Evang Com Dio W Virginia Charleston WV 1995-1996, Dioc Cmncatn Com 1994-1996, Dn, Dioc Study Prog 1993-1996, Dir, Creative Arts Camp for Yth 1992-1993. Auth: Congrl Thesis, "Mnstry in the Marketplace," *Unpublished*, SWTS, 2003. H Cross Assoc 1985. Red Ribbon for Theol Reflection Lois Leonard Ch Nwsltr Contest 2005; Blue Ribbon for Theol Reflection Lois Leonard Ch Nwsltr Contest 2001; Red Ribbon for Theol Reflection Lois Leonard Ch Nwsltr Contest 2000; Dramatic Awd SWTS 1990.

BOYER, John Paul (WNY) 3885 Teachers Ln Apt 8, Orchard Park NY 14127 **Regular Supply P S Paul's Ch Holley NY 2012-** B Niagara Falls NY 1942 s George & Ethal. BA Dart Coll 1964; MDiv EDS 1967; BA Oxf GB 1969; MA Oxf GB 1973. D 6/17/1967 Bp Lauriston L Scaife P 1/1/1968 Bp Stephen F Bayne Jr. Vic S Paul's Epis Ch Stafford NY 2007-2012; Bex Sem Columbus OH 2001-2005; R S Dav's Epis Ch Buffalo NY 1988-2004; S Jn's Ch Wilson NY 1983-1988; Dio Sthrn Ohio Cincinnati OH 1983; R H Trin Ch Cincinnati OH 1978-1982; Asst Ch Of S Mary The Vrgn New York NY 1969-1978.

BOYER, Marcia M (Vt) Po Box 494, Woodstock VT 05091 B Boston MA 1950 d Stuart & Margaret. BA Kirkland Coll 1972; MDiv EDS 1977; JD Vermont Law Sch 1988. D 6/11/1977 P 1/1/1978 Bp Robert Shaw Kerr. Ch Of The Gd Shpd Barre VT 1984; Asst R S Jas Ch Woodstock VT 1982-1988; Cathd Ch Of S Paul Burlington VT 1977-1982. Jd cl Vermont Law Sch 1988.

BOYER, William James (CFla) 126 E Palmetto Ave, Howey in the Hills FL 34737 **Asst S Jas Epis Ch Leesburg FL 2015-, P-in-c 2013-** B Rochester MN 1946 s Charles & Margaret. AA St Petersburg Jr Coll 1966; BS Florida St U 1968; MDiv Candler TS Emory U 1972. D 12/12/2009 P 6/26/2010 Bp John Wadsworth Howe. m 6/5/1982 Nancy West Boyer c 3. P-in-c S Mths Epis Ch Clermont FL 2011-2012, Asst 2010-2011; Chapl U.S. Navy 1978-1998; Pstr The Meth Ch Florida Conf 1969-2010.

BOYLE, Patton Lindsay (Spok) 1342 Bartlett Ave, Wenatchee WA 98801 B Charlottesville VA 1943 s Eldridge & Sarah. D 6/20/1970 Bp Philip Alan Smith P 5/1/1971 Bp Addison Hosea. m 10/11/2015 Eeva-Liisa Beebe-Boyle c 2. P-in-c S Lk's Epis Ch Wenatchee WA 2005-2009; Vic S Jn's By The Sea Kaneohe HI 2003-2005; P-in-c S Ptr's Ch Honolulu HI 2001-2003; Int S Ambr Epis Ch Boulder CO 1999-2001; Pstr Counslr Pastorial Counslg Cntr Corvallis OR 1993-1995; R Chr Ch Biddeford ME 1988-1993; Int Chr Ch Gardiner ME 1987-1988; Int Ch Of The Epiph Danville VA 1986-1987; Vic S Clem's Ch Arkansas City AR 1976; Emm Ch Lake Vill AR 1975-1976; Asst S Paul's Epis Ch Meridian MS 1973-1974; Int Calv Ch Golden CO 1971-1972; Part time Asst Chr Ch Cathd Lexington KY 1970-1971.

BOYLE, Peter (Nwk) 10 Lindbergh Ave, Rensselaer NY 12144 **Non-par 1986-** B Somerville NJ 1943 s William & Jane. BA Leh 1966; MA Rutgers The St U of New Jersey 1969; Cert GTS 1972. D 6/10/1972 Bp Leland Stark P 3/17/1973 Bp George E Rath. m 4/19/1969 Jeanne Evelyn Baumuller. R Ch Of The Redeem Rensselaer NY 1999-2013; Supply H Cross Perth Amboy NJ 1996-1999; P-in-c S Jas's Newark NJ 1974-1985; Vic Ch Of Our Sav Secaucus NJ 1974-1976; Non-par 1972-1974.

BOYLES, David Joseph (Fla) St Mary's Episcopal Church, PO Box 611, Madison FL 32341 **S Mary's Epis Ch Madison FL 2013-** B Arcadia FL 1948 s Eugene & Frances. BS USAF Acad 1970; MS AF Inst of Tech 1977. D 5/9/2013 Bp Charles Lovett Keyser. m 7/25/1970 Linda L Boyles c 2.

BOYNTON, Caroline Cochran (NY) B 1947 D 5/19/2001 Bp Richard Frank Grein.

BOZARTH, Alla Renée (Minn) 43222 SE Tapp Rd, Sandy OR 97055 **Fndr/Dir/P-in-c Wisdom Hse Inc. 1975-; P-in-c and Dir Wisdom Hse Inc. Minneapolis MN and Sandy 1974-** B Portland OR 1947 d René & Alvina. BSS NWU 1971; MA NWU 1972; PhD NWU 1974; Cert Gestalt Trng Cntr of San Diego 1978. D 9/8/1971 Bp James Walmsley Frederic Carman P 7/29/1974 Bp Daniel Corrigan. Auth, "This is My Body: Praying for Earth, Prayers from the Heart," iUniverse, 2003; Auth, "This Mortal Mar: Poems of Love, Lament and Loss," iUniverse, 2003; Auth, "Accidental Wisdom~ Poems by Alla Renée Bozarth," iUniverse, 2003; Auth, "Womanpriest: A Personal Odyssey," Paulist Press 1978, rev. ed. Wisdom Hse, 2002; Auth, "Moving to the Edge of the Wrld," iUniverse, 2000; Auth, "At the Foot of the Mtn: Nature and the Art of Soul Healing," iUniverse, 2000; Auth, "The Bk of Bliss~ Poems," iUniverse, 2000; Auth, "The Word's Body: An Incarnational Aesthetic of Interp," U Press of Amer/Rowman and Littlefield, 1997; Auth, "Soulfire: Love Poems in Black and Gold," Yes Intl and Wisdom Hse, 1997; Auth, "A Journey through Grief," Compcare 1989, Hazelden, 1993; Auth, "Dance for Me When I Die audio," CompCare 1989, Wisdom Hse, 1993; Auth, "Lifelines: Threads of Gr through Seasons of Change," Sheed and Ward, Rowman and Littlefield, 1993; Auth, "Six Days in St. Petersburg: A Chronicle of Return," Purple Iris Press, 1993; Auth, "A Journey through Grief audio," CompCare 1989, Wisdom Hse, 1993; Auth, "Life is Goodbye/Life is Hello: Grieving Well through All Kinds of Loss," Hazelden, rev. ed., 1993; Auth, "Wisdom & Wonderment: 31 Feasts to Nourish Your Soul," Sheed and Ward, 1993; Auth, "Water Wmn audio," Wisdom Hse, 1990; Auth, "Reading Out Loud to God audio," Wisdom Hse, 1990; Co-Auth, "Stars in Your Bones: Emerging Signposts on Our Sprtl Journeys," No Star Press of St. Cloud, 1990; Auth, "Love's Prism: Reflections from the Heart of a Wmn," Sheed and Ward, 1987. The Bp Scarlett Awd The Epis Ch Pub Co 1994.

BOZZUTI-JONES, Mark Francisco (NY) 74 Trinity Place, New York NY 10006 **Pstr Care & Cmnty Trin Par New York NY 2007-; S Bartholomews Ch 2005-** B Kingston Jamaica 1966 s Hector & Muriel. MDiv Jesuit TS 1997; MDiv Jesuit TS 1997; Doctor of Mnstry Aquinas Inst of Theol 2014. Rec 5/31/2003 as Priest Bp M(Arvil) Thomas Shaw. m 10/2/1999 Kathleen Mary Bozzuti-Jones c 1. St. Barth Ch New York NY 2005-2007; Assoc R Chr Ch Cambridge Cambridge MA 2003-2005. Auth, "The Gospel of Barack Hussein Obama According to Mk," Create Space, 2012; Auth, "The Gospel of Barack Hussein Obama According to Mk," *Hist Fiction*, Create Space, 2012; Auth, "Informed by Faith," *Educ Bk*, Cowley, 2006; Auth, "Womb of Adv," *Adv Meditation*, Cowley, 2005; Auth, "The Mitre Fits Fine: Bp Harris," *Biography*, Cowley, 2005; Auth, "Jesus the Word," *Childrens Bk*, Augsburg, 2005; Auth, "God Created," *Childrens Bk*, Augsburg, 2003; Auth, "Never Said a Mumbalin Word," *Lenten Meditation*, Augsburg, 2002.

BRACKETT, Thomas L (WNC) 13 Kent Pl, Asheville NC 28804 **Epis Ch Cntr New York NY 2008-** B Norfolk VA 1960 s Burton & Helga. BA Vermont Coll of Norwich U 1997; MDiv Bangor TS 2001. D 6/23/2001 Bp Chilton Richardson Knudsen P 12/23/2001 Bp Gethin Benwil Hughes. m 11/7/1987 Cheri A Brackett c 1. St Georges Epis Ch Asheville NC 2004-2008; Ch Of The Mssh Murphy NC 2003-2004; Brevard Epis Mssn Brevard NC 2003; Assoc S Jas By The Sea La Jolla CA 2001-2002.

BRADA, Netha Nadine (Ia) 345 Lincoln Ave, Iowa Falls IA 50126 **Supply P Gr Epis Chas City IA 2012-** B Rockwell IA 1937 d Elmer & Irene. EFM Sewanee TS 1991; EFM Sewanee: The U So, TS 1991. D 8/23/1997 P 6/20/1998 Bp Chris Christopher Epting. m 6/15/1957 Ronald Brada c 3. P S Matt's-By-The-Bridge Epis Ch Iowa Falls IA 1998-2007; D S Matt's-By-The-Bridge Epis Ch Iowa Falls IA 1997-1998.

BRADBURY, John Saferian (Ind) B 1928 D 6/14/1965 Bp John P Craine P 3/3/1966 Bp James Winchester Montgomery. m 6/10/1951 Shirley Tuttle.

BRADBURY, Stephanie (Mass) 390 Main St, North Andover MA 01845 **S Jn's Ch Beverly MA 2013-** B Boston MA 1963 d Richard & Eva-Maria. BA U of Virginia 1985; MDiv Ya Berk 1995. D 6/15/1996 P 2/15/1997 Bp Robert Wilkes Ihloff. m 4/24/2010 William John Bradbury c 2. R S Paul's Epis Ch No Andover MA 2007-2013; Exec Coun Appointees New York NY 2005-2007; Pstr Dom & Frgn Mssy Soc Klaipeda Lithuania 2004-2007; Resolutns Com Chair Dio Maryland Baltimore MD 2003-2004, COM Mem 2001-2004, Evang Com Mem 1998-2000; R All SS Epis Par Sunderland MD 1999-2004; The Ch Of The Redeem Baltimore MD 1996-1999; Chapl Cathd Hse Rentry Prog Baltimore MD 1995-1997.

BRADBURY, William John (Mass) 133 School Street, New Bedford MA 02740 **All SS Ch Chelmsford MA 2012-** B Portchester NY 1951 s John & Polly. BA U GA 1973; MDiv VTS 1978. D 6/10/1978 Bp Charles Judson Child Jr P 5/24/1979 Bp Bennett Jones Sims. c 4. R Gr Ch New Bedford MA 2006-2012; R S

Ptr's Epis Ch Washington NC 1985-2005; Assoc R S Paul's Ch Augusta GA 1982-1985; Vic S Andr's In-The-Pines Epis Ch Peachtree City GA 1979-1982; Dio Atlanta Atlanta GA 1978-1981. MDiv cl VTS 1978; AB scl U GA 1973. rev.wjbradbury@gmail.com

BRADEN, Anita (Mil) PO Box 2938, Tappahannock VA 22560 **S Marg's Sch Tappahannock VA 2014-; Vic/Urban Mssnr S Andr's Ch Milwaukee WI 2001-** B New York NY 1957 d Ernest & Marion. Mstr of Arts VTS; BA Lakeland Coll 1993; BA Milwaukee Theol Inst 1998. D 2/4/2001 P 8/4/2001 Bp Roger John White. c 2. VTS Alexandria VA 2014; Trin Ch Washington DC 2012-2014; S Fran Ch Menomonee Falls WI 2004-2010; Dio Milwaukee Milwaukee WI 2001-2004. abraden@smsapps.org

BRADFORD, Kathleen Diane Ross (Cal) 1713 Daisy Way, Antioch CA 94509 **D S Alb's Epis Ch Brentwood CA 1999-** B Oakland CA 1952 d Roderic & Marian. AA Diablo Vlly Coll 1972; BA Sch for Deacons 1998. D 6/5/1999 Bp William Edwin Swing. m 4/28/1977 Ricky Eugene Bradford. NAAD.

BRADFORD, Lawrence J (Colo) 4131 E 26th Ave, Denver CO 80207 B Oklahoma City OK 1942 s Lawrence & Bonnie. BA S Mary of The Plains Dodge City KS 1964; MEd Wichita St U 1969; PhD U CO 1979; MDiv Iliff TS 2001. D 6/9/2001 P 12/23/2001 Bp William Jerry Winterrowd. m 7/23/1994 Ann H Bradford c 2. Dio Colorado Denver CO 2013; P-in-c S Phil In-The-Field Sedalia CO 2010-2013; S Barn Of The Vlly Cortez CO 2009-2010; Ch Of S Phil And S Jas Denver CO 2009; Epis Ch Of S Ptr And S Mary Denver CO 2008-2009; H Trin Epis Ch Wyoming MI 2005-2007; R Ch Of The H Redeem Denver CO 2001-2003. lbradford59@gmail.com

BRADFORD, Lewis Gabriel (Md) 2900 E Fayette St, Baltimore MD 21224 B Ft Belvoir VA 1957 s Lewis & Helene. Essex Cmnty Coll; Townson St Coll. D 6/7/2008 Bp John L Rabb. m 8/2/1980 Francene R Bradford c 3.

BRADLEY, Carolyn Ann (NJ) 503 Asbury Ave, Asbury Park NJ 07712 B Newark NJ 1953 d Joseph & Dolores. BA Coll of St Eliz 1974; MSW Ford 1978; PhD Ford 2005. D 5/9/2015 Bp William H Stokes. m 12/1/2013 Monica Medlicott.

BRADLEY, Charles Eldwyn (Okla) D 6/13/1990 Bp Robert Manning Moody.

BRADLEY, Gary J (Los) Immanuel Mission, 4366 Santa Anita Ave., El Monte CA 91731 **Ch Of Our Sav Par San Gabr CA 2011-, 1998-2010** B Seattle WA 1947 s Francis & Marion. BA S Johns Sem Coll 1970; MA S Johns Sem Boston 1973; ISEE Mex City Sem 1974; DAS ETSBH 1988. Rec 2/26/1988 as Deacon Bp Oliver Bailey Garver Jr. m 8/23/1980 Peg Bowerman c 4. Imm Mssn El Monte CA 2010-2011; Sr Assoc Pstr Care All SS Ch Pasadena CA 1989-1998; Cmncatn Assoc Serv Rom.Cath. Franciscan Comm. Los Angeles CA 1980-1988; Mssy P Serv as Rom. Cath. Mssy PERU 1979-1980; Pstr and Assoc. Pstr Serv Rom.Cath.Dioc.of Phoenix Phoenix AZ 1973-1979. Auth, "Par: Sacr of Presence," *Par Educ Booklets*, Franciscan Cmncatn, 1983. gbradley@churchofoursaviour.org

BRADLEY, James (Ct) 95 Cornwall Ave, Cheshire CT 06410 B Welch WV 1947 s Virgil & Marian. BA W Virginia U 1969; MTS Harvard DS 1971; MDiv VTS 1975; DMin Hartford Sem 1998. D 5/24/1975 Bp Wilburn Camrock Campbell P 5/15/1976 Bp Robert Poland Atkinson. m 9/5/1970 Bernadine Bradley c 2. Middlesex Area Cluster Mnstry Higganum CT 2011-2013; R S Jn's Epis Par Waterbury CT 1989-2010; R S Paul And S Jas New Haven CT 1980-1985; Vic S Jas Ch Charleston WV 1975-1980; Chapl W Virginia St Coll Inst WV 1975-1980. Auth, *Gathering the Body Scattered*, 1998.

BRADLEY, Martha Jean (Spr) 3621 Troon DR, Springfield IL 62712 **D The Cathd Ch Of S Paul Springfield IL 1987-** B Carbondale IL 1930 d Don & Bertha. BA NWU 1952; MEd Sthrn Illinois U 1965; Coc 1989. D 11/1/1987 Bp Donald Maynard Hultstrand. Auth, "Living On". Epis Chapl Coll Chapl.

BRADLEY, Martha Mantelle (NJ) 318 Elton Ln, Galloway NJ 08205 B Newport News VA 1968 d William & Martha. BA W&M 1990; MDiv GTS 1996. D 5/25/1996 Bp Frank Harris Vest Jr P 12/7/1996 Bp Joe Doss. c 2. R Ch Of S Mk And All SS Absecon Absecon NJ 2008-2016; Vic H Sprt Bellmawr NJ 1998-2008; S Lk's Ch Westville NJ 1998-2008; Timber Creek Epis Area Mnstry Gloucester City NJ 1998-2005; Trin Ch Moorestown NJ 1996-1998.

BRADLEY, Matthew Bryant (Ky) St. John's Episcopal Church, 1620 Main St, Murray KY 42071 **Campus Min Murray St Epis Coll Fllshp Murray KY 2008-; P-in-c S Jn's Ch Murray KY 2008-** B Louisville KY 1983 s James & Judy. BSE Tul 2005; MDiv VTS 2008. D 12/21/2007 P 6/21/2008 Bp Ted Gulick Jr.

BRADLEY, Michael Lee (NH) 15 Park Court, Durham NH 03824 **Sub Dn New Hampshire Chapt AGO 2012-; Exec Com Harvard Club of New Hampshire 2006-; Adj Instr New Engl Coll 2006-; R S Geo's Ch Durham NH 1997-; Chapl U of New Hampshire Durham NH 1997-** B Taunton MA 1956 s Robert & Janet. BA U of Sthrn Maine 1979; MDiv Harvard DS 1990. Trans 4/1/1997 as Priest Bp Douglas Edwin Theuner. m 8/24/1979 Becky Lynn Bradley c 1. Chapl AGO Concord NH 2000-2002; Mem Dioc Coun Dio New Hampshire 1998-2001; Mem Harvard DS Alum/ae Com Cambridge MA 1993-1997; R Serv Angl Ch of Can Plum Point Can 1993-1997. BA mcl U of Sthrn Maine 1979.

BRADLEY, Patrick John (WNY) 505 Riverdale Ave, Lewiston NY 14092 **D S Ptr's Ch Niagara Falls NY 2001-, D 2000-; Niagara Interfaith Chapl Niagara Falls NY 1998-; Bp's Advsry Com on Deacons Dio Wstrn New York Tonawanda NY 2012-** B Niagara Falls NY 1954 s Melvin & Dorothy. BA SUNY 1976. D 5/6/2000 Bp Michael Garrison. m 11/13/1982 Linda Ann Bradley c 1. bradleypj@gmail.com

BRADLEY, Peg (Los) 619 W Roses Rd, San Gabriel CA 91775 **Ch Of Our Sav Par San Gabr CA 2009-** B Mesa AZ 1952 d Lloyd & Marlene. Arizona St U; BS Nthrn Arizona U 1978; MDiv ETSBH 2003. D 12/18/2005 P 9/8/2007 Bp Joseph Jon Bruno. m 8/23/1980 Gary J Bradley c 4. S Jas' Par So Pasadena CA 2006-2009.

BRADLEY, Raymond Earle (Ind) 15914 Blush Drive, Fishers IN 46037 **Ret 2004-** B Buffalo NY 1940 s Earle & Helen. BA SUNY 1963; Bangor TS 1966; Theol Geo Mercer Jr. Memi TS 1970; Mercer TS 1970; BA SUNY 1972; MS LIU 1984; U.S. Army War Coll 1995. D 6/22/1969 Bp Charles Waldo MacLean P 12/22/1969 Bp Lauriston L Scaife. m 8/21/1964 Franka Helen Welbourn c 2. R Trin Ch Anderson IN 2000-2004; Cn Chr Ch Cathd Indianapolis IN 1996-2000; Chapl US-A 1975-1997; Chapl Off Of Bsh For ArmdF New York NY 1975-1996; R S Alb's Ch Danielson CT 1972-1975; R Trin Ch Warsaw NY 1970-1972; Cur H Trin Epis Ch Hicksville NY 1969-1970. AUSA 1976; H Cross Monstry 1969; Mltry Chapl Assn. chappy4041@gmail.com

BRADNER, Lawrence Hitchcock (RI) 500 Angell St Apt 504, Providence RI 02906 **Assoc S Mart's Ch Providence RI 2006-; Ret 1998-** B Providence RI 1934 s Leicester & Harriet. BA Ya 1956; MAT Br 1960; STB GTS 1964; Cert Assn of Mntl Hlth Clerics 1981. D 6/20/1964 P 2/12/1966 Bp John S Higgins. m 1/2/1965 Marcia B Bradner c 3. Ch Of The Ascen Cranston RI 1990-1991; S Eliz's Ch Hope Vlly RI 1986-1987; Calv Ch Pascoag RI 1984-1985; S Matt's Par Of Jamestown Jamestown RI 1982-1983; Ch Of The Resurr Warwick RI 1980; SS Matt and Mk Barrington RI 1979-1980; Ch Of The Redeem Providence RI 1978; Dio Rhode Island Providence RI 1976-1998; Chapl Eleanor Slater Hosp Cranston RI 1976-1998; Stff The Epis Ch Of S Andr And S Phil Coventry RI 1975-1977; Chapl Bp Hare Hm Mssn SD 1971-1975; P-in-c Epiph Ch 1971-1975; P-in-c Gr Ch Soldier Creek SD 1971-1975; Trin Epis Ch Mssn SD 1971-1975; Vic S Mk's Oakes ND 1967-1971; DCE Trin Thomaston CT 1965-1967; Cur S Paul's Ch Pawtucket RI 1964-1965. Auth, *Following the Trail of the Old Narragansett Ch*, 1990; Auth, "The Plum Bch Light: Birth," *Life & Death of a Lighthouse*, LH Bradner Pub, 1989; Auth, *The Med Cntr & Publ Hlth Care in Rhode Island*. Cert Assn Mntl Hlth Cleric 1980; Felloship of St. Jn 1970.

BRADSEN, Kate (Az) **Vic S Andr's Epis Ch Tucson AZ 2011-; Tchr Imago Dei Middle Sch 2008-** B Evanston IL 1978 d William & Kathryn. BA NWU 2000; MDiv EDS 2005. D 12/18/2004 P 7/2/2005 Bp Alan Scarfe. c 3. Imago Dei Middle Sch Tucson AZ 2008-2011; Asst Gr St Pauls Epis Ch Tucson AZ 2005-2014; D Epis Chapl At Harvard & Radcliffe Cambridge MA 2005.

BRADSHAW, Charles Robbins (Me) 54 Thorsen Rd, Hancock ME 04640 **Assoc Mssy Soc of Angl Missionaries and Senders 2016-** B Lake Forest IL 1951 s Charles & Sarah. BA Harv 1973; MDiv TESM 1992; DMin TESM 2011. D 6/13/1992 Bp Arthur Edward Walmsley P 12/16/1992 Bp John Clark Buchanan. m 4/22/1984 Elizabeth W Will c 2. R Ch Of Our Fr Hulls Cove ME 1999-2012; R Emm Epis Ch Emporium PA 1994-1999; R S Agnes' Epis Ch S Marys PA 1994-1999; Assoc Chr Epis Ch S Jos MO 1992-1994; Soc Serv Off Long Island Refugee Resettlement Prog Dio of Long Isl 1983-1984; Prncpl Bp Lutaaya Theol and Vocational Coll Mityana 2013-2016; Sprtl Dir, Maine Curs Dio Maine Portland ME 2006-2012; Exam Chapl Dio NW Pennsylvania Erie PA 1996-1999. Anglicans for Life 2006; BroSA 1989; Maine Epis Curs 2000-2012.

BRADSHAW, Katie Ann (Miss) **S Columb's Ch Ridgeland MS 2015-; Other Lay Position Dio Mississippi Jackson MS 2012-** B Dothan AL 1982 d Phillip & Susan. BA Birmingham-Sthrn Coll 2004; JD Mississippi Coll Sch of Law 2008; MDiv The TS at The U So 2015. D 6/13/2015 P 1/16/2016 Bp Brian Seage.

BRADSHAW, Mark David (Los) PO Box 93096, Pasadena CA 91109 B Lodi CA 1981 s Clifford & Sally. BS Moody Bible Inst 2007; MDiv Fuller TS 2014; Angl Stds Cert CDSP 2017. D 6/3/2017 Diane Jardine Bruce. m 9/11/2010 Katherine Louise Flynn Bradshaw c 2.

BRADSHAW, Michael Ray (NC) St Paul's Episcopal Church, 520 Summit St, Winston Salem NC 27101 B Hickory NC 1954 s Everette & Joan. Angl Stds year Seabury-Wstrn; BS Mars Hill Coll 1977; MDiv SE TS 1980. D 2/18/2012 Bp Michael B Curry. m 5/3/1986 Penni Pearson Bradshaw c 1. D S Paul's Epis Ch Winston Salem NC 2012-2013.

BRADSHAW, Paul Frederick (NI) University of Notre Dame, 1 Suffolk Street, London SW1Y 4HG Great Britain (UK) **Prof of Liturg Notre Dame U IN 1990-** B Preston Lancashire UK 1945 s Reginald & Marian. BA U of Cambridge 1966; MA U of Cambridge GB 1970; PhD London U GB 1971; Oxf GB 1994. Trans 1/1/1990 Bp Francis Campbell Gray. m 12/5/1970 Rowenna Street. Hon Cn Dio Nthrn Indiana So Bend IN 1990-2012; Assoc Prof of Liturg Notre Dame U IN 1985-1990; Serv Ch of Engl 1969-1985. Auth, *Early Chr Wrshp*, SPCK, 1996; Auth, *The Search for Origins of Chr Wrshp*, SPCK/OUP, 1992;

Auth, *Ord Rites of the Ancient Ch of E and W*, Pueblo, 1990; Auth, *Daily Pryr in the Early Ch*, SPCK/OUP, 1981; Auth, *The Angl Ordinal*, SPCK, 1971. DD GTS 2005; Hon Cn Dio NI 1990.

BRADTMILLER, Katharine E (Minn) **Dio Minnesota Minneapolis MN 2015-; S Jn The Evang S Paul MN 2013-** B New Haven CT 1981 d Peter & Caron. BA Wellesley Coll 2003; MDiv EDS 2006. D 11/1/2005 P 7/22/2006 Bp Creighton Leland Robertson. m 8/6/2013 Louisa Irene Bradtmiller c 2. Stff Chapl Hennepin Cnty Med Cntr Minneapolis MN 2010-2013; Asst S Barn Ch Falmouth MA 2006-2009. kate.bradtmiller@stjohnssstpaul.org

BRADY, Amanda B Mandy (At) 1501 Ridge Ave., Evanston IL 60201 **Cbury Crt Atlanta GA 2016-** B Lewes DE 1965 d James & Amanda. BS W&M 1989; MDiv GTS 1997. D 6/7/1997 Bp Robert Wilkes Ihloff P 12/13/1997 Bp Frank Kellogg Allan. m 6/14/2012 Sarah Kathleen Fisher. All SS Epis Ch Atlanta GA 2015-2016; S Fran Ch Macon Ga 2015; Chapl to Emory U Dio Atlanta Atlanta GA 2010-2014; Int S Mk's Ch Evanston IL 2008-2010; Int S Paul's Epis Ch Newnan GA 2007-2008; P-in-c Emm Epis Ch Athens GA 1999-2007; Asst R S Mich And All Ang Ch Stone Mtn GA 1997-1999.

BRADY, Christian Mark (CPa) 18 Hampton Ct, State College PA 16803 **D S Andr's Ch St Coll PA 2007-; Dn Penn St U 2006-** B Houston TX 1968 s Charles & Martha. BA Cor 1992; MA Wheaton Coll 1994; MS Oxf GB 1999; PhD Oxf GB 2000; Locally Formed 2002. D 12/21/2005 Bp Charles Edward Jenkins III P 10/20/2007 Bp Nathan Dwight Baxter. m 8/14/1993 Elizabeth Warma Brady c 2. Int S Barth's Ch Nashville TN 2016-2017.

BRADY, Jane (NJ) **R Gr Ch Pemberton NJ 2007-; Planned Giving Com Dio New Jersey Trenton NJ 2011-, Sudan Com 2009-, Rdr, Gnrl Ord Exams 2008-, Com on Priesthood 2007-** B Englewood NJ 1950 d John & Mary. BA U of Pennsylvania 1976; MDiv PrTS 1999; ThM PrTS 2001. D 12/13/2005 P 7/8/2006 Bp George Edward Councell. Asst Ch of S Jn on the Mtn Bernardsville NJ 2006-2007.

BRADY, Susan Jane (Colo) 3250 Lee Hill Dr., Boulder CO 80302 B Salt Lake City UT 1944 d Archibald & Margaret. BA U of Nthrn Colorado 1966. D 8/21/1985 Bp William Carl Frey. D Ch Of The H Comf Broomfield CO 1985-2001. NAAD.

BRADY JR, Thomas Joseph (Chi) 5733 North Sheridan Road #16-C, Chicago IL 60660 **Died 8/19/2015** B Chicago IL 1936 s Thomas & Maxine. BA U IL 1958; STB GTS 1961. D 6/24/1961 Bp Charles L Street P 12/23/1961 Bp Gerald Francis Burrill. Ret 1995-2015; R S Clem's Ch Harvey IL 1964-1994; Cur Epis Ch Of The Atone Chicago IL 1961-1963.

BRADY II, William Donald (CFla) 10780 W Yulee Dr Unit 198, Homosassa FL 34487 B Erie PA 1943 s William & Elizabeth. AA BelHaven U 2007; Grad w/Cert Inst for Chr Stuides 2007. D 6/2/2007 Bp John Wadsworth Howe. m 7/2/1964 Wanda Tandy c 2. Sexton S Anne's Ch Crystal River FL 2007-2008; Fieldwork assignment S Marg's Ch Inverness FL 2007. skipwanda@gmail.com

BRAINARD, Mary-Lloyd (Ct) 3A Gold St, Stonington CT 06378 **S Jn's Epis Ch Essex CT 2005-** B Hartford CT 1936 d William & Kathryn. BA Connecticut Coll 1995. D 12/12/1998 Bp Andrew Donnan Smith. c 3. D Calv Ch Stonington CT 1998-2005. NAAD.

BRAINE, Beverly Barfield (Md) 1314 Second Avenue, Tybee Island GA 31328 B Atlanta GA 1946 d Elmer & Barbara. BA Georgia St U 1969; MS Indiana U 1974; MDiv Sewanee: The U So, TS 1981; MEd Towson U 1995. D 6/9/1981 P 1/1/1982 Bp William Gillette Weinhauer. c 4. Imm Epis Ch Glencoe MD 2002-2005; The Ch Of The Redeem Baltimore MD 1999-2002; S Dav's Ch Baltimore MD 1995-1996; S Paul's Par Baltimore MD 1991-1992; Trin Ch Towson MD 1986-1993; Stuart Hall Staunton VA 1981-1986; Chapl Stuart Hall Staunton VA 1981-1986.

BRAKE, Mary Wood (Va) B Fort Benning GA 1950 d Ralph & Phyllis. U NC 1972; BA Amer U 1974; MDiv VTS 1978; U of Basel Basel Ch 1983. D 8/18/1978 Bp John Alfred Baden P 3/1/1980 Bp David Henry Lewis Jr. Asst S Paul's Ch Charlottesville VA 1988-2002; Chapl Bloomfield Inc. 1985-1988; Asst S Clem's Ch 1983-1985; Non-par 1981-1982; Asst Emm Epis Ch Geneva 1201 1978-1980. EvangES.

BRAKEMAN, Lyn G (Mass) 203 Pemberton St Unit #, Cambridge MA 02140 **P Assoc S Jn's Ch Charlestown (Boston) Charlestown MA 2013-; Ret 2010-; EFM Co-Coordntr Dio Massachusetts Boston MA 2009-** B New York NY 1938 d McDonald & Margaret. BA Smith 1960; MA Col 1962; MDiv Yale DS 1982. D 6/13/1987 P 3/25/1988 Bp Arthur Edward Walmsley. m 11/23/1986 Richard John Simeone c 4. self-employed Auth 1997-2013; self-employed Pstr Counslr 1997-2010; Assoc S Jn's Epis Ch Gloucester MA 1997-2010; Assoc S Alb's Ch Simsbury CT 1991-1997; Int H Trin Epis Ch Enfield CT 1990-1991; Asst Calv Ch Suffield CT 1987-1990; Chapl Blue Ridge Cntr Bloomfield CT 1984-1990; Chapl Hartford Hosp Hartford CT 1982-1984. Auth, "Pray As You Are," *Presence*, SpiritualDirectors Intl, 2008; Auth, "The God Between Us: A Sprtlty of Relationships," Innisfree Press / Augsburg Fortress, 2001; Auth, "Sprtl Lemons, Biblic Wmn, Irreverant Laughter and Righteous Rage," Innisfree/Augsburg Books, 1997. Fell AAPC 1992; Rel Sis of Mercy, Assoc 1996; Sprtl Dir Intl 2001. Ozark Fell Coll of the Ozarks 1991; Phi Beta Kappa Smith 1960.

BRALL, Catherine Mary (Pgh) 321 Parkside Ave, Pittsburgh PA 15228 **Pittsburgh TS Pittsburgh PA 2015-; S Thos' Epis Ch Canonsburg PA 2015-; Provost Trin Cathd Pittsburgh PA 2004-** B Evergreen Park IL 1958 d Donald & Carol. BS U IL 1981; MEM NWU 1988; MDiv TESM 1995; DMin Fuller TS 2010. D 6/17/1995 Bp Frank Tracy Griswold III P 12/17/1995 Bp Alden Moinet Hathaway. Cn Dio Pittsburgh Pittsburgh PA 2013-2015, Cong Dvlp 1999-2003, Stndg Com 2003-2006, Dioc Coun, Presisent 2000-2001; Provost Trin Cathd Pittsburgh PA 2004-2013; R Ch Of The Adv Pittsburgh PA 1995-2003. Dissertation, "Using the Rule of Ben to Form and Equip Cler for Epis Par Mnstry," Fuller TS, 2010.

BRAMBILA, Gerardo Brambila (Az) 483 W. 80Th. Avenue, Denver CO 80221 **Vic S Mk's Epis Ch Mesa AZ 2014-; Stndg Com Mem Dio Colorado Denver CO 2011-** B Oaxaca Oaxaca Mexico 1958 s Miguel Angel & Ana Luisa. AE Unam/Nunez Pragosa Mex City Mx 1980; Cert Theol Stud Epis TS of the SW 2001. D 6/2/2001 Bp Joseph Jon Bruno P 1/12/2002 Bp Frederick Houk Borsch. m 4/27/2006 Viviana Elena Brambila c 5. Our Merc Sav Mnstrs Denver CO 2014; R Our Merc Sav Epis Ch Denver CO 2010-2014; Vic H Fam Mssn N Hollywood CA 2005-2009; P-in-c S Marg's Epis Ch So Gate CA 2004-2005; Assoc S Fran' Par Palos Verdes Estates CA 2001-2004.

BRAMBLE, Peter Wilkin Duke (LI) 1417 Union St, Brooklyn NY 11213 B Harris MS 1945 s Charles & Margaret. Lic Codrington Coll 1970; MA Ya 1972; STM Ya Berk 1974; PhD U of Connecticut 1976. Trans 8/1/1977 Bp David Keller Leighton Sr. m 12/28/1972 Jocelyn Cheryl Bramble. R S Mk's Ch Brooklyn NY 1997-2015; Ch Of S Kath Of Alexandria Baltimore MD 1977-1997; Asst P Ch Of The H Trin Middletown CT 1973-1976; Cur S Jn's Cathd Antigua 1972-1973.

BRAMLETT, Bob (Mil) 419 E Court St, Janesville WI 53545 B Detroit MI 1941 s Kenneth & Jane. BA NEU 1971; MDiv SWTS 1974; DMin McCormick TS 1985. D 6/8/1974 Bp Quintin Ebenezer Primo Jr P 12/14/1974 Bp James Winchester Montgomery. m 8/22/1970 Linda J Bramlett c 1. R Trin Ch Janesville WI 1991-2004; R S Andr's Epis Ch Valparaiso IN 1985-1990; R Annunc Bridgeview IN 1979-1985; Ch Of The Annunc Bridgeview IL 1979-1985; Vic S Anselm Epis Ch Lehigh Acres FL 1975-1979; Cur S Mary's Ch Pk Ridge IL 1974-1975. OHC.

BRAMLETT, Bruce Richard (ECR) 6028 El Dorado Street, El Cerrito CA 94530 **Asst to the R St. Jude's Epis Ch Cupertino Ca. 2017-** B Middletown CT 1948 s James & Olive. CDSP; Grad Theol Un; BA Cntrl 1970; MDiv EDS 1976. D 6/18/1977 P 2/1/1978 Bp Alexander D Stewart. c 2. R S Paul's Epis Ch San Rafael CA 1995-2003; S Mths Epis Ch San Ramon CA 1994-1995; S Jn The Bapt Lodi CA 1986-1988; S Mk's Ch Teaneck NJ 1979-1985; Assoc S Ptr's Ch Essex Fells NJ 1979; S Jn's Ch Williamstown MA 1977-1978. Auth, "Israel, Land & St In Tchg Jewish-Chr Relatns," *Shofar mag*, 1988. Soc Of S Jn The Evang, Epis Peace Fellowshi. Graebe Awd; Bogert Tchg Fell CDSP; Newhall Tchg Fell Grad Theol Un; Mart Luther King Awd Marin Cnty Human Rts Cmsn.

BRANCH, Caroline E (At) 2089 Ponce De Leon Ave NE, Atlanta GA 30307 **Assoc S Bede's Ch Atlanta GA 2014-** B New York City NY 1973 d James & Dianne. BS US Naval Acad 1995; MA St Jn's Coll 2001; MDiv Candler TS 2007; MDiv Candler TS Emory U 2007; JD Emory Sch of Law 2007. D 5/22/2013 Bp Robert Christopher Wright. m 7/21/2001 Daniel Bernice Branch c 3.

BRANCHE, Ronald Clifford (VI) PO Box 28, Main Street, Tortola British Virgin Islands **S Geo Mtyr Ch Tortola 2002-** B Trinidad 1946 BA U of The W Indies. Trans 5/10/2002 Bp Theodore Athelbert Daniels. m 11/26/1972 Heather Sharon Theresa Branche c 1. Reverend S Geo Sch Road Town Tortola 2002-2015.

BRANDENBURG, John Paul (SO) 56482 Boyd Avenue, Bridgeport OH 43912 **Chapl Cambridge Heights Ret Cmnty 2008-; Dn of NE Dnry Dio Sthrn Ohio Cincinnati OH 2004-** B Louisville KY 1946 s John & Betty. BA Franciscan U of Steubenville 1967; S Jn Vianney Sem 1971; Wheeling Jesuit U 2006. Rec 3/8/1992 as Deacon Bp William Grant Black. m 10/2/1971 Marian Kay Brandenburg c 1. D E Cntrl Ohio Area Mnstry Bridgeport OH 2003-2005; Assoc Chapl S Jos Orphanage Cincinnati OH 1998-2002; D Ch Of Our Sav Cincinnati OH 1991-2003. Angl Acad, Cincinnati OH 1991; EUC 1990-1994; Living Stones 2003-2007.

BRANDENBURG, Nancy Lee Hamman (SO) Saint John'S Church, Worthington OH 43085 B Sioux City IA 1938 d Lester & Letty. MS OH SU; BD Capital U 1982; Angl Acad 1994. D 11/11/1994 Bp Herbert Thompson Jr. m 8/28/1976 David Brandenburg c 4. NAAD Curs.

BRANDON, Bonnie P (Los) 1874 W Nutwood Pl, Anaheim CA 92804 **R S Andr's Par Torrance CA 2012-** B Anaheim CA 1961 d Richard & Lorraine. AA Fullerton Coll 1986; BA Chapman U 2002; MDiv ETSBH 2007. D 6/9/2007 P 1/12/2008 Bp Joseph Jon Bruno. Assoc St Andr Epis Ch Irvine CA 2007-2009; S Clem's-By-The-Sea Par San Clemente CA 2002-2007. revbonniebrandon@gmail.com

BRANDON, Karen Dale (RG) 226 Jupiter Dr, White Sands Missile Range NM 88002 B Granite City IL 1948 MDiv SW Bapt TS 1973; DMin SW Bapt TS 1984; MS U of Virginia 2005. D 11/23/2002 P 6/21/2003 Bp Terence Kelshaw. Chapl U.S. Army 1988-2008.

BRANDON II, Miles Raymond (Tex) 1501 W 30th St, Austin TX 78703 **St Julian of Norwich Epis Ch Round Rock TX 2015-** B Houston TX 1973 s Nathan & Ellen. BA U of Texas 1998; MDiv VTS 2002. D 6/22/2002 Bp Claude Edward Payne P 5/17/2003 Bp Don Adger Wimberly. m 11/3/2007 Ashley Brandon c 2. Vic The Great Cmsn Fndt Houston TX 2002-2015; Yth Min S Mart's Epis Ch Houston TX 1996-1999.

BRANDT JR, George Walter (NY) 16 Park Ave, Apt 9C, New York NY 10016 **Chair Of Stndg Cmsn On Const And Cn Epis Ch GC 1997-; Cn Ch Of The Prov Of Cntrl Afr 1995-** B New York NY 1943 s George & Lillian. BA Franklin & Marshall Coll 1965; JD Boston Coll 1968; EDS 1976; MDiv Nash 1978; Cert Col 1995. D 6/3/1978 Bp Paul Moore Jr P 12/17/1978 Bp James Winchester Montgomery. R S Mich's Ch New York NY 1994-2011; Cmsn On Black Mnstrs Epis Ch Black Mnstrs Off 1992-1994; Bd. Mem Emmaus Hse Epis Ch Atlanta GA 1991-1994; Cn For Wrshp And Cmnty Outreach Cathd Of S Phil Atlanta GA 1988-1994; P-in-c All Souls Ch New York NY 1987-1988; Mssy Exec Coun Appointees New York NY 1983-1988; Prov Secy Ch Of The Prov Of Cntrl Afr 1983-1986; Urban Mssnr Dio Wstrn New York Tonawanda NY 1982-1983; Vic S Marg's Ch Chicago IL 1978-1982. Assoc- Soc Of S Jn The Evang 1978; EUC 1987; UBE 1969. Cn Prov Ch Of Cntrl Afr 1995.

BRANDT, Robert G (LI) 414 SW Horseshoe Bay, Port Saint Lucie FL 34986 B New York NY 1938 s George & Edith. Cert Hofstra U 1963; BA Hofstra U 1963; MA U of Vermont 1966; MA St U of NY at Stony Brook 1968; MALS St U of NY at Stony Brook 1970; S Johns U 1973; Cert S Johns U 1973; Cert Theol Stud Mercer TS 1976; Cert Yashiva U 1982; Natl Endwmt for the Hmnts 1983; Fulbright Fndt 1988; Natl Endwmt for the Hmnts 1993; Milton V Brown Fndt 1995. D 6/5/1976 P 12/18/1976 Bp Jonathan Goodhue Sherman. m 6/1/1963 Jean Schwaemle. Vic Chr Ch-Epis Prt Jefferson NY 2002-2010, Asst 1983-2001; Supply P Dio Long Island Garden City NY 2000-2001; P-in-c S Mk's Epis Ch Medford NY 1995-2000, Asst 1986-1995; Asst S Jn's Ch Huntington NY 1981-1983; Chapl Hofstra U Hempstead NY 1976-1981; Asst S Ann's Ch Sayville NY 1976-1981. Auth, "Jn Ruskin & The Gld Of S Geo"; Auth, "Indn Art As A Reflection Of The Indn Wrld View"; Auth, "The Icon," *A Window Into The Byzantine Mind.* Ord Of S Lk, ERM; Tertiary Of The Soc Of S Fran. Fndt Fell Milton V Brown 1995; Fell Natl Endwmnt For Hmnts 1993; Fulbright Fellowow To India 1988; Fell Natl Endwmnt For Hmnts 1987.

BRANNOCK, Christina Combs (Lex) PO Box 27, Paris KY 40362 **S Ptr's Ch Paris KY 2010-** B Johnson City TN 1956 d Kent & Beatrice. BFA E Tennessee St U 1977; MA Emory U 1983; MDiv GTS 1983. D 6/15/1986 P 5/1/1987 Bp William Evan Sanders. c 1. S Paul's Ch Windsor VT 2010; R S Jas Ch Woodstock VT 2000-2009; Ch Of The Gd Samar Knoxville TN 1999-2000; R Thankful Memi Ch Chattanooga TN 1992-1998; Anglo-Cath Strng Com Dio E Tennessee Knoxville TN 1992-1994, Dept of Yth 1987-1992, Chair of Anglo-Cath Strng Com 1994-1995; Vic S Mk's Ch Copperhill TN 1987-1992; D Gr Ch Chattanooga TN 1986-1987.

BRANNOCK-WANTER JR, Henry Paul (Vt) 257 Us Route 5, Hartland VT 05048 B Niagara Falls NY 1949 s Henry & Vera. Van; BS Un Coll 1972; MDiv GTS 1984. D 7/1/1984 P 4/1/1985 Bp William Evan Sanders. c 1. R S Lk's Ch Chester VT 2002-2012; R S Raphael's Epis Ch Crossville TN 1995-2001, Vic 1985-1994; Dio E Tennessee Knoxville TN 1985-1994; D-In-Trng Gr Ch Chattanooga TN 1984-1985. adventcynthianaky@gmail.com

BRANNON, Kenneth Hoffman (Ida) St. Thomas Episcopal Church, PO Box 1070, Sun Valley ID 83353 **R S Thos Epis Ch Sun Vlly ID 2007-; Dep, GC Dio Idaho Boise ID 2014-, Fac, Preaching Practicum 2013-, Trnr, Safeguarding God's Chld 2012-2014, Chair, Deputation, GC 2010-2013, Pres, Stndg Com 2008-2012, Secy, Stndg Com 2008-2012** B Fort Collins CO 1968 s Richard & Judith. BA Wheaton Coll 1990; MA NYU 1997; MDiv VTS 2003. D 3/8/2003 P 9/20/2003 Bp Mark Sean Sisk. m 3/18/1995 Rachel Miller Brannon c 2. Assoc R S Barn Ch Irvington NY 2003-2007; Sem S Alb's Par Washington DC 2002-2003; CE Dir Ch Of The H Trin New York NY 1996-2000; Mem, Camp and Conf Com Dio New York New York NY 2006. Co-Auth, "Superheroes, monsters, and babies," *The Arts in Psych*, Elsevier Sci, 2002. Soc for the Increase of the Mnstry 2001. Diac Cn The Collgt Chap of S Jn, The DeKoven Cntr 2007; Evang for the 21st Century Grant Epis EvangES 2004; Sem Consult on Mssn Grant Sem Consult on Mssn 2004; Graduated cl VTS 2003; Roothbert Fell Roothbert Fund 2002; Merit Schlrshp VTS 2000; Graduated cl NYU 1997; Human First Awd Horizons Cmnty Serv 1996; Jn W. Withers Awd NYU 1995; Tchg Fell NYU 1994; Graduated cl Wheaton Coll 1990; Schlr Geo F. Baker Trust Schlr 1973. kbrannon@stthomassunvalley.org

BRANNON, Lecia Elaine (ECR) Calv Epis Ch Richmond TX 2016- D 6/4/2016 P 12/9/2016 Bp Mary Gray-Reeves.

BRANNON, Stephen Nave (NCal) 19275 Robinson Rd, Sonoma CA 95476 **Vice-Chncllr Dio Nthrn California 1995-** B Metropolis IL 1944 s William & Mary. Sthrn Illinois U 1964; BA U IL 1966; STB GTS 1969; JD U of San Francisco 1981. D 5/24/1969 P 12/1/1969 Bp Albert A Chambers. c 1. R Trin Ch Sonoma CA 1995-2005; Chncllr Prov VIII 1989-2000; Chapl Berkeley Cbury Fndt Berkeley CA 1988-1995; Vice-Chncllr Prov VIII 1984-1988; Vic S Edm's Epis Ch Pacifica CA 1984-1988; Int Trsfg Epis Ch San Mateo CA

1984; Assoc Ch Of The Adv Of Chr The King San Francisco CA 1981-1984; Assoc Trin Ch San Francisco CA 1977-1981; Vic S Andr's Ch El Paso IL 1975-1977; Int S Matt's Epis Ch Bloomington IL 1973-1974; Vic S Thos Ch Salem IL 1969-1972; Stndg Com The Epis Dio Nthrn California Sacramento CA 1991-1994, 1989-1990, 1988. Cmnty Of S Mary; OHC.

BRANSCOMB JR, William Maurice (Ala) 532 W Ariel Ave, Foley AL 36535 **Ret 1997-** B Dayton OH 1925 s William & Ada. BA Otterbein U 1960; BD VTS 1963; MDiv VTS 1964. D 6/15/1963 Bp Robert Fisher Gibson Jr P 6/1/1964 Bp Samuel B Chilton. m 5/28/1949 Joan W Branscomb c 3. Vic Imm Ch Bay Minette AL 2006-2007; R Gr Ch Birmingham AL 1988-1997; R Ch Of The H Comm Charleston SC 1984-1987; R S Andrews's Epis Ch Birmingham AL 1971-1984; Asst S Paul's Epis Ch Alexandria VA 1968-1971; Asst Min Chr Epis Ch Charlottesvlle VA 1965-1968; Gr Ch Bremo Bluff VA 1963-1965; S Jn's Columbia Columbia VA 1963-1965. Awd Cmnty Kitchen 2006; Golden Rule Awd 1997; Bro Brian Awd 1982.

BRANSCOMBE, Mike (SwFla) 1010 Charles St, Clearwater FL 33755 B Birmingham UK 1965 BA U of Durham GB 1995; DMin TESM 2008. Trans 6/14/2003 as Priest Bp John Bailey Lipscomb. m 8/27/1988 Margaret V Branscombe c 2. Assoc R Ch Of The Ascen Clearwater FL 2003-2015; Asst R S Alfred's Epis Ch Palm Harbor FL 2003; Serv Ch of Engl 1995-2001; COM (Chair) Dio SW Florida Parrish FL 2007-2011.

BRANSCOME III, Dexter Arno (Miss) 1 Oakleigh Pl, Jackson MS 39211 B Greenwood MS 1937 BA U of Mississippi 1959; MA U of Alabama 1975. D 1/4/2003 Bp Alfred Marble Jr. m 12/21/1959 Martha Branscome c 4. D S Phil's Ch Jackson MS 2011-2013.

BRANSON, John H (Ct) 827 Fearrington Post, Pittsboro NC 27312 B Concord NH 1948 s John & Virginia. BA Coll of Wooster 1971; MDiv Ya Berk 1974. D 6/5/1974 Bp Philip Alan Smith P 3/1/1975 Bp Morgan Porteus. m 6/23/1973 Judith J Branson c 1. Chr Ch Alexandria VA 2015-2016; R Chr And H Trin Ch Westport CT 1991-2012; R S Paul's Epis Ch Chatham NJ 1980-1991; Trin Epis Ch Hartford CT 1974-1980.

BRANSTETTER, Kent A (SanD) St Dunstans Episcopal Church, 6556 Park Ridge Blvd, San Diego CA 92120 **S Dunst's Epis Ch San Diego CA 2016-** B Boone IA 1950 s Robert & Geraldine. BA Oral Roberts U 1976; MA Point Loma Coll 1982; MDiv Ya Berk 1985; MA Drew U 1989. D 6/22/1985 P 12/21/1985 Bp Charles Brinkley Morton. m 8/24/1991 Rebecca A Adams c 2. R S Edw's Epis Ch Lawrenceville GA 1996-2016; P-in-c Ch Of The Atone Fair Lawn NJ 1991-1996; Int S Andr's Epis Ch Lincoln Pk NJ 1990-1991; Int S Mk's Ch W Orange NJ 1989-1990; Non-par 1987-1989; Cur S Barth's Epis Ch Poway CA 1985-1987. kbranstetter@stdunstans.org

BRANT, George Henry (Nwk) 601 Park St Apt 11-D, Bordentown NJ 08505 **Ret 1986-** B Stanton Bridge UK 1921 s William & Mary. ATCM U Tor 1937; LTh Emml Saskatoon Sask 1945; BA U Sask CA 1945; BD Emml Saskatoon Sask 1947. Trans 10/1/1950 Bp Charles Bernard Barfoot. c 3. S Jas' Epis Ch Hackettstown NJ 1969-1986; Serv Iglesia Anglicana de Mex 1966-1969; Assoc Gr Ch Madison NJ 1964-1966; P-in-c S Jn's Ch Dover NJ 1950-1952; Serv Angl Ch of Can 1945-1950.

BRANTINGHAM, Nancy Marie (Minn) 3185 County Road 6, Long Lake MN 55356 B Minneapolis MN 1954 d Robert & Sue. BA U MN 1981; MA The Coll of S Cathr 2002; Cert SWTS 2004. D 6/15/2005 P 12/15/2005 Bp James Louis Jelinek. m 4/6/1974 Henry Baldwin Brantingham c 2. Assoc R S Steph The Mtyr Ch Minneapolis MN 2009-2014; Assoc R Trin Ch Excelsior MN 2005-2009; Adj Fac Coll of St. Cathr 2004-2005.

BRATHWAITE, Christopher Ethelbert (CFla) 102 North 9Th Street, Haines City FL 33844 **R S Mk's Epis Ch Haines City FL 2011-** B Barbados 1947 s Whitley & Louise. BS U of Pheonix 2005; MTS Asbury TS 2008. D 9/7/2008 P 5/30/2009 Bp John Wadsworth Howe. m 9/26/1986 Genevieve Brathwaite c 2. Auth, "Bk," *Jude*; Auth, "Bk," *Tit*; Auth, "Bk," *Walking w Jas*.

BRATHWAITE, Percy Alphonso (NY) 17 Granada Cres Apt 6, White Plains NY 10603 **Vic S Martha's Ch Bronx NY 2002-** B BB 1940 s Percy & Octavia. MDiv Ya Berk 1989. D 7/8/1989 Bp Clarence Nicholas Coleridge P 1/1/1990 Bp Walter Decoster Dennis Jr. m 11/17/1990 Delores S Brathwaite. Dio New York New York NY 2002-2012; Gr Ch (W Farms) Bronx NY 2002-2012; Vic Calv and St Geo New York NY 1996-2002; S Andr's Ch New York NY 1993-1995; Gr Ch White Plains NY 1991-1993. Epis Black Caucus.

BRAUN, Elise (Vt) Wood Road, Box 1033, Stowe VT 05672 **Died 6/17/2016** B New Britain CT 1932 d Samuel & Julia. U of Miami; BA U NC 1954; Cert Dioc Study Prog for Lay People Middlebury VT 1991. D 10/2/1991 Bp Daniel Lee Swenson. m 4/24/1970 Robert Thompson Braun c 1. D S Jn's In The Mountains Stowe VT 1991-1999.

BRAUN, James Richard (Mil) 5900 7th Avenue, Kenosha WI 53140 B Racine WI 1949 s Jerome & Dorothy. BS U of Wisconsin 1971; MDiv Nash 1974. D 4/19/1974 P 11/9/1974 Bp Charles Thomas Gaskell. m 8/14/1976 Karen Killingstad c 2. R S Matt's Ch Kenosha WI 1985-2011, Cur 1975-1984; Asst Gr Ch Madison WI 1974-1975.

BRAUNSCHNEIDER, Karl Nicholas (CFla) 202 Pontotoc St, Auburndale FL 33823 B Rochester MI 1978 s David & Sharon. D 1/30/2017 Bp Gregory Orrin Brewer. m 9/7/2002 Kimberly M Braunschneider c 5.

BRAUZA, Ellen Lederer (WNY) 4210 Gunnville Road, Clarence NY 14031 **S Andr's Ch Buffalo NY 2013-; Pstr Buffalo CHS (emergent Grp) 2005-** B Buffalo NY 1950 d Arthur & Norma. BA Valparaiso U 1972; MA Chr the King Sem 1986; MDiv Bex Sem 2000. D 1/20/2001 P 8/19/2001 Bp Michael Garrison. m 11/12/1977 Walter Brauza c 2. Dioc Coun Epis Dio Wstrn New York 2010-2012; Pres Epis Cmnty Serv of Wstrn New York 2008; Pres Epis Cmnty Serv of Wstrn New York 2007-2008; Vic St Johns Epis Youngstown NY 2005-2013; Co-Vic Ch Of The Ascen Buffalo NY 2004-2005; Hosp Chapl Kaleida Hlth System Buffalo NY 2004-2005; Bd Dir Epis Cmnty Serv of Wstrn New York 2002-2007; Asst S Paul's Epis Ch Harris Hill Buffalo NY 2001-2003; Adj Instr Bex Sem Columbus OH 2000-2003. Buffalo CHS 2005; SCHC 2002-2011.

BRAWLEY, Anna P (Ala) 1900 Darby Drive, Florence AL 35630 **Ch Of S Jas The Less Ashland VA 2016-; R S Barth's Epis Ch Florence AL 2010-** B Greenwood SC 1965 d Robert & Jane Amelia. AB Erskine Coll 1987; MDiv Ya Berk 1992; MDiv Yale DS 1992; STM Ya Berk 1994; STM Yale DS 1994; PhD Van 1999; Cert Ang Stud SWTS 2008. D 6/6/2009 P 6/15/2010 Bp Jeff Lee. Dio Alabama Birmingham 2014-2016; Pstr Asst The Ch Hm At Montgomery Place Chicago IL 2009-2010. anna.brawley@att.net

BRAWLEY, Joan Biddles Kirby (CFla) 631 W Lake Elbert Dr, Winter Haven FL 33881 **Assoc The Epis Ch Of The Gd Shpd Lake Wales FL 2007-** B Portsmouth VA 1951 d Frank & Lucy. BA Mary Baldwin Coll 1973; MDiv Asbury TS 2007. D 6/2/2007 Bp John Wadsworth Howe. m 7/19/1975 Marion Porter Brawley c 4.

BRAXTON JR, Louis (Nwk) 480 Warwick Ave, Teaneck NJ 07666 B Paris TN 1956 s Louis & Shirley. MS No Dakota St U; SWTS; BA Concordia Coll 1978; MA EDS 1984. D 1/6/1985 Bp Harold Anthony Hopkins Jr P 9/1/1985 Bp Walter Decoster Dennis Jr. Chr Ch Teaneck NJ 1986-1993, Cur 1984-1986; Chr's Ch Rye NY 1985-1986; Asst Geth Cathd Fargo ND 1981-1982; Chapl S Lk's Hosp Fargo ND 1980-1982.

BRAY, Doris S (Be) 443 Franklin Ave, Palmerton PA 18071 **Ret 1999-** B Palmerton PA 1929 d Walter & Laura. Cert Moravian TS 1980. D 9/21/1978 P 6/2/1979 Bp Lloyd Edward Gressle. m 7/12/1952 Marvin Walter Bray c 3. Chair of Renwl and Evang Com Dio Bethlehem Bethlehem PA 1994-1998, Renwl and Evang Com 1985-1994, Search Consult 1978-1999, Cn Pstr 1996-, Stwdshp Consult 1988-1995, Sprtl Dir for Curs 1985-1987, COM 1980-1984; Assoc S Jn's Epis Ch Palmerton PA 1989-1999; Asst All SS Epis Ch Lehighton PA 1978-1999. SCHC 1993. Cn Pstr Dio Bethlehem 1996.

BRDLIK, Christopher M F (Nwk) 914 Ridge Rd, Newton NJ 07860 B Hinsdale IL 1951 s Mel & Dolores. AB Ham 1973; MDiv VTS 1977; Fell Coll of Preachers 1988. D 6/12/1977 Bp Frank S Cerveny P 1/6/1978 Bp Jackson Earle Gilliam. m 6/18/1977 Debra Cleveland c 3. Co-Chair New Bp Transition Com Dio Newark 2005-2007; Co-Chair Com to Nominate Bp Coadj Dio Newark 1996-1998; R Calv Epis Ch Summit NJ 1995-2010; Bd Trst VTS Alexandria VA 1991-1995; Dep GC Dio SW Virginia 1991-1994; Pres Stndg Com Dio SW Virginia 1987-1993; R S Jn's Epis Ch Waynesboro VA 1984-1995; Chair of COM Dio SW Virginia 1984-1992; R S Andr's Ch Clifton Forg VA 1981-1984; Cur Ch Of The Incarn Great Falls MT 1977-1981. Auth, *arts & Revs*.

BREAKEY, Pamela Jean (WMich) 54581 California Rd, Dowagiac MI 49047 B Berkeley CA 1946 d Loyd & Bethea Betty. BA MI SU 1969; BA MI SU 1969; MA MI SU 1973; MA MI SU 1973; MDiv SWTS 1996. D 6/8/1996 P 2/26/1997 Bp Edward Lewis Lee Jr. m 1/2/2002 Michael P Heidenreich c 3. Assoc R S Barn Epis Ch Portage MI 2003-2004; R S Paul's Epis Ch Dowagiac MI 2000-2003; Assoc R Chr Epis Ch No Hills Pittsburgh PA 1997-2000; Consulting Team Dio W Michigan Portage MI 1990-1993; Transition Team Dio Wstrn Michigan Kalamazoo MI 2001-2002. Contributing ABC Patient, "The Quiet War: Profiles of Wmn Facing Advncd Breast Cancer," *Documentary Film*, Affinity Films, 2006.

BRECHNER, Eric Lonell (NJ) Po Box 126, Gibbsboro NJ 08026 **Ch Of S Jn-In-The-Wilderness Gibbsboro NJ 1996-; Chapl Sch for Deacons Dio New Jersey NJ 1995-** B Los Angeles CA 1955 s Verne & Virginia. BA W&M 1977; MDiv GTS 1982; STM GTS 1990. D 6/19/1982 P 2/5/1983 Bp Robert Claflin Rusack. Chapl Coll of New Jersey Trenton NJ 1995-1997; Chapl Momentum AIDS Mnstry 1989-1990; Asst S Jas Ch New York NY 1988-1989; S Jas Epis Ch S Jas NY 1988-1989; S Jn The Evang Mssn Needles CA 1986-1988; Cur The Epis Ch Of The Blessed Sacr Placentia CA 1982-1985.

BRECHT, Laura Berger (SanD) 3425 Santa Saba Rd, Borrego Springs CA 92004 **R S Barn Ch Borrego Spgs CA 2010-** B Cincinnati OH 1949 d Carl & Martha. BA U CO 1971; MCP Harv 1976; MDiv Sewanee: The U So, TS 2008. D 6/14/2008 P 1/24/2009 Bp John L Rabb. m 8/27/1977 Lyle A Brecht c 2. Epis Campus Min Dio Maryland Baltimore MD 2002-2005.

BRECKENRIDGE, Elaine (SJ) 2927 Sweetwood Dr, Lodi CA 95242 **P-in-c S Jn The Bapt Lodi CA 2013-** B Henderson NV 1957 d Gail & Phyllis. BA Westminster Coll 1980; MDiv EDS 1987. D 4/25/1987 Bp George Edmonds

Bates P 3/25/1988 Bp Allen Lyman Bartlett Jr. m 5/12/1990 Frank G Brecken-ridge c 2. R S Dav's Ch Spokane WA 2004-2013; Gr St Pauls Epis Ch Tucson AZ 1998-2014; Vic S Jn's Epis Ch Logan UT 1994-1998; Dio Utah Salt Lake City UT 1993-1998; Int Ch Of The Resurr Centerville UT 1993-1994; Dio Kentucky Louisville KY 1992; Asst S Thos Epis Ch And Sch San Antonio TX 1991-1992; Asst Trin Ch Swarthmore PA 1989-1991; Cur S Dav's Ch Wayne PA 1987-1989. mother_elaine@comcast.net

BRECKENRIDGE, Ella Huff (WLa) 1825 Albert Street, Alexandria LA 71301 B Orlando FL 1941 d Marshall & Aileen. MS Florida St U 1981; MEd U of No Florida 1985; MDiv Epis TS of the SW 2002. D 6/15/2002 Bp Robert Jefferson Hargrove Jr P 5/29/2003 Bp D Avid Bruce Macpherson. c 1. Int Dio Rochester Henrietta 2012; Int Chr Ch Corning NY 2009-2011; Int S Thad Epis Ch Aiken SC 2006-2009; Int Ch Of The Nativ Greenwood MS 2005-2006; Chapl Dio Alabama Birmingham 2005; Asst Trin Epis Ch Florence AL 2003-2005; Cur St Mich's Epis Ch Pineville LA 2003; Fam Specialsts Vol's of Amer 2003; Cur S Tim's Ch Alexandria LA 2002.

BRECKENRIDGE, William Allen (Az) 2721 N Dos Hombres Rd, Tucson AZ 85715 B New Orleans LA 1952 s Sidney & Francis. AA Jones Cnty Jr Coll Ellisville MS 1972; BA Mississippi St U 1975; MDiv Sewanee: The U So, TS 1978. D 5/21/1978 P 6/1/1979 Bp Duncan Montgomery Gray Jr. m 8/18/1973 Donna Breckenridge. R Ch Of S Matt Tucson AZ 2001-2009; Dio Arizona Phoenix AZ 1992-2001; Dio Sthrn Virginia Newport News VA 1981-1992; Chapl Hamden-Sydney Coll Hamden Sydney VA 1981-1992; S Fran Of Assisi Ch Philadelphia MS 1978-1981; Vic S Matt's Epis Ch Kosciusko MS 1978-1981. ESMHE.

BRECKINRIDGE IV, Alexander Negus (Oly) 8398 NE 12th St, Medina WA 98039 **R S Thos Epis Ch Medina WA 2009-; Chapl S Andr's Epis Sch 2005-** B Beckley WV 1951 s Alexander & Beverly. BA U NC 1974; JD Tul 1979; MDiv Epis TS of the SW 1998. D 5/30/1998 Bp Charles Edward Jenkins III P 6/24/1999 Bp Claude Edward Payne. m 5/28/1977 Jeanne Ledoux Breckinridge c 3. Chapl S Andrews Epis Sch Austin TX 2005-2009; R S Alb's Epis Ch Austin Austin TX 1999-2005; Assoc S Mich's Ch Austin TX 1998-1999.

BREDLAU, Mary Theresa (Nev) 8520 W Hammer Ln, Las Vegas NV 89149 **P Gr In The Desert Epis Ch Las Vegas NV 2008-; Per Diem Chapl Palm Mortuary Las Vegas NV 2008-** B Milbank SD 1945 d Jerome & Avelline. AA Corbett Jr Coll Crookston MN 1966; BA Our Lady of the Lake U 1970; Cert Corpus Christi Cntr Phoenix AZ 1988; Dplma Creighton U 1988; MA S Mary U Winona MN 1991; Death Stds Cert Cntr for Loss & Life Transition 2000; 4 units CPE 2000; Cert Redemptorist Renwl Cntr Tucson AZ 2005; CT Assoc Death Ed ; Counslg 2006. D 2/14/1995 P 9/17/1995 Bp Stewart Clark Zabriskie. c 2. Dn Dio Nevada Las Vegas 2011-2013, 1990-2010, Dn 2010-2013; Chapl CompassionCare Hospice Las Vegas NV 2008-2009; P Chr Ch Las Vegas NV 2001-2008; P in Charge All SS Epis Ch Las Vegas NV 1999-2000; Chapl Palm Mortuary Las Vegas NV 1996-2008; Chapl Nathan Adelson Hospice Las Vegas NV 1990-1996. Auth, "Grief Guides," self: copyrighted, 2009. AssemblyEpHealthcareChaplaincy 1995; Assn Death Educ & Counslg 1990; Assn Of Profsnl Chapl 1991; Benedictine Oblate 1982; Interfaith Coun Nccj 1990-1996.

BREEDEN, James Pleasant (Mass) 29 Rope Ferry Rd # 3755, Hanover NH 03755 **Non-par 1966-** B Minneapolis MN 1934 s Pleasant & Florence. BA Dart 1956; Cert Grad Sch Ecum Stds 1959; MDiv UTS 1960; EdD Harv 1972. D 6/1/1961 P 12/1/1961 Bp Anson Phelps Stokes Jr. Bp'S Vic On Civil Rts Dio Massachusetts Boston MA 1963-1965; The Cathd Ch Of S Paul Boston MA 1963-1965; Cur S Jn's S Jas Epis Ch Boston MA 1961-1963. Cmsn On Ch And Race / Massachusetts Coun Of Ch 1967-1969. Man Of The Year Boston Jr ChmbrCom 1964; Roxbury Proj Awd 73; Alper Awd Ma Clu 78.

BREEDLOVE, William J (WNC) Church Of The Good Shepherd, PO Box 677, Hayesville NC 28904 **R Ch Of The Gd Shpd Hayesville NC 2013-** B Heidelberg, Germany 1962 s Harry & Linde. BS U of So Carolina 1984; MA U of So Carolina 1986; PhD The Florida St U 1993; MDiv Nash 2009. D 5/28/2009 Bp Mark Joseph Lawrence P 12/8/2009 Bp Dean E Wolfe. m 6/19/1993 Susan P Morgan c 2. Assoc S Mich And All Ang Ch Mssn KS 2009-2013. rectorgsec@brmemc.net

BREEDLOVE II, William Otis (NJ) 10 Winthrop Road, Somerset NJ 08873 **S Barn Epis Ch Monmouth Jct NJ 2001-** B Indianapolis IN 1941 s William & Bessie. BA Butler U 1963; BD U Chi 1966; MS U IL 1968; CSD GTS 1991; DAS GTS 1991. D 6/8/1991 P 1/11/1992 Bp George Phelps Mellick Belshaw. m 8/17/1968 Elizabeth Ann Breedlove. S Andr's Ch Trenton NJ 2001-2003; Int S Andr's Ch Mt Holly NJ 1997-1999; Vic Trin Epis Old Swedes Ch Swedesboro NJ 1991-1995. Third Ord, SSF 1988.

BREESE, Mary Schrom (WMo) 606 Woodcrest Dr, Saint Joseph MO 64506 B Kansas City MO 1946 d Stanley & Helen. BA Bryn 1969; MA U of Iowa 1973; Lon GB 1977; MDiv Nash 1981. D 5/24/1982 P 11/1/1982 Bp Richard Frank Grein. m 6/5/1988 Sidney Samuel Breese. Dir of Sprtl Care Living Cmnty of St. Jos 2002-2013; P-in-c S Lk's Epis Ch Excelsior Sprg MO 1995-2002; Assoc For Pstr Care Gr And H Trin Cathd Kansas City MO 1993-1995; R Gr Epis Ch Ottawa KS 1990-1993; R S Mk's Epis Ch Wadsworth OH 1988-1990; Vic Epis Ch Of S Geo Canyon TX 1984-1988; Chapl W Texas St U In Canyon

Canyon TX 1983-1988; Chapl Dio NW Texas Lubbock TX 1983; Cn To The Ordnry Dio Kansas Topeka KS 1982-1983. Auth, "Mod Liturg". Assn of Profsnl Chapl 2005; Bd ETSSw, Austin Tx 1990-1993. Mdiv cl Nash 1981. mary. breese@bhshealth.org

BREESE, Sidney Samuel (WMo) 2533 Francis St, Saint Joseph MO 64501 B Schenectady NY 1942 s Samuel & Ruth Avery. Resurr CA 1965; BA U of Waterloo 1965; MDiv VTS 1969; Washington Urban Trng Prog 1969; IAPS 1974; Ldrshp Acad for New Directions 1980; Shoresh Study Tour IL 1996. D 6/11/1969 P 6/1/1970 Bp Ned Cole. m 6/5/1988 Mary Schrom c 2. R Chr Epis Ch S Jos MO 1998-2007; P-in-c S Mary's Ch Savannah MO 1997-1998; Yth Dir Dio Kansas Topeka KS 1993-1996; R S Aid's Ch Olathe KS 1990-1995; Dio Ohio Cleveland 1987-1990; R Ch Of S Jas The Apos Clovis Curry NM 1985-1987; Archvicar Ilano Estacado Mnstry 1985-1987; R S Andr's Epis Ch Las Cruces NM 1982-1985; P-in-c Centralia Effingham Salem Bradenton FL 1980-1981; S Jn's Ch Centralia IL 1978-1980; P-in-c S Thos Ch Salem IL 1978-1980; R S Jude's Epis Ch Fenton MI 1975-1978; Asst Chr Ch Detroit MI 1973-1975; R Trin Epis Ch W Branch MI 1971-1973; Cur Emm Ch Norwich NY 1969-1971. Auth, *Chr Looks at Drugs.*

BREHE, Stephen L (Mont) 912 Stuart St., Helena MT 59601 **Asstg P Gr Epis Ch St. Geo UT 2012-** B Springfield IL 1947 s Melvin & Mildred. BA Mar 1969; MA U of Missouri 1972; MDiv SWTS 1979; DMin GTF 1986. D 9/5/1979 Bp James Winchester Montgomery P 3/24/1980 Bp Quintin Ebenezer Primo Jr. m 6/9/1969 Jacqueline Brehe c 2. Dn S Ptr's Cathd Helena MT 1991-2010; R S Paul's Ch Minneapolis MN 1986-1991; Ch of the H Sprt Belmont MI 1980-1986; Dio Wstrn Michigan Kalamazoo MI 1980-1982; Cur S Mary's Ch Pk Ridge IL 1979-1980.

✠ BREIDENTHAL, The Rt Rev Dr Thomas Edward (SO) Diocese Of Southern Ohio, 412 Sycamore St, Cincinnati OH 45202 **Bp of Sthrn Ohio Dio Sthrn Ohio Cincinnati OH 2007-** B Jersey City NJ 1951 s Leslie & Ruth. BA Portland St U 1974; MA U of Victoria 1977; MDiv CDSP 1981; PhD Oxf GB 1991. D 6/28/1981 P 6/12/1982 Bp Matthew Paul Bigliardi Con 4/28/2007 for SO. m 7/7/1984 Margaret Breidenthal c 2. Chair Angl RC Dialogue USA 2003-2009; Dn of Chap and Rel Life Pr 2002-2007; Asstg P Ch Of S Mary The Vrgn New York NY 1999-2001; Mem GBEC 1997-2001; Dir Cntr for Jewish-Chr Stds and Relatns 1994-1997; Prof of Chr Ethics and Moral Theol The GTS New York NY 1992-2001; R Trin Epis Ch Ashland Ashland OR 1989-1992; Sr Chapl Harvard-Westlake Sch Studio City CA 1986-1988; Serv Ch of Engl 1983-1986; Stdt ECF Inc New York NY 1983-1984; Asst to the R S Mich And All Ang Ch Portland OR 1981-1983. Auth, "Sacr Unions," *Sacr Unions,* Cowley, 2006; Auth, "Neighbor-Christology: Reconstructing Chrsnty Before Supersessionism," *Cross Currents,* 1999; Auth, "The Politics of Incarn," *Mod Theol,* 1998; Auth, "Chr Households: The Sanctification of Nearness," *Chr Households: The Sanctification of nearness,* Cowley, 1997; Auth, "Sanctifying Nearness," *Our Selves, Our Souls & Bodies,* Cowley, 1996. Fell ECF 1983. tbreidenthal@diosohio.org

BREINER, Bert Fredrick (NY) 401 W 24th St, New York NY 10011 B Burlington VT 1948 s Roy & Margeret. BD Geo 1970; STM GTS 1973; PhD U of Birmingham Birmingham Gb 1988. D 6/16/1973 Bp Jonathan Goodhue Sherman P 12/1/1973 Bp Robert Lionne DeWitt. Hon Assoc Chr And S Steph's Ch New York NY 2002-2004, Assoc 1994-2001, 1994-; Gr Ch Sch New York New York NY 2001-2004; Assoc Gr Epis Ch New York NY 2000-2004; Epis Ch Cntr New York NY 1993-2000; Non-par 1984-1994; Exec Coun Appointees New York NY 1976-1993; Ch Of S Mart-In-The-Fields Philadelphia PA 1973-1976. Auth, "0pus Dei"; Auth, "European Judaism"; Auth, "Nwsltr Cntr For Study Of Islam & Chr-Muslim Relatns". tapanta@gmail.com

BRELSFORD, Diane Bowyer (Oly) 507 5th Ave W, Seattle WA 98119 B Dallas TX 1930 d Hubard & Virginia. BA U Denv 1966; MA U Denv 1969; MDiv CDSP 1986. D 6/28/1986 Bp Gayle Harris P 6/6/1987 Bp William Edwin Swing. Assoc Ch Of The Ascen Seattle WA 1993-2004; Chapl Annie Wright Sch Tacoma WA 1992-1993; Chapl Vesper Hospice San Leandro CA 1989-1992; Asst The Epis Ch Of The Gd Shpd Berkeley CA 1986-1988. Assn Cmnty Of S Mary; ECW; EPF; Recovery Mnstrs. Epis Peace Fellowowship.

BRENEMEN, Betty Jo (CGC) 18 West Wright Street Street, Pensacola FL 32501 **D Chr Epis Ch Pensacola FL 2012-** B Oklahoma City OK 1942 d Jack & Gladys. BS U of Florida 1964; MS U of Florida 1964; MS U of W Florida 1971; MA U of W Florida 1999; D Sch 2010. D 2/10/2011 Bp Philip Menzie Duncan II. c 1.

BRENMARK-FRENCH, Regina Kay (Chi) 2105 Cumberland St, Rockford IL 61103 **D S Chad Epis Ch Loves Pk IL 2001-** B Chicago IL 1941 d Edward & Catherine. BA Roosevelt U 1996. D 2/3/2001 Bp Bill Persell. m 6/7/1998 Chellis F French.

BRENNEIS, Michael Joseph (Va) 2309 N Kentucky St, Arlington VA 22205 B New York NY 1955 BA SW Bapt U 1978; MA Spalding U 1982; MDiv Sthrn Bapt TS 1983; PhD Geo Mason U 2000; DAS VTS 2003. D 1/14/2004 Bp Peter J Lee P 7/24/2004 Bp David Colin Jones. m 1/1/2001 Jeanne Ziobrowski c 2. P-in-c S Mary's Epis Ch Arlington VA 2004-2005.

BRENNOM, Kesha Mai (Los) 4366 Santa Anita Ave., El Monte CA 91731 B 1974 d Howard & Linda. BA U MI 1996; MDiv VTS 2009. D 12/20/2008 P 6/21/2009 Bp Alan Scarfe. m 5/13/2000 Wade James Brennon c 1. Assoc Vic Imm Mssn El Monte CA 2011-2012; P-in-c All SS Epis Ch Oxnard CA 2009-2011; Stff Off for Chld. & CE Dom and Frgn Mssy Soc NYC NY 2005-2011; Mssnr for Chld, Yth, and YA Dio Iowa Des Moines IA 2000-2005.

BRENTLEY, David J (SO) B Pittsburgh PA 1936 s Roy & Viola. BA Duquesne U 1961. D 10/28/1995 Bp Herbert Thompson Jr. c 1.

BRENTNALL, Burden (Oly) 9086 Chickadee Way, Blaine WA 98230 **Dio Los Angeles Los Angeles CA 1992-** B La Jolla CA 1930 s Samuel & Natalie. BS USMA 1953; MS U MI 1958; MS U MI 1958; PhD Stan 1963. D 6/27/1992 Bp Chester Lovelle Talton. c 3. D Chr Epis Ch Blaine WA 2000-2010; S Paul Epis Ch Bellingham WA 1999-2000; S Columba's Par Camarillo CA 1995-1998; S Fran Of Assisi Epis Ch Simi Vlly CA 1992-1995.

BRENY, Judith Mary (WNY) 745 Ashland Ave, Buffalo NY 14222 **Assoc P Ch of the Gd Shpd 2003-; Vic Ephphatha Epis Ch Of The Deaf Eggertsville NY 2003-** B Dumont NJ 1943 d Charles & Mary. MS SUNY 1993; MDiv GTS 2003. D 6/4/2003 P 12/13/2003 Bp Michael Garrison. c 3. Dio Wstrn New York Tonawanda NY 2004-2009.

BRERETON, Thomas Frederick (Colo) 2741 Freedom Heights, Colorado Springs CO 80904 **Ret 1987-** B Rochester NY 1927 s Frederick & Charlotte. BA W Virginia Wesleyan Coll 1951; MDiv Garrett-Evang TS 1954; Command and Gnrl Stff Coll 1975. D 12/17/1958 P 6/21/1959 Bp Frederick Lehrle Barry. m 10/23/2010 Gloria J Brereton c 3. Ret - Asstg S Raphael Epis Ch Colorado Sprg CO 1989-2010; R S Paul's Lake Jas NC 1983-1987; R St Mary's and St Steph's Epis Ch Morganton NC 1983-1987; Chapl (Colonel) US-A Reserves 1972-1987; R S Jn's Ch Richfld Spgs NY 1972-1983; Chapl (Major) US-A 1960-1972; Cur S Jn's Ch Troy NY 1958-1960; Vic S Lk's Troy NY 1958-1960; Serv Methodist Ch. Bronze Star Medal US-A; Meritorious Serv Medal US-A; Army Commendation Medal US-A.

BRESCIANI, Eduardo Roberto (Los) 9037 Park St, Bellflower CA 90706 **R S Marg's Epis Ch So Gate CA 2005-** B 1951 s Eduardo & Maria. Pacific Luth TS; Pontifical Cath U of Chile; U of Chile. D 6/27/1992 Bp Chester Lovelle Talton. Assoc S Paul's Pomona Pomona CA 2003-2005; D S Phil's Par Los Angeles CA 1992-1994.

BRESNAHAN ACF, Paul B (Mass) 17 King Street, Unit 1, Lynn MA 01902 B Somerville MA 1945 s Paul & Pauline. BA Glendon Coll York U Toronto ON CA 1967; MDiv EDS 1972. D 6/24/1972 P 12/16/1972 Bp John Melville Burgess. m 10/13/1979 Cynthia Ann Saltalamacchia c 3. P-in-c S Ptr's Ch Salem MA 2007-2012; R S Mk's Epis Ch St Albans WV 1995-2006; Chapl Lawr Gnrl Hosp Lawr MA 1991-1995; R S Andr's Ch Methuen MA 1991-1995; Asst H Cross Faith Memi Epis Ch Pawleys Island SC 1991; R Of The Epiph Euclid OH 1983-1990; R Chr Ch Hyde Pk MA 1975-1983; P-in-c S Lk's Epis Ch Malden MA 1972-1975; Cur Chr Ch Quincy MA 1972-1974. Auth, "Everything You Need to Know About Sex in Ord to Get to Heaven," Xlibris, 2005; Auth, "User Friendly Evang," Forw Mvmt. Man of the Year City of S Albans, W Virginia 2006; Mountaineer of the Year Gvnr of W Virginia 2006.

BRETSCHER, Robert George (SwFla) 240 Hancock Ln, Athens GA 30605 **1969-** B New York NY 1933 s George & Christine. BA Wesl 1956; BD VTS 1963; MA U of So Florida 1971; PhD U GA 1974. D 6/11/1963 Bp Duncan Montgomery Gray P 1/1/1964 Bp Joseph Warren Hutchens. m 9/2/1961 Ann Devore Bretscher c 3. R S Mary's Ch Dade City FL 1967-1969; Asst Ch Of The Ascen Clearwater FL 1965-1967; Cur S Paul's Ch Wallingford CT 1963-1965. Eaa.

BRETTMANN, William Sims (EC) 557 Fearnington Post, Pittsboro NC 27312 **Ret 1999-** B Junction City KS 1936 s James & Jean. BA (cl) U So 1959; BA Oxf GB 1961; MA Oxf GB 1965; STM Yale DS 1965; Coolidge Resrch Collegium 1990. D 8/24/1962 P 6/1/1963 Bp Charles C J Carpenter. c 2. R S Steph's Ch Goldsboro NC 1993-1999; Asst to Bp Dio No Carolina Raleigh NC 1991-1993, Dir/Secy 1985-1990; Chapl No Carolina St U at Raleigh Raleigh NC 1985-1991; R Trin Ch Columbus OH 1978-1984; R Gr Epis Ch Orange Pk FL 1970-1978; Cn Chr Ch Cathd Louisville KY 1966-1969; Cur Trin Epis Ch Mobile AL 1962-1964; Chair of COM Dio Florida Jacksonville 1974-1975. Fellowowship Coolidge Resrch Colloguim 1990; Fell Coolidge Resrch Colloquim 90; Life Mem Citation Ohio Pastors Convoc.

BRETZ, Donald Walter Andrew (WVa) 5 Hattaras Ct, Bordentown NJ 08505 **Died 9/5/2015** B Portsmouth OH 1957 s Donald & Jean. BS U Cinc 1979; MA Webster U 1984; MDiv Epis TS of the SW 1988. D 5/25/1988 Bp John Herbert MacNaughton P 12/1/1988 Bp Earl Nicholas Mc Arthur Jr. m 3/31/1979 Darla Fay Bretz. Chapl Mcguire AF Base NJ 1998-2015; Off Of Bsh For ArmdF New York NY 1998-2015; The Memi Ch Of The Gd Shp Parkersburg WV 1994-1998; R Chr Ch Wellsburg WV 1991-1994; Ch Of The Gd Shpd Corpus Christi TX 1988-1991; Asst R S Jas Epis Sch Of Corpus Christi Inc. Crp Christi TX 1988-1991; Chapl S Jas's S Jas's Sch Corpus Christi TX 1988-1991. CBS, GAS, Soc Of S Fran.

BREUER, David R (ECR) 20 University Ave, Los Gatos CA 95030 **Cnvnr Bd Dir Santa Maria Urban Miniustry Dio El Camino Real Salinas CA 1997-** B San Mateo CA 1946 s Arthur & Ethel. AA San Mateo Coll 1965; BA Golden Gate U 1969; MBA Golden Gate U 1972; MDiv Nash 1975. D 6/28/1975 Bp Chauncie Kilmer Myers P 12/1/1975 Bp John Joseph Meakin Harte. m 4/29/1984 Nancy Barbara Breuer. R S Lk's Ch Los Gatos CA 1993-2015; R Chr Ch Sausalito CA 1979-1993; Asst Epis Par Of S Mich And All Ang Tucson AZ 1975-1979. Soc Of S Jn The Evang 1972. drbreuer3@gmail.com

BREWER, Aaron Keith (Ga) PO Box 273, Hawkinsville GA 31036 **S Lk's Epis Hawkinsville GA 2015-** B Vandenberg A.F.B. CA 1972 s James & Sandra. BA St Leo Coll 1998; MBA Webster U 2002; MDiv Emory U Candler TS 2015. D 5/1/2015 P 11/7/2015 Bp Scott Anson Benhase. m 6/15/1996 Kristi Keith Kristi Lee Keith c 2.

BREWER, Anne (NY) 1275 Summer St, Stamford CT 06905 **Non-par 1993-** B Kansas City MO 1949 d Chester & Martha. BA Br 1971; MDiv EDS 1979; MD U of Vermont 1979. D 5/22/1979 P 5/10/1980 Bp Robert Shaw Kerr. m 9/4/1976 James August Kowalski. The CPG New York NY 2006-2015; Asst Ch Of The Gd Shpd Hartford CT 1982-1993; Asst Trin Ch Newtown CT 1980-1982; Non-par 1979-1980.

BREWER, Floyd William (SwFla) 910 Murfreesboro Rd Apt 314, Franklin TN 37064 **Died 12/2/2016** B Chatanooga TN 1931 s Floyd & Ruth. BA U of Florida 1958; MDiv Sewanee: The U So, TS 1996. D 6/15/1996 Bp Rogers Sanders Harris P 1/24/1997 Bp John Bailey Lipscomb. m 2/5/1989 Anne Blake Brewer. S Cecilia's Ch Tampa FL 1999-2000; Vic S Chad's Ch Tampa FL 1997-1999; D S Alfred's Epis Ch Palm Harbor FL 1996-1997.

✠ BREWER, The Rt Rev Gregory Orrin (CFla) 1017 East Robinson St, Orlando FL 32801 **Bp of Cntrl Florida Dio Cntrl Florida Orlando FL 2012-** B Richmond VA 1951 s Robert & Olivia. BA Lynchburg Coll 1973; MDiv VTS 1976. D 6/5/1976 Bp William Henry Marmion P 1/6/1977 Bp William Hopkins Folwell Con 3/24/2012 for CFla. m 9/11/1981 Laura Lee Brewer c 5. R Calv and St Geo New York NY 2009-2012; R Ch Of The Gd Samar Paoli PA 1997-2008; Prof TESM Ambridge PA 1992-1996; R Ch Of The New Cov Winter Spgs FL 1977-1992; Cur All SS Ch Of Winter Pk Winter Pk FL 1976-1977. Auth, "Journey Through The Word". bpbrewer@cfdiocese.org

BREWER, Johnny Lyvon (CGC) 7810 Navarre Pkwy, Navarre FL 32566 B Monroe LA 1957 s Bernisc & Ira. AAS Lamar U. D 2/10/2011 Bp Philip Menzie Duncan II. m 12/31/1992 Antoinette Louise Brewer c 2.

BREWER JR, Luther Gordon (ETenn) 1417 Warpath Dr Ste B, Kingsport TN 37664 B Lumberton NC 1960 s Luther & Mary. BA Mars Hill Coll 1983; MEd E Tennessee St U 2001. D 12/5/2009 Bp Charles Glenn VonRosenberg. m 1/22/1994 Mary C Brewer c 1. Exec Coordntr EAM Kingsport TN 2010-2017.

BREWER, Richard Elliott (Okla) 6606 E 99th Pl, Tulsa OK 74133 **Vic Chr Epis Ch 2004-; Non-par 1981-** B Raton NM 1945 s Paul & Helen. BA U So 1967; MDiv GTS 1970. D 6/20/1970 P 12/1/1970 Bp Chilton R Powell. m 8/10/2013 Angela L Hock c 1. Chr Epis Ch Tulsa OK 2005-2011; Dio Oklahoma Oklahoma City OK 1991-2011, 1977-1980; Oaces Inst Oklahoma City OK 1981-1991; Vic S Aid's Epis Ch Tulsa OK 1977-1981; S Andr's Ch Stillwater OK 1971-1976; Cur S Dunst's Ch Tulsa OK 1970-1972. Auth, "Common Lessons & Parallel Guides For Efm"; Auth, "Practically Chr:"; Auth, "A Prog For Practical Chr," *Active Reflection & Pryr*; Auth, "Venture: Exploring Ideas & Images Of Chr F," *Venture: Exploring Ideas & Images Of Chr Faith*.

BREWER III, Richard Frederick (LI) Prestwick Farm, 2260 County Route 12, Whitehall NY 12887 B Johnson City TN 1947 s Richard & Anne. BA Van 1968; MHA Duke 1973; MDiv GTS 1981. D 9/14/1981 Bp Paul Moore Jr P 3/25/1982 Bp Walter Decoster Dennis Jr. m 4/28/2012 William Albert Davidson c 2. Int Deploy Off Dio Long Island Garden City NY 2010, Stndg Com 2008-2012, Dep to GC 2006-2012, Stndg Com 1994-2002; Stndg Cmsn on Hlth Epis Ch 2006-2012; Vice-Chair NEAC Brooklyn NY 1999-2003; Com on HIV/AIDS Epis Ch 1998-2003; R The Ch Of S Lk and S Matt Brooklyn NY 1986-2010; Cur Trin-St Jn's Ch Hewlett NY 1982-1986; The GTS New York NY 1982; Bd Mem NEAC Washington DC 1995-2004; Chapt Mem Cathd Of The Incarn Garden City NY 1993-1999; Bd Mem Epis Hlth Serv Far Rockaway NY 1986-1998. Hon Cn Cathd of the Incarn 2010; Trst of the Year Untd Hosp Fund of New York 2001.

BREWER, Todd H (Pgh) 4048 Brownsville Rd, Pittsburgh PA 15227 **The GTS New York NY 2015-** B Orlando FL 1984 s Gregory & Laura. BA Laf 2006; MDiv TESM 2009. D 11/12/2009 P 6/2/2010 Bp Michael Smith. m 6/3/2006 Kelly Brewer. Assoc S Ptr's Ch Morristown NJ 2014-2015; Int S Ptr's Epis Ch Brentwood Pittsburgh PA 2010.

BREWIN-WILSON, Debbie (Nwk) St Mary's Church, 85 Conestoga Trl, Sparta NJ 07871 **R S Mary's Ch Sparta NJ 2016-** B Woodbury NJ 1959 d Walter & Florence. Doctor of Mnstry VTS; BSN U of Pennsylvania 1980; MSN Seton Hall U 1983; Cert U of S Andrews 1999; MDiv VTS 2006. D 6/3/2006 P 12/16/2006 Bp George Edward Councell. m 12/20/1980 Bradford Scott Wilson c 2. R Ch Of The Incarn Uppr Marlboro MD 2009-2016; R S Thos Par Croom Uppr Marlboro MD 2009-2016; P-in-c All SS Epis Ch Lakewood NJ 2007-2009; D Trin Epis Ch Cranford NJ 2006.

BREWSTER, John Gurdon (CNY) 376 Shaffer Rd, Newfield NY 14867 **Artist in Res, Sculptor Dio Cntrl NY 2012-2022 Died 4/7/2017** B New York NY 1937 s Carroll & Blandina. Gestalt Ther Inst; BA Hav 1959; The Art Stdt League 1962; BD UTS 1962; STM UTS 1970. D 6/10/1962 P 12/1/1964 Bp Horace W B Donegan. m 6/16/1962 Martha Klippert Brewster c 4. Vic Ch Of The Epiph Trumansburg NY 2003-2017; Epis Ch At Cornell Ithaca NY 1996-1999; Asst. to MLKing Sr. & MLK Jr. Ebenezer Bapt Ch Atlanta GA 1967; Dio Cntrl New York Liverpool NY 1965-1996; Fac Mem Madras Chr Coll Madras India 1963-1964; Asst to: MLKing Sr. MLKing Jr. Ebenezer Bapt Ch Atlanta GA 1961. "No Turning Back," *My Sum w Daddy King*, Orbis Pub, 2007; Artist Sculptor, "Sculptures placed: UTS, The Vatican, Hav, Publ and Priv Collelctions"; Artist Sculptor, "Sculptures placed: UTS, The Vatican, Hav, Publ and Priv Collelctions". Epis Ch and Visual Arts, Fndr 2000-2007. Dn of All SS' Chap U So 2009. gurdonbrewster@gmail.com

BREWSTER, John Pierce (At) 1064 Can Tex Dr, Sewanee TN 37375 B Atlanta GA 1939 s Maurice & Dorothy. BS Georgia Inst of Tech 1962; MDiv VTS 1977. D 6/11/1977 Bp Bennett Jones Sims P 3/1/1978 Bp Charles Judson Child Jr. m 10/9/2010 Emily S Herman. Ch Of The Atone Sandy Sprg GA 1985-2001; R Calv Epis Ch Cleveland MS 1980-1985; Gr Ch Rosedale MS 1980-1985; S Jas Epis Ch Marietta GA 1977-1980.

BREWSTER JR, William (O) 7 Bond Rd, Kittery Point ME 03905 B Hartford CT 1934 s William & Elizabeth. BA U of Texas 1955; MDiv CDSP 1960; MA U Chi 1966; Coll of Preachers 1981. D 6/29/1960 Bp Richard Stanley Merrill Emrich P 1/1/1961 Bp Stephen F Bayne Jr. m 6/17/1966 Arlene Blank Brewster c 3. Dn of Youngstown Dnry Dio Ohio Cleveland 1995-1999, Stndg Com 1987-1994, Com on Ch and Soc 1980-1986; R S Jn's Ch Youngstown OH 1979-1999; Assoc Chr Ch Cranbrook Bloomfield Hills MI 1972-1979; Campus Min Untd Campus Mnstrs Rochester MI 1967-1972; Chapl Lake Forest Coll Lake Forest IL 1965-1966; Chapl Culver Mltry Acad Culver IN 1964-1965; Assoc Chapl Convoc of Amer Ch in Europe - Switzerland 1960-1963. Auth, *Ch Life*, 1984; Auth, *Texts of Synoptic Sources*. Acad Par Cleric, Epis Soc for Mnstry in Hig.

BREYER, Chloe Anne (NY) 1800 Adam Clayton Powell Blvd., Apartment 7B, New York NY 10026 **Assoc S Phil's Ch New York NY 2012-; The Interfaith Cntr of New York New York NY 2007-; Exec Dir The Interfaith Cntr of New York New York NY 2007-; Bd Mem Afghans4Tomorrow 2004-** B Boston MA 1969 d Stephen & Joanna. BA Harv 1992; MDiv GTS 2000. D 6/10/2000 Bp Ronald Hayward Haines P 5/24/2001 Bp Jane Hart Holmes Dixon. m 8/16/1997 Greg Scholl c 2. Assoc S Mary's Manhattanville Epis Ch New York NY 2003-2012; Cathd Of St Jn The Div New York NY 2000-2003; Vol Chapl Red Cross 2001-2002. Contrib, "Violence, Educ, and Intervention: The Human Security of Girls in Afghanistan," *The Gender Imperative: Human Security vs. St Security*, Routledge, 2010; Contrib, "Wmn, Childbearing and Justice," *Challenging the Chr Rt from the Heart of the Gospel*, Beacon Press, 2006; Contrib, "Stndg on Giant's Shoulders," *What Can One Person Do: Faith to Heal a Broken Wrld*, Ch Pub, 2002; Auth, "The Close: A Young Wmn's First Year at Sem," Basic Books, 2000. The Coun on Frgn Relatns 2013. Ba mcl Harv 1992.

BREYFOGLE, Elizabeth Elain (Dal) 511 Foote St., McKinney TX 75069 **D S Ptr's Ch Mc Kinney TX 2014-** B Bay Shore NY 1949 d Clifford & Elizabeth. BSN U of Tennessee 1971. D 11/10/2007 Bp James Monte Stanton. c 3.

BREZNAU, Jack Charles (EMich) PO Box 1882, Caseville MI 48725 B Detroit MI 1927 D 7/1/2001 P 12/29/2001 Bp Edwin Max Leidel Jr. m 9/8/1951 Nancy Ann Breznau c 2.

BREZNAU, Nancy Ann (EMich) PO Box 1882, Caseville MI 48725 B Weehauken NJ 1931 D 7/1/2001 P 12/29/2001 Bp Edwin Max Leidel Jr. m 9/8/1951 Jack Charles Breznau c 3.

BRICE, Jonathan Andrew William (Colo) Christ Episcopal Church, 536 W North St, Aspen CO 81611 **Chr Epis Ch Aspen CO 2012-** B London England 1961 s Dennis & Joyce. Art Fndt Year: Art and Design Harlow Coll 1980; BA Bath Acad of Art 1983; Theol Wycliffe Hall 1992. Trans 11/29/2012 as Priest Bp Robert John O'Neill. m 7/4/1992 Shara LC Brice c 2. rev@christchurchaspen. org

BRICE, Theresa (At) 302 West Avenue, Cedartown GA 30125 **S Jn's Atlanta GA 2017-** B Sumter SC 1948 BA Georgia St U 1995; MBA Merc 1997; MDiv GTS 2004. D 6/5/2004 P 12/11/2004 Bp J Neil Alexander. c 2. S Teresa Acworth GA 2014-2017; S Jas Ch Cedartown GA 2013-2015; S Anne's Epis Ch Atlanta GA 2013-2014; Emm Epis Ch La Grange IL 2008-2013; Assoc R S Chrys's Ch Chicago IL 2004-2008.

BRICKSON, Cynthia Jean (Minn) 905 4th Ave S, Minneapolis MN 55404 B Minneapolis MN 1962 d James & Carol. BA Coll of St Teresa 1984. D 6/20/2015 P 6/21/2016 Bp Brian N Prior. m 6/21/1985 Margaret Ann Gosar c 5.

BRIDGE, Melvin Alden (FtW) 729 Carette Dr, Fort Worth TX 76108 **Chapl All SS' Epis Sch Of Ft Worth Ft Worth TX 1996-** B Vallejo CA 1950 s Lawrence & Nellie. BS Florida St U 1972; MS Florida St U 1973; Reformed TS 1979; MDiv Columbia TS 1982; CAS SWTS 1987. D 6/29/1987 P 11/12/1987 Bp William Hopkins Folwell. m 12/31/1982 Ruth Acreman c 2. R Ch

Of The Trsfg Bat Cave NC 1993-1996; Res Min St. Albans Angl Ch Of Australia Five Dock NSW 1992-1993; Assoc R S Mk's Ch Cocoa FL 1991-1992, Assoc R 1987-1990; Assoc Pstr Raleigh Presb Ch Memphis TN 1982-1984. fatherbridge@aseschool.org

BRIDGE, Michael James (WK) B Pittsburgh PA 1978 s Charles & Loretta. BA U Pgh 2000; MDiv TESM 2004. D 6/12/2004 Bp Robert William Duncan P 12/18/2004 Bp James Marshall Adams Jr. m 7/31/2004 Bonnie F Bridge c 3. R/Vic S Jn's Ch Ulysses KS 2004-2010.

BRIDGE, Peter James (NJ) 1509 Esther Ln, Yardley PA 19067 **Assoc Trin Cathd Trenton NJ 2002-, Assoc 2002-; Clincl Dir Samar Counslg Cntr Philadelphia PA 1982-** B Johannesburg ZA 1942 s Basil & Kathleen. BA U of So Afr Pretoria ZA 1972; MSW Rutgers The St U of New Jersey 1975; DMin Lancaster TS 1984. Rec 6/21/2002 as Priest Bp David Bruce Joslin. m 8/27/1977 Jane Q Anderson c 4. Samar Counslg Cntr Blue Bell PA 2005-2013. Co-Auth, "Pstr Correspondence," *Dictionary of Pstr Care and Counslg*, Abingdon, 1990; Auth, "Documentation of Psych Supervision," *Psych in Priv Pract*, Haworth Press, 1990; Auth, "A Record Form for Psych Supervision," *Innovations in Clincl Pract*, Profsnl Resource Exch, 1988. Samar Sprt Awd Samar Counslg Cntr/ Philadelphia 2008.

BRIDGEMOHAN, Areeta D (Mich) **Cur Chr Ch Grosse Pointe Grosse Pointe Farms MI 2015-** B Georgetown Guyana 1982 d Harripaul & Dhanmatie. BA McGill U 2004; MPH U MI 2009; MDiv Trin - Toronto Sch 2015. D 6/13/2015 P 12/12/2015 Bp Wendell Nathaniel Gibbs Jr. abridgemohan@christchurchgp. org

BRIDGERS, Anne (SanD) 1114 9th St, Coronado CA 92118 **Chr Ch Coronado CA 2014-; Vic Chr Ch San Pablo FL 2006-** B Montgomery AL 1951 d Eulon & Elizabeth. U of Montevallo 1971; BS U of Alabama 1974; MDiv VTS 1998. D 5/30/1998 P 1/25/1999 Bp Charles Farmer Duvall. m 8/8/1981 John Dixon Bridgers c 4. R S Ptr's Ch In The Great Vlly Malvern PA 2008-2014; Chr Epis Ch Ponte Vedra FL 2006-2008; S Jn's Cathd Jacksonville FL 2001-2006; Trin Epis Ch Mobile AL 1998-2001. rector@christchurchcoronado.org

BRIDGES, David Leslie (Okla) **Crt-Appointed Spec Advoc for Minor Chld CASA of NE Oklahoma 2017-; Vic Dio Oklahoma Oklahoma City OK 2016-, Disciplinary Bd Mem 2016-; Vic S Andr's Ch Grove OK 2016-** D 11/1/2014 P 5/14/2015 Bp Barry Leigh Beisner.

BRIDGES, Melva Gayle (Okla) 12719 S Couts Dr, Mustang OK 73064 **D Epis Ch Of The Resurr Oklahoma City OK 1988-** B Hobart OK 1935 d Melvin & Bessie. MA Cntrl St U. D 6/20/1984 Bp Gerald Nicholas Mcallister. m 6/14/1953 John Wesley Vernon Bridges. Cleric S Jas Epis Ch Oklahoma City OK 1984-1988. Auth, "Trng Fac As Developmental Gdnc Facilitators"; Auth, "Dealing w Isolation In The Classroom Bldg The Affective Triangle: Parents," *Teachers & Kids*.

BRIDGES, Nancy Kilbourn (Okla) 408 Ridge Rd, Edmond OK 73034 **D S Mary's Ch Edmond OK 2001-** B Litchfield CT 1944 d Norton & Helen. U of Cntrl Oklahoma; BS OH SU 1967. D 6/16/2001 Bp Robert Manning Moody. m 7/6/1968 Timothy Robert Bridges.

BRIDGES, Penelope Maud (SanD) 6935 Camino Pacheco, San Diego CA 92111 **Dn Cathd Ch Of S Paul San Diego CA 2014-** B Belfast IE 1958 d Gibbon & Alice. BA U of Cambridge 1979; MDiv Ya Berk 1997. D 6/21/1997 P 2/2/1998 Bp Douglas Edwin Theuner. c 2. R S Fran Epis Ch Great Falls VA 2003-2014; Asst R Gr Epis Ch Alexandria VA 1997-2003. bridgesp@stpaulcathedral.org

BRIDGFORD, Peter W (WNY) 18 Harbour Pointe Cmn, Buffalo NY 14202 **Ret 2000-** B Indianapolis IN 1934 s Oral & Agnes. BA NWU 1956; MDiv CDSP 1968. D 6/28/1968 P 1/11/1969 Bp Lauriston L Scaife. m 7/2/1960 Belmore H Bridgford c 1. R S Jn's Gr Ch Buffalo NY 1974-2000; Vic Ch Of The H Comm Lake View NY 1970-1974; Cur S Lk's Epis Ch Jamestown NY 1968-1970.

BRIDGFORD, Richard Oliver (SVa) 707 Steiner Way, Norfolk VA 23502 **Magnolia Gardens Inc. Norfolk 2000-; Trin Woods Inc. Norfolk 1991-; Pres Partnr in Mgmt Inc. 1988-; Urban Mnstry Hsng Dvlp. Corp Norfolk VA 1981-; Norfolk Urban Outreach Mnstry 1975-** B Chicago IL 1941 s Archie & Helen. BA Old Dominion U 1965; MDiv Sewanee: The U So, TS 1968. D 6/22/1968 P 6/2/1969 Bp George P Gunn. R Ch Of The Epiph Norfolk VA 1993-2013; Int 1988-1993; Int Ch Of H Apos Virginia Bch VA 1990-1992; Norfolk Urban Outreach Mnstry Norfolk VA 1986-2013, 1975-1978; Int S Jas Epis Ch Portsmouth VA 1985-1986; Int S Thos Epis Ch Chesapeake VA 1983-1985; Int S Mk's Ch Hampton VA 1982-1983; Int S Steph's Ch Norfolk VA 1981-1982; Int S Jn's Ch Suffolk VA 1979-1980; Int S Aid's Ch Virginia Bch VA 1978-1979; Asst to R Ch Of The Gd Shpd Norfolk VA 1968-1974; Dn - Convoc III Dio Sthrn Virginia Newport News VA 2005-2011. DuBose Awd for Serv STUSo 2005.

BRIDGFORTH, David Elgin (USC) 900 Calhoun St, Columbia SC 29201 **Died 12/5/2016** B Wilmington DE 1943 s David & Grace. BA Newberry Coll 1965; MDiv VTS 1969. D 6/29/1969 P 6/25/1970 Bp John Adams Pinckney. m 8/8/1970 Sandra Ann Bridgforth. R S Tim's Ch Columbia SC 1987-2006; Dio Upper So Carolina Columbia SC 1987-1989, Chair BEC 1986, Chair Ch Pension Fund Com 1984-1985, Bp'S Coun 1979-1983, Dept Of Missions 1977-1979; S Steph's Ch S Steph SC 1977-1979; S Matt's Epis Ch Spartanburg

SC 1972-1987; Vic Ch Of The Adv Spartanburg SC 1972-1976; Vic Ch Of The Ascen Seneca SC 1970-1972. Auth, "Cats & Birds & Blessings Of God". Dio Upper So Carolina 1987-1989. stgeorgee@bellsouth.net

BRIGGLE, Justin David (Tex) **Cur S Mk's Ch Beaumont TX 2016-** B Fort Worth TX 1979 s Joe & Patricia. B.S. U of No Texas 2001; M.A. The U of Texas at Austin 2003; Ph.D. The U of Texas at Austin 2005; M.Div. Sewanee: The U So, TS 2016. D 6/25/2016 Bp C Andrew Doyle P 2/27/2017 Bp Jeff Fisher. m 1/3/2004 Rebecca Dawn Brown c 2. jbriggle@stmarksbeaumont.org

BRIGGS, Barbara K (NJ) 306 S Main St, Pennington NJ 08534 **S Matt's Ch Pennington NJ 2015-; COM Dio Connecticut Meriden CT 2012-, BEC 2008-2012** B Boston MA 1961 d Gilbert & Katharine. ABS Smith 1983; BA Universite Catholique De Lyon FR 1996. D 6/2/2007 Bp Gordon Scruton P 12/15/2007 Bp Andrew Donnan Smith. m 9/1/2002 Paul R Briggs c 1. P-in-c S Alb's Ch Simsbury CT 2011-2015; Asst R Trin Epis Ch Hartford CT 2007-2011; Mssnr for Chr Formation Dio Wstrn Massachusetts Springfield 2000-2006. bakbriggs@yahoo.com

BRIGGS, Lyn Zill (U) 661 Redondo Ave, Salt Lake City UT 84105 **Vic Dio Utah Salt Lake City UT 2009-, 2006-2007, 2006, Yth Mnstry T/F 2013-, VP, Dioc Coun 2012-2013, Stwdshp Com 2012-, Dioc Coun, Exec Com 2010-, EFM Coordntr 2007-** B Sioux City IA 1955 d Marcus & Marilyn. Concordia Coll 1974; BA U of Nebraska 1977; Epis TS at Claremont 2004; MDiv CDSP 2006. D 6/10/2006 P 1/20/2007 Bp Carolyn Tanner Irish. m 5/21/1977 Nathan H Briggs c 2. Assoc S Paul's Ch Salt Lake City UT 2007-2009; Par Adm All SS Ch Salt Lake City UT 1989-2004. Auth, "God's Word My Voice," Ch Pub, 2015.

BRIGGS, Michael (Ark) PO Box 954, Granby CO 80446 **S Barth's Epis Ch Ft Smith AR 2016-** B West Memphis AR 1964 s Jerry & Clarice. AA Shelby St Cmnty Coll 2001; BS Chr Brothers U 2002; MDiv Memphis TS 2009. D 3/11/2011 P 9/25/2011 Bp Larry Benfield. m 6/26/2010 Timothy White. P Epis Ch Of S Jn The Bapt Granby CO 2013-2016; All SS Epis Ch Paragould AR 2012-2013; Ch Of The Gd Shpd Forrest City AR 2012; S Mk's Epis Ch Jonesboro AR 2011-2012.

BRIGGS II, Paul R (Ct) 14 Melody Ln, East Longmeadow MA 01028 **Dn Hartford Dnry Manchester CT 2011-; Bd Dir Seabury Ret Cmnty Bloomfield CT 2008-** B Hartland ME 1954 s Paul & Ida. BA Mt Allison U 1976; MDiv GTS 1981. D 6/18/1981 Bp Frederick Barton Wolf P 12/18/1981 Bp Philip Alan Smith. m 9/1/2002 Barbara K King c 4. R S Mary's Epis Ch Manchester CT 2008-2015; R S Mk's Epis Ch E Longmeadow MA 1986-2008; Asst S Dav's Ch Austin TX 1983-1986; Int Par Of S Jas Ch Keene NH 1981-1983. pbriggs@doaneacademy.org

BRIGHAM, Richard Daniel (At) 208 Edgewater Way, Peachtree City GA 30269 B Kansas City MO 1940 s Richard & Mary. BA U of Missouri 1962; MA U of Missouri 1967; BD EDS 1968. D 6/14/1968 Bp Robert Rae Spears Jr P 2/1/1969 Bp Edward Randolph Welles II. m 8/29/1964 Vivian Ruth Brigham. R S Andr's In-The-Pines Epis Ch Peachtree City GA 1983-2006; All SS Ch W Plains MO 1976-1983, Vic 1974-1975; R Gr And H Trin Cathd Kansas City MO 1972-1974; Chapl St Trng Sch For Girls Chillicothe MO 1969-1972; P-in-c Gr Epis Ch Chillicothe MO 1968-1972; S Phil's Ch Trenton MO 1968-1972. Fllshp S Alb & S Sergius.

BRIGHT, Barbara Pamela (WNC) Episcopal Church of the Redeemer, 502 W Sumter St, Shelby NC 28150 B Marion NC 1959 d Hall & Barbara. BA Appalachian St U 1981; BSW Appalachian St U 2000. D 1/28/2006 Bp Porter Taylor.

BRIGHT, Carl Connell (CGC) 198 Beardsley Court, Muscle Shoals AL 35661 B Montgomery AL 1938 s Henry & Asa. BS U of Alabama 1960; MDiv Sewanee: The U So, TS 1976. D 5/31/1976 P 12/17/1976 Bp Furman Charles Stough. m 8/12/1960 Caroline Mushat Bright c 3. Int Assoc R St Thos Epis Ch Huntsville AL 2008-2009; Int S Mary's Epis Ch Jasper AL 2007-2008; Int Chr Epis Ch Albertville AL 2004-2005; Dio Cntrl Gulf Coast Pensacola FL 1999-2003, Cmncatn Com 1999-2001, Stndg Com 1995-1998, Missions Cmsn 1989-1994; R Chr The King Epis Ch Santa Rosa Bch FL 1991-2003; Non-par 1989-1990; R Gr Ch Anniston AL 1988-1989; Dept Of CE So Carolina Charleston SC 1986-1988, Dioc Coun 1985-1988; R S Jn's Ch Florence SC 1984-1988; Dioc Coun Dio Alabama Birmingham 1982-1984, Chair - Dept Of Camp Mcdowell 1981-1984; R Gr Ch Sheffield AL 1978-1984; Cur Ch Of The Ascen Montgomery AL 1976-1978.

BRIGHT SR, Dee Wellington (Okla) 511 South Cabin Lake Drive, San Antonio TX 78244 **Gr Epis Ch Ponca City OK 2013-** B River Cess LR 1961 s William & Yansawon. BA Cuttington U 1986; MA Epis TS of the SW 1999. Trans 6/1/1999 as Priest Bp James Edward Folts. m 11/7/1987 Monyue Bright c 3. S Ptr's Ch Springfield MA 2003-2012; R S Phil's Ch San Antonio TX 1999-2003.

BRIGHT, John Adams (Cal) 812 Southwest Saint Clair Ave. Apt 1, Portland OR 97209 **Ret 1989-** B Portland OR 1927 s George & Helen. BA Pr 1949; MDiv CDSP 1956. D 6/29/1956 P 1/8/1957 Bp Benjamin D Dagwell. m 4/6/1975 Sandra J Bright c 3. Int Par of St Clem Honolulu HI 1990-1991; R S Fran' Epis Ch San Francisco CA 1983-1989; Dn S Andr's Cathd Honolulu HI 1978-1983; R Chr Ch Par Lake Oswego OR 1965-1978; R Trin Ch Bend OR 1962-1965;

Serv Igreja Epis Anglicana do Brasil 1961-1962; Vic S Andr's Ch Portland OR 1957-1960; Asst S Mk's Epis Par Medford OR 1956-1957. Auth, *Carry A Story*. MDiv w hon CDSP 1956.

BRIGHT, Patrick Edmund (Okla) 11901 Maple Hollow Ct, Oklahoma City OK 73120 **Assoc R All Souls Epis Ch Oklahoma City OK 1995-** B Ottawa 1953 s John & Mona. BA U of Kings Coll Halifax NS CA 1977; MDiv U Tor CA 1980. Trans 4/1/1995 Bp Robert Manning Moody. m 6/20/1981 Rhea Nadine Bright c 5. Serv Angl Ch of Can 1989-1995; Assoc R S Jn's Ch Savannah GA 1984-1989; Serv Angl Ch of Can 1980-1984. PB Soc of Can.

BRIGHT, Wheigar J (NC) PO Box 858, Yanceyville NC 27379 **P-in-c S Lk's Ch Eden NC 2015-** B Liberia 1958 s John & Julia. BA Cuttington U 1986; MDiv Nash 1991. Trans 7/19/2010 Bp Michael B Curry. m 1/14/1995 Frances Bright c 2. S Lk's Epis Ch Yanceyville NC 2010-2013.

BRIGHTMAN, Dorothy Louise (RI) 17 N Country Club Dr, Warwick RI 02888 **D Ch of the Epiph Rumford RI 2012-** B Providence RI 1935 d Lester & Marion. BS Tufts U 1957; MA U of Connecticut 1964; EdD U NC 1979; MS Simmons Coll 1986; Rhode-Island Sch for Mnstrs 1997. D 5/25/2006 Bp Gerry Wolf. D S Lk's Epis Ch E Greenwich RI 2006-2012.

BRILL, Steven G (Oly) St Luke's Episcopal Church, PO Box 1294, Elma WA 98541 **P S Lk's Epis Ch Elma WA 1999-** B Salt Lake City UT 1957 s Paul & Geraldine. AA S Jn 1975; BA Bethany Coll 1979. D 3/15/1999 Bp Sanford Zangwill Kaye Hampton P 9/29/1999 Bp Vincent Waydell Warner. m 5/30/1992 Elizabeth Murphy.

BRIMM, Martha Carol (NC) 7 Surrey Ln, Durham NC 27707 **Assoc Chap Of The Cross Chap Hill NC 2013-; Chapl Franklin Correctional Cntr 2012-** B Macon GA 1946 d Hugh & Verna. BS Duke 1968; MS U of Washington 1972; MDiv Candler TS Emory U 2010; MDiv Candler TS at Emory U 2010; Dip Ang Stud GTS 2011; Dip Ang Stud The GTS 2011. D 6/18/2011 P 4/28/2012 Bp Michael B Curry. m 11/25/1978 Richard Clark c 1. S Jos's Ch Durham NC 2011-2013. Cert of Appreciation Franklin Correctional Cntr 2015; Vol of the Year Franklin Correctional Cntr 2012.

BRINDLEY, Thomas (Cal) 704 Sutro Ave, Novato CA 94947 B Port Arthur TX 1952 s Melvin & Geraldine. Texas A&M U 1971; BS Lamar U 1975; MDiv VTS 1978. D 6/21/1978 Bp Roger Howard Cilley P 6/1/1979 Bp James Milton Richardson. m 9/14/1991 Lorna Brindley c 3. R S Columba's Ch Inverness CA 1994-2010; R S Cuth's Epis Ch Houston TX 1981-1994; The Great Cmsn Fndt Houston TX 1978-1990; S Lk's Ch Livingston TX 1978-1980; S Paul's Epis Ch Woodville TX 1978-1980. frthomas@upwardcallministries.org

BRINKMAN, Charles Reed (Pa) 219 Hanover Rd, Phoenixville PA 19460 B Pittsburgh PA 1947 s Albert & Anna. BS Indiana U of Pennsylvania 1973; MDiv EDS 1977; DMin Sewanee: The U So, TS 2004. D 9/11/1977 Bp Robert Bracewell Appleyard P 3/18/1978 Bp William Hawley Clark. m 9/7/1975 Paula J Hansen c 2. R S Jas Ch of Kingsessing Philadelphia PA 1981-2007; Vic Ch Delaware City DE 1977-1981; Cur Imm Ch On The Green New Castle DE 1977-1981.

BRINKMANN, Mark Ransom (SC) All Saints Episcopal Church, 3001 Meeting St, Hilton Head Island SC 29926 **Assoc All SS Ch Hilton Hd Island SC 2007-; Mem, Dioc Coun So Carolina Charleston SC 2013-** B Cincinnati OH 1956 s James & Martha. BA U of Iowa 1980; MDiv SWTS 1985. D 6/14/1986 P 1/17/1987 Bp James Winchester Montgomery. m 8/20/1988 Kendell Leann Brinkmann c 3. R S Jas Epis Ch Midvale UT 1999-2007; R S Andr's Ch Chelan WA 1993-1999; Assoc S Mths' Par Whittier CA 1986-1993; Mem, Liturg and Mus Com Dio Utah Salt Lake City UT 2005-2007, Co-chair, COM 2000-2005; Chair, Mnstry Dvlpmt Com Dio Spokane Spokane WA 1997-1999, Mem, COM 1996-1999; Mem, Liturg and Mus Cmsn Dio Los Angeles Los Angeles CA 1990-1993. ADLMC, Associated Parishes. saintsassociate@hargray.com

BRINKMOELLER, Leonard Joseph (WMich) 312 Maple Street, Paw Paw MI 49079 B Cincinnati OH 1942 s Leonard & Marie. Ford; BA S Chas Sem Carthagena OH 1965; MA U of Dayton 1968. Rec 11/1/1983 as Priest Bp William Cockburn Russell Sheridan. m 5/2/1980 Marla Rae Brinkmoeller. R Trin Epis Ch Marshall MI 2000-2008; R H Trin Epis Ch Manistee MI 1993-2000; R S Steph's Epis Ch Hobart IN 1984-1993; Serv RC Ch 1965-1979.

BRINSON, Katherine Herrington (Ga) 4227 Columbia Rd, Martinez Branch GA 30907 **Gr Ch Waycross GA 2011-** B Millen GA 1952 d Edwin & Anne. BS Georgia Sthrn U 1975; MA Georgia Sthrn U 1978; EdS Georgia Sthrn U 1982; Cert Ang Stud Sewanee: The U So, TS 2007; Cert Ang Stud Sewanee: The U So, TS 2007. D 2/3/2007 P 9/8/2007 Bp Henry Irving Louttit. Epis Ch Of S Mary Magd Louisville GA 2010-2011; S Mich's Ch Waynesboro GA 2008-2010; D Ch Of Our Sav Augusta GA 2007.

BRION, Theresa Markley (Md) 5726 Colfax Ave, Alexandria VA 22311 **Goodwin Hse Baileys Crossroads Falls Ch VA 2016-; St Johns Evang Luth Cumberland MD 2016-; S Geo's Epis Ch Mt Savage MD 2012-** B Elizabethtown KY 1958 d Robert & Augusta. BS Longwood U 1980; JD W&L 1985; Cert Florida Inst of Tech 1997; MDiv EDS 2009. D 2/13/2010 Bp Neff Powell P 10/2/2010 Bp John L Rabb. m 5/26/2001 Denis J Brion. Vic Ch Of The H Cross Cumberland MD 2012-2014; Bishops' Dep for Wstrn Maryland Dio Maryland Baltimore MD 2010-2016, Cmsn on Mnstrs 2010-2015; Ldrshp Team Living Stones Partnership USA & Can 2014-2015; EAM Kingsport TN 2012-2015; Coordntr Living Stones Partnership USA & Can 2010-2015. Cert in Mnstry Dvlpmt Living Stones Partnership 2013; Bp Atwood of Arizona Prize EDS 2009; St Georges Coll--Jerusalem Schlrshp EDS and St Georges Coll 2009; Wm Ellis Scull Prize EDS 2007. tbrion@goodwinhouse.org

BRIONES, Miguel Angel (Chi) 5101 W Devon Ave, Chicago IL 60646 B Atlixco Puebla Mexico 1966 s Leonardo & Lidia. D 8/31/2011 Bp Jeff Lee. m 3/4/1995 Norma Catalina Cid c 2. Cristo Rey Chicago IL 2011-2012; S Mk's Epis Ch Glen Ellyn IL 1998-2011.

BRISBANE, Paul Owen (Colo) 513 N. Union City Rd., Coldwater MI 49036 B Kalamazoo MI 1936 s William & Viola. BA Wstrn Michigan U 1958; MDiv CDSP 1962. D 6/21/1962 Bp Charles Bennison Sr P 5/23/1963 Bp Conrad H Gesner. m 7/9/1983 Judith Elaine Meyer c 4. Supply P Dio Wstrn Michigan Kalamazoo MI 2001-2016, Supply P 2001-, Supply P 1977-2001; R S Jas' Epis Ch Meeker CO 1991-2001; Vic Ascen-On-The-Prairie Epis Ch Colby KS 1989-1991; Dn NW Epis Reg Mnstry Goodland KS 1989-1990; S Paul's Epis Ch Goodland KS 1985-1991; P-in-c St Judes Epis Cmnty Hoxie KS 1985-1991; Vic Ch Of The H Comm Lake View NY 1975-1977; Ch Of The Ascen Neodesha KS 1968-1975; Vic Ch Of The Epiph Independence KS 1968-1975; P-in-c Ch of the Gd Shpd Fredonia KS 1968-1975; R Trin Epis Ch Mineral Point WI 1965-1968; Vic Trin Epis Ch Platteville WI 1964-1968; Vic Emm Ch Lancaster WI 1964-1965; H Trin Epis Ch Prairie Du Chien WI 1964-1965; P-in-c Adv Chap Mosher SD 1963-1964; Chapl Bp Hare Mssn Hm Mssn SD 1963-1964; Chapl Of Rosebud Boarding Sch Rosebud Epis Mssn Mssn SD 1963-1964; Cur S Paul's Ch Brookings SD 1962-1963; Dep, GC Dio Wstrn Kansas Hutchinson KS 1988, Dioc Coun 1987-1991; Dioc Coun Dio Kansas Topeka KS 1972-1975, Pres, Stndg Com 1972-1975, Dn, SE Convoc 1969-1975. RWF 1964-2000.

BRISBIN, James A (Alb) 2647 Brookview Rd., Castleton NY 12033 **S Dav's Epis Ch Castleton NY 2013-** B Rotterdam New York 1961 s Phillip & Julie. D 5/10/2008 P 12/15/2012 Bp William Howard Love. m 8/18/1984 Laurie Brisbin c 5.

BRISON, William Stanly (Ct) 2 Scott Ave, Bury BL9 9RS Great Britain (UK) **Ret 1998-** B West Chester PA 1929 s William & Marion. BS Alfred U 1951; Westcott Hse Theol Coll Cambridge 1955; MDiv Ya Berk 1957; STM Ya Berk 1971. D 5/29/1957 Bp William A Lawrence P 12/1/1957 Bp Robert McConnell Hatch. m 6/16/1951 Marguerite Brison c 4. Team R Pendleton Team Mnstry 1994-1998; Serv Ch Of Engl 1972-1994; R Emm Epis Ch Stamford CT 1969-1972; Vic Chr Ch Bethany CT 1957-1959. "A Tale of Two Visits to Chechnya," Self-Pub, 2005. CMS 1992. Hon Cn Manchester Cathd 1982.

BRISSON JR, James L (Az) 868 Satinwood Ct, Fayetteville NC 28312 **Chapl US-A Chapl 1993-** B St Paul MN 1959 s James & Helen. AA City Colleges of Chicago 1985; BS U of Maryland 1987; MDiv Trin Evang DS 1990; MDiv Trin Evang DS 1990; MA Trin Evang DS 1990. D 6/6/2009 P 12/9/2009 Bp Kirk Stevan Smith. m 9/19/1981 Tina C Brisson c 4.

BRISTOL II, Henry Platt (NJ) St David's Church, 90 S Main St, Cranbury NJ 08512 **D S Dav's Ch Cranbury NJ 2012-** B Princeton NJ 1953 s Lee & Louise. BA Bow 1976; MA U of Virginia 1983; Cert Sch for Deacons 2012. D 5/5/2012 Bp George Edward Councell. m 10/22/1983 Susan Pikaart Bristol c 3.

BRISTOL, Joan Esther (Ore) 2529 Bel Abbes Ave, Medford OR 97504 **D S Lk's Ch Grants Pass OR 1988-** B Grants Pass OR 1945 d Fayette & Esther. BA OR SU 1967; BS OR SU 1969; MS U of Oregon 1982. D 6/29/1988 Bp Robert Louis Ladehoff. NAAD.

BRITCHER, Sharon Ann (CFla) 1010 Pennsylvania Ave, Fort Pierce FL 34950 B Daytona Beach FL 1946 d Clyde & Majorie. D 6/19/1999 Bp John Wadsworth Howe. m 9/16/1975 Edward Stanley Britcher c 1. D S Andr's Epis Ch Ft Pierce FL 1999-2003, D 1999-.

BRITNELL, Offie Wayne (Ak) 18609 S. Lowrie Loop, Eagle River AK 99577 B Hackleburg AL 1943 s Offie & Constance. Auburn U; U of Alaska; U of Maryland; EFM Sewanee: The U So, TS 1989; Dio Alaska 1997. D 6/20/1998 Bp Mark Lawrence Macdonald P 8/7/1999 Bp Cabell Tennis. m 12/16/1967 Gussie Mae Britnell c 3. P/R S Christophers Ch Anchorage AK 2001-2008.

BRITO, Antonio P (At) 1015 Old Roswell Rd, Roswell GA 30076 **Hisp Vic S Dav's Ch Roswell GA 2011-** B Dominican Republic 1959 s Antonio & Ramona. Santo Tomas de Aquino 1987. Rec 2/2/2011 Bp J Neil Alexander. m 6/14/2003 Roxanna Jacqueline Brito c 2.

BRITO, Napoleon Ramon (DR) Box 764, Santo Domingo Dominican Republic **Asst S Mk's Haina 1993-** B Salcedo 1944 s Jose & Maria. LTh S Thos De Aquino Sem 1972; Instituto De Catequesis 1977; LMFT San Pietro In Latere U 1985. Rec 12/1/1993 as Priest Bp Julio Cesar Holguin-Khoury. m 8/19/1990 Nelly Mercedes Martinez c 2. Dio The Dominican Republic (Iglesia Epis Dominicana) Gazcue Santo Domingo 1993-2013.

BRITT, Diane (LI) St Ann's Church, 257 Middle Rd, Sayville NY 11782 **R S Ann's Ch Sayville NY 2012-** B Greenville TX 1952 d Patrick & Teni. BS Texas A&M U 1975; BS Texas A&M U 1977; MDiv VTS 2002. D 6/22/2002 P 3/9/2003 Bp Michael B Curry. R S Lk's Ch Katonah NY 2005-2012; Asst Ch Of The Gd Shpd Rocky Mt NC 2002-2005. motherdiane@saint-anns.org

BRITT, Larry (WNC) 236 Camelot Dr, Morganton NC 28655 **Ed Advsr Sewanee U So TS Sewanee TN 1991-** B Montgomery AL 1938 s Albert & Mary-Glenn. BA Huntingdon Coll 1960; MDiv Sewanee: The U So, TS 1986. D 8/9/1986 Bp Quintin Ebenezer Primo Jr P 2/28/1987 Bp William Gillette Weinhauer. m 5/22/1976 Martha Lee Britt c 4. R St Mary's and St Steph's Epis Ch Morganton NC 1998-2006; R All Faith Epis Ch Charlotte Hall MD 1993-1998; R S Andr Mt Holly NC 1987-1993; S Andr Ch Mt Holly NC 1986-1993. Cmnty of S Mary 1987. Distinguished Flying Cross USAF 1965.

BRITT, Marc Lawrence (WA) 2 Amy Ct, Pittsfield MA 01201 B Hampton VA 1950 s Cecil & Katherine. BA U of Maryland 1973; MA W Virginia U 1976; RPI 1979; MDiv EDS 1990. D 6/9/1990 Bp Ronald Hayward Haines P 12/16/1990 Bp Otis Charles. m 10/12/2013 Frances Ann Hills. CLP Chapl Trin Wall St Cler Ldrshp Proj W Cornwall CT 2008-2011; R St Johns Broad Creek Ft Washington MD 1999-2013; R Ch Of The Redeem Lorain OH 1996-1999; R All SS Ch Oakley Av MD 1990-1996. Auth, "Bk Revs: Love Set Free," Epis Life; Auth, "Bk Revs: By Way Of The Heat The Word Is Very Near You," Epis Life; Auth, "Bk Revs: We Preach Chr Crucified," Epis Life.

BRITT, Sarah Eugenia Swiss (At) 253 Lake Somerset Dr Nw, Marietta GA 30064 B Birmingham AL 1940 d Harold & Sadie. EFM; U of Alabama; U of Florida. D 10/18/1998 Bp Onell Asiselo Soto. m 2/25/1961 Pope Patterson Britt.

BRITT, Stephen (Fla) San Jose Episcopal, 7423 San Jose Blvd., Jacksonville FL 32217 **R San Jose Epis Ch Jacksonville FL 2006-** B Fort Wayne IN 1969 s Larry & Susan. BA Erskine Coll 1991; MA U of So Carolina 1993; MDiv Sewanee: The U So, TS 1996. D 6/15/1996 Bp Rogers Sanders Harris P 2/9/1997 Bp John Bailey Lipscomb. m 12/17/1994 Carol Britt c 1. Assoc The Ch Of The Gd Shpd Augusta GA 1999-2006; Asst H Innoc Epis Ch Valrico FL 1996-1999. Auth, "Encouragement, Hope, And Relatns," From The Mtn, 2000; Auth, "All In A Days Wk For God," Living Ch, 2000; Auth, "Young Cler Discuss New Ways To Share Faith," Living Ch, 1999; Auth, "The Prophet Of Adv," Sewanee Theol Revs, 1998.

BRITTON, John Clay (Chi) 680 Madrona Ave S, Salem OR 97302 **Non-par 1986-** B Bellefonte PA 1956 s Joseph & Jean. BA Ham 1978; MDiv Ya Berk 1981; Willamette U 1988. D 6/12/1981 Bp Dean Theodore Stevenson P 1/1/1982 Bp Charlie Fuller Mcnutt Jr. m 10/18/1981 Sara Ruth Britton. Cur S Mk's Barrington IL 1982-1986; Cathd Ch Of S Steph Harrisburg PA 1981-1982; Dio Cntrl Pennsylvania Harrisburg PA 1981-1982. Auth, "Soc Sci Revs"; Auth, "Population Rel Ideology," & Economical Efficency A Case Study Of The.

BRITTON, Joseph Harp (RG) St. Michael and All Angels Church, 601 Montano Road, NW, Albuquerque NM 87107 **S Mich And All Ang Ch Albuquerque NM 2015-; Bd Mem The Friends Of Cbury Cathd In The Untd States Washington DC 2011-** B Fort Collins CO 1960 s Charles & Maxine. AB Harv 1982; MDiv GTS 1989; ThD Institut Catholique De Paris 2002. D 6/8/1989 Bp William Carl Frey P 12/9/1989 Bp Richard Frank Grein. m 7/17/1982 Karla Marie Britton c 1. Chr Ch New Haven CT 2014-2015; Pres and Dn Ya Berk New Haven CT 2003-2014; Convoc of Epis Ch in Europe Paris 2003; Cn Mssnr, Convoc of Amer Ch in Europe The Amer Cathd of the H Trin Paris 75008 1998-2003; R All Souls Par In Berkeley Berkeley CA 1993-1996; Kellogg Fell Epis Chapl At Harvard & Radcliffe Cambridge MA 1991-1993; Asst R S Paul's Ch Dedham MA 1991-1993; Assoc R S Mich's Ch New York NY 1989-1991; Advsry Bd CDSP Berkeley CA 1995-1996; Bd Mem Berkeley Cbury Fndt Berkeley CA 1994-1996; Bd Mem California Counslg Inst San Francisco CA 1994-1996. Auth, "Abraham Heschel and the Phenomenon of Piety," T & T Clark, 2013; Auth, "The Berkeley Rite," The Serious Bus of Wrshp, T & T Clark, 2010; Ed, "Toward a Theol of Ldrshp," ATR, 2009; Auth, "The Breadth of Orthodoxy: On Phillips Brooks," One Lord, One Faith, One Baptism, Eerdmans, 2006; Auth, "The Evangelicity of the Episcopate," ATR, 2003; Auth, "Piety & Moral Conciousness," ATR, 1999; Auth, "Dispersed Authority," Sewanee Theol Revs/Angl and Epis Hist, 1999. Assoc Ed, ATR 2004-2009; Coun of Epis Sem Deans 2003; Soc of S Jn the Evang 1992. Cmnty Bd Manhattan Borough Pres 2012; DD GTS 2004; Fell Allin Fellowships: Bossey Ecum Inst 1998; Fell ECF 1998; Fell Scaife Anderson 1997. joeb@all-angels.com

BRITTON SR, Judith Ann (NMich) 365 Kirkpatrick Ln, Gwinn MI 49841 **D H Innoc Epis Ch Little Lake MI 2001-** B Escanaba MI 1938 d Oren & Katherine. AD Nthrn Michigan U; Dio Nthrn Michigan 2001. D 7/1/2001 Bp James Arthur Kelsey. m 9/7/1957 Robert Britton c 3. Soc of the Comp of the H Cross 2004.

BRITTON JR, Richard (Tenn) 509 Laurel Park Dr, Nashville TN 37205 B Pittsburgh PA 1951 s Richard & Mildred. BA U Pgh 1975; MDiv GTS 1978. D 5/24/1978 Bp Robert Bracewell Appleyard P 5/5/1979 Bp William Carl Frey. m 7/20/1985 Donna F Britton c 2. R S Ann's Ch Nashville TN 2008-2017; Asst S Lk's Epis Ch Atlanta GA 1999-2008; Cn Trin Cathd Columbia SC 1996-1999; R Ch Of The Incarn Atlanta GA 1990-1996; Dio Tennessee Nashville TN 1987-1988; Part time Adj Instr Vanderbilt DS 1984-1987; Coll Epis Chapl S Anselm's Epis Ch Nashville TN 1980-1989; P-in-c Ch Of The H Redeem Denver CO 1978-1980.

BRO, Andrew Harmon (Chi) Po Box 111, Mount Carroll IL 61053 B Chicago IL 1930 s Albin & Margueritte. BA Denison U 1956; SWTS 1957; BD U Chi 1957; MA U of Iowa 1970. D 6/15/1957 Bp Charles L Street P 12/21/1957 Bp Gerald Francis Burrill. m 7/28/1956 Adalu Bro c 2. Gr Ch Boone IA 1997-1999; 1968-1996; Chapl S Katharine's Sch Davenport IA 1967-1968; Chapl Shimer Coll Waukegan IL 1959-1964; Cur S Aug's Epis Ch Wilmette IL 1957-1959.

BROACH, Merrill Kilburn (Kan) 3401 Plymouth Pl, New Orleans LA 70131 **Died 7/22/2016** B Tulsa OK 1926 s Roland & Anna. LTh Sewanee: The U So, TS 1972. D 7/1/1972 Bp Chilton R Powell P 12/1/1972 Bp Frederick Warren Putnam. m 1/30/1947 Virginia Louise Broach. Vic Mt Olivet Epis Ch New Orleans LA 1998-2016; Ret 1996-2016; P-in-c S Matt's Ch Bogalusa LA 1992-1996; R S Paul's Epis Ch Clay Cntr KS 1978-1991; Gr Ch Henryetta OK 1978; S Ptr's Ch Tulsa OK 1976-1978; Assoc Dio Oklahoma Oklahoma City OK 1976; Cur Gr Ch Muskogee OK 1972-1973. Bro of S Andr.

BROAD, Thomas Michael (WNY) 19 N Washington St, Randolph NY 14772 **R Gr Ch Randolph NY 2008-; Wrshp Cmsn Dio Wstrn New York Tonawanda NY 2013-, Actg Dn, Cattaraugus-Chautauqua Dnry 2012-, Fresh Start, Fac 2010-** B Buffalo NY 1954 BS RPI 2007; MDiv GTS 2008. D 9/2/2007 P 9/13/2008 Bp Michael Garrison. m 7/9/1977 Susan L Broad. rector@gracechurchrandolph.org

BROADFOOT III, Walter Marion (EC) 200 S. McMorrine Street, Elizabeth City NC 27909 **Chr Ch Eliz City NC 2014-; Epis Fndt Bd Mem Dio E Carolina Kinston NC 2017-; Mem Rotary Club of Eliz City NC 2014-** B Memphis TN 1962 s Walter & Anne. BS Mississippi St U 1984; MDiv Sewanee: The U So, TS 2008. D 5/14/2008 P 12/16/2008 Bp Henry Nutt Parsley Jr. m 1/26/1991 Rebecca S Broadfoot c 2. Assoc R Ch Of The Ascen Montgomery AL 2008-2014; Bd Mem Samar Counslg Cntr Montgomery AL 2013-2014; Past Participant and Current Bd Mem Ldrshp Montgomery Montgomery AL 2011-2014; Current Bd Mem Fam Promise Montgomery AL 2010-2014; Dioc Camp Bd Mem Dio Alabama Birmingham 2009-2013. Fndr Stop Hunger Now Cmnty Event 2016; Mayoral Appointee Unity at the Table 2016; Fndr Room in the Inn 2015; Grad Ldrshp Montgomery 2011. fatherchip@christchurchcity.org

BROADHEAD, Alan John (ND) 107 Heartwood Drive, Lansdale PA 19446 B Birmingham UK 1938 s Wilfred & Hilda. MD Lon GB 1962; Ripon Coll Cuddesdon 1966. Trans 11/1/1981 Bp Arthur Edward Walmsley. m 12/18/1965 Mary Patricia Broadhead. Assoc S Jn's Epis Ch Dickinson ND 1997-2005; Ch Of The Adv Devils Lake ND 1995-1997; Dio No Dakota Fargo ND 1992-2004; S Thos Ch Ft Totten ND 1992-1995; SS Mary And Mk Epis Ch Oakes ND 1991; Vic Zion Epis Ch N Branford CT 1982-1990; Serv Ch Of Engl 1966-1967.

BROADLEY, Rodger Charles (Pa) 336 S Camac St, Philadelphia PA 19107 **R Ch Of S Lk And Epiph Philadelphia PA 1980-** B Philadelphia PA 1951 s Harry & June. BA Mid 1973; MDiv EDS 1978. D 6/17/1978 P 5/1/1979 Bp Lyman Cunningham Ogilby. m 6/27/2013 Joseph Henry Quinn. Cur Ch Of The Redeem Bryn Mawr PA 1978-1980.

BROCATO, Christian (Mass) St. Peter's Episcopal Church, 838 Mass Ave., Cambridge MA 02139 **S Mk's Ch Grand Rapids MI 2017-; Epis City Mssn Bd Dio Massachusetts Boston MA 2012-, Criminal Justic Reform Taskforce 2011-2012, Liturg and Mus Com 2008-** B Helena AR 1950 s Sam & Jeannine. BM U Cinc/Coll Conservatory of Mus 1976; MFA U MN 1978; PhD U MN 1986; MA Aquinas Inst of Theol 1989. Rec 1/12/2008 Bp M(Arvil) Thomas Shaw. m 12/31/2004 Jeffrey John Hickey. Dio Massachusetts S Ptr's Epis Ch Cambridge MA 2011-2017; Dio Massachusetts All SS Ch Stoneham MA 2009-2011; Dn of Acad Affrs New Engl Coll of Bus and Fin 2008-2011; Assoc Par Of The Epiph Winchester MA 2008-2011. Mus, "March from Floridante," *Wk for Organ and Trumpets*, Augsburg Pub Hse, 1986. AGO 1975. Pi Kappy Lambda U MN 1980; Purple Heart US ARMY 1945.

BROCHARD, Philip Thomas (Cal) 2729 Kinney Dr, Walnut Creek CA 94595 **R All Souls Par In Berkeley Berkeley CA 2008-** B San Francisco, CA 1974 BA U CA. D 6/7/2003 P 12/6/2003 Bp William Edwin Swing. m 1/6/2001 Sarah Oneto c 2. Assoc R S Paul's Epis Ch Walnut Creek CA 2003-2008. rector@allsoulsparish.org

BROCK, Charles F. (Va) St. James' Episcopal Church, Alexandria VA 22309 **R S Jas' Epis Ch Mt Vernon VA 2012-** B Boston MA 1960 BA Hav 1983; MDiv VTS 2007. D 6/30/2007 P 1/18/2008 Bp Bavi Edna Rivera. m 11/22/2003 Heidi B Brock c 1. Assoc R S Barn Ch Annandale VA 2007-2012.

BROCK, Elizabeth Ann (U) HC 69 Box 630016, Randlett UT 84063 B Roosevelt UT 1959 d Frank & Evelyn. D 6/9/2012 Bp Scott Byron Hayashi. c 3. Ch Of The H Sprt Randlett UT 2012-2013. ANNB@UTETRIBE.COM

BROCK, Laurie M (Lex) 2025 Bellefont Dr, Lexington KY 40503 **R Ch S Mich The Archangel Lexington KY 2010-; Comission on Mnstry Dio Lexington Lexington 2015-, Bp Nomin Com 2011-2012, Disciplinary Com 2011-; Response Team Chapl Lexington Dept. of Police Lexington KY 2012-** B Fayette AL 1968 d Thomas & Linda. BS U of Sthrn Mississippi 1991; JD U of Alabama 1995; MDiv GTS 2002. D 6/1/2002 P 5/31/2003 Bp Philip Menzie Duncan II. Assoc S Jas Epis Ch Baton Rouge LA 2007-2010; Cur Trin Epis

Ch Mobile AL 2002-2007; Chapl Dio Cntrl Gulf Coast Pensacola FL 2002. Auth, "At the Barn," *There's a Wmn in the Pulpit*, Skylight Paths, 2015; Auth, "Where God Hides Holiness," Morehouse, 2013; Auth/Ed, "50 Days of Fabulous," Forw Mvmt, 2013; Celebrity Blogger, "Lent Madness," Forw Mvmt, 2013; Auth, "This Should Be Interesting," *Ruach*, EWC, 2011; Auth, "Christmas Fruitcakes," Ecumininet.com, 2009; Auth, "A Hm of Her Own," *Fidelia's Sis*, Young Cler Wmn, 2008; Auth, "Sex, Affrs, and the Absence of Ch," *Fidelia's Sis*, Young Cler Wmn, 2008; Auth, "Alpha Females at the Altar," *In Search of a Feminist Faith*, Pilgrim Press, 2005; Auth, "The Fifteenth Psalm," *The Adelphean*, The Adelphean, 2004. Acad of Preachers 2014. rector@saint-michaels.org

BROCK, Scott (USC) 230 Pinecrest Dr Apt 25, Fayetteville NC 28305 **P S Dav's Epis Ch Columbia SC 2012-** B Spartanburg SC 1957 s Ralph & Angeline. BA Clemson U 1979; MDiv VTS 1986. D 10/4/1986 P 5/1/1987 Bp William Arthur Beckham. m 10/15/1988 MaryAnne B Brock. S Mich And All Ang Savannah GA 1999-2012; Assoc R S Jn's Epis Ch Fayetteville NC 1993-1999; Asst R S Jas Par Wilmington NC 1990-1993; Ch Of The Nativ Un SC 1987-1990; R Nativ Un SC 1987-1990; D Ch Of The Resurr Greenwood SC 1986-1987.

BROCK, Velma Elaine (WA) 233 Cambridge St, Syracuse NY 13210 B Washington DC 1937 d James & Martha. MS Fed City Coll 1973; AS Washington Tech Inst 1975; MDiv Wesley TS 1993. D 6/11/1994 P 4/1/1995 Bp Ronald Hayward Haines. S Phil's Chap Baden Brandywine MD 2004-2007; Dio Washington Washington DC 2000-2003; Vic/Chapl U Of Maryland Mssn Coll Pk MD 2000; U Meth Ch Syracuse NY 1994-2000; Prog Asst Cathd of St Ptr & St Paul Washington DC 1993-1994; Chapl/Counslr Epis Caring Response To Aids Washington DC 1993-1994. Intl Rel Coun Cny; UBE.

BROCKENBROUGH, Sarah (SVa) PO Box 3520, Williamsburg VA 23187 **Emm Epis Ch Greenwood VA 2015-** B Savannah GA 1974 MHP U GA; BS Van 1997; MDiv VTS 2014. D 5/31/2014 Bp Scott Anson Benhase P 12/13/2014 Bp Herman Hollerith IV. m 9/20/2003 William M Brockenbrough. Assoc Bruton Par Williamsburg VA 2014-2015. sbrockenbrough@brutonparish.org

BROCKMAN, Bennett Albert (Ct) 362 Lake St, Vernon CT 06066 **P-in-c Gr Ch Stafford Sprg CT 2010-** B Greer SC 1942 s Albert & Lois. BA Furman U 1964; MA Van 1966; PhD Van 1970. D 6/13/1987 P 3/9/1988 Bp Arthur Edward Walmsley. m 6/12/1965 Linda Brockman c 2. Int Chr And H Trin Ch Westport CT 2012-2013; R S Paul's Ch Fairfield CT 1993-2008; Cur S Mich's Ch Litchfield CT 1987-1993; Asst & Assoc Prof of Engl U of Connecticut Storrs CT 1968-1995; Dioc Exec Com Dio Connecticut Meriden CT 2002-2008, Ch Missions Pub Co Bd 1994-1998, Exam Chapl Mem 1993-1999.

BROCKMAN, John Martin (Ind) 82 E. Colony Acres Dr., Brazil IN 47834 B Batesville IN 1934 s Martin & Margaret. BS Xavier U 1957; MEd Xavier U 1977; Cert Ang Stud EDS 1999. Rec 12/11/1999 Bp Douglas Edwin Theuner. m 8/29/1998 Sylvia A Brockman. S Mk's Ch Plainfield IN 2005-2006; Int S Jn's Epis Ch Crawfordsvlle IN 2004-2005; S Mk's Epis Ch Perryville MD 2000-2004. EPF 2004.

BROCKMANN, Robert John (Mass) 78 Mann Hill Rd, Scituate MA 02066 **R Gr Ch Norwood MA 2010-; Min Prov Third Ord SSF Prov. of the Americas 2012-; Min Prov Third Av Cmnty Churc Columbus OH 2011-** B New York NY 1951 s Robert & Marilyn. BA Geo 1973; MA U Chi 1974; DA U MI 1981. D 6/14/1997 P 12/13/1997 Bp Cabell Tennis. m 8/28/1993 Sarah Brockmann c 2. Int Chr Ch Delaware City DE 2005-2009; Int S Paul's Ch Camden Wyoming DE 2002-2005; Int Chapl U of Delaware 1999-2001; P-in-c Ch Without Walls (Mssn) Bear Delaware 1996-1999; Full Prof U of Delaware Dept of Engl 1984-2010. Auth, "Commodore Robert F. Stockton (1792-1867)," Cambria Press, 2009; Auth, "Twisted Rails/Sinking Ships: Rhetoric of 19th Century Accident Investigations," Baywood Pub, 2004; Auth, "Exploding Steamboats, Senate Debates, and Tech Reports," Baywood Pub, 2002; Auth, "From Millwrights to Shipwright to the 21st Century," Hampton Press, 1998; Auth, "Writing Better Computer User Documentation: From Paper to Hypertext, Version 2.0," Jn Wiley & Sons, 1990; Ed, "Ethics in Tech Cmncatn," Soc for Tech Cmncatn, 1989; Co-Auth, "Writer's Pocket Almanack," Info Books, 1988; Ed, "Case Method in Tech Cmncatn," Assn of Teachers of Tech Writing, 1985; Ed, "New Essays in Sci and Tech Cmncatn," Baywood Pub, 1983. Third Ord Soc of S Fran 1993.

BROCKMANN, Sarah (Mass) 78 Mann Hill Road, Scituate MA 02066 **R Trin Epis Ch Rockland MA 2009-** B Worcester MA 1964 d Richard & Virginia. BS Bos 1986; MDiv Harvard DS 1994. D 5/11/2000 P 2/2/2002 Bp Wayne Wright. m 8/28/1993 Robert John Brockmann c 2. Asst and Epis Campus Min S Thos's Par Newark DE 2007-2009; Yth Dir Dio Delaware Wilmington 2006; Asst Imm Ch Highlands Wilmington DE 2001-2006; Yth Dir Ch of St Andrews & St Matthews Wilmington DE 2000; D Epis Ch Of SS Andr And Matt 2000.

BROCKMEIER, Alan Lee (RG) 8516 N Prince St, Clovis NM 88101 **R Ch Of S Jas The Apos Clovis Curry NM 2013-, P-in-c 2010-2013** B Freeport IL 1948 s Lowell & Barbara. AS Estrn New Mex U 1987; BS Estrn New Mex U 2001; Dip TESM 2003. D 6/21/2003 P 7/11/2004 Bp Terence Kelshaw. m 7/8/1994 Suzanne Carroll Brockmeier c 1. Asst S Jas 2004-2010; D S Jas 2003-2004. Bro of S Andr 2007; Ord of S Lk 2007; PHI KAPPA PHI hon Soc 2001.

BROCKMEIER, Suzanne Carroll (RG) St James Episcopal Church, PO Box 249, Clovis NM 88102 B N. Kingstown RI 1955 AA Cape Cod Cmnty Coll 1975; BS Suffolk U 1977; EdM Estrn NM U 1988; Dplma Trin Sch for Mnstry 2011. D 11/30/2012 P 9/14/2013 Bp Michael Vono. m 7/8/1994 Alan Lee Brockmeier.

BRODERICK, Janet (Nwk) 268 2nd St, Jersey City NJ 07302 **R S Ptr's Ch Morristown NJ 2009-; R Gr Ch Van Vorst Jersey City NJ 2001-** B New York NY 1955 d James & Patricia. BA U MI 1977; MDiv GTS 1990. D 6/9/1990 P 12/15/1990 Bp Richard Frank Grein. c 2. Gr Ch Van Vorst Jersey City NJ 2001-2009; Vic Gr Epis Ch New York NY 1997-2001; All SS' Epis Ch Briarcliff NY 1994-1997; The Ch Of The Epiph New York NY 1990-1994; Sem S Jas Ch New York NY 1990-1991. jbroderick@stpetersmorristown.org

BRODERICK, Rosemarie (NJ) P.O. Box 326, Navesink NJ 07752 **D All SS Memi Ch Navesink NJ 2009-; Nomin Com Dio New Jersey Trenton NJ 2010-, D's Coun (Chair - 2011-12) 2009-2012, Bp's Advsry Com on Liturg 2009-, Wmn's Cmsn 2009-** B Belefonte PA 1962 d John & Diane. BS Trin and U 2001; DCW Dio New Jersey Sch for Deacons 2009. D 5/16/2009 Bp Sylvestre Donato Romero. c 2. Port Chapl Seamens Ch Inst 2008-2009.

BRODERICK Y GUERRA, Cecily (LI) 3495 Hawthorne Dr N, Wantagh NY 11793 **Epis Hlth Serv Far Rockaway NY 2008-, 2007; VP for Pstr Care Epis Hlth Serv New York 2007-; VP of Pstr Care S Jos's Epis Chap Far Rockaway NY 2007-** B Mountain Home ID 1960 d Cecil & Mercedes. Cert CPE; DMin SFTS; Cert Oxf GB 1982; BA Trin Hartford CT 1982; MDiv Ya Berk 1987. D 6/13/1987 P 1/10/1988 Bp Paul Moore Jr. m 10/22/2011 Julie Ann Bates c 2. P-in-c S Phil's Ch New York NY 2002-2006, Cur 1988-1990; R St Jn the Evang Epis Ch Lynbrook NY 1992-2002; Cn Cathd Of St Jn The Div New York NY 1990-1991; Asst S Martha's Ch Bronx NY 1987-1988. Auth, *Inheriting Our Mo's Gardens*, Fortress; Auth, *St. Jn's First 100 Years: Story as a Resource for Ch Life*, San Francisco Theol Semianry (dissertation); Auth, *Wmn Voices & Visions of the Ch*, WCC. Black Caucus; UBE. Mercer Preaching Awd Ya Berk.

BRODIE, Robert (SwVa) 1612 Valhalla Ct, Salem VA 24153 **Chapl Fed Bureau of Investigation 2005-** B Miami FL 1946 s Earle & June. BA U of Miami 1970; MDiv Sewanee: The U So, TS 1978; MA U of Miami 1980; DMin Bethany TS 1985; MEd UTC 1985; CAS S Michaels 1990; Coll of Preachers 1991; PsyD Sthrn 1999; MA Amer Mltry U 2011; MS Amer Mltry U 2013; DMin Sewanee: The U So, TS 2014; MS Amer Mltry U 2015; MA Creighton U 2016. D 6/4/1978 P 12/1/1978 Bp James Loughlin Duncan. m 4/16/1983 Linda M Brodie. Dn The Cathd Ch Of S Paul Springfield IL 2006-2013; Cn for Mnstry Dio Tennessee Nashville TN 1996-2006; Cn To Ordnry Dio E Tennessee Knoxville TN 1994-1996; Dep Chf of Security The GC Stff 1990-2009; R S Paul's Ch Athens TN 1987-1993; Chapl Tennessee Highway Patrol 1983-2006; R Chr Ch Epis S Pittsburg TN 1980-1987; Chapl Miami-Dade Cnty Florida Publ Sfty Dept 1978-1980; Cur S Phil's Ch Coral Gables FL 1978-1980; Dep Chf of Security GC- Epis Ch Cntr New York NY 1990-2009. Auth, "The Use Of Rel Lang In Suicide Attempts," *Journ of Crisis Intervention*, Sthrn Mississippi Press, 1985; Auth, "A Discussion Of Ethical Implications Of The Plcy Of Detente In View Of The Siviet Definitn Of Detente," *White Paper for U.S. Congr*, The Wackenhut Security Study Cntr, 1974. Acad Of Par Cleric Amer Mnstry Assn 1985; Amer Acad Of Homil 1987; AAR 2010; Assn of Form Intelligence Off 2003; CODE 1986-2006; Int Mnstry Ntwk 1997; Intl Conf Police Chap 1983; No Amer Dn's Assn 2006. Hon Cn The Cathd od St Paul, TEC Dio Quincy 2009; Iron Arrow Hon Soc U Miami 1969.

BRODY, Mary Ann (Roch) 190 Penarrow Rd., Rochester NY 14618 **CPE Supvsr Cath Hlth System Buffalo NY 2017-** B Shelby NC 1959 d William & Carolyn. Assoc Eductr Assn of CPE; BA Pur 1983; MA Wake Forest U 1985; MEd Leh 1988; MDiv Bex Sem 2004. D 6/5/2004 P 5/27/2006 Bp Jack Marston Mckelvey. m 2/24/2011 Nancy Jeanne Ramsay c 1. R S Steph's Ch Rochester NY 2012-2016, P-in-c 2009-2012, P-in-c 2007-2008; Dioc Coun Dio Rochester Henrietta 2012-2014, Disciplinary Revs Bd 2011-, COM 2008-2011, Dioc/SSJ Discernment Cmsn 2012-, Epis Sch Exploratory Team 2009-2012, Hosp Chapl 2005-2009, Chapl Res 2004-2005; Asst to the R S Lk And S Simon Cyrene Rochester NY 2006-2009, Asst to the R 2005-2006; Contract Chapl Strong Memi Hosp/U Roch Rochester N 2005-2006; Transitional D S Thos Epis Ch Rochester NY 2004-2005; Chapl Res Strong Memi Hosp/U Roch Rochester N 2004-2005. ACPE Supervisory Candidate, "Curiosity, Creativity, and Cmnty in ACPE Supervision," *Reflective Pract*, Assn of Profsnl Chapl, 2017. Assoc of H Cross Monstry 1996-2006; EPF 2011-2012; EWC 2005-2007. Len Cedarleaf Awd Assn of CPE (ACPE) 2017; DSA Grtr Rochester Cmnty of Ch (GRCC) 2016. mbrody@chsbuffalo.org

BROEREN, Erik Stephanus Simon (ETenn) **Assoc Gr Ch Chattanooga TN 2011-** B Roosendaal, The Netherlands 1971 s Simon & Elisabeth. BA Tilburg U 2005; MDiv Van 2010; DAS Sewanee: The U So, TS 2017. D 2/11/2017 Bp George Young III. m 7/17/2015 Mark Andrew Siedlecki.

BROGAN, Betty Jean (Mich) 17665 E Kirkwood Dr, Clinton Township MI 48038 B Marietta OH 1927 d Cornelius & Mae. BA Duke 1948; MA U of Detroit Mercy 1964; EdD Wayne 1978. D 6/15/2002 Bp Wendell Nathaniel

Gibbs Jr. D Gr Ch Mt Clemens MI 2012-2015; D S Gabr's Epis Ch Eastpointe MI 2002-2012; Dioc Tithes and Offerings Com Dio Michigan Detroit MI 2007-2009, Dioc Nomin Com 2005-2007, Bd Dir Whitaker TS 2004-2009, Dioc CESA Com 2004-2008, Bd Dir St. Anne's Mead 2004-2007.

BROGAN, Margaret C (Cal) 1432 Eastshore Dr, Alameda CA 94501 **Chapl S Andr's Epis Sch Saratoga CA 2006-** B Cleveland OH 1949 d James & Margaret. BA Guilford Coll 1971; California St U 1974; MDiv CDSP 1993. D 6/8/1994 P 6/1/1995 Bp William Edwin Swing. m 6/15/2003 Wendell Kawahara c 3. S Andr's Sch Saratoga CA 2006-2011; Cur S Clare's Epis Ch Pleasanton CA 1994-2005. Outstanding Cler Awd Natl Allnce For Mntl Illness 2002.

BROKAW, Ronald Gene (CFla) 1106 Dorchester St, Orlando FL 32803 **Ret 1990-** B Kirksville MO 1930 s Edward & Minnie. BA U of Missouri 1953; MDiv CDSP 1957; MS Emporia St U 1966. D 6/22/1957 Bp Edward Clark Turner P 12/21/1957 Bp Goodrich R Fenner. Int S Ptr's Epis Ch Lake Mary FL 1989-1990; Non-par 1968-1989; Trin Preparatory Sch Of Florida Winter Pk FL 1968-1989; R S Andr's Epis Ch Emporia KS 1959-1968; Asst S Jas Ch Wichita KS 1957-1959. Associated Parishes.

BROME, Henderson LeVere (Mass) 1201 Davenport Ave, Canton MA 02021 B Barbados 1942 s Leon & Constance. MDiv Ya Berk 1973; PhD Col 1978. Rec 1/1/1980 Bp The Bishop Of Chichester. m 10/3/1986 Deborah Brome c 2. S Cyp's Ch Boston MA 1980-2009; Vic S Andr's Ch New Haven CT 1974-1979. Auth, "The Journey of Life: Confronting, Celebrating, and Coping w Its Experiences," IUniverse Inc., 2007.

BROMILEY, Hugh Philip (CFla) 1250 Paige Pl, The Villages FL 32159 B Aldershot UK 1953 s Norman & Katherine. Tchr Cert Alexander Tchg Cntr 1980; MTh Trin Theol Coll 1989; MTh Westminster Coll Oxford UK 1999. Trans 7/3/1989 Bp Charles Shannon Mallory. R S Geo Epis Ch The Villages FL 2007-2013; R Trin Epis Ch Redlands CA 2003-2005; R S Thos Ch Savannah GA 1998-2003; R S Jas' Ch Monterey CA 1993-1997; R S Lk's Ch Auburn CA 1991-1993; Cur All SS Ch Carmel CA 1989-1991. Auth, "In Search of a Miracle," *In Search of a Miracle*, iuniverse, 2001. Chapl and Speaker Ord Of S Lk 1991.

BRONDSTED, Linda J (Eur) 1880 Taylor Ave, Winter Park FL 32789 **Chapl Arnold Palmer Hosp Orlando FL 2007-; S Richard's Ch Winter Pk FL 2004-** B New Britain CT 1944 d Harlan & Mary. Newton Hosp Sch of Nrsng 1965; BD Indiana U 1985; Inst for Chr Stds 1985. D 3/10/1986 Bp William Hopkins Folwell. c 3. D Cathd Ch Of S Lk Orlando FL 1994-2002; Archd Dio Cntrl Florida Orlando FL 1993-2010; D All SS Ch Of Winter Pk Winter Pk FL 1990-1994; Chapl Arnold Palmer Hosp Orlando FL 1989-1993; 1985-1989. NAAD 1992. Steph Mnstry Awd NAAD 2003.

BRONK JR, Harold R (Mass) 27 Curtis Road, Milton MA 02186 **Died 5/20/2017** B New York NY 1928 s Harold & Anna. BA Hofstra U 1951; MDiv Ya Berk 1954; canddrtheol. U of Tuebingen 1967; Cert U of Massachusetts 1992. D 6/2/1954 Bp Charles Francis Hall P 12/4/1954 Bp Oliver J Hart. m 12/10/1988 Joyce Caggiano c 6. Ch Of S Jn The Evang Boston MA 2005-2012, Bd Dinner Prog 2002-2005, Assoc 1986-2002; Int S Eustace Ch Lake Placid NY 2004-2005; P-in-c Gr Ch Detroit MI 2004; Int Belmont Chap at S Mk's Sch Southborough MA 1999-2000; S Jas Ch Amesbury MA 1998-2000; Int S Mk's Ch Southborough MA 1997-1998; R Ch of the Ascen Munich 1994-1996; Int S Andr's Ch Framingham MA 1992-1993; P-in-c S Paul Dusslingen Germany 1966-1968; P-in-c S Dav's Epis Ch Cambria Heights NY 1957-1959; R The Ch Of S Mary Of The Harbor Provincetown MA 1956-1957; Chapl And Headmaster Tuller Sch Barnstable MA 1955-1956; Asst S Paul Memi Overbrook PA 1954-1955; Liturg Cmsn Dio Massachusetts Boston MA 1986-2000. Auth, "Das Streben Nach Glueck," *Beitraege zur Situation....*, Rombach, Freiburg, Germany, 1981; Auth, "Bleiben Unsere Kinder Sitzen?," *Beitraege zur Situation....*, Rombach, Freiburg, Germany, 1980; Auth, "Infermiere-Didattiche," *Rapporto del seminario....*, Ministero sanitaria, Milano, Italia, 1976. Soc of Cath Priests 2011.

BRONOS, Sarah L (CFla) 7718 White Ash Street, Orlando FL 32819 **R Ch Of The Gd Shpd Maitland FL 2009-** B Doncaster Yorkshire U.K. 1952 d George & Alma. Diplome d'Etudes Francaises Inst Francais Du Royaume 1973; MDiv Nash 2007. D 6/2/2007 P 12/29/2007 Bp John Wadsworth Howe. m 10/6/1979 Patiste G Bronos c 2. Cur Ch of the Incarn Oviedo Florida 2007-2009; Dir of Chr Formation All SS Epis Ch Winter Pk Florida 1999-2006. revdsarah@goodshepherd-maitland.com

BRONSON, David Louis (NY) 414 Cottekill Rd, Stone Ridge NY 12484 **Ret 1989-** B Jackson MI 1929 s Glenn & Yetchen. BA U MI 1953; STM Ya Berk 1956. D 6/20/1956 Bp Richard Stanley Merrill Emrich P 7/6/1957 Bp Charles L Street. R Ch Of The H Cross Kingston NY 1963-1989; Cur S Paul's Ch Fairfield CT 1961-1963; Serv Ch of Engl 1957-1961; Cur Chr Ch Waukegan IL 1956-1957; Vic Our Lady Waukegan IL 1956-1957.

BROOK, Robert Charles (Mich) 6112 W Longview Dr, East Lansing MI 48823 B Canada 1937 s Charles & Jean. BA MI SU 1959; BD Bex Sem 1963; MA MI SU 1964; EdD MI SU 1968. D 6/29/1963 Bp Archie H Crowley P 1/20/1964 Bp Robert Lionne DeWitt. m 9/5/1959 Suzanne Brook c 3. Trin Epis Ch Grand Ledge MI 1998-1999; Cbury On The Lake Waterford MI 1997-2002; Counselling Psychol Stds Lansing MI 1988-2008; Assoc. Clincl prof Michigan St Univ. dept psych 1988-2002; Dir St Off /Publ Hlth and Substance abuse St of Michigan Lansing MI 1983-1988; Asst Hur-Sem Angl Ch Can 1970-1983; Reg Dir Ontario Mnstry of Hlth /ARF 1970-1983; Assoc. Clincl prof U Wstrn Ontario 1970-1983; Vic S Aug Of Cbury Mason MI 1969-1970, Vic 1963-1968.

✠ BROOKE-DAVIDSON, The Rt Rev Jennifer (WTex) 6000 Fm 3237 Unit A, Wimberley TX 78676 **Bp Suffr Dio W Texas San Antonio TX 2017-** B Corpus Christi TX 1960 d John & Sherry. AB Ya 1982; JD U of Texas Sch of Law 1985; MA Fuller TS 2009. D 6/8/2009 Bp David Mitchell Reed P 12/16/2009 Bp Gary Richard Lillibridge Con 7/29/2017 for WTex. m 8/17/1985 Charles C Brooke-Davidson c 2. S Eliz's Epis Ch Buda TX 2011-2017; Dir of Chr Ed S Steph's Epis Ch Wimberley TX 2009-2011, 2005-2009. pastorjbd@gmail.com

BROOKFIELD, Christopher Morgan (Va) 1870 Field Rd, Charlottesville VA 22903 B Rye NY 1936 s William & Louise. BA Pr 1958; MA Col 1963; BD and M. Div. UTS 1968; BD UTS 1968. D 12/19/1976 P 12/10/1977 Bp Robert Bruce Hall. m 6/8/1963 Lynne Brookfield c 2. Assoc R S Mary's Epis Ch Richmond VA 1996-2008; Chapl, Chairman Rel Dept S Cathr's Sch Richmond VA 1988-1995; The Very Reverend, The Dn Ch Schools Dio Virginia Richmond VA 1975-1989; Chairman Rel Dept The Phillips Exeter Acad Exeter NH 1963-1975; VTS Alexandria VA 1988-1994. Co-Auth, *Rel & Educ*, NAIS, 1972; Co-Auth, *Yth in Crisis*, Seabury Press, 1966; Ed/Co-Auth, *Take Off Your Shoes & Walk*, Devin-Adair, 1961. 7 Dioc Schools, Dio Virgina: Bd Mem 1975-1988; NAES: Bd Mem 1976-1984. BD cl UTS 1968.

✠ BROOKHART JR, The Rt Rev Charles Franklin (Mont) PO Box 2020, Helena MT 59624 **Bp of Montana Dio Montana Helena MT 2003-; Stndg Cmsn, Ecum Dom And Frgn Mssy Soc- Epis Ch Cntr New York NY 2012-, Co-Chair, Meth-Epis Dialog 2004-** B Parkersburg WV 1948 s Charles & Jo. BA Witt 1970; Van 1971; MDiv Luth TS 1974; DMin Untd TS 1984. D 6/1/1988 P 10/22/1988 Bp Robert Poland Atkinson Con 9/27/2003 for Mont. m 6/15/1974 Susan Jane Brookhart c 2. R The Lawrencefield Chap Par Wheeling WV 1988-2003; Serv Luth Ch 1974-1987. Auth, "Living the Resurr," Ch Pub Inc, 2012; Ed and Contrib, "Make Us One w Chr," TEC and Meth Ch, 2006. Anamchara Fllshp 2008. cfbmt@qwestoffice.net

BROOKMAN, Cathleen Anne (Chi) 29 West 410 Emerald Green Drive, Warrenville IL 60555 B Lakewod OH 1943 d Kenneth & Anne. MS Geo 1985; MS Wms 1985. D 2/5/2000 Bp Bill Persell. S Jn's Epis Ch Naperville IL 2000-2009; Counslr Publ Schools Aurora IL 1986-2005.

BROOKS, Albert (Hond) Aptd 28, La Ceiba Atlantida 31101 Honduras **P-in-c Iglesia Epis Santisima Trinidad La Ceiba At 1976-** B Tola Atlantida HN 1941 s Albert Ernest & Mary. MA Universidad Nacional Autonoma De Mex Mx 1971; Cert Inst Theologico Epis 1973; Cert Epis TS of the SW 1976. D 6/26/1971 Bp William Carl Frey P 8/24/1977 Bp Anselmo Carral-Solar. m 1/10/1973 Maria del Carmen Morales de Brooks. Dio Honduras San Pedro Sula 1972-2010.

BROOKS, Ashton Jacinto C/O Cathedral Church of the Epiphany, P O BOX 764, Santo Domingo Dominican Republic B 1942 s Eduardo & Maria. Santo Domingo Autonoma U Santo Domingo Do 1963; BA Inter Amer U of Puerto Rico 1966; STB ETSC 1969; Cert EDS 1979; STM GTS 1989; DD CDSP 1993. D 5/25/1969 P 11/1/1969 Bp Paul Axtell Kellogg. m 4/24/1969 Margaret Brooks c 1. Dn The Coun of Theol Educ in Latin Amer & Caribbean Santo Domingo 2009-2011; Dn Cathd Ch of All SS St Thos VI 2000-2008; St Mary the Vrgn Ch Vrgn Gorda VG 1150 1998-1999; Cn In Res Cathd Of St Jn The Div New York NY 1993-1998; Coordntr Centro De Reflexion Teologica San Jose Cr 1988-1993; Dio The Dominican Republic (Iglesia Epis Dominicana) Gazcue Santo Domingo 1988-1993; Novena Provincia Iglesia Epis 1988-1993; Dn Centro De Estudios Teologicos Santo Domingo Do 1979-1988; R Iglesia Epis San Andres Santo Domingo Di 1972-1979. Auth, "Eclesiologia: Presencia Anglicana En La Reg Cntrl De Amer". DD CDSP 1993.

BROOKS, Donald Edgar (WTenn) 1436 Forest Drive, Union City TN 38261 **Chapl Assoc Bapt Memi Hosp - Un City TN 2009-; Chf Chapl Unioni city Police Dept 2005-; Chapl U of Tennessee - Mart 2004-** B Alvin TX 1946 s Weldon & Edna. BA Austin Peay St U 1969; MEd U of Memphis 1975; MA U of Memphis 1982; Cert of Angl Stds TS 1987; Cert of Angl Stds Sewanee: The U So, TS 1987; U So 1987. D 11/29/1981 Bp William F Gates Jr P 12/1/1982 Bp William Evan Sanders. S Jas Epis Ch Un City TN 2004-2012; Chr Ch Brownsville TN 1995-2004; Imm Ch Ripley TN 1987-2004; Vic Imm Epis Ch La Grange TN 1987-1992; S Thos Ch Somerville TN 1987-1992; Chapl Bolivar Cmnty Hosp/Wstrn Mntl Hlth Inst 1984-1986; Asst S Jas Bolivar TN 1981-1986. Auth, "A Hist Of Temple Adas Israel Brownsville Tn w Symbology Of The Windows". Spck/Usa.

BROOKS, Dub (Tex) 1718 Wentworth St, Houston TX 77004 **Hd of Sch S Mk's Epis Sch FL 2006-** B Houston TX 1951 s James & Hazel. BFA U of Houston 1976; MA U of Houston 1978; MDiv VTS 1981. D 6/18/1981 P 3/1/1982 Bp Maurice Manuel Benitez. m 10/18/1986 Suzanne Lee Brooks c 2. Assoc Palmer Memi Ch Houston TX 2011-2016; S Mk's Epis Sch Ft Lauderd FL 2006-2011; Hd of Sch S Paul Epis Sch LA 2004-2006; S Paul's Ch New Orleans LA 2004-2006; Asst Hd of Sch Epis HS 1994-2004; Chapl Epis HS

1993-2004; Assoc Epis HS Bellaire TX 1993-2004; Asst S Fran Ch Houston TX 1981-1993.

BROOKS, James Buckingham (Ida) Po Box 36, Letha ID 83636 **D S Mich's Cathd Boise ID 1987-** B Boise ID 1938 s Orville & Frances. Boise St U; Estrn Oregon U; The Coll of Idaho. D 3/28/1987 Bp David Bell Birney IV. m 1/24/1960 Susan Jane Brooks c 2. Auth, "Treasuers Of Imagination," *The Intl Libr Of Poetry*, 2000; Auth, "Heart Sounds". Love Awd (Ldr Of Excellence) Idaho Hosp Assoc 1999; Dsa For Publ Serv.

BROOKS, Porter Harrison (Va) 9797 Kedge Ct, Vienna VA 22181 **Died 6/13/2016** B Chicago IL 1926 s Hugh & Lucy. BA McMurry U 1948; MDiv VTS 1951; US-A Chapl Sch 1962; Command and Gnrl Stff Coll 1964; Command and Gnrl Stff Coll 1966. D 1/3/1951 P 7/4/1951 Bp George Henry Quarterman. c 3. Ret 1992-2016; Ret 1992-2016; Assoc S Jn's Epis Ch Mc Lean VA 1987-1992; Int S Alb's Epis Ch Annandale VA 1986-1987; Int Trin Ch Arlington VA 1985-1986; Int S Mary's Epis Ch Arlington VA 1983-1985; Emm Epis Ch Delaplane Delaplane VA 1982; Off Of Bsh For ArmdF New York NY 1955-1969; R S Matt's Ch Pampa TX 1953-1955. Auth, "Cross, Crook, and Candle: Story of Rel at Ft Myer," *Virginia*, 1974.

BROOKS, Reverend Kimberly Brooks (CPa) 248 Seneca St, Harrisburg PA 17110 B Harrisburg PA 1956 s Jesse & Rebecca. BS Lancaster Bible Coll; Doctorate Newbern TS; MDiv Lancaster TS 2005; MD VTS Alexandria VA 2007. D 6/9/2007 P 2/9/2008 Bp Nathan Dwight Baxter. m 10/26/2013 Andrea Brooks c 3. Cn Cathd Ch Of S Steph Harrisburg PA 2015-2017; S Paul's Epis Ch Harrisburg PA 2007-2015; Fuel Inspctn Specialists Fism Ii Mack Trucks 1979-2003.

BROOKS, Richard Smith (WK) 1333 Crescent Ln, Concordia KS 66901 B Glasco KS 1924 s Earl & Leona. AA SUNY 1973; BS Cameron U 1976. D 11/21/1997 P 10/30/1998 Bp Vernon Edward Strickland. m 2/12/1944 Alve May Brooks c 2. P-in-c Ch Of The Epiph Concordia KS 1998-2005. Who'S Who In Amer Universities 1976; Phi Kappa Phi 1974.

BROOKS JR, Robert Brudon (NY) 4 Quail Ridge Rd, Hyde Park NY 12538 B Allentown PA 1936 s Robert & Elizabeth. BA Alleg 1958. D 6/4/1994 Bp Richard Frank Grein. m 9/15/1973 A Jayne Brooks c 2. D Ch Of The Mssh Rhinebeck NY 1994-2008.

BROOKS, Robert Johnson (Ct) 140 Christopher Cv, Kyle TX 78640 **Ret P Dio Connecticut 2004-; Mem, Liturg, Mus, and the Arts Mnstry Ntwk Dio Connecticut Meriden CT 2001-, Mem, Soc Justice and Advocacy Mnstry Ntwk 2001-; Cn for Intl Affrs Epis Dio El Salvador 1997-; Mem The Bretton Woods Com Washington DC 2000-; Mem, Bd Dir Cntr for Natl Plcy Washington DC 1995-** B Austin TX 1947 s Robert & Marietta. DD CDSP; BA S Edwards U Austin TX 1970; MDiv CDSP 1973; MA U of Notre Dame 1980. D 6/25/1973 Bp Scott Field Bailey P 6/22/1974 Bp James Milton Richardson. R S Paul's Epis Ch Willimantic CT 2001-2004; Bp's Mssn Strtgy Advsry Grp Dio Washington Washington DC 1994-1999; Dir of Govt Relatns Washington D.C Epis Ch Cntr New York NY 1988-1998, Mem, SLC 1985-1988; Asstg P S Thos' Par Washington DC 1984-2001; Lectr in Liturg St Mary's RC Sem Houston TX 1981-1982; Lectr in Liturg Grad TS U of St Thos Houston TX 1981-1982; Epis Chapl Lee Coll Baytown TX 1978-1983; All SS Ch Baytown TX 1973-1983; Vic All SS Baytown TX 1973-1983; Vic Dio Texas Houston TX 1973-1983; The Great Cmsn Fndt Houston TX 1973-1983; Treas, Bd Dir Generations Fam Hlth Cntr Willimantic CT 2008-2014; Chair, Chart Revs Cmsn Town of Windham CT 2001-2004; Dir Bus Partnership for a New Global Future 1999-2001; Sr Consult Washingon Wrld Grp 1999-2000; Sr Advsr to the Pres People for the Amer Way Fndt 1998-1999; Mem, Exec Panel; Chair, Resources Availability Comm. St of Texas AIDS T/F 1986-1989; Prlmntrn and Mem; Chair, Legis Com St of Texas Hlth Coordntng Coun 1984-1989. Contrib, "The Baptismal Mystery & Catechumenate," Ch Pub Inc, 1988. Coun of AP 1981; EUC 2006; Intl Consult of Angl Liturgists 1985; Most Venerable Ord of the Hosp of S Jn of Jerusalem 1998; No Amer Acad of Liturg 1981; OHC 1970; Societas Liturgica 1982; The Consult Strng Com 2004. DD CDSP 2015; Cmdr, The Most Venerable Ord of the Hosp of St. Jn of Jerusalem Queen Eliz II 1994; Rossiter Lectr Bex/Rochester, NY 1991.

BROOKS, Robert Thomas (RI) 285 W Main Rd, Little Compton RI 02837 B Washington DC 1946 s William & Katherine. mdiv eds; AB Harv 1968; MBA Harv 1973; MDiv EDS 1995. D 6/10/1995 Bp Allen Lyman Bartlett Jr P 12/19/1995 Bp J Clark Grew II. m 12/28/1968 Rhea klein c 2. S Andr's By The Sea Little Compton RI 2009-2010; R Gr Ch In Providence Providence RI 2000-2009; R Chr Epis Ch Kent OH 1995-2000. Auth, "Conjugating The Verb To Be," *Preaching Through The Year of Lk*, Morehouse Pub, 2000. Fllshp of S Jn the Evang 1995. harvard varsity club hall of fame football harvard Coll 1998.

BROOKS, Teddy (NY) 750 Kelly St, Bronx NY 10455 **Vic Dio New York New York NY 1997-; S Marg's Ch Bronx NY 1997-** B Grassfield LR 1963 d John & Ida. U Liberia LR; BA Cuttington U 1987; MDiv VTS 1992; STM GTS 2000. Trans 12/9/1996 Bp Walter Decoster Dennis Jr. m 6/22/2002 Paul Erik Block c 2.

BROOKS, Thomas Gerald (NY) 35 Cambridge Ct, Highland NY 12528 **Non-par 1967-** B Seattle WA 1939 s Thomas & Winnifred. BA U of Washington

1962; MDiv GTS 1965. D 9/11/1965 P 3/28/1966 Bp Ivol I Curtis. c 2. Vic Chr Ch Marlboro NY 2004-2011; Dio New York New York NY 2004-2011; Cur S Paul's Epis Ch Bremerton WA 1965-1967.

BROOKS, Weldon Timothy (NH) 113 Main St, Lancaster NH 03584 **S Paul's Ch Lancaster NH 2015-** B Stewartstown NH 1963 s Weldon & Brenda. BA Notre Dame Coll 1985. D 6/6/2015 P 12/5/2015 Bp A Robert Hirschfeld. c 1.

BROOKS, Zachary D (Spr) 359 W State St, Jacksonville IL 62650 B Belleville IL 1982 s Courtney & Elizabeth. BA Perdue U 2004; BA Pur 2004; MDiv Boston Coll 2013; Cert EDS 2015. D 6/4/2016 Bp Alan Gates P 12/10/2016 Bp Daniel Hayden Martins. m 8/3/2013 Leah C Brooks c 2. brooksz@gmail.com

BROOME, John Tol (NC) 3009 Round Hill Rd, Greensboro NC 27408 **Died 10/ 2/2016** B Orlando FL 1931 s Lafayette & Lillie. BA U So 1954; MDiv VTS 1958. D 8/20/1958 P 3/14/1959 Bp Thomas H Wright. m 7/11/1959 Mary Hines Broome c 3. Ret 1995-2016; R H Trin Epis Ch Greensboro NC 1972-1994; Asst S Andr's Epis Ch Coll Pk MD 1965-1968; R S Paul's Ch Beaufort NC 1962-1965; R Emm Ch Farmville NC 1960-1962; P-in-c S Barn Ch Snow Hill NC 1960-1962; P-in-c S Jas Epis Ch Belhaven NC 1958-1960; P-in-c S Matt Yeatesville NC 1958-1960. Auth, "Yth arts," *'64 EYC Notebook.*

BROOME JR, William Bridges (Chi) 504 E Earle Street, Landrum SC 29356 B Spartanburg SC 1950 s William & Grace. BA Newberry Coll 1972; MEd U of So Carolina 1974; MDiv SWTS 1979; CPE Alexian Brothers 1980; MA H Apos Sem 2005. D 6/27/1979 Bp George Moyer Alexander P 5/1/1980 Bp James Winchester Montgomery. Chapl Arlington Natl Cemetary Washington DC 2008-2009; Asstg P Basilica of the Natl Shrine of the Immac Concep 2008-2009; Chapl Quantico Marine Base Quantico VA 2008-2009; R The Annunc Of Our Lady Gurnee IL 1998-1999; P in Charge Santa Teresa de Avila Chicago IL 1997; Joliet Dnry Dio Chicago Chicago IL 1995-1997, 1985-1986; R S Raphael The Archangel Oak Lawn IL 1989-1997; Vic S Chad Epis Ch Loves Pk IL 1985-1989; Employee Assistance Counslr Motorola Corp 1984-1985; Chapl The Mather Hm Evanston IL 1982-1985; Addictions Counslr Grant Hosp of Chicago 1982-1984; Addictions Counslr Chicago's Alcoholic Treatment Cntr 1979-1982; Asst P S Alb's Ch Chicago IL 1979-1981. Missionaries of the H Apos 2003.

BROOMELL, Ann Johnson (Ct) 28 Long Hill Farm, Guilford CT 06437 **Trin Ch On The Green New Haven CT 2016-** B New Rochelle NY 1946 d John & Ethel. Cert in Int Mnstry Cler Ldrshp Inst; Buc 1966; BA Cedar Crest Coll 1968; 1 unit CPE Massachusetts Gnrl Hosp 1992; MDiv EDS 1994; DMin SWTS 2003; 3 units CPE Yale New Haven Hosp 2010. D 6/3/1995 Bp Barbara Clementine Harris P 4/26/1996 Bp M(Arvil) Thomas Shaw. c 2. Gr Epis Ch Medford MA 2017; S Andr's Ch Madison CT 2016; Chr Ch New Haven CT 2015-2016; Int The Ch Of The Redeem Beth MD 2013-2014; Int S Steph's Ch Pittsfield MA 2013; Transitional P-in-c S Paul's Ch Brunswick ME 2011-2013; Int R S Barn Epis Ch Greenwich CT 2010-2011; Int R S Paul's Ch Fairfield CT 2010; Chapl Res Yale New Haven Hosp New Haven CT 2009-2010; Assoc Wrshp/Formation Chr Epis Ch Ponte Vedra FL 2007-2009; Fin Com Dio Easton Easton MD 2003-2007; Cathd Dn Trin Cathd Easton MD 2003-2007; Dio Pennsylvania PA 2001-2003; R Ch Of S Asaph Bala Cynwyd PA 1999-2003; Dioc Coun Dio Massachusetts Boston MA 1996-1998; D/P-in-c S Paul's Epis Ch Bedford MA 1995-1998; D Ch Of The Gd Shpd Waban MA 1995. Amer Friends of the Epis Dio Jerusalem Bd Trst 2011; No Amer Com, St. Geo's Coll, Jerusa 2007-2011; Soc of Cath Priests 2009; SCHC 2012.

BROSEND II, William Frank (Ky) 335 Tennessee Ave., Sewanee TN 37383 **Prof of NT and Preaching Sewanee U So TS Sewanee TN 2006-** B Cincinnati OH 1954 s William & Lucille. BA Denison U 1976; MDiv Van 1979; PhD U Chi 1993. D 6/4/2005 P 12/10/2005 Bp Ted Gulick Jr. c 1. Exec Dir Epis Preaching Fndt 2010-2015; D Chr Ch Cathd Louisville KY 2005-2006; Louisville Presb TS Louisville KY 2005-2006; Assoc. Dir., Louisville Inst Louisville Presb TS Louisville KY 2001-2006. Ed, "Feasting on the Gospels," WJKP, 2012; Auth, "The Preaching of Jesus," WJKP, 2010; co-Auth, "Feasts of Jesus and the H Fam," *Commentary on Feasts, Fasts and H Days,* Fortress Press, 2007; Auth, "The Parables," *Conversations w Scripture,* Morehouse Pub, 2005; co-Auth, "Adv and Christmas," *New Proclamation Lectionary Commentary Year B,* Fortress Press, 2005. Acad of Homil 2003; Angl Assn of Biblic Scholars 2002; SBL 1992. Phi Beta Kappa Denison U 1976.

BROTHERTON, E Ann (Tex) 12101 Bluebonnet Ln, Manchaca TX 78652 B IL 1946 d LeRoy & Helen. BA Cntrl Methodist U 1968; RN Missouri Bapt Hosp Sch of Nrsng S Louis MO 1986; MDiv Epis TS of the SW 2008. D 5/31/2008 P 12/13/2008 Bp Robert Leroy Fitzpatrick. m 3/1/1968 Thomas James Brotherton c 2. SLEH Stff Chapl Dio Texas Houston TX 2011-2013; Stff Chapl S Lk's Epis Hosp Houston TX 2010-2011; Assoc R S Alb's Epis Ch Austin TX 2008-2009. Assn of Profsnl Chapl 2012.

BROUCHT, Mary Louise (CPa) 126 N. Water St., Lancaster PA 17603 B Lancaster PA 1935 d Joseph & Frances. Lancaster TS. D 6/16/1983 Bp Charlie Fuller Mcnutt Jr. c 2. S Jn's Epis Ch Lancaster PA 1999-2005; S Jas Ch Lancaster PA 1989-1997.

BROUGHTON, Jacalyn Irene (Eau) E4357 451st Ave, Menomonie WI 54751 **Gr Epis Ch Menomonie WI 2014-** B Lubbock TX 1955 d Jack & Bernadine.

D 5/4/2008 Bp Mark Lawrence Macdonald P 8/23/2014 Bp William Jay Lambert III. m 12/14/1979 William Broughton c 4.

BROUGHTON, William (SanD) 1830 Avenida Del Mundo Unit 712, Coronado CA 92118 B New Bedford MA 1929 s Harry & Anne. BA Wheaton Coll 1955; MA Wheaton Coll 1956; BD SWTS 1958; SFTS 1981; UTS 1981; USN 1982. D 9/27/1958 Bp Charles L Street P 4/1/1959 Bp Gerald Francis Burrill. Chapl S Geo's Coll Jerusalem IL 1986-1990; Stff Trin Par New York NY 1978-1981; Chapl USCG 1978-1981; Off Of Bsh For ArmdF New York NY 1968-1969; Asst R Chr Ch Winnetka IL 1966-1968, Cur 1958-1965. Ascalon Excavation Soc, Ecum Fraternity Of Jerusalem; Helenic Inst For Preservation Of Ancient Ships. Presidental Meritorious Serv Awd Jewish/Chr/Muslim Trialogue; Hon Cn S Paul Cathd.

BROWDER, David O'Neal (Tex) St Dunstan's Episcopal Church, 14301 Stuebner Airline Rd, Houston TX 77069 **S Thos Ch Houston TX 2013-** B Decatur AL 1972 s Ernest & Laura. BS U of Alabama 1996; MDiv TESM 2008. Trans 2/16/2012 as Priest Bp C Andrew Doyle. m 8/1/2009 Kari Heuer Browder c 3. S Dunst's Epis Ch Houston TX 2012-2013.

BROWDER III, James Wilbur (SVa) Po Box 133, Courtland VA 23837 B Richmond VA 1943 s James & Alice. BA Wake Forest U 1965; MEd U of Virginia 1969; MDiv VTS 1981. D 6/24/1982 P 3/1/1983 Bp Claude Charles Vache. S Lk's Ch Courtland VA 1982-2015; Vic S Paul's Epis Ch Surry VA 1982-1986.

BROWER, David (WMich) 7895 Adams St, Zeeland MI 49464 **Int H Trin Epis Ch Wyoming MI 2017-; Int S Paul's Epis Ch Greenville OH 2014-** B Zeeand MI 1942 s Angus & Emma. BD Grand Rapids Bapt Sem 1964; MA Wstrn Michigan U 1966; MDiv EDS 1979; DMin GTF 2001. D 6/16/1979 P 4/12/1980 Bp H Coleman Mcgehee Jr. m 7/11/1964 Clara Elizabeth Brower c 1. Int S Mk's Ch Sidney OH 2012-2013; Int P-in-c S Lk's Par Kalamazoo MI 2011; Int Ch Of The H Cross Kentwood MI 2009-2011; Int S Greg's Epis Ch Maskegan MI 2005-2009; Int S Greg's Epis Ch Norton Shores MI 2005-2008; R Gr Ch Lockport NY 2000-2005; R S Jas Ch Piqua OH 1997-2000; R Gr Epis Ch Southgate MI 1982-1996; Asst All SS Epis Ch Pontiac MI 1979-1982.

BROWER, Gary (Colo) 2050 E Evans Ave Ste 29, Denver CO 80208 **U Chapl U Denv Denver CO 2007-** B Portland OR 1955 s Robert & Selma. BA NW Chr Coll 1978; BS U of Oregon 1978; MDiv CDSP 1981; PhD Duke 1996. D 4/5/1992 Bp Huntington Williams Jr P 4/19/1993 Bp Robert Whitridge Estill. m 7/3/1982 Susan Lynn Bailey c 2. Berkeley Cbury Fndt Berkeley CA 1996-2007; Epis Campus Min U CA at Berkeley Berkeley CA 1996-2007; Dio No Carolina Raleigh NC 1994-1996; Epis Campus Min U NC at Charlotte Charlotte NC 1994-1996; Assoc S Tit Epis Ch Durham NC 1992-1994; Int Epis Chapl Duke Durham NC 1991-1992. Auth, "The Monks' Carols," The Fac Club, UC Berkeley, 2005; Auth, "Cato of Clermont-Ferraud: A Case of Charcter Assassination in Greg's Hist of the Franks?," *Medieval Perspectives,* 1991. Distinguished Ldrshp Awd YA and Higher Educ Mnstrs 2007; MDiv w dist CDSP 1981. gary.brower@du.edu

BROWER, George C (Ct) 503A Heritage Village, Southbury CT 06488 **P-in-c Imm S Jas Par Derby CT 2005-** B Port Chester NY 1930 s George & Florence. U of Bridgeport 1950; Iona Coll 1955; Concordia Coll 1960; LTh Sewanee: The U So, TS 1963; MDiv Sewanee: The U So, TS 1970. D 6/11/1963 P 12/21/1963 Bp Horace W B Donegan. m 12/30/1983 Evelyn F Brower c 4. P-in-c Chr Ch Oxford CT 1998-2002; S Jn's Ch Sandy Hook CT 1995-1997; P-in-c Chr Ch Bethlehem CT 1995-1996; Asst Litchfield Hills Reg Mnstry Bridgewater CT 1993-1995; nonparochial 1970-1993; R S Tim's Epis Ch Kingsport TN 1966-1970; P-in-c S Simon Lawrenceburg TN 1964-1966; Cur Chr Ch Of Ramapo Suffern NY 1963-1964. H Cross 1962. Paul Harris Fellowowship 1991; Paul Harris Fellowowship 1989; Geo Shettle Awd Publ Spkng 1963; Who's Who in the So 1963.

BROWER, Katherine Moore (WMich) 335 Bridge St NW Apt 2301, Grand Rapids MI 49504 **Exec Dir Southend Cmnty Outreach Mnstrs 2011-** B East Liverpool OH 1947 d Robert & Katherine. BA Albion Coll 1969. D 5/7/1994 Bp Edward Lewis Lee Jr. m 6/20/1970 Robert Brower c 3. D S Andr's Ch Grand Rapids MI 2009-2010; D Gr Ch Grand Rapids MI 1994-2008. NAAD.

BROWER, Meaghan M (RI) Episcopal Diocese of Rhode Island, 275 N Main St, Providence RI 02903 **Dio Rhode Island Providence RI 2012-** B South Kingstown RI 1978 d Thomas & Margaret. BA Rhode Island Coll 2002; MDiv VTS 2007. D 6/13/2007 P 1/5/2008 Bp Gerry Wolf. m 5/19/2007 Jonathan A Brower c 2. Asst R Emm Par Epis Ch Sthrn Pines NC 2007-2011; Switchboard Optr VTS 2004-2007.

BROWER, Sally (NC) 164 Fairview Rd, Mooresville NC 28117 **S Pat's Epis Ch Mooresville NC 2013-** B Norfolk VA 1949 d Chester & Priscilla. BFA Virginia Commonwealth U 1971; MS NC St U 1978; PhD NC St U 1988; MDIV Erskine TS 1998. Rec 5/31/2009 Bp Michael B Curry. m 6/19/1971 Allan Brent Brower c 2.

BROWN JR, Allen Webster (Va) 3625 SE 17th Pl, Cape Coral FL 33904 **Died 3/26/2016** B Cooperstown NY 1931 s Allen & Helen. BS USNA 1955; Untd States Naval Postgraduate Sch 1963; STB PDS 1966; Command and Gnrl Stff Coll 1975; DMin Trin TS 1981. D 3/20/1966 P 9/24/1966 Bp Allen Webster Brown. c 2. Ret 1997-2016; Consult For Congrl Dvlpmt Epis Ch Cntr

New York NY 1989-1996; S Hilary's Ch Ft Myers FL 1981-1987; COM Dio Virginia Richmond VA 1980-1984, Exec Asst To Bp Of Virginia 1980-1984, 1976-1984; R S Andr's Epis Ch Miami FL 1979-1980; Off Of Bsh For ArmdF New York NY 1967-1976; Cur S Jn The Evang Ch Lansdowne PA 1966-1967. Auth, "Mssn Fulfilling: Story Rural & Sm Cmnty Workk Of Epis Ch 20th Century," Morehouse Pub, 1997; Auth, "Congrl Hlth Mnstry: Challenge & Opportunity," Ch Pub Inc, 1997; Auth, "arts Theol & Mltry Pub"; Auth, "Models Of Ecum," Atr; Ed, "AltGld," Morehouse-Barlow. AFP, Conf Of Dioc Exec.

BROWN, Aston George (Tex) D 6/25/2016 Bp C Andrew Doyle.

BROWN, Barton (NJ) D 6/11/1960 P 12/17/1960 Bp Horace W B Donegan.

BROWN, Becky (Colo) 6820 W 84th Cir Unit 26, Arvada CO 80003 **P-in-c The Ch Of Chr The King (Epis) Arvada CO 2014-, P-in-c 2011-2014** B Kingston NY 1950 d Donald & Betty. Kalamazoo Coll 1969; Kalamazoo Coll 1973; BS Carnegie Mellon U 1981; Pittsburgh TS 1991; MDiv GTS 1992. D 6/6/1992 P 12/8/1992 Bp Alden Moinet Hathaway. c 3. R S Mk's Ch Foxborough MA 2001-2011; Assoc R All SS Ch Worcester MA 1995-2001; Prog Asst Assn of Theol Schools 1995; Int R The Ch Of The Redeem Pittsburgh PA 1994; Int Cmncatn Off Dio Pittsburgh Pittsburgh PA 1993-1994; Cn Trin Cathd Pittsburgh PA 1992-1994. rebecca@ctkarvada.org

BROWN, Bernard Owen (Chi) 5417 S Blackstone Ave, Chicago IL 60615 B Brooklyn NY 1930 s C Maxwell & Dorothy. Duke 1950; BD U Chi 1955; MA U Chi 1965; PhD U Chi 1973. D 6/13/1970 Bp James Winchester Montgomery P 12/1/1970 Bp Gerald Francis Burrill. m 6/13/1951 Carol Jean Brown. Serv Methodist Ch 1953-1962. Auth, "W Side Orgnztn & Ideology Of Deviance"; Auth, "Seasons Of His Mercy".

BROWN JR, Bill (Ida) 5605 Lynwood Pl., Boise ID 83706 B San Francisco CA 1948 s William & Blanche. BA OR SU 1971; MDiv CDSP 1976. D 6/26/1976 Bp Chauncie Kilmer Myers P 1/6/1978 Bp John F Conlin. m 12/21/2010 Laurel Crookston c 2. S Andr's Epis Ch Mccall ID 2004-2015; Dir Paradise Point Camp Dio Idaho Boise ID 1999-2004; Cmnty Serv Coordntr City of Boise Boise ID 1991-1998; Cn S Mich's Cathd Boise ID 1983-1989; R two point Par Andlican Ch of Can Vegreville Tofield 1979-1983; Cn, St. Matt's Cathd Angl Ch of Can Brandon 1976-1979; Engr Off USN VietNam 1971-1973.

BROWN, Charles Homer (Okla) 1416 Stoneridge Pl, Ardmore OK 73401 **Exec Dir/Chapl Ardmore Vill Sr Citizens Res 1981-** B Paris TX 1927 s Charles & Mamie. BA TCU 1948; BD Ya Berk 1952; U So 1966; U of Oklahoma 1971. D 9/9/1961 P 5/1/1962 Bp John Elbridge Hines. m 8/28/1949 Bettye C Brown. S Ptr's Ch Coalgate OK 1992-1993; Ardmore Vill Ardmore OK 1988-1994; S Mk's Par Altadena CA 1981-1994; Non-par 1972-1994; R Ch Of The Adv Houston TX 1966-1971; Assoc S Mk's Ch Houston TX 1962-1966; Serv Ch Of Engl 1958-1978.

BROWN, Christopher Aubrey (Alb) 437 Old Potsdam Parishville Road, Potsdam NY 13676 **Prov Chapl CSM Greenwich NY 2005-; R Trin Ch Potsdam NY 2000-** B Zurich CH 1955 s William & Anne. BA Amh 1977; MDiv GTS 1985; PhD UTS 2001. D 6/1/1985 P 6/20/1986 Bp John Bowen Coburn. m 6/24/1989 Starr Marie Brown c 2. Par of Chr the Redeem Pelham NY 1998-2000, Cur 1985-2000; Int S Jn's Epis Ch Kingston NY 1997-1998; Asst Gr Ch New York NY 1988-1997; Gr Epis Ch New York NY 1988-1997; Chaplian Gr Ch Sch New York NY 1988-1993. Auth, "Real Presence," *Angl Dig*, 1999; Auth, "Can Buddhism Save? Finding Resonance in Incomensurability," *Cross Currents*, 1999; Auth, "More than Affirmation: The Incarn as Judgement and Gr," *The Rule of Faith: Scripture*, Morehouse Pub, 1988.

BROWN, Cliff (Mass) 351 Pearl St # 1, Cambridge MA 02139 **R Chr Ch Quincy MA 2005-** B Cambridge MA 1955 s Herbert & Muriel. BS Estrn U 1981; Cert Bp Tucker Theol Coll 1991; MDiv Andover Newton TS 1992. D 6/15/2002 P 5/31/2003 Bp M(Arvil) Thomas Shaw. Asst S Steph's Memi Ch Lynn MA 2002-2005; Bd Mem Epis City Mssn Boston MA 2008-2014; Theol Stdt Angl Stds Vol For Mssn New York NY 1989-1990.

BROWN, Colin (Los) 1024 Beverly Way, Altadena CA 91001 B Bradford Yorkshire UK 1932 s Robert & Maud. BA U of Liverpool 1953; BD Tyndale Hall Bristol/Lon GB 1958; MA U of Nottingham 1961; PhD Tyndale Hall Bristol/Lon GB 1970; DD U of Nottingham 1994. Trans 1/4/1981 Bp Robert Claflin Rusack. c 3. Asstg S Mk's Par Altadena CA 2007-2010; Assoc R S Mk's Par Altadena CA 1981-2007; Prof Fuller TS Pasadena CA 1978-2013; Serv Ch of Engl 1958-1978. Auth, "Chrsnty & Wstrn Thought," *vol1 From the Ancient Wrld to the Age of Enlightenment*, InterVarsity Press, 1990; Auth, *Hist & Faith*, InterVarsity Press, 1987; Auth, "European," *Jesus in ProtestantThought 1778-1860*, Labyrinth, 1985; Auth, "Report," *That You May Believe*, Paternoster Press, 1985; Auth, "Report," *Miracles & the Critical Mind*, Eerdmans, 1984; Auth, *The New Intl Dictionary of NT Theol (3 volumes)*, Paternoster Press, 1978; Auth, "Hist," *Criticism & Faith (French translation)*, InterVarsity Press, 1976; Auth, *Philos & the Chr Faith*, InterVarsity Press, 1969; Auth, *Karl Barth & the Chr Message*, InterVarsity Press, 1967. AAR 1982; SBL 1982. Hensley Henson Lectures U of Oxford 1993; Awd for Excellence C Davis Weyerhaeuser 1988; Gold Medallion Evang Bk Pub Assoc 1985.

BROWN, Craig Howard (WK) 3710 Summer Ln, Hays KS 67601 B Melbourne FL 1967 BS U of Florida 1990; MEd U of Florida 1997; MDiv TESM 2004.

D 5/30/2004 Bp Samuel Johnson Howard P 12/4/2004 Bp James Marshall Adams Jr. m 7/29/2000 Elizabeth Christie Brown c 2. D S Mich's Ch Hays KS 2004-2009; Chair - COM Dio Wstrn Kansas Hutchinson KS 2007-2009.

BROWN, Daniel Aaron (NC) 936 Cannock St, Grovetown GA 30813 **Non-par 2004-** B Savannah GA 1947 s Henry & Mildred. BA Armstrong Atlantic St U 1974; MDiv Sewanee: The U So, TS 1996. D 6/8/1996 Bp Don Adger Wimberly P 12/15/1996 Bp James Gary Gloster. m 7/27/1985 Donna Jane Brown c 1. P-in-c All Souls Ch Ansonville NC 1996-2005; Calv Ch Wadesboro NC 1996-2005.

BROWN, Daniel Barnes (At) Po Box 490, Clarkesville GA 30523 **The Epis Ch Of The Adv Madison GA 2012-** B Harlan KY 1953 s Thomas & Dora. BA Furman U 1976; MDiv Sewanee: The U So, TS 1993. D 6/12/1993 Bp William Arthur Beckham P 1/21/1994 Bp Harry Woolston Shipps. m 11/24/1989 Cynthia Leigh Carson c 2. Chapl Dio Atlanta Atlanta GA 2003-2014; S Julian's Epis Ch Douglasville GA 2001-2003; R Gr-Calv Epis Ch Clarkesville GA 1998-2001; Asst The Ch Of The Gd Shpd Augusta GA 1993-1998. rector@adventmadisonga.org

BROWN, David Churchman Kirk (WNC) 500 Christ School Rd, Arden NC 28704 **Chapl Chr Sch Chap Arden NC 1995-** B Marianna FL 1953 s David & Anne. AB Davidson Coll 1975; MA U of Virginia 1977; MDiv VTS 1992. D 6/6/1992 Bp A(rthur) Heath Light. c 2. Assoc R S Jn's Ch Roanoke VA 1992-1995. kbrown@christschool.org

BROWN, David Crane (NY) 125 Prospect Ave Apt 9G, Hackensack NJ 07601 **Ret 2009-** B Englewood NJ 1947 s Percival & Katherine. BA CUNY Hunter Coll 1969; MDiv PDS 1972. D 6/3/1972 P 12/9/1972 Bp Paul Moore Jr. Morningside Hse Nrsng Hm Bronx NY 1994-2008; Dir of Pstr Care Morningside Hse Nrsng Hm Bronx NY 1994-2008; Ch Of S Mary The Vrgn Ridgefield Pk NJ 1982-1994; S Matt's Ch Bedford NY 1974-1982; Cur Ch Of The Mssh Rhinebeck NY 1972-1974. Auth, "S Fran of Assisi," *The Journ for Better Living*.

BROWN, David Wooster (Ct) 729 W Beach Rd, Charlestown RI 02813 **Ret 1989-** B Waterbury CT 1926 s Harold & Ruth. BA Ya 1948; MDiv Ya Berk 1959; Ldrshp Acad for New Directions 1975. D 6/11/1959 Bp Walter H Gray P 12/5/1959 Bp John Henry Esquirol. m 7/19/1952 Carole Brown c 6. Middlesex Area Cluster Mnstry Higganum CT 1981-1989; Grtr Hartford Reg Mnstry Dio Connecticut Meriden CT 1980-1989, 1980; R Chr Ch Montpelier VT 1966-1980; Ch Of The Resurr Norwich CT 1963-1965; R Ch of the Resurr CT 1963-1965; Vic S Andr's Norwich CT 1961-1963; Vic Trin Norwich CT 1959-1963. Auth, "Var arts & Revs". OHC 1961. The Berkeley Awd The Ya Berk 1985.

BROWN, Debbie (Minn) 1297 Wilderness Curv, Eagan MN 55123 **Chapl Metro CISM Team Minneapolis MN 2001-; Chapl City of Eagan Police Dept Eagan MN 1995-** B Carmel CA 1940 d Charles & Lois. BA Occ 1961; MDiv Epis TS of the SW 1989. D 6/22/1989 Bp Robert Marshall Anderson P 5/1/1990 Bp Anselmo Carral-Solar. m 7/6/1963 Ronald Brown c 2. Co Int S Clem's Ch S Paul MN 2005-2006, Pre Int 2005; Int S Lk's Ch Minneapolis MN 2000-2001; Int Assoc S Jn The Evang S Paul MN 1998-1999; Int S Chris's Epis Ch S Paul MN 1996-1998, Assoc 1993-1998; Chapl S Dav's Hosp Austin TX 1990-1992; Dio Minnesota Minneapolis MN 1989-2012, Coordntr, D Educ Prog 2002-2008; P Gr Epis Ch Georgetown TX 1989-1992; Chapl Austin St Hosp 1989-1990. Minnesota Epis Cler Assn.

BROWN OJN, Deborah Renee (Ore) Diocese of Oregon, 11800 SW Military Ln, Portland OR 97219 B Charlotte NC 1966 d Robert & Dorothy. BMus Eastman Sch of Mus 1989; MME Winthrop U 1998; MDiv Duke DS 2006; Cert Theol Stud SWTS 2008. D 6/6/2009 P 12/7/2009 Bp Prince Grenville Singh. R S Phil The D Epis Ch Portland OR 2012-2015; St. Phil the D Dio Oregon Portland OR 2012-2013, Epis Campus Mnstry at Portland St U 2012-; Asst Trin Ch Geneva NY 2011-2012; Presiding Yth Mssnr Dio Rochester Henrietta 2010-2011; D Tri-Par Mnstry Hornell NY 2009. Writer of one Pryr, "Anthology of Prayers," *Lifting Wmn Voices: Prayers to Change the Wrld*, Morehouse Pub, 2009. The Janet Skogen Stff Appreciation Awd SWTS 2008; Seabury-Wstrn Prize SWTS 2008.

BROWN, Dennis Roy Alfred (CGC) 306 Grant St, Chickasaw AL 36611 **Vic S Thos Ch Citronelle AL 2008-** B 1948 s Charles & Frances. S Johns Au 1979; MDiv Sewanee: The U So, TS 1983. D 7/15/1983 P 5/1/1984 Bp Charles Farmer Duvall. Wilmer Hall Mobile AL 2005-2008; Dio Cntrl Gulf Coast Pensacola FL 1996-1998; P-in-c S Mich's Ch Mobile AL 1989-2008; R S Jas Ch Eufaula AL 1985-1989; Cur S Jas Ch Fairhope AL 1983-1985.

BROWN JR, Dewey Everrett (SwFla) 37637 Magnolia Ave, Dade City FL 33523 **P S Mary's Ch Dade City FL 2009-; COM Dio SW Florida Parrish FL 2010-** B Fort Knox KY 1956 s Dewey & Dolores. BBA MI SU 1979; Cert U of Pennsylvania 1992; MDiv VTS 2001. D 6/9/2001 Bp David Conner Bane Jr P 12/18/2001 Bp Clifton Daniel III. m 4/22/1981 Deborah Bennett Brown c 3. P S Lk's Epis Ch Haworth NJ 2003-2009; P S Jn's Epis Ch Wilmington NC 2001-2003; Chair, Dioc Conv Nomin Com Dio Newark Newark NJ 2007-2009, Eccl Crt 2007-2009, Dioc Working Grp on Evang 2006-2009, Dioc Bp's Nomin

Commitee for Dio Newark 2005-2007, Dioc Revs Com 2004-2007; Dioc Exec Coun Dio E Carolina Kinston NC 2001-2003.

BROWN, Don (La) 224 Pecan Ave, New Roads LA 70760 **Chapl to the Ret S Jas Epis Ch Baton Rouge LA 2011-** B Elsberry MO 1942 s Ralph & Florence. BS U of Missouri 1964; MDiv Nash 1981. D 1/3/1981 P 7/25/1981 P Donald James Parsons. m 1/4/1997 Geraldine Brown c 2. Chapl St Jas Place 2010-2014; P-in-c S Mary's Ch Morganza LA 2006-2009; R S Paul's/H Trin New Roads LA 2006-2009; R S Jn's Epis Ch Decatur IL 2001-2006; All SS Epis Ch Russellville AR 1996-2001; R S Fran Ch Denham Spgs LA 1990-1996; Vic Ch Of The Redeem Oak Ridge LA 1984-1990; R S Andr's Epis Ch Mer Rouge LA 1984-1990; Vic S Oswald In The Field Skidmore MO 1981-1984; Vic S Paul's Ch Maryville MO 1981-1984.

BROWN, Donald Gary (Cal) 2821 Claremont Blvd, Berkeley CA 94705 **Dept of Missions San Francisco CA 2008-; non-stipendiary P Assoc All Souls Par In Berkeley Berkeley CA 2005-; Bd Mem Berkeley Cbury Fndt Berkeley CA 2005-** B Eureka CA 1946 s Donald & Ilene. BA Willamette U 1968; STB EDS 1971; DMin CDSP 1998. D 6/22/1971 P 1/22/1972 Bp James Walmsley Frederic Carman. m 7/5/1975 Carol A Brown c 2. The Epis Dio Nthrn California Sacramento CA 1993-2005, Chair Of COM 1989-1992, 1987-1988, Stndg Com 1987-1991; Dn Trin Epis Cathd Sacramento CA 1987-2005; R S Steph's Epis Ch Longview WA 1977-1987; Assoc Chr Ch Par Lake Oswego OR 1973-1977; Dio Oregon Portland OR 1971-1975; Dept Of CE S Paul's Epis Ch Salem OR 1971-1973; Chapl Wilamette U Salem OR 1971-1973; Chair Of COM Dio Olympia Seattle 1984-1987, Evaltn Com 1981-1983, Dioc Coun 1979-1980. EvangES. DD CDSP 2005.

BROWN, Donna Hvistendahl (WA) 1318 Charlottesville Blvd, Knoxville TN 37922 **Ch Of The Resurr Loudon TN 2016-** B Worthington MN 1946 d Dale & Charlotte. BA Hur 1968; MDiv VTS 1993. D 6/24/1993 Bp Craig Barry Anderson P 1/6/1994 Bp George Clinton Harris. m 5/21/1994 Kenneth E Brown c 3. All SS' Epis Ch Morristown TN 2015-2016; R S Mk's Ch Fairland Silver Sprg MD 2000-2011; Assoc R Chr Epis Ch Warren OH 1998-2000; Asst S Lk's Par Kalamazoo MI 1995-1998; Chr Epis Ch Lead SD 1994-1995; Yth Dir Dio So Dakota Pierre SD 1994-1995; Assoc S Jn's Ch Deadwood SD 1994-1995; Dioc Yth Coordntr Dio So Dakota 1993-1995; Cur Calv Cathd Sioux Falls SD 1993-1994.

BROWN, Donn H (At) 217 Booth St Apt 119, Gaithersburg MD 20878 B Albany CA 1932 s Howard & Ethel. U of Hawaii 1952; Arizona St U Flagstaff 1958; CDSP 1969; BD CDSP 1975. D 6/10/1969 Bp Edwin Lani Hanchett P 12/14/1969 Bp Edmond Lee Browning. c 3. P-in-c S Jn's Epis Ch Franklin NC 1998-2006; S Jas Epis Ch Clayton GA 1992-1996; S Andr's Priory Sch Honolulu HI 1990-1998; P Ch Of The H Cross Decatur GA 1990-1992; Vic The Epis Ch in Hawaii Honolulu HI 1985-1990, 1973-1984; S Matt's Epis Ch Waimanalo HI 1981-1983; S Andr's Cathd Honolulu HI 1981, P 1976-1979; R H Cross Malaekahana HI 1976-1985; S Ptr's Ch Honolulu HI 1976-1985; Vic Kohala Epis Mssns No Kohala HI 1971-1973; Serv St. Jn the Div Guam 1969-1971. Ed, "Adv In The Hm"; Auth, "The Euch As Preparation For Mssn"; Auth, "Bible Study Aids".

BROWN, Dorothy (At) 1197 Skyline Drive, Toccoa GA 30577 B Pittsburgh PA 1947 d Howard & Mildred. BS Indiana U of Pennsylvania 1968; MS Buc 1971; MA U of Virginia 1979; MDiv Sewanee: The U So, TS 1986. D 12/9/1986 Bp Peter J Lee P 6/29/1987 Bp Charles I Jones III. R S Mths Epis Ch Toccoa GA 2003-2009; R S Thos a Becket Epis Ch Morgantown WV 1992-2003; Ch Of The Incarn Greg SD 1989-1992; RurD Rosebud Reg Dio So Dakota Pierre SD 1989-1992; Trin Epis Ch Winner SD 1989-1992; Asst S Jas Ch Bozeman MT 1987-1989.

BROWN, Dwight (Va) 489 Ridge Rd, Moscow ID 83843 **long term supply Chr Ch Kealakekua HI 2017-; Cn, Dio Cntrl Buganda Ch of the Prov of Uganda Kasaka 1997-; Cn St. Jn's Cathd Kasaka Uganda 1995-; Vic S Mary's Memi Berryville VA 1984-** B Bridgeport CT 1954 s Ralph & Joy. BA Trin Hartford CT 1976; MDiv VTS 1981. D 5/30/1981 P 12/18/1981 Bp Alexander D Stewart. m 7/11/1981 Catherine Elizabeth Brown c 2. VTS Alexandria VA 1989-1992; Colloquy Mentor VTS Alexandria VA 1989-1992; Dn, Reg XIV Dio Virginia Richmond VA 1987-1991; R Gr Ch Berryville VA 1984-2016; Asst Min Trin Ch Arlington VA 1981-1984. BDiv w hon VTS 1981; BA w Honorsw Trin 1976; Phi Beta Kappa Trin 1976.

BROWN, Elly Sparks (WA) 5006-B Barbour Dr, Alexandria VA 22304 **1998-** B Pittsburgh PA 1950 d Clifford & Arlene. BA Seton Hill U 1972; MA CUA 1977; MDiv VTS 1984; DMin Wesley TS 1991. D 6/23/1984 Bp Peter J Lee P 6/1/1985 Bp David Henry Lewis Jr. m 10/6/1990 Hugh Eldridge Brown. Vic Chr Ch Palmyra NJ 2011-2017; R Old Fields Chap Hughesville MD 1999-2008; R Trin Epis Par Hughesville MD 1999-2007; Admin Dir of the Cntr for Arts Wesley TS Washington DC 1995-1998; Vic New Life Epis Ch Uniontown OH 1994-1995; All SS Ch Richmond VA 1990-1993; Assoc R S Lk's Ch Alexandria VA 1984-1989.

BROWN, Enrique Ricardo (WA) 5248 Colorado Ave Nw, Washington DC 20011 B Ancon Republic of Panama 1944 s Sherman & Una. U of Panama PA; BA New Sch U 1971; MDiv Ya Berk 1974. D 12/14/1974 Bp James

Stuart Wetmore P 6/28/1975 Bp Harold Louis Wright. m 6/15/1974 Irene V Jackson-Brown c 1. Int S Matt's Epis Ch Hyattsville MD 2011-2013; Int S Mk's Ch Jackson Heights NY 2006-2010; P-in-c S Paul's Rock Creek Washington DC 2002-2006; Int S Jas' Epis Ch Baltimore MD 2000-2002; Assoc Ch Of The Ascen Gaithersburg MD 2000; Latino/Hisp Mssnr Dio Washington Washington DC 1995-1999; Mssn San Juan Washington DC 1995-1999; Int Hisp Mnstry New York NY 1993-1995; Archd Reg II Dio New York New York NY 1985-1992; Inst Pstr Hispano 1977-1985; Vic S Lk's Stamford CT 1977-1980; Latino/Hisp Mssnr Dio Connecticut Meriden CT 1975-1985; Asst S Lk's/S Paul's Ch Bridgeport CT 1975-1977. Auth, "Renwl Of The Ch In The City". Consult Lambeth Conf-Archbp of Cbury 1988; Hon Cn Cathd of S Jn the Div 1985.

BROWN III, Erv (Eas) 2212 E Baltimore St, Baltimore MD 21231 **Died 12/12/2016** B Birmingham AL 1937 s Ervin & Anilee. BA U of Alabama 1958; MPA Indiana U 1961; MDiv VTS 1965. D 6/22/1965 P 6/7/1966 Bp Harry Lee Doll. m 6/4/1960 Letetia Brown c 3. Memi Ch Baltimore MD 2009-2016; Int Dn Cathd Of The Incarn Baltimore MD 2008-2009; All SS Ch Worcester MA 2007-2008; Chr Ch St Michaels Par S Mich MD 1995-2002; Stndg Com Dio Michigan Detroit MI 1994-1995, Exec Coun 1988-1995; R Chr Ch Detroit MI 1981-1995; R S Paul's Epis Ch Lynchburg VA 1973-1981; COM Dio SW Virginia Roanoke VA 1973-1976, Stndg Com 1976-1979; R S Jn's Ch Reisterstown MD 1967-1973; Chair of COM Dio Easton Easton MD 1998-2002.

BROWN, Freda Marie (Tex) St. Vincent's Episcopal House, 2817 Alfreda Houston Place, Galveston TX 77550 B Greenville MS 1956 d Leon & Marie. BS Xavier U of LA 1979; BS Xavier U of LA 1979; MTS SMU 2002; MTS SMU 2002; MAR Epis TS of the SW 2009; MA Epis TS of the SW 2009. D 6/6/2009 Bp James Monte Stanton P 3/25/2010 Bp Paul Emil Lambert. m 5/24/1981 Charles E Brown c 1. P Ch Of The Annunc Lewisville TX 2009-2014. Auth, "Call to Mnstry," *PRAISES ABOUND: Hymns & Meditations for Lent & Easter from the Epis Sem of the SW*, Ch Pub, 2012.

BROWN, Frederick Ransom (Vt) 346 Gladys Avenue, Long Beach CA 90814 **Non-par 1969-** B Springfield VT 1941 s Milton & Emmy. BA Ya 1963; BD CDSP 1966; MSW Smith 1974. D 6/29/1966 P 1/1/1967 Bp Harvey D Butterfield. Asst Cathd Ch Of S Paul Burlington VT 1966-1968.

BROWN JR, F Wilson (SwVa) 715 Sunset Drive, Bedford VA 24523 **R S Jn's Ch Bedford VA 2008-** B Richmond VA 1961 s Francis & Leslie. BA W&M 1984; MDiv VTS 1991. D 6/15/1991 Bp Claude Charles Vache P 1/1/1992 Bp William George Burrill. m 7/11/1992 Kara Suzanne Wagner Brown c 3. R H Sacr Hollywood FL 2004-2008; R S Mk's Epis Ch Le Roy NY 1994-2004; Asst S Paul's Ch Rochester NY 1991-1994. wbrownstjohns@verizon.net

BROWN, Gary N (NCal) B Monterey CA 1944 s Harold & Mildred. AA Cuesta Coll 1973; BA California St U 1998; BDS Epis Sch for Deacons 2012. D 6/9/2012 Bp Barry Leigh Beisner. m 7/6/1985 Cathy Page Brown c 3.

BROWN, Gaye (NC) 308 W Main St, Elkin NC 28621 **Vic Galloway Memi Chap Elkin NC 2010-** B Elkin NC 1943 d Dennis & Mary. BA Salem Coll Winston-Salem NC 1965; MDiv Van 1969. D 6/7/2008 P 12/14/2008 Bp William Carl Frey. c 1. Asst H Trin Epis Ch - Mssn Raton NM 2008-2009; Exec Dir The Mandala Cntr 2000-2009; Exec Dir Epis Cmnty Serv in Arizona 1990-2000; Mgr of Prog VGS Inc 1971-1990.

BROWN III, George Willcox (Dal) 409 Prospect St, New Haven CT 06511 **R Ch Of The H Cross Dallas TX 2007-** B 1979 BA U So 2001; MDiv Yale DS 2005. D 2/5/2005 P 7/9/2005 Bp Henry Irving Louttit. Ch Of S Mths Dallas TX 2006; Epis Ch At Yale New Haven CT 2005-2006.

BROWN, Greg (WMich) 1020 E Mitchell St, Petoskey MI 49770 **R Emm Ch Petoskey MI 2005-** B 1965 s David & Marilyn. BS MI SU 1989; MDiv GTS 2001. D 6/2/2001 P 12/8/2001 Bp Edward Lewis Lee Jr. m 6/24/1995 Catherine R Brown c 3. R Trin Epis Ch Grand Ledge MI 2001-2005; Dio Wstrn Michigan Kalamazoo MI 1995-1997.

BROWN, Greg (Los) St Cross Episcopal Church, 1818 Monterey Blvd, Hermosa Beach CA 90254 **Assoc St Cross Epis Ch Hermosa Bch CA 2013-** B Berkeley CA 1973 s David & Carol. BA Carleton Coll 1995; MDiv GTS 2012. D 6/2/2012 P 12/1/2012 Bp Marc Handley Andrus. m 8/22/2015 Stefanie Glenn Wilson. Assoc R for Wrshp and Formation Chr Epis Ch Ponte Vedra FL 2012-2013.

BROWN III, Henry William (CFla) Po Box 1420, Homosassa Springs FL 34447 **D S Anne's Ch Crystal River FL 1988-** B Dunedin FL 1953 s Henry & Juanita. Marion Mltry Inst 1972; BA U So 1975. D 11/17/1988 Bp William Hopkins Folwell. m 6/11/1976 Virginia Diane Brown c 2.

BROWN JR, H (Horace) Frederick (WTex) 309 S Someday Dr, Boerne TX 78006 **Cler Supply Dio W Texas 2005-** B Austin TX 1938 s Horace & Naomi. BA U So 1960; JD S Mary U San Antonio TX 1970; MDiv Houston Grad TS 1992; CAS CDSP 1996. D 6/22/1996 Bp Claude Edward Payne P 1/18/1997 Bp William Elwood Sterling. S Eliz's Epis Ch Buda TX 2005-2008; Asst S Helena's Epis Ch Boerne TX 2000-2005; The Epis Dio Nthrn California Sacramento CA 2000; Asst to R H Trin Ch Nevada City CA 1997-1999; D Chr Ch Jefferson TX 1996-1997; D Trin Ch Marshall TX 1996-1997.

BROWN III, Hugh Eldridge (NJ) 16 All Saints Rd, Princeton NJ 08540 **R All SS Ch Princeton NJ 2007-** B Roanoke VA 1959 s Hugh & Josephine. BA W&M 1981; MA U of Virginia 1985; MDiv VTS 1988; DMin Wesley TS 1999. D 6/24/1988 P 9/1/1989 Bp A(rthur) Heath Light. m 10/6/1990 Elly Sparks Brown. S Thos Par Croom Uppr Marlboro MD 2003-2007; S Phil's Chap Baden Brandywine MD 1999-2003; S Jn's Ch Lafayette Sq Washington DC 1997-1999; R Chr Epis Ch Kent OH 1993-1995; Asst Chr Epis Ch Charlottesvlle VA 1990-1993; Co-Chapl R E Lee Memi Ch (Epis) Lexington VA 1988-1990. Auth, "Vts Sem Journ". ESMHE; Iaf-Win/Apt.

BROWN, Ian Frederick (Mich) 26 Tower Dr., Saline MI 48176 B Cape Town ZA 1932 s Frederick & Dorothy. BD U Chi 1958; MS Wayne 1971. D 7/17/1966 Bp Archie H Crowley P 11/1/1966 Bp Chauncie Kilmer Myers. c 3. S Jn's Ch Clinton MI 2000-2004; Non-par 1970-1980; Vic All SS Epis Ch Marysville MI 1965-1969; Serv Bapt Ch 1958-1966.

✠ BROWN, The Rt Rev James Barrow (La) 2136 Octavia St, New Orleans LA 70115 **Ret Bp Of Louisiana Dio Louisiana New Orleans LA 1998-, Bp 1976-1998, 1971-1976, Archd 1971-1976, BEC 1967-1976** B El Dorado AR 1932 s John & Ella. BS LSU 1954; BD Austin Presb TS 1957; Goettingen U DE 1960; PrTS 1963; GTS 1965; Sewanee: The U So, TS 1976; Tubingen U Tubingen DE 1984. D 6/22/1965 Bp Girault M Jones P 12/15/1965 Bp Iveson Batchelor Noland Con 4/24/1976 for La. m 10/3/1970 Mary J Brown. Asst Dio Texas Houston TX 2000-2002; Int Trin Ch Galveston TX 1998-2000; Cur S Andr's Epis Ch New Orleans LA 1968-1971; Cur Gr Epis Ch Monroe LA 1966-1968; Cur S Geo's Ch Bossier City LA 1965-1966; Serv Presb Ch 1957-1964. DD U So 1976.

BROWN, James Louis (O) 1533 N 85th Ct, Kansas City KS 66112 B Kansas City KS 1945 s Louis & Margaret. BD Emporia St U 1967; MA Emporia St U 1968; PhD K SU 1975. D 6/4/1982 Bp Richard Frank Grein. m 8/9/1970 Neea Beth Brown c 2. D S Mich And All Ang Ch Mssn KS 1982-2001. Auth, "Origins Of Black Engl," 1979; Auth, "Tchg Engl In Cmnty Coll," *Ar Engl Bulletin*, 1979.

BROWN, James Thompson (Cal) 6225 Vine Hill School Rd, Sebastopol CA 95472 **Ret 1983-** B Salt Lake City UT 1927 s Harold & Norinne. BA Ya 1950; STB GTS 1960. D 5/20/1960 P 11/1/1960 Bp Richard S Watson. The Cathd Ch Of The Adv Birmingham AL 1985-1998; Ch Of The Ascen Knoxville TN 1977-1985; R The Epis Ch Of S Jn The Evang San Francisco CA 1977-1983; Non-par 1972-1985; Assoc Vic S Jn's 1971-1974; Dio Tennessee Nashville TN 1969-1972; Cn Chapl U Of Utah Salt Lake City UT 1964-1966; R E Lee Memi Ch (Epis) Lexington VA 1963-1969; All SS Epis Ch Norton VA 1960-1963; Asst To Dn Cathd Ch Of S Mk Salt Lake City UT 1960-1963.

BROWN, Janet Easson (CPa) 140 N Beaver St, York PA 17401 **D The Epis Ch Of S Jn The Bapt York PA 2010-** B Braintree MA 1951 d Alexander & Barbara. Diac Stds Dio Cntrl PA Sch of Chr Stds; BA Dickinson Coll 1973; MSW Virginia Commonwealth U 1978. D 10/31/2010 Bp Nathan Dwight Baxter. m 12/3/1983 Roy Drinkwater c 1.

BROWN, Janet Kelly (Vt) Po Box 351, Jericho VT 05465 B Flushing NY 1942 d Thomas & Janet. BA Swarthmore Coll 1964; MA Wesl 1965; MA Antioch U New Engl 1987. D 6/2/1974 Bp Harvey D Butterfield P 1/6/1977 Bp Robert Shaw Kerr. c 2. P-in-Partnership Gr Ch Sheldon VT 2008-2014; P-in-c Ch Of The Gd Shpd Barre VT 1998-2001; Int Trin Epis Ch E Poultney VT 1996-1998; H Trin Epis Ch Swanton VT 1988-1991; Trin Milton VT 1979-1982; S Ann's Ch Burlington VT 1978-1979; S Jas Epis Ch Essex Jct VT 1978-1979; S Matt's Ch Enosburg Fls VT 1978-1979.

BROWN, Jan Michelle (SVa) D 4/16/2016 Bp Herman Hollerith IV.

BROWN, Jennifer (NY) 1558 Unionport Rd Apt 7E, Bronx NY 10462 **Chr Ch Bronxville NY 2009-** B 1954 d Fetzgerald & Barbara. Utica Coll 1992; MSW Yeshiva U 1992; MDiv GTS 2009. D 3/7/2009 P 9/12/2009 Bp Mark Sean Sisk. m 7/8/1995 James L Lanier c 3.

BROWN, Jennifer Clarke (NC) 2212 Tyson Street, Raleigh NC 27612 **Assoc Chr Epis Ch Raleigh NC 2009-; Pstr Counslr Triangle Pstr Counslg Inc. Raleigh 2005-** B New York NY 1961 d Robert & Lynn. BA Pr 1983; JD Duke 1988; MDiv Andover Newton TS 1996. D 9/8/1996 P 3/8/1997 Bp M(Arvil) Thomas Shaw. m 11/24/2007 Davin Brown c 1. Chapl WakeMed Hosp 2004-2005; Asst S Tim's Epis Ch Cincinnati OH 1999-2004; Asst S Anne's In The Fields Epis Ch Lincoln MA 1998-1999; Asst S Jn's Ch Beverly MA 1996-1998. jbrown@christchurchraleigh.org

BROWN JR, John Ashmore (USC) 9 Sweet Branch Ct, Columbia SC 29212 B Gaffney SC 1948 s John & Bobbie. BA Wofford Coll 1970; MEd U of So Carolina 1972; MDiv VTS 1986. D 6/7/1986 P 5/1/1987 Bp William Arthur Beckham. m 6/21/1969 Pamela Hammett c 1. Asst S Mary's 1990-1996; S Lk's Ch Newberry SC 1986-1989. OHC.

BROWN, John Clive (Ore) 431-A Red Blanket Rd, Prospect OR 97536 **Vic Ch Of The Gd Shpd Prospect OR 1997-** B Riverside CA 1933 s John & Pauline. U CA. D 7/30/1996 P 2/26/1997 Bp Robert Louis Ladehoff. m 10/10/1973 Esther Gertrude Brown.

BROWN, John Daniel (Dal) 7610 Rockingham Rd, Prospect KY 40059 **P H Trin Epis Ch Garland TX 2007-** B Torrence CA 1952 BS USNA. D 6/14/2003 Bp Peter J Lee P 12/13/2003 Bp Ted Gulick Jr. m 3/6/1976 Evelyn Louise Brown c 2. Assoc S Fran In The Fields Harrods Creek KY 2003-2007.

BROWN, John Thompson (Ala) 4157 Winston Way, Birmingham AL 35213 **Ret 1998-; T/F on Stwdshp of Creation Dio Alabama Birmingham 2012-, Cmsn on the Mnstry 2001-2012** B Nashville TN 1933 s John & Vera. BA Georgia Inst of Tech 1957; MDiv VTS 1960. D 6/24/1960 P 9/22/1961 Bp William Henry Marmion. m 9/5/1959 Ann R Brown c 2. Admin The Cathd Ch Of The Adv Birmingham AL 1994-1998; Dir of Pstr Care 1985-1994; P Assoc Ch Of The Ascen Knoxville TN 1980-1985; Coordntr Chapl Trng Lakeshore Mntl Hlth Inst Knoxville TN 1972-1985; Chapl In Res S Eliz's Hosp Washington DC 1969-1972; Assoc R E Lee Memi Ch (Epis) Lexington VA 1963-1969; Vic All SS Epis Ch Norton VA 1960-1963; Vic S Steph's Nora VA 1960-1963. Auth, "Healing, Some Sci & Theol Considerations," *Sewanee Theol Revs*, 1998; Auth, "On-The-Job Profsnl Growth For Par Cler," *Assn Of Mntl Hlth Cler*; Auth, "Bowen Theory & Pstr Care," *Assn Of Mntl Hlth Cler*. Assn of Mntl Hlth Cler 1972.

BROWN, Keith B (SJ) 1776 S Homsy Ave, Fresno CA 93727 B Los Angeles CA 1945 s Delbert & Elizabeth. BA USC 1967; MBA U of Utah 1975; MDiv CDSP 1982. D 1/16/1983 P 12/9/1984 Bp Charles Shannon Mallory. m 6/7/1986 Linda Ann Brown. Proj Consult The CPG New York NY 2002-2011; Secy Prov VIII 2000-2002; Intercultural Mnstry Dvlpmt Com Prov VIII 1997-2000; Cn Mssnr Epis Dio San Joaquin Modesto CA 1995-1999, 1984-1985; Dep GC 1990-2001; Dep Prov VIII 1987-2001; Vic Our Lady of Guadalupe Fresno CA 1986-1994; Cur S Dunst's Epis Ch Carmel CA 1983-1984. Auth, "On The Road Again," *Mng Evang And Stwdshp For The Kingdom*, Ch Pub, 2001; Auth, "Numerous arts Dio Nwspr". kbbrown4545@msn.com

BROWN, Kenneth E (WA) 1318 Charlottesville Blvd, Knoxville TN 37922 **Ch Of The Resurr Loudon TN 2016-** B Evanston IL 1945 s Seth & Lydia. BA U of So Dakota 1967; STB GTS 1970. D 6/13/1970 Bp James Winchester Montgomery P 12/19/1970 Bp Gerald Francis Burrill. m 5/21/1994 Donna Hvistendahl c 3. All SS' Epis Ch Morristown TN 2015-2016; S Raphael's Epis Ch Crossville TN 2014-2015; Int S Lk's Ch Brighton Brookeville MD 2000-2002; P-in-c S Andr's Ch Akron OH 1998-2000; P-in-c S Alb's Mssn N. Muskegon MI 1997-1998; Chr Epis Ch Lead SD 1989-1995; R S Jn's Ch Deadwood SD 1989-1995; R S Marg's Ch Hazel Pk MI 1985-1989; R Trin Ch Three Rivers MI 1973-1985; Chapl Manteno St Hosp IL 1972-1973; Assoc S Mk's Ch Fairland Silver Sprg MD 1970-2011; Vic Ch Of The Gd Shpd Momence IL 1970-1973.

BROWN, Kevin S (NC) Church of the Holy Comforter, 2701 Park Rd, Charlotte NC 28209 **R Ch Of The H Comf Charlotte NC 2010-; Dep to GC Dio No Carolina Raleigh NC 2013-; Bd Dir Trin Epis Sch Charlotte NC 2012-** B Asheville NC 1968 BS Duke 1991; MBA U of W Florida Pensacola FL 1996; MDiv GTS 2007. D 6/2/2007 P 12/15/2007 Bp Don Edward Johnson. m 8/7/1993 Caroline C Brown c 2. R Gr Epis Ch Paris TN 2007-2010; Dep to GC Dio W Tennessee Memphis 2007-2009. bishop@dioceseofdelaware.net

BROWN, Lawrence Mitchell (Los) 44550 Denmore Ave, Lancaster CA 93535 **R Trin Par Fillmore CA 2010-** B Greenwood MS 1951 s Alvin & Mary. BA Rhodes Coll 1973; BS Rhodes Coll 1975; Cert ETSBH 1996; MDiv Claremont TS 1997. D 6/1/1996 Bp Frederick Houk Borsch P 1/18/1997 Bp Chester Lovelle Talton. m 7/11/1975 Nancy Edwards c 3. S Steph's Epis Ch Valencia CA 2005-2010; P Asstg Ch Of The Epiph Oak Pk CA 2001-2005; P Asstg S Aug By-The-Sea Par Santa Monica CA 1999-2000; P Asstg S Patricks Ch And Day Sch Thousand Oaks CA 1997-1998. OHC 1992; Soc of Cath Priests 2010. rector@trinityfillmore.org

BROWN, Lila Byrd (Fla) 2358 Riverside Ave. #704, Jacksonville FL 32204 **Non-par 2005-** B Jacksonville FL 1948 d Connor & Claude. BA Queens Coll 1971; MDiv VTS 1996. D 5/26/1996 P 12/8/1996 Bp Stephen Hays Jecko. S Mk's Epis Ch Jacksonville FL 2006-2008, 1999-2002; Cn Dio Florida Jacksonville 2002-2004; 1998-1999; Assc R S Jn's Epis Ch Tallahassee FL 1996-1998.

BROWN, Linda (Ark) D 6/15/2017 Bp Larry Benfield.

BROWN, Linda Josephine (Colo) 1700 W 10th Ave, Broomfield CO 80020 **D Ch Of The H Comf Broomfield CO 2011-** B Bethesda MD 1950 d Davis & Mary Josephine. BS U CO 1972; MA U CO 1977; PhD U CO 1980; MASM Iliff TS 2011. D 11/12/2011 Bp Robert John O'Neill. m 10/14/1972 Jesse James Brown.

BROWN, Lydia Huttar (Minn) 10 Buffalo Rd, North Oaks MN 55127 B Chicago IL 1954 d Charles & Joy. BA Hope Coll 1977; MA U MI 1978; MDiv Untd TS of the Twin Cities 2001; CTh SWTS 2002. D 12/20/2001 P 6/20/2002 Bp James Louis Jelinek. m 9/3/1977 Mark Leslie Brown c 4. S Paul's Ch Minneapolis MN 2016-2017; R S Anne's Epis Ch S Paul MN 2004-2015; Asst to the R Chr Ch S Paul MN 2004; D S Jn In The Wilderness S Paul MN 2002; Co-Chair, Cmsn on Liturg and Mus Dio Minnesota Minneapolis MN 2007-2010, Chair, Cler Cont Educ Com 2006-2008.

BROWN, Lyle L (Ia) 605 Avenue E, Fort Madison IA 52627 **The Reverend S Lk's Ch Ft Madison IA 2010-, The Reverend 2009-** B Davenport IA 1937 s Leslie & Edna. BA U of Iowa 1959; MA U Denv 1963. D 10/25/2009 P 5/9/2010 Bp Alan Scarfe. m 8/26/1967 Gwen Brown c 2. lbgb1008@mchsi.com

BROWN, Mac Macdonald (ETenn) Good Shepherd Episcopal Church, 211 Franklin Rd, Lookout Mountain TN 37350 **Asst Ch Of The Gd Shpd Lookout Mtn TN 2013-** B Knoxville TN 1982 s Larry & Jennifer. BA U So 2004; MDiv GTS 2013; MDiv The GTS 2013. D 6/15/2013 P 1/14/2014 Bp George Young III. m 5/25/2012 Aloyse M B Brown c 1. mac@gslookout.com

BROWN, Marilynn Marie (Ore) 332338 109Th Pl SE Apt 102, Auburn WA 98092 B Cheyenne WY 1933 d Clarence & Adah. BS USC 1956; U of Washington 1976; MDiv GTS 1991. D 12/14/1986 Bp Donald Purple Hart P 6/9/1991 Bp Allen Lyman Bartlett Jr. c 5. Asst S Mich And All Ang Ch Portland OR 2004-2005; R S Fran Of Assisi Epis Wilsonville OR 1997-2000, Assoc 1992-1996; Asst Chr Ch And S Mich's Philadelphia PA 1991, D 1989-1991; D S Ptr's Ch Glenside PA 1987-1988; Chapl S Andr Priory Sch Honolulu HI 1986-1987; D S Chris's Ch Kailua HI 1986-1987; Sunset Convoc Dn Dio Oregon Portland OR 2002-2004, Racism Cmsn 1994-1996, Dioc Coun 1993-1999.

BROWN, Marion Mackey (SwFla) 208 Ne Monroe Cir N Apt 103-C, Saint Petersburg FL 33702 **D S Giles Ch Pinellas Pk FL 1992-** B Pittsburgh PA 1935 d Thomas & Marion. Eckerd Coll; GTS; S Petersburg Jr Coll; Rider U 1959. D 6/13/1992 Bp Barbara Clementine Harris. m 9/26/1959 Harry Thomas Brown c 3. Cathd Ch Of S Ptr St. Petersburg FL 1992-1994.

BROWN SSJE, Mark (Mass) 980 Memorial Dr, Cambridge MA 02138 **Mem Soc of S Jn the Evang Cambridge MA 1997-; Asst Superior Soc of S Jn the Evang 2013-** B Peoria IL 1949 s Jesse & Naomi. BA U IL 1971; MA U IL 1976; MDiv SWTS 1994. D 5/7/1994 P 3/1/1995 Bp Peter Hess Beckwith. S Jn's Chap Cambridge MA 1997-2014; Soc-St Jn The Evang Cambridge MA 1997-2014; R Ch Of S Jn The Bapt Mt Carmel IL 1995-1997; D S Mk's Ch Hoosick Falls NY 1994-1995; Dioc Coun Dio Springfield Springfield IL 1995-1997.

BROWN, Mary K (Va) 228 Pitt St, Alexandria VA 22314 **S Dav's Ch Ashburn VA 2009-** B Kittanning PA 1959 d Glenn & Lois. BSW U Pgh 1981; MSW Case Wstrn Reserve U 1983; MDiv VTS 2008. D 5/24/2008 P 12/14/2008 Bp Peter J Lee. m 6/18/1994 Mark Eugene Boyer c 2. Asst S Paul's Epis Ch Alexandria VA 2008-2009.

BROWN, Nancy (Los) 2095 Stoneman St, Simi Valley CA 93065 **R S Paul's Par Lancaster CA 2005-** B Dyersburg TN 1947 d Harry & Opal. MDiv ETS-BH 2000. D 6/25/2000 Bp Chester Lovelle Talton P 1/6/2001 Bp Frederick Houk Borsch. m 7/11/1975 Lawrence Mitchell Brown c 3. Int S Patricks Ch And Day Sch Thousand Oaks CA 2000-2005. Soc of Cath Priests 2010. revnancy@stpaulslancaster.net

BROWN, Nancy Elisabeth (Okla) 3914 E. 37th Street, Tulsa OK 74135 **D Gd Shpd Epis Ch Sapulpa OK 2014-; Chapl Brookhaven Hosp Tulsa OK 2013-** B Flint MI 1953 d Herbert & Doris. Oral Roberts U 1973; Ord Dio Oklahoma 2000; CPE Hillcrest Med Cntr 2006. D 6/24/2000 Bp Robert Manning Moody. D Chr Epis Ch Tulsa OK 2007-2012; Chapl Hospice 2006-2011; Chapl Hillcrest Med Cntr Tulsa OK 2005-2006; Asst S Jn's Epis Ch Tulsa OK 2001-2005.

BROWN, Neva Wilkins (Md) **D S Barth's Ch Baltimore MD 2013-** B Baltimore MD 1946 d Warren & Mildred. BS Morgan St U 1973; MBA Morgan St U 1989. D 6/1/2013 Bp Joe Goodwin Burnett. m 7/2/1964 Larry Martin Brown c 1.

BROWN, Percival George (LI) 926 Dana Ave, Valley Stream NY 11580 **Died 6/24/2016** B Miami FL 1949 s Percy & Carmetta. BA U of Florida 1969; MDiv VTS 1972. D 7/9/1972 P 6/29/1973 Bp James Loughlin Duncan. m 4/9/1991 Rosalyn Ann Ferguson c 2. Ret 2005-2016; R Gr Ch Jamaica NY 1989-2005; Assoc Trin Educ Fund New York NY 1981-1988; Vic S Phil's Ch Pompano Bch FL 1977-1980; R Ch Of S Chris Ft Lauderdale FL 1972-1980; Liturg Off Trin Par New York NY 1980-1989. Outstanding Young Men Amer 1976.

BROWN, Ralph Douglas (Ind) Po Box 1596, Old Fort NC 28762 B New York NY 1934 s Ralph & Dorothy. BA Br 1956; MDiv Sewanee: The U So, TS 1984. D 2/16/1985 P 9/18/1985 Bp Craig Barry Anderson. m 5/11/1958 Ruth Evelyn Brown c 2. R S Paul's Ch Richmond IN 1988-2000; Chr Ch Chamberlain SD 1985-1988; Vic H Comf Epis Ch Lower Brule SD 1984-1988; Stwdshp Com Dio Indianapolis Indianapolis IN 1989-2000.

BROWN, Raymond Dutson (Mont) 6162 Lazy Man Gulch, Helena MT 59601 **S Ptr's Cathd Helena MT 2015-, Int 2011, Dn 1966-2011; Captain, Auxiliary Dep,Search & Rescue Sherff's Off L&C Cnty MT 2014-** B Philadelphia PA 1933 s Allen & Helen. BA Br 1959; MDiv PDS 1962. D 6/16/1962 P 12/23/1962 Bp Allen Webster Brown. m 2/10/1978 Joyce F Brown c 5. R Trin Ch Ennis MT 1997-2000; Int Ch Of The Incarn Great Falls MT 1995-1996; Bureau Cheif, Tribal Liaison Mt Dept of Transportaion Helena MT 1986-1997; Int S Jn's Ch Butte MT 1986-1987; Int S Fran Epis Ch Great Falls MT 1984-1986; Equity Coordntr Off of Publice Instrn Helena MT 1983-1986; Admin Montana Human Rts Cmsn Helena MT 1975-1983; Vic All SS Epis Ch Columbia Falls MT 1963-1966; S Matt's Ch Columbia Fls MT 1963-1966; S Mich And All Ang Eureka MT 1963-1966; Cur S Paul's Ch Schenectady NY 1962-1963; Stndg Com Dio Montana Helena MT 1993-1996, Chair of Ch and Soc Cmsn 1983-1992, EDEO 1974-1982; SSGT USMC 1951-1954. Tribal hon Blackfeet Nation 1997; Extra Mile Awd Fed Highway Adminisetration 1997; Korean Serv Medal USMC 1953.

BROWN, Raymond Francis (EC) 205 Bedell Pl, Fayetteville NC 28314 B Danville KY 1945 s Francis & Lu. BA Cntr Coll 1968; JD Duke 1974; MDiv Ya Berk 1986. D 6/24/1986 P 4/27/1987 Bp David Reed. m 5/31/1969 Judith Ann Brown c 2. R H Trin Epis Ch Fayetteville NC 2001-2013; R Ch Of The H Trin Georgetown KY 1988-2001; Asst R S Mk's Epis Ch Louisville KY 1986-1988; Dn, Upper Cape Fear Dnry Dio E Carolina 2003-2004; Pres, Stndg Com Dio Lexington Lexington 2000-2001. Archibald Prize Ya Berk 1986; Daggett Prize Ya Berk 1986; Mdiv mcl Ya Berk 1986; Julia Archibald Prize & Oliver E Daggett Prize Yale 1986; Jd w dist Law Sch, Duke 1974; Ba mcl Cntr Coll 1968.

BROWN, Reed Haller (Vt) 49 Brewer Pkwy, South Burlington VT 05403 B Cooperstown NY 1935 s Allen & Helen. BA Trin Hartford CT 1960; MDiv GTS 1963; PhD U of Vermont 1975. D 6/10/1963 Bp Allen Webster Brown P 12/21/1963 Bp Harvey D Butterfield. m 8/20/1960 Gail C Brown c 2. R S Paul's Epis Ch On The Green Vergennes VT 1997-2002; P-in-c Inter Par Coun Of Churchs Enosburg Fls VT 1995-1996; Gr Ch Sheldon VT 1994-1996; S Ann's Ch Burlington VT 1994-1996; Cn Pstr S Matt's Ch Enosburg Fls VT 1994-1996; Pscyhologist/Dr Priv Clincl Psychol Pract 1975-1997; Consulting Psychol Rock Point Sch Burlington VT 1974-1980; Ret Counslg Ctr UVM Burlington 1974-1979; Consulting Psychol Dio Vermont Burlington VT 1973-1979; Chapl Vermont St Hosp 1968-1970; Vic All SS' Epis Ch S Burlington VT 1964-1969; Asst Cathd Ch Of S Paul Burlington VT 1963-1965.

BROWN III, Richard Julius (ETenn) 1431 Armiger Lane, Knoxville TN 37932 **Died 5/4/2017** B Charleston SC 1937 s Richard & Helen. BA Furman U 1960; BD SE Bapt TS 1965; ThM SE Bapt TS 1967; MA Appalachian St U 1976; PhD U NC at Greensboro 1981. D 2/6/1994 P 10/1/1994 Bp Robert Oran Miller. m 5/11/2017 Geneva Leek Brown c 1. Int S Eliz's Epis Ch Knoxville TN 2009-2010; Cn S Jn's Epis Cathd Knoxville TN 2001-2005; Int Gr Epis Ch Pike Road AL 2000-2001; Assoc Ch Of The H Comf Montgomery AL 2000; P Epis Ch Of The Epiph Tallassee AL 1996-1997; P-in-c S Mk's Ch Prattville AL 1995-1996; P-in-c Trin Epis Ch Clanton AL 1994-1995; Chapl US AF Reserves 1968-1998; Min Sthrn Bapt Ch 1964-1970.

BROWN, Rob (USC) 531 Old Iron Works Rd, Spartanburg SC 29302 **R S Matt's Epis Ch Spartanburg SC 2003-** B Greer SC 1960 s John & Bobbie. BA U of So Carolina 1984; MDiv Sewanee: The U So, TS 1995. D 6/10/1995 P 5/18/1996 Bp Dorsey Henderson. m 4/23/1988 Sandra Dean Brown c 2. Assoc R Ch Of The Adv Spartanburg SC 1996-2003; D S Fran of Assisi Chapin SC 1995-1996; Pres, Stndg Com Dio Upper So Carolina Columbia SC 2010-2011, Vice-Pres, Stndg Com 2008-2010, Dn, Piedmont Convoc 2006-2008, Mem, Dioc Exec Coun 2003-2006, Chair, Com for YA Mnstry 1998-2001. Auth, "An Unexpected Gift," *Hub for the Holidays*, Hub City Press, 2013; Auth, "Hunting Magnolia," *Outdoor Adventures in the Upcountry*, Hub City Press, 2010; Contrib, "In Morgan's Shadow," Hub City Press, 2001.

BROWN, Robert Charles (Ark) 501 S Phoenix Ave, Russellville AR 72801 B Shreveport LA 1945 s John & Bobby. BA NW St U 1967; PhD LSU 1976; Cert Iona Inst of Arkansas 2017. D 4/1/2017 Bp Larry Benfield. m 6/8/1968 Jill Lestage Brown c 3.

BROWN, Robert Eugene (Ore) 23834 SE 248th St, Maple Valley WA 98038 **Died 8/22/2016** B Berkeley CA 1937 s Russell & Thelma. BA California St U Long Bch 1960; MDiv CDSP 1966; Cert Pstr Inst of Washington WA 1972; Cert Samar Counslg Cntr 1991. D 3/5/1966 Bp George Richard Millard P 9/7/1966 Bp Harry Sherbourne Kennedy. m 9/2/1976 Marilynn Marie Brown c 3. Ret 1999-2016; Exec Asst to Bp Dio Oregon Portland OR 1996-1999, Chair of COM 1994-1996; R S Fran Of Assisi Epis Wilsonville OR 1992-1996; R S Ptr's Ch Glenside PA 1987-1992; R S Chris's Ch Kailua HI 1979-1987; Chapl Washington St Search and Rescue 1977-1979; R S Mich And All Ang Ch Issaquah WA 1973-1979; Cn to the Ordnry Dio Olympia Seattle 1972-1973; Assoc Epiph Par of Seattle Seattle WA 1967-1972; Vic Chr Ch Kealakekua HI 1966-1967; COM Dio Pennsylvania Philadelphia PA 1988-1990; Dioc Coun The Epis Ch in Hawaii Honolulu HI 1984-1987, Stndg Committee, Chair 1980-1983.

BROWN, Robert Henry (Pa) 117 Pine Lake Dr, Whispering Pines NC 28327 **Vic S Mary Magd Ch Troy NC 2007-** B Philadelphia PA 1930 s Henry & Elizabeth. BA La Salle U 1968; MDiv Luth TS 1996. D 6/1/1996 P 6/7/1997 Bp Allen Lyman Bartlett Jr. m 11/9/1957 Jean C Brown. R S Faith Ch Havertown PA 1998-2003.

BROWN, Robert James Crawford (FdL) 778 Hillside Ter, Ripon WI 54971 **Died 1/23/2017** B Chambersburg PA 1932 s John & Sybilla. BA Ripon Coll Ripon WI 1954; BD Nash 1957. D 12/1/1956 P 6/2/1957 Bp Donald H V Hallock. Ret 1998-2017; R S Ptr Ripon 1966-1997; S Ptr's Ch (S Mary's Chap) Ripon WI 1966-1997; Chapl Epis Campus Rectory Milwaukee WI 1964-1966; Instr of NT Gk S Mk's Ch Milwaukee WI 1959-1966; Nash Nashotah WI 1959-1960; Vic Gr Epis Ch Galena IL 1958-1959; Vic S Mich Shullsburg WI 1957-1959; Vic Trin Epis Ch Platteville WI 1957-1959. CBS; Forw in Faith No Amer; GAS; SHN. Hon Cn S Paul's Cathd 1993.

BROWN, Robert Labannah (Neb) 9302 Blondo St, Omaha NE 68134 B Scotts Bluff NE 1945 s Walter & Pauline. D 9/21/2002 Bp James Edward Krotz. m 8/30/1969 Samala Kay Popp c 2. Sexton All SS Epis Ch Omaha NE 2013-2017.

BROWN, Rodney K (Eas) 32659 Seaview Loop, Millsboro DE 19966 B Richmond VA 1945 s Theron & Sarah. BA Westminster Choir Coll of Rider U 1969; MDiv VTS 1974. D 6/7/1975 P 6/1/1976 Bp John Harris Burt. m 6/1/1968 Gretchen Diane Brown c 2. R Ch Of The H Trin Oxford MD 1990-2009; Chapl S Steph's Sch Alexandria VA 1988-1990; St Steph Sch Alexandria VA 1988-1990; The Ch Of The Epiph Oak Hill VA 1987-1988; Epis HS Alexandria VA 1981-1987; Chapl Epis HS Alexandria VA 1981-1987; Truro Epis Ch Fairfax VA 1976-1986.

BROWN, Rosa Maria (Nwk) 50 N Illinois St, Indianapolis IN 46204 **Int Chr Ch Cathd Indianapolis IN 2017-; Dn Dio Los Ang 2004-** B Limon Costa Rica 1957 d Easle. Cert-Appreciative Transitional Mnstry The Appreciative Way; CPE U Med Cntr; MDiv Seminario Biblico Latino Americano 1990; STM GTS 1994. Trans 7/20/2002 Bp Joseph Jon Bruno. Dio Newark Newark NJ 2012-2013; S Paul's Epis Ch Paterson NJ 2010-2016; Dio Sthrn Ohio Cincinnati OH 2009-2010; Ch Of Our Sav Cincinnati OH 2006-2008; Vic Iglesia Epis De La Magdalena Mssn Glendale CA 2002-2006; Dio Los Angeles Los Angeles CA 2002. rosab@cccindy.org

BROWN, Royce Walter (Wyo) Central Wyoming Hospice, 319 S Wilson, Casper WY 82601 B Scottsbluff NE 1942 s Walter & Pauline. AS Scottsbluff Jr Coll 1962; BA U of Nebraska at Kearney 1964; MDiv PDS 1967. D 6/20/1967 P 12/21/1967 Bp Russell T Rauscher. m 6/4/1966 Sandra H Brown c 3. Chapl Cntrl Wyoming Hospice 2007-2016; R S Mk's Epis Ch Casper WY 1986-2004; Eccl Crt Dio Wyoming Casper 1986-2000; R S Andr's Epis Ch Liberal KS 1980-1986; Vic S Geo's Ch Oshkosh NE 1973-1980; Vic S Paul's Ch Ogallala NE 1973-1980; Vic S Pauls Epis Ch Arapahoe NE 1969-1973; D Calv Ch Hyannis NE 1967-1969; S Jos's Ch Mullen NE 1967-1969; Stwdshp Com Dio Wstrn Kansas Hutchinson KS 1981-1985; Exec Coun Dio Nebraska Omaha NE 1976-1980. Bro of S Andr 1987-2013; Intl Ord of S Lk 1987; Reg VI Dir 2000-2006.

BROWN, Ruth Ellen (Az) 9071 E Old Spanish Trl, Tucson AZ 85710 **D Ch Of S Matt Tucson AZ 2012-** B Colorado Springs CO 1937 d Lewis & Lucile. BA U GA 1957. D 7/11/2007 Bp Johncy Itty. m 4/7/2005 Richard Brown c 2.

BROWN, Sally Sims (Colo) 85 Rampart Way Uniit 510, Denver CO 80230 B Portland OR 1936 d Darwin & Doris. BA U CO 1958; Iliff TS 1978. D 7/19/1987 Bp William Carl Frey. c 4. Ret Dio Colorado Denver CO 2009-2011, 2001-2009, 1993-2001; D S Andr's Ch Denver CO 1997-2008; D S Thos Epis Ch Denver CO 1992-1996. EPF 1992; NAAD 1990. Diac Mnstry-Tradition of St. Steph No Amer Assoc.for Diac 1999.

BROWN, Scott Jeffrey (WTex) 1417 E Austin Ave, Harlingen TX 78550 **Chapl Texas Mltry Inst San Antonio TX 2004-** B Houston TX 1975 s James & Joanne. BS Victoria Coll U of Houston 1999; MDiv Sewanee: The U So, TS 2002. D 6/20/2002 Bp Robert Boyd Hibbs P 2/28/2003 Bp James Edward Folts. m 7/2/2004 Kimberly Ann Brown c 2. R S Alb's Ch Harlingen TX 2007-2017; Asst S Dav's Epis Ch San Antonio TX 2002-2004. Auth, "Just Where Does God Live?," WinePress, 2009.

BROWN, Thomas James (Mass) 70 Church St., Winchester MA 01890 **Trst Par Of The Epiph Winchester MA 2009-; Co-Chair Deputation to 78th GC Dio Massachusetts Boston MA 2015-2018; Trst Ch Pension Fund Benefici 2009-** B Bruce Crossing MI 1970 s Dennis & Suzanne. BS Wstrn Michigan U 1992; CFS OH SU 1993; MDiv CDSP 1997. D 6/28/1997 P 1/17/1998 Bp Edward Lewis Lee Jr. m 5/1/2011 Thomas Nordboe Mousin. R S Mich's Epis Ch Brattleboro VT 2000-2009; CDSP Berkeley CA 1997-2000; Dir, Alum/ae & Ch Relatns CDSP Berkeley CA 1997-2000; Assoc The Epis Ch Of S Jn The Evang San Francisco CA 1997-1999. Soc of S Jn the Evang 1994. tbrown@3crowns.org

BROWN RC, Virginia Dabney (WMo) 874 Yorkchester, # 108, Houston TX 77079 **Fac Bp Kemper Sch for Mnstry 2011-; Dn Geo Herbert Inst for Pstr Stds Dio We 2004-; Guardian Rivendell Cmnty 2000-** B Savannah GA 1948 d William & Jeanne. BS MI SU 1969; MDiv SWTS 1974; MA New Mex St U 1981; U of New Mex 1984. D 9/10/1974 P 1/28/1977 Bp Richard Mitchell Trelease Jr. c 3. P in Charge S Mk's Epis Ch Kimberling City MO 2008-2014; R Shpd Of The Hills Branson MO 2007-2010; Assoc R Chr Epis Ch Springfield MO 2000-2004; Assoc R Gr - S Lk's Ch Memphis TN 1993-2000; R S Thos A Becket Ch Roswell NM 1988-1993; Dn Dio The Rio Grande Albuquerque 1980-1988; Chapl New Mex St U at Las Cruces NM 1979-1983; Vic S Chad's Epis Ch Albuquerque NM 1976-1979. Coauthor, "Fully Alive! Explorations in the Chr Sprtl Tradition," 2012; "Bringing the Story to Life," Benedictines, 2006.

BROWN, Virginia Wood (Colo) 706 E. 3rd Avenue, Durango CO 81301 **D St. Mk's Epis Chuch 2003-** B Highland Park MI 1940 d John & Madeline. BS NWU 1962; MS U Denv 1991. D 4/26/2003 Bp William Jerry Winterrowd. m 11/1/1980 Donald Brown c 2.

BROWN JR, Walter R (Ark) 12415 Cantrell Rd, Little Rock AR 72223 **S Jn's Epis Ch Helena AR 2016-** B Wilmington NC 1954 s Walter & Betty May.

BA Pacific Chr Coll 1976; MDiv Phillips TS 1984. D 5/31/2011 P 12/12/2011 Bp Larry Benfield. m 8/17/1979 Royce Brown c 2. St Nich Ch Maumelle AR 2012-2016; S Mich's Epis Ch Little Rock AR 2011.

BROWN, Wendy (EMich) D 6/17/2017 Bp Steven Todd Ousley.

BROWN, William Garland (Lex) 311 Washington St, Frankfort KY 40601 B Lexington KY 1939 s J.A. & Mary. BA S Paul Sem 1959; MA Mt S Marys Sem 1964; PhD U of St Thos Rome Italy 1969. Rec 12/8/2003 Bp Stacy F Sauls. m 6/29/1996 Linda K Brown. Asstg P Ch Of The Ascen Frankfort KY 2008-2011, 2006-2007; Vocation Dir & Dir of Lay Formation RC Dio Lexington Lexington KY 1986-1996; Pres of Sem RC Dio Covington Covington KY 1972-1983; P RC Dio Covington Covington KY 1963-1986.

BROWN, Willis Donald (Ky) 2402 Glenview Ave, Louisville KY 40222 **Ret 1999-** B Fort Worth TX 1930 s Willis & Claire. BBA Texas Tech U 1953; MDiv VTS 1980. D 2/18/1984 P 12/17/1988 Bp David Reed. m 7/31/1983 Patricia Lou Knadler Brown. R S Jn's Ch Louisville KY 1994-1999.

BROWN III, Wm Hill (Va) 5103 Harlan Cir, Richmond VA 23226 B Washington DC 1937 s William & Charlotte. AB Pr 1959; GTS 1960; BA Oxf GB 1962; MA Oxf GB 1966. D 11/24/1962 Bp Samuel B Chilton P 11/24/1963 Bp Robert Fisher Gibson Jr. m 2/13/1965 Margaret K Brown c 2. Dn of Reg 10 Dio Virginia Richmond VA 1975-1982; Gr & H Trin Epis Ch Richmond VA 1962-2001. Ch Schools of the Dio Virginia 1975-1982; S Cathr's Sch, Richmond, VA 1978-1990; Westminster-Cbury Hse, Richmond Va 1982-1986.

BROWN DOUGLAS, Kelly Delaine (WA) 12519 Hawks Nest Ln, Germantown MD 20876 B Dayton OH 1957 d William & Mary. BS Denison U 1979; MDiv UTS 1982. D 10/9/1982 Bp William Grant Black P 9/1/1983 Bp Walter Decoster Dennis Jr. Ch Of The Intsn New York NY 1982-1986. holycomforterdc@gmail.com

BROWNE, Bliss Williams (Chi) 7743 SE Loblolly Bay Dr, Hobe Sound FL 33455 B Atlanta GA 1950 d Emory & Janet. Smith 1969; BA Ya 1971; Rockefeller Fndt 1972; MDiv Harvard DS 1974; Ya 1975; MM NWU 1978; Kellogg Fndt 1991. D 6/23/1974 Bp James Winchester Montgomery P 8/6/1977 Bp Quintin Ebenezer Primo Jr. m 2/20/1977 Howell Browne c 3. Asst Cathd Of S Jas Chicago IL 1987-1995; Asst Trin Ch Chicago IL 1978-1987; Serv Ch Of Our Sav Chicago IL 1976-1977; Cur S Paul And S Jas New Haven CT 1974-1976; D Chr Ch Winnetka IL 1974. Auth, "Wmn Alive: A Legacy of Soc Justice," Wmn Alive: A Legacy of Soc Justice, Imagine Chicago, 2004; Auth, "Ten Years of Imagination in Action," Ten Years of Imagination in Action, Imagine Chicago, 2002. Imagine Chicago 1992. Chicago Wmn Extraordinaire IWA Chicago 2008; Cranmer Cup Captain Cranmer Cup USA 2000; Mercedes Mentor Awd Chicago mag 1998; Saguaro Seminar In Civic Engagement Harvard Kennedy Sch 1998; Natl Ldrshp Fell Kellogg Fndt 1988; Fell Rockefeller Fndt 1971.

BROWNE, Frances Louise (NC) 303 Eastchester Dr, High Point NC 27262 B Atlanta GA 1954 d Robert & Virginia. BA Mars Hill Coll 1978; MDiv SE Bapt Theol Sem 1982. D 1/25/2014 Bp Anne Hodges-Copple.

BROWNE, Gayle (SO) 212 Tulane Ave, Oak Ridge TN 37830 B Bunk LA 1950 d Hubert & Marilyn. BS LSU 1971; MA U So 1992. D 2/2/1986 P 12/1/1990 Bp William Evan Sanders. m 5/28/2016 James Paul Browne c 3. Procter Conf Cntr London OH 2012-2015; Vic S Andr's Epis Ch Wshngtn Ct Hs OH 2008-2016; S Lk's Ch Knoxville TN 2002-2008; Ch Of The Resurr Loudon TN 1999-2001; S Steph's Epis Ch Oak Ridge TN 1991-1999; Dio E Tennessee Knoxville TN 1990-1991; D S Jn's Epis Cathd Knoxville TN 1986-1989.

BROWNE III, Joseph M (EC) 200 NC Highway 33 W, Chocowinity NC 27817 **Dio E Carolina Kinston NC 2016-** B Greenville NC 1977 s Joseph & Virginia. BA U NC 1999; MA U NC 2001; MDiv VTS 2004. D 6/19/2004 P 2/24/2005 Bp Clifton Daniel III. R Trin Epis Ch Chocowinity NC 2004-2016.

BROWNE, Joy Elizabeth (Ky) 922 Milford Ln, Louisville KY 40207 B Berkeley CA 1949 d Leon & Maxine. BA U of Washington 1971; MA U Chi 1976; MDiv Colgate Rochester Crozer DS 1989; MDiv CRDS 1989; PhD Emory U 1995. D 6/2/1990 Bp Charles Shannon Mallory P 1/1/1992 Bp Richard Lester Shimpfky. Dio Long Island Garden City NY 2005; St Jn the Evang Epis Ch Lynbrook NY 2004-2005; S Thos' Par Newark DE 2001-2002; Vic S Geo's Epis Ch Louisville KY 1997-2000; Dio Kentucky Louisville KY 1997-1999; Asst S Mart In The Fields Ch Atlanta GA 1993-1994; Chapl/Instr Of Rel Spelman Coll Atlanta GA 1990-1992. Auth, "Itc Journ". AAR; Black Wmn In Ch & Soc; SBL.

BROWNE, Samuel Jonathan (SeFla) 426 Cypress Dr, Lake Park FL 33403 **Died 6/29/2016** B Key West FL 1929 s John & Ruth. BA S Augustines Coll Raleigh NC 1956; Nash 1959. D 7/4/1959 Bp Henry I Louttit P 1/16/1960 Bp William Francis Moses. c 2. Ret 1995-2016; Chapl CAP W Palm Bch FL 1965-1996; S Patricks Ch W Palm Bch FL 1964-1994; P-in-c Ch Of S Jn Lake Worth FL 1964-1988; In-charge S Aug's Epis Ch St Petersburg FL 1959-1964.

BROWNELL, Leona Weiss (Del) 4830 Kennett Pike #3504, Wilmington DE 19807 **Ret 1991-** B Waterloo IA 1923 d Leonard & Anna. BA U of Nthrn Iowa 1944; MS U of Wisconsin 1948; PhD U of Delaware 1967; PDS 1974; MDiv Luth TS at Gettysburg 1976. D 6/25/1977 P 2/11/1979 Bp John Harris Burt. c 2. Supply Dio Delaware Wilmington 1991-1994; Chapl Epis Ch Hm Hockessin

DE 1988-1991; Supply P Dio No Carolina Raleigh NC 1987-1988; Dir of Pstr Care Cleveland Preaching Inst Cleveland OH 1979-1986; Dio Ohio Cleveland 1979-1986; D-in-Res S Jas Ch Painesville OH 1977-1979. Auth, *Var Books-Biology*. Coll Chapl, ACPE, 1990. BA w high hon U of Nthrn Iowa 1944.

BROWNING II, Charles Alex (SeFla) 2707 NW 37th Street, Boca Raton FL 33434 **Chap Of S Andr Boca Raton FL 2013-; Mnstry Discernment Advsr Dio SE Florida Miami 2015-, So Palm Dnry Yth Coordntr 2014-, Dioc Exam Chapl 2012-** B Memphis TN 1982 s Richard & Dorothy. BA Palm Bch Atlantic U 2007; MDiv VTS 2011. D 12/21/2010 P 6/29/2011 Bp Leo Frade. m 5/21/2011 Cainna Beth Jirikowic c 2. H Trin Epis Ch W Palm Bch FL 2011-2013.

✠ BROWNING, The Most Rev Edmond Lee (Haw) 5164 Imai Rd, Hood River OR 97031 **Died 7/11/2016** B Corpus Christi TX 1929 s Edmond & Mae. CDSP; BA U So 1952; BD Sewanee: The U So, TS 1954; Japanese Lang Sch 1965; Epis TS of the SW 1970. D 7/2/1954 P 5/23/1955 Bp Everett H Jones Con 1/5/1968 for Oki. m 9/10/1953 Patricia Alline Sparks c 5. Ret PBp of The Epis Ch Epis Ch GC 1997-2016; PBp of The Epis Ch Epis Ch Cntr New York NY 1986-1997, 1974-1976; Exec & Secy Off New York NY 1986-1989; Bp The Epis Ch in Hawaii Honolulu HI 1976-1985; Exec for Wrld Mssn Epis Ch Exec Coun 1974-1976; Bp Convoc of Epis Ch in Europe Paris 1971-1974; Bp of Okinawa Angl Comm in Japan 1968-1971; Serv Angl Comm in Japan 1959-1968; R Ch Of The Redeem Eagle Pass TX 1956-1959; Asst Ch Of The Gd Shpd Corpus Christi TX 1954-1956. Auth, *A Year of Days*; Auth, *Essay*; Auth, *No Outcast*. DD U So 1970; Hon Degree CDSP; Hon Degree EDS; Hon Degree GTS; Hon Degree SW; Hon Degree VTS.

BROWNING, Peter Sparks (Los) 2 HIdalgo, Irvine CA 92620 **Vic St Andr Epis Ch Irvine CA 2004-** B Okinawa JP 1960 s Edmond & Patricia. BA Whitworth U 1983; MDiv GTS 1991. D 6/15/1991 P 1/1/1992 Bp Frederick Houk Borsch. m 6/19/1988 Melissa C Browning c 2. R S Tim's Epis Ch Apple Vlly CA 1996-2003; S Jas' Par So Pasadena CA 1991-1996. peter@standrewsirvine.org

BROWNING JR, Robert Franklin (Nwk) Grace Church, 128 W Passaic Ave, Rutherford NJ 07070 **P-in-c Gr Epis Ch Rutherford NJ 2011-** B Jersey City NJ 1946 s Robert & Margaret. BA New Jersey City U 1974; MA Wm Paterson U 1978; MDiv Prot TS 2006. D 3/11/2006 P 9/23/2006 Bp Mark Sean Sisk. c 1. Dio New York New York NY 2007-2008; Vic S Andr's Ch Poughkeepsie NY 2006-2011.

BROWNING JR, Robert Guy Shipton (SwFla) 7038 West Brandywine Circle, Fort Myers FL 33919 B Philadelphia PA 1930 s Robert & Sara. BA Ge 1960; MDiv Nash 1963; U of Pennsylvania Wharton 2048. D 6/8/1963 P 12/14/1963 Bp Joseph Gillespie Armstrong. m 9/7/1957 Alva Barbara Browning c 5. Dio SW Florida Parrish FL 1965-1996, Chair:Archit/Construction;Fin,Bdgt,Prog Chair'Chair Dioc Yth Cmsn 1979-1985, Dioc Coun 1974-1985, CE 1974-1983, COM 1969-1996, Dioc Retreat 1969-1996, Sprtl Direction 1969-1996; R S Hilary's Ch Ft Myers FL 1965-1996, Vic 1965-1996; R S Steph's Ch Philadelphia PA 1963-1965. Angl-RC Ecclectic Relation 1965-1996. Angl-Roman Catholicc Eccl Cmsn on Religio 1965.

BROWNING, Trace (U) All Saints Episcopal Church, 1710 S Foothill Dr, Salt Lake City UT 84108 **R All SS Ch Salt Lake City UT 2014-; Chapl S Mk's Chap Salt Lake City UT 2005-** B Ogden UT 1961 s Merlin & Lois. BA Weber St U 1990; MDiv Bex Sem 1995. D 6/17/1995 Bp George Edmonds Bates P 12/10/1995 Bp William George Burrill. m 9/4/1981 Karen K Wood c 5. P S Paul's Ch Salt Lake City UT 2013-2014; Dio Utah Salt Lake City UT 2005-2014; Rowland Hall/S Mk's Sch Salt Lake City UT 2005-2014; R S Pauls Epis Ch The Dalles OR 2000-2005; Asst S Jn's Ch Portsmouth NH 1997-2000; Assoc S Ptr's Epis Ch Henrietta NY 1996-1997; R Calv/St Andr's Par Rochester NY 1995-1996; Dioc Coun Dio Estrn Oregon Cove OR 2002-2005. MDiv w dist Bex 1995; BA mcl Weber St U 1990. tracebrowning@allsaintsslc.org

BROWNLEE, Annette Geoffrian (Colo) 410 W 18th St, Pueblo CO 81003 **Wycliffe Coll Toronto ON 2008-** B Washington DC 1955 d Donald & Antoine. BA U of Iowa 1977; MS U IL 1978; MA U of Iowa 1983; MDiv GTS 1987. D 6/13/1987 Bp Walter Cameron Righter P 5/21/1988 Bp James Russell Moodey. m 1/24/1987 Ephraim Louis Radner c 2. Assoc Ch Of The Ascen Pueblo CO 1998-2007; Emm Epis Ch Stamford CT 1989-1997; Asst S Paul's Epis Ch Cleveland OH 1988-1989; Dio Ohio Cleveland 1987-1989. "Not on the Same Page," *The Angl Vol. 32(2)*, 2003; Auth, "The Dark Night of Hope," *Journ of Rel & Aging*; "The Lectionary Commentary," *Theol Exegesis for Texts*.

BROWNMILLER, David Clark (Ore) 16379 Nw Charlais St, Beaverton OR 97006 **Int All SS Ch Hillsboro OR 2008-** B Shawnee OK 1945 s William & Charlene. BA U of Oklahoma 1969; JD U Denv 1972; MDiv SWTS 1994. D 6/11/1994 P 12/3/1994 Bp William Jerry Winterrowd. m 3/29/1986 Gail Marie Brownmiller c 2. Dio Oregon Portland OR 2008-2009, 1999-2004; S Gabr Ch Portland OR 1999-2004; Vic S Eliz's Epis Ch Brighton CO 1994-1998.

BROWN-NOLAN, Virginia (WA) 12613 Meadowood Dr, Silver Spring MD 20904 B Brooklyn NY 1948 d Dillard & Sarah. BA Lake Forest Coll 1970; MS U IL 1974; MDiv CDSP 1986. D 6/29/1986 Bp Frederick Warren Putnam P 3/1/1987 Bp Donald Purple Hart. m 8/29/1992 Nathaniel Nolan c 4. All Souls Memi Epis Ch Washington DC 2016; S Mk's Ch Fairland Silver Sprg MD 2011-2013;

R S Lk's Ch Washington DC 1999-2011; Coordntr Dio Michigan Detroit MI 1995-1999; Vic Ch Of The H Comm Maywood IL 1988-1994; Asst Ch Of Our Sav Mill Vlly CA 1986-1988; Dio California San Francisco CA 1986-1987.

BROWNRIDGE, Walter Bruce Augustine (Md) The Episcopal Diocese of Maryland, 4 East Parkway Ave., Baltimore MD 21202 **Exec Coun Appointees New York NY 2011-, 2003-2006; Dn S Andr's Cathd Honolulu HI 2011-** B Toledo OH 1956 s Walter & Eunice. BA JCU 1978; MA U of San Diego 1985; JD Geo 1987; MDiv GTS 2000. D 6/24/2000 Bp J Clark Grew II P 6/9/2001 Bp Arthur Williams Jr. m 12/18/1982 Christina Marie Nader c 2. Assoc Sewanee U So TS Sewanee TN 2006-2011; Cn: Cathd Ch of St. Geo the Mtyr Appointed Mssy of TEC - Angl Ch of Sthrn Af 2003-2006; Assoc Chr Ch Shaker Heights OH 2000-2003. Auth, "How To Talk Contructively About Race," *A Toolbox & Conversation For Chr Formation in the Context of Race*, VTS - CMT, 2016; Auth, "'We'Ve Come This Far By Faith, Reflections On Anglo-Catholicism," *Fllshp Papers*, 1994. Affirming Catholicism No Amer 1997; Bd Mem: The Cmnty of the Cross of Nails - No Amer 2012; Bd Trst: The ATR 2014; EUC 2002; Hawaii St Pres: Faith Action for Cmnty Equity 2012-2016; NAACP 1994; Potomac Cltn 2004; The Soc of Cath Priests 2011; UBE 1997; Urban League 1979-1984. The Bp Walter Decoster Dennis Awd for Eccl & Cncl Ldrshp The UBE 2017; Seymour Preaching Prize For Extemp Preaching GTS 2000; Preaching Excellence Prog Fell 2000 Preaching Excellence Prog 2000; Who'S Who Among Amer Law Students Who's Who 1987; One Of The Outstanding Young Men Of Amer OYMA 1985. frwbab@gmail.com

BROYLES, Elizabeth Ruth (NY) 37 Chipmunk Hollow Rd, Kerhonkson NY 12446 **Asstg P Chr the King Epis Ch Stone Ridge NY 2011-** B Moenchweiller DE 1961 d Jerome & Ruth. BA Rutgers The St U of New Jersey 1982; MDiv UTS 1992; Cert The Haden Inst 2011. D 6/11/1994 P 12/1/1994 Bp Richard Frank Grein. P-in-res H Cross Monstry W Pk NY 2002-2007; P-in-c Ch Of The H Trin Pawling NY 1998-2002; Dio New York New York NY 1998-2002; Asst Gr Ch White Plains NY 1994-1998.

BRUBAKER GARRISON, Tasha Vache (Ore) 418 Stonewood Dr, Eugene OR 97405 B Bakersfield CA 1971 d David & Linda. BA Stan 1993; HSC London Sch of Econ 1995; MDiv GTS 2003. D 6/28/2003 Bp Vincent Waydell Warner P 1/3/2004 Bp Francis Campbell Gray. c 1. R Ch Of The Resurr Eugene OR 2008-2011; Asst Chr Ascen Ch Richmond VA 2003-2007; Chr Ch Glen Allen VA 2003-2007. "September 13 2001," Epis Dio Pittsburgh, 2002.

BRUCE, David Allison (Me) Brigham'S Cove Road, Box 243 HCR 63, West Bath ME 04530 **Chapl Peabody Hse Portland ME 1986-** B 1948 s Donald & Madelyn. AA Nthrn Essex Cmnty Coll 1968; BA U of Massachusetts 1971; BD U of Edinburgh Edinburgh Gb 1977. Trans 8/25/1983 Bp Frederick Barton Wolf. All Soul's Epis Ch Chatan Okinawa 2003-2006; Assoc Gr Memi Portland OR 1986-2008; Off Of Bsh For ArmdF New York NY 1984-1986; Chapl U Of Alberta Edmonton Alberta CA 1980-1983; Serv Angl Ch Of Can 1977-1980.

✠ BRUCE, The Rt Rev Diane Jardine (Los) 5 W Trenton, Irvine CA 92620 **Bp Suffr of Los Angeles Dio Los Angeles Los Angeles CA 2010-, Stndg Com Pres 2005-2008, Stndg Com Mem 2004-2008, Fresh Start Ldr 2002-2003, Dioc Invstmt Trust Bd Mem 1994-2002; Trst The CPG New York NY 2012-** B Pequannock NJ 1956 d Donald & Mary. BA U CA Berkeley 1979; MDiv Claremont TS 1997; DMin SWTS 2010. D 6/7/1997 Bp Robert Marshall Anderson P 1/17/1998 Bp Frederick Houk Borsch Con 5/15/2010 for Los. m 8/1/1981 Gregory S Bruce c 2. R S Clem's-By-The-Sea Par San Clemente CA 2000-2010; Assoc R Ch Of The Mssh Santa Ana CA 1997-2000; Bd Mem Bloy Hse Claremont CA 2004-2006. Emerging Ldr's Awd Assn of CPE 2012; Hood 'Hero' for Indiv Quality Ft Hood 2012; Dio Los Angeles Bp Garver Awd 2009; Dio Los Angeles Bp Garver Awd 2008; Dio Los Angeles Bp Garver Awd 2007; Yale DS Pstr of Excellence Awd 2004; Dio Los Angeles Hon Cn 2003; DD VTS 2003; Tchr of the year Multiple Radiology Prog 1980; Mem Michigan St Bd Mar Counselors 1977.

BRUCE, Jane (NC) 750 Weaver Dairy Rd Apt 1225, Chapel Hill NC 27514 B Fordyce AR 1941 d Imon & Catherine. BA Mt Holyoke Coll 1963; MA U of Arkansas 1964; MDiv GTS 1987. D 6/13/1987 Bp Ronald Hayward Haines P 6/18/1988 Bp Frank Harris Vest Jr. Vic S Dav's Epis Ch Laurinburg NC 1990-2002; Asst Ch Of The Gd Shpd Rocky Mt NC 1987-1990. OHC.

BRUCE, John Allen (Ore) 31877 SW Village Crest Ln, Wilsonville OR 97070 **1968-** B Kansas City MO 1934 s Basil & Thelma. BA Wesl 1956; MDiv GTS 1959; PhD U MN 1972. D 6/20/1959 Bp Angus Dun P 12/1/1959 Bp Horace W B Donegan. m 7/22/1989 Judith Bruce. Vic Ch Of The Resurr Windcrest TX 1967-1968; Chapl USN 1965-1967; Assoc Chr Ch Charlotte NC 1962-1964; R Ch Of The Div Love Montrose NY 1961-1962; Cur S Barn Ch Irvington NY 1959-1961. Cosmos Club. Who'sWho.

BRUCE, Todd (NCal) **R Trin Ch Folsom CA 2012-** B Snellville GA 1981 s J & V. AB U GA 2002; MDiv VTS 2007. D 12/21/2006 Bp J Neil Alexander P. Assoc R S Paul's Ch Kansas City MO 2007-2012. tbruce@trinityfolsom.org

BRUCE, Tracy Ann (Md) 5814 19th St N, Arlington VA 22205 **R S Jn's Ch Reisterstown MD 2006-** B Cincinnati OH 1952 d Dean & Faye. BS U of Kentucky 1974; MDiv GTS 1991. D 6/22/1991 P 5/28/1992 Bp William Grant Black. c 3. Assoc S Mary's Epis Ch Arlington VA 2002-2006; Asst S Lk's

Epis Ch Atlanta GA 1993-1994; Asst The Ch Of Ascen And H Trin Cincinnati OH 1991-1993. Cramer Middler Acad Awd UTS 1990; Flinchbaugh Ot/Hebr Awd UTS 1989; Sullivan Medallion U Of Kentucky 1974. tracy.bruce@stjohnsglyndon.org

BRUCKART, Robert Monroe (CFla) 2327 Saint Andrews Cir, Melbourne FL 32901 **Dir Of Pstr Care Holmes Reg Med Cntr Melbourne FL 1995-; Dir of Pstr Care Hlth First Inc. 1995-** B Columbus OH 1951 s William & Jessie. Lic St of Florida; BA Westminster Coll 1973; MDiv SWTS 1979; MA Webster U 1998. D 6/9/1979 P 12/7/1979 Bp Robert Bracewell Appleyard. m 9/10/1977 Deborah E Bruckart c 3. Assoc For Pstr Care H Trin Epis Ch Melbourne FL 1995-1998, Assoc R 1984-1994; S Jn's Epis Ch Donora PA 1979-1984; R S Paul's Ch Monongahela PA 1979-1984; Dir of Pstr Care Holmes Reg Med Cntr 1995. Lic Mntl Hlth Counslr St Of Florida.

BRUGGER, Stephanie Black (SO) 335 Lincoln Ave, Troy OH 45373 **D S Mk's Ch Sidney OH 2013-** B 1958 d William & Ruth. AD Edison St 1984. D 10/20/2001 Bp Herbert Thompson Jr. c 3.

BRUMBAUGH, Charlie (Colo) PO Box 2166, Breckenridge CO 80424 **Epis Ch Of S Jn The Bapt Breckenridge CO 2016-** B Greenville OH 1956 s Philip & Nancy. BS Mia 1978; MDiv VTS 1986. D 6/14/1986 P 1/10/1987 Bp William Grant Black. m 10/18/2003 Anne Keely Galluzzo c 2. Assoc The Ch of the Redeem Cincinnati OH 2001-2016; Dir of Marketing Forw Mvmt of the Epis Ch Cincinnati OH 2001-2002; R The Ch Of Ascen And H Trin Cincinnati OH 1994-2001; Assoc S Paul's Epis Ch Pittsburgh PA 1991-1993; R Chr Ch Cape Girardeau MO 1988-1991; Asst Calv Ch Cincinnati OH 1986-1988.

BRUNDIGE, Allyson Paige (Nwk) 333 Christian St, Wallingford CT 06492 B Ridgewood NJ 1980 d Robert & Katherine. MDiv Berk 2011; MDiv Ya Berk 2011. D 12/21/2013 P 9/14/2014 Bp Mark M Beckwith.

BRUNEAU, Betsy (NCal) 66 E. Commercial St., Willits CA 95490 **Assoc S Fran In The Redwoods Mssn Willits CA 2005-** B Rockville Center NY 1944 d Russell & Isabelle. BA Stan 1965. D 4/28/2005 P 11/26/2005 Bp Jerry Alban Lamb. m 9/5/1983 William Bruneau c 2.

BRUNELLE, Denis Charles (LI) PO Box 2733, East Hampton NY 11937 **R S Lk's Ch E Hampton NY 2009-** B Manchester NH 1951 s Ferdinand & Muriel. BA DeSales U 1974; MDiv Cath Theol Un 1977; MA Cath Theol Un 1978; MA San Diego St U 1988; ABD U IL 1988. Rec 5/26/1992 as Priest Bp Peter Hess Beckwith. Geo Mercer TS Garden City NY 2006-2009; Dir Mercer TS Garden City NY 2006-2009; R S Ptr's by-the-Sea Epis Ch Bay Shore NY 1998-2006; R The Par Ch Of S Lk Long Bch CA 1995-1998; R S Ptr's Ch Huntington WV 1992-1994; Serv RC Ch 1977-1992. Ed, "Preaching the Lectionary," Glazier Pub, 1986. Phi Kappa Phi U IL 1991. rector@stlukeseasthampton.org

BRUNETT, Harry Edgar (Md) 9855 S Iris Ct, Littleton CO 80127 B Baltimore MD 1936 s Harry & Minnie. BA W&L 1958; MA Bos 1959; BD EDS 1962; MBA Loyola U 1982; DMin SWTS 1998. D 6/26/1962 Bp Harry Lee Doll P 4/1/1963 Bp Noble C Powell. m 9/2/1961 Joan Marilyn Forsell c 3. R S Andr's Epis Ch Glenwood MD 1998-2003; Asst S Jn's Ch Ellicott City MD 1992-1997; 1967-1992; Vic S Paul's Perry Hall MD 1963-1966; Cur Ch Of S Marks On The Hill Pikesville MD 1962-1963. Auth, "Seeking the Sprt," *How to Create a Cmnty of Seekers,* Morehouse Pub, 2006; Auth, *Seeker Mnstry for Next Generation,* Seabury-Wstrn. Commision On Anti-Racism 2004; ESMA Bd; Mssn Strtgy Grp 1996.

BRUNNER, Arthur Fischer (Pa) Po Box 1190, N Cape May NJ 08204 **Ret 1997-** B Providence RI 1932 s Arthur & Esther. Br 1950; US-A 1952; BS Tem 1957; MDiv PDS 1960. D 5/14/1960 Bp Joseph Gillespie Armstrong P 11/1/1960 Bp Oliver J Hart. m 11/22/1952 Joan F Brunner. Dn Brandywine Dnry 1976-1982; Resurr Epis Ch Rockdale Aston PA 1970-1997; R S Dav Manayunk PA 1961-1970; R S Steph Wissahickon PA 1961-1963; Vic S Steph Wissahickon PA 1960-1961. Auth, *Don't Pk the Ark.* Human Rts Awd City of Philadelphia 1968.

BRUNO, James Ernest (Ark) D 3/19/2016 P 10/1/2016 Bp Larry Benfield.

BRUNO, Jean M (DR) Box 1309, Port-Au-Prince Haiti **R S Esprit Cap Haitien 1974-** B Croix des Bouquets HT 1945 s Merove & Antoinette. MDiv ETSC 1971. D 11/21/1971 P 6/1/1972 Bp Luc Anatole Jacques Garnier. m 3/29/1973 Marise Bruno. Dio The Dominican Republic (Iglesia Epis Dominicana) Gazcue Santo Domingo 1999-2007; Asst Redemp Gonaives Haiti 1972-1973; Dio Haiti Port-au-Prince HT 1971-1998.

✠ **BRUNO, The Rt Rev Joseph Jon** (Los) 3505 Grayburn Rd., Pasadena CA 91107 **Bp of Los Angeles Dio Los Angeles Los Angeles CA 2002-, Bp Coadj Of Los Angeles 2000-, Mssnr For Stwdshp And Dvlpmt 1990-1993, 1988-1993** B Los Angeles CA 1946 s Joseph & Dorothy. BA California St U 1973; MDiv VTS 1977. D 6/18/1977 P 1/14/1978 Bp Robert Claflin Rusack Con 4/29/2000 for Los. m 12/30/1984 Mary A Bruno. Cathd Cntr Of S Paul Cong Los Angeles CA 1993-1999, R 1986-1992; Cathd Cong Los Angeles CA 1986-1999; Assoc S Paul's Pomona Pomona CA 1983-1986; Vic S Matt's Epis Ch Eugene OR 1980-1983; Assoc S Mary's Epis Ch Eugene OR 1979-1980; S Patricks Ch And Day Sch Thousand Oaks CA 1977-1979. EWC; EvangES; Ord Of S Lk. bishop@ladiocese.org

BRUNO, Suzanne Lee (NC) 9528 Spurwig Ct, Charlotte NC 28278 B Los Angeles CA 1944 d Allen & Ada. BA Occ 1966; Tchr Cert Occ 1967; Cert Inst for Chr Stds 1994. D 12/18/1993 Bp John Wadsworth Howe. m 9/24/1966 Paul Michael Bruno c 2. S Marg's Epis Ch Waxhaw NC 2010-2016; D S Jn's Epis Ch Charlotte NC 2009-2010; D Epis Ch Of The Resurr Longwood FL 1993-2008; Chapl & Rel Ed Sweetwater Epis Acad Longwood FL 1993-2008; Bd, Cbury Retreat Ctr Dio Cntrl Florida Orlando FL 2006-2008. Assoc, Ord Of S Helena 1994; NAAD 1994-1999.

BRUNS, Thomas Charles (Mo) 222 Montwood, Seguin TX 78155 **Emm Epis Ch Lockhart TX 2001-; Ret 1998-** B El Paso TX 1938 s Joseph & Florence. BS U of Texas 1961; BD VTS 1964. D 7/15/1964 Bp Everett H Jones P 2/1/1965 Bp Richard Earl Dicus. m 9/24/1983 Martha Bruns c 1. Int S Phil's Ch Beeville TX 1998; R H Cross Epis Ch Poplar Bluff MO 1985-1998; Trin Mssn Pearsall TX 1978-1979; P-in-c All SS Epis Ch Pleasanton TX 1966-1985; P-in-c S Tim's Ch Cotulla TX 1966-1974; Vic Gr Ch Llano TX 1964-1966; Chapl Veterans' Admin Hosp.

BRUNSON, Catherine E (NJ) 124 Harrow Dr, Somerset NJ 08873 **D Trin Epis Ch 2004-** B New Brunswick NJ 1949 Rutgers The St U of New Jersey; AAS Mcc 1969. D 11/21/2002 Bp David Bruce Joslin. c 2. S Alb's Epis Ch New Brunswick NJ 2002-2009.

BRUSCO, Kathleen Kyle (Minn) 112 Crestridge Dr, Burnsville MN 55337 B Saint Paul MN 1970 d Richard & Jane. BA S Olaf Coll 1992; MDiv SWTS 1999. D 6/11/1999 Bp Calvin Onderdonk Schofield Jr P 12/17/1999 Bp James Louis Jelinek. m 1/14/1995 Paul J Brusco. Ch Of The Nativ Burnsville MN 2012, 2011, Assoc 1999-2003; Dio Minnesota Minneapolis MN 1999-2003.

BRUSSO, Leonard George (SeFla) 1225 Knollcrest Ct, Venice FL 34285 **Ret 1998-** B New York NY 1934 s Leonard & Ida. BA Adel 1957; MDiv GTS 1960. D 4/23/1960 P 10/29/1960 Bp James Pernette DeWolfe. m 10/16/1976 Wendy Jean Brusso. Assoc The Epis Ch Of The Gd Shpd Venice FL 1999-2007; Pres of Stndg Com Dio SE Florida Miami 1995-1996, Stndg Com 1993-1995, Com on Cn 1992-1996, Chair of Agenda Com 1989-1990, COM 1981-1982, Chair of Assessment Appeals Com 1993-1998, Cathd Chapt 1989-1992, Exec Bd 1988, Chair of COM 1982-1987, 1981; R S Andr's Epis Ch Miami FL 1981-1998; R S Paul's Ch Glen Cove NY 1968-1981; R Ch of S Jude Wantagh NY 1963-1968; Cur Epis Ch of The Resurr Williston Pk NY 1960-1963; COM Dio Long Island Garden City NY 1966-1978.

BRUST, John Costello (SwFla) 1201 Yellowstone Dr, Naples FL 34110 B Medina NY 1920 s Philip & Mary. BS SUNY 1943. D 6/30/1990 Bp Rogers Sanders Harris. m 7/2/1949 Elsie Ruth Brust c 3. D S Mary's Epis Ch Bonita Sprg FL 1990-2001. NAAD.

BRUTTELL, Susan Margaret (SeFla) 706 Glenwood Ln, Plantation FL 33317 **R S Chris's By-The-Sea Epis Ch Key Biscayne FL 2011-** B Milford CT 1949 d Harold & Margaret. Nova U Davie FL 1993; MDiv Ya Berk 2005; MDiv Yale DS 2005. D 11/15/2006 P 5/26/2007 Bp Leo Frade. m 6/14/1969 Thomas Allen Bruttell c 4.

BRUTTELL, Thomas Allen (SeFla) 706 Glenwood Ln, Plantation FL 33317 **ECBF No Chesterfield VA 2017-** B Fort Lauderdale FL 1949 D 6/21/2003 P 12/21/2003 Bp Leo Frade. m 6/14/1969 Susan Margaret Lund. Archd Dio SE Florida Miami 2008-2017, 2007-2008, Archd for Deploy 2006-; S Chris's By-The-Sea Epis Ch Key Biscayne FL 2006-2007; H Trin Epis Ch W Palm Bch FL 2003-2006.

BRUTUS, Joseph Mathieu (Hai) Box 1309, Port-Au-Prince Haiti **Admin Cathd S Trin 1995-** B Leogane HT 1947 s Dumonvert & Milosia. BA Coll S Pierre 1971; Utcwi 1976; Cntr DEtudes Theol 1977. D 9/18/1977 P 5/1/1978 Bp Luc Anatole Jacques Garnier. m 4/17/1980 Marie Victoria N Brutus. P-in-c S Pierre Par 1993-1995; P-in-c H Innoc Par Port De Paix 1983-1993; Assoc S Sauveur Cayes Hai 1982-1983; Dio Haiti Port-au-Prince HT 1977-2012.

BRYAN, Elizabeth (SD) 1521 Forest Dr, Rapid City SD 57701 B Escanba MI 1945 d Robert & Carol. Calvin Coll 1965; Hope Coll 1967; BA NW Coll 1968; MDiv VTS 1989. D 7/23/1990 Bp Craig Barry Anderson P 6/11/1991 Bp David Henry Lewis Jr. c 1. Vic Ch Of The H Sprt San Antonio TX 2001-2002; R S Jn's Ch Gap PA 1999-2001; S Jas Epis Ch Belle Fourche SD 1994-1997; R S Thos Epis Ch Sturgis SD 1994-1997; Asst The Ch Of The Epiph Oak Hill VA 1991-1992; Gr Epis Ch Alexandria VA 1990-1991. Peo Educational Soc.

BRYAN, Joan (Fla) PO Box 1584, Ponte Vedra Beach FL 32004 B Evanston IL 1944 d Charles & Anne. BA U of Florida 1966; MDiv Sewanee: The U So, TS 1990. D 6/10/1990 P 12/9/1990 Bp Frank S Cerveny. m 7/23/1966 Patrick S Bryan c 2. Assoc Chr Epis Ch Ponte Vedra FL 1991-2006; COM, Chair Dio Florida Jacksonville 2003-2007, Stndg Com, Pres 1995-1997, Stndg Com 1994-2003, Cmnty of S Mary 1990.

BRYAN, Jonathan (Va) 7815 Midday Ln, Alexandria VA 22306 B Richmond VA 1934 s Corbin & Alice. BA U of Virginia 1957; MA GW 1967; PhD Amer U 1972; VTS 1982. D 6/9/1982 Bp David Henry Lewis Jr P 5/1/1983 Bp Charles Francis Hall. m 12/28/1961 Judith M Bryan c 3. P Assoc S Aid's Ch Alexandria VA 2001-2011; R Ch Of The H Cross Dunn Loring VA 1986-1999; R S Dunst's Ch Mc Lean VA 1983-1985; Asst Ch Of The Resurr Alexandria VA 1982-1983. Auth, CreateSpace Pub, 2013; Auth, "Questings: A Parable," iUniverse Pub, 2009; Auth, "Nonetheless, God Retrieves Us," iUniverse Pub, 2006; Auth, "CrossRoads: Musings on a Fr-Son Pilgrimage," Trafford Pub, 2003; Auth, "Life of Love, Love of Life," Trafford Pub, 2002.

BRYAN, Michael John Christopher (Tenn) The School of Theology, The University of the South, 335 Tennessee Ave, Sewanee TN 37398 **Ed, Sewanee Theol Revs The U So 1990-** B London UK 1935 s William & Amy. BA Oxf GB 1957; MA Oxf GB 1959; PhD U of Exeter 1983; Hon. DD Other 2013. Trans 11/1/1983 Bp William Evan Sanders. m 7/1/1972 Wendy E Smith. C K Ben Prof of NT Sewanee U So TS Sewanee TN 1983-2007; Serv Ch of Engl 1960-1983. Auth, "Siding Star," Diamond Press, 2012; Auth, "The Resurr of the Mssh," Oxf Press, 2011; Auth, "Render to Caesar," Oxf Press, 2005; Auth, "A Preface to Romans," Oxf Press, 2004; Auth, "And God Spoke: The Authority of the Bible for the Ch Today," Cowley Pub, 2002; Auth, "A Preface to Mk," Oxf Press, 1997; Auth, "Numerous arts, Revs, etc.". Angl Assn of Biblic Scholars 1995; Cath Biblic Assn 1983; SBL 1983. DD The U So 2013; mcl Gregorian U 2001; Schlrshp and Resrch Awd Assn of Theol Schools 1989; Glanfield Exhibitioner Wadham Coll, Oxford 1958; Woodward Schlr Wadham Coll, Oxford 1954.

BRYAN, Nancy Henry (Cal) 2111 Hyde St # 404, San Francisco CA 94109 **D The Epis Ch Of S Mary The Vrgn San Francisco CA 2009-** B St Paul MN 1938 d Burt & Harriet. U CA 1960; BA Sch for Deacons 2005. D 12/3/2005 Bp William Edwin Swing. m 7/8/1961 Richard Bryan c 3. D Ch Of The Incarn San Francisco CA 2005-2009.

BRYAN, Peggy L (ECR) 5038 Hyland Ave, San Jose CA 95127 **Outreach Assoc S Andr's Ch Saratoga CA 2014-, 2010-2011; Stndg Com Mem Dio El Camino Real Salinas CA 2011-** B Santa Cruz CA 1951 d Raymond & Edith. BA USC 1973; MS USC 1975; MDiv CDSP 2007; MDiv CDSP 2007. D 12/5/2009 P 6/25/2010 Bp Mary Gray-Reeves. m 10/11/2008 Catherine Holley c 2. P-in-c S Phil's Ch San Jose CA 2012-2014.

BRYAN, Walter Lee (WNC) PO Box 1356, Columbus NC 28722 B Rutherfordton NC 1939 s James & Eula. No Carolina Agricultural & Tech St U 1960; U NC 1972; Epis TS in Kentucky 1976; Loyola Coll 1988. Trans 1/12/2004 Bp Bill Persell. m 3/8/1961 Carolyn Bryan c 2. R Ch Of The Gd Shpd Tryon NC 2003-2013; Gr Ch Pontiac IL 1991-2002; Chapl Pontiac Correctional Cntr 1986-2003; R Ch Of S Thos Chicago IL 1986-1990; Lawr Hall Sch Chicago IL 1986; Chapl Dept of Corrections Cook Country IL 1985-1986; Dio Chicago Chicago IL 1985; R Mssh-S Barth Epis Ch Chicago IL 1982-1984; Dio Louisiana New Orleans LA 1981-1982; R S Lk's Ch New Orleans LA 1981-1982; R S Phil's Ch Buffalo NY 1979-1981; Asst S Andr's Ch Lexington KY 1976-1979.

BRYANT, Bronson Howell (Miss) 5408 Vinings Lake View, SW, Mableton GA 30126 **Ret 1996-** B Ocala FL 1931 s Bronson & Martha. BA U of Florida 1953; STB Harvard DS 1958. D 12/7/1958 P 6/24/1959 Bp Edward Hamilton West. m 9/8/1956 Mildred Elizabeth Bryant c 2. R Trin Ch Epis Pass Chr MS 1985-1996; P-in-c Epis Ch Of The Epiph Leeds AL 1981-1985; Chapl S Mart-Of-The-Pines Nrsng Hm Birmingham AL 1980-1985; Chapl S Martins-In-The-Pines Ret Comm Birmingham AL 1979-1985; Asst The Cathd Ch Of The Adv Birmingham AL 1973-1979; R Gr Ch Sheffield AL 1965-1973; Asst S Paul's By-The-Sea Epis Ch Jaxville Bch FL 1961-1965; P-in-c S Mary's Epis Ch Green Cv Spg FL 1959-1961; Asst Chr Epis Ch Pensacola FL 1958-1959.

BRYANT, Julie Diane (Los) Church of the Transfiguration, 1881 South First Avenue, Arcadia CA 91006 **Ch Of The Trsfg Arcadia CA 2009-** B Houston TX 1960 d Douglas & Mary. BA U CA 1982; MDiv STC 1996; DMin Claremont TS 2009. D 6/8/1996 P 12/8/1996 Bp Gethin Benwil Hughes. c 2. The Par Of S Matt Pacific Plsds CA 2009-2012, 1999-2009; Epis Cmnty Serv Natl City CA 1997-1999; All SS Epis Ch Riverside CA 1997.

BRYANT, Katherine Seavey (Va) 14 Cornwall St NW, Leesburg VA 20176 **Sr Assoc R S Jas' Epis Ch Leesburg VA 2012-, Asst to R for Adult Mnstrs 2006-** B Washington DC 1951 d Hollis & Anne. BA The JHU 1973; MA NYU 1976; Cert Westchester Med Cntr 2003; Dip Ang Stud Ya Berk 2006; MDiv Yale DS 2006. D 3/11/2006 P 9/23/2006 Bp Mark Sean Sisk. Soc of St. Marg 2007. Bridges Awd Loudoun Interfaith Bridges 2009; Champion for Chld hon Roll So Dakota Voices for Chld 2009; St. Lk's Awd Ya Berk 2006; Frederick J. Streng Bk of the Year Awd Soc for Buddhist-Chr Stds 1995.

BRYANT, Laura Annette (At) 2456 Tanglewood Rd, Decatur GA 30033 **S Greg The Great Athens GA 2016-** B Boston MA 1958 d Dudley & Judith. BA Duke 1980; MDiv Candler TS Emory U 1987. D 11/5/1989 P 5/1/1990 Bp Frank Kellogg Allan. m 7/30/1983 John Thomas Hutton c 1. P The Ch of the Common Ground Atlanta GA 2015-2016; Dio Atlanta Atlanta GA 2011-2016; Assoc R S Bede's Ch Atlanta GA 1996-2014; Asst P Ch Of The Epiph Atlanta GA 1989-1996.

BRYANT, Peter F (Roch) 4160 Back River Rd, Scio NY 14880 **Vol S Andr's Ch Friendship NY 2004-** B Gowanda NY 1952 D 12/8/2001 P 10/26/2002 Bp Jack Marston Mckelvey. m 3/19/1977 Nancy Bryant c 2.

BRYANT, Richard Gordon (Md) 678 Dave Ct, Covington KY 41015 **Ret 2000-** B Covington KY 1946 s Gordon & Mildred. MDiv Epis TS in Kentucky; BA U of Kentucky. D 6/22/1972 P 12/23/1972 Bp Addison Hosea. Ch Of The

Adv Baltimore MD 1989-2000; R S Lk's Ch Baltimore MD 1978-1983; Asst S Geo's Epis Ch Schenectady NY 1974-1978; Cur Calv Epis Ch Ashland KY 1972-1974. CBS; SocMary.

BRYANT, Robert Harrison (Ore) 6300 Sw Nicol Rd, Portland OR 97223 **R Epis Par Of S Jn The Bapt Portland OR 2002-; Cn Theol Dio Oregon Portland OR 2011-** B Richmond VA 1957 s Francis & Catherine. BA W&M 1979; MDiv Nash 1988. D 6/4/1988 P 6/3/1989 Bp William Edwin Swing. R Ch Of Our Sav Mill Vlly CA 1990-2002; Asst Epis Ch of St Jn the Bapt Aptos Aptos CA 1988-1990.

BRYANT, Todd A (Tex) 5826 Doliver Dr, Houston TX 77057 **Ch Of The Ascen Houston TX 2011-** B Tulsa OK 1970 s Harlin & Rosemary. BS U of Oklahoma 1994; MDiv Epis TS of the SW 2006. D 6/26/2006 Bp Don Adger Wimberly P 1/12/2007 Bp Dena Arnall Harrison. m 4/28/2002 Kimberly Bryant c 3. Palmer Memi Ch Houston TX 2008-2011; Assoc R S Chris's Ch League City TX 2006-2008. kharvin@hotmail.com

BRYANT, William Reid (WLa) 715 Lewisville Rd, Minden LA 71055 **Dio Wstrn Louisiana Alexandria LA 2013-, Cn 2002-2003, Cn 2001-2003, Pres of Stndg Com 2008-2009, GC First Alt 2006-2009, GC Dep 2003-2006, COM 1995-1999; Asst S Mk's Cathd Shreveport LA 2010-; Chapl to Ret Cler Dio Wstrn Louisiana 2006-** B Minneapolis MN 1938 s Frank & Virginia. BA LSU 1964; MBA U of Dallas 1975; Lic Sacr Theol Angl TS 1988. D 6/18/1988 P 6/7/1989 Bp Donis Dean Patterson. m 9/17/1966 Judith Bayliss Bryant c 2. P-in-c S Jn's Epis Ch Minden LA 2012-2013, R 1995-2001; Dn Shreveport Convoc 2007-2010; P-in-c S Jas Epis Ch Shreveport LA 2005-2010, P-in-c 2005-2010; P-in-c S Alb's Epis Ch Monroe LA 2003-2004; P-in-c The Epis Ch Of The Gd Shpd Vidalia LA 2003; Dn Shreveport Convoc 1998-2001; Asst The Epis Ch Of The Trsfg Dallas TX 1988-1995.

BRYCE, Christopher David Francis (USC) 819 Angela Ln, Cross SC 29436 B Adrian MI 1948 s David & Elsie. BA Saginaw Vlly St U 1972; MDiv Epis TS in Kentucky 1976. D 3/19/1976 P 12/1/1976 Bp Addison Hosea. m 5/13/2000 Susan David Francis Bryce. Vic Trin Ch Abbeville SC 1998-2001; Non-par 1994-1999; R S Ptr's Ch Plant City FL 1990-1994; Int S Dav's Epis Ch Englewood FL 1990; Int S Nath Ch No Port FL 1989-1990; Vic S Jn's Pine Island FL 1982-1989; Vic S Jn's Epis Ch St Jas City FL 1980-1989; Assoc S Jn's Epis Ch Clearwater FL 1980-1982; R S Steph's Epis Ch Latonia KY 1978-1979; Vic S Alb's Ch Morehead KY 1976-1978. Outstanding Young Men Amer Awd 1985.

BRYSON, Nancy Gretchen (CFla) **D S Geo Epis Ch The Villages FL 2015-; H Trin Epis Sch Fruitland Pk FL 2014-** D 9/12/2015 Bp Gregory Orrin Brewer.

BRZEZINSKI, James (RG) The Ch Of S Anne Morrison IL 2017- B New Britain CT 1955 s Joseph & Georgia. BBA Belhaven U - Orlando Campus 2008; MDiv Nash 2012. D 5/26/2012 P 6/11/2013 Bp Gregory Orrin Brewer. m 4/17/1982 Nancy Bock c 1. P-in-c S Fran On The Hill El Paso TX 2014-2017; Asst for Pstr Care and Liturg Ch of the H Faith Santa Fe NM 2013-2014; D Nash Nashotah WI 2012-2013; S Barth's Ch Pewaukee WI 2012-2013; Mem of the Bp Search Com Dio The Rio Grande Albuquerque 2017, Mem of the Eccl Disciplinary Bd 2016-2017; Dep to 76th GC - Anaheim, California 2009 Dio Cntrl Florida Orlando FL 2009, Secy of Stndg Com 2007-2010, Dep to 75th GC - Columbus, Ohio 2006 2006, Dioc Bd 2004-2007. revjamesbski@gmail.com

BUB, Sally Letchworth (Wyo) 30 Diversion Dam Rd, Kinnear WY 82516 B Princeton NJ 1942 d James & Elizabeth. BA Smith 1964; MDiv GTS 1993. D 8/24/1993 P 2/25/1994 Bp Bob Gordon Jones. m 6/19/1993 Richard J Bub c 2. Mnstry Dvlp Dio Wyoming Casper 2010-2012; Assoc Ch Of The H Nativ Kinnear WY 2002-2012, P-in-c 1942-; Pstr St Jn Luth Ch Riverton WY 2002-2005; P S Helen's Epis Ch Crowheart WY 1997-2000; R S Thos Ch Dubois WY 1997-2000; Vic St Jn the Bapt Epis Ch Big Piney WY 1993-1996. Educ for Minitstry 1998-2007.

BUCCO, Dennis M (RI) 58 Arrowhead Ln, West Greenwich RI 02817 **R S Lk's Ch Pawtucket RI 2009-** B Warwick RI 1967 s Harry & Genevieve. Bos; BS Johnson & Wales U 1991; MDiv GTS 2007. D 6/13/2007 P 2/2/2008 Bp Gerry Wolf. m 3/17/1996 Madeline M McHenry c 2. S Lk's Epis Ch E Greenwich RI 2007-2009.

BUCHAN III, Thomas Nicholson (CFla) 1716 River Lakes Rd N, Oconomowoc WI 53066 **S Anskar's Epis Ch Hartland WI 2014-; Nash Nashotah WI 2012-; Assoc Ch of the Incarn Oviedo FL 2009-; Assoc Prof Asbury TS Orlando FL 2006-** B Rahway NJ 1972 s Thomas & Marilyn. BA Wheaton Coll 1994; MA Wheaton Coll 1995; MPhil Drew U 1999; PhD Drew U 2003. D 5/30/2009 P 12/1/2009 Bp John Wadsworth Howe. m 12/18/1993 Margaret Michelle Buchan c 2. tnbuchan3@gmail.com

BUCHANAN, Andrew (SVa) 3928 Pacific Ave, Virginia Beach VA 23451 **R Galilee Epis Ch Virginia Bch VA 2009-** B Bishop CA 1970 s James & Claudia. BA U So 1992; MDiv TESM 1997; STM Yale DS 2003. D 6/14/1997 P 12/15/1997 Bp David Mercer Schofield. m 6/28/1997 Dana Buchanan c 4. R S Paul's Ch Brookfield CT 2003-2009; Asst Trin Ch Tariffville CT 1997-2003.

BUCHANAN, Furman Lee (USC) 910 Hudson Road, Greenville SC 29615 **R S Ptr's Epis Ch Greenville SC 2010-** B Barnwell SC 1966 s Furman & Rosanne. BA Wofford Coll 1989; MDiv Sewanee: The U So, TS 2006. D 6/24/2006 P

1/20/2007 Bp Dorsey Henderson. m 7/28/1990 Kim D Buchanan c 3. Asst S Martins-In-The-Field Columbia SC 2006-2010.

BUCHANAN, H Ray (SwFla) 9650 Gladiolus Dr, Fort Myers FL 33908 **Iona Hope Epis Ch Ft Myers FL 2014-** B Waverly TN 1955 s Herman & Hilda. AA Mart Methodist Coll 1976; BS Tennessee Tech U 1978; MDiv Duke DS 1981; MA Vermont Coll of Norwich U 1994. D 11/4/1984 Bp William Evan Sanders P 10/6/1985 Bp Edward Witker Jones. m 4/1/2005 Nancy J Jacobson c 1. R The Ch Of The Redeem Mobile AL 2006-2014; P in Charge/Vic S Lk's Ch Springfield TN 1996-2006; Pstr Counslr Pstr Counslg and Consult Nashville TN 1988-1993; Assoc Trin Ch Clarksville TN 1986-1996.

✠ **BUCHANAN, The Rt Rev John Clark** (WMo) 1Bishop Gadsden Way Apt 332, Charleston SC 29412 **Prlmntrn HOB 2003-** B Laurens County SC 1933 s Dock & Ella. BA U of So Carolina 1958; JD U of So Carolina 1960; MDiv GTS 1969; DMin McCormick TS 1975; GTS 1989. D 6/25/1969 P 1/24/1970 Bp Gray Temple Con 2/25/1989 for WMo. m 11/28/1964 Peggy Annelle Brown c 2. Provsnl Bp Dio Quincy Peoria IL 2009-2013; Int Bp Dio Sthrn Virginia Newport News VA 2006-2008; Int Bp Dio Sthrn Virginia Norfolk VA 2006-2008; Asstg Bp Dio Texas Houston TX 2004-2006; Asstg Bp Dio Texas Houston TX 2004-2006; S Mich's Epis Ch Charleston SC 2000-2004; Bp, W Missouri Dio W Missouri Kansas City MO 1989-1999; R S Andr's Ch Mt Pleasant SC 1975-1989; R S Matt's Epis Ch Darlington SC 1971-1975; Vic S Barn Ch Dillon SC 1969-1971. DD GTS 1989. bpjcb@bellsouth.net

BUCHANAN, Margaret Grace (WNC) 827 Montreat Rd, Black Mountain NC 28711 **D Trin Epis Ch Asheville NC 2002-** B Rochester NY 1947 d Charles & Ruth. Asheville-Buncombe Tech Cmnty Coll 1979. D 12/9/1995 Bp Bob Johnson. m 11/29/1985 John Haywood Buchanan c 3. D S Jas Ch Black Mtn NC 2000-2002.

BUCHANAN, Susan Jill (Va) PO Box 1135, Glen NH 03838 **Chapl Meml Hosp No Conway NH 2005-; P-in-c Ch of theTransfiguration Bretton Woods NH 2002-; Convoc Cnvnr Dio New Hampshire Concord NH 2011-, GC Dep 2004-, Re-imagining Com 2003-2004, COM 2002-2009** B Orlando FL 1957 d Harry & Charlotte. BA Wheaton Coll 1985; MDiv VTS 1994. D 11/8/1994 Bp Frank Clayton Matthews P 5/14/1995 Bp Peter J Lee. m 10/16/2004 Richard A Smith c 2. R S Thos' Ch Richmond VA 2014-2017; R Chr Ch No Conway NH 2002-2014; Dir, Mid-Atlantic Par Trng Prog Dio Virginia Richmond VA 2000-2002, UTO Grant Com 1996-2002, Mid-Atlantic Par Trng Prog Bd Dir 1996-2000; Assoc R Chr Epis Ch Winchester VA 1994-2002. Polly Bond Awd of Excellence for Theol Reflection ECom 2007. sbuchanan@stthomasrichmond.org

BUCHHOLZ, Paige Randolph (ETenn) 1211 Oakdale Trl, Knoxville TN 37914 B Alexandria VA 1948 d Donald & Margaret. BA U NC 1969; MDiv VTS 1988. D 6/11/1988 P 3/1/1989 Bp John Thomas Walker. m 12/30/2014 Elizabeth Joanne Deeter. Dio E Tennessee Knoxville TN 2007-2008, 1988-2000; Assoc S Eliz's Epis Ch Knoxville TN 2001-2007; Vic S Lk's Ch Knoxville TN 1991-2008; Cleric S Steph's Epis Ch Charleston SC 1989-1991; Chapl Urban Mnstry Cntr Knoxville TN 1988-1989.

BUCHIN, Daniel Arthur (Mich) 2260 Baltic Ave, Idaho Falls ID 83404 **Gd Shpd Ft Hall ID 1996-, P 1996-** B Lansing MI 1953 s James & Nancy. BS GW 1982. Rec 6/25/1995 Bp John Stuart Thornton. m 4/1/1993 Christie Hayes.

BUCK, David E (NC) 616 Watson St., Davidson NC 28036 B Birmingham AL 1949 s David & Doris. ABS Davidson Coll 1971; MDiv New Orleans Bapt TS 1977; MDiv New Orleans Bapt TS 1977; MTh PrTS 1984; DMin Candler TS Emory U 1996; GTS 2003. D 2/16/2004 P 10/24/2004 Bp Michael B Curry. m 11/24/2009 Andrea Baker c 5. R S Alb's Ch Davidson NC 2007-2017; Assoc Ch Of The Nativ Raleigh NC 2004-2007.

BUCK, Elizabeth Salmon (EC) 744 Lakeside Dr Se, Bolivia NC 28422 B Columbia SC 1927 d Eugene & Elizabeth. BA U of So Carolina 1946; MA Appalachian St U 1969. D 5/2/1990 Bp Brice Sidney Sanders. m 11/9/1945 Robertson Williams Buck c 4. D S Jas The Fisherman Epis Ch Shallotte NC 1990-2000. Dok.

BUCK, Leonard Frank (HB) **Non-par 1967-** B Scranton PA 1940 s Leonard & Janet. BA Penn 1962; MA Penn 1963; STB PDS 1967. D 6/17/1967 Bp Frederick Warnecke P 5/31/1968 Bp Donald J Campbell. m 12/28/1966 Margaret Guyer Porter Buck.

BUCK, Martha (ECR) 651 Sinex Ave Apt L115, Pacific Grove CA 93950 B Orange NJ 1935 d Carl & Adelaide. BS Skidmore Coll 1956; BA Sch for Deacons 1997. D 12/6/1997 Bp William Edwin Swing. D S Jas' Ch Monterey CA 2001-2010; D S Mk's Par Berkeley CA 1997-2001. Contrib, "Initial Resrch on Pay Equity," *Bargaining for Pay Equity*, Natl Com on Pay Equity, 1990.

BUCK, Robert Allen (Colo) 3070 Indiana St, Golden CO 80401 **Ret 1997-** B Pasadena CA 1932 s Robert & Faith. BS U CA 1957; MDiv CDSP 1968. D 7/1/1968 P 2/12/1969 Bp C J Kinsolving III. m 8/20/1955 Mary Stuart Buck c 3. Pres Of Epis Fndt Dio Colorado Denver CO 1983-1985; R S Paul's Epis Ch Lakewood CO 1981-1997; Vic/R Epis Ch Of The Gd Shpd San Angelo TX 1972-1981; Vic S Mary's Ch Lovington NM 1968-1972.

BUCK-GLENN, Judith (Pa) 1031 N Lawrence St, Philadelphia PA 19123 **Assoc Chr Ch Epis Ridley Pk PA 2002-** B London ON CA 1947 d Conrad &

Joan. Penn; U of Wisconsin; BA U of Massachusetts 1973; MDiv Estrn Bapt TS 1991; MA Tem 1995. D 6/19/1999 P 5/20/2000 Bp Charles Ellsworth Bennison Jr. m 10/14/1989 Gary Scott Glenn. Dio Pennsylvania Philadelphia PA 1999-2001; S Anne's Ch Abington PA 1999-2001; Serv Methodist Ch 1994-1999; Serv Unitarian Ch 1987-1991. Auth, "Homilies," *Homily Serv*, 1996; Auth, "The Legend Of The Donkey'S Cross"; Auth, "One Room Sunday Sch". Hist Soc Of Pennsylvania.

BUCKINGHAM, Carole Sylmay (Wyo) PO Box 12, Kaycee WY 82639 B 1957 d Roy & Pauline. D 8/22/2008 P 3/7/2009 Bp Bruce Caldwell. m 10/13/1979 Ord Allen Buckingham c 6.

BUCKINGHAM, Karen Burnquist (Wyo) 608 6th St, Rawlins WY 82301 **P Ch Of S Thos Rawlins WY 2010-** B Taft CA 1937 d Charles & Virginia. AA Pasadena City Coll 1959. D 5/21/2009 P 1/30/2010 Bp Bruce Caldwell. m 12/27/1964 Harold Buckingham c 3.

BUCKLEY, Abigail J (ETenn) St Barnabas Episcopal Church, 822 SW 2nd St, Mcminnville OR 97128 **Dio Oregon Portland OR 2015-; The Epis Ch Of The Gd Samar Corvallis OR 2015-** B Hartford CT 1986 d Julian & Kathleen. BA Arcadia U 2008; MDiv CDSP 2013; MDiv CDSP 2013. D 4/20/2013 Bp Dan Thomas Edwards. m 6/15/2013 Christopher D Buckley c 1. S Paul's Epis Ch Holdenville OK 2015; Dio E Tennessee Knoxville TN 2014-2015.

BUCKLEY, Herbert Wilkinson (U) 1964 Colorado Gulch Dr, Helena MT 59601 **Ret 1993-** B Brooklyn NY 1927 s Herbert & Phoebe. BS Newark St Teachers Coll NJ 1950. D 12/21/1971 P 7/1/1975 Bp Jackson Earle Gilliam. m 7/27/1952 Carlee Buckley. Dio Utah Salt Lake City UT 1992; Vic S Mich's Ch Brigham City UT 1989-1992; Supply P Dio Montana Helena MT 1985-1989, Supply P 1981-1984; Int Ch Of The Incarn Great Falls MT 1985; P-in-c Gr Ch White Sulphur Sprg MT 1982-1984; P-in-c S Jn's Ch/Elkhorn Cluster Townsend MT 1982-1984; Vic St Johns Epis-Luth Ch Williams AZ 1979-1980; All SS Epis Ch Columbia Falls MT 1976-1978; Mssy Flathead Epis Fllshp Kalispell MT 1976-1978; Mssy S Matt's Ch Columbia Fls MT 1976-1978; Assoc S Ptr's Cathd Helena MT 1971-1976.

BUCKLEY, Terrence Patrick (LI) 64 S Country Rd, Bellport NY 11713 **Chr Ch Bellport NY 2017-** B Brooklyn NY 1962 s Timothy & Kathleen. D 1/14/2017 Bp Lawrence C Provenzano. m 11/27/1992 Bonnie Buckley c 2.

BUCKLIN, Lydia Kelsey (Ia) 225 37th St, Des Moines IA 50312 **S Paul's Ch Coun Blfs IA 2016-; Dio Iowa Des Moines IA 2015-, Other Lay Position 2007-2015** B Burlington VT 1980 d James & Mary. BSW U of Vermont 2002; MSW U MI 2003; MDiv EDS 2015. D 8/6/2015 P 2/6/2016 Bp Alan Scarfe. m 9/4/2010 Brandon Scott Bucklin c 2. lbucklin@iowaepiscopal.org

BUCKWALTER, Georgine (Ky) 2511 Cottonwood Dr, Louisville KY 40242 B Pt Pleasant NJ 1947 d Leonard & Charlotte. U So; BA Westminster Choir Coll of Rider U 1969; MDiv Sthrn Bapt TS 1990. D 5/8/1989 Bp David Reed P 1/1/1995 Bp Ted Gulick Jr. c 2. S Lk's Chap Louisville KY 1998-2013; H Trin Ch Brandenburg KY 1996-1998; Presb Hm & Serv Of Ky Inc Louisville KY 1993-1998. Auth, "Handbook Of Themes For Preaching"; Auth, "Weavings: Sprtlty".

BUCKWALTER, Paul William (Az) 927 N 10th Ave, Tucson AZ 85705 **Died 2/16/2016** B Orange NJ 1934 s Paul & Julia. BA Ya 1956; MA Ya 1960; MDiv EDS 1963; MCP U Cinc 1972. D 6/22/1963 Bp Robert McConnell Hatch P 12/18/1963 Bp Roger W Blanchard. m 5/7/1994 Sandra Cason c 4. Int Chapl Epis Campus Mnstrs U of Arizona Tucson 2008-2009; Ret 1997-2016; Adj Fac Seabury Wstrn TS Evanston IL 1997-2007; Serv Arizona Inter Faith Ntwk Phoenix AR 1997-2005; Exec Assoc S Phil's In The Hills Tucson AZ 1984-1996; 1973-1984; Epis Chapl Untd Chr Mnstrs U of Cincinnati Cincinnati 1969-1972; Stff Basin Mnstry Chincinnati OH 1967-1969; Asst Chr Ch Cathd Cincinnati OH 1963-1967; Int St. Geo's in the Arctic Kotzebue AZ 1962. "Bldg Power: Finding and Developing Leaders in Arizona Congregations," *Soc Plcy Sprg v.33 #3*, 2003; Auth, "Drums Along the Penobscot," *Cincinatti Horizons*, 1981. Oblate Ord of S Ben 1990.

BUDD, Dorothy Reid (Dal) 3707 Crescent Ave, Dallas TX 75205 **D Ch Of The Incarn Dallas TX 2006-** B Charlottesville VA 1958 d Rust & Jeanne. BA Colorado Coll 1980; JD Ut Law Sch 1983; MDiv SMU Perkins 2006; MDiv SMU Perkins 2006. D 12/2/2006 Bp James Monte Stanton. m 5/3/1985 Russell Budd c 2. Lawyer Var Firms 1983-1994.

BUDD, Richard Wade (SVa) 120 Cypress Crk, Williamsburg VA 23188 B Henderson MD 1934 s Bryan & Dorothea. BA Bowling Green St U 1956; MA U of Iowa 1962; PhD U of Iowa 1964. D 4/13/1985 Bp George Phelps Mellick Belshaw. m 8/28/1955 Beverly Knight c 3. R Chr The King Epis Ch Yorktown VA 2006-2009; R Ch Of The Gd Shpd Richmond VA 2002-2006; D Hickory Neck Ch Toano VA 1998-2000; D H Trin Ch So River NJ 1993-1996. Auth/Ed, "Approaches To Human Cmncatn"; Auth/Ed, "Beyond Media"; Auth, "Content Analysis". Who'S Who In Amer.

✠ **BUDDE, The Rt Rev Mariann Edgar** (WA) Diocese of Washington, Episcopal Church House-Mount St Alban, Washington DC 20016 **Bp of Washington Dio Washington Washington DC 2011-** B Summit NJ 1959 d William & Ann. MA U Roch 1982; MDiv VTS 1988. D 5/28/1988 Bp John Shelby Spong P 3/4/1989 Bp James Russell Moodey Con 11/12/2011 for WA. m 5/24/1986 Paul E Budde c 2. R S Jn The Bapt Epis Ch Minneapolis MN 1993-2011; Assoc R Trin Ch Toledo OH 1988-1993. mebudde@edow.org

BUDEZ, Jorge Horacio (WNY) **Off Of Bsh For ArmdF New York NY 2007-** B Barranquilla Colombia 1971 s Fabian & Rosalba. BA Pontificia U Javeriana 1998; MAPM Chr the King Sem 2001. Rec 9/13/2007 as Priest Bp Michael Garrison. m 1/8/2005 Erika Maria Palma.

BUDHU, Esar (Nwk) 206 Renshaw Ave, East Orange NJ 07017 **S Agnes And S Paul's Ch E Orange NJ 1987-** B Georgetown GY 1947 s Raikmoon & Ishmatie. Lic Codrington Coll 1975; BA Codrington Coll 1981. Trans 3/15/1987 Bp John Shelby Spong. m 6/26/1976 Jessica Budhu c 2. Serv Ch In The Prov Of The W Indies - Barbados 1981-1986; Serv Ch In The Prov Of The W Indies - Guyana 1975-1980.

BUDNEY, Karen Vickers (CNY) 18 Cross St., Dover MA 02030 **Pstr Assoc S Andr's Ch Wellesley MA 2007-** B Philadelphia PA 1946 d Raymond & Helen. BS W Chester St Coll 1968; MDiv Harvard DS 1991. D 6/1/1991 Bp David Elliot Johnson P 5/9/1992 Bp Barbara Clementine Harris. m 6/15/1968 Albert Joseph Budney c 2. S Ptr's Epis Ch Cazenovia NY 2005-2006; S Dav's Ch Fayetteville NY 2002; Cn Pstr St Paul's Syracuse Syracuse NY 1999-2002, Asst 1997-1998; Asst S Paul's Ch Kansas City MO 1994-1995; S Paul's Epis Day Sch Kansas City MO 1994-1995; Int Chr Ch Warrensburg MO 1993-1994; Cathd Chapt Dio Massachusetts Boston MA 1992-1993; Int The Ch Of Our Redeem Lexington MA 1992-1993; D S Jn's Ch Newtonville MA 1991-1992. Harvard DS Alum/Ae Coun 2000-2006; Harvard DS Dn's Coun 2006; Newton Wellesley Hosp Prot Chapl Coun 2009-2012; Samar Cntr Bd Dir 1998-2006.

BUECHELE, Thomas John (Haw) 15-2686 Hinalea St, Pahoa HI 96778 B Davenport IA 1942 s Carl & Dorothy. BA S Ambr U 1964; MTh Mt S Bern Sem Dubuque 1968. Rec 9/25/2002 as Priest Bp Robert Reed Shahan. m 1/23/1993 Jean Buechele. Mssnr to St. Columba S Jas Epis Ch Kamuela HI 2013; Int S Jude's Hawaiian Ocean View Ocean View HI 2012-2013; Vic Kohala Epis Mssn Kapaau HI 2005-2010; Border Mssnr Dio Arizona Phoenix AZ 2004-2005; Vic S Jn's Epis Ch Bisbee AZ 2002-2003.

BUECHNER, Deborah Ann (CFla) 1078 Coastal Cir, Ocoee FL 34761 B Mt. Clemons MI 1951 d John & Betty. AA Valencia Cmnty Coll 2000. D 12/10/2005 Bp John Wadsworth Howe. m 7/27/1991 William Buechner c 2. Epis Ch Of The Ascen Orlando FL 2007-2011.

BUECHNER, Frederick Alvin (Ga) Po Box 2626, Thomasville GA 31799 **Int R Calv Epis Ch Americus Georgia 2013-** B Saint Louis MO 1952 s Alvin & Elinor. BA U of Virginia 1974; MDiv VTS 1980. D 4/28/1980 P 1/27/1981 Bp George Paul Reeves. m 12/27/1975 Kathy Buechner c 2. R All SS Epis Ch Thomasville GA 1988-2012; R Chr Epis Ch Dublin GA 1986-1988; Dn Of Dublin Convoc Dio Georgia Savannah GA 1985-1986; Assoc S Jn's Ch Savannah GA 1981-1986; Asst Chr Ch Frederica St Simons Is GA 1980-1981.

BUEHLER, Lynnsay Anne (At) 147 Shadowmoor Dr, Decatur GA 30030 **Dir, The Julian of Norwich Ctr. S Bede's Ch Atlanta GA 2000-; Mentor, Atlanta Grp EFM Univ. of the So Sewanee 1988-** B Abington PA 1956 d Martin & Patricia. BA Duke 1978; MDiv Candler TS Emory U 1982. D 6/10/1989 P 5/25/1990 Bp Frank Kellogg Allan. m 7/25/1981 Robert Burwell Townes c 1. Cov Colleagues Retreat Ldr Candler TS Ch Min. Ed. Atlanta 2001-2008; Supvsr, Sup'd Min./Contextual Ed. Candler TS Emory Univ. Atlanta 1997-2000; Chapl, Atl. Chapt SCHC Atlanta GA 1996-2010; Pstr Counslr/Sprtl Dir S Barth's Epis Ch Atlanta GA 1994-1998; Pstr Counslr Dunwoody Counslg Cntr Atlanta GA 1992-1996; Assoc R Ch Of The Atone Sandy Sprg GA 1989-1993; Sprtl Formation Com Dio Atlanta Atlanta GA 1991-1998. AAPC 1992; EFM Mentor 1988; Green Bough Hse Of Pryr Assoc 1998; Sprtl Dir Intl 1991. MDiv cl Candler TS, Emory U 1982.

BUEHRENS, Gwen Langdoc (Mass) 1333 Gough St. Apt 1-D, San Francisco CA 94109 **P Assoc S Jas Epis Ch San Francisco CA 2014-; Chapl Beth Israel Dss Hosp 2009-; Assoc S Mary's Ch Newton Lower Falls MA 2005-** B Chicago IL 1943 d Malcolm & Mignonne. BA U CA 1968; BA U CA 1968; M.A. in Rel Yale DS 1972; MA Ya 1972. D 6/24/1972 Bp Chauncie Kilmer Myers P 11/30/1985 Bp Donis Dean Patterson. m 6/21/1972 John Buehrens c 2. P Assoc All SS Ch Carmel CA 2012-2014; Chapl W River Hospice 2006-2009; Chapl Res Hartford Hosp 2005-2006; S Andr's Ch Wellesley MA 1994-2003, Assoc 1993-2003; Assoc S Paul's Ch Dedham MA 1993-1994; Assoc Chr And S Steph's Ch New York NY 1989-1993; Epis Ch Cntr New York NY 1989-1992; Info/Cmncatn Off Epis Migration Mnstrs 1989-1991; Asst Ch Of The H Trin New York NY 1987-1989; The Epis Ch Of The Trsfg Dallas TX 1985-1986; Asst Ch Of The Epiph Richardson TX 1981-1983; Asst S Mich And All Ang Knoxville TN 1979-1981.

BUELL, Susan Davies (NwPa) 75 Perry St. 2A, New York City NY 10014 B Upper Darby PA 1939 d Frank & Mary. BA Ladycliff Coll 1968; MLS U of Texas 1974; MDiv Epis TS of the SW 1978; Cert Institut Catholique De Paris 1991; Cert Natl Archv 2003. D 9/23/1977 P 5/1/1978 Bp Richard Mitchell Trelease Jr. m 6/21/1959 William Collins Buell c 3. Dn Angl Catedral Del Redentor Madrid Spain 2004-2009; Chr Epis Ch Meadville PA 1992-2004; Non-par 1990-1991; All SS Ch Pasadena CA 1987-1990; Asst to R S Fran Ch Houston TX 1982-1987; Chapl To Epis Sch Pro Cathd Epis Ch Of S Clem El Paso TX 1980-1981; Dio The Rio Grande Albuquerque 1977-1982; Vic S Anne's El Paso TX 1977-1978. Auth, "Our Lady Of Guadalupe: A Feminine Mythology In The New Wrld," Susan Davies Buell, 1984. Doc. Honoris Causa ETSSW 1994.

BUELOW, Peggy Jean (SVa) 23397 Owen Farm Road, Carrollton VA 23314 B Pensacola FL 1947 d John & Georgia. BS U of W Florida 1969; MA U of W Florida 1979; MDiv VTS 1986. D 5/24/1986 P 4/1/1987 Bp Claude Charles Vache. m 6/1/1980 John Peter Buelow c 3. Pstr Counslr Tidewater Pstr Counslg Serv Norfolk VA 2007-2010; R S Mk's Ch Hampton VA 1992-2013; Off Of Bsh For ArmdF New York NY 1989-1992; Chapl USN 1989-1992; Asst R All SS' Epis Ch Virginia Bch VA 1986-1989.

BUENO BUENO, Francisco Javier (Colom) Kra 80 #53a-78, Medellin Colombia B 1968 s Bernardino & Ana. D 5/15/1994 Bp Bernardo Merino-Botero. Iglesia Epis En Colombia Bogota 1995-1999.

BUENTING, Julianne (Chi) 3857 N Kostner Ave, Chicago IL 60641 **Ch Of The Trsfg Palos Pk IL 2017-; Assoc S Anna's Chap Chicago IL 2013-** B Brockport NY 1960 d John & Mary Ann. BSN SUNY at Brockport 1981; MS SUNY at Buffalo 1986; DNS SUNY at Buffalo 1990; MA S Bernards TS and Mnstry 1997; MDiv SWTS 2009. D 6/6/2009 P 12/5/2009 Bp Jeff Lee. P The Ch Hm At Montgomery Place Chicago IL 2013-2017; Ch Of The H Nativ Chicago IL 2012-2013. jbuenting@hotmail.com

BUENZ JR, John Frederick (ECR) 22115 Dean Ct, Cupertino CA 95014 **Assoc Chr Epis Ch Los Altos CA 1997-** B San Antonio TX 1932 s John & Harriett. Stan; BS U of Texas 1955; MDiv CDSP 1965; DD CDSP 1996. D 6/20/1965 Bp James Albert Pike P 12/28/1965 Bp George Richard Millard. m 11/27/1975 Marilyn A Mueller. All SS Ch Carmel CA 2006-2007; Int Epis Ch in Almaden San Jose CA 2004-2005; Calv Epis Ch Santa Cruz CA 2003-2004; Int Ch of S Mary's by the Sea Pacific Grove CA 1999-2000; Vstng Chapl CDSP Berkeley CA 1996-1997; Dn Cathd Of S Jn The Evang Spokane WA 1986-1996; R Ch Of S Jude The Apos Cupertino CA 1973-1986; Vic Epis Ch in Almaden San Jose CA 1967-1973; Asst S Mk's Epis Ch Santa Clara CA 1965-1967; Chair of Futures Com Dio Spokane Spokane WA 1993-1996, Bp Search Com 1989-1992; Stndg Com Dio California San Francisco CA 1974-1979. DD CDSP 1996.

BUFFONE, Gregory James (Tex) B Steubenville OH 1948 s Harry & M'Elise. MS U of So Florida 1973; PhD U NC 1975; Iona Sch for Mnstry 2007. D 9/17/2007 Bp Don Adger Wimberly. m 5/23/1970 Janet Louise Buffone c 2.

BUHRER, Richard Albert (Oly) 2021 15th Ave S Apt 1, Seattle WA 98144 **D St Ptr's Epis Par Seattle WA 2010-** B Pasco WA 1948 s Albert & Betty. BA Gonzaga U 1970; MDiv Loyola U 1978. Rec 6/28/2002 Bp Vincent Waydell Warner. D S Paul's Ch Seattle WA 2003-2009.

BUICE, Bonnie Carl (At) 115 Maplewood Ave Sw, Milledgeville GA 31061 B East Point GA 1932 s Bonnie & Elizabeth. BA Merc 1954; JD Merc 1957; MA U of Notre Dame 1975. D 6/26/1965 Bp Randolph R Claiborne P 9/1/1975 Bp Bennett Jones Sims. m 2/18/1984 Hulane George c 4. S Jas Ch Macon GA 1992-2004; S Steph's Ch Milledgeville GA 1990-1991; Non-par 1984-1991; R S Fran Ch Macon GA 1979-1984; Cur H Trin Par Decatur GA 1975-1979; D, Asst Gr Epis Ch Gainesville GA 1965-1974.

BUICE, Samuel Walton (At) 3 Westridge Rd, Savannah GA 31411 **Gr-Calv Epis Ch Clarkesville GA 2015-; R S Ptr's Epis Ch Savannah GA 2001-** B Atlanta GA 1959 s Bonnie & Elizabeth. BA La Cen Coll 1982; MDiv VTS 1991. D 6/8/1991 P 1/26/1992 Bp Frank Kellogg Allan. m 5/24/1982 Margaret Ann Buice c 4. S Ptr's Epis Ch Savannah GA 2002-2015; R S Mths Epis Ch Toccoa GA 1994-2001; Epis Ch Of The H Fam Jasper GA 1991-1994; Vic S Tim's Epis Ch Calhoun GA 1991-1994.

BUICE, William Ramsey (Hond) 10100 Hillview Dr #4A, Pensacola FL 32514 B Atlanta GA 1926 s Bonnie & Elizabeth. BS U GA 1948; MS USAFIT 1962; MBA GW 1963; MDiv Sewanee: The U So, TS 1977; DMin Van 1985. D 10/27/1977 P 9/1/1978 Bp David Reed. m 2/3/1982 Lillian Ruth Stilwell Buice c 4. Assoc H Cross Ch Pensacola FL 2005-2015; Int S Mary's Epis Ch Milton FL 2002-2004; Trin Epis Ch Pass Chr MS 1996-1997; Int Trin Ch Pass Chr MS 1996-1997; Assoc Trin Ch Pass Chr MS 1985-1996; Cn to Ordnry Dio Honduras 1985-1989; Vic S Patricks Epis Ch Long Bch MS 1980-1985; Vic S Jn's Ch Morganfield KY 1977-1980. Cmnty of S Mary-Assoc 1975. Purple Heart U.S.A.F. 1968; Air Medal U.S.A.F. 1968; Distinguished Flying Cross U.S.A.F. 1968.

BUIE, Delinda Stephens (Ky) 2341 Strathmoor Blvd, Louisville KY 40205 **D St. Mk's Epis Ch 2005-; Assoc S Andr's 1988-** B Evansville IN 1951 d Eldee & Margaret. U of Louisiana; AA Alice Lloyd Coll 1971; BA Spalding U 1973; U of Edinburgh Gb 1974; MLS U of Kentucky 1975; Louisville Presb TS 1983. D 8/6/1987 Bp David Reed. m 9/15/1973 Gregory Lea Buie c 3.

BUISSON, Pierre-Henry (Az) 4 Clos Bardon Lagrange, Cadillac 33410 France **S Lk's Ch Prescott AZ 2014-; Assoc R St Martins-In-The-Field Ch Severna Pk MD 2012-, Chapl 2010-2014; S Mart's-In-The-Field Day Sch Severna Pk MD 2010-** B Rochefort - France 1959 s Jacques & Josette. BA Lycee Sv Etupery S Dizier FR 1978; RC Dioc Sem Poitiers France 1986; MDiv Other 1990; MTS VTS 2010. Rec 1/31/2004 as Priest Bp Pierre W Whalon. m 6/21/1997 Sophie Buisson c 3. S Dunst's Epis Ch Beth MD 2008-2010; P-in-c Mssn S Mart Convoc of Amer Ch in Eu 2004-2008; lay Pstr Ldr Mssn S Mart Convoc of Amer Ch in Eu 2001-2004; R ARCHIAC RC Dio La Rochelle France 1995-1996; P in Charge St Genis RC Dio La Rochelle France 1991-1995; Yth Chapl Dnry of Jonzac RC Dio La Rochelle France 1990-1996; Asst Mirambeau RC Dio La Rochelle France 1990-1991; Coun of Advice Convoc of Epis Ch in Europe Paris 2005-2006.

BUKER, Karen Elaine (Mil) 3380 S Jeffers Dr, New Berlin WI 53146 **D S Ptr's Ch Milwaukee WI 1995-** B Milwaukee WI 1947 d Kenneth & Isabel. U of Wisconsin - Oshkosh. D 6/3/1995 Bp Roger John White. m 12/14/1968 Lee Arthur Buker c 2. Photographer, "Var photographs and arts," *E-News*, Dio Milwaukee. Bp's Shield Awd Bp Steven Miller-Dio Milwaukee 2010.

BULL, Julian (Los) 5049 Gloria Ave, Encino CA 91436 **Headmaster Campbell Hall Vlly Vlg CA 2004-; Headmaster Campbell Hall (Epis) No Hollywood CA 2003-** B Albuquerque NM 1959 s Malcolm & Audrey. ABS Dart 1982; MA Boston Coll 1988; MDiv VTS 2007. D 2/28/2004 P 9/29/2007 Bp Joseph Jon Bruno. m 6/26/1993 Katherine Bull c 2. Chair of Suffr Search Com Dio Los Angeles Los Angeles CA 2008-2009. NAES 1995.

BULL, Terry Wayne (WNY) 633 Harrison Ave, Buffalo NY 14223 **Chapl to Ret Cler Dio Wstrn New York 2014-; R Ch Of The Adv Buffalo NY 2001-; Chapl to Ret Cler Dio Wstrn New York Tonawanda NY 2013-** B Wichita KS 1954 s Harold & Kathryn. BA California St U 1984; MDiv SWTS 1996. D 6/8/1996 P 12/20/1996 Bp Gethin Benwil Hughes. c 2. COM - Ord Grp Dio Wstrn New York 2005-2008; Sprtl Advsr - Curs Dio Wstrn New York 2004-2007; Dio. Cmsn on Const and Cannons Dio Wstrn New York 2003-2006; R Chr Ch Durham Par Nanjemoy MD 1996-2001; Epis Sr Mnstrs Dio Washington Washington DC 2000-2001.

BULLARD, Carol Ann (Neb) 1603 17th St, Mitchell NE 69357 **Trin Epis Ch Monroe MI 2015-** B 1948 D 9/12/1999 Bp Charles I Jones III P 11/7/2001 Bp Charles Glenn VonRosenberg. Ch Of The H Apos Mitchell NE 2004-2015; S Tim's Ch Gering NE 2004-2006; Dio E Tennessee Knoxville TN 2001-2004; R S Matt's Ch Dayton TN 2001-2004.

BULLARD, Jill Staton (NC) 403 E Main St, Durham NC 27701 **S Phil's Ch Durham NC 2008-; C0-Fndr, Dir Inter-Faith Food Shuttle Raleigh NC 1989-** B Winston Salem NC 1948 d W Reid & Muriel. D 6/14/2008 Bp Michael B Curry. c 3.

BULLARD, Lynn Huston (Ala) 8020 Whitesburg Dr S, Huntsville AL 35802 B Sylacauga AL 1952 d Jack & Nona. BS U of Alabama 1975. D 10/30/2004 Bp Henry Nutt Parsley Jr. m 12/8/1984 William Thomas Bullard c 2.

BULLER, Reverend Deacon Alberta Brown (Cal) P.O. Box 494, Fairfax CA 94978 **S Fran Of Assisi Ch Novato CA 2017-; Chapl Marin Gnrl Hosp Greenbrae CA 2014-** B Connecticut 1956 d Ernest & Alberta. D The Epis Sch for Deacons 2016. D 6/11/2016 Bp Marc Handley Andrus. m 7/11/2009 David Ross Buller c 3. Marin Interfaith Coun 2017. deacon@stfrancisnovato.org

BULLION, James Regis (Ga) 512 Flamingo Ln., Albany GA 31707 **Conf Cntr. Cmsn 2005-; Mem, Comm. on Mnstry Dio Georgia Savannah GA 1990-** B Homestead PA 1940 s Francis & Gertrude. BA Duquesne U 1981; MA Duquesne U 1982; DMin Sewanee: The U So, TS 2003. D 6/17/1982 P 1/21/1983 Bp George Paul Reeves. m 1/13/1984 Mary White Bullion. Mem, Bd Trst U So Sewanee TN 2002-2008; R S Patricks Ch Albany GA 1993-2008; Vic S Barn Epis Ch Valdosta GA 1989-1993; S Paul's Ch Augusta GA 1985-1988; Ch Of The H Sprt Dawson GA 1983-1985; H Trin Epis Ch Blakely GA 1983-1985; D Intern S Alb's Epis Ch Augusta GA 1982-1983.

BULLITT-JONAS, Margaret (WMass) 83 Bancroft Rd, Northampton MA 01060 B Cambridge MA 1951 d John & Sarah. BA Stan 1974; PhD Harv 1984; MDiv EDS 1988; Cert Shalem Inst for Sprtl Formation Washington DC 1988. D 6/11/1988 Bp David Elliot Johnson P 6/17/1989 Bp Barbara Clementine Harris. m 10/25/1986 Robert A Jonas c 1. Assoc Gr Ch Amherst MA 2004-2013; Chapl HOB 1998-2000; Assoc R All SS Par Brookline MA 1996-2004; EDS Cambridge MA 1996-2002, 1991-1992; Asst R Gr Ch Newton MA 1992-1996; Assoc Emm Ch Boston MA 1991-1992; Cur Par Of Chr Ch Andover MA 1988-1991. Auth, "Beauty and Advocacy," *Vstry Papers*, ECF, 2015; Auth, "I Saw an Ocean in New York," *Fllshp*, Fllshp of Recon, 2014; Auth, "The Epis Ch and Climate Change: The First Twenty-Five Years," *ATR*, ATR, 2013; Auth, "15 meditations," *SEEKING GOD DAY BY DAY: A YEAR OF MEDITATIONS*, Forw Mvmt, 2013; Auth, "JOY OF HEAVEN, TO EARTH COME DOWN," Forw Mvmt, 2012; Auth, "Putting Down the Duck," *WRITERS ON THE EDGE*, Loving Healing Press, 2012; Auth, "Made for Goodness (Bk Revs)," *Presence*, Sprtl Dir Intl , 2010; Auth, "Running to the Empty Tomb (sermon)," *Cowley*, SSJE, 2008; Auth, "The Majesty of Your Loving (Bk Revs)," *Presence*, Sprtl Dir Intl , 2008; Auth, "Conversion to Eco-Justice," *EARTH AND WORD: MEDITATIONS ON ECOLOGY, CREATION, NATURE, AND JUSTICE*, Continuum, 2007; Auth, "When Heaven Happens," *HEAVEN*, Seabury, 2007; Auth, "Missionaries to the Planet (Bk Revs)," *Sojourners*, 2007; Auth, "Marg Bullitt-Jonas (interview)," *FEEDING THE FAME*, Hazelden, 2006; Auth, "Open Your Hand: The Pract of Generosity," *Shalem News*, 2006; Auth, "The Art of Sponsorship," *Steps*, 2005; Auth, "Coming to Sense," *Epis Times*, 2003; Auth, "Chr'S PASSION, OUR PASSIONS," Cowley, 2002; Auth, "H HUNGER," Knopf; Vintage Paperback, 2000; Auth, "Faith at Our Fin-

gertips (Sermon)," *Sermons That Wk IX*, Morehouse Pub, 2000; Auth, "From Kitchen Stool To Meditation Cushion," *Sprtlty and Hlth*, 1999; Auth, "Feeling & Pain & Pryr," *Revs for Rel*, 1995; Auth, "Doubting as a Step Toward Sprtl Growth," *Human Develpment*, 1994; Auth, "Even at the Grave We Make Our Song," *Revs for Rel*, 1994; Auth, "Sprtl Direction for Adult Chld of Alcoholics," *Human Dvlpmt*, 1991. EPF 1991. Distinguished Alum/ae Awd EDS 2008; Sprtlty & Justice Awd All SS Par, Brookline, MA 2004.

BULLOCK, Debra K (Chi) St. Mark's Episcopal Church, 1509 Ridge Avenue, Evanston IL 60201 **Bexley Seabury Fed Chicago IL 2017-; R S Mk's Ch Evanston IL 2011-** B Wausau WI 1969 d Robert & Brenda. BA Luther Coll 1992; MTS Bos 1994; MDiv SWTS 2006. D 6/3/2006 P 12/16/2006 Bp Bill Persell. m 10/3/2014 Andrea M Nowack. S Barn By The Bay Villas NJ 2007-2011; Asst. to R S Mary's Epis Ch Stone Harbor NJ 2007-2011; Cur Ch Of The Trsfg Palos Pk IL 2006-2007. rector@stmarksevanston.org

BULLOCK, Jeff (Los) 3474 NW Bryce Canyon Ln, Bend OR 97703 **P-in-c Chr The King Ch Tucson AZ 2013-** B Chicago IL 1949 s Lester & Lura. BA Morningside Coll 1971; MDiv CDSP 1980; DMin CDSP 1999. D 6/28/1980 P 6/29/1981 Bp William Edwin Swing. m 6/25/2015 Kathy T Bullock c 5. R All SS-By-The-Sea Par Santa Barbara CA 2002-2012; R S Barn On The Desert Scottsdale AZ 1998-2002; Pres of Cler Assn Dio Oregon Portland OR 1994-1995; Chr Ch Par Lake Oswego OR 1991-1998; Gr Epis Ch Hutchinson KS 1986-1991; S Steph The Mtyr Ch Minneapolis MN 1984-1986; R Emm Epis Ch Alexandria MN 1982-1984; Assoc S Jn's Epis Ch Oakland CA 1980-1981; Cn Theol Dio Arizona 2013-2015; Chair of Stndg Com Dio Wstrn Kansas Hutchinson KS 1987-1992. Auth, "Practicing Chr Patience," *Bk*, Ch Pub, 2014; Auth, "sev," *arts*, Living Ch; Auth, "sev," *arts*, Living Ch; Auth, *CTI papers*, Cntr of Theol Inquiry; Auth, *Theol & Bk Revs*, Alb Inst and Theol Today; Auth, *Theol Today and Wrshp*, Princeton Sem and Liturg Press. Los Angeles Cler Assn; NECCA; Natl Rel Ldrshp Fndt; PACT. Pstr Theol Cntr of Theol Inquiry, Princeton Sem 2000; Doctor of Divnity Alberston Coll 1999; Lilly Ldrshp Lilly Fndt 1997.

BULLOCK, Kenneth R (Pa) 213 Stable Rd, Carrboro NC 27510 B Rugby ND 1944 s Ralph & Anna. BMus U CO 1968; BD SWTS 1970; MSW U of Wisconsin 1984. D 6/22/1970 Bp George T Masuda P 12/19/1970 Bp Gerald Francis Burrill. m 2/4/1967 Norma K Rice c 2. P-in-c S Dunstans Ch Blue Bell PA 2007-2010; Int Gr Epiph Ch Philadelphia PA 2005-2007; P-in-c S Aidans Ch Cheltenham PA 2001-2005; P S Ptr's Ch Northlake WI 1990-1991; Vic S Alb's Ch Sussex WI 1976-1982; S Barth's Ch Pewaukee WI 1976-1979; P Epis Ch Of S Jn The Bapt Breckenridge CO 1975-1976; P Epis Ch Of The Trsfg Vail CO 1974-1975; S Geo Epis Mssn Leadville CO 1974-1975; Cur The Ch Of Chr The King (Epis) Arvada CO 1973-1974; Cur S Tim's Epis Ch Littleton CO 1972-1973; Cur Gr Epis Ch Hinsdale IL 1970-1971.

BULLOCK, Michael Anderson (Pa) 1040 Brentwood Dr, Columbia SC 29206 **P-in-c Gr Epis Ch Camden SC 2011-** B Schenectady NY 1950 s Raymond & Gladys. BA U NC 1972; MDiv Ya Berk 1976. D 4/26/1978 Bp Joseph Warren Hutchens P 1/26/1979 Bp Morgan Porteus. m 6/16/1979 Beverly L Lyman c 3. The Epis Ch Of The Adv Kennet Sq PA 2012-2014; Cn to the Ordnry Dio Upper So Carolina Columbia SC 2008-2011; R S Martins-In-The-Field Columbia SC 1999-2008; R Chr Ch Manlius NY 1986-1999; Assoc S Paul's Ch Dedham MA 1981-1986; Kent Sch Kent CT 1978-1981.

BULLOCK, Richard (Ore) 22346 Se Hoffmeister Rd, Damascus OR 97089 **Died 6/24/2017** B Shenandoah IA 1937 s Arlan & Helen. BA U of Cntrl Missouri 1960; MDiv Ya Berk 1963; DMin Eden TS 1972; S Louis U 1974; Coll of Preachers-Fell 1978. D 6/29/1963 Bp Gordon V Smith P 12/28/1963 Bp Russell T Rauscher. m 8/6/1960 Ruthanne K Kruse c 3. Assoc S Mich And All Ang Ch Portland OR 2002-2017; Dio Oregon Portland OR 2000-2001, Dn Of Metro-E Convoc And Cler 1988-1992; Assoc Chapl Mt Hood Hosp 1987-2017; R S Lk's Epis Ch Gresham OR 1987-2000; S Thos Of Cbury Par Long Bch CA 1986-1987; Mssnr For Congrl Dvlpmt Dio Los Angeles Los Angeles CA 1985-1986; R S Paul's Epis Ch Tustin CA 1982-1985; R S Fran Epis Ch San Jose CA 1975-1981; Assoc S Mich & S Geo S Louis MO 1970-1974; P-in-c Calv Epis Ch Sioux City IA 1963-1968; Mem - Mutual Mnstry Revs Com ECF Inc New York NY 2001-2004; Proj Dir - Election of a Bp Natl Ntwk Of Epis Cler Assn Lynnwood WA 1997-1999; Alum Coun Ya Berk New Haven CT 1982-1984. Auth, "Cler Renwl: The Alb Guide To Sabbatical Plnng," Alb Inst, 1999; Auth, "Proj Mgr: The Raising Up Of Epis Ldrshp," *Manual*, Off Of Pstr Dvlpmt - HOB, 1997; Auth, "Mutual Mnstry Revs For Cler & Cong," Cornerstone Proj, 1994; Auth, "Sabbatical Plnng For Cler & Cong," The Alb Inst, 1987; Auth, "Do You Know The Way To Jan Jose: One Pstr'S Search For A Job," The Alb Inst, 1975. Assn Of Pstr Counselors 1974-1995; Natl Ntwk of Epis Cler Assn 1974. Appreciation For Serv Girl Scouts of Oregon and SW Washington 1992.

BULSON, William Lawrence (Minn) 13000 Saint Davids Rd, Minnetonka MN 55305 **St Albans Angl- Epis Ch Tokyo 2012-** B Marion OH 1965 s Leo & Jessie. Pushkin Inst Moscow USSR 1986; BA U of Kentucky 1988; MA OH SU 1990; MDiv VTS 1996. D 6/29/1996 Bp Herbert Thompson Jr. c 1. Assoc St Dav's Epis Ch Minnetonka MN 2009-2012; Vic Ch Of The H Apos S Paul MN 2004-2009, 2000-2003; Asst Geth Ch Minneapolis MN 2000-2001;

Cn Cathd Ch Of S Mk Minneapolis MN 1998-1999; Vic E Cntrl Ohio Area Mnstry Bridgeport OH 1996-1998. Oblate, Ord of Julian of Norwich 2009.

BUMGARNER, William Ray (SwVa) 605 Clay St, Lynchburg VA 24504 **D S Paul's Epis Ch Lynchburg VA 2010-** B Lynchburg VA 1953 s Abner & Alease. BS Lynchburg Coll 1977. D 12/16/2006 Bp Neff Powell. m 8/16/1986 Mary Lynne Bumgarner c 1.

BUMILLER, William Norton (SO) 320 Lonsdale Ave, Dayton OH 45419 **Ret 1996-** B Cincinnati OH 1931 s Theodore & Elizabeth. BS U Cinc 1953; MDiv CDSP 1958; U So 1960. D 6/10/1958 P 12/17/1958 Bp Henry W Hobson. c 3. S Jas Ch Piqua OH 1995-1996; S Mk's Ch Sidney OH 1995-1996; Int S Paul's Epis Ch Greenville OH 1995-1996; Int Trin Ch Hamilton OH 1993-1994; Int S Chris's Ch Fairborn OH 1991-1993; Assoc S Geo's Epis Ch Dayton OH 1976-1990; Assoc S Paul's Epis Ch Dayton OH 1963-1976; R Trin Epis Ch London OH 1958-1963.

BUMP, Anne Glass (Mich) 1708 Jamestown Place, Pittsburgh PA 15235 B East Cleveland OH 1948 d Elwood & Flora. BA Ohio Wesl 1970; MDiv Pittsburgh TS 1999. D 12/18/1999 Bp Arthur Williams Jr P 6/26/2000 Bp J Clark Grew II. c 2. R Gr Ch Mt Clemens MI 2004-2009; R Chr Epis Ch Geneva OH 2002-2004; R S Paul Epis Ch Conneaut OH 1999-2002.

BUMSTED, David S (CFla) Church Of The Redeemer, 222 S Palm Ave, Sarasota FL 34236 **R Emm Ch Orlando FL 2015-** B Oklahoma City OK 1982 s David & Lynne. AA Brevard Cmnty Coll 2003; BA Florida St U 2005; MDiv Nash 2013; MDiv Nash TS 2013. D 6/8/2013 P 12/9/2013 Bp Gregory Orrin Brewer. m 11/29/2008 Rebekah R Bumsted. Assoc Ch Of The Redeem Sarasota FL 2013-2015. dbumsted@redeemersarasota.org

BUNCH, Linda Lauren (Cal) 600 Colorado Ave, Palo Alto CA 94306 **S Mk's Epis Ch Palo Alto CA 2016-** B Columbia SC 1987 d John & Linda. BA Wofford Coll 2009; MDiv Wesley TS 2014. D 11/21/2015 Bp Mariann Edgar Budde P 6/11/2016 Bp Marc Handley Andrus. Other Lay Position S Paul's Rock Creek Washington DC 2014-2015.

BUNCH, Wilton Herbert (Ala) Samford University, Birmingham AL 35229 B Walla Walla WA 1935 s Walter & Winnifred. BA Walla Walla Coll 1956; MD Loma Linda U 1960; PhD U MN 1967; MBA U Chi 1983; MDiv CDSP 1998. D 6/7/1997 P 12/13/1997 Bp William Jerry Winterrowd. m 11/27/1983 Victoria Mae Bunch c 3. Assoc The Epis Ch of the H Apos Hoover AL 2001-2011; Assoc S Alb's Epis Ch St Petersburg FL 1998-2001; Assoc Epis Ch Of S Jn The Bapt Granby CO 1997-1998. Auth, "Ethics of Direct to Consumer Advert," *Spineline*, 2009; Auth, "On the Ethics of Reducing Pain to a Number," *Loyola Orthopaedic Journ*, 2007; Auth, "Courts should seek justice, not revenge," *The Birmingham Tribune*, 2007; Auth, "Conflict-of-Interest: The Need for Rules," *Spineline*, 2006; Auth, "Capital Punishment: A Hoax and Delusion," *Birmingham News*, 2005; Auth, "The Ethics of Indep Med Examiners," *Journ of the Amer Acad of Disabil Evaluating Physicians*, 2005; Auth, "Cloning is not Concep: But that doesn't make it Rt," *Chr Ethics Today*, 2002; Auth, "Revs: Natural and Div Law: Reclaiming the Tradition for Chr Ethics by Jean Porter," *ATR*, 2001; Auth, "Revs: Who Are We? By Jean Elstham," *ATR*, 2001; Auth, "A Theol Inclusive Of The Experience Of Disabil, Journ Of Rel," *Disabil And Hlth*, 2001; Auth, "The Ethics Of Gene Ther," *Clincl Orthapedics & Related Resrch*, 2000; Auth, "The Virtuous Orthapedist Has Fewer Malpractice Suits," *Corr*, 2000; Auth, "Moral Decisions Regarding Innovation: The Case Method," *Corr*, 2000; Auth, "Informed Consent," *Corr*, 2000; Auth, "Moral Resoning, Professionalism And Tchg Of Ethics To Orthapedic Surgeons," *Corr*, 2000.

BUNDER, Peter J (Ind) 610 Meridian St, West Lafayette IN 47906 **Chapl Dio Indianapolis Indianapolis IN 2009-, Pres Stndg Com 2006-2007** B Rochester NY 1951 s Peter & Sophia. BA S Jn Fisher Coll 1973; MDiv U Tor CA 1977; Bex Sem 1982. Rec 5/23/1982 as Priest Bp Robert Rae Spears Jr. m 6/26/1982 Kathleen Lynn Bunder c 2. Chapl Chap Of The Gd Shpd W Lafayette IN 1985-2009; R E Lee Memi Ch (Epis) Lexington VA 1982-1985; Chapl VMI Lexington VA 1982-1985; Transition Prog Dio Rochester Henrietta 1981-1982; Serv RC Ch 1977-1981. W Lafayette City Coun Dist #2 2011; W Lafayette City Coun Dist #2 2007. peter@goodshep.org

BUNKE, Jeff L (O) 871 E Boundary St, Perrysburg OH 43551 **R S Tim's Epis Ch Perrysburg OH 2013-** B Defiance OH 1954 s Walter & Margaret. BA Valparaiso U 1976; MDiv SWTS 1981. D 6/27/1981 P 1/25/1982 Bp John Harris Burt. m 10/23/1976 Kay Ann Bunke c 3. R S Anne Epis Ch W Chester OH 2007-2013; R Gr Epis Ch Inc Port Orange FL 1992-2007; R S Jn's Epis Ch Cuyahoga Fls OH 1985-1992; Asst Min S Paul's Ch Maumee OH 1981-1985. ComT 1987. rector@saint-timothy.net

BUNKER, Oliver Franklin (Kan) Grace Episcopal Church, 209 S Lincoln Ave, Chanute KS 66720 B Topeka KS 1963 s Virgil & Dorothy. BM Neosho Cnty Cmnty Jr Coll 1984; AA Neosho Cnty Cmnty Jr Coll 1985. D 6/11/2011 Bp Dean E Wolfe. m 3/13/1982 Josephine Bunker c 1.

BUNN III, George Strother (SwVa) 518 Beech Forest Rd, Bristol TN 37620 **Ret 1998-** B Pulaski VA 1932 s George & Winifred. SWTS; BS Florida St U 1954; U So 1957. D 7/13/1957 P 11/1/1959 Bp William Henry Marmion. m 3/31/1959 Barbara Bunn c 2. Emm Epis Ch Bristol VA 1975-1998; Non-par 1962-1975; Vic S Thos Epis Christiansbrg VA 1957-1962.

BUNSY, Martin (SJ) 1327 N Del Mar Ave, Fresno CA 93728 **Asst S Mart Of Tours Epis Ch Fresno CA 2005-** B Vientrane Laos 1951 s Outhai & May. Dongdok U Laos 1968; Bible Trng Sch Ft Worth TX 1984; Fresno City Coll Fresno CA 1991. D 9/10/2004 P 4/23/2005 Bp David Mercer Schofield. c 2.

BUNTAINE, Raymond Earl (NJ) 106 Palmwood Ave, Cherry Hill NJ 08003 **Died 12/5/2016** B Kalamazoo MI 1920 s Ralph & Elva. Wstrn Michigan U 1939; BA U MI 1942; MA U MI 1946; GTS 1963. D 8/18/1956 P 2/23/1957 Bp Alfred L Banyard. m 10/23/1976 Virginia Buntaine. Ret 1985-2016; Non-par 1972-1985; Vic S Ptr Woodbury Heights NJ 1970-1972; R S Jn The Evang Ch New Brunswick NJ 1959-1970; Chapl St Boys Hm Jamesburg NJ 1956-1959; Vic S Geo's Epis Ch Helmetta NJ 1956-1957.

BUNTING, Michael Andrew (Mil) 290 Quintard Rd # 19, Sewanee TN 37375 **Chapl S Andr's-Sewanee Sch Sewanee TN 2014-** B Fayetteville NC 1975 s Michael & Glyn. BA Wms 1997; MDiv Ya Berk 2002. D 12/6/2002 Bp Leo Frade P 9/6/2003 Bp Dorsey Henderson. m 6/8/2002 April L Berends c 2. P-in-c S Jas Epis Ch Milwaukee WI 2013-2014; P-in-c Epis Ch Of The Resurr Mukwonago WI 2009-2013; Assoc S Columba's Ch Washington DC 2005-2008; Cur/Chapl S Steph's Ch Coconut Grove Miami FL 2002-2005; Dio Upper So Carolina Columbia SC 1997-1999.

BUNTING SR, Norman Richard (Eas) St Paul's Episcopal Church, 3 Church St, Berlin MD 21811 B Salisbury MD 1945 s Norman & Eileen. D 5/4/2013 Bp Bud Shand. m 6/10/1967 Ellen Hudson Bunting c 2.

BUNYAN, Frederick Satyanandam (Colo) 1749 Stove Prairie Cir, Loveland CO 80538 **Chapl Loveland Police Dept 1982-; Chairman Colorado Epis Fndt Denver CO 2012-** B Jammalmadugu IN 1945 s Alfred & Shantha. BA Andhra Chr Coll 1967; BD Bishops Theol Coll Calcutta 1970; STM SMU Perkins 1972. Trans 6/1/1977 Bp William Carl Frey. m 7/15/1974 Ann S Bunyan c 3. R All SS Ch Loveland CO 1982-2010; Asst Ch Of Our Sav Colorado Sprg CO 1978-1982; Asst The Ch Of The Ascen Denver CO 1977-1978; Asst Ch Of The Resurr Austin TX 1975-1977; Serv Ch of So India 1970-1975. Colorado Epis Fndt 2002; Colorado Link, Co-Workers of Mo Teresa 1982; Loveland Police Chapl 1982; Loveland Rotary Club - Pres 1991-1992. Bp's Cross Dio Colorado 2000.

BUOTE-GREIG, Eletha A (RI) Po Box 192, North Scituate RI 02857 **Chapl U Mass Dartmouth 1986-** B Providence RI 1942 d James & Elsie. BA U of Rhode Island 1982; MDiv EDS 1986. D 6/21/1986 P 12/23/1986 Bp George Nelson Hunt III. R S Jas Epis Ch At Woonsocket Woonsocket RI 2004-2014; R S Jn's/S Steph's Ch Fall River MA 1995-2004; R S Steph's Ch Fall River MA 1992-1998; Assoc S Lk's Epis Ch E Greenwich RI 1987-1991; Chapl Dio Massachusetts Boston MA 1986-2000. Comp of the H Cross.

BUQUOR, Anthony Francis (Mass) 1357 Old Marlboro Rd, Concord MA 01742 B San Antonio TX 1946 s Anthony & Mildred. BA So Dakota St U 1968; MS Troy U 1976; MDiv SWTS 1996. D 4/10/1996 P 11/11/1996 Bp Creighton Leland Robertson. m 1/18/1970 Louann Buquor c 2. R Trin Ch Concord MA 2003-2016; Cn to the Ordnry Dio So Dakota Pierre SD 1999-2003; R Chr Epis Ch Yankton SD 1996-1999.

BURBANK, Kristina Dawn (Ore) **Reverend D S Jas Ch Lincoln City OR 2004-** B Spokane WA 1949 d Donald & B Evelyn. BA Ft Wright Coll of H Names 1976; BA Marylhurst U 1988. D 9/18/2004 Bp Johncy Itty.

BURCH, Charles Francis (Mil) D Zion Epis Ch Oconomowoc WI 1998- B Jersey City NJ 1941 s Joseph & Hazel. BS FD 1974. D 5/9/1998 Bp Roger John White. m 4/12/1969 Mary Ann Burch c 3. Phi Omega Epsilon FD 1972.

BURCH, Ian C (Mil) 1424 N Dearborn St, Chicago IL 60610 **S Mk's Ch Milwaukee WI 2016-** B Emporia KS 1978 s Philip & Susan. BA Gustavus Adolphus Coll 2000; MDiv Luth TS 2004. D 6/8/2013 P 1/5/2014 Bp Jeff Lee. m 8/5/2014 Travis J Trott. S Chrys's Ch Chicago IL 2013-2015.

BURCH, Suzanne (ETenn) 4111 Albemarle Ave, Chattanooga TN 37411 B Oak Ridge TN 1947 d Robert & Ruth. BS U of Tennessee 1992. D 12/15/2001 Bp Charles Glenn VonRosenberg. D S Tim's Ch Signal Mtn TN 2012-2015; D S Mart Of Tours Epis Ch Chattanooga TN 2002-2011; D Gr Ch Chattanooga TN 2001-2002.

BURCHARD, Russell Church (SwVa) 51 Mayapple Gln, Dawsonville GA 30534 B Jacksonville NC 1944 s Roswell & Thelma. BA Amer U 1968; MPA GW 1973; MDiv VTS 1979. D 5/27/1979 P 12/1/1979 Bp Alexander D Stewart. m 11/23/1968 Miriam S Burchard c 2. R Chr Ch Martinsville VA 2000-2002; Assoc Galilee Epis Ch Virginia Bch VA 1994-2000; R Chr Ch Par Epis Watertown CT 1987-1994; R Gr Ch Broad Brook CT 1982-1987; S Steph's Ch Pittsfield MA 1982, Asst 1979-1982; Dio Wstrn Massachusetts Springfield 1979-1982. Auth, "The Sprtl Gifts Workbook," St Andr's Mnstrs.

BURCHILL, George Stuart (SwFla) 2611 Bayshore Blvd, Tampa FL 33629 **Ret 1993-** B Newcastle New Brunswick CA 1927 s Henry & Blanche. BA Dalhousie U 1949; LTh U of Kings Coll Halifax NS CA 1952; BD U of Kings Coll Halifax CA 1961. Trans 10/1/1954 Bp Henry I Louttit. m 2/7/1952 Nancy Elizabeth Anne Burchill c 4. Headmaster S Jn Par Day Sch Tampa FL 1954-1992; St Johns Epis Ch Tampa FL 1954-1992; Serv Angl Ch Of Can 1951-1953. Auth, "arts Liturg Classics," *Var Subjects*.

BURDEKIN, Edwina Amelia (Colo) 4566 Winewood Village Dr, Colorado Springs CO 80917 **Ret 2008-; Diac Coun Dio Colorado Denver CO 1999-, BEC 1997-2002** B Twillingate NF CA 1932 d Edwin & Annie. D Formation Prog; ADN Pikes Peak Cmnty Coll 1986. D 11/2/1996 Bp William Jerry Winterrowd. c 5. S Raphael Epis Ch Colorado Sprg CO 2003-2008; D Ch Of S Mich The Archangel Colorado Spg CO 1996-2003. NAAD 1996.

BURDEN, Richard James (Mass) 2323 Lexington Rd, Richmond KY 40475 **All SS Par Brookline MA 2014-; Chair, Nomin Com for the 7th Bp of the Dio Dio Lexington Lexington 2011-** B Loveland CO 1964 s Roy & Mary Ellen. BA Colorado St U 1986; MA U CO@Denver 1996; PhD U Chi 2006; MDiv CDSP 2009. D 6/6/2009 Bp Sergio Carranza-Gomez P 12/21/2009 Bp Stacy F Sauls. m 8/15/1999 Monica J Burden c 2. P-in-c Epis Ch of Our Sav Richmond KY 2009-2013. rector@allsaintsbrookline.org

BURDEN, William Robertson (Chi) PO Box 273, Orangeville IL 61060 **Died 9/19/2015** B Rockford IL 1943 s William & Marjory. BA Bos 1965; MDiv GTS 1968; MA Loyola U 1978. D 6/15/1968 Bp James Winchester Montgomery P 12/21/1968 Bp Gerald Francis Burrill. m 9/28/1997 Irene Meros c 2. Asst Cathd Ch Of S Ptr St. Petersburg FL 2010-2015; R Trin Epis Ch Aurora IL 1975-2005; R All SS Epis Ch Chicago IL 1970-1975; Cur Chr Ch Winnetka IL 1968-1970. Auth, "High Rises For Low & Middle Income Families," *Challenge*, HUD.

BURDESHAW, Charles Abbott (Tenn) 139 Brighton Close, Nashville TN 37205 **S Ann's Ch Nashville TN 1990-** B Chattanooga TN 1940 s James & Cornelia. Emory U 1960; U of Tennessee 1961; DDS U of Tennessee 1965; U of Missouri 1968; Epis TS in Kentucky 1990. D 10/28/1989 Bp George Lazenby Reynolds Jr. m 3/18/1964 Rosemary Dean Burdeshaw c 1.

BURDETT, Audrey Brown (At) 3223 Rilman Rd Nw, Atlanta GA 30327 **Ret 1995-** B Flushing NY 1922 d Walter & Ottilie. BA Georgia St U 1984; MDiv Candler TS Emory U 1988. D 6/11/1988 P 10/12/1988 Bp Charles Judson Child Jr. m 5/25/1945 Lucien Briscoe Burdett. D Cathd Of S Phil Atlanta GA 1988-1995. Auth, "Personal Plnng Guide". DOK.

BURDETTE, Matthew E (NJ) **Ch Of The Gd Shpd Dallas TX 2017-** D 5/19/2017 Bp William H Stokes.

BURDICK II, Edward Noyes (SO) 2437 Swans Rd Ne, Newark OH 43055 **Died 11/18/2016** B Westerly RI 1923 s Harry & Prudence. BS Ya 1948; MDiv UTS 1953. D 6/13/1953 P 1/23/1954 Bp William A Lawrence. c 2. Ret 1990-2016; R S Lk's Ch Granville OH 1960-1989; Chapl U of Maryland Coll Pk MD 1957-1960; Cur S Jn's Ch Northampton MA 1953-1957.

BURDICK III, Henry C (Ct) 152 Wharf Landing Dr Unit A, Edenton NC 27932 **R Gr Epis Ch Plymouth NC 2008-** B New London CT 1943 s Henry & Eleanor. BA U of Connecticut 1970; MEd Antioch U 1982; MDiv Ya Berk 1985. D 6/8/1985 P 12/1/1985 Bp Arthur Edward Walmsley. m 8/5/1967 Kathrine Lillian Burdick. R S Dav's Ch Gales Ferry CT 1988-1999; Trin Ch Branford CT 1985-2009; Wmns Seamens Frd Soc Of Ct New Haven CT 1985-1999. Wmn Seamen's Friend Soc Of Connecticut, New Haven Ct 1983-2001.

BURG, Michael John (FdL) 2515 Lakeshore Dr, Sheboygan WI 53081 **D Gr Epis Ch Sheboygan WI 1990-** B Lena WI 1944 s Norbert & Marion. BS U of Wisconsin 1971; Diac Sch Dio Fond du Lac 1990. D 9/12/1990 Bp William Louis Stevens. c 3. D All SS Chap Elkhart Lake WI 1989-2013.

BURGDORF, David (Los) 36270 Avenida De Las Montanas, Cathedral City CA 92234 B Auburn NY 1944 s Kenneth & Rita. BA SUNY at Buffalo 1966; MDiv GTS 1969; MA U of St Thos MN 1989. D 6/21/1969 P 12/22/1969 Bp Lauriston L Scaife. Vic S Jos Of Arimathea Mssn Yucca Vlly CA 1997-1999; Mgr Betty Ford Cntr Rancho Mirage CA 1992-2010; Counslr St. Mary's Rehab Cntr Minneapolis MN 1982-1992; Vic Ch of the H Name Dolton IL 1975-1978; Cur Emm Epis Ch Rockford IL 1971-1975; Cn S Paul's Cathd Buffalo NY 1969-1971. SSF 1978-1986; Third Ord, SSF 1991.

BURGER, Charles Sherman (Ida) 9640 W. Sleepy Hollow Ln, Garden Valley ID 83714 **Ret 1997-** B Saint Louis MO 1938 s Joseph & Eleanor. BA Trin Hartford CT 1960; BD CDSP 1966. D 3/5/1966 Bp George Richard Millard P 9/4/1966 Bp Harry Sherbourne Kennedy. m 1/17/1984 Leah Diane Burger. R S Thos Epis Ch Sun Vlly ID 1985-1997; R S Thos Sun Vlly ID 1985-1997; R S Paul's Epis Ch Elko NV 1983-1985; R H Innoc' Epis Ch Lahaina HI 1973-1983; Vic S Mich And All Ang Ch Lihue HI 1966-1968.

BURGER, Douglas Clyde (RI) 214 Oakley Rd, Woonsocket RI 02895 B New Haven CT 1938 s William & Alice. Coll of Wooster 1959; BA DePauw U 1960; MA Indiana U 1963; BD SWTS 1966. D 6/11/1966 Bp John P Craine P 12/1/1966 Bp William R Moody. m 7/2/1959 Bessie Gould c 2. Assoc S Steph's Ch Providence RI 1993-2002; Vic S Phil's Ch Harrodsburg KY 1966-1967; Vic Trsfg Lawrenceburg KY 1966-1967. Auth, "A Complete Bibliography Of The Schlrshp On The Life & Works Of S Jn Chrysostem".

BURGER, Robert Franz (Wyo) Po Box 579, Estes Park CO 80517 **Asst S Barth's Ch Estes Pk CO 2001-; 1989-** B Saint Louis MO 1929 s Joseph & Eleanor. Pasadena City Coll; BA USC 1950; BD CDSP 1953. D 6/22/1953 P 2/1/1954 Bp Francis E I Bloy. R All SS Epis Ch Torrington WY 1986-1989; P-in-c S Chris's Ch Trona CA 1978-1986; 1976-1978; Epis Dio San Joaquin Modesto CA 1975-1976; Trin Meml Epis Ch Lone Pine CA 1975-1976; Vic

S Anne's Epis Ch Washougal WA 1974-1975; Vic S Jn's Epis Ch So Bend WA 1969-1974; Vic S Ptr Ilwaco WA 1969-1974; Vic S Paul's Epis Ch Port Townsend WA 1964-1969; Cur S Paul Epis Ch Bellingham WA 1962-1963; Chapl Wstrn WA St Coll 1962-1963; Vic Ch Of S Jn The Div Springfield OR 1956-1962; Cur S Mk's Epis Par Medford OR 1955-1956; Vic Chr The Gd Shpd Par Los Angeles CA 1954-1955; Cur S Jas Par Los Angeles CA 1953-1955.

BURGER, Timothy H (WMass) 11 Berkeley Pl, Glen Rock NJ 07452 **Dio Wstrn Massachusetts Springfield 2015-** B Athens GA 1978 s Raymond & Mary. BA U GA 2002; MDiv GTS 2005; STM UTS 2014. D 12/21/2004 P 6/16/2005 Bp J Neil Alexander. m 6/6/2014 Gregory C Lisby c 2. R All SS' Epis Ch Glen Rock NJ 2010-2015; Ch of the Epiph Rumford RI 2007-2010; St Mich & Gr Ch Rumford RI 2007-2010; Ch Of The Epiph Providence RI 2007-2009; Assoc S Mary's Epis Ch Ardmore PA 2005-2007.

BURGESS, Barbara Candis (NC) Po Box 1547, Clemmons NC 27012 **Ch Of The Gd Shpd Cooleemee NC 2014-; Vic S Mart's-In-The-Fields Mayfield KY 2000-; S Paul's Ch Hickman KY 2000-** B Jacksonville FL 1958 d Willard & Marian. BA U So 1981; MDiv Sewanee: The U So, TS 1996. D 6/15/1996 Bp Rogers Sanders Harris P 2/22/1997 Bp John Bailey Lipscomb. S Matt Ch Salisbury NC 2014-2016; Dio No Carolina Raleigh NC 2013; Chr Epis Ch Cleveland NC 2012, 2011; S Paul's Ch Salisbury NC 2009-2010; S Clem's Epis Ch Clemmons NC 2005-2009; S Ptr's of the Lakes Gilbertsville KY 2000-2006; Parc Area Vic Dio Kentucky Louisville KY 2000-2005; Trin Epis Ch Fulton KY 2000-2005; Dio Nthrn Michigan Marquette MI 2000; R S Jas Ch Of Sault S Marie Sault Sainte Marie MI 1998-2000; Asst to R S Andr's Epis Ch Sprg Hill FL 1996-1998.

BURGESS, Brian Kendall (NJ) The Rectory of Christ Church, 62 Delaware Street, Woodbury NJ 08096 **Convoc Dn Dio New Jersey Trenton NJ 2016-, Dioc Stndg Com 2014-2015, Dioc Coun 2009-2012, Convoc Dn 2006-2010, Stndg Cmsn on Cler Compstn 2006-2009; Cler Mem - Bioethics Com Underwood-Memi Hosp Woodbury NJ 2012-; R Chr Ch In Woodbury Woodbury NJ 2005-; Chapl Underwood-Memi Hosp Woodbury NJ 2005-** B Tampa FL 1960 s Willard & Marian. BS Ball St U 1983; MDiv Sewanee: The U So, TS 1999. D 6/12/1999 P 12/18/1999 Bp John Bailey Lipscomb. m 4/9/1985 Denise Lee Burgess c 2. Assoc P/Chapl of Par Day Sch S Lk's Ch Baton Rouge LA 2001-2005; R S Jn's Epis Ch Brooksville FL 1999-2001; Trst The U So Sewanee TN 2011-2014; Epis Cmnty Serv Bd Dio Louisiana New Orleans LA 2000-2005; Ecum and Interfaith Relatns Com Dio SW Florida Parrish FL 1999-2001. The Geo T. Shettle Prize for Excellence in Liturg Reading Sewanee: The U So, TS 1999. office@christchurch.woodburynj.org

BURGESS, Carol Jean (NC) 721 7 Lks N, Seven Lakes NC 27376 **D S Mary Magd Ch Troy NC 1999-** B Duluth MN 1939 d Stuart & Audrey. BS Hamline U 1961; MEd U of Wisconsin 1982; Reg II Dioc Minn 1987. D 10/25/1987 Bp Robert Marshall Anderson. m 6/23/1962 Timothy John Burgess c 2. Asst Chapl Penick Vill Sthrn Pines NC 2003-2006; D Emm Par Epis Ch Sthrn Pines NC 1998-1999; Chapl Pk Point Manor Duluth MN 1988-1991; D S Edw's Ch Duluth MN 1987-1998.

BURGESS, Judith Fleming (RG) 134 Hillcrest Loop, Capitan NM 88316 **Dioc Coun Dio the Rio Grande 2011-; R Epis Ch In Lincoln Cnty Ruidoso NM 2010-** B Rotan TX 1950 d Albert & Erin. BA U of Texas 1972; MA U of Washington 1975; MPhil Col 1979; MDiv VTS 1984. D 6/23/1984 Bp Peter J Lee P 4/13/1985 Bp Clarence Nicholas Coleridge. m 10/13/1990 Seth B Burgess. Vic Big Bend Epis Mssn Alpine TX 1996-2010; R Gr Epis Ch Goochland VA 1989-1993; Cur S Geo's Ch Fredericksburg VA 1986-1989; Cur S Mich's Ch Naugatuck CT 1984-1986.

BURGESS, Vicki Tucker (Tenn) 4016 Brush Hill Rd, Nashville TN 37216 **R S Phil's Ch Nashville TN 2007-** B Winter Haven FL 1954 d Arthur & Carol. BS U of Tennessee 1976; MDiv Sewanee: The U So, TS 2003. D 6/22/2003 P 4/18/2004 Bp Bertram Nelson Herlong. m 7/26/1975 John Thomas Burgess c 3. Ch Of The Gd Shpd Brentwood TN 2004-2007; Dio Tennessee Nashville TN 2003-2004, Chair, GC Deputation 2011-2014, Mem, Stndg Com 2009-2012.

BURGESS, Walter F (Eas) 105 Gay St, Denton MD 21629 **Chapl Baltimore Fire Dept 1996-** B Baltimore MD 1948 s Franklin & Helen. BS Towson U 1982; MDiv GTS 1993. D 6/12/1993 Bp Albert Theodore Eastman P 6/1/1994 Bp Charles Lindsay Longest. m 7/19/2008 Mary Eileen Menton. R Chr Ch Denton MD 2007-2014; Emm Epis Ch Chestertown MD 2006-2007; Ch Of S Paul The Apos Baltimore MD 2003-2005; P-in-c S Lk's Ch Baltimore MD 1997-2002; Cur/Asst Gr And S Ptr's Ch Baltimore MD 1993-1997.

BURGOS, Joe A (Tex) 305 Sunset Drive, North Manchester IN 46962 B Merida Yucatan MX 1937 s Alejandro & Isabel. AA Warren Wilson Coll 1958; BA Maryville Coll 1960; BD McCormick TS 1964; MA Prairie View A&M U 1984. D 6/13/1993 P 3/24/1994 Bp Maurice Manuel Benitez. m 8/25/1962 Janice Mary Burgos c 3. Supply P S Alb's Ch Houston TX 1995-1996; Ch Of The Redeem Houston TX 1993-1996.

BURGOYNE, Douglas G (Va) 11757 Triple Notch Ter, Richmond VA 23233 **Died 2/5/2017** B Orange NJ 1930 s Robert & Marion. BA Wms 1952; MDiv EDS 1958. D 5/31/1958 Bp William A Lawrence P 12/1/1958 Bp Lane W Barton. m 12/27/1952 Joanna Cutter Burgoyne c 5. Assoc St Jas Ch Richmond VA

2007-2011; Int Ch Of S Jas The Less Ashland VA 2005-2007; P-in-c S Mart's Epis Ch Richmond VA 2001-2004; R All SS Ch Richmond VA 1992-2000; R S Andr's Epis Ch Newport News VA 1975-1991; R S Jn's Ch Williamstown MA 1964-1975; R S Matt's Epis Ch Ontario OR 1958-1964; Stndg Com Dio Sthrn Virginia Newport News VA 1989-1991, Dep GC 1982-1985; Dep GC Dio Wstrn Massachusetts Springfield 1970-1973. Auth, "arts Ch mag". Hon Cn Cntrl Tanganyika 1969.

BURHANS III, Charles F (CFla) **R Gr Epis Ch Inc Port Orange FL 2008-** B Lakeland FL 1951 BA Stetson U 1975; MDiv TESM 2005. D 5/28/2005 P 12/8/2005 Bp John Wadsworth Howe. m 5/5/1985 Carolyn M Burhans c 1. Asst S Jas Epis Ch Ormond Bch FL 2005-2008. rector@egracepo.org

BURHOE, Alden Read (Mass) 54 Grant Ave, Somerset MA 02726 **Asst S Mk's Ch Marco Island FL 2002-; Ret 1995-** B Providence RI 1931 s Paul & Ruth. BA Br 1953; BD EDS 1956. D 6/23/1956 P 3/23/1957 Bp John S Higgins. c 2. Vic and R Ch Of Our Sav Somerset MA 1958-1994; Cur S Mart's Ch Providence RI 1956-1958.

BURK, John H (SJ) 599 Colton St, Monterey CA 93940 **Chapl U.S.Navy 1963-; Asstg Cler All SS Ch Carmel CA 2012-** B Binghamton NY 1940 s Donald & Ruth. BS Un Coll Schenectady NY 1960; MDiv SWTS 1966; MLS San Jose St 1992. D 6/11/1966 Bp James Winchester Montgomery P 12/1/1966 Bp Gerald Francis Burrill. m 9/5/1962 Anne Burk c 2. S Mk's Epis Ch Tracy CA 1985-1990; Epis Dio San Joaquin Modesto CA 1985; Ch Of The Resurr Clovis Clovis CA 1982-1984; R S Jn's Ch Mt Morris NY 1976-1982; Vic S Ptr's Ch Clearfield UT 1969-1976; Cur Emm Epis Ch Rockford IL 1966-1969. Phi Sigma Kappa 1956. Bp Anderson Schlr 1966; Alpha Phi Omega 1956.

BURK, William H (Va) 7159 Mechanicsville Tpke, Mechanicsville VA 23111 **R Ch Of The Creator Mechanicsvlle VA 1998-** B Washington DC 1962 s Paul & Mildred. BA California St U 1990; MDiv VTS 1996. D 10/12/1996 P 4/1/1997 Bp Frank Clayton Matthews. m 6/1/1996 Jennifer Louise Burk c 5. Pres Chapl Serv of Virginia 2008-2009; Asst R Gr Ch Kilmarnock VA 1996-1998.

BURKARDT, Jay P (Roch) St Paul Episcopal Church, 25 Westminster Rd, Rochester NY 14607 **S Paul's Ch Rochester NY 2015-** B Rochester NY 1978 s Peter & Judith. BA Mt Un Coll 2001; MDiv Epis TS of the SW 2004. D 6/5/2004 P 4/20/2005 Bp Jack Marston Mckelvey. m 5/21/2005 Leslie S Burkardt c 1. Vic S Andr's Epis Ch Corpus Christi TX 2013-2015; All SS' Epis Ch Concord NC 2011-2013; Cbury Sch Greensboro NC 2007-2010; Cur Ch Of The Gd Shpd Corpus Christi TX 2004-2007. jayburkardt@stpaulsec.org

BURKARDT, Leslie S (Roch) 2000 Highland Ave, Rochester NY 14618 **Int S Thos Epis Ch Rochester NY 2015-** B Muncie IN 1975 d John & Dana. MDiv Epis TS of the SW 2006. D 7/3/2006 Bp Barry Howe P 1/12/2007 Bp Gary Richard Lillibridge. m 5/21/2005 Jay P Burkardt c 1. S Chris's By The Sea Portland TX 2014; S Andr's Epis Ch Charlotte NC 2010-2013; S Andr's Ch Greensboro NC 2008-2010; Assoc R All SS Epis Ch Corpus Christi TX 2007; S Andr's Ch Kansas City MO 2000-2003; DCE S Andr's Epis Ch Corpus Christi TX 2000-2003. interimrector@stthomasrochester.org

BURKE, Anne B (RI) 66 Elm St Apt 1, Westerly RI 02891 B 1950 d John & Stan. AA Pine Manor Coll 1970. D 9/12/2009 Bp Gerry Wolf. c 2. D Ch Of The Ascen Cranston RI 2010-2012.

BURKE, Celine (WMich) 1033 NW Stannium Rd, Bend OR 97701 **Bp's Chapl to the Ret Dio Estrn Oregon 2010-; Ret 2008-; Cert Sprtl Dir Dominican Cntr Grand Rapids MI 2007-** B Covington KY 1946 d John & Hilda. BS Dominican Coll 1968; MS U of Wisconsin 1973; MDiv VTS 1985. D 6/22/1985 Bp Peter J Lee P 1/26/1986 Bp John Shelby Spong. m 4/9/1988 Richard M Burke c 1. R H Trin Epis Ch Manistee MI 2001-2008; R S Jn's Ch Clinton IA 1995-2001; R H Trin Ch Churchville MD 1988-1995; Asst S Ptr's Ch Morristown NJ 1985-1987; Stwdshp Com Dio Wstrn Michigan Kalamazoo MI 2003-2008; Com On Episcopate Dio Maryland Baltimore MD 1991-1994. Sprtl Dir Intl 2006.

BURKE, Cyril Casper (Ct) 26 Hoskins Rd, Bloomfield CT 06002 B Cambridge MA 1926 s Casper & Paulina. St Aug Coll CA 1946; Mercer TS 1964; DMin Hartford Sem 1982. D 6/20/1964 P 12/21/1964 Bp James Pernette DeWolfe. m 12/27/1947 Avis Gloria Burke. P-in-c S Mart's Ch Hartford CT 1999-2002; Int S Andr's Ch New Haven CT 1994-1998; Int S Ptr's Ch Springfield MA 1992-1993; Adj Prof Shaw DS Raleigh NC 1990-1991; Chapl S Aug Coll Raleigh NC 1984-1991; S Aug's Coll Raleigh NC 1984-1991; S Monica's Ch Hartford CT 1966-1984; Cur S Geo's Ch Brooklyn NY 1964-1965; Chapl VetA Hosp 1984. Auth, "Predominantly Black Middle Class Congregations Attempts To Min To Its Cmnty"; Auth, "Cmnty". ESMHE; Rel & The Intellectual Life.

BURKE, Geneva Frances (Mich) 21514 Deguindre, #202, Warren MI 48091 **D S Lk Epis Hm 1991-** B Lake City FL 1933 d James & Nancy. Cert EDS; BS Lewis Coll of Bus 1971. D 7/11/1981 Bp Quintin Ebenezer Primo Jr. D Emm Ch Detroit MI 1981-1991.

BURKE, Michael Edward (Ak) 3221 Amber Bay Loop, Anchorage AK 99515 **Mng Mem / CEO St. Mary's Epis Ch Hsng Co LLC 2014-; Dioc Invstmt Com. Epis Dio Alaska 2005-; R S Mary's Ch Anchorage AK 2000-** B Glens Falls NY 1962 s Robert & Magery. Cor 1984; BS U of Alaska 1990; MDiv Colgate Rochester Crozer DS 1995; MDiv CRDS 1995. D 8/12/1995 P 6/1/

1996 Bp Steven Charleston. m 8/19/1989 Nancy Irene Burke c 2. Dir, Sch for Mnstry Dioc Sch for Mnstry Rochester NY 1998-2000; Dio Rochester Henrietta 1998-2000; R S Geo's Ch Hilton NY 1997-2000; Assoc S Lk And S Simon Cyrene Rochester NY 1995-1997. Auth, "Gd Soil in Unlikely Places: Reflections on More Than Forty Years of Shared Mnstry in an Alaskan Cmnty," *ATR*, ATR, 2013. MDiv w dist Colgate-Rochester Div Sch 1995.

BURKE, Norman Charles (Az) 9552 West Wild Turkey Lane, Strawberry AZ 85544 **P-in-c S Paul's Epis Ch Winslow AZ 2013-, Vic 2006-2011** B Chicago IL 1934 s Benjamin & Phyllis. BA Ripon Coll Ripon WI 1956; MDiv Nash 1960. D 6/18/1960 Bp Gerald Francis Burrill P 12/1/1960 Bp Charles L Street. m 6/25/1960 Arlene Burke c 4. P-in-c S Geo's Epis Ch Holbrook AZ 2011-2014; P-in Churge St. Geo's Epis Ch Holbrook Arozona 2011-2013; Chapl CAP 2005-2011; Chairperson Bp's Search Com 2001-2004; Vic S Paul's Ch Payson AZ 1996-2006; Bd Chairperson Chap Rock Conf Cntr 1981-1994; R S Jn The Bapt Epis Ch Glendale AZ 1979-1996; Vic S Jn the Bapt Phoenix AZ 1978-1985; Int S Aug's Epis Ch Tempe AZ 1977-1978; P Dio Arizona Phoenix AZ 1976-1978, Chairman, Bishiop Search Com 2002-2003, Mem of Dioc Coun 2001-2003, Mem Dioc Coun 1994-1998, Mem Dioc Coun 1983-1986, Chairman, Camp/ Conf Com 1981-1993; Chapl Alexian Brothers Med Cntr Elk Grove Vill IL 1972-1976; Vic S Bede's Epis Ch Bensenville IL 1967-1976; Chapl St Mntl Hosp Manteno IL 1961-1974; Ch Of The Gd Shpd Momence IL 1961-1967; Asst S Paul's Ch Kankakee IL 1961-1967; Cur Chr Ch Waukegan IL 1960-1961. Cn Dio Arizona 2005.

BURKE, Richard Early (Mass) 3279 Flamingo Blvd, Hernando Beach FL 34607 B Baltimore MD 1946 s Edmund & Margaret. U CA 1965; BA Iowa Wesleyan Coll 1967; BD EDS 1970. D 7/8/1970 Bp Jose Guadalupe Saucedo P 5/8/1971 Bp John Melville Burgess. R S Aug's 1974-1994; Cur Gr Epis Ch Lawr MA 1970-1972.

BURKE, Robert Thomas (NwPa) Grace Episcopal Church, 10121 Hall Ave, Lake City PA 16423 B Union City PA 1953 s Thomas & Doris. Nrsng Mursyhurst U 2003. D 12/11/2004 P 6/12/2005 Bp Robert Deane Rowley Jr. m 8/4/1975 Wendy Louise Burke c 2.

BURKE, Sean Dennis (Ia) 201 Hollihan St, Decorah IA 52101 **Assoc Prof of Rel Luther Coll Decorah IA 2013-; S Jas Epis Ch Independence IA 2007-** B Rahway NJ 1972 s William & Lorraine. BA Concordia Coll 1994; MDiv Luth TS 1998; PhD Grad Theol Un/CDSP 2009. D 6/3/2006 Bp William Edwin Swing P 12/2/2006 Bp Marc Handley Andrus. Asst Prof of Rel Luther Coll Decorah IA 2009-2013; Instr of Rel Luther Coll Decorah IA 2007-2009; P All SS' Ch San Francisco CA 2006-2007; Assoc The Epis Ch Of The Gd Shpd Berkeley CA 2006-2007. Auth, "Queering the Ethiopian Eunuch: Strategies of Ambiguity in Acts," *Bk*, Fortress Press, 2013; Auth, "Queering Early Chr Discourse: The Ethiopian Eunuch," *Bible Trouble: Queer Readings at the Boundary of Biblic Schlrshp*, SBL, 2011; Auth, "Early Chr Drag: The Ethiopian Eunuch as a Queering Figure," *Reading Ideologies: Essays in hon of Mary Ann Tolbert*, Sheffield Phoenix Press, 2011. SBL 2002.

BURKERT-BRIST, Monica Anne (FdL) 315 E Jefferson St, Waupun WI 53963 **Vic H Trin Epis Ch Waupun WI 2016-** B New York NY 1959 d Alfred & Irene. BA U of Wisconsin 1981; JD U of Wisconsin 1987; MDiv Nash 2010. D 8/15/2015 P 6/11/2016 Bp Matthew A Gunter. m 6/16/1979 Steven C Brist c 2.

BURKETT, William Vernard (SwFla) 2902 Weset San Rafael Street, Tampa FL 33629 **R S Barth's Ch St Petersburg FL 2005-** B Huntsville AL 1960 s Vernard. BA Birmingham-Sthrn Coll 1982; MDiv SMU Perkins 1985; MS U of Alabama 1988; Sewanee: The U So, TS 2002. D 4/6/2002 Bp Duncan Montgomery Gray III P 1/4/2003 Bp John Bailey Lipscomb. m 12/21/1991 Patricia A Burkett c 2. Cur S Thos' Epis Ch St Petersburg FL 2002-2004.

BURKHART, John Delmas (Lex) 701 E Engineer St, Corbin KY 40701 B Barnesville OH 1933 s Vernon & Leota. BA St Chas 1956; The Athenaeum of Ohio 1960; MA OH SU 1969; PhD OH SU 1972. Rec 6/1/1973 as Priest Bp Addison Hosea. m 8/3/1996 Milly Alice Burkhart c 4. P-in-c S Jn's Ch Corbin KY 1994-2001; P-in-c Chr Epis Ch Harlan KY 1992-1996; Vic Chr Ch Cathd Louisville KY 1991-1994; Vic S Phil's Ch Harrodsburg KY 1983-1991; Int Supply Dio Lexington Lexington KY 1973-1982; Serv RC Ch 1960-1969.

BURKS, Bill (WTenn) 98 Jim Dedmon Rd., Dyer TN 38330 **P-in-c S Thos The Apos Humboldt TN 2004-** B Lawrenceburg TN 1939 s Royce & Willa. BS Austin Peay St U 1960; MDiv Sewanee: The U So, TS 1971. D 7/5/1971 Bp William Evan Sanders P 5/1/1972 Bp John Vander Horst. m 12/21/1969 Janice W Burks c 1. R Gr Ch Oak Pk IL 1989-1993; P-in-c S Fran's Jonesville VA 1986-1989; R S Mary's Epis Ch Middlesboro KY 1977-1989; Int Chapl U Tenn Knoxville TN 1975-1976; P-in-c Annunc Newport KY 1973-1977; Dio Tennessee Nashville TN 1973-1977; Chapl U Tenn Chattanooga 1972-1973; Mssnr Our Sav Soddy Daisey TN 1971-1973; D S Ptr's Ch Chattanooga TN 1971-1972.

BURKS, Tami Louise (NY) **S Thos Ch Mamaroneck NY 2016-** B 1967 Bachelor of Sci Penn 1989; Mstr of Arts Luth TS at Gettysburg 1991; Mstr of Sci Bank St Coll of Educ 1995; Dplma GTS 2016. D 3/5/2016 Bp Allen Shin P 10/15/2016 Bp Andrew Marion Lenow Dietsche. m 12/10/1994 Joseph Auxford Burks c 3. Other Lay Position Chr's Ch Rye NY 2012-2015. associatestthomas@gmail.com

BURLEIGH, Judith Cushing (Me) PO Box 8, Presque Isle ME 04769 **Aroostook Epis Cluster Caribou ME 2007-; D S Jn's Ch Presque Isle ME 2007-** B Presque Isle ME 1934 d Parker & Mamie. BA Wellesley Coll 1956; MEd Harv 1957; PhD U of Connecticut 1966. D 8/4/2007 Bp Chilton Richardson Knudsen.

BURLEY, Aloysius Englebert John Timothy (Minn) 615 W Tanglewood Dr, Arlington Heights IL 60004 **Asst S Dav's 1984-** B Ada MN 1928 s Andrew & Philomene Ann. BA; BA. Rec 12/1/1973. m 5/15/1965 Gisela E Burley. Nonpar 1973-1984.

BURLEY III, Clarence Augustus (ECR) 651 Broadway, Gilroy CA 95020 **R S Steph's Ch Gilroy CA 2007-** B Evanston IL 1947 s Clarence & Shirley. BA Claremont Coll 1970; MDiv CDSP 1977. D 6/25/1977 Bp Chauncie Kilmer Myers P 11/1/1978 Bp Hanford Langdon King Jr. m 7/29/2012 Dana Lee Werner Burley c 2. Int St Paul's/San Pablo Epis Ch Salinas CA 2006-2007; Int St. Paul's Salinas CA 2006-2007; Int S Barn Ch Arroyo Grande CA 2005-2006; Int St. Clare's Pleasanton CA 2004-2005; S Clare's Epis Ch Pleasanton CA 2004; S Lk's Ch Bakersfield CA 1990-2001; Int S Mich's Epis Par Ridgecrest CA 1990; S Mk's Epis Ch Idaho Falls ID 1988-1989; Dio Idaho Boise ID 1986-1989; Int S Jas Ch Burley ID 1986-1989; St Matthews Epis Ch Rupert ID 1986-1989; Int S Jn's Ch Powell WY 1981-1982; Int S Alb's Ch Worland WY 1980-1981; S Andr's Ch Basin WY 1979-1980; Assoc Ch Of The Ascen Twin Falls ID 1978-1979; Asst S Mich's Cathd Boise ID 1977-1978.

BURLINGTON, Robert Craig (RI) 2070 Homewood Blvd Apt 306, Delray Beach FL 33445 B Elizabeth NJ 1944 s Walter & Dorothy. BA Rutgers The St U of New Jersey 1966; STB GTS 1969; STM NYTS 1975; DMin NYTS 1980; GTS 1985. D 6/14/1969 Bp Leland Stark P 12/19/1969 Bp George E Rath. m 7/1/1967 Adelene Burlington. Dio Rhode Island Providence RI 2000-2003, Chair Stwdshp Cmsn 1994-1999, Dept of Chr Soc Responsibility 1975-1993; R S Lk's Epis Ch E Greenwich RI 1992-2010; Mem, Alum Bd GTS New York NY 1992-2002; Interfaith Holocaust Com Dio Newark Newark NJ 1980-1992, CE Com 1973-1979; S Geo's Epis Ch Maplewood NJ 1969-1992, Assoc 1969-1974. Epis Chars 2002-2004.

BURMAN, Susan Crandall (FdL) 315 E Jefferson St, Waupun WI 53963 B Kenosha WI 1938 d David & Virginia. RN St Lukes Sch of Nrsng 1958. D 10/3/1998 Bp Russell Edward Jacobus. m 12/14/1957 Harvey R Burman c 4. St Paul's Epis Cathd Fond Du Lac WI 1988-1997.

BURMEISTER, Melissa Lynne (Mil) 5556 E. Colonial Oaks Dr., Monticello IN 47960 B Elmhurst IL 1962 d Marvin & Veronica. BS Nthrn Illinois U 1984; MDiv SWTS 1999. D 12/2/1999 Bp Bill Persell P 7/1/2000 Bp James Barrow Brown. m 8/17/1985 Douglas W Burmeister c 1. S Mk's Epis Ch Harvey LA 2004-2005; Zion Epis Ch Oconomowoc WI 2003; S Jn In The Wilderness Elkhorn WI 2001-2003; S Paul's Ch New Orleans LA 1999-2001.

BURNARD, Karen (SO) PO Box 284, Little Switzerland NC 28749 **Chapl (CPE) The OH SU Hosp 1990-** B Columbus OH 1950 d George & Katharine. BA OH SU 1972; MS U IL 1977; MDiv Trin Luth Sem 1992. D 6/22/1991 Bp William Grant Black P 6/1/1992 Bp Herbert Thompson Jr. m 6/25/1982 Robert Duane Burnard c 1. R H Trin Epis Ch Oxford OH 2006-2014; Vic S Andr's Ch Pickerington OH 1995-2006; Trin Ch Columbus OH 1991-1995.

BURNER, Dan E (Roch) **S Mk's Epis Ch Penn Yan NY 2015-** B Bluffton OH 1948 s Howard & Marciella. BS Nthrn Arizona U 1971; MBA Houston Bapt U 1991; MDiv CDSP 2010; MDiv CDSP 2010. D 12/7/2013 P 6/14/2014 Bp Marc Handley Andrus. c 2.

✠ **BURNETT, The Rt Rev Joe Goodwin** (Neb) PO Box 540617, Omaha NE 68154 **Chair HOB Theol Com 2010-** B Jackson MS 1948 s Marshall & Mary. BA Millsaps Coll 1970; MDiv SMU Perkins 1974; DMin SMU 1985. D 6/1/1974 Bp John Maury Allin P 5/15/1975 Bp Duncan Montgomery Gray Jr Con 9/13/2003 for Neb. c 3. Int S Columba's Ch Washington DC 2014-2015; Asst Bp of Maryland Dio Maryland Baltimore MD 2011-2013; Mem HOB Theol Com 2004-2015; Bp Dio Nebraska Omaha NE 2003-2011; Prof Sewanee U So TS Sewanee TN 1999-2003; R Trin Ch Hattiesburg MS 1991-1999; R S Ptr's By The Sea Gulfport MS 1984-1991; Vic Ch Of The Creator Clinton MS 1980-1983; Asst S Jas Ch Jackson MS 1976-1980; Cur S Jn's Epis Ch Pascagoula MS 1974-1976. Auth, "Reconsidering a Bold Proposal: Reflections, Questions, and Concerns Regarding a Theol of Cnfrmtn," *ATR*, ATR, 2006; Auth, "The Marvelous Memory Of God: Pstr And Personal Reflections On Preaching Lk," *Sewanee Theol Revs*, Sewanee Theol Revs, 2001; Auth, "Always And Everywhere: BCP 1979 & The Promise Of Liturg Evang," *w Ever Joyful Hearts*, Ch Pub Inc, 1999. ATR Bd 2005-2014; Epis Ch Bd Archv 2006-2012. DD GTS 2008. joegburnett@aol.com

BURNETT, Joseph or Jody Goodwin (Miss) St. Peter's Episcopal Church, 113 S 9th St, Oxford MS 38655 **S Ptr's Ch Oxford MS 2016-** B Jackson MS 1981 s Joe & Barbara. BA U of Sthrn Mississippi 2006; MDiv VTS 2009. D 5/30/2009 Bp Joe Goodwin Burnett P 12/6/2009 Bp Shannon Sherwood Johnston. m 10/20/2012 Julia Stewart Burnett c 1. Cn for Par Mnstry S Andr's Cathd Jackson MS 2013-2016; Sr Assoc Ch Of The H Comf Vienna VA 2009-2013; Dir of Yth & YA Mnstrs Trin Ch Hattiesburg MS 2003-2006. jburnett@stpetersoxford.org

BURNETT, Richard Alvin (SO) 125 E Broad St, Columbus OH 43215 **R Trin Ch Columbus OH 1997-** B New York NY 1957 s A W & Mary. BA Dickinson Coll 1978; MDiv Ya Berk 1983. D 6/11/1983 Bp John Thomas Walker P 12/17/1983 Bp James Stuart Wetmore. m 7/30/1988 Katharine Ward Burnett. Dn Dio Sthrn Ohio Cincinnati OH 2000-2008, Dn Columbus Dnry 2000-; Fac Mercer Theol Sem Garden City NY 1996-1997; Geo Mercer TS Garden City NY 1995-1997; Econ Justice Com Dio Long Island Garden City NY 1990-1997, Dioc Coun 1991-1997; R S Jas Epis Ch S Jas NY 1990-1997; S Barth's In The Highland White Plains NY 1983-1990; Chair Dio New York New York NY 1987-1990. Auth, "The Quest For Common Lrng," Carnegie Fndt, 1981.

BURNETTE, William Marc (Ala) 1930 Fairfax Dr, Florence AL 35630 **R Cbury Chap and Coll Cntr Tuscaloosa AL 2009-** B Atlanta GA 1967 s William & Suzanne. BA U of Alabama 1990; MFA U of Alabama 1994; MDiv GTS 1999. D 5/24/1999 P 11/1/1999 Bp Henry Nutt Parsley Jr. m 11/25/1995 Jennifer Roth c 2. R S Andrew's Epis Ch Birmingham AL 2001-2009; Trin Epis Ch Florence AL 1999-2001. canterburymarc@gmail.com

BURNHAM, Frederic Bradford (NY) 556 Lakeshore Drive Ext, Asheville NC 28804 B Cambridge MA 1938 s Bradford & Anna. AB Harv 1960; MDiv EDS 1963; Dplma U of Cambridge 1964; PhD JHU 1970; DD Hobart and Wm Smith Colleges 1985. D 6/12/1965 Bp Charles Bowen Persell Jr P 9/17/1967 Bp Allen Webster Brown. m 3/17/1991 Regan Church Burnham c 2. Sr Fell Cathd Coll Washington Natl Cathd Washington 2006-2008; Sr Fell Inst for Servnt Ldrshp Hendersonville NC 2005-2010; Trin Educ Fund New York NY 1992-1994; Dir, Trin Inst Trin Par New York NY 1984-2004; Pres AEC New York 1978-1984; R Memi Ch Of All Ang Twilight Pk NY 1977-1989; Asst Chr Ch Detroit MI 1976-1978; Prof and Dn Wayne Detroit MI 1968-1978. Auth, "Links: Establishing Communities Of Dialogueon Campuses," *Educ as Transformation*, Lang, 2000; Auth, "Chaos: A New Theol," *Mundi Medicina*, 1992; Auth, "Horizons In Biblic Theol," *Maker Of Heaven & Earth: A Perspective Of Contemporary Sci*, 1990; Ed, "Postmodern Theol: Chr Faith In A Pluralist Wrld," Harper, 1989; Ed, "Love: The Fndt Of Hope," Harper, 1988; Auth, "The Bible & Contemporary Sci," *Rel & Intellectual Life*. AAR; Hist of Sci Assn 1965-1978; Soc For Values In Higher Educ. Phi Beta Kappa Phi Beta Kappa 1996; DD Hobart and Wm Smith Colleges 1985.

BURNS, Karen Lee (Colo) 2029 Pine St, Pueblo CO 81004 **Ch Of The Ascen Pueblo CO 2007-** B Cortland NY 1947 d Carl & Alice. BA Wheaton Coll 1969. D 11/11/2000 Bp William Jerry Winterrowd. D S Andr's Ch Manitou Sprg CO 2000-2006. No Amer Assn on the Diac (NAAD) 2000-2008.

BURNS, A(Nn) Lyn (Colo) PO Box 635, La Veta CO 81055 **S Paul's Epis Ch Ft Collins CO 2016-; Mem of Stndg Com Dio Colorado Denver CO 2011-** B Pretoria South Africa 1950 d Herbert & Evelyn. BA U of Witwaterstrand ZA 1972; MDiv VTS 2006. D 6/10/2006 P 12/18/2006 Bp Robert John O'Neill. c 2. P-in-c Par Ch Of S Chas The Mtyr Ft Morgan CO 2011-2015; Vic S Ben Epis Ch La Veta CO 2007-2010.

BURNS, Deborah Stansbrough (Kan) 3021 Steven Dr, Lawrence KS 66049 **D St Mart in the Fields Epis Ch 2004-** B St Louis MO 1952 d Raymond & Ruth. 1Year Full Time CPE Residency Bapt Hosp; Kansas Sch for Mnstry; BGS U of Kansas 1998. D 12/22/2001 Bp William Edward Smalley. m 5/31/1975 Garth Burns c 1.

BURNS, Duncan Adam (LI) 209 Albany Ave, Kingston NY 12401 **R S Jn's Ch Huntington NY 2014-** B Bay Shore NY 1957 s Bruce & Sue. Colg 1979; MDiv SWTS 2003. D 6/28/2003 Bp Alan Scarfe P 7/1/2004 Bp Desmond Mpilo Tutu. m 7/17/1982 Barbara M Burns c 3. R S Jn's Epis Ch Kingston NY 2005-2014; Chr Ch Alexandria VA 2003-2005. aroth@stjohnshunting.org

BURNS, Jacquelyn Mae (SO) St John's Episcopal Church, 700 High St, Worthington OH 43085 B Indianapolis IN 1947 d Jack & Dolores. D 6/23/2007 Bp Kenneth Lester Price. c 4.

BURNS, James Lee (NY) 1029 Arrowhead Rd, Camano Island WA 98282 B Indianapolis IN 1946 s David & Jessie. BA Mia 1968; MS U of Idaho 1972; MDiv Sewanee: The U So, TS 1982. D 6/27/1982 Bp William F Gates Jr P 1/5/1983 Bp William Evan Sanders. m 5/7/1976 Nancy VanderNaald c 2. R Ch Of The Heav Rest New York NY 1996-2011; Dn Chr Ch Cathd Lexington KY 1988-1996; R S Thos Epis Ch Knoxville TN 1988, R 1987-1988, 1982-1987; Dio Tennessee Nashville TN 1982-1984. Auth, *The Bible and Episcopalians*, Forw Mvmt; Auth, "The Real Chr Agenda," *The Real Chr Agenda*, Forw Mvmt; Auth, "The Real Chr Agenda," *The Real Chr Agenda*, Forw Mvmt.

BURNS, Jerome (SO) 1316 Villa Paloma Blvd, Little Elm TX 75068 B Jackson MS 1944 s Emmitt & Clara. BA Jackson St U 1966; JD Sthrn U Baton Rouge LA 1975; MDiv VTS 1978. D 6/22/1978 P 5/1/1979 Bp Duncan Montgomery Gray Jr. m 6/5/1976 Carol Lynn Burns c 1. R S Phil's Ch Columbus OH 2002-2012; Ch Of The H Cross Pittsburgh PA 1993-2002; R S Steph's Ch Petersburg VA 1986-1993; Asst S Jas Epis Ch Houston TX 1983-1986; Vic Of The Resurr Houston TX 1982-1983; The Great Cmsn Fndt Houston TX 1982-1983; S Mary's Ch Vicksburg MS 1978-1982.

BURNS JR, Jervis Oliver (Miss) 204 Donnybrook Dr, Carriere MS 39426 B New Orleans LA 1942 s Jervis & Mary. BA Tul 1964; MDiv SWTS 1968; Command and Gnrl Stff Coll 1995. D 6/25/1968 Bp Girault M Jones P 5/1/1969 Bp

Iveson Batchelor Noland. m 8/1/1964 Susan Barrow Burns c 2. Exec Dir/VP St Fran Acad Picayune MS 2002-2006; Reg VP S Fran Cmnty Serv Inc. Salina KS 2002-2004; Coordntr Epis Black Belt Mnstry Greensboro AL 1996-2001; Coordntr Trin Ch Demopolis AL 1996-2001; Hon Cn Dio Louisiana New Orleans LA 1985-1996; R S Matt's Epis Ch Houma LA 1975-1985; Chapl US-AR 1973-1996; Vic Leonidas Polk Memi Epis Mssn Leesville LA 1971-1975; Trin Epis Ch Deridder LA 1971-1975; Int S Ptr's By The Sea Gulfport MS 1969-1971; Chapl NW St Coll Natchitoches 1968-1969; S Paul's Ch Winnfield LA 1968-1969; Cur Trin Epis Ch Natchitoches LA 1968-1969. CODE 1985-1996.

BURNS, Leonetta Faye (Me) 52 Dondero Rd, Chelsea ME 04330 B Augusta ME 1945 d Warren & Evelyn. AA U of Maine 1981. D 6/19/2004 Bp Chilton Richardson Knudsen. m 6/3/1967 Robert Scottie Burns c 3. D S Giles Ch Jefferson ME 2004-2014; Com on Indn Relatns-Chair Dio Maine Portland ME 2010-2013.

BURNS, Steven Thomas (Eau) **P-in-c S Alb's Ch Spooner WI 2015-; S Alb's Ch Superior WI 2014-** B England 1969 s Bernard & Margaret. BA Intl Chr Coll 2002; PGCE Paisley U 2003; Angl Stds Cert Nash 2014. D 1/4/2014 P 9/13/2014 Bp William Jay Lambert III. m 7/19/2008 Susan Gerrette Jedlicka c 1.

BURNS, Thomas Dale (NwT) 3402 W Ohio Ave, Midland TX 79703 **D S Nich' Epis Ch Midland TX 2009-** B Huron SD 1948 D 10/27/2002 Bp C Wallis Ohl. m 12/9/1988 Gwendolyn Rae Beeler. D Ch Of The H Trin Midland TX 2002-2009.

BURR, John Terry (Roch) 594 Stearns Rd, Churchville NY 14428 **D S Lk And S Simon Cyrene Rochester NY 1969-** B Springfield OH 1932 s Irving & Priscilla. BA Gri; PhD Pur. D 4/30/1968 Bp George West Barrett. m 4/24/1993 Antoinette Marie Bradford c 2. Asst S Lk's Ch Brockport NY 1968-1973. Auth, "Var Sci Papers".

BURR, Whitney Haight (Mass) 175 Shane Dr, Chatham MA 02633 B New York NY 1943 s Vernon & Elizabeth. BS Bos 1967; MDiv Ya Berk 1971. D 6/5/1971 P 12/18/1971 Bp Horace W B Donegan. m 4/12/1969 Leslie Ellen Burr c 2. Dioc Coun Dio Massachusetts Boston MA 1990-1995, Consult 1979-2009, Stndg Com 1988-2002; R S Chris's Ch Chatham MA 1982-2001; R Trin Epis Ch Wrentham MA 1977-1981; Asst S Mary's Epis Ch Barnstable MA 1973-1977; Vic S Paul's Ch Westbrook CT 1971-1973.

✠ BURRILL, The Rt Rev William George (Az) 7550 N. 16th Street #5204, Phoenix AZ 85020 **All SS Ch Phoenix AZ 2000-; Asstg Bp Dio Arizona Phoenix AZ 2000-** B New York NY 1934 s Gerald & Elna. BA U So 1955; STB GTS 1959; GTS 1985. D 6/20/1959 P 12/1/1959 Bp Charles L Street Con 4/26/1984 for Roch. c 4. Bp Dio Rochester Henrietta 1984-1999; Bd Trst Hobart & Wm Smith Colleges Geneva NY 1984-1999; Archd The Epis Dio Nthrn California Sacramento CA 1981-1984, 1978-1980, COM 1971-1977, Stndg Com 1969-1970, Dn Sacramento Dnry 1966-1968; Joint Stndg Com Prog Bdgt and Fin Epis Ch GC 1978-1984; Ch Of S Mart Davis CA 1962-1982; Chapl U CA 1962-1981; Cur S Jn The Evang Ch Elkhart IN 1959-1962; Trst The GTS New York NY 1986-1999. Auth, *Var arts in Rel Journ*.

BURRIS, Richard R (Okla) 900 Schulze Dr., Norman OK 73071 **Bus Admin McFarlin Memi Meth Ch Norman OK 2009-** B Sheridan WY 1948 s Ralph & Julia. BS Linfield Coll 1970; MDiv Nash 1987. D 5/30/1987 Bp Charles I Jones III P 12/19/1987 Bp James Daniel Warner. m 5/18/1970 Carmelita Burris c 2. Contrllr Dio Oklahoma Oklahoma City OK 2004-2009, Chair Liturg Cmsn 1996-2001; Pres Natl Epis Curs Comm. 2004-2005; R S Mich's Epis Ch Norman OK 1992-2004; R Ch Of The H Apos Mitchell NE 1987-1992.

BURROUGHS, Joseph Parker (Md) 7236 Gaither Rd, Sykesville MD 21784 **Ret 1998-** B Wadesboro NC 1933 s Robert & Margaret. BA Davidson Coll 1955; STB EDS 1958. D 6/29/1958 Bp Edwin A Penick P 6/24/1959 Bp Richard Henry Baker. R S Barn Epis Ch Sykesville MD 1978-1998; R St Martins Ch Triangle VA 1967-1978; Asst S Paul's Ch Richmond VA 1961-1967; R Andr's By The Sea Nags Hd NC 1960-1961; P-in-c Calv Ch Tarboro NC 1958-1960; P-in-c St Ign Old Sparta NC 1958-1960.

BURROWS, Judith Anne (WNY) 106 Hickory Hill Rd Apt A, Buffalo NY 14221 **P-in-c S Ptr's Ch Niagara Falls NY 2007-** B Syracuse NY 1940 d Charles & (Mary). BA U Roch 1962; MDiv EDS 1965; MA U Cinc 1974. D 6/4/1977 P 4/8/1978 Bp Harold Barrett Robinson. c 2. R S Paul's Epis Ch Harris Hill Buffalo NY 1986-2006; R S Mart In The Fields Grand Island NY 1981-1986, P-in-c 1977-1980. SCHC 1977. Phi Beta Kappa U Roch 1962; Ab w High hon U Roch 1962.

BURROWS OSB, Paul Anthony (Cal) 474 48th Avenue, Apt 23A, Long Island City NY 11109 B Harpenden Hertfordshire UK 1955 s Reginald & Vera. BA U of Nottingham 1977; Oxf GB 1979; STM GTS 1988. Trans 6/20/1986 Bp George Phelps Mellick Belshaw. m 7/11/2008 Michael Barlowe. R Ch Of The Adv Of Chr The King San Francisco CA 2001-2014; R S Mk's Epis Ch Des Moines IA 1996-2001; The Cathd Ch Of S Paul Des Moines IA 1996-2001; R S Barn Epis Ch Temple Hills MD 1990-1995; Vic S Lk And All SS' Ch Un NJ 1985-1990; Serv Ch of Engl 1979-1985. CBS 1984; Oblate Ord of S Ben 1980. paulburrows1@mac.com

BURRUSS, John Bailey (WTenn) 8282 Macon Rd, Cordova TN 38018 **Dio W Tennessee Memphis 2015-** B Little Rock AR 1981 s George & Alice. BA Pur 2003; MDiv VTS 2013. D 6/8/2013 P 12/14/2013 Bp Don Edward Johnson. m 4/24/2010 Anne Cook Burruss c 2. Vic Ch Of The Annunc Cordova TN 2013-2015; Ch Of The H Comm Memphis TN 2004-2010. jburruss@eptiswtn.org

BURSON, Grace Pritchard (NH) 20 Winter Street, Episcopal Church of the Holy Spirit, Plymouth NH 03264 **H Trin Evang Luth Ch Newington NH 2016-; Chapl Untd Campus Mnstry Plymouth St U 2012-** B New Haven CT 1978 d Arnold & Gretchen. BA Wms 2000; Angl Dplma Ya Berk 2004; MDiv Ya Berk 2004; Cert Inst of Sacr Mus 2004; MDiv Yale DS 2004. D 6/14/2008 Bp Andrew Donnan Smith P 1/17/2009 Bp Vicky Gene Robinson. c 1. R Ch Of The H Sprt Plymouth NH 2011-2015; Cur Gr Ch Manchester NH 2008-2011. holyspiritrector@gmail.com

BURT, William R 813 Marla Dr, Point Pleasant Boro NJ 08742 B Newark, NJ 1952 s William & Jemima. BS CUNY 1996; MDiv U Tor CA 2007. Trans 6/16/2010 as Priest Bp John L Rabb. R S Jn's Ch Hvre De Gr MD 2010-2012. wburt@stjohns-northhaven.org

BURTENSHAW, Noel C (At) 2813 Greenhouse Pkwy, Alpharetta GA 30022 B Dublin IE 1936 s Frederick & Christina. BA All Hallows Coll 1960; MDiv All Hallows Coll 1962. Rec 12/1/1993 as Priest Bp Frank Kellogg Allan. m 2/23/2008 Marilynne Sue Hughes c 1. S Aid's Epis Ch Milton GA 1995-2003; S Dav's Ch Roswell GA 1994; Serv RC Ch 1962-1985.

BURTON, Anthony John (Dal) 3966 McKinney Ave, Dallas TX 75204 **R Ch Of The Incarn Dallas TX 2008-** B 1959 s Peter & Rachel. BA Trin 1983; U of Kings Coll Halifax NS CA 1985; BA Oxf GB 1987; MA Oxf GB 1992. Trans 10/10/2008 Bp James Monte Stanton. m 4/8/1989 Anna Kristine Burton c 2. Dio Bp Dio Saskatchewan 1993-2008. DD (Hon) U of King's Coll, Halifax, NS 1994.

BURTON, Bob (Az) 9502 W. Hutton Drive, Sun City AZ 85351 **R All SS Of The Desert Epis Ch Sun City AZ 2009-** B Eugene OR 1949 s Harry & Phyllis. BA Albion Coll 1971; MDiv CDSP 1974. D 6/15/1974 P 4/20/1975 Bp Robert Claflin Rusack. m 12/8/1998 Anne Marie Burton c 2. R S Paul's Epis Ch Salem OR 2005-2009; S Lk The Physcn Miami FL 1999-2005; R S Lk the Physcn Epis Ch Miami FL 1999-2005; S Jn's Epis Ch Sonora TX 1998-1999; Asst S Mk The Evang Ft Lauderdale FL 1998-1999; Assoc S Jas Epis Ch Baton Rouge LA 1991-1998; S Jas Epis Ch Ft McKavett TX 1991-1998; S Aug's Ch Ft Smith AR 1987-1991; S Jn's Epis Ch Ft Smith AR 1984-1991; R S Marg's Epis Ch Palm Desert CA 1978-1983; Asst Chr Ch Coronado CA 1976-1978; Assoc S Edm's Par San Marino CA 1974-1976.

BURTON, Cassandra Yvonne (WA) **Reg 6 Del Dioc Coun 2013-** B East Oarange NJ 1945 d William & Gwendolyn. BA U of Baltimore 1979; MDiv VTS 2007. D 6/16/2007 Bp Peter J Lee P 12/18/2007 Bp Shannon Sherwood Johnston. m 6/2/1979 Malachi Burton c 3. R Chr Epis Ch Clinton MD 2010-2017; Asst S Lk's Ch Washington DC 2007-2009.

BURTON, Christine Hazel (RI) PO Box 48, Hope Valley RI 02832 B Framingham MA 1942 d Carl & Winola. Rhode Island Sch for Deacons. D 3/28/1992 Bp George Nelson Hunt III. m 5/2/1962 Salvatore Frank Burton c 4.

BURTON, Jack C (SO) Norton Orchard Rd, PO Box 5195, Edgartown MA 02539 B Saint Louis MO 1936 s Henry & Lorine. BS Washington U 1959; MDiv EDS 1963. D 6/15/1963 P 12/22/1963 Bp Roger W Blanchard. c 3. R S Jn's Epis Ch Cambridge OH 1968-1972; Asst S Mk's Epis Ch Columbus OH 1965-1968; Asst S Tim's Epis Ch Cincinnati OH 1963-1965. Auth, "Article," *Chld's Commision*, Comm/Living Ch, 1970.

BURTON, James M (SC) 126 Taylor Cir, Goose Creek SC 29445 B Greenville SC 1939 s Theron & Mary. BA Other 1961; BA St. Mary's Coll, St. Mary, Kentucky 1961; MA CUA 1965. Rec 1/1/1995 as Priest Bp Edward Lloyd Salmon Jr. m 6/23/1984 Patricia Fosberry c 1. Supply Chr Ch Florence SC 2003-2013; Vic Ch Of The H Fam Moncks Corner SC 1996-2002; Dioc Dir of Chr Eduation So Carolina Charleston SC 1995-2002; S Steph's Ch S Steph SC 1995-1996.

BURTON, John (Ct) **Vic S Paul's Ch Windham CT 2006-** B Chicago IL 1956 BA Bard Coll 1978; DAS Ya Berk 2004; MDiv Ya Berk 2004. D 6/12/2004 Bp Andrew Donnan Smith P 12/18/2004 Bp James Elliot Curry. m 5/15/1999 Kaice Burton c 2. Cur S Mary's Epis Ch Manchester CT 2004-2006.

BURTON, John (Ark) 807 COUNTY ROAD 102, EUREKA SPRINGS AR 72632 **Mng Ed Speak Eureka Sprg AR 2001-** B Waco TX 1942 s William & Frances. BS Texas A&M U 1963; MS Baylor U 1968; Truett TS 2000. D 12/10/2006 Bp Larry Maze P 8/12/2007 Bp Larry Benfield. m 12/24/1992 Gloria Burton c 3. S Jas Ch Eureka Spgs AR 2007-2015.

BURTON, John Peter (Chi) 4839 W Howard, Skokie IL 60076 **S Richard's Ch Chicago IL 2004-** B Vienna Austria 1922 s Alfred & Elfriede. SWTS 1985. D 5/23/1970 Bp Gerald Francis Burrill P 7/1/1985 Bp James Winchester Montgomery. m 3/2/1950 Leonora Gordon c 2. Asst H Trin Ch Skokie IL 1970-1993. S Geo Medal.

BURTON, Kenneth William Fowler (Colo) 472 Crystal Hills Blvd, Manitou Springs CO 80829 **Ret 1994-** B Manchester UK 1928 s Harold & Sarah. BA U of Cambridge 1948; MA U of Cambridge 1952. D 7/14/1974 Bp Edwin B

Thayer P 11/1/1974 Bp William Carl Frey. m 8/4/1950 Mary Burton. Chr Ch Cn City CO 1992; Gr And S Steph's Epis Ch Colorado Sprg CO 1988-1992; Ch Of Our Sav Colorado Sprg CO 1987-1988; Assoc Prof Rel/Dn/Chapl Colorado Coll 1961-1994.

BURTON, Laurel Arthur (Ark) B Indianapolis IN 1943 s William & Mary. BS Indiana U 1965; ThM Bos 1970; ThD Bos 1983. D 5/14/2015 P 11/21/2015 Bp Larry Benfield. m 7/28/1968 Mary Kay Gisolo Burton c 2.

BURTON, Whitney A (SwVa) **S Jn's Ch Roanoke VA 2015-** B Fulton County GA 1989 d John & Ann. BA U of So Carolina 2012; MDiv Sewanee: The U So, TS 2015; MDiv The TS at The U So 2015; MDiv U So 2015. D 12/20/2014 Bp Robert Christopher Wright.

BURTON-EDWARDS, Grace (At) St Thomas Episcopal Church, 2100 Hilton Ave, Columbus GA 31906 **R S Thos Epis Ch Columbus GA 2014-; Cler Cont Educ Com Dio Indianapolis Indianapolis IN 2013-, GC Cler Dep 2012, Cnvnr Global Missions Cmsn 2011-2013, Alt Dep GC 2010-2012; Bd Mem Cntr for Interfaith Coop 2012-** B Raleigh NC 1967 d Robert & Lydia. BA Mississippi Coll 1989; MDiv Chr TS 1993; DMin SWTS 2005; Fllshp Other 2010; Fllshp Wabash Coll 2010; Cert - pilot Prog Indiana U Sch of Philanthropy 2013; Cert Other 2013. D 1/28/2007 P 11/18/2007 Bp Cate Waynick. m 1/6/1991 Taylor Burton-Edwards c 2. Assoc R and Sch Chapl Trin Ch Indianapolis IN 2007-2014, St. Richard's Sch Chapl 2005-2007; DCE S Matt's Ch Indianapolis IN 2004-2007; Dir of Davis Pk Mnstrs First Meth Ch Anderson IN 1998-2004; Yth Min - Ecum Adams St Kids Plymouth IN 1996-1998; Resource Consult Par Resource Cntr Mishawaka IN 1995-1998; Int Emm Bapt Ch Mishawaka IN 1995-1996; Yth Curric writer Smyth and Helwys Pub Macon GA 1991-2000. Writer, "Faith Forum," *Indianapolis Star*, Gannet News Serv, 2012; Auth, "The Screen of Common Pryr: Using Visual Media Tech in Epis Liturg," *Seabury DMin thesis*, Seabury-Wstrn, 2005; Writer/Ed, "Bookmarks Yth Curric," *Bookmarks*, Judson Press, 2000; Writer, "Intersection Yth Curric," *Intersection*, Smyth and Helwys, 1993. rector@stthomascolumbus.org

BURTS, Ann Horton (NC) 8804 Broadmore Ct, Raleigh NC 27613 B Chicago IL 1944 d James & Honora. BA Duke 1966; MAT Duke 1968; MDiv Duke DS 1993; CAS GTS 1994. D 5/11/1994 Bp Robert Whitridge Estill P 5/13/1995 Bp Charles Lindsay Longest. m 5/28/1967 Richard Burts c 2. P Assoc Ch Of The Nativ Raleigh NC 2014-2016; Int S Lk's Ch Annapolis MD 2011-2012; Int S Johns Epis Ch Wake Forest NC 2009-2010; S Jn's Ch Mt Washington Baltimore MD 2008-2009; S Dav's Ch Baltimore MD 2008; Int All Hallows Par So River Edgewater MD 2006-2007; Pstr Assoc S Anne's Par Annapolis MD 1994-2006. Soc of S Marg.

BUSBY, Lisa Jo (Ala) 37 W Main St, Norwich NY 13815 **S Lk's Ch Scottsboro AL 2016-; Emm Ch Norwich NY 2015-** B Norwich NY 1967 d Bruce & Joanne. BS Binghamton U 1998; MA Binghamton U 2001; MSW U of Albany 2001; MDiv The GTS 2015. D 6/6/2015 P 12/12/2015 Bp Gladstone Bailey Adams III. m 8/19/2006 Gary H Busby c 3. Dio Cntrl New York Liverpool NY 2015-2016; S Andr's Ch New Berlin NY 2015-2016; S Matt's Ch So New Berlin NY 2015-2016. lisajbusby@gmail.com

BUSCH, Edward Leonard (SanD) 11650 Calle Paracho, San Diego CA 92128 **Asst S Tim's Ch San Diego CA 2009-** B Chicago IL 1930 s Morris & Rose. BS U IL 1951; MD U IL 1955; Angl TS 1980. D 6/20/1981 P 6/1/1982 Bp Archibald Donald Davies. m 2/26/1994 Babs Marie Meairs c 3. Vic S Columba's Epis Ch Santee CA 2001-2008; Asst Epis Ch Of The Redeem Irving TX 1997-2000; Asst Ch Of The Gd Shpd Cedar Hill TX 1995-1997; R S Chris's Ch And Sch Ft Worth TX 1987-1992, Cur 1981-1986; Cur Ch Of The H Apos Ft Worth TX 1983-1987.

BUSCH, Glenn Edward (NC) 3024 Cardinal Pl, Lynchburg VA 24503 B Kissimmee FL 1945 s Russell & Sarah. BA Penn 1967; MDiv VTS 1971; DMin UTS 1974. D 5/22/1971 P 12/11/1971 Bp Robert Bracewell Appleyard. m 6/13/1970 Kathleen Gayle Busch c 2. S Mary's Epis Ch High Point NC 2000-2008; Adj Prof of Rel High Point U NC 1989-2007; R S Jn's Ch Bedford VA 1975-1981; Asst S Steph's Ch Richmond VA 1971-1975; Pres Stndg Com Dio No Carolina Raleigh NC 1990-1991, Stndg Com/ Pres 1990 1988-1991, Dn - Greensboro Convoc 1986-1988, Dioc Coun 1984-1987, Dioc Coun 1984-1986; City Coun / Mayor 1980 Bedford Virginia 1978-1980. Auth, "Journey to the Final Cast," Warwick Hse Pub, 2011; Auth, "101 Things You Didn't Know About Judas," Adams Media, 2007; Auth, "Portraits of the Div Presence," St. Mary's Ch Press, 2007; Auth, "Of Doves and Serpents," *Epis Life*, Dom and Frgn Mssy Soc, 2005; Auth, "Filling our Empty Nets: Encouraging," St. Mary's Ch Press, 1999; Auth, "Talking to the Devil," *PreachingThrough the Year of Mk*, Morehouse, 1999; Auth, "Look into my Eyes," *Lectionary Homil*, Lectionary Homil, 1997; Auth, "Somthing to Cling to," *The Communicant*, Dio No Carolina, 1997; Auth, "A Tale of Two Tables," *Sermons That Wk V*, Forw Mvmt, 1995; Auth, "Filling Our Empty Nets," *Sermons That Wk III*, Forw Mvmt, 1993. AAPC 1981-2008. Sermon Competition Epis Evang Fndt 1995; Sermon Competition Epis Evang Fndt 1993; S Geo Epis Awd Episcopa Ch 1987.

BUSCH, Richard Alan (Los) 4125 36th St S, Arlington VA 22206 B New York NY 1932 s Richard & Helen. BA W&L 1954; BD Ya 1959; Ripon Hall Theol Coll 1960; PhD Claremont TS 1975. D 9/14/1959 Bp Theodore N Barth P 6/3/

1960 Bp John Vander Horst. m 3/4/1972 Lewise L Busch c 2. Prof VTS Alexandria VA 1976-1999; Asst H Faith Par Inglewood CA 1970-1974; R S Paul's Epis Ch Tustin CA 1967-1970; Asst All SS Par Beverly Hills CA 1962-1967; Asst Gr Ch Chattanooga TN 1960-1962.

BUSH JR, Arnold Arlington (CGC) 1109 Bristol Way, Birmingham AL 35242 **Cordinator,Cong. Dev. & Evan. Prov IV 2008-; Ret 2002-** B Laurel MS 1937 s Arnold & Lillian. BA Millsaps Coll 1959; MDiv Sewanee: The U So, 1962; VTS 1976. D 6/29/1962 P 5/22/1963 Bp Duncan Montgomery Gray. m 3/2/2015 Nancy Ellen Guthrie c 5. R S Jude's Epis Ch Niceville FL 1995-2002; Assoc R Chr Epis Ch San Antonio TX 1990-1995; Vic S Ptr's By The Lake Brandon MS 1981-1990; Assoc Reg Assoc in Evang Prov. IV 1975-1986; Dio Georgia Savannah GA 1975-1983; R S Anne's Ch Tifton GA 1972-1981; Vic S Eliz's Epis Ch Jacksonville FL 1968-1972; Vic S Fran Of Assisi Gulf Breeze FL 1964-1968; Vic Dio Mississippi Jackson MS 1962-1990; Vic Ch Of The Redeem Brookhaven MS 1962-1964; Coordntr for Evang/Congrl Dvlpmt Prov IV Jackson MS 2007-2013; Chair Ch Growth Cmsn Dio Cntrl Gulf Coast Pensacola FL 1997-2000. Auth, "Faith Growing," FA Org. FA 1970. Liberty Bell Awd Tift Cnty Bar 1980.

BUSH, Emilie Chaudron (Los) St. Paul's, PO Box 726, Barstow CA 92312 **Pstr Shpd of the Desert Luth Ch Barstow CA 2005-; Vic S Paul's Mssn Barstow CA 2001-** B Hawkinsville GA 1952 d Fred & Rietta. ETSBH; BA Tul 1974; MDiv Claremont TS 2001. D 6/9/2001 P 1/12/2002 Bp Frederick Houk Borsch. m 6/15/1974 John Lincoln Bush c 2.

BUSH, Katherine McQuiston (WTenn) 718 Charles Place, Memphis TN 38112 **Chapl S Mary's Epis Sch Memphis TN 2010-** B Memphis TN 1975 d John & Robbie. BA Rhodes Coll 1997; MDiv VTS 2003. D 6/28/2003 P 1/10/2004 Bp Don Edward Johnson. m 11/7/1998 Stephen C Bush c 2. Assoc R Ch Of The H Comm Memphis TN 2005-2010; Cn S Mary's Cathd Memphis TN 2003-2005. Contrib, "Pstr Essays," *Feasting on the Gospels, Matt*, Westminster Jn Knox Press, 2011; Contrib, "Homiletical Essays," *Feasting on the Word, Year C, Vol 3*, Westminster Jn Knox Press, 2010. Harris Awd VTS 2003.

BUSH, Patricia (SanD) 4642 Utah Street #1, San Diego CA 92116 B National City CA 1943 d Alvin & Audrey. BA San Diego St U 1964; MDiv Claremont TS 1983. D 11/18/1983 P 6/16/1984 Bp Charles Brinkley Morton. c 2. Vic S Eliz's Epis Ch San Diego CA 1991-1999; Dir Sch for Lay Mnstry Dio San Diego San Diego CA 1988-1990; Asst S Barth's Epis Ch Poway CA 1987-1990; Cur The Epis Ch Of S Andr Encinitas CA 1984-1986. SBL 1987-2009.

BUSH, Patrick M (Ct) 11 Church St, Tariffville CT 06081 **Galilee Epis Ch Virginia Bch VA 2017-** B Englewood CO 1978 s Patrick & Elizabeth. BS U of Hartford 2000; MDiv VTS 2014. D 3/29/2014 Bp James Elliot Curry P 12/16/2014 Bp Ian Theodore Douglas. m 6/9/2001 Nicole M Nicole Marie Broyles c 2. P Trin Ch Tariffville CT 2014-2017.

BUSHEE, Grant Sartori (Cal) 1225 Rosefield Way, Menlo Park CA 94025 **D S Ptr's Epis Ch Redwood City CA 2002-** B Los Angeles CA 1945 s Grant & Joan. BS U CA 1968; MBA Stan 1974; BD Sch for Deacons 2002. D 6/1/2002 Bp William Edwin Swing. m 9/28/1968 Jean Marie Bushee c 1.

BUSHEY JR, Howard Wallace (La) 8833 Goodwood Blvd, Baton Rouge LA 70806 B Temple TX 1943 s Howard & Margaret. BA LSU 1966; MA Webster U 1980; JD LSU 1992; MA Sewanee: The U So, TS 2000. D 12/29/1999 P 8/6/2000 Bp Charles Edward Jenkins III. m 9/16/1995 Sue Bushey c 2. Dio Louisiana New Orleans LA 2010-2011, Mssnr 2000-2010; Epis Ch Of The H Sprt In Baton Rouge Baton Rouge LA 2008-2010; S Marg's Epis Ch Baton Rouge LA 2008; S Lk's Ch Baton Rouge LA 2005-2008; S Paul's/H Trin New Roads LA 2005; R S Steph's Ch Innis LA 2000-2004; Mssnr S Mary's Ch Morganza LA 1999-2000. La Bar Assn.

BUSHNELL, Peter Emerson (Ct) Holy Trinity Church, 383 Hazard Ave., Enfield CT 06082 **Pres Educational Resources for Chld Enfield CT 2008-; R H Trin Epis Ch Enfield CT 2008-; R H Trin Epis Ch Enfield CT 2007-; Pres Integrated Refugee & Immigrant Serv New Haven CT 2001-** B Winsted CT 1948 s Waldo & Helen. BA Gordon Coll 1970; MDiv PDS 1973. D 6/8/1974 P 2/24/1975 Bp Joseph Warren Hutchens. m 5/19/1973 Kathryn P Bushnell c 4. Sr Mssnr Calv Ch Suffield CT 1993-2007; Gr Ch Broad Brook CT 1993-2007; No Cntrl Reg Mnstry Enfield CT 1993-2007; S Andr's Epis Ch Enfield CT 1993-2007; Pres Curtis Hm Meriden CT 1992-1995; R All SS Epis Ch Meriden CT 1977-1992; Cur Chr Ch Ansonia CT 1974-1977; Dio Connecticut Meriden CT 1974, Exec Coun 2000-2006.

BUSHONG JR, Edward Stuart (SVa) 2806 E. Marshall St., Richmond VA 23223 B Hagerstown MD 1944 s Edward & Rachel. BA U of Maryland 1966; MDiv Ya Berk 1970; MA Antioch U 1978; PhD Un Inst & U Cincinnati OH 1990. D 6/23/1970 Bp Harry Lee Doll P 3/20/1971 Bp David Keller Leighton Sr. m 8/8/1981 Martha Menser c 2. S Jn's Ch Petersburg VA 2003-2006; R S Jn's Ch Hopewell VA 1995-2002; R S Anne's Ch Appomattox VA 1991-1995; R S Andr's Mt Harpers Ferry WV 1988-1991; S Andr's-On-The-Mt Harpers Ferry WV 1988-1991; R All SS Ch Collingdale PA 1985-1988; S Andrews Sch Of Delaware Inc Middletown DE 1983-1985; Assoc Chapl S Andr's Sch Middletown DE 1983-1985; Cn Mssnr Cathd Ch Of S Jn Wilmington DE

1981-1983; Dio Delaware Wilmington 1979-1981; Washington Co Mssn Hagerstown MD 1975-1977; Dio Maryland Baltimore MD 1970-1973.

BUSLER, George Warren (LI) P. O. Box 55, Westhampton Beach NY 11978 B Philadelphia PA 1938 s George & Kathryn. BA Ursinus Coll 1960; STB PDS 1963; ECF 1964; STM UTS 1964; Coll of Preachers 1973; Cert VTS 1983; DD Cumberland U 1999; Rotary Intl 1999. D 6/8/1963 P 12/14/1963 Bp Joseph Gillespie Armstrong. m 6/23/1962 Joy Busler c 2. Prof Geo Mercer TS Garden City NY 1994-1999; Prof, Moral Theol Dio Long Island Garden City NY 1971-1999; Exec Dir Fam Counslg Serv The Hamptons L.I. 1971-1999; R S Mk's Ch Westhampton Bch NY 1966-1999; Asst R S Lk Forest Hills Forest Hills NY 1963-1966; Exec Com,Chairman of Med Stff Committe Dio Long Island Garden City NY 1971-1999. Auth, "Abortion:Theol & Expediency," 1975; Auth, "Theol & Jurisprudence," 1966; Auth, "Legal Philos of Justice Holmes," 1964. DD Degree Cumberland U 1999; Paul Harris Fell Rotary Intl 1999; STM mcl UTS 1964; STB cl PDS 1963.

BUSSE, Mary Ruth (Fla) 3580 Pine St, Jacksonville FL 32205 B Saint Louis MO 1943 d George & Arline. Duke 1996; Oxf GB 1999; VTS 1999. D 6/11/2000 P 12/10/2000 Bp Stephen Hays Jecko. c 2. Assoc Ch Of Our Sav Jacksonville FL 2008; Bethany Ch Hilliard FL 2006-2007; Assoc R The Epis Ch Of S Ptr And S Paul Marietta GA 2001-2005; S Jn's Cathd Jacksonville FL 2000-2001.

BUSTARD-BURNSIDE, Carol (Md) 1106 Woodheights Ave, Baltimore MD 21211 B Memphis TN 1955 d Wade & Sarah. BA U of Arkansas 1979; MDiv EDS 1992. D 6/6/1992 Bp Jack Marston Mckelvey P 12/12/1992 Bp John Shelby Spong. m Barbara Bustard-Burnside. S Barn Epis Ch Sykesville MD 2014; Ch Of The Ascen Middle River MD 2006-2010; S Alb's Epis Ch Glen Burnie MD 2004-2005; R S Mary's Epis Ch Woodlawn Gwynn Oak MD 1999-2003; S Mk's Ch W Orange NJ 1994-1999; Assoc R S Jas Ch Montclair NJ 1992-1993. Newark Cler Assn.

BUSTO, Mercedes (SeFla) **Trin Cathd Miami FL 2016-; S Phil's Ch Coral Gables FL 2015-** B Havanna Cuba 1946 d Fernando & Mercedes. BA Florida Intl U 1978; Juris Doctor Columbia Law Sch 1981; MDiv GTS 2013. D 11/23/2013 P 5/31/2014 Bp Leo Frade. m 8/14/1992 William G Jennings c 3.

BUSTRIN, Robert C (Az) 118 Lafayette Ave, Brooklyn NY 11217 **Vic S Mary's Epis Ch Phoenix AZ 2010-** B Phoenix AZ 1953 s James & Mary. BA Arizona St U 1975; MDiv SWTS 1979. D 6/10/1979 Bp John Joseph Meakin Harte P 1/1/1980 Bp Charles Bennison Sr. Asst P S Mich's Ch New York NY 1986-2000; Asst H Trin Epis Ch Gainesville FL 1982-1984; Chapl Wstrn Missouri U Kalamazoo 1980-1982; Cur S Lk's Par Kalamazoo MI 1979-1982. Soc Of S Jn The Evang.

BUTCHER, Geoffrey (Ky) 607 5th Ave W, Springfield TN 37172 **P-in-c Trin Ch Russellville KY 2010-** B Orange NJ 1941 s Harold & Elizabeth. RSCM; BA Hobart and Wm Smith Colleges 1961; MDiv GTS 1965; MA New Mex Highlands U 1970; DMin McCormick TS 1979. D 5/7/1965 P 4/2/1966 Bp C J Kinsolving III. m 2/14/2017 James C Johnson c 2. Cn Chr Ch Cathd Nashville TN 2008-2010, Cn 1997-2007, Assoc for Pstr Care 1992-1997; Cn S Jn's Cathd Albuquerque NM 1968-1992; P-in-c H Trin Epis Ch - Mssn Raton NM 1966-1968; S Paul's Peace Ch Las Vegas NM 1966-1968; Cur S Andr's Epis Ch Las Cruces NM 1965-1966. Auth, "Without the Miracle There is Nothing," CreateSpace, 2014.

BUTCHER, Gerald Alfred (Okla) 1720 W Carolina Ave, Chickasha OK 73018 B Ponca City OK 1955 s Clarence & Reva. BS Oklahoma St U 1977. D 6/22/2002 Bp Robert Manning Moody. m 8/13/1977 Debra Ann Stotts. D S Lk's Ch Chickasha OK 2002-2013.

BUTCHER, Julie Ann (WMass) D 6/10/2017 Bp Doug Fisher.

BUTCHER, Kenneth Pf (Colo) 3306 Morris Ave, Pueblo CO 81008 **D Ch Of The Ascen Pueblo CO 1992-** B Snodland Kent UK 1937 s Cecil & Bessie. BA U of Southampton GB 1960; U of Reading Gb 1961; MA U of Nthrn Colorado 1971. D 10/24/1992 Bp William Jerry Winterrowd. m 8/11/1962 Barbara Rosemary Butcher c 1. Tchg Fac For Diac Formation Dio Colorado Denver CO 1996-2002. Auth, "Performance Pract Of 16th Century Part Bk," *Amer Choral Dir'S Journ*, 1985; Auth, "Contrib Ch Hymnal Series V," Ch Hymnal Corp., 1980. NAAD 1990. Hall Of Fame Colorado Mus Educators Assn 1999.

BUTERBAUGH, Matthew L (Mil) St Matthew's Church, 5900 7th Ave, Kenosha WI 53140 **R S Matt's Ch Kenosha WI 2013-** B Winfield KS 1980 s James & Charlotte. BA Oklahoma St U 2003; MDiv SWTS 2007. D 6/9/2007 P 1/7/2008 Bp Dean E Wolfe. R S Jn The Evang Ch New Brunswick NJ 2009-2013; S Dav's Epis Ch Topeka KS 2007-2009.

BUTIN, John Murray (Ga) 303 Cannon Ct, St Simons Island GA 31522 **P-in-c Gd Shpd Ch Pennick GA 2005-** B Wichita KS 1964 s James & Betty. BA U of Kansas 1986; MDiv Candler TS Emory U 1994; LLD Emory U 1994. D 8/3/2002 P 2/17/2003 Bp Henry Irving Louttit. m 12/28/1991 Mary Margaret Butin c 3. S Mk's Ch Brunswick GA 2002-2004.

BUTLER III, Andrew Garland (NY) 59 Montclair Ave, Montclair NJ 07042 **Chr Ch Riverdale Bronx NY 2014-** B Richmond VA 1967 s Andrew & Phyllis. MA Presb Sch CE Richmond VA 1999; MDiv PrTS 2001; Cert VTS 2008. D 5/24/2008 Bp Peter J Lee P 12/6/2008 Bp Edward Lewis Lee Jr. c 3. S Mk's Ch Teaneck NJ 2013-2014; Stwdshp Chair S Jn's Epis Ch Mont-

clair NJ 2011-2012, 2010-2013; Assoc R Ch Of The Redeem Bryn Mawr PA 2008-2010; Mus Min S Thos' Ch Richmond VA 2002-2007.

BUTLER, Barbara Thayer (Minn) 2324 Branch St, Duluth MN 55812 **D S Paul's Epis Ch Duluth MN 2001-** B Duluth MN 1932 d Jorice & Verna. U MN 1951; BA Carleton Coll 1954. D 10/25/1987 Bp Robert Marshall Anderson. m 10/6/1956 John Tyler Butler c 4. Dir of Acolytes The Par of St Paul's Epis Ch Duluth MN 1987-2001; Deacons' Coun Dio Minnesota Minneapolis MN 1989-1992.

BUTLER, Charles Roger (CNY) 28205 Nc 73 Hwy, Albemarle NC 28001 **Ret 1994-** B Huntington WV 1932 s Charles & Genevieve. BA Marshall U 1953; MDiv VTS 1956. D 6/11/1956 P 6/1/1957 Bp Wilburn Camrock Campbell. m 12/19/1981 Joyce Griffith Butler c 3. P Assoc All SS' Epis Ch Concord NC 2001-2011; R S Paul's Ch Watertown NY 1989-1994; Vic Ch Of The H Innoc Leechburg PA 1980-1989; Int Chr Ch New Brighton PA 1979-1980; Fell Coll of Preachers 1973; Vic S Mary Epis Ch Red Bank Templeton PA 1963-1984; S Paul's Epis Ch Kittanning PA 1963-1975; Dioc Rep., Pgh., CNY PBp's Fund 1960-1989; Assoc R Ch Of The Ascen Pittsburgh PA 1960-1963; Chapl U Pgh 1960-1963; Vic S Ann's Ch N Martinsvlle WV 1956-1960; Pres of Dioc Coun Dio Pittsburgh Pittsburgh PA 1986-1988.

BUTLER, Clarence Elliot (Roch) 19 Russell Ave., Watertown MA 02472 B Shelby MS 1941 s Robert & Addie. BA Washington U 1963; MA U of Kansas 1965; STB EDS 1967; PhD Washington U 1973. D 6/24/1967 P 6/1/1968 Bp George Leslie Cadigan. c 2. EDS Cambridge MA 2010-2011; Trin Ch Geneva NY 2006-2009, R 2006-2009, Int 1993-1995, Asst to R 1979-1992; Dn Hob Geneva NY 1979-2006; Serv Ch Of The Ascen S Louis MO 1968-1970; Dio Missouri S Louis MO 1968-1969, 1968; S Mk's Ch S Louis MO 1968. Auth, "Heinz Meyer Die Zahlenallegorese im Mittelalter," *German Quarterly*, 1977; Auth, *Rel Stds Revs*.

BUTLER, David Floyd (Kan) PO Box 65, Independence KS 67301 B Pawhuska OK 1947 s Harold & Velma. BS K SU 1973; Kansas Sch of Mnstry 2001. D 6/11/2005 Bp Dean E Wolfe. m 8/1/1970 Nora Veith Butler c 4.

BUTLER, Guy Harry (Tex) 10019 Beaverdam Creek Rd, Berlin MD 21811 **Died 3/8/2017** B Reading PA 1933 s Bruce & Elizabeth. BA Franklin & Marshall Coll 1956; MDiv PDS 1959; Coll of Preachers 1963; Coll of Preachers 1966; Coll of Preachers 1977. D 6/27/1959 Bp Earl M Honaman P 1/9/1960 Bp John Thomas Heistand. m 2/11/1961 Joanna Butler. Ret 1996-2017; The Great Cmsn Fndt Houston TX 1993-1996; Trin Ch Jacksonville TX 1993-1996; Trin Ch Natchez MS 1993-1996; Serv Angl Ch of Can 1987-1993; Dio NW Pennsylvania Erie PA 1987-1993; Tri-Dioc Stwdshp Com Winnipeg MB 1987-1992; R Chr Epis Ch Meadville PA 1978-1987; Vic S Mary's Ch Erie PA 1976-1978; Vic S Jos's Epis Ch Grand Prairie TX 1965-1976; Vic S Alb's Epis Ch Salisbury MD 1961-1965; Cur Cathd Ch Of S Steph Harrisburg PA 1959-1961.

BUTLER, Joseph Green (O) 471 Crosby St, Akron OH 44302 B Youngstown OH 1949 s Joseph & Dorothy. D 11/12/2010 Bp Mark Hollingsworth Jr. m 2/10/2006 Denise Butler c 3.

BUTLER, Marilyn M (Ida) 4251 N 1800 E, Buhl ID 83316 **P Trin Ch Buhl ID 1994-** B Twin Falls ID 1940 d Pete & Mildred. BS Colorado St U 1961; MS Colorado St U 1966. D 1/29/1994 P 8/1/1994 Bp John Stuart Thornton. m 9/9/1959 Calvin Charles Butler.

BUTLER, Mark Hilliard (LI) 225 Arbutus Ln, Hendersonville NC 28739 **P-in-c Ch of the Gd Shpd Tryon NC 2015-; Ret Dio Long Island 2005-** B Poughkeepsie NY 1945 s Frank & Alice. BA U of So Florida 1969; MDiv EDS 1976; MDiv The EDS 1976; EDS 1977; The EDS 1977. D 6/16/1985 P 12/15/1985 Bp Frank S Cerveny. m 8/12/1991 Margaret W Butler c 2. Int R Ch of the Trsfg Bat Cave NC 2012-2014; R Chr Ch Babylon NY 2003-2005; Dio Spokane Spokane WA 2000-2005, Dioc Coun 2000-2003; R Epis Ch of the Nativ Lewiston ID 2000-2003; COM w Gays And Lesbians Dio Oregon Portland OR 1994-2000, Stndg Com 1996-2000; R Gr Epis Ch Astoria OR 1994-2000; Chair Cler Fam Com Dio Upper So Carolina Columbia SC 1993-1994, Cler Fam Com 1991-1993, Cmsn Stwdshp And Dvlpmt 1992-1994; R Ch Of The Incarn Gaffney SC 1991-1994; Vic S Davids Ch Brunswick GA 1988-1991; S Mk's Ch Brunswick GA 1988-1991; Int S Paul's Epis Ch Jacksonville FL 1985-1987; Camp Dewolfe Bd Mem Dio Long Island Garden City NY 2004-2005. Auth/Ed, "Employee Assistance Prog Supervisory Trng Manual," 1985.

BUTLER, Oliver Martin (Dal) 8011 Douglas Ave, Dallas TX 75225 **S Mich And All Ang Ch Dallas TX 2015-** B Houston TX 1971 s Arthur & Lyndel. BA Baylor U 1997; MDiv VTS 2005. D 6/4/2005 P 3/4/2006 Bp James Monte Stanton. m 11/5/2011 Rachel Elizabeth Butler c 1.

BUTLER, Pauline Felton (CFla) 815 E Graves Ave, Orange City FL 32763 B Norfolk VA 1944 d George & Muriel. AS Dayton Bch Cmnty Collge 1991; AS Dayton Bch Cmnty Collge 1992; AA Dayton Bch Cmnty Collge 1994; BA U of Cntrl Florida 1995. D 12/12/2009 Bp John Wadsworth Howe. m 6/20/2009 Gary Butler c 2.

BUTLER, Robert Mitchell (Me) 35821 Pradera Dr, Zephyrhills FL 33541 **Ret 1989-** B Philadelphia PA 1925 s Freeman & Bertha. BA U of Maine 1951; GTS 1965. D 12/18/1965 P 12/17/1966 Bp Oliver L Loring. c 2. Asst S Eliz's Epis Ch Zephyrhills FL 1992-2015; R Ch of the Gd Shpd Houlton ME 1975-1989; Vic S Giles Ch Jefferson ME 1972-1975; Const and Cn Dio Maine Portland ME

1970-1975, Dir Dioc Conf Cntr 1970-1975, Prog Coordntr 1970-1975, Bp's Stff 1970-1972, Stff Dioc Conf Cntr 1963-1969; Vic Penobscot ME Missions 1968-1970; Cur Chr Ch Gardiner ME 1965-1967.

BUTLER, Susan J (ETenn) 20 Belvoir Ave, Chattanooga TN 37411 B Scranton PA 1954 d Edwin & Mildred. BA Franklin & Marshall Coll 1976; MDiv Drew U 1997. D 5/31/1997 Bp Jack Marston Mckelvey P 12/13/1997 Bp John Shelby Spong. c 2. R Gr Ch Chattanooga TN 2010-2016, P-in-c 2010; S Ptr's Ch Mtn Lks NJ 2007-2009; Trin Epis Ch of Bergen Cnty Allendale NJ 2007; Chr Ch Newton NJ 2002-2003; Asst Trin Ch Solebury PA 1999-2002; Cur S Ptr's Ch Morristown NJ 1997-1998. sbutler@saygrace.net

BUTLER, Tony Eugene (Cal) Po Box 4380, Sparks NV 89432 **Vic S Baranabas's Antioch CA 1982-** B Muskegon MI 1947 s Alfred & Joanne. BA U of Nevada at Reno 1969; MDiv CDSP 1973. D 6/6/1973 P 5/1/1974 Bp Wesley Frensdorff. m 6/5/1976 Linda Ann Jones c 1. S Geo's Epis Ch Antioch CA 1981-1983; Ch Of Coventry Cross Minden NV 1975-1981; Vic Coventry Cress Minden Nv 1975-1981; Cur Trin Epis Ch Reno NV 1973-1975. Auth, "Var arts".

BUTLER-GEE, Eve (SVa) Martin's Brandon Episcopal Church, 18706 James River Dr, Disputanta VA 23842 B Buenos Aires Argentina 1944 d Randolph & Elizabeth. 2 year Cert Sch for Mnstry Formation Dio Sthrn VA; AA Cand Trin; Cert of Completion VTS 2010. D 6/9/2012 P 12/15/2012 Bp Herman Hollerith IV. m 9/5/1992 John Thomas Gee c 2. Mnstry Intern St. Mart's Epis Ch Williamsburg Virginia 2011-2012; Intrnshp St. Mk's Epis Ch Hampton Virginia 2009-2010; Sr Verger Ch of the H Comf Vienna Virginia 1992-2005. ebutlergee@cox.net

BUTTERBAUGH, Marie (CGC) 401 Live Oak Ave, Pensacola FL 32507 **Died 3/6/2017** B Monticello FL 1957 d Charles & Margaret. BA U of W Florida 1979; MTS Sprg Hill Coll 2002; MDiv Epis TS of the SW 2010. D 12/19/2009 P 1/22/2011 Bp Philip Menzie Duncan II. m 6/25/1977 Timothy R Butterbaugh. Par Admin and Vstry Clerk S Jn's Ch Pensacola FL 2010-2017.

BUTTERWORTH, Gary Wayne (WNC) 3587 Fieldstone Dr, Gastonia NC 28056 **R All SS' Epis Ch Gastonia NC 2012-; Curs Sec Spiritil Dir Dio Sthrn Virginia Newport News VA 2010-, Exec Bd 2010-, Chair, Liturg Cmsn 2009-** B Marion OH 1956 s Wayne & Mary Louetta. BS Excelsior Coll 1996; MMAS Command and Gnrl Stff Coll 2001; MBA Touro U Intl 2004; MDiv Sewanee: The U So, TS 2008; DMin TS 2013; DMin Sewanee: The U So, TS 2013. D 2/1/2008 P 8/1/2008 Bp John Clark Buchanan. m 10/4/1983 Christina Butterworth c 2. R Emm Epis (Par Mssn) 2008-2012; R S Jn's Epis Ch Halifax VA 2008-2012; Trin Epis Ch So Boston VA 2008-2012. Auth, "The Colonial Ch, its impact and legacy in Colonial Dioceses: A Fam Systems Perspective," *Doctoral Thesis*, U So, 2013; Auth, "Was the Grp dynamic Groupthink present onboard USS Greeneville when it collided w the Ehime Maru," *Masters Thesis*, Command and Gnrl Stff Coll, 2002; Auth, "Where were the Images," *Proceedings*, Naval Inst, 1993. Magna Cumme Laude Touro U Intl 2004; Life Mem Ord of St. Vinc 1995.

BUTTON, Roger Dee (Dal) 9845 McCree Rd, Dallas TX 75238 B Dodge City KS 1956 s Richard & Peggy. BA Washington U 1979; MABS Dallas TS 1984; JD Dedman Sch of Law 1992; Dplma in Angl Stds Epis TS of the SW 2009; Dplma in Angl Stds Sem of the SW 2009. D 12/10/2011 Bp Paul Emil Lambert. m 10/17/1992 Kathryn Annette Button c 1.

BUTTS, Roger Paul (Md) 2206 Pheasant Run Dr, Finksburg MD 21048 **Died 5/29/2017** B Baltimore MD 1936 s Roger & Alice. BA McDaniel Coll 1959; MDiv Wesley TS 1962; VTS 1965. D 6/22/1965 P 6/1/1966 Bp Harry Lee Doll. m 6/25/1960 Lois Butts c 2. Ret 1998-2017; Emm Ch Baltimore MD 1994-1998; S Paul's Par Kent Chestertown MD 1993-1994; Ch Hosp Corp Baltimore MD 1985-1993; S Paul's Epis Ch Mt Airy MD 1981-1985; Vic S Paul's Poplar Sprg MD 1981-1985; Ch Of-Ascen & Prince-Peace Baltimore MD 1965-1981; Cur Ch Of The Ascen Middle River MD 1965-1968; Serv Methodist Ch 1960-1964.

BUTTS, Stephen Jack (Tex) 314 N Henderson Blvd, Kilgore TX 75662 B Placerville CA 1948 s Jack & Anna. AA Sierra Coll Rocklin CA 1973; BA Chapman U 1992; MDiv CDSP 1995. D 5/31/1995 Bp Jerry Alban Lamb P 12/1/1995 Bp Claude Edward Payne. m 7/6/1985 Eva Butts c 2. R S Paul's Ch Kilgore TX 1995-2010. OHC 1993.

BUXO, David Carlysle (Mich) 3601 W 13 Mile Rd, Royal Oak MI 48073 **Dir, Sprtl Care & CPE Beaumont Hlth System 2006-; Dir, Sprtl Care and CPE Beaumont Hlth System 1994-** B Levara GD 1939 s Ivan & Beryl. BA Lon GB 1967; MDiv GTS 1981. Trans 9/1/1993 Bp R aymond Stewart Wood Jr. m 2/14/1987 Jennifer Buxo c 2. Dir, CPE Wm Beaumont Hosp Royal Oak Michigan 2001-2006; R S Lk's Ch Utica MI 2006-2009; S Mk's Ch Detroit MI 1995-1996; R S Tim's Ch Detroit MI 1993-1994. ACPE (ACPE) Inc 1998; Assn of Profsnl Chapl 1999.

BUXTON JR, Eugene Harvey (Tex) 514 Belleair Pl, Clearwater FL 33756 B Akron OH 1931 s Eugene & Vesta. BA Coll of Wooster 1952; BD Bex Sem 1955. D 6/18/1955 Bp Nelson Marigold Burroughs P 1/6/1956 Bp Harry Sherbourne Kennedy. Trin Ch Findlay OH 2003-2004; Int NW OH Cluster 1998-1999; Extended Supply P Dio Ohio Cleveland 1992-1996; Int Dio Texas

Houston TX 1990; S Aug's Epis Ch Galveston TX 1985-1989; R Trin Ch Connersville IN 1964-1973; Vic S Jn's Epis Ch Sparta WI 1958-1964; Serv Ch of Engl 1957-1958; Int S Mary's Epis Ch Honolulu HI 1956-1957; Chapl Iolani Epis Sch Honolulu HI 1955-1957.

BUXTON-SMITH, Sarah Wallace (WNY) 100 Beard Ave, Buffalo NY 14214 **Mem, Chairs' Advsry on Ldrshp Dvlpmt Ya Berk 2015-; Trst Dio Wstrn New York Tonawanda NY 2010-, Dioc Coun: Chair of Governance 2006-2010, Deputation GC: Alt 2006-2009, Liturg Cmsn 2000-2004, Rel Leaders Forum of Buffalo: Bp's Dep 2000-2004, D's Exam Bd 2000-2002, Stndg Com: Pres 1999-2005, Stndg Com Mem 1999-2004** B Summit NJ 1949 d Horace & Ann. BA VPI 1971; MFA U NC 1977; Washington Theol Un 1986; DAS Ya Berk 1994; MDiv Yale DS 1994. D 6/11/1994 Bp Peter J Lee P 3/25/1995 Bp Clarence Nicholas Coleridge. m 6/25/1994 Stephen John Stanyon Smith. Intl Bd Compass Rose Soc of the Angl Comm 2007-2014; Natl Advsry Bd for Vital Practices ECF 2005-2010; R S Andr's Ch Buffalo NY 2002-2012; Chapl Bishops' Spouses Epis HOB 1999-2003; Assoc Trin Epis Ch Buffalo NY 1999-2001; Resrch Assoc,The Zacchaeus Proj ECF 1998-2003; Resrch Assoc ECF 1998-2002; P Assoc Calv Epis Ch Williamsville NY 1998-1999; Sr Prog Assoc Listening Hearts Mnstry 1998-1999; P Assoc S Matt's Epis Ch Wilton CT 1998; Int R Chr Ch New Haven CT 1994-1998; Chapl & Theol Tchr St. Steph's And St. Agnes Sch Alexandria VA 1990-1991; Dn's Natl Advsry Ya Berk 2004-2010; Bd Mem Natl Fed for Just Communities of WNY Inc. 2003-2009; Bd Mem Buffalo/Niagara Wrld Connect 2002-2006; Dn's Search Com Ya Berk 2002-2003; Bd Mem Buffalo/Niagara Cltn on Wmn Rts 2001-2002; Grad Soc: Vice-Pres Ya Berk 2000-2004; Fndr & Chair Interfaith Wmn of WNY 1999-2002; Bd Mem Pan-Am Wmn Rts Conf 1999-2002; Bd Mem Cmnty Soup Kitchen New Haven CT 1996-1998; Fndr & Chair Wmn Shltr Concerns New Haven CT 1995-1998; Mus Cmsn Dio Connecticut Meriden CT 1994-1998. Producer, "Walking Into Difference," *Interfaith Wmn at the Millennium*, Avocado Productions, 2002; Auth, "Fr Lady," *Magnificent: Celebrating Wmn Priests*, Buckfriars Press, 2000. Cmnty Of The Cross Of Nails 1985; Compass Rose Soc 1995; Fllshp Of S Jn 2002. Invited Observer NIFCON Conf: HIndu Diaspora in Europe 2015; Interfaith Cmnty Ldr Awd The Natl Fed of Just Communities of Wstrn New York, Inc. 2012; Preaching Awd Ya Berk 1994.

BUZZARD, Henry Lewis (NY) 71 Wayne Ave, White Plains NY 10606 B Normal IL 1923 s Robert & Alice. Estrn Illinois U 1945; BA Wabash Coll 1946; MA Clark U 1949; MLS U IL 1951. D 9/26/1996 Bp William Edwin Swing P 6/28/1997 Bp Egbert Don Taylor. m 6/9/1956 Juliet Dickinson Barnett. P S Ann's Ch For The Deaf New York NY 1997-2004. Auth, "Thos Gallaudet: Apos To The Deaf," 1989. Empire St Assn Of The Deaf; Epis Conf Of The Deaf; New York City City Assn Of The Deaf.

BWECHWA, Oswald (Mil) 3400 E Debbie Drive, Oak Creek WI 53154 **P-in-c S Mart's Ch Milwaukee WI 2008-; Asstg P St. Martins Epis Churc Brown Deer WI 2003-** B Muleba TZ 1958 s Damian & Magdalena. BA Miltown Pk Inst 1985; BS Marq 1990; MDiv Hekima Coll 1993; ThM Berkeley Jesuit TS 1998; DAS VTS 1999; MSW U of Wisconsin 2003. Rec 6/1/1999 as Deacon Bp Roger John White. m 5/29/1999 Rosemarie Nhonoli c 1. R S Nich Epis Ch Racine WI 1999-2000. APSW 2005.

BYE, Mike (NC) P.O. Box 942, wadesboro NC 28170 **R All Souls Espiscopal Ch Ansonville NC 2005-** B Harrisburg PA 1947 s Theodore & Grace. BS Campbell U 1968; VTS 1970; MDiv Ya Berk 1971. D 6/26/1971 Bp Robert Fisher Gibson Jr P 5/1/1972 Bp Robert Bruce Hall. m 11/23/2009 Judith B Brittingham. R Calv Ch Wadesboro NC 2005-2015; S Clem's Epis Ch Clemmons NC 2003-2005; Dio No Carolina Raleigh NC 2003; Vic Chap Of Chr The King Charlotte NC 1999-2003; S Paul's Ch Georgetown DE 1991-1999; Vic S Andr The Fisherman Epis Mayo MD 1981-1988; Vic St Jas Epis Ch Exch PA 1977-1982; R S Jas Ch Muncy PA 1977-1981; Asst Ch Of The Gd Shpd Burke VA 1975-1977; S Ptr's Epis Ch Arlington VA 1973-1975; St Jas Ch Richmond VA 1971-1973.

BYE, Tommy Frank (FtW) 1201 Overhill St, Bedford TX 76022 **S Lk's Ch Cypress Mill TX 2000-** B Abilene TX 1945 s Jessey & Mollya. Choir Coll of The SW 1969; AA El Centro Dallas TX 1971; U of Dallas 1990; MDiv Nash 1994. D 12/27/1993 Bp Clarence Cullam Pope Jr P 7/1/1994 Bp Jack Leo Iker. m 4/11/1980 Connie Bye c 1. R S Lk's In The Meadow Epis Ch Ft Worth TX 1997-2007; S Vinc's Cathd Bedford TX 1994-1997.

BYER, Martha Russell (WMo) 3907 Ivanhoe Blvd, Columbia MO 65203 **Asstg P Chr Ch Epis Boonville MO 2013-, D 2002-2013** B Little Rock AR 1940 d Wesley & Martha. AA All SS Epis Jr. Coll 1960; BS Texas Womans U 1964. D 2/2/2002 Bp Barry Howe P 11/1/2013 Bp Martin Scott Field. c 3.

BYERS, Mark Harrison (Ct) 38 Grove St, Thomaston CT 06787 **R S Ptr's-Trin Ch Thomaston CT 2011-** B Philippines 1965 s Clarence & Sara. BA Hav 1995; MDiv Ya Berk 1998. D 6/9/2001 Bp Andrew Donnan Smith P 12/15/2001 Bp Wilfrido Ramos-Orench. m 7/20/2002 Jessica Byers c 3. Ch of the Apos La Quinta CA 2009-2011; Cur S Jn's Epis Ch Essex CT 2001-2004.

BYERS, Sara Shovar (Ga) PO Box 925, Moultrie GA 31776 B Toledo OH 1940 d Mark & Willa. AA U of Florida 1960; BA Humboldt St U 1978. D 4/29/2012 Bp Scott Anson Benhase. c 3.

BYERS, William (WMass) 35 Nedwied Rd, Tolland CT 06084 **Non-par 1971-** B Boston MA 1936 s Douglas & Dorothy. BA Colby Coll 1961; MDiv Bex Sem 1966. D 6/22/1966 P 12/13/1966 Bp Robert McConnell Hatch. m 11/25/1978 Susan Kinsloe c 2. Chapl Tolland Ct Fire Dept 2003-2010; Asst Min All SS Ch Worcester MA 1966-1971; Chapl Worcester Ma Police And Fire Departments 1966-1971. Auth, "Sculpting Wood: Contemporary Tools & Techniques," Davis Pub, 1986; Auth, "Pollen & Archeology At Wetherill Mesa". Chapl Ord Of S Lk.

BYRD, Bear (CGC) 403 W College St, Troy AL 36081 **R S Mk's Epis Ch Troy AL 2006-, D-In-Trng 2005-2017** B Knoxville TN 1962 s Frank & Joyce. BS Austin Peay St U 1992; MS Austin Peay St U 1994; MDiv Epis TS of the SW 2005. D 6/4/2005 P 5/6/2006 Bp Philip Menzie Duncan II. m 1/9/1988 Elizabeth A Ensor c 2.

BYRD, Frederick Colclough (USC) 1115 Marion St, Columbia SC 29201 **Archd Dio Upper So Carolina Columbia SC 1979-, Archd Emer 2008-** B Augusta GA 1942 s Frederick & Addie. BS Clemson U 1964; MDiv VTS 1968. D 6/23/1968 P 5/1/1969 Bp John Adams Pinckney. Vic S Lk's Ch Newberry SC 1969-1971; Asst S Jas Epis Ch Greenville SC 1968-1969. Soc Of First Families Of So Carolina; So Carolina Huguenot Soc. Who'S Who In Amer Colleges And Universities; Personalitites Of The So; Outstanding Young Men In Amer.

BYRD, Janice Lovinggood (NwT) 430 Dallas St, Big Spring TX 79720 **Died 2/7/2016** B Breckenridge TX 1932 d Thurman & Dorothy. BS Texas Womans U 1954. D 10/27/2002 Bp C Wallis Ohl. c 2. D The Epis Ch Of S Mary The Vrgn Big Sprg TX 2002-2016.

BYRD, Katherine Hahn (Lex) 166 Market St, Lexington KY 40507 **Chr Ch Cathd Lexington KY 2014-** B Fairfax VA 1987 d Thomas & Elizabeth. BA Randolph Macon Coll 2010; MDiv VTS 2014. D 6/7/2014 Bp Shannon Sherwood Johnston P 1/24/2015 Bp Doug Hahn. m 1/12/2013 Carvus Andrew Byrd.

BYRD, Nita Charlene Johnson (NC) St Paul Episcopal Church, 221 Union St, Cary NC 27511 **S Aug's Coll Raleigh NC 2013-** B Raleigh NC 1963 d Paul & Delcie Susie Bell. BS No Carolina St U 1986; MS No Carolina St U 1989; MDiv Duke DS 2012. D 6/16/2012 P 10/14/2013 Bp Michael B Curry. m 12/20/1986 Kevin Leon Byrd c 1. S Ambroses Ch Raleigh NC 2012-2017.

BYRD, Ronald Charles (Mich) 634 Canoga, Haslett MI 48840 **R S Kath's Ch Williamston MI 2009-** B Detroit MI 1960 s Robert & Elizabeth. AA Northwood U 1980; AA Northwood U 1980; Aa Northwood U 1982; BBA Northwood U 1982; BBA Northwood U 1982; MDiv VTS 2007. D 12/16/2006 P 9/15/2007 Bp Wendell Nathaniel Gibbs Jr. m 11/28/2003 Jennifer Byrd c 8. S Paul's Epis Ch Lansing MI 2007-2009; Area Dir Wendy's Intl 2000-2004.

BYRER, Johnine Vaughn (Pa) 6 Juniper Dr, Whitehouse Station NJ 08889 **D Ch Of The H Sprt Lebanon NJ 2002-** B Ann Arbor MI 1946 d John & Laura. BS Estrn Michigan U 1968; MA Estrn Michigan U 1971. D 9/21/2002 Bp David Bruce Joslin. m 10/7/1972 Donald V Byrer c 4. NAAD 2002. S Steph Awd NAAD 2007.

BYRNE, Anne Sc (Md) 126 E. Liberty St., Oakland MD 21550 **Assoc Cler S Matt's Par Oakland MD 2008-** B Portsmouth VA 1961 d John & Anne. Garrett Cmnty Coll; MMP Wstrn Maryland Coll 2008. D 7/5/2008 P 6/27/2009 Bp John L Rabb. m 5/18/1985 William Hamilton Byrne c 3.

BYRNE, Larry (LI) 21433 40th Ave., Bayside NY 11361 **All SS Ch Bayside NY 2006-** B Wilmington DE 1962 s Richard & Beatrice. BA U of Delaware 1985; MDiv VTS 1994. D 6/25/1994 P 12/9/1995 Bp Cabell Tennis. m 5/18/1996 Susan R Byrne c 1. Asst Ch Of The Resurr Kew Gardens NY 2006-2007; Assoc S Andr's Ch Stamford CT 2003-2004; Asst S Paul's Ch Riverside CT 2002-2004; R Chr Ch Easton CT 1999-2002; Cur S Paul's Ch Fairfield CT 1994-1999; DCE and Yth Chr Ch Christiana Hundred Greenville DE 1989-1990.

BYRUM, Emory Etheridge (Nwk) Trinity Episcopal Church, 6587 Upper York Rd. PO Box 377, Solebury PA 18963 **Int Trin Ch Solebury PA 2009-** B Portsmouth VA 1933 s Daniel & Grace. Chowan Coll Murfreesboro NC 1955; BA Carson-Newman Coll 1959; MDiv SE Bapt TS 1962; DMin UTS Virginia 1981. D 3/5/1994 Bp Jack Marston Mckelvey P 9/17/1994 Bp John Shelby Spong. c 3. Vic S Mary's Epis Ch Belvidere NJ 1994-2009; S Mary's Ch Belvidere NJ 1994-2005; Serv Bapt Ch 1962-1989; Pstr Three Virginia Ch. Cbury Schlr/P of the Year Dio Newark Conv 2000.

BYRUM, Philip Robert (NC) 1207 Cambridge Rd Nw, Wilson NC 27896 **Ret 2000-; Vic La Iglesia de la Guadalupana Wilson NC 2000-; Vic S Mk's Ch Wilson NC 1991-** B Durham NC 1941 s Robert & Ada. BA Greensboro Coll 1963; BD EDS 1966. D 6/29/1966 P 6/24/1967 Bp Thomas Augustus Fraser Jr. c 2. R S Tim's Ch Wilson NC 1991-2000; Stndg Com Dio No Carolina Raleigh NC 1983-1993, Liturg Cmsn 1969-1982; S Mary Magd Ch Troy NC 1982-1983; P-in-c S Mary Magd Ch Troy NC 1981-1987; R Chr Ch Albemarle NC 1969-1991; S Mich's Ch Tarboro NC 1966-1969; M-in-c St Marys Epis Ch Speed NC 1966-1969.

BYRUM, Rick Yervant (Los) 28648 Greenwood Pl, Castaic CA 91384 **Epis Communities & Serv Pasadena CA 2008-** B Pasadena CA 1955 s Richard &

June. BA Div Word Coll Epworth IA 1979; MDiv Cath Theol Un 1990. D 6/19/1999 P 1/8/2000 Bp Frederick Houk Borsch. m 2/25/1989 Anita Byrum. Ch Of The H Trin and S Ben Alhambra CA 2005-2008; S Jas Par Los Angeles CA 2001-2005.

C

CABALLERO, Daniel (Mil) 4305 Rolla Ln, Madison WI 53711 B Mercedes TX 1935 s Arcadio & Josephine. BA Sherwood Conservatory of Mus Chicago IL 1958; MA New Mex Highlands U 1965; MDiv Nash 1986. D 5/9/1986 P 1/10/1987 Bp Roger John White. m 6/25/1966 Gretchen L Caballero c 4. Mssnr - Hisp Mnstry Off Epis Ch Cntr New York NY 1999-2005; Int S Mk's Ch Beaver Dam WI 1995-1998; Int S Lk's Ch Madison WI 1994-1995; Hisp Mnstry-P-in-c Mision San Miguel Milwaukee WI 1990-1999; Chapl Epis City Msn Of Madison Inc Madison WI 1988-1999, P 1986; Chapl Univ. of Wisconsin & Veterans Admin. Hosp. Madison WI 1988-1994; Assoc S Barn Richland Ctr WI 1987-1988. Hisp. Mins. Mssnr - Ed, "Las fiestas menores y los días de ayuno - 2003," *Lesser Feasts & Fasts - 2003 (1st Spanish Ed)*, ECC Hisp. Mnstry Off, 2005. Phi Kappa Phi 1965. Cn Reformed Epis Ch of Spain, Madrid, Spain 2002.

CABANA, Denise E (Ct) 2584 Main St, Glastonbury CT 06033 **S Jas Ch Glastonbury CT 2015-** B Northampton MA 1961 d Norman & Jean. BA No Adams St Coll 1983; MA U of Maine 1985; MDiv VTS 2002. D 6/8/2002 Bp Andrew Donnan Smith P 1/25/2003 Bp Wilfrido Ramos-Orench. m 5/7/1994 Charles D Scott. P S Jas' Ch Indn Hd MD 2006-2015, P 2006-; Assoc R Trin Ch Branford CT 2002-2006.

CABEY, Lenroy Kirtley (VI) **S Andr's Ch St Thos VI 2004-** B 1961 s John & Sarah. Trans 2/27/2004. m 3/30/2004 Donnalie Bloise Carlene Cabey c 2.

CABRERA, Amador Fredy (Hond) IMS SAP Dept 215. PO Box 523900, Miami FL 22152 Honduras B Tegucigalpa, Honduras 1963 s Fredy. D 3/11/2007 Bp Lloyd Emmanuel Allen. m 12/10/1995 Doris Estela Rubio Ercobar c 3.

CABRERO-OLIVER, Juan M (LI) 443 Maren St, West Hempstead NY 11552 **Hisp Mnstry Asst 2009-** B San Juan, PR 1948 s Juan & Awilda. BA Ford 1970; MFA U of New Mex 1977; MDiv CDSP 1988; PhD Grad Theol Un Berkeley CA 2006. D 6/4/1988 P 12/1/1989 Bp William Edwin Swing. m 5/25/2016 Johnny Lorenzo. Dir, Hisp Prog The GTS New York NY 2002-2008; Dir, Mercer Sch Dio Long Island Garden City NY 2000-2006; Gd Shpd Epis Chap Garden City NY 2000-2006; Cn Mssnr Dio New Jersey Trenton NJ 1997-2000; Dir, Hisp Prog Epis Sch For Deacons Berkeley CA 1994-1995; Assoc for Hisp Mnstry Trin Cathd San Jose CA 1994; Int The Epis Ch Of S Jn The Evang San Francisco CA 1993-1994; S Aid's Mssn Bolinas CA 1990-1992; Asst S Mk's Epis Ch Palo Alto CA 1988-1990. Auth, "Ripe Fields: the Challenge and Promise of Latino Mnstry," Ch Pub, 2009; Auth, ""Our Place: Inculturating Liturg Space."," *The Chant of Life [Liturg Stds IV]*, Ch Pub, 2003; Auth, ""Why Gay Mar?," *Journ of Men's Stds, (IV, 3, 2/1996).*, Men's Stds Press, 1996; Auth, ""Just Praise: PB Revs and Hisp/Latino Anglicanism," *Liturg Stds III*, Ch Pub, 1996; Auth, ""Lang Shaped and Shaping,"" *How Shall We Pray? [Liturg Stds II]*, Ch Pub, 1994; Auth, "Towards a Theol of Gay Sprtl Dvlpmt," *HEART*, The Parsonage, 1986. No Amer Acad of Liturg 1990; Societas Liturgica 1990-2008; The AP 1986; The Intl Angl Liturg Consult 1990. Pres The AP 1990; Doctoral Fllshp The ECF 1990; Hisp Doctoral Grant Fund for Theol Educ 1989; Tchg Assistantship Grad Theol Un 1989; Tchg Assistantship Grad Theol Un 1988; M.F.A. Dissertation Prize Ford Fndt 1977.

CABUSH, David Walter (Nwk) 2 Pond Hill Rd # 7960, Morristown NJ 07960 **Int S Jn's Memi Ramsay NJ 2005-** B Racine WI 1942 s Walter & Gladys. BA San Diego St U 1964; MS San Diego St U 1968; PhD MI SU 1971; Cert Washington Sch of Psych 1990; MDiv PrTS 1994; ThM PrTS 1995; GTS 2002. D 9/20/2003 P 3/27/2004 Bp John Palmer Croneberger. m 6/9/1990 Diane Lynn Gabrielsen c 3. P Ch Of The Trsfg Towaco NJ 2009-2014; S Andr's Epis Ch Lincoln Pk NJ 2009-2014; S Jn's Memi Ch Ramsey NJ 2005-2009; Assoc S Ptr's Ch Morristown NJ 2003-2005.

CACOPERDO, Peter Anthony (RG) PO Box 1747, Elephant Butte NM 87935 **Mem Sierra Cnty Mnstrl Allnce 2003-** B Brooklyn NY 1941 s Anthony & Lucille. AA Nassau Cmnty Coll 1974; Lic Mercer Sch Dio. of Long Island 1977; Cert Mercer TS 1977; BA SUNY 2000. D 3/22/1980 P 10/18/1981 Bp Robert Campbell Witcher Sr. m 12/8/1962 Margaret Richards c 3. Int Desert Sprg ELCA Truth or Consequences NM 2011-2015; Int St Lk's Epis Ch Anth NM 2010-2011; Int St. Ptr's ELCA Carlsbad NM 2009; P-in-c Chr Ch Hillsboro NM 2003-2008; Vic St Pauls Epis Ch Truth Consq NM 2000-2008; R H Trin Epis Ch Hicksville NY 1994-2002; Int S Bon Epis Ch Lindenhurst NY 1992-1994, Assoc 1981-1992; Pres Sierra Cnty Mnstrl Allnce 2013-2015; Mem Bp's Search Com DRG 2009-2010; Dept Of Missions Dio Long Island Garden City NY 1997-1999.

CADARET, John Michael (Va) 8411 Freestone Ave, Richmond VA 23229 **Emm Ch Woodstock VA 2016-; S Andr's Ch Mt Jackson VA 2016-** B Richmond

VA 1967 s Albert & Sharon. LTh VTS 2003. D 6/14/2003 P 12/20/2003 Bp Peter J Lee. m 11/20/1993 Cari Ann Cadaret c 2. Assoc Gr & H Trin Epis Ch Richmond VA 2009-2014; P-in-c Varina Epis Ch Henrico VA 2006-2009; Asst. R All SS Epis Ch Jacksonville FL 2004-2006; Asst. R Trin Ch Upperville VA 2003-2004.

CADDELL, Christopher Len (WTex) The Episcopal Church of the Holy Spirit, 301 Hays Country Acres Rd, Dripping Springs TX 78620 **R The Ch Of The H Sprt Dripping Spgs TX 2012-** B Odessa TX 1976 s Len & Patricia. BS Texas A & M U 1999; MDiv Sewanee: The U So, TS 2010; MDiv The U So TS 2010. D 6/8/2010 Bp Gary Richard Lillibridge P 12/19/2010 Bp David Mitchell Reed. m 1/8/2000 Bryn S Caddell c 2. Asst S Alb's Ch Harlingen TX 2010-2012.

CADE, Wendy MP (At) 1323 N Dupont St, Wilmington DE 19806 **St Benedicts Epis Day Sch Smyrna GA 2015-; Gr Ch Asheville NC 2005-** B Atlanta GA 1979 d Everett & Arlene. BS Shorter Coll 2001; MDiv GTS 2005. D 12/21/2004 P 12/21/2004 Bp J Neil Alexander. m 4/17/2010 Shaun Russell Cade c 1. H Innoc' Epis Sch Atlanta GA 2011-2015; S Edw's Epis Ch Lawrenceville GA 2009-2011; S Anne's Epis Ch Atlanta GA 2007-2009; Chr Ch Christiana Hundred Wilmington DE 2005-2007.

CADENA, Enrique (Az) 2801 N 31st Street, Phoenix AZ 85008 **Vic Iglesia Epis De San Pablo Phoenix AZ 2015-; Dioc Coun Mem Dio Wstrn New York Tonawanda NY 2005-** B Mexico City Mexico 1952 s Ignacio & Cecilia. MA Colgate DS 1989. Rec 10/4/2003 Bp Michael Garrison. c 2. Dio Arizona Phoenix AZ 2008-2015; Chr Ch Albion NY 2005-2008; R S Paul's Ch Holley NY 2004-2008. "A Quest For Freedom," Olde Ridge Bk Pub, 1999.

CADIGAN, Charles Richard (Mo) 1625 Masters Drive, DeSoto TX 75115 B Northampton MA 1937 s Charles & Elizabeth. BA Wesl 1959; BA Wesl 1959; MDiv EDS 1962. D 6/20/1962 Bp Robert McConnell Hatch P 12/15/1962 Bp George Leslie Cadigan. m 3/21/1981 Linda Renasco c 4. Headmaster The Cbury Epis Sch DeSoto TX 2004-2008; Headmaster Trin Epis Sch Galveston TX 1994-2002; Tchr,Dn of Students,Headmaster Wooster Sch Danbury CT 1970-1980; Chapl/Dn/Prncpl/Headmaster Wooster Sch Danbury CT 1970-1979; R-St Eliz's Ch Ovrs Appointee(ECUSA) Dio Natal So Afr 1967-1970; Assoc Emm Epis Ch S Louis MO 1966-1967, Asst 1962-1966; R-St Jas Ch, Dioces of Natal Ch of the Prov of So Afr 1965-1966.

CADIGAN, Katherine (Los) 1227 4th St, Santa Monica CA 90401 **S Aug By-The-Sea Par Santa Monica CA 2014-** B Detroit MI 1961 d Charles & Sally. BA Br 1983; MA Stan 1995; MDiv and Angl Dplma Ya Berk 2014. D 6/7/2014 P 1/17/2015 Bp Joseph Jon Bruno. m 9/22/1990 Mark Andrew Vickers. katie@saint-augustine.org

CADWALLADER, Doug (Tex) PO Box 35303, Houston TX 77235 B Orlando FL 1944 s Harold & Lenora. BA LSU 1966; BS LSU 1972; MDiv VTS 1977; MA LSU 1994. D 5/18/1979 Bp James Milton Richardson P 11/1/1979 Bp Roger Howard Cilley. Asst S Thos Ch Houston TX 1996-2010; Non-par 1989-1996; R S Steph's Ch Liberty TX 1986-1989; Asst Trin Ch Houston TX 1981-1986; Chapl S Lk's Epis Hosp Houston TX 1981; Chr Ch Matagorda TX 1979-1981; Vic S Jn's Epis Ch Palacios TX 1979-1981; The Great Cmsn Fndt Houston TX 1979-1981.

CADWELL, Matthew P (Mass) 94 Newbury Ave Apt 309, Quincy MA 02171 **R Emm Epis Ch Wakefield MA 2008-; Adj Fac Trin U Tor 2007-; Stndg Com Dio Massachusetts Boston MA 2016-, Bdgt Com 2012-, Dioc Coun 2011-; Co-Pres, Alum/ae Exec Com EDS Cambridge MA 2014-, Alum/ae Exec Com 2012-2014; Natl Scandinavia Advsry Bd Gustavus Adolphus Coll 2014-; Pres Wakefield Interfaith Cler Assn 2010-** B Minneapolis MN 1972 s Peter & Mary Ann. BA Gustavus Adolphus Coll 1995; MDiv EDS 1999; PhD St Mich's Coll, U Tor 2013. D 6/12/2004 Bp M(Arvil) Thomas Shaw P 1/8/2005 Bp Gayle Harris. Assoc P Serv Angl Ch of Can 2004-2008; Ch Of S Jn The Evang Boston MA 1999-2001. Auth, "God w Us: The Story of Emm Epis Ch, Wakefield," God w Us: The Story of Emm Epis Ch, Wakefield, Vstry of Emm Ch, Wakefield, 2016; Auth, "EDS: A Pioneering Voice in Progressive Theol Educ," EDS Now, EDS, 2015; Auth, "The Philadelphia 11," Journ of the Can Ch Hist Soc, 2014; Auth, "Richard Hooker: The Incarn and the Foundations of Angl Comprehensiveness," Richard Hooker: His Life, Wk, and Legacy, St. Osmund Press, 2013; Auth, "A Juggling Act," Rel Stds News, AAR, 2006; Auth, "Epis City Mssn and Hsng: 65 Years of Commitment," All Things New, Epis City Mssn, 2004; Auth, "Called as Friends: Lutherans and Episcopalians Spend Sum Together," Epis Times, Dio Massachusetts, 2004; Auth, "From Word to Table: Acton Par Goes Back to the Future," Epis Times, Dio Massachusetts, 2004; Auth, "Revealing the Kingdom of Chr: The City Mssn¿s Wk w Immigrant Parishes, 1894-1959," All Things New, Epis City Mssn, 2002; Auth, "A Hist of EDS," A Hist of EDS, Trst of EDS, 2000; Auth, "In Memoriam: Lloyd Geo Patterson," EDS News, 1999. AAR 2003; Phillips Brooks Cler Club of Boston 2015; Soc of Schlr Priests 2013. Eileen and Geo Carey Awd in Angl Stds Angl Dio Toronto 2005; Doctoral Fllshp Trin, U Tor 2003; Bp Atwood of Arizona Awd in Ch Hist EDS 1999; Geo Hall Prize for Schlrshp in Rel Gustavus Adolphus Coll 1995; Phi Beta Kappa Gustavus Adolphus Coll 1995.

CADY, Donald Holmes (Va) Grace Episcopal Church, PO Box 43, Keswick VA 22947 B Montclair NJ 1938 s Donald & Patricia. BS Un Coll 1960. D 2/11/2012 Bp Shannon Sherwood Johnston. m 9/9/1961 Diane Hartman Cady c 2. D Emm Epis Ch Greenwood VA 2012-2014.

CADY III, Mark Stone (Dal) 650 Copper Creek Circle, Alpharetta GA 30004 **Non-par 1985-; Fin Advsr 21st Century Fin 2013-** B Warren PA 1943 s Mark & Marion. BAS NWU 1965; MDiv SWTS 1968. D 6/22/1968 Bp John Raymond Wyatt P 12/1/1968 Bp Jackson Earle Gilliam. m 12/19/1964 Diana Robinson c 2. P S Thos The Apos Ch Overland Pk KS 1976-1984; R S Barn Ch Garland TX 1974-1976; Ch Of Our Lady Of Gr Dallas TX 1973-1974; Cleric Our Lady Of Gr Dallas TX 1973-1974; S Mk's Ch Evanston IL 1972-1973; Cur S Mk's Epis Ch Glen Ellyn IL 1969-1972; D S Paul's Fishtail MT 1968-1969; Calv Epis Ch Red Lodge MT 1968; Dio Montana Helena MT 1968; Our Sav Epis Joliet MT 1968.

CAFFERATA, Gail Lee (NCal) 4794 Hillsboro Cir, Santa Rosa CA 95405 **Vstng Schlr The Grad Theol Un Berkeley CA 2013-; Vstng Resrch Bos TS Boston MA 2012-; Vstng Resrch Bos TS 2012-** B Brooklyn NY 1945 d Herbert & Ruth. BA SUNY 1966; MA SUNY 1969; PhD U Chi 1974; MDiv EDS 1997. D 6/7/1997 Bp M(Arvil) Thomas Shaw P 4/14/2002 Bp Jerry Alban Lamb. m 6/10/1967 Robert Cafferata c 2. Ch Of The Incarn Santa Rosa CA 2010-2011, Asst 2002-2003, 2001-2002; P-in-c H Fam Epis Ch Rohnert Pk CA 2003-2012; Assoc Ch Of The Gd Shpd Watertown MA 1999-2000; Asst S Ptr's Ch Weston MA 1998-1999; D All SS Par Brookline MA 1997-1998. Auth, "Respect, Challenges and Stress among Prot Pastors Closing a Ch: Structural and Identity Theol Perspectives," Pstr Psychol, Pstr Psychol, 2017. gailc@bu.edu

CAFFREY, David (Los) PO Box 514, Joshua Tree CA 92252 **R Trin Epis Ch Redlands CA 2006-** B Tuscon AZ 1947 s Howard & Violet. AA California Cmnty Coll; BA California St U; MDiv EDS 1974; STM GTS 2007. D 6/15/1974 P 1/4/1975 Bp Robert Claflin Rusack. m 5/31/2008 Louisa Parker Young c 1. Trin Epis Ch Redlands CA 2005-2012; Dio Los Angeles Los Angeles CA 1999-2005, 1974-1975; P S Jos Of Arimathea Mssn Yucca Vlly CA 1999-2000; R S Fran Of Assisi Par Sn Bernrdno CA 1986-1999; Chapl Police Dept 1981-1985; R S Alb's Ch Worland WY 1981-1985; Reg Vic S Jn The Evang Mssn Needles CA 1974-1981. "The Daily Off in the Ch Today," Unpublished MS, 2007; Auth, Songs of the Desert, 1983. CREDO Fac Mem 2006; Desert Journeys 1986; Friends of St. Ben 2003; OHC 1978. Cn of Cathd Dio Los Angeles 2006.

CAGE JR, Stewart B (La) 8932 Fox Run Ave, Baton Rouge LA 70808 B Baton Rouge LA 1943 s Stewart & Eleanor. D 9/29/2000 P 11/14/2001 Bp Charles Edward Jenkins III. m 3/3/1991 Diane Thomas. P-in-c S Aug's Ch Baton Rouge LA 2007-2011; P-in-c S Mich's Ch Baton Rouge LA 2004-2011.

CAGGIANO, Diane Ruth (Ct) 11 Overvale Rd, Wolcott CT 06716 **D S Jn's Epis Ch Bristol CT 2011-** B Waterbury CT 1944 d Frederick & Ruth. BA Cntrl Connecticut St U 1990. D 9/17/2005 Bp Andrew Donnan Smith. m 6/4/1966 Robert Caggiano c 2. D S Andr's Ch Meriden CT 2005-2011.

CAGGIANO, Joyce (Mass) 27 Curtis Rd., Milton MA 02186 **Acctg Mgr, Epis City Mssn Dio Massachusetts Boston MA 2008-** B Bethpage NY 1949 d Armand & Renee. BA U of Massachusetts 1982; MDiv Yale DS 1985; Harv 1996; PhD Un Inst & U Cincinnati OH 2000. D 6/4/1986 Bp John Bowen Coburn P 6/20/1987 Bp David Elliot Johnson. c 2. Asst S Mich's Ch Milton MA 2013-2014; Epis City Mssn Boston MA 2008-2010, 1992-1993; P-in-c S Paul's Ch Peabody MA 2007-2013; Ch Of Our Sav Arlington MA 2006-2007; Exec Dir, Epis Cmnty Serv Dio Michigan Detroit MI 2002-2004; Chr Ch Grosse Pointe Grosse Pointe Farms MI 2002; Crossroads Of Michigan Mnstrs Detroit MI 2000-2002; Cathd Ch Of S Paul Detroit MI 2000; S Paul's Ch Newburyport MA 1996-2000; Serv Convoc Of Amer Ch In Europe - Germany 1994-1996; R Gr Ch Everett MA 1988-1992; The Cathd Ch Of S Paul Boston MA 1986-1989. Auth, "No God, No Mstr," Rel Socialism, 2001; Auth, "Who Will Be The Teachers?," Ch Eductr, 1979. Epis Cmnty Serv Of Amer, Treas 2002-2004; Treas EWC Mass Chapt; Treasurerurer 1999-2000; Treas Phillips Brooks Cler 1998-2000; VP Merrimack Vlly Proj 1998-2000. Merrill Fell Harvard DS 1996.

CAGUIAT, Carlos J (Mich) 10901 176 Circle NE apt 2421, Redmond WA 98052 **Assoc Ch Of The H Cross Redmond WA 2015-; Ret 2002-** B New York NY 1937 s Carlos & Carmen. BA CUNY 1958; MDiv GTS 1965; MPA NYU 1976. D 6/12/1965 P 12/18/1965 Bp Horace W B Donegan. m 8/29/1958 Julianna Skomsky c 3. P-in-c Ch Of The Gd Shpd Elizabethtown NY 1994-1996; Assoc The Ch of St Lk The Beloved Physcn Saranac Lake NY 1992-2014; S Fran Cmnty Serv Inc. Salina KS 1990-2002; Reg VP The S Fran Acad Lake Placid NY 1990-2002; S Annes Ch Dewitt MI 1987-1990; R Ch Of The Gd Shpd Wakefield Bronx NY 1976-1981; 1972-1975; Exec Dir, Proj for Human Cmnty Dio New York New York NY 1971-1973; Cur, St. Chris's Chap Trin Par New York NY 1965-1967; Fin Com Dio NY> NY 1969-1970; Chair, Chidren's Div, CE Dio NY. NY 1966-1970. SSJE Assoc 2003. Distinguished ROTC Grad ROTC Alum Assoication City Coll of NY 2014; Commendation Medal U.S. Army 1962.

CAGUIAT, Julianna (Oly) 20 Oakwood Road, Saranac Lake NY 12983 **D Asst The Ch of St Lk The Beloved Physcn Saranac Lake NY 1997-** B New York NY 1940 d William & Evelyn. BS CUNY 1975. D 12/20/1997 Bp David Standish Ball. m 8/29/1958 Carlos J Caguiat c 3. SSJE Assoc 2003.

CAHILL, Patricia Ann Bytnar (ETenn) 317 Windy Hollow Dr, Chattanooga TN 37421 B Pittsburgh PA 1944 d Leonard & Josephine. BA Seton Hill U 1965; PhD U of Tennessee 1969; MDiv VTS 1998. D 6/13/1998 P 1/25/1999 Bp Robert Gould Tharp. m 11/29/1997 Edward Eugene Cahill c 2. R Thankful Memi Ch Chattanooga TN 2000-2007; Dio E Tennessee Knoxville TN 1999; S Fran Of Assisi Epis Ch Ooltewah TN 1998-1999.

CAHOON, Vernon John (NC) 428 Pee Dee Ave, Albemarle NC 28001 B Fall River MA 1957 s Vernon & Constance. BA U of Massachusetts 1979; JD NEU 1986. D 6/19/2010 Bp Michael B Curry. m 2/27/1987 Lori Earls-Cahoon c 4.

CAIMANO, Catherine Anne (NC) 13804 Hill St, Huntersville NC 28078 **CEO Free Range P Huntersville NC 2016**- B St Louis MO 1966 d Nicholas & Barbara. BS Geo 1989; MDiv GTS 1999. D 6/19/1999 Bp James Gary Gloster P 1/22/2000 Bp Robert Carroll Johnson Jr. m 11/29/2014 Jeffrey J Haas c 1. Cn for Reg Mnstry Dio No Carolina Raleigh NC 2011-2015; R S Jn's Ch Wichita KS 2007-2011; Assoc R S Phil's Ch Durham NC 2001-2007; Cur Ch Of The H Trin New York NY 1999-2001; Fac, Kansas Sch of Mnstry Dio Kansas Topeka KS 2008-2011. Auth, "Free Range P: Ord Mnstry Reimagined in the 21st Century," Lulu Press, 2017; Auth, "Many Signs And Wonders: A Travel Guide For You," Dom & Frgn Mssy Soc, 2000; Auth, "Epis Ch Q & A'S," Fmp, 1999. Mdiv Wth hon GTS 1999. frcathie@freerangepriest.org

CAIN, Donavan G (Fla) St Mark's Episcopal Church, 4129 Oxford Ave, Jacksonville FL 32210 B Corbin KY 1974 s Billy & Debra. BS Un Coll 1997; MA Appalachian St U 2001; MDiv GTS 2007. D 6/9/2007 P 12/21/2007 Bp Stacy F Sauls. m 12/26/2013 Audrey Bridget Cain c 3. All SS Epis Ch Jacksonville FL 2013, R 2013-; S Mk's Epis Ch Jacksonville FL 2010-2012; R S Ptr's Ch Paris KY 2007-2010; Dep-GC Dio Lexington Lexington 2008-2009, Lay Coll Chapl 2003-2007. The SocMary 2008. dcain@asejax.com

CAIN JR, Everett Harrison (Tex) 7705 Merrybrook Circle, Austin TX 78731 B Humble TX 1936 s Everett & Doris. BS Lamar U 1960; BD Austin Presb TS 1963. D 11/23/1966 Bp Everett H Jones P 3/1/1967 Bp Richard Earl Dicus. m 9/2/1955 Paula Marilyn Cain c 1. The Ch of the Gd Shpd Austin TX 1986-1999; R Trin Ch Houston TX 1978-1986; R S Alb's Epis Ch Waco TX 1974-1978; Asst S Jn The Div Houston TX 1970-1974; R Trin Epis Ch Pharr TX 1969-1970; Cur S Lk's Epis Ch San Antonio TX 1966-1969; Serv Presb Ch 1963-1965.

CAIN, George Robert (SwFla) 1813 Echo Pond Pl, Wesley Chapel FL 33543 B Boston MA 1938 s Carroll & Mildred. BA Mid 1960; MDiv EDS 1964; ThM PrTS 1975. D 6/20/1964 Bp Anson Phelps Stokes Jr P 1/10/1965 Bp Lauriston L Scaife. m 12/17/1966 Polly Cain c 2. Vic Gr Ch Tampa FL 2000-2004; Dioc Stff Dio SW Florida Parrish FL 1997-2000, Chair Coll Wk Com 1988-1996; Epis Cntr Chapl and Dir U of So Florida at Tampa Tampa FL 1987-1997; Int S Paul's Ch Natick MA 1987; Ch Of Our Sav Boston MA 1986; St Albans Sch Cathd of St Ptr & St Paul Washington DC 1979-1985; Day Sch Chapl/Chair Rel Dept S Alb's Sch Washington DC 1979-1985; Pstr Assoc S Dunst's Ch Tulsa OK 1974-1979; Chapl Holland Hall Sch Tulsa OK 1973-1979; Chapl Holland Hall Sch Tulsa OK 1973-1979; Chapl Salisbury Sch Salisbury CT 1966-1973. OHC, Assoc 1975-2005.

CAIRES, Joy MarieLouise (Minn) 12671 Woodside Drive, Chesterland OH 44026 **P S Clem's Ch S Paul MN 2014-; pediatric Chapl Luth Chapl Serv Cleveland OH 2006**- B Kahului Maui HI 1978 d Gordon & Sallie. BA Smith 2000; MDiv EDS 2006. D 6/3/2006 P 1/9/2007 Bp Mark Hollingsworth Jr. m 9/4/2004 Lona Caires. Ch Of Our Sav Akron OH 2008-2011; Luth Chapl Serv Cleveland OH 2006-2008.

CAIRNS, John C (Alb) 316 Valentine Pond Road, Pottersville NY 12860 **D Vic Adirondack Mssn Pottersville NY 2015**- B Delhi NY 1956 s Leonard & Lillian. Associated New York St U 1977; Assoc New York St U 1977. D 5/31/2014 Bp William Howard Love. m 9/27/1980 Nancy L Cairns c 2.

CALAFAT, Karen A (Los) 2647 Mayflower Ave, Arcadia CA 91006 **S Lk's In The Meadow Epis Ch Ft Worth TX 2014-; Chapl Hillsides 2004**- B Texas 1964 D 6/19/2004 P 1/22/2005 Bp Joseph Jon Bruno. m 10/2/1993 Philip Paul Calafat c 2. The Reverend S Jas' Par So Pasadena CA 2004-2006; Hillsides Educ Cntr Pasadena CA 2004; Chapl Hillsides Pasadena CA 1999-2004.

CALCOTE, A(Lan) Dean (Tex) 5615 Duff St, Beaumont TX 77706 **Chair Exam Chapl Dio Texas Houston TX 1995-, COM 1995-, Chair Dioc Schools Cmsn 1978-2013** B Shreveport LA 1933 s Aucie & Patty. BA Tul 1955; MDiv GTS 1958; STM GTS 1963. D 6/21/1958 Bp Iveson Batchelor Noland P 5/8/1959 Bp Girault M Jones. c 2. Headmaster All SS Epis Sch Beaumont TX 1974-1998; Assoc S Mk's Ch Beaumont TX 1974-1998; Asst Headmaster Epis HS Baton Rouge LA 1969-1974; Asst R All SS Epis Sch Vicksburg MS 1965-1969; Chapl All SS Epis Sch Vicksburg MS 1963-1965; The GTS New York NY 1961-1963; Cur S Paul's Ch New Orleans LA 1958-1961. Auth, "The Proposed PB of 1785," *Hist mag of the Prot Epis Ch, Vol XLVI*, 1977. Citation for Outstanding Serv to Epis Schools SW Assn of Epis Schools 2007; Citation for Outstanding Serv to Epis Schools NAES 1998; STB cl GTS 1958; Phi Beta Kappa Tul 1955.

CALDBECK, Elaine S (Ia) 2400 Middle Rd, Bettendorf IA 52722 **S Ptr's Ch Bettendorf IA 2017-; Instr, Resrch Methods SWTS Evanston IL 2004**- B Des Moines IA 1957 d Velma. BS Iowa St U 1980; MS U MN 1987; MDiv

SWTS 1995; MA Garrett-Evang TS 1996; PhD NWU 2000. D 6/19/2004 P 12/18/2004 Bp Bill Persell. S Mk's Epis Ch Ft Dodge IA 2015-2016; The Epis Ch Of The Ascen Middletown OH 2009-2015; Dio Chicago Chicago IL 2006-2008, Admin, Bp Search 2006-; Asstg Cler S Matt's Ch Evanston IL 2005-2006. "The Poetry of Pauli Murray: Afr Amer Civil Rts Lawyer and P," Ruether Fortress Press, 2002. saintpetersbettendorf@gmail.com

CALDWELL, Brenda Ann (Wyo) 1167 Hidalgo Dr, Laramie WY 82072 B Tampa FL 1948 d George & Lillian. AA S Petersburg Cmnty Coll 1968; BA U of So Florida 1996. D 12/30/1999 Bp Bruce Caldwell. m 12/13/1971 Bruce Caldwell c 2. Cathd Hm For Chld Laramie WY 2003-2007; Dio Wyoming Casper 1999-2002.

✠ CALDWELL, The Rt Rev Bruce (Wyo) 104 S 4th St, Laramie WY 82070 B Painesville OH 1947 s Robert & Lois. BA U of So Florida 1973; MDiv GTS 1978; GTS 1998. D 6/22/1978 P 3/1/1979 Bp Emerson Paul Haynes Con 9/26/1997 for Wyo. m 12/13/1971 Brenda Ann Caldwell c 1. Int Cathd Ch Of S Mk Minneapolis MN 2012-2014; Ret Bp of Wyoming Dio Wyoming Casper 2010, Bp Of Wyoming 1997-2010; R S Geo's Epis Ch Bismarck ND 1991-1997; Dio Alaska Fairbanks AK 1989-1991; R S Steph's Ch Ft Yukon AK 1989-1991; R S Jas Hse Of Pryr Tampa FL 1984-1989; St Johns Epis Ch Tampa FL 1981-1984, Asst 1978-1979; S Thos Epis Christiansbrg VA 1979-1980. bishop@diolex.org

CALDWELL, Edward Frederick (Alb) 100 Farmington Dr, Camillus NY 13031 **Ret 1991**- B Rochester NY 1926 s Francis & Winifred. BA U Roch 1949; STB GTS 1959; STM GTS 1989. D 6/8/1952 P 12/1/1952 Bp Dudley S Stark. c 4. S Paul's Ch Bloomville NY 1986-1991; S Ptr's Ch Stamford NY 1982-1983; R Chr Ch Walton NY 1975-1991; R Trin Ch Gouverneur NY 1967-1975; Vic S Hilda's - S Pat's Epis Ch Edmonds WA 1964-1967; Assoc S Lk's Epis Ch Seattle WA 1963-1964; Chapl Nthrn St Hosp Sedro-Woolley WA 1958-1963; P-in-c S Jas Ch Sedro Woolley WA 1958-1963; Cur S Paul's Epis Ch Indianapolis IN 1956-1958; S Paul's Ch Angelica NY 1952-1956; P-in-c S Phil's Ch Belmont NY 1952-1956. Auth, "Chr Affirmations," 1996. Assoc, OHC 1980; Ch Cmncatn Ntwk.

CALDWELL, George M (Va) 501 Slaters Ln Apt 521, Alexandria VA 22314 B Dublin IE 1951 s Robert & Martha. BA Cor 1973; MA U CA 1974; MDiv VTS 1998. D 6/13/1998 P 4/15/1999 Bp Peter J Lee. m 7/12/2003 Kathleen G Caldwell. Assoc S Paul's Epis Ch Alexandria VA 1998-2006.

CALDWELL, James Hardy (Chi) 1307nW Logan St, Freeport IL 61032 B Chicago IL 1936 s W Wendell & Josephine. BA Cor 1958; BD VTS 1964. D 6/26/1964 Bp Philip Frederick McNairy P 3/1/1965 Bp Donald H V Hallock. c 1. The Epis Ch in Hawaii Honolulu HI 2009-2010; Asst S Fran' Par Palos Verdes Estates CA 2007-2009; Gr Epis Ch New Lenox IL 2005-2006; Int Chr Ch Joliet IL 1998-2000; Asst S Giles' Ch Northbrook IL 1984-1986; Asst S Chris Milwaukee WI 1964-1967.

CALDWELL, Margaret Caldwell (ETenn) 1264 Duane Rd, Chattanooga TN 37405 B Chattanooga TN 1952 d Christopher & Joanne. BSN Van 1975; M Div TS 1997; M Div Sewanee: The U So, TS 1997. D 5/31/1997 Bp Robert Gould Tharp. ED / Fndr The Sanctuary 2002-2007; S Ptr's Ch Chattanooga TN 1999-2002; Ch Of The Gd Samar Knoxville TN 1997-1999.

CALDWELL, Michael L (Tex) 1430 N Mound St, Nacogdoches TX 75961 **Chr Ch Nacogdoches TX 2016**- B Abilene TX 1967 s James & Ruby. BS Trin U San Antonio 1989; BS Trin U San Antonio 1989; MBA Schiller Intl U 1992; MBA Schiller Intl U 1992; MDiv Sewanee: The U So, TS 2009. D 12/20/2008 P 8/8/2009 Bp C Wallis Ohl. m 9/21/2002 Dawn M Caldwell. Zion Epis Ch Oconomowoc WI 2012-2015; Cur Trin Epis Ch Ft Worth TX 2009-2011; Trst of Funds and Endowments Epis Dio Milwaukee 2013-2015; Dnry Rep to Exec Coun Dio Ft Worth TX 2010-2011; Trst Sewanee U So TS Sewanee TN 2010-2011. michael@cc-nac.org

CALDWELL, Steve (RG) 9632 Allande Rd. NE, Albuquerque NM 87109 B Springfield OH 1938 s Russell & Cora. BA OH SU 1960; MDiv GTS 1969. D 6/7/1969 P 12/10/1969 Bp Horace W B Donegan. m 12/30/1972 Barbara J Caldwell c 3. R S Chad's Epis Ch Albuquerque NM 1989-2003; R S Agnes Ch Sebring FL 1978-1988; Assoc All SS Epis Ch Lakeland FL 1973-1978; Cur/Headmaster S Paul's Ch Winter Haven FL 1969-1973.

CALDWELL, Wallace Franklin (Mo) 1115 Woodleigh Ct, Harrisonburg VA 22802 B Saint Louis MO 1947 s Robert & Martha. BA Cor 1970; MDiv Bex Sem 1974. D 7/10/1974 P 6/1/1976 Bp Ned Cole. Trin Epis Ch Kirksville MO 2001-2009; S Jn's Ch Fremont MI 1999-2001; All SS Epis Ch Columbia Falls MT 1997-1998; P-in-c Ch Of The Gd Shpd Forrest City AR 1994-1996; Ch of the Redeem Addison NY 1989-1990; S Paul's Ch Montour Falls NY 1987-1994; P-in-c S Paul's Montour Falls NY 1986-1994; P-in-c S Mk's Ch Candor NY 1982-1986; Trin Ch Lowville NY 1978-1980; P-in-c Ch Of The Epiph Trumansburg NY 1976-1978; Non-par 1974-1976. Phi Beta Kappa.

CALER, Joshua Morgan (Tenn) 900 Broadway, Nashville TN 37203 B Sewickley PA 1982 s Jerry & Laura. BA Grove City Coll 2004; MDiv Duke DS 2011. D 6/4/2011 Bp Shannon Sherwood Johnston P 1/7/2012 Bp John Bauerschmidt. m 7/24/2004 Mary E Caler c 1. Cur Chr Ch Cathd Nashville TN 2011-2016.

CALEY BOWERS, Elizabeth Ann Ann (Fla) 9252 San Jose Blvd. Apt. 3703, Jacksonville FL 32257 **D Gr Epis Orange Pk FL 2011**- B Kingsport TN

1937 d Arthur & Helen. BA Katharine Gibbs Sch 1957. D 7/7/1993 Bp Harry Woolston Shipps. c 3. D Chr Ch San Pablo Jacksonville 2007-2011; D St. Jn's Catherdral Jacksonville FL 2005-2007; D S Paul's By-The-Sea Epis Ch Jaxville Bch FL 2002-2005; Bp's D S Marg of Scotland Moultrie GA 2000-2002; D Dio Georgia Savannah GA 1993-2002; S Thos Epis Ch Thomasville GA 1993-2000.

CALHOUN, Annie (Los) 2400 N Canal St, Orange CA 92865 **Assoc Trin Epis Ch Orange CA 2014-** B Burbank CA 1961 d Frederick & Marie. BA U CA 1984; MDiv Claremont TS 2014. D 6/7/2014 P 1/17/2015 Bp Joseph Jon Bruno. m 11/22/2016 James T Calhoun c 1. annie@trinityorange.org

CALHOUN, Dolores Moore (CPa) Po Box 32, Jersey Mills PA 17739 **D Trin 1998-** B Williamsport PA 1941 d Amos & Susan. BS Lock Haven U 1963; Denai St 1973; Cert Pennsylvania Diac Sch 1985; CPE Hershey Med Cntr 1987. D 6/10/1988 Bp Charlie Fuller Mcnutt Jr P 10/6/2007 Bp Nathan Dwight Baxter. m 7/17/1964 Larry David Calhoun c 1. D S Mk's Epis Ch Lewistown PA 1992-1993.

CALHOUN JR, Joseph William (ETenn) 9420 States View Dr, Knoxville TN 37922 **R Ch Of The Gd Samar Knoxville TN 2005-** B Omaha NE 1963 s Joseph & JoAnne. Rice U 1983; BS U of Sthrn Mississippi 1986; MDiv Epis TS of the SW 2002. D 6/1/2002 P 12/28/2002 Bp Duncan Montgomery Gray III. m 9/22/1990 Anna Calhoun c 2. Cur Ch Of The Nativ Greenwood MS 2002-2005.

CALHOUN, Nancy Ellen (Del) 31 Dresner Cir, Boothwyn PA 19061 B Hartford WI 1947 d Allen & Ann. BA U of Wisconsin 1971; MDiv SWTS 1981; DMin Chicago TS 1992. D 6/2/1983 Bp James Winchester Montgomery P 12/13/1986 Bp Frank Tracy Griswold III. Assoc The Ch Of The Ascen Claymont DE 2007-2009; S Dav's Epis Ch Wilmington DE 2002; Dio Delaware Wilmington 1998; Brandywine Epis Parishes Wilmington DE 1996-1997; R Calv Epis Ch Hillcrest Wilmington DE 1996-1997; S Gabr The Archangel Ch Vernon Hills IL 1992-1995; Pstr Assoc S Aug's Epis Ch Wilmette IL 1984-1991.

CALHOUN, Ora Albert (WK) 26627 Midland Rd, Bay Village OH 44140 B Aurora OH 1941 s Charles & Winifred. Cleveland St U; LTh VTS 1972. D 6/17/1972 P 5/12/1973 Bp John Harris Burt. c 3. S Alb Epis Ch Cleveland OH 2004-2007; LocTen S Phil's Epis Ch Topeka KS 1994-1995; S Fran Cmnty Serv Inc. Salina KS 1991-2004; Reg VP St Fran Acad Atchison KS 1991-2003; S Lk's Epis Ch Niles OH 1987-1989; Dio Ohio Cleveland 1980-1991; Asst to Bp for Yth Dio Ohio Cleveland OH 1980-1991; Exec Dir Cedar Hills Conf Dio Ohio Cleveland OH 1980-1991; Dio Ohio Cleveland OH 1977-1980; Vic S Matt's Ch Ashland OH 1973-1980.

CALHOUN, Robert Clay (Kan) D 6/17/2017 Bp George Wayne Smith.

CALHOUN, Royce (WTex) 103 Bluff Vista, Boerne TX 78006 **Psych Priv Counslg Pract San Antonio TX 2006-** B Kaufman TX 1938 s Grover & Sarah. BS E Texas Bapt U 1961; MDiv SW Bapt TS 1965; ThM SW Bapt TS 1968; ThD SW Bapt TS 1972; PhD SW Bapt TS 1975. D 3/3/1993 Bp Earl Nicholas Mc Arthur Jr P 12/20/1993 Bp John Herbert MacNaughton. m 7/7/1985 Angeline Harrington Williams. S Mich And All Ang Epis Ch Blanco TX 1994-2012; Vic S Lk's Ch Cypress Mill TX 1994-2006; Asst St Fran Epis Ch San Antonio TX 1993-1994; Clncl Dir Ecum Cntr for Rel and Hlth San Antonio TX 1990-2006; Psych Priv Counslg Pract San Antonio TX 1982-1990; Adj Instr St. Mary's Univeristy San Antonio TX 1978-1991; Counslr Trin Bapt Ch San Antonio TX 1977-1982; Adj Prof Webster U St. Louis MO 1976-2012; Pstr Care/Counslr First Bapt Ch San Antonio TX 1972-1977. Amer Assn for Mar and Fam Ther 1976; AAPC 1974; Amer Assn of Sex Educators 1978; Soc for the Advancement of Sexual Hlth 2007. Outstanding Contribution Awd SW Reg, AAPC, 1999.

CALHOUN III, William Brown (WTex) 355 Marina Dr, Port Aransas TX 78373 B Camden NJ 1933 s William & Evelyn. Leh 1952; Rutgers The St U of New Jersey 1953; Rutgers The St U of New Jersey 1959; STh Epis TS of the SW 1982. D 6/17/1982 Bp Scott Field Bailey P 1/1/1983 Bp Stanley Fillmore Hauser. m 11/29/1958 Judith Calhoun. Int Trin-By-The-Sea Port Aransas TX 1998-2001; S Helena's Epis Ch Boerne TX 1985-1998; Assoc S Lk's Epis Ch San Antonio TX 1982-1984. HSEC.

CALHOUN-BRYANT, Julie Elizabeth (CNY) Po Box 91, Camillus NY 13031 **S Alb's Ch Syracuse NY 2006-** B Albany NY 1961 d Francis & Dagmar. AAS Corning Cmnty Coll 1980; BA Hobart and Wm Smith Colleges 1982; MDiv Ya Berk 1988. D 6/18/1988 P 6/17/1989 Bp O'Kelley Whitaker. m 5/17/1986 Brian Russell Calhoun-Bryant. S Jn's Ch Marcellus NY 2006, 2002-2006; R S Lk's Epis Ch Camillus NY 1995-2002; Asst S Paul's Ch Endicott NY 1991-1995; Int Dio Cntrl New York Liverpool NY 1989-1991; D S Paul And S Jas New Haven CT 1988-1989. Ba mcl Wm Smith 1982.

CALKINS, Linda R (WA) 10617 Eastwood Ave, Silver Spring MD 20901 **S Barth's Ch Gaithersburg MD 2010-** B Long Island NY 1955 d Willis & Jeanne. MA Washington Theol Un 1999; MS Loyola Coll 2000; MDiv VTS 2001. D 6/9/2001 Bp Jane Hart Holmes Dixon P 1/19/2002 Bp Allen Lyman Bartlett Jr. c 2. Int S Jn's In The Mountains Stowe VT 2008-2009; P-in-c S Lk's Ch Washington DC 2007-2008; Asst R S Jn's Ch Olney MD 2001-2004.

CALKINS, Matthew H(amilton)) (NY) PO Box 366, Millbrook NY 12545 **Gr Ch Millbrook NY 2014-** B Los Angeles CA 1955 s Richard & Marylou. BA Mid 1977; MDiv UTS 1998. D 6/13/1998 P 12/19/1998 Bp Richard Frank

Grein. m 6/23/1984 Mary Anne Bulakowski c 1. R S Tim's Ch Fairfield CT 2001-2014; Chr And H Trin Ch Westport CT 1998-2001. Ba w hon Mid 1977.

CALLAGHAN, Alice Dale (Los) 307 E 7th St, Los Angeles CA 90014 **Las Familias Del Pueblo Los Angeles CA 1994-; Non-par 1981-** B Calgary AB CA 1947 d Henry & Olga. D 6/20/1981 P 1/1/1982 Bp Robert Claflin Rusack.

CALLAGHAN, Carol L (Eas) 308 Elm Ave, Easton MD 21601 B Baltimore MD 1946 d James & Marilynn. BA U of Charleston 1975; MA MD Consortium of Grad Wk Rockville MD 1983. D 7/23/2005 Bp Bud Shand. m 7/8/1989 Kevin Thomas Callaghan c 1. D Chr Ch S Ptr's Par Easton MD 2008-2014.

CALLAHAM, Arthur A (Tex) 6167 Olympia Drive, Houston TX 77057 **Vic Chr Ch Cathd Houston TX 2014-** B Arlington Heights IL 1975 s Arnold & Ruth Anne. BS VPI 1997; MS VPI 2000; MDiv U Chi DS 2006. D 6/24/2006 P 1/27/2007 Bp John L Rabb. m 6/14/2003 Erica L Callaham c 2. R S Cyp's Ch Lufkin TX 2009-2014. acallaham@christchurchcathedral.org

CALLAHAN, Gary Edward (ETenn) Po Box 21275, Chattanooga TN 37424 B New York NY 1943 s Frederick & Catherine. BA Col 1964; STB GTS 1969; DMin Sewanee: The U So, TS 1982. D 6/7/1969 P 12/1/1969 Bp Horace W B Donegan. m 12/27/1969 Barbara J Callahan c 2. R S Mart Of Tours Epis Ch Chattanooga TN 1998-2008; Chapl S Anne's Mead Hm Southfield MI 1977-1998; R S Dav's Ch Southfield MI 1977-1998; Vic Ch of the H Sprt Belmont MI 1974-1976; Dio Wstrn Michigan Kalamazoo MI 1974-1976; Asst S Lk's Par Kalamazoo MI 1969-1974. Auth, "Together In Life & Death".

CALLARD, Tom Adams (WMass) 35 Chestnut St, Springfield MA 01103 **Dio Wstrn Massachusetts Springfield 2013-** B Burlington VT 1967 BA U of Massachusetts. D 1/10/2004 P 9/10/2004 Bp M(Arvil) Thomas Shaw. m 7/27/2003 Sagrario C Callard c 4. R All SS Par Los Angeles CA 2007-2013; Vic S Lk's/San Lucas Epis Ch Chelsea MA 2004-2007.

CALLAWAY, James Gaines (NY) 549 W 123rd St Apt 13A, New York NY 10027 **Trst The Constable Fund 2012-; Gnrl Secy Colleges & Universities of the Angl Comm New York NY 2011-; Chair Emer Psych & Sprtlty Inst 1998-** B Kansas City MO 1944 s James & Martha-Hall. BA U So 1966; MDiv GTS 1969; DD U So 2008. D 11/28/1970 Bp Edward Randolph Welles II P 7/1/1971 Bp Paul Moore Jr. m 5/20/1972 Mary Callaway c 2. Pres CEEP San Antonio TX 2004-2007; Chair, TS Vstng Com U So Sewanee TN 2002-2003; Mem Coun of Angl Provinces in Afr CAPA Nairobi Kenya 1988-2011; Trin Par New York NY 1980-2011, Dep Emer 1980; The Ch Of The Annunc Oradell NJ 1980, 1975-1980; Asst S Paul's Ch Englewood NJ 1973-1975; Asst S Mary's Manhattanville Epis Ch New York NY 1970-1973. Auth, "How Is a Preschool Evacuated?," *Trin News*, Trin Ch, 2001; Auth, "Article," *Sprtly of Endwmt*, Consortium of Endowed Parishes, 1994; Auth, "Article," *Endwmt: Friend or Foe*, Consortiumn of Endowed Parishes, 1987. Soc of S Marg 1982. St. Aug's Cross Archbp of Cbury 2015; Hon Cn Dio Cape Coast, Ghana 2009; Chairman Emer Psychotheapy Spiritualty Inst 2008; Prov Cn Ch of the Prov of Sthrn Afr 2004. jcallaway@cuac.org

CALLAWAY, Richard H (At) 6513 Blue Creek Ct, Douglasville GA 30135 **S Mich's Ch Raleigh NC 1987-** B Bluefield WV 1946 s Murray & Ellen. BA VPI 1969; MDiv GTS 1984; Cert SWTS 2003. D 6/23/1984 Bp Peter J Lee P 6/29/1985 Bp Robert Whitridge Estill. m 12/7/1991 Cecelia Wynn White c 2. Cn To The Ordnry Dio Atlanta Atlanta GA 2001-2014, Pres Of Stndg Com 1998-2000; R S Julian's Epis Ch Douglasville GA 1991-2001; Asst Ch Of The Nativ Raleigh NC 1987-1991; Asst To R Ch Of The Gd Shpd Rocky Mt NC 1984-1987.

CALLENDER, Francis Charles (SJ) 1060 Cottage Ave, Manteca CA 95336 B Limerick IR 1948 s Francis & Alberta. BA Trin Dublin IE 1970; Trin Dublin IE 1971; MA Trin Dublin IE 1973; GOE Ireland Theol Coll Ie 1979. Trans 1/1/1989 Bp David Mercer Schofield. m 3/17/1976 Susan Elizabeth Anderson c 2. S Mary's Ch Manteca CA 1989-1990; Serv Angl Ch Of New Zeland 1982-1988; Serv Ch Of Ireland 1979-1982. Trin Theol Soc, Chr Un, ERM, SOMA, Arm, SAMS.

CALLENDER, Randy Kyle (Md) Saint Philip's Church, 730 Bestgate Rd, Annapolis MD 21401 **S Phil's Ch Annapolis MD 2012-** B Philadelphia, PA 1983 s Sereta. BA Cheyney U 2007; MDiv EDS 2010. D 6/5/2010 Bp Edward Lewis Lee Jr P 1/22/2011 Bp Charles Ellsworth Bennison Jr. m 8/4/2012 Chantale Callender c 1. The Reverend Gr Ch And The Incarn King of Prussia PA 2010-2012. saintphilips@verizon.net

CALLISON, Donald Walter (NCal) D 6/6/2015 Bp Barry Leigh Beisner.

CALLOWAY, Nancy Laine (WNC) 1119 Old Fort Sugar Hill Rd, Old Fort NC 28762 **D The Ch of the H Sprt Nars Hill NC 2006-** B Morgantown NC 1950 d James & Mildred. BA Mars Hill Coll 1973; MDiv Duke DS 1978. D 11/23/2002 Bp Bob Johnson. S Jn's Epis Ch Marion NC 2002-2005.

CALVERT, Cara J (SO) 1129 Franklin St, Hamilton OH 45013 **Died 11/15/2015** B Poplar Plains KY 1923 s Erastus & Carrie. Denison U 1943; Lic Epis TS in Kentucky 1989. D 3/14/1989 Bp Herbert Thompson Jr. c 5. Associated Parishes; NAAD.

CALVERT, George (SanD) 3990 Bonita Rd, Bonita CA 91902 **R Ch Of The Gd Shpd Bonita CA 1998-; COM Dio San Diego San Diego CA 2015-, San Diego Epis Fndt 2012-2015, Dioc Coun 2007-2010, Curs Sprtl Advsr 2003-,**

Dioc Coun 2000-2003 B San Diego CA 1956 s Lowell & Maxine. BA U CA 1979; MDiv VTS 1986; DMin Fuller TS 1997. D 6/14/1986 P 2/21/1987 Bp Charles Brinkley Morton. m 8/6/1988 Nancy Lyn Calvert c 2. S Paul's Epis Ch Lamar CO 1993-1998; Cur S Patricks Ch And Day Sch Thousand Oaks CA 1988-1990; Asst S Fran' Par Palos Verdes Estates CA 1986-1988; Exec Coun Dio Colorado Denver CO 1995-1998.

CALVO PEREZ, Antonis De Jesus (Colom) C165 No. 36 A-30, Bogota Colombia **Iglesia Epis En Colombia Bogota 2005-** B Turbana Bolivar 1963 s Humberto & Ana. Universidad Javeriana; Instituto Pstr Y Filosofia Cepaf 1999. D P. Asiste Administrativo Subqerencia Interpovig Ltda 1995-2005.

CAMERON, David Albert (SD) 2417 Holiday Ln, Rapid City SD 57702 B El Paso TX 1947 s David & Ruth. BA U So 1969; MA Oxf GB 1973; MDiv SWTS 1974. D 9/10/1974 Bp Richard Mitchell Trelease Jr P 3/14/1975 Bp Jackson Earle Gilliam. m 6/26/2004 Constance N Lane c 4. Black Hills Dnry Dio So Dakota Pierre SD 1990-1998, Exec Com (in absence of Bp.) 1992-1994, GC Dep 1991-2003, Prov VI Del 1991-2000, Stndg Com, Pres 1989-1996, Sum Camp Sprtl Dir 1988-1999, Yth Coun 1988-1999, Theol Educ Com 1988-1994, EFM/DOC C Mentor/Ldr 1987-2003; R Emm Epis Par Rapid City SD 1987-2006; R S Andr's Epis Ch New Orleans LA 1982-1987; Mem, Pres Louisiana Epis Cler Assn LA 1977-1987; R S Fran Ch Denham Spgs LA 1977-1982; Cur S Lk's Ch Billings MT 1974-1977; Yth Dir Dio Montana Helena MT 1974-1976, Stndg Com 1974-1976, Yth Dir 1974-1976; EFM Mentor Dio Louisiana New Orleans LA 1981-1987, Personl Com/ Yth Coun 1981-1986, LA. Epis Cler Assn, Bd., Pres. 1980-1987, Prov IV Educators, Strng Com 1980-1987, Sum Camp Dir 1979-1987, Bd. of Dir., Epis Cmnty Serv 1979-1986, Dept of CE, Chair 1978-1987, Dioc Exec Bd 1978-1987, LA. Epicopal Cler Assn, Pres. 1978-1983, Bd. of Trst., St. Mart Epis Sch 1977-1981. Epis Cler Assn 1977-1987.

CAMERON, Euan Kerr (NY) **P Assoc Ch Of The Heav Rest New York NY 2014-; Prof of Reformation Ch Hist UTS New York City 2002-** B St Andrews, Fife UK 1958 s JK & E Leslie. BA Oxf 1979; MA,DPhil Oxf 1982. D 3/15/2014 P 9/27/2014 Bp Andrew Marion Lenow Dietsche. m 8/9/1980 Ruth Tonkiss Cameron c 2. Ed, "The New Cambridge Hist of the Bible vol 3," Camb Press, 2015; Auth, "Enchanted Europe: Superstition, Reason and Rel 1250-1750," Oxf Press, 2010; Ed, "The Sixteenth Century," Oxf Press, 2006; Auth, "Interpreting Chr Hist," Blackwell, 2005; Auth, "Waldenses," Blackwell, 2000; Ed, "Early Mod Europe," Oxf Press, 1999; Auth, "The European Reformation," Oxf Press, 1991; Auth, "The Reformation of the Heretics," Oxf Press, 1984.

CAMERON, Jackie (Chi) 513 W Aldine Ave Apt 2h, Chicago IL 60657 B San Gabriel CA 1962 BA Wheaton Coll 1984; MA Kings Coll - Lon 1994; MD NWU Med Sch 1994; MDiv GTS 2004; MSc Queen Mary - Lon 2013. D 6/19/2004 P 12/18/2004 Bp Bill Persell. Epis Ch Of The Atone Chicago IL 2008-2010; Bp Anderson Hse Chicago IL 2005-2011; S Matt's Ch Evanston IL 2004-2005. Auth, "Minding God/Minding Pain: Chr Theol Reflection On Recent Advances In Pain Resrch," Zygon Vol.40 No. 1, 2005.

CAMERON, Krista Ann (Roch) 3345 Edgemere Dr, Rochester NY 14612 **R S Lk's Ch Brockport NY 2008-** B Indianapolis IN 1955 d Robert & Dolores. BA Ball St U 1978; MA Ball St U 1989; MDiv SWTS 1995. D 6/23/1995 Bp Edward Witker Jones P 6/15/1996 Bp John Henry Smith. P Gr Ch Lyons NY 2007-2008; Chapl Res Strong Memi Hosp 2006-2007; R S Geo's Ch Hilton NY 2002-2006; Int Ch Of The Nativ Indianapolis IN 2000-2001; P S Paul's Ch Richmond IN 2000; Chapl Boys Hm Covington VA 1999; Int Yth Mnstry Coordntr Dio SW Virginia Roanoke VA 1998-1999; Supply P Chr Ch Pearisburg VA 1997-1999; Cur S Jn's Ch Huntington WV 1995-1996.

CAMERON, Meigan Cameron (Chi) 4140 N Lavergne Ave, Chicago IL 60641 **Vic Epiph Ch Chicago IL 2004-** B Washington,DC 1957 d James & Margaret. BA U CA 1980; BS U of Idaho 1990; MDiv SWTS 1999. D 6/26/1999 Bp R aymond Stewart Wood Jr P 11/1/2001 Bp Victor Alfonso Scantlebury. m 12/31/ 2009 Jeremy Smerage c 2. Vic Ch Of The Epiph Chicago IL 2004-2010; Assoc Gr Ch Oak Pk IL 2001-2004; S Chrys's Ch Chicago IL 1999-2000. Catechesis Gd Shpd.

CAMERON JR, Robert Speir (CFla) 1200 W International Speedway Blvd, Daytona Beach FL 32114 **Ret 1995-** B Albany NY 1932 s Robert & Ruth. BD U of So Carolina 1955; MS U of Florida 1967; EdD Nova SE U 1979. D 6/15/1975 Bp William Hopkins Folwell. m 12/20/1955 Joyce Metts. Chapl Daytona Bch Cmnty Coll 1978-1994; D H Trin Daytona Bch FL 1978-1985; D S Jas Epis Ch Ormond Bch FL 1975-1978. Ees, NAAD.

CAMPBELL, Anne (Oly) 3438 161st Pl Se Apt 51, Bellevue WA 98008 **Assoc S Margeret's In Bellevue 1989-** B 1945 d Frank & Myrtle. BA NWU 1965; MA NWU 1967; MA SWTS 1978. D 11/18/1978 P 5/1/1979 Bp Otis Charles. c 3. Dio Utah Salt Lake City UT 1988-1989; Chapl S Mk's Hosp Salt Lake City UT 1981-1986; St Marks Hosp Salt Lake City UT 1981-1984; S Jas Epis Ch Midvale UT 1979-1981; R S Jas Salt Lake City UT 1979-1981; S Ptr's Ch Clearfield UT 1979.

CAMPBELL, Benjamin Pfohl (Va) 1310 Whitby Rd, Richmond VA 23227 **Pstr Emer Richmond Hill 2015-** B Washington DC 1941 s Edmund & Eliza-

beth. BA Wms 1961; MA Oxf GB 1964; MA Oxf GB 1964; MDiv VTS 1966; Grad Sch Pecos Benedictine Abbey 1987. D 11/1/1966 Bp Robert Bruce Hall P 6/15/1967 Bp Robert Fisher Gibson Jr. m 8/12/1989 Ann Elizabeth Hopkins c 2. Pstr Dir Richmond Hill Richmond VA 1988-2013; Int Ch Of The Creator Mechanicsvlle VA 1987-1988; Dio Virginia Richmond VA 1986-1988, 1970-1978; S Paul's Ch Richmond VA 1986-1987, Urban Mssnr 1979-1982, P-in-res 1979-1980; Exec Dir Hm Base Richmond Virginia 1982-1985; Exec Dir Richmond Urban Inst Richmond Virginia 1979-1982; Vic S Mary's Whitechapel Epis Lancaster VA 1966-1970; Trin Epis Ch Lancaster VA 1966-1970; Sr Pstr Richmond Hill 2013-2015. Auth, "Richmond's Unhealed Hist," Brandylane, 2011; Auth, "The Jesus Scandals," Self, 2002; Auth, "No Alien Power," Forw, 1985; Ed, "The Virginia Churchman," *The Virginia Churchman*, Dio Virginia, 1978. Doctor of Humane Letters Virginia Un U 2014; DD VTS 2010; Mdiv mcl VTS 1966; MA Oxon The Queen's Coll, Oxford 1965; Ba mcl Wms 1961; Rhodes Schlr Rhodes Schlrshp Trust 1960.

CAMPBELL, Bruce Alan (Mich) 160 Walnut St, Wyandotte MI 48192 B Highland Park MI 1945 s Edwin & Margaret. Wheaton Coll 1965; BA Wayne 1967; MDiv GTS 1971. D 6/29/1971 Bp Richard Stanley Merrill Emrich P 1/1/1972 Bp Archie H Crowley. m 7/6/1968 Sarah E Gerig. P Assoc S Jn's Ch Plymouth MI 2010-2013; R S Steph's Ch Wyandotte MI 1988-2009; Assoc R Chr Ch Dearborn MI 1982-1988; P-in-c S Mich And All Ang Brooklyn MI 1976-1981; Assoc Chapl Epis Stdt Fndt Ann Arbor MI 1973-1975; Vic All SS Houghton Lake MI 1972-1973; Vic S Eliz's Higgins Lake MI 1971-1973. frbruce@wyan. org

CAMPBELL, Catherine Mary (Va) 3420 Flint Hill Place, Woodbridge VA 22192 **Vic La Iglesia Epis de San JosÃ© Arlington VA 2006-; Vic Dio Virginia Richmond VA 2005-; Vic La Iglesia de Cristo Rey Arlington VA 2005-; Vic La Mision Hispana El Divino Salvador Sacramento CA 1995-** B Mexico City MX 1956 d David & Edith. BA U of So Florida 1977; MDiv VTS 1988. D 9/27/1990 Bp Robert Poland Atkinson P 4/27/1991 Bp Peter J Lee. VTS Alexandria VA 2011; Vic S Jas Epis Par Lincoln CA 1999-2005; Hisp Mssnr The Epis Dio Nthrn California Sacramento CA 1995-2005; Assoc Trin Par Wilmington DE 1993-1995; Ch of the Incarn Mineral VA 1990-1993.

CAMPBELL, Claude Alan (Mo) 2831 N Prospect Ave, Milwaukee WI 53211 **Died 7/13/2017** B San Antonio TX 1927 s Claude & Kate. Coll of Preachers; BS U of Texas 1950; BD VTS 1964. D 7/8/1964 Bp Everett H Jones P 1/1/ 1965 Bp Richard Earl Dicus. m 6/19/1997 Linda Ann Campbell c 2. Non-par 1989-2017; Chapl Supvsr Dss Hosp S Louis MO 1974-1989; Assoc Ch Of The Incarn Dallas TX 1970-1974; Chapl Pan-Amer Coll 1964-1968; Vic S Matt's Ch Edinburg TX 1964-1968; S Jn's Ch McAllen TX 1964-1966. ACPE.

CAMPBELL, Dana L(Ou) (Ct) 58 Greenwood St, East Hartford CT 06118 **P Ch Of The H Trin Middletown CT 2014-; Mssnr The Grtr Hartford Reg Mnstry E Hartford CT 1999-** B Tulsa OK 1948 d Colin & Helen. BA Kalamazoo Coll 1970; MDiv Ya Berk 1996. D 6/14/1997 Bp Clarence Nicholas Coleridge P 2/14/1998 Bp Andrew Donnan Smith. S Andr's Ch Meriden CT 2012-2014, Asst 1997-1999; Ch Of The Gd Shpd Hartford CT 2009-2012; Grtr Hartford Reg Mnstry E Hartford CT 1999-2009.

CAMPBELL, David W Tennessee Memphis 2016- B Fort Worth TX 1970 s Patrick & Venita. BA SW Bapt Sem 1993; MA Cov TS 2000; Doctor of Mnstry Pittsburgh TS 2014. D 6/4/2016 P 12/11/2016 Bp Don Edward Johnson. m 7/18/1994 Allyson Shandel Rippy c 2.

CAMPBELL, Dennis Gail (Ark) 1501 32nd Ave S, Seattle WA 98144 **S Jas Ch Eureka Spgs AR 2015-** B Michigan City IN 1956 s Dolan & Juanita. U of Florida 1979; BSE Arkansas St U 1983; MA Arkansas St U 1985; MDiv Memphis TS 1990; DMin Sewanee: The U So, TS 1999. D 6/23/1990 P 12/28/ 1990 Bp Herbert Alcorn Donovan Jr. c 4. P-in-c S Clem's Epis Ch Seattle WA 2010-2015; Cn Dio Arkansas Little Rock AR 2001-2009; Cn S Marg's Epis Ch Little Rock AR 2000-2009; Vic St Jas Epis Ch Sewanee TN 1995-2001; Int Chapl S Andr's Swanee TN 1995; Fac Dir Of Congrl Mnstry Sewanee U So TS Sewanee TN 1994-2002; Vic S Matt's Epis Ch Benton AR 1990-1994. Auth, "Developing Congregations As Lrng Communities:Tools To Shape Your Future," The Alb Inst, 2000; Auth, "Lrng Orgnztn Theory Applied To Congrl Dvlpmt," 1999. Ch Dvlpmt Inst Nationalntrainers Ntwk; Saccem; Soc Of Angl And Luth Theologians. Mdiv mcl Memphis TS 1990. dgc777@gmail.com

CAMPBELL, Ernest Francis (Spok) 825 Wauna Vista Dr, Walla Walla WA 99362 **Ret 1991-; R Emer S Paul's Ch Walla Walla WA 1991-, R 1969-1990** B Evanston IL 1927 s Ernest & Cecilia. BS NWU 1950; LTh SWTS 1953. D 6/6/1953 P 12/12/1953 Bp Charles L Street. m 2/4/1956 Margaret Campbell c 4. Dn The Epis Cathd Of Our Merc Sav Faribault MN 1967-1969; Assoc St Geo's Epis Ch Minneapolis MN 1960-1967; Asst S Jn The Evang S Paul MN 1956-1960; Chapl Breck Sch No Minneapolis MN 1955-1962; Cur S Mk's Ch Evanston IL 1953-1955.

CAMPBELL, Ernestina Rodriguez (NCal) 1617 32nd Ave, Sacramento CA 95822 B Long Beach CA 1947 d Isauro & Elisa. BA U CA 1969; MA California St U 1981; Cert Dio of Nthrn California Sch For Deacons at Berkeley 1985. D 2/23/1991 Bp John Lester Thompson III. m 11/27/1971 Brian Lorne Campbell. D Trin Epis Cathd Sacramento CA 1993-2011; D S Lk's Ch Woodland CA 1991-1993. NAAD.

CAMPBELL III, George Latimer (NJ) 257 4th St, South Amboy NJ 08879 B Ithaca NY 1950 s George & Jean. BA Sir Geo Wms Montreal CA 1976. Trans 2/14/1983 Bp Henry D Robinson. c 3. R Chr Ch So Amboy NJ 1998-2013; Litchfield Hills Reg Mnstry Bridgewater CT 1991-1995; S Mk's Ch Bridgewater CT 1989-1991; R Ch Of The H Trin Pawling NY 1986-1989; Estrn Dutchess Min Coun Pawling NY 1985-1988; R S Paul's Epis Ch Angola NY 1983-1986; S Alb's Ch Silver Creek NY 1983-1985; Serv Angl Ch Of Can 1979-1983.

CAMPBELL, James Donald (La) B Mountain View AR 1925 s James & Ruth. BS Hendrix Coll 1948. D 12/1/1996 P 6/1/1997 Bp James Barrow Brown. m 11/2/1954 Margaret Antoinette Cain. D Ch Of The Incarn Amite LA 1996-1997.

CAMPBELL, Janet Bragg (Oly) 6509 80th St SW, Lakewood WA 98499 B Waukegan IL 1944 d John & Mary. AB Vas 1966; MDiv GTS 1988. D 6/6/1988 Bp Robert Campbell Witcher Sr P 2/18/1989 Bp Orris George Walker Jr. m 7/9/2009 Roger Charles Campbell c 1. Chr Ch Tacoma WA 2014-2016; Cn for Liturg Dio Olympia Seattle 2010-2016, P in Charge Chr Ch Tacoma 2016-, COM 2012-2015, Liturg and Arts Cmsn 2011-2017; Int R S Steph's Epis Ch Seattle WA 2007-2010; Adj Prof Seattle U TS and Mnstry 2006-2012; Dir Of Liturg And The Arts S Mk's Cathd Seattle WA 2001-2007; Cathd Of S Jas Chicago IL 1993-2000; Dioc Liturg Dio Chicago Chicago IL 1993-2000; Assoc Vic S Ptr's Ch New York NY 1988-1992. Auth, "Through The Window Of The Ordnry: Experiences Of H Week," Ch Pub Grp, 2002. janet@ccptacoma.org

CAMPBELL OSH, Jean (NY) 42 Timberline Dr, Poughkeepsie NY 12603 B Buffalo NY 1946 d Donald & Clara. BS SUNY 1967; MA U of Notre Dame 1981; DD SWTS 1994. D 8/11/1989 P 2/24/1990 Bp Richard Frank Grein. R Trin Ch Fishkill NY 2005-2015; Assoc Zion Epis Ch Wappingers Falls NY 2000-2004; P S Mk's Epis Ch Chelsea NY 1998-2004; Supply P Hudson Vlly Mnstry 1991-2008; Adult Chr Formation Ch Of The H Apos New York NY 1982-1984; Chr Formation Calv and St Geo New York NY 1978-1981; Life-Professed Ord Of S Helena 1970-2010. Auth, "Var arts". Coun Of Associated Parishes 1984; No Amer Acad Of Liturg 1982; Ord Of S Helena - Life Professed 1974-2010. DD Seabury Wstrn TS 1994.

CAMPBELL, Karen (LI) PO Box 570, Hampton & East Union Street, Sag Harbor NY 11963 **P-in-c Chr Ch Sag Harbor NY 2012-** B Bakersfield CA 1948 d Edwin & Jean. BA cl California St U 1970; MDiv EDS 1991. D 1/8/2000 Bp Mary Adelia Rosamond Mcleod P 10/28/2000 Bp Gordon Scruton. m 7/12/1969 Graham Ross Campbell c 3. R Ch Of The Gd Shpd Fitchburg MA 2000-2010. Ba cl California St U 1970. gardenerforgod@gmail.com

CAMPBELL, Kathryn Sue (Ia) 106 3rd Ave, Charles City IA 50616 **Theol Consult Dio Iowa Des Moines IA 2006-, Mnstry Dvlpmt Consult 2005-2014, Mssnr 1991-1992, 1986-1989, Chair NE Dnry 1995-1997; Dir Hazelnut Connection 1996-** B Santa Barbara CA 1942 d Joseph & Margaret. A.B. U of Kansas; M.A. U of Kansas; U of Aberdeen Aberdeen Scotland 1964; PhD U IL 1973; U of Iowa 1978; CPE S Lukes Hosp Cedar Rapids IA 1984; CPE Cherokee Mntl Hlth Inst Cherokee IA 1985; CAS SWTS 1986; DMin CDSP 2003; No Iowa Cmnty Coll 2011. D 6/11/1986 P 12/12/1986 Bp Walter Cameron Righter. Assoc Ch Of The Sav Clermont IA 2005-2014, 1992-1999; S Jn's Ch Mason City IA 2001; Supply S Andr's Epis Ch Waverly IA 2000-2002, 2000-2001, Vic 1987-1990, Int 1986; Supply Gr Epis Ch Chas City IA 1992-2005, Int Vic 1986-1987. Auth, "Bk Revs: Jn Moschos, The Sprtl Meadow; trans. by Jn Wortley," *Cistercian Stds Quarterly*, 2016; Auth, "Bk Revs: Ihssen, Jn Moschos¿ Sprtl Meadow: Authority and Autonomy," *Cistercian Stds Quarterly*, 2016; Auth, "Bk Revs: Carl McColman, Befriending Silence," *Cistercian Stds Quarterly*, 2016; Auth, "Bk Revs: Monastic Tradition in Estrn Chrsnty," *Cistercian Stds Quarterly*, 2015; Auth, "Undinna thaettir: Structure in the Gisla Saga," *Neophilologys*, 1985; Auth, "Medieval and Mod and the Allegory of Rhetoric," *Allegorica*, 1979; Auth, "Y Gymraeg yn Iowa," *Tudalen y Dysgwyr*, Y Cymro, 1978; Auth, "Iowerth Ddu and Gwilym Pue," *Fourteenth Century Mystics Quarterly*, 1977. AAR 1986-2015; Assn for Amer Indn Affrs 1988-2007; Assn of Iowa Cistercians 1997; Interfaith Allnce, Iowa 1998; Rural Mnstrs Ntwk 2000-2005. Finalist, Iowa Bus Plan Competition Pappajohn Corp 2011.

CAMPBELL, Kenneth Stuart B (WMass) 5 Peace Lane, Box 306, South Orleans MA 02653 **Convenor Nauset Interfaith Assn 2010-; Coordntr Fllshp of Recon Cape Cod MA 2007-** B Hyannis MA 1941 s Douglas & Gwendolyn. BS Boston St Coll 1963; MA Brigham Young U 1965; MDiv EDS 1969. D 6/21/1969 P 5/26/1970 Bp John Melville Burgess. m 8/26/1967 Ruth W Campbell c 3. Int Chr Ch Epis Harwich Port MA 2007-2008; Pres Justice and Peace Cmsn Dio Wstrn Massachusett 1999-2004; Pres of the Bd Dir Citizen Advocacy Springfield MA 1995-2004; R Epis Ch Of The Epiph Wilbraham MA 1981-2005; Pres. Stndg Comm. Dio Wstrn Massachusetts Springfield 1981-2004; Sr Sprtl Dir Curs Boston MA 1975-1981; R S Anne's Ch No Billerica MA 1972-1981; The Ch Of The H Sprt Orleans MA 1969-1972; Cur Chap Of S Jas The Fisherman Wellfleet MA 1969-1971. EPF 1975; OHC 1982-2004.

CAMPBELL, Leslie R (SD) Po Box 722, Mobridge SD 57601 **Vic Rosebud Mssn 1987-** B Sisseton SD 1938 s Adelord & Alice. Flandreau Indn Sch. D 1/25/1975 P 6/1/1976 Bp Walter H Jones. m 1/1/1995 Mary Campbell c 3. S Jas

Epis Ch Mobridge SD 1995-1996; Dio Minnesota Minneapolis MN 1984-1987; Dio So Dakota Pierre SD 1976-2004; Vic Cheyenne River Mssn SD 1976-1987; S Ptr's Ch McLaughlin SD 1975-1976.

CAMPBELL, Linda Mcconnell (ECR) 2065 Yosemite St., Seaside CA 93955 **R Epis Ch Of The Gd Shpd Salinas CA 2009-** B Fresno CA 1955 d Willis & Janet. BA U CA 1979; MA PSR 1998; Cert Ang Stud CDSP 2002. D 8/10/2002 P 3/1/2003 Bp Jerry Alban Lamb. c 3. Int S Alb's Ch Albany CA 2006-2009; Asst St Johns Epis Ch Ross CA 2004-2006; Asst Ch Of The Incarn Santa Rosa CA 2002-2004.

CAMPBELL, Lynn Marie (Mass) 1132 Highland Ave, Needham MA 02494 **S Ptr's Ch Weston MA 2016-** B Reading PA 1975 d Roger & Christine. BA Coll of the H Cross 1998; MDiv Weston Jesuit TS 2003; Dip VTS 2010. D 6/25/2011 P 1/27/2012 Bp M(Arvil) Thomas Shaw. Asst Chr Ch Needham Hgts MA 2011-2016.

CAMPBELL, Maurice Bernard (SJ) 1151 Park View Ct, Sheridan WY 82801 **D S Paul's Ch Bakersfield CA 1992-** B Sheriden WY 1930 s Earl & Cecilia. BS U of Wyoming 1959. D 5/15/1972 Bp Chauncie Kilmer Myers. m 12/28/1957 Carola J Rowland c 2. S Mk's Epis Ch Santa Clara CA 1972-1992.

CAMPBELL, Patrick Alan (RI) St Paul's Church, 50 Park Pl, Pawtucket RI 02860 **Ch Of The Redeem Providence RI 2012-** B Southbridge MA 1962 s James & Louise. BFA U of Connecticut 1984; MDiv EDS 1993. D 10/8/2011 P 6/30/2012 Bp Gerry Wolf. S Paul's Ch Pawtucket RI 2000-2012.

CAMPBELL, Peter Nelson (Chi) 519 Franklin Ave, River Forest IL 60305 **Chr Ch River Forest IL 2008-, Extended Supply P 2004-2006** B Atlanta GA 1948 s Nelson & Mary. BS Trin Hartford CT 1970; MS Georgia St U 1975; MDiv SWTS 1986. D 6/14/1986 Bp James Winchester Montgomery P 12/1/1986 Bp Frank Tracy Griswold III. Extended Supply P The Epis Ch Of The H Trin Belvidere IL 2007-2008; S Ign Of Antioch Ch Antioch IL 2006-2007; R H Trin Ch Skokie IL 1992-2004; Chapl NW Mltry And Naval Acad Lake Geneva IL 1986-1992.

CAMPBELL II, Ralph (LI) 9825 Georgetown St. N.E., Louisville OH 44641 B Radford VA 1947 s Ralph & Virginia. BA Ohio U 1969; MDiv GTS 1973; Coll of Preachers 1983. D 12/22/1974 Bp Hal Raymond Gross P 11/30/1975 Bp Matthew Paul Bigliardi. c 2. Regular Sunday Supply St Andr Epis Ch Yaphank NY 2010-2011; S Ann's Ch Sayville NY 2006-2010; Mem SCLM 1994-1997; S Tim's Epis Ch Salem OR 1978-2005, Vic 1978-1979; Assoc S Barth's Ch Beaverton OR 1977-1978; Chapl Gd Samar Hosp & Med Cntr Portland OR 1975-1977; Asst, Yth Min Epis Par Of S Jn The Bapt Portland OR 1974-1977; Chapl Multnomah Cnty Wmn Jail and Jvnl Cntr 1974-1975; Stndg Com Dio Oregon Portland OR 1997-2000, Stndg Com 1991-1994. Cmnty H Sprt. Citizen Awd Marion Cnty City of Salem; Citizen Awd Drug & Alco Plannig Com.

CAMPBELL, Robert Dean (Spok) 16007 Red Fox Ln, Colorado Springs CO 80921 **Died 8/13/2016** B Alamosa CO 1936 s Edwin & Eva. BA Colorado St U 1963; MDiv Nash 1966; Cert Int Mnstry Prog 1996. D 6/6/1966 Bp William Hampton Brady P 12/21/1966 Bp Richard S Watson. c 3. Ret 2003-2016; Reg Mssnr S Anne's Ch Omak WA 1998-2002; Trin Ch Oroville WA 1998-2002, 1990-1995; Dio Spokane Spokane WA 1995-2001; Serv Angl Ch of Can Ft Vermilion/Whitewood Parishes 1973-1986; R Angl Ch in New Zealand Maniototo Par 1970-1973; R Carbon Cnty Par Dragerton UT 1967-1970; D S Christophers Ch Bluff UT 1966-1967. mcampbell@trace3.com

CAMPBELL, Ross Walton (Mich) 899 Greenhills Dr, Ann Arbor MI 48105 B Detroit MI 1923 s Ross & Ernestine. BS USMA 1945; JD U MI 1955; Cert Whitaker TS 1982. D 6/13/1981 Bp H Coleman Mcgehee Jr P 4/13/1987 Bp William Jones Gordon Jr. m 6/26/1983 Beverly Jean Taylor c 2. Asstg P S Clare Of Assisi Epis Ch Ann Arbor MI 1987-1988, D 1981-1987; Ret. Auth, "Chld Custody," *Judges Journ*, 1978; Auth, "The Atty in Jvnl Crt," *Michigan St Bar Journ*, 1965. Soc of S Paul the Tentmaker 1981-1983.

CAMPBELL, Scott Duncan (Colo) PO Box 1961, Monument CO 80132 **Area Pstr Tri-Lakes Chap 2013-** B Denver CO 1965 s Malcolm & Mary. BA U CO 1990; MDiv GTS 1997. D 6/7/1997 P 12/20/1997 Bp William Jerry Winterrowd. m 7/1/2006 Heather Campbell c 3. R S Mths Epis Ch Monument CO 2001-2012; Assoc S Matt's Ch Grand Jct CO 1997-2001; Stndg Com, VP Dio Colorado Denver CO 2007-2012; Bd Pres Tri-Lakes Cares 2005-2009.

CAMPBELL, Solomon Sebastian (SeFla) P.O. Box 50222, Nassau Bahamas **Serv Ch in the Prov of the W Indies - Bahamas 1990-** B Arthurs Town Cat Island BS 1956 s Sebastian & Almeda. DIT Codrington Coll 1980; BA U of The W Indies 1980; MA PrTS 1988. Trans 3/21/1986 Bp Calvin Onderdonk Schofield Jr. m 4/7/1980 Agatha Maria Antionette Wells c 1. S Matt's Epis Ch Delray Bch FL 1987-1988; Serv Ch in the Prov of the W Indies - Bahamas 1982-1985.

CAMPBELL, Thomas Wellman (SD) 234 W Kansas St, Spearfish SD 57783 B Deadwood SD 1939 s John & Ruberta. BA Augustana Coll 1962; MDiv GTS 1965; ABD So Dakota St U 1975; ABD So Dakota St U 1975. D 6/11/1965 P 12/20/1965 Bp Conrad H Gesner. m 9/3/1960 Elizabeth Ann Thompson c 4. Sr Chapl Trin Sch Midland TX 2011-2014; Instr Black Hills St Univ. Spearfish SD 2005-2011; R St. Jn's Deadwood SD 2002-2012; R S Thos Epis Ch Sturgis SD 1998-2001; S Fran Cmnty Serv Inc. Salina KS 1994-1998; S

Mich's Epis Day Sch Carmichael CA 1991-1994; Int S Steph's Ch Norfolk VA 1987-1989; Dir. of Counslg, Asst to Headmaster Norfolk Acad Norfolk Virgina 1986-2001; Norfolk Acad Norfolk VA 1986-1991; S Edw's Sch Vero Bch FL 1984-1986; Shattuck-S Mary's Sch Faribault MN 1982-1984; R Ch Of The Gd Shpd Sioux Falls SD 1981-1982; Locumtenens Gr Epis Ch Jamestown ND 1977-1980; Ch Of The Epiph Epis Minneapolis MN 1976; Gr Epis Ch Madison SD 1973-1976; S Steph's Ch DeSmet SD 1973-1976; P-in-c S Steph's Desmet SD 1973-1976; R Chr Epis Ch Tarrytown NY 1969-1971; R Ch Of All Ang Spearfish SD 1966-1969; Cur Calv Cathd Sioux Falls SD 1965-1966. Coun for Rel in Indep Schools 1986-1989; NAES 1989-2014; Natl. Assoc. of Indep Schools, 1984-1989.

CAMPBELL, William Edward (Spok) 1421 S Josephine Street, Denver CO 80210 **Died 5/19/2017** B Lincoln NE 1932 s Henry & Beatrice. BA Occ 1954; MDiv CDSP 1957. D 6/24/1957 P 3/6/1958 Bp Francis E I Bloy. m 6/21/1985 Anne D Campbell. Asst S Mich And All Ang' Ch Denver CO 2004-2017; R Emm Ch Kellogg ID 1993-2004; H Trin Epis Ch Wallace ID 1993-2000; Int Dio Colorado Denver CO 1987-1993; Asst Ch Of S Phil And S Jas Denver CO 1986-1987; Int, Supply and Vic All SS Of The Mtn Epis Chap Crested Butte CO 1984-1993; Asst H Apos Epis Ch Englewood CO 1984-1985; Dio Utah Salt Lake City UT 1984; S Fran Ch Moab UT 1981-1984; R H Trin Epis Ch Garland TX 1974-1980; Vic S Chris's By The Sea Portland TX 1969-1974; S Barn Epis Ch Fredricksburg TX 1968-1969; Vic S Bon Ch Comfort TX 1968-1969; R S Paul's Epis Ch Tustin CA 1960-1967; Asst S Jas Par Los Angeles CA 1957-1960; Bp Search Com Dio Spokane Spokane WA 1993-2011; Dept Of Missions Dio Dallas Dallas TX 1976-1980. Ord Of S Lk 2007.

CAMPBELL-DIXON OHC, Robert A (NY) PO Box 99, West Park NY 12493 B Corn Island NI 1934 s Frank & Susan. Inst Angl De Nicaragua Ni; S Barbara Cmnty Coll. Trans 11/22/1982. Cur S Ptr's Ch Bronx NY 1986-2004; Dio Nicaragua New York NY 1982-1986; Vic S Mk Bluefield Nicaragua 1982-1986; Serv Ch Of Bahamas 1979-1982. H Cross Monstry 1965.

CAMPBELL-LANGDELL, Alene L (Los) 144 S C St, Oxnard CA 93030 B Farmington NM 1971 d Ivan & Emma. BA Coll Ozarks Point Lookout MO 1993; MA Boston Coll 2006; MDiv CDSP 2009. D 1/31/2009 P 1/28/2010 Bp Edward Joseph Konieczny. m 1/17/2013 Melissa Christina Campbell-Langdell. Dio Los Angeles Los Angeles CA 2013-2015, Alt-Dioc Coun 2014-; S Jn's Par Sn Bernrdno CA 2009-2011.

CAMPBELL-LANGDELL, Melissa Christina (Los) 144 S. C St, Oxnard CA 93030 **Int P-in-c All SS Epis Ch Oxnard CA 2011-** B London UK 1981 d Timothy & Cheri. BA Vas 2003; MDiv CDSP 2009. D 6/6/2009 Bp Sergio Carranza-Gomez P 1/9/2010 Bp Chester Lovelle Talton. m 1/17/2013 Alene L Campbell. Cur All SS Epis Ch Riverside CA 2009-2011. Fran Toy Preaching Awd CDSP 2009. revmelissalangdell@gmail.com

CAMPBELL-PEARSON, Constance (Mont) **D S Jas Ch Bozeman MT 2014-** D 5/18/2014 Bp Charles Franklin Brookhart Jr.

CAMPO, JoAnne Crocitto (NY) 48 Spring St S, South Salem NY 10590 B Mt Pleasant NY 1946 d Pasquale & Evelyn Rose. AS Dutchess Cmnty Coll 1989; BA Concordia Coll 2005; MDiv GTS 2009. D 3/7/2009 P 9/12/2009 Bp Mark Sean Sisk. m 8/8/1998 Joseph John Campo c 3. S Lk's Ch Eastchester NY 2010-2012.

CAMPO, Joseph John (NY) **R S Jn's Ch So Salem NY 2012-; Chair of Angl/Orth Ch Sub-Com Dioc Ecum and Interfaith Committ6ee 2011-; Adj Prof. Cn Law The GTS 2009-** B New Rochelle NY 1950 s Anthony & Theresa. BA Cathd Coll of the Immac Concep 1971; MA Gregorian U 1975; JCL S Paul U Ottawa On CA 1984; Dip Ang Stud GTS 2003. Rec 6/28/2003 Bp Mark Sean Sisk. m 8/8/1998 JoAnne Crocitto Campo. P-in-c S Andr's Epis Ch Hartsdale NY 2006-2012; Assoc P Gr Ch White Plains NY 2003-2006. Com Mem, "The Ch of the Triune God: The Cyprus Agreed Statement," *Ecclesiology Vol. 9, No. 1*, p. 75-84, 2013; Auth, "Ben XVI's Apostolic Const Anglicanorum Coetibus," *The Journ of Epis Ch Cn Law Vol. 2, No. 2*, p. 29-68, 2011. Eccl Law Soc 2012; The Fllshp of St. Alb and St. Sergius 2012.

CAMPO CAMAYO, Omar Julio (Colom) **Iglesia Epis En Colombia Bogota 2017-** B Popayan 1964 s Julio & Gabina. Filosopia San Clemente Maria Hofbauer. Rec 4/17/2014 as Priest Bp Francisco Jose Duque-Gomez.

CANADY III, Hoyt Paul (EC) Christ Church, P.O. Box 1246, New Bern NC 28563 **R Chr Ch New Bern NC 2015-, Assoc 2009-2015; Stndg Com Dio E Carolina Kinston NC 2016-, Bp Transition Com 2013-2014, Title IV Disciplinary Bd 2011-2017, COM 2011-2015; Bd Managers Trin Cntr Epis Dio E Carolina Atlantic Bch NC 2015-** B Knoxville TN 1976 s Hoyt & Marilyn. BA Middle Tennessee St U 1998; VTS 2009; MDiv Wesley TS 2009. D 8/22/2009 P 4/19/2010 Bp John Bryson Chane. m 7/19/2003 Emily Gowdy c 2. CPE Intern Hebr Hm of Grtr Washington 2009; Dep for Yth Mnstry Dio Washington Washington DC 2002-2009; Yth Min S Jn's Ch Ellicott City MD 2002; Yth Min S Geo's Ch Germantown TN 1998-2002; Dioc Yth Coun Dio W Tennessee Memphis 2000-2002; Epis Yth Event Design Team Epis Ch Cntr New York NY 2000-2002; Prov IV Yth Event Prov IV Jackson MS 1998-2001. paulcanady@christchurchnewbern.com

CANAN, David A (Pa) 708 S Bethlehem Pike, Ambler PA 19002 **R Trin Epis Ch Ambler PA 1999-** B Ravenna OH 1953 s Ellsworth & Julia. BS Kent St U 1976; MDiv TESM 1990. D 6/2/1990 P 1/25/1991 Bp Alden Moinet Hathaway. m 6/30/1984 Anne Louise Canan c 2. Ch of the Gd Shpd Rahway NJ 1994-1999; Assoc S Thos' Ch Whitemarsh Ft Washington PA 1990-1994; Prog Coordntr for Yth Dept Dio Pittsburgh Pittsburgh PA 1987-1990.

CANAVAN, Mary Ann (Ct) D 5/26/1999 Bp Robert Louis Ladehoff P 12/11/1999 Bp Roger John White.

CANDLER, Samuel Glenn (At) 2744 Peachtree Rd Nw, Atlanta GA 30305 **Adj Prof Candler TS Emory U 2012-; Dn Cathd Of S Phil Atlanta GA 1998-, 1984-1991; Bd Advisors Epis Stds Prog at Candler TS 2010-; Bd Dir Magnetawan Watershed Land Trust Allnce 2010-; Bd Trst The Westminster Schools 2002-** B Panama City FL 1956 s Samuel & Beth. BA Occ 1978; MDiv Yale DS 1982. D 6/12/1982 P 5/11/1983 Bp Bennett Jones Sims. m 5/25/1980 Barbara Candler c 3. Bd Trst Ya Berk New Haven CT 1994-1998, Bd Trst 1994-2013; Dn Trin Cathd Columbia SC 1993-1998; Epis Ch Of The H Sprt Cumming GA 1988-1993; Epis Ch of the Gd Shpd Summerville SC 1985-1987; Com On Liturg And Mus Dio Atlanta Atlanta GA 1984-1991; S Jude's Ch Marietta GA 1982-1985; Vice-Pres and Bd Dir Compass Rose Soc of the Angl Comm 2003-2014; Bd Dir Wrld Pilgrims 2003-2009; Bd Dir Faith Allnce of Metro Atlanta (Interfaith) 2002-2009; Bd Dir LaGrange Coll 2000-2008; Mem Ldrshp Atlanta 2000-2001; Bd Dir Metropltn Atlanta YMCA 1999-2007; Dep GC- Epis Ch Cntr New York NY 1997-2015; Mem Gvnr's Cmsn of Race Relatns So Carolina 1996-1998; Stndg Com Dio Upper So Carolina Columbia SC 1995-1998; Bd Trst Heathwood Hall Epis Sch 1995-1998; Bd Trst Epis Media Cntr Inc Atlanta GA 1994-2003. Auth, "Var arts," 2003; Writer, "Essays," *Epis Cafe*. Associated Parishes; Assn Of Dioc Liturg & Mus Comm; Cumberland Island Preservation Soc 2005; NNECA; Rotary Club of Atlanta 1998; The Buckhead Cltn 2010. Mdiv mcl Ya Berk 1982; Phi Beta Kappa Occ 1978; Ba cl Occ 1978. scandler@stphilipscathedral.org

CANELA CANELA, Ramon (DR) Ms Digna Valdez, Box 764, Dominican Republic Dominican Republic **Dio The Dominican Republic (Iglesia Epis Dominicana) Gazcue Santo Domingo 2008-** B 1969 s Basilio & Melania. Rec 10/2/2008 Bp Julio Cesar Holguin-Khoury. m 12/20/2002 Ana Espinal Canela c 3.

CANGIALOSI, Grace Louise (Va) 2209 E Grace St, Richmond VA 23223 **Assoc Gr Ch Stanardsville VA 2011-** B Salina KS 1943 d John & Grace. BA U MI 1964; MA U of Maryland 1977; MDiv VTS 1989. D 6/10/1989 Bp Peter J Lee P 2/1/1990 Bp Robert Poland Atkinson. c 2. S Geo's Ch Stanley VA 1991-2000; Asst to R The Ch of S Clem Alexandria VA 1989-1990. Auth, "A Kairos Winter". Advoc Of The Year Page Cnty 1993. gracecan@rocketmail.com

CANHAM, Elizabeth Jean (WNC) 51 Laurel Ln, Black Mountain NC 28711 B Hatfield Herts UK 1939 d Robert & Marjorie. BD Lon GB 1972; MDiv Lon GB 1978; STM GTS 1983; DMin GTF 1990. Trans 12/1/1980 as Deacon Bp John Shelby Spong. Calv Epis Ch Fletcher NC 2004-2005; P Stillpoint Mnstrs Arden NC 1994-2002; Gr Ch Asheville NC 1994-1998; Fndr & Dir Stillpoint Mnstrs Inc 1992-2003; Dio Wstrn No Carolina Asheville NC 1992-1999; P The Sav Epis Ch Newland NC 1991-1993; Sprtlty Consult/Prog Dir H Sav Priory Pineville SC 1985-1991; St. Barth Ch New York NY 1983-1985; Asst S Dav's Ch Kinnelon NJ 1981-1982; Serv Ch of Engl 1978-1980; Prof of Biblic Stds Wilson Carlile Coll Blackheath London 1975-1980. Auth, *A Table of Delight*, Upper Room, 2005; Auth, *Heart Whispers*, Upper Room, 1999; Auth, *Pilgrimage to Priesthood*, SPCK, 1993; Auth, *Journaling w Jeremiah*, Paulist Press, 1992; Auth, *Praying By the Bible*, Cowley, 1987.

CANION, Gary Yates (Tex) 5435 Whispering Creek Way, Houston TX 77017 **1979-** B Seadrift TX 1937 s Leslie & Mae. BA Rice U 1959; BD Epis TS of the SW 1962; STM SWTS 1968; Cert Texas Inst of Rel 1969; Cert SW Paralegal Inst 1981. D 6/18/1962 Bp John Elbridge Hines P 8/21/1963 Bp Frederick P Goddard. c 4. Serv Angl Ch in Australia 1976-1979; Chapl S Mk's Pstr Care Cntr Salt Lake City UT 1972-1976; St Marks Hosp Salt Lake City UT 1972-1976; Vic S Jn's Epis Ch Carthage TX 1962-1964; Cn Sacristan Trin Cathd Trenton NJ 1965-1967.

CANNADAY, Brian W (Tex) 410 N Main St, Boerne TX 78006 **S Chris's Ch League City TX 2016-** B 1975 s Mark. BA U of Texas at San Antonio 2011; MDiv Sewanee: The U So, TS 2014; MDiv The TS at The U So 2014. D 12/29/2013 P 7/2/2014 Bp Gary Richard Lillibridge. m 7/17/1999 Crystal L Cannaday c 1. Assoc S Helena's Epis Ch Boerne TX 2014-2016; S Alb's Epis Ch Arlington TX 1999-2002.

CANNADY, Jessie Edmonia (Colo) D 6/18/2016 Bp Robert John O'Neill.

CANNAN, Andrew (EC) St Lukes Episc Church, 435 Peachtree St NE, Atlanta GA 30308 **S Paul's Epis Ch Greenville NC 2013-** B Pensacola FL 1977 s Stephen & Jane. BA Samford U 1999; MDiv Duke 2005; MDiv Duke 2005; Dplma in Angl Stds GTS 2012; Dplma in Angl Stds The GTS 2012. D 12/17/2011 P 6/24/2012 Bp J Neil Alexander. m 8/14/2004 Ashley A Cannan c 2. Dir of Yth & YA Mnstrs S Lk's Epis Ch Atlanta GA 2008-2013. andrew@stlukesatlanta.org

CANNELL, John Edward (WTex) 11107 Wurzbach Rd Ste 401, San Antonio TX 78230 B Scottsbluff NE 1952 s John & Maxine. BA U Denv 1975; MA U of

Nebraska 1977; MDiv Nash 1980; PhD U of Nebraska 1986. D 5/31/1980 P 12/1/1980 Bp James Daniel Warner. m 5/20/1978 Judith Lynne Hanse. Int S Helena's Epis Ch Boerne TX 1998-1999; Int Trin Ch San Antonio TX 1992-1993; Asst St Fran Epis Ch San Antonio TX 1983-1991; Ch Of The H Trin Lincoln NE 1980-1981. Phi Beta Kappa U Denv 1975; Pi Gamma Mu U Denv 1974.

CANNING, Michael Jacob Brinton (Ida) 2333 W Duck Alley Rd, Eagle ID 83616 B St. John's Newfoundland 1954 BA Memi U of Newfoundland. Trans 3/25/2003 Bp J Clark Grew II. m 8/25/1982 Clarissa A Canning c 3. Ch Of H Nativ Meridian ID 2009-2011; R S Paul's Ch Bellevue OH 2002-2004.

CANNON JR, Alberry Charles (USC) 51 Roper Rd, Flat Rock NC 28731 **Ret 1996-; Gr Ch Cathd Charleston SC 1967-** B Greenville SC 1936 s Alberry & Mary. BA Cit 1957; MDiv Sewanee: The U So, TS 1963. D 6/22/1963 Bp Robert E Gribbin P 5/1/1964 Bp John Adams Pinckney. c 5. Asst Ch Of S Jn In The Wilderness Flat Rock NC 2000-2005; Int Trin Ch Abbeville SC 1997-1998; R S Andr's Epis Ch Greenville SC 1991-1996; Calv Ch Pauline SC 1986-1991; R S Thos Epis Par Miami FL 1976-1985; R S Mk's Ch Cocoa FL 1973-1976; Campus Min So Carolina Charleston SC 1970-1973; R Ch of the Nativ Un SC 1963-1967. Auth, *The Maxwells of Greenville*, 1989; Auth, *Centennial Historty of the Cotillion Club of Greenville So Carolina*, 1988. S Andr's Soc of Upper SC.

CANNON, Carl Thomas (La) 10622 Masters Dr, Clermont FL 34711 B Orlando FL 1939 s Edwin & Jane. BA U of Cntrl Florida 1970; MDiv SWTS 1973. D 6/9/1973 P 12/21/1973 Bp William Hopkins Folwell. c 3. S Lk's Ch Baton Rouge LA 1996-1999; R All SS Epis Ch Memphis TN 1987-1996; R The Epis Ch Of The Mssh Pulaski TN 1982-1987; Assoc S Vinc's Epis Ch St Petersburg FL 1981-1982; Vic H Fam Ch Orlando FL 1975-1980; Stipendiary H Cross Epis Ch Sanford FL 1973-1975.

CANNON III, Charles (SwFla) 87500 Overseas Highway, Islamorada FL 33036 **P S Hilary's Ch Ft Myers FL 2014-** B Greenville SC 1958 s Alberry & Nancy. BA U of Florida 1982; MS Barry U 1985; Cert Dio SE Florida TS FL 1998; MA Sewanee: The U So, TS 2011. D 9/11/1998 Bp John Lewis Said P 6/19/2011 Bp Leo Frade. m 12/29/1984 Lauren Cannon c 2. R S Jas The Fisherman Islamorada FL 2011-2013; D S Paul's Epis Ch Chattanooga TN 2009-2010; D S Jn The Apos Ch Belle Glade FL 2008-2009; D S Dav's-In-The-Pines Epis Ch W Palm Bch 2006-2008; D S Christophers Ch W Palm Bch FL 2001-2006; D S Dav's-In-The-Pines Epis Ch W Palm Bch FL 1998-2001. Cmnty of Blessed Sacr 1975; GAS 1975; Soc of Cath Priests 2011; SocMary 1975.

CANNON, Charles Wilcken (Haw) 291 Shady Glen Ave., Point Roberts WA 98281 **P Trin Luth Ch Point Roberts WA 2001-** B Glendale CA 1935 s Charles & Irene. BS California Maritime Acad 1956; MDiv CDSP 1968; Ripon Coll Cuddesdon Oxford Gb 1968. D 8/23/1968 Bp James Albert Pike P 3/8/1969 Bp George Richard Millard. m 8/24/1984 Shirley Loraine Cannon. R H Innoc' Epis Ch Lahaina HI 1994-2001; Vic S Andr's Ch Ben Lomond CA 1970-1974; Asst Trin Cathd San Jose CA 1968-1970.

CANNON, David Lawrence (Ct) #93 Route 2-A Pouquetanuck, Preston CT 06365 **Ret 2000-** B Buffalo NY 1937 s Raymond & Marian. BS Springfield Coll 1961; STB Ya Berk 1964; MDiv Ya Berk 1964. D 6/11/1964 Bp Duncan Montgomery Gray P 12/1/1964 Bp Joseph Warren Hutchens. m 12/28/1957 Ann-Etta Cannon. S Jas Ch Preston CT 1970-1999; Cur Chr Epis Ch Norwich CT 1964-1965.

CANNON, Justin R (Cal) 911 Dowling Blvd, San Leandro CA 94577 **All SS Epis Ch San Leandro CA 2016-; Dir H Hikes 2010-** B Detroit MI 1984 s Richard & Nancy. BA Earlham Coll 2006; MDiv CDSP 2009. D 6/4/2011 P 12/3/2011 Bp Marc Handley Andrus. P-in-c S Giles Ch Moraga CA 2012-2016; Epis Chars San Francisco CA 2011-2012, 2009-2011; D S Clem's Ch Berkeley CA 2011-2012. Ed, "Homosexuality in the Orth Ch," CreateSpace, 2011; Auth, "The Bible, Chrsnty, & Homosexuality," CreateSpace, 2008; Ed, "Sanctified: An Anthology of Poetry by LGBT Christians," CreateSpace, 2008. Phi Beta Kappa 2006; Soc of S Fran (Assoc) 2009-2015. Top 25 Leading Men of 2007 INSTINCT mag 2007; Out100 People of the Year OUT mag 2006. revjustin.allsaints@gmail.com

CANNON, Thomas Kimball (Chi) 141 S Taylor Ave, Oak Park IL 60302 **Chapl Cook Cnty Dept Of Corrections 1973-** B Oak Park IL 1934 s Joseph & Mary. BS Nthrn Illinois U 1960; LTh Nash 1964. D 6/11/1966 Bp James Winchester Montgomery P 12/1/1966 Bp Gerald Francis Burrill. m 6/8/1963 Kathleen M Kirby c 2. S Andr's Ch Chicago IL 2000-2006; St Leonards Hse Chicago IL 1978-1982; Dio Chicago Chicago IL 1973-1977; Vic S Anselm's Pk Ridge IL 1968-1973; Cur Trin Epis Ch Wheaton IL 1966-1968. Amer Correctional Chapl Assn.

CANO, George Luciano (SJ) 3605 Shady Valley Ct, Modesto CA 95355 B San Mateo CA 1937 s Francis & Frances. Mennonite Brethren Biblic Sem; San Joaquin Schools For Mnstry; TESM. D 12/13/2003 Bp David Mercer Schofield. m 11/2/1968 Jeanne Cano c 5. Chr The King Ch Riverbank CA 2003-2004; Ch Of The Gd Shpd Tomball TX 2003-2004.

CANTELLA, Frances French (Los) 30015 Buchanan Way, Castaic CA 91384 **Asst St. Barn Epis Ch 2005-** B Los Angeles CA 1947 d William & Frances. BS Woodbury U 1997. D 11/14/2004 Bp Joseph Jon Bruno P 5/15/2005 Bp Chester Lovelle Talton. m 4/26/2003 Vincent Cantella c 1. R S Barn' Epis Ch Los Angeles CA 2010-2015.

CANTER, Matthew A (SanD) PO Box 127, Carlsbad CA 92018 B Zanesville OH 1983 s Robert & Kathy. BSS Ohio U 2008; MDiv Nash 2011. D 6/4/2011 Bp Mark Joseph Lawrence P 12/3/2011 Bp Jim Mathes. m 12/9/2006 Ashley D Canter c 2. Cur S Michaels By-The-Sea Ch Carlsbad CA 2011-2012.

CANTERBURY, Marion Lucille (RG) 5304 Rincon Rd Nw, Albuquerque NM 87105 B Fort Worth TX 1927 d Claude & Emma. BA New Mex St U 1976; MDiv CDSP 1979. D 8/6/1979 P 6/1/1980 Bp Richard Mitchell Trelease Jr. Chr Epis Ch Douglas WY 1997-2002; Int S Geo's Ch Lusk WY 1997-2002; S Jn The Bapt Ch Glendo WY 1997-2002; S Andr's Epis Ch Las Cruces NM 1989-1990; Nat'L Religeous Partnership New York NY 1985-1988; R S Barn Dio The Rio Grande 1984-1995; Dio The Rio Grande Albuquerque NM 1979-1985.

CANTOR, Este (Cal) 1105 High Ct, Berkeley CA 94708 **Vic The Epis Ch Of The Gd Shpd Berkeley CA 2010-** B Sandusky MI 1950 d David & Joan. Corcoran Sch of Art Washington DC 1975; BA Antioch Coll W San Francisco CA 1977; MDiv CDSP 2005. D 6/4/2005 P 12/3/2005 Bp William Edwin Swing. m 10/14/1989 Matt Geoffrey Cantor c 2. P-in-c Ch Of The H Trin Richmond CA 2010-2013; Chapl An Epis Mnstry to Convalescent Hospitals (Aemch) Fremont CA 2008-2011; Assoc R for Chld's and Yth Mnstrs Ch Of Our Sav Mill Vlly CA 2006-2009; Dioc Faith Formation Com Mem Dio California 2006-2007; Assoc P All Souls Par In Berkeley Berkeley CA 2005-2006; Intern Chaplain St. Paul's Epis Sch Oakland 2003-2004; DRE All Souls Par 1998-2006; Peace, Justice and Integrity of Creation Com Dio California San Francisco CA 2006-2007.

CANTOS DELGADO, Jose (EcuL) B Guayaquil 1962 s Emiliano & Lidia. licencia ISEDET Facultad Teologia - Buenos Aires (Argentina) 1990. D 4/3/2016 Bp Terencio Alfredo Morante-Espana. m 10/27/2007 Wilma Mercedes Garcia.

CANTRELL, Darla (Nev) PO Box 181, Austin NV 89310 B Reno NV 1954 d Chas & Shirley. D 10/24/2008 P 4/26/2009 Bp Dan Thomas Edwards. m 11/12/2008 Mitchell D Cantrell c 2.

CANTRELL, Laura (Ga) Christ Church, 1521 N Patterson St, Valdosta GA 31602 B Charleston SC 1949 d Paul & Margaret. BA Converse Coll 1971; MLS U of So Carolina 1973; MDiv Bex Sem 1992. D 6/13/1992 Bp Edward Lloyd Salmon Jr P 1/30/1993 Bp William George Burrill. m 12/15/2004 Jeffrey Whittaker Meadowcroft c 2. Int R Chr Ch Valdosta GA 2012-2014; Cn Trin Cathd Columbia SC 2006-2012; R All SS Epis Ch Clinton SC 2000-2006; S Phil's Epis Ch Greenville SC 1999; Trin Ch Abbeville SC 1998; S Paul's Epis Ch Stafford NY 1994-1996; Serv S Mk's And S Jn's Epis Ch Rochester NY 1992-1993.

CANTRELL, Patricia Martin (Miss) PO Box 316, West Point MS 39773 **D Epis Ch Of The Incarn W Point MS 2011-** B Hattiesburg MS 1954 d Fred & Miriam. BS Mississippi St U; MS Mississippi St U. D 1/15/2011 Bp Duncan Montgomery Gray III. m 8/6/2011 Jimmy Dale Harris c 2.

CAPALDO, Christopher James (La) 801 Atlantic Ave, Fernandina Beach FL 32034 **Ch Of The H Comm Plaquemine LA 2017-** B Clearwater FL 1988 s Robert & Joyce. BA Florida St U 2011; BA The Florida St U 2011; BA The Florida St U 2011; MDiv Sewanee: The U So, TS 2014; MDiv The TS at The U So 2014; MDiv The U So 2014. D 12/8/2013 P 6/15/2014 Bp Samuel Johnson Howard. Asst S Ptr's Ch Fernandina Bch FL 2016; Dio Florida Jacksonville 2014-2016. ccapaldo@stpetersparish.org

CAPELLARO, John Joseph (Los) 13029 Central Ave Unit 304, Hawthorne CA 90250 B Philadelphia PA 1951 s Leon & Jane. Penn 1971; MDiv Sewanee: The U So, TS 1995. D 6/3/1995 P 12/9/1995 Bp Richard Frank Grein. m 1/16/1971 Bernadette C Verderese c 2. Dio Los Angeles Los Angeles CA 2007-2008; R S Mich and All Ang Epis Ch Studio City CA 2004-2007; S Paul's Ch Norfolk VA 1998-2005; Asst Trin Ch Solebury PA 1995-1998. "Searching the Heart of God," Green Tree Press, 2003.

CAPITELLI, Stephen Richard (Mil) St John in the Wilderness, 13 S Church St, Elkhorn WI 53121 **S Alb's Ch Sussex WI 2013-** B Peoria IL 1954 s Richard & Mary Louise. BS SUNY 1990; MDiv Nash 2007. D 12/11/2006 P 2/5/2007 Bp Keith Lynn Ackerman. m 9/1/2001 Cathy Capitelli c 3. P-in-c S Jn In The Wilderness Elkhorn WI 2007-2013. frsteve@stalbans-sussex.org

CAPPEL, Jerry (Ky) 344 Reed Ln, Simpsonville KY 40067 **Advsry Coun on the Stwdshp of Creation ECD New York NY 2016-; Environ Ntwk Coordntr Prov IV Jackson MS 2012-** B North Platte NE 1956 s Clarence & Velda. BA Lubbock Chr U 1979; MDiv Harding Grad Sch Memphis 1983; PhD Sthrn Bapt TS 1994. D 6/4/2005 P 12/10/2005 Bp Ted Gulick Jr. m 6/24/2001 Jean Gail Hawxhurst c 2. S Jas Ch Pewee Vlly KY 2015-2016; Ch Of The Ascen Frankfort KY 2012-2014; S Matt's Epis Ch Louisville KY 2009-2011; D Resurr Ch Louisville KY 2005-2009. Auth, "Environ Advocacy and the Absence of the Ch," *Ecotheology and NonHuman Ethics in Soc*, Lexington Books, 2017; Auth, "A Life of Gr for the Whole Wrld," *Leaders Guide for Yth and Adults*, Ch Pub, 2017; Auth, "Deeper Green Ch," *Sewanee Theol Revs*, U So, 2014.

CAPPER, Steve (Tex) 4405 McKinney St, Houston TX 77023 **Vic The Great Cmsn Fndt Houston TX 2015-; Pres, Int Ex. Dir. For Houston's Kids 2013-** B Columbus OH 1953 s Robert & Barbara. BS Texas A&M U 1974; MDiv Epis TS of the SW 1980. D 8/6/1980 P 4/1/1981 Bp Richard Mitchell Trelease Jr. m

7/20/1974 Karen L Cates c 3. Exec Dir Mssn Houston 2003-2012; R Ch Of The Redeem Houston TX 1994-2003; Mem The Stndg Com Dio Indianapolis IN 1992-1994; Mem Stwdshp Cmsn Dio Indianapolis IN 1989-1991; R S Johns Ch Indianapolis IN 1987-1994; Mem Cmsn on Wrld Missions Dio the Rio Grande TX 1985-1987; Consult in Evang & Renwl Serv Angl Ch inTasmania Dio Tasmania Austra 1984-1985; Mem Cmsn on the Mnstry Dio the Rio Grande TX 1981-1983; Asst Pro Cathd Epis Ch Of S Clem El Paso TX 1980-1987. "The Marks of a Mentor," *The Mentoring Handbook*, Afr Mnstry Resources, 2005. ERM 1982-1993; SOMA 1994-2003. scapper@lordofthestreets.org

CAPPERS, Linda Frances (Me) 30 Hemlock Dr, Saco ME 04072 **Trin Ch Saco ME 2007-** B Brockton MA 1946 d Girdham & Lillian. BA Hobart and Wm Smith Colleges 1968; Rhode Island Sch for Deacons 1995. D 6/24/1995 Bp J Clark Grew II. m 8/31/1968 Stephen Roger Cappers. D Chr Ch In Lonsdale Lincoln RI 2000-2006; D S Paul's Ch Pawtucket RI 1996-2000; D S Mart's Ch Pawtucket RI 1995-1996; Dio Rhode Island Providence RI 2003-2006. Fell S Jn; NAAD; SCHC. Phi Beta Kappa Wm Smith 1968.

CAPWELL, Kim F (Del) 2400 W 17th St, Wilmington DE 19806 **R Imm Ch Highlands Wilmington DE 2008-** B Paterson NJ 1953 s Milton & Betty. AAS Bergen Cmnty Coll 1980; BS Wm Paterson U 1984; MDiv VTS 1988. D 5/28/1988 P 12/3/1988 Bp John Shelby Spong. m 8/13/1977 Sharon L Capwell c 3. Chapl Heath Vill Hackettstown NJ 1992-2008; R S Ptr's Ch Mt Arlington NJ 1992-2008; R All SS' Epis Ch Glen Rock NJ 1990-1992; R Trin Ch Irvington NJ 1988-1990. kcapwell@immanuel-highlands.org

CARABIN, Robert Jerome (WTex) 203 Panama Ave, San Antonio TX 78210 **Asstg prist S Paul's Epis Ch San Antonio TX 2006-** B San Antonio TX 1935 s Robert & Evelyn. BA Immac Concep Sem 1960; BD Immac Concep Sem 1964; BA S Marys U San Antonio TX 1966; MEd Our Lady of the Lake U San Antonio TX 1971; EdD Texas A&M U 1981. Rec 1/1/1971 as Priest Bp Scott Field Bailey. m 12/27/1974 Joan Anne Carabin. Asstg P Chr Epis Ch San Antonio TX 2001-2005, 1996-2000; Vic S Matt's Epis Ch Kenedy TX 1994-1995; S Mk's Epis Ch San Antonio TX 1992-1994; Asst S Fran Epis Ch Victoria TX 1988-1992; R Gr Ch Port Lavaca TX 1986-1988; Vic All SS Epis Ch Pleasanton TX 1986; Vic S Mths Devine TX 1983-1986; Vic S Tim's Ch Cotulla TX 1983-1986; Asst S Andr's Epis Ch San Antonio TX 1979-1982; Asst St Fran Epis Ch San Antonio TX 1977-1979. Auth, "So Common a Name," *LivCh*, 1996; Auth, "Pryr Cats," *LivCh*, 1996.

CARADINE, Billie Charles (Ala) Po Box 787, Asotin WA 99402 **Ret 1995-** B Flat Creek AL 1928 s Thomas & Cladys. BA Birmingham-Sthrn Coll 1957; MDiv Sewanee: The U So, TS 1966. D 6/16/1966 P 4/29/1967 Bp George Mosley Murray. m 8/15/1992 Lillian Francine Caradine. Int Epis Ch of the Nativ Lewiston ID 1998-2000; Exec For Mssn Plnng Epis Ch Cntr New York NY 1988-1994; Exec Coun Appointees New York NY 1987-1988; Cn Ordnry Dio Alabama Birmingham 1984-1987, 1974-1988; S Mich's Epis Ch Birmingham AL 1974-1984; Vic S Mich's Ch Ozark AL 1967-1971; Vic Ch Of The Epiph Enterprise AL 1966-1971. Auth, "Alabama Plan".

CARBERRY, Timothy Oliver (SO) 49 Dipper Cove Rd, Orrs Island ME 04066 **Ret 2002-** B Warwick NY 1944 s Oliver & Louise. BA Hobart and Wm Smith Colleges 1966; MDiv GTS 1969. D 6/11/1969 Bp John Henry Esquirol P 12/13/1969 Bp Joseph Warren Hutchens. c 2. R S Alb's Epis Ch of Bexley Columbus OH 1982-2002; Chr Ch Oxford CT 1970-1982; Vic S Ptr's Epis Ch Oxford CT 1970-1972; Cur S Mary's Epis Ch Manchester CT 1969-1970. Auth, "They Were Spoken Here (Bklet Sermons)".

CARCEL-MARTINEZ, Antonio (Hond) Apdo 52, Camino Rio Mar, Puerto Cortes Honduras **Iglesia Epis San Fernando-Rey Omoa Co 1993-; Vic Mision Epis Bola Laguna Puerto Cortes 1993-** B Los Duques Reguena ES 1943 s Dionisio & Amparo. Lic U of Barcelona Barcelona Es; U of Madrid. Rec 1/1/1995 as Priest Bp Leo Frade. m 5/11/1990 Maria Gladis Argentina Vasquez de Carcel c 1. Dio Honduras San Pedro Sula 1995-2011; Serv RC Ch 1971-1990.

CARD, Sarah June Coffey (Los) 24102 Avenida Corona, Dana Point CA 92629 **Pstr Care Co-ordinator S Marg of Scotland Epis Ch San Juan Capistr 1995-** B 1931 d Charley & Ruby. ETSBH 2006. D 12/2/2006 Bp Chester Lovelle Talton. m 11/6/1967 Jack Card c 6.

CARDEN, Larry Edward (Tenn) University Of The South, Spo, Sewanee TN 37375 **P-in-c S Agnes Cowan 1982-** B New York NY 1944 s Paul & Wynona. BA DePauw U 1967; BD Yale DS 1970; PhD Van 1980. D 2/21/1977 Bp William Evan Sanders P 3/1/1978 Bp William F Gates Jr. m 8/28/1971 Barbara F Fittz. Sewanee U So TS Sewanee TN 1982-2015; Chr Ch Cathd Nashville TN 1981, P 1977-1980. Auth, "Theol," 1988; Auth, "Waiting Sprtl Transformation & The Absence Of God," *S Lk Journ*.

CARDONE, Susan Holliday (Los) 6125 Carlos Ave, Los Angeles CA 90028 B Pasadena CA 1964 d Savino & Donna. BA DePaul U 1997; Angl Stds Bloy Hse 2014; MDiv Claremont TS 2014. D 6/3/2017 Bp Diane Jardine Bruce. c 2. St Stephens Epis Pre-Sch Los Angeles CA 2015-2016.

CARDOZA, Edward Miguel (Mass) 116 South St, Foxboro MA 02035 **S Mk's Ch Foxborough MA 2015-** B Malden MA 1972 s Arthur & Catherine. AB St Jn's Sem 1994; MA.Min St Jn's Sem 2003. D 6/6/2015 Bp Gayle Harris

P 12/11/2015 Bp Alan Gates. m 12/31/2012 Albert A Cummings. ecardoza@stillharbor.org

CARDWELL, Sarah L (ETenn) **Middleham & S Ptr's Par Lusby MD 2016-** B 1987 d Derek & Susan. B.A. Sewanee: The U So 2009; M. Div. VTS 2016. D 2/6/2016 Bp George Young III P 8/13/2016 Bp Chilton Richardson Knudsen. m 10/8/2016 Amanda Ann Akes.

CAREY, Brent (SanD) 2561 Wexford Rd, Upper Arlington OH 43221 **Chapl The OH SU Wexner Med Cntr 2017-; Emergency Dept Chapl CHRISTUS Hosp -- St. Eliz Beaumont TX 2015-; Chapl Res VA San Diego Healthcare System 2012-** B Cleveland OH 1953 s Frank & Phyllis. BA OH SU 1976; MDiv CDSP 1993. D 6/7/1997 Bp William Edwin Swing P 12/6/1997 Bp Douglas Edwin Theuner. m 4/12/1997 Elizabeth H Carey c 4. S Mk's Ch Grand Rapids MI 2015-2016; Long-Term Supply H Trin Epis Par San Diego CA 2011-2013; R S Dav's Epis Ch San Diego CA 2001-2010; Assoc R S Jn's Ch Lynchburg VA 1998-2001; Cur Chr Ch Exeter NH 1997-1998.

CAREY, Grant S (NCal) 2701 Capitol Ave Apt 302, Sacramento CA 95816 **Died 2/21/2017** B Oakland CA 1925 s Grant & Mildred. BA California St U 1951; MA California St U 1952; MDiv CDSP 1957. D 6/29/1957 Bp Archie Noel Porter P 1/18/1958 Bp Clarence Rupert Haden Jr. Cn Res Trin Epis Cathd Sacramento CA 2006-2017, 1983-2005; Headmaster Colegio San Justo PR 1963-1968; Chapl Colegio San Justo PR 1961-1963; Vic S Jn's Epis Ch Lakeport CA 1957-1961. DD CDSP 2007.

CAREY, Pamela Hann (Cal) 525 29th St, Oakland CA 94609 B Houston TX 1963 d Horace & Ann. Cert Epis Sch for Deacons 2009. D 12/3/2011 Bp Marc Handley Andrus. m 4/30/1988 Edward Joseph Carey c 2. S Cuth's Epis Ch Oakland CA 2013-2014.

CAREY, Peter M (SwFla) 5602 Cary Street Rd, Richmond VA 23226 **Berkeley Preparatory Sch Tampa FL 2014-** B Middlebury VT 1969 s Jason & Carolyn. BA Bates Coll 1991; MEd GW Washington DC 1995; MDiv VTS 2007. D 6/9/2007 Bp Charles Ellsworth Bennison Jr P 12/18/2007 Bp Peter J Lee. m 6/29/2017 Lisa E Plog c 3. P S Paul's Memi Charlottesvlle VA 2012-2014; Emm Epis Ch Greenwood VA 2009-2012; S Cathr's Sch Richmond VA 2007-2009; Upper Sch Hist&Rel Tchr The Epis Acad 2000-2004. petermcarey@gmail.com

CAREY, Peter R (NY) 150 9th Ave Apt 1, New York NY 10011 **Asstg P Ch Of The H Apos New York NY 1998-** B New York NY 1938 s Peter & Kathleen. BA Providence Coll 1962; MA S Steph Coll 1964; STL Dominican Hse of Stds 1967; MA Aquinas Inst of Theol 1970. Rec 6/1/1990 Bp Harold Barrett Robinson. m 10/6/2007 David M Natoli. Vic S Steph's Epis Ch Woodlaw Bronx NY 1998-2000, 1991-1996; Dio New York New York NY 1997.

CAREY SSF, Tom (Los) 888 N Alameda St, Los Angeles CA 90012 **Vic Ch Of The Epiph Los Angeles CA 2010-** B Santa Monica CA 1951 s Henry & Marilyn. Actors and Dir Lab 1975; BA Col 1998; MDiv CDSP 2002. D 5/27/2002 Bp Jerry Alban Lamb P 2/28/2003 Bp Orris George Walker Jr. P-in-c S Pat's Ch Deer Pk NY 2005-2010; Cur Ch Of The Redeem Astoria NY 2002-2004; Yth Dir All SS Ch Woodhaven NY 1989-1999. Auth, "Sm Crimes," Blazevox Books, 2011; Auth, "Desire: Poems 1989-1999," Painted Leaf Press, 1997. tomascarey@gmail.com

CARHARTT, Forrest Andrew (Colo) 4737 Mckinley Dr, Boulder CO 80303 **Asst P S Jn's Epis Ch Boulder CO 1997-; Chapl Boulder Cnty Ret Off Assn 1996-; Pstr Serv Presb Ch (USA) 1954-** B Denver CO 1923 s Forrest & Helen. BS USMA 1945; MDiv Pittsburgh TS 1954; DMin McCormick TS 1985; CAS Iliff TS 1997. D 6/7/1997 P 12/28/1997 Bp William Jerry Winterrowd. m 10/12/1946 Virginia Whipple c 5. Bd Trst Dio Colorado Denver CO 1997-2003. Auth, *These Days*, Presby Ch (USA), 1982; Auth, *These Days*, Presby Ch (USA), 1976; Auth, *These Days*, Presby Ch (USA), 1974. Assn of Graduates USMA W Point 1945.

CARL, Elizabeth (WA) 1414 Montague St NW, Washington DC 20011 B Houston TX 1947 d Emory & Margaret. BA Occ 1969; GW 1972; MLS CUA 1976; MDiv UTS 1990. D 6/9/1990 P 6/5/1991 Bp Ronald Hayward Haines. m 1/5/2011 Victoria C Hill. Int R S Thos' Par Washington DC 2003-2004; Int R S Phil's Epis Ch Laurel MD 2000-2001; EAP Libr of Congr Washington DC 1996-1997; Assoc. Fac The Cathd Coll Washington DC 1995-2007; Mem, Comm On Mnstry Dio Washington Washington DC 1994-2000, Mem of COM 1994-2000; Int Assoc The Ch Of The Epiph Washington DC 1993-1994, Asst 1991-1992; Bd Mem UTS NY NY 1991-1999; Epis Chapl Washington Hosp Cntr Washington DC 1991-1992; D S Mary Magd Ch Silver Sprg MD 1991, D 1990-1991. Auth, "Going Fishing," *The Bk Of Wmn Sermons*, Riverhead Books, 1999; Auth, "Bk Revs," *Chrsnty & Crisis*, 1991. EWC 1980; Integrity 1978; Washington DC Epis Cler Assoc. 1990. Maxwell Fell. for Excellence In Pstr Mnstry UTS NY NY 1990; Hudnut Preaching Prize UTS NY NY 1989.

CARLETON, Ellen Diane (Wyo) 519 E Park Ave, Riverton WY 82501 B Lander WY 1951 d Leonard & Mary. BA Goddard Coll 2012. D 6/11/2014 P 1/24/2015 Bp John Smylie. m 12/6/1980 Guy H Carleton c 3.

CARLETTA, David M (WTenn) St Andrew's Church, 17 South Ave, Beacon NY 12508 **S Andr's Ch Beacon NY 2012-; Mem Angl-RC Dialogue (ARC-NY) 2013-** B Rochester, NY 1967 s Paul & Mary Ann. PhD MI SU 2009; MDiv GTS 2010. D 5/29/2010 P 12/3/2010 Bp Wendell Nathaniel Gibbs Jr. m 8/12/

2006 Susanne K Eineigel c 1. P S Andr's Epis Ch Collierville TN 2014-2017; Dio New York New York NY 2012-2016; Asst. to the R The Ch of S Matt And S Tim New York NY 2010-2012. Prchr, "Matt 5:10," *Preaching the Beatitudes*, Preaching Excellence Prog/ Epis Preaching Fndt, 2009.

CARLIN, Christine (EC) 810 Fisher St Apt 4, Morehead City NC 28557 B Ridgewood NJ 1952 d John & Clare. BA Jas Madison U 1975; MA Kent St U 1977; MDiv VTS 1991. D 6/15/1991 Bp Ronald Hayward Haines P 2/1/1992 Bp David Reed. S Chris's Ch Havelock NC 2012-2016; Assoc R S Tim's Epis Ch Greenville NC 2000-2005; S Fran Ch Greensboro NC 1998-2001; R Gr Ch Newton MA 1996-1998; Assoc S Fran In The Fields Harrods Creek KY 1991-1996.

CARLIN II SSJE, William B (Okla) 3508 Robert Drive, Duncan OK 73533 B Jackson MS 1950 s William & Betty. BS U of Sthrn Mississippi 1972; MDiv Sewanee: The U So, TS 1996; DMin SWTS 2008. D 6/22/1996 P 12/21/1996 Bp Alfred Marble Jr. c 1. R S Andr's Epis Ch Lawton OK 2002-2010; R S Alb's Epis Ch Vicksburg MS 1998-2002; S Mary's Ch Lexington MS 1996-1998; Vic S Matt's Epis Ch Kosciusko MS 1996-1998.

CARLING, Paul Joseph (Ct) Saint Paul's Episcopal Church, 661 Old Post Road, Fairfield CT 06824 **Trin Epis Ch Trumbull CT 2016-; Epis Ch At Yale New Haven CT 2014-, Chapl & P in Charge 2014-** B New York NY 1945 s James & Mary. BA U of Pennsylvania 1971; MS U of Pennsylvania 1973; PhD U of Pennsylvania 1977; MDiv EDS 2002. D 6/16/2002 P 12/21/2002 Bp Thomas C Ely. m 6/17/1995 Cherise A Rowan c 2. Assoc R S Paul's Ch Fairfield CT 2011-2016; Assoc R S Lk's Par Darien CT 2004-2011; Assoc R S Mich's Epis Ch Brattleboro VT 2002-2004; Int Dir Bp Booth Conf Cntr Burlington VT 2002, Int Dir 2002; Exec Dir Cntr for Cmnty Change Intl 1983-1999; Dep Cmssnr Vermont Dept of Mntl Hlth 1981-1983; Asst to Dir Natl Instute of Mntl Hlth 1979-1981; Bureau Chf New Jersey Dept of Mntl Hlth & Hospitals 1977-1979; Prog Dir Horizon Hse Psychosocial Rehab Cntr 1973-1977; Chair, Title III T/F Dio Connecticut Meriden CT 2011-2012, Treas, Bridgeport Dnry 2011-2012, Mem, Title IV Eccl Cmsn 2011-, Fac, Bridgeport Mssn Ldrshp Team 2010-2012, Mem, COM 2009-2012, Bd Mem, St. Jn's Fam Cntr 2008-; Dio Vermont Burlington VT 2000-2002; Chair, T/F on Campus Mnstry Cathd Ch Of S Paul Burlington VT 2000-2001. Auth, "Multiple Bk Chapters - arts In Psychol Journ," 1998; Auth, "Coming Hm," Guilford Press, 1995. Fllshp Of The Soc Of S Jn The Evang 2000. Excellence In Liturg Reading Massachusetts Bible Soc 2001.

CARLISLE, Christopher Arthur Elliott (WMass) 758 N Pleasant St, Amherst MA 01002 B Windsor ON CA 1953 s Arthur & Elizabeth. BA Col 1975; MA Harvard DS 1978; MDiv Ya Berk 1982. D 9/26/1981 P 3/26/1982 Bp Alexander D Stewart. m 6/7/2008 Nathalie Lavoie c 5. Chapl Dio Wstrn Massachusetts Springfield 1983-2013; S Andr's Ch Longmeadow MA 1982-1983. Auth, "The Real Meaning Of The Reformation (Humor)," *The Wittenburg Door*, 1990; Auth, "The Christmas Chld," 1984; Auth, "In Memoriam," 1983. ESMHE.

CARLISLE, Michael Emerson (Lex) 85 Mikell Ln, Sewanee TN 37375 B Lexington KY 1947 s Ralph & Thelma. K SU 1967; BA U of Mississippi 1971; MDiv Sewanee: The U So, TS 1975. D 5/28/1975 P 6/21/1976 Bp Duncan Montgomery Gray Jr. m 12/31/1996 Doris Carlisle c 2. Trin Epis Ch Florence AL 2006-2007; S Ptr's Ch Paris KY 1995-2005; Dio Atlanta Atlanta GA 1989-1995, Liturg Cmsn 1984-1988; Dir Rondo Retreat Cntr Kakalega Kenya 1988-1995; Prncpl St. Philips Theol Coll Kongwa Tanzania 1988-1991; S Pat's Epis Ch Atlanta GA 1988-1989; R Ch Of The Ascen Cartersville GA 1982-1988; Assoc H Sprt Epis Ch Houston TX 1979-1982; S Mary's Ch Enterprise MS 1975-1979; Cur S Paul's Epis Ch Meridian MS 1975-1979; Trin Ch Newton MS 1975-1979.

CARLISTO OTCG, John Bradley (EC) 121 Radley Ln, Beaufort NC 28516 **Exec Coun Dio E Carolina Kinston NC 2015-2018, Trst U So 2009-2011, Evang Cmsn 2009-2010, Fin Dept 2005-2009; Grievence Revs Bd Beaufort Hsng Authority 2013-** B Jacksonville NC 1954 s John & Thelma. BS Natl U 1983; MDiv Sewanee: The U So, TS 1986. D 5/23/1986 Bp Furman Charles Stough P 12/11/1986 Bp Robert Oran Miller. m 4/16/1977 Janice Marie Skotte c 3. R S Paul's Ch Beaufort NC 2004-2017; R Chr Epis Ch Albertville AL 1988-2004; Assoc R S Jn's Ch Decatur AL 1986-1988; Mem of the Corp Bd Boys and Girls Clubs of Coastal Carolina 2010-2015. No Carolina Area Coun Bd Mem of the Year Boys and Girls Clubs of Amer 2013; Robert E. Hallman Serv Awd Boys and Girls Club of Coastal Carolina 2012; Infulential of the Year Boys and Girls Clubs of Coastal Carolina 2009; Citizen of the Year Chamber of Commerce Albertvile AL 1997; scl Natl U San Diego CA 1983.

CARLOZZI, Carl Gillman (Az) 10801 East Happy Valley Road, Lot #53, Scottsdale AZ 85255 **Chapl Phoenix Fire Dept 2003-; Ret 2002-** B Canton OH 1940 s Carl & Barbara. BA Ken 1962; MDiv EDS 1965; DMin Luther Rice TS 1977. D 6/29/1965 Bp Nelson Marigold Burroughs P 2/12/1966 Bp Plinio L Simoes. m 11/8/1985 Muriel McClellan c 4. Chapl Phoenix Fire Dept 1993-2002; R All SS Ch Phoenix AZ 1980-2002; R S Chris's Ch Chatham MA 1969-1980; Chapl Chatham Police Dept 1969-1971; Asst S Jas Ch Montclair NJ 1967-1968; Cur S Paul's Ch Maumee OH 1965-1967; Cathd Chapt Dio Arizona Phoenix AZ 1989-1992, COM 1981-1988. Auth, "Death & Contemporary Man"; Auth,

"Through Life's Window"; Auth, "Pocket Parables"; Auth, "Episcopalians & the Bible"; Auth, "The Epis Way"; Auth, "The New Epis Way"; Auth, "Prayers for Pstr & People"; Auth, "Promises & Prayers for Healing". Hon Kachina Awd for Volunteerism 1999; Hon Cn Trin Cathd 1992.

CARLSEN, Gail Melin (Az) 3756 E Marble Peak Pl, Tucson AZ 85718 **Vic All SS Epis Ch Safford AZ 2012-; Ret 2009-** B Glen Ridge NJ 1944 d Carl & Mildred. BA Wellesley Coll 1966; BFA U of Arizona 1976; MDiv Ya Berk 1991. D 6/8/1991 P 12/29/1991 Bp Joseph Thomas Heistand. m 7/9/2009 John Knox Freeman. Assoc S Phil's In The Hills Tucson AZ 2004-2009, 2003-2009, 1993-1995; S Mk's Ch New Canaan CT 1996-2002; S Alb's Epis Ch St Petersburg FL 1991-1993; Asst To Dn Ya Berk New Haven CT 1991-1992.

CARLSEN, Stephen Earl (Ind) 55 Monument Cir Ste 600, Indianapolis IN 46204 **Dn and R Chr Ch Cathd Indianapolis IN 2007-; Bd Mem CEEP Austin TX 2012-; Trst at Lg, Vice-Chair since 2014 Ya Berk New Haven CT 2009-** B Des Moines IA 1965 s Charles & Sherrian. PrTS; BA Wheaton Coll 1988; MDiv U Chi DS 1994. D 6/15/1996 P 1/17/1997 Bp Frank Tracy Griswold III. m 5/31/2012 Jennifer L Hund c 2. Sub-Dn and Cn S Jn's Cathd Denver CO 2003-2007; R Harcourt Par Gambier OH 1998-2003; Cur Chr Ch Winnetka IL 1996-1998. Auth, "A Message So Gd As To Border On Folly," *Preaching Through The Year Of Mk: Sermons That Wk Viii*, Morehouse Pub, 1999. stephenc@cccindy.org

CARLSEN, Vause Smith (EMich) 745 E Main St, Flushing MI 48433 **Died 11/18/2016** B Gallipolis OH 1932 d John & Veta. BA Marshall U 1954; MA Ohio U 1955. D 2/11/2006 Bp Edwin Max Leidel Jr. m 9/2/1955 Paul B Carlsen c 3.

CARLSON, Carol Emma (NwPa) Po Box 328, Mount Jewett PA 16740 B Bradford PA 1945 d Carl & Vivian. BA Rad 1967; MDiv EDS 1980; SUNY 1992. D 6/17/2000 P 12/17/2000 Bp Robert Deane Rowley Jr. c 2. S Mary's Ch Erie PA 2006-2007; Int Ch Of The H Cross No E PA 2003-2013; Int Chr Ch Coudersport PA 2000-2002; D Gr Epis Ch Ridgway PA 2000. Soc Of S Fran 1973.

CARLSON, Constance (Oly) St Andrew's Episc Church, 111 NE 80th St, Seattle WA 98115 B Seattle WA 1944 d Ronald & Muriel. BA Seattle Pacific U 2002; MDiv CDSP 2007. D 1/26/2008 Bp Gregory Harold Rickel. m 1/29/1965 Lawrence Carlson c 3. Assoc R S Andr's Ch Seattle WA 2009-2016.

CARLSON, David John (Mich) 28217 Edward Ave, Madison Heights MI 48071 B Detroit MI 1946 s David & Phyllis. BS Wayne 1969; MA U MI 1972; Whitaker TS 1986. D 2/2/1991 Bp R aymond Stewart Wood Jr. m 12/29/1967 Kay Frances Carlson c 2. D S Pat's Epis Ch Madison Hts MI 2011; D S Lk's Ch Ferndale MI 1997-2008; S Marg's Ch Hazel Pk MI 1997-2007; D S Andr's Ch Clawson MI 1991-1996; Chapl Wm Beaumont Hosp Royal Oak 1991-1996. Auth, "The Diac Trng Cntr of the Dio Michigan," *Diakoneo*, 2000. NAAD 1991.

CARLSON, David Lee (NY) 84 Seward Ave, Port Jervis NY 12771 **Assoc Dio New York New York NY 2008-; P Gr Epis Ch Port Jervis NY 2008-** B Rockville Centre NY 1958 s Edwin & Gwendolyn. BA Ham 1981; Cert The London Acad of Mus and Dramatic Art 1982; MDiv GTS 1992. D 3/25/1992 Bp Leigh Allen Wallace Jr P 9/1/1992 Bp Walter Decoster Dennis Jr. m 10/16/2009 Timothy Smith. R Ch Of The Gd Shpd New York NY 2005-2008; Adj Prof The GTS 2005; R S Aug's Epis Ch Croton Hdsn NY 1996-2005; Cur Ch Of S Mary The Vrgn New York NY 1992-1996. Ord Of S Jn Of Jerusalem 1996; OHC 1994. ggoldstein@hvc.rr.com

CARLSON, Geraldine Beatrice (WMich) 1287 La Chaumiere Drive # 5, Petoskey MI 46770 B Philadelphia PA 1923 d Melville & Geraldine. EFM Sewanee: The U So, TS 1996. D 7/7/1996 Bp Edward Lewis Lee Jr. m 8/14/1948 Howard Carlson c 1. D Emm Ch Petoskey MI 1996-2004.

CARLSON, Kelly B (Mo) Saint Peter's Episcopal Church, 110 N Warson Rd, Saint Louis MO 63124 **Dioc Stndg Com Dio Missouri S Louis MO 2012-, Dioc BEC 2011-** B Hannibal MO 1964 d Rodney & Carol. BA Westminster Coll Fulton MO 1987; JD Ya 1990; MA Marylhurst U 2003; MDiv CDSP 2008. D 6/7/2008 Bp Johncy Itty P 1/10/2009 Bp George Wayne Smith. Asst to the R S Ptr's Epis Ch S Louis MO 2008-2011, Assoc R 2008-.

CARLSON, Kit (Mich) 907 Southlawn Ave, East Lansing MI 48823 **R All SS Ch E Lansing MI 2007-** B Indianapolis IN 1959 d Harry & Katherine. MI SU 1978; BS U of Florida 1980; MDiv VTS 2000; DMin VTS 2015. D 6/10/2000 Bp Ronald Hayward Haines P 12/16/2000 Bp Jane Hart Holmes Dixon. m 6/14/1980 Wendell Dana Lynch c 1. Assoc Ch Of The Ascen Gaithersburg MD 2000-2007. Auth, "Working Dogs:Tales From The K9-5 Wrld," Discovery Books/ Random Hse, 2000; Auth, "Bringing Up Baby: Wild Animal Families," Crown Pub, 1998; Auth, "The Leopard Son," Mcgraw Hill, 1996. Mem Washington Epis Cler Assn 2000; SBL 1998-2000. Read Prchr/Schlr Awd Madison Av Presb Ch 2000; Mdiv cl VTS 2000.

CARLSON, Monica (Ala) 2310 Skyland Blvd E, Tuscaloosa AL 35405 **Epis Ch Of The Epiph Leeds AL 2015-** B Jackson MS 1957 d William & Ingrid. BA Duke 1979; MDiv Sewanee: The U So, TS 2012; MDiv The TS at The U So 2012. D 6/2/2012 P 12/18/2012 Bp John Bauerschmidt. S Mths Epis Ch Tuscaloosa AL 2013-2015. monicacrlsn@gmail.com

CARLSON, Philip Lawrence (Az) 7147 N 78th St, Scottsdale AZ 85258 B Moline IL 1939 s lawrence & Ruth. BS IL Wesl 1961; MDiv Garrett-Evang TS

1965. D 10/27/2001 P 6/8/2002 Bp Robert Reed Shahan. m 9/10/1983 Bonnie L Carlson c 2. Assoc S Barn On The Desert Scottsdale AZ 2002-2011.

CARLSON, Reed Anthony (Minn) D 6/26/2014 P 6/20/2015 Bp Brian N Prior.

CARLSON, Robert Bryant (Ore) 15242 Sw Millikan Way Apt 517, Beaverton OR 97006 B Springfield OR 1974 s John & Donna. D 6/24/2000 Bp Vincent Waydell Warner P 1/7/2001 Bp Robert Louis Ladehoff. Asst S Barth's Ch Beaverton OR 2000-2008, 2000.

CARLSON, Sally (Oly) 17320 97th Pl Sw Apt 603, Vashon WA 98070 **D S Lk's Epis Ch Renton WA 2013-** B Seattle WA 1943 d Edward & Florence. AA Peterson Sch of Bus; LSU 1963; Dioc Sch of Mnstry And Theol Seattle WA 2004. D 6/26/2005 Bp Vincent Waydell Warner. c 1. D S Jn The Bapt Epis Ch Seattle WA 2010-2013; D Ch Of The H Sprt Vashon WA 2006-2010. sally. carlson@gmail.com

CARLSON, Walter Donald (Nwk) 11 Avalon Ct, Somerset NJ 08873 **Died 11/6/2016** B Glen Ridge NJ 1934 s Robert & Anna. AB Rutgers The St U of New Jersey 1958; MDiv GTS 1967. D 6/10/1967 P 12/21/1967 Bp Leland Stark. m 7/18/1964 Marlene Joyce Carlson c 2. Ret 1999-2016; Non-par 1991-1999; R Ch Of The Atone Fair Lawn NJ 1977-1991; R S Mary's Ch Belvidere NJ 1974-1977; R Trin Ch Bayonne NJ 1971-1974; Asst S Steph's Ch Pittsfield MA 1968-1971; Cur Chr Ch Pompton Lake NJ 1967-1968; Dept Of Missions Dio Newark Newark NJ 1977-1990.

CARLSON, William Douglas (At) 114 Grady Ridge Dr, Ashville NC 28806 B Minneapolis MN 1931 s Carl & Gladys. BBA U MN; EFM Sewanee: The U So, TS 1981. D 1/25/1983 Bp William Gillette Weinhauer. m 3/19/1955 Helen Carlson. S Pat's Epis Ch Atlanta GA 1994-2003; D in Charge Ch Of The Mssh Murphy NC 1983-1992; S Fran Of Assisi Cherokee NC 1983-1988.

CARLTON, Cathleen Ann (Az) D 6/11/2016 Bp Kirk Stevan Smith.

CARLTON-JONES, Anne Helen (SwFla) 15608 Fiddlesticks Blvd, Fort Myers FL 33912 B Birmingham England 1934 D 6/13/1998 Bp John Bailey Lipscomb. m 10/3/1955 Dennis Carlton-Jones c 2.

CARLYON, Robert David (Be) P.O.Box 262, Orwigsburg PA 17961 **Ret 1998-** B Hazleton PA 1937 s Robert & Dorothy. BA Lycoming Coll 1959; MDiv PrTS 1963; Cert VTS 1965; DMin Untd TS 1981. D 6/26/1965 Bp Earl M Honaman P 1/1/1966 Bp Walter M Higley. m 1/20/1986 Christine E Carlyon. P-in-c Calv Ch Tamaqua PA 1978-1980; R S Jas Ch Shuykl Haven PA 1971-1997; R S Jas Ch Muncy PA 1968-1971; Cur Trin Memi Ch Binghamton NY 1965-1968. Auth, "Hlth Care & The Ch," Dayton Untd Sem, 1981.

CARMAN, Charles Churchill (RG) 94 Winterhaven Drive, Nellysford VA 22958 B Denver CO 1932 s James & Phyllis. BS L&C 1957; MDiv CDSP 1960. D 6/22/1960 P 1/4/1961 Bp James Walmsley Frederic Carman. m 11/23/1985 Mary Ann Carman c 3. Int S Jas Epis Ch Taos NM 1992-1994; Int S Jn's Epis Ch Alamogordo NM 1991-1992; Ch Of The Ascen Cloudcroft NM 1991; Int S Mart's Epis Ch Richmond VA 1989-1990; Brandon Epis Ch Disputanta VA 1988-1989; Epis Ch Of S Paul And S Andr Kenbridge VA 1987; Gibson Memi Crewe VA 1987; S Andr's Ch Victoria VA 1987; Hickory Neck Ch Toano VA 1985-1986; Calv Ch Bath Par Mc Kenney VA 1985; Int Dio Sthrn Virginia Newport News VA 1984-1989; Johns Memi Epis Ch Farmville VA 1984-1985; Int S Andr's Ch Richmond VA 1982-1983; S Thos' Ch Richmond VA 1981-1982; Vic Gr Epis Ch Lk Havasu City AZ 1977-1981; Cur Epis Par Of S Mich And All Ang Tucson AZ 1975-1977; Vic S Paul's Epis Ch Modesto CA 1973-1975; Vic S Dunstans Epis Ch Modesto CA 1970-1973; Vic S Matt's Epis Ch Browns Point WA 1966-1970; Vic Estrn Grays Harbor Elma/Montesano WA 1964-1966; Vic S Jas Epis Ch Childress TX 1960-1964; Vic S Jn The Bapt Epis Clarendon TX 1960-1964; S Mich And All Ang Ch Shamrock TX 1960-1964.

CARMICHAEL, Alisa Roberts (SwFla) 502 Druid Hills Rd, Temple Terrace FL 33617 **Mus Dir/Org St Cathr of Alexandria Epis Ch Temple Terrace FL 2008-** B Jacksonville FL 1954 d Milton & Helen. BA Florida St U 1976; MA Wstrn Kentucky U 1995. D 12/7/2013 Bp Dabney Tyler Smith. m 3/17/1974 John Charles Carmichael c 2. Chapl Dio SW Florida Parrish FL 2014-2015; St Johns Epis Ch Tampa FL 2013-2014.

CARMICHAEL, Anna R (SJ) 1528 Oakdale Rd, Modesto CA 95355 **Cn Camp San Joaquin Kings Canyon Natl Pk CA 2016-; Cn Epis Dio San Joaquin Modesto CA 2016-** B NC 1975 d Michael & Donna. BA Barton Coll 1997; MS Longwood U 1998; MTS Vanguard U 2005; MDiv CDSP 2008. D 6/7/2008 P 1/10/2009 Bp Joseph Jon Bruno. m 7/19/2008 Matthew D Carmichael. R The Par Of S Mk The Evang Hood River OR 2010-2016; Chapl S Marg Of Scotland Par San Juan Capo CA 2008-2010. DOK 2005. canonanna@diosanjoaquin.org

CARMICHAEL, Mary Jean (Oly) 1600 Marshall Cir Unit 328, Dupont WA 98327 **Ret 2003-** B Los Angeles CA 1931 d James & Esther. AA U CA 1952; BS San Diego St U 1955; Diac TS 1989; Cert Sprtl Dir Formation 1994. D 6/18/1991 Bp Vincent Waydell Warner. Asstg D S Andr's Epis Ch Tacoma WA 1998-2002, D 1991-1997; D Chr Ch Tacoma WA 1995-1997; Chapl Faith Hm 1991-1994. Assn for Epis Deacons 1986.

CARMIENCKE JR, Bayard Collier (LI) 1145 Walnut Ave, Bohemia NY 11716 **Ret 1995-** B Brooklyn NY 1933 s Bayard & Frances. BA Hofstra U 1959; MDiv PDS 1962; MEd S Johns U 1971; Coll of Preachers 1976; 1992; 1997;

Cert 1997. D 4/28/1962 P 12/21/1962 Bp James Pernette DeWolfe. Asst S Mary's Ch Ronkonkoma NY 1995-1997; Dio Long Island Garden City NY 1983-1989; P-in-c S Lukes Ch Bohemia NY 1980-1995; Ch Of The Redeem Merrick NY 1980; S Thos' Epis Ch Floral Pk NY 1968-1980; P-in-c Chr Ch Franklinville PA 1966-1968; Vic S Ambr Kensington PA 1966-1968; R S Jas Epis Ch Westernport MD 1964-1966; Asst Gr And S Ptr's Ch Baltimore MD 1962-1964.

CARMODY, Alison Cutter (Ala) 1708 Wickingham Cv, Vestavia AL 35243 B Wilmington NC 1945 d Edward & Marjorie. BS U of Tennessee 1967; MA Austin Peay St U 1970; MDiv VTS 2000. D 6/3/2000 P 12/5/2000 Bp Henry Nutt Parsley Jr. m 12/27/1968 Richard Patrick Carmody c 2. Assoc R S Steph's Epis Ch Birmingham AL 2005-2012; Assoc R All SS Epis Ch Birmingham AL 2003-2005, Asst 2000-2002.

CARMONA, Paul B (SanD) -, San Diego CA 92115 B Los Angeles CA 1947 AAGO AGO; ETSBH; STB/MA Katholieke Universiteit Leuven, Belgium; PhD Katholieke Universiteit Leuven, Belgium; BA Loyola U of Los Angeles; MMus U of Sthrn Californis. D 6/8/2002 P 12/21/2002 Bp Gethin Benwil Hughes. m 9/26/1980 Therese H Henckens. Assoc R S Mk's Ch San Diego CA 2003-2013; D Cathd Ch Of S Paul San Diego CA 2002; Cathd Of S Lk And S Paul Charleston SC 2002.

CARNAHAN, Patricia King (Pgh) 4201 Saltsburg Rd, Murrysville PA 15668 B Boston MA 1949 d Robert & Marion. BA Chatham Coll 1970; BS U Pgh 1978; MDiv Pittsburgh TS 1980; DMin GTF 1991. D 6/13/1981 P 12/20/1981 Bp Robert Bracewell Appleyard. m 11/30/1974 Byron Lee Carnaham. S Brendan's Epis Ch Franklin Pk PA 1988-1997; Dio Pittsburgh Pittsburgh PA 1983-1985, Chair 1983-1985, 1981-1982; Chr Epis Ch No Hills Pittsburgh PA 1982-1987. Soc Of S Marg.

CARNES, Ralph Lee (Chi) 4507 Dayton Blvd, Chattanooga TN 37415 **Died 10/16/2015** B Tallapoosa GA 1931 s Randal & Letitia. BA Emory U 1959; MA Emory U 1960; PhD Emory U 1965; Cert SWTS 1986; Coll Chapl 1989. D 6/1/1987 Bp James Winchester Montgomery P 12/1/1987 Bp Frank Tracy Griswold III. m 10/15/2015 Valerie Folts Bohanan. D/Stff Chapl NW Cmnty Hosp Arlington Heights IL 1989-2015; Stff Chapl Gd Shpd Hosp Barrington IL 1986-1989. Auth, "The Road To Damascus"; Auth, "Dictionary Of Intl Bios". Apha.

CARNES, Valerie Folts (Mil) 4507 Dayton Blvd, Chattanooga TN 37415 B Chattanooga TN 1940 d Ross & Valerie. MA Emory U 1963; PhD Emory U 1967; MA Loyola U 1989; MDiv SWTS 1994; CAS SWTS 1995. D 8/26/1995 Bp Roger John White P 6/1/1996 Bp Robert Gould Tharp. S Ptr's Ch Chattanooga TN 2005-2012; Asst Gr Ch Chattanooga TN 1999-2005.

CARNEY, Georgia Martyn (Roch) 350 Chili Ave, Rochester NY 14611 B Newport News VA 1959 d Terrance & Marian. BA Smith 1982; Cert - Chr Ldrshp Colgate Rochester Crozer DS 2013. D 1/10/2014 Bp Prince Grenville Singh. m 1/2/1982 Mark Donald Darling c 3.

CARNEY, Michael R (U) PO Box 55, Whiterocks UT 84085 **Vic Dio Utah Salt Lake City UT 2016-** B Osage IA 1952 s Clarence & Jacquelyn. BA U MN 1978; MDiv CDSP 1998. D 6/6/1998 P 12/5/1998 Bp William Edwin Swing. m 4/10/1982 Marsha S Heron c 2. R S Tim's Epis Ch Littleton CO 2006-2016; Vic S Geo's Epis Ch Antioch CA 2000-2006; Asst S Steph's Par Bel Tiburon CA 1998-2000. Auth, "Liturg Mus in the Postmodern Age," *The Hymn*, 1999; Auth, "Sacagawea's Story," *Many Voices: True Tales from Amer's Past*, Natl Story Telling Press, 1995. whiterocksrev@gmail.com

CARNEY, Paulette Louise (WNY) 131 Lincoln Blvd, Kenmore NY 14217 **Stff Chapl Kenmore Mercy Hosp Buffalo NY 1990-; D 1987-** B Buffalo NY 1947 d Henry & Eleanor. BS SUNY 1968; Cert Humber Coll 1981; Cert DYouville Coll 1985. D 6/13/1987 Bp Harold Barrett Robinson. m 7/18/1997 Dennis Dwyer c 1. Dio Wstrn New York Tonawanda NY 1995; Chapl Kenmore Mercy Hosp Buffalo NY 1987-1989.

CARNEY, Paul Martin (Alb) 146 1st St, Troy NY 12180 **D S Jn's Epis Ch Troy NY 2009-; D's Advsry Bd Mem Dio Albany Greenwich NY 2012-, Disciplinary Bd Mem Elected Position 2011-, Bd Mem COM 2010-; Police Off/Chapl City of Troy New York 1976-** B Troy NY 1955 s Paul & Julia. AAS Hudson Vlly Cmnty Coll 1975. D 5/30/2009 Bp William Howard Love. m 5/1/1976 Marilyn E Carney c 2.

CARNEY, Susan Roberta (RI) 9924 Pointe Aux Chenes Road, Ocean Springs MS 39564 **Off Of Bsh For ArmdF New York NY 1984-** B Ankara TR 1952 d Richard & Bernice. BS SW Missouri S U 1975; MDiv PrTS 1978; CPE Bethany Coll 1979; GTS 1979; STM Ya Berk 1984. D 6/7/1980 P 12/11/1980 Bp Albert Wiencke Van Duzer. Int S Jn's Ch Guilford CT 1983-1984; Assoc Lk's Ch Trenton NJ 1982-1983; Cur S Mart's Martinsville NJ 1980-1982; Dio New Jersey Trenton NJ 1980-1981.

CARON, Donald Raymond (NJ) 116 Forte Dr Nw, Milledgeville GA 31061 B Norwich CT 1949 s Raymond & Beatrice. BA Providence Coll 1971; MA Providence Coll 1979; MDiv Weston Jesuit TS 1984. Rec 11/21/2005 Bp J Neil Alexander. m 1/31/1998 Melanie Caron. St Jn the Bapt Epis Ch Linden NJ 2015-2016; R Chr Ch Middletown NJ 2013-2015; Int S Jos's Epis Ch Mcdonough GA 2012-2013; R S Steph's Ch Milledgeville GA 2005-2012. st.johns.linden@verizon.net

CARON II, Joseph A (Alb) 271 Stevenson Rd, Greenwich NY 12834 **Chapl Ny St Dept Of Correctional Serv 1995-** B Bay Shore NY 1936 s Joseph & Mary. BA Barrington Coll 1968; MDiv Ya Berk 1971; DMin Drew U 1993. D 6/9/1973 P 12/15/1973 Bp Paul Moore Jr. m 2/14/2013 Barbara B Simoneau c 5. Assoc Slate Vlly Mnstry Of The Dioceses Of Albany And Vermont 1997-2000; S Paul's Epis Ch Greenwich NY 1993-1994, R 1976-1983; Ch Of The H Cross Troy NY 1986-1991. Alum Achievement Stony Brook Sch 1983.

CARPENTER, Allen Douglas (Alb) 62 S. Swan St., Albany NY 12210 B Oneonta NY 1947 s Orson & Ingehorg. BA Bard Coll 1969. D 5/10/2008 Bp William Howard Love. Cathd Of All SS Albany NY 2008-2014.

CARPENTER, Catherine E (CNY) PO Box 6, Baldwinsville NY 13027 **R Gr Ch Baldwinsville NY 2015-** B Evanston IL 1958 BA S Cathr U 2007; MDiv GTS 2012. D 6/30/2011 P 6/28/2012 Bp Brian N Prior. m 8/25/2001 Jonathan David Holmer. Asst S Jas On The Pkwy Minneapolis MN 2012-2015; Regular Supply P S Paul's On-The-Hill Epis Ch Minneapolis MN 2012-2015; Ed/Consulting ECF Inc New York NY 2009-2014. rector@graceepiscopalbaldwinsville.org

CARPENTER, Charles Monroe (Ind) 91 Smiths Rd, Mitchell IN 47446 B La Grange KY 1948 s Joseph & Elizabeth. BS Indiana St U 1970; MDiv Epis TS of the SW 2000. D 6/23/2000 P 2/11/2001 Bp Cate Waynick. R S Jn's Epis Ch Bedford IN 2003-2013; Dio Indianapolis Indianapolis IN 2000-2003; S Lk's Epis Ch Cannelton IN 2000-2002.

CARPENTER, Doug (Ala) 3037 Overton Rd, Birmingham AL 35223 **Ret 2005-; Chapl to Ret Dio Alabama Birmingham 2006-, Dio Coun,Dept Fin,Stdg Com,Comp Dio Com,Dep GC,BEC 1965-2005** B Savannah GA 1933 s Charles & Alexandra. BA Pr 1955; MDiv VTS 1960; Fell Coll of Preachers 1971. D 6/24/1960 Bp Charles C J Carpenter P 3/15/1961 Bp George Mosley Murray. m 8/30/1989 Ann Carpenter c 4. R S Steph's Epis Ch Birmingham AL 1975-2005; R S Paul's Epis Ch Lynchburg VA 1969-1973; R S Steph's Epis Ch Huntsville AL 1963-1969; S Mary's Epis Ch Andalusia AL 1960-1963; R S Steph's Ch Brewton AL 1960-1963. Auth, "Camp McDowell, The Way the Wrld Could be," self Pub, 2015; Auth, "A Powerful Blessing, Chas Colcock Jones Carpenter, Sixth Bp of Alabama," *Biography of C. C. J. Carpenter, Sr.*, self Pub, 2012; Auth, "Terrifying Tales and Inspiring Stories," *Terrifying Tales and Inspiring Stories*, Self Pub, 2008; Auth, "The Story of St. Steph's," *The Story of St. Steph's*, Self Pub, 2006; Auth, "A Casserole for a Horse," *A Casserole for a Horse*, Mercy Seat Press, 2005. DSA Epis Conf of Deaf 1995.

CARPENTER, Elizabeth Kincaid (Tenn) 216 University Ave, Sewanee TN 37375 B Vicksburg MS 1946 d Robert & Elizabeth. BS LSU 1967; Dio Tennessee D Sch 2013. D 1/25/2014 Bp John Bauerschmidt. c 3. Otey Memi Par Ch Sewanee TN 2012, D 2012-.

CARPENTER, Francis Newton (Chi) 337 Ridge Rd, Barrington Hills IL 60010 B Port Chester, NY 1947 s Francis & Patricia. BA U of So Carolina 1970. D 2/6/2010 Bp Jeff Lee. m 1/18/1986 Joan May Carpenter c 1.

CARPENTER, George Harrison (Oly) Po Box 343, Medina WA 98039 **1980-** B Colusa CA 1934 s Leslie & Elizabeth. BA California St U Chico 1958; MTh CDSP 1961; MA U of Washington 1978. D 6/15/1961 P 12/21/1961 Bp Clarence Rupert Haden Jr. m 4/20/1967 Patricia Ann Carpenter. Asstg P S Thos Epis Ch Medina WA 1977-1980; 1968-1977; Asst S Jn's Epis Ch Snohomish WA 1965-1968; Vic S Mich's Ch Anderson CA 1961-1964.

CARPENTER, John Paul (Pa) 3937 Netherfield Rd, Philadelphia PA 19129 **Dio Pennsylvania Philadelphia PA 1968-** B Saint Paul MN 1936 s Edwin & Helen. BA U MN 1959; BD Nash 1962; JD Tem 1971. D 6/29/1962 Bp Hamilton Hyde Kellogg P 5/1/1963 Bp Daniel Corrigan. m 8/27/1958 Pamela Carpenter. Vic S Geo & H Redeem Philadelphia PA 1967-1968; Cn Gr Cathd Topeka KS 1964-1966; Vic S Paul's Epis Ch Two Harbors MN 1962-1963.

CARPENTER, Judith Perry (Mass) 192 N. Main Street, Rockland ME 04841 B Somerville MA 1942 d Richard & Ruth. BA U MN 1963; MDiv Andover Newton TS 1981; DMin EDS 1995. D 5/30/1981 Bp John Bowen Coburn P 6/9/1982 Bp George E Rath. m 6/5/1965 John Carpenter c 4. Pstr Counslr/Stff Greenfire Retreat Hse Tenants Harbor ME 1993-2006; Chapl Dana Hall Sch Wellesley MA 1981-1993. Auth, "Voices:Wmn of Color," *Indep Sch mag*, 1991. Phi Beta Kappa U MN 1963.

CARPENTER, Leslie Scott (Tex) 6050 N. Meridian St., Indianapolis IN 46208 **S Aid's Ch Cypress TX 2012-** B Austin TX 1979 s Scott & Eva Jean. BA W&M 2002; MDiv SWTS 2008. D 6/28/2008 Bp Bavi Edna Rivera. m 6/18/2005 Kristin RS Carpenter c 2. Asst R S Paul's Epis Ch Indianapolis IN 2008-2012.

CARPENTER II, Marion George (NI) Saint Annes, 424 W Market St, Warsaw IN 46580 B Goshen IN 1954 s Marion & Delores. D 11/16/2007 Bp Edward Stuart Little II. m 7/10/1976 DeBra Ann Carpenter c 2. D S Anne's Epis Ch Warsaw IN 2007-2012.

CARPENTER, Morton Eugene (EC) 1603 E Walnut St, Goldsboro NC 27530 B Repton AL 1948 s Morton & Sallie. BS Auburn U 1971; MDiv Sewanee: The U So, TS 1986. D 7/12/1986 P 5/9/1987 Bp Charles Farmer Duvall. m 10/9/1976 Judy Lee Carpenter c 1. R S Steph's Ch Goldsboro NC 2001-2013; R S Lk's

Ch Marianna FL 1991-2001; Vic Ch Of The H Cross No E PA 1989-1991; Cur Trin Epis Ch Mobile AL 1986-1988.

CARPENTER, Nicholas (Los) 15757 Saint Timothy Rd, Apple Valley CA 92307 **Chapl St. Mary Med Cntr Apple Vlly CA 2010-** B Dallas TX 1947 s Robert & Lottie. Cert ETSBH 2010. D 2/13/2010 Bp Chester Lovelle Talton. D S Tim's Epis Ch Apple Vlly CA 2010-2014.

CARPENTER, Stephen Morris (NCal) 1020 Westview Dr, Napa CA 94558 **R S Mary's Epis Ch Napa CA 1983-** B Santa Monica CA 1951 s Austin & Margaret. BMus Estrn New Mex U Portales NM 1974; MDiv SWTS 1979. D 5/12/1979 P 11/30/1979 Bp John Lester Thompson III. m 8/26/1974 Frances R Carpenter. P Trin Epis Cathd Sacramento CA 1979-1983.

CARPENTER, Susan M (RI) PO Box 505, Greenville RI 02828 **R S Thos Ch Greenville RI 2012-, Dir of The Epis Conf Cntr 2010-** B Providence RI 1953 d Donald & Shirly. BS Rhode Island Coll 1975; MEd Rhode Island Coll 1983; MDiv GTS 2008. D 6/14/2008 Bp Gerry Wolf. m 6/14/1975 Brian E Carpenter c 2. Dio Rhode Island Providence RI 2010-2012, Dioc Coun 2011-, Bd Dir of The Epis Conf Cntr 2010-, Congrl Dvlpmt Cmsn 2010-; Assoc R S Jn's Ch Barrington RI 2008-2010.

CARR, Clifford Bradley (Be) 526 11th Avenue, Bethlehem PA 18018 **Ret 2000-** B Newport RI 1939 s Oliver & Gladys. BA Leh 1961; MDiv GTS 1964. D 6/20/1964 P 3/27/1965 Bp John S Higgins. R Trin Ch Easton PA 1993-2000; Chair of Liturg Cmsn Dio Bethlehem Bethlehem PA 1980-1998, Ecum Off 1994-1999, Cn 1987-1993; Trin Epis Ch Pottsville PA 1980-1993; Par Of The H Fam Pen Argyl PA 1974-1980; Vic S Jos's Ch Pen Argyl PA 1974-1980; R No Par Epis Ch St. Clair PA 1968-1974; R S Jn Ashland PA 1967-1968; Asst S Mk's Ch Warwick RI 1966-1967; Cur S Lk's Epis Ch E Greenwich RI 1964-1966. AAM 1985-2005. Hon Cn Dio Bethlehem 1987.

CARR, Dale Robert (Ore) 5223 NE Everett St, Portland OR 97213 **Lead Chapl Providence ElderPlace Portland OR 2008-; Chapl Providence ElderPlace Portland OR 2005-; Assoc P S Steph's Epis Par Portland OR 2005-** B Melford OR 1957 s Robert & Karen. BS OR SU 1979; MBA Monterey Inst of Intl Stds 1989; MDiv GTS 2001. D 6/16/2001 Bp William O Gregg P 1/27/2002 Bp Pierre W Whalon. Chapl Res Portland VA Med Cntr Portland OR 2004-2005; Cur Ch of the Ascen Munich 2001-2004. Assembly of Epis Healthcare Chapl 2005; Assn of Profsnl Chapl 2007.

CARR, John Joseph (WNY) 56 Mckinley Ave, Kenmore NY 14217 B Akron OH 1937 s Owen & Mary. Maryknoll TS; Wadhams Hall Sem Coll; BA S Johns TS 1961; Lic Sacr Theol S Johns TS 1965. Trans 9/26/1984 Bp Harold Barrett Robinson. m 3/7/1969 Gloria Ann Grey c 4. S Mary's Epis Ch Gowanda NY 1984-1985.

CARR, John Philip (Tex) **Other Lay Position S Lk's Epis Ch Lindale TX 2013-** B Dallas TX 1953 s Bernard & Helen. BS U of Texas at Arlington 1977; Dplma in Theol Iona Sch for Mnstry 2015. D 6/20/2015 Bp C Andrew Doyle P 1/15/2016 Bp Jeff Fisher. m 7/30/1977 Lucy A Carr c 2.

CARR, Michael (SanD) 651 Eucalyptus Ave, Vista CA 92084 B Fayetteville NC 1956 s Peter & Margaret. BA TCU 1979; MDiv Nash 1982. D 6/26/1982 Bp Archibald Donald Davies P 7/20/1983 Bp Charles Brinkley Morton. m 8/31/1980 Kelly Elizabeth Carr c 1. All SS Ch Vista CA 2007-2014; R S Andrews Epis Ch Port Angeles WA 1994-2007; R S Swithin Forks Forks WA 1994; Vic S Richard's Epis Ch Skyforest CA 1989-1994; R S Bede's Epis Ch Los Angeles CA 1986-1989; Asst Ch Of Our Sav Par San Gabr CA 1985-1986; Asst S Jn's Epis Ch Chula Vista CA 1983-1985; Cur S Anne's Ch Ft Worth TX 1982-1983.

CARR, Michael Leo (Mich) 9132 Pine Valley Dr, Grand Blanc MI 48439 **Chf Chapl VetA Hosp 1994-** B Indianapolis IN 1940 s John & Bridget. BA S Marys Sem and U 1963; MA S Maurs Sem 1967; MDiv Immac Concep Sem 1982; BCC Natl Assn of VetA Chapl 1991; DMin GTF 1992; PhD GTF 1996. Rec 10/1/1994 as Priest Bp R aymond Stewart Wood Jr. m 12/19/1990 Karen Christine Carr. Co-R Chr The King Epis Ch Taylor MI 1998-2012; Co-R Dream Cluster Allen Pk MI 1998-2012; S Lk's Epis Ch Allen Pk MI 1998-2012; ArmdF and Fed Ministires New York NY 1994-2011; P RC Ch 1967-1992. Auth, *Psychol Importance of the Sprtl in Recovery Process ofVietnam PTSD Veterans*, Wyndham Hall Press of Indiana, 1998; Ed, *Fells Yearbook*, Wyndham Hall Press, 1992; Auth, *A Unique Journey*. ACPE; ACC; Fed Fire Chapl - Fed of Fire Chapl; Fell GTF; Michigan St Fireman's Assn; Mltry Chapl Assn; Natl Assn of VA Chapl-Bd Cert. Secy's Awd for Excellence in Chapl Secy of Veterans' Affrs 2002.

CARR, Nathan Daniel (Okla) 6400 N Pennsylvania Ave, Nichols Hills OK 73116 **Dio Oklahoma Oklahoma City OK 2016-** B Oklahoma City OK 1980 s Steven & Nancy. MA Reformed TS; BS U of Cntrl Oklahoma 2003; Angl Cert Wycliffe Coll 2013. D 11/22/2013 P 6/20/2014 Bp Edward Joseph Konieczny. m 3/16/2002 Sarah R Carr c 4. S Jas Epis Ch Oklahoma City OK 2015-2016; All Souls Epis Ch Oklahoma City OK 2014-2015.

CARR, Spencer David (Colo) 4661 Wilson Dr, Broomfield CO 80023 **Asst S Mary Magd Ch Boulder CO 2011-, Cur 2000-2001** B San Diego CA 1944 s Albert & Shirley. BA Occ 1966; PhD U MI 1970; MDiv SWTS 2000. D 6/10/2000 P 12/16/2000 Bp William Jerry Winterrowd. m 6/8/1997 Karla J Allen. R Epis Ch Of S Jn The Bapt Granby CO 2001-2011.

CARR, Timothy Patrick (Nwk) St John's Episcopal Church, 226 Cornelia St, Boonton NJ 07005 **S Jn's Epis Ch Boonton NJ 2013-** B Providence RI 1955 s Joseph & Barbara. BS Thos Edison St Coll 2010; MDiv GTS 2013; MDiv The GTS 2013. D 5/18/2013 P 12/7/2013 Bp Mark M Beckwith. m 6/21/2014 Edwin M Acevedo c 1.

CARR, Virginia Rose (WNY) 12 Elm St, Westfield NY 14787 **S Ptr's Ch Westfield NY 2010-** B Queens New York 1955 d Robert & Rose. MA S Bonaventure U 2003; Cert Ang Stud Nash 2009. D 7/2/2010 P 1/15/2011 Bp Michael Garrison. m 6/27/1992 Owen C Carr c 3. SAMS Ambridge PA 1994-1998.

✠ CARR, The Rt Rev William Franklin (USC) 4249 Cedar Grove Rd, Murfreesboro TN 37127 B Alexandria VA 1938 s Franklin & Virginia. VTS; BS E Tennessee St U 1961; MDiv VTS 1970. D 6/11/1970 P 2/1/1971 Bp Wilburn Camrock Campbell Con 6/1/1985 for WVa. m 3/19/1960 Lena Carr c 4. Asst Bp Of Upper So Carolina Dio Upper So Carolina Columbia SC 1990-1994; Bp Suffr Dio W Virginia Charleston WV 1985-1990, Asst to Bp 1981-1990, Asst to Bp 1981-1985, Chair Dept Of Mssn And Mnstry 1978-1980, Dn Of SW Convoc 1976-1980; R S Jn's Ch Huntington WV 1975-1981; Vic S Barn Bridgeport WV 1972-1975; Vic Olde S Jn's Ch Colliers WV 1970-1972. DD VTS 1980.

✠ CARRANZA-GOMEZ, The Rt Rev Sergio (Los) PO Box 512164, Los Angeles CA 90051 B Mexico City MX 1941 s Faustino & Belina. BA Universidad Nacional Autonoma De Mex 1958; BA Universidad Nacional Autonoma De Mex 1964; MDiv VTS 1967. D 5/20/1967 Bp William Foreman Creighton P 12/8/1967 Bp Jose Guadalupe Saucedo Con 8/20/1989 for Mex. Dio Los Angeles Los Angeles CA 2003-2010; Dio Mex Mex City MOR 2001-2002, 1989-1999; Bp of Mex Angl Ch of Mex 1994-2003; Bp Dio Mex Mex City Mex 1989-1993; Iglesia Epis Mexicana San Jeronimo 117 1988-1989; R San Jorge Mex City Mex 1988-1989; Dio The Dominican Republic (Iglesia Epis Dominicana) Gazcue Santo Domingo 1984-1988; R S Andr's Mex City Mex 1980-1988; Vic Mssn Universitaria Mex 1974-1980; Dn S Andr's Sem Mex City Mex 1970-1974; Dio Wstrn Mex Zapopan Jalisco 1967-1984; P-in-c H Fam Monterrey Mex 1967-1970. OHC, Jn 23 Ecum Assn. DD VTS 1990.

CARREKER, Michael Lyons (Ga) 1 West Macon Street, Savannah GA 31401 B Atlanta GA 1954 s James & Mary. Gordon-Conwell TS; BA U GA 1976; DIT Oxf GB 1978; MA Dalhousie U 1983; Cert S Lk Sem 1988; PhD Dalhousie U 1993. D 9/14/1988 P 9/20/1989 Bp Harry Woolston Shipps. m 7/30/1977 Frances Lynne Carreker c 2. R S Jn's Ch Savannah GA 1999-2006, Assoc 1989-1990; Chr Ch Frederica St Simons Is GA 1989, D 1988-1989; Dio Georgia Savannah GA 1988-1989; Killam Schlr Dalhousie U; Gk Tchg Fell Gordon-Conwell TS. Isaac Walton Killam Schlr Dalhousie U; Gk Tchg Fell Gorgon-Conwell TS.

CARRENO-GAMBOA, Bladimir Francisco (Ve) **Dio Venezuela Caracas 2004-** B 1958 D 12/16/1992 P 6/20/1993 Bp Onell Asiselo Soto.

CARRICK, Judith Trautman (LI) 4 Kenny St, Hauppauge NY 11788 **S Thos Of Cbury Ch Smithtown NY 2008-** B Flushing NY 1935 d Henry & Estelle. BA Tufts U 1957; MS Adel 1979; Cert Mercer TS 1994. D 6/23/1995 Bp Orris George Walker Jr. m 5/2/1959 Edward Bird Carrick c 2. D Caroline Ch of Brookhaven Setauket NY 2006-2008; D S Anselm's Ch Shoreham NY 2002-2005; D St Jn the Evang Epis Ch Lynbrook NY 2001-2002; D S Mk's Ch Islip NY 1999-2000; D S Ptr's by-the-Sea Epis Ch Bay Shore NY 1995-1998. Preached Ord/Consec R Michel, Suffr Long Island 1997.

CARRIERE, Anne Stone (Ark) 31 Stonecrest Ct, Mountain Home AR 72653 **Ret 2003-** B Memphis TN 1943 d Coe & Elizabeth. BA Van 1964; MDiv Memphis TS 1981. D 7/12/1981 Bp William F Gates Jr P 6/27/1982 Bp William Evan Sanders. c 2. Vic S Andr's Ch Mtn Hm AR 1998-2003; Ch of the H Apos Collierville TN 1990-1997; Gr - S Lk's Ch Memphis TN 1983-1990.

CARRINGTON, James Henry (ECR) B 1935 D 6/22/1959 P 2/16/1960 Bp Francis E I Bloy. m 7/30/1992 Rosemarie Carrington. S Steph's Epis Ch Sn Luis Obispo CA 1995-1996.

CARR-JONES, Philip (NJ) 3 Haytown Rd, Lebanon NJ 08833 **R Ch Of The H Sprt Lebanon NJ 1987-** B Plainfield NJ 1957 s William & Mary. BA Juniata Coll 1980; MDiv EDS 1984. D 6/2/1984 P 3/1/1985 Bp George Phelps Mellick Belshaw. m 8/29/1982 Janmarie Carr-Jones c 3. Cur S Ptr's Ch Perth Amboy NJ 1984-1987; Chapl Cambridge City Hosp 1982-1983. "A Survey Of Leahets," Aplm, 2004. Soc Cappodocian Fathers (Patristics).

CARROCCINO, Michael Jonathan (Oly) 541 W Morondo Ave, Ajo AZ 85321 B Montgomery AL 1979 s Larry & Jerri. BA U of Alabama at Birmingham 2000; MDiv Epis TS Of The SW 2013; MDiv Epis TS of the SW 2013. D 10/18/2012 P 6/13/2013 Bp Gregory Harold Rickel. m 11/17/2000 Kristin Carroccino c 2. S Jn The Bapt Epis Ch Seattle WA 2015-2016; Cur S Mk's Cathd Seattle WA 2013-2015. mcarroccino@gmail.com

CARROLL III, Bill William (Okla) 924 N Robinson Ave, Oklahoma City OK 73102 **Cn Dio Oklahoma Oklahoma City OK 2016-, Stndg Com Pres 2014-2016, Chair of Bp's Com on Same Gender Unions 2013, BEC 2013-, Stndg Com Mem 2013-, Assoc Dn Iona Sch in Oklahoma 2012-; Bd Mem Fam Promise Shawnee Shawnee OK 2013-** B Glendale CA 1969 AB Harv 1992; MDiv U Chi DS 1996; Cert Sewanee: The U So, TS 2002; PhD U Chi 2005. D 12/14/2002 P 1/28/2004 Bp Dorsey Henderson. m 8/14/1993 Tracey Fiore Carroll c 2. R Emm Epis Ch Shawnee OK 2012-2016; R Ch Of The Gd Shpd Athens OH 2006-2012; Vstng Asst Prof Sewanee U So TS Sewanee TN 2004-2006; Dir Of Chr Formation S Fran of Assisi Chapin SC 2003; Cnvnr Soc of Cath Priests No Amer 2011-2013; Chair of Faith in Life Cmsn Dio Sthrn Ohio Cincinnati OH 2009-2012, Bp's Ad Hoc Com on Same Sex Unions 2009, COM/Examing Chapl 2007-2012; Chair of Bd U Interfaith Assn Athens OH 2009-2012; Mem City of Athens Human Relatns Cmsn Athens OH 2008-2012; Bd Mem/Exec Cmte Rural Action Trimble Ohio 2007-2012. Auth, "Restoring the Bonds of Affection," *ATR, 87:4*, 2005. Soc of Cath Priests, No Amer 2009. canonbill@epiok.org

CARROLL, Charles Moisan (Me) PO Box 195, Brunswick ME 04011 B Anesburg MA 1940 s Marcus & Geraldine. AB Pr 1962; MA Bangor TS 2011. D 6/25/2011 Bp Stephen Taylor Lane. m 5/17/1981 Ann Carroll c 4.

CARROLL, Christian (Nwk) 173 Oakland Rd, Maplewood NJ 07040 B Brooklyn NY 1950 d Vincent & Ann. MA New Sch For Soc Resrch NY NY 1979; MS Hunter Coll Sch of Soc Wk NY NY 1988; MDiv Drew U 2005. D 6/2/2007 P 12/8/2007 Bp Mark M Beckwith. m 7/10/2004 Christine West. Clincl Soc Worker Cath Chars 1988-2001.

CARROLL, Diana E (Md) St. Luke's Church, 1101 Bay Ridge Avenue, Annapolis MD 21403 **P-in-c S Lk's Ch Annapolis MD 2013-, P-in-c 2012-2013; Chapl and Middle Sch Rel Tchr St. Anne's Day Sch Annapolis MD 2012-** B Barrington IL 1981 d Peter & Catherine. AB Ken 2004; MDiv Ya Berk 2008. D 6/7/2008 Bp David Charles Bowman P 1/10/2009 Bp Edward Lewis Lee Jr. m 1/4/2013 Sarah Rebecca Lamming. Asst to the R The Ch Of The H Trin Rittenhouse Philadelphia PA 2008-2011; COM Dio Pennsylvania Philadelphia PA 2010-2011. pastordiana@stlukeseastport.org

CARROLL, Diane Phyllis (Va) 10360 Rectory Ln, King George VA 22485 **R Hanover w Brunswick Par - S Jn King Geo VA 2006-; R Hanover-w-Brunswick Par King Geo VA 2006-** B Brooklyn NY 1948 d Lewis & Anita. BA S Leo U 1999; MDiv VTS 2003. D 6/14/2003 P 12/6/2003 Bp Carol J Gallagher. m 7/4/1974 Matthew Carroll c 3. Asst S Aid's Ch Virginia Bch VA 2003-2005.

CARROLL, Douglas James (Roch) 3387 County Route 6, Cohocton NY 14826 **Assoc Allegany Cnty Epis Mnstry 1975-** B Princeton NJ 1933 s Richard & Ida. BA Washington and Jefferson U 1960; BD EDS 1963. D 6/15/1963 Bp William S Thomas P 12/1/1963 Bp Austin Pardue. m 8/27/1954 Donna L Carroll. Allegany Cnty Epis Mnstry Belfast NY 1981-1992; Epis Tri-Par Mnstry Dansville NY 1969-1979; R Chr Epis Ch Hornell NY 1969-1975; Chr Epis Ch Indiana PA 1963-1969; P-in-c S Ptr's Epis Ch Blairsville PA 1963-1969.

CARROLL, James Earle (SanD) 3750 Amaryllis Dr, San Diego CA 92106 **Assoc All Souls' Epis Ch San Diego CA 2002-; Ret 1994-** B Tucson AZ 1929 s Glen & Margaret. BA U of Puget Sound 1951; BD SWTS 1954. D 6/29/1954 P 6/29/1955 Bp Stephen F Bayne Jr. m 11/1/1958 Lanita Carroll c 3. Vice Chair, Stndg Cmsn on Ecum Relation Epis Ch GC 1979-1982; Cathd Ch Of S Paul San Diego CA 1978-1994; Chapl Gnrl ComT 1975-1985; Dn Cathd Of S Jas Chicago IL 1972-1978; R Trin Epis Ch Reno NV 1966-1972; R All SS Par Long Bch CA 1959-1966; Assoc St Marks Epis Ch Van Nuys CA 1956-1959; Vic Chr Epis Ch Anacortes WA 1954-1956; Vic Mssion Whidbey Island 1954-1956; Chapl Gnrl CT 1975-1985. Auth, "Eucharistic Sacrifice: An Angl Consideration," Amer Ch Quarterly, 1961; Auth, "Fllshp Papers"; Auth, "PB Cn and Pstr Choices"; Auth, "Legitimate heirs 0f the Cath Mvmt"; Auth, "Bloy Hse Paper"; Auth, "Sxlty and Chr". Affirming Angl Catholicism 1994. DD SWTS 1981.

CARROLL, Kevin Charles (Mil) 3309 N Knoll Terrace, Wauwatosa WI 53222 **Dn All SS' Cathd Milwaukee WI 2010-** B Janesville WI 1960 BS U of Wisconsin 1984; MDiv Nash 2003. D 3/25/2003 Bp Chilton Richardson Knudsen P 11/1/2003 Bp Steven Andrew Miller. m 9/2/1995 Jane Vinopal c 2. P-in-c S Jas Ch W Bend WI 2006-2010; Asst S Mk's Ch Milwaukee WI 2003-2006. kevin. carroll@ascathedral.org

CARROLL, Michael Edward (Ct) 16 Church St, Waterbury CT 06702 **S Jn's Epis Par Waterbury CT 2016-; All SS Epis Ch Meriden CT 2014-** B Waterbury CT 1948 s James & Marybeth. AB St Mary's Sem 1970; MA U of St Jos 1999. Rec 12/4/2004 as Deacon Bp Andrew Donnan Smith. m 8/2/2002 Marian R Carroll c 2.

CARROLL, Steven E (NJ) 618 S Hazel Ct, Gilbert AZ 85296 **Com on Nomin Dio New Jersey Trenton NJ 2011-, Com on Priesthood 2010-, Dn of Woodbury Convoc 2010-** B Detroit MI 1949 s Edward & Helen. BA Wayne 1976; MDiv U Tor CA 1979. D 6/16/1979 Bp H Coleman Mcgehee Jr P 5/16/1980 Bp Henry Irving Mayson. m 5/26/1979 Rosemary Carroll. R S Jn's Ch Salem NJ 2009-2015; R Trin Ch Newark OH 2005-2009; S Phil And S Steph Epis Ch Detroit MI 2004-2005; R S Jas Ch Grosse Ile MI 2001-2003; P-in-c S Jn The Bapt Epis Ch Glendale AZ 1998-2001; R S Steph's Ch Sierra Vista AZ 1992-1998; Vic S Jn's Epis Ch Bisbee AZ 1989-1993; Dio Arizona Phoenix AZ 1989-1991; Vic Ch Of The H Sprt Bullhead City AZ 1988-1989; Int Trin Epis Ch Pocatello ID 1987-1988; R S Jn's Ch Howell MI 1980-1986; Asst All SS Epis Ch Marysville MI 1979-1980; Asst Gr Epis Ch Port Huron MI 1979-1980. stevenemcarroll@gmail.com

CARROLL, Tracey Fiore (Okla) 335 Tennessee Ave, Sewanee TN 37383 **Dio Oklahoma Oklahoma City OK 2013-; Vic S Dav's Ch Oklahoma City OK 2013-** B New Milford CT 1964 d Carmine & Nellie. BA Natl U 1993; MDiv SWTS 1997. D 6/14/1997 P 12/27/1997 Bp Gethin Benwil Hughes. m 8/14/1993 Bill William Carroll Iii c 2. P-in-c S Paul's Ch Chillicothe OH 2010-2012; Asst H Trin Par Epis Clemson SC 1998-2001.

CARROLL, Vincent John (SwVa) 2518 2nd St, Richlands VA 24641 B Tillson NY 1943 s Vincent & Virginia. BA Niagara U 1965; JD Ford Law 1968; MPA U of Indiana 1978. D 5/27/2006 P 12/9/2006 Bp Neff Powell. m 12/11/1982 Marilyn B Carroll c 3.

CARROLL, William Wesley (Fla) 465 11th Ave N, Jacksonville FL 32250 B Jacksonville FL 1937 s William & Margaret. D 9/27/2012 Bp Samuel Johnson Howard. m 1/7/1978 Ann C Carroll c 2.

CARROON, Robert Girard (Ct) 24 Park Pl, Apt 8F, Hartford CT 06106 **Cn Chr Ch Cathd Hartford CT 2000-; Hstgr Dio Connecticut Meriden CT 1988-, Archv 1985-2004, 1984-2004, Hstgr 1985-; Assoc Gr Epis Ch Hartford CT 1988-** B Kansas City MO 1937 s Matthew & Agnes. BA Indiana St U 1959; MDiv Nash 1962; MA U of Wisconsin 1970; DLitt U of Sussex 1977; Additional study U of Southampton 2015; Additional study U of Lecister 2016. D 4/28/1962 P 10/20/1962 Bp Donald H V Hallock. Dir of Schlrshp Prog Soc for the Increase of the Mnstry 2005-2009; Secy Bd Archv of ECUSA Epis Ch Cntr New York NY 1997-2009; Litchfield Hills Reg Mnstry Bridgewater CT 1991-2015; Vic Trin Ch Milton CT 1983-1988; Asst S Jas Epis Ch Milwaukee WI 1977-1981; Asst Trin Ch Milwaukee WI 1974-1976; Asst S Lk's Ch Racine WI 1969-1974, Cur 1962-1968; Archv/Hstgr Dio Milwaukee Milwaukee WI 1968-1981; Dn All SS' Cathd Milwaukee WI 1964-1968. Auth, *Provost Marshal of Charleston*, Between the Lakes Grp, 2007; Auth, *Un Blue: The Hist of the Mltry Ord of the Loyal Legion of the US*, White Mane Pub Co, 2000; Auth, *From Freeman's Ford to Bentonville*, White Mane Pub Co, 1998; Auth, *A New Heart and A New Sprt*, Morehouse-Barlow, 1988; Auth, *Broadswords & Bayonets*, Soc of Colonial Wars, 1984. CBS 1962; GAS 1961; Mltry Ord of the Loyal Legion of the Untd States 1977; Soc of Colonial Wars 1978; Soc of the Cincinnati 1984. Lectr US Coast Guard Acad 2014; Knight Cmdr Ord of St. Mich the Archangel Grand Duchess Maria of Russia 2012; Dep to the Gnrl Conventon Dio Connecticut 2006; Dep to the Gnrl Convetnon Dio Connecticut 2003; Ven. Ord of St. Jn HM Eliz II of Great Britain 2003; Dep to the GC Dio Connectict 2000; Dep to the GC of the Epis Ch, 1997,2000 2006, Dio Connectict 1997; Chevalier of the Ord of S Mich Grand Duke Vladimir of Russia 1992.

CARRUBBA, Amity (Chi) 1434 W Thome Ave Apt 1A, Chicago IL 60660 **Gr Ch Chicago IL 2016-; Assoc Ch Of The Redeem Elgin IL 2008-** B Syracuse NY 1975 BS U IL 1997; MDiv EDS 2006. D 6/3/2006 P 12/16/2006 Bp Bill Persell. Ch of Our Sav Chicago IL 2016; Asstg P Ch Of S Paul And The Redeem Chicago IL 2012-2016; Exec Dir Epis Serv Corps Chicago IL 2011-2016; Cur S Mary's Ch Pk Ridge IL 2006-2008. gracerector637@gmail.com

CARSKADON, Garrett Harvey (Md) 32 Main St, Westernport MD 21562 **P S Jas Epis Ch Westernport MD 2007-** B Keysen WV 1949 s Garrett & Elva. BS Frostburg St U 1971; MEd Frostburg St U 1977; MEd Frostburg St U 1981. D 12/21/2007 Bp John L Rabb P 6/29/2008 Bp Katharine Jefferts Schori.

CARSON, Boyd Rodney (SwFla) 1875 Massachusetts Ave Ne, Saint Petersburg FL 33703 B Lafollette TN 1946 s Boyd & Ireland. BS Cumberland U 1968; BS Epis TS in Kentucky 1978. D 5/15/1978 P 12/17/1978 Bp Addison Hosea. S Bede's Ch St. Petersburg FL 1983-2013; Assoc Cathd Ch Of S Ptr St. Petersburg FL 1980-1982; S Paul's Sch Clearwater FL 1978-1980. OHC.

CARSON, Julie Ann (Mass) 500 Brook St, Framingham MA 01701 **R S Andr's Ch Framingham MA 2007-** B Newton MA 1973 d Domenic & Dorothy. BA Keene St Coll 1995; MDiv Andover Newton TS 2000. D 6/7/2003 P 6/5/2004 Bp M(Arvil) Thomas Shaw. m 6/28/2003 Phillip Thomason Carson c 2. Asst R for Fam Mnstry S Andr's Ch Wellesley MA 2003-2007, 2000-2003.

CARSON, Mary Claypoole (O) 3207 Montana Ave, Cincinnati OH 45211 **R S Jas Epis Ch Cincinnati OH 2016-; R Ch Of The Redeem Lorain OH 2013-, Int R 2010-2016, P-in-c 2010-; Bd Trst Bex Sem Columbus OH 2013-** B Hillsboro OH 1964 d John & Jean. BA Ken 1986; MA Bex Sem 1989; MDiv Bex Sem 1992. D 6/13/1992 P 12/29/1992 Bp William George Burrill. Luth Chapl Serv Cleveland OH 2007-2011; Assoc/Int Exec Dir Luth Chapl Serv Cleveland OH 2007-2011; Asst to Bp for Mnstry Dvlpmt Dio Ohio Cleveland 1999-2007, Disciplinary Panel 2012-2016, GC Dep 2006-2008; Asst Gr Epis Ch Sandusky OH 1996-1999; Asst S Chris's Ch Gladwyne PA 1994-1996; Cur Trin Ch Newport RI 1992-1994; Bd Mem, Pres Lorain Coop Mnstry 2010-2016; Bd Mem Luth Chapl Serv 2001-2007. Phi Beta Kappa Ken 1985. mcarson@stjamescincy.org

CARSON, Rebecca Jayne (CGC) 1707 Government St, Mobile AL 36604 B Bessemer AL 1950 d Arthur & Lena. BS U of Sthrn Alabama 1983; MS U of Sthrn Alabama 1992. D 2/10/2011 Bp Philip Menzie Duncan II.

CARSON, Stephen Wilson (WTex) 3002 Miori Ln, Victoria TX 77901 **R S Fran Epis Ch Victoria TX 2012-** B Dallas TX 1975 s James & Kenny. BA U of Texas San Antonio; MDiv Sewanee: The U So, TS 2010. D 6/9/2010 Bp Gary

Richard Lillibridge P 12/10/2010 Bp David Mitchell Reed. m 1/11/2003 Julie L Carson c 2. Cur S Lk's Epis Ch San Antonio TX 2010-2012.

CARSWELL, Amber Brooke (Ark) 531 W College Ave, Jonesboro AR 72401 **Trin Cathd Little Rock AR 2016-; S Mk's Ch Crossett AR 2014-; S Mk's Epis Ch Jonesboro AR 2014-** B Emporia KS 1985 d Russell & Lori. BS U of Arkansas 2011; MDiv VTS 2014. D 3/15/2014 P 10/4/2014 Bp Larry Benfield.

CARTAGENA MEJIA DE AREVALO, Maria Consuelo (Hond) San Angel B-26, C4202, Tegucigalpa C Honduras B Juanita Dpto Lewpina 1944 d Belizario. Programa De Educ Teologica; Universidad Biblica Latinoamericana. D 4/15/1998 P 1/1/2000 Bp Leo Frade. m 7/15/1994 Luis Gustavo Arevalo Flores c 5. Dio Honduras San Pedro Sula 1998-2016; Vicaria San Juan Evangelista.

CARTER, Bente (Cal) 60 Pinehurst Way, San Francisco CA 94127 B Horsens DK 1950 d Gunnar & Alyss. U CA; BA U CA 1972; MDiv CDSP 1992. D 12/5/1992 P 12/1/1993 Bp William Edwin Swing. m 8/28/1971 James Carter c 3. R S Fran' Epis Ch San Francisco CA 1999-2009; Asst Trin Par Menlo Pk CA 1995-1999; Asst R S Lk's Ch San Francisco CA 1993-1995; Asst Chapl Boys Cathd Sch San Francisco CA 1992-1993.

CARTER III, Charles Alexander (Pa) 8018 Navajo St, Philadelphia PA 19118 **Died 10/31/2016** B Nashville TN 1937 s Charles & Madrienne. BA Van 1958; BD EDS 1963. D 7/15/1963 Bp William Evan Sanders P 5/1/1964 Bp John Vander Horst. m 6/19/1993 Sarah Heckscher c 3. The Ch Of The Trin Coatesville PA 2000-2011; S Ptr's Ch Phoenixville PA 1997; Ret 1996-2016; Dio Pennsylvania Philadelphia PA 1996-1998; R S Paul's Ch Chestnut Hill PA 1984-1995; S Paul's Ch Philadelphia PA 1984-1995; Cn-in-Res Cathd Of St Jn The Div New York NY 1978-1984; Urban Mssnr Dio W Tennessee Memphis 1975-1978; Memphis Urban Mnstry Memphis TN 1975-1978; Vic S Mary's Ch Jacksonville FL 1969-1975; Asst Chr Ch Cathd Nashville TN 1965-1969; Vic Ch of the H Sprt Springfield TN 1963-1965.

CARTER, David Morgan (Ct) 521 Pomfret Street (Box 21), Pomfret CT 06258 **R Chr Ch Pomfret CT 1996-** B New York NY 1953 s David & Patricia. BA Clark U 1976; MDiv UTS 1980; MA Col 1981. D 6/14/1986 P 7/25/1987 Bp Arthur Edward Walmsley. m 8/8/1981 Christine L'Abbe Amiot c 2. Cur S Jn's Ch Portsmouth NH 1988-1996; Chapl White Mtn Sch Littleton NH 1986-1988; Spec. Ed. Tchr Jr HS 118 NYC NY 1981-1988. christchurchpomfret@gmail.com

CARTER, Davis Blake (WTex) Po Box 707, Aberdeen MS 39730 **Non-par 1966-** B Luling TX 1925 s John & Lucille. BA U of Texas 1947; BD Sewanee: The U So, TS 1953. D 6/11/1953 P 12/1/1953 Bp Everett H Jones. m 7/18/1945 Mary E Busch c 2. Asst Min Cathd of St Ptr & St Paul Washington DC 1954-1964; P-in-c Gr Ch Llano TX 1953-1954; S Lk's Epis Ch San Saba TX 1953-1954; S Paul's Ch Brady TX 1953-1954.

CARTER JR, Frederick Leroy (U) 472 Gordon Cir, Tooele UT 84074 **Ret 2003-** B Roanoke VA 1935 s Frederick & Mildred. BA Bridgewater Coll 1958; MS VPI 1960. D 3/19/1979 P 9/1/1980 Bp Otis Charles. m 12/27/1958 Nancy Marie Carter. Dio Utah Salt Lake City UT 1996-2002; Presb S Barn EpiscopalChurch Tooele UT 1980-2003.

CARTER, Grayson Leigh (RG) 1602 Palmcroft Dr Sw, Phoenix AZ 85007 **Assoc Prof of Ch Hist Fuller TS SW Phoenix AZ 2002-** B San Diego CA 1953 s James & Iona. BS USC 1976; MA Fuller TS 1984; PhD Oxf GB 1990; Oxf GB 1990. Trans 12/27/1996 Bp Brice Sidney Sanders. m 9/10/1988 Catherine Louise Randall c 3. Asst Chr Ch of the Ascen Paradise Vlly AZ 2002-2008; Int Trin Ch Lumberton NC 2002; Assoc Prof of Rel Methodist U Fayetteville NC 1996-2002; Asst H Trin Epis Ch Fayetteville NC 1996-2000; Chapl and Tutor Brasenose Coll Oxf 1992-1996; Cur Ch of Engl 1990-1992. Auth, Wipf and Stock, 2013; Auth, "Miscellaneous arts," *The Oxford Dictionary of Natl Biography*, 2003; Auth, "Angl Evangelicals. Protestant Secession from the via media, c.1800-1850," Oxf Press, 2000; Auth, "Miscellaneous arts," *Rel in Geschichte und Gegenwart*, 2000; Auth, "Jn Henry Newman and Henry Bulteel," *The Angl Cath*, 2000; Auth, "The Case of the Revd Jas Shore," *Journ of Eccl Hist*, 1996; Auth, "Miscellaneous arts," *The Blackwell Encyclopedia of Evang Biography*, 1995.

CARTER, Halcott Richardson (USC) 4708 Seahurst Ave, Everett WA 98203 **Chapl USN 2017-** B Everett WA 1984 s Donald & Marla. BA U of Puget Sound 2006; MDiv Sewanee: The U So, TS 2011. D 2/15/2011 P 10/27/2011 Bp Gregory Harold Rickel. Assoc R for Outreach and Missions Ch Of The Adv Spartanburg SC 2011-2014; Chapl Candidate Prog Off USN 2011-2014.

CARTER, James Currie Mackechnie (Va) 3510 Hastings Dr, Richmond VA 23235 B Norfolk VA 1948 s Worral & Margaret. BA VPI 1971; MDiv Epis TS of the SW 1980; MA Virginia Commonwealth U 2004. D 6/8/1980 P 6/1/1981 Bp Claude Charles Vache. m 1/1/2000 Sandra Carter. S Dav's Ch Aylett VA 1996-1997, 1987-1989; S Asaph's Par Ch Bowling Green VA 1989-1992; S Ptr's Port Royal Port Royal VA 1989-1990; Asst All SS Ch Richmond VA 1982-1987; Vic S Lk's Ch Courtland VA 1980-1982; Vic S Paul's Epis Ch Surry VA 1980-1982.

CARTER, James Lee (SwFla) 9925 Ulmerton Rd Lot 40, Largo FL 33771 **Asst R Calv Ch Largo FL 1988-** B Fortville IN 1930 s John & Fern. Carroll Coll. D 10/4/1982 Bp Edward Witker Jones. m 9/1/1950 Delores Anne Carter. Calv Ch

Indn Rk Bc FL 1990-1994; Chapl S Jn's Hosp Anderson IN 1982-1988; Asst to R Trin Ch Anderson IN 1982-1988; Asst to R St Dunst's Largo FL.

CARTER JR, James Robert (Ga) 601 Washington Ave, Savannah GA 31405 B Selma AL 1938 s James & Laura. BA U So 1960; MDiv Candler TS Emory U 1968; MA Emory U 1968; CPE Emory U 1969; PhD Emory U 1977. D 2/24/1977 P 11/1/1977 Bp George Paul Reeves. m 1/26/1985 Jan Carter. Cn The Collgt Ch of St Paul the Apos Savannah GA 2002, Cn 2002-; Cn To Ordnry Dio Georgia Savannah GA 1988-2002; Vic Trin Ch Statesboro GA 1985-1988; S Barn Epis Ch Valdosta GA 1983-1985; S Jas Epis Ch Quitman GA 1980-1984; Cur Chr Ch Valdosta GA 1977-1982; Chapl Valdosta St Coll Valdosta GA 1977-1982. Auth, "Gascon Archive Materials In A British Museum Manuscript". Ord Of S Helena, Assoc.

CARTER, John Franklin (Ct) John Carter, 19 Willow Dr, Lakeville CT 06039 B New York NY 1944 s Lewis & Gertrude. BA Ya 1967; MDiv VTS 1984. D 6/1/1985 Bp John Bowen Coburn P 6/14/1986 Bp Don Edward Johnson. m 8/31/1974 Deborah S Carter c 3. R S Jn's Ch Salisbury CT 1998-2014; All SS Ch Highland Pk NJ 1998; R Chr Ch Norwalk CT 1992-1998; Asst R S Phil's Ch Brevard NC 1986-1992; Chapl White Mtn Sch Littleton NH 1984-1986. Auth,Mus, *Carry The Dream*, 1983. johnfcarter44@gmail.com

CARTER, L Susan (Mich) 1102 Portage Path, East Lansing MI 48823 **S Paul's Epis Ch Lansing MI 2015-; Prof MI SU 1991-** B Columbus OH 1950 d Edward & Jane. BA MI SU 1984; JD Wayne 1988; MA Wayne 1991; MDiv GTS 2009; DMin SWTS 2013. D 12/20/2008 Bp Wendell Nathaniel Gibbs Jr. c 1. R S Jn's Ch Howell MI 2010-2015.

CARTER, Lynda Anne (Mich) 2803 1st St, Wyandotte MI 48192 **Gr Epis Ch Southgate MI 2015-** B Detroit MI 1948 d Stanley & Elizabeth. A.S Schoolcraft Coll 1974; B.S Estrn Michigan U 1977; MDiv Ecumencial TS 2014; MDiv Ecum TS 2014. D 12/13/2014 P 6/13/2015 Bp Wendell Nathaniel Gibbs Jr.

CARTER III, Philander Lothrop (WMich) 1296 Siena Way, Boulder CO 80301 B Ann Arbor MI 1947 s Collins & Mary. BA Stan 1974; MA Amer Grad Sch of Intl Mgmt Glendal 1980; MDiv TESM 1989. D 6/12/1989 Bp John Wadsworth Howe P 12/1/1989 Bp Peter J Lee. m 8/16/1975 Gretchen Carter c 3. Chr Epis Ch Charlevoix MI 1989-1998. Bro Of S Andr.

CARTER, R Douglas (SwFla) Berkeley Preparatory School, 4811 Kelly Road, Tampa FL 33615 **Chapl Berkeley Epis Preparatory Sch 2000-** B Tampa FL 1951 s A Robert & Claire. BA Millsaps Coll 1973; MDiv VTS 1976. D 6/25/1981 Bp Duncan Montgomery Gray Jr P 5/29/1982 Bp The Bishop Of Tokyo. m 9/30/1992 Susan E Carter. Chapl S Marks Sch Of Texas Dallas TX 2014-2015; Mem, Admin Team Berkeley Preparatory Sch Tampa FL 2000-2014; R Chr Ch Epis Lomas De Chapultepec 1995-2000; R Iglesia Anglicana De Mex 1995-2000; R All Ang Ch Miami FL 1991-1995; Assoc S Dav's Epis Ch Englewood FL 1988-1991; Vic Ch Of The Ascen Brooksville MS 1986-1988; Chapl Ch Of The Resurr Starkville MS 1986-1988; Chapl Mississippi St U At Starkville 1986-1988; Serv Angl Comm In Japan 1977-1984. Auth, "Epis Identity Amidst Rel Pluralism: How One Sch Traveled Back to Its Roots," *Ntwk*, NAES.

CARTER JR, Richard Blair (ETenn) PO Box 5104, Knoxville TN 37928 **Ch Of The Gd Shpd Knoxville TN 2011-** B Auburn NY 1969 s Richard & Kathryn. BA Bos 1991; MDiv UTS 1995; MD Baylor Coll of Med 2003. D 6/4/2011 Bp Charles Glenn VonRosenberg P 5/16/2012 Bp George Young III. m 5/25/1996 Marjorie Mae Thigpen c 3.

CARTER, Stanley Edward (ETenn) 1930 Chelsea Jo Ln., Sevierville TN 37876 B Charleston WV 1944 s Garnett & Sara. BA U of Kentucky 1970; MA U of Kentucky 1976; MDiv Epis TS in Kentucky 1982. D 6/5/1982 Bp Charles Gresham Marmion P 12/1/1982 Bp Addison Hosea. m 11/9/2002 Linda E Carter. Trin Epis Ch Gatlinburg TN 1993-1999; Vic Ch of the Nativ Sarasota FL 1985-1993; Vic S Lk's Ch Newberry SC 1983-1985. SSC.

CARTER, Thomas Brooke (Md) 2860 Hill Top Dr, Salisbury NC 28147 B Baltimore MD 1946 s Harry & Edith. U of W Georgia; LTh VTS 1992. D 12/12/1992 P 6/1/1993 Bp William Arthur Beckham. m 9/18/1971 Patricia B Boring c 3. R The Ch Of The Nativ Cedarcroft Baltimore MD 2000-2012; S Mths Ch Rock Hill SC 1998-2000; Dio Upper So Carolina Columbia SC 1996-1997; P-in-c Ch Of The Ascen Hickory NC 1995-1996; Asst R Gr Epis Ch Anderson SC 1992-1993.

CARTER, Wayne Ervin (WLa) 396 Country Club Circle, Minden LA 71055 **S Mk's Cathd Shreveport LA 2014-, Int 2012; Ecum and Interreligous Off Dio Wstrn Louisiana 2003-** B Portland ME 1940 s Thomas & Florence. BS Gorham St Teachers Coll Gorham ME 1965; MA U of Maine 1967; PhD U of So Carolina 1974; Lic Sacr Theol Angl TS 1983. D 6/11/1983 Bp Robert Elwin Terwilliger P 5/22/1984 Bp Donis Dean Patterson. c 1. Tchr St. Mk's Cathd Sch 2012-2013; Dio Wstrn Louisiana Alexandria LA 2004-2005; R S Jn's Epis Ch Minden LA 2002-2012; R Trin Epis Ch Pharr TX 1996-2002; R S Paul's Epis Ch Dallas TX 1985-1996; P-in-c Dept Of Missions Dallas TX 1985; Cur S Chris's Ch Dallas TX 1983-1984; Dn - Dioc TS Dio Wstrn Louisiana 2005-2006; Ecum Off Dio W Texas 1998-2001; Ecum Off Dio Dallas 1990-1996. Auth, *Evaltn of CE*, Profsnl paper given, 1981; Auth, *A Taxon-omy of Educational Evaltn*, (PhD dissertation), 1974. CHS 1983; Dallas Ward (Chapl) 1986-1996.

CARTER-EDMANDS, Lynn (SO) 55 S Vernon Ln, Fort Thomas KY 41075 **Cn Dio Sthrn Ohio Cincinnati OH 2012-** B Modesto CA 1953 d Robert & Nancy. BA California St U 1987; MDiv GTS 1990. D 10/31/1992 P 6/3/1993 Bp William George Burrill. m 5/2/1981 Frank A Edmands. R S Jas Epis Ch Columbus OH 2006-2011; R S Andr's Epis Ch Lewisburg PA 1997-2006; Sch Min Trin-Pawling Sch Pawling NY 1994-1997; Int Mnstry Dio Rochester Henrietta 1993-1994; Asst Ch Of The Gd Shpd Webster NY 1992-1993. Soc of Cath Priests 2010. lcarter-edmands@diosohio.org

CARTIER, Fred Claire (NY) 222 Starbarrack Rd, Red Hook NY 12571 **Ret 2005-** B Morristown NJ 1940 s Harold & Antoinette. BA Moravian Coll 1965; STB PDS 1968. D 4/20/1968 P 10/26/1968 Bp Alfred L Banyard. m 6/22/1968 Rosalie Y Cartier c 2. Chr Ch Red Hook NY 1976-2005; Asst R S Geo's Ch Hempstead NY 1975-1976; Chapl S Paul Sch Garden City NY 1970-1975; Cur Gr Ch Merchantville NJ 1968-1970. fred@theservices.org

CARTWRIGHT, Gary Earle (SwFla) 2202 Wildwood Hollow Dr, Valrico FL 33594 B New Bedford MA 1938 s Earle & Dorothy. NE Inst of Indstrl Tech Boston MA 1957. D 6/14/1997 Bp Barbara Clementine Harris. m 4/11/1959 Simone Marie Martin. Dio SW Florida Parrish FL 2001-2003, Dep For Diac Mnstrs 2000-; D H Innoc Epis Ch Valrico FL 1997-2000.

CARTWRIGHT JR, Howard Mott (Los) 5825 Lincoln Ave Ste D, Buena Park CA 90620 **Dioc Yth Cmsn Dio Los Angeles Los Angeles CA 1980-** B Detroit MI 1930 s Howard & Ola. BA California St U 1964; Cert ETSBH 1968; MDiv CDSP 1969. D 9/13/1969 P 3/21/1970 Bp Francis E I Bloy. m 8/21/1986 Mary Alice Cartwright. Asstg P Trin Epis Ch Orange CA 1988-2003; Vic S Mich Ch Alturas CA 1983-1984; P-in-c S Andr Battle Mtn NV 1977-1978; P-in-c S Mary's Ch Winnemucca NV 1977-1978; Vic S Jn The Div Epis Ch Costa Mesa CA 1972-1976; Chapl GFS 1972-1973; Ch Of The H Sprt Bullhead City AZ 1971-1972; Vic S Jn The Evang Mssn Needles CA 1971-1972; Vic S Ptr-By-The-River Holiday Shores AZ 1971-1972; S Phil's Preaching Sta Parker AZ 1971-1972; Cur S Andr's Par Fullerton CA 1969-1971. Bro Of S Andr 2001; Westar Inst 1999.

CARTWRIGHT, Thomas Lisson (Ore) 1720 Ten Oaks Ln, Woodburn OR 97071 **Ret 2000-** B Lubbock TX 1935 s Thomas & Teresa. BA Duke 1957; STB GTS 1961. D 6/20/1961 Bp Charles A Mason P 12/1/1961 Bp John Joseph Meakin Harte. m 4/4/1970 Jocelyn S Cartwright. Vic S Mary's Ch Woodburn OR 1993-2000; Dio Oregon Portland OR 1992-2000; S Ptr's Epis Ch Red Bluff CA 1992; Non-par 1990-1992; R S Mk's Ch Yreka CA 1966-1990; Cur S Lk's Ch Denison TX 1964-1965; Cur S Matt's Cathd Dallas TX 1961-1964. Who'S Who In Rel.

CARTY, Shawn (Nwk) PO Box 117, Bellevue ID 83313 **S Mk's Ch Mendham NJ 2014-** B La Grange IL 1970 s John & Elaine. BA Seattle Pacific U 1992; MDiv Drew U 1996. D 6/26/2004 Bp Vincent Waydell Warner P 4/1/2005 Bp Bavi Edna Rivera. m 6/27/1992 Jeanne Alo Smith c 1. R Emm Ch Hailey ID 2005-2014; Pstr Fall City Meth Ch Fall City WA 1996-1999.

CARUSO, Cynthia Woodham (Tex) 209 W 27th St, Austin TX 78705 **All SS Epis Ch Austin TX 2013-** B Detroit MI 1949 d Alan & Anne. BA U CA 1969; MA U of Texas 1989; MDiv Epis TS Of The SW 2013; MDiv Epis TS of the SW 2013. D 6/15/2013 Bp C Andrew Doyle P 12/19/2013 Bp Michael Vono. c 2.

CARUSO, Frank (Mass) 112 Spring St, Hopkinton MA 01748 **Psychol Self-Employed 1980-** B Salem MA 1950 D Formation Prog; BS U of Massachusetts 1981; MS Suffolk U 1984; EdD Bos 1989; Massachusetts Diac Formation Prog 2006. D 6/3/2006 Bp M(Arvil) Thomas Shaw. m 7/18/1999 Sheila Reindl c 2. Trin Epis Ch Wrentham MA 2006-2007.

CARUSO, Kevin (Chi) 647 Dundee Ave, Barrington IL 60010 **R Trin Epis Ch Wheaton IL 2014-** B Hartford CT 1981 s Daniel & Betty. BA U Chi 2003; MDiv Ya Berk 2011. D 6/5/2010 P 6/28/2011 Bp Jeff Lee. m 10/9/2004 Kathryn J Caruso c 3. Assoc S Mich's Ch Barrington IL 2011-2014; Yth Dir Ch Of Our Sav Chicago IL 2004-2008. kcaruso@trinitywheaton.org

CARUTHERS, Mary C (Ark) 509 Scott St, Little Rock AR 72201 B Memphis TN 1948 D 12/21/2001 P 7/19/2003 Bp Larry Maze. m 12/31/1976 Laird D Caruthers c 3. St Peters Epis Ch St Croix VI 2012-2013; S Paul's Newport AR 2010-2011; Dio Arkansas Little Rock AR 2009-2010; Chr Epis Ch Little Rock AR 2003-2005.

CARVER, Barbara Schenkel (Spok) 1904 Browning Way, Sandpoint ID 83864 B Huntington IN 1948 d Richard & Mary. Indiana U 1970; BS U of Maryland 1981; Natl-Louis U 1994; Gonzaga U 2005. D 9/28/1994 Bp Francis Campbell Gray. m 6/4/1977 J.P. Carver. H Sprt Epis Ch Dover ID 1999-2009; D S Mary's Bonners Ferry Bonners Ferr ID 1999-2003; D H Fam Ch Angola IN 1994-1998; COM Dio Spokane Spokane WA 2002-2008. The Ord Of The DOK 1994.

CARVER, J.P. (Spok) 1904 Browning Way, Sandpoint ID 83864 **Vol Chapl Sandpoint Police Dept 2009-** B Spokane WA 1947 s Harold & Marguerite. BA U of Washington 1970; MDiv SWTS 1994. D 12/4/1993 Bp John Stuart Thornton P 7/1/1994 Bp Francis Campbell Gray. m 6/4/1977 Barbara Schenkel Carver. H Sprt Epis Ch Dover ID 2009, 1999-2000; Ret Dio Spokane Spokane

WA 2001-2008; Vic S Mary's Bonners Ferry Bonners Ferr ID 1999-2000; R H Fam Ch Angola IN 1994-1998; Dioc Coun, Mem Dio Nthrn Indiana So Bend IN 1995-1997.

CARVER, Larry A (WK) 18 E 28th Ave, Hutchinson KS 67502 **P-in-res Gr Epis Ch Hutchinson KS 2011-** B Detroit MI 1944 s Roger & Mary. AA Schoolcraft Coll Livonia MI 1966; BA Oakland U 1968; MDiv VTS 1972; Cert The Amer Coll 1985; MI SU 1992; Cert UCLA Ext 2004; MS Emporia St U 2007. D 6/29/1972 Bp Richard Stanley Merrill Emrich P 3/10/1973 Bp H Coleman Mcgehee Jr. m 4/29/1999 Joyce A Ziegelmann c 1. Chr Ch Kingman KS 1995-2008; Vic All SS Ch Pratt KS 1995-2001; S Mk's Ch Med Ldg KS 1995-2001; Gr Ch Anth KS 1995-1999; R Chr Ch Flint MI 1976-1978; R Chr Enrichment Cntr Flint MI 1976-1978; R S Paul's Epis Ch Brighton MI 1974-1976; Asst Gr Ch Mt Clemens MI 1972-1973; Ecum and Interreligious Off Dio Wstrn Kansas Hutchinson KS 2011-2017, Asst Treas 2011-. Auth, "The Vic's View," *syndicated weekly Nwspr column in Kansas*, 1997.

CARVER, Lynne (Ia) St. Peter's Episcopal Church, 2400 Middle Rd., Bettendorf IA 52722 B Radford VA 1951 d James & Ann. BS Pur 1973; MA U of No Dakota 1975; PhD U of No Dakota 1978; MDiv SWTS 1992. D 5/31/1992 Bp Thomas Kreider Ray P 12/19/1992 Bp Frank Tracy Griswold III. c 1. R S Ptr's Ch Bettendorf IA 1999-2015; S Lawr Epis Ch Libertyville IL 1997-1999; Int The Annunc Of Our Lady Gurnee IL 1996-1997; Advoc Hlth Care Oak Brook IL 1992-1999; Assoc Ch Of Our Sav Chicago IL 1992-1993; Stndg Com Pres Dio Iowa Des Moines IA 2008-2009.

CARVER, Robert Cody (Oly) 1701 N Juniper St, Tacoma WA 98406 **Assoc Chr Ch Tacoma WA 2015-** B Phoenix AZ 1946 s William & Eileen. BA California St U 1968; MDiv CDSP 1971; ADN Pierce Coll 2008; MN U of Washington Tacoma 2014. D 9/11/1971 Bp Francis E I Bloy P 3/1/1972 Bp Philip Frederick McNairy. m 6/16/1968 Kristin Elizabeth Carver c 2. RN (Psych) Wstrn St Hosp 2009-2012; Int S Cathr Enumclaw WA 2005-2007; Primary Mssnr All SS Epis Ch Williamsport PA 2002-2004; Gleam Williamsport PA 2002-2004; Ch Of Our Sav Montoursville PA 2000-2004; S Lk's Ch Tacoma WA 1994-1999; R S Simons Ch Miami FL 1985-1994; R S Andr's Epis Ch Aberdeen WA 1978-1985; Vic Emm Epis Ch Alexandria MN 1975-1978; R Ch Of The Gd Samar Sauk Cntr MN 1975-1977; Asst S Helen's Ch Wadena MN 1974-1978; Asst S Steph The Mtyr Ch Minneapolis MN 1972-1974; Vic S Mary's Ch Ely MN 1971-1972; S Steph Hoyt Lakes MN 1971-1972. Auth, *The Creator's Wrld*. Sigma Theta Tau hon Soc of Nrsng 2010. robert.carver@cptc.edu

CARVER, Sarah Frances (NC) 4795 Silver Creek Dr., Greensboro NC 27410 **Assoc H Trin Epis Ch Greensboro NC 2017-; Bd Mem UTO 2013-** B Petoskey MI 1978 d Carlos & Edwardine. BS Alma Coll 2000; MDiv GTS 2007; MSW MI SU 2013. D 6/23/2007 P 2/9/2008 Bp Steven Todd Ousley. m 1/9/2010 Peter Carver c 1. Dio No Carolina Raleigh NC 2015; Oncology Soc Worker MidMichigan Med Cntr 2014; R H Fam Epis Ch Midland MI 2010-2014; Mssnr To YA Dio Estrn Michigan Saginaw MI 2007-2010, COM 2008-2014. sarah@holy-trinity.com

CASAS, Alberto Moreno (NwT) San Miguel Arcangel, 907 N Adams Ave, Odessa TX 79761 **P Dio NW Texas Lubbock TX 2012-** B Mexico 1961 s Alberto & Teresa. BSc Universidad de San Luis Potosi 1985; BA Seminario Diocesano 1998; BTh Gregorian U 2001; MA Gregorian U 2004; Dplma Universidad de Monterrey 2007. Trans 7/3/2012 Bp James Scott Mayer. m 6/18/2005 Malgorzata Olszowka c 2. Latino Mssnr San Miguel Arcangel Odessa TX 2012-2017; Asst Dio Nthrn Mex Nuevo Leon 2009-2012; U Prof Universidad de Monterrey Nuevo Leon MX 2005-2012; Resrch in Soc Ethics Consejo Estatal de Valores y Legalidad Nuevo Leon MX 2005-2012. Auth, "Liderazgo," *Caracter del Lider*, Nueva Cultura Ediciones, 1994. Yoder Prize for Essay on Love VTS 2012; Second Place, Stdt Essay Competition LivCh 2011; cl Gregorian U 2004; mcl Gregorian U 2001.

CASE, Doris May (Mich) 10242 Joslin Lake Rd, Gregory MI 48137 **Election Cordinator, Secy Bd of Appeals, Dep Townshi Lyndon Township 1997-** B Ann Arbor MI 1935 d John & Virginia. D 12/10/2005 Bp Wendell Nathaniel Gibbs Jr. m 4/8/1961 Leon Folsome Case c 1. Dep Treas, Supvsr, Chair of employees Ret Washington Cnty Treas 1955-1995.

CASE, Jaime J (Oly) 426 E Fourth Plain Blvd, Vancouver WA 98663 **R S Lk's Epis Ch Vancouver WA 2011-; Fac CREDO (Spanish) Memphis TN 2005-; Cn The Epis Dio Texas Multi-Cultural Mnstrs Aus 2005-; Assoc Prof Epis TS of the SW Austin TX 2004-; Cntr for Hisp Mnstrs Prov VII Austin 2003-** B Kaufman TX 1957 s Norman & Thelma. BA Coe Coll 1980; MDiv Epis TS of the SW 1994. D 6/25/1994 Bp James Monte Stanton P 1/9/1995 Bp Maurice Manuel Benitez. m 12/20/1980 Amy P Case c 2. Dio Texas Houston TX 2005-2011; The Cntr For Hisp Mnstrs Austin TX 2003-2005; Iglesia San Francisco de Asis Austin TX 2000-2003; El Buen Samar Mssn Austin TX 1995-2003; The Great Cmsn Fndt Houston TX 1994-1999. "Jugar Junto a Dios (Mng Ed, Spanish of Godly Play) Vols 1-4," Living the Gd News, 2007; "La Serie del Descubrimiento (The Discovery Series, Ed, Spanish Ed)," The Epis Dio Texas, 2005; "Preparacion de Niños para la Santa Eucaristia (Comunmente Llamado Primera Comunión)," Cntr for Hisp Mnstrs, 2004. CODE 2005; Chapl, BroSA's 2003-2004; UBE (Assoc) 2005.

CASE, James J (At) Holy Innocents Episcopal Church, 805 Mount Vernon Hwy, Atlanta GA 30327 **Chr Ch Charlotte NC 2017-** B Selma AL 1977 s James & Elizabeth. BA U of Alabama 2002; MDiv Candler TS Emory U 2011; MDiv Candler TS-Emory 2011. D 12/21/2013 P 6/21/2014 Bp Robert Christopher Wright. m 6/28/2003 Laura Dawn Case c 2. H Innoc Ch Atlanta GA 2014-2017.

CASE, Margaret Timothy (RG) B Columbus OH 1949 BA U NC 1971; MDiv Nash 2005. D 7/30/2005 Bp Terence Kelshaw P 6/4/2006 Bp Jeffrey Neil Steenson. Asst S Chad's Epis Ch Albuquerque NM 2010-2013; S Jn's Cathd Albuquerque NM 2008-2009; Epis Ch Of The H Fam Santa Fe NM 2006-2007; COM Dio The Rio Grande Albuquerque 2006-2008.

CASE, Michael Allen (Ida) 704 S Latah St, Boise ID 83705 B Los Angeles CA 1966 s Ronald & Mary Ann. BA Idaho St U 1992. D 10/26/2014 P 4/26/2015 Bp Brian James Thom. m 11/15/2013 Peter Henry Haskins c 3.

CASEY, Dayle Alan (Colo) 2059 Glenhill Rd, Colorado Springs CO 80906 B Dallas TX 1937 s Lester & Wanda. BA TCU 1959; MA Duke 1960; MA Brandeis U 1962; MDiv Nash 1977. D 4/16/1977 P 10/24/1977 Bp Charles Thomas Gaskell. m 6/6/1959 Judith R Casey c 2. R Ch Of Our Sav Colorado Sprg CO 1986-2009; Vic S Mary's Epis Ch Summit WI 1977-1986. Auth, "The Rts Of Americans". Mdiv cl Nash 1977; Ba cl TCU 1959.

CASEY, Stephen Charles (CPa) 429 Camp Meeting Rd, Landisville PA 17538 **R S Edw's Epis Ch Lancaster PA 1998-** B Hull UK 1946 s James & Hilda. BA Ge 1991; MDiv VTS 1995. D 6/9/1995 Bp Charlie Fuller Mcnutt Jr P 3/16/1996 Bp Michael Whittington Creighton. m 8/13/1983 Rayelenn Sparks c 2. S Paul's Ch Lock Haven PA 1995-1998; Cnvnr of Convoc Dio Cntrl Pennsylvania Harrisburg PA 2014-2015, Chair Dioc Fin Com 2013-2015, Coun of Trst 2013-2015, Pres Stndg Com 2008-2009, Ecum Cmsn 2003-2013. Hon Cn St. Steph's Cathd, Harrisburg, PA Dio Cntrl Pennsylvania 2008; Phi Beta Kappa Ge 1991; Ba mcl Ge 1991. stedsoffice@comcast.net

CASEY-MARTUS, Sandra (WTex) St. Stephen's Episcopal Church, Wimberley TX 78676 **R S Steph's Epis Ch Wimberley TX 2012-; Exec Dir Alta Retreat Cntr 2004-** B New Rochelle NY 1948 d Charles & Patricia. BA Springfield Coll 1970; MEd Springfield Coll 1971; MTS Oblate TS 1983; CITS Epis TS of the SW 1993. D 6/16/1996 P 12/7/1996 Bp John Stuart Thornton. c 2. Assoc All SS-By-The-Sea Par Santa Barbara CA 2011-2012; R All SS Epis Ch Corpus Christi TX 2009-2011; Assoc All SS Epis Ch Austin TX 2005-2009; Vic Idaho Boise ID 2005; Epis TS Of The SW Austin TX 1998; Vic S Fran Of The Tetons Alta WY 1996-2005. Auth, "Simplicity Silence Pryr," *Teton Valley Top to Bottom (Winter)*, 2001; Contributing Auth, "Centering Pryr and Priestly Formation," *Centering Pryr in Daily Life and Mnstry*, Continuum Press Inc., 1998; Auth, "Centering Pryr & Priestly Formation," *Sewanee Theol Revs*, U So, 1997; Auth, "Concordance to the Lessons," Ex-Libris; Auth, "The Lessons: How to Understand Sprtl Principles, Sprtl Acativities and Rising Emotions," Wheatmark; Auth, "Your Other Heart," Wheatmark. 2005 Hal Brook Perry Awd Epis Sem of the SW 2005.

CASHELL, Douglas Hanson (NwT) D 11/16/2013 Bp James Scott Mayer.

CASHMAN, Patricia (Pa) 2 Riverside St, Rochester NY 14613 **H Trin Ch Lansdale PA 2016-** B SD 1953 d Henry & Verdeen. BS Widener U 1983; MS Neumann Coll Aston PA 1987; MDiv Luth TS at Gettysburg 1995. D 7/29/1995 Bp Allen Lyman Bartlett Jr P 9/28/1996 Bp Franklin Delton Turner. m 5/18/1974 Paul Cashman c 3. P Chr Epis Ch Burlington IA 2013-2016; Ch Of The Ascen Rochester NY 2011-2013; R Emm Ch Philadelphia PA 1999-2003; Int S Faith Ch Havertown PA 1997-1998.

CASILLAS, Laina Wood (Cal) 4942 Thunderhead Ct, El Sobrante CA 94803 **D S Paul's Epis Ch Walnut Creek CA 2013-; D S Mich And All Ang Concord CA 1996-** B CA 1954 d Harrell & Eleanor. BA Sch for Deacons 1990. D 12/7/1996 Bp William Edwin Swing. m 10/27/1973 Frank J Casillas.

CASKEY, Charles C (Chi) 24410 Reserve Ct Apt 103, Bonita Springs FL 34134 **Int St. Elis 2004-** B Mooresville NC 1946 s Clinton & Olive. No Carolina St U 1967; BA Wake Forest U 1968; GW 1971; MDiv VTS 1975; Indiana U 1993. D 5/22/1975 Bp Robert Bruce Hall P 12/28/1975 Bp Frederick Hesley Belden. m 5/22/1971 Elizabeth L Caskey c 2. R Chr Epis Ch S Jos MO 2011-2015; S Andr's Par Fullerton CA 2010-2011; Int S Chris's Ch Milwaukee WI 2008-2009; S Thos Epis Ch Battle Creek MI 2007-2008; R Chr Ch Waukegan IL 2006-2007; S Elis's Ch Glencoe IL 2004-2005; Int S Lk's Ch Evanston IL 2000-2004; S Jn The Div Epis Ch Burlington WI 1999-2000; H Cross Epis Ch Wisconsin Dells WI 1999; S Andr's Ch Milwaukee WI 1997-1999; Non-par 1993-1997; Chapl Indiana U 1987-1993; Trin Epis Ch Bloomington IN 1987-1993; R S Paul's Ch Marquette MI 1981-1987; R Ch Of The Gd Shpd Pawtucket RI 1979-1981; S Cathr's Sch Richmond VA 1978-1979; Chapl S Cathr's Sch Richmond VA 1978-1979; Chapl Johnson & Wales Coll Providence RI 1976-1978; Asst Min Gr Ch In Providence Providence RI 1975-1978. EPF, ESMHE, Cleric & Laity Concerned; Witness For Peace.

CASON JR, Charles Edward (FdL) 1805 Arlington Dr, Oshkosh WI 54904 **Ret 1998-** B Vidalia GA 1937 s Charles & Sarah. BS Georgia Sthrn U 1960; MDiv SWTS 1963; Coll of Preachers 1971. D 6/22/1963 P 4/25/1964 Bp Albert R Stuart. m 7/20/1963 Joan Prescott Brain. R Trin Epis Ch Oshkosh WI 1977-1997; R Zion Epis Ch Oconomowoc WI 1974-1977; P-in-c Gr Epis Ch

150

Menomonie WI 1967-1974; Vic S Fran Ch Camilla GA 1964-1967; Sem S Jas Epis Ch Quitman GA 1963-1966. CBS. Royal Ord Of Scotland 1998.

CASPARIAN, Peter (LI) 705 Snyder Hill Dr, San Marcos TX 78666 B New York NY 1951 s George & Particia. BA Rhodes Coll 1971; MDiv Sewanee: The U So, TS 1974; MA U of Missouri 1980; DMin Sewanee: The U So, TS 1988. D 6/29/1974 P 2/1/1975 Bp David Reed. m 4/16/1977 Marguerite West c 2. Epis TS Of The SW Austin TX 2016; R Chr Ch Oyster Bay NY 2004-2014; R S Jas Epis Ch Firenze 50123 1995-2004; R Ch S Mich The Archangel Lexington KY 1986-1995; Chapl Cbury At Kansas U Lawr KS 1979-1986; Chapl S Marks Sch Of Texas Dallas TX 1978-1979; Chapl/Tchr The Selwyn Sch Denton TX 1977-1978; Asst S Andr's Ch Kansas City MO 1974-1977; Tchr S Andr's-Sewanee Sch S Andrews TN 1971-1974. Photographer, "The PBp Visits Armenia," *Episcipal Life*, 2005. Consortium of Endowed Parishes 2004; EPF 1979; ESMHE 1979-1993.

CASSELL JR, John Summerfield (Md) 708 Milford Mill Rd, Baltimore MD 21208 **Ret _ 2012-** B Baltimore MD 1938 s John & Beulah. BS Loyola Coll 1961; MDiv PDS 1965. D 6/22/1965 P 6/23/1966 Bp Harry Lee Doll. m 7/29/1977 Carol Cassell c 1. Vic S Tim's Ch Frederick MD 1992-2012; Int Ch Of The Redemp Baltimore MD 1990-1991, Int 1985-1986; Int Ch Of The H Cov Baltimore MD 1987-1988; Vic H Cross Ch Baltimore MD 1967-1975, Asst to the Vic 1965-1967; Team Min SW Chr Par Inc Baltimore 1967-1975; Vic All SS Ch Baltimore MD 1967-1970; Vic S Jn's Relay MD 1967; Asst to the Vic S Jn's Relay MD 1965-1967. Maryland Epis Cler Assn 2010.

CASSELL, Jonnie Lee (Mo) 12025 Willow Ln Apt 916, Overland Park KS 66213 B Boise MS 1943 d John & Virginia. BA Mt Mercy Coll 1982; MDiv Epis TS of the SW 1996; Cont Educ Gnrl Bd Higher Educ and Mnstry 1997; Cont Educ Meth Ch 1997. D 5/17/1997 P 11/22/1997 Bp Robert Deane Rowley Jr. R S Andr's Ch S Louis MO 1998-2001; Stff Cathd Of S Paul Erie PA 1997-1998; Dio NW Pennsylvania Erie PA 1997. Auth, "Build Yourself A Future"; Auth, "Ms Lady"; Auth, "A Trip". Outstanding Performance,Outstanding Conciliatory Efforts/Results Untd States Dept Hud 1988; Mart Luther King Jr Awd, Outstanding Citizen Loc P3 Meat Cutters & Butchers Of Amer; Pi Sigma Alpha Awd Mt Mercy Coll; Wmn Of Worth Awd Older Wmn League.

CASSELL JR, Warren Michael (SeFla) 2718 Sw 6th St, Boynton Beach FL 33435 B Philadelphia PA 1934 s Warren & Ann. BS Colg 1954; U of Birmingham Birmingham GB 1954; MTh PDS 1957; MA Tem 1969. D 6/1/1957 Bp Oliver J Hart P 4/28/1958 Bp Russell S Hubbard. c 5. Speaker Food for the Poor Coconut Creek FL 2000-2015; Dn of So Palm Dnry Dio SE Florida Miami 1995-1998; R S Jos's Epis Ch Boynton Bch FL 1985-2000; Dn of Niagara Dnry Dio Wstrn New York Tonawanda NY 1978-1985; R S Ptr's Ch Niagara Falls NY 1971-1985; Chapl/Dir of Admssns DeVeaux Sch Niagara Falls NY 1966-1971; Assoc Ch Of Our Sav Jenkintown PA 1963-1966; R Ch Of Our Merc Sav Penns Grove NJ 1959-1963; Vic Chr Epis Ch Zillah WA 1957-1959. Tertiary of the Soc of S Fran 1959. ThM w hon PDS 1957.

CASSELS, Christine Helen (RI) D 6/10/2017 Bp W Nicholas Knisely Jr.

CASSEUS, Frantz Joseph (Hai) 7835 Jean Vincent, Montreal QC H1E 3C4 Canada **R Dio SE Florida Miami 2001-; Assoc P Dio Haiti Port-au-Prince HT 1990-** B Arcahaie HAITI 1947 s Andre & Anacile. MA U of Montreal 1978; BA Montreal TS CA 1981; Licence Other 1989; Licence Seminaire de Thelogie, Eglise Episcopale d'HAITI 1989; Lic Séminaire de Théologie Haiti 1990; PhD Col 1993. D 6/23/1991 P 1/1/1992 Bp Luc Anatole Jacques Garnier. m 1/27/1975 Yvrose Pierre-Casseus c 3. Eglise Du Bon Pasteur Miami FL 2003-2012; Assoc Cath S Trin Port-au-Prince 1991-2000; Serving - Vicair - Dir St-Vinc Cntr Dio Haiti Port-au-Prince 1991-2000. Auth, "Sprtlty and Psych," 2013; Auth, "Immigrant and Sch failure," 2005; Auth, "Fam and Brief Ther," 2003; Auth, "Jvnl Delinquency in CC Cmnty," 2002. Amer Coounseling Assn 2003; Can Psychol Assn 1988.

CASSINI, Mary Ellen Dakin (SeFla) 2805 Duncan Dr Apt C, Boca Raton FL 33434 **Palmer Trin Sch Palmetto Bay FL 2014-** B Miami FL 1956 d Thelus & Betty. DMin Barry U Miami; BA Barry U 1977; MA Barry U 1984; Cert The Prot Epis TS 2005. D 11/7/2006 Bp Leo Frade P 5/12/2007 Bp Calvin Onderdonk Schofield Jr. m 1/6/1978 Charles Jean-Marie Cassini c 2. S Chris's By-The-Sea Epis Ch Key Biscayne FL 2013-2014; S Mk The Evang Ft Lauderdale FL 2011-2013. maryellendakin.cassini@gmail.com

CASSON, Jordan F (Va) D 6/11/2016 Bp Shannon Sherwood Johnston.

CASSON, Lloyd Stuart (Del) 902 N Market St Apt 1327, Wilmington DE 19801 B Dover DE 1935 s Clarence & Nancy. BA U of Delaware 1961; MDiv VTS 1964. D 6/23/1964 P 6/5/1965 Bp John Brooke Mosley. c 2. Ch of St Andrews & St Matthews Wilmington DE 1997-2007, R 1969-1972, Actg R 1967-1968, Asst 1964-1967; Epis Ch Cntr New York NY 1995-1997; Cathd Of St Jn The Div New York NY 1985-1988; Cathd of St Ptr & St Paul Washington DC 1976-1985; Trin Par New York NY 1972-1993. EUC.

CASTELLAN, Megan Laura (WMo) 11 E 40th St, Kansas City MO 64111 **S Paul's Epis Day Sch Kansas City MO 2013-** B Newport News VA 1983 d Stephen & Barbara. BA W&M 2005; MDiv GTS 2008. D 2/1/2008 P 8/1/2008 Bp John Clark Buchanan. Chapl Dio Arizona Phoenix AZ 2009-2013; Cur Estrn Shore Chap Virginia Bch VA 2008-2009.

CASTELLI ACF, Paul Henry (Mich) **S Geo's Ch Milford MI 2016-** B 1987 s Ralph & Deborah. M.Div Bexley-Seabury; STM Trin Luth Sem; B.S. Mus Industry Mgmt/Marketing Ferris St U 2009. D 12/12/2015 P 6/11/2016 Bp Wendell Nathaniel Gibbs Jr. m 8/16/2015 Mechelle Alaina Sieglitz.

CASTELLON, Paul Frank (NJ) 7403 Dress Blue Cir, Mechanicsville VA 23116 B Havana Cuba 1936 s Francisco & Maria. BS U of Florida 1957; MS U CA 1971; Sch for Deacons 2007. D 6/9/2007 Bp George Edward Councell. m 8/20/1977 Patricia Castellon c 3.

CASTILLO, Guillermo Antonio (Ark) 406 W Central Ave, Bentonville AR 72712 **Assoc All SS Ch Bentonville AR 2011-** B Santa Ana El Salvador 1975 s Bernardino & Rosa. San Jose dela Montana 2001. Rec 3/11/2011 Bp Larry Benfield. m 6/9/2008 Araceli Herrera c 4.

CASTILLO, Sandra Ann (Okla) 322 N Water St, Sparta WI 54656 B Chicago IL 1948 BA U IL. D 6/19/2004 P 12/18/2004 Bp Bill Persell. c 4. S Steph's Ch Guymon OK 2013-2015; Vic S Jn's Epis Ch Sparta WI 2011-2012; St Jn's Epis Ch of Sturgis Sturgis MI 2010-2011; La Iglesia De Nuestra Senora De Las Americas Chicago IL 2006-2010; Ch Of The Adv Chicago IL 2006-2009; Cur S Ptr's Epis Ch Chicago IL 2004-2006.

CASTLEBERRY, Howard Glen (Tex) 300 N Main St, Temple TX 76501 **R Chr Ch Nacogdoches TX 2011-** B Hutchinson KS 1961 BA U of Houston 2004; MDiv Sewanee: The U So, TS 2009. D 6/20/2009 P c Andrew Doyle P 1/9/2010 Bp Dena Arnall Harrison. m 5/21/1994 Joanne Wilson Castleberry c 4. Cur Chr Epis Ch Temple TX 2009-2011. fr.castleberry@att.net

CASTLES, Charles William (Ga) 1552 Pangborn Station Dr, Decatur GA 30033 B St. Petersburg FL 1933 s David & Catherine. BA Florida Sthrn Coll 1959; BD Columbia TS 1963; MDiv Columbia TS 1971. D 2/26/2005 Bp J Neil Alexander. m 2/12/1965 Janice Louise Castles.

CASTO, David Cameron (Pgh) 9 Cliff Rd. Apt. B2, Woodland Park NJ 07424 **Ret 1993-; Asstg P S Jas Ch Montclair NJ 1990-, 1988-1989** B Wadsworth OH 1931 s Cameron & Mabelle. BA Ohio Wesl 1953; BD U Chi 1957. D 5/30/1958 P 12/6/1958 Bp Nelson Marigold Burroughs. m 7/23/2000 Doranne O'Hara c 3. Cn Res S Steph's Ch Jersey City NJ 1992-1993; St Stephens Ch Newark NJ 1992-1993; All SS Ch Bergenfield NJ 1991-1992; Cn Res Ch Of The H Innoc W Orange NJ 1990; Non-par 1985-1987; Trin Epis Ch of Bergen Cnty Allendale NJ 1984; S Steph's Ch Millburn NJ 1983-1984; Trin Epis Ch Kearny NJ 1982-1983; S Andr's Ch Harrington Pk NJ 1980-1982; Ch Of The H Comm Norwood NJ 1979; Ch Of The Trsfg Towaco NJ 1978; Int P Dio Newark Newark NJ 1974-1990, 1974-1984; Non-par 1968-1973.

CASTO, R Richard Richard (CFla) Po Box 2068, Dunnellon FL 34430 B Buckhannon WV 1926 s Ralph & Bess. W Virginia Wesleyan Coll. D 6/3/1981 P 6/1/1982 Bp Robert Poland Atkinson. Int Chr Ch S Marys GA 2007-2008; H Faith Epis Ch Dunnellon FL 1987-1997; R Chr Ch Point Pleasat WV 1984-1987; D S Mths Grafton WV 1981-1984; D S Phil's Philippi WV 1981-1984.

CASTRO, Jose Roberto (DR) **Dio The Dominican Republic (Iglesia Epis Dominicana) Gazcue Santo Domingo 2012-** B El Salvador 1983 s Jose & Dolores. Trans 6/26/2012 as Priest Bp Julio Cesar Holguin-Khoury. m 10/13/2011 Christel Bruno.

CASTRO, Mario (SwFla) Church of the Redeemer, 222 S Palm Ave, Sarasota FL 34236 **P Ch Of The Redeem Sarasota FL 2012-** B Santo Domingo DR 1960 s Jose & Ramona. BA Santo Tomas de Aquino 1987; BA Santo Tomas de Aquino 1990. Rec 2/2/2011 Bp Dabney Tyler Smith. m 2/18/1991 Lidia Castro c 2.

CASTRO, Reinel (CFla) 29655 Circle R Greens Drv, Escondido CA 92026 **Chapl Navy Chapl 2012-; Chapl Navy Chapl Naval Base Chapels San Diego CA 2012-; Chapl US Navy 2006-; Chapl Navy Chapl 2012-** B CO 1967 s Jose & Maria. Sem Mayor De Tunja CO; U of Tampa 1994; BA S Jn Vianney Sem 1995; MA S Vinc De Paul Reg Sem Boynton Bch 1995; MD S Vinc the Paul Sem 1995; Commissioned Off Navy Chapl Sch 2006; Navy Off US Navy 2006; USMC FMF Fleet Marine Force 2011; Naval War Coll JPME Joint Profsnl Mltry Educ 2014; USN Profsnl Ldrshp 2015. Rec 5/29/1987 as Priest Bp John Wadsworth Howe. m 10/31/1997 Jennifer Castro c 1. R All SS Epis Ch Deltona FL 2000-2012; P-in-c Ch Of Our Sav Okeechobee FL 1998-2000. Navy Marine Achievement M US Navy 2012; Hal Brooke Perry Awd Sem of the SW 2010.

CATALANO, Patricia (ECR) **Assoc Epiph Luth & Epis Ch Marina CA 2008-** B Bogota Colombia 1953 MDiv CDSP 2005. D 4/30/2005 Bp Sylvestre Donato Romero P 2/28/2006 Bp George Richard Millard. c 1. Assoc All SS Ch Carmel CA 2006-2008; Chld and Yth Min S Bede's Epis Ch Menlo Pk CA 2005-2006; Dio El Camino Real Salinas CA 2005.

CATCHINGS, Robert Mitchell (WA) B 1941 D 6/23/1973 Bp Milton Legrand Wood P 12/23/1973 Bp Bennett Jones Sims. m 6/16/1996 Joy L Catchings c 1. Dio Washington Washington DC 1980-1988; Trin Par New York NY 1977-1980; Dio Atlanta Atlanta GA 1973-1977.

CATE, Suzanne (USC) Holy Trinity Parish, 193 Old Greenville Hwy, Clemson SC 29631 **H Trin Par Epis Clemson SC 2016-; Bd Trst Fam Renew Cmnty Holly Hill FL 2013-** B Dimmitt TX 1962 d Roy & Charlotte. BA Florida St

1984; MDiv Sewanee: The U So, TS 2012; MDiv The TS at The U So 2012. D 6/2/2012 P 12/12/2012 Bp John Bauerschmidt. m 5/5/1984 William N Cate c 2. S Jn's Epis Ch Charlotte NC 2013-2016; S Jas Epis Ch Ormond Bch FL 2012-2013. scate@holytrinityclemson.org

CATES, Susanna (NwT) 602 Meander St, Abilene TX 79602 **S Ptr's Ch Moristown NJ 2016-** B Gainesville FL 1974 d Robert & Judith. BS Troy U 2009; MDiv Epis TS Of The SW 2013; MDiv Epis TS of the SW 2013. D 1/26/2013 P 8/3/2013 Bp James Scott Mayer. Cur Ch of the Heav Rest Abilene Abilene TX 2013-2016. scates@heavenlyrestabilene.org

CATHERS, Robert Earl (SwFla) 2291 Hebron Rd, Hendersonville NC 28739 B Wellington KS 1939 s Robert & Winfred. PhD Texas Tech U 1966; MDiv Sewanee: The U So, TS 1983. D 6/17/1977 P 12/1/1977 Bp Edward Clark Turner. m 11/27/1981 Kimberly Cathers c 3. R All Souls Epis Ch No Ft Myers FL 1987-1989; R Trin Ch Mt Airy NC 1983-1987; Assoc S Andrews Ch Derby KS 1981-1982, Vic 1978-1980.

CATINELLA, Gayle (O) 16507 S Red Rock Dr, Strongsville OH 44136 **P S Jn's Ch Youngstown OH 2014-** B Chicago IL 1962 d David & Dorothy. BA Loyola U 1984; MS U IL 1989; MA Creighton U 2001. D 12/13/2001 P 6/29/2002 Bp James Edward Krotz. m 4/8/1989 Daniel James McGuire c 6. R Ch Of S Thos Berea OH 2004-2007; Asst S Matt's Ch Lincoln NE 2002-2004; Cur S Jas' Epis Ch Fremont NE 2001-2002. stec1@sbcglobal.net

CATIR JR, Norman Joseph (FtW) 31 John St, Providence RI 02906 **Ret 1999-** B Bangor ME 1932 s Norman & Ruth. BA Trin Hartford CT 1955; MDiv Ya Berk 1958; MA Trin Hartford CT 1962. D 6/11/1958 P 12/22/1958 Bp Horace W B Donegan. m 6/6/1964 Zulette Catir. P inmates.charge Mat. Jn the Evang Newport Rhode Island 2006-2007; P in Charge St. Jn the Evang Newport RI 2006-2007; P in Charge St. Thos Camden ME 2003-2004; R Ch Of The Trsfg New York NY 1971-1998; R S Andr's Ch Stamford CT 1964-1971; Cur S Steph's Ch Providence RI 1961-1964; Cur S Paul's Ch Wallingford CT 1958-1961; Chair Liturg Cmsn Dio New York New York NY 1973-1979. Contrib, "towards a Living Liturg," *Towards A Living Liturg*, 1970; Auth, "St. Steph's Ch in Providence," *S Steph's Ch in Providence*, 1964. Amer Friends of the Angl Cntr in Rome 1991; CCU 1961; Engl Spkng Un 1965; Hope Club 2000.

CATO, Brooks (CNY) St. Thomas', 12 1/2 Madison St, Hamilton NY 13346 **R S Thos Ch Hamilton NY 2016-; Cur Chr Epis Ch Little Rock AR 2014-** B Harrison AR 1984 s Billy & Kathy. BA U of Cntrl Arkansas 2009; MDiv Sewanee: The U So, TS 2013; MDiv The TS at The U So 2013. D 3/16/2013 P 9/14/2013 Bp Larry Benfield. m 7/24/2010 Rebecca Leigh McGill. S Paul's Newport AR 2013-2014.

CATO, Phillip Carlyle (WA) 8617 Hidden Hill Ln, Potomac MD 20854 **P-in-c S Barn' Ch Leeland Uppr Marlboro MD 2012-** B Charlotte NC 1934 s Thornwell & Edna. BA Duke 1956; STB EDS 1959; Duke 1965; Sewanee: The U So, TS 1965; PhD Emory U 1977; DD S Pauls Coll Lawrenceville 1980. D 6/25/1959 P 1/2/1960 Bp Richard Henry Baker. m 7/7/1984 Sarah Maier Cato c 6. P-in-c S Ptr's Epis Ch Arlington VA 2009; P-in-c S Jn's Ch Olney MD 2005-2006; P-in-c S Mary's Epis Ch Foggy Bottom Washington DC 2002-2004; P-in-c All SS' Epis Ch Chevy Chase MD 1997-2001; P S Jas' Epis Ch Warrenton VA 1992-1997; P S Chris's Ch New Carrollton MD 1990-1992; Pagan Intl Washington DC 1987-1988; S Fran Ch Potomac MD 1982-1986; S Andr's Ch Harrington Pk NJ 1982; Gr Epis Ch Rutherford NJ 1981-1982; Dep Gc Dio Newark Newark NJ 1979-1982, Chair COM 1977-1982, Stndg Com 1981-1982, Chair, COM 1976-1982; R Ch Of The H Comm Norwood NJ 1973-1981; Asst R S Ptr's Ch Morristown NJ 1973-1981; Asst All SS Epis Ch Atlanta GA 1968-1973; Chapl (CAPT-06) Untd States Naval Reserve Chapl Corps 1963-1993; Chapl Ch Of The H Comf Charlotte NC 1960-1963; Vic S Jas Ch Mooresville NC 1959-1960; Chair, Dioc Disaster Preparedness Com Dio Washington Washington DC 2011-2012, COM 1985-1988; Adj Judge Crt of Revs Prov III 2011; Bp's Applicant Advsry Com Bp Suffr for Armed Serv and Fed Mnstrs 2010-2015; Bp's Advsry Com Dio Washington 2002-2003; Elected Mem Intl Insttute for Strategic Stds London 1984-2001; Chairman Wilks Fund St. Ptr's Ch Morristown 1974-1981; Mem and Secy of Bd Trst St. Aug's Coll Raleigh NC 1965-1973. Auth, "Not Prepared," *LivCh*, 2009; Auth, "Pandemic Influenza Plnng for Epis Parishes: Avian Flu Preparedness," *Pandemic Flu Preparedness for Epis Parishes*, 2006; Auth, "The Hidden Costs of Fertility," *Journ of Legal Commentary*, St. Jn's U Law Sch, 2005; Auth, "Cler Need Coaches , Too," *Leaven*, 2003; Auth, "Beyond Sex: A Broader Look At Cler Ethics," *Leaven: The Journ Of The Natl Ntwk Of Epis Cler*, 2002. ESMHE; Navy Chapl Fndt 2000; Sacem 2003. DD (Honoris Causa) St. Paul's Coll 1980; Omicron Delta Kappa Emory U Chapt 1971.

CATO, Vanessa Gisela (U) 2374 Grant Ave, Ogden UT 84401 **R Ch Of The Gd Shpd Ogden UT 2012-** B UK 1951 d Leonard & Dorothy. Cert Borough Road Coll and St Osyth Tchr Trng Coll 1975; CTM Westcott Hse 1993. Trans 2/1/2012 Bp Scott Byron Hayashi. c 2. revdvgc@gmail.com

CATON, Lisa Elfers (NJ) 23 E Welling Ave, Pennington NJ 08534 **Coll of NJ Chapl Dio New Jersey Trenton NJ 2008-** B Camden NJ 1954 d Robert & Lisa. BA NYU 1978; MPA NYU 1988; MDiv GTS 2007. D 6/9/2007 P 1/20/

2008 Bp George Edward Councell. m 10/1/1983 Philip Caton c 3. CE Dir All SS Ch Princeton NJ 2007-2009.

CATRON MINER, Antoinette (U) 1710 Foothill Dr, Salt Lake City UT 84108 **D All SS Ch Salt Lake City UT 2011-** B Camden NJ 1940 d Angelo & Domenica. Cert Utah Mnstry Formation Prog; BA Hood Coll 1961; MA Mid 1962. D 6/11/2011 Bp Scott Byron Hayashi. m 11/26/2011 Richard Miner.

CAUCUTT, Mary Allison (Wyo) 820 River View Dr, Cody WY 82414 **R Chr Ch Cody WY 2006-** B Lansing MI 1966 d Gregory & Amy. BA Trin U San Antonio 1988; MDiv EDS 1992. Trans 12/1/2003 Bp Bruce Caldwell. m 1/6/2001 Casey Owen Horton c 1. R S Jn's Ch Newtonville MA 2003-2006; Vic Ch Of S Andr's In The Pines Pinedale WY 1996-2003; R S Hubert The Hunter Bonduran Bondurant WY 1996-2003; Assoc S Mich & Geo S Louis MO 1994-1996; S Mich & S Geo S Louis MO 1994-1996; Chapl Heppepin Cnty Med Cntr Minneapolis MN 1992-1994.

CAUDLE, Stephen (WLa) 7714 Albany Ave Apt B, Lubbock TX 79424 B 1951 BA Austin Coll; MDiv Nash; MDiv Nash; MA U of Texas. D 6/25/1978 P 5/25/1979 Bp Robert Elwin Terwilliger. m 7/11/1980 Gaylan Carr. S Geo's Ch Bossier City LA 1989-1991; Chr Ch Epis Beatrice NE 1985-1989; Dio Ft Worth Ft Worth TX 1980-1985; All SS' Epis Ch Ft Worth TX 1978-1980.

CAUGHEY, Robert Grover (Cal) 721 E 16th Ave, San Mateo CA 94402 **Died 6/14/2017** B Salt Lake City UT 1926 s J Robert & Marian. BS U MI 1949; Profsnl Engr 1955. D 11/26/1973 Bp Chauncie Kilmer Myers. m 2/14/1961 Nancy Caughey. D S Matt's Epis Ch San Mateo CA 1999-2017; S Ptr's Epis Ch Redwood City CA 1990-2000; Pstr to Deacons (Dio) S Paul's Epis Ch Burlingame CA 1984-1990; D Trsfg Epis Ch San Mateo CA 1973-1984.

CAULFIELD, Dorothee Renee (NY) **D Chr's Ch Rye NY 2006-, Par Secy 2001-; Chair of the Prison Mnstrs Com Epis Dio New York 2007-** B Hicksville NY 1957 d Francis & Carol. D 5/6/2006 Bp Mark Sean Sisk. m 5/5/1984 Frederick C Caulfield c 3. All SS' Epis Ch Briarcliff NY 2006-2009; S Mary's Ch Of Scarborough Briarcliff NY 2006-2009; S Pauls On The Hill Epis Ch Ossining NY 2006-2009; D Trin Epis Ch Ossining NY 2006-2009. AED 2006.

CAULKINS, Rodney LeRoy (SVa) 267 Jefferson Dr, Palmyra VA 22963 **Int S Jas Epis Ch Louisa VA 2013-** B Williamsport PA 1934 s Frank & Elsie. BA Penn 1956; BD VTS 1966; MDiv VTS 1970. D 6/18/1966 P 3/11/1967 Bp Frederick Warnecke. m 4/2/1955 Janyce Caulkins c 4. P-in-c S Lk's Simeon Charlottesville VA 2000-2007; P S Jn's Ch Hampton VA 1980-1999; P S Marg's Ch Woodbridge VA 1969-1980; Vic S Barn Ch Kutztown PA 1966-1969.

CAVAGNARO, Deborah Daggett (NwPa) St Luke's Church, 600 W Main St, Smethport PA 16749 B Bradford PA 1962 d George & Catherine. BA Alfred U 1982. D 5/20/2012 Bp Sean Walter Rowe. m 10/29/1983 Scott Jackson Cavagnaro c 3.

CAVALCANTE, Jose Ivanildo (Los) 48 Old Post Rd, Mount Sinai NY 11766 B Orobo Brazil 1966 s Manoel & Inacia. Educ Lic Faculdade Paulistana de Ciências 1996; BA Pontifical Fac of Theol Our Lady of the Assumption 2008. Trans 1/29/2014 Bp Joseph Jon Bruno.

CAVALERI, Eva Maria K (WA) 3612 Woodley Rd NW, Washington DC 20016 **Cathd of St Ptr & St Paul Washington DC 2015-** B Port Huron MI 1973 d Clemens & Marjorie. BA Albion Coll 1994; MDiv EDS 2004. D 6/10/2004 Bp James Louis Jelinek P 1/22/2005 Bp Joseph Jon Bruno. m 6/12/2004 Jorma Cavaleri c 2. Chapl Shattuck-S Mary's Sch Faribault MN 2009-2015; Assoc R Trin Epis Ch Santa Barbara CA 2006-2009; Stff Assoc Ch Of Our Sav Par San Gabr CA 2004-2006; Chair, COM Dio Minnesota Minneapolis MN 2012-2015; Mem, Bd Dir River Bend Nature Cntr Faribault MN 2012-2015. Awd For Excellence In The Liturg Reading Of The Scriptures The Massachusetts Bible Soc 2003. ecavaleri@cathedral.org

CAVALIERE, Denise B (NJ) 15 Paper Mill Rd., Cherry Hill NJ 08003 **D H Apos Epis Ch Trenton NJ 2000-; Archd for Pstr Care of Deacons Dio New Jersey Trenton NJ 2014-** B Fitchburg MA 1949 d Henry & Agnes. BA S Johns U New York 1971. D 10/21/2000 Bp David Bruce Joslin. m 9/27/1975 Louis Cavaliere c 2. Fllshp of St. Jn the Evang 1993.

CAVANAGH, David Nathan (NCal) 2901 Owens Ct, Fairfield CA 94534 **P Assoc Gr Epis Ch Fairfield CA 2008-, Int 2000-2002, Assoc R 1990-2000; Ret 2000-** B Colfax WA 1943 s Nathan & Marjorie. BA WA SU 1966; MDiv Candler TS Emory U 1971. D 6/22/1977 P 7/2/1978 Bp Clarence Rupert Haden Jr. P-in-c S Andr's In The Highlands Mssn Antelope CA 2004-2006; Int S Jn's Epis Ch Marysville CA 2002-2003; Chapl VetA Hosp San Francisco CA 1992-2000; Chapl VetA Hosp Martinez CA 1980-1992; V.A. Hosp. Martinez CA Trin Epis Cathd Sacramento CA 1977-1980; Serv Methodist Ch 1971-1976. AEHC; ACPE.

CAVANAUGH, Sean Harris (Va) 1795 Johnson Ferry Rd, Marietta GA 30062 **St. Steph's And St. Agnes Sch Alexandria VA 2004-** B Chattanooga TN 1969 s Deborah. BA E Carolina U 1991; MDiv VTS 1996. D 7/14/1996 Bp Brice Sidney Sanders P 1/1/1997 Bp Clifton Daniel III. m 6/19/1993 Jennifer Maria Cavanaugh c 2. Assoc R The Epis Ch Of S Ptr And S Paul Marietta GA 1999-2004; Asst S Andr's On The Sound Ch Wilmington NC 1996-1999.

CAVANAUGH, William Jeffrey (Dal) 421 Custer Road, Richardson TX 75080 **R Ch Of The Epiph Richardson TX 2004-** B New Brunswick NJ 1954 s Vincent & Ruth. BS Drexel U 1976; MDiv GTS 1981. D 6/20/1981 Bp Lyman Cunningham Ogilby P 1/25/1982 Bp Scott Field Bailey. c 2. R S Paul's Epis Ch Salem OR 2004, R 1996-2002; Alum/ae Exec Bd GTS New York NY 1999-2006; R S Barth's Ch Corpus Christi TX 1990-1996; R S Marg's Epis Ch San Antonio TX 1984-1989; Asst S Mk's Epis Ch San Antonio TX 1981-1984; Bd Chair Ntwk of Comm. Mnstrs Richardson TX 2009-2013; Exec Bd Dio Dallas Dallas TX 2007-2009. frbill@epiphany-richardson.org

CAVANNA, Robert Charles (Minn) 6910 43rd Ave Se, Saint Cloud MN 56304 **P-in-c H Trin Epis Ch Elk River MN 2012-** B New York NY 1943 s Charles & Margaret. BA Pace U 1966; MA U of New Mex 1968; EdD U of Wyoming 1977; Dio MN Trng/Cath Sem 2002; Other 2002. D 4/6/2002 Bp Frederick Warren Putnam P 10/6/2002 Bp Daniel Lee Swenson. m 8/4/1973 Regina Clipper Cavanna c 2.

CAVE, Daniel Eugene (RG) 7052 McNutt Rd, La Union NM 88021 **R St Lk's Epis Ch Anth NM 2012-** B Rantoul IL 1955 s Norman & Beverly. M.Div TESM 2007; MDiv TESM 2007; MDiv TESM 2007. D 10/21/2006 Bp Jeffrey Neil Steenson. m 7/7/1979 Jane Kay Cave c 1. Assoc S Andr's Epis Ch Las Cruces NM 2010-2012; Dioc Yth Dir Dio The Rio Grande Albuquerque 2007-2010; Yth Dir 2007-2010; S Fran Ch Rio Rancho NM 2007-2010; Chf Corp Pilot Wrld Balloon 2000-2003.

CAVE JR, George Harold (SwFla) 14 Old Club Ct, Nashville TN 37215 **Ret 1992-** B Newton MA 1927 s George & Charlotte. Lic Untd States Maritime Serv Radio Sch 1945; BA U So 1956; STB Ya Berk 1959; STM Sewanee: The U So, TS 1964. D 6/20/1959 Bp Anson Phelps Stokes Jr P 12/21/1959 Bp Henry I Louttit. m 4/10/2005 Constance Ann Cave c 4. Asst S Mary's Par Tampa FL 2008-2012; St Johns Epis Ch Tampa FL 1985-1992; Sum Vic Ch of the Resurr Little Switzerland NC 1982-2007; 1965-1968; Mstr Rel Stds Berkeley Prep Sch 1965-1968; P-in-c S Adrian Islamorada FL 1962-1964; Vic S Columba Epis Ch Marathon FL 1962-1964; Chapl CAP 1960-1963; Vic Blessed Sacr Indiantown FL 1960-1962; Vic Ch Of Our Sav Okeechobee FL 1959-1962. AAR 1972-1992; ESMHE 1972-1992.

CAVE, Jeffrey Paull (At) D 9/16/1965 P 3/1/1966 Bp Francis E I Bloy.

CAVENDISH, John Claude (Lex) 240 Cedar Cliff Rd, Waco KY 40385 B Cleveland OH 1927 s Charle & Helene. BA JHU 1952; BD CDSP 1961; Epis TS in Kentucky 1970; DMin Lexington TS 1980; Oxf GB 1986; MA Lexington TS 1996. D 6/10/1961 P 12/1/1961 Bp James Pernette DeWolfe. Walnut Hill Epis Ch Lexington KY 1978-1979; R S Hubert's Ch Lexington KY 1973-1975; Epis TS Lexington KY 1971-1980; Chr Ch Richmond KY 1967-1971; Serv Convoc of Amer Ch in Europe - Switzerland 1963-1965; Cur Trin Ch San Francisco CA 1961-1962.

CAVIN, Barbara (EMich) Saint Paul's Episcopal Church, 711 S Saginaw St, Flint MI 48502 B Minneapolis MN 1949 d William & Dorothy. BS Colby Coll 1972; MDiv EDS 1980. D 8/18/1980 Bp Robert Marshall Anderson P 4/1/1981 Bp William Jones Gordon Jr. P-in-c S Paul's Epis Ch Flint MI 2011-2014; S Jn's Ch Plymouth MI 2010; R Ch Of The H Sprt Livonia MI 2002-2009; H Faith Ch Saline MI 1988-2002; Vic H Faith Ch Saline MI 1988-2002; S Andr's Ch Ann Arbor MI 1984-1988; S Aid's Ch Ann Arbor MI 1981; Chapl U MI Hosp 1980-1983. SCHC. holyspirit6452@sbcglobal.net

CAWTHORNE, John Harry (Md) 1597 Amberlea Dr. S, Dunedin FL 34698 B Edgewood MD 1944 s David & Lorraine. BA U of Maryland 1970; MDiv EDS 1977. D 6/25/1977 Bp William Foreman Creighton P 3/28/1978 Bp John Thomas Walker. m 7/1/1995 Bonnie Cawthorne c 3. All SS Ch Annapolis Ju MD 2000-2001; Int S Jn's Ch Hvre De Gr MD 1998-1999; Dir of Men Rescue Mssn Frederick MD 1990-1992; Asst All SS Epis Ch Frederick MD 1989-1990; All SS Ch Frederick MD 1988; R Gr Ch New Mrkt MD 1986-1988; R S Geo's Epis Ch Mt Savage MD 1981-1985; Chr Epis Ch Clinton MD 1981, Int R 1980-1981; Asst S Jn's Ch Wichita KS 1979; Vic Chr Ch Wm And Mary Newburg MD 1977-1978. Cler Assn of Maryland; NAACP Fund. NAL Awd for Creating Nonprint Media Multiple Replicating Hold USDA 1997.

CAYLESS, F(Rank) Anthony (LI) 108 Woodbridge Ln, Chapel Hill NC 27514 B Leicester UK 1933 s Frank & Hilda. BA S Davids Coll Lampeter GB 1953; LTh St Davids Coll Lampeter Wales 1955; Dplma UWI - BIMAP 1972; MA Adel 1987; DMin GTF 1995; Cert Linwood Sprtl Dir Trng 2003. Trans 2/1/1984 as Priest Bp Robert Campbell Witcher Sr. m 12/27/1956 Suzette Lily Cayless c 1. Int S Andr's Epis Ch New Paltz NY 2002-2006; S Thos Ch Farmingdale NY 2000-2001; Geo Mercer TS Garden City NY 1994-2000; Cathd Of The Incarn Garden City NY 1991-2000; Chapl S Paul's Epis Sch Garden City NY 1984-1991; St Pauls Sch Garden City NY 1984-1991; Cathd Schools Garden City NY 1984-1988; Archd Dio Barbados Barbados 1976-1984; Dioc Admin Dio Barbados Barbados 1969-1976; R St. Geo Ch Barbados 1964-1972; Vic St. Ambr Ch Barbados 1960-1964; Asst Cur/P in Charge St. Mths & St. Lawr Barbados 1955-1960. Auth, "Gk for Groups," *Gk for Groups*, 1995; Auth, "Hist of St. Geo Glebe," *Journ BMHS Vol XXXVIII # 2*, Barbados Museum and Hist Soc, 1988; Auth, "S Geo Glebe," *Barbados-An Ethnographic Study*, U.M.I. Ann Arbor MI, 1987; Draft and Edit, "Mssn and Evang," *ACC-3 Report*, London, 1976.

Ord of H Cross 2000. Bp Burgess Fllshp St. Dav's Coll 1953; Evan Jones Gk Prize St. Dav's Coll Lampeter 1953; Van Mildert Schlr St. Dav's Coll Lampeter 1951.

CAZDEN, Jan Steward (Cal) 2901 Verona Ct, Arlington TX 76012 B Dallas TX 1948 d Thomas & Ima. Diac Stds Sch for Deacons 1991; MA U of San Francisco 2000. D 12/7/1991 Bp William Edwin Swing. m 6/25/1978 Burton S Cazden c 1. California Pacific Med Cntr San Francisco CA 2007-2011; Lead Stff Chapl California Pacific Med Cntr San Francisco CA 2007-2011; D Trin Ch San Francisco CA 2007-2009; Dio California San Francisco CA 2004-2007; D S Greg Of Nyssa Ch San Francisco CA 2000-2006; Ch Of The H Innoc San Francisco CA 1998; Dir of Chapl Serv St. Lk's Hosp San Fransisco CA 1997-2007; S Lukes Hosp San Francisco CA 1997-2004; Epis Sch For Deacons Berkeley CA 1996-1997; Asst Trsfg Epis Ch San Mateo CA 1994-1996; D S Fran Of Assisi Ch Novato CA 1991-1994; St Johns Epis Ch Ross CA 1991-1992. NAAD 1991; Oblate Ord of S Ben 1990.

CEDENO MEDINA, Oscar Antonio (PR) **Died 3/31/2016** B 1937 m 5/4/1960 Ana J Jimenez De Jesus. Dio Puerto Rico Trujillo Alto PR 2004-2009, 1987-2003.

CEDERBERG, Todd Lee (SeFla) 623 SE Ocean Blvd, Stuart FL 34994 **R S Mary's Epis Ch Stuart FL 2011-** B Bay City MI 1958 s Ernest & Eleanor. BA Wheaton Coll 1981; MDiv VTS 1986; DMin Fuller TS 2005; Cert Amer Coll 2006. D 6/8/1986 Bp William Jones Gordon Jr P 12/14/1986 Bp H Coleman Mcgehee Jr. m 6/17/1982 Darla Jean Cederberg c 4. Assoc Ch Of The Gd Samar Paoli PA 1997-2011; Asst S Barth's Ch Nashville TN 1993-1997; Vic Nativ Cmnty Epis Ch Holly MI 1986-1993.

✠ CEDERHOLM JR, The Rt Rev Roy Frederick (Mass) 499 Webster St, Needham MA 02494 **Ret Bp Suffr of Massachusetts Dio Massachusetts Boston MA 2012-, Bp Suffr of Massachusetts 2001-2011** B Brockton MA 1944 s Roy & Roberta. BA Bos 1966; MDiv Bex Sem 1971. D 6/26/1971 P 5/20/1972 Bp John Melville Burgess Con 3/24/2001 for Mass. m 5/20/1966 Ruth Cederholm c 2. R Chr Ch Needham Hgts MA 1989-2001; R S Paul's Epis Ch White Riv Jct VT 1976-1989; S Steph's Ch Cohasset MA 1975-1976. DD Bex 2001.

CEKUTA, Nancee A (USC) 471 W Martintown Rd, North Augusta SC 29841 **S Barth's Ch No Augusta SC 2017-; S Jn's Epis Ch Charlotte NC 2015-** B Rochester NY 1961 d Francis & Dorothy. BA SUNY 1984; MDiv TS 2015; MDiv Sewanee: The U So, TS 2015. D 12/20/2014 P 6/20/2015 Bp Robert Christopher Wright. c 2.

CELESTIN, Jois Goursse (Hai) **Dio Haiti Port-au-Prince HT 2012-** B 1983 s Luc & Malia. D 7/29/2012 P 3/13/2014 Bp Jean Zache Duracin.

CELL, John Albert (FdL) 825 N Webster Ave, Green Bay WI 54302 **Chapl Hon Port Missions To Seamen 1983-** B Philadelphia PA 1943 s John & Clara. BS Tem 1970; MDiv Epis TS in Kentucky 1978. D 5/28/1978 Bp William R Moody P 12/16/1978 Bp Charles Bennison Sr. RurD Green Bay Dnry Dio Fond du Lac Appleton WI 2004-2007; R Ch of the Blessed Sacr Green Bay WI 1982-2010; Cur S Paul's Ch Muskegon MI 1978-1982. CBS 1989; Interfaith Seafarers Mnstry 1983; P Assoc. Of Our Lady Of Walsingham 1997; P Assoc. Of The Sis Of The H Nativ 1983; SSC 1998.

CELLA, Richard L (Colo) 4935 Hahns Peak Dr Apt 104, Loveland CO 80538 **Ret 2009-** B Baltimore MD 1933 s Emil & Susanne. BS U of Oklahoma 1968. D 2/3/1991 Bp William Harvey Wolfrum. m 6/14/1987 Mary Ann Bliss c 5. D Dio Colorado Denver CO 1991-2009; S Steph's Epis Ch Aurora CO 1991-2009. Bro of S Andr 1970; No Amer Assn Diac 1991. EFM EFM 1990; Acorn Awd Heartland Mediators Assn 1969. rlmbc2318@gmail.com

CEMBALISTY INNES, Susan Eve (Be) 108 Fern Way, Clarks Summit PA 18411 B Springfield MA 1950 d Richard & Charlotte. BA Mt Holyoke Coll 1972; U of S Andrews GB 1977; MDiv TESM 1984; U of S Andrews GB 2002. D 6/2/1984 P 1/2/1985 Bp Alden Moinet Hathaway. c 1. Int Chr Ch Indn Orchard PA 2005-2007; Gr Epis Ch Honesdale PA 2005-2007; S Lk's Ch Scranton PA 2005; Ch Of The Epiph Glenburn Clarks Summit PA 2002-2005; Consult Ch Growth and Congrl Dvlpmt Dio DE PA and NJ 2001-2002; Int Scottish Epis Ch 1999-2001; R The Ch Of The Ascen Claymont DE 1996-1999; Dio Delaware Wilmington 1995-1996; Int Ascen Wilmington DE 1994-1996; Chapl Med Cntr of Delaware Wilmington DE 1991-1994; R Trin Ch Boothwyn PA 1986-1990; 1985-1986; Chapl Allegheny Gnrl Hosp Pittsburgh PA 1984-1985; Calv Ch Pittsburgh PA 1983-1985; Chapl Southside Hosp Pittsburgh PA 1981-1983. Auth, "Soc Concerns in Calvin's Geneva," Pickwick Press, Allison Pk,PA, 1992. Commendation for Congrl Dvlpmt & Ch Growth Dio Delaware 2000.

CENCI, Daniel M (EC) 110 W Main St, Clinton NC 28328 **R S Paul's Epis Ch Clinton NC 2015-** B Towson MD 1985 s Roland & Rhonda. BA The U of Alabama 2007; MDiv VTS 2012. D 5/18/2013 Bp Santosh K Marray P 11/23/2013 Bp John Mckee Sloan Sr. m 6/1/2013 Jessica D Outlaw. S Jn's Ch Montgomery AL 2013-2015.

CENDESE, William Ivan (U) 521 9th Ave, Salt Lake City UT 84103 B Niagara Falls, Canada 1936 s James & Angela. BA CUA 1961; DeSales TS 1965; Other 1965; MEd Utah St U 1973; PhD U of Utah 1980. Rec 8/6/1989 as Priest Bp George Edmonds Bates. c 2. Assoc Dio Utah Salt Lake City UT 2012-2015,

1995-2003, Cn to the Ordnry 1995-2002; Asst S Ptr's Ch Clearfield UT 2012; P-in-c S Fran Ch Moab UT 2007-2011; Tchr Rowland Hall St. Marks HS 2005-2006; Cn Cathd Ch Of S Mk Salt Lake City UT 1993-2000, P 1990-1991; Serv RC Ch 1954-1972. icendese@gmail.com

CERRATO III, John A (WMass) 2813 Market Bridge Ln Unit 101, Raleigh NC 27608 **Int S Mart's Ch Chagrin Fall OH 2014-; Dn of the Franklin-Hampshire Dnry Dio Wstrn Massachusetts Springfield 2011-, Bement Waterfield Educational Grants 2010-** B West Chester PA 1955 s John & Blanche. BA W Chester U of Pennsylvania 1978; MDiv Gordon-Conwell TS 1983; ThM Harvard DS 1985; DPhil Oxf GB 1997. Trans 2/2/1993 Bp Cabell Tennis. m 6/26/2010 Mary E Cerrato. S Jas' Ch Greenfield MA 2008-2012; P-in-c S Bern's Ch Bernardsville NJ 2005-2008; S Thos Ch Alexandria Pittstown NJ 2004-2005; Int St. Thos Alexandria NJ 2004-2005; P-in-c Chr Ch Three Bridges NJ 2003-2004; Vic S Paul's Epis Ch Bound Brook NJ 2001-2002; Tchr, Hd of Classics The Pennington Sch 1996-2002; Chr Ch Greensburg PA 1995-1996; The Ch Of The Adv Jeannette PA 1995-1996; P-in-c All Souls Ch N Versailles PA 1994-1995; Asst Chapl Keble Coll Oxf 1991-1993; Dir Newark Yth Cltn Newark DE 1989-1991; Yth Dir S Thos's Par Newark DE 1989-1991; Yth Min Trin Ch Bolton MA 1981-1982; Ch Archit Com Dio New Jersey Trenton NJ 2007-2008, Bd Missions 2004-2007; Coordntr of The Epiph Partnership Dio Pittsburgh Pittsburgh PA 1995-1996; Yth Com Dio Delaware Wilmington 1989-1991. Auth, "Hippolytus," *Oxford Dictionary of Late Antiquity*, Oxf Press, 2013; Auth, "Revs of Aragione and Norelli, Des Eveques," *Journ of Eccl Hist*, Camb Press, 2012; Auth, "Hippolytus and Cyril of Jerusalem on the Antichrist," *Apocalyptic Thought in Early Chrsnty*, Baker Acad, 2009; Auth, "Hippolytus," *Dictionary of Major Biblic Interpreters*, IVPAcademic, 2007; Auth, "Origen's Encounter w Hippolytus," *Studia Patristica 43*, Peeters Intl , 2005; Auth, "The Assn of the Name Hippolytus w a Ch Ord, now known as The Apostolic Tradition," *St. Vladimir's Theol Quarterly*, St. Vladimir's Sem, 2004; Auth, "Hippolytus Between E and W," *Oxford Theol Monographs*, Oxf Press, 2002; Auth, "Martha And Mary In The Commentaries Of Hippolytus," *Studia Patristica 34*, Peeters Intl , 2002; Auth, "Revs of Allen Brent, Hippolytus and the Roman Ch," *Journ of Early Chr Stds*, The JHU Press, 1996; Auth, "Hippolytus On The Song Of Songs & The New Prophecy," *Studia Patristica 31*, Peeters Intl , 1996. AAR 1994-1998; No Amer Patristic Soc 1994. MDiv mcl Gordon-Conwell TS 1983; Phi Alpha Chi hon Soc Gordon-Conwell TS 1983; BA cl W Chester U 1978. stmartins@stmartinschagrinfalls.org

CERTAIN, Robert (At) 3776 Loch Highland Pkwy NE, Roswell GA 30075 **Exec Dir Mltry Chapl Assn of the USA 2012-; Mem, Med Ethics Subcommittee Defense Hlth Bd 2013-; Co-Chair, Faith Communities T/F Natl Action Allnce for Suicide Prevention 2011-; Mem VA Advsry Com on Form POWs 2008-** B Savannah GA 1947 s Glenn & Myrtle. BA Emory U 1969; MDiv Sewanee: The U So, TS 1976; DMin Sewanee: The U So, TS 1990. D 7/27/1975 P 4/28/1976 Bp Harold Cornelius Gosnell. m 5/25/1972 Robbie Lee Certain c 2. R The Epis Ch Of S Ptr And S Paul Marietta GA 2007-2012; Pres, Stndg Com Dio San Diego San Diego CA 2005-2007; R S Marg's Epis Ch Palm Desert CA 1998-2007; Assoc Pstr S Barn On The Desert Scottsdale AZ 1995-1998; R S Alb's Ch Harlingen TX 1990-1994; R Ch of the H Apos Collierville TN 1985-1989; R Trin Ch Yazoo City MS 1978-1985; Asst S Peters Epis Sch Kerrville TX 1977-1978; Chapl USAF 1976-1999; Wing Chapl Andrews AFB MD 1976-1977; Off Of Bsh For ArmdF New York NY 1975-1977; Asst Chr Ch Epis S Pittsburg TN 1974-1976; Mem DOD T/F on Suicide Prevention 2009-2010; Chair, Denominational Hlth Plan T/F Dio Atlanta Atlanta GA 2009-2010; Mem Defense Hlth Bd 2007-2011; Dioc Coun Dio Arizona Phoenix AZ 1999-2000. Auth, "Chapl and Mltry Ethics," *The Mltry Chapl*, The Mltry Chapl Assn, 2013; Auth, "Wartime Sacrifice," *The Mltry Chapl*, The Mltry Chapl Assn, 2010; Collaborator, "Yankee Air Pirates," *Yankee Air Pirates*, Deeds Pub, 2010; Auth, "Panning for Gold in the Muck of War," *The Mltry Chapl*, The Mltry Chapl Assn, 2009; Auth, ETC Pub, 2007; Auth, "Salvation Through Chr Alone," *LivCh*, LivCh, 2006; Auth, "Unchained Eagle," *Unchained Eagle*, ETC Pub, 2003; Auth, "Quite by Accident," *LivCh*, LivCh, 2001; Auth, "Charcoal 1 Delta: The Story of the First B-52 Crewmember to be captured in Vietnam," *Air & Space mag*, Smithsonian, 2000; Auth, "Trin Ch," *Trin Ch: A Sesquicentennial Hist*, Kenroe Printing, 1984; Auth, "In the Light of His Mercy," *ATR*, Seabury-Wstrn Sem, 1982. GC Prchr The Epis Ch 2013; Ord of the W Range Pi Kappa Alpha Fraternity 2008.

✠ CERVENY, The Rt Rev Frank S (Fla) 3711 Ortega Blvd, Jacksonville FL 32210 B Ludlow MA 1933 s Frank & Julia. Epis TS in Kentucky; STD Trin Hartford CT; BA Trin Hartford CT 1955; MDiv GTS 1958; GTS 1976; Sewanee: The U So, TS 1976; Trin Hartford CT 1977; STD Epis TS in Kentucky 1979. D 6/11/1958 Bp William A Lawrence P 12/17/1958 Bp Henry I Louttit Con 5/23/1974 for Fla. m 11/1/1961 Emmy Cerveny. Ret Bp of Florida Dio Florida Jacksonville 1993-2013, Bp 1974-1992, Bp Coadj 1974-1975; Exec VP/Mgr The CPG New York NY 1993-1997; SCWM Epis Ch GC 1988-1996; Chair Pb'S Com On Deans And Bishops Epis Ch PBp 1987-1992; Bd Theol Educ 1982-1988; Consult Angl/Orth 1981-1984; SCER Epis Ch GC 1979-1985; Chair Com On Evang And Renwl HOB 1974-1982; Chair Pb'S Com On Renwl

And Evang Epis Ch PBp 1974-1978; Dn S Jn's Cathd Jacksonville FL 1972-1974; R S Jn's Epis Cathd Knoxville TN 1969-1972; R S Lk's Epis Ch Jackson TN 1963-1969; Stff Trin Par New York NY 1961-1963; Asst Ch Of The Resurr Miami FL 1958-1961; Sewanee U So TS Sewanee TN 1974-1992; Trst The GTS New York NY 1974-1982. Advsry Com Chair - Cntr For Chr Sprtlty 1975-1979; Amer Friends Of Jerusalem; Bible And Common PB Soc 1992; Bible Reading Fllshp 1982-1986; Bd - AFP 1979-1988; Bro Of S Andr, Natl Bd; Caribbean Cov Com 1992-1992; Chair, Amer Del, Partnr In Mssn To Cuba 1984-1984; Chair, Strategic Plnng For Theol Educ 1983-1986; Com Of 200; Compass Rose Soc 1996-1999; Environ Stwdshp Team 1992-1996; Eub; Interfaith Coun On Christians And Jews; Irenaeus, Bd; Metropltn Coun; Urban Cltn Of Bishops; Vice Chair, Angl Coun On No Amer And The Caribbean 1980-1985.

CESAR, Gerard David (Hai) Box 1309, Port-Au-Prince Haiti **Dir H Trin Sch Ht 1995-; Dio Haiti Port-au-Prince HT 1991-** B HT 1965 s Adam & Carmicile. Law Sch 1988; BA H Trin Sem 1991. D 9/15/1991 P 4/1/1992 Bp Luc Anatole Jacques Garnier. m 3/6/1993 Kyria Evangeline Heraux-Cesar c 2. Int Admin H Trin Cathd & Ch Of H Name Ht 1994-1995; P Asst S Pierre Mirebalais Ht 1993-1994; P Asst S Bazile's Gonaives Ht 1991-1993. Soc Of S Marg.

CESARETTI, Charles Antony (NJ) Po Box 408, New Milford PA 18834 **Non-par 1996-** B Trenton NJ 1941 s Charles & Angelina. BA Rutgers The St U of New Jersey 1962; MDiv PDS 1965; ThM PrTS 1975. D 5/1/1965 P 11/6/1965 Bp Alfred L Banyard. Dio New Jersey Trenton NJ 1996; Int S Lk's Ch Gladstone NJ 1995-1996; Ch Of S Mary The Vrgn Ridgefield Pk NJ 1994-1995; Int S Matt's Ch Paramus NJ 1993-1995; Trin Par New York NY 1991-1994; Int Chr Ch Short Hills NJ 1989-1990; Dep Of Angl Relatns Epis Ch Cntr New York NY 1985-1989, Stff Off For Hunger 1976-1979; Non-par 1974-1989; Cur S Paul's Epis Ch Westfield NJ 1971-1974; R St Jn the Bapt Epis Ch Linden NJ 1967-1971; Asst Gr Epis Ch Plainfield NJ 1965-1966. Auth, "To Care Enough"; Auth, "The Prometheus Question"; Auth, "Let The Earth Bless The Lord"; Auth, "Rumors Of War".

CEYNAR, Marlene Hruby (Minn) 1811 Southbrook Ln, Wadena MN 56482 B Park Rapids MN 1947 d Lloyd & Marian. BS U MN 1969; MS Bemidji St U 1978. D 10/25/1987 Bp Robert Marshall Anderson. m 1/1/1977 Paul Julian Ceynar c 1. D S Helen's Ch Wadena MN 1987-2008.

CHABOT, Bruce Guy (Tex) 5919 Wild Horse Run, College Station TX 77845 **Cmsn Chair Epis Dio Texas ArmdF 2004-; Non-par S Mich's Acad Bryan TX 2003-** B Pomona CA 1962 s Wilfred & Belia. AA Del Mar Coll 1982; BA U of Dallas 1984; MDiv Pontifical Coll Josephinum 1988; MA Texas A&M U 1996; PhD Texas A&M U 2003. Rec 1/16/2002 as Priest Bp James Barrow Brown. m 6/8/2002 Nancy Griffin Stebbins c 4. S Paul's Ch Navasota TX 2003-2010; S Thos Epis Ch Coll Sta TX 2002-2003. Auth, "Majerista Theol: Xicana Writers Claim Liberation," *Chrsnty And Lit*, Baylor U, 2001; Auth, "Salve Deus Rex Judaeorum," Intl Literary Symposium (London, Uk), 2000; Auth, "Beginning In A Dark Room," *Scottish Rite Journ*, 1995; Auth, "Reading The Tapestry," *Revs Of Cmncatn*. Ancient Free And Accepted Masons 1992; BSA 1972. Past Mstr Sul Ross Lodge 2003; Outstanding Stdt - Frgn Lang Del Mar Coll 1982; Hall Of Fame Del Mar Coll 1982; Hall Of Fame Incarnate Wrld Acad 1982; Outstanding Stdt - Engl Dept Del Mar Coll.

CHACE, Alston Rigby (WMass) 144 Pine Bluff Rd, Brewster MA 02631 B Fall River MA 1932 s Frank & Alice. BS Tufts U 1954; CPE Boston St Hosp 1956; Harv 1956; MDiv EDS 1957; Duke 1962; U of Edinburgh New Coll Edinburgh GB 1965; USAF 1972; MS Troy U 1973. D 6/8/1957 P 1/4/1958 Bp William A Lawrence. m 6/11/1955 Beverly Chace c 3. Supply P Dio Massachusetts Boston MA 1997, Dioc Yth Coun 1957-1958; Dio Wstrn Massachusetts Springfield 1990-1997, Dn of No Worcester Ch 1990-1997, Dioc ArmdF Rep 1990-1997, Dioc Cler Response Team 1990-1997; Dio Wstrn Massachusetts Springfield MA 1990-1997; R S Paul's Epis Ch Gardner MA 1990-1997; Ecum Interfaith Coun of ECUSA for Bp of the ArmdF 1990-1997; Off Of Bsh For ArmdF New York NY 1961-1990; Asst Chr Ch Fitchburg MA 1958-1961; Cur All SS' Epis Ch Belmont MA 1957-1958. Auth, *Mar Enrichment Model Bldg Prog Gdnc for AF Chapl*, Air U, Maxwell AFB, 1973; Auth, *The AF Acad Cadet Attrition Rate*, AF Chapl's Sch, 1968; Auth, *Amer's Commitment to Freedom*, AF Chapl; Auth, *Human Goals - Fndt of our Heritage*, Freedoms Fndt; Auth, *My Responsibilities in Keeping my Country Free*, Freedoms Fndt; Auth, *Spec Occasion Pryr for AF Chapl*, AF Chapl; Auth, *What is an Amer?*, Freedoms Fndt. Bro of S Andr; Life Mem Mltry Chapl Assn of Amer 1973. Epis Bp nomination, ArmdF ArmdF Epis Ch 1989; Distinguished Eagle Scout Awd (Eagle Scout 1947) Trans Atlantic Boy Scout Coun, Europe 1987; Geo Washington hon Medal Freedom Fndt Writing Awd 1977; Geo Washington hon Medal Freedom Fndt Writing Awd 1976; Geo Washington hon Medal Freedom Fndt Writing Awd 1971; Geo Washington hon Medal Freedoms Fndt Writing Awd 1971; Mltry hon Epis Mltry Chapl.

CHACE, Brian David (EMich) Trinity Episcopal Church, PO Box 83, West Branch MI 48661 **P-in-c Trin Epis Ch W Branch MI 2012-** B New Bedford MA 1947 s Kenneth & Jessie. BSEE Worcester Polytechnic Inst 1969. D 4/21/2012 P 10/20/2012 Bp Steven Todd Ousley. m 6/14/1969 Elizabeth Marian Maxwell c 3. Trst Dio Estrn Michigan Saginaw MI 2009-2012. trinitywestbranch@gmail.com

CHACE, Elizabeth Marian Maxwell (EMich) PO Box 109, Frederic MI 49733 B Hartford CT 1947 d William & June. BA Simmons Coll 1970; Cert SUNY 1984; MDiv EDS 2002. D 3/9/2003 P 10/25/2003 Bp Edwin Max Leidel Jr. m 6/14/1969 Brian David Chace c 3. P-in-c S Barth's Epis Ch Mio MI 2003-2005, D-in-c 2003, R 2002-2003; P-in-c S Fran Epis Ch Grayling MI 2003-2005, D-in-c 2003, R 2003-; Lay Mssnr-in-Charge S Barth's Epis Ch Mio MI 2002-2003; Eccl Trial Crt Dio Estrn Michigan Saginaw MI 2008-2011. EWC 2000.

CHACON, Frank Joe (NCal) **D S Lk's Ch Woodland CA 2004-** B Sacramento CA 1947 D 9/17/2004 Bp Jerry Alban Lamb. m 8/15/1990 Susan Orsborn Chacon.

CHACON-RODRIGUEZ, Dagoberto (Hond) **Dio Honduras San Pedro Sula 1998-** B 1963 m 5/3/1988 Maria Varela.

CHADWICK, Leslie E (Va) 11290 Spyglass Cove Lane, Reston VA 20191 **Admin VTS Alexandria VA 2015-** B Valdosta GA 1971 d John & Phyllis. BA U So 1993; MA U of Virginia 1995; MDiv VTS 2004. D 2/7/2004 P 8/18/2004 Bp Henry Irving Louttit. m 12/31/2001 George Albert Chadwick c 2. Assoc R S Tim's Ch Herndon VA 2006-2015; Cler Res Chr Ch Alexandria VA 2004-2006. "In Sure and Certain Hope," *Congregations*, The Alb Inst, 2006. The Chas and Janet Harris Awd VTS 2004; The Fund for Theol Educ Mnstry Fllshp Fund for Theol Educ 2001; The Howard D. King and Ruth King Mitchell Merit Schlrshp for VTS 2001.

CHADWICK, Loring William (CFla) 11440 SW 84th Avenue Rd, Ocala FL 34481 B Providence RI 1932 s William & Laura. BA Br 1954; MDiv EDS 1957; MEd Rhode Island Coll 1975. D 6/15/1957 P 2/23/1958 Bp John S Higgins. m 7/4/1957 Muriel E Chadwick c 1. Asstg P, Org Ch Of The Adv Dunnellon FL 1999-2013; Asst Chr Ch In Lonsdale Lincoln RI 1992-1994; Assoc & Dir of Mus Emm Epis Ch Cumberland RI 1990-1992, Org/Choir 1968-1983; Assoc St Mich & Gr Ch Rumford RI 1988-1990; P-in-c Gr Ch In Providence Providence RI 1983-1988; Cn Pstr Cathd Of S Jn Providence RI 1966-1967; Asst Trin Ch Newport RI 1961-1966; Asst All SS' Memi Ch Providence RI 1959-1961; Vic H Sprt Shannock RI 1957-1959; Vic S Thos' Alton Wood River Jct RI 1957-1959; Chair Ch Mus Cmsn Dio Rhode Island Providence RI 1975-1979, 1960-1974. Auth, *Mass of the Incarn*; Auth, *Mass of the Sprt*; Auth, *Song of Mary*.

CHADWICK, Thora Louise Libbey (Vt) 267 Hildred Dr, Burlington VT 05401 **P-in-c, Borders Reg Mnstry S Lk's Ch Alburg VT 2005-** B Greenfield MA 1937 d Robert & Thelma. BA Wilson Coll 1959; MLS Rutgers The St U of New Jersey 1967; MDiv GTS 1981. D 6/6/1981 Bp Albert Wiencke Van Duzer P 12/12/1981 Bp George Phelps Mellick Belshaw. c 1. Int S Matt's Ch Enosburg Fls VT 2002-2005; Cmnty Chapl Fletcher Allen Hlth Care Burlington VT 2001-2005; R S Mk's Epis Ch Newport VT 1995-1999; Mssnr Ohio Vlly Cluster S Ann's Ch N Martinsvlle WV 1991-1994; Mssnr Ohio Vlly Cluster S Pauls Ch Sistersville WV 1991-1994; Hospice Chapl Sistersville Cmnty Hosp Sistersville WV 1991-1993; Vic Ch Of S Clem Of Rome Belford NJ 1987-1991; Assoc Chr Ch Middletown NJ 1985-1990; Dir of Pstr Care Bayshore Cmnty Hosp Holmdel NJ 1985-1987; Int All SS Ch Bay Hd NJ 1983-1984; Cur Ch Of S Mary's By The Sea Pt Pleas Bch NJ 1981-1982; CE Dir S Bern's Ch Bernardsville NJ 1976-1978; CE Coordntr S Lk's Epis Ch Metuchen NJ 1974-1976; Dir of Stds, Vocational Diac Prog Dio New Jersey Trenton NJ 1987-1990. Auth, *Var arts - Sermons - Curric*.

CHAFFEE, Adna Romanza (Ga) 302 E General Stewart Way, Hinesville GA 31313 B 1939 D 2/15/2008 Bp Henry Irving Louttit.

CHAFFEE, Barbara A (EC) 10618 Peppermill Dr, Raleigh NC 27614 B Sheboygan WI 1938 d John & Beatrice. BA Wheaton Coll at Norton 1960; MDiv SWTS 1990. D 2/23/1990 Bp Thomas Kreider Ray P 12/15/1990 Bp Frank Tracy Griswold III. c 2. Assoc R Chr Epis Ch Raleigh NC 2000-2008; COM Dio E Carolina Kinston NC 1998-2000, Congrl Dvlpmt 1996-2000, Sprtl Life Com 1995-2000, Stndg Com 1998-2000, Stndg Com 1994-2000, Stndg Com 1990-2000; S Thos' Ch Windsor NC 1993-2000; S Aug's Epis Ch Wilmette IL 1990-1993. SCHC. revbchaffee2@gmail.com

CHALAKANI, Paul Scott (NJ) 7 Lincoln Ave, Rumson NJ 07760 B Yonkers NY 1955 s John & Shirley. BA Rider U 1977; MFA GW 1979. D 5/9/2015 Bp William H Stokes. m 8/23/2008 Tara A Robles c 2.

CHALARON, Janice Belle Melbourne (USC) 144 Caldwell St, Rock Hill SC 29730 **Ch Of Our Sav Rock Hill SC 2012-** B 1953 d Roy & Viginia. BA U NC 1975; MS U NC 1982; MDiv Duke DS 1987; STM Sewanee: The U So, TS 1997. D 5/26/1990 Bp Huntington Williams Jr P 5/1/1991 Bp Robert Whitridge Estill. m 6/3/1984 Pierre Rivalier Chalaron c 3. R S Bede's Ch Atlanta GA 2004-2012; R S Andr's Ch Rocky Mt NC 1996-2004; Ch Of The H Comf Burlington NC 1990-1996. Cmnty Of S Mary 1990.

✠ CHALFANT, The Rt Rev Edward Cole (Me) PO Box 2056, Ponte Vedra Beach FL 32004 **Ret Bp of Maine Chr Epis Ch Ponte Vedra FL 2001-; Ret Bp Dio Maine Portland ME 1996-, Bp of Maine 1986-1996, Bp Coadj of Maine 1984-1986** B Pittsburgh PA 1937 s Edward & Helen. BA Wesl 1960; MDiv

VTS 1963; VTS 1985. D 6/12/1963 Bp William Loftin Hargrave P 12/18/1963 Bp Henry I Louttit Con 9/21/1984 for Me. m 10/29/1959 Marydee Wimbish c 2. R S Mk's Epis Ch Columbus OH 1972-1984; Vic S Jn's Epis Ch Clearwater FL 1967-1972; Asst Ch Of The Ascen Clearwater FL 1963-1967. Hon DD VTS 1985.

CHALFANT-WALKER, Nancy Oliver (Pgh) 33 Thorn St, Sewickley PA 15143 **R S Steph's Epis Ch Pittsburgh PA 2007-** B Pittsburgh PA 1950 d Henry & Nancy. BA Chatham Coll 1973; MBA Bos 1979; MDiv Pittsburgh TS 2002. D 6/14/2003 P 1/6/2004 Bp Robert William Duncan. m 7/8/1978 Jon Walker c 3. Int S Paul's Epis Ch Pittsburgh PA 2006-2007; S Mart's Epis Ch Monroeville PA 2004-2006; Chair, Bp Search Transition Com Dio Pittsburgh Pittsburgh PA 2011-2012, Pres, Stndg Com 2010-2011, Chair, Bp Search Transition Com 2010-, Cmsn on Racism 2004-.

CHALK, David Paul (WTex) 651 Pecan St, Canyon Lake TX 78133 **R S Fran By The Lake Canyon Lake TX 2010-** B Kansas City MO 1958 s Paul & Marie. DMin Pittsburgh TS; BA Whitman Coll 1982; MDiv Bex Sem 1990. D 6/9/1990 Bp William Harvey Wolfrum P 3/9/1991 Bp William Carl Frey. m 5/14/1983 Julie Raymond c 2. R S Jas Epis Ch Del Rio TX 2000-2010; R Ch Of The Gd Shpd Lyndhurst OH 1993-2000; Asst to R S Ptr's Epis Ch Lakewood OH 1990-1993. dpchalk@gmail.com

CHALK, Michael Dulaney (WTex) 155 El Rancho Way, San Antonio TX 78209 B Houston TX 1947 s Dulaney & Thelma. BA U of No Texas 1970; Masters VTS 1973; MS VTS 1973. D 6/24/1973 Bp Richard Earl Dicus P 1/1/1974 Bp Harold Cornelius Gosnell. m 8/15/1970 Paula Catherine Chalk c 1. R S Mk's Epis Ch San Antonio TX 1994-2013, R 1973-1976; R S Jas The Apos Epis Ch Conroe TX 1983-1994; R S Andr's Epis Ch Seguin TX 1976-1983.

CHALMERS, Glenn Burr (NY) 296 9th Ave, New York NY 10001 B Paterson NJ 1954 s Andrew & Joyce. BA Hope Coll 1976; MDiv PrTS 1980; Cert SWTS 1981; MS Rutgers The St U of New Jersey 1982. D 6/5/1982 Bp Albert Wiencke Van Duzer P 1/1/1983 Bp George Phelps Mellick Belshaw. c 3. R/Exec Dir Ch Of The H Apos New York NY 2009-2016; Ch Of The Epiph Chicago IL 2002-2003; Cathd Shltr Chicago IL 1997-2009; ReVive Cntr for Hsng and Healing Chicago IL 1997-2009; R Gr Epis Ch Lawr MA 1990-1997; Dir of Prog Dvlpmt Epis City Mssn Boston MA 1988-1990; Epis City Mssn Boston MA 1988-1990; Dio New Jersey Trenton NJ 1984-1987; Vic Gr Epis Ch Eliz NJ 1982-1987. Auth, "The Chr Mnstry"; Auth, "City Issues". Comp Ord Of Ascen.

CHAMBERLAIN, Carol Moore (Pa) 22 Pin Oak Rd, Newport News VA 23601 B Princeton NJ 1946 d Frank & Lucille. BS Syr 1968; MDiv EDS 1975. D 6/14/1975 P 1/15/1977 Bp Lyman Cunningham Ogilby. c 2. PHILADELPHIA Prot Hm Philadelphia PA 2001-2009; Chapl Philadelphia Prot Hm 2001-2009; R S Aidans Ch Cheltenham PA 1982-2001; Int Ch Of S Jn The Evang Philadelphia PA 1981; Non-par 1978-1981; Dio Pennsylvania Philadelphia PA 1977-1978; Coordntr Fairmount Team Mnstry 1975-1978; S Nathanaels Ch Philadelphia PA 1975-1977; Chapl Philadelphia Prot Hm Philadelphia PA 2001-2009.

CHAMBERLAIN, David Morrow (EC) 136 Fairway Oaks Dr, Perry GA 31069 B Chattanooga TN 1946 s Augustus & Myrle. BA U of Chattanooga 1968; MDiv VTS 1971. D 7/4/1971 Bp John Vander Horst P 1/30/1972 Bp William Evan Sanders. m 1/8/1972 Patricia Ann Magill c 2. Dio E Carolina Kinston NC 1997-2001, Sprtl Advsr for Curs 1990-1996, Int 1988-1992, 1988-1989; R S Jn's Epis Ch Fayetteville NC 1987-2002; Cathd Of S Phil Atlanta GA 1980-1987, Cn Eductr 1980-1984; R S Jn's Epis Ch Arlington VA 1976-1980; Supvsr VTS Alexandria VA 1973-1980; Asst S Andr's Epis Ch Arlington VA 1973-1976; Asst Calv Ch Memphis TN 1972-1973; P S Jn's Epis Ch Johnson City TN 1971-1972; Reg Dn Reg Three Arlington VA 1978-1980. Auth, "A Gift of God," 2015; Auth, "The Bible in Capsule Form," 1995. Who's Who in Rel 1985.

CHAMBERLAIN, Donald Fred (WMass) 340 Burncoat St, Worcester MA 01606 **Ret 1996-; Hon Cn Dio Wstrn Massachusetts Springfield 1993-, Cn 1993-** B Springfield MA 1933 s Walter & Ruby. BA Amer Intl Coll 1964; GTS 1967. D 6/22/1967 P 12/1/1967 Bp Robert McConnell Hatch. m 8/1/2005 Sylvia J Chamberlain c 4. R S Mich's-On-The-Heights Worcester MA 1973-1995; P-in-c S Mart's Ch Pittsfield MA 1971-1973; P-in-c Cntrl Berkshire Area Mnstry 1969-1973; Cur S Steph's Ch Pittsfield MA 1967-1968. Auth, "The Attitudes Of White Police Off Toward Negro Offenders"; Auth, "Transitional Par In A Sm City". Phi Beta Kappa Amer Intl 1964; Hon Cn 93 Dio Wmass.

CHAMBERLAIN, Eve Yorke (NJ) 325 Little Silver Point Rd, Little Silver NJ 07739 B Northampton MA 1951 d James & Elizabeth. BS Syr 1974. D 5/9/2015 Bp William H Stokes. c 3.

CHAMBERLAIN-HARRIS, Naomi Redman (Cal) 4467 Crestwood Cir, Concord CA 94521 **D S Anselm's Epis Ch Lafayette CA 2008-** B Oakland CA 1940 d Howard & Jean. BA Sch for Deacons 2009. D 12/5/2009 Bp Marc Handley Andrus. m 6/9/2007 Paul Richard Harris c 3.

CHAMBERS, Joseph Michael Cortright (Mo) 3906 Tropical Ln, Columbia MO 65202 **Cn Dio Missouri S Louis MO 2015-, Chapl 2006-2015** B Springfield MO 1978 s David & Dayna. BS S Louis U; MDiv GTS 2006. D 12/21/2005 P

6/29/2006 Bp George Wayne Smith. m 9/23/2005 Amy Ethel Marie Chambers Cortright c 1. jchambers@diocesemo.org

CHAMBERS, Mark Ellis (Tex) 1708 Persimmon Rd, Cedar Park TX 78613 **Cur S Lk's On The Lake Epis Ch Austin TX 2016-** B Houston 1972 s Donald & Kay. Bachelors of Sci Excelsior Coll 2011; Mstr of Div VTS 2016. D 6/25/2016 Bp C Andrew Doyle. m 2/16/1991 Ella-Marie Justine Wewer c 2. frmchambers@stlukesonthelake.org

CHAMBERS, Rex (Colo) PO BOX 237, WINDSOR CO 80550 B 1944 s Charles & Phyllis. BA California St U Sacramento 1971; MMin Iliff TS 2007. D 1/22/2000 P 8/5/2000 Bp William Jerry Winterrowd. m 8/28/1970 Dana Cherie Chambers c 2. R S Alb's Ch Windsor CO 2008-2016; St Fran Ch-Dillon Breckenridge CO 2004-2006; R St. Fran Epis Ch Dillon CO 2003-2006; P Epis Ch Of S Jn The Bapt Breckenridge CO 2000-2006.

CHAMBERS, Richard Graeff Mark (CFla) 91 Church St, Seymour CT 06483 B Middletown CT 1941 s Julian & Velma. BA U of Miami 1963; STB GTS 1967. D 6/13/1967 Bp Walter H Gray P 3/1/1968 Bp Joseph Warren Hutchens. m 10/19/1985 Ellen J Trollinger c 1. R Trin Ch Seymour CT 1989-2007; Hse of Hope Orlando FL 1985-1989; R Trin Ch Hampton NH 1982-1985; Dir. of Yth Mnstrs & Chr Ed. All SS Ch Of Winter Pk Winter Pk FL 1979-1982; R Trin Ch Brooklyn CT 1969-1979; Cur S Steph's Ch Ridgefield CT 1967-1969.

CHAMBERS, Robert Karl (NY) **Gr Epis Ch Georgetown TX 2016-** B Newfane New York 1967 s Perry & Betty. BS Rochester Inst of Tech 1990; MDiv Epis TS Of The SW 2015; MDiv Epis TS of the SW 2015. D 3/15/2014 P 9/19/2015 Bp Andrew Marion Lenow Dietsche. m 9/23/2003 Amity Angel Worrel c 2.

CHAMBERS, Stanford Hardin (Dal) PO Box 540562, Dallas TX 75354 **Ret 1997-** B Louisville KY 1934 s Loyal & Mary. BA U So 1956; MDiv GTS 1959. D 6/20/1959 P 12/21/1959 Bp Charles A Mason. Ch Of The Epiph Dallas TX 2000-2005; S Marg's Ch Bronx NY 1977-1991; Dio New York New York NY 1975-1977; Asst Cathd Of S Jn The Div New York NY 1967-1968; Assoc S Jn's Ch New York NY 1966-1975; Asst S Ptr's Ch Spotswood NJ 1964-1966; Cur Gr Ch Muskogee OK 1963-1964; Vic S Phil's Muskogee OK 1963-1964; Vic S Laurence Epis Ch Southlake TX 1960-1962; The Epis Ch Of The H Nativ Plano TX 1960-1962; Ch Of The Gd Shpd Dallas TX 1960-1961.

CHAMBLISS, Arrington (Mass) 7 Eldridge Rd, Jamaica Plain MA 02130 **Epis City Mssn Boston MA 2016-** B Winston-Salem NC 1966 d Mallory & Mary. BA U Rich 1988; MDiv Harvard DS 1999. D 6/7/2003 P 6/5/2004 Bp M(Arvil) Thomas Shaw. Exec Dir of Life Together: Diomass Intern Prog Dio Massachusetts Boston MA 2008-2016; Assoc Wyman Memi Ch of St Andr Marblehead MA 2003-2008.

CHAMPION, Peter (Cal) 703 Mariposa Avenue, Rodeo CA 94572 **Anti-Racism Trnr Dio California Anti-Racism Working Grp 2010-; Cert Anti-Racism Trnr Dio California San Francisco CA 2010-** B New York NY 1952 s Jean & Hertha. BA Br 1974; Cert Los Angeles Trade Tech Coll 1976; MDiv SWTS 1989. D 6/29/1989 Bp Robert Hume Cochrane P 1/6/1990 Bp David Charles Bowman. m 6/23/1973 Susan Manley c 2. R S Jn's Epis Ch Clayton CA 2008-2013; Int S Alb's Epis Ch Brentwood CA 2007-2008; P-in-c/Vic Emm Epis Ch Kailua HI 2001-2006; Chapl Klamath Hospice 1998-1999; Mentor P S Barn Ch Bonanza OR 1992-2001; Mentor P S Barn's Epis Ch 1992-2001; Co-R S Paul's Ch Klamath Fall OR 1992-2001; Asst S Jas' Ch Batavia NY 1989-1992; Asst S Paul's Epis Ch Stafford NY 1989-1992; COM Dio Estrn Oregon Cove OR 1993-1999. Anglimergent 2008; Bread for the Wrld 1990; EPF 1989. Whipple Schlr SWTS 1989; Preaching Excellence Conf Epis Evang Fndt 1988; Anderson Schlr SWTS 1988; Phi Beta Kappa Br 1974. peterchamp@hotmail.com

CHAMPION, Susan Manley (Cal) 703 Mariposa Ave., Rodeo CA 94572 **R Chr The Lord Epis Ch Pinole CA 2006-; Vic Chr the Lord Epis Ch Pinole CA 2006-; T/F on Socially Responsible Investing Dio California San Francisco CA 2015-** B Houston TX 1953 d John & Phyllis. BA Br 1974; Cert Pacific Luth U 1980; SWTS 1989; MDiv Bex Sem 1991. D 11/14/1991 P 5/14/1992 Bp David Charles Bowman. m 6/23/1973 Peter Champion c 2. S Andr's Priory Sch Honolulu HI 2001-2006; Chapl S Andr's Priory Sch Honolulu HI 2001-2006; Co-R S Paul's Ch Klamath Fall OR 1992-2001; S Barn Akron NY 1992; D-in-c St. Barn' Epis Ch Akron NY 1991-1992; Res Chapl Victory Memi Hosp Waukegan IL 1988-1989. ACPE 1990-2000. Allin Fllshp Bex 1990; NT Awd SWTS 1986; Hebr Awd SWTS 1986; Phi Beta Kappa Br 1974; Freshman French Awd Br 1971.

CHAMPION-GARTHE, Mo Vinck (Mont) 2101 W Broadway, #103-190, Columbia MO 65203 B Mount Vernon OH 1944 s Carl & Marie. BA Ashland U 1966; MDiv Bex Sem 1969. D 6/14/1969 P 5/7/1970 Bp John Harris Burt. m 7/22/1989 Marybeth Champion-Garthe c 3. Cn Dio Montana Helena MT 2005-2010; R Trin Ch Ennis MT 2002-2005; P-in-c New Life Epis Cluster Seward NE 2001-2002; R S Dav Of Wales Epis Ch Lincoln NE 1991-2000; Dio W Missouri Kansas City MO 1990-1991; Vic Ch of the Mssh Liberty MO 1988-1990; Vic Gr Epis Ch Liberty MO 1988-1990; S Lk's Epis Ch Excelsior Sprg MO 1988; R Ch Of The Redeem Kansas City MO 1981-1988; R Gr Ch Galion OH 1976-1981; R S Paul Epis Ch Conneaut OH 1971-1976; Cur S Matt's Epis Ch Toledo OH 1969-1971. Oblate of S Ben 1999-2013.

CHAMPLIN, Jeffrey Fletcher (Ark) 2701 Old Greenwood Rd, Fort Smith AR 72903 B Providence RI 1956 s Arthur & Julia. BA Wesl 1978; MDiv Ya Berk 1983; Ldrshp Acad for New Directions 1986. D 6/8/1985 Bp Arthur Edward Walmsley P 12/1/1985 Bp William Bradford Hastings. m 8/22/1981 Anne K Champlin c 3. R S Barth's Epis Ch Ft Smith AR 1998-2016; S Andr's Epis Ch Liberal KS 1991-1998; Asst Mssnr Middlesex Area Cluster Mnstry Durham CT 1985-1992; Middlesex Area Cluster Mnstry Higganum CT 1985-1991.

CHAN, Charles Yang-Ling Ping-Fai (Colo) Po Box 662, Mukwonago WI 53149 **P-in-c Dio So Dakota Pierre SD 2005-** B HK 1955 s Dick-Kwong & Woon-Fong. Marq; BA U Denv 1978; MDiv Nash 1981. D 4/29/1981 Bp William Harvey Wolfrum P 10/1/1981 Bp William Carl Frey. m 2/14/1998 Ewa M Chan. P-in-c Epis Ch Of Our Sav New York NY 2003-2005, P-in-c 1981-1982; Epis Ch Of The Resurr Mukwonago WI 1997-2003; S Ptr's Ch Honolulu HI 1988; S Ptr's Epis Ch Chicago IL 1983-1987; S Jas Epis Ch Milwaukee WI 1982-1983; Assoc S Jn Ch/Mision San Juan Milwaukee WI 1982-1983. Ban Zung Ci; Zhu An Ji #1:.

CHAN, Henry Albert (LI) 1212 Foulk Rd Apt 4c, Wilmington DE 19803 B Demerara GY 1946 s Clarence & Ruby. BS SUNY 1978; MBA Dowling Coll 1980; DPA Nova SE U 1981; Cert Mercer TS 1982; DMin Sewanee: The U So, TS 1987; STM GTS 1992; PhD GTF 1994; PsyD GTF 2005. D 12/21/1982 Bp Robert Campbell Witcher Sr P 12/10/1983 Bp Henry Boyd Hucles III. m 4/26/1969 Jean F Chan c 3. R S Ptr's Ch Rosedale NY 1988-2008; Dio Long Island Garden City NY 1987, Co-Chair Racial Justice Com 1995-1996, Mem Cler Conf Plnng Com 1985-1986, Mem Com on Racial Audit 1984-1989; Cur S Ch Of The Trsfg Freeport NY 1983-1987; S Andr's Ch Mastic Bch NY 1983. Auth, "Hist Models for the P As Pstr: From The Major Works of Greg the Great, Geoffrey Chaucer, et. al.," Wyndham Hall Press, Lima, Ohio, 2014; Auth, "Blog, "Christmas in Guyana,"" GTF, 2012; Auth, "The Humanity of Mediators: From A Study of the Major Concepts of Viktor E. Frankl," Wyndham Hall Press, Lima, Ohio, 2007; Auth, "The Medtr As Human Being: From A Study of the Major Concepts of Sigmund Freud, Carl Jung, Erik Erikson, et. al.," Wyndham Hall Press, Lima, Ohio, 2005; Auth, "A Primary Mssn--The Sermon Is A Vital & Important Part of the Liturg," LivCh, LivCh, 1985; Auth, "Par Computer--An Aid in Many Aspects of the Ch's Wk," LivCh, LivCh, 1983. APA 2005; Amer Soc for Publ Admin 2008-2013; C.G. Jung Fndt 1998-2007; NYS Dispute Resolution Assn 2002-2009; Viktor Frankl Inst of Logotherapy 2007. Pres Jimmy Carter Prof Emer of Mediation and Pstr Care GTF 2016; Mem of the Year Awd Assn of Chinese Professionals, Atlanta, GA 2010; Serv and Humanitarian Awd Guyana Missions/Consulate/Tri-St Allnce 2002; A Point of Light for All Americans US Congr, Hse of Representatives 2001; Who's Who in Amer Marquis 2000; Who's Who in the E Marquis 1999.

CHANCE, Robin (Wyo) 6516 Weaver Rd, Cheyenne WY 82009 B New York NY 1951 d Robert & Barbara. BA Wstrn St Coll of Colorado 1973; MDiv SWTS 1995. D 6/22/1995 Bp Bob Gordon Jones P 1/5/1996 Bp William Harvey Wolfrum. m 8/17/1974 Kenneth Leroy Chance c 3. R S Chris's Ch Cheyenne WY 2002-2013; Cbury Hse Laramie WY 1995-2002; Chapl S Matt's Epis Cathd Laramie WY 1995-1999. DOK 1996.

CHANCELLOR JR, Donald Wood (Miss) PO Box 391, Como MS 38619 **Vic H Innoc' Epis Ch Como MS 2011-** B Macon MS 1967 s Donald & Karen. BPA The U of Mississippi 1989; MDiv Sewanee: The U So, TS 2011. D 6/4/2011 P 12/14/2011 Bp Duncan Montgomery Gray III. m 6/15/2013 Marian Montgomery Chancellor.

CHANDLER, Belinda (Chi) 3025 Walters Ave, Northbrook IL 60062 **Chapl and Coordntr NorthShore U HealthSystem Glenbrook Hosp IL 1996-** B Geneva NY 1953 d Hamond & Marjorie. BA Methodist U 1978; MDiv SWTS 1998. D 9/1/2010 P 3/1/2011 Bp Jeff Lee. m 12/27/1997 Henry Austin c 3. P-in-c S Giles' Ch Northbrook IL 2011, Assoc 2010-.

CHANDLER, Gail Stearns (Me) St. David's Episcopal Church, 138 York St, Kennebunk ME 04043 B New York NY 1947 d George & Phyllis. BA U of New Hampshire 1969; MA S Jos Coll 1983. D 6/28/2008 Bp Chilton Richardson Knudsen. c 2.

CHANDLER, John Herrick (Los) 2286 Vasanta Way, Los Angeles CA 90068 **Ret 1989-** B San Francisco CA 1928 s Ralph & Gwen. BA U CA 1952; BD U Chi 1958; PhD U Chi 1963. D 6/22/1959 P 2/1/1960 Bp Francis E I Bloy. m 12/10/1955 Nancy Phillips. 1959-1989.

CHANDLER, Nan Elizabeth (EC) 301 Bretonshire Rd, Wilmington NC 28405 **R All Soul's Ch Leland NC 1995-** B Charleston WV 1943 d Obadiah & Jeannette. BS U of Kentucky 1966; MHA Xavier U 1978; MSW CUA 1980; MDiv VTS 1985. D 6/5/1985 P 12/14/1985 Bp Robert Poland Atkinson. All Souls Ch NW Leland NC 2008-2009, 1995-2005; Assoc S Mk's Ch Westhampton Bch NY 1990-1993; Asst Cleric Gr Ch Cincinnati OH 1988-1990; R S Paul's Ch Wheeling WV 1985-1987.

CHANDLER, Paul-Gordon (Spok) **Exec Coun Appointees New York NY 2003-; R St. Jn's Ch / Maadi (serving w DFMS of TEC) Cairo 2003-** B Dayton OH 1964 s Wilfred & Nancy. Cert Allnce Francaise De Paris Fr 1986; BA Wheaton Coll 1986; Chichester Theol Coll 1993. Trans 2/1/2003 Bp James E Waggoner Jr. m 1/27/1990 Lynne E Chandler c 2. Pres / CEO Partnr Intl Spokane WA 1999-2003; U.S. CEO / Exec VP Intl Bible Soc Colorado Sprg CO 1997-1999; Dir of SPCK Worldwide S.P.C.K London Untd Kingdom 1995-1997; R St. Geo's Ch Tunis/Carthage Tunisia 1993-1995. "Songs in Waiting: Reflections on the Middle Estrn Songs Surrounding Chr's Birth," Morehouse Pub (Ch Pub), 2009; "Pilgrims of Chr on the Muslim Road: Exploring a New Path Between Two Faiths," Cowley Pub (Rowman & Littlefield), 2007; "God'S Global Mosaic: What We Can Learn From Christians Around the Wrld," Intervarsity Press (IVP), 2000; "Div Mosaic," S.P.C.K. / Triangle, 1997.

CHANDLER JR, Richard Anthony (CFla) Saint Anne's Church, 9870 W Fort Island Trl, Crystal River FL 34429 **S Anne's Ch Crystal River FL 2016-; R Zion Ch Hudson Falls NY 2009-** B Schenectady NY 1958 s Richard & Carolyn. BA SUNY Potsdam 1992; MS Sage Grad Sch 1995. D 5/31/2008 P 12/7/2008 Bp William Howard Love. m 7/2/1994 Kelly W Evans-Chandler c 3. laughtersmiles1@nycap.rr.com

CHANDLER, Susan (Mass) 195 Patmos Rd., Sawyer's Island, Rowley MA 01969 B Oklahoma City OK 1952 d Joe & Martha. BA U of Oklahoma 1974; MDiv GTS 2001. D 7/28/2001 Bp Terence Kelshaw P 6/28/2002 Bp M(Arvil) Thomas Shaw. m 5/19/2001 Alfred Dupont Chandler c 2. R S Jas Ch Amesbury MA 2006-2012; Asst S Jn's Ch Beverly MA 2001-2006.

CHANDLER-WARD, Constance (Mass) 16 School St., Tenants Harbor ME 04860 B Cambridge MA 1935 d Edgar & Ruth. BA U of Dublin IE 1957; MA U of Dublin IE 1959; MDiv Yale DS 1961. D 11/15/1975 P 2/13/1977 Bp Robert Bruce Hall. c 2. Admin/Counslr Greenfire Retreat Hse 1991-2008; Chapl Wellesley Coll MA 1981-1991; Assoc Gr Ch In Providence Providence RI 1980-1981; Asst S Paul's Memi Charlottesvlle VA 1977-1979; COM Dio Virginia Richmond VA 1978-1979.

CHANDY, Sunil Kulangana (RI) 1115 New Pear St, Vineland NJ 08360 **R Chr Ch Westerly RI 2014-** B Kerala IN 1967 s Kulangana & Saramma. BS Rutgers The St U of New Jersey 1991; MDiv GTS 1995. Trans 4/27/1998 Bp John Shelby Spong. m 1/22/1994 Simi Chandy c 3. S Andr's Ch Mt Holly NJ 2006-2014; Trin Epis Ch Vineland NJ 2001-2006; Chr Ch Ridgewood NJ 1999-2001; All SS Epis Par Hoboken NJ 1998-1999. standrewschurch.mh@verizon.net

✠ CHANE, The Rt Rev John Bryson (WA) 5309 Pendleton St, San Diego CA 92109 **Lectr Wrld Against Violence and Extremism Tehran Iran 2014-; Asstg Bp Dio San Diego 2013-; Bd InspiraAction 2013-; Ctr. for Global Justice Washington Natl Cathd 2013-; participant Search for Common Ground 2011-; Bd Wrld Faith Dev. and Dia. Berkeley Ctr. Georgetown 2011-; Prncpl Chr Muslim Summit 2009-; Sr. Advsr Interfaith Affrs Washington Natl Cathd 2013-** B Washington DC 1944 s Daniel & Vivienne. BA Bos 1969; MDiv Ya Berk 1972. D 6/24/1972 Bp John Melville Burgess P 1/6/1973 Bp George E Rath Con 6/1/2002 for WA. m 1/21/1967 Karen Chane c 2. Cnvnr Brookings Us Islamic Wrld Forum 2011-2014; Prchr/Lectr Chautauqua Inst 2009-2013; Int Dn Cathd of St Ptr & St Paul Washington DC 2003-2005; Bp of Washington Dio Washington Washington DC 2002-2011; Dn Cathd Ch Of S Paul San Diego CA 1996-2002; Percept Strng Com Dio San Diego San Diego CA 1996-2002; T/F on Educ Dio Massachusetts Boston MA 1994-1996, Cn 21 Consult 1993-1996, Par Consult 1992-1996, Long-R Plnng Com 1990-1996, Chair of Gdnc and Pstr Care of Post and Candidates 1989-1996, COM 1989-1996, Mssn Prog and Plnng Com 1989-1996, T/F on Hunger 1988-1996; R S Mk's Ch Southborough MA 1987-1996; Dioc Coun Dio NW Pennsylvania Erie PA 1976-1977; Int Dn Cathd Of S Paul Erie PA 1975-1987; P in charge S Paul's Ch Montvale NJ 1972-1974. Auth, "Missing Ingredient in the Iran and P5+1 Negotiations," *CGN News Serv*, Search for Common ground, 2015; Auth, "Fear, Hatred, Slaughter, Heresy," *CNN On-Line*, Cable News Ntwk, 2015; Auth, "Peace between Christians and Muslims," *Rome, Chr Muslim Summit*, Washington a. Cathd, 2014; Writer, "Messengers of Monotheism," *Dog Ear Pub*, Dog Ear Pub, 2013; Auth, "Rel and Diplomacy," *U.S. Islamic Wrld Forum*, Brookings Inst, 2013; Auth, "The H City of Jerusalem," *Chautauqua Inst*, Chautauqua Inst, 2010; Auth, "iraq Uncensored," *Amer Security Proj*, Fulcrum Press, 2009; Auth, "Iraq Uncensored," *Speakers Corner*, Speaker's Corner, 2009; Auth, "An Easter Visionof the Moral Life's Loaves and Fishes," *Epis Life*, Dio Massachusetss, 1994; Auth, "Moral Myopia and Sport," *Int. Olympic Acad*, USOC, 1994; Auth, "The Mass Miracle, Mnstry in The 90's," *Epis Life*, Dio Massachusettssetts, 1988; Auth, "Athlete Chapl," *New Directions in Athlete Chapl & Counslg*, USOC, 1988; Auth, "Athlete Chapl," *Perspective on Olympic Chapl*, USOC, 1987; Auth, "Wmn Conscience & Priesthood," *Wit*, Wit, 1986. Bishops Working for a Just Wrld 2004-2012; Bd Ecum Coun San Diego 1997-2002; Cntr for Urban Mnstry 1996-2002; Curs 2000; EPF 1993; EWC 1978; No Amer Dn Conf 1996-2002; Soc of S Jn the Evang 1994; Soc of S Paul in the Desert 1996; TEC Natl Concerns Comm. 2002; VP, Ecum Coun San Diego 1997-2002. Lux et Veritas Awd Yale DS 2012; Global Peace and Recon Awd Search for Common Ground 2011; Global Peacemakers Awd The Rumi Forum 2011; Fndr's Medal Berea Coll 2010; DD EDS 2005; Pres Medal G.W. U GW 2005; Inter-Faith Bridge Builder Inter-Faith Coun of DC 2005; DD Ya Berk 2004; DD VTS 2003; Awd of Excellence--Humor, written ECom 2000; Awd of Excellence--Editorials ECom 1997; Schlrshp Bk Prize Ya Berk DD 1972.

CHANEY JR, Michael Jackson (Ga) 1802 Abercorn St, Savannah GA 31401 **Chapl Dio Georgia Savannah GA 2014-; Cur The Collgt Ch of St Paul the Apos Savannah GA 2013-** B Greenwood MS 1968 s Michael & Mary. BFA Art Cntr Coll of Design 1991; MFA Tufts U 1996; MDiv EDS 2013. D 6/22/2013 P 1/3/2014 Bp Scott Anson Benhase. m 10/20/2001 Nicole Koplik c 3.

CHANEY, Myrna Faye (Mont) 14 September Dr, Missoula MT 59802 **D Ch Of The H Sprt Missoula MT 1999-** B Boise ID 1940 d Nelson & Glenva. BA U of Montana 1962; MA Stan 1963. D 12/5/1999 Bp Charles I Jones III. m 6/15/1963 Robert Bruce Chaney.

CHANG, Hsin Fen (Los) 15694 Tetley St, Hacienda Heights CA 91745 **S Thos' Mssn Hacienda Hgts CA 2015-; Dio Los Angeles Los Angeles CA 2011-** B Taiwan 1965 d Wen-chang & Li-cheng. BA Tunghai U TW 1987; MA U of Wisconsin-Madison 1990; PhD U Tor 2007; MDiv Logos Evang Sem 2010. D 6/11/2011 P 1/7/2012 Bp Diane Jardine Bruce.

CHANG, Lennon Yuan-Rung (Tai) Wen-Hua 3rd Road, 4th Place #75, Pei-Tan Taiwan **D Ch Of The Gd Shpd Taipei Taiwan 1995-** B Taipei 1955 s Feng-Ji & Ging-Mei. BA Fu-Jen Cath U 1980; MA Fu-Jen Cath U 1983; Dplma Trin Theol Cntr 1994; PhD Tamkang U 1998. D 12/21/1995 Bp John Chih-Tsung Chien P. m 10/18/1980 Wei Fen-Jan c 2.

CHANG, Ling-Ling (Tai) 280 Fu-Hsing South Road, Sec 2, Taipei Taiwan **Dio Taiwan Taipei 2000-; D S Jn's Cathd Taipei Taiwan 2000-** B Chang-Hua TW 1962 d Yin-Chin & Li-Hsia. BA Chung Yuan U Chung-Li Tw 1983; MA Fu-Jen Cath U 1998. D 10/28/2000 Bp John Chih-Tsung Chien.

CHANG, Mark Chung-Moon (Nwk) 11 Foakes Drive, Ajax LIT 3K5 Canada B 1930 s Byung-Kul & Soon-Hwa. Methodist Theol Coll 1959; BA Song-Sil U Seoul Kr 1962; S Michaels TS 1964; ThM Yonsei U 1969; STM GTS 1970; PhD Pacific Wstrn U 1986. Trans 10/1/1987 Bp John Shelby Spong. m 1/10/1957 Esther Haing-Im Chang. All SS' Korean Epis Ch Bergenfield NJ 1998; Vic S Peters Ch Bogota NJ 1987-1989; Serv Angl Ch Of Can 1970-1987. Auth, "b Of A Wmn"; Auth, "Space-Time Talk".

✠ CHANG, The Rt Rev Richard Sui On (Haw) 1760 S. Beretania Street, Apt. 11C, Honolulu HI 96826 **Ret Bp of Hawaii The Epis Ch in Hawaii Honolulu HI 2007-, Bp of Hawaii 1996-2007, Exec Off 1979-1986, Archd 1970-1974, Bp's Cbnt 1968-1970, Chair HI E 1976-1979, COM 1974-1976, Dioc Coun 1970** B Honolulu HI 1941 s Dick & Flora. BA Trin Hartford CT 1963; MDiv CDSP 1966; U of Hawaii 1970. D 3/5/1966 Bp George Richard Millard P 9/4/1966 Bp Harry Sherbourne Kennedy Con 1/4/1997 for The Episcopal Church in Haw. m 8/10/1969 Delia Morrish c 2. Asst to PBp Epis Ch Cntr New York NY 1986-1996; Chr Memi Ch Kilauea HI 1974-1976; R All SS Ch Kapaa HI 1970-1978; Asst Ch Of The H Nativ Honolulu HI 1966-1970; Bd Dir Credo Inst Inc. Memphis TN 2008-2012, Advsry Bd 2006-2008. CODE 1979-1986; LAND 1976-1986. DD CDSP 1997; Cn Cathd of the H Trin, Paris FR 1993; AB cl Trin 1963; Pi Gamma Mu Trin 1963.

CHANGO, Georgianna (NwPa) Rr 6 Box 324, Punxsutawney PA 15767 B Punxsutawney PA 1940 d John & Thelma. D 11/1/1991 Bp Robert Deane Rowley Jr. m 9/28/1956 Anthony Reynold Chango c 2. D Ch Of Our Sav Dubois PA 1991-2010.

CHANNON, Ethel M (Dal) 2304 County Ave, Texarkana AR 71854 **St Mk's Epis Ch Mt Pleasant TX 2014-; Mng Ed Texarkana Gazette 1987-** B East St. Louis IL 1951 d Charles & Bernice. BA Sthrn Illinois U Edwardsville IL 1973; Cathd Cntr for Mnstry Formation Dallas TX 2006. D 12/5/2006 P 11/24/2013 Bp James Monte Stanton.

CHAPLIN, George Manton (RI) 1201 Capella South, Goat Island, Newport RI 02840 **Died 9/12/2016** B Newport RI 1923 s Arthur & Florence. Aeronautical U Chicago IL 1943; Barrington Coll 1967; EDS 1967; Providence Coll 1967; Salve Regina Coll/Univ 1968. D 3/8/1969 P 12/20/1969 Bp John S Higgins. c 4. Int The Ch Of The H Cross Middletown RI 1999-2000, Int 1992-1998; Supply Dio Rhode Island Providence RI 1993-1998, 1978-1980; Ret 1990-2016; R S Mk's Ch Warren RI 1969-1989.

CHAPMAN, Alton James (SwFla) 12905 Forest Hills Dr, Tampa FL 33612 B Negaunee MI 1940 s Ellsworth & Estelle. BA U of So Florida 1967; VTS 1970. D 6/29/1970 P 11/1/1971 Bp William Loftin Hargrave. m 4/24/1971 Elizabeth Chapman c 3. R S Clem Epis Ch Tampa FL 1998-2005; Gr Ch Cedar Rapids IA 1988-1998; Vic S Lk's Ch Land O Lakes FL 1976-1987; St Lukes Ch Ellenton FL 1976-1986; R S Jas Hse Of Pryr Tampa FL 1970-1976. DOK-Chapl.

CHAPMAN JR, Chuck (Ark) 1721 Monzingo, Magnolia AR 71753 B Memphis TN 1955 s Charles & Betty. BA Un U Jackson TN 1976; MDiv Sthrn Bapt TS 1979; CTh Epis TS of the SW 1986. D 5/28/1986 P 5/26/1987 Bp Alex Dockery Dickson. Int R S Mary's Epis Ch El Dorado AR 2009, Cur 1997-2008; R S Mk's Epis Ch Plainview TX 1992-1997; Chapl S Andr's Epis Sch Amarillo TX 1991-1992; Chapl St Andrews Sch Of Amarillo Amarillo TX 1991-1992; R Gr Epis Ch Winfield KS 1990-1991; Chapl Gr-S Lk's Epis Sch Memphis TN 1986-1990; Asst to R Gr - S Lk's Ch Memphis TN 1980-1990. Auth, "The Message Of The Bk Of Revelation," Liturg Press, 1995; Auth, "Lyrics Of Easter Hymn," GIA, 1983; Auth, "Lyrics Of H Gifts," GIA, 1983. Oblate Of St. Ben Of Subiaco Abbey 1996. Silver Beaver BSA 2009; Cross of St. Geo BSA 2007. chaschap@yahoo.com

CHAPMAN, Colin (NH) Christ Church, 2 Rectory St, Rye NY 10580 **S Ptr's Epis Ch Londonderry NH 2016-; Assoc Chr And H Trin Ch Westport CT 2014-** B Hartford CT 1984 s Michael & Diane. MA Estrn Nazarene Coll 2006; MDiv GTS 2012; MDiv The GTS 2012. D 6/9/2012 Bp James Elliot Curry P 12/15/2012 Bp Laura Ahrens. m 7/1/2006 Christie J Everett Chapman c 3. Chr's Ch Rye NY 2012-2014.

CHAPMAN, Cristi Elizabeth (Oly) **D S Mk's Cathd Seattle WA 2017-** B Lubbock TX 1971 d Stephen & Jana Cene. MPA and BBA U of Texas at Austin 1994. D 12/17/2016 P 6/20/2017 Bp Gregory Harold Rickel. m 9/5/1992 Christopher Neal Chapman c 1.

CHAPMAN, George Memory (Mass) 41 Garth Road, West Roxbury MA 02132 **Iglesia De San Juan Ch Brookline MA 1978-** B Greensboro NC 1942 s George & Elizabeth. AB W&L 1963; BD EDS 1968; BD ETS 1968. D 6/8/1968 P 12/21/1968 Bp Horace W B Donegan. m 6/26/1965 Margaret R Chapman c 3. R S Paul's Ch Brookline MA 1978-2007; Sr Cn S Paul's Cathd Buffalo NY 1972-1978; P-in-c Imm Ch Highlands Wilmington DE 1968-1972; Yth Mnstry Coordntr Prov II 1974-1978. "Will I?," *Sermons that Wk X*, Morehouse, 2001; Auth, "Revelation at the Teller Windows," *Sermons that Wk IX*, Morehouse, 2000; Auth, "Jesus is Lord," *Pulpit Dig*, 1970. Fell - SSJE 1988.

CHAPMAN, Hugh William (Fla) 13 Bb Misgunsi, St. Thomas VI 802 **S Phil's Epis Ch Jacksonville FL 2007-** B Guyana South America 1954 Trans 7/1/2001 Bp Theodore Athelbert Daniels. m 6/12/1980 Paula G Chapman c 3. P Dio Vrgn Islands Charlotte Amalie St Thom VI 2001-2007.

CHAPMAN, James Dreger (Mass) 201 Washington Ave, Chelsea MA 02150 B Burlington VT 1943 s Robert & Eleanor. AB Harv. D 6/6/2015 Bp Gayle Harris. m 6/11/1965 Ann L Ann Lovell Southwick c 2.

CHAPMAN, Jerry Wayne (Dal) 11201 Pickfair Dr, Austin TX 78750 **Asstg S Matt's Ch Austin TX 2000-, Asst 1987-1999** B Dallas TX 1943 s Wayne & Archie. BS U of Texas 1970; Sewanee: The U So, TS 1980. D 6/28/1980 Bp Archibald Donald Davies P 5/1/1981 Bp Robert Elwin Terwilliger. c 2. Asst S Geo's Ch Austin TX 1981-1987; Asst S Jn's Epis Ch Austin TX 1980-1981; Serv Gd Shpd.

CHAPMAN, Justin P (Minn) 1430 15th Ave NW, Rochester MN 55901 **The Epis Cathd Of Our Merc Sav Faribault MN 2014-** B Minneapolis MN 1979 s Dann & Linda. BS U MN 2001; MDiv CDSP 2008. D 7/26/2007 P 7/8/2008 Bp James Louis Jelinek. m 10/20/2007 Katie Virginia Brandt Chapman. P in Res S Lk's Epis Ch Rochester MN 2012-2014, P-in-c 2008-2011; S Ptr's Epis Ch Kasson MN 2008-2011.

CHAPMAN, Michael (Alb) 22 Bergen St, Brentwood NY 11717 B Miami Beach FL 1951 s Lipscomb & Mary. BA Florida Atlantic U 1972; MDiv Nash 1990. P 12/1/1990 Bp Orris George Walker Jr. m 4/17/1982 Linda Chapman c 2. Vic Chr Ch Brentwood NY 1990-1999.

CHAPMAN, Phillip (Neb) 322 S 15th St, Plattsmouth NE 68048 **D S Lk's Ch Plattsmouth NE 2003-** B Franklinville NY 1943 BA Bellevue U. D 1/6/2003 Bp James Edward Krotz P 11/11/2009 Bp Joe Goodwin Burnett. m 7/15/1963 Diana Rogerson c 2.

CHAPMAN, Rebecca Ann (CFla) **Dio Cntrl Florida Orlando FL 2017-** D 9/10/2016 Bp Gregory Orrin Brewer.

CHAPMAN, Tansy (Mass) PO Box 832, Mendocino CA 95460 **Assoc S Mich And All Ang Ch Ft Bragg CA 2006-** B St Leonard's, England 1937 d Conrad & Gillian. BA U of Leicester 1959; Oxf GB 1960; MS London Inst Gb 1961; MDiv EDS 1982. D 6/5/1982 Bp John Bowen Coburn P 5/1/1983 Bp Roger W Blanchard. m 4/3/1965 Paul H Chapman c 3. Assoc Trin Ch Topsfield MA 1997-2002; Non-par 1993-1996; S Eliz's Ch Wilmington MA 1988-1992; S Mk's Epis Ch Burlington MA 1982-1987; Sprtl Dir Bethany Hse of Pryr Arlington Ma. 1992-2000. Fell Soc Of S Jn The Evang; S Anne Cnvnt Arlington Ma.

CHAPPELL, Annette Mary (Md) **P Assoc Ch Of The Adv Baltimore MD 2014-** B Washington DC 1939 d Joseph & Annette. MA U of Maryland Coll Pk 1964; PhD U of Maryland Coll Pk 1970; MDiv GTS 2003. D 6/14/2003 P 12/13/2003 Bp Robert Wilkes Ihloff. Long-term supply St. Jn's Par Kingsville MD 2016-2017; Int R Sherwood Par Cockeysville MD 2015-2016; Long-term supply Ch of the Adv Fed Hill Baltimore 2014; Cont R Ch of the Redemp Baltimore MD USA 2011-2013; R Ch Of The Redemp Baltimore MD 2003-2011; Mem, Liturg and Mus Com Dio Maryland Baltimore MD 2006-2011, Mem, Liturg and Mus Com 2006-, Mem, Compstn and Benefits Com 2003-. Soc of Cath Priests 2009.

CHAPPELLE, Veronica Donohue (CPa) 1118 State Route 973 E, Cogan Station PA 17728 **R Trin Ch Jersey Shore PA 2006-** B Philadelphia PA 1954 d Mark & Clare. BA Tem 1987; MDiv Luth TS at Gettysburg 2009. D 6/9/2000 Bp Michael Whittington Creighton P 10/6/2007 Bp Nathan Dwight Baxter. m 10/7/1977 Daniel Elwood Chappell c 1. D Trin Epis Ch Williamsport PA 2000-2002; S Mk's Epis Ch Northumberlnd PA 2003-2004; Yoke Min S Matt's Epis Ch Sunbury PA 2003-2004. trinityjs@verizon.net

CHAPPELLE, Laurinda (Nev) 1230 Riverberry Dr, Reno NV 89509 **R St Cathr of Siena Reno NV 2009-** B Englewood NJ 1947 d James & Margaret.

BA Stetson U 1968; MEd U of Florida 1969. D 1/31/2006 P 7/31/2006 Bp Katharine Jefferts Schori. P-in-c Dio Nevada Las Vegas 2007-2008.

CHAR, Zachariah (WMich) 4232 Alpinehorn Dr Nw, Comstock Pk MI 49321 **Dio Wstrn Michigan Kalamazoo MI 2012-; Employee Kent Quality Goods 2007-** B 1982 s Mayen & Akon. AA Grand Rapids Cmnty Coll Grand Rapids MI; Kuyper Grand Rapids MI 2009. D 12/9/2006 P 6/16/2007 Bp Robert R Gepert. m 12/9/2004 Tabitha Nyawut Char c 1. Gr Ch Grand Rapids MI 2007-2011.

CHARD JR, Arthur Cameron (WVa) 1206 Maple Lane, Anchorage KY 40223 **Assoc S Lk's Ch Louisville KY 2002-** B Brainerd MN 1933 s Arthur & Kathleen. BS Minnesota St U Moorhead 1956; MDiv Epis TS in Kentucky 1967. D 5/27/1967 P 12/1/1967 Bp William R Moody. m 6/1/1968 Judy Sams c 1. R All SS Ch Charleston WV 1981-1995; P-in-c S Pat Ch Somerset KY 1968-1981; Chapl Estrn St Hosp Versailles KY 1967-1968; Cur S Jn's Ch Versailles KY 1967-1968.

CHARLES, D Maurice (Roch) 412 Euclid Avenue, Oakland CA 94610 **Ph.D. Stdt DS U Chi Chicago IL 2002-** B Cleveland OH 1963 s Henry & Jeanie. BA Case Wstrn Reserve U 1987; MDiv U Chi DS 1990; CAS CDSP 1995; U Chi 2012; PhD U Chi 2013. D 12/7/1996 P 6/7/1997 Bp William Edwin Swing. c 1. Asst Epis Ch Of The Atone Chicago IL 2008-2014; P-in-c Ch Of S Thos Chicago IL 2003-2004; Assoc Dn for Rel Life Stan Stanford CA 1996-2002; Bd Mem The Ch Hm At Montgomery Place Chicago IL 2008-2010; Search Com/Bd Mem Brent Hse (U Of Chicago) Chicago IL 2003-2007. OHC 1995. charles@hws.edu

CHARLES, Kathy (Eau) 1001 McLean Ave, Tomah WI 54660 **D Chr Ch Par La Crosse WI 2001-** B Chippewa Falls WI 1949 d George & Elizabeth. Epis Acad D Sch Menomonie WI 2002; BA Viterbo U 2002; MDiv Untd TS 2005; MDiv SWTS 2008. D 6/9/2001 P 5/19/2007 Bp Keith Whitmore. m 5/8/1971 Nicholas Robert Charles c 2. S Jn's Epis Ch Sparta WI 2013, D 2002-2004; P S Mary's Epis Ch Tomah WI 2010-2016; Hospice Chapl Mayo Clnc La Crosse WI 2001-2013; Pres Stndg Com Dio Eau Claire Eau Claire WI 2013-2014, Exec Coun 2012-2015, GC Dep 2012-2015, Prov V Exec Bd 2012-2014.

CHARLES, Leonel (SeFla) Box 1309, Port-Au-Prince Haiti **Ch Of S Chris Ft Lauderdale FL 2002-; P-in-c S Andre Hinche Ht 1990-** B Cap Haitien HT 1965 s Dieubonne & Romaine. Ceteeh 1989. D 7/30/1989 P 2/1/1990 Bp Luc Anatole Jacques Garnier. m 6/3/2015 Florence Despeignes. Dio Haiti Port-au-Prince HT 1989-1995.

CHARLES, Randolph (WA) 11178 Kilkenny Rd, Marshall VA 20115 B Florence SC 1947 s Randolph & Harriet. DMin SWTS; BA The U So 1969; MDiv GTS 1976. D 1/24/1976 P 8/6/1976 Bp Gray Temple. m 5/17/2008 Joanne F Fleming c 3. R The Ch Of The Epiph Washington DC 1994-2015; BEC Dio Sthrn Virginia Newport News VA 1989-1994, COM 1989-1994, Ldrshp Trng Prog 1988-1994; R S Paul's Ch Newport News VA 1983-1994; Gr Ch Cathd Charleston SC 1978-1983; P-in-c H Cross Faith Memi Epis Ch Pawleys Island SC 1976-1978; Asst Chr the King Pawleys Island SC 1976-1977.

CHARLES, Winston Breeden (NC) 114 East Drewry Lane, Raleigh NC 27609 B Bennettsville SC 1948 s Randolph & Harriet. BA U So 1970; MDiv VTS 1974; MA UTS 1989; PhD UTS 1995. D 6/8/1974 P 12/14/1974 Bp Gray Temple. m 12/20/1970 Judy H Charles c 1. R Chr Epis Ch Raleigh NC 1993-2008; Assoc S Jas Ch New York NY 1991-1993; P-in-c S Andr's Epis Ch Staten Island NY 1990-1991; Non-par 1985-1990; R S Geo's Epis Ch Summerville SC 1979-1985; Cur Epis Ch of the Gd Shpd Summerville SC 1977-1978; Asst Min Gr Ch Cathd Charleston SC 1976-1977; Vic Epis Ch Of The H Trin Ridgeland SC 1974-1976; The Ch Of The Cross Bluffton SC 1974-1976. "Remembrance as a Dynamic of Faith in the Theol of Mart Luther [dissertation]," 2005.

✠ CHARLESTON, The Rt Rev Steven (Okla) 2702 Silvertree Dr, Oklahoma City OK 73120 B Duncan OK 1949 s Gilbert & Billie. BA Trin Hartford CT 1971; MDiv EDS 1976; Hon Doctorate Trin Hartford CT 1992. D 8/10/1982 Bp William Charles Wantland P 3/1/1983 Bp Everett H Jones Con 3/23/1991 for Ak. m 7/28/1978 Susan Shettles Charleston c 1. Dio Oklahoma Oklahoma City OK 2012-2014; Prof S Paul TS 2011-2013; Dn of the Cathd S Paul's Cathd Oklahoma City OK 2010-2012; Asst Bp Dio California San Francisco CA 2008-2010, Asst Bp 2008-2010; Pres/Dn EDS Cambridge MA 2000-2008; Chapl Dio Connecticut Meriden CT 1998-1999; Chapl Trin Chap Hartford CT 1996; Bp of Alaska Dio Alaska Fairbanks AK 1990-1996; Prof of Systematic Theol Luther NW Theo Sem S Paul MN 1984-1990; Dir Dakota Ldrshp Prog Mobridge SD 1983-1984; Exec Dir Natl Com On Indn Wk 1980-1982. Auth, "Hope As Old As Fire"; Auth, "Cloud Walking"; Auth, "Hope As Old As Fire"; Auth, "Cloud Walking"; Auth, "Reflection On A Revival: The Native Amer Alt"; Auth, "Respecting The Cir : Sharing In Wrshp w Native Americans"; Auth, "OT Of Native Amer".

✠ CHARLTON, The Rt Rev Gordon Taliaferro (Tex) 132 Lancaster Dr Apt 310, Irvington VA 22480 B San Antonio TX 1923 s Gordon & Enid. BA U of Texas 1944; MDiv VTS 1949. D 7/5/1949 Bp Everett H Jones P 1/6/1950 Bp Clinton Simon Quin Con 8/28/1982 for Tex. c 3. Ret Bp Suffr Of Texas Dio Texas Houston TX 1989-2004, Bp Suffr 1982-1988; Dn Epis TS Of The SW Austin TX 1973-1982; Asst VTS Alexandria VA 1967-1973; R Ch of St Andrews & St

Matthews Wilmington DE 1963-1967; Serv Ch In Mex 1958-1962; Asst Secy Ovrs Dept Epis Ch Exec Coun New York NY 1954-1958; R S Matt's Epis Ch Fairbanks AK 1951-1954; Asst S Jas Epis Ch Houston TX 1949-1951. LHD Epis TS of the SW 1990; DD STUSo 1988; DD VTS 1974.

CHASE, Alexis M (At) PO Box 286, Decatur GA 30031 **Dio Atlanta Atlanta GA 2014-** B Elizabethtown KY 1978 d Robert & Audrey. BA Tufts U 2000; MDiv SFTS 2006; Angl Stds CDSP 2014. D 5/22/2013 P 6/21/2014 Bp Robert Christopher Wright. c 1. vicar@holycomforter-atlanta.org

CHASE JR, Benjamin Otis (Vt) 95 Worcester Village Rd, Worcester VT 05682 B Boston MA 1939 s Benjamin & Dorothy. BA Norwich U 1962; BD CDSP 1965. D 6/26/1965 Bp John Melville Burgess P 5/1/1966 Bp Henry Knox Sherrill. m 8/14/1965 Alberta V Chase c 2. Mssy Dio Cyprus and the Gulf- Yemen UAE Oman 2001-2011; Exec Coun Appointees New York NY 1988-1999; R Chr Ch Montpelier VT 1982-1988; Vic S Lk's Fair Haven VT 1978-1982; Vic S Mk's-S Lk's Epis Mssn Fair Haven VT 1978-1981; Vic Gr Ch Sheldon VT 1973-1978; R H Trin Epis Ch Swanton VT 1973-1978; S Jn's Ch Highgate Ctr VT 1973-1978; S Lk's Ch Alburg VT 1973-1978; Chapl USN 1970-1973; Serv Angl Ch Of Can 1967-1970; S Paul's Ch Canaan VT 1967-1970; Vic S Steph's Epis Mssn Colebrook NH 1967-1970; Cur Gr Ch Manchester NH 1965-1967; Consult St. Geo's Collage Jerusalem 2000.

CHASE, Christopher (Cal) 10885 Caminito Cuesta, San Diego CA 92131 **P Dio California San Francisco CA 2014-** B Boston MA 1960 s Harry & Norma. BA U of Nottingham 1984; MA Bos 1991; Cert EDS 1996. D 9/8/1996 P 5/18/1997 Bp M(Arvil) Thomas Shaw. m 10/2/1993 Rebecca Chase c 2. Ch Of The Gd Samar San Diego CA 2006-2014; Dio E Tennessee Knoxville TN 2002-2006; S Fran' Ch Norris TN 1998-2002; Asst to R S Anne's In The Fields Epis Ch Lincoln MA 1996-1998. chris@braidmission.org

CHASE IV, Edwin Theodore (Ted) (LI) 432 Lakeville Road, The Church of St. Philip and St. James, Lake Success NY 11042 **Vic Dio Long Island Garden City NY 2014-, Bp's Cmsn on Recovery Mnstrs 1984-1994; S Phil And S Jas Ch New Hyde Pk NY 2011-; P in Charge The Ch Of S Lk and S Matt Brooklyn NY 2011-, Vic for Pstr & Hisp Mnstrs 1993-2012** B Philadelphia PA 1947 s Edwin & Lois. BA Laf 1969; MDiv GTS 1973. D 6/23/ 1973 Bp Robert Lionne DeWitt P 12/22/1973 Bp Adrian Delio Caceres-Villavicencio. c 2. Cur for Hisp Mnstry S Geo's Par Flushing NY 2009-2010; Vic The Ch of St. Mich and St. Mk Brooklyn NY 1984-1993; Latin & Spanish Tchr Brooklyn Friends Sch Brooklyn NY 1979-2013; R Ch Of Calv And S Cyp Brooklyn NY 1979-1984; Cur & Asst Hd of Sch Chr Ch and H Fam Brooklyn NY 1975-1979; R S Nich' Ch Quito Ecuador 1973-1975; Misionero Universitario 1973-1975; Profesor del Seminario para Diáconos Indígenas 1973-1975. Transltr, "El Libro de Oración Común," Ch Pub, 1989. Soc of Cath Priests 2013. tchaseiv@aol.com

CHASE JR, John Garvey (Tex) P.O. Box 103, Crockett TX 75835 **Vic All SS Epis Ch Crockett TX 2009-, Vic 2008-2009, Lay Vic 2006-2008; Safeguarding Mstr Trnr Dio Texas Houston TX 2013-, Wrld Mssn Bd Mem 2013-; Mem/Secy Houston Cnty Chld Welf Bd 1994-** B Concord MA 1947 s John & June. BA Coll of the H Cross 1969; Cert Iona Sch for Mnstry 2008. D 6/28/ 2008 Bp Don Adger Wimberly P 1/17/2009 Bp Rayford Baines High Jr. m 7/9/ 1980 Rosalie Cooper-Chase. Lay Pstr Ldr All SS Epis Ch 2005-2008. jgchase@valornet.com

CHASE, Katharine Barnhardt (SwVa) PO Box 810, Amherst VA 24521 B Bronxville NY 1944 d Eugene & Catherine. BA Sweet Briar Coll 1967; MAT JHU 1968; EdSpec U of Virginia 1974; BS Lynchburg Coll 1984. D 8/19/2006 Bp Neff Powell. m 6/29/1968 Robert Leslie Chase c 2.

CHASE, Peter Gray Otis (Mass) 258 Concord St, Newton MA 02462 **Pres, Cler Assoc. Dio Massachussetts 2005-** B Frankfurt NY 1947 s Benjamin & Dorothy. BA Bishops U QC CA 1971; MDiv CDSP 1980. D 3/25/1982 P 2/1/ 1983 Bp Charles Shannon Mallory. m 1/29/1977 Kathleen Gowdy-Chase c 2. R S Mary's Ch Newton Lower Falls MA 1992-2009; Bountiful Cmnty Ch Bountiful UT 1983-1992; R Resurr Bountiful UT 1983-1992; S Andr's Ch Saratoga CA 1982-1983.

CHASE JR, Randall (Mass) PO Box 924, Barnstable MA 02630 B Sanford FL 1946 s Randall & Julia. BS Florida St U 1968; MDiv VTS 1972; DMin Bos 1980. D 6/1/1972 P 12/13/1972 Bp William Hopkins Folwell. c 2. EDS Cambridge MA 2007-2010, Actg Pres & Dn of Admin 2006-2009, 1984-1989; Exec Off Prov Of New Engl 2003-2006; Cn to the Ordnry Dio Rhode Island Providence RI 1997-2003; Epis Ch 1994-2000; S Eliz's Ch Sudbury MA 1991-1997; Int Par Of The Epiph Winchester MA 1990-1991; Dio Massachusetts Boston MA 1989-1990; R Chap Of S Andr Boca Raton FL 1980-1984; Epis Ch Of The H Fam Miami FL 1979-1980; Sarasota Dnry Chapl Sarasota FL 1974-1978; Asst R S Dav's Epis Ch Lakeland FL 1972-1974; Dir Credo Inst Inc. Memphis TN 2003-2012; Trst The CPG New York NY 2000-2012; Exec Coun Dom And Frgn Mssy Soc- Epis Ch Cntr New York NY 1994-2000. ECom; ESMHE; Ord Of S Anne; Soc Of S Jn The Evang. rchase@eds.edu

CHASSE, Richard P (Nwk) 176 Palisade Ave, Jersey City NJ 07306 **Chapl Vcu-Mcu Cancer Cntr 1972-** B Hartford CT 1941 s Eudore & Rita. AA Lasalette Jr Coll 1961; BA Lasalette Major Sem 1964; MA Assumption Coll 1972. Rec 11/

1/1975 as Priest Bp Robert Bruce Hall. m 9/15/1973 Jean Chasse c 1. Chr Hosp Jersey City NJ 1979-1999; Serv RC Ch 1967-1972. Auth, "Cancer Trends"; Auth, "Leukemia & The Fam".

CHASSEY JR, George Irwin (USC) 9b Exum Dr, West Columbia SC 29169 **Ret 1989-** B Bridgewater MA 1921 s George & Merriel. U of Paris FR 1945; BA Stetson U 1951; MA Stetson U 1955; Sewanee: The U So, TS 1959. D 9/12/1959 P 9/29/1960 Bp Clarence Alfred Cole. m 1/14/1943 Mary Chassey c 3. Dep GC Dio Upper So Carolina Columbia SC 1985-1989, Cn Admin 1983-1984; Cn Mssnr for Stwdshp and Dvlpmt Dio Los Angeles Los Angeles CA 1980-1983; Cn to Bp So Carolina Charleston SC 1969-1980; R H Trin Epis Ch Charleston SC 1963-1969; R Ch Of The H Apos Barnwell SC 1961-1963; Asst S Martins-In-The-Field Columbia SC 1959-1961.

CHASTAIN, Gordon Lee (Ind) 1769 Dunaway Ct, Indianapolis IN 46228 **Ret 2001-** B Indianapolis IN 1938 s Charles & Thelma. BA DePauw U 1959; STB Ya Berk 1962. D 6/17/1962 P 12/16/1962 Bp John P Craine. m 10/18/ 2011 Thomas E Honderich c 3. R All SS Ch Indianapolis IN 1994-2001; The Damien Cntr Indianapolis IN 1990-1994; Cur S Paul's Epis Ch Indianapolis IN 1969-1978; R S Andr's Epis Ch Greencastle IN 1966-1968; S Chris's Epis Ch Carmel IN 1962-1966; Vic S Ptr's Ch Lebanon IN 1962-1966; Dep GC Dio Indianapolis Indianapolis IN 2000-2003, Stndg Com 1968-1999. Bd NEAC 1995-2003; Chair, Bd Natl Epis Hlth Mnstrs 2006-2010; Oblate, Ord of Julian of Norwich 2011.

CHATFIELD, Jane Sheldon (Me) 11 White St, Rockland ME 04841 B Boston MA 1941 d John & Jane. D 6/29/2013 Bp Stephen Taylor Lane. m 6/11/1974 John Snowden Chatfield c 3.

CHATFIELD, Jenifer (Los) **P S Jas Par Los Angeles CA 2014-** B Long Beach CA 1963 d Kenneth & Kathleen. BA U CA, Irvine 1985; MFA U fo California, Los Angeles 2005; MDiv Ya Berk 2013. D 6/8/2013 Bp Mary Douglas Glasspool P 1/11/2014 Bp Diane Jardine Bruce. c 1.

CHATHAM, Charles Erwin (Az) 500 S Jackson St, Wickenburg AZ 85390 B Fort Worth TX 1942 s Charles & Martha. Sam Houston St U 1961; BS Baylor U 1964; MDiv Epis TS of the SW 1970. D 6/18/1970 Bp Frederick P Goddard P 6/24/1971 Bp James Milton Richardson. m 6/23/1961 Melynda Ann Ricketts c 3. R S Alb's Epis Ch Wickenburg AZ 2000-2004; R Gr Ch Morganton NC 1992-2000; R S Mk's Epis Ch Abilene TX 1982-1991; Vic S Steph's Epis Ch Jacksonville AR 1980-1982; Vic All SS Farmington NM 1980; Assoc S Mk's Epis Ch Little Rock AR 1976-1980; Vic S Lk's Ch Rusk TX 1975-1976; Vic Trin Ch Jacksonville TX 1975-1976; P-in-c S Jas Epis Ch Ft McKavett TX 1974; Dir S Andr's Farm Waco TX 1973-1975; Vic S Jas' Epis Ch TX 1970-1975; R S Lk's Epis Ch Salado TX 1970-1973. Alumi Assn, Epis TS of the Southw 1970; CHS 1978; Ord of S Ben 1985. cmchatham1@msn.com

CHATTIN, Mark Haney (NJ) 839 Haddon Ave., Collingswood NJ 08108 **R H Trin Ch Collingswood NJ 1998-; GC--Alt Dep Dio New Jersey Trenton NJ 2008-, Dn--Camden Convcation 2007-, Stndg Com 2005-2008** B Philadelphia PA 1953 s Lloyd & Mary. BA Glassboro St U 1975; MDiv SWTS 1978. D 6/3/1978 P 12/16/1978 Bp Albert Wiencke Van Duzer. m 6/27/1974 Theresa H Chattin c 6. S Fran Ch Dunellen NJ 1980-1998; Vic Ch Of The H Innoc Dunellen NJ 1979-1980; Chapl Greenbrook And Ashbrook Nrsng Hm 1978-1998; Vic S Andr's Ch Plainfield NJ 1978-1980; H Cross Epis Ch Plainfield NJ 1978-1979; Cur St Andrews Ch Plainfield NJ 1978-1979. OHC, Angl Soc. holytrinity1@verizon.net

CHAVEZ, Karen Sue (Los) 3160 Graceland Way, Corona CA 92882 B Pheonix AZ 1948 d William & Eula. Cert of Deaconal Stds ETSBH 1982; BS USC 1982. D 12/2/2006 Bp Joseph Jon Bruno. m 7/3/1994 Louis Chavez c 3.

CHAVEZ, Rafael (Hond) B 1941 m 8/13/1993 Eufemia Lopez De Chavez. Dio Honduras San Pedro Sula 1998-2013.

CHAVEZ, Velma (Wyo) 29 Shipton Lane, Fort Washakie WY 82514 **D Shoshone Epis Mssn Ft Washakie WY 1999-** B Fort Washakie WY 1930 d Wallace & Winnie. D 8/28/2001 Bp Bruce Caldwell.

CHAVEZ FRANCO, Juan Eloy (EcuL) Iglesia Episcopal del Ecuador-Diocesis Litoral, Amarilis Fuente 603, Avenida 09015250, Guayaquil Ecuador Ecuador B Montecristi 1960 s Fernando & Angela. D 4/13/2008 Bp Terencio Alfredo Morante-Espana. m 8/15/2007 Rosario U Serrano Castro c 3. D Litoral Dio Ecuador Guayaquil 2008-2012.

CHECO, Antonio (LI) 2510 30th Rd Apt 2L, Astoria NY 11102 **D S Mk's Ch Jackson Heights NY 2008-** B Dominican Republic 1952 s Ramon & Dolores. MDiv GTS; MDiv GTS; ScD Docmm 1981; MS Ford 1991. D 1/18/2007 P 4/ 25/2008 Bp Orris George Walker Jr. m 7/22/2014 Starlin E Fermin-Rosa.

CHEE, David T (Los) 700 Devils Drop Ct, El Sobrante CA 94803 B Singapore 1948 s Siew & Swee. BA Natl Taiwan U 1971; MA Natl Taiwan U 1973; Taipei Theol Coll Tw 1974; CDSP 1980; DMin PSR 1983. D 8/24/1975 P 6/11/1977 Bp James T M Pong. m 1/25/1975 Amy Bih-Yin Chee c 3. R S Gabr's Par Monterey Pk CA 1999-2005; Dio Los Angeles Los Angeles CA 1998-1999; Chr Epis Ch Los Altos CA 1995-1998; Chinese Mssnr Dio California San Francisco CA 1993-1998, 1993-1994; R Gd Shpd Taipei Tw 1985-1993; Vic H Trin Keelung Taipei Tw 1982-1985; Dio Taiwan Taipei 1975-1993. Auth, "Epistemology Of Tao"; Auth, "Turning To God In Taiwan: A Study Of Conversion". hsutze8@gmail.com

CHEEK, Alison Mary (Mass) Po Box 356, Tenants Harbor ME 04860 **Pstr Psych Past Couns/Cons Ctrs Gr Washington DC 1986-** B Adelaide South Australia AU 1927 d Hedley & Dora. BA U of Adelaide Au 1947; MDiv VTS 1969; DMin EDS 1990. D 1/29/1972 Bp Robert Bruce Hall P 7/29/1974 Bp Edward Randolph Welles II. m 5/8/1948 Bruce M Cheek. Fac; Dir Stds In Feminist Liberation Theol EDS Cambridge MA 1989-1995; Assoc Trin Memi Ch Philadelphia PA 1980-1982; Asst Ch Of S Steph And The Incarn Washington DC 1975-1979; Asst D S Alb's Epis Ch Annandale VA 1972-1974; Asst Chr Ch Alexandria VA 1969-1971. Auth, "Journ Of Pstr Psych"; Auth, "Time"; Auth, "Shifting The Paradigm: Feminist Bible Study," *Searching Scripture: Feminist Intro.* CHS, EWHP; Greenfire Retreat Cntr For Wmn. Paradigm Shift Awd - Courage, Faith/Change Gndr Priesthood 1999; Scarlett Awd - Courag'S Contrib'N To Life Of Ch 1994; Cover Article Time mag 1976; Mnstry To Wmn 1975.

CHEESMAN JR, Benbow Palmer (Mil) 2501 S 60th St, Milwaukee WI 53219 B Charlottesville VA 1942 s Benbow & Lucile. Mia 1963; BA Morris Harvey Coll 1964; STB GTS 1967; JD U of Wisconsin 1986. D 6/12/1967 P 12/20/1967 Bp Wilburn Camrock Campbell. m 5/17/1969 Gail Cheesman. S Paul's Epis Ch Beloit WI 2003; Non-par 1975-1998; Cur S Mk's Ch Milwaukee WI 1973-1975; Gd Shpd Epis Ch Sun Prairie WI 1971-1973; Asst Gr Ch Madison WI 1971-1973; Vic S Chad's Sun Prairie WI 1971-1973; Dio W Virginia Charleston WV 1967-1971; Vic S Dav's Ch Nitro WV 1967-1971; Vic S Jas Ch Charleston WV 1967-1971; Chapl Wvsc Inst 1967-1970; Eccl Crt Dio Milwaukee Milwaukee WI 2005-2011. Auth, "Plain Lang Legal Guide To Helping Elderly Clients," *Plain Lang Legal Guide*, Cntr for Publ Representation, 1985. Cmnty Of S Mary 1971.

CHEFFEY, Anne Davis (WMo) 3 Northwoods Dr, Kimberling City MO 65686 **Dio W Missouri Kansas City MO 2014-** B Kansas City MO 1954 d James & LaVonne. BFA Missouri St U 1980; Cert of Angl Bp Kemper Sch for Mnstry 2014. D 2/3/2001 Bp Barry Howe P 4/26/2014 Bp Martin Scott Field. m 4/25/1984 Dean C Cheffey c 2.

CHEN, Charles Chin-Ti (Tai) 23 Wu-Chuan West Road, 403, Taichung Taiwan **R Emer S Jas's Tw 2005-** B Matou TW 1935 s Lau-Kuai & LeeMian. MDiv Tainan Theol Coll and Sem TW 1969; DMin Sewanee: The U So, TS 1993. D 6/29/1969 Bp James Chang L Wong P 6/1/1970 Bp Charles P Gilson. m 1/8/1959 Mary Jo Chen c 3. Int R S Jas's Tw 2001-2005; R S Jas's Tw 1986-2001; Vic S Andr's Chading Taipei Tw 1983-1986; Vic S Mk's Pintung Taipei Tw 1977-1982; Dio Taiwan Taipei 1969-2000; Chapl & Comptroller St.Jn's & St. Mary's of S Jn's ; St. Mary's Tech U 1969-1975. Auth, "Morning Star"; Auth, "Resurr & Eternal Life"; Auth, "Introducing Chrsnty to Non-Chr In Taiwan". Apos Transformational Stewardship Awd TEN of The Epis Ch 2012; Fell Amer Coll of Dentists 1992.

CHEN, Luke Hh (Tai) No 67 Lane 314 Ming Shen Rd, Shin Hua County, Tainan Hsien 71246 Taiwan B Taiwan 1940 s Tin-Lu & Chin. BS Kaohsiung Med U 1965; MDiv Tainan Theol Coll and Sem TW 1983. D 7/25/1979 Bp James T M Pong P 7/1/1983 Bp Poi-Yeung Cheung. m 5/20/1967 Su-yuan Lin c 3. P-in-c S Lk's Hualien Tw 1999-2000; P-in-c S Paul's Kaoshiung Tw 1989-1999; P-in-c S Andr's Kaoshiung Hsien Tw 1986-1989; Cur S Jas' Taichung Tw 1984-1985; Dio Taiwan Taipei 1983-2000; P-in-c S Lk's Hualien Tw 1983-1984; D S Mich's Chap Tainan Tw 1980-1983.

CHEN, Samuel Ta-Tung (Tai) 7 Lane 105, South Hangchow R, Taipei Taiwan **Died 9/25/2015** B 1924 s Sung-Lu & Pei-Lan. Oxf GB; BD Tainan Theol Coll and Sem TW 1964. D 9/19/1962 Bp Harry Sherbourne Kennedy P 9/1/1963 Bp Charles P Gilson. m 11/1/1965 Hsio-Hua Chen c 3. Dn So Cathd Taipei Tw 1975-1986; Cn To The Ordnry So Cathd Taipei Tw 1973-2015; P-in-c S Ptr's Ch Chiayi Tw 1964-1971; Dio Taiwan Taipei 1962-1990; Vic S Ptr's Ch Chi-ayi Tw 1962-1964. Auth, "Hist Of 1st 20 Years Of Tai Epis Ch".

CHENEY III, Arthur Milton (WMass) 38 Barnes Ln, West Greenwich RI 02817 **Supply P Ch Of The Redeem Sarasota FL 2014-; Ret Ret 2003-** B Worcester MA 1936 s Arthur & Helen. BA Hobart and Wm Smith Colleges 1958; LTh Ya Berk 1961; MA Providence Coll 1996. D 6/20/1961 P 12/23/1961 Bp Robert McConnell Hatch. m 4/19/1986 Lois B Cheney c 3. Dio Wstrn Massachusetts Springfield 1996-2003; R S Jn's Ch Athol MA 1996-2003; R S Mary's Ch Warwick RI 1975-1996; Asst Chr Ch Fitchburg MA 1967-1975; P-in-c S Andr's Woonsocket RI 1961-1967; P-t Asst S Jas Woonsocket RI 1961-1967; Vic S Jn's Ch Millville MA 1961-1967. GAS 2011; NOEL 1975; New Engl CCU 1961-2010.

CHENEY, Barbara T (Ct) 90 Rogers Rd, Hamden CT 06517 B Fort Lauderdale FL 1943 d Robert & June. BA Connecticut Coll 1963; MDiv VTS 1980; DMin SWTS 2000. D 6/2/1980 Bp Frederick Barton Wolf P 12/27/1980 Bp H Coleman Mcgehee Jr. m 9/26/1981 Knight Dexter Cheney c 2. Stndg Com Dio Connecticut Meriden CT 1997-2002; R S Paul And S Jas New Haven CT 1993-2010; Dio Michigan Detroit MI 1992-1993, Long Range Plnng Com 1985-1986, Bd Exam Liturgists 1981-1988; Chapl E Detroit Police And Fire

Departments 1988-1993; S Gabr's Epis Ch Eastpointe MI 1985-1993; Asst S Jn's Ch Royal Oak MI 1980-1985; Bd Pres VTS Alexandria VA 1998-1999. Auth, *H Baptism: A Rite for the Reconstituting of Sacr Commun,OPEN*, AP, 2003. Ecam Dio Michigan 1989-1990; Soc of Comp of the H Cross 2001. Hon Cn Chr Ch Cathd Hartford CT 2010.

CHENEY SR, Bruce David (SVa) St Paul Episcopal Church, 221 34th St, Newport News VA 23607 **S Paul's Ch Newport News VA 2016-; Chapl Legacy Hospice Sikeston MO 2012-; Asst P S Paul's Epis Ch Sikeston MO 2012-** B Manchester NH 1960 s George & Claire. BS New Sch U 1986; MPS Loyola U 2000; MDiv VTS 2006. D 6/24/2006 P 2/7/2007 Bp Peter J Lee. m 2/17/1979 Nancy S Allen c 2. Vic H Cross Epis Ch Olive Branch MS 2006-2011.

CHENEY, Knight Dexter (Ct) 90 Rogers Rd, Hamden CT 06517 **P-in-c Ch of the H Sprt W Haven CT 2007-** B Cleveland OH 1941 s Thomas & Anne. BBA Nichols Coll 1964; MBA U of Oregon 1969; MDiv EDS 1980. D 6/14/1980 Bp David Henry Lewis Jr P 1/1/1981 Bp H Coleman Mcgehee Jr. m 9/26/1981 Barbara T Cheney. Ch of the H Sprt W Haven CT 2007-2008, 2005-2006; Dio Connecticut Meriden CT 2006; Ch Of S Jn By The Sea W Haven W Haven CT 2005-2006; All SS' Epis Ch E Hartford CT 2002-2008; Grtr Hartford Reg Mnstry E Hartford CT 2002-2004; S Mk's Chap Storrs CT 2001-2002; Int S Mich's Ch Naugatuck CT 2000-2001; S Geo's Ch Middlebury CT 1998-2000; Middlesex Area Cluster Mnstry Higganum CT 1998; St Gabr's Ch E Berlin CT 1997; Interfaith Coop Mnstrs New Haven CT 1994-1996; All SS Ch Ivoryton CT 1993-1995; Admin Dio Michigan Detroit MI 1985-1993; S Columba Ch Detroit MI 1980-1985; Mssnr in Charge Grtr Hartford Reg Mnstry E Hartford CT; Int St. Mk's Chap Storrs CT. Auth, *Checkpoint*. Testimonial Resolution & Sprt of Detroit Awd Detroit City Coun.

CHENEY, Michael Robert (Mass) 117 Forest St, Malden MA 02148 **Fac S Mich Conf For Yth 1980-** B New Haven CT 1960 s Milton & Leanne. BA Hobart and Wm Smith Colleges 1982; MDiv GTS 1992. D 6/13/1992 P 12/19/1992 Bp Andrew Frederick Wissemann. m 5/1/1999 Dana L Neptune c 1. R S Paul's Ch Malden MA 1996-2000; Assoc Ch Of The Nativ Northborough MA 1992-1996; Dio Wstrn Massachusetts Springfield 1992-1996, Chair Yth Com 1984-1986; Ecum Yth Min Trin Epis Ch Ware MA 1983-1985. Fllshp Of The Way Of The Cross.

CHENEY, Peter Gunn (Az) 5090 N Via Gelsomino, Tucson AZ 85750 **Sr Search Consult Carney Sandoe and Assoc 2008-; Chapl S Ann's Ch Kennebunkport ME 2002-** B Worcester MA 1947 s Francis & Winona. BA Transylvania U 1969; MDiv VTS 1975; DD Sewanee: The U So, TS 2003. D 6/11/1975 P 3/25/1976 Bp Lloyd Edward Gressle. m 10/6/2012 Kirsten S Fenik. Int Headmaster St. Richard's Sch Indianapolis IN 2007-2008; Natl Assoc of Epis Schools New York NY 1998-2007; Natl Assoc Of Epis Schools- Epis Ch New York NY 1998-2007; Assoc S Phil's In The Hills Tucson AZ 1993-1998; Int S Andr's Epis Ch Contoocook NH 1984-1987; Chapl and Admssns Dir S Paul's Sch 1983-1992; S Paul's Sch Concord NH 1983-1992; R S Geo's Epis Ch Hellertown PA 1977-1983; Asst Ch Of The Gd Shpd And S Jn Milford PA 1975-1977; Asst Gr Epis Ch Port Jervis NY 1975-1977. Auth, "Three Truths of the Sprtl Life," *NAES Pamphlet*, 2002; Auth, "Schools and Parents: Partnr in Lrng and Dvlpmt," *NAES Pamphlet*, 2000; Auth, "Gd Schools," *Ntwk*, 2000; Auth, "The Epis Sch Trst as Ambassador," *Ntwk*, 2000; Auth, "Ldrshp," *Educational Directions*, 1999. Amer Associations of Pstr Counselors, Clincl Mem 1982. Jn D. Verdery Awd NAES 2014.

CHENEY II, Reynolds (WTenn) 60 Eastland Dr, Memphis TN 38111 **Died 7/10/2017** B Jackson MS 1936 s Reynolds & Winifred. BA Millsaps Coll 1957; U of Pennsylvania 1960; BD EDS 1961. D 6/16/1961 Bp Duncan Montgomery Gray P 12/1/1961 Bp John Maury Allin. m 11/26/1999 Stephanie Cheney c 3. S Mary's Cathd Memphis TN 2002; Ch Of The H Comm Memphis TN 1981-2002; R S Jas Ch Greenville MS 1968-1981; Vic Ch Of The Redeem Greenville MS 1968-1971; R S Jn's Ch Aberdeen MS 1963-1968; Vic S Mich & All Ang' Amory MS 1963-1968; D Gr Ch Carrollton MS 1961-1963; D-in-c S Clem's Ch Vaiden MS 1961-1963; S Mary's Ch Lexington MS 1961-1963; S Matt's Epis Ch Kosciusko MS 1961-1963; Cn Chapl to Cler Families and Ret Cler Dio W Tennessee Memphis 2007-2017.

CHENG, Chen Chang (Tai) 499, Sec 4 Tam King Rd, Tamsui Dist, New Taipei City Taiwan 25135 Taiwan **Dio Taiwan Taipei 2012-** B Ping Tung Taiwan 1961 MA Natl Taipei U of Tech 2004; MA Fu Jon Cath U 2011. D 4/27/2012 Bp Jung-Hsin Lai. m 9/18/1988 Yun Line Yao c 2.

CHENG, Ching-Shan (Tai) 40 Ta Tung Rd, Wu Feng, Taichung County 852 Taiwan **Dio Taiwan Taipei 2007-** B Tainan Taiwan 1953 s Kao & Bi-Yun. MDiv Tainan Theol Coll And Sem; MDiv Tainan Theol Coll And Sem; BA Taiwan Normal U. D 3/31/2007 P 3/29/2008 Bp Jung-Hsin Lai. m 12/19/1977 Kuo-Li Chi c 2.

CHENG, Patrick S (NY) 19 E 34th St, New York NY 10016 **Affiliated Assoc Prof of Theol Chicago TS Chicago IL 2015-; Assoc P Ch Of The Trsfg New York NY 2015-; Chf Compliance Off The CPG New York NY 2014-** B Kowloon Hong Kong 1968 s Richard & Deanna. BA Ya 1990; JD Harv 1993; MA UTS 2001; MPhil UTS 2009; PhD UTS 2010. D 6/7/2014 Bp M(Arvil) Thomas Shaw P 1/10/2015 Bp Alan Gates. m 7/27/2011 Michael J Boothroyd.

Asstg P St. Barth Ch New York NY 2015; Assoc Prof of Hist and Systematic Theol EDS Cambridge MA 2014.

CHERBONNEAU, Allen Robert (Ala) 4367 East River Road, Box 282, Mentone AL 35984 B Springfield MA 1944 s Vincent & Rita. BA U of Massachusetts 1967; MDiv TESM 1995. D 11/22/1995 P 5/1/1996 Bp Keith Lynn Ackerman. m 6/23/1973 Jan Cynthia Barket. R S Jos's On-The-Mtn Mentone AL 1996-2000.

CHERBONNIER, Edmond La Beaume (Mo) 843 Prospect Ave, Hartford CT 06105 **Died 3/7/2017** B Saint Louis MO 1918 s Edward & Adelaide. BA Harv 1939; BD UTS 1947; BA U of Cambridge 1948; PhD Col 1951; U of Vermont 1959. D 5/28/1947 Bp William Scarlett. m 4/11/2017 Phyllis White Cherbonnier c 1. Ret 1990-2017; D Dio Connecticut Meriden CT 1947-1990; Dio New York New York NY 1947-1990. Auth, "Hardness Of Heart".

CHERISME, Charles M. (Hai) 472 Beech St, Roslindale MA 02131 **Assoc Ch Of The H Sprt Mattapan MA 1989-; R H Sprt Lascabobas 1967-** B Port-de-Paix 1936 s Joseph & Derina. Coll of S Pierre HT 1962; ETSC 1966. D 12/4/1965 P 6/4/1966 Bp Charles Alfred Voegeli. c 4. R Our Lady Port-au-Prince Ht 1986-1988; R H Cross Leogane Ht 1970-1986; R S Paul's Montrouis Ht 1968-1970; Cur S Ptr's Mirebalais Ht 1966-1968; Dio Haiti Port-au-Prince HT 1965-1990. Ord Of S Marg 1968.

CHERRY, Charles Shuler (Minn) 734 7th St S, Breckenridge MN 56520 B Durham NC 1934 s Albert & Tommie. BA Wake Forest U 1956; STB GTS 1967; MA Spalding U 1973; MA No Dakota St U 1993. D 10/14/1967 P 11/1/1968 Bp Charles Gresham Marmion. m 5/29/1993 Shirley Cherry c 2. S Jn's Ch Moorhead MN 1995-1998, P-in-c 1991-1995; Non-par 1988-1989; R Trin Ch Wahpeton ND 1985-1988; R S Jas' Epis Ch Fergus Falls MN 1985-1987; R St Georges Epis Ch Asheville NC 1979-1985; Vic S Mart's-In-The-Fields Mayfield KY 1978-1979; Vic S Ptr's of the Lakes Gilbertsville KY 1978-1979; R Ch Of Our Merc Sav Louisville KY 1972-1977; Vic S Ptr's-In-The-Vlly Vlly Sta KS 1967-1972.

CHERRY, Jacqueline Ann (Cal) 1076 De Haro St, San Francisco CA 94107 **D Beekeeper Julian Apiaries San Francisco CA 2011-; D Beekeeper The Epis Ch Of S Jn The Evang San Francisco CA 2009-** B San Diego CA 1961 d William & Mary. BA U CA Santa Cruz 1983; RN San Francisco St U 2000; BA California Sch for Deacons 2008. D 6/6/2009 Bp Marc Handley Andrus. m 10/23/2008 Elizabeth Freeman c 1.

CHERRY, Mary Jane (Ky) Episcopal Church Home, 7504 Westport Rd, Louisville KY 40222 **S Lk's Chap Louisville KY 2015-, D 2015-** B Louisville KY 1951 d Lee & Mary. (All but dissertation completed) U of Louisville; BA U of Kentucky 1978; MA U of Louisville 1996. D 4/17/2010 Bp Ted Gulick Jr. m 8/12/1978 Stephen Cherry. D S Andr's Ch Louisville KY 2012-2015, D 2012-2015; Dio Kentucky Louisville KY 2010-2011, D 2010-2011.

CHERRY, Timothy B (Dal) 56 Cedar Ln, Osterville MA 02655 **R Ch Of The Apos Coppell TX 2009-** B Portsmouth VA 1965 s Aaron & Kay. BS USNA 1988; MDiv VTS 1997. D 6/14/1997 Bp Peter J Lee P 3/13/1998 Bp Frank Clayton Matthews. m 11/25/1989 Jennifer L Cherry c 3. Ch Of The H Cross Paris TX 2007-2009; R S Ptr's Ch Osterville MA 2000-2007; Cur Chr Ch St Michaels Par S Mich MD 1997-2000. Mdiv cl VTS 1997.

CHERY, Jean (Hai) B Haiti 1982 s Maccena & Marie. D 11/1/2009 P 6/29/2010 Bp Jean Zache Duracin. m 4/7/2011 Emilie Milord Chery c 1. Dio Haiti Port-au-Prince HT 2009-2016.

CHERY, Marie Carmel (Hai) **Dio Haiti Port-au-Prince HT 2012-** B 1983 d Edward & Clercia. Undergradute Publ Libr System 2005; Grad Sem of Theol 2011. D 7/29/2012 P 3/13/2014 Bp Jean Zache Duracin.

CHESHIRE, Grady Patterson (WNC) 1131 S Edgemont Ave, Gastonia NC 28054 B Charlotte NC 1950 s John & Phyllis. BA Erskine Coll 1972. D 12/21/1996 Bp Bob Johnson. m 10/13/1984 Kathy Ann Bailey. D All SS' Epis Ch Gastonia NC 1996-2005.

CHESNEY, Jonathan C (Ala) 608 Harper Ave, Auburn AL 36830 B Charlottesville VA 1983 s James & Valerie. BA Trin 2005; MDiv VTS 2014. D 6/7/2014 Bp John Mckee Sloan Sr P 12/4/2014 Bp Santosh K Marray. Asst H Trin Epis Ch Auburn AL 2014-2017; Ch Of The Ascen Montgomery AL 2008-2011.

CHESNUT, Mark Douglas (Alb) **Dio Albany Greenwich NY 2015-** D 5/31/2014 P 12/14/2014 Bp William Howard Love.

CHESS, Jean D (Pgh) 1500 Cochran Rd Apt 901, Pittsburgh PA 15243 **D St Andrews Epis Ch Pittsburgh PA 2001-** B Pittsburgh PA 1958 d James & Nolly. BS Denison U 1980; MS Carnegie Mellon U 1988. D 6/10/2000 Bp Robert William Duncan. Dio Pittsburgh Pittsburgh PA 2014-2015; Chapl Forbes Hospice 2001-2003; D Calv Ch Pittsburgh PA 2000-2002. jchess@episcopalpgh.org

CHESTERMAN JR, Thomas Charles (DR) 2418 Hidden Valley Dr, Santa Rosa CA 95404 **Vic Emer True Sunshine Par San Francisco CA 2003-, Mssn Vic 1960-2002; Ret 1994-; Dep GC 1991-** B San Francisco CA 1931 s Charles & Helen. AB Harv 1953; MDiv Epis TS of the SW 1956; D.Phil Toledo E P ES 1978. D 7/1/1956 P 1/26/1957 Bp Karl M Block. c 3. Hisp Mssnr S Paul's Ch Healdsburg CA 2012; Speaker/Homilist Food for the Poor Natl Untd States 1999-2011; R & Dn Cathd Ch of St. Mich & All Ang Cuernavaca More 1993-1994; R Iglesia Epis Epifania Santo Domingo Di 1989-1992; Pstr Un Ch of Santo Domingo Dominican Republic 1989-1992; Prog. Host/Cmnty Affrs Dir. KUNR Reno Nevada 1988-1989; Headmaster Nova Acad Lake Tahoe California 1987-1988; Assoc Trin Epis Ch Reno NV 1981-1989; Chapl S Jn's Mltry Sch Salina KS 1978-1979; R Ch Of The Gd Shpd Silver City NM 1975-1977; Int S Cyp's Ch San Francisco CA 1975; Vic S Chris's Ch San Lorenzo CA 1966-1975; R S Barn Ch Arroyo Grande CA 1959-1960; Vic S Edm's Epis Ch Pacifica CA 1956-1959; Stndg Com Mem Dio The Dominican Republic (Iglesia Epis Dominicana) Gazcue Santo Domingo 1990-1992; Dioc Coun Mem Dio Wstrn Kansas Hutchinson KS 1978-1979; Supvsr Wstrn Par Trng Prog 1963-1973. Auth, "Records of Fest Celebration," *(Translation)*, La Hermandad Mozarabica, 1977. NNECA 1966-1975. Vic Emer True Sunshine Ch, San Francisco CA.

CHEVES, Henry Middleton (SC) 635 Foredeck Lane, Edisto Island SC 29438 B La Jolla CA 1944 s Henry & Chilton. BS U of So Carolina 1967; MBA Cit 1976; MDiv Sewanee: The U So, TS 1992. D 5/30/1992 P 11/30/1992 Bp John Clark Buchanan. m 7/27/1984 Susan Cheves c 4. Assoc R Epis Ch on Edisto Edisto Island SC 2003-2009; R S Paul's Ch Bennettsville SC 2000-2003; Vic S Paul's Epis Ch Lees Summit MO 1996-2000; Vic Trin Epis Ch Lebanon MO 1992-1996.

CHILD, Kendrick H (Mass) Po Box 2085, New London NH 03257 **Died 10/14/2016** B Brockton MA 1943 s Ralph & Lois. BA Bates Coll 1965; BD Yale DS 1965; DMin Bos 1990. D 6/21/1969 Bp Anson Phelps Stokes Jr P 12/21/1969 Bp Frederick Barton Wolf. m 8/23/1987 Pamela J Child c 2. S Aug's Ch Lawr MA 2005-2006; Assoc The Cathd Ch Of S Paul Boston MA 1993-1996; Asst S Paul's Ch Malden MA 1989-1993; Ch Of The Trsfg Derry NH 1982-1987; Reg Assoc for Evang and Renwl Prov I 1978-1989; R S Matt's Epis Ch Lisbon Falls ME 1970-1982; Cur Trin Epis Ch Portland ME 1969-1970; Serv Methodist Ch 1967-1968. Auth, "Don't Be Afraid To Say A Gd Word for Jesus," *Sem Dvlpmt News*, 1997; Auth, "One Among Many: Sem Dvlpmt in a U Setting," *Sem Dvlpmt News*, 1992.

CHILDERS, Robert T J (ETenn) Church of the Good Shepherd, P.O. Box 145, Lookout Mountain TN 37350 **R Ch Of The Gd Shpd Lookout Mtn TN 2008-; COM Dio Alabama Birmingham 2002-, Dioc Coun 1995-2001** B Selma AL 1954 s Benjamin & Hallie. BA Van 1978; JD U of Alabama 1981; MDiv GTS 1991. D 6/18/1991 P 12/21/1991 Bp Robert Oran Miller. m 10/28/1981 Teresa Childers c 2. R Gr Ch Anniston AL 1995-2008; R S Jos's On-The-Mtn Mentone AL 1993-1995; Cur Chr Ch Tuscaloosa AL 1991-1993. robert@gslookout.com

CHILDRESS JR, John (Ark) 10702 Crestdale Ln, Little Rock AR 72212 B Canton MS 1952 s John & Virginia. BS Mississippi St U 1974; MDiv SWTS 1989. D 6/3/1989 P 12/21/1989 Bp Duncan Montgomery Gray Jr. m 8/11/1978 Pamela DeGraw c 2. Epis Collgt Sch Little Rock AR 2004-2016; R S Paul's Newport AR 1996-2004; R S Paul's Ch Abbeville LA 1995-1996; S Fran Of Assisi Ch Philadelphia MS 1989-1995; Vic S Matt's Epis Ch Kosciusko MS 1989-1995.

CHILES, Bob (USC) The Reverend Robert L Chiles, 103 Underwood Dr, Hendersonville NC 28739 **Curs Coun Dio Upper So Carolina Columbia SC 2013-, Sch for Mnstry Com 2003-2010, COM 2008-2011; Assoc Chr Ch Greenville SC 2011-** B Greenville SC 1952 s Jack & Margaret. BA Furman U 1974; MDiv SWTS 1990. D 6/9/1990 P 5/16/1991 Bp William Arthur Beckham. m 5/3/1975 Christine Z Chiles c 2. R S Dav's Epis Ch Columbia SC 1996-2011; COM Dio Nthrn Indiana So Bend IN 1993-1995; Asst S Jn The Evang Ch Elkhart IN 1991-1996; D S Barth's Ch No Augusta SC 1990-1991. BA cl Furman U 1974.

CHILESE, Sandra Lee (Az) **SS Phil And Jas Morenci AZ 2015-** B Gross Pointe MI 1954 d William & Dorothy. B.S Arizona St U 1984; Dplma of Angl Stds Epis TS Of The SW 2015; Dplma Sem of the SW 2015. D 6/6/2015 Bp Kirk Stevan Smith. m 2/23/1985 Alfred Joseph Chilese c 1.

CHILLINGTON, Joseph Henry (Ind) 215 N 7th Street, Terre Haute IN 47807 **Invstmt & Fin Com Dio Indianapolis Indianapolis IN 2001-, Const & Cn 2000-2011** B Whittier CA 1947 s Joseph & Edwardine. BA Occ 1970; DIC Imperial Coll London GB 1972; MS Lon GB 1972; MDiv VTS 1984. D 6/9/1984 P 1/6/1985 Bp Arthur Edward Walmsley. c 1. R S Steph's Ch Terre Haute IN 1993-2012; Int All SS Epis Ch Meriden CT 1993; Int S Jn's Epis Ch Essex CT 1992-1993; St Gabr's Ch E Berlin CT 1984-1991; Cur Gr Ch Newington CT 1984-1986.

CHILTON, Bruce (NY) Bard College, Annandale-on-Hudson NY 12504 **Chapl Chap at Fairthorne Manor Fairthorne Manor 1976-; Chapl Elko Lake Camps 1971-** B Roslyn NY 1949 s Bruce & Virginia. BA Bard Coll 1971; MDiv GTS 1974; PhD Camb 1976. Trans 6/29/1975 Bp Willian F Wall Jr. m 6/28/1982 Odile Chilton c 2. Bard Coll Annandale On Hudson NY 2008-2015; R Ch Of S Jn The Evang Red Hook NY 1987-2015; Cur St. Jas CT 1985-1987; Cur St. Aug's Ch Eudcliffe Untd Kingdom 1980-1985; Cur St. Paul's Ch Norton Lees Untd Kingdom 1976-1980; Cur St. Mary Cambridge Untd Kingdom 1975-1976. Auth, *Rabbi Jesus*, Doubleday, 2000; Auth, *Galilean Rabbi & His Bible*; Auth, *Jesus & the Ethics of the Kingdom*; Auth, *Jesus' Pryr & Jesus' Euch*; Auth, *Profiles of A Rabbi*; Auth, *Pure Kingdom: Jesus' Vision of God*;

Auth, *Targumic Approaches to the Gospels*; Auth, *The Isaiah Targum*. Inst for Biblic Resrch; Inst of Advncd Theol; SBL; Studiorum Novi Testamenti Societas.

CHILTON, Frank Eugene (Fla) 107 Golf Course Ln, Crescent City FL 32112 **Ret 2002-** B Dayton OH 1925 s Alfred & Lestie. D 5/28/1997 P 12/1/1997 Bp Stephen Hays Jecko. m 10/14/1950 Martha Lucille Brown. Asst S Mk's Ch Palatka FL 2000-2002; Vic Emm Ch Welaka FL 1997-2000.

CHILTON, Mary Habel (Alb) 3 Woods Edge Ln, West Sand Lake NY 12196 **Dio Albany Albany NY 2002-** B Newport News VA 1941 d John & Margaret. BA Utica Coll 1975; MA SUNY 1977; EdD Syr 1991; MDiv GTS 1995. D 2/25/1995 Bp David Bruce Joslin P 12/1/1997 Bp Robert William Duncan. m 7/1/1962 R Hunter Chilton. Cn to the Ordnry Dio Albany Greenwich NY 1999-2002; S Andr's Ch Schenectady NY 1999-2000; Supply P Dio Pittsburgh Pittsburgh PA 1998-1999; Int TESM Ambridge PA 1997-1998; Asst Trin Epis Ch Beaver PA 1995-1997. Auth, *Our Mssy God: Perspectives in Wrld Missions*, Trin Epis Sem, 1997.

CHILTON, William Parish (Eas) 214 Wye Ave, Easton MD 21601 B Birmingham AL 1939 s John & Virginia. BA Ya 1961; BD VTS 1966. D 6/18/1966 Bp Charles C J Carpenter P 6/10/1967 Bp George Mosley Murray. m 6/5/1965 Kathleen Chilton c 2. Ed, Dioc Nwspr Dio Easton Easton MD 1981-1994; R St Lk's Par Ch Hill MD 1979-2005; Grtr Birmingham Mnstrs Birmingham AL 1975-1979, 1970-1974; Dio Nicaragua New York NY 1975-1977; S Jas' Ch Livingston AL 1968-1970; Assoc Cbury Chap and Coll Cntr Tuscaloosa AL 1966-1970. Hon Cn, Trin Cathd Dio Easton 2005.

CHIN, Mary Louise (Ll) Po Box 650397, Fresh Meadows NY 11365 B Jamaica NY 1946 d John & Eleanor. Cert Mercer TS 1986; MS Adams St Coll 1992; Advncd Inst for Analytic Psych Jamaica NY 1997. D 12/15/1986 Bp Robert Campbell Witcher Sr. m 9/10/1972 Philip Chin. Asst S Ptr's by-the-Sea Epis Ch Bay Shore NY 1999-2001; 1994-1999; Asst S Marg's Ch Plainview NY 1986-1994; S Johns Epis Hosp Far Rockaway NY 1986-1991; Chapl Vill of St. Jn Smithtown NY 1986-1991; Asst Chapl St. Jn's Episcopal Hosp Smithtown NY 1986-1989.

CHINERY, Edwin Thomas (NJ) 165 Essex Ave Apt 102, Metuchen NJ 08840 **Ch Of The Ascen New York NY 2013-** B Plainfield NJ 1957 s Edwin & Helen. BA Thos Edison St Coll 2007; Certification - Sprtl Direction GTS 2010; MDiv GTS 2010. D 11/14/2009 P 6/19/2010 Bp George Edward Councell. Gr Epis Ch Plainfield NJ 2010-2013; S Mk's Epis Ch Keansburg NJ 2010-2013.

CHINLUND, Stephen James (NY) 445 W 19th St Apt Ph-D, New York NY 10011 B New York NY 1933 s Edwin & Helen. BA Harv 1955; BD UTS 1958. D 6/14/1958 P 12/8/1958 Bp Benjamin M Washburn. m 12/24/1966 Caroline Chinlund c 3. Sheltering Arms Chld and Fam Serv Inc New York NY 1988-2004; R Trin Epis Ch Southport CT 1982-1988; Cur H Trin Epis Ch Inwood New York NY 1963-1966; Cur S Aug's Ch New York NY 1960-1963; Cur Gr Epis Ch New York NY 1958-1960. Auth, "Lrng by Going Inside," *Rel and Mntl Hlth*, 2003; Auth, *A Way to Measure Success in Rehab of Drug Addicts*; Auth, *Alt Pursuits for Amer's 3rd Century*; Auth, *Healing & Hell: The Contradiction*. stephenchinlund@yahoo.com

CHIPPS, Kathleen Dawn (Va) 3604 Secret Grove Ct, Dumfries VA 22025 B Mansfield OH 1945 d Norman & Mary. BA GW 1968; MDiv VTS 1984; Cert Virginia Tech U 1994; Int Basic Trng 2000. D 7/25/1984 Bp Robert Bruce Hall P 10/26/1985 Bp Peter J Lee. P-in-c S Marg's Ch Woodbridge VA 2007-2012; Int Chr Epis Ch Gordonsville VA 2003-2004; Int S Steph's Epis Ch Culpeper VA 2000-2001; Int Little Fork Epis Ch Rixeyville VA 1999-2000; Int Dio Washington Washington DC 1997-1998; Int S Barn' Epis Ch of The Deaf Chevy Chase MD 1997-1998; Assoc S Dav's Ch Ashburn VA 1995-1998; Trin Epis Ch Washington VA 1994; Int S Lk's Ch Remington VA 1992-1993; Chapl H Trin Mnstry Of The Deaf Richmond VA 1986-1992; Mssnr For The Deaf Olivet Epis Ch Alexandria VA 1986-1992; DRE S Jn's Ch Chevy Chase MD 1984-1985. Auth, "A Litany Of Wholeness".

CHIRAN QUINONEZ, Jairo Ernesto (EcuL) Santiago Apostol, Parroquia La Pila Calle Mexico, La Pila 593 Ecuador B Pazz Y Bien 1984 s Richard & Lourdes. Licensia Enfermeria Tecnica De Manabi 2012. D 4/3/2016 Bp Terencio Alfredo Morante-Espana. m 9/8/2009 Janeth Toala Menendez c 2.

CHIRICO, Carey D (Va) 905 Princess Anne St, Fredericksburg VA 22401 **S Geo's Ch Fredericksburg VA 2013-, CE Dir 2007-2013** B Charleston WVA 1963 d Hugh & Barbara. BA U Rich 1984; MEd Virginia Commonwealth 1986; D Formation Inst 2012. D 2/23/2013 Bp Shannon Sherwood Johnston. m 7/3/1984 Bernardo M Chirico c 2. carey.chirico@stgeorgesepiscopal.net

CHIRINOS-HERNANDEZ, Jose A (Hond) **Dio Honduras San Pedro Sula 2001-** B 1961 m 2/13/1997 Darling Nunez.

CHISHAM, Anne Beardsley (SanD) 47568 Hawley Boulevard, San Diego CA 92116 B San Diego CA 1934 d John & Florence. ETSBH; BA Mills Coll 1955. D 12/19/1992 Bp Gethin Benwil Hughes. c 2. D All Souls' Epis Ch San Diego CA 1994-2007; Serv S Tim's Ch San Diego CA 1993-1994.

CHISHOLM, Alan Laird (NY) 209 S Broadway, Nyack NY 10960 B Washington DC 1937 s Robert & Margaret. BA Amh 1958; Drew U TS 1960; M. Div. GTS 1960; MDiv GTS 1961; Cert Blanton-Peale Grad Inst 1973; Cert Natl

Assn for the Advancement of Psychoanalysis 1995. D 6/10/1961 Bp Horace W B Donegan P 12/14/1961 Bp Francis E I Bloy. m 2/3/1962 Linda A Armstrong c 3. Hon Assoc Gr Epis Ch Nyack NY 1981-2002; Supply Chr Ch Of Ramapo Suffern NY 1979-1980; Pstr Psych Psych and Sprtlty Inst 1975-2014; Area Dir; Psych Psych and Sprtlty Inst 1974-2012; Vic All SS Epis Ch Vlly Cottage NY 1970-1976; Dio New York New York NY 1970-1976; R S Jn's Ch So Salem NY 1965-1970; Cur Chr Ch Bronxville NY 1962-1965; Cur S Jas Par Los Angeles CA 1961-1962. Cert Psychoanalyst NAAP 1995; Clincl Mem AAMFT 1975-2007; Diplomate AAPC 1973.

CHITTENDEN, Nils Philip (NY) St Stephens Church, 50 Bedford Rd, Armonk NY 10504 **P-in-c S Steph's Ch Armonk NY 2015-** B Folkestone England 1969 s John & Kirsten. BA St Chads Coll U of Durham UK 1991; CTM Westcott Hse U of Cambridge UK 1995; MA Northumbria U Newcastle-upon-Tyne UK 1999. Trans 3/28/2011 as Priest Bp Michael B Curry. m 7/9/2010 Kelly D Skaggs. Mssnr for YA Mnstry Dio No Carolina Raleigh NC 2011-2015, Mem of Cmsn of Mnstry (P Track) 2012-, Mem of Botswana Dioc Link Com 2011-, Mem of Coun of Advice, Sch of Mnstry 2011-, Chapl, Epis Cntr at Duke 2010-, Mem of COM in Higher Educ 2010-, Mssnr for YA 2010-; Minor Cn, Durham Cathd Dio Durham Co Durham 2004-2008; Serv Ch of Engl 1993-2010. Auth, "Traidcraft Cov Serv," *Cov Pryr*, Traidcraft Exch Ltd, 2008; Auth, "Is half a loaf better than no bread?," *Ch Times*, Hymns Ancient & Mod Grp, 2000; Compsr, "The Consult Mass," *Durham Dioc Consult Wrshp*, Dio Durham, 1998; Co-Transltr, "Speeches and Sermons from the 500th Anniv Fest of the Convoc of Uppsala," *Svenska Kyrkans Jubelfest (Jubilee of the Ch of Sweden)*, Ch of Sweden, 1995.

CHO, Francis Soonhwan (NJ) 16 Rodak Cir, Edison NJ 08817 **H Cross Perth Amboy NJ 1999-; Chapl Intl Seafarers' Cntr 1985-** B 1939 s Byung & Myung. Presb TS; S Michaels Angl Sem. D 4/1/1970 P 7/1/1970 Bp The Bishop Of Seoul. m 7/17/1972 Beatrice Cho. Port Chapl Seamens Ch Inst New York NY 1985-2005; Serv Ch Of Korea 1970-1985.

CHOATE JR, Horace (NY) 4 Gateway Rd., Unit 1-D, Yonkers NY 10703 B Macon GA 1950 s Horace & Sally. BA U of Mississippi 1973; MDiv GTS 1998. D 7/2/1998 P 1/31/1999 Bp Alfred Marble Jr. m 11/12/1988 Yamily Sierra c 2. Chr Ch Bronxville NY 2012; The Ch Of S Jos Of Arimathea White Plains NY 2010-2013; R Zion Epis Ch Wappingers Falls NY 2005-2010; Assoc S Columb's Ch Ridgeland MS 2001-2005; Vic/P-in-c S Mary's Ch Lexington MS 1999-2001; Vic/P-in-c S Matt's Epis Ch Kosciusko MS 1999-2001; Ch Of S Mary The Vrgn New York NY 1998-1999; Media Spec Epis Ch Cntr New York NY 1998-1999.

CHOI, Beryl Turner (WNY) 51 Virginia Pl, Buffalo NY 14202 **Ret 1993-** B 1926 d Alfred & Nellie. BA S Christophers Coll Gb 1947; Wm Temple 1950; STh Lon GB 1952. D 10/19/1973 P 1/1/1977 Bp Robert Bracewell Appleyard. c 3. The Fork Ch Doswell VA 2003-2005; Asst P Trin Epis Ch Buffalo NY 1996-1998; Int Trin Epis Ch Fredonia NY 1995-1996; Int The Epis Ch Of The Gd Shpd Buffalo NY 1994-1995; Calv Epis Ch Williamsville NY 1986-1994; P Eductr The Par Ch Of S Lk Long Bch CA 1984-1986; Asst Min Calv Ch Pittsburgh PA 1976-1983; Ch Of The Ascen Pittsburgh PA 1974-1976. Wmn Of The Year In Rel Awd U Pgh 1978; Archbp Of C'Bury Cmsn As Tchr Of Theol.

CHOI, Stephen Young Sai (NY) 5 77th St # 7047, North Bergen NJ 07047 **Died 4/10/2016** B 1945 s In & Boo. BA U of Korea Kr 1970; MA S Michaels Angl Sem 1974. Trans 7/1/1991 Bp Walter Decoster Dennis Jr. m 10/26/1974 Young H Choi. Dio New York New York NY 1997-2000; Korean-Amer Epis Ch New York NY 1992-1996; Vic S Jn's Korean-Amer Ch New York NY 1992-1996; Serv Ch Of Korea 1974-1991. Auth, "Korea U Engl Nwspr".

✠ CHOI, The Rt Rev William Chul-Hi (Los) 8105 232nd St Se, Woodinville WA 98072 **Dir/Chapl Epis Maritime Mnstry Seattle WA 1991-** B Um Song KR 1930 s Basil & Busilla. BA S Mich Seoul Kr 1954; LTh S Fran Coll Brisbane AU 1962; MA Rikkyo U Tokyo Jp 1972; Concordia TS 1974; CDSP 1984. Trans 12/10/1988 Bp Frederick Houk Borsch Con 1/1/1974 for Anglican Church Of Korea. m 7/16/1980 Catherine Misao Choi. Sup Ch Of The H Apos Bellevue WA 1997-2000; Dio Olympia Seattle 1991-2002; Sci San Pedro CA 1988-1991; Bp Of Pusan Dio Pusan Pusan Korea 1974-1987; Serv Ch Of Korea 1954-1973. Auth, "Future Of Martime Mssn In The Far Estrn Perspective," Intl Assn For Study Of Martime Missions., 2002; Auth, "Bridges Toward Effective Multicultural Mnstry, Pontifical Coun For The Pstr Care," *Rome In People On The Move.*, Vatican City, 1999; Auth, "A Survey Of Chr Growth," Korea Chr Pub., 1996; Auth, "Buddhism And It'S Influence In Korea," Intl Chr Martime Assn Paper, 1989.

CHOI, Young Kwon Kwon (Va) 1830 Kirby Rd, Mclean VA 22101 **St Fran Korean Ch McLean VA 2011-** B Seoul Korea 1961 s Kyungsoo & Yanghee. BA Cath U 1986; DMA U of Maryland 1997; MDiv Wesley TS 2000; Angl Study VTS 2009. D 6/4/2011 P 12/10/2011 Bp Shannon Sherwood Johnston. m 3/30/1992 Mina Choi c 1. Peace Epis Ch Rockport IN 2011-2016.

CHOLLET, Mariclea Joaquim (Mo) 232 South Woods Mill Rd., Chesterfield MO 63017 **Assoc Dir of Pstr Care St Lk's Hosp Chesterfield MO 2007-; Chapl S Lk's Hosp Chesterfield MO 2006-** B Curitiba Brazil 1971 d Jose & Teresa. MDiv Luth Fac of Theol - FLT Brazil 1993; No Brazil Bapt TS 1996;

Tuiuti U Brazil 2000; Supervisory CPE 2004. D 12/20/2006 P 6/29/2007 Bp George Wayne Smith. m 1/20/1996 Sidnei Chollet c 2. Clincl Pstr Eductr/Chapl St Lk's Hosp Chesterfield MO 2002-2006. mari.chollet@stlukes-stl.com

CHORNYAK, Christopher John (Me) 3 Spring House Ln, Ellsworth ME 04605 B Boulder CO 1951 s John & Dorothy. BA U of Massachusetts 1973; MDiv Nash 1977. D 11/1/1977 P 12/1/1978 Bp Alexander D Stewart. m 11/26/1977 Joyce Ann Chornyak c 3. R S Dunst's Ch Ellsworth ME 1994-2012; Int Chr Epis Ch Eastport ME 1988-1989; S Anne's Ch Calais ME 1982-1994; Vic St Lukes Ch Woodland ME 1982-1987, 1982-1986; S Paul's Ch Milwaukee WI 1980-1982; Cur Gr Ch Amherst MA 1977-1979. BA cl U of Massachusetts, Amherst 1973.

CHOYCE, George (ETenn) 27 Cool Springs Rd, Signal Mountain TN 37377 B 1963 Georgia Sthrn U; BA Georgia St U 1985; MDiv VTS 1992. D 6/20/1992 Bp John Wadsworth Howe P 1/30/1993 Bp Charles Farmer Duvall. m 8/3/1985 Anne Statham Choyce c 4. S Tim's Ch Signal Mtn TN 2002-2012; Gr Ch Newington CT 1997-2002; Calv Ch Pittsburgh PA 1994-1997; S Andr's Epis Ch Panama City FL 1992-1994; Trin Ch Vero Bch FL 1987-1989.

CHRISMAN JR, John Aubrey (RI) 7118 Treymore Ct, Sarasota FL 34243 **P in Res S Bon Ch Sarasota FL 2005-** B Charlotte NC 1933 s John & Alice. No Carolina St U 1952; BS USNA 1958; Westcott Hse CambridgeUK 1988. Trans 5/1/1991 Bp George Nelson Hunt III. m 9/19/1959 Donna Lee Chrisman c 3. Chapl Navy League of US Sarasota FL 2009; Assoc Emm Ch Newport RI 2002-2005; Chapl Newport Fire Dept 1991-2001; R S Geo's Ch Newport RI 1991-2001; Serv Ch of Engl 1988-1990. Fed of Fire Chapl 1993-2001.

CHRISMAN, Robert (Oly) 1214 184th Pl, Long Beach WA 98631 B Lindsay CA 1944 s Edwin & Garnet. BA Marylhurst U 1983; MDiv CDSP 1985. D 7/3/1985 P 1/1/1986 Bp Rustin Ray Kimsey. m 8/5/2005 Mary Etta Ewing c 4. Chr Ch Tacoma WA 2008-2010; Dio Oregon Portland OR 2005-2007; Int S Lk's Epis Ch Vancouver WA 2004-2005; S Jn's Ch Hermiston OR 2003-2004; R The Par Of S Mk The Evang Hood River OR 1996-2002; R S Jas Epis Ch Laconia NH 1989-1993; Vic Epis Ch Of The Trsfg Sis OR 1985-1989.

CHRISNER, Marlen Ronald (At) 6517 SW 85th St, Ocala FL 34476 B Jackson MI 1936 s Marlen & Rosa. BS Wayne 1970; MDiv Ya Berk 1973. D 6/30/1973 P 10/31/1974 Bp H Coleman Mcgehee Jr. m 8/23/1958 Marcella A Chrisner c 3. R Gd Shpd Epis Ch Austell GA 1999-2000; H Innoc Ch Atlanta GA 1994-2001; Chapl/Rel Instr H Innoc Epis Sch Atlanta GA 1994-2001; H Innoc' Epis Sch Atlanta GA 1994-2001; R S Paul's Ch Sharpsburg MD 1993-1994; Chapl/Rel Instr S Jas Epis Sch S Jas MD 1991-1994; St Jas Sch Hagerstown MD 1991-1994; Chapl / Rel Instr Epis HS of Jacksonville Jacksonville FL 1985-1991; Jacksonville Epis HS Jacksonville FL 1985-1991; Asst P S Paul's Epis Ch Jacksonville FL 1985-1991; Chapl / Rel Instr Queen Anne Sch Upper Marlboro MD 1976-1985; Queen Anne Sch Uppr Marlboro MD 1976-1985; S Dunst's Epis Ch Davison MI 1973-1976.

CHRISTENSEN, Bonniejean Mcguire (ND) 4001 Beneva Rd Apt 334, Sarasota FL 34233 B Los Angeles CA 1931 d Robert & Elsa. Ndea; MA Claremont TS 1953; BA USC 1953; PhD USC 1969. D 6/26/1978 Bp George T Masuda. m Francis Christensen c 3. D/Asst S Wlfd's Epis Ch Sarasota FL 1985-1988; Chapl 1978-1985. Auth, "New Rhetoric"; Auth, "The Christensen Method". ESMHE. Phi Beta Kappa USC 1953; Phi Kappa Phi; Doctoral Fell Ndea.

CHRISTIAN, Carol Jean (SO) 5701 Makati Cir Apt E, San Jose CA 95123 B Cincinnati OH 1950 Cert Sch for Deacons 2004. D 6/12/2004 Bp George Richard Millard.

CHRISTIAN, Charles Ellis (Ind) 3627 E Crystal Valley Dr, Vincennes IN 47591 B Gadsden AL 1953 s Ellis & Charlotte. AS Gadsden St Jr Coll 1973; BS Lacrosse U 2004. D 6/24/1994 Bp Edward Witker Jones. m 2/23/1974 Mary Elizabeth Christian c 4.

CHRISTIAN, David Victor (WTenn) 8282 Macon Rd, Cordova TN 38018 B Northampton MA 1948 s Jack & Zipporah. NR Duke 1979; MMS Nova SE U 2005. D 6/26/2010 Bp Don Edward Johnson. m 9/1/1972 Marilee Christian c 2.

CHRISTIAN, Earl Rix (SVa) 25 Tripp Ter, Hampton VA 23666 B New York NY 1944 s Ernest & Mary. Cert Germain Sch of Photography New York NY 1979; AAS CUNY 2000. D 4/26/1997 Bp Richard Frank Grein. m 8/26/1981 Claire Evans c 1. D Emm Epis Ch Hampton VA 2002-2004.

CHRISTIAN JR, Frank Stanaland (Ga) 212 W Pine St, Fitzgerald GA 31750 **P-in-c S Matt's Epis Ch Fitzgerald GA 2011-, P-in-c 2011-** B Valdosta GA 1948 s Frank & Carolyn. Dplma U of Freiburg 1969; BA Stetson U 1970; MDiv Sthrn Bapt TS 1973; PhD Sthrn Bapt TS 1977. D 2/7/2009 P 8/29/2009 Bp Henry Irving Louttit. m 8/7/1971 Charlotte Rostron Christian c 3.

CHRISTIANSEN, Anthony D 6/10/2017 Bp Robert John O'Neill.

CHRISTIANSON, Regina (Vt) PO Box 57, Underhill VT 05489 **Emm Epis Ch Chatham VA 2016-; Calv Ch Underhill VT 2012-** B Panama Canal Zone 1948 d Charles & Dorothy. BA Excelsior Coll; MDiv EDS 2006. D 11/29/2006 P 4/12/2008 Bp Thomas C Ely. m 6/20/1987 Stephen D Whiteley. S Ptr's Mssn Lyndonville VT 2009-2010; D S Mary's Epis Par Northfield VT 2007; Intern Chapl Fletcher Allen Heath Care 2006-2007. rector.emmanuelchatham@gmail.com

CHRISTIANSSEN, Paul Jerome (NCal) 1016 W. Arrow Hwy, Apt. C, Upland CA 91786 B Chicago IL 1939 s Einar & Ida. BA Wheaton Coll 1961; MDiv UTS 1964; STM GTS 1965; PhD U of Texas 1970; U of Texas 1970; Claremont Coll 1995; PhD Claremont Coll 1998. D 6/6/1964 P 12/19/1964 Bp Horace W B Donegan. m 10/15/1966 Sarah Louise Christianssen c 2. S Steph's Epis Ch Colusa CA 1981-1994; S Mich's Epis Ch Carmichael CA 1976-1981; The Epis Dio Nthrn California Sacramento CA 1971-1976; Asst St. Martins Epis Ch Davis CA 1971-1973; Chapl U CA Davis Davis 1971-1973; Chapl All SS Epis Ch Austin TX 1968-1970; S Steph's Epis Sch Austin TX 1968; Cur Ch Of The Ascen New York NY 1965-1968, 1965-1967; All SS Ch Bayside NY 1964-1965, Cur 1964-1965; Yth Worker S Lk's Cnvnt Av New York NY 1962-1964; Yth Worker St. Annes Ch Bronx NY 1961-1962; Instr, Dept. of Philos Yuba Cmnty Coll Yuba City CA 1982-1985; Instr, Dept. of Rel U CA Davis Davis 1976-1977; Instr, Dept. of Rel Sacramento St Coll Sacramento CA 1972-1976. oliverivanboris@aol.com

CHRISTIE, Robert Lusk (Oly) 6350 Portal Way Unit 72, Ferndale WA 98248 B Olympia WA 1936 s Elmer & Margaret. U of Washington 1964; Everett Jr Coll 1965; BA Seattle Pacific U 1967; MDiv CDSP 1970. D 8/6/1970 P 6/29/1971 Bp Ivol I Curtis. m 9/28/1957 Marjorie A Christie c 3. Asst S Paul Epis Ch Bellingham WA 1998-2003; S Geo's Ch Seattle WA 1990-1998; COM Dio Olympia Seattle 1987-1993, Dep GC 1988-2003, Stndg Com 1983-1987; Vic All SS' Epis Ch Vancouver WA 1979-1990; Vic Estrn Grays Harbor Mssn Montesano WA 1972-1979; S Mk's Epis Ch Montesano WA 1972-1979; Cur S Jas Epis Ch Kent WA 1970-1972. Chapl COP 1992-1995.

CHRISTOFFERSEN, Timothy Robert (Cal) 611 Foxwood Way, Walnut Creek CA 94595 B Los Angeles CA 1942 s Daniel & Betty. BA Stan 1964; MDiv UTS 1967. D 6/2/2001 P 12/1/2001 Bp William Edwin Swing. m 7/24/1965 Susan Griffiths Gray c 1. S Anselm's Epis Ch Lafayette CA 2001-2002. Phi Beta Kappa Stan 1964.

CHRISTOPHER JR, Charles Harry (EO) 19529 Sugar Mill Loop, Bend OR 97702 B Denver CO 1946 s Charles & Margaret Ann. BA U CO 1968; MDiv SWTS 1971; DMin CDSP 2000. D 12/27/1970 P 6/1/1971 Bp Edwin B Thayer. m 8/19/1967 Patsy P Port c 2. Transition Consult S Alb's Epis Ch Redmond OR 2008-2010; Transition P Trin Ch Bend OR 2006-2008; Transition Consult S Fran Of Assisi Epis Wilsonville OR 2005-2006; Transition Consult S Paul's Epis Ch Salem OR 2004-2005; Assoc St. Mk's Epis Ch Medford OR 1999-2006; S Mk's Epis Par Medford OR 1999-2001; R All SS Ch Richland WA 1991-1999; R S Barn Ch Glenwood Spgs CO 1987-1991; R Calv Ch Golden CO 1980-1987; R Ch Of The Gd Samar Gunnison CO 1973-1980; Vic S Jas Ch Lake City CO 1973-1980; Cur S Paul's Epis Ch Lakewood CO 1971-1973; S Andr's Ch Manitou Sprg CO 1962-1964; Chair COM Dio Spokane Spokane WA 1996-1999.

CHRISTOPHER, Cynthia Ann (Md) Holy Trinity Episcopal Church, 1131 Mace Ave, Essex MD 21221 B Baltimore MD 1959 d William & Marie. D 6/11/2016 Bp Eugene Taylor Sutton. m 1/18/1981 Thomas Albert Christopher c 2.

CHRISTOPHER, John S (Az) 5143 E Karen Dr, Scottsdale AZ 85254 **Vic St Judes Epis Ch Phoenix AZ 2015-; CE Dir Epiph On The Desert Gila Bend AZ 2011-** B South Plainfield NJ 1957 s Robert & Martha. not completed Rio Salado Cmnty Coll. D 5/5/2012 P 10/11/2014 Bp Kirk Stevan Smith. m 8/12/2010 Lisa Christopher c 2.

CHRISTOPHER, Mary (Ia) 2110 Summit St, Sioux City IA 51104 **P S Mich's Ch Mt Pleasant IA 2010-** B New York NY 1950 AA Brookdale Cmnty Coll 1987; BA Monmouth U 1990; MDiv GTS 1995. D 5/21/1995 Bp Joe Doss P 1/1/1996 Bp Craig Barry Anderson. c 2. R S Thos' Epis Ch Sioux City IA 1997-2005; Asst Chr Ch Epis Shrewsbury NJ 1995-1997.

CHRISTOPHER, Melanie (Colo) 371 Upham St, Lakewood CO 80226 **Mng Dir St. Claires Mnstrs Denver CO 2002-; Bilingual Chapl Vol Swedish Med Cntr Denver CO 1999-; D Dio Colorado Denver CO 2000-** B Santiago CU 1937 d Jesus & Melania. BA FD 1977. D 12/18/1999 Bp Bob Johnson. m 10/11/1979 Leonard Henry Christopher c 3. D S Jos's Ch Lakewood CO 2011; D Epis Ch Of S Ptr And S Mary Denver CO 2005-2008; Ch Of S Phil And S Jas Denver CO 2000-2005. Auth, "Wake Up Call!," *Colorado Epis*, Dio Colorado, 2000; Auth, "Servnt Mnstry," *Highland Epis*, Dio WNC, 1999. Dio WNC Hisp Ministers Com 1995-2000; Dio Colorado Hisp Minstry Com 2002; Dio Colorado Mssn Strtgy Com 2006. Vol of the Year St of NC Hlth Dept. 1998.

CHRISTOPHERSON, Paul Conrad (Minn) Wildlife Run, New Vernon NJ 07976 **Non-par 1974-** B Minneapolis MN 1946 s Paul & Edna. BA Wms 1968; MDiv EDS 1971; MBA Col 1974. D 6/29/1971 P 4/1/1972 Bp Horace W B Donegan. m 7/3/1971 Elizabeth Jean Christopherson. Asst S Thos Ch New York NY 1971-1973.

CHRISTY, Christine Lavon (Az) D 6/11/2016 Bp Kirk Stevan Smith.

CHRISTY, Stephen James (Wyo) D 6/11/2014 P 1/10/2015 Bp John Smylie.

CHRONISTER, Lisa Marie (Okla) **D S Jn's Ch Oklahoma City OK 2014-** B Camp Lejeune NC 1971 d Hershel & Rose. BArch U of Oklahoma 1994; MArch Pratt Inst 2006. D 5/12/2012 Bp Mark Sean Sisk. m 5/28/2005 Aaron Mooney c 1. D S Chris's Ch Midwest City OK 2012-2014.

CHRYSTAL, Susan (Nwk) 33 Woodstone Cir, Short Hills NJ 07078 **Pstr Psych Gr Counslg Cntr Madison NJ 2007-; Psych Gr Counslg Cntr Madison NJ 2005-; COM Dio Newark Newark NJ 2010-** B Shaker Hgts OH 1958 d Robert & Susanne. BA Ya 1980; MBA U Chi 1984; MDiv UTS 1990; Cert Blanton-Peale Grad Inst 2003. D 6/2/1990 Bp John Shelby Spong P 12/1/1990 Bp Walter Cameron Righter. c 1. Pstr Psych Montclair Counslg Cntr Montclair NJ 2002-2007; Min S Mary The Vrgn Primrose Hill London Uk 1996-1999; Cur S Paul's Epis Ch Morris Plains NJ 1992-1995; Cur S Eliz's Ch Ridgewood NJ 1990-1991.

CHUBB JR, Donald Allen (Kan) 1011 SW Cambridge Ave, Topeka KS 66604 **D Gr Cathd Topeka KS 1976-** B Topeka KS 1946 s Donald & Elisabeth. BS U of Kansas 1968. D 9/26/1976 Bp Edward Clark Turner. m 9/2/1967 Janet Anderson c 1.

CHUBOFF, Esther Lois (Ct) 83 E Main St, Clinton CT 06413 B North Bergen NJ 1932 d Peter & Lydia. BS Rutgers The St U of New Jersey 1952; Colgate Rochester Crozer DS 1986; CRDS 1986. D 6/21/1986 P 6/29/1987 Bp O'Kelley Whitaker. Int Chr Ch Sharon CT 2000-2002; Ch of the H Sprt W Haven CT 2000; Ch Of The Gd Shpd Shelton CT 1999-2000; Ch Of The H Adv Clinton CT 1998-1999; Chr Ch Oxford CT 1992-1998; Trin Ch Boonville NY 1988-1989; S Paul's Ch Windham CT 1986-2006; D S Mk The Evang Syracuse NY 1986-1987.

CHUMBLEY, Kenneth Lawrence (WMo) 601 E Walnut St, Springfield MO 65806 **R Chr Epis Ch Springfield MO 1995-** B Louisville KY 1953 s Gilbert & Anine. BA U of Louisville 1976; MDiv GTS 1986; Cert Coll of Preachers 2000; Oxf GB 2012; M.A. Missouri St U 2013; M.A. (expected) Missouri St U 2013. D 6/24/1986 P 3/1/1987 Bp David Reed. m 8/14/1976 Penelope G Chumbley c 1. R All SS Epis Ch Johnson City NY 1989-1994; Asst. R Chr Epis Ch Bowling Green KY 1986-1989; Chapl Wstrn KY U 1986-1989; Mem, Cmncatn Com Dio W Missouri Kansas City MO. Auth, "Revs," *Sojourners*; Auth, "Revs," *The Chr Century*; Auth, "Three chapters," *The Chr Source Bk*; Auth, "arts," *The Other Side*; Auth, "monthly Rel/ethics column," *The Springfield (MO) News-Ldr*. Soc of S Marg 1991.

CHUN, Franklin (Haw) 1163 Lunaanela St, Kailua HI 96734 **Chapl to Ret Cler & Spouses /Partnr, and Surviving Spouses The Epis Ch in Hawaii Honolulu HI 2009-, COM 2001-2009** B Honolulu HI 1942 s Ahee & Margaret. BA U of Hawaii 1965; MDiv CDSP 1968. D 5/10/1968 Bp Edwin Lani Hanchett P 12/8/1968 Bp Harry Sherbourne Kennedy. m 6/19/1966 Norma F Fung c 3. R Ch Of The Epiph Honolulu HI 2003-2008; Chapl S Alb's Chap Honolulu HI 1996-2002; Cn S Andr's Cathd Honolulu HI 1992-1996; Chapl S Andr's Priory Sch Honolulu HI 1981-1992; R S Ptr's Ch Honolulu HI 1973-1981, Assoc 1968-1970; Vic St. Jn's Eleele and St. Paul's Kekaha 1970-1973; Camp Dir Camp Mokuleia Waialua HI 1968-1970. Co-Transltr, *Da Jesus Bk (Hawaii Pidgin NT)*, Wycliffe, 2000. Chinese Chr Assn 1968. Awd of Recognition Kaimuki Bus & Profsnl Assn 2008; Hon Cn S Andr Cathd 1996; HS Tchr of the Year S Andr Priory 1991.

CHUN, Malcolm N (Haw) **S Andr's Cathd Honolulu HI 2015-; S Jn's By The Sea Kaneohe HI 2013-; Bd Dir ITTI 2013-** B Honolulu HI 1954 s Albert & Thelma. BA U of Hawaii 1976; St Johns Theol Coll 1984; MA U of Hawaii 1985; Other 1989; Vancouver TS 1989; PhD Wananga@Awanuiarangi 2012. D 10/28/2011 P 6/10/2012 Bp Robert Leroy Fitzpatrick. Calv Epis Ch Kaneohe HI 2015; The Epis Ch in Hawaii Honolulu HI 2013-2014. Auth, "No Na Mamo," *Hawaiian Traditional and Contemporary Virtues and Values*, U of Hawaii Press, 2011.

CHUNG, Jae W (LI) 262 Middle Rd, Sayville NY 11782 **Died 12/16/2015** B Seoul Korea 1973 s Yong & Yang. BS Dankook U 1999; MDiv GTS 2014; MDiv The GTS 2014. D 1/11/2014 P 7/19/2014 Bp Lawrence C Provenzano. m 9/12/2006 Shin Young Y Shin Young Kang c 4. P S Ann's Ch Sayville NY 2014-2015; Mem of COM Dio Long Island Garden City NY 2014-2015. fatherjae@saint-anns.org

CHURCH, Susan Campbell (Ore) Po Box 605, John Day OR 97845 **S Lk's Ch Waldport OR 1989-; Vic S Steph's Ch Newport OR 1989-** B Oregon City OR 1953 d McGregor & Linda. BA U of Oregon 1977; MA U of Oregon 1977; MDiv CDSP 1985. D 6/22/1985 Bp Matthew Paul Bigliardi P 5/30/1986 Bp Robert Louis Ladehoff. Dir of Field Educ NW Hse of Theol Educ Salem OR 2003-2008; Asst The Epis Ch Of The Gd Samar Corvallis OR 1985-1989. CHS. stmavis@gmail.com

CHURCH, Susan Jean (NMich) Christ Church, 3906 5th St, Calumet MI 49913 B Detroit MI 1946 d George & Mary. Detroit Coll of Bus Dearborn MI; Ferris St Coll Big Rapids MI; Mutual Mnstry Calumet MI. D 11/28/2006 Bp James Arthur Kelsey P 9/18/2007 Bp Thomas Kreider Ray. m 6/23/1989 Alan Jeffrey Church c 4.

CHURCHILL, Gregg Hardison (Los) Po Box 1082, Lompoc CA 93438 B Los Angeles CA 1935 s Edwin & Coralynn. BS Colorado St U 1957; BD Fuller TS 1964; ThD Claremont TS 1972. D 3/12/1966 P 9/1/1966 Bp Francis E I Bloy. m 10/3/1992 Patricia Kiphut. S Steph's Epis Ch Valencia CA 1991; S Mary's Par Lompoc CA 1990-2001; Non-par 1968-1999; Cur S Mk's Par Downey CA 1966-1968.

CHURCHMAN, Michael Arthur (Neb) 300 W Broadway Ste 108, Council Bluffs IA 51503 B Council Bluffs IA 1928 s Henry & Teresa. BA S Paul Sem 1950; MA Creighton U 1955. Rec 1/1/1981 as Deacon Bp James Daniel Warner. Assoc R S Andr's Ch Omaha NE 1991-2003; Vic S Pauls Epis Ch Arapahoe NE 1984-1990; S Ptr's In The Vlly Lexington NE 1982-1990; Vic S Christophers Ch Cozad NE 1981-1990; Chapl Mercy Hosp Coun Bluffs IA 1979-1980; Serv RC Ch 1981.

CHURCHMAN, Nina Wood (Colo) 3224 S Eudora St, Denver CO 80222 B The Hague Holland NL 1952 d Michael & Jean. BA U of Pennsylvania 1974; MS Pur 1978; MDiv Ya Berk 1995. D 6/8/1996 P 1/18/1997 Bp William Jerry Winterrowd. c 2. All SS Ch Loveland CO 2014-2016; P-in-c S Laurence's Epis Mssn Conifer CO 2009-2013; S Paul's Epis Ch Ft Collins CO 2008, 2008, Supply 2007-2008; Assoc R S Tim's Epis Ch Littleton CO 2001-2007; R Epis Ch Of S Ptr And S Mary Denver CO 1999-2001; Asst R Gd Shpd Epis Ch Centennial CO 1996-1999.

CHURCHWELL, Katherine C (SwFla) PO Box 1581, St Petersburg FL 33731 **Cathd Ch Of S Ptr St. Petersburg FL 2016-** B Douglas WY 1985 d Kent & Christine. BA L&C 2007; MDiv VTS 2012. D 6/11/2011 P 12/15/2012 Bp Kirk Stevan Smith. m 1/21/2012 Logan Choate Churchwell c 2. Cur S Mary's Epis Ch Cypress TX 2013-2016.

CIANNELLA, Domenic Kenneth (LI) 320 Great River Rd, PO Box 586, Great River NY 11739 **Died 12/11/2015** B Far Rockaway NY 1921 s Vito & Adeline. BA U So 1943; MDiv Sewanee: The U So, TS 1945. D 12/24/1944 P 7/1/1945 Bp James Pernette DeWolfe. m 11/27/1945 Annette Ciannella c 5. Int All SS Ch Pleasant Ridge OH 2003-2015; Int H Trin Ch Hicksville NY 2003-2004; Chr Ch Babylon NY 2002-2013, Int R 1994-2001; Int S Fran Epis Ch Springboro OH 2001-2002; Int Calv Ch Cincinnati OH 1998-2000; Int H Trin Epis Ch Oxford OH 1997-1998; Int Trin Ch Columbus OH 1995-1997; Ret 1993-2015; Int S Jn's Ch Huntington NY 1993-1994; P-in-c Emm Epis Ch Great River NY 1992-1993; Prof of Pstr Theol, Theory & Pract of Mnstry Geo Mercer TS Garden City NY 1990-1992; R H Trin Epis Ch Hicksville NY 1959-1992; R S Paul's Ch Patchogue NY 1951-1959; P-in-c S Mary's Ch Ronkonkoma NY 1947-1951; P-in-c S Mich's & All Ang' Gordon Heights NY 1947-1951; Chapl Cntrl Islip St Hosp Cntrl Islip NY 1945-1951; P-in-c Ch Of The Mssh Cntrl Islip NY 1945-1951; S Mk's Epis Ch Medford NY 1945-1947. Dubose Awd for Serv The Schoo of Theol 2005; Hon Cn Cathd Incarn Garden City New York 1989.

CIANNELLA, J oseph Domenic Kennith (Mass) 13 Park Dr, West Springfield MA 01089 **Chapl Wing Hospice Palmer MA 2006-** B Mineola NY 1946 s Domenic & Annette. BA LIU 1973; MDiv SWTS 1998. D 6/20/1998 P 1/16/1999 Bp Herbert Thompson Jr. m 9/12/1998 Elizabeth Ciannella c 2. R Ch Of The Gd Shpd W Springfield MA 2002-2006; R S Phil's Ch Circleville OH 1999-2002; Cur S Matt's Epis Ch Westerville OH 1998-1999. AAPC 2014; Assn for Death Educ and Counslg 2013.

CICCARELLI, Sharon Lynn (Mass) 13 Turner Ter, Newton MA 02460 B Boston MA 1955 d Eugene & Margaret. BA Ya 1977; MDiv Epis TS of the SW 1993. D 6/5/1993 P 6/11/1994 Bp David Elliot Johnson. c 2. Assoc Trin Par of Newton Cntr Newton Cntr MA 1998-2004; Assoc Chr Ch Cambridge MA 1994-1998; D Chr Ch Cambridge Cambridge MA 1993-1994.

CICORA, Julie Anne (Roch) 556 Forest Lawn Dr, Webster NY 14580 **Gr Ch Lyons NY 2017-; S Mk's And S Jn's Epis Ch Rochester NY 2016-** B Laconia NH 1958 d Kenneth & Betty. AA Colby-Sawyer Coll 1977; BA Wellesley Coll 1979; MDiv Bex Sem 1999. D 6/5/1999 Bp William George Burrill P 5/27/2000 Bp Jack Marston Mckelvey. m 10/8/1994 F Scott Cicora c 5. Cn Dio Rochester Henrietta 2009-2016; R S Ptr's Epis Ch Henrietta NY 2006-2009; Assoc S Jn's Ch Canandaigua NY 2003-2016; Assoc S Lk's Ch Fairport NY 1999-2003. julie@episcopaldioceseofrochester.org

CIESEL, Barbara Bitney (SD) 126 N Park St Ne, Wagner SD 57380 **D S Ptr's Ch Lake Andes SD 2000-; Woniya Wakan/Ch Of The H Sprt Wagner SD 2000-** B Ann Arbor MI 1939 d Dewey & Barbara. BS MI SU 1963; MS MI SU 1965; MA Mt Marty Coll Yankton SD 2006. D 6/12/2000 Bp Creighton Leland Robertson. m 8/24/1968 Conrad Henry Ciesel. Sis of the H Nativ - Assoc 1973.

CIESEL, Conrad Henry (SD) Po Box 216, Lake City SD 57247 **Semi-Ret Asstg Sisseton Epis Missions Sisseton SD 2008-** B Buffalo NY 1941 s Henry & Irene. BA SUNY 1968; ETSBH 1975; MDiv GTS 1977. D 6/18/1977 P 1/1/1978 Bp Robert Claflin Rusack. m 8/24/1968 Barbara Bitney Ciesel c 1. Dio So Dakota Pierre SD 1994-2007; Vic Yankton Epis Missions Yankton SD 1994-2007; Vic Chr The King Quincy CA 1988-1994; S Richard's Epis Ch Skyforest CA 1982-1988; Vic St Columbas Epis Ch Big Bear City CA 1977-1988; Vic S Alb's Epis Ch Yucaipa CA 1977-1980. Auth, "Measurement Of Kidney Parenchyma P02 & Pc02 During In Vitro," Perfusion; Auth, "Direct Measurement Of Renal Cortical Oxygen & Carbon Dioxide," Pressures; Auth, "Induced Seizures As Ther Of Experimental Strokes In Dogs". Ord Of S Lk, SHN.

CIHAK, Susan Elizabeth (Az) 12990 E Shea Blvd, Scottsdale AZ 85259 **D S Anth On The Desert Scottsdale AZ 2009-** B La Jolla CA 1970 d George &

Doris. BS U of Arizona 1995. D 1/24/2009 Bp Kirk Stevan Smith. m 10/25/1997 Stephen Cihak c 2.

CILLEY, Norman H (CFla) 23 E Hampton Dr, Auburndale FL 33823 B North Danville VT 1932 s H Norman & Florance. D 12/3/1988 Bp Arthur Edward Walmsley. m 2/14/1954 Mona Nadine Stewart. D Dio Connecticut Meriden CT 1988-1993.

CIMIJOTTI, Jerry Anthony (SD) 2822 S Division St, Spokane WA 99203 **R Chr the King Ch Spokane WA 2005-** B Mason City IA 1964 s Raymond & Rosemary. TESM 1999. D 6/10/2000 Bp Robert William Duncan P 12/10/2000 Bp Edwin Max Leidel Jr. m 8/27/1999 Courtney Kathryn Cimijotti c 3. R S Mary's Epis Ch Mitchell SD 2002-2005; D S Jn's Epis Ch Midland MI 2000-2001; Assoc St Johns Epis Ch Midland MI 1999-2001.

CINTRON, Julio A (PR) B Yauco, PR 1935 s Gumersindo & Filomena. D 6/14/1991 P 6/6/1992 Bp David Andres Alvarez-Velazquez. c 4. Vicario Mision La Santa Cruz Lares PR 2010; Dio Puerto Rico Trujillo Alto PR 2004-2007, 1992-2003; Prncpl Colegio San Andres Mayaguez 1994-2005. Educadores Puertoriqueños 1983.

CIOSEK, Scott Andrew (Mass) 351 Elm St, South Dartmouth MA 02748 **S Mart's Epis Ch New Bedford MA 2013-; P-in-c S Ptr's Ch Dartmouth MA 2013-** B Fall River MA 1971 s Andrew & Donna. BA U of Massachusetts 1993; MDiv St Jn's Sem 2000; Angl Stds EDS 2013. Rec 6/22/2013 as Priest Bp M(Arvil) Thomas Shaw. m 6/11/2008 Elizabeth Ciosek c 3. sac371@comcast.net

CIPOLLA, Angela Marie (NJ) 650 Rahway Dr., Woodbridge NJ 07095 **Trin Ch Woodbridge NJ 2015-** B Lawrence MA 1982 d Raymond & Elaine. BA St Jos's Coll of Maine 2004; MDiv GTS 2014; MDiv The GTS 2014. D 6/14/2014 P 2/14/2015 Bp A Robert Hirschfeld. m 8/8/2014 Jenna Cipolla. parishoffice@trinitywoodbridge.org

CIRIELLO, Mary Anne (Ct) 3768 Anslow Drive, Leland NC 28451 B New York NY 1950 d Albert & Gertrude. BA Bennington Coll 1973; BS U of Massachusetts 1976; MDiv TESM 1982. D 6/9/1984 Bp Arthur Edward Walmsley P 1/1/1985 Bp William Bradford Hastings. m 6/27/1992 John Louis Ciriello. R Gr Ch Broad Brook CT 1988-1991; Asst to R S Jas's Ch W Hartford CT 1984-1988; Intern Chr Ch Cathd Hartford CT 1982-1984.

CIRILLO, James Hawthorne (Va) Po Box 847, Buckingham PA 18912 **R Gr Ch Casanova VA 2004-** B Alexandria VA 1953 s John & Ada. BA Emory and Henry Coll 1976; MDiv TESM 1983; VTS 1983. D 8/16/1983 Bp David Henry Lewis Jr P 3/15/1984 Bp Walter H Jones. m 7/7/1979 Dale Cirillo c 3. R Trin Ch Buckingham PA 1996-2003; Assoc Ch Of The Gd Samar Paoli PA 1988-1996; Asst S Lk's Epis Ch Hilton Hd Island SC 1985-1988; Cur Emm Epis Par Rapid City SD 1983-1985; Pstr Intern Truro Epis Par Fairfax VA 1981-1982. Bd Mem Widows & Orphans Corp.

CIRVES, Judith Melanie (Mil) 510 Ludington Ave, Madison WI 53704 B Milwaukee WI 1940 d John & Pearl. U of Wisconsin. D 9/10/1988 Bp Roger John White. D S Lk's Ch Madison WI 2000-2009; D Ch Of The Gd Shpd Sun Prairie WI 1988-1990.

CISNEROS, Hilario (WNC) 2657 Chimney Rock Rd, Hendersonville NC 28792 **Dio Wstrn No Carolina Asheville NC 2013-; Latino Mssnr Dio WNC 2013-; R La Capilla De Santa Maria Hendersonvlle NC 2013-; Latino Mssnr Dio WNC 2013-** B Michoacan Mexico 1957 s Luis & Maria. Salesian Sch of TH Guadalajara MX 1992. Rec 11/1/2009 as Priest Bp Dan Thomas Edwards. m 3/9/2006 Ruth A. Flores Torres. Disciliary Cmsn Dio Nevada Las Vegas 2010-2013; R S Lk's Epis Ch Las Vegas NV 2009-2013. Las Vegas Vlly Interfaith S Com 2009.

CIVALIER, Gordon Richard (NJ) 161 Lakebridge Dr., Deptford NJ 08096 **Ret 2008-** B Camden NJ 1947 s Gordon & Anna. BA Morningside Coll 1969; MDiv PDS 1972. D 4/22/1972 P 10/28/1972 Bp Alfred L Banyard. Ch Of The Ascen Gloucester City NJ 2006-2008, R 1980-1996; H Sprt Bellmawr NJ 1997-2007; S Lk's Ch Westville NJ 1997-2007; Timber Creek Epis Area Mnstry Gloucester City NJ 1997-2005; Serv Ch of Can NL 1974-1980; Cur Chr Ch Middletown NJ 1972-1974. Bd Mem & Secy for the Cmnty Plnng & Advocacy 1989-2002. R Emer Ch of the Ascen 2012; Vol of the Year Sthrn NJ AIDS Cltn 1989.

CLAASSEN, Scott Allen (Los) 714 Mission Park Dr, Santa Barbara CA 93105 **S Mich's U Mssn Isla Vista CA 2015-** B Monterey CA 1979 s Roy & Barbara. BA Van 2001; MDiv Yale DS 2011; Angl Stds Bloy Hse Epis Sem 2013. D 4/28/2014 P 10/26/2014 Bp Joseph Jon Bruno. m 4/13/2013 Mary Elizabeth Schroeder c 2. P Thads Santa Monica CA 2014. gauchopriest@gmail.com

CLABUESCH, Ward Henry (Mich) 3176 Topview Ct, Rochester Hills MI 48309 B Bad Axe MI 1927 s Ernst & Bertha. BA MI SU 1950; STB GTS 1953. D 6/27/1953 Bp Richard Stanley Merrill Emrich P 12/27/1953 Bp Russell S Hubbard. c 2. Asst All SS Epis Ch Pontiac MI 1991-1992, Cur 1953-1990; R Chr Ch Dearborn MI 1971-1991; R S Lk's Epis Ch Allen Pk MI 1961-1971; R S Paul's Epis Ch Corunna MI 1955-1961.

CLADER, Linda Lee (NCal) 5555 Montgomery Dr Apt N201, Santa Rosa CA 95409 B Evanston IL 1946 d Carl & Geraldine. BA Carleton Coll 1968; MA Harv 1970; PhD Harv 1973; MDiv CDSP 1988. D 6/23/1988 P 1/25/1989 Bp Robert Marshall Anderson. m 4/6/1991 Robert Nicholas Ristad. Prof Homil

Dn of Acad Affrs CDSP Berkeley CA 1991-2013; Adv Ch Farmington MN 1989-1990. Co-Auth, "The Formation of a Eucharistic Prchr," *Preaching at the Double Feast, ed. Monshau,* Liturg Press, 2006; Auth, "Voicing the Vision: Imagination and Prophetic Preaching," Morehouse, 2003; Auth, "Preaching the Liturg Narrative: The easter Vigil and the Lang of Myth," *Wrshp,* 1998; Co-Auth, "At the Wedding of Peleus & Thetis: Trans of Catullus 64," Black Oak, 1981; Auth, "Helen: Evolution from Div to Heroic in Gk Epic Tradition," E.J. Brill, 1976. Phi Beta Kappa 1968.

CLAGGETT III, Thomas West (Md) 1123C Jefferson Pike, Knoxville MD 21758 B Baltimore MD 1938 s Thomas & Blanche. BS JHU 1966; MA St Marys Sem & U 1974. D 5/12/1979 Bp David Keller Leighton Sr. m 6/11/1960 Lucy Margaret Claggett c 2. D Gr Ch Brunswick MD 2011-2014; D S Paul's Epis Par Pt Of Rocks MD 2011-2013; D All SS Ch Frederick MD 1979-2011.

CLANCE, Bennett Bolton (Fla) D 5/23/2010 Bp Samuel Johnson Howard.

CLAPP JR, Schuyler Lamb (EMich) 2830 Arborview Dr Apt 2, Traverse City MI 49685 B Oceanside NY 1931 s Schuyler & Florence. BA Yankton Coll 1952; STM SWTS 1955; MSW Wayne 1968. D 6/23/1955 Bp Archie H Crowley P 12/1/1955 Bp Conrad H Gesner. c 5. Archd Dio Michigan Detroit MI 1992-1994, 1965-1968; R S Andr's Epis Ch Gaylord MI 1987-1997; LocTen S Jas Epis Ch Belle Fourche SD 1981-1987; Chapl Henry Ford Hosp Detroit MI 1964-1966; R Calv Memi Epis Ch Saginaw MI 1960-1964; Cur All SS Ch Detroit MI 1959-1960; Vic Chr Epis Ch Gettysburg SD 1955-1959; Dn, Nthrn Convoc Dio Estrn Michigan Saginaw MI 1995-2001. Auth, *Video: Sons of Single-Parent Mothers,* 1991.

CLARK, Adelaide (NY) 45 Miami Dr. Unit B, Monroe OH 45050 B Logan WV 1944 d John & Josephine. Witt 1963; BS OH SU 1965; Untd TS 1986; MDiv GTS 1988. D 6/18/1988 P 12/18/1988 Bp William Grant Black. m 8/28/1965 Larry Edward Clark c 2. The Ch Of S Jos Of Arimathea White Plains NY 1997-2009; Dio Indianapolis Indianapolis IN 1991-1996; Vic S Lk's Epis Ch Shelbyville IN 1990-1996; D S Lk's Ch Marietta OH 1988-1989.

CLARK, Anthony Patrick (Tex) 5525 N Circuit Dr, Beaumont TX 77706 **S Mk's Ch Beaumont TX 2016-; Chapl Florida Army NG FL 1995-** B Springfield MA 1961 s John & Patricia. BA Stetson U 1983; MDiv VTS 1992; Dplma US Army Command and Gnrl Stff Coll 2009. D 6/14/1992 Bp Frank S Cerveny P 12/16/1992 Bp John Wadsworth Howe. m 6/17/1989 Laurie Boss Clark c 2. Dn Cathd Ch Of S Lk Orlando FL 2006-2016; Epis Ch Of The H Sprt Apopka FL 2003-2006, 2003, 1999-2003; Pension Fund Mltry New York NY 2003; R Epis Ch Of S Mary Belleview FL 1994-1999; Asst All SS Ch Of Winter Pk Winter Pk FL 1992-1994. Auth, "Commentary on Jas," *The Journey: God's Word for Daily Living,* The Bible Reading Fllshp, 2007; Auth, "Commentary on 1 and 2 Tim," *The Journey: God's Word for Daily Living,* The Bible Reading Fllshp, 2000; Auth, "Commentary on Philippians and Colossians," *The Journey: God's Word for Daily Living,* The Bible Reading Fllshp, 1998; Auth, "Commentary on Ephesians," *The Journey: God's Word for Daily Living,* The Bible Reading Fllshp, 1997; Auth, "Commentary on Matt 8-17," *The Journey: God's Word for Daily Living,* The Bible Reading Fllshp, 1995. Abbey of S Greg 1995. Min of the Year Stetson U 1996. tclark@stmarksbeaumont.org

CLARK, Audrey Hansen (Ala) **The Epis Ch of the H Apos Hoover AL 2015-** D 5/18/2015 Bp John Mckee Sloan Sr P 12/9/2015 Bp Santosh K Marray.

CLARK, Beatryce Arlene (NCal) 581 Ridgewood Dr, Vacaville CA 95688 **Archd The Epis Dio Nthrn California Sacramento CA 2010-; D Epiph Epis Ch Vacaville CA 2004-** B Newark NJ 1935 d Edward & Margaret. BBA Ups 1957; BTA Sch for Deacons 2004. D 7/4/2004 Bp Jerry Alban Lamb. m 8/15/1981 Philip T Clark c 3.

CLARK, Bradford Duff (Mass) Po Box 25, Arlington VT 05250 **R Ascen Memi Ch Ipswich MA 2006-** B Providence RI 1960 s Donald & Ruth. BA Hobart and Wm Smith Colleges 1982; MA U Chi 1985; Cert SWTS 1989. D 8/19/1989 P 3/22/1990 Bp Edward Cole Chalfant. m 12/13/2013 Erica Ann Fuller. S Jas Epis Ch Arlington VT 1994-2006; R Confederation For N.W. Area Mnstry Swanton VT 1992-1994; Dio Vermont Burlington VT 1992-1994; Asst S Alb's Ch Cape Eliz ME 1989-1991.

CLARK, Carole Sue (Okla) Hc 67 Box 82, Indianola OK 74442 B Cushing OK 1946 BA Oklahoma St U. D 5/30/1998 Bp Robert Manning Moody. m 2/6/1970 Bill Clark c 2. D Trin Ch Eufaula OK 1998-2012.

CLARK, Carol Ruth (NMich) 10401 V.05 Rd, Rapid River MI 49878 **Non-par 1990-** B Dayton OH 1930 d Bailey & Jessie. RN Miami Vlly Hosp Sch Dayton OH 1951. D 9/30/1990 P 4/14/1991 Bp Thomas Kreider Ray. m 8/24/1951 Donald Eugene Clark. Ord Of S Lk.

CLARK, Cathy A (NMich) P.O. Box 601, Ishpeming MI 49849 **P Estrn Reg Sault Sainte Marie MI 2013-** B Ishpeming MI 1960 d John & Sally. BS Nthrn Michigan U 2006. D 11/4/2007 Bp Rustin Ray Kimsey. S Jas Ch Of Sault S Marie Sault Sainte Marie MI 2012. cclarkupnorth@gmail.com

CLARK, Charles Halsey (NH) 5 Timber Ln Apt 228, Exeter NH 03833 B New York NY 1926 s Alfred & Martha. BA Ya 1948; BD VTS 1952; MA Ya 1956; STD Ya Berk 1982; LHD Mid 1991. D 6/8/1952 P 12/22/1952 Bp Horace W B Donegan. m 5/15/1953 Priscilla Clark. P-in-c Ch Of S Jn The Evang Dunbarton NH 1999-2011; R S Paul's Sch Concord NH 1982-1992; Dn Ya Berk New

Haven CT 1977-1982; Interseminary Prog Field Educ Manip Pi 1967-1972; P-in-c Serv Ch in Singapore 1962-1967; Dn St. Andrews TS Manila Philippines 1956-1977; P-in-c Serv Ch in Singapore 1956-1957; Instr Trin Ts Singapore 1956-1957; Asst Chapl Ya 1953-1956; Asst Gr And S Ptr's Epis Ch Hamden CT 1952-1953. Fndt For Theol Educ In SE Asia; Soc For Values In Higher Educ; Untd Bd For Chr Higher Educ In Asia.

CLARK, Cheryl L (Ark) 1106 Deer Run N, Pine Bluff AR 71603 B Saint Louis MO 1950 d Terry & Dorothy. BA W&M 1972; MA U of York 1975; EdD Bos 1982; MDiv VTS 2002. D 12/22/2001 P 6/22/2002 Bp Larry Maze. Exec Com Dio Arkansas Little Rock AR 2010-2013, First Cler Alt, GC 2007-2010, Nomin Ctte for Election of a Bp 2005-2006, T/F on Dioc. Conv Representation 2005-2006, Curric Cttee. for Loc Ord to Priesthood 2011-, 2008-2011, 2005-2008, 2005; R Gr Ch Pine Bluff AR 2002-2012.

CLARK, Cindy Lou (Tex) 501 E Gregg St, Calvert TX 77837 B Ft Worth TX 1948 d Billy & Evelyn. Dplma Iona Sch for Mnstry; BS Sthrn Illinois U in Carbondale; MS U of Houston Clear Lake 1984; MARE SW Bapt TS 1987. D 6/20/2015 Bp C Andrew Doyle P 1/8/2016 Bp Jeff Fisher.

CLARK, Constance Lee (Va) PO Box 183, Earlysville VA 22936 **Vic Buck Mtn Epis Ch Earlysville VA 2008-; S Paul's Epis Ch Evanston WY 2005-, 2002-2005** B Alexandria VA 1954 d Harry & Edna. BA U Chi 1976; MA S Stephens Coll 2008. D 9/23/2005 P 4/1/2006 Bp Bruce Caldwell. m 5/20/1978 Guy A Lushin. Chapl Wyoming St Hosp Evanston WY 2002-2007; Chapl Nthrn Virginia Mntl Hlth Inst Falls Ch VA 1999-2002; Gr Epis Ch Alexandria VA 1991-2002. "Faith," Salt Lake Tribune, 2006; "The Faith Factor: Proof of the Healing Power of Pryr," Viking Penguin, 1998; "H Meeting Ground," Shalem Inst, 1993; "In the Line of Duty," Potomac Pub, 1988.

CLARK, Darrah Corbet (Oly) 11520 Sw Timberline Dr, Beaverton OR 97008 **Chapl Oregon Epis Sch Portland OR 2011-; Assoc Gr Memi Portland OR 1998-; Chapl, Instr Or Epis Sch OR 1988-** B Seattle WA 1951 s Irving & Anne. BA Harv 1972; MA Ya 1974; Coll of the Resurr Mirfield Gb 1976; MDiv GTS 1977; DMin VTS 2011. D 7/26/1977 P 6/29/1978 Bp Robert Hume Cochrane. m 8/7/1976 Myra Florence Waite c 2. Dio Oregon Portland OR 2014, 2011; VTS Alexandria VA 2014; Assoc S Jas Epis Ch Portland OR 1989-1998; Int Epis Chapl Ft Lewis WA 1984-1986; Int Chapl/Instr Chas Wright Acad Tacoma WA 1983-1987; Chr Ch Tacoma WA 1980-1984; Int Dio Olympia Seattle 1979; Cur Ch Of The Ascen Seattle WA 1977-1979. Auth, "Amer Wines Of The NW," Wm Morrow, 1989; Auth, "The Frugal Gourmet Cooks w Wine," Wm Morrow, 1986. Phi Beta Kappa 1972.

CLARK, David Norman (Md) 12265 Boyd Rd, Clear Spring MD 21722 B Lewisburg PA 1949 s Vance & Elva. BA McDaniel Coll 1971; MDiv VTS 1976. D 5/22/1976 P 12/4/1976 Bp David Keller Leighton Sr. m 6/10/2000 Colleen Clark c 4. Vic S Andr's Ch Clear Sprg MD 2001-2007; 1980-2001; Dio Cntrl Pennsylvania Harrisburg PA 1980-1981; R S Mary's Ch Williamsport PA 1978-1980; Asst S Ptr's Epis Ch Ellicott City MD 1976-1977.

CLARK, Diana Doyle (Nwk) 59 Montclair Ave, Montclair NJ 07042 B Bridgeport CT 1945 d Harrison & Carolyn. BA Ge 1967; MDiv Drew U 1987. D 5/28/1988 P 12/18/1988 Bp John Shelby Spong. m 7/15/1967 Charles P Clark c 2. S Jn's Epis Ch Montclair NJ 1991-2010; Assoc R S Geo's Epis Ch Maplewood NJ 1988-1991; Ethics Com Dio Newark Newark NJ 1986-1997, Com 1983-1984; Strng Com Chair Cntr For Chr Sprtlty Nyc 1986-1987.

CLARK, Diane Catherine FitzGerald (WA) 13 Eleanor Avenue, Saint Albans, Hertfordshire AL35TA Great Britain (UK) **Chapl (Full-time) St. Albans HS for Girls St Albans Hertfordshire 1998-; Associated Cler The Cathd & Abbey Ch of St. Alb St. Albans Hertfo 1998-** B Attleboro MA 1954 d Paul & Blanche. BA U of Rhode Island 1976; MDiv GTS 1986. D 6/21/1986 P 2/28/1987 Bp George Nelson Hunt III. m 7/31/1982 Charles Graham Clark. Asst P (NSM) Emm Ch W Hampstead London 1996-1998; P-in-c S Pat's Ch Washington DC 1994-1995; Supply P Dio Washington Washington DC 1993-1994; All SS' Epis Ch Chevy Chase MD 1989-1992; Tutor The GTS New York NY 1987-1989; Cur S Mich's Ch New York NY 1986-1989. Auth, *QUEST*, 1989; Auth, *The Angl*, 1989. Cmsn Liturg & Mus Dio Washington DC 1990-1992.

CLARK, Douglas Burns (SeFla) 116 Prospect Park W # 2r, Brooklyn NY 11215 **Hon Assoc S Mary's Manhattanville Epis Ch New York NY 1987-; Asst 1973-1986** B Los Angeles CA 1948 s Martin & Beverly. AAPC; BA Amh 1970; MDiv GTS 1973; Cert Blanton-Peale Grad Inst 1976; Cert Blanton-Peale Grad Inst 1977. D 6/9/1973 Bp Paul Moore Jr P 5/1/1974 Bp Harold Louis Wright. m 9/5/1970 Eleanor Preston. Assoc S Mary's Ch Brooklyn NY 1988-2008. Auth, "Cler As Systems Analyst (The Guide To Pstr Counslg And Care)," Psychosocial Press, 2000; Auth, "Aspects Narcissistic Revenge Elicited In Grp Psych". Aamft. Tchg Fell Inst Of Rel & Hlth 1976; Fell Agpa; Fell Egps.

CLARK, Frances M (NJ) 201 Penbryn Rd, Berlin NJ 08009 **D The Ch Of The Gd Shpd Berlin NJ 2008-** B Philadelphia PA 1949 D 9/21/2002 Bp David Bruce Joslin. D S Ptr's Ch Medford NJ 2002-2007.

CLARK, Frank H (Az) 7810 W Columbine Dr, Peoria AZ 85381 **S Phil's In The Hills Tucson AZ 2015-** B Pontiac MI 1941 s Harold & Dorothy. BS MI SU 1964; MDiv Nash 1971; Cert Cler Ldrshp Inst 2008. D 3/5/1971 P 9/11/1971 Bp Donald H V Hallock. m 7/30/1966 Carolyn C Christiansen c 2. S Lk's Ch

Prescott AZ 2013-2014; P-t Assoc P All SS Ch Phoenix AZ 2008-2009; R All SS Of The Desert Epis Ch Sun City AZ 1997-2008; Dn Geth Cathd Fargo ND 1986-1997; R Trin Epis Ch Pierre SD 1976-1985; Chapl Platteville Wisconsin Police Dept 1972-1976; S Jn The Bapt Epis Ch Glendale AZ 1971-2010; Trin Epis Ch Mineral Point WI 1971-1976; Trin Epis Ch Platteville WI 1971-1976; Chapl Univerity of Wisconsin-Platteville 1971-1976; Pres of the Stndg Com Dio No Dakota Fargo ND 1988-1996, Liturg Off 1986-1997; Secy of the Stndg Com Dio So Dakota Pierre SD 1978-1985, Liturg Off 1976-1985; Rep Untd Mnstrs in Higher Educ - Wisconsin Dio Milwaukee Milwaukee WI 1971-1976. Auth, "Out Of The Ashes," *Faith & Form*, Interfaith Forum on Rel, Art & Archetecture, 1995. Hon Cn Dio Arizona/Trin Cathd, Phoenix 2007; Silver Beaver BSA 1994; St Geo Awd The Epis Ch 1985.

CLARK, Jacqueline (Mass) St Elizabeth's Episcopal Church, 1 Morse Rd, Sudbury MA 01776 **S Eliz's Ch Sudbury MA 2013-** B Oak Park IL 1984 d John & Karen. BA U of Notre Dame 2006; MDiv/MSW U Chi-DS 2012. D 6/8/2013 Bp Jeff Lee P 1/4/2014 Bp M(Arvil) Thomas Shaw. m 10/5/2013 Andrew Goldhor. All SS Epis Ch Chicago IL 2012-2013. jacqueline_clark@st-elizabeths.org

CLARK II, James Boyd (Az) 6715 N Mockingbird Lane, Paradise Valley AZ 85253 **R S Barn On The Desert Scottsdale AZ 2004-** B Oklahoma City OK 1951 s Jack & Anne. BA Oral Roberts U 1985; MDiv Fuller TS 1991. D 6/15/1991 P 1/11/1992 Bp Frederick Houk Borsch. m 12/8/1978 Betsy Clark c 4. Assoc Ch Of Our Sav Par San Gabr CA 1991-2004.

CLARK, Jane Alice (Chi) 1608 W Plymouth Dr, Arlington Heights IL 60004 **Vol Chapl Grayslake Fire Dept 2011-; R S Andr Ch Grayslake IL 2006-; Mem Dio Chicago Congregations Cmsn 2017-; Mem Dio Chicago Bdgt Com 2009-** B Joliet IL 1953 d Francis & Sarah. BSN IL Wesl 1975; MSN CUA 1981; MDiv SWTS 2005; DMin GTF 2010. D 6/18/2005 P 12/17/2005 Bp Bill Persell. m 6/11/1977 Michael Alan Clark c 2. Independant Vendor, Chapl Sabbatical Replacement Montgomery Place 2005; Night Nurse Supvsr Evanston Hosp Corp 1989-2004.

CLARK, Joan Bonnell (CFla) 231 Waters Edge Dr, Kissimmee FL 34743 **D Shpd Of The Hills Epis Ch Lecanto FL 1996-** B Highland NY 1931 d Walter & Viola. BA U IL 1954; MS U IL 1967; Cert Sewanee: The U So, TS 2002. D 2/3/1996 Bp Frank Tracy Griswold III. m 7/4/1991 Sherman Clark c 4. S Chad Epis Ch Loves Pk IL 1971-1998. Auth, "Along the Way: 60 Poems Through the Christain Years," CHB Media, 2014; Auth, *Glimpses of God & Seasonal Chr Poems*, First Books Libr, 2003. Amer Benedictine Acad 1998-2005; Benedictine Secular Cn 1998; NAAD 1996; Ord Julian of Norwich 1995. Beta Phi Mu Intl Libr hon Soc 1967; Zeta Phi Eta Natl Speech hon Soc 1954.

CLARK, John E (CFla) 414 Pine St, Titusville FL 32796 **D Dio Cntrl Florida Orlando FL 2016-; No Amer Bd Mem/Florida Dir Intl OSL the Physcn San Antonio T 2016-; Mnstry Dir No One Hungry Titusville FL USA 2015-** B Columbus OH 1951 s Earl & Juanita. D 9/10/2016 Bp Gregory Orrin Brewer. m 12/27/1999 Jacqueline Bailey.

CLARK, John Leland (SO) #1712 - 8888 Riverside Dr E, Windsor ON N8S 1H2 Canada **1965-** B Saint Louis MO 1933 s John & Marian. BA Ken 1955; BD EDS 1958; MCP U Cinc 1967; PhD U Cinc 1970. D 6/20/1958 Bp Frederic Cunningham Lawrence P 12/7/1958 Bp Henry W Hobson. m 3/7/2007 Janet Finlay c 3. Asst Calv Ch Cincinnati OH 1960-1964; Asst S Jn's Ch Worthington OH 1958-1960.

CLARK SR, Johnny (John) Warren (WLa) 321 Horseshoe Drive, Crowley LA 70526 **Assoc P S Lukes Ch Jennings LA 2011-** B Roswell NM 1947 s Jim & Madeline. BS New Mex St U 1971; MDiv Epis TS of the SW 2000. D 6/3/2000 P 12/9/2000 Bp Robert Jefferson Hargrove Jr. m 11/18/1977 Phyllis Clark c 3. Assoc P S Barn Epis Ch Lafayette LA 2011-2015, Int P 2009-2011, Assoc P 2008-2015; R Trin Ch Crowley LA 2000-2009; Pres of Stndg Com Wstrn Louisiana Alexandria LA 2007-2009, Dn of Convoc 2007-, Mem of Stndg Com 2006-2009, Hd of Anti-Racism Com 2004-2009, Mem of COM 2000-2003.

CLARK, Joseph Madison (WA) 402 Grove Ave, po box 1098, Washington Grove MD 20880 B Wichita KS 1940 s Howard & Vera. BA NWU 1963; BA NWU 1963; MDiv VTS 1966; U of Maryland 1970; STM GTS 1993. D 6/11/1966 Bp Edward Clark Turner P 3/1/1967 Bp Hamilton Hyde Kellogg. m 7/10/1999 Meredith Myers c 3. R Ch Of The Ascen Gaithersburg MD 1991-2006; R Trin Ch Torrington CT 1986-1991; R S Alb's Epis Ch Salisbury MD 1977-1986; R S Mary's Woodlawn MD 1974-1976; Cmnty organizer St of Maryland 1972-1977; assistand Dir Grtr Baltimore Com 1970-1972; Cur S Jn The Evang S Paul MN 1966-1967.

CLARK, Judith (Mass) 10 Ida Rd., Worcester MA 01604 B Southbridge MA 1949 d Milton & Lillian. BA U of Massachusetts 1978; MA U of Massachusetts 1984; MDiv Bos TS 1999. D 5/29/1999 P 11/30/1999 Bp Douglas Edwin Theuner. m 5/12/1984 Robin E Clark c 2. R S Jn's Epis Ch Westwood MA 2006-2011; Vic Gr Epis Ch Concord NH 2001-2005; Int P Ch Of The H Sprt Plymouth NH 2000-2001; Asst to the R S Andr's Ch New London NH 1999-2000. Auth, "Encyclopedia of Chld Abuse," *3rd Ed.*, Facts on File, Inc., 2007; Auth, "Encyclopedia Of Chld Abuse," *2nd Ed.*, Facts On File, Inc., 2000; Auth, "Awesome Facts To Blow Your Mind," Price Stern Sloan, Inc., 1993; Auth, "Amer'S Gilded Age," Facts On File, Inc., 1992; Auth, "Disciplines 1989

- 2002," Upper Room Pub, 1989; Auth, "Almanac Of Amer Wmn Of The 20th Century," Prentice Hall Press, 1987; Auth, "From Colony To Commonwealth: and Illustrated Hist of Massachusetts," Windsor Books, 1987; Auth, "I Remember," *Yankee mag*, 1985.

CLARK, Katherine Hampton (Los) 3969 Bucklin Pl, Thousand Oaks CA 91360 B San Francisco CA 1939 d Robert & Jane. BA Mills Coll 1961; Cert ETSBH 1986; MA ETSBH 1987. D 6/20/1987 P 5/14/1988 Bp Oliver Bailey Garver Jr. c 2. Asst Prince Of Peace Epis Ch Woodland Hls CA 2006-2012, Assoc 1997-2004, Assoc R 1988-1995; Asst S Patricks Ch And Day Sch Thousand Oaks CA 1987-1988; Trin Par Fillmore CA 1987. DOK 1992. Asst, Emeritaus Prince of Peace Epis Ch, Woodland Hills, CA 2012.

CLARK, Marlene M (Mich) 1180 S Durand Rd, Lennon MI 48449 B Manistique MI 1933 d Walter & Rhea. U of New Mex 1957; MDiv SWTS 1989. D 6/24/1989 Bp H Coleman Mcgehee Jr P 4/21/1990 Bp R aymond Stewart Wood Jr. c 1. P-in-c S Matt's Epis Ch Saginaw MI 2009-2016; R S Mk's Epis Ch Guadalajara Mex 1998-2003; R Engl Spkng Cong H Cross Acapulco Mex 1993-1998; S Jn's Ch Chesaning MI 1993-1994; R S Andr's Epis Ch Flint MI 1989-1993; Par Admin S Paul's Epis Ch Corunna MI 1973-1982.

CLARK, Martha K (WA) 600 M St SW, Washington DC 20024 **S Aug's Epis Ch Washington DC 2005-** B New Haven CT 1957 d Charles & Priscilla. BA Harv 1982; MDiv Duke DS 1992. D 2/14/1993 Bp Huntington Williams Jr P 2/1/1994 Bp Robert Whitridge Estill. c 3. S Marg's Ch Washington DC 1999-2001; Asst Emm Epis Ch Geneva 1201 1997-1998; S Phil's Ch Durham NC 1994-1995; Vic S Andrews Ch Durham NC 1993-1995; Dio No Carolina Raleigh NC 1993. Auth, "Sthrn Exposure".

CLARK, Paula E (WA) 3001 Orion Ln, Upper Marlboro MD 20774 B Washington DC 1962 BA Br. D 6/12/2004 P 1/22/2005 Bp John Bryson Chane. c 1. Dio Washington Washington DC 2013, Cn 2013-; P-in-c S Jn's Epis Ch Zion Par Beltsville MD 2008-2013; Asst S Pat's Ch Washington DC 2004-2007. pclark@edow.org

CLARK, Philip C (Minn) 128 Canterbury Cir, Le Sueur MN 56058 B Syracuse NY 1933 s Henry & Catherine. BS Syr 1954; MS Syr 1958. D 11/21/1993 P 6/18/1994 Bp Sanford Zangwill Kaye Hampton. m 5/2/1957 Shirley A Welsh. Loc P Dio Minnesota Minneapolis MN 1994-2002.

CLARK, Ralph (EC) 801 Bobby Jones Drive, Fayetteville NC 28312 **Chapl Mltry Chapl US Army VA 2005-** B Latrobe PA 1965 s Harry & Gretchen. BA Cit 1987; MDiv Sewanee: The U So, TS 2001; MA Webster U 2011. D 6/16/2001 P 11/25/2003 Bp Clifton Daniel III. c 2. R H Trin Epis Ch Hertford NC 2001-2005.

CLARK JR, Richard Johnston (Fla) 1623 7th St, New Orleans LA 70115 **Cn Dio Florida Jacksonville 2014-; Chapl Ch Of The Incarn Gainesville FL 2011-** B Rantoul IL 1970 s Richard & Helen. BA LSU 1992; MBA Nimbas 2001; MDiv Wycliffe Coll Toronto CA 2009. D 12/27/2008 P 6/27/2009 Bp Charles Edward Jenkins III. m 12/31/2004 Cinda L Clark c 1. S Mich's Ch Gainesville FL 2011-2015; Mssnr Dio Louisiana New Orleans LA 2009-2011.

CLARK, Richard Neece (WMich) 900 Pivot Rock Rd, Eureka Springs AR 72632 **Ret 1999-** B Kingsville TX 1944 s Ralph & Willie. BMus SMU 1966; MDiv Nash 1969. D 6/18/1969 P 12/22/1969 Bp Charles A Mason. m 12/31/1972 Kimberly P Pulley c 1. R Trin Ch Three Rivers MI 1986-1999; S Andr's Ch Mtn Hm AR 1985-1986; Vic S Jas Ch Eureka Spgs AR 1977-1984; Asst Trin Cathd Little Rock AR 1971-1977; Cur S Alb's Epis Ch Arlington TX 1969-1971. Abbey of S Greg - Oblate 1983. rnclarktx@gmail.com

CLARK, Richard Tilton (Mass) 16 Timothy St, Fairhaven MA 02719 **Non-par 1982-** B Portsmouth NH 1934 s Bradley & Helen. BA U of New Hampshire 1956; MDiv Andover Newton TS 1961. D 11/13/1963 Bp Dudley S Stark P 3/1/1964 Bp Charles Francis Hall. m 5/20/1983 Dianne Clark. Supplement Accounts Boston MA 1972-1977; Vic Ch Of The Gd Shpd Fairhaven MA 1967-1982; Cur S Mart's Epis Ch New Bedford MA 1965-1967; Cur Ch Of The Gd Shpd Nashua NH 1963-1965.

CLARK, Robbin (Cal) 36 Larkhay Road, Hucclecote Gloucester AE GL3 3NS Great Britain (UK) B Washington DC 1945 d Alonzo & Elizabeth. BA Mt Holyoke Coll 1967; BS Col 1970; MS U CA 1975; Cert Oxf GB 1980; MDiv CDSP 1981. D 6/27/1981 P 5/29/1982 Bp William Edwin Swing. R S Mk's Par Berkeley CA 1993-2010; R S Bede's Epis Ch Santa Fe NM 1985-1993; Cur S Mk's Epis Ch Upland CA 1981-1984.

CLARK, Susan Mccarter (EMich) W180N7890 Town Hall Rd Apt D315, Menomonee Falls WI 53051 B Madison WI 1934 d John & Jean. Nash; VTS; BA Whitman Coll 1956. D 5/10/1980 Bp Charles Thomas Gaskell P 5/28/1987 Bp Roger John White. c 2. R S Paul's Epis Ch S Clair MI 1992-2001; Sr Assoc Chr Ch Milwaukee WI 1988-1992, Asst to R 1983-1987, DRE 1971-1982; Adj Fac Nash Nashotah WI 1981-1991.

CLARK, Taylor Brooks (Ore) 991 Normandy Ave S, Salem OR 97302 B Joplin MO 1950 s Richard & Gladys. BS Portland St U 2005; MSW Portland St U 2007. D 9/16/2000 Bp Richard Sui On Chang. c 2.

CLARK, Vance Norman (CPa) 925 S. Lincoln Ave., Apt. G, Tyrone PA 16686 **Ret 1986-** B Canton OH 1926 s Harold & Loretta. BA Dickinson Coll 1947; STM Wesley TS 1950; U So 1956. D 6/16/1957 P 2/1/1958 Bp Albert R Stuart.

c 3. P-in-c Ch Of The H Trin Houtzdale PA 1992-1997; Int H Trin Epis Ch Hollidaysburg PA 1989-1990; S Lk's Epis Ch Altoona PA 1980-1982; Dio Cntrl Pennsylvania Harrisburg PA 1978-1984; Trin Epis Ch Tyrone PA 1972-1986; P-in-c S Jn's Epis Ch Huntingdon PA 1972-1976; Chapl US-A 1962-1971; R S Anne's Ch Tifton GA 1958-1962; Cur S Mk's Ch Brunswick GA 1957-1958; Serv Methodist Ch 1950-1956. Meritorious Achievement Medal 1978; Bronze Star 1968.

CLARK, Vanessa E B (O) St. James Episcopal Church, 131 N State St, Painesville OH 44077 **Dio Ohio Cleveland 2016-, Mem COM 2013-2017, Chapl to Ord of the DOK 2009-; R S Jas Ch Painesville OH 2009-** B Lexington KY 1973 d Kenneth & Vivian. BA U CO 1995; Mstr of Div Bex Sem 2007. D 12/2/2006 P 6/16/2007 Bp Kenneth Lester Price. m 2/23/2002 Mark D Clark c 2. P-in-c S Paul's Epis Ch Greenville OH 2007-2009; Lay Admin S Jn's Ch Worthington OH 2001-2004; Rep to Ohio Coun of Ch Faith and Ord Com Dio Sthrn Ohio Cincinnati OH 2007-2009, Clerk to Faith in Life Com 2004-2007. CT Assoc 2009. rector@stjamesoh.org

CLARK, William Roderick (WTex) 1417 E Austin Ave, Harlingen TX 78550 **St Ptr & St Paul Ch Mssn TX 2016-** B Ft Worth TX 1977 s William & Patricia. BA U of Texas 2011; BA U of Texas at Austin 2011; MDiv Epis TS Of The SW 2014; MDiv Epis TS of the SW 2014. D 12/13/2013 Bp David Mitchell Reed P 7/1/2014 Bp Gary Richard Lillibridge. m 10/28/2006 Andrea Brown c 2. S Alb's Ch Harlingen TX 2014-2016.

CLARK, William Whittier (Alb) Po Box 56, Medusa NY 12120 B Albany NY 1949 s Richard & Jane. AAS Paul Smiths Coll 1969; BS Syr 1978. D 5/14/1994 Bp David Standish Ball. m 6/15/1974 Kathleen Loraine Clark c 2.

CLARKE, Anne Elizabeth (NCal) **The Epis Dio Nthrn California Sacramento CA 2015-** D 8/27/2016 P 3/25/2017 Bp Barry Leigh Beisner.

CLARKE, Barbara Jean (Me) 11 Daisey Ln, Brewer ME 04412 **R S Pat's Brewer ME 2005-** B Ellsworth ME 1941 d John & Vivian. BA U of Maine 1963; MS U of Maine 1965; PhD Tul 1974; Cert EDS 1995; MDiv Wesley TS 1996. D 6/17/1995 Bp Jane Hart Holmes Dixon P 5/9/1996 Bp Ronald Hayward Haines. R S Pat's Ch Brewer ME 2008; Int S Aug's Epis Ch Washington DC 2004-2005; P-in-c S Lk's Ch Trin Par Beth MD 2001-2003; Int S Matt's Epis Ch Hyattsville MD 1999-2001; S Marg's Ch Washington DC 1996-1997; Ch Of The Ascen Gaithersburg MD 1995-1996; Assoc Prof Amer U Washington DC 1974-2000. Auth, "Healing Power of Anger," *Through Eyes of Wmn:Insights in Pstr Care*, 1996.

CLARKE, Charles Ray (Wyo) 796 Garner Dr, Lander WY 82520 B Hebron NE 1943 s Darrell & Margaret. BS U of Wyoming 1971; EFM Sewanee: The U So, TS 1990. D 1/24/1993 Bp Bob Gordon Jones P 11/30/2002 Bp Bruce Caldwell. m 8/29/1969 Cheryl Ann Caufman. NAAD.

CLARKE JR, Daniel L (SC) 94 Willow Oak Cir, Charleston SC 29418 B Sumter SC 1955 s Daniel & Una. BA Belmont Abbey Coll 1976; MA Cit 1980; MDiv Nash 1999. D 6/17/1999 P 12/19/1999 Bp Edward Lloyd Salmon Jr. m 4/19/2009 Lisa S Clarke. Cur Ch Of The H Comm Charleston SC 2013-2015, 1999-2011; H Cross Stateburg Sumter SC 2011-2013. Assn Our Lady Of Walsingham; CBS, GAS, SocMary; Living Rosary Our Lady Of S Dominic Soc King Chas Mtyr.

CLARKE, Debra M (NJ) 187 Aster Ct, Whitehouse Station NJ 08889 **D S Thos Ch Alexandria Pittstown NJ 2009-; Dir of Yth Mnstry Dio New Jersey Trenton NJ 2005-** B Plainfield NJ 1959 d David & Ellen. D 9/21/2002 Bp David Bruce Joslin. m 9/5/1981 Stephen R Clarke c 2.

CLARKE, Gervaise Angelo Morales (Nwk) 34 Orane Ave, Meadowbrook Mews Kingston 19 Jamaica **Chapl Police & Fire Departments Orange NJ 1987-** B Kingston JM 1940 s Vincent & Maude. LTh Untd Theol Coll of The W Indies Kingston Jm 1968; BA U of The W Indies 1971; MTh PrTS 1981; PhD Thornewood U Amsterdam Nl 2001. Trans 2/1/1987 Bp The Bishop Of Jamaica. m 7/13/1968 Joan F Clarke c 2. Cathd Chapt Dio Newark Newark NJ 2004-2012, Const & Cn Com 2004-2012, Cathd Chapt 1989-1992; Cn Ch Of The Epiph Orange NJ 1987-2007; Serv Ch Of Belize 1984-1986; Serv Ch Of Jamaica 1966-1984. "Intl & Jamaican Track And Field," *Track And Field Jamaica (Quarterly)*, 1998. Fell Of The Royal Geographical Soc 1983; Lions Club Of Kingston 1969-1984; Rotary Club Of Orange 1987. Paul Harris Fell In Rotary Rotary Club Of Orange 2000; Off Of The Ord Of dist (O.D) Govt Of Jamaica 1998; Hon Cn Dio Belize 1984.

CLARKE, James Munro (Alb) Po Box 405, Downsville NY 13755 B Newport RI 1951 s David & Claudia. BA Muskingum Coll 1974; MDiv Yale DS 1978. D 6/17/1978 P 12/17/1978 Bp Frederick Hesley Belden. m 12/6/1997 Janet G Clarke c 3. S Marg's Ch Margaretville NY 2001-2002; S Mary's Ch Downsville NY 2001-2002; All SS Epis Ch Kansas City MO 1999-2001; Dioc Coun Dio Albany Greenwich NY 1996-1999, Prov Syn 1998-1999, Co-Chr Yth Mnstry Metropltn Dnry 1990-1997, Chair Yth Com 1988-1989; R S Andr's Ch Schenectady NY 1988-1999; Assoc R All SS Ch Tarpon Spgs FL 1987-1988, Asst R 1984-1986; Ce Com Dio SW Florida Parrish FL 1987-1988, Yth Com 1985-1988; Cmsn Chr Formation Dio Cntrl Florida Orlando FL 1982-1984, Epis Sch Assn 1981-1984; Chapl S Edwards Sch Vero Bch FL 1981-1984; S

Edw's Sch Vero Bch FL 1981-1984; Epis HS Alexandria VA 1978-1981; Asst Chapl Epis HS Alexandria VA 1978-1981.

CLARKE, Janet Vollert (SeFla) 33406 Fairway Rd, Leesburg FL 34788 **D S Thos Epis Ch Eustis FL 1996-** B New York NY 1931 d Rudolph & Ada. Rutgers The St U of New Jersey 1953; Barry U 1984; Cert Diac Sch Mnstry Miami FL 1988; AA Miami-Dade Cmnty Coll 1988. D 6/4/1988 Bp Calvin Onderdonk Schofield Jr. m 4/22/1979 Ronald Clarke c 5. D S Andr's Epis Ch Miami FL 1991-1996; Ret DRE St. Andr's Epis Ch 1983-1996. NAAD 1989. McKnight Schlrshp Acad Excellence MDCC.

CLARKE, John David Blackmore (NY) 790 11th Ave Apt 29a, New York NY 10019 B Providence RI 1939 s Kenneth & Ruth. AA Bos 1960; BS U of Arizona 1969. D 5/19/2001 Bp Richard Frank Grein. m 5/28/1978 Maria Antonia Velez c 2. St. Barth Ch New York NY 2001-2009.

CLARKE, John Robert (Mass) 2 Ridgewood Rd, Malden MA 02148 **P-in-c S Paul's Ch Malden MA 2004-** B Boston MA 1948 s Buell & Anne. BA Wheaton Coll 1970; MDiv Weston Jesuit TS 1997. D 6/6/1998 P 5/29/1999 Bp M(Arvil) Thomas Shaw. m 9/29/2007 William James Theisen. Par Of The Mssh Auburndale MA 2001-2003; Int Ascen Memi Ch Ipswich MA 1999-2000; Asst S Steph's Epis Ch Boston MA 1998-1999. Affirming Cath; Alpha Sigma Nu; Human Rts Cmpgn Fund; MECA; Rel Cltn for the Freedom to Marry.

CLARKE, Julian Maurice (VI) 123 Circle Dr, Saint Simons Island GA 31522 **Cn to the Ordnry Dio the Vrgn Islands Vrgn Islands (U.S.) 2006-; Ret 1999-** B Tortola VI 1938 s Cardigan & Elsa. Cert ETSC 1969; Advncd CPE 1973; MDiv ETSC 1974; Fell VTS 1988; VTS 1990; Bd Cert Clincl Chapl, Pstr Counslr Coll of Pstr Supervision & Psych 2012. D 6/27/1969 P 1/1/1970 Bp Cedric Earl Mills. m 12/27/1961 Esther Alicia Clarke c 2. Cur S Paul's Epis Ch Orangeburg SC 1999; S Geo Mtyr Ch Tortola 1993-1999; R S Geo's Ch 1993-1999; R S Athan Ch Brunswick GA 1990-1993; R S Andr's Ch St Thos VI 1979-1990, Vic 1975-1978; Cn to Bp of VI Dio Vrgn Islands Charlotte Amalie St Thom VI 1976-1977; Vic Ch of the H Sprt St Thos VI 1974-1987; Cur Cathd Ch of All SS St Thos VI 1969-1972; Cur The Cathd Ch of All SS UsVirgin Islands 1969-1972. Auth, "The Test," *Ten Who Tithe*, The Epis Ch Cntr, 1980; Auth, "Culture and Sprtl Aspects of Aging," *Proceedings of the First Caribbean Inst on Gerontology*, Coll of the Vrgn Islands, 1979. Cn Cathdral Ch of All SS 2006; Off of the British Empire Eliz II, Queen of Engl 1999; League of British Vrgn ISlands Awd League of British Vrgn Islands 1998; Legis Awd for Dedicated Serv to People of VI 1990; Soc Worker of Achievement NASW VI Chapt 1987. jmc38@aol.com

CLARKE, Kenneth Gregory (SO) 3090 Montego Ln. Apt. 1, Maineville OH 45039 B Chicago IL 1929 s Arthur & Leta. BA Denison U 1952. D 6/13/2009 Bp Thomas Edward Breidenthal. c 1.

CLARKE, Richard Kent (WMass) 162 Laurelwood Dr, Hopedale MA 01747 **Ret 1996-** B Springfield MA 1935 s Louis & Hazel. BA Wesl 1957; UTS 1958; BD EDS 1960. D 6/28/1960 Bp Robert McConnell Hatch P 12/29/1960 Bp William Jones Gordon Jr. m 6/12/1965 Katherine W Clarke. Int S Andr's Ch No Grafton MA 1996-1997; Pres Montachusett Coun Of Ch 1993-1996; Natl Bd EME Dio Wstrn Massachusetts Springfield 1984-1986, Bd Mgr 1972-1983, Bement/Waterfield Grants Com 1985-2010; R The Chap Of All SS Leominster MA 1981-1996; Assoc Chr Ch Fitchburg MA 1979-1981; R Trin Epis Ch Whitinsville MA 1970-1979; Mssnry Mssnry Dist Of Alaska 1960-1970. Ord Lectio Divina.

CLARKE, Robert (Chi) 524 Sheridan Sq Apt 3, Evanston IL 60202 B Chicago IL 1952 s Thomas & Thelma. BA Luther Coll 1982; MDiv SWTS 1982; DMin Chicago TS 1995. D 6/11/1983 Bp Quintin Ebenezer Primo Jr P 12/1/1983 Bp James Winchester Montgomery. m 7/8/2010 Laurel J Clarke c 1. S Mich And All Ang Ch Albuquerque NM 2013-2014; Gr Epis Ch Sheboygan WI 2010-2011; S Dav's Ch Glenview IL 2008-2010; The Cathd Ch Of S Paul Springfield IL 2004-2006; St Paul's Epis Cathd Fond Du Lac WI 2001-2003; Int Chr Ch River Forest IL 2000-2001; P-in-c Ch Of S Ben Bolingbrook IL 1986-1987; P-in-c S Bride's Epis Ch Oregon IL 1985-1986; Asst S Aug's Epis Ch Wilmette IL 1984-2000. rdrbclarke@aol.com

CLARKE, Sheelagh Alison (Nwk) 119 Main St, Millburn NJ 07041 **R S Steph's Ch Millburn NJ 2011-** B Aylesbury UK 1956 d Anthony & Joan. BEd U of Reading Reading GB 1977; MA Open U Milton Keynes GB 1990; MDiv GTS 2005. D 6/11/2005 P 1/14/2006 Bp George Edward Councell. m 6/19/2003 Michael Christopher Clarke c 1. Int S Barn Epis Ch Monmouth Jct NJ 2009-2011; Asst S Paul's Epis Ch Westfield NJ 2007-2009; Asst S Lk's Ch Gladstone NJ 2005-2007.

CLARKE, Thomas George (Los) 1549 E Lobo Way, Palm Springs CA 92264 **Consult Epis Schools 2003-; Trst VTS Alexandria VA 2001-** B Los Angeles CA 1945 s Thomas & Majory. BA U of Redlands 1967; MDiv VTS 1970. D 9/13/1970 Bp Francis E I Bloy P 3/1/1971 Bp Victor Manuel Rivera. Headmaster Campbell Hall Sch/Argyll Acad No Hollywood CA 1983-2003; Dn & Pres Campbell Hall Sch/Argyll Acad No Hollywood CA 1972-1982; Campbell Hall Vlly Vlg CA 1971-2004; Chapl Campbell Hall Sch/Argyll Acad No Hollywood CA 1971-1972; Asst The Ch Of The Epiph Washington DC 1970-1971; Pres Natl Assoc Of Epis Schools- Epis Ch New York NY 1990-1992, Trst

1987-2003. Distinguished Alum Awd Campbell Hall/Argyll Acad Alum Assn 2008; The Jn Verdery Awd Nat. Assoc. of Epis Schools 2008.

CLARKSON, Frederick C (Tex) 4401 Statesville Blvd., Salisbury NC 28147 B Bogota Colombia 1970 s Frederick & Gwinneth. MA U of St Andrews 1993; MDiv VTS 2008. D 5/24/2008 Bp Peter J Lee P 11/29/2008 Bp William O Gregg. Cur Dio Texas Houston TX 2017; S Tim's Epis Ch Houston TX 2013-2017; Vic Ch Of The Gd Shpd Cooleemee NC 2008-2013; Dio No Carolina Raleigh NC 2008-2013. fclarkson@yadtel.net

CLARKSON, J (WNC) **Cur Calv Epis Ch Fletcher NC 2017-** D 12/17/2016 Bp Jose Antonio McLoughlin.

CLARKSON, Julie Cuthbertson (NC) 1420 Sterling Rd, Charlotte NC 28209 B Charlotte NC 1929 d William & Julia. BA Agnes Scott Coll 1951; MDiv Duke DS 1984; Cert GTS 1987. D 8/30/1987 Bp Frank Harris Vest Jr P 9/1/1988 Bp Robert Whitridge Estill. c 3. S Ptr's Epis Ch Charlotte NC 1996-1998; Gr Epis Ch Lexington NC 1993-1995; S Chris's Epis Ch High Point NC 1987-1992.

CLARKSON, Ted Hamby (Ga) Po Drawer 929, Darien GA 31305 **R S Andr's Ch Darien GA 2006-; Vic S Cyp's Ch Darien GA 2006-; Dn, SE Convocataion Dio Georgia Savannah GA 2011-, Dep, GC 2011-, Stndg Com 2011-, Bp's Search Com 2009-2010, Eccl Trial Crt 2008-2011, Chairman, C&C Commision 2007-2010** B Augusta GA 1958 s Allen & Mary. BS Wofford Coll 1979; JD U GA 1982; MDiv Sewanee: The U So, TS 2006. D 2/4/2006 P 8/9/2006 Bp Henry Irving Louttit. m 6/28/1980 Allison H Clarkson c 3.

CLARKSON IV, William (WA) 1424 W Paces Ferry Rd Nw, Atlanta GA 30327 **Cler Assoc All SS Epis Ch Atlanta GA 2002-; Pres The Westminster Schools Atlanta GA 1991-; Non-par 1984-** B Corsicana TX 1947 s William & Mary. BA Duke 1970; MDiv GTS 1973; DMin SMU 1982. D 6/11/1973 P 12/1/1973 Bp Archibald Donald Davies. m 5/27/1972 Lucile McKee c 2. Asst Hd/Headmaster The Potomac Sch McClean VA 1983-1991; Asst Chr Ch Georgetown Washington DC 1981-1983; Cur S Mich And All Ang Ch Dallas TX 1978-1981; Chapl S Mk's Sch Dallas TX 1975-1980; S Marks Sch Of Texas Dallas TX 1975-1978; Cur S Alb's Epis Ch Arlington TX 1973-1975; Chapl U Of Texas-Arlington 1973-1975.

CLASSEN, Ashley Molesworth (Dal) 635 N Story Rd, Irving TX 75061 B El Paso TX 1944 s Ashley & Hilda. BS Baylor U 1974; DO UNT Hlth Sci Cntr 1978; Cert The Stanton Cntr For Mnstry Formation 2010. D 6/11/2011 P 5/19/2012 Bp James Monte Stanton. m 11/24/1977 Eva Jobailey c 4.

CLAUSEN, Kathryn (SO) 3623 Sellers Drive, Millersport OH 43046 B Dayton OH 1941 d George & Katherine. BA OH SU 1962; MD OH SU 1966; MS OH SU 1968; MTS Trin Luth Sem 2001. D 10/28/2000 P 6/23/2001 Bp Herbert Thompson Jr. c 2. P-in-c S Jas Epis Ch Zanesville OH 2006-2009; Int Trin Epis Ch London OH 2005-2006; Assoc Dn Bex Sem Columbus OH 2003-2006, Assoc Dn 2003-2006; P-in-c Trin Ch Newark OH 2001-2005. Auth, "Numerous Med arts In," *Numerous Med arts In Var Pub.* Sprt of Wmn Awd OH SU Med Ctr 1999; Tchg Awards x 4 OH SU Med 1986; Alum Achievement Awd OH SU Med 1986; Prof of Year OH SU Med 1976; AOA hon Med Soc OH SU 1966; Med awards Var 1961.

CLAUSEN, Ruth Lucille (Mich) 100 N. College Row Apt. 165, Brevard NC 28712 **Ret 1997-** B Mansfield OH 1930 d Ray & Florence. Baldwin-Wallace Coll 1949; BS OH SU 1952; MSW U MI 1969; CDSP 1988. D 6/25/1988 Bp Henry Irving Mayson P 1/28/1989 Bp H Coleman Mcgehee Jr. c 1. Trin Ch Detroit MI 1992-1997; S Mich's Ch Grosse Pointe MI 1991-1992; R S Geo's Ch Warren MI 1988-1992.

CLAVIER, Anthony Forbes Moreton (Spr) 193 Summit Avenue, Glen Carbon IL 62034 B Worsbrough Dale UK 1940 s Forbes & Ethel. Bern Gilpin Soc Durham Gb 1960; Inst of Theol London Gb 1964; BD Geneva TS 1974; STD Geneva TS 1975; Nash 1994. Trans 2/15/2004 Bp Creighton Leland Robertson. c 3. S Paul's Epis Ch Laporte IN 2008-2012; Int S Thos a Becket Epis Ch Morgantown WV 2005-2008; Convoc of Epis Ch in Europe Paris 2004-2005; Exec Coun Appointees New York NY 2004; Dio Arkansas Little Rock AR 2001-2004; Dio So Dakota Pierre SD 2001-2004; R Trin Epis Ch Watertown SD 2001-2004; Trin Ch Pine Bluff AR 1999-2001; Serv Amer Epis Ch 1970-1995.

CLAWSON, Donald Richard (SeFla) 1605 Paseo Del Lago Ln, Vero Beach FL 32967 **Ret FL 1998-** B Pittsburgh PA 1933 s Richard & Hannah. BA U Pgh 1955; MDiv GTS 1958. D 6/14/1958 Bp William S Thomas P 12/21/1958 Bp Austin Pardue. m 1/3/1988 Stacey Hanna c 3. S Paul's Epis Ch New Smyrna Bch FL 1983-1998; Dn So Palm Bch Dnry 1979-1983; R S Paul's Ch Delray Bch FL 1977-1998; R S Jn's Ch Hollywood FL 1975-1976; Dio Cntrl Gulf Coast Pensacola FL 1970-1975; Chapl S Paul Day Sch Mobile AL 1970-1975; R S Paul's Ch Mobile AL 1970-1975; Instr Epis HS Jacksonville FL 1967-1970; R Gr Epis Ch Orange Pk FL 1963-1970; P-in-c S Phil's Ch Coraopolis PA 1958-1963; Chair - Duncan Conf Cntr Bd Dir Dio SE Florida Miami 1984-1987; DeptCE Dio Pittsburgh Pittsburgh PA 1959-1963. Hon HLD El Shaddai Sem 1996.

CLAWSON, Jeffrey David (Los) 3 Bayview Ave., Belvedere CA 94920 **P-in-c S Anselm Of Cbury Par Garden Grove CA 2012-** B Garden Grove CA 1959 s David & Suzanne. BA California St U 1984; MS California St U 1986; MDiv

CDSP 2008. D 6/7/2008 P 1/10/2009 Bp Joseph Jon Bruno. All SS Par Los Angeles CA 2009-2010; Assoc R S Steph's Par Bel Tiburon CA 2008-2009.

CLAXTON, Constance Colvin (Minn) 312 Church St, Audubon IA 50025 B Tulsa OK 1940 d Richard & Muzetta. BA S Cathr U 1981; MDiv SWTS 1985. D 6/24/1985 P 1/1/1986 Bp Robert Marshall Anderson. m 1/2/1989 Roger C Claxton c 3. R S Lk's Epis Ch Hastings MN 2004-2010, 1994-2003; P-in-c Trin Ch Litchfield MN 1999-2000; P-in-c S Jas Ch Marshall MN 1995-1998; P-in-c Emm Epis Ch Alexandria MN 1989-1994; Asst Chr Ch S Paul MN 1986-1989; P-in-c S Mary's Basswood Grove Hastings MN 1985-1989; Bp's Stff Dio Minnesota Minneapolis MN 1994-1999.

CLAXTON, Leonard Cuthbert (Minn) RR #2, Box 207, Truman MN 56088 Mentor EFM 1977- B Superior WI 1923 s Cuthbert & Mary. Minnesota St U Mankato 1959; U MN 1962; U of No Dakota 1970. D 2/24/1966 P 9/1/1966 Bp Russell T Rauscher. m 4/24/1948 Shirley Claxton. Supply S Andrews Epis Ch Waterville MN 1996-2011; S Andr's Ch Cloquet MN 1985-1989; S Steph's Epis Ch Stevensville MT 1982-1985; Exec Counsel Dio Montana Helena MT 1981-1985, Chair 1979-1985, Chair 1970-1975, Bd Trst 1974-1981; Vic S Paul's Ch Hamilton MT 1974-1985; Cur S Lk's Ch Billings MT 1971-1974; Vic S Thos Ch Hardin MT 1970-1971; Ch Of The Gd Shpd Bridger MT 1969-1971; Vic S Alb's Epis Ch Laurel MT 1969-1971; Vic S Ptr And S Jas Ch Grafton ND 1966-1969; Vic S Ptr's Pk River ND 1966-1969. Ord Of S Lk.

CLAY, Thomas Davies (WA) 15003 Reserve Rd, Accokeek MD 20607 Ret 1998- B Huntington WV 1938 s Earl & Mary. BA Marshall U 1960; MDiv Epis TS in Kentucky 1963. D 6/1/1963 P 12/1/1963 Bp William R Moody. m 4/5/1997 Kathleen Jenkins O'Day c 2. P-in-c Chr Ch Wm And Mary Newburg MD 1998-2002; R S Andr Leonardtown MD 1994-1998; S Andr's Ch Leonardtown California MD 1994-1998; R Calv Epis Ch Front Royal VA 1978-1994; R S Mk's Epis Ch Lagrange GA 1969-1978; Asst S Ptr's Epis Ch Washington NC 1966-1969; Chapl Berea Coll Berea KY 1963-1966; Chr Ch Richmond KY 1963-1966.

CLAYTON JR, Paul Bauchman (NY) 4 Townsend Farm Rd, Lagrangeville NY 12540 B Port Arthur TX 1939 s Paul & Bernice. BA U of Texas 1961; STB GTS 1964; STM GTS 1968; MA UTS 1975; PhD UTS 1985. D 6/18/1964 P 12/18/1964 Bp Theodore H McCrea. m 6/1/1988 Sharon Hoffman Chant c 2. Adj Prof of Patristics The GTS New York NY 1992, Asst Zion 1966-1991; Lectr in Anglicanism UTS NY 1988-1993; R S Andr's Ch Poughkeepsie NY 1971-2005; Asst Zion Epis Ch Wappingers Falls NY 1966-1971; Vic Ch of the Mssh White Settlement TX 1965-1966; Vic Ch Of The H Apos Ft Worth TX 1964-1966; Asst All SS' Epis Ch Ft Worth TX 1964-1965. Auth, "The Christology of Antiochene," *Theo of Cyrus: Late Antiochene Christology*, Oxf Press, 2007; Auth, "arts," *Encyclopedia Amer*, 1972. Alcuin Club 1964-2005; Amer Soc Ch Hist 1964; Angl Soc 1964; HSEC 1964; No Amer Acad Ecumenists 1987; No Cmsn Patriotics Soc 2009; Oxford Intl Conf of Patristic Stds 1971; Soc of Angl and Luth Theologians 1988. Fell ECF 1971; Phi Beta Kappa U of Texas 1961.

CLAYTON, Sharon Hoffman Chant (NY) 4 Townsend Farm Rd, Lagrangeville NY 12540 B New York NY 1946 d Bernard & Geraldine. Premier Degree U of Paris FR 1967; BA CUNY 1968; MDiv GTS 1986. D 6/7/1986 Bp Paul Moore Jr P 12/13/1986 Bp Walter Decoster Dennis Jr. m 6/1/1988 Paul Bauchman Clayton. Vic S Paul's And Trin Par Tivoli NY 2007-2016; R Gr Ch Millbrook NY 1999-2000; Cur S Andr's Ch Poughkeepsie NY 1989-2005; Asst Chr's Ch Rye NY 1986-1988. Auth, *Joining the Conversation*.

CLAYTON, Vikki (WA) 20100 Fisher Ave, Poolesville MD 20837 S Lk's Ch Brighton Brookeville MD 2016-; Chapl Frederick Memi Hosp 2014- B Bethesda MD 1957 d John & Marie. BA U of Maryland 1982; MA U of Maryland 1986; MDiv VTS 2014. D 12/7/2013 P 6/14/2014 Bp Mariann Edgar Budde. m 9/19/1981 John S Clayton c 2.

CLAYTOR, Susan Quarles (CPa) 310 Elm Avenue, Hershey PA 17033 R All SS' Epis Ch Hershey PA 2009-; R St. Jas' Epis Ch Lake CIty Florida 2007- B Atlanta GA 1961 d Willie & Ethel. BA U of No Florida 2001; MDiv VTS 2004. D 5/30/2004 Bp Stephen Hays Jecko P 12/5/2004 Bp Samuel Johnson Howard. m 8/4/1979 Francis Parr Claytor c 7. S Jas' Epis Ch Lake City FL 2007-2008; Trin Epis Ch St Aug FL 2004-2007; Asst R Trin Epis Par S Aug Florida 2004-2007; Ch Of Our Sav Jacksonville FL 1991-2001. revclaytor@gmail.com

CLEAVER-BARTHOLOMEW, Dena Marcel (CNY) 4566 Stoneledge Ln, Manlius NY 13104 R Chr Ch Manlius NY 2010- B Chinon FR 1960 d Bruce & Jeanene. BA Tem 1983; MDiv Ya Berk 1988; ThM Candler TS Emory U 1994. D 6/10/1988 P 7/6/1989 Bp Charlie Fuller Mcnutt Jr. m 8/22/1987 David G Cleaver-Bartholomew c 2. Assoc R S Paul's Ch Akron OH 2006-2010; Assoc R New Life Epis Ch Uniontown OH 2005-2006; Assoc R S Jas' Epis Ch Dexter MI 2000-2005; P Ch Of The Epiph Atlanta GA 1993-1995; Assoc R H Trin Par Decatur GA 1991-1993; Assoc R S Ptr's Par San Pedro CA 1989-1991; D S Lk's Epis Ch Atlanta GA 1988-1989; Chair, Cler Cont Educ Team Dio Cntrl New York Liverpool NY 2011-2012; Dioc Coun Dio Ohio Cleveland 2008-2010, Congrl Dvlpmt Cmsn 2006-2010.

CLEAVES JR, George Lucius (EMich) 9020 South Saginaw Road, Grand Blanc MI 48439 B Needham MA 1942 s George & Marie. BS Bentley Coll 1976; MDiv EDS 1984. D 6/3/1989 Bp David Elliot Johnson P 6/14/1990 Bp Robert Rae Spears Jr. S Christophers Epis Ch Grand Blanc MI 2014-2015, R 1992-2014; Dioc Treas Dio Estrn Michigan Saginaw MI 1995-2004; Assoc S Jas Ch New York NY 1990-1992; Stndg Com Mem Dio Estrn Michigan Saginaw MI 1995-2001.

CLECKLER, Michael Howard (Ala) 1513 Edinburgh Way, Birmingham AL 35243 Non-par 1995- B Birmingham AL 1947 s Robert & Kathleen. BA Samford U 1969; JD Cumberland Sch of Law 1972; MDiv Epis TS of the SW 1989. D 6/7/1989 P 12/1/1989 Bp Robert Oran Miller. m 4/24/1992 Mary Rogers c 3. St. Matt's Epis Ch Madison AL 1992-1994; Dio Alabama Birmingham 1991-1992; Chr Ch Tuscaloosa AL 1989-1991.

CLEGHORN, Charlotte Dudley (WNC) 37 Cherry St., Arden NC 28704 B Ocala FL 1949 d Edward & Bettie. AA Bennett Coll 1969; BA Bos 1971; MRE Gordon-Conwell TS 1975; MDiv VTS 1986. D 6/4/1986 Bp John Bowen Coburn P 6/6/1987 Bp James Russell Moodey. m 1/17/2015 Elizabeth Holland. The Cathd Of All Souls Asheville NC 2005-2010; Ch Of The H Fam Mills River NC 2004-2005; Int S Jas Epis Ch Hendersonvlle NC 2002-2004; Assoc P S Geo's Epis Ch Laguna Hills CA 1998-2001; Dio Los Angeles Los Angeles CA 1997-2001; R S Ann's Epis Ch Windham Windham ME 1989-1996; Asst S Paul's Epis Ch Cleveland OH 1986-1989; Chapl/Tchr The Gvnr's Acad Byfield MA 1979-1984; Reg Dir FOCUS Greenwich CT 1975-1979.

CLEGHORN, Maxine Janetta (NY) 4401 Matilda Ave, Bronx NY 10470 S Mk's Epis Ch Yonkers NY 2012- B Jamaica 1963 d Noel & Urdella. MDiv NYTS; BA Untd TS. Trans 3/2/2010 Bp Mark Sean Sisk. Asst Ch Of the Gd Shpd Wakefield Bronx NY 2010.

CLELAND, Carol Elaine (Cal) 1550 Portola Avenue, Palo Alto CA 94306 B Malden MA 1940 d Robert & Della. BS Bos 1965; MA FD 1979; MDiv CDSP 1991; MA U of San Francisco 2003; Psychoanalytic Inst of Nthrn California 2009. D 12/7/1991 P 12/5/1992 Bp William Edwin Swing. m 9/4/1965 Alan Stuart Cleland. S Anne's Ch Fremont CA 1994-2006; Int Ch Of The Epiph San Carlos CA 1993-1994; Asst S Lk's Ch San Francisco CA 1991-1993.

CLEM, Stewart Douglas (Okla) 616 Lincolnway E, Mishawaka IN 46544 Asstg P S Paul's Ch Mishawaka IN 2013-; Asstg P - WECHT Com Ch Of The H Trin So Bend IN 2014- B Oklahoma City OK 1982 s Timothy & Deborah. BA Oklahoma St U 2005; BA Oklahoma St U 2005; MA Oklahoma St U 2008; MDiv Duke DS 2013; PhD Other 2018; PhD U of Notre Dame 2018; PhD U of Notre Dame 2018. D 12/21/2012 P 11/22/2013 Bp Edward Joseph Konieczny. m 7/1/2006 Molly Jeanine Clem c 3. D S Tim's Ch Raleigh NC 2013.

CLEMENT, Betty Cannon (Dal) 4120 Jasmine St, Paris TX 75462 B Paris TX 1937 d Bill & Bessie. Angl TS 2001. D 12/19/2001 Bp James Monte Stanton. m 6/2/1957 Wayne Clement c 2. D Ch Of The H Cross Paris TX 2001-2014.

CLEMENT, James Marshall (Chi) 222 Somonauk St, Sycamore IL 60178 Int S Ptr's Epis Ch Sycamore IL 2016- B Charleston SC 1967 s Samuel & Anne. BA Coll of Charleston 2001; MA Coll of Charleston Grad Sch 2005; BA CR Mirfield Yorks GB 2006; MDiv Nash 2007. D 12/8/2007 P 6/14/2008 Bp Keith Lynn Ackerman. Int The Ch Of S Anne Morrison IL 2015-2016; Cn Asst St Paul's Epis Ch Peoria IL 2012-2015; R S Jn's Epis Ch Kewanee IL 2010-2012; Credo Inst Inc. Memphis TN 2010; D Gr Epis Ch Galesburg IL 2007-2008; Pres of Stndg Com Dio Quincy Peoria IL 2012-2013, Dep, GC 2012, Stndg Committee 2011-2013, Dioc Coun 2009-2011. jclement@sycamorestpeters.org

CLEMENTS, C(Harles) Christopher (USC) 1523 Delmar St, West Columbia SC 29169 B Cleveland TN 1939 s Charles & Mary. BS U of Tennessee 1961; STB GTS 1964. D 6/29/1964 Bp John Vander Horst P 5/22/1965 Bp William Evan Sanders. Asstg P S Mary's Ch Columbia SC 2002-2012; Vic S Steph's Epis Ch Ridgeway SC 1989-2001; P S Jn's Ch Winnsboro SC 1987-1988; R S Jn's Epis Ch Johnson City TN 1975-1986; Chapl E Tennessee St U 1968-1975; R S Johns Ch Old Hickory TN 1966-1968; Cur S Lk's Epis Ch Jackson TN 1965-1966.

CLEMENTS, Elaine Gant (La) St Andrew's Episcopal Church, 1101 S Carrollton Ave, New Orleans LA 70118 B Ft Worth TX 1950 d Roy & Helen. BA U of No Texas 1972. D 12/1/2007 Bp Charles Edward Jenkins III. m 11/27/1977 John Clements c 2.

CLEMENTS, Robert (Ct) PO Box 809, Litchfield CT 06759 Chr Ch Bethany CT 2017-; Chapl Rumsey Hall Sch 2007- B Xenia OH 1956 s Carl & Mary. BA Thiel Coll 1978; MDiv GTS 1985; DMin PrTS 2000. D 6/15/1985 Bp James Russell Moodey P 9/15/1986 Bp Donald James Davis. m 6/24/1989 M Jennings Jennings Matheson. R Chr Ch Roxbury CT 2009-2016, Int 1999-2001; R Trin Ch Lakeville CT 2006-2009, 1998-1999, Int 1998-1999; Int S Paul's Epis Ch Shelton CT 2005-2006; Adj Prof Hartford Sem 2004-2006; Transition Consult S Mart's Ch Providence RI 2004; Int Trin Epis Ch Hartford CT 2002-2004; Int S Jas's Ch W Hartford CT 2001-2002; Pstr Assoc S Paul's Epis Ch Bantam CT 1998-1999; Ch Of The Gd Shpd So Lee MA 1998; Transition Consult Dio Wstrn Massachusetts Springfield 1998; Int S Paul's Epis Sum Chap Otis MA 1997-1998; Int S Geo's Ch Lee MA 1996-1997; Asst Headmaster Berkshire Sch 1993-1997; P-in-c All SS Ch Hoosick Falls NY 1988-1993; Chapl Hoosac Sch Hoosick NY 1988-1993; Chapl Hoosac Sch Hoosick NY

1988-1993; Vic S Aug Of Cbury Ch Edinboro PA 1986-1988; S Ptr's Ch Waterford PA 1986-1988; Chapl Edinboro U Edinboro PA 1985-1988. Auth, *Ten Ways From Sunday: Raising a Faithful Teenager*, Eschaton, 2003; Auth, *Stdt Perceptions of Indep Sch Chapl Prog*, Princeton, 2000.

CLEMMONS, Geraldine Dobbs (Alb) 105 23rd St., Troy NY 12180 B Memphis TN 1943 d James & Marguerite. MA U of Memphis 1982; BS Med U of So Carolina 1995; MDiv TESM 2008. D 5/31/2008 P 11/8/2009 Bp William Howard Love. m 10/9/1982 Byard Q Clemmons c 3. D-in-c S Jn's Ch Cohoes NY 2009-2015.

CLEMONS, D David (NCal) 8148 Emerson Ave, Yucca Valley CA 92284 B Oklahoma City OK 1937 s William & Lelah. BA U of Oklahoma 1959; BD SWTS 1963; CDSP 1974; Cert CPE 1978; Untd States-Army Chapl Sch 1982; Command and Gnrl Stff Coll 1983; DMin SWTS 2001. D 6/11/1963 P 12/16/1963 Bp Chilton R Powell. m 12/29/1979 Kathryn L Clemons c 2. Res P-in-c St. Jos of Arimathea Yuca Vlly CA 2004-2006; Gr Epis Ch Wheatland CA 2002; R S Lk's Ch Auburn CA 1994-2002; R H Trin-S Andr's Pocatello ID 1988-1993; Trin Epis Ch Pocatello ID 1988-1993; Asst S Paul's Epis Ch Ventura CA 1983-1988; S Dunst's Epis Ch San Diego CA 1982-1983; Assoc S Marg's Epis Ch Palm Desert CA 1980-1982; P-in-c H Trin Epis Ch Elk River MN 1977-1978; Chapl NW Hosp MN 1977-1978; 1974-1977; Chapl US-Army TPU (LTC) 1967-1990; Vic S Andr's Broken Arrow OK 1965-1973; Gr Ch Henryetta OK 1963-1965. "Dining w Jesus Then & Now," *The Commensality of Jesus Chr and Congrational Dvlpmt:*, doctoral thesis on file at Seabury Wstrn/NW U., 2001; "Last Supper Soliloquies". RACA 1975. Meritorious Serv Medal 90 Dept of the Army 1991; Commendation Medal 88 US-A 1988; Jas Mills Fllshp Dio Okla 1973.

CLEMONS, Earlie R (NJ) 132 S Adelaide Ave Apt 1b, Highland Park NJ 08904 **P S Aug's Ch Camden NJ 2006-** B Austin TX 1946 s Earlie & Velma. BS Texas Sthrn U 1969; MDiv Epis TS of the SW 1982. D 10/22/1987 Bp Maurice Manuel Benitez P 2/27/1988 Bp Gordon Taliaferro Charlton. m 1/19/2008 Catherine E Dabney-Clemons c 3. S Wilfrid's Ch Camden NJ 2009-2011; All SS Ch Highland Pk NJ 2004-2006; S Phil's Ch New York NY 1998-2003; Exec Bd Dio Texas Houston TX 1994-1997, Chair Csmn Black Mnstry 1991-1998, Epis Black Mnstry Csmn 1989-2000; S Fran Of Assisi Epis Prairie View TX 1990-1998; The Great Cmsn Fndt Houston TX 1987-1998; S Jas Ch Austin TX 1987-1990. Distinguished Awd Black Cultural Workshop 1986.

CLENDENIN, Evan Graham (Oly) 719 West 2nd St, Erie PA 16507 **S Andr's Epis Ch Aberdeen WA 2014-** B Meadville PA 1980 s John & Dona. BA Reed Coll 2002; Pittsburgh TS 2008; MDiv VTS 2011. D 12/4/2010 P 9/25/2011 Bp Sean Walter Rowe. m 8/8/2009 Amy L Seese-Bieda. Cathd Of S Paul Erie PA 2011-2014.

CLENDINEN JR, James H (Ga) 2621 Cotuit Ln, Tallahassee FL 32309 B Rockledge FL 1955 s James & Mary. AA Brevard Cmnty Coll 1974; BA Florida St U 1976; MS Florida St U 1978; MTS Candler TS Emory U 1980; Emory U 1983; CAS Nash 1990. D 6/17/1990 P 12/21/1990 Bp Harry Woolston Shipps. m 1/14/1978 Anne Clendinen c 3. Chapl Heartland Hospice 2014-2017; R The Epis Ch Of The Annunc Vidalia GA 2009-2013; R S Jn's Epis Ch Bainbridge GA 2003-2009; P-in-c S Thos Aquinas Mssn Baxley GA 1999-2002; R S Paul's Epis Ch Jesup GA 1994-2002; Vic S Eliz's Epis Ch Richmond Hill GA 1992-1994; R S Phil's Ch Hinesville Hinesville GA 1990-1994. Phi Beta Kappa Alpha Chapt, Florida St U 1976.

CLERKIN OJN, Shawn Jeffrey (NwPa) 662 Silliman Ave, Erie PA 16510 **Vic S Mary's Ch Erie PA 2009-; Assoc Prof Gannon U 1989-** B Ridgway PA 1963 s Charles & Violet. BA Gannon U 1986; MFA Virginia Commonwealth U 1989; MDiv Bex Sem 2008. D 12/12/2004 P 6/26/2005 Bp Robert Deane Rowley Jr. m 6/15/1985 Almitra Clemente Clerkin c 1. Cathd Of S Paul Erie PA 2007-2009; Dioc Coun Dio NW Pennsylvania Erie PA 2008-2011.

CLEVELAND, Jennifer B (Oly) 125 SW Eckman St, McMinnville OR 97128 **Chapl Oregon Epis Sch Portland OR 2009-** B Seattle WA 1961 d Richard & Nancy. BA Smith 1983; MDiv PSR 1991; CAS CDSP 1993. D 11/12/1993 P 7/11/1994 Bp Vincent Waydell Warner. m 6/25/1988 Stewart Rule Stout c 2. Assoc Trin Epis Cathd Portland OR 2008-2009; Assoc S Barth's Ch Beaverton OR 2001-2008; Assoc S Lk's Ch Evanston IL 1997-2000; Assoc S Tim's Epis Ch Yakima WA 1995.

CLEVELAND, Thomas Grover (Mass) 28 Grover Ln, Tamworth NH 03886 **Ret 1997-** B Baltimore MD 1927 s Richard & Ellen. BA Pr 1949; BD VTS 1954. D 6/5/1954 Bp Robert Fisher Gibson Jr P 12/1/1954 Bp William Jones Gordon Jr. m 7/6/1996 Ruth Elaine Cleveland c 4. The Milton Acad Milton MA 1965-1997; P-in-c S Jas Ch Tanana AK 1961-1965; P-in-c S Barth's Ch Palmer AK 1960-1961; M-in-c S Paul's Holikachuk AK 1954-1958.

CLEVELEY, Susan Lynn (Spok) 1005 E B St, Moscow ID 83843 **Dio Spokane Spokane WA 2012-; Sprtl Care Coordntr and Chapl Gentiva Hospice Pullman Washington 2011-** B Honolulu HI 1964 d David & Phyllis. BFA U of Idaho 1987. D 6/7/2008 P 12/13/2008 Bp James E Waggoner Jr. m 11/27/1986 Charles Brian Cleveley c 1.

CLEVENGER, Mark R (U) PO Box 606, Shoreham NY 11786 **Int Dio Utah Salt Lake City UT 2015-; Cn to the Ordnry Dio Upper So Carolina Co-**lumbia SC 2005-; Prov Crt of Revs, Mem Prov II 2011-; Katrina Mssnr Ecusa / Mssn Personl New York NY 2007-** B Fort Wayne IN 1960 s Elmer & Iris. BA U MI 1983; MDiv Ya Berk 1986; JD U of Kansas 1989. D 5/16/1986 Bp William Cockburn Russell Sheridan P 1/10/1987 Bp Richard Frank Grein. R S Anselm's Ch Shoreham NY 2008-2015; Dio Upper So Carolina Columbia SC 2005-2007; Dioc Stwdshp Com, Chair Dio Long Island Garden City NY 2002-2004, Eccl Crt, Mem 2009-2010, Bp's Dep for Stwdshp 2002-2004, Bp's Dep for Stewarship 2002-2004, Const and Cn Com, Mem 2002-2004, Dioc Stwdshp Com, Chair 2002-2004; Dio Mssn Dev Dio Chicago Chicago IL 2000-2002; Epis Hse of Pryr Collegeville MN 1998-2000; Cn Mssn Strat Dio Minnesota Minneapolis MN 1996-2000, Joint Plnng Cmsn Epis/Luth Concordat 1998-1999; Vic Ch Of The Nativ Burnsville MN 1996-1998; Adj Fac, hon Wstrn Civilization U of Kansas Lawr KS 1994-1996; Dioc Coun, Mem Dio Kansas Topeka KS 1993-1994, 1986-1989, Dioc Trst Mem 1992-1996, Apportnmt Com, Chair 1988-1992, Alt Dep to GC 1988, Alt Dep to GC 1988-; S Marg's Ch Lawr KS 1991-1996; Trin Ch Lawr KS 1989-1991, 1987-1988; Co-Chapl Cbury At Kansas U Lawr KS 1986-1991; Bd Dir, Mem Hse of Pryr Collegeville MN 1998-2000. Auth, "Seasons of Stwdshp Series," *The Dominion*, Dio Long Island, 2002; Ed/Auth, "Pstr's Tool Box Series," *Mssn Matters*, Dio Chicago, 2001; Ed/Auth, "Congrl Dvlpmt - Ch Coach Series," *The Great Cmsn*, Dio Minnesota, 2000; Creator, "Gratitude Mangament". mclevenger@gracestgeorge.org

CLIFF, Frank Graham (Be) 15 Bede Circle, Honesdale PA 18431 **P-in-c S Jas-S Geo Epis Ch Jermyn PA 2009-** B Melton Mowbray UK 1938 s Frank & Florence. Cert S Paul Tchr Coll GB 1960; Chilton TS 1966; DIT Lon GB 1966. Trans 6/1/1972 Bp James Milton Richardson. m 6/9/1990 Mary-Jo Cliff c 4. R Chr Ch Honesdale PA 1994-2005; R Gr Epis Ch Honesdale PA 1994-2005; R Ch Of The Adv Pittsburgh PA 1987-1994; St Philips Mssn Pittsburgh PA 1987; Vic S Philips Ch Pittsburgh PA 1986-1987; Dio Pittsburgh Pittsburgh PA 1986; Dn - Middle Convoc Dio Easton Easton MD 1983-1984, Vice-Pres - Dioc Coun 1981-1984, R 1978-1983, Asst to the Bp 1978-1982; Chr Ch Denton MD 1978-1985; Asst S Jas Ch Potomac MD 1974-1978; S Alb's Epis Ch Waco TX 1972-1978; Asst S Thos Ch Houston TX 1971-1972; Serv Ch of Engl 1966-1971.

CLIFF, Wendy Dawson (Cal) 77 Kensington Rd, San Anselmo CA 94960 **Epis Sr Communities Lafayette CA 2016-** B Greenbrae CA 1963 d William & Judith. BA U CA 1985; Tchg Cred Dominican U 1992; MDiv CDSP 2015. D 6/13/2015 Bp Marc Handley Andrus P 12/5/2015 Bp Chester Lovelle Talton. m 9/16/1989 Ivan Spaulding Cliff c 2. S Steph's Par Bel Tiburon CA 2015-2017; Other Lay Position St Johns Epis Ch Ross CA 2005-2008.

CLIFFORD III, George Minott (Haw) **P-in-c Ch Of The H Nativ Honolulu HI 2016-; Assoc Ch Of The Nativ Raleigh NC 2011-; Vstng Prof of Ethics and Publ Plcy Naval Postgraduate Sch Monterey CA 2008-** D 8/3/1992 P 2/1/1993 Bp Charles Lovett Keyser.

CLIFT, Jean Dalby (Colo) 2130 E Columbia Pl, Denver CO 80210 **Chair, Pstr Counslg, Guidelines for Cler Ethics Dio Colorado Denver CO 1991-, Pstr Intervention Team 1989-** B Naples TX 1930 d Roy & Willie. BA U of Texas 1950; JD U of Texas 1952; CG Jung Inst 1966; MA U Denv 1972; PhD U Denv 1978. D 6/11/1988 P 12/13/1988 Bp William Carl Frey. m 1/23/1954 Wallace B Clift c 3. Angl Stds Prog Iliff Sch of Theol Denver CO 1989-2002; Assoc S Jn's Cathd Denver CO 1988-2011; Adj Prof Iliff Sch of Theol & St Thos Sem Denver CO 1980-2002; Dir, Cntr for Rel Meaning Loretto Heigts Coll Denver CO 1975-1980. Auth, "The Myster of Love and The Path of Pryr," Amazon.com, 2008; Auth, "Where Would You Be Now?," *Journeys*, AAPC, 2006; Co-Auth, "The Archetypd of Pilgramage: Outer Journey w Inner Meaning," Paulist Press, 1996; Auth, "Core Images of the Self," Crossroad, 1992; Co-Auth, "The Hero Journey in Dreams," Crossroad, 1988; Auth, "Theory & Pract in Clincl Supervision in Pstr Counslg," *Jnl of Supervision and Trng*, 1988; Auth, "An Excerpt from Responses to Ord Questions," *Jnl of Wmn & Rel*, 1988; Auth, "Pstr Mnstry: A Macedonian Plea," *Jml of Wmn Mnstrs*, 1985; Co-Auth, "Symbols of Transformation in Dreams," Crossroad, 1984; Auth, "15 poems," *LivCh*, 1967. AAPC 1982; Pres, AAPC 1994-1996. Cn Pstr Emer Bp of Colorado 2002.

CLIFT, Joe Walter (Ga) 343 Gander Rd, Dawson GA 39842 B Chattanooga TN 1940 s Walter & Ray. BA Bethel U 1962; MDiv Van 1965; DMin Sewanee: The U So, TS 1989. D 3/18/1989 P 9/17/1989 Bp Harry Woolston Shipps. m 7/11/1964 Sandra Clift c 2. P-in-c Ch Of The H Sprt Dawson GA 1995; R The Epis Ch Of S Jn And S Mk Albany GA 1993-2007; Vic Chr Epis Ch Cordele GA 1989-1993; D S Paul's Ch Albany GA 1989. Amer Assn of Mar and Fam Therapists 1996; Amer Soc of Clincl Hypnosis 1998.

CLIFT JR, Wallace B (Colo) 2328 Lakemoor Dr SW, Olympia WA 98512 **Cn Theolgian Dio Colorado Denver CO 1992-, Pres, Stndg Com 1989-1990** B Robert Lee TX 1926 s Wallace & Ruth. BA U of Texas 1949; JD Harv 1952; MDiv CDSP 1960; CG Jung Inst 1966; MA U Chi 1967; PhD U Chi 1970; CDSP 2003. D 6/24/1960 P 5/26/1961 Bp John Elbridge Hines. m 1/23/1954 Jean Dalby Clift c 3. S Jn's Cathd Denver CO 1992-2002; Dio Colorado Denver CO 1976-1992; Dio Colorado Denver CO 1964-1996; 1964-1992; Ch Of The Resurr Houston TX 1960-1964; Vic Gr Resurr Houston 1960-1964. Auth,

The Archetype of Pilgrimage: Outer Action w Inner Meaning, Paulist Press, 1996; Auth, *Journey into Love*, Crossroad, 1990; Auth, *The Hero Journey in Dreams*, Crossroad, 1988; "Four arts," *Encyclopedia of Rel*, Macmillan, 1987; Auth, *Symbols of Transformation in Dreams*, Crossroad, 1984; Auth, *Jung & Chrsnty: Challenge of Recon*, Crossroad, 1982. AAPC, Amer Acad o 1982. D.D., honorus causa CDSP 2003; Study Grant - 6 year Farish Fndt 1964.

CLIFTON JR, Ellis Edward (Mich) St. Clement'S Episcopal Church, 4300 Harrison Road, Inkster MI 48141 **R S Clem's Epis Ch Inkster MI 2007-** B Detroit MI 1953 s Ellis & Marie. BS Cntrl St U 1974; OH SU 1975; MDiv TESM 1991. D 6/6/1992 P 8/1/1993 Bp Alden Moinet Hathaway. m 7/26/1975 Wanda Agee. Ch Of The Resurr Ecorse MI 2004-2006; P-in-c S Mary's Epis Ch Boston MA 2000-2004; Assoc S Mich's Ch Milton MA 1998-2000; S Andr's Epis Ch Cincinnati OH 1998; Vic Ch Of S Mich And All Ang Cincinnati OH 1995-1997; Int Ch Of The H Innoc Leechburg PA 1994-1995; Cur Ch Of The H Cross Pittsburgh PA 1993-1994. Bro S Andr 1988; Mercy Of God Cmnty Assoc 1999; UBE 1994.

CLIFTON, Steve (CFla) 3137 Denham Ct, Orlando FL 32825 **Epis Ch Of The Resurr Longwood FL 2015-; Sweetwater Epis Acad Longwood FL 2015-; Bd Trst Sewanee U So TS Sewanee TN 2011-** B Savannah GA 1960 s Gay & Joan. BMusEd Troy St U Troy AL 1981; MDiv Nash 1984; DMin Sewanee: The U So, TS 2000. D 5/16/1984 Bp George Paul Reeves P 5/10/1985 Bp Harry Woolston Shipps. m 6/14/2003 Sonia Tutan c 2. R Chr The King Epis Ch Orlando FL 2003-2015; P-in-c S Barn Epis Ch Valdosta GA 2001-2003; R S Geo's Epis Ch Bradenton FL 1996-2000; Assoc S Thos Ch Savannah GA 1993-1996; Vic S Jn's Epis Ch Bainbridge GA 1985-1993; Assoc S Aug Of Cbury Ch Augusta GA 1984-1985; Dioc Coun Dio Georgia Savannah GA 1989-1992.

CLINEHENS JR, Hal (NCal) 714 Lassen Lane, Mount Shasta CA 96067 **Int All SS Epis Ch Redding CA 2013-; Chair, Haiti T/F Epis Dio San Joaquin Modesto CA 2011-, Dioc Exec Coun 2010-2011** B Fayetteville AR 1947 s Harold & Virginia. USMA 1966; BS U of Arkansas 1971; MDiv CDSP 1979. D 6/9/1979 P 2/23/1980 Bp Christoph Keller Jr. m 1/6/2007 Beverley Charlotte Clinehens c 2. R S Jn The Bapt Lodi CA 2009-2012; Int Gr St Pauls Epis Ch Tucson AZ 2008-2014; Int S Anth On The Desert Scottsdale AZ 2007-2008; R S Wilfrid Of York Epis Ch Huntington Bch CA 1999-2007; Stndg Com The Epis Dio Nthrn California Sacramento CA 1997-1999, Stndg Commitee 1997-1999; R S Paul's Epis Ch Benicia CA 1991-1999; R S Paul's On The Plains Epis Ch Lubbock TX 1985-1991; Assoc S Andr's Epis Ch Amarillo TX 1982-1985; Vic Calv Epis Ch Osceola AR 1980-1982; Cur S Jn's Ch Harrison AR 1979-1980; Stndg Com Dio NW Texas Lubbock TX 1985-1988; Dioc Coun Dio Arkansas Little Rock AR 1981-1982. Auth, "Sermons That Wk IV". Prize Winning Sermon Epis Evang Fndt 1994.

CLINGENPEEL, Ronald H (La) 1911 Cypress Creek Road #222, New Orleans LA 70123 B Chadron NE 1953 s Harvey & Luella. BS U of Nebraska 1975; MDiv GTS 1978; Montana St U 1982; U So 1986. D 6/3/1978 P 12/21/1978 Bp James Daniel Warner. c 4. S Jn's Epis Ch Thibodaux LA 2011-2013; Dn Chr Ch Cathd S Louis MO 2002-2008; Cn Ordnry Dio Louisiana New Orleans LA 1998-2002, 1996-2002; Chapl Ch Of The H Sprt New Orleans LA 1987-1998; Dio Kansas Topeka KS 1983-1987; Vic K SU Manhattan KS 1982-1987; Chapl K SU Manhattan KS 1982; Chapl S Jas Ch Bozeman MT 1980-1982; Asst Trin Cathd Omaha NE 1978-1979. Contributing Auth, "Disorganized Rel," Cowley Press, 1998; Ed/Contrbuting Auth, "In the Great Hall," Plumbline/ESMHE, 1993. CODE 1996-2002; ESMHE 1978-2002; NAAD 2000; No Amer Conf of Deans 2002.

CLIVER, Stanley Cameron (Wyo) Po Box 176, Sundance WY 82729 B Saint Louis MO 1924 s Benjamin & Elsie. Eden TS 1963. D 6/15/1963 P 3/1/1964 Bp George Leslie Cadigan. m 12/24/1943 Marceline Cliver. Vic S Jn's Upton WY 1971-1981; Ch Of The Gd Shpd Sundance WY 1971-1980; St Johns Ch 1971-1980; R S Andr's Normandy MO 1965-1971; Cur S Jn's Ch S Louis MO 1963-1965.

CLODFELTER, Jonathan Norwood (Pa) 4442 Frankford Ave, Philadelphia PA 19124 **R S Mk's Ch Philadelphia PA 2002-** B Saint Louis MO 1954 s Robert & Jean. BS SUNY 1993; MDiv VTS 1999. D 12/17/1999 Bp Peter J Lee P 6/25/2000 Bp James Gary Gloster. m 8/31/1985 Alice G Clodfelter c 4. Chapl Charlotte-Mecklenburg Police Dept 2000-2002; Thompson Chld's Hm Matthews NC 1999-2002.

CLOSE, David Wyman (Ore) 7990 Headlands Way, Clinton WA 98236 B Seattle,WA 1947 s Donald & Ruth. BS U of Washington 1969; MDiv CDSP 1973; DMin VTS 1997. D 7/17/1973 P 7/6/1974 Bp Ivol I Curtis. m 2/24/1979 Wendy Boyd c 3. R S Mk's Epis Par Medford OR 1987-2004; Vic No Skagit Mssns WA 1979-1987; S Jas Ch Sedro Woolley WA 1979-1987; Asst S Steph's Epis Ch Seattle WA 1973-1979.

CLOSE, Leroy Springs (RI) 316 W Main Rd, Little Compton RI 02837 **D S Steph's Ch Providence RI 2012-; Pres/Fndr 1000 Jobs/Haiti Inc. 2009-; Exec Dir Geo Hunt HELP Cntr 2006-; Chair Hisp Mnstry Com 2006-** B Charlotte NC 1950 s Hugh & Anne. BA Tul 1972. D 5/20/2000 Bp Richard Frank Grein. m 8/14/1971 Lucy Garrett Close c 3. D S Geo And San Jorge Cntrl Falls RI 2008-2011; D S Andr's By The Sea Little Compton RI 2005-2008; D S Mk's Ch Mt Kisco NY 2000-2004.

CLOSE, Patrick Raymond (NJ) Grace Episcopal Church, 19 Kings Hwy E, Haddonfield NJ 08033 **R Gr Ch In Haddonfield Haddonfield NJ 1997-** B Elmira NY 1952 s Julion & Myrtie. BA U of Maryland 1974; MDiv VTS 1984; DMin Drew U 1994. D 6/23/1984 P 6/8/1985 Bp Peter J Lee. m 1/4/1975 Diane D Close c 2. Dn Camden Convoc Haddonfield NJ 2004-2007; Chapl Vstng Nurse Assoc Hospice Morristown NJ 1995-1997; Adj Fac Drew U Madison NJ 1995-1996; R S Ptr's Ch Mtn Lks NJ 1991-1997; Dn Montclair Aids T/F Montclair NJ 1987-1990; R S Jn's Epis Ch Montclair NJ 1986-1991; Assoc S Tim's Ch Herndon VA 1984-1986; Cmsn on Stwdshp Dio New Jersey Trenton NJ 2010-2011, Curs Sprtl Dir 2007-, COM 2003-2010, 1998-2002; Coun Dio Newark Newark NJ 1995-1997, Pres-Epis Cmnty Servs 1986-1994. Assoc P, Convenor of St. Jn Bapt 1991-2009; Chapl, Haddonfield Fire Dept 2006; Chapl, Hospice-Vstng Nurses Assn 1995-1996; Chapl, Nj Assn Of Deaf 1991-1997; Pres, Haddonfield Coun Of Ch 1999-2000. Haddonfield Haddonfield Human Rts Cmsn 2006; Herndon Times Citizen Year Herndon Times Citizen Year 1984.

CLOSE ERSKINE, Christine Elaine (Ore) 60960 Creekstone Loop, Bend OR 97702 **Emm Ch Coos Bay OR 2014-** B Seattle WA 1956 d Donald & Ruth. BS U of Puget Sound 1979; MBA U of Washington 1987; MDiv Ya Berk 1994. D 1/4/1994 P 7/9/1994 Bp Vincent Waydell Warner. m 6/8/1996 Jack Arthur Erskine c 4. Dio Oregon Portland OR 2014; R Trin Ch Bend OR 2008-2013; Assoc P Ch Of The Gd Shpd Vancouver WA 1994-2008.

CLOTHIER, Tamara A (Tex) 5001 Hickory Rd, Temple TX 76502 **D S Fran Par Temple TX 2013-** B New York 1955 d Elwood & Betty. BA San Diego St U 1978; BA San Diego St U 1978; Iona Sch of Mnstry 2013. D 6/15/2013 Bp C Andrew Doyle.

CLOUD, Vernon Luther (SD) 13696 448th Ave, Waubay SD 57273 B Sisseton SD 1942 s Iver & Gertrude. AA Sthrn Arkansas U 1967; AA Nthrn St Coll 1969. D 9/10/2011 Bp John Tarrant. m 6/7/1964 Sharon Lee Cloud c 3.

CLOUGHEN JR, Charles Edward (Md) PO Box 313-, Hunt Valley MD 21030 **Dir of Planned Giving, Stwdshp and Dvlpmt,Dio Maryland Dio Maryland Baltimore MD 2009-; Alum Relatns Ya Berk 2008-** B Teaneck NJ 1942 s Charles & Anna. BA Hobart and Wm Smith Colleges 1964; STB Ya Berk 1969; Cert Hartford Sem 1990. D 6/14/1969 Bp Leland Stark P 12/22/1969 Bp Charles P Gilson. c 2. R S Thos Epis Ch Towson MD 1990-2008; R S Andr's Ch Pasadena MD 1986-1990; Int Spec Dio Dallas Dallas TX 1985-1986; Int S Mary's Epis Ch Manchester CT 1984-1985; Asst S Jn's Epis Par Waterbury CT 1982-1984; R S Matt's Par Of Jamestown Jamestown RI 1973-1982; Asst S Mart's Ch Providence RI 1969-1973. Auth, "Sixty-Second Stwdshp Serv," Liturg Press, 2000; Auth, "One Minute Stwdshp Sermons," Morehouse, 1997. Ord of St Jn 2005; Pres, Amer Friends of the Epis Dio Jerusal 2004-2007. Distinguished P Awd Dio Maryland 2006; Resrch Fell Ya 1983.

CLOWERS, Grantland Hugh (Kan) 2007 Miller Dr, Lawrence KS 66046 B Joplin MO 1956 s Ted & Alline. BA U of Missouri 1978; MDiv GTS 1983. D 10/18/1983 P 5/1/1984 Bp Richard Frank Grein. m 5/27/1997 Peggy Wichman. S Andr's Ch Ft Scott KS 1997-1998; S Lk's Epis Ch Shawnee KS 1993-1994; Asst Trin Ch Lawr KS 1986-1992; Calv Ch Yates Cntr KS 1983-1986; Vic S Tim & Calv Yates Cntr KS 1983-1986; S Tim's Ch Iola KS 1983-1986.

CLUETT JR, Richard Ide (Be) 119 W. Johnston St., Allentown PA 18103 **Int Dn Cathd Ch of the Nativ Bethlehem PA 2005-; Mem SCMD 2000-** B New York NY 1942 s Richard & Jane. BA Hobart and Wm Smith Colleges 1965; Ya Berk 1967; MDiv VTS 1970. D 6/27/1970 Bp William Foreman Creighton P 2/13/1971 Bp John Thomas Walker. m 4/12/1969 Patricia K Cluett c 3. Cathd Ch Of The Nativ Bethlehem PA 2010-2016; Ch Deploy Bd New York NY 1997-2000; Archd Dio Bethlehem Bethlehem PA 1984-2004; R S Marg's Ch Emmaus PA 1978-1984; Dio Rochester Henrietta 1975-1976; Assoc Chr Ch Corning NY 1972-1978; Asst S Lk's Ch Trin Par Beth MD 1970-1972. rick@diobeth.org

COAN, Barbara Frances Smith (Haw) 1311 Nahele Pl, Kapaa HI 96746 B Hackensack NJ 1923 d Frank & Marie. Art Students League of New York; Bos; Maine Diac Formation Prog; Queensland U. D 7/19/1993 Bp Edward Cole Chalfant. D S Mich And All Ang Ch Lihue HI 1996-2009; Dio Cnvnr S Dunst's Ch Ellsworth ME 1995-1996; D Ch Of Our Fr Hulls Cove ME 1993-1996; Chair Bd Dio Maine Portland ME 1999-2000, Prov I Rep Untd Thenk Off 1985-1998. Fllshp Soc Of S Jn The Evang; NAAD. One-Person Art Shows Intl.

COATS, Bleakley Irving (Ida) B Ft Riley KS 1948 s Robert & Dorothy. D 12/19/2010 P 6/19/2011 Bp Brian James Thom. m 2/14/1981 Christine Coats.

COATS, Christopher Vincent (CGC) Wharf Marina Slip #38, Orange Beach AL 36561 B Coral Gables FL 1950 s Hall & Clotilda. BA U of W Florida 1983; MDiv VTS 1987. D 6/27/1987 P 2/14/1988 Bp Charles Farmer Duvall. m 4/3/1971 Barbara A Coats c 2. R H Sprt Epis Ch Gulf Shores AL 2006-2014; Chapl 530th MP BN Deployed to Iraq w US Army in Spprt of OIF 2003-2004; R S Geo's Ch Belleville IL 2002-2006; R S Steph's Ch Brewton AL 1994-2002; Vic S Jn's Ch Pensacola FL 1987-1994. Alabama NG Chapl; US Army Reserve Chapl.

171

C

COATS, John Rhodes (Cal) 15814 Champion Forest Dr, Spring TX 77379 **Non-par 1981-** B Pasadena TX 1946 s W R & Doris. BA Steph F Austin St U 1969; MDiv VTS 1973. D 6/21/1973 Bp Scott Field Bailey P 6/1/1974 Bp James Milton Richardson. m 1/2/1986 Pamela Faye Coats. S Anne's Ch Fremont CA 1978-1981; Vic S Anne's Freemont CA 1978-1981; Assoc H Sprt Epis Ch Houston TX 1975-1978; Asst Chr Epis Ch Tyler TX 1973-1975. Auth, "Journ Of Acad Of Par Cler". OHC.

COATS, William Russell (Nwk) 19 Elmwood Ave., Ho Ho Kus NJ 07423 **Asst Chr Ch Ridgewood NJ 2002-** B New Rochelle NY 1936 s Guy & Marjorie. BA U CA Los Angeles 1959; STB GTS 1964. D 8/23/1964 Bp Daniel Corrigan P 6/1/1965 Bp David Shepherd Rose. m 5/24/2005 Deborah K Coats c 2. Int S Paul's Epis Ch Chatham NJ 2010-2011; Int Ch Of The Epiph Orange NJ 2008; Int Ch Of The H Comm Norwood NJ 2006-2007; Int S Jn's Ch Un City NJ 2002; R S Clem's Ch Hawthorne NJ 1988-2002; Int Trin Ch Long Green MD 1987-1988; Int Ch Of The Redeem Morristown NJ 1986-1987; R The Ch Of The Redeem Pittsburgh PA 1978-1986; Chapl U Of Wisconsin-Milwaukee 1971-1977; Chapl U CA-San Diego 1969-1971; Chapl U NC-Chap Hill 1965-1969; Assoc Min S Cyp's Epis Ch Hampton VA 1964-1965. Auth, "God In Publ". ESMHE 1968-1978.

COBB, Christina Rich (Mo) 1212 Ringo St, Mexico MO 65265 **R S Matthews Epis Ch Mex MO 2006-** B Unionville MO 1971 d James & Frances. BS U of Missouri 1993; Cntrl Bapt TS 1996; MS U of Missouri 1996; Epis Sch for Mnstry 2006. D 5/31/2006 P 12/9/2006 Bp George Wayne Smith. m 8/10/2002 Michael William Cobb c 2. Dio Missouri S Louis MO 2011-2013.

COBB, David (Chi) 34 Running Knob Hollow Rd, Sewanee TN 37375 **Sewanee U So TS Sewanee TN 2017-** B Mobile AL 1955 s Hiram & Gladys. DMin The U So, The TS; BA U of Alabama 1978; MDiv SWTS 1983. D 6/2/1983 P 12/6/1983 Bp Furman Charles Stough. m 11/21/1981 Ruth S Sheridan c 3. Chr Of The Ascen Chicago IL 2014-2016; R Chr Ch New Haven CT 2002-2014; R S Paul's Par Baltimore MD 1996-2002; R S Chris's Epis Ch Oak Pk IL 1987-1996; Cur Ch Of Our Sav Chicago IL 1984-1987; Cur S Paul's Ch Selma AL 1983-1984; R S Paul's Carlowville AL 1983-1984. Revised, "St Aug's PB," Forw Mvmt, 2016. Pres SWTS Alum Assn 1986-1987; Soc for the Increase of the Mnstry, Pres of the Bd 2014-2016; Soc of Cath Priests, Prov Cnvnr 2009-2011. dccobb@sewanee.edu

COBB JR, Harold James (SVa) 1931 Paddock Rd, Norfolk VA 23518 **R Gr Ch Norfolk VA 1995-** B Burlington NC 1958 s Harold & Armadia. Morehouse Coll 1979; BA U NC 1982; MDiv VTS 1990; D.D. S Paul's Coll 1999. D 11/15/1990 Bp Robert Whitridge Estill P 11/1/1991 Bp Huntington Williams Jr. m 6/29/1991 Sheliah Cobb c 1. R S Steph's Epis Ch Winston Salem NC 1990-1995; Serv Bapt Ch 1978-1987. Auth, "Black Seminarians In The Epis Ch". UBE, Black Epis Seminarians. Who's Who In Black Amer.

COBB, John Pierpont (SO) 36 Ledge Rd, Gloucester MA 01930 **Died 9/25/2016** B Chicago IL 1923 s Evelyn & Daphne. BA Harv 1948; BD CDSP 1961. D 6/25/1961 Bp James Albert Pike P 2/1/1962 Bp Roger W Blanchard. c 5. S Mk's Epis Ch Dayton OH 1969-1995; Asst Chr Ch Cathd Cincinnati OH 1961-1963.

COBB, Julia Kramer (NwT) St Barnabas Episcopal Church, 4141 Tanglewood Ln, Odessa TX 79762 B Odessa TX 1939 d Richard & Marjorie. U of Texas Austin; EFM course U So TS. D 10/29/2000 Bp C Wallis Ohl. m 9/3/1966 James Vance Cobb.

COBB, Matthew M (Kan) 1915 Montgomery Dr, Manhattan KS 66502 **Hse of Pryr Collegeville MN 2017-; R/Campus Min S Fran Of Cbury Manhattan KS 2001-** B Statesboro GA 1968 s Marvin & Linda. BA Rockhurst U 1993; MDiv Epis TS of the SW 1996; MA Creighton U 2001. D 6/8/1996 P 1/18/1999 Bp John Clark Buchanan. m 8/3/1991 Erica J Olson-Cobb c 2. S Lk's Ch Wamego KS 2008-2016; Dio Kansas Topeka KS 2001-2005, Chapl - Cbury Hse 1997-1998; Dio Iowa Des Moines IA 1999-2001; Asst/Campus Min Epis Par of Ames Ames IA 1999-2001; Dio W Missouri Kansas City MO 1998, 1997, 1996; Trans D S Jn's Ch Kansas City MO 1997-1999; Trans D S Andr's Ch Kansas City MO 1996-1997; St Lk's So Chap Overland Pk KS 1996-1997.

COBB-ANDERSON, Vienna (Va) 1138 West Ave, Richmond VA 23220 B Richmond VA 1935 d Robert & Vienna. Schlr London Acad of Mus & Dramatic Arts; AAS Briarcliff Coll 1955; Shakespeare Inst Stratford-on-Avon gb 1957; Yale Sch of Drama 1958; The London Acad of Mus and Dramatic Art 1959; BFA Richmond Profsnl Inst 1964; MFA Ya 1967; Spec Mnstry Prog Washington DC 1977; DMin PrTS 1986; LHD Lynchburg Coll 1988. D 6/25/1977 Bp William Foreman Creighton P 2/26/1978 Bp John Thomas Walker. S Paul's Ch Richmond VA 1996-2001; Adj Prof VTS Alexandria VA 1996, 1982-1994; R S Marg's Ch Washington DC 1987-1996; S Marg's Ch Woodbridge VA 1987-1996; R Cmnty of Hagar 1984-1987; Chapl Washington Hm Hospice 1984-1987; Assoc S Alb's Par Washington DC 1977-1984. Auth, "H Faces, H Places," *H Faces, H Places*, Dimenti Milestone Pub, 2008; Auth, "Prayers of Our Hearts," *Prayers of Our Hearts*, Crossroad Continuum, 2001; Auth, "Celebrations of Life," *Celebrations of Life*, Morehouse Barlow; Auth, "Create & Celebrate," *Create & Celebrate*, Morehouse Barlow; Auth, "The People & P Make Euch," *The People & P Make Euch*, U Micro Films. Associated Parishes 1968. L.H.D. 1988; Fulbright Schlr 1957.

COBDEN JR, Edward Alexander Morrison (Mich) Po Box 295, South Egremont MA 01258 **Ret 1997-** B Larchmont NY 1935 s Edward & Clementine. BA Wms 1957; MDiv EDS 1960; MA Assumption Coll 1974; DMin VTS 1983. D 6/25/1960 P 2/11/1961 Bp Robert McConnell Hatch. c 2. R Chr Ch Grosse Pointe Grosse Pointe Farms MI 1982-1997; Assoc Chr Ch Greenwich CT 1979-1982; R H Trin Epis Ch Southbridge MA 1967-1979; Chapl (Capt) US-A 1963-1967; Cur All SS Ch Worcester MA 1960-1963.

COBDEN III, Edward Alexander Morrison (NY) 374 Sarles St, Bedford Corners NY 10549 B Worcester MA 1960 s Edward & Evelyn. BA Wms 1982; MDiv VTS 1988. D 6/6/1988 Bp Robert Campbell Witcher Sr P 1/1/1990 Bp William Bradford Hastings. m 8/13/1983 Cynthia Ann Graves. All Ang' Ch New York NY 1994-1997; S Barth's Ch In The Highland White Plains NY 1992-1994; Assoc S Lk's Par Darien CT 1988-1989.

COBLE JR, John Reifsnyder (Be) 1929 Pelham Rd, Bethlehem PA 18018 **Ret 1997-** B Lebanon PA 1933 s John & Pauline. BS Rider U 1960; MDiv PDS 1963. D 6/15/1963 P 3/10/1964 Bp Frederick Warnecke. m 8/26/1961 Patricia Ann Coble c 1. R Trin Ch Bethlehem PA 1984-1997; Dio Bethlehem Bethlehem PA 1976-1984, Cn Ordnry 1976-1984; Vic S Geo's Epis Ch Hellertown PA 1970-1976; R S Jas Ch Shuykl Haven PA 1968-1970, D 1963-1967; Chr Ch Frackville Frackville PA 1963-1968.

COBLE, Robert Henry (Pa) 36 Crescent Cir, Harleysville PA 19438 B Lebanon PA 1944 s John & Pauline. BA Salem Coll Salem WV 1967; MDiv PDS 1970. D 6/27/1970 P 5/1/1971 Bp Frederick Warnecke. m 7/28/1979 Barbara Coble c 1. R All SS Ch Norristown PA 1978-2009; R S Steph's Epis Ch Norwood PA 1972-1978; Asst Trin Ch Easton PA 1970-1972.

COBURN, Ann Struthers (Mass) PO Box 1988, Berkeley CA 94709 B Portchester NY 1949 d William & Lilly. BA Georgian Crt Coll 1972; MDiv CDSP 1977; DMin Georgian Crt U 2009; DMin Georgian Crt U 2009. D 6/11/1977 Bp Paul Moore Jr P 12/17/1977 Bp John Bowen Coburn. c 2. Dir of Alum/ae and Ch Relatns CDSP Berkeley CA 2005-2012; Int Gr Ch New Bedford MA 2003-2005; R S Mart's Ch Providence RI 1998-2003; R S Jas Epis Ch Danbury CT 1982-1998, Asst 1977-1979; Cn Chr Ch Cathd Hartford CT 1979-1981.

COBURN, Michael (RI) 55 Linden Road, Barrington RI 02806 **P-in-c Ch Of The Ascen Cranston RI 2010-** B Northampton MA 1949 s John & Ruth. BA Pr 1972; MDiv CDSP 1977. D 6/11/1977 Bp Paul Moore Jr P 12/17/1977 Bp John Bowen Coburn. m 3/4/2005 Carol Lewis c 3. P-in-c All SS' Memi Ch Providence RI 2009-2010; Homeless Outreach Case Mgr The Providence Cntr Providence RI 2007-2008; Outreach worker McAuley Hse Soup Kitchen 2004-2007; S Mart's Ch Providence RI 1998-2002; R S Jas Epis Ch Danbury CT 1982-1998, Asst 1977-1979; Cn Chr Ch Cathd Hartford CT 1979-1981.

COCHRAN, Elizabeth Jane (Oly) St Matthew's Episcopal Church, 412 Pioneer Ave, Castle Rock WA 98611 **R S Matt Ch Castle Rock WA 2004-** B Hiawatha KS 1937 d Virgil & Helen. BS Emporia St U 1959. D 2/28/2004 Bp Sanford Zangwill Kaye Hampton P 11/13/2004 Bp Vincent Waydell Warner. m 6/1/1959 Jere Cochran c 4.

COCHRAN, Joseph M (Md) **S Jn's Ch Reisterstown MD 2013-** B Muncie IN 1962 s Henry & Janie. BA Virginia Tech; JD Washington & Lee U Sch of Law; MDiv Sewanee TS 2013; MDiv Sewanee: The U So, TS 2013. D 6/8/2013 Bp Shannon Sherwood Johnston P 1/4/2014 Bp Eugene Taylor Sutton. m 4/24/1999 Pamela D.H. Cochran c 2.

COCHRAN, Laura (Va) 1700 Wainwright Dr, Reston VA 20190 **Asst S Anne's Epis Ch Reston VA 2012-** B Washington DC 1976 d Richard & Frances. BBA Belmont U 1998; MDiv VTS 2012. D 6/2/2012 Bp Ted Gulick Jr P 12/15/2012 Bp Shannon Sherwood Johnston. m 6/6/2009 John Wilson Cochran c 1. laura@stannes-reston.org

COCHRAN, Lottie (SVa) 713 Seagrass Reach, Chesapeake VA 23320 **S Thos Epis Ch Chesapeake VA 2016-** B Norfolk VA 1957 d Charles & Mary. BS Mia 1982; MDiv VTS 1993. D 6/5/1993 Bp O'Kelley Whitaker P 1/25/1994 Bp Frank Harris Vest Jr. m 3/25/1978 Thomas Hale Cochran c 2. Asstg Cler Old Donation Ch Virginia Bch VA 2011-2014, Asstg Cler 2007-2008; Assoc for Pstr Care S Dav's Ch Wayne PA 2009-2010; Int Gd Samar Epis Ch Virginia Bch VA 2004-2006; R Time Certain S Paul's Epis Ch Suffolk VA 2004-2006; Exec Dir AFP Orlando FL 2002-2003; Assoc Chr and S Lk's Epis Ch Norfolk VA 1999-2002; Assoc S Jn's Ch Roanoke VA 1993-1999; Bd Trst; Exec Com VTS Alexandria VA 1995-2007, Pres of Alum/ae Assn 1994-1995, AAEC 1993-1995. Auth, "Pstr Pract Seeking Understanding," 1995. AFP - Exec Dir 2002-2004.

COCHRAN, Paul Coleman (Be) 40 S. Laurel St., Hazleton PA 18201 **Died 10/14/2016** B Detroit,MI 1941 s Maurice & Ellanna. BA S Johns Coll Annapolis MD 1963; STB GTS 1970; ThD GTS 1976; GTS 1982. D 6/14/1970 Bp Harold Cornelius Gosnell P 12/1/1970 Bp Richard Earl Dicus. m 9/21/1966 Effie Cochran. S Ptr's Epis Ch Hazleton PA 2002-2003; Dio Long Island Garden City NY 2000-2001; Ch of S Jude Wantagh NY 1999-2000; Int S Geo's Ch Hempstead NY 1998-1999; P-in-c S Aug's Epis Ch Croton Hdsn NY 1994; Non-par 1988-1991; Int All Ang' Ch New York NY 1987-1988; R Holyrood Ch New York NY 1980-1987; Non-par 1978-1979; Ch Of The H Apos New

York NY 1976-1977; Non-par 1973-1974; The GTS New York NY 1972-1976; Vic Ch Of The H Cross San Antonio TX 1970-1972. Fell Ecf 1978.

COCKBILL, Douglas J (Chi) 3310 Coventry Ct, Joliet IL 60431 **Vic S Andr's Harrow Engl 1990-** B Joliet IL 1953 s William & Margaret. BA U Chi 1975; MDiv GTS 1978. D 6/17/1978 Bp Quintin Ebenezer Primo Jr P 10/1/1979 Bp Edward Clark Turner. c 2. S Lk's Epis Ch Wenatchee WA 2010; Asst Epis Ch Of The Atone Chicago IL 1989-1990; Non-par 1984-1986; Vic S Jn's Harbour Island Bahamas 1980-1983; Chapl S Dunst's Sch S Croix VI 1979-1980; Cur S Paul's Ch S Croix VI 1979-1980. Auth, "Update Of The Mvmt For The Reform Of Infant Baptism," 1996.

COCKE, Reagan Winter (WTex) 2450 River Oaks Blvd, Houston TX 77019 **Assoc R S Jn The Div Houston TX 2002-** B San Antonio TX 1962 s Bartlett & Winifred. BA U of Pennsylvania 1985; MA U of Pennsylvania 1988; DIT Oxf GB 1999. D 8/23/2000 P 3/6/2001 Bp James Edward Folts. m 6/21/1986 Stephanie H Cocke c 2. Asst Ch Of The Adv Brownsville TX 2000-2002. rcocke@sjd.org

COCKRELL, Ernest William (ECR) 1538 Koch Ln, San Jose CA 95125 **Cnvnr of The Eccl Coun The Sovereign Ord of S Jn of Jerusalem Knights Hosp 2008-** B Port Arthur TX 1938 s Herman & Laverne. BA Oklahoma City U 1960; STM Harvard DS 1963; Cert EDS 1964. D 6/20/1964 P 1/9/1965 Bp Anson Phelps Stokes Jr. m 8/24/1963 Jill S Cockrell c 2. The Stndg Com Dio El Camino Real Salinas CA 2000-2004; R S Andr's Ch Saratoga CA 1992-2007; Sum Dir Camp Mishawaka Grand Rapids MN 1975-1981; Chapl Tabor Acad Marion MA 1974-1976; R S Gabr's Epis Ch Marion MA 1967-1992; Cur Ch Of The Redeem Chestnut Hill MA 1964-1967; Chair Dio Mass Ltrgc Cmsn Dio Massachusetts Boston MA 1986-1990. Auth/Compsr, "The Heav Host"; Auth, "Samson'S Shadow"; Auth, "Sama (Listening) Voices Of Palestinians/Israeli Peacemakers". The Bp's Cross Dio El Camino Real 2005.

COCKRELL, John Grafton (SC) 275 Warden Ave, Bluefield WV 24701 B Ophelia VA 1937 s Dandridge & Retha. BA Randolph-Macon Coll 1959; MDiv Duke DS 1962; ThM Duke 1963; CAS EDS 1965. D 6/29/1965 P 6/29/1966 Bp Thomas Augustus Fraser Jr. c 3. R S Steph's Epis Ch N Myrtle Bch SC 1997-2001; Ch Of The Cross Columbia SC 1992; So Carolina Epis Min To The Aging Columbia SC 1987-1991; R Ch Of Our Sav Rock Hill SC 1973-1987; Chapl Winthrop Coll Rock Hill SC 1973-1987; Assoc Chr Ch Charlotte NC 1969-1972; Vic S Mk's Epis Ch Raleigh NC 1967-1969; Ch Of The Ascen At Fork Advance NC 1965-1967; Vic Ch Of The Gd Shpd Cooleemee NC 1965-1967. Pi Delta Epsilon R.M. Coll 1958.

COCKRELL, Richard (USC) 8700 N La Cholla Blvd Apt 2137, Anderson SC 29625 B Madison WI 1925 s Frank & Grace. Newberry CollegeNewberrySC 1944; Tulane UniversityNew orleans LA 1945; BA U of Wisconsin 1949; MA MI SU 1953; MDiv CDSP 1957; STM Yale DS 1974. D 6/30/1957 Bp Richard Stanley Merrill Emrich P 1/1/1958 Bp Archie H Crowley. c 4. Asst-Ret Chr Ch Greenville SC 1991-1995; Int Gr Epis Ch Anderson SC 1989-1990; Int S Jn's Epis Ch Troy NY 1987-1988; Dio New Jersey Trenton NJ 1987; Asst Chr Ch Ridgewood NJ 1986; Int Trin Ch Paterson NJ 1985; Int R Ch Of The Epiph Newport NH 1983-1984, 1982-1983; Int S Andr's Ch Manchester NH 1983-1984; Asst Dio New Hampshire Concord NH 1982-1984; Calv Epis Ch Williamsville NY 1982-1983; Tchr Sch Rel Dio Vermont Burlington VT 1979-1981; Cmnty Serv 1974-1981; Ecum Coun Peace T/F 1974-1981; S Jas Ch Woodstock VT 1974-1981; S Jas's Ch W Hartford CT 1974-1981; Trin Ch On The Green New Haven CT 1971-1973; Ch Of The Gd Shpd Hartford CT 1967-1970; Chapl Armsmear Hm for Aged 1966-1971; Asst S Andr's Ch Ann Arbor MI 1959-1966; Dio Michigan Detroit MI 1958-1965; Dept CSR Chr Ch Grosse Pointe Grosse Pointe Farms MI 1958-1959; Vic S Barn' Ch Chelsea MI 1957-1958; Mus & Liturg y Com Dio Connecticut Meriden CT 1971-1974. Auth-Coordntr, "An Amer Renaissance," 7 *Videos: Healing our Professions*, Anderson U,And. SC, 2005; Auth, "Mnstry Proposal for NJ Dio," *Study of the Ch of Atlantic City,NJ*, DioceseNJ, 1987. Anderson TS for Lay Persons, Anderson, SC 1989; Cntr for Progressive Chrsnty 1998; Inst of Servnt Ldrshp 1995; Untd Rel Initiative-URI 1999. Citation of Faithful Serv Downtown Coop Mnstry,New Haven, CT 1974; Citation of Faithful Serv Sage Advocates-Trin Ch.New haven, CT 1974; Citation of Faithful Serv Cntr city Ch, Hartford, CT 1971.

CODE, David Arthur (NJ) 729 Partridge Ln, State College PA 16803 B Redvers Canada 1965 s Arthur & Alice. BA Ya 1987; PrTS 1999; MDiv GTS 2002. D 6/22/2002 Bp David Bruce Joslin P 1/11/2003 Bp James Elliot Curry. m 4/26/1997 Karen Bysiewicz c 2. Caroline Ch Of Brookhaven E Setauke NY 2004-2005; Asst S Steph's Ch Ridgefield CT 2002-2003.

CODY, Daphne C (Chi) 380 Hawthorn Ave, Glencoe IL 60022 **R S Elis's Ch Glencoe IL 2005-** B Parkersburg WV 1966 d Cecil & Constance. BA Coll of Wooster 1989; MS NWU 1991; MDiv SWTS 1996. D 6/15/1996 Bp Frank Tracy Griswold III P 5/1/1998 Bp Herbert Alcorn Donovan Jr. m 8/10/1991 Jason Andrew Cody c 2. Assoc S Mary's Ch Pk Ridge IL 1999-2004.

COE III, Frank S (WVa) 74 Rhodes Court, Harpers Ferry WV 25425 **P Assoc Trin Ch Shepherdstown WV 2010-, P Assoc 2006-2009** B East Orange NJ 1937 s Frank & Hazel. BS VPI 1960; U of Houston 1964. D 6/13/1998 P 6/12/1999 Bp John Henry Smith. m 8/20/1960 Wilma Cassell Coe c 2. Int Mt Zion Epis Ch Hedgesville WV 2009-2010; S Mk's Epis Ch Berkeley Spg WV 2009-2010; Exec Dir Peterkin C&C Dio W Virginia Charleston WV 1997-2003.

COE, Wayland Newton (Tex) 5934 Rutherglenn Dr, Houston TX 77096 B Austin TX 1960 s Gordon & JoeAnn. Drury U 1981; BBA U of Texas 1983; MDiv TESM 1990. D 6/16/1990 Bp Maurice Manuel Benitez P 1/30/1991 Bp William Elwood Sterling. m 6/23/1984 Janet Lynn Coe c 2. Chapl Air NG 1995-2003; S Thos Ch Houston TX 1993-2005; The Great Cmsn Fndt Houston TX 1991-1993; Chr Ch Nacogdoches TX 1990-1993; Asst to R Dio Texas Houston TX 1990; Chapl Steph F. Austin St U Nacogdoches TX. PB Soc of the USA 1993.

COENEN, Susan Ann (FdL) B Oshkosh WI 1949 d Robert & Annabelle. D 8/27/2005 Bp Russell Edward Jacobus. D S Ptr's Ch (S Mary's Chap) Ripon WI 2013-2014; D Trin Epis Ch Oshkosh WI 2005-2013.

COERPER, Becky (CNY) 98 East Genesee St, Skaneateles NY 13152 **R S Jas Ch Skaneateles NY 2010-** B New Rochelle NY 1956 d David & Marion. BA Coll of Wooster 1978; MDiv Sewanee: The U So, TS 2003; DMin Luther Sem 2012. D 5/29/2003 P 11/29/2003 Bp Edward Lloyd Salmon Jr. m 7/1/1978 Milo Wilson Coerper c 2. Assoc R Epis Ch of the Gd Shpd Summerville SC 2003-2010.

COERPER, Milo George (Md) 7315 Brookville Rd, Chevy Chase MD 20815 **Ret MD 2010-** B Milwaukee WI 1925 s Milo & Rose. BS USNA 1946; LLB U MI 1954; MA Geo 1957; PhD Geo 1960; ST Sewanee: The U So, TS 1980. D 7/5/1978 Bp William Jackson Cox P 5/6/1979 Bp David Keller Leighton Sr. m 4/11/1953 Lois Hicks c 3. Cathd Chapl Cathd of St Ptr & St Paul Washington DC 1986-2010; Sprtl Counslr Cathd Washington D.C 1986-2010; R S Andr's Ch Clear Sprg MD 1979-1985. Auth, "A Deeper Dimension," *Experience*, ABA, 1995. Actg Chair Cbury Cathd Trust in Amer 1991-1991; Advsry Bd, Camaldolese Benedictines 1991-2001; Advsry Coun, Shalem Inst for Sprtl Formation 2000; Bd Dir, Shalem Inst for Sprtl Formation 1980-2000; Bd Dir, The Jn Main Inst, Ltd 1991-1999; Bd Dir, Treas, the Evelyn Underhill Assn 1991-2010; Bd Dir, Wrld Cmnty for Chr Meditation 1997-1999; Fllshp of Contemplative Pryr 1975; Mem, Coun, Friends of Cbury Cathd in US 1999-2005; Mem, Living Ch Fndt 1989-2004; Oblate Camaldolese Benedictines 1995; Oblate S Anselm Benedictine Abbey 1989; Off Most Venerable Ord of the Hosp of S Jn Jeru 1989-2010; Pres Natl Assn for the Self-Supporting Active M 1981-1983; Trst, Friends of Cbury Cathd in US 2005-2010; V-Chair Cbury Cathd Trust in Amer 1981-1997. Patron Wrld Cmnty for Chr Meditation 1999; Patron Friends of S Ben 1997.

COFFEY, Bridget (Va) 2112 Harvest Dr, Winchester VA 22601 **Asst Chr Epis Ch Winchester VA 2011-** B Greenville NC 1979 d John & Marlene. BS Chris Newport U 2003; MDiv GTS 2009. D 6/13/2009 Bp Bud Shand P 12/21/2009 Bp Stacy F Sauls. Chr Ch Cathd Lexington KY 2009-2010; S Aug's Chap Lexington KY 2009-2010.

COFFEY, E Allen (Va) 10231 Fenholloway Dr, Mechanicsville VA 23116 B New York NY 1947 s Edward & Rosa. BA Randolph-Macon Coll 1969; MDiv VTS 1973; DMin UTS Richmond 1986. D 5/26/1973 P 5/11/1974 Bp Robert Bruce Hall. m 4/27/2002 Deborah Waters c 1. R S Paul's Epis Ch Millers Tavern VA 2008-2013; Int R Buck Mtn Epis Ch Earlysville VA 2007; R Abingdon Epis Ch White Marsh VA 2002-2007; Stndg Comm Dio Virginia Richmond VA 1996-1999, Conv Plnng Com 1980-1982, Rgstr 1979-2001, Exec Bd 1978-1981, Mssns Com 1978-1981; R Emm Ch At Brook Hill Richmond VA 1991-2002; Assoc R S Jas Ch Richmond VA 1988-1991; P-in-c Imm Ch Old Ch VA 1981-1982; R S Ptr's Par Ch New Kent VA 1973-1988. Auth, *A Hist of the Dio Virginia & Its Bishops*; Auth, *S Ptr's Par 1679-1979: 300 Years*; Auth, *Some Thoughts on Chr Stwdshp*; Auth, *Video- (videotape tour) S Ptr's Par Ch 1701*. EvangES 1974-1998.

COFFEY, Gary Keith (WNC) 23 Forest Knoll Dr, Weaverville NC 28787 **R Gr Ch Asheville NC 2001-** B Shelby NC 1953 s James & Hannah. BA U NC 1977; MDiv TESM 1983. D 6/25/1983 P 5/23/1984 Bp William Gillette Weinhauer. m 8/11/1973 Astrid Coffey c 2. R S Jn's Ch Cedar Rapids IA 1987-2001; R S Jn's Cedar Rapids IA 1987-1997; Asst Trin Ch Myrtle Bch SC 1983-1987.

COFFEY JR, Jonathan Bachman (Fla) 4903 Robert D Gordon Rd, Jacksonville FL 32210 **R St Marks FL 2006-** B Chattanooga TN 1950 s Jonathan & Mary. DMin S Vladimirs Orth TS; BA Goddard Coll 1972; MDiv SWTS 1977; STM GTS 1984. D 6/22/1977 Bp William Hopkins Folwell P 12/21/1977 Bp Charles Bennison Sr. m 7/6/1974 Julia G Gibson c 2. S Mk's Epis Ch Jacksonville FL 2006-2015; R S Anth On The Desert Scottsdale AZ 1998-2006; R Ch Of S Jas The Less Scarsdale NY 1992-1998; R S Paul's Ch Fayetteville AR 1989-1991; R S Richard's Ch Winter Pk FL 1983-1989; Dn Lakeland Dnry 1981-1983; R St Alb's of Auburndale Inc Auburndale FL 1980-1983; Vic S Christophers Ch Northport MI 1977-1980; S Paul's Epis Ch Elk Rapids MI 1977-1980; Grand Traverse City Area Mssn Traverse City MI 1977-1979. Auth, "9/11: A Wakeup Call to the Ch," *Living Ch*, 2002; "Var arts," *Living Ch*. OHC- Assoiate 2004. Whipple Schlr SWTS.

COFFEY, Kevin Patrick Joseph (Nwk) 2-06 31st St, Fair Lawn NJ 07410 **R Ch Of The Atone Fair Lawn NJ 2000-, 1996-2000; Chf, Crisis Response Team Off of Emergency Mgmt Rochelle Pk NJ 1998-; Chapl Rochelle Pk Fire Dept Rochelle Pk NJ 1996-; Disciplinary Bd Dio Newark Newark NJ 2015-, Dioc Coun 2013-, Dioc Coun 1999-2004, Wmn Cmsn 1997-2005, Cathd Chapt 1997-2001; Chf, Crisis Mgmt Team Rochelle Pk Off of Emergency Mgmt 2002-; Chapl Rochelle Pk Fire Dept Rochelle Pk NJ 1997-** B Lackawanna NY 1954 s William & Frances. BS Quinnipiac Coll 1982; Ya Berk 1983; MDiv GTS 1988. D 6/4/1988 Bp Harry Woolston Shipps P 3/11/1989 Bp Charles Lee Burgreen. m 8/4/1977 Kathy Propst c 2. Co Mssnr Bergen Epis Area Mnstry Maywood NJ 1996-2000; Int R Ch of the Ascen Munich 1996-2000; S Mart's Ch Maywood NJ 1996-2000; S Ptr's Ch Rochelle Pk NJ 1996-2000; Assoc R The Angl/Epis Ch Of Chr The King Frankfurt am Main 60323 1992-1996; Spec Ministeries, 104th ASG, Hanau, DE Off Of Bsh For ArmdF New York NY 1992-1995, Spec Mnstry, 104th ASG, Hanau, Germany 1992-1995; Pstr Ch Of The Gd Shpd Newburgh NY 1989-1992; Cler Team Hudson Vlly Mnstrs New Windsor NY 1989-1992; Asst to the Epis Chapl USMA W Point NY 1988-1992; Assoc R S Phil's Ch Garrison NY 1988-1989. Cmnty of St Jn Bapt (Assoc) 1998; Soc of Cath Priests 2009. rector@atonement-fairlawn.org

COFFEY, Paris (Chi) 240 S. Marion St., 1N, Oak Park IL 60302 B Lynchburg VA 1950 d William & Margaret. BA U of Missouri 1973; MA Eden TS 1988. D 5/18/1995 P 5/29/1996 Bp Hays H. Rockwell. m 10/11/1975 Robert Michael Coffey c 2. R S Chris's Epis Ch Oak Pk IL 1998-2015; Assoc S Tim's Epis Ch S Louis MO 1995-1997; Dir of Sprtl Formation S Mich & S Geo Epis Ch S Louis MO 1986-1995. Cathd Chapt 1995-1997; Cathd Shltr Bd 2005; Dioc Coun 2003-2005; SSJE Sprtl Dir Trng 1986-1987; Sprtl Dir Intl 1988-1995.

COFFIN, Peter R (NH) 35 Woodbury St, Keene NH 03431 B Salem MA s Lloyd & Martha. BA Bos 1982; MDiv SWTS 1988. D 6/11/1988 P 5/6/1989 Bp David Elliot Johnson. m 12/31/1994 Tania Coffin c 2. R Par Of S Jas Ch Keene NH 2000-2007; R S Paul's Ch Lancaster NH 1994-2000; Cn Res Cathd Ch Of S Steph Harrisburg PA 1990-1994; Cur Ch Of The H Cross Tryon NC 1988-1990. Soc Of S Jn The Evang 1988.

COFFMAN, Daniel Brian (Neb) Holy Trinity Episcopal Church, 6001 A St, Lincoln NE 68510 **D Ch Of The H Trin Lincoln NE 2013-** B Durango CO 1951 s Robert & Helen. BS/SW U of Wyoming 1974. D 5/9/2013 Bp Scott Scott Barker. m 8/30/1986 Nancy Lynette Coffman.

COGAN, Timothy Bernard (NJ) 38 The Blvd/RFD659, Edgartown MA 02539 **P The Epis Ch Of Beth-By-The-Sea Palm Bch FL 2005-; Ret Ret 2002-** B Boston MA 1935 s Bernard & Mary. AB Harv 1956; MDiv VTS 1959; DD VTS 2004. D 6/10/1959 P 5/30/1963 Bp Anson Phelps Stokes Jr. m 5/20/1967 Ruth M Mitchell c 2. Asst S Paul's Epis Ch No Andover MA 1988-2002; Int S Andr's Ch Edgartown MA 1987; Brooks Sch Chap No Andover MA 1985-2002; Strng Com ESMHE 1977-1980; Instr PrTS Princeton NJ 1972-1985; Chapl Pr Princeton NJ 1972-1985; Chapl The Wm Alexander Procter Fndt Trenton NJ 1972-1985; Chapl Trin Sch New York NY 1970-1972; Dir Indep Schools' Opportunity Proj New York NY 1969-1972; Asst Gr Epis Ch New York NY 1966-1969; Cur S Phil's Ch New York NY 1965-1966; Hd Theol, Chapl Lenox Sch Leuox MA 1961-1965; Ch Of The Gd Shpd Fairhaven MA 1960-1961; Min S Andr's Ch New Bedford MA 1960-1961; Cur S Jn's Ch Beverly MA 1959-1960. Auth, "Let all the Peoples Praise Him," *Let all the Peoples Praise Him*; Auth, "The Ch Boarding Sch," *The Ch Boarding Sch*; Auth, "The Story & the Meal," *The Story & the Meal*; Auth, "Worshiping on the Margin," *Worshiping on the Margin*. Sr Mem/Assoc Kings Coll, Camb 2004; DD VTS 2004.

COGAR, Carolyn Christine (SO) 541 2nd Ave, Gallipolis OH 45631 B Gallipolis OH 1942 d Virgil & Pearl. AB Marshall U 1965. D 6/7/2014 Bp Thomas Edward Breidenthal. c 2.

COGGI, Lynne Marie Madeleine (NY) 3206 Cripple Creek St Apt 39b, San Antonio TX 78209 B New York NY 1933 d Herbert & Hilda Rebecca. BA CUNY 1963; CUNY 1965; MDiv UTS 1985. D 10/25/1985 Bp Walter Decoster Dennis Jr P 12/7/1988 Bp Edmond Lee Browning. c 2. Co-Int Cn Mssnr Cntrl Convoc (3 Ch) San Antonio TX 2004-2005; Supply S, Sthrn Partnership (4 Ch) Dio W Texas 2002-2005; Supply P Dio W Texas San Antonio TX 1999-2002, Supply P 1995-1998; Int S Phil's Ch San Antonio TX 1998-1999; Supply P Dio Long Island Garden City NY 1992-1995; P-in-c S Steph's Epis Ch Jamaica NY 1990-1992; AIDS Consult Epis Ch Cntr New York NY 1985-1988; S Ptr's Ch Bronx NY 1985-1986. Auth, "A Time for Caring," Epis Ch Cntr, 1985.

COGGIN, Bruce W (FtW) 3700 Ellsmere Ct, Fort Worth TX 76103 **1989-** B Lafayette LA 1941 s Ross & Martha. BA U of Texas 1962; MA Col 1964; MDiv SWTS 1966; PhD U of Texas 1982. D 6/15/1966 Bp Charles A Mason P 12/21/1966 Bp Theodore H McCrea. c 3. All SS' Epis Ch Ft Worth TX 1990; S Simon Of Cyrene Epis Ch Ft Worth TX 1990; Gd Shpd Granbury TX 1989; R S Tim's Ch Ft Worth TX 1987-1989; Nash 1985-1995; Ch Of The H Comf Cleburne TX 1979-1987; Asst All SS Epis Ch Austin TX 1974-1977; R S Ptr's Ch Mc Kinney TX 1969-1974; Vic S Mary's Ch Hamilton TX 1966-1969; S Matt's Ch Comanche TX 1966-1969. The Philadelphia Soc 1978. Phi Beta Kappa U of Texas 1962.

COGILL, Richard Leonard (Minn) Cathedral of St George the Martyr, 5 Wales St, Cape Town 8001 South Africa **Serving Ch of the Prov of Sthrn Afr 2012-** B Capetown ZA 1966 s Henry & Veronica. BA Gustavus Adolphus Coll 1994; MDiv Luther TS 1997; STM GTS 2002. D 6/15/2002 P 12/17/2002 Bp James Louis Jelinek. Dio Minnesota Minneapolis MN 2002-2003; Cur Trin Ch Excelsior MN 2002-2003.

COGSDALE, Michael H (WNC) 845 Cherokee Place, Lenoir NC 28645 **Int S Jn's Epis Ch Marion NC 2017-; Dep Genral Conv Dio Wstrn No Carolina Asheville NC 2009-, Dioc Coun 2005-2008, Asst Bp For Yth Mnstry 1992-2004** B Norfolk VA 1956 s Alvin & Charlotte. BS Appalachian St U 1979; MDiv VTS 1987. D 5/15/1987 P 12/19/1987 Bp William Gillette Weinhauer. m 7/18/1987 Elizabeth Gartman Cogsdale c 2. Pres No Carolina Coun of Ch Raleigh NC 2006-2007; R S Jas Epis Ch Lenoir NC 2005-2015; R Ch Of The Epiph Newton NC 2001-2005; Exec Bd No Carolina Coun of Ch Raleigh NC 1998-2008; COM Dio E Carolina Kinston NC 1998-2000; Gr Epis Ch Plymouth NC 1998-2000, R 1998-2000, Int 1995-1996; P S Paul's Ch Vanceboro NC 1997-1998; R S Fran By The Sea Bogue Banks NC 1996-1997; S Fran by the Sea Bogue Banks Salter Path NC 1996-1997; Valle Crucis Conf Cntr Valle Crucis NC 1990-1995; Chapl Patterson Sch Patterson NC 1988-1990; The Patterson Sch Lenoir NC 1988-1990; Cur Gr Ch Morganton NC 1987-1988.

COHEE, William Patrick (Az) 114 W Roosevelt St, Phoenix AZ 85003 B Phoenix AZ 1955 s William & Patricia. D 1/26/2008 Bp Kirk Stevan Smith.

COHEN, David Michael (NCal) 310 W North St, Alturas CA 96101 **Gd Shpd Epis Ch Susanville CA 2014-; S Mich Ch Alturas CA 2014-** B Raleigh NC 1970 s Harris & Priscilla. BA U Coll - Santa Cruz CA 1992; PhD California Sch Prof. Psychol 1998; Cert of Angl Stds Ch DS Pacific 2014. D 6/28/2014 P 3/28/2015 Bp Barry Leigh Beisner. m 10/26/1997 Wendy Dier c 3.

COHEN, Georgia S (NJ) Po Box 5, Blawenburg NJ 08504 B Cleveland OH 1946 d Raymond & Elaine. BA U MI 1967; AMLS U MI 1968; MDiv VTS 1976; PhD PrTS 1987. D 6/26/1976 P 3/9/1977 Bp H Coleman Mcgehee Jr. Ch Of The Annunc Lawnside NJ 2002-2005; S Ptr's Ch Medford NJ 1993-1997; Dio Michigan Detroit MI 1987-1989; Dioc Bd S Mich's TS 1980-1982; Asst Chapl VTS Alexandria VA 1977-1981; Asst Imm Ch-On-The-Hill Alexandria VA 1977-1980; VTS Alexandria VA 1976-1981; Instr VTS Alexandria VA 1976-1981; Com Dio Virginia Richmond VA 1980-1981. Atla.

COHOON, Frank Nelson (Kan) 44 Sw Pepper Tree Ln, Topeka KS 66611 **Died 5/25/2016** B Oklahoma City OK 1925 s Cecil & Sally. Phillips U 1945; BA TCU 1947; STB GTS 1954. D 6/22/1954 P 12/21/1954 Bp Chilton R Powell. c 3. Ret 1993-2016; Planned Giving Off Dio Kansas Topeka KS 1992-2000, Exec Off 1987-1992, Dvlpmt Off 1985-1993, Archd Mssn 1978-1992, CDO 1978-1987, Chair Cmsn Strtgy & Cong Dvlpmt 1978-1987, 1976-1992, COM 1961-1987, Chair Liturg Cmsn 1965-1970; Vic Calv Ch Yates Cntr KS 1976-1978; S Tim's Ch Iola KS 1976-1978; Dio Nthrn Mex Nuevo Leon 1974-1976; Asst. to Bp of Wstrn Mex S Mk's Ch Guadalajara Mex 1974-1976; R S Dav's Epis Ch Topeka KS 1966-1974; R Ch Of The Cov Jct City KS 1961-1965; Chapl (Maj) USAR 1958-1968; Vic S Chris's Ch Midwest City OK 1956-1961; R Chr Memi Epis Ch El Reno OK 1954-1956; Admin Asst. to the Dn S Paul's Cathd Oklahoma City OK 1947-1951. Angl Soc; Associated Parishes; RWF.

COHOON, Richard Allison (CPa) 500 E Guardlock Dr, Lock Haven PA 17745 **Ret 1994-** B Worcester MA 1929 s Charles & Barbara. Coll of Preachers; BA Coll of Wooster 1951; BD EDS 1954. D 6/24/1954 P 12/1/1954 Bp Dudley S Stark. m 5/17/1952 Diana Rees Cohoon c 2. R S Paul's Ch Lock Haven PA 1985-1994; Chr Ch Stroudsburg PA 1985; Chapl Lehigh Cnty Prison 1977-1984; Vic S Anne's Epis Ch Trexlertown PA 1971-1975; Assoc The Epis Ch Of The Medtr Allentown PA 1967-1975; S Jn's Ch Sodus NY 1959-1967; R Chr Ch Sodus NY 1959-1962; R Gr Ch Lyons NY 1954-1959. AAMFC 1974.

COIL, John Albert (WMo) 7917 Lamar Ave, Prairie Village KS 66208 **Vic S Lk's Epis Ch Excelsior Sprg MO 2002-** B Kendallville IN 1951 s John & Virginia. Sewanee: The U So, TS; Valparaiso U 1970; BA Phillips U 1973; MDiv Sewanee: The U So, TS 1977. D 6/18/1977 P 1/8/1978 Bp Gerald Nicholas Mcallister. m 8/12/1973 Janette Coil c 3. Epis Ch Of The H Sprt Kansas City MO 1996-2001; Int S Aug's Ch Kansas City MO 1993-1994; Admin R S Andr's Ch Kansas City MO 1986-1991; Vic S Jn's Ch Woodward OK 1979-1986; Dn, Reg 4 Dio Oklahoma Oklahoma City OK 1978-1986; S Steph's Alva Alva OK 1978-1981; S Paul's Cathd Oklahoma City OK 1977-1978; COM Dio W Missouri Kansas City MO 2000-2006. Auth, "Yes, But How Do I Become a Nonanxious Presence?," *Congregations*, The Alb Inst; Auth, "Effective Del Skills Promote Vital Congregations," *Congregations*, The Alb Inst. Ord of S Ben.

COIL, Paul Douglas (At) 4141 Wash Lee Ct Sw, Lilburn GA 30047 **Chr Ch Norcross GA 2015-; Chapl Eastside Hosp 2015-** B Washington DC 1945 s Everett & Mary. BA Salem Coll Salem WV 1970; MDiv Ya Berk 1973. D 6/23/1973 Bp William Foreman Creighton P 2/22/1975 Bp Wilburn Camrock Campbell. m 7/24/1971 Carolyn Coil c 2. R The Ch Of S Matt Snellville GA 1992-2013; R H Trin Epis Ch Bartow FL 1981-1992; Vic Chr Memi Ch Williamstown WV 1974-1981; Asst S Pat's Ch Washington DC 1973-1974;

Liturg Com Dioces of W Virginia Charleston WV; Chapl Dio Cntrl Florida Orlando FL; Exec Bd Dio Atlanta Atlanta GA, Stwdshp Cmsn. Auth, "Two Curric Guides for CE". OHC 1972.

COKE III, Henry Cornick (Dal) 5433 N Dentwood Dr, Dallas TX 75220 **Ret 1992-** B New Haven CT 1928 s Henry & Ethel. BA Ya 1950; MDiv GTS 1954; STM SMU 1971. D 6/16/1954 Bp Harry Tunis Moore P 12/1/1954 Bp Charles A Mason. m 6/26/1954 Anne Coke. S Mich And All Ang Ch Dallas TX 1961-1980; Vic S Mich's U Mssn Isla Vista CA 1958-1961; Chapl U CA-Santa Barbara 1958-1961; Vic S Alb's Electra TX 1954-1958. Auth, "Why Baptize Babies?".

COKE, Paul Tyler (Tex) 9426 Peabody Ct, Boca Raton FL 33496 **Ret & Prof Emer ETSSw 1998-** B Long Beach CA 1933 s Paul & Beatrice. BA Pomona Coll 1954; BA Oxf GB 1958; STB GTS 1959; MA Oxf GB 1962; ThD GTS 1971. D 6/22/1959 P 2/16/1960 Bp Francis E I Bloy. m 4/30/1960 Ethel Coke. Prof NT ETSSw 1974-1998; Epis TS Of The SW Austin TX 1974-1998; Assoc Prof ETSC Puerto Rico 1968-1974; Mssy Dio Liberia 1963-1966; Chapl Bp's Sch La Jolla CA 1960-1963; Cur S Jas Par Los Angeles CA 1959-1960. Auth, *Mtn & Wilderness: Pryr & Wrshp in the Biblic Wrld & Early Ch.* Fell Royal Soc of Arts.

COLANGELO, Preston Hart (Ala) 1663 Bradford Ln, Bessemer AL 35022 **VP Estrn Vlly Fire Dist 2008-; Ther team and animal handler Delta Soc 2005-; D Dio Alabama Birmingham 2004-; R.N. NY St 1980-; Vol Fireman, Pres Live Hose Co. #4 N. Tonawanda NY 1975-** B Lockport NY 1951 s Anthony & Carolyn. AAS SUNY 1980. D 10/30/2004 Bp Henry Nutt Parsley Jr. m 8/25/1972 Denise Colangelo c 2. Auditor, Corp Lead Quality Systems Delphi Harrison Lockport NY 1995-2000; Acolyte Fr; Vstry; Chris. Edu. Dir;SLEM St Mk Epis Ch No Tonawanda NY 1976-1996; Emergency Med Tech N. Tonawanda NY and NY St 1976-1986; Adv. Chrmn. Dist Eagle Chairman Boy Scouts Buffalo NY 1975-1997; Interpreter and SLEM Epathatha Mssn to the Deaf Buffalo NY; Dir, Police Acad Niagara Cnty Police Aux. Lockport NY; Captain Niagara Cnty Police Auxilliary Lockport NY; Pres Nrsng Assn; Squadron Educ Off U.S. Power Squadron Lockport NY. Delta Soc 2005; Natl Italian Amer Fed 2009.

COLAVINCENZO, Sue (EMich) St Dunstan's Episcopal Church, 1523 N Oak Rd, Davison MI 48423 **P-in-c S Dunst's Epis Ch Davison MI 2012-; Bd Dir Ballard Vill 2011-; Bd Dir Braidwood Manor/taeckens Terrace 2010-** B Steubenville OH 1942 d Thomas & Naomi. BA W Virginia U 1964; Coppage-Gordon Sch for Mnstry 2012. D 4/21/2012 P 10/20/2012 Bp Steven Todd Ousley. c 3. Lay Dir Epis Curs Dio Mich / E Mich 2001-2006; Chairperson Evang Connection Dio Mich 1998-2003.

COLBERT, Paul (SJ) 230 S Church St, Grass Valley CA 95945 B Louisville KY 1954 s George & Jean. BS No Carolina St U 1978; MS U NC 1985. D 10/11/2002 P 4/26/2003 Bp Katharine Jefferts Schori. m 11/5/2016 Rebecca Marie Goodwin. Vic St Raphael's Epis Ch Oakhurst CA 2014-2015; Vic St Nich Epis Ch Atwater CA 2010-2012; Chr Ch Las Vegas NV 2006-2008; P S Lk's Epis Ch Las Vegas NV 2006-2008; Pres, Dioc Revs Com Dio Nevada Las Vegas 2004-2008, P 2003-2008; Disciplinary Bd Epis Dio San Joaquin Modesto CA 2011-2016, Dioc Coun 2010-2016, GC Dep 2010-, Mssnr for Madera/MerceCounties 2008-2013, COM 2008-2011. Cmnty of Solitude 2010. pcolbert@diosanjoaquin.org

COLBOURNE, Albert George (Cal) 136 Manzanita Dr., Vallejo CA 94590 **Died 10/1/2015** B Baie Verte NF Canada 1915 s Alfred & Bertha. BEd Seattle U 1955; BD Nash 1958; MS California St U 1972; MDiv Nash 1974. D 11/30/1945 P 8/24/1946 Bp Benjamin F P Ivins. m 4/17/1991 Martha Copeland. Assoc S Lk's Mssn Calistoga CA 1995-2000; Sprtl Dir Priv Pract CA 1994-2015; Assoc S Mary's Epis Ch Napa CA 1990-1995; Asst Trsfg Epis Ch San Mateo CA 1986-1989; Ascen Epis Ch Vallejo CA 1978-1989, R 1955-1977; Vic Ch of the Ascen Burlingame CA 1978-1986; 1968-1978; P-in-c Gr Epis Ch Fairfield CA 1967-1968; R S Clem's Epis Ch Seattle WA 1950-1955; R Gr Ch Cedar Rapids IA 1947-1950; Emm Ch Lancaster WI 1945-1950; Vic Emm Epis Ch Lancaster WI 1945-1947; Sprtl Dir, Bp's Ranch Dio California San Francisco CA 1994-1999. Sprtl Dir Intl 1985.

COLBURN, Suzanne (Mass) Po Box 185, Boothbay Harbor ME 04538 B New York NY 1946 d Merton & Edna. BA Bow 1987; MTS Harvard DS 1990; MDiv EDS 1996. D 6/7/1997 P 6/1/1998 Bp M(Arvil) Thomas Shaw. c 2. P-in-c Ch Of S Thos Camden ME 2016-2017; S Paul's Ch Lynnfield MA 2014-2015; Int Chr Ch Needham Hgts MA 2013-2014; Int Par Of The Mssh Auburndale MA 2011-2017; Int S Jn's Ch Beverly MA 2009-2011; P-in-c S Columba's Epis Ch E Boothbay ME 2007-2009; Dio Maine Portland ME 2004-2009; Chr Ch Biddeford ME 2004-2006; Dn Dio Massachusetts Boston MA 2002-2004; Assoc Emm Ch Boston MA 1998-2003; D S Ptr's Epis Ch Cambridge MA 1997-1998; Chapl Sherrill Hse Boston MA 1997-1998; Stff Asst Rad Cambridge MA 1996-1998. SBL; Soc Of S Jn The Evang. Phi Beta Kappa Bow 1987; Cum Honoribus PDS 1971.

COLBURN, Therese Jean (Colo) D 6/18/2016 P 6/10/2017 Bp Robert John O'Neill.

COLBY, Richard Everett (Me) 3702 Haven Pines Dr, Kingwood TX 77345 **Assoc Un Ch Vina del Mar Chile SA 2006-; Non-par 1996-** B Bath ME 1937 s Earl & Madeline. BA Indiana U 1959; STB Ya Berk 1962; Spanish Stds CostaRica 1965; Cntr Intercultural Formation Mex 1966. D 6/2/1962 P 12/6/1962 Bp Oliver L Loring. m 8/14/1965 Janet Meredith Colby c 3. Pstr Un Ch Vina del Mar Chile SA 2001-2004; Assoc R S Matt's Epis Ch Lisbon Falls ME 1990-1995; R Ch Of The Epiph Avalon PA 1984-1990; Vic S Steph The Mtyr Epis Ch Waterboro Cntr ME 1980-1984; Assoc Trin Epis Ch Portland ME 1978-1979, Assoc 1971-1977; Assoc Gd Shpd San Jose Cr 1969-1971; Assoc San Marcos Limon Cr 1966-1969. Authoir, "The Recycled Pharisee," Westbow Press, 2012; Auth, "Sm Ch Are Beautiful," Hartford Sem Fndt.

COLE, Allan Hunter (Colo) 9200 W 10th Ave, Lakewood CO 80215 **R S Paul's Epis Ch Lakewood CO 2007-** B Atlanta GA 1966 s Willis & Betty. BA U NC 1996; MDiv Sewanee: The U So, TS 2000. D 12/16/2000 Bp Charles Glenn VonRosenberg. c 3. Heathwood Hall Epis Sch Columbia SC 2003-2005; D S Andr's Ch Maryville TN 2000-2003.

COLE, Anson Dean (O) 565 S Cleveland Massilon Rd, Akron OH 44333 B Kansas City MO 1931 s Anson & Helen. BS U of Kansas 1952; U CO 1957; MDiv Nash 1960. D 6/21/1960 P 12/1/1960 Bp Joseph Summerville Minnis. m 6/11/1960 Gail Cole. Assoc R S Lk's Epis Ch Akron OH 1987-1997; S Andr's Epis Ch Toledo OH 1987; Assoc R S Paul's Ch Maumee OH 1986; St Johns Ch Temperance MI 1978-1986; Vic S Jn's Temperance MI 1978-1985; Ch Of The Mssh Detroit MI 1971-1978; Colorado St U Cortez CO 1970-1971; Cur S Andr's Ch Denver CO 1970-1971; R S Barn Of The Vlly Cortez CO 1963-1970; Dn Wstrn Slope Ch Camp Ilium CO 1963-1970; Vic Epis Ch Of S Jn The Bapt Granby CO 1960-1963; Trin Ch Kremmling CO 1960-1963.

COLE, Anthony Richard (Eur) D 1/24/2009 Bp Pierre W Whalon.

COLE, Brian Lee (Lex) Church of the Good Shepherd, 533 E Main St, Lexington KY 40508 **R Ch Of The Gd Shpd Lexington KY 2012-; Cn The Cathd Of All Souls Asheville NC 2005-, Assoc 2002-2012** B Hayti MO 1967 s Bruce & Betty. BS Murray St U 1989; MDiv Sthrn Bapt TS 1992. D 6/8/2002 P 12/7/2002 Bp Bob Johnson. m 9/5/1998 Susan P Weatherford c 1. Vic Ch Of The Advoc Asheville NC 2002-2005. Affirming Catholicism 2002; Assoc Of The OHC 2002. bcole@goodshepherdlex.org

COLE JR, C Alfred (CFla) 125 Larkwood Dr, Sanford FL 32771 **Ret 2004-** B Charlotte NC 1942 s Clarence & Catharine. BS U of So Carolina 1965; CPA - 1967; CPA So Carolina 1967; MDiv VTS 1984; MDiv VTS 1984; VTS 1992; VTS 1992. D 6/8/1985 P 5/10/1986 Bp William Arthur Beckham. m 2/1/1969 Mary B Cole c 2. R H Cross Epis Ch Sanford FL 1993-2004; Exec Asst to Bp Dio Albany Greenwich NY 1992-1993; Reg Dn So Carolina Charleston SC 1989-1992, Trst 1987-1992, Dioc Coun (Ex officio) 1989-1992, Trst 1988-1992; R The Ch Of The Epiph Eutawville SC 1987-1992; Asst to the R S Fran Ch Greenville SC 1985-1987; Epis Ch Of The Redeem Greenville SC 1985.

COLE JR, Cecil T (Mass) 2210 E Tudor Rd, Anchorage AK 99507 **S Jn's Ch Jamaica Plain MA 2015-** B New York NY 1968 s Cecil & Jean. BA Mid 1990; MTS Harvard DS 1993; PhD Bos 2007. D 6/4/2005 Bp M(Arvil) Thomas Shaw P 1/7/2006 Bp Roy Frederick Cederholm Jr. m 7/9/2013 Sage S Cole c 1. Assoc S Mary's Ch Anchorage AK 2009-2015; Int Chr Ch Par Plymouth MA 2005-2009, Cur 2005-2008.

COLE, Christopher Alan (At) Holy Innocents Episcopal Church, 805 Mt Vernon Hwy NW, Atlanta GA 30327 B Greenville SC 1985 s Gary & Robin. BSBA U NC Charlotte 2007; MDIV VTS 2012. D 12/17/2011 P 7/14/2012 Bp Porter Taylor. Assoc Emm Epis Ch Athens GA 2013-2017; H Innoc Ch Atlanta GA 2012-2013. associaterector@emmanuelathens.org

COLE, Christopher Owen (WTex) 5909 Walzem Rd, San Antonio TX 78218 **R Ch Of The Resurr Windcrest TX 2008-** B Philadelphia PA 1966 s Raymond & Cornelia. BA U of Kansas 1988; MDiv SWTS 1998. D 6/20/1998 Bp Chilton Richardson Knudsen P 1/18/1999 Bp Robert Louis Ladehoff. m 10/19/1991 Laura G Cole c 2. R All SS Ch Hillsboro OR 2001-2008; S Paul's Epis Ch Salem OR 1998-2001.

COLE, Dennis Curtis (Oly) 3917 Ne 44th St, Vancouver WA 98661 **Assoc Chapl Salmon Creek Hosp Vancouver WA 2009-; Assoc S Lk's Epis Ch Vancouver WA 1998-** B Portland OR 1946 s Howard & Ruth. BA Willamette U 1968; MDiv Yale DS 1971; Tubingen U Tubingen DE 1972. D 6/20/1998 P 12/1/1998 Bp Vincent Waydell Warner. m 6/1/1968 Susan Joyce Cole c 3. Res Chapl Emanuel Hosp Portland OR 2008.

COLE, Elaine Agnes (SwFla) 330 Forest Wood Ct, Spring Hill FL 34609 **D S Mart's Epis Ch Hudson FL 2005-** B Central Falls RI 1950 d William & Elmira. D 6/26/1993 Bp George Nelson Hunt III. m 11/15/1969 Raymond Cole c 2.

COLE, Ethan J (WNY) 5083 Thompson Rd, Clarence NY 14031 B Dunkirk NY 1979 BA Hobart and Wm Smith Colleges. D 12/20/2003 P 11/6/2004 Bp Michael Garrison. m 6/1/2012 Frank J Cannata c 1. Calv Epis Ch Williamsville NY 2007-2014; All Souls Memi Epis Ch Washington DC 2006-2007; Cn S Paul's Cathd Buffalo NY 2004-2006. ethan.cole@calvaryepiscopal.net

COLE, Frantz (Hai) Box 1309, Port-Au-Prince Haiti **Dio Haiti Port-au-Prince HT 1987-** B 1958 s Roger & Genevieve. U 2 Yrs; Sem 1986. D 2/8/1987 P 11/1/1987 Bp Luc Anatole Jacques Garnier. Soc Of S Marg.

COLE JR, Howard Milton (Pa) 2001 S. 40th Court, West Des Moines IA 50265 B Newport News VA 1944 s Howard & Susie. W&M; BS Virginia Commonwealth U 1970; MA U of The Dist of Columbia 1975; MDiv GTS 1982; Cert Cuernavaca Lang Inst Mex Mx 1992; Lang Inst of Mex Mx 1992. D 6/29/1983 P 5/31/1984 Bp Claude Charles Vache. m 1/6/1999 Mary Duvall Cole-Duvall c 1. Dio Pennsylvania Philadelphia PA 1998; S Paul's Ch Elkins Pk PA 1994-1998; Int S Andr's By The Sea Nags Hd NC 1992-1994; Exec Coun Appointees New York NY 1989-1992; Vic S Andr Philippine Sea Agat GU 1989-1992; Chapl Servs Va Prisons 1987-1989; Cur Trin Ch Portsmouth VA 1983-1989. Auth, "Resolution Of Commendation Ecec 92". Peacemaker Among Us Pacem In Terris 1999; Resolutn Of Commendation Ecec 1992; Gd Samar Awd Cath Fam Serv 1987.

COLE, Judith Hampton Poteet (WNC) 8015 Island View Ct, Denver NC 28037 **D Epis Ch Of S Ptr's By The Lake Denver NC 1996-; Chapl Lakewood Care Cntr Denver NC 1996-** B South Charleston WV 1940 d Russell & Virginia. BS Morris Harvey Coll 1962; MS Marshall U 1968. D 12/21/1996 Bp Bob Johnson. m 7/24/1959 David Ray Cole c 2. Sis of the Trsfg 1993.

COLE, Marguerite June (Nev) 5268 Jodilyn Ct Apt 150, Las Vegas NV 89103 **D St. Fran-on-the-Hill El Paso TX 1985-** B Washington PA 1936 d Gustav & Margaret. BS W Virginia U 1958; EFM Sewanee: The U So, TS 1980; Cert Prchr Lewis Sch of Mnstry 1982. D 4/29/1985 Bp Richard Mitchell Trelease Jr. m 2/9/1973 John Wyatt Cole c 4. D Gr In The Desert Epis Ch Las Vegas NV 2008-2009; Par Admin Chr Epis Ch 2006-2007.

COLE, Michael George (SC) 1202 Stonegate Way, Crozet VA 22932 **Died 5/13/2016** B Sudbury Suffolk UK 1935 s Bertie & Elsie. LTh Lichfield Theol Coll 1960; DMin Wesley TS 1989. Trans 12/1/1982 Bp John Thomas Walker. m 8/2/1962 Valerie Hart c 4. H Cross Faith Memi Epis Ch Pawleys Island SC 2002-2004; Ret 1998-2016; R S Jn's Epis Ch Halifax VA 1994-1998; R The Memi Ch Of The Prince Of Peace Gettysburg PA 1990-1994; Chr Ch Chaptico MD 1983-1990; Serv Ch of Engl & Can 1960-1982. UN Peace Keeping Medal Untd Nations 1976; Can Decoration Can ArmdF 1974.

COLE JR, Raymond Elden (WTex) 3614 Hunters Dove, San Antonio TX 78230 B Newburyport MA 1938 s Raymond & Emily. BA Leh 1960; MDiv GTS 1963. D 6/8/1963 P 12/1/1963 Bp Joseph Gillespie Armstrong. m 8/31/1963 Cornelia Cole. R S Geo Ch San Antonio TX 1996-2004; R S Mk's Epis Ch Glen Ellyn IL 1979-1996; Asst R Ch Of The Gd Samar Paoli PA 1973-1979; Chapl Montgomery Hall Jvnl Detention Cntr 1971-1973; Vic Ch Of The Epiph Royersford PA 1966-1973; Cur Gr Ch Mt Airy PA 1963-1966.

COLE, Roy Allen (NY) 1333 Bay St, Staten Island NY 10305 **Adj Asst. Prof of Rel Hunter Coll CUNY 2005-; COM Dio New York New York NY 2015-; Exec Com RIchmond Inter-Par Coun 2010-** B San Diego CA 1956 s Roy & Alice. BA Warner Pacific U 1984; MA U of Nevada at Reno 1995; GTS 2003; STM GTS 2004; DMin SFTS 2007. D 8/6/2003 Bp Egbert Don Taylor P 7/26/2004 Bp Catherine Scimeca Roskam. R S Jn's Ch Staten Island NY 2008-2016; P in Charge S Mk's Epis Ch Yonkers NY 2004-2008; P-in-c S Paul's Ch Yonkers NY 2004-2008; Bd Dir and Chair of the Advsry Com Epis Chars of the Dio NY New York NY 2009-2017.

COLE III, Roy W (USC) 184 Clifton Ave, Spartanburg SC 29302 B El Paso TX 1939 s Roy & Nancy. BS USMA 1962; MDiv EDS 1974; MA Rhode Island Coll 1983. D 6/15/1974 P 12/1/1974 Bp Frederick Hesley Belden. m 6/9/2000 Mary Barbara Dorsey c 3. Asst R Ch Of The Adv Spartanburg SC 2007-2009; P-in-c Nativ Un SC 2005-2006; Int St. Marg's Boiling Sprg SC 2003-2005; S Marg's Epis Ch Boiling Spgs SC 2003-2004; Int S Matt's Ch Charleston WV 2000-2003; Int S Steph's Epis Ch And U Columbus OH 1999-2000; Int S Thos Epis Ch Towson MD 1998-1999; Int H Trin Ch Churchville MD 1995-1997; Int S Geo's Ch Perryman MD 1992-1995; P-in-c S Lk's Epis Ch Las Vegas NV 1989-1991; R Emm Ch Newport RI 1976-1985; Asst S Jas Epis Ch At Woonsocket Woonsocket RI 1974-1976. Fell 85 Coll of Preachers 1985; Adams Prize for Preaching Epis TS 1974.

COLE, Sue (Me) 41 Gardiner Pl, Walton NY 13856 **Ch Of Our Fr Hulls Cove ME 2014-** B Northport NY 1957 d Richard & Barbara. BS SUNY 1979; MA S Bernards TS and Mnstry 2003. D 6/2/2002 Bp David John Bena P 12/8/2002 Bp Daniel William Herzog. m 10/20/1979 Jack R Cole c 3. R Chr Ch Walton NY 2002-2014.

COLE, Timothy Alexander Robertson (WA) Christ Church, 3116 O St NW, Washington DC 20007 **S Jn's Ch Georgetown Par Washington DC 2016-** B Edinburgh Scotland 1960 s Donald & Shisna. MA The U of Aberdeen 1983; BD Coates Hall 1986; MTh Cardiff U 2002. Trans 9/8/2016 as Priest Bp Mariann Edgar Budde. m 4/22/1989 Lorraine K Cole c 2.

COLE-DUVALL, Mary Duvall (Ia) 2001 S 40th Ct, West Des Moines IA 50265 **R S Tim's Epis Ch W Des Moines IA 2004-** B Saint Louis MO 1959 d Harmann & Vilma. BA Col 1981; MDiv Epis TS of the SW 1996. D 6/3/1997 Bp James Monte Stanton P 1/17/1998 Bp Robert William Duncan. m 1/6/1999 Howard Milton Cole c 2. Asst Chr Ch Christiana Hundred Wilmington DE 1997-2004; Com Dio Delaware Wilmington 1999-2004. Corp Individual Awd Aids Delaware 2002; Citizenship Awd City Of Wilmington 2002; Peacemaker Among Us Pacem In Terris 2001. sttimsepis@msn.com

COLEGROVE, Jerome Higgins (O) 475 Laurel Drive, Kent OH 44240 **P-in-c Ch Of Our Sav Salem OH 2009-; Trin Ch Allnce OH 2009-** B Fort Lewis WA 1948 BS Geo 1972; MDiv SWTS 1977; MA U of Virginia 1989; CSD The Open Door Inc Charlottesville VA 1991. D 4/28/1996 P 12/11/1996 Bp Martin Gough Townsend. m 8/14/1982 Julie Blake Fisher. Int R S Jas Ch Painesville OH 2007-2009; R S Mary's Ch Nebraska City NE 1999-2006; R S Mk's Epis Ch Perryville MD 1996-1999.

COLEMAN, Bernice (LI) 10206 Farmers Blvd, Hollis NY 11423 B Claremont Saint Ann JM 1935 d George & Susan. Cert Coll of Arts Sci & Tech 1978; Cert Merc TS 1989. D 6/17/1989 P 6/1/1990 Bp Orris George Walker Jr. Epis Hlth Serv Far Rockaway NY 1992-2007; Dir Pstr S Jn's Epis Chap Brooklyn NY 1992-1997; Cur All SS' Epis Ch Long Island City NY 1990-1992, Asst 1989-1990. AEHC; Black Caucus; Bd Cert Mem Coll Chapl; UBE.

COLEMAN, Betty Ellen Gibson (SO) 4325 Skylark Dr, Englewood OH 45322 **R Chr Ch Cathd Cincinnati OH 2005-** B Dayton OH 1943 d Isaac & Ellen. BS Wilberforce U 2000; MDiv Bex Sem 2005. D 1/23/1993 P 6/25/2005 Bp Herbert Thompson Jr. c 4. Chr Ch Cathd Cincinnati OH 2005-2007; S Marg's Ch Dayton OH 2001-2005; S Andr's Ch Dayton OH 1993-2007.

COLEMAN, Brian Ray (WMich) 252 Chestnut St, Battle Creek MI 49017 **R S Thos Epis Ch Battle Creek MI 2008-; Pres JONAH Battle Creek MI 2012-; Prov Chapl Soc of Cath Priests (NA) 2012-** B Fort Worth TX 1971 s Ray & Rebecca. U So 1991; Fullerton Coll 1992; BA California St U 1994; MDiv SWTS 1998. D 6/13/1998 Bp Chester Lovelle Talton P 1/9/1999 Bp Frederick Houk Borsch. m 8/26/2014 John Michael Moore. Vice-Pres, Dioc Coun Dio Wstrn Michigan Kalamazoo MI 2011-2016, Dn 2014-, Chairman, Estrn Deanry 2011-2014; P-in-c Ss. Ptr and Oswald Abbeydale and Millhouses (CofE) 2003-2008; Serv Ch of Engl 2001-2008; Assoc Vic St. Leonard's Par Ch Norwood (CofE) 2000-2003; Assoc R S Jas Par Los Angeles CA 1998-2000. Soc of Cath Priests 2005.

COLEMAN, Carolyn (Tenn) Holy Cross Episcopal Church, 1140 Cason Land, Murfreesboro TN 37128 **S Dav's Epis Ch Nashville TN 2016-; Contingent Fac Sewanee U So TS Sewanee TN 2011-** B Nashville TN 1970 d Robert & Rodalyn. BA U of Tennessee 1992; MA Mia 1994; MDiv Bos TS 2007. D 6/12/2007 P 12/15/2007 Bp Chilton Richardson Knudsen. m 7/12/1997 Joe H Bandy c 2. Vic Ch of the H Cross Murfreesboro TN 2011-2016; Asst. Yth Mssnr Cathd Ch Of S Lk Portland ME 2007-2010; Dio Maine Portland ME 2007-2010; Stdt Bos Boston MA 2004-2007; Par Admin S Alb's Ch Cape Eliz ME 1998-2004.

COLEMAN JR, Dale D (Spr) 105 E. D St., Belleville IL 62220 **R S Geo's Ch Belleville IL 2007-** B Hillsdale MI 1954 s Dale & Eva. BA U of Wisconsin 1976; MDiv Nash 1980. D 3/22/1980 P 9/27/1980 Bp Charles Thomas Gaskell. m 8/7/2010 M Joan Wood c 3. Dn Dio The Rio Grande Albuquerque 1997-2007, RurD 1999-2007; R Ch of the H Faith Santa Fe NM 1996-2007; Dn Dio Wstrn Louisiana Alexandria LA 1992-1996, Pres of Stndg Com 1994-1995; Stndg Com 1992-1995; R S Mths Epis Ch Shreveport LA 1990-1996; R S Thos Of Cbury Ch Greendale WI 1983-1990; Assoc Gr Ch Madison WI 1980-1983; RurD Dio Springfield Springfield IL 2012-2016; COM Dio Milwaukee Milwaukee WI 1985-1990. Auth, "The Angl Sprt, revised," Ch Pub, 2004; Auth, "Taking Conversion Seriously," LivCh, 1994; Auth, "The Angl Sprt," Cowley, 1991; Auth, "Our Great Angl Heritage," St. Geo's Ch; Auth, "Easter w St. Pat," St. Geo's Ch; Auth, "Journey in Faith," St. Geo's Ch. Fr. Dale Coleman Day- Oct. 14 City of Santa Fe, NM 2005; Chapl Ord of St. Jn of Jerusalem 2002; Adj Prof of Ch Hist TESM 2000; Adj Prof of Wrshp TESM 2000; Hon Cn Dio The Rio Grande 1998.

COLEMAN, Dennis E (Pa) 121 Church St, Phoenixville PA 19460 B Philadelphia PA 1951 s Eugene. D 6/14/2014 Bp Clifton Daniel III. m 7/9/1992 Joan Coleman.

COLEMAN, Edwin Cabaniss (Tenn) 4715 Harding Pike, Nashville TN 37205 B Jackson MS 1929 s John & Edna. BA LSU 1950; MDiv Sewanee: The U So, TS 1953. D 6/25/1953 Bp Iveson Batchelor Noland P 5/1/1954 Bp Girault M Jones. m 11/26/1954 Mary Alexandra Parker. Assoc R S Geo's Ch Nashville TN 1985-1995; Chair Com So Carolina Charleston SC 1970-1980, Exec Bd 1967-1984, Chair Deptce 1967-1970, Bec 1966-1980; R S Mich's Epis Ch Charleston SC 1965-1985; Chapl Prov IV Dok 1964-1965; R S Jn's Atlanta GA 1958-1965; R Mt Olive Pineville LA 1954-1958; P-in-c S Phil's Boyce LA 1954-1958; Cur Calv Ch Bunkie LA 1953-1954.

COLEMAN JR, Fred George (NY) 2048 Lorena Ave., Akron OH 44313 **Ch Pension Fund Benefici 2005-; Non-par 1981-** B Bronx NY 1936 s Fred & Marion. BD Stevens Inst of Tech 1957; MDiv GTS 1964. D 6/6/1964 P 12/1/1964 Bp Horace W B Donegan. Asst S Andr's Ch Akron OH 1977-1981, Asst 1968-1976; Asst S Paul's Ch Akron OH 1973-1977, Asst 1970-1972; Vic S Jn The Evang Ch Napoleon OH 1971-1973; Cur S Ptr's Ch Freehold NJ 1967-1968; Cur Chr Ch Schenectady NY 1966-1967; Cur S Andr's Ch Baltimore MD 1965-1966; Cur S Geo's Par Flushing NY 1964-1965.

COLEMAN, Henry Douglas (NY) 39 W Lewis Ave, Pearl River NY 10965 **Died 4/13/2016** B 1936 s Henry & Gladys. BA Trin 1958; STB GTS 1961. D 6/10/1961 P 12/1/1961 Bp Horace W B Donegan. m 6/27/2004 Marilyne Faye Coleman. Gr Ch Bronx NY 1980-2004; St Pauls Ch New Rochelle NY 1966-1987; Cur S Jn's Ch Getty Sq Yonkers NY 1961-1966.

✠ COLEMAN, The Rt Rev James Malone (WTenn) 3052 Tyrone Dr, Baton Rouge LA 70808 **Ret Bp of WTenn Dio W Tennessee Memphis 2001-, Bp of WTenn 1994-2001, Bp Coadj of WTenn 1993-1994, Dep GC 1979-1993** B Memphis TN 1929 s Fredrick & Dorris. BS U of Tennessee 1953; MDiv Sewanee: The U So, TS 1956; DMin Wake Forest U 1975; Sewanee: The U So, TS 1994. D 7/3/1956 Bp John Vander Horst P 5/5/1957 Bp Theodore N Barth Con 11/13/1993 for WTenn. m 3/30/2005 Emily Douglass Coleman. R S Jn's Epis Ch Memphis TN 1989-1993; R S Jas Epis Ch Baton Rouge LA 1975-1989; R Chr Ch Martinsville VA 1972-1975; R S Jn's Epis Ch Johnson City TN 1966-1972; R Ch Of The Gd Shpd Knoxville TN 1962-1966; Chapl GA Institute Tech Atlanta Agnes Scott Coll Decatur GA 1960-1962; Ch Of Our Sav Gallatin TN 1957-1960; P-in-c The Ch Of The Epiph Lebanon TN 1957-1960; Trst Sewanee U So TS Sewanee TN 1986-1989, Pres Alum Assn 1969-1985; COM Dio Tennessee Nashville TN 1968-1972.

COLEMAN, James Patrick (CFla) 4820 Lake Gibson Park Rd, Lakeland FL 33809 B Chicago IL 1932 s John & Sarah. BA S Mary of the Lake Sem 1955; MA U of S Mary of the Lake Mundelein Sem 1959. Rec 3/1/1984 as Deacon Bp William Hopkins Folwell. m 10/26/1975 Beth M Coleman. S Ptr's Epis Ch Charlotte NC 2000; S Dav's Epis Ch Lakeland FL 1984-1998. Auth, "The Sacr Of Recon". Profsnl Softball Wrld Champions 1951.

COLEMAN, John Charles (CGC) 2 Chateau Place, Dothan AL 36303 **Dir Coleman Wrld Grp Fndt 2013-** B Hutchinson KS 1968 s James & Janice. BA U of Alabama 1991; JD U of Alabama 1994; MDiv GTS 2005. D 6/4/2005 P 5/20/2006 Bp Philip Menzie Duncan II. m 8/29/1998 Mary J Coleman c 3. S Lk's Ch Marianna FL 2014-2015; R Ch Of The Ascen Montgomery AL 2007-2013; S Mary's Epis Ch Andalusia AL 2005-2007; Alabama Epis Fndt Trst Dio Alabama Birmingham 2011-2013, Dioc Fin Com Mem 2011-2013, Bp Search Nomination Com 2010-2011, Dept of Camp McDowell Mem 2008-2011; Bd Dir Chld's Museum of Alabama 2009-2013; Bd Dir The Samar Counslg Cntr 2009-2013; Bd Dir Success by Six 2008-2012; Dept of Fin Dio Cntrl Gulf Coast Pensacola FL 2006-2007, Dioc Fin Com Mem 2006-2007.

COLEMAN, Karen (Mass) 59 Fayerweather St # 2138, Cambridge MA 02138 **Bos Epis Chap Brookline MA 2016-; Chapl Dio Massachusetts Boston MA 2016-; R S Jas Epis Ch Teele Sq Somerville MA 2010-; Dioc Coun Mem Dio MA 2005-** B Detroit MI 1957 BA U MI. D 2/14/2004 P 9/11/2004 Bp John Palmer Croneberger. m 12/2/2006 James F Reamer. Trin Ch Randolph MA 2007-2010; Chr Ch Needham Hgts MA 2004-2007; Epis City Mssn Boston MA 2004. clergy@stjamessomerville.org

COLEMAN, Kim Latice (Va) 912 S Veitch St, Arlington VA 22204 **Adj Prof VTS 2006-; Trin Ch Arlington VA 2002-; Advsry Bd Mem Mary Marshall Assisted Living Res 2012-** B Hampton VA 1958 d Warren & Carole. BA Penn 1980; MDiv VTS 2001. D 6/23/2001 P 12/29/2001 Bp Peter J Lee. VTS Alexandria VA 2013-2014; S Geo's Epis Ch Arlington VA 2001-2002; Exec Bd Mem Dio Virginia Richmond VA 2008-2012, UTO Grant Screening Com 2006-2011.

COLEMAN, M Joan (Spr) 9 Teakwood Dr, Belleville IL 62221 B Santa Fe NM 1960 d H Joe & Mary. TESM. D 5/10/2002 Bp Terence Kelshaw. m 8/7/2010 Dale D Coleman c 2. D S Geo's Ch Belleville IL 2011-2016; D S Barth's Ch Granite City IL 2010-2011; S Thos Epis Ch Glen Carbon IL 2010-2011; D/Par Admin Ch of the H Faith Santa Fe NM 2002-2007, Par Admin 1994-2002.

✠ COLERIDGE, The Rt Rev Clarence Nicholas (Ct) 29 Indian Rd, Trumbull CT 06611 **Ret Bp of Connecticut Dio Connecticut Meriden CT 1999-, Bp of Connecticut 1993-1999, Exec Coun 1981-2000, Bp Suffr 1981-1993** B Georgetown 1930 s Charles & Ina. BA How 1954; MDiv Drew U 1960; GTS 1961; Amer Fndt of Rel & Psych 1966; MS U of Connecticut 1973; DMin Andover Newton TS 1977; STD Ya Berk 1984; GTS 1984. D 1/27/1961 P 1/1/1962 Bp Leland Stark Con 10/23/1981 for Ct. m 9/8/1962 Euna Idris Volda Coleridge c 2. Ret Bp of Connecticut Dio Pennsylvania Philadelphia PA 1999-2000; Com Pstr Dvlpmt HOB 1988-2000; Epis Soc Serv Ansonia CT 1974-1981; Soc Concerns Com; T/F On Hunger; Vim Educ Com 1968-1981; R S Mk's Ch Bridgeport CT 1966-1981; Cur S Geo's Ch Brooklyn NY 1962-1966. DD Berkeley TS; DD GTS; DD Trin.

COLES, Clifford Carleton (NC) 3927 Napa Valley Dr, Raleigh NC 27612 **Chapl S Aug Coll 2004-** B Brooklyn NY 1928 s Walter & Clara. BA Shaw U 1952; MS Col 1961; EdD No Carolina St U 1982. D 7/18/1992 Bp Huntington Williams Jr P 7/11/1993 Bp Robert Whitridge Estill. m 11/21/1981 Marsha Coles. Chapl S Aug's Coll Raleigh NC 2004-2008; Ch Of The Redeem Greensboro NC 2000; R S Steph's Epis Ch Winston Salem NC 1996-2000; Dio No Carolina Raleigh NC 1995-1996; Vic Ch Of The Epiph Rocky Mt NC 1993-1996. Auth, "Princeville Centennial," 1985; Auth, "Persistence In Engr: Selected Variables And Participation In Acad Spprt Prog (Doctoral Dissertation)," 1983; Auth, "Perception Of Ncsu By Upward Bound Students," 1979; Auth, "A Study Of Accessibility Of Ncsu To The Handicapped," 1979; Auth, "Soc Welf Attitudes Among Selected Ldrshp In Montclaire, Nj," 1961. Rocke-

feller Intrnshp In Higher Educ 1975; Fllshp Natl Prog For Educational Ldrshp 1971; Fllshp Nation Urban League 1959.

COLES, Constance C (NY) 73 Waterside Lane, Clinton CT 06413 **Fin Com Cathd Of St Jn The Div New York NY 2014-, Trst 1994-2016; Bd Dir, 1993-Present Metropltn Japanese Mnstry Dio New York NY 1993-** B Brooklyn NY 1945 d Robert & Edna. BA Wells Coll 1967; MRE UTS 1970; MDiv UTS 1978. D 6/3/1978 P 1/14/1979 Bp Paul Moore Jr. m 12/21/1968 William B McKeown c 2. Cn for Mnstry Dio New York New York NY 2001-2013, Stndg Com, Pres 1999, Stndg Com mbr 1996-1999, Dn, Shore Cler 1993-2001; R All SS Ch Harrison NY 1986-2001; Asst The Ch Of The Epiph New York NY 1978-1986. Wider Quaker Fllshp 1980.

COLETON, John M (Kan) 7224 Village Dr, Prairie Village KS 66208 B Troy NY 1924 s John & Anna. SUNY 1948. D 12/13/1968 Bp Edward Clark Turner. c 4. D S Thos The Apos Ch Overland Pk KS 1996-1997; D S Lk's Epis Ch Shawnee KS 1978-1984.

COLLAMORE JR, Harry Bacon (Ct) 899 Turtle Ct, Naples FL 34108 B Hartford CT 1928 s Harry & Dorothy. BA Pr 1950. D 12/3/1988 Bp Arthur Edward Walmsley. m 6/23/1951 Elizabeth Caldwell Collamore c 3. Bp'S Awd For Ch And Cmnty Dio Connecticut 1998.

COLLEGE, Philip Anthony (SO) 5691 Great Hall Ct, Columbus OH 43231 **R S Jn's Ch Worthington OH 2007-, 2004-2006** B Biloxi MS 1953 s Conrad & Alice. BS Morehead St U 1975; BA U of Kentucky 1978; MS Cntrl Michigan U 1987; MDiv GTS 1994. D 6/17/1994 P 5/1/1995 Bp Herbert Thompson Jr. c 2. Int S Mk's Epis Ch Columbus OH 2006-2007; Int S Jas Epis Ch Columbus OH 2004-2005; R S Jas Epis Ch Zanesville OH 1999-2002; Supply Dio Sthrn Ohio Cincinnati OH 1997-1999; Asst S Alb's Epis Ch Of Bexley Columbus OH 1994-1997. pacollege11@yahoo.com

COLLER, Patricia Marie (Ct) Church Pension Group, 19 E 34th St, New York NY 10016 **P Chr Ch Norwalk CT 2013-** B Philadelphia PA 1951 d Harry & Margaret. BS Kutztown U 1987; MDiv Ya Berk 1991. D 9/14/1991 Bp Cabell Tennis P 9/29/1992 Bp Andrew Frederick Wissemann. c 3. Exec VP, Chf Eccl Off The CPG New York NY 2000-2014; Cn to the Ordnry Dio Wstrn Massachusetts Springfield 1995-2000; Assoc R S Jn's Ch Northampton MA 1994-1995, Cur 1991-1994. mompat101@aol.com

COLLEY-TOOTHAKER, Sam Scott (WNY) 437 Hawthorne Drive, Danville VA 24541 **Gr Ch Lockport NY 2016-** B Portland ME 1960 s Clifford & Erna. BA Vermont Coll of Norwich U 2003; MDiv EDS 2004. D 4/3/2005 P 10/27/2005 Bp Chilton Richardson Knudsen. m 10/13/1984 Linda L Colley c 2. Int S Ptr's Epis Ch Chicago IL 2015-2016; Cathd Of S Jas Chicago IL 2014-2015; Ch Of S Ben Bolingbrook IL 2014; S Andr's Ch Downers Grove IL 2014; R Ch Of The Epiph Danville VA 2007-2013; S Andr's Epis Ch Newport News VA 2005-2007.

COLLIER, Catherine Hudson (Ala) 605 Lurleen B Wallace Blvd N, Tuscaloosa AL 35401 **Assoc Chr Ch Tuscaloosa AL 2009-** B Jacksonville NC 1954 d Willard & Patricia. BS Troy U 1980; MS Troy U 1981; EdS Troy U 1982; PhD U of Alabama 1992; MDiv Sewanee: The U So, TS 2009. D 5/20/2009 P 12/18/2009 Bp Henry Nutt Parsley Jr. m 12/10/1988 Samuel D Collier c 4.

COLLIER, Daniel R (NH) 155 Salem Rd, Billerica MA 01821 B Lynn MA 1959 s Raymond & Claire. Cert EDS; MA Weston Jesuit TS 1991; PhD NEU Boston MA 2003. D 6/4/2002 P 1/7/2006 Bp M(Arvil) Thomas Shaw. m 7/30/2004 W Michael Hamilton. 25 Hrs/Week S Andr's Ch Manchester NH 2007-2012; D S Paul's Epis Ch Bedford MA 2005-2007.

COLLIER, Mary Anne (NwT) 1605 W Pecan Ave, Midland TX 79705 **Patient Counslr Us Oncology 2000-** B Pittsburgh PA 1959 d Delwood & Mary. BA Texas St U San Marcos 1982; MA Lon GB 1989. D 10/31/2004 Bp C Wallis Ohl. m 7/9/1983 Patrick Collier c 2.

COLLIN, Winifred Nohmer (Roch) 2696 Clover St, Pittsford NY 14534 B New York NY 1944 d Fritz & Martha. D 6/22/1988 P 1/1/1989 Bp William George Burrill. m 6/3/1967 Dwight R Collin c 2. R Chr Ch Pittsford Pittsford NY 1999-2012; R The Ch Of The Epiph Gates NY 1995-1998, 1989-1990; S Paul's Ch Rochester NY 1990-1995.

COLLINS, Aaron Paul (O) 2387 Edgerton Rd, University Heights OH 44118 **R Ch Of The Gd Shpd Lyndhurst OH 2012-** B Arakonam INDIA 1954 s Abraham & Mary. BS U of Madras 1979; BD Un Biblic Sem/Serampore U Pune Maharas 1993; MTh Untd Theol Coll Serampore U Bangalore IN 1997. Trans 7/26/2004 as Priest Bp Stacy F Sauls. m 11/12/1982 Anita P Collins c 3. R S Alb's Epis Ch Louisville KY 2006-2012; P-in-c S Andr's Ch Lexington KY 2004-2006; Asst To The R Ch Of The Ascen Frankfort KY 2002-2004; Int S Raphael's Ch Lexington KY 2002; Presb St. Jn's Ch Pune India 2000-2001; Sr Lectr Un Biblic Sem Pune India 1997-2001. Biblic Lit Soc 2006.

COLLINS, Charles Blake (WTex) 431 Richmond Pl Ne, Albuquerque NM 87106 B Silver City NM 1953 s Charles & Nancy. TESM; BA U of Texas 1976; MDiv Epis TS of the SW 1980. D 8/6/1981 P 5/3/1982 Bp Richard Mitchell Trelease Jr. m 7/9/1979 Ellen Collins c 4. R Chr Epis Ch San Antonio TX 2001-2010; R S Mk's On The Mesa Epis Ch Albuquerque NM 1990-2001; R H Fam Ch Orlando FL 1985-1990; Asst R Trin Ch Vero Bch FL 1983-1985; S Fran On The Hill El Paso TX 1982-1983; Dio The Rio Grande Albuquerque NM 1981-1982.

177

Auth, "Separated By Love"; Auth, "A R Should Learn To Wk w The Vstry"; Auth, "No Hope For Sick Paradigm," *Living Ch*; Auth, "Helen W & The Three Legged Stool," *Mssn & Mnstry*; Auth, "Sin," *Not Promiscuous Genes*.

COLLINS, David Browning (At) 132 Hearthstone Dr, Woodstock GA 30189 **Died 12/29/2016** B Hot Sprgs AR 1922 s Charles & Agnes. BA U So 1943; BD Sewanee: The U So, TS 1948; S Augustines Coll Cbury GB 1961; STM Sewanee: The U So, TS 1962. D 6/16/1948 P 3/11/1949 Bp Richard B Mitchell. m 10/14/1945 Maryon Virginia Collins c 4. Pres HOD - GC 1985-1991; Ret 1984-2016; VP Hse Deps Dio Atlanta 1976-1985; Dio Atlanta 1973-1975; Bd Cler Deploy Dio Atlanta 1971-1976; Dep GC Dio Atlanta 1967-1988; Dn Cathd Of S Phil Atlanta GA 1966-1985; Chapl and Assoc Prof of Rel Sewanee U So TS Sewanee TN 1953-1966; P-in-c Ch Of The H Cross W Memphis AR 1949-1953; D-in-c S Andr's Ch Marianna AR 1948-1949; Coll Wk Cmsn Dio Tennessee Nashville TN 1957-1959. Auth, *Memoirs: There is Lad Here*, Privately Pub see Amazon.com. DD U So 1974.

COLLINS, David William (SeFla) 365 La Villa Dr., Miami Springs FL 33166 **Dir for Sprtl Care Memi Reg & Joe DiMaggio Chld's Hospitals 2011-** B Abington PA 1963 s John & Evelyn. BA Gordon Coll 1981; MDiv Ya Berk 2003. D 12/10/2008 Bp Leo Frade. Ch Of The Intsn Ft Lauderdale FL 2011; H Sacr Hollywood FL 2010; S Lk's Epis Ch Stuart FL 2009.

COLLINS, Diana Garvin (Vt) 535 Woodbury Rd, Springfield VT 05156 B Rahway NJ 1943 d Lester & Barbara. Vermont Dio Study Prog VT; ADN Vermont Coll 1963; BD Vermont Coll 1985. D 6/15/1993 Bp Daniel Lee Swenson. m 8/10/1963 Christian Collins c 3. D S Paul's Epis Ch White Riv Jct VT 1993-2002.

COLLINS, Emily Selden (NMich) 1628 W Town Line Rd, Pickford MI 49774 B 1946 d Gilbert & Nancye. D 11/28/2005 P 5/28/2006 Bp James Arthur Kelsey. c 1. P S Jas Ch Of Sault S Marie Sault Sainte Marie MI 2006-2012.

COLLINS, Gary David (Los) 2720 Colt Rd, Rancho Palos Verdes CA 90275 **Died 1/4/2016** B Oakland CA 1952 s Ronald & Lola. BA San Francisco St U 1974; MDiv CDSP 1977. D 6/25/1977 Bp Chauncie Kilmer Myers P 6/7/1978 Bp CE Crowther. m 7/28/1984 Heather Kaye Shawhan c 1. S Ptr's Par San Pedro CA 1988-1992; S Paul's Epis Ch Walnut Creek CA 1988; S Anne's Ch Fremont CA 1982-1987; S Paul's Epis Ch San Rafael CA 1980-1982; S Andr's Ch Saratoga CA 1977-1980.

COLLINS, Gerald (Pa) 4700 City Avenue, Apt. 11310, Philadelphia PA 19131 B Baltimore MD 1949 s William & Evelyn. BS Morgan St U 1976; MPS NYTS 1994; MDiv UTS 1996; CTh Oxf GB 2001. D 6/1/1996 P 12/7/1996 Bp Richard Frank Grein. S Paul's Ch Doylestown PA 2015-2017; S Geo S Barn Ch Philadelphia PA 2014-2015; S Mary's Ch Hampton Bays NY 2012-2014; Int Emm Ch Baltimore MD 2010-2011; R Ch Of S Mary The Vrgn Baltimore MD 2005-2010; Int S Chris's Ch Fairborn OH 2005; S Andr's Epis Ch Cincinnati OH 2003-2005; R S Jn's Epis Ch Sprngfld Gdnd NY 1998-2003; Assoc R S Aug's Ch New York NY 1996-1998. Auth, "Absalom Jones Sermon," *Wrshp That Works*, 2003; Auth, "A Witness For The Lamb Of God," *Wrshp That Works*, 2002; Auth, "Finding A Way Out Of The Wifinding A Way Out Of The Wilderness," *Wrshp That Works*, 2002. Bd Dir New Fed Theater Ny 1996-1998; Bro Of S Andr; Chair, Dept Of Bdgt 1999-2003; COM 2008; Curs #56 Dio Li 2002; Dioc Coun Li 1999; Epis Black Caucus Dio Ny 1996-1998; EUC 2009; Geo Freeman Bragg Fell 1996-1998; Liturg and Wrshp 2005-2008; Prog and Bdgt 2008; UBE 1996.

COLLINS, Guy J(Ames) D(Ouglas) (NH) 9 W Wheelock St, Hanover NH 03755 **R and Epis Chapl to Dartmouth S Thos Ch Hanover NH 2007-; Stndg Com Dio New Hampshire Concord NH 2014-** B Runnymede England 1974 MTh U of St Andrews 1996; PhD Peterhouse, U of Cambridge 2000. Trans 10/30/2003 Bp Charles Ellsworth Bennison Jr. m 11/29/2002 Kristin A Bornholdt-Collins c 2. R S Jn's Ch Huntingdon Vlly PA 2003-2007; Cur Barnes Team Mnstry (Ch of Engl) 2000-2003. Auth, "Faithful Doubt: The Wisdom of Uncertainty," *Cascade*, 2014; "Defending Derrida: A Response To Milbank And Pickstock," *Scottish Journ of Theol*, T Clark, 2001; "Questioning Theol: Affirming Culture," *Theol*, Spck, 2001; "Thinking The Impossible: Derrida And The Div," *Lit and Theol*, Oxf Press, 2000. guy.collins@dartmouth.edu

COLLINS, James Edward (ECR) 615 Santa Paula Dr, Salinas CA 93901 B Pittsburgh PA 1949 s Kenneth & Dorothea. BA Gordon Coll 1971; MDiv Gordon-Conwell TS 1974; DMin Gordon-Conwell TS 1985. Trans 3/1/2007 Bp Sylvestre Donato Romero. c 6. Serv Angl Ch of Can 1974-1997. "One Man's Mile," *Gnrl Store Pub Hse, Renfrew, Ontario*, 2004.

COLLINS, Jean Griffin (Mont) 1000 Fountain Terrace, 402, Lewistown MT 59457 **P-in-c S Jas Ch Lewistown MT 2013-, 2011-2013** B Denver CO 1956 d John & Virginia. BA U of Montana 1980; MDiv VTS 1983. D 8/25/1983 P 1/31/1985 Bp Jackson Earle Gilliam. c 2. P-in-c S Paul's Ch Hamilton MT 1997-2003; P-in-c S Steph's Epis Ch Stevensville MT 1994-2009; Ch Of The H Sprt Missoula MT 1994-1996; Int Trin Ch Moorestown NJ 1991; R S Paul's Ch Chittenango NY 1986-1990; Asst Gr Epis Ch Utica NY 1985-1986; Geriatric Min Trin Ch Uppr Marlboro MD 1984-1985; Intern Chapl S Eliz's Hosp Washington DC 1983-1984; COM Dio Montana Helena MT 2006-2010, COM 2006-2010, Dioc Coun 2006-2009, Stndg Com, Pres 2002-2003, GC Dep, 2000,2003,2009, 2015 2000-2009, Stndg Com 2000-2003, Dioc Coun 1996-1999.

COLLINS III, John Milton (SanD) 701 Kettner Blvd Unit 94, San Diego CA 92101 **Ret 1999-** B Washington DC 1933 s John & Josephine. BA U of Maryland 1959; BD EDS 1962; MDiv EDS 1972. D 6/16/1962 P 12/22/1962 Bp William Foreman Creighton. m 2/20/1999 Janet Elizabeth Kopf c 4. For Pstr Care Cathd Ch Of S Paul San Diego CA 2002-2015; S Anne's Epis Ch Oceanside CA 1995, Int R 1994-1995; Ch Of The Gd Samar San Diego CA 1992-1995; Asst to R S Barth's Epis Ch Poway CA 1990-1999; Chapl U. S. Navy Off Of Bsh For ArmdF New York NY 1963-1990; Chapl (CAPT) USN 1963-1990; S Andr's Ch Leonardtown California MD 1962-1963; P-in-c The Ch Of The Ascen Lexingtn Pk MD 1962-1963. SSP 1975. Geo Washington Hon Medal Freedoms Fndt.

COLLINS, John Robert (EO) PO Box 130, Sisters OR 97759 B Houston TX 1946 s Eldon & Isla Mae. BA U of Texas 1969; MA Oklahoma St U 1971. D 8/10/2014 P 6/6/2015 Bp Bavi Edna Rivera.

COLLINS, Judith Tindall (RI) 84 Benefit St # 3, Providence RI 02904 B Somerville MA 1940 d Frederick & Esther. BA Guilford Coll 1962. D 6/20/1992 Bp George Nelson Hunt III. c 3. D S Mary's Ch E Providence RI 2013-2014; D Ch Of The Redeem Providence RI 2005-2012; D Trin Ch Cranston RI 2000-2005; D Ch Of The Ascen Cranston RI 1996-2000; D S Geo's Ch Newport RI 1995-1996; D S Barn Ch Warwick RI 1992-1995.

COLLINS, Loretta L (CPa) 21 S Main St, Lewistown PA 17044 **D S Mk's Epis Ch Lewistown PA 2010-** B Lancaster PA 1952 d Lester & Elva. BA Estrn Mennonite U 1975; MA CUA 1978. D 10/31/2010 Bp Nathan Dwight Baxter. m 7/8/1989 Patrick A Collins.

COLLINS, Lynn Arnetha (LI) 21 Eldridge Ave, Hempstead NY 11550 **R St Jn the Evang Epis Ch Lynbrook NY 2005-** B New York NY 1953 d James & Elsie. AA Queensborough Cmnty Coll 1974; BA CUNY 1976; MDiv NYTS 1989; DMin NYTS 2000; Harvard DS 2002. D 7/9/1990 Bp Richard Frank Grein P 3/2/1991 Bp Arthur Williams Jr. c 1. R St Johns Pro-Cathd Los Angeles CA 2003-2005; P-in-c S Steph's Epis Ch Jamaica NY 2003; Nat'l Off Epis Ch Cntr New York NY 1995-2003; R S Paul's Epis Ch Of E Cleveland Cleveland OH 1992-1995; Urban Missions Dio Ohio Cleveland 1990-1992; Yth Advsr Dio New York 1988-1990.

COLLINS, Mac (SanD) 3847 Balsamina Dr, Bonita CA 91902 **R S Mk's Ch San Diego CA 2006-, R 1998** B San Diego CA 1952 s Arthur & Mary. BA Point Loma Coll 1977; MA Fuller TS 1978; MA Point Loma Coll 1978; PhD Fuller TS 1986. D 11/22/1986 P 6/22/1987 Bp Charles Brinkley Morton. m 8/15/1992 Constance Elizabeth Collins. Dio San Diego San Diego CA 1997-2005, 1995; S Barth's Epis Ch Poway CA 1996-1997; S Mary's In The Vlly Ch Ramona CA 1995; Int Assoc Pastr Incarn Luth Ch San Diego 1992-1997; Luth Ch Of The Incarn Poway CA 1991-1992; Min Ce Cathd Ch Of S Paul San Diego CA 1987-1990. Auth, "God & Evil In The Process Thought Of An Whitehead". Comp Bsp; Soc Of S Paul.

COLLINS, Mark R (Nwk) 40 Central Ave, Glen Rock NJ 07452 **All SS' Epis Ch Glen Rock NJ 2015-** B Memphis TN 1959 s Vernon & Peggy. BA City Coll of New York 1997; MDiv GTS 2008. D 3/15/2008 P 9/20/2008 Bp Mark Sean Sisk. m Denton Stargel. Int Ch Of The H Trin New York NY 2012-2015. Epis Response to AIDS 2008.

COLLINS, Patrick A (Eas) 640 N 67th St, Harrisburg PA 17111 **All Faith Chap Miles River Par Easton MD 2016-; Cn Dio Easton Easton MD 2016-; Bd Dir Camp Mt Luther Mifflinburg PA 2008-; Convenor, Altoona Convoc Dio Cntrl Pennsylvania Harrisburg PA 2010-, Coun of Trst 2010-, Stndg Com 2010-, Instr, Sch of Chr Stds 2009-, Chair, Chld's Cmsn 2007-, Dir, BASIC camping Prog 2006-, Partnr in Mssn Cmsn 2006-** B Washington DC 1965 s Robert & Andrea. AA Ferrum Coll 1985; BS Ferrum Coll 1988; MDiv GTS 2006. D 6/3/2006 Bp Michael Whittington Creighton P 12/13/2006 Bp Nathan Dwight Baxter. m 7/8/1989 Loretta L Lehman. R S Jn's Epis Ch Huntingdon PA 2009-2012; Cur Cathd Ch Of S Steph Harrisburg PA 2006-2009. patrick@dioceseofeaston.org

COLLINS, Paul Michael (Oly) PO Box 1204, Summerland CA 93067 **Dep Dir Snohomish Cnty Corrections Dept 2002-** B Colfax WA 1947 s Robert & Elsie. MDiv CDSP 1972. D 8/26/1972 Bp Ivol I Curtis P 5/1/1981 Bp Robert Hume Cochrane. m 5/15/1981 Dorothy Kathleen Deviny. R Trin Par Seattle WA 1998-2012; Vic S Hilda's - S Pat's Epis Ch Edmonds WA 1988-1998; Int S Andr's Ch Seattle WA 1984-1988; Dep Dir Snohomish Cnty Corrections Dept 1974-1984.

COLLINS, Stanley Penrose (SJ) 1401 Locke Rd, Modesto CA 95355 B Philadelphia PA 1935 s Berry & Lillian. BA Tem 1959; MDiv Epis TS of the SW 1983. D 6/22/1983 P 1/30/1984 Bp Gordon Taliaferro Charlton. m 6/17/1967 Carole Schweizer Collins c 6. Supply St.Nich Epis Ch Atwater CA 2013; Vic S Mk's Epis Ch Tracy CA 2004-2007; Int Vic S Mary's Ch Manteca CA 2002-2004; Int R Chr The King Ch Riverbank CA 2002; R S Paul's Epis Ch Modesto CA 1994-2002; Vic S Lukes Ch Deer Pk TX 1989-1994; R Gr Epis Ch Galveston TX 1984-1989; Asst to R Ch Of The Gd Shpd Friendswood TX 1983-1984; Pres Nthrn Dnry Epis Dio San Joaquin Modesto CA 2012-2013,

VP Nthrn Dnry 2011-2012, Dn, Yosemite Dnry 1996-2002, Dn Yosemite Dnry 1995-2002, Dioc Coun 1995-2001, Dioc Invstmt Trust 1994-1995; Chair, Bldg Com S Vincents Hse Galveston TX 1985-1986; CE Plcy Bd Dio Texas Houston TX 1983-1986. "Motivational Messages on Faith & Renwl," *Dear Par Fam*, 2003; "Column on Sprtl Direction," *Texas Epis Churchmen*, 1986; "Var arts," *The Angl Dig*, 1986. Chapl Ord of S Lk 1985; OHC 1983.

COLLINS, Victoria Lundberg (CFla) 688 Ebony St, Melbourne FL 32935 **D H Trin Epis Ch Melbourne FL 2006-, D 2005-2011** B Orlando FL 1940 d Henric & Edna. BS Richmond Profsnl Inst; NO SWTS 1975; Cert Inst For Chr Stds/Sch of Diac Stds 1995. D 3/23/1996 Bp John Wadsworth Howe. m 12/26/1972 Perry William Collins c 1. D Epis Ch Of The H Apos Satellite Bch FL 1996-2005.

COLLINS, William Gerard (Ga) 209 Maple St, Saint Simons Island GA 31522 **Assoc/Chapl S Thos Ch Savannah GA 2009-** B IE 1945 s Michael & Sara. MA S Patricks Coll 1971; MA Merc 1994. Rec 6/1/1996 Bp Henry Irving Louttit. m 11/20/1994 Mary Collins. The Collgt Ch of St Paul the Apos Savannah GA 2009-2010; R S Mk's Ch Brunswick GA 2003-2008, Assoc 1996-2002.

COLLINS-BOHRER, Padraic Michael (Roch) 111 East Ave Apt 330, Rochester NY 14604 B Rochester NY 1977 s Thomas & Mary. Dplma in Angl Stds Bexley-Seabury; M.Div Colgate Rochester Crozer DS; B.S. Medaille Coll. D 6/3/2017 Bp Prince Grenville Singh. CPE Intern Chapl U Roch Med Cntr 2015; Chapl Eastman Sch of Mus Genesee Area Campus Mnstrs Rochester NY 2014-2016. Trost Awd Colgate Rochester Crozer DS 2017.

COLLINS REED, Charlotte Collins (O) 409 E High St, Springfield OH 45505 **Chr Ch Epis Hudson OH 2016-; Bd Mem Bex Sem Columbus OH 2010-; COM-Chair Dio Sthrn Ohio Cincinnati OH 2010-, COM 2007-, Stndg Com Pres 2006-2007, COM 2005-, Stndg Com Mem 2004-2007, Stndg Com 2003-2007, Com on Congrl Life 1998-2005** B Dothan AL 1959 d Richard & Ann. BA Hendrix Coll 1981; MA Van 1985; Trin Luth Sem 1995; MDiv SWTS 1997. D 6/21/1997 P 1/24/1998 Bp Herbert Thompson Jr. m 1/2/1982 Donald Collins Reed c 2. R Chr Epis Ch Of Springfield Springfield OH 2000-2016; P S Jas Ch Piqua OH 1997-2000; S Mk's Ch Sidney OH 1997-2000; P S Paul's Epis Ch Greenville OH 1997-2000.

COLLINSWORTH, Beverly (NI) B Glendale CA 1942 d Delbert & Evelyn. Rec 3/19/2016 as Priest Bp Edward Stuart Little II. c 2.

COLLIS, Geoffrey (NJ) 32 Lafayette St, Rumson NJ 07760 **Ret 2007-** B Red Bank NJ 1950 s Harry & Margaret. BS Rider U 1972; MDiv GTS 1976. D 6/5/1976 P 12/18/1976 Bp Albert Wiencke Van Duzer. Int Epis Ch Of The Epiph Ventnor City NJ 2006-2007; S Dav's Ch Cranbury NJ 2005; Int Trin Epis Ch Cranford NJ 2003-2004; Vic S Ptr's At The Light Epis Barnegat Light NJ 2001-2002; Int Chr Ch Somers Point NJ 1999-2000; S Jas Ch Long Branch NJ 1981-1999; Asst Chr Ch Toms River Toms River NJ 1976-1981.

COLLIS, Shannon Jane (Los) 11305 Hesperia Rd., Hesperia CA 92345 B San Diego CA 1956 d John & Shirley. BA San Diego St U 1986; MA San Diego St U 1992; MDiv CDSP 2008. D 6/7/2008 P 1/10/2009 Bp Joseph Jon Bruno. S Fran On The Hill El Paso TX 2012-2014; S Hilary's Epis Ch Hesperia CA 2009-2012; Assoc S Paul's Par Lancaster CA 2008-2009.

COLMENAREZ, Gustavo Adolfo (Ve) Iglesia Episcopal de Venezuela, Colinas de Bello Monte, Centro Diocesano Av. Caroní No. 100, Caracas 1042-A Venezuela B 1968 s Gladys. Educ Universidad Nacional Experimental Simón Rodríguez. D 10/19/2013 Bp Orlando Jesus Guerrero. Dio Venezuela Caracas 2014-2015.

COLMORE III, Charles Blayney (SanD) Po Box 516, Jacksonville VT 05342 B Orange NJ 1940 s Charles & Margaret. BA U of Pennsylvania 1963; MDiv EDS 1966. D 6/25/1966 Bp Anson Phelps Stokes Jr P 12/5/1966 Bp Nelson Marigold Burroughs. m 12/26/1979 Lacey J Colmore c 3. R S Jas By The Sea La Jolla CA 1987-1996; R S Paul's Ch Dedham MA 1973-1987; St. Jn's, Lafayette Sq, Washington, D.C. S Jn's Ch Lafayette Sq Washington DC 1969-1973; Cur S Paul's Ch Akron OH 1966-1969; Pres/Stndg Com Dio San Diego San Diego CA 1992-1993, Chair 1988-1991. Auth, "Meander: Wooing Ms. Maudie," *Novel*, Xlibris, 2010; Auth, "God Knows; It's Not About Us," *Novel*, Xlibris, 2004; Auth, "In The Zone; Notes on Wondering Coast To Coast," *Fiction/Non-fiction Collection*, Xlibris, 2000; Auth, "Notes From Zone 4 & 10," *Zone Notes*, Internet, 1995; Auth, "arts," *Epis Ch Times/Various Pub*, 1966.

COLON TORRES, Lydia (PR) PO Box 902, Saint Just PR 00978 Puerto Rico B Adjuntas PR 1942 d Antonio & Angelica. AA Hostos Cmnty Coll 1974; BA Universidad Catolica 1980; MA Universidad Catolica 1986; MDiv Seminario San Pedro-Pablo 2010. D 11/22/2009 P 8/15/2010 Bp David Andres Alvarez-Velazquez. m 11/21/2004 Daniel Guadalupe Mendoza c 2.

COLTON, Elizabeth Wentworth (Pa) 966 Trinity Lane, King of Prussia PA 19406 **All SS Ch Philadelphia PA 2017-** B Albany NY 1951 d James & Ruth. BA Elmira Coll 1973; MA H Names U 1978; Cert Pennsylvania Diac Sch 1992; MTS EDS 2004. D 9/19/1992 Bp Wilson Mutebi P 5/29/2004 Bp Charles Ellsworth Bennison Jr. Trin Ch Gulph Mills Kng Of Prussia PA 2014-2016; R Gr Ch And The Incarn King of Prussia PA 2004-2014; D/Par Admin Ch Of The H Sprt Harleysville PA 2000-2002; D Cathd Ch of Our Sav Philadelphia PA 1998-2000; Dio Pennsylvania Philadelphia PA 1995-1998; D S Mary's Ch Hamilton Vill Philadelphia PA 1992-1994.

COLVILL, Lea Nadine (Mont) **Emm Ch Hailey ID 2017-** D 12/21/2014 Bp Charles Franklin Brookhart Jr P 9/29/2015 Bp Cate Waynick.

COLVIN, Jeremi Ann (Mass) 160 Rock St, Fall River MA 02720 **Asst R for Mssn in Homeless Mnstry Ch of the H Sprt Fall River MA 2011-; Fndr/co-Ldr The Bayside Fllshp (St Ch) Fall River MA 2011-** B Mineola NY 1958 d Donald & Jeannette. BA SUNY at New Paltz 1980; MDiv EDS 2009. D 6/5/2010 Bp Gayle Harris P 1/8/2011 Bp M(Arvil) Thomas Shaw. m 7/11/2005 Lynn Colvin c 1.

COLVIN, Myra Angeline (Mich) 226 Spring Lake Dr, Chelsea MI 48118 B Lima Ohio 1921 d Samuel & Myrtle. D 12/10/2005 Bp Wendell Nathaniel Gibbs Jr. c 4.

COLVIN, Sarah M (Va) 131 Waterbury Court, Charlottesville VA 22902 **S Patricks Ch Falls Ch VA 2016-** B Galveston TX 1966 d Arthur & Josephine. BS Cor 1987; MD UT SW Med Cntr 1991; MDiv VTS 2014. D 12/7/2013 P 6/14/2014 Bp Mariann Edgar Budde. m 6/7/2002 Richard David McFarland c 2.

COLWELL, Charles Richard (NY) 172 Ivy St, Oyster Bay NY 11771 **Ret Epis Ch 2008-** B Ellsworth ME 1937 s George & Dorothy. BA U of Maine 1960; MDiv GTS 1963; NYTS 1967; Postgraduate Cntr for Mntl Hlth 1967; DMin Drew U 1977. D 6/8/1963 Bp Oliver L Loring P 12/21/1963 Bp Horace W B Donegan. m 8/29/1964 Judith Colwell c 3. Int Chr Ch Garden City NY 2016-2017; Int Chr Ch Oyster Bay NY 2014-2015; Int Chr Ch Manhasset NY 2013-2014; Gr Epis Ch Massapequa NY 2013; Int S Jn's Of Lattingtown Locust Vlly NY 2011; Int S Mary's Ch Ronkonkoma NY 2011; Int S Steph's Ch Prt Washington NY 2011; Int S Lk's Ch Sea Cliff NY 2009-2011; R S Barn Ch Irvington NY 1972-2008; Assoc Ch Of The H Trin New York NY 1967-1972; Chapl Rikers Island Prison 1967-1968; Chapl Camp LaGuardia 1966-1967; Cur S Marg's Ch Bronx NY 1963-1966; Stndg Com Dio New York New York NY 2002-2003, Mem of the Eccl Crt 2000-2003, Bp Co-adjutor Transition Team, Chair 1998-, Chair, Commisson on Ministy 1986-1989, Stndg Com 1984-1989, Reg II Advsry Bd 1975-2003; Stff Mem Grp's Living (Grp Ther Prog) 1971-1973. Auth, "Collision of Worlds: A P's Life," *Bk*, 2008; Producer, "An Island in Time," *Video*, 2002; Producer (of Segment), "Will the Dust Praise You?," *Video*, 1989; Producer, "The Power of Touch," *Video*, 1988; Auth, "arts," *Living Ch, The Epis New Yorker*; Auth, "arts," *Personal Journey, Guideposts mag*. Irvington Vol Ambulance Corps. 1988-1992; The Cntr for Jewish-Chr-Muslim Understanding, Fndr a 2002-2009; The Holocaust and Human Rts Cmsn Advsry Bd 2006-2008. Muslim Wmn Assn 2008; Excellence in Pstr Care Ord of S Jn the Theol, Bp of New York 1998.

COLWELL II, Kirby Price (O) 4449 Lander Rd, Chagrin Falls OH 44022 B Amarillo TX 1949 s Kirby & Olga. W Texas A&M U; TESM 1997. D 2/21/1998 Bp Terence Kelshaw. m 12/24/1984 Gail Gatewood. S Paul's Epis Ch Cleveland OH 2002-2014. Sons of the Amer Revolution 1995.

COMBS, Carrie Anne (Ct) **Sewanee U So TS Sewanee TN 2014-** D 6/10/2017 Bp Ian Theodore Douglas.

COMBS, Jaqueline Suzanne (WNC) D 1/21/2017 Bp Jose Antonio McLoughlin.

COMBS, Leslie David (NY) 123 Franklin St., Concord NH 03301 **Non-par 1986-** B KC City MO 1948 s Josef & Lois. U of Missouri 1967; BA U of Kansas 1970; MDiv SWTS 1976. D 4/25/1976 Bp Quintin Ebenezer Primo Jr P 11/1/1976 Bp James Winchester Montgomery. c 2. R Gr Ch Millbrook NY 1983-1986; R Ch Of The Ascen Buffalo NY 1978-1983; Cur S Ptr's Epis Ch Chicago IL 1976-1978.

COMBS, Nikolaus Michael (Ida) **Sewanee U So TS Sewanee TN 2013-** B Vienna Austria 1986 s Paul & Ellen. D 12/18/2016 Bp Brian James Thom. m 1/2/2016 Carrie Anne Combs.

COMBS, William (At) 2920 Landrum Education Dr, Oakwood GA 30566 **Ch Of The Redeem Greensboro GA 2016-** B 1961 BS Emory U 1983; DMD Harv Sch of Dental Med 1988; MDiv VTS 2003. D 6/7/2003 P 1/18/2004 Bp J Neil Alexander. m 1/1/2001 Jennifer W Combs c 2. R S Gabr's Epis Ch Oakwood GA 2007-2015; Asst S Thos Epis Ch Columbus GA 2003-2007.

COMEAU, Molly Stata (Vt) 70 Poor Farm Rd, Alburg VT 05440 B Burlington VT 1948 d Cyrus & June. BS Trin Burlington VT 1983. D 5/29/1982 P 5/12/1983 Bp Robert Shaw Kerr. m 5/6/1967 Joseph Kerry Vaughn Comeau c 3. Grand Isle Cnty Crt Diversion 2006-2008; P-in-c S Jas Epis Ch Essex Jct VT 2000-2003; Cn Ordnry Dio Vermont Burlington VT 1994-2000; Bp Booth Conf Cntr Burlington VT 1993-1994; R S Jas Epis Ch Arlington VT 1990-1993; Assoc S Jn's In The Mountains Stowe VT 1989; H Trin Epis Ch Swanton VT 1985-1989. OHC.

COMEAUX, Andrew Anthony (WLa) 3728 Sabine Pass Dr, Bossier LA 71111 **Chapl Willis-Knighton Hlth System 2009-** B Plaquemine LA 1948 s Wilmot & Aline. BA S Jos Sem Coll 1970; MDiv Notre Dame Sem Grad TS 1974; MS Tul 1998. Rec 2/1/1999 as Priest Bp Charles Edward Jenkins III. m 7/13/1996 Eydie G Comeaux c 6. Cn S Mk's Cathd Shreveport LA 2002-2009; R S Jas Epis Ch Shreveport LA 2000-2002; R Ch Of The H Comm Plaquemine LA 1999-2000; Serv RC Ch 1973-1998.

COMEGYS JR, David Pierson (Dal) 25721 Weston Dr, Laguna Niguel CA 92677 **Died 2/8/2016** B Shreveport LA 1932 s David & Harriet. BA W&L 1954; Epis TS of the SW 1957; MDiv CDSP 1966. D 6/24/1957 Bp Iveson Batchelor Noland P 5/8/1958 Bp Girault M Jones. m 11/3/1960 Elizabeth Miller Hemphill c 3. Non-par 1981-1997; R S Lk's Epis Ch San Antonio TX 1975-1981; R Trin Epis Ch Ft Worth TX 1972-1975; Asst S Mich And All Ang Ch Dallas TX 1966-1972; R S Geo's Ch Bossier City LA 1963-1966; Assoc S Paul's Epis Ch Shreveport LA 1960-1963; Cur Epis Ch Of The Gd Shpd Lake Chas LA 1957-1960. Auth, "Collar," *Collar*, Auth Hse, 2005.

COMER, Harold Leroy (WMich) 1231 Fran Dr, Frankfort MI 49635 B Goshen IN 1949 s Harold & Evelyn. LTh Nash 1983. D 5/13/1983 P 11/30/1983 Bp William Cockburn Russell Sheridan. m 6/21/1985 Molly A Comer c 1. R S Phil's Ch Beulah MI 1998-2015; R S Alb's Epis Ch Ft Wayne IN 1986-1998; Cur Trin Ch Ft Wayne IN 1983-1986.

COMER, John Fletcher (Ala) 898 Running Brook Dr, Prattville AL 36066 B Memphis TN 1946 s John & Bettie. Sewanee: The U So, TS 1966; BS Auburn U 1968; MBA Auburn U 1969; MDiv Sewanee: The U So, TS 1975. D 6/1/1975 P 12/1/1975 Bp Furman Charles Stough. m 3/15/1969 Judith Walton c 2. Assoc S Phil's Ch Ft Payne AL 2010-2013; Int Ch Of The Mssh Heflin AL 2008-2010; Int S Lk's Ch Scottsboro AL 2006; P Epis Black Belt Mnstry Greensboro AL 1998-2005; Chapl Marion Millitart Inst 1998-2005; R S Wilfrid's Ch Marion AL 1998-1999; R S Mk's Ch Prattville AL 1985-1996; Cn The Cathd Ch Of The Adv Birmingham AL 1979-1985; Chapl US-AR 1976-1980; R S Andr's Epis Ch Sylacauga AL 1975-1979; R S Andr's Childersburg AL 1975-1979; S Mary's Epis Ch Childersburg AL 1975-1979; GC Dep Dio Alabama Birmingham 1994-1997. co-Auth, "Pstr Partnerships for Excellence," Resource Cntr for Pstr Excellence, 2005. Co-Fndr Birmingham Downtown Corperative Mnstrs 1992; Co-Fndr Noah, Outreach Mnstry & Par Spprt 1988; Co-Fndr, Sm Par Assn 1976. Who's Who Among Amer Teachers 1999; Who's Who Among Amer Teachers 1999; Who's Who in Rel 1992; Who's Who in Rel 1992; Paul Harris Fell Rotary Intl 1992; Who'S Who So & Sw 90 1990; Algernon Sydney Sullivan Awd 1968.

COMER, Judith Walton (Ala) 2813 Godfrey Ave NE, Fort Payne AL 35967 **Mentor EFM SOT U So 2011-; Chair of Hisp Cmsn Dio Alabama Birmingham 2011-** B 1947 d James & Margaret. BS Auburn U 1969; MA Auburn U 1971; MDiv Sewanee: The U So, TS 2008. D 5/17/2008 Bp Henry Nutt Parsley Jr P 12/16/2008 Bp John Mckee Sloan Sr. m 3/15/1969 John Fletcher Comer c 4. P-in-c S Phil's Ch Ft Payne AL 2008-2015. Freeman Awd for Merit TS, Sewanee 2006. stphilipsrector@boonlink.net

COMER, Kathleen Susan (La) 4105 Division St, Metairie LA 70002 B New Orleans LA 1947 d Sidney & Margaret. BA SE Louisiana U 1970; Cert Sch for Mnstry Dio Louisiana 2002. D 2/23/2002 Bp Charles Edward Jenkins III. D Chap Of The H Comf New Orleans LA 2011-2015; D S Mart's Epis Ch Metairie LA 2002-2009.

COMER, Susanne Darnell (Tex) 1941 Webberville Rd, Austin TX 78721 **S Mary's Epis Ch Inc Lampasas TX 2012-** B Quito Ecuador 1959 d James & Susanne. BA Rice U 1981; MDiv Columbia TS 1984; ThM Harvard DS 1990; MSW Simmons Coll 1996; Dip Ang Stud Epis TS of the SW 2010. D 6/19/2010 Bp C Andrew Doyle. c 2. S Mk's Ch Austin TX 2011-2012; Asst R S Jas Ch Austin TX 2010-2011.

COMFORT, Alexander Freeman (WNC) 105 Sunny Ln, Mars Hill NC 28754 **Non-par 1996-** B Cleveland OH 1948 s William & Anne. BA U So 1970; MA Duke 1971; MDiv Sewanee: The U So, TS 1978. D 6/17/1978 Bp Hunley Agee Elebash P 1/13/1979 Bp Gray Temple. m 6/20/1987 Sarah Comfort c 1. Trin Ch Spruce Pine NC 2009-2010; Mt Olivet Epis Ch New Orleans LA 1989-1995; Non-par 1986-1988; R S Lk's Epis Ch Jackson TN 1983-1986; Asst Trin Ch New Orleans LA 1980-1983; Asst Par Ch of St. Helena Beaufort SC 1978-1980. Auth, "Temptation At Geth," *Ch Eductr*, 1986. Outstanding Fund Raising Exec Assn of Fundraising Professionals 1995.

COMINOS, Peter Mitchell (EMich) 508 Hart St, Essexville MI 48732 B Salinas CA 1940 s Mitchell & Argero. Hartnell Coll; Cert USALS 1961; BA Golden Gate U 1987; MDiv CDSP 1990. D 2/21/1986 Bp Charles Shannon Mallory P 6/1/1990 Bp David Mercer Schofield. c 2. R Trin Epis Ch Bay City MI 1996-2006; R S Paul's Ch Altus OK 1993-1996; Vic Ch Of The Resurr Clovis Clovis CA 1990-1993; Soledad St Prison California 1988-1990; D Epis Ch Of The Gd Shpd Salinas CA 1986-1987. OHC 1978. fpc10@charter.net

COMMINS, Gary (Los) 954 Avenue C, Bayonne NJ 07002 **Ch Of The Incarn Jersey City NJ 2016-** B Los Angeles CA 1952 s Richard & Marcia. BA U CA 1974; MDiv CDSP 1980. D 6/21/1980 P 12/21/1980 Bp Robert Claflin Rusack. c 1. R The Par Ch Of S Lk Long Bch CA 2001-2016; R H Faith Par Inglewood CA 1990-2001; Vic S Mich's U Mssn Isla Vista CA 1983-1990; Chapl U CA Santa Barbara Ca 1983-1990; Asst S Geo's Epis Ch Laguna Hills CA 1980-1983. Auth, "If Only We Could See: Mystical Vision and Soc Transformation," Cascade, 2015; Auth, "Is Suffering Redemptive?," *Hist and Theol Reflection of Mart Luther King, Jr.*, Sewanee Theol Revs, 2008; Auth, "Becoming Bridges," *The Sprt and Pract of Diversity*, Cowley, 2007; Auth, "Thos Merton's Three Epiphanies," *Theol Today*, 1999; Auth, "Death & The Circus: The Theol Of Wm Stringfellow," *ATR*, Atr, 1997; Auth, "Harlem And Eschaton, Robert Slocum'S:Prophet Of Justice," *Prophet Of Life*, Ch Pub Inc, 1997; Auth, "Sprtl People/Radical Lives," *Internationl Scholars Press*, 1996; Auth, "Woody Allen's Theol Imagination," *Theol Today*, 1987. Cn The Rt. Rev. J. Jon Bruno 2010; Hon DD CDSP 2001.

COMPIER, Don Hendrik (Kan) 835 SW Polk St, Topeka KS 66612 **The Bp Kemper Sch for Mnstry Topeka KS 2014-** B Oklahoma City OK 1956 s Hendrik & Phyllis. BA U Pac 1978; MDiv Equivalent Nazarene TS 1988; PhD Emory U 1992. D 6/7/2014 Bp Dean E Wolfe. m 1/7/1983 Yolanda Compier c 1. Dio Kansas Topeka KS 2014.

COMPTON, William Hewlett (Miss) 674 Mannsdale Rd, Madison MS 39110 **The Chap Of The Cross Madison MS 2015-** B Meridian MS 1986 s John & Ann. BBA Mississippi St U 2008; MDiv VTS 2015. D 6/13/2015 P 1/16/2016 Bp Brian Seage. m 12/12/2009 Sarah Spengler Sarah Annie Spengler c 1. Dio Mississippi Jackson MS 2012-2015. wcompton@chapelofthecrossms.org

CONANT, Louise Ritchey (Mass) 24 Bowdoin St, Cambridge MA 02138 B Cincinnati OH 1937 d Hugh & Mary. BA Smith 1959; MAT Ya 1960; MDiv EDS 1984. D 6/1/1985 Bp John Bowen Coburn P 5/1/1986 Bp David Elliot Johnson. m 6/27/1964 Loring Conant c 2. Ch Of The Gd Shpd Waban MA 2000-2003; Assoc R Chr Ch Cambridge Cambridge MA 1988-1999; S Paul's Ch Brookline MA 1985-1988; Dio Massachusetts Boston MA 1985-1986, COM Mem 1992-. MECA 1985.

CONATY, Peter (Tex) 404 Buena Vista Ln, West Columbia TX 77486 B New York NY 1948 s Peter & Anna. AA S Peters Coll Baltimore MD 1968; BA S Pauls Coll Washington DC 1971; Washington Theol Un 1974; Cert Theol Stud Epis TS of the SW 1987. Rec 5/1/1987 as Priest Bp Gordon Taliaferro Charlton. m 11/24/1994 Susan Melinda Conaty c 1. R S Mary's Ch W Columbia TX 1999-2017; Chapl Ben Taub Gnrl Hosp Houston TX 1990-2005; S Jn's Epis Ch Sealy TX 1990-1999; The Great Cmsn Fndt Houston TX 1990-1999; Asst S Mk's Ch Houston TX 1987-1990; Serv RC Ch 1974-1986. "Yo-Yo Inspires VBS," *Faith @ Wk*, Faith At Wk, Inc, 2004. stmaryswc@centurylink.net

CONAWAY, Arthur Clarence (Lex) 1403 Providence Rd, Richmond KY 40475 **Supply S Alb's Ch Morehead KY 2008-; PINC Supply S Jas' Prestonburg KY 2006-; Chapl Hospice of KY KY 1995-** B Kent OH 1927 s Charles & Clara. AA U of Baltimore 1960; BA U of Baltimore 1965; MDiv Epis TS in Kentucky 1969; U of Kentucky 1971. D 12/15/1968 P 5/15/1969 Bp William R Moody. m 4/6/1946 Martha Agnes Smith c 2. S Thos Ch Beattyville KY 2008-2010; PINC Supply Ascen Mt Sterling KY 2005-2006; Adv Ch Cynthiana KY 2004-2005; PINC Supply Our Savoir Richmond KY 2003-2004; PINC Supply S Phil's Harrodsburg KY 2002-2003; PINC Supply S Alb's Morehead KY 1999-2002; Supply S Mk's Ch Hazard KY 1995-1996; Asst Chr Ch Columbia MD 1980-1995; Asst S Pat Ch Somerset KY 1976-1979; D S Jas Epis Ch Prestonsburg KY 1968-1969; Chapl Scottish Highland Games Glasgow KY 1964-2005. Life Mem Bro of S Andr 1994.

CONDON, Joshua T (Tex) Holy Spirit Episcopal Church, 12535 Perthshire Rd, Houston TX 77024 **Vic H Sprt Epis Ch Houston TX 2013-** B Louisville, KY 1978 BA U GA 2000; MDiv VTS 2003; STM GTS 2009. D 6/7/2003 P 1/4/2004 Bp J Neil Alexander. m 10/14/2006 Sarah Taylor Sarah Ferguson Taylor c 2. R Dio New York New York NY 2009-2013; S Steph's Ch Armonk NY 2009-2013; P-in-c S Lk's Ch Eastchester NY 2008-2009; Asst Chr And S Steph's Ch New York NY 2006-2008; Asst Gr Epis Ch Gainesville GA 2003-2006.

CONDON, Sarah Taylor (Tex) **S Mart's Epis Ch Houston TX 2014-** B Nashville TN 1982 d Owen & Debra. MDiv Yale DS 2013; MDiv Yale DS 2013. D 3/2/2013 Bp Andrew Marion Lenow Dietsche. m 10/14/2006 Joshua T Condon c 1. Dio Texas Houston TX 2013-2014; Dio New York New York NY 2007-2009.

CONES, Bryan Matthew (Chi) 1140 Wilmette Ave, Wilmette IL 60091 **Bd Mem The Ch Hm At Montgomery Place Chicago IL 2015-** B Knoxville TN 1973 s Marvin & Margaret. BA Concep Sem Coll Concep 1996; MA Cath Theol Un 2001; Advncd Cert in Theol Stds EDS 2013. D 6/28/2014 Bp John Clark Buchanan P 1/22/2015 Bp Jeff Lee. m 8/6/2014 David Alan Lysik. Asst S Aug's Epis Ch Wilmette IL 2014-2016; Res Chapl NW Memi Hosp 2014. Auth, "Daily Mass Intercessions 2015," Wrld Libr Pub, 2014; Coauthor, "A PB for the Twenty-First Century?," *ATR 96:4 (Fall 2014)*, 2014. bryan.cones@staschurch.org

CONGDON, William Hopper (Ct) B 1934 D 6/13/1961 Bp Walter H Gray P 3/24/1962 Bp Joseph Warren Hutchens. S Paul's Ch Schenectady NY 1967-1968; S Lk's Ch Chatham NY 1965-1967; S Mk's Ch Philadelphia PA 1962-1965; S Paul's Ch Wallingford CT 1961-1962.

CONGER, George AM (CFla) 3086 N Barton Creek Cir, Lecanto FL 34461 **Shpd Of The Hills Epis Ch Lecanto FL 2014-; Correspondent Ch Of Engl Nwspr London Engl 1998-; Dn, NW Dnry Dio Cntrl Florida Orlando FL 2016-, Dioc Bd Mem 2008-2011; Dir Angl.TV Milford CT 2011-; Hon Cn S Matt's Cathd Dallas TX 1998-** B Camp Lejeune NC 1962 s Oliver & Cynthia. BA Duke 1984; MBA Duke 1985; MDiv Yale DS 1995; Oxf GB 1997. D 9/20/1997 P 5/21/1998 Bp Robert William Duncan. m 6/8/1985 Susan B Baxter c 2. P-in-c The Epis Ch Of The Redeem Avon Pk FL 2011-2014; Chapl Treasure Coast Hospice Ft Pierce FL 2006-2011; Correspondent LivCh 2003-2009; R S Eliz's Epis Ch Sebastian FL 2000-2002; Chapl Serv Ch of Engl 1997-2000; Chapl Thos Jefferson U Hosp Philadelphia PA 1996-1997. Bd Cert Chapl Assn of Profsnl Chapl 2008; Resrch Fell Yale DS 1999. george.conger@aya.yale.edu

CONGER, George Mallett (NY) 9 Angel Rd, New Paltz NY 12561 B New York NY 1934 s Frederic & Elizabeth. BA Harv 1956; MDiv GTS 1959; MEd Boston Coll 1974. D 6/13/1959 P 12/1/1960 Bp Horace W B Donegan. m 9/23/1973 Jane Conger c 1. Ch Of The Gd Shpd New York NY 1983-1986; Assoc Ch Of The Gd Shpd Wakefield Bronx NY 1982-1986; Tri-Cnty Epis Area Mnstry Monticello NY 1982; S Jn's Memi Ch Ellenville NY 1977-1981; Hoosac Sch Hoosick NY 1975-1977; Asst R S Geo's Epis Ch Newburgh NY 1969-1973; Asst The Ch Of The Adv Boston MA 1962-1964; Asst S Ptr's Ch New York NY 1960-1962. Auth, "Chelsea Revs".

CONGER, John Peyton (Cal) B 1935 D 10/28/1961 Bp Anson Phelps Stokes Jr P 11/6/1965 Bp Alfred L Banyard. m 12/27/1961 Judith Donovan.

CONIGLIO, Robert Freeman (SVa) 21313 Metompkin View Lane, Parksley VA 23421 **P-in-c Emm Ch Cape Chas VA 2013-** B Nashville TN 1950 s John & Carmen. VTS; BA Emory and Henry Coll 1972; Cert Med U of So Carolina 1980; Cert Dio Sthrn Virginia Sch for Mnstry Formation 2010; Cert Other 2010. D 6/12/2010 P 12/18/2010 Bp Herman Hollerith IV. m 8/14/1976 Joanne Coniglio c 3. Chapl Hermitage of the Estrn Shore 2011-2013. robertconiglio@mac.com

CONKLIN, Andrea Caruso (Tex) 1819 Heights Blvd, Houston TX 77008 B Englewood NJ 1950 d Andrew & Elizabeth. BA Roa 1972; Iona Sch for Mnstry 2010. D 6/19/2010 Bp C Andrew Doyle. m 10/25/1986 George Conklin c 1. D St Andrews Epis Ch Houston TX 2010-2012.

CONKLIN, Caroline Elizabeth (Mont) 13231 15th Ave N.E., Seattle WA 98125 B Tucson AZ 1935 d Warren & Blanche. BA Rad 1957; MA U of Montana 1971. D 6/24/1991 Bp Charles I Jones III. m 8/23/1958 William Conklin c 4. D Ch Of The Incarn Great Falls MT 1991-2006. Auth, *MEDITATIONS FOR Alt-Gld MEMBERS*, Morehouse Pub, 2000.

CONKLIN, Daniel (Oly) Neue Jakob Str 1, Berlin 10179 Germany **Pfarrer im Ruhestand Kirchenkreis Berlin Stadt Mitte 2011-** B Phoenixville PA 1943 s Henry & Evelyn. BA Penn 1965; MDiv PDS 1968; Tubingen U Tubingen DE 1973. D 6/8/1968 P 12/21/1968 Bp Robert Lionne DeWitt. m 10/17/2007 Genuady A Kurbat. Int P Imm Luth Ch Berlin 2012-2013; Shpd for Pstr Care S Mk's Cathd Seattle WA 2009-2010; Assoc R Epiph Par of Seattle Seattle WA 1997-2008; Pstr German Untd Ch Chr Seattle WA 1994-1997; Pstr German Untd Ch Of Chr Seattle WA 1994-1997; P in Charge German Old Cath Ch Hannover Germany 1984-1993; Scholarships Secy German Luth Cmnty Serv Stuttgart Germany 1977-1983; Tchr Eugen Bolz Gymnasium Rottenburg a.N. Germany 1972-1977; Cur S Paul's Ch Philadelphia PA 1968-1970; Docent for OT - TS Dio Olympia Seattle 1996-2009. Auth, "Jesus and ET," *Bangalore Theol Journ*, Bangalore TS, 2007; Auth, "The Virtues," *Forw Series*, Forw Mvmt, 2002; Transltr, "Icons - The Facination & the Reality," *Bk*, Riverside, 1998; Contrib, "Var Sermons in German," *Homiletische Monatshefte*, Vanderhoek und Ruprecht, 1978.

CONKLIN, Edward Wilbur (NC) 980 N May St Apt 7, Southern Pines NC 28387 **Died 10/30/2015** B Jamaica NY 1922 s Leonard & Bessie. BS USNA 1944; BD VTS 1949; Coll of Preachers 1965; VTS 1982. D 6/19/1949 P 1/1/1950 Bp Benjamin M Washburn. m 9/12/1953 Lila Conklin c 2. Ret 1994-2015; Chapl Penick Vill Sthrn Pines NC 1985-1994; The Bp Edwin A Penick Vill Sthrn Pines NC 1985-1994; R Trin Ch Athens PA 1980-1985; Dio Bethlehem Bethlehem PA 1970-1980; Chapl Talbot Hall Jonestown PA 1970-1980; R Resurr Ch Louisville KY 1953-1967; Asst Trin And S Phil's Cathd Newark NJ 1949-1953; USN 1939-1946. Auth, "Thirsting on That Hewn Tree," *Fleet St Poet*, 1984; Auth, "The Hewn Tree," *Seabury in Memoriam*, 1983. First Hlth MRH Outstanding Vol 2004; Outstanding Moore Cnty Vol Serv Awd 2002.

CONKLING JR, Allan Alden (WTex) PO Box 314, Bandera TX 78003 **S Chris's Ch Bandera TX 2011-; R Emm Epis Ch San Angelo TX 2004-** B Temple TX 1952 s Allan & Alice. BA Texas St U San Marcos 1974; MA S Marys U San Antonio TX 1978; MDiv Sewanee: The U So, TS 1985. D 6/18/1985 Bp Stanley Fillmore Hauser P 1/1/1986 Bp Scott Field Bailey. m 1/8/2000 Kelly S Schneider c 4. Emm Epis Ch San Angelo TX 2005-2011; Assoc R S Thos Epis Ch And Sch San Antonio TX 1998-2004; Ch Of The Epiph Kingsville TX 1996-1998; S Fran By The Lake Canyon Lake TX 1993-1996; R Chr Ch Epis Larèdo TX 1988-1993; Asst R Ch Of The Gd Shpd Corpus Christi TX 1985-1988.

CONKLING, Kelly S (WTex) 10642 Newcroft Pl, Helotes TX 78023 **Asst Ch Of The H Sprt San Antonio TX 2015-, 2011-2014; Int S Chris's by the Sea Portland TX 2004-** B Beeville TX 1955 s Joseph & Virgina. BFA Sam Houston St U 1977; Cert Texas St U San Marcos 1984; MS Texas A&M U 1991; MDiv Epis TS of the SW 1997. D 6/26/1997 Bp Robert Boyd Hibbs P 12/1/1997 Bp C Wallis Ohl. m 1/8/2000 Allan Alden Conkling c 2. P Dio NW Texas Lubbock TX 2010-2012; Calv Luth Ch San Angelo TX 2009; The Epis Ch Of S Mary The Vrgn Big Sprg TX 2007-2008; Asst. R Emm Epis Ch San Angelo TX 2005-2006; S Chris's By The Sea Portland TX 2004; Asst S Andr's Epis Ch San

Antonio TX 2000-2003; Ch of the Heav Rest Abilene Abilene TX 1997-1999; S Mk's Epis Ch Abilene TX 1997. Auth, "Pryr of the Heart," Moorehouse Pub, 2006.

CONLEY, Alan Bryan (WTex) P.O. Box 350, 231 Cave Springs Dr. W., Hunt TX 78024 **Fndr PFLAG-Kerr Cnty TX 2009-; Ret 2001-** B Pampa TX 1934 s Elmer & Fern. BA Texas Tech U 1956; MDiv VTS 1959. D 6/22/1959 P 4/1/1960 Bp George Henry Quarterman. m 8/26/1956 Corinne Conley c 3. S Peters Epis Sch Kerrville TX 1988-2001; R S Ptr's Epis Ch Kerrville TX 1988-2001; Asst R/Headmaster Ch Of The Gd Shpd Corpus Christi TX 1975-1988; Cur S Andr's Epis Ch Amarillo TX 1964-1975; Vic All SS Ch Colorado City TX 1959-1964.

CONLEY, Joan Frances (Nwk) 169 Fairmount Rd, Ridgewood NJ 07450 **Cler Assoc S Eliz's Ch Ridgewood NJ 2010-** B Brockton MA 1964 d John & Marian. BA U of Notre Dame 1986; MDiv Drew U 2010. D 6/5/2010 P 12/11/2010 Bp Mark M Beckwith. c 2.

CONLEY, Kristina Mellor (Me) 17 Littlefield Dr, Kennebunk ME 04043 **Early Intervention Spec Chld Dvlpmt Serv Arundel ME 1992-** B Buffalo NY 1947 BSW U of Sthrn Maine 1992. D 6/24/2006 Bp Chilton Richardson Knudsen. m 1/28/1969 Greg Conley c 2.

CONLEY, Patricia Ann (Chi) 1993 Yasgur Dr, Woodstock IL 60098 B Modesto CA 1951 d Charles & Ruth. BA Regis U 1997; MDiv SWTS 2000. D 6/15/2002 P 12/21/2002 Bp Bill Persell. m 7/16/2012 Roma Karon Simons. R S Ann's Ch Woodstock IL 2005-2016; Dir of Par Hlth Mnstrs S Matt's Ch Evanston IL 2002-2005. Suma cl Regis U.

CONLEY, Thomas Herbert (At) 2215 Cheshire Bridge Road NE, Atlanta GA 30324 **Died 8/25/2016** B Jacksonville FL 1937 s Thomas & Mary. BA Furman U; MDiv Sthrn Bapt TS 1962; ThM Sthrn Bapt TS 1964. D 6/10/1995 Bp Frank Kellogg Allan P 12/16/1995 Bp Onell Asiselo Soto. m 8/16/1959 Helen Elizabeth Conley. Fndr, Dir, Psych The Thos H. Conley Cntr: Care Counslg Psych 2001-2016; Cathd Of S Phil Atlanta GA 1999-2002; Ch Of The Annunc Marietta GA 1996-1999; S Bede's Ch Atlanta GA 1995-1996. Auth, "The Common Cup," Trafford Press, 2005; Auth, "Wrshp & The Diakonic Task," Hm Mssn Bd, 1982; Auth, "Pstr Care For Personal Growth," Judson Press, 1977; Auth, "Two In Pulpit-Sermons In Dialogue," Word, 1973.

CONLIFFE, Mario Romain Marvin (Md) 2434 Capehorn Rd, Hampstead MD 21074 **Other Lay Position S Geo Ch Hampstead MD 2013-** B Bahamas 1977 s Randy & Eleanor. BA U of the W Indies 2001; STM Nash 2006; MS Loyola U 2015. Trans 10/6/2015 as Priest Bp Eugene Taylor Sutton. m 2/4/2006 Barbara Za Franks. info@saintgs.com

CONN JR, Doyt Ladean (Oly) 1805 38th Ave, Seattle WA 98122 **R Epiph Par of Seattle Seattle WA 2008-** B Rochester MN 1967 s Doyt & Gracia. BS NWU 1989; MBA Case Wstrn Reserve U 1997; MDiv VTS 2003. D 6/14/2003 P 12/30/2003 Bp J Clark Grew II. m 7/23/1994 Kristin Leigh Conn c 2. Assoc R For Pstr Care All SS Par Beverly Hills CA 2003-2008.

CONN, John Hardeman (Mass) 4 Alton Court, Brookline MA 02446 B Norfolk VA 1935 s John & Virginia. BA Lander U 1966; MDiv EDS 1969. D 6/21/1969 Bp Anson Phelps Stokes Jr P 5/1/1971 Bp John Melville Burgess. c 2. Int Emm Ch Braintree MA 1996-1998; Int Trin Ch Bridgewater MA 1995; Int S Eliz's Ch Sudbury MA 1984-1986; Int Dio Massachusetts Boston MA 1976-1999; 1973-1976; R S Paul's Epis Ch Hopkinton MA 1971-1973; Cur Trin Par Melrose MA 1969-1971. jconnh@yahoo.com

CONN, Rodney Carl (Be) 108 N. 5th St., Allentown PA 18102 **Gr Epis Ch Allentown PA 2008-; Chapl Dio Bethlehem Bethlehem PA 2008-** B Willoughby OH 1962 s Carl & Patricia. BS U of Akron 1986. D 2/2/2008 Bp Paul Victor Marshall. m 7/18/1999 Sarabel Ryan Conn.

CONNELL, George Patterson (Ky) 11 Saint Lukes Ln, San Antonio TX 78209 B Belle Glade FL 1952 s Hueston & Betty. BA Shorter Coll 1974; MDiv Epis TS of the SW 1981. D 6/24/1981 Bp Wesley Frensdorff P 1/1/1982 Bp Scott Field Bailey. m 8/5/1977 Diana H Connell c 2. R Trin Epis Ch Owensboro KY 1998-2017; S Lk's Epis Ch San Antonio TX 1995-1998; S Andr's Epis Ch Seguin TX 1989-1995; R Gr Ch Cuero TX 1984-1989; Asst Trin Ch Victoria TX 1981-1984.

CONNELL, John Baade (Haw) 95-1050 Makaikai St. Apt. 17M, Mililani HI 96789 B Waukegan IL 1930 s John & Phillis. BA U of Hawaii 1959; MDiv CDSP 1985. D 7/18/1985 Bp Edmond Lee Browning P 5/1/1986 Bp Frederick Warren Putnam. m 12/17/1960 Carol Connell c 3. S Lk's Epis Ch Honolulu HI 2006-2007; S Geo's Epis Ch Honolulu HI 2004-2005; S Ptr's Ch Honolulu HI 2003-2004; Int Epis Ch on W Kauai Eleele HI 2001-2003; Int Vic Kohala Epis Mssn Kapaau HI 1998-2001; S Alb's Chap Honolulu HI 1987-1988; Vic S Nich Epis Ch Aiea HI 1985-1998. Hawaii Epis Cler Assn. 1985; Int Mnstry Ntwk, 1995.

CONNELL, Susan Lee Clare (Okla) 57200 E Hwy 125, Unit 3431, Monkey Island OK 74331 B Traverse City MI 1949 d Chester & Garie. BA Bethany Coll 1971; Gordon-Conwell TS 1973; MDiv EDS 1976; LPN Middlesex Vocational HS 1977. D 6/18/1977 Bp Alexander D Stewart P 12/8/1990 Bp Walter Decoster Dennis Jr. c 2. R All SS Epis Ch Miami OK 2006-2012; R Ch Of The Gd Samar Gunnison CO 2003-2006; Int Epis Ch Of S Mk The Evang Bellmore

NY 2000-2003; Vic Trin Epis Ch Vincentown NJ 1998-1999; Chapl Cmnty Med Cntr Hospice Toms River NJ 1990-1999; Assoc S Raphael The Archangel Brick NJ 1990-1998; D S Mk's Ch Hammonton NJ 1979-1983; Chapl The Epis Campus Mnstry at Rutgers New Brunswick NJ 1977-1978. Sis of S Greg 1989-2007. First Superior, Sis of S Greg Sis of S Greg 1999.

CONNELLY III, Albert Pinckney (CFla) 16 Hawks Lndg, Weaverville NC 28787 **1994-** B Orlando FL 1940 s Albert & Frances. BSA U of Florida 1962; STB Ya Berk 1965; MTh Duke DS 1977; MBA Florida Inst of Tech 1984. D 6/29/1965 Bp James Loughlin Duncan P 12/29/1965 Bp Henry I Louttit. m 8/17/1963 Lillian Judith Brown c 2. Chapl (Ret) USN 1968-1994; Off Of Bsh For ArmdF New York NY 1968-1979; Cur S Thos' Epis Ch St Petersburg FL 1966-1968; Vic Ch of Our Sav Palm Bay FL 1965-1966.

CONNELLY, Charles Evans (SwFla) 2401 Bayshore Blvd., Unit 505, Tampa FL 33629 **Assoc R & Chapl to the Sch St Johns Epis Ch Tampa FL 2007-; Stndg Com Dio SW Florida Parrish FL 2014-, COM 2011-2014, Eccl Trial Crt 2008-2011; Conflict of Interest Com U of So Florida Tampa FL 2014-; Trst and Treas The GTS New York NY 2013-, Asst Treas 2011-2013** B Toledo OH 1948 s Jack & Elizabeth. BS U NC 1970; MBA Col 1972; MDiv GTS 2007. D 6/2/2007 P 12/9/2007 Bp Dabney Tyler Smith. Chapl Cbury Tower Ret Cmnty 2012-2013; Chapl S Jn's Epis Par Day Sch Tampa FL 2007-2014; Instnl Revs Bd U of So Florida Tampa FL 2009-2014. cconnelly@stjohnstampa.org

CONNELLY, Constance R (NC) 1950 S Wendover Rd, Charlotte NC 28211 B Morganton NC 1944 d Benjamin & Isbel. BA Converse Coll 1967; MDiv GTS 2001. D P 7/10/2002 Bp Michael B Curry. c 2. S Simon's On The Sound Ft Walton Bch FL 2011-2012; Chr Epis Ch Raleigh NC 2009-2010; Chr Ch Greenwich CT 2005-2009; S Mart's Epis Ch Charlotte NC 2003-2004; Dio No Carolina Raleigh NC 2001-2003.

CONNELLY, John Vaillancourt (Chi) 2327 Birchwood Ave, Wilmette IL 60091 **Assoc S Lk's Ch Evanston IL 1996-; Cn for the Bp's Endwmt Fund Dio Chicago Chicago IL 2011-** B Syracuse NY 1958 s William & Shirley. BA Wheaton Coll 1981; MA U of Rhode Island 1983; MDiv Yale DS 1986. D 6/21/1986 P 12/1/1986 Bp George Nelson Hunt III. m 8/27/1983 Mary Connelly c 3. R S Ann's Epis Ch Old Lyme CT 1992-1994; Assoc R S Andr's Ch Downers Grove IL 1989-1992; Asst R S Mart's Ch Providence RI 1986-1989.

CONNELLY JR, Walter (Mass) 231 Bowdoin St, Winthrop MA 02151 **P-in-c S Jn's Ch Winthrop MA 2008-, R 2008-** B Boston MA 1965 AB Geo 1990; MDiv Weston Jesuit TS 1996. D 6/7/2003 P 6/5/2004 Bp M(Arvil) Thomas Shaw. m 8/20/2005 Daniel Frederick Dalo. extended supply S Matt And The Redeem Epis Ch Boston MA 2005-2008; Asst Bristol Cluster No Easton MA 2004.

CONNER, Georgene Davis (SwFla) 2926 57th Street S, Gulfport FL 33707 B Tampa FL 1944 d Thomas & Marian. U of Detroit Mercy; U of Mississippi; U of Mississippi 1963; U of Detroit 1987; MDiv EDS 1991. D 6/21/1991 Bp Henry Irving Mayson P 2/1/1992 Bp R aymond Stewart Wood Jr. c 2. Cler Cathd Ch Of S Ptr St. Petersburg FL 1999-2009; S Mich's Ch New York NY 1995-1999; Asst R S Paul's Washington DC 1991-1996; S Paul's Rock Creek Washington DC 1991-1995. Bp Pk Matsumoto Prize; Frederick Mcghee Adams Prize In Homil. revgigiconner@gmail.com

CONNER, Lu-Anne (Mo) Church Of The Transfiguration, 1860 Lake Saint Louis Blvd, Lake St Louis MO 63367 **Ch Of The Trsfg Lake S Louis MO 2016-** B Boston MA 1962 d Malcolm & Luella. BA Connecticut Coll 1984; MDiv UTS 2001. D 6/23/2001 P 2/2/2002 Bp Chilton Richardson Knudsen. m 5/10/2013 Kathryn A McCormick. Chr Ch Gardiner ME 2016; R S Andr's Ch Newcastle ME 2010-2016; Assoc S Eliz's Ch Ridgewood NJ 2001-2010. lu-anne.conner@transfigurationchurch.org

CONNER, Martha (Az) 11102 W. Kolina Lane, Sun City AZ 85351 B Spokane WA 1957 d Edgar & Eula. BS Troy U 1978; MS U of Sthrn Mississippi 1985; MDiv VTS 2000; DMin VTS 2006. D 6/3/2000 P 2/24/2001 Bp Charles Farmer Duvall. m 6/11/1977 Michael Conner c 2. S Chris's Ch Sun City AZ 2008-2012; Chapl Still Hopes Epis Ret Cmnty Columbia SC 2007-2008; Still Hopes Epis Ret Cmnty W Columbia SC 2007-2008; Ch Of The Epiph Danville VA 2006-2007; Asst. R S Thad Epis Ch Aiken SC 2004-2006; R S Mk's Epis Ch Troy AL 2002-2004; Asst R S Jude's Epis Ch Niceville FL 2000-2002.

CONNER, Sarah A (Mass) 4 Ernest Rd # 3, Arlington MA 02474 B Boston MA 1962 d Malcolm & Luella. BA Connecticut Coll 1984; MDiv Harvard DS 1988. D 6/5/1996 P 5/17/1997 Bp M(Arvil) Thomas Shaw. Trin Ch Concord MA 2016-2017; Ch Of The Gd Shpd Waban MA 2015-2016; Chr Ch Swansea MA 2014-2015; Int All SS Par Brookline MA 2012-2014, 1998-2000; Int S Mich's Ch Milton MA 2010-2012; Int S Ptr's Ch On The Canal Buzzards Bay MA 2007-2010; Int S Dunstans Epis Ch Dover MA 2005-2007; P-in-c Chr Ch Quincy MA 2002-2005.

CONNERS, John H (EC) 14703 Dorset Dr, Noblesville IN 46062 B Menominee MI 1950 s Harold & Luella 'Sis'. BMus U MI 1972; MDiv GTS 1990. D 12/30/1989 P 7/18/1990 Bp William Louis Stevens. m 7/23/2014 Hugh King McGlaughon c 1. Gr Epis Ch Hartford CT 2015-2016; Vic S Mich's Ch Trenton NJ 2000-2004; Weekend Pstr Asst The Ch of St.Mary the Vrgn 1996; Int Trin

Ch Lawrenceburg IN 1994; Int S Thos' Ch Windsor NC 1991-1993; Assoc Ch Of S Mary The Vrgn New York NY 1990-1991, 1989-1990.

CONNOLLY, Emma French (WTenn) 480 S. Greer St., Memphis TN 38111 **Exec Dir WriteMemphis Inc. 2010-** B Hattiesburg MS 1949 Millsaps Coll; U of Sthrn Mississippi. D 1/15/2005 Bp Duncan Montgomery Gray III. m 12/11/1999 Robert P Connolly c 4. D S Jn's Epis Ch Memphis TN 2007-2014; S Andr's Cathd Jackson MS 2005-2007.

CONNOR, Alice Elizabeth (SO) 5751 Marmion Ln, Cincinnati OH 45212 **Gd Shpd Luthern Ch Cincinnati OH 2009-; Cur, YA Mnstrs Ch of the Redeem Hyde Pk Cincinnatti 2004-** B Portland OR 1977 d Thomas & Nancye. BA Transylvania U 1999; MDiv Bex Sem 2005. D 5/22/2004 P 6/25/2005 Bp Herbert Thompson Jr. m 9/11/1999 Leighton Lewis Connor c 1. The Ch of the Redeem Cincinnati OH 2004-2009. Auth, "Fierce: Wmn of the Bible and their Stories of Violence, Mercy, Bravery, Wisdom, Sex, and Salvation," Fortress Press, 2017.

CONNORS, Barbara Mae (Ct) 35350 E Division Rd, Saint Helens OR 97051 **Died 6/3/2017** B Portland OR 1936 d John & Ethel. RN Emm Hosp Sch Nrsng 1959; BA New Engl Coll 1985; MA Andover Newton TS 1988. D 12/29/1996 Bp Robert Louis Ladehoff.

CONRAD JR, James Wallace (Az) 2540 Ontario Dr, Las Vegas NV 89128 B Phoenix AZ 1948 s James & Anna. BA Humboldt St U 1970; MDiv CDSP 1973; DMin Jesuit TS 1979. D 7/14/1973 P 2/1/1974 Bp Victor Manuel Rivera. m 9/12/1981 Donna K Mosby c 4. Ch Of The Apos Oro Vlly AZ 1993-2005; Dio Arizona Phoenix AZ 1991-1992; R S Alb's Epis Ch Tucson AZ 1987-1991; Ch Of Coventry Cross Minden NV 1981-1987; S Alb's Ch Los Banos CA 1973-1979; Epis Dio San Joaquin Modesto CA 1973-1977.

CONRAD, John William (Los) All Saints Episcopal Church, 3847 Terracina Dr, Riverside CA 92506 **R All SS Epis Ch Riverside CA 2006-** B Victorville CA 1952 s Lloyd & Eva. BA Thos Edison St Coll 1993; MDiv CDSP 1996; DMin CDSP 2005. D 6/8/1996 Bp Robert Marshall Anderson P 1/18/1997 Bp Frederick Houk Borsch. m 8/23/2009 Shannon M Murphy c 2. Int Ch Of The Gd Samar San Diego CA 2005-2006; R S Alb's Epis Ch El Cajon CA 1999-2005; S Mk's Par Glendale CA 1996-1999. Auth, "To The Least of These: A better Chr Response to Homelessness," Trade Bk, Create Space/Amazon, 2017; Auth, "Getting Unstuck: An Intervention Strtgy for Dysfunctional Congregations," Trade Bk, Berkeley U Press, 2005; Auth, "Hundreds," Aviation/Travel mag, Numerous; Auth, "Var arts," Sermons That Wk. Sis of the Perpetual Indulgence 1996.

CONRAD JR, Larry Brown (NC) D 2/20/2016 Bp Anne Hodges-Copple.

CONRAD, Matthew McMillan (ECR) 5318 Palma Ave., Atascadero CA 93422 **R S Lk's Ch Atascadero CA 1984-; Stndg Com Dio El Camino Real Salinas CA 2010-, COM 1998-2009** B Exeter CA 1954 s James & Anna. BA Humboldt St U 1976; MDiv CDSP 1980. D 8/2/1980 P 7/18/1981 Bp Victor Manuel Rivera. m 9/3/1977 Diana Conrad c 3. Cur S Mk's Epis Ch Santa Clara CA 1982-1983; Cur Epis Ch Of S Anne Stockton CA 1980-1982.

CONRAD, Pamela Gales (Md) 105 1st Ave SW, Glen Burnie MD 21061 B Washington DC 1952 d Edward & Priscilla. BA The GW 1974; MMus The GW 1987; MPhil The GW 1995; PhD The GW 1998; MDiv EDS 2017. D 1/15/2017 Bp Chilton Richardson Knudsen. m 12/12/2012 Nina Catherine Barratt.

CONRADO VARELA, Victor Hugo (Chi) **P S Mk's Epis Ch Glen Ellyn IL 2011-** B Colombia 1975 s Victor & Carmen. BA Jesuit TS. Rec 7/6/2011 Bp Jeff Lee. m 10/11/2008 Lucia E Conrado c 2.

CONRADS, Alexandra (Los) D 6/23/2001 P 12/29/2001 Bp Peter J Lee.

CONRADS, Nancy Alice (Chi) 4801 Spring Creek Rd, Rockford IL 61114 B Rockford IL 1941 d Paul & Beatrice. BA Lawr 1963; MSW U IL 1969. D 2/7/2009 Bp Jeff Lee.

CONRADT, James Robert (FdL) W1693 Echo Valley Rd, Kaukauna WI 54130 B Lessor WI 1937 s Elmer & Irene. W&M; U of Wisconsin. D 9/6/1996 P 10/4/2001 Bp Russell Edward Jacobus. m 12/24/1983 Nancy F Conradt c 2. Vic S Paul's Epis Ch Suamico WI 2009-2017, Vic 2002-2009, D 2000-2001; D S Anne's Epis Ch De Pere WI 1996-2000.

CONROE, Jon Wallace (RG) **Chapl U.S. Navy Chapl 1999-** B 1960 s Wallace & Marie-Anne. MDiv Concordia Sem St Louis 1993; MS U of San Diego 2005; MA U of San Diego 2011. D 11/19/2015 P 7/27/2016 Bp James Beattie Magness. m 6/12/1982 Ronda Olguin Riggs c 2.

CONROY, Mary E (SeFla) 1121 Andalusia Ave, Coral Gables FL 33134 **R S Phil's Ch Coral Gables FL 2009-; S Phil's Epis Sch Coral Gables FL 2009-; Stndg Com Dio SE Florida Miami 2014-; Bd Trst The ATR 2005-** B Pittsfield MA 1963 d Edward & Anne. BS Marymount Coll 1985; MS Ford 1988; MDiv SWTS 1996; DMin SWTS 2009. D 6/8/1996 Bp Robert Reed Shahan P 6/7/1997 Bp Claude Edward Payne. Int Ch Of The Ascen Pueblo CO 2008-2009; Assoc R Trin Ch Epis Boston MA 1999-2008; Asst Palmer Memi Ch Houston TX 1997-1999; Chapl Chr Ch Greenville SC 1996-1997; D Chr Ch Epis Sch Greenville SC 1996; Bd Trst Bexley Seabury Fed Chicago IL 2013-2015. mconroy@saintphilips.net

CONSIDINE, H James (NwPa) 11733 SW 17th CT, Miramar FL 33025 B Baraboo WI 1944 s Harvey & Ruth. Sterling Coll 1964; BMus U of Wisconsin

1967; MM MI SU 1968; MDiv Nash 1975. D 4/26/1975 Bp Charles Thomas Gaskell P 11/1/1975 Bp Frederick Hesley Belden. m 12/28/1971 Linda M Considine. R S Jn's Epis Ch Sharon PA 1986-1992; R Trin Epis Ch Logansport IN 1977-1986; Cur S Barn Ch Warwick RI 1975-1977.

CONSTANT, Donna Rittenhouse (Pa) 167 Hermit Hollow Lane, Middleburg PA 17842 **Ret 1998-** B Geneva IL 1937 d John & Angela. Beloit Coll; U CO; U of New Mex; BA CUA 1987; MDiv VTS 1991. D 6/15/1991 Bp Peter J Lee P 2/12/1992 Bp Robert Poland Atkinson. m 8/29/1959 Richard E Constant c 2. Supply P Dio Cntrl Pennsylvania Harrisburg PA 1998-2000; R Calv Ch Germantown Philadelphia PA 1995-1998; Asst Ch Of The H Cross Dunn Loring VA 1991-1994.

CONSTANT, Joseph (WA) 701 Oglethorpe St NW, Washington DC 20011 **S Jn's Epis Ch Zion Par Beltsville MD 2015-; Dir of Racial and Ethnic Mnstrs VTS Alexandria VA 2005-** B Haiti 1967 s Murat & Marie Therese. BS NEU 1991; MDiv VTS 2003. D 6/7/2003 P 2/9/2004 Bp M(Arvil) Thomas Shaw. m 6/28/1997 Sarah Christine Constant c 1. Ch Of The H Comf Washington DC 2014-2015; Spec Coordntr for Haiti Epis Ch Cntr New York NY 2010-2014; Asst S Tim's Epis Ch Washington DC 2003-2004. Auth, "Bk," *No Turning Back: The Black Presence at VTS*, Evergreen Press, 2009. UBE 2004. Bp's Awd Dio Virginia 2010.

CONTESTABLE, Christine Marie (U) 673 Wall St, Salt Lake City UT 84103 **P S Paul's Ch Salt Lake City UT 2011-; Adj Instr of Cmncatn Westminster Coll Salt Lake City UT 2009-; Adj Instr Utah Vlly U Orem UT 2003-** B San Pablo CA 1964 d Robert & Rita. BA U of Tulsa 1989; MDiv CDSP 1995; PhD U of Utah 2010. D 6/10/1995 Bp Robert Reed Shahan P 6/7/1997 Bp William Edwin Swing. m 12/23/2013 Stacy D Waddoups. Adj Instr and Tchg Fell U of Utah Salt Lake City UT 2005-2010; Coordntr, Mnstry w YP Dio Utah Salt Lake City UT 1999-2002, Int U Chapl, Epiph Hse 1998-1999; CDSP Berkeley CA 1995-1998; P S Paul's Ch Oakland CA 1995-1998; Hosp Chapl, San Francisco Gnrl Hosp Sojourn Multifaith Chapl San Francisco CA 1993-1994; Chapl Intern Virginia Mason Hosp Seattle WA 1993-1994. Auth, "Becoming-Lrng: Rethinking Transformative Educ by Reconceptualizing Learner Agcy and Illuminating the Immanent Dynamism of Classrooms," Proquest, 2010; Co-Auth, "Dancing w the enemy? A man and Wmn talk turkey," *Rocky Mtn Cmncatn Revs*, 2006.

CONWAY, J Cooper (NY) 1514 Palisade Ave, Union City NJ 07087 **Trin Epis Ch Ossining NY 2011-** B New York NY 1949 d James & Mary. Carnegie Mellon U 1967; Webster Coll 1969; ADS Culinary Inst of Amer 1979; MDiv GTS 1998. D 5/30/1998 Bp John Shelby Spong P 12/12/1998 Bp Jack Marston Mckelvey. m 10/5/1974 Peter J Madison c 1. S Cuth's Epis Ch Oakland CA 2015-2016; Chr Ch Poughkeepsie NY 2014-2015; S Steph's Ch Millburn NJ 2010-2011; S Alb's Ch Oakland NJ 2008-2010; R S Jn's Ch Un City NJ 2003-2008; All SS Ch Harrison NY 2002-2003; Int All SS Ch Harrison NY 2001-2003; Dio Newark Newark NJ 1999; Gr Ch Newark NJ 1998-2002; Asst Yth Dir Dio Neward Newark NJ 1998-1999. ACTS-VIM Bd, Dio Newark 2005-2008; Dio Nwk Yth Cmsn 1998-2001.

CONWAY, Nancy (CPa) 6 Watch Tower Ct, Salem SC 29676 **Ret 2000-** B Dedham MA 1933 d Walter & Elinor. BS U of Massachusetts 1954; MA W Virginia U 1979; MA VTS 1989. D 2/21/1993 P 12/11/1993 Bp Charlie Fuller Mcnutt Jr. Pstr Asst H Trin Par Epis Clemson SC 2002-2012; R Trin Ch Jersey Shore PA 1994-2000; Asst R Trin Epis Ch Williamsport PA 1993-1997. Cleric Assn.

CONWAY, Natalie Hall (Md) **D S Jn's Ch Huntingdon Baltimore MD 2014-** B Baltimore MD 1947 d Nathaniel & Bernice. D 6/1/2013 Bp Joe Goodwin Burnett. c 1. Jubilee Off Ch Of The H Cov Baltimore MD 2013-2014; Dio Maryland Baltimore MD 2000-2011, Jubilee Off 2013-.

CONWAY, Thomas Bradley (NJ) 22 Wickapecko Dr, Interlaken NJ 07712 **Ret 2001-** B Indianapolis IN 1940 s John & Jomyla. BA Indiana U 1963; MDiv Ya Berk 1966; MS Rutgers The St U of New Jersey 1975. D 6/11/1966 Bp John P Craine P 12/18/1966 Bp Albert Wiencke Van Duzer. c 2. Int Trin Ch Asbury Pk NJ 2003-2004; Trin Cathd Trenton NJ 2001-2004; Non-par Dept. Human Serv St of New Jersey 1971-2001; Vic Ch Of The H Sprt Lebanon NJ 1968-1971; Cur/Dce Trin Epis Ch Cranford NJ 1966-1968.

CONYERS, Kacei (NCal) **S Mary's Ch Anchorage AK 2016-** B 1991 D 6/26/2016 Bp Mark A Lattime P 1/27/2017 Bp Barry Leigh Beisner.

COOK, Ashley Michele (Tex) 919 S John Redditt Dr, Lufkin TX 75904 B Rota Spain 1971 d Gary & Linda. BS Steph F Austin St U 2004; Dplma Iona Sch for Mnstry 2011. D 6/18/2011 Bp C Andrew Doyle P 6/27/2014 Bp Jeff Fisher. m 8/18/1990 Lloyd Steven Cook c 2.

COOK, Carol Lee (Cal) 2235 3rd St, Livermore CA 94550 B San Jose CA 1949 d Donn & Barbara. BA Macalester Coll 1971; MA San Francisco St U 1974; MDiv CDSP 1991. D 12/8/1990 P 12/1/1991 Bp William Edwin Swing. Adj Prof of Rel Las Positas Coll Livermore CA 2002-2010; R S Barth's Epis Ch Livermore CA 1996-2010; Int S Mk's Epis Ch Palo Alto CA 1993-1995; S Paul's Epis Ch Walnut Creek CA 1991-1993.

COOK, Charles James (Tex) Po Box 2247, Austin TX 78768 **Asstg Epis Ch of the Gd Shpd Austin TX 2000-; Bd Mem Cntr for Par Dvlpmt Chicago IL 1995-; Chapl Advsry Bd Brackenridge Hosp 1993-** B Pampa TX 1944 s Charles & Jeanee. BA Drake U 1966; Ecumencial Inst 1973; MDiv Epis TS of the SW 1974. D 6/8/1974 P 4/1/1975 Bp Willis Ryan Henton. m 6/12/1965 Christine Cook c 3. The Ch of the Gd Shpd Austin TX 1993-2008; Bd Mem S Andr's Sch 1992-2000; Dir Field Ed Epis TS Of The SW Austin TX 1985-2008; Pres The Educational Cntr 1982-1985; Dio No Carolina Raleigh NC 1979-2009, ExCoun 1979-1985, Chair St Ch Com 1978-1979; R Ch Of The Gd Shpd S Louis MO 1979-1984; Chap Of The Cross Chap Hill NC 1975-1979; Mssn Funding Com Dio Texas Houston TX 1996-2009. ATFE 1985; Assn Practical Theol 1985; Cntr for Par Dvlpmt 1995; PEALL 2005. Sub Chapl Venerable Ord S Jn 1994.

COOK, Charles Robert (Neb) 2666 El Rancho Rd, Sidney NE 69162 **D Chr Ch Sidney NE 2004-; Pres Cook & Assoc. Inc. Sidney Cheyenne NE 1982-** B Potlatch ID 1930 s Robert & Lena. BS Chadron St Coll; MEd U of Nthrn Colorado. D 9/19/2004 Bp Joe Goodwin Burnett. m 6/7/1953 Marian Elizabeth Cook c 2. Pres C.A. Assoc. Story Agcy Sidney Cheyenne NE 1966-1982.

COOK, Debbie (NJ) 202 Navesink Avenue, Atlantic Highlands NJ 07716 **All SS Memi Ch Navesink NJ 2014-** B Ft Dix NJ 1961 d John & Marilyn. BS Trenton St Coll 1983; MDiv GTS 2007. D 6/9/2007 P 12/22/2007 Bp George Edward Councell. m 7/14/1984 James R Cook c 2. Assoc R Gr Ch In Haddonfield Haddonfield NJ 2007-2010; Part time Acct DHD Mgmt Little Silver NJ 1997-2005. mother.debbie@comcast.net

COOK, Diane Elizabeth (O) 2521 W Stockwell Ln, Clinton IA 52732 **Died 12/19/2015** B Morristown NJ 1960 d Richard & Virginia. BS Iowa St U 1982; MDiv SWTS 1995. D 4/1/1995 P 10/1/1995 Bp Chris Christopher Epting. m 10/9/2005 Douglas M Thibaut. Trin Ch Coshocton OH 2009-2015; R S Paul's Ch Mt Vernon OH 2000-2005; Chr Epis Ch Clinton IA 1995-1999. Ord Of S Helena.

COOK, Edward Richard (NJ) 130 Stoneham Dr, Glassboro NJ 08028 **Died 6/13/2017** B Pennsgrove NJ 1923 s Edward & Frances. BA Cbury Coll 1950; Ya Berk 1958; Ext Educ Prog Trenton NJ 1961. D 4/29/1961 P 10/28/1961 Bp Alfred L Banyard. c 2. R S Lk's Ch Woodstown NJ 1993-2017; Ret 1989-2017; R Gr St Pauls Ch Trenton NJ 1969-1989; R Chr Ch So Amboy NJ 1964-1969; P-in-c S Steph's Ch Mullica Hill NJ 1962-1964; D-in-c/P-in-c S Ptr's Ch Clarksboro NJ 1961-1964. OHC. cookykay@aol.com

COOK, Ellen Piel (SO) 2768 Turpin Oaks Ct, Cincinnati OH 45244 B Woodbury NJ 1952 d Gerhardt & Mary. BA U of Toledo 1973; PhD U of Iowa 1977; Angl Acad 2006. D 5/13/2006 Bp Kenneth Lester Price. m 5/31/1980 David Piel Cook c 2.

COOK II, Harry Theodore (Mich) 3114 Vinsetta Blvd, Royal Oak MI 48073 B Detroit MI 1939 s Harry & Bessie. BA Albion Coll 1961; BD Garrett-Evang TS 1964. D 12/23/1967 Bp Richard Stanley Merrill Emrich P 4/27/1968 Bp Archie H Crowley. m 11/3/1979 Susan M Chevalier c 2. R S Andr's Ch Clawson Mi 1988-2009; Non-par 1979-1987; R Emm Ch Detroit MI 1969-1979; Asst R Chr Ch Detroit MI 1967-1969; Asst Chapl NWU Evanston IL 1963-1964. Auth, "Resonance," Polebridge Press, 2011; Auth, "A Humanist Manifesto," Polebridge Press, 2011; Auth, "Asking," WIpf & Stock, 2010; Auth, "Findings," Ch Pub Grp, 2003; Auth, "Seven Sayings Of Jesus," Vintage Press, 2001; Auth, "Devoted Heretic," Cntr For Rational Chrsnty, 1999; Auth, "Chrsnty Beyond Creeds," Cntr For Rational Chrsnty, 1997. Civil Libertarian of the Year Michigan ACLU 1998; Civil Libertarian of the Year Michigan ACLU 1998; Marg Sanger Awd Planned Parenthood of Michigan 1995; Loundy Prize in Hebr Garrett TS 1962.

COOK, Harvey Gerald (Lex) 20129 N Painted Sky Dr, Surprise AZ 85374 **Ret 1998-** B Chester PA 1933 s Walter & Elsie. BS Penn 1955; MEd Penn 1956; MDiv SWTS 1965; DMin McCormick TS 1975. D 6/29/1965 P 6/29/1966 Bp Thomas Augustus Fraser Jr. m 11/8/1960 Betty Lou Cook c 3. R Chr Ch Of The Ascen Paradise Vlly AZ 1989-1998; Stndg Com So Carolina Charleston SC 1978-1987, Dioc Coun 1982-1989, Dioc Coun 1975-1981; R Trin Ch Myrtle Bch SC 1970-1989; Chapl USN 1968-1970; Asst S Lk's Ch Salisbury NC 1965-1968. Auth, "Vietnam," *Living Ch*.

COOK, James Bonham (Okla) Saint Andrew's Church, 516 W 3rd Ave, Stillwater OK 74074 **R S Andr's Ch Stillwater OK 2013-; Congrl Dvlpmt Cmsn Dio Kansas Topeka KS 2004-** B Charlottesville VA 1957 s Henry & Nancy. BS Trin U San Antonio 1980; MDiv VTS 1989. D 6/4/1989 Bp John Herbert MacNaughton P 12/10/1989 Bp Earl Nicholas Mc Arthur Jr. m 4/28/1984 Peggy L Roper c 2. R S Lk's Epis Ch Shawnee KS 1994-2013; Asst R St Fran Epis Ch San Antonio TX 1989-1994; Happ Advsry Bd Dio W Texas San Antonio TX 1990-1992.

COOK, James Harrison (Minn) 317 Franklin St, Red Wing MN 55066 **Ret 1986-** B Red Wing MN 1920 s Harry & Alvida. BA U MN 1942; Untd TS of the Twin Cities 1977. D 6/30/1969 Bp Hamilton Hyde Kellogg P 6/25/1977 Bp Philip Frederick McNairy. c 3. Long Term Supply S Matt's Epis Ch Chatfield MN 1990-1998; Asst Chr Ch Red Wing MN 1969-1986.

COOK, Jim (SeFla) 3395 Burns Road, Palm Beach Gardens FL 33410 **R S Mk's Ch Palm Bch Garden FL 2007-** B Elkhorn WI 1958 s Robert & Verone. BA U of Wisconsin 1980; MA U of Wisconsin 1982; MDiv Sewanee: The U So, TS 1993. D 6/19/1993 P 1/8/1994 Bp Don Adger Wimberly. m 10/29/1983 Karen

A Cook c 2. St Dav's Epis Ch Minnetonka MN 2004-2007, R 1998-2002; R S Lk's Ch Whitewater WI 1995-1998; Assoc R Ch Of The Ascen Frankfort KY 1993-1995.

COOK JR, Joe (Mass) 28 Highland Ave, Roxbury MA 02119 B 1946 D 6/5/1972 Bp Robert Lionne DeWitt P 8/1/1976 Bp Morris Fairchild Arnold. m 9/1/1968 Angela Brooks.

COOK, Johnny Walter (CGC) 206 Fig Ave, Fairhope AL 36532 **Cn S Matt's Cathd Dallas TX 2003-** B Corpus Christi TX 1946 s Homer & Floris. BA U of Texas 1967; MDiv Epis TS of the SW 1984. D 6/26/1984 Bp Gordon Taliaferro Charlton P 1/28/1985 Bp Maurice Manuel Benitez. m 1/27/1968 Mary E Cook c 4. Stndg Com Dio Cntrl Gulf Coast Pensacola FL 2005-2009; Dn Chr Ch Cathd Mobile Mobile AL 2003-2013; Stndg Com Dio Dallas Dallas TX 2002-2003, Exec Coun 1998-2002; R S Lk's Epis Ch Dallas TX 1997-2003; R S Cyp's Ch Lufkin TX 1989-1997; Pres. Alum Assn. '86, Bd Trst '85-'96 Epis TS Of The SW Austin TX 1986-1996; R Trin Epis Ch Jasper TX 1986-1989; Asst R S Jas The Apos Epis Ch Conroe TX 1984-1986; Exec Bd Dio Texas Houston TX 1988-1996. Ord of St. Jn 2001.

COOK, Kay Kellam (U) 2425 Colorado Ave, Boulder CO 80302 **Assoc S Aid's Epis Ch Boulder CO 2008-** B Houston TX 1939 d Glenn & Amy Geraldine. BA Lamar U 1968; MA Lamar U 1972; PhD U CO 1991. D 6/9/2007 P 1/12/2008 Bp Carolyn Tanner Irish. m 6/22/1991 Douglas Burger c 3.

COOK, Lilian Lotus Lee (RG) 2114 Hoffman Dr Ne, Albuquerque NM 87110 B San Francisco CA 1932 d Frank & Eleanor. AA Monterey Peninsula Coll 1953. D 5/23/1988 Bp William Davidson. m 4/20/1974 Pleas M Cook. D S Chad's Epis Ch Albuquerque NM 1988-2005. DOK.

COOK, Nancy Bell (Ark) 1112 Alcoa Rd, Benton AR 72015 B Beverly MA 1938 d Charles & Helen Virginia. BA California St U 1977; MS California St U 1979. D 10/25/2014 Bp Larry Benfield. c 3. nancybcook@gmail.com

COOK, Patricia Ann (NAM) PO Box 85, Bluff UT 84512 **Assoc S Christophers Ch Bluff UT 2011-; S Jn The Baptizer Montezuma Creek UT 2010-; Assoc S Mary Of-The-Moonlight Oljato UT 2010-; Assoc St. Chris's Mssn Bluff UT 2010-; Utah Reg Bluff NM 2010-; Faith-Based Fac Gentle Ironhawk Shltr Blanding UT 2005-; Var roles San Juan Cnty Publ Sfty Bldg Monticello UT 2000-** B Chicago IL 1941 d William & Linda. D 12/13/2005 Bp Mark Lawrence Macdonald P 8/28/2010 Bp David Earle Bailey. m 5/20/1994 John Bond c 5.

COOK, Paul Raymond (WMo) 4 Burton Rd, Kingston KT25TE Great Britain (UK) B Gloucester UK 1943 s George & Margaret. LTh Jn Wollaston Theol Coll Au 1966. Trans 2/1/2000 Bp Barry Howe. m 8/9/1986 Yvonne Elizabeth Baker. S Mary's Epis Ch Kansas City MO 2000-2002; Serv Ch Of Australia 1967-2000.

COOK, Peter John Arthur (WLa) 4100 Bayou Rd, Lake Charles LA 70605 B Cambridge UK 1942 s Alan & Elizabeth. BA Reading U 1964; MA Brandeis U 1966; Trin TS 1971; PhD Queens U 1981. Trans 7/1/1988 as Priest Bp James Barrow Brown. m 7/24/1971 Nancy Jo Cook c 5. R S Mich And All Ang Lake Chas LA 1991-2014; Epis HS Baton Rouge Baton Rouge LA 1988-1991; Chapl Epis Hs Baton Rouge LA 1987-1991; Serv Ch Of Engl 1971-1987. Auth, "Wolfhard Pannenberg: A Post Enlightenment Theol," *Churchman*; Auth, "Wolfhard Pannenberg," *New Dictionary Of Theol.*

COOK JR, Robert (NC) 8400 Goose Landing Ct, Browns Summit NC 27214 B Attleboro MA 1943 s Robert & Elizabeth. BS Nthrn Michigan U 1967; Wayne 1970; MDiv EDS 1973; DMin Sewanee: The U So, TS 1979. D 6/30/1973 P 6/25/1974 Bp H Coleman Mcgehee Jr. m 11/1/1987 Sandra Cook c 3. Int S Andr's Ch Greensboro NC 2009-2010; Int S Mary's Epis Ch High Point NC 2008-2009; R Ch Of The Epiph Eden NC 2003-2008; Chapl Cbury Sch (Epis) Greensboro NC 2001-2003; R Gr Epis Ch Lexington NC 1997-2001; Assoc S Fran Ch Greensboro NC 1986-2003; R S Dav's Epis Ch Lakeland FL 1980-1986; Asst To Bp - Yth Mnstry & Ce Dio SE Florida Miami 1977-1980; Cur S Mary's Par Tampa FL 1975-1977; Chapl S Ptr Hm For Boys Detroit MI 1973-1975; Asst S Jn's Ch Plymouth MI 1973-1975; Chair of Mnstry and Mssn Event Dio No Carolina Raleigh NC 2006-2008, Chair of Sprtl Formation Cmsn 1991-1996, Sprtl Advsr Curs 1990-2006; Alco & Substnce Abuse Com Dio Cntrl Florida Orlando FL 1983-1986; Educ Com Dio SW Florida Parrish FL 1975-1977. Auth, "Practical Aspects Rel Educ In Parishes," Sewanee/Vanderbelt Press, 1979; Auth, "Mgmt Theory & Pract," Wayne Press, 1969. Rea.

COOK, Thomas R (Minn) 4439 W 50th St, Edina MN 55424 **S Steph The Mtyr Ch Minneapolis MN 2015-** B Eustis FL 1963 s Robert & Katherine. BA U of Florida 1985; MDiv Sewanee: The U So, TS 1997. D 5/31/1997 P 2/10/1998 Bp Charles Farmer Duvall. m 8/11/1990 Britton B Cook c 3. R Trin Ch Swarthmore PA 2007-2015; R Gr Epis Ch Medford MA 2001-2007; Asst R All SS Epis Ch Mobile AL 1997-2001. tcook@ststephens.com

COOK, William E (Tex) 11245 Shoreline Dr., Apt 308, Tyler TX 75703 B DeQueen AR 1938 s William & Edith. BA Rice U 1960; BS Rice U 1961; PhD Van 1969; MDiv Epis TS of the SW 1983. D 6/21/1983 Bp Gordon Taliaferro Charlton P 1/1/1984 Bp Maurice Manuel Benitez. m 4/19/1963 Joan Cook c 2. Vic S Lk's Epis Ch Lindale TX 2009-2012; R S Fran Epis Ch Tyler TX 1986-2004; All SS Epis Ch Crockett TX 1983-1986; Vic H Innoc' Epis Ch

Madisonville TX 1983-1986; The Great Cmsn Fndt Houston TX 1983-1986. Auth, "A Digital Data Acquisition System for use in Nuclear Med," Van Press, 1969; Auth, "Lot Plot Method of Quality Control," *Quality Control mag*, 1963.

COOK OJN, Winifred Rose (Mich) PO Box 287, Onsted MI 49265 **D S Mich And All Ang Brooklyn MI 2011-** B Jackson MI 1956 d Benjamin & Joyce. Whitaker Inst 2011. D 5/24/2011 Bp Wendell Nathaniel Gibbs Jr. m 8/3/1991 Michael Garry Cook.

COOKE, Barbara Jane (NC) 5205 Ainsworth Dr, Greensboro NC 27410 B Buffalo NY 1950 d James & Katherine. MS OH SU 1979; MDiv Methodist TS in Ohio 1994; DAS VTS 2002. D 6/22/2002 Bp Michael B Curry P 4/5/2003 Bp James Gary Gloster. m 6/9/1973 James L Baker c 3. S Chris's Epis Ch High Point NC 2016; Gr Epis Ch Lexington NC 2015; R The Epis Ch Of Gd Shpd Asheboro NC 2009-2013; Int S Thos Epis Ch Sanford NC 2007-2009; Chapl Res Alamance Reg Med Cntr Burlington NC 2006-2007; Int S Paul's Epis Ch Smithfield NC 2006-2007; Dioc Coun Mem Dio No Carolina 2004-2007; Vic S Jn's Ch Henderson NC 2002-2006; Chapl Hospice of Greensboro Greensboro NC 2000-2001; Min Unitarian Universalist Ch of Greensboro 1996-2000; Min Unitarian Universalist Fllshp of Wayne Cnty 1992-1996.

COOKE, Bruce Henry (Va) 117 Wagon Wheel Trl, Moneta VA 24121 **Died 3/6/2017** B Flint MI 1923 s Herschel & Alena. BA U MI 1946; STM EDS 1949; Cert U of Maryland 1985; MEd U of Maryland 1985. D 7/24/1949 P 2/3/1950 Bp Richard Stanley Merrill Emrich. m 7/14/1984 Janice M Cooke c 7. Ret 1988-2017; Organizing Pstr Trin Ecum Ch Moneta VA 1988-1991; Asst S Ptr's Epis Ch Arlington VA 1983-1988; ArmdF and Fed Ministres New York NY 1975-1980; Dio Iowa Des Moines IA 1970-1980, Excoun 1970-1975; Dn Trin Cathd Davenport IA 1969-1973; R Calv Ch Columbia MO 1965-1969; Assoc S Ptr's Epis Ch S Louis MO 1962-1965; Chapl USAFR 1957-1980; Excoun S Alb's Ch Worland WY 1955-1962; R S Jas Ch Riverton WY 1952-1955; Cur Chr Ch Detroit MI 1949-1950; Dio Wyoming Casper WY 1955-1962. Legion Of Merit USAF 1980.

COOKE, Catherine Cornelia Hutton (Vt) 500 South Union, Burlington VT 05401 B San Antonio TX 1944 d William & Catherine. U MI 1963; AS Pur 1965; BS Bos 1967; U of Pennsylvania 1974. D 8/24/1988 Bp Daniel Lee Swenson. m 1/20/1968 Roger Lee Cooke c 3. Actg Chapl Epis/Luth Campus Mnstry 1989-1992; Serv Ch of Engl 1988-1989; Archd Cathd Ch Of S Paul Burlington VT 1986-2010. NAAD.

COOKE, C(Hester) Allen (ETenn) 2124 Carpenter's Grade Road, Maryville TN 37803 **Died 2/21/2016** B Memphis TN 1931 s H Brent & Dorothy. BA Rhodes Coll 1953; MDiv EDS 1956; Coll of Preachers 1967. D 7/3/1956 Bp Theodore N Barth P 1/1/1957 Bp John Vander Horst. m 2/2/1960 Sara Dee Goodloe c 3. Ret 1994-2016; R Trin Epis Ch Florence AL 1986-1994; R S Geo's Ch Germantown TN 1971-1985; R S Andr's Ch Maryville TN 1967-1971; Ch Of The Gd Shpd Lookout Mtn TN 1961-1963; Asst S Thaddaeus' Epis Ch Chattanooga TN 1961-1963; Cur Chr Ch Cathd Nashville TN 1959-1961; P-in-c S Mk's Ch Copperhill TN 1956-1959.

COOKE, Douglas Tasker (Ct) 19 Ridgebrook Dr, West Hartford CT 06107 **Ret 1995-** B Stamford CT 1934 s Tasker & Evelyn. BA Hobart and Wm Smith Colleges 1956; MDiv Ya Berk 1959. D 6/11/1959 Bp Walter H Gray P 3/5/1960 Bp John Henry Esquirol. m 4/11/1970 Ann B Cooke c 2. Cur Dio Connecticut Meriden CT 1969-1995; R All SS Epis Ch Oakville CT 1962-1970; Cur S Jn's Ch New Milford CT 1959-1962. Hon Cn Chr Ch Cathd 1995.

COOKE, Hilary (Ind) **Assoc St Johns Epis Ch Lafayette IN 2008-** B Burlington VT 1977 d Roger & Catherine. BA Bryn 1998; MDiv PrTS 2002; DMin Chr TS 2012. D 6/4/2005 P 5/1/2006 Bp Thomas C Ely. m 8/7/2004 Gregery Thomas Buzzard c 2. Dio Indianapolis Indianapolis IN 2006-2007.

COOKE, Hugh Mabee (SJ) 67 W Noble St, Stockton CA 95204 B Omaha NE 1923 s Layton & Margaret. BS U of Nebraska 1948; Arizona St U 1965; MS Utah St U 1973; BTh Sch for Deacons 1985. D 6/21/1987 Bp Victor Manuel Rivera. m 6/5/1965 Mildred S Cooke. D H Cross Epis Mssn Stockton CA 1987-1999.

COOKE JR, James Coffield (EC) 309 Mary Lee Ct, Winterville NC 28590 **Supply P St Jn Epis Ch Grifton NC 2004-** B Kinston TN 1940 s James & Iris. MA UNC 1962; MDiv Sewanee: The U So, TS 1967. D 6/29/1967 P 1/6/1968 Bp Thomas H Wright. m 12/22/1962 Bonnie Lynn Jones c 2. Supply P Trin Epis Ch Chocowinity NC 2001-2004; R S Anne's Epis Ch Jacksonville NC 1987-2000; Cn for Mnstry Dio Maryland Baltimore MD 1981-1987; Assoc R S Anne's Par Annapolis MD 1975-1981; R S Paul's Epis Ch Clinton NC 1972-1975; Asst R S Jn's Epis Ch Wilmington NC 1967-1972; Chair, Com on Constitutions and Cn Dio E Carolina Kinston NC 2001-2007, Dep GC 1991-1997.

COOKE, James Daniel (Ct) 23 Parsonage Road, HIgganum CT 06441 **Dir of Pstr Serv, ACPE Supvsr Hartford Hosp 2011-** B New Brunswick NJ 1967 s George & Priscilla. BS Boston Coll 1989; MDiv PrTS 1993; CAS Ya Berk 1996; ThM Yale DS 1996. D 6/20/1998 Bp Herbert Thompson Jr P 1/9/1999 Bp Clarence Nicholas Coleridge. m 11/13/1993 Judith Marie Meyers c 1. Chr Ch Cathd Hartford CT 2016; Chapl, ACPE Supvsr in Trng Bridgeport Hosp

2001-2011; Asst S Jn's Epis Ch Essex CT 2000-2001; Cur S Mary's Epis Ch Manchester CT 1998-2000. Assn of CPE 2002; Assn of Profsnl Chapl 2002.

COOKE, Peter Stanfield (NJ) 16 Brandywyne, Brielle NJ 08730 **Ret 1996-** B New York NY 1926 s John & Cecilia. USNA 1948; Drew U 1951; BA Monmouth U 1962. D 4/19/1969 P 10/25/1969 Bp Alfred L Banyard. m 9/10/1994 Mary Elizabeth Cooke c 2. Int St Michaels Epis Ch Wall Township NJ 1995-1996; Vic S Mk's Epis Ch Keansburg NJ 1992-1995; Int Chr Ch So Amboy NJ 1989-1991; Int S Jn's Ch Eliz NJ 1988-1989; Vic S Jn's Ch Sewaren NJ 1984-1986; R S Raphael The Archangel Brick NJ 1974-1981; Asst The Ch Of S Uriel The Archangel Sea Girt NJ 1969-1973. Lambda Sigma Tau 1962.

COOKE, Philip Ralph (ECR) 17740 Peak Ave, Morgan Hill CA 95037 **R S Jn The Div Epis Ch Morgan Hill CA 2001-** B Chicago IL 1950 s Ralph & Celesta. BA U MN 1976; MDiv Nash 1981. D 6/20/1981 P 6/10/1982 Bp Archibald Donald Davies. m 11/23/1977 Karen G Cooke c 2. S Greg's Epis Ch Mansfield TX 1990-2001, 1983-1984; Instr Angl Sch Theol Dallas TX 1982-1999; Cur S Jn's Ch Ft Worth TX 1981-1983.

COOL, Opal Mary (Neb) 3525 N. 167Th Cir. Apt. 206, Omaha NE 68116 B Scotts Bay Canada 1926 d Truman & Ruth. EFM Sewanee: The U So, TS 1996. D 4/7/1999 Bp James Edward Krotz. c 2. D H Fam Epis NE 1999-2003.

COOLEY, Andrew A (Colo) 1315 Figueroa St, Walla Walla WA 99362 **S Paul's Ch Walla Walla WA 2016-** B Meeker CO 1957 s Frank & Carolyn. BA U MN 1980; MDiv GTS 1985. D 6/14/1985 P 12/18/1985 Bp William Carl Frey. m 5/18/1985 Teresa J Trimboli c 1. Gr And S Steph's Epis Ch Colorado Sprg CO 2014-2016; Int R S Mary Magd Ch Boulder CO 2013-2014; Int R S Lk's Epis Ch Ft Collins CO 2011-2013; Int Chr Epis Ch Aspen CO 2011; Dep GC Dio Colorado Denver CO 2005-2011, 1987-1993; Reg Mssnr Dio Colorado Durango CO 2005-2011; R S Mk's Epis Ch Durango CO 1995-2011; Vic S Nich Epis Ch Littleton CO 1991-1995; Vic S Pat's Epis Ch Pagosa Sprg CO 1985-1987. IMEC Int Ministers in the Epis Ch 2011; Int Mnstry Ntwk 2011. andrewc@stpaulsww.org

COOLIDGE, Edward Cole (Ct) 43 Spruce Ln, Cromwell CT 06416 B Beverly MA 1929 s William & Eleanor. BA Dart 1952; MDiv UTS 1955; Cert GTS 1963. D 6/11/1963 Bp Walter H Gray P 3/21/1964 Bp Joseph Warren Hutchens. m 8/23/1952 Joy Searle Coolidge c 4. Sr. Mentor Annand Prog Ya Berk New Haven CT 1991-1999; Asst Ch Of S Jn By The Sea W Haven W Haven CT 1989-1991; Asst R Ch Of The H Trin Middletown CT 1983-1989; Assoc Missnr Middlesex Cluster Mnstry 1980-1983; Prog Dir Cmnty Action Middletown CT 1971-1983; Cmnty Action For Grtr Middletown Inc E Hampton CT 1971-1983; R Chr Epis Ch Middle Haddam CT 1968-1971; Asst S Paul And S Jas New Haven CT 1963-1968; Serv Presb Ch 1955-1962.

COOLIDGE, Robert T (Cal) PO Box 282, Westmount QC H3Z 2T2 Canada **Fndr and Dir Montreal Fund for the Diac 1980-; Serv Ch in Can 1971-** B Boston MA 1933 s Lawrence & Victoria. BA Harv 1955; MA U CA 1957; BLitt Oxf GB 1966; Cert Montreal TS CA 2002. D 7/29/1967 Bp John Melville Burgess. m 9/10/1960 Ellen Osborne c 3. Serv Ch in Engl 1970-1971; Serv Ch in Can 1967-1969; Assoc Prof of Hist Concordia U Montreal 1963-1988; Hon Asst Cur St. Mary Par London Engl 1970-1971. Auth, "Adalbero, Bp of Laon," *Stds in Medieval & Renaissance Hist*, U of Nebraska Press, 1965. Amer Soc of Ch Hist 1968; Compass Rose Soc 2013; Eccl Hist Soc 1967; Integrity Inc 1996; NAAD 1968; RACA 1985. Fell Royal Hist Soc 1968.

COOLIDGE, William Mccabe (NC) 118 Cumberland Ave, Asheville NC 28801 **Non-par 1994-** B Battle Creek MI 1943 s John & Alice. U CO 1963; BA MI SU 1965; MBA MI SU 1966; MDiv VTS 1972. D 6/24/1972 P 6/23/1973 Bp Thomas Augustus Fraser Jr. m 4/1/2003 Karen Elizabeth Day c 3. R S Barth's Ch Pittsboro NC 1981-1993; R S Paul's Epis Ch Cary NC 1975-1981; Asst Chap Of The Cross Chap Hill NC 1973-1975.

COOLING, David Albert (USC) 280 Holcombe Way, Lambertville NJ 08530 B Los Angeles CA 1939 s Arthur & Lois. BA Occ 1961; MS USC 1968; MA U CA 1969; MDiv CDSP 1971; EdD GTF/Oxford 2004. D 10/3/1971 P 4/10/1972 Bp Edwin Lani Hanchett. c 2. P Assoc S Paul's Epis Ch Westfield NJ 1992-2004; P Assoc Trin Ch Columbus OH 1986-1991; R Trin Cathd San Jose CA 1981-1985; Dn Gr Cathd San Francisco CA 1978-1979, Cn Chncllr & Vice Dn 1976-1981; Headmaster S Andr's Ch Saratoga CA 1973-1976; Headmaster Ch Of The H Nativ Honolulu HI 1971-1973; Chair, Cont Educ Com CDSP Berkeley CA 1983-1985; Co-Chair, VIM Dio El Camino Real Salinas CA 1982-1985; COM Dio California San Francisco CA 1977-1981; Anglical Consult Cmsn The Epis Ch in Hawaii Honolulu HI 1972-1973. Nomin Com Natl Philanthropy Day 2007; Bd Dir Trin Epis Acad 2004; Advancement Dir of the Year Natl Methodist Hosp and Hlth Assn 2001; V.P. Advancement Meth Hm of N.J. 1992; Corp V.P. Ward, Dreshman and Reinhardt 1986; Bd Chairman The Hamlin Sch 1978; Tchr Corp Untd States Govt 1966; Crossroads Afr Riverside Ch 1961.

COOMBER, Matthew J.M. (ND) B 1974 s James & Eleanor. PhD U of Sheffield; MDiv U Tor CA 2005. D 6/15/2005 P 12/17/2005 Bp Michael Smith. m 7/31/2004 Sarah Allison Coomber c 1. Auth, "Amos and Micah Through the Centuries.," Wiley-Blackwell, 2018; Co-Ed, "Fortress Commentary on the Bible: The OT and Apocrypha," Fortress Press, 2014; Ed, "Bible and Justice: Ancient Texts, Mod Challenges," Routledge, 2011; Auth, "Prophets to Profits: How Prophetic Lit Can Address Landownership Abuse in Corp Globalization," *Bible and Justice: Ancient Texts, Mod Challenges*, Equinox, 2010; Guest Ed, "(Spec Ed of Political Theol)," *Political Theol*, Equinox, 2010; Auth, "Exegetical Notes on 1 Kgs. 17.8-16: The Widow of Zarephath," *Expository Times*, Sage Pub, 2007. Cath Biblic Assn of Amer 2014; European Assn of Biblic Stds 2006; SBL 2004; Soc of OT Stds 2007. The Chas K. & Mary Ellen Wilber Awd for Resrch in Peace and NonViolence St. Ambr U 2012; Sheffield Grad Awd U of Sheffield, UK 2010; Gvnr Gnrl's Silver Medal for highest overall Stndg Trin, U Tor 2005; Gordon Kent Steph Memi Prize for highest Stndg in thir Trin, U Tor 2005; McDonald Prize for Gnrl knowledge of the Engl Bible Trin, U Tor 2005; U of Sheffield OSRS full tuition fee waiver U of Sheffield, UK 2005; Trin Prize for highest Stndg in Hebr Trin, U Tor 2004.

COON, David Paul (Haw) Po Box 690, Kamuela HI 96743 **Ret 1993-** B Flint MI 1928 s Elmer & Jane. BA Estrn Michigan U 1949; CDSP 1954; MA MI SU 1967. D 6/18/1954 Bp Richard Stanley Merrill Emrich P 12/21/1954 Bp Harry Sherbourne Kennedy. m 9/11/1953 Joanne F Coon c 4. Int S Jas Epis Ch Kamuela HI 1996-1998, Vic 1954-1996; Headmaster Iolani Sch Honolulu HI 1970-1992; S Alb's Chap Honolulu HI 1960-1993; Asst. Headmaster Iolani Sch Honolulu HI 1960-1970; Vic St Jn the Bapt Epis Ch Waianae HI 1957-1963; Var Iolani Sch Honolulu HI 1957-1960; Coach Hawaii Epis Acad Kamuela HI 1954-1957; Tchr Hawaii Epis Acad Kamuela HI 1950-1951. DD CDSP 1971.

COON, Nancy Galloway (WTex) 200 Crossroads Drive, Dripping Springs TX 78620 B Gulfport MS 1942 d Morris & DruEtta. BS Sam Houston St U 1964; MA Sam Houston St U 1965; MDiv Epis TS of the SW 1994. D 5/22/1994 P 12/3/1994 Bp John Herbert MacNaughton. R The Ch Of The H Sprt Dripping Spgs TX 1997-2010; Asst/Assoc S Jn's Ch McAllen TX 1994-1997.

COONEY, James Francis (O) 384 Burr Oak Dr, Kent OH 44240 **P-in-c Chr Ch 2004-** B Lancaster OH 1928 s Paul & Mildred. BA S Chas Sem Columbus OH 1950; Lic Sacr Theol Gregorian U 1954; PhD OH SU 1966. Rec 8/2/1974 as Priest Bp John Harris Burt. m 6/16/1968 Sondra Louise Miley. Ch Of S Thos Berea OH 2000-2004; 1974-1999; Serv RC Ch 1953-1967.

COOPER JR, A(Llen) William (Alb) 1365 County Route 60, Onchiota NY 12989 **P-in-c S Jn In The Wilderness (Sum Chap) Paul Smiths NY 2009-; P-in-c S Thos Ch Tupper Lake NY 2003-; Sprtl Dir to the Cler & their families Dio Albany Greenwich NY 2015-, Chapl 2004-2015** B Syracuse NY USA 1942 s Allen & A June. BS SUNY 1965; MDiv Ya Berk 1969. D 6/11/1969 P 6/18/1970 Bp Ned Cole. m 7/23/1966 Margo Cooper c 2. The Ch Of The Mssh Glens Falls NY 1994-2003; R S Jn's Ch Essex NY 1982-1994; Trin Ch Rochester NY 1979-1982; R S Matt's Epis Ch Horseheads NY 1972-1979; Dio Cntrl New York Liverpool NY 1969-1979; Asst Seneca/Tompkins Mssn Field Romulus NY 1969-1973. Auth, "Evang: Presenting Chr w Clarity," *(Video w Study Guide)*, Dio Alb, 1989; Auth, "When to Baptize Infants and Young Chld," *LivCh*, 1988; Auth, "The Positive Aspects of Evang," *S Andr's Cross*, 1987. Franciscan OHC 2004.

COOPER, Cricket S (WMass) 67 East Street, Pittsfield MA 01201 **R Dio Wstrn Massachusetts Springfield 2013-; S Steph's Ch Pittsfield MA 2013-** B Baltimore MD 1961 d Robert & Marilyn. BA NWU 1983; GTS 1987; MDiv SWTS 1989. D 6/14/1989 Bp Daniel Lee Swenson P 12/15/1989 Bp Robert Marshall Anderson. m 11/27/1999 Thomas Tuthill. R S Andr's Ch New London NH 2003-2011; Assoc S Ptr's Epis Ch S Louis MO 2000-2003; Cn for Liturg, Educ and Admin Chr Ch Cathd S Louis MO 1996-2000; Assoc Ch Of The Redeem Chestnut Hill MA 1995-1996; Assoc S Andr's Ch Wellesley MA 1991-1994; Assoc S Jn The Evang S Paul MN 1989-1990; Cn for Liturg Dio New Hampshire Concord NH 2007-2011. Auth, "Chemo Pilgrim," *February 14, 2017*, Ch Pub Inc., 2017; Auth, "assorted meditations," *Finding God Day By Day*, Forw Mvmt, 2010. Preaching Awd SWTS 1989; Prize For Liturg Chanting SWTS 1989. cricketuvm@gmail.com

COOPER, Deborah Silas (Ark) B 1948 M.Ed U of Arkansas at Little Rock 2000; IONA 2016. D 8/6/2016 Bp Larry Benfield. c 1. dcooper@trinitylittlerock.org

COOPER IV, Francis Marion (CGC) Po Box 1677, Santa Rosa Beach FL 32459 **Stndg Com Dio Cntrl Gulf Coast Pensacola FL 2012-, Rgstr, Sch for Deacons 2008-2011** B Fort Myers FL 1948 s Frank & Mary. AA S Petersburg Jr Coll 1968; BA U of W Florida 1970; MDiv Nash 1973; PhD U of St Andrews 1981. D 6/24/1973 P 12/28/1973 Bp William Loftin Hargrave. m 8/22/1969 Martha Virginia Cooper c 2. R Chr The King Epis Ch Santa Rosa Bch FL 2004-2014; R S Jn's Epis Ch Johnson City TN 1997-2004; Dn S Mary's Cathd Memphis TN 1990-1997, Assoc 1981-1983; BEC Dio W Tennessee Memphis 1984-1990, 1983-1991, Dep, GC 1985-1997, chair, COM 1983-1997; Serv Ch in Scotland 1978-1981; Vic S Chad's Ch Tampa FL 1975-1978; Cur St Johns Epis Ch Tampa FL 1973-1975; Dep, GC Dio E Tennessee Knoxville TN 2003-2006, Bp & Coun 2003-2004, BEC 1998-, chair, Dio Theol Com 1997-2004. Auth, "Faith Dvlpmt in Chld: A Strtgy for CE"; Auth, "Blessed are the Peacemakers: A Curric for Chld & Adults"; Auth, "The Background & Dvlpmt of Evang Catholicism". Rutherford Prize for Hist Resrch S Mary's Coll 1981.

COOPER, Gale Hodkinson (NC) 1636 Headquarters Plantation Drive, Charleston SC 29455 **Asstg Chapl Bp Gadsden Ret Cmnty Charleston SC 2013-; Chapl Coastal Crisis Chapl Charleston SC 2010-** B Windsor UK 1944 d Sydney & Elizabeth. AA Sullins Coll 1965; BA U Rich 1967; MDiv UTS Richmond 1990; Cert VTS 1990. D 6/2/1990 P 4/6/1991 Bp Peter J Lee. m 11/23/1968 Elliot Cooper c 2. S Jn's Epis Ch Charlotte NC 2004-2009, Assoc 1996-2001, Assoc 1991-1995; Assoc Epiph Epis Ch Richmond VA 1991-1995; Chapl Med Coll of VA Hospitals Richmond VA 1990-1991.

COOPER, James Herbert (Fla) 1314 Ponte Vedra Blvd, Ponte Vedra Beach FL 32082 B Orange NJ 1944 s Herbert & Catharine. BA W&L 1967; MDiv VTS 1970; DMin VTS 1993. D 6/13/1970 Bp Leland Stark P 12/27/1970 Bp Allen Webster Brown. m 9/10/1966 Peggy Octavia Wood c 2. Trin Par New York NY 2004-2015; Chr Epis Ch Ponte Vedra FL 1972-2004; Asst Min S Ptr's Ch Albany NY 1970-1972. Auth, "Liturg and Wrshp: An Invitation to Cmnty," *Bldg Up The Ch*, Forw Mvmt Press, 1997; Auth, "Chr Piety," *Study & Action in the Hm*, 1993; Auth, "Trng Model for Chal Br," *Aware*, 1981. Compass Rose Soc 1982; Intl Rectors and Deans 2006; OHC 1985.

COOPER, Joseph Wiley (EC) 4925 Oriole Dr, Wilmington NC 28403 B Windsor NC 1944 s John & Rachel. BA Barton Coll 1967; MDiv VTS 1970. D 6/27/1970 P 3/27/1971 Bp Hunley Agee Elebash. Ch Of The Servnt Wilmington NC 1982-2006; S Paul's In The Pines Epis Ch Fayetteville NC 1976-1982; Dio E Carolina Kinston NC 1971-1976; Chapl Chowan Coll Murfreesboro NC 1971-1974; P-in-c S Barn Murfreesboro NC 1971-1974; P-in-c S Mary's Ch Gatesville NC 1971-1974; Vic S Ptr's Sunbury NC 1971-1974; Asst R S Steph's Ch Goldsboro NC 1970-1971.

COOPER, Michael Francis (Los) 4018 Vista Ct, La Crescenta CA 91214 **R S Nich Par Encino CA 2010-; DRE And Yth Dio Los Angeles Los Angeles CA 2005-, 2004-2009, Dir Of Yth Mnstrs 2002-** B Burbank CA 1964 MTh Loyola U 2000. D 6/19/2004 P 1/22/2005 Bp Joseph Jon Bruno. m 6/26/1999 Leslie Anne Cooper c 2.

COOPER, Michael Scott (CPa) 181 S 2nd St, Hughesville PA 17737 B New York NY 1952 s Samuel & Mildred. NYU 1978; BA CUNY Hunter Coll 1984; MDiv UTS 1987. D 6/13/1987 P 1/1/1988 Bp Paul Moore Jr. c 4. R S Jas Ch Muncy PA 1995-2000; Int S Jas' Ch Drifton PA 1993-1995; Assoc R S Steph's Ch Whitehall PA 1991-1993; Int S Anth Of Padua Ch Hackensack NJ 1989-1990; R S Paul's And Resurr Ch Wood Ridge NJ 1988-1991. Ord Of S Ben, Probationer Assn H Cross. Un Schlrshp Uts 1985.

COOPER, Miles Oliver (CFla) 423 Forest Ridge Dr, Aiken SC 29803 **Ret 1997-** B Saint Paul MN 1932 s Miles & Olive. BA U MN 1954; MDiv Bex Sem 1966. D 6/29/1966 Bp Philip Frederick McNairy P 3/1/1967 Bp Hamilton Hyde Kellogg. m 10/27/1956 Nancy A Cooper c 3. S Aug Of Cbury Epis Ch Vero Bch FL 1993-1997; Trin Ch Vero Bch FL 1989-1992; Assoc S Paul's Epis Ch New Smyrna Bch FL 1987-1988; R S Mths Epis Ch Toccoa GA 1985-1987; Int S Paul's Epis Ch Jesup GA 1984-1985; Supply Cler Dios Fla & GA 1968-1985; Asst Ch Of The Gd Shpd Jacksonville FL 1967-1968; Cur Geth Ch Minneapolis MN 1966-1967.

COOPER, Milton Norbert (SeFla) 11201 Sw 160th St, Miami FL 33157 **R Ch Of The Ascen Miami FL 1989-** B 1948 s Milton & Enid. BA S Aug 1973; MDiv Nash 1976. Rec 1/1/1982 as Priest Bp The Bishop Of Nassau. m 2/24/1979 Beryl Cooper c 2. Vic S Mary Epis Ch Chester PA 1986-1989; R S Ptr's Epis Ch Key W FL 1982-1986; St. Andrews Pentecost Epis Ch Evanston IL 1982; Serv Ch Of Bahamas 1975-1978. church_ascension@bellsouth.net

COOPER, Richard Randolph (Tex) 4805 E Columbary Dr, Rosenberg TX 77471 **Ret 1996-** B Ashland KY 1940 s Francis & Marian. BA U So 1964; MDiv Sewanee: The U So, TS 1966. D 6/24/1966 Bp William Loftin Hargrave P 1/6/1967 Bp Henry I Louttit. m 7/10/1965 Susan T Cooper c 2. Cn Dio Texas Houston TX 1986-1995; R S Geo Ch San Antonio TX 1976-1986; R Trin Epis Ch Baytown TX 1972-1976; R S Chris's Ch Tampa FL 1969-1972, Cur 1968-1969; Vic St. Chris's Epis Ch Tampa FL 1968-1969; Asst Gr Epis Ch Of Ocala Ocala FL 1966-1968. Chapl Ord of S Lk 1970; Reg Wrdn 1975-1982; Treas 1983-1987.

COOPER, Robert Norman (WLa) 108 Blue Ridge, Site 41, Comfort TX 78013 B New Orleans LA 1937 s John & Mildred. BS U of Louisiana 1959; MS U of Louisiana 1963; PhD Texas A&M U 1973; Advncd Theol Study Sewanee: The U So, TS 1999. D 6/7/1999 P 12/11/1999 Bp Robert Jefferson Hargrove Jr. m 12/16/1989 Sallie C Cooper c 4. Chr Ch St Jos LA 2001-2009; Gr Ch S Jos LA 2001-2009; The Epis Ch Of The Gd Shpd Vidalia LA 1999-2001.

COOPER, Stephenie Rose (ECR) 1205 Pine Ave, San Jose CA 95125 **D H Fam Epis Ch San Jose CA 2010-; D S Fran Epis Ch San Jose CA 2010-; Asst Secy of Conv Epis Dio El Camino Real 2008-** B Oakland CA 1952 Theol Stds Epis Sch for Deacons 2006; Diac Stds Epis Sch for Deacons 2006. D 6/5/2010 Bp Mary Gray-Reeves. Assn of Epis Deacons 2006.

COOPER-WHITE, Pamela (NY) Union Theological Seminary, 3041 Broadway, New York NY 10027 **Christiane Brooks Johnson Prof of Psychol & Rel UTS 2015-; Prof of Pstr Theol, Care & Counslg Columbia TS Decatur GA 2008-** B Lynn MA 1955 d Thomas & Constance. BA Bos 1977; MA Harv 1979; MDiv Harvard DS 1983; PhD Harv 1983; MA H Name U 1994; MA H Names U 1994; PhD Inst for Clincl Soc Wk Chicago IL 2001. D 6/6/1992 P 12/5/1992 Bp William Edwin Swing. m 4/26/1986 Michael Lee Cooper c 3. Asst H Trin Par Decatur GA 2011-2014; Asst S Barth's Epis Ch Atlanta GA 2008-2010; Prof of Pstr Theol Luth TS at Philadelphia 2004-2008; Asst Ch Of S Mart-In-The-Fields Philadelphia PA 1999-2008; Assoc Prof of Pstr Theol Luth TS Philadelphia 1999-2004; Prof Bexley Seabury Fed Chicago IL 1998-1999; Pstrl Cnslng Luth Gnrl Hosp 1995-1997; Assoc S Mary's Ch Pk Ridge IL 1994-1998; Asst S Paul's Ch Oakland CA 1992-1993; Dir Cntr Wmn & Rel Grad Theol Un 1989-1994; Dir/Min San Francisco Partnership Mnstry 1984-1986. Auth, "The Cry of Tamar: Violence Against Wmn, 2nd Ed," *Bk: The Cry of Tamar: Violence Against Wmn, 2nd ed.*, Fortress Press, 2012; Auth, "The Wiley-Blackwell Comp to Practical Theol," *Chapt: Suffering*, Wiley-Blackwell, 2012; Auth, "The Wiley-Blackwell Comp to Practical Theol," *Suffering*, Wiley-Blackwell, 2012; Auth, "Pastoralpsychologie und Religionspsychologie im Dialog," *A Critical Tradition: Psychoanalysis*, Kohlhammer, 2011; Auth, "Braided Selves: Collected Essays on Multiplicity, God & Persons," *Bk: Braided Selves: Collected Essays on Multiplicity, God & Persons*, Cascade Books, 2011; Auth, "Pastoralpsychologie und Religionspsychologie im Dialog," *Chapt: A Critical Tradition: Psychoanalysis*, Kohlhammer, 2011; Auth, "In Search of the Self: Interdisciplinary Perspectives on Personhood," *Chapt: Reenactors: Theol and Psychol Reflections on "Core Selves," Multiplicity, and the Sense of Cohesion*, Eerdmans, 2011; Auth, "Concise Dictionary of Pstr Care and Counslg," *ENTRY: Intersubjectivity, Countertransference, and Use of the Self in Pstr Care and Counslg*, Abingdon Press, 2010; Auth, "Cambridge Dictionary of Chrsnty," *ENTRY: Pstr Theol*, Camb Press, 2010; Auth, "Concise Dictionary of Pstr Care and Counslg," *Intersubjectivity, Countertransference, and Use of the Self in Pstr Care and Counslg*, Abingdon Press, 2010; Auth, "Cambridge Dictionary of Chrsnty," *Pstr Theol*, Camb Press, 2010; Auth, "Wmn Out of Ord: Risking Change and Creating Care in a Multi-Cultural Wrld," *Chapt: Complicated Wmn: Multiplicity and Relationality across Gender, Race, and Culture*, Fortress Press, 2009; Auth, "Healing Wisdom: Mnstry in Depth," *Chapt: Sacr Space and the Psyche: Reflections on Potential Space and the Sacr Built Environ*, Eerdmans, 2009; Auth, "Many Voices: Pstr Psych in Relational and Theol Perspective," *Bk: Many Voices: Pstr Psych in Relational and Theol Perspective*, Fortress Press, 2007; Auth, "The Formation of Pstr Counselors: Challenges and Opportunities," *Chapt: Thick Theory: Psychol, Theoretical Models, and the Formation of Pstr Counselors*, Haworth Press, 2006; Auth, "Shared Wisdom: Use of the Self in Pstr Care & Counslg," *Bk: Shared Wisdom: Use of the Self in Pstr Care & Counslg*, Fortress Press, 2004; Auth, "Human Dvlpmt and Faith," *Chapt: Human Dvlpmt in Relational and Cultural Context*, Chalice Press, 2004; Auth, "Human Dvlpmt and Faith," *Human Dvlpmt in Relational and Cultural Context*, Chalice Press, 2004; Auth, "Clincl Handbook of Pstr Counslg Vol. 3," *Chapt: Sexual Exploitation and Other Boundary Violations in Pstr Mnstrs*, Paulist Press, 2003; Auth, "Clincl Handbook of Pstr Counslg Vol. 3," *Sexual Exploitation and Other Boundary Violations in Pstr Mnstrs*, Paulist Press, 2003; Auth, "In Her Own Time: Wmn and Developmental Issues in Pstr Care," *Chapt: Opening the Eyes: Understanding the Impact of Trauma on Dvlpmt*, Fortress, 2000; Auth, "In Her Own Time: Wmn and Developmental Issues in Pstr Care," *Opening the Eyes: Understanding the Impact of Trauma on Dvlpmt*, Fortress, 2000; Auth, "Schoenberg & the God-Idea: Moses & Aaron," *Bk: Schoenberg & the God-Idea: Moses & Aaron*, UMI Resrch Press, 1985. AAR 1990; AAPC 1989; Assn of Epis Healthcare Chapl (AEHC) 1988; ECF (ECF) Fell 1995; IARPP Intl Assn for Relational Psychoanalysis 2007; Resrch Assoc of the Amer Psychoanalytic Assn 2000; Soc for Pstr Theol 1993; Soc of Angl and Luth Theologians (SALT) 2000; Sprtl Dir Intl (SDI) 2009. Fulbright-Freud Schlr of Psychoanalysis Fulbright Fndt 2013; Natl Cert Counslr Natl Bd Cert Counselors 2007; Sprt Awd for Cmnty Serv Samar Counslg Cntr Philadelphia 2007; Distinguished Achievement in Resrch & Writing (Natl Awd) AAPC 2005; Awd of Excellence--Feature Writing ECom 2004; Fac Writing Prize Inst for Clincl Soc Wk 1999; Cert Fell AAPC 1998; Awd of Excellence--News Writing ECom 1997; Top 10 Bk Awd Acad of Par Cler 1995.

COOTER, Eric Shane (SwFla) 4309 Trout River Xing, Ellenton FL 34222 **Wing Chapl USAF Aux - CAP Florida Wing HQ 2016-; Cn for Mnstry Dvlpmt Dio SW Florida Parrish FL 2013-, Mem Dioc Coun 2010-2012; Dep - SW Florida GC 2016-** B Greeneville TN 1965 s Haskell & Minnie. BBA E Tennessee St U 1988; MDiv Sewanee: The U So, TS 2010. D 12/20/2009 P 6/20/2010 Bp Dabney Tyler Smith. m 5/8/1999 Terri Lynn Eros c 1. R S Dav's Epis Ch Englewood FL 2011-2012, P-in-c 2010-2011, Asst P 2010; Admin Lamb Of God Epis Ch Ft Myers FL 2005-2007; Pres CODE - CODE 2015-2016; Pres St. Lk's Cmnty Sewanee U So TS Sewanee TN 2009-2010. Auth, "Fresh Expressions: Evangelisme for Our Culture," *Mnstry Matters*, 2013; Auth, "21st Century Wells: Chr Cmnty in the Third Place," *Mnstry Matters*, 2013. CODE - CODE 2014; Gathering of Leaders 2012. ecooter@episcopalswfl.org

COPE, Jan Naylor (WA) Washington National Cathedral, 3101 Wisconsin Avenue, NW, Washington DC 20016 **Provost Cathd of St Ptr & St Paul Wash-**

ington DC 2015-, Vic 2010-2015; Gvnr Wesley TS 2012-; Cler Dep GC-Epis Ch Cntr New York NY 2011-; Resolutns Com Dio Washington Washington DC 2010- B Corpus Christi TX 1956 d Glen & Jeannine. BA Trin U San Antonio 1978; MDiv Wesley TS 2007; DMin VTS 2013. D 6/9/2007 P 1/19/2008 Bp John Bryson Chane. m 5/22/1993 John Cope. Assoc R S Dav's Par Washington DC 2007-2010; Bd Mayor's Interfaith Coun 2011-2012; Mem Sibley Hosp Pstr Care Com 2009-2011; Trst Washington Theol Consortium 2009-2011; Trst Prot Epis Cathd Fndt 2004-2010. Auth, "A Budding YA Mnstry: Tending God's Garden at Washington Natl Cathd," *Doctoral Thesis*, 2013; Contrib, "Commentaries," *The Bible Challenge*, Forw Mvmt, 2012; Commentary Writer, "Commentaries," *The Bible Challenge*, Forw Mvmt, 2012. Compass Rose Soc 1999. Garfield Soc Fell Hiram Coll 2011. jcope@cathedral.org

COPE, Marie S (USC) 101 St. Matthew's Ln, Spartanburg SC 29301 B Fletcher NC 1976 d William & Brenda. BA Furman U 1998; MDiv VTS 2002. D 6/8/2002 P 12/21/2002 Bp Bob Johnson. m 6/15/2002 Hayne Carlisle Cope c 2. S Ptr's Epis Ch Greenville SC 2013-2014; Asst S Matt's Epis Ch Spartanburg SC 2009-2010; Assoc Ch Of The H Cross Tryon NC 2006-2008; Ch Of The Redeem Shelby NC 2006, 2002-2004.

COPELAND, Richard (Dal) 1141 N Loop 1604 E, Suite 105-614, San Antonio TX 78232 B San Angelo TX 1938 s Gay & Ester. BA Baylor U 1960; MDiv Nash 1974; DMin Pittsburgh TS 1988. D 6/20/1974 Bp Theodore H McCrea P 12/21/1974 Bp Archibald Donald Davies. c 2. R The Epis Ch Of The Resurr Dallas TX 1989-1999, Cur 1974-1977; R S Andr's Epis Ch Panama City FL 1985-1989; R Gr Epis Ch Of Ocala Ocala FL 1981-1985; R Ch Of The Annunc Lewisville TX 1977-1981. Cmnty Cross Of Nails 1980; OSL 1974; Trsfg Retreat Monstry 1975.

COPELAND, Wanda Ruth (CNY) St Matthews Episcopal Church, 408 S Main St, Horseheads NY 14845 **Trin Ch Elmira NY 2016-; S Matt's Epis Ch Horseheads NY 2012-; Dioc Coun Mem Dio Cntrl New York Liverpool NY 2015-** B Opelika AL 1956 d Charles & Ina. BA Judson Coll 1977; Cert U MN 1984; MDiv SWTS 1994. D 6/29/1994 Bp James Louis Jelinek P 1/7/1995 Bp Sanford Zangwill Kaye Hampton. m 12/20/2014 Melody G Graham c 2. Asst S Chris's Epis Ch S Paul MN 2007-2012; Chapl Guardian Ang Care Cntr Elk Elk River MN 1994-2006; H Trin Epis Ch Elk River MN 1994-2006. pastorwanda@stny.rr.com

COPENHAVER, Robert Thomas (SwVa) 50 Draper Place, Daleville VA 24083 **Ret 1998-; Chapl Dio SW Virginia Roanoke VA 2000-** B Roanoke VA 1932 s Marion & Rena. BA Roa 1954; BD VTS 1962; DMin S Marys Sem & U Baltimore 1984. D 6/25/1962 P 6/6/1963 Bp William Henry Marmion. m 1/30/1954 Margaret Copenhaver c 4. Int S Mk's Ch Fincastle VA 2010-2011; Int Trin Epis Ch Rocky Mt VA 2005-2007; Int S Jn's Ch Bedford VA 1998-2000; R S Paul's Epis Ch Salem VA 1969-1997; Assoc The Falls Ch Epis Falls Ch VA 1968-1969; Chr Epis Ch Buena Vista VA 1962-1968; R S Jn's Epis Ch Glasgow VA 1962-1966. Auth, "Aging Together In The Faith Cmnty". Cmnty Builders Awd Untd Way Of Roanoke Vlly 2002; Distinguished Bd Mem Awd Virginia Assn Of Chld'S Hm 1999. aypiper@aol.com

COPLAND, Edward Mark (SwFla) 5462 Shadow Lawn Dr, Sarasota FL 34242 **Consult Coach and Consult for Epis Ch 2011-; Mssnr Dio Pretoria Pretoria 1999-** B Stamford CT 1943 s Edward & Marjorie. BA Cor 1965; MDiv GTS 1968; S Josephs 1972. D 6/11/1968 P 3/25/1969 Bp Walter H Gray. m 6/12/1965 Judith M Mix c 2. R S Bon Ch Sarasota FL 1991-2011; Pres and Fndr Casa Ave Maria Masaya Nicaragua 1990-2004; Bd Mem, Mssy Ecum Refugee Coun Milwaukee WI 1984-1990; R S Matt's Ch Evanston IL 1976-1991; Chapl Miss Porter's Sch Farmington CT 1972-1975; Via Media Exec Comm Dio SW Florida Parrish FL 2003-2008, COM Chair 2001-2008; Dioc Coun Dio Chicago Chicago IL 1976-1982. Cert in Appreciative Inquiry Cler Ldrshp Inst 2010.

COPLEY, David Mark (NY) 10 West Elizabeth Street, Tarrytown NY 10591 **Dom And Frgn Mssy Soc- Epis Ch Cntr New York NY 2006-; Epis Ch Cntr New York NY 2006-; Mssn Personl Off Epis Ch Cntr New York NY 2006-** B Notingham England 1960 s Gordon & Bridget. RGN/RSCN Sheffield Sch of Nrsng Sheffield GB 1984; VTS 2003. D 6/14/2003 Bp Carol J Gallagher P 12/6/2003 Bp David Conner Bane Jr. m 12/17/1993 Susan Kay Leckrone c 1. S Jn's Ch Hampton VA 2003-2006; Exec Coun Appointees New York NY 2003-2005.

COPLEY, Susan Kay (NY) 10 W Elizabeth St, Tarrytown NY 10591 **R Chr Epis Ch Tarrytown NY 2007-** B Belleville IL 1954 d Charles & Margaret. BA U of Puget Sound 1976; RN S Vincents Sch of Nrsng 1986; MDiv VTS 2003. D 6/14/2003 Bp Carol J Gallagher P 12/6/2003 Bp David Conner Bane Jr. m 12/17/1993 David Mark Copley c 1. Asst S Jn's Ch Hampton VA 2003-2007.

COPP, Ann Humphreys (Md) 444 Garrison Forest Rd, Owings Mills MD 21117 **S Mths' Epis Ch Baltimore MD 2011-; Chapl Cathd Sch for Boys 1998-** B Memphis TN 1946 d Edward & Ann. BA Connecticut Coll 1968; MA U of Memphis 1980; MDiv Ya Berk 1995. D 11/30/1997 P 5/1/1998 Bp Stewart Clark Zabriskie. c 2. Ch Of The Gd Shpd Towson MD 2010-2011; Asst S Thos' Ch Garrison Forest Owings Mills MD 1999-2010. annhcopp@gmail.com

COPPEL JR, Stanley Graham (SJ) Po Box 1431, Twain Harte CA 95383 B Berkeley CA 1942 s Stanley & Frances. BA U of San Francisco 1977; BTh DiocCalif Sch for Deacons 1987; CDSP 2009. D 12/3/1988 Bp William Edwin Swing P 2/28/2009 Bp Jerry Alban Lamb. m 5/9/1972 Rebecca Coppel c 1. P Epis Dio San Joaquin Modesto CA 2010-2013; P St Jas Epis Ch Sonora CA 2009-2012; D S Mich And All Ang' Epis Ch Sonora CA 2000-2004; D S Eliz's Epis Ch S San Fran CA 1990-1999; S Ptr's Epis Ch Redwood City CA 1990; Chapl Seton Med Cntr 1989-1990; Police Chapl So. San Francisco Police Dept 1988-1990. Auth, "Police Chapl - Notification of Death," *Diakonia Nwsltr*, 1989.

COPPEN, Christopher J (Spok) 5108 W Rosewood Ave, Spokane WA 99208 **Non-par 1998-** B Ottawa CA 1959 s Peter & Edith. BA U of Arizona 1981; MDiv EDS 1988; MS Estrn Washington U 2000. D 6/2/1988 P 2/1/1989 Bp Joseph Thomas Heistand. m 6/16/1990 Mary Joan Cowley. R S Ptr's Ch Beverly MA 1995-1998; Vic S Thos Ch Dubois WY 1991-1995; Emm Epis Ch S Louis MO 1988-1991. "None". None.

COPPICK, Glendon Cleon (Ky) 851 Live Oak Pl, Owensboro KY 42303 **Died 4/18/2017** B Stigler OK 1926 s Cleo & Gertie. BA TCU 1952; MDiv CDSP 1955; STD SFTS 1987. D 6/21/1955 P 12/21/1955 Bp Charles A Mason. m 11/21/1954 Shirley Jane Coppick c 3. Ret 1991-2017; R Trin Epis Ch Owensboro KY 1959-1991; R Ch Of The Gd Shpd Dallas TX 1955-1959. "The Legacy of Trin Epis Ch," 2008; Auth, "Var arts," 2003.

COPPINGER, Tim (WMo) 107 W Perimeter Dr, San Antonio TX 78227 **P Dio W Missouri Kansas City MO 2012-** B Neosho MO 1965 s Fred & Jennie. BS K SU 1988; MDiv TESM 1997. D 6/7/1997 P 12/6/1997 Bp John Clark Buchanan. c 3. Ch Of S Jn The Div Burkburnett TX 2007-2008; P-in-c The Epis Ch of Wichita Falls Wichita Falls TX 2004-2007; R S Geo Epis Ch Camdenton MO 1997-2004. timothyrcoppinger@gmail.com

CORAM, James M (NC) 12109 Park Shore Ct, Woodbridge VA 22192 B 1939 BA Amer U; BD VTS. D 6/8/1968 Bp Robert Bruce Hall P 5/31/1969 Bp Samuel B Chilton. m 8/27/1966 Donna Jean Coram. Dio No Carolina Raleigh NC 1973-1976; S Chris's Epis Ch High Point NC 1972-1985.

CORBETT, Ian Deighton (NAM) Po Box 28, Bluff UT 84512 **Serv Ch of Engl 2009-; Ret 2008-** B Birmingham England 1942 s Jack & Marjorie. BA U of Cambridge 1964; MA U of Cambridge 1967; Westcott Hse Cambridge 1969; MS U of Salford Manchester GB 1983. Trans 9/1/2001 Bp Steven Tsosie Plummer Sr. U.R. Vic Navajoland Area Mssn Farmington NM 2001-2008; Utah Reg Bluff NM 2001-2008; Serv Angl Ch of Can 1999-2001; Serv Ch of Ireland 1997-1999; Serv Ch of the Prov of Sthrn Afr 1995-1996; Serv Ch of the Prov of Cntrl Afr 1992-1995; Serv Ch of the Prov of Sthrn Afr 1988-1992; Serv Ch of Engl 1969-1988; Serv Ch of Engl 1969-1988. "Vanishing Lesotho," *Guardian*, Newspapers, 1991; *Love of the Wrld*, Churchman (UK), 1986.

CORBETT, James Bd (Los) 10819 SE Rex St, Portland OR 97266 B Indianapolis IN 1940 s James & Louise. AB USC 1963; MDiv PDS 1968. D 9/7/1968 P 3/8/1969 Bp Francis E I Bloy. m 5/7/1966 Karen Corbett c 1. Asst All SS Ch Portland OR 2009-2013; Int S Jas Epis Ch Midvale UT 2007-2008; Int S Paul's Ch Akron OH 2006-2007; Int S Mk's Epis Ch Casper WY 2005-2006; Int S Steph's Ch Durham NC 2003-2005; Int S Thos Ch Franklin IN 2002-2003; Int The Epis Ch Of The Epiph So Haven MI 2001-2002; Int S Mk's Ch Yreka CA 2000-2001; P-in-c S Augustines In-The-Woods Epis Par Freeland WA 1999; Dio Los Angeles Archv 1994-1998; R S Andr's Epis Ch Ojai CA 1977-1993; LocTen S Jn's And H Chld Wilmington CA 1974-1975; Asst S Mary's Par Laguna Bch CA 1971-1973; P-in-c Gr Epis Ch Lk Havasu City AZ 1970-1971; Cur S Patricks Ch And Day Sch Thousand Oaks CA 1968-1970.

CORBETT, John Philip (NwT) P.O. Box 334, Brownfield TX 79316 **Serv The Epis Ch of the Gd Shpd Brownfield TX 2003-; D The Epis Ch Of The Gd Shpd Brownfield TX 2002-** B Phoenix AZ 1935 s Harry & Miriam. BA Estrn New Mex U 1960; MA Estrn New Mex U 1967. D 10/4/1989 Bp Terence Kelshaw P 10/18/2008 Bp C Wallis Ohl. m 9/4/1994 Eunice F Dickey c 2. D S Paul's Ch Artesia NM 1997-2002; D S Thos A Becket Ch Roswell NM 1989-1996. NAAD 1989-2008. nigo@nwtdiocese.org

CORBETT-WELCH, Kathy (WA) 2218 Hillhouse Rd, Baltimore MD 21207 B Boston MA 1952 d Thomas & Ellen. Jn Hopkins Hosp; Mt Auburn Hosp Sch of Nrsng Cambridge MA 1974; MDiv Harvard DS 1993. D 10/3/1997 Bp Gerry Wolf P 6/15/1998 Bp Jane Hart Holmes Dixon. m 9/15/2005 Ellen Corbett Welch. R S Lk's Ch Brighton Brookeville MD 2002-2016; Asstg P Ch Of The Gd Shpd Towson MD 2001-2002; Palliative Care Chapl U of MD Med Cntr Baltimore MD 2001-2002; Palliative Care Dio Maryland Baltimore MD 1999-2017; Epis Chapl/CPE Supvsr in Trng Johns Hopkins Hosp Baltimore MD 1999-2001; Asstg P Ch Of S Steph And The Incarn Washington DC 1997-1999; Dir, Pstr Care Epis Caring Response To Aids Washington DC 1997-1999; Dir of Pstr Care Epis Caring Response to AIDS Washington DC 1997-1999.

CORBIN, Portia Renae (SD) 500 S Main Ave, Sioux Falls SD 57104 **P Dio So Dakota Pierre SD 2013-** B Rapid City SD 1987 d Timothy & Dawn. AA Cottey Coll 2007; BA Creighton U 2009; MDiv Ya Berk 2013. D 6/22/2013 Bp John Tarrant. m 7/13/2013 Christopher W Corbin c 1. youth.diocese@midconetwork.com

CORBISHLEY, Frank J. (SeFla) 921 Sorolla, Coral Gables FL 33134 **Coll Chapl & P in Charge Chap of the Venerable Bede Coral Gables FL 1994-; Mem COM 2013-; Trst Palmer Trin Sch Palmetto Bay FL 2006-** B Syracuse NY 1956 s Bernard & M Kathleen. BS Geo 1978; MS Amer Grad Sch of Intl Mgmt Glendal 1980; MIM Thunderbird Grad Sch of Intl Mgmt 1980; MDiv GTS 1990. D 6/25/1990 P 12/21/1990 Bp Calvin Onderdonk Schofield Jr. m 11/19/1994 Deborah S Corbishley c 3. Assoc S Andr's Epis Ch Miami FL 1990-1994. fcorbishley@miami.edu

CORDINGLEY, Saundra Lee (Roch) 23 Seneca Road, Rochester NY 14622 **Assoc S Lk And S Simon Cyrene Rochester NY 2010-** B Sodus NY 1944 d Edward & Betty Jane. Monroe Cmnty Coll; BA S Jn Fisher Coll 1976; MDiv Colgate Rochester Crozer DS 1980; MDiv CRDS 1980. D 6/22/1985 P 4/19/1986 Bp William George Burrill. c 3. R Chr Ch W River MD 1996-2010; R Chr Epis Ch Jordan NY 1990-1996; P-in-c S Jn's Ch Sodus NY 1985-1990. AAPC 1992; EPF.

CORDOBA, Guillermo (Fla) 2961 University Blvd N, Jacksonville FL 32211 B San Jose Costa Rica 1954 s Guillermo & Maruja. Rec 11/1/2010 as Deacon Bp Samuel Johnson Howard. stlukesjax@bellsouth.net

CORIOLAN, Simpson (Hai) Box 1309, Port-Au-Prince Haiti **P-in-c S Simeon Croix-Des-Bouquets 1975-** B Port-au-Prince Haiti 1947 s Paul & Lise. MDiv ETSC 1974. D 9/29/1974 P 5/1/1975 Bp Luc Anatole Jacques Garnier. m 1/29/1977 Marie Carmen Gilberte Archin c 2. Other Cler Positon Jqes-Juste (St Jacques Le Juste) Petionville Haiti 2001-2004; Other Cler Positon St. Bazile Le Grand Gonaives Haiti 1990-1994; P in charge Notre Dame Port-au- Prince Haiti 1975-1990; Dio Haiti Port-au-Prince HT 1974-2004.

CORKERN, Matthew Thomas Locy (Nwk) 41 Woodland Avenue, Summit NJ 07901 **R Calv Epis Ch Summit NJ 2011-; Trst for FOCCUS Cbury Cathd 2009-** B Brookhaven MS 1972 s Thomas & Rebecca. BA U Rich 1995; Cert Ang Stud Ya Berk 2001; MDiv Ya Berk 2001; MA U Rich 2001. D 6/23/2001 P 12/29/2001 Bp Peter J Lee. m 8/16/2012 Alice Coke-Corkern c 1. R Trin Epis Ch Mobile AL 2008-2011; Cn Res Chr Ch Cathd Nashville TN 2004-2008; Assoc R For Adult Educ S Jn's Epis Ch Mc Lean VA 2001-2004. The Amer Priory Ord of St. Jn 2004; Vergers' Gld of The Epis Ch 2011.

CORKLIN, Stanley Earl (Vt) 744 Parker Road, West Glover VT 05875 **Ret 2002-** B Cheyenne WY 1941 s Jack & Alsie. BA U of Nthrn Colorado 1964; MDiv Nash 1969. D 6/19/1969 Bp James Winchester Montgomery P 12/20/1969 Bp Gerald Francis Burrill. m 2/10/2012 Richard A Pugliese. P-in-c St. Chris's Ch 2004-2010; R S Matt's Ch Enosburg Fls VT 1998-2001; Int S Jn's In The Mountains Stowe VT 1993-1994; 1991-1993; R Gr Ch Sterling IL 1983-1992; R Chr Ch Streator IL 1978-1983; Vic S Jn The Evang Lockport IL 1972-1978; Cur Chr Ch Waukegan IL 1969-1972. Auth, "Hist of S Matt's Ch Enosburg Falls VT," S Matthews Press, 2002. Benedictine Oblate: St. Benoit du lac 2015; CBS; OHC. loonsongoldenpond@hotmail.com

CORL, James Alexander (CNY) 2435 Fleming Scipio Town Line Road, Auburn NY 13021 B Syracuse NY 1943 s John & Jane. BA Syr 1965; MDiv EDS 1968; DMin VTS 1992. D 6/10/1968 Bp Walter M Higley P 5/28/1969 Bp Ned Cole. m 6/18/1966 Nancy Jane Duckett c 3. R Chr Ch Manlius NY 2001-2008; R S Paul's Ch Endicott NY 1980-2001, Assoc 1970-2001; Dep GC Dio Cntrl New York Liverpool NY 1982-1997, No Country Mssn Field 1968-1981. Soc of S Marg 1983.

CORLETT, Diane Bishop (NC) 6901 Three Bridges Cir, Raleigh NC 27613 **R Ephphatha Ch For The Deaf Raleigh NC 1992-; Coordntr Of Deaf Mnstry Dio No Carolina Raleigh NC 1986-** B Durham NC 1950 d David & Rachel. U Durham Durham NC; BS Barton Coll 1972; MEd U NC 1980; MDiv GTS 1986. D 6/29/1986 Bp Frank Harris Vest Jr P 6/1/1987 Bp Robert Whitridge Estill. m 8/28/1971 Donald F Corlett c 1. R Ch Of The Nativ Raleigh NC 1992-2009; Chr Epis Ch Cleveland NC 1989-1992; Asst to R All SS' Epis Ch Concord NC 1986-1988. Auth, "Joining The Conversation". P Assoc, CHS. Aclu W.W. Finlater Awd Wale Co. Aclu 2002.

CORLEY, Kathryn S (CNY) 97 Underhill Rd, Ossining NY 10562 B Decatur IL 1957 d Kenneth & Carol. D 3/18/2000 P 9/16/2000 Bp Richard Frank Grein. m 6/17/1978 David Wayne Corley c 2. Int S Lk's Epis Ch Camillus NY 2015-2017; Gr Ch Baldwinsville NY 2012-2015; S Mary's Ch Of Scarborough Briarcliff NY 2008-2010; Gr Ch Hastings Hds NY 2007-2008; S Lk's Ch Somers NY 2006-2007; Dio New York New York NY 2005-2006, 2001-2003; DCE Ch Of S Mary The Vrgn Chappaqua NY 2000-2001.

CORLEY, Robert M (Dal) 10837 Colbert Way, Dallas TX 75218 **R S Mk's Ch Irving TX 2012-** B Dallas TX 1970 s Jerry & Jerilyn. BA U of Texas; MDiv Sewanee: The U So, TS 2006. D 6/24/2006 P 3/26/2007 Bp James Monte Stanton. m 5/14/1994 Laura N Corley c 2. Cur S Jn's Epis Ch Dallas TX 2006-2011.

CORNEJO, Quirino H. (Colo) 193 Bristlecone St, Brighton CO 80601 **Dio Colorado Denver CO 2016-** B Leon Guanajuato, Mexico 1963 s J Jesus & Maria. Rec 6/18/2016 as Priest Bp Robert John O'Neill. m 3/18/2016 Margarita Garza c 2.

CORNELL, Allison Lee (Az) 2252 Cherry Hills Dr, Sierra Vista AZ 85635 **All SS Epis Ch Safford AZ 2016-** B Greensboro NC 1963 d John & Delores. BA MWC 1985; MSSI Joint Mltry Intelligence Coll 2000; Cert of Theol Stds Bloy

Hse - The Epis Theological Sch at Claremont 2014; MDiv EDS 2014. D 6/7/2014 P 1/17/2015 Bp Joseph Jon Bruno. Dio Arizona Phoenix AZ 2016; P H Cross Epis Ch Carlsbad CA 2014-2015; Chapl Veterans Affrs Med Cntr San Diego CA 2014-2015. alcornell5@gmail.com

CORNELL, Amy S (NJ) **P Gr St Pauls Ch Trenton NJ 2012-** B New Brunswick NJ 1966 d Thomas & Joan. BA Douglass Coll 1989; MDiv GTS 2012. D 12/7/2011 P 6/14/2012 Bp George Edward Councell. acornell@gts.edu

CORNELL, Charles Walton (NCal) 813 Mormon St, Folsom CA 95630 B Marysville CA 1948 s Woodrow & Helen. AA Yuba Coll 1968; BS California St U 1971; MDiv Nash 1989. D 6/21/1989 Bp John Lester Thompson III P 12/1/1989 Bp James Barrow Brown. Trin Ch Folsom CA 1998-2011; S Geo's Ch Bossier City LA 1992-1998; R S Jn's Ch Kenner LA 1989-1992.

CORNELL, Lucinda Sims (WNY) Church of the Asencion, 16 Linwood Ave, Buffalo NY 14209 **D Ch Of The Ascen Buffalo NY 2011-** B Lockport NY 1952 d Harry & Ruth. BS Cor 1974; MEd Niagara U 1981. D 2/13/2011 Bp Michael Garrison. c 1.

CORNELL, Peter Stuart (NJ) 5 Paterson St, New Brunswick NJ 08901 **D Chr Ch New Brunswick NJ 2007-; Archd Dio New Jersey Trenton NJ 2012-; Mem, Cler Cmsn for Liturg 2010-** B Mt Holly NJ 1955 BS Trenton St Coll 1977; MBA Rutgers The St U of New Jersey 1996. D 6/9/2007 Bp George Edward Councell. m 10/11/1980 Nancy Cornell c 2. Cmncatn Chairperson Epis Transition Commitee 2012-2013. deacon@christchurchnewbrunswick.org

CORNER, Cynthia Ruth (Mich) PO Box 287, Onsted MI 49265 **D S Mich And All Ang Brooklyn MI 2011-** B Detroit MI 1948 d Albert & Ida. MA Siena Heights U; Total Mnstry Trng in Dio Michigan; BA Adrian Coll 1970. D 5/24/2011 Bp Wendell Nathaniel Gibbs Jr.

CORNEY, Richard Warren (NY) 12 Hartford Ave Apt B, Glens Falls NY 12801 B Poughkeepsie NY 1932 s Richard & Mabel. BA Leh 1954; STB GTS 1957; ThD UTS 1970. D 6/11/1957 P 12/21/1957 Bp Horace W B Donegan. m 6/21/1958 Susan S Corney c 4. Asstg P S Jn's Ch New York NY 2001-2009; Prof The GTS New York NY 1971-2000, Asst Prof 1964-1971, Instr 1960-1964, Fell; Tutor 1957-1960. Contrib, "Bible Challenge," Forw Mvmt, 2012; Auth, "The Bk of Job," *Bible Briefs*, Virginia Theol Seminay, 2012; Auth, "The Bk of Amos," Forw Mvmt, 2008; Auth, "Rod And Stff: A Double Image," *On The Way To Nineveh*, Scholars Press, 1999; Auth, "What Does Literal Meaning Mean," *The ATR*, 1998; Contrib, "Mysteries of the Bible," Readers Dig, 1988; Co-Auth, "Responsible Use of the Scriptures," *Pro and Con on the Ord of Wmn*, Seabury, 1976; Auth, "Isaiah L 10," *Vetus Testamentum*, 1976; Contrib, "Interpreter's Dictionary of the Bible," Abingdon, 1962. Amer Schools Of Oriental Resrch 1964-2000; Col Fac Seminar on the Hebr Bible 1971; SBL 1957-2000.

CORNILS, Calvin Stanley (NCal) D 8/13/2016 Bp Barry Leigh Beisner.

CORNMAN, Jane Elizabeth (Me) Po Box 105, Northeast Harbor ME 04662 **The Par Of S Mary And S Jude NE Harbor ME 2014-; Yth Advsry Bd Dio Pennsylvania Philadelphia PA 2010-** B Beverly MA 1967 d John & Elizabeth. BA Mssh Coll 1989; MDiv Ya Berk 2005. D 6/4/2005 P 12/17/2005 Bp Charles Ellsworth Bennison Jr. m 10/19/1991 Douglas E Cornman c 2. Assoc R S Mary's Ch Wayne PA 2005-2013.

CORNNER, Robert Wyman (Los) 8170 Manitoba St., Unit #1, Playa Del Rey CA 90293 B Wichita KS 1946 s William & Charlotte. BA California St U 1969; ETSBH 1982. D 6/19/1982 P 1/22/1983 Bp Robert Claflin Rusack. m 7/17/1992 Madelyn Rosen c 2. R Chr Ch Par Redondo Bch CA 2001-2015; S Geo's Mssn Hawthorne CA 1991; Supply P Dio Los Angeles Los Angeles CA 1990-2001; S Fran' Par Palos Verdes Estates CA 1989-1990; Asst S Fran' 1988-1990; Chapl Chart Pacific Hosp 1987-1988; Asst St Cross Epis Ch Hermosa Bch CA 1982-1987; Chapl Suncrest Hosp.

CORNTHWAITE, Hannah Elyse (Ia) B Wrangell AK 1986 d Otto & Deborah. BA NW Coll 2010; MDiv Ch of the Sav 2016. D 12/7/2013 P 5/30/2015 Bp Alan Scarfe.

CORNWELL, Marilyn M (Oly) Church of the Ascension, 2330 Viewmont Way Weat, Seattle WA 98199 **R Ch Of The Ascen Seattle WA 2010-; Outdoor Mnstrs Cmsn Dio Olympia Seattle 2011-, Stndg Com 2010-, Anti-Racism T/F 2007-** B Davenport IA 1952 BA U of Texas 1979; PhD U of Texas 1984; MDiv CDSP 2006. D 6/24/2006 Bp Vincent Waydell Warner P 1/11/2007 Bp Bavi Edna Rivera. m 3/10/1979 Robert Earl Cornwell c 1. S Mk's Cathd Seattle WA 2007-2010; Emm Epis Ch Mercer Island WA 2006-2007; Epiph Par of Seattle Seattle WA 2006. co-Auth, "Programmatic Stff Care in an Outpatient Setting," *The Journ of Pstr Care & Counslg*, Journ of Pstr Care Pub, 2005.

CORREA, Trino Cortes (SJ) 3345 Sierra Madre, Clovis CA 93619 B MX 1950 s Rogelio & Concepcion. Rec 4/19/1997 Bp David Mercer Schofield. m 1/18/1983 Robertina A Correa c 4. Vic Our Lady of Guadalupe Fresno CA 1997-2008.

CORREA AMARILES, Maria Ofelia (Colom) Parroquia San Lucas, Cr 80 No 53A-78, Medellin Antioguia Colombia B Valdivia - Antioquia 1942 d Javier & Rosario. D 6/16/2007 Bp Francisco Jose Duque-Gomez. m 9/15/1972 Horacio Velez c 3.

CORREA GALVEZ, Jose William (Colom) Carrera 6 No 49-85, Piso 2, Bogota Colombia B Casabianca Tolima 1965 s Fabio & Maria. Theol Rhema Cebco 2008. D 3/22/2009 Bp Francisco Jose Duque-Gomez.

CORRELL, Ruth E (Va) 15639 John Diskin Cir, Woodbridge VA 22191 **Asst to the R Pohick Epis Ch Lorton VA 2012-; Tchr Epiph Assn Pittsburgh PA 2004-** B Decatur IN 1947 d George & Esther. BS Kent St U 1969; MEd Kent St U 1971; MA Trin Evang DS 1975; EdD NYU 1987; TESM 1995; Cert Epiph Assn 2004. D 6/12/1999 P 2/24/2000 Bp Robert William Duncan. Chapl Hospice Greenspring Erickson Living Springfield VA 2008-2012; Asst to the R S Fran Ch Potomac MD 1999-2008. Auth, "That We May Be One: The Power of Gender in God's Story," *Trin Journ for Theol and Mnstry*, Trin Sch for Mnstry, 2009; Auth, "Tell Me the Old, Old Story: Uncovering Sprtl Formation in Biblic Narratives," *Epiph Intl* , Epiph Assn, 2007; Auth, "Why Use Bible Stories in the Classroom," *NAES Journ*, NAES, 1992. rcorrell@pohick.org

CORRIGAN, Candice Lyn (Oly) 506 21st St SW, Austin MN 55912 **Supply Cler St. Paul's Winona Chr Ch 2010-** B Bayshore NY 1948 d Robert & Arnella. BA Pur 1972; MS Pur 1973; BS U of Kentucky 1979; MS Idaho St U 1985; PhD U of Kentucky 1988; MDiv GTS 2010. D 7/23/2009 Bp James Louis Jelinek. m 7/18/2000 Johanna Rose Leuchter c 2. Dio Olympia Seattle 2012-2016; P Chr Ch Austin MN 2011; P Calv Ch Rochester MN 2010-2011. ACPE (ACPE) 2010; Assn of Profsnl Chapl 2010; Beatitudes Soc 2008; Soc for Anthropology & Rel 1993; Soc for Applied Anthropology 1982; Sprtl Dir Intl 2005. cl GTS 2010.

CORRIGAN, Gertrude Lane (NMich) 809 Michael St, Kingsford MI 49802 **Died 10/29/2015** B 1927 D 2/29/2004 Bp James Arthur Kelsey.

CORRIGAN, Michael (Mass) Northfield Mount Hermon School, 1 Lamplighter Way #4702, Mt. Hermon MA 01354 **Chapl Northfield Mt. Hermon Sch Mt. Hermon MA 2005-** B Baltimore MD 1945 s Daniel & Elizabeth. BA Col 1970; MDiv EDS 1973. D 6/9/1973 Bp Paul Moore Jr P 12/9/1973 Bp Daniel Corrigan. c 4. R Ch Of Our Sav Brookline MA 1988-2005; Dio Massachusetts Boston MA 1986-1987, Urban Mssn Com 1986-1987, 1979-1983; R S Jn's Epis Ch Westwood MA 1983-1988; Chapl Bos Boston MA 1979-1983; R Ch Of The Gd Shpd Granite Spgs NY 1975-1979; Cur The Ch Of The H Sprt Lake Forest IL 1973-1975. ESMHE.

CORRIGAN, Michael Edward (Los) 1500 State St, Santa Barbara CA 93101 B Northfield MN 1955 s Robert & Mary. BA The Evergreen St Coll 1977; MBA U of Washington 1978; MDiv CDSP 2015. D 6/6/2015 Bp Mary Douglas Glasspool P 1/16/2016 Bp Joseph Jon Bruno. m 7/6/2015 Tine Sloan c 5.

CORRY, Lisa Marie (Ark) **Trin Cathd Little Rock AR 2017-** D 6/15/2017 Bp Larry Benfield.

CORRY, Richard Stillwell (Va) 214 E King St, Quincy FL 32351 **Ret 1989-** B Quincy FL 1919 s Arthur & Constance. BA U So 1941; MDiv Sewanee: The U So, TS 1944; MS Bos 1958. D 12/21/1943 P 11/1/1944 Bp Frank A Juhan. c 3. R Gr Ch Millers Tavern VA 1974-1988; R S Paul's Epis Ch Millers Tavern VA 1974-1988; Asst Truro Epis Ch Fairfax VA 1966-1973; 1962-1966; M-in-c Ch Of Our Sav Arlington MA 1960-1962; Chapl Crittenton-Hastings Maternity Hm 1953-1960; Ch Of The Gd Shpd Watertown MA 1950-1953; R Ch of the Gd Shpd Boston MA 1950-1953; Vic S Mary's Ch E Providence RI 1949-1950; Vic S Mary's Epis Ch Honolulu HI 1948-1949; Asst Ch Of The Gd Shpd Jacksonville FL 1944-1947; Vic S Steph's Jacksonville FL 1944-1947.

CORSELLO, Dana Colley (Cal) 1755 Clay St, San Francisco CA 94109 **S Lk's Ch San Francisco CA 2009-** B Midland TX 1963 d Jack & Reba. BA U of Missouri 1985; MDiv GTS 1999. D 6/5/1999 P 12/1/1999 Bp C Wallis Ohl. m 6/26/1999 Andrew K Corsello c 2. St Jas Ch Richmond VA 2001-2009; S Mary's-In-Tuxedo Tuxedo Pk NY 1999-2001; Intern / Consult Epis Ch Cntr New York NY 1997-1998.

CORT, Aubrey Ebenezer (SwFla) 2507 Del Prado Blvd S, Cape Coral FL 33904 **TLC-Mnstrs Ch Of The Epiph Cape Coral FL 2009-, TLC-Mnstrs 2009-** B 1941 s Charles & Hilda. Cert Adel 1981; Cert Mercer TS 1997. D 10/10/2009 Bp Dabney Tyler Smith. m 8/26/1967 Jean Cort c 2. TLC-Mnstrs St.Jn's Epis Ch . St.Jas City Pine Is. FL 2009-2000.

CORTINAS, Angela M (SeFla) 333 Tarpon Dr, Fort Lauderdale FL 33301 **Yth Dir S Greg's Ch Boca Raton FL 2012-** B Coral Gables, FL 1970 d Enrique & Teodora. BA Florida Intl U 1992; MA U of Memphis 1995; MDiv Epis TS of the SW 2010. D 12/18/2009 Bp Leo Frade P 7/10/2010 Bp Calvin Onderdonk Schofield Jr. m 7/27/2017 Phelan J Holmes c 2. Asst P All SS Prot Epis Ch Ft Lauderdale FL 2010-2012. angelacortinas@gmail.com

CORTRIGHT, Amy Ethel Marie Chambers (Mo) Christ Church Cathedral, 1210 Locust Street, St. Louis MO 63103 **S Jn's Ch S Louis MO 2016-** B Washington DC 1976 MDiv GTS 2004. D 3/13/2004 P 9/18/2004 Bp Mark Sean Sisk. m 9/23/2005 Joseph Michael Cortright Chambers c 2. Vic Chr Ch Cathd S Louis MO 2010-2016; Assoc Calv Ch Columbia MO 2006-2010; Asst Ch Of The Incarn New York NY 2004-2006. amy@towergrovechurch.org

COSAND, Dale Wayne (CFla) Box 228, Radio City Station, New York NY 10101 **Died 9/7/2015** B Saint Charles IA 1922 s Floyd & Vava. BA U of Nthrn Iowa 1942; BD SWTS 1945; MS CUNY 1962; PhD Col 1964. D 11/30/1945 P 10/4/1946 Bp Elwood L Haines. Ret 1991-2015; Ass't Headmaster Kew-For- est Sch Forest Hills NY 1981-1991; Asst S Paul's Ch-In-The-Vill Brooklyn NY 1971-1989; Serv Chr Ch Eliz NJ 1965-1968; S Eliz's Ch Eliz NJ 1965-1968; Dir of Gdnc Rhodes Sch New York NY 1960-1980; Serv S Matt's Ch Woodhaven NY 1959-1971; Serv Ch Of S Alb The Mtyr S Albans NY 1956-1959; Gr Epis Ch Inc Port Orange FL 1950-1954; R S Paul's Epis Ch New Smyrna Bch FL 1950-1954; Assoc R Ch Of The H Comf Kenilworth IL 1948-1950; Vic S Steph's Ch Spencer IA 1945-1948.

COSBY, Arlinda W (Cal) 36458 Shelley Ct, Newark CA 94560 B Oakland CA 1942 d Richard & Marjorie. BA San Jose St U 1963; MA San Jose St U 1973; MDiv CDSP 1979. D 6/30/1979 Bp Chauncie Kilmer Myers. c 2. D H Cross Epis Ch Castro Vlly CA 1989-2008; D S Jas Ch Fremont CA 1984-2007, D 1979-1983; Chapl An Epis Mnstry to Convalescent Hospitals (Aemch) Fremont CA 1981-2007; Chapl Epis Mnstry To Convalescent Hospitals 1981-2007. Associated Parishes; NAAD. S Steph'S Awd Naad 1999.

COSENTINO, Eric Fritz (NY) 719 Hudson Ave, Peekskill NY 10566 B Queens NY 1956 s Jerry & Helga. BA CUNY 1979; MDiv GTS 1984. D 6/9/1984 Bp James Stuart Wetmore P 12/16/1984 Bp Walter Decoster Dennis Jr. m 6/28/1980 Melinda Cosentino c 4. R Ch Of The Div Love Montrose NY 1987-2014; Cur S Eliz's Ch Ridgewood NJ 1984-1987.

COSMAN, Sandra Lee (Ct) 220 Prospect St, Torrington CT 06790 **S Jn's Ch Pine Meadow CT 2015-; R Dio Connecticut Meriden CT 2014-** B Manchester CT 1963 d Gerald & Shirley. MDiv EDS 2007. D 6/14/2008 Bp Andrew Donnan Smith P 1/31/2009 Bp Laura Ahrens. c 1. S Jn's Ch E Windsor CT 2012-2014; Grtr Hartford Reg Mnstry E Hartford CT 2010-2012; Cur Trin Ch Torrington CT 2008-2010; S Jn's Epis Ch Vernon Rock Vernon Rockville CT 1990-1994.

COSSLETT, Ashley Cosslett (WNC) 449 Crowfields Dr, Asheville NC 28803 B Hitchin UK 1952 d Kenneth & Margot. Bard Coll 1972; U of Paris-Sorbonne FR 1973; BA U of San Francisco 1982; MDiv Ya Berk 1991. D 6/8/1991 Bp John Shelby Spong P 12/14/1991 Bp Jack Marston Mckelvey. Assoc S Paul's By-The-Sea Epis Ch Jaxville Bch FL 2000-2001; R All SS' Epis Ch Glen Rock NJ 1993-1999; P-in-c S Eliz's Ch Ridgewood NJ 1991-1993; Ecum Off Dio Newark Newark NJ 1991-1999.

COSTA, Steven James (Haw) St Timothy's Episcopal Church, 98-939 Moanalua Rd, Aiea HI 96701 B Honolulu HI 1952 s Charles & Jetta. D 10/25/2013 Bp Robert Leroy Fitzpatrick. m 10/11/2008 Rae M Costa c 2.

COSTAS, Catherine Stephenson (Cal) 905 W Middlefield Rd Apt 946, Mountain View CA 94043 **Assn for Epis Deacons Providence RI 2016-; OSSCR Prog The CPG New York NY 2016-, ECD Prog 2010-2016; D Chr Ch Sausalito CA 2012-** B Ames IA 1965 d James & Naomi. BMus U of Iowa 1987; US Army Intrnshp 1989; BTS Sch for Deacons 2003. D 12/4/2004 Bp William Edwin Swing. Supply D Dio California San Francisco CA 2007-2012, Deacons' Exec Coun 2007-2009; Assoc D in Res S Ptr's Epis Ch Redwood City CA 2007-2012; Vol Chapl Sojourn Chapl SF Gnrl Hosp San Francisco 2007-2008; D Gd Shpd Epis Ch Belmont CA 2004-2007. Assn for Epis Deacons (NAAD) 2000. ccostas@cpg.org

COSTAS, J Kathryn (Ind) 838 Ridgewood Dr NE, Lenoir NC 28645 **Int S Jas Epis Ch Lenoir NC 2015-** B Gary IN 1952 d William & Angie. MDiv Ya Berk 1991; MSW Bos 1996. D 5/6/2006 P 2/25/2007 Bp Porter Taylor. c 2. Int S Mary Anne's Epis Ch No E MD 2013-2015; P-in-c S Steph's Epis Ch New Harmony IN 2011-2013; R S Mk's Epis Ch Aberdeen SD 2007-2011. revkat@mac.com

COSTELLO, Elizabeth R (Colo) St John's Cathedral, 1350 Washington St, Denver CO 80203 B Virginia Beach VA 1984 d Thomas & Donna. MDiv Duke DS 2009; STM Yale DS 2013. D 6/29/2013 Bp Michael B Curry P 6/14/2014 Bp Robert John O'Neill. m 7/15/2006 Joseph Geoffrey Wolyniak c 1. Chr Ch Ridgewood NJ 2016-2017; Cur S Jn's Cathd Denver CO 2013-2016; Ch Of The H Comf Burlington NC 2010-2012.

COSTIN, Richard Banks (CFla) 1601 Alafaya Trl, Oviedo FL 32765 **D Ch Of The Gd Shpd Maitland FL 2014-** B Asheville NC 1941 s Alpheus & Alice. BA U of Washington 1967; MS Pace U 1981. D 12/11/2010 Bp John Wadsworth Howe. m 10/14/1995 Sandra Costin c 3. D Ch of the Incarn Oviedo FL 2011-2014.

COTTER, Barry Lynn (SO) 1864 Sherman Ave Apt 5SE, Evanston IL 60201 B Los Angeles CA 1943 s Lawrence & Frankie. BA USC 1964; PhD Indiana U 1970; MDiv SWTS 1986. D 6/28/1986 Bp James Russell Moodey P 4/1/1987 Bp Duncan Montgomery Gray Jr. m 6/10/1967 Joan Cotter c 1. Area Mssnr E Cntrl Ohio Area Mnstry Bridgeport OH 2000-2006; S Jn's Epis Ch Cambridge OH 2000-2006; area Mssnr, eco cluster S Paul's Ch Martins Ferry OH 2000-2006; Trin Ch Bellaire OH 2000-2006; R S Ptr's By The Lake Brandon MS 1992-2000; R S Thos Epis Ch Diamondhead MS 1989-1991; R S Thos' Bay S Louis MS 1989-1991; Cur S Jn's Epis Ch Ocean Sprg MS 1986-1989. co-Auth, "Pith, Heart, and Nerve: Truman M. Smith: Horticulture as the Way Back," *Ramsey Cnty Hist*, Ramsey Cnty Hist Soc, 2009; co-Auth, "Pith, Heart, and Nerve: Truman M. Smith: From Banker to Mrkt Gardener," *Ramsey Cnty Hist*, Ramsey Cnty Hist Soc, 2008.

COTTRELL, Jan M. (Lex) 1445 Copperfield Court, Lexington KY 40514 B Covington KY 1955 d Harry & Joan. BA U of Kentucky 1977; MA U of Louisville 1981; MDiv Lexington TS 1991; DMin Sewanee: The U So, TS 2000. D 6/9/1991 P 1/1/1992 Bp Don Adger Wimberly. m 5/15/2010 Kenneth Wayne Cottrell c 2. R Ch Of The Resurr Nicholasville KY 1993-2014; Ch S Mich The Archangel Lexington KY 1991-1993; Sem Asst S Jn's Ch Versailles KY 1990-1991. jancottrell.cfr@gmail.com

COTTRILL, C David (SO) 3724 Mengel Dr, Kettering OH 45429 **Affiliate S Geo's Epis Ch Dayton OH 2010-** B Columbus OH 1941 s Charles & Ruby. Methodist TS in Ohio 1963; BS OH SU 1963; MDiv Bex Sem 1966; DMin Untd TS Dayton OH 1994. D 6/25/1966 Bp Roger W Blanchard P 12/17/1966 Bp William S Thomas. m 12/16/1962 Martha J Cottrill c 2. Affiliate S Fran Epis Ch Springboro OH 2007-2010; Chapl Epis Ret Serv Cincinnati OH 1996-2007; Asst R Chr Epis Ch Dayton OH 1992-1996; Chapl, USAF Dio Arizona Phoenix AZ 1973-1993; Chapl, USAF Off Of Bsh For ArmdF New York NY 1973-1993; R S Andr's Ch Glendale AZ 1971-1973; Asst R All SS Ch Cincinnati OH 1967-1971; Cur S Steph's Epis Ch Mckeesport PA 1966-1967; Trst Dio Sthrn Ohio Cincinnati OH 1993-1996. Auth, "A Liturg for Celebration of Ret as Redirection," *Untd TS*, 1994. BSA 1948; Epis Hosp & Chapl Assn 1996-2007; Interfaith Com on Scouting 1988; Miami Vlly Epis Russian Ntwk 2008; NOEL 1980; SO Affirmative Aging Cmsn 1989-2000. Hon Cn Dio Los Angeles 2013; St. Geo Awd, BSA Epis Ch 1984; Meritorious Serv Medal w 5 Oak Leaf Clusters USAF 1981; Commendation Medal w Oak Leaf Cluster USAF 1976.

COUDRIET, Alan P (NwPa) 10 Woodside Ave, Oil City PA 16301 **Vic Gr Epis Ch Ridgway PA 2015-, Int 2014-2015; Disciplinary Bd Dio NW Pennsylvania Erie PA 2011-, Mem, Bp Search Com, 2007 - 2008 2007-2011, Mem, Dioc Coun, 2005 - 2008 2005-2011, Alt to GC, 3x's 2004-2012** B Clearfield PA 1954 s Carl & Helen. D. Min. Trin Luth Sem; D. Min. Trinty Luth Sem, Columbus, Ohio; BA Clarion U of Pennsylvania 1976; MDiv Nash 1995. D 3/22/1995 P 10/4/1995 Bp William Charles Wantland. m 10/7/1989 Karen Schmidt. P-in-c Emm Ch Corry PA 2011-2013; Int Ch Of Our Sav Dubois PA 2010-2011; Int Trin Memi Ch Warren PA 2009-2010; R Chr Epis Ch Oil City PA 2003-2008; Cluster S Lk's Ch Springbrook WI 2002-2003; Epis Acad Admin Dio of Eau Claire 1999-2003; Cluster S Alb's Ch Spooner WI 1995-2003; Cluster S Steph's Shell Lake WI 1995-2000; Dep to GC, 2003 Dio Eau Claire Eau Claire WI 2001-2003, Admin & Fac, Epis Acad, 2000 - 2003 2000-2003, Exam Chapl, 2000 - 2003 2000-2003, Cler Rep to Dom Mssy Partnership 1999-2003, Pres, Stndg Com, 1999 - 2001 1999-2001, VP of Dio, 1999 1998-1999, Chapl/Instr, Sum Yth Camps, 1997 - 2002 1997-2003, Chair, Cmte on New & Existing Congregations, 1996 - 2000 1996-2001, Mem, Exec Coun, 1995 - 2001 1995-2001. fralancoudriet@gmail.com

COUFAL, M(ary) Lorraine (Ind) 3819 Green Arbor Way #812, Indianapolis IN 46220 **S Ptr's Ch Lebanon IN 2009-; Dio Indianapolis Indianapolis IN 2005-; Chapl Indiana U Hosp 1998-** B Atkinson NE 1938 s Edward & Helen. BA Regis U 1964; MA Webster U 1973; MA Seattle U 1980; MDiv Cntrl Bapt TS 1985; DMin GTF 1989; U So 1991. D 11/8/1992 P 6/23/1993 Bp Craig Barry Anderson. S Alb's Ch Indianapolis IN 2004-2005; Intern S Tim's Ch Indianapolis IN 2001-2002; Int S Lk's Epis Ch Shelbyville IN 2000-2003; Assoc Calv Cathd Sioux Falls SD 1992-1998; Chapl Sioux Vlly Hosp Sioux Falls SD 1983-1998. Auth of article, ""God's Messages,"" *GTF Fellows YearBook*, GTF, 1989. AEHC 1993; Assn of Profsnl Chapl - Cert Chapl 1982; Int Mnstry Ntwk 2001; Sprtl Dir of Cntrl Indiana Ntwk 2007. Friend of Nrsng Awd Sioux Vlly Hosp 1994.

COUGHLIN, Christopher Anthony (O) 7640 Glenwood Ave, Boardman OH 44512 **S Jn's Epis Ch Cuyahoga Fls OH 2013-** B Youngstown OH 1977 s John & Julie. BA The Coll of Wooster 1999; SWTS 2008; MDiv Bex Sem 2010. D 6/5/2010 Bp Mark Hollingsworth Jr P 4/16/2011 Bp Arthur Williams Jr. m 10/8/2005 Lisa M Coughlin c 1. S Jn's Epis Ch Bowling Green OH 2011-2013; Chr Epis Ch Warren OH 2011; Assoc R S Jas Epis Ch Boardman OH 2010-2011. fatherzeke@gmail.com

COUGHLIN, Clark Fay (Ct) 400 Seabury Dr., Apt. 2126, Bloomfield CT 06002 B Holyoke MA 1932 s Patrick & Edna. AS U of New Haven 1952; BS Quinnipiac U 1954; EDS 1980; MDiv Gordon-Conwell TS 1980. D 10/17/1980 Bp Wilbur Emory Hogg Jr P 6/18/1981 Bp Arthur Edward Walmsley. m 10/4/1969 Joy Coughlin. R S Jas' Epis Ch Winsted CT 1983-2000; Asst R Chr Ch Par Epis Watertown CT 1980-1983; Field Educ S Ptr's Ch Beverly MA 1978-1980; Yth, Mus, Tchg S Paul's Ch Brookfield CT 1974-1977. Phi Theta Kappa 1953. Bachelor of Sci Quinnipiac Coll 1954.

COULSON, Mary Lynn (WMo) 16275 Pomerado Rd, Poway CA 92064 **Cur S Barth's Epis Ch Poway CA 2016-** B Kansas City MO 1989 d Richard & Alison. BA St. Olaf Coll 2011; MDiv VTS 2016. D 3/17/2016 P 9/24/2016 Bp Martin Scott Field. mlcoulson@stbartschurch.org

COULTAS OJN, Amy Carol Real (Ky) 612 Myrte St, Louisville KY 40208 **Int Dn Chr Ch Cathd Louisville KY 2013-, Cn Mssnr 2009-2013; Dio Kentucky Louisville KY 2013-, Trst & Coun 2013-, COM 2007-2011; Presb-Epis Dialog Ecusa / Mssn Personl New York NY 2010-; Joint Nomin Com for the Election of a PBp Prov IV Jackson MS 2009-** B Louisville KY 1975 d Paul & Hollis. BFA U of Louisville 1999; MDiv GTS 2006. D 2/24/2006 P 9/9/2006 Bp Ted Gulick Jr. m 9/25/1999 Kevin Michael Coultas. Campus Min Epis Campus Mnstry Louisville KY 2006-2013; S Jas Ch Shelbyville KY 2006-2009. Soc of Cath Priests 2010. amy@episcopalky.org

COULTER, Clayton Roy (Ore) 7430 Sw Pineridge Ct, Portland OR 97225 B Hartney MT CA 1931 s Thomas & Mabel. BA Wstrn Washington U 1952; MDiv SWTS 1955; BD SWTS 1955. D 6/29/1955 P 6/29/1956 Bp Stephen F Bayne Jr. m 12/26/1965 Sharon Towne Coulter c 3. R Dio Oregon Portland OR 2000-2001, Dn 1993-2000; Dn Epis Par Of S Jn The Bapt Portland OR 1981-2000; R S Paul's Ch Seattle WA 1968-1981; Vic Ch Of The Redeem Kenmore WA 1957-1968; Cur Trin Par Seattle WA 1955-1957. Sis Of S Jn The Bapt 1982; SSJE 1953.

COULTER, Elizabeth (Ia) 3148 Dubuque St. NE, Iowa City IA 52240 **P in Res New Song Epis Ch Coralville IA 2005-** B Champaign IL 1942 d Lyle & Elizabeth. BA U of Iowa 1975; MSW U of Iowa 1976; MDiv SWTS 1993. D 9/21/1993 P 4/18/1994 Bp Chris Christopher Epting. m 12/16/1961 Charles Roy Coulter c 1. P New Song Epis Ch Coralville IA 2001-2004; Assoc S Andr's Epis Ch Waverly IA 2001; P in Res St. Andrews Episocpal Ch Waverly IA 2001; Assoc Dio Iowa Des Moines IA 1994-2000; D Trin Ch Muscatine IA 1993-1994.

COULTER, Sherry Lynn (At) 681 Holt Rd Ne, Marietta GA 30068 B Memphis TN 1961 d James & Ellen. AA Shelby St Cmnty Coll 1983; BA U of Memphis 1988; MDiv Sewanee: The U So, TS 2000. D 12/16/2000 Bp James Malone Coleman. S Cathr's Epis Ch Marietta GA 2002-2007; Dio W Tennessee Memphis 2000-2002; S Mary's Cathd Memphis TN 2000-2002.

✠ COUNCELL, The Rt Rev George Edward (NJ) Diocese of New Jersey, 808 West State Street, Trenton NJ 08618 **Chapl Doane Acad Burlington NJ 2014-** B Detroit MI 1949 s Graham & Jeannie. BA U CA 1971; MDiv EDS 1975; DD GTS 2010. D 6/21/1975 P 12/21/1975 Bp Robert Claflin Rusack Con 10/18/2003 for NJ. m 1/10/1971 Ruth Councell c 2. Bp of New Jersey Dio New Jersey Trenton NJ 2003-2014; R The Ch Of The H Sprt Lake Forest IL 1995-2003; Cn to Ordnry Dio Wstrn Massachusetts Springfield 1986-1995; R S Geo's Ch Riverside CA 1977-1985; Chapl U CA-Riverside 1977-1985; Vic Gr Ch Colton CA 1975-1977; Vic S Lk's Mssn Fontana CA 1975-1977. Phi Beta Kappa. gcouncell@aol.com

COUNSELMAN, Robert Lee (NJ) 119 S Hondo St, P O Box 1478, Sabinal TX 78881 B Ottawa KS 1948 s George & Corrine. BA U of New Mex 1974; MDiv GTS 1976. D 8/6/1976 P 2/15/1977 Bp Richard Mitchell Trelease Jr. m 6/5/1970 Sharon Counselman c 2. R Trin Ch Woodbridge NJ 1981-2014; Cur Chr Ch Middletown NJ 1976-1980. bob.counselman@outlook.com

COUNTRYMAN, L(Ouis) William (Cal) 5805 Keith Avenue, Oakland CA 94618 **Assoc The Epis Ch Of The Gd Shpd Berkeley CA 1985-** B Oklahoma City OK 1941 s Louis & Bera. BA U Chi 1962; STB GTS 1965; Hebr Un Coll 1968; MA U Chi 1974; PhD U Chi 1977. D 6/20/1965 Bp Chilton R Powell P 12/29/1965 Bp Frederick Warren Putnam. m 10/27/2008 John David Vieira c 1. Sherman E. Johnson Prof Emer in Biblic Stds CDSP Berkeley CA 1983-2007; Asst Prof. NT TCU Ft Worth TX 1979-1983; Chapl SW MO Ecum Cntr Springfield MO 1977-1979; Asst Prof SW MO St U Srpingfield MO 1976-1979; 1972-1976; R S Paul's Epis Ch Logan OH 1968-1972; Asst St Phil's Epis Ch Ardmore OK 1965-1967. Auth, "The Psalms," Morehouse, 2013; Auth, "Calling on the Sprt in Unsettling Times," Morehouse, 2012; Auth, "Lovesongs and Reproaches," Morehouse, 2010; Auth, "Dirt, Greed & Sex," Fortress Press, 2007; Auth, "Love, Human and Div," Morehouse, 2005; Ed, "Run, Shepherds, Run," Morehouse, 2005; Auth, "Interpreting the Truth," Trin Press Intl , 2003; Auth, "Gifted by Otherness," Morehouse, 2001; Auth, "The Poetic Imagination," Orbis, 2000; Auth, "Living on the Border of the H," Morehouse Pub, 1999; Auth, "Forgiven & Forgiven," Morehouse Pub, 1998; Auth, "The Mystical Way in the Fourth Gospel," Trin Press Intl , 1994; Auth, "Gd News of Jesus," Trin Press Intl , 1993. D.D. (hon.) CDSP 2012.

COUPER, David Courtland (Mil) 5282 County Road K, Blue Mounds WI 53517 **Supply Vic St Peters Epis Ch No Lake WI 2009-** B Little Falls MN 1938 s John & Elsa. BA U MN 1968; MA U MN 1970; CAS Nash 1994; MA Edgewood Coll 2005. D 12/16/1994 P 6/27/1995 Bp Roger John White. m 12/29/1981 Sabine Lobitz c 3. Vic S Ptr's Ch Northlake WI 2005-2008; P-in-c S Jn The Bapt Portage WI 1996-2004. Auth, "Arrested Dvlpmt: One man's Mssn to improve our nation's police," Dog Ear Pub, 2012; Auth, "Forgiveness In The Cmnty," *Exploring Forgiveness*, U of Wisconsin Press, 1998; Auth, "Quality Policing: The Madison Experience," PERF, Washington DC, 1992; Auth, "How to Rate Your Loc Police," PERF, Washington DC, 1983.

COUPLAND, Geoffrey D (Va) 5110 Park Ave., Richmond VA 23226 B Ottawa CA 1954 s James & Eileen. BA Carleton U 1978; MDiv U Tor CA 1981. Trans 6/1/1996 Bp David Standish Ball. m 12/20/2008 Patricia C Coupland c 1. S Barth's Ch No Augusta SC 2015-2017; S Paul's Ch Abbeville LA 2014-2015; R Ch Of The H Comf Richmond VA 2009-2013; Int All SS Ch S Louis MO 2007-2009; Int S Lk's Ch Powhatan VA 2006-2007; Brooke-Hancock Cluster Weirton WV 2005-2006; R S Mary's Epis Ch Bonita Sprg FL 2002-2004;

R S Jn's Ch Ogdensburg NY 1996-2002; Serv Angl Ch Of Can 1981-1996. interimrector@saintbart.org

COURTNEY, Michael David (Ark) 235 Caroline Acres Road, Hot Springs AR 71913 **P-in-c Ch Of The Gd Shpd Little Rock AR 2010-** B Hawthorne CA 1958 s Alvin & Frances. AA SUNY; BS Sthrn California U of Hlth Sciences 1978; DC Sthrn California U of Hlth Sciences 1981; STD Sem of the Amer Ch of the E San Jose 1995; Cert in Theol and Mnstry PrTS 2014; Cert in Theol and Mnstry PrTS 2014. Rec 7/18/2006 as Priest Bp Larry Maze. m 4/28/1990 Johnna Courtney c 3. Emm Ch Lake Vill AR 2006-2009; Vic S Paul's Ch Mc Gehee AR 2006-2009. SocMary 2014.

COURTNEY, Peter (At) 339 Reeds Landing, 807 Wilbraham Rd, Springfield MA 01109 **Int Cathd Ch of All SS St Thos VI 2012-; Ret 2005-** B Boston MA 1943 s Paul & Julia. BA Hobart and Wm Smith Colleges 1965; STB Ya Berk 1968; Nash 1976. D 6/22/1968 P 12/28/1968 Bp George West Barrett. m 11/28/1986 Deborah T Perry c 2. Int S Alb's Ch Elberton GA 2012; Int S Alb's Ch Monroe GA 2012; Int S Aug Of Cbury Ch Augusta GA 2010; Int S Mk's Epis Ch E Longmeadow MA 2008-2009; Int S Dav's Ch Baltimore MD 2007-2008; Int Chr Ch Las Vegas NV 2006-2007; Int S Teresa Acworth GA 2005-2006; R Emm Epis Ch Athens GA 2000-2005; Dn S Andr's Cathd Honolulu HI 1996-2000; R Emm Ch Virginia Bch VA 1984-1996; R Gr Epis Ch Elmira NY 1977-1984; R S Ptr's Epis Ch Henrietta NY 1972-1977; R S Paul's Ch Angelica NY 1970-1972; S Phil's Ch Belmont NY 1970-1972; Asst Ch Of The Incarn Penfield NY 1968-1970.

COURTNEY II, Robert Wickliff (La) 1025 Beverly Garden Drive, New Orleans LA 70002 **P-in-c S Paul's Ch New Orleans LA 2014-, P-in-c 2012-2014** B Crowley LA 1972 s Robert & Linda. BS U of Phoenix 2006; MDiv Sewanee: The U So, TS 2009. D 12/27/2008 P 6/27/2009 Bp Charles Edward Jenkins III. m 5/27/2000 Catherine Davis Courtney c 2. R Trin Epis Ch Morgan City LA 2009-2012; Par Admin Chr Ch Cathd New Orleans LA 2003-2006. rcourtney@stpauls-lakeview.org

COURTNEY JR, Robin Spencer (Tenn) 7872 Harpeth View Dr, Nashville TN 37221 **Chapl & Bereavement Dir Gateway Hospice 2011-; P-in-c S Jas The Less Madison TN 2008-** B Columbia TN 1961 s Robin & Lucille. BA Van 1984; MDiv VTS 1996. D 6/16/1996 P 4/6/1997 Bp Bertram Nelson Herlong. P Gr Epis Ch Sprg Hill TN 2007; Assoc S Mk's Ch Antioch TN 2007; Chapl & Bereavement Dir Aseracare Hospice 2006-2008; CRA/Low Income Hsng Off Capital Bank & Trust Co 2003-2005; Int Dio Tennessee Nashville TN 2003; Field Supvsr U So TS 1998-2003; R S Bede's Epis Ch Manchester TN 1996-2003.

COURTRIGHT, Alice Hodgkins (NH) B New York City NY 1988 d Robin & Margaret. BA Ya 2011; MDiv Sewanee TS 2014; MDiv Sewanee: The U So, TS 2014. D 10/22/2013 Bp George Edward Councell P 10/2/2014 Bp William H Stokes. m 8/11/2012 Andrew Michael Courtright.

COUVILLION, Brian Neff (Chi) 4370 Woodland Ave, Western Springs IL 60558 B Alexandria LA 1945 s Arthur & Eugenia. BS Louisiana Tech U 1968; MDiv Epis TS of the SW 1987. D 6/13/1987 P 12/12/1987 Bp Willis Ryan Henton. m 7/14/1967 Judith Ebright Couvillion c 3. R All SS Ch Wstrn Sprgs IL 2002-2013; R S Jas Ch Dundee IL 1997-2002; Asst R Gr Epis Ch Hinsdale IL 1990-1997; Assoc R S Paul's Epis Ch Shreveport LA 1988-1990; Cur Epis Ch Of The Gd Shpd Lake Chas LA 1987-1988.

COUZZOURT, Beverly Schmidt (NwT) 2516 4th Ave, Canyon TX 79015 B Roswell NM 1958 d William & Frances. BGS W Texas St U 1981; Cert Primary Montessori Certification 1992. D 9/30/2006 P 4/14/2007 Bp C Wallis Ohl. m 11/6/1982 James Edward Couzzourt c 2. Sacramental P Epis Ch Of S Geo Canyon TX 2011-2016. mob@suddenlink.net

COVENTRY, Donald Edgar (Spr) 246 Southmoreland Pl, Decatur IL 62521 **D St.Johns 2004-** B Shelbyville IL 1937 s Kenneth & Lelia. U IL 1975; AAS Rickland Cmnty Coll Decatur IL 1976; Other 2004; Springfield Sch for Mnstry 2004. D 6/29/2004 Bp Peter Hess Beckwith. m 7/8/1989 Delores Ann Moyer. Lieutenant Police Dept. Decatur IL 1969-2001.

COVER, Michael Benjamin (Dal) 616 Lincolnway E., Mishawaka IN 46544 **S Paul's Ch Mishawaka IN 2009-** B Boston MA 1982 s Robin & Janet. AB Harv 2004; MST Oxf GB 2005; MDiv Ya Berk 2008. D 6/6/2009 Bp James Monte Stanton P 2/13/2010 Bp Paul Emil Lambert. m 8/4/2007 Susanna Cover c 1. D Dio Nthrn Indiana So Bend IN 2009.

COVERSTON SSF, Harry Scott (ECR) 630 Roberta Ave, Orlando FL 32803 **Fran-Clare Cmnty Orlando 1998-** B West Palm Beach FL 1953 s Samuel & Marjorie. Living Sch for Action and Contemplation; AA Lake-Sumter Cmnty Coll 1973; BA U of Florida 1976; JD U of Florida 1981; MDiv CDSP 1995; PhD Florida St U 2000. D 12/21/1994 P 6/22/1995 Bp Richard Lester Shimpfky. m 8/13/2010 Andy Mobley. Asst Chapl Florida St U Tallahassee Tallahassee 1995-1997; Chapl California St U Hayward Hayward 1994-1995. "Conversation of Content," *Revs of Religous Resrch*, 2008; Auth (Chapt), "Evang Cartons, the Gd and the Bed," *Selling Jesus, Visual Culture and the Mnstry of Chrsnty*, Ed. Dominic Janes, 2008; Auth, "Revs: Deep in Our Hearts," *Turning Wheel*, 2001; Auth, "Sarah," *Living Ch*. Tertiary Ord, Soc of S

Fran 1990. Fulbright-Hays Schlr US Dept of Educ 2011; Bridges Awd Loudoun Interfaith Bridges 2009.

COVERT, Edward Martin (SwVa) Po Box 126, Fort Defiance VA 24437 **Ret 1999-** B Raleigh NC 1944 s Otis & Ruth. BA U NC 1966; MDiv VTS 1969. D 6/24/1969 P 6/29/1970 Bp Thomas Augustus Fraser Jr. m 6/26/1970 Nan Taylor Covert c 1. P-in-c Emm Ch Staunton VA 1999; R Chr Ch Martinsville VA 1980-1999; P-in-c S Steph's Epis Ch N Myrtle Bch SC 1974-1980; Asst S Mich's Epis Ch Charleston SC 1971-1974; Asst Ch Of The H Comf Burlington NC 1969-1971; Dep Gc Dio SW Virginia Roanoke VA 1991-1994, Chair Com 1984-1990. Auth, "Epis".

COVINGTON, John E (NY) 410 West 24th Street, Apartment 8K, New York NY 10011 **Pstr Gr Ch Bronx NY 2017-** B Charlotte NC 1946 s William & Winona. STM GTS; MDiv GTS; No U NC; BA Trin Hartford CT 1968. D 5/26/1973 P 11/24/1973 Bp George Alfred Taylor. Int Chr Ch Riverdale Bronx NY 2003-2004; Dio New York New York NY 2001-2003; Int Trin Ch Mt Vernon NY 2000-2003; Int S Ptr's Ch Bronx NY 1997-2001; R S Alb's Epis Ch Staten Island NY 1977-1997; Asst S Jn's Ch Larchmont NY 1975-1977; Cur Chr Ch S Ptr's Par Easton MD 1974-1975.

COWANS, William Marsden (ECR) 10101 Double R Blvd Apt B10, Reno NV 89521 **Died 11/3/2016** B Redlands CA 1931 s William & Agnes. BA San Diego St U 1958; MDiv CDSP 1961. D 6/25/1961 P 6/15/1962 Bp James Albert Pike. c 2. R S Thos Epis Ch Sunnyvale CA 1974-1994; P-in-c S Mk's Par Crockett CA 1963-1968; Cur S Mk's Epis Ch Palo Alto CA 1961-1963; COM Dio El Camino Real Salinas CA 1982-1994. billcowans@gmail.com

COWARDIN, Eustis Barber (ND) 510 E Lake County Rd, Jamestown ND 58401 B Philadelphia PA 1935 d William & Margaret. BA Wellesley Coll 1956; LPN No Dakota St Coll of Sci Wahpeton ND 1981. D 12/2/1995 P 6/25/1999 Bp Andrew Fairfield. m 6/23/1956 Lewis Cowardin c 4.

COWARDIN, Stephen Paul (SVa) 8525 Summit Acres Dr, Richmond VA 23235 B Richmond VA 1947 s John & Maude. HS S Jn Vianney Sem; BS Old Dominion U 1987; MDiv VTS 1992; DMin VTS 2007. D 6/7/1992 P 12/20/1992 Bp Frank Harris Vest Jr. m 9/11/1980 Susan Malligo c 2. R Ch Of The Redeem Midlothian VA 1992-2014.

COWART, Alan B (SwVa) 1021 New Hampshire Ave, Lynchburg VA 24502 **Gr Memi Ch Lynchburg VA 2017-** B Elizabeth NJ 1970 s John & Sheila. BA Georgia St U 2005; MDiv VTS 2015. D 12/20/2014 P 6/20/2015 Bp Robert Christopher Wright. m 7/11/2002 Lauren K Robertson. Gr Epis Ch Gainesville GA 2015-2017. alan@gracechurchgainesville.org

COWDEN, Matthew D (NI) 8385 Luce Ct, Springfield VA 22153 **S Mich And All Ang Ch So Bend IN 2009-** B Washington DC 1969 s Arthur & Marie. BFA Florida St U 1991; MFA U CA 1994; MDiv VTS 2006; MDiv VTS 2006. D 4/1/2006 P 11/1/2006 Bp Leo Frade. m 7/11/1992 Melissa T Cowden c 3. Assoc R Chr Ch Alexandria VA 2006-2009.

COWELL, Curtis Lyle (Kan) 2601 Sw College Ave, Topeka KS 66611 B Bluefield WV 1938 s Joseph & Theodosia. BS VPI 1960; MDiv VTS 1969. D 6/11/1969 P 6/1/1970 Bp Wilburn Camrock Campbell. m 6/24/1966 Elinor Kathryne Schadt c 1. Gr Cathd Topeka KS 1995-2000; The Wheeling Cluster Wheeling WV 1989-1995; R S Andr's Ch Oak Hill WV 1983-1989; The New River Epis Mnstry Pratt WV 1983-1989; Vic Gr Ch Welch WV 1978-1983; Vic S Lk's Epis Ch Welch WV 1978-1983; Vic S Mk's War WV 1978-1983; Vic S Barn Bridgeport WV 1976-1978; Dio W Virginia Charleston WV 1969-1976; Vic S Dav's Crosslanes WV 1969-1976.

COWELL, Frank Bourne (Nev) 7300 W Van Giesen St, West Richland WA 99353 **Asst S Mich's Epis Ch Yakima WA 2007-** B Los Angeles CA 1944 s Henry & Olive. AB California St U Long Bch 1966; MDiv VTS 1983. D 6/21/1983 P 1/20/1984 Bp Leigh Allen Wallace Jr. c 1. R S Paul's Epis Ch Elko NV 2001-2004; Vic Epis Ch On W Kaua'i Eleele HI 1994-2001; Rgnl Dn The Epis Ch in Hawaii Honolulu HI 1993-1995; S Jn's Ch Eleele HI 1992-1994; RurD H Trin Epis Ch Sunnyside WA 1987-1992; Vic S Jas Epis Ch Brewster WA 1985-1987; S Anne's Ch Omak WA 1983-1987; Ch Of The Trsfg Omak WA 1983-1985.

COWELL, Mark Andrew (WK) 501 W 5th St, Larned KS 67550 **Stndg Com, Pres Dio Wstrn Kansas Hutchinson KS 2009-, 2004-; SS Mary And Martha Of Bethany Larned KS 2004-** B Washington DC 1965 D 11/29/2003 P 6/12/2004 Bp James Marshall Adams Jr. m 11/27/1999 Julie Ann Cowell c 2.

COWPER, Judith Ann (Ct) 54 Dora Dr, Middletown CT 06457 B Cambridge MA 1942 d Harold & Dorothy. BA Carleton Coll 1964; MA U of Connecticut 1973; CAS Ya Berk 1992; MDiv Yale DS 1992. D 6/13/1992 Bp Arthur Edward Walmsley P 1/25/1993 Bp Jeffery William Rowthorn. m 9/13/1975 G Clive Cowper. R S Thos Epis Ch Morgantown PA 1999-2002; Int All SS Epis Ch Meriden CT 1999; Int Gr Epis Ch Trumbull CT 1997-1999; P-in-c Ch Of The H Adv Clinton CT 1992-1997. Ord of S Lk, Chapl 1993. judithcowper@sbcglobal.net

COWPERTHWAITE, Robert W (Fla) 7001 Charles St., St. Augustine FL 32080 B New Brunswick, NJ 1948 s William & June. BA W&L 1970; MDiv VTS 1973. D 6/13/1973 P 5/8/1974 Bp Edward Hamilton West. m 9/28/1974 Susan L Cowperthwaite c 2. R S Paul's Ch Franklin TN 1988-2014; Pstr Off Trin Par

191

New York NY 1981-1988; Assoc San Jose Epis Ch Jacksonville FL 1976-1981; Dio Florida Jacksonville 1973-1976; S Cathr's Ch Jacksonville FL 1973-1976; Vic S Jas Ch Macclenny FL 1973-1976.

COX, Amy Eleanor (WMo) St. Francis of Assisi in the Pines, 17890 Metcalf Ave, Overland Park KS 66085 B San Luis Obispo CA 1975 d James & Loretta. BA California Polytechnic St U; MDiv PrTS 2000. D 4/28/2013 P 11/1/2013 Bp Martin Scott Field. m 3/23/2000 David Cox c 2. S Fran Of Assisi Stilwell KS 2015-2016.

COX, Anne Elizabeth (Mich) 8 Ridge Rd, Tenants Harbor ME 04860 **Non-par Hedgerow 1997-** B Downey CA 1960 d Donald & Judith. BEDA No Carolina St U 1981; MLa U MI 1984; MDiv UTS 1987. D 6/27/1987 Bp H Coleman Mcgehee Jr P 3/12/1988 Bp Jose Agustin Gonzalez. m 7/28/2013 Julie Ann Wortman. Econ Justice Cmsn Dio Michigan Detroit MI 1992-1997, Asst Bp Serv Cmsn 1992-1994; R Nativ Epis Ch Bloomfield Township MI 1991-1997; Bible T/F Dio Newark Newark NJ 1989-1991, Cntr For Food Action 1988-1991; Asst R S Paul's Ch Englewood NJ 1987-1991.

COX IV, Brian (Los) 871 Serenidad Pl, Goleta CA 93117 **Dir PACIS Proj in Faith-Based Diplomacy Straus Inst 2008-; Sr VP Intl Cntr for Rel and Diplomacy Wash. DC 1999-; R Chr The King Epis Ch Santa Barbara CA 1992-; Dio Los Angeles Los Angeles CA 2001-** B Chicago IL 1950 s Milton & Mary. BS USC 1972; MDiv EDS 1975; Doctor of Mnstry Prog Fuller TS 1985; MDR Pepperdine U 2000; Harv Kennedy Sch of Gov't 2002. D 6/21/1975 P 12/21/1975 Bp Robert Claflin Rusack. m 6/16/1973 Ann Cox c 2. Assoc R Ch Of The Apos Fairfax VA 1986-1992; Assoc R St Jas the Great Epis Ch Newport Bch CA 1977-1986; Vic S Agnes Mssn Banning CA 1975-1977; R S Steph's Par Beaumont CA 1975-1977. Auth, "Faith-Based Recon," *A Rel Framework for Peace Making and Conflict Resolution*, 2011; Auth, "Recon Basic Seminar," *Abrahamic Ed*, 2008; Auth, "Recon Basic Seminar," *Gandhian Ed*, 2008; Auth, "Faith-Based Recon," *A Moral Vision that Transforms People and Soc*, 2007. Intl Fndt 1986-2000; Mem of the Ara Pacis Initiative of Rome 2010. Peace Maker of the Year Awd Natl Assn of Conflict Resolution 2011; Mahatma Gandhi Peace Prize Awd Com 2007; Melvin Jones Fell Lions Clubs Intl 2007; Illinois St Schlrshp St of Illinois 1962. briancox@cox.net

COX, Catherine Susanna (WMo) 365 E 372nd Rd, Dunnegan MO 65640 **Retreat Dir Rivendell Cmnty Dunnegan MO 2003-; Vic S Alb's In The Ozarks Ch Bolivar MO 2003-** B NC 1947 d Clifford & Florence. BS Loretto Heights Coll 1971; MDiv Nazarene TS 1981. D 2/1/2003 P 9/6/2003 Bp Barry Howe. c 5. The Rivendell Cmnty Retreat Hse Dunnegan MO 2003-2015.

COX, Celeste O'Hern (Del) 568 Willowwood Dr, Smyrna DE 19977 B Pittsburgh PA 1949 d John & Anna. BS Sthrn Illinois U 1982; CPE 1992; MA S Vinc De Paul Sem 1992; STM GTS 1996. D 9/21/1992 P 9/21/1996 Bp Calvin Onderdonk Schofield Jr. m 11/8/1975 Louis E Cox. R Chr Ch Dover DE 1999-2013; Assoc The Epis Ch Of Beth-By-The-Sea Palm Bch FL 1994-1999; Dio SE Florida Miami 1993-1994; Chapl Jackson Memi Hosp Miami FL 1993-1994. Bd Cert Mem Assn Profsnl Chapl. celeste127@verizon.net

COX, Christopher Edward (NJ) 801 W State St, Trenton NJ 08618 **D Trin Cathd Trenton NJ 2009-** B 1957 s Edward & Joyce. BS U of Liverpool 1978; New Jersey Sch for Deacons 2009. D 5/16/2009 Bp Sylvestre Donato Romero. m 10/7/1978 Hilary Cox c 2.

COX, David (Kan) 1455 E 37th St, Sedalia MO 65301 **Asst S Mich And All Ang Ch Mssn KS 2013-** B Johnson City TN 1972 s Samuel & Sue. BA Carson-Newman Coll 1995; MDiv PrTS 1998; MA E Tennessee St U 2001; PhD Van 2007. D 3/24/2012 P 12/1/2012 Bp Martin Scott Field. m 3/23/2000 Amy Eleanor Hutchinson c 2.

COX, Edwin Manuel (NC) 4510 Highberry Rd, Greensboro NC 27410 B Ponce PR 1944 s Oral & Alicia. BS USCG Acad 1966; MDiv Sewanee: The U So, TS 1979; MEd Coll of Idaho 1987. D 2/24/1984 P 11/17/1984 Bp David Bell Birney IV. m 7/11/1998 Frances Fosbroke c 3. Int Assoc R S Fran Ch Greensboro NC 2004-2007; Supply for Med Angl Ch of Can 2003-2004; Int R S Sav's Par Bar Harbor ME 1999-2002; Int R S Jn's Ch Hvre De Gr MD 1997-1999; Int R S Paul's Epis Ch Prnc Frederck MD 1996-1998; Int R S Jn's Ch Olney MD 1994-1995; Dir Pstr Care Ch Hosp Corp Baltimore MD 1993; Int R S Paul's Par Kent Chestertown MD 1992-1993; R S Marg's Epis Ch Parkville MD 1989-1992; Tri-Ch Par S Mk's Ch Lake City MN 1987-1988; P-in-c H Trin Vale OR 1986-1987; P-in-c S Lk's Ch Weiser ID 1985-1987; Int R Sts Clare & Frances Epis Ch Boise ID 1985-1986; D & P S Steph's Boise ID 1984-1986; Dn, Greensboro Convoc Dio No Carolina Raleigh NC 2009-2012, Curs Sprtl Advsr 2007-2009; T/F on Assessment Revs Dio Maine Portland ME 2001-2002, Dioc Coun 2000-2002; EFM Mentor Dio Maryland Baltimore MD 1998-1999, Dioc Coun 1993-1998, Secy of Conv 1992-1996, Secy of Conv 1992-1996, Plnng Cmte 1991-1996, D Formation Fac 1990-1999, Liturg & Mus Cmte 1990-1996; D Formation Fac Dio Idaho Boise ID 1985-1987, EfM Cordinator & Mentor 1985-1987, Dioc Coun 1985-1986, Cmncatn Cmte Chair 1985, Liturg Cmte Chair 1984-1986. Contrib, "Monograph," *The Ord of Mnstry: Reflections on Direct Ord*, Assn for Ep Deacons (then N Amer Assn for Diac/NAAD), 1996. Assn for Ep Deacons (was NAAD) 1984; Assoc Parishes for Liturg & Mus (AP) 1977-2001; Cmnty of S Mary 1978; Curs 1982;

EWC (EWC) 1977; Int Mnstry Ntwk 1994-2004; Md Cler Ass'n, Bd then Pres. 1990-1992; Nat'l Ntwk of Ep Cler Ass'ns 1989-2004; Towson (MD) Area Mnstrl Assn, Pres. 1992-1993; UBE 2005.

COX, Frances Fosbroke (Md) 4510 Highberry Rd, Greensboro NC 27410 **S Matt's Epis Ch Kernersville NC 2015-** B Boston MA 1948 d Gerald & Kay. BSN U of Maryland 1974; Cert U of Kentucky 1977; MDiv VTS 1981; Cert VTS 1991. D 6/27/1981 Bp David Keller Leighton Sr P 5/11/1985 Bp Albert Theodore Eastman. m 7/11/1998 Edwin Manuel Cox. Int R Ch Of The Epiph Eden NC 2009-2010; Int Ch Of The Redeem Greensboro NC 2007-2008; Int R S Fran Ch Greensboro NC 2004-2007; Serv Angl Ch of Can Par of Woodstock Woodstock 2003-2004; Int R The Par Of S Mary And S Jude NE Harbor ME 2001-2002; Ch Of The Gd Shpd Houlton ME 2000; Mssnr Ch of the Gd Shpd Houlton ME 1999-2004; Chapl Johns Hopkins Hosp Baltimore MD 1994-1999; R Ch Of The Redemp Baltimore MD 1992-1999; Assoc R S Jn's Ch Reisterstown MD 1985-1991; D Assoc H Trin Epis Ch Bowie MD 1984-1985; D Assoc Ch Of The Mssh Baltimore MD 1981-1984; Sprtl Advsr to Curs Secretariate Dio No Carolina Raleigh NC 2007-2011; Green Cler Ntwrk, ME Coun of Ch Dio Maine Portland ME 2001-2004, Mutual Mnstry Consult 2001-2004, Case Maager for Response Team 2000-2004, Safe Ch Trnr 2000-2004; Cathd Chapt Dio Maryland Baltimore MD 1997-1999, Comp Dio Relatns - Tokyo 1995-1999, Dir, Living into Ptiestly Vocation Prog 1994-1999, Coordntr, Educ for D Formation 1992-1999, Sprtl Advsr to Curs Secretariate 1992-1998, Chair, Post-Ord Com of COM 1992-1994, Eccl Crt 1991-1998, COM 1988-1994, COM 1988-1994, Cntrl Maryland Eccumenical Com 1988-1992, NW Reg Pres 1987-1989, Cnvnr, Clerica Femina 1986-1999, Pstr Counslg & Consult Cntr Bd 1986-1992, U of Maryland at Baltimore Chapl Bd 1986-1989, NE Reg Pres 1984-1985, Pres Hargor Reg 1982-1995, NE Reg VP 1981-1983. Associated Parishes 1980-1999; Assn of Epis Deacons (Form NAAD) 1978; Cler Families of Lesbians and Gays 1999-2011; Clerica Femina (Dio MD) 1981-2000; EWC 1978; Integrity 1982; Maryland Cler Assn 1987-1998; No Amer Maritime Mnstry Assn 1992-2006; NE Mnstrl Assn 1981-1984; UBE 2007.

COX, Gary Robert (Chi) **Pstr Calv Luth Ch 2017-; Vic Santa Teresa de Avila Chicago IL 2009-** B Chicago IL 1967 s Maurice & Lorraine. BA Beloit Coll 1989; MA NE Illinois U 1997; MEd Chicago St U 1999; MDiv Epis TS of the SW 2006. D 6/3/2006 P 12/16/2006 Bp Bill Persell. Asst La Iglesia De Nuestra Senora De Las Americas Chicago IL 2011; Chr Ch Waukegan IL 2008; Cur Nuestra Senora De Guadalupe Waukegan IL 2006-2008.

COX, James Richard (WK) Po Box 827, Salina KS 67402 B Garden City KS 1934 s Harold & Pheobe. BA U of Nthrn Colorado 1959; MDiv Nash 1990. D 5/26/1990 P 11/30/1990 Bp John Forsythe Ashby. m 7/20/1977 Ruth M Cox. Ch Of The Trsfg Bennington KS 1992-2004; Armstrong Memi Chap of S Jn the Evang Salina KS 1990-2004; S Jn's Mltry Sch Salina KS 1990-2004; Asst Chr Cathd Salina KS 1990-1991. CHS; Skcm; SocMary; SocOLW; SSC. Phi Delta Kappa; Phi Alpha Theta.

COX JR, James Stanley (Ga) 1805 Jeanette St, Valdosta GA 31602 **Chapl U So Wstrn LA 1982-; Assoc Prof U So Wstrn LA 1970-** B Washington DC 1936 s Anna. BA Pr 1958; BD CDSP 1961; MA Florida St U 1967; PhD Florida St U 1970. D 6/24/1961 P 12/1/1961 Bp Richard Henry Baker. m 6/25/1960 Juanita Oglesby Cox. S Barn Epis Ch Valdosta GA 1999-2000; S Matt's Epis Ch Houma LA 1995-1996; R S Paul's Ch Abbeville LA 1983-1984; P-in-c S Jas Epis Ch Quitman GA 1966-1970; Vic Gr Ch Pine Bluff AR 1962-1965; Asst Ch Of The Gd Shpd Rocky Mt NC 1961-1962; S Jn's Ch Battleboro NC 1961-1962. Auth, "Rel Literacy Criticism". Danforth Assn 1979.

COX, Jason (Los) 8201 16th St Apt 1024, Silver Spring MD 20910 **Assoc S Columba's Ch Washington DC 2011-; Mem, Strategic Fin Resources Cmsn Dio Washington Washington DC 2017-** B Silsbee TX 1978 BA U of Houston 2001; MDiv VTS 2007. D 5/19/2007 P 1/12/2008 Bp Joseph Jon Bruno. m 3/1/2017 James N Obomsawin. Jubilee Consortium Los Angeles CA 2009-2011; Chapl Cbury Westwood Fndt Los Angeles CA 2009-2010; Epis Urban Intern Prog Los Angeles CA 2007-2009. Auth, "Serving Skid Row: Urban Mssn as Theol Educ," *VTS Journ*, VTS, 2010. jcox@columba.org

COX, Mildred Louise (Minn) 1210 Washburn Ave N, Minneapolis MN 55411 **D Deaconio MN 1992-** B Knoxville TN 1935 d Clyde & Katie. Msn 1963; Mph 1974; Cert 1981; D Formation Prog 1992. D 11/14/1992 Bp Sanford Zangwill Kaye Hampton P 12/17/1999 Bp James Louis Jelinek. m 4/15/1961 Walter A Cox.

COX, Nancy L J (NC) 525 Lake Concord Road NE, Concord NC 28025 **R All SS' Epis Ch Concord NC 2013-, R, Time-Certain 2010-2013** B Honolulu HI 1962 d Richard & Suzanne. BA Pr 1984; Mstr of Publ Affrs U of Texas at Austin-LBJ Sch 1987; MDiv VTS 1995. D 7/8/1995 P 1/10/1996 Bp Peter J Lee. m 11/8/1986 Lee Forrest Cox c 4. R S Mk's Chap Storrs CT 2002-2010; Asst Trin Epis Ch Southport CT 1998-2002; Asst S Paul's Epis Ch Alexandria VA 1995-1998. ncox@allsaintsconcord.org

COX, Raymond L (Ct) 461 Mill Hill Ter, Southport CT 06890 **P Comp Trin St. Mich's 2010-** B London UK 1933 s Alfred & Ellen. BA U of Hartford 1970; MDiv Sewanee: The U So, TS 1979. D 6/9/1979 P 12/15/1979 Bp Morgan Porteus. m 11/13/1954 Dorothy T Cox c 2. P In Charge (Pt) Trin Ch 2003-2006;

Calv St Geo's Epis Ch Bridgeport CT 1982-1995; Cur S Mk's Ch New Britain CT 1979-1982.

COX, R. David (SwVa) 107 Lee Ave., Lexington VA 24450 **R S Lk's Ch Hot Sprg VA 2009-, R 2006-2009; Adj Fac Souhern Virginia U Buena Vista VA 2008-; Adj Prof of Hist Sthrn Virginia U Buena Vista VA 2007-; SCWM, PHOD rep. Epis Ch 2012-; PHOD Rep SCWM TEC 2012-** B Washington DC DC 1947 s W Russell & Muriel. BA U of Virginia 1969; MDiv Ya Berk 1972; STM Ya Berk 1987; PhD Fndt Hse Oxford/GTF 2001. D 6/10/1972 P 12/16/1972 Bp Joseph Warren Hutchens. m 6/30/1973 Melissa Anne Cox c 3. Dn, Augusta Convocatio Dio SW Virginia Roanoke VA 2010-2013, Dep, GC 1999-2002, Dep, GC 2008-2014, Exec Bd 2008-2011, Dep, GC 1999-2002; Mem, City Coun City of Lexington VA 2009-2013; Mem City Coun Lexington VA 2009-2012; Adj Instr in Ethics Dabney S. Lancaster Cmnty Coll Clifton Forge VA 2006-2010; Adj Fac Dabney Lancaster Cmnty Coll Rockbridge Co. VA 2006-2009; Int S Alb's Epis Ch Annandale VA 2003-2004; Int Emm Ch At Brook Hill Richmond VA 2002-2003; Int S Mich's Epis Ch Arlington VA 2001-2002; R R E Lee Memi Ch (Epis) Lexington VA 1987-2000; R S Dav's Ch Gales Ferry CT 1975-1987; Stff Cler S Mk's Ch New Canaan CT 1972-1975; Mem/chair Rockbridge (VA) Area Cmnty Serv Bd 2006-2014; Co-Chair Wrld Mssn Com Dio Connecticut Meriden CT 1984-1987, Dn Seabury Deanry 1978-1983. Auth, "Priesthood In A New Millennium," Ch Pub Inc, 2003; Auth, "Bond And Cov," Ch Pub Inc, 1999; Auth, "Misc. arts". Merrill Fell Harvard DS 2001; Woods Fell VTS 2000. david.cox@svu.edu

COX, Sean Armer (NCal) 3601 Sudbury Rd, Cameron Park CA 95682 **R Faith Epis Ch Carmeron Pk CA 2012-; Chapl US Navy Reserve 1994-** B Phoenix AZ 1970 s George & Mary. BA U of Arizona 1992; MDiv Epis TS of the SW 1996; DMin VTS 2005. D 6/15/1996 P 6/14/1997 Bp Robert Reed Shahan. m 12/28/1996 Katherine Shaw Cox c 2. R S Andr's Ch Bryan TX 2006-2012; Vic S Thos Epis Ch Temecula CA 2006; Assoc R S Marg's Epis Ch Palm Desert CA 1998-2000; Int Assoc R S Barn On The Desert Scottsdale AZ 1997-1998; Cur Trin Cathd Phoenix AZ 1996-1997; Alt, GC The Epis Dio Nthrn California Sacramento CA 2014-2015, Chair, Stwdshp Cmsn 2014-; Pres of Stndg Com Dio Texas Houston TX 2011-2012, Chair, ArmdF Cmsn 2009-2012, Mem of Stndg Com 2009-2012, Stndg Com 2009-2012; COM Dio San Diego San Diego CA 2000-2006. sean@faithec.org

COX, Sharron Leslie (Tex) 601 Columbus Ave, Waco TX 76701 **S Paul's Ch Waco TX 2014-** B Texas City TX 1960 d John & Nancy. BS Texas A & M U 1982; MBA The U of Texas 1986; MDiv Sewanee: The U So, TS 2014; MDiv The TS at The U So 2014. D 6/21/2014 Bp Dena Arnall Harrison P 1/29/2015 Bp C Andrew Doyle. Prize for Excellence in Hist Stds The U So-Sewanee TS 2014. sharron@stpaulswaco.org

COYNE, Margaret (Vt) 14 Church St, Bellows Falls VT 05101 **Died 2/10/2016** B Skowhegan ME 1943 d Robert & Margaret. BA Johnson St Coll 1980; MDiv EDS 1994. D 5/31/1994 Bp Mary Adelia Rosamond Mcleod P 12/20/1994 Bp Thomas Kreider Ray. m 12/30/2006 Anthony Coyne c 2. R Imm Ch Bellows Falls VT 2003-2016; Imm Ch Bellows Falls VT 1995-2007; Dio Vermont Burlington VT 1994-1995.

COYNE, William (SC) 1615 Ellsworth St, Mount Pleasant SC 29466 **S Steph's Epis Ch Charleston SC 2015-** B Plainfield NJ 1953 s Hugh & Miriam. BA W Virginia Wesleyan Coll 1975; MDiv GTS 1978. D 6/3/1978 Bp Albert Wiencke Van Duzer P 12/16/1978 Bp Alexander D Stewart. m 6/25/1977 Janet S Smith c 3. P-in-c Ch of the Gd Shepard W Springfield MA 2014-2015; Int Epis Ch Of The Epiph Wilbraham MA 2013-2014; Archd Dio Wstrn Massachusetts Springfield 1998-2013, Dioc Coun 1998-2011, GC Dep 1988-2012; Cn Chr Ch Cathd Springfield MA 1989-1995; R Trin Epis Ch Ware MA 1981-1989; Assoc Ch Of The Atone Westfield MA 1978-1981. whcoyne@gmail.com

COZZOLI, John David (Md) 17524 Lincolnshire Rd, Hagerstown MD 21740 **D S Mk's Ch Lappans Boonsboro MD 1999-** B Hagerstown MD 1937 s Michael & Vera. EFM Sewanee: The U So, TS; U of Mississippi. D 6/17/1989 Bp Albert Theodore Eastman. m 12/20/1969 Ruth Cozzoli c 2. D S Anne's Epis Ch Smithsburg MD 1995-1998; Sm Ch Developmennt Dio Maryland Baltimore MD 1993-1994; D S Thos' Par Hancock MD 1989-1993.

CRABTREE, David R (NC) PO Box 28024, Raleigh NC 27611 B 1949 s Jesse & Sarah. BS Middleton St U 1972. D 6/13/2004 Bp Michael B Curry. c 2. D Ch Of The Gd Shpd Raleigh NC 2004-2009.

CRAFT, Bernadine Louise (Wyo) Po Box 567, Rock Springs WY 82902 B Rock Springs WY 1950 d Ralph & Agnes. BA U of Utah 1972; MA U of Utah 1974; PhD U of Nthrn Colorado 1990. D 8/20/2013 P 4/5/2014 Bp John Smylie. c 1. bcraft@wyoming.com

CRAFT, Carolyn Martin (SVa) 1702 Briery Rd, Farmville VA 23901 B Boston MA d James & Carolyn. Other; BA Agnes Scott Coll 1964; MA U of Pennsylvania 1965; PhD U of Pennsylvania 1973; Ya 1975; U of Virginia 1977. D 4/8/1983 P 4/24/1984 Bp Lyman Cunningham Ogilby. Sprtl Dir Ch Of The Epiph Danville VA 2009-2012; S Jas Ch Cartersville VA 1998-2009; Chr Ch Amelia Ct Hs VA 1998-2004; Assoc. R; R Emm Epis Ch Powhatan VA 1998-2004; Serv Longwood & Hampden-Sydney Epis Campus Mnstrs VA 1992-1994; P-in-Chg, Vic S Jas Chuch Warfield VA 1989-1996; S Jas

Ch Emporia VA 1989-1996; Asst.Prof., Assoc.Prof., Prof. Longwood U Farmville VA 1968-2005; Asst.Prof., Assoc.Prof., Prof. Longwood U Farmville VA 1968-2005. Ed Bd, 1976, 2013; Reviewer, 1976, 2013. AAR 1975-2013. UVA Vstng Schlr U of Virginia 1977; Yale PD Fllshp Ya 1974; Phi Kappa Phi.

CRAFT, John Harvey (La) 4505 S Claiborne Ave, New Orleans LA 70125 B Hattiesburg MS 1953 s Harvey & Mary Beth. BA Tul 1975; JD Tul 1979; MPS Loyola U - New Orleans 2008. D 2/2/2011 P 8/27/2011 Bp Morris King Thompson Jr. m 12/21/1974 Nancy Craft c 5.

CRAFT, Stephen Frank (La) 3101 Plymouth Pl, New Orleans LA 70131 **S Phil's Ch New Orleans LA 2004-; R S Phil's Ch New Orlenas LA 2004-** B Hattiesburg MS 1958 s Harvey & Mary. BD Tul 1985; MDiv Epis TS of the SW 1992. D 6/13/1992 P 12/13/1992 Bp James Barrow Brown. Vic S Andr's Ch Clinton LA 1992-2000; S Pat's Ch Zachary LA 1992-2000.

CRAFTON, Barbara Cawthorne (NY) 53 McCoy Ave, Metuchen NJ 08840 B Mora MN 1951 d David & Aida. BA, cl Rutgers The St U of New Jersey 1977; MDiv, cl GTS 1980. D 6/7/1980 Bp Albert Wiencke Van Duzer P 12/1/1980 Bp George Phelps Mellick Belshaw. m 11/25/1989 Richard Edgecomb Quaintance c 2. Int S Lk's Epis Ch Metuchen NJ 2012-2015, 1981-1983; Int S Jas Epis Ch Firenze 50123 2008-2009; Dir The Geranium Farm Metuchen NJ 2003-2015; R S Clem's Ch New York NY 1996-2002; Chapl Seamens Ch Inst New York NY 1993-1996, Chapl 1983-1989; Assoc Trin Par New York NY 1990-1991; Int Ch Of The Atone Laurel Sprg NJ 1985; Dio New Jersey Trenton NJ 1980-1981; Stndg Com Dio New York New York NY 2000, COM 2000-. Auth, "Jesus Wept," Jossey-Bass, 2009; Auth, "Yes! We'll Gather at the River," Ch Pub, 2001; Auth, "Meditations on the Psalms," Morehouse, 1997; Auth, "The Sewing Room," Morehouse, 1997; Auth, "Numerous books"; Auth, "Numerous other books". Cmnty H Sprt. Fisher Fac Tchg Awd Claremont TS 2011; D.D.(Hon) Sewanee 2011.

CRAFTS JR, Robert (SanD) 13030 Birch Ln, Poway CA 92064 **Ret 2000-; Port Chapl Mssn To Seafarers San Diego CA 1998-; Port Chapl The Mssn to Seafarers - San Diego San Diego CA 1998-** B Cleveland OH 1935 s Robert & Glenna. BA Ya 1957; MD Case Wstrn Reserve U 1962; MDiv Nash 1989. D 6/24/1989 P 12/27/1989 Bp Charles Brinkley Morton. m 7/6/1963 Carol Ann Crafts c 3. Vic S Eliz's Epis Ch San Diego CA 2001-2007; Mssnr S Mk's Ch San Diego CA 1999-2001; S Mary's In The Vlly Ch Ramona CA 1999; Asst All SS Ch Vista CA 1998; Dio San Diego San Diego CA 1992-2000; P-in-c S Jn's Ch Indio CA 1989-1998; Bd Of Trst Nash Nashotah WI 2000-2004. Conf Of S Ben 1978.

CRAGON JR, Miller M. (Chi) 5555 N Sheridan Rd Apt 810, Chicago IL 60640 **Died 3/19/2016** B Ruston LA 1924 s Miller & Lou. BA Tul 1944; MDiv Sewanee: The U So, TS 1947; S Augustines Coll Cbury GB 1954; MA SMU 1960. D 12/29/1946 Bp John L Jackson P 12/21/1950 Bp Girault M Jones. m 9/6/2011 Gregorio Alvarado. Ret 1990-2016; Coordntr Sch for Diac Mnstry Dio Chicago Chicago IL 1984-1989, Cn Ordnry 1978-1989; Seamens Ch Inst New York NY 1970-1978; Exec Dir DeptCE Dio New York New York NY 1961-1969; DRE S Mich And All Ang Ch Dallas TX 1954-1961; R Chr Ch Covington LA 1950-1953; Cur S Andr's Epis Ch New Orleans LA 1947-1948. Auth, *Rel Educ.*

CRAIG, Carrie (EC) 820 Lake Park Dr Apt 101, Davidson NC 28036 B Sewanee TN 1957 d Claude & Nancy. BA U CO 1985; Harvard DS 1988; Duke DS 1990; MDiv CDSP 1992. D 6/20/1992 Bp Hunley Agee Elebash P 5/1/1993 Bp Brice Sidney Sanders. Dir of Chr Formation and Educ S Paul's Epis Ch Greenville NC 2007-2011; Int S Tim's Epis Ch Greenville NC 2006-2007, 2005-2007, DCE 1994-1996; Chapl Dio E Carolina Kinston NC 2005-2006, Compstn and Benefits 2010-2012, Chr Formation Com 2008-2012, COM 2003-2008; P S Paul's Ch Vanceboro NC 2000-2003; Chapl Pitt Cnty Memi Hosp Greenville NC USA 1992-2004; Chair of Lifelong Chr Formation Com Dio Wstrn No Carolina Asheville NC 2014-2016, Lifelong Chr Formation Com 2012-2016. lilly031@gmail.com

CRAIG SR, Claude Phillip (EC) 214 Twain Ave, Davidson NC 28036 B Oklahoma City OK 1936 s Harold & Mary. BA U So 1958; BD Sewanee: The U So, TS 1962. D 6/29/1962 Bp Thomas Augustus Fraser Jr P 6/29/1963 Bp Richard Henry Baker. m 9/8/1956 Nancy Dibble c 3. Cdo Dio E Carolina Kinston NC 2000-2011, Cn Ordnry 1998-2000, 1997-1999, Chair 1990-1998; Mem Dep Gc Liturg Cmsn 1991-1997; R S Mary's Ch Kinston NC 1986-1997; Chair Dept Msnns Dio No Carolina Raleigh NC 1983-1985, Const & Cns Cmsn 1984-1985, Educ & Trng Com 1978-1983; R The Epis Ch Of Gd Shpd Asheboro NC 1981-1985; R Emm Ch Warrenton NC 1978-1980; S Matt's Ch Pampa TX 1974-1976. Oblate Ord Julian Of Norwich 1994. nanphilc@gmail.com

CRAIG JR, Claude Phillip (Ore) 6300 SW Nicol Road, Portland OR 97223 **P Ascen Par Portland OR 2011-; Chapl Oregon Epis Sch Portland OR 2011-; Chapl Epis Hs Alexandria VA 1997-** B Greensboro NC 1967 s Claude & Nancy. BA U NC 1991; MDiv VTS 1995. D 6/3/1995 P 12/10/1995 Bp Brice Sidney Sanders. m 9/24/1994 Jennifer Lynn Bosworth. Chapl Epis HS Alexandria VA 1997-2000; Asst R S Jn's Epis Ch Wilmington NC 1995-1997.

CRAIG JR, Harry Walter (Kan) 5041 Sw Fairlawn Rd, Topeka KS 66610 **D S Dav's Epis Ch Topeka KS 1986-** B Lawrence KS 1939 s Harry & Lola. BA

U of Kansas 1961; LLB U of Kansas 1964. D 10/24/1986 Bp Richard Frank Grein. m 4/30/1960 Karen May Craig c 4.

CRAIG, Hugh Burnette (NC) **Died 10/15/2015** B 1936 D 6/29/1962 P 6/29/1963 Bp Richard Henry Baker. m 4/22/1962 Sally Emerson.

CRAIG, Idalia S (NJ) 85 Stone Rd, Mcdonough GA 30253 B Goldsboro NC 1952 d Clifton & Etla. BA Carleton Coll; MDiv PrTS; Mstr of Arts in Tchg The Coll of New Jersey. D 5/20/2000 P 12/9/2000 Bp David Bruce Joslin. c 2. S Thos' Epis Ch Glassboro NJ 2006-2016; Assoc R S Ptr's Ch Freehold NJ 2000-2006.

CRAIG III, James (WMass) 11 Cotton St, Leominster MA 01453 **R S Mk's Ch Leominster MA 1996-; VP of Bd Dir Beacon of Hope Leominster MA 2017-; VP of Bd Dir Our Fr's Hse Fitchburg MA 2010-** B Manchester CT 1953 s James & Ruth. BA Southampton Coll Southampton NY 1976; MDiv Bex Sem 1992. D 6/13/1992 P 12/19/1992 Bp William George Burrill. m 8/16/1975 Cynthia Keough c 4. D/R S Geo's Ch Hilton NY 1992-1996; Dioc Coun Dio Wstrn Massachusetts Springfield 2007-2012, Dn, No Worcester Dnry 1998-2007.

CRAIG, Jo Roberts (NwT) 2401 Parker St, Amarillo TX 79109 **R S Andr's Epis Ch Amarillo TX 2011-, Assoc 2002-2016; Chapl St. Andr's Epis Sch Amarillo Texas 2002-** B Wichita Falls TX 1945 d William & Eleanor. Rice U; U of St Thos; BS U of Texas 1967; MDiv Epis TS of the SW 1985. D 4/22/1985 Bp Gordon Taliaferro Charlton P 12/1/1985 Bp Maurice Manuel Benitez. m 6/1/2014 Richard Clifton Craig c 3. Assoc R S Steph's Ch Lubbock TX 1994-2002; Chapl All SS Epis Sch Lubbock TX 1992-1994; Chapl Dio NW Texas Lubbock TX 1990-1994; Cbury Chapl Texas Tech U In Lubbock 1990-1992; Assoc R S Paul's On The Plains Epis Ch Lubbock TX 1988-1990; Cbury Chapl Texas Tech U In Lubbock 1988-1990; Assoc R S Mich's Ch Austin TX 1985-1988. jmann@standrewsamarillo.org

CRAIG III, Richard Edwin (Mil) 4417 Westway Ave, Racine WI 53405 **Cler Assoc S Jas Ch W Bend WI 2013-, Long Term Supply 2010-2013** B Atlanta GA 1945 s Richard & Nettie. BA Georgia St U 1969. D 6/3/1990 Bp Earl Nicholas Mc Arthur Jr P 2/17/1991 Bp John Herbert MacNaughton. m 6/23/1967 Marie Pascoe Craig c 3. R S Jn The Bapt Portage WI 2008-2010; Int R S Mk's Ch Milwaukee WI 2007-2008; R S Lk's Ch Racine WI 2002-2006; Vic S Andr's Epis Ch Corpus Christi TX 2001-2002; Ch Of Our Sav Aransas Pass TX 1998-2001; Vic S Thos And S Mart's Ch Crp Christi TX 1998-2001; Asst to R S Andr's Epis Ch San Antonio TX 1990-1997. Auth, "Questions of the Bible: Who? What? Where? When? Why?," PublishAmerica, 2006; Auth, "What Do We Do w Lk 6?," PublisherAmerica, 2004.

CRAIGHEAD JR, J. Thomas (Oly) 23404 107th Ave SW, Vashon WA 98070 **Hospice Chapl Franciscan Hospice Tacoma WA 2001-** B New York NY 1951 s John & Mary. Coll of Wooster 1971; BA U of Montana 1975; MDiv GTS 1982; MSW Syr 1994. D 6/5/1982 Bp William Moultrie Moore Jr P 12/9/1982 Bp Harold Barrett Robinson. m 11/26/1983 Lorna Walker c 2. St Bede Epis Ch Port Orchard WA 1995-2001; 1992-1994; S Andr's Epis Ch Colchester VT 1986-1992; Cn S Paul's Cathd Buffalo NY 1982-1985. Sprtl Dir Intl 2001.

CRAIGHEAD, Thomas Gray (Chi) St Andrew's Church, 1125 Franklin St, Downers Grove IL 60515 **D S Andr's Ch Downers Grove IL 2012-** B Denver CO 1951 s Joseph & Shirley. BA Carleton Coll 1973; MAT Colg 1974. D 2/4/2012 Bp Jeff Lee. m 5/19/1979 Susan Glover Craighead c 2.

CRAIGHILL, Peyton Gardner (Pa) 25 Sycamore Lane, Lexington VA 24450 B Nanchang China 1929 s Lloyd & Marian. BA Ya 1951; BD VTS 1954; STM GTS 1965; PhD PrTS 1973. D 7/10/1954 P 3/31/1955 Bp Lloyd Rutherford Craighill. m 4/24/1962 Mary Roberts Craighill c 2. Assoc Ch Of The Redeem Bryn Mawr PA 2004-2008; P-in-c S Mart's Ch Boothwyn PA 1998-2000; Engl-Lang Chapl S Jas' Ch Taichung W Dist Taiwan 1995-1997; Epis Cmnty Serv Philadelphia PA 1989-1994; Dio Pennsylvania Philadelphia PA 1988-1994; Assoc The Ch Of The H Trin Rittenhouse Philadelphia PA 1988-1989; The Epis Acad Newtown Sq PA 1983-1988; Sewanee U So TS Sewanee TN 1980-1982; Resrch Assoc Epis Ch Cntr New York NY 1978-1980; Archd Dio Taiwan Taipei 1978; Prof and Vice-Pres Tainan Theol Coll and Sem Tainan Taiwan 1961-1978; Vic St Jn Cathd Taipei 1959-1960; P-in-c All Soul's Epis Ch Chatan Okinawa 1957-1959; Asst The Ch Of The Redeem Baltimore MD 1954-1957. Ed, "Diac Mnstry, Past, Present and Future," NAAD, 1998. Cntr for Baptismal Living 1998-2008; Episcopalians on Baptismal Mssn 2010; Mem Mssn 2006; NAAD 1989-1998; SE Asia Assn for Theol Educ 1961-1978; Taiwan Chr Consultative Coun 1961-1978.

CRAIN II, Lee Bryan (LI) 518 Brooklyn Blvd, Brightwaters NY 11718 **D S Ptr's Bay Shore 1987-** B Flushing NY 1951 s Michael & Norma. D 7/19/1987 Bp Henry Boyd Hucles III. m 7/30/1983 Allison Jill Crain.

CRAIN, William Henry (WMo) 9208 Wenonga Rd, Leawood KS 66206 **Bp Spencer Place Inc Kansas City MO 2004-; Chapl Bp Spencer Place Inc. 2004-** B Atlanta GA 1941 s William & Dorothy. BA Olivet Nazarene U 1963; MS Creighton U 1968. D 2/7/2004 Bp Barry Howe. m 6/29/1985 Rebecca A Andes c 1. St Lk's Chap Kansas City MO 2004-2013; St Lk's So Chap Overland Pk KS 2004-2013.

CRAM, Donald Owen (RG) Po Box 45000, Rio Rancho NM 87174 B Glendale CA 1949 s Owen & Doris. BS USC 1971; MDiv NW Bapt Sem 1976; Brigham Young U 1996. D 11/17/1999 P 4/25/2001 Bp Terence Kelshaw. m 6/13/1970 Carol Linda Cram c 4. Cn S Jn's Cathd Albuquerque NM 2006-2007; Vic Hope Epis Ch Albuquerque NM 2005-2006; Hope in the Desert Eps Ch 2004-2005; Vic Epis Ch Of The H Fam Santa Fe NM 2004; R Epis Ch in Lincoln Cnty 2003-2004; Vic Epis Ch Of The Epiph Socorro NM 2001-2003; D S Fran Ch Rio Rancho NM 1999-2001. Bro of S Andr.

CRAM JR, Norman Lee (NCal) Po Box 224, Vineburg CA 95487 B Waukegan IL 1937 s Norman & Charlotte. MDiv CDSP; BA Wms 1959; BD CDSP 1962; MA Grad Theol Un 1976. D 8/12/1962 P 5/1/1963 Bp William F Lewis. m 7/21/1962 Deirdre Elizabeth Field c 2. P-in-c St Johns Epis Ch Petaluma CA 2007-2009, 1996-2007; P-in-c S Steph's Epis Ch Sebastopol CA 1999-2000; Chapl Off Of Bsh For ArmdF New York NY 1964-1994; Captain, US NAVY USN 1964-1994; Cur S Jn's Epis Ch Olympia WA 1962-1964. Norman Cram Hall S Jn's, Petaluma, CA 2012; Distinguished Alum Antioch U Seattle 2006; 5 Meritorious Serv Medals US Navy 1994; USCoast Guard Commendation Medal US Coast Gaurd 1986; St. Geo Awd, BSA Epis Ch 1984; Joint Serv Commendation Medal US Navy 1969; 2 Navy Commendation Medals US Navy 1967.

CRAMER, Alfred Anthony (Vt) 47 Morningside Commons, Brattleboro VT 05301 **Ret 1997-** B Somerville MA 1933 s Alfred & Irene. BA Bos 1957; MDiv EDS 1962; MSW Smith 1991. D 7/15/1962 P 1/25/1963 Bp William F Lewis. m 6/18/1988 Janet French Cramer c 4. R Chr Epis Ch Burlington IA 1978-1983; R S Lk's Ch Des Moines IA 1969-1978; Chapl Drake U Des Moines IA 1968-1978; Chapl U of Washington-Seattle 1965-1968; Vic S Matthews Auburn WA 1964-1965; Cur S Mk's Cathd Seattle WA 1962-1964. Amer Assn for Marriages Fam Ther 1979.

CRAMER, Barry Barry (Ind) B Kenton OH 1951 s James & Mary Ruth. BA The OH SU 1973; JD Intl Sch of Law 1977; MDiv Earlham Sch of Rel 1999; MDiv Earlham Sch of Rel 1999. D 10/26/2013 Bp Cate Waynick. m Jeffrey Lee Bessler.

CRAMER, Jared C (WMich) 524 Washington Ave, Grand Haven MI 49417 **R S Jn's Epis Ch Grand Haven MI 2010-** B Owosso MI 1981 s Gerald & Susan. BS Rochester Coll 2004; MDiv Abilene Chr U 2007; STM Sewanee: The U So, TS 2008; D.Min. Sewanee: The U So, TS 2008. D 4/20/2008 P 12/14/2008 Bp C Wallis Ohl. m 11/8/2008 Bethany A Switter c 1. Dn (of Dnry) Dio Wstrn Michigan Kalamazoo MI 2010-2016, Chair, COM 2012-2015; Cler Res Chr Ch Alexandria VA 2008-2010; Faith & Ord Cmssnr Natl Coun Of Ch New York NY 2011-2014. Auth, "Safeguarded by Glory: The Ecclesiology of Mich Ramsey Applied Today," Lexington, 2010. Soc of Cath Priests in the Epis Ch and the Angl Ch of Can 2008. rector@stjohnsepiscopal.com

CRAMER, Roger Weldon (Mass) 16 Aubin Street, Amesbury MA 01913 B Mansfield OH 1944 s Stanley & Annabel. Drew U; BA OH SU 1966; MTh U Chi 1969; DMin U Chi 1971. D 6/18/1972 P 12/9/1972 Bp David Keller Leighton Sr. m 3/29/2014 Kirsten Joan Helgeland c 2. R S Paul's Ch Newburyport MA 1979-2005; Assoc Trin Ch Princeton NJ 1976-1979; Chr Ch Columbia MD 1973-1976.

CRAMMER, Margaret Corinne (Chi) 927 Scott Blvd Apt 205, Decatur GA 30030 **Cler Assoc All SS Epis Ch Atlanta GA 2007-** B Omaha NE 1950 d Adrain & Ruth. Emory U; Garrett-Evang TS; U Chi; BA NWU 1980; MA NWU 1983; MDiv Ya Berk 1995. D 6/17/1995 P 12/1/1995 Bp Frank Tracy Griswold III. Int S Paul's Epis Ch Newnan GA 1997-2000; Asst to R S Jos's Epis Ch Mcdonough GA 1996-1997. Norenberg Preaching Prize Yale - Berkely DS 1994.

CRAMPTON, Barbara Amelia (Ga) 703 E 48th St, Savannah GA 31405 **Died 9/13/2015** B Monticello NY 1925 d Chester & Winifred. BS The Coll of S Rose 1975; Dio Albany Diac Prog Albany NY 1983. D 6/18/1983 Bp Wilbur Emory Hogg Jr. m 5/15/1948 Gordon Kelsey Crampton c 2. D S Mich And All Ang Savannah GA 2000-2015; D The Epis Ch Of S Jn Bapt Thomaston ME 1984-2000; D S Andr's Ch Schenectady NY 1983-1984. NAAD 1982.

CRAMPTON, Susan H (WMass) 16595 Warren Ct Apt 305, Chagrin Falls OH 44023 B Denver CO 1938 d Jack & Ellen. BA Smith 1960; MDiv EDS 1977. D 6/18/1977 P 2/4/1978 Bp Alexander D Stewart. m 12/29/1961 Stuart Crampton c 3. R Chr Epis Ch Sheffield MA 1994-2003; Assoc R S Andr's Ch Longmeadow MA 1991-1993; Dio Wstrn Massachusetts Springfield 1984-2003; Vic S Jn's Ch Ashfield MA 1984-1991; Asst The Amer Cathd of the H Trin Paris 75008 1982-1983; Assoc S Jn's Ch Williamstown MA 1978-2015; Intern Gr Ch Amherst MA 1977-1978. Fllshp of the Way of the Cross 1982; SCHC 1978. scrampto@williams.edu

CRANDALL, Harry Wilson (SVa) PO Box 275, 9115 Franktown Road, Franktown VA 23354 **R Emer Hungars Par Machipongo VA 2002-, R 1983-2002** B Portland ME 1932 s Harry & Ada. BS USMA 1956; MDiv Sewanee: The U So, TS 1983. D 7/6/1983 P 4/7/1984 Bp Claude Charles Vache. m 9/7/1963 Catherine Crandall c 2. Treas ECom 1989-1998; Dn Dio Sthrn Virginia Newport News VA 1987-1991. Treas Natl ECom 1989-1998. Janette Pierce Awd ECom 1998; Polly Bond Awd ECom 1998.

CRANDALL, John Davin (Mass) 404 Juniper Way, Tavares FL 32778 **Asst S Edw The Confessor Mt Dora FL 2008-; Ret 1999-** B Harrisburg PA 1937 s John & Elizabeth. BA Trin Hartford CT 1958; MDiv VTS 1969. D 6/4/1969 P 12/6/1969 Bp Dean Theodore Stevenson. m 10/6/2007 Mary Beth Beth Whitcher c 3. Par Dev Comm Dio Massachusetts Boston MA 1986-1989; R All SS Epis Ch Attleboro MA 1984-1999; R Chr Ch Albert Lea MN 1979-1984; Dn Lay Acad Dio Bethlehem Bethlehem PA 1976-1979; Cn Cathd Ch Of The Nativ Bethlehem PA 1975-1979; Vic Chr Ch Berwick PA 1971-1975; Cur The Epis Ch Of S Jn The Bapt York PA 1969-1971; Dioc Coun Dio Minnesota Minneapolis MN 1980-1984. ACPE; Bd Dir Acad Par Cleric.

CRANDELL, Herbert Charles (EMich) 3191 Hospers St, Grand Blanc MI 48439 **Ret 1993-** B Ann Arbor MI 1931 s Herbert & Vera. BS U MI 1953; MDiv VTS 1963. D 6/29/1963 Bp Archie H Crowley P 2/29/1964 Bp Richard Stanley Merrill Emrich. m 12/6/1986 Janet Crandell c 3. R S Jude's Epis Ch Fenton MI 1965-1974; Asst S Paul's Epis Ch Flint MI 1963-1965.

CRANE, Charles Tarleton (Haw) 6220 E Broadway Rd # 309, Mesa AZ 85206 **Died 12/7/2015** B Honolulu HI 1928 s Ezra & Frances. BD Iowa St U 1951; MDiv CDSP 1957; Chichester Theol Coll 1977. D 6/23/1957 Bp Russell S Hubbard P 12/23/1957 Bp Harry Sherbourne Kennedy. m 9/1/2012 Marilyn Dorothy Snyder c 3. Ret 1988-2015; Ch Of The H Nativ Honolulu HI 1968-1988; R All SS Ch Kapaa HI 1959-1966; Mem, Dioc Coun The Epis Ch in Hawaii Honolulu HI 1986-1988, Trst 1981-1985; CDSP Berkeley CA 1981-1988; Yth DCE S Andr's Cathd Honolulu HI 1957-1959. Auth, "The Cler Search Dilemma," 1991.

CRANE, Linda Sue (EMich) 1213 6th St, Port Huron MI 48060 **D Gr Epis Ch Port Huron MI 2010-** B St Clair MI 1953 d James & Ruth. St Clair Cnty Cmnty 1980. D 11/18/2006 Bp Edwin Max Leidel Jr. c 4.

CRANE, Rebecca Mai (Mass) 13 Trinity St., Danvers MA 01923 B Salem MA 1965 d Barney & Shirley. BA U of Massachusetts 1987; MEd Salem St Coll Salem MA 2003; Cert Ang Stud D Progam Dio Massachusetts 2008. D 6/7/2008 Bp M(Arvil) Thomas Shaw. m 6/6/1987 Eric Crane c 2.

CRANSTON, Dale L (NY) 21 Stone Fence Road, Mahwah NJ 07430 **R Chr Ch Of Ramapo Suffern NY 2010-, 2004-2009** B Paterson NJ 1946 s Lawrence & Marie. BA Grove City Coll 1968; MDiv EDS 1972. D 6/10/1972 Bp Leland Stark P 4/26/1975 Bp George E Rath. Dio New York New York NY 2004-2009, Dioc Conv Com 2007-; 1982-2003; Assoc All SS' Epis Ch Glen Rock NJ 1972-1988.

CRANSTON, Pamela Lee (Cal) 207 Taurus Ave, Oakland CA 94611 B New York NY 1950 d Day & Nancy. Stetson U; Cert Ch Army Trng Coll 1972; BA San Francisco St U 1984; MDiv CDSP 1988. D 6/3/1989 P 6/9/1990 Bp William Edwin Swing. m 8/18/1984 Edward E Cranston. Vic S Cuth's Epis Ch Oakland CA 2008-2016, 2001-2003; Epis Sr Communities Lafayette CA 2006-2017, Chapl 2001-2005; Chapl Hope Hospice Dublin CA 1998-2013; Assoc P S Cuth's Epis Ch Oakland CA 1998-2006; Field Educ Supvsr CDSP Berkeley CA 1995-2004; Assoc R All Souls Par In Berkeley Berkeley CA 1995-1997; Asst R S Tim's Ch Danville CA 1990-1994; Asst to Cn Pstr Gr Cathd San Francisco CA 1989-1990; Exeuctive Dir Haight-Ashbury Alco Treatment Serv 1984-1985; Hospice Chapl Vstng Nurses Assn Oakland CA 1984-1985; Nun CSF UK and San Francisco CA 1974-1978; Exec Dir - Vol Corps Epis Ch Cntr New York NY 1972-1973; Exec Dir The Vol Corps 1972-1973; Cler Wellness Cmsn, Chair Dio California San Francisco CA 1992-2009. Auth, "Sunrise Liturg: A Poem Sequence by Mia Anderson," *ATR*, ATR, Inc., 2013; Auth, "Rosing From the Dead: Poems of Paul J. Willis," *ATR*, ATR, Inc., 2010; Auth, "Bach Concerto - poem," *ATR*, ATR, Inc., 2010; Auth, "Carriers of Strange Fire - Poem," *Pacific Ch News*, Dio California, 2010; Auth, "Love Was His Meaning: An Intro to Julian of Norwich," Forw Mvmt, 2008; Auth, "Psalm Writing - A Playbox for Bldg Beloved Cmnty," *Playbox CD - for Bldg the Beloved Cmnty*, Dio CA, 2008; Auth, "Essay: Poetry and Priesthood," *The Angl: A Journ of Angl Identity*, Angl Soc - GTS, 2006; Auth, "Coming to Treeline: Adirondack Poems," St. Huberts Press, 2005; Auth, "Poem For Chr the King," *The Angl*, Angl Soc - GTS, 2005; Auth, "The Poet as Archbp: The Poems of Rowan Williams," *The Angl: A Journ of Angl Identity*, Angl Soc - GTS, 2005; Auth, "Two Portraits of Wm Jas," *Blueline*, SUNY Potsdam, 2004; Auth, "The Madonna Murders," St. Huberts Press, 2003; Auth, "Coming To Treeline - poem," *Blueline Anthology*, Syr Press, 2003; Auth, "Poetry," *Penwood Revs*, 2002; Auth, "A Sprtl Journey w Jn Donne," Forw Mvmt, 2001; Auth, "Searching For Nova Albion," *ATR*, ATR, Inc., 2001; Auth, "Cler Wellness & Mutual Mnstry," O'Brien & Whitaker Pub, 2000; Auth, "Poetry," *Adirondack Revs*, 2000; Auth, "Resurr," *Wmn Healing and Empowering*, ELCA Pub, 1996. Amer Acad of Poets 2000-2005; Cal Cler Assn Bd Mem 1995-1997; Dio Cal Cleric Compnstn T/F Mem 1996-2000; Kilvert Soc 1993. MDiv w hon CDSP 1988.

CRAPSEY II, Marc (Mass) 77 L Drew Rd, Derry NH 03038 **Int Trin Epis Ch Tilton NH 2012-** B New York NY 1950 s Marcus & Rosemary. BA U of Connecticut 1972; MSW U of Connecticut 1976; MDiv GTS 1979. D 6/9/1979 Bp Morgan Porteus P 5/10/1980 Bp Richard Beamon Martin. m 8/12/1972 Linda E Ericsson c 2. Int S Jn's Epis Ch Gloucester MA 2010-2011; Int S Mary's Epis Par Northfield VT 2009; R Trin Epis Ch Haverhill MA 1989-2009; Vic S Geo's Ch Middlebury CT 1982-1989; Coordntr Hamptons Coun Ch Fam Cnslng W Hampton Bch NY 1979-1982; Asst S Mk's Ch Westhampton Bch NY 1979-1982.

CRARY, Kathleen (Cal) 733 Baywood Rd, Alameda CA 94502 **Assoc S Fran Of Assisi Ch Novato CA 2012-** B Lawrence KS 1951 Rec 12/1/2001 Bp William Edwin Swing. m 10/12/2013 Carol A Graham. R Chr Ch Alameda CA 2010-2012; Int S Jas Ch Fremont CA 2008-2010; Assoc Ch Of The H Trin Richmond CA 2005-2008; Assoc Chr The Lord Epis Ch Pinole CA 2002-2005.

CRASE, Jane L (Los) P.O. Box 1989, 56312 Onaga Trail, Yucca Valley CA 92284 **Died 1/10/2016** B Pasadena CA 1945 d Gladys & Gladys. Cert USC 1976; AA Mt San Antonio Coll 1986. D 6/4/2011 P 12/10/2011 Bp Joseph Jon Bruno. m 1/8/1983 Gary Crase. P S Jos Of Arimathea Mssn Yucca Vlly CA 2011-2016. dmtjane@aol.com

CRAUN, Christopher (Ore) 3236 NE Alberta St., Portland OR 97211 **R S Mich And All Ang Ch Portland OR 2009-** B Berkeley CA 1980 d Raymond & Carol. BA U CA 2002; CTh CDSP 2003; MDiv GTS 2006. D 6/3/2006 Bp William Edwin Swing P 12/2/2006 Bp Marc Handley Andrus. m 11/5/2015 Carrie M Struss c 1. Asst S Jas's Ch W Hartford CT 2006-2009; Dio California San Francisco CA 2002-2003.

CRAVEN III, James Braxton (NC) 17 Marchmont Ct, Durham NC 27705 **P Assoc S Lk's Epis Ch Durham NC 1992-; Prison Cmsn Dio No Carolina Raleigh NC 2010-, Chair, Dioc Cmsn on the ArmdF 1992-2009** B Portsmouth VA 1942 s James & Mary. Coll of Preachers; USNA 1960; BA U NC 1964; JD Duke 1967; MDiv Duke DS 1981. D 12/14/1985 Bp Robert Whitridge Estill P 12/29/1995 Bp Charles Lovett Keyser. m 8/22/1964 Sara Ann Harris c 3. Coun of Advice Bp of the ArmdF 1990-1997; Asst S Jos's Ch Durham NC 1985-1992; Epis Chapl Fed Prisons 1983-2000. Auth, "arts," *Living Ch*, Living Ch, 1985. LCDR, USN(Ret) US Navy 1996.

CRAVEN, Samuel Harold (Tex) 6221 Main St, Houston TX 77030 **Vice-R Palmer Memi Epis Ch Houston TX 2005-** B Andalusia AL 1946 s Harold & Virginia. BS U of Alabama 1968; JD Loyola U 1971; MDiv Epis TS of the SW 2003. D 6/7/2003 P 4/1/2004 Bp D Avid Bruce Macpherson. m 2/14/1987 Irma Louise Craven c 3. Palmer Memi Ch Houston TX 2005-2012; S Cuth's Epis Ch Houston TX 2003-2005.

CRAVENS, James Owen (Spr) 4 Canterbury Ln, Lincoln IL 62656 **Ch Of S Jn The Bapt Elkhart IL 1996-** B Pueblo CO 1954 s Jackson & Barbara. BA Ft Lewis Coll 1976; MDiv UTS 1980. D 6/14/1980 P 12/1/1980 Bp John Shelby Spong. m 10/23/2010 Mary Cravens c 2. Trin Ch Lincoln IL 1996-2010; R S Mart's Ch Pawtucket RI 1987-1996; Assoc S Steph's Ch Ridgefield CT 1982-1987; Cur Chr Ch Ridgewood NJ 1980-1982. Auth, "Recent Trends In Epis Stwdshp".

CRAVER III, Marshall P (CGC) 613 Highland Woods Dr E, Mobile AL 36608 **Assoc R S Paul's Ch Mobile AL 2003-** B Brewton AL 1953 s Marshall & Ellen. BS Auburn U 1977; MDiv Sewanee: The U So, TS 1984. D 6/1/1984 P 5/1/1985 Bp Charles Farmer Duvall. m 12/16/1978 Jan Denise Craver c 3. Int S Steph's Ch Brewton AL 2002-2003; R S Jas' Epis Ch Alexander City AL 1995-2002; Chr The Redeem Ch Montgomery AL 1988-1995; Vic The Ch Of The Redeem Mobile AL 1988-1995; Asst Chr Ch Cathd Mobile Mobile AL 1984-1988.

CRAWFORD, Alicia Leu Lydon (Chi) 550 N Green Bay Rd, Lake Forest IL 60045 B Saint Louis MO 1950 d Alicia. BA Amer U 1972; MDiv SWTS 1986. D 6/14/1986 Bp James Winchester Montgomery P 12/12/1987 Bp Frank Tracy Griswold III. m 12/22/1969 James Ellis Crawford c 2. Cur S Mk's Ch Evanston IL 1986-1987. Soc of S Jn the Evang.

CRAWFORD, Gerald Gene (Ark) D 7/18/2004 Bp Larry Maze P 6/21/2017 Bp Larry Benfield.

CRAWFORD JR, Grady J (At) 2602 Oglethorpe Cir NE, Atlanta GA 30319 **H Innoc Ch Atlanta GA 2014-** B Waycross GA 1959 s Grady & Patricia. BA U of So Alabama; MDiv Candler TS Emory U 2009. D 12/20/2008 P 6/28/2009 Bp J Neil Alexander. m 9/12/2014 Eric Trevena. S Lk's Epis Ch Atlanta GA 2011-2014; Cathd Of S Phil Atlanta GA 2009-2011.

CRAWFORD, Hayden G (SeFla) 701 45th Ave S, Saint Petersburg FL 33705 B Gainesville FL 1948 s Jackson & Marion. BS Florida A&M U 1973; MDiv Interdenominational Theol Cntr 1978. D 5/3/1980 P 12/17/1980 Bp Furman Charles Stough. m 4/8/1989 Alexis M Crawford c 2. R Ch Of The Incarn Miami FL 2010-2012; P-in-c S Alb's Epis Ch St Petersburg FL 2009-2010; Assoc Ch Of S Mich And All Ang Sanibel FL 2007; Assoc Chr Ch Bradenton FL 2005-2007; R S Aug's Epis Ch St Petersburg FL 1996-2005; R S Aug And S Mart Ch Boston MA 1992-1996; R Ch Of Our Merc Sav Louisville KY 1987-1992; R S Mk's Ch Jackson MS 1984-1987; R S Simon The Cyrenian Ch Philadelphia PA 1983-1984; Vic Gd Shpd Ch Montgomery AL 1980-1983; Jubilee Mnstry Advsry Exec Coun Appointees New York NY 2000-2003; Stndg Com Dio SW Florida Parrish FL 1997-2003; Exec Coun Dio Mississippi Jackson MS 1985-1986. CPE Advsry Bd; NAACP; UBE. Cntrl Cmnty Cntr Awd 1987; Ldrshp Awd Naacp 1982; Young Men Of Amer 1979; Rel Awd Phi Beta Sigma.

CRAWFORD, Karen Graham (Ia) 223 E 4th St N, Newton IA 50208 **P-in-c S Steph's Ch Newton IA 2015-** B Kansas City 1946 d William & Aloha. BA Drake U 1968; MA Drake U 1997; MDiv Epis TS Of The SW 2014; MDiv Sem of the SW 2014. D 12/7/2013 P 6/21/2014 Bp Alan Scarfe. c 1. ststephn@pcpartner.net

CRAWFORD JR, Kelly (Los) 450 NW Ivy Ave, Dallas OR 97338 B Farmington NM 1946 s Kelly & Evelyn. BD U of New Mex 1982; MDiv CDSP 1989. D 7/22/1989 Bp Terence Kelshaw P 5/15/1990 Bp Donald Purple Hart. c 2. Exec Dir Seamens Ch Inst Of Los Angeles San Pedro CA 1991-2011; Vic Epis Ch On W Kaua'i Eleele HI 1989-1991.

CRAWFORD, Lee (Vt) POB 67, Plymouth VT 05056 **Ch of Our Sav Killington VT 2013-; Mem Epis Ch Exec Coun 2006-; Cn Iglesia Anglicana Epis De El Salvador 2004-; GC Dep Dio Vermont Burlington VT 1997-** B Norwalk CT 1957 d Arthur & Jean. BA Smith 1979; MA Pr 1983; PhD Pr 1991; MDiv GTS 1993. D 6/12/1993 Bp George Phelps Mellick Belshaw P 1/29/1994 Bp Joe Doss. m 8/15/2012 Anne Clarke Brown. P-in-c Trin Ch Rutland VT 2008-2011; R S Mary's Epis Par Northfield VT 1994-2008; Gr St Pauls Ch Trenton NJ 1993-1994; Asst H Trin Ch So River NJ 1993-1994; Asst Seamens Ch Inst New York NY 1993-1994. Auth, "The Mtn Echo"; Auth, "Wit". Cler Ldrshp Proj Class Ix 1997-2000; EWC 1988; Fundacion Cristosal 2000; Integrity; Ord Of S Helena 1988. Pilgrim Min to Israel Knights Templar 2011.

CRAWFORD, Leo Lester (SwFla) 2694 Grove Park Rd, Palm Harbor FL 34583 **Ret 2008-; Asst Ch Of The Ascen Clearwater FL 2008-** B Jonesville LA 1941 s Leo & Mabel. BD LSU 1964; MDiv Nash 1988. D 6/4/1988 P 12/10/1988 Bp Willis Ryan Henton. m 4/28/1973 Ann R Crawford c 3. R Gd Samar Epis Ch Clearwater FL 2000-2008; Chr Ch Bastrop LA 1988-2000.

CRAWFORD, Malia (Mass) 21 Marathon St., Arlington MA 02474 **R Ch Of Our Sav Arlington MA 2011-** B Honolulu HI 1974 d James & Nola. SB MIT 1996; MDiv Harvard DS 2005. D 6/7/2008 Bp M(Arvil) Thomas Shaw P 1/10/2009 Bp Roy Frederick Cederholm Jr. m 10/4/2008 Amy LaVertu c 1. Cur Gr Ch New Bedford MA 2008-2011; Admin Asst for Wrshp and Pstr Care Trin Ch Epis Boston MA 2005-2008.

CRAWFORD, Mark Taylor (Tex) PO Box 20269, Houston TX 77225 B New Orleans LA 1954 s William & Jeanette. BA SMU 1976; BA Oxf GB 1978; MA Oxf GB 1983; MA Wycliffe Hall Oxford 1983; Cntrl Texas Pstr Cntr TX 1992; DMin Austin Presb TS 2001; DMin Austin Presb TS 2001; BCC Assn of Profsnl Chapl 2013. D 12/21/1980 P 9/16/1981 Bp The Bishop Of Paraguay. m 6/16/1979 Jean Crawford c 3. S Tim's Epis Ch Lake Jackson TX 2016-2017; S Mk's Ch Beaumont TX 2014-2015; Hosp Chapl Dio Texas Houston TX 2011-2014, GBEC 1997-2009; S Lk's Epis Hosp Houston TX 2008-2011; Campus Mssnr Palmer Memi Ch Houston TX 2004-2008; R Gr Epis Ch Alvin TX 1999-2003; Chapl Cbury Assn Texas A & M U 1996-1999; The Great Cmsn Fndt Houston TX 1996-1999, 1985-1990; R Epis Ch Of The H Sprt Waco TX 1990-1996; S Jas' Ch Taylor TX 1987-1990, 1985-1986; Vic Gr Epis Ch Georgetown TX 1985-1987; Asst Ch Of The Ascen Houston TX 1983-1985; Mssy Angl Ch of Paraguay 1980-1982. Auth, "Doctoral Proj," *Called To Serve: /Exam The Process Of Ord*, Austin Presb TS, 2000; Auth, "Bk Revs," *Susana Wesley: The Complete Writings*, 1999. Assn of Epis Hlth Care Chapl 2008. mcrawford@stmarksbeaumont.org

CRAWFORD, Nancy Rogers (Ore) 1595 E 31st Ave, Eugene OR 97405 B Agana Guam 1949 d James & Virginia. BS U of Louisiana Monroe 1971. D 10/21/2006 Bp Johncy Itty. m 3/19/1982 Phillip Crawford c 2. S Mary's Epis Ch Eugene OR 2010-2012, D 2006-; Dio Oregon Portland OR 2006-2008.

CRAWFORD, Robert Lee (NY) Po Box 1415, Camden ME 04843 B Toledo OH 1938 s Lee & Dorcas. BA NWU 1960; STB GTS 1966; MA U of Pennsylvania 1971. D 6/4/1966 P 12/1/1966 Bp Horace W B Donegan. m 6/18/1960 Kathryn Shearer c 2. Ch Of The Gd Shpd Waban MA 1994-2004; 1970-1993; S Geo's Ch Newport RI 1966-1969; Assoc Chapl S Geo's Sch Newport RI 1966-1969.

CRAWFORD, Sidnie White (Neb) 925 Piedmont Rd, Lincoln NE 68510 **P Assoc S Mk's On The Campus Lincoln NE 2011-; Prof U of Nebraska-Lincoln Lincoln NE 1997-** B Greenwich CT 1960 d Earle & Mildred. MA Harv 1984; PhD Harv 1988. D 9/2/2004 P 10/15/2005 Bp Joe Goodwin Burnett. m 6/11/1994 Dan Duvall Crawford. Angl Assn of Biblic Scholars 2003.

CRAWFORD, Stephen Howard (La) 3552 Morning Glory Ave, Baton Rouge LA 70808 **S Mary's Ch Franklin LA 2015-** B Chillicothe OH 1986 s Timothy & Louise. Philos LSU 2008; MDiv Duke DS 2014. D 12/28/2013 P 7/19/2014 Bp Morris King Thompson Jr. m 8/7/2010 Amanda Lela Loucke Crawford c 2. Trin Epis Ch Baton Rouge LA 2014. stephen.h.crawford@gmail.com

CRAWFORD, Susan Kaye (Miss) 1026 S Washington Ave, Greenville MS 38701 B Kennett MO 1948 d Carl & Marie. BS Evangeligal 1970; MDiv Sewanee: The U So, TS 1989. D 6/3/1989 P 3/24/1990 Bp Alex Dockery Dickson. S Jas Ch Greenville MS 2009-2013; Int S Mart's Ch Ellisville MO 2007-2009; S Lk's Epis Ch Jackson TN 2004-2006; Assoc S Geo's Ch Germantown TN 1992-2004; Dio W Tennessee Memphis 1989-1992; D-In-Trng S Jn's Ch Mart TN 1989-1990. Auth, "mag'S 2000 List Of Wmn Who Make A Difference". Dioc Coordntng Cmsn; Wmn Kairos Prison Mnstry.

CRAWLEY, Clayton D (ECR) 20 Pine St Apt 2106, New York NY 10005 **EVP Chf Info Off The CPG New York NY 2010-, SVP, Chf Info Off 2004-2010, VP 1999-2003; Non-Stipendiary Cler Trin Par New York NY 2007-; Non-Stipendiary Cler St. Barth Ch New York NY 2002-** B Atlanta GA 1964 s Harvey & Beverly. BMus Samford U 1987; CAS CDSP 1990; MDiv CDSP 1994. D 4/23/1994 P 11/12/1994 Bp Richard Lester Shimpfky. m 9/23/2011 Roy Kim. Non-Stipendiary Cler The Ch Of S Lk In The Fields New York NY 2000-2002; Assoc R All SS Epis Ch Palo Alto CA 1997-1999, D 1994-1995; Non-Stipendiary Cler The Epis Ch Of S Jn The Evang San Francisco CA 1996-1997; Bd Mem EDS Cambridge MA 2008-2016. Associated Parishes Coun, Exec Com 1999-2001; Associated Parishes Coun, Pres 2001-2003; AP, Coun Mem 1996-2005; GTNG Core Team 1998-2000. ccrawley@cpg.org

CREAMER JR, Francis Bunnell (LI) 715 Friendship Rd, Waldoboro ME 04572 **Died 2/27/2016** B Detroit MI 1937 s Francis & Margaret. BA Trin Hartford CT 1958; STB Ya Berk 1963; U Tor CA 1964. D 6/11/1963 Bp Walter H Gray P 6/1/1964 Bp John Henry Esquirol. m 11/28/1959 Ann L Lichty c 2. Chapl Miles Memi Hosp Damariscotta ME 2002-2016; Bd Chapl Dartmouth-Hitchcock Med Cntr Lebanon NH 1998-2001; Ret 1997-2016; R S Lk's Ch E Hampton NY 1978-1997; R S Andr's Ch New London NH 1971-1978; Asst Ch Of The Heav Rest New York NY 1966-1971; Cur S Jas's Ch W Hartford CT 1964-1966. Sidney Chld Fell Trin, U Tor, Can 1964.

CREAN, Charleen (Los) 931 E. Walnut St. #114, Pasadena CA 91106 **Dio Los Angeles Los Angeles CA 2014-, Mem, COM 2012-2013; Par D All SS Ch Pasadena CA 2012-** B Fort Rucker AL 1951 d Frank & Frances. BA U of Hawaii 1985; MSW U of Hawaii 1995. D 12/14/1986 Bp Donald Purple Hart. m 9/19/1985 John Edward Crean. Par D Gr Ch Grand Rapids MI 2009-2010; Par D Ch of the H Sprt Belmont MI 2004-2009; Chapl Iolani Sch Honolulu HI 1987-1993; Mem, Stndg Com Dio Wstrn Michigan Kalamazoo MI 2009-2016. ccrean@ladiocese.org

CREAN JR, John Edward (Los) 1735 La Paz Rd, Altadena CA 91001 **Int R St Gregorys Epis Ch Long Bch CA 2015-; Ecum & Interfaith Prog Grp Dio Los Angeles Los Angeles CA 2014-, 2012-, Dioc Coun 2011-** B New York NY 1939 s John & Agnes. BA H Cross Coll 1962; MA Ya 1964; PhD Ya 1966. D 4/28/1974 P 11/30/1974 Bp Edwin Lani Hanchett. m 9/19/1985 Charleen Mccoy c 5. Int S Lk's Epis Ch Monrovia CA 2012-2013; Chapl Scripps-Kensington Epis Hm Cmnty 2011; R-under-Contract S Jn the Apos Epis Ch Ionia MI 2008-2010; R-under-Contract S Alb's Mssn N. Muskegon MI 2007; R S Paul's Epis Ch Grand Rapids MI 1996-2005; Dn Grand Vlly Dnry 1996-2000; Dn - W Oahu Dnry The Epis Ch in Hawaii Honolulu HI 1989-1993, Stndg Com 1985-1988, Dioc Sprtl Dir 1980-1984, Dioc Sprtl Dir 1980-1990; R S Geo's Epis Ch Honolulu HI 1983-1996; Asst Par of St Clem Honolulu HI 1977-1982; Assoc S Steph's Ch Wahiawa HI 1974-1977; Dir of Vocational Formation Dio Wstrn Michigan Kalamazoo MI 2005-2009. Auth, "arts," *Magistra:Wmn Sprtlty In Hist*, 1995; Auth, "Altenburg Rule Of Ben (Ed)," Eos Verlag, Germany, 1992; Auth, "arts," *LivCh*, 1971. Confrater, Ord Of S Ben 1996; Mem, Soc of Cath Priests 2012; Oblate, Benediktinerabtei Sankt Bonifaz, Munich, Germany 2004; P Assoc, OHC 1974.

CREASY, James Arthur (Ala) 3228 Lee Road 56, Auburn AL 36832 **Ret 2007-** B Florence AL 1947 s James & Nancy. BA U of No Alabama 1970; PDS 1973; MDiv EDS 1975. D 5/31/1975 P 12/20/1975 Bp Furman Charles Stough. m 4/8/1972 Charleen Marie Creasy c 1. Calv Ch Oneonta AL 2005-2006; Trin Epis Ch Bessemer AL 2004-2005; R Emm Epis Ch Opelika AL 1997-2002; R S Jn's Ch Bedford VA 1992-1997; R Chr Epis Ch Marion VA 1987-1992; Cur S Andr's Epis Ch Miami FL 1985-1987; Cur S Geo's Epis Ch Griffin GA 1982-1985; Dio Micronesia Tumon Bay GU 1980-1981; Cur Exec Coun Appointees New York NY 1980-1981; Chapl S Jn Epis Prep Sch Tumon Bay GU 1980-1981; R S Mk's Ch Prattville AL 1976-1980; D S Barth's Epis Ch Florence AL 1975-1976; Exec Bd Dio SW Virginia Roanoke VA 1989-1992.

CREASY, William Charles (O) 65 E Maple Ave, New Concord OH 43762 **Ret 1989-** B Massillon OH 1927 s Steven & Ella. BA Coll of Wooster 1949; Kent St U 1950; BD Ob 1954; Van 1971. D 3/27/1960 P 10/16/1960 Bp Nelson Marigold Burroughs. c 1. Serv Meth Ch 1969-1989; R All SS Ch Cleveland OH 1963-1968; D/R Adv Epis Ch Westlake OH 1960-1963; Serv Evang Untd Brethren Ch 1953-1959. Auth, "Popular Motives of the Early Disciples of Chr," 1971.

CRECCA, Kimberly Diane (Az) D 6/11/2016 Bp Kirk Stevan Smith.

CREED, Christopher Duflon (ECR) 501 Portola Rd Apt 8185, Portola Valley CA 94028 B Baltimore MD 1943 s Eugene & Jeanne. BA JHU 1965; JD Harv 1968; MBA Stan 1975; MDiv CDSP 1993. D 6/3/1995 P 6/1/1996 Bp William Edwin Swing. m 6/10/1967 Barbara Creed. R S Fran Epis Ch San Jose CA 2000-2011; Asst Chr Ch Portola Vlly CA 1999-2000; Int 1996-1998; Int Trin Par Menlo Pk CA 1998-1999; Asst R S Ambr Epis Ch Foster City CA 1995-1996; Chapl Stan Hosp Stanford CA 1993-1996; Chapl Stan Hosp Stanford CA 1993-1995. Phi Beta Kappa JHU 1965.

✠ **CREIGHTON, The Rt Rev Michael Whittington** (CPa) 2716 Gingerview Lane, Annapolis MD 21401 **Ret Bp of Cntrl Pennsylvania Dio Cntrl Pennsylvania Harrisburg PA 2006-, Bp 1995-2006** B Saint Paul MN 1940 s

William & Marie-. BA Trin Hartford CT 1962; MDiv EDS 1968. D 6/29/1968 Bp William Foreman Creighton P 1/25/1969 Bp Chauncie Kilmer Myers Con 11/18/1995 for CPa. m 12/30/1966 Elizabeth G Goodridge c 2. R S Steph's Epis Ch Seattle WA 1981-1995; R Epis Ch in Almaden San Jose CA 1973-1981; Assoc The Epis Ch Of S Mary The Vrgn San Francisco CA 1968-1973. Auth, *For Starters Volumes I & II*, Forw Mvmt, 1988.

CREIGHTON, Susan (Oly) 15 Huckleberry Court, Bellingham WA 98229 **Anchorite Anchorite Dio Olympia 2004-; Anchorite Dio Olympia Seattle 1995-, TS 1990-1995, Trial Crt 1985-1987** B Flagstaff AZ 1943 d Carroll & Edith. BS Colorado St U 1965; MDiv CDSP 1979. D 6/24/1979 Bp Matthew Paul Bigliardi P 6/1/1981 Bp Paul Moore Jr. Campus Mnstry Dio Wstrn Michigan Kalamazoo MI 1987-1989; Vic Ch Of The H Apos Bellevue WA 1984-1987; S Marg's Ch Seattle WA 1984-1987; Nun / P OSH Seattle WA 1982-1984; P / Nun The Ord Of St Helena No Augusta SC 1979-1984; Nun / P OSH Vails Gate NY 1979-1982. Auth, "DeepLight: A Memoir of the Soul," *DeepLight: A Memoir of the Soul*, Anchorhold Press, Bellingham, WA, 2017; Auth, "poetry, essays," *Voices Weaving*, Anchorhold Press, Bellingham, WA, 1996; Auth, "Revs," *Cntr Bulletin*, Theol & Natural Sciences Cntr, Berkeley, CA, 1993; Auth, "DeepLight Hill--A Personal Sprtlty of Creation," *Earth Letter*, Earth Mnstry, Seattle, WA, 1993; Auth, "Wmn Ways of Knowing-Sprtl Gifts of Wisdom & Knowledge," *The Royal Cross- DOK*, DOK--The Royal Cross, 1992; Auth, "essays," *St Helena*, OSH, Vales Gate, NY, 1979. Ord of S Helena, D 1979-1981; Ord of S Helena, P 1981-1984. Beta Beta Beta Coll of Agriculture-Colo.St.Univ. 1965; Gamma Sigma Delta Coll of Agriculture-Colo.St.Univ. 1965. anchorite@holydwelling.com

CRELLIN, Timothy Edward (Mass) 25 Boylston St, Jamaica Plain MA 02130 **Dio Massachusetts Boston MA 1999-; Vic S Steph's Epis Ch Boston MA 1999-** B Oswego NY 1968 s David & Barbara. BA Br 1990; MDiv Harvard DS 1996. D 9/8/1996 Bp M(Arvil) Thomas Shaw P 4/13/1997 Bp Robert Wilkes Ihloff. m 6/29/1996 Jennifer A Sazama c 1. Assoc Ch Of The Redeem Chestnut Hill MA 1996-1999. SSM 2008. Robert Tobin Awd for Soc Justice Epis City Mssn, Boston 2008. tim@ststephensbos.org

CRERAR, Patrick T (Los) 202 Avenida Aragon, San Clemente CA 92672 **R S Clem's-By-The-Sea Par San Clemente CA 2012-** B Ft Leavenworth KA 1968 s John & Katherine. BS Geo Mason U 1991; MDiv VTS 2008. D 5/24/2008 P 12/14/2008 Bp Peter J Lee. m 5/6/2000 Christina A Crerar c 1. Assoc Gr Epis Ch Alexandria VA 2008-2012. cl VTS 2008. frpatrick@scbythese.org

CRESPO, Willy (SanD) 10125 Azuaga St, San Diego CA 92129 **R S Tim's Ch San Diego CA 2007-** B New York NY 1952 s Joseph & Gladys. BA Coll of New Rochelle 1980; MA NYU 1984; MDiv NYTS 1986; MA U of Phoenix 1999; DMin SWTS 2005. D 3/17/1994 P 9/21/1994 Bp Gethin Benwil Hughes. m 6/24/2000 Maria Tillmanns c 2. Fed Bureau of Prison Off Of Bsh For ArmdF New York NY 1995-2008; Chapl Fed Bureau Prisons 1988-2008. Amer Assn of Profsnl Chapl; Coll Of Chapl, Amer Correctional Chapl Assn.

CRESS, Katherine Elizabeth (Mass) 28 Pleasant St., Medfield MA 02052 **Ch Of Our Sav Somerset MA 2009-** B Fairborn OH 1960 d Donald & Diana. BA Geo 1982; MAT Br 1984; EdD Harvard Grad Sch of Educ 2000; MDiv Bos TS 2009. D 6/6/2009 Bp M(Arvil) Thomas Shaw. m 12/29/1989 Samuel Kauffmann c 2.

CRESSMAN, Lisa Suzanne Kraske (Minn) 3 Blue Iron Dr, Missouri City TX 77459 **Asstg P Epis Ch of the Epiph Houston Tx 2015-; Fndr and Steward Back Story Preaching 2014-** B Detroit MI 1962 d Robert & Elizabeth. BSN U of Wisconsin 1985; MDiv CDSP 1992; DMin Chr TS 2000. D 5/31/1992 Bp George Edmonds Bates P 3/13/1993 Bp Edward Witker Jones. m 9/26/1987 Erik N Cressman c 2. Adj Facility Epis TS Of The SW Austin TX 2015; Assistanting P S Mary's Basswood Grove Hastings MN 2008-2012, Assoc P 2006-2007; R S Thos Ch Franklin IN 1999-2002; Assoc R Trin Ch Indianapolis IN 1992-1999. Auth, "Journey Into Compassion (sermon)," *Preaching through the Year of Mk: Sermons that Wk VIII*, Morehouse Pub, 1999; Auth, "How Can This Be ? (sermon), Preaching as Image," *Story and Idea: Sermons that Wk VII*, Morehouse Pub, 1998.

CRESSMAN, Louise A (NJ) 25 Lakeshore Dr, Hammonton NJ 08037 **D S Mk's 1985-** B Philadelphia PA 1948 d Louis & Elizabeth. BA Juniata Coll 1971; MS Bryn 1991. D 4/13/1985 Bp George Phelps Mellick Belshaw. m 12/31/1976 David Michael Watral c 4. The Evergreens Moorestown NJ 1988-1989.

CRESSMAN, Naomi May (NJ) 305 Main St, Riverton NJ 08077 B Camden NJ 1962 d Joseph & Naomi May. D 5/9/2015 Bp William H Stokes.

CRESWELL, Carl Edward (NwT) 2113 S Lipscomb St, Amarillo TX 79109 **Chapl VA Hosp Amarillo TX 2001-** B Toledo OH 1934 s George & Ruth. BA Cntrl Michigan U 1961; BD Bex Sem 1964; MA Cntrl Michigan U 1974; JD Texas Tech U 1981. D 6/13/1964 P 12/1/1964 Bp Roger W Blanchard. c 5. S Jn The Bapt Epis Clarendon TX 1987-2000; 1972-1985; R S Andr's Epis Ch Emporia KS 1969-1971; Actg R S Mk's Epis Ch Dayton OH 1968-1969; Chapl (Lieutenant Colonel) US-A 1966-1968; Cur Chr Epis Ch Dayton OH 1964-1966. Auth, *Privileged Communicants & The Mltry Chapl*; Auth, *Substituted Judgement For The Terminally Ill Incompetent*; Auth, *The Short Term Counslg Contract*. Conf of Ord of S Ben 1964.

CRESWELL, Jennifer M (Ore) 4411 NE Beech St., Portland OR 97213 B Portland OR 1979 d Jeffrey & Sarah. BA Mt Holyoke Coll 2001; MDiv Ya Berk 2005. D 10/8/2005 Bp Johncy Itty P 4/8/2006 Bp Catherine Scimeca Roskam. m 8/4/2002 Ian H Doescher c 2. S Lk's Epis Ch Gresham OR 2008-2016; Assoc Gr Ch Millbrook NY 2005-2007.

CRETEN, Claude Daniel (NMich) E4929 State Highway M35, Escanaba MI 49829 B Escanaba MI 1941 D 5/4/2003 Bp James Arthur Kelsey. m 7/24/1965 Kathleen La Porte. D S Steph's Ch Escanaba MI 2003-2010.

CREWDSON, Robert (SwVa) 6 Miley Ct, Lexington VA 24450 **Ret 1998-** B Ridley Park PA 1933 s Henry & Kathryn. BS VPI 1955; MDiv VTS 1960; STM UTS Richmond 1971; DMin UTS Richmond 1974. D 6/28/1960 Bp Frederick D Goodwin P 7/1/1961 Bp Samuel B Chilton. m 8/5/1956 Lois Perkins c 2. Chapl R E Lee Memi Ch (Epis) Lexington VA 2008-2011; Coordntr of EDEIO's Prov III 2005-2007; R S Andr's Ch Clifton Forg VA 2000-2008; Ecum Off Dio SW Virginia Roanoke VA 1999-2009; Dio Wstrn No Carolina Asheville NC 1993-1997; R Par Of The H Comm Glendale Sprg NC 1989-1998; Prince Geo Winyah Epis Preschool Georgetown SC 1985-1989; R Prince Geo Winyah Epis Ch Georgetown SC 1985-1989; R S Paul's Ch Haymarket VA 1970-1985; R Chr Epis Ch Brandy Sta VA 1964-1970; S Lk's Ch Remington VA 1964-1970; R Lynnwood Par Port Republic VA 1960-1964. Auth, "Love & War: A Sthrn Soldier's Struggle Between Love & Duty," *Love and War*, Mariner Companies, Inc., 2009; Auth, "Ecum & the Corinthian Correspondence," *Ch Unity and the Corinthian Correspondence*, Mariner Companies, Inc., 2007. Woods Fell VTS 1996; Rec The Allin Fllshp 1992.

CREWS, Norman Andrew (SwVa) 1125 Spindle Xing, Virginia Beach VA 23455 **Ret 1998-** B Sapulpa OK 1935 s Norman & Mildred. BS U of Nebraska 1970; MDiv GTS 1985. D 5/25/1985 P 3/1/1986 Bp Claude Charles Vache. m 6/7/1996 Nordleen S Crews c 3. Chapl Boys Hm Covington VA 1997-1998; R Emm Ch Covington VA 1988-1997; R Calv Ch Bath Par Mc Kenney VA 1985-1988; R Ch of the Gd Shpd Mc Kenney VA 1985-1988.

CREWS, Norman Dale (CPa) 201 Porter Dr, Annapolis MD 21401 **Asst S Anne's 1972-** B Louisville KY 1937 s Maurice & Alleta. BS Ball St U 1959; LTh Sewanee: The U So, TS 1964. D 7/20/1964 P 1/1/1965 Bp Joseph Thomas Heistand. m 7/11/1964 Dianne Crews. Annapolis Yth Ctr Inc Annapolis MD 1975-1976; R S Jn's Epis Ch Huntingdon PA 1965-1972; Cur S Andr's Epis Ch York PA 1964-1965.

CREWS, Warren Earl (Mo) 2 Algonquin Wood, Saint Louis MO 63122 **Adj Prof Eden TS 2000-** B Guthrie OK 1940 s Earl & Judith. BA Ya 1962; MDiv EDS 1965; BD EDS 1965; MAT Oklahoma City U 1976; MA Oklahoma City U 1976; PhD S Louis U 1995. D 6/20/1965 P 12/1/1965 Bp Chilton R Powell. m 7/28/1967 Mary Crews c 2. Assoc Emm Epis Ch Webster Groves MO 2003-2007; Epis Sch for Mnstry Dio Missouri S Louis MO 1998-2003, Chair, Dioc BEC 2010-2009, Chair, Dioc Nomin Com 2009-2013, Dn, Epis Sch for Mnstry 1998-2005; Assoc Emm Epis Ch S Louis MO 1996-2007; Int Ch Of The Epiph Kirkwood S Louis MO 1996; P Asst Emm Epis Ch Webster Groves MO 1995-2003; R S Tim's Epis Ch S Louis MO 1986-1991; Sub-Dn Trin Cathd Little Rock AR 1981-1986; Cn to the Ordnry Dio Arkansas Little Rock AR 1977-1981; Dio Arkansas Little Rock AR 1977-1980; Vic S Mths Oklahoma City OK 1974-1976; Asst S Jn's Ch Oklahoma City OK 1971-1974; Asst Chapl Casady Sch Oklahoma City OK 1967-1976; Asst Vic S Edw Chap Oklahoma City OK 1967-1976; S Paul's Cathd Oklahoma City OK 1967-1971; R S Thos Ch Pawhuska OK 1966-1967; Vic S Clare's Mssn Fairview OK 1965-1966; S Matt's Ch Enid OK 1965-1966; Vic S Steph's Alva Alva OK 1965-1966. Pres Interfaith Partnership of St. Louis 2002; Pres EDEO 1982.

CREWS, William Eugene (Colo) 4042 Xerxes Ave. S., Minneapolis MN 55410 B Tulsa OK 1933 s Ira & Ruth. W&L 1953; BA U of Oklahoma 1955; BD CDSP 1958; Grad Theol Un 1982. D 5/16/1958 P 11/29/1958 Bp Chilton R Powell. m 11/8/1958 Ann H Crews c 2. P-in-c Trin Epis Ch Kingman AZ 2003-2007; Colorado Epis Fndt Denver CO 1987-1997; P-in-c Epis Ch Of S Ptr And S Mary Denver CO 1987-1997; Exec Dir Colorado Epis Fndt Denver CO 1987-1997; R S Dav's Epis Ch Topeka KS 1982-1986; Post Grad Stdt Grad Theol Un 1981-1982; Chapl: at U of N.M. S Thos Of Cbury Epis Ch Albuquerque NM 1973-1981; Chaplin New Mex Legislature Santa Fe. NM 1962-1968; R S Bede's Epis Ch Santa Fe NM 1962-1967; Asst Ch of the H Faith Santa Fe NM 1961-1962; Inter Sem Mvmt NCC. New York City 1959-1961; P-in-c S Edm's Ch Bronx NY 1959-1961; Vic S Barn Ch Foreman AR 1959; Vic S Jas Ch Antlers OK 1958-1959; S Lk The Beloved Physcn Idabel OK 1958-1959, Vic 1958-1959; Vic S Mk's Ch Hugo OK 1958-1959, Vic 1958-1959; Vic St. Barn Forman AK 1958-1959; Chapl Kansas Legislature Topeka KS 1983; Chapl New Mex Legislature Santa Fe. NM 1962-1968. Associated Parishes Coun. Commencement Speaker CDSP 1963. williamcrews5@gmail.com

CRICHLOW, Neville Joseph (CFla) 381 N Lincoln St, Daytona Beach FL 32114 **P-in-c S Tim's Epis Ch Daytona Bch FL 2013-** B Port-of-Spain Trinidad 1940 s Hubert & Rosie. Lic of Theol Coll of Emm and Saskatoon 1972; BA Advncd U Sask 1983; Post Grad Dplma U Sask 1985; MDiv Coll of Emm and Saskatoon 1987; MDiv Coll of Emm and Saskatoon 1987; DMin GTF 1996.

Trans 12/17/2013 Bp Gregory Orrin Brewer. m 4/24/1998 Dawn McDonald c 2. crichlow@cfl.rr.com

CRIDER, Dion Gregory (Okla) B Dayton OH 1970 s IIa. Diac Formation Iona Sch of Formation 2017. D 6/30/2017 Bp Edward Joseph Konieczny. m 12/28/1998 Linda Kay DeWitt c 3.

CRIGLER, Meredith (Tex) 1115 36th St, Galveston TX 77550 **R Gr Ch Galveston TX 2012-** B Newport RI 1985 d Thomas & Diane. BA Claremont McKenna Coll 2007; MDiv VTS 2010. D 6/19/2010 P 1/6/2011 Bp C Andrew Doyle. m 4/22/2016 Timothy Daniel Crigler. Assoc S Mary's Epis Ch Cypress TX 2010-2012.

CRIM, Marcus Jacob (Cal) 385 Eddy St Apt 613, San Francisco CA 94102 B Lewisburg PA 1958 s Jack & Janet. AA City Coll of San Francisco 1990; BDS Epis Sch for Deacons 2013. D 12/7/2013 Bp Marc Handley Andrus. maccrim@gmail.com

CRIMI, Lynne B (Alb) 7 Sweet Rd, Stillwater NY 12170 B Virginia 1944 d William & Doris. BA Russell Sage Coll 1966; MS Rutgers The St U of New Jersey 1989. D 6/11/2005 Bp Daniel William Herzog. m 8/7/1965 Dennis Crimi c 3. Masters In Soc Wk, Soc Worker Morristown Meml Hosp 1989-1998.

CRIPPEN, David Wells (ETenn) 4617 County Road 103, Florence CO 81226 B Chester PA 1936 s Lynn & Mildred. BS U of Tampa 1962; MA U of So Florida 1965; MA Scarritt Coll 1967; PhD Peabody Coll 1973; MDiv Sewanee: The U So, TS 1986. D 6/10/1986 Bp William Hopkins Folwell P 5/31/1987 Bp George Lazenby Reynolds Jr. m 7/23/1961 Karen Lou Crippen c 3. S Mart Of Tours Epis Ch Chattanooga TN 2008-2010; R S Jos's On-The-Mtn Mentone AL 2001-2008; S Mich And All Ang Anniston AL 1999-2001; S Jas Epis Ch of Greeneville Greeneville TN 1998-1999; S Andr's Epis Ch Douglas GA 1998; 1992-2001; Hosanna Wildwood GA 1992-1997; Chr Epis Ch Tracy City TN 1989-1992; Dio Tennessee Nashville TN 1987-1992; Dio Cntrl Florida Orlando FL 1986-1987. Auth, "Was that a Coincidence or What!," 2013; Auth, "2 Sides of the River," Abingdon Press, 1976; Auth, "New Approaches in Rel Educ"; Auth, "Written Lesson: 4 Methods of Presentation," Elem Sch Journ.

CRIPPEN, Stephen Daniel (Oly) 2631 Jamestown Ln Apt 104, Alexandria VA 22314 B Worthington MN 1970 s Gary & Nancy. BA Augsburg Coll 1992; MA Pacific Luth U 1999; Cert Diac Stud Seattle U 2011. D 10/29/2010 Bp Gregory Harold Rickel. m 9/13/2003 Andrew Stone. D S Paul's Ch Seattle WA 2014-2017; D S Mk's Cathd Seattle WA 2011-2014; D S Steph's Epis Ch Seattle WA 2010-2011.

CRIPPS, David Richard (Roch) 139 Lake Bluff Rd, Rochester NY 14622 **Nonpar 1991-** B Rochester NY 1955 s Richard & Florence. BA S Jn Fisher Coll 1977; MDiv TESM 1980; MS Nazareth Coll 1983. D 8/10/1991 P 5/1/1992 Bp William George Burrill. m 12/15/1984 Kathleen Ann Dobberstein.

CRISE, Rebecca Ann (WMich) Saint Mark's Episcopal Church, PO Box 307, Paw Paw MI 49079 **R S Mk's Epis Ch Paw Paw MI 2007-** B Chicago IL 1951 d Roger & Helen. DVM Pur 1975; MDiv SWTS 2005. D 4/15/2005 P 11/18/2005 Bp Edward Stuart Little II. Cur Chr Ch Waukegan IL 2005-2007; Dn St Jos Dnry 2010-2017; Mem, Dioc Coun Dio Wstrn Michigan Kalamazoo MI 2010-2016.

CRISP, Justin Ernest (ETenn) 111 Oenoke Rdg, New Canaan CT 06840 **Admin S Mk's Ch New Canaan CT 2014-** B Knoxville TN 1989 s Joe & Sherry. BA U of Tennessee 2011; MDiv Berk 2014; Dplma in Angl Stds Ya Berk 2014; MDiv Yale DS 2014. D 6/14/2014 Bp George Young III P 2/1/2015 Bp Richard Frank Grein. m 5/21/2016 Jewelle Bickel.

CRISP, Sheila La (Oly) PO Box 88550, Steilacoom WA 98388 **Died 11/16/2016** B Coronado CA 1960 d Daniel & Jo Ann. AA So Puget Sound Cmnty Coll 2004; BA U of Washington 2006; MDiv CDSP 2010. D 4/17/2010 P 2/3/2011 Bp Gregory Harold Rickel. c 1. P-in-c S Jos And S Jn Ch Lakewood WA 2011-2016; D Chr Ch Tacoma WA 2010-2011; Asst CDSP Berkeley CA 2010.

CRISS, Carthur Paul (Kan) 4138 E 24th St N, Wichita KS 67220 **asssociated P S Jas Ch Wichita KS 2003-, Int 2001-2003** B Kansas City KS 1932 s Paul & Ellen. BA U IL 1954; MDiv SWTS 1957; STM Sewanee: The U So, TS 1971. D 7/11/1957 P 11/1/1958 Bp William Henry Marmion. m 6/3/1977 Marybeth True Criss c 2. Int S Andrews Ch Derby KS 1998-2001; Cn To Ordnry Dio Kansas Topeka KS 1983-1994, Chapl to Ret Cler SW Conv. 2012-; R S Alb's Epis Ch Wichita KS 1978-1997; Chapl Wichita St Univ Campus Mssn Wichita KS 1970-1978; R Gr Epis Ch Winfield KS 1961-1965; Vic Nelson Par Nelson Cnty VA 1957-1961. EFM, Mentor, Trnr 1974-2012. Cn Dio Kansas 2008; Vigil hon Ord of the Arrow, BSA 1978.

CRIST, John Frederick (Chi) P.O. Box, 131 Fifth St., McNabb IL 61335 B Muncie IN 1942 s Robert & Armella. BA MI SU 1965; BD SWTS 1968; MA Edgewood Coll 1991. D 6/29/1968 Bp Archie H Crowley P 3/15/1969 Bp Richard Stanley Merrill Emrich. m 9/2/1967 Maryfrances Crist. S Paul's Ch La Salle IL 2000-2010; Chr Epis Ch Ottawa IL 1999-2010; Chr Ch Streator IL 1998-2010; Assoc Pstr P-t/ Sr. Pstr Epis Mnstry LaSalle Cnty IL 1998-2008; Chr Educ Coordntr Prov VI 1995-1998; R S Mart's Epis Ch Fairmont MN 1990-1998; Prov V 1986-1989; R Trin Ch Janesville WI 1984-1990; R Ch Of The Epiph Washington DC 1980-1984; Asst S Thos Epis Ch Battle Creek MI 1976-1980; Cur Trin Ch Indianapolis IN 1973-1976; Asst S Lk's Epis Ch

Rochester MN 1971-1973; Assoc Min Chr Ch Cathd Eau Claire WI 1969-1971; S Lk's Ch Altoona WI 1969-1971; D-in-c S Jn Bedford MI 1968-1969. Auth, "Change in the Ch," *Acad of Par Cler Journ*, 1970.

CRIST, Mary Frances (Los) St Michael's Episcopal Church, 4070 Jackson St, Riverside CA 92503 **Lead conversion of Ch to outreach Mnstry Cntr S Mich's Epis Ch Riverside CA 2012-; Sum Chapl Intern for Licensing, will complete 4th unit 2013 Gd Samar Hosp Los Angeles CA 2010-; Christmas, Easter, Sum Missions to Native Villages Dio Alaska Fairbanks AK 2005-; Com on Indigenous Mnstry Exec Coun Appointees New York NY 2013-; Dio Los Angeles Los Angeles CA 2012-, Mem, Native Amer Prog Com 2006-2012** B Texas 1944 d Paul & Frances. AB U CA 1966; MEd Pan Amer U 1973; EdD Col 1990; MDiv Claremont TS 2011. D 6/11/2011 P 1/7/2012 Bp Diane Jardine Bruce. m 6/4/1977 William Harold Crist c 2. Sum Chapl Intern - 3 units Gd Samar Hosp Los Angeles CA 2010-2013; Dn, Sch of Educ, Prof California Bapt U Riverside CA 1992-2012; Exec Dir Acad Hill Cntr for Gifted Chld Wilbraham MA 1981-1992; Asst. Hd of Sch St. Lk's Epis Sch San Antonio TX 1979-1981; Hd of Sch St. Matt's Epis Sch Edinburg TX 1976-1979. GC Prchr The Epis Ch 2013; Jonathan R. Davis Awd for Soc Justice, Given in Recognition for Mssn Wk in Alaska ETS at Claremont (Bloy Hse) 2010; Extra Class Amateur Lic FCC 2010; Black Belt Larry Tatum Kenpo Karate 2005. mcristusa@gmail.com

CRIST, Roy Gene (WVa) Box 602, 19958 Midland Trail, Ansted WV 25812 **Died 6/23/2017** B Beckley WV 1939 s Eugene & Hazel. BA W Virginia Inst of Tech 1987. D 12/12/1987 P 12/4/1988 Bp Robert Poland Atkinson. m 4/6/1978 Jane Crist c 3. P-in-c S Andr's Ch Oak Hill WV 2002-2017; Mssnr New River Mnstrs Oak Hill WV 2002-2011; Mssnr The New River Epis Mnstry Pratt WV 1990-2011; P-in-c Ch Of The Redeem Ansted WV 1988-2017. Land 1992.

CRIST JR, William Harold (Los) 2091 Business Center Dr Ste 130, Irvine CA 92612 B Edinburg TX 1946 s William & Larayne. BA TCU 1969; MDiv EDS 1974; MA U of Massachusetts 1988. D 5/23/1974 Bp Harold Cornelius Gosnell P 11/1/1974 Bp Richard Earl Dicus. m 6/4/1977 Mary Frances Crist. Assoc S Geo's Epis Ch Laguna Hills CA 1992-1994; Dio Wstrn Massachusetts Springfield 1991-1992, 1989-1990, Supply P 1988-1989; Asst S Mk's Epis Ch San Antonio TX 1978-1981; Chapl Trin U San Antonio TX 1978-1981; Vic S Matt's Ch Edinburg TX 1974-1977. Klingenstein Fllshp Col 1984.

CRISTE-TROUTMAN, Robert Joseph (Be) 137 Trinity Hill Rd., Mt. Pocono PA 18344 B Bourne MA 1951 s Lawrence & Dorothy. AA Concordia Coll 1971; BA Concordia Coll 1973; MDiv Luth TS at Gettysburg 1979. D 3/21/1998 Bp Jack Marston Mckelvey P 10/31/1998 Bp John Shelby Spong. m Neil I Criste-Troutman c 2. P-in-c Trin Epis Ch Mt Pocono PA 2011-2016; R S Ptr's Ch Washington NJ 2001-2011, Supply 2000-2001; D S Jas Ch Montclair NJ 1998-1999.

CRISTOBAL, Robert S (Chi) 1000 West Rt 64, Oregon IL 61061 **P S Geo/S Mths Ch Chicago IL 2014-** B Moline IL 1979 s Reynaldo & Maria Paz. BA Monmouth Coll 2001; MDiv SWTS 2005. D 6/3/2006 P 12/16/2006 Bp Bill Persell. P-in-c S Bride's Epis Ch Oregon IL 2008-2014. rfs.cristobal@gmail.com

CRITCHFIELD, Margot Dunlap (Mass) PO Box 524, Cohasset MA 02025 B Huntington CT 1955 d Wallace & Margaret. BA GW 1978; MDiv VTS 2001. D 6/9/2001 P 2/9/2002 Bp Jane Hart Holmes Dixon. m 5/31/1987 Donald D Critchfield c 1. R S Steph's Ch Cohasset MA 2008-2017; Assoc S Alb's Par Washington DC 2001-2008.

CRITCHLOW II, Fitzgerald St Clair Jerry (Tex) 3700 Kingwood Dr Apt 1806, Kingwood TX 77339 B Brooklyn NY 1944 s Fitzgerald & Frances. BA Natl U 1985; Cert Natl U 1986; MA Natl U 1988; BA D Formation Prog 1995. D 6/3/1995 Bp Jerry Alban Lamb. m 7/29/1983 Mary Jo Alfonso Critchlow c 2. Serv All SS Meml Sacramento CA 2001-2005; D S Matt's Epis Ch Sacramento CA 1995-2000. Prince Hall Masons 1973; Prince Hall Shiners 1978; Scotish Rite Masons 1976.

CRITELLI, Robert J (NJ) 13 King Arthurs Ct, Sicklerville NJ 08081 **Chr Ch Magnolia NJ 2006-** B Jersey City NJ 1937 s John & Irene. Epiph Apostolic Coll; BA Immac Concep Sem 1959; MS Iona Coll 1971. Rec 6/26/1985 as Deacon Bp Vincent King Pettit. m 11/4/1972 Victoria Hughes c 2. Chr Ch Magnolia NJ 2007-2009; Chr Ch Oaklyn NJ 2004; R Ch Of The Atone Laurel Sprg NJ 1985-1990.

CRITES, Becky (SwVa) St Johns Episcopal Church, P O Box 607, Glasgow VA 24555 **Int R Ch Of The Epiph Danville VA 2014-** B Arlington VA 1957 d Anthony & Elnora. BS Longwood U 1979; Virginia Commonwealth U 1982; MDiv VTS 2007; Cert SMU 2011. D 6/10/2007 Bp A(rthur) Heath Light P 12/15/2007 Bp Neff Powell. m 8/13/1977 James W Crites c 3. R S Jn's Epis Ch Glasgow VA 2008-2014; S Thos Ch Bedford VA 2008-2014; S Jas Ch Roanoke VA 2007; Admin Asst VAFC 2002-2004.

CRITES, Karry D (Nev) 1035 Munley Dr, Reno NV 89503 B Louisville KY 1953 s Cyrus & Joycelynn. BS U of Missouri 1987; MDiv CDSP 1990. D 4/25/1990 P 11/6/1990 Bp Stewart Clark Zabriskie. m 4/7/1979 Dale Crites c 2. ELM Cmnty Ch Reno NV 2002-2009; Gr-St Fran Cmnty Ch Lovelock NV 1990-1996; Dio Nevada Las Vegas 1990-1994. Angl Comm Ntwk; ERM.

CRITTENDEN, Tom Thomas Glasgow (SwVa) 123 W. Washinton St., Lexington VA 24450 **R R E Lee Memi Ch (Epis) Lexington VA 2007-** B Honolulu HI 1953 s William & Conde. BA Lawr 1976; MDiv CDSP 1984. D 6/5/1984 P 12/18/1984 Bp Furman Charles Stough. m 10/8/1988 Christianna H Crittenden c 4. R H Comf Epis Ch Tallahassee FL 1994-2007; Assoc S Mart's Ch Ellisville MO 1991-1994; R Trin Ch Wetumpka AL 1986-1990; Cur Chr Ch Tuscaloosa AL 1984-1986.

CRITTENDEN, William S (WNY) Po Box 93, Chautauqua NY 14722 B Hazelton PA 1932 s William & Eleanor. BA Gannon U 1961; MTh Hur CA 1964. D 6/13/1964 P 3/1/1965 Bp William Crittenden. m 9/7/1963 Charlotte Victoria Crittenden c 2. P-in-c S Lk's Epis Ch Smethport PA 2007-2013; Supply P Dio NW Pennsylvania Erie PA 1991-1999; Cluster Mnstry Clearfield PA 1990-1991; Vic S Barn Ch Franklinville NY 1989-1990; Vic S Jn's Epis Ch Ellicottville NY 1989-1990; Non-par 1976-1989; Vic Ch Of The H Cross No E PA 1974-1976; R S Matt's Epis Ch Horseheads NY 1969-1971; P-in-c S Andr's Rome NY 1966-1969; Assoc Zion Ch Rome NY 1966-1969; Stff S Mk's Ch New Canaan CT 1964-1966.

CROCKER, Byron Grey (Tex) 2025 Hanover Cir, Beaumont TX 77706 B Newton KS 1935 s H Mason & Florabel. BA U of Texas 1957; MDiv CDSP 1966; Oxf GB 1984. D 7/11/1966 Bp Everett H Jones P 1/1/1967 Bp Richard Earl Dicus. m 7/8/2016 Terry Crocker c 1. Trin Epis Ch Jasper TX 2005-2011; S Mk's Ch Beaumont TX 1992-1998; Pstr Assoc. St Marks Epis Ch Beaumont TX US 1991-2005; The Great Cmsn Fndt Houston TX 1991-1992; R S Steph's Ch Beaumont TX 1971-1991; Assoc S Mk's Epis Ch San Antonio TX 1968-1971; Asst Ch Of The Adv Brownsville TX 1966-1968.

CROCKER, Edna Irene (Fla) 10560 Fort George Rd, Jacksonville FL 32226 B Louisville KY 1939 d Reese & Ethel. D 9/23/2012 Bp Samuel Johnson Howard. c 1.

CROCKER, George Neville (Ct) 29 Powder Horn Hl, Brookfield CT 06804 **P-in-c Chr Ch Quaker Farms 2005-; R Emer S Paul's Ch Brookfield CT 2003-, R 1970-2002** B New York,NY 1933 s Neville & Katherine. BS Sthrn Connecticut St U 1964; MDiv Ya Berk 1967; MS Iona Coll 1982; DMin Ecum Theol Cntr Detroit MI 1987. D 6/13/1967 Bp Walter H Gray P 4/6/1968 Bp Joseph Warren Hutchens. Vic Imm Ch Ansonia CT 1969-1970; Cur Chr Ch Ansonia CT 1967-1970; Chapl (LtC) US Army. CHS 1980; OHC.

CROCKER JR, John Alexander Frazer (U) 3541 Ocean View Dr, Florence OR 97439 **Asst S Andr's Epis Ch Florence OR 1996-; Ret 1995-** B Detroit MI 1935 s John & Marjorie. AB Ken 1957; MDiv CDSP 1960; MSW U of Utah 1974; DMin GTF 1992. D 6/29/1960 Bp Richard Stanley Merrill Emrich P 12/30/1960 Bp Gordon V Smith. m 6/4/1977 Diana Crocker c 2. Exec Dir Epis Soc & Pstr Mnstrs Dio Utah Salt Lake City UT 1991-1995, Bp Of U Dep For Pstrl Care & Mnstry Enablement 1988-1990; Epis Cmnty Serv Inc Salt Lake City UT 1991-1995; Chapl St Marks Hosp Salt Lake City UT 1983; Chapl St Prison Draper UT 1968-1974; R S Mary's Ch Provo UT 1967-1972; Assoc R Gr Ch Jamaica NY 1964-1967; Vic S Paul's Indn Mssn Sioux City IA 1961-1964; Cn Trin Cathd Davenport IA 1960-1961. Cath Fllshp Epis Ch; OHC.

CROCKER, Ronald Conrad (Va) 3 Hamilton Court, Uxbridge MA 01569 B Quincy MA 1944 s Rendell & Margaret. BA U of Massachusetts 1965; MDiv CDSP 1968. D 6/30/1968 Bp Frederic Cunningham Lawrence P 5/17/1969 Bp Anson Phelps Stokes Jr. m 8/19/1967 Donna G Crocker c 4. R S Geo's Epis Ch Arlington VA 1997-2009; Cn to Ordnry Dio Rhode Island Providence RI 1991-1997; R Chr Ch In Lonsdale Lincoln RI 1979-1990; R S Ptr's Ch Dartmouth MA 1970-1979; Cur S Paul's Ch Brockton MA 1968-1970. Auth, *Passion & Death of Jesus*, Priv, 1971; Auth, "Psalm 80," *Psalm 80*, Priv, 1968.

CROCKETT, Daniel L (SVa) PO Box 102, Conyers GA 30012 **Hungars Par Machipongo VA 2014-** B Ottawa KS 1954 s James & Leta. BA Coll of the Ozarks 1991; MDiv VTS 1994. D 6/4/1994 Bp John Clark Buchanan P 1/6/1995 Bp Ted Gulick Jr. m 6/24/1995 Star A Crockett c 2. Chr Epis Ch Eastville VA 2014; R S Simon's Epis Ch Conyers GA 2003-2014; R S Mk's Epis Ch Jonesboro AR 2000-2003; R S Ptr's Epis Ch Monroe CT 1996-2000; Area Mssnr Barren River Area Russellville KY 1994-1996; Epis Chapl Wstrn Kentucky St U Bowling Green KY 1994-1996. Weekly Rel Columnist, *Rockdale Citizen*, 2004 - 2008. Davis Awd for Soc Justice ETS at Claremont (Bloy Hse) 2010; Ord of the W Range Pi Kappa Alpha Fraternity 2008; Burger Schlrshp Burger Fndt 1991; Ozark Fell Coll of the Ozarks 1991.

CROCKETT, Jennie L (SO) 2700 Kenview Rd S, Columbus OH 43209 B Franklin County 1939 d Helen. BA Capital U 1985; MDiv The Angl Acad Columbia 2006. D 5/13/2006 Bp Kenneth Lester Price. m 7/15/1961 Kenneth L Crockett c 2.

CROCKETT, Larry Joe (Minn) 4525 Alicia Dr, Inver Grove Heights MN 55077 **hon Dir/ Prof Augsburg Coll Minneapolis MN 1988-** B Dayton OH 1949 s Fred & Amelia. BA Pacific Luth U 1971; MDiv Luther TS 1977; PhD U MN 1990. D 12/17/1999 Bp James Louis Jelinek P 8/10/2000 Bp Daniel Lee Swenson. m 3/21/1981 Cheryl Diane Crockett c 2. P-in-c S Mary's Basswood Grove Hastings MN 2001-2010. Auth, *Turing Test and the Frame Problem*, Ablex, 1994; Auth, *Universal Assembly Lang*, McGraw-Hill, 1986. Honored Fac Awd Augsburg Coll 1996; Outstanding Tchg Awd Metro St U 1987.

CROES, John Rodney (NJ) 20 Claremont Ave, South River NJ 08882 B New Brunswick NJ 1942 s John & Evelyn. BA Rutgers The St U of New Jersey 1966; MDiv PDS 1974. D 4/27/1974 P 12/1/1974 Bp Albert Wiencke Van Duzer. m 9/1/2008 Margaret P Croes c 3. R S Ptr's Ch Perth Amboy NJ 1977-2008, Cur 1974-1977; R St Jn the Bapt Epis Ch Linden NJ 1976-1977; Captain, Disaster Control Off USAF 1956-1971.

CROFT, Charles Carter (RG) 615 N Texas St, Silver City NM 88061 B Lohngsthal NY DE 1955 s Eldred & Mary. BA Acadia U 1977; MDiv Nash 1990; Cert Advncd CPE 1991. D 6/30/1990 P 2/1/1991 Bp Rogers Sanders Harris. m 9/11/1999 Ann H Croft c 1. R Ch Of The Gd Shpd Silver City NM 2008-2010; Int Epis Ch Of The Sav Hanford CA 2007-2008; Asst S Jas Epis Cathd Fresno CA 2003-2007; S Mary's Ch Charleroi PA 2001-2003; S Andr's Ch Breckenridge TX 1996-2001; Ch Of The Redeem Sarasota FL 1991-1996; Dio SW Florida Parrish FL 1990-1991; Res Chapl S Lk's Cntr Milwaukee WI 1990-1991.

CROFT, Jay Leslie (WA) 5595 Teakwood Ct, Frederick MD 21703 **P Assoc Ch Of The H Comf Montgomery AL 2011-** B Hartford CT 1942 s Enoch & Lila. BA Simpson Coll 1965; MDiv UTS 1970. D 6/7/1969 P 12/10/1969 Bp Horace W B Donegan. m 8/7/1968 Frances Ralston Croft c 2. P-in-c S Mk's For The Deaf Mobile AL 2006-2009; Archd Deaf Dio Alabama Birmingham 1996-2005; R S Jn's Epis Deaf Ch Birmingham AL 1996-2005; Dio Washington Washington DC 1996; Vic S Barn' Epis Ch of The Deaf Chevy Chase MD 1980-1995; Vic For Deaf Wk Dio Ohio Cleveland 1974-1979; Vic S Ann's Ch For The Deaf New York NY 1969-1974. Epis Conf Of The Deaf Of The Epis Ch In The 1984. Meritorious Serv Awd ECD 1992.

CROMEY, Edwin Harry (NY) St. Luke's Church, 850 Wolcott Ave. Box 507, Beacon NY 12508 **Vic S Lk's Ch Beacon NY 2006-** B Brooklyn NY 1934 s Edward & Helen. BA Adel 1956; MDiv GTS 1962; DMin Drew U 1997. D 4/28/1962 P 12/21/1962 Bp James Pernette DeWolfe. m 8/11/1972 Pamela Cromey c 2. R S Mary's-In-Tuxedo Tuxedo Pk NY 1981-2006; P-in-c S Jn's Arden NY 1980-2006; Int Ch of S Jn on the Mtn Bernardsville NJ 1979-1980; St Jn The Bapt Sch Mendham NJ 1978-1980; Headmaster S Jn the Bapt Sch Mendham NJ 1975-1980; P-in-c S Jn Jersey City NJ 1973-1976; Headmaster Luth Par Sch of Hudson Cnty Jersey City NJ 1972-1975; R S Ann's Ch Sayville NY 1964-1970; Asst Cathd Of The Incarn Garden City NY 1962-1964. Auth, "Faith is There," *Let Us Get on w the Works*; Auth, *S Jn Bapt Sch 1880-1980*; Auth, *Ultimate in Educ*. Cmnty of S Jn the Bapt 1975.

CROMEY, Robert Warren (Cal) 3839 - 20th, San Francisco CA 94114 B Brooklyn NY 1931 s Edward & Helen. Coll of Preachers; Esalen Inst; BA NYU 1953; MDiv GTS 1956. D 6/3/1956 P 12/17/1956 Bp Horace W B Donegan. m 8/14/1983 Elizabeth Garbett c 3. R Trin Ch San Francisco CA 1981-2002; S Eliz's Epis Ch S San Fran CA 1981; 1970-1981; Vic S Aid's Ch San Francisco CA 1965-1970; Cn Ordnry Dio California San Francisco CA 1962-1965; R Ch Of The H Nativ Bronx NY 1958-1962; Cur Chr Ch Bronxville NY 1956-1958. "So You Want to Get m," *Self-Pub*, Lulu.com, 2007; Auth, *In God's Image*, Alamo Sq Press, 1992; Auth, "Feeding Prog," *Wit*, 1972; Auth, "Sex and the Unmarried," *Wit*, 1972; Auth, "Soc Relatns as Evang," *Wit*, 1968; Auth, "I Can't Pray," *Wit*, 1968; Auth, "Mnstry to Homosexuals," *LivCh*, 1964. Bd Trst, GTS 1991-1994; Ethics Com U CA Med Cntr San Francisco CA 1997-1999. SS Alive Awd MCC, San Francisco 1995; Ldrshp in GLT Rts Cable Car Awards 1990; Care of Homeless Awd San Francisco Bd. of Supervisors 1985.

CROMMELIN-DELL, Sally Huntress (SVa) 500 Court St., Portsmouth VA 23704 B San Diego CA 1938 d Henry & Sally. BA Wellesley Coll 1960; MSW U of Houston Grad Sch of Soc Wk 1978; MDiv EDS 2008. D 2/1/2008 P 8/1/2008 Bp John Clark Buchanan. m 1/26/1980 Paul F Dell c 4. Assoc Estrn Shore Chap Virginia Bch VA 2010-2013.

CROMWELL, Peggy Lynn (Ark) **D S Ptr's Ch Conway AR 2016-** B Helena AR 1960 D 8/6/2016 Bp Larry Benfield.

CROMWELL, Richard (NJ) 322 Aoloa St Apt 1103, Kailua HI 96734 B Bronx NY 1947 s Richard & Corinne. BA Drew U 1970; MDiv PDS 1973; Andover Newton TS 1985. D 6/9/1973 Bp Leland Stark P 6/1/1974 Bp George E Rath. m 6/6/1970 Margaret Monahan c 1. P-in-c S Geo's Ch Pennsville NJ 2011-2012; Int S Ptr's At The Light 2003-2004; Assoc S Dav's Ch Cranbury NJ 1997-2004; Non-par 1983-1997; Chapl New Hampshire Yth Dvlpmt Cntr 1981-1984; Asst Ch Of The Gd Shpd Waban MA 1981-1982; Int All SS Ch Stoneham MA 1979-1980; R Ch Of The H Comm Norwood NJ 1975-1979; Cur S Paul's Epis Ch Morris Plains NJ 1973-1974. ACPE, AAPC, Ord Of S Lk.

CRON, Ian Morgan (Ct) 226 5th Ave S, Franklin TN 37064 **S Aug's Chap Nashville TN 2017-** B Bronxville NY 1960 s John & Anne. BA Bow 1982; MA Denver Sem 1994; MDiv NYTS 1997. Trans 1/26/2012 as Priest Bp Ian Theodore Douglas. m 6/20/1987 Anne Rankin Cron c 3. Asst Chr Ch Greenwich CT 2012-2017.

✠ CRONEBERGER, The Rt Rev John Palmer (Be) 1079 Old Bernville Rd, Reading PA 19605 **Ret Bp Dio Newark Newark NJ 2007-** B Pottsville PA 1938 s Robert & Ethel. BA Leh 1960; MDiv VTS 1963. D 6/15/1963 P 3/1/1964 Bp Frederick Warnecke Con 11/21/1998 for Nwk. c 5. Bp of Newark Dio Newark Newark NJ 2000-2007, Ret Bp of Newark 1998-2007, Bp Coadj of Newark

1998-2000, Pres, Newark Cler Assn 1992-1998, Dep, GC 1991-1997, Stndg Com 1993-1998, Dioc Coun 1983-1985; R Ch Of The Atone Tenafly NJ 1980-1998; R S Mary's Epis Ch Reading PA 1974-1980; S Mk's Epis Ch Moscow PA 1966-1980; R S Mk's Ch Dunmore PA 1964-1974; Vic S Geo's Ch Olyphant PA 1963-1966; Chair, Evang Com Dio Bethlehem Bethlehem PA 1977-1979, Dep, GC 1973-1979, Exec Coun 1967-1976. Auth, "Spkng the Truth About Doing the Truth," *The Voice of Integrity*. DD VTS 1999; Hon Lifetime Cn Dio Newark 1996; Dioc Cbury Schlr Dio Newark 1992.

CRONIN, Audrey Ann (WMass) D 10/28/2006 Bp Gordon Scruton.

CROOK II, Jerry V (Ga) 4027 Dumaine Way, Memphis TN 38117 B Memphis TN 1946 s Jerry & Mary Francis. BS Lambeth Coll 1969; MDiv GTS 1976. D 4/21/1976 P 11/1/1976 Bp George Paul Reeves. Consult No Amer Cousel St. Geo's Coll Jerusalem 2013-2015; Asst S Geo's Ch Germantown TN 2006-2014; S Eliz's Epis Ch Richmond Hill GA 2004-2005; S Phil's Ch Hinesville Hinesville GA 1985-1990; Non-par 1979-1983; Calv Ch Americus GA 1978-1983; The Ch Of The Gd Shpd Augusta GA 1976-1978.

CROOK, Senter Cawthon (WTenn) 2796 Lombardy Ave, Memphis TN 38111 **Assoc Gr St.Lukes 2005-; Pstr Counslr Samar Cnslng Cntr 1991-** B Memphis TN 1943 d Jere & Janie. Bradford Coll; Pacifica Grad Inst; BA Rhodes Coll 1965; MDiv Sewanee: The U So, TS 1988. D 6/26/1988 P 5/20/1989 Bp Alex Dockery Dickson. c 3. S Geo's Ch Germantown TN 2012-2013; Asstg P S Mary's Cathd Memphis TN 1996-1998; Assoc S Elis's Epis Ch Memphis TN 1993-1995; Int Ch of the H Apos Collierville TN 1990, Assoc 1988-1989.

CROOM, James (WMich) 2795 Riley Ridge Road, Holland MI 49424 **S Anne's Ch Winston Salem NC 2016-** B Fort Hood TX 1949 s Horace & Irene. BMus U NC 1973; MMus U NC 1977; MDiv CDSP 2001; DMin Wstrn Theol Seminsry 2013. D 6/2/2001 P 12/1/2001 Bp William Edwin Swing. m 4/8/1995 Stephanie B Croom c 1. Ch of the H Sprt Belmont MI 2015-2016; Dn Dio Wstrn Michigan Kalamazoo MI 2010-2016, COM 2008-2011; R H Trin Epis Ch Wyoming MI 2008-2016; Gr Ch Grand Rapids MI 2008-2010; Int S Lk's Par Kalamazoo MI 2007-2008; Dir of Sprtl Care Epis Hm Fndt Lafayette CA 2006-2007; Epis Sr Communities Lafayette CA 2006-2007; Ch Of Our Sav Mill Vlly CA 2004-2006; Int Gr Ch Martinez CA 2002-2004; Cur S Bede's Epis Ch Menlo Pk CA 2001-2002.

CROSBY, David Malcolm (Va) Immanuel Church-on-the-Hill, 3606 Seminary Rd, Alexandria VA 22304 **Assoc Imm Ch-On-The-Hill Alexandria VA 2012-** B Norfolk VA 1958 s Derrill & Margaret. Lic MDiv VTS 2012. D 6/2/2012 Bp Ted Gulick Jr P 12/15/2012 Bp Shannon Sherwood Johnston. m 1/2/1981 Christine McFadden Crosby c 1. VTS Alexandria VA 2013-2014. dcrosby@icoh.net

CROSBY, Derrill Plummer (NH) 11 Central St, Peterborough NH 03458 **Ret 1991-** B Providence RI 1923 s Gordon & Florence. BA U of Maryland 1971; MDiv VTS 1977; Ldrshp Acad for New Directions 1981. D 5/21/1977 Bp Robert Bruce Hall P 11/1/1977 Bp Charles Gresham Marmion. m 2/20/1988 Janice Crosby c 3. R Ch Of The Epiph Newport NH 1983-1990; Dn Roanoke Cler Dio SW Virginia Roanoke VA 1978-1981; R Trin Ch Buchanan VA 1977-1983; Chair - Dioc Subcommittee Ret Cler & Fams Dio New Hampshire Concord NH 1991-1995, Dioc Renwl & Evang Com 1988-1990, Sprtl Dir Curs Sec 1984-1987, Exec Dir Newport Area Assn Chs 1983. Auth, "arts". Bro Of S Andr; Ord Of S Lk.

CROSBY, Karen Ann (Md) 52 S Broadway, Frostburg MD 21532 **P-in-c S Jn's Ch Frostburg MD 2013-** B Cumberland MD 1956 d Ernest & Ruth. BA Frostburg St U 1978; MSW W Virginia U 1980; Luth TS Gettysburg PA 2011. D 7/6/2008 P 2/14/2009 Bp John L Rabb. m 8/8/1981 Anthony E Crosby.

CROSIER, Allen Duane (Spok) D 12/15/2002 Bp James E Waggoner Jr.

CROSKEY, Christine Lucille (CFla) Holy Apostles Episcopal Church, 505 Grant Ave, Satellite Beach FL 32937 B Bryn Mawr PA 1949 d Ralph & Margaret. D 9/10/2016 Bp Gregory Orrin Brewer. m 10/15/2005 Brian M Nemeth c 2.

CROSS II, Eugenia Sealy (NC) 1032 Wessyngton Rd, Winston Salem NC 27104 B Marion NC 1949 d Oliver & Eugenia. BA Meredith Coll 1974; MDiv VTS 1992. D 6/15/1992 Bp Robert Whitridge Estill P 6/1/1993 Bp Huntington Williams Jr. m 2/7/2014 Georgena H Clayton. Vic Ch Of The Ascen At Fork Advance NC 2007-2014; Assoc R S Tim's Epis Ch Winston Salem NC 1992-2006.

CROSS JR, Freeman Grant (Ga) 5424 Hill Rd, Albany GA 31705 B Knoxville TN 1935 s Freeman & Jean. BS USMA 1957; MS U IL 1962; MDiv SWTS 1989. D 6/10/1989 P 3/1/1990 Bp Harry Woolston Shipps. m 12/6/1961 Emilie Cross c 2. Ch Of The H Sprt Dawson GA 1997-2007; S Marg Of Scotland Epis Ch Moultrie GA 1995-1996; S Fran Ch Camilla GA 1993-2007; Vic S Matt's Epis Ch Fitzgerald GA 1989-1993; Vic S Marg-Scotland Moultrie S Fran.

CROSS, Kevin Michael (Eas) P.O. Box 387, Oxford MD 21654 **Chapl (Vol) The Natl Cathd 2011-; R Ch Of The H Trin Oxford MD 2010-; Pres Recovery Mnstrs of the Epis Ch 2009-; Coun Yth Shpd Dio Easton Easton MD 2012-** B Grosse Pointe Shores, MI 1952 s Harold & Loretta. BA Tufts U 1974; MSW Boston Coll 1977; MDiv EDS 2008. Trans 3/31/2010 Bp Bud Shand. m 8/18/1974 Barbara A Cross c 2. Soc Justice Awd EDS 2008.

CROSS, Myrick Tyler (SO) 52 Pleasant St., Freedom ME 04941 **P-in-c S Pat's Ch Brewer ME 2014-, Int 2004-2005** B Belfast ME 1943 s Stephen & Hazel. BA Wheaton Coll 1965; MEd U of Maine 1969; EdD Ball St U 1976; MDiv GTS 1983. D 5/28/1983 P 12/1/1983 Bp Frederick Barton Wolf. c 2. Cn Vic Chr Ch Cathd Cincinnati OH 2005-2010; Int S Jas Ch Old Town ME 2005; R St Fran By The Sea Epis Ch Blue Hill ME 2001-2003; R Ch Of The Mssh Woods Hole MA 1989-2001; Assoc The Ch Of The Redeem Baltimore MD 1986-1989; R Chr Ch Biddeford ME 1983-1986.

CROSS, Samuel Otis (NY) 330 Fletcher Hollow Rd, Collierville TN 38017 B Memphis TN 1947 s Ruben & Annie. BS U of Memphis 1971; MDiv GTS 1976; STM GTS 1981. D 6/26/1976 Bp John Vander Horst P 4/24/1977 Bp William Evan Sanders. Assoc P S Jn's Ch New York NY 1993-2017; Vic Ch Of The H Apos Brooklyn NY 1991-1993, Vic 1986-1989; Epis Mssn Soc New York NY 1989-1991; R S Paul's Ch Brooklyn NY 1985-1986, Vic 1982-1984; Dio Long Island Garden City NY 1983-1984; Bp Otey Memi Ch Memphis TN 1977-1979; Dio Tennessee Nashville TN 1977-1979; D-in-Trng Ch Of The Gd Shpd Lookout Mtn TN 1976-1977.

CROSSETT, Judith Hale Wallace (Ia) 320 E College St, Iowa City IA 52240 **D Trin Ch Iowa City IA 2009-; CPE Advsry Com U of Iowa Hospitals 2000-** B Chicago IL 1947 d David & Joan. BA Gri 1968; MA U Tor Toronto ON CA 1970; PhD U of Iowa 1977; MD U of Iowa 1984; MS U of Iowa 1988; none Nash 2003. D 2/8/2009 Bp Alan Scarfe. c 1.

CROSSNOE, Marshall E (Mo) 217 ADAMS ST, JEFFERSON CITY MO 65101 **S Alb's Epis Ch Fulton MO 2008-** B Abilene TX 1960 s Floyd & Barbara. MA Dallas TS 1986; MA U of Texas 1989; PhD U of Wisconsin 1996. D 12/21/2007 P 6/21/2008 Bp George Wayne Smith. m 12/19/1987 Debra Sue Crossnoe c 2. Part Time S Mk's Epis Ch Portland MO 2008-2015.

CROSSWAITE, John (CNY) 700 Quinlan Dr., Pewaukee WI 53072 **Cn Dio Cntrl New York Liverpool NY 2017-** B Elkhorn WI 1949 s John & Mary. MDiv S Fran Sem 1978; MA U of San Francisco 1984. Rec 7/8/2008 as Priest Bp Steven Andrew Miller. c 2. Chr Ch Clayton NY 2013-2017; St Jn's Ch Cape Vinc NY 2013-2017. jcrosswaite@cnyepiscopal.org

CROTHERS, John-Michael (NY) 214 Burntwood Trl, Toms River NJ 08753 **Ret 1999-** B Vancouver BC CA 1938 s Donald & Helene. BA Concordia U 1963; MDiv GTS 1966. D 6/16/1966 P 12/21/1966 Bp Jonathan Goodhue Sherman. Chapl AGO Staten Island NY 1979-1990; R S Jn's Ch Staten Island NY 1978-1999; P-in-c Ch Of S Alb The Mtyr S Albans NY 1977; Asst Zion Ch Douglaston NY 1976-1978; Admin Ord of S Vinc Pelham Manor NY 1974-1978; Asst ACU Pelham Manor NY 1974-1976; Cur S Paul's Ch Brooklyn NY 1968-1974; Cur S Thos' Epis Ch Floral Pk NY 1967-1968; Curage St Andr's Williston Pk NY 1966-1967. CCU 1968; GAS 2001; SocMary 1999; SSC 1991. DD Ign U, Indianapolis, IN 1999.

CROTHERS, Kenneth Delbert (Ida) Po Box 374, Shoshone ID 83352 **D Chr Ch Shoshone ID 1988-** B Jerome ID 1925 s Delbert & Olive. BS Idaho St U 1949; MS U of Idaho 1955. D 11/6/1988 Bp David Bell Birney IV. m 8/27/1950 Inez Marie Crothers c 3.

CROUCH, Billy Gene (NY) 3604 Balcones Dr, Austin TX 78731 **Ret 1995-** B Port Lavaca TX 1930 s Lemuel & Lillian. BS Baylor U 1954; MS Baylor U 1955; PhD U of Tennessee 1958. D 12/24/1961 Bp James Albert Pike. Asst Ch Of The Resurr New York NY 1965-1995; Asst S Jn's Ch Cohoes NY 1964-1965; Asst Gr Cathd San Francisco CA 1961-1963.

CROUCH, Emily Schwartz (Ky) 821 S 4th St, Louisville KY 40203 B Tallahassee FL 1980 d Geoffrey & Victoria. BA Rhodes Coll 2002; MS Louisville Presb Sem 2007; MDiv GTS 2008. D 9/5/2008 P 3/25/2009 Bp Ted Gulick Jr. m 5/30/2010 Zachary James Crouch c 1. Assoc S Matt's Epis Ch Louisville KY 2009-2016; Assoc Calv Ch Louisville KY 2008-2009.

CROW, Lynda D (Los) 1145 W Valencia Mesa Dr, Fullerton CA 92833 **Assoc R Emm Par Fullerton CA 1995-** B Toronto Ontario Canada 1947 d Leslie & Bessie. AS Mt San Antonio Coll 1967; BA U of La Verne 1984; MDiv CDSP 1995. D 6/10/1995 Bp Robert Marshall Anderson P 1/13/1996 Bp Chester Lovelle Talton. c 2.

CROW, Robert B (CGC) St. Andrews By-the-Sea Episcopal Church, PO Box 1658, Destin FL 32540 **R S Andr's By The Sea Epis Ch Destin FL 2011-** B Jackson MS 1963 s Robert & Margaret. BS U of Alabama Birmingham 1986; MBA Samford U 1993; MDiv Sewanee: The U So, TS 2011. D 5/14/2011 Bp Scott Anson Benhase P 2/11/2012 Bp Philip Menzie Duncan II. m 6/20/1992 Kathryn Ann Brymer Crow.

CROWDER, James Robert (Md) 13801 York Rd Apt E9, Cockeysville MD 21030 **Ret 1996-; Dio Maryland Baltimore MD 2002-, Chair, T/F of Corp 1998-2001, Human Sxlty Com 1990-1997, Dioc Coun 1971-1989** B Ellisville MS 1933 s Walter & Sadie. BS Mississippi St U 1955; MDiv VTS 1959. D 6/16/1959 P 12/17/1959 Bp Duncan Montgomery Gray. m 6/6/1958 Suzanne Crowder c 4. Exec Secy Corporations for Widows and Chld of Cler in Maryland 2001-2012; S Jn's Ch Ellicott City MD 1996; Sr Assoc The Ch Of The Redeem Baltimore MD 1989-1996; R S Jas Epis Ch Farmington CT 1976-1989; Epiph Ch Dulaney Vlly Luthvle Timon MD 1966-1976; R S Jn's Ch Mt Washington Baltimore MD 1961-1966; Asst S Paul's Epis Ch Meridian MS 1959-1961;

Fin Com Dio Connecticut Meriden CT 1984-1986, Chair Structure Evaltn Com 1980-1983.

CROWE, Amy Beth (Haw) **H Innoc' Epis Ch Lahaina HI 2015-** B Wilmington DE 1975 d Charles & Sue. BA Estrn U 1997; MDiv PrTS 2000. D 10/28/2011 P 5/12/2012 Bp Robert Leroy Fitzpatrick. m 9/24/2011 James K Crowe c 2.

CROWE, Kathleen A (ECR) The Rev Kathleen Crowe, 4271 N 1st St Spc 74, San Jose CA 95134 **D S Andr's Ch Saratoga CA 2013-; Chapl Chapl San Jose St U 2012-** B Sioux City Iowa 1945 d William & Helen. Unviersity of California Santa Cruz Cert in Behavioral Sci 1998; BA California Sch for Deacons 2007. D 9/8/2007 Bp Sylvestre Donato Romero. D Ch Of The H Sprt Campbell CA 2007-2014; D Gd Samar Epis Ch San Jose CA 2007-2009; Sr. Software Engr IBM 1969-2002.

CROWELL, Larry A (SO) B Philipsburg PA 1953 s Jules & Helen. BBA Elizabethtown Coll 1976; MPA Penn 1985; MDiv TESM 2004. D 6/12/2004 P 12/12/2004 Bp Robert William Duncan. m 3/2/1974 Deborah Crowell. S Lk's Ch Powhatan VA 2007-2011; Galilee Epis Ch Virginia Bch VA 2005-2007; Angl Comm. Ntwk Of Dio And Parishes Pittsburgh PA 2004-2005.

CROWELL, Paul L (Az) 2800 Huntsman Ct, Jamestown NC 27282 **Ret 2006-** B Denver CO 1942 s Paul & Mary. BA Cornell Coll 1965; MDiv Nash 1981; DMin Fuller TS 1997. D 5/26/1981 P 11/30/1981 Bp Walter Cameron Righter. m 8/15/1965 Patricia Crowell c 4. R S Lk's Ch Prescott AZ 1990-2006; Assoc R All SS Ch Of Winter Pk Winter Pk FL 1985-1990; Vic S Geo's Ch Oshkosh NE 1981-1985; Vic S Paul's Ch Ogallala NE 1981-1985. Auth, *BRF SALT*. OHC 1981.

CROWLE, Wesley Edward (Minn) 1545 Northeast 7 1/2 Avenue NE, Rochester MN 55906 **Died 5/26/2017** B Three Hills AB CA 1922 s Harold & Ida. BA U of Alberta Edmonton AB CA 1948; LTh U Tor 1951; CPE Advncd CPE 1962. Trans 9/1/1965 as Priest Bp Hamilton Hyde Kellogg. m 1/21/1956 Dorothy I Crowle c 4. Pstr Asst S Lk's Epis Ch Rochester MN 1990-2017, Int 1988-1989; Chapl Asst Hosp Rochester MN 1990-1991; Ret 1988-2017; Epis Cmnty Serv Inc Minneapolis MN 1982-1986; Dio Minnesota Minneapolis MN 1965-1988; Epis Chapl Hosp Rochester MN 1965-1988; Serv Ch of Can 1951-1965. APHA 1971-1989; Assembly of Epis Hosp & Chapl 1981-1989; Assn of Profsnl Chapl 1998-1989; Coll of Chapl 1971-1989. Chapl Emer Coll of Chapl APHA 1989.

CROWLEY, Daniel Fenwick (Mass) 76 Olde Towne Lane, West Chatham MA 02669 B Lawrence MA 1940 s Archie & Jean. BA Wms 1962; MA Col 1963; BD EDS 1970. D 6/20/1970 P 1/29/1971 Bp Archie H Crowley. m 8/17/1963 Susan L Crowley c 3. Int S Jn's Epis Ch Saugus MA 2008-2010; Int S Paul's Epis Ch No Andover MA 2006-2007; Yth Dir S Jn's Epis Ch Westwood MA 2004-2006; Assoc Ch Of The H Sprt Mattapan MA 2000-2004; Assoc R S Jn's Ch Ellicott City MD 1997-2000; R S Jn's Ch Bridgeport CT 1984-1997; R S Mart's Epis Ch New Bedford MA 1974-1984; Cur S Ptr's Epis Ch Lakewood OH 1970-1974. Phillips Brook Soc 2000-2003.

CROWSON, Steven Franklin (LI) 1778 Hallowell Rd, Litchfield ME 04350 B Birmingham AL 1939 s Cecil & Selamarie. BS Auburn U 1963; MDiv Gordon-Conwell TS 1974; DMin Bos 1987. D 6/9/1976 P 12/5/1976 Bp Morris Fairchild Arnold. c 1. R Dio Maine Portland ME 2008-2016; R Trin Epis Ch Lewiston ME 2008-2016; R S Mary's Epis Ch Shltr Island NY 1995-2006; R Gr Ch Salem MA 1979-1995; Cur S Paul's Ch Brockton MA 1976-1978.

✠ **CROWTHER, The Rt Rev CE** (Los) 289 Moreton Bay Ln Apt 2, Goleta CA 93117 **Asstg Bp Dio Los Angeles 1988-; Psych Priv Pract Santa Barbara 1975-** B Bradford Yorkshire UK 1929 s Joseph & Margaret. BA U of Leeds Gb 1950; LLB U of Leeds Gb 1952; LLM U of Leeds Gb 1953; GOE Cuddesdon Theol Coll Oxford 1956; PhD U CA 1975. Trans 4/1/1959 as Priest Bp Francis E I Bloy. m 12/18/1994 Claudette Y Crowther. Collegial Bp Of Ecr Dio El Camino Real Salinas CA 1984-1986; Dio California San Francisco CA 1971-1977; Dir Allnce Labor Action Santa Barbara CA 1969-1971; Fell Cntr for the Study of Democratic Institutions 1967-1969; Bp Of Kimberley & Kuruman (Deported) Kimberley & Kuruman 1965-1967; Dn S Cyp's Cathd 1964-1965; Lectr in Black Stds UCLA 1959-1964; Serv Ch Of Engl 1956-1958. Auth, "Where Rel Gets Lost In The Ch," Morehouse Barlow; Auth, "Face Of Apartheid," U Of New Zealand Press; Auth, "Rel Trusts: Their Dvlpmt," *Scope & Meaning*, Geo Ronald - Oxford; Auth, "Intimacy," *Strtgies For Successful Relationships*, Capra Press. Dplma AAPC, Life Clini.

CROWTHER JR, James Pollard (Ga) 398 Laurel Mountain Trl # 999, Saluda NC 28773 **Died 9/9/2015** B New York NY 1933 s James & Lottie. BS Florida St U 1954; Harv 1966; MDiv Sewanee: The U So, TS 1971; MS Sewanee: The U So, TS 1973. D 6/17/1957 P 2/1/1961 Bp Albert R Stuart. Ret 1983-2015; S Fran Ch Camilla GA 1983-1986; Cur All SS Epis Ch Thomasville GA 1982-1983; Chr Ch Greenville SC 1978-1980; S Steph's Ch S Steph SC 1968-1977; Trin Epis Ch Pinopolis SC 1968-1977; Cur H Trin Epis Ch Charleston SC 1966-1968; Assoc Chapl S Mk's Sch Southborough MA 1963-1966; Cur The Ch Of The Gd Shpd Augusta GA 1960-1963; Serv Ch In Liberia 1958-1960; Ch Of The Gd Shpd Swainsboro GA 1957-1958; Vic The Epis Ch Of The Annunc Vidalia GA 1957-1958. Auth, "How To Teach Rel (The Old-Fashioned And Proven Way)"; Auth, "A Study Course On The Miracles In The NT," *A Few Portraits Of Jesus Chr In The NT*; Auth, "A Study Course On The Bk Of Revelation," *H Cross*; Auth, "A Study Course On The Original Twelve Apos - Plua Study Course On The Original Twelve Apos - Plus One," *What Happened At The Reformation (An Ang*.

CROZIER, Richard Lee (USC) 125 Pendleton St Sw, Aiken SC 29801 **Still Hopes Epis Ret Cmnty W Columbia SC 2016-** B San Diego CA 1956 s Robert & Carolyn. BA San Diego St U 1981; MDiv SWTS 1984. D 8/24/1984 Bp Charles Brinkley Morton P 5/1/1985 Bp Richard Mitchell Trelease Jr. m 6/25/1982 Rita Ann Crozier. S Barn Ch Jenkinsville SC 2001; S Thad Epis Ch Aiken SC 1998-2000; Off Of Bsh For ArmdF New York NY 1993-1998; Vic S Mk's Ch Chester SC 1987-1993; Vic S Ptr's Ch Great Falls SC 1987-1993; R S Mk's Epis Ch Pecos TX 1985-1986; Cur S Andr's Ch Roswell NM 1984-1985. SHN.

CRUIKSHANK, Charles Clark (CPa) 208 W Foster Ave, State College PA 16801 **D S Andr's Ch St Coll PA 2013-** B Sewickley PA 1956 s Charles & Lois. BS Penn 1979. D 10/31/2010 Bp Nathan Dwight Baxter. m 10/27/1979 Patricia Cruikshank c 2.

CRUM JR, George Milton (USC) 9 Bumblebee Court, Helena MT 59601 **Died 6/27/2017** B Orangeburg SC 1924 s George & Sadelle. Clemson U 1943; BS U of Nebraska 1945; MDiv Sewanee: The U So, TS 1951; Dip S Augustines Coll Cbury GB 1957; Cert CUA 1970. D 6/28/1951 P 2/1/1952 Bp Thomas N Carruthers. Ret 1989-2017; Prof VTS Alexandria VA 1972-1989, Asst Prof 1966-1969; Chapl H Trin Par Epis Clemson SC 1961-1966; Chapl Clemson U Clemson SC 1960-1966; R Ch Of The H Comm Allendale SC 1951-1960. Auth, "Bereavement: Long Term," *PlainViews*, HealthCare Chapl Ntwk, 2015; Auth, "On frailty and facing death," *AgingToday*, Amer Soc on Aging, 2014; Auth, "I'm Old," *Lifelong Faith Fndt Resources*, Cntr for Sprtl Resources, 2011; Auth, "Evil, Anger, and God," WingSpan Press, 2008; Auth, "Confessions of a Recovering Racist," *The Virginia Sem Journ*, VTS, 1997; Auth, "The Sundays after Pentecost," *Breaking the Word*, Ch Hymnal Corp, 1994; Auth, "Manual on Preaching," Morehouse-Barlow, 1988; Auth, "If Ordnry People Had Gone to Ch," *St. Lk's Journ of Theol*, Sewanee TS, 1984; Co-Auth, "Lesser Festivals 3: SS' Days and Spec Occasions," Fortress Press, 1981; Auth, "Manual on Preaching," Judson Press, 1977; Auth, "Our Approach to the Ch Year," *Wrshp*, St Johns Abbey, 1977.

CRUM, Robert James Howard (EO) 700 SW Eastman Pkwy Ste B110, Gresham OR 97080 **Ret 1991-** B Portland OR 1945 s Howard & Mary. BA Mt Ang Abbey 1967; MDiv S Thos Sem 1971. Rec 1/25/1984 as Priest Bp Matthew Paul Bigliardi. m 11/29/1975 Gayle Frances Spulniak. Dio Estrn Oregon Cove OR 1989-1991; S Alb's Epis Ch Redmond OR 1989-1991; Vic S Mk's Epis and Gd Shpd Luth Madras OR 1989-1991; Vic Cmnty of the Epiph Saipan 1986-1988; Vic Exec Coun Appointees New York NY 1985-1989; Vic S Andr Philipines Sea Agat GU 1985-1988; St Andrews Ch Agat GU 1985-1988; Assoc S Fran Of Assisi Epis Wilsonville OR 1982-1984.

CRUMB, Lawrence Nelson (Ore) 1674 Washington St, Eugene OR 97401 **Vic S Andr's Ch Cottage Grove OR 2015-, P in charge 2009-2014, Asst 1980-1981, P-in-c 1979-1981** B Palo Alto CA 1937 s Fred & Esther. BA Pomona Coll 1958; MDiv Nash 1961; GTS 1962; MA U of Wisconsin 1967; STM Nash 1973. D 9/7/1961 Bp Francis E I Bloy P 6/16/1962 Bp Daniel Corrigan. m 7/31/1968 Ellen Adele Locke c 1. Int S Tim's Epis Ch Salem OR 2005-2007; Int S Geo's Epis Ch Roseburg OR 2003-2004; Int Trin Ch S Louis MO 2000-2001; Dio Oregon Portland OR 1999, Instr Sch Theol & Mnstry 1990-1992; Int S Alb's Epis Ch Tillamook OR 1999, Int 1995-1999; Vstng P-Libr Pusey Hse Oxford UK 1998; Asst S Mary's Epis Ch Eugene OR 1989-1995; P-in-c S Mary Ch Gardiner OR 1981-1982; P-in-c S Dav's Ch Drain OR 1980-1981; Asst S Lk's Ch Racine WI 1978; Asst S Steph's Ch Racine WI 1970-1978; Asst Libr, NT Gk Instr Nash Nashotah WI 1965-1970; Cur St Johns Epis Ch Lafayette IN 1964-1965; Cur S Jn The Evang Ch Elkhart IN 1962-1964; Asst Gr Ch Un City NJ 1961-1962. Auth, "2nd ed. (Oxford Mvmt)," *2nd ed. (Oxford Mvmt)*, Scarecrow, 2009; Auth, "Supplement (Oxford Mvmt)," *Supplement (Oxford Mvmt)*, Scarecrow, 1993; Auth, "The Oxford Mvmt & Its Leaders," *The Oxford Mvmt & Its Leaders*, Scarecrow, 1988; Auth, "Historic Preservation in the Pacific NW," *Historic Preservation in the Pacific NW*, Coun of Plnng Librarians, 1979. Affirming Catholicism; HSEC. Phi Beta Kappa Pomona Coll 1958.

CRUMBAUGH III, Frank (NJ) 410 S Atlantic Ave, Beach Haven NJ 08008 **R The Ch Of The H Innoc Bch Haven NJ 1997-** B Memphis TN 1953 s Frank & Jennie Sue. BA Cntr Coll 1974; MDiv GTS 1984. D 2/20/1988 P 9/28/1988 Bp John Shelby Spong. m 8/11/1984 Gretchen Densmore Zimmerman c 3. R S Tim's Epis Ch S Louis MO 1992-1997; R S Mary's Ch Belvidere NJ 1988-1992; S Ptr's Ch Washington NJ 1988-1992; The Stndg Com Dio New Jersey Trenton NJ 2014-2015, Necrologist of Conv 2013-, Chairperson, Nets for Life Cmpgn 2012-2013, COM 2011-, Intake Off 2010-2012, T/F on Restructure 2009-2010, Trial Crt 2007-2010, Com on Const & Cn 2004-2010, Loan & Grant Com 2004-2006. Auth, "Letters from the Bch," 2012; Auth, "Pilgrim's Journ," 2012; Auth, "Stwdshp Notes, 2nd Ed," 2011; Auth, "Stwdshp Notes," 2001. CLP 2000-2003; F&AM 1977; OGS 1995; Phi Delta Theta 1971; SAR 2002. Eagle Scout BSA 1968.

CRUMLEY, Carole Anne (WA) 3039 Beech St Nw, Washington DC 20015 **Co-Exec Dir Shalem Inst For Sprtl Formation 2002-** B Johnson City TN 1944 d Harry & Margaret. BA Duke 1966; MA U NC 1969; MDiv Inter/Met Sem 1976. D 6/26/1976 P 1/8/1977 Bp William Foreman Creighton. m 2/4/1995 Clark E Lobenstine. Shalem Inst For Sprtl Formation Washington DC 1999-2015; Prog Dir Shalem Inst For Sprtl Formation 1997-2002; Cathd of St Ptr & St Paul Washington DC 1981-1997; S Jn's Ch Georgetown Par Washington DC 1980-1982; Ch Of The Ascen Gaithersburg MD 1979-1980; Cur Chr Ch Capitol Hill Washington DC 1976-1978. Auth, "Meaning In The Midst Of Chaos".

CRUMMEY, Rebecca (Colo) 967 Marion St Apt 7, Denver CO 80218 **Dio Colorado Denver CO 2016-; Colorado Epis Serv Corps Denver CO 2013-; Vic Epis Ch Of S Ptr And S Mary Denver CO 2013-** B London England 1967 BA U IL. D 6/8/2003 Bp Peter Hess Beckwith P 3/25/2004 Bp Robert John O'Neill. m 6/18/2011 Richard Morris. S Jn's Cathd Denver CO 2010-2012, Cur 2003-2009.

CRUMP, Carl Calvin (ETenn) St Martin's/ St Stephen's, 15801 US Highway 19, Hudson FL 34667 B Bakersfield CA 1944 s George & Ruby. Cert St Meinrad Sem 2004. Rec 6/5/2010 as Deacon Bp Dabney Tyler Smith. m 12/30/2008 Kathleen W Crump. D S Steph's Ch New Prt Rchy FL 2010-2013.

CRUMP, David Archelaus (Los) Po Box 371645, Montara CA 94037 **Died 2/29/2016** B Saugerties NY 1927 s Benjamin & Frances. BA Alfred U 1950; MDiv VTS 1953. D 6/23/1953 P 12/23/1953 Bp Dudley S Stark. m 5/22/1983 Anne Crump c 1. 1971-2016; Assoc R St Jas the Great Epis Ch Newport Bch CA 1966-1970; Vic Ch Of S Jude The Apos Cupertino CA 1962-1965; Chapl Hob Geneva NY 1957-1961; R S Lk's Ch Brockport NY 1953-1956. Auth, *Forth*.

CRUMPTON IV, Alvin Briggs (Ga) 6230 Laurel Island Pkwy, Kingsland GA 31548 **King Of Peace Kingsland GA 2013-** B Americus GA 1970 s Alvin & Brenda. Bachelor of Bus Admin (BBA) Georgia SW St U 1994; Mstr of Div (MDiv) Sewanee: The U So, TS 2011. D 2/11/2011 P 10/1/2011 Bp Scott Anson Benhase. m 12/4/2006 Valerie T Crumption c 1. P S Mk's Ch Brunswick GA 2011-2013. acrumpton@kingofpeace.org

CRUPI OJN, Hilary (FdL) Our Lady of the Northwoods Monastery, W704 Alft Rd, White Lake WI 54491 **Guardian of the Ord The Ord of Julian of Norwich 2010-** B San Diego CA 1961 d Robert & Kathleen. BA California St U 1986. D 5/10/2002 P 12/21/2002 Bp Russell Edward Jacobus.

CRUSE, John Woolfolk (Ala) 4941 Montevallo Rd, Birmingham AL 35210 **Gr Ch Birmingham AL 2002-** B Tuscaloosa AL 1945 s Joseph & Johnnie. BA U So 1967; MA U of Virginia 1968; MDiv Sewanee: The U So, TS 1973. D 6/8/1973 P 12/1/1973 Bp Furman Charles Stough. P Assoc S Martins-In-The-Pines Ret Comm Birmingham AL 2002-2009; Trin Ch Wetumpka AL 2001; S Paul's Epis Ch Lowndesboro AL 1996-1999; Chapl S Dunst's: The Epis Ch at Auburn U Auburn AL 1995-2000; All SS Ch Montgomery AL 1995-1996; H Comf Ch Gadsden AL 1987-1995; R S Alb's Ch Hoover AL 1983-1986; R Gr Epis Ch Pike Road AL 1981-1983; S Paul's Ch Selma AL 1980-1981; Dio Alabama Birmingham 1978-1999; Chapl To Angl Bp Jersualem & Middle E 1978-1980; Ch Of The H Comf Montgomery AL 1973-1978; Cur H Comm Montgomery AL 1973-1978. Kappa Sigma; Omicron Delta Kappa; Phi Beta Kappa.

CRUSE, William Clayton (NH) PO Box 382, North Conway NH 03860 B Cleveland OH 1961 s Donald & Marialice. BMus Ohio U 1985; MMus Ohio U 1986; MDiv EDS 2015. D 6/6/2015 P 1/21/2016 Bp A Robert Hirschfeld. m 12/29/2012 John Robert Deuel.

CRUSOE, Lewis D (EMich) **S Jas' Epis Ch Cheboygan MI 2016-, P-in-c 2016-** B Cheboygan MI 1948 s James & Dolores. BA Sacr Heart Sem 1970; Ord St. Johns Prov Sem 1973; MSPA Walsh Coll 1986. Rec 6/1/2015 as Deacon Bp Steven Todd Ousley.

CRUZ, Hector (PR) B 1934 m 11/20/1979 Teresa Cedeño. Dio Puerto Rico Trujillo Alto PR 2004-2006, 2001-2003, 1980-1996.

CRUZ-DIAZ, Nora (At) 5148 Victor Trail, Norcross GA 30071 B Dorado PR 1942 d Juan & Margarita. BA Interamerican U 1973. D 8/6/2011 Bp J Neil Alexander. m 5/19/1995 Wilfredo Diaz c 3.

CRYSLER JR, Fred (Ct) PO Box 9324, Louisville KY 40209 B Wabash IN 1941 s Frederick & Emma. BA Br 1963; MDiv EDS 1968. D 6/6/1968 P 3/1/1969 Bp Robert Lionne DeWitt. m 5/18/2014 Joan Dodge c 2. R Chr Ch Sharon CT 2003-2006; R Resurr Ch Louisville KY 1988-2002; Vic S Chad's Ch Tampa FL 1983-1988; Int Trin Ch Covington KY 1982-1983; Assoc S Jn's Ch Bala Cynwyd PA 1976-1977; Assoc Chapl for Prison Mnstry Dio Pennsylvania Philadelphia PA 1972-1975; Cur The Epis Ch Of The Adv Kennet Sq PA 1968-1970. EPF, WON, Natl Assn for the S 1968-1975.

CRYSLER, Kenneth W (EO) B 1939 s Kenneth & Lucille. MA Estrn Oregon St Coll; BA Indiana St U 1968; Spec Stds Epis TS of the SW 1976. D 9/29/1976 P 6/19/1977 Bp William Benjamin Spofford. m 7/18/1964 Sabra J Crysler c 2. D Ch Of The Redeem Pendleton OR 1999-2004, P 1995-2007, P 1977-1995; P-in-c S Steph's Baker City OR 1997-2001.

CUBILLAS, Angelito Conde (Az) PO Box 8667, Phoenix AZ 85066 **S Lk's At The Mtn Phoenix AZ 2015-** B Butuan City Philippines 1953 s Juan & Timotea. AB St Fran Xavier Coll Sem 1975; AB St Fran Xavier Coll Sem 1975;

Liturg San Anselmo Inst of Liturg 1989. Rec 3/1/2015 as Priest Bp Kirk Stevan Smith. m 7/24/2008 Louise Holt.

CUBINE, James W (WTenn) 7910 Gayle Ln, Memphis TN 38138 B Chattano GA 1947 s Thomas & Jo. BA U of Tennessee 1971; MA U of Kansas 1973; MDiv SWTS 1981. D 6/21/1981 Bp William F Gates Jr P 5/1/1982 Bp William Evan Sanders. m 4/26/2014 Patricia K Horton c 2. S Anne's Ch Millington TN 2004-2010; S Andr's Epis Ch Collierville TN 1988-2000; S Jas Epis Ch Zanesville OH 1987-1988; Dio W Tennessee Memphis 1986-1987; S Geo's Ch Germantown TN 1981-1983.

CUDD, Anne Grover (Ida) 3024 SW 98th Way, Gainesville FL 32608 B Troy NY 1940 d Horace & Alice. BS Denison U 1961; MD OH SU 1967; MS U of Delaware 1975; MDiv Sewanee: The U So, TS 1991. D 11/22/1986 P 8/4/1990 Bp David Bell Birney IV. m 8/28/1969 Kermit George Cudd. Asst S Fran Epis Ch Coll Sta TX 2007-2010; Vic S Dav's Epis Ch Caldwell ID 1999-2005; P-in-c S Agnes' Mssn Cowan TN 1990-1999; D Trin Epis Ch Pocatello ID 1986-1988. Phi Beta Kappa Denison U 1961.

CUDWORTH, Robert Wallace (Ct) 400 Seabury Dr Apt 3142, Bloomfield CT 06002 **Ret 2001-** B West Hartford CT 1923 s Abel & Ruth. BA Trin Hartford CT 1949; U of Connecticut 1956; S Josephs Coll 1986. D 12/1/1990 Bp Arthur Edward Walmsley. m 7/29/1978 Dorothy Jorgensen Cudworth c 4. D St Johns Ch W Hartford CT 1996-2001; D Gr Ch Newington CT 1993-1996; D Trin Ch Portland CT 1991-1993; Chapl Inst Liv Psych Hosp Hartford CT 1990-2006; D S Jn The Evang Yalesville CT 1990-1991. "Anglicanism," *Understanding Your Neighbor's Faith*, KTAV Pub Hse, 2004.

CUEVAS FELIZ, Pedro G (RG) Blvd Benitez #99, El Pedregal Tijuana BC 22104 Mexico **S Bede's Epis Ch Santa Fe NM 2016-** B Dominican Republic 1973 s Alejandro & Carmen. Licenciatura en Derecho Universidad Autónoma de Santo Domingo 2002; Postgrado en Gestión Cultural Universidad Autónoma de Santo Domingo 2003. D 12/9/2013 Bp Lino Rodriguez-Amaro. m 10/29/2009 Yanensy Volquez de Cuevas c 2. Dio Wstrn Mex Zapopan Jalisco 2013-2015.

CUFF, Stephen (SO) 2140 Grandview Ave, Portsmouth OH 45662 **Sum Camp Dir Dio Sthrn Ohio Cincinnati OH 2014-, Vic 1999-2002; P-in-c All SS Epis Ch Portsmouth OH 2013-** B Buffalo NY 1960 s Robert & Dessie. BA SUNY at Buffalo 1982; Nash 1991; MDiv Sewanee: The U So, TS 1993. D 6/19/1993 Bp John Wadsworth Howe P 6/11/1994 Bp John Henry Smith. m 2/4/1984 Beth E Cuff c 2. Dir of Sprtl Serv Epis Ret Hm Cincinnati OH 2007-2013; Epis Ret Serv Cincinnati OH 2007-2013; Chapl Marjorie P Lee Ret Cmnty Cincinnati OH 2007-2013; Chapl Marjorie P Lee Ret Cmnty Cincinnati OH 2007-2013; S Andr's Epis Ch Wshngtn Ct Hs OH 1999-2007; R S Mk's Epis Ch Berkeley Spg WV 1994-1999; Cur Trin Ch Parkersburg WV 1993-1994. Assn of Profsnl Chapl 2009-2014.

CUFF, Victoria Slater Smith (NJ) 45 2nd St, Keyport NJ 07735 **D Chr Ch Epis Shrewsbury NJ 2013-; Archd Dio NJ NJ 2005-** B Orange NJ 1943 d William & Constance. BS Simmons Coll 1965. D 10/31/1998 Bp Joe Doss. m 12/21/1966 William Cuff c 3. D Chr Ch Middletown NJ 1998-2011, Archd 1995-2012; Trin Ch Princeton NJ 1986-1994. NACED 2006; NAAD; Rel Educ Assn.

CUFFIE, Karen Ann (ECR) 2094 Grant Rd, Mountain View CA 94040 **S Tim's Epis Ch Mtn View CA 2016-** B San Diego CA 1960 d Edward & Isabelle. BME Shenandoah Coll & Conservatory of Mus 1982; BME Shenandoah Coll and Cons. of Mus 1982; BME Shenandoah Coll and Cons. of Mus 1982; MDiv CDSP 2015. D 6/6/2015 P 1/23/2016 Bp Mary Gray-Reeves. m 10/16/1982 Craig Cuffie c 5. rector.sttims@gmail.com

CULBERTSON, David Paul (CPa) 210 S Washington St, Muncy PA 17756 **R-Full Time S Jas Ch Muncy PA 2004-** B Carlisle PA 1968 BA Wilson Coll. D 6/20/2004 P 1/29/2005 Bp Michael Whittington Creighton. m 10/6/1994 Diane L Culbertson c 2. dculbertsonrector@windstream.net

CULBERTSON, Thomas Leon (Md) 6 Yearling Way, Lutherville MD 21093 **Prof Ecum Inst of Theol St Mary's Sem (Baltimore) 1987-** B Oil City PA 1939 s Russell & Frances. BA Baldwin-Wallace Coll 1962; Oberlin Grad Sch 1963; MDiv EDS 1966; DMin Ashland TS 1977; PhD GTF 2000. D 6/25/1966 P 1/27/1967 Bp Nelson Marigold Burroughs. m 6/11/1966 Deborah R Culbertson c 2. Bd Epis Soc Mnstrs 1993-1998; Emm Ch Baltimore MD 1986-2005; R S Paul's Epis Ch Lynchburg VA 1982-1985; Assoc S Paul's Epis Ch Cleveland OH 1972-1982; R S Paul's Ch Oregon OH 1968-1972; Cur S Michaels In The Hills Toledo OH 1966-1968; Com on Cn, Dn, Exam Chapl Dio Maryland Baltimore MD 2000-2005; Ecum Off Dio SW Virginia Roanoke VA 1983-1985; Dioc Coun Dio Ohio Cleveland 1976-1979. Auth, "Mntl Illness and Psych Treatment A Guide for Pstr Counselors," The Haworth Press, 2003. The Soc for Values in Higher Educ 2007.

CULBREATH, Leeann Drabenstott (Ga) PO Box 889, Tifton GA 31793 B Painesville OH 1972 d Earle & Patricia. BA Wheaton Coll 1996; MA U of Montana 1998. D 9/14/2013 Bp Scott Anson Benhase. m 10/11/2003 Albert Kipple Culbreath c 2.

CULHANE, Suzanne M (NY) **Chr Ch Greenwich CT 2015-** D 3/7/2015 P 9/19/2015 Bp Andrew Marion Lenow Dietsche.

CULLEN, Kathleen Mary (NH) St. Andrew's Episcopal Church, 102 N Main St., Manchester NH 03102 B Manchester NH 1948 d Edward & Dorothy. BA U of New Hampshire 1973; MDiv Andover Newton TS 2003; EDS 2005; Cert Shalem Inst for Sprtl Formation 2006. D 8/26/2007 P 6/4/2008 Bp Vicky Gene Robinson. m 8/5/2013 Mary Janet Young. P-in-c S Andr's Ch Manchester NH 2013-2015; P-in-c Chr Ch Portsmouth NH 2011-2012; Trin Ch Hampton NH 2011-2012; Assoc P Gr Ch Manchester NH 2011; Pstr Assoc S Matt's Ch Goffstown NH 2008-2011; Chapl Beacon Hospice Inc 2007-2010; Chapl Elliot Hosp 2005-2006; Chapl Manchester VNA Hospice 2003-2005. Pryr Grp & Retreat Ldrshp Shalem Inst of Sprtl Formation 2006; mcl Andover Newton Theol 2003.

CULLEN, Peter (LI) 199 Carroll St, Brooklyn NY 11231 **R S Paul's Ch Brooklyn NY 1987-** B Ancon PA 1951 s James & Evelyn. BA Florida Sthrn Coll 1973; MDiv GTS 1978; STM GTS 1982. D 6/24/1978 P 6/1/1979 Bp William Gillette Weinhauer. Assoc R S Ptr's by-the-Sea Epis Ch Bay Shore NY 1982-1987; Int Ch Of The Ascen Hickory NC 1980-1981, D-In-Trng 1978-1979. rector@stpaulscarrollst.org

CULLINANE, Kathleen Jean (Haw) 1515 Wilder Ave, Honolulu HI 96822 **Par of St Clem Honolulu HI 2016-** B Cape May Courthouse NJ 1955 d Daniel & Jeanette. U CA, Irvine 1974; Goldenwest Huntington Bch CA 1975; BS Loyola Marymount U 1977; Cert Theol Stud Bp Tucker Theol Coll Mukono Ug 1988; STM GTS 1989; MDiv GTS 1989. D 6/10/1989 P 1/13/1990 Bp Frederick Houk Borsch. Cn to the Ordnry Epis Dio San Joaquin Modesto CA 2011-2016; Int S Fran In The Fields Zionsville IN 2009-2010; Chapl S Vinc Hosp Indianapolis IN 2008-2011; Assoc Dn Chr Ch Cathd Indianapolis IN 2000-2008; R S Mary's Epis Ch Los Angeles CA 1989-2000; Exec Dir St Anselm Immigrant & Refugee Cmnty Cntr Garden Grove 1980-1985. katec@stclem.org

CULLIPHER III, James Robert (USC) 800 Stillpoint Way, Balsam Grove NC 28708 **Ret 2000-** B Monroe LA 1934 s James & Lois. BS U of Louisiana Monroe 1957; MDiv Sewanee: The U So, TS 1970. D 6/30/1970 Bp William Evan Sanders P 5/30/1971 Bp John Vander Horst. c 3. Journey into Wholeness Inc. Greenville 1988-2000; Journey Into Wholeness Inc Balsam Grove NC 1988-1999; Asst R Chr Ch Greenville SC 1984-1987; R The Epis Ch of The Redeem Jacksonville FL 1977-1984; Dio Florida Jacksonville 1976; Asst S Ptr's Ch Jacksonville FL 1975-1976; P-in-c S Mary Magd Ch Fayetteville TN 1971-1975; D-in-trng S Jn's Epis Cathd Knoxville TN 1970-1971.

CULMER, Ronald D (Cal) 3350 Hopyard Rd, Pleasanton CA 94588 **R S Clare's Epis Ch Pleasanton CA 2004-** B Mildenhall UK 1964 s Henry & Sonia. DMin SWTS; BA California Luth U 1990; MDiv CDSP 1994. D 6/4/1994 Bp Chester Lovelle Talton P 1/14/1995 Bp Frederick Houk Borsch. m 8/5/1995 Diana H Culmer c 2. R S Mart-In-The-Fields Par Winnetka CA 1997-2004; Asst S Steph's Epis Ch Valencia CA 1994-1996; Chair of the Eastmund Fund Dio California San Francisco CA 2008-2010, The Stndg Com 2006-2010; Trst CDSP Berkeley CA 2004-2006; Alum Coun 2003-2006.

CULP JR, Robert S (Roch) 19 Arbor Ct, Fairport NY 14450 **Ret 2001-** B Long Beach CA 1938 s Robert & Margaret. BS USMA 1962; MEd Bos 1976; MDiv Bex Sem 1980. D 3/22/1981 P 5/1/1982 Bp Robert Rae Spears Jr. m 11/16/2002 Karen Joyce Culp c 3. Epis Ch Hm Rochester NY 1998-2000; Chapl The Chap of the Gd Shpd Rochester NY 1998-2000; S Jn's Ch Mt Morris NY 1986-1998; P-in-c The Ch Of The H Apos - Epis Perry NY 1986-1998; Chapl Epis Ch Hm.

CULPEPPER, Charles Leland (Miss) 1832 Saint Ann St, Jackson MS 39202 **S Alexis Epis Ch Jackson MS 2006-; Vic S Alexis' Epis Ch Jackson MS 2006-** B Meridian MS 1950 s Arlas & Virginia. BA Millsaps Coll 1972; JD U of Mississippi 1978; MDiv Epis TS of the SW 1989. D 5/30/1998 P 1/30/1999 Bp Alfred Marble Jr. m 12/30/1978 Katherine Culpepper c 1. Dio Mississippi Jackson MS 2001-2005, Cn to Yth & Col Mnstrys 2000-2006; Cur S Paul's Epis Ch Meridian MS 1998-2000.

CULPEPPER, Judith Anne (Ind) 6736 Prince Regent Ct, Indianapolis IN 46250 B Fort Jackson SC 1952 d Julius & Evelyn. BS U of So Carolina 1973; MD U of Virginia 1977; MDiv Chr TS 1994; CAS SWTS 1994. D 6/24/1994 P 6/1/1995 Bp Edward Witker Jones. S Paul's Epis Ch Gas City IN 2005-2007; Vic S Steph's Elwood IN 1999-2008; Asst Trin Epis Ch Bloomington IN 1997-1999; Med Dir St. Thos Clnc Franklin IN 1996-2007; S Thos Ch Franklin IN 1994-2008. judithculpepper@gmail.com

CULPEPPER, Polk (Ind) 1301 Summit Ave, Washington NC 27889 B Alexandria LA 1948 s W A & Thelma. BA LSU 1970; JD LSU 1973; MDiv Sewanee: The U So, TS 1987. D 6/20/1987 P 12/15/1987 Bp Willis Ryan Henton. m 4/7/1973 Catherine C Culpepper c 2. R S Paul's Epis Ch New Albany IN 2005-2010; S Jas Ch Shelbyville KY 2004-2005; Calv Ch Louisville KY 2001-2003; Ch Of The Gd Shpd Cashiers NC 1994-2001; R Ch Of The Ascen Mt Sterling KY 1988-1994; Asst Gr Epis Ch Monroe LA 1987-1988. polecat793@gmail.com

CULTON, Douglas (Del) 1212 E Holly St, Goldsboro NC 27530 **P-in-c S Fran Ch Goldsboro NC 2011-** B Providence RI 1950 s Donald & Melva. BA Drury U 1973; MDiv GTS 1977; Cert St Marys Sem Univ Baltimore MD 1987. D 9/10/1977 P 3/1/1978 Bp Robert Bracewell Appleyard. c 3. Int S Anne's Epis Ch Jacksonville NC 2007; Int Chr Epis Ch Tarrytown NY 2004-2006; Int Chr Epis Ch Tarrytown NY 2003-2006; R S Ptr's Ch Lewes DE 1984-2003; R S Jas Epis Ch Arlington VT 1979-1983; Asst Fox Chap Epis Ch Pittsburgh PA 1977-1979.

CULVER, Carson Kies (Mil) 590 N Church St, Richland Center WI 53581 **P-in-c H Trin Epis Ch Prairie Du Chien WI 2002-** B Detroit MI 1944 s Ernest & Genevieve. BS U of Wisconsin 1967; MS U of Wisconsin 1979; MDiv U of Dubuque 1985; Cert Nash 1989. D 8/6/1989 P 2/1/1990 Bp Roger John White. m 8/19/1967 Marilyn Culver c 2. P-in-c Trin Epis Ch Platteville WI 1991-2000; S Barn Richland Ctr WI 1989-2009; Serv Meth Ch 1980-1988. Richland Cnty Mnstry Assn 1989.

CULVER, Esme Jo R (Ore) Grace Memorial Church, 1535 Ne 17th Ave, Portland OR 97232 **Gr Memi Portland OR 2007-, Assoc. For Mssn & Mnstry 1982-2001** B Cheltenham Brigtain 1943 d Geoffrey & Kathleen. BA Portland St U 1981; MDiv CDSP 2007. D 7/13/2006 P 4/14/2007 Bp Johncy Itty. c 3. Ceo Pro Team Profsnl Stff Serv.

CUMBIE II, Walter Kenneth (CGC) 172 Hannon Ave, Moile AL 36604 **S Lk's Epis Ch Mobile AL 2005-** B San Antonio TX 1952 s Walter & Joyce. BA U of Mobile 1974; MDiv MidWestern Bapt TS 1980; CPE CPE 1983; DMin GTF 1989. D 1/23/1993 P 7/24/1993 Bp John Clark Buchanan. m 8/29/2007 Joan Cumbie c 1. Dep to GC The Epis Ch 2003-2009; R H Sprt Epis Ch Gulf Shores AL 2000-2005; Mem, Bd Dir Wilmer Hall Birmingham AL 2000-2005; R Ch Of The Gd Shpd Mobile AL 1996-2000; 1993-1996; Dir of Pstr Care Cox Hlth Systems Springfield MO 1991-1996; Chapl Beth Naval Hosp Washington DC 1988-1991; Chapl Supvsr U Hosp Augusta GA 1983-1988; Mem Stndg Com Dio Alabama Birmingham 2006-2009. Cert Fell Coll of Chapl 1985; Cmdr, US Navy (Reserves) 1986.

CUMMER, Edwin West (SwFla) B 1917 D 6/29/1972 Bp William Loftin Hargrave.

CUMMING, Jane (NY) 163 Todd Road, Katonah NY 10536 **Died 5/22/2016** B Basingstoke Hampshire UK 1927 d Leslie & Esther. BA SUNY 1982; MDiv GTS 1983. D 6/4/1983 Bp Paul Moore Jr P 7/1/1984 Bp James Stuart Wetmore. m 2/2/1957 Ian J Cumming c 2. Dio New York New York NY 1997; Mnstry Of Persons w Disabil Rye NY 1987-1988; Dir, Min. w/ People w/ Disabil, Reg 2 Dio New York New York NY 1985-1988.

CUMMINGS, Carolsue J (NJ) 322 So Second St, Surf City NJ 08008 **Chapl, Bereavement Grp Coordntr, and Counslr Meridian Hospice So Manahawkin NJ 2000-** B Camden NJ 1944 d John & Mary. BS Penn Hall Coll Chambersburg PA 1966; Basic Certification Amer Inst of Bereavement Counslg 2004; Advncd Certification Amer Inst of Bereavement Counslg 2006. D 6/9/1990 Bp George Phelps Mellick Belshaw. m 4/29/1967 Donald Cummings c 3. D S Steph's Ch Waretown NJ 1999-2009.

CUMMINGS, Patricia L (Cal) 110 Wood Rd Apt C-104, Los Gatos CA 95030 B Palo Alto CA 1935 d Howard & Dorothy. BA California St U 1957; MDiv CDSP 1980. D 9/15/1980 P 1/6/1982 Bp William Edwin Swing. c 3. S Aug's Ch Oakland CA 1999-2004; Int S Aid's Ch San Francisco CA 1984-1985; Asst H Cross Epis Ch Castro Vlly CA 1982-1984; Assoc S Paul's Ch Oakland CA 1980-1982. Hesed Comm Oakland 1990; OHC 1980.

CUMMINGS, Sally Ann (Minn) 520 N Pokegama Ave, Grand Rapids MN 55744 B Minneapolis MN 1957 d John & Ruth. AS No Hennepin Cmnty Coll 1978. D 6/21/2009 Bp James Louis Jelinek. m 5/21/1988 Gary Cummings c 2.

CUMMINGS, Sudduth R (NC) 3990 Meandering Ln., Tallahassee FL 32308 **Ret FL 2010-; Adj Gorgon Conwell Sem 2009-** B Kansas City MO 1946 s Robert & Pamelia. BA Phillips U 1968; MDiv GTS 1971; DMin SMU 1979. D 6/29/1971 P 12/21/1971 Bp Chilton R Powell. m 6/6/1969 Charlotte Cummings. Int S Jn's Epis Ch Charlotte NC 2008-2009; Int S Jn's Ch New Haven CT 2006-2008; Int S Paul's By-The-Sea Epis Ch Jaxville Bch FL 2002-2006; Int S Lk's Ch Ft Myers FL 2001-2002; Prof TESM Ambridge PA 1998-2001; R S Tim's Ch Catonsville MD 1991-1998; R S Mk's Epis Ch San Antonio TX 1980-1991; Asst Ch Of The Incarn Dallas TX 1977-1980; R S Jn's Ch Durant OK 1974-1976; Int Gr Ch Muskogee OK 1971-1972. Auth, "Bible Stds," *Journey in the Word*, BRF. Paul Harris Fell Rotary Club Intl 1986.

CUMMINS, James Michael (Kan) B 1954 D 6/11/2016 Bp Dean E Wolfe. m 7/27/1991 Margaret Montello.

CUMMINS, Thomas W (Ore) 11100 Sw Riverwood Rd, Portland OR 97219 **Ret 1993-** B New York NY 1918 s John & Florence. BS U of Connecticut 1943; STD CDSP 1971; DMin Jesuit TS 1984. D 6/17/1973 P 10/4/1974 Bp George Richard Millard. m 7/31/1943 Emily Murray c 4. Chr Ch Par Lake Oswego OR 1998-2000, 1991-1997, Assoc 1975-1990; R S Fran Of Assisi Epis Wilsonville OR 1987-1991, P 1979-1986; S Andr's Ch Saratoga CA 1974-1976; R Emeritis St. Fran of Assisi Wilsonville OR. Collegiality in Ch Ldrshp Jesuit TS 1976.

CUNIFF, Wanda Wood (Tex) Christ Episcopal Church, 1320 Mound St., Nacogdoches TX 75961 **D Chr Ch Nacogdoches TX 2007-** B Galveston TX 1949 d Robert & Dorothy. BA Steph F Austin St U 1970; MLS U of Texas 1974; Cert Iona Sch of Mnstry 2007. D 2/9/2007 Bp Don Adger Wimberly. m 1/31/1970 Troy Cuniff c 2. Sch Libr Nacogdoches ISD 1979-2004. The OSL 1998.

CUNNINGHAM, Arthur Leland (Mil) 1320 Mill Rd, Delafield WI 53018 **Ret 2000-** B Kingfisher OK 1941 s James & Pauline. BA Coll of Emporia 1963; MDiv SWTS 1968. D 6/1/1968 Bp Edward Clark Turner P 5/16/1969 Bp

Chauncie Kilmer Myers. m 8/24/1968 Mary Cunningham c 3. Prov Syn Dio Milwaukee Milwaukee WI 1995-1998, Ecum Com/Dioc Coun 1996-2000, Dn, Nash Deanry 1989-1995; R Zion Epis Ch Oconomowoc WI 1989-2000; R S Matt's Ch Enid OK 1981-1989; Epis Dio San Joaquin Modesto CA 1978-1980; S Dunstans Epis Ch Modesto CA 1978-1980; R S Jas' Ch Monterey CA 1971-1978; Cur All SS Ch Carmel CA 1968-1971; Dioc Coun Dio Oklahoma Oklahoma City OK 1981-1983.

CUNNINGHAM, Chris (SVa) 400 High St, Farmville VA 23901 **Mem, Exec Coun Dom And Frgn Mssy Soc- Epis Ch Cntr New York NY 2012-** B Frankfurt DE 1961 s Richard & Elisabeth. BA GW 1983; MDiv Wesley TS 2005. D 6/18/2005 P 12/18/2005 Bp Peter J Lee. m 10/4/2013 Leigh Anna Christine Cunningham c 3. P-in-c S Jas Epis Ch Birmingham MI 2013-2014; R Johns Memi Epis Ch Farmville VA 2008-2013; Vic Ch Of The Gd Shpd Bluemont VA 2007-2008; Asst S Ptr's Epis Ch Purcellville VA 2005-2008; D Trin Ch Manassas VA 2005; Dir of Info Tech VTS Alexandria VA 1996-2000; Dep to GC Dio Sthrn Virginia Newport News VA 2012-2014, Prog & Bdgt Com 2011-2013, COM 2011-, Dn, Convoc VIII 2010-2013, Mem, Prog, Bdgt and Revs Cte 2010-2013.

CUNNINGHAM, James Earl (Tex) 2227 Woodland Springs Dr, Houston TX 77077 **D S Mart's Epis Ch Houston TX 2007-** B Cleveland OH 1928 s Thomas & Dorothy. BS U of Texas 1957; MS SMU 1966; Iona Sch for Mnstry 2007. D 2/9/2007 Bp Don Adger Wimberly. c 3. Fac-The Cmnty of Hope St Lk's Epis Hosp 1997-2004.

CUNNINGHAM, Joyce Corbin (NC) B Newport News VA 1947 d Jessie & Eula. BA Hampton U 1970; MDiv VTS 2015. D 6/20/2015 Bp Michael B Curry P 12/20/2015 Bp Anne Hodges-Copple. m 9/18/2015 Dennis Arturo Allen Anderson.

CUNNINGHAM, Lynn Edward (Wyo) 3403 Ordway St Nw, Washington DC 20016 B Ithaca NY 1944 s Lowell & Marie. BA Cor 1966; BD UTS 1969; JD Col 1972. D 2/10/1970 Bp Leland Stark P 12/12/1970 Bp George E Rath. Adj S Marg's Ch Washington DC 1986-1997; Asst Ch Of S Steph And The Incarn Washington DC 1975-1986; Asst S Mary's Manhattanville Epis Ch New York NY 1970-1975.

CUNNINGHAM, Marcus T (FdL) 309 W Elm St, Sedan KS 67361 **R S Ptr's Ch (S Mary's Chap) Ripon WI 2017-** B Evergreen Park IL 1963 s Marcus & Elizabeth. Marq 1983; BS U of Wisconsin 1987; MDiv Sewanee: The U So, TS 2006. D 1/25/2006 P 9/11/2006 Bp Edward Stuart Little II. m 7/22/1989 Anne-Marie D Cunningham c 5. R Trin Epis Ch Oshkosh WI 2013-2015; Ch Of The Epiph Sedan KS 2009-2013; New Life Epis Ch Uniontown OH 2009; D S Matt's Epis Ch Brecksville OH 2006-2009; S Jn The Evang Ch Elkhart IN 2000-2003. fmstpeter@yahoo.com

CUNNINGHAM, Margaret Taylor (Pa) 1122 Wabash St, Pasadena CA 91103 B Pasadena CA 1940 d Daniel & Sarah. Vas 1961; BA U CA Los Angeles 1982; MA U CA Los Angeles 1984; MDiv EDS 1996. D 6/18/1996 P 1/18/1997 Bp Frederick Houk Borsch. c 3. Ch Of The Redeem Bryn Mawr PA 2001-2004; All SS Ch Pasadena CA 1996-2001.

CUNNINGHAM, Michael Ray (Los) St Marys Episcopal Church, 2800 Harris Grade Rd, Lompoc CA 93436 **R S Mary's Par Lompoc CA 2007-** B Dallas TX 1954 s Donald & Irene. BFA U of Texas 1976. D 5/2/2007 P 11/17/2007 Bp Joseph Jon Bruno. c 2. Dio Los Angeles Los Angeles CA 2007, 1994-2007; Mssnr For Mssn Con Dio Los Angeles 1994-2007.

CUNNINGHAM, Philip John (WTex) 2500 N. 10th St., McAllen TX 78501 **Ch Of S Jn Chrys Delafield WI 2014-; Nash Nashotah WI 2013-** B Fresno CA 1970 s Daniel & Melinda. BA Santa Clara U 1992; MBA Van 1996; MDiv Nash 2008. D 6/25/2008 Bp David Mitchell Reed P 6/8/2009 Bp Gary Richard Lillibridge. m 6/15/1996 Amy Cunningham c 2. Vic S Marg's Epis Ch San Antonio TX 2010-2013; Asst S Jn's Ch McAllen TX 2008-2010.

CUNNINGHAM, Trish (Cal) 1668 Bush St, San Francisco CA 94109 **P-in-c Trin Ch San Francisco CA 2014-** B Vancouver BC 1958 d Edward & Daisy. MA Emory U 2000; MS The London Sch of Econ and Political Sci 2002; MA Berkeley Bapt DS 2007. D 6/9/2007 P 12/15/2007 Bp Andrew Donnan Smith. m 5/27/1984 David Epp Cunningham c 4. Int S Jn's Epis Ch Boulder CO 2011; Chr Epis Ch Norwich CT 2009-2010; Chr Ch Roxbury CT 2008-2009; Cur S Paul's Ch Riverside CT 2007-2008. patriciastarrscunningham@gmail.com

CUNNINGHAM, William Wallace (Ala) **Chaplin Jackson Hosp Montgomery AL 2003-** B Nashville TN 1942 s William & Elizabeth. Diac Sch Birmingham AL; EFM; BBA Lamar U. D 10/30/2004 Bp Marc Handley Andrus. m 10/4/1964 Sharrell Cunningham c 5.

CUPP, Jean Carol (EO) 1239 Nw Ingram Ave, Pendleton OR 97801 **D Ch Of The Redeem Pendleton OR 1999-** B Chicago IL 1943 D 9/26/1999 Bp Rustin Ray Kimsey. m 9/26/1964 William Cupp c 3.

CURL, James Fair (WNC) 461 Crowfields Dr., Asheville NC 28803 **Allegany Cnty Mnstry Belmont NY 2002-** B Millen GA 1944 s William & Carolyn. BA Davidson Coll 1966; MA NWU 1968; PhD U Pgh 1974; Cert Dioc Sch for Total Common Mnstry 2002. D 12/8/2001 P 10/22/2002 Bp Jack Marston Mckelvey. m 8/23/1968 Kathryn W Curl c 2. U Chapl Alfred Epis Campus Mnstry 2003-2007.

CURNS, Mary S (WMass) All Saints Episcopal Church, PO Box 374, North Adams MA 01247 **Dio Wstrn Massachusetts Springfield 2015-** B Elmira NY 1956 d Andrew & Berdena. BS Mansfield U of Pennsylvania 1979; MS Elmira Coll 1985; MDiv GTS 2004. D 6/9/2004 Bp Gladstone Bailey Adams III P 1/6/2005 Bp Clifton Daniel III. c 2. R S Anne's Epis Ch Jacksonville NC 2009-2015; Asst Chr Ch New Bern NC 2004-2009.

CURRAN JR, Charles Daniel (SwVa) 1011 Francisco Road, Henrico VA 23238 **Died 6/12/2017** B Ancon Panama 1934 s Charles & Virginia. AB Earlham Coll 1958; Amer U 1960; MDiv Sewanee: The U So, TS 1967. D 6/21/1967 Bp Henry I Louttit P 12/22/1967 Bp James Loughlin Duncan. m 9/10/1977 Anne Gordon Curran c 6. Int Kingston Par Epis Ch Mathews VA 1992-1993; Assoc P S Steph's Ch Richmond VA 1991-1995; Int Asst Gr & H Trin Epis Ch Richmond VA 1988-1989; Supply P Dio Virginia Richmond VA 1980-2008; P-in-c Gd Shpd Folly Mills VA 1976-1980; Asst S Marg's Ch Woodbridge VA 1974-1975; Vic S Dav's Manassas VA 1971-1974; R S Jn's Epis Ch Homestead FL 1968-1971; Cur H Trin Epis Ch W Palm Bch FL 1967-1968.

CURRAN, Michael Joseph (Ak) 4024 Ridge Way, Juneau AK 99801 B Derby CT 1947 s Robert & Ruth. Cert U So 1999. D 12/18/1999 P 6/18/2000 Bp Mark Lawrence Macdonald. m 8/6/1977 Cynthia Ann Curran c 2. S Ptr's Ch Seward AK 2010-2012; S Brendan's Epis Ch Juneau AK 2004-2005; R S Phil's Ch Wrangell AK 2000-2004.

CURREA, Luis Alejandro (SwFla) Po Box 9332, Tampa FL 33674 B Bogota CO 1934 s Alejandro & Elisa. Cert Sem Mayor De Bogota 1960; BA Florida Intl U 1977; DIT VTS 1986. Rec 9/1/1986 as Priest Bp Calvin Onderdonk Schofield Jr. c 3. S Fran Ch Tampa FL 1992-1999; Dio SW Florida Parrish FL 1988-1991; Iglesia Epis De Todos Los Santos Miami FL 1988; Cur All Ang Ch Miami FL 1986-1988.

CURRIN JR, Beverly Madison (CGC) 510 N 20th Ave, Pensacola FL 32501 **Died 1/7/2016** B Greensboro NC 1931 s Beverly & Gertrude. BA Elon U 1953; MDiv Duke DS 1956; ThM UTS Richmond 1957; PhD UTS Richmond 1958. D 10/26/1958 Bp Frederick D Goodwin P 11/1/1959 Bp Robert Fisher Gibson Jr. m 8/4/1962 Eleanor McCall Lachicotte c 3. R Chr Epis Ch Pensacola FL 1966-2002; R Cathd Of S Lk And S Paul Charleston SC 1961-1963; Asst Gr & H Trin Epis Ch Richmond VA 1958-1961. Auth, *The Chr Ch Bk*, 2002; Auth, *Search for the Lost Rectors*, 1999; Auth, *The Vision Glorious*, 1996; Auth, *Decision in Crisis*, 1995; Auth, *The Faith That Never Disappoints*, Abingdon, 1983; Auth, *From One Generation to Another*, 1979; Auth, *If Man is to Live*, Abingdon, 1969. DECONS 1977-1997. Hon Cn The Cathd Ch of St. Lk and St. Paul 2003; Fell Coll of Preachers 1980.

CURRY, Dorothy Reed (Cal) 4351 Ridgeway Dr, San Diego CA 92116 B Seattle WA 1934 d Elmer & Elise. BA U of Washington 1956; MDiv CDSP 1982. D 11/22/1981 P 12/11/1982 Bp William Edwin Swing. c 2. Cn for Pstr Care Cathd Ch Of S Paul San Diego CA 2006-2015; Asst The Epis Ch Of S Andr Encinitas CA 1999; R Ch Of The H Trin Richmond CA 1986-1996; Asst Chr Ch Portola Vlly CA 1984-1986; Asst S Jas Ch Fremont CA 1983-1984; Asst S Edm's Epis Ch Pacifica CA 1982-1983.

CURRY, Gene E (Mich) 2735 Manchester Rd, Ann Arbor MI 48104 B Colville WA 1936 s Elliot & Jessie. BS California St Polytechnic U 1958; MDiv Bex Sem 1961. D 6/25/1961 Bp James Albert Pike P 1/25/1962 Bp George Henry Quarterman. m 10/14/2004 Ruth Evelyn Vogt c 2. P-in-c S Mich And All Ang Epis Ch Lincoln Pk MI 2002-2007; Vic S Matt's Epis Ch Flat Rock MI 1990-1999; P-in-c S Jn's Ch Westland MI 1988; P-in-c S Clem's Epis Ch Inkster MI 1987-1988; P-in-c S Columba Ch Detroit MI 1986-1987; P-in-c S Hilda's Epis Ch River Rouge MI 1975-1979; Assoc S Mart Ch Detroit MI 1966-1975; Vic Epiph Mt Moris MI 1964-1966; Cur S Nich' Epis Ch Midland TX 1964-1964.

CURRY, Glenda (Ala) 2670 Southgate Dr, Birmingham AL 35243 **R All SS Epis Ch Birmingham AL 2004-** B Fort Stockton TX 1953 d Dalton & Mac. MDiv Sewanee: The U So, TS 2002. D 5/29/2002 P 12/3/2002 Bp Henry Nutt Parsley Jr. R Epis Ch Of The Epiph Leeds AL 2002-2004.

✠ **CURRY, The Rt Rev James Elliot** (Ct) 14 Linwold Dr, West Hartford CT 06107 B Oak Park IL 1948 s Warren & Clemence. BA Amh 1970; MEd U of Massachusetts 1979; MDiv Ya Berk 1985. D 6/8/1985 Bp Arthur Edward Walmsley P 12/10/1985 Bp Clarence Nicholas Coleridge Con 10/14/2000 for Ct. m 1/17/1970 Kathleen McIntosh c 3. Cn Ordnry Dio Connecticut Meriden CT 1998-2014; R Trin Ch Portland CT 1988-1998; Asst Trin Ch Torrington CT 1985-1988. DD Berk 2006.

✠ **CURRY, The Most Rev Michael B** 200 W Morgan St Ste 300, Raleigh NC 27601 **PBp of The Epis Ch Dom And Frgn Mssy Soc- Epis Ch Cntr New York NY 2015-; Epis Ch Cntr New York NY 2015-** B Chicago IL 1953 s Kenneth & Dorothy. BA Hobart and Wm Smith Colleges 1975; MDiv Yale DS 1978; Ya Berk 2001; U So 2001. D 6/3/1978 Bp Harold Barrett Robinson P 12/1/1978 Bp John Melville Burgess Con 6/17/2000 for NC. m 6/20/1981 Sharon C Curry c 1. Bp of NC Dio No Carolina Raleigh NC 2000-2015; R S Jas' Epis Ch Baltimore MD 1988-2000; Chapl Bethany Sch 1984-1988; R S Simon Of Cyrene Epis Ch Cincinnati OH 1982-1988; R S Steph's Epis Ch Winston Salem NC 1978-1982. Auth, *Sermons That Wk*. Soc Trsfg.

CURT, George (SwFla) 1204 Westlake Blvd, Naples FL 34103 **Assoc S Mary's Epis Ch Bonita Sprg FL 2002-; Ret 1990-** B Detroit MI 1927 s Karl & Margaret. LTh Sewanee: The U So, TS 1975; MDiv Sewanee: The U So, TS 1987. D 5/18/1975 P 11/1/1975 Bp Addison Hosea. m 11/18/1975 Vivi Curt. R S Dav's Epis Ch Englewood FL 1983-1990; Vic S Chad's Ch Tampa FL 1978-1983; Vic S Bede's Ch St. Petersburg FL 1977-1978; All SS Ch Newport KY 1975-1977; Vic All SS' Cold Sprg KY 1975-1977. Ord Of S Lk.

CURTIN, Anne Fahy (Alb) Healing a Woman's Soul, Inc., 68 S.Swan St., Albany NY 12210 **Chr Ch Coxsackie NY 2007-; Exec Dir Healing a Wmn's Soul Inc. 2007-** B Southampton NY 1947 d James & Anna. BS Le Moyne Coll 1968; MA Colg 1970; JD Albany Law Sch Un U 1982; MTh S Bernards TS and Mnstry 2002. D 6/9/2001 P 12/8/2001 Bp Daniel William Herzog. c 2. R Ch Of The H Cross Troy NY 2001-2007; Lead Cooordinator Prevent Chld Abuse Dio Albany Greenwich NY 2007-2010. Captial Dist Wmn Bar Assn 1983; Healing a Wmn's Soul, Inc. 2007; Wmn Bar Assn of New York St 1983.

CURTIN JR SHN, Ernest Albert (Pa) St Luke's Episcopal Church, 100 E Washington Ave, Newtown PA 18940 **R S Lk's Ch In The Cnty Of Buck Newtown PA 2007-** B Trenton NJ 1949 s Ernest & Doris. BA W&M 1971; MTS VTS 1973; MAT Coll of NJ 1975. D 9/2/2006 Bp Keith Lynn Ackerman P 12/16/2006 Bp Charles Ellsworth Bennison Jr. Dioc Coun Dio Pennsylvania Philadelphia PA 2010-2013. SocMary 1975-2021.

CURTIS, Chuck (EMich) 3260 E Midland Rd, Bay City MI 48706 **P-in-c S Eliz's Epis Ch Roscommon MI 2013-; Bp's Chapl to Ret Cler and Surviving Spouses Dio Estrn Michigan Saginaw MI 2003-** B Cooperstown NY 1943 s Edward & Lucy. BA MI SU 1964; STB EDS 1967. D 6/29/1967 Bp Richard Stanley Merrill Emrich P 3/26/1968 Bp Archie H Crowley. m 1/17/1981 Jayne N Curtis c 1. Asst S Paul's Epis Ch Flint MI 2009-2011; Int Trin Epis Ch Flushing MI 2004-2008; Int S Jn's Epis Ch Saginaw MI 2003-2004; Int Trin Epis Ch W Branch MI 2002-2003; R S Albans Epis Ch Bay City MI 1986-2001; R All SS Ch Nevada MO 1980-1986; Asst S Jn's Ch Royal Oak MI 1977-1980; Vic Chr The King Epis Ch Taylor MI 1969-1977; Asst S Thos Ch Trenton MI 1967-1969. The Alcuin Club 1968. cecpr68@yahoo.com

CURTIS, David (Va) D 4/16/2016 Bp Shannon Sherwood Johnston.

CURTIS, Edward W (Chi) 637 S Dearborn St Ste 1, Chicago IL 60605 **S Jn's Ch Wichita KS 2016-** B Cambridgeshire UK 1953 s Douglas & Beryl. BA W&L 1975; EdM Bos 1979; MDiv GTS 1984; DMin SWTS 2001. D 6/2/1984 Bp Claude Charles Vache P 12/7/1984 Bp Charles Thomas Gaskell. m 6/19/2013 Alfred Leopold Papillon. R Gr Ch Chicago IL 1991-2015; Cn Trin Cathd Cleveland OH 1987-1991; S Paul's Ch Milwaukee WI 1984-1987. EPF 1988.

CURTIS, Frederick L (Alb) 262 Main St N, Southbury CT 06488 B Norwalk,CT 1947 s Frederick & Nancy. MDiv EDS 1974. D 6/8/1974 P 2/22/1975 Bp Joseph Warren Hutchens. m 7/19/1969 Phyllis R Curtis. R Ch Of The Epiph Southbury CT 1977-2004; Cur S Andr's Ch Meriden CT 1974-1977. SSC.

CURTIS, James Dabney (At) 1100 Hampton Way NE, Atlanta GA 30324 B Memphis TN 1938 s Dana & Virginia. BA Rhodes Coll 1960; BD VTS 1964; CPE Georgia Mntl Hlth Inst Atlanta GA 1971; ThD Emory U 1975; Oxf GB 1976. D 6/22/1964 Bp John Vander Horst P 5/29/1965 Bp William Evan Sanders. c 2. Int S Jn's Atlanta GA 2007-2010; Artist in Res EDS Cambridge MA 2004-2005; S Bede's Ch Atlanta GA 2002-2004; S Barth's Epis Ch Atlanta GA 2001-2002; All SS Epis Ch Atlanta GA 1999-2001; Dio Atlanta Atlanta GA 1998-1999; Int S Jas Epis Ch Marietta GA 1996-1998; Int S Edw's Epis Ch Lawrenceville GA 1995-1996; S Jos's Epis Ch Mcdonough GA 1995; R Gr Ch Chattanooga TN 1979-1994; Chapl Lovett Sch Atlanta GA 1972-1979; Chapl Webb Sch Knoxville TN 1969-1970; Vic Ch Of The Gd Samar Knoxville TN 1965-1969; D Ch Of The Ascen Knoxville TN 1964-1965. ECVA 2003. Procter Fllshp Epis Div. Sch 2004; Braitmyer Fllshp Natl. Assn Indep Schools 1978.

CURTIS, Kenton (NY) 200 Bennett Ave #3G, New York NY 10040 **D Cathd Of St Jn The Div New York NY 2012-** B Loveland CO 1960 s James & Geraldine. BA U of Nthrn Colorado 1985; MSW Colorado St U 1989; Dio Colo Diac Prog CO 1996. D 11/2/1996 Bp William Jerry Winterrowd. D All SS Ch New York NY 1999-2012; D S Lk's Ch Denver CO 1997-1999. Assn for Epis Deacons 2014. kcurtis@actorsfund.org

CURTIS, Lynne Marsh Piret (Alb) 912 Route 146, Clifton Park NY 12065 B New York City NY 1945 d George & Pauline. BA Hobart and Wm Smith Colleges 1967; MSW Sch fo Soc Welf 1982. D 11/30/1991 Bp David Standish Ball. m 6/24/1967 Clark Sanford Curtis c 4.

CURTIS, Mary Page (NC) 212 Edinboro Dr, Southern Pines NC 28387 B Montgomery AL 1942 d William & Mary. BS Geo Mason U 1987; MDiv VTS 1991. D 6/15/1991 P 2/2/1992 Bp Peter J Lee. m 2/8/1999 Frank Curtis c 2. Assoc R S Thos Epis Ch Sanford NC 2000-2008; Asst R Emm Par Epis Ch Sthrn Pines NC 1993-1999; Assoc R S Andr's Epis Ch Ft Pierce FL 1991-1993.

CURTIS, Patricia H (WNC) St John's Episcopal Church, PO Box 175, Sylva NC 28779 **R S Jn's Ch Sylva NC 2007-** B Jacksonville FL 1951 d John & Mary. BA U of Cntrl Florida 1982; JD Florida St U Coll of Law Tallahassee FL 1986; MA U NC 1996; MDiv GTS 2007. D 6/9/2007 Bp Porter Taylor. Assitant To Mgr Unc- Asheville 2003-2004.

CURTIS, Sandra King (Roch) 10 Shether St # 272, Hammondsport NY 14840 B Corning NY 1943 d Leland & Honor. BS SUNY 1965; MEd Nazareth Coll 1979; MDiv S Bernards TS and Mnstry 1991. D 8/10/1991 P 2/23/1992 Bp William George Burrill. m 6/15/1963 Crocker Curtis c 2. S Jas Ch Hammondsport NY 1995-2012; Ch of the Redeem Addison NY 1991-2005. Auth, "The Cursive Approach To Readiness & Reading," 1981.

CURTIS, Sandra O (Ark) Episcopal Collegiate School, 1701 Cantrell Rd, Little Rock AR 72201 **Dn Dio Arkansas Little Rock AR 2013-; Epis Collgt Sch Little Rock AR 2013-** B Cologne Germany 1976 d Maurice & Lea. BA Trevecca Nazarene U 1999; MTS Duke DS 2004; MLS No Carolina Cntrl U 2005; Dplma Angl Stds hool of Theol at The U So 2013. D 8/17/2013 P 2/14/2014 Bp Larry Benfield. m 6/2/2001 Randall D Curtis c 1.

CURTIS III, William L (Ind) 2407 Cascade Rd SW, Atlanta GA 30311 **Cn Chr Ch Cathd Indianapolis IN 2015-** B Cape Canaveral FL 1988 s William & Alison. BA Florida St U 2009; MDiv Candler TS 2013; MDiv Candler TS Emory U 2013. D 5/22/2013 P 12/21/2013 Bp Robert Christopher Wright. m 10/13/2011 Hannah E Jacobs c 2. R Ch Of The Incarn Atlanta GA 2015, 2013-2014. leec@cccindy.org

CURTIS JR, William Shepley (Nev) 1654 County Rd, Minden NV 89423 B Abilene TX 1943 s William & Frances. BA Dart 1965; U CO 1966; MDiv CDSP 1969; Advncd CPE 1980. D 6/24/1969 P 10/28/1970 Bp Edwin B Thayer. m 4/4/1982 Joy Marcia Curtis c 4. Ch Of Coventry Cross Minden NV 2007-2008; Wkr P All SS So Lake Tahoe CA 1984-1988; All SS Of The Sierras S Lake Tahoe CA 1984-1988; Trin Ch Trinidad CO 1983-1984; Cur S Lk's Ch Billings MT 1978-1979; Asst Ch Of S Phil And S Jas Denver CO 1975-1977; Vic Gr Ch Olathe CO 1971-1975; S Mich's Ch Telluride CO 1971-1975; S Paul's Ch Montrose CO 1971-1975; S Jn's Epis Ch Ouray CO 1971-1974; Cur Ch Of Our Sav Colorado Sprg CO 1969-1970.

CURTIS, Yvonne Marie (WNY) PO Box 14, Dunkirk NY 14048 B Gowanda NY 1942 d Lawrence & Bernice. BS U of Nevada at Reno 1964; MS U of Nevada at Reno 1966; PhD U CA 1972. D 4/14/2009 P 11/8/2009 Bp Michael Garrison. c 2.

CURTISS, Geoff (Nwk) 202 3RD AVE, Bradley Beach NJ 07720 **Sprtl Counslr Hudson Cnty Correctional Cntr 2014-; Theol-in-Res Trin Cathd Cleveland OH 2015-; Mem Prison Mnstry Com Dio Newark 2014-; Mem Jersey City Together 2005-; Bd Mem, Past Pres Epis Ntwk for Econ Justice 1990-; Co-Pres Interfaith Cmnty Orgnztn 1986-** B Paterson NJ 1948 s Edgar & Ann. BA Ge 1970; MDiv Gettysburg Luth TS 1975. D 6/14/1975 P 12/14/1975 Bp George E Rath. m 2/6/1971 Linda Wiggins Curtiss c 2. All SS Epis Par Hoboken NJ 1984-2013; Hoboken Urban Mssn And Dioc Yth Hoboken NJ 1980-1983; Mssnr Hoboken NJ 1980-1983; Vic S Paul's Hoboken NJ 1980-1983; Asst Trin And S Phil's Cathd Newark NJ 1975-1979; Founding Pres Hoboken Shltr 1983-2013. Auth, "Mnstry in the Gentrifying Cosmopolis," *Faithfulness in the City*, Monad Oress, 2003. lindacurtiss@gmail.com

CUSANO, William Alan (NY) 2500 Jerome Ave, Bronx NY 10468 **D S Jas Epis Ch Fordham Bronx NY 2013-** B Astoria NY 1954 s Arthur & Marion. D 5/4/2013 Bp Andrew Marion Lenow Dietsche. m 10/26/1991 Kathleen Marcella Cusano.

CUSHING, Nan Chenault Marshall (NC) 69 Crystal Oaks Ct, Durham NC 27707 **D Dio No Carolina Raleigh NC 2002-, Archd 2001-2006, D 1995-; Mem Pstr Response Team Dio NC 2002-** B New York NY 1935 d Gerard & Nan. BFA Rhode Island Sch of Design 1957; Cert Appalachian Mnstry Educ Resource Cntr 1986; MA TESM 1989. D 4/29/1995 Bp Huntington Williams Jr. c 2. S Andr's Ch Haw River NC 2004-2006, D 2002-2009; Chapl Res Duke Med Cntr 2001-2002; D S Tit Epis Ch Durham NC 1995-1998. NAAD 1994.

CUSHINOTTO, Susan Elizabeth (NJ) 9425 3rd Ave, Stone Harbor NJ 08247 **D S Barn By The Bay Villas NJ 2013-** B Camden NJ 1956 d Frank & Margaret. D 5/16/2009 Bp Sylvestre Donato Romero. m 1/10/1976 Richard Cushinotto c 3. D S Mary's Epis Ch Stone Harbor NJ 2009-2013.

CUSHMAN, Mary Toohey (NY) PO Box 211, Chebeague Island ME 04017 B New York NY 1942 d John & Virginia. BS U of Sthrn Maine 1976; MDiv Ya Berk 1988. D 6/4/1988 P 5/1/1989 Bp Edward Cole Chalfant. m 6/1/1985 Thomas Spaulding Cushman. Assoc S Jas Ch New York NY 1993-1997; Assoc To R Chr Ch Alexandria VA 1988-1993.

CUSHMAN, Thomas Spaulding (NY) PO Box 211, Chebeague Island ME 04017 B Meriden CT 1942 s Robert & Barbara. BA Randolph-Macon Coll 1967; MEd U of Maine 1976; MDiv Ya Berk 1988. D 6/4/1988 P 5/1/1989 Bp Edward Cole Chalfant. m 6/1/1985 Mary Toohey Cushman c 2. Sr Assoc S Jas Ch New York NY 1993-1997; Assoc To R Chr Ch Alexandria VA 1988-1993.

CUSIC, Georgeanne Hill (FdL) 1510 N Broadway Ave, Marshfield WI 54449 B Dayton OH 1946 Dio Fond Du Lac; BA U of Wisconsin 1969; Sch of Chr Stds 2003. D 6/19/2004 Bp Russell Edward Jacobus. m 9/3/1966 Marshall Edward Cusic c 3. D S Alb's Epis Ch Marshfield WI 2004-2013.

CUSTER, Dale (SVa) 14404 Roberts Mill Court, Midlothian VA 23113 **R S Jn's Ch Chester VA 2004-** B South Boston VA 1970 s Raymond & Emily. BS VPI 1994; MS VPI 1996; MDiv VTS 2000. D 5/27/2000 Bp Donald Purple Hart P 12/7/2000 Bp David Conner Bane Jr. m 12/5/2004 Doris Delauder Custer c 1.

Asst S Mart's Epis Ch Williamsburg VA 2002-2004; Asst Ch Of The Redeem Midlothian VA 2000-2002.

CUSTER, Margaret (Peg) Gardiner (NH) 356 Deer Hill Road, Chocorua NH 03817 B Washington DC 1930 d Donald & Margaret. MRE CUA 1979; MDiv S Marys Sem and U 1983; CAS VTS 1986. D 6/14/1986 Bp John Thomas Walker P 6/14/1987 Bp Ronald Hayward Haines. c 5. Search Consult St. Mk's Ashland NH 2012; Chr Ch Portsmouth NH 2010-2011, Vic 2003-2010; P-in-c Trin Epis Ch Tilton NH 2005-2007; R S Andr's-In-The-Vlly Tamworth NH 1992-2002; Int S Paul's Epis Ch Piney Waldorf MD 1991-1992; Int R S Jn Deer Pk MD 1990-1991; Int S Jn's Ch Oakland MD 1990-1991; Int S Edw's Epis Ch Lancaster PA 1989-1990; Int Epis Ch Of Our Sav Midlothian VA 1988-1989; Asst Gr Epis Ch Silver Sprg MD 1986-1988; Mssn Resources Cmsn Dio New Hampshire Concord NH 2006-2012, COM 1994-2005. Co-Auth/Ed, "Act Now"; Auth, "Young At Heart; Ideas & Illustrations".

CUTAIAR, Michael Louis (NMich) B Detroit MI 1957 s Donald & Elaine. D 6/4/2006 Bp James Arthur Kelsey P 11/23/2014 Bp Rayford J Ray. m 2/19/2007 Luann Cutaiar.

CUTIE, Albert R (SeFla) 11173 Griffing Blvd, Miami FL 33161 **S Benedicts Ch Ft Lauderdale FL 2014**- B San Juan PR 1969 s Alberto & Yolanda. BA S Johns Vianney Sem 1991; MA St Vinc DePaul Reg Sem 1994; MDiv St Vinc DePaul Reg Sem 1995; DMin Sewanee: The U So, TS 2014. Rec 5/29/2010 Bp Leo Frade. m 6/26/2010 Ruhama Buni Cutie c 3. P-in-c Ch Of The Resurr Miami FL 2010-2014, LP 2009-2010; P-in-c St. Fran de Sales Cath Ch 2005-2009; Admin San Isidro Mssn 2002-2004; Auth Columnist - Daily Advice Self-help 2001-2009; Pres CEO/Gnrl Dir. Pax Cath Cmncatn Inc. 2001-2009; Par Vic/Asst. St. Pat Ch 1998-2002; Host Telemundo Ntwk 1998-2001; Par Vic/Asst. St. Clem Ch 1995-1998; D St. Mary Star of the Sea 1994-1995. Auth, "Dilemma," Penguin USA, 2011; Auth, "Var Columns," *Huffington Post / AOL LATI-NO*, 2011; Auth, "Real Life, Real Love," Penguin USA, 2006.

CUTLER, Donald Robert (NY) 38 Chestnut St, Salem MA 01970 **Ret 1991**- B Sharon PA 1931 s John & Elmo. BA Penn 1953; MTh VTS 1957; PhD Harv 1965. D 6/7/1957 P 12/14/1957 Bp John Thomas Heistand. m 6/20/1958 Virginia Cutler c 3. R The Ch Of S Jos Of Arimathea White Plains NY 1971-1991; Non-par 1966-1971; Dir The Ch Soc For Coll Wk Cambridge MA 1963-1966; Non-par 1962-1963; Chapl Harvard & Radcliffe 1959-1962; Asst S Andr's Ch St Coll PA 1957-1959. Fell Harv 1959; Phi Beta Kappa.

CUTLER, E Clifford (Pa) 18 E Chestnut Hill Ave, Philadelphia PA 19118 **R S Paul's Ch Philadelphia PA 2006**- B Philadelphia PA 1949 s Edward & Catherine. BS Trin 1971; MDiv EDS 1976. D 6/12/1976 P 5/1/1977 Bp Lyman Cunningham Ogilby. m 12/22/1973 Amy L Cutler c 2. R S Steph's Ch Cohasset MA 1985-2006; Vic S Lk's Kensington Philadelphia PA 1978-1985; St Lukes Ch Philadelphia PA 1978-1985; Cur Nevil Memi Ch Of S Geo Ardmore PA 1976-1978. Fllshp S Alb & Sergius, Philadelphia Cler.

CUTLER, Howard Taylor (HB) 1124 Westhampton Glen Dr, Richmond VA 23238 **1973**- B Princess Ann County VA 1935 s Julian & Rena. BS E Carolina U 1959; BD VTS 1962. D 6/28/1962 P 1/1/1963 Bp Thomas H Wright. m 8/2/1991 Joy Cutler c 5. R St Fran Epis Ch Charleston SC 1967-1973; R H Innoc' Lenoir Cnty NC 1962-1967.

CUTLER, Paul Colman (NMich) Hc 1 Box 646, Wetmore MI 49895 B Buffalo NY 1928 s Paul & Frances. BS Baldwin-Wallace Coll 1952; MS Case Wstrn Reserve U 1954. D 9/8/1996 Bp Thomas Kreider Ray. m 2/22/1952 Shirley Jane Hanson.

CUTOLO, Mark Anthony (WNY) 351 E 74th St, New York NY 10021 B Buffalo NY 1983 s Anthony & Laudi. BA SUNY at Buffalo 2005; MDiv Yale DS 2008. D 12/22/2007 P 6/21/2009 Bp Michael Garrison.

CUTSHALL, Jason Edward (Va) D 6/10/2017 Bp Shannon Sherwood Johnston.

CUTTER IV, Irving Taylor (Okla) 4200 S Atlanta Pl, Tulsa OK 74105 **R S Jn's Epis Ch Tulsa OK 2006-; Trst Holland Hall Sch Tulsa OK 2013-; Trst S Simeons Epis Hm Tulsa OK 2007**- B Austin TX 1966 s Irving & Hilde. BA Rice U 1987; MDiv VTS 1998. D 6/20/1998 Bp Claude Edward Payne P 6/26/1999 Bp Leopoldo Jesus Alard. m 10/12/2002 Andrea Cutter c 2. R S Jas Epis Ch Houston TX 2001-2006; S Mk's Ch Beaumont TX 1998-2001; Stndg Com Dio Oklahoma Oklahoma City OK 2009-2012, COM 2009-. Dudley Speech Prize VTS 1998. icutter@sjtulsa.org

CYR, Gary A (Me) 3 J St, Bangor ME 04401 **S Jas' Ch Clinton NY 2017-** B Caribou ME 1962 s Alphy & Viola. BA S Josephs Coll 2008; MDiv Bangor TS 2010. D 6/19/2010 P 6/23/2012 Bp Stephen Taylor Lane.

CYR, Mark Bernard (Eas) 25 Addy Road, P.O. Box 191, Bethany Beach DE 19930 **The Ch Of The H Sprt Ocean City MD 2016**- B Van Buren ME 1956 s Bernard & Aline. Concordia U 1977; BA U of Utah 1984; MDiv EDS 1988; DMin SWTS 2005. D 9/9/1989 P 6/10/1990 Bp Otis Charles. m 8/21/1993 Margie Kirby c 5. Ch Of S Paul's By The Sea Ocean City MD 2014-2015; Int S Martha's Epis Ch Bethany Bch DE 2010-2011; P-in-c Gr Epis Ch - Wicomico Par Princess Anne MD 2009-2010; Dioc Stff Dio New York New York NY 2000-2009; R Chr Ch Warwick NY 1993-2000; R S Jn's Epis Ch Holbrook MA

1991-1993; Chapl McLean Hosp Belmont MA 1990-1991; Asst to R Par Of The Epiph Winchester MA 1989-1991.

CZARNETZKY, Sylvia Yale (Miss) 148 French Br, Madison MS 39110 **Calv Epis Ch Cleveland MS 2012-; P Gr Ch Rosedale MS 2012**- B Greenville MS 1958 d James & Sylvia. BA U So 1980; JD Tul 1984; MA U of Mississippi 1993; MDiv SWTS 1998. D 8/29/1998 P 3/24/1999 Bp Alfred Marble Jr. m 9/25/1999 John M Czarnetzky. S Jn's Ch Aberdeen MS 2009-2012; The Chap Of The Cross Madison MS 2006-2009; D Ch Of The Adv Sumner MS 1998-2006.

CZARNIECKI, Lynn (Pa) 30 Gildersleeve Pl, Watchung NJ 07069 B 1947 BSN Hunter Coll 1969; MSN U of Pennsylvania 1976; MTS Drew TS 2004; MTS Drew U 2004. D 6/5/2004 Bp John Palmer Croneberger.

CZOLGOSZ, Joseph Tamborini (NI) 707 S Chester Ave, Park Ridge IL 60068 **Trng Trnr, Safeguarding God's People Epis Dio Chicago IL 2005-; Affiliated Cler S Mary's Ch Pk Ridge IL 2003-; Mem/Supply P S Mary's Ch Pk Ridge IL 1999**- B Saginaw MI 1950 s Joseph & Edna. BA U of St Thos 1972; MA CUA 1975; MDiv Anderson U TS 1992; Full Supvsr Certification ACPE (ACPE) 1999; Bd Cert Chapl Assn of Profsnl Chapl 2000; DMin SWTS 2008. Rec 9/24/2003 as Priest Bp Bill Persell. m 9/4/1993 Susan T Tamborini c 1. S Chas Ch St. Chas IL 2015-2016. "Healing Stories, Past, Present and Future: A Framework for Par Nrsng," *Proceedings of the Eighth Annual Westberg Symposium*, Natl Par Nurse Resource Cntr, 1994. ACPE 1991; Assn of Profsnl Chapl 1998; BroSA 2002-2010; St. Mary's Men's Grp 2011. Summit Ldrshp Advoc Hlth Care 2005. czolgosz.jt@gmail.com

D

DAGG, Margaret K (Kan) 1427 SW Macvicar Ave, Topeka KS 66604 B Topeka KS 1949 d Richard & Margaret. BA Washburn U 1975; MA U of Kansas 1986; MDiv VTS 2002. D 4/6/2002 P 10/5/2002 Bp William Edward Smalley. m 9/26/1992 Adam Leroy Dagg c 2. P-in-c S Andr's Epis Ch Emporia KS 2015-2017; Int S Mart-In-The-Fields Edwardsville KS 2008-2012; P-in-c S Phil's Epis Ch Topeka KS 2004-2007; Vic S Aid's Ch Olathe KS 2002-2004.

DAGGETT, Paul (SO) 115 North 6th Street, Hamilton OH 45011 **P-in-c S Paul's Ch Chillicothe OH 2013**- B Providence RI 1943 s Edward & Myra. BA Bos 1965; MDiv Epis TS of the SW 1970. D 6/19/1970 Bp Frederick P Goddard P 6/1/1971 Bp James Milton Richardson. m 12/21/1969 Mary Jane Daggett c 2. Dio Sthrn Ohio Cincinnati OH 2006-2009; Trin Ch Hamilton OH 2000-2012; R S Alb's Ch Wilmington DE 1991-2000; S Paul's Ch Mt Vernon OH 1984-1991; R Chr Ch Point Pleasat WV 1977-1983; R S Thos' Epis Ch Weirton WV 1973-1977; Vic-in-c Chr Ch Epis San Augastine TX 1970-1973; Dio Texas Houston TX 1970-1973; Vic-in-c S Jn's Epis Ch Carthage TX 1970-1973; Vic-in-Charge S Jn's Epis Ch Cntr TX 1970-1973; Bdgt Comm Dio Sthrn Ohio Cincinnati OH 2003-2008; Stndg Cmsn Dio Delaware Wilmington 1993-1999; Plnng Com Dio Ohio Cleveland 1984-1988; Chair - Dept. of Mssn & Mnstry Dio W Virginia Charleston WV 1982-1983, Yth Dir 1976-1981. Paul Harris Fell 1991.

DAHARSH, Floyd Arthur (Okla) 112 West 9th Street, Hugoton KS 67951 **S Jn's Ch Ulysses KS 2003-; Ret 2000**- B Americus KS 1936 s Frank & Della. BS Emporia St U 1960; MS Emporia St U 1966. D 9/9/1990 P 11/30/1991 Bp John Forsythe Ashby. m 3/1/1963 Edwina Berniel Daharsh. S Steph's Ch Guymon OK 2003-2011; Cluster Mssnr SW Area Reg Mnstry Guymon OK 2001-2003; Loc P Asstg the Cluster Mnstry SW Area Reg Mnstry Guymon OK 1991-2001; 1990-2000.

DAHILL, Laurel Anne (Mich) Saint Mary's-In-The-Hills Church, 2512 Joslyn Ct, Lake Orion MI 48360 **R S Mary's-In-The-Hills Ch Lake Orion MI 2012**- B Arlington MA 1971 d Charles & Eileen. BA SUNY 1994; MFA VPI 1997; MDiv SWTS 2007; MTS SWTS 2008. D 6/7/2008 Bp Jeff Lee P 12/6/2008 Bp Robert R Gepert. m 2/14/2014 Elisabeth A Gurney. R S Andr's Ch Big Rapids MI 2008-2012. Contrib, "Freedom and Liberty," *Recon & Healing*, Preaching Excellence Prog, 2007.

DAHL, Joan Elizabeth (Spok) 8991 State Route 24, Moxee WA 98936 **D Chr Epis Ch Zillah WA 2000**- B Seattle WA 1946 d William & Dorothy. U of Washington; AS Shoreline Cmnty Coll 1968. D 10/16/1999 Bp John Stuart Thornton. m 8/17/1968 Joseph Miller Dahl c 2. Lower Yakima Vlly Mutual Mnstry 2000.

DAHLIN, James G (WNC) 140 Saint Marys Church Rd, Morganton NC 28655 B Arlington Heights IL 1977 s Rodney & Barbara. BS Wheaton Coll 1999; MDiv Duke DS 2007; Dplma in Angl Stds Epis TS Of The SW 2015. D 5/16/2015 P 11/21/2015 Bp Porter Taylor. St Mary's and St Steph's Epis Ch Morganton NC 2015, R 2015-. jamesgdahlin@gmail.com

DAHLMAN, Thomas A (Okla) 4250 W Houston St, Broken Arrow OK 74012 **R Emm Epis Ch Shawnee OK 2017**- B Tulsa OK 1977 s Gordon & Emma. BA Freed-Hardeman U 1999; MA Oklahoma Chr U 2008; MDiv Epis TS Of The SW 2015; MDiv Epis TS of the SW 2015. D 1/10/2015 P 8/1/2015 Bp Edward Joseph Konieczny. m 8/31/2002 Alexis Dawn Sander c 2. Cur S Pat's

Epis Ch Broken Arrow OK 2015-2017; Sem S Alb's Epis Ch Austin Austin TX 2013-2015.

DAIGLE, Deborah Heft (Tex) PO Box 1344, Madisonville TX 77864 B Cleveland OH 1948 d Ronald & Mary. Iona Sch of Mnstry 2010. D 6/19/2010 Bp C Andrew Doyle. c 2.

DAILEY, Beulah Huffman (Dal) 2929 Hickory St, Dallas TX 75226 B Marion NC 1936 d Aaron & Lola. Clevenger Coll of Bus; Lic Sacr Theol GTS 1985. D 6/14/1986 Bp Donis Dean Patterson P 3/1/1996 Bp James Monte Stanton. Asst S Jas Ch Dallas TX 2002-2011, 1998-2000; Asst S Paul's Epis Ch Waxahachie TX 1992-1998; Asst Ch Of The Gd Shpd Cedar Hill TX 1986-1992. DOK 1989; Ord Of S Lk 1976; S Steph Mnstry 1999. High Profile Dallas Morning News 2002; Serv To Mankind Awd Sertoma Club Of Dallas Texas 2002; Ex. Dir Of The Year Texas Homeless Ntwk 2002; Participated In Pres. G.W. Bush Inaguration Serv 2000; Heart Of Gold Awd Leukemia Soc 1997.

DAILEY, Douglas G (At) 3603 Tradition Drive, Gainesville GA 30506 **S Andr's Ch St Coll PA 2015-** B Columbus OH 1956 s Alan & Vivian. Emory U 1977; LTh Lincoln Theol Coll, UK 1988; BTh U of Nottingham, UK 1988. Trans 4/1/1992 Bp Bob Johnson. m 8/23/1980 Judith Ann Dailey c 3. S Matt's Epis Cathd Laramie WY 2012-2013; R Gr Epis Ch Gainesville GA 2002-2012; R Trin Epis Ch Statesville NC 1993-2002; Assoc R Ch Of The Ascen Hickory NC 1991-1993; Serv Ch of Engl 1988-1991; Stndg Com Pres Dio Atlanta Atlanta GA 2009, Assessment Appeal Bd Chair 2007-2012, Stndg Com Mem 2007-2009, NE Georgia Convoc Dn 2006-2012; Ecum Off Dio No Carolina Raleigh NC 1997-2002, Chr Formation Com Mem 1995-1998; Catechumenate Commisssion Mem Dio Wstrn No Carolina Asheville NC 1991-1993, Liturg and Mus Cmsn Mem 1991-1993. douglasdailey@charter.net

DAILY JR, Charles W (FdL) N 6945 Ash Road, Shawano WI 54166 **Chapl (Hosp & Hospice) Shawano Med Cntr Shawano WI 2002-** B Oakland CA 1943 s Charles & June. BA U Denv 1969; MSW U Denv 1971; MA Creighton U 1990. Rec 4/12/2003 as Deacon Bp Russell Edward Jacobus. m 8/6/2002 Pamela Kerry. St Ambr Epis Ch Antigo WI 2012-2015; D S Jn's Ch Shawano WI 2003-2011; Ther-Soc Worker Luth Soc Serv Wittenberg WI 1999-2002. Angl Comm Ntwk 2006.

DAILY, Teresa Wooten (Ark) 925 Mitchell St, Conway AR 72034 **D-in-c S Ptr's Ch Conway AR 2008-** B Atlanta GA 1966 d Ernest & Virginia. BS Duke 1988; MD Ya Sch of Medecine 1992; MDiv Epis TS of the SW 2008. D 3/15/2008 P 9/20/2008 Bp Larry Benfield. m 6/7/1992 David W Daily c 2.

DAISA IV, George Donald John (Los) PO Box 37, Pacific Palisades CA 90272 **S Patricks Ch And Day Sch Thousand Oaks CA 2016-** B Bakersfield CA 1974 s George & Deborah. BFA U CA, Los Angeles 1996; MDiv Claremont TS 2013. D 6/8/2013 Bp Joseph Jon Bruno P 1/11/2014 Bp Mary Douglas Glasspool. m 5/8/1999 Karen Garvey Daisa c 1. The Par Of S Matt Pacific Plsds CA 2013-2016, 2013. daisageorge@gmail.com

DAKAN, Karen Nugent (SwFla) 14 Sandy Hook Rd N, Sarasota FL 34242 B Chicago IL 1942 d Martin & Marie. BA Br 1964; MA U of So Florida 1975. D 11/30/1986 Bp Emerson Paul Haynes. m 4/20/1963 Stephen Lee Dakan c 2. Asst S Bon Ch Sarasota FL 1986-2000.

DALBY, Marti (Ark) **S Fran Ch Heber Sprg AR 2009-** B Little Rock AR 1958 d Edward & Mary. BS LSU 1981; MDiv Sewanee: The U So, TS 2006. D 7/9/2005 P 2/4/2006 Bp Larry Maze. m 4/27/1985 Robert E Dalby c 2. Dio Arkansas Little Rock AR 2009, Exec Coun 2010-, Del to ECW Trien 2009, Camp Mitchell Bd Trst 2009-, Bd Trst 2008-, Del to ECW Trien 2006, ECW Bd 2002-; S Jn's Epis Ch Ft Smith AR 2006-2009.

D'ALCARAVELA, Joao A (Mass) Palmoinho, Serra do Louro, Palmela 2950-305 Portugal **MA Dioc Del El Salvador 1990-** B Sardoal Portugal 1931 s Antonio & Patrocinia. Cert Seminario da Luz Lisbon PT 1958; BD Dominican U Ottawa CA 1974; MEd U of Montreal 1976; PhD U of Montreal 1987; EDS 1988. Rec 9/29/1990 as Priest Bp David Bell Birney IV. m 6/13/1987 Carol Blanchard c 2. Vol for Mssn, Dir. Missao Lusa: Prof. of Theol ECUSA/Lusitanian Ch PT Partnr in Mssn Portugal 1994-2001; Ethno Fam Serv New Bedford MA 1993-1994; Dio Massachusetts Boston MA 1990-1993, Portico, Mssnr and Dir for Portuguese; Bd Mem Inter-Ch Coun New Bedford MA 1990-1993; Assoc P St Ptr's St Gabr's St Thos 1990-1993; Mem Wider Mssn Com Dio. MA Boston 1990-1993; OFM RC Ch Portugal 1950-1988. Auth, "A Minority in a Changing Soc:The Portuguese Communities of Quebec," *in Engl*, U of Ottawa Press, 1980.

DALE, Anne (SVa) **The Epis Ch Of The Adv Norfolk VA 2013-** B Norfolk VA 1955 d James & Coraleigh. BA Meredith Coll 1977; MEd No Carolina St U 1983; MDiv VTS 2011. D 6/11/2011 P 2/18/2012 Bp Clifton Daniel III. m 4/17/1982 Roland Ward Dale c 2. annedale4@gmail.com

DALE, Cortney H (EC) **Assoc Chr Ch New Bern NC 2015-** B Bowling Green KY 1984 d James & Mary. BA Bellarmine U 2007; MDiv VTS 2015. D 11/7/2014 P 5/27/2015 Bp Terry Allen White. m 5/25/2013 James Gillespie Gilmore.

DALE, Kathleen Askew (Los) St. Margaret's Episcopal Church, 47-535 HWY 74 at Haystack Rd., Palm Desert CA 92260 **Dir of Counslg S Marg's Epis Ch Palm Desert CA 2008-; Non-par 1990-** B Hahira GA 1948 d Robert & Hazel. BA Bos 1970; MDiv Harvard DS 1977; MA Antioch U 1985. D 6/11/1978 Bp

Morris Fairchild Arnold P 2/11/1979 Bp Robert Claflin Rusack. Assoc All SS Par Beverly Hills CA 1984-1990; Assoc S Mich and All Ang Epis Ch Studio City CA 1980-1984; Cur All SS Ch Pasadena CA 1978-1980.

DALES, Randolph Kent (NH) PO Box 1363, Wolfeboro NH 03894 **Chapl to the Ret Dio New Hampshire Concord NH 2013-, Cn to the Ordnry 2012-2013, Bd Trst 2010-; Asstg Chapl The Holderness Sch Plymouth NH 2013-, Bd Trst 2008-, Chapl 1971-1978** B Los Angeles CA 1941 s John & Freda. BA Stan 1963; MDiv VTS 1966. D 9/10/1966 P 3/11/1967 Bp Francis E I Bloy. m 4/15/1994 Marilyn A Tyler c 4. R All SS Epis Ch Wolfeboro NH 1978-2012; S Gabr's Epis Ch Marion MA 1977-1978, 1976, 1976; Vic Trin Ch Meredith NH 1972-1978; Chapl Holderness Sch Plymouth NH 1971-1978; Cur Chr Ch Exeter NH 1969-1971; Cur S Dav's Par N Hollywood CA 1967-1969.

D'ALESANDRE, Peter John (O) 84 Lake Washington Dr # 2814, Chepachet RI 02814 **Died 5/16/2017** B New York NY 1943 s John & Marie. BA Leh 1965; BD Nash 1970; MA U of Connecticut 1998; Natl Taiwan Normal U 1999. D 6/6/1970 Bp Horace W B Donegan P 12/21/1970 Bp Donald H V Hallock. m 12/21/1968 Janet D'Alesandre c 4. Vic Gr Epis Ch Yantic CT 2006-2017, Vic 2005-2017; Int St Mary 's Epis Ch Warwick RI 2004-2005; Lectr in Philos Gd News Coll Taichung Taiwan 2003; S Steph's Ch Providence RI 2000-2017; Engl Chapl S Jas Par Taichung Taiwan 1999-2003; Dio Taiwan Taipei 1999-2001; Engl Chapl S Jn's Cathd Taipei Taiwan 1998-1999; R S Matt's Ch Ashland OH 1988-1996; Cur S Barn Ch Warwick RI 1981-1988; Vic Chr The King Epis Ch Huntington IN 1975-1980; Cur All SS Epis Ch Kansas City MO 1971-1975; Chr Epis Ch Of Delavan Delavan WI 1970-1971. CCU, CBS; P AssociateCom-Transfiguration 1992.

DALEY, Alexander Spotswood (Mass) 81 Mill Pond, North Andover MA 01845 **Epis Commissary (for USA) Dio W Newfoundland 1999-** B Boston MA 1935 s Robert & Louisa. BA Harv 1957; STB EDS 1971; DMin Pittsburgh TS 1984; D.D. Queens Coll of New Foundland 2011; D.D. Queens Coll of Newfoundland, Can 2011. D 6/26/1971 P 1/20/1972 Bp John Melville Burgess. Chapl Soc Of Colonial Wars In Massachusetts 1999-2009; Cler Convenr Dio Massachusetts Boston MA 1994-1999; S Aid's Chap So Dartmouth MA 1991-1995; R S Paul's Epis Ch No Andover MA 1976-2005; R Angl Par Stephenville Nf Can 1975-1976; Chapl Dios Fulham & Gilbratar 1973-1975; Asst S Geo's Epis Ch Dayton OH 1971-1973; Lt. CDR US Naval Chapl 1964-1995; Lt. CDR US Navy Reserve 1957-1995; Chapl to the Bp of Gibraltar Ch of Engl 1973-1975. Ord Of S Lk 2000.

DALEY, Joy Anne (Dal) 13355 Pandora Cir, Dallas TX 75238 **The Epis Ch Of S Thos The Apos Dallas TX 2014-; Vic The Epis Ch Of The Trsfg 2005-** B Beverly MA 1953 d Henry & Theresa. BA Bridgewater Coll 1975; MA Assumption Coll 1980; MDiv Brite DS 2001. D 6/9/2001 P 5/25/2002 Bp James Monte Stanton. c 2. Vic The Epis Ch Of The Trsfg Dallas TX 2001-2014.

DALFERES, Craig Douglas (La) 624 Winfield Blvd, Houma LA 70360 **R S Matt's Epis Ch Houma LA 2004-** B Baton Rouge LA 1968 s Joseph & Linda. BS Centenary Coll 1990; MDiv Nash 1998. D 5/30/1998 P 12/12/1998 Bp Charles Edward Jenkins III. m 9/24/1994 Jennifer Dalferes c 2. Assoc R Trin Epis Ch Baton Rouge LA 1998-2004; Pres of Stndg Com Dio Louisiana New Orleans LA 2008-2009.

DALGLISH, William Anthony (Tenn) 1911 Hampton Dr, Lebanon TN 37087 B Saint Paul MN 1941 s James & Mary. BA S Paul Sem 1963; MA Scarritt Grad Sch 1969; MDiv S Meinrad TS 1971; DMin Van 1979; CFP Coll for Fin Plnng 1983; Sewanee: The U So, TS 1985. Rec 6/1/1985 as Priest Bp William Evan Sanders. m 11/2/1974 Carol Dalglish c 2. Int Vic Ch of the H Cross Murfreesboro TN 2008-2011; Pstr Faith Evang Luth Ch Lebanon TN 2001-2005; Dir Affirmative Aging Dio Tennessee Nashville TN 1999-2000, Dandridge Trust - Trst, Treas 1987-1999; Chapl Cumberland U Lebanon TN 1996-1998; Vic S Jn's Epis Ch Mt Juliet TN 1996-1998; Vic The Ch Of The Epiph Lebanon TN 1989-1998; Dir Glenmary Missioners Rel Ed. Dept. 1968-1982. Auth, "Models For Catechetical Mnstry In The Rural Par," Conf Of Cath Bishops, 1982; Auth, "Fam Centered Model As Option For CE," Meth Bd Discipleship, 1974; Auth, "Media For Chr Formation (3 Volumes)," Pflaum, 1970. First Epis P In Tennessee appointed as Pstr Of Luth (ELCA) Ch Luth Syn (SE) and Epis Dio TN 2001.

DALLMAN, Matthew Christian (Spr) **All SS Ch Morton IL 2016-; S Paul's Epis Ch Pekin IL 2016-** B Washington, D.C. 1974 s Robert & Katherine. BA Washington U in S Louis 1997; MA Cath Theol Un 2014; MTS Nash 2015. D 6/11/2016 P 12/13/2016 Bp Daniel Hayden Martins. m 7/24/1999 Hannah Irene Pendzich c 4. rector@tazewellparish.org

DALLY, John Addison (Chi) 2650 N Lakeview Ave Apt 2501, Chicago IL 60614 **Tchr Bexley Seabury Fed Chicago IL 2015-, 2011-2015, 2006-2009, 1995-2005; Ch Of Our Sav Chicago IL 2015-** B Park Ridge IL 1957 s Addison & Betty. BA U CA 1978; MDiv Yale DS 1981; PhD U Chi 1994. D 6/19/1982 P 1/20/1983 Bp Robert Claflin Rusack. m 8/1/2008 Todd Marcus Young. Assoc Prof of Preaching and Missional Ldrshp Garrett-Evang TS Evanston IL 2009-2013; Exec Dir Seabury Inst Seabury Inst Evanston IL 2000-2005; R S Dunst's Epis Ch Westchester IL 1995-2000; Chapl Epis Luth Mnstry Evanston IL 1994-1995; Assoc S Mary's Ch Pk Ridge IL 1989-1992; Yth Dir Dio Chicago Chicago IL 1989; Prof Bloy Hse Claremont CA 1986-1987; P-in-c S Paul's Epis Ch Tustin CA 1986-1987; Assoc R Trin Epis Ch Santa Barbara CA 1982-1986; Lectr Yale DS 1981-1982. Auth, "Choosing the Kingdom: Missional Preaching for the Household of God," Alb Inst, 2008; Auth, "Myths And Fictions," E. J. Brill, 1993; Ed, "Monasticism & The Arts," Syr Press, 1983; Compsr, "Var Choral Works"; Auth, "Var Plays". Galler Prize U Chi 1994; Fllshp Inst For The Advncd Study Of Rel, Unversity Of Chic 1992; Fell ECF 1988; B.A. mcl U CA, Irvine 1978; Phi Beta Kappa U CA, Irvine 1978. jdally@bexleyseabury.edu

DALMASSO, Gary Lee (Chi) 215 29th Ave, East Moline IL 61244 **Non-par 1994-** B Canton IL 1942 s Joseph & Maxine. BA U of Iowa 1964; BA GTS 1967. D 4/1/1967 P 10/28/1967 Bp Francis W Lickfield. m 6/28/1969 Judith Connie Dalmasso c 4. Chr Epis Ch Clinton IA 2003-2005; Renwl In Chr Mnstrs E Moline IL 1995-2003; Vic S Jn's Epis Ch Preemption IL 1990-1994; Non-par 1975-1985; Vic S Mk's Epis Ch Silvis IL 1967-1975. Fllshp Of Epis Evangelicals, Pews Action.

DALMASSO, Judith Connie (Ia) Renewal in Christ Ministries, PO Box 94, East Moline IL 61244 **Asst Trin Cathd Davenport IA 2010-; Renwl In Chr Mnstrs E Moline IL 2007-** B Moline IL 1946 d Conrad & Marion. BA Augustana Coll 1987; MTS Nash 2006. D 6/23/2007 P 1/6/2008 Bp Alan Scarfe. m 6/28/1969 Gary Lee Dalmasso c 4.

DALRYMPLE, Sharon Gladwin (ECR) 5147 Show Low Lake Rd, Lakeside AZ 85929 B San Antonio TX 1946 d Carl & Margaret. BA Arizona St Univesity 1968. D 6/22/2013 Bp Kirk Stevan Smith.

DALTON, Harlon L (Ct) Episcopal Diocese of Connecticut, 1335 Asylum Avenue, Hartford CT 06105 **Prof (Adj) of Law and Rel Yale DS/Berk New Haven CT 2006-** B Cleveland OH 1947 s John & Louise. read for Ord; BA Harv 1969; JD Ya 1973; Cert Ang Stud Ya Berk 2001. D 6/8/2002 P 1/4/2003 Bp Andrew Donnan Smith. m 9/6/1986 Jill M Dalton. Chr Ch Cathd Hartford CT 2012-2015; Cn Dio Connecticut Meriden CT 2011-2014, Com 2, COM 2011, Stndg Com 2007-2011, Prog & Bdgt Com 2006-2011, Com 1, COM 2005-2011; Int S Ann's Epis Ch Old Lyme CT 2010; Assoc R S Paul And S Jas New Haven CT 2002-2010. "Racial Healing," Doubleday, 1995.

DALTON JR, James Albert (Ark) 94 Cherrywood Dr., Cabot AR 72023 **P S Steph's Epis Ch Jacksonville AR 2006-** B Charleston AR 1953 s James & Doris. BSE Arkansas Tech U 1975; MSE U of Cntrl Arkansas 1989. D 6/3/2006 P 12/9/2006 Bp Larry Maze. m 6/16/1973 Joyce Foley Dalton c 2.

DALTON, Joyce Foley (Ark) St Stephen's Episcopal Church, 2413 Northeastern Ave, Jacksonville AR 72076 B Ft Smith AR 1953 d Charles & Loretta. BA Arkansas Tech U 1975; MEd U of Arkansas 1983. D 6/3/2006 Bp Larry Maze. m 6/16/1973 James Albert Dalton c 2.

DALTON, William Thomas (Dal) 311 W. 5th St., Bonham TX 75418 **Died 3/22/2017** B University City MO 1933 BA U of No Texas 1958; MDiv Epis TS in Kentucky 1964. D 6/18/1964 Bp Theodore H McCrea P 9/18/2004 Bp James Monte Stanton. m 11/23/1967 Lois Charlene Forbus c 1. Ret Ch Of The H Trin Bonham TX 2004-2008.

DALY JR, Herbert T (Pgh) 209 E. Adkins St., Starke FL 32091 **R S Mk's Ch Starke FL 2017-** B Arcadia FL 1958 s Herbert & Adrienne. MDiv TESM 2014. D 6/21/2014 P 1/17/2015 Bp Dorsey McConnell. P-in-c S Paul's Epis Ch Kittanning PA 2015-2017, P 2015.

DALY, Joseph Erin (WLa) 1030 Johnston St, Lafayette LA 70501 **R Ch Of The Ascen Lafayette LA 2009-** B Truro NS CA 1971 s George & Carol. PhD McGill U; Regent Coll Vancouver CA 1996; MDiv Samford U 1998. D 10/26/2002 P 6/3/2003 Bp Daniel William Herzog. m 6/30/1995 Angela A Daly c 2. R S Andr's Epis Ch Douglas GA 2003-2009; Asst Trin Ch Plattsburgh NY 2002-2003.

DALY III, Raymond Ernest (Fla) 160 Sea Island Dr, Ponte Vedra Beach FL 32082 B Chicago IL 1929 s Raymond & Catherine. Nash; BA DePaul U 1950; PhD Unversity of Lausanne Ch 1972. D 4/19/1986 Bp Charles Brinkley Morton. m 5/23/1980 Suzanne Morgan. Assoc S Geo Epis Ch Jacksonville FL 2000-2014; Assoc - Mssn Hse Dio Florida Jacksonville 1995-2000; Assoc S Mary Of The Hills Epis Par Blowing Rock NC 1992-1995; Asst To Bp Dio Wstrn No Carolina Asheville NC 1990-1992; Assoc S Ptr's Epis Ch Del Mar CA 1986-1989; Consult To Congs Dio Olympia Seattle 1983-1984. Auth, "Intl Money Mgmt". Compass Rose Soc 1999.

DALY, Richard R (Dal) 5323 N Mulligan Ave, Chicago IL 60630 **Par Vic S Paul's Par Riverside IL 2002-** B Chicago IL 1962 s Ernest & Lucille. BA Loyola U 1985; MDiv Nash 1991; Cntr for Rel & Psych Chicago IL 1995. D 12/1/1990 P 6/14/1991 Bp William Louis Stevens. m 10/23/2004 Diana Lyn Daly c 3. Int S Raphael The Archangel Oak Lawn IL 1999-2002; R S Steph's Epis Ch Sherman TX 1996-1998; R S Ptr's Epis Ch Sheboygan Falls WI 1993-1996; Cur Trin Ch Milwaukee WI 1991-1993; Asst S Anskar's Epis Ch Hartland WI 1990-1991; Dn Lake Shore Dnry Dio Fond du Lac Appleton WI 1993-1995, Stndg Com 1993-1995. Socitey of the H Cross 1997; Sovereign Mltry Ord of the Temple of Jerusalem 2012.

DALY JR, Robert Edmund (Md) 13801 York Rd Apt D5, Cockeysville MD 21030 B Baltimore MD 1936 s Robert & Virginia. BS JHU 1966; MDiv EDS 1969. D 6/23/1969 Bp David Keller Leighton Sr P 6/3/1970 Bp Harry Lee Doll. m 12/30/1967 Anne Elizabeth Limpert c 2. R Ch Of The Mssh Baltimore MD 1981-2001; Int St Matthews Epis Ch Washington MD 1980-1981; P in Charge S Jn's Ch Chevy Chase MD 1979-1980, Asst 1973-1980; Exch St. Jn's Broadbridge Heath Horsham Par 1977; R S Thos' Par Hancock MD 1971-1973; Asst S Geo's Ch Perryman MD 1969-1971; Endwmt Grants Comittee Dio Maryland Baltimore MD 1997-2000, Stndg Com 1991-1997, Chair - Stwdshp Com 1988-1990, Dioc Coun 1983-1987.

DALZON, Wilfrid (Hai) **Non-par 1967-** B 1940 STB ETSC 1964. D 5/14/1964 Bp Charles Alfred Voegeli P 12/1/1964 Bp James Loughlin Duncan. Vic S Mart's Of Tours Port-Au-Prince Haiti 1964-1967.

D'AMARIO, Matthew Justin (Eas) 302 North Baltimore Avenue, Ocean City MD 21842 **Ch Of S Paul's By The Sea Ocean City MD 2016-** B Westminster MD 1970 s Raymond & Evelyn. BA JHU 1992; BA JHU 1992; MDiv S Marys Sem and U 1998; MDiv S Marys Sem and U 1998. Rec 9/29/2009 as Deacon Bp John L Rabb. m 7/13/2013 Craig G D'Amario. P in Charge Copley Par: The Ch Of The Resurr Joppatowne MD 2012-2016; Asst Ch Of The H Nativ Baltimore MD 2012; Asst S Jn's Ch Mt Washington Baltimore MD 2011-2012, D 2009-2011; Math Tchr Archbp Spalding HS 2005-2016; Instr of Philos and Rel Stevenson U 2004-2012.

D'AMICO, Samuel Robert (Los) 23442 El Toro Rd # 368, Lake Forest CA 92630 **Ret 1986-** B Wakefield MA 1918 s Anthony & Annie. BA Harv 1939; MDiv EDS 1943; Harv 1943; PhD Grad Theol Un 1972. D 9/15/1943 P 5/31/1944 Bp Raymond A Heron. c 3. Netwk Off PBFWR Epis Ch Cntr New York NY 1982-1985; Chapl S Jas Wilshire Sch Los Angeles CA 1979-1982; S Jas Par Los Angeles CA 1963-1982; H Faith Par Inglewood CA 1953-1963; Exec DRE Dio Los Angeles Los Angeles CA 1953-1958; R Cathd Cong Los Angeles CA 1947-1953; Exec DRE Cathd Of S Jn Providence RI 1944-1947; Dio Rhode Island Providence RI 1944-1947; Asst Chapl S Mk's Sch Southboro MA 1943-1944.

DAMON, David Reid (Fla) 7930 Bellemeade Blvd S, Jacksonville FL 32211 **Died 3/21/2016** B Baltimore MD 1926 s Samuel & Jeannie. BS USMMA 1947; BS Pur 1950; MDiv Sewanee: The U So, TS 1950; DMin Van 1974; DMin Van 1974. D 6/16/1955 Bp Frank A Juhan P 2/1/1956 Bp Edward Hamilton West. c 3. Ret 1987-2016; R S Andr's Ch Jacksonville FL 1969-1979; D H Nativ Epis Ch Panama City FL 1955-1956. Auth, *JD*; Auth, *TA & Some Rel Applications*.

DAMON, Robert Edward (SeFla) 3329 Wilson St, Hollywood FL 33021 B Milford CT 1950 s Eugene & Jennie. Miami Dade Coll 1974; AS/AA Miami Dade Coll 1974; BBA Florida Intl U 1981. D 5/30/2015 Bp Leo Frade. m 10/9/1970 Karin Jean Steinbach c 2.

DAMROSCH, Thomas Hammond (WMass) PO Box 612, Stockbridge MA 01262 B Manila Phillipines 1949 s Leopold & Elizabeth. Dplma NYU 1979; BA SUNY 1986; MDiv GTS 1989. D 6/10/1989 Bp Paul Moore Jr P 12/9/1989 Bp Richard Frank Grein. m 2/12/1977 Marthe Emily Turner c 1. R S Paul's Epis Ch Stockbridge MA 2007-2014; R S Paul's Ch Naples FL 2001-2007; Cn Mssnr Dio Cntrl New York Liverpool NY 1999-2001, Precentor 1996-1998, Mem Liturg & Mus Cmsn Precentor 1995-2001, Mem, Liturg and Mus Cmsn, Precentor 1995-2001; R S Paul's Ch Brownville NY 1995-2001; Shared Mnstry Of Nthrn NY Brownville NY 1995-2001; Dio Wstrn Massachusetts Springfield 1991-1995; R Gr Ch Dalton MA 1991-1995; Tri-Cnty Epis Area Mnstry Monticello NY 1989-1991; Prog Coordntng P Tri-Cnty Epis Area Mnstry Monticello NY 1989-1991; Mem, Liturg and Mus Cmsn Dio New York New York NY 1989-1991.

DAMUS, Pierre Gasner (LI) 1227 Pacific St, Brooklyn NY 11216 **P-in-c S Barth's Ch Brooklyn NY 2005-; Asstg P S Paul's Ch-In-The-Vill Brooklyn NY 1998-** B 1961 s Prince & Victorie. BA Sem Theol of Haiti 1989. D 7/30/1989 P 2/14/1990 Bp Luc Anatole Jacques Garnier. m 9/22/1998 Magdala Damus c 4. Asstg P Gr Ch Jamaica NY 2001-2005; P-in-c S Matthieu Grande Riviere 1990-1997; P-in-c Dio Haiti Port-au-Prince HT 1989-1997.

DANAHER JR, William Joseph (Mich) 470 Church Rd, Bloomfield Hills MI 48304 **Chr Ch Cranbrook Bloomfield Hills MI 2014-** B Torrington CT 1965 s William & Jeanne. BA Br 1988; MDiv VTS 1994; MA Ya 2001; PhD Ya 2002. D 6/10/1995 P 2/4/1996 Bp Clarence Nicholas Coleridge. m 6/23/1990 Claire B Danaher c 2. The GTS New York NY 2006-2008; P Asst Gr Ch New York NY 2006-2007; Sewanee U So TS Sewanee TN 2000-2006; Asstg P U So Sewanee TN 2000-2006; Supply P Dio Connecticut CT 1998-1999; Cur Gr Ch New York NY 1997-1998; Gr Epis Ch New York NY 1997-1998; Epis Ch At Yale New Haven CT 1995-1997; Asst Chapl Epis Ch at Ya CT 1995-1997. "Towards a Pachal Theol of Restorative Justice," *ATR*, 2007; "Renewing the Angl Moral Vision," *ATR*, 2005; "The Trinitarian Ethics of Jonathan Edwards," *Columbia Series in Reformed Theol*, Westminster/Jn Knox, 2004. Fllshp of the Soc of S Jn the Evang 2001. Bp Hines Preaching Awd VTS 2004. wdanaher@christchurchcranbrook.org

DANCER, Kathleen Ruth (WMich) 501 Se 50th Ave, Ocala FL 34471 B Baltimore MD 1945 d George & June. BS MI SU 1965; MA U of Kansas 1967; PhD Cor 1971; Bex Sem 1983; Cert Onondaga Pstr Counslg Cntr 1983. D 6/11/1983 Bp Ned Cole P 5/31/1984 Bp O'Kelley Whitaker. c 3. Chapl Franciscan

Ord of Celi De 1997-2003; R S Alb's Mssn N. Muskegon MI 1993-1996; Fndr/ Dir S Fran Sprtl Renwl Cntr Ithaca NY 1989-1993; R Ch Of The Epiph Trumansburg NY 1986-1993; Assoc Schuyler Cnty Episc Parishes Watkins Glen NY 1984-1986; S Jas' Epis Ch Watkins Glen NY 1983-1986; Dir S Jn's Epis Ch Odessa NY 1983-1986; S Paul's Ch Montour Falls NY 1983-1986; S Jn's Ch Ithaca NY 1983-1985. Assn Chr Therapists 1985; Ord Of S Lk 1978.

DANDRIDGE, Robert Floyd (WLa) 702 Elm St, Minden LA 71055 B Minden LA 1937 s Floyd & Nellie. Sewanee: The U So, TS; BS NW St U 1959; U So 1989; Int Mnstry Prog 2002. D 3/1/2000 P 11/12/2000 Bp Robert Jefferson Hargrove Jr. m 8/4/1961 Evelyn Virginia Greene.

DANFORD, Nicholas C (NY) 4 Fountain Sq, Larchmont NY 10538 **Gr Epis Ch New York NY 2015-** B Corsicana TX 1982 s Jimmy & Dana. BA Rice U 2004; MDiv VTS 2011. D 6/18/2011 Bp C Andrew Doyle P 12/17/2011 Bp Catherine Scimeca Roskam. m 2/21/2015 Giuliano Argenziano. S Jn's Ch Larchmont NY 2011-2013.

DANFORTH, John Claggett (Mo) 911 Tirrill Farms Rd, Saint Louis MO 63124 B Saint Louis MO 1936 s Donald & Dorothy. BA Pr 1958; BD Ya 1963. D 9/15/1963 P 3/1/1964 Bp George Leslie Cadigan. m 9/7/1957 Sally Baird Dobson. Assoc Ch Of The H Comm S Louis MO 2009-2010; Assoc S Alb's Par Washington DC 1977-1994; Assoc Gr Ch Jefferson City MO 1969-1976; Nonpar 1966-1969; Asst The Ch Of The Epiph New York NY 1963-1966.

DANGELO, Michael B (Mass) 10600 Preston Rd, Dallas TX 75230 **Ch Of The Redeem Chestnut Hill MA 2014-** B Harrogate North Yorkshire UK 1976 BA Wheaton Coll 1998; DAS Ya Berk 2004; MDiv Ya Berk 2004. D 6/12/2004 P 1/8/2005 Bp M(Arvil) Thomas Shaw. m 6/10/2000 Faye Dangelo c 1. S Marks Sch Of Texas Dallas TX 2012-2014; S Mich And All Ang Ch Dallas TX 2012-2014; S Paul's Ch Lynnfield MA 2008-2012; Trin Ch Epis Boston MA 2004-2008.

D'ANGIO, Peter David (Lex) 16 E 4th St, Covington KY 41011 **R Trin Ch Covington KY 2012-** B Boston MA 1959 s Giulio & Jean. BA U of Pennsylvania 1981; MA U of Pennsylvania 1985; MDiv GTS 1994; MS Coll of Preachers 2000. D 6/29/1994 Bp Sanford Zangwill Kaye Hampton P 1/6/1995 Bp James Louis Jelinek. m 8/24/2012 Gregory Scott Hinson. P-in-c S Lk's Ch Scranton PA 2007-2012; Int Trin Epis Ch Pottsville PA 2006; Indep Consulting Silver Sprg MD 2005-2006; Int S Andr's Epis Ch Glenwood MD 2003-2004; Int S Jas Ch Lancaster PA 2002-2003; Int Imm Epis Ch Glencoe MD 2001-2002; Int Chr Ch Columbia MD 1999-2001; R S Mths' Epis Ch Baltimore MD 1997-1999; Non-par 1996-1997; Vic Chr Ch Harrison NJ 1995-1996. Auth, "Liturg Conf". Epis Carmel of St. Teresa (Assoc) 2007. RECTOR@ TRINITYCHURCHCOVKY.COM

D'ANGIO-WHITE, Sara (Roch) Christ Church, 36 S Main St, Pittsford NY 14534 B Philadelphia PA 1984 d Carl & Donna. BA Bryn Maur Coll 2007; MDiv VTS 2012. D 10/21/2012 P 5/11/2013 Bp Prince Grenville Singh. m 7/19/2008 Andrew D'Angio Andrew Sexton White c 1. Assoc Gr Ch Lyons NY 2015-2016; Assoc S Jn's Ch Sodus NY 2015-2016; S Mk's Ch Newark NY 2015-2016; Chr Ch Pittsford Pittsford NY 2013-2014.

✠ **DANIEL III, The Rt Rev Clifton** (Pa) 1047 Amsterdam Ave, New York NY 10025 **Bd Trst CPG 2016-; Chair GTS Bd Trst 2015-; Mem Epis Ch Exec Coun 2012-; Bd Mem / Chair GTS 2009-** B Goldsboro NC 1947 s Clifton & Evelyn. BA U NC at Chap Hill 1969; MDiv VTS 1972; S Georges Coll, Jerusalem 1977; Coll of Preachers 1980; Grad Theol Un 1984; St Petersburg Theol Acad, Russia 1992; Angl Cntr In Rome 1993. D 6/29/1972 P 4/14/1973 Bp Hunley Agee Elebash Con 9/21/1996 for EC. m 8/19/1978 Anne M Miller c 3. Provsnl Bp of Pennsylvania Dio Pennsylvania Philadelphia PA 2013-2016; Pres PBp's Coun of Advice 2007-2012; VP Prov IV 2006-2012; Mem SCSC 2006-2011; Presiding Judge Crt of Revs for the Trial of a Bp 2000-2009; Chair Cler Deploy Bd 1997-2003; Bp of E Carolina Dio E Carolina Kinston NC 1996-2013, Chair, Dept, Chr Educ 1977-1980; Pres Epis Chars of RI 1985-1988; R S Mich's Ch Bristol RI 1984-1996; Rdr Gnrl Ord Examinations 1984-1995; Dir Mid-Atlantic Par Trng Prog 1980-1984; Assoc S Paul's Epis Ch Dayton OH 1980-1984; R S Thos' Epis Ch Ahoskie NC 1975-1980; Asst S Mary's Kinston NC 1972-1975; Dep GC Dio Rhode Island Providence RI 1991-1996, Chair, COM 1990-1996, Pres, Epis Chars 1989-1994. St Jn of Jerusalem 2013. DD St. Lk's TS U So 1997; DD VTS 1997. ddaniel@ stjohndivine.org

DANIEL, Wilfred Arthnel (VI) 112 Estate La Reine, Christiansted, Saint Croix VI 00823 B Saint Kitts West Indies 1945 s Alfred & Albertha. Trans 9/1/2000 Bp Theodore Athelbert Daniels. m 10/17/1968 Gwendolyn Daniel c 2. R S Jn's Ch Christiansted St Croix VI 2000-2009.

DANIEL JR, William Otis (Roch) St James School, 17641 College Rd, St James MD 21781 **S Mich's Ch Geneseo NY 2015-** B Augusta GA 1977 s William & Fay. MTS Duke DS 2004; MTS Duke DS 2004; STM Nash 2012; PhD U of Nottingham 2012. D 6/2/2012 Bp Dabney Tyler Smith. m 1/8/2000 Amanda K Kelley c 2. St Jas Sch Hagerstown MD 2012-2015; S Andr's Epis Ch Tampa FL 2010-2011; Ch Of The Gd Shpd Raleigh NC 2002-2005. wdaniel@ stmikesgeneseo.org

DANIELEY, Teresa Kathryn Mithen (Mo) 3664 Arsenal St, Saint Louis MO 63116 B St Louis MO 1977 d Francis & Phyllis. BA Ya 1998; MA U Chi 2001; MDiv GTS 2004. D 12/19/2003 P 6/25/2004 Bp George Wayne Smith. m 9/14/2009 Jonathan Danieley c 1. R S Jn's Ch S Louis MO 2004-2016. YA Cmnty Serv Awd Untd Ch Wmn of Connecticut 1998.

DANIELS, Janet (NJ) St Mary's by the Sea, 804 Bay Ave, Point Pleasant NJ 08742 B Teaneck NJ 1949 d Alfred & Annamarie. AD Ocean Cnty Coll 1985; Graduated NJ Sch for Deacons 2012. D 5/5/2012 Bp George Edward Councell. m 5/17/1985 William Louis Daniels c 3.

DANIELS, Joel C. (NY) 1 W. 53rd St., New York NY 10019 **Cur S Thos Ch New York NY 2014-, Asst 2013-2014** B St. Augustine FL 1978 s James & Ginger. BA Col 2000; MDiv GTS 2007; PhD Bos 2015; PhD Bos 2015. D 3/10/2007 P 9/15/2007 Bp Mark Sean Sisk. m 9/19/2003 Lystra Batchoo c 2. Tchg Fell Bos 2010-2011; Int S Barn Ch Irvington NY 2007-2009; Dir Instinet Grp 2000-2004. Auth, "Christology, Evolution, and Cultural Change," *ATR*, 2014; Auth, "Rowan Williams on Sharia, Secularism, and Surprise," *Journ of Ecum Stds*, 2014.

DANIELS, John D (WA) 1001 E Lincoln Hwy, Exton PA 19341 **Wrld Rel Tchr CFS The Sch At Ch Farm Exton PA 2011-** B Doylestown PA 1960 s Beverly & Winifred. W Los Angeles Coll; BS U of Phoenix 2002; MDiv VTS 2007. D 6/4/2011 Bp John Bryson Chane P 1/21/2012 Bp Mariann Edgar Budde. m 11/6/1993 Lori L Martin c 3.

✠ DANIELS, The Rt Rev Theodore Athelbert (VI) 3208 Prairie Clover Path, Austin TX 78732 **Ret 2005-** B Ancon PA 1944 s Ethelridge & Carlotta. AA Canal Zone Coll 1971; MDiv ETSC 1975; BS Florida St U 1976; Oklahoma St U 1978; Cntr for Addiction Trng and Educ 1989; St Eliz Hosp 1989; Bowie St U 1990; Institue for Pstr Psych 1994; Fielding Grad Inst 1998; GTS 2002; Dispute Resolution Cntr 2005; Dispute Resolution Cntr 2008; Employer Spprt of Guard and Reserve ESGR 2008; Employer Spprt of Guard and Reserve ESGR 2010. D 6/7/1969 P 12/1/1969 Bp Reginald Heber Gooden Con 6/30/1997 for VI. m 10/21/1972 Cristina Daniels c 3. Asst Bp Dio Texas Houston TX 2003-2005; Mem of Abundance Com Ch Pension Fund 2001-2002; Exec Coun Epis Ch 1999-2005; Hse. Bp. Theol Com HOB 1999-2004; Hse. Bp. Pstr Com HOB 1998-2005; Bp Of VI Dio Vrgn Islands Charlotte Amalie St Thom VI 1997-2003; Chair Ecum Com Dio The Republic Of Panama & The Canal Zone 1995-1997; Chapl CAP 1994-2003; R Calv Ch Washington DC 1992-1997; Mentor VTS 1987-1988; Vic H Redeem Landover Hills MD 1986-1992; Vic H Redeem Mssn Capitol Hgts MD 1985-1992; Chapl at Ben & Allen Universities Dio Upper So Carolina 1980-1985; R S Lk's Epis Ch Columbia SC 1980-1985; Dep Prov IX Syn Dio The DRepublic of Panama & TheCanal Zone 1978-1980; Com Dio The Republic Of Panama 1975-1979; Exam Chapl Dio The Republic Of Panama & The Canal Zone 1975-1979; Fin Com Dio The Republic Of Panama & The Canal Zone 1974-1979; Chair Cmncatns Com Dio Panama & The Canal Zone 1972-1979; Com Const & Cns Dio Panama & The Canal Zone 1972-1979; R S Chris Pqe Lefevre RP 1972-1979; Chapl U Cntr Rep. of Panama 1972-1973; R St Christophers Ch 1971-1980; P-in-c 5 Missions Wstrn Bocas del Toro 1971-1972; P-in-c Ch Of The Trsfg 1971-1972; St Georges Ch 1971-1972; Dio Panama 1969-1980; Asst R/ Dir Yth Wk S Chrisopher Panama City ReP. of Panama 1969-1970; Abundance Com The CPG New York NY 2001-2003; Chapl, CAP ArmdF and Fed Ministires New York NY 1994-2004. Life Mem Ord S Vinc Gld of Acolytes 1970; Ord Of S Lk, Bro Of S Andr 1974. DD The GTS 2002; Citation from Coun of Dist of Columbia Coun of Dist of Columbia 1997; Citation from Gvnr of St of Maryland Gvnr of St of Maryland 1997; Citation from Maryland Gnrl Assembly Maryland Gnrl Assembly 1997; Citation from Maryland Hse of Representatives Maryland Hse of Rep 1997; Proclamation of Theo A. Daniels Day Mayor of the Dist of Columbia 1997; Ord of the Palmeto Gvnr of the St of So Carolina 1985; Phi Theta Kappa Delta Omega Chapt, Canal Zone Coll 1964; Natl Hon Soc Copley HS 1962. theodore. daniels@sbcglobal.net

DANIELSON JR, Paul Everett (ECR) 22481 Ferdinand Dr, Salinas CA 93908 **Died 3/1/2016** B Santa Barbara CA 1938 s Paul & Katharine. BA Pr 1960; MDiv UTS 1963; CAS EDS 1964. D 6/6/1964 Bp Walter M Higley P 6/16/1965 Bp Ned Cole. m 6/25/1966 Margaret E Entwisle c 3. Ret 2001-2016; Chapl All SS' Epis Day Sch 1984-2001; All SS' Epis Day Sch Carmel CA 1984-2001; R Epis Ch Of The Gd Shpd Salinas CA 1969-1984; Chapl York Sch Monterey CA 1969-1974; Cur Calv Epis Ch Santa Cruz CA 1967-1968; Cur S Paul's Scotts Vlly CA 1967-1968; Mssy-In-Charge S Mich's & All Ang' W Endicott NY 1964-1967; Cur S Paul's Ch Endicott NY 1964-1967.

DANIEL-TURK, Patricia (Fla) 15 East Manor, Beaufort SC 29906 B Goldsboro NC 1949 d Clifton & Evelyn. BA No Carolina Wesleyan Coll 1971; MDiv VTS 1985. D 12/18/1986 Bp Frank Harris Vest Jr P 12/21/1987 Bp Robert Whitridge Estill. m 12/30/1983 James M Turk c 1. R St Pat's Epis Ch S Johns FL 2008-2010; Assoc Ch Of Our Sav Jacksonville FL 2001-2008; S Mk's Epis Ch Jacksonville FL 1994-2001; Asst Emm Ch Orlando FL 1989-1993; S Jn's Epis Ch Charlotte NC 1987-1988.

D'ANIERI, Margaret C (O) 18369 State Route 58, Wellington OH 44090 **Cn Dio Ohio Cleveland 2015-, Stndg Cmsn on Sm Congregations GC 2013-, Stndg**

Com 2012-, Sem Field Educ Supvsr 2010-2012, Dn 2007-, Trst 2003-2008, COM 2003-2007; R S Paul Epis Ch Norwalk OH 2009- B Schenectady NY 1960 d John & Mary. BA U of Virginia 1982; Bex Sem 2001; Trin Luth Sem 2001; MDiv GTS 2002. D 6/8/2002 P 12/14/2002 Bp Arthur Williams Jr. m 5/23/1992 Chester John Bowling. R No Cntrl Epis Shared Mnstry Port Clinton OH 2002-2009, Assoc R 2002-2004; Pres Norwalk Mnstrl Assn 2009-2011. mdanieri@dohio.org

DANITSCHEK, Thomas K (Colo) 6930 E 4th Ave, Denver CO 80220 B Omaha NE 1962 s Edgar & Alice. TESM; BS U CO 1987. D 6/9/2001 P 12/29/2001 Bp William Jerry Winterrowd. Calv Ch Golden CO 2014-2015; Assoc Chr Epis Ch Denver CO 2001-2011.

DANKEL, Susan Rainey G (Mass) 233 Clarendon St., Boston MA 02115 **Assoc Trin Ch Epis Boston MA 2012-** B Whitmire SC 1946 d Connolly & Melba. BA Mary Baldwin Coll 1968; Cert Ang Stud Ya Berk 2011; MDiv Yale DS 2011. D 6/12/1999 P 6/18/2011 Bp Clifton Daniel III. D Ch Of The Servnt Wilmington NC 1999-2008; Bd Trst Ya Berk New Haven CT 2009-2011. rdankel@trinitychurchboston.org

DANNALS, James Clark (SC) 1979 Long Branch Rd, Marshall NC 28753 **Int R Ch of The Trsfg Saluda NC 2017-** B Huntsville AL 1953 s George & Cortez. BS Florida St U 1975; MDiv Yale DS 1979. D 6/25/1979 P 1/6/1980 Bp William Hopkins Folwell. m 9/7/1974 Carolyn Hoffman Dannals c 3. Int R Gr Ch in the Mountains Waynesville NC 2016-2017; Vic St. Mk's Port Royal SC 2014-2015; R S Geo's Ch Fredericksburg VA 2004-2013; Dio Wstrn Massachusetts Springfield 2002-2004; R S Steph's Ch Pittsfield MA 2002-2004; R S Lk's Ch Boone NC 1997-2002; R Ch Of The Gd Shpd Jacksonville FL 1989-1997; Vic Ch of Our Sav Palm Bay FL 1982-1989; Asst S Jn's Ch Melbourne FL 1979-1982; Stndg Com So Carolina Charleston SC 2014-2015; Stndg Com Dio Wstrn No Carolina Asheville NC 1999-2002; Stndg Com Dio Florida Jacksonville 1994-1997. Auth, "Love That Endures," *LivCh*, 1988. Publ Spkng Berk 1979. jdannals@gmail.com

DANNALS, Robert S (Dal) 8011 Douglas @ Colgate, Dallas TX 75225 B Orlando FL 1955 s George & Corky. BA Florida St U 1977; MDiv VTS 1981; DMin Drew U 1989; PhD Grad Theol 2005. D 6/21/1981 P 1/17/1982 Bp William Hopkins Folwell. m 6/23/1991 Valerie Robie c 3. St. Barth Ch New York NY 2015-2016; R S Mich And All Ang Ch Dallas TX 2007-2015; R Chr Ch Greenville SC 1997-2007; R Chr Ch New Bern NC 1992-1997; R Trin Epis Ch Statesville NC 1985-1992; Assoc R Chr Ch Charlotte NC 1981-1985. "Aspects Of The Imitation Of Chr In The Moral Christology Of Dietrich Bonhoeffer," Grad Theol Press, 2005; "A Theol Chr Mar," Drew U Press, 1989. Compass Rose Soc; Spck/Usa.

DANNELLEY, James Preston (Tex) 1205 Flag St, Llano TX 78643 **Ret 1985-** B Laredo TX 1928 s Preston & Bernice. MDiv Epis TS of the SW 1961. D 7/18/1961 Bp Everett H Jones P 1/1/1962 Bp Richard Earl Dicus. m 6/3/1950 Laura Eloise Dannelley c 2. R Gd Shpd Houston TX 1977-1985; Ch Of The Gd Shpd Houston TX 1977-1984; S Phil's Ch Hearne TX 1974-1977; The Great Cmsn Fndt Houston TX 1974-1977; P-In-C S Mk's Guadalajara Mex 1969-1974; Vic Chr & S Andr's Guadalajara Mex 1966-1969; Dio Nthrn Mex Nuevo Leon 1965-1974; R Chr Ch Eagle Lake TX 1962-1965; D-in-c Trin Ch Jct TX 1961-1962.

DANNER, David Lawrence (SwFla) All Angels by the Sea Episcopal Church, 563 Bay Isles Rd, Longboat Key FL 34228 **R All Ang By The Sea Longboat Key FL 2005-** B Rockford IL 1951 s Edward & Olive. BA Lawr 1973; MDiv Trin, Toronto, ON 1976; MA U Tor 1978; DMin Luth TS at Gettysburg 1997. Trans 12/1/1986 as Priest Bp Emerson Paul Haynes. m 8/25/1979 Wafa Danner c 2. R Trin Par of Newton Cntr Newton Cntr MA 1995-2005; R Emm Ch Quakertown PA 1988-1995; Asst Calv Ch Indn Rk Bc FL 1986-1988; Chapl York Cntrl Hosp Richmond Hill ON 1981-1986; Serv Angl Ch Of Can 1976-1986; Disciplinary Bd Dio SW Florida Parrish FL 2011-2016, Eccl Crt 2007-2010; Pres Phillips Brooks Club of Boston 2000-2005; Dioc Coun Dio Massachusetts Boston MA 1998-2005. Auth, "Immigration and the Epis Ch: An Ever-changing Face," *ATR*, 2013; Auth, "Lutherans and Anglicans Together: On to Mssn at Last," *Open: Journ of the AP*, 2003; Auth, "The Parting Of The Ways For Lutherans & Episcopalians," *Angl & Epis Hist*, 1999; Auth, "Flo-A Study In Hope," *Journ Of Humane Med*, 1986; Auth, "Gown," *Trin Revs*, 1976. Phi Beta Kappa 1973. OFFICE@ALLANGELSLBK.ORG

DANNHAUSER, Adrian (NY) St James' Church, 865 Madison Ave, New York NY 10021 **Ch Of The Incarn New York NY 2015-; Ch Of The Intsn New York NY 2013-** B Meridian MS 1978 BA Duke 1999; JD Van Law Sch 2003; MDiv Ya Berk 2013; MDiv Yale and Berkeley 2013. D 3/2/2013 P 9/7/2013 Bp Andrew Marion Lenow Dietsche. m 4/30/2005 Jess Brandon Dannhauser c 1. S Jas Ch New York NY 2013-2015.

DANSDILL, Dorothy Newton (NMich) 501 N Ravine St, Sault Sainte Marie MI 49783 B 1947 d Arthur & Dortothy. BA U MI 1969; MA U MI 1970. D P 5/28/2006 Bp James Arthur Kelsey. m 7/28/1973 John Newton Dansdill c 2. P S Jas Ch Of Sault S Marie Sault Sainte Marie MI 2006-2012.

DANSON, Michelle Anne (Colo) 7776 Country Creek Dr, Longmont CO 80503 **Supply P CO 2006-; Fac Sprtl Dir Benet Hill Monstry Colorado Sprg CO**

2004- B Bradford England 1952 d John & Kathleen. BS Dur Engl 1973; PGCE Dur Engl 1974; MDiv Iliff TS 2002; CCS GTS 2007. D 6/8/2002 P 6/22/2003 Bp William Jerry Winterrowd. m 8/7/2004 David Alan Plume c 4. H Apos Epis Ch Englewood CO 2005-2006, D/part time 2002-2003; Asst P/ Par Sprtl Dir Ch Of The H Trin New York NY 2003-2004; D/ part time The Epis Ch of the Resurr 2002-2003.

DANTONE, Jan (WTex) **Ch Of The Epiph Kingsville TX 2017-; Assoc S The Div Houston TX 2006-** B Sherman, TX 1959 d Thomas & Paula. BS US-AF Acad 1981; MS Troy St U 1984; MDiv TESM 2006. D 6/24/2006 P 1/25/2007 Bp Don Adger Wimberly. m 8/2/2008 Harold Dantone c 3.

DANZEY, Charles (Oly) St Peter's Episcopal Church, 621 W Belmont Ave, Chicago IL 60657 **Gd Samar Epis Ch Sammamish WA 2015-; Ch of the Redeem Irving TX 2007-** B Fort Jackson SC 1957 s Charles & Opal. BA Samford U 1980; PhD SW Bapt TS 1995; MDiv SW Bapt TS 1998. D 6/24/2006 Bp James Monte Stanton P 11/6/2008 Bp Paul Emil Lambert. c 1. S Ptr's Epis Ch Chicago IL 2012-2015; Asst Epis Ch Of The Redeem Irving TX 2008-2012; Ch Of The Incarn Dallas TX 2006, 2005-2006. steve_danzey@yahoo.com

D'AOUST, Jean J (Colo) 1515 W 28th St Apt 114, Loveland CO 80538 **Asst All SS Ch Loveland CO 2002-** B Alfred ON CA 1924 s Henri & Aurore. BA U of Ottawa 1946; MA S Vincents Sem 1957; Pontifical Inst For Mediaeval Stds CA 1963; MA Ya 1966; MA Ya 1967; PhD Ya 1968; MA Slippery Rock U 1987. Rec 12/26/1966 as Deacon Bp John Melville Burgess. m 10/31/1987 Susan D'Aoust. Int S Andr's in the Vill Ch Barboursville WV 1996-2001; Assoc R Trin Ch Huntington WV 1994-1996; Fox Chap Epis Ch Pittsburgh PA 1983-1987; Asst R Fox Epis Ch Fox Chap PA 1983-1987; Ch Of The Epiph Grove City PA 1981-1982; Dio Maryland Baltimore MD 1978-1980; Shared Cmnty Mnstry Cortland A A Homer NY 1975-1978; Chapl Slippery Rock St Coll. Auth, "The Wrld Of Teilhard De Chardin," 1960; Auth, "Energetics Of Cosmic Love". AAR 1967; APA 1987; Amer Psychol Soc 1987; Soc For Values In Higher Educ 1964; Wester Inst 1999. Natl Tchg Fllshp 1967; Can Coun Fllshp 1966; Kent Fllshp 1964; Fllshp Ya 1964.

DARBY, Steven Lanier (Ga) 114 W Mockingbird Ln, Statesboro GA 30461 **Chapl Ogeechee Area Hospice Statesboro GA 2005-** B Jacksonville FL 1947 s Jack & Jean. BA Georgia Sthrn U 1971; Non-degree GTS 1974; MA Georgia Sthrn U 1978. D 2/22/2006 Bp Henry Irving Louttit. m 6/6/1976 Regina Darby c 1.

DARDEN, John Webster (Dal) 1852 E Mulberry, PPrescott Valley AZ 89314 **Asst S Ptr's 1971-** B Tyler TX 1932 s Robert & Willie. BBA U of Texas 1959; GTS 1963. D 9/21/1963 P 3/1/1964 Bp Theodore H McCrea. m 6/15/1957 Helen Darden. Rural D Dio Dallas Dallas TX 1967-1971; R Ch Of The Gd Shpd Brownwood TX 1966-1971; Vic Ch Of The Gd Shpd Dallas TX 1964-1966; Vic Ch Of The H Cross Burleson TX 1963-1964.

DARISME, Joseph Wilkie (Hai) Boite Postale 1309, Port-Au-Prince Haiti **Non-par 1970-** B Arcahaie HT 1943 s Adopted & Alvert. STB ETSC 1969. D 11/30/1968 Bp Charles Alfred Voegeli. Mssy Haiti 1968-1970.

DARKO, Daniel Dodoo (WA) 1510 Erskine St, Takoma Park MD 20912 B Accra GH 1942 s Wallestine & Paulina. Cert U of Ibadan Ibadan NG 1965; Cert Ghana Inst of Mgmt & Publ Administrion Legon 1982; Dip Theol Stud U of Ghana Sem Legon GH 1982; BA SUNY 1985; MA SUNY 1988. Trans 2/1/1987 as Priest Bp Paul Moore Jr. m 4/25/1970 Juliana E Darko c 3. R S Monica's Epis Ch Washington DC 1992-2007; Asst All SS Ch Staten Island NY 1990-1991; UTO Grants Admin Epis Ch Cntr New York NY 1989-1992; R Hse Of Pryr Epis Ch Newark NJ 1987-1989; Cur The Ch of S Matt And S Tim New York NY 1986-1987; R Angl Ch in Trinidad and Tobago 1984-1985; P in Charge Angl Ch in Ghana 1982-1984. OHC 1980. Hon Cn and Commissary Dio Cape Coast 1994.

DARLING, Beth (WNC) 118 Clubwood Ct, Asheville NC 28803 **Pediatric Chapl Mssn Hospitals 2003-** B Ann Arbor MI 1954 d James & Mary. MDiv McCormick TS 1982; MLS U Chi 1982; ThM Luth TS at Chicago 1985; CAS EDS 1992. D 10/8/1992 Bp William Walter Wiedrich P 6/5/1993 Bp Bob Johnson. St Georges Epis Ch Asheville NC 2013-2017; Assoc R & Int S Jas Ch Black Mtn NC 1999-2003; Assoc R S Mk's Ch Gastonia NC 1992-1999.

DARLING, Laura Toepfer (Cal) 724 Valle Vista Avenue, Vallejo CA 94590 **Epis Sr Communities Lafayette CA 2013-** B Berkeley CA 1968 d Louis & Janet. BA Ob 1990; AAS Rochester Inst of Tech 1993; MDiv CDSP 2001. D 6/23/2001 P 5/4/2002 Bp Jack Marston Mckelvey. m 8/3/2013 Mary Darling. Sabbatical Int All SS Epis Ch San Leandro CA 2010; Assoc R Chr Ch Alameda CA 2003-2008; Asst R & Chapl to Ken Dio Ohio Cleveland 2001-2002.

DARLING, Mary (Roch) 2704 Darnby Dr, Oakland CA 94611 B Corning NY 1964 d Arthur & Anne. BA Hav 1986; MBA NWU 1993; MDiv CDSP 1999. D 6/5/1999 Bp William George Burrill P 9/29/2000 Bp Jack Marston Mckelvey. m 8/3/2013 Laura Toepfer Darling. S Jn's Epis Ch Oakland CA 2001-2010.

DARLINGTON, Diane Lillie (NMich) 301 N 1st St, Ishpeming MI 49849 B Montreal Quebec 1944 d Harold & Doris. BA U of Nthrn Michigan 2014. D 5/4/2014 Bp Rayford J Ray. m 7/23/1988 John Thomas West c 2.

DARROW, Robert Michael (Colo) 3275 S Pontiac St, Denver CO 80224 **Ret 1999-** B Denver CO 1937 s Robert & Alice. Wms 1957; BA U Denv

1959; MDiv Nash 1962; Int Mnstry Prog 1998. D 6/18/1962 P 12/21/1962 Bp Joseph Summerville Minnis. Trst Coll of Preachers (Natl Cathd) Washington DC 1991-1997; chair Com on Mnstry Dio Milwaukee Milwaukee WI 1985-1995; R S Jas Ch W Bend WI 1980-1999; chair Com on Mnstry Dio Colorado Denver CO 1977-1980; R S Tim's Epis Ch Littleton CO 1967-1979; Vic S Alb's Monticello IN 1966-1977; Reorgnztn Com Dio Nthrn Indiana So Bend IN 1965-1967; S Ptr's Ch Rensselaer IN 1965-1967; Cur S Lk's Epis Ch Ft Collins CO 1962-1965.

DARVES-BORNOZ, Derek Yves (NY) Church Pension Group, 19 E 34th St, New York NY 10016 **Assoc R S Steph's Ch Millburn NJ 2014-** B Montreal Canada 1978 s Gilles & Bonnie. BA Reed Coll 2001; MS U of Oregon 2003; PhD U of Oregon 2006; MDiv GTS 2009; BCC Assn of Profsnl Chapl 2010. D 5/30/2009 Bp Sanford Zangwill Kaye Hampton P 12/4/2009 Bp Catherine Scimeca Roskam. c 1. P Assoc S Phil's Ch Garrison NY 2012-2014; Mgr of Ch Resrch The CPG New York NY 2011-2017; P Assoc The Ch Of The Epiph New York NY 2010-2011; Stff Chapl New York Presb Hosp 2009-2011. Coauthor, "Corp Unity in Amer Trade Plcy: A Ntwk Analysis of Corp-Dyad Political Action," *Amer Journ of Sociol*, U Chi Press, 2011. ddarves@cpg.org

DASS, Stephen (CFla) 1108 SE 9th Ave, Ocala FL 34471 **Dio Cntrl Florida Orlando FL 2014-; Mssy DCF Mssy Outreach Sao Paulo Brazil 2013-** B Singapore 1968 s Francis & Daisy. LTh Montreal Dioc Theol Coll 2004; BA Lon 2012. Trans 5/1/2009 as Priest Bp John Wadsworth Howe. m 8/19/1995 Mary Dass. P-in-c Coventry Epis Ch Ocala FL 2009-2012.

DATOS-ROBYN, Richard James (Pa) St Mary's-in-Tuxedo, PO Box 637, Tuxedo Park NY 10987 **R Trin Ch Oxford Philadelphia PA 2009-** B Kalamazoo MI 1974 s John & Linda. AA Kalamazoo Vlly Cmnty Coll 1995; BA Loyola U New Orleans 1997; MDiv GTS 2007. D 7/1/2007 Bp Charles Edward Jenkins III P 6/11/2008 Bp Egbert Don Taylor. m 8/15/2010 Peter Datos. Hon Cur Ch Of The Resurr New York NY 2007-2009; Sem Asst Ch Of The Trsfg New York NY 2005-2007; Vice Chair, Dioc Coun Dio Pennsylvania Philadelphia PA 2016-2017, COM 2011-2016; Bd Dir Philadelphia Prot Hm Philadelphia PA 2015-2017; Bd Trst Epis Cmnty Serv Philadelphia PA 2012-2017. CBS 2008; Soc of Cath Priests 2009; US Friends of Walsingham 2008; US SocMary 2008; Un League of Philadelphia 2010. frrobyn@stmarysintuxedo.org

DAUER-CARDASIS, Joade (NY) 227 E 87th St Apt 1B, New York NY 10128 **R S Ptr's Ch Bronx NY 2008-** B New York NY 1947 d John & Adeline. BA Marymount Coll 1968; Iona Coll 1974; NYU 1976; MDiv Ya Berk 1990. D 6/9/1990 P 2/1/1991 Bp Arthur Edward Walmsley. m 10/17/1970 James J Cardasis c 4. Dio Long Island Garden City NY 2001-2002; S Ann And The H Trin Brooklyn NY 1999-2001; Dio Vermont Burlington VT 1997-1999; S Jn's In The Mountains Stowe VT 1994-1999; S Fran Ch Stamford CT 1990-1994.

DAUGHERTY, Jennifer King (Oly) 1245 Tenth Ave E, Seattle WA 98102 **Cur S Mk's Cathd Seattle WA 2014-** B Ventura CA 1964 d David & Judith. BA Pr 1986; BA Pr 1986; MBA NYU 1990; MBA NYU 1990; MDiv Seattle U TS and Mnstry 2014. D 12/21/2013 P 7/22/2014 Bp Gregory Harold Rickel. m 12/31/1988 William Henry Daugherty c 3. D S Clem's Epis Ch Seattle WA 2013-2014. jkdaugherty@saintmarks.org

DAUGHTRY, James Robert (RG) 205 Augusta Way, Melbourne FL 32940 **Ret 1994-** B Roswell NM 1931 s Robert & Blaine. BS Geo 1954; STB GTS 1960. D 6/26/1960 Bp William Francis Moses P 12/29/1960 Bp Henry I Louttit. Asstg Cler S Mary's Epis Ch Albuquerque NM 1993-1994; Ch of the H Faith Santa Fe NM 1989-1991; S Paul's Par Washington DC 1974-1989; R S Paul's Rock Creek Washington DC 1974-1989; Vic Chap of th Resurr Tucson AZ 1963-1974; Ch Of The Resurr Tucson AZ 1963-1974; Cur S Phil's Ch Coral Gables FL 1960-1963. Hon Cn S Cyp the Mtyr 1983.

DAUGHTRY, Susan (Minn) 1325 Nottoway Ave, Apt. A, Richmond VA 23227 **Dio Minnesota Minneapolis MN 2014-** B Waynesboro VA 1981 d Robert & Judith. BA U of Virginia 2003; MDiv VTS 2006. D 6/24/2006 P 2/3/2007 Bp Peter J Lee. m 6/9/2012 Brian E Dowdy c 1. S Steph The Mtyr Ch Minneapolis MN 2013-2014; Asst S Thos' Ch Richmond VA 2008-2013; Tchr Seven Hills Sch Richmond VA 2008-2010; Assoc R Ch Of The H Comf Vienna VA 2006-2008; Stndg Com Dio Virginia Richmond VA 2007-2010.

DAUNT, Francis Thomas (La) 815 E Guenther St, San Antonio TX 78210 B Enniskeane County Cork IE 1945 s Albert & Hilda. BA U So 1967; MDiv GTS 1970. D 6/11/1970 Bp George Paul Reeves P 3/24/1971 Bp Albert R Stuart. m 2/4/1995 Jane L Bowles c 3. R S Mary's Ch Franklin LA 1994-2010; R S Jas Epis Ch Baton Rouge LA 1989-1993; Dio Atlanta 1982-1989; Stwdshp Dept Dio Atlanta 1981-1984; R H Trin Par Decatur GA 1980-1989; Stwdshp Consult Dio Georgia 1977-1988; Dio Georgia 1976-1978; R S Mk's Ch Brunswick GA 1975-1980; Vic Trin Ch Statesboro GA 1972-1975; Vic S Ptr Eastman GA 1970-1972; Vic Trin Ch Cochran GA 1970-1972; Stndg Com Dio Louisiana New Orleans LA 1992-1995.

DAUPHIN, Joanne Coyle (Eur) 51 rue d'Amsterdam, Paris 75008 France **Ecum Off for France Convoc of Epis Ch in Europe Paris 2003-, Ecum Rep 2003-** B White Plains NY 1936 d Hugh & Marie. BA Wellesley Coll 1957; MA Tufts U 1958; MA Tufts U 1959; PhD Tufts U 1963; Cert U of Wales Bangor 2003.

D 6/7/2003 Bp Pierre W Whalon. m 7/13/1963 Patrick Dauphin. D Amer Cathd of the H Trin 2005-2010.

DAUTEL, Terrence Pickands (O) Po Box 62, Gates Mills OH 44040 B Cleveland OH 1943 s Charles & Seville. BA Kenyon Adelbert 1968; MA Wstrn Carolina U 1973; MA Wstrn Carolina U 1975; MDiv Bex Sem 1978. D 3/4/1979 P 9/1/1980 Bp John Harris Burt. Assoc S Mart's Ch Chagrin Fall OH 2008-2015, 1981-1983; The Cluster Of Ch In NE OH Ashtabula OH 1997-1999; S Hubert's Epis Ch Mentor OH 1980-1996; S Barth's Ch Cleveland OH 1979-1980; S Barth's Mayfield Vill OH 1979-1980; Cur S Barth's Mayfield Vill OH 1978-1979.

DAVENPORT, Anetta Lynn (Wyo) Holy Trinity Episcopal Church, PO Box 950, Thermopolis WY 82443 **Admin H Trin Epis Ch Thermopolis WY 2011-** B Thermopolis WY 1953 d Rex & Donna. AA Coconino Cnty Cmnty Coll 1998. D 8/31/2013 P 3/29/2014 Bp John Smylie. c 2. Dio Wyoming Casper 2016.

DAVENPORT, Carrol Kimsey (Mo) 17 Broadview, Kirksville MO 63501 **Chapl/Bereavement Coordntr Hospice of NE Missouri 2006-; Assoc Trin Epis Ch Kirksville MO 2006-, Assoc 2005-2007** B Norfolk VA 1959 d Aubrey & Mary Louise. BA Averett U 1981; MDiv Sthrn Bapt TS 1986. D 12/21/2005 P 6/29/2006 Bp George Wayne Smith. m 1/7/1984 William Michael Ashcraft c 2. davenport1959@yahoo.com

DAVENPORT JR, Charles Richard (NH) PO Box 85, Colebrook NH 03576 **P Dio New Hampshire Concord NH 2011-** B Levelland TX 1959 s Charles & Bobbie. BS U of Texas 1982; Dplma in Angl Stds GTS 2010. D 11/6/2011 P 5/13/2012 Bp Vicky Gene Robinson.

DAVENPORT, David Wendell (SVa) 6051 River Road Pt, Norfolk VA 23505 B Miami FL 1948 s Luther & Dorothye. BA Furman U 1970; MDiv VTS 1973. D 6/23/1973 Bp Milton Legrand Wood P 4/1/1974 Bp Bennett Jones Sims. m 8/5/1988 Lillian H Davenport c 2. R Ch Of The Ascen Norfolk VA 1997-2013, Asst 1976-1978; Pres Charitable Giving Inc. 1988-1996; Dir Dio Sthrn Virginia Newport News VA 1978-1986, Campus Min 1975-1986; Asst R Chr Ch Macon GA 1973-1975.

DAVENPORT, Elizabeth Jayne Louise (Chi) 5850 S. Woodlawn Ave, Chicago IL 60637 **Dn U Chi Chicago IL 2008-** B Potters Bar Hertfordshire UK 1955 d Ian & Esme. BA Oxf GB 1977; MA Oxf GB 1981; DIT Nthrn Ord Course Manchester Gb 1982; ThM Fuller TS 1989; PhD USC 2003. Trans 1/1/1991 Bp Frederick Houk Borsch. m 6/22/2008 Anne Cecilia Benvenuti. Sr. Assoc Dn USC Los Angeles CA 2003-2008; Stdt Affrs USC Los Angeles CA 1993-2003; Asst St Johns Pro-Cathd Los Angeles CA 1991-2008; Chapl Dio Los Angeles Los Angeles CA 1991-1993; Chapl USC Los Angeles CA 1991-1993; Asst All SS Ch Pasadena CA 1991; Cur Ch Of Engl 1982-1988.

DAVENPORT, Marcia EM (SwFla) 1606 Chickasaw Rd, Arnold MD 21012 B Detroit MI 1947 d Jay & Elizabeth. Antioch Coll 1967; BA Bloomfield Coll 1973; MA Montclair St U 1975; MS Loyola U 1984; MDiv VTS 1990; Cert Loyola U 1997. D 6/16/1990 P 1/30/1991 Bp Albert Theodore Eastman. m 5/26/1995 Robert Davenport c 1. Chapl/Asst St Johns Epis Ch Tampa FL 2002-2009; Gr Ch Brunswick MD 2000-2002; St. Anne's Day Sch Annapolis MD 1999-2000; R S Paul's Ch Trappe MD 1996-1999; Int Trin Cathd Easton MD 1994-1995; Pstrl Assoc S Anne's Par Annapolis MD 1990-1994. Int Mnstry Ntwk 1996-2000.

DAVENPORT, Robert A (SVa) 1509 N Shore Rd, Norfolk VA 23505 **Trin Ch Portsmouth VA 2017-** B Salem MA 1951 s Stephen & Susan. BA U So 1973; MDiv VTS 1985. D 9/15/1985 Bp David Reed P 4/1/1986 Bp A(rthur) Heath Light. m 1/3/2004 Elizabeth Allen c 5. Chap Of The Cross Chap Hill NC 2015-2016; Int Emm Par Epis Ch Sthrn Pines NC 2015; R Ch Of The Gd Shpd Norfolk VA 2004-2013; R Trin Ch Upperville VA 1993-2004, Assoc 1990-1992; R Nelson Par Arrington VA 1986-1990; Nelson Par Cluster Lovingston VA 1985-1989; D Nelson Par Arrington VA 1985-1986.

DAVENPORT III, Stephen Rintoul (WA) 4700 Whitehaven Pkwy Nw, Washington DC 20007 B Charlottesville VA 1942 s Stephen & Susan. BA W&L 1964; MDiv VTS 1970. D 7/23/1970 P 7/1/1972 Bp Charles Gresham Marmion. m 12/27/1997 Tracy Ann Bruce. Assoc R S Pat's Ch Washington DC 1980-1993; S Jn's Ch Murray KY 1975-1980; The Untd Campus Mnstry Murray KY 1975-1980; Mssn Partnr Dio Haiti Port-au-Prince HT 1970-2003; Untd Campus Mnstry Murray KY 1970-1980. Rgnl Serv Awd Murray St U 1976.

DAVID, Charles Wayne Laskin (Mass) 6390 Sagewood Way, Delray Beach FL 33484 B Klamath Falls OR 1949 BA Goddard Coll 1979; MDiv EDS 2003. D 6/7/2003 P 6/5/2004 Bp M(Arvil) Thomas Shaw. S Jn's Chap Cambridge MA 2005-2014; Soc-St Jn The Evang Cambridge MA 2005; S Mary's Epis Ch Boston MA 2004-2005.

DAVID, Christopher Leyshon (LI) PO Box 110, 482 County Route 30, Salem NY 12865 **S Jas Epis Ch Arlington VT 2015-** B Llwyn-y-pia, Glamorgan, Wales UK 1947 s Stanley & Mary. NYU; BA NYU 1969; MDiv GTS 1972. D 6/2/1972 P 12/9/1972 Bp Paul Moore Jr. m 4/29/1978 Kathleen David c 3. Int Trin Ch Rutland VT 2012-2014; R S Mk's Ch Westhampton Bch NY 2001-2011; Migrant Mnstry Consult The ECEC New York NY 1997-2001; R Ch Of The Gd Shpd Midland Pk NJ 1987-2001; R S Jn's Epis Ch Kingston NY 1978-1987; S Anne's Ch Washingtonville NY 1975-1978; Vic S Dav's Ch

Highland Mls NY 1975-1978; Asst Min Gr Epis Ch New York NY 1972-1975; Dir Gr Opportunity Proj New York NY 1972-1975; Dn of Peconic Dio Long Island Garden City NY 2003-2010, Dn of Peconic 2003-2010; Chairperson, The Migrant Mnstry Com Ecusa / Mssn Personl New York NY 1988-2002; Pres Mid Hudson Catskill Rural and Migrant Min Poughkeepsie NY 1980-1987.

DAVID, Jacob Thandasseril (Nwk) 1 Paddock Court, Dayton NJ 08810 B Kottayam Kerala IN 1941 s Thandasseril & Mariamma. BS U Kerala IN 1961; MDiv VTS 1984. Trans 5/1/1991 Bp John Shelby Spong. m 1/20/1972 Shanta P David. S Paul's And Resurr Ch Wood Ridge NJ 1991-2011; Serv Ch Of So India 1984-1991.

DAVID, John Spencer (WMich) 157 Lost Creek Lane, Kalispell MT 59901 **P S Matt's Epis Ch Fairbanks AK 2013-** B Aurora IL 1943 s John & Blanche. BA DePauw U 1965; MDiv Sewanee: The U So, TS 1983. D 6/24/1983 P 1/1/1984 Bp William Hopkins Folwell. m 6/15/1968 Susan Lewis Carr c 4. R Chr Epis Ch Charlevoix MI 2006-2012; R S Greg's Epis Ch Norton Shores MI 1995-2005; R S Ptr's By-The-Sea Sitka AK 1991-1994; R Ch Of The Redeem Ruston LA 1987-1991; Epis Chapl Lousiana Tech U Ruston LA 1987-1991; R S Fran' Ch Norris TN 1984-1987; Asst All SS Epis Ch Lakeland FL 1983-1984.

DAVID, Ronald (Los) 1225 Wilshire Blvd, Los Angeles CA 90017 **Chapl Gd Samar Hosp Los Angeles CA 2007-; Chapl Hosp of the Gd Samaritans 2006-** B New York NY 1948 s Reginald & Hentlyn. BA SUNY 1971; MD SUNY 1975; MDiv VTS 2003. D 12/19/2005 P 7/15/2006 Bp Joseph Jon Bruno. m 12/30/2000 Deborah David c 3. Prof Pstr Care Bloy Hse Claremont CA 2012-2013.

DAVIDSON, Charles Alexander (Pa) 814 N 41st St, Philadelphia PA 19104 B Mackenzie GY 1954 s Albert & Marjorie. BA Codrington Coll 1977. Trans 2/10/1998 as Priest Bp Joe Doss. m 6/22/1996 Maureen Davidson. Calv St Aug Epis Ch Philadelphia PA 2014-2015; R S Monica's Ch Hartford CT 2007-2014; R S Vinc's Epis Ch St Petersburg FL 2003-2007; R S Aug's Epis Ch Asbury Pk NJ 1997-2003; P in Charge All Souls Ch New York NY 1996-1997; Serv Ch In Prov Of W Indies 1977-1996. AFP 1987.

DAVIDSON, Donald F (EMich) 9020 S Saginaw Rd, Grand Blanc MI 48439 **P-in-c S Christophers Epis Ch Grand Blanc MI 2015-; Chapl Kansas St Senate 2013-** B Bellefontaine OH 1957 s George & Thelma. OH SU; BS Rio Grande Rio Grande OH 1981; MDiv SWTS 1984; DMin SWTS 1996. D 9/9/1984 Bp William Grant Black P 5/4/1985 Bp John Forsythe Ashby. m 5/20/2006 Marcella Davidson. R S Dav's Epis Ch Topeka KS 2004-2015; US-A Pension Fund Mltry New York NY 2002-2003; R S Thos The Apos Ch Overland Pk KS 1997-2004; Vic S Lk's Ch Wymore NE 1992-1997; R Chr Ch Epis Beatrice NE 1989-1997; Vic Epis Ch Of The Incarn Salina KS 1988-1989; Chapl (Colonel) US NG 1984-2012; Chapl S Jn Mltry Sch Salina KS 1984-1989; Chapl S Jn's Mltry Sch Salina KS 1984-1989. Ord of S Helena - Assoc 1984. The Bp's Cross Dio Kansas 2011.

DAVIDSON, Jon Paul (Nev) PO Box 8822, Incline Village NV 89452 B Los Angeles CA 1935 s Paul & Celo. BA U CA 1959; MDiv CDSP 1962; MA U of Pennsylvania 1970. D 6/30/1962 Bp Charles Francis Hall P 6/5/1963 Bp George Richard Millard. m 6/27/1964 Elizabeth Simmons c 1. Web Ed Dio Nevada NV 2004-2008; S Paul's Epis Ch Sparks NV 2001-2006; S Pat's Ch Incline Vlg NV 1984-1986; Gnrl Mgr Cmnty Television Channel 20 Knoxville TN 1976-1978; VP & Co-Fndr Ecumedia Inc Baltimore 1971-1973; Radio-TV Dir Maryland Coun of Ch Baltimore MD 1969-1971; Vic S Mich & All Ang Ch Suncook NH 1964-1966; Cur Gr Ch Manchester NH 1962-1964. Auth, "Living A Biblic Story," *TV (Video) Prog*, CDSP, 1986; Auth, "Introducing Students to the Natural Sciences," *TV (Broadcast & Video) Prog*, U.S.D.A. Forest Serv, 1985; Auth, "We Gather Together," *TV (Video) Prog*, The Epis Ch Gnrl Conv., 1982; Auth, "Your Leaders Are Listening," *TV (Video) Prog*, The Epis Ch (Hse of Bps), 1981; Auth, "Welcome to the Dio Nevada," *Website*, www.nvdiocese.org/profile, 1970.

DAVIDSON, Mark Alan (NC) 3205 S Main St, Winston Salem NC 27127 B Washington DC 1963 s Roger & Joan. D 1/28/2017 Bp Anne Hodges-Copple. m 6/4/1983 Sherry Cook Davidson c 2.

DAVIDSON, Patricia Foote (Ct) 118 Bill Hill Rd, Lyme CT 06371 **Ret 1995-** B Brooklyn NY 1929 d Merrill & Ruth. BA Mt Holyoke Coll 1951; MDiv GTS 1983. D 6/13/1983 Bp Robert Campbell Witcher Sr P 6/17/1984 Bp Arthur Edward Walmsley. m 4/7/1956 Robert Treat Hooker Davidson c 1. Assoc P S Ann's Epis Ch Old Lyme CT 1998-2009, Int 1991-1992; Middlesex Area Cluster Mnstry Higganum CT 1993-1994; Int The Par Of Emm Ch Weston CT 1987-1988; Asst Dio Connecticut Meriden CT 1983-1987. Auth, "Jewelry in the Brooklyn Museum," *The Brooklyn Museum*, 1984; Auth, "The Bastis Gold," *The Brooklyn Museum Annual*, 1967; Auth, "Gk Gold Jewelry from the Age of Alexander," Museum of Fine Arts, 1965.

DAVIDSON, Robert Michael (Pa) 22 E Chestnut Hill Ave, Philadelphia PA 19118 **Alum Bd Luth TS Philadelphia PA 2010-; D S Paul's Ch Philadelphia PA 2010-; Liturg Cmsn Dio Pennsylvania Philadelphia PA 2011-, Disciplinary Bd 2009-, 1990-2011** B Philadelphia PA 1941 s William & Sarah. BA Leh 1963; MDiv Luth TS 2008. D 6/6/2009 Bp Edward Lewis Lee Jr. m

12/17/1966 Pamela Davidson c 4. D Calv St Aug Epis Ch Philadelphia PA 2009-2010. Vergers Gld of the Epis Ch 2002.

DAVIDSON, Robert Paul (Colo) 1005 Cimmaron Dr, Loveland CO 80537 B Lewistown MT 1952 s William & Mary. BSW U of Kentucky 1976; MSW U of Kentucky 1978; Dioc Theol Cert. Epis Theol Inst 1981; Dioc Theol Cert. Epis Theol Inst 1981; Dioc Theol Cert. Other 1981. D 12/5/1981 Bp William Carl Frey P 12/16/2001 Bp William Jerry Winterrowd. m 5/27/1972 Linda L Davidson c 3. S Alb's Ch Windsor CO 2015; S Jas Epis Ch Wheat Ridge CO 2012-2013, 2012; Int The Ch Of The Ascen Denver CO 2011-2012; R S Paul's Epis Ch Ft Collins CO 2003-2005; Vic Santiago Lafayette CO 2001-2002; Assoc Trin Ch Greeley CO 1999-2000; D S Barth's Ch Estes Pk CO 1993-1997; D All SS Ch Loveland CO 1986-1992; D H Cross Epis Mssn Sterling CO 1981-1985; Prov Coun Secy Dio Colorado Denver CO 2000-2004, BEC 1994-1997, COM 1989-1993, Stndg Com 1985-1988, GC Dep 1970-2003. EPF 1970; Int Mnstry Ntwk 2006; RWF 1982. Soc Wk Hon Alpha Delta Tau 1976; Phi Beta Kappa U Of Kentucky 1976.

DAVIDSON, Susan La Mothe (Ct) 61 Hunter Ct, Torrington CT 06790 **P-in-c All SS Ch Wolcott CT 2011-** B Buffalo NY 1942 d Theodore & Helen. BA SUNY at Buffalo 1965; SMM UTS 1969; MDiv GTS 1994. D 8/15/1994 P 2/24/1995 Bp Larry Maze. m 5/21/1969 Jerry Frank Davidson c 2. Mem GTS Alum/ae Exec. Comm. 2004-2010; Exec Bd Dio Louisiana 2004-2008; Chair, Liturg & Mus Dio Louisiana 2003-2008; R All SS Epis Ch New Orleans LA 1998-2008; Vic S Mich's Epis Ch Little Rock AR 1994-1998; Dn, Jefferson Dnry Dio Louisiana New Orleans LA 2005-2008, Chair, Liturg Cmsn 2003-2008; Exec Coun Dio Arkansas Little Rock AR 1996-1998. AGO 1963-1992.

DAVIDSON, Thomas Walter (Az) 4041 N 164th Dr, Goodyear AZ 85395 B Denver CO 1937 s Norris & Ruth. BA Indiana U 1959. D 6/11/1994 Bp Robert Reed Shahan P 1/23/2005 Bp Kirk Stevan Smith. m 6/12/1999 Jacynth C Davidson c 2. Assoc Chr Ch Of The Ascen Paradise Vlly AZ 2008-2009; All SS Ch Phoenix AZ 2000-2007; Dio Arizona Phoenix AZ 1994-1996, Chair, Stwdshp Cmsn 1968-1993, Trst, Epis Cmnty Serv 1996-2007; Chairman of the Bd S Paul's Preparatory Academiy Phoenix AZ 1994-1996. ESMA 1995-2005; NAAD 1996-2005.

DAVIDSON, William Albert (Vt) Prestwick Farm, 2260 County Route 12, Whitehall NY 12887 **Vic S Paul's Epis Ch Wells VT 2009-** B Pittsburgh PA 1939 s William & Ruth. BA U Pgh 1961; MDiv Nash 1964; Cert Inst for Advncd Supervision 1979. D 6/20/1964 P 12/21/1964 Bp James Pernette DeWolfe. m 4/28/2012 Richard Frederick Brewer. Int S Paul's Epis Ch On The Green Vergennes VT 2006-2008; Int S Mk's Ch Springfield VT 2004-2006; Int Consult Dio New York New York NY 1993-1997, Chair Jewish-Chr Comm. 1994-2002; R Chr Ch Riverdale Bronx NY 1985-2002; Prof The GTS New York NY 1976-1985; R Ch Of The Ascen Greenpoint Brooklyn NY 1966-1976; Cur S Paul's Ch-In-The-Vill Brooklyn NY 1964-1966; Trst Cathd Of St Jn The Div New York NY 1997-2000.

DAVIDSON-METHOT, David G (Los) 2945 Bell Rd Pmb 325, Auburn CA 95603 B Dearborn MI 1953 s Theodore & Maxine. BA Nthrn Arizona U 1975; MDiv CDSP 1979; PhD Pacifica Grad Inst, Carpinteria CA 2000. D 6/17/1979 Bp Thomas Heistand P 12/21/1979 Bp William Edwin Swing. c 2. P-in-c S Clem's Ch Rancho Cordova CA 2014-2017; P-in-c S Mich's Ch Coolidge AZ 2011-2012; Assoc All SS Epis Ch Oxnard CA 1999-2001; R S Patricks Ch And Day Sch Thousand Oaks CA 1990-1998; St Of The Ch The Epis Dio Nthrn California Sacramento CA 1988-1990; R Emm Epis Ch Grass Vlly CA 1983-1990; Int Epis Ch Of Our Sav Placerville CA 1982-1983; Cur S Paul's Epis Ch Walnut Creek CA 1979-1982; Cler Chapl Dio Arizona 2006-2013; COM Dio Los Angeles Los Angeles CA 1992-1994. Auth, "Compass? What Compass?," *Residential Treatment for Chld & Yth*, Am Assoc of Chld's Residential Centers, 2004; Auth, "Calibrating the Compass," *Residential Treatment for Chld & Yth*, Am Assoc of Chld's Residential Centers, 2004; Auth, "An Early Amer Sampler: Being A Collection Of Early Amer Hymns For Use In Publ Wrshp," All SS Press. San Francisco, 1981; Auth, "Log Bldg In The San Francisco Peaks Area Of Nthrn Arizona," SW Folklore, 1979. APA 1995; Arizona Psychol Assn 2007-2013; California Psychol Assn 2012. drdavesierrahills@gmail.com

DAVIES, Ian E (Los) 7501 Hollywood Blvd, Los Angeles CA 90046 **R S Thos The Apos Hollywood Los Angeles CA 2002-; R S Thos The Apos Hollywood Los Angeles CA 2002-** B Merthyr Tydfil Wales 1964 s John & Edith. BD U of Wales GB 1985; Cert Ang Stud U of Cambridge 1988; Cert Ang Stud U of Cambridge 1988. Trans 1/16/2002 as Priest Bp Joseph Jon Bruno. "Club" (for Theol Stds) Athenaeum, London 1998; British & European Societies for Philos of Rel 1987-2002; Mem of the Royal Inst of Philos 1985-2002; Soc for the Study of Theol 1986.

DAVIES JR, Richard Wood (Pgh) 300 Madison Ave, Apt 309, Pittsburgh PA 15243 **Vic Old St. Lk's Ch Scott Twp. PA 1988-; Vic St Lk's Epis Ch Pittsburgh PA 1988-; P-in-c Old St. Lk's Ch Pittsburgh PA 1988-** B Pittsburgh PA 1927 s Richard & Hannah. BA U Pgh 1952; MDiv VTS 1955; MEd U Pgh 1972. D 6/25/1955 P 12/21/1955 Bp Austin Pardue. m 8/18/1951 Doris J Davies c 2. Asst S Paul's Epis Ch Pittsburgh PA 1987-2010; Cn Dio Pittsburgh Pittsburgh PA 1983-1990, Cn to Ordnry 1983-; R S Ptr's Epis Ch Brentwood Pittsburgh PA 1957-1982; Min in charge S Paul's Ch Monongahela PA 1955-1957. Auth, "Hist of the Cong," *Rebellion & Revelation - The Hist of Old S Lk Ch*, 1996; Auth, "One act play," *A Burning Faith- The 1794 Whiskey Rebellion*, 1995.

DAVIES-ARYEEQUAYE, Eliza Ayorkor (NY) 23 Water Grant St. Apt. 9E, Yonkers NY 10701 **D S Martha's Ch Bronx NY 2008-** B Accra Ghana 1949 d Daniel & Alice. BA U of Houston 1986; NY Dio Deaconate Trng 2005. D 5/14/2005 Bp Mark Sean Sisk. c 1. D S Paul's Ch Yonkers NY 2005-2008; Mem Bp's Com S Jas Epis Ch Fordham Bronx NY 1992-2002. New York AltGld 2009.

DAVILA, Mary Fisher (Va) 117 Rivana Terr SW, Leesburg VA 20175 B Lexington NC 1976 d Donald & Talmadge. BA U Rich 1998; MDiv VTS 2005. D 6/18/2005 P 12/18/2005 Bp Peter J Lee. m 8/7/2004 Christopher Davila. Int Chr Epis Ch Raleigh NC 2013-2014; S Jas' Epis Ch Leesburg VA 2005-2012; Dir. Chld'S Mnstrs S Steph's Ch Richmond VA 1999-2002.

DAVILA, Willie Rodriguez (SeFla) 1063 Haverhill Rd N, Haverhill FL 33417 **S Christophers Ch W Palm Bch FL 2010-** B San Antonio TX 1951 s Guadalupe & Reducinda. BS Trin U San Antonio 1977; MDiv Epis TS of the SW 1986. D 6/15/1986 Bp John Herbert MacNaughton P 1/1/1987 Bp Stanley Fillmore Hauser. m 12/29/1973 Teresita G Davila c 2. Vic The Ch Of The Recon Corpus Christi TX 1991-2010; Chapl Coll 1987-1993; Asst R Ch Of The Gd Shpd Corpus Christi TX 1987-1991; Dio W Texas San Antonio TX 1986-1991; Asst R S Mk's Ch San Marcos TX 1986-1987. Auth, "Moments Of Gr," *Ratherview*, Ets-Austin, 1987.

DAVILA COLON, Angel Michael (PR) **Dio Puerto Rico Trujillo Alto PR 2013-** B Catano PR 1975 s Miguel & Olga. Cert Estudio Religioso Seminario del Caribe 1996; BA Universidad Cntrl de Bayamon 1997; MDiv Seminario San Pedro y San Pablo 2010. D 2/5/2012 P 1/20/2013 Bp David Andres Alvarez-Velazquez.

DAVILA FIGUEROA, Wilson Jaime (Colom) c/o Diocese of Colombia, Cra 6 No. 49-85 Piso 2, Bogota, BDC Colombia B 1947 s Luis & Florinda. Filosofo-Teologo Seminario Diocesano 1972; Licenciado Educae U of Mariana 1973; Psicologo Soc Unad 2001. Rec 7/1/1973 as Priest Bp Francisco Jose Duque-Gomez. m 9/20/1991 Gloria Calderon Lopez c 1.

DAVINICH, George Lawrence (Mich) 945 Palmer St, Plymouth MI 48170 **Dnry Rep Dio Michigan Dioc Coun 2012-; Bd Dir New Morning Sch Plymouth MI 2011-** B Detroit MI 1953 s Michael & Rachel. Assoc Applied Sci Oakland Cmnty Coll 1979; BGS U MI 1994; MDiv SWTS 2004. D 12/20/2003 P 6/26/2004 Bp Wendell Nathaniel Gibbs Jr. m 2/1/1985 Mary Davinich c 3. P-in-c S Steph's Ch Wyandotte MI 2012-2015; Cmsn Mem COM Detroit MI 2007-2011; Bd Chairperson Whitaker TS Detroit MI 2007-2011; R Gr Epis Ch Southgate MI 2006-2015; Asst R All SS Ch E Lansing MI 2004-2006.

DAVIOU, Albert G (At) 432 Noelle Lane, Dahlonega GA 30533 B Hackensack NJ 1948 s Albert & Evelyn. BA Calvin Coll 1972; MDiv SWTS 1984. D 6/11/1984 Bp Charles Ellsworth Bennison Jr P 12/21/1984 Bp Howard Samuel Meeks. m 5/26/2017 Patricia P Prince c 2. R S Eliz's Epis Ch Dahlonega GA 2007-2015; The Ch Of The Gd Shpd Acton MA 2004-2005; Dio Atlanta Atlanta GA 1996; Ch Of The Annunc Marietta GA 1994-1996; Assoc S Mk's Ch Grand Rapids MI 1988-1993; R S Jn the Evang Fremont MI 1984-1988; S Jn's Ch Fremont MI 1984-1988; R S Mk's Ch Newaygo MI 1984-1988.

DAVIS JR, Albin P (Los) 209 S. Detroit St., Los Angeles CA 90036 **1963-** B Baltimore MD 1920 s Albin & Irene. JD U of Maryland 1951; ETSBH 1963. D 9/5/1963 P 3/1/1964 Bp Francis E I Bloy. m 8/28/1943 Martha C Davis c 3. Assoc S Jas Par Los Angeles CA 1988-2007; Asst St Thos the Apos Hollywood CA 1968-1988; Asst/Worker P St Fran Palos Verdes Est CA 1964-1968.

DAVIS, Alice Downing (Va) P.O. Box 622, Luray VA 22835 B Richmond VA 1940 d John & Evelyn. BFA Richmond Profsnl Inst 1963; MDiv VTS 1984; DMin VTS 1993. D 1/6/1985 Bp Peter J Lee P 10/1/1985 Bp Albert Theodore Eastman. m 10/12/1974 Joseph Claiborne Davis. Vic S Paul's Ch Shenandoah VA 2000-2003; Dio Virginia Richmond VA 2000-2001; Vic Chr Epis Ch Lucketts Leesburg VA 1995-1998; Non-par 1990-1995; Vic Ch Of The Gd Shpd Bluemont VA 1987-1990; D S Paul's Epis Par Pt Of Rocks MD 1985-1986.

DAVIS, Angus Kenneth (Pa) PO Box 329, Kimberton PA 19442 B Charleston SC 1948 s Kenneth & Judith. BA Col 1971; MA U of Delaware 1973; MDiv GTS 1985; MA Tem 1990. D 6/15/1985 P 6/1/1986 Bp Lyman Cunningham Ogilby. m 6/23/1985 Tamara Rose Burk c 2. The Epis Ch Of The Adv Kennet Sq PA 1998; Asst S Christophers Epis Ch Oxford PA 1995-1997; Vic S Geo S Barn Ch Philadelphia PA 1993-1995, 1988-1990; Dio Pennsylvania Philadelphia PA 1990-1995; Vic S Barn' Philadelphia PA 1990-1993; Pres S Barn' Mssn To Homeless 1990-1993; Vic S Geo's Philadelphia PA 1988-1993; Asst to R The Ch Of The H Trin Rittenhouse Philadelphia PA 1986-1988; D-In-Trng Ch Of S Jn The Evang Philadelphia PA 1985-1986. Soc Of S Jn The Evang.

DAVIS, Bancroft Gherardi (Pa) 419 Chandlee Dr, Berwyn PA 19312 **Psychol Caron Fndt Wernersville PA 2013-; Stff Psychol Caron Treatment Cntr 2013-** B New York NY 1950 s Bancroft & Marguerite. BA JHU 1973; MLS

Wesl 1984; MDiv Ya Berk 1991; MSW Virginia Commonwealth U 2001; PsyD Chestnut Hill Coll 2010. D 6/13/1992 Bp Arthur Edward Walmsley P 6/20/1993 Bp Jeffery William Rowthorn. m 9/3/1977 Rebecca Davis c 2. PostDoctoral Intern Delaware Vlly Psychol Serv 2010-2013; Pre-Doctoral Intern Tuttleman Counslg Cntr Tem 2009-2010; Assoc R Ch Of The Redeem Bryn Mawr PA 2004-2007; P-in-c S Dunstans Ch Blue Bell PA 2001-2004; Pstr Assoc Trin Luth Ch 1999-2001; Virginia Epis Sch Lynchburg VA 1996-1999; Assoc R S Paul's Epis Ch Lynchburg VA 1993-1996; S Thos's Ch New Haven CT 1992-1993; Chapl S Thos's Day Sch New Haven CT 1992-1993; Chapl S Tim's Ch Fairfield CT 1992-1993. Auth, "The Role of Mindfulness Meditation in Preventing Cler Burnout," 2010. bgdavis1015@gmail.com

DAVIS, Calvin Lee (SwFla) 725 Nokomis Ave S, Venice FL 34285 B Staunton VA 1939 s Reuben & Mary. AA Palm Bch Jr Coll 1960; BS Jas Madison U 1962; MA Jas Madison U 1965; MDiv Bex Sem 1968. D 6/23/1968 Bp James Loughlin Duncan P 12/1/1968 Bp Albert Ervine Swift. m 6/26/1965 Sandra Davis c 2. Assoc The Epis Ch Of The Gd Shpd Venice FL 1993-2015; S Mk's Epis Ch Venice FL 1970-1990; Cur S Mary's Par Tampa FL 1968-1970.

DAVIS, Catherine Ward (EC) St James Parish, 25 S 3rd St, Wilmington NC 28401 **S Jas Par Wilmington NC 2014-** B Wilmington NC 1952 d Edward & Adelaide. BA Duke 1974; MA U NC Wilmington 1999. D 6/3/2006 Bp Clifton Daniel III. m 10/11/1975 Michael C Davis c 2.

DAVIS, Charles Lee (Ak) ST MATTHEW'S EPISCOPAL CHURCH, 1030 2ND AVE, FAIRBANKS AK 99701 **P S Matt's Epis Ch Fairbanks AK 2007-** B Anchorage AK 1940 s Edward & DeEtte. LLB U of Idaho 1966. D 7/23/2006 P 6/28/2007 Bp Mark Lawrence Macdonald. m 1/1/1963 Mary Margaret Davis c 1.

DAVIS JR, Charles Meyer (USC) 3709 Greenbriar Dr, Columbia SC 29206 B Decatur GA 1955 s Charles & Wilmarose. BA Valdosta St U 1979; MDiv GTS 1985. D 6/8/1985 P 5/31/1986 Bp Charles Judson Child Jr. m 12/28/1985 Alicia P Davis c 2. Trin Cathd Columbia SC 2001-2017; S Chris's Ch Spartanburg SC 1997-2001; R S Jn's Epis Ch Ocean Sprg MS 1993-1996; R S Simon's Epis Ch Conyers GA 1989-1993; Asst S Thad Epis Ch Aiken SC 1986-1989; Asst S Mk's Ch Dalton GA 1985-1986. davis@trinitysc.org

DAVIS SR, Charles Meyer (USC) 232 Elstow Rd, Irmo SC 29206 **Assoc Trin Cathd Columbia SC 2009-; P S Ptr's Ch Great Falls SC 2002-** B Macon GA 1932 s James & Hilda. BS U GA 1958; MDiv Sewanee: The U So, TS 1973. D 6/25/1973 P 2/25/1974 Bp George Paul Reeves. c 2. P-in-c Epis Ch Of S Simon And S Jude Irmo SC 2004-2008; R S Jn's Epis Ch Congaree Hopkins SC 1994-2001; R S Mths Epis Ch Toccoa GA 1988-1992; Mikell C&C Toccoa GA 1979-1987; Dir Mikell C&C Toccoa GA 1979-1987; Georgia Epis Conf Cntr At Honey Creek Waverly GA 1976-1979; Vic H Cross Ch Thomson GA 1973-1976; Trin Ch Harlem Harlem GA 1973-1976.

DAVIS, Charlotte Murray (NC) 3120 Sunnybrook Dr, Charlotte NC 28210 **D S Andr's 1992-** B Huntington NY 1946 d Andrew & Alice. BA Mt Holyoke Coll 1969. D 5/31/1992 Bp Robert Whitridge Estill. m 9/20/1969 John Macnutt Davis.

DAVIS III, Chip A lfred (WTenn) 2225 Jefferson Ave, Memphis TN 38104 **Cn Dio W Tennessee Memphis 2010-** B Little Rock AR 1947 s Z A & Mary. JD U of Mississippi Law Sch; BS Mississippi Coll 1969; MDiv SWTS 1990. D 5/12/1990 P 12/5/1990 Bp Duncan Montgomery Gray Jr. m 5/26/1973 Cathleen C Davis c 2. Dio Atlanta Atlanta GA 2010; Vic St Ben's Epis Ch Smyrna GA 2009-2010; R Trin Ch Natchez MS 1997-2009; Vic H Innoc' Epis Ch Como MS 1992-1997; Vic Ch Of The Redeem Greenville MS 1990-1992; Cur S Jas Ch Greenville MS 1990-1992.

DAVIS, Clifford Bruce (Kan) 1070 W Antelope Creek Way, Tucson AZ 85737 **D S Thos The Apos Ch Overland Pk KS 2000-** B Edina MO 1957 s Bert & Fonda. BTh Hannibal-Lagrange Coll 1979; MDiv SW Bapt TS 1981; Midwest TS Kansas City MO 1988. D 10/19/1998 Bp William Edward Smalley. m 8/19/1978 Terri Cusimano. Auth, "Working Grief".

DAVIS, David Joseph (EC) 208 Country Club Dr., Shallotte NC 28470 B New York NY 1951 s David & Marilyn. BA VMI 1973; Dplma Command and Gnrl Stff Coll 1986; Command and Gnrl Stff Coll 1986; MBA Webster U 1988; Cert Dio EC Diac Trng Sch 1996; MDiv Sewanee: The U So, TS 2004. D 4/26/1997 Bp Brice Sidney Sanders P 7/19/2004 Bp Clifton Daniel III. m 12/29/1972 Patricia Jean Davis c 2. R S Jas The Fisherman Epis Ch Shallotte NC 2004-2017; D Ch Of The H Comf Monteagle TN 2001-2004; D H Trin Epis Ch Fayetteville NC 1997-2001. BroSA 1991; Ord Of S Lk, Bro Of S Andr; OSL 1994. fatherdave@stjamesthefisherman.net

DAVIS, Donald Henry Kortright (WA) 11414 Woodson Ave, Kensington MD 20895 B 1941 s Cecil & Florence. BD Codrington Coll 1965; MA U of The W Indies 1976; PhD U of Sussex 1979. Trans 11/1/1986 Bp John Thomas Walker. m 1/18/1967 Joan Ianthe Davis c 3. R Ch Of The H Comf Washington DC 1987-2013. Auth, "Mssn For Caribbean Change"; Auth, "Emancipation Still Comin". Arcic Ii, Uspg.

DAVIS, Doyal (Okla) P.O. Box 1905, Shawnee OK 74802 B Midlothian OK 1940 s William & Grace. MA U of Hawaii; BA U of Hawaii. D 6/20/2009 Bp Edward Joseph Konieczny.

DAVIS, Elizabeth Hill (Okla) **P-in-c S Mk's Ch Seminole OK 2015-; P-in-c S Paul's Epis Ch Holdenville OK 2015-** D 6/20/2014 P 1/10/2015 Bp Edward Joseph Konieczny.

DAVIS, Emily (Mo) 9441 Engel Ln, St. Louis MO 63132 **Asst S Mart's Ch Ellisville MO 2011-; Vic S Thos Ch For The Deaf Kirkwood MO 2011-** B Richmond VA 1967 d David & Catherine. BA Indiana U 1989; MA Washington U 1992; PhD Washington U 2002; MDiv Eden TS 2007. D 12/20/2006 P 6/29/2007 Bp George Wayne Smith. m 12/29/1990 Warren Davis c 3. Asst Gr Ch S Louis MO 2007-2011.

DAVIS, Gail E (Kan) 1228 Auburn Village Dr, Durham NC 27713 **Assoc Int S Steph's Ch Durham NC 2013-** B Saint Louis MO 1945 d William & Mary. BFA U of Kansas 1970; BA U of Kansas 1978; MS Nova SE U 1990; MDiv Epis TS of the SW 2001. D 3/17/2001 P 10/27/2001 Bp William Edward Smalley. m 11/16/1996 Jeffrey Benson Stephens c 2. R Int Emm Epis Ch San Angelo TX 2011-2012; Philos Instr Ottawa U Ottawa Kansas 2010; R Gr Epis Ch Ottawa KS 2007-2010; P-in-c Gr Epis Ch Ottawa KS 2007-2008; Executuve Dir S Fran Acad Atchison KS 2002-2006; S Fran Cmnty Serv Inc. Salina KS 2001-2007; Chapl Sain Fran Acad Atchison KS 2001-2002; Trst Dio Kansas Topeka KS 2009-2011, Trst 2008-2011; Trst Epis TS Of The SW Austin TX 2004-2008, Trst 2004-2008. Fllshp of SSJE 1996.

DAVIS, Gale Ann (Mass) 25 Central St, Andover MA 01810 B Pasadena CA 1946 d Richard & Dorothy. Scripps Coll 1966; BS U of San Francisco 1983; MDiv CDSP 1989; DMin SWTS 1998. D 6/24/1989 P 6/1/1990 Bp Charles Shannon Mallory. m 6/22/2012 Ernest Lloyd Frohring c 4. S Paul's Ch In Nantucket Nantucket MA 2014-2015; Int Par Of Chr Ch Andover MA 2012-2014; Int Ch Of The Adv Medfield MA 2011; R The Ch Of The Gd Shpd Acton MA 1998-2011; Int S Andr's Ch Milwaukee WI 1995-1998; R S Paul's Ch Milwaukee WI 1994-1998; Cn Cathd Ch Of S Mk Minneapolis MN 1991-1994; Assoc S Fran Epis Ch San Jose CA 1989-1991; Dn, Metro Dnry Dio Milwaukee Milwaukee WI 1995-1998.

DAVIS, Gena Lynn (Tex) 5010 N Main St, Baytown TX 77521 **Vic Gr Epis Ch Houston TX 2011-, Vic 2011-** B Kingsville TX 1963 d Richard & Margie. BBA U of Houston 1985; MBA U of Texas 1990; MDiv Epis TS of the SW 2009. D 6/20/2009 P 1/10/2010 Bp C Andrew Doyle. m 2/22/1999 Gary Richard Davis c 1. Cur Trin Epis Ch Baytown TX 2009-2011.

DAVIS, Gordon Bell (Va) 1201 Rothesay Cir, Richmond VA 23221 B Beaufort NC 1926 s Clarence & Claudia. BS E Carolina U 1948; VTS 1954; S Augustines Coll Cbury Gb 1965. D 6/4/1954 P 6/1/1955 Bp George P Gunn. m 2/16/1963 Virginia Davis c 2. Par Assoc Chr and S Lk's Epis Ch Norfolk VA 1992-2006; R Chr Epis Ch Gordonsville VA 1971-1989; Assoc All SS Ch Richmond VA 1965-1971; R Gr Ch Yorktown Yorktown VA 1957-1964; D S Jn's Ch Chester VA 1954-1957. Who'S Who Rel; Stdt/P Awd Amer Com 64-65 S Aug Coll Engl.

DAVIS, Holly (Az) All Saints' Episcopal Church and Day School, 6300 N Central Ave, Phoenix AZ 85012 **Assoc for Chld, Yth, & Fam Mnstrs All SS Ch Phoenix AZ 2014-** B Norfolk VA 1967 d Peter & Kay. BA Transylvania U 1989; MDiv VTS 2008. D 1/24/2008 Bp Stacy F Sauls P 10/18/2008 Bp Sean Walter Rowe. R S Jn's Ch Franklin PA 2008-2014. hdavis@allsaints.org

DAVIS, James Howard (Ida) 4705 Savannah Ln., Boise ID 83714 B Saint Louis MO 1928 s Robert & Lee. BSME U of Nevada at Reno 1951; MDiv CDSP 1954. D 7/29/1954 P 2/9/1955 Bp William F Lewis. c 2. R S Steph's Boise ID 1963-1989; R S Mary's Ch Emmett ID 1956-1962; Cur Trin Epis Ch Reno NV 1954-1956.

DAVIS, James Lloyd (Ia) 6617 Romford Ct, Johnston IA 50131 B Wilkes-Barre PA 1951 s William & Hannah. U of Wisconsin; BA Wilkes Coll 1976; MDiv Bex Sem 1981; DMin Estrn Bapt TS 1989. D 6/13/1981 P 3/17/1982 Bp Lloyd Edward Gressle. m 6/2/1978 Mary Davis c 1. Dio Iowa Des Moines IA 2003-2006; S Andr's Ch Madison WI 1989-1996; S Gabr's Epis Ch Philadelphia PA 1985-1989; No Par Epis Ch St. Clair PA 1984-1985; Trin Ch Newtown CT 1982-1984; Ch Of The Epiph Glenburn Clarks Summit PA 1981-1982; Non-par. Auth, "Boundaries: The Pstr'S Role," *Integration.*

DAVIS, Jane Lowe (VI) PO Box 7386, St Thomas VI 00801 **S Andr's Ch St Thos VI 2011-** B Wadesboro NC 1941 d Thomas & Jane. Non Degree Study Gnrl Theol; Non Degree Study GTS; BA Duke 1963. D 3/5/2011 P 3/3/2012 Bp Edward Gumbs. c 2.

DAVIS, John Bartley (ND) 7940 45r Street Southeast, Jamestown ND 58401 B Aberdeen SD 1948 s Edwin & Mary. BS No Dakota St U 1974. D 12/1/1995 P 10/1/1996 Bp Andrew Fairfield. m 6/25/1977 Katherine Mcelroy.

DAVIS JR, Johnnie Manly (USC) PO Box 2959, West Columbia SC 29171 **Dioc Exec Coun Dio Upper So Carolina Columbia SC 2011-** B Hartsville SC 1944 s Johnie & Lucy. U of So Carolina 1969; BS Fran Marion U 1972; MDiv SE Bapt TS 1976; CAS Sewanee: The U So, TS 1997. D 6/1/1997 P 12/7/1997 Bp Edward Lloyd Salmon Jr. m 5/15/1965 Carol P Davis c 1. Still Hopes Epis Ret Cmnty W Columbia SC 2009-2016; Vic And P-in-c Epis Ch Of The H Trin Ridgeland SC 1997-2009. OHC - Assoc 1988. frjdavis@gmail.com

DAVIS, John William (Be) Church of the Good Shepherd, 1780 N Washington Ave, Scranton PA 18509 B Scranton PA 1971 s Robert & Janet. CJA Mansfield U of PA 1995. D 12/21/2012 Bp Paul Victor Marshall. m 9/25/2004 Wendy Lee Davis c 3.

DAVIS, Jon (CFla) 1412 Palomino Way, Oviedo FL 32765 **Cbury Retreat And Conf Cntr Oviedo FL 2009-** B Fort McPherson GA 1959 s Millard & June. BA Berry Coll 1982; MDiv Reformed TS 2000; TESM 2000. D 3/3/2001 P 10/20/2001 Bp John Wadsworth Howe. m 12/27/1991 Beth B Davis. Vic Ch of the Incarn Oviedo FL 2006-2014; All SS Ch Of Winter Pk Winter Pk FL 2003-2006; Dio Cntrl Florida Orlando FL 2001-2003, Cn for Yth Mnstry 1991-2003.

DAVIS, Joseph N (Tenn) 8215 Planters Grove Dr, Cordova TN 38018 **Gr Epis Ch Sprg Hill TN 2017-** B Nashville TN 1957 s Maclin & Dorothy. BA U So 1979; W&L 1980; MDiv Nash 1986. D 6/21/1986 Bp George Lazenby Reynolds Jr P 1/1/1987 Bp Donis Dean Patterson. m 5/26/1984 Cynthia Hill Davis c 2. Ch Of The Redeem Shelbyville TN 2016; Calv Epis Ch Cumberland Furnace TN 2015; Dio Tennessee Nashville TN 2015; Ch Of The Adv Nashville TN 2014; The Epis Ch Of The Resurr Franklin TN 2007-2014; R S Phil Ch Memphis TN 1994-2007; Assoc R S Jn's Epis Ch Memphis TN 1990-1994; R Ch Of The H Sprt Graham TX 1988-1990; Vic S Ptr By The Lake Graford TX 1988-1990; Yth Min Ch Of The Incarn Dallas TX 1986-1988.

DAVIS, Joy Ruth (Ga) St Patrick's Episcopal Church, 4800 Old Dawson Rd, Albany GA 31721 B Albany GA 1956 d John & Barbara. D 6/2/2012 Bp Scott Anson Benhase. m 8/14/1982 Timothy Ott Davis c 2.

DAVIS, Judith Anne (Mass) 671 Route 28, Harwich Port MA 02646 **R Chr Ch Epis Harwich Port MA 2008-** B Henderson NC 1947 d Herbert & Estelle. BS High Point U 1969; PhD U of Florida 1980; Ds Duke 1989; MDiv Ya Berk 1991; STM Yale DS 1995. D 6/22/1991 Bp Huntington Williams Jr P 6/27/1992 Bp George Nelson Hunt III. m 12/30/2009 Anne Elizabeth Gilson c 1. COM Dio Washington 2005-2008; Chair, Exam Chapl Dio Washington Washington DC 2003-2008, Washington Natl Cathd 1997-2008, Chair of Cmsn on Liturg 1998-2006; R Chr Ch Capitol Hill Washington DC 1996-2008; Stndg Com Dio Rhode Island Providence RI 1992-1996, Instr, D's Sch 1994-1996, Chair of Cmsn on Liturg 1993-1996; Asst S Mich's Ch Bristol RI 1992-1996; Ch Of S Jas The Apos New Haven CT 1991-1992; Cur S Jas' Ch New Haven CT 1991-1992; S Thos's Day Sch New Haven CT 1991-1992; Chapl S Thos Epis Sch New Haven CT 1990-1992; Trst and Secy of Bd Trst Ya Berk New Haven CT 1994-2008. Contrib, "two chapters," *Visio Divina: A Rdr in Faith and Visual Arts,* LeaderResources, 2009. Cape Cod Bird Club Off 2012; Christians in the Visual Arts 2000; Epis Ch and the Visual Arts -artist Mem 1996; Gld of Harwich Artists Off 2008. Phi Kappa Phi U of Florida 1977. motherjude@comcast.net

DAVIS, Judy (Va) 236 S Laurel St, Richmond VA 23220 **Asst All SS Ch Richmond VA 2015-** B Charlotte NC 1959 d William & Grace. BA Salem Coll 1982; MDiv VTS 2014. D 6/7/2014 Bp Shannon Sherwood Johnston. m 4/5/1986 Cyril Douglas Davis c 2. Asst S Andr's Ch Richmond VA 2015.

DAVIS, Malcolm Fletcher (WMass) 4490 Smugglers Cove Rd, Freeland WA 98249 **Trin Par Seattle WA 2011-; Mem Bp's Com for the Environ 2005-; Ret 2000-; Assoc S Augustines In-The-Woods Epis Par Freeland WA 2000-; Mbr, Form Chair Commitee for Israel/Palestine 1998-; Mbr - 3 terms Cler Assn Dio Olympia 1990-** B Cleveland OH 1935 s Kenneth & Carol. AB Harv 1958; MDiv CDSP 1961. D 6/12/1961 P 12/16/1961 Bp Sumner Walters. m 8/15/1959 Jane Elizabeth Davis c 4. R S Thos Epis Ch Medina WA 1989-2000; R & Headmaster S Patricks Ch And Day Sch Thousand Oaks CA 1984-1989; Del Prov Syn 1980-1989; Cmssnr Epis Asiamer Cmsn 1980-1986; Wstrn Field Off PBp's Fund for Wld Relief New York City 1980-1984; R S Anselm Of Cbury Par Garden Grove CA 1978-1984; Dep GC 1969-1994; R S Columba Ch Fresno CA 1969-1978; Mssy Mmadinare Botswana Cntrl Afr 1968-1969; R S Jn's Par Porterville CA 1964-1968; Vic Chr Ch Lemoore CA 1961-1964. Auth, "How to Resettle A Refugee Fam," Forw; Auth, "Of Foxes & Birds & the s Man," Forw. OHC 1962.

DAVIS, Margaret Callender (CFla) 19924 W Blue Cove Dr, Dunnellon FL 34432 B Ashtabula OH 1951 d Robert & Florence. BA Meryhurst U 1986; MA Xavier U 1994; DMin GTF 2012. D 9/12/2015 Bp Gregory Orrin Brewer. m 5/21/2005 William L Davis c 2.

DAVIS, Mary Alice (Okla) 3200 Shady Brook Rd, Woodward OK 73801 **Vic S Jn's Epis Ch Woodward OK 1996-** B Berwyn IL 1953 d Chester & Mabel. BD U MN 1980; MDiv SWTS 1992. D 6/24/1992 P 3/6/1993 Bp Robert Marshall Anderson. m 9/6/1998 Mac Benbrook. Dio Oklahoma Oklahoma City OK 1996-2012; Int S Bede's Ch Westport OK 1994-1996; Chapl Cancer Treatment Cntr Tulsa 1994-1995; Chapl New Hope Hospice Tulsa 1993-1994; Chapl Abbott NW Hosp Minneapolis MN 1992-1993.

DAVIS, Maryan Elizabeth (NH) D 6/12/2016 Bp A Robert Hirschfeld.

DAVIS, Mary Elizabeth (Nwk) 200 Main St, Chatham NJ 07928 **R S Paul's Epis Ch Chatham NJ 2011-** B Ashland KY 1966 d Stephen & Elizabeth. BA U So 1988; MA Col Teachers Coll 1992; MDiv Drew U 2009. D 6/5/2010 P 12/11/2010 Bp Mark M Beckwith. m 6/18/1988 Walter J Davis c 3. Asst R Calv Epis Ch Summit NJ 2010-2011.

DAVIS, Matthew Steven (SJ) 1710 Verde St, Bakersfield CA 93304 B Gardena CA 1951 s William & Christine. BA California St U 1973; Sewanee: The

214

U So, TS 1983; MA U of Greece 1983; TS Fresno 2005. Rec 5/21/2006 Bp David Mercer Schofield. m 9/10/1998 Christine Davis. S Mk's Ch Shafter CA 2006-2008; Gk Orth P Dio San Francisco 1984-1999.

DAVIS, Michael McKean (WTex) 8401 Kearsarge Dr, Austin TX 78745 **1994-** B Chicago IL 1938 s David & Margaret. BA Ken 1960; MDiv CDSP 1966; MA U of Texas 1974. D 7/14/1966 Bp Everett H Jones P 1/25/1967 Bp Richard Earl Dicus. m 12/27/2008 Patricia Ann Rose c 2. Supply S Tim's Ch Cotulla TX 1998-2013; Supply S Andr's Ch Brackettville TX 1998; Supply S Mich's Ch Lake Corpus Christi TX 1997-1998; Chapl Texas Mltry Inst San Antonio TX 1992-1994; Supply S Geo Ch San Antonio TX 1991; Chapl Tx Mltry Inst San Antonio TX 1990-1994; Supply S Matt's Epis Ch Universal City TX 1988-1990; Supply S Matt's Epis Ch Kenedy TX 1987-1989; Supply S Steph's Ch Goliad TX 1987-1988; R All SS Epis Ch San Benito TX 1983-1987; Asst Trin Ch Marshall TX 1982-1983; Hdmstr Trin Day Sch Marshall TX 1979-1983; Chapl Trin Epis Sch Marshall TX 1979-1983; Hdmstr Par Day Sch Houston TX 1977-1979; Asst Ch Of The Ascen Houston TX 1976-1979; Hdmstr Chr Luth Sch San Antonio TX 1975-1976; Chapl Tx Mltry Inst San Antonio TX 1968-1974; Asst Ch Of The Epiph Kingsville TX 1966-1968.

DAVIS, Milbrew (WTex) 338 Hub Ave, San Antonio TX 78220 B La Grange TX 1930 s George & Victoria. BA Prairie View A&M U 1952; MS Our Lady of the Lake U San Antonio TX 1960; MDiv Epis TS of the SW 1970; DMin SFTS 1985. D 6/2/1970 Bp Harold Cornelius Gosnell P 12/1/1970 Bp Richard Earl Dicus. m 7/25/1953 Shirley M Davis c 3. S Phil's Ch San Antonio TX 1975-1997; D S Thos And S Mart's Ch Crp Christi TX 1970-1972. Auth, *Hist of S Phil's Epis Ch San Antonio TX 1895-1985*, 1985. Coll of Chapl 1973; Natl Assn of Soc Wk 1960; Phi Beta Sigma Fraternity, Inc. 1952.

DAVIS, Orion Woods (Nwk) 2 Pasadena St, Canton NC 28716 B Aiken SC 1943 s Orion & Ruth. BA Clemson U 1965; MDiv Sewanee: The U So, TS 1968. D 6/23/1968 P 5/15/1969 Bp John Adams Pinckney. m 9/3/1966 Pamela N Davis c 2. R S Mary's Ch Sparta NJ 2004-2006; R S Jas Ch Montclair NJ 1994-2004; R Trin Epis Ch of Bergen Cnty Allendale NJ 1989-1994; R S Elis's Epis Ch Memphis TN 1982-1989; R S Steph's Ch Pearl River NY 1976-1982; R Chr Ch Red Hook NY 1971-1976; Asst Gr Epis Ch Nyack NY 1969-1971; Asst Ch Of The Resurr Greenwood SC 1968-1969.

DAVIS, Patricia Rhoads (Ga) 215 Grimball Point Rd, Savannah GA 31406 **D Chr Ch Epis Savannah GA 2013-; Chapl Riverview Nrsng and Rehab 2012-** B Macon GA 1948 d Walter & Genevieve. BA Roa 1970; Cert EFM 1992; Cert Virginia Inst for Sprtl Dir Smithfield VA 1995; Cert D Formation Prog NC 1999. D 6/19/1999 Bp David Conner Bane Jr. m 7/10/1971 Rodney Michael Davis c 2. D Chr and S Lk's Epis Ch Norfolk VA 2009-2012; D, Int Galilee Epis Ch Virginia Bch VA 2008-2009; D The Epis Ch Of The Adv Norfolk VA 2003-2008; COM Mem Dio Sthrn Virginia Newport News VA 2002-2008; D Westminister Cbury Virginia Bch VA 1999-2012; D S Paul's Ch Norfolk VA 1999-2003; D / Sr Chapl Beacon Shores Nrsng Hm Virginia Bch VA 1995-2012. Auth, Amazon, 2011; Auth, "What Chld is This?," self, 2011; Co-Auth, "Searching the Heart of God," Greene Tree Press, 2003; Auth, "Reflections of Jesus," *Prisms of the Soul*, Morehouse Pub, 1996. Alzheimers Assn 1999-2001; Dio SVa Cmsn on Aging 1999-2001; NAAD 1999; Sthrn Virginia Epis Cler Assn 2000-2012. Jn Hines Preaching Awd VTS 2006.

DAVIS, Philip Arthur (SwFla) 1603 52nd St W, Bradenton FL 34209 **D Manasota Misssion 1997-** B Salem MA 1935 s Chester & Esther. BS NEU 1958; BA NEU 1958. D 6/14/1997 Bp Rogers Sanders Harris. m 6/10/1969 Janet E Halverson.

DAVIS, Rodney (NCal) 2140 Mission Ave., Carmichael CA 95608 **Assoc for Adult Sprtl Formation S Mich's Epis Ch Carmichael CA 2009-; Assoc Ord of Julian of Norwich 2000-; Trst Bd Trst Grad Theol Un 2012-; Mem, Chr Formation Cmsn The Epis Dio Nthrn California Sacramento CA 2011-, Chair, Const & Cn Com 2010-; Trst CDSP Berkeley CA 2010-; Advsry Bd Mem UC Davis Clincl Pstr Serv 2010-** B Sacramento CA 1949 s Lester & Pauline. BA U CA Davis 1971; JD UC Hastings Coll of Law 1974; MPA USC 1979; MDiv CDSP 2009. D 6/13/2009 P 1/9/2010 Bp Barry Leigh Beisner. m 8/10/1974 Susan Davis c 2.

DAVIS, Ronald C. (Fla) B Jacksonville Fl 1938 D 6/24/1965 P 3/30/1966 Bp Edward Hamilton West. m 8/15/1964 Jean P Davis. Ch Of The Adv Tallahassee FL 1988-1993; All SS Epis Ch Lakeland FL 1979-1988; S Chris's Ch Pensacola FL 1975-1978.

DAVIS, Ronald Lee (WA) Saint Anne's Church, 25100 Ridge Rd, Damascus MD 20872 **R S Anne's Ch Damascus MD 2012-** B Abingdon VA 1969 s Ronald & Suzane. BB Amer Intl 2004; MDIV Bex 2009; MDIV Bex Sem 2009; MDiv Bex Sem 2009. D 12/27/2008 P 6/27/2009 Bp Leo Frade. m 10/11/2013 Daniel Anthony Lonteen. S Andr's Epis Ch Of Hollywood Hollywood FL 2010-2012; Bd Dir THe Jubilee Cntr Hollywood FL 2010-2012; Chapl Vitas Palliative Care 2009-2011; Cur S Mart's Epis Ch Pompano Bch FL 2009-2010; Chapl Vitas Hospice 2009; Bd Dir Jubilee Cntr of So Broward 2010-2012; Cler In Charge - New Beginnings Dio SE Florida Miami 2009-2012, Cler In Charge-Yth Conv 2009-2012; Bd Dir St. Laurence Chap Pompano Bch FL 2009-2010. rector@stannesdamascus.org

DAVIS, Roy Jefferson (Tex) D 6/20/2015 Bp C Andrew Doyle P 12/22/2015 Bp Dena Arnall Harrison.

DAVIS, Thomas Anthony (Spr) 5063 Cartter Rd, Kell IL 62853 **Died 8/30/2015** B New York NY 1939 s Thomas & Roxanna. AS Kaskaskia Coll 1984; BS Sthrn Illinois U 1986; MS Sthrn Illinois U 1999. D 10/23/1998 P 6/8/2003 Bp Peter Hess Beckwith. m 8/19/1978 Karen Burton c 2. Vic S Thos Ch Salem IL 2002-2010. NAAD.

DAVIS JR, Thomas Clark (USC) 102 Carteret Court, Clemson SC 29631 B Forty-Fort PA 1929 s Thomas & Frances. BA Brothers 1951; MDiv Drew U 1954. D 12/17/1957 P 6/17/1958 Bp Frederick Warnecke. c 4. Int S Jas Epis Ch Greenville SC 2007-2008, Int 1999-2007; Int S Fran Ch Greenville SC 2001-2002; Int Gr Epis Ch Anderson SC 1998-1999; Int Ch Of The Resurr Greenwood SC 1996-1997; R H Trin Par Epis Clemson SC 1970-1995; Chapl Serv US-A 1967-70 Untd States 1967-1970; R Our Sav Roslindale Boston 1961-1967; Asst S Steph's Epis Ch Wilkes Barre PA 1957-1958.

DAVIS, Thomas Preston (USC) 30 Lyme Bay Road, Columbia SC 29210 **Int Chr Ch Milford DE 2013-; Asst Chr Ch 1974-** B South Bend IN 1945 s Daniel & Mary. MDiv UTS; BS U Cinc. D 9/10/1972 Bp Frederick Warren Putnam P 3/1/1973 Bp John Mc Gill Krumm. m 12/17/1966 Judith Baston. Ccn.

DAVIS, Vicki M (Ct) 4551 Pennsylvania Ave Unit 1523, Kansas City MO 64111 B Highland IL 1954 d Thomas & Mary. BA U of Missouri 1976; JD Col 1981; MDiv Ya Berk 1999. D 6/9/2001 P 5/25/2002 Bp Andrew Donnan Smith. c 3. Assoc Trin Ch On The Green New Haven CT 2012-2014; Chapl Gr Ch Sch New York NY 2008-2011; Cur S Mk's Ch New Canaan CT 2002-2007; Chapl/Dir Of Pstr Care Silver Hill Hosp New Canaan CT 2001-2002; Asst Chr Ch Stratford CT 1999-2001.

DAVIS, West Richard (Oly) 790 Smugglers Cove Rd, Friday Harbor WA 98250 B Minneapolis MN 1936 s West & Evelyn. BA San Jose St U 1961; MDiv EDS 1965; Cert SWTS 2005. D 12/18/1965 P 7/1/1966 Bp James Albert Pike. m 5/2/1970 Martha Suzanne Davis. R The Epis Par of St Dav Friday Harbor WA 1993-2001; R S Andr's Epis Ch Tacoma WA 1978-1993; R Gd Samar Epis Ch San Jose CA 1969-1971; Assoc S Andr's Ch Saratoga CA 1965-1969. R Emer S Davids 2000.

DAVIS-HELLER, Lisa Ann (WVa) **Reverend Ohio Vlly Episc. Mnstrs St. Marys WV 2002-; Ohio Vlly Epis Cluster Williamstown WV 2002-** B 1957 D 9/20/2001 Bp Claude Charles Vache P 6/8/2002 Bp William Michie Klusmeyer. m 4/5/1986 Richard C Heller c 2.

DAVIS-LAWSON, Karen Dm (LI) 1420 27th Ave, Astoria NY 11102 **P-in-c S Geo's Ch Astoria NY 2014-, P-in-c 2011-2014** B 1961 d Beresford & Eileen. MA Brooklyn Coll; BA Brooklyn Coll 1982; MS Brooklyn Coll 1997; MDiv GTS 2009. D 6/22/2009 Bp James Hamilton Ottley P 1/16/2010 Bp Lawrence C Provenzano. m 8/18/2007 Noel Lawson. D Ch Of The Redeem Astoria NY 2009-2011. stgeorge.astoria@gmail.com

DAVISON, Arienne Siu Ling (Oly) 2151 4th St, Bremerton WA 98312 **Vic St Bede Epis Ch Port Orchard WA 2014-; Cn for Multicultural Mnstrs Dio Olympia Seattle 2011-** B Seattle WA 1979 d Eric & Sara. BS U of Washington 2002; MDiv VTS 2007. D 6/30/2007 P 1/26/2008 Bp Bavi Edna Rivera. m 12/8/2009 Douglas Peters c 2. S Matthews Auburn WA 2015-2016; S Alb's Ch Edmonds WA 2013-2014; Assoc Gr Ch Bainbridge Island WA 2010-2013; Assoc R for Fam Mnstrs Emm Epis Ch Mercer Island WA 2007-2010.

DAVISSON, Mary Thomsen (Md) 2363 Hamiltowne Cir., Baltimore MD 21237 **Exec Dir/Port Chapl Baltimore Intl Seafarers' Cntr Inc Baltimore MD 2005-, Asst Dir 2004; Assoc Ch Of The Redemp Baltimore MD 2004-; Mem, Bd Dir No Amer Maritime Mnstry Assn 2009-; Cnvnr Ord of Urban Missioners Maryland Chapt 2005-** B Baltimore MD 1952 d John & Helen. AB Br 1974; MA Br 1974; PhD U CA Berkeley 1979; MDiv VTS 2004. D 6/12/2004 Bp John L Rabb P 1/8/2005 Bp Robert Wilkes Ihloff. m 3/22/1980 Edwin Orlando Davisson c 3. Mem Dio Maryland Mssn Strtgy Grp 2005-2009. "Chapl to Seafarers," *Virginia Sem Journ*, 2007; "The Observers of Daedalus in Ovid," *Classical Wrld 90*, 1997; "Mythological Examples in Ovid's Remedia," *Phoenix 50*, 1996; "Tristia 5.13 and Ovid's Use of Epistolary Form," *Classical Journ 80*, 1985. Ord of Urban Missioners 1999. Wmn of the Year Port of Baltimore 2007.

DAVIS-WILSON, Lillian Juanita (WNY) St Philip's Episc Church, 15 Fernhill Ave, Buffalo NY 14215 **Other Lay Position S Phil's Ch Buffalo NY 1999-** B New York City 1943 d Charles & Elva. BA The City Coll 1974; MPA NYU 1976; Cert Colgate Rochester Crozer Div Schol 2016; Cert Colgate Rochester Crozer Div Schol 2016; Cert Colgate Rochester Crozer DS 2016. D 8/29/2015 Bp Ralph William Franklin. m 7/12/1986 Herman E Wilson c 2.

DAVY, Brian Kendall (At) 589 Martins Grove Rd, Dahlonega GA 30533 **S Lk's Ch Ft Vlly GA 2008-; S Thos Of Cbury Thomaston GA 2004-** B 1947 s Martin & Dorothy. BA Georgia St U 1982; MDiv Sewanee: The U So, TS 1991. D 6/6/1991 P 1/1/1992 Bp Frank Kellogg Allan. m 12/15/1990 Susan Callender c 1. Chr Ch Macon GA 2002-2003; S Eliz's Epis Ch Dahlonega GA 1994-2001; Asst R Ch Of The Epiph Atlanta GA 1991-1993.

DAW JR, Carl Pickens (Ct) 171 Highland Ave, Watertown MA 02472 B Louisville KY 1944 s Carl & Sara. BA Rice U 1966; MA U of Virginia 1967;

PhD U of Virginia 1970; MDiv Sewanee: The U So, TS 1981. D 6/14/1981 P 3/18/1982 Bp Claude Charles Vache. m 5/31/1969 May Bates c 1. The Hymn Soc in Untd States & Can 1996-2009; Int S Thos Memi Epis Ch Oakmont PA 1993-1994; Ed Advsry Comm. Hymnal 1982 Comp 1986-1990; Vic/ Chapl S Mk's Chap Storrs CT 1984-1993; Asst Chr And Gr Ch Petersburg VA 1981-1984; Text Com Hymnal 1982 1980-1982. Auth, "Pryr Rising into Song: Fifty New and Revised Hymns," Hope Pub Co., 2016; Auth, "Glory to God: A Comp," WestminsterJohn Knox Press, 2016; Co-Auth, "A HymnTune Psalter, RCL Ed, v. 1-2," Ch Pub, Inc., 2007; Co-Auth, "Liturg Mus for the RCL, Years A,B,C," Ch Pub, Inc., 2007; Auth, "Gathered for Wrshp," Hope Pub Co., 2006; Co-Auth, "A HymnTune Psalter v. 1-2," Ch Pub, Inc., 1998; Auth, "New Psalms and Hymns and Sprtl Songs," Hope Pub Co., 1996; Auth, "Breaking the Word," Ch Pub Inc., 1994; Auth, "To Sing God's Praise," Hope Pub Co., 1992; Auth, "A Year of Gr," Hope Pub Co., 1990. Hymn Soc US & Can 1982. D.D. U So 2012; Fell RSCM 2011; D.D. VTS 2009; Fell Hymn Soc in the US & Can 2007.

DAWSON, Adrien P (Md) 4412 Eastway, Baltimore MD 21218 **All SS Ch Frederick MD 2016-** B Charlottesville VA 1975 d Richard & Susan. BA St Johns Coll Annapolis MD 1996; MDiv GTS 2002. D 6/8/2002 Bp John L Rabb P 12/6/2002 Bp Robert Wilkes Ihloff. m 5/20/2000 Sean Frederick Dawson. R Ch Of S Marks On The Hill Pikesville MD 2007-2016; Asst Trin Ch Towson MD 2002-2007.

DAWSON, Barbara Louise (Cal) 399 Gregory Ln, Pleasant Hill CA 94523 **D Ch Of The Resurr Pleasant Hil CA 1988-** B Omaha NE 1952 d Charles & Harriet. BS San Diego St U 1975. D 3/14/1985 Bp Otis Charles. m 6/9/1973 David Lanford Dawson c 2. D Dio Utah Salt Lake City UT 1985-1988.

DAWSON, Eric Emmanuel (VI) B Saint Thomas VI 1937 s Joseph & Ann. BS NYU 1964. D 3/25/1974 Bp Edward Mason Turner. m 6/11/1966 Betty J Vanterpool c 2.

DAWSON JR, Frank Prescott (Md) 9422 Penfield Rd N, Columbia MD 21045 **Assoc Chapl Howard Cnty Gnrl Hosp Columbia MD 1993-; Voc D Dio Maryland Baltimore MD 1983-** B Chicago IL 1924 s Frank & Kathryn. U of Wisconsin 1948; BS Roosevelt U 1954. D 6/26/1983 Bp David Keller Leighton Sr. m 11/12/1977 Mickey Dawson. Voc D S Ptr's Epis Ch Ellicott City MD 1991-1993; Asst Chapl Fairhaven Epis Ret Cntr Sykesville MD 1987-1990; D Ch Of The H Cov Baltimore MD 1986-1987. Irenaeus Soc Of Priests & Deacons.

DAWSON, George Henry (WTex) 4426 Dolphin Pl, Corpus Christi TX 78411 B Baltimore MD 1932 s George & Anna. BS Duke 1954; MDiv VTS 1961. D 7/11/1961 Bp Everett H Jones P 1/1/1962 Bp Richard Earl Dicus. m 12/3/1955 Lorraine Dawson c 2. Int S Jas Epis Ch Hebbronville TX 1990-1993; P-in-c Ch Of Our Sav Aransas Pass TX 1987-1990; P-in-c Ch Of The Ascen Refugio TX 1986-1990; P-in-c S Mart's Ch Corpus Christi TX 1973-1987; P-in-c S Thos And S Mart's Ch Crp Christi TX 1973-1987; 1971-1973; Actg/Assoc. R Ch Of The Gd Shpd Corpus Christi TX 1969-1971, Asst R 1965-1968; S Chris's By The Sea Portland TX 1965-1968; Asst S Lk's Ch Alexandria VA 1964-1965; Vic S Chris's Ch Bandera TX 1961-1964; Vic S Dav Hondo TX 1961-1964. Auth, *A Plan for Bldg an Integrated Total Distribution Co*, Self, 1972; Auth, "Transportation Concerns," *Choices Facing Corpus Christi*, 1972. Mssn to Seafarers 1976; Rotary Club of Corpus Christi, Texas 1969. Alum of the Year Lambda Chi Alpha Sigma-Epsilon Chapt 2012; Dist Gvnr Rotary Dist 5930 2004; Meritorious Publ Serv Citation Commandant, U.S. Coast Guard 1994.

DAWSON, Margaret G (La) 320 Sena Dr, Metairie LA 70005 B 1942 D 9/13/2003 Bp Charles Edward Jenkins III. m 7/29/1989 Anthony Michael Dawson. D S Mart's Ch Metairie LA 2003-2014.

DAWSON JR, Marshall Allen (Lex) 1375 Weisenberger Mill Rd, Midway KY 40347 B Versailles KY 1938 s Marshall & Mary. BS U of Kentucky 1960; MD U of Kentucky 1964; Epis TS in Kentucky 1986. D 6/4/1985 Bp Don Adger Wimberly. m 8/5/1961 Nancy Ann Barnett c 2.

DAWSON, Paul Sweeting (Md) 145 Main St., Apt. A1, Vineyard Haven MA 02568 B Baltimore MD 1930 s Jesse & Blanche. MS Loyola U; BA McDaniel Coll 1953; Drew U 1956; GTS 1957. D 3/29/1958 P 1/1/1959 Bp Noble C Powell. c 1. S Judes Epis Ch Franklin NH 1996-1999; P-in-c Trin Epis Ch Tilton NH 1996-1998; R S Paul Poplar Sprg MD 1989-1996; Fairhaven Sykesville MD 1982-1991; Chapl Fairhaven Par Sykesville 1982-1989; Chapl Ch Hm & Hosp Baltimore MD 1972-1982; Ch Hosp Corp Baltimore MD 1972-1982; Cur S Mich And All Ang Ch Baltimore MD 1969-1972; R S Jn's Ch Kingsville MD 1962-1969; R S Jn Shady Side MD 1959-1962. Auth, "Poems: After Tao," *Tryst-ATR*, 1976; Auth, "A Hospice Handbook Chapt 7"; Auth, "Hospice: Complete Care For Terminally Ill Chapt 5".

DAWSON JR, Tucker Edward (La) 321 State St, Bay Saint Louis MS 39520 **Chr Ch Bay S Louis MS 2015-; Ret 1998-** B Baton Rouge LA 1934 s Tucker & Evelyn. BS LSU 1957; MDiv Sewanee: The U So, TS 1962; MEd U of New Orleans 1971. D 6/29/1962 Bp Girault M Jones P 6/1/1963 Bp Iveson Batchelor Noland. m 2/27/1965 Margene Dawson c 1. R S Andr's Epis Ch New Orleans LA 1988-1998; R S Thos The Apos Ch Overland Pk KS 1975-1988; R

Chr Ch Slidell LA 1969-1975; Cur and Headmaster S Paul's Sch New Orleans LA 1962-1969; Mem, Stndg Com Dio Kansas Topeka KS 1981-1985.

DAWSON, Walter (Mich) 18017 Grand Lake Blvd, Presque Isle MI 49777 B Detroit MI 1945 s Donald & Lois. BS Cntrl Michigan U 1968; MDiv VTS 1973. D 9/2/1973 P 6/23/1974 Bp H Coleman Mcgehee Jr. m 2/27/1971 Laura J Dawson c 3. R S Geo's Ch Milford MI 1997-2011; R S Jas Epis Ch Hibbing MN 1990-1997; R Emm Ch Staunton VA 1986-1990; Chapl Epis U Mnstry Johnson City TN 1986; S Jn's Epis Ch Johnson City TN 1980-1985; Vic S Fran Epis Ch Grayling MI 1975-1980; Cur All SS Ch E Lansing MI 1973-1975. Pi Kappa Delta (Hon Forensics).

DAY III, Charles V. (Be) 1006 Eisenhower Way, Tobyhanna PA 18466 **Reserve Asso. Chapl St. Lk's U Healthcare Ntwk 1999-** B Cartersville GA 1936 s Charles & Mary. BS & BA Stetson U 1965; MDiv Sewanee: The U So, TS 1967. D 6/13/1967 Bp James Loughlin Duncan P 12/20/1967 Bp William Loftin Hargrave. m 3/31/1981 Virginia Rex c 4. Chapl Kirkland/Westminster Vill Bethlehem/Allentown PA 1995-1999; R S Geo's Epis Ch Hellertown PA 1986-1995; Vic S Tim's Ch Macedonia OH 1982-1986; R Aug Par Chesapeake City MD 1981-1982; R S Jn's Ch Naples FL 1976-1981; R H Innoc Epis Ch Valrico FL 1969-1976; Asst Ch Of The Gd Shpd Dunedin FL 1967-1969; Strng Com Epis Peace & Justice Netwrk Dio Bethlehem Bethlehem PA 1989-1993. Auth, "The Chapl Becomes a Patient," *Chapl Today*, Asso. of Profsnl Chapl, 2008; Auth, "Bk Revs," *Living Ch*, Living Ch Fndt, 2006; Ed, "Nwsltr - Assembly Of Epis Hospitals And Chapl," *Assembly of Epis. Hosps. & Chapl*, AEHC, 1975; Assoc Ed, "S Lk Journ Of Theol," *St. Lk's Journ of Theol*, TS, Univ of So, 1965. Assn Of Profsnl Chapl - Bd Cert Chaplai 1999. Bd Cert Chapl Assn of Profsnl Chapl 1999.

DAY, Christine Jane (CNY) 35 Second St, Johnson City NY 13790 **R All SS Epis Ch Johnson City NY 2004-** B North Tonawanda NY 1953 d Elmer & Mary Jane. BA Cor 1975; MS Indiana U 1977; MDiv GTS 1999. D 6/12/1999 P 12/18/1999 Bp David Bruce Joslin. St Paul's Syracuse Syracuse NY 2004; Int Assoc St. Paul's Catherdral Syracuse NY 2003-2004; S Dav's Ch Fayetteville NY 2002; Campus Mnstry Mssnr Dio Cntrl New York Liverpool NY 2001-2003, 1999-2003, Spec Asst to Bp 1999-2001, Dn 2017-, Stndg Com, Pres 2012-2017, Stndg Com, Secy 2010-2012, Bd Mem 2004-2010; Consult ECF New York NY 1996-1999. Bd Nazareth Proj 1995-2007; ESMHE 1999-2003.

DAY, Dennis Lee (CGC) PO Box 2066, Fairhope AL 36533 **Cn Regular Coll of S Jean-Marie Vianney Dio of Cent Gulf Coast 2013-; Assoc S Paul's Chap Magnolia Sprgs AL 2011-; Ret Unknown 1996-** B Chicago IL 1936 s Elden & Leona. BA Pr 1958; Nash 1960; BD SWTS 1961; MA U of Wisconsin 1970; PhD U of Wisconsin 1975; MEd U of So Alabama 1980; EdS U of So Alabama 1989. D 6/10/1961 P 12/1/1961 Bp Horace W B Donegan. m 11/17/1979 Marjorie Day c 2. Assoc Trin Epis Ch Mobile AL 1996-2004; Assoc All SS Epis Ch Mobile AL 1993-1996, Assoc 1982-1992; Unknown 1984-1990; Serv S Jn The Evang Robertsdale AL 1978-1981; Unknown 1976-1977; P-in-c H Cross Epis Ch Wisconsin Dells WI 1972-1975; Unknown 1970-1971; Assoc S Matt's Ch Kenosha WI 1967-1969; R S Andr's Ch Kenosha WI 1963-1966; Cur S Jn The Evang Ch Elkhart IN 1961-1963; Chapl US-AR 1960-1969. Coll of St Jean-Marie Vianney (Cn Regular) 2013. Tchr of the Year 1995 AL St Brd of Educ 1995; Woodrow Wilson Fndt Fllshp 1992.

DAY, Jeremiah (EC) 109 Skipper Circle, Oriental NC 28571 **P S Thos Ch Oriental NC 1999-** B Fort Knox KY 1953 s Jeremiah & Anna. BS USNA 1975; MDiv VTS 1990. D 6/16/1990 P 12/22/1990 Bp Brice Sidney Sanders. m 6/7/1975 Marian Day c 3. Chapl, Reserve USN 1999-2008; Chapl Off Of Bsh For ArmdF New York NY 1994-2000; Trin Epis Ch Chocowinity NC 1990-1994; P-in-c Zion Epis Ch Washington NC 1990.

DAY, John Edward (SJ) 9843 Derby Way, Elk Grove CA 95757 **Dio Los Angeles Los Angeles CA 1999-** B Salt Lake City UT 1951 s Jack & Frances. BS U of Utah 1988; MDiv CDSP 1991; DMin SWTS 2001. D 6/2/1991 P 12/7/1991 Bp George Edmonds Bates. m 9/11/1973 Gail K Day c 2. R S Mk's Epis Ch Moscow ID 2004-2006; R S Geo's Par La Can CA 1995-2004; Dio Utah Salt Lake City UT 1993-1995; Vic Gr Epis Ch St Geo UT 1992; Cur Cathd Ch Of S Mk Salt Lake City UT 1991-1992. Assoc, OHC. Hon Cn Dio Los Angelels 2003.

DAY JR, John Warren (Wyo) 441 Highland Dr, Bellingham WA 98225 **Ret 1987-** B Sapulpa OK 1922 s John & Harriet. BA Antioch Coll 1949; BD UTS 1958; Brigham Young U 1974. D 9/16/1958 P 3/1/1959 Bp James W Hunter. c 2. R S Jas Ch Riverton WY 1960-1970; All SS Ch Wheatland WY 1958-1960; In-Charge Ch Of Our Sav Hartville WY 1958-1960; S Jn The Bapt Ch Glendo WY 1958-1960.

DAY, Kate Lufkin (CNY) 106 Ardsley Dr, Syracuse NY 13214 **Assoc S Dav's Ch Fayetteville NY 2015-; Mng Chapl, Crouse Hosp InterFaith Works of Cntrl New York Syracuse NY 2009-** B Saint Paul MN 1954 d James & Rosemarie. BA S Johns Coll 1976; MA Untd TS 1983; MDiv GTS 1989; Bd Cert Assn of Profsnl Chapl 2015. D 6/10/1989 Bp Paul Moore Jr P 12/9/1989 Bp Douglas Edwin Theuner. m 6/23/1979 William Blaine Day c 2. R Chr Epis Ch Jordan NY 1997-2010; R H Trin Ch So River NJ 1994-1997; Assoc S Lk's Ch

Gladstone NJ 1991-1993; Asst S Andr's Ch New London NH 1989-1991. Assoc, Cmnty S Jn Bapt 1992. revkatherineday@crouse.org

DAY, Margaret Ann (Me) 777 Stillwater Ave Lot 63, Old Town ME 04468 **Serv Dio Maine Portland ME 1990-** B Bangor ME 1951 d William & Jean. BSW U of Maine 1990; MS U of Maine 1996. D 10/25/1990 Bp Edward Cole Chalfant. m 6/9/1973 Lloyd Wesley Day. Auth, *Discerning the Call to Soc Mnstry*, Alb Inst. St. Steph's Awd NAAD 2005.

DAY, Marshall Benjamin (At) 2089 Ponce de Leon Ave NE, Atlanta GA 30307 **R Chr Epis Ch Kennesaw GA 2016-** B Seneca SC 1988 s Derek & Alice. BS U NC 2009; MDiv Candler TS Emory U 2013; MDiv Emory U - Candler Thelology 2013. D 5/22/2013 P 12/21/2013 Bp Robert Christopher Wright. m 10/9/2013 Amanda Day. S Columba Epis Ch Suwanee GA 2016; Asst Ch Of The Epiph Atlanta GA 2013-2014. fatherben@epiphany.com

DAY, Michael Henry (SwFla) 1070 54th St N, Saint Petersburg FL 33710 **Ret 2002-** B Tampa FL 1941 s Frank & Winfred. BA U of So Florida 1964; MDiv GTS 1967. D 6/17/1967 Bp William Loftin Hargrave P 12/1/1967 Bp Henry I Louttit. m 11/16/2006 Julianna V Day c 2. S Vinc's Epis Ch St Petersburg FL 1976-2001; R S Mary's Epis Ch Palmetto FL 1970-1976; Cur S Mich's Ch Orlando FL 1967-1970.

DAY, Randall Carl Kidder (Los) 2901 Nojoqui Avenue, P.O. Box 39, Los Olivos CA 93441 **R S Mk's-In-The-Vlly Epis Los Olivos CA 2008-** B Brazil IN 1955 s Robert & Marion. BA Oral Roberts U 1977; MA U of Tulsa 1980; MDiv Nash 1985; DMin SWTS 2010. D 6/15/1985 Bp Frank Tracy Griswold III P 12/19/1985 Bp James Winchester Montgomery. m 3/18/2012 William R Hurbaugh. R S Mk's Ch Teaneck NJ 1998-2008; Asstg Cler Cathd of St Ptr & St Paul Washington DC 1993-1997; Int S Monica's Epis Ch Washington DC 1991-1992; Assoc Fac Coll Prchrs Wdc 1990-1997; Cbury Cathd Trust In Amer 1989-1997; Exec Dir The Friends Of Cbury Cathd In The Untd States Washington DC 1989-1997; Int S Geo's Ch Glenn Dale MD 1989-1990; P-in-c S Andr's Ch Downers Grove IL 1985-1988; COM Dio Newark Newark NJ 2006-2008, GC Alt Dep 2006, Bp Nomin Com 2005-2006, Profile Com Co-Chair 2005-2006, COM Lay Mnstry Com 2004-2008, Ward J. Herbert Fund Bd 2004-2008. Auth, "Sewanee Theol Revs," 1994. Mem Bd, Los Olivos Bus Orgnztn 2011; Mem Bd, Santa Ynez Vlly Cottage Hosp Fndt 2011; Lee Reid Awd Bergen Cnty Mart Luther King, Jr. Com 2006; Coun Mem Township of Teaneck 2006; Mem Med Ethics Com, H Name Hosp 2004; Pres Teaneck Interfaith Cler Coun 2000; Hon Chapl Untd States Hse Of Representatives 1995. randallday@mac.com

DAY, Robert Charles (Mass) 47 Willow Tree Hollow, PO Box 3000 PMB 3124, West Tisbury MA 02575 **Ret 1995-** B Hackensack NJ 1927 s Harvey & Sophie. BA U of Delaware 1949; MA Oxf Engl 1959; MDiv EDS 1965. D 6/12/1965 Bp Charles Francis Hall P 12/1/1965 Bp John Melville Burgess. m 12/21/1963 Barbara Day c 3. Hd of Sch The Adv Sch Boston MA 1965-1995; Asst The Ch Of The Adv Boston MA 1965-1977.

DAY, Stephen Crayton (Mont) PO Box 1526, Miles City MT 59301 **D Dio Montana Helena MT 2016-** B Charleston WV 1979 s Phillip & Susan. BA Hampden¿Sydney Coll; MDiv VTS. D 6/26/2016 P 1/14/2017 Bp Charles Franklin Brookhart Jr. Yth Dir Dio W Virginia Charleston WV 2011-2014. sday@wvdiocese.org

DAY, Thomas Leighton (Tex) 320 N Kansas Ave, League City TX 77573 B Bristol VA 1950 s Frank & Sarah. BS U of Tennessee 1973; MDiv Sewanee: The U So, TS 1990; DMin SWTS 2001. D 6/16/1990 P 1/9/1991 Bp Maurice Manuel Benitez. m 6/9/1973 Kim McVeigh Day c 3. R S Chris's Ch League City TX 2002-2016; R S Tim's Epis Ch Houston TX 1992-2002; Asst to the R Adv Epis Ch Stafford TX 1990-1992; All SS Epis Ch Stafford TX 1990-1992. OSL 1985.

DAY, Virginia Rex (Be) 1006 Eisenhower Way, Tobyhanna PA 18466 **COM Dio Bethlehem Bethlehem PA 2013-, Dioc Coun 2007-2012, Evang Cmsn 2002-2012** B Holyoke MA 1940 d Percy & Ruth. BA Smith 1962; Moravian TS 1993; MDiv GTS 1994; STM GTS 2006. D 4/23/1994 P 10/29/1994 Bp James Michael Mark Dyer. m 3/31/1981 Charles V. Day c 2. R Trin Epis Ch Mt Pocono PA 1999-2008; Cn Mssnr Cathd Ch Of The Nativ Bethlehem PA 1994-1999; Bkkeeper ESMA Bethlehem PA 1989-1993; Hd Teller First Fed Savings Northfield Ohio 1982-1986; Customer Serv SE Bank Naples Florida 1978-1981; Classroom Tchr Elem Tchr Naples Florida 1966-1972.

DAYTON, Douglas Kennedy (NwPa) 3600 Mcconnell Rd, Hermitage PA 16148 **Assoc Trin Epis Ch New Castle PA 2011-** B North Tonawanda NY 1942 s William & Virginia. BS SUNY 1964; MS SUNY 1969; MDiv TESM 1989. D 6/29/1989 Bp Christopher FitzSimons Allison P 4/1/1991 Bp Robert Deane Rowley Jr. m 8/16/1969 Kathleen Dayton c 2. Stndg Com Dio NW Pennsylvania Erie PA 1998-2003, Dioc Coun 2006-2008, Dioc Coun 1997-2005; S Jn's Epis Ch Sharon PA 1989-2009.

DAYTON-WELCH, Matthew H (WA) 763 Valley Forge Rd, Wayne PA 19087 B Oklahoma City OK 1981 s James & Elizabeth. BA U of Oklahoma 2003; MDiv GTS 2015. D 11/8/2014 P 6/13/2015 Bp Mariann Edgar Budde. m 6/15/2016 Paul Cr Dayton-Welch. Assoc S Dav's Ch Wayne PA 2015-2017. mwelch@stdavidschurch.org

DE ACETIS, Joseph Lewis (Be) 58 Deer Path Dr, Flanders NJ 07836 **Died 11/21/2016** B Brooklyn NY 1927 s Fiore & Margaret. BS S Mary Coll Leaven-

worth KS 1951; Mt St Alphonsus 1955. Rec 6/1/1997 as Priest Bp Paul Victor Marshall. m 7/18/1970 Joan B De Acetis. Trin Ch Easton PA 1997-2002. Fed Of Chr Ministers.

DEACON JR, Charles Alexander (WNY) 84 Rosedale Blvd., Amherst NY 14226 **Ret 2002-** B Quincy MA 1932 s Charles & Winnifred. BA Bos 1954; MDiv PDS 1962. D 10/13/1962 Bp Anson Phelps Stokes Jr P 4/27/1963 Bp Lewis B Whittemore. c 3. Mem Alum Exec Coun EDS 2003-2006; Int S Jn's Gr Ch Buffalo NY 2000-2002; S Matt's Ch Buffalo NY 1997-1998; Epis Chapl Lockport Hosp NY 1985-1989; All SS Ch Lockport NY 1970-1979; R All SS Lockport NY 1970-1979; Cur Ch Of The Adv Buffalo NY 1966-1970; S Andr's Ch Friendship NY 1965-1966; Vic S Paul's Ch Angelica NY 1965-1966; Cur Chr Ch Rochester NY 1962-1965; Stndg Com Dio Wstrn New York Tonawanda NY 2001-2002, VP Niagara Dnry 1992-2000, Dioce Coun 1982-1991. Toastmasters Intl Soc 2001. deaconac@roadrunner.com

DEACON, Jonathan (NJ) 12 Bryan Dr, Voorhees NJ 08043 **Supply P Dio New Jersey 2011-; Pres/Pstr and PsychoSocial Counslr Safe Haven Pstr Counslg Serv Inc. NJ 1999-; Ret 1998-; Chapl Intl Police Chapl Voorhees NJ 1997-; P-t P in Charge The Ch Of The Gd Shpd Berlin NJ 2013-** B Auckland NZ 1949 s Owen & Joyce. BA U of Auckland Nz 1969; BTh S Jn Angl Sem 1978; BS U of Auckland Nz 1979; MDiv S Jn Angl Sem 1995; PhD S Jn Angl Sem/ Auckland U 2000. Trans 2/1/1996 Bp Joe Doss. m 4/18/1998 Margaret Deacon c 2. Trin Epis Ch Vineland NJ 1997-1999; Dio New Jersey Trenton NJ 1997-1998; R Trin Epis Old Swedes Ch Swedesboro NJ 1996; Serv Ch of New Zealand 1978-1996. Intl Police Chapl Conf Untd States of Ameri 1992-1995. Hon Cn Trin Cathd 1995. safehavenpcs@aol.com

DEADERICK, Dianna LaMance (USC) 1300 Pine St, Columbia SC 29204 B Pontiac MI 1958 d Ralph & Nancy. BA Berea Coll 1980; MA U of So Carolina 1996; Sch for Mnstry 2008. D 5/21/2011 Bp W illiam Andrew Waldo. m 1/17/1981 Douglas Deaderick c 2.

DEAKLE, David Wayne (La) 4350 SE Brooklyn St, Portland OR 97206 **Ret 2005-** B Mobile AL 1955 s Jackson & Katherine. BA U of Mobile 1977; MDiv New Orleans Bapt TS 1979; MA U of New Orleans 1982; ThD New Orleans Bapt TS 1985; MA Notre Dame Sem Grad TS 1987; PhD S Louis U 1991. D 6/17/1989 P 1/18/1990 Bp James Barrow Brown. m 11/17/1979 Guadalupe Brenes. Prof of NT & Patristics Nash Nashotah WI 1992-2005; P-in-c S Ptr's Ch Northlake WI 1992-2005; Asst R S Jn's Ch Norristown PA 1989-1992. Cath Biblic Assn 1990.

DEAN BSG, Aelred B (Lex) PO, 131 Edgewood Rd, Middlesboro KY 40965 **S Mary's Epis Ch Middlesboro KY 2016-** B Peoria, Illinois 1961 s Howard & Elizabeth. Masters Valdosta St U; Masters of Div Sewanee: The U So, TS 2016. D 12/19/2015 P 6/25/2016 Bp Robert Christopher Wright. m 5/31/2011 James M Elledge. Sexton Ch Of The Epiph Atlanta GA 2007-2012. The Bro of S Greg 1992. st.marys.mboro@gmail.com

DEAN, Bobby Wayne (CGC) PO Box 1677, Santa Rosa Beach FL 32459 B Wake County NC 1938 s Hursel & Mary. BA Wstrn Carolina U 1964. D 2/10/2011 Bp Philip Menzie Duncan II. m 8/8/1981 Patricia Dean c 3.

DEAN JR, Edward Carroll (RI) St Davids Episcopal Church, 200 Meshanticut Valley Pkwy, Cranston RI 02920 B Hartford CT 1953 s Edward & Margaret. AS Cmnty Coll of the AF; BS Johnson & Wales U. D 6/11/2016 Bp W Nicholas Knisely Jr. m 11/23/1996 Martha H Lefoley c 3.

DEAN, Gordon Joy (WMass) 10 Fox Rd, Shelburne Falls MA 01370 **Trin Ch Shelburne Falls MA 2013-; Ret St Lk Epis Ch Darien CT 1995-** B Fall River MA 1932 s Arthur & Gladys. BU; BMus Bos 1954; MMus Bos 1955; MDiv EDS 1961. D 6/25/1961 Bp Anson Phelps Stokes Jr P 1/5/1962 Bp Roger W Blanchard. c 4. Chair, Prison Mnstry T/F Coun of Ch Springfield MA 2013; Vic S Jn's Ch Ashfield MA 1999-2002; Dir of Mus S Lk's Par Darien CT 1988-1995; Massachusetts Coun Of Ch Boston MA 1977-1979; R S Barn And All SS Ch Springfield MA 1973-1977; Assoc for Lay Mnstry Gr Ch Amherst MA 1969-1973; Assoc S Steph's Epis Ch And U Columbus OH 1961-1969; Chair, Dioc Revs Com, Dioc Coun Dio Wstrn Massachusetts Springfield 1976-1977; Chair, Prison Mnstry T/F Coun of Ch Springfield MA 1973-1975; Coun on Aging Amherst MA 1970-1972. Auth, "Sermon As Intervention: A Tool for Change," ACC, 1976; Auth, "Yth Culture," *Resrch Paper as Fell, Coll of Preachers*, 1967; Auth, "Theol Of Hymnal 1940," *Thesis, ETS*, 1961. Associated Parishes; ACC: Cert Practitioner; Orgnztn Dvlpmt Ntwk. Fell Coll Of Preachers 1967.

DEAN, Jay Judson (Me) 33 Baker St, Dover NH 03820 **1980-** B Ipswich MA 1930 s William & Amy. BS U of New Hampshire 1953; MDiv Ya Berk 1964; MS U of Maine 1976; DMin Bos 1980. D 6/20/1964 Bp Anson Phelps Stokes Jr P 6/12/1965 Bp Oliver L Loring. m 2/12/1981 Claire Hope Elliott c 4. Int Chr Ch Norway ME 1979-1980; P-in-c S Ann's Epis Ch Windham Windham ME 1974-1976; P-in-c S Steph The Mtyr Epis Ch Waterboro Cntr ME 1966-1974; Cur Trin Epis Ch Portland ME 1964-1965. Auth, *How Damage is Done in Name of Chr!*.

DEAN, Rebecca Anderson (SVa) 985 Huguenot Trl, Midlothian VA 23113 **D Manakin Epis Ch Midlothian VA 2007-** B Salem OR 1947 d Gene & Betty.

Dioc of No Carolina D Formation Prog Durham NC. D 6/9/2007 Bp John Clark Buchanan. m 8/26/1967 Kerry Dean c 2.

DEAN, Steve (Los) 25211 Via Tanara, Santa Clarita CA 91355 B Tacoma WA 1945 s Jay & Ruth. BS California St U 1972; MDiv Claremont TS 1998. D 6/15/1996 P 1/1/1997 Bp Chester Lovelle Talton. m 12/17/1966 Dorothy Dean c 3. Vic S Fran Of Assisi Epis Ch Simi Vlly CA 2002-2011; S Marg's Epis Ch So Gate CA 1998-2002; S Simon's Par San Fernando CA 1996-1998.

DEAN, Susan Chanda (Oly) 3714 90th Avenue SE, Mercer Island WA 98040 **Exec Dir Underhill Hse Seattle WA 2012-; Assoc S Lk's Epis Ch Renton WA 2010-** B Washington DC 1945 d John & Ruth. BA Clark U 1967; MDiv CDSP 2002. D 6/29/2002 Bp Sanford Zangwill Kaye Hampton P 1/25/2003 Bp Vincent Waydell Warner. m 6/10/1978 David Dean c 1. Exec Dir - Underhill Hse Dio Olympia Seattle 2012-2017; D/P Assoc Emm Epis Ch Mercer Island WA 2002-2004.

DE ANAYA, Nilda Lucca (PR) 2100 Washington Ave Apt 2c, Silver Spring MD 20910 B 1927 D 8/15/1982 P 2/8/1983 Bp Francisco Reus-Froylan. Dio Puerto Rico Trujillo Alto PR 1982-1997.

DEANE JR, William Boyd (Pa) 812 Lombard St, Philadelphia PA 19147 **Nonpar 1974-** B Fort Bragg NC 1947 s William & Alma. MDiv EDS; BS Oklahoma St U; PhD U of Pennsylvania. D 6/23/1973 P 3/22/1974 Bp Robert Lionne DeWitt. Auth, "The Runaway & The Law".

DEAR, Tyrrel (CFla) Po Box 668, New Smyrna FL 32170 B Hackensack NJ 1938 s Arthur & Dorothea. BS Florida St U 1960; STB GTS 1963; Ntl Profsnl Dvlpmt Prog 1974. D 6/10/1963 Bp Henry I Louttit P 12/1/1963 Bp James Loughlin Duncan. m 12/27/1958 Roxanna Dear. Int Ch Of S Dav's By The Sea Cocoa Bch FL 1997-1998; Int S Edw The Confessor Mt Dora FL 1996; Assoc Gr Epis Ch Inc Port Orange FL 1993-2010; Int Chr Ch Ft Meade FL 1990-1992; Int Ch of Our Sav Palm Bay FL 1989-1990; Owner - Fin Planner ATD & Assoc Fin Serv 1988-2009; Vic S Ptr The Fisherman Epis Ch New Smyrna FL 1987; Asst S Paul's Epis Ch New Smyrna Bch FL 1985-1986; S Jas Epis Ch Ormond Bch FL 1982-2004; Asst S Matt's So Miami FL 1978-1981; Asst S Phil's Ch Coral Gables FL 1977-1978; Comty Srvcs/ Off Dade Cnty FL METROBUS 1975-1978; R St Margarets and San Francisco de Asis Epis Ch Hialeah FL 1975-1977; Cn Dio SE Florida Miami 1969-1975; Vic Ch Of The Incarn Miami FL 1966-1969; Asst S Steph's Ch Coconut Grove Miami FL 1963-1966. Who'S Who Rel Amer 1975.

DEARING, Trevor (Oly) 4 Rock House Gardens, Radcliffe Road, Stamford PE9 1AS Great Britain (UK) **Ret 1983-** B Hull Yorkshire UK 1933 s Walter & Hilda. BD Lon GB 1956; MA U of Birmingham GB 1963. Trans 4/22/1981 Bp Robert Hume Cochrane. c 4. R S Lk's Epis Ch Seattle WA 1981-1983; Serv Ch of Engl 1961-1981. Auth, *A People of Power*; Auth, *God & Healing of the Mind*; Auth, *Its True*; Auth, *Supernatural Healing Today*; Auth, *Supernatural Superpowers*; Auth, *Total Healing*; Auth, *Wesleyan & Tractarian Wrshp*. Chapl Ord of S Lk Physcn 1996.

DEARMAN, David (Tex) 90 Island Psge, Galveston TX 77554 B Baton Rouge LA 1960 s William & Melvie. BS U So 1982; MDiv VTS 1987; MEd Mississippi Coll 1994. D 6/11/1987 P 4/28/1988 Bp James Barrow Brown. m 8/15/1981 Corey Layne Morgan c 3. Hd of Sch Trin Ch Galveston TX 2002-2017; Hd of Sch All SS' Epis Sch Morristown TN 1996-2002; Dn of Students All SS' Epis Sch Vicksburg MS 1990-1996; Chapl Chr Ch Covington LA 1987-1990. Dn Calcote Awd SW Assn of Epis Schools 2015.

DEARMAN JR, William Benjamin (NY) 7 Oakridge Pkwy, Peekskill NY 10566 **Vic Chap of S Jn the Div Tomkins Cove NY 2004-** B Lumberton MS 1926 s William & Maxie. BS Tul 1949; MDiv Epis TS of the SW 1958. D 4/9/1960 P 10/18/1960 Bp Charles Francis Hall. m 6/30/1962 Mary J Dearman c 3. Asst Mssn Epis Shared Mnstry of Rockland Cnty 1999-2008; P in charge S Jn's In The Wilderness Stony Point NY 1997-2003; Chapl S Mary's Cnvnt Peekskill NY 1974-1999; St Marys Sch Peekskill NY 1974-1977; Vic Ch Of The Epiph Lisbon Lisbon NH 1971-1973; Chapl S Mary's Sch Littleton NH 1965-1971; Vic S Dav's Ch Salem NH 1961-1965; Assoc Gr Ch Manchester NH 1959-1961.

DEASY, James Scott (Az) Epiphany Episcopal Church, 423 N Beaver St, Flagstaff AZ 86001 B Colfax WA 1950 s James & Jaine. BA DePauw U 1973; MD Indiana U 1976. D 5/5/2012 Bp Kirk Stevan Smith. m 8/5/1972 Kathy Scott Deasy c 3.

DEATON JR, Charles Milton (Miss) 1616 52nd Ct, Meridian MS 39305 **S Fran Of Assisi Ch Philadelphia MS 2016-** B Greenwood MS 1970 s Charles & Mary. BA Millsaps Coll 1992; MDiv Sewanee: The U So, TS 1997. D 5/29/1997 P 2/1/1998 Bp Alfred Marble Jr. m 5/18/1996 Jennifer Deaton Melnyk c 1. R S Ptr's By The Lake Brandon MS 2006-2013; S Paul's Epis Ch Meridian MS 2005-2006; S Jn's Ch Laurel MS 2004-2005; Asst S Aug's Epis Ch Croton Hdsn NY 2003-2004; The GTS New York NY 2002-2004; S Ptr's Ch Oxford MS 1997-2001.

DEATON, Jennifer Deaton (Miss) PO Box 23107, Jackson MS 39225 **S Andr's Cathd Jackson MS 2012-; Coordntr of Yth Mnstrs Allin Dioc Hse Jackson MS 2006-** B Heidelberg Germany 1971 d Walter & Catherine. BA Emory U 1996; MEd U of Mississippi 1999; MDiv GTS 2004. D 6/24/2004 P 2/5/2005

Bp Duncan Montgomery Gray III. m 5/18/1996 Charles Milton Deaton c 1. S Andr's Epis Sch Ridgeland MS 2007-2011; Cur S Paul's Epis Ch Meridian MS 2004-2006.

DEATRICK, George Edward (NJ) 215 Philadelphia Blvd, Sea Girt NJ 08750 **Ret Dio New Jersey 2007-** B Defiance OH 1952 s John & Alma. BA Heidelberg U 1973; MDiv SWTS 1976. D 6/19/1976 Bp John Harris Burt P 1/18/1977 Bp James Winchester Montgomery. m 9/15/2001 Jean Harden Rodgers. P-in-c Ch Of S Mk And All SS Absecon Absecon NJ 2005-2007; R S Helena's Ch Burr Ridge IL 2001-2005, Int R 1996; Int R Ch Of The Medtr Chicago IL 2000-2001; Int R The Ch Of S Uriel The Archangel Sea Girt NJ 1998-2000; Int R Bexley Seabury Fed Chicago IL 1995-1998; Dio Chicago Chicago IL 1995-1998; R St Michaels Epis Ch Wall Township NJ 1993-1995; Cn St Paul's Epis Ch Peoria IL 1992-1993; R S Jas Epis Ch Newport Newport DE 1990-1992; Vic S Dunst's Epis Ch Westchester IL 1988-1990; Int R Gr Epis Ch Hinsdale IL 1987-1988; R S Andr's Ch Downers Grove IL 1980-1987, Assoc 1978-1980; Cur The Epis Ch Of S Jas The Less Northfield IL 1976-1978. Bro Of S Andr 1982.

DEATS, Cathy (NC) 6625 Battleford Dr, Raleigh NC 27613 **Cn Dio No Carolina Raleigh NC 2016-** B Greenwich CT 1949 d William & Irene. BS U of Connecticut 1971; BS U of Connecticut 1971; MSW U of Connecticut 1977; MS U of Connecticut 1977; DSW CUNY 1990; MDiv Drew U 1996. D 6/1/1996 Bp John Shelby Spong P 12/6/1996 Bp Jack Marston Mckelvey. m 5/14/1977 Theodore L Deats c 1. Assoc S Paul's Epis Ch Cary NC 2014-2016; Ch Of The Gd Shpd Rocky Mt NC 2014; R S Jas' Epis Ch Hackettstown NJ 2001-2013; Consult Adjustment to Vision Loss Proj 2000-2010; Cur S Paul's Ch Englewood NJ 1996-2001; Psych Montclair NJ 1990-1996; Pres Stndg Com Dio Newark Newark NJ 2011-2013, Pres Stndg Com 2009-2010, Dep to GC 2008-2013, COM 1998-2004, Co-Chair Deaf Mnstry 1993-2013. CHS 1991; NASW 1976. Preaching Awd Drew Univ TS 1996; Preaching Awd Drew Univ TS 1996. cathydeats@episdionc.org

DEAVOURS, Cipher A (NJ) 112 Union St, Montclair NJ 07042 B Lebanon TN 1941 s Burns & Lucille. M.S. Applied Mathematics Br 1966; ScD U of Virginia 1969. D 6/4/2005 Bp George Edward Councell. m 6/19/2004 Lyn Headley-Deavours. D S Jn's Ch Eliz NJ 2005-2011.

DE BARY, Edward Oscar (Miss) 11 Wakefield Dr Apt 2105, Asheville NC 28803 B Antwerp Belgium 1938 s Edmond & Anne Marie. BA U So 1961; MDiv Sewanee: The U So, TS 1968; STL U of Louvain 1978; PhD U of Louvain 1983; STD U of Louvain 1984. D 6/22/1968 Bp George P Gunn P 9/21/1969 Bp David Shepherd Rose. m 5/29/1974 Marcia H De Bary. R S Paul's Ch Columbus MS 2005; Trin Ch Winchester TN 2001; S Barn Ch Tullahoma TN 1997-1998; S Bede's Epis Ch Manchester TN 1995-1996; Dir EFM Sewanee U So TS Sewanee TN 1982-2004; Vic Epis Ch Of The Incarn W Point MS 1978-1982; Ch Of The Resurr Starkville MS 1974-1976; Ch Of The Ascen Brooksville MS 1971-1976; P-in-c Ch Of The Nativ Macon MS 1971-1976; Chapl Mississippi St U 1971-1976; Asst Exec Dir Epis Radio/TV Fndt Atlanta GA 1969-1971. "Theol Reflection," Liturg Prfess, 2003; Gnrl Ed, *EFM Year 4*, 2002; Auth, "EFM," *Creative Transformation*, 2001; Gnrl Ed, *EFM Year 3*, 2001; Gnrl Ed, *EFM Year 2*, 2000; Gnrl Ed, *EFM Year 1*, 1999; Auth, "A Hist of the EFM Prog," *Sewanee Theol Revs*, 1999; Auth, "Common Lessons and Supporting Materials," *EFM*, 1998.

DEBBOLI, Walter Anthony (Ct) 80 Rockwell Ave, Plainville CT 06062 **1986-** B Troy NY 1929 s Anthony & Eleanor. BA Siena Coll 1952; MDiv Ya Berk 1955; DMin Bible Inst Sem 1979; MS U of Hartford 1983. D 5/29/1955 P 12/1/1955 Bp David Emrys Richards. Ch of our Sav Plainville CT 1960-1984; R S Ptr's Plymouth 1956-1960; Cur S Jn's Ch Larchmont NY 1955-1956; Chapl Connecticut St Police. Auth, *Systematic Phoebic Desensitization*.

DE BEER, John Michael (Mass) 2905 Wynnewood Drive, Greensboro NC 27408 **R S Mk's Epis Ch Burlington MA 2008-, R 2000-2005** B Johannesburg ZA 1945 s Charles & Sheila. BS U of Witwaterstrand ZA 1967; MA Oxf GB 1969; DMin SWTS 2005. D 12/17/1972 P 12/1/1973 Bp The Bishop Of Johannesburg. m 7/10/1970 Patricia Jean Worrell c 1. Int S Ptr's Ch Weston MA 2005-2006; R St Martins-In-The-Field Ch Severna Pk MD 1992-2005; Congrl Dvlpmt Dio SE Florida Miami 1991-1992; Int Hd of Sch S Phil's Ch Coral Gables FL 1988-1990; S Phil's Epis Sch Coral Gables FL 1988-1989; Dir of Educ for EfM Sewanee U So TS Sewanee TN 1980-1988. Auth, "The Art of Theol Reflection," Crossroad, 1994; Auth, "Until We Are Free-A Study Guide on So Afr," Friendship Press, 1988; Auth, "Everyday Theol," *Chicago Stds*, 1983. EPF.

DE BEER, Patricia Jean (Mass) 2905 Wynnewood Dr., Greensboro NC 27408 **Chapl Life Together 2011-** B Los Angeles CA 1949 d Jack & Frances. BA U CA 1971; MDiv Chicago TS 1980; Cert Shalem Inst Washington DC 1984; DMin Sewanee: The U So, TS 1990. D 4/24/1987 P 12/4/1987 Bp George Lazenby Reynolds Jr. m 7/10/1970 John Michael De Beer c 1. Int The Cathd Ch Of S Paul Boston MA 2012-2015; R The Ch Of Our Redeem Lexington MA 2005-2009; Int Ch Of Our Sav Arlington MA 2000-2010; R St Martins-In-The-Field Ch Severna Pk MD 1992-2005; Int S Phil's Ch Coral Gables FL 1988-1992; P in Charge Dio Tennessee Nashville TN 1987-1988; Chair, Cmsn of Mnstry Dio Maryland Baltimore MD 1994-2000; Bd Trst Sewanee U So TS Sewanee TN 1990-1992. Auth, "Forming a People," *Chicago TS Register*, 1980; Auth, *Plnng for Mnstry*; Auth, *Study Guide on So Afr*; Auth, *Until We Are Free*. EPF; Ord of S Lk.

DEBENHAM JR, Warren Warren (Cal) 143 Arlington Ave, Berkeley CA 94707 **Non-par 1985-** B San Francisco CO 1933 s Martin & Josephine. BA Stan 1955; BD CDSP 1958. D 6/29/1958 Bp Henry H Shires P 3/1/1959 Bp James Albert Pike. m 5/25/1957 Sally F Debenham c 3. R S Alb's Ch Albany CA 1975-1985, P-in-c 1973-1974; Vic S Thos Epis Ch Sunnyvale CA 1960-1965; Asst Trin Cathd San Jose CA 1958-1960. "Laughter On Record," Scarecrow Press, 1988.

DEBLASIO, Diane L (LI) 100 46th St, Lindenhurst NY 11757 **P-in-c S Bon Epis Ch Lindenhurst NY 2015-** B Kew Gardens NY 1960 d Charles & Joan. Long Island; LIU; The Geo Mercer, Jr. Memi TS; BS Stony Brook U 1982; MS Long Island 1987; MS Polytechnic U 1987; BA LIU 2005; LIU 2005. D 1/31/2015 P 9/12/2015 Bp Lawrence C Provenzano. c 2.

DEBOW, Rebecca Stephenson (Ala) 3519 W Lakeside Dr, Birmingham AL 35243 **S Lk's Epis Ch Birmingham AL 2006-** B Omaha NE 1955 d Ottis & Sarah. BA Huntingdon Coll 1977; MDiv Candler TS Emory U 1995. D 2/25/1995 P 8/1/1995 Bp Robert Oran Miller. m 8/29/1981 Michael Eugene DeBow c 2. R The Epis Ch Of S Fran Of Assisi Pelham AL 1996-2006; Cur S Steph's Epis Ch Birmingham AL 1995-1996.

DEBUSSY, Muriel S (NJ) 825 Summerset Dr, Hockessin DE 19707 B Scranton PA 1936 d Ellson & Virgina. AA Keystone Jr Coll 1956; BS Rutgers The St U of New Jersey 1987; MDiv GTS 1994. D 6/11/1994 Bp George Phelps Mellick Belshaw P 12/1/1994 Bp Joe Doss. m 8/6/2005 Robert Paul deBussy c 1. R S Thos' Epis Ch Glassboro NJ 2001-2005; Asst S Ptr's Ch Spotswood NJ 1994-2001.

DEBUYS III, John Forrester (Ala) 2501 Country Club Cir, Birmingham AL 35223 B Tuscaloosa AL 1966 s John & Maida. BA Hampden-Sydney Coll 1988; MDiv Sewanee: The U So, TS 2004. D 5/21/2005 P 12/13/2005 Bp Henry Nutt Parsley Jr. m 5/1/1993 Katherine DeBuys c 3. All SS Epis Ch Birmingham AL 2005-2007.

DECAMPS, Walin (Hai) **Dio Haiti Port-au-Prince HT 2003-** B 1967 D. m 4/27/2005 Marie Kenite Drouillard c 2.

DECARLEN, Marya Louise (Mass) same, Boxford MA 01921 **All SS Epis Ch of the No Shore Inc Danvers MA 2014-** B Green Bay WI 1956 d Clifford & Carla. BA Stephens Coll 1977; MDiv EDS 1983. D 6/8/1983 P 1/1/1984 Bp Walter Cameron Righter. m 2/24/2012 John Quinn c 2. R S Jas Ch Groveland Groveland MA 2003-2014; Wyman Memi Ch of St Andr Marblehead MA 1999-2003, 1992-1995; Vic S Mk's Ch Maquoketa IA 1985-1989; Asst R S Thos' Epis Ch Sioux City IA 1983-1985. mdecarlen@comcast.net

DECARVALHO, Maria Elena (RI) 18 Vassar Ave, Providence RI 02906 B Providence RI 1954 d Manuel & Mary. BA Ya 1976; MDiv Boston Coll TS and Mnstry 1990. D 6/23/1990 P 2/9/1991 Bp George Nelson Hunt III. m 10/17/1981 Ashbel Tingley Wall c 2. Dn Cathd Of S Jn Providence RI 1998-2004; Asst R Gr Ch In Providence Providence RI 1990-1996.

DE CHAMBEAU, Franck Alsid (Ct) 163 Belgo Rd, P.O. Box 391, Lakeville CT 06039 **Assoc Cler St. Marg's Ch Palm Desert CA 2004-; Assoc Cler St. Marg's Ch Palm Desert CA 2004-** B Marinette WI 1936 s Alsid & Viola. BS U of Wisconsin 1958; STB GTS 1961; MA Col 1976; EdD Col 1977. D 6/18/1961 Bp William Hampton Brady P 4/7/1962 Bp Joseph Warren Hutchens. m 11/17/2008 Richard D Spoor. Int St Thos Ch Armenia Un New York NY 2006-2007; Asst S Jn's Ch Salisbury CT 2002; Trin Ch Lakeville CT 2002; Cur S Mk's Ch Jackson Heights NY 1963-1964; Cur S Ptr's Epis Ch Cheshire CT 1961-1963. Auth, "Keeping the Corp Tall Ships Afloat," *Bus Week*; Auth, "Concrete Approaches to a Philos of Adult Lrng," *Doctoral Thesis*; Auth, "Positioning Multi-Nationals for New Global Strategies," *Leaders*. Acad of Mgmt 1985; HR Plnng Soc 1977; Strategic Mgmt Soc 1990; The Berkshire Choral Fest 2000; The Conf Bd, Orgnztn & Mgmt Coun 1982; The Grp for Strategic Orgnztn Effectiveness 1983; The Salisbury Forum 2005.

DECHAMPLAIN, Mitties (NY) 175 9th Ave, New York NY 10011 B Pasadena CA 1948 d Edgar & Caroline. AA Palomar Coll 1968; BS NWU 1970; MA NWU 1971; PhD USC 1987. D 6/10/1995 P 1/1/1996 Bp Frederick Houk Borsch. The GTS New York NY 2014-2016, 1998-2014; S Clem's Ch New York NY 2009-2014; Assoc Prof Of Homil Fuller TS CA. mittiesd@gmail.com

DECKER, Clarence Ferdinand (SO) 545 Woodsfield Dr, Columbus OH 43214 **Ret 1990-** B Taintor IA 1925 s Richard & Marie. BS Wstrn Michigan U 1950; MS MI SU 1952; PhD MI SU 1954; MDiv SWTS 1967. D 6/12/1965 Bp James Winchester Montgomery P 12/18/1965 Bp Gerald Francis Burrill. m 8/15/1948 Lucile E Decker c 2. Int Trin Ch Newark OH 1997-1998; Int S Paul's Ch Marion OH 1996-1997; Int S Paul's Ch Chillicothe OH 1992-1993; Supply P Dio Sthrn Ohio Cincinnati OH 1990-1991; Epis Ret Serv Cincinnati OH 1984-1990; Chapl Whetstone Convalescent Cntr Columbus OH 1982-1990; Ch Of S Edw Columbus OH 1982-1983; S Phil's Ch Columbus OH 1979-1981; Cur Trin Ch Highland Pk IL 1965-1967; Cmsn Higher Educ Dio Pittsburgh Pittsburgh PA 1970-1975. Auth, *arts Sci Journ*. Soc of St. Mary 1965; Soc of St. Simeon and St. Anna 1995.

DECKER, Dallas B (Haw) 18218 Paradise Mountain Rd Spc 88, Valley Center CA 92082 B Elmira NY 1939 s George & Theodora. BS SUNY 1975; Mercer TS 1977. D 6/5/1976 P 12/21/1976 Bp Jonathan Goodhue Sherman. m 8/21/1960 Cynthia P Decker c 4. Vic S Jude's Hawaiian Ocean View Ocean View HI 2008-2011; Int Ch Of The Recon Webster MA 2006-2008; Supply S Mich And All Ang Seaford NY 2000-2006; Assoc S Ann's Ch Sayville NY 1997-2000, Assoc 1990-1996; Int S Paul's Ch Glen Cove NY 1996-1997, Assoc 1995-1996; Assoc Trin Rslyn NY 1995-1996; Assoc S Thos Ch Farmingdale NY 1994-1997; R Zion Ch Douglaston NY 1987-1990; R Ch Of The H Sprt Gallup NM 1983-1987; Vic Ch Of The Gd Shpd Bridger MT 1978-1983; S Alb's Epis Ch Laurel MT 1978-1983; S Thos Ch Hardin MT 1978-1983; Vic S Mths Epis Ch Bellmore NY 1977-1978; S Paul's Ch Roosevelt NY 1977-1978; Asst S Mk's Ch Westhampton Bch NY 1976-1977. Ord Of Ascen; OHF.

DECKER, Georgia Ann (WK) 509 16th Ter, Hutchinson KS 67501 **Gr Epis Ch Hutchinson KS 2003-** B Hutchinson KS 1936 D 11/29/2003 Bp James Marshall Adams Jr. c 3.

DECKER, Linda McCullough (Haw) 307 S Alu Rd, Wailuku HI 96793 **Assoc The Par Of Gd Shpd Epis Ch Wailuku HI 2013-** B Wichita Falls, TX 1937 d Marvin & Adaline. Rad 1958; MDiv Weston Jesuit TS 1981. D 5/16/2010 P 12/4/2010 Bp Robert Leroy Fitzpatrick. m 12/30/1957 John A Decker c 1.

DECKER, Margaret Sharp (SanD) 1651 S Juniper St Unit 26, Escondido CA 92025 **R Trin Ch Escondido CA 1995-, Cur 1990-1993; Dioc Corp Dio San Diego San Diego CA 2005-** B Reno NV 1962 d Milton & Beverly. BA U of Nevada at Reno 1984; MDiv CDSP 1990. D 5/1/1990 P 11/15/1990 Bp Stewart Clark Zabriskie. c 1. Asst S Dunst's Epis Ch San Diego CA 1993-1995.

DECKER, Prince A (WA) 3918 Wendy Ln, Silver Spring MD 20906 **Ch Of The Epiph Washington DC 2012-** B Freetown Sierra Leone 1952 s Jonathan & Millicent. Mindolo Ecumenical Coll; HNDIP London Inst of Commerce 1975; Fbc U of Sierra Leone 1980. Trans 1/3/2005 Bp John Bryson Chane. m 12/29/1984 Kadi Decker c 3. Calv Ch Washington DC 2007-2012; S Paul's Rock Creek Washington DC 2005-2007. calvary.episcopaldc@verizon.net

DECOSS, Donald Albion (Cal) 26 Overlake Ct, Oakland CA 94611 **Ret 1990-** B Oakland CA 1920 s Bertram & Alma. Golden Gate U. D 12/24/1960 Bp James Albert Pike. m 10/3/1947 Catherine Francis Scheimer c 1. D/Asst S Clem's Ch Berkeley CA 1962-1989; S Anne's Ch Fremont CA 1960-1962; D/Asst S Jn's Epis Ch Oakland CA 1960-1962.

DEDDE, Joseph Colin (WNY) 233 Brantwood Rd, Amherst NY 14226 **Ret Buffalo NY 2001-** B Mount Kisco NY 1939 s Joseph & Grace. AS Dn Coll 1960; BA Juniata Coll 1963; MDiv Ya Berk 1966. D 6/4/1966 P 12/1/1966 Bp Horace W B Donegan. m 12/31/1966 Cynthia Margaret Kirby. R S Mich And All Ang Buffalo NY 1977-2001; R S Mk's Epis Ch Yonkers NY 1969-1977; Asst S Mary's Ch Mohegan Lake NY 1967-1969; Cur Gr Ch In Providence Providence RI 1966-1967. Cwc.

DEDEAUX JR, James Terrell (Miss) 5303 Diamondhead Cir, Diamondhead MS 39525 B Riverside CA 1954 s James & Guadalupe. MA U of Sthrn Mississippi 1978; MA U of Sthrn Mississippi 1989. D 1/11/2014 Bp Duncan Montgomery Gray III. m 6/24/2005 Ella H DeDeaux c 3.

DEDMON JR, Robert Aaron (Chi) 1804 Sycamore Circle, Manchester TN 37355 **Chair, Com to Reorganize Dio Quincy Peoria IL 2009-, Stndg Com 2006-2008** B Dyersburg TN 1947 s Robert & Mary. BA Un U Jackson TN 1969; MA U of Tennessee 1970; PhD U of Tennessee 1975; MDiv Sewanee: The U So, TS 1982. D 6/20/1982 P 4/20/1983 Bp William Evan Sanders. m 8/30/1969 Judy S Dedmon c 3. Dn And R St Paul's Epis Ch Peoria IL 2005-2014; Cn To Ordnry Dio Tennessee Nashville TN 1994-2005, 1983-1988; R S Mk's Ch Antioch TN 1989-1994; Vic S Bede's Epis Ch Manchester TN 1983-1986; D S Paul's Epis Ch Chattanooga TN 1982-1983; Trst Sewanee U So TS Sewanee TN 1982-1987. Auth, "Job As Holocaust Survivor," *S Lk Journ Of Theol*, 1984.

DEERY, Laurel Pierson (Mass) 44 School St, Manchester MA 01944 **Math Tchr Tower Sch MA 1986-2996** B Stamford CT 1948 BA Buc 1970; MEd U of New So Wales 1986. D 6/3/2006 Bp M(Arvil) Thomas Shaw. m 1/24/1970 Craig Deery c 2.

DEETHS, Margaret Edith (Cal) 576 Cedarberry Ln, San Rafael CA 94903 B London England 1934 d George & Edith. BA Sch for Deacons 2003. D 12/6/2003 Bp William Edwin Swing. c 3. D Gr Cathd San Francisco CA 2003-2011.

DEETS, Sherry (Pa) 2717 Shelburne Road, Downingtown PA 19335 **The Widows Corp Philadelphia PA 2014-; Police Chapl Coatesville City Police Dept Coatesville PA 2004-; R The Ch Of The Trin Coatesville PA 2003-** B Hanover PA 1964 d Barry & Nancy. AS Brandywine Coll 1984; BS Widener U 1990; MDiv GTS 2002; MS Neumann U 2011. D 6/22/2002 P 5/31/2003 Bp Charles Ellsworth Bennison Jr. m 10/8/2011 Stuart Curtis Nelson Deets c 1. Dio Pennsylvania Philadelphia PA 2002-2003, Stndg Com 2012-.

DEETZ, Susan Maureen (Minn) 4210 Robinson St, Duluth MN 55804 B 1955 D 6/17/2001 Bp James Louis Jelinek. m 6/23/1978 William Harold Deetz c 3. The Par of St Paul's Epis Ch Duluth MN 2001-2004.

DE FONTAINE-STRATTON, James Bruce (NY) 161 Mansion St, Poughkeepsie NY 12601 B Farnborough Kent UK 1932 s Eric & Winifred. Cert London St

Mk & St Jn 1959; Cert London St Mk & St Jn 1965; BA London Univ Golsmiths Coll 1971; Dip London Univ Inst of Educ 1972; MA Col TC NYC 1975; MEd Columbia Univercity TC NYC 1977. D 1/14/1979 P 1/16/1980 Bp Charles Lee Burgreen. m 10/1/1967 Dorothy Elaine De Fontaine-Stratton c 3. Int P S Lk's Ch Somers NY 2005-2006; Dio New York New York NY 1998-2004, Dn 1993-1994; P-in-c S Paul's Ch Poughkeepsie NY 1998-2004; Int Ch Of The Gd Shpd Wakefield Bronx NY 1997-1998; Ch Of The H Nativ Bronx NY 1990-1994, Asst 1982-1983; Chapl Montefiore Med Cntr NY 1990-1994; S Steph's Epis Ch Woodlaw Bronx NY 1988-1990; S Hilda's And S Hugh's Sch New York NY 1985-1988; S Hilda & S Hugh Sch NY 1982-1988; Assoc Ch Of The Atone Bronx NY 1982-1983; Assoc The Epis Ch of S Jn the Div Tamuning GU 1980-1982; Dio Micronesia Tumon Bay GU 1979-1982; Chapl S Jn's Sch Agana GU 1979-1982.

DEFOOR II, Allison (Fla) 325 N Market St, Jacksonville FL 32202 **Cn Dio Florida Jacksonville 2015-** B Coral Gables FL 1953 s James & Marjorie. BA U of So Florida 1976; JD Stetson U Coll of Law 1979; MA U of So Florida 1979; MDiv Florida Cntr for Theol Stds 2001; DMin Florida Cntr for Theol Stds 2005. D 9/9/2006 P 3/6/2007 Bp Leo Frade. m 1/27/2017 Randle P DeFoor c 6. Asst Pstr Gr Mssn Ch Tallahassee FL 2013-2015; Chapl Wakula Correctional Inst Crawfordville FL 2007-2015. STD Florida Cntr for Theol Stds 1999. adefoor@diocesefl.org

DEFOREST, John William (Tex) 3535 Whittaker Ln, Beaumont TX 77706 B Sewanee TN 1946 s John & Anne. BS SW U Georgetown TX 1969; MA U of Houston 1972; MDiv VTS 1996. D 6/22/1996 Bp Claude Edward Payne P 1/6/1997 Bp William Elwood Sterling. m 8/30/1969 Nancy P Van Kleef c 2. Int R S Jas Epis Ch Houston TX 2007-2008; Int R S Chris's Ch Houston TX 2005-2007; P-t Supply H Trin Epis Ch Dickinson TX 2005; Chapl S Lk's Epis Hosp 2004-2005; S Lk's Epis Hosp Houston TX 2004-2005; R S Jn's Ch La Porte TX 2003-2004; Vic Ch Of The Incarn Houston TX 1998-2003; The Great Cmsn Fndt Houston TX 1998-2003; Asst R S Steph's Epis Ch Houston TX 1996-1998.

DEFOREST, Nancy P (Tex) 3535 Whittaker Ln, Beaumont TX 77706 B Minneapolis MN 1948 d William & Alfhild. U of Texas 1967; BS U of Houston 1970; MS U of Houston Clear Lake 1978; MDiv VTS 1996. D 6/22/1996 Bp Claude Edward Payne P 1/6/1997 Bp William Elwood Sterling. m 8/30/1969 John William Deforest c 2. R S Steph's Ch Beaumont TX 2008-2016; S Lk's Epis Hosp Houston TX 2007-2008; Chapl St. Lk's Epis Hosp 2007-2008; Chapl/Bp's Fell St. Lk's Epis Hosp Houston TX 2007-2008; S Ptr's Epis Ch Brenham TX 2007; Asst R S Jn The Div Houston TX 1996-2006.

DE FRANCO JR, Peter (Nwk) 396 Clifton Ave, Clifton NJ 07011 **R S Ptr's Ch Clifton NJ 2005-** B Paterson NJ 1952 s Peter & Gisella. BA Don Bosco Coll 1975; MDiv Drew U 2002; GTS 2002. D 5/31/2003 Bp John Palmer Croneberger P 12/6/2003 Bp Rufus T Brome. m 12/29/2015 Carl Alan Gincley. Gr Ch Nutley NJ 2004-2005; Assoc for Chr Formation Gr Ch Madison NJ 2003-2004.

DEFRIEST, Jeannette (Chi) 400 Main St Apt 5A, Evanston IL 60202 **R S Lk's Ch Evanston IL 2006-, P-in-c 2004-; Dep GC Dio Newark Newark NJ 2003-** B Pasadena CA 1956 d J & M. California St Polytechnic U; MDiv EDS 1988; Cert The Ch Dvlpmt Inst 1998; DMin SWTS 2004; Cert Kellogg Sch of Mgmt 2011. D 12/22/1990 P 6/22/1991 Bp Daniel Lee Swenson. m 7/15/2011 Diane R Todd. Adj. Fac SWTS Evanston IL 2006-2010; R Ch Of The Mssh Chester NJ 2002-2004; Asst R S Lk's Epis Ch Montclair NJ 1991-1993; Alum Exec Com EDS Cambridge MA 1993-2004.

DEGAVRE, Susan Williams (Va) 7120 S. Wenatchee Way Unit C, Aurora CO 80016 **Trst, Treas Colorado Epis Fndt Denver CO 2009-** B San Antonio TX 1942 d William & Hazel. BA Randolph-Macon Coll 1963; MDiv VTS 1991. D 6/15/1991 Bp Peter J Lee P 1/12/1992 Bp Frank Harris Vest Jr. c 3. Int S Steph's Epis Ch Aurora CO 2007-2008; Int S Jas Epis Ch Essex Jct VT 2004-2007; Assoc Ch Of S Jn The Evang Hingham MA 2001-2004; R Imm Ch King and Queen Courthouse VA 1997-2001; R S Jn's Ch W Point VA 1997-2000; Assoc R S Thos' Ch Whitemarsh Ft Washington PA 1996-1997; Asst R Estrn Shore Chap Virginia Bch VA 1991-1996.

DEGENHARDT, Terri Walker (Ga) St Michael's Episcopal Church, 515 S Liberty St, Waynesboro GA 30830 B Washington DC 1959 d Ralph & Elisabet. BA Augusta Coll 1981; MEd Augusta Coll 1987. D 9/30/2009 Bp Henry Irving Louttit P 5/13/2017 Bp Scott Anson Benhase. m 11/23/2004 Walter Perkins Degenhardt c 1.

DEGIORGIS, Richard John (NCal) **Died 1/12/2017** D 6/6/2015 P 9/29/2016 Bp Barry Leigh Beisner.

DEGOOYER, Bruce Underwood (Haw) 2816 Greenfield Rd, Bloomington IL 61704 **Trin Ch By The Sea Kihei HI 2016-; Asstg P S Matt's Epis Ch Bloomington IL 2012-, Asstg D 2004-2012** B Fort Leavenworth KS 1952 s Louis & Mary. BA WA SU 1974; MPA The Evergreen St Coll 1986; Olympia TS 1993. D 6/29/2004 Bp Peter Hess Beckwith P 10/4/2012 Bp Daniel Hayden Martins. m 10/9/1976 Sylvia Hoffman c 2. No Amer Assoc. for the Diac 2004.

DE GRAVELLES, Charles Nattons (La) 3651 Broussard St, Baton Rouge LA 70808 B Lafayette LA 1949 s Charles & Mary. BA LSU 1971. D 6/10/1995 Bp James Barrow Brown. m 12/19/1970 Angela Margaret De Gravelles c 3. Epis HS Baton Rouge Baton Rouge LA 2002-2016.

DEGWECK, Stephen William (Ala) 1336 Round Hill Rd, Birmingham AL 35216 B Staten Island NY 1949 s William & Elaine. BA Wag 1970; MDiv Trin Luth Sem 1975; DMin GTF 1988. D 6/13/1992 P 1/8/1993 Bp Robert Oran Miller. m 3/30/1972 Dawn Louise Asquith c 2. Assoc S Lk's Epis Ch Birmingham AL 2004-2015; R S Mk's Ch Prattville AL 1996-2004; Chapl Off Of Bsh For ArmdF New York NY 1992-1996; Chapl USAF 1978-1996; Serv H Trin Luth Ch Falls CH VA 1975-1978.

DEHART, Benjamin Robert (NY) Calvary and St George, 61 Gramercy Park N Fl 2, New York NY 10010 **Calv and St Geo New York NY 2014-** B Red Bank NJ 1985 s Robert & Lisa. BA Grove City Coll 2008; MDiv TESM 2012. D 6/15/2013 P 1/11/2014 Bp Dorsey McConnell. Chapl Dio Pittsburgh Pittsburgh PA 2014; Ch Of The Nativ Pittsburgh PA 2013-2014; Trin Cathd Pittsburgh PA 2012-2013.

DEHART, Elsa Arp (Ak) St James the Fisherman, PO Box 1668, Kodiak AK 99615 B Davenport IA 1958 d August & Mary. MS U of Alaska 2005; DNP U of Massachusetts 2013. D 10/20/2012 Bp Mark A Lattime. m 4/9/1979 Steven Lloyd DeHart c 4.

DEHART, Steven Darrell (Mont) D 6/26/2016 Bp Charles Franklin Brookhart Jr.

DEHETRE, Donna (Chi) 31 Edgehill Rd, New Haven CT 06511 B Washington DC 1941 d William & Mildred. BA Wheaton Coll 1962; MDiv SWTS 1980. D 6/15/1981 Bp James Winchester Montgomery P 11/19/1983 Bp Quintin Ebenezer Primo Jr. m 12/22/2005 Claudia R Libertin c 3. Ch Of S Jn By The Sea W Haven W Haven CT 2001-2003; No Cntrl Reg Mnstry Enfield CT 1997; Assoc S Thos's Ch New Haven CT 1996-2001; Int Ch Of The H Fam Lake Villa IL 1990-1994; Int S Chad Epis Ch Loves Pk IL 1989-1990; Int S Bride's Epis Ch Oregon IL 1988-1989; Asst The Epis Ch Of S Jas The Less Northfield IL 1981-1986; Asst To Dir Field Educ Bexley Seabury Fed Chicago IL 1981-1983. AAPC 1990.

DEHLER, Debra Rae (Ind) St Albans Episcopal Church, 4601 N Emerson Ave, Indianapolis IN 46226 **S Alb's Ch Indianapolis IN 2016-** B Minneapolis MN 1962 d Darwin & Nancy. AA Normandale Cmnty Coll 1982; BA Winona St U 1985; MDiv Untd TS 2015; MDiv Untd TS 2015. D 6/26/2014 P 6/20/2015 Bp Brian N Prior. m 5/9/1987 Jeffrey A Dehler c 2. rector@st-albans.org

DEJARDIN, Wisnel (Hai) **Dio Haiti Port-au-Prince HT 2009-** B Hinche Haiti 1977 BTh Seminaire de Theologie EEH 2007. D 11/1/2009 P 6/29/2010 Bp Jean Zache Duracin.

DE JESUS, Gerardo James (CFla) 6316 Matchett Rd, Orlando FL 32809 B New York City 1958 s Frank & Blanca. BA The Kings Coll 1980; MDiv Fuller TS 1984; PhD TS at Claremont 2007. D 1/16/2014 P 7/20/2014 Bp Gregory Orrin Brewer. m 2/1/2015 Lourdes De Jesus. S Mary Of The Ang Epis Ch Orlando FL 2014-2016.

DE JESUS-JIMENEZ, Justo (PR) Parroquia Santo Nombre de Jesus, 806 Calle Jesus T Pineiro, Ponce PR 00728 Puerto Rico **Dio Puerto Rico Trujillo Alto PR 2014-** B 1956 s Felix & Francisca. Maestria Mstr Alta Gerencia; Certificado de Estudio Anglicano San Pedro y San Pablo. Rec 6/14/2014 as Priest Bp Wilfrido Ramos-Orench. m 12/10/1994 Julie Burnep c 2.

DE JESUS LAGARES, Jose Joaquin (DR) **Dio The Dominican Republic (Iglesia Epis Dominicana) Gazcue Santo Domingo 2014-** B 1975 s Bernardo & Ysabel. Licenciado Sagrada Teogia Centro de Estudios Teologicos; Licenciado Potificia Universidad; Especilista UTE. D 2/16/2014 P 2/15/2015 Bp Julio Cesar Holguin-Khoury. m 6/19/2015 Monica Yanirisdel Carmen Encarnacion.

DEJOHN, Kathleen Ann Gillespie (NJ) 138 Rector St, Perth Amboy NJ 08861 **D S Ptr's Ch Perth Amboy NJ 1998-** B Perth Amboy NJ 1951 d William & Audrey. Allentown Hosp Sch of Nrsng 1972. D 10/31/1998 Bp Joe Doss. m 6/9/1973 Gennaro De John.

DE KAY, Charles Augustus (Chi) 901 Forest Avenue 1E, Evanston IL 60202 **R S Matt's Ch Evanston IL 2011-** B New York NY 1963 s George & Mary. New Sch U; Vas; BA Tem 1988; MDiv SWTS 2004. D 6/19/2004 Bp Carolyn Tanner Irish P 12/18/2004 Bp Bill Persell. m 9/18/2004 Christina Teresa Padilla c 3. R Trin Epis Ch Aurora IL 2006-2011; Cur The Epis Ch Of S Jas The Less Northfield IL 2004-2006.

DEKKER, Robert Peter (Chi) 15145 Smarty Jones Drive, Noblesville IN 46060 B Sheboygan WI 1944 s Peter & Bernice. BA California St U Los Angeles 1972; MEd California St U SB 1979; MA Claremont TS 1986. D 6/22/1986 Bp Robert Claflin Rusack P 1/17/1987 Bp Oliver Bailey Garver Jr. m 6/29/1968 Helen Dekker c 1. Dn - Elgin Dnry Dio Chicago Chicago IL 2008-2011, Dn - Elgin Dnry 1996-2008, Mem at Lg 1995-1998, Mem, COM 2003-2011; R S Simons Ch Arlington Hts IL 1991-2011; Asst R All SS-By-The-Sea Par Santa Barbara CA 1988-1991; Cur St Gregorys Epis Ch Long Bch CA 1986-1988. Ord of H Cross, Assoc 2003.

DE LA CRUZ, Luis Manuel (CFla) 1709 N John Young Pkwy, Kissimmee FL 34741 **S Jn's Epis Ch Of Kissimme Kissimmee FL 2015-** B La Vega DR 1950 s Luis & Maria. Rec 7/27/2014 as Priest Bp Gregory Orrin Brewer. m 3/17/1990 Ramona Antonia Perez c 3.

DELAFIELD, Audrey Sawtelle (Me) 32 Ship Channel Rd, South Portland ME 04106 B Boston MA 1941 d Egerton & Muriel. AA Bradford Jr Coll 1962; BA McGill U 1964. D 5/20/1988 Bp Edward Cole Chalfant. m 11/27/1965 Joseph Livingston Delafield c 3. Epis Chapl Maine Med Cntr Portland ME 1989-2006; D S Alb's Ch Cape Eliz ME 1988-2000.

DELAMATER, Joan (Minn) 6287 Crackleberry Trl, Woodbury MN 55129 **Bd Mem Epis Hse of Pryr Collegeville MN 2011-** B Cadillac MI 1953 d James & Mariette. BA S Cathr U 1975; MA U of St Thos 1977; MDiv SWTS 2001; MDiv Untd TS of the Twin Cities 2001. D 12/20/2001 P 6/20/2002 Bp James Louis Jelinek. m 9/22/1979 James R Delamater c 2. S Anne's Epis Ch S Paul MN 2015-2016; Assoc S Jn In The Wilderness S Paul MN 2004-2012; Assoc Ch Of The Ascen Stillwater MN 2002-2004; Bd Mem Epis Cmnty Serv Minneapolis MN 2002-2004; COM Bd Mem Dio Minnesota Minneapolis MN 2003-2009. The OSL 2002.

DELANCEY, Mary Louise (CFla) 510 SE Broadway St, Ocala FL 34471 **D Gr Epis Ch Of Ocala Ocala FL 2012-** B Poughkeepsie NY 1947 d Raymond & Louise. BSN U of the St of New York 1981; MS San Francisco St U 1989; Cert Inst for Chr Stds 2010; Cert Other 2010. D 12/8/2012 Bp Gregory Orrin Brewer. marydelancey@gmail.com

DE LANEROLLE, Nihal Chandra (Ct) 500 Prospect St Apt 2-F, New Haven CT 06511 **Chapl In Res Epis Ch At Ya New Haven CT 2002-** B Colombo LK 1945 s Leslie & May. BS U of Ceylon Colombo Lk 1967; PhD U of Sussex 1972; BA U of Cambridge 1974; MA U of Cambridge 1981. D 5/31/1977 Bp Philip Frederick McNairy P 7/11/1978 Bp Robert Marshall Anderson. Middlesex Area Cluster Mnstry Higganum CT 2000-2012, 1996-1998; P S Paul And S Jas New Haven CT 1987-1993; P S Matt's Epis Ch Minneapolis MN 1977-1978. Dsc U Of Sussex 1995.

DELANEY, Conrad Todd (WA) B Jackson TN 1971 s Conrad & Ann. BA Un U 1999; MDiv Memphis TS 2007. D 7/26/2015 P 8/6/2016 Bp James Beattie Magness. m 10/12/2013 Heather Melendez DeLaney c 3.

DELANEY, James William (Nwk) 26 Prescott Rd, Ho Ho Kus NJ 07423 **Died 2/ 12/2016** B Passaic NJ 1928 d John & Vera. BBA Pace U 1951. D 12/21/1975 Bp Leland Stark. m 12/12/2016 Janet Kirwan Delaney c 1. Gr Epis Ch Westwood NJ 1988-2016; D Ch Of The H Comm Paterson NJ 1975-1990.

DELANEY, Mary Joan (Az) 5611E Alta Vista St, Tucson AZ 85712 **Assoc Gr S Paul's AZ 2006-** B Faribault MN 1931 d Hobson & Marguerite. BA California St U 1980; MA Azusa Pacific U 1982; MDiv Fuller TS 1992. D 6/13/1992 Bp Chester Lovelle Talton P 1/1/1993 Bp Frederick Houk Borsch. m 4/19/1952 Daniel Delaney c 7. Assoc S Andrews Par 2004-2005; Assoc S Jn's Cathd Denver CO 1996-2013; Assoc Ch Of Our Sav Par San Gabr CA 1992-1993.

DELANEY, Mary Timothea Kathleen (EMich) 1038 W Center St, Alma MI 40001 B Detroit MI 1937 d George & Dorothy. BSN U of Detroit Mercy 1961; MSN Wayne 1972; PhD NWU 1991; Cert Theol Stud SWTS 2002. D 5/4/2002 P 11/2/2002 Bp Edwin Max Leidel Jr. R S Jn's Epis Ch Alma MI 2005-2009; Chr Epis Ch E Tawas MI 2002-2005; P-in-c Leap Harrisville MI 2002-2005; P-in-c S Andrews-By-The-Lake Epis Ch Harrisville MI 2002-2005.

DELANEY, Michael F (NY) 191 Kensington Road, Garden City NY 11530 **Asst Cathd Of The Incarn Garden City NY 2014-** B Jersey City NJ 1957 s Keiran & Marie. BA Seton Hall U 1994; MDiv UTS 1998. Trans 9/29/2003 Bp John Palmer Croneberger. Dio Long Island Garden City NY 2015; Int Dn/R Trin And S Phil's Cathd Newark NJ 2013-2014; R S Andr's Epis Ch Staten Island NY 2001-2013; Chapl Chr Hosp Jersey City NJ 1999-2001; Dir Pstr Care Chr Hosp Jersey City NJ 1999-2001; P-in-c S Ptr's Ch Washington NJ 1998-1999. Co-Auth, "Rel Educ," *Exploring the Pathways of Faith*, Brown-Roa, 1997. Natl Assn of Pstr Mus 1977. mdelaney@incarnationgc.org

DELANEY, Ryan Ray (Alb) 340 S Elm St, Oconomowoc WI 53066 B Tomah WI 1976 s Leo & Valerie. Fox Vlly Tech Coll 1995; U of Wisconsin - Stevens Point 1995; MDiv Nash 2014. D 10/25/2013 Bp William Howard Love. m 2/ 19/2000 Melanie M Delaney c 2. Dio Albany Greenwich NY 2014.

DE LA TORRE, Carlos Enrique (Ct) **Dio Connecticut Meriden CT 2015-** B 1990 s Juan & Adelaida. BA Manhattanville Coll 2012; MDiv VTS 2015. D 4/ 16/2015 P 11/21/2015 Bp Ian Theodore Douglas.

DE LA TORRE, William Jhon (SwFla) 8271 52nd St N, Pinellas Park FL 33781 **S Giles Ch Pinellas Pk FL 2015-; S Mary's Epis Ch Palmetto FL 2015-** B Peru 1956 s Manuel & Elizabeth. BA U Mayor de San Marcos 1980; MA Ministerio de Educacion 1982; MDiv Centro de Estudios Teologicos 2006. D 10/ 4/2007 Bp Julio Cesar Holguin-Khoury P 3/3/2013 Bp Dabney Tyler Smith. m 10/30/1978 Zully Andrea De la Torre c 3.

DELAURA, Gilbert Frank (Alb) Church of the Messiah, 296 Glen St, Glens Falls NY 12801 B Rockville Centre NY 1946 s Gil & Frances. BBA Marq 1968; MA S Louis U Grad Sch 1970; JD Duquesne U Sch of Law 1982. D 6/2/2012 Bp William Howard Love.

DELAUTER, Joseph Halvor (CPa) 598 Longbarn Rd, State College PA 16803 **D S Andr's Ch St Coll PA 2005-** B State College PA 1945 s Joseph & Lettie. BS Penn 1976. D 9/19/2005 Bp Michael Whittington Creighton. m 12/22/1965 Sandra DeLauter c 2. Soc of Cert Sr Advisors 2011.

DE LA VARS, Gordon (Md) 115 S Erie St, Mayville NY 14757 **Ch Of The Trsfg Braddock Heights MD 2012-** B Elyria OH 1950 s Gordon & Elizabeth. BS Kent St U 1974; MA U of Akron 1980; PhD OH SU 1985; MDiv Bex Sem 1998. D 6/6/1998 P 12/19/1998 Bp David Charles Bowman. m 5/27/2006 Barbara Baxter. S Paul's Epis Ch Mayville NY 1999-2012; R Chap Of The Gd Shpd Chautauqua NY 1999; Ch Of The Adv Buffalo NY 1998-1999. Auth, "Testament Of Yth"; Auth, "Heritage Restored: Franciscanism In The Angl Comm". Conf On Chrsnty & Lit. fr.gordoncott@gmail.com

DEL BENE, Ronald Norman (Ala) 2841 Floyd Bradford Rd, Trussville AL 35173 **Sprtl Dir The Hemitage 1980-** B Warren OH 1942 s Donald & Virginia. BA Gannon U 1963; MA Marq 1966; Sewanee: The U So, TS 1979; DMin U of Creation Sprtlty Oakland CA 2002. D 3/9/1979 P 12/11/1979 Bp Emerson Paul Haynes. m 7/6/1968 Eleanor M Del Bene c 2. Int Chr Ch Cathd Cincinnati OH 2010-2013; Int Gr - S Lk's Ch Memphis TN 2008-2010; Int S Mary's Cathd Memphis TN 2006-2007; Int Ch Of The H Comm Memphis TN 2005-2006; Int The Chap Of The Cross Madison MS 2004-2005; Int All SS Epis Ch Birmingham AL 2002-2004; R S Mich's Epis Ch Birmingham AL 1996-2002; Exec S Lk's Epis Ch Birmingham AL 1988-1992; Mssnr Dio Alabama Birmingham 1987-1990; R H Cross Trussville AL 1980-1986; Asst S Bon Ch Sarasota FL 1979-1980. Auth, *Into the Light*, Wipf&Stock, 2007; Auth, *Alone w God*, Wipf&Stock, 2005; Auth, *Hunger of the Heart*, Wipf&Stock, 2005; Auth, *The Breath of Life*, Wipf&Stock, 2005.

DEL CASTILLO, Gloria R (Cal) 622 Lois Lane, El Sobrante CA 94803 B 1950 d Jorge & Berthina. BA U Fed erico Villarreal 1975; MA U Federico Villarreal 1977; BS Contra Costa Coll 1984; CDSP 1996; BTh The Sch for Deacons 1996. D 6/6/1998 P 12/5/1998 Bp William Edwin Swing. Chr Ch Cathd Indianapolis IN 2014; Dio California San Francisco CA 2012-2014; Vic Iglesia Epis Del Buen Samaritano San Francisco CA 2002-2011.

DELCUZE, Mark Stewart (Eas) 623 Cloverfields Dr, Stevensville MD 21666 **P-in-c Chr Ch Par Kent Island Stevensville MD 2013-** B Quantico VA 1958 s Godfrey & Patricia. BA U of Virginia 1980; MDiv EDS 1985. D 6/5/1985 P 1/ 6/1986 Bp Robert Poland Atkinson. m 9/10/1983 Mary Jerome c 2. R S Jn's Ch Beverly MA 2010-2013; R S Steph's Ch Ridgefield CT 2005-2010; Assoc Estrn Shore Chap Virginia Bch VA 1997-2005; R Ch Of The Ascen Norfolk VA 1992-1997; Asst R Gr Ch Kilmarnock VA 1989-1992; Chapl Reynolds Memi Hosp Glen Dale WV 1986-1989; R Trin Ch Moundsville WV 1986-1989; Asst R Trin Ch Parkersburg WV 1985-1986. frmark@ccpki.org

DELEERY, Seth Mabry (Tex) 9002 Clithea Cv, Austin TX 78759 B Galveston,TX 1946 s Joseph & Mildred. BA U of Houston 1969; MDiv Epis TS of the SW 1974; MS U of Houston 1980; ThM Harvard DS 1990. D 6/19/ 1974 Bp Scott Field Bailey P 6/18/1975 Bp James Milton Richardson. m 11/ 14/1992 Elizabeth Deleery c 2. R S Richard's Of Round Rock Round Rock TX 1993-2004; Cn To Ordnry Dio Texas Houston TX 1991-1993; The Great Cmsn Fndt Houston TX 1991-1993, 1981-1989; Chapl U Of Texas Austin 1984-1989; Vic S Jn's Epis Ch Austin TX 1981-1984; R S Mich's Ch La Marque TX 1978-1981; Locten Trin Ch Houston TX 1977-1978; Mssy Iran 1976-1977; Trin Ch Jacksonville TX 1976-1977; Dio Iran New York NY 1976; Asst S Mart's Epis Ch Houston TX 1974-1976. Auth, "Chr Socialist Mvmt In Engl 1848-1854". Hal Perry Awd Epis TS 2004.

DE LEEUW, Gawain (NY) 95 Ralph Ave, White Plains NY 10606 **Epis Chapl Manhattanville Coll Purchase NY 2003-; R S Barth's Ch In The Highland White Plains NY 2001-** B Rochester NY 1969 s Hendrik & Shreela. BA Ob 1991; MDiv U Chi DS 1995; CAS GTS 1996; DMin SWTS 2010. D 12/9/ 1995 P 6/15/1996 Bp William George Burrill. Cur Gr Ch White Plains NY 1998-2001; Assoc P Santa Rosa Mssn at Gr Ch White Plains NY 1998-2001; Vic Angl Cathd Seoul Korea 1996-1998. Auth, "Counting Treasures," *Volume 89*, ATR, 2007. Affirming Catholicism; OA 2012; SBL; Soc of Cath Priests 2011. Wm Coolidge Awd Cross Currents 2013; Afr Amer Art Lifetime Achievement Awd Howard Univerity 2012; Luce Schlr Henry Luce Schlr 1996.

DELEUSE, Betsey W (Me) 27 Arlington St. Unit 1, Portland ME 04101 B Lexington KY 1936 d Newell & Gertrude. BA Hartwick Coll 1958; EFM The U So Sch of Theoloby 1999. D 12/1/2001 Bp Chilton Richardson Knudsen. c 3. Chapl, Mercy Hosp Dio Maine 2004-2011; D Cathd Ch Of S Lk Portland ME 2001-2011; Cler Mem, Com on H Ord Dio Maine Portland ME 2001-2011.

DELFS SSG, Carin Bridgit (SO) 11 Rosemary Run, Delaware OH 43015 B Holyoke MA 1944 d Bernard & Ruth. Hudson Vlly Cmnty Coll; BA Salem Coll Winston-Salem NC 2002; MDiv Wake Forest U 2005. D 10/10/1994 Bp David Standish Ball P 10/29/2005 Bp Michael B Curry. c 2. Int Harcourt Par Gambier OH 2014-2015; Asst S Ptr's Epis Ch Delaware OH 2011-2014; Vic S Paul's Ch Louisburg NC 2007-2010; Dio No Carolina Raleigh NC 2005-2007, D Asst 2001-2002; P Asst Winston-Salem Area Colleges Mnstry Winston Salem NC 2005-2007; Asst S Paul's Epis Ch Winston Salem NC 2002-2007; Asst S Anne's Ch Winston Salem NC 1999-2000; Asst Cathd Of All SS Albany NY 1997-1998; Asst S Paul's Epis Ch Albany NY 1994-1997. Odk 2001; SSG/ The Sis of S Greg 1999; Theta Alpha Kappa Natl hon Soc For Rel Stds 2002.

DELGADO, Joseph Anthony (Cal) 2220 Cedar St, Berkeley CA 94709 **P All Souls Par In Berkeley Berkeley CA 2012-** B Guam 1962 s Jose & Anita. Psycholodgy/Philos St Jos's Coll Sem 1989; MDiv St Pat's Sem 1994. Rec 12/1/2012 as Priest Bp Marc Handley Andrus. m 11/1/2008 Michael E Lemaire.

DELGADO-MARKSMAN, Adams Felipe (Ve) **Dio Venezuela Caracas 2004-** B 1957 D P. m 5/12/1994 Antonia Francisco de Delgado.

DELGADO-MILLER, Diego (NY) 260 W 231st St, Bronx NY 10460 **Hisp Vic H Trin 1990-** B 1944 s Mario & Amanda. Inst Comercial 1962; Jr Coll 1966; Universidad Autonoma De Santo Domingo Santo Domingo Do 1969; NYTS 1982; Inst Pstrl Hispano 1986. D 11/23/1987 Bp Paul Moore Jr P 11/1/1989 Bp Walter Decoster Dennis Jr. m 5/4/2012 Dulce Maria S Silverio Mariano c 2. Dio New York New York NY 2007-2016, 1998-2004, 1997; Ch Of The Medtr Bronx NY 2004-2006, 2004; Asst P S Jas Epis Ch Fordham Bronx NY 1998-2001; Hisp Mnstry New York NY 1990-1992. ndelgado512@gmail.com

DELGADO-VERA, Ramiro Mario (WTex) 697 W White Ave, Raymondville TX 78580 **D Epis Reynosa Tamps 1984-** B Monterrey MX 1950 s Ramiro & Maria. BA 1969; Fashion Sch 1979; Sem 1983. D 7/21/1984 P 2/3/1985 Bp Leonardo Romero-Rivera Con 1/1/2004 for Diocese Of Cuernavaca. Ch Of The Redeem Eagle Pass TX 2012-2015; Dio Cuernavaca 2003-2008; Epiph Epis Ch Raymondville TX 2002; Dio W Texas San Antonio TX 1998-2001; Hisp Mssnr S Matt's Mcminnville TN 1997-1998; Ch Of The Epiph Kingsville TX 1996-1997; Dio Nthrn Mex Nuevo Leon 1989-1996; Dio Mex Mex City MOR 1984-1988.

DELICAT, Joseph Kerwin (Hai) **Dio Haiti Port-au-Prince HT 2002-** B 1974 D. m 4/10/2007 Jeanne Rholcie Delicat c 1.

DELINGER, Ian Michael (ECR) **S Steph's Epis Ch Sn Luis Obispo CA 2016-** Trans 5/4/2016 as Priest Bp Mary Gray-Reeves.

DE LION, Lawrence Raymond (LI) 15 Greenwich Rd, Smithtown NY 11787 **R S Thos Of Cbury Ch Smithtown NY 2003-; Cathd Chapt Dio Long Island Garden City NY 2008-, Cn Com 2007-, Dn of Suffolk No Shore 2007-, Revs Com 2007-, Asst Secy to Dioc Conv 2006-2009, Asst Secy to Dioc Coun 2006-2009** B Alliance OH 1952 s Carl & Ruth. BA Mt Un Coll 1974; MDiv Yale DS 1977. D 6/25/1983 P 11/1/1983 Bp John Harris Burt. Supvsr for Lay Chapl Bp Anderson Inst S Alb's Ch Chicago IL 1989-2003; S Greg's Epis Sch Chicago IL 1989-2003; R S Andr Ch Canfield OH 1985-1989; P S Paul's Epis Ch Goodland KS 1984-1985; Asst Chr Epis Ch Warren OH 1983-1984; Chair of Yth Issues Com Dio Chicago Chicago IL 1992-1994, Dioc Coun 1991-1994, Dioc Yth Com 1990-1994, Dioc Yth Coun 1990-1993, Dnry Chair for CE 1989-2003, 1989-1996, Cmsn on EFM and Mssn 1989-1994, Cmsn on Racism 1989-1994, EUC 1989-1994; Ldrshp Trng Div Dio Ohio Cleveland 1986-1989, Reg Assoc in CE 1986-1989, Com on CE 1985-1989; EFM Mentor Dio Wstrn Kansas Hutchinson KS 1984-1985. Co-Chair Crop Walk for Wrld Hunger 1990-1994; HIV/AIDS Pstr Care 1989-2003.

DELK, Michael (SVa) 205 Castle Ln, Williamsburg VA 23185 **S Lk's Ch Louisville KY 2014-** B Russellville KY 1972 s Clyde & Nancy. BA Transylvania U 1994; MDiv VTS 1997. D 6/21/1997 P 12/22/1997 Bp Don Adger Wimberly. m 6/6/1998 Stephanie L Delk c 2. R Hickory Neck Ch Toano VA 2002-2014; Cn for YA & Cmncatn Cathd Of S Phil Atlanta GA 1999-2002; Asst to the R Ch Of The Gd Shpd Lexington KY 1997-1999.

DELL, Jacob William (NY) 504 E 79th St Apt 4H, New York NY 10075 **Vic Dio New York New York NY 2015-; Chapl U.S. Navy Reserve 2013-** B Orange NJ 1973 s William & Joanne. BA Ya 1995; MA Nash 2008; Cert Ang Stud Nash 2010. D 12/12/2009 Bp William Howard Love P 11/12/2013 Bp Stacy F Sauls. c 3. Mgr, Digital Marketing and Advert Dom And Frgn Mssy Soc- Epis Ch Cntr New York NY 2012-2015; Epis Ch Cntr New York NY 2011-2015.

DELL, Mary Lynn (O) 2741 Sherbrooke Road, Shaker Heights OH 44122 B Valley Forge PA 1959 BS Milligan Coll 1981; MD Indiana U 1985; MTS Candler TS Emory U 1993; MTh Candler TS Emory U 1995; DAS VTS 2002. D 6/14/2003 P 12/20/2003 Bp Peter J Lee. m 5/29/1999 David John Vandermeulen c 2. VTS Alexandria VA 2004; Chr Ch Alexandria VA 2003-2004.

DELLARIA, Kevin (Pa) Saint Francis-In-The-Fields, 689 Sugartown Rd, Malvern PA 19355 **S Fran-In-The-Fields Malvern PA 2016-; BEC Dio W Texas San Antonio TX 2012-, Mustang Island Strng Com 2012-, Ins Com 2009-** B Houston TX 1972 s Charles & Shirley. BA Hardin-Simmons U 1996; MA Hardin-Simmons U 2001; MDiv Epis TS of the SW 2008. D 12/20/2007 Bp C Wallis Ohl P 7/11/2008 Bp Gary Richard Lillibridge. m 11/23/1996 Donna K Dellaria c 3. R S Andr's Epis Ch Seguin TX 2009-2016; Asst Trin Ch Victoria TX 2008-2009. Co-Auth, "The Bible and the 'Other': Fndt for Theologizing in a Global Context," *Revs & Expositor*, 1997. rectorstfrancisfields@verizon.net

DELLENBARGER, Leslie Ann (Ga) D 5/27/2017 Bp Scott Anson Benhase.

DELMAS, Hailey Lynne (Cal) 28 Cobblestone Ln, Belmont CA 94002 **D Ch Of The Epiph San Carlos CA 2000-** B Redwood City CA 1967 d Daniel & Judith. BA U CA 1989; Cert Mercer TS 1999. D 6/23/1999 Bp Orris George Walker Jr. Epis Chapl Stanford Hosp and Clinics 2004-2011; D Ch Of The Adv Westbury NY 1999-2000. Assn for Epis Deacons 1999.

DEL PRIORE, Dorian (USC) 910 Hudson Rd, Greenville SC 29615 **Trin Cathd Columbia SC 2017-** B Columbia SC 1978 s Johnny & Debra. Coll of Charleston; BA U of So Carolina 2003; MDiv VTS 2014. D 6/7/2014 P 1/23/

2015 Bp W illiam Andrew Waldo. m 5/22/1999 Lauren M Del Priore c 2. Assoc S Ptr's Epis Ch Greenville SC 2014-2017; S Jn's Epis Ch Columbia SC 2008-2011. rev.dorian@gmail.com

DEL VALLE-ORTIZ, Efrain Edgardo (PR) 557 Calle Plinio Peterson, Vieques RP 00765 Puerto Rico **Dio Puerto Rico Trujillo Alto PR 2016-** B San Juan PR 1957 s Efrain & Fidelina. Maestria Biologia Universidad Puerto Rico 1980; Doctor Medicina UNPHU 1985; Cert Estudio Anglicanos San Pedro y San Pablo 2007. D 6/30/2007 P 7/6/2008 Bp David Andres Alvarez-Velazquez. m 8/6/2010 Nancy Alicea Marin c 4.

DEL VALLE-TIRADO, Jose A (PR) **Dio Puerto Rico Trujillo Alto PR 1973-** B 1944 m 10/21/1972 Margarita Boria.

DELZELL, Constance Kay Clawson (Colo) 3 Calle de Montanas, Santa Fe NM 87507 **P-in-c S Steph's Epis Ch Espanola NM 2013-** B Carmi IL 1941 d Darrell & Gertrude. SWTS; BA U CO 1979; MA Iliff TS 1981. D 6/4/1983 Bp William Carl Frey P 12/1/1983 Bp William Harvey Wolfrum. m 2/23/1962 David Delzell. S Andr's Ch Denver CO 1999-2007; S Jn's Cathd Denver CO 1992-1998; Vic S Mary Magd Ch Boulder CO 1986-1990; S Jn's Epis Ch Boulder CO 1983-1987. AAPC.

DEMAREST, Richard Alan (Ida) 518 N. Eighth Street, Boise ID 83702 **Dn S Mich's Cathd Boise ID 1998-** B Paterson NJ 1956 s Harrison & Ruth. BA Montclair St U 1984; MDiv Colgate Rochester Crozer DS 1987; MDiv CRDS 1987; MA Geo Fox U Newburgh Oregon 2004. D 5/30/1987 P 12/5/1987 Bp John Shelby Spong. m 1/4/1986 Diane Lorraine Demarest c 2. Cn Trin Cathd Pittsburgh PA 1993-1998; R S Andr's Ch Harrington Pk NJ 1989-1993; Asst Calv Epis Ch Summit NJ 1987-1989; Dioc Coun Dio Idaho Boise ID 2004-2006; Bp's T/F on the Bible Dio Newark Newark NJ 1987-1988. Boise Downtown Rotary. Inter-Angl Stds Prog Oxford 1991; Rossiter Fell Bex 1990.

DEMBI, Megan E (Be) 6030 Grosvenor Ln, Bethesda MD 20814 **S Thos Epis Ch Morgantown PA 2015-** B Nampa ID 1988 d Nick & Ionicia. BA Coll of Idaho 2010; MDiv VTS 2014. D 12/22/2013 P 6/18/2014 Bp Brian James Thom. m 6/21/2014 Dennis Joseph Reid. S Lk's Ch Trin Par Beth MD 2014-2015.

DE MEL, Chitral Suranjith (Mass) **Ch Of The Gd Shpd Dedham MA 2015-** B Sri Lanka 1957 LLD Law Coll Colombo Lk 1984; MS Clarion U of Pennsylvania 1992; MDiv EDS 2005. D 6/4/2005 P 1/7/2006 Bp M(Arvil) Thomas Shaw. m 12/29/1984 Vyonni De Mel c 1. Urban Res S Anne's Ch Lowell MA 2011-2012, 2008-2011; S Mary's Epis Ch Boston MA 2006.

DEMENT, Thomas Erik (Oly) 1118 E Baldwin Ave, Spokane WA 99207 **Ret 2008-** B Portland OR 1946 s Karl & Margaret. Willamette U 1966; BA Stan 1968; MA Stan 1974; MDiv CDSP 1977. D 6/25/1977 Bp Chaunchie Kilmer Myers P 5/17/1978 Bp Matthew Paul Bigliardi. c 1. Dio Olympia Olympia WA 2000-2006; Dio Olympia Olympia WA 1992-1996; S Dunst-The Highlands Shoreline WA 1986-2008; R S Dunst's Ch w the Henry Memi Chap Seattle WA 1986-2008; Dio Oregon Portland OR 1984-1986; Vic S Tim's Ch Brookings OR 1980-1986; Cur S Barth's Ch Beaverton OR 1979; Stff Chapl Gd Samar Hosp Portland OR 1977-1979; Legacy Gd Samar Hosp Portland OR 1977-1978. A.B. "w dist" andDepartmental hon (Hist) Stan 1968.

DEMING, Nancy James (Pa) 518 Hilaire Rd, Saint Davids PA 19087 **Chr Ch Media PA 2017-; S Gabr's Epis Ch Philadelphia PA 2004-** B Lynn MA 1957 BA Simmons Coll 1979; MA Luth TS 2000; GTS 2004. D 6/24/2000 P 5/29/2001 Bp Charles Ellsworth Bennison Jr. m 6/20/1981 Philip S Deming. Dio Pennsylvania Philadelphia PA 2004-2017; S Ptr's Ch Phoenixville PA 2002-2003; Trin Ch Gulph Mills Kng Of Prussia PA 2000-2002.

DEMING, Robert (Ct) 20 Shepherd Ln, Orange CT 06477 B Providence RI 1942 s Edwin & Violet. BA Wag 1964; MDiv GTS 1967. D 6/17/1967 P 3/1/1968 Bp John S Higgins. m 5/18/1968 Carolyn Deming c 2. R Ch Of The Gd Shpd Orange CT 1974-2008; S Mk's Ch Groveton NH 1970-1974; R S Paul's Ch Lancaster NH 1970-1974; Cur S Paul's Ch Pawtucket RI 1967-1970. Paul Harris Fell Rotary Intl.

DE MIRANDA, Mario Eugenio (SeFla) 15650 Miami Lakeway N, Miami Lakes FL 33014 B 1945 s Jose & Juana. Trans 10/20/1993 Bp Julio Cesar Holguin-Khoury. m 8/28/1968 Romelia Calviz c 3. San Francisco de Asis Miami Lakes FL 2006-2009.

DEMLER, Maureen Ann (Alb) 912 Route 146, Clifton Park NY 12065 B Yonkers NY 1949 d Margaret. MA SUNY 1972; BS Albany Coll of Pharm 1979. D 5/30/2009 Bp William Howard Love. m 5/31/1971 Randall Demler c 3.

DEMMLER, Mary Reynolds Hemmer (At) 995 E Tugalo St, Toccoa GA 30577 **R S Mths Epis Ch Toccoa GA 2009-; Dn, NE Georgia Convoc Dio Atlanta Atlanta GA 2013-** B Greenvile SC 1977 d John & Jane. BA W&L 1999; MDiv Duke DS 2003. D 9/8/2003 P 3/30/2004 Bp Henry Irving Louttit. m 9/30/2005 Derek J Demmler c 3. Assitant R S Ptr's Epis Ch Arlington VA 2009; Chr Ch Valdosta GA 2004-2006; Epis Campus Min, Valdosta St U Chr Epis Ch Valdosta GA 2004-2006; S Barn Epis Ch Valdosta GA 2004-2006. Rotary Club of Toccoa 2010.

DEMMON, Michael David Scott (Colo) 407 Club Drive, Hinesville GA 31313 **Battalion Chapl 3-69 AR 1HBCT 3rd Infantry Div 2011-** B Norfolk VA

1983 s William & Elisabeth. BA U CO 2005; MDiv TESM 2008. D 5/31/2008 P 1/10/2009 Bp Robert John O'Neill. m 8/23/2007 Elizabeth Demmon c 1. Assoc R S Lk's Epis Ch Ft Collins CO 2008-2011; Sem S Paul's Ch Monongahela PA 2006-2007.

DEMO, Gar R (Kan) 8144 Rosehill Rd, Lenexa KS 66215 **R S Thos The Apos Ch Overland Pk KS 2006-** B Austin TX 1969 s Jerry & Sondra. MBA Friends U; BA Wichita St U 1994; MDiv Epis TS of the SW 1997. D 6/7/1997 P 12/1/1997 Bp William Edward Smalley. m 6/4/1994 Kelly Marie Hamilton c 2. Vic S Ptr's Ch Conway AR 2002-2006; Asst R S Mich And All Ang Ch Mssn KS 1998-2002; Dioce Yth Coordntr 1997-1998; Dio Kansas Topeka KS 1997-1998. gdemo@stthomasop.org

DEMO, Kelly Marie (Kan) 8144 Rosehill Rd, Lenexa KS 66215 **Dir of Faith Intiatives Chld Intl Kansas City 2010-** B Topeka KS 1968 d Hudson & Carol. BD U of Kansas 1993; Epis TS of the SW 1997. D 6/7/1997 P 12/6/1997 Bp William Edward Smalley. m 6/4/1994 Gar R Demo c 2. Cn Dio Arkansas Little Rock AR 2002-2006; Dio Kansas Topeka KS 2000-2002, Yth Off 1999-2000; Assoc R Trin Ch Lawr KS 1997-1999.

DE MONTMOLLIN, Dee Ann Ann (SwFla) 394 N. Main Street, Rutherfordton NC 28139 B Lawtey FL 1947 d Ina. BD Barry U 1988; MS St Thos U Miami FL 1991; MDiv Ya Berk 2001. D 6/16/2001 P 12/15/2001 Bp Leo Frade. m 8/10/1968 Phil de Montmollin c 2. R Ch Of The Annunc Holmes Bch FL 2010-2015; R S Fran' Epis Ch Rutherfordton NC 2003-2010; Asst R S Thos Epis Par Miami FL 2001-2003. revdee@tampabay.rr.com

DEMOTT, Richard Arthur (Va) 784 Alpine Dr, Seven Devils, Banner Elk NC 28604 **Adj Cler S Mary Of The Hills Epis Par Blowing Rock NC 1999-** B Rockville Center NY 1930 s Arthur & Eva. BS Un Coll Schenectady NY 1952; MDiv Yale DS 1955; STM Luth TS 1966; GTS 1975. D 8/21/1976 Bp George E Rath P 12/21/1976 Bp John Shelby Spong. c 5. P-in-c The Sav Epis Ch Newland NC 1996-2001; S Matt's Epis Ch Sterling VA 1979-1995; Assoc S Tim's Ch Herndon VA 1977-1979; Serv Untd Presb Ch U.S.A 1955-1976.

DEMPESY-SIMS, Catherine Biggs (WNY) St Pauls Cathedral, 128 Pearl St, Buffalo NY 14202 **Dio Wstrn New York Tonawanda NY 2016-; P-in-c Ch Of The Ascen Buffalo NY 2012-** B Chicago IL 1961 d George & Elaine. BA Lawr 1982; MS Benedictine U 1989; MDiv Bex Sem 2008. D 12/1/2007 Bp Michael Garrison. m 1/6/2013 Lucinda Jean Dempesy-Sims. The Epis Ch Of The Gd Shpd Buffalo NY 2010-2015; S Paul's Cathd Buffalo NY 2008-2010. cdsims@episcopalwny.org

DEMPZ, Julia A (Mich) 61 Grosse Pointe Blvd, Grosse Pointe Farms MI 48236 B Jackson MI 1948 d Williard & Barbara. BA Mia 1970; S Johns Prov Sem 1988; MDiv U Tor CA 1989; DMin Ecum TS 1997. D 6/23/1990 P 1/5/1991 Bp R aymond Stewart Wood Jr. m 8/8/1987 Charles Dempz. Nativ Epis Ch Bloomfield Township MI 2002-2009; Assoc Chr Ch Grosse Pointe Grosse Pointe Farms MI 1994-2002; S Jas Epis Ch Birmingham MI 1990-1994.

DEMURA, Christine A (Oly) 10042 Main St Apt 410, Bellevue WA 98004 **Assoc S Marg's Epis Ch Bellevue WA 2002-** B Seattle WA 1954 d Betty. Trans 6/10/2002 Bp Vincent Waydell Warner. c 2.

DE MUTH, Steven H (Los) Holy Trinity Parish, PO Box 4195, Covina CA 91723 **H Trin Epis Ch Covina CA 2014-, P-in-c 2016-; Chapl Masonic Hm of Covine 2016-** B Milwaukee WI 1964 s Herbert & Jean. BM Mt St Mary's Coll; MDiv CDSP 2013. D 6/8/2013 Bp Mary Douglas Glasspool P 1/11/2014 Bp Diane Jardine Bruce. m 7/4/2013 Francisco Cisneros Garcia. holytrinitycovina@yahoo.com

DENARO, John (LI) 157 Montague St, Brooklyn NY 11201 **R S Ann And The H Trin Brooklyn NY 2013-, P-in-c 2011-** B Bronx NY 1963 s Gabriel & Elisa. BA Wms 1981; MDiv Ya Berk 1991. D 1/25/1992 Bp Walter Decoster Dennis Jr P 7/29/1992 Bp Richard Frank Grein. m 1/23/2015 Joel G Van Liew. Int Asst Ch Of The H Apos New York NY 2008-2009; Int S Mk's Ch In The Bowery New York NY 2007-2008; Epis Ch Cntr New York NY 2003-2011; Trin Par New York NY 2001-2003; Pstr The Ch of S Edw The Mtyr New York NY 1998-2001; Int Chr And S Steph's Ch New York NY 1997-1998; Int Gr Ch Middletown NY 1996-1997; Vic Calv and St Geo New York NY 1994-1996; Assoc S Ptr's Ch New York NY 1992-1993. Berk Grad Soc 2005.

DENDTLER, Robert Blanchard (At) 1011 Cedar Ridge, Greensboro GA 30642 **Ret 2000-** B Buffalo NY 1936 s Hilmar & Genevieve. BS U of Pennsylvania 1958; MS U of Tennessee 1963; MDiv VTS 1983; ThM PrTS 1990. D 6/18/1983 Bp Robert Bruce Hall P 12/20/1983 Bp John Shelby Spong. m 6/18/1960 Charlotte W Dendtler c 3. Int S Jn's Ch Christiansted St Croix VI 2009-2010; All Ang Epis Ch Eatonton GA 2000-2007; R Chr Epis Ch Kennesaw GA 1993-2000; R S Mary's Ch Sparta NJ 1986-1993; R Trin Epis Ch Kearny NJ 1983-1986.

DENEAU, Elizabeth Ann (NMich) 500 Ogden Ave, Escanaba MI 49829 B St Louis MO 1943 d Norman & Norma. BS Nthrn Michigan U 1978. D 9/19/2010 Bp Thomas Kreider Ray. m 8/27/1962 Walter Deneau c 2.

DENEKE, Bill (At) 515 E Ponce De Leon Ave, Decatur GA 30030 B San Antonio TX 1943 s William & Ella. BS U of Texas 1965; MDiv Sthrn Bapt TS 1969; ThM Sthrn Bapt TS 1970; VTS 1971. D 6/13/1971 Bp Charles Gresham Marmion P 12/1/1971 Bp William G Wright. m 1/27/1990 Deborah Lee Sil-

ver c 1. R H Trin Par Decatur GA 2000-2010; R Ch Of Our Sav Augusta GA 1979-2000; R All SS Ch Alexandria VA 1977-1978; P-in-c All Souls' NW NC 1974-1977; R S Phil's Ch Southport NC 1974-1977; Asst S Ptr's Epis Ch Washington NC 1971-1974.

DENG DENG, William (Oly) 4759 Shattuck Pl S Unit B101, Renton WA 98055 B Sudan 1977 s Deng & Amir. Masters of Div TESM 2011. Trans 3/13/2003 Bp Vincent Waydell Warner. m 7/31/2012 Achol Deng Deng c 1. Dio Olympia Seattle 2011-2012.

DENHAM, John (WA) 767 N Cambridge Way, Claremont CA 91711 B Jacksonville FL 1930 s Thompson & Leila. BA U NC 1952; MDiv VTS 1956; MS CUA 1981. D 6/12/1956 Bp Richard Henry Baker P 8/10/1957 Bp Edwin A Penick. Pstr Counslr S Alb's Par Washington DC 1988-1990; Pstr Counslr Ch Of The Resurr Alexandria VA 1987-1990; Exec Dir Mid-Atlantic Assoc For Train & Consult Washington DC 1968-1979; Dir of Chr Trng & Educ Dio Maryland Baltimore MD 1961-1968; Assoc S Jn's Par Hagerstown MD 1959-1961; P-in-c Ch Of The Mssh Mayodan NC 1957-1959; Asst S Phil's Ch Durham NC 1956-1957. Diplomate NASW 1986-1990; Diplomate-Amer Bd Examiners in Clincl Soc Wk 1988-1990.

DENISON, Charles Wayne (Wyo) 2502 Overland Road, Laramie WY 82070 B Arlington TX 1961 s Michael & Donnie. BBA Texas Wesl 1984; MDiv Fuller TS 1987; PhD U Denv 1994. D 6/24/1996 Bp Bob Gordon Jones P 1/28/1997 Bp William Harvey Wolfrum. m 1/7/1984 Bodwin W Denison c 2. S Matt's Epis Cathd Laramie WY 2000-2002. Auth, "The Chld Of Est".

DENISON JR, Raleigh Edmond (Dal) 1504 S Ash St, Georgetown TX 78626 **Non-par 1982-; Ch Of S Andr's In The Pines Pinedale WY 1971-; P-in-c S Hubert's Bondurant 1971-** B Alpine TX 1935 s Raleigh & Carolyn. BA U of Texas 1956; STB Ya Berk 1959; MA U of Texas 1964. D 6/21/1959 Bp John Elbridge Hines P 12/1/1959 Bp James W Hunter. m 6/9/1956 Mary Bert Hewitt c 2. P-in-c H Trin Ch Eastland TX 1971-1982; P-in-c Trin Ch Dublin TX 1967-1982; Cleric St Jn the Bapt Epis Ch Big Piney WY 1959-1962.

DENMAN, Scott (Cal) 7917 Outlook Ave, Oakland CA 94605 **Founding Chair Gamaliel of California 2010-; Co-Fndr Genesis 2007-; Fndr Confirm not Conform 2006-; R S Jn's Epis Ch Oakland CA 1996-** B Denver CO 1955 s Victor & Janet. BA Colorado Coll 1978; MA Harvard DS 1981; MDiv Gordon-Conwell TS 1992; EDS 1994. D 6/4/1994 Bp David Elliot Johnson P 6/24/1995 Bp Barbara Clementine Harris. m 5/12/2011 Kendace M O'Donnell c 2. Dio Massachusetts Boston MA 1994-1996; Cox Fell The Cathd Ch Of S Paul Boston MA 1994-1996.

DENNEY, Curtis Stetson (Alb) 8101 State Highway 68, Ogdensburg NY 13669 **Died 11/1/2015** B Utica NY 1932 s Daniel & Stephanie. Hist SUNY 1960; BA SUNY 1960; MDiv GTS 1963. D 6/15/1963 Bp Allen Webster Brown P 12/21/1963 Bp Charles Bowen Persell Jr. m 1/27/1951 Mary Elizabeth Pickett c 3. Chr Ch Morristown NY 1989-1992; Chapl SLPC 1988-1997; R Gr Epis Ch Canton NY 1969-1988; R S Lk's Ch Mechanicville NY 1967-1969; Assoc Chr Ch Cooperstown NY 1963-1967; Camps and Conf Dio Albany Greenwich NY 1980-1986, COM 1980-1986, Curs Pres 1980-1986, Mar Cmsn 1980-1986, RurD 1980-1986, Stndg Com 1980-1986, Stndg Com 1970-1979. H Cross Affiliate 1991-2011; Soc of S Marg 1991-2011. Hon Cn Cathd of All SS 2003.

DENNEY, Robin (ECR) B Fresco CA 1981 d Robert & Shelley. D 12/17/2016 Bp Mary Gray-Reeves.

DENNEY, Shawn W (Spr) 3813 Bergamot Dr, Springfield IL 62712 **Cmssnr Illinois Exec Ethics Cmsn 2004-; Archd Dio Springfield Springfield IL 2003-, Stndg Com 2008-; Vic S Lk's Ch Springfield IL 2003-, Vic 1999-2003, P-in-c 1998-1999** B Jacksonville IL 1951 s Ray & Marilyn. BA MacMurray Coll 1973; JD U IL 1976. D 6/1/1997 P 5/26/1998 Bp Peter Hess Beckwith. m 2/8/1997 Mary Ann Denney c 1. CBS; SKCM; SocMary. archdeacon@episcopalspringfield.org

DENNEY, Shelley Booth (ECR) PO Box 1317, Lake Arrowhead CA 92352 **Epis Ch in Almaden San Jose CA 2015-; Bd Mem Global Epis Mssn Ntwk 2011-; Mem Prog Grp on Wrld Mssn Dio Los Angeles 2011-** B Nashville TN 1950 d John & Edith. BA U CA 1972; MA San Jose St U 1975; MDiv CDSP 2008. D 6/21/2008 Bp Mary Gray-Reeves P 12/21/2008 Bp Chester Lovelle Talton. m 10/4/2008 David H Starr c 3. P-in-c S Richard's Epis Ch Skyforest CA 2008-2015. priest@strichardsweb.org

DENNEY-ZUNIGA, Amy E **Gr Ch S Helena CA 2016-; Mssnr/Vol In Mssn Fundacion Cristosal W/ Mssn Personl Episc Ch Cntr 2007-** B Los Gatos CA 1977 d Robert & Shelley. BS U CA 2001; BA U CA 2001; MDiv Yale DS 2005; MDiv Yale DS 2005. D 6/24/2005 Bp Jerry Alban Lamb P 12/27/2005 Bp Martin De Jesus Barahona-Pascacio. m 8/21/2004 Vince Michael Zuniga c 3. P-in-c S Lk's Ch Hollister CA 2009-2016; Dom And Frgn Mssy Soc- Epis Ch Cntr New York NY 2008; Exec Coun Appointees New York NY 2008; Mssnr Fundacion Cristosal 2005-2006. revamy@grace-episcopal.com

DENNIS, Alan Godfrey (NY) 45 orchard lane, Torrington CT 06790 **Ch Of S Mary The Vrgn Chappaqua NY 2016-** B Cape Town Cape ZA 1955 s Benjamin & Mary. ThD S Peters Coll Fed TS 1978. Trans 7/30/1999 Bp Clarence Nicholas Coleridge. m 4/16/1979 Jennifer Dennis c 2. S Jn's Ch New York NY 2015-2016; Assoc Par of Chr the Redeem Pelham NY 2013-2015, 2009-2010;

P-in-c S Ptr's Ch New York NY 2010-2013; Sub-Dn Cathd Of St Jn The Div New York NY 2006-2009; Dn S Jn's Cathd Albuquerque NM 2003-2006; R S Jn's Ch Bridgeport CT 1999-2003; Asst R S Lk's Par Darien CT 1996-1999; R Ch of the Prov of Sthrn Afr 1978-1996. Auth, "Towers Of Hope (1 Chapt)," 2002; Auth, "Life & Teachings Of S Aug," 1992; Auth, "Between Sea & Mtn," 1986; Auth, "Suffering Servnt As Contemporary Figure," 1977. Assoc OHC 2004; Comp Cmnty Of The Resurrect 1976; Comp Cmnty Of The Resurrect.

DENNIS, Fredrick Hogarth (Alb) 455 Park Ave, Saranac Lake NY 12983 B Washington DC 1939 s Lynwood & Muriel Ellen. BA U of Virginia 1962; MDiv VTS 1965. D 6/9/1965 P 12/15/1965 Bp Wilburn Camrock Campbell. m 6/23/1977 Dorothy Dennis. R The Ch of St Lk The Beloved Physcn Saranac Lake NY 1985-2005; Assoc R The Cathd Of All Souls Asheville NC 1975-1985; R S Jn Wheeling WV 1973-1975; Asst Trin Ch Huntington WV 1967-1973.

DENNIS, Loretta Anne (Roch) 240 S 4th St, Philadelphia PA 19106 **Non-par 1987-** B Rochester NY 1947 d Bernard & Carmella. BA Nazareth Coll 1970; MDiv CDSP 1980. D 9/29/1980 P 10/1/1981 Bp Robert Rae Spears Jr. Int La Iglesia De La Santa Nativdad Rochester NY 1985-1987; Assoc Ch Of The Ascen Rochester NY 1984-1986; Cleric Iglesia Epis Dominicana 1983-1984; Asst S Paul's Ch Rochester NY 1980-1983.

DENNIS, William J (WLa) 501 Springfield Ave, Eutaw AL 35462 **Ret 2000-** B Rockford IL 1933 s Joseph & Winona. LTh Epis TS in Kentucky 1964; BA U of Wisconsin 1970; MDiv Epis TS in Kentucky 1973. D 5/30/1964 Bp William R Moody P 3/25/1965 Bp Albert A Chambers. c 1. R Chr Ch St Jos LA 1995-2000; R Gr Ch S Jos LA 1995-2000; S Lk's Ch Hot Sprg VA 1992-1995; S Patricks Ch Albany GA 1986-1991; R S Lk's Epis Ch Jacksonville AL 1983-1986; R S Steph's Ch Eutaw AL 1974-1982; R S Andr's Ch Kenosha WI 1967-1974; Cn/Cur The Cathd Ch Of S Paul Springfield IL 1964-1967. The Franciscan Ord of the Div Compassion (Oblate P) 1997; The SocMary (Mem).

DENNISON JR, Bryant Whitman (Mich) PO Box 3974, Ann Arbor MI 48106 B Oberlin OH 1945 s Bryant & Mary. BA Ob 1968; MDiv EDS 1971. D 6/26/1971 P 5/3/1972 Bp John Harris Burt. m 8/24/1974 Joyce Dennison c 2. Int R S Paul's Ch Fairfield CT 2009-2010; Int R Gr Epis Ch Traverse City MI 2007-2009; Int R S Andr's Ch Ann Arbor MI 2006-2007; Int R S Tim's Epis Ch Perrysburg OH 2004-2006; Int Pstr Cross Of Glory Luth Ch Detroit MI 2004; Dio Michigan Detroit MI 2003; Int R S Clare Of Assisi Epis Ch Ann Arbor MI 2002-2003; Assoc R Chr Ch Grosse Pointe Grosse Pointe Farms MI 1983-2002; R H Fam Epis Ch Midland MI 1979-1983; Assoc R S Jn's Epis Ch Saginaw MI 1973-1979; Asst R S Paul's Ch Akron OH 1971-1973. bwd45@juno.com

DENNISTON, Marjanne Manlove (Spok) 6232 E English Point Rd, Hayden Lake ID 83835 **Died 9/20/2015** B Newburgh NY 1927 d Stanley & Marjorie. Gonzaga U; AA Ladycliff Coll; BA U CA. D 4/29/1981 Bp Leigh Allen Wallace Jr P 1/8/1997 Bp Frank Jeffrey Terry. m 6/6/1946 Clyde R Denniston, Jr. Asst S Lk's Ch Coeur D Alene ID 1992-1997; Asst S Steph's Epis Ch Spokane WA 1984-1992; Asst Ch Of The H Sprt Vashon WA 1981-1983. Auth, "Prism Of The Soul," Morehouse Pub.

DENNLER, William David (Tenn) 615 6th Ave. S., Nashville TN 37203 **D in Charge Ch Of The H Trin Nashville TN 2009-** B Middletown CT 1954 s Albert & Sally. AA Los Angeles City Coll 1977; BA Indiana U 2005; MDiv Nash 2009. D 6/6/2009 P 12/6/2009 Bp John Bauerschmidt. c 2.

DENNY, Stephen Michael (Ore) 10143 Se 49th Ave, Milwaukie OR 97222 **D S Jn The Evang Ch Portland OR 1993-** B Portland OR 1953 s John & Rosalie. Cert Clackamas Cmnty Coll 1973; Oregon Cntr for the Diac 1993. D 10/4/1993 Bp Robert Louis Ladehoff. m 11/21/1973 Betty Wills.

DENSON JR, John Eley (Ind) 5 Granite St, Exeter NH 03833 **R S Paul's Epis Ch Indianapolis IN 2011-** B Richmond VA 1962 s John & Barbara. BA W&M 1984; MDiv SWTS 1992; DMin SWTS 2009. D 6/13/1992 Bp Allen Lyman Bartlett Jr P 12/19/1992 Bp Frank Tracy Griswold III. m 8/16/1986 Stephanie W Denson c 2. R Chr Ch Exeter NH 1999-2011; Ch Of The H Comf Kenilworth IL 1992-1999. Auth, "For God Alone My Soul in Silence Waits," *New Hampshire Epis News*, 2009; Auth, "The Chr Pract of Hosp," *New Hampshire Epis News*, 2008. Henry Benjamin Whipple Schlr SWTS 1992; Dramatics Awd SWTS 1992; HN Moss Bk Awd SWTS 1991.

DENTON, Edna Marguerite (SO) 1021 Crede Way, Waynesville OH 45068 B Chicago IL 1932 d Thomas & Edna. Angl Acad 2002. D 10/26/2002 Bp Herbert Thompson Jr. m 1/31/1953 John Louis Denton. D S Fran Epis Ch Springboro OH 2002-2009.

DENTON, Jean Margaret (Ind) 607 Alden Rd, Claremont CA 91711 B Brooklyn NY 1946 d Cornelius & Janet. BSN Cor 1968; MA Col 1971; Dio Indianapolis Sch of Mnstry IN 1992. D 6/24/1992 Bp Edward Witker Jones P 7/17/2005 Bp Cate Waynick. c 2. Sr. Assoc S Paul's Epis Ch Indianapolis IN 2006-2012, Dir of Hlth Mnstrs 1992-2005; Hlth Fac CREDO Memphis TN 1999-2008; Nat'l Epis Hlth Mnstrs Indianapolis IN 1996-2006; Par Nrsng Consult to Congreg Mnstrs Cluster Epis Ch Cntr New York NY 1996-2001. Auth, "Gd is the Flesh," Morehouse, 2005; Auth, "An Epis Answers Questions about Par Nrsng," *Natl Epis Hlth Mnstrs*, 2001; Auth, "Steps to a Hlth Mnstry in Your Epis Cong," *Natl Epis Hlth Mnstrs*, 2001. Hlth Mnstrs Assn 1989; US Friends of Gladstone's Libr 2009.

DENTON, Maria Anna (Colo) 7068 Kiowa Rd, Larkspur CO 80118 B Boston MA 1940 D 11/10/2001 Bp William Jerry Winterrowd. m 11/10/2001 James Denton c 2.

DEOKARAN, Teresa Jean (WK) 209 S Walnut St, Medicine Lodge KS 67104 B Mt Carmel IL 1958 d Lester & Virginia. BA SE Louisiana U 1980; MPS Loyola Inst for Mnstry 2010; Angl Prog Bp Kemper Sch for Mnstry 2015. D 12/12/2015 P 7/9/2016 Bp Mike Milliken. c 2. terryrose12@yahoo.com

DEPHOUSE, John R (Los) 1325 Monterey Rd, South Pasadena CA 91030 **Thads Santa Monica CA 2016-; Assoc All SS Ch Pasadena CA 2013-** B Muskegon MI 1980 s James & Cathleen. BA Cornerstone U; MA Fuller TS 2005; MDiv VTS 2009. D 6/6/2009 P 1/9/2010 Bp Sergio Carranza-Gomez. m 12/23/2005 Sarah L Dephouse c 2. Assoc D S Jas' Par So Pasadena CA 2009-2013. jondephouse@gmail.com

DEPPE, Jimmie Sue Marie (Roch) 3285 Buffalo Rd, Rochester NY 14624 **The Ch Of The Epiph Gates NY 2016-** B Mt Clemens MI 1970 d Guy & Linda. BS St Mary's U 1999; MDiv EDS 2014. D 3/16/2014 P 10/13/2014 Bp Thomas C Ely. m 9/2/2009 Amy M Deppe c 2. S Mich's Ch Grosse Pointe MI 2014-2016. coerector1@frontier.com

DEPPE, Thomas W (SVa) 2020 Laskin Rd, Virginia Beach VA 23454 **R Estrn Shore Chap Virginia Bch VA 2013-** B Carthage TX 1958 s Walter & Nell. BS USNA 1980; MA Naval War Coll 1993; MDiv Epis TS of the SW 2003. D 6/21/2003 P 5/15/2004 Bp Philip Menzie Duncan II. m 7/17/1982 Deborah S Deppe c 3. R All SS Epis Ch Jacksonville FL 2006-2013; D-In-Trng/P Associte S Paul's Ch Mobile AL 2003-2006. Masters w dist Naval War Coll 1993.

DEPPEN, G(ehret) David (NJ) 35 Queens Way, Wellfleet MA 02667 **Ret 1994-** B Reading PA 1931 s Charles & Helen. BA Cor 1953; MA U of Wisconsin 1956; STB GTS 1959; STM GTS 1964. D 6/20/1959 P 12/19/1959 Bp Charles L Street. c 2. Int Gr Ch New Bedford MA 1993-1994; Gr Ch Newton MA 1986-1994; Dio New Jersey Trenton NJ 1984-1987; R S Paul's Epis Ch Westfield NJ 1982-1992; Ch Of The H Comm S Louis MO 1970-1982; R H Comm S Louis 1970-1982; Dio Missouri S Louis MO 1970-1979; Vic S Lk's Ch Madison WI 1964-1965; Cur The Ch Of S Jn The Evang Flossmoor IL 1959-1962. Auth, *My Dear People: Letters to a Cong*, Mnstry Press, 1990.

DEPRIEST, Sandra Moss (Miss) 510 7th St N, Columbus MS 39701 **Vic The Epis Ch Of The Gd Shpd Columbus MS 2007-, 2001-2003** B 1954 d Charles & Edith. BS K SU 1976; JD Washburn U 1978; MDiv VTS 1999. D 8/6/1999 Bp Alfred Marble Jr P 2/11/2000 Bp Henry Nutt Parsley Jr. m 1/21/1984 Donald DePriest c 3. Vic S Jn's Ch Aberdeen MS 2001-2003; Asst R Chr Ch Tuscaloosa AL 1999-2001.

DEPUE, Karen Lynn Joanna (NY) 7 Heather Ln, Orangeburg NY 10962 **D Chr Epis Ch Sparkill NY 2013-, D 1994-2013; D The Geranium Farm Metuchen NJ 2005-** B Morristown NJ 1950 d Harold & Constance. Dio New York D Trng Prog NY 1993. D 6/15/1993 Bp Walter Decoster Dennis Jr. D S Barth's Ch In The Highland White Plains NY 2002-2005; D Gr Ch Hastings Hds NY 1996-1998; Chapl Friedman Rehab Inst For Chld Ossining 1993-1995. NAAD 1994.

DE PUY KERSHAW, Susan Lynn (NH) P.O. Box 485, Walpole NH 03608 **R S Jn's Ch Walpole NH 2004-** B Lakewood NJ 1954 BA Tem 1976; MDiv Estrn Bapt TS 1980; ThM PrTS 1985; CAS EDS 2002. D 3/27/2004 P 11/6/2004 Bp Vicky Gene Robinson. Par Of S Jas Ch Keene NH 2013-2014.

DERAGON, Russell Lelan (Ct) 871 N Indian River Dr, Cocoa FL 32922 **Died 2/4/2017** B Worcester MA 1927 s Lelan & Margaret. BA McDaniel Coll 1951; MDiv Ya Berk 1954; MA U of Rhode Island 1974. D 6/2/1954 Bp Walter H Gray P 12/18/1954 Bp Robert McConnell Hatch. m 6/12/1954 Desdemona Alice Deragon c 2. Asst Bp Seabury Ch Groton CT 1997-2005; Ret 1995-2017; S Paul's Ch Westbrook CT 1974-1979; Dio Connecticut Meriden CT 1974-1977; R Cathd Of S Jn Providence RI 1970-1972; Chapl Yale New Haven Hosp New Haven CT 1968-1969; R Trin Epis Ch Bristol CT 1962-1970; R S Jas Ch The Par Of N Providence RI 1959-1961; Chr Ch Stratford CT 1954-1956.

DERAVIL, Jean-Jacques (Hai) Diquini 63b #8, Carrefour Haiti **Dio Haiti Port-au-Prince HT 2002-** B Haiti 1959 LTh Codrington Coll. D 10/18/1998 P 4/25/1999 Bp Jean Zache Duracin. m 5/29/1993 Marie Fenide T Deravil c 1. Peace Epis Ch Rockport IN 2002-2007; St. Croix Par Ch Leogane 2002-2007; R S Thos Arcahai Haiti.

DERBY, Roger Sherman (Mich) 2441 Mulberry Sq Apt 25, Bloomfield Hills MI 48302 **Died 3/19/2016** B Brooklyn NY 1935 s Irving & Helen. BA Ham 1957; BD EDS 1960. D 6/15/1960 P 3/25/1961 Bp Dudley S Stark. m 1/7/1961 Nancy T Tyner c 2. Ret 1998-2016; Int Nativ Epis Ch Bloomfield Township MI 1997-1998; Int S Jn's Ch Plymouth MI 1995-1997; Int S Jas Ch Grosse Ile MI 1993-1994; Int Chr Ch Dearborn MI 1992-1993; R All SS Epis Ch Pontiac MI 1974-1992; R Calv Ch Utica NY 1969-1974; R The Ch Of The Epiph Gates NY 1964-1969; S Andr's Ch Friendship NY 1962-1964; Vic S Paul's Ch Angelica NY 1962-1964; Cur Chr Ch Pittsford Pittsford NY 1960-1962.

DERBY, William Vinton (NY) 14 E 109th St, New York NY 10029 **R The Ch of S Edw The Mtyr New York NY 2010-, R 2010-** B 1946 s William & Julia.

MDiv EDS 1972; STM GTS 1988; STM GTS 1988. D 6/3/1972 Bp Paul Moore Jr P 1/6/1973 Bp James Stuart Wetmore. Dio New Westminster Vancouver BC 2009-2010; S Thos Angl Ch Vancouver BC 2007-2009; Int S Jas Ch Vancouver BC 2004-2006; St Mich All Ang Ch 1994-2004. OGS 1991. PhiBetaKappa Rutgers U 1967.

DERBYSHIRE, John Edward (CNY) 229 Twin Hills Dr, Syracuse NY 13207 **Chapl Dio Cntrl New York Syracuse NY 1988-** B New York NY 1927 s Ivan & Madeline. BS Wayne 1951; MDiv Bex Sem 2003. D 12/9/1989 Bp David Charles Bowman. m 2/9/1952 Cynthia Derbyshire c 6. D St Paul's Syracuse Syracuse NY 1998-2003; D S Paul's Cathd Buffalo NY 1991-1998; D S Mary's on the Hill Buffalo NY 1990-1991; D S Mich And All Ang Buffalo NY 1989-1990.

DE RIJK OSB, Cornelis Johannes (Az) 28 W Pasadena Ave, Phoenix AZ 85013 **Died 9/24/2016** B Utrecht Holland NL 1936 s Godefridus & Cornelia. BA Arizona St U 1971; MS Arizona St U 1973; MDiv Nash 1976. D P 1/18/1977 Bp John Joseph Meakin Harte. Ret 1985-2016; Assoc S Mary's Epis Ch Phoenix AZ 1982-1985; Prog Dir S Jude's Ranch for Chld Boulder City NV 1979-1982; Vic Ch Of The Resurr Tucson AZ 1977-1979; Epis Par Of S Mich And All Ang Tucson AZ 1977-1979; Epis Cmnty Serv Phoenix AZ 1976-1977. "factors during hemodialysis and their implications of Soc Wk"; *Mstr Thesis - Identification of Specific stress factors during hemodia lysis and their implications for Soc Wk.*

DERKITS III, J James (WTex) Trinity by the Sea Episcopal Church, PO Box 346, Port Aransas TX 78373 **Vic Trin-By-The-Sea Port Aransas TX 2012-** B Beaumont TX 1977 s John & Bonnie. BS Texas St U San Marcos 1999; MDiv VTS 2006. D 6/24/2006 P 1/6/2007 Bp Don Adger Wimberly. m 1/8/2000 Laura Keelan Derkits c 1. Assoc S Mk's Ch Houston TX 2008-2012; Asst R S Mary's Epis Ch Cypress TX 2006-2008; Dir of Yth and YA Mnstry Chr Ch Cathd Houston TX 2000-2003.

DEROSE, Kathryn Pitkin (Los) 2621 6th St Apt 5, Santa Monica CA 90405 **D S Aug By-The-Sea Par Santa Monica CA 2009-; D H Faith Par Inglewood CA 1998-** B Iowa City IA 1963 d Roy & Marcia. PhD U CA; BA Duke 1985; MA U CA 1992. D 6/27/1998 Bp Chester Lovelle Talton. m 4/10/1999 Stephen Francis Derose. Auth, "Dealing w Diversity: Recruiting Ch & Wmn For Randomized Trial Of Mam"; Auth, "Breast Cancer Screening Adherence: Does Ch Attendan," *Breast Cancer Screening Adherence: Does Ch Attendance Matter*; Auth, "Ch-Based Telephone Mamography Counslg w Peer Counselors," *Hlth Cmncatn*; Auth, "Networks Of Care: How Latina Immigrants Find Their Way To & Through A Cmnty Hosp," *Journ Of Immigrant Hlth*; Auth, "Limited Engl Proficiency & Latinos' Use Of Physicians Serv," *Med Care Resrch & Revs.* Hlth Ministers Assn, Caucus On Publ Hlth & The 4th Cmnty.

DERRICK, John Burton (Ga) 1512 Meadows Ln, Vidalia GA 30474 B Germany 1949 s John & Margaret. Assoc Georgia Mltry Coll 1969; PA Med U of So Carolina 1975. D 11/14/2014 Bp Scott Anson Benhase. m 1/11/1970 Johanna Fletcher Derrick c 1.

DERSNAH, Donald L (Mich) 4354 Weber Rd, Saline MI 48176 **D H Faith Ch Saline MI 2009-** B Gladwin MI 1947 s William & Ruth. BA U MI 1969; U MI 1974; Cert Whitaker TS 1997. D 10/11/1997 Bp R aymond Stewart Wood Jr. m 12/21/1968 Patricia M McCoy c 2. D S Jn's Ch Howell MI 2001-2009; D S Clare Of Assisi Epis Ch Ann Arbor MI 1997-2001.

DE RUFF, Elizabeth Anslow (Cal) PO Box 1137, Ross CA 94957 B Boston MA 1962 d Robert & Carolyn. BS USC 1984; MDiv CDSP 1998. D 6/5/1999 P 11/26/1999 Bp William Edwin Swing. m 5/28/1988 David Alan DeRuff c 3. Vic Dio California San Francisco CA 2010, Liturg and Mus Cmsn 1998-; Vic The Macrina Cmnty Larkspur CA 2006-2010; Assoc P Chr Ch Sausalito CA 2001-2003; P S Greg Of Nyssa Ch San Francisco CA 1999-2000. Auth, "Including Henry," *God's Friends.* Creative Mnstrs Grant Dio California Creative Mnstrs Dept 2005.

DESALVO, David P (Del) 350 Noxontown Rd, Middletown DE 19709 **S Andrews Sch Of Delaware Inc Middletown DE 2011-** B Winchester MA 1953 BA U So. D 12/13/2003 P 1/15/2005 Bp Wayne Wright. m 7/19/1981 Mary P Park c 2. Assoc S Andr's Sch Chap Middletown DE 2003-2011. ddesalvo@ standrews-de.org

DESAULNIERS, John Joseph (Va) 406 Haven Lake Ave, Milford DE 19963 **P-in-c S Paul's Ch Camden Wyoming DE 2011-; Pstr St. Paul's Camden DE 2011-** B Boston MA 1931 s George & Genevieve. BS U of Maryland 1972; MDiv VTS 1985. D 6/22/1985 P 4/1/1986 Bp Peter J Lee. m 8/26/1978 Charlotte Elizabeth Desaulniers c 3. S Steph's Ch Harrington DE 2003-2009; Assoc Chr Ch Dover DE 2002-2003; P-in-c All SS Epis Ch Delmar DE 2000-2003; Little Fork Epis Ch Rixeyville VA 1985-1999.

DESCHAINE, Thomas Charles (Me) Po Box 467, Augusta ME 04332 **D St.Lk's 2004-** B Augusta ME 1943 BS U of Maine 1965; MEd Providence Coll 1973; Cert Sewanee: The U So, TS 2001. D 6/5/2004 Bp Chilton Richardson Knudsen. m 8/13/1966 Carlene Preble c 2.

DESHAIES, Robert Joseph (SeFla) Rec 10/4/1991 as Priest Bp Calvin Onderdonk Schofield Jr.

DESHAW OJN, Glen Allen John (Oly) 11380 NE 36th Pl Apt B135, Bellevue WA 98004 **Died 1/14/2017** B Seattle WA 1949 BA U of Washington 1983; MDiv Nash 2005. D 6/25/2005 Bp Vincent Waydell Warner P 12/18/2005 Bp Jeffrey Neil Steenson. m 3/18/1972 Rebecca S DeShaw c 2. S Jn's Ch Kirkland WA 2008-2017; S Jn's Epis Ch Olympia WA 2008-2011; R S Paul's Ch Artesia NM 2007-2008; Vic S Thos A Becket Ch Roswell NM 2005-2006. Auth, "Stem Cell Confusion," *Nwsltr of NOEL*, Nat'l Org. of Episcopalians for Life, 2007. Assoc, Ord of Julian of Norwich, 2004; Mem, Ord of St Lk 2005. rdeshaw@ outlook.com

DE SHEPLO, Louis John (NJ) 551 Saint Kitts Dr, Williamstown NJ 08094 **D S Thos' Epis Ch Glassboro NJ 2009-** B Long Beach NJ 1943 s John & Caroline. BA Glassboro St U 1972; MA Rowan U 1974. D 10/31/1998 Bp Joe Doss. m 10/26/1968 Marie Grant c 3. D S Mk's At The Crossing Ch Williamstown NJ 1998-2008.

DE SILVA, Sumith Sreeman (Az) 9533 E. Kokopelli Circle, Tucson AZ 85748 B Kotte LK 1942 s Edward & Silta. Wesley Coll 1964; DIT Theol Coll of Lanka 1973; Dip Coll of Preachers Washington DC 1991. Trans 9/26/1984 Bp Jackson Earle Gilliam. m 8/31/1974 Shanthi Malani De Silva c 2. Assoc S Alb's Epis Ch Tucson AZ 2000-2013; R S Jn The Bapt Globe AZ 1995-1999, R 1994-1999; Vic S Paul's Ch Ft Benton MT 1989-1999; R S Fran Epis Ch Great Falls MT 1989-1992, R 1986-1993; Assoc Ch Of The Incarn Great Falls MT 1986-1989; Assoc Area Min Upper Missouri Area Mnstry 1986-1989; Vic Calv Epis Ch Roundup MT 1984-1986, Vic 1983-1986; Curs Mvmt Sprtl Dir Dio Arizona Phoenix AZ 2009-2011; RurD Big Sky Dnry Dio Montana Helena MT 1990-1992, Chair of Ch and Soc Com and Comp Dio 1988-1992; P Counslr Epis Cmnty Serv Phoenix AZ 1980-1982. Ch & Soc Cmsn Ntwk, PBFWR.

DESIR, Jean Nephtaly (DR) Iglesia Episcopal Dominicana, Apartado 764, Santo Domingo Dominican Republic **Dio The Dominican Republic (Iglesia Epis Dominicana) Gazcue Santo Domingo 1992-** B Gressier Port-au-Prince HT 1960 s Aurel & Servilia. 1986; TS Grad 1991; Licenciado Sociologia 2008. D 6/7/1992 P 12/1/1993 Bp Julio Cesar Holguin-Khoury. m 4/25/1993 Maria Redman c 1.

DESIR, Saint Clair Roger (Hai) Box 13224, Port-Au-Prince Haiti **Died 11/17/2016** B 1929 s Alphonse & Emmanuella. BA Lycee Petion Hai Ht 1947; ETS-BH 1951; Epis TS 1951; MA Wayne 1953. D 6/17/1951 P 8/1/1953 Bp Charles Alfred Voegeli. m 6/8/1962 Marie Mathilde Desir c 3. Ret 1992-2016; Gladwyne Presb Ch Gladwyne PA 1990-1992; ABS New York NY 1969-1989; P-in-c H Innoc' Port-De-Paix Haiti 1962-1969; Dn H Trin Cathd Port-Au-Prince Haiti 1959-1961; Cn H Trin Cathd Port-Au-Prince Haiti 1957-1959; P-in-c Bainet-Jacmel Haiti 1953-1954; Asst S Thos' Arcahaie Haiti 1952-1953; Asst S Matthius' Mirebalais Haiti 1951-1952. Auth, "The Process Of Urbanization At Port-Au-Prince"; Auth, "Etudes Creoles"; Auth, "The Other Side"; Auth, "Tetansanm/Comm". Haitian Bible Soc, Untd Bible Soc.

DESIRE, Fritz (Hai) **Dio Haiti Port-au-Prince HT 2002-** B 1970 D. m 7/2/2005 Adeline Eliassaint Desire c 1.

DESMARAIS, Susanna (Neb) 4545 S 58th St, Lincoln NE 68516 **R Ch Of The H Trin Lincoln NE 2010-; Bp and Trst Dio Nebraska Omaha NE 2011-** B Boston MA 1954 d Paul & Phoebe. BA California St U 1978; MBA California St U 1984; MLS San Jose St U 1992; MDiv CDSP 2003. D 6/28/2003 P 1/12/2004 Bp Richard Lester Shimpfky. c 2. R S Paul's Ch Endicott NY 2006-2010; Assoc All SS Epis Ch Omaha NE 2003-2006; Liturg Cmsn Dio Cntrl New York Liverpool NY 2007-2010, Mem, Eccl Trial Crt 2007-2010.

DESMITH, David John (Nwk) 90 Kiel Ave, Kinnelon NJ 07405 B Canandaigua NY 1951 s Elmer & Ruth. BA SUNY 1973; MDiv Bex Sem 1990. D 6/16/1990 Bp William George Burrill P 2/2/1991 Bp Andrew Frederick Wissemann. m 7/12/2014 James R Alden c 2. R S Dav's Ch Kinnelon NJ 2003-2017; Int Trin Cathd Easton MD 2002-2003; Dio Wstrn Massachusetts Springfield 2000-2002, 1998-1999, 1990-1997; Assoc S Steph's Ch Pittsfield MA 1998-2000; R Chr Ch Rochdale MA 1993-1997; Cur Ch Of The Atone Westfield MA 1990-1993.

DESROSIERS JR, Norman (CFla) St Sebastian By The Sea, 2010 Oak St, Melbourne Beach FL 32951 B Fall River MA 1946 s Norman & Rose. BA Barrington Coll 1975; MDiv EDS 1980; MS Command and Gnrl Stff Coll 1999. D 6/7/1980 Bp Morris Fairchild Arnold P 6/1/1981 Bp George Nelson Hunt III. m 5/31/1969 Barbara Lorraine Desrosiers c 2. S Sebastian's By The Sea Melbourne Bch FL 2012-2016; R Epis Ch Of The H Apos Satellite Bch FL 2006-2012; Off Of Bsh For ArmdF New York NY 1989-2006; Chapl USAF 1989-2006; Vic S Mths Ch Coventry RI 1984-1989; S Paul's Ch N Kingstown RI 1980-1984; Asst S Paul's Wickford RI 1980-1984.

DESUEZA, Edmond (NY) 271 Broadway, Newburgh NY 12550 B San Pedro de Macoris DO 1934 s Frank & Ellen. D 6/10/1961 P 1/14/1962 Bp Paul Axtell Kellogg. m 8/17/1979 Isha Rojas Delgado c 3. P-in-c Ch Of The Gd Shpd Newburgh NY 2002-2006; Dio New York New York NY 2001-2006; Cntrl Epis Dnry New Britain CT 2000-2001; Grtr Hartford Reg Mnstry E Hartford CT 2000; P S Matt's Ch Henderson TX 1998-2002; P S Chris's Ch League City TX 1997-1998; P S Fran Ch Houston TX 1996-1997; Dio The Dominican Repub-

D

225

lic (Iglesia Epis Dominicana) Gazcue Santo Domingo 1994-2000, 1973-1976; Novena Provincia Iglesia Epis 1994-2000; Dio El Salvador Ambato Tu 1993.

DESUEZA-SAVINON, Edmond (PR) Urb. Fairview, D11 Calle 10, San Juan PR 00926 **Dio Puerto Rico Trujillo Alto PR 2004-, 1995-2003** B Santo Domingo Dominican Republic 1961 s William & Carmen. BA 1979; MD 1984; BTh 1987. D 5/3/1987 P 5/29/1988 Bp Telesforo A Isaac. m 7/14/1987 Hortensia Marina Cabreja. Dio The Dominican Republic (Iglesia Epis Dominicana) Gazcue Santo Domingo 1987-1995.

DETTWILLER II, George Frederick (Tenn) 108 Savoy Cir., Nashville TN 37205 **Cn Dio Tennessee Nashville TN 2006-** B Memphis TN 1932 s Edgar & Elsie. BA Van 1954. D 2/14/2004 P 10/24/2004 Bp Bertram Nelson Herlong. m 6/19/1987 Kathryn King c 4. Int The Ch of Our Sav Gallatin TN 2005-2006; Asst S Phil's Ch Nashville TN 2004-2005. fred.dettwiller@episcopaldiocese-tn.org

DEUEL, Ellen Mighells Cook (SanD) 1212 H St Spc 219, Ramona CA 92065 **Died 7/19/2016** B Buffalo NY 1932 d Harold & Harriet. Mt Holyoke Coll; Pratt Inst. D 6/10/1995 Bp Calvin Onderdonk Schofield Jr. m 12/30/1961 Starr Alfred Deuel. D S Mary's In The Vlly Ch Ramona CA 2000-2016; D S Fran' Epis Ch Turlock CA 1995-2016. Ed, "California Quarterly," Orange Cnty Geneological Soc. CT 1960.

DEVALL IV, Frederick D (La) St. Martin's Episcopal Church, 2216 Metairie Road, Metairie LA 70001 **R S Mart's Epis Ch Metairie LA 2004-** B New Orleans LA 1969 s Frederick & Ruth. BS U So 1991; MDiv VTS 1996. D 6/15/1996 P 12/21/1996 Bp James Barrow Brown. m 6/22/1996 Lisa J Devall c 2. Vic Chap Of The H Comf New Orleans LA 1998-2000; Cur S Lk's Ch Baton Rouge LA 1996-1998; Chair, Bd Trst of St. Mart's Epis Sch Dio Louisiana New Orleans LA 2011-2013, Exec Bd the Dio 2010-2013, Pres, Stndg Com 2005-2006; Chairman, Bd Trst S Mart's Epis Sch Metairie LA 2010-2012.

DEVATY, Jean M (Alb) 508 4th Ave, Beaver Falls PA 15010 **S Jas' Epis Ch Lake Geo NY 2015-; Chapl DOK of So Carolina 2013-** B Pittsburgh PA 1958 d Joseph & Dorothy. BA Wheaton Coll 1980; MA Wheaton Grad Sch 1991; MDiv TESM 2005. D 6/11/2005 P 12/11/2005 Bp Robert William Duncan. Assoc R S Lk's Epis Ch Hilton Hd Island SC 2008-2012; Asst. R Ch Of The Ascen Pittsburgh PA 2005-2007.

DEVAUL, Philip H (Los) 31641 La Novia Ave, San Juan Capistrano CA 92675 **The Ch of the Redeem Cincinnati OH 2016-; S Jn The Div Epis Ch Costa Mesa CA 2012-** B Orange CA 1979 s Gary & Marcia. BA Tufts U 2001; MDiv VTS 2010. D 6/12/2010 Bp Diane Jardine Bruce P 1/8/2011 Bp Mary Douglas Glasspool. m 7/19/2008 Krista W DeVaul c 1. Chapl S Marg Of Scotland Par San Juan Capo CA 2010-2012. philip.hpredeemer@gmail.com

DEVEAU, Peter (WMo) 5916 Oak St, Kansas City MO 64113 **The Very Reverend Gr And H Trin Cathd Kansas City MO 2012-, Assoc 1990-1996** B Rye NY 1953 s Richard & Marie. BA SUNY 1982; MDiv Ya Berk 1986. D 6/7/1986 Bp Paul Moore Jr P 12/14/1986 Bp Arthur Anton Vogel. m 10/4/1980 Mary A Deveau c 1. COM Dio Olympia 2004-2010; R S Jn The Bapt Epis Ch Seattle WA 1997-2011; Asst Chr Epis Ch Springfield MO 1986-1990. pdeveau@kccathedral.org

DEVENS, Philip (RI) 111 Greenwich Ave # 2886, Warwick RI 02886 **R All SS Ch Warwick RI 2000-; Prot Chapl Bryant Coll 1992-** B Boston MA 1952 s Richard & Sylvia. BA Roa 1975; MDiv EDS 1984. D 6/2/1984 Bp John Bowen Coburn P 6/22/1985 Bp George Nelson Hunt III. Ch Of The H Sprt Charlestown RI 1986-2000; Cur S Paul's Ch Pawtucket RI 1984-1986. Soc Of S Jn The Evang 1980.

DEVINE, Michael Francis (WMass) 47 Ruskin St, Springfield MA 01108 **Int S Ptr's Ch Springfield MA 2013-** B Davenport IA 1946 s Ralph & Elizabeth. Concordia Coll 1966; BA Augustana Coll 1968; MDiv VTS 1977. D 9/10/1977 P 1/6/1979 Bp George Phelps Mellick Belshaw. m 12/23/1972 Mariana M Bauman c 2. Cn Chr Ch Cathd Springfield MA 2003-2012; R S Geo And San Jorge Cntrl Falls RI 1989-2003; Vic Ch Of S Andr The Apos Camden NJ 1981-1989; Hisp Mssnr Dio New Jersey Trenton NJ 1977-1980. Fllshp of the Way of the Cross 2010.

DEVINE, Taylor (Va) D 6/10/2017 Bp Shannon Sherwood Johnston.

DEVINE, Whitney Alford Jones (Oly) 4420 - 137th Avenue Northeast, Bellevue WA 98005 B Memphis TN 1957 d Frank & Dorothy. BD Van 1980; ThM Fuller TS 1986; MDiv VTS 1988. D 6/18/1988 Bp Alex Dockery Dickson P 6/26/1991 Bp Vincent Waydell Warner. m 6/25/1988 Craig Richard Devine c 4. Assoc Ch Of The Resurr Bellevue WA 2001-2007; Vic Gr Ch Duvall WA 1997-2000; Asst Epiph Par of Seattle Seattle WA 1992-1997; Assoc S Fran Epis Ch Bothell WA 1989-1992; Cur Chap of S Martha and S Mary of Bethany Seattle WA 1988-1989.

DE VOLDER, Luk Jozef (Ct) 950 Chapel St Fl 2, New Haven CT 06510 **Trin Ch On The Green New Haven CT 2011-** B Brussels, Belgium 1971 s Louis & Almée. Bachelors Degree Sem Educ Malignes Belgium 1997; Ph.D. Cath U of Louvain Belgium 2003; Ph.D. Other 2003. Rec 6/1/2005 as Priest Bp Pierre W Whalon. m 6/5/2004 Tiffany Israel c 1. Chr Ch Clermont-Ferrand France Royat 63130 2005-2011; Tchr, Dr St Johns Intl Sch 2004-2005.

DEVORE, Kirk Eugene (Md) 2 E High St, Hancock MD 21750 B Decatur GA 1968 s Richard & Karen. D 6/14/2014 Bp Joe Goodwin Burnett. m 10/18/1997 Elizabeth Starrett DeVore.

DEWEES, Herbert Reed (Dal) 9511 Meadowknoll Dr, Dallas TX 75243 **Ret S Jn's Epis Ch Dallas TX 2011-** B Stockton CA 1942 s Russell & Aletha. BS Austin Coll 1965; MDiv TESM 2000. D 6/3/2000 Bp D Avid Bruce Macpherson P 6/7/2001 Bp Clifton Daniel III. m 7/1/1965 Emily Dewees. Assoc R Ch Of The Gd Shpd Dallas TX 2003-2010; Cur S Lk's Epis Ch Dallas TX 2000-2003.

DE WETTER, Robert Emerson (Colo) PO Box 5310, Snowmass Village CO 81615 **Sr Pstr Snowmass Chap Snowmass Vill CO 2009-** B El Paso TX 1960 s Peter & Margaret. BA U CA 1981; MA U CA 1985; PhD U CA 1987; MDiv Sewanee: The U So, TS 1999. D 5/23/1999 Bp Terence Kelshaw P 12/11/1999 Bp Douglas Edwin Theuner. m 4/1/1989 Regina Ann de Wetter c 3. R S Jas Ch Skaneateles NY 2002-2009; Asst to R S Paul's Ch Concord NH 1999-2002. Woods Ldrshp Awd U So 1997.

DEWEY, Edward Robinson (SC) 598 E Hobcaw Dr, Mount Pleasant SC 29464 **Sr Chapl/CEO Atffbi/Police 1991-; Natl Coordntr For Disaster Response ECUSA 1991-** B Memphis TN 1952 s Edward & Laurie. BA Mars Hill Coll 1977; MDiv TESM 1983; U So 1983; FBI Chapl Trng 1993. D 6/25/1983 P 5/1/1984 Bp Alex Dockery Dickson. m 4/20/2001 Kathryn R Dewey. Coastal Crisis Chapl N Charleston SC 2001-2017; So Carolina Charleston SC 1991-1997; Asst R S Jn's Epis Par Johns Island SC 1989-1991; Assoc R Chr Epis Ch San Antonio TX 1987-1989; Assoc R All SS Epis Ch Birmingham AL 1985-1986; Assoc R Gr - S Lk's Ch Memphis TN 1983-1985. Auth, "Pstr Crisis Intervention II," Icisf/Chevron, 2002; Auth, "Pstr Crisis Intervention I," Icisf/Chevron, 2001. Chr Rotary Club 1994; Intl Conf Of Police Chapl 1991. Citizen Of Year Breakfast Rotary Club 1995.

DEWEY JR, Sanford Dayton (NY) B908 New Providence Wharf, 1 Fairmont Ave, Docklands, London E14 9PB U.K. Great Britain (UK) **Serving Ch Of Engl 1986-** B Hampton VA 1944 s Sanford & Betty. BA Syr 1967; MA Syr 1972; MDiv GTS 1979. D 6/2/1979 Bp Paul Moore Jr P 3/1/1980 Bp Ned Cole. Asst Chr Ch Hampstead 1992-1996; Asst S Mary's Le Bow Engl 1986-1992; Assoc Dir Of Rel Serv Roosevelt Hosp New York NY 1981-1986; Dio New York New York NY 1980-1986; S Lk's-Roosevelt Hosp Cntr New York NY 1980-1986; Assoc Chapl Roosevelt Hosp New York NY 1980-1981. Auth, "Living," *Lrng & Loving.*

DEWITT, Edward Leonard (NMich) 90 Croix St Apt 2, Negaunee MI 49866 B 1935 s William. BS Nthrn Michigan U 1995. D 11/4/2007 Bp Rustin Ray Kimsey. m 11/20/1954 Phyllis M DeWitt c 4.

DEWITT, Phyllis M (NMich) 301 N 1st St, Ishpeming MI 49849 B Detroit MI 1934 d Henry & Alma. Nthrn Michigan U. D 5/2/2007 Bp James Arthur Kelsey P 11/4/2007 Bp Rustin Ray Kimsey. m 11/20/1954 Edward Leonard DeWitt c 4.

DEWITT, William Henry (NMich) 301 N 1st St, Ishpeming MI 49849 B Ishpeming MI 1964 s Edward & Phyllis. BA Nthrn Michigan U 1996. D 5/4/2014 Bp Rayford J Ray. m 2/1/1999 Jennifer DeWitt c 2.

DEWLEN, Janet Marie (Colo) 2500 22nd Drive, Longmont CO 80503 B Minneapolis MN 1954 d Clifford & Alice. Cert Sch of Radiologic Tech Denver CO 1974; Colorado Sch of Diac Trng Denver CO 1999. D 11/6/1999 Bp William Jerry Winterrowd. m 5/14/1977 Gerald Dewlen c 2. Mem COM Dio Colorado Denver CO 2007-2011. NAAD (NAAD) 1998.

DE WOLF, Mark Anthony (Ct) 9 Weetamoe Farm Druve, Bristol RI 02809 **R S Andr's 1975-** B Flushing NY 1932 s Mark & Elizabeth. BA Ripon Coll Ripon WI 1955; MDiv Ely Theol Coll Cambridge UK 1959. P 6/1/1960 Bp The Bishop Of London. m 6/5/1965 Jennifer M De Wolf c 3. S Andr's Ch Stamford CT 1975-1997; R S Mary's Ch Amityville NY 1967-1975; P-in-c Emm Epis Ch Of Sheepshead Bay Brooklyn NY 1964-1966; S Jn's Epis Chap Brooklyn NY 1964-1966; Serv Ch Of Engl 1959-1964.

DEWOLFE, Robert F (WTex) 3412 Pebblebrook Dr, Tyler TX 75707 **Int S Fran Epis Ch Tyler TX 2010-; Gr Ch Port Lavaca TX 1996-** B Providence RI 1939 s Fred & Amy. So Dakota St U; BEd Rhode Island Coll 1965; MA Chapman U 1974; MDiv Sewanee: The U So, TS 1980; DMin SMU 1998. D 6/18/1980 Bp Stanley Fillmore Hauser P 12/19/1980 Bp Scott Field Bailey. m 10/28/1961 Jo-Anne De Wolfe c 4. Vic S Marg's Epis Ch San Antonio TX 2005-2009; Partnr In Mnstry Estrn Convoc Kenedy TX 2000-2005; Cn Mssr- Partnr in Mnstry Dio W Texas San Antonio TX 1995-2005, 1995-1999; R Trin Epis Ch Pharr TX 1990-1995; Vic S Chris's By The Sea Portland TX 1985-1990; St Andrews Ch Robstown TX 1982; Vic H Comf Sinton TX 1980-1989; Vic Ch Of Our Sav Aransas Pass TX 1980-1987; Vic S Andr's Epis Ch Corpus Christi TX 1980-1982. Bro Of S Andr 1993; OHC 1976.

DEXTER, Beverly Liebherr (SanD) 325 Kempton St Apt 400, Spring Valley CA 91977 B Toledo OH 1943 d Richard & Georgiana. BS OH SU 1961; MEd Georgia St U 1969; EdS Georgia St U 1973; EdD Duke 1975; MDiv Ya Berk 1990. D 6/16/1990 P 12/15/1990 Bp Charles Brinkley Morton. Assoc R S Ptr's Epis Ch Del Mar CA 2005-2010; Asstg P The Epis Ch Of S Andr Encinitas CA 2005; Asst R S Barth's Epis Ch Poway CA 2002-2005, 2001-2002; Assoc R S

226

Dunst's Epis Ch San Diego CA 1999-2000; Chapl S Jas By The Sea La Jolla CA 1998-1999; Priory Sch Chapl S Andr's Cathd Honolulu HI 1992-1998; Chapl S Andr's Priory Sch Honolulu HI 1992-1998; Asst to R Ch Of The Gd Samar San Diego CA 1990-1992. Auth, *Spec Educ & the Classroom Tchr*, Chas C. Thos, 1977. CT 1994.

DEYOUNG, Lily April (Mass) 12408 Main Campus Drive, Lexington MA 02421 **R Ch of Our Sav Arlington MA 2007-** B Red Bank NJ 1955 d Roderick & Lois. BA Rutgers The St U of New Jersey 1978; JD Seton Hall U 1983; MDiv EDS 2000; MA Weston Jesuit TS 2001. D 6/10/2000 P 2/24/2001 Bp John Palmer Croneberger. m 5/10/2013 Katherine Moira Clarke. R Ch Of Our Sav Arlington MA 2007-2010; Assoc St. Mary the Vrgn San Francisco CA 2003-2005; The Epis Ch Of S Mary The Vrgn San Francisco CA 2003-2005; Asst Trin Ch Concord MA 2001-2003.

DEZHBOD, Esmail Shahrokh (Ct) 294 Main St S, Woodbury CT 06798 **S Jn's Epis Ch Bristol CT 2016-** B Iran 1959 s Ebrahim & Shokuuh. Chr Theol Study St Jn Cath Acad 1999; BS Post U 2006. Trans 6/1/2007 as Priest Bp Andrew Donnan Smith. m 2/1/1992 Monireh Malmasi c 3.

DIAS, Krista K (Colo) Church Of Our Saviour, 8 4th St, Colorado Springs CO 80906 **Ch Of Our Sav Colorado Sprg CO 2015-** B Portland OR 1984 d Mark & Doreen. BA Sarah Lawr Colleg 2006; MDiv GTS 2013. D 3/2/2013 P 9/7/2013 Bp Andrew Marion Lenow Dietsche. m 7/25/2009 John S Dias c 2. Chr Ch Short Hills NJ 2013-2015.

DIAZ, George (NY) 257 Clinton St Apt 19n, New York NY 10002 **D St. Matt And St. Tim New York NY 2005-; D The Ch of S Matt And S Tim New York NY 2005-; Admin Mgr D.A. Kings Cnty Brooklyn NY 1980-** B New York NY 1950 s Domingo & Paulita. BA SUNY 1975. D 5/14/2005 Bp Mark Sean Sisk. m 9/9/1977 Magdalena Perez c 2.

DIAZ, Gladys (NY) Po Box 617, Bronx NY 10473 **Int Dio New York New York NY 2016-, 2010-2016** B Puerto Rico 1957 BS SUNY 2004; MDiv GTS 2006. D 3/11/2006 P 9/23/2006 Bp Mark Sean Sisk. Gr Ch White Plains NY 2009-2010.

DIAZ, Jose (Pa) 3554 N 6th St, Philadelphia PA 19140 B Fajardo Puerto Rico 1951 s Gregorio & Rosa. Cert ETSC 1985; BBA U of Puerto Rico 1989; MBA U of Phoenix 1993. Trans 11/4/2003 Bp Andrew Donnan Smith. c 2. Dio Pennsylvania Philadelphia PA 2012-2016; Mssnr Dio Connecticut Meriden CT 2003-2012; Dio Puerto Rico Trujillo Alto PR 1990-2003.

DIAZ, Joseph Herbert (SwFla) 3396 Deerfield Ln, Clearwater FL 33761 B Tampa FL 1939 s Sergio & Evelia. AA U of Tampa 1967; BS U of Tampa 1981; MDiv Sewanee: The U So, TS 1985. D 6/22/1985 P 12/28/1985 Bp Emerson Paul Haynes. m 9/13/1959 Janet Diaz c 1. H Trin Epis Ch In Countryside Clearwater FL 2010-2012, R 1989-2012, R 1989-2010; Dn Clearwater Dnry 1998-2002; Cathd Ch Of S Ptr St. Petersburg FL 1985-1989.

DIAZ, Juan Jose (Hond) **Dio Honduras San Pedro Sula 1998-** B 1960 P 5/1/2004 Bp Lloyd Emmanuel Allen. m 5/30/1993 Nora Colindres c 4.

DIAZ, Narciso Antonio (Chi) 400 E Westminster Rd, Lake Forest IL 60045 **Nuestra Senora De Guadalupe Waukegan IL 2000-** B DO 1965 s Jose Juaquin & Rita E. BA Universidad Del Valle Mx 1997; BA San Andres Angl Sem Mex City Df Mx 1998. Trans 1/1/2000. m 7/14/1994 Olivia Diaz c 1. Dio Chicago Chicago IL 2000-2002.

DIAZ ESTEVEZ, Manuel (DR) **Dio The Dominican Republic (Iglesia Epis Dominicana) Gazcue Santo Domingo 2012-** B Santiago DR 1965 s Candido & Elna. D 2/14/2011 P 2/20/2012 Bp Julio Cesar Holguin-Khoury. m 10/28/2001 Angelina Sosa Garcia.

DIBENEDETTO, Aileen Elizabeth (WMass) 8 Cedar Rd, Shrewsbury MA 01545 **Dio Wstrn Massachusetts Springfield 2016-** B Worcester MA 1977 d Robert & Genevieve. BA Fairfield U 1999; MDiv Weston Jesuit TS 2003. D 6/6/2015 Bp Gayle Harris P 1/30/2016 Bp Alan Gates. m 10/26/2013 Anthony Joseph DiBenedetto c 1. The Ch Of The Gd Shpd Acton MA 2015-2016.

DICARLO, Michael Joseph (Los) 1400 W. 13th St. Spc 139, Upland CA 91786 **Chapl Vitas Innovative Hospice 2011-** B Los Angeles CA 1948 s Donald & Muriel. BA California St U 1974; MDiv GTS 1980; AS Coll of Canyons 1996; MHA U of La Verne 2004. D 6/21/1980 P 1/1/1981 Bp Robert Claflin Rusack. m 5/26/2001 Cheryl Reid c 2. R S Nich Par Encino CA 1982-1993; Assoc Prince of Peace Epis Ch Woodland Hls CA 1980-1982. OHC.

DICE, Daniel (At) 2833 Flat Shoals Rd, Decatur GA 30034 **Epis Ch Of The Atone Chicago IL 2017-** B Columbus OH 1972 s Gary & Janet. BA and BS Mia 1995; JD The U of Dayton Sch of Law 1998; MDiv GTS 2008; MDiv The GTS 2008. D 9/28/2011 P 6/24/2012 Bp J Neil Alexander. m 5/31/2017 Manapat Kachingtagsa. S Tim's Decatur GA 2013-2017.

DICK, Brandt (Miss) 1026 S. Washing Ave, Greenville MS 38701 **S Jas Ch Greenville MS 2014-** B McComb MS 1968 s Donald & Shirley. BS Mississippi Coll 1990; MDiv Sewanee: The U So, TS 2005. D 6/1/2005 P 12/14/2005 Bp Duncan Montgomery Gray III. m 6/27/1998 Erica Pope Dick c 1. Vic S Jn's Ch Aberdeen MS 2012-2014; Int Headmaster Trin Epis Day Sch Natchez MS 2011-2012, Chapl 2009-2012; Cur Trin Ch Natchez MS 2005-2008; Tchr Mccomb Publ Schools Mccomb MS 1990-2000.

DICKERSON, Shawn Evan (O) 7640 Glenwood Ave, Boardman OH 44512 **S Jas Epis Ch Boardman OH 2014-** B Silver Spring MD 1972 s John & Gail. BA K SU 1994; MDiv Bexley Seabury 2014; MDiv Bexley-Seabury 2014. D 11/7/2014 P 5/15/2015 Bp Mark Hollingsworth Jr.

DICKEY, Michael Patrick (CGC) D 12/3/2016 Bp Russell Kendrick.

DICKEY, Robert William (Va) 108 Forest Garden Rd, Stevensville MD 21666 **Ret 1987-** B Lexington VA 1932 s Robert & Elizabeth. W&L 1952; BA Duke 1956; BD VTS 1960. D 5/21/1960 Bp John Brooke Mosley P 11/22/1960 Bp James W Hunter. m 6/22/1957 Carolyn Dickey c 3. Reg Dn Dio Virginia Richmond VA 1976-1978; R S Thos Epis Ch Mclean VA 1969-1987; R S Phil's Ch Laurel DE 1965-1969; Assoc S Marg's Ch Washington DC 1963-1965; Vic Ch Of The Gd Shpd Sundance WY 1960-1963; Vic S Jn Upton WY 1960-1963. Reg Dn Dio Virginia 1976.

DICKINSON, Albert Hugh (Pa) 2510 Lake Michigan Dr, NW Apt. A-205, Grand Rapids MI 49504 **Assoc S Mk's Ch Grand Rapids MI 2011-** B Wilmington DE 1934 s Albert & Margaret. BA Trin Hartford CT 1955; STB EDS 1958; DMin Estrn Bapt TS 1981. D 5/31/1958 P 6/6/1959 Bp John Brooke Mosley. m 7/30/2005 Margery Livingston c 3. Supply P S Phil's Epis Ch Grand Rapids MI 2009-2012; Supply P Emm Ch Hastings MI 2007-2009; Gr Ch Grand Rapids MI 2006-2008; Int S Barn By The Bay Villas NJ 1999-2002; Serv Ch of Ireland 1997-1999; R S Jn The Evang Ch Lansdowne PA 1976-1997; R Chr Ch Baltimore MD 1964-1976; R S Phil's Ch Laurel DE 1960-1964; Cur S Jas Ch Wilmington DE 1958-1960.

DICKINSON, Garrin William (Dal) 3804 Carrizo Dr, Plano TX 75074 **R The Epis Ch Of The H Nativ Plano TX 2005-** B Ann Arbor MI 1969 s Robert & Ann. BA U Pgh 1995; MDiv TESM 2000. D 11/9/2001 P 5/25/2002 Bp Robert William Duncan. m 9/4/1999 Jennifer Elizabeth Dickinson c 3. Nthrn Convoc Chairman Dio Dallas Dallas TX 2006-2008, COM 2006-2008; Cur The Ch Of The Gd Shpd Rosemont PA 2001-2002. "The Subversion of Middle-Earth," *Touchstone*, The Fllshp of St. Jas, 2002.

DICKS, Paul Richard (Spr) 422 E 1st South St, Carlinville IL 62626 B Oto IA 1937 s Paul & Edith. BA Morningside Coll 1959; BD EDS 1962. D P 12/1/1962 Bp Gordon V Smith. m 9/24/1988 Christine Ann Dicks c 2. Vic S Ptr's Ch Chesterfield IL 1996-2002; S Paul's Epis Ch Carlinville IL 1996-2001; P Ch Of The Gd Shpd Sun Prairie WI 1993-1996; Gd Shpd Epis Ch Sun Prairie WI 1988-1993; Vic S Chad's Sun Prairie WI 1988-1993; R S Anskar's Epis Ch Hartland WI 1981-1988; Chr Ch Cathd Eau Claire WI 1978-1981; S Lk's Ch Altoona WI 1978-1981; Non-par 1973-1978; R S Alb's Ch Superior WI 1972-1973; P-in-c S Andr's Clear Lake IA 1969-1972; R S Jn's Ch Shenandoah IA 1966-1969; R S Barth's Ch Granite City IL 1964-1966; S Thos Epis Ch Glen Carbon IL 1964-1966; Vic S Alb's Ch Sprt Lake IA 1962-1964; Vic S Steph's Sprt Lake IA 1962-1964. SHN, SocMary, Amer Angl Coun.

✠ DICKSON, The Rt Rev Alex Dockery (WTenn) 1 Bishop Gadsden Way Apt 356, Charleston SC 29412 **Bp in Res for Angl Essentials S Mich's Epis Ch Charleston SC 2008-; Ret Bp of W Tennessee Dio W Tennessee Memphis 1994-, Bp of WTenn 1983-1994** B Alligator MS 1926 s Alex & Georgie. BBA U of Mississippi 1949; MDiv Sewanee: The U So, TS 1958; MEd Mississippi Coll 1971; Sewanee: The U So, TS 1985. D 5/31/1958 P 12/2/1958 Bp Duncan Montgomery Gray Con 4/9/1983 for WTenn. m 1/2/1999 Jane Dickson c 2. Chapl CDM 1985-1988; HOB 1983-1992; SLC SLC 1983-1985; ECEC ECEC 1982-1983; St of Ch Com Dio Mississippi Jackson MS 1976-1982, 1965-1968, 1964-1982, COM Hse Deps 1976-1982, Chair Dept Yth 1963-1975; R All SS Sch Vicksburg MS 1968-1983; R/Headmaster All SS' Epis Sch Vicksburg MS 1968-1983; R S Columb's Ch Ridgeland MS 1962-1968; R Chap Of The Cross Rolling Fork MS 1958-1962; S Paul's Ch Leland MS 1958-1962.

DICKSON JR, Elton Robert (Mass) 6102 Buckhorn Rd, Greensboro NC 27410 B Binghamton NY 1929 s Elton & Florence. BA Binghamton U 1952; STB EDS 1957. D 6/29/1957 Bp Walter M Higley P 6/13/1958 Bp Malcolm E Peabody. c 4. R S Jn's Epis Ch Holbrook MA 1964-1988; Asst Zion Ch Rome NY 1960-1964; S Jas Ch Cleveland NY 1957-1960; Mssy-in-c Trin Ch Camden NY 1957-1960.

DICKSON, Patricia Joan (Va) **P Assoc For Wrshp Cathd of St Ptr & St Paul Washington DC 2002-** B Somers Point NJ 1952 d Richard & Bernice. BS Mt St Marys Sem 1975; MA Mt St Marys Sem 1976; MDiv S Vinc Sem Latrobe 1985. D 11/17/2001 Bp Peter J Lee P 5/18/2002 Bp Duncan Montgomery Gray III. m 3/20/1987 Christopher Patrick Hoff. S Jas Ch Potomac MD 2007-2008; Chapl Geo Hosp 2001-2002.

DIEBEL, Mark H (Alb) 68 Troy Rd., East Greenbush NY 12061 **R Chr Ch Greenville NY 2010-** B Colorado Springs CO 1955 s Wendel & Thayer. Non-completed Barry U; BS Colorado St U 1979; MDiv Epis TS of the SW 1988. D 6/11/1988 Bp William Carl Frey P 12/14/1988 Bp James Daniel Warner. m 8/12/1978 Beth Ann Kasic c 2. Par Admin S Andr's Epis Ch Albany NY 2007-2010; R S Jn The Evang Stockport NY 1991-2007; Cur S Matt's Ch Lincoln NE 1988-1991; RurD - Hudson Vlly Dnry Dio Albany Greenwich NY 1997-2005; Bd Pres Hawthorne Vlly Waldorf Sch 1995-1998. Auth, "A Contemporary Theol Anthropology of Two Jesus Chld," *Sthrn Cross Revs*, 2014; Auth, "Human Nature and Truthfulness in Adoption and Donor Concep Pract,"

Journ of Chr Legal Thought, Chr Legal Soc, 2012. Theta Alpha Kappa hon Soc 2010. christchurchgreenville@gmail.com

DIEFENBACHER, Fred H (SwFla) 3824 Twilight Dr, Valrico FL 33594 B Mineola NY 1932 s Carl & Marie. BA Juniata Coll 1954; MDiv Dubuque TS 1958; MS U of Iowa 1968. D 6/1/1979 Bp Edward Mason Turner P 11/1/1980 Bp Emerson Paul Haynes. m 7/29/1956 Anne Shoeman. S Cecilia's Ch Tampa FL 1991-1992; Dio SW Florida Parrish FL 1986-1991; S Barth's Ch St Petersburg FL 1985-1986; Asst Ch Of The Epiph Cape Coral FL 1983-1985. Mnstrl Fllshp.

DIEGUE, Joseph Tancrel (Hai) Box 1309, Port-Au-Prince Haiti **Dio Haiti Port-au-Prince HT 1983-** B Leogane HT 1954 Epis TS. D 1/23/1983 P 7/1/1983 Bp Luc Anatole Jacques Garnier. m 9/14/1995 Marie Carole V Diegue c 2.

DIEHL, Jane Cornell (EMich) 3201 Gratiot Ave, Port Huron MI 48060 **D S Paul's Epis Ch Port Huron MI 2008-** B Durham NC 1946 d William & Milared. BA Wayne 1975; MSW MI SU 1989. D 12/13/2008 Bp Steven Todd Ousley. m 5/1/1971 Robert Edward Diehl c 2.

DIEHL, Robert Edward (EMich) 3201 Gratiot Ave, Port Huron MI 48060 **Assoc S Paul's Epis Ch Port Huron MI 2008-** B Detroit MI 1941 s Robert & Mary-Louise. BA Wayne 1964; MA Estrn Michigan U 1973. D 6/7/2008 P 12/13/2008 Bp Steven Todd Ousley. m 5/1/1971 Jane Cornell Diehl c 2.

DIELY, Elizabeth Barrett Hanning (Be) 629 Glenwood St, Emmaus PA 18049 **Asstg P S Marg's Ch Emmaus PA 2002-** B York PA 1942 d Norman & Eva. BA Wilson Coll 1964; MA GW 1968. D 10/23/2001 P 10/6/2002 Bp Paul Victor Marshall. m 6/21/1969 Paul Rockwell Diely c 1. S Mary's Epis Ch Reading PA 2004.

DIERICK, F Lorraine (Oly) 102 Glenn Ln, Montesano WA 98563 **P S Mk's Epis Ch Montesano WA 1993-** B Aberdeen WA 1936 d George & Lena. Gn Coll. D 8/29/1992 P 3/27/1993 Bp Vincent Waydell Warner. m 11/4/1954 Robert Louis Dierick. Montesano Mnstrl Assn.

DIETEL, Robert G. (Oly) 1331 Rucker Ave, Everett WA 98201 **Died 12/17/2015** B Palo Alto CA 1944 s Howard & Lila. BA Walla Walla Coll 1966; PhD U of Washington 1986; MDiv CDSP 1992. D 6/26/1992 P 6/22/1993 Bp Vincent Waydell Warner. m 7/22/1978 Lorraine Cecille Meier c 2. Vic S Aid's Epis Ch Stanwood WA 1999-2013; S Mart And S Fran Epis Rockport WA 1994-2015; P-in-c Ch Of The Trsfg Darrington WA 1994-2002; Asst S Hilda's - S Pat's Epis Ch Edmonds WA 1992-1994. Auth, "Ancient Akkadian Grammatical Concepts," 1986; Auth, "Current Issues in Linguistics," 1985; Auth, "Salix of Alaska," *Flora No Amer*, 1973. Cath Biblic Assn; SBL. Who's Who in Amer Botany Carnegie-Mellon U 1973.

DIETER, David D (Mich) 847 Grand Marais St, Grosse Pointe Park MI 48230 B Easton MD 1954 s Paul & Clara. BS Indiana Wesl 1976; MDiv GTS 2003; DMin GTF/Oxford Prog 2009. D 12/21/2002 P 6/24/2003 Bp Wendell Nathaniel Gibbs Jr. m 7/11/2015 Richard Paul Thomas. Sr Assoc Chr Ch Grosse Pointe Grosse Pointe Farms MI 2003-2013. Epis Soc for Mnstry on Aging 1988-1997. Sprt of Detroit Awd Detroit City Coun, Mayor, MI Gvnr 2009.

DIETERLE, Ann M (WNC) 200 W Cowles St, Wilkesboro NC 28697 **R S Paul's Ch Wilkesboro NC 2014-** B Patchogue NY 1976 BS Florida St U 1998; MDiv Sewanee: The U So, TS 2005. D 6/5/2005 Bp Samuel Johnson Howard P 12/10/2005 Bp David Conner Bane Jr. P St Jas Ch Richmond VA 2010-2014; Assoc R Ch Of The H Comf Kenilworth IL 2008-2010; Assoc Hickory Neck Ch Toano VA 2005-2008.

DIETRICH, Seth A (Mil) 4234 N Larkin St, Milwaukee WI 53211 **Chr Ch Milwaukee WI 2007-; Cur Chr Ch Whitefish Bay WI 2007-** B Austin TX 1974 s William & Elizabeth. BA Wheaton Coll 1996; MDiv VTS 2007. D 6/2/2007 P 1/12/2008 Bp Steven Andrew Miller. m 7/27/1996 Margaret Dietrich c 2.

✠ DIETSCHE, The Rt Rev Andrew Marion Lenow (NY) 1047 Amsterdam Ave, New York NY 10025 **Dio New York New York NY 2013-, Bp of New York 2013-, Bp Coadj 2012-2013, Cn For Pstr Care 2001-2013; Bp Visitor OHC New York NY 2014-; Hon Cn S Paul's Cathd London Engl 2014-** B Frankfurt DE 1953 s Raymond & Jane. California St Polytechnic U 1974; BA U CA 1976; MDiv SWTS 1987. D 6/13/1987 Bp Charles Brinkley Morton P 12/12/1987 Bp Frank Tracy Griswold III Con 3/10/2012 for NY. m 3/26/1977 Margaret Dietsche c 2. P S Mk's Epis Ch Chelsea NY 2005-2012; R Ch Of The Gd Shpd W Springfield MA 1990-2001; Asst to the R Chr Ch Winnetka IL 1987-1990; Cn Chr Ch Cathd Springfield MA 1996-2001. DD GTS 2013; DD SWTS 2012. bpdietsche@dioceseny.org

DIETZ, Joseph Bland (Pa) 2619 N Charlotte St, Pottstown PA 19464 **D S Ptr's Ch Phoenixville PA 2010-, D 1999-2010, D 1994-1999** B Easton PA 1937 s Luther & Mary. BS Lebanon Vlly Coll 1960; AA Penn 1980; Cert Pennsylvania Diac Sch 1994. D 10/8/1994 Bp Allen Lyman Bartlett Jr. m 7/15/1961 Shirley Ann Dietz c 2. D Trin Epis Ch Ambler PA 2009-2010; Chapl Montgomery Hosp Hm Care and Hospice 2007-2012; D Ch Of The Epiph Royersford PA 2006-2009; D Emm Ch Quakertown PA 2003-2006; Chapl Manatawny Manor Nrsng & Rehab Cntr 2002-2005; D The Ch Of The Trin Coatesville PA 1996-1999. NAAD 1994.

DIETZ-ALLEN, Doyle (Az) Saint Alban's Episcopal Church, 3738 N Old Sabino Canyon Rd, Tucson AZ 85750 **Asst S Alb's Epis Ch Tucson AZ 2013-** B Austin TX 1957 d Oscar. BA SMU 1979; MDiv Perkins TS 2008; MDiv SMU Perkins 2008. D 4/21/2012 P 10/27/2012 Bp C Wallis Ohl. m 12/7/2007 Thomas Fenton Allen.

DIGGS, Thomas Tucker (USC) 2313 Kestrel Dr, Rock Hill SC 29732 B Richmond VA 1934 s John & Dorothy. BBA U of Miami 1956; MDiv VTS 1959. D 11/14/1959 Bp Charles L Street P 6/18/1960 Bp John S Higgins. m 6/10/1959 Doris R Diggs c 2. Vic S Mk's Ch Chester SC 1995-2002; CT Cathd Chapt Dio Connecticut Meriden CT 1987-1990, Dioc Coun 1989-1992; R Chr Ch Stratford CT 1986-1994; Dn E Worcester Dnry Dio Wstrn Massachusetts Springfield 1980-1984, Dioc Coun 1979-1985, Chair Stwdshp Com 1982-1986; Dept Evang Ch Of The Gd Shpd Clinton MA 1977-1986; Chapl Day Sch WDC 1975-1977; Assoc S Pat's Ch Washington DC 1975-1977; Vic Gr Epis Ch Sandersville GA 1972-1975; Asst Trin Ch Newport RI 1965-1970; R Ch Of The Resurr Warwick RI 1962-1965; R Ch Of The H Trin Tiverton RI 1959-1962; Dioc Coun Dio Georgia Savannah GA 1973-1975.

DILEO, John (Fla) 1505 NW 91st Ter, Gainesville FL 32606 B Port Chester NY 1955 s Joseph & Emily. BA Duke 1977; MEd U of Florida 1980; MDiv VTS 1989. D 6/24/1989 Bp Gerald Francis Burrill P 12/1/1989 Bp Rogers Sanders Harris. m 1/3/1981 Lucinda Field Dileo c 1. R S Jos's Ch Newberry FL 1994-2009; Asst to R St Johns Epis Ch Tampa FL 1989-1994.

DILG, **Arthur Charles** (Pgh) 1371 Washington St, Indiana PA 15701 **Ret Chr Epis Ch Indiana PA 1998-; Chapl to the Ret Dio Pittsburgh Pittsburgh PA 2000-** B New York NY 1936 s Charles & Emma. BA Bethany Coll 1959; BD Bex Sem 1962; MA Duquesne U 1990. D 6/16/1962 Bp William S Thomas P 12/22/1962 Bp Austin Pardue. m 9/9/1961 Marilyn A Dilg c 2. Regular Supply P S Mich's Wayne Township Wayne Township PA 2005, Regular Supply P 2005-; Int S Alb's Epis Ch Murrysville PA 2002-2004, Int 1998-2001; Int S Thos Ch In The Fields Gibsonia PA 1999-2002; R Chr Epis Ch Indiana PA 1969-1998; Asst R Ch Of The Ascen Pittsburgh PA 1965-1969; P-in-c S Thos Ch Nthrn Cambria PA 1962-1965; P-in-c Trin Patton PA 1962-1965. Alb Inst, AFP, Trustsee 1997-2003; Assoc, All SS Sis of the Poor 2005; Int Mnstry Ntwk 1998-2005.

DILL, David S (Colo) Church of the Good Shepherd, 3809 Spring Avenue SW, Decatur AL 35603 **Ch Of Our Sav Colorado Sprg CO 2017-** B Birmingham AL 1970 s Ralph & Peggy. BA Birmingham-Sthrn Coll 1992; MDiv Ya Berk 2008. D 6/14/2008 P 1/24/2009 Bp John Bryson Chane. m 5/3/1997 Mary Alexandra A Dill c 2. R Gd Shpd Decatur AL 2011-2017; Asst Trin Ch Epis Boston MA 2008-2011. dsdill@me.com

DILL, Todd R (NC) 8515 Rea Rd, Waxhaw NC 28173 **S Marg's Epis Ch Waxhaw NC 2008-** B Portsmouth VA 1966 s H & Helen. BMus U Cinc 1991; MM U Cinc 1994; MDiv Sewanee: The U So, TS 2004. D 6/5/2004 P 1/15/2005 Bp J Neil Alexander. m 8/24/1991 Regina O Dill c 2. S Dav's Ch Roswell GA 2004-2008.

DILLARD, Walter Scott (Va) 9 Deerfield Dr, Luray VA 22835 B Greenville SC 1939 s Walter & Mildred. BS USMA 1961; MA U of Washington 1969; PhD U of Washington 1972; MDiv VTS 1993. D 6/12/1993 P 12/1/1993 Bp Peter J Lee. m 6/13/2012 Elizabeth Lester Dillard c 2. R Wicomico Par Ch Wicomico Ch VA 1993-2011; Dn, Reg 2, Dio Virginia Dio Virginia Richmond VA 2001-2005, Mem, Dio Virginia COM 2000-2008. Auth, NDU Press, 1981. Int Mnstry Ntwk; RWF.

DILLER, Sallie Winch (NMich) 733n E Gulliver Lake Rd, Gulliver MI 49840 B Hartford CT 1930 d Winch & Josephine. D 9/30/2006 Bp James Arthur Kelsey. c 2. Homehealth Nurse, Rn.C Lmas Hlth Dept 1976-1997.

DILLEY, John S (HB) B 1928 Bachelor of Arts Ken 1952; Mstr of Div Bex 1955; Mstr of Div Bex Sem 1955. D 5/19/1955 Bp William Crittenden P 12/21/1955 Bp Stephen E Keeler. m 4/30/1949 Frances A Dilley.

DILLIPLANE, Nancy Burton (Pa) PO Box 245, Buckingham PA 18912 **Trin Ch Buckingham PA 2015-** B Abington PA 1961 d Kenneth & Marjorie. DMin The Luth Sem at Philadelphia; BA Swarthmore Coll 1983; MS Nova SE U 1987; Cert of Study The Luth Sem at Philadelphia 2005; MDiv GTS 2006. D 6/10/2006 P 12/16/2006 Bp Charles Ellsworth Bennison Jr. m 6/30/1984 Steven C Dilliplane c 3. R Gr Memi Ch Darlington MD 2010-2015; Asst S Paul's Ch Philadelphia PA 2007-2010; Asst Chr Ch Prince Geo's Par Rockville MD 2006-2007; Dir of Chr Formation S Andr's Ch Yardley PA 2000-2004. rector@trinitybuckingham.org

DILLON, Gwendolyn J (Chi) 446 E 95th St, Chicago IL 60619 **D S Geo/S Mths Ch Chicago IL 1989-** B Minneapolis MN 1926 d Henry & Lillian. D 12/2/1989 Bp Frank Tracy Griswold III. m 8/31/1958 Webster Dillon. Tertiary Of The Soc Of S Fran.

DILLON, John Lawrence (U) 8738 Oakwood Park Cir, Sandy UT 84094 **Asstg P S Jas Epis Ch Midvale UT 2000-, Sexton 1985-1999** B UK 1935 s Joseph & Mabel. D 3/14/1985 P 5/26/1996 Bp George Edmonds Bates. m 12/14/1963 Mary Lilian Shutter.

DILLON II, **Tommy J** (La) 1715 Saint Rose Ave Apt 3, Baton Rouge LA 70808 **S Marg's Epis Ch Baton Rouge LA 2016-; Dioc Disaster Coordntr Dio California San Francisco CA 2012-, SOJOURN Chapl to SF Gnrl Hosp 2006-2012** B Baton Rouge LA 1969 s Tommy & Linda. MDiv Yale DS; BA

LSU 1992; Angl Dplma Ya Berk 1995; STM GTS 1996. D 7/24/2003 Bp Charles Edward Jenkins III P 2/20/2004 Bp Robert Campbell Witcher Sr. Gr Ch Bainbridge Island WA 2015-2016; R S Aid's Ch San Francisco CA 2006-2015; R S Aug's Ch Baton Rouge LA 2003-2005; Chair, Undoing Racism Com Dio Louisiana New Orleans LA 2003-2005.

DILLS, Robert Scott (Oly) 919 - 21st Avenue East, Seattle WA 98112 B Tulsa OK 1935 s Robert & Evelyn. BA Harv 1957; MDiv CDSP 1965. D 8/29/1965 Bp Hal Raymond Gross P 6/1/1966 Bp Russell S Hubbard. m 6/25/1965 Eleanor Louise Pollock c 2. Admin S Mk's Cathd Seattle WA 1993-1996; Non-par 1970-1973; R Epis Ch of the Nativ Lewiston ID 1968-1970; Asst R S Tim's Epis Ch Yakima WA 1965-1968.

DI LORENZO, Anthony (LI) 40 Warren Avenue, Lake Ronkonkoma NY 11779 P-in-c Chr Ch-Epis Prt Jefferson NY 2011- B Brooklyn NY 1939 s Antonio & Angelina. Pratt Inst 1957; S Mary Coll S Mary KY 1962; BA Mt St Marys Sem 1964; MDiv Mt S Marys Sem 1968; DAS GTS 1993. Rec 2/1/1994 as Priest Bp Orris George Walker Jr. m 5/21/1994 Myriam Di Lorenzo c 3. R S Mary's Ch Ronkonkoma NY 1998-2011; P-in-c S Paul's Ch Coll Point NY 1995-1998; St Jn's Epis Ch Flushing NY 1995-1998; Vic Ch Of The H Cross Brooklyn NY 1994-1995; Dio Long Island Garden City NY 1994-1995; Assoc S Ann And The H Trin Brooklyn NY 1993-1994.

DIMARCO, Thomas Edgar (USC) PO Box 206, Trenton SC 29847 S Alb's Ch Lexington SC 2015-; Vic Trin Ch Edgefield SC 2011- B Spartanburg SC 1959 s Joseph & Caroline. BA The Coll of Charleston 1981; MDiv Sewanee: The U So, TS 2011. D 6/4/2011 P 12/7/2011 Bp W illiam Andrew Waldo. m 3/21/1982 Miranda Gail Somers DiMarco c 2. Vic Ch Of The Ridge Trenton SC 2011-2015. stalbanspriest@gmail.com

DIMMICK, Kenneth Ray (Tex) Lorenzstaffel 8, Stuttgart 70182 Germany Dio Mssnry, Vic, St Cathr's Ang Chplncy, Stuttgart Dio Texas Houston TX 2009-; Vic St. Cathr's Angl Chapl Stuttgart Germany 2006-; S Jas Hse Of Baytown Baytown TX 2005- B Douglas WY 1955 s Raymond & Janet. BA Texas A&M U 1977; MDiv Nash 1984. D 6/9/1984 P 12/21/1984 Bp Willis Ryan Henton. The Great Cmsn Fndt Houston TX 2005-2006; Assoc R Palmer Memi Ch Houston TX 2000-2005; Dn Baton Rouge Dnry 1989-1993; Gr Ch Of W Feliciana St Francisvlle LA 1987-2000; Vic S Jn Mssn Laurel Hill St Francisvlle LA 1987-1999; Cur S Mths Epis Ch Shreveport LA 1984-1986. Auth, "A Letter From Engl," Angl & Epis Hist, Hist Soc Of The Epsicopal Ch, 2001. CAECG [Coun of Angl and Epis Ch in Germany] 2006; HSEC 1987; SHN 1983; SocMary 1996.

DINGES, John Albert (Mil) Box 27671, West Allis WI 53227 Non-par 1978- B Chicago IL 1938 s Charles & Grace. Nash 1975. D 2/2/1976 Bp Charles Thomas Gaskell. m 3/1/1958 Marlene Elza c 2. Conf Of S Ben, S Greg Abbey.

DINGLE, John Hausman (NY) 143 Kent I, Century Village, West Palm Beach FL 33417 Ret 1986- B Runnemede NJ 1921 GTS 1956. D 3/24/1956 P 12/1/1956 Bp Benjamin M Washburn. m 2/1/1973 Suni Hatil c 2. Fndr & Dir Lupus Mssn Washington DC 1978-1986; Non-par 1975-1978; Vic S Steph's Guaynabo PR 1974-1975; Non-par 1962-1974; Cur Chr Ch Franklinville PA 1960-1962; R Ch Of The Crucif Philadelphia PA 1958-1959; Vic S Fran' Elmsford NY 1957-1958. Chapl Ord Of S Lk.

DINGLEY, Alison M. (Haw) 1255 Nuuanu Ave., #E1513, Honolulu HI 96817 B Hilo HI 1949 d Leighton & Helen. BA Shimer Coll 1970; MDiv Untd TS of the Twin Cities 1976. D 4/25/1978 Bp Philip Frederick McNairy P 11/1/1978 Bp Robert Marshall Anderson. m 8/15/1998 Willis H A Moore. Int Ch Of The Redeem Pendleton OR 2011-2015; P-in-c S Paul's Ch Klamath Fall OR 2008-2011; Int S Pauls Epis Ch The Dalles OR 2006-2008; P-in-c S Steph's Ch Wahiawa HI 2001-2006; R S Lk's Epis Ch Honolulu HI 1999-2000; Vic Waikiki Chap Honolulu HI 1996-1999; Addictions Prog Mgr Hawaii St Dept of Publ Sfty 1995-1999; Dir, Outpatient Treatment Salvation Army Additions Treatment Serv 1993-1995; Shltr Mgr Inst for Human Serv 1991-1993; Mgr, Addictions Treatment Cntr The Queen's Med Cntr 1989-1991; Vic S Matt's Epis Ch Waimanalo HI 1987-1989; Fam Counslr Womens Addictions Treatment Cntr 1987-1989; Pastr Asst S Eliz's Ch Honolulu HI 1986-1987; Mgr Kalihi-Palama Immigrant Serv Cntr 1985-1987; Kauai Interfaith Coun 1984-1985; Non-par Addictions Counslr 1980-1984; Chapl Chem Dependency Cntr Anoka St Hosp 1980-1981; Consult Twin Cities Metropltn Ch Com 1976-1980; Ascen Sch Bd Dio Estrn Oregon Cove OR 2012-2015, Alt Dep to GC 2009-2013, Dioc Coun 2008-2011, Stndg Com 2008-2011; Bd Dir and Publ Plcy Com Ecum Mnstrs of Oregon Portland OR 2012-2015; Dioc Coun The Epis Ch in Hawaii Honolulu HI 2001-2005, Alt Dep to GC 2000-2009, Dioc Coun 1998-2004, COM 1997-2000, Bp's Search Com 1994-1996, Bp's Search Com 1994-1996; Hawaii Advsry Cmsn of Drug and Alco Serv St of Hawaii Honolulu HI 2000-2006.

DINGMAN, Joel (Wyo) 419 Circle Dr, Gillette WY 82716 Cn for Ch Growth and Increase of Mnstry Dio Wyoming Casper 2012-, Mnstry Dvlp 2010-, Apostolic P 2008-2010 B Jackson MN 1957 s Donald & Carol. D 8/23/2000 P 3/17/2001 Bp Bruce Caldwell. m 2/21/1976 Nancy J Dingman c 3. P All SS Ch Wheatland WY 2001-2007.

DINNERVILLE, Robert Raymond (CFla) 6400 N Socrum Loop Rd, Lakeland FL 33809 D Chr The King Ch Lakeland FL 2015- B Chicago IL 1943 s Ray-

mond & Betty. BGS Roosevelt U 1973; MA Cntrl Michigan U 1975. D 9/12/2015 Bp Gregory Orrin Brewer. m 2/20/1965 Janice Darlene Dinnerville c 4.

DINOTO, Anthony Charles (Ct) PO Box 810, Niantic CT 06357 S Jn's Epis Ch Niantic CT 2014-; Int Ch Of The Epiph Durham CT 2011- B Westerly RI 1950 s Angelo & Irene. AS Amer Acad McAllister Inst of Funeral Serv 1977; BS SUNY 1998; MDiv GTS 1990. D 6/12/1999 Bp Clarence Nicholas Coleridge P 1/8/2000 Bp Andrew Donnan Smith. m 10/1/1977 Susan Stockwell Payne c 3. Int Chr Ch Guilford CT 2008-2010; Vic S Alb's Ch Danielson CT 2002-2008; Asst Chr Ch Greenwich CT 1999-2000; Asst R Chr Ch. st. johnsoffice@yahoo.com

DINOVO, Darlyn Rebecca (SanD) St John The Evangelist Episcopal Church, 2036 SE Jefferson St, Milwaukie OR 97222 S Jas By The Sea La Jolla CA 2016- B Sacramento CA 1972 BA Whitworth U 1995; MDiv Nash 2000; STM Nash 2003. D 4/30/2003 P 11/23/2003 Bp Wendell Nathaniel Gibbs Jr. c 2. Dio Oregon Portland OR 2013-2016; R S Jn The Evang Ch Portland OR 2013-2014; Assoc Gr Ch S Louis MO 2011-2013; R S Alb's Epis Ch El Cajon CA 2007-2011; Assoc R S Jn's Ch Worthington OH 2004-2007; Cbury Hse Laramie WY 2003-2004; Epis Stdt Fndt Ann Arbor MI 2003-2004.

DINSMORE, Taylor Whitehead (ETenn) 9125 Candlewood Dr, Knoxville TN 37923 Assoc S Tim's Ch Signal Mtn TN 2016- B Chattanooga TN 1952 d James & Mary. BA U of Tennessee 1975; MDiv Sewanee: The U So, TS 2005. D 6/18/2005 P 1/6/2006 Bp Charles Glenn VonRosenberg. m 7/28/1979 Ervin Lewis Dinsmore c 2. Asst R Ch Of The Gd Samar Knoxville TN 2005-2016. tdinsmore@sttimsignal.com

DINSMORE, Virginia Carol (Nwk) 681 Prospect Ave, West Orange NJ 07052 Coordntr for Missional Ch Strtgy Dio Newark Newark NJ 2013- B Lynchburg VA 1960 d Clyde & Kathleen. AS Cleveland St Cmnty Coll 1993; BA Tennessee Wesleyan Coll 2000; MDiv Drew U 2003; Cert GTS 2004; STM GTS 2005. D 9/11/2005 P 3/26/2006 Bp John Palmer Croneberger. c 1. P-in-c S Dunst's Epis Ch Succasunna NJ 2008-2014; Asst to the R & Coordntr for Chr Formatio S Mary's Ch Portsmouth RI 2005-2008. gdinsmore@dioceseofnewark.org

DINWIDDIE, Donald H (Fla) 1113 Fleet Landing Blvd, Atlantic Beach FL 32233 B Crawfordsville IN 1934 s Ernest & Catharine. BA Wabash Coll 1956; Oral Roberts TS 1968; MDiv Epis TS of the SW 1972; MEd U of No Texas 1994. D 7/1/1972 Bp Chilton R Powell P 12/20/1972 Bp Frederick Warren Putnam. m 2/13/2016 Frances Moredock Parker c 5. P-in-c S Paul's Fed Point E Palatka FL 2013-2015; Int Ch Of The H Comf Cres City FL 2001-2010; R S Paul's Epis Ch Greenville TX 1995-2001; R Chr The King Epis Ch Ft Worth TX 1986-1995; Vic St Mart of Tours Epis Ch Pryor OK 1983-1986; Vic S Bede Westport OK 1975-1978; Vic S Matt's Ch Sand Sprg OK 1975-1976; Vic Serv Dio Nicaragua Managua Nicaragua 1973-1975; Cur St Phil's Epis Ch Ardmore OK 1972-1973; Capt USMC 1956-1968. BroSA 2010. donaldhdinwiddie@bellsouth.net

DINWIDDIE, Philip Matthew (Mich) 25150 East River, Grosse Ile MI 48138 R S Jas Ch Grosse Ile MI 2004- B Beeville TX 1974 s Brian & Lucy. Illinois Inst of Tech 1992; BSW Jane Addams Coll of Soc Wk at U IL 1997; MS U MI 1998; MDiv VTS 2002. D 12/22/2001 P 6/26/2002 Bp Wendell Nathaniel Gibbs Jr. m 4/15/2010 Elizabeth K Dinwiddie c 3. Asst All SS Ch E Lansing MI 2002-2004. Cmnty of Celebration 2001.

DIRADDO, Joseph Andrew (WTex) 1 Bishop Gadsden Way #329, Charleston SC 29412 Int S Jn's Ch Charleston SC 2002-; Ret 1996- B Camden NJ 1929 s Nicholas & Florence. BA U of Pennsylvania 1951; STB GTS 1954. D 5/8/1954 Bp Wallace J Gardner P 11/15/1954 Bp Alfred L Banyard. m 7/15/1954 Mary G Di Raddo c 5. R S Lk's Epis Ch San Antonio TX 1982-1996; Dept Stwrdshp Dio Texas Houston TX 1977-1982; R Ch Of The Epiph Houston TX 1969-1982; R S Paul's Epis Ch Orange TX 1966-1969; Ch Of The Resurr Austin TX 1963-1965; R S Jas Ch Austin TX 1963-1964; Asst Trin Cathd Columbia SC 1962-1963; R All SS Ch Florence SC 1958-1960; Asst S Jn's Ch Florence SC 1957-1958; Vic S Andr's Epis Ch Lincoln Pk NJ 1954-1957.

DIRBAS, Joseph James (SanD) 1475 Catalina Blvd, San Diego CA 92106 All Souls' Epis Ch San Diego CA 2014-; Exec Coun Dio San Diego San Diego CA 2015-, Disciplinary Bd 2014-, Liturg Com 2013-, Chair, Cler Enrichment and Fllshp Com 2012- B Livonia MI 1966 s George & Tajmahal. BS California Polytechnic St U 1988; MSEE California St U Fullerton 1992; MDiv GTS 2010. D 6/19/2010 P 12/18/2010 Bp Jim Mathes. m 8/15/2009 Terry Shields c 2. Assoc S Ptr's Epis Ch Del Mar CA 2010-2014. jdirbas@allsoulspointloma.org

DIRBAS, Terry Shields (SanD) 1114 9th St, Coronado CA 92118 B Fayetteville NC 1983 d Alfred & Pawley. BA Duke 2006; MDiv GTS 2010. D 6/12/2010 Bp Clifton Daniel III P 12/18/2010 Bp Jim Mathes. m 8/15/2009 Joseph James Dirbas. Assoc Chr Ch Coronado CA 2010-2012.

DIRGHALLI, S George (CNY) 131 Durston Ave, Syracuse NY 13203 Died 10/29/2016 B Detroit MI 1926 s George & Lulu. Drew U; Harv; BS U of Florida 1950; MS U of Florida 1951; MDiv EDS 1964. D 6/17/1964 P 12/21/1964 Bp John P Craine. m 4/22/1967 Kira S Dirghalli c 2. S Jn's Epis Ch Oneida NY 1991-1993; Ret 1988-2016; Chapl Bp's Chapl to Ret Cler/Spouses 1988-2016;

R Calv Ch Syracuse NY 1968-1988; R Calv Syracuse NY 1968-1988; Chapl Cortland St Coll 1964-1968; Coll Chapl Gr Epis Ch Cortland NY 1964-1968; Coordntr Provinces I & II The CPG New York NY 1996-2016. Auth, *A Theol of Mnstry*; Auth, *The Origin & Dvlpmt of Creedal Confession in the Life of the Primitive Ch.*

DISBROW, Jimme Lynn (Okla) 1737 Churchill Way, Oklahoma City OK 73120 B Blackwell OK 1938 s James & Lilla. GTS; BS Oklahoma Bapt U 1960; MEd NWU 1965; EdD Oklahoma St U 1971; MA Epis TS of the SW 1985; MEd Cntrl St U 1988. D 6/20/1973 Bp Chilton R Powell P 7/1/1985 Bp Gerald Nicholas Mcallister. m 8/25/1966 Laura Lou Disbrow c 2. Dio Oklahoma Oklahoma City OK 1985-1995; Vic S Tim's Epis Ch Pauls Vlly OK 1978-1983; D S Lk's Epis Ch Ada OK 1974-1978; P-in-c H Fam. Auth, *Abstracts of Engl Stds.* Sigma Tau Delta.

DISCAVAGE, Thomas Damian (Los) 2563 Sale Pl, Walnut Park CA 90255 **Dio Los Angeles Los Angeles CA 2016-** B Buffalo NY 1962 s Robert & Lillian. BS Canisius Coll 1984; MDiv Chr the King Sem 1988. Rec 5/3/2002 as Priest Bp Michael Garrison. m 11/28/2016 Francis Brant Quijada-Discavage. Int R/P-in-c S Jas Par Los Angeles CA 2014-2015, Vic for Admin 2008-2014; R S Barn' Epis Ch Los Angeles CA 2004-2008; Actg R Chr Ch Albion NY 2002-2003. tdiscavage@ladiocese.org

DISHAROON, Susan Clay (Miss) 3030 Highway 547, Port Gibson MS 39150 B Champaign IL 1935 d Robert & Mary. BA Sweet Briar Coll 1956. D 1/4/2003 Bp Alfred Marble Jr. m 6/10/1959 Benjamin Magruder Disharoon c 4. D Chr Epis Ch Vicksburg MS 2005-2010.

DISTANISLAO, Virginia Gates (SVa) 512 S. Broad St., Kenbridge VA 23944 **P-in-c Epis Ch Of S Paul And S Andr Kenbridge VA 2008-** B Richmond VA 1962 d Ernest & Virginia. BS Mary Baldwin Coll 1984; Cert Sch of Mnstry Formation 2008. D 2/1/2008 P 8/1/2008 Bp John Clark Buchanan. m 10/26/1985 Phillip Thomas DiStanislao c 2.

DITTERLINE, Richard Charles (Pa) 1350 Spring Valley Rd, Bethlehem PA 18015 **Ret Dio Pennsylvania 2000-** B Bethlehem PA 1937 s Roy & Anna. BA Moravian TS 1967; MDiv Berkeley Bapt DS 1970; DMin Drew U 1996. D 6/27/1970 Bp Frederick Warnecke P 3/13/1971 Bp Richard Stanley Merrill Emrich. m 6/19/1965 Susan Y Ditterline c 2. Int S Marg's Ch Emmaus PA 2015-2017; Int S Geo's Epis Ch Hellertown PA 2009-2010; Int Trin Ch Bethlehem PA 2006-2007; Sec and Sprtl Dir Dio Pennsylvania Philadelphia PA 1994-1997, Sec 1985-1988, Chart Sec 1977-1979, Curs Stff Coordntr 2000-2003, Secy Curs 1997-2000, Chair of Lower Bucks Cnty Chapl Coun 1996-2000, Dn Bucks Deanry 1982-1995, Secy Curs 1977-1981; Mem Bd Fam Srv Assoc. of Bucks Cnty 1993-1999; Assoc. Chapl Lower Bucks Hosp 1980-2000; R Gr Epis Ch Hulmeville PA 1976-2000; Cn Geth Cathd Fargo ND 1974-1976; Vic S Paul's Epis Ch Harsens Island MI 1970-1974. Auth, *Trng Lay Visitation Team for Par Shut-Ins*, UMI, 1996.

DITZENBERGER, Christopher Steven (Colo) 6190 E. Quincy Avenue, Englewood CO 80111 **Dio Colorado Denver CO 2015-, St. Fran Cntr Bd Mem 2013-, Discernment Com Trnr 2012-, Congrl Dvlpmt Consult 2011-, Mssn Strtgy Com 2010-2011; R St Gabr the Archangel Epis Ch Englewood CO 2005-** B Denver CO 1966 s James & Joanne. BA Gordon Coll 1988; MA Gordon-Conwell TS 1995; MDiv VTS 1999. D 6/19/1999 P 2/19/2000 Bp Peter J Lee. m 8/27/1993 Chungjoo L Ditzenberger c 2. Asst Chr Ch Greenville SC 2001-2005; S Mary's Fleeton Reedville VA 1999-2001; Cur S Steph's Ch Heathsville VA 1999-2001; Lrng Cmnty Participant Integral Not Incidental - at Denver Sem 2013; Participant and Sm Grp Ldr Emerging Angl Cler Grp 2012-2013; Lrng Cmnty Participant Washington Inst on Faith Vocation and Culture 2012-2013; Loc Outreach Rotary Club 2011-2012.

DIVINE, Elizabeth Baird (Tex) 1616 Fountainview Dr #203, Houston TX 77057 **Jubilee Off Epis Dio Texas 2011-; D S Jas Epis Ch Houston TX 2010-** B Houston TX 1944 d Russell & Lucy. BS U of Texas 1966; MEd U of St Thos 1999; Iona Sch for Mnstry 2007. D 2/9/2007 Bp Don Adger Wimberly. m 1/16/1999 Thomas McCallie Divine c 3. D S Mk's Ch Houston TX 2007-2010.

DIVIS, Mary Lou (Be) 408 E Main St, Nanticoke PA 18634 **R S Ptr's Epis Ch Tunkhannock PA 2012-** B Buffalo NY 1949 d Robert & Alice. BEd Hastings Coll 1972; MEd Sacr Heart U 1992; MTh U of Scranton 2003; Cert Ang Stud GTS 2006. D 5/17/2006 P 5/18/2012 Bp Paul Victor Marshall. m 9/23/2000 Wayne George Divis c 4. S Paul's Ch Montrose PA 2016-2017; S Geo's Ch Nanticoke PA 2008-2009.

DIXON III, David Lloyd (SwVa) 42 E Main St, Salem VA 24153 **D S Paul's Epis Ch Salem VA 2010-** B Kinston NC 1950 s David & Josephine. BS Davidson Coll 1972; MD Wake Forest U Sch of Med 1976. D 9/6/2008 Bp Neff Powell. m 6/9/1973 Nancy Warren c 2.

DIXON JR, John Henry (RG) Av. C. Leon de Nicaragua 1, Esc. 3, 1-B, Alicante 03015 Spain **Mssy SAMS Ambridge PA 1989-** B Fort Hood TX 1949 s John & Mary. BA U of Texas 1971; MDiv Trin Evang DS 1979; MA U of Texas 1989. D 8/6/1979 P 5/1/1980 Bp Richard Mitchell Trelease Jr. m 8/6/1976 Ninfa Duran Dixon c 3. SAMS Ambridge PA 1991-2009; Dio The Rio Grande Albuquerque 1990-1991; Global Teams Forest City NC 1988-1989; R S Paul's Mtn El Paso TX 1981-1987; S Paul's Ch El Paso TX 1979-1987; Cur All SS Epis Ch El Paso TX 1979-1981. SAMS 1989.

DIXON, Mary Lenn (Tex) 1101 Rock Prairie Rd, College Station TX 77845 **Dio Texas Houston TX 2016-** B Hamilton TX 1947 d Robert & Mavis. Iona Sch for Mnstry 2011. D 6/18/2011 Bp C Andrew Doyle. m 2/10/1975 Warren A Dixon c 2.

DIXON, Robert Keith (Nwk) 73 Fernbank Ave, Delmar NY 12054 B Albany NY 1936 s Harry & Rebekah. BA Ham 1958; STB GTS 1961. D 6/10/1961 P 12/1/1961 Bp Leland Stark. m 7/8/1961 Linda Dixon c 3. S Jn's Ch Cohoes NY 1997-2002; Cathd Of All SS Albany NY 1994-1997; R S Jn's Ch Passaic NJ 1966-1981; Cur Ch Of The H Trin New York NY 1963-1966; Cur Calv Epis Ch Summit NJ 1961-1962; P-in-c Chr & S Barn'. lintimdix@gmail.com

DIXON, Robert P (CGC) Saint Stephen's Church, 1510 Escambia Ave, Brewton AL 36426 **H Cross Ch Pensacola FL 2016-** B Mobile AL 1976 s David & Rose. BS Auburn U 2000; MDiv Epis TS Of The SW 2012; MDiv Epis TS of the SW 2012. D 12/21/2011 P 6/23/2012 Bp Philip Menzie Duncan II. m 11/28/2008 Amanda E Dixon c 3. S Mart's Epis Ch Houston TX 2015-2016; R S Steph's Ch Brewton AL 2012-2015; Chr Epis Ch Pensacola FL 2008.

DIXON, Valerie Wilde (Ct) 23 Bayview Ave, Niantic CT 06357 **Vol Coordntr Chrysalis Prog York Correctional Inst Niantic CT 06357 2004-** B Berkeley CA 1944 d Robert & Mary. BA Stan 1966; MA CUA 1970; MDiv EDS 2002. D 6/8/2002 P 6/21/2003 Bp Andrew Donnan Smith. m 4/1/1968 Gregg W Dixon c 3. Assoc S Jn's Epis Ch Niantic CT 2009-2012; S Jas Ch Preston CT 2002-2008.

DOAR, Katherine Baginski (ECR) 1225 Pine Ave, San Jose CA 95125 **D S Fran Epis Ch San Jose CA 2002-** B Washington DC 1967 d Joseph & Linda. BA U CA 1990; BA U CA, Santa Cruz 1990; MTS Harvard DS 1998; MA Harvard DS 1998; CAS CDSP 2002. D 6/22/2002 P 3/1/2003 Bp Richard Lester Shimpfky. m 4/22/1995 Matthew Doar c 3.

DOBBIN, Robert A (Cal) 24 Van Gordon Pl, Danville CA 94526 **Asst. Gen. Counsel Asyst Technologies Inc 1999-** B Baltimore MD 1946 s Tilton & Julia. BA Dart 1967; JD Willamette U 1975; LLM Geo 1978; BD The Sch For Deacons Berkeley 2006. D 12/2/2006 Bp Marc Handley Andrus. m 7/10/1971 Patricia A Dobbin c 3.

DOBBINS, Burford C (WTex) 1501 N. Glass St., Victoria TX 77901 **S Barn Epis Ch Fredricksburg TX 2016-** B 1961 BA U So 1984; JD So Texas Coll of Law 1987; MDiv Sewanee: The U So, TS 2003. D 6/9/2003 Bp Robert Boyd Hibbs P 1/6/2004 Bp James Edward Folts. m 4/9/2005 Melissa Gallander Dobbins c 2. Ch Of The Annunc Luling TX 2013-2016; Trin Ch Victoria TX 2006-2013; St Ptr & St Paul Ch Mssn TX 2003-2006.

DOBBINS JR, David David (RI) 205 Lindley Ave, North Kingstown RI 02852 **P in Charge S Aug's Ch Kingston RI 2012-** B Torrington CT 1956 s William & Agatha. BS U of Virginia 1978; Oak Hill Theol Coll 1981; STM GTS 1987; MDiv GTS 1987; Cert Blanton-Peale Grad Inst 1992. D 6/13/1987 Bp Arthur Edward Walmsley P 2/26/1988 Bp Jeffery William Rowthorn. m 4/23/1994 Jane R Reid. Int R S Paul's Ch N Kingstown RI 2010-2012; Int R Trin Ch Newport RI 2008-2010; Int R S Mich's Ch Bristol RI 2005-2008; Int R S Jn's Ch Walpole NH 2004, Int R 2003-2004; Fndr and Exec Dir Greenwoods Counslg Serv Litchfield CT 1994-1995, Exec Dir 1992-2002; Asst to R S Jn's Of Lattingtown Locust Vlly NY 1987-1989; Mem, Chapt of Cathd of St. Jn Dio Rhode Island Providence RI 2015-2017, Vice Chair, Cntr for Recon 2015-2017, Mem, Dioc Coun 2015-, Pres, Disciplinary Bd 2013-2016, Same-Sex Blessing T/F 2013. AAPC 1991; Int Mnstry Ntwk 2001. therevdobbins@gmail.com

DOBBINS, Timothy (Pa) 292 Militia Dr, Radnor PA 19087 B Camp Lejeune NC 1954 s Peter & Christine. BA U of Florida 1976; MDiv VTS 1981. D 6/7/1981 Bp Frank S Cerveny P 12/1/1981 Bp John Thomas Walker. c 2. Ch Of The Redeem Bryn Mawr PA 1990-1998; R S Jn's Epis Ch Gloucester MA 1984-1990; Asst S Jn's Ch Lafayette Sq Washington DC 1981-1984. Auth, *,Stepping Up: Bus Decisions That Matter*, Harper Collins, 2006; Auth, *,Bus Comp*, Random Hse, 2002; Auth, "Aware"; Auth, "Signs Of Gr: Mnstry For The 21st Century".

DOBSON, Marc A (Dal) 6021 Shady Valley Court, Garland TX 75043 **R Ch Of The Gd Shpd Cedar Hill TX 2013-** B Pittsburgh PA 1959 s Edward & Helen. AA Edinboro U 1987; BS Geneva Coll 1991; MDiv TESM 2003. D 6/12/2004 Bp Robert William Duncan P 12/19/2004 Bp Henry W Scriven. m 12/8/2012 Elizabeth A Dobson c 3. Vic Resurr Gr Epis Ch Dallas TX 2008-2013; R S Mary's Ch Warwick RI 2005-2007; Assoc R Prince Of Peace Epis Ch Aliquippa PA 2004-2005; Min of Mus Prince of Peace Epis Ch Aliquippa PA 2001-2004; Chr Ch Greensburg PA 1999-2001; Min of Mus St. Phil's Epis Ch Moon TWP PA 1998-1999.

DOBYNS, N(ancy) (Ind) 1021 Sw 15th St, Richmond IN 47374 B Charleston WVa 1949 d Samuel & Julia. AAS Seattle Cmnty Coll 1972; BA Fairhaven Coll 1975; MDiv Earlham Sch of Rel 1997; CAS Bex Sem 2005. D 6/18/2005 P 7/8/2006 Bp Cate Waynick. m 3/19/1972 R(ichard) Dobyns c 3. Exec Coun Mem Dio Indianapolis Indianapolis IN 2009-2012, 2008-2012; Asst Gr Ch Muncie IN 2006-2008; D S Lk's Epis Ch Shelbyville IN 2005-2006; Sem Stdt Bex 2003-2005.

DOBYNS, R(ichard) (Ind) 1021 Sw 15th St, Richmond IN 47374 B Bethesda MD 1949 s Donald & Kathleen. BS Wstrn Washington U 1976; DO Des Moines U 1978; MDiv Earlham Sch of Rel 1998; CAS Bex Sem 2005. D 6/18/ 2005 P 7/8/2006 Bp Cate Waynick. m 3/19/1972 N(ancy) Lawrence c 2. Dio Indianapolis Indianapolis IN 2008-2012; Asst Gr Ch Muncie IN 2006-2008; Transitional D Gr Ch IN 2005-2006.

DOCKERY, Nancy Lynn (Nev) 501 Bianca Bay St, Las Vegas NV 89144 B Colorado Springs CO 1956 d Eldon & Billie. AAS Comm Coll of S Nevada 1992. D 12/3/1995 Bp Stewart Clark Zabriskie. m 9/27/1980 Jan Theodore Dockery c 2.

DOCTOR, Virginia Carol (Ak) P.O. Box 93, Tanana AK 99777 **Angl Ch of Can Toronto ON 2012-** B Syracuse NY 1950 d Alfred & Birdie. Onondaga Cmnty Coll 1971; SUNY 1973. D 9/2/2000 P 7/15/2001 Bp Mark Lawrence Macdonald. Exec Coun Appointees New York NY 2005-2008; Dio Alaska Fairbanks AK 2001-2011, Cn To The Ordnry 2000-. gindoctor@aol.com

DOD, David Stockton (ECR) 8294 Carmelita Ave, Atascadero CA 93422 B Klamath Falls OR 1944 s Donald & Annabelle. AA Warren Wilson Coll 1964; BA Trin U San Antonio 1966; MDiv ETSC 1971. D 5/31/1971 P 12/21/1971 Bp Francisco Reus-Froylan. m 6/19/1966 Judith Dod c 2. Chapl Marin Interfaith Hmless 1993-1994; Hisp Min Sthrn Reg Dio El Camino Real Salinas CA 1990-1992; Vic S Mk's Ch King City CA 1986-1990; Chr And S Ambr Ch Philadelphia PA 1981-1986; Asst To Hisp Mnstry Dio Pennsylvania Philadelphia PA 1981-1986; Dio Panama 1979-1981; R S Margarita Rp 1979-1981; Chr Ch By The Sea 1978-1981; P Ch Of S Mths Asheville NC 1975-1977; Non-par 1971-1975; Prot Chapl Atascadero St Hosp Atascadero CA 93423 1994-2009.

DODD, Debra (Dee) Anne (Ct) 37 Bailey Dr, North Branford CT 06471 **S Paul's Ch Wallingford CT 2009-** B Pineville WV 1958 d Robert & Rosemary. BS Ohio U 1980; MDiv UTS 1988; STM GTS 1991. D 6/10/1989 P 3/24/1990 Bp Arthur Edward Walmsley. m 7/20/1983 Brad Schide c 2. Vic Zion Epis Ch N Branford CT 1994-2009; Asst R S Mary's Epis Ch Manchester CT 1989-1994; Dir Wrld Hunger Globl Dlpmt Amer Friends Serv 1982-1985; Rgnl Org Bread For The Wrld Nyc 1981-1982. Producer/Co-Writer, "Let Them Eat Missiles," 1985; Writer/Ed, "Hunger & Militarism: A Guide To Study Reflection & Action," 1984.

DODD, Jean Carrison (Fla) 1860 Edgewood Ave S, Jacksonville FL 32205 **D S Jn's Cathd Jacksonville FL 2011-** B Tampa FL 1941 D 9/21/2003 Bp Stephen Hays Jecko. m 2/8/1991 Arthur Robert Dodd c 3. Hd of Sch San Jose Epis Ch Jacksonville FL 2000-2010.

DODDEMA, Peter (Lex) 118 West Poplar Street, Harrodsburg KY 40330 **S Phil's Ch Harrodsburg KY 2011-; Fin Asst for the Cathd Domain Dio Lexington Lexington 2015-, Int Dir of the Ntwk for Pstr Ldrshp & Congrl Dvlpmt 2013-2014** B Cedar Falls IA 1973 s Paul & Margaret. BA U of Kansas 2001; MDiv VTS 2011. D 6/11/2011 Bp Dean E Wolfe P 12/21/2011 Bp Chilton Richardson Knudsen. m 7/10/1999 M Nicole Burchinal Doddema c 1. Rotary Intl 2014. saintphilip@bellsouth.net

DODGE, Jeffrey A (Cal) 1944 Trinity Ave, Walnut Creek CA 94596 **Assoc S Paul's Epis Ch Walnut Creek CA 2016-** B Dade City FL 1981 s Richard & Joy. BA Middle Tennessee St U 2005; MDiv CDSP 2014; MA CDSP 2015. D 6/7/2014 Bp M(Arvil) Thomas Shaw P 1/10/2015 Bp Alan Gates. Dio California San Francisco CA 2015; S Lk's Ch San Francisco CA 2015. jdodge@ stpaulswc.org

DODGE, Robin Dennis (RG) Church Of The Holy Faith, 311 E Palace Ave, Santa Fe NM 87501 **R Ch of the H Faith Santa Fe NM 2016-** B Springfield VT 1958 s Kenneth & Bea. BA Cor 1980; JD Bos 1983; MDiv VTS 1999. D 4/14/1998 P 5/22/1999 Bp Leo Frade. m 9/20/1986 Therese Saint-Andre c 2. R S Dav's Par Washington DC 2005-2016; Assoc Vic/P-in-c St Mary Redcliffe Ch Bristol Engl 2002-2005; Assoc R S Mary's Epis Ch Arlington VA 1999-2002; Com on Const and Cn Dio Washington Washington DC 2012-2016, Cmsn on Ecum and Interreligious Relatns 2011-2016, Fin Com 2009-2012. fr.robin@ holyfaithchurchsf.org

DODSON, Wayne J (NY) 9 W 130th St, New York NY 10037 **R S Ambr Epis Ch New York NY 1999-** B BB 1952 s Darnley & Eula. BS CUNY 1981; MDiv GTS 1994; STM GTS 1996. D 2/14/1994 P 9/1/1994 Bp Orris George Walker Jr. m 8/29/1993 Maurina Dodson c 1. Asst to R Gr Ch Jamaica NY 1994-1999.

DOERR, Nan (Tex) 901 S. Johnson, Alvin TX 77511 **Int R S Jn's Ch La Porte TX 2011-** B San Antonio TX 1944 d Andrew & Jimmie. BME Sam Houston St U 1967; MDiv Epis TS of the SW 2000. D 6/17/2000 Bp Claude Edward Payne P 6/17/2001 Bp Leopoldo Jesus Alard. m 4/27/1968 Samuel Doerr c 2. R Ch Of The Redeem Houston TX 2006-2010; Asst & Mssnr Campus Mnstry S Steph's Ch Huntsville TX 2000-2006. "Praying w Beads," Eerdmans, 2007.

DOGARU, Vickie A (Oly) 22465 Ne 182nd Ave, Battle Ground WA 98604 B Salem Oregon 1951 d Dale & Violet. BS U of Oregon 1973; MDiv Seattle U 2005; MDiv Seattle U 2005. D 6/24/2006 Bp Vincent Waydell Warner P 2/17/ 2007 Bp Bavi Edna Rivera. m 9/9/1978 Emil Dogaru c 2. Assoc. Adult Sprtl Dvlpmt and Yth Mnstry S Lk's Epis Ch Vancouver WA 2007-2013.

DOGGETT, William Jordan (WA) 1209 East Capitol Street SE, Washington DC 20003 B Woodland CA 1956 s James & Muriel. BA U CA 1978; MDiv CD-

SP 1995; PhD Grad Theol Un 2005. D 12/2/1995 P 12/6/1996 Bp William Edwin Swing. m 6/26/2010 Matthew Braman c 2. S Jas Ch Potomac MD 2015-2017; S Jas Epis Ch Mt Airy MD 2014-2015; Emm Epis Ch Alexandria VA 2012; Gr Ch Washington DC 2011-2013; Chr Ch Capitol Hill Washington DC 2001-2010; Adj Fac SFTS CA 1998-1999; Liturg And Mus Dir S Ptr's Epis Ch Redwood City CA 1997-1998. Compsr, "Mus By Heart: Paperless Songs for Evening Wrshp," Ch Pub, 2008; Auth, "New Proclamation Commentary on Feasts: H Days and Other Celebrations," Augsburg/Fortress, 2007; Auth, "Make Believe," Klutz Press, 1991.

DOHERTY, Anna Clay (Minn) 670 E Monroe Ave, Hartford WI 53027 **Chr Ch S Paul MN 2016-; Chapl Res Aurora Sinai Med Cntr Milwaukee WI 2008-; Mem Cmsn on Mssn and Dvlpmt 2010-** B Fort Madison IA 1983 d Jerry & Sheila. BA Cornell Coll 2005; MDiv Ya Berk 2008. D 7/26/2007 P 7/8/2008 Bp James Louis Jelinek. m 6/23/2007 Jeremy R Deaner c 1. S Jas Ch W Bend WI 2013-2015; Vic S Aidans Ch Hartford WI 2009-2016, Pres of Stndg Com, Dio Milwaukee 2011-; Asst S Paul's Ch Milwaukee WI 2008-2009; D S Mk's Ch New Britain CT 2007-2008. pastoranna@staidans-hartford.org

DOHERTY, Jerry Clay (Minn) 201 Bayberry Avenue Ct, Stillwater MN 55082 **Chapl U Epis Cmnty Minneapolis MN 2008-; Total Mnstry Mentor St. Lk's Epis Ch Hastings MN 2012-** B Des Moines IA 1949 s Joe & Nia. BS Iowa St U 1971; MDiv SWTS 1974; DMin SWTS 1998. D 6/14/1975 P 12/ 1/1975 Bp Walter Cameron Righter. m 4/23/1982 Sheila Maybanks c 2. R Ch Of The Ascen Stillwater MN 1992-2008; R Ch Of The Incarn Great Falls MT 1985-1992; R S Lk's Ch Ft Madison IA 1979-1985; Cur S Tim's Epis Ch W Des Moines IA 1978-1979; Vic S Andr's ClearLake IA 1975-1978; Asst S Jn's Ch Mason City IA 1975-1978; Chapl U Epis Ch Minneapolis MN 2011-2014. Auth, *A Celtic Model of Mnstry*, The Liturg Press, 2003; Auth, *Crossroads*.

DOHERTY, John S (Ia) CATHEDRAL CHURCH OF ST PAUL, 815 HIGH ST, DES MOINES IA 50309 **Dio Iowa Des Moines IA 2014-, Epis Corp Bd, Chapt Rep. 2011-, One Wrld One Ch Cmsn 2010-, COM 2007-; Coord. of Fin & Mnstry The Cathd Ch Of S Paul Des Moines IA 2008-** B Des Moines IA 1953 s Joe & Nia. D 10/8/2007 Bp Alan Scarfe. m 6/8/1974 Janet C Doherty c 2. OSL 2009. jdoherty@iowaepiscopal.org

DOHERTY, Maureen Catherine (Ia) 417 Olive St, Cedar Falls IA 50613 B Albuquerque NM 1946 d Jerome & Margaret. Xavier U; BA Coll of Mt St Jos 1971; MDiv Epis TS of the SW 2001. D 6/29/2002 P 1/18/2003 Bp Robert Manning Moody. m 5/8/2009 Joan Elizabeth Farstad c 1. no Trin Epis Par Waterloo IA 2011-2013; Dir New City Mnstrs 2010-2013; Chapl Dio Iowa Des Moines IA 2009-2015; Campus Min U of Nthrn Iowa Cedar Falls IA 2009-2015; R S Andr's Epis Ch Waverly IA 2002-2009; D S Aid's Epis Ch Tulsa OK 2001-2002; Campus Min Epis Ch NM 1996-1998.

DOHERTY, Noel James (Okla) 6910 E 62nd St, S, Tulsa OK 74133 B Redding CA 1941 s Robert & Ella. BA Bethany Coll 1963; MDiv GTS 1971. D 6/29/ 1971 P 12/19/1971 Bp Chilton R Powell. R S Dunst's Ch Tulsa OK 2001-2008; R All SS Epis Ch Miami OK 1980-2001; Dio Oklahoma Oklahoma City OK 1980; Cur S Jn's Epis Ch Tulsa OK 1973-1979; Cur Trin Ch Tulsa OK 1971-1973.

DOHERTY, Tyler Britton (U) 231 E 100 S, Salt Lake City UT 84111 **Cathd Ch Of S Mk Salt Lake City UT 2015-** B Toronto Ontario 1973 BA McGill U 1996; MFA Naropa U 2001; MEd Arcadia U 2003; MDiv VTS 2014; MDiv Virginia Theol Sem 2014; MDiv Virginia Theol Sem 2014. D 1/17/2015 Bp Clifton Daniel III P 6/17/2015 Bp Scott Byron Hayashi. m 6/3/2001 Michelle Veronica Isaac-Doherty c 3.

DOHERTY-OGEA, Kathleen Lambert (WLa) 206 South Street, Bastrop LA 71220 B Battle Creek MI 1944 d Glenn & Edith. D 6/3/2000 P 12/16/2000 Bp Robert Jefferson Hargrove Jr. m 4/2/1994 Herman Joseph Ogea. D Chr Ch Bastrop LA 2000-2002.

DOHLE, Robert Joseph (Tex) St Paul's Episcopal Church, 1307 W 5th St, Freeport TX 77541 **Vic S Paul's Epis Ch Freeport TX 2008-** B Steelville MO 1947 s Robert & Venita. Iona Sch for Mnstry. D 6/23/2007 Bp Don Adger Wimberly P 1/26/2008 Bp Rayford Baines High Jr. m 10/15/1971 Patricia Anne Dohle c 2.

DOHONEY, Edmund Luther (WTex) 14906 Grayoak Frst, San Antonio TX 78248 **Int Deploy Off Dio W Texas 2008-** B Shreveport LA 1941 s Alfred & Sally. BA U of Arkansas 1964; MDiv Sewanee: The U So, TS 1977. D 6/14/ 1977 P 5/1/1978 Bp James Barrow Brown. m 3/31/1978 Christine Dohoney c 3. R The Epis Ch Of The Epiph New Iberia LA 1999-2001; Int Epis Ch Of The Mssh Gonzales TX 1993, 1979-1983, R 1979-1983; Int All SS Epis Ch Corpus Christi TX 1990-1991; Cn to the Ordnry Dio W Texas San Antonio TX 1988-1999, COM 1985-1988, Chair, Compstn Com 1984; R S Andr's Epis Ch Seguin TX 1983-1988; S Jas Ch Hallettsville TX 1979-1982; Asst S Lk's Epis Ch San Antonio TX 1978-1979; Cur S Phil's Ch New Orleans LA 1977-1978. CODE 1989-1998. ed.dohoney@dwtx.org

DOING JR, Robert Burns (SwFla) 36 Barkley Circle Apt 205, Fort Myers FL 33907 **Ret 1995-** B Brooklyn NY 1929 s Robert & Louisa. BA Trin Hartford CT 1951; LTh GTS 1954. D 4/24/1954 P 11/13/1954 Bp James Pernette De-Wolfe. c 3. R S Anselm Epis Ch Lehigh Acres FL 1982-1994; R S Jas' Epis Ch

231

Winsted CT 1962-1982; Vic S Johns' Epis Ch Bristol CT 1956-1962; Cur Trin Epis Ch Roslyn NY 1954-1956.

DOLACK, Craig A (Ga) Saint Michael And All Angels, 3101 Waters Ave, Savannah GA 31404 B Cortez CO 1971 s Gary & Elizabeth. BA No Carolina St U 1994; MDiv Sewanee: The U So, TS 2006. D 5/11/2006 Bp Richard Sui On Chang P 11/15/2006 Bp Henry Irving Louttit. m 12/16/2000 Sharon W Dolack c 2. S Mich And All Ang Savannah GA 2013; S Mk's Ch Fincastle VA 2008-2011; Asst S Thos Ch Savannah GA 2006-2008. One Epis 2007; The Epis Majority 2007; The Epis Publ Plcy Ntwk 2007.

DOLAN, John Richard (Chi) 3925 Central Ave, Western Springs IL 60558 **Died 10/8/2016** B Oxford UK 1942 s Walter & Joan. BS Lon GB 1969. D 2/3/1996 Bp Frank Tracy Griswold III. m 7/5/1975 Karen Joyce Dolan c 2. D Trin Epis Ch Aurora IL 2011-2016; D All SS Ch Wstrn Sprgs IL 2011-2013; D Emm Epis Ch La Grange IL 1996-2011. Auth, "The Black Dog," *The Black Dog*, Signalman Pub, 2012; Auth, "The Mushroom Farm," *The Mushroom Farm*, Signalman Pub, 2011. Inst Chart Acct 1968.

DOLAN, Mary Ellen Teresa (Eur) Frankfurter Strasse 3, Wiesbaden 65189 Germany **Pres, Disciplinary Borad 2011-; 1st Alt Dep, GC 2012 2010-** B Framingham MA 1944 d Matthew & Helen. BS S Jos Sem & Coll 1968; Dplma Inst De Médecine Tropicale BE 1972; Dplma Inst D'Enseignement Med-RDC 1974; MA S Johns U 1986; Cert GTS 1990; STM GTS 1990; Cert Sprtl Direction 1990. D 6/24/1995 Bp J Clark Grew II P 12/30/1995 Bp Craig Barry Anderson. Int R Ch Of The Gd Shpd And S Jn Milford PA 2012-2014; Int R All SS Epis Ch Braine-l'Alleud 2010-2012; Int R Ch of S Aug of Cbury 65189 Wiesbaden 2007-2010; Convoc of Epis Ch in Europe Paris 2007-2010; Asst to the R Chr Ch Westerly RI 2002-2006; St Mich & Gr Ch Rumford RI 2000-2001; Asst to the R S Mary's Ch Portsmouth RI 1997-1998; Asst to the Dn Cathd Of S Jn Providence RI 1995-1996. Coun of Angl/Epis Ch Germany 2007-2010; Epis Partnership for Global Mssn 1998-2006; Int Mnstrs of TEC, Bd 2012; Réseau Francophone de la Comm Anglicane 1998.

DOLAN, Pamela E (Mo) 9 S Bompart Ave, Saint Louis MO 63119 **Ch Of The Gd Shpd S Louis MO 2011-** B Oakland CA 1968 d David & Patricia. BA U CA Berkeley 1990; MTS Harvard DS 1995. D 12/18/2009 P 6/19/2010 Bp George Wayne Smith. m 7/16/1994 John J Dolan c 2. Dir of Chr Formation/ Cmncatn Asst Emm Epis Ch S Louis MO 2010-2011.

DOLAN-HENDERSON, Susan Mary (Tex) 3104 Harris Park Ave, Austin TX 78705 B Flushing NY 1957 d Michael & Irene. BD Boston Coll 1979; MDiv Ya Berk 1985; PhD Emory U 1994. D 11/1/1994 Bp Maurice Manuel Benitez P 5/1/1995 Bp Claude Edward Payne. m 10/27/1990 Alvin Augustus Dolan-Henderson c 1. Epis TS Of The SW Austin TX 1995-2007. Auth, "Our Common Life & Heritage"; Auth, "Dictionary Feminist Theologies". AAR, Soc Chr Ethics.

DOLEN, William Kennedy (Ga) 605 Reynolds St, Augusta GA 30901 **Chapl Georgia Hlth Sciences U 2010-** B Memphis TN 1952 s William & Dorothy. BS Rhodes Coll 1974; MD U of TN Cntr for Hlth Serv 1977. D 2/6/2010 P 8/21/2010 Bp Scott Anson Benhase. m 12/21/1974 Carolyn Dolen c 2. D S Paul's Ch Augusta GA 2010, Asstg P 2010-.

DOLL, Gregory Allen (Kan) **Chapl Meadowlark Hospice 2016-; D S Paul's Ch Manhattan KS 2016-; D 2016-** B 1954 D 6/11/2016 Bp Dean E Wolfe P 6/17/2017 Bp George Wayne Smith. m 8/5/1977 Elizabeth A Koepke.

DOLLAHITE, Damian DeWitt Gene (Dal) 226 Oakhaven Dr, Grand Prairie TX 75050 B Yukon OK 1939 s Louis & Mabel. AA Coll of Marin 1971; BA Antioch Coll W San Francisco CA 1976; MDiv CDSP 1981. D 10/24/1973 Bp Chauncie Kilmer Myers P 5/1/1981 Bp William Edwin Swing. c 1. R S Mary's Epis Ch And Sch Irving TX 1995-2008; R S Phil's Ch Beulah MI 1987-1995; P-in-c S Geo's Ch Valley WY 1986-1987; Ch Of S Andr's In The Pines Pinedale WY 1982-1985; Vic Epis Ch Bridge Wilderness Area WY 1982-1985; Vic S Hubert The Hunter Bonduran Bondurant WY 1982-1985; St Jn the Bapt Epis Ch Big Piney WY 1982-1985; Exec Coun Dio Wstrn Michigan Kalamazoo MI 1988-1995; Yth Min Ch Of The H Innoc Corte Madera CA 1961-1978. Angl Eucharistic League; Chapl Ord Of S Lk, Ohca, CBS, NOEL, Epis Untd.

DOLLHAUSEN, Matthew Mark (CGC) 6849 Oak St, Milton FL 32570 **R S Mary's Epis Ch Milton FL 2015-** B Fond du Lac WI 1951 s John & Ruth. BLS Barry U 1992; MDiv Luth Sthrn TS 1996. Rec 12/1/2014 as Priest Bp Philip Menzie Duncan II. m 12/27/2009 Vickie E Dollhausen c 3.

DOLNIKOWSKI, Edith Wilks (Mass) The Episcopal Diocese Of Massachusetts, 138 Tremont St, Boston MA 02111 **Ord Vocations Dio Massachusetts Boston MA 2013-** B Pittsburgh PA 1959 d Joseph & June. BA Coll of Wooster 1981; MA MI SU 1984; PhD MI SU 1989; MDiv EDS 1994. D 6/3/1995 Bp Barbara Clementine Harris P 5/23/1996 Bp M(Arvil) Thomas Shaw. m 12/30/1980 Gregory G Dolnikowski. Assoc St. Andr's Ch Wellesley MA 2003-2013; Par Admin S Andr's Ch Wellesley MA 1998-2013; Asst Ch Of Our Sav Brookline MA 1995-2003. Amer Soc of Ch Hist 1990; MA Epis Cleric Assn 1995. edie@ diomass.org

DOLPH, Scott Marshall Michael (Ore) 4233 S. E. Ash Street, Portland OR 97215 **Assoc Chapl Legacy Gd Samar Hosp Portland OR 1995-** B Tucson AZ 1957 s Wilbert & Shirley. BArch U of Arizona 1980; BA U of Arizona 1980;

MDiv GTS 1985; MDiv GTS 1995. D 6/11/1985 Bp Joseph Thomas Heistand P 12/27/1985 Bp Emerson Paul Haynes. S Aid's Epis Ch Portland OR 2000-2014, R 1995-2000; Dio Oregon Portland OR 1995; San Pablo Hillsboro OR 1994-1995; Cur Trin Epis Cathd Portland OR 1988-1993; Cur S Jn's Epis Ch Clearwater FL 1985-1987. Auth, "Maintenance," *Tucson Preservation Primer*.

DOLS, Timothy Walters (Va) 5705 Oak Bluff Ln, Wilmington NC 28409 B Baltimore MD 1942 s William & Isabel. BA W&L 1964; MDiv VTS 1967; DMin Wesley Sem 1985; DMin Wesley TS 1985. D 6/20/1967 P 6/1/1968 Bp Harry Lee Doll. m 8/22/1964 Anne S Dols c 2. S Phil's Ch Holly Ridge NC 2003-2015; R S Ptr's Epis Ch Arlington VA 1975-2001; R Sherwood Epis Ch Cockeysville MD 1969-1975; Asst S Tim's Ch Catonsville MD 1967-1968.

DOLS JR, William Ludwig (Va) 300 Aspen St, Alexandria VA 22305 **Ret 2001-** B Baltimore MD 1933 s William & Isabel. BA W&L 1955; MDiv VTS 1958; Coll of Preachers 1983; PhD Grad Theol Un 1988. D 6/17/1958 Bp Harry Lee Doll P 1/1/1959 Bp Noble C Powell. m 9/7/1957 Shirley Dols c 2. Serv Bapt Ch 1996-2001; Ed The Bible Workbench 1992-2001; Dir The Educational Cntr St. Louis MO 1987-1995; R Imm Ch-On-The-Hill Alexandria VA 1972-1983; R S Jas Par Wilmington NC 1965-1972; Vic S Jn's Epis Ch Arlington VA 1961-1965; Cur S Thos' Ch Garrison Forest Owings Mills MD 1958-1960; BEC; Exec Coun Dio Virginia Richmond VA 1972-1983; Exec Coun Dio E Carolina Kinston NC 1967-1969. Auth, "Finding Jesus, Discovering Self," Morehouse, 2006; Auth, "Just Because It Didn'T Happen: Sermons And Prayers As Story," Myers Pk Bapt Ch, 2001; Auth, "Awakening The Fire Within: A Primer For Issue-Centered Educ," The Educational Cntr, 1994; Auth, "The Ch As Crucible For Transformation," *Jung's Challenge To Contemporary Rel*, Chiron, 1987; Auth, "3-Dimensional Man: A Collection Of Sermons," 1968.

DOMBEK, Timothy M (Az) 11242 N 50th Ave, Glendale AZ 85304 **Ch Of The Adv Sun City W AZ 2016-** B Warsaw IN 1958 s Wladyslaw & Olive. Anderson U; BA Bethel U 1989; MDiv SWTS 1992. D 4/25/1992 P 12/9/1992 Bp Francis Campbell Gray. m 6/9/1990 Beth Ann Dombek c 1. Cn to the Ordnry Dio Arizona Phoenix AZ 2007-2016; R S Jas Epis Ch Greenville SC 2000-2007; Chapl Heathwood Hall Epis Sch Columbia SC 1996-2000; P-in-c S Barn Ch Jenkinsville SC 1996-2000; Assoc The Epis Ch Of The Trsfg Dallas TX 1992-1996. Co-Auth, "Making the Annual Pledge Drive Obsolete," *Making the Annual Pledge Drive Obsolete*, CommonWealth Consulting, 2013; Auth, "E-Prime & Euch: Theol/Semantic Consideration," *E-Prime III! Third Anthology*, Int'l Soc for Gnrl Semantics, 1997. Natl Forensic League 1997-2000. timothy@adventaz.org

DOMENICK JR, W(arren) L(ee) (Minn) St Luke's Church, 4557 Colfax Ave S, Minneapolis MN 55419 **S Lk's Ch Minneapolis MN 2013-** B Fort Ord CA 1966 s Warren & Elaine. BA Shaw U 1997; MDiv Sewanee: The U So, TS 2000. D 6/24/2000 P 2/17/2001 Bp Clifton Daniel III. m 5/16/2016 Jeffrey Luke c 1. R S Paul's Epis Ch Jesup GA 2008-2013; R Ch Of The Ascen Lakewood OH 2002-2008; Asst to R Chr Ch New Bern NC 2000-2002. CE Awd For Creativity And Excellence In Biblic Tchg ABS 2000. saintlukesfatherlee@gmail. com

DOMIENIK, Steven B (Mich) St. John's Episcopal Church, 555 S Wayne Rd, Westland MI 48186 **Nativ Epis Ch Bloomfield Township MI 2016-; S Jn's Ch Westland MI 2015-** B Detroit MI 1961 s Bernard & Katherine. BA U of Detroit Mercy 1984; MA U Cinc 1991; MDiv EDS 2009. D 6/14/2008 P 6/20/2009 Bp Thomas Edward Breidenthal. c 2. P-in-c S Andr's Ch Madison CT 2010-2015; Cur Ch Of The Gd Shpd Athens OH 2009-2010. frsteve@ stjohnswestland.com

DONAHOE, Melanie (Cal) Church of the Epiphany, 1839 Arroyo Avenue, San Carlos CA 94070 **R Ch Of The Epiph San Carlos CA 2009-** B San Rafael CA 1953 d Stephen & Virginia. BA Stan 1975; MA Geo 1987; MA Washington Theol Un 1989; CAS CDSP 2004. D 4/30/2005 P 11/12/2005 Bp Sylvestre Donato Romero. m 5/29/1983 Henry L Tenenbaum c 3. Assoc Trsfg Epis Ch San Mateo CA 2005-2009.

DONAHUE, Lawrence Charles (NwPa) 204 Jackson Ave, Bradford PA 16701 B Bronx NY 1941 s Lawrence & Grace. BA Niagara U 1966; MDiv Niagara U 1970. Rec 5/1/1979 as Priest Bp Robert Campbell Witcher Sr. m 11/13/1982 Patricia Ann Rielly Donahue. R Ch Of The Ascen Bradford PA 1998-2007; Dio Long Island Garden City NY 1983; S Cuth's Epis Ch Selden NY 1982-1998; Cur H Trin Epis Ch Hicksville NY 1979-1982.

DONAHUE, Ray Lawrence (Alb) 24929 State Highway 206, Downsville NY 13755 **Chapl (post Ret/current) Lake Delaware Boys Camp Delhi NY 2001-, Chapl 1989-2001** B Elmira NY 1929 s James & Laura. BA Hobart and Wm Smith Colleges 1951; STB GTS 1954. D 6/6/1954 Bp Frederick Lehrle Barry P 12/18/1954 Bp David Emrys Richards. P-in-c S Marg's Ch Margaretville NY 1956-2001; S Mary's Ch Downsville NY 1956-2001; S Paul's W Middleburgh NY 1954-1956; Asst The Ch Of The Gd Shpd Canajoharie NY 1954-1956.

DONALD, David Seth (WLa) 715 Kirkman St, Lake Charles LA 70601 **S Mich And All Ang Lake Chas LA 2016-** B Jennings LA 1975 s David & Brenda.

BA Rhodes Coll 1997; MBA Centenary Coll 2008; MDiv Sewanee: The U So, TS 2015; MDiv The TS at The U So 2015. D 12/27/2014 P 7/25/2015 Bp Jacob W Owensby. m 7/3/1999 Amy Parratt Amy Marie Parratt c 3. Epis Ch Of The Gd Shpd Lake Chas LA 2015-2016. donalds0@sewanee.edu

DONALD, James (WA) 1 Peachtree Battle Ave. , NW #5, Unit #5, Atlanta GA 30305 **Cler Assoc All SS Epis Ch Atlanta GA 2007-** B Hackensack NJ 1944 s Joseph & Marion. BA S Michaels Coll Vermont 1966; MAT U of Notre Dame 1967; MDiv cl GTS 1978; DMin Fuller TS 1997. D 6/9/1978 Bp Robert Shaw Kerr P 2/9/1979 Bp John Thomas Walker. m 6/10/1967 Kathryn Donald c 2. R S Columba's Ch Washington DC 1995-2005; R S Matt's Ch Charleston WV 1984-1995; Dep to the Bp So Carolina Charleston SC 1981-1984; Asst Gr Epis Ch Silver Sprg MD 1979-1981; St. Albans Sch Cathd of St Ptr & St Paul Washington DC 1978-1979; Chapl S Alb Sch WDC 1978-1979; Mem, Stwdshp Cmsn Dio W Virginia Charleston WV 1984-1994. Auth, "arts," 2003. Jn Hines Preaching Awd VTS 2000.

DONALDSON, Audley (LI) 1345 President St, Brooklyn NY 11213 **R Ch Of SS Steph And Mart Brooklyn NY 2010-; Vic S Phil's Chap 1987-** B Negril Jama CA 1957 s Lester & Lena. BA U of The W Indies 1980; DMin W Indies Untd Theol Coll Kingston Jm 1980; STM Ya Berk 1985; Ya 1985. Trans 1/1/1987 Bp Christopher FitzSimons Allison. m 9/7/2011 Kendra A Donaldson c 1. Ch Of The Redeem Brooklyn NY 2007-2010; S Mk's Ch Brooklyn NY 2004-2007, Asst 1985-1986; Voorhees Coll Charleston SC 1987; Chapl Kings Cnty Hosp Brooklyn NY 1986-1987; R Mortan Bay Cure S Thos Jamaica 1982-1984.

DONALDSON, Walter Alexander (Los) 7631 Klusman Ave, Rancho Cucamonga CA 91730 **Ret 1998-; Asst Chr Ch Par Ontario CA 1975-** B New Castle PA 1937 s Harold & Dorothy. BA U CA 1966; MEd U of Redlands 1971; DIT ETSBH 1976. D 6/18/1977 P 1/14/1978 Bp Robert Claflin Rusack. m 4/20/1966 Dolly Ruth Thacker. Tchr to the Handicapped San Bernandino Cnty Schools 1967-1998. Auth, *Chance to be a Chld.*

DONATELLI, Todd M (WNC) Cathedral of All Souls, 9 Swan St, Asheville NC 28803 **Dn The Cathd Of All Souls Asheville NC 1997-** B Oak Park IL 1956 s Henry & Audrey. ABJ U GA 1979; MDiv VTS 1987. D 6/6/1987 P 4/23/1988 Bp Charles Judson Child Jr. m 12/29/1979 Rebecca Louise Ferguson c 2. Dio Wstrn No Carolina Asheville NC 1999-2002; Dio Mississippi Jackson MS 1996-2002, Dioc Educ Cmsn 1990-1995; Cn S Andr's Cathd Jackson MS 1990-1997; Asst to R S Barth's Epis Ch Atlanta GA 1987-1990. Auth, "The Fruitful Mar," *Mississippi mag*, 1995. Guest Prchr "The Prot Hour" Series Of Four Sermons 2001.

DONATHAN, William Larry (WA) 105 15th Street SE, Washington DC 20003 **Epis Chapl Knollwood Mltry Ret Res 2005-; Eductr Dist of Columbia Publ Schools 2003-; COM Dio Washington Washington DC 2012-, Dioc Coun 2000-2012** B Alexandria VA 1966 s Foley & Frances. BA Geo Mason U 1989; MDiv VTS 1994; MA Amer U 2005. D 6/11/1994 P 12/14/1994 Bp Peter J Lee. R S Jn's Epis/Angl Ch Mt Rainier MD 1997-2003; Asst R S Mary's Ch Wayne PA 1995-1997; Asst R Gr Ch Anniston AL 1994-1995. SocMary 1989. Highly Effective Eductr Awd DC Publ Schools 2013; Jn Hines Preaching Awd VTS 2013; Highly Effectuve Eductr Awd DCPublic Schools 2012; Highly Effective Eductr Awd DC Publ Schools 2011; Winner Winifred H. Clark Prize, Gnrl Sem 2011; Highly Effective Eductr Awd DC Publ Schools 2010; Mentor EFM, Sewanee, TN 2006; Coll Bus Fraternity Delta Sigma Pi 1951.

DONCASTER CT, Diana (NCal) 495 Albion Ave, Cincinnati OH 45246 B Alturas CA 1956 d Rodney & Jeane. BA California St U 1981; MA U of Iowa 1986; CAS CDSP 2014. D 10/2/2014 P 5/7/2015 Bp Barry Leigh Beisner. srdianact@gmail.com

DONDERO, Christina Downs (At) 879 Clifton Rd Ne, Atlanta GA 30307 B Doylestown PA 1948 d Raymond & Elizabeth. BA Connecticut Coll 1969; Candler TS Emory U 1999. D 8/6/2006 Bp J Neil Alexander. m 7/6/1968 Timothy Joseph Dondero c 5. D S Barth's Epis Ch Atlanta GA 2006-2014.

DONECKER, Paul Clayton (CPa) 351 Bull Run Crossing, Lewisburg PA 17837 **All SS Ch Selinsgrove PA 2011-** B Philadelphia PA 1948 s John & Mary. BA Buc 1970; MDiv VTS 1976. D 6/11/1977 P 7/9/1978 Bp Lyman Cunningham Ogilby. m 12/22/1973 Leigh D Donecker c 2. Sabbatical Supply P Chr Epis Ch Williamsport PA 2011; Int R Trin Memi Ch Binghamton NY 2007-2011; Archd Congrl Dev & Deplymt Dio Cntrl Pennsylvania Harrisburg PA 1996-2007; Chapl Com Evang Cmnty Hosp 1990-1996; R S Andr's Epis Ch Lewisburg PA 1979-1996; Cur Chr Ch Stratford CT 1978-1979; Chapl Walter Reed Army Med Cntr 1977-1978. Cler Asociation 1979; Int Mnstry Ntwk 2008.

DONEHUE, Robertson Carr (SC) **St Anne's Epis Ch Conway SC 2016-** B 1979 s John & Virginia. BA U of So Carolina 2001; MA Dur 2004; MDiv Sewanee: The U So, TS 2016. D 5/14/2016 Bp Charles Glenn VonRosenberg P 11/19/2016 Bp Gladstone Bailey Adams III. m 2/8/2015 Davis Du Bose Donehue. Other Lay Position Gr Ch Cathd Charleston SC 2010-2013. Contrib, "Sermon," *Tell the Story: Narrative and Preaching*, The Epis Preaching Fndt, 2015. Isaac Marion Dwight Medal for Biblic and Philos Gk The TS at the U So 2016; Prize in Biblic Stds The TS at the U So 2016.

DONELSON JR, Frank Taylor (WTenn) 475 N Highland St Apt 7e, Memphis TN 38122 B Memphis TN 1924 s Frank & Mildred. BA Van 1948. D 3/25/1969

Bp William F Gates Jr. m 8/26/1950 Virginia Donelson c 3. D S Jn's Epis Ch Memphis TN 1969-2009.

DONNELLY, Frances (Nwk) 852 Bullet Hill Rd, Southbury CT 06488 **P-in-c S Ptr's Epis Ch Oxford CT 2012-** B Pittsburg CA 1944 d William & Mary. BA U MI 1969; MDiv VTS 1982. D 6/27/1982 P 4/1/1983 Bp Robert Rae Spears Jr. m 10/31/1981 John Allen Donnelly c 2. S Mich's Epis Ch Wayne NJ 2002-2011, R 1991-1998; R Calv Ch Stonington CT 1986-1991; Asst Min Chr Ch Greenwich CT 1983-1986; Asst S Thos Epis Ch Rochester NY 1982-1983.

DONNELLY, Jeffrey Joseph (Cal) B Albany NY 1963 s Joseph & Betty. BA Gordon Coll 1990; MA Tem 1995; MDiv U Tor CA 2006. D 6/3/2006 Bp William Edwin Swing P 12/2/2006 Bp Marc Handley Andrus.

DONNELLY, John Allen (Ct) 470 Quaker Farms Road, Oxford CT 06478 **R Chr Ch Oxford CT 2011-; Dept Chapl The Oxford Fire Dept Oxford CT 2014-** B Cincinnati OH 1953 s Cecil & Jean. BA U Cinc 1976; BS U Cinc 1976; MDiv VTS 1981; DMin Kingsway Chr Coll and Sem 1999; Cert Drew U 2000. D 6/27/1981 Bp William Grant Black P 6/27/1982 Bp Robert Rae Spears Jr. m 10/31/1981 Frances Donnelly c 2. Chapl Hospice Paramus NJ 2001-2011; R S Mich's Epis Ch Wayne NJ 1991-2011; R Calv Ch Stonington CT 1986-1991; Asst Min Chr Ch Greenwich CT 1983-1986; P-in-c S Thos Epis Ch Rochester NY 1981-1983; Chapl The Wayne Police Dept Wayne NJ 2010-2013. Auth, "Its A Miracle," *A Journ of Chr Healing*, 2006; Auth, "The Healing Continues," *A Journ of Chr Healing*, 2000. DD Chr Ldrshp U 2014; NJ Hospice Chapl of the Year NJ Hospice and Palliative Care Orgnztn 2011; US Congressional Cert of Spec Recognition 2001; Phi Beta Kappa 1976.

DONNELLY, Richard Colonel (Ct) 430 Quaker Drive, York PA 17402 **Non-par Dir 1987-** B Albany NY 1927 s Henry & Lena. Berea Coll 1955; BA Hartwick Coll 1957; MA Syr 1958; BD Harvard DS 1961; MDiv EDS 1972. D 6/16/1962 Bp Allen Webster Brown P 12/22/1962 Bp Donald MacAdie. m 1/14/2006 Frances Allison Donnelly c 3. R Chr Ch Ansonia CT 1982-1987; Assoc S Jas Epis Ch Danbury CT 1979-1982; Chapl Wstrn Ct S U-Danbury 1977-1979; R Zion Epis Ch Wappingers Falls NY 1971-1977; R S Andr's Epis Ch York PA 1965-1971; Asst Trin Epis Ch Roslyn NY 1963-1965; Cur Chr Epis Ch E Orange NJ 1962-1963. The AAPC 1975.

DONOHUE, Mary Jane (Mass) 51 Ryder Ave, Melrose MA 02176 B Manchester CT 1968 d Ralph & Judith. BS NWU 1994; MA TESM 1994; MDiv Yale DS 2004. D 6/9/2007 Bp Andrew Donnan Smith P 2/16/2008 Bp Laura Ahrens. m 8/12/2009 Lauren Lea Patalak c 1. Chapl Dio Massachusetts Boston MA 2010-2013; Asst S Ann's Epis Ch Old Lyme CT 2007-2010. Meuhl Preaching Prize Berkeley Grad Soc 2004.

DONOHUE-ADAMS, Amy (Oly) 11703 Oakwood Dr, Austin TX 78753 **Chapl Round Rock Med Cntr Round Rock TX 1996-** B Chicago IL 1946 d Daniel & Bernice. BS S Mary of the Woods Coll 1969; MDiv Epis TS of the SW 1993; Bd Certification Assn of Profsnl Chapl 2007. D 6/21/1993 Bp William Jackson Cox P 3/14/1994 Bp Claude Edward Payne. m 6/3/1995 William Seth Adams. Chapl S Jas Ch Austin TX 1998-2010; Vic S Ptr's Epis Ch Leander TX 1995-1996; The Great Cmsn Fndt Houston TX 1995-1996; Asst S Fran Ch Houston TX 1993-1995.

✠ **DONOVAN, The Rt Rev Herbert Alcorn** (NY) 152 Broadway # 8, Dobbs Ferry NY 10522 **Chapl AEC and Universities Bd Mem 2003-; Dio New York New York NY 1993-** B Washington DC 1931 s Herbert & Marion. BA U of Virginia 1954; MDiv VTS 1957; Coll of Preachers 1976; Harvard DS 1987. D 6/10/1957 Bp Frederick D Goodwin P 12/10/1957 Bp James W Hunter Con 9/22/1980 for Ark. m 7/7/1959 Mary Sudman c 3. Cnslt to Prvsnl Bp Epis Ch Cntr New York NY 2011-2013, Cnslt to Provsnl Bp 1990; Int R Trin Ch Epis Boston MA 2005-2006; Provsnl Bp of NJ Dio New Jersey Trenton NJ 1999-2000; Provsnl Bp of Chi Dio Chicago Chicago IL 1998-1999; Ret Bp of Ark Dio Arkansas Little Rock AR 1993-2003, Bp of Arkansas 1984-1992, Bp Coadj of Ark 1980-1983; Vic Trin Par New York NY 1993-1997; Secy HOB 1986-1998; R S Lk's Epis Ch Montclair NJ 1970-1980; COT and Exec Off Dio Kentucky Louisville KY 1959-1964, Exec Off 1964-1970; Vic S Andr's Ch Basin WY 1959-1964; R S Jn's Ch Green River WY 1957-1959; Chapl / Captain US Naval Reserve 1955-1992; Angl Observer to the Untd Nations Dom And Frgn Mssy Soc- Epis Ch Cntr New York NY 2001-2003; DD Berk atYale New Haven CT 2003; DD U So Sewanee TN 1984; DD VTS Alexandria VA 1981.

DONOVAN, John Carl (Tex) 2908 Avenue O Apt 1, Galveston TX 77550 **Ret 1995-** B Muncie IN 1930 s Carl & Eleanor. BA U of Texas 1952; LLB U of Texas 1954; BD Epis TS of the SW 1957; Coll of Preachers 1970. D 6/20/1957 P 5/24/1958 Bp James Parker Clements. m 2/3/1962 Joal Donovan c 3. R Trin Ch Galveston TX 1976-1995, Assoc 1963-1965; Serv Ch in Mex 1971-1976; R St. Paul's Iglesia Epis San Miguel de Allende 1971-1976; R S Steph's Ch Beaumont TX 1965-1971; Chapl Baylor U 1957-1962; Vic Chr Epis Ch Mexia Mexia TX 1957-1962; BEC Dio Texas Houston TX 1971-1995. Phi Beta Kappa.

DONOVAN, Nancy Lu (SD) 9412 Saint Joseph St, Silver City SD 57702 B Hot Springs SD 1935 d Glenn & Verda. Stephens Coll; U Denv 1957. D 5/24/1996 Bp James Edward Krotz. m 2/1/1958 Uhl Dean Donovan c 3. Oblate Ord Of S Ben.

DONOVAN, William Patrick (Minn) 684 Mississippi River Blvd S, Saint Paul MN 55116 B Saint Louis MO 1929 s John & Dorothy. BA Washington U 1951; MA Washington U 1952; PhD U Cinc 1961; Westcott Hse Cambridge 1968. D 5/10/1971 P 2/13/1972 Bp Philip Frederick McNairy. m 6/15/1955 Patricia Ann O'Keefe c 2. Cn Cathd Ch Of S Mk Minneapolis MN 1978-2013; Asst St Geo's Epis Ch Minneapolis MN 1971-1974. Auth, *Excavations at Nichoria*; Auth, *Palace of Nestor*.

DOOLEY, Martha Mae (NJ) 4735 Cedar Ave, Philadelphia PA 19143 **D Ch Of S Jn-In-The-Wilderness Gibbsboro NJ 2005-** B York Harbor ME 1949 d George & Eugenia. BSN U of Maryland 1972; MSN U of Pennsylvania 1983. D 6/11/2005 Bp George Edward Councell. m 5/30/2013 Kathleen Murray. Gr Ch Pemberton NJ 2005. Integrity 1994.

DOOLING, Thomas Alexander (Mont) 511 N Park Ave, Helena MT 59601 B Montana 1942 s John & Dorothea. AB Harvard Coll 1963; Juris Doctor Geo Washington 1972. D 10/2/1999 P 4/8/2000 Bp Charles I Jones III. c 4.

DOOLITTLE, Geoffrey Douglas (CNY) 117 Main St, Owego NY 13827 **R S Paul's Ch Owego NY 2010-** B Binghamton NY 1960 s Raymond & Barbara. AAS Broome Cmnty Coll 1980; MDiv VTS 2010. D 12/19/2009 P 11/3/2010 Bp Gladstone Bailey Adams III. m 5/24/1980 Joann E Doolittle c 3.

DOPP, William Floyd (SwFla) 818 Chamise Ct, San Marcos CA 92069 B Watertown WI 1942 s William & June. San Diego St U; BS Indiana U 1990; MDiv Claremont TS 1994; DMin SWTS 2001. D 6/11/1994 P 2/24/1995 Bp Gethin Benwil Hughes. m 9/8/1962 Janet Dopp. R S Mart's Epis Ch Hudson FL 2005-2009; Cmncatn Off Dio San Diego San Diego CA 1999-2002, 1994-2005; Vic S Columba's Epis Ch Santee CA 1995-1999; Trin Ch Escondido CA 1994. Auth, "Tale of Two Ch," 2009; Auth, "The Archd's Column," *The Ch Times*, 2002; Auth, "The Ed'S Notebook," *The Ch Times*, 1994; Auth, "Copy Writers Idea Bk," 1982. Bro Of S Andr 1982; OSL 2006. Ord Of Constantine Sigma Chi Fraternity Alum 2001; Polly Bond Cert For "Spec Lambeth Ed" ECom 1998.

DORAN, Judith Ann (Chi) 1350 N Western Ave Apt 111, Lake Forest IL 60045 **The Ch Of The H Sprt Lake Forest IL 2015-** B Chicago IL 1953 d Walter & Catherine. BA Chapman U 1983; MDiv Bex Sem 2006. D 5/14/2005 Bp Herbert Thompson Jr P 6/24/2006 Bp Kenneth Lester Price. m 5/6/1978 Patrick George Doran c 2. Trin Ch Highland Pk IL 2014-2015; All SS Ch Wstrn Sprgs IL 2013-2014; P Trin Epis Ch Troy OH 2011-2012; P S Andr's Ch Dayton OH 2011; P S Jas Ch Piqua OH 2010; Asst S Paul's Epis Ch Dayton OH 2006-2010. rev.judithdoran@gmail.com

DORAN, Michelle Stuart (Md) All Saints, PO Box 40, Sunderland MD 20689 **D All SS Epis Par Sunderland MD 2011-; Archd for Formation Dio Maryland Baltimore MD 2012-, Mem COM 2011-** B Oil City PA 1947 d Charles & Mary. BA SUNY 1969; MEd U of Maryland 1975. D 6/2/2007 Bp John L Rabb. m 8/25/1973 Richard Doran c 2. A.E.D. 2007.

DORN, Christy (WMo) 13134 Lamar Ave, Overland Park KS 66209 **Assoc Gr And H Trin Cathd Kansas City MO 2012-** B Oakland CA 1949 d Lewis & Eleanor. BA U of Arizona 1972; MDiv CDSP 1991. D 12/5/1992 Bp William Edwin Swing P 11/1/1993 Bp John Lester Thompson III. m 6/11/1994 Lawrence G Ehren. Assoc S Wilfrid Of York Epis Ch Huntington Bch CA 2006-2011; Assoc S Mk's Ch Grand Rapids MI 2002-2005; Assoc Ch Of The Gd Shpd Lexington KY 2001-2002; Assoc Komo Kulshan Cluster Mt Vernon WA 2000; Assoc S Andr's Ch Seattle WA 1998-1999; Assoc S Paul Epis Ch Bellingham WA 1995-1997; Cn Chr Ch Cathd Cincinnati OH 1993-1995; Chapl In Res California Pacific Med Cntr San Francisco CA 1991-1992. cdorn@kccathedral.org

DORN III, James M (CFla) 574 West Montrose St, Clermont FL 34711 **R S Mths Epis Ch Clermont FL 2013-; Trst Sewanee U So TS Sewanee TN 2014-** B Charleston SC 1961 s James & Mary. BS Presb Coll 1983; MDiv Sewanee: The U So, TS 2002. D 12/14/2002 Bp Dorsey Henderson P 12/19/2003 Bp Henry Irving Louttit. m 1/4/1986 Janette Sue McIntosh c 3. R S Mk's Ch Palatka FL 2005-2012; Asst R S Thos Ch Savannah GA 2002-2005. rector@stmatthiasfl.com

DORNEMANN, Deanna Maxine (EC) 60 Bethlehem Pike Rm 1401, Philadelphia PA 19118 B 1944 d Alton & Maudine. BS Wesl 1966; MDiv Sewanee: The U So, TS 1990. D 6/16/1990 P 12/27/1990 Bp Brice Sidney Sanders. S Paul Ch Exton PA 2008-2016; Ch Of The Incarn Morrisville PA 2001-2003; S Paul's Ch Philadelphia PA 1993-1999; Asst To R S Jn 1990-1993.

DORNER, Mary Anne (SwFla) 27127 Fordham Dr, Wesley Chapel FL 33543 **Vol Chapl Florida Hosp Wesley Chap Wesley Chap FL 2012-; Adj Prof of Theol Barry U Univ. Partnership Prog Seminole 2005-** B Chicago IL 1945 d James & Anne. Cert Coll of Preachers; Lancaster TS; BA Neumann Coll Aston PA 1984; MDiv VTS 1989. D 6/24/1989 P 6/22/1991 Bp Cabell Tennis. m 8/1/1964 Theodore M Dorner. S Jn The Div Epis Ch Sun City Cntr FL 2004-2006; Vic Resurr Epis Ch Naples FL 1998-2002; Assoc R Ch Of The Gd Shpd Dunedin FL 1994-1998; Asst Gr Epis Ch Wilmington DE 1990-1991; D & DRE S Mart's Ch Wayne PA 1989-1990; Dioc Coun Dio Delaware Wilmington 1991-1994. Auth, "Brandywine Baptism Progran Ldr'S Manual & Parents Guide". Epis Soc For Mnstry To Aging 1992-1995.

DORNHECKER, Douglas Boyd (Oly) 114 20th Ave SE, Olympia WA 98501 B Dallas Oregon 1950 s Robert & Frances. D 12/17/2016 P 6/3/2017 Bp Gregory Harold Rickel. m 6/10/1972 Kathleen Anne Connolly c 3.

DOROW, Robert M (NI) 1007 Moore Rd, Michigan City IN 46360 **S Andr's By The Lake Epis Ch Michigan City IN 2012-; Chapl Helen DeVos Chld's Hosp 2011-** B Pittsburgh PA 1969 s Ernest & Arlene. MDiv TESM 2002. D 6/14/2003 P 3/6/2005 Bp Robert William Duncan. c 2. Int Bread of Life Luth Ch Hudsonville MI 2008-2011; P-in-res Trin Cathd Pittsburgh PA 2005-2007. robdorow@hotmail.com

DORR JR, Erwin John (Ind) 256 51st St Cir E, Palmetto FL 34221 B Farina IL 1930 s Erwin & Edna. BA U IL 1952; MA Ya 1955. D 10/14/1959 P 5/5/1960 Bp Chilton R Powell. m 12/31/1991 Marion Dorr c 2. P-in-c S Mths Ch Rushville IN 1974-1982; R S Jas Ch New Castle IN 1970-1973; R Gr Epis Ch Chadron NE 1962-1970; Vic Ch Of The Ascen Pawnee OK 1959-1962; S Andr's Ch Stillwater OK 1959-1962; Ret.

DORR, Kathleen (Ct) 39 Whalers Pt, East Haven CT 06512 B Wyandotte MI 1952 d Robert & Beatrice. BA OH SU 1977; MDiv Ya Berk 1989. D 6/23/1995 Bp Orris George Walker Jr P 9/1/1996 Bp Charles Lovett Keyser. c 2. Seabury Ret Cmnty Bloomfield CT 2003-2008; Epis Ch At Yale New Haven CT 1999-2002; Int Chr Ch Bay Ridge Brooklyn NY 1998-1999; Asst S Matt's Cathd Dallas TX 1996-1998.

DORRIEN, Gary John (NY) Union Theological Seminary, 3041 Broadway, New York NY 10027 **Non-par 1988-** B Midland MI 1952 s John & Virginia. Harv; BA Alma Coll 1974; MA PrTS 1978; MDiv UTS 1978; ThM PrTS 1979; PhD Un Grad Sch New York NY 1989. D 6/19/1982 P 12/1/1982 Bp Wilbur Emory Hogg Jr. Dio Albany Greenwich NY 1986-1987; S Andr's Epis Ch Albany NY 1982-1987; Doane Stuart Sch Albany NY 1982-1985. Auth, "The Making Of Amer Liberal Theol: Idealism, Realism," *And Modernity 1900-1950*, 2003; Auth, "The Making Of Amer Liberal Theol: Imagining Progressive Rel 1805-1900," 2001; Auth, "The Barthian Revolt In Mod Tech," 2000; Auth, "The Neoconservative Mind," 1993; Auth, "The Democratic Socialist Vision," 1986; Auth, "Logic & Consciousness"; Auth, "Reconstructing The Common Gd"; Auth, "Soul In Soc"; Auth, "The Word As True Myth"; Auth, "Remaking Evang Theol". Omicron Delta Kappa hon Soc 1973; Phi Beta Kappa, Sw Mi Chapt 1999. Florence J. Lucasse Awd For Outstanding Schlrshp Kalamazoo Coll 1994; U Chi Prog On Secondary Sch Tchg 1987.

DORSCH, Kenneth John (Ore) 15625 Nw Norwich St, Beaverton OR 97006 **Dio Oregon Portland OR 2017-** B Newark NJ 1945 s Harold & Marie. BA Rutgers The St U of New Jersey 1967; Fulbright Schlr 1968; MDiv Ya Berk 1971; ECF Fllshp 1979; DMin SWTS 2005. D 6/12/1971 Bp Leland Stark P 12/1/1971 Bp George E Rath. m 6/11/1977 Joy A Swickard c 1. Int Chr Ch Par Lake Oswego OR 2013-2014; Int All SS Ch Portland OR 2010-2012; S Barth's Ch Beaverton OR 2000-2009, 1999-2000; S Jn's Par Hagerstown MD 1992-1999; R S Jn The Div Ch Saunderstown RI 1990-1992; Ch Of The H Comf Kenilworth IL 1985-1990; Asst & Dir Of Mus Trin Epis Ch Wheaton IL 1979-1984; Int Mssh-S Barth Epis Ch Chicago IL 1978-1979; Nash Nashotah WI 1975-1978; Cur Par of St Paul's Ch Norwalk Norwalk CT 1971-1975. Soc Of S Jn The Evang 1970-1991. Fllshp ECF 1979; Fulbright Schlr U. S. Govt 1967.

DORSEE, Ballard (Ct) 461 Mill Hill Ter, Southport CT 06890 **Died 3/28/2016** B Detroit MI 1929 s Edmund & Alice. LTh VTS; BA U of Maryland 1951. D 6/24/1967 P 6/1/1969 Bp William Foreman Creighton. m 11/9/1974 Roberta Dorsee c 5. P in charge Ch Of The Gd Shpd Shelton CT 1999-2016; Clerk of the Works St Johns Ch W Hartford CT 1993-1996; R Gr Epis Ch Norwalk CT 1977-1991; R St Jas Epis Ch Hartford CT 1969-1977; Asst S Phil's Epis Ch Laurel MD 1967-1969; Stndg Com Dio Connecticut Meriden CT 1982-1987.

DORSEY, Laura Miller (Eas) 28333 Mount Vernon Rd, Princess Anne MD 21853 B Catonsville MD 1950 D 9/15/2001 Bp Martin Gough Townsend P 10/5/2002 Bp Charles Lindsay Longest. c 1. stmarystyaskin@peoplepc.com

DORSEY, Martha June Hardy (O) 3602 Hawthorne Ave, Richmond VA 23222 **P S Andr's Epis Ch Elyria OH 2013-** B Russellville KY 1958 d Robert & Mavis. BA Berea Coll 1980; MDiv Sthrn Bapt TS 1988. D 6/4/2011 P 12/10/2011 Bp Shannon Sherwood Johnston. m 12/10/1988 David FH Dorsey c 1. Asst S Thos' Ch Richmond VA 2011-2013.

✠ DOSS, The Rt Rev Joe (NJ) 15 Front St, Mandeville LA 70448 **Form Bp of New Jersey Dio New Jersey Trenton NJ 2001-, Bp 1993-2001** B Mobile AL 1943 s Morris & Frances. BA LSU 1965; JD LSU 1968; STB GTS 1971; GTS 1981. D 6/21/1971 P 1/1/1972 Bp Iveson Batchelor Noland Con 10/31/1993 for NJ. m 2/15/1975 Susan T Doss c 2. S Mk's Epis Ch Palo Alto CA 1985-1993; R Gr Ch New Orleans LA 1973-1985; D Epis Ch Of The Gd Shpd Lake Chas LA 1971-1973; Dep GC Dio Louisiana New Orleans LA 1969-1979. Auth, *Law & Morality: Capital Punishment*; Auth, *Let the Bastards Go: From Cuba to Freedom--Or God's Mercy*; Auth, *The Songs of the Mothers: Messages of Promise for the Future Ch*.

DOSTAL FELL, Margaret Ann (Minn) 1765 Upper 55th St E, Inver Grove Heights MN 55077 B Jackson MN 1947 d Louis & Clara. BA U MN 1970; MDiv Untd TS 2002. D 6/12/2003 P 12/18/2003 Bp James Louis Jelinek. m 12/

31/2002 George Mansfield Fell. Assoc St. Jas on the Pkwy Minneapolis MN 2003-2010.

DOSTER, Daniel Harris (Ga) 724 Victoria Cir, Dublin GA 31021 B Moultrie GA 1934 s Percy & Juanita. BA Florida St U 1961; MS Ft Vlly St U 1984. D 12/3/1980 Bp George Paul Reeves P 11/22/1997 Bp Henry Irving Louttit. m 3/29/1964 Robin Baker. D'S Advsry Com Dio Georgia Savannah GA 1996-1997, Cmsn Alcosm & Drug Abuse 1985-1988; Human Servs Provider Cmnty Mntl Hlth Cntr 1987-1996; Chapl Parkside Ladge Alco Treatment Hosp 1984-1992; D Chr Epis Ch Dublin GA 1980-1997.

DOTY, D(Avid) Michael (WNC) 143 Caledonia Rd, Landrum SC 29356 B Greeneville TN 1952 s Isaac & Opal. BA Carson-Newman Coll 1976; MDiv Sewanee: The U So, TS 1990; DMin Sewanee: The U So, TS 1997. D 6/18/1990 P 12/21/1990 Bp William Evan Sanders. m 5/20/1972 Pamela Doty c 1. R Ch Of The H Cross Tryon NC 2002-2013; Dio E Tennessee Knoxville TN 2000-2002, Sm Ch Off 1990-1996, Vic 1990-1994, Archd 2000-2002, Stndg Com 1997-2000, Alt Dep to GC 1994-1996, Wm E. Sanders Minorities Schlr-shp Fund, Chair 1992-2002, Bp and Coun 1990-1993; R S Paul's Ch Athens TN 1994-2000; S Thos Ch Elizabethton TN 1990-1994; Deerfield Bd Dir Dio Wstrn No Carolina Asheville NC 2005-2009, Dn, Hendersonville Dnry 2004-2012; Bd Dir and Chair EAM Kingsport TN 1992-1995. Auth, "Anglicanism in Appalachia: The Formation of the Epis Ch in E Tennessee," *DMin Dissertation Proj STUSo*, Dio E Tennessee, 1997; Auth, "Anglicanism in Appalachia," *Appalachian Stds Conf*, Virginia Tech, Blacksburg, VA, 1995; Auth, "Epis Ch & Baptismal Tradition: Examination of Faith Perspectives," *Sewanee Theol Revs*, U So, 1995. CODE 2000-2001.

DOTY, Phyllis Marie (Fla) P.O. Box 4366, Dowling Park FL 32064 **D S Lk's Epis Ch Live Oak FL 2009-** B Colorado Springs CO 1940 d Theodore & Isabel. Angl TS; BA Col Bible Coll 1969; MA Uta-Arlington 1981; Lic Angl Sem 1991. D 6/20/1992 Bp Donis Dean Patterson. D for Hisp Mnstrs S Matt's Cathd Dallas TX 2000-2004; Ch Of The Gd Shpd Cedar Hill TX 1992-1994.

DOUBLEDAY, William Alan (NY) 31 Croton Avenue, MOUNT KISCO NY 10549 **P-in-c S Mk's Ch Mt Kisco NY 2012-; Assoc S Lk's Ch Forest Hills NY 2005-** B Northamton MA 1951 s Elwyn & Margret. BA Amh 1972; MDiv EDS 1976. D 6/14/1980 P 12/12/1980 Bp Alexander D Stewart. Dn Bex Sem Columbus OH 2006-2011; The GTS New York NY 1986-2006; Dio New York New York NY 1983-1986; S Lk's-Roosevelt Hosp Cntr New York NY 1983-1986; Morningside Hse Nrsng Hm Bronx NY 1980-1982; Cur Gr Ch Great Barrington MA 1979-1980. Auth, "Fighting Aids & Hiv Together," *Envisioning The New City: A Rdr On Urban Mnstry*, Westmin/Jknox, 1992; Contrib, "The Gospel Imperative In The Midst Of Aids," Morehouse-Barlow, 1988; Contrib, "Aids: Facts & Issues," Rutgers U Pr, 1986. Hon Cn Dio the Highveld, So Afr 2003. billdoubleday@stmarksmtkisco.org

DOUCETTE OSB, Lee Francis (Minn) 7213 W Shore Dr, Edina MN 55435 **Died 8/31/2015** B Minneapolis MN 1936 s Clifford & Frances. BS U MN 1973; MA Untd TS of the Twin Cities 1983; DMin Untd TS of the Twin Cities 1986. Rec 6/22/1978 as Deacon Bp Robert Marshall Anderson. m 7/14/1956 Vivian E Thielman c 2. Dio Minnesota Minneapolis MN 2003-2004, Dir of D Formation 1984, Dioc Screening Com 1981-1984; Int Mssh Epis Ch S Paul MN 2003-2004; S Steph The Mtyr Ch Minneapolis MN 1993-2003, Asst 1993-2003; Asst Geth Ch Minneapolis MN 1991; Serv S Nich' Minneapolis MN 1978-1983; Serv Roman Catcholic Ch 1976-1978. Comp of St. Lk/OSB 2005.

DOUGHARTY, Philip Wilmot (WNY) 427 Loma Hermosa Dr NW, Albuquerque NM 87105 B Fort Worth TX 1950 s Bernard & Margaret. BME Oklahoma Bapt U 1972; MM U of New Mex 1982; MDiv UTS 1995. D 6/10/2000 P 2/10/2001 Bp John Palmer Croneberger. m 3/7/1984 Adrian Maurice Goodwin c 1. R S Jn's Gr Ch Buffalo NY 2002-2012; Asst Trin And S Phil's Cathd Newark NJ 2001-2002.

DOUGHERTY JR, Edward Archer (SeFla) 10 Eighth St., Biddeford Pool ME 04006 **Chairman of the Bd Hoosac Sch Hoosick NY 2010-; Assoc S Paul's Epis Ch Albany NY 2010-** B Glen Ridge NJ 1939 s Edward & Elizabeth. BA Wms 1962; BD Harvard DS 1965; MEd Ohio U 1969; PhD U MI 1972. D 6/26/1965 P 1/16/1966 Bp Roger W Blanchard. m 6/17/1961 Barbey Dougherty c 3. Asst Cathd Of All SS Albany NY 1995-1998; Hdmstr Doane Stuart Sch 1993-1998; Hdmstr Trin Sch Miami FL 1983-1993; Asst S Clare Of Assisi Epis Ch Ann Arbor MI 1974-1983, 1972; Serv 1969-1972; Untd Campus Mnstry Athens OH 1968-1972; Vic Ch Of The Epiph Nelsonville OH 1966-1968; Ch Of The Gd Shpd Athens OH 1965-1968; Campus Min Gd Shpd Athens OH 1965-1968. ned.dougherty@gmail.com

DOUGHERTY, Janet Hayes (Minn) 5844 Deer Trail Cir, Woodbury MN 55129 B Mount Pleasant IA 1940 d Ernest & Ruth. Pomona Coll 1960; BS U of Iowa 1962. D 1/5/1989 Bp Robert Marshall Anderson. m 8/26/1961 Richard Dougherty c 4. D Cathd Ch Of S Mk Minneapolis MN 1997-2013; D S Martha & S Mary 1989-1997.

DOUGHERTY, Katherine G (Va) **Sewanee U So TS Sewanee TN 2014-** D 6/10/2017 Bp Shannon Sherwood Johnston.

DOUGLAS, Alan David (Colo) 5409 Fossil Creek Dr, Fort Collins CO 80526 B San Antonio TX 1936 s Leslie & Avis. BA Stetson U 1958; MDiv Brite DS 1961; ThM TCU 1965. D 6/26/1966 Bp Everett H Jones P 12/1/1966 Bp Richard Earl Dicus. m 4/27/1957 Patricia Pipkin c 6. S Lk's Epis Ch Ft Collins CO 1982-1999; R Ch Of The Gd Shpd Brownwood TX 1971-1982; P-in-c Ch Of Our Sav Aransas Pass TX 1968-1971; Trin-By-The-Sea Port Aransas TX 1968-1971; Assoc R S Dav's Epis Ch San Antonio TX 1966-1968.

DOUGLAS, Ann Leslie (NY) 201 Scarborough Rd, Briarcliff Manor NY 10510 **D All SS' Epis Ch Briarcliff NY 2011-** B 1946 d Gordon & Constance. EFM completion sewannee TS 2008. D 5/2/2009 Bp Mark Sean Sisk. m 10/14/1967 Dwight Hendee Douglas c 4. D S Jn's Ch Cornwall NY 2009-2011.

DOUGLAS, Carole Robinson (Md) 7521 Rockridge Rd, Pikesville MD 21208 **Asstg P S Jas' Epis Ch Baltimore MD 2009-, Asst 1997-1999** B Fort Meade MD 1958 d John & Catherine. BD U of Maryland 1984; MDiv VTS 1997. D 6/7/1997 P 12/1/1997 Bp Robert Wilkes Ihloff. m 11/1/1996 John Allen Douglas c 1. Ch Of The H Nativ Baltimore MD 2006-2008; S Mich And All Ang Ch Baltimore MD 2001.

DOUGLAS, Dorothy Ruth (CGC) 5904 Woodvale Dr, Mobile AL 36608 **Dio Cntrl Gulf Coast Pensacola FL 2004-** B Birmingham AL 1941 d Ralph & Mildred. Birmingham-Sthrn Coll 1962; BA Emory U 1963; MA U of Alabama 1966; EdD U of Alabama 1969; Cert Sewanee: The U So, TS 1997. D 8/24/1997 P 3/21/1998 Bp Charles Farmer Duvall. Ch Of The Gd Shpd Mobile AL 2005-2008; S Mk's For The Deaf Mobile AL 2005-2006; S Thos Ch Citronelle AL 2005-2006, 1998-2002, Vic 1997-2002; S Ptr's Ch Jackson AL 2002-2004; Vic S Ptr's Jacksonville AL 2002-2004; Dio Cntrl Gulf Coast Pensacola FL 1997-1998.

DOUGLAS JR, Harry Bell (SeFla) 33 Kathy Ann Dr, Crawfordville FL 32327 B Augusta GA 1925 s Harry & Frances. BA U So 1948; MDiv Sewanee: The U So, TS 1952. D 6/23/1952 P 12/17/1952 Bp Frank A Juhan. m 7/31/1971 Lianne Heckman Douglas c 3. Vic Ch Of The Ascen Carrabelle FL 2005-2009; Asst to R S Jn's Epis Ch Tallahassee FL 1993-2000; R All SS Prot Epis Ch Ft Lauderdale FL 1978-1988; R Ch Of The Gd Shpd Jacksonville FL 1968-1970; Vic Ch Of The Adv Tallahassee FL 1959-1962; Exec Dir Yth And Camp Weed Dio Florida Jacksonville 1954-1959; S Jas' Epis Ch Port St Joe FL 1952-1954; S Jn The Bapt Epis Ch Wewahitchka FL 1952-1954. Hon Cn Dio Florida 2006.

✠ DOUGLAS, The Rt Rev Ian Theodore (Ct) Episcopal Diocese Of Connecticut, 290 Pratt Street, Box 52, Meriden CT 06450 **Bp of Connecticut Dio Connecticut Meriden CT 2010-** B Fitchburg MA 1958 s Duncan & Gladys. BA Mid 1980; EdM Harv 1982; MDiv Harvard DS 1983; PhD Bos 1993. D 6/11/1988 P 6/24/1989 Bp Andrew Frederick Wissemann Con 4/17/2010 for Ct. m 10/13/1984 Kristin Harris c 3. Angus Dun Prof of Mssn and Wrld Chrsnty EDS Cambridge MA 1991-2010, Adj Prof 1989-1991; S Jas' Epis Ch Cambridge MA 1989-1990. "Inculturation and Angl Wrshp," *Oxford Guide to BCP*, Oxf Press, 2006; "Authority, Unity and Mssn in the Windsor Report," *ATR 87*, 2005; Auth, "GThankful for their Offerings: Wmn in the Frgn Mssn of the Epis Ch in the 20th Centur," *Deeper Joy: Laywomen and Vocation in the 20th-Century Epis Ch*, Ch Pub, 2005; "An Amer Reflects on the Windsor Report," *Journ of Angl Stds 3.2*, 2005; "Anglicans Gathering for Gods Mssn: A Missiological Ecclesiology for the Angl Comm," *Journ of Angl Stds 2.2*, 2004; Auth, *Waging Recon: God's Mssn in a Time of Globalization and Change*, Ch Pub, 2002; Co-Ed, *Beyond Colonial Anglicanism: The Angl Comm in the Twenth-First Century*, Ch Pub Inc, 2001; Auth, "Angl Identity and the Missio Dei: Implications for the Amer Convoc of Ch in Europe," *ATR 82*, 2000; Auth, "Whither the Natl Ch? Reconsidering the Mssn Structures of the Epis Ch," *A New Conversation: Essays on the Future of Theol and th*, Ch Pub Inc, 1999; Auth, "Baptized into Mssn: Mnstry and H Ord Reconsidered," *Sewanee Theol Revs 40*, Michaelmas, 1997; Auth, "Lambeth 1998 and the Challenge of Pluralism," *The Angl 26*, 1997; Auth, *Fling Out the Banner: The Natl Ch Ideal and the Frgn Mssn of the Epis Ch*, Ch Hymnal, 1996. Amer Soc for Missiology 1986; Angl Contextual Theologians Ntwk 2003; Dep to GC 2000-2006; Epis Partnership for Global Mssn 1990; EWHP 1993; Hist Soc of Epis Ch 1992; HOB Theol Com 2000-2006; Inter-Angl Stndg Cmsn on Mssn and Evang 2001-2006; Sem Consult on Mssn 1994; SCWM, The GC of 1992-1997. Stndg Com Angl Comm 2009; St. Aug's Cross Archbp of Cbury 2008; Angl Consultative Coun Exec Coun 2007; Spec Cmsn on the Epis Ch and the Angl Com GC 2006; Execuive Coun GC 2006; Design Grp for Lamberth Conf of Angl Bishops 2008 Archbp of Cbury 2005; Ed Bd Journ of Angl Stds 2002; Fllshp Epis Ch Foundations 1986. itdouglas@episcopalct.org

DOUGLAS, Jeff (EC) 907 Colony Ave N, Ahoskie NC 27910 **S Thos' Epis Ch Ahoskie NC 2002-** B Eugene OR 1957 s Allen & Phyllis. BA U So 1979; MDiv GTS 1989. D 6/10/1989 Bp John Thomas Walker P 1/1/1990 Bp Brice Sidney Sanders. m 6/12/1982 Elizabeth Douglas c 1. R Ch of the H Cross Mt Holly NC 1998-2002; R S Andr Ch Mt Holly NC 1998-2001; R H Trin Epis Ch Hampstead NC 1993-1998; P-in-c Ch Of The H Innoc Seven Sprg NC 1991-1993; Asst to R S Mary's Ch Kinston NC 1989-1993. jeff@saintthomasahoskie.com

DOUGLAS, Michael John (Az) 400 S Old Litchfield Rd, Litchfield Park AZ 85340 B Appleton WI 1951 s Richard & Shirley. AAS Milwaukee Area Tech

Colleg 1975; AAS Milwaukee Tech 1975; AAS Milwaukee Tech 1975; BA U of Phoenix 1995. D 6/6/2015 Bp Kirk Stevan Smith. m 1/10/2000 Katherine Douglas c 2.

DOUGLAS, Robert Charles (SwFla) **S Mary's Epis Ch Bonita Sprg FL 2016-** B 1964 s Charles & Gloria. Bachelor of Sci Franklin Pierce U 1994; Mstr of Div Nash 2016. D 12/5/2015 P 7/16/2016 Bp Dabney Tyler Smith. m 9/21/1985 Elaine K Couture c 2.

DOUGLAS, Roger Owen (Az) 47280 Amir Dr, Palm Desert CA 92260 B New York NY 1932 s Milton & Veola. BA Trin 1953; STB Ya Berk 1956; STM Ya Berk 1971; Ya 1972; DMin VTS 1979. D 6/9/1956 P 12/1/1956 Bp Benjamin M Washburn. m 10/25/1958 Margaret Douglas c 4. R S Marg's Epis Ch Palm Desert CA 2007-2009; R S Phil's In The Hills Tucson AZ 1977-2001; R S Matt's Epis Ch Wilton CT 1966-1977; Vic The Ch Of The Sav Denville NJ 1960-1966; Assoc Ch Of The Intsn New York NY 1959-1961; Asst Gr Ch Orange NJ 1956-1959. Auth, "The Pilgrim Season," Forw Mvmt; Auth, "Letters To Mk," Amazon; Auth, "Letters To Mk," Amazon; Auth, "Selected Sermons"; Auth, "Chapt From Chap To Reg Ch," *Cntr City Ch: The New Urban Frontier*.

DOUGLASS, David George (NI) 6085 N 190 W, Howe IN 46746 **D All SS Chap Howe IN 2003-; S Mk's Par Howe IN 2003-** B East Cleveland OH 1942 s David & Jessadale. Montreal TS CA; BA Heidelberg U 1964; MA Kent St U 1971. D 1/8/2003 Bp Edward Stuart Little II. m 4/19/1969 Nancy Jo Douglass c 3.

DOUGLASS, James Herford (La) Po Box 523900, Miami FL 33152 **Ret 1991-** B DeQuincy LA 1927 s Robert & Frankie. BA Centenary Coll 1950; BTh Sewanee: The U So, TS 1953; MS Tul 1972. D 6/23/1953 Bp Girault M Jones P 5/1/1954 Bp Iveson Batchelor Noland. c 1. S Jas Place Baton Rouge LA 1984-1991; Chapl S Jas' Place Baton Rouge LA 1984-1991; Vic S Mich's Ch Baton Rouge LA 1984-1991; R S Jn The Bapt Puerto Cortes Honduras 1982-1984; Vic S Aug's Barbacheles 1975-1982; Vic S Jn The Bapt Puerto Cortes Honduras 1973-1984; Exec Coun Appointees New York NY 1972-1984; Vic All SS' New Orleans LA 1966-1971; Chr Ch St Jos LA 1963-1966; P-in-c Gr Ch S Jos LA 1963-1966; R S Steph's Santo Domingo Dr 1957-1963; P-in-c S Anna's Mssn Gibson LA 1955-1957; R Trin Epis Ch Morgan City LA 1955-1957; P-in-c S Andr's Bayou Du LA 1954-1955.

DOULOS, William Lane (Los) 535 W Roses Rd, San Gabriel CA 91775 **Other Lay Position Ch Of Our Sav Par San Gabr CA 2003-** B Johnstown PA 1943 s William & Miriam. N/A Gordon DS 1565; N/A Gordon DS 1965; BA Westminster Coll 1965; MDiv Fuller TS 1974. D 5/17/2014 Bp Joseph Jon Bruno. c 1.

DOVER III, John Randolph (SC) 231 Cedar Berry Ln, Chapel Hill NC 27517 **Ret 1984-** B Shelby NC 1927 s John & Elaine. BA U NC 1960; JD U NC 1962; Cert GTS 1978. D 6/1/1978 P 5/1/1979 Bp William Gillette Weinhauer. c 3. P Assoc Ch Of Our Sav Johns Island SC 1992-2003, Int 1991; Trin Epis Ch Orange CA 1978-1984.

DOVER, Sara Harned (Be) 226 Ridings Cir, Macungie PA 18062 **Died 5/13/2016** B Allentown PA 1935 d Robert & Estelle. BA Cedar Crest Coll 1983; MDiv VTS 1987. D 6/30/1987 P 2/1/1988 Bp James Michael Mark Dyer. c 2. Asst S Anne's Epis Ch Trexlertown PA 1999-2000; Int Trin Ch Bethlehem PA 1997-1998; R/Mentor Blue Ridge Cluster Mnstry 1990-1996; Chr Epis Ch Buena Vista VA 1990-1995; Asst H Sprt S Clair PA 1987-1990; No Par Epis Ch St. Clair PA 1987-1990.

DOW, Neal Hulce (Colo) 3296 S Heather Gardens Way, Aurora CO 80014 **Ret St. Stepehn's Aurora CO 1985-** B Washington DC 1933 s Carl & Alice. BS Cntrl Michigan U 1958; MDiv Nash 1964. D 6/17/1964 Bp John P Craine P 12/21/1964 Bp Donald H V Hallock. m 12/13/1952 Marjorie H Dow c 5. R S Steph's Epis Ch Aurora CO 1972-1985; R S Alb's Ch Sussex WI 1966-1972; Vic S Ptr's Ch Northlake WI 1966-1972; Cur S Matt's Ch Kenosha WI 1964-1966. CCU 1972; Clowns Of Amer, Intl 1990-2000; Fllshp Of Chr Magicians 1990; Fllshp Of Merry Christians 1974; Wrld Clown Assn 1990-2000. S Geo Awd 1980; God And Serv Awd BSA 1980; Silver Beaver Awd BSA 1971.

DOWARD, Amonteen Ravenden (VI) PO Box 486, Christiansted VI 00821 B Anguilla, BWI 1941 d Alfred & Isolen. BA U of the Vrgn Islands 1984. D 3/6/2010 P 4/6/2013 Bp Edward Gumbs. c 3.

DOWDESWELL, Eugenia Hedden (WNC) Po Box 132, Flat Rock NC 28731 B Fort Bragg NC 1944 d Julius & Elizabeth. BA Mary Baldwin Coll 1966. D 10/27/1990 Bp Bob Johnson. m 6/26/1970 Robert Horton Dowdeswell c 2. Archd The Cathd Of All Souls Asheville NC 2005-2011; D S Jas Epis Ch Hendersonvlle NC 1990-2004. Honored Wmn Awd Natl ECW at Trienniel 2000.

DOWDLE, Catherine Ellen (SanD) 726 2nd Ave, Chula Vista CA 91910 **Sr. Account Mgr Miro Technologies La Jolla CA 1994-** B Salem OR 1955 d Gordon & Iris. BA L&C 1977; MDiv ETSBH 2007. D 12/21/2006 P 6/9/2007 Bp Jim Mathes. m 9/23/1978 Timothy Dowdle. Dio San Diego San Diego CA 2014-2015; P-in-c The Ch Of Chr The King Alpine CA 2007-2013.

DOWELL, Elizabeth Ruth (Tex) PO Box 746, Columbus TX 78934 **Dio Texas Houston TX 2016-** B 1981 d Bruce & Virginia. Pyschology U of Phoenix 2010;

Dplma Iona Coll 2014. D 6/21/2014 Bp Dena Arnall Harrison P 1/6/2015 Bp Jeff Fisher. m 5/28/2005 Matthew Scott Dowell c 3.

DOWER, Ronny W (NJ) 3500 Penny Ln, Zanesville OH 43701 **Ret 2009-** B Huntington WV 1943 s Frederick & Deanie. BA Marshall U 1975; MDiv Sewanee: The U So, TS 1980; DMin Sewanee: The U So, TS 1993. D 6/4/1980 P 6/3/1981 Bp Robert Poland Atkinson. m 6/27/1964 Vivion M Mullins c 3. P-in-c S Jn's Epis Ch Maple Shade NJ 2002-2009; Trin Ch Moorestown NJ 2001-2002; S Mary's Ch Haddon Heights NJ 1997-2000; S Steph's Epis Ch Forest VA 1994-1997; Geth Epis Ch Marion IN 1990-1994; S Ann's Ch N Martinsvlle WV 1981-1990; S Jn's Ch Huntington WV 1980; CE Com Dio W Virginia Charleston WV 1984-1990. Auth, "Common Pryr In Concord: A Practical Approach To The L/E Concordat". Dowerrw80@yahoo.com

DOWER, Sandra Nichols (WNY) B Westerly RI 1935 d Thomas & Helen. BA Edinboro U 1973; MS SUNY 1985; MDiv Bex Sem 2004. D 12/20/2003 P 11/13/2004 Bp Michael Garrison. m 5/21/1955 David M Dower c 3. P-in-c S Ptr's Ch Westfield NY 2009-2010; P-in-c Gr Ch Randolph NY 2006-2007; Infant/Toddler Spec Coi Early Headstart Dunkin NY 1995-2001; Retailer 1989-1994; Educ Spec Cao Headstart 1984-1989; Priv Consult 1981-1984; Day Care Dir Ywca 1973-1981; Hd Start Trng Dir Edinboro St Coll Edinboro PA 1970-1973.

DOWLING, Shelley (Ia) D 5/9/2010 Bp Alan Scarfe.

DOWLING-SENDOR, Elizabeth (NC) 6 Davie Cir, Chapel Hill NC 27514 **Assoc. Dir Angl Epis Hse Duke DS 2012-; Co-Chair - COM Dio No Carolina Raleigh NC 2002-, Pstr Response Team 2002-, COM 2000-2007, 2000-2006** B Beaufort SC 1952 d Grafton & Edith. BA Harv 1973; MDiv Duke DS 1998; Cert VTS 1998. D 6/20/1998 Bp Robert Carroll Johnson Jr P 5/1/1999 Bp James Gary Gloster. m 6/18/1978 Benjamin Dowling-Sendor c 3. Ch Of The Advoc Chap Hill NC 2005-2008; Assoc Ch Of The H Fam Chap Hill NC 2002-2004; Assoc R S Phil's Ch Durham NC 1998-2001.

DOWNER, Gretchen Marie (Ida) 1419 Butte View Cir, Emmett ID 83617 **P-in-c S Mary's Ch Emmett ID 1999-, P 1997-, D 1996-1999** B Livingston MT 1942 d Alfred & Doris. TS; Sewanee: The U So, TS; L&C 1962; BS The Coll of Idaho 1964; MA Cntrl Michigan U 1978. D 12/15/1996 P 11/29/1997 Bp John Stuart Thornton. m 9/4/1962 Larry Vinton Downer c 2. stmarysemmett@gmail.com

DOWNES, Richard Hill (Mass) 71 Saint Marys St Apt 1, Brookline MA 02446 **Died 12/24/2016** B Haverhill MA 1938 s Richard & Irene. BA Bow 1960; MDiv GTS 1967. D 6/24/1967 P 5/25/1968 Bp Anson Phelps Stokes Jr. m 3/19/1976 Sherrell B Downes. P Par Of The Epiph Winchester MA 2012-2016; Assoc Ch Of S Jn The Evang Boston MA 2004-2006; Ret 2003-2016; R Ch Of The Redeem Chestnut Hill MA 1995-2003; S Paul's Ch Brunswick ME 1993; S Pat's Ch Washington DC 1986-1987; Cathd Sch For Boys San Francisco CA 1980-1984; Cathd of St Ptr & St Paul Washington DC 1969-1978. Soc Of S Jn The Evang.

DOWNEY, John (NwPa) 220 W 41st St, Erie PA 16508 **Dn Cathd Of S Paul Erie PA 1987-** B Corry PA 1954 d John & Jean. BA Grove City Coll 1975; MDiv SWTS 1980. D 6/11/1980 P 12/20/1980 Bp Donald James Davis. m 6/7/2002 Sharon Ann Downey c 3. R Gr Epis Ch Ridgway PA 1983-1986; Vic Ch Of The H Trin Houtzdale PA 1980-1982; St Laurence Epis Ch Osceola Mills PA 1980-1982.

DOWNIE, Elizabeth Morris (EMich) 668 Elder Ln, Winnetka IL 60093 B Columbus OH 1935 d Donald & Mary. BA Wellesley Coll 1957; Ya Berk 1959; MA U MI 1973; U So 1991. D 6/21/1991 Bp Henry Irving Mayson P 2/1/1992 Bp R aymond Stewart Wood Jr. c 2. Assoc S Christophers Epis Ch Grand Blanc MI 2004-2013; R S Jude's Epis Ch Fenton MI 1993-2004; All SS Ch E Lansing MI 1992-1993; Pres Dio Estrn Michigan Saginaw MI 1996-1998; Sccm Epis Ch Cntr New York NY 1975-1994. Auth, "The Hymnal 1982 Serv Mus"; Auth, "A Guide For The Selection & Employment Of Ch Mus"; Auth, "A Survey Of Serv Mus," *The Hymnal 1982 Comp*. Associated Parishes 1980; AAM 1977; Assn Of Dioc Liturg & Mus Committees 1976; Epis Ntwk For Economical Justice; EPF 1980; EWC 1994; Naac; NNLP; Oblate Of S Ben 1981.

DOWNING, John W (Mil) B 1932 D 5/27/1958 P 12/19/1958 Bp William F Lewis. m 4/15/1973 Nancy Downing c 2. S Mk's Par Glendale CA 1989-1990; Dio Milwaukee Milwaukee WI 1986-1989; Trin Epis Ch Platteville WI 1986-1989; S Mk's Ch King City CA 1985-1986.

DOWNING, LaRue (WNC) 21 Indigo Way, Hendersonville NC 28739 B Jacksonville FL 1944 s Frank & Doris. BA Marshall U 1968; MDiv VTS 1971. D 6/11/1971 P 2/1/1972 Bp Wilburn Camrock Campbell. m 9/14/1963 Marsha R Racer. Imterim R Ch Of The H Nativ Honolulu HI 2002-2006; Assoc Calv Ch Memphis TN 2001-2002; Ch Of The Ridge Trenton SC 1996-2001; Dio Upper So Carolina Columbia SC 1996-2001; Our Sav Epis Ch Trenton SC 1993-2001; Vic Trin Ch Edgefield SC 1993-2001; R The Ch Of The Gd Shpd Augusta GA 1982-1992; Kanuga Conferences Inc Hendersonvlle NC 1980-1982; R S Jn's Epis Ch Wilmington NC 1976-1980; Assoc S Jas Par Wilmington NC 1973-1976; R S Ptr's Ch Huntington WV 1972-1973.

DOWNING, Patricia S (Del) 1108 N Adams St, Wilmington DE 19801 **R Trin Par Wilmington DE 2008-; Stndg Com Dio Delaware Wilmington 2013-, Eccl Trial Crt Judge 2011-2012, Fin Com 2010-; Vice Chairman Dioc Coun**

Inc Wilmington DE 2012- B Cheverly MD 1966 d Charles & Maureen. BA U of Vermont 1988; MDiv GTS 1995. D 6/17/1995 Bp Jane Hart Holmes Dixon P 1/18/1996 Bp Ronald Hayward Haines. m 10/8/1995 Richard E Downing. R Gd Shpd Epis Ch Silver Sprg MD 1997-2008; Asst S Paul's Epis Ch Piney Waldorf MD 1995-1997.

DOWNING, Richard E (WA) 2602 N Harrison St, Wilmington DE 19802 B Allegan MI 1944 s Ernest & Donna. STB GTS; BD Geo 1966. D 6/28/1969 P 6/14/1970 Bp William Foreman Creighton. m 10/8/1995 Patricia S Steinecke. R Par of St Monica & St Jas Washington DC 1976-2008; R S Paul's Par Prince Geo's Cnty Brandywine MD 1972-1976; D-in-Trng Nativ Epis Ch Temple Hills MD 1969-1971. Capitol Hill Grp Mnstry; Pres/Secy, Cath Fllshp Epis Ch 1986-1994.

DOWNS, Alice Lacey (NJ) 14 Winding Lane, Southwest Harbor ME 04679 B Hartford CT 1952 d Norton & Mary. AA Bradford Jr Coll 1972; BA Bradford Coll 1973; MA Geo 1982; MDiv GTS 1987. D 6/6/1987 P 2/1/1988 Bp Edward Cole Chalfant. m 10/1/1988 Dean Henry. S Anne's Ch Calais ME 2012; P-in-c S Mk's Epis Ch Keansburg NJ 2001-2010; Int S Lk's Epis Ch Metuchen NJ 1998-2000; Int S Jn's Ch Somerville NJ 1996-1998; New Jersey Coun Of Ch Trenton NJ 1995-1996; Assoc Chr Ch Middletown NJ 1994-1996; New Jersey Coun Of Ch 1994-1996; The GTS New York NY 1991-1994; Aids Chapl Jersey City Med Cntr 1990-1991; Assoc Chr Ch Epis Shrewsbury NJ 1989-1993; S Peters Luth Ch New York NY 1988-1990. Auth, "Leaven For Our Lives: Conversations On Faith," Cowley, 2002; Auth, "Jubilee," 1985.

DOWNS, Andrew D (Ind) Saint Stephen's Church, 215 N 7th St, Terre Haute IN 47807 **S Steph's Ch Terre Haute IN 2014-; Asst S Dav's Ch Lansing MI 2007-** B Wyanndotte 1978 s Joseph & Merrill. BA Alma Coll 1999; Emerson Coll Boston MA 2000; MDiv Hur, U of Wstrn Ontario, Can 2007. D 6/16/2007 P 5/17/2008 Bp Steven Todd Ousley. m 5/20/2005 Rose R McKellar c 2. S Paul's Epis Ch S Clair MI 2012-2014; S Paul's Epis Ch Newnan GA 2009-2011. rector@ststephensth.org

DOWNS, Dalton Dalzell (WA) 703 Carmel Lane, Poinciana FL 34759 B Corn Island NI 1936 s Alexander & Brunella. CPA Escuela Practica de Comercio PA 1957; BA U Nacl Panama 1961; MDiv ETSC 1964. D 6/20/1964 P 1/1/1965 Bp Reginald Heber Gooden. m 6/8/1968 Ana Jo Downs c 2. R S Tim's Epis Ch Washington DC 1986-2006; ACPE Supvsr/Trng Off St. Elizabeths Hosp WDC 1979-2003; R Emm Cleveland OH 1968-1980; Ch Of The Trsfg Cleveland OH 1967-1980; Asst Emm Cleveland OH 1967-1968; Asst S Andr's Ch Cleveland OH 1967-1968; Asst Chr Sea Colon 1964-1966. Hon Cn 89 Gd Shpd San Pedro 1989; Urban Consult/Orgnzr Campbell Awd CS4 Ohio Coun of Ch 1977.

DOWNS, Donna (Ct) 64 Philip Dr, Shelton CT 06484 B Bridgeport CT 1955 BS Marketing U of New Haven 1983; MDiv Ya Berk 1987. D 6/21/2003 Bp Andrew Donnan Smith P 1/3/2004 Bp James Elliot Curry. m 8/29/1981 Allen Gybbon Downs c 3. R All SS Epis Ch Oakville CT 2013-2016; R S Paul's Ch Woodbury CT 2009-2012; Assoc Par of St Paul's Ch Norwalk Norwalk CT 2004-2009; Cur S Ptr's-Trin Ch Thomaston CT 2003-2004.

DOWNS JR, Joseph Thomas (EMich) 3225 N Branch Dr, Beaverton MI 48612 **P-in-c S Paul's Epis Ch Gladwin MI 2009-** B Morenci AZ 1948 s Joseph & Harriet. BS Cntrl Michigan U 1970; MDiv VTS 1974. D 6/15/1974 P 6/1/1975 Bp H Coleman Mcgehee Jr. m 9/7/1969 Merrill L Faustman c 2. P-in-c H Fam Epis Ch Midland MI 2008-2009; Cmncatn Dir Dio Estrn Michigan Saginaw MI 2000-2010, GC, Pension Com, VP 2009, GC Dep, chair of deputation 1997-2010; Chapl Michigan St Police 1993-2000; R Trin Epis Ch Alpena MI 1981-2000; Vic Gr Epis Ch Southgate MI 1977-1981; Asst S Paul's Epis Ch Lansing MI 1974-1977.

DOWNS, Lee Daniel (Mil) N77W17700 Lake Park Dr Apt 311, Menomonee Falls WI 53051 B Richland Center WI 1944 s Dan & Alice. BS U of Wisconsin 1968; ThM Bos 1972; DMin Bos 1975. D 9/12/1986 P 1/10/1987 Bp Roger John White. m 10/21/1995 Susan Downs c 3. R Chr Ch Milwaukee WI 2002-2009; Supply S Jn In The Wilderness Elkhorn WI 1999-2001; P-in-c S Nich Epis Ch Racine WI 1995-1998; P-in-c S Andr's Ch Kenosha WI 1991-1994; Asst S Matt's Ch Kenosha WI 1986-1991; Serv Methodist Ch 1966-1986.

DOWNS, Thomas Alexander (CFla) 390 Lake Lenelle Drive, Chuluota FL 32766 **(Ret) R Emer St. Richard's Epis Ch Winter Pk FL 2003-** B Superior WI 1938 s Alexander & Eleanor. BA S Paul Sem 1960; MA S Paul Sem 1964; MA S Paul Sem St Paul MN 1964; MA U of Notre Dame 1970; DMin Grad Theol Un 1978. Rec 9/21/1982 as Priest Bp William Hopkins Folwell. m 7/3/1970 Bernice A Downs c 3. R S Richard's Ch Winter Pk FL 2004-2010; R S Paul's Ch Albany GA 1992-2003; Cn to the Ordnry Dio Cntrl Florida Orlando FL 1986-1993; Cn Dio Cntrl Florida Orlando FL 1985-1992, Cn 1982-1985; Cn Cathd Ch Of S Lk Orlando FL 1982-1985; Exec Dir Florida Coun of Ch Orlando 1980-1983. Auth, *The Par as Lrng Cmnty*, Paulist, 1979; Auth, *A Journey to Self Through Dialogue (23rd Pub)*, 23rd Pub, 1977. Serv to Mankind Sertoma 1994.

DOYLE, Ann K (Ky) Calvary Episcopal Church, 821 S 4th St, Louisville KY 40203 **S Thos Epis Ch Louisville KY 2016-; Chair of Chr Formation Dio Kentucky Louisville KY 2011-** B Charlottesville VA 1968 d William & Bar-

bara. BA U of Virginia 1990; MS Augusta St U 1994; MDiv Louisville Presb TS 2011; Angl Stds Seabury 2012. D 5/19/2012 P 12/8/2012 Bp Terry Allen White. m 12/18/1993 Christopher R Doyle c 4. Cur Calv Ch Louisville KY 2012-2015.

✠ DOYLE, The Rt Rev C Andrew (Tex) 1225 Texas Ave, Houston TX 77002 B Carbondale IL 1966 s Charles & Sylvia. BFA U of No Texas 1990; MDiv VTS 1995. D 6/17/1995 Bp Claude Edward Payne P 1/23/1996 Bp William Elwood Sterling Con 11/22/2008 for Tex. m 5/19/1990 Joanne C Doyle c 2. Bp Coadj Dio Texas Houston TX 2008-2009, Bp of Texas 2003-2008, 2003-, 1997-2003; The Great Cmsn Fndt Houston TX 1997-2003; Cur Chr Epis Ch Temple TX 1995-1997; Dir Of Stdt Activities S Steph's Epis Sch Austin TX 1990-1992. adoyle@epicenter.org

DOYLE, Henry Lovelle (Minn) 1000 Shumway Ave, Faribault MN 55021 **P-in-c Chr Ch Albert Lea MN 2012-; Chapl Shattuck-S Mary's Sch Faribault MN 1989-** B Tampa FL 1951 s Robert & Muriel. BA Colorado Coll 1973; MEd Colorado St U 1981; MDiv Nash 1989. D 7/17/1989 Bp William Harvey Wolfrum P 1/27/1990 Bp Sanford Zangwill Kaye Hampton. Auth of the Pub, "Freshman Drinking Patterns," *Freshman Drinking Patterns*, 1981. SHN 1987.

DOYLE, Margaret E (Ala) 429 Cloudland Dr, Hoover AL 35226 **R S Alb's Ch Hoover AL 2014-** B Boston MA 1952 d Andrew & Margaret. BS Bridgewater St Coll; MA St Mary of the Woods; Grad Murray St U 1990; Angl Stds Seabury 2012. D 3/16/2013 P 11/23/2013 Bp Larry Benfield. c 1.

DOYLE, Ralph Thomas (Mo) 1432 Kearney St, El Cerrito CA 94530 **Dir The Metanoia Mnstry El Cerrito California 2003-** B Boston MA 1944 s Ralph & Marion. CDSP 1975; Notre Dame Coll 1978; U of Name Coll 1978; Instnl Admin U of Notre Dame 1979; Cert Managmnt Consult 1980. D 6/28/1975 P 5/9/1976 Bp Chauncie Kilmer Myers. P-in-c Dio Missouri S Louis MO 2000-2002; Cn to the Ordnry Dio San Diego San Diego CA 1989-1995; Founding Vic S Ben's Par Los Osos CA 1986-1988; Int S Jas Ch Paso Robles CA 1985-1986; Assoc S Columba Retreat Hse Inverness 1975-1987; Assoc S Fran' Epis Ch San Francisco CA 1975-1985; Treas Prov of the Pacific 1976-1994. Coauthor, "Rev: 3 Critical Questions," *Imagery in the Bk of Revelation*, Peeters, 2011; Coauthor, "Audio-Visual Motif in Apocalypse of Jn," *Journ of Biblic & Pneumatological Resrch*, Wipf & Stock, 2011; Coauthor, "Lion/Lamb in Revelation," *Currents in Biblic Resrch*, Sage, 2009; Coauhor, "Violence in the Apocalypse of Jn," *Currents in Biblic Resrch*, Sage, 2007. Amer Assn of Chr Counselors 1985; Cath Conf on Alcosm 1990. Hon Cn St. Paul's Cathd, San Diego 1990.

DOYLE, Seamus (Ark) 1802 W Cambridge Dr, Harrison AR 72601 B Bellaghy County Derry IE 1946 s Harry & Annie. MDiv H Ghost Mssy Coll Dublin IE 1973; Cert Catechetical & Pstr Cntr Dundalk IE 1974; DMin Sewanee: The U So, TS 1997. Rec 5/1/1991 as Priest Bp David Reed. c 2. R S Jn's Ch Harrison AR 2005-2011; Vic S Barn Ch Moberly MO 2003-2004; Mid Missouri Cluster Fulton MO 2000-2005; S Alb's Epis Ch Fulton MO 2000-2005; S Mk's Epis Ch Portland MO 2000-2005; Pstr S Matthews Epis Ch Mex MO 2000-2002; Purchase Area Reg Mnstry Mayfield KY 1992-1999; S Mart's-In-The-Fields Mayfield KY 1992-1999; S Paul's Ch Hickman KY 1992-1999; S Ptr's of the Lakes Gilbertsville KY 1992-1999; Vic / Area Min Trin Epis Ch Fulton KY 1992-1999. Auth, *Do this in Remembrance of Me*, Liquori, 2003; Auth, *A Way of Life: Fourteen Moments in the Life of Jesus*, Liquori, 2002; Auth, "Magdala-The Wmn of the Well," *Chr Singles mag*, 1987; Auth, "Short Stories," *The Best of Lafayette*, 1976. CASA 2008; Ecum Mnstrs, Chair of Bd 2000; Rotary Intl 2001.

DRACHLIS, David Bernard (Ala) 1103 Shades Cir Se, Huntsville AL 35803 **St Thos Epis Ch Huntsville AL 2004-** B Los Angeles CA 1948 s Irving & Virginia. D 10/30/2004 Bp Henry Nutt Parsley Jr. m 2/27/1988 Sharon Fay Drachlis. Cmncatn Coordntr Dio Alabama Birmingham 2009-2016, Co-hcair Comp Dio Cmsn 2007-, Asst Disaster Rresponse Coodrdinator 2006-. dave@stthomashuntsville.org

DRAEGER JR, Walter Raymond (WMich) 3957 Sherwood Forest Dr, Traverse City MI 49686 B Racine WI 1929 s Walter & Lulu. Marq; U of Arizona; U of Wisconsin; LTh SWTS 1979. D 6/9/1979 Bp Quintin Ebenezer Primo Jr P 12/1/1979 Bp James Winchester Montgomery. m 1/5/1952 Sally Draeger c 5. S Eliz's Epis Ch Roscommon MI 2006-2013; Int R S Phil's Ch Beulah MI 1995-1998; S Fran Epis Ch Grayling MI 1994-1995; Emm Ch Petoskey MI 1990-1994; R S Jn's Ch Howell MI 1987-1990; S Dav's Ch Lansing MI 1981-1987; Cur S Simons Ch Arlington Hts IL 1979-1981; Ret.

DRAESEL JR, Herbert Gustav (NY) 215 W 84th St #515, New York NY 10024 B Jersey City NJ 1940 s Herbert & Irene. BA Trin Hartford CT 1961; BD GTS 1964. D 6/13/1964 Bp Dudley S Stark P 12/1/1964 Bp George E Rath. m 1/1/1967 Ada Draesel c 2. R Ch Of The H Trin New York NY 1984-2003; R Gr Ch White Plains NY 1975-1984; R Ch Of S Mary The Vrgn Chappaqua NY 1972-1975; Cur Hse Of Pryr Epis Ch Newark NJ 1964-1965; SCCM Dio New York New York NY 1988-1990. Auth, *Celebration*; Auth, *Everyman: The Mus*; Auth, *Praise & Jubilee*; Auth, *Rejoice*; Auth, *Troubadour*.

DRAKE, Betty L (Fla) 100 S Palmetto Ave, Green Cove Springs FL 32043 B Charleston WV 1931 d Leonard & Beatrice. Marshall U; S Fran Sch Nrsng San

Fran WV; W Virginia St Fire Sch. D 2/18/1990 Bp Frank S Cerveny. m 4/12/1949 Robert Theodore Drake c 4. Cn S Jn's Cathd Jacksonville FL 1991-2001.

DRAKE, Deborah Rucki (Nwk) 380 Clifton Ave, Clifton NJ 07011 **D S Agnes Ch Little Falls NJ 2013-** B Jersey City NJ 1954 d Zigmunt & Dorothy. Cert Rel Stud Felician Coll 1996; MPA Seton Hall U 2000. D 6/9/2007 Bp Mark M Beckwith. m 6/11/1983 Theodore Drake. All SS' Epis Ch Glen Rock NJ 2010-2011.

DRAKE, Jo-Ann Jane (RI) 104 Lafayette St, Pawtucket RI 02860 B Providence RI 1949 d Daniel & Edith. AS Johnson & Wales U 1971; BA Rhode Island Coll 1974; MDiv EDS 1977. D 8/27/1977 P 10/1/1978 Bp Frederick Hesley Belden. R Ch Of The Redeem Providence RI 1993-2012; Assoc R S Matt's Ch Maple Glen PA 1989-1993; Psych Asst NW Psych Inst 1985-1989; Spec Asst S Paul's Ch Elkins Pk PA 1985-1989; Vic S Gabr's Epis Ch Philadelphia PA 1982-1985; Asst S Mary Epis Ch Chester PA 1981; Asst Par Of S Jas Ch Keene NH 1979-1981; Asst S Ptr's Ch Glenside PA 1977-1979. Soc of Cath Prists 2009.

DRAKE, Lesley-Ann (At) 2160 Cooper Lake Rd SE, Smyrna GA 30080 B Norbury England 1958 d Derek & Judith. OND E Surrey Coll 1977. D 8/6/2011 Bp J Neil Alexander. m 6/11/1989 Bob Drake c 2. D St Ben's Epis Ch Smyrna GA 2011-2014.

DRAKE, Leslie Sargent (USC) 1630 Silver Bluff Rd., Aiken SC 29803 B Melrose MA 1947 s Edward & Emily. BA Bos 1969; BA Bos 1969; BA Bos 1969; MTh Bos 1972; BPhil Other 1974; BPhil U of Hull, UK 1974; BPhil Coll of the Resurr, Mirfield, W Yorkshire UK 1978; Other 1978. Trans 7/2/2009 Bp Dorsey Henderson. m 9/6/2006 Yolande Patricia Stewart. S Aug Of Cbury Aiken SC 2009-2012.

DRAPER, Richard Thorp (Ind) 11974 State Highway M26, Eagle Harbor MI 49950 B Rocky Mount NC 1947 s William & Mildred. BA U NC 1969; MDiv VTS 1973; S Georges Coll Jerusalem 1986. D 6/23/1973 Bp Thomas Augustus Fraser Jr P 1/13/1974 Bp William Jones Gordon Jr. m 9/6/1993 Sherry Mattson c 3. P Chr Ch Madison IN 1998-2010; Vic Trin Ch So Hill VA 1995-1997; Int R Chr Ascen Ch Richmond VA 1994; Int Vic Trin Epis Ch Highland Sprg VA 1992-1993; Emm Ch Callaville Freeman VA 1976-1992; R S Andr's Epis Ch Lawrenceville VA 1976-1992; Trin / S Mk's Alberta VA 1976-1987; Dio Alaska Fairbanks AK 1974-1976; Vic S Geo In The Arctic Kotzebue AK 1973-1976.

DRAZDOWSKI, Edna Jean (Neb) 1217 10th Ave, Sidney NE 69162 **P-in-c Chr Ch Sidney NE 2014-** B Arlington VA 1955 d Joseph & Ellen. U of Maryland 1974; BS Valdosta St U 1979; M.Ed Valdosta St U 1988; M.Ed Valdosta St U 1992; Valdosta St U 1995; Sewanee: The U So, TS 2002; M.Div Vancouver TS CA 2012. D 2/4/2006 P 11/11/2006 Bp Henry Irving Louttit. m 9/11/1977 James Drazdowski c 2. Asst Chr Ch Valdosta GA 2009-2014. tardraz@gmail.com

DREBERT, Kay Marie (CNY) 227 W Walnut Dr, Sturgeon Bay WI 54235 **D Trin Memi Ch Binghamton NY 2011-** B Plymouth WI 1957 BA Lakeland Coll 1984. D 10/2/1998 Bp Russell Edward Jacobus. m 6/24/2000 Rebecca Ellen Drebert c 2. S Anskar's Epis Ch Hartland WI 2006-2009; D Ch Of Chr The King.

DREBERT OJN, Rebecca Ellen (CNY) St. Peter's Episcopal Church, 1 Church St, Bainbridge NY 13733 **P in Charge St. Ptr's Epis Ch 2016-** B Cambridge MA 1949 d William & Lillian. BA U of Vermont 1970; MS U of Vermont 1973; MBA U of Sthrn Maine 1991; MTS SWTS 2002; DMin SWTS 2008. D 9/11/1998 P 12/15/2001 Bp Russell Edward Jacobus. m 6/24/2000 Kay Marie Halle c 2. R Trin Memi Ch Binghamton NY 2011-2016; S Jas Epis Ch Milwaukee WI 2010-2011; Int All SS' Cathd Milwaukee WI 2009-2010; R S Anskar's Epis Ch Hartland WI 2006-2010; Vic Chr the King/H Nativ (Sturgeon Bay) Sturgeon Bay WI 2002-2006; D S Paul's Ch Marinette WI 1998-2001. Ord of Julian of Norwich 2003. kestreldave@yahoo.com

DREIBELBIS, John LaVerne (Chi) 3317 Grant St, Evanston IL 60201 **Died 3/10/2017** B Miles City MT 1934 s John & Regina. U Chi 1956; MDiv SWTS 1959; PhD U Chi 1990. D 6/20/1959 P 12/1/1959 Bp Charles L Street. m 6/11/1960 Patricia A Dreibelbis c 4. Prof Emer SWTS Evanston IL 2005-2017; Prof Chr Mnstry SWTS Evanston IL 2003-2004; Bexley Seabury Fed Chicago IL 1994-2004; Epis Ch Coun U Chi Chicago IL 1976-1977; R Gr Epis Ch Huron SD 1971-1975; Ch Of Chr The King Chicago IL 1964-1971; S Chrys's Ch Chicago IL 1964-1971; Vic Gd Samar Oak Pk IL 1960-1963; Cur S Matt's Ch Evanston IL 1959-1960. "Beyond Wish Lists for Pstr Ldrshp," *Theol Educ, Vol. 40 Supplement*, 2005. Serv Awd Seabury-Wstrn Alum/AE Assn 2004; Prncpl Investigator Lilly Endwmt Resrch Proj "Toward A Higher Quality" 1999; Seabury Cross, honoris causa Seabury-Wstrn Stdt body 1999.

DREISBACH, Christopher (Md) Old St. Paul's Episcopal Church, Charles & Saratoga, Baltimore MD 21201 B Brooklyn NY 1957 s Frank & Christine. BA Hamline U 1979; MA JHU 1981; PhD JHU 1988. D 6/2/2012 Bp Joe Goodwin Burnett P 6/26/2013 Bp Eugene Taylor Sutton. m 5/25/2013 Rebecca Anne Dreisbach c 2. Auth, "Abortion ethics not so simple," Baltimore Sun, 2012; Auth, "Vicious duty: The ethics of Osama bin Laden," *Think*, 2011; Auth, "The ethics of the ethics of belief," *Proceedings of the 14th Wrld Multi-Conf on Sys-* tematics, Cybernetics and Informatics, 2010; Auth, "Chrsnty: Not a Theol of tears," Maryland Ch News, 2009; Auth, "Collingwood on the Moral principles of Art," Susquehanna U Press, 2009; Auth, "Dreams and Div: A critical look at Kelsey," *Dreaming*, 2008; Auth, "The ethics of belief: Elements of a course," *Proceedings of the Third Annual Intl Conf on Ethics in the Intelligence Cmnty*, 2008; Auth, "Collingwood on dreams and art," *Collingwood and British Idealism Stds*, 2007; Auth, "Just war and the descendants of Abraham," *Proceedings of the Fifth Annual Intl Conf on Arts and Hmnts*, 2006; Auth, "Dreams in the Hist of Philos," *Dreaming*, 2000; Ed, "R.G. Collingwood: A bibliographic checklist.," Philos Documentation Cntr, 1993; Auth, "Making the upper-level course 'upper-level,'" Educational Resources Info Cntr, 1991; Co-Auth, "TUTORIALS: A software package to accompany Copi's Intro to logic.," Macmillan, 1988; Co-Auth, "ALICE – An Intro to formal logic," MUSE Software, 1982. Outstanding Fac Mem California Cmsn on Peace Off Standards and Trng 2010; Ord of St. Geo Epis Ch/ BSA 2008; Magna Cumme Laude Touro U Intl 2004; Dunning Distinguished Lectr Ecum Inst of Theol, St. Mary's Sem & U 1997. dreisbach@jhu.edu

DRENNEN, Zachary Polk (WVa) c/o Katakwa Diocese, PO Box 68, Amagoro 50244 Kenya **Coalfield Dvlpmt Corp Wayne WV 2016-** B Washington DC 1970 s William & Sarah. BA Colorado Coll 1993; MDiv Harvard DS 2002. D 6/8/2002 P 12/14/2002 Bp William Michie Klusmeyer. Exec Coun Appointees New York NY 2008-2016; The Memi Ch Of The Gd Shpd Parkersburg WV 2002-2004.

DRESBACH, Michael (ECR) 490 Vivienne Dr, Watsonville CA 95076 **All SS Epis Ch Watsonville CA 2012-; El Cristo Rey Seaside CA 2012-; Appointed Mssy The Epis Ch of the U.S.A. Panama Panama 1999-** B Oakland CA 1954 s James & Constance. BS U of San Francisco 1994; MDiv CDSP 2000; MA Grad Theol Un 2000; DD (Honoris causa CDSP 2012. D 6/21/1997 P 12/22/1997 Bp Richard Lester Shimpfky. m 3/18/1978 Mona L Dresbach c 2. Exec Coun Appointees New York NY 2002-2012; Dio Panama 1999-2011; S Phil's Ch San Jose CA 1998-1999, 1997.

DRESSEL, Marilyn Kaye (EMich) 3725 Woodside Dr, Traverse City MI 49684 B Cass City MI 1939 d Keith & Mildred. MI SU 1961; BS Cntrl Michigan U 1962; Cert Whitaker TS 1978; Bex Sem 1989. D 10/22/1978 Bp William Jones Gordon Jr P 7/15/1989 Bp H Coleman Mcgehee Jr. m 8/21/1960 Joseph Charles Dressel c 3. Supply P Gr Ch Traverse City MI 2000-2002, 1997-1998; Epis Tri Par Cluster Gladwin MI 1994-1995; Gr Epis Ch Standish MI 1994-1995; P/Admin S Paul's Epis Ch Gladwin MI 1994-1995; Asst S Jn's Epis Ch Midland MI 1989-1993, Asst 1978-1989.

DRESSER, Deborah Metcalf (NY) 105 Grand St, Newburgh NY 12550 B Boston MA 1943 d Richard & Elizabeth. BA Manhattanville Coll 1980; MDiv UTS 1984; DMin NYTS 1994. D 6/9/1984 Bp James Stuart Wetmore P 1/13/1985 Bp Paul Moore Jr. c 2. S Geo's Epis Ch Newburgh NY 2010, 1997-2009; Dio New York New York NY 1997-2009; Chr Epis Ch Sparkill NY 1995-1996; Chap Of S Jn The Div Tomkins Cove NY 1992-1996; Reg II Yth Mnstrs Tomkins Cove NY 1990-1992; Gr Ch White Plains NY 1987-1990; Int S Mary's Ch Mohegan Lake NY 1986-1987; Cur S Andr's Ch Brewster NY 1984-1986. Auth, "Into The Wrld," *Reflections*. Leaveners.

DREWRY, John Colin (EC) 2513 Confederate Dr, Wilmington NC 28403 B Raleigh NC 1932 s John & Mary. BA U NC 1959; U NC 1959. D 10/21/1998 Bp Clifton Daniel III. m 8/27/1955 Gail Farthing c 3.

DRINKWATER, Michael (RG) PO Box 1246, Albuquerque NM 87103 **Cn S Jn's Cathd Albuquerque NM 2012-** B Pensacola FL 1988 s Frederick & Amanda. AA Pensacola Jr Coll 2007; BSBA U of W Florida 2009; MDiv GTS 2012; MDiv The GTS 2012. D 7/29/2012 P 2/2/2013 Bp Philip Menzie Duncan II. m 6/24/2014 Sarah Rachel Drinkwater.

DRINO, Jerry William (ECR) 14801 Whipple Ct, San Jose CA 95127 **Ret 2007-; Exec Dir Hope w Sudan San Jose CA 2007-; Sudanese Mnstry Trin Cathd San Jose CA 2002-** B Monterey Park CA 1941 s Louie & Winifred. BA U CA 1963; MDiv CDSP 1967; CDSP 2002. D 9/10/1966 P 9/11/1967 Bp Francis E I Bloy. m 6/25/1966 Marilyn Drino c 2. Exec VP Amer Friends of the Epis Ch in Sudan 2005-2008; Exec Dir Prov VIII San Diego CA 1999-2006; R S Phil's Ch San Jose CA 1971-1999; Chapl/Yout Dir S Andr's Ch Saratoga CA 1967-1971; Yth Dir S Steph's Par Bel Tiburon CA 1966-1967; Stndg Com Dio El Camino Real Salinas CA 1987-1991, Alt Dep GC 1984-1987; Dept of Missions Dio California San Francisco CA 1975-1979. Auth, "Meeting on New Ground," *Cultural Sensitivity in the Ord Process*, Ch Pub, 2007; Contributing Auth, "Celtic Liturg," *From Shore to Shore*, Soc for the Propagation of the Gospel, 2003; Contributing Auth, "Vision for Mssn in Matt & Lk," *Global Mssn*, Untd Soc for the Propagation of theGospel, 2002; Co-Auth, "Mart Luther King Day Dialogues," *(Same)*, Ch Pub, 1999; Auth, "Reclaiming The Beloved Cmnty," *(Same)*, Prov Viii, 1998; Auth, "Resource In Cultural Sensitivity in the Ord Process," *(Same)*, Ch Pub, 1992; Contributing Ed, "Records Of The Life Of Jesus (Rsv)," *(Same)*, Gld For Psychol Stds, San Francisco, 1991. Amer Friends of the Epis Ch in the Sudan 2005; Four Sprg Seminars 1998; Gld For Psychol Stds 1971-1992; Hope w Sudan 2003. Jefferson Awd 2010; Jefferson Awd for

Publ Serv Natl Jefferson Awards 2010; Jefferson Awd for Publ Serv Natl Jefferson Awards 2010; Bp's Cross Dio El Camino Real 2008; DD CDSP 2002.

DRISCOLL, Jeanine (NC) D 6/17/2017 Bp Anne Hodges-Copple.

DRISKILL, Lorinda Elizabeth (Tex) Trinity Episcopal Church, PO Box 777, Anahuac TX 77514 B Houston TX 1960 d Franklin & Linda. BA Rice U 1983; MA Rice U 1986; Graduated Iona Sch for Mnstry 2013. D 6/15/2013 Bp C Andrew Doyle P 12/19/2013 Bp Jeff Fisher. m 3/15/1998 Michael Albert Miles.

DRIVER, Bess D (Az) 2137 W. University Ave., Flagstaff AZ 86001 **D Ch Of The Epiph Flagstaff AZ 2004-** B Muskegon MI 1935 d Edgar & Bonnie. D 10/14/2006 Bp Kirk Stevan Smith.

DROBIN, Frederick A (NY) PO Box 126, Hopewell Junction NY 12533 B Utica NY 1941 s Joseph & Stella. BA S Anth Coll Hudson NH 1966; BD Capuchin TS 1969; MA Maryknoll TS 1970; MA NYU 1978; Cert Inst of Relatns Ther New York NY 1985; Cert Inst of Relatns Ther New York NY 1986; MPhil UTS 1992; PhD UTS 1996. Rec 6/1/1985 as Priest Bp Paul Moore Jr. S Andr's Epis Ch New Paltz NY 2012-2013; P-in-c Chr Ch Patterson NY 2011-2012; Dio New York New York NY 2007-2009; Vic La Misión Epis Santiago Apóstol [La MESA] Dover Plains NY 2007-2009; P-in-c Ch Of The Gd Shpd Greenwood Lake NY 2005-2007; Assist Gr Epis Ch Nyack NY 1989-2004; Assist S Jas Ch New York NY 1981-1982; Pstr Counslr & Dir Fndt For Rel & Mntl Hlth Rockland Cnty 1977-1995; Chapl Vas Poughkeepsie 1971-1979; Chapl Vassar Bros Hosp 1970-1971; Chapl No Shore U Hosp 1970. Auth, "Recovery, Sprtlty, and Psych," *J. of Rel & Hlth,* 2014; Auth, "Sprtlty, the New Opiate," *J. of Rel & Hlth,* 1999; Auth, "Reflections of a Psychoanalyst at Mass," *J. of Rel & Hlth,* 1997; Auth, "Tribute To Ann Belford Ulanov," *Un Sem Quarterly Revs A Festschrift For Ann Ulanov,* 1997; Auth, *Tribute to Ann Belford Ulanov,Un Sem Quarterly Revs: A festschrift for Ann Ulanov.* nyresurrection@gmail.com

DROPPERS, Thomas (NC) 1503 Pepper Hill Rd, Greensboro NC 27407 **Died 7/21/2017** B Albany NY 1931 s Seton & Margaret. BA Ham 1953; STB GTS 1956; MALS U NC 1998. D 5/27/1956 P 12/8/1956 Bp Frederick Lehrle Barry. m 6/27/1959 Mary Ellen Droppers c 4. P-in-c S Andr's Ch Greensboro NC 2000-2001; Ret 1994-2017; R All SS Ch Greensboro NC 1984-1994; R S Mk's Epis Ch Huntersville NC 1969-1984; R S Jas Ch Black Mtn NC 1964-1969; P-in-c Trin Ch Kings Mtn NC 1959-1964; Asst S Geo's Epis Ch Schenectady NY 1956-1959; Chair Person for Dioc Com for Environ Mnstry Dio No Carolina Raleigh NC 2005-2017.

DROST, Pat (Eas) **S Mk's Epis Ch Perryville MD 2012-** B Indianapolis IN 1947 d Alton & Lucy. BS SUNY at Buffalo 1970; MS Rochester Inst of Tech 1978; JD GW 1982; MDiv VTS 2003. D 6/14/2003 Bp Robert Wilkes Ihloff P 1/6/2004 Bp John L Rabb. Int S Paul's Epis Ch Mt Airy MD 2010-2011; Int Gr Memi Ch Darlington MD 2008-2009; P-in-c Imm Epis Ch Glencoe MD 2006-2008; Admin Asst Homecoming Proj 2006; Cur S Mary's Ch Abingdon MD 2004-2005; Assoc Atty Priv Law Pract 1984-2000; Tech Law Clerk U.S. Crt of Appeals for the Fed Circuit 1982-1984; Patent Agt, Instr, and Chem Eastman Kodak Co 1970-1982; Compstn and Benefits Com Dio Maryland Baltimore MD 2011-2012, Eccl Crt 2007-2011. Integrity Baltimore 2004; Other Sheep 2010. Phi Beta Kappa SUNY at Buffalo 1970.

DROSTE, Robert E (NJ) 911 Dowling Blvd, San Leandro CA 94577 **Dio New Jersey Trenton NJ 2014-** B Syracuse NY 1962 s Ronald & Susan. BA Coll of Charleston 1984; MDiv CDSP 2000; DMin SWTS 2010. D 6/2/2000 Bp Robert Louis Ladehoff P 12/2/2000 Bp William Edwin Swing. m 5/13/1995 Karla J Droste. R All SS Epis Ch San Leandro CA 2002-2014; Assoc Trin Ch San Francisco CA 2000-2002.

DRUBE, Bruce James (Ala) 1219 Quail Run Dr Sw, Jacksonville AL 36265 B Clearlake SD 1952 s Donald & Frances. D 10/30/2004 Bp Henry Nutt Parsley Jr. m 8/7/1976 Sharon Lynn Drube c 3. D S Mich And All Ang Anniston AL 2005-2011.

DRUCE, Glenn Edward (NJ) 1450 Iris Ave Unit 14, Imperial Beach CA 91932 B Camden NJ 1947 s Albert & Margaret. BS Alderson-Broaddus Coll 1969; MDiv GTS 1972. D 6/5/1972 P 2/16/1973 Bp Wilburn Camrock Campbell. Dio New Jersey Trenton NJ 1998-2003, Cn To Ordnry 1998-2003; Ch Of S Mk And All SS Absecon Absecon NJ 1974-1997; Vic S Andr's Ch Beckley WV 1972-1974.

DRUMM, Elizabeth Prentice (Kan) B Baltimore MD 1944 d Angus & Mellicent. BA Elmira Coll 1966. D 6/11/2011 Bp Dean E Wolfe. c 1.

DRURY, Susan R (Kan) 7311 Legler Road, Shawnee KS 66217 B Boston MA USA 1943 d Charles & Phyllis. BSN Ferris St U 1987; MA Webster U 1992. D 2/2/1997 Bp William Edward Smalley. m 9/30/2006 Ronald Ellis Donnelly c 2. D S Mich And All Ang Ch Mssn KS 2004-2012, D 1997-2003; D S Dav's Epis Ch Topeka KS 2002-2004. NAAD 1997; PEO 2005; Sigma Theta Tau 1989. Ord of the Bp's Cross Dio Kansas 2012; Archd's Cross Dio Kansas, Topeka, KS 2008; Vision Awd Bp, Dio Kansas 2004; Phi Beta Kappa Smith 1960.

DRYMON, John A (O) Trinity Church, 128 W Hardin St, Findlay OH 45840 **Trin Ch Findlay OH 2016-** B Little Rock AR 1984 s John & Patricia Ann. AB Colg 2006; MDiv GTS 2009. D 3/21/2009 Bp Larry Maze P 9/22/2009 Bp Larry Benfield. m 4/20/2013 Annie B Stricklin. R S Paul's Epis Ch Batesville AR

2009-2016; Dn of the NE Convoc Dio Arkansas Little Rock AR 2014-2016, Cmsn on Const and Cn 2012-2016, Secy of Exec Coun and Dioc Conv 2012-2016, BEC 2011-2016. Phi Beta Kappa 2006; Rotary Intl 2009. trinfinrector@att.net

DRYNAN, Thomas Steele (Ore) 6431 Ganon St Se, Salem OR 97317 **D Chr The King Mssn 1990-** B Salem OR 1937 s Thomas & Dehlia. OR SU; AS Chemeketa Cmnty Coll Salem OR 1970. D 6/10/1990 Bp Robert Louis Ladehoff. m 8/31/1957 Marilynne Drynan c 2. Silver Beaver BSA; Eagle Scout BSA.

DRYSDALE, Jessie Cookson (Me) 136 Butterfield Landing Rd., Weston ME 04424 **D Ch Of The Gd Shpd Houlton ME 2003-** B Framingham MA 1935 d Frederick & Andrena. Lic Katharine Gibbs Sch. D 5/3/2003 Bp Chilton Richardson Knudsen. m 9/2/1955 David Thomas Drysdale c 2.

DRYSDALE-SCHRUTH, Sherry (Minn) Grace Memorial Episcopal Church, PO Box 27, Wabasha MN 55981 B Wabasha MN 1965 d Peter & Jean. D 6/20/2015 P 6/21/2016 Bp Brian N Prior. m 10/14/1989 Mitchell Lynn Schruth.

DUBAY, Joseph Arthur (Ore) 1805 NW 34th Ave, Portland OR 97210 B Cambridge MA 1931 s Joseph & Jessie. BA Harv 1953; MA Harv 1954; MDiv CDSP 1963. D 6/24/1963 P 1/5/1964 Bp James Walmsley Frederic Carman. m 7/8/1959 Inga S Dubay c 3. Trin Epis Cathd Portland OR 1996-2011, Adj Cler 1996-, 1989-1996, 1976-1977; Int All SS Ch Hillsboro OR 1994-1996; Dir Wm Temple Hse Portland OR 1992-1993; Wm Temple Hse Portland OR 1992-1993; Chapl Dio Oregon Portland OR 1968-1976; Chapl Portland St Coll Portland OR 1968-1976; R Trin Epis Ch Ashland Ashland OR 1965-1968; Cur Emm Ch Coos Bay OR 1963-1965. Peace Awd Jewish Cmnty Cntr, Portland OR 1972; Phi Beta Kappa Harvard Coll 1953.

DUBOIS, Charles Holgate (NJ) 33509 Anns Choice Way, Warminster PA 18974 **Ret 1997-** B Woodbury NJ 1932 s Carl & Margaret. BA Dickinson Coll 1955; STB Ya Berk 1958; Cert Pstr Trng Inst Philadelphia PA 1980; DMin Estrn Bapt TS 1983. D 4/26/1958 P 11/1/1958 Bp Alfred L Banyard. m 6/9/1960 Ruth Jarvis DuBois c 2. Sewanee U So TS Sewanee TN 1986-1997; Dio New Jersey Trenton NJ 1981-1984; Alt / Dep GC Dio New Jersey Trenton NJ 1979-1985, COM 1983-1986, Dept. GC 1982-1985, Chairman, Stndg Com - N.J. 1884-1985; R Ch Of The Gd Shpd Pitman NJ 1968-1986; R Dio NW Pennsylvania Erie PA 1964-1968; Cur Trin Ch Moorestown NJ 1958-1964.

DUBOSE, Georgia (WVa) Po Box 999, Harpers Ferry WV 25425 **S Andr's Epis Ch Florence OR 2014-; Chapl Washington Natl Cathd 2010-; Nelson Cluster Of Epis Ch Rippon WV 2005-** B Rockford IL 1947 d Henry & Christina. BA U of Missouri 1969; Cert Pstr Stud Bex Sem 2003. D 12/10/2005 P 6/10/2006 Bp William Michie Klusmeyer. m 1/3/1998 Robert Du Bose c 2. Dio Oregon Portland OR 2014; S Barth's Leetown Kearneysville WV 2012-2014; St Johns Epis Ch Harpers Ferry WV 2008-2014. Columnist, "Pilgrim's Process," *Sprt of Jefferson,* Jefferson Pub Co., Inc., 2013.

DUBOSE, Jerry Davis (USC) 50 Keoway Dr Apt F7, Seneca SC 29672 B Manning SC 1954 s Kelly & Talberta. BA Clemson U 1977; MBA Duke 1992; MDiv Sewanee: The U So, TS 2003. D 6/14/2003 P 6/3/2004 Bp Dorsey Henderson. m 6/5/1999 Anna DuBose c 1. Ch Of The H Apos Barnwell SC 2005-2010; Asst R St. Thad Epis Ch Aiken SC 2004-2005; Chapl Mead Hall Epis Day Sch Aiken SC 2003-2005; S Thad Epis Ch Aiken SC 2003-2005; Transitional D St.Thad Epis Ch Aiken SC 2003-2004. OSL 2007.

DUCKWORTH, Bonnie Wagner (NC) **D S Lk's Ch Salisbury NC 2016-; Dir, Arts Acad at Gr Gr Epis Ch Lexington NC 2006-; D Gr Epis Ch Lexington NC 2005-, Lay Par Asst 2005-** B Lexington NC 1949 d Belford & Bennie. D 6/13/2004 Bp Michael B Curry. c 2. D Yadkin Vlly Cluster Salisbury NC 2004-2005. bduckworth@stlukessalisbury.net

DUCKWORTH, Penelope (Cal) Trinity Cathedral, 81 North Second Street, San Jose CA 94115 **S Lk's Ch Los Gatos CA 2016-; Vic Chr Ch Sei Ko Kai San Francisco CA 2006-** B Columbus OH 1947 d Benton & Alice. BA U CA 1970; MDiv CDSP 1978; MFA SFSU 1998. D 5/29/1982 Bp Charles Shannon Mallory P 9/1/1983 Bp William Edwin Swing. m 11/19/1983 Dennis Gordon c 1. Chr Epis Ch Sei Ko Kai San Francisco CA 2006-2008; S Ambr Epis Ch Foster City CA 2005-2006; Chapl St. Ambr Ch and Sea Breeze Sch Foster City CA 2005-2006; R Calv Epis Ch Santa Cruz CA 2002-2004; R Calv Epis Ch Santa Cruz CA 2002-2004; Stanford Cbury Fndt Palo Alto CA 1985-2002; Chapl The Epis Chapl at Stan Stanford CA 1985-2002; Asst to the R S Paul's Epis Ch Burlingame CA 1983-1985. Auth, *Mary: The Imagination of Her Heart,* Cowley, 2004; Auth, *I Am: Sermons On the Incarn,* Abingdon, 1996; Auth, "Disbelief for Joy," *Best Sermons III,* Harper and Row, 1990; "poetry," *The Amer Schlr, The ATR, The Chr Century, Theol Today, Poetry NW, and others.* EPF 2005; ESMHE 1985-2002.

DUDLEY, Michael Devere (O) 28 Perry Place, Canandaigua NY 14424 B Sandusky OH 1941 s William & Doris. BS Otterbein U 1964; MA U of Mississippi 1969; MDiv SWTS 1981. D 6/27/1981 P 1/26/1982 Bp John Harris Burt. m 2/14/2006 David Hefling. Assoc S Paul's Epis Ch Cleveland OH 2003-2005; Int Gr Ch Madison WI 2002-2003; Vic Cathd Of S Jas Chicago IL 2001-2002; R Ch Of Our Sav Akron OH 1991-2001; R S Paul's Ch Steubenville OH 1987-1991; Asst S Lk's Ch San Francisco CA 1984-1987; P-in-c S Jas Epis

Ch Teele Sq Somerville MA 1981-2006; Asst R S Jn's Ch Youngstown OH 1981-1984. Soc Of S Jn The Evang.

DUDLEY JR, Thomas Lee (USC) 134 Boscawen, Winchester VA 22601 **R S Mich's Epis Ch Easley SC 2011-; Chapl Serv Of Virginia 1984-** B Fayetteville NC 1950 s Thomas & Josephine. BA U of Maryland 1976; MDiv VTS 1982. D 6/7/1982 Bp Hunley Agee Elebash P 5/1/1983 Bp David Henry Lewis Jr. m 1/29/1977 Martha E Dudley c 1. Off Of Bsh For ArmdF New York NY 1985-2011; Chr Epis Ch Winchester VA 1982-1985.

DUER, Don Rey (CFla) 2005 Harrison Ave, Orlando FL 32804 **D Cathd Ch Of S Lk Orlando FL 2000-** B Ocala FL 1936 s Roy & Margaret. BA U of Florida 1966; Cert Inst for Chr Stds Florida 1990. D 12/9/2000 Bp John Wadsworth Howe. m 2/14/1985 Christine Eleanor Duer c 1. "Bldg for Chr," *Cntrl Flordia (Series of arts),* 2002.

DUERR, Robert Edward (Mass) 15 Millbrook Rd, Beverly MA 01915 **Non-par 1978-** B Pittsburgh PA 1949 s Elmer & Philomena. BA U Pgh 1971; PDS 1974; MDiv EDS 1976. D 8/29/1976 P 4/1/1977 Bp Robert Bracewell Appleyard. m 12/19/1970 Nancylee P Cunningham. Cur S Paul's Ch Newburyport MA 1976-1978.

DUFF, Eric Towle Moore (NCal) 524 Old Wagon Road, Trinidad CA 95570 B Cincinnati OH 1957 s Edward & Janet. BA Colby Coll 1979; MS Col 1984; MDiv UTS 1984; Lic LCSW CA 1990. D 6/8/1985 P 1/25/1986 Bp William Grant Black. m 6/17/1994 Betty J Duff c 3. Epis Cmnty Serv Sacramento CA 2009-2010; Dir, ECS The Epis Dio Nthrn California Sacramento CA 2006-2009; R S Alb's Ch Arcata CA 1990-2006; Assoc Chr Ch Eureka CA 1989-1990; Apos Hse Newark NJ 1985-1988; Assoc Hse Of Pryr Epis Ch Newark NJ 1984-1988. Columnist, "From Time to Time," *Weekly Column,* Times-Standard.com, 2015; Interview, "Eric Duff," *Do Unto Others,* Westview Pres, 2003. Cmnty of theTransfiguration 1990. Cmndatn Nwk City Coun 1988.

DUFF, Lyndie (Wyo) 1117 West Ramshorn Boulevard, Box 844, Dubois WY 82513 **D S Thos Ch Dubois WY 1991-** B San Francisco CA 1940 d John & Norma. Sewanee: The U So, TS 1987; Ldrshp Acad for New Directions 1990; S Lukes Hosp Aberdeen SD 1990. D 1/25/1991 Bp Bob Gordon Jones. m 11/15/1958 Carroll Duff c 4.

DUFFEY, Ben Rosebro (SVa) 1401 N High St., Apt. 102, Franklin VA 23851 **R S Mk Ch Roanoke Rapids NC 1991-; Ret 1989-** B Richmond VA 1927 s Parks & Frances. U of Virginia 1951; VTS 1966. D 6/24/1966 P 6/1/1967 Bp George P Gunn. m 7/15/1977 Suzanne Duffey c 3. Emm Ch Franklin VA 1970-1989; Cur Estrn Shore Chap Virginia Bch VA 1966-1970.

DUFFEY, Bill (Pa) 3300 Darby Rd, Cottage 304, Haverford PA 19041 B Lincoln NE 1937 s Floyd & Lorna. BS U of Nebraska 1960; MA U of Nebraska 1967; MEd Col 1972; EdD Col 1976; Cert Ang Stud GTS 1983. D 6/11/1983 P 6/12/1984 Bp Lyman Cunningham Ogilby. c 2. Assoc R S Dav's Ch Wayne PA 2008-2014; Cleric Nevil Memi Ch Of S Geo Ardmore PA 1996-2008; R S Jas Epis Ch Prospect Pk PA 1990-1996; Asst S Mart's Ch Wayne PA 1985-1990; Asst S Clements Ch Philadelphia PA 1984-1985; Cur The Ch Of The Trin Coatesville PA 1984. Auth, "Living Ch". Cmnty Of S Mary, CBS.

DUFFIELD, Suzanne (U) St Eliizabeth Episcopal Church, PO Box 100, Whiterocks UT 84085 **Tutor for Indigenous Prog Dio New Caledonia B.C. Vancouver TS 2012-** B Darien CT 1942 d Roland & Doris. U of Connecticut 1960; BA Florida Atlantic U 1988; MDiv Sewanee: The U So, TS 1992. D 6/29/1992 P 12/19/1992 Bp Calvin Onderdonk Schofield Jr. m 10/28/1961 James Duffield c 2. P Dio Utah Salt Lake City UT 2014-2016, Stndg Commitee, VP 2008-2014; Int S Mths Epis Ch Toccoa GA 2002; Int Gr-Calv Epis Ch Clarkesville GA 2001; Int S Jas Epis Ch Clayton GA 2000-2001; Assoc Ch of the Resurr Sautee Nacoochee GA 1999-2000; Assoc The Epis Ch Of S Ptr And S Paul Marietta GA 1992-2000; Dioc Coun Dio Utah Salt Lake City UT. US. 2003-2007. Eli Lilly Endwmt Grant 2008; Eli Lilly Endwmt Grant 2008.

DUFFTY, Bryan (ECR) 3020 Daurine Ct, Gilroy CA 95020 B Leeds Yorkshire UK 1933 s John & Olive. Leeds Coll of Tech Gb; BA Sch for Deacons 1983. D 5/26/1985 Bp Charles Shannon Mallory. m 2/7/1959 Ann Russell c 2. D S Steph's In-The-Field Epis Ch San Jose CA 1996-1999; D S Jn The Div Epis Ch Morgan Hill CA 1985-1990.

DUFFUS, Cynthia Slaughter (EC) 48 W High St, Mt Sterling KY 40353 **S Anne's Epis Ch Jacksonville NC 2016-; Exec Coun Dio Lexington Lexington 2011-, Cler Event Plnng Com 2010-, Dep Ecum Off 2010-, Ldrshp Team 2009-** B Pittsburgh PA 1954 d Pendleton & Mary. BA U of Virginia 1976; MS Virginia Commonwealth U 1991; MDiv Sewanee: The U So, TS 2009. D 6/13/2009 Bp Herman Hollerith IV P 12/21/2009 Bp Stacy F Sauls. m 8/25/1979 Gordon Douglas Duffus c 1. Reverend Ch Of The Ascen Mt Sterling KY 2009-2015.

DUFFY, Christopher Gregory (NJ) 338 Ewingville Rd., Trenton NJ 08628 **Ret 2001-** B Staten Island NY 1943 s Gregory & Rose. BA S Fran Coll Brooklyn NY 1965; MA Indiana U 1966; EdD Indiana U 1970; PrTS 1979; GTS 1982; Cert Coll of NJ 1983; GTF 1987. D 6/4/1983 P 1/14/1984 Bp George Phelps Mellick Belshaw. m 8/13/1967 Barbara M Duffy c 1. S Matt's Ch Pennington NJ 2001; S Thos Ch Alexandria Pittstown NJ 1999-2000; Trin Cathd Trenton NJ 1994-1995; Assoc S Lk's Ch Trenton NJ 1988-1994; Chapl Yci Bordentown

NJ 1987-1997; R Ch Of Our Merc Sav Penns Grove NJ 1985-1987; Int The Ch Of The H Innoc Bch Haven NJ 1985; Assoc Dir Ecs Philadelphia PA 1984-1985; Epis Cmnty Serv Philadelphia PA 1984-1985; Asst Ch Of The H Sprt Lebanon NJ 1983-1984; Chapl Yci Annandale NJ 1981-1984. Honoray Cn Trin Cathd 1995; Phi Delta Kappa.

DUFFY, Glenn Alan (Eas) 63 Battersea Rd., Berlin MD 21811 B Jamaica NY 1940 s Philip & Ernestine. Mercer TS 1975. D 6/29/1974 P 1/25/1975 Bp Jonathan Goodhue Sherman. m 7/2/1960 Marie D Dietrich c 2. R S Pat's Ch Deer Pk NY 1998-2003; R Chr Epis Ch Lynbrook NY 1981-1998; D Par Of S Jas Of Jerusalem By The Sea Long Bch NY 1974-1975; Who'S Who In Rel 1981; Who'S Who In Fin And Industry 1979.

DUFORD, Donald John (Mich) 16889 Club Drive, Southgate MI 48195 B Detroit MI 1944 s George & Florence. Sacr Heart Sem 1986; BA Madonna U 1992; MBA GTF 1993; DMin GTF 1995. Rec 6/1/1995 as Deacon Bp R aymond Stewart Wood Jr. m 7/7/1965 Kathleen M Duford c 3. R Ch Of The Resurr Clarkston MI 2004-2007; Asst Chr Ch Cranbrook Bloomfield Hills MI 2002-2004; R S Dav's Ch Southfield MI 2000-2002; R Dream Cluster Allen Pk MI 1998-2000; Dir of Pstr Care Riverside Hosp 1998-1999; Chapl VA Med Cntr Detroit MI 1996-1998; P-in-c Gr Epis Ch Southgate MI 1996-1997; Chapl Off Of Bsh For ArmdF New York NY 1995-1998; Chapl VA Med Cntr Allen Pk MI 1995-1996. Auth, "Addiction," *Peacemaker Bible,* Intl Bible Soc, 2007. Amer Counslg Assn 1996; Mltry Chapl Associations 1995; SSC 2005. Mem Mortuary Sci Exam Bd-Michigan 2004.

DUFOUR, Matthew John (Ak) PO Box 773223, Eagle River AK 99577 B Michigan 1977 s Lorrie. BA U of Alaska 2005. D 5/10/2014 P 5/13/2017 Bp Mark A Lattime. m 8/5/2000 Leann J DuFour.

DUGAN II, Haynes Webster (Okla) 305 Camino Norte, Altus OK 73521 B Shreveport LA 1939 s Haynes & Helen. BBA Texas A&M U 1961; MDiv VTS 1968. D 6/24/1968 Bp Girault M Jones P 1/1/1969 Bp Iveson Batchelor Noland. m 3/30/1998 Emilie Dugan c 2. Pstr Our Sav Luth Ch 1998-2006; R S Paul's Ch Altus OK 1998-2006; Off Of Bsh For ArmdF New York NY 1978-1998; R S Geo's Ch Bossier City LA 1976-1978; P Dio W Texas San Antonio TX 1974-1976; R Trin Epis Ch Pharr TX 1971-1974; Cur Epis Ch Of The Gd Shpd Lake Chas LA 1970-1971; Cur Ch Of The Incarn Amite LA 1968-1970; Gr Memi Hammond LA 1968-1970. Legion Of Merit. Legion Of Merit Us Army 1998.

DUGAN, Jeffrey Scott (Ct) 102 Seabury Drive, Bloomfield CT 06002 B Boston MA 1954 s Michael & Priscilla. BA Dart 1976; MDiv Ya Berk 1980. D 5/31/1980 Bp Frederick Barton Wolf P 11/29/1980 Bp H Coleman Mcgehee Jr. m 7/6/2002 Elizabeth Hall c 4. R S Jas Epis Ch Farmington CT 1990-2010; Int Chr And H Trin Ch Westport CT 1989-1990; Int S Jn's Epis Par Waterbury CT 1988-1989; Sprtl Advsr Hospice Williamsburg VA 1984-1987; Assoc R Bruton Par Williamsburg VA 1983-1987; Assoc R Chr Ch Grosse Pointe Grosse Pointe Farms MI 1980-1983. Auth, "Chris's Sum," Cumberland Hse, 2001.

DUGAN, Raymond Paul (Az) 534 W Wilshire Dr, Phoenix AZ 85003 B Temuco Chile South America 1935 s Walter & Marguerita. BS Arizona St U 1957; MDiv Epis TS of the SW 1960. D 6/12/1960 P 12/11/1960 Bp Arthur Kinsolving. m 6/9/1954 Nancy H Dugan c 2. Int S Andr's Ch Glendale AZ 2010-2012; Assoc Trin Cathd Phoenix AZ 2008-2010, Cn Pstr 1964-2007; Asst Gd Shpd Of The Hills Cave Creek AZ 2006-2007; Int S Ptr's Ch Casa Grande AZ 2003-2006; 1996-1997; R Epis Ch Of The Trsfg Mesa AZ 1994-2002; Int S Ptr's Ch Litchfield Pk AZ 1992-1993; Vic S Lk's At The Mtn Phoenix AZ 1979-1992; Dioc Plnng Cmsn 1973-1977; 1972-1975; Cmnty Coun Phoenix AZ 1970-1976; Secy 1966-1971; Pres Phoenix Untd Mnstry Fllshp 1965-1966; 1962-1966; Pres No Arizona Coun Of Ch 1962-1963; Vic S Chris Grand Canyon AZ 1960-1964; S Dav's Epis Page AZ 1960-1964; Vic St Johns Epis-Luth Ch Williams AZ 1960-1964.

DUGARD, Debra Harris (WTenn) Emmanuel Episcopal Church, 4150 Boeingshire Dr, Memphis TN 38116 B Memphis TN 1952 d Albert & Thelma. BA Bethune-Cookman U 1975; MEd Trevecca Nazarene U 1990; MAR Memphis TS 2012. D 1/14/2012 Bp Don Edward Johnson.

DUGGAN, Joe F (NCal) 1644 Shadow Wood Road, Reno NV 93103 **P-in-c S Fran Epis Ch Fair Oaks CA 2012-** B Bronx NY 1956 d James & Catherine. BS Manhattan Coll 1978; MA EDS 2006; PhD 2010. D 6/3/2006 P 1/6/2007 Bp Joseph Jon Bruno. "The Postcolonial Paradox," *Journ of Angl Stds,* Camb Press, 2009. Acad Fllshp Partnr ECF 2008.

DUGGAR, Marilyn Elaine (Ak) St Mark's Episcopal Church, PO Box 469, Nenana AK 99760 **Dio Alaska Fairbanks AK 2013-** B Fairbanks AK 1954 d Robert & Gladys. BA U of Alaska 1976. D 4/25/2007 Bp Mark Lawrence Macdonald P 7/29/2009 Bp Rustin Ray Kimsey. m 12/22/1984 Morgan Hilton Duggar c 2.

DUGGER, Clinton George (Alb) Po Box 148, New Lebanon NY 12125 **Pres- Bd Samaratan Shelters Albany NY 2001-; P-in-c Ch Of Our Sav New Lebanon NY 2000-; Ret 1997-** B Beacon NY 1929 s William & Mary. BA S Aug 1959; STB PDS 1962; MS SUNY 1967. D 6/9/1962 Bp Horace W B Donegan P 12/15/1962 Bp Allen Webster Brown. m 11/24/1962 Virginia McLean c 1. Chapl Albany Cnty Jail Albany NY 1993-1997; Dn, Metroplitn Dnry Dio Albany

1987-1993; Ch Of The Redeem Rensselaer NY 1985-1997; Chapl Hoosac Sch Hoosac NY 1982-1986; Vic S Lk's Ch Chatham NY 1973-1985; Cur Trin Ch Albany NY 1962-1964; Cathd Chapt Dio Albany Greenwich NY 1998-2002. Sigma Rho Sigma 1958. Chapl Emer Hoosac Sch 1988; Who's Who in Rel 1975; Man of the Year Awd Nthrn Columbia Rotarians 1975; Hon Cn All SS Cathd 1968.

DUGGER, Rita Jacqueline Carney (WNY) 24 Linwood Ave, Buffalo NY 14209 B Buffalo NY 1927 d John & Anne. Basic Interp Trng Prog; Rochester Inst of Tech Natl Tech Institu 1986. D 6/7/1980 Bp Harold Barrett Robinson. m 6/21/1946 Raymond Emerson Dugger c 4. Cwc; Natl Epis Ch Of The Deaf.

DUGGER, Tracy Michelle (CFla) 241 N Main St, Winter Garden FL 34787 **Ch Of The Mssh Winter Garden FL 2016-** B Indianapolis IN 1986 d Craig & Teresa. BA Pur 2008; MDiv Asbury TS 2014; Cert Angl Stds Nash 2015. D 5/23/2015 P 11/29/2015 Bp Gregory Orrin Brewer. m 2/12/2009 William Daniel Dugger c 1.

DUGGIN, Sarah Helene (WA) 3240 O St NW, Washington DC 20007 **Asst R S Jn's Ch Georgetown Par Washington DC 2009-** B Philadelphia PA 1954 d John & Kathryn. AB Smith 1976; JD U of Pennsylvnia Law Sch 1979; MDiv Wesley TS 2009. D 6/13/2009 P 1/16/2010 Bp John Bryson Chane. m 9/8/1984 Bruce Kirkby Renaud c 2.

DUGGINS, Amy E (NC) **Cur Dio Nebraska Omaha NE 2016-** D 6/11/2016 P 1/14/2017 Bp Anne Hodges-Copple.

DUGGINS, Gordon Hayes (NY) P.O. Box 670, Colfax NC 27235 **Assoc S Mary's Manhattanville Epis Ch New York NY 1993-** B Winston-Salem NC 1950 s Hayes & Pencie. BA Duke 1973; MDiv VTS 1976; ThM Harvard DS 1977; ThD Harvard DS 1982. Trans 6/1/1985 Bp Paul Moore Jr. m 11/26/2008 Armando Tejeda Dunn c 1. Vic Trin Ch Litchfield CT 1988-1992; Cur S Thos Ch New York NY 1981-1984. Rec Campbell Schlrshp, Harvard 1978; Fell ECF 1978; Rec WN Reynolds Schlrshp, Duke 1969.

DUGHI, Lorraine Mazuy (Nwk) B Newton NJ 1925 D 6/12/2004 P 3/25/2006 Bp John Palmer Croneberger.

DUGUID-MAY, Deborah Lee (Roch) 3450 W Ridge Rd, Rochester NY 14626 B Greytown South Africa 1972 d Hugh & Mareth. MTh U of Kwazulu Natal 2010; DMin Colgate Rochester Crozer DS 2015. Trans 2/22/2016 as Priest Bp Prince Grenville Singh. m 12/9/2009 Melanie Duguid-May c 4. Dn Dio Rochester Henrietta 2016; P-in-c Trin Ch Rochester NY 2011-2016.

DUH, Michael Yung-Che (Tai) 952 Sec 2 Chading Road Chading, Kaohsiung Hsien 85202, Taiwan China **P-in-c S Lk's Hualien 1985-** B 1955 s Dau-Sheng & Shyuee-Lii. BA Natl Cheng-Chi U 1979; MDiv Tainan Theol Coll and Sem TW 1984. D 7/15/1984 P 8/1/1985 Bp Poi-Yeung Cheung. m 7/23/1981 Shiang-Ling Lee Duh. Dio Taiwan Taipei 1984-1990; D S Lk's Hualien Taipei Tai 1984-1985.

DUKE, Brandon (At) Saint Julian's Episcopal Church, 5400 Stewart Mill Rd, Douglasville GA 30135 **Dn of the SW Convoc The Epis Dio Atlanta 2017-; S Julian's Epis Ch Douglasville GA 2014-** B Tyler TX 1978 s James & Brenda. BBA Merc 2001; MDiv Candler TS 2011; MDiv Candler TS Emory U 2011; DAS Sewanee TS 2014. D 12/21/2013 P 6/21/2014 Bp Robert Christopher Wright. m 12/17/2005 Leann Giraud Duke c 1. frbrandon@saintjulians.org

DUKE, Ceci (At) 597 Haralson Dr Sw, Lilburn GA 30047 **R Chr Ch Norcross GA 2009-** B Richmond VA 1953 d Joseph & Catherine. BA VPI 1975; MEd Georgia St U 1981; EdS Georgia St U 1991; MDiv Candler TS Emory U 1999. D 6/5/1999 Bp Onell Asiselo Soto P 2/5/2000 Bp Frank Kellogg Allan. m 8/12/1978 David H Duke c 2. Assoc R The Epis Ch Of S Ptr And S Paul Marietta GA 2005-2008; S Mich And All Ang Ch Stone Mtn GA 2001-2005; S Pat's Epis Ch Atlanta GA 1999-2001; Stndg Commision on Educ Dio Atlanta Atlanta GA 2000-2003. Bd Emmaus Hse 2009; Delta Kappa Gamma 1979-1994; EFM 2002; Green Bough Hse of Pryr, Adrian, GA 1993; Kappa Delta Phi 1983-1995; Ldrshp Trng Inst 2000-2005; The SSAP 2006.

DUKES, John (At) 626 Mississippi Ave, Signal Mountain TN 37377 **S Eliz's Epis Ch Knoxville TN 2015-** B Montgomery AL 1950 s Arthur & Flora. BA Auburn U 1972; MDiv Sewanee: The U So, TS 1981. D 5/28/1981 P 12/1/1981 Bp Furman Charles Stough. m 12/12/1987 Ethel L Dukes c 2. All SS' Epis Ch Morristown TN 2014-2015; Int S Tim's Ch Signal Mtn TN 2012-2014; Vic S Anth's Epis Ch Winder GA 2002-2005; Int S Edw's Epis Ch Lawrenceville GA 1996; Vic S Mary And S Martha Ch Buford GA 1993-1995; Dio Atlanta Atlanta GA 1992-1993; Asst to R The Ch Of S Matt Snellville GA 1990-1992; Non-par 1986-1989; R S Phil's Ch Ft Payne AL 1982-1984; Cur Ch Of The H Comf Montgomery AL 1981-1982; Vic S Mary & S Martha.

DUKES, Lynne Adair Slane (WMich) 115 3rd St S Apt 913, Jacksonville Beach FL 32250 B Los Angeles CA 1941 d Henry & Jean. BA Jacksonville U 1997; MDiv Epis TS of the SW 2000. D 6/11/2000 P 12/10/2000 Bp Stephen Hays Jecko. c 2. P Trin Ch Three Rivers MI 2001-2006.

DULFER, John Guidi (NY) 110 W 15th St Apt 1, New York NY 10011 B Broken Hill NSW AU 1937 s Jack & Maybell. TSTC Ballarat & Melbourne Art Schools Melbourne Au 1957; Lichfield Theol Coll 1964. Trans 10/1/1984. m 6/22/2009 Shung Lung Chen. P-in-c S Mary's Castleton Staten Island NY 2001-2002; Int Ch Of The Resurr New York NY 2000-2001; Non-par 1986-2000; S Jn Jer-sey City NJ 1985-1986; S Matt's Ch Jersey City NJ 1985-1986; Dio Newark Newark NJ 1984; Serv Ch Of Engl 1964-1983.

DULGAR, Sandra Lee (Nev) P.O. Box 3522, Tonopah NV 89049 B Sandpoint ID 1941 d Guy & Louise. D 11/15/1997 Bp Stewart Clark Zabriskie. m 7/20/1984 James R Dulgar. D S Mk's Ch Tonopah NV 1997-2002.

DULL, Stanley Lynn (Pa) 2215 Palm Tree Dr, Punta Gorda FL 33950 B Midland MI 1942 s Orville & Barbara. BS Cntrl Michigan U 1969; MDiv PDS 1974; MA Immaculata U 1993; PsyD Immaculata U 1999. D 6/15/1974 P 8/15/1975 Bp Lyman Cunningham Ogilby. c 5. Ch Of The Epiph Cape Coral FL 2003-2008; R Ch of the Epiph Cape Coral FL 2003-2008; Ch Of The Ascen Parkesburg PA 1975-2000.

DUMKE, Barbara A (Colo) 11684 Eldorado St Nw, Coon Rapids MN 55433 B Oshkosh WI 1946 d Robert & Florence. BA U of Wisconsin 1968; MA U Pgh 1970; MDiv Untd TS of the Twin Cities 1985; MA CDSP 1987. D 6/24/1987 P 5/1/1988 Bp Robert Marshall Anderson. m 9/17/1988 Eugene Richard Wahl. Ch of the Gd Shpd Colorado Spg CO 2007-2012; Trin Ch Anoka MN 1992-2000; The Epis Cathd Of Our Merc Sav Faribault MN 1992; Assoc R St Johns Epis Ch Ross CA 1989-1992; Asst S Aid's Ch San Francisco CA 1987-1988. Auth, "Cath Dig"; Auth, "Soundings".

DUMKE, Edward John (Cal) 805 Barneson Ave, San Mateo CA 94402 B San Mateo CA 1946 s Donald & Dorothy. San Francisco St U; BA San Francisco St U 1968; MDiv CDSP 1975. D 6/28/1975 Bp Chauncie Kilmer Myers P 4/1/1976 Bp Clarence Rupert Haden Jr. Trin Epis Cathd Sacramento CA 1975-1977; Field Worker Trsfg Epis Ch San Mateo CA 1974-1975.

DUMOLT, Elizabeth Ann (Los) 122 S. California Ave., Monrovia CA 91016 **D S Lk's Epis Ch Monrovia CA 2013-** B San Diego, CA 1956 d Raymond & Gloria. B.A. U of San Diego 1979; Cert ETS at Claremont (ETSC) 2010; MDiv Claremont TS & ETSC 2014; MDiv ETSBH 2014. D 5/22/2010 Bp Chester Lovelle Talton. D Gr Epis Ch Glendora CA 2010-2013. Assn for Epis Deacons 2007. Guja MemorialScholarship ETS Claremont 2012. deaconann@saintlukesmonrovia.org

DUNAGAN, Joe K (SwVa) 116 Alabama Ave, Macon GA 31204 **Emm Epis Ch Bristol VA 2014-** B Haw Kinsville GA 1955 s Joe & Bettie. BA Berry Coll 1976; M. Div. Candler Schoo of Theol, Emory U 1980; M. Div. Other 1980; D. Min. Other 2012; D. Min. STUSo: Sewanee 2012. D 12/19/2009 Bp J Neil Alexander. m 10/25/2009 Katherine K Katherine Torbert Kelly c 1. S Jn's Ch Roanoke VA 2013-2014; R Ch Of The Trsfg Rome GA 2012-2013; P in Charge S Chris's At-The-Crossroads Epis Perry GA 2010-2012; Elder The Meth Ch So Georgia Conf 1978-2007. jdunagan@stjohnsroanoke.org

DUNAGAN, Katherine K (SwVa) 1 Mountain Ave SW, Roanoke VA 24016 B Bristol TN 1962 d John & Janet. BA U NC - Greensboro 1985; MDiv Candler TS 1990; MDiv Candler TS Emory U 1990. D 2/23/1999 Bp Henry Irving Louttit P 12/13/2014 Bp Mark Bourlakas. m 10/25/2009 Joe K Dunagan c 1. S Thos' Epis Ch Abingdon VA 2015-2016; D Dio SW Virginia Roanoke VA 2014, Cn Mssnr 2014-. kdunagan@dioswva.org

DUNBAR, Donald Machell (Mass) 160 Longmeadow Rd, Fairfield CT 06824 **1980-** B New York NY 1934 s Howard & Alice. BA Colby Coll 1956; MDiv EDS 1959; MLS Wesl 1973; Med Boston Coll 1980. D 6/20/1959 P 12/1/1959 Bp Anson Phelps Stokes Jr. m 8/27/1966 Susan Morrill Dunbar c 1. Chapl S Paul's Sch Concord NH 1966-1970; Chapl Bp Brent Sch Baguio 1961-1962; Cur Trin Par Melrose MA 1959-1961; Chapl Phillips Acad Andover MA 1979-1983; Dir Chr Ch Waltham MA 1976-1979; Dir S Ptr's Ch Weston MA 1970-1979, Asst Min 1963-1969. "What You Don't Know Can Keep You Out of Coll," Penguin-Gotham, 2007. St. Jn's Soc 2007.

DUNBAR, Gavin Gunning (Ga) 1 W Macon St, Savannah GA 31401 **Assoc S Jn's Ch Savannah GA 1997-** B Toronto ON CA 1961 s Addison & Phyllis. Dalhousie U; BA U Tor 1984; MDiv U Tor CA 1991. Trans 7/1/1997 Bp Henry Irving Louttit. R Ch Of Can Ecum Secum 1991-1997. PB Soc of the U. S. A. 2000.

DUNBAR, Julia Brown (WMass) 20 Whitney Ave, Cambridge MA 02139 B Washington DC 1949 D 6/12/2004 P 1/8/2005 Bp M(Arvil) Thomas Shaw. c 2. Assoc All SS Par Brookline MA 2011-2012.

DUNBAR, Pamela (Dal) 9221 Flickering Shadow Dr, Dallas TX 75243 B San Francisco CA 1947 d Noble & Isabelle. Dio NW TS For Deacons; Texas Tech U; BA California St U 1969. D 10/25/1985 Bp Sam Byron Hulsey. m 5/1/1970 David W Dunbar c 2. Mssnr Dio Dallas Dallas TX 1999-2016; Dio NW Texas Lubbock TX 1996-1999; D S Nich' Epis Ch Midland TX 1985-1999. CHS 1981.

DUNBAR, Philip Craig (CFla) 2505 Gramercy Dr, Deltona FL 32738 **D All SS Epis Ch Deltona FL 2001-, Asst 1977-2000** B Brockton MA 1942 s Donald & Hazel. BA Florida St U 1970; Inst For Chr Stds Orlando FL 1976; MA Rol 1983. D 5/14/1977 Bp William Hopkins Folwell. m 7/3/1966 Judy Ann Dunbar c 4. D S Barn Ch Deland FL 1981-2000.

DUNBAR, Robert Barron (USC) PO Box 36155, Rock Hill SC 29732 B Chester SC 1932 s James & Louise. BA Davidson Coll 1954; MDiv UTS Richmond 1957; MA Presb Sch CE Richmond VA 1964; Sewanee: The U So, TS 1965; Harvard DS 1987. D 4/2/1966 P 4/1/1967 Bp John Adams Pinckney. c 1. P-in-c

Ch Of Our Sav Rock Hill SC 2007-2008, Asst 1995-2007; Int R Par Ch of St. Helena Beaufort SC 1994, Assoc 1989-1993; R S Ptr's Epis Ch Cambridge MA 1980-1989; Vic Ch Of S Jn The Evang Boston MA 1977-1980; Cn Dio Upper So Carolina Columbia SC 1968-1977; Vic Calv Ch Pauline SC 1968-1976; D Epis Ch Of The Redeem Greenville SC 1966-1967.

DUNBAR, Timothy Andrew (Colo) D 6/18/2016 Bp Robert John O'Neill.

DUNBAR ACF, Veronica (Mich) D 6/10/2017 Bp Wendell Nathaniel Gibbs Jr.

DUNCAN, Barbara Tompkins (WA) 8103 Langley Dr, Glen Allen VA 23060 B Richmond VA 1942 d Brown & Ada. BS Virginia St U 1962; MM W Chester U of Pennsylvania 1979; MDiv Lancaster TS 1987; DMin GTF 1992. D 2/28/1987 P 2/1/1988 Bp Cabell Tennis. c 4. S Nich' Epis Ch Newark DE 2002; Cn Mssnr/Pstr Cathd of St Ptr & St Paul Washington DC 1997-2002; Coordntr, Criminal Justice Epis Comm. Serv Philadelphia PA 1995-1997; Epis Cmnty Serv Philadelphia PA 1995-1997; Assoc R S Columba's Ch Washington DC 1993-1995; Assoc R Chr Ch Christiana Hundred Wilmington DE 1990-1992; Int Ch of St Andrews & St Matthews Wilmington DE 1988-1990; Dio Delaware Wilmington 1987-1990; Bp's D to City Cathd Ch Of S Jn Wilmington DE 1987-1988. NAAD 2005.

DUNCAN, Carol (Pa) 503 W Springer St, Philadelphia PA 19119 **D Ch Of S Mart-In-The-Fields Philadelphia PA 2012-** B Macon GA 1945 d William & Catherine. BA Hobart and Wm Smith Colleges 1967. D 11/8/1996 Bp J Clark Grew II. m 10/28/1967 James Robert Duncan c 1. D S Paul's Ch Canton OH 2000-2011; D Trin Ch Allnce OH 1996-1999.

DUNCAN, Carrie Barnes (Miss) **Epis TS Of The SW Austin TX 2016-** D 6/10/2017 Bp Brian Seage.

DUNCAN, Christopher Ray (Tex) PO Box 5176, Austin TX 78763 **S Paul's Ch Katy TX 2012-** B Houston TX 1981 s Mark & Dianne. BA Texas A&M U 2004; MDiv VTS 2009. D 6/20/2009 Bp C Andrew Doyle P 1/20/2010 Bp Dena Arnall Harrison. m 6/24/2006 Casey Duncan c 1. Cur The Ch of the Gd Shpd Austin TX 2009-2012.

DUNCAN, David (Los) 6700 Woodland Hills Rd, Rushville IL 62681 B Brooklyn NY 1948 s Donald & Jean. 1 year full-time doctoral study Claremont Grad Sch; BA Swarthmore Coll 1969; MA Claremont Grad Sch 1974; MA Claremont Grad Sch 1976; MDiv GTS 1979. D 6/23/1979 P 1/12/1980 Bp Robert Claflin Rusack. m 1/15/2011 Sarah Korkowski c 2. Ch Of The H Trin and S Ben Alhambra CA 2004-2005; Int (Var parishes) Dio Los Angeles Los Angeles CA 2002-2005; S Martha's Epis Ch W Covina CA 2001-2004; Chr Ch Par Redondo Bch CA 2000-2001; S Thos The Apos Hollywood Los Angeles CA 2000; S Mk's Par Downey CA 1997-2000; Cathd Cntr Of S Paul Cong Los Angeles CA 1995-1997; Assoc St Cross Epis Ch Hermosa Bch CA 1994-1995; R The Par Ch Of S Lk Long Bch CA 1992-1994; S Anselm Of Cbury Par Garden Grove CA 1989-1992; Trin Epis Par Los Angeles CA 1982-1989; Bloy Hse Claremont CA 1981-1991; Dio Los Angeles Los Angeles CA 1979-1982. Auth, "Sm parishes," *Wit*.

DUNCAN, Hugh C (Ida) 5120 W Overland Rd PMB-276, Boise ID 83705 **Ret 1998-** B Greenville NC 1938 s Fitzhugh & Elizabeth. BS USNA 1961; MDiv Epis TS of the SW 1981. D 6/24/1981 P 1/1/1982 Bp Leigh Allen Wallace Jr. c 2. R All SS Epis Ch Boise ID 1989-1998; COM Dio Spokane Spokane WA 1982-1988; S Mart's Ch Moses Lake WA 1981-1989; S Mk's Ch Ritzville WA 1981-1982; Stndg Com Dio Idaho Boise ID 1988-1993.

DUNCAN, James Bruce (Los) 45 Chestnut St Unit A, North Adams MA 01247 **Pstr Assoc All S's Ch of the Berkshires No Adams MA 2003-; Dio Wstrn Massachusetts 2003-; Ret 2002-** B Elgin IL 1937 s Delbert & Elizabeth. U CO 1957; BA San Francisco St U 1959; Cert Sewanee: The U So, TS 1987; Cert Sewanee: The U So, TS 1987; MDiv GTS 1990; Nash 1992; STM GTS 1994; U Tor 1996; Cert The Ch Dvlpmt Inst 1998; Cert The Ch Dvlpmt Inst 1998. Trans 11/1/1996 Bp Frederick Houk Borsch. m 7/13/1973 Ruth K Duncan. Supply Cler Dio Wstrn Massachusetts Springfield 2002; St Fran Cong Alhambra CA 2000-2001; Dio Los Angeles Los Angeles CA 1999-2001; Int Epis Chap Of S Fran Los Angeles CA 1999-2001; Vic S Alb's Epis Ch Yucaipa CA 1996-1999; Serv Angl Ch of Can 1991-1996. AAR 1990-2014; Angl Soc 1996; Integrity Inc 1990; SBL 1990. Seymour Prize Extemporaneous Preaching GTS 1988.

DUNCAN, John L (NCal) 110 San Benito Avenue, Aptos CA 95003 **Assoc (Ret) St. Jn the Bapt Seacliff (Aptos) CA 2006-; Ret 2000-** B San Jose CA 1939 s John & Frances. CDSP; BA San Jose St U 1962; MDiv PSR 1966. D 6/29/1966 P 5/19/1967 Bp Clarence Rupert Haden Jr. m 4/8/1961 Janet G Duncan c 3. S Phil's Mssn Scotts Vlly CA 2000-2006; R Gr Epis Ch Fairfield CA 1983-2000; Assoc All SS Epis Ch Watsonville CA 1970-1983; Vic S Andr's In The Highlands Mssn Antelope CA 1967-1969; Cur Trin Epis Cathd Sacramento CA 1966-1967; Serv Methodist Ch 1962-1966.

✠ DUNCAN II, The Rt Rev Philip Menzie (CGC) 7208 Mitra Dr, Austin TX 78739 B Glen Cove NY 1944 s Philip & Jessie. BA Baldwin-Wallace Coll 1967; MDiv GTS 1970; St Georges Coll Jerusalem 1977; PrTS 1984; DMin VTS 1990. D 6/13/1970 P 12/19/1970 Bp Jonathan Goodhue Sherman Con 5/12/2001 for CGC. m 6/20/1970 Kathlyn Duncan c 2. Dio Texas Houston TX 2011; Bp Dio Cntrl Gulf Coast Pensacola FL 2001-2015; Dn S Matt's Cathd Dallas TX 1993-2001; TV Advsry Bd Sea of Faith 1986-1993; Cler Advsry Horizon

Hosp Clearwater MPH 1985-1993; Profnsl Comprehensive Addictive Serv Inc 1985-1993; R S Jn's Epis Ch Clearwater FL 1972-1993; Cur Chr Ch Ridgewood NJ 1970-1972; Bd Angl TS Dio Dallas Dallas TX 1993-2000; Chair Epis Migration Mnstry Dio SW Florida Parrish FL 1990-1993, VP Ecum Bd 1982-1989, Dioc Coun 1979-1981. Fllshp of the Soc of S Jn the Evang 1978; Ord of S Jn of Jerusalem 1996. DD The U So TS 2003; DD The GTS 2002; DD The VTS 2002. bishopduncan@diocgc.org

DUNCAN, Rosemarie Logan (WA) 1329 Hamilton St Nw, Washington DC 20011 **Cathd of St Ptr & St Paul Washington DC 2016-** B Washington DC 1959 d William & Falva. BS How 1985; MS How 1989; PhD How 1999; MDiv VTS 2005; DMin VTS 2013. D 6/11/2005 P 1/21/2006 Bp John Bryson Chane. m 8/24/2010 Judith S Hutchinson. Assoc S Columba's Ch Washington DC 2005-2016.

DUNCAN, Rudolph Atherton (Haw) 46-082 Puulena St Apt 1221, Kaneohe HI 96744 **Ret 1991-** B Honolulu HI 1926 s Rudolph & Gladys. BS U CA 1949; MDiv CDSP 1968. D 5/10/1968 Bp Edwin Lani Hanchett P 12/18/1968 Bp Harry Sherbourne Kennedy. m 6/9/1951 Kathleen U Duncan c 3. Treas The Epis Ch in Hawaii Honolulu HI 1979-1991; S Mary's Epis Ch Honolulu HI 1968-1978.

DUNCAN, Shawn P (LI) 722 E 22nd St, Brooklyn NY 11210 B Anaheim CA 1962 s Fred & Linda. BA U CA 1985; MDiv CDSP 1992. D 5/26/1992 P 12/4/1992 Bp Jerry Alban Lamb. m 6/30/1991 Victoria D Duncan c 2. Ch Of The Ascen Staten Island NY 2015-2016; Cn for Media and Mssn Dio Long Island Garden City NY 2012-2014; Committe on Cn 2012-2014; Int S Geo's Par Flushing NY 2010-2012; Int All SS' Epis Ch Briarcliff NY 2009-2010; R Trin Epis Ch Hamburg NY 1999-2009; Elko Emergency Chapl Inc Elko NV 1997-1999; R S Paul's Epis Ch Elko NV 1995-1999; S Mich's Epis Ch Carmichael CA 1992-1995; Const & Cn Com - Chair Dio Wstrn New York Tonawanda NY 2008-2009, Mssn Ldrshp and Mgmt Team - Chair 2008-2009, Stndg Com 2008-2009, Reg Dn 2007-2009, Dn, Sthrn Erie Dnry 2007-, Dep - GC 2006-, Dep to GC 2004-2009; Dioc Coun Dio Nevada Las Vegas 1995-1998. sd@shawnduncan.org

DUNCAN, Victoria D (LI) 722 E 22nd St, Brooklyn NY 11210 B Berkeley CA 1958 d Dawson & Ruth. Albert Einstein Coll of Med; BA Mt Holyoke Coll 1980; MDiv CDSP 1991. D 10/6/2000 P 4/7/2001 Bp Michael Garrison. m 6/30/1991 Shawn P Duncan c 2. Chr Ch New Brighton Staten Island NY 2015-2017; Ch Of S Mary's By The Sea Pt Pleas Bch NJ 2014-2015; Mssnr for Transition Mnstry Epis Ch Cntr New York NY 2009-2013; Cn for Mssn & Mnstry and Dioc Deploy Off Dio Wstrn New York Tonawanda NY 2003-2009, Dn, Bp Brent Sch for Mnstry 2001-2009; Dn Bp Brent Sch for Mnstry Buffalo NY 2001-2009; Assoc R S Mk's Ch Orchard Pk NY 2000-2002; COM Dio Nevada Las Vegas 1996-1997; COM The Epis Dio Nthrn California Sacramento CA 1992-1995.

DUNCAN-O'NEAL III, William McKinley (Ark) 9669 Wedd St, Overland Park KS 66212 **Ret 1995-** B Cleveland OH 1934 s William & Mary. BA U of Texas 1956; BD VTS 1962; MDiv VTS 1970; MLS U of Texas 1971. D 7/20/1962 Bp Everett H Jones P 2/15/1963 Bp Richard Earl Dicus. m 2/14/1994 Janet O'Neal c 2. Dn, SW Convoc Dio Arkansas Little Rock AR 1968-1969; R S Jn's Ch Camden AR 1966-1969; Cur The Falls Ch Epis Falls Ch VA 1964-1966; Dn, Sthrn Convoc Dio W Texas San Antonio TX 1963-1964; Vic S Andr Robstown TX 1962-1964.

✠ **DUNCAN-PROBE, The Rt Rev Dr DeDe** (CNY) 2 Audubon Drive, Cazenovia NY 13035 **Dio Cntrl New York Liverpool NY 2016-** B Ft Worth TX 1962 Doctor of Philos Theol; BS Steph F Austin St U 1985; MA Pepperdine U 1993; MDiv GTS 2003. D 6/28/2003 Bp Richard Lester Shimpfky P 1/19/2004 Bp David Colin Jones Con 12/3/2016 for CNY. m 2/12/1994 Christopher A Probe c 3. Vic S Peters-In-The-Woods Epis Ch Fairfax Sta VA 2009-2016; P-in-c All SS Ch Stoneham MA 2007-2008; Int S Jn's Epis Ch Mc Lean VA 2006-2007; Assoc R Ch Of The H Comf Vienna VA 2003-2006; All SS Par Beverly Hills CA 1992-1994. Hon Doctorate of Div The GTS 2017. cnybishop@gmail.com

DUNEVANT, Emily Hope (Va) 2955 River Rd W, Goochland VA 23063 **Gr Epis Ch Goochland VA 2016-** B Forth Worth TX 1972 d Derrell & Joyce. BA Winthrop U 1994; MDiv UTS 2010. D 11/21/2015 Bp Susan Goff P 6/14/2016 Bp Ted Gulick Jr. m 5/28/2016 Michael Dwayne Dunevant c 2.

DUNFEE, Mikayla Suzanne (SD) **Cur Dio So Dakota Pierre SD 2016-** D 12/19/2015 P 6/25/2016 Bp John Tarrant.

DUNHAM, Richard Eldon (WTex) 4137 Harry St, Corpus Christi TX 78411 B Corpus Christi TX 1949 s Walter & Virginia. BA U of Texas 1972; MDiv Epis TS of the SW 1979. D 6/12/1979 Bp Scott Field Bailey P 12/12/1979 Bp Stanley Fillmore Hauser. m 3/10/2012 Debra W Dunham c 1. R S Chris's Ch Bandera TX 2002-2010; S Mk's Epis Ch Moscow ID 1988-2002; The Epis Ch Of The Adv Alice TX 1983-1988; S Peters Epis Sch Kerrville TX 1979-1983; S Ptr's Epis Ch Kerrville TX 1979-1983.

DUNKERLEY, James Hobson (Chi) 6033 N Sheridan Rd Apt 44B, Chicago IL 60660 B Manchester UK 1939 s James & Elsie. Kelham Theol Coll 1964; BD SWTS 1969; STM SWTS 1970. Trans 10/28/1970 as Priest Bp Gerald Francis Burrill. Dn Dio Chicago Chicago IL 2004-2006, Dioc Coun Mem 2000-2005,

Dioc Coun Mem 1984-2003; R S Ptr's Epis Ch Chicago IL 1970-2007; Serv Ch Of Engl 1964-1968. CCU 1965; Soc of the Sacr Mssn (Assoc) 1958.

DUNKLE, Kurt Hughes (Fla) **The GTS New York NY 2013-; Gvnr Angl Cntr in Rome Rome ITALY 2012-** B Saint Petersburg FL 1961 s Harry & Caroline. BA Duke 1983; JD U of Florida 1987; MDiv GTS 2004. D 5/30/2004 P 12/5/2004 Bp Samuel Johnson Howard. m 5/16/1987 Cathleen B Dunkle c 2. Gr Epis Ch Orange Pk FL 2008-2013; Cn Dio Florida Jacksonville 2004-2008. Auth, "Stwdshp," *LivCh*, 2008. dunkle@gts.edu

DUNKS, Andrew A (Va) Saint Bartholomew's Church, 10627 Patterson Ave, Richmond VA 23238 **R S Barth's Ch Richmond VA 2012-** B Bryan TX 1962 s Wallace & Ginger. BA Texas A&M U 1984; MA U of Notre Dame 1986; MDiv Epis TS of the SW 1989. D 2/8/1990 Bp William Elwood Sterling P 8/1/1990 Bp Earl Nicholas Mc Arthur Jr. m 1/20/1990 Julia D Dunks c 2. Chapl Christchurch Sch Christchurch VA 2010-2012; Chapl Virginia Epis Sch Lynchburg VA 2002-2010; Vic S Mich's Epis Ch San Antonio TX 1994-2002; Asst R S Barth's Ch Corpus Christi TX 1990-1993. ERM. dunks.andy@gmail.com

DUNLAP, Daniel K (Eas) 715 Carrell St., Tomball TX 77375 **Old Trin Ch Ch Creek MD 2014-** B Philadelphia PA 1963 s David & Patricia. BS Penn 1986; MDiv Biblic TS 1989; PhD Wycliffe Hall 2001. D 6/23/2007 Bp Don Adger Wimberly P 1/9/2008 Bp Rayford Baines High Jr. m 6/27/1987 Donna G Dunlap c 3. Actg R Ch Of The Gd Shpd Tomball TX 2009-2014.

DUNLAP, Dennis Joe (Chi) 326 W. Northland Ave, Peoria IL 61614 B Bloomington IL 1949 s Everett & Gladys. BA Illinois St U 1970; MA Illinois St U 1971; MDiv Nash 1974. D 5/14/1974 P 5/24/1975 Bp Albert William Hillestad. R S Paul's Ch Mchenry IL 2004-2006; R All SS Ch Morton IL 1996-2004; R Ch of St Jn the Evang Wisconsin Rapids WI 1983-1996; Cn St Paul's Epis Cathd Fond Du Lac WI 1977-1983; Vic Chr The King Guayaquil Ecuador 1975-1977; Mssy Appointee by PB Iglesia Epis Del Ecuador Quito 1975-1977; Cur Ch Of The Trsfg Freeport NY 1974-1975; Dom And Frgn Mssy Soc- Epis Ch Cntr New York NY 1975-1977. AGO 1976; GAS 1971; OSB, Confrater 1968; Organ Hist Soc 1977; SHN 1978.

DUNLAP, Eunice R (Del) 403 Northview Dr, Fayetteville NC 28303 **All SS and St Georges Ch Rehoboth Bch DE 2014-** B New York NY 1961 d John & Margarete. MDiv Bangor TS 1997; BS SUNY 1997; DAS VTS 2002. D 4/10/2002 P 2/25/2003 Bp Clifton Daniel III. m 8/11/1984 George Mackenzie Dunlap c 3. Asst R S Jas Epis Ch Hendersonvlle NC 2007-2014; H Trin Epis Ch Fayetteville NC 2002-2006.

DUNLAP, Garland Edward (Va) 537 Chattooga Place Dr, Wilmington NC 28412 B Winchester VA 1942 s Charles & Anna. BA Virginia Commonwealth U 1969; MDiv VTS 1972. D 5/27/1972 Bp Charles Francis Hall P 5/1/1973 Bp Robert Fisher Gibson Jr. m 12/18/1966 Donna Ploss c 1. R S Paul's On-The-Hill Winchester VA 2000-2003; R Varina Epis Ch Henrico VA 1997-2000; S Paul's Epis Ch Wilmington NC 1995-1996; Imm Ch Mechanicsvlle VA 1994-1995; R S Fran Ch Goldsboro NC 1980-1994; R S Phil's Ch Southport NC 1978-1980; Asst S St Jas Ch Richmond VA 1974-1978.

DUNLAP, Mary Balfour (NC) Emmanuel Parish Episcopal Church, 340 S Ridge St, Southern Pines NC 28387 **Emm Par Epis Ch Sthrn Pines NC 2016-** B Greenville MS 1977 d Polk & Mary. MDiv Epis TS of the SW 2014; MDiv Epis TS of the SW 2014. D 5/31/2014 Bp John Mckee Sloan Sr P 1/10/2015 Bp Santosh K Marray. m 10/25/2016 Murray Wheeler Dunlap. Chr Ch Fairfield AL 2016; S Mich's Epis Ch Fayette AL 2014-2016.

DUNLOP, William Henry (Mil) 413 S 2nd St, Watertown WI 53094 B Hackensack 1954 s William & Muriel. BSCE U of New Hampshire 1976; MCE U of Florida 1984. D 6/13/2015 Bp Steven Andrew Miller. m 8/29/1976 Amy Morgan Amy Ruth Morgan c 2.

DUNN, Carlton Willard (NJ) St Andrew's Church, 121 High St, Mount Holly NJ 08060 B Salem NJ 1947 s Carlton & Carolyn. BS Philadelphia Coll of Bible 1969; MA Glassboro St Coll 1972. D 5/5/2012 Bp George Edward Councell. m 10/22/2005 Eleanor H Dunn c 4.

DUNN III, D(ouglas) (SVa) 2000 Huguenot Trl, Powhatan VA 23139 **Ch Of The Redeem Midlothian VA 2015-** B Norfolk VA 1951 s Douglas & Nira. UTS Richmond; U Sydney Moore Theol Coll 1972; BS Old Dominion U 1974; Med Coll of Virginia 1976; S Georges Coll Jerusalem IL 1977; MDiv VTS 1978; S Jn Coll GB 1986. D 5/25/1978 P 11/1/1978 Bp Claude Charles Vache. m 12/27/1989 Mary S Dunn c 1. S Jas' Epis Ch Warrenton VA 2012-2013; Int Gr Epis Ch Hinsdale IL 2010-2012; Int Epiph Epis Ch Richmond VA 2009-2010; Vic H Fam Ch Midlothian VA 2005-2008; Cn Dio Sthrn Virginia Newport News VA 2003-2005; S Paul's Ch Petersburg VA 1999-2006, P-in-c 1999-2005, Int 1992-1994; Int S Lk's Ch Powhatan VA 1998-1999; Int S Mart's Epis Ch Richmond VA 1997; Int S Mk's Ch Richmond VA 1995-1997; Int S Barn Epis Ch No Chesterfield VA 1994-1995; Int The Fork Ch Doswell VA 1992; Int S Lk's Ch Blackstone VA 1990-1991; Int Ch Of The Gd Shpd Richmond VA 1989-1990; Int Gr Ch Yorktown Yorktown VA 1988-1989; Glebe Ch Suffolk VA 1987-1988; Int S Jn's Ch Suffolk VA 1987-1988; R Trin Epis Ch Beaver PA 1982-1983; Assoc All SS Ch Richmond VA 1979-1982; Chr Ch Amelia Ct Hs VA 1978-1979; Emm Epis Ch Powhatan VA 1978-1979; Int Pac Cure Par

Cartersville VA 1978-1979; D S Jas Ch Cartersville VA 1978-1979. Societas Liturgica. Woods Fell VTS 1985.

DUNN, Douglas Robert (Colo) 1270 Poplar St, Denver CO 80220 **R S Lk's Ch Denver CO 1993-** B Sioux Falls SD 1953 s Robert & Shirley. BS So Dakota St U 1979; MDiv Nash 1984; DMin SWTS 2001. D 5/31/1984 Bp Conrad H Gesner P 11/30/1984 Bp Craig Barry Anderson. m 8/11/1979 Janet Dunn c 3. Reg Mssnr Dio Colorado Denver CO 2005-2009; R S Dav Of Wales Ch New Berlin WI 1985-1993; Vic Ch Of The Incarn Greg SD 1984-1985; Supvsr Mnstry Dvlpmt Prog Dio So Dakota Pierre SD 1984-1985; Educ Coordntr S Paul's Ch Milwaukee WI 1983-1984.

DUNN, Frank (WA) St Stephen and the Incarnation Parish, 1525 Newton St NW, Washington DC 20010 **Sr P Ch Of S Steph And The Incarn Washington DC 2010-** B Conway, SC 1945 s Otis & Dora. BA Randolph-Macon Coll 1967; BD PrTS 1970; GTS 1971. D 6/4/1971 P 12/1/1971 Bp William Henry Marmion. m 5/20/2011 Joseph Casazza c 2. R S Jn's Ch Lynchburg VA 1992-2004; R Trin Ch Newtown CT 1979-1992; R S Andr's Epis Ch Charlotte NC 1975-1979; Cur S Mart's Epis Ch Charlotte NC 1971-1974. Auth, "Bldg Faith In Families," Morehouse, 1986.

DUNN, George Mervyn (Ga) 8 Woodbridge Crescent, Kanata ON K2M 2N6 Canada **Assoc Chr Ch Frederica St Simons Island 2007-** B Belfast Northern Ireland 1941 s George & Alice. LTh Ch of Ireland Theol 1973. Trans 2/1/1998 as Priest Bp Edward Lloyd Salmon Jr. m 2/1/1964 Margaret Dunn c 3. Assoc R Chr Ch Frederica St Simons Is GA 2007-2010; Asst R Ch Of The Ascen Knoxville TN 2001-2006; Vic S Barn Ch Dillon SC 1998-2001; Serv Angl Ch of Can Ontario Can 1982-1998; Serv Ch of Ireland Nthrn Ireland 1973-1982.

DUNN, Matilda Eeleen Greene (ETenn) 7013 Rocky Trl, Chattanooga TN 37421 B Greenville LR 1952 d Judson & Rachel. BA Bloomfield Coll 1974; MS Sthrn Illinois U 1976; MDiv Sewanee: The U So, TS 1994. D 8/6/1994 Bp Bertram Nelson Herlong P 5/1/1995 Bp Robert Gould Tharp. m 1/30/1970 Daniel Elwood Dunn. Dio E Tennessee Knoxville TN 2001-2005; Epis. Comm. Of Se Tennessee Signal Mtn TN 1998-2001; Gr Ch Chattanooga TN 1996-1998; Assoc S Ptr's Ch Chattanooga TN 1995-1996. Cmnty Cross Nails; Cmnty Of S Mary; EWHP; Eshme; UBE.

DUNN, Patrick Hall (Miss) 4030 Perch Point Dr, Mobile AL 36605 **Supply S Ptr's Ch Jackson AL 2010-** B Florence AL 1938 s Julius & Emma. BA U of Alabama 1960; BD VTS 1968. D 6/14/1968 P 6/1/1969 Bp George Mosley Murray. m 7/14/1963 Phyllis Dunn c 2. Int S Paul's Epis Ch Daphne AL 2008; Gd Shpd 2004-2008; Int S Jas Ch Fairhope AL 1999-2002; Par Of The Medtr-Redeem Mccomb MS 1985-1993; R S Andr's Ch Mobile AL 1969-1984; Vic H Cross Trussville AL 1968-1969. "Mullet -Mugill Cephalus Manuscript," Self Pub, 2000; Auth, "Theol of Water"; Auth, "Theol of Water".

DUNN, Prentiss Carroll (La) 422 W Hickory Ave, Bastrop LA 71220 B Bastrop LA 1944 s Prentiss & Bennie. BA Baylor U 1967; Acad Mus & Dramatic Arts Vienna at 1972; MA Indiana U 1973. D 6/6/1982 P 12/1/1983 Bp James Barrow Brown. Trin Epis Ch Baton Rouge LA 1983-1984; Trin Ch New Orleans LA 1982-1983.

DUNN, Robert Ellis (Oly) Po Box 1377, Granite Falls WA 98252 **Int R St Alb's Epis Ch 2014-** B Bloomington IL 1938 s William & Lillie. Dplma Burnley Sch of Art 1960; BTh Vancouver TS CA 1973. D 7/17/1973 P 7/10/1974 Bp Ivol I Curtis. c 4. Asst Trin Epis Ch Everett WA 2007-2010, Cur 1973-1975; Asst S Phil Ch Marysville WA 2002-2007; Vic Ch Of Our Sav Monroe WA 1997-1998; R S Steph's Epis Ch Spokane WA 1991-1997; R S Fran' Par Palos Verdes Estates CA 1988-1991; R S Jn's Ch Kirkland WA 1978-1988; R Ch Of The H Trin Hoquiam WA 1975-1978; R H Trin Ch Seattle WA 1975-1978; S Christophers Epis Ch Westport WA 1975-1978. bob@bobdunnartist.com

DUNN, Sarah Amelia (WMass) 14 Boltwood Ave, Amherst MA 01002 **Dio Wstrn Massachusetts Springfield 2015-** B Fort Belvoir VA 1989 d Robert & Kaaren. BA Mt Holyoke Coll 2011; MDiv Ya Berk 2015. D 12/6/2014 P 10/3/2015 Bp Doug Fisher. m 11/5/2016 Nathan G Syer.

DUNN, Sharon Kay Estey (Nev) 3500 San Mateo Ave, Reno NV 89509 **P S Steph's Epis Ch Reno NV 1995-** B Bartlesville OK 1937 d Clarence & Irma. BA U of Kansas 1959; MA Stan 1963; U of Arizona 1979; CDSP 1993. D 8/14/1994 P 2/17/1995 Bp Stewart Clark Zabriskie. m 9/6/1959 Peter Graves Dunn. Edtr Dio Nevada Las Vegas 1992-1995. Auth, "Pryr," *Race And Pryr*, Morehouse, 2003; Auth, "Poem And Pryr," *Wmn Uncommon Pryr*, Morehouse, 2000. Ord Of S Lk 1986.

DUNN, William Edward (Los) 1803 Highland Hollow Dr # 559, Conroe TX 77304 **S Steph's Par Beaumont CA 2010-** B Freeport TX 1957 s John & Ella. BA Steph F Austin St U 1978; Texas St U San Marcos 1987; MDiv Epis TS of the SW 1998. D 6/20/1998 Bp Claude Edward Payne P 6/22/1999 Bp Leopoldo Jesus Alard. m 2/1/1991 Sharron H Dunn c 4. S Mich's Epis Ch Riverside CA 2009-2010; S Lk's Epis Hosp Houston TX 2005-2007; The Great Cmsn Fndt Houston TX 2005; Chr The King Epis Ch Humble TX 2001-2005; Asst S Jas The Apos Epis Ch Conroe TX 1998-2001.

DUNNAM, Thomas Mark (Eur) Via Bernardo Rucellai 9, Firenze 50123 Italy **S Jas Epis Ch Firenze 50123 2009-** B Mobile AL 1946 s Ernest & Kitty. BA Birmingham-Sthrn Coll 1969; MDiv GTS 1972. D 6/11/1972 P 4/1/1973

Bp John Maury Allin. m 1/3/1981 Emily Dunnam c 1. Dioc Coordntr Dio Cntrl Gulf Coast Pensacola FL 1987-2009; S Mk's For The Deaf Mobile AL 1982-1987; R Ch Of The Gd Shpd Mobile AL 1981-1987; Cleric S Greg's Abbey Three Rievers MI 1976-1980; Cur S Andr's Epis Ch New Orleans LA 1973-1976; Dio Mississippi Jackson MS 1972-1973; Cur S Jn's Epis Ch Pascagoula MS 1972-1973.

DUNNAN, Donald Stuart (Md) Saint James School, Saint James MD 21781 **P St Jas Sch Hagerstown MD 1992-** B Washington DC 1959 s Weaver & Diana. MA Harv 1981; BA Oxf GB 1985; Cert GTS 1986; MA Oxf GB 1990; PhD Oxf GB 1991. D 6/21/1986 P 1/1/1987 Bp Oliver Bailey Garver Jr. Chapl Lincoln Coll Oxford 1990-1992; R Libr Pusey Hse Oxford 1987-1990; Harvard-Westlake Sch Studio City CA 1986-1987.

DUNNAVANT, Charles Randall (Tenn) 817 Stonebrook Blvd, Nolensville TN 37135 **R Ch Of The Gd Shpd Brentwood TN 1998-** B Pulaski TN 1953 s Charles & Bettye. BS Middle Tennessee St U 1985; MDiv Sewanee: The U So, TS 1988. D 6/25/1988 P 1/21/1989 Bp George Lazenby Reynolds Jr. m 2/14/1976 Lannette I Ikard c 1. Vic Dio Tennessee Nashville TN 1995-1997, 1988; R S Mary Magd Ch Fayetteville TN 1992-1995, D-in-Trng 1988-1991; Chapl Lincoln Co. Hospice 1991-1995. Citizen of Year 94 Natl Grand Elks Lodge 1994; Silver Beaver Awd for Distinguished Serv BSA 1993.

DUNN CUNNINGHAM, Deborah (Los) 402 S Lincoln St, Santa Maria CA 93458 **Died 4/20/2017** B Angleton TX 1951 d John & Ella. BFA U of Texas 1976; California St U 1987; ETSBH 1988; MDiv GTS 1991. D 6/15/1991 P 1/11/1992 Bp Frederick Houk Borsch. m 4/20/2017 Michael Ray Cunningham c 2. R S Ptr's Par Santa Maria CA 2007-2017; Vic S Thos' Mssn Hacienda Hgts CA 1999-2007; Assoc The Par Of S Matt Pacific Plsds CA 1995-1999; Dio Los Angeles Los Angeles CA 1993-1995; Asst St Cross Epis Ch Hermosa Bch CA 1992-1993; Cur S Fran' Par Palos Verdes Estates CA 1991-1992.

DUNNETT, Walter McGregor (Chi) 2127 Hallmark Ct, Wheaton IL 60187 **Asstg P S Mk's Epis Ch Glen Ellyn IL 1998-** B Tayport Scotland GB 1924 s Daniel & Jemima. BA Wheaton Coll 1949; MA Wheaton Coll 1950; BD Wheaton Coll 1953; PhD Case Wstrn Reserve U 1967; STM Luther TS 1980; DWS Inst for Wrshp Stds Orange Pk FL 2004. D 6/24/1991 Bp Robert Marshall Anderson P 1/22/1992 Bp Sanford Zangwill Kaye Hampton. m 7/8/1944 Dolores R Eddy c 2. Adj Prof Bible Bethel Coll S Paul MN 1996-1997; P Mssh Mssh Epis Ch S Paul MN 1992-1997; Prof Bible & Gk NoWstrn Coll S Paul MN 1976-1992; Prof Bible & Gk Moody Bible Inst Chicago IL 1972-1976; Prof Bible Trin Deerfield IL 1969-1972; Prof Bible Wheaton Coll Wheaton IL 1966-1969; Prof Bible & Gk Moody Bible Inst Chicago IL 1958-1966. Auth, "NT Survey," *NT Survey*, Eerdmans, 1985; Auth, "The Interp of H Scripture," *The Interp of H Scripture*, Thos Nelson, 1984; Auth, "The Bk of Acts," *The Bk of Acts*, Baker, 1981; Auth, "Revelation," *Revelation: God's Final Word to Man*, Meridian, 1967; Auth, "NT Survey," *NT Survey*, E.T.T.A., 1963; Auth, "An Outline of N.T. Survey," *An Outline of NT Survey*, Moody Press, 1960. Evang Theol Soc, Pres 1987. Pi Gamma Mu Wheaton Coll 1948.

DUNNING, Jane Romeyn (WMass) 44 Main St, Shelburne Falls MA 01370 **Chapl Shelburne Falls Fire Dist Shelburne Falls MA 2013-; P Assoc, St. Jas, Greenfield Dio Wstrn Massachusetts Springfield 2012-, Chapl to the Ret 1997-** B Detroit MI 1938 d Hendrik & Margery. BA Manhattanville Coll 1987; MDiv GTS 1991. D 6/8/1991 P 12/14/1991 Bp Richard Frank Grein. m 2/13/1960 Harry Martin Dunning c 2. Vic S Jn's Ch Ashfield MA 2002-2006; Int S Mk's Ch Adams MA 2000-2006; Vic St Helenas Chap Lenox MA 1993-2000; Cur S Jn's Ch Larchmont NY 1991-1993.

DUNNING, William (Md) 1612 Trebor Ct, Lutherville MD 21093 **Assoc for Pstr Care Ch Of The H Comf Luthvle Timon MD 2012-; Chapl Ret Cler Spouses of Cler Baltimore 2009-; Chapl to Ret Cler Dio Maryland Baltimore MD 2006-** B Worcester MA 1936 s Elmer & Marion. BA Bos 1959; MDiv GTS 1962. D 6/22/1962 Bp Robert McConnell Hatch P 12/22/1962 Bp Leland Stark. m 8/6/1965 Margaret S Dunning. Int R S Thos Epis Ch Towson MD 2008-2011; P-in-c Ch Of S Marks On The Hill Pikesville MD 2004-2007; Int Imm Ch Highlands Wilmington DE 2002-2004; Int S Jas' Epis Ch Downingtown PA 2001-2002; Int S Fran-In-The-Fields Malvern PA 1999-2001; Int The Ch Of The H Trin W Chester PA 1998-1999; R S Mich And All Ang Ch Baltimore MD 1988-1998; R Trin Epis Ch Haverhill MA 1981-1988; R Chr Ch Waterbury CT 1975-1981; Asst No Lackawanna Vlly Mnstry Carbondale PA 1972-1975; Asst S Thos Epis Ch Rochester NY 1966-1971; Vic Gr Ch Oxford MA 1964-1966; Cur S Jn's Ch Dover NJ 1962-1964.

DUNNINGTON, Michael Gerard (Mo) 1620 Forestview Ridge Ln, Ballwin MO 63021 **Dioc Chapt Rep Chr Ch Cathd 2011-; P-in-c All SS Ch S Louis MO 2010-** B Saint Louis MO 1946 s Joseph & Olive. BA S Louis U 1969; MA S Louis U 1970; MBA Sthrn Illinois U 1975; MDiv Sewanee: The U So, TS 1996. D 6/29/1996 P 6/1/1997 Bp Robert Carroll Johnson Jr. m 8/3/2000 Leslie Holdsworth Dunnington c 2. P-in-c Ch Of The Ascen S Louis MO 2004-2007; All SS Epis Ch St. Louis MO 2003-2004; R The Ch Of The H Innoc Henderson NC 1998-1999; Asst Ch Of The H Comf Burlington NC 1996-1998. Cath Fllshp of the Epis Ch 1993-1997. pastorallsaints@yahoo.com

DUNPHY, Martha-Jane (NY) 190 Pinewood Rd Apt 78, Hartsdale NY 10530 **Gr Ch White Plains NY 1997-; D Santa Rosa Mssn at Gr Ch White Plains NY 1997-** B White Plains NY 1945 d William & Jane. SUNY; The Coll of Westchester 1968. D 4/26/1997 Bp Richard Frank Grein. NAAD.

DUNST, Earl Walter (Mil) 8121 N Seneca Rd, Milwaukee WI 53217 **Ret 1996-** B Milwaukee WI 1915 s Albert & Marie. D 12/22/1956 Bp Donald H V Hallock. m 10/19/1946 Jane Lango c 3. Asst S Paul's Ch Milwaukee WI 1956-1996.

DUPLANTIER, David Allard (La) 2037 South Carrollton Avenue, New Orleans LA 70118 **Dn Chr Ch Cathd New Orleans LA 2002-** B Louisville KY 1961 s Donald & Lucy. BA Mia 1983; MDiv GTS 1993. D 6/26/1993 P 9/21/1994 Bp Herbert Thompson Jr. m 11/26/2011 Karla Sikaffy duPlantier c 2. Asst The Ch of the Redeem Cincinnati OH 1997-2002; R Gr Ch Pomeroy OH 1994-1997; Cur Ch Of The Gd Shpd Athens OH 1993-1994. CT (assoc) 1995; Soc of the Cincinnati (Virginia) 2011. Distinguished Alum Gnrl Sem 2009.

DUPLESSIE, Thomas Frederick (Me) 27 Butters Rd, Exeter ME 04435 **Treas St. Mart's Literacy Prog Palmyra 1998-; Dioc Coun Mem Dio Maine Portland ME 2002-** B Waterville ME 1942 s Emile & Christine. AA Thos Jr Coll 1963; BA U of Maine 1971; MS SUNY 1993; Cert Bangor TS 2002. D 6/20/2004 Bp Chilton Richardson Knudsen. c 2. NADD 2004.

DUPREE, Charlie (Ind) 111 S. Grant St., Bloomington IN 47408 **R Trin Epis Ch Bloomington IN 2008-** B Tarboro NC 1969 s Joseph & Sara. BFA E Carolina U 1993; MDiv VTS 1999. D 6/12/1999 P 5/2/2000 Bp Clifton Daniel III. m 10/12/2011 Matthew Cole. Dio New York New York NY 2004-2008; S Greg's Epis Ch Woodstock NY 2004-2008; Assoc R S Paul's Epis Ch Greenville NC 1999-2004.

DUPREE, Hugh Douglas (Ga) 325 N Market St, Jacksonville FL 32202 **Dio Florida Jacksonville 2015-; Dn Balliol Coll Univ. of Oxford Oxford 2007-; Chapl & Fell Balliol Coll Univ. of Oxford Oxford 1987-** B Dothan AL 1950 s Hubert & Ann. BA U So 1972; MDiv VTS 1975; MA Oxf GB 1986; PhD Oxf GB 1988. D 6/8/1975 Bp Frank S Cerveny P 2/25/1976 Bp George Paul Reeves. Chapl HM Prison Oxford Oxford Untd Kingdom 1988-1996; Asst Chapl & Fell Balliol Coll Univ. of Oxford Oxford 1984-1987; Cleric Chr Ch Oxford Untd Kingdom 1980-1984; Assoc S Jn's Ch Savannah GA 1975-1980. Hon Cur S Mich's Ch/Oxford 1980.

DUPREY, David Luke (Wyo) 1 S Tschirgi St, Sheridan WY 82801 **USN Off Of Bsh For ArmdF New York NY 2008-** B Norwich CT 1962 s Richard & Mary. Wright St U 1980; OH SU 1983; BD Capital U 1985; MDiv TESM 1988. D 6/24/1988 P 1/6/1989 Bp Bob Gordon Jones. c 3. R S Ptr's Epis Ch Sheridan WY 1992-2008; St Jn the Bapt Epis Ch Big Piney WY 1988-1992. "Full of Gr and Truth," *self Pub*, self Pub, 1998.

DU PRIEST, Travis Talmadge (Mil) 508 DeKoven, Racine WI 53403 B Richmond VA 1944 s Travis & Mildred. BA U Rich 1966; PhD U of Kentucky 1972; Studied at St Chads Coll U of Durham 1973; MTS Harvard DS 1974; U of Cambridge 1982. D 6/1/1974 P 6/16/1975 Bp Addison Hosea. m 9/1/1972 Mabel B Du Priest c 2. Exec Dir Dekoven Fndt for Ch Wk Racine WI 1991-2006; Vice Pres & Exec Dire DeKoven Fndt Racine WI 1990-2006; Bk Ed/Ed Asst. LivCh mag 1990-2003; Asstg P S Lk's Ch Racine WI 1988-1997; Chapl CSM (Wstrn Prov) 1985-2012; Prof of Engl Carthage Coll 1974-1999. Auth, "To Hear Celestial Harmonies: Jas DeKoven and The DeKoven Cntr," *Co-edited*, Foreward Mvmt Pub, 2002; Ed, "Poems by Kath Philips," *Intro*, Schlr's Facsimiles and Reprints, 1988; Auth, "Measure & Off of Friendship by Jeremy Taylor," *Intro*, Schlr's Facsimiles and Reprints, 1986; "numerous poems and arts," TLC, ATR, and others; "A Heart for the Future," *Chapt*, Ch Pub; Ed, "A New Conversation," *Chapt*, Ch Pub; Co-Ed, "Engaging the Sprt," *Chapt*, Ch Pub; "Sum Storm on the Jas," *Long Poem*, Telstar Pub; "Noon at Smyrna," *Poetry Chapbook*, Can; "Soapstone Wall," *Poetry Chapbook*, Wolfsong Pub. Cmnty of S Mary, P Assoc. 1977; Natl Huguenot Soc, Hon. Pres. Gnrl 1985; Venerable Ord of S Jn 1995. Distinguished Tchr Year Awd Carthage Coll 1980; Fell Danforth 1977; Fell Rockerfeller 1971; Fell NDEA 1967; Vstng Fell Cntr for Renaissance & Reformation Stds, Victoria Coll,; Best Paper at Conf Chrsnty & Lit: SE Reg; Fell Coll of Preachers; Moon Fell Dio Milwaukee Fllshp; Mid-W Fac Fllshp Univ. of Chicago; Allin Fllshp U So; Resrch Fell Wm. A. Clark Libr, UCLA.

✠ **DUQUE-GOMEZ, The Rt Rev Francisco Jose (Colom)** Calle 122-A #1211, Bogota Colombia **Bp Of Colombia Iglesia Epis En Colombia Bogota 2002-** B 1950 s Jose & Oliva. Cert ETSC; JD Universidad Libre De Colombia; Unv Javeriana. D 12/8/1988 P 12/1/1991 Bp Bernardo Merino-Botero Con 7/14/2001 for Colom. m 12/16/1983 Blanca Echeverry.

✠ **DURACIN, The Rt Rev Jean Zache (Hai)** Box 1309, Port-Au-Prince Haiti **Bp of Haiti Dio Haiti Port-au-Prince HT 1977-** B Leogane, Haiti 1947 s Montas & Camenise. BD Lycee A Petion; BD Lycee A Petion 1972; Untd Theol of W Indies 1976; Sem Epis Ch Hai 1977; Sem Epis Ch Haiti 1977. D 9/18/1977 P 5/1/1978 Bp Luc Anatole Jacques Garnier Con 6/2/1993 for Hai. m 12/18/1979 Marie Edithe Louis-Jean c 3. R H Trin Cathd Port-Au-Prince Haiti 1990-1993; R S Andr Hinche Haiti 1982-1990. Hon Doctorate in Div Sewanee: The U So

2010; St. Geo's Coll The Bible and the H Land 1997; Hon Degree GTS 1996. epihaiti@yahoo.com

DURAIKANNU, Yesu (Colo) St.James' Church, 1 St. James' Place, Goshen NY 10924 **S Andr's Ch Bronx NY 2013-** B Eachambadi IN 1958 s S & A. BD Bishops Theol Coll Calcutta IN; BTh So India Biblic Sem Bangarpet Ks IN; DMin Sewanee: The U So, TS 2003. Trans 3/14/2001 Bp Bertram Nelson Herlong. m 12/27/1994 Suchita Yesupatham c 2. Int Ch Of S Mary The Vrgn Chappaqua NY 2013; R Ch Of The Ascen Salida CO 2007-2012; Mem -Fin Com Dio New York New York NY 2002-2006; P-in-c St Fran of Assisi Montgomery NY 2002-2006; P-in-c S Andr's Ch Walden NY 2001-2006; Asst R S Ptr's Ch Columbia TN 2001-2002.

DURAND, Sally Elaine (Az) 7813 N. Via De La Luna, Scottsdale AZ 85258 **D/ Admin Iglesia Epis De San Pablo Phoenix AZ 2015-** B Santa Fe NM 1953 d Harvey & Gratia. BA New Mex St U 1975; MA U of San Diego 1992; Cert Theol Stud ETSBH 2000. D 6/9/2001 Bp Gethin Benwil Hughes. Epis Cmnty Serv Phoenix AZ 2012-2015; Hisp Mnstrs Trin Cathd Phoenix AZ 2009-2013; Dio Arizona Phoenix AZ 2009-2012; Asst S Lk's Ch San Diego CA 2004-2007, 2002-2004; Dio San Diego San Diego CA 2001-2005; Chapl Mssn to Seafarers 2000-2005. Soc of S Jn the Evang (Assoc) 1996. sunburst1.spablophx@gmail.com

DURANT, Jack Davis (NC) 3001 Old Orchard Rd, Raleigh NC 27607 **D St. Mich's 2000-; Ret 1998-** B Birmingham AL 1930 s Kyle & Benalie. BA Maryville Coll 1953; MA U of Tennessee 1955; PhD U of Tennessee 1963. D 4/29/1995 Bp Huntington Williams Jr. c 2. Nativ 1995-1998.

DURANY, Helen Marie (Colo) D 6/18/2016 P 6/10/2017 Bp Robert John O'Neill.

D'URBANO, Faith Jeanne (Be) 340 W. Orange Street, Lancaster PA 17603 B Bryn Mawr PA 1950 d John & Susanne. BA W Chester U of Pennsylvania 1971; MA Villanova U 1976; MDiv GTS 2000. D 4/29/2000 P 3/26/2001 Bp Paul Victor Marshall. c 2. Asst S Gabr's Ch Douglassville PA 2000-2005.

DURBIDGE, Andrew John (LI) 50 Cathedral Ave, Garden City NY 11530 **Dio Long Island Garden City NY 2015-** B Sydney Australia 1962 s Jack & Maisie. MPM U of Techology 1996; MDiv GTS 2014. D 6/6/2015 P 12/5/2015 Bp Lawrence C Provenzano. adurbidge@dioceseli.org

DURE, Lucy Ann (Nwk) 46 Montrose Ave, Verona NJ 07044 B Fort Sill OK 1954 d Richard & Mary. BA Ford 1987; MDiv Ya Berk 1991. D 5/30/1998 Bp Jack Marston Mckelvey P 12/5/1998 Bp John Palmer Croneberger. m 12/30/1989 Davis Oakford Dure. R Ch Of The H Sprt Verona NJ 2000-2013; Asst S Lk's Epis Ch Montclair NJ 1998-2000.

DURGIN, Ralph Thayer (Ct) 250 Old Field Ln # 823, Eastham MA 02642 **Died 10/9/2015** B Weymouth MA 1928 s Chester & Emma. BA Bos 1952; Cert Merc TS 1973. D 6/17/1972 P 12/1/1972 Bp Jonathan Goodhue Sherman. m 4/21/1947 Kathleen Durgin. Int Ch Of The Ascen Fall River MA 2000-2002; Int Gd Shpd Fair Haven MA 1996-1997; R S Jas' Ch New Haven CT 1980-1994; R S Jas Ch Old Town ME 1975-1980; S Jas Ch Old Town ME 1974-1980; S Pat's Ch Brewer ME 1974-1980; Asst S Bon Epis Ch Lindenhurst NY 1972-1974. Int Mnstry Ntwk 1998.

DURHAM, Eugenia M (Az) 1275 S Heritage Pl, Safford AZ 85546 B Little Rock AR 1939 d Paul & Marjorie. BA Maryville Coll 1961; MA Luther TS 1990; CAS SWTS 1993; DMin SWTS 2006. D 6/24/1993 Bp Robert Marshall Anderson P 1/6/1994 Bp Sanford Zangwill Kaye Hampton. c 2. Dio Arizona Phoeniz AZ 1999-2006; Dioc Coun Dio Arizona Phoenix AZ 1996-1999, 1993-2011, Pres of Stndg Com 2005-2006, Pres of Stndg Com 2000-2004; All SS Epis Ch Safford AZ 1993-1995; S Matt's Ch S Paul MN 1993-1995; P Mssnr SS Phil And Jas Morenci AZ 1993-1995; Ch Of S Matt Tucson AZ 1993.

DURHAM, Martha Hemenway (Chi) St Mary's Episcopal Church, 306 S Prospect Ave, Park Ridge IL 60068 **D S Mary's Ch Pk Ridge IL 2007-, Dir Rel Educ 1993-2006** B Westfield NY 1955 d Richard & Marjorie. BSS Cornell Coll 1978; Sch for Deacons Dio Chicago 2007. D 1/19/2008 Bp Victor Alfonso Scantlebury. m 5/5/1984 Thomas Durham c 2.

DURNING, Michael Peter (SwFla) 12002 Summer Meadow Dr, Bradenton FL 34202 **Cn to the Ordnry Dio SW Florida Parrish FL 2001-, Cn 1997-, Cong Dvlpmt 1997-** B Philadelphia PA 1951 s Francis & Catherine. BFA U of the Arts Philadelphia PA 1973; MDiv GTS 1987. D 6/11/1988 Bp Allen Lyman Bartlett Jr P 5/27/1989 Bp Frank S Cerveny. m 11/17/1973 Bonnie Jean Durning c 3. S Mk's Ch Marco Island FL 1992-1997; Asst S Jn's Ch Naples FL 1988-1992; S Fran-In-The-Fields Malvern PA 1987-1988. CODE 1997. mdurning@episcopalswfl.org

DURREN, Paula Ellen (WMich) 19 S Jameson St, New Buffalo MI 49117 **R Ch of the Medtr Harbert MI 2002-** B Columbus IN 1953 d Charles & Marjorie. BSW Geo Wms 1976; MS Indiana U 1985; MDiv SWTS 2002. D 5/26/2002 Bp Edward Lewis Lee Jr P 12/14/2002 Bp Robert R Gepert. m 1/6/1973 Michael Jerry Durren c 2. mediatorrector@isp.com

DURST, Lester Earle (CGC) 5409 Twin Creeks Dr, Valrico FL 33596 **Died 6/22/2016** B Sarasota FL 1951 s Marion & Mildred. BA Stetson U 1973; JD U of Florida 1976; MDiv VTS 1990. D 6/30/1990 P 1/18/1991 Bp Rogers Sanders Harris. m 6/9/1973 Carolyn Fleischman c 2. Asst S Mary's Par Tampa FL 2010-2016; R S Chris's Ch Pensacola FL 2002-2008; R S Ptr's Ch Plant City FL 1995-2002; Asst St Johns Epis Ch Tampa FL 1993-1995; Asst Ch Of The Redeem Sarasota FL 1990-1992. Contrib, *Gd News Daily.* Chapl Ord of S Lk 1992.

DURST, Ted (Chi) 4900 N Marine Dr Apt 411, Chicago IL 60640 **Asstg Epis Ch Of The Atone Chicago IL 2011-; Chapl Methodist Hosp of Chicago 2010-** B Brady TX 1952 s Clinton & Anna. BBA Angelo St U 1974; MDiv SWTS 1995. D 6/12/1995 Bp James Edward Folts P 12/16/1995 Bp Frank Tracy Griswold III. m 8/6/2012 Mark Damon Britt c 1. Chapl Methodist Hosp of Chicago Chicago IL 2010-2016; Dir of Sprtl Care Norwegian Amer Hosp 2006-2009; Dir of Pstr Care and Chapl Norwegian Amer Hosp Chicago IL 2006-2009; Sprtl Care Coordntr Bonaventure Hse Chicago IL 2005-2006; P-in-c The Ch Of The H Innoc Hoffman Schaumburg IL 2004-2006; R Trin Epis Ch Houghton MI 2001-2004; Asstg S Ptr's Epis Ch Chicago IL 2000-2001; Sprtl Care Coordntr AIDS Pstr Care Ntwk 1999-2001; Corp Relatns Coordntr The Night Mnstry 1997-1999; Assoc R Emm Epis Ch Rockford IL 1996-1997; Exec Dir Shltr Care Mnstrs Emm Epis Ch Rockford 1996-1997; Asst to Exec. Dir. ReVive Cntr for Hsng and Healing Chicago IL 1995-1996. Bd Cert Chapl Assn of Profsnl Chapl 2013.

DUTCHER, Katherine Grant (Okla) St Andrew's Episcopal Church, PO Box 1256, Lawton OK 73502 **D S Andr's Epis Ch Lawton OK 2007-** B Ft Arbuckle OK 1934 d Thomas & Katie. D 6/16/2007 Bp Robert Manning Moody. m 3/29/1956 Joe Blake Dutcher c 4.

DUTTON-GILLETT, Matthew Richard (Cal) 330 Ravenswood, Menlo Park CA 94025 **R Trin Par Menlo Pk CA 2009-** B Cleveland OH 1966 s Carl & Marilyn. BA MI SU 1987; MDiv EDS 1991. D 6/21/1991 Bp Henry Irving Mayson P 1/18/1992 Bp R aymond Stewart Wood Jr. m 9/2/1989 Katherine Sydney Dutton-Gillett c 2. R S Eliz's Epis Ch Knoxville TN 1999-2009; Chapl Vencor Hosp Sycamore IL 1996-1999; R S Ptr's Epis Ch Sycamore IL 1995-1999; Assoc To R S Ptr's Epis Ch S Louis MO 1991-1995. "Homilies On A Gd Life," (Priv Pub), 2004. matthew@trinitymenlopark.org

DUVAL, Linda Marie (NY) 16 Boulder Ave, Kingston NY 12401 B Newburgh NY 1955 d Norman & Helen. D 5/20/2000 Bp Richard Frank Grein. m 6/4/1977 Gary Joseph Duval.

DUVAL JR, Richard Henri (SJ) 813 Lassen View Dr, Lake Almanor CA 96137 **Ret 1993-** B Buffalo NY 1930 s Richard & Isobel. BA Claremont Coll 1951; MDiv CDSP 1956. D 6/25/1956 Bp Francis E I Bloy P 2/26/1957 Bp Donald J Campbell. m 12/20/1952 Bernice A Duval c 7. Int S Matt's Ch San Andreas CA 1999-2001; R S Mich The Archangel Par El Segundo CA 1972-1992; Vic All SS Epis Ch Brawley CA 1966-1972; Vic S Mk Holtville CA 1966-1972; Civilian Chapl to the Epis Cong Edwards AFB 1957-1966; Vic S Paul's Par Lancaster CA 1957-1966; Cur S Mk's Par Altadena CA 1956-1957.

DUVAL, Robert Joseph (Ct) 3121 St. Stephens Ln., Whitehall PA 18052 **Died 3/13/2017** B Bristol CT 1939 s Joseph & Juliette. BA Trin Hartford CT 1960; MDiv Sewanee: The U So, TS 1986. D 6/14/1986 Bp Arthur Edward Walmsley P 12/20/1986 Bp Clarence Nicholas Coleridge. m 5/2/1959 Gloria C Duval c 2. R S Ptr's Epis Ch Hebron CT 1997-2003; R Chr Ch Trumbull CT 1986-1997.

✠ DUVALL, The Rt Rev Charles Farmer (CGC) 104 Wildeoak Trl, Columbia SC 29223 **Ret Bp Of Cntrl Gulf Coast Dio Cntrl Gulf Coast Pensacola FL 2001-, Bp 1981-2001** B Bennettsville SC 1935 s Henry & Elizabeth. BA Cit 1957; MDiv VTS 1960. D 6/18/1960 Bp Albert S Thomas P 3/24/1961 Bp Gray Temple Con 4/11/1981 for CGC. m 6/2/1957 Nancy Duvall c 3. Epis Media Cntr Chair 2003-2006; Bd Rgnts Sewanee U So TS Sewanee TN 1995-2001; Chair No Amer Rgnl Com S Geo Jerusalem 1994-1997; Kanuga Conf Bd 1987-1993; R Ch Of The Adv Spartanburg SC 1977-1980; R H Trin Epis Ch Fayetteville NC 1970-1977; Dep Gc So Carolina Charleston SC 1967-1969, Chair, Dept. of CE 1964-1967; R S Jas Ch Charleston SC 1962-1970; In-C H Trin Grahamville SC 1960-1962. EvangES. Hon Doctor TS, U fo the So 1986; Hon Doctor VTS 1982.

DUVALL, Robert Welsh (Va) 704 Holloway Circle N, North Myrtle Beach SC 29582 **Died 12/31/2016** B Cheraw SC 1928 s Gideon & Mary. BS Clemson U 1951; MDiv Sewanee: The U So, TS 1962. D 7/11/1962 Bp Clarence Alfred Cole P 6/24/1963 Bp Robert E Gribbin. c 3. Ret No Myrtle Bch SC 2005-2016; Ret Ret Highlands NC 1993-2005; Non-par Richmnd VA 1976-1993; Chapl Virginia Commonwealth U Richmond VA 1967-1976; Asst Trin Cathd Columbia SC 1964-1967; S Ptr's Ch Great Falls SC 1963-1964; Vic S Steph's Epis Ch Ridgeway SC 1963-1964. EPF 2003.

DUVEAUX, Irnel (Hai) Box 1309, Port-Au-Prince Haiti **Dio Haiti Port-au-Prince HT 2002-, 1989-1998; Non-par 1988-** B Cap Haitien HT 1961 s Marie. Montrouis TS 1987. D 6/12/1988 P 12/1/1988 Bp Luc Anatole Jacques Garnier. m 8/15/1996 Mireille Duveaux c 1.

DUVERT, Pierre-Andre (NY) 331 Hawthorne St, Brooklyn NY 11225 **S Lk's Epis Ch Bronx NY 2012-** B 1964 s Andre & Paunie. BA SUNY 1989; MDiv GTS 1992; STM GTS 1996. D 6/8/1991 P 12/1/1991 Bp Richard Frank Grein. m 4/25/1992 Elourdes Isidore Duvert c 3. Epis Ch of Gr and Resurr E Elmhurst NY 2013-2015, 1999-2012; S Gabr's Ch Brooklyn NY 1995-1999; Non-par 1991-1999.

DVARISHKIS, Dorcie Della Kafka (Mont) Church Of The Holy Spirit, 130 S 6th St E, Missoula MT 59801 B Havre MT 1959 d Lada & Sylvia. BS Rocky Mtn Coll. D 6/26/2016 Bp Charles Franklin Brookhart Jr. m 8/22/1981 Paul Curtis Polzin c 2.

DWARF, Lindsey Craig (ND) PO Box 45, Cannon Ball ND 58528 **Asst S Lk's Ch Ft Yates ND 2003-** B Fort Yates ND 1962 D 6/12/2003 P 12/13/2003 Bp Andrew Fairfield. m 7/1/2002 Kimberly Crow c 4. Asst Dio No Dakota Fargo ND 2006-2017.

D'WOLF JR, James Francis (Kan) 6976 Pintail Dr # 113, Fishers IN 46038 **Died 2/6/2017** B Saint Louis MO 1927 s James & Leone. BA U of Missouri 1950; STB ETS Cambridge MA 1955. D 6/18/1955 P 12/18/1955 Bp Arthur C Lichtenberger. m 4/18/1958 Jean Lee Sampson c 3. Assoc R S Mich & S Geo S Louis MO 1990-2005; S Judes Ch Monroe City MO 1989-1990; S Paul's Ch Palmyra MO 1989-1990; Int S Matt's Epis Cathd Laramie WY 1985-1986; Int S Steph's Ch Casper WY 1984-1985; R S Paul's Ch Manhattan KS 1971-1983; R Trin Epis Ch El Dorado KS 1963-1971; Vic S Lk and S Jn's Caruthersvlle MO 1955-1962. Auth, "Heav Food II," 1995; Auth, "Heav Food I," 1978.

DWYER, Beatrice Mary (Eau) Christ Church Cathedral, 510 S Farwell St, Eau Claire WI 54701 B Sparta WI 1949 d William & Beatrice. BA U MN 1987; MA,OT Coll of St Scholastica 2000; MDiv Ya Berk 2011. D 12/15/2012 Bp Edwin Max Leidel Jr. c 4.

DWYER, John F (Minn) 2300 Hamline Ave N, Roseville MN 55113 **Treas Dio Minnesota Minneapolis MN 2016-; R S Chris's Epis Ch S Paul MN 2011-** B Mt Vernon NY 1960 s James & Mary. BA Fairfield U 1982; JD St Johns Univ Sch of Law 1986; MDiv VTS 2007. D 3/10/2007 P 9/15/2007 Bp Mark Sean Sisk. m 4/30/2016 Benjamin M Riggs. P-in-c S Anne's Ch Damascus MD 2011; Asst S Thos' Par Washington DC 2007-2010; Mem, Fin Com Dio Washington Washington DC 2008-2011. Auth, "Those 7 References: A study of the 7 References to Homosexuality in the Bible," Amazon, 2007. fr.john@stchristophers-mn.org

DWYER, Martin James (Ida) 3 Park Pl, Garden Valley ID 83622 **Ret 1988-** B South Bend IN 1926 s Martin & Martha. BA Ripon Coll Ripon WI 1954; STM Ya Berk 1957; MA U of Nthrn Iowa 1972. D 6/29/1957 P 1/25/1958 Bp Conrad H Gesner. m 6/21/1980 Rebecca Ann Dwyer c 1. Dn S Mich's Cathd Boise ID 1979-1988; R S Andr's Epis Ch Minneapolis MN 1973-1979; R Trin Epis Par Waterloo IA 1968-1973; R S Steph's Epis Ch Aurora CO 1964-1967; Cur Emm Epis Par Rapid City SD 1961-1964; P-in-c Geth Epis Ch Sisseton SD 1957-1961; Cmdr/ Chapl USNR 1959-1983. OHC 1958-1994. Fulbright Sr Spec Fulbright Assn 2008; Dn Emer St. Mich's Cathd - Boise, ID 1988.

DWYER, Michael William (NI) 1101 Park Drive, Munster IN 46321 **P-in-c S Barn-In-The-Dunes Gary IN 2012-; S Paul's Epis Ch Munster IN 2012-; Co Dn of Wstrn Dnry Dio Nthrn Indiana So Bend IN 2012-** B Chicago IL 1948 BA Loyola U 1972; MHA Gvnr St U 1979; Masters/Pstr Stds Cath Theol Un 2011; Masters/Pstr Stds Other 2011. D 9/2/2011 P 3/3/2012 Bp Edward Stuart Little II. m 7/4/1996 Jane Ann Dwyer c 5.

DWYER, Patricia Marie (Be) B Waterbury CT 1939 d George & Kathleen. BS Alverno Coll 1961; MA La Salle U 1983; DMin Estrn Bapt TS 1985; MA La Salle U 1985. D 4/17/2004 P 10/31/2004 Bp Paul Victor Marshall. c 2. S Jos's Ch Pen Argyl PA 2006-2009; R S Mary's Epis Ch Wind Gap PA 2006-2009; supply P Trin Epis Ch Pottsville PA 2005-2006; Intern Chr Ch 2004-2005.

DWYER, Thomas Patrick (CGC) 800 22nd St, Port St Joe FL 32456 **R S Jas' Epis Ch Port St Joe FL 2009-; Cmsn on Fin Dio Cntrl Gulf Coast Pensacola FL 2011-, Dioc Disciplinary Bd 2011-, Disciplinary Bd 2010-, Cmsn of Fin 2009-** B Dorchester MA 1949 s Robert & Barbara. BS Palm Bch Atlantic U 1998; MDiv VTS 2003. D 12/18/2003 Bp James Hamilton Ottley P 7/17/2004 Bp Leo Frade. m 12/7/1968 Lynn Anne Dwyer. Vic S Steph's Epis Ch Ridgeway SC 2004-2009; Chapl Dio SE Florida 2004; D Epis Ch Of The Adv Palm City FL 2004. BSA 2010; Rotary Intl 2010.

DYAKIW, Alexander Raymond (CPa) St John's Episc Ch, 120 W Lamb St, Bellefonte PA 16823 B New York City NY 1951 s Mykola & Anna. D 6/9/2007 Bp Nathan Dwight Baxter. m 11/25/1972 Ellen P Dyakiw.

DYCHE, Bradley Callaway (NY) 6 Old Post Road North, Croton on Hudson NY 10520 **R S Aug's Epis Ch Croton Hdsn NY 2006-** B Enid OK 1976 s Steven & Kathie. BA U of Oklahoma 1998; MDiv GTS 2002. D 6/29/2002 Bp Robert Manning Moody P 12/28/2002 Bp Catherine Scimeca Roskam. Cur S Jn's Ch Larchmont NY 2002-2006. Mnstry Fell The Fund For Theol Educ 1999.

DYER, Alex (WA) 51 Crown St, New Haven CT 06510 **S Thos' Par Washington DC 2016-** B Kingsport TN 1979 s Charles & Carol. MDiv GTS; BA Randolph-Macon Coll. D 6/15/2005 Bp James Louis Jelinek P 1/7/2006 Bp Egbert Don Taylor. m 10/1/2010 Ryan DeLoach c 1. Old S Andr's Ch Bloomfield CT 2015-2016; P S Paul And S Jas New Haven CT 2010-2015; Epis Ch Cntr New York NY 2009, 2008, 2007, 2007, 2005-2007, Web Serv Spec 2005-2007; Assoc Trin Ch On The Green New Haven CT 2007-2010; The Ch Of S Lk In The Fields New York NY 2006. ECom 2005-2007.

DYER, Susan Jeinine (Wyo) PO Box 399, Saratoga WY 82331 B Denver CO 1946 D 11/11/2000 Bp William Jerry Winterrowd P 12/3/2011 Bp John Smylie. m 10/29/1994 Stephen Dyer c 3. sandsdyer@aol.com

DYER, Timothy D (NwPa) 444 Pennsylvania Ave W, Warren PA 16365 **Assoc Trin Memi Ch Warren PA 2015-** B Warren PA 1966 s Donald & Linda. BA Clarion U 2014. D 2/8/2015 P 12/11/2016 Bp Sean Walter Rowe. m 5/5/2001 Noreen J Jones c 1.

DYER-CHAMBERLAIN, Margaret Elizabeth (Cal) **Archd Dio California San Francisco CA 2016-** B Cleveland OH 1958 d John & Sylvia Ann. BA Smith-Northampton MA 1980; MALD Fletcher Sch of Law and Diplomacy 1983; BA Epis Sch for Deacons 2013. D 6/8/2013 Bp Marc Handley Andrus. m 8/22/1981 Charles Page Chamberlain c 2.

DYKE, Nicolas Roger David (Tex) 3815 Echo Mountain Dr, Humble TX 77345 **Int Trin Woodlands TX 2007-** B London UK 1937 s John & Mary. BBA Texas A&M U 1961; So Texas Coll of Law 1967; MDiv Epis TS of the SW 1977. D 6/30/1977 Bp Roger Howard Cilley P 6/1/1978 Bp James Milton Richardson. m 6/2/1984 Kathleen Karoline Dyke c 2. Trin Ch Houston TX 2006; S Dunst's Epis Ch Houston TX 2004-2005; R S Andr's Ch Bryan TX 1988-2004; S Phil's Ch Hearne TX 1988-2003; H Comf Epis Ch Sprg TX 1986-1988, 1977-1986, R 1977-1986; The Great Cmsn Fndt Houston TX 1977-1979.

DYKES, Deborah White (Miss) 3524 Old Canton Rd, Jackson MS 39216 B Shreveport LA 1951 d Ruben & Elizabeth. MA Mississippi St U 1977; Cert Dio Colorado Diac Formation Prog 2001; Iliff TS 2001. D 11/10/2001 Bp William Jerry Winterrowd. m 12/9/1992 David R Dykes c 4. Dir of Cntr for Formation & Mssn Dio Mississippi Jackson MS 2005-2009; Cn for Sprtl Formation for Adults & Chld S Andr's Cathd Jackson MS 2002-2005; Dir of Yth Mnstry S Jn's Cathd Denver CO 2001-2002, Dir of Yth Mnstry 1992-2002.

DYKSTRA, Danny Jon (Ky) 9616 Westport Rd, Louisville KY 40241 **Urban Mssn D Dio Kentucky Louisville KY 2014-** B Redlands CA 1958 s Harold & Jean. BA U CA, Berkeley 1981; MEd Spalding U 2001; MAS Louisville Presb TS 2007; Sch of Mnstry 2013. D 6/24/2014 Bp Terry Allen White. m 6/4/2004 Catheryn O Dykstra c 1.

DYNER, Marthe Fillman (NH) Po Box 347, Charlestown NH 03603 **S Lk's Ch Charlestown NH 2004-** B New York NY 1937 d Jesse & Elizabeth. Rad 1956; BA Bryn 1958; U of Utah 1976; MDiv EDS 1988. D 6/12/1988 Bp George Edmonds Bates P 5/8/1989 Bp Douglas Edwin Theuner. m 6/17/1989 Charles Meader. R Un-St. Lk's Epis Ch Claremont NH 2004-2016; Int S Ptr's Epis Ch Londonderry NH 2004; Assoc S Paul's Ch Concord NH 1998-2003; Cn for Mnstry Resources Dio New Hampshire Concord NH 1993-2004; Asst R Ch Of The Gd Shpd Nashua NH 1988-1993.

DYSON, Elizabeth Wheatley (Mass) 451 Birchbark Dr, Hanson MA 02341 **Dn So Shore Dnry Dio Massachusetts Boston MA 2011-** B New Bedford MA 1956 d William & Alice. BA U of Massachusetts 1978; MA Bridgewater St Coll 1992; MDiv Andover Newton TS 2002. D 6/15/2002 P 5/31/2003 Bp M(Arvil) Thomas Shaw. m 7/14/1984 David Dyson c 3. R S Andr's Ch Hanover MA 2007-2016, Dn of So Shore 2011-; Asst R S Steph's Ch Cohasset MA 2002-2007.

DYSON, Martha Lynn (Vt) 123 Caroline St, Burlington VT 05401 B Houston TX 1958 d Jeff & Shirley. U of Houston 1980; BFA Steph F Austin St U 1981; MA Oral Roberts U 1987; MA Drew U 1992. D 6/5/1993 Bp John Shelby Spong P 4/23/1994 Bp Jack Marston Mckelvey. Cathd Ch Of S Paul Burlington VT 1997-2001.

DYSON, Thack Harris (CGC) 28788 N Main St, Daphne AL 36526 **R S Paul's Epis Ch Daphne AL 2001-** B Pensacola FL 1955 s Bromley & Nina. BA U of Alabama 1977; JD Cumberland Law Sch Samford U 1982; MHLP Cumberland Sch of Law, Samford U 1982; MDiv VTS 1996. D 6/1/1996 P 2/2/1997 Bp Charles Farmer Duvall. m 8/13/1977 Rebecca Ann Dyson c 1. R S Mk's Epis Ch Troy AL 1999-2001; Adj Prof Of Ethics Troy U Troy AL 1999-2001; Assoc R S Chris's Ch Pensacola FL 1996-1999; GC Dep Dio Cntrl Gulf Coast Pensacola FL 2015, Stndg Com 2014-, GC Dep 2012, Stndg Com 2009-2012, GC Dep 2009, GC Dep 2006-2009.

E

EADE, Christopher K (Los) 1031 Bienveneda Ave, Pacific Palisades CA 90272 **R S Mart-In-The-Fields Par Winnetka CA 2004-** B San Jose CA 1952 s Kenneth & Doris. New Mex St U 1975; MDiv Nash 1978. D 6/3/1978 Bp John Alfred Baden P 5/1/1979 Bp Robert Bruce Hall. m 6/18/2005 Saralloyd Truax c 4. S Mk's Par Downey CA 1995-1996; The Par Of S Matt Pacific Plsds CA 1991-1995; Asst P All SS Par Beverly Hills CA 1989-1991; Harvard-Westlake Sch Studio City CA 1987-1991; R S Ptr's Ch Altavista VA 1984-1987; Virginia Epis Sch Lynchburg VA 1982-1987; Chapl Virginia Epis Sch Lynchburg VA 1982-1987; Vic S Lk's Epis Hawkinsville GA 1980-1982; Asst Pohick Epis Ch Lorton VA 1978-1980; Chapl Harvard Sch. st-martins@roadrunner.com

EADE, Kenneth Charles (Va) 6465 Calamar Dr, Cumming GA 30040 **Died 6/27/2016** B Hanna AB CA 1921 s Charles & Maud. BA Occ 1948; BD, MDiv CDSP 1951; BD CDSP 1951; Claremont Coll 1953; S Augustines Coll Cbury

Gb 1959; S Augustines Coll Cbury UK 1959. D 8/4/1951 P 2/1/1952 Bp Karl M Block. m 8/20/1951 Doris Church c 3. R S Mary's El Paso TX 1972-2016; S Mary's Epis Ch Arlington VA 1972-1983; R St Lk's Epis Ch Anth NM 1962-1972; Cur Ch Of The H Trin Midland TX 1958-1962; Chapl/Admin Epis Day Sch Midland TX 1958-1962; Vic S Thos Epis Ch Sunnyvale CA 1952-1953.

EADES, Susan Tindall (Mont) 218 E Chapman St, Dillon MT 59725 **R St Jas Epis Ch Dillon MT 2011-** B Lewistown MT 1953 d Herbert & Betty. NW Cmnty Coll 1995; BTh The Coll of Emm and S Chad CA 2000; U of Great Falls 2003. D 12/11/1999 P 6/17/2000 Bp Charles I Jones III. c 2. R Chr Epis Ch Clinton IA 2005-2010; Assoc Ch Of The Incarn Great Falls MT 2003-2004; Dio Montana Helena MT 2000-2005, Congrl Dvlpmt Com 2017-, Pres of the Stndg Com 2015-2016, Stwdshp Chair 2004-2005, Ecum Off 2001-2005; Vic S Fran Epis Ch Great Falls MT 2000-2004; Congrl Developement Com Dio Iowa Des Moines IA 2006-2008. stjamesdillon@live.com

EADS, Charles Carroll (Md) 16 Swantamont Rd, Swanton MD 21561 **Died 9/17/2016** B Baltimore MD 1924 s John & Rosina. BA U of Maryland 1947; MDiv VTS 1947. D 3/17/1947 P 6/1/1948 Bp Noble C Powell. Ret 1989-2016; Chr Ch Forest Hill MD 1949-1989; H Cross Ch St MD 1949-1989; Cur Ascen & Prince Of Peace Balt 1947-1949.

EAGER, Donald Bates (SO) 2102 Scenic Dr Ne, Lancaster OH 43130 **Pres Donald B. Eager And Assoc. 1991-** B Clarksville TN 1946 s Orlo & Mary. BS Kent St U 1976. D 6/12/2004 Bp Herbert Thompson Jr. m 1/1/1997 Linda Eager c 3.

EAGLEBULL, Harold L (Minn) Po Box 1149, Cass Lake MN 56633 B Pine Ridge SD 1945 s Ross & Emma. Cert Cook Coll & TS Tempe AZ 1981; Rio Salado Coll 1981; MDiv Untd TS of the Twin Cities 1983. D 6/23/1984 Bp Harold Stephen Jones P 3/1/1986 Bp Harold Anthony Hopkins Jr. m 5/14/1999 Charlette Eaglebull c 4. Int. Vic S Johns/Epis Ch Onigum Mssn Walker MN 2002-2012; S Ptr's Ch Cass Lake MN 2002-2012; Dio Wyoming Casper 1999-2002; Mssr Our Fr's Hse Lander WY 1999-2001; S Alb's Epis Ch Porcupine SD 1988-1999; Supply P S Julia's Epis Ch Porcupine SD 1988-1999; S Thos Ch Porcupine SD 1988-1999; Dio No Dakota Fargo ND 1986-1988; S Jas Ch Ft Yates ND 1985-1988; Vic Dio Minnesota Minneapolis MN 1985-1986; Ch Of The Mssh Prairie Island Welch MN 1984-1985; D Ch of the Mssh Mssn Sioux Falls SD 1984. 82nd Airborne Div Assn; Airborne Static Line; Amer Indn Veterans; Nata Alum.

EAKINS, Bill (Ct) 25 Scarborough St, Hartford CT 06105 **Assoc S Mk's Ch New Britain CT 2013-** B Atlanta GA 1944 s William & Ruth. BA Trin 1966; BA Oxf GB 1968; BD EDS 1970; MA Oxf GB 1972. D 6/20/1969 Bp Robert McConnell Hatch P 1/1/1970 Bp Donald J Campbell. m 5/11/1996 Hope Howlett c 3. St Johns Ch W Hartford CT 2014-2015; Int S Jas Epis Ch Farmington CT 2010-2012; Chapl Trin Chap Hartford CT 2007; R Trin Epis Ch Hartford CT 1984-2002; R All SS Ch So Hadley MA 1980-1984; Vic Ch Of The Nativ Northborough MA 1973-1980; D-Intern Chr Ch Cathd Springfield MA 1969-1971. "Faith and Hearing," *Faith and Form*, 2007; Auth, *Lord Ptr Wimsey Cookbook*, Ticknor and Fields, 1982.

EAKINS, Hope Howlett (Ct) 25 Scarborough St, Hartford CT 06105 **Int St Johns Ch W Hartford CT 2013-** B Wilmington DE 1942 d Harold & Helen. BA NWU 1963; MS Sarah Lawr Coll 1971; MDiv Yale DS 1989. D 6/10/1989 Bp Arthur Edward Walmsley P 12/19/1989 Bp Jeffery William Rowthorn. m 5/11/1996 Bill Eakins c 3. Int S Jas Epis Ch Farmington CT 2010-2012; Int S Alb's Ch Simsbury CT 2008; Chapl Trin Chap Hartford CT 2007; Int S Lk's Epis Ch E Greenwich RI 2006; R S Jn's Epis Ch Essex CT 1993-2002; Assoc Trin Epis Ch Hartford CT 1989-1993.

EAMES, Marc Gilbert (Mass) 28 Pleasant St., The Church of the Advent, Medfield MA 02052 **Ch Of The Adv Medfield MA 2011-** B Springfield MA 1979 s John & Guylene. BA U of Connecticut 2001; MDiv Berkeley Bapt DS 2007; MDiv Ya Berk 2007. D 6/2/2007 P 1/12/2008 Bp M(Arvil) Thomas Shaw. m 9/21/2002 Gretchen Eames c 2. Cur Ch Of The Redeem Chestnut Hill MA 2007-2011; Chap Min Berkley DS At Yale 2006-2007. rector@adventmedfield.org

EANES II, William Raymond (SwVa) St James Episcopal Church, 4515 Delray St NW, Roanoke VA 24012 **D S Jas Ch Roanoke VA 2013-** B Roanoke Va 1948 s William & Phyllis. BA Emory and Henry Coll 1970; D Formation Prog D Sch Dio No Carolina 2010. D 7/25/2012 Bp A(rthur) Heath Light. m 6/6/1970 Carol Friski Eanes c 2.

EARL, John Keith (WNC) 1650 5th St Nw, Hickory NC 28601 B Tulsa OK 1946 s Gene & Marjorie. MD U of Oklahoma 1968; U of Virginia 1976. D 11/10/1985 Bp William Gillette Weinhauer. m Jane Sarah c 4. D S Alb's Ch Hickory NC 1985-2010.

EARLE, Charles Douglas (WTex) 7302 Robin Rest Dr, San Antonio TX 78209 B San Antonio TX 1949 s Charles & Nila. BBA U Americas Puebla MX 1972; MDiv Epis TS of the SW 1984. D 6/8/1984 P 12/11/1984 Bp Scott Field Bailey. m 8/21/1971 Mary Colbert c 2. R S Paul's Epis Ch San Antonio TX 1999-2012; Vic S Paul's Ch Brady TX 1998; R Ch Of Recon San Antonio TX 1995-1998; Dir of MHE Dio W Texas San Antonio TX 1990-1996; Chair COM Dio W

Texas San Antonio TX 1990-1994; Vic S Mths Devine TX 1989-1990; Vic All SS Epis Ch Pleasanton TX 1987-1990; Area Mssnr S Matt's Epis Ch Kenedy TX 1984-1987; S Steph's Ch Goliad TX 1984-1987; Mssnr Trin Ch Victoria TX 1984-1987; Trin Epis Ch Edna TX 1984-1987. Hal Brooke Perry Awd Sem of the SW 2010.

EARLE, Leigh Christensen (Wyo) 1745 Westridge Cir, Casper WY 82604 **D Chr Epis Ch Glenrock WY 2010-; Chapl Wyoming Med Cntr Casper WY 2003-; Field Educ Supvsr Chr Epis Ch Glenrock WY 2012-** B TX 1952 d Joe & Dorothy. AS Casper Coll 1987; BS U of Wyoming 1990; MS U of Wyoming 1996; Cert CDSP 2013; Cert CDSP 2013. D 5/31/2005 Bp Bruce Caldwell. m 5/31/1986 Ralph Theodore Earle. D S Mk's Epis Ch Casper WY 2005-2009; Stff Chapl Wyoming Med Cntr Casper WY 2003-2015. Auth, "Benefits and Barriers to Well-Chld Care: Perceptions of Mothers in a Rural St," *Publ Hlth Nrsng*, Blackwell Sci, Inc., 1998. Amer Acad of Nurse Practitioners 1996; Assn of Epis Deacons 2004; Natl Epis Hlth Mnstrs 2004; Off of Bp Suffr for Chaplaincies 2006; OSL the Physcn 2003.

EARLE, Mary Colbert (WTex) 7302 Robin Rest Dr, San Antonio TX 78209 B San Antonio TX 1948 d Gene & Mary. BA U of Texas 1970; MA U of Texas 1975; MA Epis TS of the SW 1984; MDiv Epis TS of the SW 1986. D 2/2/1987 P 9/4/1987 Bp John Herbert MacNaughton. m 8/21/1971 Charles Douglas Earle c 2. Instr in Pstr Mnstry Epis TS Of The SW Austin TX 2000-2008; Asst R S Mk's Epis Ch San Antonio TX 1999-2004; Assoc R Ch Of Recon San Antonio TX 1990-1998; Chapl & Dn of Students Texas Mltry Inst San Antonio TX 1989-1990; Chapl Texas Mltry Inst San Antonio TX 1989-1990; Vic S Mths Devine TX 1987-1989. Auth, "Julian of Norwich," SkyLight Paths, 2013; Auth, "Marvelously Made: Gratefulness and the Body," Morehouse, 2012; Auth, "Celtic Chr Sprtlty," SkyLight Paths, 2011; Auth, "Days of Gr: Meditations and Practices for Living w Illness," Morehouse, 2009; Auth, "The Desert Mothers," Morehouse, 2007; Auth, "Beginning Again: Benedictine Wisdom for Living w Illness," Morehouse, 2004; Auth, "H Comp: Sprtl Practices from the Celtic SS," Morehouse, 2004; Auth, "Broken Body, Healing Sprt: Lectio Divina and Living w Illness," Morehouse, 2003; Auth, "Praying w the Celtic SS," S Mary's Press, 2000. Soc for the Study of Chr Sprtlty 1997; Sprtl Dir Intl 1997. Phi Beta Kappa U of Texas at Austin 1970.

EARLE, Patty Ann Trapp (NC) Po Box 1103, Statesville NC 28687 B Akron OH 1931 d Edward & Geneva. MA Kent St U 1958; PhD U NC 1978; MDiv Duke DS 1989; CAS VTS 1989. D 6/3/1989 Bp Robert Whitridge Estill P 6/1/1990 Bp Huntington Williams Jr. S Anne's Ch Winston Salem NC 2000-2001; Ch Of The Mssh Mayodan NC 1989-2000; Sem Asst S Andr's Ch Greensboro NC 1987-1988. Auth, "Var arts," *Pub & Books 64-88*. Vts Mssy Soc.

EARLE III, Richard Tilghman (SwFla) 555 13th Avenue NE, Saint Petersburg FL 33701 **D Cathd Ch Of S Ptr St. Petersburg FL 2002-; Const and Cn Com Dio SW Florida Parrish FL 2003-** B Saint Petersburg FL 1942 BA The U So 1963; JD The U of Forida 1966; Mstr of Div EDS 2013. D 1/18/2002 Bp John Bailey Lipscomb P 2/22/2017 Bp Dabney Tyler Smith. m 5/13/1989 Shirley Sipe c 2.

EARLS, John Greeley (USC) B Gaffney SC 1962 s Larry & Rose. BS Clemson U 1984; MDiv VTS 2004. D 6/12/2004 P 5/12/2005 Bp Dorsey Henderson. m 5/30/2012 Edward Gettys Meeks. Asst S Jn's Ch Columbus OH 2004-2011; S Barth's Ch No Augusta SC 2004-2005.

EARLY, Nancy Davis (WA) 402 Montrose Ave, Catonsville MD 21228 B New York NY 1958 d John & Eleanor. BA U of Vermont 1982; MDiv Harvard DS 1986. D 6/11/1988 Bp David Elliot Johnson P 5/1/1989 Bp John Thomas Walker. c 2. Assoc R S Columba's Ch Washington DC 2000-2002; R S Lk's Ch Brighton Brookeville MD 1992-2000; S Jn's Ch Georgetown Par Washington DC 1988-1991; Ecclesiastical Mem Dio Washington Washington DC 1993-1998, ECRA/ Chair of Healing Serv 1992-1998.

EARLY, Thomas M (Ia) B Harlan IA 1989 s William & Sara. BA The U of Nthrn Iowa 2012; MDiv Sewanee: The U So 2017. D 12/10/2016 P 6/17/2017 Bp Alan Scarfe. m 6/7/2013 Sara Michelle Lee Andino.

EARLY THOMPSON JR, Will (USC) 16 Bernwood Dr, Taylors SC 29687 **Died 7/17/2017** B Macon GA 1952 s William & Neva. BA Furman U 1974; MS Virginia Commonwealth U 1979; MDiv EDS 1983. Trans 11/17/2003 Bp Chilton Richardson Knudsen. m 2/2/2002 Nicki Thompson c 5. Dir The Cler Coach 2004-2017; S Mich's Epis Ch Easley SC 2003-2004; S Matt's Epis Ch Spartanburg SC 2002-2003; Int Olivet Epis Ch Alexandria VA 2000-2002; Int The Ch of S Clem Alexandria VA 1999-2000; Int Assoc S Mk WDC 1997-1999; S Mk's Ch Washington DC 1997-1999; 1986-1997; Downeast Epis Cluster Deer Isle ME 1985-1986; Vic Downeast Cluster ME 1985-1986; Cur Trin Ch Torrington CT 1984-1985. "The Power of Play: The ABC's of Living w Wonder and Exuberance," Auth Hse, 2006.

EASLEY, Alexandra (WTex) **Palmer Memi Ch Houston TX 2015-** B 1990 d Robert & Felicia. B.A. Psychol U of Texas at Austin 2012; M.Div Epis TS of the SW 2015. D 6/20/2015 P 1/20/2016 Bp C Andrew Doyle.

EASLEY, Barbara Ann (Ia) 605 Avenue E, Fort Madison IA 52627 B Brookfield MO 1934 d Eugene & Marjorie. D 10/25/2009 Bp Alan Scarfe. c 3.

E

EASLEY, Julia Kathleen (Ia) 26 E Market St, Iowa City IA 52245 B Fort Madison IA 1963 d Norris & Barbara. BA U of Notre Dame 1985; MDiv SWTS 1990. D 5/12/1990 P 12/14/1990 Bp Chris Christopher Epting. c 1. U Of Iowa Chapl Iowa City IA 1992-2008; Dio Iowa Des Moines IA 1992-2007; Int Cbury At Kansas U Lawr KS 1991-1992; Dio Kansas Topeka KS 1991-1992; S Paul's Ch Milwaukee WI 1990-1991. Auth, "Evang w YA," Plumbline. ESMHE 1991-2005.

EASTER, James Hamilton (Okla) 11308 N Miller Ave, Oklahoma City OK 73120 D All Souls Epis Ch Oklahoma City OK 2004- B Baltimore MD 1931 s James & Mary. BA Bowling Green St U 1953. D 7/14/1968 Bp Chilton R Powell. m 1/31/1953 Colleen Jean Easter c 2. D S Jas Epis Ch Oklahoma City OK 1993-2004; Asst S Aug Of Cbury Oklahoma City OK 1982-1993; Asst S Geo's Oklahoma City OK 1968-1982.

EASTER, Mary Kathleen (WMo) 973 Evergreen Ave, Hollister MO 65672 B Londonderry IE 1947 d Leslie & Margaret. BSW Missouri Wstrn St U 1987. D 2/1/1997 Bp John Clark Buchanan. m 10/19/1991 James Dennis Easter.

EASTER, William Burton (Chi) 594 Eastlake Dr Se, Rio Rancho NM 87124 B Grosse Pointe Farms MI 1926 s William & Marvel. BA Ripon Coll Ripon WI 1953; BD VTS 1959. D 6/20/1959 P 12/19/1959 Bp Charles L Street. c 6. Int St. Chad's Epis Ch Albequerque NM 2004-2005; Int Epis Ch Of The Epiph Socorro NM 1995-1996; Int Gr Ch Sterling IL 1992-1993; Int Ch Of The Trsfg Palos Pk IL 1991; S Jn The Evang Lockport IL 1990; Assoc S Paul's On The Plains Epis Ch Lubbock TX 1965-1970; R S Alb's Ch Harlingen TX 1962-1965; R S Thos And S Mart's Ch Crp Christi TX 1960-1962; Cur Gr Ch Oak Pk IL 1959-1960; ExCoun Dio W Texas San Antonio TX 1963-1965. Auth, "The Professionalizing Process," Journ of Par Cler; Auth, "Time for a Hse of P?," Profsnl Supplement Epis Life Predecessor. Associated Parishes; Silver Eagles; Westar Inst.

EASTERDAY, Pamela Kay (CFla) 1830 S. Babcock St, Melbourne FL 32901 Co-R H Trin Epis Ch Melbourne FL 2006- B Marion IN 1961 d James & Betty. Manchester Coll 1982; BS Indiana St U 1984; MDiv CDSP 1992. D 5/26/1992 Bp Edward Witker Jones P 11/29/1992 Bp John Stuart Thornton. m 6/2/1982 Stephen Wayne Easterday c 2. Dn Geth Cathd Fargo ND 1998-2006; Cn Ordnry Dio Idaho Boise ID 1997-1998; Epis Ch In Minidoka & Cassia Cnty Rupert ID 1994-1997; S Jas Ch Burley ID 1992-1997; Co-Vic St Matthews Epis Ch Rupert ID 1992-1997; Cntrl Dnry Cluster Shoshone ID 1992-1993. FA 2009; Ord of S Lk 2000.

EASTERDAY, Stephen Wayne (CFla) 1830 S. Babcock St., Melbourne FL 32901 Co-R H Trin Epis Ch Melbourne FL 2006- B Marion IN 1962 s Wayne & Dorothy. BS Rose-Hulman Inst for Tech 1984; MDiv CDSP 1992. D 5/26/1992 Bp Edward Witker Jones P 11/29/1992 Bp John Stuart Thornton. m 6/2/1982 Pamela Kay Oakerson c 2. Dn Geth Cathd Fargo ND 1998-2006; Dio Idaho Boise ID 1997; Epis Ch In Minidoka & Cassia Cnty Rupert ID 1994-1998; S Jas Ch Burley ID 1992-1997; Co-Vic St Matthews Epis Ch Rupert ID 1992-1997; Cntrl Dnry Cluster Shoshone ID 1992-1993. EvangES; Ord of S Lk 2000. frsteve@holytrinitymelbourne.org

EASTERLING JR, Richard Brooks (La) 4600 St. Charles Avenue, New Orleans LA 70115 Vic S Geo's Epis Ch New Orleans LA 2013- B Alexandria LA 1977 s Richard & Michelle. BA LSU 1999; MDiv SWTS 2003. D 12/28/2002 P 7/6/2003 Bp Charles Edward Jenkins III. Int Chr Ch Slidell LA 2011; Int S Lk's Ch New Orleans LA 2007-2010; Sch Chapl Trin Ch New Orleans LA 2006-2012; Cur S Augustines Ch Metairie LA 2003-2005. CBS 2008; Our Lady of Walsingham 2008. richard@stgeorge-nola.org

EASTERLING SR, William Ramsay (WLa) 504 Tech Dr, Ruston LA 71270 B Little Rock AR 1948 s Thomas & Gladys. BS LSU 1975; BS Iowa Wesleyan Coll 1986; MTS Nash 2007. D 12/7/2006 P 6/30/2007 Bp Keith Lynn Ackerman. m 8/9/1975 Catherine G Easterling c 3. Int Gr Epis Ch Monroe LA 2011; Assoc Nash Nashotah WI 2007-2011.

EASTES, Suzanne Hardey (Mo) 312 Clayton Crossing Dr., #108, Ellisville MO 63011 Assoc S Tim's Epis Ch S Louis MO 2005- B Indianapolis IN 1936 d Karl & Jane. BS Pur 1958; MBA U MN 1977; MDiv Nash 1985. D 6/24/1985 Bp Robert Marshall Anderson P 2/2/1986 Bp William Augustus Jones Jr. c 2. Assoc Gr Ch S Louis MO 1993-2005; Assoc S Augustines Ch S Louis MO 1991-1993; Int S Andr's Epis Ch Edwardsville IL 1990-1991; Asst Trin Ch S Louis MO 1985-1987.

EASTHILL, Christopher Mark (Eur) Schuetzenstrasse 2, Wiesbaden 65195 Germany R Ch of S Aug of Cbury 65189 Wiesbaden 2016-, P-in-c 2014-2016 B Singapore 1960 s Eric & Betty. BA U of Leeds 1982; Fndt Degree St Jn's Theol Coll 2012; MDiv VTS 2013. D 3/16/2013 P 11/17/2013 Bp Pierre W Whalon. m 9/22/1989 Heidi Grau c 2. Convoc of Epis Ch in Europe Paris 2014; Ch of the Ascen Munich 2013-2014. ceasthill@gmail.com

✠ EASTMAN, The Rt Rev Albert Theodore (Md) 3440 S Jefferson St, #1481, Falls Church VA 22041 B San Mateo CA 1928 s Carl & Inette. BA Hav 1950; MDiv VTS 1953; Epis TS of the SW 1963; Coll of Preachers 1972; Epis TS of the SW 1980. D 7/15/1953 Bp Henry H Shires P 1/25/1954 Bp Karl M Block Con 6/26/1982 for Md. m 6/13/1953 Sarah T Eastman c 3. Vic Washington Natl Cathd Washington DC 2003-2004; Exec VP Prot Epis Cathd Fndt Washington DC 2001-2002; Chair Coll for Bps 1993-1997; Co-Chair A-RC USA 1992-1994; Chair SCER 1992-1994; Bp of MD Dio Maryland Baltimore MD 1986-1994, Bp Coadj of MD 1982-1985; Mem SCER 1985-1994; V-Chair SCWM 1979-1982; R S Alb's Par Washington DC 1973-1982; Dir PBFWR 1973-1978; R The Epis Ch Of The Medtr Allentown PA 1969-1973; Consult HOB 1968-1969; Exec Secy Ovrs Mssn Soc WDC 1957-1968; Exec Secy, Ovrs Mssn Soc Dio Washington Washington DC 1956-1979; Chapl Soledad St Prison 1954-1956; Vic Trin Ch Gonzales CA 1953-1956. Auth, "The Mssn of Chr in Urban Amer," Crossroads are for Meeting, SPCK/USA, 1986; Auth, "The Baptizing Cmnty: Chr Initiation and the Loc Cong," Seabury Press, 1982; Auth, "Mssn: In or Out," Friendship Press, 1967; Auth, "Chr Responsibility in One Wrld," Seabury Press, 1965; Auth, "Chosen And Sent: Calling the Ch to Mssn," Eerdmans, 1965; Auth, "Letters from the Rim of E Asia," The Natl Coun, 1963. DD S Mary Sem & U 1994; DD VTS 1983; LHD Epis TS of the SW 1982.

EASTMAN, Susan Grove (NC) 4604 Brodog Ter, Hurdle Mills NC 27541 Fac Duke DS Durham NC 2003- B Tucson AZ 1952 d George & Patricia. BA Pomona Coll 1974; MDiv Yale DS 1978; PhD Duke DS 2003. D 6/5/1982 Bp Paul Moore Jr P 1/29/1983 Bp George Clinton Harris. m 7/20/1986 Edward Eastman c 2. Asst S Steph's Ch Durham NC 1997-1998; The Epis Ch Of The Prince Of Peace Salem OR 1991-1995; Dio Oregon Portland OR 1991-1993; Vic Dio Alaska Fairbanks AK 1982-1986; S Andr's Epis Ch Petersburg AK 1982-1986; Non-par. Auth, "Incarn as Mimetic Participation," Journ for the Study of Paul and His Letters, Journ, 2011; Auth, "Israel and the Mercy of God: a re-reading of Galatians 6:16 and Romans 9-11," NT Stds, Journ, 2010; Auth, "Imitating Chr Imitating Us," The Word Leaps the Gap, Eerdmans, 2008; Auth, "Recovering Paul's Mo Tongue," Bk, Eerdmans, 2007; Auth, "Cast out the slave Wmn and her son," Journ for the Study of the NT, Journ, 2006; Auth, "The Foolish Fr and the Econ of Gr," The Expository Times, Journ, 2006; Auth, "Whose Apocalypse? The Identity of the Sons of God in Romans 8:19," Journ of Biblic Lit, Journ, 2002.

EASTON, Elizabeth Lavender (Neb) 9302 Blondo St., Omaha NE 68134 R Dio Nebraska Omaha NE 2014- B Seattle WA 1983 d David & Marilyn. BA Wstrn Washington U 2005; MDiv CDSP 2009. D 4/17/2009 Bp Gregory Harold Rickel P 11/17/2009 Bp Joe Goodwin Burnett. Cur All SS Epis Ch Omaha NE 2009-2014. leaston@episcopal-ne.org

EASTON, Stanley Evan (Ala) 1104 Church Avenue Northeast, Jacksonville AL 36265 B Spokane WA 1936 s Arthur & Nellie. BA WA SU 1958; MEd LSU 1967; EdD LSU 1970. D 10/6/1990 Bp Charles I Jones III. m 5/30/1981 Tien-Han Easton c 1. S Lk's Epis Ch Jacksonville AL 1998-1999. Assn for Epis Deacons 1990.

EASTWOOD, John Harrison (Cal) 30 Ogden Ave, San Francisco CA 94110 B Chester PA 1943 s John & Margaret. BA Pur 1966; STB GTS 1971; DMin Chr TS 1981. D 6/12/1971 P 12/15/1971 Bp John P Craine. m 9/12/1970 Judith A Eastwood c 2. R S Paul's Ch Oakland CA 1993-2007; R The Epis Ch Of S Jn The Evang San Francisco CA 1985-1993; Assoc R All SS Ch Indianapolis IN 1973-1985; Asst S Thos Ch Franklin IN 1971-1973; S Tim's Ch Indianapolis IN 1971-1973; Pres Prov VIII San Diego CA 2006-2012. AAPC. R Emer Epis Ch of St Jn the Evang 2008; Bachillerato mcl Universidad de Puerto Rico 1968.

EATON, Bert (EC) PO Box 337, Swansboro NC 28584 R S Ptr's By-The-Sea Swansboro NC 2004- B Pittsburgh PA 1946 s Edward & Judith. Leh; BS Indiana U 1968; MBA Indiana U 1970; MDiv Sewanee: The U So, TS 1995. D 5/24/1995 P 12/2/1995 Bp Bob Johnson. m 7/15/1967 Carol Ann Lusher c 3. S Andr's Ch Bessemer City NC 1997-2004; Ch Of The Redeem Shelby NC 1995-1996.

EATON, Carol Ann (EC) St Francis By the Sea Church, 920 Salter Path Rd, Salter Path NC 28512 B Philadelphia PA 1945 d Wilfred & Mary. BA Indiana U Bloomington. D 6/20/2015 Bp Robert Stuart Skirving. m 7/15/1967 Bert Eaton c 3.

EATON, Cornelia Kay (NAM) PO Box 720, Farmington NM 87499 B Shiprock NM 1970 d Yazzie & Alice. AA San Juan Coll 2009. D 12/21/2013 P 2/7/2015 Bp David Earle Bailey. m 9/21/1991 Fred Eaton c 2. Navajoland Area Mssn Farmington NM 2013-2015, 2012-2013. ceaton@ec-n.org

EATON, Karen A (Oly) PO Box 753, Port Townsend WA 98368 B Port Townsend WA 1964 d William & Patricia. BA WA SU 1985; Cert U of Washington 1996. D 10/17/2009 Bp Gregory Harold Rickel. m 5/9/2015 Elizabeth Faragher Appling c 1. D S Paul's Epis Ch Port Townsend WA 2009, Resource Mgr 2009.

EATON, Laura Mary (NMich) Assoc Chr Ch Calumet Larium MI 2006-; Assoc Trin Epis Ch Houghton MI 2006- B Laurium MI 1948 d Beverly. Michigan Tech U; Non Sem/Stds Through Dio N Michigan; AD Nthrn Michigan U 1970. D 8/17/2005 P 2/28/2006 Bp James Arthur Kelsey. c 4. Epis P S Ptr's-By-The-Sea Eagle Harbor MI 2006-2012; Prog Dir Keweenaw Acad 1998-2004.

✠ EATON, The Rt Rev Peter David (SeFla) 525 NE 15th Street, Miami FL 33132 Bp Coadj of SE Florida Dio SE Florida Miami 2015-; Mem Stndg Cmsn on Ecum and Interfaith Relatns 2009-; Mem, Bd the Corp Anlgican Theol Revs 2009-; Mem, Advsry Bd Wayne Morse Cntr for Law and Politics Eugene OR 2008- B Washington DC USA 1958 s Alfred & Judith. CLI Fell Shalom Hartman Inst Jerusalem; BA Lon GB 1982; BA U of Cambridge 1985; CTh Westcott Hse Cambridge 1986; MA U of Cambridge 1989; MA Oxf GB 1990; Fell-in-Res Sewanee: The U So, TS 1995; Fell-in-Res Sewanee: The U So, TS 2014. Trans 5/20/1991 as Priest Bp George Edmonds Bates Con 5/9/2015 for SeFla. m 9/25/2004 Katherine K Gleason. Adj Fac Iliff TS Denver CO 2005-2015; Dn S Jn's Cathd Denver CO 2002-2015; R S Jas Ch Lancaster PA 1995-2001; Assoc R S Paul's Ch Salt Lake City UT 1991-1995; Serv Ch of Engl 1986-1991; Fell, Chrsitian Ldrshp Initiative Shalom Hartman Inst Jerusalem 2008-2009; Mem, Stndg Com Dio Cntrl Pennsylvania Harrisburg PA 1997-2000. Contrib, "Remembering Jn Krumm," *Remembering Jn Krumm*, Forw Mvmt, 1998; Contrib, "Oxf Dictionary of the Chr Ch 3rd Ed," *Oxf Dictionary of the Chr Ch 3rd Ed*, OUP, 1997; Ed, "Bp Paul Jones," *Bp Paul Jones*, Forw Mvmt, 1992; Ed, "The Trial of Faith," *The Trial of Faith*, Morehouse, 1988; Auth, "Journ," *arts & Revs*, Var. Alcuin Club 1985; Assoc OHC 1975; Eccl Law Soc 2008; Nikaean Club 1985; Soc of Cath Priests 2010. Advancing Lrng in Lancaster Sch Dist of Lancaster 2002; Publ Serv Awd Utah AIDS Fndt 1994. bishop@diosef.org

EATON, Robert G (SJ) 1571 E Glenwood Ave, Tulare CA 93274 **Dio San Joaquin Fresno CA 2007-** B Portland OR 1955 s Donald & Joan. BMus U of Oregon 1977; MDiv CDSP 1984. D 6/29/1984 Bp Robert Hume Cochrane P 6/1/1985 Bp Matthew Paul Bigliardi. m 6/23/1978 Shirley M Eaton c 2. S Dunst's Epis Ch San Diego CA 2014-2016; S Jas Ch Paso Robles CA 2013-2014; Dio San Joaquin Fresno CA 1997-2006; Dioc. Yth Dir Epis Dio San Joaquin Modesto CA 1994-1995, Exam Chapl & Tutor 2001-2007, Chair, Dept of Cmncatn 2000-2007, Yth Prog Dir 1996-2000; R S Jn's Epis Ch Tulare CA 1989-2013; Co-Mssnr Prince of Peace Epis Ch W Salem OR 1987-1989; Assoc S Paul's Epis Ch Salem OR 1984-1989, Yth Min 1984-1989; Sem Intern St Johns Epis Ch Roseville CA 1982-1983. Auth, "How to Motivate, Train and Nurture Acolytes," Morehouse, 2002; Auth, *Sm Ch Wk Series*, HOWS website, 1999. ERM 1983; Fllshp of S. Jn Evang 1978-1985; OSL 1975-1989. interimrector@stdunstans.org

EATON, William Albert (SeFla) 10914 Nw 8th Ct, Plantation FL 33324 **Asstg H Sacr Hollywood FL 2002-** B Pittsburgh PA 1934 s William & Edith. Muskingum Coll; Pittsburgh Pstr Inst 1977; Pittsburgh Tpm 1977; TESM 1984. D 6/25/1977 Bp Robert Bracewell Appleyard P 12/1/1984 Bp Alden Moinet Hathaway. m 10/2/1954 Ruthmary H Eaton c 3. Ch Of The Resurr Cranberry Twp PA 1984-1995; Asst S Mart's Epis Ch Monroeville PA 1977-1984. Ord Of S Lk.

EAVES, Lindon John (Va) 10835 Old Prescott Rd, Richmond VA 23238 B 1944 s Kenneth & Winifred. BS U of Birmingham Gb 1966; GOE Ripon Coll Cuddesdon 1968; PhD U of Birmingham Birmingham Gb 1970; MA Oxf GB 1979; Ds Oxf GB 1980. Trans 1/1/1995 Bp Peter J Lee. m 6/29/1968 Susan Nuthall Eaves. P S Thos' Ch Richmond VA 2002-2013; P-In-Res Ch Of The H Comf Richmond VA 1985-1997; Serv Ch Of Engl 1968-1981. Auth, "Genes Culture & Personality," 1989. Pres Behavior Genetics Assn 1993. Doctor, Honoraryoris Causa Vrije Universiteit 2000; Dobzhansky Lifetime Achievement Awd Behavioral Genetics Assn 1998; Paul Hoch Awd Amer Psych Assn 1992.

EAVES, Susan Nuthall (Va) 3207 Hawthorne Ave, Richmond VA 23222 B Birmingham UK 1947 d Norman & Lilian. Cert Lady Spencer Churchill Coll of Educ 1968; Cert VTS 1991; MA U Rich 1992. D 12/12/1991 P 9/1/1992 Bp Peter J Lee. m 6/29/1968 Lindon John Eaves c 3. R S Thos' Ch Richmond VA 2001-2013; GC Dep Dio Virginia Richmond VA 2000-2009, 2000, Stndg Com 1998-2000; St Jas Ch Richmond VA 1996-2001; P-in-res Ch Of The H Comf Richmond VA 1991-1994; St. Cathr's Epis Sch Richmond VA 1991-1994.

EBEL, Ann Teresa (PR) B 1940 D 12/23/1978 Bp Chauncie Kilmer Myers P 6/5/1980 Bp William Edwin Swing. m 12/23/1967 William Ebel. S Mk's Par Berkeley CA 1987-1990; Epis Ch Of Our Sav Oakland CA 1979-1980, 1978-1979.

EBENS, Richard Frank (Mass) 4-C Autumn Dr, Hudson MA 01749 **Ret 1990-** B Somerville MA 1929 s Frank & Dorothy. BS NEU 1952; BS NEU 1952; STB Ya Berk 1958. D 6/21/1958 Bp Frederic Cunningham Lawrence P 12/1/1958 Bp Anson Phelps Stokes Jr. m 6/5/1965 Mary J Comings c 2. R S Lk's Ch Hudson MA 1966-1990; Assoc S Jn's Ch Norristown PA 1965-1966; Chapl Wstrn Maryland Coll 1963-1965; Vic S Geo Ch Hampstead MD 1961-1965; Cur Ch Of S Jn The Evang Hingham MA 1958-1961.

EBERHARDT, Karen Anne (Nwk) 18 Ute Ave., Lake Hiawatha NJ 07034 B Denver CO 1947 d Friend & Doris. U of New Mex; BA Thos Edison St Coll 1995; MDiv Drew U 1999; MDiv Drew U 1999. D 12/9/2006 Bp Carol J Gallagher. c 2. D S Paul's Epis Ch Morris Plains NJ 2007-2009.

EBERHARDT, Timothy Charles (Vt) 2460 Braintree Hill Rd, Braintree VT 05060 **Sprtl Care Coordntr Gifford Med Cntr Randolph VT 05060 2013-** B Morristown NJ 1945 s Charles & Dorothy. BA Bow 1968; BA Bow 1968; MDiv Bangor TS 1977; MDiv Bangor TS 1977. D 6/4/1977 P 12/5/1977 Bp Frederick Barton Wolf. m 5/20/1995 Mary Ellen Bean c 2. R S Jn's Epis Ch Randolph VT 1981-2010; R S Barn Ch Rumford ME 1977-1980.

EBERLE, William Edward (Va) P.O. Box 367, Rixeyville VA 22737 B Orange NJ 1947 s Edward & Jane. Asbury TS; BA Ya 1970; MDiv UTS 1974. D 6/

8/1974 Bp George E Rath P 1/26/1975 Bp David Keller Leighton Sr. m 6/21/1969 Linda Sue Eberle c 3. R Little Fork Epis Ch Rixeyville VA 2008-2014; R S Thos Ch Lancaster PA 1998-2008; R Gd Samar Epis Ch San Jose CA 1983-1998; R S Lk's Ch Phillipsburg NJ 1978-1983; Asst The Ch Of The Redeem Baltimore MD 1974-1978; Stndg Com Dio El Camino Real Salinas CA 1988-1990; Dioc Coun Dio Maryland Baltimore MD 1976-1978.

EBERLY, George Douglas (NJ) 500 19th St, Ocean City NJ 08226 **Ret 2006-** B Philadelphia PA 1946 s Charles & Charlotte. Westminster Coll 1965; BA SMU 1968; MDiv SWTS 1971. D 6/22/1971 Bp Archibald Donald Davies P 12/23/1971 Bp Theodore H McCrea. R Epis Ch Of The Epiph Ventnor City NJ 1997-2005; Asst H Trin Epis Ch Ocean City NJ 1995-1997, Assoc 1995-1997; R Gr Epis Ch Glendora CA 1991-1995; R Epis Ch Of The Redeem Irving TX 1976-1991; R S Ptr's Ch Mc Kinney TX 1974-1976; P-in-c S Jas Ch Dallas TX 1973-1974, Cur 1972-1973. AAM 1976-1995; Dioc Liturg & Mus Commissions 1980-1991; SocMary 1997. Fr. Tom Schiavo Bro Awd Judea-Chr 2005; Who'S Who In Amer Rel 1972.

EBERMAN, John Fowler (WA) 703 Agawam St, Elizabeth City NC 27909 **Died 1/17/2016** B Norfolk VA 1933 s John & Eloise. BS VPI 1958; MDiv VTS 1961. D 6/26/1961 P 6/27/1962 Bp William Henry Marmion. c 2. S Ptr's Epis Ch Sunbury NC 2005-2011; Gr Epis Ch Plymouth NC 2001-2002; Int St. L:uke's/St. Anne's Epis Ch Roper NC 2001-2002; Int P S Thos Ch Oriental NC 1998-1999; Supply P S Andr's Ch Columbia NC 1997-2011; Ret 1996-2016; R S Paul's Par Prince Geo's Cnty Brandywine MD 1989-1996; R S Jn's Epis Ch Crawfordsvlle IN 1981-1989; Vic Chr Ch Elizabethtown KY 1975-1981; H Trin Ch Brandenburg KY 1968-1979; Asst S Jn's Ch Roanoke VA 1964-1968; Vic Ch Of The Gd Shpd Lynchburg VA 1963-1964; Vic S Lk's Ch Pedlar Mills VA 1962-1964; Vic Emm Epis Ch Madison Heights VA 1961-1964.

EBERT, Bernhard (Colo) 802 Raton Ave, La Junta CO 81050 B Port Colborne Ontario CA 1958 s Erich & Emma. BMus U of Wstrn Ontario CA 1980; MDiv U Tor CA 2000. D 6/9/2001 P 12/1/2001 Bp William Jerry Winterrowd. m 6/5/1993 Angelika Ebert c 1. R St Andr Epis & H Cross Luth Ch La Junta CO 2001-2011, 2000-2001.

ECCLES, Mark Eldon (Ia) 1619 21st St Nw, Cedar Rapids IA 52405 **Stff Hosp Chapl Mercy Med Cntr Cedar Rapids IA 2002-; Stff D Chr Ch Cedar Rapids IA 1996-, Deaon on Stff 1995-** B Fort Dodge IA 1951 s Guy & Mary. BA U of Nthrn Iowa 1973; Mstr or Arts Other 2008; Mstr or Arts St. Mary's MN 2008. D 12/3/1995 Bp Chris Christopher Epting. m 8/28/1971 Sandra Fay Walkenhauer c 1.

ECCLES, M E (Chi) 311 N. Westgate Rd., Mount Prospect IL 60056 **Equity Stage Mgr Freelance 1991-** B Tucson AZ 1969 d Robert & Margot. BA Lake Forest Coll 1991; MTS SWTS 2003; MAPC Loyola U 2005; MDiv SWTS 2007. D 6/2/2007 Bp Bill Persell P 12/15/2007 Bp Victor Alfonso Scantlebury. m 9/23/1990 Kathleen E DeBock. S Mart's Ch Des Plaines IL 2013, R 2013-; Int S Simons Ch Arlington Hts IL 2011-2013, Assoc 2007-2013; Bd Mem Cathd Counslg Cntr Chicago IL 2007-2011. rev.m.e.eccles@gmail.com

ECHAZABAL, Livan (SwFla) 6709 N Nebraska Ave, Tampa FL 33604 **Vic S Fran Ch Tampa FL 2014-** B Habana Cuba 1967 s Jose & Miriam. Trans 3/10/2014 Bp Dabney Tyler Smith. m 7/22/1993 Lazara Yudith Jimenez c 1. isanfrancisco@tampabay.rr.com

ECHOLS, Mary W (SwFla) 917 11th St N, Naples FL 34102 **Off Of Bsh For ArmdF New York NY 1994-** B Pittsfield IL 1942 d Roy & Elma. BS U IL 1964; USC 1965; Lic Sacr Theol Angl TS 1986. D 6/13/1987 Bp Donis Dean Patterson. m 7/6/1965 Ronald Echols c 2. D Trin By The Cove Naples FL 2004-2013; Cbury Hse SMU Dallas TX 1994-1996; Asstg D Ch Of The Annunc Lewisville TX 1992-1994; Asstg D Epis Ch Of The Redeem Irving TX 1987-1992. Epis Cleric Un.

ECHOLS, William Joseph (WLa) 104 Ingram St, Lake Providence LA 71254 **Gr Ch Lk Providence LA 2012-, 1995-2003; Trin Ch Tallulah LA 1999-** B Monticello AR 1951 s Don & Betty. BBA NE Louisiana U 1978; MDiv Sewanee: The U So, TS 1987. D 5/30/1987 P 12/1/1987 Bp Willis Ryan Henton. m 12/29/1999 Linda Gail Mcdonald Echols c 3. R S Thos' Ch Monroe LA 1990-1994; Cur S Mths Epis Ch Shreveport LA 1987-1990.

ECKARDT, Robert Remick (At) 720 Whitemere Ct Nw, Atlanta GA 30327 **Died 5/22/2017** B Brooklyn NY 1933 s Richard & Ruth. BA Amh 1955. D 10/28/1995 Bp Frank Kellogg Allan. m 6/1/1996 Eve Eckardt c 4. D S Anne's Epis Ch Atlanta GA 1996-2014.

ECKART JR, Richard Joseph (Roch) 38 Dale Rd, Rochester NY 14625 B New York NY 1934 s Richard & Mary. BA Ya 1956; MDiv VTS 1961; Cert Onondaga Cmnty Coll 1982. D 10/14/1961 Bp William Foreman Creighton P 4/1/1962 Bp Angus Dun. m 9/16/1961 Renate Gertrude Eckart c 2. Assoc S Mich's Ch Geneseo NY 2000-2010; R S Mk's And S Jn's Epis Ch Rochester NY 1980-1999; Emm Ch E Syracuse NY 1980; Dio Cntrl New York Liverpool NY 1979-1980; Chapl S Andr Sch Jackson MS 1978-1979; S Andr's Epis Sch Ridgeland MS 1978-1979; Groton Sch Groton MA 1970-1976; R Ch Of The H Comf Washington DC 1963-1970; Cur S Tim's Epis Ch Washington DC 1961-1963. Auth, "To Complete A Par," *Aware*.

ECKEL, Malcolm David (Mass) 11 Griggs Ter., Brookline MA 02446 **Assoc Ch Of Our Sav Boston MA 1995-, Assoc 1991-; Prof of Rel Bos 1990-** B Albany NY 1946 s Malcolm & Mary. BA Harv 1968; EDS 1969; BA Oxf GB 1971; MA Oxf GB 1976; PhD Harv 1980. D 3/31/1974 P 3/1/1975 Bp Alexander D Stewart. m 6/25/1995 Leslie Arenas c 1. Auth, "Bhaviveka and His Buddhist Opponents," Harv Press, 2008; Auth, "Buddhism," Oxf Press, 2002; Auth, "To See The Buddha," Pr Press, 1994; Auth, "Jnanagarbha on The dist Between The Two Truths". Distinguished Tchg Prof of the Hmnts Bos 2003; Metcalf Awd for Tchg Excellence Bos 1998.

ECKIAN, Deirdre (WA) 4000 Tunlaw Road NW Apt 1005, Washington DC 20007 B Orlando FL 1975 BA Ya 1997; MDiv Ya Berk 2003. D 6/10/2006 P 1/20/2007 Bp John Bryson Chane. m 5/24/2008 James Leslie c 1. Asst to the R Chr Ch Georgetown Washington DC 2006-2014.

EDDY, Charles H. (Ak) P.O. Box 747, Willow AK 99688 B Cincinnati OH 1939 s William & Catherine. BA Hanover Coll 1962; MDiv VTS 1966. D 6/5/1966 Bp William R Moody P 12/1/1966 Bp William Jones Gordon Jr. c 2. S Mary's Ch Anchorage AK 1972-2000; Asst The Ch Of The H Trin Juneau AK 1966-1969; Ret.

EDDY, Diane Lynn (Ia) 1458 Locust St, Dubuque IA 52001 **D S Jn's Epis Ch Dubuque IA 2009-** B Mendota IL 1960 d Eugene & Margaret. D 2/22/2009 Bp Alan Scarfe. m 7/28/1990 David Ross Eddy c 1.

EDDY, Elizabeth (NJ) 913 Fassler Ave, Pacifica CA 94044 **Supply P Dio California San Francisco CA 2014-** B Sullivan's Island SC 1943 d Robert & Vada. BA Florida St U 1964; MA Florida St U 1968; PhD Florida St U 1970; MDiv Nash 1982. D 6/20/1982 Bp H Coleman Mcgehee Jr P 3/2/1984 Bp John Shelby Spong. c 1. S Jn's Ch Eliz NJ 2001-2009; S Jn's Ch Fords NJ 1994-1997; Ch Of The Atone Tenafly NJ 1984-1986; Asst S Paul's Ch Englewood NJ 1984-1985; Asst S Steph's Ch Hamburg MI 1982-1983; Supply P Dio Newark Newark NJ 2009-2011, 1997-2001; Supply P Dio New Jersey Trenton NJ 1997-2001. Contemplative Outreach 1986; Curs 1977; DOK 1977; Kairos 1987; Tres Dias 1984.

EDDY, William Welles (Mass) PO Box 3615, Waquoit MA 02536 B Hartford CT 1946 s Welles & Elizabeth. BA Ya 1968; Epis TS of the SW 1975; New York Inst of Tech 1976. D 6/11/1977 P 6/28/1978 Bp Paul Moore Jr. m 4/8/1994 Eileen E Walsh c 2. Int S Andr's Ch Wellesley MA 2012-2013; S Mary's Epis Ch Barnstable MA 2011-2012, 2004; Int Trin Epis Ch Wrentham MA 2009-2011; Int Par Of The Epiph Winchester MA 2008-2009; Int S Paul's Ch In Nantucket Nantucket MA 2007-2008; Int Ch Of S Jn The Evang Duxbury MA 2005-2007; Int Trin Epis Ch Weymouth MA 2002-2004; Int Chr Ch Epis Harwich Port MA 2000-2002; Int S Andr's Ch Hanover MA 1998-2000; Sabbatical P S Steph's Ch Cohasset MA 1997; Int Ch Of The Gd Shpd Wareham MA 1995-1997; Int S Jn's Ch Sandwich MA 1994-1995; Int All SS Par Whitman MA 1992-1994; R S Andr's Ch Edgartown MA 1987-1991, 1984-1986, Int R 1984-1986; Int S Ptr's Ch On The Canal Buzzards Bay MA 1987; R S Jn's Ch Jamaica Plain MA 1982-1984; Chapl Colorado Coll Colorado Sprg CO 1979-1980; Cur Gr Ch Vineyard Haven MA 1977-1978.

EDELMAN, Walter Lucian (SanD) 17427 Gibraltar Ct, San Diego CA 92128 **Ret 1999-** B White Plains NY 1937 s Walter & Mary. BA Ken 1958; U of Paris-Sorbonne Fr 1958; U of Strasbourg Fr 1959; MDiv GTS 1962. D 6/9/1962 P 12/22/1962 Bp Horace W B Donegan. P-in-c H Cross Epis Ch Carlsbad CA 1996-1999; R Chr Ch Coronado CA 1978-1995, Assoc 1973-1976; Chapl Bishops Sch La Jolla CA 1976-1978; The Bp's Sch La Jolla CA 1976-1978; R Ch Of The Medtr Bronx NY 1967-1973; Cur S Lk's Chap New York NY 1965-1967; Cur Chr Epis Ch Tarrytown NY 1962-1965.

EDEN, Holly (CNY) 120 W 5th St, Oswego NY 13126 B Utica NY 1947 d William & Kathryn. AA Mohawk Vlly Cmnty Coll 1966; BA Utica Coll 1968; MS SUNY 1973; MDiv Bex Sem 1979. D 6/23/1979 P 5/28/1980 Bp Ned Cole. R Ch Of The Resurr Oswego NY 2000-2009; Vic S Paul's Ch (Sum Chap) Parishville NY 1992-2000; R S Steph's Ch New Hartford NY 1992-2000; Ch Of The Gd Shpd Rangeley ME 1984-1992; St Andrews Epis Ch Rome NY 1981-1984; R S Andr Rome NY 1981-1983; Cur Trin Memi Ch Binghamton NY 1979-1981.

EDEN, Jonathan T (Mass) 865 Madison Ave, New York NY 10021 **Chr Ch Cambridge Cambridge MA 2009-** B Chicago, IL 1974 s Charles & Anne. BS Bates Coll 1996; MBA Boston Coll 2002; MDiv Andover Newton TS 2006. D 6/2/2007 P 1/12/2008 Bp M(Arvil) Thomas Shaw. Lilly Fell S Jas Ch New York NY 2007-2009.

EDENS III, Henry Harman (NC) 8011 Douglas Ave, Dallas TX 75225 **R Chr Ch Charlotte NC 2006-** B Richmond VA 1970 s Henry & Jane. BA Hampden-Sydney Coll 1992; MDiv Ya Berk 1996. D 6/15/1996 Bp Peter J Lee P 1/1/1997 Bp Frank Clayton Matthews. m 2/10/2000 Beverly T Edens c 2. Assoc R S Mich And All Ang Ch Dallas TX 2002-2006; Assoc R S Paul's Ch Charlottesville VA 1998-2002; Asst R S Paul's Ch Augusta GA 1996-1998; Par Assoc R E Lee Memi Ch (Epis) Lexington VA 1994-1995.

EDINGTON, Mark David Wheeler (Mass) PO Box 455, Hardwick MA 01037 Dominican Republic **R S Jn's Ch Newtonville MA 2009-** B Lansing MI 1961 s Edgar & Patricia. MDiv Harvard DS 2000; MALD Fletcher Sch of Law and Diplomacy 2007. D 5/27/2000 Bp M(Arvil) Thomas Shaw P 5/26/2001 Bp Barbara Clementine Harris. m 8/20/1983 Judith Hadden. R S Dunstans Epis Ch Dover MA 2007-2009, D 2000-2009; Assoc. Min and Dir of Admin The Memi Ch Harv 2000-2007. Coun on Frgn Relatns 1995.

EDLEMAN JR, Samuel Warren (Md) 1257 Weller Way, Westminster MD 21158 B Savannah GA 1936 s Samuel & Adelaide. BA Oglethorpe U 1957; STB GTS 1960. D 6/5/1960 P 4/25/1961 Bp Albert R Stuart. m 6/7/1960 Margaret Frances Edleman c 3. Asst Ch Of The Ascen Westminster MD 1999; Int S Phil's Ch Annapolis MD 1997-1999; Int S Lk's Ch E Hampton NY 1996-1997; Int Gr Ch Brunswick MD 1994-1995; S Andr's Ch Leonardtown California MD 1993-1994; Int S Andr's Leonardtown MD 1993-1994; Garrett Cnty Epis Ch Oakland MD 1992; P-in-c All SS Ch Annapolis Ju MD 1982-1991; R S Mk's Ch Highland MD 1975-1981; Asst R S Paul's Ch Augusta GA 1965-1975; P-in-c Chr Epis Ch Dublin GA 1961-1965; Gr Epis Ch Sandersville GA 1961-1965; S Lk's Epis Hawkinsville GA 1960-1961; P-in-c Trin Ch Cochran GA 1960-1961.

EDMAN, David Arthur (FtW) 47 Acorn Hollow Ln, Ardmore OK 73401 **Ret 1992-** B Worcester MA 1930 s Victor & Edith. BA Wheaton Coll 1955; MA Col 1958; BD UTS 1959. D 1/10/1959 P 7/1/1959 Bp Charles Francis Boynton. m 9/14/1987 Rita J Hayward. Int S Paul's Epis Ch Gainesville TX 2008-2010; R Ch Of S Thos Camden ME 1984-1991; R Gr Ch Scottsville NY 1969-1984; Cn Chr Ch Rochester NY 1965-1968; Chapl Rochester Inst of Tech Rochester NY 1965-1968; Cur Chr Ch Bronxville NY 1959-1962. Auth, "Your Weaknesses Are Your Strengths," Loyola U Press, 1993; Auth, "Once Upon an Eternity," Resource Pub, 1984; Auth, "Of Wise Men & Fools: Realism in the Bible," DoubleDay, 1972.

EDMAN, Elizabeth Marie (Nwk) 690 Fort Washington Ave., apt 1L, New York NY 10040 B Fort Smith AR 1962 d Norman & Martha. BA Franklin & Marshall Coll 1985; MDiv UTS 1991. D 6/4/2005 P 8/5/2006 Bp Thomas C Ely. c 2. Assoc R All SS Epis Par Hoboken NJ 2012-2013; Epis Coun At Nthrn Illinois U Sycamore IL 2006-2009; Chapl NWU Evanston IL 2006-2009; Cathd Ch Of S Paul Burlington VT 2005-2006. Auth, "Queer Virtue: What LGBTQ People Know About Life and Love and How it Can Revitalize Chrsnty," Beacon Press, 2016. Louie Crew Schlrshp OASIS Newark 2014.

EDMANDS II, Frank A (SO) 55 S Vernon Lane, Fort Thomas KY 41075 **P Trin Epis Ch London OH 2010-** B Newton MA 1946 s Lawrence & Dorothy. AA Fullerton Coll 1972; BA California St U 1976; BA California St U Fullerton 1976; MA California St U 1981; MA California St U Fullerton 1981; MA California St U Fullerton/ 1981; MDiv GTS 1990. D 6/16/1990 Bp Frederick Houk Borsch P 1/18/1991 Bp William George Burrill. m 5/2/1981 Lynn Carter-Edmands. P-in-c S Andr's Ch Pickerington OH 2007-2008; R Chr Memi Epis Ch Danville PA 2000-2006; Asst All SS Epis Ch Williamsport PA 1998-2000; Trin Epis Ch Williamsport PA 1998-1999; Tchr/Chapl Trin-Pawling Sch Pawling NY 1994-1997; Ch Of The Gd Shpd Savona NY 1992-1994; Vic S Jas Ch Hammondsport NY 1992-1994; Asst R Chr Ch Pittsford Pittsford NY 1990-1992. teclondon@sbcglobal.net

EDMINSTER, Beverley Beadle (Az) 1810 E Camino Cresta, Tucson AZ 85718 **D S Phil's In The Hills Tucson AZ 2000-** B Atlantic IA 1931 d Howard & Frances. BA U of Tulsa 1953; MEd U of Arizona 1966. D 10/14/2000 Bp Robert Reed Shahan. c 2. Benedictine Ord 1993-2003; Ssje,Cambridge Mass 1994.

EDMISTER, Jeffery Ray (WNY) Christ Episcopal Church, 7145 Fieldcrest Dr, Lockport NY 14094 **D Chr Ch Lockport NY 2011-** B Newfane NY 1963 s David & Alexandra. D 6/4/2011 Bp Ralph William Franklin. m 2/28/2001 Lisa L Edmister c 2. D Gr Ch Lockport NY 2011-2013.

EDMISTON, Alan James (LI) 3939 Ocean Dr, Vero Beach FL 32963 **Ret 1999-** B Bay Shore NY 1940 s Ralph & Helen. BS Rider U 1963; STB PDS 1967. D 4/22/1967 P 10/1/1967 Bp Alfred L Banyard. R All SS Ch Bayside NY 1982-1999; S Ptr's by-the-Sea Epis Ch Bay Shore NY 1970-1982; Cur Gr Epis Ch Plainfield NJ 1967-1970.

EDMONDS, Curtis M (Nev) Po Box 70342, Las Vegas NV 89170 B Des Moines IA 1944 s Augustus & Leone. BS U of Nevada at Reno 1980. D 5/18/1987 P 12/1/1987 Bp Stewart Clark Zabriskie. m 8/27/1966 Geraldine Slomka. Assoc S Tim's Epis Ch Henderson NV 1987-1992; Dioc P.

EDMONDS, John B (NY) Po Box 1535, Blue Hill ME 04614 B Concord NH 1942 s John & Katherine. BA Carleton Coll 1964; BD EDS 1968. D 6/22/1968 P 6/14/1969 Bp Anson Phelps Stokes Jr. S Jn The Evang Mansfield MA 2000-2002; Assoc P S Mk's Ch No Easton MA 1998-2002; Supt Seaman's Ch Inst Newport RI 1994-2002; Supt Seamens Ch Inst Newport RI 1994-2002; Pstr Co-ordinator Tri-Cnty Epis Area Mnstry Monticello NY 1993-1994; Pstr Coordntr TEAM Monticello NY 1992-1994; Vic S Eliz's Ch Hope Vlly RI 1987-1992; S Thos' Alton Wood River Jct RI 1987-1992; Dir/Sch for Deacons Dio Rhode Island Providence RI 1982-1992; Chapl Delaware St Hosp New Castle DE 1975-1977; CPE CPE 1974-1978; Chapl Pomfret Sch Pomfret CT 1970-1974; Cur Ch Of The H Nativ S Weymouth MA 1968-1970.

EDMONDSON, Emily F (SwVa) **P-in-c Chr Epis Ch Marion VA 2012-** B New Milford, CT 1951 d Benjamin & Anne. BS U of Tennessee 1973. D 3/13/2010

P 10/2/2010 Bp Neff Powell. m 6/15/2002 Keith Everett Edmondson c 2. Asst The Tazewell Cnty Cluster Of Epis Parishes Tazewell VA 2010-2012.

EDMUNDS, Robert Douglas (Mass) PO Box 9000, Edgartown MA 02539 **Middle E Partnership Off Dom And Frgn Mssy Soc- Epis Ch Cntr New York NY 2011-** B Boston MA 1955 s Verne & Carolyn. AA Quinsigamund Cmnty Coll 1975; BA U of Massachusetts 1977; MDiv Yale DS 1984. D 6/13/1984 P 2/27/1985 Bp Andrew Frederick Wissemann. m 8/20/1977 Deborah Schuller c 2. Epis Ch Cntr New York NY 2011-2014; P in Charge Trin Epis Ch Wrentham MA 2011-2014; Secy to the Meetings of the Heads of Ch Heads of Ch Jerusalem 2010-2011; Chapl to the Angl Bp in Jerusalem Exec Coun Appointees New York NY 2008-2011; R S Andr's Ch Edgartown MA 1992-2008; Dioc Coun Mem Dio Wstrn New York Tonawanda NY 1989-1992, Dir - Hunger T/F 1985-1990, Cler Compstn Cmsn 1990-1992, Vic, Chap of the Gd Shpd, Chautauqua Inst 1987-1992, Hosp Chapl Cmsn 1986-1990; R S Paul's Epis Ch Mayville NY 1987-1992; Cur S Lk's Epis Ch Jamestown NY 1984-1987; Bp's Rep to Havenside Elderly Hsng Dio Massachusetts Boston MA 2005-2008, Lay Eucharistic Mnstry Instr 1997-2005; Mem/Pres, Bd Dir Island Elderly Hsng Martha's Vineyard 2003-2008; Mem, Ethics Com Martha's Vineyard Hosp MA 1997-2005; Mem, Cmnty Action Team Edgartown MA 1997-2000; Mem, Bd Dir Edgartown Coun on Aging Edgartown MA 1993-2006; Mem, Bd Dir Martha's Vineyard Hunger Com MA 1993-1996; Mem, Cmsn on Fam Violence and Neglect Chautauqua Cnty NY 1989-1992; Mem, Bd Dir Westfield Memi Hosp Westfield NY 1989-1992. "Selective Divestment: Bringing Econ pressure on the Govt of Israel," *LivCh*, LivCh Fndt, 2006; "Israel's Actions Can't be Ignored," *LivCh*, LivCh Fndt, 2005. redmunds@episcopalchurch.org

EDSON, Heidi L (Vt) 6795 W 19th Pl Apt 304, Lakewood CO 80214 **R S Lk's Ch Chester VT 2015-** B Germany 1955 d Marshall & Ella. AA Young Harris Coll 1975; BMus Georgia Sthrn U 1977; MDiv CDSP 2010. D 6/12/2010 P 12/11/2010 Bp Robert Leroy Fitzpatrick. m 4/29/2000 Douglas A Edson. Cler-in-Charge Gr Ch Hoolehua HI 2010-2012.

EDSON, John B (CPa) 622 S York Rd, Dillsburg PA 17019 **Died 3/14/2016** B West Point,NY 1938 s Holt & Elizabeth. BA Tusculum Coll 1966; STB Ya Berk 1970. D 6/27/1970 Bp William Foreman Creighton P 3/13/1971 Bp John Harris Burt. c 1. Int S Jn's Luth Ch New Freedom PA 2007-2008; Int H Trin Evang Luth Ch York Sprg PA 2005-2007; Int St. Paul's Evang Luth Ch Carlisle PA 2004-2005; Hope Epis Ch Manheim PA 2001-2003; R Trin Epis Ch Monroe MI 1998-2001; S Lk's Epis Ch Mechanicsburg PA 1997-1998; Dio Wstrn Massachusetts Springfield 1996-1997; Int S Jas Epis Ch At Woonsocket Woonsocket RI 1995-1996; Trin Ch Potsdam NY 1994-1995; Zion Ch Hudson Falls NY 1992-1994; Int S Jas Epis Ch Essex Jct VT 1991-1992; Int S Paul's Ch Winona MN 1990-1991; Int Chr Ch Austin MN 1989-1990; R Chr Ch Albert Lea MN 1986-1989; Dio Spokane Spokane WA 1980-1985; R All SS Ch Spokane WA 1979-1986; R S Lk's Epis Ch Niles OH 1974-1979; P-in-c S Paul's Ch Bellevue OH 1972-1974; Cur S Barn Ch Bay Vill OH 1970-1972; Mem, Comm. on Chr Ed. Dio Ohio Cleveland 1973-1975, Mem, COM 1971-1974. "In Gratitude for Lutherans," *LivCh*, January 23, 2007, 2007. Citation ARC 1976.

EDSON, Lawrence Neil (Eau) 608 Madison St, Stanley WI 54768 B Kansas City MO 1939 s James & Edythe. BS U of Cntrl Missouri 1965; MS U of Cntrl Missouri 1966; DO Kirksville Coll 1974. D 11/30/1989 Bp William Charles Wantland P 3/29/2003 Bp Keith Whitmore. m 9/17/1960 Marilyn June Edson c 3. H Trin Ch Conrath WI 2005-2009. ESA.

EDSON, Robert Bruce (Mass) 4 Home Meadows Ln, Hingham MA 02043 **Assoc (part time) Emm Ch W Roxbury MA 2011-** B West Point NY 1941 s Holt & Elizabeth. BA Tusculum Coll 1963; MDiv EDS 1966. D 6/25/1966 P 5/27/1967 Bp William Foreman Creighton. c 2. Part Time S Jn's Ch Franklin MA 2008-2011; full time Ch Of S Jn The Evang Hingham MA 1981-2007; full time Trin Ch Washington DC 1976-1981; full time S Jn's Ch Cornwall NY 1970-1976; full time S Jn's Ch Chevy Chase MD 1966-1970; Chair Recently Ord Cler Dio Massachusetts Boston MA 1985-1996. Chapl to Ret Cler and Surviving Spouses 2007; Marg Coffin PB Soc 1995; Phillips Brooks Cler 1981; Soc for Relief of Aged and Disabled Cler and Widows, Widowers and Orphans of Cler of Epis Ch 2012.

EDWARD, Baskaran John (NY) 8 Sunnyside Ave, Pleasantville NY 10570 B Kelang Malaysia 1964 s Edward & Sushila. BTh Un Biblic Sem Pune India 1988; MDiv Un Biblic Sem Pune IN 1990; ThM PrTS 2002. Trans 5/3/2004 Bp John Palmer Croneberger. m 8/28/1995 Addaline Princet Suja Godwin c 3. P S Jn's Ch Pleasantville NY 2006-2010; Ch Of The H Trin W Orange NJ 2004-2006.

EDWARD, Gadi M (ND) 120 8th St S, Moorhead MN 56560 B Sudan 1963 s Michael & Yomama. D 6/23/2007 Bp Michael Smith. m 10/28/1998 Charity Justin Baringwa c 2.

EDWARDS, Bonnie (RG) 4908 Corrales Rd Ste B, Corrales NM 87048 **San Gabr the Archangel Epis Ch Corrales NM 2017-** B Tyler TX 1961 d Tilton & Mildred. BA U of No Texas 1987; MDiv Epis TS of the SW 2007. D 6/23/2007 Bp Don Adger Wimberly P 8/8/2009 Bp Joseph Jon Bruno. R S

Barn Epis Ch Portage MI 2012-2016; P-in-c S Thos Of Cbury Par Long Bch CA 2010-2011; Transitional D S Clem's-By-The-Sea Par San Clemente CA 2008-2009; CPE Chapl Res Vitas Innovative Hospice Care 2008-2009; Cur S Steph's Ch Huntsville TX 2007-2008.

EDWARDS, Carl Norris (Md) 201 Box Turtle Trl, Chapel Hill NC 27516 **Assoc S Matt's Epis Ch Hillsborough NC 2011-** B Asheville NC 1933 s Lee & Elia. BA Duke 1955; MDiv UTS 1960. D 6/29/1965 P 5/1/1966 Bp Thomas Augustus Fraser Jr. m 9/3/1955 Janet P Edwards c 3. Vic S Barth's Ch Pittsboro NC 2007-2011; P-in-c S Paul's Ch Louisburg NC 2002-2007; R Imm Epis Ch Glencoe MD 1979-2001; Asst S Paul's Par Baltimore MD 1976-1979. Soc for Values in Higher Educ 1961. Bp's Awd for Outstanding Ord Mnstry Dio Maryland 2000. carljanet@bellsouth.net

✠ EDWARDS, The Rt Rev Dan Thomas (Nev) 9480 S Eastern Ave Ste 236, Las Vegas NV 89123 **Bp of Nevada Dio Nevada Las Vegas 2008-** B Texarkana AR 1950 s Jewel & Verdi. BA U of Texas 1972; JD U of Texas 1975; MDiv GTS 1990; STM GTS 1992. D 8/6/1990 Bp David Bell Birney IV P 5/1/1991 Bp Frank Kellogg Allan Con 1/5/2008 for Nev. m 10/31/1977 Linda H Holdeman c 2. R S Fran Ch Macon GA 1994-2007; Asst to R Chr Ch Macon GA 1990-1994. Auth, "Study Guides Pb Sprtlty Reflections On"; Auth, "Tx Law Revs". AAR. dan@episcopalnevada.org

EDWARDS, Douglas Brian (Los) 4255 Harbour Island Ln, Oxnard CA 93035 **Angl Ch of Ghana 2000-; Chapl Claremont Colleges 1991-; Chair Immigration & CitizenshipComm Dio Los Angeles Los Angeles CA 1987-, Stwdshp & Fin 1985-, 1993-; Asst S Paul's Epis Ch Ventura CA 1984-** B Orange CA 1956 s Harold & Mary. MDiv GTS 1984; BS Newport U 1984; DMin GTF 1997. D 6/16/1984 P 12/19/1984 Bp Robert Claflin Rusack. m 4/18/1982 Lynn Stopher Edwards c 2. R S Ambr Par Claremont CA 1990-2004; Trin Epis Ch Orange CA 1984-1990. "Questions from the Pew," *LA Times Weekly Column*, 2003; Auth, "Abortion: Does the Epis Ch Have a Plcy?," *Living Ch*, 1984. Hon Archd Dio Senyani 2004.

EDWARDS, Dwight Woodbury (ECR) Po Box 853, Pacific Grove CA 93950 **Died 11/24/2016** B Oakland CA 1930 s Maurice & Ruth. BA U CA 1951; CDSP 1955. D 6/12/1955 P 12/17/1955 Bp Karl M Block. m 1/1/1991 Rose J Edwards. Pres, Stndg Com Dio California San Francisco CA 1976-1977; R Ch of S Mary's by the Sea Pacific Grove CA 1973-1998; R S Tim's Epis Ch Mtn View CA 1963-1973, Vic 1955-1963; Vol Chapl for Ret Cler Dio El Camino Real Salinas CA 2006-2016. DD CDSP 1993; Par Hall Named Dedication S Mary, Pacific Grove CA 1993; Par Hall Named Dedication S Tim, Mtn View CA 1976.

EDWARDS, Fitzroy Foster (NY) 72 Carnegie Ave, Elmont NY 11003 **D S Phil's Ch New York NY 1998-** B Saint John's Antigua AG 1941 s Joseph & Susanna. BS CUNY 1965; MS U of the Incarnate Word 1970. D 5/16/1998 Bp Richard Frank Grein. m 7/16/1966 Yvonne Monica Edwards c 3. Auth, "Journ Of Clincl Microbiology". Amer Soc For Microbiology; Med Mycology Soc Of New York; Norad.

EDWARDS, Halbert D (Okla) 1728 NW 42nd St, Oklahoma City OK 73118 B Oklahoma City OK 1940 s Joseph & Clara. BA U of Oklahoma 1961; BD Nash 1964; DDS U of Oklahoma 1982. D 6/20/1964 P 12/21/1964 Bp Chilton R Powell. m 8/12/1967 Lillian Ann Edwards c 2. Dio Oklahoma Oklahoma City OK 1978-2001; Dio Colorado Denver CO 1971-1978; Chapl U CO CO 1971-1978; Asst S Mary's Ch Edmond OK 1968-1971; Vic S Barn Ch Poteau OK 1964-1968.

EDWARDS, James Dennison (LI) 4 S Aspen Pl, Lewisburg PA 17837 B Endicott NY 1940 s Floyd & Marguerite. AAS SUNY 1960; BA Dakota Wesl 1964; MDiv GTS 1970; MSW Yeshiva U 1982. D 3/14/1970 P 12/19/1970 Bp Frederick Warnecke. Vic Ch Of The Redeem Mattituck NY 1990-2002; Dio Long Island Garden City NY 1986-1990; Sr. Ther Epis Cmnty Serv Long Island 1927 Bay Shore NY 1985-1986; Assoc Gr Epis Ch Massapequa NY 1981-1984; Vic St Christophers Ch Massapequa NY 1976-1981; Cur S Lk's Ch Forest Hills NY 1972-1974; Cur Ch of St Andrews & St Matthews Wilmington DE 1971-1972; D-in-trng Trin Ch Bethlehem PA 1970-1971. SocMary 1990.

EDWARDS, James Paul (Nev) 1400 Ebbetts Dr, Reno NV 89503 B Salinas CA 1931 s Joseph & Catherine. MA U of San Francisco; W Baden Coll; BA Gonzaga U 1955; BA Gonzaga U 1956. D 2/12/2002 P 9/14/2002 Bp Katharine Jefferts Schori. m 2/2/1963 Joan Irene Vertin. Assoc Trin Epis Ch Reno NV 2002-2008.

EDWARDS, Jamie L (NC) 1902 N Holden Rd, Greensboro NC 27408 **S Clem's Epis Ch Clemmons NC 2009-** B New Orleans LA 1967 d Howard & Julia. BA LSU 1989; MDiv Duke DS 1993; STM GTS 1994. D 11/30/1995 Bp Huntington Williams Jr P 6/1/1996 Bp Robert Carroll Johnson Jr. m 1/4/2014 Frank B Edwards c 1. Asst S Fran Ch Greensboro NC 2007-2009; Cbury Sch Greensboro NC 2003-2007; Asst H Trin Epis Ch Greensboro NC 1998-2003; S Paul's Epis Ch Winston Salem NC 1995-1998, 1994-1995. Soc Of S Jn The Evang.

EDWARDS, John Garry (CFla) 102 N 9th St, Haines City FL 33844 B St Peter Barbados 1961 s John & Jerminica. MDiv GTS 2017. D 1/30/2017 Bp Gregory Orrin Brewer. m 5/5/2007 Lisa A Edwards.

EDWARDS JR, John Richard (Ark) 6850 Rosefield Dr, La Mesa CA 91941 **Died 8/10/2015** B Beloit WI 1929 s John & Thelma. BA Beloit Coll 1951; MDiv Nash 1960. D 10/31/1953 P 6/1/1954 Bp Donald H V Hallock. m 6/24/1950 Doris Koebel c 3. Int S Mk's Epis Ch Jonesboro AR 1999-2000; Int S Paul's Epis Ch Batesville AR 1997-1998; Int Trin Epis Ch Mineral Point WI 1996-1997, P-in-c 1954-1995; Non-par 1994-1995; Int S Paul's Ch Fayetteville AR 1991-1993; S Barn' Epis Ch Los Angeles CA 1986-1989; Assoc R S Paul's Epis Ch Tustin CA 1983-1986; Off Of Bsh For ArmdF New York NY 1961-1969; P-in-c S Thos Hales Corners WI 1956-1961; D S Chad Okauchee WI 1953-1954. Angl Priests Euch League; Oblate OHC; Soc Of S Mary.

EDWARDS II, Justin Sargent (SJ) 765 Mesa View Dr Spc 98, Arroyo Grande CA 93420 **Ret 1995-** B Denver CO 1933 s Justin & Virginia. BA U of Washington 1955; MDiv CDSP 1966; DMin Fuller TS 1988. D 6/29/1966 Bp Ivol I Curtis P 3/17/1967 Bp George Richard Millard. m 7/3/1994 Nancy Edwards c 3. R Calv Epis Ch Kaneohe HI 1978-1995; R S Steph's Ch Gilroy CA 1969-1978; Asst All SS Epis Ch San Leandro CA 1966-1969. Auth, *Hm Groups in Ch Renwl*, 1988.

EDWARDS, Kathleen Louise (Minn) B Wabasha MN 1949 d Richard & Elizabeth. D 6/20/2015 Bp Brian N Prior. m 9/25/1971 Roger James Edwards c 3.

EDWARDS, Laura MacFarland (WA) 13118 Collingwood Ter, Silver Spring MD 20904 **Chapl Montgomery Hospice Rockville MD 2011-** B Dallas TX 1956 d Robert & Phoebe. Hobart and Wm Smith Colleges 1976; BA U of Pennsylvania 1979; MDiv GTS 1984. D 6/2/1984 P 4/25/1985 Bp George Phelps Mellick Belshaw. c 3. Chapl Pen Bay Hlth Care/Kno-Wal-Lin Hm Hlth & Hospice Rockpo 2004-2009; Chapl Augusta Mntl Hlth Inst Augusta ME 1994-1996; 1988-1994; Asst S Steph's Ch Newport News VA 1986-1988; Chapl Columbia-Presb Hosp New York NY 1984-1985; Assoc S Mk's Ch In The Bowery New York NY 1984-1985.

EDWARDS, Lloyd (USC) 4628 Datura Rd, Columbia SC 29205 B Morgan City LA 1941 s James & Nelwya. BS LSU 1962; PhD LSU 1971; MDiv Nash 1974. D 6/30/1974 Bp William Evan Sanders P 5/1/1975 Bp John Vander Horst. m 6/25/1988 Curry Harrison c 1. P-in-c Ch Of The Cross Columbia SC 1993-2011; Cn Pstr Trin Cathd Columbia SC 1982-1993; Vic Dio Tennessee Nashville TN 1978-1982; Vic S Thos Epis Ch Knoxville TN 1978-1982; Asst S Geo's Ch Nashville TN 1974-1978. Auth, "How We Belong, Fight and Pray," The Alb Inst, 1993; Auth, "Discovering Your Sprtl Gifts," Cowley Press, 1988.

EDWARDS, Lydia Alice (NJ) 81 Hillside Ave, Metuchen NJ 08840 B Baltimore MD 1950 d Jack & Jeter. BA U of Maryland 1972; U of Wisconsin 1974; MDiv GTS 1982; BA Rutgers The St U of New Jersey 2001. D 6/5/1982 Bp Albert Wiencke Van Duzer P 1/22/1983 Bp George Phelps Mellick Belshaw. m 6/20/1971 Paul Clemens c 2. Int S Lk And All SS' Ch Un NJ 1990-1991; Assoc S Lk's Epis Ch Metuchen NJ 1987-2000; Urban Mssnr New Brunswick Epis Ch New Brunswick NJ 1984-1986; New Brunswick Episurban Wk Com No Brunswick NJ 1984-1986; The Wm Alexander Procter Fndt Trenton NJ 1983, 1982-1983; The Epis Campus Mnstry at Rutgers New Brunswick NJ 1982-1984. Auth, "Study guide for The Mtn That Loved a Bird," 1985. OHC 1990.

EDWARDS, Lynn Chester (Pgh) 611 West St, Pittsburgh PA 15221 **Died 6/5/2017** B Pittsburgh PA 1940 s Chester & Eleanor. BS U of Pennsylvania 1963; MDiv GTS 1966. D 5/28/1966 Bp William S Thomas P 12/1/1966 Bp Austin Pardue. P Assoc S Matt's Epis Ch Homestead PA 2006-2010; P Assoc All SS Epis Ch Brighton Heights Brighton Heights PA 2006; P Assoc Chr Epis Ch No Hills Pittsburgh PA 2005-2006; P Assoc Trin Cathd Pittsburgh PA 2003-2004; Supply P 1998-2017; Vic Ch Of The Gd Shpd Pittsburgh PA 1971-1998; Vic S Jn's Epis Ch Donora PA 1966-1971; COM Dio Pittsburgh Pittsburgh PA 2010-2017. CBS, ECF, GAS; Ord Of S Ben, Comt, SocOLW; Sheperd Wellness Cmnty Fndr 1987.

EDWARDS, Nancy Beltz (NCal) Po Box 10202, Bainbridge Is WA 98110 **Ret 1989-** B Tillamook OR 1927 d Fredrich & Naomi. BA U of Oregon 1949; MDiv CDSP 1984. D 6/10/1984 P 1/6/1985 Bp John Lester Thompson III. Organizing Vic S Jas Of Jerusalem Epis Ch Yuba City CA 1985-1986; Asst Min S Jn's Epis Ch Marysville CA 1984-1986; Chapl Chas Wright Acad Eugene 1980-1988.

EDWARDS JR, Otis Carl (WNC) 115 Murphy Hill Rd, Weaverville NC 28787 **Adj P Epis Ch Of The H Sprt Mars Hill NC 2002-; P Assoc S Mary's Ch Asheville NC 1999-; Ret 1993-** B Bienville LA 1928 s Otis & Margaret. BA Centenary Coll 1949; STB GTS 1952; STM SMU 1962; MA U Chi 1963; PhD U Chi 1971; Nash 1976; U So 2006. D 5/28/1953 Bp Iveson Batchelor Noland P 4/28/1954 Bp Girault M Jones. m 2/19/1957 Jane T Edwards c 3. Dn Bexley Seabury Fed Chicago IL 1974-1993; Prof Nash Nashotah WI 1964-1974; Vic Gr Ch Chicago IL 1961-1963; Vic S Paul's Epis Ch Waxahachie TX 1960-1961; S Thos Ch Ennis TX 1960-1961; Vic S Anna Gibson LA 1957-1960; R Trin Epis Ch Morgan City LA 1957-1960; Vic S Paul's Ch Abbeville LA 1954-1957; Chapl U SW LA-Lafayette 1954-1957; Cur Trin Epis Ch Baton Rouge LA 1953-1954. Auth, *Elements of Homil*, Pueblo, 1981; Auth, *Lk's Story of Jesus*, Fortress, 1981; Auth, *The Bible for Today's Ch*, Seabury, 1980. Jos Cardinal Bernardin Natl Coun of Ch 2008; Lifetime Achievement

Acad of Homil 2007; Bk of the Year Acad of Par Cler 2005; Raven Mystery Writers of Amer 1965.

EDWARDS, Paul David (Los) 734 W Maplewood Ave, Fullerton CA 92832 B New York NY 1932 s George & Louise. BA U So 1954; BD UTS 1957; STM Sewanee: The U So, TS 1968; MA Chapman U 1981. D 6/17/1957 P 12/21/1957 Bp Horace W B Donegan. m 6/22/1957 Anita Edwards c 3. Assiting Cler Trin Epis Ch Orange CA 2002-2007; Emm Par Fullerton CA 1963-1994; Chapl Sewanee Mltry Acad 1960-1963; Chapl (1stlt) US-Army 1958-1960; Cur S Jn's Ch Getty Sq Yonkers NY 1957-1958. Auth, "Sprtl Intelligence Handbook," Morris Pub, 1998. Aamft.

EDWARDS, Rebecca (Cal) 4321 Eastgate Mall, San Diego CA 92121 **P Dio California San Francisco CA 2014-** B Reno NV 1978 d James & Georgia. BA Wellesley Coll 2001; MDiv VTS 2011. D 6/4/2011 Bp Charles Glenn Von-Rosenberg P 1/7/2012 Bp Jim Mathes. m 11/26/2003 Joshua Edwards. Ch Of The Gd Samar San Diego CA 2011-2014. rebecca@braidmission.org

EDWARDS, Robert Daniel (Los) 31641 La Novia, San Juan CA 92675 **R/Hd Chapl S Marg Of Scotland Par San Juan Capo CA 1999-, Chapl 1987-1990** B Augusta GA 1959 s Paul & Anita. BA California St U 1982; MDiv GTS 1987. D 6/20/1987 Bp Oliver Bailey Garver Jr P 5/1/1988 Bp William Carl Frey. m 8/6/1988 Michele A Edwards c 4. R Chr Ch Par Redondo Bch CA 1990-1999. robedwards@smes.org

EDWARDS, Terry Ann (SVa) 2515 Marshall Ave, Newport News VA 23607 **R S Aug's Epis Ch Newport News VA 2015-, 2014-2015** B Winston-Salem NC 1948 d Willie & Kabirda. BA No Carolina Cntrl U; MA Regent U 2005; MA VTS 2012. D 6/9/2012 P 12/15/2012 Bp Herman Hollerith IV. m 1/29/1972 John Henry Edwards c 2. revterryedwards9@gmail.com

EDWARDS JR, Theodore Whitfield (SwFla) 114 John Pott Dr, Williamsburg VA 23188 B Glen Ridge NJ 1947 s Theodore & Dorothy. BA Hobart and Wm Smith Colleges 1970; MDiv VTS 1977; MA Webster U 1985; STM Yale DS 2001. Trans 9/10/2003 Bp Stephen Hays Jecko. m 1/3/1970 Carol J Henseler c 2. P-in-c S Geo's Epis Ch Bradenton FL 2006-2010; R S Jn's Ch Ogdensburg NY 2003-2005; Chapl Off Of Bsh For ArmdF New York NY 1983-2003; Navy Chapl U. S. Navy Chapl Corps 1982-2003; Vic Ch Of The Trsfg Towaco NJ 1980-1983; Asst to R Lower Luzerne Par Hazleton PA 1977-1980; S Ptr's Epis Ch Hazleton PA 1977-1980. Auth, "Refuge and Strength," *Refuge and Strength*, Ch Pub Grp, 2008. Mltry Chapl Assn 1983-2004. NATO Medal US Marine Corps 1997; Meritorious Serv Medal (3) US Navy 1997; NATO Medal Royal Navy 1993; Coast Guard Commendation Medal US Coast Guard 1991; Coast Guard Achievement Medal (2) US Coast Guard 1991; Navy Commendation Medal (2) US Navy 1989.

EDWARDS III, Tilden Hampton (WA) 9615 Page Ave, Bethesda MD 20814 **Fndr and Sr Fell Shalem Inst for Sprtl Formation Beth MD 2001-** B Austin TX 1935 s Tilden & Marie. BA Stan 1957; MDiv Harvard DS 1961; CAS EDS 1962; PhD Un Grad Sch Cincinnati OH 1979. D 6/16/1962 P 12/16/1962 Bp William Foreman Creighton. m 7/3/1999 Mary Edwards c 2. Shalem Inst for Sprtl Formation Washington DC 1978-2000; Shalem Inst For Sprtl Formation Washington DC 1967-2000; Dio. of Wash. Metropltn Ecum Train. Ctr. Washington 1967-1978; Cur Ch Of S Steph And The Incarn Washington DC 1962-1966. Auth, "Sprtl Dir, Sprtl Comp," Paulist Press, 2001; Auth, "Living Simply Through the Day (Revised; 1st Ed 1977)," Paulist Press, 1998; Auth, "Sabbath Time (revised 1st. ed 1980))," Upper Room, 1992; Auth, "Living in the Presence," Harper San Francisco, 1987; Ed, "Living w Apocalypse," Harper San Francisco, 1984; Auth, "All God's Chld," Abingdon Press, 1982; Auth, "Sprtl Friend," Paulist Press, 1980. DD VTS 2002; Phi Beta Kappa Stan 1957.

EDWARDS, Whitney (Ct) St Jame's Episcopal, 1205 W Franklin St, Richmond VA 23220 **S Chris's Sch Richmond VA 2016-** B Richmond VA 1976 d Eric & Karen. BA U of Pennsylvania 1998; MDiv Ya Berk 2007; MDiv Ya Berk 2007. D 6/16/2007 P 12/18/2007 Bp Peter J Lee. m 5/28/2011 Christopher A Edwards c 2. Chr And H Trin Ch Westport CT 2013-2016; Epis Par Of S Jn The Bapt Portland OR 2011-2013; St Jas Ch Richmond VA 2007-2011; Prison Mnstry Asst Cath Dio Richmond 2001-2004.

EDWARDS, William Glover (WNC) 38 Wildwood Ave, Asheville NC 28804 B Tarboro NC 1933 s Solomon & Elizabeth. BA U NC 1955; MDiv GTS 1958; DMin GTF 1996. D 6/29/1958 Bp Edwin A Penick P 5/23/1959 Bp Richard Henry Baker. m 5/5/1972 Margaret M Edwards c 2. Int P S Lk's Epis Ch Asheville NC 2004-2005; Int P Trin Ch Spruce Pine NC 2002-2003; Int P S Fran' Epis Ch Rutherfordton NC 2000-2001, R 1961-1999; Chair - Prov Iv Commisions on Min Dio Wstrn No Carolina Asheville NC 1988-1994, Dioc Conv Secy 2001-2008, Dep - GC 1969-2000; Coun for Dvlpment of Mnstry The Epis Ch New York NY 1988-1994; R Gr Ch Asheville NC 1968-1999; Vic Chap Of Hope Charlotte NC 1958-1961. Intl Enneagram Assn; Intl Transactional Analysis Assn; Sprtl Dir Intl .

EDWARDS, William Patrick (LI) St John's Episc Ch, Po Box 5069, Southampton NY 11969 **R S Jn's Epis Ch Southampton NY 2016-; Epis HS Baton Rouge Baton Rouge LA 2011-** B Melbourne FL 1962 s Gerald & Bernice. BA Oglethorpe U; MDiv Nash 2011. D 6/4/2011 Bp Steven Andrew Miller P 12/8/

2011 Bp Morris King Thompson Jr. m 8/3/2003 Deborah Abbott Edwards c 4. P-in-c S Marg's Epis Ch Baton Rouge LA 2011-2016.

EDWARDS-ACTON, Jaime Kendall (Los) 727 Olympic Ave, Costa Mesa CA 92626 **Jubilee Consortium Los Angeles CA 2006-; R St Steph Epis Ch Los Angeles CA 1999-** B Hemet CA 1964 s Sidney & Jane. BS U CA 1994; MDiv Epis TS of the SW 1997. D 6/7/1997 Bp Chester Lovelle Talton P 1/1/1998 Bp Frederick Houk Borsch. m 5/14/1994 Suzanne Marie Edwards. S Mich And All Ang Par Corona Dl Mar CA 1997-1999. hopeinhollywood@gmail.com

EFFINGER, Richard W (SeFla) 141 S County Rd, Palm Beach FL 33480 **Assoc S Jn's Epis Ch Tallahassee FL 2015-** B Cleveland OH 1951 s Richard & Helen. BA OH SU 1974; MA OH SU 1978; MDiv GTS 2010; MDiv GTS 2010. D 12/18/2009 P 6/19/2010 Bp Leo Frade. S Ptr's Epis Ch Key W FL 2013-2015; The Epis Ch Of Beth-By-The-Sea Palm Bch FL 2010-2012.

EGAN, Adam DJ (Alb) 16 Elsmere Ave, Delmar NY 12054 B Baltimore MD 1980 s Colleen. Bangor TS; BA La Roche Coll; Savonarola Sem 2008. Rec 2/27/2010 Bp William Howard Love. m 8/17/2002 Jeanne Novak-Egan c 1. R S Steph's Ch Delmar NY 2010-2016.

EGBERT, David (Okla) 2817 Natchez Trl, Edmond OK 73012 B 1941 s David & Ada. BS SW Oklahoma St U 1963; MDiv SWTS 1969. D 6/17/1969 Bp Frederick Warren Putnam P 12/1/1969 Bp Chilton R Powell. m 6/1/1963 Norma Egbert c 2. S Jn's Epis Ch Tulsa OK 2005-2006; S Jn's Ch Oklahoma City OK 2004; Int R S Jn's Ch Norman OK 2003-2004, Asst 1972-2002; Gr Epis Ch Monroe LA 2002-2003; Int R S Mich's Epis Ch Norman OK 2000-2001; S Mary's Ch Edmond OK 1981-2001; R Ch Of The Redeem Kansas City MO 1975-1981; Dio W Missouri Kansas City MO 1975-1981; Chapl U of Oklahoma 1972-1975; Ecum Chapl E Cntrl Oklahoma St U Ada OK 1969-1972. Int Mnstry Ntwk 2000. Distinguished Mnstry Awd Dio Oklahoma 2002; Cn Dio Oklahoma 2001.

EGBERT, Paula Sue (Ida) 5780 Millwright Ave, Boise ID 83714 **D Ch Of H Nativ Meridian ID 1989-** B Monterey CA 1944 d Paul & Betty. LPN Boise St U 1977. D 5/6/1989 Bp David Bell Birney IV. m 10/23/1987 Richard G Egbert.

EGERSTROM, Marisa (Mass) D 6/4/2016 P 1/19/2017 Bp Alan Gates.

EGERTON, Karen (CFla) 1404 Chapman Cir, Winter Park FL 32789 B Steubenville OH 1945 d Alfred & Phyllis. Reformed TS; BA U of Florida 1967; MDiv Sewanee: The U So, TS 2002. D 12/13/1997 P 6/29/2002 Bp John Wadsworth Howe. m 6/15/1968 Charles Egerton c 4. Asst All SS Ch Of Winter Pk Winter Pk FL 2002-2007; D Epis Ch Of The Ascen Orlando FL 1997-2001.

EGGER, Jon Anthony (WMo) 4334 Northern Avene Apt 2911, Kansas City MO 64133 B Virginia MN 1958 s Joseph & Margaret. ADN Hibbing Cmnty Coll 1979; Dip W Missouri Sch of Mnstry 2002. D 2/1/2003 Bp Barry Howe. m 10/13/2007 Dawn Ann Tish c 3. D Trin Ch Independence MO 2009-2015; D Ch Of The Resurr Blue Sprg MO 2003-2006. NAAD 2003; RACA 2006. D Emer Trin Epis Ch, Independence, MO 2015.

EHMER, Joseph Michael (NwT) Diocese of Northwest Texas, 1802 Broadway, Lubbock TX 79401 **Cn to the Ordnry Dio NW Texas Lubbock TX 2012-, Cn to the Ordnry 1999-2006** B Miami FL 1952 s Joseph & Virgilee. BS U of Florida 1974; MBA RPI 1982; MDiv Epis TS of the SW 1999. D 3/13/1999 P 10/2/1999 Bp C Wallis Ohl. m 4/19/1975 Sue-Ann W Ehmer c 2. Assoc Dir Credo Inst Inc. Memphis TN 2007-2012; S Jn's Ch Andrews TX 1999-2003; S Lk's Epis Ch Levelland TX 1999-2003; The Epis Ch Of the Gd Shpd Brownfield TX 1999-2003. mehmer@nwtdiocese.org

EHRICH, Thomas Lindley (NC) 505 W 54th St Apt 812, New York NY 10019 **Pres Morning Wall Media 2004-; Non-par 1995-** B Evansville IN 1945 s William & Sarah. BA Wms 1967; MS Col 1968; MDiv EDS 1977. D 6/18/1977 Bp John P Craine P 12/1/1977 Bp Edward Witker Jones. m 6/11/1977 Helen Ehrich c 3. St. Barth Ch New York NY 2007-2008; R S Paul's Epis Ch Winston Salem NC 1993-1995; R S Mart's Epis Ch Charlotte NC 1988-1993; R S Steph's Ch S Louis MO 1985-1988; Vic S Fran In The Fields Zionsville IN 1979-1985; Dio Indianapolis Indianapolis IN 1977-1979; Vic S Steph's Elwood IN 1977-1979. Auth, "Ch Wellness," Ch Pub Corp., 2008; Auth, "Just Wondering, Jesus," Ch Pub Corp., 2005; Auth, "w Scripture as My Compass," Abingdon Press, 2003; Auth, "Journey," Crossroad Pub, 1995; Auth, "New Perspectives On Epis seminaries"; Auth, "Foward Day-By-Day," FMP; Auth, "On A Journey 93-," Morning Walk Media Inc.

EIBIN, Julian Raymond (Nwk) 284 Island Ave., Ramsey NJ 07446 **S Mk's Ch Orchard Pk NY 2016-; Mem Int Mnstry Ntwk 2015-** B Amersham UK 1951 s Karol & Janina. BA S Marys Sem & U Baltimore 1973; MA CUA 1977; Cert SWTS 2003. Rec 5/28/1983 as Priest Bp Otis Charles. m 8/6/2005 Deborah J Eibin c 3. R S Jn's Memi Ch Ramsey NJ 2009-2016; R S Paul's Ch Mt Vernon OH 2006-2009; Extended Supply Ch of the Nativ-St Steph Newport PA 2005; Ch Planter / Mssnr So Mtn Epis Cmnty Dillsburg PA 2003-2004; Ch Planter Dio Cntrl Pennsylvania Harrisburg PA 2002-2005; Dio Arkansas Little Rock AR 2002; Vic S Thos Ch Springdale AR 1999-2002; R Ch Of The Trsfg Braddock Heights MD 1991-1999; R S Andr's Epis Ch Enfield CT 1985-1991; Asst To Bp For Mnstry Dio Utah Salt Lake City UT 1983-1985; Pstr Team S Steph's Ch W Vlly City UT 1983-1985; Co-Conveener, Disctrict 10 Dio Newark Newark NJ 2011-2015, COM-Commitee on the Priesthood

2011-, Newark ACTS Bd Dir 2010-; Congrl Dvlpmt Commision Dio Ohio Cleveland 2006-2009. julian.eibin@stmarksop.org

EIBNER, Susan (NH) 97 Halls Mill Rd, Newfields NH 03856 **Gr Ch Vineyard Haven MA 2017-** B Salem MA 1950 BS U of Maine. D 6/14/2003 Bp Douglas Edwin Theuner P 12/20/2003 Bp Vicky Gene Robinson. m 5/17/2017 James J Eibner c 2. All SS Epis Ch Littleton NH 2015-2016; S Thos Ch Dover NH 2008-2014; Asst R S Jn's Ch Portsmouth NH 2003-2007.

EICH III, Wilbur Foster (Ala) St Bartholomew's Episcopal Church, 1600 Darby Dr, Florence AL 35630 **Assoc S Barth's Epis Ch Florence AL 1981-** B Tuskegee AL 1938 s Wilbur & Lula. BA Huntingdon Coll 1960; MD Tul 1964. D 6/6/1980 P 12/15/1981 Bp Furman Charles Stough. m 5/31/1963 Eugenia Graves Eich c 3.

EICHELBERGER JR, J Gary (USC) 10 N Church St, Greenville SC 29601 **S Andr's Epis Ch Greenville SC 2016-; Chr Ch Greenville SC 2014-** B Charleston SC 1972 s John & Kathryn. BA Furman U 1994; MTS Duke DS 1999; JD Duke Law Sch 1999. D 6/21/2014 Bp Anne Hodges-Copple P 1/23/2015 Bp Michael B Curry. m 10/27/2001 Kacey Young Kacey Elizabeth Young c 3. rector@standrewsgreenville.org

EICHENLAUB, Patricia (Mich) 2745 Lake Pine Path Apt 219, Saint Joseph MI 49085 B South San Gabriel CA 1940 d Arthur & Bette. BA U CA Santa Barbara 1961; MA Arizona St U 1967; EdD Utah St U 1974; MDiv SWTS 1977. D 6/11/1977 Bp James Winchester Montgomery P 2/5/1978 Bp William Henry Marmion. m 3/19/1967 Frank J Eichenlaub c 2. R S Geo's Epis Ch Warren MI 1998-2003; R S Pat's Epis Ch Madison Hts MI 1998-2003; Vic Ch Of The Gd Shpd Dearborn MI 1987-1998; Dir Whitaker TS Detroit MI 1984-1998; The Whitaker Inst of Theol Detroit MI 1979-1998; Assoc Whitaker TS Detroit MI 1979-1984; Chapl Stuart Hall Staunton VA 1977-1979. Ed, Quarterly Revs.

EICHLER, Stephen (ETenn) 1151 Gudger Rd, Sewanee TN 37375 B New York NY 1950 s Frederick & Dorothy. BA Florida Atlantic U 1975; MDiv Sewanee: The U So, TS 1984. D 6/11/1984 P 12/21/1984 Bp Calvin Onderdonk Schofield Jr. m 2/22/1979 Dolores Eichler c 3. Chr Ch Epis S Pittsburg TN 2004-2010; R S Mary Magd Epis Ch Pompano Bch FL 1993-2002; R S Alb's Epis Ch Hixson TN 1986-1993; Asst To Dn Trin Cathd Miami FL 1984-1986.

EICHNER, James F (Oly) **R Ch Of The H Cross Redmond WA 2002-** D 8/18/1996 Bp Andrew Fairfield P 4/8/1997 Bp Edward Lloyd Salmon Jr.

EICK, John David (WMo) 8030 Ward Pkwy, Kansas City MO 64114 B Niagara Falls NY 1939 s Norman & Laura. BS U MI 1963; MS GW 1966; PhD SUNY 1971. D 10/28/1988 Bp Richard Frank Grein. m 7/10/1960 Mary Elizabeth Eick c 3. D Healing Mnstrs. EFM, NAAD.

EICK, Mary Herron (Ore) 11511 SW Bull Mountain Rd, Tigard OR 97224 B Cincinnati OH 1941 d James & Mary. Cert OH SU 1967; MEd U of Portland 1976. D 10/8/2005 Bp Johncy Itty. m 9/11/1967 William Charles Eick c 1.

EIDAM JR, John Mahlon (SVa) 224 S Military Hwy, Norfolk VA 23502 **R S Ptr's Epis Ch Norfolk VA 1997-** B West Reading PA 1948 s John & Jeanette. BS W Chester U of Pennsylvania 1970; MEd W Chester U of Pennsylvania 1976; MDiv VTS 1990. D 6/16/1990 Bp Allen Lyman Bartlett Jr P 9/28/1991 Bp Donis Dean Patterson. c 2. Assoc R Ch Of The Gd Shpd Norfolk VA 1993-1997; Asst R Chr Epis Ch Plano TX 1990-1993.

EIDSON, Robert George (Mich) 6257 Telegraph Road, Apt. 102, Bloomfield Hills MI 48301 **Ret 1991-** B Niles MI 1929 s Duane & Helen. BBA U MI 1950; LLB U MI 1952; BD VTS 1961. D 6/29/1961 Bp Richard Stanley Merrill Emrich P 1/1/1962 Bp Archie H Crowley. m 9/20/1958 Margaret H Eidson c 3. R S Jn's Ch Royal Oak MI 1973-1990; R Trin Epis Ch Flushing MI 1967-1973; R S Paul's Epis Ch Brighton MI 1961-1967.

EIMAN, Amanda B (Pa) St Davids Church, 763 Valley Forge Rd, Wayne PA 19087 **Assoc S Dav's Ch Wayne PA 2014-** B Ridgewood NJ 1981 d Stephen & Alice. BA Drew U 2004; MDiv VTS 2007. D 9/6/2008 Bp Mark M Beckwith. m 8/3/2012 Christopher Bishop c 1. H Trin Ch Lansdale PA 2012-2014; S Jas Ch Wichita KS 2010-2012; Asst Emm Epis Ch Alexandria VA 2008-2010. aeiman@stdavidschurch.org

EINERSON, Dean Alfred (FdL) 29 S Pelham St, Rhinelander WI 54501 B Dubuque IA 1948 s Dean & Mary. BS U of Wisconsin 1971; MDiv SWTS 1999. D 8/25/1984 Bp Charles Thomas Gaskell P 5/29/1999 Bp Roger John White. m 8/14/1971 Barbara J Portman c 2. R S Aug's Epis Ch Rhinelander WI 2002-2015; P-in-c Trin Epis Ch Platteville WI 1999-2002; D S Jas Ch W Bend WI 1984-1996.

EISENSTADT-EVANS, Elizabeth Anne (Pa) 50 Fleming Drive, Glenmoore PA 19343 B New York NY 1955 d Abraham & Paulette. BA Kirkland Coll 1976; MDiv PrTS 1980; GTS 1984. D 6/16/1984 P 7/1/1985 Bp Lyman Cunningham Ogilby. m 9/19/1992 Haydn Barry Evans c 2. S Jas' Epis Ch Downingtown PA 2015; S Mk's Ch Honey Brook PA 2010-2011; Int R Resurr Epis Ch Rockdale Aston PA 2009; Dio Pennsylvania Philadelphia PA 2002; Assoc Ch Of The Gd Samar Paoli PA 1995-2002; Int Calv And S Paul Philadelphia PA 1993-1995; The Philadelphia Theo Inst Lansdowne PA 1992; S Dav's Ch Philadelphia PA 1990-1992, 1984-1985; P-in-c S Dav's Manayunk PA 1990-1992; Epis Ch Cntr New York NY 1988-1990; Campus Mnstry U Of Pennsylvania-Philadelphia 1986-1988; S Mary's Ch Hamilton Vill Philadelphia

PA 1985-1987. Online Contrib, "GetReligion," *www.getreligion.org.* Assoc of SSM. Polly Bond Awd 1992; Polly Bond Awd For Merit 1989; Awd For Merit Associated Ch Presses 1989.

EKBERG, Sean Armington (Okla) 210 E 9th St, Bartlesville OK 74003 **P-in-c S Lk's Epis Ch Bartlesville OK 2017-, Cur 2015-2017** B Aransas Pass TX 1980 s Steven & Tricia. AA Nthrn Oklahoma Coll; BA NW Oklahoma St U 2012; MDiv Epis TS Of The SW 2015; MDiv Epis TS of the SW 2015. D 1/10/2015 P 8/1/2015 Bp Edward Joseph Konieczny. m 10/20/2007 Nicole R Ekberg.

EKEVAG, Ellen Poole (Chi) 209 N Pine St, New Lenox IL 60451 **Emm Epis Ch La Grange IL 2016-; S Paul's Ch Hickman KY 2006-; Vic Trin Epis Ch Fulton KY 2006-** B Fulton KY 1980 d John & Roslyn. BA Ham 2002; MDiv VTS 2006. D 2/24/2006 P 9/9/2006 Bp Ted Gulick Jr. m 5/23/2006 Per Ekevag. Vic Gr Epis Ch New Lenox IL 2010-2016; Trin Epis Ch Fulton KY 2010; Asst Gr Ch Paducah KY 2006-2009. eekevag@gmail.com

EKIZIAN, Hagop J (NY) 137 N Division St, Peekskill NY 10566 B New York NY 1926 s Mardiros & Vehanoush. BS Hartwick Coll 1950. D 6/8/1968 Bp Horace W B Donegan. m 8/30/1947 Grace Link c 4. D S Ptr's Epis Ch Peekskill NY 1968-2007.

EKLO, Thomas (Minn) 8064 Golden Valley Rd, Golden Valley MN 55427 B Minneapolis MN 1951 MA S Cathr U 1993; MDiv GTS 2004. D 6/10/2004 P 12/16/2004 Bp James Louis Jelinek. m 3/12/2017 Stephen Charles Ingerson. R S Nich Ch Minneapolis MN 2005-2017; Int S Matt's Ch S Paul MN 2004-2005; Int Assoc P St. Matt's Epis Ch St. Paul MN 2004-2005.

EKLUND, Carolyn Hassig (Me) Episcopal Church St Paul, PO Box 195, Brunswick ME 04011 **R S Paul's Ch Brunswick ME 2013-** B Kansas City KS 1955 d Robert & Carol. M.Div. The GTS; BA U of Kansas 1978; BS U of Kansas 1979; MDiv GTS 1998. D 6/20/1998 P 6/19/1999 Bp Robert Carroll Johnson Jr. R Gr Epis Ch Plainfield NJ 2001-2013; Asst Yth & Ce Ch Of The Gd Shpd Rocky Mt NC 1998-2001. Ord Of S Helena 1999. carolyneklund@stpaulsmaine.org

EKLUND, Virginia Jane Rouleau (Lex) 130 Winterhawk Rd, Danville KY 40422 **D NonParochial/Dio Lexington 2006-** B Clinton MA 1943 d Robert & Emeline. BA Mid 1965; MA U MN 1969; MS U of Kentucky 1992. D 6/12/1988 Bp Don Adger Wimberly. m 8/9/1969 Neil Andrew Eklund c 2. D St. Andr's Epis Churc Lexington KY 2005-2006; D Epis Ch of Our Sav Richmond KY 1990-1998; D Trin Epis Ch Danville KY 1988-1990.

EKREM, Katherine Boyle (Mass) 12 White Pine Ln, Lexington MA 02421 **R The Ch Of Our Redeem Lexington MA 2009-** B Greenwich CT 1969 d Howarth & Esther. BA Wms 1991; MDiv GTS 2000. D 3/18/2000 P 9/16/2000 Bp Richard Frank Grein. m 5/13/1995 David N Ekrem c 3. R Gr Ch Norwood MA 2003-2009; Asst S Barn Ch Irvington NY 2000-2002.

EKSTROM, Ellen Louise (Cal) 1017 Virginia Street, Berkeley CA 94710 **D The Epis Ch Of The Gd Shpd Berkeley CA 2012-** B Vallejo CA 1953 d Alvin & Jeannette. AA Contra Costa Coll 1975; BA Sch for Deacons 2002. D 12/7/2002 Bp William Edwin Swing. m 6/28/1982 Carlos A Fernandez c 3. D S Mk's Par Berkeley CA 2002-2011; Eccl Crt Dio California San Francisco CA 2010-2011. Auth, "Scarborough," Cntrl Av Pub, 2012; Auth, "A Knight on Horseback," Cntrl Av Pub, 2011; Auth, "Tallis' Third Tune," Cntrl Av Pub, 2011; Auth, "Armor of Light," ireadiwrite Pub LLC, 2009; Auth, "The Legacy," *Digital Ed,* ireadiwrite Pub LLC, 2009; Auth, "The Legacy," Trivium Pub, 2004. The Iona Cmnty 2007-2011. Chr Ethics Sch for Deacons 2001; Chr Mythos Sch for Deacons 2000.

EKUNWE, Sylvester Osa (Nwk) B Benin City Nigeria 1958 s Joseph & Maria. BSc New Jersey City U 1984; MDiv New Brunswick Theol 2013; Angl Stds CDSP 2016. D 12/10/2016 P 6/17/2017 Bp Mark M Beckwith. c 2.

ELAM III, Walter L (CGC) 153 Orange Ave, Fairhope AL 36532 B Birmingham,AL 1946 s Walter & Virginia. BA Jacksonville St U 1978; MDiv Sewanee: The U So, TS 1982; DMin Sewanee: The U So, TS 1994. D 6/2/1982 P 12/1/1982 Bp Furman Charles Stough. m 6/28/2008 Anne Elam c 1. S Fran Ch Dauphin Islnd AL 2000-2008; Ch Of The H Comf Montgomery AL 1985-1999; R S Jas' Ch Livingston AL 1982-1985. Auth, "Pstr Or Profsnl"; Auth, "The Use Of Psychotherapeutic Technique In The Priestly Off". AAPC; Assn For Sprtl Ethical & Rel Values In Counslg; Lic Profsnl Counslr, Lic Mar Fam Ther.

ELBERFELD, Katherine Ann Fockele (At) 123 Church St NE # 150, Marietta GA 30060 **Pres/Fndr Gabr Cntr for Servnt-Ldrshp 2008-; Pres Servnt-Ldr Pub Inc. 2004-; Pres Servnt-Ldr Pub 2002-** B Daytona Bch FL 1949 d Louis & Jean. Coll of Preachers; Stetson U 1969; BA U So 1971; MA Amer U 1974; MDiv VTS 1993. D 6/19/1993 P 1/6/1994 Bp Don Adger Wimberly. c 1. PBp'S T/F On Ldrshp Epis Ch Cntr New York NY 2001; Servnt-Ldr Dvlpmt Cntr Inc Alexandria VA 1999-2000; Adj Instr VTS Alexandria VA 1999; Coordntr Servnt-Ldr Dvlpmt Cntr Alexandria VA 1998-2002; Fndr Servnt-Ldr Dvlpmt Cntr Alexandria VA 1998; Assoc S Geo's Epis Ch Arlington VA 1997-1998; Asst S Aid's Ch Alexandria VA 1993-1996; Dio Lexington Lexington 1986-1989, COM 1987-1990. Co-Auth, "Green by Design," *Green by Design,* Gabr Cntr for Servnt-Ldrshp, 2008; Auth, "In the Midst of Sunflowers," *In the Midst of Sunflowers,* Servnt-Ldr Publicatioons, 2006; Auth, "Reaching For Peace," *Concepts In Human Dvlpmt,* 2003; Auth, "To Speak of Love," *To Speak of Love,* Servnt-Ldr Pub, 2003; Auth, "To Speak Of Love," *Concepts In Human Dvlpmt; Var Dioc Newspapers,* 2002; Auth, "Serv Is The Truest Form Of Ldrshp," *Ldrshp In Action,* 2002; Auth, "Servnt-Ldrshp: The Doorway To Cmnty," *New Ther; Concepts In Human Dvlpmt,* 2002; Auth, "The Hats," *Appalachian Heritage,* 1987; Auth, "Brotherly Love," *Appalachian Heritage,* 1986; Auth, "Jordan To Jerusalem," Forw Mvmt Pubs, 1979. Bd Trst Uso Sewanee Tn 1999-2002; Solo Flight, Stff Mem 1999-2000. Nomin For 1993 Dav H.C. Read Prchr/Schlr Awd VTS 1993; Poly Bond Awd ECom 1989; Phi Beta Kappa U So 1971; Ord Of The Gownsmen, Acad hon Soc U So 1969.

ELBERFELD, Richard (NwPa) 3105 Springland Terrace, Erie PA 16506 **Dn of NW Dnry Dio NW Pennsylvania Erie PA 2006-, Coun 1996-** B Columbus OH 1948 s Richard & Mildred. BA U So 1970; MDiv VTS 1977; DMin Sewanee: The U So, TS 1987. D 5/21/1977 Bp Robert Bruce Hall P 12/18/1977 Bp Arthur Anton Vogel. m 2/8/1997 Sung Hui Elberfeld c 4. Vic Chr Epis Ch Meadville PA 2010-2014; P-in-c Ch Of The H Sprt Erie PA 2007-2010; Vic S Mary's Ch Erie PA 1998-2005; R S Mk's Ch Erie PA 1996-2009; P-in-c Trin Epis Ch Clanton AL 1995-1996; Chapl Off Of Bsh For ArmdF New York NY 1990-1996; R Epis Ch of Our Sav Richmond KY 1985-1990; Dio W Missouri Kansas City MO 1981-1985, Dn of Cntrl Dnry 1982-1985; Chr Ch Epis Boonville MO 1981-1984; Asst Gr And H Trin Cathd Kansas City MO 1979-1981; Chapl US AF/Air NG 1977-2007; Cur St Ptr & All SS Epis Ch Kansas City MO 1977-1979; Chair Liturg Cmsn Dio Lexington Lexington 1985-1987.

ELCOCK, Frank Ulric (LI) 257 Leaf Ave, Central Islip NY 11722 **Vic Ch Of The Mssh Cntrl Islip NY 2003-, D 1991-2002** B Panama City PA 1931 s Clyde & Edith. Cert Mercer TS 1986; BS Liberty U 1990; MA Liberty U 1999. D 1/16/1991 P 1/4/1992 Bp Orris George Walker Jr. m 2/27/1960 Elvia Jesticia Blake c 4. Asst Caroline Ch Of Brookhaven E Setauke NY 2000-2004; Int 1992-1999; Vic S Mths Epis Ch Bellmore NY 1999-2004; Assoc S Ann's Ch Sayville NY 1993-1997; Chapl Pilgrim Psych Hosp 1988-1990.

ELDER, Clayton L (Dal) 311 E Corpus Christi St, Beeville TX 78102 **S Phil's Epis Ch Frisco TX 2016-** B Victoria TX 1972 s Donald & Elizabeth. BA SMU 1995; MAIB Webster U 1998; MDiv SMU Perkins 2008. D 10/18/2008 Bp James Monte Stanton P 4/18/2009 Bp Paul Emil Lambert. m 8/16/2003 Jodie L Elder c 2. R S Phil's Epis Ch Beeville TX 2010-2016; Cur S Lk's Epis Ch Dallas TX 2008-2010. clayton@stphilipsfrisco.org

ELDER, Paul Robert (Los) 580 Hilgard Ave, Los Angeles CA 90024 B London England 1937 s George & Joyce. Diac Cert Bloy Hse. D 12/20/2014 Bp Joseph Jon Bruno. m 2/24/1958 Barbara Ann Elder.

ELDER, Robert Macrum (Va) 218 2nd St, Huntingdon PA 16652 B Baltimore MD 1925 s George & Anna. BA Washington Coll 1951; BD Bex Sem 1954. D 6/25/1954 P 3/1/1955 Bp Noble C Powell. R Angl Par of Flower's Cove 1996-2002; R Angl Par Ramea Can 1991-1996; R Emm Ch Rapidan VA 1985-1990; Off Of Bsh For ArmdF New York NY 1958-1969; Cur S Thos' Baltimore MD 1955-1958; Cur S Jas Ch Monkton MD 1954-1955; S Jas' Epis Ch Parkton MD 1954-1955.

ELDER, Ruth Annette (Md) 4238 Pimlico Rd, Baltimore MD 21215 B Los Angeles CA 1958 d Edward & Naomi. BA The U of Maryland, Baltimore Cnty 1980; MA St Mary's Sem 2012. D 6/13/2015 Bp Eugene Taylor Sutton. c 2.

ELDER-HOLIFIELD, Donna Ellen Carter (ECR) 64 San Pedro St, Salinas CA 93901 B Chicago IL 1940 d Herbert & Elizabeth. MA U of Arkansas 1960; U MI 1963; Cert U of Paris-Sorbourne Paris FR 1983; BS Sch for Deacons 1992. D 6/22/1994 Bp Richard Lester Shimpfky. m 7/7/2003 Richard C Holifield. CA Teachers of Frgn Languages; NAAD. Dedicated Unionist Awd CA Fed of Teachers 2002.

ELDRIDGE, Barbara Adelle (CFla) 2143 Kings Cross St, Titusville FL 32796 **D S Giles Chap Deerfield Asheville NC 2000-** B Ardsley PA 1938 d Newton & Eva. BA Barry U 1959. D 12/18/1993 Bp John Wadsworth Howe. m 1/29/1960 Radford Washington Eldridge. D S Tim's Epis Ch Daytona Bch FL 1993-2000. Ord Dok; Ord Of S Lk.

ELDRIDGE JR, Robert William (USC) Hq Forscom, 1777 Hardee Ave Sw, Fort Mcpherson GA 30330 B Melrose MA 1946 s Robert & Florence. BA Bos 1965; MTh Bos 1973. D 11/14/1998 P 5/1/1999 Bp Henry Irving Louttit. m 8/17/1968 Leona Marion Haskell. Off Of Bsh For ArmdF New York NY 1999-2003; Chapl US-A. eldridgebbe@aol.com

ELEK, Hentzi (Pa) 3625 Chapel Rd, Newtown Square PA 19073 **Trin Ch Moorestown NJ 2015-** B Philadelphia PA 1965 s Peter & Mary. BA Harv 1988; MDiv Ya Berk 1995. D 6/10/1995 Bp Allen Lyman Bartlett Jr P 1/10/1996 Bp Peter J Lee. m 12/28/1990 Sarah F Barton c 2. H Trin Ch Lansdale PA 2015; R S Alb's Ch Newtown Sq PA 2001-2015; Asst R S Fran Epis Ch Great Falls VA 1997-2000; Asst R S Paul's Epis Ch Alexandria VA 1995-1997. Soc Of S Jn The Evang 1985.

ELEY, Gary W (Vt) 33 Adams Ct, Burlington VT 05401 **Non-par 1990-** B Altus OK 1944 s Carl & Margaret. BA Oklahoma St U 1966; MDiv Drew U 1969; Cert CDSP 1970; MEd U of Vermont 1980. D 5/31/1970 Bp George Richard Millard P 12/1/1970 Bp Leland Stark. c 1. R All SS' Epis Ch S Burlington VT

254

1973-1989; Cur S Ptr's Ch Morristown NJ 1970-1973; CEO and Fndr Eley Fin Mgmt Burlington Vermont 1989-2013. Chart Fin Analysts Soc 1994-2013.

ELFERT, Martin (Ore) 127 E 12th Ave, Spokane WA 99202 **Gr Memi Portland OR 2015-; COM Dio Spokane Spokane WA 2012-** B Vancouver BC 1972 s Frank & Helen. BFA U of British Columbia Vancouver BC CA 1995; MDiv CDSP 2011. D 8/14/2011 Bp Michael Hanley P 3/23/2012 Bp James E Waggoner Jr. m 4/7/2004 Phoebe R Macrae c 3. Cur Cathd Of S Jn The Evang Spokane WA 2011-2015. Blogger, "Fr Knows Best," *spokanefaithandvalues.com*, Spokane Faith and Values, 2013; Homilist/Contrib, "Sample Sermon," *How to Get Your Sermon Heard by Wm Hethcock*, Plateau Books, 2012; Homilist/Contrib, "Sample Sermon," *Preaching Jesus: Sermons, Reports and Comments From the 2010 Preaching Excellence Prog*, Epis Preaching Fndt, 2010. Brave Prchr Awd Beatitudes Soc 2012; D.D. (hon.) CDSP 2012; AABS Stdt Paper Winner Angl Assn of Biblic Scholars 2011; Bp Richard Millard Preaching Prize CDSP 2011; Open Water Certification PADI 2008; Burger Schlrshp Burger Fndt 1991.

ELFRING-ROBERTS, Jess (Chi) Church of our Saviour, 530 W Fullerton Pkwy, Chicago IL 60614 **Ch Of Our Sav Chicago IL 2013-** B St Charles IL 1986 d Gary & Mary Elizabeth. BA Columbia Coll Chicago 2008; Cert Dioc Sch for Deacons 2012. D 1/17/2013 Bp Chris Christopher Epting. m 12/20/2013 Rebecca J Elfring-Roberts. Dio Chicago Chicago IL 2013-2016; S Jn's Epis Ch Chicago IL 2009-2013.

ELFVIN, Robert Roger (Ia) 8 Poinciana Lane, Palm Coast FL 32164 B Charleston SC 1945 s Charles & Gloria. BA OH SU 1966; MDiv Ya Berk 1969. D 6/14/1969 P 5/8/1970 Bp John Harris Burt. m 3/5/1966 Karon Elfvin c 4. R S Lk's Ch Des Moines IA 1978-2009; R Trin Ch Findlay OH 1971-1978; Asst Chr Ch Lima OH 1969-1971.

ELIN, Darren Richard Strawn (SO) 100 Miami Ave, Terrace Park OH 45174 **R S Thos Epis Ch Terrace Pk OH 2010-; Dioc Coun Dio Sthrn Ohio Cincinnati OH 2011-** B Stockton CA 1970 s Rhoderick & Andrea. BA California St U 1992; DAS Ya Berk 1998; MDiv Yale DS 1998; Cert Yale Inst of Sacr Mus 1998. D 6/26/1999 Bp Sanford Zangwill Kaye Hampton P 12/17/1999 Bp Andrew Donnan Smith. m 6/27/1998 Sarah Julie S Elin c 2. R S Jn's Epis Ch Saginaw MI 2004-2010; Assoc S Jn's Ch Barrington RI 2002-2004; P-in-c S Dav's Epis Ch Halifax MA 2000-2002; Assoc S Matt's Epis Ch Wilton CT 1999-2000; Mutual Mnstry Dvlpmt Team Dio Estrn Michigan Saginaw MI 2007-2010, Pstr Response Team 2007-2010, Personl Com 2005-2010. Thos Philips Memi Awd in Liturg Ya Berk 1998.

ELIOT, Mary (Md) 1930 Brookdale Rd, Baltimore MD 21244 **R Epis Ch Of Chr The King Baltimore MD 2009-** B Evanston IL 1967 d John & Sylvia. BS U of Maryland 1989; EdM Harv 1993; MA Theol Washington Theol Un 1998; DAS GTS 1999. D 6/26/2004 Bp Peter J Lee P 1/15/2005 Bp Robert Wilkes Ihloff. m 1/29/2005 Jeffrey K Staples c 1. Assoc R Chr Ch Columbia MD 2004-2009; S Dunst's Ch Mc Lean VA 1999-2004.

ELISEE, Jean R (Hai) 33 Mount Pleasant Ave Rm 120, West Orange NJ 07052 B Haiti 1927 D 6/8/1952 P 12/8/1952 Bp Charles Alfred Voegeli Con 1/1/1972 for Hai. m 12/20/1961 Anita Elisee. Dio New York New York NY 1988-1989; Exec Coun Appointees New York NY 1980-1987.

ELKINS-WILLIAMS, Stephen John (NC) 100 Black Oak Pl, Chapel Hill NC 27517 **R Chap Of The Cross Chap Hill NC 1985-, Assoc 1982-2015** B Bakersfield CA 1944 s Harold & Agnes. BA Gonzaga U 1969; MDiv Regis Coll Toronto CA 1975. Rec 5/26/1982 as Priest Bp Robert Hume Cochrane. m 12/20/1978 Elizabeth C Elkins-Williams c 2. Asst S Steph's Epis Ch Seattle WA 1982, 1978-1982. Auth, "Oh It's You Again! in Preaching Through the Years of Lk," *Sermons That Wk IX*, 2000; Auth, "Lost in Wonder, Love and Praise," *Angl Dig*, 1999; Auth, "Ch-Going," *Angl Dig*, 1999.

ELL, Marianne Sorge (Del) 4751 Highway 1804, Williston ND 58801 **Epis Mnstrs To The Aging Eldersburg MD 2014-; S Lk's Epis Ch Seaford DE 2014-; VP Prov VI 2004-** B Fargo ND 1963 d Elliott & Marjorie. BA DePauw U 1984; MDiv Epis TS of the SW 1989. D 6/3/1989 P 1/6/1990 Bp Elliott Lorenz Sorge. m 12/1/1990 John William Ell c 1. Dio No Dakota Fargo ND 2000-2010; R S Ptr's Epis Ch Williston ND 1995-2013; R S Mich's and All Ang' Ch Cartwright ND 1995-1999; Dioc Res Chapl (summers) Camp Wright 1993-1995; Vic S Paul's Ch S Jn's Hillsboro ND 1990-1995; Cur Chr Ch S Ptr's Par Easton MD 1989-1990. revmariell@gmail.com

ELLEDGE II, Charles Clyde (Mass) 54 Robert Road, Marblehead MA 01945 **R Wyman Memi Ch of St Andr Marblehead MA 2011-** B Tacoma WA 1962 s C Ray & Marjorie. BA U of Kansas 1986; MDiv SWTS 1993. D 6/27/1993 Bp Peter Hess Beckwith P 5/1/1994 Bp Donald Purple Hart. m 6/10/1995 Kathryn Elledge c 2. R The Annunc Of Our Lady Gurnee IL 2000-2011; Asst S Chris's By-The River Gates Mills OH 1997-2000; R All SS Ch Brooklyn MI 1995-1997; Chapl S Andr's Priory Sch Honolulu HI 1993-1995; Chapl St. Andr's Priory Sch Honolulu HI 1993-1995. Contrib, "Effective Orgnztn for Congrl Renwl," Acta Pub., 2008.

ELLEDGE, Kathryn (Mass) 54 Robert Road, Marblehead MA 01945 **All SS Ch Stoneham MA 2012-** B Arlington IL 1962 d Robert & Janet. BA U of Missouri 1982; MDiv & MSW U Chi DS 1990; CAS SWTS 1991. D 6/15/1991 P 12/1/

1991 Bp Frank Tracy Griswold III. m 6/10/1995 Charles Clyde Elledge c 2. The Annunc Of Our Lady Gurnee IL 2007-2011; Long-term supply Dio Ohio Cleveland 1997-2001; Long-term supply Dio Michigan Detroit MI 1995-1997; Fam crisis Counslr Families First Adrian MI 1995-1997; Seabury Hall Makawao HI 1992-1995; Chapl/Counslr Seabury Hall Sch 1991-1995. Massachusetts Epis Cler Assn 2012.

ELLER, Ruth Elizabeth (U) 700 S Silver Ridge St Spc 85, Ridgecrest CA 93555 **Asstg P All Souls' Epis Fllshp Ridgecrest CA 2009-** B Tac WA 1943 d Henry & Victoria. BA Vas 1965; MA Smith 1967; PhD U CA 1980; MDiv CDSP 1989. D 6/3/1989 P 6/9/1990 Bp William Edwin Swing. Int Pstr Ch Of The Resurr Centerville UT 2008-2009; R S Jn's Epis Ch Logan UT 1999-2008; Dioc Mssnr Dio California San Francisco CA 1996-1999; Int Pstr S Thos Epis Ch Sunnyvale CA 1995-1996; Int Pstr Epis Ch of St Jn the Bapt Aptos Aptos CA 1994-1995; Int Pstr All SS Epis Ch Palo Alto CA 1993-1994; Int Pstr S Lk's Ch Los Gatos CA 1992-1993, Pstr Assoc 1990-1993, Pstr Asst 1989-1990.

ELLERY, Celia (NwT) 2661 Yale Ave, San Angelo TX 76904 **R Epis Ch Of The Gd Shpd San Angelo TX 2009-, P-in-c 2007-2009, Asst 2005-; P-t Pstr Chr Luth Ch ELCA San Angelo TX 2007-; Dn, Eagle Cove Dnry Dio NW Texas Lubbock TX 2010-, Ecum Off 2008-2009** B Tulsa OK 1955 BA Arkansas Tech U 1977; MA Texas St U San Marcos 1982; MDiv Epis TS of the SW 2005. D 12/18/2004 P 6/18/2005 Bp C Wallis Ohl. m 8/9/1975 Jon Christopher Ellery c 3. EDEIO 2008-2009. goodshepherdepiscopal1@gmail.com

ELLESTAD, Charles Dwight (Lex) 837 Isaac Shelby Cir E, Frankfort KY 40601 **Asstg P S Hubert's Ch Lexington KY 2009-; Chapl Hospice of the Bluegrass 2006-** B Madison WI 1945 s Elver & Eleanor. BS U of Wisconsin 1967; MA U of Wisconsin 1971; MA Westminster TS 1977; MDiv Nash 1983. D 11/27/1982 Bp Charles Thomas Gaskell P 6/1/1983 Bp Addison Hosea. m 4/24/1981 Jean Rowley Ellestad c 2. S Jos Mssn Salvisa KY 1993-2006; R Ch Of The Ascen Frankfort KY 1989-2006; Cn To Ordnry Dio Easton Easton MD 1987-1989; Assoc Chr Ch Cathd Lexington KY 1983-1987.

ELLEY, Eric M (WMass) PO Box 528, Somersville CT 06072 B Trenton NJ 1970 s Svend & Irene. AAS Pennco Tech Bristol PA; D Formation Prog 2000. D 10/21/2000 Bp David Bruce Joslin. m 2/18/2005 Graham Van Keuren. D S Jn's Ch Northampton MA 2006-2015; Dio New Jersey Trenton NJ 2000-2005.

ELLGREN SHEPLEY, Neysa A (Ore) 11800 SW Military Ln, Portland OR 97219 **Cn Dio Oregon Portland OR 2010-; Reg VI, Dn Dio MN MN 2007-** B Blue Earth MN 1959 d Stanley & Mary. MDiv Iliff TS; BS Minnesota St U Mankato; DMin SWTS; BS Minnesota St U Mankato 1981; MDiv Iliff TS 1997; DMin SWTS 2005. D 6/7/1997 P 1/3/1998 Bp William Jerry Winterrowd. m 5/7/2015 William Bruce Shepley c 4. Int S Jn The Evang S Paul MN 2010; R Ch Of The Epiph Epis Minneapolis MN 2004-2010, 2000-2003; Dept. of Congrl Dvlpmt, Chair Dio MN MN 2003-2005; COM - Advsr for H Ord for Young Vocations Dio MN MN 2001-2003; Assoc S Aid's Epis Ch Boulder CO 1997-1999. Epis Publ Plcy Ntwk 2004; ESMHE/Strng Com 1997-1999; Epis Soc of Mnstry for Higher Educ Strng Com 1997-1999; Minnesota Epis Cler Assn (ECAM) 2000; NNECA (NNECA) 2008; Natl Nework of Epis Cler Associations (NNECA) 2007-2013. neysae@diocese-oregon.org

ELLINGBOE, Shirley Kay (RG) 5794 Ndcbu, Taos NM 87571 **Int St Thos Ch Hanalei HI 2009-** B Colfax WI 1940 d Lawrence & Marie. BSW Avila Coll 1989; MDiv SWTS 1993. D 1/25/1984 Bp Robert Marshall Anderson P 5/8/1993 Bp William Edward Smalley. m 4/15/1977 John Ellingboe c 2. Dioc Coun Dio The Rio Grande Albuquerque 1998-2000, Growth & Effective Cmte 1995-2000; R S Jas Epis Ch Taos NM 1995-2006; Assoc S Thos The Apos Ch Overland Pk KS 1993-1995, D 1987-1993; D Sprt of Gr Luth Epis Ch W Bloomfield MI 1984-1987. scl Avila Coll 1989.

ELLINGTON, Meta Louise Turkelson (NC) 521 Marlowe Rd, Raleigh NC 27609 **D S Mich's Ch Raleigh NC 2008-** B Reidsville NC 1945 d Richard & Lillian. BA U NC 1966. D 10/2/1988 Bp Robert Whitridge Estill. m 8/6/1966 William Woolcott Ellington c 2. D Ch Of The Gd Shpd Raleigh NC 1998-2008; Chr Epis Ch Raleigh NC 1994-1998; D S Mary's Chap Sch Raleigh NC 1994-1998; S Mary's Sch Raleigh NC 1994-1998; D-In-C St Elizabeths Epis Ch Apex NC 1993-1994; D S Cyp's Ch Oxford NC 1992-1993; D S Tim's Ch Raleigh NC 1988-1992.

ELLINGTON, William Ferrell (Cal) 303 N West St, McAlester OK 74501 **P-in-c Trin Ch Eufaula OK 2008-** B Arlington TX 1934 s Bennett & Irene. MDiv SWTS; BA U of Texas 1961; U of Oklahoma 1974; PhD Pacific Grad Inst 1998. D 6/18/1964 P 12/1/1964 Bp Theodore H McCrea. m 6/18/1977 Patricia D Ellington c 2. R Trin Par Fillmore CA 1995-2000; Vic S Paul's Mssn Barstow CA 1991-1995; Int S Jn The Bapt Par Corona CA 1990-1991; R S Jos's Par Buena Pk CA 1987-1990; R S Paul's Epis Ch Evanston WY 1979-1987; Vic St Mart of Tours Epis Ch Pryor OK 1973-1977; Vic S Jn's Epis Ch Vinita OK 1973-1974; R S Jas Epis Ch Oklahoma City OK 1970-1972; Chapl Untd States Naval Reserve 1969-1982; R S Andr's Ch Breckenridge TX 1966-1969; Vic S Philips Epis Ch Sulphur Spgs TX 1965-1966. Hon Cn S Matt Cathd 1969.

ELLIOTT, Annie (Miss) 370 Old Agency Rd, Ridgeland MS 39157 **Sch Chapl S Andr's Epis Sch Ridgeland MS 2012-; Coordntr for Yth Mnstrs Dio Mississippi Jackson MS 2009-, Coordntr for Yth Mnstrs 2009-** B Meridian MS

1981 d Luke & Susan. BA Van 2003; MDiv VTS 2008. D 6/7/2008 P 2/1/2009 Bp Duncan Montgomery Gray III. m 9/24/2010 Gates Safford Elliott. All SS Ch Inverness MS 2012-2013; Assoc S Andr's Cathd Jackson MS 2008-2011.

ELLIOTT, Barb (Minn) St Paul's Episcopal Church, 1710 E Superior St, Duluth MN 55812 **Chapl Essentia St Mary's Med Cntr Duluth MN 2002-2022** B Grand Rapids MN 1948 d William & Ramona. BA U MN 1969; PhD U MN 1983; MDiv EDS 2012. D 6/28/2012 P 1/6/2013 Bp Brian N Prior. m 5/30/1969 Thomas Edward Elliott c 2. Journ Article, "Rel Beliefs and Practices in ESRD: Implications for Clinicians," *Journ of Pain and Symptom Mgmt*, 44(3):400-409, 2012; Journ Article, "Forgiveness Ther: A Clincl Intervention for Chronic Disease," *Journ of Rel and Hlth*, 50(2):240-247, 2011.

ELLIOTT, Beverley Florence (At) 5458 E Mountain St, Stone Mountain GA 30083 **S Barth's Epis Ch Atlanta GA 2002-** B Hobart Tasmania AU 1952 d John & Joan. DAS Queensland U 1982; MDiv Candler TS Emory U 1997; GTS 2001. D 6/9/2001 Bp Robert Gould Tharp P 1/21/2002 Bp J Neil Alexander. m 10/11/1980 Paul Alexander Elliott.

ELLIOTT, Bianca Lynn (Kan) D 6/17/2017 Bp George Wayne Smith.

ELLIOTT III, David Augustus (Miss) 205 Autumn Ridge Dr, Jackson MS 39211 B Meridian MS 1940 s David & Mary. BA U So 1961; MDiv/optime merins Sewanee: The U So, TS 1969. D 6/23/1969 P 5/24/1970 Bp John Maury Allin. m 4/27/1959 Gay Elliott c 4. Int S Andr's Cathd Jackson MS 2016-2017; Cn 1975-1980; S Ptr's Ch Oxford MS 2015-2016; Assoc R S Jas Ch Jackson MS 2000-2007; R Ch of the H Trin Vicksburg MS 1994-2000; R S Jas Ch Greenville MS 1984-1994; R S Tim's Ch Signal Mtn TN 1980-1983; Chapl/Tchr All SS' Epis Sch Vicksburg Ms 1971-1972; Chapl U Mississippi 1969-1971. Auth, "Var Bk Revs," *S Lk Journ*.

ELLIOTT, Diane Lynn (Minn) B Buffalo NY 1959 d Kenneth & Jeanne. D 6/21/2016 Bp Brian N Prior. m 2/10/2001 Dale Stephen Elliott c 3.

ELLIOTT, Gates Safford (Miss) 4130 Crestview Dr, 118 N Congress St, Jackson MS 39201 **Exec Com Dio Mississippi Jackson MS 2015-; Dir of Dvlpmt and Planned Giving Dio Mississippi 2015-; Chairman, Bd Managers Duncan M. Gray Epis Camp And Confer Canton MS 2015-** B Houston TX 1973 s David & Elizabeth. BBA U of Houston 2001; MDiv VTS 2009. D 6/20/2009 Bp C Andrew Doyle P 1/7/2010 Bp Rayford Baines High Jr. m 9/24/2010 Annie Elliott c 2. Assoc The Chap Of The Cross Madison MS 2010-2015; Cur S Steph's Ch Beaumont TX 2009-2010. gelliott@dioms.org

ELLIOTT III, Harry Arnold (Ct) Grace Episcopal Church, 311 Broad St, Windsor CT 06095 **R Gr Epis Ch Windsor CT 2011-** B Buffalo NY 1953 s Harry & Joy. BA SUNY 1976; MDiv Bex Sem 1990. D 2/28/1987 P 5/12/1990 Bp David Charles Bowman. m 8/28/1976 Susan E Minch c 3. R S Mary's Epis Ch Manchester CT 1998-2007; GOE Rdr ECUSA 1996-1998; Chapl Fire Dept 1994-1997; Chapl Police Dept Chapl 1990-1998; R S Ptr's Ch Westfield NY 1990-1998; Prison Chapl Dio Wstrn New York Tonawanda NY 1986-1988, Cmncatn Com 1991-1998, Outreach Grants Com 1991-1998, COM 1991-1997, Fin Com 1987-1991; Asst Ch Of The Adv Buffalo NY 1984-1988; Dn, Hartford Dnry Dio Connecticut Meriden CT 1999-2000. "From Death Comes Life," The Journ/Hearst, 1994; "The Real Meaning of All Souls and All SS," Westfield Republican/Hearst, 1991. BDEC Dio Connecticut 2013; Bp's Cross Dio Kansas 2011; Cler Conf Plnng Com Dio Ct 1999; Dn Dio Ct 1999; Supvsr, OTP Prog Dio Ct 1998.

ELLIOTT JR, James Edward (Ala) 2714 Hilltop Cir, Gadsden AL 35904 B Fayette AL 1942 s James & Ruby. BS Auburn U 1963; MDiv Candler TS Emory U 1967; U of Alabama 1986; CAS Sewanee: The U So, TS 1987. D 5/26/1987 Bp Robert Oran Miller P 12/17/1987 Bp Furman Charles Stough. m 6/6/1962 Jane P Pinkston c 2. Int Chr Epis Ch Albertville AL 2008; Int S Paul's Ch Selma AL 2008; R H Comf Ch Gadsden AL 1996-2008; R H Cross Trussville AL 1990-1996; P-in-c Calv Ch Oneonta AL 1987-2013; R S Mich And All Ang Millbrook AL 1987-1990; Ecum and Interfaith Off Dio Alabama Birmingham 2005-2010, Dn of Mtn Convoc 2002-2008, Secy of the Dio 1994-1997. Jim2714@icloud.com

ELLIOTT, James Lawrence (Ga) PO Box 864, Quitman GA 31643 **P-in-c S Jas Epis Ch Quitman GA 2011-** B Thomasville GA 1959 s William & Walton. None - Read for H Ord TS; None - Read for H Ord Sewanee: The U So, TS; AB Davidson Coll 1982; JD U GA Sch of Law 1985. D 11/7/2009 Bp Henry Irving Louttit P 8/21/2010 Bp Scott Anson Benhase. m 5/25/1985 Susan Thomas Elliott c 3. Asstg P Chr Ch Valdosta GA 2010-2013. jelliott@ebbglaw.com

ELLIOTT, Jim (NCal) 1407 N Anderson St, Tacoma WA 98406 **Ret 1995-** B Bremerton WA 1935 s George & Alma. BMus U of Puget Sound 1957; SMM UTS 1961; MDiv CDSP 1965; DMin SFTS 1992. D 9/11/1965 P 3/26/1966 Bp Ivol I Curtis. m 9/17/1994 Anne Scholes c 2. Int S Matt's Epis Ch Sacramento CA 1986; R Epiph Epis Ch Vacaville CA 1978-1985; Chapl Campus Chr Mnstry Univ of WashingtonSeattle WA 1974-1975; Chapl Campus Chr Mnstry Univ of Washington Seattle WA 1969-1970; Vic S Geo's Ch Seattle WA 1968-1978; Cur S Jn's Epis Ch Olympia WA 1965-1968; DRE First Congrl Ch Tacoma WA 1957-1959.

ELLIOTT, Luz Adriana (Dal) St Anne Episcopal Church, 1700 N Westmoreland Rd, Desoto TX 75115 B Mexico City 1961 d Roberto & Maria. D 6/4/2016 Bp George Robinson Sumner Jr. m 7/4/1987 Robert Leonard Elliott c 3.

ELLIOTT, Norman Henry Victor (Ak) 2401 Galewood St, Anchorage AK 99508 **Died 9/9/2016** B Plymouth England 1919 s Sidney & Laura. BA Detroit Inst of Tech 1948; BD VTS 1951; S Augustines Coll 1956; MDiv VTS 1971; Oxf GB 1986. D 6/30/1951 Bp Russell S Hubbard P 2/17/1952 Bp William Jones Gordon Jr. c 3. Archd So Cntrl Alaska AK 1996-2016; R Emer All SS' Epis Ch Anchorage AK 1990-2016, R 1962-1989; Pres and Mem Stndg Com AK 1990-1993; Hon Chapl Port of Anchorage AK 1980-2016; Dep GC AK 1979-2016; Dep GC AK 1970-2016; Dep GC AK 1969-2016; Hon Chapl to the ArmdF of Alaska ArmdF and Fed Ministires New York NY 1963-2016; R S Jn's Ch Ketchikan AK 1958-1962; Archd of the Yukon Dio Alaska Fairbanks AK 1957-1958; Archd of the Yukon Mssy Dist of Alaska AK 1957-1958; R S Matt's Epis Ch Fairbanks AK 1954-1955; Dist Mssnr Mssy Dist of Alaska AK 1952-1957; Mssy-in-charge S Steph's Ch Ft Yukon AK 1952-1953; D S Mk's Ch Nenana AK 1951-1952. Auth, *Living Ch*. Mssn to Seafarers, U.K. 1962; SSC 1989. Soc of SS Simeon and Anna Epis Dio Alaska 1990; Hon Chapl ArmdF Chapl 1963.

ELLIOTT, Paul Alexander (At) 5458 E Mountain St, Stone Mountain GA 30083 B 1952 BA Cntrl Queensland U Rockhampton Qld Au 1981; Dip U of Sthrn Queensland Brisbane Qld Aus 1982; BTh Brisbane Coll of Theol AU 1985; ThD Candler TS Emory U 2004. Trans 10/31/2000 Bp Frank Kellogg Allan. m 10/11/1980 Beverley Florence Elliott. R S Mich And All Ang Ch Stone Mtn GA 2000-2015.

ELLIOTT, Paul C (At) 3131 Dale Dr Ne, Atlanta GA 30305 **S Andr's In-The-Pines Epis Ch Peachtree City GA 2007-** B Huntsville AL 1968 s Paul & Judith. BA Birmingham-Sthrn Coll 1990; MDiv GTS 1996. D 6/8/1996 P 12/1/1996 Bp Frank Kellogg Allan. m 5/4/2013 Allegra Maria Elliott c 5. S Mart In The Fields Ch Atlanta GA 1996-2002.

ELLIOTT III, Richard G (EC) 2322 Metts Ave, Wilmington NC 28403 **R S Andr's On The Sound Ch Wilmington NC 2002-** B Lexington KY 1953 s Richard & Virginia. BA Cntr Coll 1975; MDiv Sewanee: The U So, TS 1979. D 5/13/1979 Bp Addison Hosea P 5/19/1980 Bp William Arthur Beckham. m 8/28/1982 Giles Singleton c 2. R S Geo Ch Anderson SC 1995-2001; Chapl U Of Kentucky Lexington KY 1986-1995; Vic S Aug's Chap Lexington KY 1985-1995; Asst R S Mk's Epis Ch Venice FL 1983-1985; Cur H Trin Par Epis Clemson SC 1979-1983.

ELLIOTT, Robert James (O) 4141 Bayshore Blvd Apt 101, Tampa FL 33611 **Ret 1985-** B Coshocton OH 1924 s Frank & Ruby. BA Muskingum Coll 1953; Cert Bex Sem 1956; Accredited Int Spec 1990. D 6/23/1956 P 12/23/1956 Bp Nelson Marigold Burroughs. m 10/31/1981 Janis L Ford c 2. Int S Clem Epis Ch Tampa FL 1996-1997; Asst St Johns Epis Ch Tampa FL 1995-2005; Int All SS Ch Cleveland OH 1994-1995; Int Chr Epis Ch Warren OH 1992-1994; Int Ch Of The Epiph Euclid OH 1990-1992; Int S Ptr's Epis Ch Ashtabula OH 1989-1990; Int Gr Epis Ch Willoughby OH 1987-1988; S Mk's Ch Cleveland OH 1974-1984; R S Paul's Ch Marion OH 1961-1973; Chf Chapl St Hosp Toledo OH 1959-1961; Min in charge Gr Ch Galion OH 1956-1959. Auth, *Evang in the Epis Ch*, 1950. Natl Int Mnstry Ntwk 1987-1997.

ELLIOTT, Rodger Neil (Minn) 1262 Birch Pond Trail, White Bear Lake MN 55110 **Acquiring Ed Augsburg Fortress (ELCA Pub Hse) Minneapolis 2005-; Schlr in Res St. Paul's Ch on the Hill St. Paul MN 2005-** B Newton KS 1956 s Rodger & Mary. BA Pepperdine U 1978; MDiv PrTS 1983; PhD PrTS 1989; CAS SWTS 2002. D 6/15/2002 P 12/17/2002 Bp James Louis Jelinek. m 8/22/1998 Mary Ellen Elliott c 2. Chapl U Epis Cntr Minneapolis MN 2004-2005; U Epis Ch Minneapolis MN 2000-2004. Coeditor, "Documents and Images for the Study of Paul," Fortress Press, 2010; Auth, "Paul and Marxist Interp," *Paul in Postcolonial Perspective*, Forttress Press, 2010; Auth, "Ideology and the Chr Event," *S Paul's Journey into Philos*, Wipf & Stock, 2009; Auth, "The Arrogance of Nations: Reading Romans in the Shadow of Empire," Fortress Press, 2008; Auth, "A Famine of the Word: Stringfellowian Reflection," *The Bible in the Publ Sq*, Fortress Press, 2008; Auth, "The Bible and Empire," *The Peoples' Bible*, Fortress Press, 2008; Auth, "The Rhetoric of Romans," Sheffield 1990; Fortress Press, 2006; Auth, "Liberating Paul: The Justice of God and the Politics of the Apos," Orbis 1994; Fortress Press, 2005. Assn of Angl Biblic Scholars 1998; EPF 1990. Breaking the Silence Awd GLBT Prog Off, U MN 2005.

ELLIOTT, Scott Fuller (Chi) 2222 W Belmont Ave, # 205, Chicago IL 60618 **D S Greg's Epis Ch Deerfield IL 2012-** B Norfolk VA 1955 s George & Dorothy. AA Harper Cmnty Coll Palatine IL 1975; BA U of Iowa 1977. D 2/7/1998 Bp Herbert Alcorn Donovan Jr. m 5/21/2005 Cynthia Ann Cheski. D S Alb's Ch Chicago IL 2010-2012; D S Ptr's Epis Ch Chicago IL 1998-2010. CBS 2008; Soc of Cath Priests 2014.

ELLIOTT, William Tate (EMich) 6757 Middle Rd, Hope MI 48628 **Ret 1984-** B Detroit MI 1924 s Chester & Bessie. BA Wayne 1950; MDiv VTS 1951. D 7/7/1951 Bp Richard Stanley Merrill Emrich P 1/19/1952 Bp Russell S Hubbard. c 2. R S Jn's Epis Ch Midland MI 1960-1984; R Trin Epis Ch Flushing MI

1957-1960; S Paul's Epis Ch Gladwin MI 1951-1956; Vic Gr Epis Ch Standish MI 1951-1954. Auth, "25 Days to Christmas," *An Adv Journey*, Forw Mvmt, 2003; Auth, *The Forty Days of Lent*, Forw Mvmt, 2002.

ELLIS JR, Bill (Spok) 128 E 12th Ave, Spokane WA 99202 **Dn Cathd of St. Jn the Evang Spokane WA 2006-; Stndg Com Dio Spokane Spokane WA 2009-, Dep, GC 2008-, COM 2007-** B Portland OR 1954 s William. BA U of Oregon 1976; MDiv CDSP 1982. D 6/29/1982 P 5/25/1983 Bp Matthew Paul Bigliardi. m 6/24/1978 Beth Ellis c 2. Dn Cathd Of S Jn The Evang Spokane WA 2006-2017; R Trin Ch Bend OR 1992-2006; Vic S Bede's Ch Forest Grove OR 1984-1988; Vic Emm Ch Coos Bay OR 1982-1984; S Mary Ch Gardiner OR 1982-1984; COM Dio Estrn Oregon Cove OR 2002-2005, Dep, GC 1997-2006, Stndt Com 1994-2001; Dioc Coun Dio Oregon Portland OR 1990-1992. DD CDSP 2009; Phi Beta Kappa Alpha of Oregon Chapt 1976. bellis@stjohns-cathedral.org

ELLIS, Jane Fielding (Ala) 556 Mohave Cir, Huntington CT 06484 B Montgomery AL 1947 d Frank & Dorothy. BA Judson Coll 1970; MS Troy U 1976; Grad Spec U of Alabama 1985; MPA Auburn U 1987. D 12/9/2000 Bp Andrew Donnan Smith. D S Jn's Ch Bridgeport CT 2002-2005. Wmn Of dist Awd GSA 2002; Wmn Of Substance 2001; hon Soc Pi Sigma Alpha 1987; Outstanding Young Wmn Of Amer 1981; hon Soc Chi Delta Phi 1970. revdeaconjellis@gmail.com

ELLIS, Kassinda Rosalind Tabia (LI) **P-in-c S Jos's Ch Queens Vlg NY 2015-** B Long Island, NY 1979 d Randolph & Perpetua. BA Hofstra U 2001; MDiv SWTS 2005; MDiv SWTS 2005. D 1/25/2006 Bp Rodney Rae Michel P 6/14/2007 Bp Orris George Walker Jr. P-in-c Dio Long Island Garden City NY 2012-2015; P-in-c Ch Of S Thos Brooklyn NY 2009-2012; S Aug's Epis Ch Brooklyn NY 2006-2009; Bexley Seabury Fed Chicago IL 2002-2005.

ELLIS, Malcolm A (Md) 232 Saint Thomas Ln, Owings Mills MD 21117 **R S Thos' Ch Garrison Forest Owings Mills MD 2009-** B Durban Natal ZA 1951 s Leslie & Kathleen. DIT S Paul Theol Coll 1974; MDiv Chicago TS 1978; DMin Chicago TS 1979. Trans 7/1/1989 Bp Frank Tracy Griswold III. m 7/3/1976 Teresa A Ellis c 5. R S Lk's Epis Ch San Antonio TX 2002-2009; R Mssh Epis Ch S Paul MN 1994-2002; R S Mary's Epis Ch Palmetto FL 1990-1994; Assoc The Ch Of The H Sprt Lake Forest IL 1987-1990; Serv Ch Of So Afr 1974-1987.

ELLIS, Michael Elwin (Fla) 6126 Cherry Lake Dr N, Jacksonville FL 32258 **R St Fran in the Field 2005-; St Fran in the Field Ponte Vedra FL 2005-** B Cocoa FL 1951 s Basil & Doris. BS Florida St U 1976; MDiv SWTS 1981. D 6/7/1981 P 12/20/1981 Bp Frank S Cerveny. m 2/11/2006 Joan Barnwell Ellis c 2. S Eliz's Epis Ch Jacksonville FL 2004-2005; R S Barth's Ch Nashville TN 1999-2003; Epis Ch Of H Sprt Tallahassee FL 1985-1999; Ch Of The Epiph Jacksonville FL 1981-1985.

ELLIS, Michael Warren (Md) 4803 Leybourne Dr, Hilliard OH 43026 **Ret 1997-; Dio Sthrn Ohio Cincinnati OH 1997-** B Cambridge MA 1937 s Stanley & Frances. BA Pr 1959; STB GTS 1962; MSW Wayne 1973. D 6/23/1962 Bp Anson Phelps Stokes Jr P 6/1/1963 Bp George West Barrett. m 8/31/1963 Anice R Ellis c 2. R S Jn's Ch Frostburg MD 1988-1997; Supply P Dio Cntrl Pennsylvania Harrisburg PA 1974-1988; Asst Chr Ch Grosse Pointe Grosse Pointe Farms MI 1967-1968; S Jas Ch S Clair MO 1964-1967; R St. Jas Ch St. Clair MO 1964-1967; Cur Chr Ch Corning NY 1962-1964. Curs 1982-1997.

ELLIS, Nana Kwasi (Md) All Saints Episcopal Church, Po Box 279, Reisterstown MD 21136 B Accra Ghana 1962 s Benjamin & Helena. Trans 10/20/2016 as Priest Bp Eugene Taylor Sutton. m 9/16/2015 Elizabeth Nketia Ellis c 4.

ELLIS, Richard Alvin (Ct) 15 Piper Rd Apt J313, Scarborough ME 04074 **Ret 1992-** B Medford MA 1930 s Lewis & Doris. BA Dart 1952; MS Ya Berk 1955. D 2/23/1957 Bp Charles Francis Hall P 2/26/1958 Bp Robert McConnell Hatch. m 6/28/1958 Monica Ellis c 3. Chr Ch Harwinton CT 1974-1978; S Jn's Ch Pine Meadow CT 1971-1992; Dio Connecticut Meriden CT 1971-1981; Vic Ch Of The H Comm Lake View NY 1964-1970; Vic S Mart's Ch Pittsfield MA 1960-1964; Cur All SS Ch Worcester MA 1957-1960.

ELLIS, Russell Ray (Vt) 328 Shore Rd, Burlington VT 05408 **Ret 1992-** B Plymouth VT 1927 s Ray & Hyldanna. BA Lawr 1950; BD SWTS 1954; STM UTS 1965. D 6/19/1954 P 12/20/1954 Bp Gerald Francis Burrill. m 6/14/1955 Nancy E Ellis c 4. Headmaster Rock Point Sch 1969-1992; Rock Point Sch Burlington VT 1969-1992; R S Steph's Ch Middlebury VT 1956-1969; Cur S Paul's By The Lake Chicago IL 1954-1956. Phi Beta Kappa Lawr Coll.

ELLIS, Steven MacDonald (ECR) 1408 Beaumont St NW, Salem OR 97304 B Fresno CA 1951 s Donald & Virginia. BA California St U 1974; MDiv CDSP 1978. D 7/2/1978 P 6/1/1979 Bp Victor Manuel Rivera. m 2/22/2003 Robin K MacDonald c 4. R Epis Ch of St Jn the Bapt Aptos Aptos CA 1995-2015; R Epis Ch Of S Anne Stockton CA 1986-1995; Cur S Paul's Epis Ch Modesto CA 1978-1985. silleevets@gmail.com

ELLIS, Walter L (Tex) 2419 Lansing Cir, Pearland TX 77584 B McKinney TX 1941 s Erwin & Mary. BA U of No Texas 1964; MA U of No Texas 1966; MDiv VTS 1977; DMin Auston Presb TS 1993. D 6/17/1977 Bp Roger Howard Cilley P 6/12/1978 Bp James Milton Richardson. m 11/23/1960 Susan E Elder c 3. Chairman Ascen Epis Ch Endwmt Fund Houston TX 2008-2010; Bd Chair-

man Ascen Epis Sch Houston TX 2001-2010; R Ch Of The Ascen Houston TX 2001-2010; R S Chris's Ch League City TX 1982-2001; S Mich And All Ang' Epis Ch Longview TX 1977-1982; R S Mk's Ch Gladewater TX 1977-1979; Bd Mem Pastors Bd for W Houston Assistance Mnstry 2001-2010; Dioc Fin Com Dio Texas Houston TX 1998-1999, Dioc Stndg Com Pres 1998-1999, Dioc Curs Sec 1997-1998, Dioc Stndg Com 1996-1998, St. Vinc's Hse Bd Dir 1996-1997, Bp Quin Fndt Bd Dir 1990-1993, St. Jas Hse Bd Dir 1990-1992, Dioc Exec Bd 1989-2001, Liturg Cmsn 1989-1998, Dn Galveston Convoc 1989-1997, FA Coordntr 1987-1989, Camp Allen Bd Dir 1986-1990, St. Jas Hse Bd Dir 1984-1985, Dept of Evang and Renwl 1981-1984, Dept of Stwdshp 1978-1998; Bd Mem League City InterFaith Caring Mnstrs 1993-1994; Bd Mem and Pres Rotary Club of League City 1986-1990; Exec Bd & Advancement Chair Bay Area Coun of BSA 1983-1985. Auth, "Baptismal Study Text"; Auth, "Numerous Rel & Sci arts Baptismal Study Text". First Families of Tennessee 2016; Gnrl Soc of the War of 1812 2012; Loc Mnstrl Associations 1977-2010; Sons of the Amer Revolution 2011. Paul Harris Fellowowship Rotary Club of Westchase Houston 2009; Paul Harris Fellowowship Rotary Club of Space Cntr 1988; Skylab Med Team Grp Achievement Awd NASA Houston 1974; Apollo Achievement Awd NASA Houston 1969.

ELLIS, William Joseph (NwPa) 222 Brisbin St, Houtzdale PA 16651 **Vic - nonstipendiary Ch Of The H Trin Houtzdale PA 2008-** B Philipsburg PA 1951 s Joseph & Gail. Other; DNWPA Sch of Mnstry 2007. D 11/17/2006 Bp Arthur Williams Jr P 1/19/2008 Bp Sean Walter Rowe. m 5/15/1971 Donna Marie Ellis c 2.

ELLISON, Andrew Duncan (FtW) 4321 Us Highway 80 W, Marshall TX 75670 **Trin Ch Marshall TX 2016-** B 1983 s Dyke & Jeanne. Bachelor Texas Tech U 2007; Mstr Epis TS of the SW 2016. D 12/16/2015 Bp James Scott Mayer P 9/22/2016 Bp Rayford Baines High Jr. m 6/29/2007 Casie Fruin c 3.

ELLISON, Monique (Md) 6060 Charles Edward Terrace, Columbia MD 21045 **R S Chris Epis Ch Linthicum Hts MD 2011-; COM Dio Maryland Baltimore MD 2013-** B Wayne MI 1970 d James & Della. BS U of Detroit Mercy 1994; MDiv SWTS 2002. D 12/22/2001 P 6/27/2002 Bp Wendell Nathaniel Gibbs Jr. m 8/7/2014 Katrina Yvette Colleton. S Ptr's Ch Philadelphia PA 2005-2007; Asst S Paul's Epis Ch Lansing MI 2002-2005. rector@stchris.org

ELLISTON, Mark (NwPa) D 5/7/2017 Bp Sean Walter Rowe.

ELLSWORTH, Anne (Az) 6300 N Central Ave, Phoenix AZ 85012 **S Jas The Apos Epis Ch Tempe AZ 2016-** B Phoenix AZ 1976 d Barry & Loretta. BA Arizona St U 1999; MA Jesuit TS 2007; CAS CDSP 2015; CAS CDSP 2015. D 6/7/2014 P 12/13/2014 Bp Kirk Stevan Smith. m 1/20/2001 Matthew Jerome Ellsworth c 2. All SS Ch Phoenix AZ 2014-2016; Admin S Aug's Epis Ch Tempe AZ 2010-2013.

ELLSWORTH, Bradford Edwin (WMo) Po Box 160, Cabool MO 65689 **Vic Ch Of The Trsfg Mtn Grove MO 1997-** B Oakland CA 1939 s George & Edwina. U CA; BA U CA 1961; W Missouri Sch of Mnstry 1994. D 2/4/1995 P 8/31/1997 Bp John Clark Buchanan. m 6/13/1959 Jean Elaine Ellsworth. NAAD.

ELLSWORTH, Eleanor L (SanD) 2205 Caminito Del Barco, Del Mar CA 92014 **P-in-res St Jas By-The-Sea Epis Ch 2005-; Chapl Cathd of St Ptr & St Paul Washington DC 1993-** B Biloxi MS 1948 d John & Mary Eleanor. BA U of Tennessee 1970; MLS U of Tennessee 1972; MPA U of Tennessee 1976; MDiv VTS 1990. D 6/9/1990 P 12/9/1990 Bp Ronald Hayward Haines. c 2. S Thos Epis Ch Temecula CA 2016-2017; Assoc S Jas By The Sea La Jolla CA 2007-2016, 2005-2006; S Mary's Epis Sch Memphis TN 2000-2002; Sr Chapl & Dir Of Rel Stds S Mary's Epis Sch Memphis TN 2000-2002; Chr Ch Par Kensington MD 1996-1999; S Paul's Epis Par Pt Of Rocks MD 1995-1996; Assoc R & Chapl Chr Ch Prince Geo's Par Rockville MD 1990-1994. Auth, "Column Ed," *Journ Of Rehab*, 1983; Auth, "Motivation And Stff Dvlpmt," *Journ Of Libr Admin*, 1982; Auth, "Natl Rehab Info Cntr," *Rehab Journ/ Newsletters*, 1980; Auth, "Photograph," *Sch Libr Journ*, 1973. Cathd Fund (Chair: 1997)/ Washington Natl Cathd 1996-2000; Cath Fllshp Of The Epis Ch 1990-1994; Friends Of S Ben 1996; NAES, Bd Gvnr 2001; OSL (Chapl, 1997-8) 1996-1999; Sead 1990-1996. Shirley Olefson Awd Jr Members Round Table/ Amer Libr Assn 1972.

ELLSWORTH JR, Phillip C (Cal) 10033 River Rd, Potomac MD 20854 **S Steph's Par Bel Tiburon CA 2016-; Cler Supply S Jn's Ch Harbor Spgs MI 2003-** B El Paso TX 1959 s Phillip & Akiko. BA Wheaton Coll 1982; MA Wheaton Coll 1987; Dip Ya Berk 1995; MDiv Yale DS 1995. D 6/24/1995 Bp J Clark Grew II P 1/6/1996 Bp Craig Barry Anderson. m 6/28/1980 Victoria M Ellsworth c 4. Assoc R S Fran Ch Potomac MD 1998-2016; Assoc R St. Barth Ch New York NY 1995-1998. The Wolcott Calkins Prize Ya 1995. fr. ellsworth@ststephenschurch.org

ELLSWORTH, Scott Anthony (Ida) 2887 Snowflake Dr, Boise ID 83706 **D S Steph's Boise ID 1998-** B Mankato MN 1956 s Richard & Nancy. U MN; BS OR SU 1981. D 1/31/1998 Bp John Stuart Thornton. m 12/28/1981 Susan Ann Ellsworth c 3. COM Dio Idaho Boise ID 2003-2009. NAAD 1998.

ELMER-ANTHONY, Betty Lou (Ak) 11641 Hebron Dr, Eagle River AK 99577 **Ret 2007-; D H Sprt Epis Ch Eagle River AK 1998-** B San Diego CA 1929 d Joseph & Isabell. Anchorage Cmnty Coll; U of Alaska; EFM Sewa-

E

nee: The U So, TS 1986. D 6/1/1984 Bp George Clinton Harris. m 5/18/1990 Richard David Anthony c 3. D S Christophers Ch Anchorage AK 1984-1997; Chapl Alaska Native Med Cntr 1979-2003; Chapl Providence Extended Care 1979-2001. Auth, "We have a whale!," *Alaska mag*; Auth, "A Century of Faith: Centennial Commemorative, 1885-1995, Epis Dio Alaska," *Centennial Press*. Soc of S Anne and S Simeon 1992. Recognition of Dioconical Mnstry in the tradion of St. Steph (Represented Dio Alaska) NAAD 2010.

ELMIGER-JONES, Mary Kathleen (Cal) St Timothy's Church, 1550 Diablo Rd, Danville CA 94526 B Elizabeth NJ 1954 d Frederick & Margaret. BA Kean U 1977; BTh Sch for Deacons - Berkeley 2011. D 6/2/2012 Bp Marc Handley Andrus. m 8/18/1979 Matthew T Jones c 1.

ELPHEE, David T (SwVa) B Melbourne Australia 1939 s Leon & Iva. Case Wstrn Reserve U; St U of NY at Delhi; BA U So 1960; M Div GTS 1965. D 6/12/1965 Bp Beverley D Tucker P 12/21/1965 Bp Nelson Marigold Burroughs. m 4/27/2013 Nancy Harris c 3. Dir of Mus Third Presb Ch Staunton VA 1994-2014; Org & Chrmstr Gr Memi Ch Port Republic VA 1988-1994; Trin Ch Staunton VA 1982-1987; S Jn's Ch Delhi NY 1972-1982; Cler Dir Curs of SW VA 1987-1988. AGO 2011-2013; Pi Gamma Mu 1959.

ELSBERRY, Terence Lynn (NY) PO Box 293, Bedford NY 10506 **Bd Mem Epis Charties New York NY 1998-; Bd Mem Epis Chars of the Dio NY New York NY 1999-; Bd Mem The Woodland Fndt 1999-** B Marshalltown IA 1943 s Lynn & Adaline. BA Drake U 1966; MDiv VTS 1984. D 5/26/1984 Bp Walter Cameron Righter P 12/16/1984 Bp William Foreman Creighton. m 11/23/1989 Nancy O Elsberry c 2. R S Matt's Ch Bedford NY 1994-2015; Sr Assoc R Chr Ch Greenwich CT 1986-1994; Asst Min S Jn's Ch Lafayette Sq Washington DC 1984-1986. Auth, "The Power of Doing the Rt Thing"; Auth, "The Bible in 60 Minutes," *Bk*; Auth, "The Power of Doing the Rt Thing," *Bk*; Auth, "The Bible in 60 Minutes," *Bk*; Auth, "Marie of Romania," *Bk*. Annual Epis Dio New York Awd for outstanding Serv to the Dio Epis Dio New York 2009; cl Gregorian U 2004.

ELSE, John David (Pgh) 272 Caryl Dr, Pittsburgh PA 15236 **Non-par 1988-** B Pittsburgh PA 1933 s Harry & Esther. BS Penn 1955; Nash 1965. D 5/22/1965 Bp William S Thomas P 12/18/1965 Bp Austin Pardue. m 6/6/1953 Patricia Else c 3. Supply The Ch Of The Adv Jeannette PA 2005-2012; Supply S Jn's Epis Ch Donora PA 2000-2005; Emer Dir Cntr For Sprtlty In 12-Step Recovery Pittsburgh PA 1988-2008; Consult Trin Cathd Pittsburgh PA 1984-1988; Addictions Ther/ Consult Addictions Ther/ Consult 1970-1988; Min In Charge S Geo's Ch Waynesburg PA 1965-1970; S Thos' Epis Ch Canonsburg PA 1965-1968. Auth, "Recovering Recovery, Journ Of Mnstry In Addiction And Recovery," *Volume 6 (2)*, 1999; Auth, "In Giving We Rescue: The View From Russia, Journ Of Mnstry In Addiction And Recovery," *Volume 1 (2)*, 1994; Auth, "Life Is A Journey Back Hm," *Centering*, 1993; Auth, "Two Plus Two Equals One," *Chem People Inst*, 1984. Pres Of NECAD 1985-1987.

ELSENSOHN, David Dirk (Ak) 1714 Edgecumbe Dr, Sitka AK 99835 B Portland OR 1948 s Harold & Patricia. BA Marylhurst U 1988; Cert Marylhurst U 1988; Cert Dio AK Prog Juneau AK 1993; MDiv Vancouver TS CA 2001. D 4/11/1993 P 12/6/1993 Bp Steven Charleston. m 3/14/1981 Bonnie M Elsensohn c 2. Bd Mem Sitka Counslg and Prevention Serv 2008-2011; Chapl U.S. Coast Gurad Air Sta Sitka Alaska 2008-2011; Pres Brave Hart Vol (Vol respite care org.) 2001-2006; Pres Sitka Mnstrl Assn Sitka Alaska 1996-1998; R S Ptr's By-The-Sea Sitka AK 1995-2011; Asst to R The Ch Of The H Trin Juneau AK 1993-1995; Tutor in the M.Div. Progam Vancouver TS 2001-2006; Dep to GC Dio Alaska Fairbanks AK 1999-2011, Pres Stndg Com 1996-2008.

ELVIN, Peter Thurston (WMass) 35 Park St, Williamstown MA 01267 **S Jn's Ch Williamstown MA 1978-** B Cranston RI 1947 s Arthur & Margaret. BA Trin Hartford CT 1969; MDiv GTS 1973. D 6/16/1973 Bp Frederick Hesley Belden P 1/5/1974 Bp Conrad H Gesner. m 6/22/1974 Diana M Elvin c 2. Dep Gc Dio Wstrn Massachusetts Springfield 1988-2000, Dn 1988-1994, Com 1985-1995, Bec 1983-1990, Chair Ce Cmsn 1979-1982; R S Lk's Ch Worcester MA 1978-1986; R S Phil's Ch Easthampton MA 1976-1978; Asst S Andr's Ch Longmeadow MA 1973-1976.

ELWELL, Pamela (SO) 321 East Kanawha Ave, Columbus OH 43214 **D S Steph's Epis Ch And U Columbus OH 2006-** B Richmond VA 1941 d Horace & Isabel. BA W&M 1963; MLS Case Wstrn Reserve U 1970. D 5/13/2006 Bp Kenneth Lester Price. m 8/24/1963 William Edwin Elwell c 2.

ELWOOD, Frederick Campbell (Mich) 1334 Riverside Dr, Buhl ID 83316 B Wichita KS 1948 s Harold & Mary. BA Wichita St U 1970; MA U CA 1975; MDiv GTS 1979; STM GTS 1988. D 6/23/1979 P 1/12/1980 Bp Robert Claflin Rusack. m 5/29/1971 Alice A Akin c 2. Chapl St. Lk's Magic Vlly Reg Med Cntr Twin Falls 2011-2017; R S Jas Epis Ch Birmingham MI 2001-2011; R S Jn's Epis Ch Olympia WA 1993-2001; R S Andr's Epis Ch Staten Island NY 1991-1993; R Ch Of The Ascen Twin Falls ID 1988-1991, R 1982-1988; Assoc S Paul's Epis Ch Ventura CA 1979-1982; Chld's Trust Fund Bd St of Idaho 1985-1990. Auth, "Sharing Biblic Dialogues: Lectionary Readings for Groups," *Sharing Biblic Dialogues: Lectionary Readings for Groups*, Ch Pub, 2002; Auth, "In the Shadows of H Week: The Off of Tenebrae," *In the Shadows of H Week: The Off of Tenebrae*, Ch Pub, 1996.

ELWOOD, Richard Hugh (Tex) 308 E San Antonio St, Fredericksburg TX 78624 **R S Barn Epis Ch Fredricksburg TX 2004-** B Fort Riley KS 1939 s Ernest & Madeline. BA Baylor U 1961; BD Sewanee: The U So, TS 1966. D 6/26/1966 Bp James Milton Richardson P 6/6/1967 Bp Frederick P Goddard. m 8/10/1990 Ellen Jane Elwood c 2. S Fran Ch Houston TX 2012-2016; S Mart's Epis Ch Houston TX 2000-2005; S Mk's Ch Beaumont TX 1984-2000; Bd Trst S Steph Sch Austin TX 1980-1984; Ch Of The Gd Shpd Kingwood TX 1979-1984; R Palmer Memi Ch Houston TX 1977-1979, Asst 1966-1970; R Chr Epis Ch Tyler TX 1971-1977; Chapl S Jos's Chap at the Kent Sch Kent CT 1970-1971. Auth, "Mart in the Narthex by Mart the Dog," *Shearer Pub*, 2011; Auth, "Rel Column Kingwood Observer". Moonbeam Chld's Bk Awd Indep Pub Assn of Amer 2011; Moonbeam Chld's Bk Awd Indep Pub Assn of Amer 2011. relwood@sfch.org

ELY, Elizabeth Wickenberg (NC) Dunwyck, 64 Peniel Road, Columbus NC 28722 B Columbia SC 1953 d Charles & Margaret. BA Agnes Scott Coll 1975; MS Col 1976; MDiv GTS 1989; PhD GTF 2012; PhD GTF 2013. D 5/19/1989 Bp Allen Lyman Bartlett Jr P 5/23/1990 Bp Huntington Williams Jr. m 6/14/1984 Duncan C Ely c 1. Cn for Reg Mnstry Dio No Carolina Raleigh NC 2009-2014, GC Deputation Chair 2010-2014, Suffr Com Search Com Secy 1995-1996, Dioc Coun Secy 1993-1996, COM, Secy 1991-1996; Vic S Phil's Epis Ch Greenville SC 2000-2009; Bereavement Coordntr Luth Hospice Greer SC 2000-2003; Instr U of So Carolina Upstate Spartanburg SC 2000-2003; Assoc R Ch Of The Adv Spartanburg SC 1996-2000; S Pat's Epis Ch Mooresville NC 1994-1995, Vic 1992-1993; Vic All SS Epis Ch Charlotte NC 1993-1995; Assoc R S Jn's Epis Ch Charlotte NC 1989-1992; Prov IV, Eccl Crt Epis Ch Cntr New York NY 2009-2012, GBEC Ed 2005-; Dn of Reedy River Convoc Dio Upper So Carolina Columbia SC 2000-2004, Dioc Coun 1999-2003, Dioc BEC 1998-2009, GC Dep 1998-2009, Dioc Cmncatns Com Chair 1998-2000, Stndg Com, Pres 1998-1999, Stdng Com Pres 1997. Auth, "Chrsnty and Politics: A Consideration of Apartheid," *Fndt Theol Monograph 2009*, GTF, 2009; Auth, "It's Your Turn to Carry the Chld," *Preaching as the Art of Sacr Conversation: Sermons that Wk VI*, Morehouse, 1997; Auth, "A Manual for Eucharistic Visitors," Morehouse, 1991. ECom 1997-2000. Oxford Fndt Fell GTF 1999; Sewanee Fell U So 1999.

ELY, James Everett (Tex) 1700 Golden Ave, Bay City TX 77414 B Stillwater OK 1946 s Delbert & Lohoma. BS U of Missouri 1978; MD U of Missouri 1983. D 2/3/2002 Bp Claude Edward Payne P 11/16/2002 Bp Don Adger Wimberly. m 6/28/1968 Linda Louise Ely c 3.

✠ **ELY, The Rt Rev Thomas C** (Vt) 11 Rock Point Rd, Burlington VT 05408 **Bp of Vermont Dio Vermont Burlington VT 2001-** B Norwalk CT 1951 s Leonard & Shirley. BA Wstrn Connecticut St U 1976; MDiv Sewanee: The U So, TS 1980. D 6/14/1980 Bp Morgan Porteus P 12/13/1980 Bp Arthur Edward Walmsley Con 4/28/2001 for Vt. m 5/22/1976 Martha A Wiggins c 2. Mssnr Grtr Hartford Reg Mnstry Grtr Hartford Reg Mnstry E Hartford CT 1991-2001; Dir of Yth Mnstrs Dio CT Dio Connecticut Meriden CT 1985-1991, 1980; Asst Mssnr Middlesex Area Cluster Mnstry Middlesex Area Cluster Mnstry Higganum CT 1981-1984; Trst EDS Cambridge MA 2009-2014. CB Open 2005; Cranmer Cup 2000; LAND 1981; Living Stones 2001; Porter Cup 2001. Cranmer Cup Captain Cranmer Cup USA 2006; Wall of hon Norwalk HS 2002; Hon Doctorate of Mnstry U So 2002. tely@dioceseofvermont.org

EMANUEL, Philip Grantham (Nev) PO Box 990, Pawleys Island SC 29585 B Lancaster SC 1956 s Philip & Gloria. BA Furman U 1978; MDiv The Luth TS 1987. Rec 5/8/2011 as Priest Bp Dan Thomas Edwards. c 1.

EMBLER, Liz (ETenn) **S Paul's Ch New Orleans LA 2017-; Sewanee U So TS Sewanee TN 2016-** D 2/11/2017 Bp George Young III.

EMENHEISER, David Edward (WMich) 174 Wakulat Ln, Traverse City MI 49686 B Hanover PA 1941 s Paul & Esther. BA U So 1963; MDiv GTS 1966. D 4/16/1966 P 10/18/1966 Bp Francis W Lickfield. m 6/11/1966 Ann Emenheiser c 2. R Gr Epis Ch Traverse City MI 1994-2007; R H Trin Epis Ch Wyoming MI 1976-1994; S Jn's Epis Ch Kewanee IL 1975-1976; Dio Quincy Peoria IL 1974-1976, 1966-1972; H Trin Epis Ch Geneseo IL 1974-1976; Sabbatical Washington DC 1972-1974; Vic Trin Epis Ch Monmouth IL 1969-1972; Vic S Fran Epis Ch Chillicothe IL 1966-1969; S Jn's Ch Henry IL 1966-1969.

EMERSON, Angela Angela (Vt) Gates Briggs Blgd. Ste. 315, White River Junction VT 05001 B Knoxville TN 1952 d Samuel & Elmarie. BA U of Tennessee 1974; JD Woodrow Wilson Coll of Law 1977; MDiv Epis TS of the SW 2006. D 12/21/2005 P 6/25/2006 Bp J Neil Alexander. Min of Stwdshp Dvlpmt Dio Vermont Burlington VT 2008-2015; Cur and Sch Chapl Epis Par Of S Mich And All Ang Tucson AZ 2006-2007. Lettie Pate Whitehead Evans Awd for Lay Ldrshp VTS 2001. aemerson@dioceseofvermont.org

EMERSON, James Carson 1625 Hershey Ct, Columbia MO 65202 B Quincy IL 1939 s James & Dorothy. BA U of Missouri 1962; MDiv VTS 1969; Ldrshp Acad for New Directions 1984. D 6/21/1969 Bp Lauriston L Scaife P 12/21/1969 Bp Harold Barrett Robinson. Vic S Jas Epis Ch Griggsville IL 1996-1999; Cn to the Ordnry Dio Quincy Peoria IL 1988-1995, Dioc Healthcare Mssn Co-ordntr/Chapl 1987-1995; R S Ptr's Ch Canton IL 1985-1995; Vic S Andr's Ch Hays Hays KS 1982-1985; Admin Arnold M. Lewis Conf Cntr Dio Wstrn

Kansas 1980-1985; Vic Dio Wstrn Kansas Hutchinson KS 1980-1985; S Eliz's Ch Russell KS 1980-1985; Vic Dio W Missouri Kansas City MO 1973-1980; Chapl Marshall St Sch/Hosp Marshall MO 1973-1980; S Mary's Ch Fayette MO 1973-1980; Trin Epis Ch Marshall MO 1973-1980; S Andr's Ch Newfane Burt NY 1971-1973; Vic S Jn's Ch Wilson NY 1971-1973; Chapl Chld's Hosp Buffalo NY 1969-1971; Cur S Jn's Gr Ch Buffalo NY 1969-1971. Alum Recognition Awd Missouri Chapt of Delta Upsilon Intl Fraternity 2010; Man-Of-Yr Finalist Russell Cnty Ks 1983.

EMERSON, Jason Daniel (Neb) 9932 Bedford Ave., Omaha NE 68134 **R Ch Of The Resurr Omaha NE 2009-** B Corinth MS 1976 s Isaac & Eula. BA Middle Tennessee St U 1999; MA U Cinc 2001; MDiv GTS 2005. D 5/30/2005 P 1/21/2006 Bp Joe Goodwin Burnett. m 6/12/2004 Jodie L Emerson. Assoc All SS Epis Ch Omaha NE 2007-2009; Min for Yth and YA Dio Nebraska Omaha NE 2005-2007.

EMERSON, Keith Roger (SVa) St. Paul's Church, 213 N. Main Street, Suffolk VA 23434 **R S Paul's Epis Ch Suffolk VA 2007-** B Pittsburgh PA 1959 s Roger & Jane. BA Grove City Coll 1982; Gordon-Conwell TS 1985; MDiv VTS 1987; DMin Un Theol Seminaunion TS & Presbyt 2005. D 6/27/1987 P 5/13/1988 Bp James Russell Moodey. c 2. R Epiph Epis Ch Richmond VA 1997-2007; R S Jn's Ch Keokuk IA 1993-1997; Asst Chr Ch Epis Hudson OH 1989-1993; Asst S Ptr's Epis Ch Lakewood OH 1987-1989.

EMERSON, Mary Beth (Va) 8991 Brook Rd, McLean VA 22102 B Newark NJ 1955 d Joseph & Christina. MA U GA 1986; Cert Epis Sem of the SW 2002; Advncd Certification Epis TS of the SW 2003; Diac Formation Inst Dio Virginia 2010. D 2/5/2011 Bp Shannon Sherwood Johnston. m 5/20/1983 Warren K Emerson c 3. Fam Mnstry S Thos Epis Ch Mclean VA 2012-2017; D Trin Ch Arlington VA 2010-2012.

EMERSON, Richard Clark (ECR) 1412 Maysun Ct, Campbell CA 95008 **Asst S Lk's Ch Los Gatos CA 1985-** B Los Angeles CA 1945 s George & Irma. AA Foothill Coll 1964; BA San Jose St U 1966; Cert San Jose St U 1967; MDiv CDSP 1972. D 6/24/1972 P 1/6/1973 Bp George Richard Millard. Asst St Johns Pro-Cathd Los Angeles CA 1976-1985; Asst S Fran' Par Palos Verdes Estates CA 1972-1976.

EMERY, Dana Karen (Minn) 1400 Corbett Rd, Detroit Lakes MN 56501 B Fargo ND 1947 d Marvin & Helen Marie. BA U MN 1988; Cert Engl Sch of Gardening 1996; MDiv Untd TS of the Twin Cities 2008. D 12/11/2008 P 6/27/2009 Bp James Louis Jelinek. m 8/12/1967 John Richard Emery c 3.

EMERY, Harold Alfred (SVa) 2363 Chapel Ridge Pl Apt 2B, Salina KS 67401 **Ret 1997-** B Scranton PA 1932 s Harold & Ellen. BA Un Coll Barbourville KY 1953; STB PDS 1960. D 6/16/1960 P 12/22/1960 Bp Frederick Warnecke. m 1/13/2007 Karen Anne Emery c 5. Cntrl Mecklenburg Cure Chase City VA 1992-1997; Gr Epis Ch Drakes Branch VA 1992-1997; R S Jn's Epis Ch Chase City VA 1992-1997; S Tim's Epis Ch Clarksville VA 1992-1997; R S Phil's Ch Coraopolis PA 1982-1992; S Fran Cmnty Serv Inc. Salina KS 1974-1982; R S Jn's Epis Ch Bellefonte PA 1968-1973; Asst Ch Of The Gd Samar Paoli PA 1962-1965; In-C Epis Par Of S Mk And S Jn Jim Thorpe PA 1960-1962.

EMGE, Kevin Ray (Ia) **D S Paul's Epis Ch Grinnell IA 2012-** B 1959 Mstr of Arts in Mnstry Nash 2015. D 7/1/2012 Bp Alan Scarfe. Ord of St. Lukes 2012; Recovery Mnstrs of the Epis Ch 2012; Soc of Cath Priests 2012.

EMMERT, John Howard (CPa) 648 Laurel View Dr., Manheim PA 17545 **Ch Consult Samar Counslg Cntr 2012-; Wellness Initiative Co-Ldr Dio Cntrl Pennsylvania Harrisburg PA 2011-, Stndg Com 1998-2011; Cler Colleagues Grp Mentor Samar Counslg Cntr 2011-** B Kendallville IN 1941 s Howard & E Gwendolyn. Frgn Stdt U of Madrid 1962; BA U MI 1963; MDiv VTS 1970; DMin Palmer TS 1995. D 6/29/1970 Bp George P Gunn P 5/1/1971 Bp David Shepherd Rose. m 12/19/1964 Kathryn Klontz Emmert c 2. R S Jn's Epis Ch Lancaster PA 1996-2004; R Old Donation Ch Virginia Bch VA 1985-1996; Asst Galilee Epis Ch Virginia Bch VA 1980-1985; Campus Min Longwood/Hampden-Sydney Colls Farmville VA 1975-1980; P-in-c Ch Of The Epiph - Luth Valdez AK 1973-1975; Wm & Mary Dio Sthrn Virginia Newport News VA 1970-1980, GC Dep 1987-1994; Bruton Par Williamsburg VA 1970-1973; Chapl Wm & Mary Williamsburg VA 1970-1973. Lifetime Distinguished Serv Dio Cntrl PA 2013; Acad Fell ECF 2013.

EMPSALL, Glenda Mascarella (Spok) 501 E Wallace Ave, Coeur D Alene ID 83814 B 1954 BS U of Arizona 1976; MS MIS U of Arizona 1983. D 10/19/2014 Bp James E Waggoner Jr. m 5/6/1978 John S Empsall.

EMRICH III, Frederick Ernest (WMass) 7 Smith St, P.O. Box 318, North Haven ME 04853 **Assoc All Ang By The Sea Longboat Key FL 2010-; S Paul's Epis Ch No Andover MA 2002-** B Boston MA 1940 s Richard & Beatrice. BA Harv 1961; BD EDS 1968. D 6/22/1968 Bp Anson Phelps Stokes Jr P 5/1/1969 Bp Richard Stanley Merrill Emrich. m 6/7/2008 Diana Cable c 4. Brooks Sch Chap No Andover MA 2002-2008; Sch Min Brooks Sch No Andover MA 2002-2008; Sch Min Trin-Pawling Sch Pawling NY 1999-2002; Ch Of The H Trin Pawling NY 1999-2000; Dio Wstrn Massachusetts Springfield 1987-1998; R S Jas' Ch Greenfield MA 1987-1998; R Trin Ch Washington DC 1982-1987; R Ch Of The Gd Shpd Reading MA 1971-1982; Cur S Ptr's Ch Beverly MA 1968-1971.

EMRICH III, Richard S M (Chi) 755 Hinchman Rd, Baroda MI 49101 B Boston MA 1938 s Richard & Beatrice. BA Harvard Coll 1960; JD The U MI Law Sch 1964; MDiv SWTS 1992. D 6/27/1992 Bp Richard Stanley Merrill Emrich P 1/10/1993 Bp Henry Irving Mayson. m 1/22/1980 Mary Emrich c 3. R Chr Ch River Forest IL 2006-2007; R Zion Ch Rome NY 1994-2002; Asst To Dn Cathd Ch Of S Paul Detroit MI 1992-1994.

EMRY, Anne D (Ore) 1444 Liberty St SE, Salem OR 97302 **R S Paul's Epis Ch Salem OR 2014-** B Greenwich CT 1958 d Tibo & Nancy. BA NWU 1980; MDiv CDSP 2010. D 6/5/2010 Bp Marc Handley Andrus P 1/8/2011 Bp M(Arvil) Thomas Shaw. m 7/31/1988 Steve Emry. Cur Ch Of S Jn The Evang Hingham MA 2010-2014.

ENCARNACION-CARABALLO, Felix Antonio (DR) C/Santiago 114, Santo Iomingo Dominican Republic **Dio The Dominican Republic (Iglesia Epis Dominicana) Gazcue Santo Domingo 2000-** B La Romana 1966 D 4/10/1999 P 5/13/2000 Bp Julio Cesar Holguin-Khoury. m 8/29/1998 Berkys Herrera c 3.

ENCINOSA, Christina (SeFla) 68 Paxford Ln, Boynton Beach FL 33426 B Miami FL 1978 d Jose & Dolores. BA U of Miami 1999; MDiv GTS 2004. D 4/17/2004 P 10/17/2004 Bp Leo Frade. m 5/14/2011 Gerhardt Meyer Witt. P-in-c Ch Of The H Redeem Lake Worth FL 2004-2015. Ch And Soc Prize The GTS 2004.

ENDICOTT, Rachel Faith (Oly) 15114 SE 48th Dr., Bellevue WA 98006 **R Chr Epis Ch Puyallup WA 2016-, P-in-c 2014-2015** B London UK 1963 d Oliver & Yvonne. BA Scripps Coll 1985; MBA Natl U 1987; MDiv VTS 1997. D 6/14/1997 P 12/21/1997 Bp Gethin Benwil Hughes. m 7/20/2012 Gary T Irvin c 5. Int Chr Ch Seattle WA 2012-2014; Assoc R Trin Par Seattle WA 2006-2009; Int S Alb's Ch Edmonds WA 2005-2006; Visitation Pstr Cross Of Chr ELCA Ch Bellevue WA 2003-2006; Assoc R S Marg's Epis Ch Bellevue WA 1997-2003. Auth, "The Many Faces Of Rachel," *Wmn Uncommon Prayers: Our Lives Revealed, Nurtured, Celebrated*, Morehouse Pub, 2000.

ENGDAHL JR, Frederick Robert (Mich) 6490 Clarkston Rd., Clarkston MI 48346 B Escanaba MI 1956 s Frederick & Margaret. BS Cntrl Michigan U 1980; LTh SWTS 1983; MDiv SWTS 1985. D 6/29/1985 Bp H Coleman Mcgehee Jr P 12/15/1985 Bp Frank S Cerveny. m 6/21/1980 Gail Engdahl c 2. Ch Of The Resurr Clarkston MI 2008-2009; S Lk's Ch Marietta OH 2005-2008; R Gr Ch Rice Lake WI 2000-2005; R S Mk's Epis Ch Aberdeen SD 1997-1998; S Mk's Ch Lake City MN 1994-1997; Non-par 1991-1993; R S Paul's Epis Ch S Clair MI 1989-1991; R S Steph's Baker City OR 1987-1989; Asst Chr Epis Ch Ponte Vedra FL 1985-1987.

ENGELHARDT, Hanns Christian Joachim (Eur) Stephanienstrasse, 72, Karlsruhe 76133 Germany B Frankfurt on Main Germany 1934 s Christian & Clara. DR. IUR. Goethe U 1961. D 6/7/1999 P 6/17/2000 Bp Jeffery William Rowthorn. m 12/4/1981 Rosa Maria Engelhardt c 2. Eccl Law Soc 1992. PRIEST@ST-COLUMBAN.DE

ENGELHORN, Paula Elaine (Chi) B 1939 BA Long Bch St U 1962; Grad year Long Bch St U 1963; MA Sonoma St U 1980; MDiv Epis TS of the SW 2011; MDiv Sem of the SW 2011. D 5/11/2011 P 12/10/2011 Bp John Clark Buchanan. m 7/13/1963 John Robert Engelhorn c 2.

ENGELS, Allen Robert (Colo) 3081 Evanston Ave, Grand Junction CO 81504 **Assoc St. Matthews Epis Ch Grand Jct CO US 2010-** B Martinez CA 1939 s Allen & Ann. Cmnty Coll of Af; Other 2004; EFM U So 2004. D 1/22/2000 P 7/29/2000 Bp William Jerry Winterrowd. m 6/16/1962 Carolyn Beatrice Engels c 3. P Ch Of The Nativ Grand Jct CO 2000-2007.

ENGELS, Jimichael (Mass) 1190 Adams St Apt 213, Dorchester Center MA 02124 B Salt Lake City UT 1936 s Kenneth & Rebecca. BA Dart 1958; MA U Tor 1963; Nash 1967; MDiv U Tor CA 1968. D 9/7/1968 P 3/8/1969 Bp Francis E I Bloy. m 11/22/2014 Manoel Airton Ximenes-Engels c 4. Gr Ch Everett MA 1998-2002; Supply P Dio Massachusetts Boston MA 1991-1997; St Johns Ch Taunton MA 1989-1992; R S Jn The Evang Mansfield MA 1989-1991; Int S Jn's Epis Ch Preemption IL 1988-1989; Trin Ch Muscatine IA 1985-1987; R S Steph's Par Whittier CA 1977-1985; Serv Ch In New Zealand 1975-1977; Assoc S Jas Par Los Angeles CA 1972-1975; P-in-c Ch Of The Ang Pasadena CA 1970-1972; Chapl (Capt) US-Army 1969-1978; Cur All SS Par Long Bch CA 1968-1970. ,Auth, Verse Drama, "GOD's Mantra, Steps to Paradise, A Circular Song," *GOD's Mantra, Steps to Paradise, A Circular Song*, Self-Pub, 1997.

ENGFER, Michael John (Nev) 4201 W Washington Ave, Las Vegas NV 89107 **All SS Epis Ch Las Vegas NV 2015-** B Tacoma WA 1972 s Oscar & Virginia. DMin The Luth TS; BS Summit U 1995; MDiv Summit U 2002. D 10/24/2015 P 11/19/2016 Bp Dan Thomas Edwards. m 10/14/2011 Katherine Alison Ramer c 4. priest@allsaintslv.com

ENGLAND, Edward Gary (ETenn) 408 Oak Ave, South Pittsburg TN 37380 **Dir and Vice-Pres Marion Cnty Cmnty Mnstrs 2001-** B Springfield IL 1939 s Edward & Pauline. BS Georgia St U 1967. D 1/7/2006 Bp Charles Glenn VonRosenberg. m 6/15/1963 Virginia Stanley c 3.

ENGLAND, Gary William (Ky) 7404 Arrowwood Rd, Louisville KY 40222 B Birmingham AL 1952 s William & Laura. BS U of Alabama 1974; MA U of Alabama 1975; JD Cumberland Sch of Law at Samford U 1981. D 9/27/2011 Bp Terry Allen White. m 11/11/1989 Maria Nicolette Sorolis c 3.

ENGLAND, Loy David (WTex) Po Box 1025, Pflugerville TX 78691 **Ret 1988-** B Texarkana AR 1931 s Loy & Natalie. BS U of Arkansas 1953; MDiv Epis TS of the SW 1960; MA U of Texas 1966. D 6/6/1974 Bp Harold Cornelius Gosnell P 12/1/1974 Bp Richard Earl Dicus. m 12/31/1955 Margaret Penelope Carsen. P-in-c S Mich And All Ang Epis Ch Blanco TX 1974-1988. Auth, "Var Tech arts". Apwa.

ENGLAND, Margaret Jefferson (Az) 11058 Portobelo Dr, San Diego CA 92124 B Liverpool UK 1930 d Herbert & Margaret. Cert Avery Hill Coll 1955; Lon GB 1955; Cert Westminster Coll 1955; Cert Theol Stud Claremont TS 1980. D 11/7/1992 Bp Robert Reed Shahan. m 4/5/1958 James Norman England c 2. D S Dav's Epis Ch San Diego CA 1998-1999; D S Steph's Ch Scottsdale AZ 1993-1998; S Steph's Ch Phoenix AZ 1993-1997. SCHC 1982.

ENGLAND, Nicholas B (SO) 134 N Broad St, Lancaster OH 43130 B Lancaster OH 1950 s Harold & Janet. D 6/6/2015 Bp Thomas Edward Breidenthal. m 6/26/1976 Joan Marie England c 5.

ENGLAND JR, Nick Arnold (WVa) 411 Prichard St, Williamson WV 25661 **P S Pauls Epis Ch Williamson WV 2005-, D 2004-2005; P St. Paul's Epis Ch Williamson WV 2005-** B Pikeville KY 1945 s Nick & Nanna. BS Pikeville Coll 1968; DMD U of Louisville 1977. D 11/22/2004 P 11/5/2005 Bp William Michie Klusmeyer. m 5/21/1983 Mary Jane England c 3.

ENGLAND, Otis Bryan (WMo) 315 E Partridge Ave, Independence MO 64055 B Mammoth Sprg AR 1949 s Otis & Lola. Weatherford Coll 1974; BA U of Texas at Arlington 1976; MA U of Texas at Arlingrton 1981. D 4/10/1994 Bp Chris Christopher Epting. m 8/16/1986 Linda Marie England c 2. D Gr And H Trin Cathd Kansas City MO 2003-2010; Chapl Missouri St Highway Patrol Lee's Summit MO 2002-2010; Chapl Bettendorf Police Dept Bettendorf IA 1998-2001; D Chr Epis Ch Clinton IA 1998-2000; D S Ptr's Ch Bettendorf IA 1994-2002; S Alb's Ch Davenport IA 1994-1998; COM Dio W Missouri Kansas City MO 2006-2010; COM Dio Iowa Des Moines IA 1996-2001. Assn for Epis Deacons 1994; Intl Conf of Police Chapl 1998-2010.

ENGLE, Cynthia L (Tex) 414 E. McAlpine, Navasota TX 77868 **S Fran Of Assisi Epis Prairie View TX 2011-; P S Paul's Ch Navasota TX 2011-** B Waco TX 1953 d Harvey & Neal. BMus Texas A&M U 1983; MDiv TESM 1995; PhD U of Cambridge 2006. D 12/6/2008 Bp Kirk Stevan Smith P 12/9/2009 Bp Dena Arnall Harrison. c 2. D S Mk's Ch Beaumont TX 2009-2011; Adult Educ Dir Chr Ch Of The Ascen Paradise Vlly AZ 2008-2009; Asst Gd Shpd Of The Hills Cave Creek AZ 1995-1997. cynthiaengle13@gmail.com

ENGLE SR, Mark Christoph (NMich) 22975 Pine Lake Rd, Battle Creek MI 49014 B Denver CO 1948 s Vernon & Catharine. BA Alma Coll 1970; MDiv SWTS 1973; DMin Sewanee: The U So, TS 1982. D 5/19/1973 Bp Charles Ellsworth Bennison Jr P 1/26/1974 Bp Charles Bennison Sr. m 3/20/1970 Sharon Engle c 3. S Andr's Ch Lexington KY 2000-2007; S Paul's Ch Marquette MI 1988-2006; S Paul's Jeffersonvlle IN 1981-1988; Cn S Paul's Cathd Buffalo NY 1978-1981; Chapl S Andr's Sch TN 1975-1978; S Andr's-Sewanee Sch Sewanee TN 1975-1978; Chapl Kemper Hall Kenosha WI 1974-1975; Cur S Lk's Par Kalamazoo MI 1973-1974.

ENGLEBY, Matt (NJ) 379 Mount Harmony Rd, Bernardsville NJ 07924 **Exec Coun Appointees New York NY 2011-** B Roanoke VA 1962 s Jane. BA U So 1984; MDiv GTS 1991. D 6/9/1991 Bp Arthur Edward Walmsley P 5/1/1992 Bp Allen Lyman Bartlett Jr. m 8/4/1990 Linda Nash Engleby c 3. The Ch Of The Sav Denville NJ 2009-2011; R Ch of S Jn on the Mtn Bernardsville NJ 1999-2009; S Andr's Epis Sch Potomac MD 1998-1999, 1993-1998; Asst Ch Of The Redeem Bryn Mawr PA 1991-1993.

ENGLISH, Allison Rainey (Los) 504 N Camden Dr, Beverly Hills CA 90210 **Assoc R All SS Par Beverly Hills CA 2013-** B Franklin IN 1982 d Phillip & Judith. BA Hanover Coll 2004; MDiv Claremont TS 2008. D 6/7/2008 P 1/10/2009 Bp Joseph Jon Bruno. m 10/11/2008 Robert D English c 2. Assoc for Yth S Wilfrid Of York Epis Ch Huntington Bch CA 2008-2013; Stdt Mnstry Intern The Ch Of The Ascen Sierra Madre CA 2006-2008; BEC Dio Los Angeles Los Angeles CA 2012-2015, 2010-; Mem and Com Chair Grtr Huntington Bch Interfaith Coun 2009-2013; Bd Mem Natl Assn of Interfaith and Interchurch Families 2009-2012; 76th GC Yth Prog- Asst Dir Ecusa / Mssn Personl New York NY 2008-2009. aenglish@allsaintsbh.org

ENGLISH, Ann Cantwell (Spok) Rr 1 Box 241-B, Touchet WA 99360 B Indianapolis IN 1943 d John & Betty. BA U GA. D 3/19/1987 Bp Leigh Allen Wallace Jr. m 11/26/1964 Weyman English c 2. Chapl S Mary's Med Cntr.

ENGLISH, John Lyle (WMich) 1045 Woodrow Ave Nw, Grand Rapids MI 49504 **Contract Cler S Phil's Epis Ch Grand Rapids MI 2003-; Ret 1995-** B Detroit MI 1930 s William & Viola. BA MI SU 1955; LTh SWTS 1959. D 5/29/1959 Bp Charles L Street P 11/28/1959 Bp William W Horstick. m 8/25/1956 Jeanette M English c 4. R S Paul's Epis Ch Grand Rapids MI 1980-1995, R 1963-1975; R S Andr's Ch Big Rapids MI 1975-1980; R S Kath's Ch Owen WI 1959-1963.

ENGLISH, Linda (WK) 114 W Roosevelt, Phoenix AZ 85003 **Chapl The S Fran Acad Inc. Salina KS 2004-** B Kansas City MO 1946 d Rodger & Lila. BS Upper Iowa U 2001; MDiv SWTS 2004. D 12/20/2003 P 6/26/2004 Bp Dean E Wolfe. m 11/9/1991 Robert Cook c 3. S Mich's Ch Hays KS 2010-2011; Dio Arizona Phoenix AZ 2007-2009; Vic S Geo's Epis Ch Holbrook AZ 2007-2009; S Fran Cmnty Serv Inc. Salina KS 2004-2007. EPF 2006.

ENGLISH, Rev Carrie (Fla) 11601 Longwood Key Dr W, Jacksonville FL 32218 **R Resurr Epis Ch Jacksonville FL 2013-, D 2006-2012** B Jacksonville FL 1948 d James & Myrtle. BS Tennessee St U 1970; MA U of No Florida 1979; Angl Inst Live Oak FL 2004. D 6/5/2005 P 6/17/2012 Bp Samuel Johnson Howard. m 11/27/1976 Jeffery A English c 2.

ENGLISH, Thomas Ronald (Ore) 2530 Fairmount Blvd, Eugene OR 97403 **Chapl Ln Cnty Jail 2000-; Transition Chapl Or St Prison 2000-; D S Mary's Epis Ch Eugene OR 2000-; Chapl Ln Cnty Oregon Adult Corrections 1999-; Co-Chair Jail & Prison Mnstry Cmsn Dio Oregon Portland OR 2011-** B Salt Lake City UT 1943 s Thomas & Rosemary. BA U of Oregon 1966; MA U of Oregon 1978; Cert Cntr for the Diconate 1999. D 10/4/1999 Bp Robert Louis Ladehoff. m 5/26/1984 Nancy Alice English c 2. Rotary Intl 2001; W Cascade Returned Peace Corps Vol 2000. Vol of the Year-Civic and Cmnty Cmnty Leaders Together 2014; Voulenteer of the year Ln Cnty Sheriff 2005.

ENGLISH, Tristan Clifford (Minn) Christ Church, 321 West Ave, Red Wing MN 55066 **Chr Ch Red Wing MN 2016-** B Decorah IA 1971 s Clifford & Martha. BA Ursinus Coll 1994. D 3/13/2010 Bp Bruce Caldwell P 9/29/2010 Bp John Smylie. m 2/10/2001 Debra L English. Cn for Congrl Enrichment Dio Wyoming Casper 2010-2015, COM 2011-, HR Camp Fndt 2010-. trisenglish@hotmail.com

ENGLISH, William H (Roch) 248 Commons Lane, Foster City CA 94404 B Corning NY 1939 s Floyd & Marian. BS SUNY at Buffalo 1961; JD St Univ of NY at Buffalo Law Sch 1964; MDiv EDS 1969. D 6/21/1969 P 12/1/1969 Bp George West Barrett. m 8/18/1962 Elizabeth Margaret English c 1. R Zion Ch Avon NY 1991-1994; Asst for Pstr Mnstry S Paul's Ch Rochester NY 1972-1991; Chr Ch Sodus NY 1969-1972; P-in-c S Steph's Ch Wolcott NY 1969-1972.

ENGLISH, William Lawson (NY) 605 Radiance Dr, Cambridge MD 21613 **Died 8/25/2015** B Cambridge MD 1936 s William & Mary. BA Amer U 1960; STB GTS 1965. D 6/12/1965 P 12/21/1965 Bp Allen J Miller. S Mary's Castleton Staten Island NY 1967-1999; R Ephiphany Preston MD 1965-1967; R S Andr's Hurlock MD 1965-1967; S Steph's Epis Ch E New Mrkt MD 1965-1967.

ENGLUND, David (NCal) 1624 10th St, Oroville CA 95965 **P-in-c S Paul's Epis Ch Oroville CA 2007-** B Kansas City MO 1949 s Vernon & Emma. BA Azusa Pacific U 1971; MDiv Fuller TS 1979; DMin SWTS 2009. D 4/18/2004 P 10/17/2004 Bp Jerry Alban Lamb. m 12/31/1998 Susan Jean Doughty c 2.

ENGLUND, Henry C (NJ) 90 Dillon Way, Washington Crossing PA 18977 B Trenton NJ 1943 s Gustaf & Louise. BS U of Virginia 1965; MDiv PDS 1968; STM NYTS 1980; MBA La Salle U 1984. D 4/20/1968 P 10/26/1968 Bp Alfred L Banyard. m 8/30/2001 Judith R Goodman c 1. Trin Ch Moorestown NJ 1995-2004; The Evergreens Hm Moorestown NJ 1979-2004; Evergreens Chap Moorestown NJ 1979-2003; The Evergreens Moorestown NJ 1979-2003; R S Paul's Epis Ch Bound Brook NJ 1972-1979; Vic S Barn Mantua NJ 1968-1972.

ENGSTROM, Marilyn Jean (Wyo) 1714 Mitchell St, Laramie WY 82072 B Rawlins WY 1950 d Louis & Mary. BA U of Wyoming 1973; MDiv TESM 1989. D 6/14/1989 P 12/5/1989 Bp Bob Gordon Jones. Dn S Matt's Epis Cathd Laramie WY 2002-2012; R H Trin Epis Ch Gillette WY 1994-2002; Dio Wyoming Casper 1991-1994; Bd Chapl ECW 1990-1996; R S Geo's Ch Lusk WY 1989-1991.

ENGWALL, Douglas Brian (Ct) Trinity Episcopal Church, 55 River Rd, Collinsville CT 06019 B Manistee MI 1949 s Delbert & Dorothy. BA Albion Coll 1971; PhD Suny at Buffalo 1976. D 9/15/2007 Bp Andrew Donnan Smith. m 8/31/1975 Karen Block Engwall c 2.

ENNIS, Kathleen Knox (SwFla) 6180 Golden Oaks Ln, Naples FL 34119 B Wichita KS 1938 d Van & Katherine. Smith-Study Abroad Madrid ES 1959; BA Sweet Briar Coll 1960. D 6/13/1998 Bp John Bailey Lipscomb. m 10/14/1961 Hugh Richard Ennis c 4. Iona Hope Epis Ch Ft Myers FL 1998-2009; Campus Min Florida Gulf Coast U Ft Myers FL 1997-2000. Auth, "Washed Clean: the Value of Sacramental Confession," LivCh, LivCh Fndt, Inc., 12-10-2000; Auth, "The Atone," LivCh, LivCh Fndt, Inc., 3-5-2000.

ENSOR, Amelia Jeanne (Oly) 8235 36th Ave Ne, Seattle WA 98115 B Seattle WA 1948 d Glenn & Maxine. AA Shoreline Cmnty Coll 1982. D 7/9/1994 Bp Vincent Waydell Warner. m 11/4/1967 Harold Carl Ensor c 2. D Chr Ch Seattle WA 2007-2009; D Resurr. Hlth Ministers Assn; NAAD.

ENSOR, Peter Crane (Los) 111 Westview Drive, Dubois WY 82513 B Cambridge MA 1938 s Howard & Florence. BA Ham 1960; BD EDS 1963. D 6/22/1963 Bp Anson Phelps Stokes Jr P 5/1/1964 Bp John Brooke Mosley. m 6/30/1962 Jean D Ensor. R S Thos Ch Dubois WY 2000-2002; S Jas' Par So Pasadena CA 1989-1999; Vic S Marg Of Scotland Par San Juan Capo CA 1985-1989; R Epis Ch Of The Ascen Dallas TX 1981-1985; The Oakridge Sch Ft Worth TX 1979-1981; White Lake Sch Ft Worth TX 1978; S Mk's Cathd Shreveport LA 1975-1978.

EOYANG JR, Thomas (Pa) 6622 Germantown Ave Unit 3A, Philadelphia PA 19119 B New York NY 1951 s Thomas & Ellen. BA Harvard Coll 1972; MA Stan 1975; MDiv EDS 2003; DMin EDS 2014. D 6/19/2004 P 12/18/2004 Bp

Charles Ellsworth Bennison Jr. EDS Cambridge MA 2015-2017; Chair, COM Dio Pennsylvania Philadelphia PA 2010-2015; R Gr Epiph Ch Philadelphia PA 2007-2015; Int Trin Memi Ch Philadelphia PA 2005-2007; S Ptr's Ch Glenside PA 2004-2005. Auth, "Why This Story Yet Again," *Sermons That Wk XIII: Preaching as Pstr Caring*, Morehouse Pub, 2005; Auth, "The Ethics Of Healthcare For Profit (Guest Ed)," *Journey Of Profsnl Nrsng*, Saunders, 2001; Auth, "The Illness Experience," *Sorensen & Luckmann'S Basic Nrsng*, Saunders, 1994. Jas Arthur Muller Prize EDS 2014; Frederick Meggee Adams Prize EDS 2003; Wm C. Winslow Prize EDS 2003; Wm H. Lincoln Prize EDS 2002; Class Of 1936 Prize EDS 2001.

EPES, Gail E (Va) 1200 N Quaker Ln, Alexandria VA 22302 B Lawrence KS 1946 d Edward & Louise. BA GW 1968; MEd U of Virginia 1969; MDiv VTS 1987. D 6/13/1987 P 4/27/1988 Bp Peter J Lee. m 8/24/1968 William P Epes. Epis HS Alexandria VA 2012-2013; Asst Chapl Epis HS Alexandria VA 1991-2007; P Ch Of The Gd Shpd Burke VA 1987-1991.

EPPERSON, Christopher Larry (SVa) PO Box 3520, Williamsburg VA 23187 **R Bruton Par Williamsburg VA 2011-; R S Columbas Middletown RI 2006-** B Cleveland TN 1970 s Robert & Armen. BS U of Tennessee 1996; MDiv GTS 1999. D 6/19/1999 P 2/26/2000 Bp Charles Glenn VonRosenberg. m 12/31/1996 Laura B Epperson c 3. S Columba's Chap Middletown RI 2006-2011; Assoc R - Adult Formation / Pstr Care All SS Epis Ch Atlanta GA 2001-2006; S Jn's Epis Ch Johnson City TN 1999-2001. cepperson@brutonparish.org

EPPLE, Jogues Fred (Okla) 1830 University Ave W, Apt 201, Saint Paul MN 55104 **Ret 1992-** B Cleveland OH 1930 s Fred & Caroline. MDiv Cath Theol U 1957; MA CUA 1967. Rec 6/24/1983 as Priest Bp James Daniel Warner. Vic S Paul's Ch Clinton OK 1987-1989; Dio Oklahoma Oklahoma City OK 1987-1988; R Calv Ch Hyannis NE 1984-1987; Vic S Jos's Ch Mullen NE 1984-1987; Chr Ch Cntrl City NE 1983-1984. Auth, *Exploring Gray: Value of Depression*; Auth, *Gigapop Opportunities of Aging*; Auth, *Tour: Intro to Internet 2*.

EPPLY-SCHMIDT, Joanne (NJ) 26 Nelson Ridge Rd, Princeton NJ 08540 **Non-par 2000-** B Hartford CT 1955 d William & Loraine. BA Pr 1982; MDiv Ya Berk 1988. D 6/10/1989 Bp George Phelps Mellick Belshaw P 10/27/1990 Bp Albert Wiencke Van Duzer. m 5/17/1986 Paul Erick Epply-Schmidt c 2. Epis Ch at Pr Princeton NJ 2016; Assoc Trin Ch Princeton NJ 2005-2011; Asst S Matt's Ch Pennington NJ 1990-2000; Asst S Bern's Ch Bernardsville NJ 1989-1990.

✠ **EPTING, The Rt Rev Chris Christopher** (Ia) 86 Broadmoor Ln, Iowa City IA 52245 B GreenvilleSC 1946 s Carl & Margaret. BA U of Florida 1969; MDiv SWTS 1972; STM GTS 1984. D 4/29/1972 Bp James Winchester Montgomery P 11/8/1972 Bp William Hopkins Folwell Con 9/27/1988 for Ia. m 11/9/2001 Susanne K Freyermuth c 3. Asstg Bp Dio Chicago Chicago IL 2012-2015; Int Dn Trin Cathd Davenport IA 2009-2011; Ecum Off Epis Ch Cntr New York NY 2001-2009; Ret Bp of Iowa Dio Iowa Des Moines IA 1988-2001; R S Mk's Ch Cocoa FL 1981-1988; Cn S Jn's Cathd Jacksonville FL 1978-1980; Vic S Lk The Evang Ch Mulberry FL 1974-1978; Vic S Steph's Ch Lakeland FL 1974-1978; Dir Inst for Chr Stds Orlando FL 1974-1977; Cur H Trin Epis Ch Melbourne FL 1972-1974. Auth, "w Gladness and Singleness of Heart," *Amazon Kindle*, Amazon Kindle, 2016; Auth, "Jn Mk: A Gospel Novel," *Red Moon Pub*, Red Moon Pub, 2013. Bp Visitor - Cmnty of Celebration 1998; Bp Visitor - CT Cincinnati Oh 1995-2015. DD Wartburg TS 2001; DD SWTS 1988.

ERB, Edward Kenneth (Be) 827 Church St., Honesdale PA 18431 **R Gr Epis Ch Honesdale PA 2008-** B Lock Haven PA 1957 s Walter & Margaret. BA Lycoming Coll 1979; MDiv GTS 1997. D 6/6/1997 P 6/27/1998 Bp Michael Whittington Creighton. m 8/17/1980 Susan Renee Shadle. S Jn's Epis Ch Hamlin PA 1998-2007; CPE Hershey Med Cntr PA 1997-1998; Hon Cn for Liturg and Mus Dio Bethlehem Bethlehem PA 2002-2004. H Cross Monstry in W Pk, NY. St. Geo Awd BSA 2012. rector@gracechurchhonesdale.org

ERDELJON, Lisa Michele (Va) 647 Dundee Ave, Barrington IL 60010 **S Mich's Ch Barrington IL 2017-** B Silver Spring MD 1985 d Barry & Mary. BS Old Dominion U 2007; MS Geo Mason U 2011; MDiv Yale DS 2017. D 6/10/2017 Bp Shannon Sherwood Johnston. lerdeljon@stmichaelsbarrington.org

ERDMAN, Daniel Le Roy (Mich) 929 E Hawthorne Loop, Webb City MO 64870 **Chapl S Lk Nrsng Cntr Carthage MO 2008-; P-in-c S Jn's Ch Neosho MO 2007-** B York PA 1944 s Marlin & Mabel. BA Wheaton Coll 1968; MA Yale DS 1971; MDiv Yale DS 1973. D 6/8/1973 P 12/15/1973 Bp Dean Theodore Stevenson. m 12/31/1974 Susan C Erdman c 1. R Trin Epis Ch Farmington MI 2001-2006; R S Phil's Ch Joplin MO 1996-2001; R Chr Ch Rolla MO 1992-1996; R S Lk's Epis Ch Mt Joy PA 1984-1992; R Chr Memi Epis Ch Danville PA 1981-1984; Chr Ch Berwick PA 1975-1981; Vic All SS Ch Selinsgrove PA 1974-1975; S Mk's Epis Ch Northumberlnd PA 1974-1975.

ERDMAN, Nathan (Md) St Thomas Episcopal Church, 232 Saint Thomas Ln, Owings Mills MD 21117 **Asst S Thos' Ch Garrison Forest Owings Mills MD 2013-** B Mahoning Twp PA 1976 s Daniel & Susan. BA Sewanee: The U So, TS 2000; BA The TS at The U So 2000; MDiv Sewanee: The U So, TS 2013; MDiv The TS at The U So 2013. D 1/19/2013 Bp Joe Goodwin Burnett P 7/21/2013 Bp Eugene Taylor Sutton. m 12/28/2002 Rachel Ryan Bush Erdman c

2. Chr Ch Georgetown Washington DC 2008-2010; S Jn's Ch Ellicott City MD 2005-2008; Ch Of The Ascen Clearwater FL 2002-2005.

ERHARD, Michael Edward Charles (Cal) 2421 Day Dr, The Villages FL 32163 **Non Par Epis Ch 2015-; D Gr Ch S Helena CA 2004-** B Chicago IL 1953 s Edward & Mary. BA NWU 1975; MPA NWU 1977; BA Sch for Deacons 1984. D 12/7/1985 Bp William Edwin Swing. S Jn's Ch Mason City IA 2015, 2014-2015; Int Assoc S Mk's Epis Ch Palo Alto CA 1994-1996; S Lk's Ch San Francisco CA 1993-2004; D S Clem's Epis Ch Seattle WA 1990-1992; D Gr Cathd San Francisco CA 1987-1989; Trsfg Epis Ch San Mateo CA 1985-1987.

ERICKSON, David L (Los) 1818 Monterey Blvd, Hermosa Beach CA 90254 **Cn S Jn's Cathd Jacksonville FL 2015-** B Decorah IA 1976 s Kenneth & Carol. BFA U CO at Boulder 2001; MDiv VTS 2011. D 6/21/2011 P 1/7/2012 Bp Mary Douglas Glasspool. m 7/1/2006 Heather B Erickson c 2. Assoc St Cross Epis Ch Hermosa Bch CA 2011-2015. derickson@jaxcathedral.org

ERICKSON, Frederick David (Los) 10700 Keswick St, Garrett Park MD 20896 B Rhinelander WI 1941 s Lennart & Marie. EDS; BA NWU 1963; MA NWU 1964; PhD NWU 1969. D 6/14/1975 Bp John Melville Burgess. m 8/31/1968 Joanne Straceski c 2. Archd Dio Los Angeles Los Angeles CA 2005-2010, Hon Cn, Cathd Cntr of St. Paul 2010-; D St Mary in Palms Los Angeles CA 1999-2011; G.F. Kneller Prof of Anthropology and Educ U CA Los Angeles 1998-2011; D Nevil Memi Ch Of S Geo Ardmore PA 1997-1998; D Ch Of S Mart-In-The-Fields Philadelphia PA 1990-1996; Prof of Educ and Pediatrics MI SU 1978-1986; D Ch Of S Jn The Evang Boston MA 1975-1978; Asst/ Assoc Prof of Educ Harv 1971-1978; Asst Prof of Educ U IL Chicago Cir 1968-1971; Prof of Educ and Dir of the Centerer for Urba U of Pennsylvania 1966-1998; Asst S Mart's-Fields. Auth, "Talk and Soc theory: Ecologies of Spkng and listening in everyday life," Polity Press, UK, 2004; Auth, "The Counslr As Gatekeeper: Interaction In Counslg Encounters," Acad Press, 1982; Auth, "Qualitative Methods In Resrch On Tchg". Annual Outstanding Dissertation Awd named in hon of Frederick Erickson Coun on Anthropology and Educ, Amer Anthropological Assn 2015; Elected Fell Amer Educational Resrch Assn 2007; Elected Mem Natl Acad of Educ 2000; Geo and Louise Spindler Awd Coun on Anthropology and Educ, Amer Anthropological Assn 1991. ferickson@gseis.ucla.edu

ERICKSON, Gregory Charles (WNC) 1359 Lamb Mountain Rd, Hendersonville NC 28792 B Jamestown NY 1952 s Frank & Carol. BS Cit 1974. D 1/28/2006 Bp Porter Taylor. m 8/13/1977 Robin Erickson c 1.

ERICKSON, Heather B (Los) St Margaret's Episcopal Church, 31641 La Novia Ave, San Juan Capistrano CA 92675 B Los Angeles CA 1978 d Roderick & Lynn. BA U CA, San Diego 2001; MDiv VTS 2011. D 6/21/2011 P 1/7/2012 Bp Mary Douglas Glasspool. m 7/1/2006 David L Erickson c 1. S Marg Of Scotland Par San Juan Capo CA 2013-2015; All SS Par Beverly Hills CA 2005-2008.

ERICKSON JR, Joseph Austin (Los) 764 Valparaiso Dr, Claremont CA 91711 **1971-** B Cambridge MA 1924 s Joseph & Esther. BA Harv 1945; STB EDS 1951; ThD Claremont TS 1965. D 1/6/1951 Bp Raymond A Heron P 7/15/1951 Bp Donald J Campbell. m 6/13/1970 Catherine Henley Erickson c 4. Pstr Coun S Martha's Epis Ch W Covina CA 1964-1971; Chapl Gd Samar Hosp Los Angeles CA 1963-1964; R S Mk's Epis Ch Upland CA 1953-1963; Cur All SS Ch Pasadena CA 1951-1953.

ERICKSON, Kenneth L (Mich) 711 Wooddale Rd, Bloomfield Hills MI 48301 B Chicago IL 1966 s Richard & John. BA Wheaton Coll 1988; MDiv Duke DS 1995; GTS 2001. D 6/23/2001 Bp Michael B Curry P 1/20/2002 Bp Robert Louis Ladehoff. m 10/20/1990 Katherine J Erickson c 1. R S Jas Epis Ch Birmingham MI 2012-2013; Asst Chr Ch Winnetka IL 2011-2012; Instnl Advancement H Fam Sch 2010-2012; Asst S Greg's Epis Ch Deerfield IL 2008-2012; R S Greg's Epis Sch Chicago IL 2008-2010; Assoc Ch Of The H Comf Kenilworth IL 2005-2007; R S Ann's Ch Woodstock IL 2004-2005; S Paul's Epis Ch Salem OR 2004, Assoc 2001-2002.

ERICKSON, Lori Jean (Ia) **D Trin Ch Iowa City IA 2005-** B Waukon IA 1961 BA Luther Coll 1983; MA U of Iowa 1985. D 4/16/2005 Bp Alan Scarfe. m 9/5/1987 Robert Sessions c 2.

ERICKSON, Mary Cobb (Wyo) PO Box 1690, Jackson WY 83001 B Berkeley CA 1963 d Miles & Beth. BA U CA Berkeley 1988; MDiv Harvard DS 1994; MDiv Harvard DS 1994. D 11/1/2009 Bp Bruce Caldwell P 8/10/2010 Bp John Smylie. m 8/29/1999 Bruce Alan Erickson c 2. Ch Of The Trsfg Jackson WY 2009-2014; Asst S Jn's Epis Ch Jackson WY 2007-2009.

ERICKSON, Mary Kahrs (At) 4 Jones St, Cartersville GA 30120 **R Ch Of The Ascen Cartersville GA 2010-** B Traverse City MI 1953 d Edward & Eunice. BSN U MI 1976; MBA Berry Coll 1983; MDiv Candler TS Emory U 2004. D 6/5/2004 P 2/12/2005 Bp J Neil Alexander. m 11/28/1981 Stephen W Erickson c 4. Assoc S Mart In The Fields Ch Atlanta GA 2005-2010. merickson@ascensioncartersville.org

ERICKSON, Richard Paul (Alb) 901 Ridge View Circle, Castleton-On-Hudson NY 12033 **D The Cathd of All SS Albany NY 2006-** B Hudson NY 1964 s Richard & Elaine. AA Columbia-Greene Cmnty Coll 1984; AS Columbia-

Greene Cmnty Coll 1986; AAS Maria Coll 1996. D 6/10/2006 Bp Daniel William Herzog. m 5/30/1998 Theresa Erickson. richard.theresa@verizon.net

ERICKSON, Scott (Cal) 420 Eureka St, San Francisco CA 94114 **Hd of Sch The Phillips Brooks Sch Menlo Pk CA 2011-** B Fort Dodge IA 1967 s Rubert & Doris. BA No Pk U 1989; MDiv No Pk TS 1993; ThD Uppsala U 1996; Vstng Schlr Harv 1998. D 11/1/2001 P 5/19/2002 Bp Douglas Edwin Theuner. m 9/9/2010 Ryan Banks-Erickson. Middle Sch Hd & Dir of Stds Natl Cathd Sch Washington DC 2007-2011; Prot Epis Cathd Fndt Washington DC 2007; Hmnts Div Hd and Chapl St. Paul's Sch Concord NH 1998-2007; Cn Liturg Dio New Hampshire Concord NH 2004-2007. Ed, "Sch Chap Serv & Prayers," Ch Pub, 2007; Auth, "The Anatomy of Immigrant Hymnody," *Hymnody in Amer Protestanism*, Oxf Press, 2003; Auth, "Immigrants, Pilgrims and People of Faith," *Essays in Memory of Zenos Hawkinson*, Cov Press, 2001; Auth, "Ethnicity and Rel in the Twin Cities," *Swedes in the Twin Cities*, Minnesota Hist Press, 2001; Auth, "The Ch as Ext of the Homeland," *Migrants and the Homeland*, Cntr for Multiethnic Resrch, 2000; Auth, "The Ch w the Soul of a Nation," *The Cov Quarterly*, 2000; Auth, "The Nature of Amer Rel Influences on the Swedish Mssn Cov Ch," *Amer Rel Influences in Sweden*, Ch of Sweden Resrch Dep't, 1996. AAR 1993; Amer Soc of Ch Hist 1993; Cbury Shaker Vill 2000; Cmnty of the Cross of Nails 1999; HSEC 1999; NAES 1998. Doctoral Fllshp Ecum Fund for the Stds of the Swedish Free Ch Move 1993; Alfred Ahnfeldt Medallion for Acad achievement No Pk TS 1993.

ERICKSON, Winifred Jean (NMich) 1506 Us #2 Highway West, Crystal Falls MI 49920 B London UK 1922 d Robert & Harriet. D 5/20/1990 Bp Thomas Kreider Ray. m 11/6/1971 Donald Arnold Erickson c 3. S Mk's Ch Crystal Falls MI 1990-2008; D Dio Nthrn Michigan Marquette MI 1990-2002.

ERICSON, Bill (Mich) Po Box 267, Dewitt MI 48820 **Supply P Emm Ch Hastings MI 2009-; Ret 2004-** B Glenwood Sprgs CO 1939 s Earl & Dagmer. Mesa Cmnty Coll 1965; BA Wstrn St Coll of Colorado 1967; MDiv SWTS 1977. D 7/3/1977 P 1/6/1978 Bp William Hopkins Folwell. m 6/12/1964 Mildred P Powe c 3. S Mich's Epis Ch Lansing MI 2002; S Aug Of Cbury Mason MI 1999-2001; Dio Michigan Detroit MI 1999; S Annes Ch Dewitt MI 1991-1999; Chr Epis Ch Owosso MI 1990-1991; Assoc S Paul's Epis Ch Lansing MI 1987-1989; R S Matt's Epis Ch Saginaw MI 1983-1987; Asst S Andr Epis Ch Mentor OH 1978-1983; Cur All SS Ch Of Winter Pk Winter Pk FL 1977-1978.

ERIXSON, Lorna Lloyd (At) 316 Spyglass Hill Dr, Perry GA 31069 **P-in-c S Chris's At-The-Crossroads Epis Perry GA 2013-** B Northern Ireland 1952 d Gilbert & Jean. BA U of Ulster 1974; PGCE Camb 1975; MSc Troy U 1987; MDiv Sewanee: The U So, TS 2010. D 12/19/2009 P 6/26/2011 Bp J Neil Alexander. c 2. Assoc S Thos Epis Ch Columbus GA 2011-2012.

ERQUIAGA, Trudel Nada (Nev) 1128 Green Valley Drive, Fallon NV 89406 **R H Trin Epis Ch Fallon NV 2003-** B White Pine County NV 1957 d Robert & Katherine. BS U of Nevada at Reno 1979. D 10/11/2002 P 5/24/2003 Bp Katharine Jefferts Schori. m 8/15/1981 David Erquiaga c 2. D H Trin Epis Ch Fallon NV 2002-2003.

ERSKINE, Jack Arthur (EO) 69787 Pine Ridge Road, Sisters OR 97759 **Chapl (Full time Feb 2014 St. Chas Med Ctr. Bend OR 2010-** B Lewiston ID 1949 s Sewell & Juliana. Cert Chapl (4 units of CPE) APC; BEd Wstrn Washington U 1972; MDiv CDSP 1976; Cert Ripon Coll Cuddesdon Oxford GB 1989. D 12/5/1979 P 1/10/1981 Bp Robert Hume Cochrane. m 6/8/1996 Christine Elaine Close c 3. Ch Of The H Sprt Episco Battle Ground WA 2006; Ch Of The Gd Shpd Vancouver WA 1998-2008; S Steph's Epis Ch Longview WA 1997; S Columba's Epis Ch Kent WA 1994-1995, Vic 1992-1994; Asst R S Barn Epis Ch Bainbridge Island WA 1989-1992; Chapl Chas Wright Acad Tacoma WA 1984-1985; Chapl Chas Wright Acad Tacoma WA 1979-1983. Auth, "Mare's Tails: Forewarnings of a Storm," *Novel*, Self Pub, 2016; Auth, "Portrait of an Artist by a Young Dog," *YA Novel*, Self Pub, 2009; Auth, "A Gd Day at White Rock," *Novel*, Self Pub, 2007. Croix de Candlestick 1987-1988; Ord of S Ben 1983; Ord of the Bore: Storyteller 1957; Quilting Partnership Extraordinaire 1997. Novel in a Month NanoWriMo 2016; Novel in a Month NanoWriMo 2014; Bd Cert Chapl APC 2013; Novel in a Month NanoWriMo 2009; Novel in a Month NanoWriMo 2008; Novel in a Month NanoWriMo 2007. jack@thresholdjourney.com

ERVOLINA, Timothy Mark (USC) 120 Ridgewood Cir, Greenwood SC 29649 **D Ch Of The Resurr Greenwood SC 2002-** B Pt Hueneme CA 1954 s Kenneth & Dorothy. BA SE Coll Assembly of God Lakeland FL 1989; MA Faith Evang Luth Sem 1994. D 12/11/1999 Bp John Wadsworth Howe. m 6/25/1994 Suzanne Phillips Smith c 3. D S Dav's Epis Ch Lakeland FL 1999-2002.

ERWIN, Ginny (Los) 2157 Birdie Dr, Banning CA 92220 B Long Island NY 1945 d John & Ruth. BS U of Nevada at Reno 1967; MS Pepperdine U 1975; MA ETSBH 1986. D 6/22/1986 Bp Robert Claflin Rusack P 1/11/1987 Bp Oliver Bailey Garver Jr. c 2. R Trin Epis Ch Orange CA 1991-2006; Archd for Cler Deploy & Dvlpmt Dio Los Angeles Los Angeles CA 1988-1991; Cur S Jas Par Los Angeles CA 1986-1988.

ERWIN JR, James Walter (NY) 5 Second St, Warwick NY 10990 **R Chr Ch Warwick NY 2012-** B Savannah, GA 1960 s James & Harriet. AA Young Harris Jr Coll 1980; BA U GA 1982; MDiv GTS 2009. D 12/15/2009 Bp Michael

B Curry P 6/26/2010 Bp Ian Theodore Douglas. c 2. Cur S Paul's Ch Riverside CT 2010-2012.

ERWIN, William Portwood (Mich) 5316 Heritage Ct, Rocklin CA 95765 **Died 11/23/2015** B Dallas TX 1927 s William & Constance. MDiv Epis TS of the SW; MS Wayne; BA Harv 1950; MA Westminster Choir Coll of Rider U 1952. D 6/27/1957 P 4/1/1958 Bp Edward Hamilton West. m 12/14/1985 Yong Joo Erwin c 4. Non-par 1979-2015; R S Matthius' Detroit MI 1974-1979; St Mths Ch Detroit MI 1974-1978; LocTen S Matthius' Detroit MI 1973-1974; R S Paul's Ch Muskegon MI 1966-1972; Vic S Mary's Epis Ch Green Cv Spg FL 1963-1965; Cn Precentor S Jn's Cathd Jacksonville FL 1962-1963; Vic S Andr's By The Sea Epis Ch Destin FL 1957-1962; Vic S Thos' Sea Laguna Bch FL 1957-1960. Auth, "Carol Of S Jos'S Dream".

ESBENSHADE, Burnell True (Mo) 1116 E Linden Ave, Saint Louis MO 63117 **Activities Dir Luth Sr Serv 2006-** B Louisville KY 1943 d Burlyn & Nell. BA Cntr Coll 1965; MA Van 1966; Epis Sch for Mnstry 2006. D 2/7/2007 Bp George Wayne Smith. m 6/26/1971 Donald H Esbenshade c 2.

ESCALERA, Jose Refugio (Okla) 8400 S Pennsylvania Ave, Oklahoma City OK 73159 B Sta Elena 1960 s Jose & Clotilde. Zoology Escuela Superior de Agri 1979. D 6/30/2017 Bp Edward Joseph Konieczny. m 8/16/2002 Miriam Reyes c 4.

ESCOTT, Raymond Philip (WNC) 12 Misti Leigh Ln, Waynesville NC 28786 B Warren OH 1950 s Phillip & Janice. D 1/28/2006 Bp Porter Taylor. m 9/2/1972 Peggy Escott c 3. S Andr's Epis Ch Canton NC 2006-2015. SSF, Third Ord 1994.

ESKAMIRE-JACKSON, Joyce (La) 1313 Esplanade Ave, New Orleans LA 70116 B Natchez MS 1944 d William & Willa. D 12/1/2007 Bp Charles Edward Jenkins III. m 5/22/1994 Ralph A Jackson c 2.

ESONU, Clinton Chukwuemeka (WA) 2031 Powhatan Rd, Hyattsville MD 20782 B Nigeria 1951 s Christopher & Cathrine. BS U of Nigeria 1979; BA London TS 1987; MA London TS 1988; MA VTS 1998. Trans 1/3/2005 Bp John Bryson Chane. m 10/3/1981 Ngozi Esonu c 3. All SS Igbo Angl Ch Coll Pk MD 2007-2016; S Mich And All Ang Hyattsville MD 2005-2016; Asst R S Jn's Epis Ch Mt Ranier MD 2000-2003; Serv Angl Ch of Nigeria 1990-1996.

ESPESETH, Cynthia A. (Oly) 13613 178TH Ave NE, Redmond WA 98052 **Vic S Hilda's - S Pat's Epis Ch Edmonds WA 2007-** B Durango CO 1959 d Ernest & Dorothy. BA U CO 1981; MDiv SWTS 2001. D 6/23/2001 P 1/13/2002 Bp Vincent Waydell Warner. c 2. Dio Olympia Seattle 2007-2009, 2003-2006, Cler Assn Bd 2002-2005, Chapl, Oprtns Com for Huston C&C 2002-, Stndg Com 2014-; Asst S Steph's Epis Ch Seattle WA 2006-2007; P-in-c All SS Ch Bellevue WA 2004-2005, Asst 2001-2006. cynthia.espeseth@gmail.com

ESPINOSA-AREVALO, Carlos (EcuC) Apartado Postal 10-04-21, Atuntaqui-Imbabura Ecuador B Tabacundo Pichincha EC 1937 s Jose & Ana. BA. D 6/30/1973 P 6/30/1974 Bp Adrian Delio Caceres-Villavicencio. m 2/17/1964 Teresa E Solorzano Espinosa-Arevalo c 5. Iglesia Del Ecuador Quito 1973-1996; Mssy Rural Mssn Of No Imbabura Ecuador 1971-1973. Auth, "The Ch & The Dynamics Of Evang".

ESPOSITO, Catherine Patricia (NJ) 14 Edgemere Dr, Matawan NJ 07747 **Naturalist Monmouth Cnty Parks System NJ 2003-** B Kearny NJ 1955 d Charles & Patricia. BA Rutgers The St U of New Jersey 1984. D 6/11/2005 Bp George Edward Councell. m 4/26/1991 Phillip M Esposito c 1. S Ptr's Ch Freehold NJ 2000-2013.

ESTES, Diane Manguno (La) **Chapl & Coord. Of Cmnty Serv St. Andr's Epis. Sch New Orleans LA 2002-** B Fort Eustis VA 1956 d Larry & Arlene. BA U of Texas 1978; PhD U of Texas 1985; Sch For Mnstry Dio Louisiana 2002. D 7/24/2003 P 5/23/2004 Bp Charles Edward Jenkins III. m 7/30/1977 David Anderson Estes c 3. S Andr's Epis Ch New Orleans LA 2005-2010; S Andr's Epis Sch New Orleans LA 2003-2016; Co-Dir, Chr Formation All SS Epis Ch New Orleans LA 1997-1999; Adjuct Prof; Co-Dir Sch Of Allied Hlth Prof Lsu Med Cntr New Orleans LA 1992-2004; Adj Asst Prof Univ. Of New Orleans New Orleans LA 1990-1991; Vstng Prof Of Psych. Tulane Univ. New Orleans LA 1990; Sch Psychol Orleans Par Sch Bd New Orleans LA 1984-1986; Sch Psychol St. Bern Par Sch Bd Chalmette LA 1983-1984.

ESTES, James Gray (SanD) 1427 Rimrock Dr, Escondido CA 92027 B Concord NH 1934 s Josiah & Della. BA New Engl Coll 1958; MDiv Yale DS 1961. D 6/10/1961 P 12/13/1961 Bp Charles Francis Hall. m 3/18/1961 Virginia Estes c 3. Chair Wrld Mssn Com Dio San Diego San Diego CA 1988-1990, Chair Cler 1988-1989, COM 1986-1992; S Fran Ch Pauma Vlly CA 1985-2002; Chair Dio The Rio Grande Albuquerque 1978-1981, Chair 1976-1981, Prov VII CE Com 1976-1981, Stndg Com 1981-1982; R Gr Ch Carlsbad NM 1977-1985; Untd Campus Mnstry Silver City NM 1976-1977; Chapl S Steph's Coll Stanley Hong Kong 1966-1975; Mssy Hong Kong & Macao 1964-1975; Mssy No Borneo 1963-1966; Cur Par Of S Jas Ch Keene NH 1961-1963; S Jn's Ch Walpole NH 1961-1963. Auth, *Does Your Par Need a Columbarium?*. Valedictorian New Engl Coll 1958.

ESTES, Robert Theodore (WMo) 425 East Cherry St, Nevada MO 64772 **Assoc Gr Ch Carthage MO 2012-** B Joplin MO 1955 s Robert & Josephine. BSE Missouri Sthrn St Coll 1977; MS Pittsburg St U 1983. D 6/7/2008 Bp Barry

Howe. m 11/7/2003 Melinda Estes c 3. D in Charge All SS Ch Nevada MO 2008-2014; S Lk Nrsng Cntr Carthage MO 2005-2008.

ESTES, William Thomas (FtW) Grace Church, 405 Glenmar Ave, Monroe LA 71201 B Memphis TN 1966 s Thomas & Carol. AS Jas H Faulkner St Cmnty Coll 1992; BA U of Memphis 1995; MA Nash 2006. D 9/30/2006 P 6/25/2007 Bp Jack Leo Iker. m 6/20/1992 Lisa M Estes c 5. Cur Gr Epis Ch Monroe LA 2006-2008; Vol - Sem Asst St. Jn Chrys Delafield WI 2004-2006. Angl Comm Ntwk 2006; CBS 2005; Forw in Faith 2005; Pusey Gld 2005-2006.

ESTEY, Lawrence Mitchell (Me) 3 Greenhead Lane, PO Box 646, Stonington ME 04681 B Trenton NJ 1941 s Lawrence & Audree. BS Col 1966; MDiv UTS 1969. D 6/7/1969 P 12/20/1969 Bp Horace W B Donegan. m 4/25/2009 Elizabeth Singer c 1. R S Brendan's Epis Ch Deer Isle ME 2003-2006, Vic 2000-2003; R S Jn's Epis Ch Troy NY 1988-2000; Assoc The Ch Of The Redeem Baltimore MD 1977-1988; R Ch Of The Gd Shpd Wareham MA 1972-1977; Cur Chr Ch S Hamilton MA 1969-1971. Fell Coll of Preachers 1982.

ESTIL, Colbert (Hai) c/o Diocese of Haiti, Boite Postale 1309, Port au Prince Haiti B 1972 s Is & Avril. D 1/25/2006 P 2/18/2007 Bp Jean Zache Duracin. m 4/22/2008 Rene Marie Monese c 3.

✠ ESTILL, The Rt Rev Robert Whitridge (NC) 8601 Cypress Lakes Dr # A302, Raleigh NC 27615 **Bd Mem Duke Marine Lab 1997-; Bd Duke Marine Lab Advsry Bd 1985-** B Lexington KY 1927 s Robert & Elizabeth. BA U of Kentucky 1949; BD EDS 1952; STM Sewanee: The U So, TS 1960; DMin Sewanee: The U So, TS 1970; VTS 1973; VTS 1980; Sewanee: The U So, TS 1984; Duke DS 1986; LHD S Augustines Coll Raleigh NC 1992. D 6/27/1952 P 12/12/1952 Bp William R Moody Con 3/15/1980 for NC. m 6/17/1950 Joyce Estill c 3. Chair Bd of Theol Ed ECUSA 1992-1994; Pres Prov IV Dio No Carolina Raleigh NC 1990-1994, Bp of No Carolina 1983-1994, Bp Coadj of No Carolina 1980-1982; Fac Duke DS Durham NC 1990-1993; Pres NC Coun of Ch 1990-1992; PBp Com of Dns & Bps 1989-1994; Chair Bd Kanuga 1989-1992; R S Mich And All Ang Ch Dallas TX 1976-1980; Fac VTS Alexandria VA 1971-1976; R S Alb's Par Washington DC 1969-1973; R Chr Ch Cathd Lexington KY 1955-1963; R S Mary's Epis Ch Middlesboro KY 1952-1955; Bd Trsts The GTS New York NY 1985-1992; Chair Kentucky Human Rts Cmsn 1959-1990. Fell, Soc of S Jn the Evang; OHC. Doctor of Humane Letters S Augustines Coll Raleigh NC 1992; Jessie Ball DuPont Awd 1989; Hall of Fame Kentucky Human Rts 1985; Doctor of Sacr Theol Sewanee: The U So, TS 1984; DD VTS 1980.

ESTRADA, Carolyn Sullivan (Los) 2516 E Willow St Unit 108, Signal Hill CA 90755 B Dallas TX 1942 d Glenn & Jessie. BA Whittier Coll 1963; MA Whittier Coll 1976; MDiv Claremont TS 2001. D 6/9/2001 Bp Joseph Jon Bruno P 1/12/2002 Bp Frederick Houk Borsch. Assoc R Ch Of The Mssh Santa Ana CA 2001-2012.

ESTRADA, Richard Roger (Los) 2808 Altura St, Los Angeles CA 90031 B 1942 s Enrique & Josephine. BA Claretian Missionaries 1995; MA The Grad Theol Un 1997. Rec 5/13/2015 as Priest Bp Joseph Jon Bruno.

ESWEIN, Nancy G (Cal) 5040 E Timrod St, Tucson AZ 85711 **D S Jn's Epis Ch Clayton CA 2013-** B San Mateo CA 1955 d Bruce & Janet. BA U CA, Berkeley 1978; BA Sch for Deacons 1993; MTS CDSP 1997. D 6/4/1994 Bp William Edwin Swing. m 12/20/2012 Angela G Guida. An Epis Mnstry to Convalescent Hospitals (Aemch) Fremont CA 2012-2015; Dio California San Francisco CA 2012-2015, 1999-2002; CDSP Berkeley CA 2004-2012; D Ch Of The H Innoc San Francisco CA 2001-2004; Sojourn Multifaith Chapl San Francisco CA 1999-2004; Ch Of The Adv Of Chr The King San Francisco CA 1996-1999. Auth, "When Worlds Collide: An Encounter between an Anglo-Cath Par & a Homeless Shltr," 1997; Auth, "The Use of Absurdity as a Corrective to Biblic Literalism: Practical Theol Tools at Wk in a Homeless Shltr". ATR, Bd Dir 2005-2017.

ETEMAD CT, Sandra L (Pa) 535 Haws Ave, Norristown PA 19401 **R All SS Ch Norristown PA 2010-; Mem of Dioc Coun Dio Pennsylvania Philadelphia PA 2012-, Mem, Anti-Racism Cmsn 2011-** B Eureka California 1962 d Jon & Louise. BA Humboldt St U 1992; MDiv VTS 2006. D 6/3/2006 Bp Jerry Alban Lamb P 12/9/2006 Bp Robert Wilkes Ihloff. m 7/26/2008 Majid Etemad c 2. Assoc R The Ch Of The Redeem Baltimore MD 2006-2010; Mem, Maryland Epis Cler Assoc. Bd Dio Maryland Baltimore MD 2006-2010. fathermom@gmail.com

ETHELSTON, Frank Geoffrey (Oly) 17543 102nd Ave NE Apt 138, Bothell WA 98011 **Died 12/14/2015** B 1927 s Frank & Hilda. TS Dio Olympia 1969. D 5/26/1973 Bp Lane W Barton P 1/1/1980 Bp Robert Hume Cochrane. c 4. Ret 1996-2015; P-in-c Gr Ch Duvall WA 1993-1996; Dio Olympia Seattle 1991-1992; D & P Assoc S Jn's Ch Kirkland WA 1974-1990.

ETHEREDGE, Anne B (WLa) 905 Dafney Drive, Lafayette LA 70503 **Ch Of The Epiph Opelousas LA 2015-; Chapl Epis Sch of Acadiana Cade LA 2006-** B New Iberia LA 1964 d Gordon & Martha. BA LSU 1986; MDiv Epis TS of the SW 2005. D 6/4/2005 P 5/20/2006 Bp D Avid Bruce Macpherson. m 11/24/2012 James Newton Etheredge c 1. Epis Sch Of Acadiana Inc. Cade LA

2013-2015; P for Fam & Yth S Barn Epis Ch Lafayette LA 2007-2012; Cur Ch Of The Ascen Lafayette LA 2005-2006.

ETHRIDGE, Forrest Eugene (Ga) 2408 Forest Ave NW, Fort Payne AL 35967 **Ret 1994-; Assoc S Phil's Ch Ft Payne AL 1992-** B Atlanta GA 1923 s Eugene & Addie. Cert U Chi 1943; BS Georgia Inst of Tech 1949; MDiv Nash 1967. D 6/10/1967 P 1/25/1968 Bp Albert R Stuart. c 1. H Cross Ch Thomson GA 1983-1991; Vic Trin Ch Harlem Harlem GA 1983-1991; S Mich's Ch Waynesboro GA 1969-1983; Vic S Phil's Ch Hinesville Hinesville GA 1968-1969; Dioc Coun Dio Georgia Savannah GA 1973-1976.

ETTENHOFER, Karen Ruth (NMich) 500 Ogden Ave, Escanaba MI 49829 B Escanaba MI 1952 d Lloyd & Laverne. D 9/19/2010 Bp Thomas Kreider Ray. m 4/8/1972 Francis Ettenhofer c 2.

ETTLING, Albert John (Tex) 4383 Varsity Ln, Houston TX 77004 **Died 11/16/2015** B Lake Charles LA 1919 s Albert & Dorothy. BA Washington U 1940; UTS 1942; MDiv EDS 1943. D 5/29/1942 P 2/27/1943 Bp William Scarlett. m 1/30/1943 Emily Tucker c 5. Ret 1986-2015; Chapl U of Houston Houston TX 1969-1985; Chapl Texas Sthrn U Houston TX 1969-1973; Chair, COM Dio Texas Houston TX 1964-1971, Mem, COM 1956-1971; The Great Cmsn Fndt Houston TX 1960-1985; Gr Epis Ch Houston TX 1960-1969; Vic S Pat's Ch Houston TX 1960-1969; S Geo's Epis Ch Texas City TX 1953-1960; S Andr's Ch Stillwater OK 1949-1953; H Cross Epis Ch Poplar Bluff MO 1943-1949.

EUNSON, Lisa Kei (Cal) St Ternan's Rectory, High Street, Banchory - AB31 5TB Great Britain (UK) **Died 6/17/2017** B Tokyo Japan 1954 d Robert & Katherine. BA San Francisco St U 1978; MDiv CDSP 2001. D 12/1/2001 P 6/1/2002 Bp William Edwin Swing. R serving in Scottish Episcoal Ch Banchory (Dio Abe 2006-2017; Assoc R S Paul's Epis Ch Burlingame CA 2001-2006.

EUSTACE, Warren Paul (ECR) 1604 E. Nectarine Ave., Lompoc CA 93436 B San Jose CA 1955 s Warren & Lynda. BA Sch for Deacons 2005. D 6/18/2005 Bp Sylvestre Donato Romero. m 7/17/1993 Kindra L Fish c 1. D S Thos Epis Ch Sunnyvale CA 2005-2010.

EUSTIS, Patricia Anne (Oly) 2200 Koch Dr Apt 313, Bismarck ND 58503 **P-in-c All SS Ch Milan NM 2013-** B Philadelphia PA 1945 d George & Anna. U of Maryland; MDiv EDS 1998. D 6/5/1999 P 6/3/2000 Bp M(Arvil) Thomas Shaw. c 3. Dio Olympia Seattle 2010-2012; R St Steph's Epis Ch Oak Harbor WA 2010; Int R S Barn Ch Falmouth MA 2007-2009; R Trin Epis Ch Cranford NJ 2004-2007; Assoc S Phil's Epis Ch Laurel MD 2003-2004; R Sherwood Epis Ch Cockeysville MD 2001-2003; Asst R Trin Ch Concord MA 1999-2001. Co-Auth, "Dom Violence T/F Report," *Med Educ Journ*, City of Boston, 1996; Co-Auth, "Dom Violence & The Healer's Responsee:Strategies for Identifying and Treating People Who Experienced Dom Violence," *Ohio St Med Assn Journel*, Ohio St Med Assn, 1996; Co-Auth, "Intimate Violence and the Healer's Response," *Harv Ldrshp Forum*, Harv, 1995; Auth, "hon You, hon Me ,Conflict Resolution," *Safe Nbrhd*, City of Boston, 1993. Co-Cnvnr Concord River Dnry 2000-2001; Dio Ma Wmn Crisis Com; Chair 1997-2001; Ma Epis Cleric Assn; Bd Mem 1999. Allison Cheek Feminist Liberation Theol Prize EDS.

EVANCHO, Nicholas (NwPa) D 5/7/2017 Bp Sean Walter Rowe.

EVANS, Aaron Jay (WMich) 1115 W Summit Ave, Muskegon MI 49441 **St Jn's Epis Ch of Sturgis Sturgis MI 2013-; COM Dio Wstrn Michigan Kalamazoo MI 2012-** B San Antonio TX 1977 s Robbie & Nan. BA E Texas Bapt U 1999; MALS Valparaiso U 2003; MDiv Sewanee: The U So, TS 2008. D 12/15/2007 P 7/2/2008 Bp Edward Stuart Little II. m 4/6/2002 Rachael Nichole Johnson c 1. R Trin Epis Ch Grand Ledge MI 2010-2013; Supply P Leonidas Polk Memi Epis Mssn Leesville LA 2008-2009. The Soc of Cath Priests 2010.

EVANS, Amber (Cal) 1357 Natoma St, San Francisco CA 94103 **Chapl S Matt's Epis Day Sch San Mateo CA 2008-; S Matt's Epis Ch San Mateo CA 2006-** B Topeka 1979 BA Washington U 2001; MDiv CDSP 2005; MA CDSP 2007. D 6/3/2006 Bp William Edwin Swing P 12/2/2006 Bp Marc Handley Andrus. m 10/8/2005 Colin H Evans. Assoc S Greg Of Nyssa Ch San Francisco CA 2008-2014; Assoc Ch Of The Epiph San Carlos CA 2006-2008.

EVANS, Bill (Ga) 675 Holly Drive, Marietta GA 30064 B Kalamazoo MI 1944 s Robert & Mabel. BA MI SU 1966; SAIS JHU 1967; Cntr for European Stds Bologna IT 1968; MDiv Hur CA 1974. D 6/15/1974 P 6/9/1975 Bp H Coleman Mcgehee Jr. m 12/23/1967 Karen Evans c 2. S Paul's Epis Ch Chattanooga TN 2006-2008; Int Ch Of The H Cross Decatur GA 2004-2005; Int H Sprt Epis Ch Cumming GA 2003-2004; Int Chr Ch Macon GA 2002-2003; Epis Ch Of The H Sprt Cumming GA 2001-2002; S Dav's Ch Roswell GA 2000-2001; Int S Mich And All Ang Ch Stone Mtn GA 1999-2000; Int S Anne's Epis Ch Atlanta GA 1998-1999; Int Ch Of Our Sav Silver Sprg MD 1997-1998; Int Gr Epis Ch Silver Sprg MD 1995-1997; Int Imm Ch-On-The-Hill Alexandria VA 1994-1995; Int Ch Of The H Comf Vienna VA 1993-1994; Int S Jas' Epis Ch Mt Vernon VA 1992-1993; S Ptr's Epis Ch S Louis MO 1986-1991; Assoc S Ptr's Ladue MO 1986-1991; R S Andr's Ch Waterford MI 1979-1986; Asst S Jas Ch Grosse Ile MI 1976-1979; Cur Trin Epis Ch Alpena MI 1974-1976.

EVANS III, Boyd Mccutchen (ETenn) Church of St Thomas, 124 E Main St, Abingdon VA 24210 **S Thos' Epis Ch Abingdon VA 2016-** B Marion, VA 1966 s Boyd & Martha. B.S. Tennessee Tech U 1989; M.S. Tennessee Tech U 1991; Ph.D. U of Tennessee 2007; M.Div. Sewanee: The U So, TS 2016. D 2/

E

6/2016 Bp George Young III P 11/30/2016 Bp Mark Bourlakas. m 12/16/1995 Kathy Lynn Nichols c 2.

EVANS, Carol S (O) 246 Cedar Ave, Ravenna OH 44266 **R Gr Ch Ravenna OH 1998-** B Hannibal MO 1957 d Virgil & Virginia. BA Truman St U 1988; MA Louisville Presb TS 1991; MDiv CDSP 1995. D 6/24/1995 P 12/27/1995 Bp Richard Lester Shimpfky. m 6/7/1991 Maynard B Evans. P S Steph's Epis Ch Sn Luis Obispo CA 1995-1996. Aamft.

EVANS, Caryllou Deedee (Kan) St. James Episcopal Church, 3750 E. Douglas, Wichita KS 67208 **Ret 2002-; D S Jas Ch Wichita KS 1986-** B Everett WA 1936 d William & Bellva. BS Friends U 1993. D 10/24/1986 Bp Richard Frank Grein. m 1/28/1955 Dennis Leigh Evans c 2. Chapl Harry Hynes Memi Hospice 1989-2002. OHC 1984-2004.

EVANS II, C David (NwPa) 506 Young Rd, Erie PA 16509 **Int S Ptr's Epis Ch Ashtabula OH 2007-; Eccl Crt 2003-; Stwdshp T/F 1999-; Resolutns Com 1998-** B Elkhart IN 1945 s Clifford & Flora. BS Pur 1968; MDiv Nash 1989; The Ch Dvlpmt Inst 1999; Ncd Trng Level 1 & 2 2005; Clp Class 17 2006. D 12/17/1988 P 6/20/1989 Bp Francis Campbell Gray. m 6/19/1966 Lorraine S Evans c 4. Dio NW Pennsylvania Erie PA 2004-2007; Cn To The Bp Dio NW PA 2004-2007; Dioc Coun 2003-2006; Bd Exam Chapl 1998-2000; R Ch Of The H Sprt Erie PA 1992-2004; S Ptr's Ch Bainbridge NY 1990-1992.

EVANS, David Hugh (Mich) 1926 Morris St, Sarasota FL 34239 **Non-par 1978-** B Detroit MI 1934 s Robert & Doris. BA U MI 1957; MDiv SWTS 1964. D 6/29/1964 Bp Chauncie Kilmer Myers P 4/10/1965 Bp Richard Stanley Merrill Emrich. m 2/21/1983 Nancy Ann Evans. R Gr Ch Mt Clemens MI 1967-1977; Vic S Barth's Ch Swartz Creek MI 1964-1966.

EVANS, Dolores Elaine (Be) 184 Meadow Lane, Conestoga PA 17516 B Lancaster PA 1944 d Franklin & Beatrice. D 9/29/2007 P 8/15/2008 Bp Paul Victor Marshall. c 2.

EVANS, Gareth Clive (Mass) 148 Newtown Rd, Acton MA 01720 **R The Ch Of The Gd Shpd Acton MA 2010-; Chairperson Acton/Boxborough/Stowe Interfaith Cler Assoc. 2012-** B Lancashire England 1968 s Reginald & Freda. Bachelor of Theol Oxf 1997; Mstr of Theol Stds Harvard DS 2002. Trans 6/25/2004 Bp M(Arvil) Thomas Shaw. m 6/1/2010 Frances E Bean c 2. R S Jn's Ch Charlestown (Boston) Charlestown MA 2004-2010; Int S Ptr's Epis Ch Cambridge MA 2002-2004; Chapl Pensions and Ovrs Benefits Agcy Newcastle UK 1997-2000; Cur All SS' Ch Newcastle-upon-Tyne UK 1996-2000; Chapl Sanderson Elderly Care Hosp Newcastle UK 1996-2000; Bdgt Com Dio Massachusetts Boston MA 2004-2010, Dioc Coun 2004-2010, Dioc Coun Exec Com 2004-2010.

EVANS, Gary T (NMich) 1000 Bluff View Dr Apt 112, Houghton MI 49931 B El Paso TX 1940 s Thomas & Evelyn. BA U of Montevallo 1962; MA SWTS 1967; MDiv SWTS 1980. D 7/27/1985 P 2/1/1986 Bp Thomas Kreider Ray. 1991-2002; P-in-res Ch Of The Trsfg Ironwood MI 1988-1991; Reg Mssnr Wstrn Reg Nthrn Michigan MI 1988-1991; Asst to Bp Dio Nthrn Michigan Marquette MI 1984-1988. Contrib, "Living Simply," Seabury Press, 1981; Co-Auth, "Equipping God's People," Seabury Press, 1979. Epis Mnstry Dvlpmt Cltn 1986-1989.

EVANS, Geoffrey Parker (Ala) 1727 Post Oak Ct., Auburn AL 36830 **R H Trin Epis Ch Auburn AL 2014-** B Huntsville AL 1984 s Ronald & Claudia. BA U of Alabama Birmingham 2006; MDiv VTS 2010. D 6/2/2010 Bp John Mckee Sloan Sr P 12/7/2010 Bp Henry Nutt Parsley Jr. m 6/26/2010 Emily Robertson Evans c 1. Asst to the R S Mary's-On-The-Highlands Epis Ch Birmingham AL 2010-2014. geoff@holytrinitychurch.info

EVANS, Haydn Barry (Pa) 214 New Street, 4N, Philadelphia PA 19106 B Washington DC 1936 s Haydn & Laura. BA Br 1959; Westcott Hse Cambridge 1961; MDiv VTS 1962. D 10/6/1962 Bp Alexander Blankingship P 1/1/1964 Bp William Foreman Creighton. m 9/19/1992 Elizabeth Anne Eisenstadt c 4. Int The Ch Of The H Comf Drexel Hill PA 2006-2007; Int S Mart's Ch Wayne PA 2005-2006; S Paul Ch Exton PA 2003-2005; Int St. Paul's Epis Ch W Whiteland PA 2003-2005; Int Trin Ch Gulph Mills Kng Of Prussia PA 2001-2003; S Alb's Ch Newtown Sq PA 2001; Int S Mary's Ch Wayne PA 1999-2000; Int Trin Epis Ch Ambler PA 1996-1999; The Grubb Inst Wayne PA 1994-1999; Pres Grubb Inst USA Washington DC 1984-1997; The Grubb Inst Washington DC 1984; Cathd of St Ptr & St Paul Washington DC 1970-1983; Dir of Prog Coll of Preachers Washington DC 1970-1983; Cur Ch Of S Steph And The Incarn Washington DC 1963-1970. Auth, "Excellence in Mnstry," Personal & Profsnl Dvlpmt Needs of Cler of the Epis Ch, ECF, 1988; Auth, "Success & Failure of a Rel Club," Bldg Effective Mnstry, Harper & Row, 1983; Auth, "Homil," A Revs of Rel Cmncatn, Acad of Homil, 1976.

EVANS, Holly Sue (CNY) PO Box 319, Copenhagen NY 13626 **Gr Ch Copenhagen NY 2009-** B Dover NH 1949 d David & Ruth. Formation Prog of The Dio Cntrl New York; BA Hobart and Wm Smith Colleges 1971; MEd SUNY 1988. D 10/7/2006 Bp Gladstone Bailey Adams III. c 2. Shared Epis Mnstry E Lowville NY 2006-2009.

EVANS, Jacob Joseph (Alb) 5 Simpson Ave, Round Lake NY 12151 **S Matt's Ch Latham NY 2017-** B Exeter NH 1961 s John & Dorothy. BS U of New

Hampshire 1983; MA Nash 2014; MA Nash TS 2014. D 5/31/2014 P 1/6/2015 Bp William Howard Love. m 9/29/1990 Carlene Hirsch Evans c 2.

EVANS, James Eston (Pa) 1013 Balfour Cir, Phoenixville PA 19460 B Grand Rapdis MI 1942 s James & Helen. BA IL Wesl 1965; BD Nash 1968. D 6/15/1968 P 12/1/1968 Bp James Winchester Montgomery. m 3/30/1964 Nancy Barclay Evans c 4. Int S Mary's Ch Wayne PA 1999-2002; P-in-c Chr Ch Bridgeport PA 1990-1998; St Peters Place Phoenixville PA 1990-1998; R S Ptr's Ch Phoenixville PA 1974-1990; Vic Ch of the Blessed Sacr Green Bay WI 1970-1974; Cur S Thos Ch Menasha WI 1968-1970. j.evans@churchhousing4u.org

EVANS, James W (Dal) 401 S. Crockett, Sherman TX 75092 **P-in-c S Steph's Epis Ch Sherman TX 2014-; P The Epis Ch Of The H Nativ Plano TX 2012-; Coll Mnstry Cmsn Dio Dallas TX 2015-** B Durham NC 1981 s Jim & Melinda. BS U NC; ThM Dallas TS 2009; Cert Ang Stud Nash 2010. D 1/25/2011 P 4/3/2013 Bp James Monte Stanton. m 7/22/2007 Alicia J Marsh. Cur Ch Of The Gd Shpd Terrell TX 2011-2012. Auth, "Have Faith?," The Angl Dig, SPEAK, inc., 2016; Auth, "On Wrath and Hell: A Thomistic Dialog," LivCh, LivCh Fndt, 2011. GAS 2011; OSL the Physcn 2010.

EVANS, Jeffrey Keith (Ala) St Timothy's Episcopal Church, 207 E Washington St, Athens AL 35611 **S Tim's Epis Ch Athens AL 2012-** B Birmingham AL 1966 s Clarence & Annette. BA U of Alabama Birmingham 1989; MDiv GTS 2012. D 5/22/2012 P 12/12/2012 Bp John Mckee Sloan Sr. m 5/18/1996 Isabel Thomas Evans c 2.

EVANS, John Frederick (WA) 10450 Lottsford Rd Apt 3115, Mitchellville MD 20721 **Ret 1988-** B Dunmore PA 1921 s Clarence & Marguerite. BA Ob 1943; MA Harv 1947; MDiv VTS 1962. D 6/9/1962 Bp Robert Fisher Gibson Jr P 6/22/1963 Bp Samuel B Chilton. m 8/27/1943 Mary R Evans c 2. P-in-c Ch Of Our Sav Silver Sprg MD 1998-1999; Int Gr Epis Ch Silver Sprg MD 1996-1997; Int S Mary's Epis Ch Foggy Bottom Washington DC 1988-1990; Dio Washington Washington DC 1979-1988; Asst Soc Mnstrs Washington DC 1979-1988; R Ch Of The Ascen Silver Sprg MD 1975-1979; R Ch Of Our Sav Washington DC 1968-1975; Asst Min S Jn's Ch Lafayette Sq Washington DC 1965-1968. Natl Interfaith Cltn on Aging 1980. Sprtlty and Aging Awd Natl Interfaith Cltn of Aging 2004; Phi Beta Kappa.

EVANS, John Howard (NH) 1215 Main Rd Apt 211, Tiverton RI 02878 **Died 5/31/2016** B Providence RI 1917 s Irving & Emily. BA Br 1940; MDiv Ya Berk 1943. D 10/24/1943 Bp James D Perry P 6/11/1944 Bp William A Lawrence. Ret 1980-2016; S Lk's Ch Charlestown NH 1970-1979; Un-St. Lk's Epis Ch Claremont NH 1970-1979; R S Jas Ch The Par Of N Providence RI 1964-1970; Vic S Matt's Ch Paramus NJ 1960-1964; R Ch Of The H Cross Troy NY 1957-1960; Asst S Paul's Ch Englewood NJ 1954-1956; Chapl Seamens Ch Inst New York NY 1948-1954; Vic Ch Of The Gd Shpd Fitchburg MA 1945-1948; The Chap Of All SS Leominster MA 1945-1948; Asst S Steph's Ch Pittsfield MA 1943-1945. Auth, Vignettes of New Engl, Connell Sullivan Press, 1958.

EVANS, John Miles (Md) PO Box 1272, PO Box 1272, Portsmouth NH 03802 **Hon Assoc S Ign of Antioch NY NY 2012-** B Chicago IL 1939 s Mydrim & Gladyce. BA Ya 1961; BA U of Cambridge 1964; JD Ya 1967; MA U of Cambridge 1968; MDiv NYTS 1993. Trans 4/1/1999 Bp Robert Wilkes Ihloff. m 12/17/2016 Douglas Michael Allen c 1. R All Hallows Par So River Edgewater MD 1999-2006; Int Chr Epis Ch Lynbrook NY 1998-1999; Trst Nash 1980-1992; Vice Chair S Hilda & S Hugh Sch NY NY 1979-1990; Com Cn Dio New York New York NY 1979-1983. Bd Mem Affirming Catholicism 2001; Ecum Soc Blessed Vrgn Mary 1993; Knight of Justice, Ord of of St. Jn 1973; Soc for Values in Higher Educ 1961; Soc of Cath Priests 2010.

EVANS, Jonathan W (SwFla) **S Bon Ch Sarasota FL 2017-** D 12/3/2016 Bp Dabney Tyler Smith.

EVANS, Karen (At) 675 Holly Drive, Marietta GA 30064 B Memphis TN 1944 d Kurt & Edna. BA Wilson Coll 1965; MA JHU 1967; MDiv S Johns Prov Sem 1984. D 6/30/1984 Bp Henry Irving Mayson P 5/25/1985 Bp H Coleman Mcgehee Jr. m 12/23/1967 Bill Evans c 2. R S Jas Epis Ch Marietta GA 1998-2009; R Emm Epis Ch Alexandria VA 1991-1998; R S Paul's Ch S Louis MO 1989-1991; Asst S Steph's Ch S Louis MO 1986-1988; Asst S Mich's Ch Grosse Pointe MI 1984-1986.

EVANS, Katharine Cope (Mass) 18 Lafayette Rd, Ipswich MA 01938 B Bryn Mawr PA 1946 d Francis & Rachel. BA Wellesley Coll 1968; MAT Br 1969; MDiv EDS 1995. D 9/8/1996 Bp M(Arvil) Thomas Shaw P 5/8/1997 Bp Donald Purple Hart. c 2. R Emm Epis Ch Wakefield MA 1999-2005; Asst S Paul's Ch Dedham MA 1996-1999. Fllshp of S Jn 1992; SCHC 1985. NDEA Fell Br 1968; Durant Schlr Wellesley Coll 1968; Pendleton Schlr Wellesley Coll 1964.

EVANS, Leonard D (U) 515 S 1000 E Apt 506, Salt Lake City UT 84102 B Jacksonville FL 1943 s Leonard & Margaret. BA Arizona St U 1965; MDiv PDS 1968. D 6/22/1968 Bp Russell S Hubbard P 7/1/1969 Bp John Joseph Meakin Harte. m 2/7/1981 Vicki C Evans c 1. Asst S Paul's Ch Salt Lake City UT 2009-2013; Int All SS Ch Phoenix AZ 2008-2009; Int S Barn EpiscopalChurch Tooele UT 2007-2008; Dio Utah Salt Lake City UT 2004-2008, 2001-2004; Int Gr Epis Ch St Geo UT 2004-2005; Int S Mary's Ch Provo UT

2004; Int Ch Of The Resurr Centerville UT 2002-2004; S Mich's Ch Brigham City UT 2001-2002; Dio Arizona Phoenix AZ 2001; R S Paul's Ch Phoenix AZ 1993-2001; Cn Gr Cathd Topeka KS 1989-1993; R Trin Epis Ch El Dorado KS 1984-1989; S Geo's Epis Ch Holbrook AZ 1977-1984; Vic S Paul's Epis Ch Winslow AZ 1977-1984; S Raphael In The Vlly Epis Ch Benson AZ 1976-1977; R S Andr's Epis Ch Nogales AZ 1973-1975; Cur S Jas Epis Ch Danbury CT 1970-1973; Cur S Andr's Ch Stamford CT 1969-1970; D S Clements Ch Philadelphia PA 1968-1969; Chapl U Pa Med Cntr 1968-1969.

EVANS, Maria Louise (Mo) B Macon MO 1960 d William & Georgia. D 12/17/2016 P 6/29/2017 Bp George Wayne Smith.

EVANS, Mark E (Spr) 402 Pekin St., P.O. Box 386, Lincoln IL 62656 **R Trin Ch Lincoln IL 2011-** B Mason City IA 1959 s E Eugene & Dorothy. BA Luther Coll 1981; MBA Drake U 1983; MDiv Nash 2009. D 12/20/2008 P 6/27/2009 Bp Russell Edward Jacobus. m 7/29/2006 Sandra Moore c 2. Dir. of Ch Relatns Nash Nashotah WI 2010-2011. rector@trinitylincolnil.org

EVANS, Noah H (Pgh) 240 Woodhaven Dr., Pittsburgh PA 15228 **S Paul's Epis Ch Pittsburgh PA 2017-** B Lansing MI 1977 s Richard & Carol. BA Washington U 2000; MDiv GTS 2004. D 6/12/2004 Bp M(Arvil) Thomas Shaw P 1/8/2005 Bp Gayle Harris. m 2/15/2003 Sara Irwin c 2. R Gr Epis Ch Medford MA 2008-2017; Dir, Micah Proj Dio Massachusetts Boston MA 2008-2009, Together Now Capital Cmpgn Com 2011-2012, Life Together Ldrshp Team 2010-2017, VP, Barbara C. Harris C&C 2009-2012, Bd Memeber, Barbara C. Harris Camp and Confernce Cntr 2006-2012; Assoc R S Anne's In The Fields Epis Ch Lincoln MA 2004-2008; Sem Trin Ch Of Morrisania Bronx NY 2003-2004; Sem Ch Of S Mary The Vrgn New York NY 2002-2003; Bd Chair Epis City Mssn Boston MA 2011-2017, Bd Mem 2005-2011. Wallace H. Kountze Cmnty Serv Awd Mystic Vlly NAACP 2016; Seymour Prize for Preaching GTS 2003. noah@stpaulspgh.org

EVANS, Norman Dean (Pa) 304 Lexington, Media PA 19063 B Springfield PA 1925 s Norman & Mae. BA Ursinus Coll 1948; MS U of Pennsylvania 1951; EdD Tem 1958; MA PrTS 1975. D 1/11/1958 Bp Andrew Y Tsu P 10/28/1972 Bp Alfred L Banyard. m 6/23/1951 Jacqueline Lentz. Supply P Dio Pennsylvania Philadelphia PA 1997-2003, Chair Pa Cmsn For Mnstry In Higher Educ 1990-1996; Int The Epis Ch Of The Adv Kennet Sq PA 1996-1997; Int Ch Of S Mart-In-The-Fields Philadelphia PA 1994-1995; Int R S Jn Concord PA 1992-1993; Int The Ch Of The H Trin Rittenhouse Philadelphia PA 1983-1984; Dce Dio New Jersey Trenton NJ 1973-1978; Assoc S Ptr's Ch Medford NJ 1972-1978; Asst Ch Of The Redeem Springfield PA 1958-1967. Auth, "Plnng & Dvlpmt Of Innovative Cmnty Colleges," Prentice Hall, 1973; Auth, "Handbook For Effective Curric Dvlpmt," Prentice Hall, 1967; Auth, "Handbook For The Effective Supervision Of Instrn," Prentice Hall, 1964. OHC 1970. Bp Albert Van Duzer Bp'S Medal Dio New Jersey 1973.

EVANS, Paul Fredric (Cal) 23 Seward St Apt C2, Saratoga Springs NY 12866 **P Assoc Ch Of Beth Saratoga Spg NY 2016-, P Assoc 1999-2016, 1982-1984** B Elizabeth NJ 1937 s Paul & A Mildred. BA SUNY at Buffalo 1960; STB (EL) Ya Berk 1963. D 6/15/1963 Bp Lauriston L Scaife P 6/22/1968 Bp Chauncie Kilmer Myers. Aux P Adirondack Mssn Brant Lake NY 1984-1999; Int Trin Ch San Francisco CA 1980-1981; n/a Angl Bibliopole Saratoga Sprg 1979-2011; Assoc The Epis Ch Of S Jn The Evang San Francisco CA 1976-1982; Vic S Barn Antioch CA 1969-1975; Ed, Pacific Churchman Dio California CA 1969-1970; Assoc Gr Cathd San Francisco CA 1968-1982; Spec Asst to Bp Suffr Dio California San Francisco CA 1968-1969; Cur S Paul's Cathd Buffalo NY 1963-1964. Auth, "Art Pottery of US," *Art Pottery of US*, Scribner's, 1987; Ed, "Pacific Churchman," *Pacific Churchman*, 1969; Auth, "Living Ch," *Living Ch*; Auth, "Var Museum and Resrch Pub," *Var Museum and Resrch Pub*. Angl Soc 2017; Ch Hist Soc 2017. Resrch Libraries in hon Of: Winterthur Museum, Del. 2000; Who's Who Amer Art Oakland CA Art Museum 1991.

EVANS, Rachael Nichole (WMich) 1115 W Summit Ave, Muskegon MI 49441 B Eau Claire WI 1980 d David & Karen. BA Valparaiso U 2002; MDiv Sewanee: The U So, TS 2008. D 12/15/2007 P 7/2/2008 Bp Edward Stuart Little II. m 4/6/2002 Aaron Jay Evans c 1. Howe Mltry Sch Howe IN 2016; S Mk's Par Howe IN 2016; Trin Ch Three Rivers MI 2014; R S Greg's Epis Ch Norton Shores MI 2009-2013; Cur St Jas Epis Ch and Sch Alexandria LA 2008-2009; Co-Yth Pstr S Jn The Evang Ch Elkhart IN 2003-2005. The Soc of Cath Priests 2010.

EVANS JR, Ralph Easen (CFla) 2804 Coral Shores Dr, Fort Lauderdale FL 33306 B Harrisburg PA 1948 s Ralph & Jean. BA Penn 1976; MDiv Nash 1980. D 6/13/1980 P 12/1/1980 Bp Dean Theodore Stevenson. m 7/24/1971 Patricia Evans c 2. R S Sebastian's By The Sea Melbourne Bch FL 2005-2010; R S Mk The Evang Ft Lauderdale FL 1990-2005; R S Steph's Ch Longmont CO 1983-1990; Vic S Aug's Ch Creede CO 1981-1983; Vic S Steph The Mtyr Epis Ch Monte Vista CO 1981-1983; Cur S Mary's Ch Wayne PA 1980-1981.

EVANS, Scott Charles (Alb) 15 W High St, Ballston Spa NY 12020 **All SS Ch Round Lake NY 2014-** B Newton NJ 1967 s John & Helen. BS Virginia Tech U 1990; MS U of Connecticut 1998; PhD Rensselaer Polythecnic Inst 2003; MA Nash 2009. D 5/30/2009 P 1/9/2010 Bp William Howard Love. m 7/13/1991 Stephanie Beth Evans c 4.

EVANS, Steven A (Ga) 4625 Sussex Pl, Savannah GA 31405 **Dir Forerunner Mnstrs Savannah GA 2005-** B Wilmington DE 1949 s Evan & Barbara. BA Duke 1984; MDiv Sewanee: The U So, TS 1992. D 6/20/1992 Bp Brice Sidney Sanders P 1/25/1993 Bp Harry Woolston Shipps. m 7/19/2008 Eunice Evans c 2. Forerunner Mnstrs Inc Savannah GA 2006-2009; Asst R Chr Ch Epis Savannah GA 1992-2005. Auth, "Matters of the Heart," *A Workbook for Personal Transformation*, Forerunner Press, 2009. SAMS 1985-1986.

EVANS, Theodore H. (WMass) 235 Walker St. Apt. 236, Lenox MA 01240 **Vstng P All SS Par (Ch of Engl) Bakewell Derbys 1996-; Ret 1995-** B Tuscaloosa AL 1933 s Theodore & Jean. AB Harv 1957; MDiv VTS 1961. D 6/23/1961 Bp Robert Fisher Gibson Jr P 4/19/1962 Bp The Bishop Of Hong Kong. m 10/31/1963 Valerie Evans c 3. Assoc S Ptr's Ch Weston MA 1999-2008, Vstng P 1996-1998; Vstng P All SS Par Bakewell Derbys 1997-1998; Dio Wstrn Massachusetts Springfield 1974-1995; R S Paul's Epis Ch Stockbridge MA 1974-1995; Epis Chapl At Harvard & Radcliffe Cambridge MA 1967-1974; Assoc Chapl Harvard Radcliffe Coll Cambridge MA 1967-1974; P-in-c S Chris Saigon Vietnam 1963-1967; Fac S Jn Coll Hong Kong 1961-1963. Contrib, "The Application of Love," *The Vietnam War: Chr Perspectives*, Eerdmans, 1967. tadevans33@gmail.com

EVANS JR, V Creighton (SwFla) All Souls Episcopal/Anglican Church, 101 Yoshihara, Chatan, Okinawa 904-0105 Japan **All Soul's Epis Ch Chatan Okinawa 2013-** B Charleston SC 1953 s V Creighton & Joan. BS Coll of Charleston 1977; MDiv TESM 1994. D 6/18/1994 P 1/4/1995 Bp Edward Lloyd Salmon Jr. m 7/1/1978 Nina Elizabeth Evans c 2. The Ch Of The Epiph Eutawville SC 2010-2011; Vic All Souls Epis Ch No Ft Myers FL 1998-2010; Vic S Mths Epis Ch Summerton SC 1994-1998.

EVENSON, Bruce John (SC) 34 Krier Ln, Mt Pleasant SC 29464 B New York NY 1946 s Swen & Aina. BA Witt 1968; MDiv Luth TS at Chicago 1972. D 1/21/1998 P 9/1/1998 Bp Edward Lloyd Salmon Jr. m 8/15/1987 Johanna Helander c 1. S Johannes Ch Charleston SC 2007-2011; Chapl Engl Ch Dio in Europe C.O.E. Stockholm 2002-2005; Chapl Porter-Gaud Sch Charleston SC 2001-2002; Chapl Porter-Gaud Sch Charleston SC 2001-2002; Assoc Gr Ch Cathd Charleston SC 2001, Assoc 1998-2000; Dir of Pstr Care Roper Hosp Charleston SC 1992-2001; Dir of Pstr Care Hosp for Spec Surgery New York City NY 1983-1992; Serv Luth Ch Westchester NY and NYC 1972-1982; Mem, Bd Trst So Carolina Charleston SC 2013. The Coll of Chapl 1983-2001.

EVERETT, Isaac J (Mass) 138 Tremont St, Boston MA 02111 **Dio Massachusetts Boston MA 2016-; Other Lay Position S Paul's Ch Brockton MA 2010-** B Indianapolis IN 1981 s Paul & Adele. BM NYU 2004; MDiv UTS 2008. D 6/4/2016 Bp Alan Gates P 3/31/2017 Bp Gayle Harris. m 10/11/2008 Katherine Everett. Other Lay Position S Geo's Epis Ch York ME 2014-2016.

EVERETT, Sherman Bradley (SO) 3206 Brandon Rd, Columbus OH 43221 B Portland OR 1936 D 10/30/1999 Bp Herbert Thompson Jr. m 8/30/1963 Joan Losingwoe c 2. Trin Ch Columbus OH 1999-2006.

EVERHARD, Darby Oliver (NC) 520 Summit Street, Winston Salem NC 27101 **Assoc S Paul's Epis Ch Winston Salem NC 2009-; S Jas Ch Dundee IL 2004-** B Natick MA 1949 BS Indiana U 1971; MDiv Bex Sem 2004. D 10/25/2003 Bp Herbert Thompson Jr P 6/19/2004 Bp Kenneth Lester Price. m 5/29/1999 Thomas C Everhard c 3. Cur S Thos Epis Ch Terrace Pk OH 2004-2009; Pres Bexley Soc 2003-2004.

EVERSLEY, Walter VL (Md) 214 Lambeth Rd, Baltimore MD 21218 B Georgetown GY 1940 s Walter & Gwendolyn. BA Moravian TS 1969; MA Harv 1974; PhD Harv 1976; JD Col 1981. D 6/11/1988 P 12/11/1988 Bp Paul Moore Jr. m 8/5/1963 Daphne Eversley c 3. R S Mich And All Ang Ch Baltimore MD 2001-2009; Theo-in-Res S Mary's Epis Ch Foggy Bottom Washington DC 2000-2001; Int Trin Ch Washington DC 1998-2000; Prof VTS Alexandria VA 1996-2001, Asst Prof 1988-1991; Assoc S Mary's Epis Ch Arlington VA 1989-1998; Prof NYTS New York NY 1975-1985; Instr Harvard DS Cambridge MA 1973-1975; Serv Moravian Ch of Amer 1972-1988. "Answered Prayers," *In Pursuit of a Useful Life*, New Visions Inst Pub, 2008; Auth, "The Pstr (Jonathan Edwards) as Revivalist," *Edwards in Our Time*, Erdman, 1999; Auth, *Handbook of Angl Theol*, 1998; Auth, "Jn Donne," *Soc of Promoting Chr Knowledge Handbook Angl Theol*, 1998; Auth, "Jesus & Culture," *Truth About Jesus*, 1998. AAR; Angl Theol Conf; SEAD, Jn Donne Soc. Resrch Fell Oxf 1996.

EVERSMAN, Karen Lynn (O) 2041 W. Reserve Cir., Avon OH 44011 **math tutor Cuyahoga Cmnty Coll 2003-** B Bethesda MD 1952 d James & Mary. BBA Ohio U 1973; MDiv EDS 1976. D 11/25/1978 P 11/4/1979 Bp John Mc Gill Krumm. P Calv Ch Sandusky OH 2000-2002; Int S Ptr's Epis Ch Lakewood OH 1999-2000; P Epis Shared Mnstry Of NW Ohio Sherwood OH 1998; P S Jas Bucyrus OH 1991-1995; math Instr/tutor No Cntrl Tech Coll 1990-1997; Int Chr Ch Lima OH 1988-1989; R Gr Ch Galion OH 1983-1987; Assoc S Ptr's Epis Ch Delaware OH 1980-1983; Serv Gr Ch Cincinnati OH 1978-1980.

EVERSON, Charles Webster (Kan) 4224 Charlotte St, Kansas City MO 64110 B Kansas City MO 1980 s Charles & Lori. Masters of Bus Admin Baker U; Cert of Presbyteral Stds Bp Kemper Sch for Mnstry; Bachelor of Arts Ouachita Bapt U. D 6/11/2016 P 1/7/2017 Bp Dean E Wolfe. m 1/17/2014 Jeremy Lee Wolf.

Cur S Lk's Epis Ch Shawnee KS 2016-2017, Cur 2016-. Soc of Cath Priests of The Epis Ch and the Angl Ch of Can 2016. charleseverson@gmail.com

EWART, Craig Kimball (NY) B Columbus OH 1943 s Cyril & Helen. BA Coll of Wooster 1965; STB PDS 1968; PhD Stan 1978. D 2/10/1969 P 12/1/1969 Bp Horace W B Donegan. m 6/1/1974 Anne Huntington Dunham c 2. P-t Asst St. Barth Ch New York NY 1971-1974; Cur S Aug's Ch New York NY 1969-1971. Homil Awd Chr Ch, Oxford, PA 1968.

EWING, Elizabeth (CNY) St Andrew's Episcopal Church, 4512 College Ave, College Park MD 20740 **Chr Ch Binghamton NY 2015-** B Lawrence KS 1956 d James & Ruth. BA U NC 1979; MSFS Geo Town U 1985; MDiv VTS 2012. D 5/12/2012 P 12/8/2012 Bp Pierre W Whalon. m 5/30/1987 Theodore H Andrews c 2. S Andr's Epis Ch Coll Pk MD 2012-2015. christchurch1810@gmail.com

EWING, Judith Lynette (SC) 203 Magnolia Bluff Dr, Columbia SC 29229 B Scarborough UK 1941 d Philip & Veronica. BEd Manchester Coll 1976; BSW Limestone Coll 1996; MS U of So Carolina 2003. D 12/14/2002 Bp Dorsey Henderson. Chr Epis Ch Mt Pleasant SC 2006-2013.

EWING, Ward Burleson (ETenn) P O Box 6, 213 Baker Cemetery Road, Ten Mile TN 37880 **Chair of Bd Gnrl Serv Bd AA 2009-; Trst Gnrl Serv Bd AA 2004-** B Johnson City TN 1942 s John & Frances. BA Trin 1964; STB GTS 1967. D 7/1/1967 Bp William F Gates Jr P 4/1/1968 Bp William Evan Sanders. m 5/11/1968 Jennings Ewing c 3. Dn & Pres The GTS New York NY 1998-2009; R Trin Epis Ch Buffalo NY 1985-1998; Vic S Ptr's Epis Ch Louisville KY 1975-1985; Cn S Jn's Cathd Jacksonville FL 1973-1975; Vic S Columba's Epis Ch Bristol TN 1968-1972; D-In-Trng Calv Ch Memphis TN 1967-1968. Auth, "Acts: Turning the Wrld Upside Down," *DOCC Educ series*, U So, 1998; Auth, "Mnstry, Power & Chr," *DOCC Educ series*, U So, 1995; Ed, "Disciples of Chr in Cmnty," *DOCC Educ series*, U So, 1993; Auth, "The Power Of The Lamb: Revelations Theol Of Liberation For You," Cowley, 1991; Auth, "Job: A Vision Of God," Seabury, 1975. D.D. U So 1999.

EXLEY, Lori Tucker (Pa) D 6/11/2016 Bp Clifton Daniel III P 12/17/2016 Bp Daniel Gutierrez.

EXNER, William Edward (NH) 19 W Union St, Goffstown NH 03045 **Natl Exec Com/VP EPF Ithaca NY 2002-** B Clifton Sprgs NY 1954 s Edward & Elizabeth. Rochester Inst of Tech 1974; Rochester Inst of Tech 1974; Cor 1975; Cor 1975; BA Ithaca Coll 1976; BA Ithaca Coll 1976; MDiv EDS 1982. D 6/26/1982 P 5/1/1983 Bp Robert Rae Spears Jr. m 7/12/1975 Jane B Bluhm c 4. R S Matt's Ch Goffstown NH 1985-2016; Vic Chr Ch Sackets Hbr NY 1982-1985; Cur Trin Epis Ch Watertown NY 1982-1985; Eccl Crt Dio New Hampshire Concord NH 2009-2012, Chair, Resolutns Com 2009-, Chair, Outreach Cmsn 2003-, Dioc Coun 2003-, Dep GC 1988-. EPF.

EYER-DELEVETT, Aimee E S (Los) All Saints By The Sea, 83 Eucalyptus Lane, Santa Barbara CA 93108 **R All SS-By-The-Sea Par Santa Barbara CA 2014-** B Indianapolis IN 1972 D 6/5/2004 P 12/10/2004 Bp J Neil Alexander. m 7/6/2014 Alyson Michele Eyer-Delevett c 1. R Ch Of The H Nativ Clarendon Hls IL 2006-2014; S Mary's Ch Pk Ridge IL 2004-2006. aimee@asbts.org

EYLERS, David Edward (NY) PO Box 352, Harwinton CT 06791 B Poughkeepsie NY 1940 s Dirk & Emily. BA Mar 1962; MDiv GTS 1965. D 6/12/1965 P 12/18/1965 Bp Horace W B Donegan. m 8/5/1967 Carla P Eylers c 3. R S Lk's Ch Beacon NY 1999-2006, 1980-1998; R S Mary's Ch Mohegan Lake NY 1971-1980; R S Thos Epis Ch New Windsor NY 1967-1971; Cur S Alb's Ch Simsbury CT 1965-1967.

EYTCHESON, Gerald Leonard (Kan) 2400 Gary Ave, Independence KS 67301 **Ch Of The Ascen Neodesha KS 1993-; Vic Ch Of The Epiph Independence KS 1993-** B Independence KS 1944 s Benjamin & Rose. AA Independence Cmnty Coll 1964; BS Pittsburg St U 1966; MS Pittsburg St U 1973; Bp Kemper Sch of Mnstry 1993; Dio Kansas Sch For Mnstry KS 1993. D 10/30/1987 Bp Richard Frank Grein P 6/23/1993 Bp William Edward Smalley. c 5. indespicopal@sbcglobal.net

EZELL II, Jim (ECR) 105 Dogwood Trl, Elizabeth City NC 27909 **R St Paul's/San Pablo Epis Ch Salinas CA 2007-** B Tulsa OK 1952 s James & Carol. BA Alfred U 1975; MDiv SWTS 1979. D 6/9/1979 P 12/1/1979 Bp Robert Bracewell Appleyard. m 11/20/2007 Marylyn L Ezell. The Morgan Sch Lenoir NC 1991-1993; S Lk's Epis Ch Asheville NC 1985-1991; Trin Epis Ch Asheville NC 1982-1985; Asst Chr Ch Greensburg PA 1979-1982; S Barth's Ch Scottdale PA 1979-1982; Vic S Barth's Scottsdale PA 1979-1982. Ord Of S Lk.

F

FAASS, Peter (O) 3566 Avalon Rd, Shaker Heights OH 44120 **R Chr Ch Shaker Heights OH 2006-** B Delft NL 1954 s Cornelius & Margaret. BA Wstrn Connecticut U 1977; MDiv GTS 1999. D 6/12/1999 Bp Clarence Nicholas Coleridge P 12/18/1999 Bp Andrew Donnan Smith. m 8/12/2013 Anthony F Kastellic. R The Epis Ch Of S Jn The Bapt Sanbornville NH 2001-2006;

Cur Trin Ch Torrington CT 1999-2001; Pres, Stndg Com Dio Ohio Cleveland 2011-2012. priest@cometochristchurch.org

FABIAN, Rick (Cal) 2525 Lyon St, San Francisco CA 94123 **Founding Dir All SS Co San Francisco CA 1974-** B Evanston IL 1942 s Francis & Gretchen. BA Ya 1965; MA U of Cambridge 1967; Coll of the Resurr 1969; MDiv GTS 1970. D 6/18/1970 Bp Theodore H McCrea P 1/30/1971 Bp Paul Moore Jr. m 2/25/2017 Greg Of Nyssa Ch San Francisco CA 1980-2007; Lectr Sch for Deacons San Francisco CA 1976-2000; Chapl Bp of California 1976-1977; Chapl Dio California San Francisco CA 1976-1977, Ch Growth & Evang Cmsn 1976-1990, Liturg & Mus Cmsn Chair 1976-; Chapl Episc Ch at Yale New Haven CT 1970-1976; Epis Ch At Yale New Haven CT 1970-1976. Auth, "The Scandalous Table," *Water Bread and Wine*, LeaderResource, 2012; Auth, "Norris's Razor," *ATR*, ATR, 2008; Compsr, "Mus in," *Mus for Liturg II*, All SS Co, 1999; Compsr, "Mus in," *Ch Hymnal Series 5: Congrl Mus for Euch*; Compsr, "Mus Hymnal 82, Mus in Wonder," *Love & Praise*. All SS Comp Founding Dir 1974; Intl Angl Liturg Consult 1989; NAAL 1981; Societas Liturgica 1987; Soc of Oriental Liturg 2010. Jones Lectures Sewanee DS 2006; Distinguished Alum GTS 2004.

FABRE, John P (Az) 18083 W Douglas Way, Surprise AZ 85374 **P-in-c S Chris's Ch Sun City AZ 2011-, Hisp Mnstry 2010-2016** B Mexico City 1944 s Gabriel & Virginia. BS Florida Sthrn Coll 1981; DTS Epis TS of the SW 2009. D 6/6/2009 P 1/3/2010 Bp Kirk Stevan Smith. m 7/24/1967 Barbara Fabre c 3. Hisp Mnstry Trin Cathd Phoenix AZ 2010, Hisp Mnstry 2009-2010.

FABRE, Julie Kilbride (U) 38105 Redwood Road #2191, West Valley City UT 84119 **Vstng Pstr To The Elderly 1997-** B 1953 d Harold & Jo. BA Harv 1979; MDiv CDSP 1985. D 5/25/1996 Bp George Edmonds Bates. m 7/17/2003 John Dickson Stewart. Epis Cmnty Serv Inc Salt Lake City UT 2002-2003, 1994-1996, 1993-1994; Dio Utah Salt Lake City UT 1996-2002.

FACCIO, David Franceschi (Pa) The Free Ch Of S Jn Philadelphia PA 2016- B Yauco 1969 s Jacinto & Alma. Trabajo Soc SUNY Empire St Coll 2006; Cert. Esp. Teologia San Pedro y San Pablo 2014. D 1/20/2013 P 8/16/2014 Bp David Andres Alvarez-Velazquez. Dio Puerto Rico Trujillo Alto PR 2014-2016.

FACKLER, Phillip Joseph Augustine (Pa) 1104 Mayberry Place, Raleigh NC 27609 B St Louis MO 1980 s James & Joan. BS U IL 2003; MDiv CDSP 2008; MA Grad Theol Un 2009. D 6/7/2008 P 12/6/2008 Bp Jeff Lee. m 9/4/2005 Callie E Swanlund. Chapl Dio No Carolina Raleigh NC 2017, Chapl 2016; Asst Ch Of The H Innoc San Francisco CA 2008-2009; Intern Cbury NW Evanston IL 2004-2005; Asst Dioc Yth Coordntr Dio Sthrn Malawi Blantyre 2003-2004. Auth, "Adversus Adversus Iudaeos: Countering Anti-Jewish Polemics in the Gospel of Nicodemus," *Journ of Early Chr Stds*, Johns Hopkins, 2015. Traebert-Graebner Gk Scriptural Scholars Awd CDSP 2006; Mercer Schlrshp Mercer Schlrshp Fund 2006; Soc for Increase in Minstiry Schlrshp Soc for the Increase in Mnstry 2006.

FACTOR, Beverly A (Los) 2620 Catherine Rd, Altadena CA 91001 B Paden City, WV 1939 d Charles & Geraldine. MDiv GTS 1995; BS Rgnts Coll SUNY Albany 1995; DMin SWTS 2004. D 7/25/1992 P 5/15/1993 Bp Herbert Thompson Jr. m 9/13/2007 Joseph Joel Elterman c 2. On-call Chapl BJC Med Cntr St. Louis MO 2004-2007; New Ch Plant - Mssnr for Monroe Cnty Dio Springfield Springfield IL 2002-2003; Sexual Misconduct Off Dio Los Angeles Los Angeles CA 2001-2002, Prevention of Misconduct and Chld Sexual Abuse Workshop Fac 1999-2002; Int S Patricks Ch And Day Sch Thousand Oaks CA 2001-2002; Int S Ptr's Par Santa Maria CA 2000-2001; Int S Mary's Par Lompoc CA 1998-2000; Vic S Fran Epis Ch Eureka MO 1995-1997; Cur Gr Ch Cincinnati OH 1992-1994; Advsry Com on Pension and Benefits Dio Sthrn Ohio Cincinnati OH 1994-1995, Lay Eucharistic Min Trnr 1994-1995, Prevention of Chld Sexual Abuse Workshop Fac 1994-1995, COM 1993-1995, Exec Com Capital Cmpgn 1993-1995.

FADELY, Diane Camille (Md) Trinity Episcopal Church, 120 Allegheny Ave, Towson MD 21204 **D Trin Ch Towson MD 2012-** B Roanoke VA 1943 d Abraham & Edna. BA U of Mary Washington 1965; MEd Loyola U 1976; CASE Loyola U 1982; DEd JHU 1989. D 6/2/2012 Bp Joe Goodwin Burnett. m 8/27/1966 Milton Harmon Fadely c 2.

FAETH, Margaret Ann (Va) 4529 Peacock Ave, Alexandria VA 22304 B Washington DC 1959 d William & Mary. BS U of Florida 1981; MBA MWC 1988; MDiv VTS 1996. D 6/15/1996 P 1/1/1997 Bp Peter J Lee. m 8/29/1981 Paul Eugene Faeth c 2. VTS Alexandria VA 2010-2011, 2001; Asst R Imm Ch-OnThe-Hill Alexandria VA 1996-2012.

FAGEOL, Suzanne Antoinette (Oly) Po Box 303, Langley WA 98260 B Akron OK 1949 d William & Suzanne. BA U of Vermont 1971; Hartford Sem 1973; U Chi 1977; MDiv SWTS 1987; Cert Heythrop Coll, Lon 1987; U of Aberdeen Aberdeen UK 1987; Cert Heythrop Coll, Lon 1988; Cert Inst for Somatic Transformation 2009; Cert Inst for Sprtl Ldrshp, Chicago Theo Sem 2009; MSD Lorian Cntr for Incarnational Sprtlty 2010; MSD Other 2010; Cert Aptitude Acad Netherlands 2011. D 6/4/1979 Bp James Winchester Montgomery P 7/11/1980 Bp Leland Stark. Emm Ch Orcas Island Eastsound WA 2007-2010; Assoc S Augustines In-The-Woods Epis Par Freeland WA 1996-2003; P Eductr Mvmt for the Ord of Wmn London UK 1985-1991; P St Hilda Experimental Wrshp

Cmnty London UK 1985-1991; Chapl/ Chair Dept Theol Cuttington U Coll Suakoko Liberia 1981-1984; Assoc / Dicesan Chair Chr Ed Trin Cathd Monrovia. Liberia W Afr 1981; Assoc S Andr's Ch St Thos VI 1980-1981; Asst to Archbp Angl Prov of Cntrl Afr 1980; Missions - Nigeria Prov V ECUSA 1980; Cur The Epis Ch Of S Jas The Less Northfield IL 1979-1980. Auth, "What to expect from an Interspiritual Sprtl Dir," *Presence: An Itnl Journ of Sprtl Direction 14:1*, Sprtl Dir Intl , 2008; Ed, "Who Are You Looking For," Wmn In Theol, 1998; Auth, "Sprtl Direction For The New Millenium," *Convergence 11:2*, Spr, 1998; Auth, "How To Set Up And Maintain A Sprtl Pract," *Convergence 8:2*, Spr, 1995; Auth, "Celebrating Experience," *Wmn Included*, Spck, 1990. Sprtl Dir Intl 1995; Wmn In Theol, Mvmt For The Ord Of Wmn 1984-1991. Fellowowship Heythrop Coll Of The Lon 1990.

FAGG, Randy Jay (Ida) PO Box 324, Rupert ID 83350 **P St Matthews Epis Ch Rupert ID 2007**- B 1948 s Ronald & Gladyce. BS U of Idaho 1971. D 10/22/2006 P 5/4/2007 Bp Harry Brown Bainbridge III.

FAHRNER, Pamela Henry (SC) Saint John's Episcopal Church, 5234 Maryland Hwy, Deer Park MD 21550 **Chapl Garrett Cnty Memi Hosp 2009-; P S Jn's Ch Oakland MD 2009-, D 2008-2009; Fac for Agape A Gathering of Wmn S Matt's Par Oakland MD 2008**- B Chicago IL 1946 d Clyde & Janis. AA Cerritos Coll Norwalk CA/UCLA 1977. D 7/5/2008 P 6/27/2009 Bp John L Rabb. m 11/27/1963 Jeffrey Fahrner c 2.

FAIN, Beth Ann Jernigan (Tex) 10515 Laneview Dr, Houston TX 77070 **R S Mary's Epis Ch Cypress TX 1997-; COM, Chair Dio Texas Houston TX 2008-, San Jacinto Convoc, Dn 2008-, Com for the Diac, Chair 2003-2008, Exam Chapl 1995-2003** B Waco TX 1951 d Austin & Elizabeth. BS Texas Womans U 1973; MEd Texas Womans U 1976; U of St Thos 1983; Cert Epis TS of the SW 1992; MDiv Houston Grad TS 1992. D 6/27/1992 P 1/25/1993 Bp Maurice Manuel Benitez. c 2. Asst to R S Dunst's Epis Ch Houston TX 1992-1997. DOK, Steph Mnstry. revdbeth@stmaryscypress.org

FAIN, Robert Duncan (Ga) 2230 Walton Way, Augusta GA 30904 B Hendersonville NC 1955 s James & Thomasina. BA Cit 1977; MDiv Sewanee: The U So, TS 1983. D 6/25/1983 P 2/24/1984 Bp William Gillette Weinhauer. m 12/31/1977 Debra A Fain c 2. Asst The Ch Of The Gd Shpd Augusta GA 1983-1992, R 1983-. Auth, "Christmas," *The Chorister(Dec/Jan)*, 2002; Auth, "Reservists Help Bridge the Gap," *Proceedings (June)*, US Naval Inst, 2000. Bd Dir Kanuga Conferences 2009; Bd Rgnts, the UOS 2004-2007; Chair Kanuga Conferences Prog Com 2009; Chair Search Com for the 10th Bp of Georgia 2008-2009; Dn Augusta Convoc 2003-2009; Naval Reserve Chapl 1985-1999; Trst Univ. Of the So 2011; V-P Ch Relatns- Assoc Alumuni UOS 2002-2005.

FAIR, Verna M (Chi) 1134 Highpointe Dr, Dekalb IL 60115 **R S Jn's Epis Ch Naperville IL 2006**- B Chicago IL 1954 d Walter & Dorothy. BS U IL 1977; MDiv McCormick TS 1982; MS Nthrn Illinois U 2003. D 6/19/1982 P 3/1/1983 Bp Quintin Ebenezer Primo Jr. m 10/16/1996 Rodney Dana Fair c 1. Gr Ch Sterling IL 2003-2006; P-in-c S Lk's Ch Dixon IL 2003-2006; Chapl Off Of Bsh For ArmdF New York NY 1994-1999; R Ch Of The H Cross Chicago IL 1985-1994; Cur S Geo & Mths 1982-1984. Chi Alpha Epsilon hon Soc 2003; Golden Key Intl hon Soc 2008; Kappa Delta Pi Intl hon Soc for Educators 2007. Navy Achievement Medal U. S. Navy 1999; Meritorious Unit Commendation U. S. Marine Corps 1996; Natl Defense Medal U. S. Navy 1994; Ldrshp Awd U. S. Navy 1994.

FAIRBANKS, Barbara Jean (Minn) 3044 Longfellow Ave, Minneapolis MN 55407 **Chapl One in the Sprt Mnstry 2008**- B Wagner SD 1954 d Phillip & Eva. BS Dakota Coll 1979; MEd So Dakota St U 1980; MDiv Untd TS of the Twin Cities 2009. D 12/11/2008 P 6/27/2009 Bp James Louis Jelinek. m 6/9/2001 Guy Fairbanks c 2.

FAIRFIELD, Roger Louis (EO) 69793 Pine Glen Rd, Sisters OR 97759 B Long Beach CA 1942 s Robert & Margaret. BS OR SU 1964; MS U CA 1966. D 6/10/2006 Bp William O Gregg. m 6/13/1964 Dixie Fairfield c 2.

FAIRLESS, Caroline (NH) 8 Whispering Pines Rd, Wilmont NH 03287 **retreat Fac The Cntr for Courage and Renwl Seattle WA 2007-; writer Writer and blogger 2000-; Dir The Cntr for Chld at Wrshp Wilmot NH 1999**- B Pittsburgh PA 1947 d Blaine & Caroline. AA Centenary Coll 1967; BA Barnard Coll of Col 1971; MDiv CDSP 1989. D 6/3/1989 P 6/9/1990 Bp William Edwin Swing. m 12/8/2001 James R Sims. S Andr's Ch New London NH 2008-2012; S Jas Epis Ch Bowie MD 2004-2007; S Jn's Ch Roanoke VA 1999-2000; Vic Ch Of The H Fam Fresno CA 1993-1999; Assoc S Paul's Epis Ch San Rafael CA 1989-1992. Auth, "The Space Between Ch & Not-Ch ~ A Sacramental Vision for the Healing of our Planet," U Press of Amer, 2011; Auth, "Hambone," Ch Pub, 2001; Auth, "New Voices/Ancient Words: Dramatic Adaptions Of Scripture," Ch Pub, 2001; Auth, "Confessions Of A Fake P," Ch Pub, 2001; Auth, "Chld At Wrshp: Congregations In Bloom," Ch Pub, 2001.

FAIRLEY, Pamela Sue (Dal) D 6/24/2017 Bp George Robinson Sumner Jr.

FAIRMAN, Henry Francis (RI) 73 Touisset Ave, Swansea MA 02777 **Ret 1999-; 1987**- B Providence RI 1934 s John & Emily. BA Bos 1956; MDiv Ya Berk 1959; MS Marywood U 1980. D 6/20/1959 P 12/19/1959 Bp John S Higgins. m 6/6/1958 Janis L Fairman c 4. Neponset Cmnty Serv Boston MA 1994-1995; Admin/COO Neponset Cmnty Serv 1989-1999; Int S Lk's Ch Pawtucket RI

1985-1986; S Mk's Epis Ch Riverside RI 1985, Int 1982-1983; Dir Edlerly Fam Serv Assn 1980-1989; 1978-1982; R Calv Wilkes Barre PA 1974-1978; H Cross Epis Ch Wilkes Barre PA 1974-1978; S Jas-Dundaff Carbondale PA 1974-1978; Trin Epis Ch Pittston PA 1974-1978; R Calv Wilkes Barre PA 1972-1973; Coordntr Dio Bethlehem Bethlehem PA 1972-1973; R S Lk's Ch Lebanon PA 1970-1972; R S Ptr's Epis Ch Hazleton PA 1965-1970; S Steph's Epis Ch Wilkes Barre PA 1962-1965; Vic The Epis Ch Of S Clem And S Ptr Wilkes Barre PA 1962-1965; Vic S Thos' Alton Wood River Jct RI 1959-1961. Who's Who in Rel 1976.

FAIRWEATHER, Carolynne Marie (Ore) 4061 Hayes St. #28, Newberg OR 97132 **Asst Chr Ch Par Lake Oswego OR 2005-; Ecum Off Dio Oregon Portland OR 2013-; Prov VIII Coordntr Epis Dioc Ecum and Interreligious Off 2013-; Cnvnr - Ecum and Interfaith Cmsn Dio Oregon Portland OR 2011**- B Grimsby England 1945 d Robert & June. BA Paterson St Coll 1966; BA Wm Paterson U 1982; MDiv Drew U 1986; DMin Drew U 1995. D 4/30/2003 Bp Robert Louis Ladehoff P 10/18/2003 Bp Johncy Itty. m 9/7/1996 Roger Weeks c 2. Trin Epis Cathd Portland OR 2004-2005; S Jas Epis Ch Portland OR 2003-2004; Chapl Legacy Meridian Pk Hosp Tualatin OR 1997-2010. Assembly of Epis Healthcare Chapl 2004; Assn of Profsnl Chapl 2000. Robert E. Hallman Serv Awd Boys and Girls Club of Coastal Carolina 2012; Natl Outstanding Loc Ldr Awd Assn of Profsnl Chapl 2011.

FAISON, Dee Doheny (Pa) 405 Warren Rd, West Chester PA 19382 B Darby PA 1947 d Joseph & Dorothy. BA Rosemont Coll 1979; MDiv Luth TS 1987; Samar Counslg Cntr 1993; Pennsylvania Coun Relationships 1997. D 6/20/1987 Bp Allen Lyman Bartlett Jr. c 3. Dir of Chapl Norristown St Hosp Norristown PA 1998-2013; Dir of Chapl Haverford St Hosp Haverford 1993-1998; S Jn The Evang Ch Lansdowne PA 1991-2004; D Ch Of The Redeem Bryn Mawr PA 1990-1991; D S Mart's Epis Ch Upper Chichester PA 1987-1989.

FAISON, Diane Elizabeth (Pa) **D Incarn H Sacr Epis Ch Drexel Hill PA 2017**- D 6/17/2017 Bp Daniel Gutierrez.

FAIT JR, Harold Charles (Minn) D 11/30/1974 Bp Philip Frederick McNairy P 2/24/1993 Bp Sanford Zangwill Kaye Hampton.

FALCIANI CCHS, Justin Anthony (NJ) 16 W. Wilmont Ave, Somers Point NJ 08244 **R Chr Ch Somers Point NJ 2010**- B Vineland NJ 1976 s Anthony & Mary Ann. BA Cabrini U 1999; MA UTS, New York City 2001; MDiv VTS 2008. D 6/7/2008 Bp George Edward Councell P 12/7/2008 Bp Sylvestre Donato Romero. Vic S Mk's At The Crossing Ch Williamstown NJ 2008-2010. Contrib, "Ecum in the 21st Century: Discovering out Common Baptism," *Ecum Trends*, Graymoor Ecum and Inter-Rel Inst, 2007. Phi Alpha Theta- Intl hon Soc for Hist 1998; Theta Alpha Kappa- Natl hon Soc of Rel Stds/Theol 1999. 2007 Natl Sem Essay Contest Epis Dioc Ecum and Inter-Rel Off 2007. ccsprector@verizon.net

FALCONE, John Francis (O) 7513 W 33rd St, Tulsa OK 74107 **Non-par 1990**- B Washington DC 1931 s Anthony & Minerva. BA S Marys Coll Raleigh NC 1953; MDiv U of Louvain BE 1957; MA GW 1968; EDS 1970; DMin Oral Roberts U 2000. Rec 7/1/1980 Bp Robert Bruce Hall. m 4/17/1976 Diana Wright Falcone c 1. Vic S Anne's In The Field Madison OH 1987-1989; R S Jn's Epis Ch Arlington VA 1980-1987; Serv RC Ch 1958-1980.

FALCONER, Allan (Miss) 11593 Avondale Dr, Fairfax VA 22030 B Derby UK 1944 s Allan & Ada. BS U of Durham GB 1965; PhD U of Durham GB 1970; DIT S Fran Coll Brisbane AU 1982. Trans 8/10/1991 Bp George Edmonds Bates. m 1/2/1967 Renee Cowley c 2. Truro Epis Ch Fairfax VA 2005-2006; Vic S Eliz's Mssn Collins MS 2003-2004; Permission to officiate Ch Of The Ascen Hattiesburg MS 1998-2006; Assoc Jn's Epis Ch Logan UT 1991-1997; Serv Ch of Kenya 1979-1989; Serv Ch of Australia 1978-1979.

FALES, Stephen Abbott (Ind) 1402 W Main St, Carmel IN 46032 B Providence RI 1952 s Lester & Virginia. BA Hartwick Coll 1974; MDiv Yale DS 1978. D 6/17/1978 P 12/17/1978 Bp Frederick Hesley Belden. m 5/8/1976 Marian F Fales c 2. R S Chris's Epis Ch Carmel IN 2002-2017; R S Ptr's Epis Ch Cheshire CT 1990-2002; R S Andr The Apos Rocky Hill CT 1982-1990; Asst Ch Of The H Comf Vienna VA 1981-1982; Chapl Rhode Island Veterans' Hm 1978-1981.

FALLIS, Robert Keith (Okla) 10901 S Yale Ave, Tulsa OK 74137 B Tulsa OK 1962 s Gordon & Mary. BS NSU 1985. D 6/30/2017 Bp Edward Joseph Konieczny. c 4.

FALLON, Amy L (Chi) Grace Place Campus Ministry, 401 Normal Rd, Dekalb IL 60115 **Gr Place Campus Mnstry Dekalb IL 2013-; Assoc S Ptr's Epis Ch Sycamore IL 2013**- B Nashua NH 1962 d John & Kathleen. BA Bryn 1984; MDiv Weston Jesuit TS 1988. D 7/25/1998 Bp Arthur Edward Walmsley P 2/20/1999 Bp Douglas Edwin Theuner. Old Trin Epis Ch Tiffin OH 2010-2012; Vic S Mk's Chap Storrs CT 2001-2010; Trin Epis Cathd Hartford CT 1998-2001. amy.fallon08@gmail.com

FALLOWFIELD, William Harris (Md) 2622 N Calvert St, Baltimore MD 21218 B Chestertown MD 1938 s Harry & Sara. BS Towson U 1960; BD VTS 1965. D 6/22/1965 P 6/1/1966 Bp Harry Lee Doll. m 10/18/1986 Faye Fallowfield c 2. S Jas Ch Irvington Baltimore MD 1994-1998; Int S Geo's And S Matthews Ch Dundalk MD 1993-1994; Dir Bp Claggett Cntr Buckeystown MD 1989-1993;

F

Bp Claggett Cntr Adamstown MD 1974-1989; R S Mary's Epis Ch Woodlawn Gwynn Oak MD 1967-1974; Asst S S Jn's Par Hagerstown MD 1966-1967. Auth, "Sacr Ground, Sacr Stories: Slave Monologues from 1840," 2011; Auth, "Lectionary Bible Plays for Chld and Yth," 2004; Auth, "Claggett Cntr: A Personal View & Guide," 1980. Bp's Awd For Distinguished Serv 1989.

FALLS, Michael Lee (Tex) 5831 Secrest Dr, Austin TX 78759 **Ret 1992-** B Bemidji MN 1934 s Harry & Agnes. U MN; Epis TS of the SW 1970. D 6/17/1970 Bp Scott Field Bailey P 7/1/1971 Bp James Milton Richardson. m 7/12/1997 Beth W Falls. S Dav's Ch Austin TX 1990-1993; Chapl Cbury Assn 1975-1989; The Great Cmsn Fndt Houston TX 1975-1989; Asst R Palmer Memi Ch Houston TX 1970-1975.

FAMULARE JR, Joseph Anthony (Alb) 119 Southern Ave, Little Falls NY 13365 **Trin And S Michaels Ch Middleville NY 2005-** B Herkimer NY 1967 s Joseph & Jean. D 6/15/2002 P 4/22/2006 Bp David John Bena. m 10/3/1992 Christine Leskovar-Famulare c 1.

FAN, Peter Sheung-Mau (Haw) St Elizabeth Episcopal Church, 720 N King St, Honolulu HI 96817 B Hong Kong 1946 s King Sui & Kit Ching. Dplma of Educ Granthon Coll of Educ 1967; Dplma of Theol Theol Sch - The Dio Hong Kong and Macau 1969; BA Chung Chi Coll 1972; Profsnl Trng Grad Sch Theol Div 1974. Trans 5/2/1988 as Priest Bp Donald Purple Hart. m 5/28/1977 Kei Shui Doris Lam c 1.

FANGUY, Mabel Matheny (Pgh) 1114 1st St, Canonsburg PA 15317 B Poughkeepsie NY 1958 d James & Dania. BS California St U 1982; MDiv VTS 1999. D 2/28/1999 Bp Charles Edward Jenkins III P 9/11/1999 Bp Robert William Duncan. m 11/26/1986 David L Fanguy c 2. Asst S Paul's Epis Ch Pittsburgh PA 2009-2012; R S Thos' Epis Ch Canonsburg PA 1999-2004.

FANNING, Thomas H (Miss) 24 Greystone Dr, Madison MS 39110 **S Jn's Epis Ch Pascagoula MS 2014-** B Jackson MS 1962 s William & Marjorie. BS Belhaven Coll 1985; MDiv Sewanee: The U So 2006. D 5/31/2006 P 2/17/2007 Bp Duncan Montgomery Gray III. m 8/2/1986 Marjorie Goodsell Fanning c 1. R S Lk's Ch Brandon MS 2006-2014.

FARABEE, Allen Waldo (WNY) 310 Norwood Ave, Buffalo NY 14222 **S Dav's Epis Ch Buffalo NY 1975-** B Fort Myers FL 1946 s A Waldo & Marion. BS Indiana U 1969; MDiv Yale DS 1972; STM Nash 1979; JD U of Connecticut 1993. D 6/2/1974 Bp Albert Ervine Swift P 3/1/1975 Bp James Loughlin Duncan. m 6/29/1968 Galen G Farabee. S Jas' Ch Batavia NY 2005-2006; S Paul's Cathd Buffalo NY 1995-2005; R S Mich's Ch Litchfield CT 1985-1995; S Paul's and Trin Chap Alton IL 1981-1984; R S Paul's Ch Marinette WI 1977-1981; Asst All SS Prot Epis Ch Ft Lauderdale FL 1975-1977; Serv Methodist Ch 1972-1974. Phi Eta Sigma; Pi Kappa Lamda.

FARAMELLI, Norman Joseph (Mass) 29 Harris St, Waltham MA 02452 **Non-par 1976-** B Wilkes-Barre PA 1932 s Guido & Clara. BS Buc 1955; STB PDS 1960; PhD Tem 1967. D 5/14/1960 P 12/1/1960 Bp Oliver J Hart. m 4/27/1957 Lucie Marie Faramelli c 2. Int S Lk's/San Lucas Epis Ch Chelsea MA 2000, 1995-1998; S Paul's Ch Newburyport MA 1994; S Lk's And S Marg's Ch Allston MA 1992-1993; S Eliz's Ch Sudbury MA 1990-1991; Gr Epis Ch Lawr MA 1989-1990; Gr Ch Newton MA 1983-1984; Epis City Mssn Boston MA 1981; Dio Massachusetts Boston MA 1980-1993; S Dunstans Epis Ch Dover MA 1979; Boston Indstrl Mssn Cambridge MA 1967-1976; R S Mart's Philadelphia PA 1963-1967; Dir S Paul's Epis Ch Westfield NJ 1960-1963. Auth, "Technethics: Chr Mssn In An Age Of Tech".

FARBER, Joseph W (EO) 1420 E Dewey Ave, Sapulpa OK 74066 **Epis Ch Of The Trsfg Sis OR 2017-** B Oklahoma City OK 1957 s Clyde & Clara Fay. BA U Chi 1980; JD U of Oklahoma 1984; MDiv Sewanee: The U So, TS 2010. D 1/23/2010 P 7/24/2010 Bp Edward Joseph Konieczny. m 8/7/2004 Janice F Farber c 3. Vic Gd Shpd Epis Ch Sapulpa OK 2010-2017. jwfarber@gmail.com

FARGO, David Rolland (La) 17 Hastings Ct, Asheville NC 28803 **Ret 2000-** B Memphis TN 1945 s Robert & Mary. BA Van 1967; MDiv GTS 1970. D 6/24/1970 Bp William F Gates Jr P 3/28/1971 Bp William Evan Sanders. m 8/26/1967 Sally Fargo c 2. R Chr Ch Slidell LA 1982-2000; Assoc H Trin Epis Ch Greensboro NC 1977-1982; Dio No Carolina Raleigh NC 1973-1976; Vic S Anne's Ch Winston Salem NC 1972-1977; D-in-trng S Steph's Epis Ch Oak Ridge TN 1970-1971; COM Dio Louisiana New Orleans LA 1993-1996, Stndg Com 1988-1992; Vice-Chairman, Bd Dir Slidell Memi Hosp Slidell LA 1990-1998. fargo.dr@gmail.com

FARGO, Valerie Mae (EMich) **D Dio Estrn Michigan Saginaw MI 2015-, Admin 2014-2015** B Hartford CT 1949 d Alburn & Arleen. BA Ge 1971; PhD U Chi 1979; MDiv McCormick TS 1986. D 3/8/2015 P 9/26/2015 Bp Steven Todd Ousley. m 7/31/1982 John Anderson Roper c 1. vfargo@eastmich.org

FARIA III, Manuel P (Mass) 4 Ocean St, Beverly MA 01915 **R S Ptr's Ch Beverly MA 1999-; Mssnr Amer Friends of the Dio Jerusalem Darien CT 2015-; Co-chair, Middle E Working Grp Dio Massachusetts Boston MA 2014-, VP, Stndg Com 2009-2010, Congrl Coach 2006-2011, Stndg Com 2006-2010** B Danbury CT 1954 s Manuel & Mary. BS Bos 1976; Dplma Ya Berk 1996; MDiv Yale DS 1996. D 6/8/1996 Bp Clarence Nicholas Coleridge P 12/21/1996 Bp Gordon Scruton. m 10/22/1988 Louise Seelig c 2. Asst S Steph's Ch Pittsfield MA 1996-1999. manny@stpetersbeverly.org

FARINA, Gaspar Miran (Mil) 154 Club Wildwood, Hudson FL 33568 **Non-par 1976-** B Beloit WI 1915 s Michael & Sarah. BD U of Wisconsin-Whitewater 1938; MS Marq 1950. D 12/22/1956 Bp Donald H V Hallock. m 6/21/1941 Jane K Lord c 4. Asst S Edmunds Ch Milwaukee WI 1963-1976; Asst St Mths Epis Ch Waukesha WI 1956-1963.

FARKAS, Hazel Daphne Martin (SVa) 111 Montrose, Williamsburg VA 23188 B Saint Albans Hertfordshire UK 1937 d George & Lucie. Maryland; MBChB U of Edinburgh Edinburgh GB 1962; Cert Sewanee: The U So, TS 1979. D 6/26/1983 Bp David Keller Leighton Sr. m 4/27/1963 Hanson Farkas c 3. D S Mart's Epis Ch Williamsburg VA 2000-2005; D Gr Epis Ch Utica NY 1988-1998; D S Jas' Ch Clinton NY 1985-1989; D The Ch Of The H Apos Halethorpe MD 1983-1984; Consult Psych S Tim's Ch Catonsville MD 1973-1984. Auth, "Var arts," *Psych Journ*, Amer Psych Assn. Ord of S Lk 1985.

FARLEY, Nancy Stone (Lex) 151 Vine St, Sadieville KY 40370 B Burbank CA 1955 d Robert & Eugenia. BD U of Kentucky 1977; MA Estrn Kentucky U 1981; MDiv GTS 1994. D 6/25/1994 P 1/18/1995 Bp Rogers Sanders Harris. c 2. R Ch Of The H Trin Georgetown KY 2002-2005; R S Eliz's Epis Ch Zephyrhills FL 1997-2002; Asst & Sch Chapl S Mary's Par Tampa FL 1996-1997; S Andr's Epis Ch Tampa FL 1994-1996.

FARMER, Edward Dean (Wyo) **S Alb's Ch Worland WY 2011-** B Cody WY 1950 D 8/27/2005 Bp Bruce Caldwell. m 6/28/1974 Rita Faye Farmer c 1.

FARMER, Eyleen Hamner (WTenn) 102 N 2nd St, Memphis TN 38103 **Assoc Calv Ch Memphis TN 2010-, Assoc R 2006-2008** B Boulder CO 1950 d Martin & Barbara. BA U of Memphis 1983; MA U of Memphis 1986; MDiv Van 1992. D 6/10/2006 P 1/6/2007 Bp Don Edward Johnson. m 11/13/2004 Thomas A Momberg c 2. Int S Jn's Par Hagerstown MD 2010; Assoc Gr - S Lk's Ch Memphis TN 2008-2009.

FARMER, Gary Clayton (WNC) Po Box 633, Arden NC 28704 B Hickory NC 1934 s Earl & Mattie. New Sch U; BA Duke 1957; MDiv GTS 1965. D 6/22/1965 Bp William Loftin Hargrave P 12/28/1965 Bp James Loughlin Duncan. c 2. Deerfield Hm Asheville NC 1984-2000; S Steph's Ch Richmond VA 1975-1977; ExCouncil Dio Wstrn No Carolina Asheville NC 1972-1973; P-in-c Ch Of The Epiph Newton NC 1967-1976; Asst Ch Of The Gd Shpd Dunedin FL 1965-1967. Amer Assn for Counslg and Develpment; Clincl Memi Intl Acad of Behavioral Med; Dplma for Amer Psych Assn.

FARMER, Jennie Marietta (EMich) 453 S 26th St, Saginaw MI 48601 B Saginaw MI 1921 d James & Irene. Delta Coll U Cntr MI; Cert Michigan TS 1982. D 6/15/1982 Bp William Jones Gordon Jr. m 6/14/1942 Thomas Owen Farmer c 1. Asst S Paul's Epis Ch Saginaw MI 1982-1990. Ord Of S Lk.

FARNES, Joseph E (Ida) 67 East St, Pittsfield MA 01201 **Dio Wstrn Massachusetts Springfield 2015-** B Idaho Falls ID 1986 s Mark & Kimberly. BA Whitman Coll 2008; MDiv Epis TS of the SW 2015. D 12/21/2014 P 6/21/2015 Bp Brian James Thom. rev.joseph.farnes@gmail.com

FARONE, Martha Jeanette (WNY) 7145 Fieldcrest Dr, Lockport NY 14094 B Lockport NY 1956 d Frederick & Virginia. D 6/20/2015 Bp Ralph William Franklin. m 10/22/1977 William Michael Farone c 2.

FARQUHAR-MAYES, Alice F(ay) (Ida) 1560 Lenz Ln, Boise ID 83712 B Passaic NJ 1945 d William & Frances. RN New Engl Bapt Hosp 1965; BA U of Hartford 1973; MS Ya 1975; Ya 1975; MDiv GTS 1982. D 6/12/1982 P 5/6/1983 Bp Arthur Edward Walmsley. m 5/16/1981 Thomas Farquhar-Mayes. Ch Of H Nativ Meridian ID 2007-2009; Cn S Mich's Cathd Boise ID 2001-2007; Serv S Steph's Boise ID 1992-2001; Hosp Chapl S Lk's Rmc Boise ID 1988-2001; S Jas Ch Mtn Hm ID 1988; Assoc S Lk's Par Darien CT 1985-1987; Cur S Paul's Ch Fairfield CT 1982-1985. Auth, "Ethical Considerations In Use Of Neuromuscular Blockades," *Ccnq*. Amer Soc For Bioethics & Hmnts 1999; Assn Of Profsnl Chapl 1989; Bd Cert Chapl 1989. Pres'S Awd S Lk'S Rmc 1994; Outstanding St Ldr Assn Of Profsnl Chapl.

FARQUHAR-MAYES, Thomas (Ida) 1115 W Clarinda Dr, Meridian ID 83642 B St. Louis MO 1938 D 11/12/1983 P 6/13/1984 Bp David Bell Birney IV. m 5/16/1981 Alice F(ay) Farquhar-Mayes c 1. Emm Epis Ch Stamford CT 1984-1986.

FARR, Beau Anthony (At) B Winder GA 1960 D 6/5/2004 P 10/1/2005 Bp J Neil Alexander. S Anth's Epis Ch Winder GA 2005-2009.

FARR, Curtis Andrew (Ct) St James' Church, 19 Walden St, West Hartford CT 06107 **Asst R S Jas's Ch W Hartford CT 2013-** B Vancouver WA 1986 s Richard & Sharon. BA WA SU 2009; MDiv VTS 2013. D 10/18/2012 P 6/13/2013 Bp Gregory Harold Rickel. m 8/16/2014 Jose Antonio A Rocha.

FARR, Matthew R (ETenn) Cur Dio Tennessee Nashville TN 2017-; Sewanee U So TS Sewanee TN 2015- B Chattanooga TN 1985 s Robert & Margaret. MDiv Sewanee: The U So, TS; BA The U So. D 2/11/2017 Bp George Young III. m 8/30/2008 Margaret Elizabeth Langford c 1. Other Lay Position Dio Virginia Richmond VA 2007-2010.

FARR, Meghan J (CFla) St Luke's Episcopal Church, PO Box 605, Gladstone NJ 07934 **H Trin Epis Ch Melbourne FL 2015-** B Providence RI 1979 d Richard & Constance. Transfered Asbury TS; AA Brevard Cmnty Coll 2000; BA U of Florida 2003; MDiv Nash 2013. D 6/8/2013 Bp Gregory Orrin Brewer P 1/14/

2014 Bp William H Stokes. m 5/1/2003 Daniel Alan Farr c 3. Cur S Lk's Ch Gladstone NJ 2013-2015.

FARRAND, Gregory C (NC) **Assoc H Trin Epis Ch Greensboro NC 2016-** D 6/11/2016 P 12/17/2016 Bp Anne Hodges-Copple.

FARRAR, Charles Thomas (Me) 2390 Rfd 201, Gardiner ME 04345 **Non-par 1984-; Chapl/Intern Cntrl Islip Psych Cntr NY 1976-** B New York NY 1941 s Clayton & Elisabeth. MDiv GTS; BA U So. D 6/7/1968 P 12/1/1969 Bp Horace W B Donegan. m 6/15/1996 Michelle Farrar c 1. S Matt's Epis Ch Hallowell ME 1979-1983; S Johns Epis Hosp Far Rockaway NY 1973-1976; Chapl S Jn's Hosp Smithtown NY 1973-1976; Chapl/Intern Cntrl Islip Psych Cntr NY 1971-1973; Asst S Paul And S Jas New Haven CT 1970-1971; Asst Min S Jn's Ch Stamford CT 1968-1970.

FARRAR III, Dean (Los) 4091 E La Cara St, Long Beach CA 90815 **Asst The Par Ch Of S Lk Long Bch CA 2007-** B San Diego CA 1949 s Holway & Bonnie. BA`U CA San Diego 1971; MDiv EDS 1975. D 6/21/1975 P 2/21/1976 Bp Robert Claflin Rusack. R S Fran' Par Palos Verdes Estates CA 1993-2006; Vic S Thos' Mssn Hacienda Hgts CA 1979-1993; Asst S Geo's Epis Ch Laguna Hills CA 1976-1979; Dio Los Angeles Los Angeles CA 1975-1976.

FARRELL, John T (LI) 1155 Warburton Ave, Apt 4D, Yonkers NY 10701 **Prof Mercer TS Garden City NY 2015-; Int S Fran Assisi And S Martha White Plains NY 2012-** B Glen Cove NY 1948 s Daniel & Lydia. BA Belmont Abbey Coll 1970; MA Ball St U 1972; PhD U of Delaware 1983; Dplma Ya Berk 1990; MDiv Yale DS 1990. D 6/8/1991 P 6/13/1992 Bp Cabell Tennis. Vic Dio Long Island Garden City NY 2008-2010; S Jas Ch Elmhust NY 2008-2010; Regimental Chapl SUNY Maritime Coll Throggs Neck NY 2005-2010; Chapl and Prof SUNY Maritime Coll Throggs Neck NY 2004-2011; P-in-c Chr Ch Bay Ridge Brooklyn NY 2003-2008; Epis Chapl Ford Bronx NY 2002-2004; Epis Chapl Ford Bronx NY 2002-2004; R S Paul's Epis Ch Prnc Frederck MD 1998-2003; Vic Mt Olivet Epis Ch New Orleans LA 1996-1998; Chapl S Mart's Epis Sch Metairie LA 1995-1998; Asst Chr Ch Cathd New Orleans LA 1995-1996; P-in-c S Dav's Ch Philadelphia PA 1992-1995. Auth, "Sought Through Pryr and Meditation," Cntrl Recovery Press, 2013; Auth, "Guide Me in My Recovery," Cntrl Recovery Press, 2011; Auth, "Writing for Bus: A Casebook," Kendall Hunt, 1995; Auth, "Numerous arts". Ord Of Urban Missioners 1999-2014. Awd of Merit The Associated Ch Press 2011; Who's Who in Amer 2010; Paul Harris Fell rotary Intl 2001.

FARRELL JR, Reid Dwyer (Vt) PO Box 273, Swanton VT 05488 **Cler Dep to GC 2012 Dio Vermont Burlington VT 2010-, First Alt Cler Dep to GC 2009 2008-2010** B New Orleans LA 1952 s Reid & Adelaide. PhD U of Florida; BS U of Florida 1977; MDiv GTS 1982. D 5/31/1982 P 1/1/1983 Bp Emerson Paul Haynes. m 10/20/2009 Dale L Willard. R H Trin Epis Ch Swanton VT 2004-2013; R Gr Epis Ch Southgate MI 1999-2004; P-in-c S Thos Ch Mamaroneck NY 1999; P-in-c Gr Ch Cincinnati OH 1997-1999; Assoc R S Bon Ch Sarasota FL 1986-1997; Asst H Trin Epis Ch Gainesville FL 1985-1986; Cur Ch Of The Gd Shpd Punta Gorda FL 1982-1984. Auth, "Var arts & Presentations". Soc Of S Jn The Evang 1979. reidndale@gmail.com

FARRELL, Wayne (SwFla) 1700 Keystone Rd, Tarpon Springs FL 34688 **P-in-c S Bon Ch Sarasota FL 2016-; R All SS Ch Tarpon Spgs FL 2011-** B Sarasota FL 1958 s Reid & Adelaide. BBC U of Florida 1980; MDiv Sewanee: The U So, TS 2011. D 2/27/2011 P 10/8/2011 Bp Dabney Tyler Smith. m 1/28/1984 Patrcia Case Farrell c 2. wfarrell@bonifacechurch.org

FARSTAD, Joan Elizabeth (Ia) 2410 Melrose Dr, Cedar Falls IA 50613 B Buffalo NY 1949 d Dan & Margaret. BA Canisius Coll 1971; MA St Jn's U TS 1983; MA U of Iowa 1991. D 2/11/2017 Bp Alan Scarfe. m 5/8/2009 Maureen Catherine Doherty.

FARWELL JR, James William (At) Virginia Theological Seminary, Alexandria VA 22304 **Prof of Theol and Liturg VTS Alexandria VA 2013-, Assoc Prof of Theol and Liturg 2012-2013** B Jacksonville FL 1960 s James & Dorothy. BA CUA 1984; MDiv GTS 1989; PhD Emory U 2001. D 6/11/1989 P 12/10/1989 Bp Frank S Cerveny. c 2. T.W. Phillips Chair, Prof of Relig Stds & Phil Bethany Coll Bethany WV 2010-2012; T.W. Phillips Chair, Assoc Prof of Relig Stds & Phil Bethany Coll Bethany WV 2007-2010; Assoc Prof of Liturg The GTS New York NY 2002-2007; Cn Theol Cathd Of S Phil Atlanta GA 1999-2002; Asst S Barth's Epis Ch Atlanta GA 1995-1997; S Steph's Ch Coconut Grove Miami FL 1990-1993; Chapl S Steph's Epis Day Sch Miami FL 1990-1993; Asst R S Andr's Ch Jacksonville FL 1989-1990. Auth, "On Whether Christians Should Participate in Buddhist Pract," *Journ of Interreligious Stds and Intercultural Theol*, 2017; Auth, "Theorizing Ritual for Interreligious Pract," *Ritual Participation and Interreligious Dialogue*, Bloomsbury, 2015; Auth, "Developments and Hopes for Interreligious Dialogue," *Ecum Trends*, Graymoor, 2014; Auth, "The Liturg Explained," *The Liturg Explained*, Morehouse, 2013; Auth, "The Study of Liturg and Postmodernism," *Proceedings of the NAAL*, 2005; Auth, "This Is the Night: Suffering, Salvation, and the Liturgies of H Week," *This Is the Night: Suffering, Salvation, and the Liturgies of H Week*, T & T Clark/Continuum, 2005; Auth, "Baptism, Euch, and the Hosp of Jesus," *ATR*, 2004; Auth, "Salvation, Bishops, FD Maurice," *Encyclopedia of Protestantism*, Routledge, 2003. AAR 1995; No Amer Acad of Liturg 2006;

Soc for Buddhist-Chr Stds 1997-2009; Soc for Comparative Theol 2011. Fell, Comparative Theol and Rel Pluralism AAR/ Luce Fndt 2010. jfarwell@vts.edu

FASEL, William Jay (WMo) 824 W 62nd St, Kansas City MO 64113 **Cn Dio W Missouri Kansas City MO 2012-, Mnstry Dvlp, NE Epis Reg Mnstry 2012-** B Wharton TX 1954 s Joseph & Lois. BS USCG Acad 1976; Geo Mason U 1981; MBA U of Texas San Antonio 1985; MDiv Sewanee: The U So, TS 1990; DMin SWTS 1998. D 5/26/1990 Bp Earl Nicholas Mc Arthur Jr P 12/2/1990 Bp John Herbert MacNaughton. m 7/3/1985 Michelle P Fasel c 4. NE Reg Mnstry Lexington MO 2001-2011; R Shpd Of The Hills Branson MO 1993-2001; All SS Epis Ch Pleasanton TX 1990-1993; Vic S Mths Devine TX 1990-1993. nerm@diowestmo.org

FAST SR, Todd Howard (Oly) 8756 Sylvan Pl Nw, Seattle WA 98117 **Ret 1991-** B Lima OH 1926 s Harley & Rose. BA Denison U 1949; Cert ETSBH 1967. D 9/10/1966 P 3/1/1967 Bp Francis E I Bloy. c 6. Asstg P S Lk's Epis Ch Seattle WA 1994-1995, Assoc 1974-1977; Int S Chas Angl Par Poulsbo WA 1989-1991; Non-par 1988-1989; Vic S Marg's White Cntr WA 1979-1984; Ch Of The H Apos Bellevue WA 1979-1983; R S Clem's Mssn Huntington Pk CA 1970-1974; Asst S Anselm Of Cbury Par Garden Grove CA 1966-1970.

FAUCETTE, Louis H (At) 2998 Kodiak Ct, Marietta GA 30062 **D The Epis Ch Of S Ptr And S Paul Marietta GA 2006-** B Chattanooga TN 1947 s Robert & Betty. BS U of Tennessee 1970. D 8/6/2006 Bp J Neil Alexander. c 3. Bro of St. Andrewsd 2001.

FAULKNER, David M (Dal) The Episcopal Church of the Good Shepherd, 200 West College Street, Terrell TX 75160 **Ch Of The Gd Shpd Terrell TX 2017-** B Dallas TX 1983 s Albert & Rebecca. BA Wheaton Coll 2005; MDiv Beeson DS, Samford U 2008; DAS Epis TS of the SW 2010. D 6/26/2010 P 4/8/2011 Bp Paul Emil Lambert. m 12/30/2006 Laura C Jones. P-in-c Trin Ch Epis Pass Chr MS 2015-2016; Cur S Jas Epis Ch Texarkana TX 2011-2015; Cur H Trin Ch Rockwall TX 2010-2011. rector@goodshepherdterrell.org

FAULKNER, Tom (NY) 131 E 66th St Apt 10b, New York NY 10065 B Nyack NY 1943 s John & Viola. BA Dart 1967; MDiv EDS 1974; MFA Pratt Inst 1978. D 6/8/1974 P 12/1/1977 Bp Paul Moore Jr. m 7/29/1995 Brenda G Husson c 1. Vic Chr Epis Ch Sparkill NY 2010-2015; Dio New York New York NY 2006-2009, 1982-1984; Supervising Chapl Red Cross New York City NY 2001-2002; Assoc S Jas Ch New York NY 2000-2005; Ch Of The Ascen Mt Vernon NY 1997-1998; Int H Innoc Highland Falls NY 1995-1997; S Thos Epis Ch New Windsor NY 1995-1996; Int Mnstry Gr White Plains NY 1994-1995; Gr Ch White Plains NY 1994; Assoc S Lk Nyc 1991-1993; S Ann And The H Trin Brooklyn NY 1978-1982; Trin Par New York NY 1978; Asst S Phil's Ch Brooklyn NY 1977-1978; Asst Gr Epis Ch Nyack NY 1976-1977; Non-par 1974-1976. Contrib, "On the Ground After 9/11," Haworth Press, 2005.

FAULSTICH, Christine Marie (Tex) 9600 South Gessner Rd., Houston TX 77071 **P Ch Of The Epiph Houston TX 2014-; Mem, Stndg Com Dio Texas Houston TX 2016-, Mem, COM 2011-2016** B Olympia Fields IL 1984 d John & Lynne. BA Rice U 2006; MDiv VTS 2010. D 6/19/2010 Bp C Andrew Doyle P 1/6/2011 Bp Dena Arnall Harrison. Assoc S Matt's Ch Austin TX 2010-2014. Contrib, "The New Atheists," *Controversies in Contemporary Rel, vol. 2*, Praeger, 2014.

FAULSTICH, Matthew (SeFla) 1704 Buchanan St, Hollywood FL 33020 B Winamac IN 1951 s Lawrence & Rita. BA Pur 1973; S Meinrad RC Sem 1974; MDiv S Vinc De Paul Reg Sem Boynton Bch 1977; Moreau RC Sem at U of Notre Dame 1978; CAS SWTS 1989. Rec 5/19/1989 Bp Francis Campbell Gray. m 9/17/1983 Cheryl Faulstich c 3. R S Jn's Ch Hollywood FL 1997-2017; Vic S Jn's Ch Centralia IL 1989-1997; S Thos Ch Salem IL 1989-1997. M Div cl St. Vinc de Paul Sem 1977.

FAUPEL, David William (SwFla) 7447 Emilia Ln, Naples FL 34114 **P-in-c S Paul's Ch Naples FL 2015-; Int R S Jn's Ch Versailles KY 2002-, Asst R 2000-2001, LocTen 1990-1999, Cur 1980-1989** B Cass City MI 1944 s David & Clara. BA Cntrl Bible Coll Springfield MO 1966; BA Evang Bible Coll 1968; MDiv Asbury TS 1971; MS U of Kentucky 1972; PhD U of Birmingham Birmingham Gb 1989. D 12/17/1978 P 12/22/1979 Bp Addison Hosea. m 6/27/1992 Bonnie Elliott. P-in-c S Phil's Ch Harrodsburg KY 1996-1999; Asst P Ch Of The Gd Shpd Lexington KY 1992-1993; Supply P S Jas Epis Ch Prestonsburg KY 1991-1992; Asst P Chr Ch Cathd Lexington KY 1987-1988; P-in-c S Andr's Ch Lexington KY 1985-1986; Asst Trin Epis Ch Danville KY 1978-1979. Auth, "Amer Pentecostal Mvmt: A Biblographical Essay"; Auth, "The Everlasting Gospel"; Auth, "The Higher Chr Life". Amer Theol Libr Assn 1967; Kentucky Libr Assn 1974; Soc For Pentecostal Stds 1970; Weslyan Theol Scoiety 1979; Wrld Methodist Hist Soc 1998. frbill@saintpaulsnaples.org

FAUSAK, Frederick Emil (NY) 41 Alter Ave, Staten Island NY 10304 **D S Andr's Epis Ch Staten Island NY 2002-, D 1997-2001** B Jersey City NJ 1936 s Albert & Martha. BA CUNY 1979. D 4/26/1997 Bp Richard Frank Grein. m 6/6/1961 Theresa Ann Fausak c 3. D S Mary's Castleton Staten Island NY 2001.

FAY, Michael (Colo) 8010 W Us Highway 50, Salida CO 81201 **R Ch Of The Ascen Salida CO 2013-** B Denver CO 1946 s John & Gladys. BS USMA 1968; MD Geo 1977; BS USMA 1977; GD Trin Melbourne AUS 2003; DMin Sewanee: The U So, TS 2010. D 10/2/1999 P 4/1/2000 Bp Charles I Jones III. m 6/

14/1970 Samar Fay c 2. Hosp Chapl Frances mahon Dss Hosp Glasgow MT 2007-2013; S Matt's Ch Glasgow MT 2000-2013. fr.mike.fay@gmail.com

FAY, Susan D (NCal) 3878 River Rd, Colusa CA 95932 **S Paul's Epis Ch Oroville CA 2002-** B Oxford MI 1963 d Louis & Alice. MDiv Sewanee: The U So, TS 1991. D 6/22/1993 P 5/1/1994 Bp John Stuart Thornton. Mssnr S Steph's Epis Ch Colusa CA 2002-2003; The Epis Dio Nthrn California Sacramento CA 1999-2013; Mssnr H Trin Epis Ch Willows CA 1999; S Tim's Ch Gridley CA 1999; S Geo's Ch Lusk WY 1996-1999; Dio Idaho Boise ID 1993-1999. Auth, "I Call Them Ang". Ord Of S Helena. info@allsaintssacramento.org

FAYETTE, Shelly Lynn (Oly) 805 SE Ellsworth Rd, Vancouver WA 98664 **R Chr Ch Seattle WA 2014-** B Yakima WA 1980 d Fred & Louise. BA Seattle U 2003; MDiv UTS 2009. D 4/17/2009 Bp Gregory Harold Rickel P 1/9/2010 Bp Bavi Edna Rivera. m 1/18/2012 Aaron Scott c 1. Dio Oregon Portland OR 2014; Assoc Pstr Ch Of The Gd Shpd Vancouver WA 2009-2013; Dioc Intern Dio Estrn Oregon Cove OR 2009.

FEAGIN JR, Jerre Willis (WNY) 3751 N Franklin Ave, Loveland CO 80538 B Macon GA 1944 s Jerre & Frances. BS Auburn U 1966; MDiv GTS 1973. D 6/5/1973 P 12/21/1973 Bp William Henry Marmion. m 10/9/2010 Amy Elizabeth Reed c 2. Bp's Asst for Congrl Spprt Dio Wstrn New York Tonawanda NY 2012-2017, Exec Dir COM 1979-1985; Int S Mths Epis Ch E Aurora NY 2011-2012; R St Mk Epis Ch No Tonawanda NY 1999-2010; Chapl Hospice Buffalo Inc Cheektowaga 1993-2012; Vic S Ptr's Epis Ch Buffalo NY 1993-1999; R Calv Epis Ch Williamsville NY 1985-1992, Assoc R 1982-1985; R The Epis Ch Of The Gd Shpd Buffalo NY 1978-1982; Asst S Jn's Of Lattingtown Locust Vlly NY 1975-1978; Asst S Jn's Ch Roanoke VA 1973-1975.

FEAMSTER JR, Thomas Otey (NC) 1805 Virginia Ct, Tavares FL 32778 **Ret 1996-** B Newport News VA 1930 s Thomas & Gladys. Florida St U 1956; MDiv Sewanee: The U So, TS 1972. D 6/16/1972 P 6/13/1973 Bp Edward Hamilton West. m 1/8/1983 Betty Feamster c 3. P-in-c S Mths Ch Louisburg NC 1986-1995; R S Paul's Ch Louisburg NC 1985-1995; R Chr Ch Hackensack NJ 1983-1985; R Gr Epis Ch Paris TN 1979-1982; Dio Florida Jacksonville 1972-1979; S Anne's Epis Ch Keystone Hgts FL 1972-1979.

FEATHER, Mark Randolph (Va) 14 Cornwall St NW, Leesburg VA 20176 **R S Jas' Epis Ch Leesburg VA 2014-** B Troy NY 1955 s Arthur & Wanda. BS U of Kentucky 1977; JD Stan 1980; MDiv VTS 2001. D 6/3/2001 P 6/8/2002 Bp Ted Gulick Jr. m 8/22/1981 Marilyn S Feather c 2. R S Paul's Ch Louisville KY 2003-2013; Asst S Mk's Epis Ch Louisville KY 2002-2003; Asst Dio Kentucky Louisville KY 2001-2003, Dn Bluegrass Dnry 2013, Mem Bdgt Com 2013, Mem Trst and Coun 2012-2013, Mem Ch Archit Com 2011-2013, Mem Eccl Crt 2008-2011; Ch Of The Adv Louisville KY 2001. Kentucky Bar Assn 1980. mark@stjamesleesburg.org

FEATHERSTON, William Roger (Eur) Via B. Rucellai 09, Florence 50123 Italy B Melbourne Australia 1943 s William & Ada. ThL S Michaels Hse Crafers Au 1967; BA U of Melbourne 1987. Trans 5/22/2005 Bp Pierre W Whalon. m 12/15/1969 Finola Elizabeth Featherston c 3. S Jas Epis Ch Firenze 50123 2005-2008; Coll Chapl St Geo's Coll JERUSALEM 1999-2000; Dir, Victoria Australian Bd Missions Vic AUSTRALIA 1981-1985; Mssy Serv St Ptr's Lautoka FIJI 1974-1976; Vic Var Parishes Dio Melbourne AUSTRALIA 1968-2005.

FECHT, Dustin Michael (Mil) St John's Episcopal Church, 405 N Saginaw Rd, Midland MI 48640 **P S Mich's Epis Ch Racine WI 2013-** B Davenport IA 1978 s James & Travis. BA Indiana Wesl 2007; MDiv Duke DS 2012. D 12/21/2011 P 8/28/2012 Bp Edward Stuart Little II. m 8/11/2006 Natalie Caye Fecht c 1. S Jn's Epis Ch Midland MI 2012-2013.

FEDEWA, Mike (WMich) 1025 3 Mile Rd Ne, Grand Rapids MI 49505 **R S Andr's Ch Grand Rapids MI 1992-** B Lansing MI 1955 s Vernon & Beverly. Aquinas Coll; BA S Thos Sem 1977; STB Gregorian U 1980; Cert GTS 1986. Rec 9/7/1986 Bp Howard Samuel Meeks. m 6/22/1984 Linda Ann Fedewa c 1. R Chr Ch Lockport NY 1990-1992; Asst S Thos Epis Ch Battle Creek MI 1986-1990. mfedewa@sbcglobal.net

FEDOCK, Maria Michele (Md) 2115 Southland Rd, Baltimore MD 21207 **D S Barth's Ch Baltimore MD 1984-** B Baltimore MD 1942 d Michael & Thelma. Cmnty Coll of Baltimore Baltimore MD 1961; Loyola Coll 1976. D 5/12/1979 Bp David Keller Leighton Sr. D Ch Of The H Nativ Baltimore MD 1979-1983.

FEDORCHAK, Karen Christina Russell (Ct) 48 S Hawthorne St, Manchester CT 06040 **D S Mary's Epis Ch Manchester CT 2002-, D 1990-2001** B Wilmington DE 1936 d Francis & Dorothy. BS U of Delaware 1958. D 12/1/1990 Bp Arthur Edward Walmsley. m 5/16/1959 John Adam Fedorchak c 3. D Grtr Hartford Reg Mnstry Off E Hartford CT 2001-2002; D S Jas's Ch W Hartford CT 1996-2001.

FEDOSUK, James Henry (Spr) 415 N Plum St, Havana IL 62644 **Died 5/9/2017** B Hillsdale MI 1931 s George & Mary. MDiv Nash; BA Bradley U 1962. D 3/13/1965 P 9/1/1965 Bp Francis W Lickfield. Ret 1994-2017; S Jas Epis Ch Lewistown IL 1985-1994; R S Barn Ch Havana IL 1968-1994; Asst Trin Epis Ch Rock Island IL 1965-1968. S Ben's Abbey (Oblate) 2003. brotherandrewosb@yahoo.com

FEELY, Mary Josephine (Minn) 8055 Morgan Ave N, Stillwater MN 55082 B Saint Cloud MN 1956 d Francis & Ludmila. BSN U MN 1978; Dio Minnesota Diac Prog MN 1994. D 9/8/1994 Bp Sanford Zangwill Kaye Hampton. m 9/2/1978 John Patrick Feely c 2. D La Mision El Santo Nino Jesus S Paul MN 1998-2001; D Chr Ch S Paul MN 1994-1998; Mssnr for the Diac Dio Minnesota Minneapolis MN 2009-2012. Intl OSL the Physcn 2005; Natl Epis Hlth Mnstrs 2005.

FEHR, Thomas James (SO) Community of the Transfiguration, 495 Albion Ave., Cincinnati OH 45246 **The Epis Ch Of The Ascen Middletown OH 2016-; Chapl The Soc of the Trsfg Cincinnati OH 2015-** B Shelbyville KY 1959 s James & Joyce. BS U of Kentucky 1982; MAR Athenaeum of Ohio 1999; MDiv Bex Sem 2009. D 6/14/2008 P 6/20/2009 Bp Thomas Edward Breidenthal. P-in-c Gr Ch Pomeroy OH 2011-2014; Asst S Lk's Ch Granville OH 2009-2011; D All SS Ch Cincinnati OH 2008-2009; Chair, Natl & Wrld Mssn Cmsn Dio Sthrn Ohio Cincinnati OH 2014-2016.

FEHR, Wayne L (Mil) 8220 Harwood Ave Apt 334, Wauwatosa WI 53213 B Covington KY 1938 s Peter & Bernetta. BA Xavier U 1959; MA Loyola U 1966; STL Hochschule Sankt Georgen Frankfurt DE 1970; PhD Yale DS 1978. Rec 6/21/1988 as Priest Bp Roger John White. R S Thos Of Cbury Ch Greendale WI 1999-2005, 1998; P-in-c S Jn The Div Epis Ch Burlington WI 1999; P-in-c S Paul's Ch Ashippun Oconomowoc WI 1995-1998; Int S Paul's Ch Milwaukee WI 1993-1994; Dir Sprtl Care S Barn Cntr Oconomowoc WI 1988-1993; Dir of Sprtl Care Rogers Meml Hosp Oconomowoc WI 1987-1993. Auth, "Tracing the Contours of Faith," Dog Ear Pub, 2013; Auth, *Sprtl Wholeness for Cler*, Alb Inst, 1993; Auth, *The Birth of the Cath Tubingen Sch*, Scholars Press, 1981.

FEIDER, Paul A (FdL) 1511 Cedarhurst Dr, New London WI 54961 B Sheboygan WI 1951 s Wilmer & Marcella. BA U of Innsbruck AT 1973; MA S Fran Sem 1977; Cert Ang Stud Nash 1995. Rec 5/21/1995 as Priest Bp Russell Edward Jacobus. m 5/27/1995 Julie J Feider c 2. Vic S Jn's Epis Ch New London WI 1997-2016; Vic S Jn's Ch Shawano WI 1997-2003; Vic Ch Of The Heav Rest Princeton WV 1995-1997. Auth, "Resting in the Heart," 2001; Auth, "Sacraments: Encountering the Risen Lord," 1986; Auth, "Journey to Inner Peace," 1984; Auth, "Paul's Letters for Today's Chr," 1982; Auth, "Healing & Suffering," 1980. Assn of Chr Therapists 1979; Ord of S Lk 1996.

FELICETTI, Elizabeth Marshall (SVa) 1217 Yarbrough Way, Virginia Beach VA 23455 **R S Dav's Epis Ch No Chesterfield VA 2011-** B Phoenix AZ 1968 d James & Betty. BA U of Arizona 1990; MDiv VTS 2007. D 6/9/2007 P 12/8/2007 Bp John Clark Buchanan. m 10/19/1996 Gary Felicetti. Assoc Old Donation Ch Virginia Bch VA 2007-2011.

FELLHAUER, Edward William (Miss) 9B Deans Court, Santa Fe NM 87508 **Asstg P S Bede's Epis Ch Santa Fe NM 2016-** B Kansas City MO 1946 s William & Maxine. BA U of Missouri 1968; MA U of Missouri 1970; MDiv Epis TS of the SW 1987. D 6/3/1987 Bp Richard Frank Grein P 12/21/1987 Bp John Herbert MacNaughton. m 1/28/1989 Sheila Rose Barber c 2. Pres/CEO S Fran Cmnty Serv Inc. Salina KS 2002-2014, Chapl 1993-2014; Reg VP S Fran Acad Inc. Salina KS 1994-2002; Int Pres MHA Tulsa OK 1992-1993; St. Bede's Vic Dio Oklahoma Oklahoma City OK 1991-1994; Pstr Counslr MHA Tulsa OK 1991-1993; Int S Matt's Ch Enid OK 1989-1990; Asst R S Alb's Ch Harlingen TX 1987-1989. Auth, "Column," *SFCS Web-site Highlights*, St. Fran Com Serv, 2011; Auth, "Column," *SFCS Web-site*, St. Franics Com Serv, 2010; Auth, "Pres's Report," *Highlights*, St. Fran Com Serv, 2009; Auth, "Pres's Column," *Highlights*, St Fran Com Serv, 2008; Auth, "Pres's column," *Highlights*, St Fran Cmnty Serv, 2007; Auth, "Cir ," *Highlights*, St. Fran Com Serv, 2006; Auth, "Cir ," *Highlights*, St. Fran Com Serv, 2005; Auth, "Cir ," *Highlights*, SFA, 2004; Auth, "Cir ," *Highlights*, SFA, 2003; Auth, "Pres's Cir ," *Highlights mag*, The S Fran Acad, 2002; Auth, "Preventing Abuse," *Preventing Chld Sexual Abuse: Creating Safer Environ*, The S Fran Acad, 1997; Auth, "Developmental Disabil," *Paradigm mag*, The S Fran Acad, 1995; Auth, "Corporal Punishment - Blistering Issue or Wrong Tool?," *AHEC News*, AHEC, 1991. Chld Welf League of Amer 2002; Epis Cmnty Serv 2002; MS Assn Chld Care Agencies 1995-2003; Natl Assn Hm & Serv for Chld 1996-2000. Excellence In Action St. Fran Cmnty Serv 2010; Excellence In Action St. Fran Cmnty Serv 2010; Serv Awd The S Fran Acad 2004; Serv Awd St. Matt's Enid Okalhama 1991; Bd Awd The Shpd Cntr,Texas 1989.

FELLHAUER, Sheila Rose (Miss) 9B Deans Court, Santa Fe NM 87508 **Asstg P S Bede's Epis Ch Santa Fe NM 2016-** B Saint Louis MO 1945 d George & Alpha. MA U of Missouri 1967; BA U of Missouri 1967; MDiv Epis TS of the SW 1987. D 6/20/1987 P 3/1/1988 Bp Gerald Nicholas Mcallister. m 1/28/1989 Edward William Fellhauer c 2. Int P St. Dav's Epis Ch Nashville TN 2015-2016; P-in-c Epis Ch Of The Incarn Salina KS 2004-2008; R S Paul's Ch Picayune MS 2000-2003; S Fran Cmnty Serv Inc. Salina KS 1999-2014; Int The Epis Ch Of The Medtr Meridian MS 1997-1998; Chapl S Fran Acad Inc. Salina KS 1996-1999; S Dunst's Ch Tulsa OK 1991-1995; Dio Oklahoma Oklahoma City OK 1987-1991; Vic S Jn's Epis Ch Woodward OK 1987-1991. Auth, "Come Join in The Search: Lenten Meditations," *S Fran Cmnty Serv*, SFCS Pub, 2011; Auth, "Can I Walk My Dog In Heaven?: Chld's Spiritually,"

S Fran Cmnty Serv, SFCS Pub, 2010; Auth, "Alleluia! Chr Is Risen!: Eastertide Meditations," *S Fran Cmnty Serv*, SFCS Pub, 2009; Auth, "Ther In Chr," *S Fran Cmnty Serv*, SFCS Pub, 2009; Auth, "Unto Us A Chld is b: Christmastide Mediations," *S Fran Cmnty Serv*, SFCS Pub, 2007; Auth, "On the Path of God's Ways/ A Lenten Journey: Lenten Mediations," *S Fran Cmnty Serv*, SFCS Pub, 2007; Auth, "All Creatures of Our God and King, Lift Up Your Voices, Let us Sing!," *The S Fran Acad*, The S Fran Acad, 2006; Auth, "Sing Alleluia Above the Treetops! Sing Alleluia to the Sun!," *The S Fran Acad*, The S Fran Acad, 2005; Auth, "Lord Make Me an Instrument of your Peace," *The S Fran Acad*, The S Fran Acad, 2004; Auth, "Twelve Gifts of Christmas: Christmastide Mediations," *The S Fran Acad*, The S Fran Acad, 2004. Phi Beta Kappa U Of Missouri 1967.

FELLOWS, Richard Greer (SwFla) 15801 Country Lake Drive, Tampa FL 33624 **Chapl Tampa Police Dept. 2010-; Chapl Tampa Police Dept. 2009-** B Douglas AZ 1958 s William & Helen. Mem Intl Conf of Police Chapl; BS U of Arizona 1980; MDiv VTS 1983. D 5/29/1983 P 12/14/1983 Bp Joseph Thomas Heistand. m 1/17/2006 Laura M Magnon c 3. Cur S Mary's Par Tampa FL 2005-2010; R Ch Of The Annunc Holmes Bch FL 1989-2000; S Jn's Ch Centralia IL 1985-1988; Vic S Thos Ch Salem IL 1985-1988; Assoc R Chr Ch Springfield IL 1983-1985.

FELLOWS, Robert Hayden (Okla) 5820 W Garden Pointe Dr, Stillwater OK 74074 B Tulsa OK 1944 s Charles & Evelyn. BA U of Tulsa 1967; MDiv Epis TS of the SW 1970. D 6/20/1970 P 12/20/1970 Bp Chilton R Powell. m 6/21/1968 Kathryn Fellows c 2. R S Andr's Ch Stillwater OK 1988-2011; Dio Oklahoma Oklahoma City OK 1978-1988, 1976-1977; R The Epis Ch Of The H Apos Oklahoma City OK 1978-1988; S Elis's Ch Oklahoma City OK 1971-1975; Cur S Lk's Epis Ch Bartlesville OK 1970-1978.

FELS, Charles Wentworth Baker (ETenn) B Cincinnati OH 1943 s Rendgis & Beatrice. VTS; BA Stan 1965; MA Van 1972; JD Van 1974; MDiv EDS 2005. D 6/18/2005 P 1/28/2006 Bp Charles Glenn VonRosenberg. m 5/20/2005 Susan Sgarlat-Fels c 2. R Ch Of The Gd Shpd Knoxville TN 2006-2016; Adj D and P St. Barth Ch New York NY 2005-2006; Sem S Alb's Par Washington DC 2003-2005.

FELSOVANYI, Andrea (NCal) 4 Bishop Ln, Menlo Park CA 94025 B Chicago IL 1947 d Anthony & Shirley. BS MI SU 1973; JD Antioch Sch Law 1976; MDiv Ya Berk 1995; STM Ya Berk 1998. D 6/13/1998 Bp Clarence Nicholas Coleridge P 1/1/1999 Bp Richard Lester Shimpfky. Epis Sr Communities Lafayette CA 2007-2016; Ch Of Our Sav Mill Vlly CA 2005-2006; S Aid's Ch San Francisco CA 2004-2005; Ascen Epis Ch Vallejo CA 2003-2005; H Cross Epis Ch Castro Vlly CA 2001-2002; S Lk's Ch Los Gatos CA 1999-2001. SCHC.

FELTNER, Allan L (EMich) 1210 S Fell Ave, Normal IL 61761 **D S Barth's Epis Ch Mio MI 2014-** B Peoria IL 1947 s George & Pauline. D 6/29/2002 Bp Peter Hess Beckwith P 5/30/2015 Bp Steven Todd Ousley. m 9/9/1967 Sue Ann Feltner c 4.

FELTON, Paul Dunbar (Tex) 707 Venice St, Sugar Land TX 77478 **Died 6/19/2016** B Chicago IL 1924 s Henry & Lucy. BA Ripon Coll Ripon WI 1949; BD Nash 1952; PhD Marq 1968. D 7/1/1952 P 12/1/1952 Bp Wallace E Conkling. m 6/7/1952 Mary Felton c 5. Ret 1993-2016; Asst R Adv Stafford TX 1992-1993; All SS Epis Ch Stafford TX 1992-1993; Ch Of The Redeem Houston TX 1982-1992, Asst 1972-1974; Cur The Ch Of The H Sprt Lake Forest IL 1952-1954. Auth, "Renwl," *Theol Renwl & Towards Renwl*.

FELTY, Rose Ann (Alb) PO Box 114, Columbiaville NY 12050 B San Antonio TX 1954 d Fred & Erma. BA S Marys U 1977; MDiv Nash 2010. D 6/5/2010 P 1/8/2011 Bp William Howard Love. St Fran Epis Ch San Antonio TX 2016-2017; S Jn The Evang Stockport NY 2010-2015.

FENLON, Mathew Charles (Tex) 2450 River Oaks Blvd, Houston TX 77019 B Dayton OH 1979 s William & Linda. BSS Ohio U 2003; MDiv TESM 2008. D 5/31/2008 Bp John Wadsworth Howe P 5/2/2009 Bp George Edward Councell. m 10/8/2010 Jessica Fenlon. S Thos Ch Houston TX 2014-2017; S Jn The Div Houston TX 2010-2014; Cur S Lk's Ch Gladstone NJ 2008-2010.

FENN, Richard Kimball (Pa) 43 Hibben Rd, Princeton NJ 08540 B Oberlin OH 1934 s Percy & Caroline. BA Ya 1955; BD EDS 1958; MTh PrTS 1966; PhD Bryn 1970. D 5/30/1958 P 12/1/1958 Bp Nelson Marigold Burroughs. m 6/1/1956 Caroline Yale White c 3. P-in-c S Phil's Ch New Hope PA 1966-1970; Dio Pennsylvania Philadelphia PA 1963-1969; Vic Ch Of The Epiph Royersford PA 1963-1966; All SS' Cathd Nagpur India 1961-1962; Cur Ch Of Our Sav Akron OH 1958-1960. Auth, "Time Exposure," Oxf Press; Auth, "Key Thinkers in the Sociol of Rel," Continuum; Auth, "Beyond Idols," Oxf Press; Auth, "TThe Persistence of Purgatory," U of Cambridge Press; Auth, "The Death of Herod," U of Cambridge Press; Auth, "The End Of Time". richard.fenn@ptsem.edu

FENN, Richard Lewis (WNY) 19 Pradas Way, Edgartown MA 02539 **Ret 1999-** B Cleveland OH 1934 s Fred & Sarah. Oxf GB; BA Ken 1957; BD EDS 1964. D 6/20/1964 P 1/1/1965 Bp Robert McConnell Hatch. c 2. Dn Dio Wstrn New York Tonawanda NY 1984-1998; R S Lk's Epis Ch Jamestown NY 1976-1998;

Dn Dio Wstrn Massachusetts Springfield 1972-1973; Epis Ch Of The Epiph Wilbraham MA 1967-1976; Cur S Steph's Ch Pittsfield MA 1964-1967.

FENNER, Renee Lynette (Mo) **R S Barn Ch Florissant MO 2010-; Stndg Com Dio Missouri S Louis MO 2011-** B Saint Louis MO 1954 d Walter & Irene. BA Webster U 1976; MDiv GTS 2005. D 12/22/2004 P 6/24/2005 Bp George Wayne Smith. Cn Pstr, Liturg, Adult Formation Chr Ch Cathd S Louis MO 2005-2010.

FENTON, Arnold Aidan (SanD) 9815 Circa Valle Verde, El Cajon CA 92021 **P-in-c Chr the King Alpine CA 2006-; Ret 1990-** B Westfield NJ 1927 s Arnold & Carla. BA Laf 1948; MDiv GTS 1951. D 6/10/1951 Bp Horace W B Donegan P 12/15/1951 Bp William A Lawrence. m 12/4/1974 Barbara B Fenton c 3. P-in-c S Dav's Epis Ch San Diego CA 2000-2001; R The Par Of S Matt Pacific Plsds CA 1979-1990; R All Souls' Epis Ch San Diego CA 1973-1979; R Chr Ch Grosse Pointe Grosse Pointe Farms MI 1969-1973; R Chr Ch Tacoma WA 1961-1969; R S Steph's Epis Ch Longview WA 1955-1961; Chapl Untd States Naval Reserve 1953-1955; Cur Chr Ch Cathd Springfield MA 1951-1953.

FENTON, David Henry (SanD) 3962 Josh St, Eugene OR 97402 **Ret 1996-** B Los Angeles CA 1931 s Melville & Helen. BA U of Redlands 1952; MDiv Nash 1969. D 9/13/1969 P 3/21/1970 Bp Francis E I Bloy. m 8/23/1952 Jean B Fenton c 2. Cler Salary Revs Dio San Diego San Diego CA 1974-1994; R S Jn's Ch Fallbrook CA 1972-1996; Cur S Lk's Of The Mountains La Crescenta CA 1969-1972. Auth, "The 1940-1982 Hymnal Cross-Reference"; Auth, *Bdgt Press Calendar*; Auth, *Liturg Desk Calendar*, Franklin X. McCormick. Cert of Recognition City of Los Angeles 2007; R Emer St. Jn's, Fallbrook, CA. 1996.

FENTON, Eric Denis (WTex) 606 W Cleveland St, Cuero TX 77954 **Mem Dio W Texas Wrld Missions Com 2013-** B Croswell MI 1948 s Omar & Jeane. BA MI SU 1975; MDiv TESM 1981. D 6/21/1981 P 5/9/1982 Bp Charles Farmer Duvall. m 7/2/1988 Janet Fenton c 6. R Gr Ch Cuero TX 2011-2014; P-in-c Chr Ch in the Hill Country Bulverde TX 2008-2009; Asst R Chr Epis Ch San Antonio TX 2003-2007; Chapl Off Of Bsh For ArmdF New York NY 1987-2003; Chapl USAF Lk AFB AZ 1987-2003; Vic All SS Ch Prudenville MI 1983-1986; S Eliz's Epis Ch Roscommon MI 1983-1986; Cur S Andr's Epis Ch Panama City FL 1981-1983. Meritorious Serv Medal USAF 2001.

FENTON, Fred (Cal) 1670 Interlachen Rd Apt 43g, Seal Beach CA 90740 **Retire Epis Ch 2001-; Dep GC ECUSA 1979-** B Los Angeles CA 1935 s Melville & Helen. BA Harv 1958; STB EDS 1961. D 9/7/1961 P 3/27/1962 Bp Francis E I Bloy. m 9/12/1954 Billie L Loit c 3. R S Jas Epis Ch Baton Rouge LA 1994-2001; Pres Westside Ecum Conf Los Angeles CA 1990-1992; Pres, Alum Assoc EDS Cambridge MA 1988-1989; Bd Trst Crossroads Sch Santa Monica CA 1971-1994; R S Aug By-The-Sea Par Santa Monica CA 1971-1994; R S Mk's Epis Ch Upland CA 1969-1971; R S Jn's Epis Ch Chula Vista CA 1966-1969; Vic S Mary's/Santa Maria Virgen Imperial Bch CA 1962-1966; Cur S Jude's Epis Par Burbank CA 1961-1962; Gift Plnng Dept Dio California San Francisco CA 2006-2009; Dn, Baton Rouge Dnry Dio Louisiana New Orleans LA 1997-2000; Prog Grp on Stwdshp Dio Los Angeles Los Angeles CA 1990-1992. Auth, "Make invisible visible," *Epis Life*, 2009; Auth, "Foreword," *Beyond Words*, Morehouse, 2004; Auth, "Nuts and Bolts of a Stwardship Cmpgn," *The Livivng Ch*, 1996; Auth, "A New Approach for Bishops," *LivCh*, 1992; Auth, "Decade of Evang: Something seems to be Missing," *LivCh*, 1992; Auth, "Baby Boomers: How have people of this Generation been brought back to Ch?," *LivCh*, 1988; Auth, "Age of the Laity," *The Epis News*, 1973. OHC 1962; Our Lady of Walsingham 1982; SHN 1964. Fr Fred Fenton Day City of Baton Rouge 2000; Sch Chair w Plaque Crossroads Sch 1994; L.A. Cnty Recognition Bd Supervisors 1991; Mayor's Commendation City of Santa Monica 1991; Sch Chair w Plaque EDS 1989.

FENTON, G Douglas (NY) 1410 Nanton St, Vancouver V6H 2E2 Canada **Exec Archd Dio New Westminster Vancouver BC 2013-, Dir for Mssn & Mnstry 2011-2012** B Fort Frances Ontario CA 1956 s James & Ethel. DD St Jn's Coll; BA U of Manitoba 1977; Cert Smith Clnc St Josephs Hosp Thunder Bay ON 1981; MDiv St Johns Coll Winnipeg CA 1981. Trans 12/11/2002 Bp Mark Sean Sisk. m 9/27/2013 Keith Scott Landherr. Assoc Chr And S Steph's Ch New York NY 2009-2011; Asst The Ch Of S Lk In The Fields New York NY 2004-2008; Prog Off for YA & Campus Mnstrs Epis Ch Cntr New York NY 2002-2011; Campus Mnstry Com Dio New York New York NY 2005-2011. Auth, "In the Batey," *People of God*, Angl Ch of Can, 1994; Auth, "When the Words Stop Working," *Plumbline*, Journ of MHE, 1994; Auth, "Hope is Found in the Struggle," *People of God*, Angl Ch of Can, 1993; Auth, "From the Down Side Up," *In Lumine*, St Jn's Coll, 1992; Co-Auth, "The Jos Proj," *The Jos Proj*, Angl Ch of Can, 1984. Affirming Angl Catholicism 1998-2010; Conf of St Ben 1979; Fllshp of St Jn the Evang 2004; Friends of the Angl Cntr-Rome 2006; Soc of Cath Priests 2013. Distinguished Ldrshp Awd Epis Campus Chapl 2011.

FENTON, Graham R C (Minn) 4720 Zenith Ave S, Minneapolis MN 55410 B Kroonstad ZA 1949 s Albert & Izetta. BS U of Natal 1971; GOE S Johns TS 1974. Trans 5/1/1984. m 6/15/1974 Gillian M Fenton c 2. Assoc S Steph The Mtyr Ch Minneapolis MN 1993-2009; R Chr Epis Ch Grand Rapids MN 1984-1993; P-in-c S Jn Wynberg Cape Town Soafr 1977-1984; Cur Chr Ch Addington Durban Soafr 1974-1977.

FENWICK, Robert Donald (SO) 6439 Bethany Village Dr., Box 307, Centerville OH 45459 B Great Falls MT 1930 s John & Amy. BS Winona St U 1953; MDiv Bex Sem 1959; S Pauls Coll 1979. D 6/20/1959 P 12/21/1959 Bp Hamilton Hyde Kellogg. m 8/3/1952 Lois Fenwick c 2. R S Paul's Epis Ch Dayton OH 1975-1995; Dn Rochester Dnry 1966-1970; R S Lk's Epis Ch Rochester MN 1964-1975; Assoc R Calv Ch Rochester MN 1962-1963; Vic Gr Ch Montevideo MN 1959-1962. Hon DD S Paul'S Collete 1979.

FEREBEE, Randy (WNC) 127 42nd Avenue Dr NW, Hickory NC 28601 P-in-c Epis Ch Of The Mssh Myrtle Bch SC 2014-; Dir Epiph Inst + Consulting 2003- B Spartanburg SC 1947 s Curtis & Sara. BA Belmont Abbey Coll 1969; MDiv VTS 1973; DMin Sewanee: The U So, TS 1999. D 5/20/1973 Bp Matthew George Henry P 11/25/1973 Bp William Gillette Weinhauer. m 5/1/1970 Judith Anne Ferebee c 2. R S Alb's Ch Hickory NC 1975-2009, R Emer 2009-; Assoc Ch Of The Ascen Hickory NC 1973-1975. Auth, "Cultivating the Missional Ch," Morehouse Pub, 2012.

FEREGRINO, Alfredo (Oly) Dio Olympia Seattle 2014- B Mexico City MX 1966 s Alfredo & Soledad. Philos Natl Auto U of Mex 1990; MDiv Seattle U 2013; MDiv Seattle U 2013. D 10/18/2012 Bp Gregory Harold Rickel P 6/13/2013 Bp Bavi Edna Rivera. m 1/9/1997 Jenifer L Feregrino c 2. S Paul's Ch Seattle WA 2013.

FERGUESON, John Frederick (Oly) 14449 90th Ct Ne, Bothell WA 98011 B Jackson MI 1944 s Carl & Doris. BA Albion Coll 1966; MDiv SWTS 1972. D 5/27/1972 Bp Charles Ellsworth Bennison Jr P 12/1/1972 Bp Charles Bennison Sr. m 2/4/1967 Virginia Fergueson. R Ch Of The Redeem Kenmore WA 1983-2014; R Emm Ch Hastings MI 1979-1983; Cn Cathd Of Chr The King Kalamazoo MI 1976-1979; Dio Wstrn Michigan Kalamazoo MI 1972-1979; S Mich's Ch Grand Rapids MI 1972-1976; Vic S Mich's Mssn Ada Cascade MI 1972-1976. Auth, "A Man Of Sorrows," Familar w Suffering. Natl Conf Viet Nam Veteran Ministers. office@redeemer-kenmore.org

FERGUSON, Anthony David Norman (Fla) 5128 Falling Water Rd, Nolensville TN 37135 B London UK 1951 s Norman & Stella. HNC1 Ewell Coll 1972; Cert Theol Stud Oxf GB 1978. Trans 7/1/1980 as Priest Bp William Gillette Weinhauer. m 9/7/1985 Norma Glennon Ferguson c 3. Reg Cn Dio Florida Jacksonville 2012-2015, Chairman, Bdgt Com 2004-2014, Chair, Prog and Bdgt Com 2004-2013, Chair -Prog,Bdgt and Audit Cttee 2004-; R S Ptr's Ch Jacksonville FL 1993-2016; Sm Ch Cmsn Dio No Carolina Raleigh NC 1984-1993; R S Marg's Epis Ch Waxhaw NC 1984-1993; R S Jn's Epis Ch Marion NC 1980-1984; Chapl SAMS USA Un Mills NC 1979-1980; D Ch of Engl Tipton Untd Kingdom 1978-1979; Chair -Yth at Risk Cmsn Dio Wstrn No Carolina Asheville NC 1982-1984.

FERGUSON, Dina McMullin (Los) St. Michael the Archangel, El Segundo CA 90245 S Mich The Archangel Par El Segundo CA 2014-; Vic S Geo's Mssn Hawthorne CA 2012-, Asst 2009-2012 B Inglewood CA 1951 d Everett & Patricia. BA USC 1973; MS USC 1977; DMin Untd TS 2007; CAS CDSP 2008. D 1/21/2009 P 7/25/2009 Bp Joseph Jon Bruno. m 7/2/1972 David Ferguson c 2. StMichaelsElSegundo@gmail.com

FERGUSON, Dru (NwT) 510 Newell Ave, Dallas TX 75223 B Las Vegas NM 1943 d Cloma & Nancy. BA Arizona St U 1965; MEd Arizona St U 1969; MDiv Epis TS of the SW 1994. D 6/25/1994 P 6/24/1995 Bp James Monte Stanton. m 11/10/1973 Ronald Ferguson c 1. S Ptr's Epis Ch Amarillo TX 2007-2009; S Andr's Epis Ch Amarillo TX 2004-2006; S Paul's Epis Ch Dallas TX 2003-2004, 1994-1996, Cur 1994-1996; Cbury Epis Sch Desoto TX 1998-2003; Chapl The Cbury Epis Sch Desoto TX 1998-2003; Int S Mths' Epis Ch Athens TX 1998-1999; Asst The Epis Ch Of The Trsfg Dallas TX 1996-1998. DOK 1992; NECA 1994-2000; NEAC 1994-2001; Ord Of S Lk 2000.

FERGUSON, Fred-Munro (Alb) 6 Spences Trce, Harwich MA 02645 Ret 1993- B Montclair NJ 1934 s Allan & Gizella. BA Westminster Choir Coll of Rider U 1956; PDS 1958. D 5/23/1959 P 12/19/1959 Bp Donald MacAdie. Bd S Fran Hms for Boys & Girls 1981-1985; Ch Of S Sacrement Bolton Landing NY 1980-1993; Trst Dio Dio Albany Greenwich NY 1980-1984, Mus Cmsn 1975-1979, Secy to Bp 1974-1979, COM 1980-1983; Trst Abba Hse of Pryr 1979-1982; R S Mk's Epis Ch Philmont NY 1975-1979; Cur S Lk's Ch Catskill NY 1971-1975; Chair Trsts Trsfg Day Care Cntr Inc 1971-1972; Bd Chr Hosp Jersey City NJ 1969-1971; Ch Of The Trsfg No Bergen NJ 1966-1971, 1960-1965; Vic Ch of the Trsfg No Bergen NJ 1966-1971; OSF 1964-1965; Vic Ch of the Trsfg No Bergen NJ 1960-1962; Cur S Jas Ch Montclair NJ 1959-1960. Osf 1964-1965; SSC 1984; Ssc.

FERGUSON, Judith Ann (NY) 391 Main St, Highland Falls NY 10928 R H Innoc Highland Falls NY 2001-; Epis Civilian Chapl USMA W Point NY 2001- B Drexel Hill PA 1952 d Robert & Pauline. BS Philadelphia Coll of Bible 1974; MFA NYU 1980; MDiv Sewanee: The U So, TS 1996. D 6/1/1996 P 12/7/1996 Bp Richard Frank Grein. Dio New York New York NY 2001-2005, Congrl Spprt Plan Com 2010-2016, Com to Elect a Bp 2010-2011, Assessment Adjustment Bd 2008-2009, Congrl Spprt Plan Com 2006-2008, Mid-Hudson Reg Coun 2003-2004, Prov Syn Dep 2002-2004, Com for Campus Mnstry--Chapl to USMA 2002-; Cur S Jn's Ch Larchmont NY 1997-2001; Cur Ch Of

S Mary The Vrgn Chappaqua NY 1997; D S Mk's Ch Honey Brook PA 1996. holyinnocents@verizon.net

FERGUSON JR, Lawrence C (EO) Po Box 1344, Prineville OR 97754 Ret 1996- B Pittsfield MA 1934 s Lawrence & Effie. BA Hav 1957; STB EDS 1960. D 6/4/1960 Bp William A Lawrence P 12/9/1960 Bp Lane W Barton. c 3. Cntrl OR Mssnr Dio Estrn Oregon Cove OR 1992-1996, 1991-1996, COM 1988-1994; S Andr's Epis Ch Prineville OR 1986-1991; Vic S Chris Wishram OR 1968-1986; R The Par Of S Mk The Evang Hood River OR 1968-1986; Pstr Cmnty Ch Antelope OR 1964-1968; Vic S Mk's Epis and Gd Shpd Luth Madras OR 1960-1968; S Alb's Epis Ch Redmond OR 1960-1961.

FERGUSON, Les (SVa) 5537 Greenefield Dr S, Portsmouth VA 23703 R S Jn's Ch Suffolk VA 2010- B Long Beach CA 1962 s Michael & Carolyn. BS OR SU 1985; MS Naval Post Grad Sch 1993; MA NAVAC War Coll 2002; MDiv VTS 2010. D 6/12/2010 P 12/18/2010 Bp Herman Hollerith IV. m 10/1/1983 Kathleen Mary Thomas. Chairman Cltn Against Pvrty in Suffolk Suffolk VA 2012-2015. rectorstjohns1755@verizon.net

FERGUSON SR, Michael Blackburn (SVa) 900 Fleet Drive #287, Virginia Beach VA 23454 Died 6/10/2016 B Baker City OR 1939 s Harold & Vivienne. BS Estrn Oregon U 1960; MDiv VTS 1993. D 6/12/1993 Bp Peter J Lee P 12/18/1993 Bp Donald Purple Hart. m 12/27/1959 Carolyn Rose Muller c 3. Co-Pstr Ch Of H Apos Virginia Bch VA 2009-2016; R S Anne's Ch Appomattox VA 1996-2008; Vic S Annes Ch Mililani HI 1993-1995; Stndg Com Dio Sthrn Virginia Newport News VA 2008-2011; Dioc Sprtl Dir Curs in Sthrn Virginia 2007-2014. Auth, "Ethical Implications of Fetal Tissue Cell Resrch & Ther," Harris Prize Essay, 1994; Auth, ATR.

FERGUSON, Ronald L (Chi) B Chicago IL 1935 s Earl & Lucile. AA Gateway Tech Kenosha WI 1964; Sem Chicago IL 1991. D 12/7/1991 Bp Frank Tracy Griswold III. m 8/15/1981 Christine Ferguson.

FERGUSON, Ruth (Roch) 377 Rector Pl Apt 95, New York NY 10280 R Chr Ch Rochester NY 2008- B Murfreesboro TN 1968 d Franklin & Elizabeth. BA Warren Wilson Coll 1991; MDiv GTS 1997. D 5/31/1997 P 4/1/1998 Bp William George Burrill. m 6/22/1991 Sam A Sommers c 2. The Ch Of S Lk In The Fields New York NY 1999-2002; Asst R S Jn's Ch Olney MD 1997-1999.

FERGUSON, Sheila Saward (Chi) 1709 Indian Knoll Rd, Naperville IL 60565 P-in-c Calv Ch Lombard IL 2006- B Windsor ON CA 1944 d Eric & Mary. Cert London Teachers Coll GB 1964; BS U MI 1969; MA U MI 1971; MDiv SWTS 1989. D 8/19/1989 Bp William Grant Black P 3/8/1990 Bp Frank Tracy Griswold III. m 8/29/1970 Ronald J Ferguson c 3. Calv Ch Lombard IL 2006-2008; Int St. Mk's Glen Ellyn IL 2005-2006; S Mk's Epis Ch Glen Ellyn IL 2004-2006; Assoc Dio Chicago Chicago IL 2003-2004, Cong Dvlpmt 1998-2002; S Hugh Of Lincoln Epis Ch Elgin IL 1990-1991; S Barn' Epis Ch Glen Ellyn IL 1989-1997.

FERGUSON, Stephen Keith (Tex) 20171 Chasewood Park Drive, Houston TX 77070 B Shreveport LA 1949 s Mason & Willadene. BS NE Louisiana U 1971; MDiv Epis TS of the SW 1994. D 6/17/1995 Bp Claude Edward Payne P 1/11/1996 Bp William Elwood Sterling. m 8/9/1969 Sandra W Willis c 3. St. Lk's Epis Hosp Dio Texas Houston TX 2011-2015, Sprtl Dir - Curs 1997-2011, Sprtl Dir for Curs 2001-2007; R H Comf Epis Ch Sprg TX 1998-2011; Assoc S Lk's On The Lake Epis Ch Austin TX 1995-1998; Asst Chr Epis Ch Temple TX 1994-1995; Chapl Scott & White Hosp 1994-1995. 0rder of St. Lk the Physcn 1987; Assn of Profsnl Chapl 2011; BroSA 1995; The Assembly of Epis Healthcare Chapl 2012. sferguson1@stlukeshealth.org

FERGUSON, Thomas C (Mass) 583 Sheridan Ave, Columbus OH 43209 S Jn's Ch Sandwich MA 2016-; Dn Bex Sem Columbus OH 2011- B Weymouth MA 1969 s Donald & Barbara. BA Wesl 1991; MDiv Ya Berk 1994; ThM H Cross TS 1997; PhD Ch DS of Pacific 2002. D 6/6/2009 Bp Steven Andrew Miller. m 9/4/1999 Shannon Kelly c 1. Epis Ch Cntr New York NY 2009-2011; Assoc Dep Dom And Frgn Mssy Soc-Episc Ch Cntr 2001-2009.

FERGUSON, Vergie Rae (Az) 1650 W Glendale Ave Apt 4103, Phoenix AZ 85021 D All SS Ch Phoenix AZ 2013- B Phoenix AZ 1929 d Arthur & Garnet. U of Arizona; BS Nthrn Arizona U 1979. D 11/7/1992 Bp Joseph Thomas Heistand. m 6/11/1947 Jay Edward Ferguson. D S Jn The Bapt Globe AZ 1999-2006; D Ch Of The Epiph Flagstaff AZ 1992-1999. DOK 1992.

FERGUSON, Virginia Alice (Nev) 6773 W Charleston Blvd, Las Vegas NV 89146 B San Francisco CA 1932 d George & Virginia. D 5/28/1983 Bp Wesley Frensdorff. D S Thos Ch Las Vegas NV 1983-1988.

FERLO, Roger Albert (NY) 1700 E 56th Street, Apartment 2601, Chicago IL 60637 Bexley Seabury Fed Chicago IL 2013-, 2012-2013; Bd Mem ATR Evanston IL 2005- B Rome NY 1951 s Albert & Nathaline. AB Colg 1973; MA Ya 1974; MPhil Ya 1975; PhD Ya 1979; Cert Ang Stud GTS 1985. D 6/8/1985 P 2/5/1986 Bp Arthur Edward Walmsley. m 7/31/1977 Anne C Harlan c 1. Assoc Dn and Dir for the Inst for Chr VTS Alexandria VA 2004-2012; Trst Colg 2002-2011; Cathd Of St Jn The Div New York NY 2000-2005; Dep GC Dio New York New York NY 2000-2003; Bd Gvnr (Pres 2008-2011 NAES 1995-2011; Bd Trst S Lk's Sch New York NY 1994-2003; R The Ch Of S Lk In The Fields New York NY 1994-2003; Pres Dioc Coun Dio Pittsburgh Pittsburgh PA 1989-1990; R The Ch Of The Redeem Pittsburgh PA 1987-1993;

Asst and Day Sch Chapl The Ch Of The Gd Shpd Augusta GA 1985-1987. Ed, "Heaven," Seabury Press, 2007; Auth, "Sensing God," Cowley Press/Rowman and Littlefield, 2002; Auth, "This Christmas in New York," *The Tablet*, 2001; Auth, "Opening The Bible," Cowley Press/Rowman and Littlefield, 1997. DD Colg 2010; Cler Renwl Grant Lilly Endwmt 2000; Distinguished Tchg Prize Ya 1981; Whiting Fllshp in Hmnts Mrs. Giles Whiting Fndt 1976; Danforth Grad Fell Danforth Fndt 1973; Phi Beta Kappa Colg 1972.

FERNANDEZ, Jose Pascual (NY) 107 Se Superior Way, Stuart FL 34997 B Guantanamo-Oriente CU 1929 s Manuel & Carmen. BTh Seminar Pont S Basilio Magno; BTh Semina Rio U 1954; Epis TS of the SW 1982. Rec 6/1/1982 as Priest Bp Calvin Onderdonk Schofield Jr. m 9/11/1977 Olga Fernandez c 2. P H Faith Epis Ch Port St Lucie FL 2006-2012; Vic Chr Ch Trenton NJ 1988-1994; Hisp Epis Cntr San Andres Ch Yonkers NY 1983-1988; Chr Epis Ch Tarrytown NY 1982-1988; Hisp Vic Gr Ch White Plains NY 1982-1988; Santa Cruz-Resurr Epis Ch Biscayne Pk FL 1982, Asst 1978-1981; Serv RC Ch 1955-1977. Auth, "Catechism For Sunday Sch At The Epis Ch"; Auth, "Conozca La Iglesia Epis"; Auth, "The Mssn". Assn Of Natl Profsnl Hispanics.

FERNANDEZ, Linda Jean Pell (Md) 1930 Brookdale Rd, Baltimore MD 21244 **Bethany Luth Ch Brunswick MD 2014-** B Exeter NH 1955 d Arthur & Beryle. BS Cntr Coll 1977; MDiv SWTS 1981; MS U IL 1984. D 6/13/1981 Bp Addison Hosea P 7/1/1982 Bp Quintin Ebenezer Primo Jr. m 9/5/1980 Rodolfo Fernandez c 3. R Gr Ch Brunswick MD 2014; S Thos Epis Ch Towson MD 2009-2011; Gr Luth Ch Westminster MD 2004-2005; R Epis Ch Of Chr The King Baltimore MD 1997-2004; P-in-c Gr Ch Everett MA 1992-1996; Assoc S Paul's Ch Malden MA 1990-1992; Ch Of The H Trin Marlborough MA 1989; Assoc S Paul's Ch Lynnfield MA 1988-1990; R S Bride's Epis Ch Oregon IL 1986-1988; St Barn Urban Cntr Chicago IL 1985; Assoc & Counslr S Barn' Ch & Urban Cntr Chicago IL 1983-1985; Counslr & Chapl Cathd Shltr Chicago IL 1981-1983; ReVive Cntr for Hsng and Healing Chicago IL 1981-1983; Asst S Mart's Ch Chicago IL 1981-1983. Auth, "A Handbook On Dom Violence For Cler". Mec Sec Convenor. Natl Assn Female Execs. ecctk@erols.com

FERNANDEZ-LIRANZO, Hipolito Secundino (DR) Calle 10 No. 30, Villa Olga, Santiago Dominican Republic B Salcedo 1929 s Secundino & Ana. BTh Sem Pontificio Sto Tomas De Aquino 1958; U Nacl Pedro Henriquez Urena 1972. Rec 10/1/1984 as Priest Bp Telesforo A Isaac. m 12/25/1971 Dulcina Natividad Reina c 3. Vic Iglesia Epis Cristo Salvador Santiago 1992-2002; Vic Iglesia Epis San Lucas Santiago 1989-2002; Dio The Dominican Republic (Iglesia Epis Dominicana) Gazcue Santo Domingo 1984-2000; Iglesia Epis Cristo el Rey Puerto Plata 1984-1988; Serv RC Ch 1958-1970.

FERNANDEZ-POLA, Rosali (PR) B Ponce Puerto Rico 1945 s Francisco & Emma. D 8/12/1972 P 5/5/1993 Bp Francisco Reus-Froylan. Dio Puerto Rico Trujillo Alto PR 2004-2014, 1980-2003, 1972-1979.

FERNANDEZ-REINA, Hipolito (SwFla) **S Monica's Epis Ch Naples FL 2015-** B Santiago DR 1974 s Hipolito. D 2/5/2005 P 2/12/2006 Bp Julio Cesar Holguin-Khoury. m 12/25/1996 Lilian M Perez De Fernandez c 3. Dio The Dominican Republic (Iglesia Epis Dominicana) Gazcue Santo Domingo 2006-2015. padrehipolito@stmonicasnaples.org

FERNER, David Raymond (Ind) 180 Red Coat Ln, Stoddard NH 03464 **Vic H Cross Epis Ch Weare NH 2017-** B Newark NJ 1947 s Arthur & Hazel. BA Montclair St U 1969; MDiv EDS 1972; DMin Bos 1995. D 6/10/1972 Bp Leland Stark P 12/20/1972 Bp Morris Fairchild Arnold. m 8/29/1970 Betty Ferner c 3. Int S Jn's Epis Ch Crawfordsvlle IN 2012; R S Thos Ch Franklin IN 2003-2011; Dio Upper So Carolina Columbia SC 1998-2003; R H Trin Par Epis Clemson SC 1998-2003; S Paul's Pendleton Clemson SC 1998-2003; R All SS Ch Chelmsford MA 1988-1998; R All SS Epis Ch Lehighton PA 1981-1988; S Jn's Epis Ch Palmerton PA 1981-1988; R Trin Ch Marshfield MA 1976-1981; Asst Chr Ch Needham Hgts MA 1972-1975; COM - Chair Dio Indianapolis Indianapolis IN 2007-2009, Dnry Dn 2006-2011, COM 2003-2009; COM Dio Bethlehem Bethlehem PA 1984-1987; Dioc Coun Dio Massachusetts Boston MA 1979-1981. Fllshp Soc Of S Jn The Evang 1992.

FERREIRA-SANDOVAL, Wilson (Ore) 372 NE Lincoln St, Hillsboro OR 97124 **S Jas Epis Ch Portland OR 2017-; Todos Los Santos Hillsboro OR 2013-; Dio Oregon Portland OR 2009-** B 1965 s Gabriel & Alvina. Teologia Other; Teologia Seminario De Teologia, San Bernardo, Diocesis Epis. D P. m 3/5/1998 Adela Sanchez-Layton c 2. Dio Puerto Rico Trujillo Alto PR 2005-2013. wilsonham@hotmail.com

FERREL, Artis Louise (Ia) 15102 Pinehurst Dr, Council Bluffs IA 51503 B Council Bluffs IA 1929 d Arthur & Olga. Mnstry Formation Prog 2000. D 6/3/2000 P 12/9/2000 Bp Chris Christopher Epting. m 10/7/1974 Carl Dewayne Ferrel.

FERRELL, Davis Marion (NCal) 515 Nursery St, Nevada City CA 95959 **D H Trin Ch Nevada City CA 1998-** B Long Beach CA 1937 s Harold & Ruth. BA California St U 1966; MA Chapman U 1972; CDSP 1986. D 5/10/1998 Bp Jerry Alban Lamb. m 8/8/1959 Doretta Gladys Ferrell c 3.

FERRELL, Nathan Wilson (Me) 41 Foreside Road, Falmouth ME 04105 **R Epis Ch Of S Mary The Vrgn Falmouth ME 2012-; Bd Dir Camp Bishopswood Hope ME 2013-** B Mount Holly New Jersey 1972 s Robert & Desma.

BA U of Vermont 1995; MDiv Bapt TS at Richmond 1998. D 6/15/2002 P 12/16/2002 Bp Peter J Lee. m 6/25/1994 Erin M McGee c 3. Vic of Shared Mnstry Ch Of The Ascen Gloucester City NJ 2011-2012; H Sprt Bellmawr NJ 2009-2012; Vic of Shared Mnstry S Lk's Ch Westville NJ 2009-2011; Supply Cler Dio New Jersey 2005-2009; R Trin Ch Topsfield MA 2003-2005; Assoc R S Geo's Ch Fredericksburg VA 2002-2003; Asst Min First Bapt Ch Of Winchester Winchester VA 1998-2002. Lieutenant: Navy Reserve Chapl The USN 2017. nathanferrell@smary.org

FERRELL, Sean Daniel (Spr) 2018 Boudreau Dr, Urbana IL 61801 **R Chap Of S Jn The Div Champaign IL 2013-** B Kansas City KS 1972 s Max & Kay. BA Ottawa U 1996; MDiv Sewanee: The U So, TS 1999. D 6/26/1999 Bp Barry Howe P 2/5/2000 Bp Frank Kellogg Allan. m 2/6/1999 Kiezha N Smith-Ferrell c 3. S Lk's Epis Ch Jackson TN 2006-2013; Chapl Cbury MI SU E Lansing MI 2003-2006; Chapl Emm Epis Ch Athens GA 1999-2002; Chapl S Mary's Chap Athens GA 1999-2002. rector@chapelsjd.org

FERRER, Gabriel V (Los) All Saints Parish, 504 N Camden Dr, Beverly Hills CA 90210 **S Mart-In-The-Fields Par Winnetka CA 2014-** B Santa Monica CA 1957 s Jose & Rosemary. D 6/3/2006 P 1/6/2007 Bp Joseph Jon Bruno. m 9/1/1979 Deborah Boone Ferrer c 4. Sr Assoc R All SS Par Beverly Hills CA 2006-2012, Assoc 1997-2006. vicar@stmartinswinnetka.org

FERRIANI, Nancy Ann (Ind) 5010 Washington Blvd, Indianapolis IN 46205 B Winthrop MA 1938 d George & Elinor. Cert SWTS; BD U of Kansas 1982; MDiv Chr TS 1986. D 6/24/1986 P 4/4/1997 Bp Edward Witker Jones. m 7/27/1956 Robert Ferriani. Trin Ch Indianapolis IN 1986-2009; Stndg Com Dio Indianapolis Indianapolis IN 1986-1998, Dep Gc 1994-2000. OA.

FERRITO, Michael Louis (ECR) 1391 Market St, Santa Clara CA 95050 **Gd Samar Epis Ch San Jose CA 2014-** B San Jose CA 1951 s Joseph & Josephine. Doctorate in Chr Counslg Newburgh TS; BA San Jose St U 1971; MDiv CDSP 2001. D 6/26/1999 P 6/14/2000 Bp Richard Lester Shimpfky. m 1/20/1972 Gwen S Ferrito c 3. Vic Ch Of The H Sprt Campbell CA 2001-2013; Assoc S Thos Epis Ch Sunnyvale CA 1999-2001.

FERRO, Mauricio (Colom) Carrera 16 #94-A-30, Bogota Colombia B Bogota CO 1942 s Cesar & Isabel. Harv; MTh Leopold Franzens U at; ThD Pontifical Liturg Inst Rome It; U De Comillas Es. Rec 8/1/1995. m 3/15/1997 Olga Moreno.

FERRY, Daniel Whitney (NH) 1465 Hooksett Rd Unit 280, Hooksett NH 03106 B Hackensack NJ 1937 s Arthur & Agnes. BS VPI 1960; BD EDS 1965; MBA Rivier Coll 1998. D 6/26/1965 Bp John Melville Burgess P 6/1/1966 Bp Frederic Cunningham Lawrence. m 10/5/1996 Janet Conway Ferry c 4. Ch Of The Epiph Newport NH 2002-2010; P Northwood Epis Mssn Northwood NH 1993-1995; P Dio New Hampshire Concord NH 1991-1993; P Gr Ch Manchester NH 1988-1989; Faith Epis Ch Merrimack NH 1988; R Ch Of Our Sav Milford NH 1968-1986; Cur S Chrys's Wollaston MA 1965-1968.

FERRY, Margaret Lee (Vt) 7297 Vt Route 14, Hardwick VT 05843 B Abington PA 1950 d John & Margaret. MDiv EDS; AB Mid; MSLIS Simmons Grad Sch of Libr and Info Sci. D 6/17/1976 P 5/1/1977 Bp Lloyd Edward Gressle. m 7/21/1984 Charles C Wohlers. P-in-c S Jn The Bapt Epis Hardwick VT 2009-2012; Int S Thos' Epis Ch Brandon VT 2006-2009; S Jn The Evang Mansfield MA 2006, 1998-2005; S Dav's Epis Ch Halifax MA 1993-1997; S Jn's/S Steph's Ch Fall River MA 1984-1985; S Steph's Ch Fall River MA 1984-1985; Dio Massachusetts Boston MA 1983-1986; Trin Ch Concord MA 1979-1983; Hd Chapl Middlesex Cnty Hse Of Corrections Billerica MA 1978-1980; Mssnr To YA All SS Par Brookline MA 1978-1979; Prot Chapl Middlesex Cnty Hse Of Corrections Billerica MA 1977-1980; Chapl In Res Methodist Hosp Brooklyn NY 1976-1977; Int S Steph's; Chapl SE Massachusetts U No Dartmouth. eleeovt@gmail.com

FESQ, John Alfred (Mass) 2708 Salem Church Rd Apt 217, Apt 222, Fredericksburg VA 22407 **Ret 1997-** B Bronx NY 1931 s Robert & Emilie. BA FD 1964; MDiv VTS 1967. D 6/10/1967 Bp Leland Stark P 12/13/1967 Bp George E Rath. m 6/13/1964 Joan E Fesq c 1. Supplement Accounts Boston MA 1976-1977; R Ch Of The Gd Shpd Dedham MA 1969-1997; Cur Chr Ch Quincy MA 1967-1969.

FESSLER, Robert H (Mil) 2275 De Carlin Dr, Brookfield WI 53045 B Milwaukee WI 1939 s Henry & Jeanette. BA S Fran Sem 1961. Rec 10/1/1986 Bp Roger John White. m 8/17/1974 Patricia Fessler. S Tim's Ch Milwaukee WI 1991-2011; 1986-1990; R Serv RC Ch 1965-1974.

FETTERMAN, James Harry (WLa) 1755 Ne 46th St, Oakland Park FL 33334 B Bloomsburg PA 1945 s Lawrence & Eleanor. BA Bloomsburg U of Pennsylvania 1978; MDiv VTS 1981. D 6/12/1981 Bp Dean Theodore Stevenson P 12/19/1981 Bp Charlie Fuller Mcnutt Jr. m 9/10/2011 Ildefonso Gonzalez-Rivera c 1. Int Trin Epis Ch Roslyn NY 2003; Cn S Mk's Cathd Shreveport LA 1998-2002; R Chr Memi Epis Ch Danville PA 1985-1998; Vic All SS Ch Selinsgrove PA 1981-1985; S Mk's Epis Ch Northumberlnd PA 1981-1985.

FETTERMAN, John J (Pgh) 1446 Maple Ave, Verona PA 15147 **Died 3/19/2017** B Harrisburg PA 1937 s John & Frances. BA S Chas Borromeo Sem 1959; Lic Sacr Theol Gregorian U 1963; MA U Pgh 1972; MLS U Pgh 1975. Rec 3/23/1978 as Priest Bp Robert Bracewell Appleyard. m 10/20/1975 Catherine Fetterman c 1. Ret 2002-2017; R Gr Ch Madison WI 1991-2002; Pres/CEO Epis Elder Care Serv Pittsburgh PA 1981-1991; Serv RC Ch 1961-1974.

FETZ, Robert Derrick (WMass) 30 Warren Ter, Longmeadow MA 01106 **Dio Wstrn Massachusetts Springfield 2011-; R S Andr's Ch Longmeadow MA 2011-** B Springfield OH 1980 s Robert & Sheila. BA Otterbein U 2004; MDiv SWTS 2007; MDiv SWTS 2007. D 5/13/2006 Bp Kenneth Lester Price P 6/16/2007 Bp Thomas Edward Breidenthal. m 6/21/2008 Jamie Ann Fetz. Vic S Mary Magd Ch Maineville OH 2009-2011; E Cntrl Ohio Area Mnstry Bridgeport OH 2007-2008.

FEUERSTEIN, John Mark (Pgh) 1066 Washington Rd, Mt Lebanon PA 15228 B Teaneak NJ 1970 s Paul & Kathleen. D 1/10/2015 Bp Dorsey McConnell. m 8/20/2001 Stefanie D Ruff c 2.

FEUERSTEIN, Paul Bruck (NY) 431 E 118th St, New York NY 10035 **Pres/CEO Barrier Free Living New York NY 2009-; Assoc Ch Of The H Trin New York NY 1977-, Asst 1974-1976** B Jersey City NJ 1947 s Charles & Helen. BA Concordia Sr Coll 1969; Concordia TS 1970; MA NYU 1971; STM GTS 1973; MSW CUNY 1982. D 6/9/1973 Bp Paul Moore Jr P 12/7/1973 Bp James Stuart Wetmore. m 9/15/1979 Rebecca Feuerstein c 3. Chapl S Albans Sch Washington DC 1976-1977; Cur Ch Of S Mary The Vrgn Chappaqua NY 1973-1974. Auth, "Disabled Wmn and Dom Violence: Notes from the Field," *Serv Delivery for Vulnerable Populations*, Springer Pub Co, 2011; Auth, "9/11 and People w Disabil," *On the Ground After September 11: Mntl Hlth Responses and Practical Knowledge Gained*, Haworth Maltreatment and Trauma Press, 2005; Auth, "Empowering Fam Ther," *Sometimes You Just Want To Feel Like a Human Being: Case Stds of Empowering Psych w People w Disabil*, Paul H Brooks, 1995; Auth, "Wmn and Chld w Disabil and Dom Violence," Milbank Memi Fund, 1986. Assoc of OHC 1971. Fell Brookdale Cntr For The Aging 1989.

FEUS, William Frederick (USC) St. Mark's Church, 132 Center Street, Chester SC 29706 B Englewood NJ 1965 s Frederick & Gloria. BA New Sch U 1992; MDiv GTS 2004; Grad Cert The U NC, Charlotte 2013. D 6/12/2004 Bp John Palmer Croneberger P 12/18/2004 Bp Vincent King Pettit. m 9/8/1990 Kimberly Mary Feus c 2. S Mk's Ch Chester SC 2015-2016; R S Bern's Ch Bernardsville NJ 2008-2012; Cur S Geo's-By-The-River Rumson NJ 2004-2008. Reviewer, "Bk Revs: Pilgrims of Chr on the Muslim Road," *LivCh*, LivCh, 2008. stmarksec@truvista.net

FEYERHERM, Elise Anne (Mass) 3400 Calumet St, Columbus OH 43214 **Trin Epis Ch Wrentham MA 2015-; Assoc S Jas Epis Ch Columbus OH 2009-** B Camden NJ 1960 d Marvin & Miriam. AB Earlham Coll 1982; MDiv Ya Berk 1986; PhD Boston Coll 2001. D 6/13/2009 P 6/19/2010 Bp Thomas Edward Breidenthal. m 8/15/1998 John Clabeaux. Chr Ch Westerly RI 2014; Prof Bex Sem Columbus OH 2009-2013.

FEYRER, David Allport (Ct) 70 S. Dogwood Trail, Southern Shores NC 27949 B Allentown PA 1941 s Albert & Margaret. ABS Muhlenberg Coll 1963; MDiv PDS 1969. D 6/29/1969 P 5/16/1970 Bp Frederick Warnecke. m 5/9/1964 Sandra Feyrer c 6. R The Par Of Emm Ch Weston CT 2002-2010; P-in-c Chr Ch Norwalk CT 1998-2002; Chapl (COL) US-Army 1975-2003; Assoc S Steph's Epis Ch Wilkes Barre PA 1973-1980; Asst Lower Luzerne Par Hazleton PA 1969-1973.

FHUERE, Brenda Lee (Colo) 520 Jaylee St Unit A, Clifton CO 81520 B Oberlin KS 1942 d Melvin & Lois. BA Mesa St Coll 1995. D 1/22/2000 P 7/29/2000 Bp William Jerry Winterrowd. c 3. Ch Of The Nativ Grand Jct CO 2005-2007; Epis Par Of S Jn The Bapt Portland OR 2005.

FICHTER JR, Richard E (Va) 10360 Rectory Ln, King George VA 22485 **Hanover w Brunswick Par - S Jn King Geo VA 2017-** B Fairfax VA 1968 s Richard & Suzanne. BS VPI 1990; MDiv VTS 2001. D 6/23/2001 P 12/29/2001 Bp Peter J Lee. P-in-c Chr Epis Ch Gordonsville VA 2008-2016; Int Asst R Chr Epis Ch Winchester VA 2006-2008; Asst R Gr Ch Kilmarnock VA 2002-2006; Assoc S Paul's Ch Beaufort NC 2001-2002. rector@hwbkgva.org

FICKS III, Robert Leslie (Ct) 8166 Mount Air Place, Columbus OH 43235 B Cincinnati OH 1944 s Robert & Virginia. BA Ken 1970; MDiv Ya Berk 1984. D 6/9/1984 P 4/25/1985 Bp Arthur Edward Walmsley. m 8/16/1969 Ann L Longbotham c 4. P-in-c Ch Of The Epiph Urbana OH 2012-2014; P-in-c Our Sav Ch Mechanicsburg OH 2012-2014; R S Andr's Ch Millinocket ME 2007-2010; Coll of Preachers Washington DC 1998-2004; R S Jn's Ch Washington CT 1988-2007; Trst Ya Berk New Haven CT 1987-1997; Asst R Chr And H Trin Ch Westport CT 1984-1988; Com for Pstr Care Cler Dio Connecticut Meriden CT 1986-1990.

FIDDLER, Andrew (Ct) 215 Highland St, New Haven CT 06511 B New York NY 1943 s Charles & Hannah. BA Pr 1964; MDiv EDS 1968. D 6/8/1968 P 12/15/1968 Bp Leland Stark. m 2/16/1974 Paulann T Fiddler c 1. Trin Ch On The Green New Haven CT 1970-2009; Cur Chr Ch Ridgewood NJ 1968-1970; Asst Chapl Cbury Hse Ann Arbor MI 1966-1967.

FIDLER, Brian Ernest (SanD) The Bishop's School, 7607 La Jolla Blvd, La Jolla CA 92037 **Chapl The Bp's Sch La Jolla CA 2011-** B Plainfield NJ 1955 s William & Beryl. BA Coll of Wooster 1977; MDiv Ya Berk 1981. D 6/6/1981 Bp Albert Wiencke Van Duzer P 1/16/1982 Bp George Phelps Mellick

Belshaw. m 6/21/1980 Joanne Shirley Blake. Chapl Groton Sch Groton MA 2000-2011; Chapl S Mk's Sch Dallas TX 1993-2000; Chapl Trin-Pawling Sch Pawling NY 1984-1993; Asst Trin Ch Moorestown NJ 1981-1984. Auth, "The Prophetic Voice," CRIS, 1991.

FIEBKE, Edward John (Alb) 6014 7th Ave W, Bradenton FL 34209 **Ret 1996-** B Antigo WI 1933 s Nicholas & Ruth. BA SUNY 1955; STB GTS 1959. D 5/23/1959 P 11/28/1959 Bp Frederick Lehrle Barry. m 4/25/1998 Linda M Dubay Fiebke c 2. Asst S Mary Magd Bradenton FL 2009-2015; Asstg Chr Ch Bradenton FL 1997-2003; R S Paul's Ch Kinderhook NY 1967-1995; R S Mk's Ch Malone NY 1961-1967; Cur S Jn's Ch Ogdensburg NY 1959-1961.

FIELD, Claire Cowden (NwT) 1601 S Georgia St, Amarillo TX 79102 **Cur S Andr's Epis Ch Amarillo TX 2015-** B Austin TX 1963 d James & Susan. BA SMU 1986; BS Texas Tech U Hlth Sciences Ctr 1992; MA Epis TS Of The SW 1996; MA Epis TS of the SW 1996; Dplma in Angl Stds Epis TS Of The SW 2015; Dplma in Angl Stds Epis TS of the SW 2015. D 12/13/2014 P 6/13/2015 Bp James Scott Mayer. m 5/13/2017 Steven J Field.

✠ **FIELD, The Rt Rev Martin Scott** (WMo) 420 W. 14th St, Kansas City MO 64105 **Bp of W Missouri Dio W Missouri Kansas City MO 2011-** B Salem OH 1956 s Lewell & Helen. BA Bethany Coll 1978; MDiv Lexington TS 1983. D 10/10/1991 Bp Charles Lovett Keyser P 5/2/1992 Bp Donald Purple Hart Con 3/5/2011 for WMo. m 8/4/1979 Donna JC Cassarino c 2. Asst to Bp for Congrl Life Dio Estrn Michigan Saginaw MI 2005-2010; R S Paul's Epis Ch Flint MI 2003-2011; Assoc S Lk's Epis Ch Jackson TN 1998-2003; Int S Anne's Ch Millington TN 1996-1997; Int S Matt's Ch Covington TN 1994-1996; U. S. Navy Off Of Bsh For ArmdF New York NY 1992-1996; Chapl US Navy 1989-1996; Yth Dir S Jn's Ch Chevy Chase MD 1985-1989. bishopfield@diowestmo.org

FIELD, Norman Grover (NwPa) 747 E 41st St, Erie PA 16504 B Erie PA 1948 s Claud & Beautrice. D 3/30/1996 P 12/1/1996 Bp Robert Deane Rowley Jr. m 11/22/1969 Joyce Mosier.

FIELD, Rachel E (Eas) **Dio Connecticut Meriden CT 2017-** B 1989 d Robert & Claire. Mstr of Div Ya Berk 2016. D 6/4/2016 Bp Henry Nutt Parsley Jr P 12/10/2016 Bp W Nicholas Knisely Jr. Dio Easton Easton MD 2017; S Mary's Ch Portsmouth RI 2016.

FIELD, Robert Durning (WNC) 256 E. Main St., Brevard NC 28712 **Fresh Start Fac Dio Wstrn No Carolina Asheville NC 2010-, 1994-2010** B Brunswick ME 1963 s John & Elizabeth. BA Dart 1985; MDiv Sewanee: The U So, TS 1993; DMin Sewanee: The U So, TS 2008. D 6/29/1993 P 12/1/1993 Bp Bob Johnson. m 8/22/1987 Jayne G Field c 2. R S Phil's Ch Brevard NC 1997-2016; Assoc S Alb's Ch Hickory NC 1993-1997. rdfield.rector@gmail.com

FIELD, William Overstreet (Del) 1611 Spring Dr Apt 5B, Louisville KY 40205 B Lexington KY 1933 s Robert & Helen. BA S Marys Sem & U Baltimore 1955; STB S Marys Sem and U 1957; MEd Xavier U 1970; JD U of Kentucky 1984; DAS Sewanee: The U So, TS 1999. Rec 3/11/2000 Bp Robert Jefferson Hargrove Jr. m 3/6/1973 Barbara H Field. Ch Of The Adv Cincinnati OH 2009-2010; Int S Lk's Ch Marietta OH 2009; Asst Chr Ch Christiana Hundred Wilmington DE 2004-2005; Assoc Ch Of The Gd Shpd Towson MD 2002-2004; Asst St Jas Epis Ch and Sch Alexandria LA 2000-2002. Auth, *Breach of Faith: A Cath Betrayal*, Vantage Press, 2008.

FIELDS, Kenneth L (Tex) 1227 Wellshire Dr, Katy TX 77494 B Tampa FL 1945 s Eugene & Pauline. BA U of Florida 1966; MA U of Florida 1968. D 6/29/1981 Bp Emerson Paul Haynes P 3/25/1988 Bp Robert Oran Miller. m 12/20/1969 Mary Alice Fields c 1. Vice R S Mart's Epis Ch Houston TX 2008-2012; R Cbury Chap and Coll Cntr Tuscaloosa AL 1997-2008; Dio Alabama Birmingham 1992-1997, 1991-1992, Stndg Com 2002-2006; S Thos Epis Ch Birmingham AL 1992-1996; S Jn's Ch Montgomery AL 1988-1991; Coordntr Educ Progs Ch Of The H Comf Montgomery AL 1982-1984. Auth, "The Apos," 1997; Auth, "Trausept Trivia"; Ed, "Dio Nwspr". fields45@comcast.net

FIELDS, Laddie B (Tex) 431 Pace Rd, Hendersonville NC 28792 B Sentinel OK 1925 s Ross & Tressie. Epis TS of the SW; BS U of Oklahoma 1948. D 1/3/1982 Bp William Carl Frey P 9/28/1982 Bp Gordon Taliaferro Charlton. m 5/13/1990 Ellen H Fields c 4. P-in-c S Paul's Ch Edneyville NC 1997-2004; Serv Presb Ch 1996-2006; Int S Alb's Ch Houston TX 1994-1995; Ch Of The Redeem Houston TX 1982-1993; Admin Redeem Dio Texas Houston TX 1982-1984.

FIELDSTON, Heidi A (Mass) 24 Court St, Dedham MA 02026 B Boston MA 1946 d Joseph & Rosely. BA Smith 1968; MBA Ya 1980; Harvard DS 1993; MDiv EDS 1996. D 6/6/1998 P 5/1/1999 Bp M(Arvil) Thomas Shaw. m 5/22/1983 Howard Ostroff c 1. Int Trin Ch Randolph MA 2010-2011; P Assoc Chr Ch Needham Hgts MA 2007-2011; S Eliz's Ch Sudbury MA 2006; Int Luth Ch Malden MA 2005; Assoc S Paul's Ch Dedham MA 1999-2005; Assoc S Dunstans Epis Ch Dover MA 1998-1999.

FIFE, Richard (SwVa) 2250 Maiden Ln Sw, Roanoke VA 24015 B Charlottesville VA USA 1953 s Francis & Virginia. BA U of Virginia 1975; AAS Piedmont Virginia Cmnty Coll 1980; Cert St Georges Coll Jerusalem Israel 1984; MDiv VTS 1985; Cert Int Mnstry Ntwk 1994; VTS 2005; Cert Cler Ldrshp Inst 2006. D 6/22/1985 Bp Peter J Lee P 5/8/1986 Bp O'Kelley Whitaker.

m 6/12/1999 Jenny G Fife c 2. Chr Epis Ch Pulaski VA 2014-2015; St. Eliz's Epis Day Sch S Eliz's Ch Roanoke VA 2001-2005, After Sch Acceleration Prog Bd Chair 2000-2007, R 1999-2014; Chr Ch Palmyra NJ 1998-1999; R Riverfront Epis Team Mnstry Riverside NJ 1998-1999; R S Steph's Ch Riverside NJ 1995-1999; R H Trin Ch Collingswood NJ 1990-1995; Ch of the Gd Shpd Oriskany Fls NY 1985-1990; Paris Cluster/Area Mnstry Cler Team Dio Cntrl New York Liverpool NY 1985-1990; R Gr Epis Ch Waterville NY 1985-1990; Disciplinary Bd Revs Pres Dio SW Virginia Roanoke VA 2011-2015, Ldrshp Dvlpmt Com 2010-2012, Long Range Plnng Com 2007-2010, Mutual Mnstry Revs Com 2006-2007, Roanoke Convoc Cler Cnvnr 2005-2009, Dn of the Roanoke Convoc 2005-2008, Exec Bd 2001-2006, Exec Bd Personl Com 2001-2004. Alb Inst 1986-1996; Associated Parishes 1986-1995; Assn of Dioc Liturg & Mus Commisions 1990-1995; Int Mnstry Ntwk 1994-1999; Ldrshp Acad for New Directions 1986-1990; Liturg done well Ntwk 2001; Natl Ntwk of Epis Cler 1990-1994; Sophia Ntwk 2001-2005.

FIGGE, Diane (RG) 3900 Trinity Dr, Los Alamos NM 87544 **S Phil's Ch Rio Communities NM 2012-** B St Louis MO 1951 d Harold & Anita. BSN Avila; Cert Dio Rio Grande Sch fro Mnstry. D 9/19/2009 P 9/24/2010 Bp William Carl Frey. Trin On The Hill Epis Ch Los Alamos NM 2010-2012. revdianemf@yahoo.com

FIKE, Christopher John (Mass) 24 Oakland St, Medford MA 02155 **S Eliz's Ch Wilmington MA 2014-** B Minneapolis MN 1965 s David & Mary. BA Ken 1987; MS Simmons Coll 1993; MDiv EDS 1999. D 6/5/1999 P 6/3/2000 Bp M(Arvil) Thomas Shaw. c 2. Chr Ch Somerville MA 2006-2012; Dio Massachusetts Boston MA 2004, 1999-2003; Cox Fell The Cathd Ch Of S Paul Boston MA 1999-2002.

FIKES, Gerald David (Tex) PO Box 100014, Arlington VA 22210 B Pine Bluff AR 1954 s Conley & Berta. BA U of Arkansas 1976; MDiv Candler TS Emory U 1981. D 6/7/1986 P 11/15/1986 Bp Charles Judson Child Jr. m 9/20/2008 Lisa Elizabeth Fikes c 2. The Ch of the Gd Shpd Austin TX 2000-2007; R Gr - S Lk's Ch Memphis TN 1992-2000; Asst All SS Epis Ch Atlanta GA 1987-1991; D S Anne's Epis Ch Atlanta GA 1986-1987. Theta Pi 1981.

FILBERT, Brandon Lee (Ore) 2090 High St. SE, Salem OR 97302 **S Tim's Epis Ch Salem OR 2008-, R 2007; Stndg Com Dio Oregon Portland OR 2008-** B Corvallis OR 1964 s John & Genevieve. BA Willamette U 1986; MDiv GTS 1993. D 5/30/1993 P 11/30/1993 Bp Robert Louis Ladehoff. m 5/17/1986 Pamela Athearn Filbert c 2. Vic S Bede's Ch Forest Grove OR 1993-2007; Fulltime Sem intern Gr Ch Brooklyn NY 1991-1992.

FILER, Judy Kathleen (Tex) St John's Episcopal Church, 514 Carter St, Marlin TX 76661 **R S Jn's Epis Ch Marlin TX 2007-** B Boise ID 1947 d Charles & Mary. BS OR SU 1969; Iona Sch of Mnstry 2006. D 6/24/2006 Bp Don Adger Wimberly P 1/20/2007 Bp Rayford Baines High Jr. m 7/10/1971 Wesley Joseph Filer c 1.

FILL CCHS, Michael (Be) 151 Prospect Ave Apt 16d, Hackensack NJ 07601 **Ret 1994-** B Passaic NJ 1938 s Michael & Mary. BS U of Scranton 1962; MDiv PDS 1965. D 6/26/1965 P 3/5/1966 Bp Frederick Warnecke. Int S Ptr's Epis Ch Tunkhannock PA 2001-2003; Int Ch of the Epiph Glenborn PA 1999; Int Ch Of The Gd Shpd Scranton PA 1997; Vic S Jn's Epis Ch Hamlin PA 1993-1994; R Chr Ch Indn Orchard PA 1975-1992; R Gr Epis Ch Honesdale PA 1975-1992; R E Berks Mnstry: St Lukes Ch Reading PA 1974-1975; R S Mich's Epis Ch Birdsboro PA 1974-1975; Vic St Lukes Ch Reading PA 1965-1975. Soc of S Jn the Evang 1993.

FILLER, John Arthur (U) 514 Americas Way #4603, Box Elder SD 57719 B Grass Valley CA 1938 s John & Mayme. BA U of Hawaii 1971; MDiv CDSP 1974. D 2/16/1975 Bp Chauncie Kilmer Myers P 10/16/1976 Bp Edmond Lee Browning. c 1. R S Ptr's Ch Clearfield UT 2000-2004, Vic 1993-2000, Int 1990-1993, Int 1990-1992; Int S Edm's Epis Ch Pacifica CA 1988-1989; All Souls Par In Berkeley Berkeley CA 1984-1990; Vic S Pat's Epis Ch El Cerrito CA 1984-1987; Int S Geo's Epis Ch Antioch CA 1984; St Columbas Epis Ch Paauilo HI 1982-1984; Vic Kohala Epis Mssn Kapaau HI 1976-1984; Vic Kohala Missions Kapaau HI 1976-1984; Vic S Aug Epis Ch Kapaau HI 1976-1984; D-in-c S Aug's Epis Ch Kapaau HI 1975-1976; COM Dio Utah Salt Lake City UT 1999-2002. RACA 1972. johnfiller@icloud.com

FINAN, A(lice) Jeanne (Vt) Cathedral Church of St. Paul, 2 Cherry St, Burlington VT 05401 **Dn & R Cathd Ch Of S Paul Burlington VT 2014-** B Tokyo JP 1949 d John & Mary. BA U NC 1970; MDiv VTS 2003; MA U of Wales 2005. D 5/31/2003 P 12/20/2003 Bp Bob Johnson. m 3/4/1975 Thomas W Eshelman c 2. R S Jn's Ch Asheville NC 2007-2014; Assoc R S Mary Of The Hills Epis Par Blowing Rock NC 2003-2007; Chair, COM Dio Wstrn No Carolina Asheville NC 2005-2011. Auth, "Remember Your Baptism: Ten Meditations," Cowley, 2004. Dir's Awd Epis EvangES 2002. jeannefinan@gmail.com

FINCH, Barbara Jo (Ore) 11865 SW Tualatin Rd Apt 45, Tualatin OR 97062 B Eugene OR 1952 d Douglas & Lucille. BS U of Oregon 1974. D 11/1/1996 Bp Robert Louis Ladehoff. D Chr Ch Par Lake Oswego OR 1996-2011; 1996-1998.

FINCH JR, Floyd William (SC) 1 Bishop Gadsden Way Apt 119, Charleston SC 29412 **Ret 1993-** B Arden NC 1929 s Floyd & Annie. BA Berea Coll 1951;

MDiv VTS 1954; MA Appalachian St U 1968. D 6/8/1954 P 6/10/1955 Bp Matthew George Henry. m 9/4/1954 Leona Iris Finch c 4. Chapl Bp Gadsden Ret Cmnty Charleston SC 2001-2007; Assoc S Jas Ch Charleston SC 1996-2003; Int Vic Ch Of The H Fam Moncks Corner SC 1993-1996; Chrmn St of Ch Comm So Carolina Charleston SC 1992-1994, Chapl to Ret Cler and spouses 2007-2013, Bp's Rep to Curs 1993-2007; All SS Epis Ch Hampton SC 1988-1993; R Epis Ch Of The H Trin Ridgeland SC 1988-1993; R Trin Epis Ch Columbus GA 1981-1986; R Epis Ch of the Gd Shpd Summerville SC 1976-1981; Hd Mstr The Patterson Sch Lenoir NC 1968-1976; Stndg Com, Trst F Crittenden Hm Dio No Carolina Raleigh NC 1966-1967, Com Evang 1965-1967, Pres Mecklenburg Convoc 1960-1961; R Ch Of The H Comf Charlotte NC 1959-1967; R S Jas Epis Ch Lenoir NC 1956-1959; P-in-c Trin Ch Kings Mtn NC 1955-1956; P-in-c S Andr's Ch Bessemer City NC 1954-1956; P-in-c S Jn's Ch High Shoals NC 1954-1956. Natl Register of Prominent Americans 1973; Personalities of the So 1972; 1,000 Men of Achievement 1969; Who's Who in the So and SW 1969; Royal Blue Bk, London 1968; Who's Who in Rel 1968; Dictionary of Intl. Biography 1967; Who's Who in Amer Colleges and Universities 1951. fwfjr01@gmail.com

FINCH, Robin Lee (Ida) All Saints' Episcopal Church, 704 S Latah St, Boise ID 83705 B Lewiston ID 1955 d Gordon & Alice. Boise St U; BS U of Idaho 1979. D 1/6/1996 Bp John Stuart Thornton P 5/22/2005 Bp Harry Brown Bainbridge III. m 2/29/1992 Douglas Finch.

FINCHER, Michael (Los) 1242 E 4th St Unit 8, Long Beach CA 90802 **St Gregorys Epis Ch Long Bch CA 2016-** B Las Vegas NV 1961 s Nelson & Mary. BA U CA 1984; MDiv SWTS 2006. D 6/3/2006 P 1/6/2007 Bp Joseph Jon Bruno. P-in-c S Paul's Epis Ch Santa Paula CA 2013-2016; Assoc R Trin Epis Ch Redlands CA 2009-2013; Cur Cbury Westwood Fndt Los Angeles CA 2006-2009; S Alb's Epis Ch Los Angeles CA 2006-2009. rector@stgregoryschurch.com

FINEANGANOFO, Sosaia Ala (Cal) 2565 Redbridge Rd, Tracy CA 95377 **Asst S Mk's Epis Ch Tracy CA 2008-** B Nukualofa To GA 1935 s Mosese & Susana. S Johns TS Fj. Trans 9/1/1993 Bp Jl Bryce. m 6/27/1959 Lavinia Iongi c 4. P Assoc S Paul's Epis Ch Burlingame CA 2000-2003; Serv Ch Of Polynesia 1965-1993.

FINEOUT, William High (Mich) 630 Moorland Dr, East Lansing MI 48823 **Died 6/14/2016** B Lansing MI 1947 s Donald & Jane. BA Estrn Michigan U 1969; MA Estrn Michigan U 1974. D 6/21/2008 Bp Wendell Nathaniel Gibbs Jr. m 6/14/1985 Shannon Drotar c 2. Chapl Intl OSL the Physcn 2009-2016; D S Paul's Epis Ch Lansing MI 2008-2013; Chapl Doane Fam Assoication of Amer 2004-2016.

FINKENSTAEDT JR, Harry Seymour (WMass) 13761 Charismatic Way, Gainesville VA 20155 **Ret 1988-** B Grosse Pt E MI 1923 s Harry & Eliza. BA Ya 1948; BD EDS 1953; MA U of Massachusetts 1968; Cert U of Massachusetts 1970. D 5/31/1953 Bp Horace W B Donegan P 1/6/1954 Bp Harry Sherbourne Kennedy. m 4/19/1960 Anne M Finkenstaedt c 4. Serv Ch in Engl 1967-1988; R S Jn's Ch Athol MA 1962-1967; Serv Ch in Bahamas 1960-1962; Epis Chapl US AF 1957-1960; Asst Ch Of The H Trin New York NY 1956-1957; Mssy The Epis Ch in Hawaii Honolulu HI 1953-1958, 1953-1956; Vic S Matt's Epis Ch Waimanalo HI 1953-1954.

FINLEY IV, John Huston (Mass) 717 Atlantic Ave Apt 3B, Boston MA 02111 **Epiph Sch Dorchester MA 2010-; S Mary's Epis Ch Boston MA 2008-; Unknown Epiph Sch Dorchester MA 1997-** B Boston 1970 s John & Margot. BA Harv 1992. D 1/7/2006 Bp M(Arvil) Thomas Shaw P 1/6/2007 Bp Gayle Harris. m 11/12/2005 Carl Stanley Mcgee. Assoc P S Mk's Ch Dorchester MA 2008-2011; S Mich's Epis Ch Holliston MA 2006-2008; Ch Of The Redeem Chestnut Hill MA 2005-2006.

FINLEY, Rosamond Stelle (Los) 212 W Franklin St, Tucson AZ 85701 B Kansas City KS 1979 BA Van 2001; MDiv Claremont TS 2005. D 6/11/2005 Bp Chester Lovelle Talton. Asst S Ptr's Par San Pedro CA 2005.

FINN, Anne Marie (NwT) 2630 S 11th St, Abilene TX 79605 B Houston TX 1941 d Edwin & Marie. BA Dominican Coll 1967; MA S Thos U Miami FL 1972; MA S Mary U 1985; Cert Theol Stud Epis TS of the SW 1989. D 1/20/1989 Bp Earl Nicholas Mc Arthur Jr P 7/1/1989 Bp John Herbert Mac-Naughton. S Mk's Epis Ch Abilene TX 1994-1996; S Mk's Epis Ch Coleman TX 1993-1994; R Epis Ch Of The Mssh Gonzales TX 1989-1993. Assn Rel & Value Issues In Counslg; Sw Ntwk Womens Ministers, Amer Assn Counslg And Dvlpmt. Distinguished Grad S Mary U 1985.

FINN, Emilie Aurora (Az) 13150 W Spanish Garden Dr, Sun City West AZ 85375 **P-in-c Dio Arizona Phoenix AZ 2015-** B Prescott AZ 1981 d Douglas & Kristine. BA Prescott Coll 2009; MDiv Ya Berk 2013. D 5/5/2012 P 6/29/2013 Bp Kirk Stevan Smith. Ch Of The Adv Sun City W AZ 2013-2015.

FINN, Michael John (Roch) 1245 Culver Rd, Rochester NY 14609 **D S Mk's And S Jn's Epis Ch Rochester NY 2011-** B Rochester NY 1947 s John & Helen. BA S Jn Fisher Coll 1974; MPA SUNY at Brockport 1994. D 5/2/2009 Bp Prince Grenville Singh. m 5/14/1983 Jane Finn c 3.

FINN, Patrick Shawn (WMich) 1006 3rd Street, Muskegon MI 49440 **Off Of Bsh For ArmdF New York NY 2008-** B Detroit MI 1958 s Bernard & Marie. Trin

Dublin IE 1978; BA U MI 1982; MDiv EDS 1987. D 6/27/1987 Bp H Coleman Mcgehee Jr P 2/27/1988 Bp David Charles Bowman. m 5/24/1980 Leslie Finn c 3. R S Paul's Ch Muskegon MI 2015-2017; S Paul's Ch Norfolk VA 2014; Spec Mobilization Spprt Plan Washington DC 2009; Pension Fund Mltry New York NY 2008; Command Chapl Us Navy 2002-2008; R Ch Of Our Sav Johns Island SC 2002-2007; R S Lk's Ch Pk City UT 1995-2012; Dio Utah Salt Lake City UT 1995-2002; R S Mk's Ch Alexandria VA 1989-1995; R Trin Ch Warsaw NY 1987-1989. Chapl, "Sprtl Resiliency," *Warrior Resiliency/Staying Green*, US NAVY, 2008. Aikido Shodan (Black Belt) Tokyo Japan 2001. Meritorious Serv Medal UnitedStates Navy 2011.

FINN, Robert Patrick (EMich) PO Box 83, West Branch MI 48661 **D Trin Epis Ch W Branch MI 2008-** B Detroit MI 1936 s Patrick & Ethel. MS Cntrl Michigan U 1970. D 9/13/2008 Bp Steven Todd Ousley. m 8/12/1961 Janet Finn c 2.

FINNERUD, Margaret A (EC) St Philip's Episcopal Church, 205 E Moore St, Southport NC 28461 **Asst S Barn Epis Ch Greenwich CT 2013-** B Winston-Salem NC 1965 d Marcus & Amanda. AB Duke 1987; MDiv Wake Forest U 2010; MDiv Wake Forest U 2010; STM GTS 2013. D 1/25/2014 Bp Anne Hodges-Copple P 8/21/2014 Bp Ian Theodore Douglas. m 2/3/2007 Kenneth Percival Finnerud c 3. S Phil's Ch Southport NC 2015-2017.

FINNIN, Nathan Mcbride (NC) Canterbury School, 5400 Old Lake Jeanette Rd, Greensboro NC 27455 **Assoc H Trin Epis Ch Greensboro NC 2016-; Chapl Cbury Sch Greensboro NC 2010-; P Assoc S Mary's Epis Ch High Point NC 2010-** B Boston MA 1982 s Timothy & Laura. BA U NC 2004; BA U NC 2004; Dplma Ya Berk 2008; MDiv Yale DS 2008. D 6/14/2008 P 2/21/2009 Bp Clifton Daniel III. m 6/11/2011 Heather Kaitlin Barker Finnin. Asst R S Mary's Ch Kinston NC 2008-2010. nathan@holy-trinity.com

FINSTER, Mary Ruth (NI) 1817 W Monroe St, Kokomo IN 46901 B Fort Wayne IN 1922 d Charles & Mary. BS Manchester Coll 1944; MA Colorado St U 1949. D 5/8/1990 Bp Francis Campbell Gray. D S Andr Epis Ch Kokomo IN 1990-2005.

FIRESTINE, Susan Lee (WNY) D 12/10/2016 Bp Ralph William Franklin.

FIRTH, Harry Warren (WMo) 4024 W 100th Ter, Overland Park KS 66207 B Topeka KS 1934 s Charles & Edna. BA Emporia St U 1956; BD SWTS 1959; Tchr Cert Can Montessori Assn Calgary CA 1964. D 6/6/1959 P 12/5/1959 Bp Edward Clark Turner. Cn to the Ordnry Dio W Missouri Kansas City MO 1995-1998; Hon Cn Gr And H Trin Cathd Kansas City MO 1994-1995; R All SS Epis Ch Kansas City MO 1970-1994; R Trin Ch Arkansas City KS 1968-1970; Cur S Mich And All Ang Ch Mssn KS 1964-1968; Vic Ch Of The Ascen Neodesha KS 1959-1964. Bp's Shield Dio W Missouri 1993.

FISCHBECK, Lisa Galen (NC) 8410 Merin Rd, Chapel Hill NC 27516 **Bd Trst UNC Hlth Care System 2011-; Founding Vic Ch Of The Advoc Chap Hill NC 2004-** B Philadelphia PA 1956 d Kenneth & Rita. BA Duke 1977; MA U of Virginia 1981; MDiv Duke DS 1991; Cert VTS 1992. D 1/18/1992 Bp Robert Whitridge Estill P 1/23/1993 Bp Huntington Williams Jr. m 9/2/1989 Robert Lamar Bland c 1. Gathering P Chap Of The Cross Chap Hill NC 2002-2003, Campus Min 1989-2002; Bd of Epis Farmworker Mnstry Dio No Carolina Raleigh NC 1999-2002, D 1992, Dioc Coun 2011-, Dep to GC 2008-2011, Stndg Com 2007-2010, Mssn Implementation Team Chair 2005-2006, Strategic Plnng Com 2003-2005, Dn of Durham Convoc 1998-2005, Chair Dept Mnstry & Higher Educ 1996-1998, Dioc Coun 1996-1998; Asst to R Ch Of The H Fam Chap Hill NC 1997-2002; Asst to R S Steph's Ch Durham NC 1992-1997; Bd Dir -Chair 2001 Epis Farmworker Mnstry Newton Grove NC 1999-2002. Auth, "Liturg in the Publ Sq," *Faith and Ldrshp*, Ldrshp Educ at Duke Div, 2013; Auth, "Epistle for Christmas and Epiph," *Feasting on the Word: Year A, Volume One*, Westminster-Knox, 2010; Auth, "Baptism by Immersion," *LivCh*, LivCh, 2007.

FISCHER III, Charles L (At) St. Paul's Episcopal Chur, 294 Peyton Rd., SW, Atlanta GA 30311 **R S Paul's Epis Ch Atlanta GA 2011-; Bd Trst H Innoc' Epis Sch Atlanta GA 2014-** B Neptune NJ 1975 s Charles & Marilyn. BA Morehouse Coll 1997; MDiv VTS 2009. D 12/20/2008 P 6/28/2009 Bp J Neil Alexander. m 10/9/2004 Rhonda D Pelham c 2. Asst S Jas Ch Irvington Baltimore MD 2010-2011; Dir of Alum VTS Alexandria VA 2009-2011. cfischer@stpaulsatl.org

FISCHER, Evelyn (O) 127 W. North Street, Wooster OH 44691 **R S Jas Epis Ch Wooster OH 1998-** B Perth Amboy NJ 1960 s Carmen & Irene. BA SUNY 1982; BA SUNY 1986; MDiv GTS 1992. D 6/6/1992 P 12/1/1992 Bp David Charles Bowman. R H Trin Epis Ch Swanton VT 1994-1998; Cur Gr Ch Lockport NY 1992-1994; R S Jn's Ch Wilson NY 1992-1994.

FISCHER, John Denny (Mil) 920 E Courtland Pl, Milwaukee WI 53211 **Asst S Andr Madison 1966-** B 1932 s Percy & Mabel. BA S Ambr U 1953; MA U IL 1954; PhD U IL 1958. D 5/27/1965 P 6/1/1966 Bp Donald H V Hallock. Chr Ch Milwaukee WI 1996-2000.

FISCHER, Sara (Oly) 2800 SE Harrison Street, Portland OR 97214 **R S Paul's Ch Seattle WA 2015-; Cn for Congrl Vitality Dio Oregon Portland OR 2012-, 2009-2010, COM 2006-2010, 2004-2012, GC Dep 2012-** B Redwood City CA 1959 d George & Elinor. BA U of Massachusetts 1984; MDiv GTS 2003. D 6/14/2003 Bp Robert Louis Ladehoff P 12/17/2003 Bp Johncy Itty.

m 7/27/1996 Mark G Faust c 1. R S Dav's Epis Ch Portland OR 2005-2015; R S Jn The Evang Ch Portland OR 2005-2009; Assoc Gr Memi Portland OR 2003-2005; Bp Search Com Dio Oregon 2008-2010.

FISCHER, Sarah Motley (WA) Grace Episcopal Church, 1041 Wisconsin Ave NW, Chevy Chase MD 20815 **Asst Gr Ch Washington DC 2013-, 2012** B Sacramento CA 1952 d Edward & Cecily. BA U CA 1974; MDiv Harvard DS 1988; M. Advncd Ecum Theol Univ. Geneva/Wrld Coun ChurchesEcumenical Inst. 2009. D 6/9/1979 P 11/30/1980 Bp John Bowen Coburn. m 11/25/1989 Christopher Fischer c 3. P-in-c La Mision Hispana El Divino Salvador Sacramento CA 2006-2008; Dioc Chapl For Higher Educ Higher Educ 2005-2007; UC Davis The Epis Dio Nthrn California Sacramento CA 2000-2007; Assoc Ch Of S Mart Davis CA 1997-1999; Assoc S Andr's Ch Trenton NJ 1995-1996; Pstr Asst Trin Ch Princeton NJ 1990-1991, Cur 1981-1984; Coordntr Liturg Cmsn Supplemental Texts 1985-1991; Dio New Jersey Trenton NJ 1985-1987; Chapl Epis Ch at Pr Princeton NJ 1985-1986; Princeton Univ. The Wm Alexander Procter Fndt Trenton NJ 1985-1986; D The Cathd Ch Of S Paul Boston MA 1979-1980. Contrib, "Bk Revs," *Ecum Revs*, WCC, 2009; Writer-in-Res, "UC Davis Bioregional Proj," 1999; Ed, "Via Media," *Via Media*, Dio New Jersey, 1985. Epis Soc For Mnstry In Higer Educ 1986-1988; SCHC 1988. Yale Medal Yale Univerity 2012; Citizen of the Year -- Cmnty Serv City of Davis, California 2006; Writer-In-Res UC Davis Bioregional 1998. assistant@gracedc.org

FISCHER-DAVIES, Clare (RI) 50 Orchard Ave, Providence RI 02906 B Saint Louis MO 1956 d George & Mary. BA New Engl Conservatory of Mus 1977; MDiv EDS 1983. D 6/5/1983 P 12/1/1983 Bp A(rthur) Heath Light. c 2. R S Mart's Ch Providence RI 2005-2013; R Chr Ch Blacksburg VA 1994-2005; Asst Gr Ch Manchester NH 1990-1994; R S Andr's-In-The-Vlly Tamworth NH 1986-1990; Cur S Lk's Epis Ch Metuchen NJ 1983-1986.

FISH, Cameron Hoover (CNY) 6 Canberra Ct, Mystic CT 06355 **Off Of Bsh For ArmdF New York NY 1997-** B Wilmington DE 1958 s Floyd & Jean. BA Cor 1982; Mstr of Div VTS 1989; MDiv VTS 1989; Mstr of Theol PrTS 2003; ThM PrTS 2003; Doctor of Mnstry Fuller TS 2014. D 6/17/1989 P 6/23/1990 Bp O'Kelley Whitaker. m 5/27/1995 Paulette Elaine Fish c 3. Gr Ch Carthage NY 1991-1997; R S Jn's Ch Black River NY 1991-1997; Dioc Intern Dio Cntrl New York Liverpool NY 1989-1991; Dioc Intern Gr Ch Baldwinsville NY 1989-1991. Cbury Way CNY 1993-1997. cameron.fish@c7f.navy.mil

FISH, Charles (Tad) Cramer (Ct) PO Box 67724, Albuquerque NM 87193 **Chapl Heartland Hopice Albuquerque NM 2006-** B San Jose CR 1950 s Charles & Cecil. BS Estrn New Mex U 1972; MA Fuller TS 1984; MDiv Sewanee: The U So, TS 1991. D 6/29/1991 Bp Terence Kelshaw P 1/18/1993 Bp Reginald Heber Gooden. m 8/4/1991 Sonnie Fish. All SS Ch Wolcott CT 2003-2005; Asst Grtr Waterbury Mnstry Waterbury CT 2003-2005; S Geo's Ch Middlebury CT 2003-2005; Int Calv Epis Ch Bridgeport CT 2001-2002; Int Calv St Geo's Epis Ch Bridgeport CT 2001-2002; R H Trin Epis Ch Hollidaysburg PA 1999-2000; Dio San Diego San Diego CA 1998-1999; R S Anth Of The Desert Desert Hot Sprg CA 1998-1999; S Jn's Ch Indio CA 1998-1999; Asst S Mary's Epis Ch Manchester CT 1995-1998; Dio NW Texas Lubbock TX 1993-1995; Reg Vic Llano Estacado Missions Lubbock TX 1993-1995; Asst S Jn's Epis Ch Odessa TX 1992-1993; Yth Min/ CE Par Ch of St. Helena Beaufort SC 1991-1992.

FISH, Gloria Hoyer (Roch) 46 Azalea Rd, Rochester NY 14620 **Assoc S Steph's Ch Rochester NY 1980-** B Dayton OH 1941 d Albert & Z Roberta. BS Kent St U 1963; MDiv Bex Sem 1979; DMin Colgate Rochester Crozer DS 1990; DMin CRDS 1990. D 6/30/1979 P 5/1/1980 Bp Robert Rae Spears Jr. m 10/13/1984 Wilfred Kenneth Cauthen. Chapl Loretto Geriatric Cntr Syracuse NY 1988-1990; CPE Supvsr Unc Memi Hosp Chap Hill 1985-1987; Prot Chapl Nazareth Coll 1978-1983. EWC.

FISH, Sonnie (Ct) PO Box 67724, Albuquerque NM 87193 **Pstr Luth Ch of the Servnt ELCA Santa Fe 2007-; All SS Ch Wolcott CT 2001-** B Brooklyn NY 1952 d Erik & Sonny. BA Florida Intl U 1973; MS Florida Intl U 1979; MDiv Sewanee: The U So, TS 1992. D 6/28/1992 Bp Joseph Thomas Heistand P 1/18/1993 Bp Reginald Heber Gooden. m 8/4/1991 Charles (Tad) Cramer Fish. Luth Ch Of The Servnt Santa Fe NM 2007-2016; Chapl Zia Hospice Albuquerque NM 2006-2007; Grtr Waterbury Mnstry Waterbury CT 2001-2005; S Geo's Ch Middlebury CT 2001; Mt Zion Ch Glasgow PA 2000-2001; Pstr Zion Luth Ch ELCA Glasgow 1999-2001; Dio San Diego San Diego CA 1998-1999; S Anth Of The Desert Desert Hot Sprg CA 1998-1999; Asst Vic S Jn's Ch Indio CA 1998-1999; Asst Mssnr Grtr Hartford Reg Mnstry E Hartford CT 1995-1998; Grtr Hartford Reg Mnstry E Hartford CT 1995-1998; Assoc Vic Llano Estacado Lubbock TX 1993-1999; Dio NW Texas Lubbock TX 1993-1995; S Jn's Epis Ch Odessa TX 1993.

FISHBAUGH-LOONEY, Kristen Fishbaugh (Md) 11232 Falls Rd, Timonium MD 21093 **S Paul's Sch Brooklandville MD 2008-** B Carthage NY 1967 d James & Roslyn. BA Coll of Wooster 1989; MDiv Yale DS 1994. D 10/29/2005 Bp Robert Wilkes Ihloff P 4/29/2006 Bp John L Rabb. m 8/17/1991 Mark Looney c 2. S Pauls Sch for Girls Lutherville MD 2008-2012; S Tim's Sch Stevenson MD 2005-2008.

FISHBECK, Nadine B (Tenn) **P-St. Mary's Chap Sis of St Mary Sewanee TN 2008-** B Plattsburgh NY 1951 d Howard & Braunda. BA Indiana St U 1973; BS

U of No Dakota 1984. D 3/29/2003 P 6/12/2004 Bp William Michie Klusmeyer. P Asst Loc Congregations Nelson Cluster WV 2005-2007; Nelson Cluster Of Epis Ch Rippon WV 2004-2007; P Intern Loc Congregations Nelson Cluster WV 2004-2005.

FISHBURNE, Donald Allston (ETenn) 57 Sweet Water Ct, Pawleys Island SC 29585 **Ongoing Ldrshp including Chair, Mem Retention and Rec CEEP 2017-; P Assoc H Cross Faith Memi Epis Ch Pawleys Island SC 2017-** B Charleston SC 1951 s Henry & Amy. BA U So 1973; MDiv VTS 1979; DMin Sewanee: The U So, TS 1998. D 6/16/1979 P 12/21/1979 Bp Gray Temple. m 5/24/1986 Sarah V Vann c 2. Asst S Jn's Epis Ch Tallahassee FL 2015-2017; Bd Trst (Pres) CEEP 2011-2017; Bp Search Com Dio E Tennessee Knoxville TN 2011; R S Paul's Epis Ch Chattanooga TN 2008-2015; Bd Rgnts Sewanee U So TS Sewanee TN 2008-2014; R Ch Of S Mich And All Ang Sanibel FL 2001-2008; Dioc Congrl Dvlpmt Cmns Dio Georgia Savannah GA 1996-1998; R S Paul's Ch Augusta GA 1990-2000; Assoc R Chr Ch Charlotte NC 1987-1990; R S Matt's Epis Ch Darlington SC 1984-1987; Dioc Dept C Ed So Carolina Charleston SC 1982-1985; Asst R S Mich's Epis Ch Charleston SC 1981-1984; P S Mths Epis Ch Summerton SC 1979-1981; Bd Dio Conf Cntr Dio No Carolina Raleigh NC 1988-1990. Auth, "New Cler Dvlpmt Handbook". The Ord of S Jn of Jerusalem, Priory in the Untd States 2016. donald@donaldfishburne.net

FISHER, Barbara Anne (Eas) D 6/24/2017 Bp Chilton Richardson Knudsen.

FISHER, David Hickman (Chi) 1012 Churchill Dr, Naperville IL 60563 B San Bernadino CA 1943 s Hickman & Julia. MA in Rel Col; BA Carleton Coll 1965; MA UTS 1967; MA Van 1973; PhD Van 1976. D 2/24/1973 Bp William F Gates Jr P 9/23/1973 Bp John Vander Horst. m 6/1/1990 Sarah B Fowler c 3. Asst Trin Epis Ch Wheaton IL 2002-2006; LocTen Ch of the H Nativ IL 1999-2001; Ch Of The H Nativ Clarendon Hls IL 1999-2000, 1998-1999; S Chris's Epis Ch Oak Pk IL 1996-1997; Prof No Cntrl Coll Naperville IL 1995-2014; Emm Epis Ch La Grange IL 1989-1993; Assoc Prof Santa Clara U Santa Clara CA 1986-1988; LocTen S Phil's Epis Palatine IL 1985-1986; LocTen All SS Ch Wstrn Sprgs IL 1983-1985; LocTen S Jn's Epis Ch Chicago IL 1980-1982; Ch Of The H Cross Chicago IL 1979-1980; S Annes Epis Ch Caseyville IL 1979-1980; LocTen S Gabr Wood River IL 1979-1980; Emm Ch Hastings MI 1977-1978; LocTen S Jn the Apos Epis Ch Ionia MI 1977-1978; LocTen S Mary Magd Ch Fayetteville TN 1975-1976; Instr Theol & Asst to Dn Sewanee U So TS Sewanee TN 1974-1976; Asst S Geo's Ch Nashville TN 1973-1974. Auth, "Theory," *Oxford Encyclopedia of Aesthetics*, 1998; Auth, *Loyalty Tolerance & Recognition in J Val Inq*, 1997; Auth, "Self in Text," *Text in Self in Semeia*, 1990.

FISHER, Davis Lee (Chi) 430 SW 13th Ave, #1015, Portland OR 97205 **P Assoc S Paul's Par Oregon City OR 2014-** B Oak Park IL 1942 s Frank & Helen. Cert Goethe Inst 1963; BA Lawr 1964; MDiv GTS 1967; MBA U Chi 1972; MTS Garrett-Evang TS 1998. D 6/17/1967 Bp James Winchester Montgomery P 12/16/1967 Bp Gerald Francis Burrill. c 3. Assoc S Lk's Ch Evanston IL 2007-2013; Assoc S Raphael The Archangel Oak Lawn IL 2005-2006; Assoc S Aug's Epis Ch Wilmette IL 1996-2005; Int Exec Dir Cathd Shltr Chicago IL 1996-1997; ReVive Cntr for Hsng and Healing Chicago IL 1996-1997; Assoc S Matt's Ch Evanston IL 1980-1995; Asst Ch Of Our Sav Chicago IL 1969-1980; Cur Ch Of The H Comf Kenilworth IL 1967-1969.

✠ FISHER, The Rt Rev Doug (WMass) 37 Chestnut St, Springfield MA 01103 **Bp of Wstrn Massachusetts Dio Wstrn Massachusetts Springfield 2012-** B Baltimore MD 1954 s Thomas & Louisa. BA S Johns U 1976; MDiv Immac Concep Sem 1980. Rec 6/8/1997 as Priest Bp Catherine Scimeca Roskam Con 12/1/2012 for WMass. m 7/1/1984 Elizabeth B Fisher c 3. R Gr Ch Millbrook NY 2000-2012; Dio New York New York NY 1997-2000; Pstr H Innoc Highland Falls NY 1997-2000. dfisher@diocesewma.org

FISHER, Elizabeth B (NY) Po Box 974, Millbrook NY 12545 **St Thos Ch Amenia NY 2010-; Asst. Min 2004-** B Rockville Centre NY 1956 d William & Eileen. BA Amer U 1978; MPS New York Inst of Tech 1986; MDiv Ya Berk 2004. D 3/13/2004 P 9/18/2004 Bp Mark Sean Sisk. m 7/1/1984 Doug Fisher c 3. Dio New York New York NY 2007-2009, 2004-2005; Asst. Min S Matt's Ch Bedford NY 2005-2007.

FISHER, Ernest Wilkin (SwFla) 550 1st Ave S Apt 514, #514, Saint Petersburg FL 33701 B Sheridan WY 1942 s Ernest & Helen. BA Col 1965; MEd Natl-Louis U 2000; BA Eckerd Coll 2012. D 10/22/1988 Bp Gerald Francis Burrill. c 4. D S Barth's Ch St Petersburg FL 2001-2006; D S Matt's Ch St Petersburg FL 1998-2000; D S Aug's Epis Ch St Petersburg FL 1994-1997; Chapl BayFront Med Cntr 1988-2000; Chapl Bayfront Med Cntr 1988-2000.

FISHER, James Alfred (NJ) 15 Maple Street, South Seaville NJ 08246 B Los Angeles CA 1942 s Alfred & Angela. BS USNA 1963; MDiv Sewanee: The U So, TS 1981; DMin Estrn Bapt TS 1991. D 6/15/1981 Bp William Grant Black P 12/15/1981 Bp A(rthur) Heath Light. m 9/16/1989 Gail Diane Fisher c 2. Ch Of The Adv Cape May NJ 1995-2007; H Trin Epis Ch Ocean City NJ 1990-1992; Chapl Cathd of St Ptr & St Paul Washington DC 1989-1990; R All Hallow's Ch Snow Hill MD 1984-1989; R Chr Ch Pearisburg VA 1981-1984. AAPC 1991-2011; Fell.

✠ FISHER, The Rt Rev Jeff (Tex) 2695 S Southwest Loop 323, Tyler TX 75701 **Bp Suffr of Texas Dio Texas Houston TX 2012-, Stndg Com 2011-2012** B Houston TX 1964 s Nelson & Nancy. BBA U of Texas 1986; MDiv VTS 2004. D 6/12/2004 P 12/21/2004 Bp Don Adger Wimberly Con 10/6/2012 for Tex. m 6/17/1989 Susan S Fisher c 2. R S Alb's Epis Ch Waco TX 2006-2012; Assoc R S Mary's Epis Ch Cypress TX 2004-2006. DD VTS 2013. jfisher@epicenter.org

FISHER, Jerry William (NC) 635 Galashiels Place, Wake Forest NC 27587 B Cleveland OH 1945 s Fred & Helen. BA OH SU 1969; MDiv VTS 1978. D 6/24/1978 P 5/19/1979 Bp John Harris Burt. m 12/20/1967 Sarah Fisher c 5. Int Calv Ch Tarboro NC 2011-2012, P-in-c 2011; Int S Anne's Ch Winston Salem NC 2009-2011, Int 2009-2011; R S Johns Epis Ch Wake Forest NC 1993-2009; Int S Steph's Ch Goldsboro NC 1992-1993; Int Emm Par Epis Ch Sthrn Pines NC 1991-1992; Int S Tim's Ch Wilson NC 1990-1991; Int S Steph's Epis Ch Erwin NC 1989-1990; R S Matt's Epis Ch Hillsborough NC 1984-1989; Asst S Thos' Ch Whitemarsh Ft Washington PA 1981-1984; Asst S Chris's By-The River Gates Mills OH 1978-1981.

FISHER, Jill Carmen (ETenn) 1175 Pineville Rd Apt 85, Chattanooga TN 37405 **D Thankful Memi Ch Chattanooga TN 2006-** B Bahia Blanca Argentina 1935 d Cecil & Rosina. Cert U of Cambridge 1948; Dioc Sch for Diac TN 1994. D 9/18/1994 Bp Robert Gould Tharp. c 2. D S Ptr's Ch Chattanooga TN 2001-2006; D S Alb's Epis Ch Hixson TN 1999-2001; D S Tim's Ch Signal Mtn TN 1994-1999.

FISHER, John Coale (SC) 8244 Crooked Creek Ln, Edisto Island SC 29438 B New York NY 1945 s Bernard & Virginia. AB Pr 1967; MS Col 1989. D 6/3/1978 Bp Paul Moore Jr P 12/21/1978 Bp Horace W B Donegan. m 7/14/2001 Susan Sage Leigh Fisher c 2. S Jas Ch Montclair NJ 1991-1997; Priv Pstr Counslr & Psych 1989-2008; Int S Dav's Ch Kinnelon NJ 1989-1990; Assoc Ch Of The Epiph New York NY 1986-1989; R Ch Of The H Comm Norwood NJ 1982-1985; R S Andr's Ch Harrington Pk NJ 1982-1985; Asst The Amer Cathd of the H Trin Paris 75008 1980-1982; Assoc Ch Of The Heav Rest New York NY 1978-1980, Affiliate 1998-2008; Affiliate Gr Ch Cathd Charleston SC 2009-2012.

FISHER, John R(Aymond) (SO) Po Box 29064, Columbus OH 43229 **Died 3/20/2016** B Shreveport LA 1929 s John & Hazel. BFA U of New Mex 1953; MDiv Epis TS of the SW 1964. D 6/9/1964 Bp Frederick P Goddard P 6/1/1965 Bp James Milton Richardson. m 3/21/1991 Mary Alice Fisher c 3. Ret 1991-2016; S Jas Epis Ch Columbus OH 1988-1990; R S Steph's Ch Billings MT 1980-1987; S Paul's Epis Ch Lewiston NY 1973-1980; R S Mary's Epis Ch Texarkana TX 1969-1973; Chapl Tx Police 1969-1973; R S Paul's Epis Ch Greenville TX 1966-1969; Chr Ch Matagorda TX 1964-1966; Vic S Jn's Epis Ch Palacios TX 1964-1966. Journalism Awd: Top Dio Pub Dio Upper So Carolina 1980; Hon Cn Dio Texas 1964.

FISHER, Joy (Ga) 147 SouthSecond Street, Cochran GA 31014 **Chairperson, Together We Grow Dio Georgia 2005-; P Trin Ch Cochran GA 2005-** B Macon GA 1945 d James & Sheila. AA Middle Georgia Coll 1964; BA U GA 1966; MEd Merc 1977; JD Merc 1982. D 2/5/2005 P 8/7/2005 Bp Henry Irving Louttit. m 2/10/1973 Thomas Wilmore Fisher c 3. Dioc Coun Mem Dio Georgia 2006-2007; Dioc Stndg Com Dio Georgia Savannah GA 2005-2009.

FISHER, Julie Blake (O) 475 Laurel Drive, Kent OH 44240 **R Chr Epis Ch Kent OH 2006-** B Buffalo NY 1961 BA U of Virginia 1983; MDiv VTS 1998. D 2/23/2005 P 9/14/2005 Bp Joe Goodwin Burnett. m 8/14/1982 Jerome Higgins Colegrove. Cur Ch Of The H Sprt Bellevue NE 2005-2006.

FISHER, Margaret Jo (Spok) 522 West Park Place, Spokane WA 99205 **S Andr's Ch Spokane WA 2011-** B Butler PA 1955 d Roy & Patricia. BA Chatham Coll 1977; MDiv Candler TS Emory U 1997. D 6/2/2001 P 10/26/2002 Bp James E Waggoner Jr. c 3. P Assoc Cathd Of S Jn The Evang Spokane WA 2008-2011; Gr Ch Ellensburg WA 2002-2007. rector@standrewsspokane.org

FISHER, Mary Carlton (NCal) 72 Mill Creek Dr, Willits CA 95490 **Assoc S Fran In The Redwoods Mssn Willits CA 1991-** B Brooklyn NY 1928 d Charles & Margaret. BA Mid 1949; JD U MI 1957; MA U CA 1970; MDiv CDSP 1984. D 12/11/1982 Bp William Edwin Swing P 12/27/1990 Bp John Lester Thompson III. D Ch Of The Incarn Santa Rosa CA 1988-1991; D S Christophers Ch Anchorage AK 1986-1987; D Gr Cathd San Francisco CA 1984-1986; D The Epis Ch Of S Jn The Evang San Francisco CA 1982-1984.

FISHER, Paige Ford (Mass) 206 Clarendon St, Boston MA 02116 B Nashville TN 1970 d Fred & Patience. BA U So 1993; MDiv EDS 2004. D 6/26/2004 P 1/8/2005 Bp Peter J Lee. m 8/12/2000 Peter Christopher Fisher c 2. R S Paul's Ch Natick MA 2014-2016; Assoc R Trin Ch Epis Boston MA 2004-2011.

FISHER, Richard Lingham (WNC) 175 Vinal St, Rockport ME 04856 **Non-par 1982-** B Brockton MA 1947 s Robert & Jean. BA U NC 1975; MDiv Chicago TS 1978; PsyD Illinois Sch of Profsnl Psychol 1986. D 6/19/1978 P 5/12/1979 Bp William Gillette Weinhauer. m 12/27/1975 Doree Koontz Fisher c 1. P-in-c S Jn's Ch Asheville NC 1978-1982. Auth, "The Intentional Sapling," *Openings Into Mnstry*. APA; Mepa.

FISHER, Robert William (ECR) PO Box 101, Carmel Valley CA 93924 **R S Dunst's Epis Ch Carmel CA 2010-** B South Laguna CA 1975 BA Ya 1998;

MDiv Ya Berk 2005. D 6/11/2005 Bp Chester Lovelle Talton P 1/14/2006 Bp Joseph Jon Bruno. m 12/31/2004 Sarah Ellen Wood c 1. Assoc R All SS-By-The-Sea Par Santa Barbara CA 2007-2010; S Edm's Par San Marino CA 2005-2007.

FISHER, Ronald Spencer (Md) 24 Evergreen Trail, Severna Park MD 21146 B Baltimore MD 1950 BS RPI 1972; MDiv VTS 1975; Cert SWTS 2006. D 1/8/1983 P 5/26/1983 Bp David Keller Leighton Sr. m 6/12/1976 Rebecca Sue Willaman c 2. R Ch Of The Ascen Westminster MD 1988-2013; Asst S Thos' Ch Garrison Forest Owings Mills MD 1983-1988; Pstr Serv in the Meth Ch S Leonard MD 1976-1982; Chapl Geo 1974-1976. Auth, *When Chld Receive Comm*, Forw Mvmt, 1987. rectorca@gmail.com

FISHER JR, Russell Ellsworth (FtW) Po Box 192, Santa Anna TX 76878 **P-in-c S Mk's Epis Ch Coleman TX 2004-** B Clairon County PA 1937 s Russell & Louise. BS U of Memphis 1959; MA U of Memphis 1966; MDiv Nash 1969; PhD Louisiana Bapt U 1997. D 12/10/1975 P 12/19/1976 Bp Bennett Jones Sims. m 8/5/1972 Louann Fisher. Int S Anne's Ch Ft Worth TX 2003-2004; R S Jn's Epis Ch Brownwood TX 1997-2003; Dept Assn Dio Dallas Dallas TX 1993-1997, Excoun 1993-1994; R S Mary's Epis Ch Texarkana TX 1992-1997; Mssnr Great Plains Epis Cluster Dio Oklahoma Oklahoma City OK 1986-1991, Mssn Coun 1986-1991, Ch Educ Field Team Coordntr 1984-1990, Com 1981-1991, Deptce 1980-1991, Cmsn Mnstry Accountability 1981-1985; Chapl Cameron U Lawton OK 1986-1990; Vic S Marg's Ch Lawton OK 1986-1990; Volntr Chapl Ok St Penit 1980-1986; R All SS Ch Mcalester OK 1979-1986; P-in-c The Epis Ch Of The Adv Madison GA 1977-1979. Auth, "Abortions Aftermath: Need For Healing & Wholeness w Pstr Serv".

FISHER, Sarah Kathleen (At) 4755 N Peachtree Rd, Atlanta GA 30338 **S Cathr's Epis Ch Marietta GA 2017-** B 1971 MDiv GTS 2005. D 12/21/2004 P 6/16/2005 Bp J Neil Alexander. m 6/14/2012 Amanda B Mandy Brady. Assoc S Pat's Epis Ch Atlanta GA 2014-2017; Int Gr-Calv Epis Ch Clarkesville GA 2013-2014; R S Ptr's Epis Ch Chicago IL 2007-2012; Asst Ch Of S Paul And The Redeem Chicago IL 2005-2007; Emm Epis Ch Athens GA 2000-2002.

FISHER, Scott Owen (Ak) 1030 2nd Ave, Fairbanks AK 99701 B Troy NY 1948 s Radm & Kitson. BA Ken 1970; MDiv Epis TS of the SW 1976. D 6/27/1976 P 3/1/1977 Bp David Rea Cochran. m 10/11/2005 Elisabeth Ljungkull c 3. R S Matt's Epis Ch Fairbanks AK 1991-2015; Asst To Bp Dio Alaska Fairbanks AK 1979-1991; P-in-c S Matt's Ch Beaver AK 1977-1979; Asst S Steph's Ch Ft Yukon AK 1976-1977; Vol Lay worker, Interior Dio Alaska Fairbanks Alaska 1970-1973. Auth, "Epis Life," Ikantha.

FISHER, William A (Colo) 200 Elk Run Dr, Basalt CO 81621 **S Ptr's Ch Basalt CO 2013-** B Buffalo NY 1971 s John & Judith. BA Br 1994; MDiv GTS 2004. D 2/7/2004 P 8/25/2004 Bp Henry Irving Louttit. m 4/24/2004 Leann Beth Fisher c 1. S Thos Ch Mamaroneck NY 2010-2013; Assoc The Epis Ch Of S Andr Encinitas CA 2008-2009; Vic S Lk's Ch Eastchester NY 2004-2008. willfisher@msn.com

FISHER-STEWART, Gayle Antoinette (WA) 820 6th St Ne, Washington DC 20002 **Calv Ch Washington DC 2016-** B Washington DC 1951 d Harvey & Geneva. MS Amer U 1983; MS U of Maryland 1987; MS U of Maryland 1990; PhD U of Maryland 1992; MTS Wesley Sem 2010. D 2/28/2015 P 11/21/2015 Bp Mariann Edgar Budde. c 1.

FISHWICK, Jeffrey Palmer (Va) 1260 River Chase Ln, Charlottesville VA 22901 B Madison WI 1946 s Marshall & Lucy. BA U of Virginia 1968; MA U of Delaware 1974; MDiv Yale DS 1976. D 6/19/1976 Bp William Hawley Clark P 3/26/1977 Bp Alexander D Stewart. m 7/29/1978 Carol Lichtenberger c 2. Int Chr Ch Glen Allen VA 2014-2015; Int S Barth's Ch Pewaukee WI 2012; P-in-c S Ptr's Epis Ch Purcellville VA 2011; Int S Andr's Ch Longmeadow MA 2009-2011; Int S Thos Ch Lancaster PA 2008; Fac Credo 1997-2006; R Chr Epis Ch Charlottesvlle VA 1995-2008; Dn Orangeburg Dnry 1992-1994; R Epis Ch of the Gd Shpd Summerville SC 1988-1994; R Ch of S Jas The Less Ashland VA 1982-1987; Asst S Paul's Ch Richmond VA 1979-1982; S Cathr's Sch Richmond VA 1977-1979; Asst Chapl S Cathr's Sch Richmond VA 1977-1979; Asst Ch Of The Atone Westfield MA 1976-1977.

FISKE, Thomas W (Wyo) 123 Linden Avenue, Fairmont MN 56031 **R H Trin Epis Ch Gillette WY 2007-** B Santa Fe NM 1954 s Eugene & Elizebeth. BA Metropltn St Coll of Denver 1981; MDiv Epis TS of the SW 2002. D 6/15/2002 P 12/17/2002 Bp James Louis Jelinek. m 7/12/1981 Mary Catherine C Fiske c 2. S Mart's Epis Ch Fairmont MN 2004-2007; Dio Minnesota Minneapolis MN 2002-2003.

FITCH, William Babcock (USC) 6342 Yorkshire Dr, Columbia SC 29209 **1986-** B Charlotte NC 1943 s Augustus & Vida. USNA; BA U So 1966; STB GTS 1969; MA CUA 1972; MA Salve Regina Coll 1988. D 6/29/1969 P 7/1/1970 Bp John Adams Pinckney. m 8/31/1968 Margaret Ancrum Fitch c 2. S Thos Ch Eastover SC 1993-1998; Chapl Naval Hosp Newport RI 1988-1991; Stff Chapl NAS Memphis 1983-1986; Chapl Navy Chapl 1977-1991; Off Of Bsh For Armdf New York NY 1977-1991; R S Andr's Epis Ch Canton NC 1974-1977; Asst Gr Epis Ch Camden SC 1970-1971; Assoc S Thad Epis Ch Aiken SC

1969-1970. Auth, *Liturg: Journ of the Litergical Conf*, Auth, *Naval War Coll Revs*. Alcuin Club; No Amer Acad of Liturg.

FITE, Robert Cotton (Chi) 1350 NE 17th Ave., 2D, Portland IL 60025 **Assoc S Lk's Ch Evanston IL 1977-** B New Rochelle NY 1938 s Robert & Mary. BA Wms 1960; MDiv GTS 1965; Urban Trng Cntr 1968; PhD NWU 1981. D 6/19/1965 Bp Charles Ellsworth Bennison Jr P 1/15/1966 Bp Robert Lionne DeWitt. m 10/14/1989 Diane H Fite c 2. Clincl Psychol Luth Gnrl Hosp Cnsling Cntr 2003-2008; Dir, Cnsling Cntr Advoc Hlth Care Luth Gnrl Hosp 1979-2003; Asst Trin Ch Princeton NJ 1973-1976; Dir, Conf. Cntr. Dio Pennsylvania 1971-1973; Dir, Conf. Cntr. Dio Pennsylvania 1970-1973; Stff Metropltn Chr Cncl Phila. PA 1968-1970; Cur S Paul's Ch Philadelphia PA 1965-1967. Auth, "The Cong as a Workplace," *Par Nrsng*, Sage Publ, 1999; Auth, "Becoming m," *Fam Living in Pstr Perspective*, WestminsterJohn Knox Press, 1993. cottonfite@me.com

FITTS, Ronald Sheldon (Eas) 21103 Striper Run, Rock Hall MD 21661 **Died 1/26/2016** B Buffalo NY 1928 s William & Dorothy. Coll of Preachers; BA Hobart and Wm Smith Colleges 1952; BD EDS 1956; MA Colg 1972. D 6/29/1956 P 6/1/1957 Bp Lauriston L Scaife. m 3/1/1984 Nancy Lee Weber c 3. Ret 1994-2016; R Chr Ch Denton MD 1990-1993; Chr Epis Ch Great Choptank Par Cambridge MD 1989-1990; Int S Mary's Ch Portsmouth RI 1989; Int S Ptr's By The Sea Narragansett RI 1988; Bruton Par Williamsburg VA 1983-1988; Chapl Coll of Wm & Mary 1983-1988; Dio Sthrn Virginia Newport News VA 1983-1988; R S Jas Epis Ch Newport Newport DE 1978-1983; Dio Cntrl New York Liverpool NY 1975-1978; R S Thos Ch Hamilton NY 1971-1978; P-in-c S Andr's Ch New Berlin NY 1966-1970; S Matt's Ch So New Berlin NY 1966-1970; P-in-c S Jn's Epis Ch Elmira NY 1962-1966; Assoc Chapl U MN 1959-1962; Cur S Jas' Ch Batavia NY 1956-1959. Fell Coll of Preachers 1968.

FITZGERALD III, John H (Mich) 1350 Berkshire Rd, Grosse Pointe Park MI 48230 **D S Phil And S Steph Epis Ch Detroit MI 1985-** B Brooklyn NY 1933 s John & Gertrude. Whitaker TS; BS Ya 1955. D 3/9/1985 Bp Henry Irving Mayson. m 8/10/1958 Beverly Byrne Fitzgerald c 3.

FITZGERALD, John Paul (HB) 1551 10th Ave E, Seattle WA 98102 **Non-par 1972-** B Seattle WA 1934 s Joseph & Rosalind. BA U of Washington 1958; BD CDSP 1961. D 10/13/1961 P 12/1/1962 Bp William F Lewis. m 12/26/1961 Carolyn Hope Gilfilen c 1. R S Geo's Epis Ch Warren MI 1970-1972; R S Andr's Epis Ch Wshngtn Ct Hs OH 1964-1965; Asst S Steph's Epis Ch Seattle WA 1961-1964.

FITZGERALD, Joseph Michael (Az) 2288 W Silverbell Tree Dr, Tucson AZ 85745 **Chapl Supvsr The U of Arizona Med Cntr Tucson AZ 2009-** B Los Angeles CA 1956 s Harold & Carmel. BA U CA Los Angeles 1978; MA Washington Theol Un 1986; MA Loyola U, Chicago 1996. Rec 4/30/2011 as Priest Bp Kirk Stevan Smith. m 11/8/2008 Deanna Fitzgerald. Stff Chapl The U of Arizona Med Cntr Tucson AZ 2005-2009; Assoc Pstr Sacr Heart Cath Ch Tucson AZ 2002-2005; Campus Min/Tchr Crespi Carmelite HS Encino CA 1996-2002; Campus Min/Tchr Salpointe Cath HS Tucson AZ 1986-1994; Yth Min St. Bernadette Cath Ch Houston TX 1980-1982. Contrib, "The Sprt in the OT from the Perspective of Liberation Theol," *Sword*, Ord of Carmelites, 1987. Acad of Magical Arts / The Magic Castle 1977-1988; Alpha Sigma Nu hon Soc 1996; Theta Xi Fraternity 1974; Tucson Chapl Assn 2005. Honored Alum Crespi Carmelite HS 2001.

FITZGERALD, Todd Robert (Tex) St Stephens School, 6528 Saint Stephens Dr, Austin TX 78746 **S Steph's Epis Sch Austin TX 2012-** B Shreveport LA 1969 s Robert & Patsy. BA Texas A&M U 1991; MDiv SWTS 1998. D 6/24/1998 Bp Robert Jefferson Hargrove Jr P 6/23/1999 Bp Claude Edward Payne. m 7/29/1995 Amy M FitzGerald c 2. Chapl St Jas Sch Hagerstown MD 2005-2012; Chapl S Andrews Epis Sch Austin TX 2000-2005; Asst R S Dav's Ch Austin TX 1998-2000. Ord of H Cross - Assoc 2012.

FITZGERALD, William Thomas (Ga) 3168 Seed Lake Rd, Lakemont GA 30552 **Died 4/30/2017** B Augusta GA 1927 s William & Martha. BS Cit 1949; MS U GA 1953; BD Sewanee: The U So, TS 1960. D 6/28/1960 Bp Henry I Louttit P 1/10/1961 Bp William Francis Moses. m 6/14/1952 Martha Fitzgerald c 11. Ret 1992-2017; R Chr Ch Frederica St Simons Is GA 1978-1992; Vic S Ign Mssn St Simons Island GA 1978-1992; R Ch Of The Redeem Sarasota FL 1960-1978.

FITZGIBBONS, Michael John (Spok) 8505 W Hood Ave, Kennewick WA 99336 B Salt Lake City UT 1941 s James & Virginia. BA U of Washington 1964; MDiv CDSP 1970; U of Utah 1972; WA SU 1977; Idaho St U 1978; Lsi #1 & 2 78 79 1980; Fam Ther Trng 1981; Var Trng & Vocational Courses 1993. D 12/21/1970 Bp Norman L Foote P 6/1/1971 Bp William Benjamin Spofford. Dio Spokane Spokane WA 2004-2009, 1986-1994, Supply P 1981-1986; Asst All SS Ch Richland WA 1995-2002; Int Lower Yakima Vlly Epis Mnstry 1993-1995; P-in-c S Jn's Ch Yakima WA 1982-1985; Asst S Mk's Epis Ch Moscow ID 1976-1981; P-in-c H Trin Epis Ch Grangeville ID 1974-1975; Supply P Epis Ch of the Nativ Lewiston ID 1972-1974; Wood Rivers Epis Par Shoshone ID 1970-1972; R Woodriver Par Shoshone Gooding ID 1970-1972.

FITZGIBBONS, Sabeth S (NwPa) 1706 NW 60th St, Seattle WA 98107 **Emm Epis Ch Mercer Island WA 2016-** B Cheyenne WY 1969 d Kerry & Edith. BA Seattle U 1990; MSW Boston Coll 1996; MA Boston Coll 1996; MDiv CD-

SP 2006. D 6/24/2006 Bp Vincent Waydell Warner P 1/11/2007 Bp Bavi Edna Rivera. m 9/21/1996 Julien R Goulet c 2. P In Charge S Steph's Ch Fairview PA 2012-2016; Asst R The Ch Of Our Redeem Lexington MA 2008-2012; Cur Trin Ch Topsfield MA 2006-2008; Stndg Com Mem Dio NW Pennsylvania Erie PA 2014-2016, COM Mem 2013-2016, Disciplinary Bd Mem 2013-2016, GC Dep, Cler 2013-2016; GC Dep, Lay Ord Dio Olympia Seattle 2003-2006, Dioc Coun Mem 1999-2003.

FITZHUGH, Bobbe Kay (Wyo) PO Box 1419, Douglas WY 82633 B Thermopolis WY 1955 d Robert & Barbara. BA U of Wyoming 1977; MPA U of Wyoming 1979. D 6/6/2015 P 12/19/2015 Bp John Smylie. m 9/21/1985 Gordon Dana Fitzhugh c 2.

FITZHUGH, Mark L (LI) 325 Lattingtown Road, Locust Valley NY 11560 **R S Jn's Of Lattingtown Locust Vlly NY 2015-** B Mobile AL 1961 s William & Dorothea. BA U of So Alabama 1985; MDiv GTS 2001. D 6/2/2001 Bp Onell Asiselo Soto P 12/4/2001 Bp Henry Nutt Parsley Jr. m 8/5/1995 Cheri Smith c 2. R S Simon's On The Sound Ft Walton Bch FL 2010-2015; Chapl CPE intern Greenwich Hosp Greenwich CT 2006-2008; Asst Chr Ch Greenwich CT 2003-2010; R Ch Of The Mssh Heflin AL 2001-2003; Gr Ch Anniston AL 2001-2003. frmark@stjlat.org

FITZPATRICK, Michael Carl (Mich) 24699 Grand River Ave, Detroit MI 48219 B Wayne County MI 1956 s Carl & Rosa. D 12/16/2010 P 7/14/2011 Bp Wendell Nathaniel Gibbs Jr.

FITZPATRICK, Robert 179 East Main st, Washingtonville NY 10992 **R S Ptr's Ch Clarksboro NJ 2016-** B Newark NJ 1964 s Robert & Dorothy. BA Rutgers The St U of New Jersey 1989; MA Rutgers The St U of New Jersey 1990; MDiv GTS 2010. D 11/14/2009 P 6/19/2010 Bp George Edward Councell. m 7/8/1989 Catherine M Hawn c 1. Dio New York New York NY 2010-2016; S Anne's Ch Washingtonville NY 2010-2013. rector@stpetersclarksboro.org

✠ FITZPATRICK, The Rt Rev Robert Leroy (Haw) Office of the Bishop, 229 Queen Emma Sq, Honolulu HI 96813 **Bp of Hawaii The Epis Ch in Hawaii Honolulu HI 2007-; Bp in Charge Dio Micronesia Tumon Bay GU 2009-** B Decatur IL 1958 s Kenneth & Mary. BA DePauw U 1981; MDiv GTS 1986; DMin SWTS 1999. D 6/24/1986 P 5/9/1987 Bp Edward Witker Jones Con 3/10/2007 for The Episcopal Church in Haw. m 5/1/1982 Beatrice Fitzpatrick c 2. P-in-c S Lk's Epis Ch Honolulu HI 2003-2006; Vic S Barn' Ch Kapolei HI 2000-2003; S Nich Epis Ch Aiea HI 2000-2003; R Gr Epis Ch Ft Wayne IN 1990-2000; Asst R S Ptr's Ch Morristown NJ 1986-1990. DD SWTS 2008; DD GTS 2007. rlfitzpatrick@episcopalhawaii.org

FITZSIMMONS, Daniel (Be) 16 Allenberry Dr, Wilkes Barre PA 18706 **R S Mart-In-The-Fields Mtn Top PA 2009-; Asst Epis Mnstry Of Unity Palmerton PA 2000-** B Hazleton PA 1947 s Steve & Beatrice. BA Wilkes Coll 1986; MA Marywood U 1989. D 4/29/2000 P 12/2/2000 Bp Paul Victor Marshall. Asst All SS Epis Ch Lehighton PA 2000-2006; Asst S Jn's Epis Ch Palmerton PA 2000-2004.

FITZSIMMONS, James (Az) 1741 North Camino Rebecca, Nogales AZ 85621 B Los Angeles CA 1932 d Charles & Carrie. Stan 1953; AA Contra Costa Coll 1962; Cert U of So Carolina 1975; BA Sch for Deacons 1984. D 6/3/1989 Bp William Edwin Swing. m 4/11/1953 Lee Sherwin Vellom c 1. Serv Ch Of The H Trin Richmond CA 1989-1996. Ord Of Dok 1997; Professed Tertiary Of The Soc Of S Fran 1989.

FITZSIMMONS, James Patrick (Az) 969 W Country Club Dr, Nogales AZ 85621 **D S Andr's Epis Ch Nogales AZ 2010-** B Urbana IL 1945 s William & Opal. D 1/23/2010 Bp Kirk Stevan Smith. m 8/2/1986 Vicki Ruth Fitzsimmons c 2.

FLAGSTAD, Judith Marie (SD) 101 W Prospect Ave Apt 3, Pierre SD 57501 B Webster SD 1950 d Alvin & Marie. BS Nthrn St U Aberdeen SD 1973; MDiv Vancouver TS CA 2005. D 11/15/1996 P 10/23/2004 Bp Creighton Leland Robertson. Int Trin Epis Ch Pierre SD 2009-2010, 2005, Assoc 2004-.

FLAHERTY, Jane (SVa) 614 E 7th St, Alton IL 62002 **Ret 2004-** B Alton IL 1939 d Francis & Julia. BS Notre Dame Coll 1961; MA S Louis U 1971; EdD Rutgers The St U of New Jersey 1978; MDiv GTS 1991. D 6/8/1991 P 2/15/1992 Bp George Phelps Mellick Belshaw. Ecum Off Dio Sthrn Virginia Newport News VA 1999-2002, 1992-2002; R S Chris's Epis Ch Portsmouth VA 1995-2004; Asst Trin Ch Moorestown NJ 1991-1995.

FLAHERTY, Jessica Barbara (Mass) B Boston MA 1947 d Robert & Jenette. BA U of Massachusetts 1974; MSW Bos 1977; MDiv EDS 2012. D 6/2/2012 Bp Gayle Harris P 1/13/2013 Bp M(Arvil) Thomas Shaw. m 10/31/1981 Edward Francis Flaherty c 3.

FLAHERTY, Philip John (Mass) 44 Park Ave, Whitman MA 02382 B Weymouth MA 1948 s Leonard & Lauretta. Cert Dio Massachusetts Diac Formation; BA U of Massachusetts. D 6/4/2016 Bp Alan Gates. m 7/10/1971 Constance Kimpton.

FLANAGAN, Carol Cole (WA) St. Barnabas' Episcopal Church, 4801 Ravensworth Rd, Annandale VA 22003 **Int R S Barn Ch Annandale VA 2017-; T/F to Update Sexual Misconduct Policies Exec Coun Appointees New York NY 2015-, Stndg Cmsn on Const & Cn 1997-2000, Com on the Full Participation of Wmn in the Ch 1985-1988, T/F on the Washington**

Off 1985-1988 B Hartford CT 1947 d Quintin & Joan. BA Villa Maria Coll 1983; MDiv VTS 1986. D 6/28/1986 Bp Henry Irving Mayson P 5/28/1987 Bp William George Burrill. c 2. R S Jn's Ch Olney MD 2008-2014; Int Chr Ch Detroit MI 2007-2008; Cn Dio Washington Washington DC 2003-2007, Com on Cn 2011-2014; R S Ptr's Epis Ch Lakewood OH 1999-2003; Int S Barth's Ch Baltimore MD 1998-1999; Int S Geo Ch Hampstead MD 1996-1998; Bp's Pstr Dio Maryland Baltimore MD 1995, Chair Stwdshp Com 1990-1993, Chair Liturg & Mus Cmsn 1986-1990, Trst, Epis Hsng Corp 1997-1999, Gvnr's T/F on Sexual Misconduct 1994-1995; Vic Ch Of The H Evangelists Baltimore MD 1990-1995; On-call Chapl Bon Secours Hosp 1989-1999; Asst Chr Ch Pittsford Pittsford NY 1986-1989; Asst H Trin Epis Ch Bowie MD 1986; Judicial Panel/ Eccl Crt Dio Ohio Cleveland 2000-2003, Com on Cn, Chair 1999-2003; Trst Bex Sem Columbus OH 1986-2001. AP 1986; AAM 1987; Consult, Washbhington Off 1986-1986; EPF 1985; EUC 1987; EWC 1977; RCRC 1985. Alice Meynell Literary Awd Villa Maria Coll 1982.

FLANAGAN, Jakki Renee (Ct) B North Dakota 1964 d Patrick & Mary. Tem 1988; Mansfield U 1992; MDiv CDSP 2013; MDiv CDSP 2013. D 12/23/2012 P 7/20/2013 Bp Thomas C Ely. m 12/6/2009 Keri T Aubert c 1.

FLANAGAN, Michael P (USC) 104 Brockman Dr, Mauldin SC 29662 **R H Cross Epis Ch Simpsonville SC 1995-** B Charlotte NC 1955 s Clifford & Pearl. BSIE No Carolina St U 1977; MDiv Nash 1991. D 5/19/1991 P 5/30/1992 Bp Roger John White. m 5/22/1982 Deborah Anne Patch c 2. S Mich And All Ang' Columbia SC 1991-1994; Dep to GC Dio Upper So Carolina Columbia SC 2012-2016, Dep to GC 2010-2013, Dioc Exec Coun 2007-2012. Auth, *Come to the Wilderness (Mus CD)*, Indep, 2002. BroSA 2006. rector@holycrossep.org

FLANAGAN, Robert D (NY) PO Box 267, Bridgewater CT 06752 **Chr's Ch Rye NY 2016-; Sch Min Brooks Sch Chap No Andover MA 2008-** B Stanford CT 1963 BA Trin 1985; MDiv VTS 2003. D 3/8/2003 P 9/20/2003 Bp Mark Sean Sisk. m 5/13/1989 Elaine B Flanagan c 3. Ch Of S Jas The Less Scarsdale NY 2015-2016; S Paul's Ch Pleasant Vlly NY 2014-2015; Assoc R S Matt's Ch Bedford NY 2003-2008. Auth, "The Chronicles of Ragg," *Novel*, Abbott Press, 2013; Auth, "Growing a Soul," *Bk*, Wine Press Pub, 2008. stpaulspv@verizon.net

FLANDERS, Alden Beaman (Mass) 145 Weyland Cir, North Andover MA 01845 B Cincinnati OH 1945 s Wilmont & Nancy. BA Hobart and Wm Smith Colleges 1967; MA U of Maine 1969; MDiv EDS 1972; MFA Brandeis U 1973. D 6/24/1972 Bp Robert Rae Spears Jr P 5/1/1973 Bp Albert A Chambers. m 6/17/1968 Birgitte Dyrlov Flanders c 1. R The Ch Of Our Redeem Lexington MA 1986-2003; P-in-c Emm Ch Dublin NH 1984-1985; Vic H Cross Epis Ch Weare NH 1977-1984; S Paul's Sch Concord NH 1975-1986; Asst R The Ch Of The Adv Boston MA 1974-1975. Auth, "There Will Always Be A Goody Glover".

FLANDERS JR, James W (WA) 3714 Harrison St Nw, Washington DC 20015 **1968-** B New Haven CT USA 1933 s James & Helen. BA Ya 1957; MDiv VTS 1962. D 9/29/1964 Bp Charles Francis Hall P 8/1/1966 Bp Paul Moore Jr. m 4/30/2005 Susan Mann Flanders c 4. Chapl U of Maryland MD 1966-1968; Asst Min S Mk's Ch Washington DC 1966-1967; Asst Chr Epis Ch Winchester VA 1964-1965. Auth, *Fishers of Men*; Auth, *Love is a Verb*; Auth, *Sweet Love Remembered*; Auth, *That Time of Year*; Auth, *To Walk the Sea*.

FLANDERS, Susan Mann (WA) Susan Flanders, 3714 Harrison St., NW, Washington DC 20015 B Philadelphia PA 1943 d Robert & Betty. Wellesley Coll 1963; BA GW 1968; MDiv VTS 1985. D 6/8/1985 P 12/18/1985 Bp John Thomas Walker. m 4/30/2005 James W Flanders c 3. R S Jn's Ch Chevy Chase MD 1998-2008; P-in-c S Johns Broad Creek Ft Washington MD 1997-1998; Int Pstr Gr Cathd San Francisco CA 1997; Assoc R S Mk's Ch Washington DC 1987-1997; Stndg Com Dio Washington Washington DC 1999-2003, Dioc Coun 1994-1999. Washington Dc Epis Cleric Assn Bd 1998-2002.

FLANIGEN, John Monteith (Ida) Po Box 71027, Tuscaloosa AL 35407 **Ret 1990-** B Warren,OH 1925 s John & Hannah. BA Oglethorpe U 1950; MDiv SWTS 1957. D 7/26/1957 P 5/24/1958 Bp Thomas N Carruthers. m 8/16/1947 Almeda Jacqueline McGehee. Int S Thos Epis Ch Knoxville TN 1998-2002; Int S Fran' Ch Norris TN 1997-1998; Vic S Jn's Epis Ch Amer Fls ID 1990-1996; Emm Ch Hailey ID 1987-1990; R Gr-Calv Epis Ch Clarkesville GA 1977-1980.

FLECK, Timothy R (Me) Saint Saviour's Parish, 41 Mount Desert St, Bar Harbor ME 04609 **S Andr And S Jn Epis Ch SW Hbr ME 2012-; P-in-c S Sav's Par Bar Harbor ME 2012-; Bd Mem Loc Solutions Mt Desert Island 2015-; Trst SW Harbor Publ Libr 2015-; Dioc Coun Dio Maine Portland ME 2013-, Com on Ch Pension Fund 2012-; Jubilee Off Dio Lexington Lexington 2011-, Chair, Justice and Peace Cmsn 2010-2012, Dioc Ldrshp Team 2010-2012** B Columbia City IN 1964 AB Harv 1986; MA Col 1990; MDiv Chr TS 2008; MDiv Bex Sem 2009. D 6/20/2009 Bp Cate Waynick P 12/21/2009 Bp Stacy F Sauls. m 2/12/2013 Robert Allan Schmeler. P-in-c St Martha's Epis Ch Lexington KY 2009-2012; D S Paul's Epis Ch Indianapolis IN 2009; Luth-Epis Campus Mnstry Bd Dio Indianapolis Indianapolis IN 2005-2009.

FLEENER SR, William Joseph (WMich) 297 W Clay Ave Apt 214, Muskegon MI 49440 **Ret 1993-** B Amarillo TX 1931 s Frank & Clara. BA SMU 1951;

STM Ya Berk 1954. D 6/2/1954 P 4/2/1955 Bp Charles A Mason. m 10/14/1961 Judith Fleener c 4. P-in-c S Jn's Ch Fremont MI 2012-2016, Int 1995-2012; Int Pstr H Trin Epis Ch Manistee MI 2008-2009; R S Greg's Epis Ch Norton Shores MI 1971-1993; Cur Ch Of Our Sav Elmhurst IL 1968-1971; Vic S Paulinus Ch Watseka IL 1964-1968; Vic S Pat's Franklin Pk IL 1962-1964; Vic S Alb's Ch Hubbard TX 1954-1960. Auth, "Var arts," *Color Computer News*, 1982. EWC - Bus Mgr 1994-2006; Int Mnstry Ntwk 1992; Ord Of Julian Of Norwich - Assoc 1995. The Jos Awd EWC, Inc. 2006.

FLEENOR, David (NY) 4310 48th Ave Apt 2f, Woodside NY 11377 **Mgr, Chapl Serv & CPE Supv at NYULMC HealthCare Chapl New York NY 2010-** B Roanoke VA 1974 s Hubert & Dorothy. BA Mssngr Coll 1996; MDiv Ch of God TS 1999; STM GTS 2006. D 6/3/2006 Bp Marc Handley Andrus P 12/18/2006 Bp Henry Nutt Parsley Jr. The Healthcare Chapl Inc New York NY 2012-2015; Assoc CPE Supvsr HealthCare Chapl New York NY 2010; Assoc P Ch Of The Trsfg New York NY 2006-2016; CPE Supvsr-in-Trng HealthCare Chaplainicy New York NY 2006-2010. Co-Auth, "The who, what, where, and how of Pryr.," *Pstr Psychol*, Springer, 2012; Auth, "Ten questions for the first day of CPE.," *PlainViews*, HealthCare Chapl, 2011; Auth, "Smartphone applications for Chapl.," *PlainViews*, HealthCare Chapl, 2011; Co-Auth, "To pray or not to pray: considering gender and Rel concordance in Pryr w the ill.," *Journ of Healthcare Chapl*, Taylor & Fran Online, 2010. ACPE (ACPE) 2006; Assn of Profsnl Chapl (APC) 2011. Emerging Ldr's Awd ACPE 2012.

FLEENOR, Ryan C (NY) 865 Madison Ave, New York NY 10021 **Assoc R S Jas Ch New York NY 2013-, Lilly Fell 2010-** B Atlanta GA 1984 s Donald & Marguerite. BA U of Virginia 2006; MDiv Ya Berk 2010. D 6/5/2010 Bp Shannon Sherwood Johnston P 1/30/2011 Bp Peter J Lee. m 11/3/2012 Daniel S Noble.

FLEETWOOD, Zachary William Maddrey (Eur) 28 Castle Terrace, Edinburgh EH1 2EL Great Britain (UK) **R, St. Columba's by the Castle Scottish Epis Ch Edinburgh 2011-, Gnrl Syn Rep 2012-** B Farmville VA 1950 s James & Hallie. BA Guilford Coll 1973; MEd U of Virginia 1980; MDiv VTS 1987. D 6/13/1987 P 4/1/1988 Bp Peter J Lee. m 5/12/1973 Donna Fleetwood c 1. S Ptr's Epis Ch Savannah GA 2015-2016; Dn and R The Amer Cathd of the H Trin Paris 75008 2003-2011; Bd S Mart's Hse Fund 1997-2003; R S Ptr's Ch Morristown NJ 1997-2003; Bd Trst Highland Sch 1995-1997; Pres - Bd Mid-Atlantic Par Trng Prog 1992-1995; R Gr Ch The Plains VA 1990-1997; Asst to R Chr Ch Georgetown Washington DC 1989-1990; Asst to R S Mary's Epis Ch Arlington VA 1987-1989; Coun of Advice Convoc of Epis Ch in Europe Paris 2004-2006, COM 2003-2006; Cmsn on Planned Giving Dio Newark Newark NJ 2000-2003, COM 1998-2002; Stndg Com Dio Virginia Richmond VA 1995-1997, Eccl Crt 1992-1997, Cmsn on Liturg and Mus 1990-1995. Human Rts Awd City of Bloomington Human Rts. Cmsn 2012.

FLEISCHER, Marie Moorefield (NC) 8241 Allyns Landing Way Apt 304, Raleigh NC 27615 B Baltimore MD 1944 d George & Virginia. BA Wake Forest U 1966; UTS 1967; MDiv Van 1970. D 6/9/1973 Bp Paul Moore Jr P 7/29/1974 Bp Robert Lionne DeWitt. Cn to Ord Dio No Carolina Raleigh NC 2001-2006; Int Trin Ch Portsmouth VA 2000-2001; Int Trin Epis Ch Buffalo NY 1998-1999; Cn/Dep for Mnstry Dio Wstrn New York Tonawanda NY 1992-1996; Int St Stephens Romney WV 1991-1992; Admin Stff Dio Maryland Baltimore MD 1988-1990; Vic S Andr's Ch Clear Sprg MD 1987-1988; Cur Trin Ch Shepherdstown WV 1985-1987; Chapl Supvsr Richmond Memi Hosp Richmond VA 1977-1979; Chapl Meth Ret Hm Topeka KS 1975-1976; Chapl Topeka St Hopital Topeka KS 1973-1975. BP Wm Scarlett Awd Wit mag 1994; Citation Unitarian Universalist Wmn Fed 1975.

FLEISCHER, Scott (USC) 2827 Wheat St, Columbia SC 29205 **Assoc P S Jn's Epis Ch Columbia SC 2011-** B Minnesota MN 1970 s Ronald & Sandra. BA California St U 1993; MDiv TESM 2002. D 6/8/2002 Bp John Wadsworth Howe P 12/8/2002 Bp Edward Lloyd Salmon Jr. m 1/18/1997 Victoria L Fleischer c 3. P Assoc/ Vol Ch Of The Gd Shpd York SC 2010; Chapl Epis Ch Hm at York Place Inc Columbia SC 2006-2010; Prince Geo Winyah Epis Ch Georgetown SC 2002-2006; Yth Min Epis Ch Of The Resurr Longwood FL 1997-2000.

FLEISCHMAN, Donald M (Mil) 297 N Main St, Richland Center WI 53581 **S Lk's Ch Madison WI 2017-** B Danville KY 1972 s Donald & Willette. BA Wstrn Michigan U 1995; MA Gordon-Conwell TS 2000; MAR Gordon-Conwell Theol Seminry 2001; Cert Ang Stud VTS 2009. D 6/6/2009 P 3/13/2010 Bp Steven Andrew Miller. m 12/30/1992 Gypsy Free Fleischman c 4. S Barn Richland Ctr WI 2010-2016.

FLEMING, Carol Ann Spayd (NI) 70865 Wayne St, Union MI 49130 B Sandusky OH 1955 d Gary & Carolyn. BS Bowling Green St U 1979; MEd U of Toledo 1988; Cert Ang Stud SWTS 2004. D 3/21/1999 Bp David Mercer Schofield P 6/18/2004 Bp Edward Stuart Little II. m 10/14/1978 Charles Walter Fleming. Chapl Howe Mltry Sch Howe IN 2011-2015, 2010-2011; P in Charge S Jn Of The Cross Bristol IN 2011-2014; P in Charge S Mk's Epis Ch Wadsworth OH 2008-2010; Assitant Gr Epis Ch Sandusky OH 2007-2008; P-in-c S Andr's by the Lake Epis Ch Michigan City IN 2004-2006; P in Charge S Andr's By The Lake Epis Ch Michigan City IN 2003-2006; D S Paul's Epis Ch Laporte IN 2001-2002; D No Cntrl Dnry Dio Ohio Cleveland 1999-2001. NAAD. SW Dist Elem. Phys. Ed. Tender of the Year SWAHPER 1996; California/Physical Educ Elem Tchr of the Year CAHPER 1995.

FLEMING, Christie Shelburne (SanD) **Chr Ch Bastrop LA 2017-** D 6/17/2017 Bp Jim Mathes.

FLEMING JR, Huett Maxwell (Pgh) 3000 William Penn Hwy, Pittsburgh PA 15235 **R Ch Of The Gd Shpd Pittsburgh PA 2013-, 1998-2009, R 1998-** B Pittsburgh PA 1947 s Huett & Marsolete. BS Indiana U 1977; MDiv TESM 1997. D 6/21/1997 Bp Alden Moinet Hathaway P 12/27/1997 Bp Robert William Duncan. m 7/27/1991 Donna Fleming. S Steph's Epis Ch Mckeesport PA 1997-1998, Int R 1997-1998.

FLEMING, Joan (NJ) 183 Hartley Ave., Princeton NJ 08540 **Ret 2004-** B London UK 1938 d Arthur Charles & Wynifred. BA Oxf GB 1960; MA Oxf GB 1965; MDiv PrTS 1979; ThM PrTS 1991. D 6/14/1986 P 3/21/1987 Bp George Phelps Mellick Belshaw. m 6/2/1962 John V Fleming c 3. R Chr Ch New Brunswick NJ 1991-2004; Assoc S Paul's Epis Ch Bound Brook NJ 1986-1991.

FLEMING, John C (Mo) 638 Huntwood Ln, Kirkwood MO 63122 B Saint Louis MO 1938 s Raymond & Rose. BA Glennon Coll St Louis MO 1960; Kenrich TS 1964; MEd Washington U 1970. Rec 3/24/1999 as Priest Bp Hays H. Rockwell. m 1/1/1994 Patricia A Fleming c 1. Int S Mary Epis Ch Crystal Lake IL 2012-2014; R S Tim's Epis Ch S Louis MO 1999-2010; Serv RC Ch 1964-1994.

FLEMING, Linda Lee (Wyo) St Paul's Episcopal Church, PO Box 68, Dixon WY 82323 B Rawlins WY 1941 d George & Reba. BS U of Wyoming 1963. D 12/12/2012 P 7/6/2013 Bp John Smylie. m 8/14/1965 John Charles Fleming c 1. lfleming22@yahoo.com

FLEMING JR, Peter Wallace (SwFla) 1 Beach Dr SE Apt 2214, Saint Petersburg FL 33701 **Ret 1996-** B Augusta GA 1930 s Peter & Sara. AB U GA 1951; Sewanee: The U So, TS 1953; MDiv VTS 1954. D 6/24/1954 Bp Middleton S Barnwell P 3/25/1955 Bp Albert R Stuart. m 6/9/1960 Marion Courtney Fleming c 3. S Thos' Epis Ch St Petersburg FL 1976-1994; R S Dav's Epis Ch Lakeland FL 1961-1976; Vic The Epis Ch Of The Annunc Vidalia GA 1955-1958; Vic S Paul's Epis Ch Jesup GA 1954-1955.

FLEMING JR, Raymond Edgar (Los) 484 Cliff Dr Apt 10, Laguna Beach CA 92651 B Worcester MA 1940 s Raymond & Betty. BA MacMurray Coll 1963; MDiv SWTS 1966. D 6/11/1966 P 12/17/1966 Bp Albert A Chambers. m 2/16/1963 Marcia R Fleming c 2. R S Mary's Par Laguna Bch CA 1989-2004; R H Faith Par Inglewood CA 1976-1989; R Gr Epis Ch Norwalk CT 1972-1976; Cur Emm Memi Epis Ch Champaign IL 1966-1969.

FLEMISTER, Ernestein (SwFla) 212 W Idlewild Avenue, Tampa FL 33604 **R S Jas Hse Of Pryr Tampa FL 2009-** B Monrovia Liberia 1952 d Arthur & Cora. BD Franklin U Columbus OH 1985; MBA Xavier U 1990; MDiv Bex Sem 2007. D 5/13/2006 Bp Kenneth Lester Price P 6/16/2007 Bp Thomas Edward Breidenthal. Vic Gr Ch Cincinnati OH 2007-2009; Night Auditor Columbus Marriott No 2004-2005.

FLEMMING, Leslie (SO) 1 Kent Dr, Athens OH 45701 B Brooklyn NY 1943 d Michael & Pauline. BA Carleton Coll 1965; MA U of Wisconsin 1968; PhD U of Wisconsin Madison 1973; MDiv Bex Sem 2008. D 6/23/2007 P 6/28/2008 Bp Thomas Edward Breidenthal. m 6/7/1969 John C Flemming c 3. P S Ptr's Ch Gallipolis OH 2008-2015; Gr Ch Pomeroy OH 2008-2010; D S Alb's Epis Ch Of Bexley Columbus OH 2007-2008. Assc, Comm. of the H Sprt 2003.

FLENTJE, Gregory Laurence (WMich) 4210 Honey Creek Ave Ne, Ada MI 49301 **D St. Paul's Ch 2003-** B Quincy IL 1962 s Laurence & Donna. BS W&L 1984; MD U IL 1992; PhD U IL 1994; Cert Br 1999. D 8/24/1992 Bp Peter Hess Beckwith. m 5/29/1993 Janice Marie Flentje. D S Mk's Ch Grand Rapids MI 2001; D S Thos Epis Ch Rochester NY 1999-2001; D Ch Of The Redeem Providence RI 1994-1997; D Chap Of S Jn The Div Champaign IL 1992-1994; Asstg Chapl U Of IL 1992-1994. Integrity; NAAD.

FLES, Jacob C (Me) 2 Dresden Ave, Gardiner ME 04345 B Patterson NJ 1954 s Jacob & Joan. MA Oral Roberts U 1977; Gordon-Conwell TS 1984; Cert Epis TS of the SW 1990; Cler Ldrshp Inst 1998; PrTS 2000. D 7/6/1990 Bp William Harvey Wolfrum P 1/20/1991 Bp Alpha Mohammed. m 4/7/1985 Rebecca Fles c 3. R Chr Ch Gardiner ME 1994-2011; S Alb's Epis Ch Arlington TX 1992-1994; Gr And S Steph's Epis Ch Colorado Sprg CO 1990-1992. Auth, "Living Unit Grp Manuel," *Campus Life*.

FLETCHER, Margaret Ann Laurie (Vt) St. Peter's Episcopal Church, 300 Pleasant St., Bennington VT 05201 B Butterworth South Africa 1943 d Harnish & Margaret. BA SUNY 1995; MDiv Yale DS 2000. D 2/2/2008 P 4/18/2009 Bp Thomas C Ely. m 3/14/1967 Alan Fletcher c 2. S Thos' Epis Ch Brandon VT 2009-2015.

FLETCHER JR, Richard James (WTenn) 108 N King Ave, Dyersburg TN 38024 **Imm Ch Ripley TN 2016-; Mem, Bp & Coun Dio W Tennessee Memphis 2014-** B Utica NY 1952 s Richard & Margaret. Memphis TS; MHA Duke 1979; MA Naval War Coll 1989. D 1/14/2012 Bp Don Edward Johnson. m 1/29/1982 Diane L Fletcher c 2. S Mary's Epis Ch Dyersburg TN 2012-2016.

FLETCHER, Wayne Alexander (NJ) **The GTS New York NY 2017-** D 6/23/2017 Bp William H Stokes.

FLETT, Carol (WA) retired, Washington DC 20016 **Chair of Bd Inter-Faith Conf of Metropltn Washington DC 2012-; Ecum & Inter-Rel Off Dio Washington DC 2011-** B White Plains NY 1947 d Harold & Helen. BA U of Connecticut 1969; Untd TS of the Twin Cities 1985; MDiv EDS 1988; DMin EDS 2000. D 6/23/1988 Bp Robert Marshall Anderson P 1/14/1989 Bp David Elliot Johnson. m 6/14/1969 George S Flett c 2. Assoc S Alb's Par Washington DC 2010-2012; Interfaith Prog Coordntr Cathd of St Ptr & St Paul Washington DC 2007-2010; R S Barth's Ch Gaithersburg MD 2007-2010; P-in-c Par Of S Paul Newton Highlands MA 2005-2007; R S Ptr's Ch Weston MA 1997-2005; R S Mk's Epis Ch Burlington MA 1992-1997; Assoc The Ch Of Our Redeem Lexington MA 1988-1992. Fllshp of the Soc of St. Jn 2000.

FLEXER, Katharine Grace (NY) 225 W 99th St, New York NY 10025 **R S Mich's Ch New York NY 2014-, Assoc 2005-2010; Dn, Manhattan Cntrl Cler Dio New York New York NY 2015-** B Bellevue WA 1971 d James & Susan. BA Whitman Coll 1993; MDiv CDSP 1997; Ripon Coll Cuddesdon Oxford GB 1998. D 1/23/2000 Bp Vincent Waydell Warner P 9/9/2000 Bp William Edwin Swing. m 5/21/2005 Jim K Hinch c 2. R Epis Ch in Almaden San Jose CA 2011-2014; Assoc R S Clem's Ch Berkeley CA 2002-2005; Dir of Alum & Ch Relatns CDSP Berkeley CA 2000-2002; Yth Min S Aid's Ch San Francisco CA 2000-2001; COM Dio El Camino Real Salinas CA 2011-2014; Chair, Dept of Yth & YA Dio California San Francisco CA 2003-2005, COM 2003-2005. kflexer@saintmichaelschurch.org

FLICK, Robert Terry (Tex) 1410 Cambridge Dr, Friendswood TX 77546 B Cincinnati OH 1947 s Robert & Anna. BA Duns Scotus Coll 1971; MS Wright St U 1979; MDiv S Leonard Coll Dayton 1981; MBA Our Lady of the Lake U 1999. Rec 11/19/2003 Bp Don Adger Wimberly. m 10/10/1992 Sarah R Robinson c 1. P The Great Cmsn Fndt Houston TX 2013-2015; Assoc S Steph's Epis Ch Houston TX 2011-2013; Vic Lord Of The St Epis Mssn Ch Houston TX 2010-2013; R S Mich's Ch La Marque TX 2004-2011.

FLINTOM, Jack Glenn (Md) 2030 Marshall Ln, Hayes VA 23072 **Supply Dio Sthrn Virginia Newport News VA 1998-** B Greensboro NC 1949 s Albert & Rachel. AA Truett Mcconnell Jr Coll 1969; BA Merc 1971; MDiv Harvard DS 1977. D 6/25/1977 P 5/18/1978 Bp William Gillette Weinhauer. m 10/31/1981 Marjorie Flintom. Cur S Tim's Ch Catonsville MD 1982-1987; Vic S Andr's Ch Bessemer City NC 1980-1982; Vic Trin Ch Kings Mtn NC 1980-1982; Asst S Lk's Ch Salisbury NC 1978-1979; Gr Ch Morganton NC 1978.

FLOBERG, John Fredrick (ND) Po Box 612, Fort Yates ND 58538 **P-in-c Dio No Dakota Fargo ND 2016-, Cn 1991-2016; Ch Of The Cross Selfridge ND 2005-; Cn The Epis Dio 2004-** B Moorhead MN 1959 s Vincent & Alice. Cert Luth Bible Inst 1984; BA Concordia Coll 1985; MDiv Bex Sem 1991. D 4/5/1991 P 10/6/1991 Bp Andrew Fairfield. m 7/16/1993 Sloane R Floberg c 4. P-in-c All SS Ch Minot ND 2007-2013; R/Cn Mssnr S Lk's Ch Ft Yates ND 1991; Asst Trin Ch Rochester NY 1988-1991. Allen Fellowowship 1990.

FLOBERG, Sloane R (ND) 820 West Central Ave, Bismarck ND 58501 **D S Lk's Ch Ft Yates ND 2003-** B Valley City ND 1971 BS No Dakota St U 1993. D 6/12/2003 Bp Andrew Fairfield. m 7/16/1993 John Fredrick Floberg c 3. D Dio No Dakota Fargo ND 2003-2014.

FLOCKEN, Robin (CNY) 1721 Stanley Rd, Cazenovia NY 13035 B Oxnard CA 1950 s Walter & Norma. BA Rutgers Coll 1972; MDiv GTS 1978. D 6/17/1978 P 2/24/1979 Bp Alexander D Stewart. m 8/17/1974 Patricia S Flocken c 2. Ret S Ptr's Epis Ch Cazenovia NY 1988-2012; Dio Wstrn Massachusetts Springfield 1981-1988; S Jn's Ch Athol MA 1981-1988; Cur Gr Epis Ch Utica NY 1978-1980.

FLOOD, Charles Ta (Pa) 19 S 10th St, Philadelphia PA 19107 B Windsor ON CA 1944 s Patrick & Margaret. BD Wayne 1968. D 6/11/1977 P 6/3/1978 Bp Lyman Cunningham Ogilby. m 9/21/2011 Mark J Yurkanin. S Steph's Ch Philadelphia PA 1988-2016; Ch Of The H Apos Wynnewood PA 1980-1982; Non-par 1979-1989; Epis Cmnty Serv Philadelphia PA 1977-1979; Stff Chapl Epis Cmnty Serv Philadelphia PA 1977-1979. Doctor Of Sci In Med (Medsc) Thommas Jefferson U 2003.

FLOOR, Marjorie Jacobsen (Alb) 77 Sabbath Day Point Rd, Silver Bay NY 12874 **Died 3/1/2017** B Brooklyn NY 1933 d Trygve & Gladys. BS SUNY 1954; MS Hofstra U 1962; DFA Inchbald Sch of Design London GB 1976; Cert Theol Stud Mercer TS 1990. D 6/17/1989 Bp Orris George Walker Jr P 5/20/1999 Bp Daniel William Herzog. m 4/17/1954 William Howard Floor c 2. Vic The Epis Ch Of The Cross Ticonderoga NY 1999-2017; D Chr Ch Babylon NY 1989-1994.

FLORES, Katherine Doris (Wyo) 4700 S Poplar St, Casper WY 82601 **Yth Dir Dio Wyoming Casper 2015-; P S Steph's Ch Casper WY 2010-** B Cheyenne WY 1956 d Lloyd & Janet. AA Laramie City Cmnty Coll 1989; BS U of Wyoming 1991. D 3/13/2010 Bp Bruce Caldwell P 9/29/2010 Bp John Smylie. c 3. kaydflores@gmail.com

FLORES, Nydia (NY) 630 Water St Apt 4-C, New York NY 10002 **Died 5/3/2017** B 1931 d Pedro & Carlota. Inst Pstr Hispano. D 4/26/1997 Bp Richard Frank Grein. Par D Mision San Pablo New York NY 1997-2000.

FLORY, Carol Inez (Fla) 9645 Old Baymeadows Rd Apt 750, Jacksonville FL 32256 B Coalmont TN 1954 d George & Hazel. BS Jacksonville U 1993; MDiv Sewanee: The U So, TS 1998. D 6/13/1999 Bp Stephen Hays Jecko.

FLORY, Phyllis Brannon (WK) 1551 Briargate Dr, Salina KS 67401 **S Fran Cmnty Serv Inc. Salina KS 2015-; Stff Chapl St. Fran Commuity Serv 2015-; Marketing & Dvlpmt St. Fran Cmnty Serv 2011-; Vol Chapl Salina Reg Hosp Salina KS 2008-; Vic H Apos Ch Ellsworth KS 2007-** B Dermott AR 1950 d Phillip & Cynthia. BS Friends U 1991; MS Friends U 1993. D 9/1/2007 P 12/13/2008 Bp James Marshall Adams Jr. m 4/20/1985 Michael G Flory. Cn Dio Wstrn Kansas Hutchinson KS 2014-2017, GC Dep 2010-2012, Prov VII Rep 2010-2012, Chrm. Bp Search Com 2010, Dioc Coun/Stndg Com 2008-2012; Vic S Jn's Ch Great Bend KS 2011-2017. tec.wks2011@gmail.com

FLOWERS JR, James Byrd (CGC) **R All SS Epis Ch Mobile AL 2004-** B Dothan AL 1955 D 6/12/2004 P 5/27/2005 Bp Philip Menzie Duncan II. m 7/21/1979 Katharine B Flowers c 3.

FLOWERS JR, James Edgar (WLa) 946 Ockley Dr, Shreveport LA 71106 **Con-voc Dn S Geo's Ch Bossier City LA 2007-** B Shreveport LA 1955 s James & Elizabeth. BS LSU 1977; MDiv VTS 1983. D 6/23/1983 P 1/1/1984 Bp Maurice Manuel Benitez. m 10/17/2008 Denise Flowers. R S Tim's Ch Alexandria LA 1999-2006; Exec Dio Wstrn Louisiana Alexandria LA 1997-2003; R Chr Memi Ch Mansfield LA 1994-1999; Non-par 1988-1993; Assoc S Mk's Ch Beaumont TX 1986-1988; Chapl NW Texas Hosp Amarillo TX 1985-1986; Asst to R S Jn The Div Houston TX 1983-1984.

FLOWERS, Lauren F (Ga) 3 Ridge Rd, Savannah GA 31405 **S Fran Of The Islands Epis Ch Savannah GA 2015-** B Lawton OK 1958 d John & Barbara. MA U So 1980; MDiv Sewanee: The U So, TS 2012; MDiv The TS at The U So 2012. D 11/24/2012 P 6/28/2013 Bp Philip Menzie Duncan II. m 6/9/2015 Samuel Russell Byrd c 3. S Ptr's Epis Ch Savannah GA 2014-2015; S Jn's Ch Monroeville AL 2013-2014; The Epis Ch Of The Nativ Dothan AL 2005-2013.

FLOWERS, Mary Miller (WA) D 11/21/2015 P 6/11/2016 Bp Mariann Edgar Budde.

FLOYD JR, Charles K(amper) (Miss) 4400 King Road, Meridian MS 39305 **Assoc The Epis Ch Of The Medtr Meridian MS 2007-** B Meridian MS 1942 s Charles & Mabel. BBA U of Mississippi 1964; MDiv Sewanee: The U So, TS 1967; DMin Sewanee: The U So, TS 1980; Cert GTS 1992. D 6/24/1967 P 5/1/1968 Bp John Maury Allin. m 6/1/1996 Helen Whitener c 4. Int S Jas Epis Ch Port Gibson MS 2006-2007; Int S Lk's Ch Brandon MS 2005-2006; Vic H Trin Ch Crystal Sprg MS 1999-2001, Vic 1967-1998; Cn Dio Mississippi Jackson MS 1993-2001, Pres, Stndg Com 1980-1983; R S Mk's Ch Houston TX 1982-1993; R S Paul's Ch Columbus MS 1978-1982; R Trin Ch Yazoo City MS 1975-1978; Vic Epis Ch Of The Incarn W Point MS 1971-1975; Cur S Jas Ch Jackson MS 1969-1971; Vic S Steph's Hazelhurst MS 1967-1969. Amer Soc of Clincl Hypnosis 2010; Diplomate, AAPC 2003; Lic Mar & Fam Therapists 2003.

FLOYD, Charles Rhein (CGC) 117 Rusty Gans Dr, Panama City Beach FL 32408 **Ret Dio Cntrl Gulf Coast 2003-** B Minneapolis MN 1931 s Oliver & Laura. BA U Pgh 1954; Sewanee: The U So, TS 1990. D 7/25/1990 P 4/20/1991 Bp Charles Farmer Duvall. c 2. Vic S Thos By The Sea Panama City Bch FL 1996-2003, Vic 1992-2003, D 1990-1991; Chapl and Lieutenant Colonel Civilian Air Patrol USAF Aux 1992-2004; Dioc Cmsn Ecum & Interfaith Rela Dio Cntrl Gulf Coast Pensacola FL 1991-1997, Mem, Cmsn on Dioc Mssn 1995-1998, Ecum Off 1994-1997, Mem, Dioc Cmsn on Ecum and Interfaith Relatns 1991-1997. Distinguished Mltry Grad US AF 1954.

FLOYD, Donna (Tenn) D 6/4/2016 Bp John Bauerschmidt.

FLOYD, Michael Hinnant (DR) 5505 B Stuart Cir Unit B, Austin TX 78721 B Kingstree SC 1946 s Eldra & Eugenia. BA Trin Hartford CT 1968; BD EDS 1971; MA Claremont Grad U 1977; PhD Claremont Grad U 1982. D 7/31/1971 P 3/29/1973 Bp Frederick Barton Wolf. m 2/1/1975 April Floyd c 3. Pstr Adv-St. Nich Ch Quito Ecuador 2010-2013; Assoc Vic Iglesia de la Epifanía Santo Domingo Dom Rep 2008-2010; Prof Centro de Estudios Teológicos República Dominicana 2007-2010; Prof OT Epis TS Of The SW Austin TX 1982-2007; Asst S Jn's Ch Ft Worth TX 1981-1982; Prof Bloy Hse Claremont CA 1977-1979; Asst S Mk's Epis Ch Upland CA 1972-1979. Auth, "Minor Prophets Part 2," *Forms Of The OT Lit*, Eerdmans, 2000. Angl Assn Of Biblic Schlars 1991; SBL 1976. michaelhfloyd@yahoo.com

FLOYD, Michael Stephen (O) 120 Ohio St, Huron OH 44839 **Chr Epis Ch Huron OH 2015-** B Bulli N.S.W Australia 1954 s John & Agnes. MDiv Trin Sch for Mnstry 2014. D 10/20/2015 Bp Mark Hollingsworth Jr P 4/5/2016 Bp Arthur Williams Jr. m 7/10/1982 Fiona Mary McKenzie c 2.

FLOYD, Peter M (Colo) 7408 Tudor Rd, Colorado Springs CO 80919 **R Ch Of S Mich The Archangel Colorado Spg CO 2013-** B Tullahoma TN 1975 s Richard & Melody. BS U of Tennessee 1998; MDiv Nash 2008. D 6/21/2008 P 1/16/2009 Bp John Bauerschmidt. m 10/3/1998 Jeneen Jensen Floyd c 2. Vic S Anskar's Epis Ch Hartland WI 2010-2013; Assoc R Gr Epis Ch Hinsdale IL 2008-2010; . rector@stmikeschurch.com

FLOYD, Peter Winslow (Ct) 18 Hidden Lake Rd, Higganum CT 06441 **Mssnr, Middlesex Area Cluster Mnstry Dio Connecticut Hartford CT 2006-** B New

York,NY 1937 s Rolfe & Frances. BA U of New Hampshire 1961; U CA 1964; STM Ya Berk 1965; Bos 1970. D 6/12/1965 Bp Charles Francis Hall P 1/6/1966 Bp Harvey D Butterfield. c 4. S Dunst's Epis Mssn Waitsfield VT 1992-2002; Asst Mssnr, Middlesex Area Cluster Mnstry Dio Connecticut Meriden CT 1982-1986; R Ch Of S Mary The Vrgn Chappaqua NY 1976-1979; Vic S Ptr's Mssn Lyndonville VT 1974-1976; S Andr's Epis Ch St Johnsbury VT 1971-1976; Chapl Cmnty Corrections Cntr S Johnsbury VT 1971-1974; Chapl New Hampshire St Legislature Concord NH 1967-1968; Cur S Paul's Ch Concord NH 1965-1968; Dioc Coun Dio Vermont Burlington VT 1994-1996. "Let's Talk Wk monthly columns," *Rutland Herald (Rutland, VT)*. Leaveners (Founding Mem) 1995-1996; Living Stones 1996-2000.

FLOYD, Theresa Ann (Ore) 4177 Nw Thatcher Rd, Forest Grove OR 97116 B Waukegan IL 1951 d Norman & Gisella. AA Coll of the Redwoods 1973; Humboldt St U 1974; Dioc Cntr For The Diacon Eugene OR 1983; Pacific U 1995. D 2/14/1988 Bp Robert Louis Ladehoff. m 9/14/1974 Kenneth King Floyd c 2. Dir Renew Dio Oregon Portland OR 1990-1993, Bursar/Secy 1987-1989; D S Bede's Ch Forest Grove OR 1988-2000; Chapl Gd Samar Hosp 1988-1990. Auth, "Renew Curric For Angl Sprtlty," Dio Ore, 1992.

FLY, David Kerrigan (Mo) 4400 Lindell Blvd Apt 11n, Saint Louis MO 63108 **Ret 1998-** B Monett MO 1941 s Jack & Kathryn. BS SW Missouri St U 1963; MDiv Nash 1966. D 12/28/1965 P 8/21/1966 Bp Edward Randolph Welles II. m 6/9/1990 Adrienne Anderson Fly c 5. Gr Ch S Louis MO 1981-1998; R Gr S Louis MO 1981-1998; Loc Ten S Lk's Ch Wamego KS 1979-1980; Dio Kansas Topeka KS 1973-1981; Chapl K SU Manhattan KS 1973-1981; Chapl Mankato St Coll Mankato MN 1971-1973; Chapl Sw Missouri St Coll Springfield MO 1969-1971; Cn Pstr Gr And H Trin Cathd Kansas City MO 1966-1969. Auth, "My Life Under the Big Top," Xlibris, 2017; Auth, "Faces of Faith," *Re-Pub*, Xlibris, 2017; Auth, "An Epis P's Reflections on the Kansas City Riot of 1968," *Missouri Hist Revs*, The St Hist Soc of Missouri, 2006; Auth, "Faces of Faith: Reflections in a Rearview Mirror," Ch Pub, Inc, 2004; Auth, "Faces In The Rearview Mirror," Walsworth, 2002; Auth, "Journey To Jerusalem," 1989. ESMHE 1968-1981.

FLYNN, Anne Regina (Kan) 21 Copperfield Ln, Charleston IL 61920 **D Trin Epis Ch Mattoon IL 2013-, D 2013-** B 1956 D 2/12/2005 Bp Michael Whittington Creighton. m 12/14/2009 Patrick Early. D S Paul's Epis Ch Harrisburg PA 2011-2012; Exec Dir St. Barn Cntr for Mnstry 2011-2012; Exec Dir St. Barn Cntr for Mnstry 2011-2012; D S Jn's Epis Ch Carlisle PA 2005-2011. Assn of Epis Deacons 2007; Campus Mnstry Assn, Estrn Illinois U 2013; Charleston Area Inter-Faith Assn 2012.

FLYNN, Michael T (Los) 4406 El Corazon Ct, Camarillo CA 93012 **Dir Fresh-Wind Mnstrs 1996-** B Glendale CA 1940 s James & Inez. BA U CA 1963; MDiv Sewanee: The U So, TS 1966. D 9/10/1966 P 3/11/1967 Bp Francis E I Bloy. m 2/12/1961 Linda Sue McCambridge c 4. Asst All SS Epis Ch Oxnard CA 2000-2005; Assoc P Chr Epis Ch Denver CO 1996-2000; R S Jude's Epis Par Burbank CA 1981-1996; Vic Imm Mssn El Monte CA 1970-1981; Chapl Cal St Fullerton 1968-2015; Vic Geth Brea CA 1968-1970; Cur S Mk's Par Altadena CA 1966-1968. Auth, *How To Be Gd Without Really Trying*, Chosen, 2004; Auth, *Making Disciples*, FreshWind, 1997; Auth, *The Mustard Seed Bk*, Chosen, 1995; Auth, *Inner Healing*, InterVarsity, 1993; Auth, *H Vulnerability*, Chosen, 1990.

FLYNN, Peggy Rishel (Kan) D 6/2/2012 Bp Dean E Wolfe.

FODOR, Luke (WNY) 410 N Main St, Jamestown NY 14701 **S Lk's Epis Ch Jamestown NY 2014-; Bd Examing Chapl Dio Wstrn New York Tonawanda NY 2014-; Bd Mem Forma 2013-** B Akron OH 1978 s Frank & Heidi. BA Moody Bible Inst 1999; MA Dur 2002; MA NYU 2004; MDiv Bex Sem 2011. D 2/6/2011 P 9/10/2011 Bp Lawrence C Provenzano. m 5/22/1999 Willow M Fodor c 2. Asst R St Jn's Ch Cold Sprg Harbor NY 2011-2014; Sem Trin Ch Columbus OH 2010-2011; Ntwk Coordainator Epis Relief & Dvlpmt New York NY 2008-2011; Ntwk Coordntr Epis Relief & Dvlpmt 2007-2011; Yth Min Chr Ch Oyster Bay NY 2006-2008; Prog Asst for YA Mnstrs Dom & Frgn Mssy Soc New York NY 2004-2008; Prog Asst for YA & Higher Educ Min Epis Ch Cntr (DFMS) 2004-2007; Bd Mem The Bd Managers of Camp De Wolfe Garden City NY 2011-2014; Bex Sem Bd Trst, Stdt Rep Bex Sem Columbus OH 2009-2011. Auth, "Marked for Mssn: Yth in Action," *Marked for Mssn: Yth in Action*, Ch Pub, 2014; Auth, "Pause. Moments to reflect," *Pause. Moments to reflect*, Brimingham, AL: Passport Media., 2013; Auth, "The Occasional Theol and Constant Sprtlty of Rowan Williams," *ATR*, ATR, 2012; Auth, "Changing Diapers, Changing Lives: Reflections for New Parents," *Changing Diapers, Changing Lives: Reflections for New Parents*, Forw Mvmt, 2012; Auth, "What Can One Person Do?: The Millennium Dvlpmt Goals," *What Can One Person Do?: The Millennium Dvlpmt Goals*, Forw Mvmt, 2009. 2011 The Chas Hefling Prize ATR 2011. luke.fodor@stlukesjamestown.org

FOERSTER III, Frederick Henry (CNY) 183 Capn Crosby Rd, Centerville MA 02632 **Non-par 1977-** B Saginaw MI 1945 s Frederick & Ellen. USNA 1965; BA MI SU 1968; MDiv PDS 1971. D 5/30/1971 P 3/1/1972 Bp Ned Cole. m 5/29/1999 Anne Foerster c 3. R Chr Epis Ch Jordan NY 1976-1977; P-in-c S

Paul's Warners NY 1976-1977; St Pauls Ch Baldwinsville NY 1976-1977; Vic S Ptr's Ch So Windsor CT 1973-1976; Cur Chr Ch Binghamton NY 1971-1973.

FOGELQUIST, Albin Hilding (Spok) 1307 Regents Blvd Apt D, Fircrest WA 98466 **Spec Serv Evang Luth Ch in Amer 2009-; Sup Hisp Mnstry S Jn's Epis Ch Olympia WA 2009-** B Spokane WA 1947 s Albin & Helen. BS Whitworth U 1969; MA Whitworth U 1969; MDiv Assn Free Luth TS 1972; CDSP 1974; ThD Grad Theol Un 1977; LHD Faith Sem 1989. D 12/19/1990 P 4/4/1991 Bp Vincent Waydell Warner. c 2. P-in-c W Cntrl Epis Mssn Spokane WA 1997-2007; LocTen Ch Of The H Apos Bellevue WA 1996-1997; Instr Dioc Theol Sch Dio Olympia Seattle 1994; P-in-c St Ptr's Epis Par Seattle WA 1991-1995; P-in-c Ch Of The H Trin Hoquiam WA 1991; DRE The Ch Of S Dav Of Wales Shelton WA 1982-1997; Prof/Rgstr Faith Sem Tacoma WA 1982-1990; Pstr Luth Ch 1972-1990. Alcuin Club 1972; Fllshp SSJE 1995. Hon Alum CDSP 1993.

FOISIE, Dawn Ann Campbell (Oly) 5757 Solomons Island Rd, Lothian MD 20711 **Chr Epis Ch Blaine WA 2016-** B Alexandria VA 1968 d Gerald & Sheila. BA Notre Dame of Maryland U 2007; MDiv VTS 2012. D 4/15/2012 Bp Joe Goodwin Burnett P 11/4/2012 Bp Eugene Taylor Sutton. m 8/22/2015 Stephen D Foisie. S Jas' Par Lothian MD 2012-2015.

FOISIE, Stephen D (Oly) 228 Wall St, Camano Island WA 98282 **S Aid's Epis Ch Stanwood WA 2014-** B Bellingham WA 1977 s Charles & Karen. BA Cntrl Washington U 2000; MDiv VTS 2010. D 4/17/2010 P 12/18/2010 Bp Gregory Harold Rickel. m 8/22/2015 Dawn Ann Campbell. Old Donation Ch Virginia Bch VA 2010-2014.

FOLEY, Kristen C (NJ) 2136 Woodbridge Ave, Edison NJ 08817 **S Jas Ch Edison NJ 2014-; Dioc Coun Dio New Jersey Trenton NJ 2015-; Chair, LGBTQ Cmsn Dio New Jersey Trenton NJ 2015-** B Denville NJ 1977 d Theodore & Kathryn. Angl Stds GTS; BA Loyola U 1995; MDiv Wesley TS 2006. D 6/8/2013 Bp George Edward Councell P 12/17/2013 Bp William H Stokes. info@stjamesedison.org

FOLEY, Michael (Pgh) 5700 Forbes Ave, Pittsburgh PA 15217 **The Ch Of The Redeem Pittsburgh PA 2014-** B San Diego CA 1964 s James & Susan. MS Fuller TS; BS U CA, Santa Barbara 1986; MDiv GTS 2013; MDiv The GTS 2013. D 6/8/2013 Bp Joseph Jon Bruno P 1/11/2014 Bp Mary Douglas Glasspool. m 2/17/2015 Chad W Tanaka Pack. D French Ch Of S Esprit New York NY 2013.

FOLEY, Theodore Archer (NJ) Christ Church, 415 Washington St, Toms River NJ 08753 **D Chr Ch Toms River Toms River NJ 2012-** B Portchester NY 1951 s Kenneth & Eleanor. BS Ford 1973; MBA FD 1981. D 5/5/2012 Bp George Edward Councell. m 10/20/1973 Kathryn Megroz c 2.

FOLSOM, Henry Titus (NH) 62 Durand Rd, Randolph NH 03593 **Ret 1987-** B Orange NJ 1927 s Henry & Anna. BA Ya 1950; MDiv Ya Berk 1957. D 6/15/1957 P 12/21/1957 Bp Benjamin M Washburn. m 10/29/1995 Clare Folsom c 3. Int S Barn Ch Berlin NH 1988-1991; R Gr Ch Old Saybrook CT 1969-1987; R Chr Ch Pompton Lake NJ 1965-1969; Vic S Ptr's Ch Washington NJ 1959-1964; Cur S Jas Ch Montclair NJ 1957-1959. *Rendezuous In The Bush*, Trophy Room Books, 1999. ERM (inactive); Episcopalians Untd (inactive).

✠ FOLTS, The Rt Rev James Edward (WTex) PO Box 6885, San Antonio TX 78209 B San Antonio TX 1940 s Alexander & Ethel. BA Trin U San Antonio 1962; MDiv VTS 1965. D 7/13/1965 Bp Everett H Jones P 1/25/1966 Bp Richard Earl Dicus Con 2/17/1994 for WTex. m 6/21/1964 Sandra Pauline Folts c 2. Ret Bp of W Texas Dio W Texas San Antonio TX 2006, 1994-2005, 1969-1979; R S Mk's Epis Ch San Antonio TX 1992-1993; R Ch Of The Adv Brownsville TX 1985-1992; R Ch of the Heav Rest Abilene Abilene TX 1979-1985; R S Mk's Ch San Marcos TX 1968-1979; Assoc S Fran Epis Ch Victoria TX 1967-1968; P-in-c Gr Falfurrias TX 1965-1967; P-in-c S Jas Epis Ch Hebbronville TX 1965-1967. DD U So TS 1994; DD VTS 1994.

FOLTS, Jonathan (Ct) 3 Windswept Ridge Road, Ivoryton CT 06442 **Chapl Essex Vol Fire Dept 2013-; R S Jn's Epis Ch Essex CT 2004-** B Victoria TX 1968 s James & Sandra. BA U of No Texas 1991; MDiv VTS 1996; DMin VTS 2013. D 6/11/1996 P 2/14/1997 Bp James Edward Folts. m 11/2/1996 Kimberly S Folts c 3. R S Fran Epis Ch Victoria TX 1999-2004; Vic S Eliz's Epis Ch Buda TX 1996-1999; The Ch Of The H Sprt Dripping Spgs TX 1996-1997; Asst Dir Of Homeless Ministers Prog St. Barth Ch New York NY 1990-1991. "Listening And Taking Action," LivCh, 2005; "The Daily Diet," LivCh, 2004.

FOLTS, Kimberly S (Ct) 40 Main St, Essex CT 06426 B Durango CO 1968 BA Dickinson Coll 1990; MDiv VTS 1994. P 5/13/1995 Bp Charlie Fuller McnuttJr. m 11/2/1996 Jonathan Folts c 3. DCE S Fran Epis Ch Victoria TX 2000-2004; S Steph's Epis Ch Wimberley TX 1997-1998; Asst S Ptr's Epis Ch Washington NC 1995-1996; All SS' Epis Ch Hershey PA 1994-1995.

FOLTZ, Marvin Lee (Mo) 12424 Cape Cod Dr, Saint Louis MO 63146 **R S Tim's Epis Ch S Louis MO 2013-; Chair - Mssn Beyond the Ch The Epis Ch in Hawaii Honolulu HI 2011-, Dep to GC 2010-, Chair - COM 2009-2011, Chair - Fin and Real Estate 2000-2009, Bd - Camp Mokule'ia 2000-, Dioc Coun 1998-2002** B El Paso TX 1954 s Carl & Marilyn. BA SW Bapt U 1975; MDiv MidWestern Bapt TS 1982; SWTS 1992. D 11/24/1992

P 5/25/1993 Bp William Walter Wiedrich. m 6/20/1987 Cynthia S Foltz c 4. R The Par Of Gd Shpd Epis Ch Wailuku HI 1998-2013; R Ch Of The Nativ Maysville KY 1993-1998; Serv Sthrn Bapt Ch 1982-1992; Exec at Lg Faith Action for Cmnty Equity 2009-2010; Chapl Maui Police Dept 1999-2008; Exec Coun Dio Lexington Lexington 1994-1998. Faith Action for Cmnty Equity 2008-2013. marvinleefoltz@gmail.com

✠ FOLWELL, The Rt Rev William Hopkins (CFla) 600 Carolina Village Rd Unit 25, Hendersonville NC 28792 B Port Washington NY 1924 s Ralph & Sara. BCE Georgia Inst of Tech 1947; LTh SWTS 1952; BD SWTS 1953. D 6/22/ 1952 P 12/22/1952 Bp Henry I Louttit Con 2/9/1970 for CFla. m 4/22/1949 Christine Folwell c 3. Chair Wrld Mssn Com ECEC 1976-1982; Bp Dio Cntrl Florida Orlando FL 1970-1989, 1967-1969, 1961-1962, Chair Dept Mssn & Ch Ext 1962-1965; Hon Cn Cathd Ch Of S Lk Orlando FL 1966-1990; R All SS Ch Of Winter Pk Winter Pk FL 1959-1970; R S Gabriels Ch Titusville FL 1956-1959; Pres FL Assn Epis Schs 1956-1957; Vic S Augustines Ch Metairie LA 1955-1956; Chapl S Mart's Sch New Orleans 1955-1956; P-in-c S Lk The Evang Ch Mulberry FL 1954-1955; Vic S Ptr's Ch Plant City FL 1952-1955. DD SWTS 1970; DD U So TS 1970.

FONCREE, Rose Mary Ivas (Miss) 4526 Meadow Hill Road, Jackson MS 39206 B Pascagoula MS 1942 d Arthur & Mamie. BA Valdosta St U 1982; MA Valdosta St U 1986. D 1/6/2001 Bp Alfred Marble Jr. c 1. The Epis Ch Of The Gd Shpd Terry MS 2006-2012.

FONDER SR, Kim Michael (SD) Holy Comforter/Messiah, PO Box 242, Lower Brule SD 57548 P-in-c Dio So Dakota Pierre SD 2013- B Browns Valley MN 1954 s Floyd & Marvel. D 6/19/2010 P 12/18/2010 Bp John Tarrant. m 10/27/ 1990 Tamara Jean Fonder c 4. fondersr@aol.com

FONES, Peter Alden (Ore) 723 S. 48th St, Springfield OR 97478 Chapl Oregon St Police-Critical Incident Response Team 2015-; Mem COM-B Dio Oregon 2014- B Portland OR 1950 s Hamilton & Helen. BEd U of Oregon 2001; Cert NW Hse of Theol Stds 2004; MDiv CDSP 2005. D 4/20/2006 P 10/21/ 2006 Bp Johncy Itty. m 11/1/1980 Leah Baker-Fones c 4. Dio Oregon Portland OR 2015-2017, Mem Dioc Coun 2007-2010; Chapl Epis Campus Mnstry Eugene OR 2006-2008; D in Charge Ch Of S Jn The Div Springfield OR 2006; Fac Fresh Start Dio Oregon 2008-2015.

FONTAINE, Ann Kristin (Wyo) PO Box 1354, Cannon Beach OR 97110 B Portland OR 1941 d Gustav & Dorothy. BA L&C 1963; MDiv Harvard DS 1995. D 6/22/1995 Bp Bob Gordon Jones P 1/6/1996 Bp William Harvey Wolfrum. m 3/9/1963 James Fontaine c 3. Int Gr Epis Ch Astoria OR 2013; Int S Cathr Of Alexandria Epis Ch Nehalem OR 2011-2012; Dioc Coordntr Epis Relief and Dvlpmt 2004-2007; Jt Nomin Com for the Next PB Epis Ch 2003-2006; Int Ch Of The Trsfg Jackson WY 2001-2003; Int S Jn's Epis Ch Jackson WY 2000-2006; DDO Dio Wyoming Casper 1998-2000; Int Shoshone Epis Mssn Ft Washakie WY 1998-1999; Int S Steph's Ch Casper WY 1997-1998; Int S Thos Ch Dubois WY 1996; Cur Trin Ch Lander WY 1995-1996; Exec Coun Epis Ch 1985-1991. Auth, "Streams of Mercy: a meditative commentary on the Bible," Bk, Auth Hse, 2005; Contrib, "Contrib," EFM Mentor Manual, Sewanee: The U So; Contrib, "essays and reporting," Epis Café, Epis Café; Auth, "arts," LivCh; Contrib, "Green Lent," http://greenlent.blogspot.com, Blog; Contrib, "what the tide brings in," http://seashellseller.blogspot.com, Blog. Epis Wmn Caucus; Integrity.

FONTAINE, H(oward) Douglas (Minn) 3940 Auburn Dr, Minnetonka MN 55305 Died 2/23/2017 B Charleston WV 1931 s Howard & Elizabeth. BA W Virginia U 1958; BD VTS 1959; SWTS 1975. D 6/11/1959 P 9/14/1960 Bp Wilburn Camrock Campbell. c 5. Ret 1994-2017; Dn Cathd Ch Of S Mk Minneapolis MN 1971-1994; R Chr Epis Ch Tyler TX 1965-1971; Assoc Chr Ch Cathd Houston TX 1961-1962; In-c Trin Ch Shepherdstown WV 1958-1961.

FOOSE, Elizabeth Boutwell (Miss) 6697 Bee Lake Rd, Tchula MS 39169 Gr Epis Ch Canton MS 2013-; Chapl S Andr's Epis Sch 1990- B Mobile AL 1957 d Charles & Mary. U So 1977; BA Mississippi Coll 1979; MDiv SWTS 1990. D 5/31/1990 P 5/8/1991 Bp Duncan Montgomery Gray Jr. m 10/25/1997 Robert Michael Foose c 1. Dio Mississippi Jackson MS 2013-2016; S Jas Ch Jackson MS 1993-1997, 1990-1992; S Jn's Cathd Denver CO 1992; Non-par. bfoose5@gmail.com

FOOTE, Beth (Cal) 705 Grand St, Alameda CA 94501 S Alb's Ch Albany CA 2015- B Oakland CA 1958 d Richard & Beth. BA U CA 1980; MDiv CDSP 2006; MDiv CDSP 2006. D 9/15/2007 P 6/14/2008 Bp Marc Handley Andrus. m 9/10/1983 Robert Hale Foote c 3. S Anne's Ch Fremont CA 2015-2017; S Lk's Ch Walnut Creek CA 2014; Assoc Trin Par Menlo Pk CA 2007-2013.

FOOTE, Margaret Lloyd Foster (SO) 334 Burns Ave, Wyoming OH 45215 B Nashua NH 1947 d Frank & Victoria. BA The OH SU 2011; MDiv CDSP 2016. D 7/11/2016 P 6/10/2017 Bp Thomas Edward Breidenthal. m 1/2/2016 Andrea Sparrow Foote. Dio Sthrn Ohio Cincinnati OH 2016, Other Lay Position 2013; DCE Chr Epis Ch Of Springfield Springfield OH 2011-2013.

FOOTE, Nancy Burns (Md) 1 Holmes Ave, Baltimore MD 21228 Died 2/18/ 2017 B Baltimore MD 1936 d Paul & Dorothy. BA Towson U 1976; MS Loyola Coll 1989. D 6/26/1983 Bp David Keller Leighton Sr. c 2. Dn of D Trng Dio Maryland Baltimore MD 1989-2003, Archd 1986-2003, COM 1985-2003, Archd/Dn of Trng 1989-2006; D Cathd Of The Incarn Baltimore MD 1987-2000; D H Trin Ch Churchville MD 1983-1986. NAAD 1980.

FOOTE, Roger Lee (SO) 7 E Interwood Pl, Cincinnati OH 45220 B Cincinnati OH 1948 s Gordon & Esther. BA U Cinc 1970; MDiv VTS 1981. D 6/22/1981 Bp William Grant Black P 12/1/1981 Bp Frank S Cerveny. m 7/5/2003 Ruth S Foote c 3. R Chr Ch - Glendale Cincinnati OH 1991-2014; R All SS Ch Alexandria VA 1984-1991; Assoc R Chr Epis Ch Ponte Vedra FL 1981-1984. Sis Of Trsfg, Ord Of S Lk.

FOOTE, Stephen Williams (Me) 574 Turner Rd, Bremen ME 04551 Ret 2003- B Hartford CT 1942 s Dwight & Helen. BA Bard Coll 1965; STB GTS 1968. D 6/ 11/1968 Bp Walter H Gray P 3/15/1969 Bp John Henry Esquirol. Dn Cathd Ch Of S Lk Portland ME 1990-2003; Archd Dio Maine Portland ME 1986-1989; Epis Ch Of S Mary The Vrgn Falmouth ME 1969-1986.

FORAKER, Greg (Colo) St Luke's Episc Ch, 2000 Stover St, Fort Collins CO 80525 S Lk's Epis Ch Ft Collins CO 2015-; Fac, Sprtl Dir Hesychia Sch of Sprtl Direction Tucson AZ 2004- B Wichita KS 1960 s John & Linda. BA U CO 1999; MA Washington Theol Un 2005; Cert ETS at Claremont 2010. D 11/ 21/2010 P 6/25/2011 Bp Kirk Stevan Smith. Asst to the R S Phil's In The Hills Tucson AZ 2011-2015.

FORAKER-THOMPSON, Jane (Nev) P.O. Box 2665, Gardnerville NV 89410 B Alhambra CA 1937 d Field & Margaret. BA U CA 1959; MA U CA 1965; PhD Stan 1985; MDiv CDSP 1997. D 1/29/1994 Bp John Stuart Thornton P 4/10/1999 Bp Stewart Clark Zabriskie. c 4. P Ch Of Coventry Cross Minden NV 2007-2008; Prison Chapl Nevada Dept of Corrections Carson City NV 2003-2008; P Dio Nevada Las Vegas 2000-2011, Del to GC 2009, Soc Justice Coordntr 2002-2008, Bd Mem of Rel Allnce of Nevada 2000-2008; P Gr-St Fran Cmnty Ch Lovelock NV 1999-2000; D All SS' Ch San Francisco CA 1995-1997; D S Mich's Cathd Boise ID 1994-1999. Auth, "Numerous arts And Papers On Var Aspects Of Criminal Justice (1971-2000): Soc Justice, Sentencing, Corrections, Alter," se Vita. OHC 1997. Who's Who of Amer Cambridge Who's Who 2008; Who's Who in the Wrld Marquis 1996; Vstng Fell at Cntr for Intergroup Stds U of Cape Town, So Afr 1990; Boise St U Alum Awd for Outstanding Fac Boise St U Alum 1989; Intl Leaders of Achievement Cambridge, Engl 1988; Biographical Historiette on Men and Wmn of Achievement and dist Biography Intl , Delhi, India 1987; Intl Who's Who of Profsnl and Bus Wmn Intl Biographical Cntr, Cambridge, Engl 1987; Dictionary of Inernational Biography Cambridge, Engl 1986; Can Stds Resrch Grant Can Govt, Ottawa 1986; Who's Who of Amer Wmn Marquis 1986; Directory of Distinguished Americans 1985; Directory of Distinguished Americans 1985; Intl Who's Who in Crime Prevention Cambridge, Engl 1985; Fell at 1985 Seminar Global Security & Arms Control, UC Irvine 1985; Who's Who in Amer Law Marquis 1985; Wrld Who's Who of Wmn Cambridge, Engl 1984; Cmnty Leaders of the Wrld Cambridge, Engl 1984; Who's Who of the Amer W Marquis 1984; Wmn of the Year Awd Soroptomists, Santa Fe 1981.

FORBES, Bruce Willard (NY) 109 E 50th St, New York NY 10022 Died 5/31/ 2016 B Allegany NY 1921 s R Norman & Jessie. BA U MI 1942; MA Harv 1943; STB GTS 1961. D 6/23/1961 P 2/24/1962 Bp Lauriston L Scaife. Asst St. Barth Ch New York NY 1964-1990; Cur S Lk's Epis Ch Jamestown NY 1961-1964.

FORBES JR, Charles Alvin (Oly) 4510 123rd Pl NE, Marysville WA 98271 Ret 1989- B San Francisco CA 1926 s Charles & Alice. BA U of Washington 1949; BD Bex Sem 1952. D 6/24/1952 P 6/29/1953 Bp Stephen F Bayne Jr. m 7/1/1955 Carolyn Forbes c 3. Vic S Geo's Ch Seattle WA 1984-1988; R S Mary Tacoma WA 1978-1983; S Mary's Ch Lakewood WA 1978-1983; Vic S Phil Ch Marysville WA 1971-1978; Serv Angl Ch In Uruguay 1967-1970; R S Eliz's Ch Seattle WA 1959-1967; Chapl U Wa-Seattle 1958-1959; Vic S Jn's Ch Kirkland WA 1954-1957; Ch Of The Redeem Kenmore WA 1954-1955; S Augustines In-The-Woods Epis Par Freeland WA 1952-1954; Vic St Steph's Epis Ch Oak Harbor WA 1952-1954.

FORBES, David Reineman (Cal) 22 Delmar St, San Francisco CA 94117 B Palo Alto CA 1926 s Francis & Eleanor. BS Stan 1949; MS Stan 1950; MDiv VTS 1953. D 6/28/1953 Bp Henry H Shires P 1/1/1954 Bp Karl M Block. c 3. Int The Epis Ch Of S Jn The Evang San Francisco CA 2003-2004; Assoc Pstr Gr Cathd San Francisco CA 1991-2000, Vice-Dn 1966-1990, Cn Sacrist & Precentor 1954-1965, Asst 1953; Dio California San Francisco CA 1988-1991; S Paul's Epis Ch Walnut Creek CA 1987-1988; S Matt's Epis Ch San Mateo CA 1985-1987; S Paul's Ch Oakland CA 1975-1985.

FORBES, Elizabeth Faye (Ga) 3321 Wheeler Rd, Augusta GA 30909 D S Aug Of Cbury Ch Augusta GA 2008- B Wilmington DE 1941 d Stephen & Grace. BA Brandywine Coll 1963; BS U of Delaware 1972; BS Med Coll of Georgia 1976. D 3/27/2009 Bp Henry Irving Louttit.

FORBES, Mark S (Ala) 156 Lavender Bloom Loop, Mooresville NC 28115 S Steph's Epis Ch Birmingham AL 2016- B Winston-Salem NC 1971 s Charles & Edna. BA U NC 1994; MDiv VTS 2004. D 5/28/2004 Bp Bob Johnson P 5/8/ 2005 Bp Robert Marshall Anderson. m 8/4/2001 Kristen T Forbes c 2. R S Pat's Epis Ch Mooresville NC 2008-2016; Asst P and Sch Chapl S Marg Of Scotland Par San Juan Capo CA 2004-2008.

FORBES, Michael Philip (Minn) 402 31st St Ne Apt 224, Rochester MN 55906 **Non-par 1982-** B Brooklyn NY 1946 s Alfred & Eleanor. BA S Piux X Sem 1968; MDiv Bex Sem 1974. D 2/5/1975 P 4/26/1976 Bp Philip Frederick McNairy. m 1/16/1971 Louise G Glass c 2. Supply Chr Ch Frontenac MN 1988-2000; P-in-c Ch Of The Mssh Prairie Island Welch MN 1987-1991; Chapl Choir Sch 1980-1982; Non-par 1975-1980; Res Rochester Med Mnstry 1974-1975. Auth, "The Ch Year," 1975; Auth, "Dio AltGld Manual"; Auth, "Amer Indn Sunday Resources & Curric"; Auth, "Lesser Festivals For Mn"; Auth, "85 Unit Cnfrmtn Curric". ADLMC 1984; Grand (Natl) Assoc Chapl 1999; Priory Chapl 1997; Sovereign & Mltry Ord Of The Temple Of Jerusalem 1997. Advncd Stndg Acpe 1975.

FORD, Austin Mcneill (At) 569 Cherokee Ave Se, Atlanta GA 30312 **Ret 1996-** B DeKalb Co GA 1929 s Harold & Elizabeth. BA Emory U 1950; BD Sewanee: The U So, TS 1953. D 6/11/1953 P 12/1/1953 Bp Randolph R Claiborne. Dio Atlanta Atlanta GA 1967-1996; Vic S Barth's Epis Ch Atlanta GA 1955-1956; Cur S Lk's Epis Ch Atlanta GA 1953-1954; Dir Emmaus Hse Epis Ch Atlanta GA 1967-1996.

FORD, Calvin Berkley (SVa) 68 Market Street, Onancock VA 23417 **H Trin Prot Epis Ch Onancock VA 2010-** B Baltimore MD 1952 s Calvin & Rosemary. Loyola U 1971; BA U of Maryland 1986; MDiv Sewanee: The U So, TS 1989. D 6/17/1989 P 5/1/1990 Bp Albert Theodore Eastman. m 6/15/1974 Marian E Ford c 3. R Chr and S Lk's Epis Ch Norfolk VA 2007-2010; R Middleham & S Ptr's Par Lusby MD 1991-2006; Asst to R Ch Of The Ascen Westminster MD 1989-1991.

FORD, Charles Allan (NY) 205 Stone Rd, West Hurley NY 12491 **Dio New York New York NY 2008-; Vic S Marg's Ch Staatsburg NY 2008-; Ret 2006-** B New York NY 1938 s Charles & Eleanor. BA CUNY 1962; STB Ya Berk 1965; MS Iona Coll 1970; DMin NYTS 2005. D 6/12/1965 P 12/18/1965 Bp Horace W B Donegan. m 6/25/2005 Leslie Ford. R S Ptr's Epis Ch Peekskill NY 1999-2006; Int S Geo's Epis Ch Antioch CA 1998-1999; Exec Dir Henry Ohlhoff Hse San Francisco CA 1993-1998; Assoc S Paul's Ch Oakland CA 1993-1998; Vic S Steph's In-The-Field Epis Ch San Jose CA 1991-1993; 1987-1991; S Cyp's Ch San Francisco CA 1978-1986; Chapl Greer Sch Millbrook NY 1968-1978; Cur S Mk's Ch In The Bowery New York NY 1965-1968. AAPC 2001.

FORD, Cheri Lynn (NMich) Rr 2 Box 939-A, Newberry MI 49868 B Pontiac MI 1950 d Stanley & Gloria. Dio No Michigan TS MI; BA Cntrl Michigan U 1972. D 7/11/1993 P 1/1/1994 Bp Thomas Kreider Ray. m 5/22/1971 Steven E Ford. Non-par. Newberry Mnstrl Assn.

FORD, Denis B (Colo) 3231 Olive St., Jacksonville FL 32207 B Jacksonville FL 1946 s Thomas & Shirley. BA Jacksonville U 1968; MDiv VTS 1972. D 6/18/1972 P 6/13/1973 Bp Edward Hamilton West. m 7/3/2005 Joann Tomlin c 1. Vic S Paul's Ch Montrose CO 2009-2011; R Gr Epis Ch Ottawa KS 1999-2006; Dio Wstrn Massachusetts Springfield 1986-1998; P-in-c S Paul's Epis Sum Chap Otis MA 1985-1997; R Ch Of The Gd Shpd So Lee MA 1985-1986; S Geo's Ch Lee MA 1985-1986; R S Barn And All SS Ch Springfield MA 1978-1985; Asst R Pohick Epis Ch Lorton VA 1975-1978; Cur S Andr's Epis Ch Tampa FL 1974-1975; Vic Chr Ch Old Town FL 1973-1974; Vic Chr Ch Cedar Key FL 1972-1974.

FORD, Janet Carol (Nev) B Ogden UT 1939 D 5/3/2003 Bp Katharine Jefferts Schori. m 12/28/1967 Don Nelson Ford c 1.

FORD, Janice Celeste (WMass) **R Ch Of The Recon Webster MA 2008-; Dn, Cntrl and W Worcester Dnry Dio Wstrn Massachusetts Springfield 2014-, Trst of the Dio 2014-, Co-chair, Dioc Elctns Com 2009-2014, Mem, Stndg Com 2008-2013** B Albany NY 1952 d Dominick & Grace. BA Coll of S Rose 1975; AS Maria Coll 1980; BS SUNY 1986; MS U of New Hampshire 1989; MDiv Andover Newton TS 2008. D 12/29/2007 P 6/7/2008 Bp Gordon Scruton. m 10/3/1981 Rodney Ford c 1. Mssnr for Hlth Mnstrs Dio Wstrn Massachusetts 2000-2005. pastor@reconciliationweb.org

FORD, Joan B (SanD) 838 4th St, Encinitas CA 92024 B Youngstown OH 1933 d Joseph & Louise. BA Stan 1975; MA Stan 1976; PhD Stan 1980; MDiv CDSP 1989. D 12/8/1989 P 12/1/1990 Bp William Edwin Swing. m 6/26/1954 Thomas Ford c 4. Cn for Cmncatn Cathd Ch Of S Paul San Diego CA 2002-2014; Dir of Telecommunications Angl Comm Off 1996-1999; R S Cyp's Ch San Francisco CA 1991-1996; P-in-c S Aid's Ch San Francisco CA 1991; Transitional D Chr Ch Portola Vlly CA 1989-1990. Dio California Cler Assn 1989. Ch Div D. D. (Honoris Causa) CDSP Berkeley Ca 2004.

FORD, Joann (Colo) 3231 Olive St, Jacksonville FL 32207 B Wichita Falls TX 1943 d Ronald & Ione. Wichita St U 1964; BA Merc 1980; Luther NW TS 1989; MDiv Sewanee: The U So, TS 1991. D 6/24/1991 P Bp Robert Marshall Anderson P 1/25/1992 Bp Frank Kellogg Allan. m 7/3/2005 Denis B Ford c 2. R S Jn's Epis Ch Ouray CO 2009-2011, P-in-c 2006-2011; Cn to the Ordnry Dio Kansas Topeka KS 2002-2006; R Ch Of The Cov Jct City KS 1998-2002; Asst S Pat's Epis Ch Atlanta GA 1993-1998; Asst Chr Ch Norcross GA 1991-1993.

FORD, John Mark (Ala) PO Box 614, Chelsea AL 35043 **P-in-c S Cathr's Chelsea AL 2007-** B Barnsville OH 1960 s Nolan & Mildred. BA Samford U 1982; MDiv Sewanee: The U So, TS 2006. D 6/15/2006 P 12/12/2006 Bp Henry

Nutt Parsley Jr. m 5/27/2000 Charlene P Ford c 4. S Lk's Epis Ch Birmingham AL 2015-2016; R St. Cathr's Epis Ch Chelsea AL 2007-2015; P-in-c S Alb's Ch Hoover AL 2006-2007.

FORD, Richard Barlow (Cal) 2165 West Dry Creek Road, Healdsburg CA 95448 **Ret 1990-** B Ontario CA 1930 s George & Verna. BA Pomona Coll 1952; MDiv Yale DS 1955. D 6/18/1955 P 12/17/1955 Bp Angus Dun. m 8/15/1953 Patricia L Ford c 3. Int S Tim's Epis Ch Mtn View CA 1992-1993, P-in-c 1980; Int Chr Epis Ch Los Altos CA 1990, Int 1985-1989; S Mk's Epis Ch Palo Alto CA 1985; Dir Hospice Min of Mid-Peninsula 1982-1987; R S Bede's Epis Ch Menlo Pk CA 1971-1980; Trin Par Menlo Pk CA 1971-1980; Assoc S Mk's Epis Ch Santa Clara CA 1967-1971; Assoc & Headmaster, Par Sch S Andr's Ch Saratoga CA 1963-1967; Assoc Trin Cathd San Jose CA 1960-1963; Vic S Barth's Epis Ch Livermore CA 1957-1960; Assoc S Marg's Ch Washington DC 1955-1957. Cont Educ Fell VTS 1970.

FORD, Robert Lawrence (Oly) PO Box 3276, Bellevue WA 98009 **Asstg P S Marg's Epis Ch Bellevue WA 1997-** B Saint Louis MO 1937 s Samuel & Margaret. U of Missouri 1958; BS Washington U 1961; MDiv Ya Berk 1968. D 10/18/1968 P 6/29/1969 Bp Chilton R Powell. m 8/26/1967 Margaret A Ford c 2. P All SS Ch Bellevue WA 1996-1997; Int All SS Epis Ch Seattle WA 1994-1996; P Dio Olympia Seattle 1993; Vic S Dav Seattle WA 1988-1994; Vic S Dav Emm Epis Ch Shoreline WA 1988-1993; Int S Matthews Auburn WA 1988; Int S Catherines Ch Enumclaw WA 1986-1987; Assoc S Paul's Ch Marion OH 1984-1986, 1974-1979; R All SS Epis Ch Miami OK 1971-1974. NASSAM.

FORD, Russell Wayne (CGC) Po Box 5853, Gulf Shores AL 36547 B Chicago IL 1932 s George & Marie. BA Lake Forest Coll 1964; MDiv Nash 1967. D 6/17/1967 Bp James Winchester Montgomery P 12/1/1967 Bp Gerald Francis Burrill. m 7/28/1956 Julie Clare Proctor. Non-par 1970-1995; Vic The Ch Of The H Innoc Hoffman Schaumburg IL 1968-1970; Chapl Of Hse Correction S Leonards Oratory Chicago IL 1967-1968; Assoc H Sprt. Auth, "Nashotah Theol Revs". Kairos Prison Mnstry. Annual Awd For Valor Il St Police 1983.

FORD, Stanley Eugene (Spok) B Walla Walla WA 1930 s John & Marion. BA Whitworth Coll 1953; Mdiv Drew U 1956. D 10/19/1959 P 4/14/1960 Bp Russell S Hubbard. m 11/19/1950 Joyce Lindstrom c 2.

FORD, Steven E (NMich) Rr 2 Box 939-A, Newberry MI 49868 B Sault Saint Marie MI 1949 s Clayton & Elizabeth. BS Cntrl Michigan U 1970; JD U MI 1975. D 9/20/1992 P 1/1/1994 Bp Thomas Kreider Ray. m 5/22/1971 Cheri Lynn Ford. Assoc All SS Ch Newberry MI 1992-2006.

FORD, Steven Richard (Az) 3436 N 43rd Pl, Phoenix AZ 85018 B Stamford NY 1953 s Winfred & Jean. BA Hobart and Wm Smith Colleges 1975; MDiv GTS 1980. D 6/7/1980 Bp Paul Moore Jr P 12/1/1980 Bp Herbert Thompson Jr. m 10/16/1976 Karen Louise Ford. Assoc S Aug's Epis Ch Tempe AZ 1998-2013; S Paul's Ch Phoenix AZ 1987-1992; S Barn On The Desert Scottsdale AZ 1980-1987; Cur S Barn' Desert Paradise Vlly AZ 1980-1987. Auth, "The Place Of Catechesis In The Early Ch"; Auth, "S Lk Journ"; Auth, "Pstr Psychol". CCU, OHC, ECM.

FORDHAM, James Frederick (EC) 1579 Bayview Rd, Bath NC 27808 **Ret 1995-** B Kinston NC 1932 s James & Lena. BS E Carolina U 1959; MA VTS 1965. D 6/29/1965 P 2/1/1966 Bp Thomas H Wright. c 2. Gr Epis Ch Plymouth NC 1975-1994; S Lk's/S Anne's Epis Ch Roper NC 1975-1976; P-in-c Calv Swanquarter NC 1973-1975; P-in-c Ch Of H Cross Aurora NC 1973-1975; R S Jas Epis Ch Belhaven NC 1968-1973; R S Matt Yeatsville NC 1968-1973; P-in-c All Souls NW NC 1966-1968; S Jas The Fisherman Epis Ch Shallotte NC 1966-1968; P-in-c S Phil's Ch Southport NC 1966-1968; Com Dio E Carolina Kinston NC 1978-1979.

FOREMAN JR, Harold Vandon (Ala) 3013 Boundary Oaks Dr SE, Owens Cross Roads AL 35763 - **Ret 2012-** B Gadsden AL 1952 s Harold & Rosemary. BA Birmingham-Sthrn Coll 1975; Tubingen U Tubingen DE 1977; MDiv Yale DS 1980; Nash 1981; MA Jacksonville St U 2008. D 5/27/1981 P 12/15/1981 Bp Furman Charles Stough. m 10/14/2006 Heidi B Foreman. R Ch Of The Resurr Rainbow City AL 2008-2012; R Chr Epis Ch Albertville AL 2005-2008; R S Simon Ptr Ch Pell City AL 1985-2005; Cur S Jn's Ch Decatur AL 1981-1985. Fndt Fell Rotary 1976.

FORESMAN, R Scott (Ia) Po Box 306, Bishop CA 93515 B Oskaloosa IA 1954 s Gerald & Arloene. BD U of Nebraska 1978; MDiv Epis TS in Kentucky 1982. D 5/7/1983 P 11/7/1983 Bp James Daniel Warner. m 9/16/2015 Cynthia Foreman c 5. S Tim's Ch Bp CA 2003-2007; S Paul's Ch Coun Blfs IA 1999-2003; S Mary's Ch Nebraska City NE 1988; Vic S Matt's Ch San Ardo CA 1985-1987; Cur S Lk's Ch Kearney NE 1984-1985; R S Jn's Ch Broken Bow NE 1983-1984. SocMary 2001.

FORHAN, Carol Lynn (Spok) 9327 E Leavenworth Rd, Leavenworth WA 98826 **Wenatchee Dnry Rep Dioc Nomination Com Cashmere WA 2007-; Mentor EFM Cashmere WA 2006-; D S Jas Epis Ch Cashmere WA 2006-; Co-Owner Advert Mgr NCW Media Inc.Leavenworth WA 2000-** B Minneapolis MN 1947 d Howard & Sally. CDSP 2006; DCOTE 2006. D 10/8/2006 Bp James E Waggoner Jr. m 11/25/1967 William Edward Forhan c 2. DOK 1994; NorthAmerican Assoc. for the Diac 2006.

FORINASH JR, Joseph Lynn (Colo) PO Box 1026, Eagle CO 81631 **D Epis Ch Of The Trsfg Vail CO 1999-** B Kansas City KS 1943 s Joseph & Mary. BS USAF Acad 1965; MA U of Oklahoma 1971; MBA Wichita St U 1971. D 11/6/1999 Bp William Jerry Winterrowd. m 10/7/1989 Kathleen LaNor Bishop c 1.

FORISHA, Martha Lee (CNY) 102 Delaware St, San Antonio TX 78210 **Died 11/1/2016** B Corpus Christi TX 1954 d Arthur & Marilyn. BD Texas Womans U 1976; MDiv Epis TS of the SW 1993. D 6/12/1993 P 10/8/1994 Bp James Monte Stanton. m 8/23/1975 Donnie Forisha c 3. Supply S Andr's Ch Brack-ettville TX 2011-2012; R Trin Epis Ch Seneca Falls NY 2000-2010; Cur Ch Of The Annunc Lewisville TX 1996-2000; Asst Ch Of The Gd Shpd Cedar Hill TX 1995; Cur Epis Ch Of The Ascen Dallas TX 1993-1995.

FORMAN, John P (Oly) 1005 S.W. 152nd Street, Burien WA 98166 **S Eliz's Ch Seattle WA 2014-** B Ironwood MI 1958 s Bernard & Mary. Journalism U of Washington 1984; MDiv Seattle U 2014; MDiv Seattle U 2014. D 12/21/2013 P 7/22/2014 Bp Gregory Harold Rickel. m 1/17/1987 Jennifer Marie Forman c 2. Assoc Ch Of The Redeem Kenmore WA 2014, D 2013-2014. Auth, "Integral Ldrshp," *Integral Ldrshp: The Next Half-Step*, SUNY Press, 2013.

FORNALIK, Barbara Horn (Roch) 1130 Webster Rd, Webster NY 14580 B Jersey City NJ 1939 d John & Lillian. Dplma Katharine Gibbs Sch 1959. D 3/29/2008 Bp Jack Marston Mckelvey. m 4/29/1961 Anthony Fornalik c 3.

FORNARO, Francis (Mass) 11 Alaska Ave, Bedford MA 01730 **Int Dio Massachusetts Boston MA 2011-, 1996-1999** B Boston MA 1942 s Simone & Grace. BS Boston St Coll 1964; MS Boston St Coll 1967; MDiv EDS 1996. D 9/8/1996 P 5/17/1997 Bp M(Arvil) Thomas Shaw. m 10/9/2004 Charles Frates. R S Paul's Epis Ch Bedford MA 1999-2010.

FORNEA, Stanley Wayne (EC) 2111 Jefferson Davis Hwy Apt603S, Arlington VA 22202 **Chapl US Navy 1996-** B Bogalusa LA 1958 MTh Duke DS; BA SE Louisiana U; DMin Van. D 12/5/2001 P 4/10/2002 Bp Clifton Daniel III. m 5/22/1982 Belinda Diane Fornea c 2.

FORNEY, John C (Los) 316 W Green St., Claremont CA 91711 B Long Beach CA 1942 s Daniel & Lillian. BA California St U Los Angeles 1969; RelD Claremont TS 1975; Cert CDSP 1986; Tchr Cred Mills Coll 1987. D 6/7/1986 Bp William Edwin Swing P 3/1/1987 Bp Rogers Sanders Harris. m 6/11/1966 Eleanor Forney c 2. S Ambr Par Claremont CA 2004-2005; Assoc St. Ambr Claremont CA 2003-2005; Dio Alaska Fairbanks AK 1987-1994; Vic S Andr's Petersburg AK 1987-1994. Cert of Recognition for Soc Justice Wk St of CA Senate 2010; The Crucis Cross Camp Crucis, Granbury, TX 1973.

FORREST, Louise Louise (Mass) 41 Hall Ave, Watertown MA 02472 B Santa Monica CA 1947 d John & Janet. BA Whittier Coll 1969; MDiv EDS 1980; Cert Rad 1996. D 5/28/1983 P 12/3/1983 Bp Frederick Barton Wolf. m 8/12/2004 Leslie Horst. S Anne's Ch No Billerica MA 2015-2016; Temporary Asst to the R The Ch Of Our Redeem Lexington MA 2007-2008; Assoc Gr Ch Newton MA 2002-2004; Assoc Dio Massachusetts Boston MA 1999-2002; The Cathd Ch Of S Paul Boston MA 1999; Ch Of S Jn The Evang Boston MA 1997-1999, 1991; P-in-c S Dav's Epis Ch Halifax MA 1992-1993; S Paul's Ch Brookline MA 1989-1991; Assoc S Paul's Ch Natick MA 1984-1986; Dir of Soup Kitchen Old W Ch (UMC) Boston MA 1980-1984.

FORREST OSB, William (FdL) 56500 Abbey Rd, Three Rivers MI 49093 **St Greg's Abbey Three Rivers MI 2014-; Monk S Greg Abbey 1973-** B Marion NC 1950 s William & Rose. BA S Andrews Presb Coll 1972. D 6/18/1992 P 12/1/1992 Bp William Louis Stevens.

FORREST, William Clifford (Az) 24922 S Lakewood Dr, Sun Lakes AZ 85248 **P S Matt's Ch Chandler AZ 2005-** B Baltimore MD 1945 s Nelson & Marguerite. BA Bridgewater Coll 1969; MDiv CDSP 1972. D 6/18/1972 P 6/17/1973 Bp John Joseph Meakin Harte. m 6/5/1983 Julia L Forrest c 2. Dio Arizona Phoenix AZ 2000-2004; S Chris's Ch Sun City AZ 2000-2004; S Aug's Epis Ch Tempe AZ 1992-2001; S Mary's Epis Ch Tomah WI 1990-1991; R Chr Ch S Paul MN 1984-1990; Gr St Pauls Epis Ch Tucson AZ 1981-1984; All SS' Epis Day Sch Phoenix AZ 1979-1981; All SS Epis Ch Torrington WY 1977-1979; R S Alb's Epis Ch Wickenburg AZ 1973-1977; Cur Trin Cathd Phoenix AZ 1972-1973.

FORREST, William Fred (Dal) 3029 Frances Dr, Denison TX 75020 **Died 1/25/2017** B Woodbury NJ 1931 s Fred & Maude. BA Westminster Choir Coll of Rider U 1954; MDiv PDS 1961. D 4/29/1961 P 10/28/1961 Bp Alfred L Banyard. c 3. Asstg P S Steph's Epis Ch Sherman TX 2002-2017; Ret 1989-2017; S Jn's Epis Ch Pottsboro TX 1988-2017, 1983; Dept Of Missions Dallas TX 1984-1987; Ch Of The H Trin Bonham TX 1983-1985; S Lk's Ch Denison TX 1978-1982; S Vinc's Cathd Bedford TX 1973-1978; S Mk's On The Mesa Epis Ch Albuquerque NM 1969-1973; Vic St Johns Epis Ch Farmington NM 1969-1973; Asst To Dn S Matt's Cathd Dallas TX 1965-1969; P-in-c S Jn's Ch Sewaren NJ 1964-1965; Vic S Marks Ch Carteret NJ 1961-1965. Amer Hymn Soc.

FORRESTER, Shelley (Okla) St. Andrew's Church, PO Box 1256, 1313 SW D Ave, Lawton OK 73502 **R S Andr's Epis Ch Lawton OK 2012-** B Cheyenne WY 1963 d William & Edwina. AAS Laramie Cnty Cmnty Coll 1987; BA U of Texas-Arlington 1989; MDiv Epis TS of the SW 2008. D 12/16/2007 Bp

Bruce Caldwell P 12/6/2008 Bp Jeff Lee. Asst R S Andr's Ch Downers Grove IL 2008-2012. sforrester@standrewslawton.org

FORSHAW, Lee (Ct) 2000 Main St, Stratford CT 06615 B Dobbs Ferry NY 1951 s Edward & Elizabeth. BA LIU 1973. D 9/15/2007 Bp Andrew Donnan Smith. m 11/23/1974 Valerie D Forshaw c 2.

FORSYTHE, Margaret Ann Kroy (NJ) 687 Donald Dr S, Bridgewater NJ 08807 **D S Fran Ch Dunellen NJ 2010-; Chapl Chelsea Assisted Living Bridgewater NJ 2006-; Chapl Chelsea Assisted Living Bridgewater NJ 2005-** B Detroit MI 1941 d Walter & Anne. BA U MI 1963; BA U MI 1963; AAS Raritan Vlly Cmnty Coll 1985; AA Raritan Vlly Cmnty Coll 1985. D 10/31/1998 Bp Joe Doss. c 2. D Chr Ch New Brunswick NJ 2005-2006; Chapl Hagedorn Psych Hosp Glen Gardner NJ 2003-2012; Chapl Res Robert Wood Johnson Hosp 2002; Chapl Res Robert Wood Johnson Hosp New Brunswick NJ 2002; Chapl Res Robert Wood Johnson Med Cntr New Brunswick NJ 2002; Chapl Seaman's Ch Inst Port Newark NJ 2002; Chapl Seamens Ch Inst New York NY 2002; Chapl Res Robert Wood Johnson Hosp New Brunswick NJ 2000-2001; Res Chapl Robert Wood Johnson Hsopital 2000-2001; Chapl Res Robert Wood Johnson Med Cntr New Brunswick NJ 2000-2001; Chapl INS Detention Cntr Eliz NJ 2000; Chapl INS Detention Cntr Port Newark NJ 2000; D S Mart's Ch Bridgewater NJ 1998-2005. DOK; NAAD.

FORSYTHE, Mary Louise (Neb) 420 Shorewood Ln, Waterloo NE 68069 **D Ch Of The Resurr Omaha NE 1988-** B Sioux City IA 1933 d Byron & Helene. BA U of Iowa 1955; MS U of Nebraska 1968; EFM Sewanee: The U So, TS 1984. D 5/7/1988 Bp James Daniel Warner. c 2.

FORTE, Jeanne (NCal) 700 Wellfleet Dr, Vallejo CA 94591 **R S Paul's Epis Ch Benicia CA 2005-** B Victoria BC 1951 d David & Margaret. BA U of Calgary Ab CA 1983; MDiv CDSP 1999. Trans 7/16/2005 Bp Jerry Alban Lamb. c 2. rector@stpaulsbenicia.org

FORTI, Nicholas (Va) 1700 University Ave, Charlottesville VA 22903 **The Fork Ch Doswell VA 2014-** B Richmond VA 1981 s Kenneth & Avis. BS Radford U 2004; MDiv VTS 2010. D 6/12/2010 P 12/11/2010 Bp Herman Hollerith IV. m 8/2/2008 Eleis M Lester. Assoc R S Paul's Memi Charlottesvlle VA 2010-2013. knicholasforti@gmail.com

FORTKAMP, Frank (Md) 1840 Canvasback Lane, Columbus OH 43215 **Died 2/26/2017** B Columbus OH 1938 s Herman & Freda. BA Josephinum 1960; MA OH SU 1968; PhD OH SU 1971. Rec 5/5/2002 as Priest Bp John L Rabb. m 1/15/1975 Deborah Fortkamp c 1. R Gr Ch Brunswick MD 2002-2009.

FORTNA, Robert Tomson (NY) 720 W End Ave Apt 818, New York NY 10025 **Died 2/6/2017** B Lincoln NE 1930 s Ralph & Gertrude. BA Ya 1952; BD CDSP 1955; MA U of Cambridge 1959; ThD UTS 1965. D 10/13/1956 P 4/1/1957 Bp Sumner Walters. m 8/27/1960 Evelyn Nelson Fortna c 3. Asst Chr Ch Poughkeepsie NY 1963-1995; Prof of Rel Vassar 1963-1993; Asst S Mary's Manhattanville Epis Ch New York NY 1960-1963; Vic S Mary's Ch Manteca CA 1956-1958; Tutor/Instr CDSP Berkeley CA 1955-1960. Auth, "Scholars Bible: Matt," Polebridge Press, 2005; Auth, "Fourth Gospel & Its Predecessor," Fortress, 1987; Auth, "Gospel of Signs," Cambridge, 1970. SBL 1954; Soc of NT Stds 1968. Annual Prof Albright Archeological Inst 1979; Fllshp Ecum Inst of Advncd Theol Study 1972.

FORTNER, Marian Dulaney (Miss) 509 W Pine St, Hattiesburg MS 39401 **R Trin Ch Hattiesburg MS 2009-** B Tunica MS 1956 d John & Dorothy. BA U of Mississippi 1978; JD U of Mississippi 1981; MDiv GTS 1996. D 6/22/1996 P 2/15/1997 Bp Alfred Marble Jr. m 6/9/2001 Thomas M Fortner c 1. Assoc R/P-in-c All SS Ch Phoenix AZ 2005-2009; P-in-c S Chris's Ch Jackson MS 2004-2005; Chapl S Andr's Epis Sch Ridgeland MS 1999-2005; Cur S Jas Ch Greenville MS 1996-1999; Title IV Disciplinary Bd Dio Mississippi Jackson MS 2011-2012, Co-Fac of Post Ord Consult 2011-, Co-Fac of Post Ord Consult 2011-.

FORTUNA, Lisa (Mass) Christ Church Iglesia San Juan, 1220 River St, Hyde Park MA 02136 B Carolina PR 1969 d Antonio & Maria. BA Yale Coll 1991; MD U of Med and Dentistry of New Jersey 1996; MDiv EDS 2012. D 6/2/2012 Bp Gayle Harris P 1/13/2013 Bp M(Arvil) Thomas Shaw. m 7/6/2006 Michelle Vicki Porche c 1. Iglesia De San Juan Hyde Pk MA 2012-2015.

FORTUNA BSG, Virgilio (Mass) 2112 County St, Somerset MA 02726 **D Ch Of Our Sav Somerset MA 2012-** B Portugal 1957 s Jose & Deodete. D 6/16/2012 Bp M(Arvil) Thomas Shaw. m 6/5/2004 Barry Turley.

FORTUNATO, Susan Boykin (NY) 82 Ehrhardt Rd, Pearl River NY 10965 **Chr Ch Poughkeepsie NY 2015-** B Nacogdoches TX 1967 d Richard & Mitylene. Sweet Briar Coll 1987; BA Seton Hall U 1996; MDiv Drew U 1999. D 6/5/1999 Bp John Palmer Croneberger P 12/11/1999 Bp John Shelby Spong. m 1/10/2015 Catherine E Gorlin c 1. R S Steph's Ch Pearl River NY 2001-2015; Asst S Jas Ch Montclair NJ 1999-2001.

FORTUNE, Dwight Chapman (Mass) 246 Mount Hope St, North Attleboro MA 02760 **Ret 1989-** B Fitchburg MA 1927 s John & Gladys. BA Amer Intl Coll 1958; MDiv Ya Berk 1962. D 6/16/1962 P 5/26/1963 Bp William A Lawrence. c 5. Int S Mart's Ch Pawtucket RI 2000-2002; S Jn The Evang Mansfield MA 1978-1989; R S Jn's Epis Ch Tauton MA 1978-1989; All SS Epis Ch Attleboro MA 1976-1978, Int R 1976-1978, 1974-1975; Int S Paul's Ch Malden MA

1975-1976; R S Jn's Ch Sharon MA 1965-1974; Cur S Ptr's Ch Beverly MA 1962-1965.

FOSS, Charles Sanford (USC) 1646 SW Spence Ave, Troutdale OR 97060 B Danville VA 1949 s Robert & Olive. BA Ya 1971; MDiv Sewanee: The U So, TS 1978; PhD Grad Theol Un Berkeley CA 1989. D 6/3/1978 P 5/23/1979 Bp George Moyer Alexander. m 4/21/1974 Gwendolyn F Foss c 2. R Ch Of Our Sav Rock Hill SC 1997-2011; Asst S Jas By The Sea La Jolla CA 1988-1997; Asst S Jas Epis Ch Greenville SC 1978-1982. Auth, "Karl Barth & the Word of God in the So," *S Lk's Journ of Theol*, 1985.

FOSTER III, Andrew William (NY) 790 Plymouth Rd, Claremont CA 91711 B Rockville Centre NY 1944 s Andrew & Doris. BS Mt Un Coll 1966; STB GTS 1970. D 6/27/1970 P 2/21/1971 Bp William Foreman Creighton. m 5/28/1969 Lynda A Foster c 2. R Ch Of The Ascen New York NY 1999-2012; R S Paul's Ch In Nantucket Nantucket MA 1993-1999; Chapl Ken Gambier OH 1986-1993; Chapl Ken Gambier OH 1986-1993; Pres ESMHE 1984-1986; Strng Com ESMHE 1981-1986; Chapl Epis Stdt Fndt Ann Arbor MI 1972-1986; Cur Gr Ch Washington DC 1970-1972. Auth, "Epis Chapl On Campus: Observations Of The Ch'S MHE," 1983. Fllshp Soc Of S Jn The Evang.

FOSTER, Craig Arthur (SO) 508 Thistle Dr, Delaware OH 43015 **Mgr Honda Of Amer Mfg 1986-** B Hastings MI 1954 s John & Juliette. BS U of Iowa 1977. D 6/23/2007 Bp Thomas Edward Breidenthal. m 8/10/2002 Kathleen Foster. S Jn's Ch Columbus OH 2007-2017.

FOSTER, Guy Roland (NY) 12408 Cambridge Village Loop, Apex NC 27502 **Ret 1990-** B Beckley WV 1925 s Walter & Dorothy. BA Tusculum Coll 1946; BD UTS 1949; STM GTS 1957; PhD U of Edinburgh Edinburgh Gb 1963; DD Nash 1974; Nash 1974; ThD U of Glasgow Glasgow Gb 1977. D 6/7/1950 P 12/1/1950 Bp Theodore N Barth. m 9/16/1950 Anna Foster. Dn/Prof of Ch Hist The GTS New York NY 1973-1989; SubDean/Prof of Ch Hist Nash Nashotah WI 1964-1973; SubDean/Prof of Ch Hist Dom And Frgn Mssy Soc- Epis Ch Cntr New York NY 1952-1964; P-in-c S Paul's Ch Athens TN 1950-1952. Auth, "Role Of Presding Bp," Forw Mvmt, 1982; Auth, "Reformation & Revolution," *The Ch Before the Covenants*, Scottish Acad Press, 1975; Auth, "Bp & Presb," S.P.C.K., 1957.

FOSTER, Katharine K (SO) 7919 N Coolville Ridge Rd, Athens OH 45701 **S Geo's Ch Clifton Pk NY 2000-; P S Jn's Ripley WV 2000-; Team Chr Ch Point Pleasat WV 1998-** B Akron OH 1941 d Arthur & Virginia. BS Kent St U 1963; MLS Case Wstrn Reserve U 1965; Cert Dio So Diac Sch 1991. D 5/4/1991 Bp William Grant Black P 6/26/2002 Bp David Colin Jones. m 8/1/1970 Theodore S Foster. D Ch Of The Gd Shpd Athens OH 1993-1998.

FOSTER JR, Kenneth Earl (Mil) 1418 Valley Dr, Wisconsin Dells WI 53965 **D H Cross Epis Ch Wisconsis Dells WI 2001-** B Kilbourn (Wisconsin Dells) WI 1933 s Kenneth & Blanche. BBA U of Wisconsin 1955. D 1/13/2001 Bp Roger John White. m 10/7/1967 Lucille Mae Foster c 3.

FOSTER, Malcolm Lysle (LI) 5 Riverside Drive, Apt 8D, New York NY 10023 **Died 9/11/2016** B Valley NE 1927 s Edwin & Frances. BMus U MI 1949; SMM UTS 1951; MDiv GTS 1955. D 6/5/1955 P 12/18/1955 Bp Horace W B Donegan. m 6/16/1956 Marilyn Foster c 2. P-in-c S Andr's Dune Chap Southampton NY 1969-1988; P-in-c S Andr's Dune Ch Southampton 1969-1988; R S Jn's Epis Ch Southampton NY 1966-1988; R S Ptr's Epis Ch Peekskill NY 1959-1966; Cur Ch Of The Resurr New York NY 1955-1959. Pi Kappa Lambda U MI 1949.

FOSTER, Margaret Reidpath (WNY) 1088 Delaware Ave Apt 5a, Buffalo NY 14209 **Chapl Epis Ch Hm 1992-** B New York NY 1930 d James & Dorothy. AA Cazenovia Jr Coll 1950. D 11/23/1991 Bp David Charles Bowman. c 3. AEHC; Curs, EFM.

FOSTER, Pamela LaMotte (Mass) 19 Warren Point Rd, Wareham MA 02571 B Danville PA 1941 d William & Mary. BA U CA 1963; MDiv Pittsburgh TS 1984. D 6/2/1984 P 1/12/1985 Bp Alden Moinet Hathaway. m 8/24/1963 Donald Foster c 3. Assoc R Trin Ch Epis Boston MA 2000-2008; Sr Assoc Chr Ch Alexandria VA 1995-2000; Asst Calv Ch Pittsburgh PA 1987-1995; Int R Ch Of The Adv Pittsburgh PA 1986-1987.

FOSTER, Penelope Hope (WNY) 54 Delaware Rd, Kenmore NY 14217 **D Ch Of The Adv Buffalo NY 2008-** B Lachine Canada 1947 d Donald & Dorothy. D 10/18/2008 Bp Michael Garrison. m 5/24/1969 Ronald Foster c 2.

FOSTER, Randal Arthur (NC) 105 Pettingill Pl, Southern Pines NC 28387 **Emm Par Epis Ch Sthrn Pines NC 2009-, Asst/Day Sch Chapl 1990-1991** B Asheboro NC 1956 s Albert & Virginia. BA U NC 1979; MDiv VTS 1988; MA U NC 1999; DMin GTF 2004; PhD GTF 2009; PhD Other 2009. D 6/30/1990 Bp Robert Whitridge Estill P 6/29/1991 Bp Huntington Williams Jr. m 5/21/1994 Roberta M Adams. S Paul's In The Pines Epis Ch Fayetteville NC 2001-2005; All SS Ch Hamlet NC 1993-1999; R Ch Of The Mssh Rockingham NC 1993-1999; Asst S Mary's Epis Ch High Point NC 1991-1993. Conf Of S Ben 1999.

FOSTER, Simon (LI) 808 Driggs Ave Apt 5B, Brooklyn NY 11211 B 1963 Cert Chichester Theol Coll; BA U of Kent. Trans 1/1/2006 Bp Orris George Walker Jr. R S Jn's Of Lattingtown Locust Vlly NY 2009-2014, P-in-c 2006-2009, Int 2003-2006, Assoc R 2002-2003.

FOSTER, Steve Leslie (LI) 13728 244th St, Rosedale NY 11422 **Cathd Chapt - Mem S Ptr's Ch Rosedale NY 2013-; Cathd Of The Incarn Garden City NY 2013-; Black Cler Caucus - VP Dio Long Island Garden City NY 2012-, The Dept of Mssn 2008-2009, The Dioc Revs Com 2005-2010** B Barbados 1976 s Marcia. BS CUNY- Brooklyn Coll 2001; MDiv GTS 2004. D 5/26/2004 P 2/21/2004 Bp Orris George Walker Jr. m 4/30/2011 Krisann F Foster c 1. P-in-c S Bon Epis Ch Lindenhurst NY 2006-2013; Cur S Geo's Ch Hempstead NY 2004-2006; Bd Trst - Treas/Mem Geo Mercer TS Garden City NY 2007-2011. 100 Black Men of Long Island Inc 2010; Rotary Club of Lindenhurst 2012.

FOSTER, Todd (Oly) **Epiph Par of Seattle Seattle WA 2016-** B 1974 s James & Joan. B.S. Virginia Tech 1995; M.S. Abilene Chr U 1999; M.Div. Abilene Chr U 2006. D 12/12/2015 P 6/21/2016 Bp Gregory Harold Rickel. m 5/31/1997 Rebecca Sue Barnhill c 2. Other Lay Position S Paul Epis Ch Bellingham WA 2014-2015.

FOSTER, Willis Renard (SVa) 228 Halifax St, Petersburg VA 23803 **R S Steph's Ch Petersburg VA 2010-** B Greensboro NC 1948 s Willis & Linnie. BS No Carolina A&T St U 1970; MS Troy U 1991; MDiv VTS 2010. D 6/12/2010 P 12/18/2010 Bp Herman Hollerith IV. m 6/23/2007 Duanne Foster c 4.

FOTCH JR, Charlton Harvey (Cal) 681 S Eliseo Dr, Greenbrae CA 94904 **Asst St Johns Epis Ch Ross CA 1989-** B Buffalo NY 1945 s Charlton & Dolores. BA Baldwin-Wallace Coll 1967; MDiv GTS 1970. D 6/29/1970 P 1/9/1971 Bp Harold Barrett Robinson. m 4/6/1991 Sheila Dutton c 1. Chapl Manatee Cmnty Coll 1978-1987; Sarasota Dnry Chapl Sarasota FL 1978-1987; R S Mk's Epis Ch Moscow PA 1974-1978; P-in-c S Paul's Epis Ch Stafford NY 1972-1974; Asst S Jas' Ch Batavia NY 1970-1974. Auth, "Growing Pains (Poem)," 1984.

FOTINOS, Dennis George (Tex) 248 Birchbark Dr., Mills River NC 28759 B Dayton OH 1945 s Dennis & Frances. BA U of Miami 1967; STB GTS 1971. D 5/31/1971 P 5/27/1972 Bp James Loughlin Duncan. m 5/26/1973 Barbara Hemphill c 2. R Ch Of The Gd Shpd Kingwood TX 1993-2008; R Trin Cathd Pittsburgh PA 1987-1993; R S Tim's Ch Alexandria LA 1983-1987; Vic Epis Ch Of S Ptr's By The Lake Denver NC 1983; Chapl CT Lincolnton NC 1979-1983; Vic S Andr Ch Mt Holly NC 1974-1982; Asst S Mk The Evang Ft Lauderdale FL 1971-1974. CT - Assoc 1980-1993.

FOUGHTY, Donna (Va) 7414 Heatherfield Ln, Alexandria VA 22315 **S Mk's Ch Alexandria VA 2017-, Assoc 1998-2002** B Ridgewood NJ 1953 d Domenica & Clara. BA Ramapo St Coll 1978; EFM 1984; MDiv VTS 1995. D 10/10/1987 Bp Craig Barry Anderson P 6/26/2002 Bp David Colin Jones. m 6/22/1974 Michael Arthur Foughty c 2. S Thos Epis Ch Mclean VA 2013; P-in-c The Ch Of The Epiph Oak Hill VA 2009-2012; Cleric Pohick Epis Ch Lorton VA 2007-2008; Asst Olivet Epis Ch Alexandria VA 2005; long term supply S Patricks Ch Falls Ch VA 2005; long term supply All SS Ch Alexandria VA 2004; Int S Marg's Ch Woodbridge VA 2003-2004; Int S Geo's Epis Ch Arlington VA 2002-2003; D Emm Epis Par Rapid City SD 1989-1992; Vol Chapl US-AF Chap Florennes Belgium 1987-1988; Diocesion Evang Com Dio So Dakota Pierre SD 1990-1992. All SS Sis of the Poor 2007; Ord Of S Lk; Ord Of S Lk.

FOUKE, Scherry Vickery (ETenn) 1601 Forest Dr, Morristown TN 37814 B Royston GA 1945 d Paul & Louise. MDiv Candler TS Emory U 1988. D 10/19/1988 P 5/1/1989 Bp William Arthur Beckham. Stndg Com Dio E Tennessee Knoxville TN 2010-2013, Chapl, All SS' Epis Sch 2004-2011, Bp's Com on Inclusivity 2010-2013; R All SS' Epis Ch Morristown TN 2004-2013; Assoc R The Epis Ch Of The Adv Kennet Sq PA 2001-2004; R S Dunstans Ch Blue Bell PA 1995-2001; Assoc R Ch Of S Mart-In-The-Fields Philadelphia PA 1990-1995; Cur Ch Of The Resurr Greenwood SC 1988-1990; Dioc Liturg Cmsn Dio Pennsylvania Philadelphia PA 1996-1999, Dioc Stwdshp Com 1996-1999, Middle E Study Grp 1993-2002.

FOULKE, Mary Lona (NY) 521 West 126th Street, New York NY 10027 B Dayton OH 1962 d Kenneth & Madeline. BA Earlham Coll 1980; MDiv UTS 1989; EdD Col 1996. D 5/20/2001 P 1/12/2002 Bp Frederick Houk Borsch. m 10/12/1991 Renee Leslie Hill c 2. Sr. Assoc The Ch Of S Lk In The Fields New York NY 2002-2014; All SS Ch Pasadena CA 2002; Sr. Assoc for Chld & Families All SS Ch Pasadena CA 1998-2002; Consult for Educ St. Mary's Manhattanville Harlem NY 1993-1996. mlf.stmarysharlem@gmail.com

FOUNTAIN, Timothy Logan (SD) 2707 W. 33rd St, Sioux Falls SD 57105 **P-in-c Dio So Dakota Pierre SD 2016-** B Los Angeles CA 1958 s Erman & Mary. BA USC 1982; MDiv GTS 1987. D 6/27/1987 P 1/23/1988 Bp Oliver Bailey Garver Jr. m 5/26/1990 Melissa Ann Fountain c 2. R Ch Of The Gd Shpd Sioux Falls SD 2004-2015; Vic S Jn Chrys Ch Rcho Sta Marg CA 1995-2004; Vic S Alb's Epis Ch Yucaipa CA 1991-1995; Assoc R S Nich Par Encino CA 1989-1991; Cur S Ptr's Par San Pedro CA 1987-1989; US-A 1977-1980. Host, "Nthrn Plains Anglicans," http://northernplainsanglicans.blogspot.com, 2007; Auth, "Imperious Control," *Orange Cnty Register*, 2002; Auth, "Deeds Of Evil Men," *Orange Cnty Register*, 2001. Outstanding Sermon Epis Ntwk For Stwdshp 1999; Us Army Achievement Medal Us Army 1982. rector.gsc@midconetwork.com

FOUT, Jason A (WMich) 591 Sheridan Ave, Bexley OH 43209 **Prof Bex Sem Columbus OH 2009-** B Waukegan IL 1971 s Glenn & Janice. BA U IL 1992; MTS SWTS 2001; MDiv SWTS 2001; PhD Camb 2010. D 6/16/2001 Bp Bill

Persell P 12/15/2001 Bp Edward Lewis Lee Jr. m 12/16/1995 Kristen G Gurga c 2. Cur S Paul's Epis Ch St Jos MI 2001-2005.

FOUTS, Guy (WA) 603 Ramapo Ave, Pompton Lakes NJ 07442 **P-in-c Gr Ch Un City NJ 2012-** B Panama 1944 s Ben & Aura. BA U of Washington 1972; GOE U of Cambridge 1981; DMin SWTS 1998. Trans 11/1/1989 Bp William Grant Black. m 7/31/2017 Carol L Martin c 4. P-in-c S Paul's Epis Par Pt Of Rocks MD 1999-2000; R S Mary Magd Ch Silver Sprg MD 1991-2000; Int S Mk's Ch Warren RI 1990-1991; Int S Pat's Epis Ch Dublin OH 1988-1989; Serv Ch In Engl 1981-1989. Int Mnstry Ntwk 1987-1998; Natl Assn Of Epis Int Mnstry Spec 1999-2001.

FOWLE, Elizabeth Heller (WMass) 15 Old Hancock Rd., Hancock NH 03449 B Pittsburgh PA 1942 d Milton & Suzanne. BA Smith 1964; MA S Jos Coll W Hartford CT 1987; MDiv Ya Berk 1993. D 6/12/1993 P 2/2/1994 Bp Arthur Edward Walmsley. m 6/20/1964 Stephen Parker Fowle c 3. R All SS Ch So Hadley MA 2000-2008; Assoc R Chr Ch Winnetka IL 1996-2000, Cur 1993-1995; Dioc Coun Dio Wstrn Massachusetts Springfield 2006-2008, Chair, COM 2003-2006, COM 2001-2008; Search and Nomin Cmte for Bp Dio Chicago Chicago IL 1997-1998.

FOWLER, Anne Carroll (Mass) 39 Prospect Street, Portland ME 04103 **Bd Mem Planned Parenthood of Nthrn New Engl 2015-** B Portland ME 1946 d Alexander & Sally. BA Rad 1968; MA Bos 1971; PhD Bos 1979; MDiv EDS 1984; Cert Boston Coll 2013. D 6/1/1985 Bp John Bowen Coburn P 5/3/1986 Bp David Elliot Johnson. m 1/18/1992 Samuel Miller Allen c 3. R S Jn's Ch Jamaica Plain MA 1992-2013; R All SS Ch Stoneham MA 1988-1992; Asst S Dunstans Epis Ch Dover MA 1985-1988; Pres Maine Rel Cltn Against Discrimination 2015-2016. Auth, "The Case of the Restless Redhead," Antrim Hse Books, 2015; Auth, "What I Could," Pudding Hse Press, 2009; Auth, "Whiskey Stitching," Pudding Hse Press, 2007; Auth, "Sum of Salvage," Pudding Hse Press, 2007; Auth, "Five Islands," Pudding Hse Press, 2002; Auth, "Liz, Wear Those Pearl Earrings," Frank Cat Press, 2002; Ed, "Models For Writing". AAPC 2014. Barbara C. Harris Awd A Wmn Committed to Soc Transformation 2013; Distinguished Alum EDS 2013; Abigail Adams Awd Massachusetts Womens' Political Caucus 2002.

FOWLER, Arlen Lowery (Okla) 817 Virginia Ln, Ardmore OK 73401 **Vic S Mk's Ch Hugo OK 2002-; Ret 1995-; Ret 1995-** B Bartlesville OK 1928 s Benjamin & Emma. BA Oklahoma St U 1952; MDiv PrTS 1957; PhD WA SU 1968. D 11/20/1971 P 3/1/1972 Bp Albert A Chambers. m 11/25/1950 Mary Fowler c 4. R S Phil's OK 1983-1995; R St Phil's Epis Ch Ardmore OK 1983-1995; Assoc R S Dunst's Ch Tulsa OK 1982-1983; Serv as Presb and Ecum Campus Chapl WA SU 1963-1966; Serv as Presb Campus Chapl Texas A&M 1960-1963. "Facing Auschwitz, A Chr Imperative," iUniverse, 2003; Auth, "The Black Infantry in the W, 1869-1891," U of Oklahoma Press, 1996; "From Blinking Lights to Stdt Rts," *Dialog, Vol l, No. 2*, The U of Tulsa, 1977; "The Black Cavalry in the W," *The Dictionary of Amer Hist*, Chas Scribner' Sons, 1976; "The Black Infantry in the W," *The Dictionary of Amer Hist*, Chas Scribner's Sons, 1976; "Chapl D. Eglington Barr: A Lincoln Yankee," *The Hist mag of the Prot Epis Ch*, 1976; Auth, "The Black Infantry in the W," Greenwood,Publ, 1974.

FOWLER, Connetta Bertrand (NwT) 430 Dallas St, Big Spring TX 79720 **D The Epis Ch Of S Mary The Vrgn Big Sprg TX 2002-** B Mamou LA 1943 BS McNeese St U; MS U of Texas. D 10/27/2002 Bp C Wallis Ohl.

FOWLER, Daniel Lewis (Oly) 4335 NE Rhodes End Rd, Bainbridge Island WA 98110 **D S Barn Epis Ch Bainbridge Island WA 2008-** B Visalia CA 1943 s Geroge & Ruth. BS San Jose St U 1966; BA Sch for Deacons 1983. D 2/21/1986 Bp Charles Shannon Mallory. m 6/12/1966 Patricia Anne Fowler c 3. The Ch Of The H Sprt Lake Forest IL 1997-2005; Archd Dio El Camino Real Salinas CA 1986-1997.

FOWLER III, Robert (Ala) St Margaret's Episcopal Church, 606 Newnan St, Carrollton GA 30117 **S Lk's Epis Ch Jacksonville AL 2015-** B Atlanta GA 1960 s Robert & Laura. BSBC Georgia Inst of Tech 1982; MHer.Pres. Georgia St U 1989; MBA Georgia SW St U 2002; MDiv Sewanee: The U So, TS 2013; MDiv The TS at The U So 2013. D 12/15/2012 P 6/22/2013 Bp Robert Christopher Wright. c 2. Cur S Marg's Ch Carrollton GA 2013-2015.

FOWLER, Stanley Gordon (Cal) 111 Ne 80th St, Seattle WA 98115 B Los Angeles,CA 1946 s Gordon & Olga. BA U CA 1967; MDiv SFTS 1971; MA Santa Clara U 1976. D 6/24/1972 Bp George Richard Millard P 4/29/1973 Bp Chauncie Kilmer Myers. m 6/15/1968 Jeanne S Fowler c 1. R S Andr's Ch Seattle WA 1982-2004; Vic S Jn The Div Epis Ch Morgan Hill CA 1976-1982; Non-par 1974-1976; Assoc Gd Samar Epis Ch San Jose CA 1972-1974.

FOWLER IV, William Young (Tex) Po Box 292, Buda TX 78610 **S Paul's Ch Waco TX 2016-; Chr Epis Ch Temple TX 2014-** B Broadwater County MT 1952 s William & Mary. BA U of Texas 1974; JD U of Texas 1977; MDiv Sewanee: The U So, TS 2000. D 6/1/2000 P 2/9/2001 Bp James Edward Folts. m 5/11/2002 Deborah F Fowler. Ch Of The Epiph Houston TX 2013-2014; H Sprt Epis Ch Houston TX 2012-2013; Trin Ch Galveston TX 2009-2011; R S Thos Epis Ch Coll Sta TX 2005-2009; Vic S Eliz's Epis Ch Buda TX 2000-2005.

FOWLKES, Tyrone (Cal) 530 W Fullerton Pkwy, Chicago IL 60614 **P-Consult Ch Of The H Cross Chicago IL 2012-** B Indianapolis IN 1970 s Thomas & Rosie. BFA Indiana U 1988; MDiv Chr TS 2000; MAM Columbia Coll Chicago 2008; Cert SWTS 2008. D 6/7/2008 P 12/6/2008 Bp Jeff Lee. R S Aug's Ch Oakland CA 2013-2015; Dir. of Sprtl Formation UCAN - Chicago Il 2010-2012; Asstg P Ch Of Our Sav Chicago IL 2008-2009. FCREATOR2002@YAHOO.COM

FOX, Carol Rogers (NY) 312 West 22nd Street, New York NY 10011 B Roxboro NC 1941 d Nathaniel & Vera. BA Duke 1963; BD Duke 1966; STM UTS 1974; MPhil UTS 1984; Cert Blanton-Peale Grad Inst 1996; Cert Blanton-Peale Grad Inst 1996; CAS GTS 2001; STM GTS 2002. D 3/16/2002 P 9/21/2002 Bp Mark Sean Sisk. c 1. Psychoanalyst Riverside Counslg Cntr 1997-2012. "Modesty & Mystery," Un Sem Quarterly Revs, 1984; "Liberation to Wholeness," The Chr Hm, 1974; "Male & Female - He Created Them," The Chr Hm, 1974.

FOX, Cheryl Lynn (NY) 175 9th Ave # 262, New York NY 10011 B Glendale CA 1952 d James & Mazie. BA USC 1973; MDiv GTS 2009. D 10/24/2008 P 8/15/2009 Bp Dan Thomas Edwards. m 7/17/1988 Tex L Fox. The Ch Of The Epiph And S Simon Brooklyn NY 2010-2013. epiphanysimon@verizon.net

FOX, David Coblentz (Okla) 2455 Sulphur Creek St, Cody WY 82414 **Assoc Chr Ch Cody WY 2005-** B Wyandotte MI 1941 s Arthur & Helen. BA Heidelberg U 1963; BD Bex Sem 1966. D 6/29/1966 Bp Archie H Crowley P 3/4/1967 Bp Richard Stanley Merrill Emrich. m 6/26/1965 Lynn Usher c 3. R S Jn's Epis Ch Tulsa OK 1979-2004; R S Ptr's Ch Tecumseh MI 1973-1979; Chapl St Prison Jackson MI 1970-1973; R Chr Ch Pleasant Lake MI 1967-1973; Cur S Tim's Ch Detroit MI 1966-1967.

FOX, Deborah (NC) 2208 Hope St, Raleigh NC 27607 **Epis Campus Mnstry No Carolina St U Raleigh NC 2004-** B Crisfield MO 1949 d Harry & Dorothy. D 6/24/2000 P 3/24/2001 Bp Clifton Daniel III. Chapl Dio No Carolina Raleigh NC 2003-2017, 2003; Ch Of The Gd Shpd Wilmington NC 2000-2003; Asst S Phil's Ch Southport NC 2000.

FOX, Donald Allan (Cal) 185 Baltimore Way, San Francisco CA 94112 **Assoc P S Aid's Ch San Francisco CA 2009-; Mem, China Friendship Com Dio California San Francisco CA 1990-, Mem, Asian Cmsn 1986-1995, Mem, Dept of Wrld Mssn 1973-1976** B Waterloo IA 1940 s Robert & Fern. U of Nthrn Iowa 1960; AB U Chi 1962; DB U Chi DS 1966; DB U Chi DS 1966; Gesamteuropaisches Studienwerk Germany 1968; Cuddesdon Theol Coll Engl 1969. D 4/4/1970 P 4/21/1971 Bp Ivol I Curtis. San Francisco Night Mnstry San Francisco CA 1995-2006; True Sunshine Par San Francisco CA 1986-1995; San Rafael Canal Mnstry San Rafael CA 1983-1984; Asst Prof Simpson Coll San Francisco CA 1982-1987; Asst P S Paul's Epis Ch San Rafael CA 1982-1986; Instr Dominican Coll San Rafael CA 1982; Epis Chapl Stanford Cbury Fndt Palo Alto CA 1976-1979; Assoc R S Fran' Epis Ch San Francisco CA 1973-1976; Cur S Thos Epis Ch Medina WA 1972-1973; Cur S Jn's Epis Ch Olympia WA 1970-1972. EPF 1970-1982; Integrity 1980-1982.

FOX III, Frederick Carl (Nwk) 441 Lockhart Mountain Rd Unit 4, Lake George NY 12845 **Ret 1996-** B Poughkeepsie NY 1936 s Frederick & Ann. BA Un Coll Schenectady NY 1958; STB Ya Berk 1961; NYU 1981. D 6/10/1961 P 12/16/1961 Bp Horace W B Donegan. m 12/28/1957 Norma F Fox c 3. Asian Mnstrs Coun Dio Newark Newark NJ 1990-1996, Comp Dioc Relatnpshp W Hong Kong & Macao 1987-1992, Mnstry To Persons Of Chinese Hertiage 1987-1992, Secy & Treas 1969-1996, Dept Ce 1967-1996, Dioc Coun 1992-1996; R S Paul's Ch N Arlington NJ 1968-1996; R All SS' Epis Ch Glen Rock NJ 1965-1968; R Ch Of S Mary The Vrgn Ridgefield Pk NJ 1963-1965; Cur Gr Epis Ch Utica NY 1961-1963. AAR; Rel Educ Assn Of The Untd States And Can; SBL.

FOX, Jed (Oly) 6345 Wydown Blvd, Saint Louis MO 63105 **R Ch Of The Redeem Kenmore WA 2015-** B Helena MT 1982 s John & Sarah. BA Carroll Coll 2006; MDiv GTS 2009. D 10/5/2008 P 5/31/2009 Bp Charles Franklin Brookhart Jr. m 5/27/2006 Mary E Jager c 1. Cur S Mich & S Geo S Louis MO 2009-2014.

FOX, Loren Charles (CFla) Tang-Lin, Minden Road 24881 Singapore **R Ch of Our Sav Palm Bay FL 2007-** B Hartford CT 1962 s Calvin & Mildred. BS U Roch 1984; MA Fuller TS 1988; MDiv TESM 1993. D 7/10/1993 Bp David Mercer Schofield P 2/1/1994 Bp John Wadsworth Howe. m 7/12/1986 Linda Susan Pan c 2. St Georges Ch Tanglin 2000-2005; Angl Frontier Missions Richmond VA 1997-2000; Trin Ch Vero Bch FL 1993-1997.

FOX, Matthew Timothy (Cal) 287 17th St Ste 400, Oakland CA 94612 B Madison WI 1940 s George & Beatrice. BA Aquinas Inst of Theol 1961; MA Aquinas Inst of Theol 1963; MA Aquinas Inst of Theol 1967; PhD Institut Catholique De Paris 1970. Rec 12/1/1994 as Priest Bp William Edwin Swing. Pres U Of Creation Spuirituality Oakland CA. Auth, "Creativity: Where The Div And The Human Meet," Tarcher, 2002; Auth, "Original Blessing," Tarcher, 2000; Auth, "One River," *Many Wells: Wisdom Springing From Global Paths*, Tarcher, 2000; Auth, "Sins Of The Sprt," *Blessings Of The Flesh*, Harmony, 1999; Auth, "Confessions: The Making Of A Post-Denominational P," Harper San Francisco, 1996; Auth, "Natural Gr (w Rsheldrake)," Doubleday, 1996; Auth, "The Physics Of Ang," Harper San Francisco, 1996; Auth, "Wrestling w

The Prophets: Essays In Creation," Tarcher, 1995; Auth, "Reinvention Of Wk," Harper San Francisco, 1995; Auth, "In The Beginning There Was Joy," Godfield, 1995; Auth, "Sheer Joy:Conversations w Thos Aquinas On Creat," *Sheer Joy:Conversations w Thos Aquinas On Creation Sprtlty*, Tarcher, 1992; Auth, "Creation Sprtlty: Liberating Gifts For Peoples Of Earth," Harper San Francisco, 1991; Auth, "Coming Of Cosmic Chr," Harper & Row, 1988; Auth, "Hildegard Of Bingen'S Bk Of Div Wk," *w Letters & Songs (Edited)*, Bear & Co, 1987; Auth, "Illuminations Of Hildegard Of Bingen," Bear & Co, 1985; Auth, "A Sprtlty Named Compassion," Inner Traditions, 1984; Auth, "Meditations w Meister Eckhart," Inner Traditions, 1982; Auth, "Manifetso For Global Civilization (w Bswimme)," Bear & Co, 1982; Auth, "Wstrn Sprtlty: Hist Roots," *Ecum Routes (Edited)*, Bear & Co, 1981; Auth, "Whee! We," *Wee All The Way Hm*, Inner Traditions, 1981; Auth, "Breakthrough," Image, 1980; Auth, "On Becoming A Mus," *Mystical Bear: Sprtlty Amer Style*, Paulist Press, 1972. Doctor Of Letters (Hon) U Of Cape Breton 2002; Courage Of Conscience Awd Peace Abbey 1995; 10th Anniv Awd New York Open Cntr 1994; Tikkun Natl Ethics Awd Tikkun.

FOX, Ralph Steven (U) 136 E 57th St Ste 405, New York NY 10022 **Non-par 1985-** B Fort Campbell KY 1955 s Ralph & Martha. BA Indiana U 1980; MDiv UTS 1984. D 6/6/1984 Bp Otis Charles. Sprtl Care Counslr Beth Israel Med Cntr New York NY 1987-1988; D S Lk's Ch Pk City UT 1984-1985. Auth, "Visions & Voices Of The New Midwest"; Auth, "Crowley On Drugs". EUC, AAR, Cg Jung Fndt.

FOX, Richard George (Mil) South 24 West 26835 Apache Pass, Waukesha WI 53188 **Chapl Waukesha Memi Hosp Waukesha WI 2006-; D St Mths Epis Ch Waukesha WI 1994-; St Philips Epis Ch Waukesha WI 1994-; Non-par assignment, Stff Jas Place Waukesha WI 2010-** B Michigan City IN 1943 s Edward & Mildred. Cert U of Wisconsin; BS Wstrn Michigan U 1965; MA Wstrn Michigan U 1967; PhD U of Kansas 1974; Cert Inst for Chr Stuides 1993; Cert Inst for Chr Stuides 1993. D 10/22/1994 Bp Roger John White. m 6/24/1976 Catherine A Fox c 2. Assn of Epis Healthcare Chapl; NAAD.

FOX, Ronald Napoleon (SeFla) 3464 Oak Ave, Miami FL 33133 B Fort Pierce FL 1944 s Rufus & Iris. BA S Augustines Coll Raleigh NC 1966; MDiv GTS 1969. D 6/18/1969 Bp Henry I Louttit P 12/21/1969 Bp James Loughlin Duncan. m 8/26/1967 Anita Fox c 3. R S Bern De Clairvaux N Miami Bch FL 1996-2010; Asst To Bp For Soc Concerns & Yth Mnstrs Dio SE Florida Miami 1992-1996; R Chr Epis Ch Miami FL 1982-1992; Chapl S Aug Coll Raleigh NC 1979-1982; S Aug's Coll Raleigh NC 1979-1982; S Tim's Epis Ch Daytona Bch FL 1974-1979; Vic S Mary's Epis Ch Of Deerfield Deerfield Bch FL 1969-1971; S Matt's Epis Ch Delray Bch FL 1969-1971. Hon Doctor Of Civil Laws S Aug'S Coll 1993; Mary Mccloud Bethune Awd Bethune Cookman Coll.

FOX, Sarah (Mich) 8500 Jackson Square Blvd Apt 5D, Shreveport LA 71115 B Ferriday LA 1939 d Joseph & Dorothy. LSU 1959; BS S Marys Dominican 1960; MDiv Epis TS of the SW 1984. D 6/25/1988 Bp Henry Irving Mayson P 2/1/1989 Bp R aymond Stewart Wood Jr. c 4. Assoc Int R S Mk's Ch Houston TX 2007, 2006; Asst S Steph's Epis Ch Houston TX 1996-2006, Asst to R 1984-1987; Int S Michaels In The Hills Toledo OH 1992-1993; COM Dio Michigan Detroit MI 1989-1992; Assoc S Jn's Ch Royal Oak MI 1988-1992.

FOX, Susann (Pa) 76 S Forge Manor Dr, Phoenixville PA 19460 **Non-par 2002-; Chapl Vitas Healthcare Corp. 2002-** B Hillsboro IL 1947 d Kenneth & Margaret. BS Estrn Illinois U 1969; MDiv Luth TS 1995; Cert Thos Jefferson U 2002; Lic Thos Jefferson U 2006. D 1/6/1988 Bp Allen Lyman Bartlett Jr. m 9/18/1971 Terrence M Fox c 1. Chap Samar Car Hospice Blue Bell PA 1997-2002; Serv Methodist Ch Thorndale PA 1995-2000; D/Asst S Giles Ch Upper Darby PA 1992-1995; Stff Chap Cathcart/Hutchinson Hse Presb Hm Inc 1991-1997; S Andr's In The Field Ch Philadelphia PA 1991; S Mary 's Ch Elverson PA 1990. Assembly Of Epis Hosp & Chapl; Soc Of Chapl.

FOX SR, Wesley D (ND) HC 2, Box 176, Garrison ND 58540 B Elbowoods ND 1940 s Robert & Naomi. Ft Lewis Coll 1968; Brigham Young U 1969; Minot St U 1977; MDiv Untd TS 1983. D 6/26/1988 P 5/1/1989 Bp Harold Anthony Hopkins Jr. m 12/27/1959 Yvonne Elizabeth Fox c 1. Vic S Paul's Ch Garrison ND 1995; Dio No Dakota Fargo ND 1989-2005; Vic S Sylvan Ch Dunseith Dunseith ND 1988-1995.

FOXWORTH, George Marion (NCal) 4338 Walali Way, Fair Oaks CA 95628 **Assoc S Mich's Epis Ch Carmichael CA 2006-; S Lk's Ch Woodland CA 2000-; Ret 1998-** B Sumter SC 1939 s George & Emma. BS Austin Peay St U 1963; MDiv VTS 1967. D 6/27/1967 P 6/1/1968 Bp Gray Temple. m 3/10/2010 Donita Foxworth c 3. R All SS Memi Sacramento CA 1986-1997; Ch Of The Resurr Pleasant Hil CA 1986; Cn Pstr Gr Cathd San Francisco CA 1980-1986; Chr Ch Greenville SC 1975-1980; P-in-c Ch Of The Gd Shpd Sumter SC 1970-1974; S Chris's Ch Sumter SC 1970-1974; Vic All SS Epis Ch Hampton SC 1967-1970; Ch Of The H Comm Allendale SC 1967-1970. Auth, "hon Friend Cdsp Alum 94," 1998; Auth, "You Are The Body," 1978. OHC 1988.

FOXX, Louis N (Mass) 397 Putnam Ave., Cambridge MA 02139 B Boston MA 1951 s Peace & Mildred. BA U of Massachusetts 1978; MDiv EDS 1981;

Advncd Cert EDS 2006; Cert Cler Ldrshp Inst 2011; Cert Cler Ldrshp Inst 2011. D 5/15/1982 Bp John Bowen Coburn P 5/1/1983 Bp John Melville Burgess. m 7/28/1973 Debre Foxx c 2. R S Barth's Epis Ch Cambridge MA 1988-2008; Vic S Mathias' Philadelphia PA 1984-1988; S Mths Ch Philadelphia PA 1984-1988; Parttime Asst S Cyp's Boston MA 1982-1984; parttime St. Paul's Cathd 1982-1984; Dio Massachusetts Boston MA 1982-1983. Fell AAMFT 2010; Partnr in Excellence Massachusetts Gnrl Hosp 2009; Polly Bond Awd ECom 2004; Cert of Appreciation St. Barth's Ch 1998; citizen of the year Omega Psi Phi Fraternity 1994; citizen of the year City of Cambridge 1992.

✠ FRADE, The Rt Rev Leo (SeFla) 525 NE 15th St, Miami FL 33132 B Havana CU 1943 s Leopoldo & Angela. BD Candler Coll De Marianao 1960; MDiv Sewanee: The U So, TS 1977; BA Biscayne Coll 1978. D 4/17/1977 P 10/17/1977 Bp James Loughlin Duncan Con 1/25/1984 for Hond. m 12/22/1987 Diana L Dillenberger c 2. Bp of SE Florida Dio SE Florida Miami 2000-2015, Secy - Hisp Cmsn 1977-1980; Dio Honduras San Pedro Sula 1984-2000; Bp of Honduras Iglesia Epis San Pablo Apostol San Pedro Sula 1984-2000; Dio Cntrl Florida Orlando FL 1982-1983; Dio Louisiana New Orleans LA 1978-1982; P-in-c Hisp Min Gr Ch New Orleans LA 1978-1982; Cur Santa Cruz-Resurr Epis Ch Biscayne Pk FL 1977-1978; Trst The GTS New York NY 1995-2000. "Winds of Change," *Memories of Wesley Frensdorff*, 1990. Alum Coun TS U So; Bro of S Greg; Fell Fund Theol Educ. D.D. Florida Cntr for Theol Stds 2006; DD ETSS 2001; DD STUSo 1989; DD GTS 1982. bishopfrade@aol.com

FRAIOLI, Karen Ann (Mass) 20 Rhodes Ave, Sharon MA 02067 B Oak Park IL 1946 d Wayland & Lois. BA Br 1968; MDiv Harvard DS 1993. D 6/18/1994 P 12/20/1994 Bp George Nelson Hunt III. m 8/17/1968 Edward Fraioli c 2. S Jn's Epis Ch Westwood MA 2011-2014, P-in-c 2011; Ch Of The Epiph Providence RI 1997-2009; Dio Rhode Island Providence RI 1997; Asst Gr Ch In Providence Providence RI 1994-1996. Catechesis Of The Gd Shpd 2000; Soc of Cath Priests 2010. Phi Beta Kappa.

FRALEY, Anne (Tenn) 1500 Hickory Ridge Rd, Lebanon TN 37087 B Hartford CT 1957 d Arthur & Anne. BA Earlham Coll 1979; MDiv Ya Berk 1994. D 12/10/1994 Bp Clarence Nicholas Coleridge P 6/24/1995 Bp David Reed. m 3/24/2006 Kenneth Fraley. P-in-c The Ch Of The Epiph Lebanon TN 2008-2011, 1999-2002, Vic/R 1999-2002; Int S Paul's Epis Ch Murfreesboro TN 2007-2008; Int S Jas The Less Madison TN 2006-2007; Wolfcraft Arts Mnstry 2005-2007; Mssnr Stem SE Tennessee Episc Mnstry Monteagle TN 2003-2005; Int S Jos Of Arimathaea Ch Hendersonvlle TN 2002-2003; Assoc S Ptr's Epis Ch S Louis MO 1995-1999; Asst Chr Ch Cathd Hartford CT 1994-1995.

FRANCE JR, Andrew Menaris (CPa) 651 Harding Ave, Williamsport PA 17701 B Baltimore MD 1937 s Andrew & Anna. BA Drew U 1962; BD VTS 1966; DMin Pittsburgh TS 1987. D 6/21/1966 P 6/8/1967 Bp Harry Lee Doll. m 8/12/1972 Dorothy D France c 3. R Trin Epis Ch Williamsport PA 1984-2007; R S Thos Ch In The Fields Gibsonia PA 1977-1984; Spec Asst S Marg's Ch Annapolis MD 1976-1977; Mid-Atlantic Career Cntr Inc Washington DC 1973-1977; Chapl Res St Hosp Sprg Grove MD 1971-1973; Asst Ch Of The Gd Shpd Towson MD 1967-1969; Asst Min S Anne's Par Annapolis MD 1966-1967. Auth, "Dvlpmt of Alternative Models of Direction for a Growing Par"; Auth, "Personal Plnng Mgmt for Leaders"; Auth, "Whole Life & Vocational Prog Manuals"; Auth, "Participant through Mid Atlantic Trng Cmsn"; Auth, "Whole Life & Vocation Prog Manuals". APC 1973-1990; AAPC 1973-1988; ACPE 1973-1988. Hon Cn of the Cathd Dio Cntrl Pennsylvania 1991.

FRANCE, Robert Lyle (Miss) 1050 Shady Ln, Tunica MS 38676 **Died 8/20/2015** B Memphis TN 1947 s Hulbert & Ruth. BS U of Mississippi 1969; MD U Cinc 1973; BA Trin Bristol GB 2003. Trans 5/1/2005 Bp Duncan Montgomery Gray Jr. m 1/29/1978 Betty France c 2. R Ch Of The Epiph Tunica MS 2005-2011.

FRANCES, Martha (Tex) 6405 Westward #65, Houston TX 77081 **R Hope Epis Ch Houston TX 2005-** B Dallas TX 1946 d Clarence & Frances. MA U of Houston 1977; MRE U of St Thos 1985; CAS Epis TS of the SW 1999; MDiv SMU Perkins 1999. D 11/30/2000 Bp Claude Edward Payne P 6/29/2001 Bp Leopoldo Jesus Alard. c 3. Hope Epis Ch Houston TX 2006-2010, 2005; Ch Of The Incarn Houston TX 2005; Vic Lord Of The St Epis Mssn Ch Houston TX 2000-2005; Pstr Asst S Paul's Ch Houston TX 1999-2000. Ord of S Helena - Assoc 1983.

FRANCIS SR, Alric H (VI) PO Box 7974, Christiansted VI 00823 Virgin Islands (U.S.) **St Peters Epis Ch St Croix VI 2014-** B 1963 s Ashley & Olga. BA Codrington Coll 2002. Trans 9/1/2014 Bp Edward Gumbs. m 2/19/1994 Gillian Diane Francis c 2.

FRANCIS, Desmond C (Alb) 2011 Trotter Ln, Bloomington IL 61704 B Madras IN 1953 s James & Constance. Dip Inst of Catering Tech Chennai 1974; BTh So India Biblic Sem Karnataka St 1978; MAR Asbury TS 1984; MDiv Asbury TS 1986; MTh Asbury TS 1987; DMiss Asbury TS 1989. Trans 6/1/1999 Bp Don Adger Wimberly. m 6/1/2016 Jean M Francis c 3. Chr The King Epis Ch Normal IL 2002-2015; S Mary's Epis Ch Middlesboro KY 1999-2001, P 1995-1999; S Andr's Ch Lexington KY 1995-1996; Serv Ch Of So India 1978-1983. Rotary Intl .

FRANCIS, Elaine Consuela (VI) PO Box 1148, St Thomas VI 00804 B St Thomas Virgin Islands 1937 d Ector & Ruth. Julian Richman HS 1954. D 6/28/2008 Bp Edward Gumbs. m 8/5/1961 Bernard G Francis c 1.

FRANCIS, Everett Warren (Be) 3200 Baker Circle Unit I131, Adamstown MD 21710 **Died 3/19/2016** B Taylor PA 1927 s Everett & Agnes. BA Duke 1946; GTS 1955. D 6/25/1955 P 1/1/1956 Bp Richard Stanley Merrill Emrich. m 4/14/2012 Elizabeth Dougherty c 5. Ret 1992-2016; S/C Ch in Metro Areas 1985-1991; Pres Ch & City Conf 1985-1988; R S Lk's Ch Scranton PA 1977-1992; Publ Affrs Dir Epis Ch Cntr New York NY 1967-1977; Publ Affrs Off Exec Coun Epis Ch NY 1967-1977; Asst Prog Dir Dio Michigan Detroit MI 1964-1967; Vic Ch Of The Gd Shpd Dearborn MI 1955-1964. Auth, "Medium of Soc Responsibility," *ATR*; Auth, "Whither Soc Involvement," *The Epis*; Auth, "UTO Story," *UTO*.

FRANCIS, James Woodcock (Mich) 1404 Joliet Pl, Detroit MI 48207 B Hamilton BM 1928 s Thomas. BA Wilberforce U 1956; BD Payne Sem 1958; Bex Sem 1959. D 6/24/1959 Bp Henry W Hobson P 12/1/1960 Bp Roger W Blanchard. m 8/30/1956 Audrie Arletha Smith. S Cyp's Epis Ch Detroit MI 1974-1985; Dio Ohio Cleveland 1971-1974; Vic S Simon Of Cyrene Epis Ch Cincinnati OH 1962-1971; Dio Sthrn Ohio Cincinnati OH 1959-1962; Cur S Andr's Epis Ch Cincinnati OH 1959-1962.

FRANCIS, John Robert (Be) 435 Court St, P.O. Box 1094, Reading PA 19603 **Chr Ch Reading PA 2005-; Chair of Benefits Com Dio Pennsylvania Philadelphia PA 2011-, Chair of CE Cmsn 1995-1996** B Syracuse NY 1956 s George & Rosemary. BS Richard Stockton Coll Pomona NJ 1978; MDiv GTS 1986; ThM New Brunswick TS 1991. D 6/14/1986 Bp George Phelps Mellick Belshaw P 12/1/1986 Bp Vincent King Pettit. m 11/17/1979 Erminia Francis c 2. R S Paul's Ch Philadelphia PA 1997-2004; Chr Ch Media PA 1990-1997; Vic Trin Epis Old Swedes Ch Swedesboro NJ 1986-1990; Cur S Jn's Ch Salem NJ 1986-1988. Soc Of S Jn The Evang.

FRANCIS, Mary Jane Jane (Oly) 725 9th Ave., Apt. 2109, Seattle WA 98104 **P Assoc St. Paul's Seattle WA 2010-; Sprtl Dir Within the dioceses of Tennessee & Olympia 1984-** B New York NY 1937 d Thomas & Dorothy. BA Wellesley Coll 1958; PhD U MI 1970; MDiv Sewanee: The U So, TS 1984. D 6/24/1984 Bp William Evan Sanders P 4/24/1985 Bp Girault M Jones. Dn of Dioc Sch of Mnstry and Theol Dio Olympia Seattle 2002-2004, Mentor & Prog Design-Total Mnstry Congregations 1997-2001, P doing extended supply, vacation & sabbatical coverage 1996-2002, Convenor & Grant Mgr-Team for Sprtl Formation 1996-, Bd Mem & Fac - Dio Schl of Mnstry and Theol 1999-2004, Dio. Olympia Rep. - Natl Consult on Sprtl Formation in Congregations 1996-1997, Mem - Cmsn for Congregations 1995-2000, Mem - Dioc Coun 1994-1998, Bd Mem [elected] - Cler Assn of the Dio Olympia 1994-1997; Consult UTO Natl Bd 2001; Design Team Sindicators 2000-2003; P-in-c Ch Of The Ascen Seattle WA 1997; Assoc S Marg's Epis Ch Bellevue WA 1992-1995; Design Team- Natl Ch's 'Families 2000' Conf 1988-1990; Dep-GC Dio Tennessee Nashville TN 1988, Dep [elected] - GC 1987-1989, Chair - Ch Consultants T/F 1987-1988, Sec'y & Chair - COM 1985-1992; Vic S Jn's Epis Ch Mt Juliet TN 1987-1992; Asst Chr Ch Cathd Nashville TN 1984-1987. Auth, "Bk Revs/article on retreat," *Regula*, The Friends of St. Ben; Auth, "Bk Revs," *Sewanee Theol Revs*. Cmnty of S Mary - Sewanee Prov, Assoc 1986.

FRANCKS, Robert Christopher (NY) 360 W 21st St, New York NY 10011 **Non-par 1981-** B New York NY 1948 s William & Olive. BA Trin Hartford CT 1970; MDiv GTS 1973. D 6/9/1973 Bp Horace W B Donegan P 12/1/1973 Bp Paul Moore Jr. R Chr Epis Ch Sparkill NY 1976-1981; Cur Gr Ch Newark NJ 1973-1975.

FRANCO ESTEVEZ, Juan Bautista (PR) Iglesia Episcopal Puertorriquena, PO Box 902, Saint Just PR 00978 Puerto Rico **Dio Puerto Rico Trujillo Alto PR 2010-** B Dominican Republic 1957 s Juan & Herninia. Lic en filosofia Universidad Catolica Madre y Maestr 1983; Lic en Teologia Pontificio Santo Tomas de Aquino 1986. Rec 6/21/2009 Bp David Andres Alvarez-Velazquez. m 7/27/2001 Rosaina A Guzman Reyes c 3.

FRANCOIS, Yvan Gesner (Hai) Box 1309, Port-Au-Prince Haiti **P-in-c S Croix Taifer 1971-** B 1943 s Gesner & Flora. Cert; BLitt Coll of S Pierre HT 1964; BTh ETSC 1968. D 12/2/1967 P 6/1/1968 Bp Charles Alfred Voegeli. m 11/28/1995 Cecile Francois. Chapl Coll-S Pierre 1968-1971; Dio Haiti Port-au-Prince HT 1967-1999.

FRANDSEN, Charles Frederick (WMich) 509 Ship St, Saint Joseph MI 49085 **Ret 1987-** B Ord NE 1921 s John & Muriel. BS Creighton U 1949; SWTS 1961. D 5/31/1961 Bp Howard R Brinker P 12/1/1961 Bp Russell T Rauscher. c 4. Vic Ch of the Medtr Harbert MI 1981-1986; R S Aug Of Cbury Epis Ch Benton Harbor MI 1971-1986; Ed S Davids Par Lancing MI 1967-1981; Dio Wstrn Michigan Kalamazoo MI 1967-1978; Vic S Dav's Ch Lansing MI 1967-1971; Ed S Thos Ch Fall City Nebraska 1962-1967; R S Thos' Epis Ch Falls City NE 1961-1967.

FRANK, Anna (Ak) 1578 Bridgewater Dr, Fairbanks AK 99709 **Archd Interior Dio Alaska Fairbanks AK 1990-, 1989-2007** B Minto AK 1939 d Jonathan & Rosie. D 3/28/1974 Bp William Jones Gordon Jr P 10/1/1983 Bp George Clin-

ton Harris. c 4. Asst S Matt's Epis Ch Fairbanks AK 1984-1989; D S Barn Ch Minto AK 1974-1981.

FRANK, Beth (O) New Life Episcopal Church, 13188 Church Ave NW, Uniontown OH 44685 **S Andr's Epis Ch Toledo OH 2016-; New Life Epis Ch Uniontown OH 2013-** B Akron OH 1959 d Paul & Elizabeth. AB Pr 1981; JD Case Wstrn Reserve U Sch of Law 1988; MDiv Bex 2013; MDiv Bex Sem 2013. D 6/1/2013 Bp Mark Hollingsworth Jr P 12/6/2013 Bp Arthur Williams Jr. bfrank@cometonewlife.org

FRANK, Richard Lloyd (U) 13640 N 21st Ave, Phoenix AZ 85029 **D 1987-** B Ravenna OH 1939 s Earle & Eileen. Hiram Coll. D 8/9/1987 Bp George Edmonds Bates. m 1/23/1960 Esther Frank c 2. Dio Utah Salt Lake City UT 1990-1996.

FRANK, Travis Ray (Ark) 14 Haslingden Ln, Bella Vista AR 72715 **Ch Of The Gd Shpd Forrest City AR 2016-** B Houston TX 1958 s Henry & Francis. BA Howard Payne U 1985; MDiv SW Bapt TS 1989. D 2/8/1997 Bp Larry Maze. S Jn's Epis Ch Helena AR 2005-2013; S Andr's Ch Marianna AR 2001-2005; Cur S Theo's Epis Ch Bella Vista AR 1999-2001; Cert Stdt ETSSw TX.

FRANK JR, William George (Va) 11 Wakefield Dr Apt 2004, Asheville NC 28803 **1960-** B Chicago IL 1926 s William & Helen. BA U of Louisiana 1949; BD VTS 1952; MD GW 1964. D 1/27/1952 P 10/1/1952 Bp Charles Clingman. m 4/16/1977 Melba Frank c 2. Asst Prof Pstr VTS Alexandria VA 1956-1960; S Paul's Ch Bailey's Crossroads Falls Ch VA 1954-1956; S Paul's Epis Ch Alexandria VA 1954-1956; R S Paul's Ch Hickman KY 1952-1954.

FRANKEN, Robert Anton (Colo) PO Box 2073, 101 E Main Street, Unit 204, Frisco CO 80443 **Sr Ldrshp Advsr THEO Exec Grp LLC 2004-; D Chr Ch Cathd S Louis MO 2002-; Mgmt Consult Strataventure LLC 2001-; Mem, PBp Transition/Installation Com Exec Coun Appointees New York NY 2013-; Mem T/F to Reimagine the Epis Ch (TREC) 2012-; Mem, Asst Treas The Fund for the Diac New York NY 2006-** B S'Gravenange Holland NL 1950 s John & Ann. BBA U of Texas 1979; MA U of Texas 1980. D 6/1/1984 Bp George Clinton Harris. m 11/4/1995 Nancy Theresa Kinney c 5. Archd Dio Missouri S Louis MO 2005-2007; Exec Dir Thompson Cntr S Louis MO 2001-2003; Chf Admin Off Dio Colorado Denver CO 1998-2001, D 1996-1998; D Ch Of S Jn Chrys Golden CO 1988-1995; D H Sprt Epis Ch Eagle River AK 1986-1987; Mem PBp's T/F on Accessability 1984-1994; D S Christophers Ch Anchorage AK 1984-1986; Mem, T/F to Reimagine the Epis Ch Dom And Frgn Mssy Soc- Epis Ch Cntr New York NY 2012-2014; Mem PBp's T/F on Accessibility 1984-1994. Auth, "Cost Efficient Adaptation of Sharp Portfolio Model for Sm Investors," *Thesis*, Self, 1980; Auth, "An Examination of the Unemployment Index: The Ability to Estimate and the Impact on the Econ," *Orgnztn of U.S. Border Cities and Counties, Inc.*, Orgnztn of U.S. Border Cities and Counties, Inc., 1979. Joint Resolution Alaska St Legislature 1987.

FRANKFURT, Dawn M (Kan) 3750 E Douglas Ave, Wichita KS 67208 **R S Jas Ch Wichita KS 2011-** B Syracuse NY 1966 d William & Kristin. BA U of Oklahoma 1988; MDiv Ya Berk 2004. D 9/10/2004 Bp Richard Sui On Chang P 5/5/2005 Bp Neff Powell. Int All SS' Epis Ch Duncan OK 2010-2011; Int St Phil's Epis Ch Ardmore OK 2009-2010; Int Trin Ch Staunton VA 2007-2008; Assoc Trin Ch Staunton VA 2004-2008.

FRANKLIN, Ann Hope (Mass) 143 Gillespie Circle, Brevard NC 28712 B Mount Airy NC 1943 d Robert & Ida. MDiv EDS 1986; DMin EDS 1991. D 6/28/1986 Bp Henry Irving Mayson P 9/7/1987 Bp H Coleman Mcgehee Jr. c 2. EDS Cambridge MA 2001-2010, 1991-1992, 1988-1990; Co-Pres MECA 2001-2003; Dn Alewife Dnry 1997-2005; R Ch Of The Gd Shpd Watertown MA 1994-2010.

FRANKLIN, Arthur Alden (SanD) 2404 Loring St # 190, San Diego CA 92109 **Ret 1996-** B Spokane WA 1930 s Arthur & Catharine. BA Gonzaga U 1952; MDiv SWTS 1955. D 6/18/1955 P 12/21/1955 Bp Russell S Hubbard. Cn Litur Emer Cathd Ch Of S Paul San Diego CA 1997-2006, Dn 1994-1996, Asst 1979-1993; Headmaster S Jn's Epis Ch Chula Vista CA 1972-1979; Asst H Trin Epis Par San Diego CA 1970-1979; Vic S Barth's Mssn Pico Rivera CA 1966-1970; Asst All SS Par Long Bch CA 1964-1966; Vic S Columba's Epis Ch Kent WA 1960-1964; Asst All SS Ch Spokane WA 1957-1960; H Trin Epis Ch Wallace ID 1955-1957; Vic S Andr's Epis Ch Mccall ID 1955-1957.

FRANKLIN, Cecil Loyd (Colo) 2250 E Columbia Pl, Denver CO 80210 **Died 2/16/2016** B El Reno OK 1927 s Marion & Mary. BA Phillips U 1947; STB Harvard DS 1950; STM Harvard DS 1951; CDSP 1956; PhD Harv 1961. D 3/13/1957 P 11/1/1957 Bp Joseph Summerville Minnis. m 6/20/1981 Priscilla Ann Franklin c 2. Ret 1989-2016; Vic S Andr's Ch Denver CO 1984-1986; Rel Studs U Denv 1966-1986; R The Ch Of Chr The King (Epis) Arvada CO 1962-1965, Vic 1960-1962; Cur All SS' Epis Ch Belmont MA 1959-1960; Cur Trin Par of Newton Cntr Newton Cntr MA 1958-1959; Asst S Jn's Cathd Denver CO 1957-1958. Auth, "Two arts," *Iliff Revs*.

FRANKLIN JR, Denson (Ala) 517 Mayfair Cir, Birmingham AL 35209 **Died 5/29/2017** B Bessemer AL 1937 s Denson & Lottie. BA Birmingham-Sthrn Coll 1958; MDiv Candler TS Emory U 1961; Drew U 1965. D 4/17/1991 P 8/25/1991 Bp Robert Oran Miller. m 11/24/1977 Carolyn Franklin c 2. Int P Ch Of

F

The Incarn Highlands NC 2010-2011; Ret Cbury Chap Tuscaloosa AL 2009; Int P S Steph's Epis Ch Birmingham AL 2005-2006; Int S Steph's Epis Ch 2004-2006; Int Shades Vlly Luth Birmingham 2003; Assoc R S Lk's Epis Ch Birmingham AL 1996-2002, P Assoc 1995; R S Barn' Epis Ch Hartselle AL 1991-1994; Serv Meth Ch 1958-1989.

FRANKLIN III, Gus Lee (Spr) 6508 Willow Springs Rd, Springfield IL 62712 **Ret 1998-; P The Cathd Ch Of S Paul Springfield IL 1998-, Cn 1979-1984, Asst 1975-1979, Cur 1967-1970** B Covington KY 1938 s Gus & Ruth. BS Estrn Kentucky U 1959; MSEd Indiana U 1960; MA U IL 1964; MDiv Nash 1967. D 6/3/1967 P 12/9/1967 Bp Albert A Chambers. Dioc Coordntr LPMSSC Dio Quincy Peoria IL 1995-1998; R S Andr's Ch Peoria IL 1986-1998; Vic Chr The King Epis Ch Normal IL 1984-1986; 1970-1975. CBS 1957; GAS 1957; SSC 1983. R Emer St Andr's, Peoria 2001; Dn Emer Bp KL Ackerman 1998.

FRANKLIN III, James (NC) Winston Salem Young Adult Ministry, PO Box 7204, Winston Salem NC 27109 B Orlando FL 1984 s James & Edith. Hist/Rel U NC 2007; MDiv Epis TS of the SW 2013. D 6/29/2013 P 1/5/2014 Bp Michael B Curry. m 12/31/2010 Samantha C Franklin c 3. YA Mssnr and Chapl at Wake Forest U Dio No Carolina Raleigh NC 2015, YA Mssnr and Chapl at Wake Forest U 2015, YA Mssnr and Chapl at Wake Forest U 2015-; P S Jas Par Wilmington NC 2013-2015. frankljd@wfu.edu

FRANKLIN, John Thomas (Mich) 2933 Dunsary Ln, Brighton MI 48114 **R S Steph's Ch Hamburg MI 2007-** B Mt. Sterling IL 1935 s Lawrence & Anna. BA S Mary of the Lake Sem 1957; Lic Sacr Theol Gregorian U 1961; MA U IL 1971; PhD U MI 1986. Rec 7/1/2006 Bp Wendell Nathaniel Gibbs Jr. m 6/1/1972 Cheryl Cunningham c 2. Psychol Brighton Hosp 1990-2008; Prof U Of Detroit Mercy 1978-2011. Co-Auth, "For When I Am Weak, The I Am Strong," *Bk of the same name*, Mercy Coll Press, 1988. OSL the Physcn 2011. Prof Emer U of Detroit Mercy 2011; Distinguished Prof U of Detroit Mercy 1998.

✠ FRANKLIN, The Rt Rev Ralph William (WNY) 1064 Brighton Road, Tonawanda NY 14150 **Bp of Wstrn New York Dio Wstrn New York Tonawanda NY 2011-; Dn Emer Berk New Haven CT 2002-** B Brookhaven MS 1947 s Ralph & Dorothy. BA NWU 1969; MA Harv 1971; PhD Harv 1975. D 3/19/2005 P 9/17/2005 Bp Mark Sean Sisk Con 4/30/2011 for WNY. m 6/19/1971 Carmela Vircillo Franklin c 2. Sr Assoc P S Mk's Ch Philadelphia PA 2010-2011; Assoc P All SS' Ch 2005-2010; Assoc Dir Amer Acad Rome Italy 2005-2010; Assoc R Trin Ch Epis Boston MA 2003-2005; Bp'S Schlr Dio New York 2002-2003; Dn Ya Berk New Haven CT 1998-2002; Assoc Dn The GTS New York NY 1993-1998; Sprw Prof. Of Hist And Mssn The GTS New York NY 1993-1998; Mich Blecker Prof. Of Hmnts S Jn Univ Collegeville MN 1975-1993. rwfranklin@episcopalwny.org

FRANKLIN, Sarah Claire (USC) 7128 Caggy Ln, Fort Mill SC 29707 **R S Paul's Epis Ch Ft Mill SC 2004-** B Athens GA 1960 d Samuel & Glenn. BS Clemson U 1983; MA U GA 1984; MDiv VTS 1994. D 6/4/1994 Bp Huntington Williams Jr P 6/4/1995 Bp Robert Carroll Johnson Jr. Chr Epis Ch Dublin GA 1998-2004; Asst S Mary's Epis Ch High Point NC 1994-1998.

FRANKLIN-VAUGHN, Robyn (WA) 319 Bryant St Ne, Washington DC 20002 **S Barn' Ch Leeland Uppr Marlboro MD 2015-** B Boston MA 1965 MDiv EDS. D 6/15/2002 P 5/31/2003 Bp M(Arvil) Thomas Shaw. m 10/21/1989 Raymond J Franklin-Vaughn. Chapl How Dio Washington Washington DC 2003-2014.

FRANKS, Laurence Edward Alexander (FdL) 299 Corey St, Boston MA 02132 B Houston TX 1943 s Verlan & Adela. BS U CA 1965; MA UWA Washington DC 1966; MLitt U of Cambridge 1972; MDiv CDSP 1980. D 6/13/1981 Bp H Coleman Mcgehee Jr P 6/30/1982 Bp Henry Irving Mayson. AIDS T/F Interfaith Mnstry Newton MA 1990-2006; Dio Massachusetts Boston MA 1990-2005; Interfaith Aids Mnstry W Newton MA 1990-2005; Jubilee Mnstry Asst Epis Ch Cntr New York NY 1985-1989; R S Ptr's Epis Ch Sheboygan Falls WI 1983-1985; Asst Chapl Wayne Detroit MI 1980-1982. Auth, "L. Edw Alexander Franks," *An Aid to Wrshp in the H Euch*, 2000; Auth, "L. Edw Alexander Franks," *Meaning & Pattern of the H Euch*, 2000.

FRANSON, Marna (Ark) **St Nich Ch Maumelle AR 2016-** B 1958 d Howard & Irene. Bachelor of Arts Gordon Coll 1980; Bachelor of Arts Gordon Coll 1980; Mstr of Arts in Theol Stds Gordon-Conwell TS 1983; Mstr of Arts in Theol Stds Gordon-Conwell TS 1983; Mstr of Arts K SU 1998; Mstr of Arts K SU 1998; Post Grad Dplma in Angl Stds VTS 2016; Post Grad Dplma in Angl Stds VTS 2016. D 8/6/2016 P 2/17/2017 Bp Larry Benfield. c 3.

FRANTZ-DALE, Heidi Hallett (NH) 247 Pound Road, Madison NH 03849 **Chapl Lakeview Neurological Rehab Cntr 2004-; Vice Chair Bp Election /Transition Com Dio New Hampshire Concord NH 2011-, Dioc Coun Mem 2007-** B Hartford CT 1950 d David & Margaret. BA Swarthmore Coll 1972; MEd U of Massachusetts 1973; MDiv EDS 2000. D 6/10/2000 P 12/17/2000 Bp Gordon Scruton. m 9/23/1978 Duane Danroy Dale c 2. R S Andr's-In-The-Vlly Tamworth NH 2004-2016; Dio Wstrn Massachusetts Springfield 2000-2004; S Jas' Ch Greenfield MA 2000-2004; Vic S Andr's Ch Turners Fall MA 2000-2003.

FRANZ, Marcia Wheatley (NMich) **Presider,Prchr,Eucharistic Vistor/Prayerchain S Paul's Ch Marquette MI 1986-** B Marquette MI 1943 d James & Harriet. BA MI SU 1965. D 5/9/2006 P 5/27/2007 Bp James Arthur Kelsey. c 2. Stndg Com Dio Nthrn Michigan Marquette MI 2006-2009.

FRASER, Ann Benton (Miss) St. Paul's Episcopal Church, P.O. Box 1225, Corinth MS 38835 **R S Paul's Epis Ch Corinth MS 2009-; GC Alt Dep Dio Mississippi Jackson MS 2017-, GC Alt Dep 2014-2017, Stndg Com 2013-2017, Disciplinary Bd 2011-2013** B Baton Rouge 1980 d James & Susan. BA LSU 2002; MDiv Sewanee: The U So, TS 2007. D 12/30/2006 P 8/19/2007 Bp Charles Edward Jenkins III. m 1/3/2004 Andrew Edwin Fraser c 2. Lilly Fell S Jas Ch New York NY 2007-2009; (Int) Yth Dir 2004.

FRASER, Joan Grimm (LI) 124 Jerusalem Ave, Hicksville NY 11801 **Died 5/23/2016** B Berea OH 1947 BS Alleg 1969; MDiv EDS 1973; MS U of Arizona 1978; BFA U NC 2000. D 6/16/1973 P 3/5/1977 Bp John Harris Burt. m 7/7/1979 Donald Ross Fraser. R H Trin Epis Ch 2004-2016; R H Trin Epis Ch Hicksville NY 2004-2016; Non-par 1996-2016; Cn Dio Wstrn Massachusetts Springfield 1996-1998; Vic S Paul's Epis Ch Thomasville NC 1994-1996; Vic S Clem's Epis Ch Clemmons NC 1989-1991; Assoc S Paul's Epis Ch Lakewood CO 1985-1988; Non-par 1977-1985; Chapl Ken Gambier OH 1974-1976; Assoc Chapl Ken OH 1974-1976.

FRASER, Richard Trent (Colo) 1400 S University Blvd, Denver CO 80210 **R S Mich And All Ang' Ch Denver CO 2013-** B North Bay ON CA 1965 s Hugh & Lillian. BA Laurentian U No Bay CA 1987; MDiv Trin, U Tor CA 1990. D 10/28/1992 P 5/18/1993 Bp Edward Harding MacBurney. R S Jn The Evang Ch Newport RI 2009-2012; P-in-c The Ch Of The Redeem Southfield MI 2001-2009; Dio Pennsylvania Philadelphia PA 2001; Cur S Clements Ch Philadelphia PA 1993-2001; Mssn and Bdgt Com Dio Michigan Detroit MI 2005-2006, Secy, Stndg Com 2005-2006. CCU 1993-2006; CBS 1993; GAS 1993; Living Rosary of Our Lady & S. Dominic 1993-2009; P Assoc of the H Hse, Walsingham, UK 1999; Societas Sanctae Crucis 2000; Soc of King Chas the Mtyr 1993-2016; SocMary 1993.

FRASER, Thomas A (Chi) 60 Akenside Rd, Riverside IL 60546 B Alexandria VA 1945 s Thomas & Marjorie. BA No Carolina St U 1967; STB GTS 1972. D 6/17/1972 P 12/1/1972 Bp James Winchester Montgomery. R S Paul's Par Riverside IL 1975-2017; Cur Ch Of The H Comf Kenilworth IL 1973-1975; Cur S Mk's Epis Ch Glen Ellyn IL 1972-1973. Bd Dir Living Ch 1989-2015.

FRASER SR, William Carson (ETenn) 4487 Post Place, #129, Nashville TN 37205 **Ret 1997-** B Nashville TN 1935 s William & Margaret. BA U of Tennessee 1958; STB Ya Berk 1960. D 7/6/1960 Bp Theodore N Barth P 5/1/1961 Bp John Vander Horst. m 12/27/2008 Mary Carl Roberts c 3. R S Andr's Ch Harriman TN 1988-1997; S Matt's Ch Dayton TN 1983-1988; Vic S Paul's Epis Ch Chattanooga TN 1983-1988; R Ch Of The Gd Samar Knoxville TN 1978-1983; R S Ann's Ch Nashville TN 1965-1978; P-in-c S Andr's Epis Ch Collierville TN 1961-1965; Chapl Barth Hse Memphis TN 1961-1963; D S Ptr's Ch Chattanooga TN 1960-1961.

FRAUSTO, Nancy Aide (Los) 861 S Mariposa Ave, Los Angeles CA 90005 **The Par Ch Of S Lk Long Bch CA 2017-; Trin Epis Par Los Angeles CA 2013-** B Mexico 1983 d Manuel & Catalina. Dplma of Theol Bloy Hse 2013; MDiv Claremont TS 2013. D 6/8/2013 Bp Mary Douglas Glasspool P 1/11/2014 Bp Diane Jardine Bruce. S Mary's Epis Ch Los Angeles CA 2014-2017. frausto. nancy@gmail.com

FRAZELLE, David C (NC) 304 E Franklin St, Chapel Hill NC 27514 **S Chris's Epis Ch Garner NC 2016-** B Asheville NC 1975 s Charles & Donna. BA U So 1997; Institut Catholique De Paris 1999; MDiv VTS 2004. D 6/19/2004 P 6/4/2005 Bp Michael B Curry. m 1/5/2002 Emily Crowder Frazelle c 1. Assoc for Par Mnstry Chap Of The Cross Chap Hill NC 2004-2016.

FRAZER, Candice Burk (Ala) St John's Episcopal Church, 113 Madison Ave, Montgomery AL 36104 **S Jn's Ch Montgomery AL 2013-** B Selma AL 1971 d Richard & Margaret. BA The U of Alabama 1993; MDiv Sewanee: The U So, TS 2013; MDiv The TS at The U So 2013. D 5/16/2013 Bp Santosh K Marray P 11/23/2013 Bp John Mckee Sloan Sr. m 7/30/1994 Charles Stephen Frazer. S Paul's Ch Selma AL 2005-2010. candice@stjohnsmontgomery.org

FRAZIER JR, Allie Washington (SVa) 1124 Dryden Lane, Charlottesville VA 22903 **Fndr Thesis/Antithesis/Synthesis (TAS) Charlottesville VA 2005-; Ret 1996-; Co-Fndr Thesis/Antithesis/Synthesis (TAS) Charlottesville VA 2005-** B Stanardsville VA 1931 s Allie & Virginia. BA U Rich 1956; MDiv VTS 1961; DMin Drew U 1992. D 6/23/1961 Bp Robert Fisher Gibson Jr P 6/13/1962 Bp Frederick D Goodwin. m 6/18/1978 Carolyn Gills Frazier c 3. R Johns Meml Epis Ch Farmville VA 1985-1996; Chr Ch Amelia Ct Hs VA 1980-1985; Emm Epis Ch Powhatan VA 1980-1985; R Pac Cure Par Cartersville VA 1980-1985; S Jas Ch Cartersville VA 1980-1985; Dn Dio Virginia Richmond VA 1970-1972; R Gr Ch Keswick VA 1968-1975; R Emm Ch Staunton VA 1966-1968; Assoc R Chr Ch Epis Savannah GA 1964-1966; R Wicomico Par Ch Wicomico Ch VA 1962-1964; Exec Bd; Dn Farmville Convoc Dio Sthrn Virginia Newport News VA 1983-1985. Auth, *Informed Chr Living*, Dissertation - Drew U, 1992; Auth, *Take Care of Your Wrld*, Dio Virginia, Stwdshp Dept., 1970. Fllshp Coll of Preachers, Washington DC 1970.

FRAZIER, John T (EC) 5324 Bluewater Pl, Fayetteville NC 28311 **R S Paul's In The Pines Epis Ch Fayetteville NC 2005-** B Nashville TN 1948 s Evelyn.

MDiv VTS; BS Pk U 1993; MA Webster U 2002. D 6/25/2005 P 4/8/2006 Bp Clifton Daniel III. m 2/14/1980 Veronica L Frazier. office@stpaulsinthepines.net

FRAZIER, Jonathan E (WMo) 516 S Weller Ave, Springfield MO 65802 **R St Ptr & All SS Epis Ch Kansas City MO 2016-** B Kansas City MO 1963 BA Rockhurst Jesuit U 1985; MDiv Sewanee: The U So, TS 2004. D 6/5/2004 P 12/6/2004 Bp Barry Howe. m 9/4/1999 Ann M Frazier c 3. Chr Epis Ch Springfield MO 2004-2016; GC Dep, C3 Dio W Missouri Kansas City MO 2010-2012, Assessment Revs Cmte 2009-2010, Bp Search and Nomin Cmte 2009-2010, Hisp Mnstry Cmte 2008-, Comp Dio Cmte 2007-2009, Dn, Sthrn Dnry 2007-2009, Dioc Coun 2007-2009, Fin Cmte 2007-2009, GC Dep, Alt 2007-2009, Chapl, Missouri St U 2007-, COM 2006-2014, Conv Committees, chair and Mem 2005-2011, Bd Dir, Acad for Lay Educ and Mnstry 2004-2007.

FRAZIER, Mark W (SwVa) 905 Highland Ave, Bristol VA 24201 **S Thos Epis Christiansbrg VA 2016-** B Memphis TN 1961 s William & Jean. BS U of Tennessee 1983; PhD Van 1989; MDiv Sewanee: The U So, TS 2001. D 5/26/2001 Bp James Malone Coleman P 12/15/2001 Bp David Bruce Joslin. m 7/9/1988 Amy LB Frazier c 4. S Paul's Ch Saltville VA 2016; R Emm Epis Ch Bristol VA 2008-2011; R S Dav's Ch Fayetteville NY 2003-2008; Asst S Matt's Ch Pennington NJ 2001-2003. Soc for Biblic Lit 2000-2003.

FRAZIER, Raymond Malcom (SwFla) 8017 Fountain Ave, Tampa FL 33615 **D S Chris's Ch Tampa FL 1993-** B Riverside CA 1949 s Clarence & Geraldine. BA U of So Florida 1976. D 6/26/1993 Bp Rogers Sanders Harris. m 6/5/1971 Donna Marie Frazier c 3. NAAD.

FRAZIER JR, Samuel Kindley (NC) 500 N Duke St. #55-202, Durham NC 27701 **Died 5/26/2017** B High Pt NC 1936 s Samuel & Mabel. BA U NC 1959; STB Ya Berk 1962. D 6/29/1962 P 6/29/1963 Bp Richard Henry Baker. m 5/17/1991 Arthur Johnson c 3. S Andr's Ch Haw River NC 1995-2008; Vic S Phil's Ch Chas Town WV 1975-1976; Vic S Phil The Evang Washington DC 1965-1970; Vic Galloway Memi Chap Elkin NC 1962-1965; Liturg Asst S Jas' Epis Ch Leesburg VA 1977-1983. Auth, "Straight Like Me: The Journey of a Gay P in the Epis Ch," Amazon Books, 2013; Auth, "Worthy Of The Nation-The Hist Of The Plnng & Dvlpmt Of Washington Dc," 1977.

FREARSON, Andrew Richard (At) 3136 Lynnray Dr, Doraville GA 30340 B Birmingham UK 1957 s George & Kathleen. Cert Oxf GB; BA U of Wolverhampton 1980. Trans 2/27/1997 Bp Frank Kellogg Allan. m 5/30/1992 Lesleigh Henderson Frearson. Assoc Chr Ch Norcross GA 1997-2004; P-in-c S Jn's Clivber Uk 1989-1996; Sr Cur S Mary's Moseley Uk 1986-1989; Cur S Mary's Acocks Green Uk 1983-1986.

FREDERIC, Eliot Garrison (Eas) 51 Columbine Ave N, Hampton Bays NY 11946 B Brooklyn NY 1941 s Eliot & Dorothy. BA Adel 1964; STB PDS 1967; STM NYTS 1979. D 6/17/1967 P 12/23/1967 Bp Jonathan Goodhue Sherman. m 9/7/1968 Barbara Frederic c 2. Supply P Chr Epis Ch Lynbrook NY 2008-2012; R Chr Ch Denton MD 1996-2004; R Chr Ch Sag Harbor NY 1982-1995; R S Mary's Ch Brooklyn NY 1975-1982; Cur S Steph's Ch Prt Washington NY 1970-1975; Cur H Apos And Medtr Philadelphia PA 1967-1970.

FREDERICK, John Bassett Moore (Ct) 32 Chestnut St, Princeton NJ 08542 **Assoc All SS Ch Princeton NJ 1996-; Ret 1995-** B New York NY 1930 s Karl & Anne. BA Pr 1951; MDiv GTS 1954; PhD U of Birmingham Birmingham GB 1973. D 6/9/1954 Bp Walter H Gray P 4/30/1955 Bp Robert McConnell Hatch. c 2. R, RurD Ch of Engl 1972-1995; R S Jn's Ch New Haven CT 1961-1971; Chapl Cheshire Acad Cheshire CT 1954-1956; Cur S Ptr's Epis Ch Cheshire CT 1954-1956; Secy, Liturg Cmsn Dio Connecticut Meriden CT 1971-1974, Secy Liturg Cmsn 1967-1971. Auth, "A Royal Amer, a New Jersey Off in the King's Serv During the Revolution," Dog Ear Pub, 2009; Compiler, "Fam Histories 1880-2005," *Turner Fam Assn*, Amer Libr Press, 2005; Auth, "The Future of Liturg Reform," Morehouse-Barlow Press, 1987; Auth, "Lineage Bk Brittish Land Forces," Microform Acad Pub, 1984; Auth, "Lineage Bk of the Brittish Army 1660-1968," Hope Farm Press, 1969. OHC (Assoc) 1956.

FREDERICK, Robert John (Md) 1930 Brookdale Rd, Baltimore MD 21244 B Troy NY 1944 s William & Emma. PhD MI SU; BS Un Coll (Schenectady); MS U of Rhode Island. D 6/14/2014 Bp Joe Goodwin Burnett. m 6/17/1967 Barbara Ann Inglis Frederick c 4. D Epis Ch Of Chr The King Baltimore MD 2014-2016; Sr Sci US Enviornmental Protection Agcy 1984-2014. frederrj@aol.com

FREDERICK, Sherman Richardson (Nev) 2724 Brienza Way, Las Vegas NV 89117 **Assoc Preist Gr In The Desert Epis Ch Las Vegas NV 1992-** B Bloomington IL 1951 s Sherman & Christine. BS Nthrn Arizona U 1977. D 2/6/1994 P 10/1/1994 Bp Stewart Clark Zabriskie. m 11/13/1971 Christina L Secker.

FREDERICK, Warren Charles (WMass) 19 Rydal St, Worcester MA 01602 **R St Mich's-on-the-Heights Worcester MA 2004-** B Johnstown PA 1947 s Morris & Betty. Trans 9/24/2000 Bp Robert Wilkes Ihloff. m 8/29/2009 Molly Carolyn Edelen c 4. S Mich's-On-The-Heights Worcester MA 2004-2013; R Ch Of The H Cross Cumberland MD 2000-2004; Serv Ch of Engl Worcester 1988-2000.

FREDERIKSEN III, Victor (EC) Po Box 7672, Wilmington NC 28406 **Supply P and P-in-res S Mk's Ch Wilmington NC 2006-; R S Paul's Epis Ch Wilm-** ington NC 1998-, 1996-2005 B Owosso MI 1943 s Victor & Elizabeth. BA Capital U 1966; MDiv Bex Sem 1969. D 6/28/1969 P 1/5/1970 Bp Roger W Blanchard. c 2. R Chr Ch Macon GA 1989-1996; Assoc Chr Ch Charlotte NC 1976-1979; S Jn's Epis Ch Charlotte NC 1976-1979; Assoc Chr Ch Cathd Cincinnati OH 1969-1976. Auth, "Mnstry In An Intensive Care Unit"; Auth, "The Approach To Parents Of A Brain Dead Chlid In"; Auth, "Requesting Organ Donation For Transplantation"; Auth, "When A Chld Dies: Helping Parents & Siblings". Aape, AAPC; Amer Assoc. of Mar and Fam Ther; Amer Assoc. Griep Counselors 1980; Amer Assoc. of CPE, Amer Assoc. of Suicideugy. Firestone Schlr Bex 1969.

FREDHOLM, Everett Leonard (Tex) 201 Nicholas Dr, Asheville NC 28806 B Lynn MA 1943 s Bror & Lois. Wentworth Inst of Tech 1961; BA Bob Jones U 1965; MDiv Conservative Bapt TS 1969; Epis TS of the SW 1970; U of Houston 1984; Asheville Buncombe Tech Cmnty Coll 2010. D 11/20/1970 Bp James Milton Richardson P 6/8/1971 Bp Frederick P Goddard. m 12/28/1968 Rebekah Able c 1. R S Fran Of Assisi Epis Prairie View TX 2000-2005; Chapl Jail Chapl Mnstrs Harris Cnty Jail 1991-1999; Other Cler Position The Great Cmsn Fndt Houston TX 1991-1999; R S Paul's Epis Ch Freeport TX 1990-1991; Chapl Jail Chapl Mnstrs Harris Cnty Jail 1987-1990; Houston Metropltn Mnstrs Houston TX 1979-1986; R Ch Of The Adv Houston TX 1977-1979; S Matt's Ch Henderson TX 1972-1977; S Paul's Ch Kilgore TX 1972-1977; Asst to R Trin Ch Longview TX 1970-1972; Instnl Revs Bd-Mem Prairie View A & M U 2003-2005; Bd Mem Houston Emmaus Cmnty 1985-1999. Natl Assn Alcosm And Drug Abuse Counselors, Amer Prot Correctional Chapl Assn. efredholm@gmail.com

FREDIE JR, Julian Von Kessel (Mass) **D S Cyp's Ch Boston MA 2012-** B Boston MA 1939 s Julian & Winona. D 6/16/2012 Bp M(Arvil) Thomas Shaw. m 5/4/1963 Deanna Wilson c 2.

FREDRICK, Lawrence Edward (EO) 1220 Tasman Dr Spc 1k, Sunnyvale CA 94089 B Joplin MO 1942 s Cecil & Ruth. BS U of Montana at Billings 1963; MA U of Montana Missoula 1966; MDiv VTS 1975; Cert Mssn Coll Santa Clara CA 1999. D 8/3/1975 P 9/26/1976 Bp William Benjamin Spofford. Serv Trin Cathd San Jose CA 1991-1994; Vic S Chris Goldendale WA 1975-1978; S Pauls Epis Ch The Dalles OR 1975-1978; The Par Of S Mk The Evang Hood River OR 1975-1978.

FREDRICKS, John Raymond (Cal) Po Box 296, San Mateo CA 94401 B Paterson NJ 1922 s Raymond & Anna. BS New Jersey St Teachers Coll 1946; GTS 1949. D 4/23/1949 Bp Robert E Campbell P 12/14/1949 Bp William F Lewis. c 4. Assoc Gd Shpd Epis Ch Belmont CA 1970-2002; Asst S Matt's Epis Ch San Mateo CA 1966-1970; Vic S Edm's Epis Ch Pacifica CA 1958-1966; Asst S Ptr's Epis Ch Redwood City CA 1956-1958; Vic S Andr Battle Mtn NV 1955-1956; Vic S Mary's Ch Winnemucca NV 1955-1956; Vic S Chris's Epis Ch Boulder City NV 1951-1954; H Trin Epis Ch Fallon NV 1949-1951; D-in-c S Paul's Ch Virginia City NV 1949-1951.

FREDRICKSON, David A (Mass) 149 Court Street, Plymouth MA 02360 **Adj Fac Andover Newton TS Newton MA 2013-; R Chr Ch Par Plymouth MA 2010-** B Colorado Springs CO 1963 s Robert & Carol. BS U CO 1986; MDiv PrTS 1994; STM TESS 1999. D 6/24/2000 P 5/12/2001 Bp Charles Ellsworth Bennison Jr. m 8/25/1997 Johnna Lee Fredrickson c 2. R Ch Of The Gd Shpd Wareham MA 2002-2009; Cur Trin Ch Buckingham PA 2000-2002. rector. christchurchplymouth@gmail.com

FREE JR, Horace D (NY) PO Box 125, Johns Island SC 29457 **S Mary's Castleton Staten Island NY 2015-** B Bamberg SC 1964 s Horace & Lynn. BA Wofford Coll 1986; MDiv Nash 2010. D 6/2/2010 P 12/4/2010 Bp Mark Joseph Lawrence. m 7/21/1990 Sallie M Free c 2. Cur S Jn's Epis Par Johns Island SC 2010-2013.

FREEBERN, Douglas Wayne (Okla) 210 E 9th St, Bartlesville OK 74003 B Yonkers NY 1939 s Ralph & Eleanor. BA Oklahoma City U 1962. D 6/24/2006 Bp Robert Manning Moody. m 12/23/1993 Connie Catherine Freebern c 4.

FREEMAN, Ashley B (La) **R S Pat's Ch Zachary LA 2016-** D 11/22/2014 P 7/16/2015 Bp Philip Menzie Duncan II.

FREEMAN, Bruce A (Los) 2944 Erie Ave, Cincinnati OH 45208 **The Par Of S Matt Pacific Plsds CA 2015-** B Boston MA 1959 s William & Carol. BA Ken 1981; MDiv EDS 1986. D 6/24/1987 P 12/28/1987 Bp Robert Marshall Anderson. m 9/3/1983 Dana J Dahlgren c 3. R The Ch of the Redeem Cincinnati OH 2003-2015; R Ch Of The Epiph San Carlos CA 1994-2003; Dio Wstrn Massachusetts Springfield 1989-1994; R S Jn's Ch Athol MA 1989-1994; Asst S Chris's Epis Ch S Paul MN 1987-1989. bafreeman@stmatthews.com

FREEMAN JR, Denson F (CGC) St James Church, 860 N Section St, Fairhope AL 36532 **S Jas Ch Fairhope AL 2016-** B Mobile AL 1969 s Denson & Mary. BA Auburn U 1993; MDiv Epis TS of the SW 2007. D 6/2/2007 P 5/17/2008 Bp Philip Menzie Duncan II. m 5/1/1993 Stephanie P Freeman c 3. R Ch Of Our Sav Colorado Sprg CO 2011-2016; Vic Ch Of The Epiph Crestview FL 2007-2011; Gnrl Mgr Davco Profsnl Collision Serv Inc Foley 1993-2004; Stndg Com Mem Dio Cntrl Gulf Coast Pensacola FL 2010-2011, Fresh Start Fac 2009-2011; Bd Mem/Mgmt Com Beckwith C&C Fairhope AL 2008-2011. dfreeman@chapelofoursaviour.com

FREEMAN, Diana Gail Burnham (Dal) 6400 Stonebrook Pkwy, Frisco TX 75034 **Ch Of Our Merc Sav Kaufman TX 2016-** B Kansas City MO 1955 d Arlan & Ruby Lee. BFA Pacific Luth U 1980; MDiv VTS 1995. D 7/21/2000 P 3/3/2001 Bp Charles Farmer Duvall. m 6/15/1974 Paul Loyd Freeman c 3. P-in-c Ch Of The Gd Shpd Terrell TX 2009-2016; S Phil's Epis Ch Frisco TX 2007-2009; R S Lk's Ch Catskill NY 2005-2007; Cur H Nativ Epis Ch Panama City FL 2000-2003; Sem Intern/Dir of Chr Ed St Johns Broad Creek Ft Washington MD 1993-1997. DOK 2006. revdifreeman@att.net

FREEMAN, John (WMass) **Dio Wstrn Massachusetts Springfield 2016-** B 1956 D P. m 1/22/1994 Josephine Freeman c 4. Dio Liberia Monrovia 2005-2012.

FREEMAN, Len (Minn) 190 Cygnet Pl, Long Lake MN 55356 **Chapl to Ret Cler & Surviving Spouses Epis Ch in Minnesota Minneapolis MN 2015-; Asst St Dav's Epis Ch Minnetonka MN 2012-; Cmncatn Stff Lambeth Conf 1988-; Mem Hennepin Cnty Adult MentalHealthAdvisory 2014-** B Lawrence MA 1943 s Wilbur & Gertrude. BA NEU 1964; NEU 1965; MDiv VTS 1969; Coll of Preachers 1972; Tem 1975. D 6/21/1969 Bp Anson Phelps Stokes Jr P 1/10/1970 Bp George E Rath. m 11/4/1989 Lindsay Hardin c 6. Int Trin Ch Excelsior MN 2010-2011; R S Mart's By The Lake Epis Minnetonka Bch MN 1998-2009; R Chr Ch Short Hills NJ 1991-1998; Dir Cmncatns Cathd of St Ptr & St Paul Washington DC 1987-1991; Dir Cmncatns Trin Par New York NY 1981-1987; Cmncatn Stff GC 1976-1994; R S Jas Ch Collegeville PA 1975-1981; Int S Aidans Ch Cheltenham PA 1974-1975; Non-par Temple Univ Doctoral Prog Philadelphia PA 1972-1975; Asst Min S Paul's Ch Montvale NJ 1969-1972; GC, Alt Dio Minnesota Minneapolis MN 2009-2012, Dioc Trst 2000-2006; VP Epis Grp Hm 2000-2009; Planned Giving Com Dio Newark Newark NJ 1996-1998; Bd CEEP Austin TX 1994-2000; Cmncatn Stff Lambeth Conf 1990; Chair, Cmncatn Com Dio Pennsylvania Philadelphia PA 1976-1979. Auth, "Ashes and the Phoenix," *2017 Lenten Bk*, Forw Mvmt, 2017; Auth, "Hawai'i: Poems From A Promised Land," CreateSpace - Amazon, 2014; Collaborator, "The Spy on Noah's Ark," Forw Mvmt, 2013; Auth, "Gd Lord Deliver Us," *2011 Lenten Bk*, Forw Mvmt, 2011; Contrib, "Praying Day by Day," *A Year of Meditations*, Forw Mvmt, 2010; Auth, "Hildegard Of Bingen Video Series," Morehouse Pub, 1990; Ed, "Cathd Age," *Cathd Age*, Washington Natl Cathed, 1989; Producer/Host, "Searching TV series," *Searching - 1981-87*, Trin Wall St NYC, 1987; Auth, "Theol Of Hope Moltman Video," Harper & Row, 1986; Producer/Host, "The H Land: A Pilgrimage," *WNYC TV, (PBS, NYC)*, Trin Wall St, NYC, 1984; Ed, "Trin News," *Trin News*, Trin Wall St, NYC, 1981; Auth, "Forw Day By Day Lent," *Forw Day by Day*, Forw Mvmt, 1980; Cont Ed, "Film & Media Critic," *The Epis & EpiscopalLife 1972-85*, Epis Ch USA, 1972; Auth, "Var Aticles In," *Epis; Living Ch; Cathd Age; Epis Life; Trin News*. CEEP 1990-2009; ECom 1972-1990; Evang Educ Soc 1975-2009. Polly Bond Awd ECom 1990; Polly Bond Awd ECom 1989; Loc Emmy Awd Loc NYC TV Emmy Com 1984; Fell Coll of Preachers 1972.

FREEMAN, Lindsay Hardin (Minn) 190 Cygnet Pl, Long Lake MN 55356 **Cler Consult Dio Minnesota Minneapolis MN 2012-, Chapl to Ret Cler 2015-, Mem, Cmsn on Mssn 2011-2013; Adj Cler St Dav's Epis Ch Minnetonka MN 2011-; Bd Dir Imara Intl Minnesota/Kenya 2012-** B Minneapolis MN 1954 d Franklin & Florence. BS Minnesota St U Mankato 1977; MA EDS 1980; MDiv EDS 1984. D 7/24/1984 Bp Robert Marshall Anderson P 6/9/1985 Bp John Bowen Coburn. m 11/4/1989 Len Freeman c 2. Int R Trin Ch Excelsior MN 2010-2011; Asst R S Mart's By The Lake Epis Minnetonka Bch MN 2007-2009; Ed, Vstry Papers ECF Inc New York NY 2002-2010, Sr. Cmncatn Consult. 1988-2001; P Assoc Chr Ch Short Hills NJ 1992-1998; Asst R Ch Of S Mart-In-The-Fields Philadelphia PA 1986-1989; Cathd Asst Dio Massachusetts Boston MA 1984-1986; The Cathd Ch Of S Paul Boston MA 1984-1986; Chapl Mem Cathd Ch Of S Mk Minneapolis MN 2011-2012. Writer, "Living Discipleship," Forw Mvmt, 2015; Auth, "Bible Wmn: All Their Words and Why They Matter," Forw Mvmt, 2014; Auth, "The Spy on Noah's Ark," Forw Mvmt, 2013; Auth, "Day by Day," *Forw, Day by Day*, Forw Movment, 2013; Auth, "Gd Lord, Deliver Us: A Lenten Journey," Forw Mvmt/Ch Pub, 2011; Ed, "Wisdom Found: Stories of Wmn Transfigured by Faith," Forw Mvmt, 2011; Auth, "The Scarlet Cord," Jn Hunt Pub, 2010; Ed, "Funding Future Mnstry," ECF, 2010; Contributing Auth, "Praying Day by Day: A Year of Meditations," Forw Mvmt, 2009; Auth, "Tips for Vestries," Forw Mvmt, 2008; Ed, "Doing H Bus: The Best of Vstry Papers," Ch Pub, 2006; Ed, "Mnstry on the Frontier," ECF, 2000; Auth, "Theol Educ: A Changing Blueprint," *Epis Life*, Epis Life, 2000; Contributing Ed, "The Zacchaeus Proj," ECF, 1999; Ed, "The Times and Timeliness of Henry Knox Sherrill," ECF, 1999; Ed, "Involuntary Termination of Cler within The Epis Ch," Epis Ch Foundaiton, 1996; Ed, "Report of PBp and Exec Coun," ECUSA, 1994; Ed, "Vstry Papers," *2001-2010*, ECF. ECom 1980. Gold Medal, Bible Study Illumination Awards 2015; Polly Bond Awards (30) ECom (1981-2009) 2009; Awd of Excellence (2) Associated Ch Press 1995; Cox Fllshp Dio Massachusetts 1986; Fllshp No Amer Mnstrl Assn 1980.

FREEMAN JR, Monroe (NC) 1706 Highlands Vw SE, Smyrna GA 30082 **Supply P Var Parishes 2001-** B Chattanooga TN 1936 s Monroe & Bessie. BA Cn-

trl St U 1958; Cert U Dijon 1966; MA Montclair St U 1970; Rutgers The St U of New Jersey 1977; MDiv GTS 1985. D 6/7/1985 P 4/26/1986 Bp John Shelby Spong. m 12/14/1980 Marjorie Freeman c 2. Int S Barth's 1999-2000; S Tit Epis Ch Durham NC 1992-1998; R S Paul's Epis Ch Greenwich NY 1989-1991; R S Steph's Ch Schuylerville NY 1988; R Trin Ch Irvington NJ 1986-1988. Auth, "Resurr Dioc Chr Nwsltr," 1990. Life Mem UBE, OHC.

FREEMAN JR, Norman (Los) St George's Church And Academy, 23802 Avenida de la Carlota, Laguna Hills CA 92653 **Timpanist The New York Pops Orchestra 1983-** B Orange NJ 1952 s Norman & Jane. BA Juilliard Sch 1974; MA Juilliard Sch 1975; CPE Bellevue Hosp 1995; MDiv GTS 1997. D 5/3/1997 Bp Joe Doss P 11/15/1997 Bp Vincent King Pettit. c 2. R and Headmaster S Geo's Epis Ch Laguna Hills CA 2006-2015; Vic S Mich's U Mssn Isla Vista CA 2000-2006; Chapl U CA At Santa Barbara Isla Vista Ca 2000-2006; Cur S Paul's Ch Riverside CT 1997-2000; Cur The Ch Of S Uriel The Archangel Sea Girt NJ 1997; Dept Chair Mannes Coll of Mus New York NY 1989-2000. Auth, "Barbara Streisand: The Concert," 1994. Grammy Awd, w Ny Philharmonic Acad Of Rcrdng Sciences 1987.

FREEMAN, Reed H (Miss) 12614 Muirfield Blvd S, Jacksonville FL 32225 **R H Trin Epis Ch Gainesville FL 2016-; S Paul's By-The-Sea Epis Ch Jaxville Bch FL 2015-; Int St. Pauls by the Sea Epis. Ch Jacksonville Bch FL 2015-** B Milton MA 1940 s Reed & Elizabeth. SB MIT 1961; SM MIT 1963; MDiv Sewanee: The U So, TS 1996; DMin Sewanee: The U So, TS 2005; DMin GTF 2012. D 6/29/1996 P 6/21/1997 Bp Robert Carroll Johnson Jr. m 6/17/1961 Nancy Bruce Freeman c 3. Int Ch of the Annunc Vidalia GA 2014-2015; Int Gr Epis Ch Orange Pk FL 2013-2014; P-in-c Resurr Epis Ch Jacksonville FL 2011-2012; Int S Mk's Ch Dalton GA 2010-2011; Int S Paul's Ch Macon GA 2010; Int S Andr's Epis Ch Douglas GA 2009-2010; Int H Comf Epis Ch Tallahassee FL 2007-2009; Int S Andr's Ch Jacksonville FL 2005-2007; R Trin Ch Hattiesburg MS 2001-2004; R S Mk's Epis Ch Huntersville NC 1998-2001; Vic All SS Epis Ch Charlotte NC 1996-1998.

FREEMAN, Robert Arthur (NH) Po Box 182, Poultney VT 05764 B Lynn MA 1932 s Robert & Miriam. BA Br 1957; MEd Bridgewater Coll 1963; BD EDS 1969. D 6/26/1969 Bp Robert McConnell Hatch P 1/1/1970 Bp Donald J Campbell. m 6/25/1966 Barbara E Freeman. S Jn's Ch Walpole NH 1993-2002; Dio Wstrn Massachusetts Springfield 1984-1988, 1969-1970, Intern 1969-1970; R S Phil's Ch Easthampton MA 1984-1988; P-in-c S Paul's Epis Sum Chap Otis MA 1978-1984; Ch Of The Gd Shpd So Lee MA 1974-1984; S Geo's Ch Lee MA 1974-1984; P-in-c Chr Ch Island Pond VT 1971-1974.

FREEMAN, Robert W (Vt) 38 Beaman St # 235, Poultney VT 05764 **Died 12/21/2015** B London UK 1931 s William & Margaret. U of Vermont 1970; MA Antioch Coll 1988. D 1/28/1973 P 11/1/1973 Bp Harvey D Butterfield. m 9/21/1957 Ivy Allan c 3. Trin Epis Ch E Poultney VT 1981-1996; S Paul's Epis Ch Wells VT 1981-1990; R S Jn's 1980-2015; Asst Chr Ch Montpelier VT 1973-1980.

FREEMAN, Sarah B (Colo) 726 W Elati Cir, Littleton CO 80120 B Kermit TX 1949 d Richard & Rose. Santa Rosa Jr Coll 1968; Lic St of California 1968; Colorado NW Cmnty Coll 1985; EFM Sewanee: The U So, TS 2000; Colorado Chr U 2004. D 8/10/1996 P 4/12/1997 Bp William Jerry Winterrowd. m 8/17/2002 Lyndle Freeman. S Paul's Epis Ch Cntrl City CO 2003-2014; D S Tim's Epis Ch Rangely CO 1996-2015. "Pryr for Erin," Wmn Uncommon Prayers/Morehouse Pub, 2000; "Cheryl's Pryr," Wmn Uncommon Prayers/Morehouse Pub, 2000.

FREEMAN, Sollace Mitchell (At) 5194 Glenstone Ct, Gainesville GA 30504 **Ret 2006-** B Gainesville FL 1940 s Sollace & Frances. BA Cntr Coll 1962; MDiv VTS 1965. D 7/19/1965 P 5/21/1966 Bp Frank A Juhan. m 7/7/1990 Patricia G Freeman c 3. Int S Mary And S Martha S Buford GA 2006-2007; R S Gabr's Epis Ch Oakwood GA 1999-2006; Assoc Gr Epis Ch Gainesville GA 1990-1999; R S Eliz's Epis Ch Dahlonega GA 1990-1994; Chapl USNR 1970-2000; R Gr Ch Paducah KY 1967-1973; Cur Gr Ch Paducah KY 1965-1967; Com on Aging Dio Cntrl Gulf Coast Pensacola FL 1984-1988; Ex-Coun Dio Kentucky Louisville KY 1968-1970.

FREEMAN, T.J. (NI) 611 W Berry St, Fort Wayne IN 46802 **Trin Ch Ft Wayne IN 2017-** B Lafayette IN 1980 s Terry & Cynthia. BA Hanover Coll 2003; MDiv Epis TS Of The SW 2014; MDiv Epis TS of the SW 2014. D 3/8/2014 P 8/29/2014 Bp Cate Waynick. m 6/5/2010 Anne M Freeman c 2. Calv Ch Pittsburgh PA 2014-2017. tjfreeman@trinityfw.org

FREEMAN, Warren Gray (Mass) 77 Lakeside Trailer Park, Mashpee MA 02649 **Died 4/7/2017** B Attleboro MA 1937 s Lawrence & Irene. BA Trin 1959; STB EDS 1963. D 6/22/1963 Bp Anson Phelps Stokes Jr P 6/10/1965 Bp Frederic Cunningham Lawrence. c 4. Asst S Barn Ch Falmouth MA 1994-1998; 1980-2017; Asst S Jn's Ch Sandwich MA 1978-1979; Assoc Chr Ch Needham Hgts MA 1965-1970; Cur Trin Par Melrose MA 1963-1965.

FREES, Mooydeen Claire (SO) 3826 Portrush Way, Amelia OH 45102 B Hays Kansas 1938 d Jack & Orpha. BA SW Coll Winfield KS 1960; RN Jewish Hosp of Cincinnati 1978; MEd Xavier U 1988; MA The Athenaeum of Ohio 1994; Cert Sthrn Ohio Sch For The Diac 1999. D 10/30/1999 Bp Kenneth Lester Price. S Tim's Epis Ch Cincinnati OH 2008-2010.

FREGEAU, Stephen Alfred (Mass) 7719 SE Sugar Sand Cir, Hobe Sound FL 33455 **Asst S Mary's Epis Ch Stuart FL 2007-** B Boston MA 1943 s Alfred & Thelma. BA Bos 1969; MA Estrn Nazarene Coll 1983; MDiv EDS 1988. D 6/4/1986 Bp John Bowen Coburn P 7/11/1987 Bp David Elliot Johnson. c 2. Assoc S Greg's Ch Boca Raton FL 2005, 2001; Assoc S Paul's Ch Delray Bch FL 2004; Int Gr Ch W Palm Bch FL 1999-2000; Jas L Duncan Conf Cntr Delray Bch FL 1998-2007; Dio Massachusetts Boston MA 1992-1994; Vic Trin Epis Ch Rockland MA 1987-1998; Asst All SS Par Whitman MA 1986-1987; Chapl Metropltn St Hosp Waltham MA 1983-1988. ACPE 1988-2003; Epis Camps & Conf Centers 1998; IACCA 1998. Cert Conf Cntr Profsnl IACCA 2007; Cert Int Mnstry IMN 2005. safregeau@aol.com

FREGOSO, Krista (Cal) 1707 Gouldin Rd, Oakland CA 94611 **S Jn's Epis Ch Oakland CA 2011-** B Akron OH 1975 d Dale & Susan. BEd U NC at Chap Hill 1999; MDiv CDSP 2008. D 6/28/2008 Bp Alfred Marble Jr P 1/7/2009 Bp Michael B Curry. Assoc S Fran' Par Palos Verdes Estates CA 2008-2010.

FREIRE-SOLORZANO, Luis Hernan (EcuC) Barrio El Tambo Sector Bomba De Aqua, Pelileo 24 Ecuador B Riobamba Chimborazo EC 1969 s Mecias & Gloria. Universidad Abjerta De Loja. D 4/16/1994 Bp Jose Neptali Larrea-Moreno. m 11/1/1990 Maria Isabel Nunez Valencia.

FRELUND, Warren F (Ia) 1029 W State St, Mason City IA 50401 B Mason City IA 1943 No Iowa Area Cmnty Coll; U of Iowa. D 5/26/1994 Bp Chris Christopher Epting. m 6/10/1962 Susan Frelund c 3. Dio Wyoming Casper 2007-2010; Dio Iowa Des Moines IA 2003-2007.

FRENCH, Alan C (NJ) 237 Summer Winds Cir, Aiken SC 29803 B New York NY 1952 s Seth & Frederica. BA Duke 1975; MDiv GTS 1979; MS NYU 2011. D 6/23/1979 Bp Robert Campbell Witcher Sr P 1/10/1980 Bp Paul Moore Jr. m 2/13/1988 Mary French c 3. Full Time Gr Epis Ch Rutherford NJ 2008-2009; Int S Jas Ch Long Branch NJ 2007; Int All SS Ch Princeton NJ 2004-2007; R S Andr's Epis Ch New Providence NJ 1985-2004; Cur S Geo's-By-The-River Rumson NJ 1981-1985; Asst Trin Ch Moorestown NJ 1979-1981; Secy Dio Conv Dio New Jersey Trenton NJ 1989-1995.

FRENCH, Clarke (NC) 814 Churchill Dr, Chapel Hill NC 27517 **R Ch Of The H Fam Chap Hill NC 2011-** B Toronto Canada 1974 s Donald & Gale. BA U Tor 1996; MDiv Trin, Toronto 1999; DMin VTS 2012. Trans 10/26/2006 as Priest Bp Gladstone Bailey Adams III. m 7/31/2004 Sally Johnson c 2. R Trin Epis Ch Watertown NY 2006-2011; Int Chr Ch New Brighton Staten Island NY 2005-2006; Serv Angl Ch of Can 1999-2005. OGS 2000-2004.

FRENCH, Jonathan D (CFla) 2304 SE 12th ST, Ocala FL 34471 **R Gr Epis Ch Of Ocala Ocala FL 2007-** B Los Angeles CA 1972 s Michael & Lisa. BA U of Florida 1995; MDiv Sewanee: The U So, TS 2006. D 5/27/2006 P 12/2/2006 Bp John Wadsworth Howe. m 11/19/2009 Maurica W French c 4. Asst Gr Epis Ch Ocala FL 2006-2008.

FRENCH, Peter (NJ) 53 University Pl., Princeton NJ 08540 B England 1972 s Michael & Christine. BA U of Melbourne Melbourne Australia 1992; BTh Untd Fac of Theol Melbourne Australia 1998; PhD U of Melbourne Melbourne Australia 2014. Trans 12/24/2008 Bp George Edward Councell. m 2/9/1999 Robyn Whitaker. Chapl Epis Ch at Pr Princeton NJ 2008-2016; P Gr Epis Ch Hinsdale IL 2007-2008; P Mssh-S Barth Epis Ch Chicago IL 2007; Chapl Trin U of Melbourne Australia 2004-2015.

FRENCH, Richard Clement (Oly) 23500 Cristo Rey Dr Unit 520G, Cupertino CA 95014 **Ret 1997-** B Lynchburg VA 1932 s C Clement & Helen. BA WA SU 1954; Dplma Oxf GB 1957; Wycliffe Hall 1957; MDiv CDSP 1959; MEd Gonzaga U 1969. D 6/9/1959 P 2/29/1960 Bp Russell S Hubbard. c 2. Vic S Jos And S Jn Ch Lakewood WA 1988-1997; Int S Marg's Epis Ch Bellevue WA 1987-1988; Int S Jn's Epis Ch Gig Harbor WA 1985-1986; Asst S Jas Epis Ch Kent WA 1983-1988; Asst All SS Ch Opportunity WA 1968-1969; All SS Ch Richland WA 1968-1969; Vic S Dunst's Epis Ch Grand Coulee WA 1963-1968; Vic S Jn Bapt Ephrata WA 1961-1968; S Paul's Ch Walla Walla WA 1959-1961. CADO 1985-2012; Curs Mvmt 1979-2012; Pastors Pryr Summit 1995-2012. hon CDSP/ Berkeley, CA 1959; Phi Beta Kappa/ scl WA SU/ Pullman, WA 1954.

FRENCH, Sally (NC) 407 E. Seneca St., Manlius NY 13104 **S Phil's Ch Durham NC 2014-** B 1970 d Herbert & Elizabeth. BA U Tor 1999; MDiv U Tor CA 2001. Trans 11/15/2008 as Priest Bp Gladstone Bailey Adams III. m 7/31/2004 Clarke French c 1. All SS Ch Hamlet NC 2013-2014; Shared Mnstry Of Nthrn NY Brownville NY 2010-2011; Int Chr Ch Manlius NY 2008-2009; Int S Mk The Evang Syracuse NY 2007-2008.

FRENCH, William A (NwPa) 42 Oak St, Brookville PA 15825 **Int St.Jas Epis 2004-** B Williamson WV 1933 s Marcellus & Margrette. BS Indiana U of Pennsylvania; BS Edinboro U 1957. D 11/1/1991 P 12/6/1992 Bp Robert Deane Rowley Jr. m 8/9/1959 Andrea Lynne McManigle. Int P Chr Epis Ch Oil City PA 2001-2003; Int S Jn's Ch Franklin PA 1999-2000; Int Chr Ch Punxsutawney PA 1997-1998; Int Ch Of Our Sav Dubois PA 1996-1997; Int S Lk's Epis Ch Smethport PA 1995-1996; Emm Epis Ch Emporium PA 1993-1995; Int S Agnes' Epis Ch S Marys PA 1993-1995.

FRENS, Mary Jean (WMich) 934 Clubview Dr, Fremont MI 49412 B Fremont MI 1949 d Authur & Geraldyne. BA Calvin Coll 1971; MA Wstrn Michigan U 1973; Angl Stds SWTS 1999; MDiv Wstrn TS 1999. D 6/17/2000 P 12/16/2000 Bp Edward Lewis Lee Jr. m 5/20/1980 Richard F String c 2. R S Mk's Ch Newaygo MI 2002-2016; Assoc S Jn's Ch Fremont MI 2001-2003, D 2000-2001.

FRENSLEY, James Monroe (Colo) 3506 Armstrong Ave, Dallas TX 75205 **Ret 1987-** B Duncan OK 1925 s Frank & Nancy. BFA U of Oklahoma 1950; MDiv Sewanee: The U So, TS 1961. D 6/20/1961 Bp Charles A Mason P 12/1/1961 Bp John Joseph Meakin Harte. Cleric S Jn's Cathd Denver CO 1984-1987; Asst S Mich And All Ang Ch Dallas TX 1976-1983; Assoc S Jas Epis Ch San Francisco CA 1974-1976; P-in-c Ch Of S Mths Dallas TX 1961-1965.

FREW, Randolph Lloyd (NY) 332 Bleecker St #K80, New York NY 10014 **Fndr, Exec Off AIDS Action Intl 1994-; Asst Cathd Ch of S Jn the Div New York NY 1987-** B Parsons KS 1947 s Everett & Alice. BA U of Nevada at Las Vegas 1969; MDiv GTS 1972. D 6/29/1972 P 2/8/1973 Bp Wesley Frensdorff. Epis Ch Cntr New York NY 1992-1994; Stff Off for AIDS Mnstry ECEC New York NY 1988-1994; Fndr, Exec Off H Apos Soup Kitchen New York NY 1981-1984; R Ch Of The H Apos New York NY 1978-1984; S Barth's Ch Ely NV 1976-1978; Vstng P S Jas Epis Ch Eureka NV 1976-1978; Instr Bp Gorman HS Las Vegas NV 1974-1975; S Matt's Ch Las Vegas NV 1973-1978; Asst Chr Ch Las Vegas NV 1973-1974; Field Educ Supvsr The GTS New York NY 1978-1984. Auth, *Praying w HIV/AIDS*, Forw Mvmt, 2002.

FREY, Louane Florence Virgilio (NC) 801 Footbridge Pl, Cary NC 27519 **Hlth Care Chapl The Forest at Duke 2009-; Assoc for Chld's & Yth Mnstry S Steph's Ch Durham NC 2008-** B Jamaica NY 1945 d Michael & Geraldine. BA Limestone Coll 1967; Cert D Formation Prog 2000. D 10/21/2001 Bp David Bruce Joslin. m 10/25/1970 Robert Alden Frey c 2. Yth Dir All SS Ch Princeton NJ 2006-2007; D S Fran Ch Dunellen NJ 2002-2006; D S Paul's Epis Ch Bound Brook NJ 2000-2002.

FREY, Matthew Vincent (WTex) 2620 Crestview Dr, Edinburg TX 78539 **Ch Of The Redeem Eagle Pass TX 2015-** B Leadville CO 1958 s William & Barbara. BA U of Nthrn Colorado 1981; MA U of Nthrn Colorado 1989; MDiv TESM 2002. D 6/8/2002 P 12/8/2002 Bp William Jerry Winterrowd. m 6/12/1983 Katharine A Frey c 2. R S Matt's Ch Edinburg TX 2012-2015; Asst R S Geo Ch San Antonio TX 2008-2012; R Ch Of The Adv Pittsburgh PA 2005-2007; Asst Trin Epis Ch Washington PA 2002-2005.

FREY, Paul Anthony (WTex) 139 Kentucky St, Laredo TX 78041 **Chr Ch Epis Laredo TX 2004-; Dn of Wstrn Convoc Dio W Texas San Antonio TX 2017-, Stndg Com 2017-, GC Dep 2012-2013, Exam Chapl 2009-** B Philadelphia PA 1955 s William & Barbara. none Red Rocks Cmnty Coll 1973; none U of Houston 1980; BA Loretto Heights Coll 1987; MDiv TESM 1992. D 6/20/1992 Bp William Jerry Winterrowd P 12/16/1992 Bp Peter J Lee. m 8/10/1980 Anne R Frey c 2. R Ch Of The Redeem Eagle Pass TX 1998-2004; Asst Truro Epis Ch Fairfax VA 1992-1998. christchurchlaredo@gmail.com

✠ FREY, The Rt Rev William Carl (Colo) 23315 Eagle Gap, San Antonio TX 78255 **Int R Chr Ch San Antonio 2010-** B Waco TX 1930 s Harry & Ethel. BA U CO 1952; BTh PDS 1955. D 6/29/1955 P 1/25/1956 Bp Joseph Summerville Minnis Con 11/26/1967 for Gua. c 5. Int Chr Epis Ch San Antonio TX 2010-2012, Int 2000-2010; Asstg Bp of the Rio Grande Dio The Rio Grande Albuquerque 2008-2010, Chair CSR 1960-2007; Dn/Pres TESM Ambridge PA 1990-1996; Dio Colorado Denver CO 1972-1990; Chapl U AR-Fayetteville 1971-1972; Pres Prov IX 1969-1972; Bp of Gua Dio Guatemala 1967-1972; Chair BEC Dio Costa Rica 1963-1967; Serv Ch in Costa Rica 1962-1964; Dn Santa Fe Convoc 1959-1962; R Trin On The Hill Epis Ch Los Alamos NM 1958-1962; Vic Timberline Circuit Mssns CO 1955-1958. Auth, "Cancelada," *Why They Threw Us Out of Guatemala*, Kindle, 2012; Auth, "The Dance of Hope," Waterbrook Press, 2003. DD VTS 1997; DD PDS 1970.

FRIAS, Miguel (Chi) 941 W Lawrence Ave, Chicago IL 60640 B 1949 s Nicolas & Cruz. S Andrews TS Manila PH; Universidad Autonoma De Santo Domingo Santo Domingo Do; LCA U Cntrl Del Este Do 1977; LST Centro de Estudios Teologicos 1980; MDiv McCormick TS 1985. D 3/1/1981 P 8/1/1982 Bp Telesforo A Isaac. m 9/26/1981 Rosa Frias. Dio Chicago Chicago IL 1989-1991; Ch Of Chr The King Chicago IL 1984-1993; S Marg's Ch Bronx NY 1983-1984; Dio The Dominican Republic (Iglesia Epis Dominicana) Gazcue Santo Domingo 1981-1983.

FRIBOURGH, Cynthia Kaye (Ark) 11123 Bainbridge Dr, Little Rock AR 72212 **Sewanee U So TS Sewanee TN 2015-; Admin Inst for Theol Stds at St. Marg's 2011-; D S Mk's Epis Ch Little Rock AR 2010-** B Iowa City IA 1956 d James & Cairdenia. BA U of Arkansas 1978; MPS Loyola U-Chicago 2006. D 10/28/2000 Bp Larry Maze. m 10/15/1988 Richard Scott Schreiber. Dio Arkansas Little Rock AR 2003-2008; D S Marg's Epis Ch Little Rock AR 2000-2010. Assn for Epis Deacons 1998.

FRICK, Matthew M (Dal) 2627 Horseshoe Dr, Alexandria LA 71301 **S Mths' Epis Ch Athens TX 2014-** B Harvey IL 1980 s Robert & Mary. BA Concordia U 2003; MDiv Nash 2008. D 6/14/2008 Bp Keith Lynn Ackerman. S Tim's Ch Alexandria LA 2011-2014; Cur Trin Ch Marshall TX 2008-2011.

FRIDAY, Roxanne (Wyo) D 6/25/2016 P 5/26/2017 Bp John Smylie.

FRIEDEL, James (WTex) 11905 E Maple Dr, Claremore OK 74019 **S Ptr's Epis Ch Rockport TX 2008-** B Cuero TX 1955 s James & Helen. Texas A&M U 1975; BBA Texas St U San Marcos 1978; MDiv Epis TS of the SW 1994. D 6/24/1994 P 4/1/1996 Bp James Edward Folts. m 4/19/1980 Christine Friedel c 3. R S Paul's Ch Claremore OK 2002-2008; Dio Oklahoma Oklahoma City OK 2000-2008; Dio Missouri S Louis MO 2000-2002; Cn to the Ordnry Epis Dio MO S Louis MO 2000-2002; Asst Emm Epis Ch S Louis MO 1997-2000; Asst R S Geo Ch San Antonio TX 1994-1997.

FRIEDMAN, Anna Russell (Ala) PO Box 27, Minter AL 36761 **All SS Epis Ch Birmingham AL 2012-** B Nashville TN 1983 d Mark & Mary. BA Lake Forest Coll 2005; MDiv Van 2008; Dip Ang Stud Sewanee: The U So, TS 2010. D 6/5/2010 P 2/19/2011 Bp John Bauerschmidt. m 5/29/2010 Christopher K Friedman c 2. D-in-c S Paul's (Carlowville) Carlowville AL 2010-2011.

FRIEDMAN, Maurice Lane (WTex) 4934 Lakeway Dr, Brownsville TX 78520 B Philadelphia PA 1952 s Donald & Joyce. BA Penn 1974; MDiv EDS 1979. D 6/16/1979 Bp Lyman Cunningham Ogilby P 6/15/1980 Bp Albert Ervine Swift. m 12/27/2008 Mary Louise B Friedman c 5. R Ch Of The Adv Brownsville TX 2009-2014; Vic Ch Of The H Sprt San Antonio TX 2002-2009; R S Ptr's Epis Ch Rockport TX 1997-2002; Stff Chapl Wilford Hall Med Cntr Lackland AFB TX 1996-1997; Hosp Chapl CPE Wilford Hall Med Cntr Lackland AFB TX 1995-1996; Chapl Peterson AFB Colorado Sprg CO 1992-1995; Chapl Off Of Bsh For ArmdF New York NY 1988-1997; P in charge S Alb's Cong US-AF Ramstein AB Germany 1988-1992; Int Ch Of The Trsfg No Bergen NJ 1988; Counslr New Views Treatment Cntr Greystone NJ 1987-1988; Counslr The Shire Mendham NJ 1986-1987; Cn Cathd Ch Of The Nativ Bethlehem PA 1985-1986; R Memi Ch Of S Lk Philadelphia PA 1981-1985; Cur S Mk's Ch Philadelphia PA 1979-1981; Chapl Police Chapl Rockport TX 1998-2002. SS-JE 1979-1995.

FRIEDRICH, James Louis (Los) 4685 Taylor Ave Ne, Bainbridge Island WA 98110 **Video, Liturg, Tchg Rel Imagineer Bainbridge Island WA 2005-** B Los Angeles CA 1944 s James & Elaine. BA Stan 1966; MDiv EDS 1969. D 9/13/1969 P 9/17/1970 Bp Francis E I Bloy. m 5/21/2005 Martha Karen Haig. Asst S Barn Epis Ch Bainbridge Island WA 2010-2013; Asst Gr Ch Bainbridge Island WA 2005-2010; Writer/Dir/Producer Cathd Films And Video Los Angeles CA 2003-2005; Writer/Dir/Producer Cathd Films And Video Clinton WA 1995-2002; Asst Chr Ch Par Ontario CA 1990-1995; Asst S Aug By-The-Sea Par Santa Monica CA 1984-1989; Writer/Dir/Producer Cathd Films And Video Los Angeles CA 1982-1995; Dio Los Angeles Los Angeles CA 1975-1976; Asst St Johns Pro-Cathd Los Angeles CA 1973-1984; Chapl U Michigan Cbury Hse Ann Arbor MI 1969-1970. Auth, "A Thin Place: Iona & The Celtic Way," Cathd Films And Video, 1998; Auth, "The Greening Of Faith," Cathd Films And Video, 1994; Auth, "The Electronic Campfire," Cathd Films And Video, 1993; Auth, "The Story Of Anglicanism," Cathd Films And Video, 1988; Auth, "The Story Of The Epis Ch," Cathd Films And Video, 1986.

FRIEDRICH JR, Robert E (Ct) 23 Friend Ct, Wenham MA 01984 **Lic Dio Bangor Wales UK 2017-; Lic Dio St. Asaph 2015-; Chapl Beacon Hospice 2007-; Pres, Consult Natl Ch Consulting Fndt Laconia NH 1997-** B Pittsburgh PA 1948 s Robert & Mary. BA Houghton Coll 1970; MDiv Gordon-Conwell TS 1974; GTS 1986; DMin GCTS 1996. D 6/7/1986 Bp Paul Moore Jr P 10/18/1986 Bp Andrew Frederick Wissemann. m 6/19/1971 Sandra B Friedrich c 2. S Steph's Ch Olean NY 2006-2007; The Ekklesia Inst Inc W Hartford CT 2006-2007; Int Gr In The Desert Epis Ch Las Vegas NV 2004-2006; Ch Of S Jn By The Sea W Haven W Haven CT 2004; All SS Epis Ch Meriden CT 1999-2002; Dio Wstrn Massachusetts Springfield 1997-1999, 1986-1988; R Ch Of The Epiph Newport NH 1992-1997; R Ch Of The Incarn Penfield NY 1988-1992; Sr Chapl Mid Hudson Psych Cntr New Hampton NY 1984-1986; Serv Presb Ch 1982-1986. Auth, "Discerning Your Cong's Future: Strategic & Sprtl Approach," Alb Inst, Inc, 1996. Ord of S Helena 1984.

FRIEDRICH, Roger Paul (SVa) 1136 Quintara St, San Francisco CA 94116 **1968-** B Long Branch NJ 1937 s Paul & Florence. BS Penn 1959; MDiv VTS 1965. D 1/17/1966 Bp David Shepherd Rose P 1/25/1967 Bp George P Gunn. Cur Chr And Gr Ch Petersburg VA 1966-1968.

FRIEND, Robert Douglas (Va) 4011 College Valley Ct, Richmond VA 23233 **Int S Jn's Epis Ch Richmond VA 2013-** B Long Beach CA 1951 s Sidney & Janice. BA U of Virginia 1973; MDiv VTS 1976; DMin VTS 1998. D 5/22/1976 Bp John Alfred Baden P 12/18/1976 Bp David Shepherd Rose. m 8/20/1977 Susan Friend c 1. R All SS Ch Richmond VA 2001-2011; R S Fran Epis Ch Great Falls VA 1987-2001; Assoc S Anne's Par Annapolis MD 1983-1986; Asst Estrn Shore Chap Virginia Bch VA 1976-1983. Auth, "Stndg Between Generations," *Honoring Fr And Mo As They Mature Into Elderhood*, 1998.

FRIESE JR, Walter Edward (WLa) 107 Shady Ave., Pineville LA 71360 B Saint Louis MO 1947 s Walter & Dorothy. BS Missouri Bapt U 1975; SW Bapt TS 1978; MS Amberton U 1985; TESM 1999. D 6/19/1999 P 3/2/2000 Bp James Monte Stanton. m 11/23/1983 Paulette Friese. R S Tim's Ch Alexandria LA 2007-2009, R 2006-; Cn to the Ordnry Dio Wstrn Lousiana Pineville LA 2004-2007; Dio Wstrn Louisiana Alexandria LA 2004-2006; R All SS Epis Ch Russellville AR 2002-2004; S Jas Epis Ch Texarkana TX 1999-2002; The Epis Ch of the Intsn Carrollton TX 1999; Chr Epis Ch Plano TX 1995-1998.

FRINK, James Phillip (RI) 3a Grouse Trl, Smithfield RI 02917 B Saint Johnsbury VT 1929 s Clarence & Beatrice. BA U of Vermont 1951; MA Br 1957; MDiv Nash 1959. D 6/20/1959 P 12/19/1959 Bp John S Higgins. m 9/3/1962 Caryl S Frink c 2. R Trin Ch N Scituate RI 1971-1996; R S Mary's Ch E Providence RI 1962-1971; In-c S Ptr Manton RI 1959-1962.

FRISCH, Floyd Charles (ECR) 2 N Santa Cruz Ave, Los Gatos CA 95030 **Assoc S Andr's Ch Saratoga CA 1981-** B Buffalo NY 1933 s Floyd & Pearl. Oxf GB; BS SUNY 1955; BD Yale DS 1958; JD U of San Francisco 1965. D 4/12/1969 Bp Chauncie Kilmer Myers P 2/1/1971 Bp George Richard Millard. m 9/10/1967 Leilani Ann Frisch c 2. P-in-c Chr Ch Alameda CA 1980-1981; P-in-c S Fran Epis Ch San Jose CA 1979-1980; P-in-c S Tim's Epis Ch Mtn View CA 1973-1979; Asst Gd Samar Epis Ch San Jose CA 1969-1971; Chancelor Dio El Camino Real San Jose CA. Auth, *Common Law & Cn Law at the End of the 13th Century*, Oxford Press, 1984.

FRITCH, Charles Oscar (CFla) 324 S Lost Lake Ln, Casselberry FL 32707 B Rock Island IL 1944 s Leo & Alice. BA S Meinrad Coll 1966; MDiv S Meinrad TS 1970; MA U of W Florida 1976. Rec 5/20/1986 Bp William Hopkins Folwell. m 1/8/1977 Patricia Fritch c 3. R S Matt's Epis Ch Orlando FL 1989-2010; Asst Emm Ch Orlando FL 1986-1988.

FRITSCH, Andrew John (WMo) 3702 Poplar Dr, Joplin MO 64804 B Joplin MO 1932 s John & Norval. MD S Louis U 1957. D 12/7/1991 Bp John Clark Buchanan. m 7/7/1956 Martha Ann Barratt c 2. D S Steph's Ch Monett MO 1997-2005; D S Phil's Ch Joplin MO 1991-1997. "Panlobular and Centulobular Emphysema," Annuals of Internal Med, 1961. NAAD.

FRITSCH, Peter Louis (Ore) 6310 W Ford Ave, Las Vegas NV 89139 B Redwood City CA 1953 s Stephen & Joyce. BA U Pac 1975; MDiv CDSP 1992. D 6/12/1992 P 1/22/1993 Bp Jerry Alban Lamb. m 12/21/1974 Brenda Gayle Fritsch c 3. Dio Oregon Portland OR 2010-2013; Dio Wstrn Massachusetts Springfield 2002-2003; R S Dav's Ch Feeding Hills MA 2002-2003; R S Paul's On The Plains Epis Ch Lubbock TX 1999-2002; S Aug Of Cbury Rocklin CA 1994-1999; Mssnr The Epis Dio Nthrn California Sacramento CA 1992-1999, 1992-1993. CT; Natl Ntwk Of Epis Cler Assns 1992.

FRITSCHE, Janet Yvonne (NMich) 122 Hunter Rd, Iron River MI 49935 B Geneseo IL 1945 d Herman & Mary. D 3/12/2006 Bp James Arthur Kelsey. m 9/21/1968 Jere Fritsche c 3.

FRITSCHNER, Annie (WNC) Po Box 2818, Hendersonville NC 28793 B Louisville KY 1955 d William & Eleanor. BA Connecticut Coll 1977; Cert Assn of Fundraising Professionals Alexandria VA 2001. D 11/23/2002 Bp Bob Johnson. m 9/23/1995 Samuel Hunt Fritschner c 2. Ch of the Advoc Asheville NC 2005-2008; Dio Wstrn No Carolina Asheville NC 2005-2006; D Ch Of S Jn In The Wilderness Flat Rock NC 2002-2008.

FRITSCHNER, John B (Ky) Saint Luke's Church, 1206 Maple Ln, Anchorage KY 40223 **Chapl Seamens Ch Inst New York NY 2016-; Asst Ch Of The Adv Louisville KY 2015-; Bd Trst Epis Ret Serv Cincinnati OH 2017-** B Indianapolis IN 1951 s Charles & Elizabeth. BA U of Kentucky 1973; MA U of Iowa 1978; MDiv Sewanee: The U So, TS 1985. D 6/1/1985 Bp Addison Hosea P 12/7/1985 Bp Don Adger Wimberly. m 6/27/1981 Nancy N Fritschner c 2. Int Gr Ch Paducah KY 2014-2015; Int S Lk's Ch Louisville KY 2013-2014; R H Trin Epis Ch Auburn AL 1995-2013; R S Dav's Ch Cheraw SC 1988-1995; Cur Ch Of The Gd Shpd Lexington KY 1985-1988. SSJE 1999. frjohn@adventky.org

FRITTS, John Clinton (WTex) St Paul's Episcopal Church, PO Box 1148, Brady TX 76825 **R S Jas Epis Ch Del Rio TX 2013-** B Tyler TX 1958 s John & Marilyn. BA Texas A&M U 1981; MDiv Epis TS of the SW 2006. D 3/2/2008 Bp David Mitchell Reed P 9/24/2008 Bp Gary Richard Lillibridge. m 10/28/1983 Lynda A Fritts c 2. R S Paul's Ch Brady TX 2008-2013.

FRITTS, Julia Anne (Ct) 702 Brookwood Rd, Baltimore MD 21229 B Washington DC 1956 d Lowell & Barbara Ann. BS U of Maryland 1985; MA Traditional Acupuncture Inst 1999; MDiv GTS 2008. D 6/14/2008 Bp John L Rabb P 1/24/2009 Bp Andrew Donnan Smith. c 1. S Jn's Ch E Windsor CT 2015-2017; The Epis Ch Of The Gd Samar Corvallis OR 2013-2014; Assoc R S Jn's Ch Stamford CT 2008-2010.

FRITZ, Janice Vary (CPa) 109 Hope Dr, Boiling Springs PA 17007 B Bethlehem PA 1951 d Samuel. BS Millersville U; MS Shippensburg U 1979. D 6/19/2004 Bp Michael Whittington Creighton. m 9/28/1996 John David Fritz. D S Andr's Epis Ch Shippensburg PA 2004-2013.

FRIZZELL, Judith Ann (Dal) 5200 Fairway Circle, Granbury TX 76049 B Navasota TX 1940 d Arthur & Louetta. U of Houston; BA Rice U 1962; Cert Angl TS 1991. D 6/27/1998 Bp James Monte Stanton. m 7/21/1962 Wesley Everett Frizzell c 4. Ch Of The Incarn Dallas TX 2003-2012.

FRNKA, Virginia H (WTex) 314 W Gayle St, Edna TX 77957 **Partnr In Mnstry Estrn Convoc Kenedy TX 2010-** B San Antonio TX 1952 d Edward & Annie. BA U of Texas 1974; MA Epis TS of the SW 2002; Cert Iona Sch for Mnstry 2010. D 6/10/2010 Bp David Mitchell Reed P 12/12/2010 Bp Gary Richard Lillibridge. c 2. D Partnr In Mnstry 2010.

FROEHLICH, Burt H (SeFla) 406-B Coopers Cove Rd, St Augustine FL 32095 B Cincinnati OH 1950 s Fredrick & Margaret. BA Morehead St U 1974; MDiv VTS 1978. D 5/27/1978 P 3/1/1979 Bp John Mc Gill Krumm. m 8/14/1993 Sharon Froehlich c 1. R / Headmaster S Chris's By-The-Sea Epis Ch Key Biscayne FL 2008-2011; S Thos Flagler Cnty Palm Coast FL 2006-2008; Reg Cn Dio Florida Jacksonville 2001-2008; Ch Of The Recon S Aug FL 2001-2006; Cn - Int Ch Of The H Comf Cres City FL 2000-2001; Cn - Int Emm Ch Welaka FL 2000-2001; S Mk's Ch Palatka FL 1999; Int S Cathr's Ch Jacksonville FL 1998-1999; Pres BMG Commercial Real Estate Jacksonville FL 1992-2006; Pres BMG Commercial Real Estate Inc. Jacksonville Florida 1990-2005; Gd Samar Epis Ch Orange Pk FL 1990-1991; VP Florida Properties Bramalea Intl Real Estate Ontario Can 1986-1992; R S Ptr's Epis Ch Ashtabula OH 1985-1988; Assoc R S Thos Epis Ch Terrace Pk OH 1983-1985; Asst R S Ptr's Ch Jacksonville FL 1980-1982; Asst & P-in-c S Jas Ch Potomac MD 1978-1980; Soc Worker Counslr Cave Run Comprehensive Care Cntr Morehead KY 1974-1978.

FROEHLICH, Meghan F (O) Presiding Bishop's Staff, 815 2nd Ave, New York NY 10017 Epis Ch Cntr New York NY 2015-; Dom And Frgn Mssy Soc- Epis Ch Cntr New York NY 2014-; Consult Consult / Exec Ldrshp Coach 2013-; Consult Consult / Exec Ldrshp Coach 2011-; Chapl Great Lakes Caring Hospice OH 2011- B Mountain View CA 1964 d Kenneth & Barbara. BA Old Dominion U 1986; MDiv Duke DS 1997. D 12/12/1999 P 6/11/2000 Bp Bob Johnson. Dio Kansas Topeka KS 2013-2014; Chapl Hospice of Medina Cnty 2011; Chapl Hospice of Medina Cnty OH 2011; R Ch Of Our Sav Akron OH 2003-2011; Assoc Ch Of The Gd Shpd Dallas TX 2000-2003; Asst Ch Of The Redeem Shelby NC 1999-2000; Chapl/Bereavement Coordntr Hospice of Cleveland Cnty NC 1997-1998; Grant Rec Calvin Inst for Chr Wrshp 2013-2014; Grant Rec Calvin Instutitue for Chr Wrshp 2010-2011; Grant Rec, Sabbatical Grant for Pstr Leaders Lousiville Inst 2009; Fresh Start Natl Fac Credo Inst Inc. Memphis TN 2007-2011; Trst Dio Ohio Cleveland 2006-2011, Fresh Start Coordntr 2004-2011. "An Incarnational Approach to Eucharistic Participation," *Questions Liturgiques/Stds in Liturg, Vol 81, 3-4*, Peeters, 2000; Auth, "What Defines Cler Compstn: Mssn or Mrkt?," *Questions for 21st Century Ch*, Abingdon, 1999.

FROILAND, Paul Vincent (Minn) 12525 Porcupine Ct, Eden Prairie MN 55344 1978- B Minneapolis MN 1947 s Jack & Harriet. BA S Olaf Coll 1969; MDiv Nash 1972; MA U MN 1978. D 6/29/1972 P 4/1/1973 Bp Philip Frederick McNairy. m 12/19/1970 Laurel Ann Froiland c 2. P-in-c S Ptr's Shakopee MN 1976-1978; Chapl Breck Sch Minneapolis MN 1974-1976; Assoc St Dav's Epis Ch Minnetonka MN 1972-1974. Auth, "Alzheimer's Disease A Case Study"; Auth, *Best Short Stories*; Auth, *Holt Guide to Engl*.

FROLICK, Betty Roberson (NI) 6334 Bennington Dr, Fort Wayne IN 46815 B Richmond VA 1942 d Andrew & Elizabeth. BS Ohio U 1964; CTh Whitaker TS 1990; Cert Theol Stud SWTS 1994. D 5/26/1990 Bp William Jones Gordon Jr P 9/1/1994 Bp R aymond Stewart Wood Jr. m 3/14/1964 Peter Frolick c 3. Assoc R Trin Ch Ft Wayne IN 2002-2014; R S Ptr's Epis Ch Hillsdale MI 1994-2001; Gr Epis Ch Standish MI 1990-1993; H Fam Epis Ch Midland MI 1990-1993; D S Paul's Epis Ch Gladwin MI 1990-1993.

FROLICK, Paul Michael (Roch) St George's Episcopal Chruch, 635 Wilder Rd, Hilton NY 14468 P-in-c S Geo's Ch Hilton NY 2012- B Pensacola FL 1968 s Peter & Betty. BM Eastman Sch of Mus 2000; MDiv Colgate Rochester Crozer DS 2012; Cert Angl Stds GTS 2012; Cert Angl Stds Gnrl Thoelogical Sem 2012. D 2/12/2012 P 8/18/2012 Bp Prince Grenville Singh. Chr Ch Pittsford Pittsford NY 2012, D 1998-2013.

FROMBERG, Paul D (Cal) 500 De Haro Street, San Francisco CA 94107 R S Greg Of Nyssa Ch San Francisco CA 2008-, R 2008-, Assoc 2004-2008; Dep to GC Dio California San Francisco CA 2015-, Alt Dep to GC 2012-2015 B Houston TX 1960 s Henry & Flora. Abilene Chr U 1980; BA Rhodes Coll 1984; MDiv Fuller TS 1987; CTh Epis TS of the SW 1990; DMin CDSP 2014. D 6/16/1990 Bp Maurice Manuel Benitez P 2/3/1991 Bp William Elwood Sterling. m 7/18/2008 Naurice Grant Martin. R St Andrews Epis Ch Houston TX 2000-2004; Cn Chr Ch Cathd Houston TX 1991-2000, D 1990-2000. Coun of AP 2008-2011. paul@paulfromberg.com

FRONTJES, Richard A (Chi) 910 Normal Rd, DeKalb IL 60115 Ch Of The Redeem Elgin IL 2015- B Saginaw Michigan 1972 s Richard & Leslie. BA Hope Coll 1995; PrTS 1996; MDiv Epis TS of the SW 2006; ThM Luth TS at Chicago 2012; ThM Other 2012; PhD Luth TS at Chicago 2014. D 12/18/2005 P 7/22/2006 Bp Edwin Max Leidel Jr. m 7/29/2000 Stacy Walker c 2. S Lk's Ch Dixon IL 2012-2015; Int S Paul's Ch Mchenry IL 2011-2012; P-in-c Mssh-S Barth Epis Ch Chicago IL 2009-2010; R S Matt's Ch Saginaw MI 2006-2009. rfrontjes@yahoo.com

FROST, Gregory Hayden (Los) 18354 Superior St, Northridge CA 91325 R Epis Ch Of S Andr And S Chas Granada Hills CA 1992- B Medford MA 1949 s Charles & Hazel. BA NEU 1973; MDiv Candler TS Emory U 1980; MDR Pepperdine U 2005. D 6/14/1980 P 5/2/1981 Bp Bennett Jones Sims. m 8/27/1976 Janice Mary Frost. Assoc H Innoc Ch Atlanta GA 1983-1992; Asst S Ptr's Ch Rome GA 1980-1983.

FROST, Jeffrey Louis (Cal) Saint Timothy's Church, 1550 Diablo Rd, Danville CA 94526 S Aug's Ch Oakland CA 2017- B San Jose CA 1957 s Robert & Elizabeth. BA California St U 1983; MDiv CDSP 1987. D 6/26/1987 Bp Charles Shannon Mallory P 5/22/1988 Bp Robert Louis Ladehoff. m 5/22/1982 Ellen Page Frost c 2. Gr Ch Martinez CA 2015-2017; R S Tim's Ch Danville CA 2013-2015; R All SS Epis Ch Redding CA 1997-2013; Calv Epis Ch Jerome ID 1994-1997; Vic Trin Ch Buhl ID 1994-1996; Cur Trin Epis Ch Ft Worth TX 1990-1994; Chapl Legacy Gd Samar Hosp Portland OR 1987-1990; Reg Dn The Epis Dio Nthrn California Sacramento CA 2008-2013. revjeff@gracechurchmtz.org

FROST-PHILLIPS, Lisa A (NC) 128 Creekview Cir, Carrboro NC 27510 Asst S Matt's Epis Ch Hillsborough NC 2003- B Atlanta GA 1967 BA U So 1989; MDiv Duke DS 1996; CAS VTS 1996. D 6/29/1996 Bp James Gary Gloster P 6/1/1997 Bp Robert Carroll Johnson Jr. m 7/7/1990 James Dickson Phillips c 3. Assoc S Lk's Epis Ch Durham NC 1996-2000. Wilkin'S Schlr U So 1985. frostphillips@gmail.com

FROTHINGHAM, Christen Struthers (Mass) 6 Sunset Ave, North Reading MA 01864 B New York NY 1950 d Alan & Sara. Bryn 1970; BA Brandeis U 1978. D 6/5/1993 P 6/12/1994 Bp David Elliot Johnson. m 1/5/1985 William Scott Wheeler c 2. Ch Of Our Sav Brookline MA 1994-2007; D All SS Par Brookline MA 1993-1994. Parsons Club 1994.

FROWE, Jeanne Shelton (Nev) 384 Sunset Dr, Reno NV 89509 R H Sprt 1983- B Athens AL 1922 d Oscar & George. BA U of Miami 1964. D 6/12/1983 P 12/1/1983 Bp Wesley Frensdorff. m 12/20/1941 Warren John Frowe.

FROYEN, Jeremy Craig (SeFla) Holy Sacrament Episcopal Church, 2801 N University Dr, Pembroke Pines FL 33024 H Sacr Hollywood FL 2016- B Memphis, TN 1974 s Robert & Janet. BA Florida Atlantic U 2011; MDiv VTS 2016. D 12/10/2015 Bp Leo Frade P 6/4/2016 Bp Peter David Eaton. frjeremy@holysacrament.org

FRUEHWIRTH OJN, Robert Alan (FdL) 66 Ella Road, Norwich NR1 4BS Great Britain (UK) S Mich's Ch Raleigh NC 2016- B Phoenix AZ 1969 s Gregory & Joan. D 1/25/1997 P 8/15/1997 Bp Russell Edward Jacobus. m 12/18/2010 Jane Fruehwirth. Rel Superior The Ord of Julian of Norwich Waukesha WI 2003-2010. Auth, "Words for Silence," Paraclete Press, 2008.

FRY, Gwenneth Jeri (Ark) 7604 Apache Road, Little Rock AR 72205 B Covington KY 1960 d Ralph & Melanie. BS Nthrn Kentucky U 1986; MDiv VTS 1990. D 6/17/1990 P 12/23/1990 Bp Don Adger Wimberly. m 6/10/1989 Lisa D Fry c 1. P-in-c Gr Ch Pine Bluff AR 2013-2014; Transitional Mnstry/Supply P Dio Arkansas Little Rock AR 2011-2013; R S Steph's Ch Phoenix AZ 2007-2011; Vic S Edm's Epis Ch Arcadia FL 2006-2007; Assoc R S Marg Of Scotland Epis Ch Sarasota FL 2003-2006; Int The Epis Ch Of S Jas The Less Northfield IL 2003; Assoc R S Bon Ch Sarasota FL 1998-2003; Vic S Jn's Ch Powell WY 1992-1994; Cur Calv Epis Ch Ashland KY 1990-1991; P-in-c S Alb's Ch Morehead KY 1990-1991.

FRY, Lisa D (Ark) 1000 N Mississippi St, Little Rock AR 72207 R Ch Of S Thos Camden ME 2017- B York ME 1959 d Gerald & Peggy. BA Colby Coll; MTS VTS 1989. D 6/11/2011 Bp Kirk Stevan Smith P 12/19/2011 Bp Larry Benfield. m 6/10/1989 Gwenneth Jeri Fry c 1. Cur S Mk's Epis Ch Little Rock AR 2011-2017.

FRY III, William Nall (WTenn) 10 N Highland St, Memphis TN 38111 Asst The Ch Of The Gd Shpd (Epis) Memphis TN 1969- B Memphis TN 1931 s William & Polly. U of Memphis 1953; U of Tennessee 1963. D 3/29/1969 Bp John Vander Horst P 2/1/1994 Bp Alex Dockery Dickson. m 9/22/1955 Catherine Dwyer. info@churchofthegoodshepherd.us

FRYE, Don Jay (Chi) 2843 Gypsum Cir, Naperville IL 60564 Registry Chapl Advoc Gd Samar Hosp 2010-; R S Jas Ch Dundee IL 2009- B Akron OH 1960 s Vernon & Onaline. BA Mt Vernon Nazarene Coll Mt Vernon OH 1982; MDiv Nazarene TS 1988; Angl Stds SWTS 2005; SWTS 2005. D 6/18/2005 P 12/17/2005 Bp Bill Persell. m 11/20/2010 David L Shallow c 3. Asst Ch Of The H Nativ Clarendon Hls IL 2005-2006.

FRYE III, Jacob Wade (ETenn) 332 Essex Dr, Knoxville TN 37922 Died 10/15/2016 B Newton NC 1947 s Jacob & Francis. Georgia St U; U of Maryland. D 12/15/2001 Bp Charles Glenn VonRosenberg. m 6/9/1972 Helen Lucille Frye. D Non-par 2005-2016; S Jn's Epis Cathd Knoxville TN 2005-2008; D S Andr's Ch Maryville TN 2001-2013. Fllshp of S Jn the Evang 2002.

FRYE, Linda Lou (Eau) 21836 Gladestone Ave, Tomah WI 54660 B Carlisle PA 1948 d Carl & Anna. D 6/29/1995 Bp William Charles Wantland. m 9/27/1997 Lyle Lavern Frye. D S Mary's Epis Ch Tomah WI 1995-2007.

FUESSEL JR, Paul A (Ia) 2585 Hurricane Loop Rd, Tennessee Ridge TN 37178 B New York NY 1940 s Paul & Ruby. BA Benedictine Coll 1974; LTh SWTS 1983. D 6/25/1983 Bp William Edwin Swing P 12/27/1983 Bp James Daniel Warner. m 12/30/1961 Chere Fuessel c 3. R Gr Ch Cedar Rapids IA 1999-2009; Chr Ch Collinsville IL 1991-1996; R Chr Ch Collinsville IL 1991-1996; Halifax-Pittsylvania Cure Java VA 1990-1991; Emm Ch Halifax VA 1988-1991; Vic S Jn's Mt Airy VA 1988-1991; Vic S Paul's Ch Peytonsburg Java VA 1988-1991; Dio Sthrn Virginia Newport News VA 1988-1989;

Vic S Aug's Ch De Witt NE 1983-1988; S Chas The Mtyr Fairbury NE 1983-1988; Vic S Chas Fairbury NE 1983-1988; 1999. Cmnty of Celebration.

FULFORD, David Edward (NwPa) **Vic S Aug Of Cbury Ch Edinboro PA 1995-** D 12/2/1995 P 12/1/1996 Bp Robert Deane Rowley Jr.

FULGHUM, Charles Benjamin (At) 759 Loridans Dr Ne, Atlanta GA 30342 B Selma NC 1926 s Charles & Alice. Candler TS Emory U; BS U NC 1950; MD U NC 1954. D 2/14/1965 Bp Randolph R Claiborne P 5/1/1984 Bp Charles Judson Child Jr. m 4/14/1977 Carole M Fulghum. S Mart In The Fields Ch Atlanta GA 1991-1995; Asst S Matt's Atlanta GA 1984-1988; Asst S Bede's Ch Atlanta GA 1983-1984; Asst S Alb's & S Andr's 1982-1983; Asst Ch Of The Atone Sandy Sprg GA 1970-1982; Asst H Innoc Ch Atlanta GA 1965-1970. Auth, "Sermons That Wk". AAPC.

FULGHUM, Peter Clopper (Md) 13007 Still Meadow Rd, Smithsburg MD 21783 **Ret 1996-** B Washington DC 1934 s James & Frances. BA Hampden-Sydney Coll 1958; BD Epis TS in Kentucky 1964. D 6/23/1964 P 5/30/1965 Bp William Henry Marmion. m 8/25/1956 Joan F Fulghum c 4. S Chris Epis Ch Linthicum Hts MD 1994-1995; All SS Ch Frederick MD 1992-1994; S Matt's Par Oakland MD 1990-1992; Trin Ch Elkton MD 1989-1990; Chr Ch Par Kent Island Stevensville MD 1988-1989; Ch Of S Marks On The Hill Pikesville MD 1987-1988; S Alb's Epis Ch Salisbury MD 1986-1987; Ch Of The H Trin Oxford MD 1985-1986; Emm Ch Cumberland MD 1985; Assoc Jn's Par Hagerstown MD 1982-1984; Int Dio Easton Easton MD 1981-1996; Int Mnstry Spec Dio Maryland Baltimore MD 1981-1996, 1980-1981; Dir Washington Cnty Mssn Proj 1975-1981; Washington Co Mssn Hagerstown MD 1975-1980; Vic S Chris's Ch New Carrollton MD 1972-1974; Vic S Andr The Fisherman Epis Mayo MD 1968-1970; Vic Chr Epis Ch Big Stone Gap VA 1965-1967; All SS Epis Ch Norton VA 1964-1967; Vic S Steph's Ch Norfolk VA 1964-1965.

FULGONI, Dina Loreen (Los) PO Box 1681, Big Bear Lake CA 92315 B Pasadena CA 1966 d Dino & Dorothy. BA Azusa Pacific U 1988; MS California St U 1990; MDiv CDSP 2007. D 4/25/2015 Bp Joseph Jon Bruno.

FULK, Michael Thomas (NI) 909 S. Darling St., Angola IN 46703 **R All SS Ch 2017-** B Fort Wayne IN 1943 s Clifton & Bertha. TS; AB Indiana U 1965; MSEd U of St Fran 1968. D 12/15/2007 P 6/27/2008 Bp Edward Stuart Little II. m 11/27/1965 Micaela Diane Bowers c 4. P-in-c S Mk's Par Howe IN 2010-2015; P-in-c H Fam Ch Angola IN 2007-2015. allsaintssanbenito@yahoo.co

FULKS, William B (Pa) 112 Elite Hts, Hurricane WV 25526 B Huntington WV 1938 s Fenton & Mary. BA Marshall U 1961; BD Bex Sem 1964. D 6/11/1964 P 12/1/1964 Bp Wilburn Camrock Campbell. m 6/3/1961 Joanne Sterrett Fulks c 2. Emm Ch Quakertown PA 1996-2000; R Trin Epis Ch So Boston VA 1990-1996; The No Cntrl Cluster Buckhannon WV 1990; R S Barn Bridgeport WV 1982-1990; Exec Coun Appointees New York NY 1979-1982; Mssy Tanzania 1979-1982; S Ptr's Ch Huntington WV 1974-1979; Vic Calv Ch Montgomery WV 1969-1974; Vic Gd Shpd Hanford WV 1969-1974; Vic Epis Ch of the Trsfg Buckhannon WV 1964-1969.

FULLER, Betty WL Works (WTex) 823 S Water St Apt 3G, Corpus Christi TX 78401 **Auth Seedlings Inc. 1978-** B North Conway NH 1951 d David & Lucy Robb. AB Sweet Briar Coll 1972; MDiv VTS 1975. D 6/20/1975 Bp Philip Alan Smith P 1/17/1993 Bp Earl Nicholas Mc Arthur Jr. m 5/18/1974 William RL Fuller c 2. Chapl All SS Epis Sch Beaumont TX 2013-2014, 2012-2013, 2011-2012, 2010-2011, 2009-2010, 2008-2009, 2008; CE Dir S Mk's Ch Beaumont TX 2009-2014; R The Epis Ch Of The Adv Alice TX 1997-2007; Ch Of The Gd Shpd Corpus Christi TX 1996-1997; S Thos And S Mart's Ch Crp Christi TX 1996-1997; Dio W Texas San Antonio TX 1993-1995; Chapl SW Texas St U San Marcos TX 1993-1995; Ch Of The Annunc Luling TX 1989-1994; Seedlings Inc. Crp Christi TX 1985-2014; Asst S Mk's Ch San Marcos TX 1982-1988. Auth, "Engrafting the Word," 2014; Auth, "Food for His Friends," 1986; Auth, "La Familia de Dios," 1984; Auth, "The Seedlings Curric," 1981. Bp Elliott Soc 2003. Samuel Shoemaker Awd Epis Recovery Minstries 2015.

FULLER, Edward Beaty (At) 3826 Courtyard Drive, Atlanta GA 30339 **Chapl Fulton Cnty Georgia Sheriff's Dept 2011-** B 1943 MA Nash 2011. D 4/20/2006 Bp J Neil Alexander. c 1. Pres/CEO Optilogistics Inc. 2003-2009.

FULLER JR, Frank (WLa) B Dallas TX 1946 BA McMurry U 1968; MEd U of No Texas 1976; PhD U of No Texas 1980; Dplma Dioc Sch for Mnstry 2006; Dplma Sch for Mnstry 2006. D 4/30/2016 P 11/19/2016 Bp Jacob W Owensby. m 2/3/2000 Jane Elisabeth Newcomer.

FULLER III, Frank E (Tex) 823 S Water St #3G, Corpus Christi TX 78401 B Marshall TX 1949 s Frank & Joan. BA U of Texas 1971; MDiv VTS 1974. D 6/18/1974 Bp Scott Field Bailey P 10/15/1975 Bp James Milton Richardson. m 5/18/1974 Betty WL Works c 2. R S Mk's Ch Beaumont TX 2007-2014; Asst Ch Of The Gd Shpd Corpus Christi TX 1995-2007; Secy Dio W Texas San Antonio TX 1991; R S Mk's Ch San Marcos TX 1980-1995; R S Jas' Epis Ch La Grange TX 1975-1980; Chapl Intrn S Eliz Hosp Washington DC 1974-1975. Auth, *Foundations for Mature Faith*, Seedlings, 1991; Auth, *Engrafting the Word*, Seedlings, 1986; Auth, *The Passion of S Jas*, 1976. Angl Comm Inst 2007; The Bp Elliott Soc 1993. fef3t@aol.com

FULLER, Glen C (WNY) B 1946 s Charles & Elena. BS SUNY 1968; MA SUNY 1985; MDiv Bex Sem 2004. D 12/20/2003 P 11/20/2004 Bp Michael Garrison. m 7/4/1970 Babette Fuller. Vic St Mk Epis Ch No Tonawanda NY 2010-2014; Ch Of The H Comm Lake View NY 2006-2010.

FULLER IV, Ham (WNC) 205 Waterford Dr, Mills River NC 28759 **Died 4/10/2017** B Deland FL 1947 s Paul & Julia. BS Florida St U 1969; MEd Stetson U 1975; PhD U of Florida 1978; MDiv Sewanee: The U So, TS 1986. D 6/8/1986 Bp Frank S Cerveny P 12/1/1986 Bp Furman Charles Stough. m 4/25/1981 Lynne Fuller c 1. Vic Ch of the Advoc Asheville NC 2008-2017; R Emm Epis Ch Bristol VA 1999-2007; S Mk's Epis Ch Jacksonville FL 1995-1999; S Paul's Epis Ch Wilmington NC 1989-1995; Asst S Andr's Epis Ch Tampa FL 1987-1989; Cur Ch Of The H Comf Montgomery AL 1986-1987. Auth, "Parent Participation In The Sch System Its Relatns To"; Auth, "Parent Self-Concepts & Internal-External Locus Of Control". Compass Rose Soc 1997; Ord Of S Lk, Ord S Mary. hamfuller@aol.com

FULLER, Jan (SwVa) 2247 Saddle Club Rd, Burlington NC 27215 **U Chapl Elon U 2011-** B Oakland CA 1956 d James & Frances. BA Hollins U 1978; MDiv Ya Berk 1982; MDiv Yale DS 1982; DMin Wesley TS 1999. D 2/21/2010 Bp A(rthur) Heath Light P 10/7/2010 Bp Neff Powell. c 1. P Assoc Chr Epis Ch Roanoke VA 2010-2011, transitional D 2010; U Chapl Hollins U 1987-2011; Bapt Chapl Ya 1982-1987.

FULLER, John Paul (Los) 940 Ivywood Dr, Oxnard CA 93030 **Ret 1991-** B El Reno OK 1929 s Joseph & Irma. Oklahoma St U 1948; BS USNA 1952; MDiv CDSP 1961. D 9/7/1961 P 3/1/1962 Bp Francis E I Bloy. m 2/11/1994 Jarrell Lynn Fuller c 4. Trin Par Fillmore CA 2007-2012; Asstg S Dav's Par Santa Paula CA 2002-2007; Asst S Columba's Par Camarillo CA 1995-2002; Peace & Justice Com Dio Los Angeles Los Angeles CA 1982-1991, Evang Cmsn 1978-1981, Hunger T/F 1978-1981, Hisp Cmsn 1976-1979, 1974-1991; R All SS Epis Ch Oxnard CA 1971-1991; Dn, San Luis Obispo Convoc Dio El Camino Real Salinas CA 1968-1970; Chapl California St Polytechnic Coll San Luis Obispo CA 1964-1971; R S Steph's Epis Ch Sn Luis Obispo CA 1964-1971; Cur All SS-By-The-Sea Par Santa Barbara CA 1961-1963. Auth, "Var arts," *LivCh*, LivCh Fndt.

FULLER, Lynnette Burley (NJ) 8 Sargent Street, #4, Nutley NJ 07110 B Detroit MI 1945 d John & Edith. BA Chatham Coll 1966; MDiv GTS 1980; STM NYTS 1983. D 6/11/1980 P 2/1/1982 Bp Albert Wiencke Van Duzer. m 11/30/1985 Frederick H Fuller c 2. S Mary's Epis Ch Rockport MA 2001; Dio Chicago Chicago IL 1992-2000; P-in-c Trin Ch Harvard IL 1992-1993; S Jn's Ch Fords NJ 1983-1986; Pstr Affiliate S Bern's Ch Bernardsville NJ 1983; Trin Epis Ch Cranford NJ 1981-1982; Dio New Jersey Trenton NJ 1980-1981.

FULLER SR, Steven George (Vt) 10 South St # 5101, Bellows Falls VT 05101 **P Assoc Imm Ch Bellows Falls VT 2003-** B Windsor VT 1959 s George & Sally. D 11/19/2002 P 6/7/2003 Bp Thomas C Ely. m 7/21/1979 Jean Parrott c 2.

FULLER, Walter Harry (LI) 1692 Bellmore Ave, North Bellmore NY 11710 B Freeport NY 1947 s Harry & Olga. D 1/31/2015 Bp Lawrence C Provenzano. m 9/25/1982 Christine S Scalzo c 2.

FULLMER, Janet (Colo) 1700 Esther Way, The Dalles OR 97058 **S Phil In-The-Field Sedalia CO 2014-** B Canton OH 1951 BA OH SU 1973; JD Franklin Pierce Law Cntr 1984; MDiv CDSP 2006. D 6/10/2006 P 12/9/2006 Bp Robert John O'Neill. m 11/18/1972 Ronald P Fullmer. R S Pauls Epis Ch The Dalles OR 2008-2014; Asst The Ch Of The Ascen Denver CO 2007-2008; Employment Off Stff Mem St. Fran Cntr 2003. janetfuller@msn.com

FULTON JR, Charles Britton (Fla) 1580 Murdock Rd, Marietta GA 30062 B West Palm Beach FL 1938 s Charles & Imogene. BS Stetson U 1960; MDiv Ya Berk 1964; ThD Intl Sem 1985. D 6/19/1964 Bp William Loftin Hargrave P 12/21/1964 Bp Henry I Louttit. c 3. P-in-c S Jude's Ch Marietta GA 2007-2016; Acts 29 Mnstrs Thomasville GA 1993-2000; Pres and CEO Acts 29 Mnstrs Atlanta GA 1987-2007; R S Ptr's Ch Jacksonville FL 1987-1993; R Ch Of The H Sprt Osprey FL 1981-1987; Assoc S Wlfd's Epis Ch Sarasota FL 1978-1980; Assoc S Mary's Ch Wayne PA 1975-1976; Asst Hdmstr Chap Of S Andr Boca Raton FL 1973-1974; R S Andr's Epis Ch Ft Pierce FL 1969-1973; Vic S Mary's Epis Ch Palmetto FL 1966-1969; Cur S Bon Ch Sarasota FL 1964-1966. Auth, "Touched By The Sprt," ERM Press, 2001; Auth, "Step Into the River of Healing," ERM Press, 2001; Auth, "Reflections On The Run". Omicron Delta Kappa; Scabbard And Blade; Sigma Nu.

FULTON III, Charles Newell (NY) 815 2nd Ave, New York NY 10017 B Memphis TN 1942 s Charles & Ellenor. BA Auburn U 1965; STB GTS 1968. D 6/16/1968 Bp John Vander Horst P 5/24/1969 Bp William Evan Sanders. m 6/12/1965 Donna Fulton c 2. Exec Dir Mssn Fund Epis Ch Cntr New York NY 2008-2009, Dir of Cong Dev 2001-2008, VP 1987-2000; Pres ECBF No Chesterfield VA 1987-2008; R S Paul's Ch Franklin TN 1972-1987; Cur S Geo's Ch Nashville TN 1968-1969. Auth, "Truth and Hope"; Auth, "Ch Sites & Buildings," *Process Guide for Cong*; Auth, "The Ch for Common Pryr," *The Ch for Common Pryr*; Auth, "Ch for Common Pryr," *Video*.

FULTON, Jennifer (NI) **P-in-c S Jn Of The Cross Bristol IN 2014-** D 2/14/2014 P 9/20/2014 Bp Edward Stuart Little II.

FULTON, John Gary (EC) 307 N Main St, Farmville NC 27828 **long term supply P Trin Ch Scotland Neck NC 2007-** B Canton OH 1937 s John & Margaret. BS U of Akron 1972; MDiv VTS 1972. D 5/25/1972 Bp John Harris Burt P 12/1/1972 Bp Furman Charles Stough. c 2. P-in-c Emm Ch Farmville NC 2002-2005; S Thos' Epis Ch Bath NC 1988-1999; P-in-c Downeast Cluster Dio Of E Carolina 1988-1994; R Ch Of The H Fam Chap Hill NC 1980-1988; Assoc Chr Ch Grosse Pointe Grosse Pointe Farms MI 1976-1980; Assoc Ch Of The Nativ Epis Huntsville AL 1975-1976; H Cross-St Chris's Huntsville AL 1972-1975. Auth, "A Short Hist Of S Thos Epis Ch Bath Nc".

FULTON, Nancy Casey (WMich) 807 South University, Mt Pleasant MI 48858 **D S Jn's Ch Mt Pleasant MI 2007-, D 1997-2005; Chapl Assn for Interfaith Mnstrs Mt. Pleaant MI 2005-; Assoc Coordntr for Mnstry Assn for Interfaith Mnstrs 2005-** B Escanaba MI 1948 d Robert & Louise. AA Bay De Noc Cmnty Coll 1969; BA Cntrl Michigan U 1971; MA Cntrl Michigan U 1973. D 9/27/1997 Bp Edward Lewis Lee Jr. m 7/13/1974 Henry Levan Fulton c 1. D S Jn's Epis Ch Alma MI 2005-2006; Sprtl Care Coordntr Woodland Hospice Mt. Pleasant MI 1998-2013. Auth, "Serving the Differently Abled," *Diakoneo*, NAAD, 2006; Auth, "20 columns on Rel Page," *The Morning Sun*, Nwspr Mt. Pleasant, MI, 2006; Auth, "Decorating the Easter Tree," *Preaching Through H Days and Holidays: Sermons*, Morehouse, 2003; Auth, "Journey: Confession and Supplication," *Race and Pryr*, Morehouse, 2003; Auth, "Reflections," *Diakoneo*, No Amer Associaton for the Diac, 2001; Auth, "For Those Who are Abused," *Wmn Uncommon Prayers*, Morehouse Pub, 2000. NAAD 1995.

FULTON, Norman Hamilton (NY) Macaulay Road, Rd #2, Katonah NY 10536 B Tarrytown NY 1941 s Norman & Dorothy. BS SUNY 1987; MA NYTS 1991. D 5/30/1992 Bp Richard Frank Grein. m 10/12/1963 Leslie Ann Fulton c 2.

FULTON, Sharline Alahverde (Pa) 1207 Foulkeways, Gwynedd PA 19436 B Ardmore PA 1934 d Evany & Rose. BA Villanova U 1977; MDiv Luth TS 1982; MA Creighton U 2002. D 6/1/1982 P 6/1/1983 Bp Lyman Cunningham Ogilby. c 2. R S Andr's Ch Yardley PA 1990-1997; Int Ch Of The Redeem Springfield PA 1989-1990; Int S Ptr's Ch Philadelphia PA 1987-1989; Ch Of S Asaph Bala Cynwyd PA 1984-1985; Asst Ch Of S Mart-In-The-Fields Philadelphia PA 1982-1984.

FULTON, William Riggs (Oly) 32 NE Tracy Hill Way, Bremerton WA 98311 **Vic S Antony Of Egypt Silverdale WA 2008-** B Wichita KS 1953 s William & Jean. BA Evergreen St Coll 1977; MDiv Sewanee: The U So, TS 1995. D 6/26/1995 P 1/8/1996 Bp William Edward Smalley. m 7/22/1984 Kathryn Anne Smith c 2. S Andr's Epis Ch Florence OR 2000-2008, Vic 1999; R Gr Epis Ch Winfield KS 1995-1999; Trin Ch Arkansas City KS 1995-1999.

FUNK, Delmar Gerald (Neb) 3668 - 18th, Columbus NE 68601 B Wichita KS 1930 s Delmar & Dorothy. BFA U of Kansas 1959; MDiv Nash 1982. D 6/18/1982 Bp Jackson Earle Gilliam P 12/1/1982 Bp James Daniel Warner. m 6/9/1956 Carolyn Ruth Funk c 2. Chr Ch Cntrl City NE 1988-2000; S Jn's Ch Albion Columbus NE 1987-1989; P-in-c S Jn's Epis Ch Albion IL 1987-1989; R Gr Ch Par -Epis Columbus NE 1985-2000; Vic Chr Ch Sidney NE 1982-1985; Vic Ch Of The Gd Shpd Bridgeport NE 1982-1985.

FUNK, Jeffrey Lawrence (Be) 46 S Laurel St, Hazleton PA 18201 **Assoc S Alb's Epis Ch Reading PA 2013-** B Rockville Centre NY 1955 s Arthur & Elizabeth. SUNY 1974; Cert Geo Mercer Jr Memi TS 1987; BA Adel 1997; SWTS 2000. D 12/15/1986 Bp Robert Campbell Witcher Sr P 9/29/2001 Bp Paul Victor Marshall. R S Jas' Ch Drifton PA 2003-2012; R S Ptr's Epis Ch Hazleton PA 2003-2012; R S Mary's Epis Ch Reading PA 2001-2002; S Elis's Epis Ch Floral Pk NY 2000-2001; Asst S Thos' Ch Bellerose NY 2000-2001; S Geo's Ch Hempstead NY 1987-1999. EAM 2005-2008; Episcopalians Untd 1989-1992; Hempstead Nrsry Co-op - Advsry Bd 1991-1999; Long Island D's Gld 1989-2001; NAAD 1989-2001.

FUNK, Nicholas (RG) 5125 Rock House Rd, Las Cruces NM 88011 **R S Jas' Epis Ch Las Cruces NM 2008-** B St Petersburg FL 1965 BA U So 1987; MDiv Sewanee: The U So, TS 2005; DMin St Petersburg TS 2009. D 6/18/2005 P 12/17/2005 Bp John Bailey Lipscomb. m 3/25/2001 Laura Funk. P-in-c S Alb's Epis Ch St Petersburg FL 2006-2007; Assoc R S Jn's Ch Naples FL 2005-2006; Area Dn Dio The Rio Grande Albuquerque 2011-2012.

FUNK, Peter Van Keuren (NJ) 4825 Province Line Rd, Princeton NJ 08540 **Died 9/20/2016** B Glenridge NJ 1921 s Wilfred & Eleanor. BA Pr 1942. D 10/31/1998 Bp Joe Doss. m 11/25/1942 Eleanor Funk. Auth, "Var arts, 15 Books," *6 Audio Books*; Auth, "My Six Loves: Love and Consequences. Fiction On Story Of Six Orphans," *Film-My Six Loves*; Auth, "It Pays To Enrich Your Word Power, 4 books on words," *Rdr'S Dig*. Tertiary Of The Soc Of S Fran. Distinquisleed Alum Awd Montclair Kimberley Acad 1995; Min Gnrl'S Awd Soc Of St Fran 1985.

FUNKHOUSER, David Franklin (Pa) 456 66th St, Oakland CA 94609 B New Market VA 1945 s Roscoe & Carrie. BS Heidelberg U 1967; MDiv VTS 1972. D 5/27/1972 P 5/18/1973 Bp Robert Bruce Hall. Ch Of S Jn The Evang Philadelphia PA 1996-2003; P-in-c S Giles Ch Upper Darby PA 1994-1996; The White Mtn Sch Bethlehem NH 1976-1977; Chapl White Mtn Sch Littleton NH 1975-1977; Asst S Dunst's Ch Mc Lean VA 1972-1975.

FUNSTON, A Patrick K (Kan) 601 Poyntz Avenue, Manhattan KS 66502 **S Paul's Ch Manhattan KS 2013-; Coun of Trst Liaison to the COM Dio Kansas Topeka KS 2012-** B San Diego CA 1983 s Charles & Evelyn. BBA U of Missouri - Kansas City 2007; MDiv VTS 2011. D 6/11/2011 P 1/7/2012 Bp Dean E Wolfe. m 8/22/2009 Michael Johanna Knoll-Funston c 2. Chapl Bp Seabury Acad Lawr KS 2011-2013. stpauls@stpaulsmanhattan.org

FUNSTON, Charles Eric (O) St. Paul's Episcopal Church, 317 E. Liberty Street, Medina OH 44256 **Congrl Dvlpmt Dio Ohio Cleveland OH 2005-; R S Paul's Epis Ch Medina OH 2003-** B Las Vegas NV 1952 s Raymond & Betty. BA U CA San Diego 1974; MBA U of Nevada at Las Vegas 1979; JD California Wstrn Sch of Law 1983; Cert CDSP 1991; DMin SWTS 1998. D 5/8/1990 P 6/21/1991 Bp Stewart Clark Zabriskie. m 4/12/1980 Evelyn Walther c 2. Dio Kansas Topeka KS 2002, Bdgt Com 1994-2001, Const & Cn 1993-2003; R S Fran Of Assisi Stilwell KS 1993-2003; Assoc R Chr Ch Las Vegas NV 1991-1993; Dio Nevada Las Vegas 1991-1993, Asst Chncllr 1989-1990, Asst Chncllr 1991-1993, Chncllr 1986-1990, Asst Chncllr 1983-1986; D Ch Of The Resurr Pleasant Hil CA 1990-1991; Const & Cn Dio Ohio Cleveland 2016-2005, Provsnl Dep, GC 2014-2016. Auth, "One Hour of the Millenium," *Songlines*, 1996; Auth, "Mnstry to the Legal Profession: A Suggested Co-dependency Model," *Journ of Pstr Care*, 1991; Auth, "Made Out of Whole Cloth: A Const Analysis of the Cler Malpractice Concept'," *California Wstrn Law Revs*, 1983. cfunston@stpauls-medina.org

FURGERSON, John Arthur (SwVa) 11 Whitmore St, Lexington VA 24450 **Ret 1996-** B Louisville KY 1931 s William & Dorothy. BS USNA 1953; BS Untd States Naval Postgraduate Sch 1965; MDiv VTS 1976. D 5/22/1976 Bp John Alfred Baden P 2/13/1977 Bp William Henry Marmion. m 6/20/1953 Alice C Furgerson c 5. S Jn's Epis Ch Glasgow VA 1988-1996; R Chr Epis Ch Buena Vista VA 1981-1988; Asst R R E Lee Memi Ch (Epis) Lexington VA 1976-1981; LtCmdr USN 1953-1973; Com Elctns Dio SW Virginia Roanoke VA 1995-1996, Stndg Com 1990-1994, Dn 1986-1989, Exec Bd 1977-1985.

FURLOW, Mark D (SwVa) The Episcopal Diocese of Southwestern Virginia, PO Box 2279, Roanoke VA 24009 **Dio SW Virginia Roanoke VA 2014-** B Tacoma Park MD 1978 s Terrance & Karen. MBA Lynchburg Coll; BA Cntr Coll 2001; MDiv GTS 2006. D 6/10/2006 Bp Stacy F Sauls P 2/3/2007 Bp Peter J Lee. m 12/2/2006 Siobhan Byrns c 1. Trin Ch Arrington VA 2013, 2012; R Ch Of The H Trin Georgetown KY 2008-2010; Cler Res Chr Ch Alexandria VA 2006-2008. mfurlow@dioswva.org

FURMAN, James Edmund (Los) 13131 Moorpark St Apt 412, Sherman Oaks CA 91423 B Long Beach CA 1947 s Alfred & Elizabeth. BA Claremont Coll 1969; MA Stan 1970; MDiv CDSP 1973. D 6/23/1973 Bp Chauncie Kilmer Myers P 4/1/1974 Bp Robert Claflin Rusack. R S Nich Par Encino CA 1995-2007; R S Ptr's Ch Honolulu HI 1986-1995; S Andr's Ch La Mesa CA 1985-1986; R Sts Ptr And Paul Epis Ch El Centro CA 1980-1985; Assoc Chr Ch Coronado CA 1979-1980; Asst S Mary's Epis Ch Los Angeles CA 1977-1979; Asst S Mk's Par Glendale CA 1973-1977. Auth, "Sand & Stars: A Possibility Bk for CE"; Auth, *Coptic Ch Revs*; Auth, *Homegrown*; Auth, *Living Ch*. Chapl, Can Soc of Sthrn California; CBS; Pres, Inter-Angl Study Prog.

FURNISS III, Robert Hosmer (Minn) 2132 Cameron Dr, Woodbury MN 55125 **Chapl Lakeview Hosp & Hospice Stillwater MN 2007-; Chapl St Croix Chapl Assn Stillwater MN 2007-** B Chicago IL 1958 s Robert & Margaret. BA Ripon Coll Ripon WI 1980; MDiv Sewanee: The U So, TS 1988; DMin Luther TS 2004. D 6/18/1988 Bp Frank Tracy Griswold III P 1/6/1989 Bp Robert Marshall Anderson. m 11/5/1983 Jean Marie Diehl c 3. R Chr Ch S Paul MN 1998-2006; R S Lk's Ch Willmar MN 1991-1998; P-in-c Ch Of The Gd Samar Sauk Cntr MN 1991-1993; Asst to R Ch Of The Epiph Epis Minneapolis MN 1988-1991. robert.h.furniss@lakeview.org

FURRER, Thomas (Ct) 5 Trout Drive, Granby CT 06035 B Ravenna OH 1950 s George & Katherine. BA Wesl 1981; MDiv Ya Berk 1986. D 6/14/1986 Bp Arthur Edward Walmsley P 12/1/1986 Bp William Bradford Hastings. m 10/16/1976 Maryjane Furrer c 3. R Trin Ch Tariffville CT 2000-2016, Cur 1986-1988; R S Paul's Epis Ch Shelton CT 1988-2000. Auth, "Living Word of The Living God: A Beginner's Guide To Reaing and Understanding The Bible," *Bk*, Winged Lion Press, 2011. Bro of S Andr Bd, Pres Habitat for Humani 1987-2007. Cn - St Mich's Cathd Dio Kaduna, Nigeria 2004; Cn - St Andr's Cathd Dio W. Tanganyika, Tanzania 2002.

FUSELIER, Donald Paul (ECR) 1017 Alameda St, Monterey CA 93940 B Fresno CA 1946 s Paul & Irene. BA Golden Gate U 1982; BA Sch for Deacons 1984; MPA Golden Gate U 1986. D 6/3/1996 Bp Richard Lester Shimpfky. m 10/29/1990 Margo L Fuselier c 3.

FUSSELL, Stacey Marie (NwPa) 462 Congress St, Bradford PA 16701 **R Ch Of The Ascen Bradford PA 2010-** B Jacksonville FL 1965 d William & Joan. AA Houston Cmnty Coll 1993; BA U of St Thos 1995; MDiv VTS 1998. D 6/20/1998 Bp Claude Edward Payne P 6/20/1999 Bp Leopoldo Jesus Alard. c 2. Vic St. Cathr Of Sienna Missouri City TX 2009-2010; The Great Cmsn Fndt Houston TX 2001-2008; Assoc Trin Epis Ch Baytown TX 1998-2001; Stndg Com Dio NW Pennsylvania Erie PA 2012-2015, Chair - Exam Chapl 2011-, Dn - NE Convoc 2011-, Dioc Strategic Plnng Com 2011-, Dn - NE Dnry 2010-; Exec Bd

Dio Texas Houston TX 2008-2009, Seafarer's Cntr Bd 1999-2001, Wrld Mssn Bd 1999-2001. DOK 1990; VTS Mssy Soc 1995-1998. Harris Awd for Acad Brilliance and Ldrshp VTS 1998; Tachau Biblic Lang Prize VTS 1997.

G

GABAUD, Pierre Simpson (SeFla) St Paul et Les Martyrs d'Haiti, 6744 N Miami Ave, Miami FL 33150 **Exec Coun Appointees New York NY 2014-** B Haiti 1960 s Antenor & Fiance. MA U of Haiti 1988; PhD Universite Laval 1996; MDiv Sewanee: The U So, TS 2011; MDiv U So TS 2011. D 3/25/2012 Bp Leo Frade P 10/17/2012 Bp Jean Zache Duracin. m 10/3/1987 Marie Lourdes Gabaud c 3.

GABB, James Neil (Neb) 21724 Oldgate Rd, Elkhorn NE 68022 B Marshall MO 1943 s James & Eugenia. BS U of Missouri 1966; MA U of Missouri 1968; MDiv Phillips TS 1986; CAS SWTS 1986. D 6/14/1986 Bp William Jackson Cox P 2/27/1987 Bp James Daniel Warner. m 5/30/1973 Betsy S Shofstall c 2. Assoc All SS Epis Ch Omaha NE 2014-2015; Int S Jas' Epis Ch Fremont NE 2009-2014; R St Aug of Cbury Epis Ch Elkhorn NE 2000-2008; Dir of Dvlpmt Imm Sr Living Omaha NE 2000-2004; Exec Dir Coun Bluffs Cmnty Hlth Cntr CB Iowa 1998-2000; Dir of Ethics Alegent Hlth System 1996-1998; Dir of Pstr Care Imm Med Cntr Omaha NE 1994-1996; Int Ch Of The H Sprt Bellevue NE 1993-1994; R S Lk's Ch Plattsmouth NE 1992-1993; Chapl Clarkson Hosp Omaha NE 1991-1993; Asst to Dn Trin Cathd Omaha NE 1988-1991; Cur/Asst Ch Of The H Trin Lincoln NE 1986-1988; Trin Memi Epis Ch Crete NE 1986-1988; Chapl to the Ret Cler & Families Dio Nebraska Omaha NE 2009-2012. fr.jayg@gmail.com

GABBARD, Justin E (Lex) **D Trin Ch Covington KY 2016-; Dioc YA Cmsn Dio Lexington Lexington 2014-** B 1978 s Gary & Diane. BA Sewanee: The U So 2002; MDiv Ya Berk 2011. D 1/9/2016 Bp Doug Hahn P 9/17/2016 Bp Bruce Caldwell. Other Lay Position Chr Ch Cathd Cincinnati OH 2003-2006.

GABEL, Mark Francis (CFla) 5139 Marbella Isle Dr, Orlando FL 32837 B Syracuse NY 1952 D 12/13/2003 Bp John Wadsworth Howe. m 8/19/1995 Charmaine Kreider.

GABLE, David Lee (Nwk) 24 Harmony Dr, Pt Jefferson Station NY 11776 B Anniston AL 1943 s Carl & Lena. BA Jacksonville St U 1965; MS U of Mississippi 1967; PhD U of Memphis 1977; MDiv VTS 1980. D 6/22/1980 Bp William F Gates Jr P 5/4/1981 Bp William Evan Sanders. R Gr Epis Ch Rutherford NJ 2002-2008; Int S Paul's Epis Ch Chatham NJ 2000-2002; Int Chr Ch Epis Ridley Pk PA 1999-2000; Int Emm Epis Ch Stamford CT 1997-1999; Int S Mark's Epis Ch Louisville KY 1996-1997; Int Ch Of The Gd Shpd S Louis MO 1995-1996; R S Andr's Epis Ch Edwardsville IL 1991-1995; R Chr Ch - Epis Chattanooga TN 1987-1990; R S Andr's Ch Harriman TN 1981-1987; D St Jas Epis Ch at Knoxville Knoxville TN 1980-1981. stamman2@aol.com

GABLE, Stephen Louis (Ind) 1045 E Sassafras Cir, 1129 Linden Dr, Bloomington IN 47408 **1976-** B Yonkers NY 1942 s Harry & Mildred. BA Butler U 1964; MDiv Epis TS of the SW 1967; MA U of St Thos 1994. D 6/24/1967 P 12/26/1967 Bp John P Craine. m 6/3/1978 Marcia Lynn Brown Bryan c 1. P-in-c Trin Ch Connersville IN 1973-1975; All SS Ch Seymour IN 1967-1969; S Thos Ch Franklin IN 1967-1969. Soc of Cert Property & Casualty Underwriters.

GADDY, Anna Lee (RG) Po Box 648, Ruidoso Downs NM 88346 B Canyon TX 1925 d Burt & Ora. W Texas A&M U. D 2/3/1986 P 8/1/1986 Bp Richard Mitchell Trelease Jr. m 6/13/1975 Randolph Gaddy. Non-par 1984-1986; Asst H Mt.

GADSDEN, Carol D (NY) 168 W Boston Post Rd, Mamaroneck NY 10543 **R S Thos Ch Mamaroneck NY 2014-; Fac Dio New York New York NY 2017-, COM 2016-2017; Bd Mem At Hm on the Sound 2015-; Chapl Mamaroneck Fire Dept Mamaroneck NY 2015-; Bd Mem The Summit Mamaroneck NY 2015-; Mem, Municipal Allnce Town of Sparta Sparta New Jersey 2012-** B Syracuse NY 1951 d Gordon & Jean. BA Keuka Coll 1972; MA Col Teachers Coll 1975; M Ed Col Teachers Coll 1976; MDiv GTS 1985; Grad Cert Radcliffe Seminars, Harv 1993. D 6/8/1985 Bp Paul Moore Jr P 1/18/1986 Bp James Stuart Wetmore. m 5/5/2005 Linda A March c 2. R S Mary's Ch Sparta NJ 2011-2014; Int S Dav's Ch Philadelphia PA 2009-2011; Int S Jn's Ch Bala Cynwyd PA 2007-2009; Non-par Healthcare 2004-2007; P-in-c S Lk's And S Marg's Ch Allston MA 2002-2004; Non-par 1995-2001; Pstr-in-Charge S Jn's Epis Ch Franklin MA 1992-1995; Vic S Nich-by-the-Sea Hull MA 1990-1992; Ther Epis Soc Serv Ansonia CT 1989; Assoc R S Fran Ch Stamford CT 1985-1989; Missions Strtgy Com Dio Newark Newark NJ 2012-2014, Reg Mnstrs Cmsn 2012-2014, Ward J. Herbert Fund 2012-2014, Constitutions and Cn 2012-2013. Mem and Chair of the Bd, Burn Fndt 2006-2011. Homilist, Ord of Deacons The Epis Dio Pennsylvania 2011. rectorstthomas@gmail.com

GAEDE, Lee A (Chi) 342 Custer Ave. Apt. 2, Evanston IL 60202 **D St. Andrews Pentecost Epis Ch Evanston IL 2014-** B Waukegan IL 1947 d Leon & Lorraine. BA Concordia Tchr Coll River Forest IL 1969; JD Washington U 1984; Chicago Deacons Sch 1999. D 2/5/2000 Bp Bill Persell. m 6/7/

1969 Bruce John Gaede c 1. D S Giles' Ch Northbrook IL 2011-2014; Bd S Mary's Serv Arlington Heights IL 2001-2006; D S Mk's Ch Evanston IL 2000-2010; Dvlpmt Assoc Cathd Shltr of Chicago 1998-2001; Deacons' Coun Dio Chicago Chicago IL 2012-2013, Cler Alt, 2012 GC 2011-2012, Deacons' Coun 2011-2012, 3rd Cler Alt, GC 2010-, Co-chair Millenium Dvlpmt Goals T/ F 2008-2011, Millenium Dvlpmt Goals T/F 2005-2011, COM 2002-2008, Sprtl Dir, Happ 2001-2015, COM 2001-2007, Deacons' Coun 2001-2004. Assoc of the CSM 1981; Assn for Epis Deacons 1997; EPF 1995; Epis Publ Plcy Ntwk 1998. The Pro Bono Awd The Missouri Bar Assn 1992.

GAEDE, Sarah Harrell (Ala) 830 Willingham Rd, Florence AL 35630 B Raleigh NC 1951 d Miller & Suzanne. BA Eckerd Coll 1972; MDiv Sewanee: The U So, TS 1994; DMin SWTS 2005. D 7/25/1995 Bp Henry Irving Louttit P 3/2/1996 Bp John Wadsworth Howe. m 12/5/1981 Henry Frazer Gaede c 1. S Paul's Epis Ch Corinth MS 2013; R S Barth's Epis Ch Florence AL 2003-2008; Supply Chr The King Epis Ch Orlando FL 2002-2003; Cn Cathd Ch Of S Lk Orlando FL 1998-2001; Chapl Res FL Hosp 1997-1998; Cur S Mich's Ch Orlando FL 1995-1996. "The Princess in the Pulpit: Preaching Like a Girl," DMin. thesis, 2005.

GAESTEL, Robert J (Los) 1100 Avenue 64, Pasadena CA 91105 **Chapl Pasadena Police Dept 2003-; R Ch Of The Ang Pasadena CA 1983-** B Neptune NJ 1953 s Herbert & Helen. BA Chapman U 1975; MDiv CDSP 1979. D 6/23/1979 P 1/12/1980 Bp Robert Claflin Rusack. m 7/9/1977 Tracy A Gaestel c 2. Assoc R S Geo's Par La Can CA 1980-1983; Cur S Mich and All Ang Epis Ch Studio City CA 1979-1980. Norman Cram Hall S Jn's, Petaluma, CA 2012; Apos Transformational Stewardship Awd TEN of The Epis Ch 2012; Grad Citizens FBI Acad 2011; Highly Effective Eductr Awd DC Publ Schools 2010; Extra Class Amateur Lic FCC 2010; Open Water Certification PADI 2008; Distinguished Vol Serv Awd Pasadena Police Dept 2008; Black Belt Larry Tatum Kenpo Karate 2005; Chf's Awd for Excellence Pasadena Police Dept 2008; Fell Amer Ldrshp Forum 1996; Profsnl Merit ScholarshipWayne St U Wayne Sch of Soc Wk 1982; Dav E. Finley Fell Natl Gallery of Art 1981.

GAFFORD, Donna Elizabeth Goodman (Ala) 38 Longview Ct, Seale AL 36875 **S Matthews In The Pines Seale AL 2011-** B Meridian MS 1957 d William & Mildred. BA Valparaiso U 1980; MDiv SWTS 1984. D 6/25/1984 Bp Edward Witker Jones P 4/1/1985 Bp William Evan Sanders. m 11/25/1977 Alexander Thomas Gafford. Trin Epis Ch Columbus GA 2005-2014, Mssnr 2003, 1995-1998; S Thos Of Cbury Thomaston GA 2000-2003; Assoc P Trin Ch Epis Pass Chr MS 1993-1994; Non-par 1992-1994; Asst Resurr Williamson Cnty TN 1990-1992; Chr Ch Cathd Nashville TN 1988; S Dav's Epis Ch Nashville TN 1984-1987. agafford2@bellsouth.net

GAFFORD, Happy Lawton (CFla) 1330 Arthur St, Orlando FL 32804 B Orlando FL 1942 d Joseph & Madalyne. BA Brenau U 1964; Inst for Chr Stds 1990; Diac Trng Sch 1992; CPE 1994; DOCC Trng 1995; CPE 1997. D 11/7/1992 Bp John Wadsworth Howe. m 6/11/1966 George Louis Gafford c 2. D S Mich's Ch Orlando FL 2002-2004, Min of Pstrl Care 1997-2002, 1993-1994; S Andr's Epis Ch Colchester VT 1995-1997; D's Coun Dio Cntrl Florida Orlando FL 1993-1994, Mentor 1988-1992. NAAD.

GAFNEY, Wilda Clydette (Pa) 7301 Germantown Ave, Philadelphia PA 19119 **Assoc Prof Of Hebr And OT Luth TS 2003-** B South Hill VA 1966 d Willie & Louvenia. BA Earlham Coll 1987; MDiv How 1997; PhD Duke 2006. D 6/9/2007 Bp Charles Ellsworth Bennison Jr P 12/15/2007 Bp Franklin Delton Turner. D Trin Epis Ch Ambler PA 2007.

GAFOUR, Ayyoubawaga Bushara (Colo) Sudanese Community Church, 1350 Washington St, Denver CO 80203 B Salara Sudan 1945 s Bushara & Toona. MDiv U of Emml 1981; MDiv U of Emml 1981; BA U Sask 1981; STM Trin, U Tor 1986; STM Trin, U Tor 1986; PhD U of Wales 1999. P 8/28/2010 Bp Robert John O'Neill. Dio Colorado Denver CO 2010-2016.

GAGE, Bartlett Wright (Ct) 26 Edmond St, Darien CT 06820 **Asst S Andr's Ch Stamford CT 2008-** B Geneva IL 1935 s Nevin & Helen. BA Ya 1957; BD Yale DS 1961; MA U Chi 1968. D 6/10/1989 Bp Arthur Edward Walmsley P 6/1/1990 Bp Clarence Nicholas Coleridge. m 6/2/1961 Faye Gage c 2. Assoc R S Jn's Ch Stamford CT 1990-2007; Pstr Intern S Mk's Ch New Canaan CT 1989-1990. "Faith, Hope and Stories," *Ben's Press*, Hound of Heaven Pub, 1999; "Faith and More Stories," *Ben's Press*, Hound of Heaven Pub, 1998; "Faith and Stories," *Ben's Press*, Hound of Heaven Pub, 1996.

GAGE, Nancy Elizabeth (Ct) Grace Church, 5958 Main St, Trumbull CT 06611 B Lynn MA 1940 d Chesley & Marian. D 9/15/2007 Bp Andrew Donnan Smith. m 7/27/1976 David Adams Gage c 3.

GAHAGAN, Susan Elisabeth (Ga) 1802 Abercorn St, Savannah GA 31401 **D The Collgt Ch of St Paul the Apos Savannah GA 2009-** B Pottsville PA 1947 d Oscar & Nedra. BSW U of Sthrn Indiana 1999. D 10/28/2009 Bp Henry Irving Louttit. c 2.

GAHAN III, W(Illiam) Patrick (WTex) Christ Episcopal Church, 510 Belknap Pl, San Antonio TX 78212 **R Chr Epis Ch San Antonio TX 2012-** B Birmingham AL 1954 s William & Lillian. Trin U San Antonio; U of Alabama; BS U of Mary Hardin-Baylor 1981; U of Tennessee 1987; MDiv Epis TS of the SW 1994; DMin SWTS 2000. D 4/15/1988 Bp Robert Oran Miller P 10/28/

1991 Bp Maurice Manuel Benitez. m 11/26/1975 Marian Kay Gahan c 3. R S Steph's Epis Ch Wimberley TX 2005-2012; Hd Chapl S Jas Sch S Jas MD 2001-2005; St Jas Sch Hagerstown MD 2001-2005; R S Steph's Ch Beaumont TX 1996-2001; SPCK Sewanee TN 1995-1996; Exec Dir Spck/Usa Sewanee TN 1995-1996; Chapl S Steph's Epis Sch Austin TX 1992-1995; Hd Chapl / Tchr / Coach S Steph Epis Sch Austin TX 1990-1995; Int Chr Epis Ch Tyler TX 1990. Auth, "Foundations of Discipleship," *Bk*, Lulu, 2010; Auth, "Daring to be a Different Ch," *LivCh*, 2007; Auth, "The Seeds of My Faith," *LivCh*, 1997; Auth, "Envisioning a Great Ch Sch," *NAES*, 1996; Auth, "Namelessness and Facelessness: Opportunities for Evil," *New Oxford Revs*, 1994; Auth, "The Secret of Abundant Living," *New Cov*, 1984. Who's Who in Amer Educ 1992; Who's Who So and SW 1988; Stokely Fell 1987.

GAHLER, Robert Edward (NY) 67 Woodmere Rd, Stamford CT 06905 **Trin S Paul's Epis New Rochelle NY 2009-** B Waseca MN 1948 s James & Henrietta. BA NWU 1978; MDiv EDS 1982. D 10/31/1982 P 6/1/1983 Bp George Nelson Hunt III. m 2/2/2009 James Michael Hull. R Epis Ch of Chr the Healer Stamford CT 1986-2006; Asst Cathd Of S Jn Providence RI 1982-1986; Dio Rhode Island Providence RI 1982-1986. EUC, EPF, Assn Of Angl Of Mus.

GAILLARD, Ann Schwarberg (Alb) **R Ch of St. Lk the Beloved Physcn Saranac Lake NY 2008-; P The Ch of St Lk The Beloved Physcn Saranac Lake NY 2008-** B Whittier CA 1960 BA Stan 1982; MA Stan 1983; MDiv GTS 2005. D 6/4/2005 P 12/17/2005 Bp Charles Ellsworth Bennison Jr. m 7/9/1985 Lee Gaillard. Assoc R Chr Ch Media PA 2005-2007.

GAINES, Elizabeth Juliet (NCal) D 8/13/2016 Bp Barry Leigh Beisner.

GAINES, Mary Moore Thompson (Cal) 128 Beaumont Ave, San Francisco CA 94118 B Fort Worth TX 1931 d James & Caroline. BA Vas 1979; MDiv CDSP 1989. D 6/3/1989 P 6/1/1990 Bp William Edwin Swing. m 8/16/1951 George Chilton Gaines c 6. S Jas Epis Ch San Francisco CA 1997-2003, Assoc R 1991-1996, P 1990, D 1989-1990.

GAINES, Winifred B (NCal) 630 Wilhaggin Dr, Sacramento CA 95864 **Died 9/30/2015** B Sacramento CA 1928 d Marshal & Winifred. BS U CA 1950; MDiv CDSP 1978; MA U of San Francisco 1982. D 5/1/1979 P 11/30/1980 Bp John Lester Thompson III. m 2/24/1951 Robert Gaines c 5. Cn Trin Epis Cathd Sacramento CA 1989-2000; Chapl Mercy San Juan Hosp & Hospice Sacramento CA 1979-1989. Assoc of the Trsfg 1980; Assn of Epis Chapl 1979-1989. Hon DD CDSP 2000; Hon Cn Trin Cathd 1984; Phi Beta Kappa U.C. Berkeley 1950.

GAISER, Ted J (Me) 641 Allen Ave, Portland ME 04103 **Dio Maine Portland ME 2016-; Gr Epis Ch Bath ME 2016-; Dom And Frgn Mssy Soc- Epis Ch Cntr New York NY 2012-; Cn Catedral de San Pablo Bogota 2015-** B Bluffton IN 1961 s Noel & Grace. BA Sthrn Connecticut S U 1986; MTS Bos TS 1988; MBA Boston Coll 1994; PhD Boston Coll 2000. D 10/6/2001 Bp M(Arvil) Thomas Shaw P 2/9/2013 Bp Francisco Jose Duque-Gomez. m 6/18/2004 Charles Hornberger. Exec Coun Appointees New York NY 2012-2015; D The Ch Of Our Redeem Lexington MA 2008-2011; D Gr Epis Ch Medford MA 2005-2008; D S Andr's Ch Framingham MA 2001-2004; D, Global Partnerships Dio Massachusetts Boston MA 2004-2010. Auth, "A Guide to Conducting On-Line Resrch," *A Guide to Conducting On-Line Resrch*, Sage Pub, Inc., 2009; Auth, "Online Cmnty: An Evaltn of the Emerging Soc Forms in Cyberspace," *Online Cmnty: An Evaltn of the Emerging Soc Forms in Cyberspace*, VDM Verlag Dr. Muller, 2009; Auth, "Conducting On-Line Focuse Groups," *The Sage Hand Bk of On-Line Resrch Methods*, Sage Pub, Inc., 2008; Auth, "Conducting On-Line Focus Groups: A Methodological Discussion," *Soc Sci Computer Revs*, Sage Pub, Inc., 1997. Cntr for Dvlpmt in Cntrl Amer 1997-2011; Global Epis Mssn Ntwk 2008; Massachusetts Epis Cler Assn 2008; NAAD 1998; Witness for Peace 1987-2000. Dissertation Fllshp Boston Coll 1997; Dissertation Fllshp Awd Boston Coll 1996; Fndr's Awd of Merit Soc Sci Computing Assn 1996; Who's Who in Amer Universities and Colleges Sthrn Connecticut St U 1986; hon Soc Mem Tau Pi Sigma 1985. gracerector@gwi.net

GAITHER, Gayle Lee (Spok) 416 E Nelson Rd, Moses Lake WA 98837 **P S Mart's Ch Moses Lake WA 2008-** B Alamosa CO 1938 s Lyle & Virginia. Big Bend Cmnty Coll; Colorado St U 1956; Dioc Cmsn Theol Educ 2006. D 11/19/2006 P 6/9/2007 Bp James E Waggoner Jr. m 7/26/1958 Mavis McCormack c 3. Chapl Chaplancy- Fresenius Moses Lake Wa. 2008-2010.

GALAGAN, Christine Kay (Wyo) PO Box 1718, Cody WY 82414 B Wichita KS 1960 d Billy & Doris. MEd Lesley U 1999. D 10/25/2014 Bp John Smylie. m 6/20/1981 Michael Paul Galagan c 3.

GALAGAN, John Michael (SJ) 21105 Carriage Dr, Tehachapi CA 93561 **Died 8/14/2016** B Milwaukee WI 1928 s Thomas & Kathryn. BA U Pac 1950; MDiv CDSP 1955. D 6/12/1955 P 12/1/1955 Bp Karl M Block. m 3/2/1957 Madeline Galagan c 4. Ret 2001-2016; S Judes In The Mountains Ch Tehachapi CA 1987-2000; Kern Hospice Servs Bakersfield CA 1984-1987; R S Lk's Ch Bakersfield CA 1981-1984; R S Jas Ch Riverton WY 1975-1980; R S Barn Par McMinnville OR 1967-1975; Vic S Jas Epis Ch Portland OR 1964-1967; Asst S Lk's Epis Ch Vancouver WA 1961-1964; S Dunst's Epis Ch Grand Coulee WA 1958-1961; Vic S Mk's Ch Ritzville WA 1958-1961; Chapl Soledad St Prison

1956-1958; Vic Trin Ch Gonzales CA 1956-1958; Vic S Mk's Epis Ch Santa Clara CA 1955-1957; Serv Methodist Ch 1950-1953.

GALANTOWICZ, Deena McHenry (Fla) 49 Ocean Ct, Saint Augustine FL 32080 B Buffalo NY 1937 d Charles & Beatrice. BS Syr 1958; MDiv GTS 1980; STM GTS 1982. D 6/14/1980 P 12/19/1980 Bp John Shelby Spong. m 8/9/1958 Richard E Galantowicz c 2. Assoc R Trin Epis Ch St Aug FL 1993-2002; R S Steph's Epis Ch Bloomfield CT 1984-1990; Wooster Sch Danbury CT 1982-1984; Chapl Wooster Sch Danbury CT 1982-1984; Int S Lk's Epis Ch Montclair NJ 1982; Asst Min Chr Ch Glen Ridge NJ 1980-1981. Auth, "Sci Article". Ord Julian Of Nowich; Chapl Ord Of S Lk 1994.

GALAZ, Ernest M (Az) 969 W Country Club Dr, Nogales AZ 85621 **R S Andr's Epis Ch Nogales AZ 2013-** B Tucson AZ 1961 s Ernesto & Marie Anoniette. BA U of Arizona 1985; MA Prescott Coll 2000. D 9/8/2012 P 4/13/2013 Bp Kirk Stevan Smith. m 11/12/1995 Elizabeth Ruth Campbell c 2. ernie@standrewsaz.com

GALBRAITH, James MacAlpine (Miss) 2196 Saint James Blvd, Gulfport MS 39507 **Died 9/1/2016** B Concord NH 1936 s Hugh & Marjorie. BS U of Oklahoma 1958; MBA U of Oklahoma 1963; MDiv Nash 1977. D 6/24/1977 Bp Robert Elwin Terwilliger P 1/6/1978 Bp Archibald Donald Davies. m 6/25/1960 Dorothy Daniels c 6. Ret 2002-2016; R S Andr's Epis Ch Las Cruces NM 1987-2002; R H Trin Ch Rockwall TX 1981-1986; R S Wm Laud Epis Ch Pittsburg TX 1979-1981; Cur S Dav's Ch Garland TX 1977-1978. OHC 1977. jimg04@bellsouth.net

GALBREATH, Janet Louise (CFla) 01236 Miller Blvd, Fruitland Park FL 34731 B Sewanee TN 1951 d George & Sammie. Inst for Chr Stds; Lake-Sumter Cmnty Coll. D 11/11/1995 Bp John Wadsworth Howe. m 1/4/1978 Donald Leonard Galbreath c 4. D H Trin Epis Ch Fruitland Pk FL 1995-2009; Chapl Reg Med Cntr Leesburg FL.

GALEANO FRANCO, Gustavo Adolfo (SeFla) **Our Little Roses Miami FL 2013-** B 1970 m 7/5/2003 Keevyn Geraldine Gabourel-Hernandez c 2. Dio Honduras San Pedro Sula 1998-2013.

GALGANO, Hollis H (NY) 311 Huguenot St, New Rochelle NY 10801 **D Trin S Paul's Epis New Rochelle NY 2009-** B Rocky Ford CO 1955 d Frank & Greta. U of Dallas; BA Oral Roberts U 1977. D 5/2/2009 Bp Mark Sean Sisk. m 5/8/1982 Dennis Michael Galgano c 3.

GALGANOWICZ, Henry C (Pa) 432 Bluestone Ct, PO Box 714, Lake Harmony PA 18624 B Hamburg, Germany 1947 s Joseph & Nina. BA Ken 1969; MDiv Bex Sem 1975; MDiv Bex Sem 1975. D 6/22/1975 Bp Robert Rae Spears Jr P 3/13/1976 Bp John Mc Gill Krumm. m 7/1/2006 Sandra L Galganowicz c 2. R H Innoc S Paul's Ch Philadelphia PA 2001-2014; Prot Campus Chapl UWH Milwaukee WI 2000-2001; St Gabr's Ch E Berlin CT 1999-2000; R The Par Of Emm Ch Weston CT 1988-1998; Vic S Paul's Ch Windham CT 1981-1988; Asst Calv Ch Pittsburgh PA 1979-1981; Asst S Alb's Epis Ch Of Bexley Columbus OH 1975-1978; Interfaith Off Dio Pennsylvania Philadelphia PA 2003-2006. hankcg@aol.com

GALICIA, Kathryn K (SJ) 3308 Swallow Dr, Modesto CA 95356 **S Fran' Epis Ch Turlock CA 2013-, P-in-c 2008-** B Buffalo NY 1952 d Denis & Norma. AA Las Positas Coll 1992; BA Chapman U 2001; MDiv Mennonite Brethren Biblic Sem 2005. D 6/3/2006 Bp William Edwin Swing P 12/2/2006 Bp Marc Handley Andrus. m 10/6/1979 Alfonso Kitchen Galicia c 1. Epis Dio San Joaquin Modesto CA 2009-2012, Exam Chapl 2011-, COM, Vice Chair 2008-.

GALINDO-PAZ, Elvia Maria (Hond) **Dio Honduras San Pedro Sula 2004-** B Juticalpa Olancho 1959 d Jose & Juana. MD Universidad Nacional Autonoma De Honduras 2000; DIT Epis 2005; Dip Theol Stud Universidad Biblica 2005; ThD Universidad Nacional 2005. D 4/22/1998 Bp Leo Frade P 5/8/2004 Bp Lloyd Emmanuel Allen. c 1.

GALIPEAU, Steven Arthur (Los) 8805 Azul Drive, West Hills CA 91304 **Pres and Exec Dir Coldwater Counslg Cntr Inc Studio City 1995-** B Summit NJ 1948 s Arthur & Theresa. BA Boston Coll 1970; MA U of Notre Dame 1972; MDiv CDSP 1977. D 6/18/1977 P 1/14/1979 Bp Robert Claflin Rusack. m 4/22/1984 Linda Holmwood c 2. Counslg Cntr Dir S Mich and All Ang Epis Ch Studio City CA 1983-1994; Assoc R S Edm's Par San Marino CA 1978-1982; Vic S Lk's Mssn Fontana CA 1977-1978. Auth, "Transforming Body & Soul: Therapeutic Wisdom In The Gospel Healing Stories," Fisher King Press, 2011; Auth, "The Journey Of Lk Skywalker: An Analysis Of Mod Myth And Symbol," Open Crt, 2001. C.G. Jung Inst Of Los Angeles 1993; California Assn Of Mar And Fam Therapists 1987; Intl Assn For Analytical Psychol 1993; Natl Assn For The Advancement Of Psychoanalysis 1993-2006.

✠ GALLAGHER, The Rt Rev Dr Carol J (NY) 40 Charlotte St, Haverhill MA 01830 **Bp for Native Amer Mnstrs and Asst Bp Dio Montana Helena MT 2014-** B San Diego CA 1955 d Donald & Elizabeth. BA Antioch Baltimore MD 1976; MDiv EDS 1989; ThM PrTS 1998; PhD U of Delaware 2004. D 6/17/1989 P 5/12/1990 Bp Albert Theodore Eastman Con 4/6/2002 for SVa. m 5/15/1975 Mark P Gallagher c 3. Dom And Frgn Mssy Soc- Epis Ch Cntr New York NY 2013; Epis Ch Cntr New York NY 2013, 2012; Int S Ptr's By-The-Sea Sitka AK 2012-2014; Dio New York New York NY 2011; R All SS Ch Harrison NY 2009-2011; Asstg Bp of No Dakota Dio No Dakota Fargo ND 2008-2014; VTS

Alexandria VA 2006; Asstg Bp Dio Newark Newark NJ 2005-2008; Bp Suffr Dio Sthrn Virginia Newport News VA 2003-2005, 2002-2005; Chapl ECW Trien 1997; R St Annes Epis Ch Middletown DE 1996-2001; P-in-c Trin Ch Boothwyn PA 1995-1996; Asst S Mart's Ch Wayne PA 1991-1994, Chapl 1989-1991; Asst Cathd Of The Incarn Baltimore MD 1989-1991.

GALLAGHER, Daniel P (NY) 29 Halcyon Rd, Millbrook NY 12545 **Dio New York New York NY 1998-** B Waverly IA 1936 s Paul & Genevieve. BA U of Houston 1966; MDiv GTS 1969. D 6/7/1969 P 12/20/1969 Bp Horace W B Donegan. m 1/10/1981 Merellyn Gallagher c 2. Dio New York New York NY 1996-1997, 1971-1995, Supply P 1971-1988, Reg Pstr Care Coordntr 1997-1998; P-in-c St Thos Ch Amenia NY 1991-1996; Assoc Gr Ch Millbrook NY 1988-1991; Asst Gr Epis Ch Monroe NY 1970-1971; S Anne's Ch Washingtonville NY 1970-1971; S Paul's Ch Chester NY 1970-1971; Asst S Jas Ch Hyde Pk NY 1969-1970.

GALLAGHER, Elvin Ross (Ida) 5605 Randolph Dr, Boise ID 83705 **Ret Epis Ch 1988-** B Grand Junction CO 1922 s George & Annie. BS U of Utah 1951; MDiv CDSP 1954. D 6/14/1954 P 12/21/1954 Bp Richard S Watson. m 8/20/1953 L Margaret Gallagher c 4. Dioc Trial Crt Dioc Trial Crt 1985-1988; Emm Epis Ch Placerville ID 1982-2003; Dioc VIM Com 1981-1984; Pstr Care Com S Alphonsus Hosp 1974-1977; All SS Epis Ch Boise ID 1971-1987; Assoc Ch of the H Faith Santa Fe NM 1969-1971; Vic S Jas Ch Tanana AK 1966-1969; Chapl/Headmaster Par Sch 1963-1966; Assoc R All SS Ch Phoenix AZ 1960-1966; Aux Chapl Dugway Mltry Post UT 1957-1960; Vic All SS Ch Salt Lake City UT 1955-1957; Asst-to-Dn Cathd Ch Of S Mk Salt Lake City UT 1954-1955. Hon Masters Degree Cumberland U 2012; Honoary Cn Dio Idaho/ St. Mich's Cathd 2007.

GALLAGHER, Gerald J (NY) 1001 Leesburg Dr, Leland NC 28451 B Flushing NY 1941 s George & Jessica. BA Cathd Coll of the Immac Concep 1964; STB Gregorian U 1966; STL Gregorian U 1968. Rec 5/22/1980 Bp James Stuart Wetmore. m 2/16/1974 Joyce A Kane c 4. R Ch Of The Mssh Rhinebeck NY 1985-2009; P-in-c Ch Of The H Trin Pawling NY 1981-1984; Zion Epis Ch Wappingers Falls NY 1980.

GALLAGHER, John Merrill (Cal) 212 Riviera Cir, Larkspur CA 94939 B San Francisco CA 1929 s Thomas & Merrill. BA Stan 1951; STB EDS 1965; MA SFTS 1983. D 6/20/1965 Bp James Albert Pike P 2/12/1966 Bp George Richard Millard. m 7/10/1971 Nancy Gallagher. Asst S Jas Epis Ch San Francisco CA 1984-2010; CA Counslg Inst 1984-1991; Dir California Counslg Inst San Francisco CA 1984-1987; Asst S Lk's Ch San Francisco CA 1982-1983; Vic Chr Epis Ch Sei Ko Kai San Francisco CA 1978-1981; Archd Personl Dio California San Francisco CA 1975-1978, Exec 1970-1975, Dept Urban Mnstrs 1968-1974; Asst The Epis Ch Of S Mary The Vrgn San Francisco CA 1965-1968.

GALLAGHER, Mary Ellen Turner (Ida) 13118 W Picadilly St, Boise ID 83713 B Dallas TX 1950 d Clarence & Ruth. Steph F Austin St U 1970; BTh California Sch for Deacons 1994; California St U 2000. D 7/18/1994 Bp William Edwin Swing. m 7/18/1994 Charles Frederick Gallagher. D S Jas Ch Fremont CA 2001-2003; D S Anne's Ch Fremont CA 1996-2000; D S Bede's Epis Ch Menlo Pk CA 1994-1996. Natl St. Steph'S Awd For Mnstry Naad 2001.

GALLAGHER, Nancy Elizabeth (Ore) 1800 Lakewood Ct, Spc 58, Eugene OR 97402 **Ch Of The H Sprt Sutherlin OR 2015-; Dio Oregon Portland OR 2015-; Assoc P Ch Of The Resurr Eugene OR 2014-** B Ontario OR 1950 d Martin & Dorothy. MDiv CDSP 2010; MDiv CDSP 2010. D 10/15/2011 P 6/9/2012 Bp Michael Hanley. m 12/7/2014 Kathleen A Smith c 2. Chapl Res Penrose Hosp Colorado Sprg CO 2013-2014; Ch Of S Jn The Div Springfield OR 2012.

GALLAGHER, Patricia Marie-Portley (Ct) 9134 Town Walk Dr, Hamden CT 06518 B Bronx NY 1946 d Donald & Sylvia. BSN U of Bridgeport 1976; MA S Jos Coll 1981; MDiv Ya Berk 1989. D 6/9/1990 Bp Arthur Edward Walmsley P 2/1/1991 Bp Jeffery William Rowthorn. c 3. P-in-c S Paul's Epis Ch Willimantic CT 2004-2008; P-in-c Chr Ch Waterbury CT 2002-2004; Int S Ptr's Epis Ch Monroe CT 2000-2002; Vic Ch Of S Jn By The Sea W Haven W Haven CT 1991-1998.

GALLAGHER, Robert (Me) 1640 18th Ave, Apt 2, Seattle WA 98122 **P Assoc S Clem's Epis Ch Seattle WA 2012-; Dir Ch Dvlpmt Inst Seattle WA 2002-** B Philadelphia PA 1944 s Thomas & Dorothy. BS Penn 1966; MDiv PDS 1971; MA Goddard Coll 1976. D 11/7/1970 P 5/1/1971 Bp Robert Lionne DeWitt. Assoc P for Ascetical and Practical Theol Trin Par Seattle WA 2008-2012; Assoc St. Paul's Ch 2005-2007; R Trin Ch Castine ME 2002; Dir Ch Dvlpmt Inst The GTS New York NY 1996-1999; Vic S Andr's Ch Trenton NJ 1988-1996; S Mich's Ch Trenton NJ 1988-1996; Congrl Dvlpmt Off Dio Connecticut Meriden CT 1981-1988; Vic S Elis's Ch Philadelphia PA 1975-1981. Auth, "In Your H Sprt: Shaping the Par Through Sprtl Pract," Ascen Press, 2011; Auth, "Fill All Things: The Sprtl Dynamics of the Par Ch," Ascen Press, 2008; Auth, "Power From On High: A Model For Par Life & Mnstry," Ascen Press, 1983; Auth, "Stay In The City," Forw Mvmt, 1981; Auth, "Mnstry Of Laity As Agents Of Instnl Change," Audenshaw Papers, 1978. OA 1983.

GALLAGHER, Robert Joseph (Mich) 78 Nason St, Maynard MA 01754 **Sr Mem C.A.P. CAP (U.S.A.F.) 2009-; Cert Tchr ONLINE TUTORING IN MATH/Engl/SOC ST/LATIN 2004-** B Lowell MA 1941 s Joseph & Margaret. BA Merrimack Coll 1963; MEd Salem St Coll Salem MA 1966; MA Salem St Coll Salem MA 1977; MDiv Weston Jesuit TS 1981; DMin Iaps Detroit 1986; JD Massachusetts Sch of Law at Andover 1998. D 4/3/1982 Bp Henry Irving Mayson P 4/1/1983 Bp H Coleman Mcgehee Jr. S Mk's Ch Southborough MA 2001-2004; S Lk's Ch Hudson MA 1998-2000; Ch Of The H Trin Marlborough MA 1995-1997; S Steph The Mtyr Epis Ch Waterboro Cntr ME 1986-1988; Howe Mltry Sch Howe IN 1985-1986; R Trin Ch St Clair Shrs MI 1983-1985; S Columba Ch Detroit MI 1982-1983.

GALLEHER, Stephen Cary (Nwk) 7855 Kennedy Blvd E, Apt. 21D, North Bergen NJ 07047 B Richmond VA 1942 s Frank & Dorothy. BA U of Virginia 1964; U of Edinburgh GB 1967; MDiv VTS 1970. D 6/20/1970 Bp Philip Alan Smith P 1/1/1971 Bp William Henry Marmion. m 10/2/2015 Mynor Barillas. Prod Mgr Brownstone Pub New York NY 1995-1999; Video Producer Presb Ch (U.S.A.) New York NY 1987-1989; Archd Dio Newark Newark NJ 1982-1986; Dio Newark Newark NJ 1982-1985; R Emm Epis Ch Delaplane Delaplane VA 1975-1982; Asst R S Jn's Ch Lynchburg VA 1971-1975. Auth, *The Voice*, The Dio Newark, 1983. EvangES 1975-1982; Shalem Bd 1977-1982. Rec Video Prod Awds Dio Newark 1983.

GALLETLY, David P (NwT) 1412 W Illinois Ave, Midland TX 79701 **R Ch Of The H Trin Midland TX 2015-, Assoc 1991-1992** B Burbank CA 1960 s Robert & Patricia. BA U CA 1982; MDiv GTS 1983; MDiv CDSP 1991. D 5/19/1991 Bp John Lester Thompson III P 1/22/1992 Bp Sam Byron Hulsey. m 12/14/1985 Michele Simmons c 2. R S Patricks Ch And Day Sch Thousand Oaks CA 2002-2015; H Fam Epis Ch Omaha NE 1996-2002; St Aug of Cbury Epis Ch Elkhorn NE 1996-1999; Vic Gr Epis Ch Liberty MO 1992-1996.

GALLIGAN, Joseph Edward (Wyo) PO Box 950, Thermopolis WY 82443 **R H Trin Epis Ch Thermopolis WY 2011-, R 1996-2008; Chapl Law Enforcement Thermopolis WY 1996-** B Hartford CT 1947 s Edward & Marie. BS Montana St U 1974; Cert Montana St U 1976; Sewanee: The U So, TS 1987; Ldrshp Acad for New Directions XXII 1992; VTS 1998. D 5/23/1984 P 12/12/1984 Bp Jackson Earle Gilliam. m 12/20/1969 Ellen Galligan c 1. Mnstry Dvlp: Reg I Dio Wyoming Casper 2009-2016, COM 1998-2013; R S Alb's Ch Worland WY 2004-2009; Land Stff Land XXXIII Bayard NE 1998-1999; Dioc Mssnr Dio Montana Helena MT 1996, Dioc Mssnr 1993-1995; S Andr's Ch Livingston MT 1995-1996; Dioc Mssnr S Jn's Ch Emigrant MT 1995-1996; Vic Trin Epis Ch Harlowton MT 1989-1996; Calv Epis Ch Red Lodge MT 1989-1995; S Alb's Epis Ch Laurel MT 1989-1995; Dioc Mssnr S Paul's of the Stillwater Ch Absarokee MT 1989-1995; Vic S Mk's Ch Big Timber MT 1989-1992; Chapl Hospice Townsend & Big Timber MT 1984-1996; Vic S Jn's Ch/Elkhorn Cluster Townsend MT 1984-1989. Wyoming Law Enforcement Chapl Assn 2001.

GALLOWAY, David Alan (At) 845 Edgewater Dr Nw, Atlanta GA 30328 B Atlanta GA 1954 s Mitchell & Doris. BA Emory U 1976; MDiv Candler TS Emory U 1979; Emory U 1982; DMin Sewanee: The U So, TS 1984. D 2/23/1985 P 8/11/1985 Bp Charles Judson Child Jr. m 8/7/1981 Mary Galloway c 2. H Innoc Ch Atlanta GA 2002-2007; Cn Dio Texas Houston TX 1995-2001; Chr Epis Ch Tyler TX 1992-2001; Cathd Of S Phil Atlanta GA 1985-1990; Serv Bapt Ch 1977-1982. Auth, "Sprtl Direction In Mssn & Mnstry"; Auth, "Journ Pstr Care"; Auth, "Growing Your Ch Through Evang & Outreach"; Auth, "Ldrshp Journ". Assn Cistercian Monstry Of The H Sprt; Cmnty Of The Cross Of Nails, Assn Of S Mary, Soc Of S Jn The Evang, Ch Uniting In Global Mssn.

GALLOWAY, Denise Althea (LI) 35 Cathedral Ave, Garden City NY 11530 B McKenzie Guyana 1961 BA and MSW Adel 1999; MPA Baruck Coll 2002. D 1/30/2016 Bp Lawrence C Provenzano. c 1.

GALLOWAY, Richard Kent (Ky) 120 Mauldin Rd, Greenville SC 29605 **P S Jas Ch Shelbyville KY 2014-** B Gainesville FL 1959 s Kenneth & Faye. BA Col 1982; MDiv GTS 2010; MA U of So Carolina 2010. D 6/3/2010 Bp W illiam Andrew Waldo P 10/29/2011 Bp Terry Allen White. Trin Epis Ch Fulton KY 2011-2014.

GALVIN, Kathleen M (Ore) 2293 NW Mcgarey Dr, McMinnville OR 97128 B Saint Paul MN 1945 d Michael & Irene. BS Minnesota St U Mankato 1968; MS Minnesota St U Mankato 1972; Cert SWTS 1994; MDiv Untd TS of the Twin Cities 1994; DMin SWTS 2005. D 6/29/1994 Bp James Louis Jelinek P 1/7/1995 Bp Sanford Zangwill Kaye Hampton. c 4. R S Barn Par McMinnville OR 2007-2015; R Epis Ch Of The Trsfg Mesa AZ 2002-2006; R S Jn's Epis Ch Mankato MN 1998-2002; Dio Minnesota Minneapolis MN 1995-2002; Vic Ch Of The Mssh Prairie Island Welch MN 1995; D Mazakute Memi S Paul MN 1994-1995.

GALVIN, Mike Joseph (Ind) 9621 Claymount Ln, Fishers IN 46037 **Pres, Stndg Com Dio Indianapolis Indianapolis IN 2012-, Stndg Com Mem 2010-2012, Personl, Plcy and Compstn Bd 2009-, Disaster Response Coordntr 2008-2009, Dn, No-Cntrl Dnry 2007-2013; Mem, Crisis Response Team Indiana St Dept of Mntl Hlth and Addictions 2012-** B Madison IN 1961 BS U Cinc 1984; MEd U Cinc 1986; MDiv Chr TS 2004; Advncd Theol Stds SWTS

2005. D 6/18/2005 P 1/29/2006 Bp Cate Waynick. m 6/28/1986 Rachelle J Galvin c 2. R H Fam Epis Ch Fishers IN 2007-2017; Assoc R S Fran In The Fields Zionsville IN 2005-2007. Liggett Schlr Chr TS 2001; Creativity Awd Harvard Bus Sch 1974.

GAMBLE, Deborah E (SO) 4234 Hamilton Ave, Cincinnati OH 45223 B Bowling Green OH 1955 d Carl & Virginia. BS Mia 1977; MS U of Maine 1982; MDiv TESM 1991. D 8/22/1993 P 4/23/1994 Bp Don Adger Wimberly. c 1. S Phil's Ch Cincinnati OH 2002-2010, 2001-2002; All SS Epis Sch Lubbock TX 1997-1998; R All S's Sch Lubbock TX 1997-1998; D S Andr's Ch Ft Thos KY 1993-1995.

GAMBLE, John Robert (SwFla) 1005 Sleepy Hollow Rd, Venice FL 34285 B Philadelphia PA 1936 s John & Lillian. U of Scranton; BS U of Pennsylvania 1967. D 9/11/1991 P 9/27/1992 Bp James Michael Mark Dyer. m 10/10/1964 Janette M Gamble. P-in-c St. Jas - St. Geo Epis Ch Jermyn PA 2002-2007; P Ch Of The Epiph Glenburn Clarks Summit PA 2000-2001; R S Jas-S Geo Epis Ch Jermyn PA 1996-2000; R S Mart-In-The-Fields Mtn Top PA 1992-1996; D Epiph Glenburn PA 1991-1992.

GAMBLE, Robert David (Ia) ul. Pasieka 24, Poznan 61657 Poland Serv Ch of Engl Chapl Warsaw Poland 2005- B Philadelphia PA 1937 s Clarence & Sarah. BA Harv 1960; MA Harv 1963; BD EDS 1966. D 6/25/1966 Bp Anson Phelps Stokes Jr P 6/1/1967 Bp Wilburn Camrock Campbell. m 5/9/1973 Antonina Gamble c 1. Asst Chapl S Paul's Cathd 1981-1992; Chapl Morgan Memi Boston MA 1980-1981; Chapl NE Dss Hosp 1979-1980; S Paul's Epis Ch Grinnell IA 1974-1979; Dio Iowa Des Moines IA 1974; Asst S Paul's Ch Pawtucket RI 1970-1974; Cur Gr Epis Ch Lawr MA 1966-1970.

GAMBLING, Paul (SanD) 5079 E 30th Pl, Yuma AZ 85365 Sts Ptr And Paul Epis Ch El Centro CA 2016-; Chapl Hospice of Yuma 2002-; Assoc S Paul's Ch Yuma AZ 1999- B Tredegar Gwent Wales 1950 s William & Amelia. BA U Sask CA 1973; Dip. Ed. The Coll of Educ, Saskatoon CA 1974; MDiv Hur CA 1986. Trans 5/15/2001 as Priest Bp Gethin Benwil Hughes. m 6/8/1974 Nora Kathleen Marlowe c 2. gfrpaul@gmail.com

GAMBRILL, James Howard (Nwk) PO Box 1929, York Beach ME 03910 B Boston MA 1940 s Howard & Mary. BA Ya 1962; MDiv UTS 1965; Bos 1969; JD Rutgers The St U of New Jersey 1988. D 6/26/1965 P 5/19/1966 Bp John Melville Burgess. m 2/11/1984 Sally Gambrill c 4. Affiliate S Geo's Epis Ch York ME 1993-2002; Non-par 1984-1993; Dio Newark Newark NJ 1979-1983, Vic Gnrl 1978-1983; R Gr Ch In Providence Providence RI 1974-1978; R S Steph's Memi Ch Lynn MA 1967-1974, Asst 1965-1966. Auth, "Bridge Of The Cross," Forw Mvmt, 1982.

GAME, Paul Richard (At) Trinity Episcopal Church, 1130 First Ave, Columbus GA 31901 R S Pat's Epis Ch Atlanta GA 2010- B Tampa FL 1961 s Paul & Suzanne. BA Van 1983; JD The U of Floriday Gainesville FL 1986; MDiv Candler TS Emory U 2007. D 12/21/2006 P 7/17/2007 Bp J Neil Alexander. m 5/30/1992 Anne Game c 3. Cur Trin Epis Ch Columbus GA 2007-2010; Partnr Bondurant Mixson & Elmore 1989-2005.

GAMEZ-CARDONA, Rosa Angelica (Hond) Dio Honduras San Pedro Sula 1998- B 1975 m 11/30/2013 Angel Roberto Vallejo Montiel c 1.

GAMMONS JR, Edward Babson (NJ) 7 Oak St, Warren RI 02885 Supply Cler Var Var RI 2001- B Cohasset MA 1934 s Edward & Betty. BA Harv 1956; BD EDS 1959. D 6/24/1959 Bp Anson Phelps Stokes Jr P 1/3/1960 Bp Leland Stark. m 6/26/1965 Gretchen R Gammons c 3. Assoc S Mich's Ch Bristol RI 2004-2007; Dn Monmouth Convoc 1995-1998; All SS Ch Bay Hd NJ 1988-2000; Dn Dn of Bucks Dio Pa 1976-1982; R S Andr's Ch Yardley PA 1974-1988; Asst Ch Of The Redeem Bryn Mawr PA 1972-1974; Chapl-Tchr St. Andr's Sch Middletown DE 1961-1972; Cur S Lk's Epis Ch Montclair NJ 1959-1961. Associated Parishes 1982-1999; Assn of Dioc Liturg & Mus Commissions 1982-1989; OHC 1977.

GANDARA-PEREA, José Roberto (Oly) PO Box 8, Eastsound WA 98245 Emm Ch Orcas Island Eastsound WA 2014- B Mayaguez, Puerto Rico 1964 s Jose & Graciela. BA Universidad Cntrl Bayamon Puerto Rico 1987; BA Universidad Cntrl Bayamon Puerto Rico 1987; MDiv Other 1991; MDiv Seminario Pontificio Sto Tomas Aquino D.R. 1991; Dplma Institut Lumen Vitae Brussels Belgium 1997; Dplma Other 1997; STB and STL Other 1999; STB and STL Universidad Pontificia Salamanca Spain 1999; Cert Ang Stud GTS 2006; Cert Ang Stud GTS 2006. Rec 4/18/2009 as Priest Bp Mark Sean Sisk. m 7/11/2009 Hugh M Grant. P-in-c Ch of the Intsn Ch Of The Intsn New York NY 2010-2013; P-in-c Ch of the Intsn Dio New York New York NY 2009-2013; Dir of Field Educ The GTS New York NY 2009-2010.

GANDELL, Dahn Dorann Dean (Roch) 21 Warwick Dr, Fairport NY 14450 Dio Rochester Henrietta 2016-; R Ch Of The Ascen Rochester NY 2015- B New Orleans LA 1965 d David & Bette. BS Van 1987; MA U of Mobile 1991; MDiv Yale DS 1995. D 3/4/1998 P 10/31/1998 Bp William George Burrill. m 9/27/1997 David Lee Gandell c 2. R S Jn's Epis Ch Honeoye Falls NY 2001-2013; D Ch Of The Gd Shpd Webster NY 1998-2001; S Ptr's Memi Geneva NY 1995-1998. "Shoveling Snow and Stolen Silver," Living Water/Epis Dio Rochester, 2004. The Polly Bond Awd of Merit ECom 2005.

GANN, Judith Fara Walsman (Okla) 6335 S 72nd East Ave, Tulsa OK 74133 D Chr Epis Ch Tulsa OK 2011- B Kansas City MO 1951 d John & Alice. BA U of Missouri 1973. D 6/24/1995 Bp Robert Manning Moody. m 4/18/1998 Randy Lee Gann c 2. Dio Oklahoma Oklahoma City OK 2005-2007, 1995-2000; Trin Ch Tulsa OK 2000-2006.

GANNON, Kathleen (SeFla) 2014 Alta Meadows Ln Apt 302, Delray Beach FL 33444 Cur S Paul's Ch Delray Bch FL 2005- B Oceanside NY 1953 d John & Patricia Ann. BBA Pace U 1980; MDiv VTS 2005; MDiv VTS 2005. D 4/17/2005 Bp Leo Frade P 11/6/2005 Bp James Hamilton Ottley. Chap Of S Andr Boca Raton FL 1991-2002.

GANNON, William Sawyer (Nwk) 11 French Dr, Bedford NH 03110 B Manchester NH 1936 s Eugene & Marion. BA Norwich U 1958; STM Epis TS of the SW 1962; MDiv Epis TS of the SW 1962. D 4/1/1962 Bp John Elbridge Hines P 10/4/1962 Bp Charles Francis Hall. m 6/21/1980 Barbara Gannon c 4. Int S Jas Epis Ch Laconia NH 2004-2005; R S Andr's Ch Harrington Pk NJ 1999-2003; R Chr Ch Glen Ridge NJ 1991-1999; Int Gr Ch Hastings Hds NY 1989-1991; St Marys Sch Peekskill NY 1974-1977; 1969-1991; R S Andr's Ch Manchester NH 1964-1969; Co-Dir Yth Cmssn Dio New Hampshire Concord NH 1963-1969; Cur All SS Ch Peterborough NH 1962-1964. Auth, Findings. Rotary Club 1992-2005.

GANTER, G David (Vt) 12 Beechwood Lane, Jericho VT 05465 D S Jas Epis Ch Essex Jct VT 2011- B Watertown New York USA 1943 s Charles & Florence. BS New York St Coll of Environ Sci And Forestry 1965; MBA Syr 1966; MS Binghamton U 1986. D 11/19/2005 Bp Gladstone Bailey Adams III. m 9/12/1964 Frances Thompson c 2. Asstg D S Matt's Ch Enosburg Fls VT 2006-2011.

GANTER-TOBACK, Gail Sage (NY) 32 Center St, New Paltz NY 12561 D S Jas Ch Hyde Pk NY 2012-, 1985-1994; Mem - Advsry Com Epis Chars of the Dio NY New York NY 2017- B Hartford CT 1944 d John & Lillian. BS Keuka Coll 1966. D 6/4/1994 Bp Richard Frank Grein. m 8/21/2004 Arnold Toback c 2. D Ch Of The H Cross Kingston NY 2005-2012; D Chr Ch Red Hook NY 1998-2005; D Ch Of The Regeneration Pine Plains NY 1994-1995; Global Mssn Cmsn Dio New York New York NY 2011-2014, Epis Relief and Dvlpmt Dioc Coordntr - Mid-Hudson Reg 2005-2015, D 2004-, D 1994-2003. Assn for Epis Deacons 1994.

GANTZ, Jay John (EMich) 10095 E Coldwater Rd, Davison MI 48423 S Andr's Epis Ch Flint MI 1998- B Buffalo NY 1954 s Frank & Janet. BA Wadhams Hall Sem Coll 1979; MDiv Cath Theol Un 1988; DMin SWTS 2004. Rec 2/1/1998 as Priest Bp Edwin Max Leidel Jr. m 5/20/2006 Patricia A Gantz c 3. Dio Estrn Michigan Saginaw MI 2002; Nativ Cmnty Epis Ch Holly MI 1998-2004; Serv RC Ch 1974-1993. "Gr in the Ghetto," Seabury-Wstrn/No Wstrn U, 2001.

GARAFALO, Robert Christopher (Los) 19988 Promenade Cir, Riverside CA 92508 B New York NY 1948 BA Oblate TS 1978; MA CUA 1980; MDiv CUA 1981; STL Pontifical Marian U Rome It 1986; SSL Pontifical Gregorian U 1989; PhD Pontifical Marian U 1993. Rec 11/19/2002 Bp Joseph Jon Bruno. m 11/15/1991 Maria Garafalo c 5. P S Mich's Epis Ch Riverside CA 2003-2004. "Hist Theol And Symbol: The Cana Narrative In Mod Exegesis," Marianum, 1994; "Through A Glass Darkly: Models Of The Loc Ch Twenty-Five Years After Vatican Ii," Sprtl Life, 1990; "The Fam Of Jesus In Mk'S Gospel," Irish Theol Quarterly, 1989; "Dogma And Consciousness In The Works Of Bern Lonergan," New Blackfriars (London), 1988.

GARBARINO, Harold William (Mass) 2038 Laurel Park Hwy, Laurel Park NC 29739 B Jamaica NY 1942 s Harold & Dorothy. BA Hobart and Wm Smith Colleges 1964; MDiv PDS 1967. D 6/17/1967 P 12/23/1967 Bp Jonathan Goodhue Sherman. m 8/6/1967 Ellen Close Cowling c 4. R Ch Of The Gd Shpd Reading MA 1984-2006; R S Jas' Epis Ch Watkins Glen NY 1980-1983; R S Jn's Epis Ch Catharine NY 1980-1983; S Jn's Epis Ch Odessa NY 1980-1983; R Schuyler Cnty Episc Parishes Watkins Glen NY 1980-1983; R Gr Ch Lyons NY 1972-1980; R S Paul's Ch Montour Falls NY 1972-1980; Asst S Lk's Par Darien CT 1970-1972; Cur Epis Ch of The Resurr Williston Pk NY 1967-1970.

GARCEAU, John Earle (Alb) 2050 N San Clemente Rd, Palm Springs CA 92262 B Cohoes NY 1955 s Alfred & Martha. RPI 1976; BS SUNY 1990. D 5/31/1988 Bp David Standish Ball. D Trin Ch San Francisco CA 1998; D Cathd Of All SS Albany NY 1994-1997; D S Steph's Ch Delmar NY 1991-1993; Secy of the Dio Dio Albany 1990-1993; D Ch Of The H Cross Troy NY 1988-1991. NAAD, Curs.

GARCES TORRES, Gilberto Goen (PR) Iglesia Episcopal Puertorriquena, PO Box 902, Saint Just PR 00978 Puerto Rico Dio Puerto Rico Trujillo Alto PR 2011- B Buenaventura Colombia 1961 s Juan & Maria. BA Instituto de Misiones Extranjeras 1991; Angl Stds Seminario San Pedro y San Pablo 2010. Rec 10/24/2010 Bp David Andres Alvarez-Velazquez. m 11/19/2011 Marilu Roman Rodriguez c 1. Mssy Misioneros De Yarumal 1992-2001.

GARCIA, Christine Joyce (Va) 1704 W Laburnum Ave, Richmond VA 23227 B MecKlenburg County VA 1951 d Arthur & Mary. AA Vance Granville Cmnty Colelge 1979; Cosmetology Johnston Tech Coll 1990. D 2/11/2012 Bp Shannon Sherwood Johnston. c 2.

G

301

GARCIA, Christopher (Va) Emmanuel Church, Greenwood Parish, PO Box 38, Greenwood VA 22943 **Emm Epis Ch Greenwood VA 2013-** B Frankfurt Germany s Charles & Barbara. AB Cor 1981; MBA Cor 1982; JD cl Cor 1990; LLM w dist The Judge Advoc Generals Sch US Army 1995; MDiv cl VTS 2010. D 6/5/2010 P 12/11/2010 Bp Shannon Sherwood Johnston. m 9/15/1990 Cheryl Garcia c 2. VTS Alexandria VA 2012; Asst to the R Chr Ch Georgetown Washington DC 2010-2013.

GARCIA, David Allen (PR) 165 Hoyt St, Brooklyn NY 11217 B Marquette MI 1944 s Abraham & Barbara. BD Bex Sem; BS Nthrn Michigan U. D 7/15/1969 Bp George R Selway P 1/1/1970 Bp Paul Moore Jr. m 2/1/1970 Migdalia De Jesus Torres c 1. Vic Mision San Rafael Arcangel Yauco PR 2010-2011; Dio Puerto Rico Trujillo Alto PR 2004-2011, 2000-2003; Mision San Juan Apostol y Evangelista Yauco PR 2004-2011; Epis City Mssn Boston MA 1994-1999; Cleric A Wrld of Difference ADL 1991-1993; S Mk's Ch In The Bowery New York NY 1969-1991. Revson Fell Col 1991.

GARCIA, Emily J (Mass) 379 Hammond St, Chestnut Hill MA 02467 B Anaheim 1987 d Roland & Ann. BA Pr 2010; Angl Cert Berkeley Div 2017; MDiv Yale DS 2017. D 6/3/2017 Bp Gayle Harris. families@redeemerchestnuthill.org

GARCIA JR, Francisco J (Los) Holy Faith Episcopal Church, 260 N Locust St, Inglewood CA 90301 **H Faith Par Inglewood CA 2015-** B Monterey Park CA 1979 Joint Mdiv w ETSC Bloy Hse Claremont TS; MA U CA, Los Angeles; BA U CA, Los Angeles 2001; MA U CA, Los Angeles 2004; MDiv The ETS At Claremont 2013. D 6/8/2013 Bp Joseph Jon Bruno P 1/11/2014 Bp Mary Douglas Glasspool. m 9/1/2001 Rebekah Christine Garcia c 3. D All SS Ch Pasadena CA 2013-2015. Auth, "Cheer Our Spirits, Make Safe the Way: Meditations for Adv and Christmas," *Forw Mvmt*, Forw Mvmt, 2012. fgarcia608@gmail.com

GARCIA, Hope Jufiar (ECR) Po Box 3994, Salinas CA 93912 B Roseville CA 1924 d Filoteo & Josefina. BTh Dio Ecr Sch For Deacons 1991. D 8/22/1992 Bp Richard Lester Shimpfky.

GARCIA, Louis Fernando (ETenn) 10 Fort Stephenson Pl, Lookout Mountain TN 37350 B Tampa FL 1926 s Alejandro & Carmen. U of Tennessee; BD Georgia Inst of Tech 1950. D 7/9/1989 Bp William Edwin Swing. m 6/17/1950 Grace Zuue Garcia. D Ch Of The Gd Shpd Lookout Mtn TN 1989-2010.

GARCIA, Michael George (Az) **D Ch of the Resurr in Gilbert Gilbert AZ 2016-** B 1958 D 6/11/2016 Bp Kirk Stevan Smith. m 2/16/2016 Juditha Flores c 2.

GARCIA, Ruth Anne (NY) Grace Episcopal Church, 116 City Island Avenue, Bronx NY 10464 **Gr Ch Middletown NY 2016-; P Gr Ch Bronx NY 2012-** B Peoria IL 1968 d Joseph & Sharon. NW Coll St Paul MN; BS Montana St U 1991; MDiv GTS 1998. D 6/20/1998 Bp Charles I Jones III P 4/15/1999 Bp Peter J Lee. m 8/19/2010 Jeremy Bacon. Trin Par New York NY 2006-2009; S Columba's Ch Washington DC 2002-2005; Dio Montana Helena MT 2002; S Paul's Sch Concord NH 2000-2001; S Tim's Ch Herndon VA 1998-2000. t_thetruth@hotmail.com

GARCIA, Sixto Rafael (SeFla) 150 SW 13th Ave, Miami FL 33135 **P-in-c Ch Of The H Comf Miami FL 2009-** B 1972 s Candido & Barbara. Trans 8/5/2009 Bp Leo Frade. m 2/10/2003 Anaysa Calderin c 2. S Phil's Ch Coral Gables FL 2008-2009. priestrafael@yahoo.es

GARCIA, Teodosio R (HB) **Non-par 1966-** B Echarri ES 1928 Trin U San Antonio. Rec 8/1/1963 as Deacon Bp Richard Earl Dicus. P-in-c Santa Fe Mssn San Antonio TX 1964-1966.

GARCIA-APONTE, Jorge (PR) B 1940 m 12/18/1965 Maria Rondon-Viera.

GARCIA CARDENAS, Pastor Elias (Colom) B 1968 Rec 12/8/2016 Bp Francisco Jose Duque-Gomez. m 7/24/2015 Ines Ricciuti.

GARCIA CORREA, Luis Alberto (DR) **Dio The Dominican Republic (Iglesia Epis Dominicana) Gazcue Santo Domingo 2015-** B 1987 s Luis & Gladys. Artes Bellas Artes; Teologia Centro de Estudios Teologicos C.E.T; Psicologia UASD. D 2/15/2015 Bp Julio Cesar Holguin-Khoury. m 6/1/2016 Edelmira Bonifacio Grullon.

GARCIA DE JESUS, Juan (PR) **Dio Puerto Rico Trujillo Alto PR 2010-, 2004-2006; Vic Mision Cristo Rey Caguas PR 2009-** B Caguas PR 1968 s Jenaro & Candida. D 11/22/2009 P 6/27/2010 Bp David Andres Alvarez-Velazquez. m 6/6/2003 Sarahi Alvarado c 2.

GARCIA DE LOS SANTOS, Ramon Antonio (DR) Guarionex #19, Ensanche Quisqueya, La Romana Dominican Republic **Dio The Dominican Republic (Iglesia Epis Dominicana) Gazcue Santo Domingo 1993-** B La Romana DO 1964 s Leopoldo & Manuela. U 2 Yrs; Cert Diac Mnstry 1992. D 6/7/1992 P 12/1/1993 Bp Julio Cesar Holguin-Khoury. m 5/24/1992 Iris Margarita de Garcia c 3.

GARCIA-PEREZ, Jose Rafael (PR) B 1947 m 12/28/1968 Ann Lind.

GARCIA-TUIRAN, Carlos Alfredo (SanD) 2660 Hardy Drive, Lemon Grove CA 91945 **S Phil The Apos Epis Ch Lemon Grove CA 2010-; Vic Santa Rosa Del Mar Desert Shores CA 2005-** B Barranquilla CO 1957 s Christian & Carmen. U Del Litoral Barranquilla CO 1979; MDiv Pacific Luth TS 1995. D 7/13/1996 P 1/18/1997 Bp Frederick Houk Borsch. m 10/26/1991 Christine Garcia c 2. Dio San Diego San Diego CA 2006-2013, 2003-2005, Curs Cmnty Sprtl

Advsr 2004-, Hisp Mnstry Comittee Mem 2003-2004; All SS Epis Ch Brawley CA 2006-2009, Vic 2003; Sts Ptr And Paul Epis Ch El Centro CA 2003; Dioc Coun Mem Dio Los Angeles Los Angeles CA 1998-2000, Hospice Chapl 1996-1999, 1992-1995; Vic Ch Of The Epiph Los Angeles CA 1997-2002; S Paul's Pomona Pomona CA 1996-2000.

GARD, Mary Anne (Ore) 147 NW 19th Ave, Portland OR 97209 B Pendleton OR 1951 d Joe & Dorothy. BA Marylhurst Coll 1974; MSPT Pacific U 1990; MDiv CDSP 2011; MDiv CDSP 2011. D 6/29/2013 P 1/4/2014 Bp Michael Hanley. m 12/14/2013 Kathryn Nell Keller. Trin Epis Cathd Portland OR 2013-2014.

GARDE, Mary Ann (LI) 573 Roanoke Ave, Riverhead NY 11901 B Joplin MO 1951 d Christopher & Anna. BA Benedictine Coll 1975; MSW Wstrn Michigan U 1986; MDiv Epis TS of the SW 1999. D 6/26/1999 P 1/2/2000 Bp Robert Manning Moody. R Gr Ch Riverhead NY 2002-2017.

GARDNER, Albutt Lorian (Pa) 600 E. Cathedral Rd., # H-304, Philadelphia PA 19128 **Ret 1994-** B Southampton County VA 1929 s Albutt & Ruby. AA Mars Hill Coll 1949; BA U Rich 1951; BD Crozer TS 1955; MDiv Crozer TS 1972; CPE Presb/ U of Pennsylvania Hosp 1983. D 2/28/1965 P 6/5/1965 Bp John Brooke Mosley. c 5. Adj P Ch Of S Mart-In-The-Fields Philadelphia PA 2004-2007; Int The Ch Of Emm And The Gd Shpd Philadelphia PA 2001-2003; Assoc Trin Ch Gulph Mills Kng Of Prussia PA 1996-2001; Vic All SS Crescentville Philadelphia PA 1983-1994; R S Paul's Ch Elkins Pk PA 1970-1981; R Chr Ch Milford DE 1966-1970; Asst Dn Cathd Ch Of S Jn Wilmington DE 1965-1966; Dioc Liturg Com Dio Pennsylvania Philadelphia PA 1975-1980. Auth, "Roots In Colonial Virginia: Wm Leonard Joyner & His Descendants," 1992.

GARDNER, Anne (Mass) Phillips Academy, 180 Main Street, Andover MA 01810 **Dir of Sprtl and Rel Life Phillips Acad Andover MA 2008-** B Boston MA 1960 d Theodore & Elizabeth. BA Fairfield U 1982; MS U Roch 1988; MDiv Harvard DS 2005. D 6/2/2007 P 1/12/2008 Bp M(Arvil) Thomas Shaw. m 9/29/2006 Beth White c 2. Assoc S Ptr's Ch Weston MA 2007-2008; Chapl/ Dir of Cmnty Serv Endicott Coll Beverly MA 2006-2008.

GARDNER, Bruce Norman (Eau) 221 Twin Oak Dr, Altoona WI 54720 B Duluth MN 1948 s Norman & Beatrice. BA U MN 1981; MA U MN 1983; MDiv Nash 1986. D 9/29/1985 P 5/25/1986 Bp William Charles Wantland. Dio Eau Claire Eau Claire WI 2007-2008, Int 1990-1995; Chr Ch Cathd Eau Claire WI 2005-2007; Ch Of The Ascen Hayward WI 1995-2005; S Alb's Ch Superior WI 1994-1995; Chr Ch Par La Crosse WI 1992-1993; Chr Ch Chippewa Fls WI 1991-1992; S Simeon's Ch Chippewa Falls WI 1991-1992; S Alb's Ch Spooner WI 1990-1991; St Stephens Ch Spooner WI 1990-1991; Vic Campus Mnstry Dio W Missouri Kansas City MO 1987-1990; S Lk's Ch Springbrook WI 1986-2002; Cur S Paul's Epis Ch Flint MI 1986-1987; Nash Nashotah WI 1985-1986; Sr D Chap S Mary's Epis Ch Summit WI 1985-1986. Csss 1983-1999; Esmhe 1986. canonitchy@gmail.com

GARDNER, Calvin George (SVa) 1405 Bruton Ln, Virginia Beach VA 23451 B Decatur IL 1925 s George & Edna. BA Bob Jones U 1950; MDiv Nthrn Bapt TS 1953. D 4/24/1994 P 11/6/1994 Bp Alden Moinet Hathaway. m 7/20/1951 Naoma Viriginia Lovelady. All SS Ch Warrenton NC 2004-2005; Asst R Galilee Epis Ch Virginia Bch VA 1996-2002; D Dio Pittsburgh Pittsburgh PA 1994-1996; Serv S Steph's Ch Sewickley PA 1989-1996; S Andr Port-Au-Prince Haiti 1979-1981; Serv Bapt Ch 1971-1977; Chapl USN 1953-1971. Ord Of S Lk.

GARDNER, Carol Hartsfield (WTenn) 215 Windsor Terrace Dr, Nashville TN 37221 B Memphis TN 1935 d Orville & Juanita. MA U of Memphis 1978; Memphis TS 1999. D 3/4/2000 Bp James Malone Coleman. m 8/13/1971 Lawrence Gale Gardner c 1. Gr - S Lk's Ch Memphis TN 2000-2003.

GARDNER, Daniel Wayne (EO) 571 Yakima St S, Vale OR 97918 **P S Thos Ch Canyon City OR 2007-** B Bend OR 1939 s Harvey & Gertrude. BS Portland St U 1962; MS U of Oregon 1971. D 3/9/1995 P 12/1/1995 Bp Rustin Ray Kimsey. m 6/20/1959 Vonna Jean Gardner c 2. Loc P - Mnstry Spprt Grp H Trin Vale OR 1995-2007; Dep 1988, 1991, 1997, 2000, 2003 GC Dio Estrn Oregon; COM Mem Dio Estrn Oregon Cove OR 1998-2003, Dioc Coun Mem 1997-2003.

GARDNER, Edward Morgan (WNC) 118 Clubwood Ct, Asheville NC 28803 B Gordonsville VA 1949 s Edward & Lorraine. BS Appalachian St U 1972; MDiv VTS 1976; VTS 1989; Cert Luther Sem Ctr for Aging Rel & Sprtlty 2006. D 6/12/1976 P 6/9/1977 Bp William Gillette Weinhauer. c 1. Mem, Exec Coun Dio Wstrn No Carolina Asheville NC 2006-2009, Mem, Stndg Com 1996-1999, Mem, Exec Coun 1984-1987, Mem, Stndg Com 2010-2014, Dep, GC 1984-, 1980-1984, 1978-1979; Dir of Pstr Care S Giles Chap Deerfield Asheville NC 2000-2015; Int Ch Of The Epiph Newton NC 2000; R S Mk's Ch Gastonia NC 1984-2000; R S Jas Ch Black Mtn NC 1979-1984; Vic S Andr's Ch Bessemer City NC 1977-1979; Vic Trin Ch Kings Mtn NC 1976-1979. Star of Merit Medal No Carolina Fire Dept 1997.

GARDNER, Elizabeth (WA) St John's Church, 6715 Georgetown Pike, McLean VA 22101 **Dio Washington Washington DC 2016-** B Pueblo CO 1965 d Anthony & Nancy. BA U CA 1987; MDiv VTS 2013. D 1/26/2013 P 7/27/2013

Bp Mariann Edgar Budde. m 6/17/2000 Christopher Kerr Gardner c 2. The Ch Of The Epiph Washington DC 2015-2016; Pstr Care S Jn's Epis Ch Mc Lean VA 2013-2015; Prog Cathd of St. Ptr & St. Paul 2012-2013. egardner@stjohnsmclean.org

GARDNER, E Ugene Clifton (Dal) 6505 Brook Lake Dr., Dallas TX 75248 B Champaine IL 1949 s Malcolm & Lillian. OH SU 1970; BS Sthrn Illinois U 1982; MDiv TESM 1986. D 6/15/1986 P 5/24/1987 Bp Christopher FitzSimons Allison. m 1/3/1973 Clarice Ann Gardner c 2. R S Jas Ch Dallas TX 2002-2017; R Epis Ch Of The Gd Shpd San Angelo TX 1993-2002; P-in-c Ch Of The H Fam Moncks Corner SC 1986-1993.

GARDNER, Harry Huey (Ala) 1910 12th Ave. South, Birmingham AL 35205 **R S Mary's-On-The-Highlands Epis Ch Birmingham AL 2002-; COM Dio Alabama Birmingham 2011-** B Fairfield AL 1959 s Harry & Saidee. BS Auburn U 1982; MDiv VTS 1991. D 5/28/1991 P 12/21/1991 Bp Robert Oran Miller. m 6/27/1992 Irene T Gardner c 2. R Chr Ch Macon GA 1998-2002; Asst Calv Ch Memphis TN 1993-1998; Asst Gr Ch Anniston AL 1991-1993.

GARDNER, James Edward (CPa) 839 Fraternity Rd, Lewisburg PA 17837 **Ret 1995-** B Philadelphia PA 1931 s Francis & Josephine. BS Carnegie Mellon U 1953; MS Carnegie Mellon U 1954; STB PDS 1961; STM GTS 1963; U of Pennsylvania 1965. D 5/13/1961 P 11/1/1961 Bp Oliver J Hart. m 7/11/1953 Patricia Ruth Gardner c 2. R S Ptr's Epis Ch Livingston NJ 1990-1995; Asst H Apos And Medtr Philadelphia PA 1966-1968; Cur S Paul's Chestnut Hill PA 1963-1966. Alb Inst. Fell Ecf; Fell Underwood (Danforth).

GARDNER III, James W (Ala) **Calv and St Geo New York NY 2017-; The GTS New York NY 2016-** D 5/13/2017 Bp John Mckee Sloan Sr.

GARDNER, Joan Margiotta (ECR) 1970 Cerra Vista Dr, Hollister CA 95023 B Hoboken NJ 1947 d Eugene & Theresa. BS California St Polytechnic U 1975; MS W Coast U Los Angeles CA 1977; MDiv CDSP 1984. D 6/10/1984 P 1/19/1985 Bp John Lester Thompson III. S Lk's Ch Hollister CA 1988-2008, R 1987-2008; Int S Anselm's Epis Ch Lafayette CA 1985-1986; Chapl Dio El Camino Real Salinas CA 1984-2008.

GARDNER, John (Pa) Ch Of The Ascension & Holy Trinity, 420 W 18th St, Pueblo CO 81003 **The Ch Of The H Trin Rittenhouse Philadelphia PA 2016-** B Abingdon VA 1973 s Philip & Betty. BS W&M 1995; MDiv VTS 2002. D 6/15/2002 P 12/15/2003 Bp Carol J Gallagher. m 2/8/2003 Rachel E Wenner Gardner c 3. P-in-c Ch Of The Ascen Pueblo CO 2012-2016; Co-R Trin Epis Ch Rocky Mt VA 2006-2012; Assoc Chr Ch Milwaukee WI 2003-2006; Chapl St. Jn's NW Mltry Acad Delafield WI 2002-2003.

GARDNER, John (Cal) 1340 Dolores St, San Francisco CA 94110 B Oakland CA 1949 s Herbert & Alice. BA San Jose St U 1972; MDiv CDSP 1978. D 5/25/1979 P 11/1/1979 Bp William Arthur Dimmick. Consult Sanctuary Design Consult: Lighting acoustics etc. 2006-2011; Gudiance Luth/Epis Pryr Grp Shep Of Hills Tiburon 2005-2011; Owner Mnstry of Hosp for Cler in my guest room SF CA 1995-2011; Asst Shpd Hills Luth Ch Tiburon CA 1994-1997; Int Mssy Lae Papua New Guinea 1990-1994; Int Ch Of The Nativ San Rafael CA 1989-1990; Asst S Mk's Ch Mt Kisco NY 1984; Cur Gr Ch Newark NJ 1983-1984; Vic Ch Of The Gd Shpd S Ignace MI 1979-1983; Dio Nthrn Michigan Marquette MI 1979-1983.

GARDNER, Mark William (Los) 1031 Lanza Ct, San Marcos CA 92078 B Union City TN 1956 s Roland & Leonore. U CA 1974; BA California St U 1978; ETSBH 1983; MDiv CDSP 1988. D 6/4/1988 P 12/1/1988 Bp Charles Brinkley Morton. c 4. Vic S Mich's U Mssn Isla Vista CA 1991-1999; Chapl U CA-Santa Barbara 1991-1999; Cur S Dav's Epis Ch San Diego CA 1988-1991. markgar33@gmail.com

GARDNER, Randal B. (Cal) Grace Cathedral Church, 1100 California St, San Francisco CA 94108 B Denver CO 1953 s Robert & Betty. BA Seattle Pacific U 1975; MDiv CDSP 1984; CTh Ripon Coll Cuddesdon Oxford Gb 1985; DMin VTS 2005. D 6/30/1984 P 10/12/1985 Bp Robert Hume Cochrane. m 6/21/1975 Cathy June Gardner c 2. CDSP Berkeley CA 2016, Trst, Treas 2008-; Cn Gr Cathd San Francisco CA 2013-2017; VTS Alexandria VA 2013; R S Jas By The Sea La Jolla CA 2006-2013; R Emm Epis Ch Mercer Island WA 1996-2006; Ch Of The Gd Shpd Fed Way WA 1988-1996; Asst R S Barn Epis Ch Bainbridge Island WA 1985-1988; D Serv Ch of Engl Oxford 1984-1985; Dir Epis Cmnty Serv Natl City CA 2006-2009; Exam Chapl Dio Olympia Seattle 1994-1998.

GARDNER, Van Howard (Md) 89 Murdock Rd, Baltimore MD 21212 B Baltimore MD 1946 s Edward & Annie. BS Frostburg St U 1968; MS Morgan St U 1973; MDiv VTS 1977. D 5/21/1977 P 11/1/1977 Bp David Keller Leighton Sr. m 11/23/1969 Kathleen K Gardner c 2. Dn Cathd Of The Incarn Baltimore MD 1987-2008; R Ch Of S Marks On The Hill Pikesville MD 1979-1987; Asst Ch Of The Mssh Baltimore MD 1977-1979. Auth, "Sermons That Wk". Natl First Prize For Best Sermon Epis Evang Fndt.

GARDNER-SMITH, Fran (Cal) 2217 Koa Ct, Antioch CA 94509 **Gr Ch Berryville VA 2016-; S Mary's Memi Berryville VA 2016-; Vic S Jn's Epis Ch Clayton CA 2013-** B Worcester MA 1966 d Francis & Barbara. AB Mt Holyoke Coll 1988; MAT Mt Holyoke Coll 1990; MDiv VTS 2006. D 3/13/2006 P 10/7/2006 Bp James Arthur Kelsey. m 7/31/2010 David A Smith. Co-Vic of ECCC Shared Mnstry Dio California San Francisco CA 2013-2016; R S

Barn Ch Berlin NH 2008-2013; Dio New Hampshire Concord NH 2008-2010; Mnstry Dvlp Intern Dio Nthrn Michigan Marquette MI 2006-2008, Mssnr 2006-2008. fbgardner@me.com

GARFIELD, Elizabeth Ann (Colo) St Luke's Episcopal Church, 1270 Poplar St, Denver CO 80220 B Minneapolis MN 1959 d Theodore & Mary. BA Iowa St U 1981. D 11/17/2007 Bp Robert John O'Neill. D S Lk's Ch Denver CO 2007-2010.

GARFIELD, Liston Alphonso (Ala) 2060 Mohican Dr, Auburn AL 36879 B Saint Thomas VI 1952 s Franz & Cassilda. BS Tuskegee Inst 1974; MEd Tuskegee Inst 1976; MDiv VTS 1985. D 1/3/1985 P 7/12/1985 Bp Edward Mason Turner. m 5/9/1987 Jacquelyn B Garfield c 1. Emm Epis Ch Opelika AL 2014-2015; Chapl Dio Alabama Birmingham 1994-2014, Mem, Disciplinary Bd 2015-, Pres of Stndg Com 2012-2013; R S Andr's Ch Tuskegee Inst AL 1993-2013; S Geo Mtyr Ch Tortola 1985-1993; Chairman, Sch Bd S Geo Sch Road Town Tortola 1985-1993; Chapl US-A Reserves 1982-2012.

GARGIULO, Mariano (Nwk) 384 Hilltop Ave # 7605, Leonia NJ 07605 **R S Jas' Ch Ridgefield NJ 2003-** B Positano Italy 1954 s Michele & Rosa. BA S Thos Aquinas Coll 1976; MDiv Immac Concep Sem 1980. Rec 11/20/2001 Bp John Palmer Croneberger. m 3/21/2014 William A Borrelli. Long Term Supply S Thos Ch Lyndhurst NJ 2001-2003; Dioc Coun Mem Dio Newark Newark NJ 2005-2009.

GARLAND III, John G (Tex) 1002 South Main Street, Greenville SC 29611 B Houston TX 1974 BA Alma Coll 1997; MDiv Sewanee: The U So, TS 2002. D 6/22/2002 Bp Claude Edward Payne P 6/4/2003 Bp Don Adger Wimberly. P-in-c Gr Epis Ch Georgetown TX 2012-2015; R S Andr's Epis Ch Greenville SC 2008-2012; Asst to R Trin Epis Ch Marble Falls TX 2006-2008; Assoc. Chapl St. Chad's Coll - Univ. of Durham Durham Untd Kingdom 2004-2006; Asst to R Ch Of The Gd Shpd Tomball TX 2002-2004.

GARLICHS, Richard Walbridge (Oly) 900 University St Apt 6G, Seattle WA 98101 **Ret 1985-; Chapl Emer Coll Chap APHA 1985-** B Saint Joseph MO USA 1923 s Lorren & Sarah. BS U of Pennsylvania 1943; GTS 1948; MDiv Ya Berk 1949. D 6/22/1949 P 12/22/1949 Bp Robert N Spencer. c 3. Int S Jas Epis Ch Kent WA 1988-1989; Asst Supvsr CPE - ACPE 1976-1983; Virginia Mason Hosp Seattle WA 1974-1983; Stndg Com Dio Olympia Seattle 1974-1977, Dioc Hosp Chapl 1972-1976, Rgnl Archd 1969-1972, Stndg Com 1965-1968, Chair DeptCE 1958-1960; Ch Of The H Cross Redmond WA 1963-1972; P-in-c Ch of the H Cross Pe Ell WA 1963-1972; S Tim's Epis Ch Chehalis WA 1963-1972; Vic S Alb's Ch Edmonds WA 1957-1963; S Hilda's - S Pat's Epis Ch Edmonds WA 1957-1963; Vic S Jn's Epis Ch So Bend WA 1953-1957; Vic S Ptr's Ilwaco WA 1953-1957; Vic S Mary's Ch Savannah MO 1949-1953; S Oswald In The Field Skidmore MO 1949-1953; S Paul's Ch Maryville MO 1949-1953. Clincl Pstr Ed. Asst Supvsr, ACPE 1976-1983.

GARMA, Joann Marie (La) 1014 Marigny Ave, Mandeville LA 70448 **Int Dir of Pstr Care E Jefferson Gnrl Hosp 2017-** B New Orleans LA 1942 d Roman & Geihade. BA Centenary Coll of Louisiana, Shreveport, LA 1964; MRE SMU, Dallas, TX 1967; EdD New Orleans Bapt TS 1984; Certification Granted, Dallas, TX Orleans Par Criminal Sheriff's Off, New Orleans, LA 1985; Full Certification Granted, Baltimore, MD Chld's Hosp, New Orleans, LA 1990. D 8/22/1982 Bp James Barrow Brown. Dir/ACPE Supvsr E Jefferson Gnrl Hosp Metairie LA 2007-2014; ACPE Supvsr VetA Hosp of Dallas Dallas TX 2006-2007; ACPE Supvsr Seton Healthcare Ntwk Austin TX 2003-2006; D All SS Epis Ch New Orleans LA 2001-2003; D S Mich's Epis Ch Mandeville LA 2000-2002; Dir/ACPE Supvsr The McFarland Inst Bapt Com. Min. New Orleans 1996-2003; Dir/ACPE Supvsr Chld's Hosp New Orleans LA 1983-1996; D Gr Ch New Orleans LA 1982-1999; Chapl/Chf Chapl Orleans Par Criminal Sheriff's Off New Orleans 1976-1982; Educ Dir Mulholland Meth Ch 1971-1976; Sch Soc Worker Trainee New Orleans Par Schools 1968-1970. Writer, "A Cry of Anguish: The Battered Wmn," *Wmn in Travail & Transition: A New Pstr Care*, Fortress Press, 1991.

GARMAN, Cynthia (Mich) 426 Cottonwood Ln., Saline MI 48176 **Int S Pat's Epis Ch Mooresville NC 2017-** B Kingston PA 1950 d Richard & Marjorie. BA Prescott Coll 1990; MDiv EDS 1995; BSci Wichita St U 2000. D 11/1/2000 P 6/28/2001 Bp William Edward Smalley. c 1. R S Phil's Epis Ch Rochester MI 2013-2016; P-in-c Ch Of The Resurr Clarkston MI 2010-2012; R S Jas' Epis Ch Dexter MI 2006-2010; R S Ptr's Epis Ch Tunkhannock PA 2003-2006; Assoc R S Paul's Ch Kansas City MO 2001-2002; Transitional D S Matt's Epis Ch Newton KS 2000-2001. Assoc of the OHC 2008.

GARMAN, Gerald Roger (Oly) 11758 Meridian Ave N, Seattle WA 98133 **Died 6/15/2016** B Seattle WA 1938 s Roger & Frances. BS U of Washington 1962. D 6/26/2004 Bp Sanford Zangwill Kaye Hampton. m 2/1/1963 Sherry Kay Roberts c 3. Gd Samar Epis Ch Sammamish WA 2004-2016.

GARNER, Evan D (Ala) 2411 13th St SE, Decatur AL 35601 **R S Jn's Ch Decatur AL 2011-; Mem of HOD Com on the St of the Ch GC- Epis Ch Cntr New York NY 2015-, Mem of Stndg Cmsn for Lifelong Chr Formation and Educ 2012-2015** B Atlanta GA 1980 s Douglas & Emily. BA Birmingham-Sthrn Coll 2002; BS Birmingham-Sthrn Coll 2002; MA U of Cambridge GB 2005; VTS 2006; MBA Troy U 2010. D 5/22/2006 P 12/12/2006 Bp Henry

Nutt Parsley Jr. m 9/17/2005 Elizabeth G Graffeo c 4. Assoc R S Jn's Ch Montgomery AL 2006-2011; Stndg Com Dio Alabama Birmingham 2013-2017, GC Dep 2012-, Dioc Coun 2010-2011. evan@stjohnsdecatur.org

GARNER, Jeffery Ray (CGC) **R H Sprt Epis Ch Gulf Shores AL 2014-** B Mobile AL 1957 s Earl & Audrey. BS Wm Carey U 1979; MS Golden Gate U 2000; MDiv Epis TS of the SW 2005. D 5/26/2005 P 12/13/2005 Bp Henry Nutt Parsley Jr. m 12/30/1977 Angela Louise Garner c 2. R S Simon Ptr Ch Pell City AL 2007-2012; R S Phil's Ch Ft Payne AL 2005-2007. hsfrjeff@gmail.com

GARNER, Mary P (Eas) 302 S Liberty St, Centrevillle MD 21617 **R S Paul's Ch Centreville MD 2015-, P-in-c 2014-2015** B Philadelphia PA 1961 d Frank & Margaret. S Johns Coll Annapolis MD; BA S Josephs U 1999; MDiv EDS 2006. D 6/3/2006 Bp Robert Carroll Johnson Jr P 1/6/2007 Bp John Clark Buchanan. m 6/21/1986 Stephen G Garner c 2. Chapl Heron Point 2013-2015; Assoc Chr Ch St Michaels Par S Mich MD 2009-2012; S Ptr's Ch Salisbury MD 2009; Asst To R Ch Of The Epiph Norfolk VA 2006-2008; Norfolk Urban Outreach Mnstry Norfolk VA 2006-2007. thegarnerfamily@aol.com

GARNER, Terry (Mil) 10328 N Stanford Dr, Mequon WI 53097 **D S Bon Ch Thiensville WI 2013-** B Covington KY 1955 s Billy & Wilma. AS U of Kentucky 1978; BA U of Wisconsin 1989. D 10/18/1986 Bp Roger John White. m 7/22/1978 Loraine Garner. D S Jas Epis Ch Milwaukee WI 1986-2013. NAAD 1987.

GARNIER, Maryellen (NCal) 1800 Wildcat Blvd, Rocklin CA 95765 **Assoc P S Aug Of Cbury Rocklin CA 2014-** B Minneapolis MN 1947 d Thomas & Ellen. RN S Barn Sch for Nrsng 1970; BS U of Notre Dame 1982; BA Dio El Camino Real Sch for Deacons 1993; MDiv CDSP 2001. D 11/30/1993 P 6/14/2001 Bp Richard Lester Shimpfky. m 4/20/1974 Gary Eldon Garnier c 1. S Andr's Ch Saratoga CA 2004-2013; COM Dio El Camino Real Salinas CA 2001-2009; D S Lk's Ch Los Gatos CA 1996-2001; D Ch Of S Jude The Apos Cupertino CA 1993-2001. Excellence in Action El Camino Hosp 2005; Fran Toy Multicultural Awd CDSP 2000; S Steph's Awd Sch for Deacons 1995.

GARNO, Arthur Scott (Alb) 5828 State Highway 68, Ogdensburg NY 13669 **S Jn's Ch Ogdensburg NY 2005-** B Gardensburg NY 1958 s Donald & Marie. AAS SUNY 1978. D 6/11/2005 Bp Daniel William Herzog. m 8/11/1979 Tammy Garno c 2.

GARNO, Scott (Alb) Po Box 537, Unadilla NY 13849 **S Paul's Ch Franklin NY 2011-** B Ogdenburg NY 1980 s Arthur & Tammy. BA SUNY 2002; MDiv TESM 2006. D 6/10/2006 P 12/16/2006 Bp Daniel William Herzog. m 5/24/2003 Sarah E Garno c 3. R S Matt's Ch Unadilla NY 2006-2017.

GARNSEY, Elizabeth H (NY) Church of the Heavenly Rest, 2 E 90th St, New York NY 10128 B Greeley CO 1970 BA U CO 1992; MDiv Yale DS 2005. D 3/11/2006 P 9/23/2006 Bp Mark Sean Sisk. S Hilda's And S Hugh's Sch New York NY 2014-2017; Assoc Ch Of The Heav Rest New York NY 2008-2015, 2007-2008; St. Barth Ch New York NY 2006-2008. ehgarnsey@hotmail.com

GARRAMONE, Laurie Marie (Alb) 28 S. Market Street, Johnstown NY 12095 **S Jn's Ch Johnstown NY 2010-** B Mahopac NY 1960 d Robert & Gertrude. BS SUNY 1982; MA U of Delaware 1986; MDiv S Bernards TS and Mnstry 2011. D 6/21/2003 Bp Daniel William Herzog P 5/12/2007 Bp William Howard Love. m 4/3/2016 Alistair James Morrison c 2. Cur S Geo's Ch Clifton Pk NY 2007-2010; Chr Ed Coord. Dio Albany Greenwich NY 2003-2009. stjohnschurch@frontiernet.net

GARRATT, Steve (Oly) 19247 40th Pl NE, Lake Forest Park WA 98155 B Louisville KY 1951 s Rowland & Loris. BA U of Washington 1973; MDiv SWTS 1980; MA Seattle U 1992; DMin SWTS 2005. D 7/25/1980 P 7/22/1981 Bp Robert Hume Cochrane. m 7/25/1987 Margaret A Niles c 3. Int Trin Par Seattle WA 2012; R Chr Ch Seattle WA 1995-2012, Asst 1988-1994; Chapl U WA 1988-1997; Asst R S Steph's Epis Ch Seattle WA 1983-1988; Cur S Barn Epis Ch Bainbridge Island WA 1980-1983. Auth (D Min. Thesis), "Treas in Earthen Vessels: Contemplative Mnstry in Congrl Settings," 2005; Auth, "Meditation As A Therapeutic: Tool Measuring Effects Of Centering Pryr On Anxiety," 1992. ESMHE 1988-1997; Intl Thos Merton Soc 1997.

GARREN, Ben (Az) **Chapl Epis Campus Mnstry - U of Arizona Tucson AZ 2014-** D 6/14/2014 Bp Stephen Taylor Lane P 2/15/2015 Bp Kirk Stevan Smith.

GARRENTON, Linwood Wilson (Roch) 599 E 7th St Apt 6E, Brooklyn NY 11218 **Ret 2006-** B Portsmouth VA 1941 s Cecil & Mary. BS VPI 1964; MDiv GTS 1970; DMin Bos 1984. D 6/27/1970 Bp William Foreman Creighton P 2/13/1971 Bp Harry Lee Doll. Chapl Eastman Sch Of Mus Rochester NY 1992-2006; Chair-Soc Mnstry Dio Rochester Henrietta 1992-1997, Dn 1983-1991; R Chr Ch Rochester NY 1982-2006; R Ch Of The H Trin Baltimore MD 1972-1982; Cur Mt Calv Ch Baltimore MD 1970-1972; V-Chair Com Cmsn Dio Maryland Baltimore MD 1974-1982.

GARRETT, David (ETenn) 515 5th St, Newport TN 37821 B Memphis TN 1951 s James & Edna. BA Rhodes Coll 1973; MDiv Sewanee: The U So, TS 1977. D 6/26/1977 Bp William F Gates Jr P 4/1/1978 Bp William Evan Sanders. m 6/19/1971 Virginia Ruth Garrett c 1. All SS' Epis Sch Morristown TN 2007; R Ch Of The Annunc Newport TN 1998-2016, Vic 1978-1998; Dio E Tennessee Knoxville TN 1985-1998; Dio Tennessee Nashville TN 1978-1984; D S Mart

Of Tours Epis Ch Chattanooga TN 1977-1978. Auth, "Living Ch". Cmnty Of S Mary, RWF, Me.

GARRETT, George Kenneth (Mass) 12 Academy Ave, Fairhaven MA 02719 **Ret 1993-** B Somerville MA 1929 s George & Myrtle. BA Tufts U 1953; STB Ya Berk 1957. D 6/22/1957 P 12/21/1957 Bp Anson Phelps Stokes Jr. m 7/26/1958 Mary Garrett c 4. R Gr Ch New Bedford MA 1991-1992, Assoc R 1959-1988; Gr Ch Newton MA 1981-1992; Min in charge S Jas Ch Groveland Groveland MA 1958-1959; Min in charge All SS Mssn Georgetown MA 1957-1959.

GARRETT, Jane Nuckols (Vt) 206 Fairway Vlg, Leeds MA 01053 **Gc Sec Ecusa 2000-** B Dover DE 1935 d David & Edna. Hartford Sem; BA U of Delaware 1957; DLitt Mid 1997. D 6/11/1980 P 6/6/1981 Bp Robert Shaw Kerr. S Steph's Ch Middlebury VT 1986-1987, Cur 1980-1983; Stndg Cmsn Ecusa 1985-1991; Dep Gc Dio Vermont Burlington VT 1979-1997. Auth, "Pamphlets On The Amer Revolution," Harv Press, 1965; Auth, "Philadelphia And Baltimore, 1790-1840: A Study Of Intra-Reg Unity," *Maryland Hist mag*, 1960; Auth, "Delaware Coll Lotteries 1815-1845," *Delaware Hist*, 1957. EPF; Integrity.

GARRETT, Kathy A (Dal) 511 Foote St, McKinney TX 75069 **Asst S Ptr's Ch Mc Kinney TX 2010-** B Bridgeport CT 1963 d Stephen & Dorothy. BA W Virginia Wesleyan Coll 1985; MDiv Ya Berk 1993. D 6/12/1993 Bp Arthur Edward Walmsley P 12/1/1993 Bp Jeffery William Rowthorn. m 9/13/1997 Sam Y Garrett c 2. S Steph's Ch Richmond VA 1995-1999; Asst Min S Mk's Ch New Canaan CT 1993-1995. kgarrett@stpetersmckinney.com

GARRETT, Mary Ann (La) PO Box 126, Baton Rouge LA 70821 **Assoc R S Jas Epis Ch Baton Rouge LA 2009-, Cntr for Sprtl Formation 2012-** B Grand Saline TX 1951 d William & Maxine. BA U of Texas 1976; MA U The Incarnate Word 1999; MDiv SWTS 2002. Trans 4/28/2008 as Priest Bp C Wallis Ohl. m 6/1/2002 William F Ashby. P S Jn's Epis Ch Odessa TX 2008-2009; P Dio SE Mex 2005-2007, Transitional D 2004-2005. lapadrecita@me.com

GARRETT, Paul (Colo) 2530 Leyden St., Denver CO 80207 **R S Barn Epis Ch Denver CO 2008-; Trst Colorado Epis Fndt Denver CO 2008-** B Denver CO 1956 s Richard & Ruth. BA Colorado St U 1981; MDiv EDS 1988. D 5/22/1989 Bp William Carl Frey P 6/29/1991 Bp Barbara Clementine Harris. m 9/5/1999 Mary Ellen Garrett. R S Barth's Ch Estes Pk CO 1997-2008; Int Wyman Memi Ch of St Andr Marblehead MA 1995-1997; Int Ch Of The H Trin Marlborough MA 1992-1993; Assoc S Lk's And S Marg's Ch Allston MA 1989-1992. Iona Cmnty 1999.

GARRIGAN, Joseph Edward (Pa) PO Box 1681, Doylestown PA 18901 **Int H Apos And Medtr Philadelphia PA 2011-; Ret 2004-** B New York NY 1947 s Thomas & Jo Ann. BA Wabash Coll 1968; STB LTS 1972; MA Yale DS 1972. D 6/24/1972 Bp Charles Gresham Marmion P 6/29/1973 Bp Charles Alfred Voegeli. m 12/6/1984 Jan Trimbur Garrigan. R S Paul's Ch Doylestown PA 1979-2004; R Chr Ch Totowa NJ 1974-1979; Cur S Ptr's Ch Springfield MA 1972-1974.

✠ GARRISON, The Rt Rev Michael (WNY) 207 Pineneedle Dr, Bradenton FL 34210 **Asstg Bp Dio SW Florida Parrish FL 2011-** B Philadelphia PA 1945 s Jack & Rosemary. BA Pontifical Coll Josephinum 1967; MRE Pontifical Coll Josephinum 1970; DD GTS 1999; GTS 1999. Rec 4/1/1975 as Priest Bp Wesley Frensdorff Con 4/24/1999 for WNY. m 1/20/1990 Carol Garrison c 6. Bp of WNY Dio Wstrn New York Tonawanda NY 1999-2011; Reg Vic Dio Nevada Las Vegas 1980-1999, Vic Team Mnstry Cntrl NV 1975-1979; S Matt's Ch Las Vegas NV 1979-1980; S Mk's Ch Tonopah NV 1975-1978; S Philips-in-the-Desert Hawthorne NV 1975-1978; Asstant R S Paul's Epis Ch Sparks NV 1974-1975; D and P RC Ch 1970-1974. Hse of Initia Nova OSB 2009; Sis Of Charity Boulder City Nv 1982-1999.

GARRISON, Thomas Martin (Minn) D 6/26/2014 P 6/20/2015 Bp Brian N Prior.

GARRISON, William (Los) 7056 Washington Ave, Whittier CA 90602 **R S Mths' Par Whittier CA 2011-** B Walla Walla WA 1950 s William & Juanita. BS U of Phoenix 2004; MDiv ETSBH 2008. D 6/7/2008 P 1/10/2009 Bp Joseph Jon Bruno. m 10/25/1986 Sherry D Garrison c 4. S Marg Of Scotland Par San Juan Capo CA 2008-2011; Asst S Marg's Epis Sch San Juan Capo CA 2008-2011. frbill@stmatthiaswhittier.com

GARRISON, William Brian (CFla) 212 Brevity Ln, DeLand FL 32724 **R S Barn Ch Deland FL 2012-; Dn of the NE Dnry Dio Cntrl Florida Orlando FL 2010-, Dio Bd 2010-, Comission on Mnstrs 2009-** B 1973 Asburry Orlando 2004; MDiv Nash 2005. D 3/12/2005 Bp Hugo Luis Pina-Lopez P 10/9/2005 Bp John Wadsworth Howe. m 6/28/1997 Susan D Garrison c 5. Vic The Ch Of The H Presence Deland FL 2005-2012.

GARRITY, Clelia Pinza (CGC) 3081 Margarita Ave, Pahrump NV 89048 **D Gr In The Desert Epis Ch Las Vegas NV 2010-** B New York, NY 1941 d Ezio & Doris. BA Col 1969; MSW Yeshiva U 1972. D 4/10/2010 Bp Dan Thomas Edwards. c 1. Chairman, Com on Soc Justice and Mercy Dio Nevada Las Vegas 2011-2013.

GARTIG, William George (SO) 2146 Cameron Ave Apt 5, Cincinnati OH 45212 **Substitute P CT 2000-; Hebr Tchr CT 1999-** B Detroit MI 1952 s Derry & Joanne. BA U of Texas 1974; MDiv Epis TS of the SW 1977; MA Hebr

G

Un Coll 1990; PhD Hebr Un Coll 1994. D 6/30/1977 P 6/1/1978 Bp Roger Howard Cilley. m 4/29/1984 Barbara Evans Rees. Gk & Hebr Tchr Lebanon Correctional Inst 1998-2001; Supply P S Lk Ch Cincinnati OH 1995-2000; Int S Phil's Ch Cincinnati OH 1986-1991; The Great Cmsn Fndt Houston TX 1983, 1977-1980; Asstg P Trin Ch Covington KY 1982-1984; All SS Epis Ch Hitchcock TX 1977-1980; S Mart's Epis Ch Houston TX 1977. "The Attribution Of The Ibn Ezra Supercommentary Avvat Nefesh To Asher Ben Abraham Crescas Reconsidered.," *Hebr Un Coll Annual*, 1995. Comt. Phi Beta Kappa Comt.

GARTON, Mary Pamela (CFla) 190 Interlachen Rd, Melbourne FL 32940 B Philadelphia PA 1955 d George & Mary. BA Cabrini Coll 1978; BS Cabrini Coll 1990. D 12/11/2010 Bp John Wadsworth Howe. m 9/19/1987 Harry Luther Garton c 2.

GARVIN, Grayson Barry (CFla) 3000 Nw 42nd Ave Apt B401, Coconut Creek FL 33066 **Ret 1998-** B Greenwood SC 1937 s Grayson & Sara. BA Lander U 1959; STM GTS 1964. D 6/27/1964 P 6/29/1965 Bp John Adams Pinckney. P-in-c St. Jas Epis Ch Leesburg FL 2006-2007; P-in-c S Jas Epis Ch Leesburg FL 2004-2005; P-in-c S Lk's Epis Ch Merritt Island FL 1998-2003; R S Richard's Ch Winter Pk FL 1989-1998; R S Ptr's Ch Plant City FL 1975-1989; R Epis Ch of the Gd Shpd Charleston SC 1967-1975; P-in-c Calv Ch Glen Sprgs 1965-1967; Assoc Epiph Ch Spartanburg SC 1965-1967; S Matt's Epis Ch Spartanburg SC 1965-1967. Outstanding Young Man Year Awd 1972.

GARWOOD, Martha Jayne (SD) 4640 Sturgis Rd Lot 49, Rapid City SD 57702 **S Andr's Epis Ch Rapid City SD 2002-** B Deadwood SD 1953 d Harold & Eileen. BA So Dakota St U 1975. D 6/16/2002 Bp Creighton Leland Robertson.

GARY, Hobart Jude (Ct) 2855 West Commericial Blvd, Apartment 354, Fort Lauderdale FL 33309 **Ret 1981-** B Evanston IL 1923 s Hobart & Elizabeth. BA Carleton Coll 1944; MDiv SWTS 1947. D 6/2/1947 Bp Edwin J Randall P 12/20/1947 Bp Oliver L Loring. m 8/22/1950 Elizabeth Gary c 4. Int S Mart's Epis Ch Pompano Bch FL 1996-1998; Int S Jn's Ch Hollywood FL 1994-1996; Int S Andr's Epis Ch Of Hollywood Hollywood FL 1992-1994; S Anne's Epis Ch Hallandale Bch FL 1992-1994; Volntr Poverello Cntr Pompano Bch FL 1989-1992; Volntr All SS Prot Epis Ch Ft Lauderdale FL 1981-1989; Chapl Southhampton Coll 1975-1981; Lectr U Bridgeprt 1970-1981; R Calv St Geo's Epis Ch Bridgeport CT 1966-1981; R S Jn's Epis Ch Southampton NY 1957-1966; Ch Of S Fran Of Assisi Levittown NY 1950-1957; P S Jas Ch Old Town ME 1950-1957; R Penobscot Mssns ME 1947-1948.

GARY, Richard Ellis (NY) Po Box 106, Heath MA 01346 **Died 11/11/2015** B Wichita KS 1924 s Paul & Marietta. BA Phillips U; BD Yale DS. D 4/15/1954 P 12/1/1954 Bp Angus Dun. m 6/13/1954 Dorothy Gary c 3. Ret 1989-2015; Epis Ch Cntr New York NY 1977-1989; Dio New York New York NY 1956-1977; P-in-c S Mary's Manhattanville NY 1956-1967; Asst Trin Ch Washington DC 1953-1956. Auth, "Episcopalians & Roman Catholics: Can They Ever Get Together?".

GARZA JR, Frederico Eloy (Va) 2900 Hanes Ave, Richmond VA 23222 B Clovis NM 1964 s Frederico & Celia. D 2/11/2012 Bp Shannon Sherwood Johnston. m 5/12/2007 Mary Alice Garza c 3.

GASKILL JR, John Joseph (EC) 174 Windy Point Rd, Beaufort NC 28516 B New Bern NC 1942 s John & Sophia. BA Wake Forest U 1964; MEd Wake Forest U 1965. D 6/3/2006 Bp Clifton Daniel III. m 11/27/1964 Donna A Gaskill c 3.

GASQUET, Mark Cordes (La) 308 Central Ave, Jefferson LA 70121 B Shreveport LA 1934 s John & Mabel. BA LSU 1958; MDiv PDS 1961; MA Bos 1973; DMin McCormick TS 1979; PhD Somerset U Gb 1992. D 10/5/1961 Bp Girault M Jones P 6/1/1962 Bp Iveson Batchelor Noland. m 8/9/1980 Marylin Gasquet c 2. Chapl (Colonel) US-AR 1985-1991; Chf Chapl Orleans Par Prison 1981-1983; R The Ch Of The Annunc New Orleans LA 1973-2000; Chapl (Major) US-A 1962-1973; Vic H Comf Lecompte LA 1961-1962; Vic Trin Epis Ch Cheneyville LA 1961-1962. Auth, "Healthy New Orleans Cuisine," 2007; Auth, "Ch-St Relatns In Soviet Bloc," 1973. AAPC, Ord Of The H 1959; Amer Personal & Priv Chefs Assoc. 1996; Bcdac 1993.

GASTON, Katherine Elizabeth (Neb) 7625 Lafayette Ave, Omaha NE 68114 **Asstg Cler S Peters Epis Sch Kerrville TX 2001-; D Omaha Indn Cmnty Ch 1988-** B Omaha NE 1918 d William & Myrtle. BS Nebraska Wesl 1943; CPT Washington U 1948; EFM Sewanee: The U So, TS 1987. D 5/7/1988 Bp James Daniel Warner. c 2.

GASTON III, Paul Lee (O) 2389 Brunswick Lane, Hudson OH 44236 B Hattiesburg MS 1943 s Paul & Ruth. SMU 1963; BA SE Louisiana U 1965; MA U of Virginia 1966; PhD U of Virginia 1970. D 11/11/1990 Bp William Evan Sanders P 4/10/2010 Bp Mark Hollingsworth Jr. m 6/29/1968 Eileen Margaret Gaston c 1. S Paul's Ch Akron OH 2014-2015; Int S Jn's Ch Youngstown OH 2013; D Chr Ch Epis Hudson OH 2012-2013, 2011-2012; S Mk's Ch Canton OH 2010-2011; Trin Ch Covington KY 1993-1999; D S Alb's Epis Ch Hixson TN 1990-1993. Prncpl Co-Auth, "Revising Gnrl Educ," AAC&U, 2009; Auth, "Bologna," *Liberal Educ*, 2008; Auth, "Geo Herbert & Angl Hymns," *Jn Donne Journ*, 2006; Auth, "W.D. Snodgrass," E. G. Hall, 1978.

GAT, Maggie (Nwk) 4230 Cascade Falls Dr, Sarasota FL 34243 **Dio SW Florida Parrish FL 2008-** B Callao PE 1940 d John & Katherine. BA Mt Holyoke Coll 1961; MA Amer Intl Coll 1978; Cert Consulting Psychologists Inc 1989; Drew U 1991; Ya Berk 1993; MDiv Yale DS 1993; Cert Cntr fo Prevention of Sexual Misconduct Seattle WA 1995; Cert Consulting Psychologists Inc 2007; Cert Int Mnstry Ntwk 2007; Cert Epis ChurchSafeguarding Chld 2011. D 6/4/1994 Bp John Shelby Spong P 12/4/1994 Bp Jack Marston Mckelvey. c 2. Assoc S Geo's Epis Ch Bradenton FL 2008-2011, Hisp/Latino Mnstry Cmsn 2008-2011; R S Jn's Ch Dover NJ 1999-2008, Int 1997-1998; Int S Agnes Ch Little Falls NJ 1996-1997; Vic Trin Ch Paterson NJ 1994-1996; Stndg Com Dio Newark Newark NJ 2005-2008, Sexual Misconduct Prevention and Chld Sfty Trng, Chair from 1999-08 1995-2008, Wmn Cmsn, Chair last 3 years 1994-2000, Hisp Mnstry Cmsn, chair 2000-2005 1993-2008; Bd, Chair last 3 years ACTS/VIM Newark NJ 1999-2005. Prchr, "Thanksgiving Day: Spreading The Cloth At The Table Of Thanks," *Sermons That Wk 1998*, Morehouse Pub, 1999.

GATCH JR, Milton Mccormick (NY) 575 W End Ave Apt 7C, New York NY 10024 **Asstg Cler The Ch Of S Lk In The Fields New York NY 2006-; P-in-c Chap Of S Jas The Fisherman Wellfleet MA 1980-** B Cincinnati OH 1932 s Milton & Mary. BA Hav 1953; U Cinc 1955; BD EDS 1960; MA Ya 1961; PhD Ya 1963. D 6/22/1960 P 6/1/1961 Bp Roger W Blanchard. m 8/25/1956 Ione Georganna White c 3. Cleric Calv and St Geo New York NY 2000-2005; Dir, Prof Burke Libr UTS 1988-1998; Dn, Provost, Prof UTS 1978-1988; Assoc Clare Hall Cambridge 1974-1975; Prof U of Missouri--Columbia 1968-1978; Assoc Prof Engl Nthrn Illinois U 1967-1968; Chapl Shimer Coll 1964-1966; Chapl Wooster Sch Danbury CT 1963-1964; Assoc S Paul And S Jas New Haven CT 1960-1963. Auth, ""Till the Break of Day": Phil Gatch and Some Descendants Through Three Centuries," Little Miami Pub, 2015; Co-Auth, "A Little Dust: Gatch Collection of Yeats," Maggs Bros Ltd, 2012; Auth, "The Libr of Leander van Ess and the Earliest Amer Collections of Reformation Pamphlets," Bibliographical Soc of Amer, 2007; Auth, "The Yeats Fam and the Bk," Grolier Club, 2000; Auth, "Eschatology and Chr Nurture (collected essays)," Ashgate (Variorum Series), 2000; Auth, "So Precious A Fndt: Libr Of Leander Van Ess," Grolier Club, 1996; Auth, "Anglo-Saxon Stds: The 1st 3 Centuries," G.K. Hall, 1982; Auth, "Preaching & Theol In Anglo-Saxon Engl: Aelfric & Wufstan," U Tor Press, 1977; Auth, "Loyalties & Traditions: Man & His Wrld In Old Engl Lit," Pegasus/Bobbs Merrill, 1971; Auth, "Death: Meaning & Mortality In Chr Thought & Contemporary Culture," Seabury Press, 1969; Auth, "Numerous arts in Journ". Fell Medieval Acad of Amer 1998; Fell Soc of Antiquaries of London 1992; Quatercentenary Vstng Fell Emml, Cambridge 1991.

GATCHELL, Lois Harvey (Okla) 8222 S Yale Ave Apt 321, Tulsa OK 74137 **D S Dunst's Ch Tulsa OK 1977-** B Fort Pierre SD 1920 d Guy & Edythe. U of So Dakota 1939; BA U of Arizona 1943; U of Oklahoma 1977. D 6/26/1977 Bp Gerald Nicholas Mcallister. m 11/27/1942 Donald Gatchell c 2. NAAD. Cert For Outstanding Serv Natl Conf Of Cathd Chars 1983; Awd For Most Innovative Prog Publ Hlth Assn 1973.

GATELEY, Gail Nicholson (Dal) 15264 SW Peachtree Drive, Tigard OR 97224 B San Augustine TX 1948 d Elton & Mary. BA Austin Coll 1970; MA U of Texas Arlington 1975; MDiv Epis TS of the SW 1995. D 12/14/1996 P 11/11/1997 Bp James Monte Stanton. m 5/31/1970 Richard H Gateley c 3. R Epis Ch Of The Redeem Irving TX 2004-2014; Assoc S Anne's Epis Ch Desoto TX 1997-2004. Ord Of S Lk.

✠ GATES, The Rt Rev Alan (Mass) Episcopal Diocese of Massachusetts, 138 Tremont St, Boston MA 02111 **Dio Massachusetts Boston MA 2014-; Bd Dir Bex Sem Columbus OH 2010-** B Springfield MA 1958 s J & Marion. Cert Pushkin Inst Moscow 1979; BA Mid 1980; Geo 1983; MDiv EDS 1987. D 6/13/1987 Bp Ronald Hayward Haines P 3/26/1988 Bp David Elliot Johnson Con 9/13/2014 for Mass. m 6/3/1980 Patricia J Harvey c 2. R S Paul's Epis Ch Cleveland OH 2004-2014; P-in-c The Ch Of The H Sprt Lake Forest IL 2003-2004, Assoc 1996-2004; R Trin Epis Ch Ware MA 1990-1996; Cur Ch Of S Jn The Evang Hingham MA 1987-1990; Chair, COM Dio Ohio Cleveland 2009-2012. Compass Rose Soc 2005; Epis Preaching Fndt Fac 2008-2008; Teleios Russian Fndtn 1994-2006. agates@diomass.org

GATES, Alan K (Cal) **Ch Of The Epiph San Carlos CA 2011-** B Portland OR 1975 BA Seattle U 2000; MDiv VTS 2005. D 6/25/2005 P 1/15/2006 Bp Vincent Waydell Warner. m 4/23/2016 Bernadette Marie Gates c 2. Ch Of The H Trin Tiverton RI 2007-2011; Asst S Paul's Ch N Kingstown RI 2005-2007.

GATES, Mary May (Ct) 16 Church St, Waterbury CT 06702 **Chap of All SS Cornwall CT 2010-; Asst Chr Ch Par Epis Watertown CT 2009-; Cur S Johns On The Green Waterbury CT 1999-** B Bridgeport CT 1954 d Charles & Edna. BS U of Connecticut 1993; MS U of Connecticut 1996; MDiv Ya Berk 1997. D 6/12/1999 Bp Clarence Nicholas Coleridge P 1/22/2000 Bp Andrew Donnan Smith. m 5/26/1974 Daniel P Gates c 3. Dio Connecticut Meriden CT 2009-2016; Cur S Jn's Epis Par Waterbury CT 1999-2002.

GATES JR, Robert J (Okla) B Ardmore OK 1945 s Robert & Dorothy. BA Oklahoma City U 1968; CSS Epis TS of the SW 1978. D 6/17/1978 P 5/29/1979 Bp Gerald Nicholas Mcallister. m 4/26/2008 Georgia L Gates c 2. Int Gd Shpd Epis Ch Sapulpa OK 2007-2010; Dio Oklahoma Oklahoma City OK 1988-1994, 1979-1982; Vic St Mart of Tours Epis Ch Pryor OK 1987-1994; S Lk's Ch Tulsa OK 1982-1985; Vic S Mk's Epis Ch Weatherford OK

1979-1982; S Paul's Ch Clinton OK 1979-1982; Cur S Matt's Ch Enid OK 1978-1979.

GATREL, Larry Gene (Ia) 1602 Edgewood Dr, Carroll IA 51401 **Died 6/25/2017** B Seymour IA 1933 s Thomas & Lena. LTh Epis TS in Kentucky 1977. D 8/6/1977 P 10/1/1978 Bp Walter Cameron Righter. m 7/26/1953 Janice Gatrel c 3. S Alb's Ch Sprt Lake IA 1985-1999; P-in-c S Steph's Ch Spencer IA 1985-1997; P-in-c Trin Ch Carroll IA 1977-1985; Ch Of The H Trin Sac City IA 1977-1982.

GATTA, Julia Milan (Ct) 243 Tennessee Ave, Sewanee TN 37375 **Prof Sewanee U So TS Sewanee TN 2004-** B New York NY 1948 d Thomas & Margaret. BA S Marys Coll Notre Dame IN 1970; MA Cor 1973; PhD Cor 1979; MDiv EDS 1979. D 6/14/1980 Bp Morgan Porteus P 5/30/1981 Bp Arthur Edward Walmsley. m 7/11/1970 John Joseph Gatta c 1. Vic S Paul's Ch Windham CT 1991-2004; Int S Paul's Ch Plainfield CT 1990-1991; Assoc Ch Of The Resurr Norwich CT 1986-1990; Lectr Yale DS New Haven CT 1986-1990; Sprtl Dir Ya Berk New Haven CT 1984-1989; Asst Middlesex Area Cluster Mnstry Higganum CT 1982-1985; Cur S Paul's Epis Ch Willimantic CT 1980-1982. Co-Auth, "Go in Peace: The Art of Hearing Confessions," Morehouse, 2012; Auth, "The Nearness of God: Par Mnstry as Sprtl Pract," Morehouse, 2010; Auth, "The Pstr Art of the Engl Mystics; rpt. of Three Sprtl Dir for our Time," Wipf & Stock (2004); Cowley, 1986; Auth, "The Cath Feminism of H Mo Ch," *Sewanee Theol Revs*, 1985. Assoc of SSJE 1978. One of Ten Winners in Best Sermon Competition Epis Evang Fndt 1995. jugatta@sewanee.edu

GATTIS, Larry R (Chi) 20326 Harding Ave, Olympia Fields IL 60461 B Harvey IL 1942 s Thomas & Modena. Transylvania U 1961; BA Lake Forest Coll 1966; MDiv Nash 1975; Cert Rutgers The St U of New Jersey 1987; Cert U of Utah 1990; Chicago Sch of Profsnl Psychol Chicago IL 1995. D 6/14/1975 Bp John P Craine P 12/20/1975 Bp Donald James Davis. m 5/19/1984 Linda S Gattis. Ch Of The Medtr Chicago IL 1999-2000; S Raphael The Archangel Oak Lawn IL 1998; Santa Teresa de Avila Chicago IL 1998; Ch Of The Gd Shpd Momence IL 1993-1999; S Tim's Ch Griffith IN 1991-1996; Chr Ch Streator IL 1989-1990; Int Dio Chicago Chicago IL 1982-2004; Trin Ch Lincoln IL 1981; R S Paul's Epis Ch Dowagiac MI 1977-1980; Cur Trin Ch New Castle PA 1975-1977.

GATZA, Mark Francis (Md) Po Box 628, Bel Air MD 21014 **R Emm Ch Bel Air MD 2009-** B Buffalo, NY 1955 s James & Marie. BA Hampshire Coll 1977; MDiv Ya Berk 1980; ThM S Mary Seminar/U Baltimore MD 1988; DMin SWTS 2003. D 6/12/1982 Bp Arthur Edward Walmsley P 1/25/1983 Bp David Keller Leighton Sr. m 9/5/1981 Jan Elizabeth Hamill c 2. Mssnr for Cong Dev & Deploy Dio Maryland Baltimore MD 2003-2009, Stndg Com 2001-2002, COM 1993-2001, Chair, Prog & Bdgt Com 2013-, Stndg Com 2000-2003, Eccl Crt 1998-2001, COM 1993-1999, Dir of Aspirancy Prog 1986-2003; Chr Ch Forest Hill MD 1990-2002; R H Cross Ch St MD 1990-1993; Asst S Anne's Par Annapolis MD 1987-1990; Asst to R Ch Of S Paul The Apos Baltimore MD 1985-1987; R S Geo's Ch Perryman MD 1983-1985; S Paul's Par Baltimore MD 1982-1987; Chapl S Paul Sch Brooklandville MD 1981-1987. Auth, "Another Look at the 1928 Euch," *Living Ch*, 2007; Auth, "Baltimore Declaration Still Has Much To Offer," *Living Ch*, 1996; Forw to, "Joy & Wonder In All God'S Works," Forw Mvmt Press, 1994; Auth, "Another Sunday For Red," *Living Ch*, 1994.

GAUMER, Susan Salot (La) 7820 Jeannette St., New Orleans LA 70118 B Washington DC 1942 d Nevin & Helen. BA Mt Holyoke Coll 1964; MA JHU 1965; MDiv Sewanee: The U So, TS 1993. D 5/23/1993 P 12/4/1993 Bp James Barrow Brown. c 2. R S Andr's Epis Ch New Orleans LA 1999-2014; Asst S Augustines Ch Metairie LA 1993-1999; Chapl S Mart's Epis Ch Metairie LA 1977-1990. Auth, "From Costly Silence To Sprtl Hlth, Presence:The Journ Of Sprtl Dir'S Intl Volume 6:No 3," *September*, 2000. Epis Dioc Ecamenical and Interreligious Off 1995. Woods Ldrshp Awd U So 1991.

GAUVIN, Joseph Henri Armand (NJ) 25 Southwood Drive, St Catharine'S L2M 4M5 Canada B Montreal QC CA 1930 s Pierre & Rose. McGill U; LTh Montreal TS CA. D 5/1/1963 P 3/8/1964 Bp The Bishop Of Montreal. m 11/9/1963 Gloria P Gauvin c 1. R Ch of the Gd Shpd Rahway NJ 1968-1993; Cur S Ptr's Ch Spotswood NJ 1967-1968; Serv Ch Of Can 1963-1967.

GAVENTA, Sarah Kinney (Va) **Austin Presb TS Austin TX 2017-** B Los Angeles CA 1977 d Martin & Pamela. BS U Rich 1999; MDiv VTS 2005. D 6/18/2005 P 12/19/2005 Bp Peter J Lee. m 6/8/2007 Matthew R Gaventa c 1. Assoc S Paul's Ch Charlottesville VA 2013-2017; Asst Trin Ch Princeton NJ 2009-2013; Asst Emm Epis Ch Greenwood VA 2005-2009.

GAVIN, Craig Edmonds (Ark) St Andrews Episcopal Church, PO Box 339, Rogers AR 72757 **S Andr's Ch Rogers AR 2015-; Bp's Trst Dio Nebraska Omaha NE 2009-** B Chicago IL 1949 s John & Evelyn. Nebraska Wesl 1971; BS Nebraska Wesl 1991; MDiv Epis TS of the SW 1994. D 5/1/1994 Bp James Edward Krotz P 11/6/1994 Bp Larry Maze. m 5/22/1971 Linda Kay Gavin c 1. R S Matt's Ch Lincoln NE 2007-2015; R The Epis Ch Of The Nativ Dothan AL 2004-2007; R S Theo's Epis Ch Bella Vista AR 1996-2004; Asst R Chr Epis Ch Little Rock AR 1994-1996. Ord Of S Lk 1996.

GAVIN, Timothy (Pa) The Episcopal Academy, 1785 Bishop White Dr, Newtown Square PA 19073 **The Epis Acad Newtown Sq PA 2012-** B Philadelphia PA 1963 s Francis & Kathleen. BS Tem 1987; MEd Tem 1988. D 6/9/2012 Bp Charles Ellsworth Bennison Jr P 1/12/2013 Bp Edward Lewis Lee Jr. m 6/24/1990 Joyce A Gavin c 2.

GAVIT, Sara B (Me) 2222 E Tudor Rd, Anchorage AK 99507 **R S Anne's Ch Calais ME 2016-; Pstr Min S Mary's Ch Anchorage AK 2013-, 2011-, 2005-2011** B Norfolk NE 1960 d Richard & Anne. U of Alaska; U of Nebraska; MDiv St Johns U TS 2011. D 6/4/2011 P 1/5/2013 Bp Mark A Lattime. m 4/25/2009 Patricia K Mcdaid c 2. Lay Pstr Min St. Mary's Epis Ch 2005-2011.

GAY, Jean Ricot (SeFla) 465 Ne 100th St, Miami Shores FL 33138 B HT 1957 s Joseph & Solange. MBA Pacific Wstrn U 1991; MS Nova SE U 1997; MDiv Sewanee: The U So, TS 2002. D 6/16/2002 P 12/21/2002 Bp Leo Frade. m 4/12/2013 Olanyine Mercedes Ventura Gay c 2. R Ch Of The Resurr Miami FL 2002-2009.

GAY, Judith S (Mass) 59 Fenno St, Cambridge MA 02138 **Assoc P S Jas' Epis Ch Cambridge MA 2001-** B New York NY 1933 d George & Orpha. BA Wellesley Coll 1954; MA UTS 1957; PhD U of Cambridge 1980. Trans 11/27/2002 Bp M(Arvil) Thomas Shaw. m 6/11/1954 John H Gay c 3. Serv Ch of the Prov of Sthrn Afr Lesotho 1994-2000. Phi Beta Kappa Wellesley Coll 1954.

GAY, Karen (La) Episcopal Church of the Holy Communion, P. O. Box 474, Plaquemine LA 70764 **Mem Stndg Com 2009-; Dio Louisiana, Sprtl Dir Curs Louisiana Baton Rouge LA 2008-; Stndg Com Pres Dio Louisiana New Orleans LA 2012-** B Fort Polk LA 1957 d James & Mary. BS LSU 1979; Cert Ldrshp Prog for Musicians of Sm Congregations 2000; Dplma Dioc Sch for Mnstry Louisiana 2002. D 1/25/2004 P 8/8/2004 Bp Charles Edward Jenkins III. m 8/16/1980 John Gay c 4. R Ch Of The H Comm Plaquemine LA 2008-2015; Chapl of Day Sch Trin Epis Ch Baton Rouge LA 2007-2009, Cur 2007-2008; Tchr-Chapl Epis HS Baton Rouge Baton Rouge LA 2007, 2006; Vic Ch Of The Nativ Rosedale LA 2006-2007, Lay Vic 2003-2005; Tchr Epis HS Baton Rouge LA 2006-2007; Vic Ch of the Nativ Rosedale LA 2004-2007; Assoc. Pstr/launch team Chr Ch Prairieville LA 2003-2004. Louisiana Epis Cler Assn 2006.

GAY, Margaret Worcester (CNY) **D Trin Epis Ch 2007-** B New York NY 1940 d Maurice & Edith. ABS U of Pennsylvania 1962; Cor 1963; Loc Formation & Bex 2006. D 10/7/2006 P 5/30/2007 Bp Gladstone Bailey Adams III. m 4/20/1968 A Edward Gay c 2. Trin Ch Camden NY 2006-2012; Ed, Tech Serv Nys Tech Corp 1998-2001.

GAY, Robert George (SVa) B Oak Park IL 1944 s George & Veronica. BS Loyola U 1966. D 4/24/2010 Bp Herman Hollerith IV. m 12/31/1971 Mary Esther Gay c 3. D Bruton Par Williamsburg VA 2012-2015.

GAYLE JR, William Gedge (La) 227 Helios Avenue, Metarie LA 70005 **Assoc Chr Ch Cathd New Orleans LA 2006-; Assoc Chr Ch Cathd 2005-** B Lake Charles LA 1939 s William & Shirley. BS Tul 1960; Edinburgh Theol Coll 1962; MDiv Sewanee: The U So, TS 1963; STM Sewanee: The U So, TS 1976. D 6/20/1963 Bp Iveson Batchelor Noland P 5/1/1964 Bp Girault M Jones. m 7/25/1990 Susan D Upham c 2. Int Trin Ch New Orleans LA 2007; Pres Bd Trst S Mart Epis Sch 1983-1985; R S Mart's Epis Ch Metairie LA 1976-2004; R S Paul's Ch Albany GA 1970-1976; Cur St Jas Epis Ch and Sch Alexandria LA 1966-1970; Cur S Andr's Epis Ch New Orleans LA 1963-1966. Louisiana Epis Cler Assn 1976-2002. Dorothy Porter Serv Awd St Mart's Epis Sch 2005; DuBose Serv Awd Sewanee 1994.

GAYLOR, Pamela Elaine (SO) 3149 Indian Ripple Rd, Dayton OH 45440 **S Mary's Ch Waynesville OH 2013-; Dio Sthrn Ohio Cincinnati OH 2003-** B Mariemont OH 1952 d Clifford & Flora. BA Morehead St U 1975; MA Mia 1989; MDiv VTS 1995. D 6/24/1995 P 5/4/1996 Bp Herbert Thompson Jr. c 1. Dioc Sprtl Dir - Curs Sec Dio Sthrn Ohio Cincinnati OH 2002-2004, 2002, COM 1999-, Natl & Wrld Mssn Com 1995-1998; R Chr Ch Xenia OH 2001-2009; R All SS Epis Ch Portsmouth OH 1997-2001; Asst R S Fran Epis Ch Springboro OH 1995-1997. CT 1988. Hon Pi Kappa Lambda Mia Chapt 1987. apeace@stmary.org

GDULA, Peter Mark (CPa) St Luke's Episcopal Church, 8 E Keller St, Mechanicsburg PA 17055 B Johnstown PA 1957 s Peter & Helen. D 4/22/2012 Bp Nathan Dwight Baxter. m 3/18/2006 Sherrill L Gdula c 2.

GEARHART, Robert James (Neb) 665 4th St., PO Box 56, Syracuse NE 68446 **Ret Ret 2003-** B Camden NJ 1938 s Curven & Isabelle. BS S Jos 1970; MDiv Nash 1973. D 6/23/1973 P 12/1/1973 Bp Robert Lionne DeWitt. c 2. Vic S Aug's Ch De Witt NE 1988-2003; R S Chas The Mtyr Fairbury NE 1988-2003; Vic S Jn's Ch Valentine NE 1978-1988; S Jn's Epis Ch Cody NE 1978-1988; Vic S Johns Ch Albion NE 1977-1978; Vic S Mk's Ch Creighton NE 1975-1978; S Ptr's Ch Neligh NE 1975-1978; R S Steph's Epis Ch Clifton Hgts PA 1973-1975.

GEARING, Charles Edward (At) 6525 Gardenia Way, Stone Mountain GA 30087 B Charleston WV 1928 s Raymond & Winifred. BS Georgia Inst of Tech 1952; MS Pur 1964; PhD Pur 1966. D 10/23/1993 Bp Frank Kellogg Allan. m 9/4/1952 Carol Leyh Gearing c 3. Archd Dio Atlanta Atlanta GA 2004-2010; Dir of Dioc Prog ECF Atlanta GA 1999-2005; Field Rep ECF Atlanta GA 1996-1999; D S Barth's Epis Ch Atlanta GA 1993-2010; Planned Giving Advsr Dio Atlanta Atlanta GA 2005-2010, Chair, Stwdshp Cmsn 1995-2000; Stwdshp Consult Epis Ch Cntr New York NY 1991-1996. Auth, "Dioc Gift Plnng Prog," ECF/Morehouse, 2002; Auth, "Funding Future Mnstry," ECF/Morehouse, 2000. Apos in Stwdshp The Epis Ntwk for Stwdshp 2003; Golden Rule Awd Untd Way 1994.

GEARS, Wallace E (Minn) 3240 Jersey Ave S, Minneapolis MN 55426 B Minneapolis MN 1920 s Charles & Artie. BA U MN; MA Minneapolis Coll Mus Minneapolis MN 1950. D 12/21/1959 Bp Philip Frederick McNairy. c 2. Asst S Geo's S Louis Pk MN 1959-1967. Auth, "Chr The Lord Is Risen".

GEDDES, Robert Douglas (Va) 269 Johnson Point Road, Hallieford VA 23068 B Wichita KS 1947 BGS Capital U, Columbus, OH; AAB Columbus Tech Inst, Columbus, OH 1973; MS Untd States Intl U, San Diego, CA 1980; MDiv Sewanee: The U So, TS 1997. D 6/14/1997 Bp Frank Harris Vest Jr P 12/13/1997 Bp David Conner Bane Jr. m 8/9/1969 Karen Geddes c 1. R Kingston Par Epis Ch Mathews VA 2005-2011; R S Jn's Epis Ch Chase City VA 1997-2005; S Tim's Epis Ch Clarksville VA 1997-2005; Gr Epis Ch Drakes Branch VA 1997-2000.

GEDRICK III, John Paul (At) 700 Route 22, Pawling NY 12564 **Chapl Trin-Pawling Sch Pawling NY 2004-** B West Point NY 1968 AB Colg 1990; BA Colg 1990; AM U Chi 1991; MA U Chi 1991; MDiv Yale DS 1998. D 6/5/2004 P 2/2/2005 Bp J Neil Alexander. St Johns Ch W Hartford CT 2015-2016. jgedrick@trinitypawling.org

GEEN, Russell Glenn (HB) 4 Shad Bush Dr, Columbia MO 65203 B Ironwood MI 1932 s William & Minnie. BA MI SU 1954; BD Ken 1957; MA U of Wisconsin 1964; PhD U of Wisconsin 1967. D 6/30/1957 Bp Herman R Page P 1/1/1958 Bp Richard Ainslie Kirchhoffer. m 9/9/1960 Barbara June Geen c 2. Prof U of Missouri 1967-2000; Vic S Barth's Epis Ch Bemidji MN 1959-1963; Cur Trin Ch Indianapolis IN 1957-1959. Auth, "Soc Motivation," Wadsworth, 1995; Auth, "Human Agression," Wadsworth, 1991; Auth, "Human Motivation," Allyn & Bacon, 1984; Auth, "Personality," Mosby, 1976. APA 1967-1996. Fell APA 1986.

GEER, Christine Groves (Md) 23 Briar Patch Rd, Stonington CT 06378 **Died 5/1/2017** B New York NY 1935 d Alpheus & Lillian. BA GW 1983; MDiv CDSP 1989; Cert Basic Trng Int Mnstry Ntwk 1992. D 1/21/1990 P 9/1/1990 Bp Stewart Clark Zabriskie. c 3. P All SS Of The Mtn Epis Chap Crested Butte CO 2002-2003; Ret 1998-2017; Supply P Dio Connecticut Meriden CT 1997-2002; S Marks Pintler Cluster Anaconda MT 1997-1998; Int S Paul's Par Prince Geo's Cnty Brandywine MD 1995-1997; Co-R S Geo's Ch Perryman MD 1994-1995; H Cross Epis Ch Sanford FL 1993-1994; Int S Marg's Coventry 1992-1994; Dio Albany Greenwich NY 1992-1993; Chapl Police Dept Santa Fe NM 1990-1992; So Carolina Charleston SC 1989-1992; Assoc Pstr S Lk's Epis Ch Las Vegas NV 1989-1990; R The Ch Of The Epiph Eutawville SC 1987-1992; Asst S Fran Ch Greenville SC 1985-1987; Asst Epis Ch Of The Redeem Greenville SC 1984-1985; Chapl, Wrld Trade Cntr Dio New York New York NY 2001. OHC 1983-2003.

GEER, Francis Hartley (NY) Po Box 158, Garrison NY 10524 **R S Phil's Ch Garrison NY 1987-; Bd Mem Hastings Cntr 2008-; Pres Hartley Corp 2004-; Mem New York St T/F on Life and the Law 1992-** B Aiea Oahu HI 1948 s Francis & Miriam. BA Rutgers The St U of New Jersey 1970; MDiv CDSP 1976. D 6/12/1976 Bp Paul Moore Jr P 9/1/1977 Bp Harold Louis Wright. m 9/9/1972 Sarah Geer c 2. Dio New York New York NY 1992-2001; Dir of Rel Serv S Lk's-Roosevelt Hosp Cntr New York NY 1992-2001; Asst Min Trin Ch Epis Boston MA 1984-1987; Asst Dn Memi Ch Stanford CA 1980-1984; Chapl Stanford Med Cntr CA 1980-1984; Stff Chapl S Mary's Hosp San Francisco CA 1977-1978; Chapl Intern U CA Hosp San Francisco 1976-1977; Pres Hartley Hse 1996-2004. Co-Auth, "Where Was God on 9/11?," 2002; Auth, "Encyclopedia Of Environ Awareness". ACPE, Fell Coll Of Chapl. stphilips@highlands.com

GEERDES, Patricia Seney (WVa) 900 Hillsborough St, Raleigh NC 27603 **R H Innoc' Key W FL 1993-** B Richmond VA 1938 d John & Audry. BA Virginia Commonwealth U 1978; DMin UTS Richmond 1983. D 6/11/1983 Bp Robert Bruce Hall P 5/1/1984 Bp David Henry Lewis Jr. Trin Ch Moundsville WV 2002-2009; S Mary's Sch Raleigh NC 1999-2002; S Paul's Ch Key W FL 1996-1999; H Innoc Key W FL 1993-1996; P-in-c S Ptr's Epis Ch Key W FL 1993; Non-par 1990-1993; Ch Of Our Sav Montpelier VA 1984-1989; Asst Chr Ascen Ch Richmond VA 1983-1984. Phi Kappa Phi.

GEHLSEN, Tom (Minn) 1232 Lakemoor Dr., Woodbury MN 55129 B Davenport IA 1946 s William & Andorothy. BA S Ambr U 1968; MDiv S Thos Univ Sch of Theo St Paul 1972; MA U of Iowa 1976; PhD Iowa St U 1998. Rec 5/4/1995 as Priest Bp Chris Christopher Epting. m 5/11/1990 Susan K Gehlsen c 6. Calv Ch Rochester MN 2016-2017; P S Steph The Mtyr Ch Minneapolis MN 2014-2015; R S Mart's Ch Perry IA 2008-2013; Transition Off Dio Iowa Des Moines IA 2004-2013; R Gr Ch Boone IA 2004-2013; Asst S Lk's Ch Des Moines IA 2001-2003; R S Anne's By The Fields Ankeny IA 1998-2001; R S Paul's Ch Durant IA 1995-1998. "Day Treatment: Behavioral Disordered Adolescents," *Dissertation*, Iowa St U, 1998.

GEHRIG, Stephen James (Oly) 1828 Field Place NE, Renton WA 98059 B Spokane WA 1951 s James & Mary. BA U of Washington 1974; MDiv Colgate Rochester Crozer DS 1979; MDiv CRDS 1979; MEd Natl U 2008. D 8/2/1979

P 6/11/1980 Bp Robert Hume Cochrane. R S Marg's Epis Ch Bellevue WA 1988-2005; R Ch Of The H Sprt Vashon WA 1983-1988; Asst S Steph's Epis Ch Longview WA 1979-1983.

GEIB, Lanny Roland (Tex) 5087 Galileo Dr, Colorado Springs CO 80917 B Harrisburg PA 1942 s Roland & Ruth. U of Nthrn Colorado; BA VMI 1965; MDiv TESM 1989. D 6/29/1989 Bp Christopher FitzSimons Allison P 6/1/1990 Bp Edward Lloyd Salmon Jr. m 10/27/1975 Thella Geib c 2. R S Paul's Ch Katy TX 1999-2004; R S Chris's Ch Killeen TX 1991-1999; D Ch Of The Heav Rest Estill SC 1989-1990; Ch Of The H Comm Allendale SC 1989-1990.

GEIGER, Clifford T (Me) 2800 Se Fairway W, Stuart FL 34997 **Non-par 1986-** B Syracuse NY 1940 s John & Mildred. BA Davis & Elkins Coll 1963; MDiv GTS 1966. D 6/4/1966 P 12/1/1966 Bp Horace W B Donegan. m 9/7/1963 Anne Joyce Geiger c 1. S Dav's Epis Ch Kennebunk ME 1968-1985; Cur Epis Ch Of S Mary The Vrgn Falmouth ME 1966-1968. Outstanding Young Men Of Amer 1970.

GEIGER, William Linwood (Pgh) 3079 Warren Rd, Indiana PA 15701 **R Chr Epis Ch Indiana PA 1999-; Faith Communities working Grp of Hlth & Human Serv Emergency Plnng Com Indiana Cnty PA 2002-; InterFaith Coun Mem Indiana U of Pennsylvania Indiana PA 2000-** B Darby PA 1957 s Linwood & Glenna. BA U of Pennsylvania 1979; MDiv TESM 1987. D 6/6/1987 Bp Alden Moinet Hathaway P 4/23/1988 Bp Charles Farmer Duvall. m 10/8/1983 Kathleen K Kearney c 2. R Ch Of The Epiph Jacksonville FL 1992-1999; Cur H Cross Ch Pensacola FL 1987-1992; GC, Alt Dep Dio Pittsburgh Pittsburgh PA 2014-2016, Stndg Com Mem 2013-2016, Disciplinary Bd 2012-, GC, Alt Dep 2011-2013, Epis search Com 2011-2012, Dioc Coun Pres 2010-2011, Dioc Coun Mem 2009-2012, sexual misconduct prevention Trnr 2001-; Bd Dir Indiana Cnty CareNet Indiana PA 2000-2012; COM Dio Florida Jacksonville 1998-1999. Indiana Rotary Club 1999. Helen S. Appelberg Vision in Ldrshp Awd Cmnty of Hope Intl 2009; Indiana Cnty Male Civic Ldr of the Year nominee Indiana Cnty Serv Orgnztn 2009. ccrector902@comcast.net

GEISLER, Mark Alexander (Chi) 113 E. Lafayette St., Ottawa IL 61350 **Assoc Chr Epis Ch Ottawa IL 2012-; P S Paul's Ch La Salle IL 2012-; P-in-c Lasalle Cnty Epis Mnstry Ottawa IL 2010-, 2009-2010** B Waukegan IL 1963 s John & Jane. BA Nthrn Illinois U 1986; MDiv VTS 1994. D 6/18/1994 Bp Frank Tracy Griswold III P 3/25/1995 Bp William Walter Wiedrich. m 4/25/1987 Varsie Ann Geisler c 1. Dn of the Rockford Dnry Dio Chicago Chicago IL 2002-2006, 2002, Dioc Stwdshp Cmpgn 2000-2001, Dioc Coun 1995-1999, Comm on Yth and Yng Adlt 2000-2002; R S Paul's Ch Dekalb IL 2000-2008; Cur Trin Ch Ft Wayne IN 1996-2000; Cur Trin Epis Ch Wheaton IL 1994-1996.

GEISLER, William Fredric (Cal) PO Box 2624, San Anselmo CA 94979 B Cleveland OH 1935 s Fredric & Dorothy. AB Harv 1957; MBA Harv 1960; MDiv CDSP 1968. D 6/22/1968 P 1/4/1969 Bp Chauncie Kilmer Myers. m 9/16/1967 Barbara Geisler c 2. Int S Columba's Ch Inverness CA 2010-2011; Ch Of The H Innoc Corte Madera CA 1998; Serv (non-stipendiary) S Paul's Epis Ch San Rafael CA 1984-1995; Serv (non-stipendiary) St Johns Epis Ch Ross CA 1982-1984; Contrllr Dio California San Francisco CA 1968-1998; Serv (non-stipendiary) S Fran' Epis Ch San Francisco CA 1968-1982; Chapl San Francisco Towers (Epis Hm Fdn.) 2000-2006; Consult CPG 1999. "Tax Guide for Epis Ministers and Ch," *Ch Pension Fund*, 1998. California Soc of CPA's 1963.

GEISLER, William Joseph (Pgh) 1283 Earlford Drive, Pittsburgh PA 15227 **TESM Ambridge PA 2016-; Cn S Ptr's Epis Ch Brentwood Pittsburgh PA 2011-** B Pittsburgh PA 1956 s William & Elizabeth. BA La Roche Coll 1979; MA Pontifical Coll 1985; MDiv Pontifical Coll Josephinum 1985; DMin Pittsburgh TS 1999. Rec 6/1/1997 as Priest Bp Alden Moinet Hathaway. m 10/13/1990 Jennie Elizabeth Geisler c 2. Cn Dio Pittsburgh Pittsburgh PA 2011-2015, Cn of Formation 2011-; S Steph's Epis Ch Mckeesport PA 2003-2010; R S Jas Epis Ch Pittsburgh PA 1998-2003; S Paul's Ch Monongahela PA 1997-1998.

GEISSLER-O'NEIL, Susan (Mass) 3350 Hopyard Rd, Pleasanton CA 94588 **S Tim's Ch Danville CA 2016-** B Valdosta GA 1956 d Arthur & Ruth. BA Smith 1978; MDiv Ya Berk 1982. D 6/5/1982 Bp John Bowen Coburn P 9/25/1983 Bp Morgan Porteus. m 5/14/1988 Stephen O'Neal c 3. S Clare's Epis Ch Pleasanton CA 2012; S Jn The Evang Mansfield MA 1995-1996; Assoc S Mk's Ch No Easton MA 1989-1996; S Mk's Ch Foxborough MA 1989-1995; S Jn's Epis Ch Westwood MA 1988-1989; The Ch Of Our Redeem Lexington MA 1986-1987; All SS Ch Chelmsford MA 1983-1985.

GEITZ, Elizabeth Rankin (NJ) 431 Twin Lakes Rd, Shohola PA 18458 **Fndr & Chair Gd Shpd Sustainable Lrng Fndt 2014-** B Clarksville TN 1953 d Oscar & Dorothy. BS Van 1974; MAT U of So Carolina 1979; PrTS 1991; MDiv GTS 1993. D 6/12/1993 Bp George Phelps Mellick Belshaw P 12/11/1993 Bp Joe Doss. m 6/8/1974 Michael Meyer Geitz c 2. Calv Epis Ch Summit NJ 2016-2002, P Assoc. & Cn for Global Mssn 2016-; P Assoc Ch Of The Gd Shpd And S Jn Milford PA 2011-2014; Cn For Mnstry Dvlpmt and Deploy Dio New Jersey Trenton NJ 2001-2009; Int Vic S Fran Ch Dunellen NJ 1998-2000; Assoc S Lk's Epis Ch Metuchen NJ 1996-1998; Theol-In-Res Trin Cathd Trenton NJ 1996; Assoc S Paul's Epis Ch Westfield NJ 1993-1995; Bd Trst, 2nd Vice-Chair The GTS New York NY 2011-2016; Sprtlty Fac Credo Inst Inc.

Memphis TN 2005-2011. Auth, "I Am That Chld," Morehouse Pub, 2012; Ed/Con., "Lifting Wmn Voices," Ch Pub, 2009; Contrib, "All Shall be Well," Ch Pub, 2009; Auth, "Calling Cler," Ch Pub, 2007; Auth, "Fireweed Evang," Ch Pub, 2004; Ed/Con., "Wmn Uncommon Prayers," Morehouse Pub, 2000; Auth, "Soul Satisfaction," Morehouse Pub, 1998; Auth, "Gender & Nicene Creed," Morehouse Pub, 1995; Auth, "Entertaining Ang," Morehouse Publising, 1993. 2nd Vice-Chair, Bd Trst GTS 2011; Bd Trst GTS 2009; Distinguished Alum Awd GTS 2007; Polly Bond Awd ECom 2003; Whipple Prize GTS 1993; Seymour Prize GTS 1993. egeitz@imaginingtomorrow.org

GELDERT, Maurice William (RG) 121 Mescalero Tr, Ruidoso NM 88345 **Vic S Paul's Ch Artesia NM 2008-** B New Orleans LA 1944 s Maurice & Doris. Cert Rel Stud Rio Grande Sch For Mnstry Tesm; BS U GA 1972; OD Sthrn Coll of Optometry Memphis TN 1976. D 12/19/2006 P 5/6/2007 Bp Jeffrey Neil Steenson. m 5/30/1992 Mary Geldert c 2.

GELFER, Miriam Carmel (Mass) 8 Saint Johns Rd, Cambridge MA 02138 B Blue Point NY 1951 d George & Genevieve. BS Concord Coll 1975; MA U of Sthrn Mississippi 1976; MA Presb Sch CE 1986; MDiv EDS 1994. D 8/7/1994 Bp Orris George Walker Jr P 3/17/1995 Bp M(Arvil) Thomas Shaw. m 6/25/2005 Lisa M Garcia. Dn of Stdt and Cmnty Life EDS Cambridge MA 2011-2014; Mem COM Dio MA MA 2000-2006; R Gr Ch Newton MA 1998-2001; Asst Par Of The Epiph Winchester MA 1994-1998. mgelfer@3crowns.org

GELIEBTER, Phillip Lincoln (Pa) 4442 Frankford Ave, Phila PA 19124 B Brooklyn NY 1959 s David & Joan. D 1/11/2014 Bp Clifton Daniel III. m 5/1/1982 Lynne Ryan Geliebter c 3.

GELINEAU, Francoise (Mich) P.O. Box 351, Roscommon MI 48653 **P-in-c Ch Of The Gd Shpd Silver City NM 2011-** B Quebec CA 1942 d Joseph & Marcelle. BS U of No Texas 1965; MDiv Ya Berk 1990. D 6/18/1983 Bp Wilbur Emory Hogg Jr P 5/1/1991 Bp Steven Charleston. m 1/2/2009 Michael Fleming Ray c 3. R S Eliz's Epis Ch Roscommon MI 2007-2009; R S Steph's Ch Hamburg MI 2001-2004; R S Ptr's Ch Pittsburg KS 1998-2001; P-in-c Trin Ch Whitehall NY 1994-1996; Int S Jas The Fisherman Kodiak AK 1992-1993; Int S Dav's Epis Ch Wasilla AK 1991-1992; D S Augustines' Epis Ch Homer AK 1990-1991. Ord Of Ascen.

GELLER, Maggie (Mass) 160 Farm St, Millis MA 02054 **D Chr Ch Medway MA 2010-** B Alexandria VA 1953 D 6/5/2004 Bp M(Arvil) Thomas Shaw. c 1. D S Paul's Epis Ch Hopkinton MA 2010-2014; The Ch Of The Gd Shpd Acton MA 2006-2009, D 2006-2009; Jub Dio Massachusetts Boston MA 2004-2012, Jub 2004-2012; S Paul's Ch Brockton MA 2004-2006. MECA 2004; NAAD 2001.

GELLERT, Alan Cranston (SeFla) 2303 NE Seaview Dr, Jensen Beach FL 34957 **D All SS Epis Ch Jensen Bch FL 2013-** B Abington PA 1941 s Walter & Mary Jane. BA U of Pennsylvania 1964; MSW U of Pennsylvania 1968; Cert of Completion Dioc Sch for Chr Stds 2013. D 11/23/2013 Bp Leo Frade. c 2.

GEMIGNANI, Michael Caesar (Tex) 1816 Dublin Dr., League City TX 77573 **Asstg P H Trin Epis Ch Dickinson TX 2014-; Asstg P H Trin Epis Ch Dickinson TX 2013-** B Baltimore MD 1938 s Hugo & Dorothy. BA U Roch 1959; MS U of Notre Dame 1964; PhD U of Notre Dame 1965; JD Indiana U 1980. D 10/14/1973 P 1/8/1974 Bp John P Craine. c 2. Assoc S Mich's Ch La Marque TX 2007-2011; R S Paul's Epis Ch Freeport TX 1993-2007; Asst to R S Chris's Ch League City TX 1989-1991; P-in-c S Johns Epis Ch Brownville ME 1986-1988; Vic S Fran In The Fields Zionsville IN 1974-1979. Auth, "Making Your Ch a Hse of Healing," Judson, 2008; Auth, "Sprtl Formation for Pastors: Tending the Fire Within," Judson, 2002; Auth, "To Know God: Sm Grp Experiences in Sprtl Formation," Judson, 2001.

GEMINDER, Randolph Jon (LI) 175 Broadway, Amityville NY 11701 **Chapl Brunswick Psych Hospiital Amityville NY 2011-; Chapl Police Assn of Suffolk Cnty NY 2004-; Chapl Fire Dept Amityville NY 2000-; Chapl So Oaks Hosp Amityville NY 1992-; R S Mary's Ch Amityville NY 1975-** B Brooklyn NY 1947 s John & Ruth. BA S Fran Coll Brooklyn NY 1968; MDiv GTS 1971. D 6/12/1971 P 12/1/1971 Bp Jonathan Goodhue Sherman. m 6/27/1970 Donna Geminder c 2. Assoc S Geo's Epis Ch Schenectady NY 1973-1975; Cur S Jn's Of Lattingtown Locust Vlly NY 1971-1973; Chair, BEC Dio Long Island Garden City NY 1986-1988, Chair, Angl/RC Cmsn 1983-1985, Secy, Dioc Coun 1979-1982.

GENEREUX, Patrick Edward (Ia) 3700 S Westport Ave #530, Sioux Falls SD 57106 B Warren MN 1947 s Arthur & Bernice. BS Wm Carey U 1973; MDiv Sewanee: The U So, TS 1978. D 5/18/1978 P 5/4/1979 Bp George Mosley Murray. m 7/6/1968 Susan Genereux c 2. Dioc Disaster Coordntr Dio Iowa Des Moines IA 2008-2011, Coordntr, Dio Disaster Relief & Recovery 2008-2011; Chapl USAFR Whiteman AFB MO 1995-1999; R Chr Epis Ch Burlington IA 1994-2008; Chapl Air NG Sioux Falls SD 1992-1995; Dn Calv Cathd Sioux Falls SD 1992-1994; Cn for Mnstry Dio So Dakota Pierre SD 1985-1992; Chapl USAFR Ellsworth AFB SD 1984-1992; Vic Chr Epis Ch Milbank SD 1984-1988; USAF Off Of Bsh For ArmdF New York NY 1982-1985; Lv of Absence Dio Cntrl Gulf Coast Pensacola FL 1981-1982; Cur SS Mary & Nich Spalding Great Britain (UK) 1981-1982; Chapl USAFR RAF Lakenheath Great Britain (UK) 1980-1982; Vic S Anna's Ch Atmore AL 1979-1981; R Trin Episcopal Ch Atmore AL 1979-1981; Cur Trin Epis Ch Mobile AL 1978-1979.

GENNETT JR, Paul William (Del) 413 Terra Dr, Newark DE 19702 **R S Thos's Par Newark DE 2008-** B Camden NJ 1949 s Paul & Cora. BA Grove City Coll 1971; MDiv VTS 1992. D 6/6/1992 P 12/9/1992 Bp Alden Moinet Hathaway. m 7/10/1971 Mariyn A Gennett c 2. Assoc S Dav's Ch Wayne PA 2000-2008; R S Mk's Ch Johnstown PA 1996-2000; S Jas Epis Ch Pittsburgh PA 1994-1996; R S Jas' Penn Hills PA 1994-1996; Asst to the R Calv Ch Pittsburgh PA 1992-1994.

GENNUSO JR, George (WLa) 500 Edgewood Dr, Pineville LA 71360 B Opelousas LA 1947 s George & Hilda. BS Louisiana Tech U 1970; MDiv Nash 1989. D 6/17/1989 Bp Willis Ryan Henton P 12/16/1989 Bp Robert Jefferson Hargrove Jr. m 3/5/1973 Grace Gennuso c 1. R St Mich's Epis Ch Pineville LA 1998-2017; Chapl S Mk's Cathd Sch 1992-1998; S Mk's Cathd Shreveport LA 1991-1998; Vic Calv Ch Bunkie LA 1989-1991; Trin Epis Ch Cheneyville LA 1989-1991. BroSA 2007; Ord to St. Lk 2008.

GENSZLER, Mark (Vt) **P-in-c S Fran Epis Ch No Bellmore NY 2015-; Ch Of Chr The King E Meadow NY 2014-** B Philadelphia PA 1971 s David & Barbara. BA Marlboro Coll 1995; MLIS Kent St U 2006; MDiv GTS 2014; MDiv The GTS 2014. D 2/28/2014 P 9/3/2014 Bp Thomas C Ely. m 7/16/2016 Christopher Allegra.

GENTLE, Judith Marie (Pgh) 315 Turnpike St, North Andover MA 01845 B Birmingham AL 1947 BS Auburn U 1970; MDiv Candler TS Emory U 1987; MA U of San Francisco 1992; PhD Boston Coll 2001. D 6/6/1987 P 5/12/1988 Bp Charles Judson Child Jr. m 8/20/1983 Jerry Edward Hardy. Ch Of The Adv Pittsburgh PA 2004; Ch Of The H Trin Marlborough MA 1998-1999; S Lk's Ch Hudson MA 1994-1997; S Bede's Ch Atlanta GA 1987-1990. 2003.

GENTRY, Bryan Massey (Tex) 209 Orange Avenue, Fairhope AL 36532 **P-in-c S Ptr's Epis Ch Bon Secour AL 2010-** B Birmingham AL 1945 s George & Dorys. BA Birmingham-Sthrn Coll 1967; MDiv Chicago TS 1970; MDiv Sewanee: The U So, TS 1976. D 6/11/1978 P 12/1/1978 Bp Furman Charles Stough. m 12/28/1968 Janeth H Gentry c 1. Exec Dir Beckwith C&C Fairhope AL 2010-2014; Int S Fran Of Assisi Gulf Breeze FL 2009; S Mart's Epis Ch Houston TX 2006-2008; R Chr Ch Las Vegas NV 1997-2006; S Jn's Ch Birmingham AL 1993-1996; Cn To Ordnry Dio Alabama Birmingham 1989-1997, 1982-1996; The Epis Ch Of S Fran Of Assisi Pelham AL 1986-1988; Trin Ch Wetumpka AL 1978-1986; Urban Mssnr Grtr Birmingham Mnstrs Birmingham AL 1973-1977; Chapl Birmingham So Coll 1970-1971.

GENTRY, Keith Alan (Nwk) 11 Hinchman Avenue, Wayne NJ 07470 **Int S Mich's Epis Ch Wayne NJ 2012-** B Evansville IN 1950 s Robert & Lois. Certification Lombard Mennonite Peace Cntr; Cert Jn Hopkins Hosp Sch of Radiologic Tech 1971; AB Loyola U Maryland 1976; MDiv GTS 1979. D 6/19/1979 Bp David Keller Leighton Sr P 2/9/1980 Bp Charles Shannon Mallory. m 4/22/2012 Carlene Gentry c 2. P-in-c Ch Of The Gd Shpd Forrest City AR 2011-2012; P S Andr's Ch Marianna AR 2010-2012; R S Lk's Epis Ch N Little Rock AR 2003-2010; Assoc S Matt's Epis Ch Westerville OH 2001-2003; R S Jas Epis Ch Columbus OH 1992-1997; Assoc S Paul's Epis Ch Modesto CA 1990-1992; Cn St Paul's Epis Ch Peoria IL 1987-1990; R S Lk's Epis Ch Niles OH 1981-1987; Cur Gr Epis Ch Massapequa NY 1979-1981. Co-Auth, "Par Guidelines for use of Seder Meal," Dioc Nwspr, Dio Ohio. OSL 1980; P Assoc - All SS Sis of the Poor 1979; SocMary 1985; SocOLW 1985. Theta Alpha Kappa Loyola U Maryland 1976; Rev DJ McGuire Theol Medal Loyola U Maryland 1976. frkeith@stmichaelswayne.org

GENTY, Marc Daniel (Colo) St Luke's Episcopal Church, 2000 Stover St, Fort Collins CO 80525 **Exec Dir Common Cathd Longmont CO 2008-; Chair Dio Colorado Denver CO 2008-, Diac Coun Mem 2008-, D 2008-** B Pueblo CO 1957 s Francois & Susannah. BS CSU 1980. D 11/17/2007 Bp Robert John O'Neill. m 11/21/1981 Heidi Genty c 3.

GEORGE, Allen Winnie Sie (NY) 781 Castle Hill Ave, Bronx NY 10473 **The Ch Of The Epiph And S Simon Brooklyn NY 2013-** B Harper Maryland Co Liberia WA 1963 s Anthony & Dolly. BA Cuttington U 1988. Trans 9/22/1996 Bp Edwin Max Leidel Jr. m 11/21/1997 Spring Y George c 3. S Andr's Ch Bronx NY 2002-2007, R 2002-; S Mich's Ch Baton Rouge LA 2000-2002; R S Jn's Epis Ch Alma MI 1996-2000, 1996-1999; Serv Ch Prov Of W Afr 1989-1994.

GEORGE, Amy Martin (WTenn) Grace - Saint Luke's Church, 1720 Peabody Ave, Memphis TN 38104 **Cur Gr - S Lk's Ch Memphis TN 2016-** B Memphis TN 1963 BA U of Memphis 1985; MEd U of Memphis 1988; Mdiv Sewanee: The U So, TS 2016. D 6/4/2016 P 12/11/2016 Bp Don Edward Johnson. amy@gracestlukes.org

GEORGE, Clarence Davis Dominic (NY) 797 Corbett Ave Apt 3, San Francisco CA 94131 **Assoc S Fran' Epis Ch San Francisco CA 1995-** B Memphis TN 1942 s Clarence & Frances. CUNY; U of Memphis; DIT Mercer TS 1974; RN S Lk Sch Nrsng San Francisco CA 1984; BD SUNY 1999. D 6/22/1974 Bp Jonathan Goodhue Sherman. Min Prov Amer Prov 1989-1993; Guard S Damiano Friary San Francisco 1984-1993; Guard Bp's Ranch Healdsburg CA 1979-1981; Bro-in-c San Andres Ch Yonkers NY 1978-1979; Serv Angl Ch of the W Indies 1974-1978; Guard S Anth Friary Trinidad W Indies 1974-1978. Professed Soc of S Fran 1967-1999; Professed Tertiary of the Soc of S Fran 1999.

GEORGE, Eldred (Chi) B Dominican Republic 1945 m 7/11/1992 Odilia N George c 3. R Gr Epis Ch Freeport IL 2013-2017, 2009-2012; P Santa Teresa de Avila Chicago IL 2004-2009; Dio Panama 1992-2004; Dio The Dominican Republic (Iglesia Epis Dominicana) Gazcue Santo Domingo 1975-1977, 1972-1973.

GEORGE, Erminie A (VI) PO Box 1148, Charlotte Amalie VI 00804 B Tortola VI 1955 d Henry & Adena. AA U of Vrgn Islands 1988; BA U of Vrgn Islands 2005. D 6/14/2008 P 3/5/2011 Bp Edward Gumbs. m 6/19/1976 Garfield Joseph George c 3. Cathd Ch of All SS St Thos VI 2016.

GEORGE JR, Jay Charles (WTex) 7714 Moss Brook Dr, San Antonio TX 78255 **Vic Gr Epis Ch San Antonio TX 2011-** B Boynton Beach FL 1970 s Jacob & Marjorie. BA Texas Tech U 1992; MDiv Sewanee: The U So, TS 2000. D 8/23/2000 P 2/27/2001 Bp James Edward Folts. m 12/18/1993 Jamie George c 3. Ch Planter Dio W Texas San Antonio TX 2008-2010; R S Andr's Epis Ch Seguin TX 2003-2008; Asst S Mk's Epis Ch San Antonio TX 2000-2003.

GEORGE, Joanna Elizabeth (Dal) St Philip's Episcopal Church, 6400 Stonebrook Pkwy, Frisco TX 75034 B St Louis MO 1940 d Francis & Catherine. D 6/9/2007 Bp George Edward Councell. m 11/19/1960 Donald Horton George c 3.

GEORGE, Johannes Mark Philip (Tex) 15325 Bellaire Boulevard, Houston TX 77083 **Chr The King Ch Houston TX 2008-; Vic The Great Cmsn Fndt Houston TX 2004-, 2001-2004** B Freetown SL 1960 s Philip & Mariama. BA S Pauls Sem LR 1982; BD S Pauls Sem LR 1985; MA Texas Sthrn U 2001; PhD Wstrn Advncd Cntrl U 2008. Rec 1/21/2001 as Priest Bp Claude Edward Payne. c 2. S Lk's Epis Hosp Houston TX 2004; St. Jos's Epis Ch Houston TX 2001-2004. Untd Chapters of Alpha Kappa Delta Intl Sociol 2000. DD GTS 2013.

GEORGE, John C (CGC) **R Ch Of The Gd Shpd Mobile AL 2016-** B St Thomas US VI 1956 s Sidney & Niresta. BSEE FD 1986; MS-ISE Polytechnic U 1990; MDiv VTS 2013. D 4/7/2013 P 7/19/2014 Bp Edward Gumbs. m 7/26/1980 Caren A King c 5. Cathd Ch of All SS St Thos VI 2014-2015. jcg@cgs.edotcgc.org

GEORGE, Juan (Del) Trinity Episcopal Church, 1108 N Adams St, Wilmington DE 19801 **Vic Santa Rosa Mssn at Gr Ch White Plains NY 1999-** B San Pedro de Macoris DO 1945 s Jacinto & Maria. BS CUNY 1978; MA Adel 1980. D 6/14/1997 P 12/1/1997 Bp Richard Frank Grein. m 6/3/1973 Joy Mentie George c 3. Assoc Trin Par Wilmington DE 2007-2017; Gr Ch White Plains NY 1998-2005.

GEORGE, Mitzi (WLa) 1020 Sutherland Rd., Lake Charles LA 70611 **Assoc S Barn Epis Ch Lafayette LA 2012-** B Onslow County NC 1957 d James & Shirley. BA McNeese St U 1982; MA Loyola U 1993; MPS Loyola U 1993; MEd McNeese St 2000; EdS McNeese St 2001; DMin U So 2003; DMin U So 2003; DMin U So 2003. D 1/24/1994 P 5/12/2001 Bp Robert Jefferson Hargrove Jr. m 3/15/1980 Kevin Dale George c 2. Dio Wstrn Louisiana Alexandria LA 2014-2016, Pres Stndg Com 2009-2010; Convocatioanl Rep. Dioc Exec Coun 2001-2003; P-in-c S Andr's Ch Lake Chas LA 1999-2013; Epis Chapl McNeese St Lake Chas LA 1994-2002; D S Mich And All Ang Lake Chas LA 1994-1998; Yth Dir Dioc Yth Dir Alexandria LA 1990-2004. NAAD.

GEORGE, Reverend Cathy Hagstrom George (Mass) 409 Prospect St., New Haven CT 06511 **Ya Berk New Haven CT 2015-** B Saint Paul Minnesota 1955 d Robert & Diane. Doctorate in Mnstry in Transformational Ldrshp Bos; BA Macalester Coll 1979; MDiv Harvard DS 1984. D 6/4/1986 Bp John Bowen Coburn P 6/1/1987 Bp Roger W Blanchard. m 6/15/1985 Michael S George c 2. Int Ch Of The Redeem Chestnut Hill MA 2012-2014; Dio Massachusetts Boston MA 2008-2011; P-in-c S Mary's Epis Ch Boston MA 2008-2011; R S Anne's In The Fields Epis Ch Lincoln MA 1996-2008; Assoc Trin Ch Epis Boston MA 1994-1995; Asst S Jn's Ch Beverly MA 1990-1993; Asst S Paul's Ch Newburyport MA 1989; R Emm Ch Dublin NH 1988-1999; Asst All SS' Epis Ch Belmont MA 1987-1988. Auth, "Howard Thurman and the Role of Intimacy in Bldg Cmnty," *Journ of Pstr Theol*, 2016; Auth, "Minding the Gap," *ATR*, ATR, 2015; Auth, "You Are Already Praying; Stories of God at Wk," *Bk*, Epis Ch Pub, 2013; Auth, "The Stillness We Seek: Meditations for Adv," Morehouse, 2011. SSJE 2015; The Soc for Schlr Priests 2017. Billings Prize for Preaching Harvard DS 1984. cathy.george@yale.edu

GEORGE, Susanne T (Cal) 60 Brunswick Park, Melrose MA 02176 B Los Angeles CA 1946 d Robert & Frances. BA U CA 1972; MA California St U 1975; BA Sch for Deacons 2005. D 12/2/2006 Bp Marc Handley Andrus. c 3. D Chr Ch Alameda CA 2005-2011; D S Cuth's Epis Ch Oakland CA 2003-2004; Chapl Summit Hosp Oakland CA 2002-2003; Docent - AIDS art Proj from Afr Gr Cathd San Francisco CA 2009.

GEORGE-HACKER, Nina (Alb) PO Box 125, Cornwall PA 17016 **S Jn's Ch Gap PA 2016-** B Washington DC 1954 d Panos & Mary. BA Connecticut Coll 1976; MA Geo 1979; MDiv Lancaster TS 1993; DMin TESM 2011. D 12/15/2008 P 6/24/2009 Bp William Howard Love. m 5/14/1994 Richard James Hack-

er. Adj Prof Coll of St. Rose Albany NY 2015; P-in-c S Paul's W Middleburgh NY 2012-2013; R St Chris's Epis Ch Cobleskill NY 2009-2016; D Chr Ch Coxsackie NY 2008-2009; Pstr Wesley Grove Meth Ch Gaithersburg MD 2000-2004; Pstr Ross St Meth Ch Lancaster PA 1993-1995; Pstr Pomeroy Meth Ch Pomeroy PA 1991-1993; Fac, D Formation Sch Epis Dio Albany NY 2015. Auth, "Daily Devotions for May 3-9, 2015," *Gd News Daily*, Bible Reading Fllshp, 2015; Auth, "Daily Devotions for June 5-11, 2016," *Gd News Daily*, Bible Reading Fllshp, 2015; Auth, "Daily Devotion for March 3, 2015," *Lenten Devotions*, Epis Dio Albany, 2015; Auth, "Ways to Use and Enjoy the Dioc Cnfrmtn Curric," *The Albany Epis, Vol. 11:4*, Epis Dio Albany, 2014; Auth, "Daily Devotion for February 16, 2013," *Lenten Devotions*, Trin Sch for Mnstry, 2013; Auth, "Resurr Comes to a Tiny Par in the Flood-Ravaged Schoharie Vlly," *The Albany Epis, Vol. 9:3*, Epis Dio Albany, 2012; Auth, "Franciscan Cmnty of the H Cross Admits New Members," *The Albany Epis, Vol. 9:3*, Epis Dio Albany, 2012; Auth, "Daily Devotion for December 8, 2009," *Adv Devotions*, Trin Sch for Mnstry, 2009; Auth, "Walking in the Word: Losing the Ball and Chain," *UM Connection*, Baltimore-Washington Conf of the UM Ch, 2009. Phi Beta Kappa 1977. Anne Askew Schlr TESM 2005; Fauth Prize for Acad Excellence Lancaster TS 1993; Georgia Harkness Awd for Female Stdt Committed to Soc Justice Lancaster TS 1992; Connecticut Stdt Poet Connecticut Poetry Circuit 1977; Chas A. Dana Schlr Connecticut Coll 1974; Marshall Prize for Poetry Connecticut Coll 1973.

GEORGES, Esther Mathilda (VI) B Trinidad West Indies 1945 d Leslie & Nella. CSLT B.C. Cancer Inst 1970; Exec Dplma U of WI 2004; HYCAS CDSP 2013. D 3/6/2010 P 3/3/2012 Bp Edward Gumbs. m 8/27/1970 James Edward William Georges c 3.

GEORGI, Geoffrey Mack (NC) Po Box 13, Rougemont NC 27572 **Clincl Dir Koala Cntr 1988-** B San Bernardino CA 1948 s Howard & Mary. Duke; PDS. D 4/27/1974 P 12/1/1974 Bp Albert Wiencke Van Duzer. m 8/26/1972 Mary Georgi. Chapl Res Coun Duke Hosp 1974-1979; Yth Min Ch Of The H Fam Chap Hill NC 1974-1979. Auth, "The Source". Chapl Assn.

✠ GEPERT, The Rt Rev Robert R (WMich) Episcopal Diocese of Central Pennsylvania, 101 Pine St, Harrisburg PA 17101 **Provsnl Bp Dio Cntrl Pennsylvania Harrisburg PA 2014-** B Pittsburgh PA 1948 s Robert & LaVerne. BS Point Pk U 1974; MDiv VTS 1985. D 6/8/1985 P 12/22/1985 Bp John Thomas Walker Con 4/27/2002 for WMich. m 9/13/1997 Anne L Labat-Gepert c 3. Bp of Wstrn Michigan Dio Wstrn Michigan Kalamazoo MI 2002-2013; Dn of Trin Cathd, Dio Easton Trin Cathd Easton MD 1996-2002; R St. Mich's S Mich's Epis Ch Birdsboro PA 1988-1996; R St. Paul's, Baden and St. Mary's, Aquasco S Paul's Par Prince Geo's Cnty Brandywine MD 1985-1988. DD VTS 2003. rrgepert@gmail.com

GERBASI, Virginia Kaye (WA) 1525 H St., N.W, St. John's Church, Lafayette Square, Washington DC 20005 **S Jn's Ch Georgetown Par Washington DC 2014-** B Harrisburg PA 1964 d John & Judith. BA W&M 1986; JD W&M 1989; MDiv Wesley TS 2007; MDiv Wesley TS 2007. D 6/9/2007 P 1/19/2008 Bp John Bryson Chane. m 5/9/1992 Joseph Gerbasi c 2. Asst R S Jn's Ch Lafayette Sq Washington DC 2012-2014; Assit R Chr Ch Par Kensington MD 2007-2012; Sr Prog Analyst USDA Food & Nutrition Serv 1994-2000.

GERBER, Ronald D (Alb) 36 General Torbert Dr, Milford DE 19963 **P-in-c Chr Ch Dover DE 2009-** B Canton OH 1939 s Dale & Mildred. BA Heidelberg U 1961; BD Lancaster TS 1964. Rec 1/29/1972. c 3. S Andr's Epis Ch Albany NY 1993-2004; R St Fran Mssn Albany NY 1977-1993; Cur S Jn's Epis Ch Troy NY 1976-1977; R H Trin Epis Ch Hollidayburg PA 1972-1976.

GERBRACHT-STAGNARO, Madge (NH) 106 Lowell St, Manchester NH 03101 **R Gr Ch Manchester NH 2011-** B Mineola NY 1970 d Frederick & June. BA U So 1992; MDiv GTS 1995; DMin SWTS 2008. D 6/23/1995 Bp Orris George Walker Jr P 5/5/1996 Bp James Russell Moodey. m 6/16/2000 Brent Joseph Stagnaro c 2. Assoc R/Day Sch Chapl S Pat's Ch Washington DC 1998-2011; Chapl S Pat's Epis Day Sch Washington DC 1998-2011; Cn Chr Ch Cathd Cincinnati OH 1995-1998.

GERDAU, Carlson (Chi) 305 W End Ave Apt 1214, New York NY 10023 **Died 5/27/2017** B New York NY 1933 s Carl & Kathryn. AB Harv 1955; STB GTS 1959; Hon GTS 2012; Hon Bexley Sem 2013; Hon Virginia Sem 2013. D 6/20/1959 Bp Anson Phelps Stokes Jr P 12/19/1959 Bp Herman R Page. Ret 2008-2017; Cn to the PBp Epis Ch Cntr New York NY 1998-2005; Trst Ch Pension Fund New York NY 1997-2009; Cn to Ordnry Dio Chicago Chicago IL 1988-1997; Int S Greg's Epis Ch Deerfield IL 1987; Archd Dio Missouri S Louis MO 1979-1986; Trst Stndg Cmsn of Sm Communities 1973-1985; R Trin Epis Ch Houghton MI 1971-1979; Vic S Jn's Ch Munising MI 1965-1971; Ch Of The Nativ Lanse MI 1962-1964; St Davids Ch Sidnaw MI 1960-1965; Vic Ch Of The Ascen Ontonagon MI 1959-1965; S Marks Ch Ewen MI 1959-1965; Dep GC- Epis Ch Cntr New York NY 1964-1997. Chairman of the Bd Bex Sem 2013; Awd for Excellence Associated Ch Press 2001.

GERDING, Susan Ann (Tex) 836 W. Jones St., Livingston TX 77351 B Oak Park IL 1957 d Robert & Patricia. MA U of Virginia 1978; MLS Rutgers 1979; Cert Iona Sch for Mnstry 2008. D 6/28/2008 Bp Don Adger Wimberly P 1/3/2009

Bp C Andrew Doyle. m 12/29/1979 Mark S Gerding c 3. R S Lk's Ch Livingston TX 2009-2012.

GERDSEN, Elizabeth Jane (SO) 1219 Amherst Pl, Dayton OH 45406 **Assoc Dio Sthrn Ohio Cincinnati OH 2011-** B Cincinnati OH 1978 d Stephen & Sally. BA Mt Holyoke Coll 2000; MDiv EDS 2006. D 5/14/2005 P 6/24/2006 Bp Kenneth Lester Price. m 8/2/2003 Robert R Konkol c 2. P-in-c S Andr's Ch Dayton OH 2006-2011.

GERHARD, Ernest J (Neb) 14214 Briggs Cir, Omaha NE 68144 B Omaha NE 1933 s August & Cornelia. BA Omaha U 1960. D 8/26/1989 Bp James Daniel Warner. m 9/29/1969 Deanna Pearl Gerhard c 1. D S Jas' Epis Ch Fremont NE 1989-2000.

GERHARD, Kurt Joseph (WA) Saint Patrick's Episcopal Church, 4700 Whitehaven Pkwy NW, Washington DC 20007 **R S Pat's Ch Washington DC 2011-** B Omaha NE 1973 s Ernest & Deanna. BS U of Nebraska 1995; MDiv Epis TS of the SW 2000; DMin VTS 2009. D 5/21/2000 P 12/13/2000 Bp James Edward Krotz. S Pat's Epis Day Sch Washington DC 2010-2011; Asst The Ch of the Gd Shpd Austin TX 2003-2010; Chapl S Andrews Epis Sch Austin TX 2001-2010; Asst to R Ch Of The H Trin Lincoln NE 2000-2001; Chair of Bp's Evaltn Com Dio Washington Washington DC 2017, Chair of COM 2015-2017, Conv Resolutns Com 2014-2015, COM 2014, Dioc Coun 2011-2014. NAES 2001. kurt@stpatrickschurchdc.org

GERHARDT, Michael Joseph (NJ) 171 Larch Ave., Bogota NJ 07603 **Chr Ch Hackensack NJ 2012-; Chapl Somerset Med Cntr Sommerville NJ 2009-** B Flushing NY 1952 s Andreas & Ann. BA S Johns U 1974; MPA NYU 1980; MDiv Drew U 1997. D 5/31/1997 Bp John Shelby Spong P 12/13/1997 Bp Jack Marston Mckelvey. m 10/2/1993 Donna Linley Gerhardt c 2. S Mk's Ch Teaneck NJ 2008-2011; Chapl Res Westchester Med Cntr Valhalla NY 2007-2008; Vic Chr Ch Teaneck NJ 1999-2007; S Paul's Epis Ch Paterson NJ 1997-1998.

GERHART JR, John James (CFla) 4315 Longshore Dr, Land O Lakes FL 34639 **P-in-c H Faith Epis Ch Dunnellon FL 2009-; Chapl HPH Hospice 2007-** B Philadelphia PA 1950 s John & Kathryn. AS Sprg Garden Coll 1972; BS Sprg Garden Coll 1974; MDiv Epis TS in Kentucky 1977. D 5/15/1977 P 5/1/1979 Bp Addison Hosea. Int Gd Samar Epis Ch Clearwater FL 1992; Asst S Andr's Epis Ch Sprg Hill FL 1991-1992; St Lukes Ch Ellenton FL 1987-1990; Vic S Eliz's Epis Ch Zephyrhills FL 1983-1986; R S Steph's Epis Ch Latonia KY 1980-1983; Cur S Raphael's Ch Lexington KY 1978-1979; Cur Ch S Mich The Archangel Lexington KY 1977-1978; Asst S Clem's. Soc Of S Jn The Evang. wa3dit@tampabay.rr.com

GERHART, Stacey Pecaut (Ia) 1308 S Cleveland St, Sioux City IA 51106 B Sioux City, IA 1958 d Richard & Dorothy Ann. BME Morningside Coll 1981; MPA The U of So Dakota 1988. D 3/2/2011 Bp Chris Christopher Epting P 10/22/2011 Bp Alan Scarfe. c 3.

GERHART, William James (NJ) 2131 Woodbridge Ave, PO Box 1286, Edison NJ 08817 **Chapl The Middlesex Cnty Auxilliary Police Acad 2000-** B Philadelphia PA 1950 s David & Ruth. BA La Salle U 1972; MDiv Epis TS in Kentucky 1975. D 5/18/1975 Bp Addison Hosea P 4/10/1976 Bp Albert Wiencke Van Duzer. m 11/26/1977 Karen L Gerhart c 1. R S Jas Ch Edison NJ 1978-2013; Asst Gr Ch Merchantville NJ 1976-1978. Auth, Forw Mvmt; Auth, "An Adv Meditation," *Sharing, LivCh*. Chapl Ord of S Lk, Convenor Cntrl Jersey Chapt 1983-1987. sjec@edisonstjames.org

GERLACH, Aaron R (O) 125 East Market St, Tiffin OH 44883 **R Old Trin Epis Ch Tiffin OH 2014-** B Mitchell SD 1974 s Bobby & Laura. BS Estrn Illinois U 1996; MDiv Bex Sem 2009. D 6/6/2009 Bp Jeff Lee P 12/8/2009 Bp Victor Alfonso Scantlebury. P-in-c S Jas Ch Piqua OH 2013-2014; P-in-c S Mk's Ch Sidney OH 2010-2014. revgerlach@oldtrinityepiscopal.com

GERMAN, Kenneth L (SJ) 329 Mannel Ave, Shafter CA 93263 B Los Angeles CA 1930 s Alfred & Margrethe. BA California St U Northridge 1962; CDSP 1965. D 6/29/1966 Bp Robert Claflin Rusack P 3/11/1967 Bp Francis E I Bloy. m 12/31/1950 Charlotte German c 5. S Mk's Ch Shafter CA 1997-2002, R 1989-1996; P S Thos Ch Avenal CA 1994-2006; P S Phil's Ch Coalinga CA 1992-1993; Chapl Epis Cong Edwards AFB CA 1989-1992; Epis Dio San Joaquin Modesto CA 1980-1981; S Andr's Epis Ch Mariposa CA 1980-1981; 1979-1989; P Chr The King A Jubilee Mnstry Palmdale CA 1971-1979; S Andr's Epis Ch Ojai CA 1969-1970, 1966-1967; Dio Los Angeles Los Angeles CA 1966-1968.

GERMINO, Carmen (Va) 1205 W Franklin St, Richmond VA 23220 **P St Jas Ch Richmond VA 2014-, P 2011-2014** B Nashville TN 1981 d Mark & Christine. BA U of So 2004; MDiv Ya Berk 2007; Cert Ang Stud Ya Berk 2011. D 6/11/2011 Bp Laura Ahrens P 12/10/2011 Bp Shannon Sherwood Johnston. m 6/11/2013 Matthew W Presson. cgermino@doers.org

GERNS, Andrew Timothy (Be) 14 Midland Dr, Easton PA 18045 **Chair, Evang Cmsn Dio Bethlehem Bethlehem PA 2004-, Dioc Coun 2003-2008, Pres, Stndg Com 2011-, 2004-2011; R Trin Ch Easton PA 2002-** B Washington DC 1957 s William & Frances. BA Drew U 1979; MDiv GTS 1982; Andover-Newton TS 1989. D 6/12/1982 P 12/18/1982 Bp Arthur Edward Walmsley. m 6/12/1979 Maugarette L Gerns c 2. Chapl S Jos's Hosp Parkersburg WV 1994-2001; Ohio Vlly Epis Cluster Williamstown WV 1994-1997; Dir of Pstr Care S Josephs Hosp Parkersburg WV 1994-1995; R Trin Ch Parkersburg WV 1992-1994; Int S Alb's Ch Danielson CT 1991-1992; Chapl Windham Hosp Willimantic CT 1987-1992; Int Ch Of The Resurr Norwich CT 1987-1989; Chapl Intern Hartford Hosp Hartford CT 1986-1987; Int Chr Ch Stratford CT 1984-1986; Cur S Paul's Epis Ch Willimantic CT 1982-1984; Dioc Coun Dio W Virginia Charleston WV 1997-2001; Cmsn on the Mnstry Dio Connecticut Meriden CT 1986-1991. Columnist, "Occaisional Columnist," *Allentown Morning Call*, Allentown Morning Call, 2002; Columnist, "Rel Columnist," *Parkerburg News and Sentinel*, Parkersburg News & Sentinel, 1996. Assembly Of Epis Healthcare Chapl 1986-2003; ACPE 1986-2002; Assn Of Profsnl Chapl 1994-2003; Intl Critical Incident Stress Fndt 1996. Bd Cert Chapl Assn of Profsnl Chapl 1998; Basic And Advncd Trnr Intl Critical Incident Stress Fndt 1996.

GEROLD, Donna (Ala) St Stephen's Episcopal Church, 3775 Crosshaven Dr, Vestavia AL 35223 **S Steph's Epis Ch Birmingham AL 2013-** B Bronxville NY 1956 AA Fashion Inst of Tech 1978; BS Framingham St Coll 1978; MDiv Epis TS Of The SW 2013; MDiv Epis TS of the SW 2013. D 5/19/2013 Bp John Mckee Sloan Sr P 12/18/2013 Bp Santosh K Marray.

GERTH JR, Stephen Shea (NY) Church of Saint Mary the Virgin, 145 West 46th Street, New York NY 10036 **R Ch Of S Mary The Vrgn New York NY 1999-** B Norfolk VA 1954 s Stephen & Barbara. BA U of Virginia 1976; AM U Chi 1979; MDiv Nash 1983. D 6/11/1983 Bp Quintin Ebenezer Primo Jr P 12/21/1983 Bp Robert Elwin Terwilliger. R Trin Ch Michigan City IN 1988-1999; Cur S Lk's Ch Baton Rouge LA 1985-1988; Asst Ch Of The Incarn Dallas TX 1983-1985. sgerth@stmvnyc.org

GERVAIS JR, Sidney Joseph (Tex) 1210 E Mesa Park Dr, Round Rock TX 78664 B New Orleans LA 1927 s Sidney & Clarita. BBA U of Houston 1951; MDiv VTS 1966. D 6/28/1966 Bp James Milton Richardson P 6/28/1967 Bp Scott Field Bailey. m 5/9/2015 Leatitia Vance Gervais c 4. Chapl St. Dav's Hosp Round Rock TX 2007-2012; Chapl to Ret Cler Dio Texas 2000-2002; Ret Ret 1993-1995; R Emer S Richard's Of Round Rock Round Rock TX 1978-1992; Vic The Great Cmsn Fndt Houston TX 1978-1986; R Ch Of The Ascen Houston TX 1971-1978; Assoc Trin Ch Houston TX 1968-1971; Vic S Lk El Campo TX 1966-1968. EvangES 1964-1966.

GESTON, Alejandro Sumadin (Haw) 91-1746 Bond St, Ewa Beach HI 96706 B Bontoc PH 1938 s Geston & Dorotea. BTh S Andrews TS Manila PH 1967; BA U of the Philippines 1968; MA Fuller TS 1990. D 8/13/1967 P 11/1/1968 Bp Benito C Cabanban. m 1/2/1965 Simeona B Geston c 4. R S Steph's Ch Wahiawa HI 1993-2000; S Tim's Ch Aiea HI 1992-1993; Chapl The Epis Ch in Hawaii Honolulu HI 1992-1993, Mem-Compstn Revs Com 1986-1987, Mem-COM 1985-1988, Chairman-Kauai Island Cler for VIM 1979-1980; Vic S Ben's Mssn W Covina CA 1989-1992; Vic S Jn's Ch Eleele HI 1980-1989; Vic Ch Of The Resurr Hilo HI 1976-1979; Actg Chapl S Steph's Epis Mssn Sch Dio Cntrl P 1971-1972; Mssn P/CE Tchr Dio No Cntrl Philippines 1968-1971.

GETCHELL, Philip Armour (ECR) 6524 Hercus Ct, San Jose CA 95119 **Dn Latino Acad San Jose CA 2000-** B Medford OR 1934 s Bayard & Myra. BD CDSP; BA Stan; DD CDSP 1990. D 6/17/1959 P 12/29/1959 Bp James Walmsley Frederic Carman. m 4/23/1960 Claudia Jean Getchell c 3. Int Mision Nuestra Sra De Guadalupe San Jose CA 2000-2005; Interrim R Nuestra Senora de Guadalupe Par San Jose CA 2000-2005; Dn Trin Cathd San Jose CA 1992-1999; R S Mk's Par Berkeley CA 1979-1992; Assoc / Int R Trin Epis Cathd Portland OR 1975-1979; R Santissima Trindade Catedral Recife Br. 1970-1975; R Sao Lucas Par Londrina Brasil 1965-1970; Mssnr Missoes Brazil-Parana Fndr 1960-1975; Cur S Matt's Epis Ch Portland OR 1959-1960; Co.chair, CDSP Cenntenial Dio California San Francisco CA 1985-1990, Mem, COM 1985-1990, Chair, Dept of Wrld Mssn 1983-1987; Natl Fin Cmsn Igreja Epis Brasil 1965-1970. Auth, "Faces from Prison," *Witness mag*, 1978. DD CDSP.

GETLEIN, Greta (RI) Saint Paul's Church, 50 Park Pl, Pawtucket RI 02860 **S Paul's Ch Pawtucket RI 2014-** B Derby CT 1961 d Edward & Olive. BSN Sthrn Connecticut St U 1986; MDiv Ya Berk 2009. D 6/13/2009 P 1/16/2010 Bp John Bryson Chane. m 5/23/2009 Wanda Strickland. Ya Berk New Haven CT 2010-2014; Assoc Dn Chr Ch New Haven CT 2010-2014; Cur 2009-2010.

GETREU, David Edward (SO) 127 W Mound Street, Circleville OH 43113 **R S Phil's Ch Circleville OH 2016-, P-in-c 2014-2016; Bd Dir Hospice of Cntrl Ohio 2012-; Bd Dir Mntl Hlth Amer of Licking Cnty 2010-; Bd Gvnr Robbins Hunter Museum 2009-; Mem Granville Kiwanis 2005-** B Colombus OH 1966 s James & Mary. BA Pontifical Coll 1989; STB CUA 1994; Cert in Angl Stds Bex 2011. Rec 9/4/2012 as Priest Bp Thomas Edward Breidenthal. m 11/11/2000 Paula Jean Getreu. S Jn's Epis Ch Cambridge OH 2012-2013; Assoc P St. Matt the Apos Ch 1996-1998; Assoc P St. Fran de Sales Ch 1994-1996. dgetreu@alink.com

GETTEL, Becky (Mass) Trinity Church, 81 Elm St, Concord MA 01742 **Asst Trin Ch Concord MA 2012-** B Houston TX 1977 d David & Cherie. BS Rhode Island Coll 2001; MDiv EDS 2012. D 6/16/2012 Bp Gerry Wolf P 2/10/2013 Bp W Nicholas Knisely Jr. m 9/24/2005 Michael G Gettel c 2. Dir of Chld and Yth Mnstrs S Jn's Ch Barrington RI 2004-2009.

GETTS, Sarah Jane (Az) B Maidstone UK 1955 d Reginald & Mary Jane. Brooks U 1975; Westminster Hosp 1978. D 5/5/2012 Bp Kirk Stevan Smith. m 6/23/1984 David H Getts c 3.

GETTYS, Jeannette Cooper (USC) 308 College Dr., Gaffney SC 29340 **Ch Of The Incarn Gaffney SC 2008-** B Charlotte NC 1963 d Thomas & Jeannette. BA Davidson Coll 1985; MFA U So Carolina Columbia SC 1988; MDiv Sewanee: The U So, TS 2006. D 6/4/2006 Bp Samuel Johnson Howard P 12/16/2006 Bp Don Edward Johnson. m 1/22/2011 Miles Gettys III. Assoc Ch of the H Apos Collierville TN 2006-2008.

GETTYS, Laura (WTenn) 692 Poplar Ave, Memphis TN 38105 **S Mary's Cathd Memphis TN 2011-** B Memphis TN 1975 D 6/26/2005 P 1/7/2006 Bp Michael B Curry. m 9/2/2000 Joseph C Gettys c 1. S Ptr's Ch Oxford MS 2007-2011; Chr Ch Alexandria VA 2005-2007.

GETZ, Peter Richard Remsen (Dal) 808 Oak Hollow Lane, Rockwall TX 75087 B Kerrville TX 1947 s Henry & Emily. BA U of the Incarnate Word 1977; MDiv Epis TS of the SW 1981; MEd Trin U San Antonio 1990; CTh SWTS 2004. D 6/29/1981 Bp Scott Field Bailey P 10/25/1982 Bp Stanley Fillmore Hauser. m 5/2/1975 Gay Esther Getz c 2. R H Trin Ch Rockwall TX 2006-2013; S Lk's Epis Hosp Houston TX 2005-2006; Pstr Fell S Lk's Epis Hosp Houston TX 2005-2006; Mem Dioc Sch Cmsn TX 2002-2005; Dn SW Convoc TX 2002-2004; Sprtl Advsr FA TX 2001-2006; Mem Exec Bd the SW Assn of Epis 1999-2005; R Ch Of The H Comf Angleton TX 1998-2005; R S Matt's Ch Henderson TX 1993-1998; Headmaster Adv Epis Sch Stafford TX 1989-1992; Ass't R and Headmaster Adv Par and Sch Epis Day Sch Stafford TX 1989-1992; Instr and Chapl Texas Mltry Inst San Antonio TX 1988-1989; Chapl Texas Mltry Inst San Antonio TX 1987-1989; Headmaster Resurr Sch San Antonio TX 1985-1986; Cur Ch Of The Resurr Windcrest TX 1983-1986; Gr Ch Falfurrias TX 1981-1983; Vic S Jas Epis Ch Hebbronville TX 1981-1983; Tchr S Lk's Epis Sch San Antonio TX 1977-1978; Sprtl Dir Bps Happ Mvmnt Dio W Texas San Antonio TX 1985-1987. Auth, "More than I asked for," *Sharing mag*, 1999. Ord of S Lk 1980.

GHEEN, Stephen Harris (Minn) D 6/21/2016 P 6/27/2017 Bp Brian N Prior.

GIACOBBE, Georgia Bates (EO) 3564 E. Second St. #26, The Dalles OR 97058 **D S Pauls Epis Ch The Dalles OR 2011-** B Camden NJ 1954 d Robert & Lillian. BA S Marys Coll of Maryland 1992. D 6/3/2000 Bp Robert Wilkes Ihloff. m 3/10/1980 Peter B Speight. D S Mich And All Ang Ch Haines AK 2003-2011; D Middleham & S Ptr's Par Lusby MD 2000-2003.

GIACOMA, Claudia Louder (U) 7362 Tall Oaks Dr, Park City UT 84098 **Chapl S Mk's Hosp Salt Lake City UT 2000-** B Park City UT 1935 d Admiral & Fanny. BS U of Utah 1972; Certificte Pecos Benecitcinte Monstry, New Mex 1989; Cert Dio Tennessee/Scarrit Benet Cntr 1991; Cert U of Utah 1996; Cert Ang Stud CDSP 2000; 5 units S Marks Pstr Care Cntr Clincl Pstr Educatio 2001. D 1/11/2001 P 12/8/2007 Bp Carolyn Tanner Irish. m 8/23/1957 Joseph Louis Giacoma. Epis Cmnty Serv Inc Salt Lake City UT 2006-2007, 2001-2006, Stff Chapl/P 2001; D S Lk's Ch Pk City UT 2001.

GIANNINI, Robert Edward (Ind) 55 Monument Cir Ste 600, Indianapolis IN 46204 B New York NY 1940 s Mario & Elizabeth. BA U So 1964; MDiv GTS 1967; PhD U of St Andrews 1977; GTS 1986. D 6/21/1967 Bp Henry I Louttit P 12/27/1967 Bp James Loughlin Duncan. m 6/12/1965 Josephine Giannini. Dn & R Chr Ch Cathd Indianapolis IN 1990-2005; Scer 1988-1993; Dn Sch Of Theol Sewanee U So TS Sewanee TN 1986-1990, Trst 1982-1986; Gbec 1982-1991; Dn Cathd Ch Of S Ptr St. Petersburg FL 1981-1986; Dio SW Florida Parrish FL 1976-1981; Asst S Andrews S Andrews Scotland 1973-1976; Vic S Simons Ch Miami FL 1968-1973; Cur S Bon Ch Sarasota FL 1967-1968. Auth, "arts & Revs".

GIANSIRACUSA JR, Michael (Pa) 225 S 3rd St, Philadelphia PA 19106 **P S Mary's Epis Ch Ardmore PA 2012-; Epis Cmnty Serv 2010-** B Philadelphia, PA 1968 s Michael & Caroline. BA La Salle U 1990; MA Villanova U 1993; DMin EDS 2010. D 6/5/2010 Bp Edward Lewis Lee Jr P 1/22/2011 Bp Charles Ellsworth Bennison Jr. m 6/23/2001 Renee J Malnak-Giansiracusa c 1. S Jn's Ch Glen Mills PA 2011-2012; Epis Cmnty Serv Philadelphia PA 2010-2011. mike.gian86@gmail.com

GIARDINA, Denise Diana (WVa) B Bluefield WV 1951 BA W Virginia Wesleyan Coll 1973; MDiv VTS 1979. D 6/6/1979 Bp Robert Poland Atkinson. Gr Ch Welch WV 1979-1980. Auth, "Emily's Ghost," *novel*, W.W. Norton, 2009; Auth, "SS and Villains," *novel*, W.W. Norton, 1998; Auth, "The Unquiet Earth," *novel*, W.W. Norton, 1992; Auth, "Storming Heaven," *novel*, W.W. Norton, 1987; Auth, "Gd King Harry," *novel*, Harper and Row, 1984. Hon doctorate W Virginia Wesleyan Coll 1998.

GIBBES, Joseph A (Fla) 12236 Mandarin Rd, Jacksonville FL 32223 **R Ch Of Our Sav Jacksonville FL 2015-** B Columbia SC 1974 BA Wake Forest U 1996; MDiv TESM 2006; MDiv TESM 2006. D 7/1/2006 P 1/6/2007 Bp Edward Lloyd Salmon Jr. m 8/15/1998 Amanda P Poindexter c 2. Cn The Cathd Ch Of The Adv Birmingham AL 2010-2015; S Jn's Epis Par Johns Island SC 2006-2010; Capital Area Ymca 1999-2003. jgibbes@oursaviourjacksonville.org

GIBBONS, David Austen (Chi) 339 Ridge Rd, Barrington IL 60010 **R S Mk's Barrington IL 2008-; Mem Pres's Coun for Interfaith Initiatives 2013-** B Westminster UK 1963 s Kenneth & Margaret. MSc U of York UK 1984; Cert Theol Stud CDSP 1994; Cert Theol Stud Ripon Coll Cuddesdon UK 1994; MA Oxf GB 1996; MA Sarum Coll U of Llampeter 2005. Trans 10/21/2008 Bp Jeff Lee. m 3/11/1995 Susan D Gibbons c 2. R St Faith's Ch of Engl Havant Portsmouth 2001-2008; R Chr Ch Ch of Engl Gosport Portsmouth 1997-2001; Off for Further Educ Colleges Dept of Educ Dio Portsmouth UK 1997-2001; Cur H Trin Ryde and St Mich's Swanmore Portsmouth 1994-1997; Co-Chair Barrington Mnstrl Assn 2011-2012.

GIBBONS, Ro (CPa) 64 Mayflower Ln, Mansfield PA 16933 **Stndg Com Mem Dio Cntrl PA 2007-; R S Jas Ch Mansfield PA 2005-** B Wilmington NC 1962 d Thomas. BA Queens Coll 1984; MDiv Sewanee: The U So, TS 2003. D 5/24/2003 P 12/1/2003 Bp John Wadsworth Howe. m 12/12/1992 William M Gibbons c 2. Stndg Com-VP Dio Cntrl Pennsylvania Harrisburg PA 2008-2009; Coun of Trst 2007-2009; Asst All SS Ch Hilton Hd Island SC 2003-2005.

GIBBS, Charles Philip (Cal) 9900 Kensington Pkwy, Kensington MD 20895 B Socorro NM 1951 s Harold & Ruth. BA Pomona Coll 1975; MA U MN 1982; MDiv CDSP 1987; DDiv honoris causa CDSP 2003. D 6/24/1987 Bp Robert Marshall Anderson P 1/1/1988 Bp William Edwin Swing. m 3/30/1975 Deborah Paul c 2. Untd Rel Initiative San Francisco CA 2007-2013; Dio California San Francisco CA 1996-2006; R Ch Of The Incarn San Francisco CA 1990-1996; Asst S Steph's Par Bel Tiburon CA 1987-1990; Exec Dir San Rafael Canal Mnstry San Rafael CA 1987-1990. Poet, "Light Reading: Poems From A Pilgrim Journey," *Light Reading: Poems From A Pilgrim Journey*, Create Space, 2015; Auth, "Reflection on Ezzeddin Nasafi's 'Oh, my friend,'" *Leading From Within -- Poetry That Sustains the Courage to Lead*, Jossey-Bass, 2007; Auth, "Opening the Dream," *Deepening the Amer Dream*, Jossey-Bass, 2005; Co-Auth, "Birth of a Global Cmnty," *Birth of a Global Cmnty*, Lakeshore Pub, 2004; Auth, "(Chapt)," *Interfaith Dialogue And Peacebuilding*, US Inst Of Peace, 2002; Auth, "A Chr Experience Of Adoration," *Prabuddha Bharata*, Ramakrishna Ord, 2002; Auth, "Interreligious Understanding: A Chr Perspective," *Prabuddha Bharata*, Ramakrishna Ord, 2001. Sri Swami Satchidananda Awd for Fostering Interfaith Harmony Satchidananda Ashram 2016; Wk for Wrld Peace Intl Assn of Sufism 2010; Interfaith Visionary Temple of Understanding 2010; DD CDSP 2003; Distinguished Alum Holland Hall Sch 2003; Cn Of Gr Cathd Bp Of California 2001. cgibbs@revcharlesgibbs.net

GIBBS, Dennis (Los) 840 Echo Park Ave, Los Angeles CA 90026 **Chapl Dir Dio Los Angeles Los Angeles CA 2010-, 2007-2010** B Nampa, ID 1954 s Robert & Evelyn. Cert Diac Stud ETSBH 2010. D 5/23/2010 Bp Chester Lovelle Talton. c 2. Ch Of Our Sav Par San Gabr CA 2012-2015.

GIBBS, Lee Wayland (O) 2413 Weymouth Dr, Springfield VA 22151 B Natchitoches LA 1937 s Norman & Virginia. BA Macalester Coll 1959; STB Harvard DS 1962; ThD Harvard DS 1968. D 6/28/1980 P 11/1/1981 Bp John Harris Burt. m 6/16/1960 Joan Brownlee Lawler c 3. Hon Assoc Chr Ch Shaker Heights OH 1995-2008. Auth, "H Days & Holidays," Forw Mvmt Press, 1995; Ed, "Folger Ed Of The Works Of Richard Hooker," 1993; Co-Ed, "Myth & The Crisis of Hist Consciousness"; Transltr, "Willam Ames," *Technometry*; Co-Ed, "The Middle Way," *Voices Of Anglicaism*. AAR; Sixteenth Century Stds Soc.

✠ GIBBS JR, The Rt Rev Wendell Nathaniel (Mich) 19594 Renfrew Rd, Detroit MI 48221 **Bp of Michigan Dio Michigan Detroit MI 2000-** B Washington DC 1954 s Wendell & Lillian. S Marys Sem & U Catonsville MD; BA Towson U 1977; MDiv SWTS 1987. D 6/1/1987 Bp James Winchester Montgomery P 12/12/1987 Bp Frank Tracy Griswold III Con 2/5/2000 for Mich. m 8/19/1989 Karlah A Gibbs. P-in-c Ch Of S Mich And All Ang Cincinnati OH 1997-1998; R S Andr's Epis Ch Cincinnati OH 1993-1999; Ch of the Gd Shpd Oriskany Fls NY 1991-1993; Paris Cluster Chadwicks NY 1991-1993; S Geo's Epis Ch Chadwicks NY 1991-1993; R S Mk's Ch Clark Mills NY 1991-1993; Chapl CNY Psych Cntr 1990-1992; Assoc Gr Epis Ch Utica NY 1989-1991; Cur Emm Epis Ch Rockford IL 1987-1989; Bd Trst Bexley Seabury Fed Chicago IL 1998-2011; BEC Dio Sthrn Ohio Cincinnati OH 1994-1999; CE Cmsn CNY Dio Cntrl New York Liverpool NY 1990-1992. Soc of Cath Priests 2010. Hon DD SWTS 2000. bishop@edomi.org

GIBLIN, Keith Fredrick (Tex) 1401 W Park Ave, Orange TX 77630 B Beaumont TX 1958 s Gordon & Evolyn. JD So Texas Coll of Law 1989; LLM U of Houston 2010; Iona Sch for Mnstry 2014. D 6/21/2014 Bp Dena Arnall Harrison P 12/21/2014 Bp Jeff Fisher. m 4/25/1981 Joyce Gale Honeycutt c 4. keith_giblin@txed.uscourts.gov

GIBSON, Alan Glen (Mich) St Andrew Episcopal Church, 306 N Division St, Ann Arbor MI 48104 **R S Andr's Ch Ann Arbor MI 2008-** B Memphis TN 1961 s Jess & Evelyn. BA NWU 1982; MDiv Yale DS 1991. D 6/8/1991 P 12/14/1991 Bp Richard Frank Grein. R Trin Ch Rutland VT 2004-2008; R All SS Memi Ch Navesink NJ 1995-2004; Vic Ch Of The H Sprt Tuckerton NJ 1992-1995; Cur The Ch of S Ign of Antioch New York NY 1991-1992. Auth, "The Sunday After 9/11," *The Day Our Wrld Changed: Chld'S Art Of 9/11*, Abrams, 2002. agibson@standrewsaa.org

GIBSON RC, Barbara Jean (Kan) 400 Sutton Dr, Newton KS 67114 **D S Stephens Epis Churchrch Wichita KS 2016-; Vol Chapl Epis Soc Serv Inc. Wichita KS 2015-** B Newton KS 1945 d Doyle & Irene. BS Wichita St U 1967; MS Cntrl Michigan U 1990; Cert Bp Kemper Sch for Mnstry 2010. D 1/8/2011 Bp Dean E Wolfe. c 3. D S Jn's Ch Wichita KS 2011-2015.

GIBSON, Beverly Findley (CGC) 24 Blacklawn St, Mobile AL 36604 **Sub-Dn Chr Ch Cathd Mobile Mobile AL 2005-** B Andalusia AL 1961 d Grover & Anne. BA Converse Coll 1983; MA U of Virginia 1985; PhD Auburn U 2000; MDiv GTS 2005. D 6/4/2005 P 5/13/2006 Bp Philip Menzie Duncan II. m 5/31/ 1987 James Michael Gibson c 2. deangibson@christchurchcathedralmobile.org

GIBSON, Catharine (Va) **Chr Ch Durham Par Nanjemoy MD 2017-** B 1964 AB Harvard Coll 1986; MSc Lon 1987; MDiv VTS 2016. D 6/11/2016 P 12/10/ 2016 Bp Shannon Sherwood Johnston. m 10/27/1990 Robert Gibson c 2. Assoc S Jas Ch Potomac MD 2016-2017.

GIBSON, Catherine S (ETenn) Carlene Cottage, Tarland, Aboyne, Aberdeen-shire, Scotland AB34 4YX Great Britain (UK) **P In Charge St. Andr's Scot-tish Epis Ch 2017-** B Philadelphia PA 1939 d Robert & Dorothea. Art Students League of New York 1958; Parsons Sch of Design 1958; Cert Aberdeen Tfm Gb 1985; Cert Edinburgh Theol Coll 1993. Trans 10/9/2008 Bp Charles Glenn VonRosenberg. c 3. Asst P Gr Epis Lrng Cntr W Palm Bch FL 2010; P-in-c S Matt's Ch Dayton TN 2009; Chapl/P-in-c The Ch of Engl Dio in Europe Lugano Switzerland 2006-2007; R -5 Ch The Ch of Ireland Fermoy Un of Parishes Cnty Cork 2004-2006; for Pstr Care The Epis Ch Of Beth-By-The-Sea Palm Bch FL 2000-2004; Assoc All SS Prot Epis Ch Ft Lauderdale FL 1999-2000; Asst The Angl Ch In Qatar Doha Qatar 1998-1999; R The Scottish Epsicopal Ch Upper Deeside Ch Aberde 1994-1998; Hosp Chapl The Scottish Epis Ch Aberdeen Scotland 1988-1993. Scottish Assn For Pstr Care And Coun-selling.

GIBSON, Earl Dodridge (Az) 31641 La Novia Ave., San Juan Capistrano CA 92675 **Assoc S Marg Of Scotland Par San Juan Capo CA 2010-; Yth Co-ordntr Prov VIII San Diego CA 2010-** B San Gabriel Valley CA 1971 s John & Jacqueline. BA California St U 1995; MDiv Claremont TS 2000. D 4/27/ 2002 Bp Robert Marshall Anderson P 1/11/2003 Bp Joseph Jon Bruno. c 3. Assoc S Mk's Par Glendale CA 2007-2009; Yth Dir Dio Arizona Phoenix AZ 2004-2006; Yth Dir S Jn's Mssn La Verne CA 2002-2004.

GIBSON, Emily Stearns (Me) 732 Nottingham Rd, Wilmington DE 19805 B Salem MA 1953 d William & Jane. BS U of Sthrn Maine 1975; MDiv EDS 1983; STM GTS 2000. D 5/28/1983 Bp Frederick Barton Wolf P 12/9/1983 Bp John Shelby Spong. m 8/11/1984 David Tallmadge Andrews. Int Gr Epis Ch Wilmington DE 2010-2014; Int S Pat's Ch Brewer ME 2008-2010; Int S Bren-dan's Epis Ch Deer Isle ME 2006-2008; Pres of the Bd InterReligious Coun of Cntrl New York 1999-2001; R S Alb's Ch Syracuse NY 1991-2006; Asst Chr Ch Corning NY 1986-1991; Asst S Paul's Epis Ch Chatham NJ 1983-1986. Soc of S Jn the Evang 1992.

GIBSON, Gregory H (VI) St John's Episcopal Church, PO Box 486, Christianst-ed 00821 Virgin Islands (U.S.) **S Jn's Ch Christiansted St Croix VI 2014-** B Barbados 1959 s Eleazar & Petrolene. Dplma Codrington Coll 2008; BA U of the W Indies 2008. Trans 3/27/2014 Bp Edward Gumbs. m 5/28/1994 Anthia M Gibson c 2.

GIBSON, John Kenneth (NC) 1520 Canterbury Rd, Raleigh NC 27608 **Iglesia El Buen Pstr Durham NC 2015-; Gr Epis Mssn Clayton NC 2013-** B Roanoke VA 1958 s Thomas & May. BA U NC 1982; MDiv Ya Berk 1990; DMin SWTS 2004; ThM Duke DS 2010. D 11/10/1990 P 11/16/1991 Bp Huntington Williams Jr. m 8/2/2002 Cindy H Gibson c 1. Assoc S Mich's Ch Raleigh NC 2005-2013; R St Elizabeths Epis Ch Apex NC 1999-2005; Asst S Paul's Epis Ch Cary NC 1991-1999.

GIBSON, John Noel Keith (VI) Box 65, Valley, Virgin Gorda VI British Virgin Islands **Ret 1992-; Serv Ch of W Indies 1957-** B Reigate England 1922 s John & Evelyn. BA U of Cambridge 1944; MA U of Cambridge 1948; BD Lon GB 1959. Trans 4/1/1964 Bp Cedric Earl Mills. m 2/4/1959 Iris Alma Gibson c 3. Pres Stndg Com VI 1981-1983; St Mary the Vrgn Ch Vrgn Gorda VG 1150 1978-1992; Vic S Mary's Vrgn Gorda British VI 1976-1992; Dio Vrgn Islands Charlotte Amalie St Thom VI 1974-1977; COM 1971-1973; Vic H Cross S Croix VI 1966-1976; BEC VI VI 1965-1970; BEC Antigua VI 1960-1971; R S Geo's Tortola British VI 1956-1966; Serv Ch of Engl 1947-1951. Mem Most Excellent Ord British Empire H.M. Queen Eliz II 1990; Cn Emer 92; Hon Cn 90-92, All SS Cathd.

GIBSON, Justin Thomas (NwT) D 6/4/2016 P 6/15/2017 Bp James Scott Mayer.

GIBSON, Libby (Mass) Saint Mary's Episcopal Church, 3055 Main St, Barnstab-le MA 02630 **R S Mary's Epis Ch Barnstable MA 2012-; Adj Instr VTS Alexandria VA 2008-; Exam Chapl Dio Massachusetts Boston MA 2013-, Mem of Bp Coadj Nomin Com 2013-** B Baltimore MD 1971 d Lawrence & Sally. BA U of Virginia 1993; PhD U of Virginia 2004; MDiv VTS 2008. D 11/16/2008 Bp Shannon Sherwood Johnston P 5/17/2009 Bp Peter J Lee. m 5/ 25/1997 Miles Gibson c 4. VTS Alexandria VA 2011-2012, 2011; Assoc Ch Of The H Comf Vienna VA 2008-2012. Auth, "Ethics from the Other Side:

Postcolonial, Lay, and Feminist Contributions to Angl Ethics," *ATR*, 2012. libbygibson@gmail.com

GIBSON III, Owen S (HB) 2926 Maple Springs Blvd, Dallas TX 75235 **Non-par 1968-** B Hominy OK 1937 s Owen & Florence. BA U of Oklahoma 1959; BD Epis TS of the SW 1963. D 6/11/1963 P 6/1/1964 Bp Chilton R Powell. Asst Chr Epis Ch Dallas TX 1965-1968; Vic The Epis Ch Of The H Apos Oklahoma City OK 1963-1965. Turtle Creek Chorale.

GIBSON, Robert Burrows (At) 20 Lucky Ln, Blairsville GA 30512 B Rochester NY 1943 s Frederick & Harriette. BA Ohio Wesl 1965; STB Ya Berk 1968; STM Ya Berk 1970; CDSP 1971; Columbia TS 1980; SE Inst for Grp & Fam Ther 1985. D 6/22/1968 P 12/22/1968 Bp George West Barrett. m 7/5/1969 Joy H Gibson c 2. Chapl Med Cntr of Cntrl Georgia Macon GA 1994-2010; Asst Chr Ch Macon GA 1991-2003; Sprtl Dir Coliseum Psych Hosp Macon GA 1990-1994; Vic S Jas Ch Macon GA 1974-1990; Dio Atlanta Atlanta GA 1974-1981; Chapl Woodward Acad Coll Pk GA 1971-1974; Asst Trin Ch Branford CT 1969-1970.

GIBSON, Thomas William (CFla) Po Box 320026, 139 S. Atlantic Avenue, Co-coa Beach FL 32932 B Elgin IL 1949 s Stanley & Thelma. Cor 1969; MDiv SWTS 1972; BA U of Nthrn Colorado 1972. D 6/8/1991 P 12/15/1991 Bp John Wadsworth Howe. c 1. R S Mk's Ch Cocoa FL 1997-2015; R Ch Of S Dav's By The Sea Cocoa Bch FL 1993-1997; Asst R S Jn's Ch Melbourne FL 1991-1993; Interfaith Emergncy Servs Ocala FL 1983-1988.

GIBSON, Webster S (Va) 111 Stonebrook Rd, Winchester VA 22602 **R Chr Epis Ch Winchester VA 2007-** B Alexandria VA 1967 s Churchill & Dorothy. BA U of Virginia; MDiv Epis TS of the SW 1997. D 6/14/1997 P 12/13/1997 Bp Frank Harris Vest Jr. m 7/6/1991 Rebecca N Gibson c 3. R Imm Ch Hanover Cnty VA 1999-2007; Imm Ch Mechanicsvlle VA 1999-2007; Int Bruton Par Williamsburg VA 1997-1999.

GIDDINGS, Monte Carl (Kan) 26755 W 103rd St, Olathe KS 66061 **Archd Dio Kansas KS 2006-; D S Mich And All Ang Ch Mssn KS 2000-** B Beloit KS 1950 s Carl & Mildred. BS U of Kansas 1972. D 5/26/1999 Bp William Edward Smalley. m 12/23/1972 Jill Huebner c 2.

GIEGLER, Carl Esten (Chi) 414 Gaspar Key Ln, Punta Gorda FL 33955 **Died 11/7/2016** B Oak Park IL 1939 s Harry & Eunice. BA Trin Hartford CT 1961; STB GTS 1964; MEd Estrn Illinois U 1970. D 6/11/1964 Bp Walter H Gray P 5/1/1965 Bp Joseph Warren Hutchens. m 6/11/1960 Beverley Pamela Giegler c 2. Ret 1990-2016; Secy Dio Chicago Chicago IL 1987-1990, Mssnr 1975-1976; Vic Gr Epis Ch New Lenox IL 1976-1991; P-in-c Ch Of S Ben Bolingbrook IL 1975-1976; Chapl Estrn Il U Charleston IL 1968-1975; Vic Trin Epis Ch Mat-toon IL 1968-1975; Cur S Jn's Ch New Milford CT 1964-1968; Chair, Coll Wk Dio Springfield Springfield IL 1969-1974.

GIERLACH, David Joseph (Haw) 231 Miloiki Pl, Honolulu HI 96825 **S Eliz's Ch Honolulu HI 2009-, 2006-2007** B Binghamton NY 1957 s Joseph & Jacquelyn. BA SUNY 1977; MA Maryknoll TS 1981; JD U of Hawaii 1989. D 8/19/2006 Bp Richard Sui On Chang P 5/19/2007 Bp Robert Leroy Fitzpatrick. m 8/11/2001 Ida Teiti c 3. S Jn's By The Sea Kaneohe HI 2007-2009; Transi-tional D S Eliz Ch Honolulu HI 2006-2007.

GIESELER, Mary Morgret (Miss) B McClure OH 1936 RN St Jos Sch of Nrsng 1972; BBA U of Memphis 1978; MBA U of Memphis 1979. D 1/6/2001 Bp Al-fred Marble Jr. c 2. S Jn's Epis Ch Pascagoula MS 2001-2006.

GIESELMANN, Robert K (ETenn) Church of the Ascension, 800 S. Northshore Drive, Knoxville TN 37919 **Ch Of The Ascen Knoxville TN 2015-** B Knoxville TN 1958 s Paul & Nancy. BS Auburn U 1979; MS Auburn U 1985; JD U of Tennessee 1987; MDiv Sewanee: The U So, TS 1999. D 6/19/1999 P 2/ 5/2000 Bp Charles Glenn VonRosenberg. c 2. R S Steph's Par Bel Tiburon CA 2010-2015; R Chr Ch Sausalito CA 2005-2010; R S Paul's Par Kent Chester-town MD 2001-2005; Assoc S Lk's Ch Cleveland TN 1999-2001. Auth, "A Walk through the Churchyard," *(a Sprtlty of Chr death)*, CreateSpace, 2013; Auth, "The Epis Call to Love," Apcryphile, 2008.

GIFFORD II, Gerald Gerard (Haw) 446 Kawaihae St Apt 119, Honolulu HI 96825 **Ret 1989-** B Columbus OH 1924 s Gerald & Gertrude. BS OH SU 1948; MS EDS 1952; DMin SFTS 1973. D 6/29/1952 P 1/18/1953 Bp Henry W Hobson. c 5. R S Eliz's Ch Honolulu HI 1978-1989; S Nich Epis Ch Aiea HI 1978; Chapl Iolani Sch Honolulu 1966-1978; S Alb's Chap Honolulu HI 1966-1978; R S Jn's Ch Worthington OH 1957-1966; Vic S Steph's Ch Wahi-awa HI 1954-1957; Asst St. Barth Ch New York NY 1952-1954; DCE Trin Ch Columbus OH 1948-1949. HI Epis Cleric Assn.

GIFFORD, Lance Allen Ball (Md) 1700 South Rd, Baltimore MD 21209 B Bal-timore MD 1944 s Robert & Caroline. BA W&L 1966; STB GTS 1969. D 6/ 23/1969 Bp David Keller Leighton Sr P 6/22/1970 Bp Harry Lee Doll. m 6/26/ 1976 Margaret McCampbell c 2. R S Jn's Ch Mt Washington Baltimore MD 1986-2008; Chapl S Tim Sch Stevenson MD 1983-1986; Asst S Barth's Ch Baltimore MD 1977-1979, Asst 1969-1971; LocTen Ch Of S Kath Of Alexan-dria Baltimore MD 1976; 1974-1976; Epis Chapl Ecum Campus Mnstrs UMBC Baltimore 1971-1974. Chapl Epis Fac Conf 1978-2000; Maryland Instnl Revs Bd 1987-2003.

GIFFORD-COLE, Irene Margarete (Minn) 225 Hoylake Rd W, Qualicum Beach V9k 1k5 Canada **Serving Angl Ch of Can 1998-** B Rosthern Sask. Canada 1932 d Herman & Marie. BA U of Manitoba 1954; BD U Mb 1955; MA U MN 1972; MDiv LNTS 1990; DMin TESM 2006. D 8/6/1976 Bp Philip Frederick McNairy P 5/1/1989 Bp Robert Marshall Anderson. m 1/4/1998 David Henry Cole c 3. Mssh Epis Ch S Paul MN 1989-1997; Asst S Pat's Bloomington MN 1976-1982.

GILBERT, Brenda Marie (WNC) 8433 Fairfield Forest Rd, Denver NC 28037 B Topeka KS 1963 d Bennie & Mary. D 1/9/2016 Bp Porter Taylor. m 6/30/1986 Daniel Jay Gilbert c 2.

GILBERT, Carol Beverly (NJ) 34 Mystic Way, Burlington NJ 08016 **D Trin Cathd Trenton NJ 2005-** B Camden NJ 1946 d Charles & Mollye. BS Fsr U Nashville TN 1968. D 6/11/2005 Bp George Edward Councell. c 2. Educational Consult Voyager Expanded Lrng Dallas TX.

GILBERT JR, George Asbury (CGC) 10100 Hillview Dr Apt 432, Pensacola FL 32514 **S Jn The Evang Robertsdale AL 2010-** B Providence RI 1925 s George & Charlotte. BS U of Rhode Island 1950; Dio California Sch for Mnstry 1978; Bachelor Theol. Stds California Sch for Deacons 1984. D 9/9/1978 Bp Chauncie Kilmer Myers P 11/8/1980 Bp William Edwin Swing. m 10/14/1950 Judith Ann Gilbert c 2. Int S Monica's Cantonment FL 2007-2009; Int Ch Of The Epiph Crestview FL 2004-2007; Int S Mary's Epis Ch Milton FL 2001-2003; Int S Mk's Epis Ch Kimberling City MO 1992-2000; Ch of the Epiph Rumford RI 1986-1991; St Mich & Gr Ch Rumford RI 1986-1991; Vic Ch Of The Mssh Foster RI 1983-1986; Int S Steph's Par Bel Tiburon CA 1982-1983; Asst Ch Of The Redeem San Rafael CA 1978-1980. Auth, "Through the Seasons in Meditation, Homily, and Verse," *Bk*, LuLu.Com, 2010. OSL 2008. R Emer St. Mich & de Ch 1994.

GILBERT, Marilynn D (Ct) 28 Windemere Pl, Grosse Pointe Farms MI 48236 B Detroit MI 1942 d James & Anne. BS U MI 1965; MDiv SWTS 1994. D 7/11/1998 P 4/5/2003 Bp Edwin Max Leidel Jr. c 3. Asst Chr Epis Ch Norwich CT 2003-2006; Intern and Transitional D S Christophers Epis Ch Grand Blanc MI 1997-2000; Lay Vic All SS Epis Ch Fair Haven MI 1994-1997.

GILBERT, Paul (LI) 1760 Parc Vue Ave, Mount Pleasant SC 29464 **Gr Ch Cathd Charleston SC 2012-; Dir The LIttle Sch at Gr Ch Chas. SC 2012-** B Bay Shore NY 1944 s Robert & Louise. BA Wesl 1966; MDiv VTS 1980. D 6/14/1980 P 12/28/1980 Bp John Shelby Spong. m 9/17/2005 Jeanette Marie Herrmann c 3. R S Jn's Of Lattingtown Locust Vlly NY 1996-2004; R The Par Of S Mary And S Jude NE Harbor ME 1982-1996; Cur Chr Ch Short Hills NJ 1980-1982. Auth, "The Mar Quest," *Mar Preparation*, self, 2010; Auth, "Personally Spkng," *Collected sermons*, self, 1996. Chapl Natl Inst of Soc Sci 1998-2003.

GILBERT, Shedrick Edward (SeFla) 3368 Nw 51st Ter, Miami FL 33142 B Miami FL 1922 s Rufus & Ethel. BS Hampton U 1954. D 3/3/1984 Bp Calvin Onderdonk Schofield Jr. m 1/22/1947 Wilma Jacqueline Wake c 3. Asst S Agnes Ch Miami FL 1984-2010.

GILBERT, Thomas F (Me) 118 Morrill St, Pittsfield ME 04967 B Valleyfield Quebec 1951 s Eugene & Norma. BS U of Maine 1973. D 6/23/2007 Bp Chilton Richardson Knudsen. m 11/1/1975 Veronica Gilbert c 3.

GILBERT, Trimble (Ak) General Delivery, Arctic Village AK 99722 **D Bp Rowe Ch 1974-** B Artic Village AK 1935 s James. D 5/19/1974 Bp William Jones Gordon Jr P 7/6/1975 Bp David Rea Cochran.

GILBERTSEN, George Eugene (Lex) Courthouse Sq, Tiffin OH 44883 **Asst Trin 1982-** B Detroit MI 1931 s George & Marie. Epis TS in Kentucky; Illinois Coll 1952. D 5/30/1970 Bp William R Moody P 12/1/1970 Bp Jonathan Goodhue Sherman. m 8/28/1954 Carolyn V Gilbertsen c 2. P-in-c S Paul's Kenton OH 1971-1982; Cur S Andr's Ch Oceanside NY 1970-1971.

GILBERTSON, Gary Raymond (WMo) 12301 West 125th Terr, Overland Park KS 66213 B New Ulm Minnesota 1938 s Herbert & Olivene. PhD Stds U of No Dakota; BS Minnesota St U Mankato 1960; MDiv SWTS 1963; MA No Dakota St U 1971. D 6/29/1963 P 5/12/1964 Bp Hamilton Hyde Kellogg. m 5/15/1993 Patricia A Thomas c 3. Int S Matt's Ch Kansas City MO 2008-2010; Int S Mich And All Ang Ch Mssn KS 2006-2008; Owner & Trnr Epis Mediation 2004-2012; Owner and CEO GRG Consulting and Coaching for Cler and Congregations 2003-2012; Int S Andr's Ch Kansas City MO 2000-2003; Int Memi Ch Baltimore MD 1998-2000; Int S Lk's Ch Washington DC 1995-1998; Int Ch Of The Ascen Silver Sprg MD 1994-1995; Chf of ANG Chapl Off Of Bsh For ArmdF New York NY 1985-1994; Dioc Coun Dio No Dakota Fargo ND 1978-1981, Dioc Coun 1974-1976, Pres of Stndg Com 1974-1976, Dioc Coun 1970-1972, Chair Dio Assessment Comm & Fin Comm 1971-2011, Chair Dio Assessment Comm & Fin Comm 1971-2011; Dn Geth Cathd Fargo ND 1973-1985; Chf Exec Off Gilbertson & Assoc 1971-2000; Chf of Chapl Serv (Col) USAF Pentagon Washington 1971-1998; HR Consult Blue Cross and Blue Shield of No Dakota 1971-1985; R S Steph's Ch Fargo ND 1969-1971; R S Mart's Epis Ch Fairmont MN 1965-1969; Vic Samuel Memi Naytahwaush MN 1963-1965; Mssn Strtgy Com Dio W Missouri Kansas City MO 2000-2002; Dioc Misconduct Prevention Trnr Dio Maryland Baltimore MD 1998-2000; Dioc Misconduct Prevention Trnr Dio Washington Washington DC

1996-1998; Cass Lake Camp Bd and Stff Dio Minnesota Minneapolis MN 1964-1969. Aircraft Owners and Pilos Associaion 2000-2012; Amer Socity for Trng and Dvlpmt 1972-1997; Assn for Conflict Resolution 2001-2005; Mltry Oficers Assn of Amer 1985-2012; The Ombudsman Assn 1997-2000. Paul Harris Fell Rotary Intl 2009.

GILCHRIST, James Edwin (Neb) 124 1st Ave Se, Ronan MT 59864 **Nonpar 1976-** B Denver CO 1939 s James & Ethel. BS U Denv 1962; MDiv Nash 1967. D 6/5/1967 P 12/1/1967 Bp Joseph Summerville Minnis. m 12/16/1961 Gail Fairley c 2. Supply P Dio Nebraska Omaha NE 1974-1976; Asst Trin Cathd Omaha NE 1972-1974; Asst S Barn On The Desert Scottsdale AZ 1971-1972; Vic S Andr's Epis Ch Ft Lupton CO 1969-1971; Vic W Brighton CO 1969-1971; Vic Ch Of The H Comf Broomfield CO 1967-1969.

GILCHRIST, James F (Colo) 5478 S Idalia Ct, Centennial CO 80015 B Brunswick GA 1950 s Howard & Sarah. AA Brunswick Coll 1975; MDiv Sewanee: The U So, TS 2006. D 6/10/2006 P 12/9/2006 Bp Robert John O'Neill. m 2/20/1970 Glenna Fabian Gilchrist. R S Mart In The Fields Aurora CO 2007-2017; Cur/Asstg S Lk's Ch Denver CO 2006-2007.

GILCHRIST, John Richard (Ct) Po Box 361, Winter Harbor ME 04693 B Montgomery AL 1938 s William & Ann. Westminster Choir Coll of Rider U 1959; BS U of Alabama 1962; MDiv VTS 1967; CG Jung Inst 1976. D 6/10/1967 P 6/1/1968 Bp George Mosley Murray. m 8/27/1982 Gail G Gilchrist c 2. Ch Of S Thos Camden ME 2005-2013; Int Trin Ch New Orleans IA 2003-2005; Dio Maine Portland ME 2003; R S Steph's Ch Ridgefield CT 1990-2003; Dio Connecticut Meriden CT 1989-1990; Congrl Dvlpmt Dio Connecticut CT 1989-1990; Dio Missouri S Louis MO 1987-1989, Dep for Congrl Dvlpmt 1987-1989; R S Dunst's: The Epis Ch at Auburn U Auburn AL 1982-1987; R S Barth's Epis Ch Florence AL 1969-1982; S Paul's Chap Magnolia Sprgs AL 1967-1969; Vic S Ptr's Epis Ch Bon Secour AL 1967-1969. Auth, *Evalution of One Cong's Experience w Par Dvlpmt Consultants*.

GILDERSLEEVE, Robert K (Be) 435 Center Street, Jim Thorpe PA 18229 **Supply P Calv Ch Tamaqua PA 1993-** B Pittsburgh PA 1942 s Brunson & Jean. BS California U of Pennsylvania 1971; MDiv Nash 1976. D 5/29/1976 P 4/1/1978 Bp Robert Bracewell Appleyard. m 5/15/1965 Karen L Gildersleeve c 3. Dio Bethlehem Bethlehem PA 1993-2005; R Epis Par Of S Mk And S Jn Jim Thorpe PA 1985-1992; Vic S Jos's Ch Port Allegan PA 1978-1984; Vic S Matt's Epis Ch Eldred PA 1978-1984; Nash Nashotah WI 1976-1977.

GILES, James D (CFla) **S Pat's Ch Ocala FL 2015-; Short Term Mssn Coordntr Ch Amry USA 2005-** B Winter Haven FL 1960 AS Indn River Cmnty Coll 2000; BD Florida Atlantic U 2002; MDiv TESM 2005. D 5/28/2005 P 11/11/2005 Bp John Wadsworth Howe. m 8/2/1980 Mary C Giles c 4. Vic Coventry Epis Ch Ocala FL 2013-2015; The Ch Army Usa Beaver Falls PA 2005-2012. wherdeego@gmail.com

GILES, Richard Stephen (Pa) 105 Lansdowne Ct, Lansdowne PA 19050 B Birmingham UK 1940 s Donald & Gladys. BA Newcastle U 1963; MLitt Newcastle U 1988. D 12/1/1965 P 9/1/1996 Bp The Bishop Of Peterborough. m 7/29/1977 Susan Giles c 1. Dn Cathd Ch of Our Sav Philadelphia PA 1999-2008; Serv Ch of Engl 1965-1999. Auth, *Mk My Word*, Cowley Pub, 2005; Auth, *Creating Uncommon Wrshp*, Liturg Press, 2004; Auth, *Repitching the Tent*, Liturg Press, 2004. Hon.Vstng Fell Jn's Coll, Durham UK 2007.

GILES, Walter Crews (FtW) 1649 Park Ln, Alvarado TX 76009 B Dallas TX 1960 s Charles & Mildred. U of Texas 1980; Richland Jr Coll Decatur IL 1981; BBA U of No Texas 1983; MDiv Nash 1994. D 12/27/1993 Bp Jack Leo Iker P 7/2/1994 Bp Clarence Cullam Pope Jr. m 1/7/1989 Becky Lynn Giles. P-in-c S Anth's Ch Alvarado TX 1998; Cur S Michaels By-The-Sea Ch Carlsbad CA 1997-1998; Cur S Jn's Ch Ft Worth TX 1995-1997; Cur All SS' Epis Ch Ft Worth TX 1994-1995.

GILES, Walter Edward (CNY) 12914 US Route 11, Adams Center NY 13606 B Watertown NY 1932 s Clarence & Florence. BA Hobart and Wm Smith Colleges 1954; BD VTS 1957. D 6/22/1957 Bp Malcolm E Peabody P 6/11/1958 Bp Walter M Higley. m 3/3/1978 Patricia A Clark c 2. Chr Ch Sackets Hbr NY 1991-1994, Vic 1976-1978; S Paul's Ch Brownville NY 1991-1994; Dio Albany Greenwich NY 1986-1998; Trin Epis Ch Watertown NY 1976-1990; Dn, Finger Lakes Dist Dio Cntrl New York Liverpool NY 1968-1991, 1967-1991, Dept of CE 1966-1991, Dept of Missioners 1957-1991, Dn, No Country Dist 1986-1995; R Epis Ch Of SS Ptr And Jn Auburn NY 1966-1976; Supvsr Tioga/Tompkins Mssn Candor NY 1958-1966; Asst Tioga/Tompkins Mssn Candor NY 1957-1958.

GILFEATHER, Gordon Grant (Az) 12990 E Shea Blvd, Scottsdale AZ 85259 **D S Anth On The Desert Scottsdale AZ 2009-** B Great Falls MT 1938 s Patrick & Margaret. BS Montana St U 1961; MA WA SU 1970. D 1/24/2009 Bp Kirk Stevan Smith. m 12/18/1971 Susan L Gilfeather.

GILHOUSEN, Dennis Ray (Kan) 6501 Mapel Dr, Mission KS 66202 **Assoc P St. Mich and All Ang 2009-; Chair, Bd Dir St. Fran Cmnty Serv Salina KS 2013-** B 1942 BA Kansas Wesl; MS U Pittsburgh Sch of Publ Hlth; U of Kansas. D 11/27/1977 P 12/8/1978 Bp William Davidson. m 3/28/1969 Melissa Meyer. P-in-c Ch Of The Trsfg.

GIL JIMENEZ, Ramon Antonio (DR) **Dio The Dominican Republic (Iglesia Epis Dominicana) Gazcue Santo Domingo 2010-** B 1949 s Jose & Juana. D 2/14/2010 P 2/20/2011 Bp Julio Cesar Holguin-Khoury. m 7/3/1980 Francia Kenia Sanchez Hernandez c 3.

GILKES, Overton Weldon (Ct) B 1933 s Christopher & Zulieka. BA Dur 1956; Codrington Coll 1957; MA Dur 1985. D 12/1/1956 P 12/31/1957 Bp The Bishop Of Barbados. m 12/17/1980 Yvonne Gilkes c 4. S Andr's Ch New Haven CT 1989-1992; P-in-c S Ptr's Ch Rosedale NY 1985-1987; Asst Gr Epis Ch Plainfield NJ 1983-1985; R Ch Of The H Sprt Brooklyn NY 1980-1983; Chapl The Lodge Sch Barbados W Indies 1974-1979.

GILKEY JR, Sam (CFla) 3670 Northgate Dr Apt 1, Kissimmee FL 34746 B Hopkinsville KY 1937 s Sam & Pauline. Bethel Coll; U of Kentucky. D 6/9/1979 Bp William Hopkins Folwell. m 6/4/1960 Jean Gilkey c 2. D The Ch Of S Lk And S Ptr S Cloud FL 2004-2015; D S Jn's Ch Morganfield KY 1998-2003; D S Mary's Ch Madisonville KY 1986-1997; D St Barn Angl Limassol & St Anth Angl Paphos 1984-1986; D S Jn's Epis Ch Of Kissimme Kissimmee FL 1979-1984.

GILKS, Cyntha Ann (Okla) 903 E Main St, Holdenville OK 74848 **D S Paul's Epis Ch Holdenville OK 2013-** B Hoidenville OK 1953 d Pete & Jessie. AA Seminole St Coll; Iona Sch of Mnstry 2013. D 6/15/2013 Bp Edward Joseph Konieczny.

GILL JR, Charles Henry (Eur) 3451 South Washington Ave., Titusville FL 32780 **Pres The Gabr Fndt Gambier OH 1986-** B Mount Vernon OH 1936 s Charles & Virginia. BA Ohio Wesl 1958; BD Ken 1963; MDiv Bex Sem 1972; Fell Harv 1973; MDiv Colgate Rochester Crozer DS 1975; MDiv CRDS 1975; ScD Buxton U 1995; MS Methodist TS in Ohio 2003. D 6/29/1963 P 1/11/1964 Bp William Foreman Creighton. c 3. Dio Sthrn Ohio Cincinnati OH 1982-2002; 1977-2009; Med Cmsn WCC Geneve Switzerland 1977-1982; Emm Epis Ch Geneva 1201 1975-1976; R Emm Epis Ch Geneva Switzerland 1972-1977; Chapl Hlth Affrs Cathd of St Ptr & St Paul Washington DC 1971-1974; R St Johns Broad Creek Ft Washington MD 1965-1971; Asst S Jn's Ch Chevy Chase MD 1963-1965. Chas Gill, "The Attack upon the NE Kingdom," Wrld Pub, Vermont, 2003; Chas Gill, *Ch's Role in Healing*, WCC, 1973; Chas Gill, *Tonkin Gulf*, The Amer Friends Serv Com, 1970; Chas Gill, "Hlth for the Americans," *Hlth for the 70s*, Tul, 1969. Dn, The Geneve Consult 1984-1985; ES-MA 1976; Wrld Hlth Assembly on Aging 1985-2010. Addiction Contract St of Maine 1992; Clincl Fell and Fac Harv, Sch of Med 1971; Mem, Acad of Med Acad of Med, Washington, D.C. 1966. gill@swissmail.or

GILL, Cynthia Elizabeth (SeFla) 2750 Mcfarlane Rd, Miami FL 33133 **S Mary Magd Epis Ch Pompano Bch FL 2007-** B Pampa TX 1955 d John & Wanda. BA Trin U San Antonio 1977; Cert The Drama Studio-London 1981; MDiv Nash 1988. D 6/22/1988 Bp Clarence Cullam Pope Jr P 6/1/1989 Bp Richard Frank Grein. S Mk The Evang Ft Lauderdale FL 2000-2004; S Steph's Ch Coconut Grove Miami FL 1993-1999; Cur The Ch of S Matt And S Tim New York NY 1988-1993. Cmnty H Sprt.

GILL, Jeffrey Shilling (Oly) Trinity Parish, 609 8th Ave, Seattle WA 98104 **Trin Par Seattle WA 2012-** B Muncie IN 1955 s Harold & Virginia. Fletcher Sch of Law and Diplomacy Tufts U; BA Indiana U 1982; MDiv Harvard DS 1985. D 6/11/1988 P 5/20/1989 Bp David Elliot Johnson. m 8/7/1976 Carolyn Shilling Gill c 2. R Par Of Chr Ch Andover MA 2002-2012; Dn No Shore Deanry Dio Massachusetts Boston MA 1998-2000; R Trin Ch Topsfield MA 1990-2002; Asst R Gr Epis Ch Lawr MA 1988-1990. Bk Reviewer, "A Ch for the Future: So Afr as the Crucible for Anglicanism in a New Century," *ATR*, 2011. Fellows of the ECF 2000; Massachusetts Epis Cler Assn 1988; Phillips Brooks Cler Club of Boston, Pres 1998-2000; Phillips Brooks Cler Club of Boston, Treas 1992-1998. Fell ECF 2000. fatherjeff@trinityseattle.org

GILL, Jim (Be) PO Box 214, East Winthrop ME 04343 **Ret 1991-** B Newark NJ 1929 s William & Anna. BA Leh 1951; STB GTS 1954; STM GTS 1964; MA Ateneo De Manila U 1968; MA Moravian TS 1989. D 6/12/1954 P 12/18/1954 Bp Benjamin M Washburn. c 3. R Trin Ch Easton PA 1968-1991; Dir of Coll Wk Epis Ch in the Philippines 1966-1968; Fac S Andr's Sem Manila 1960-1966; Vic S Matt's Ch Paramus NJ 1954-1960.

GILL JR, John Nicholas (SO) 3429 Live Oak Place, Columbus OH 43221 **Ret 1996-** B Chattanooga TN 1940 s John & Marie. BA Newberry Coll 1964; MDiv GTS 1967. D 7/10/1967 Bp John Vander Horst P 5/13/1968 Bp William F Gates Jr. m 9/10/1975 Marsha Gill c 4. Dio Sthrn Ohio Cincinnati OH 1996; P-in-c S Nich Of Myra Epis Ch Hilliard OH 1995; R S Paul's Ch Columbus OH 1991-1995; R H Trin Epis Ch Oxford OH 1977-1991; Chapl NE Cmnty Mntl Hlth Memphis TN 1974-1978; Intern Inst Med & Rel Memphis TN 1972-1974; R Ch Of The Gd Samar Knoxville TN 1971-1972; R S Johns Ch Old Hickory TN 1968-1972; D S Geo's Ch Nashville TN 1967-1968.

GILL, Jule Carlyle (WA) 4 Milford Ave, Lewes DE 19958 **P Assoc S Ptr's Ch Lewes DE 2007-** B Baltimore MD 1945 d William & Eleanor. BA Queens Coll 1967; MA Col 1970; MDiv VTS 1976. D 5/22/1976 Bp John Alfred Baden P 4/1/1977 Bp Robert Bruce Hall. Assoc R S Alb's Par Washington DC 1997-2006; R Ch Of S Steph And The Incarn Washington DC 1987-1997; Assoc R S Aug

By-The-Sea Par Santa Monica CA 1979-1987; Asst U Chapl Sewanee U So TS Sewanee TN 1976-1979.

GILL, Robert Clarence (CPa) 139 N Findlay St, York PA 17402 **Semi-Ret 2002-** B Pittston PA 1927 s Clarence & Ruth. BS Penn 1953; U MI 1974. D 6/15/1979 Bp Dean Theodore Stevenson. m 4/16/1966 Jean A Gill c 1. D S Paul's Ch Columbia PA 1998-2000; D The Epis Ch Of S Jn The Bapt York PA 1979-1997.

GILLARD, Gary Laverne (Md) B 1945 D 5/22/1971 P 12/11/1971 Bp Robert Bracewell Appleyard. Dio Washington Washington DC 1971-1974.

GILLEN, Marguerite Webb (Ct) **Died 12/10/2016** B Tampa FL 1936 d William & Marguerite. BS Chart Oak St Coll 1991. D 9/17/2005 Bp Andrew Donnan Smith. c 5. D S Mk's Ch Bridgewater CT 2005-2010. The OSL the Physcn 2008.

GILLESPIE, Ann Hazard (Va) Christ Church, 118 N Washington St, Alexandria VA 22314 **Assoc R Chr Ch Alexandria VA 2007-** B Auburn NY 1957 d David & Joanna. MFA Seattle Pacific U; Ya; BA Goddard Coll 2003; MDiv VTS 2007. D 6/9/2007 P 12/17/2007 Bp Joseph Jon Bruno. m 12/29/1984 Jeffrey E Allin c 2. VTS Alexandria VA 2012-2013.

GILLESPIE, David Marston (RI) 2206 N Hollow Rd, Rochester VT 05767 **Asst S Phil's In The Hills Tucson AZ 1992-** B Morristown NJ 1925 s Samuel & Margaret. BA Ya 1950; MDiv Yale DS 1954. D 6/13/1954 P 12/19/1954 Bp Angus Dun. m 9/1/1951 Joanna Gillespie c 2. P-in-c S Lk's Epis Ch E Greenwich RI 1986-1991; Pres Urban Ministers Allnce San Francisco CA 1980-1985; Dn Gr Cathd San Francisco CA 1978-1985; R S Paul's Ch Englewood NJ 1962-1978; R S Jas Ch Skaneateles NY 1957-1962; Asst S Alb's Par Washington DC 1954-1957; ExCoun Dio Newark Newark NJ 1963-1978. Ord of S Jn of Jerusalem 1981.

GILLESPIE, Harold Stanley (Az) 501 S. La Posada Cir., Apt. 116, Green Valley AZ 85614 **Died 7/9/2017** B Rochester MN 1920 s William & Vivian. BS U of Iowa 1957; MS Baylor U 1962. D 10/17/1992 Bp Sanford Zangwill Kaye Hampton. m 8/10/1946 C Anne Gillespie c 3. D Epis Ch Of S Fran-In-The-Vlly Green Vlly AZ 1992-2000.

GILLESPIE JR, Robert Schaeffer (WA) 14702 W Auburn Rd, Accokeek MD 20607 B Toronto ON CA 1937 s Robert & Helen. BS Tem 1959; STB GTS 1962. D 6/9/1962 Bp Oliver J Hart P 12/15/1962 Bp Joseph Gillespie Armstrong. m 9/26/1964 Charlotte D Gillespie c 2. P-in-c Chr Ch Wm And Mary Newburg MD 2011-2012; P-in-c All Faith Epis Ch Charlotte Hall MD 2008-2009; Chapl Capital Hospice 2000-2007; Chapl Mid Atlantic Hospice 1998-2000; Chapl Hospice of Prince Georges Cnty 1991-1998; Vic S Jas Epis Ch Bowie MD 1989-2002; P-in-c S Paul's Epis Ch Hebron MD 1982-1989; Chapl Hospice of Nthrn Virginia VA 1981-1982; Chapl S Eliz Hosp WDC 1979-1981; R Chr Ch S Jn's Par Accokeek MD 1968-1978; Vic St. Jn's Chap Pomonkey MD 1968-1978; Cur S Lk's Ch Philadelphia PA 1962-1968.

GILLETT, Elizabeth Rosa Hamliton (CNY) 1213 River Rd, Hamilton NY 13346 **Pres The McNeiece Fndt Hamilton NY 2004-** B 1945 d James & Monica. BA Col 1969; MDiv GTS 1983. D 6/26/1983 P 5/8/1984 Bp David Keller Leighton Sr. Epis Soc Mnstrs Baltimore MD 1998-2004; Epis Cmnty Serv of Maryland Baltimore MD 1998-2004; R S Thos Ch Hamilton NY 1988-1998; Cn St Paul's Syracuse Syracuse NY 1985-1988; Assoc The Ch Of The Redeem Baltimore MD 1983-1985. Ord Of S Helena 1982. limey4519@hotmail.com

GILLETT, Richard Walker (Oly) 719 N 67th St, Seattle WA 98103 **Ret 1996-; Hon Cn Cathd Cntr Of S Paul Cong Los Angeles CA 2000-** B El Paso TX 1931 s Irvin & Caroline. BA U So 1952; MDiv Harvard DS 1960; EDS 1974. D 4/14/1960 P 12/1/1960 Bp Frederic Cunningham Lawrence. m 11/18/1960 Anne Bartlett Gillett c 3. Vic Imm Mssn El Monte CA 1986-1996; Vic H Fam Mssn N Hollywood CA 1986; Assoc The Epis Ch Pub Co Scranton PA 1980-1986; Dir Par Prog All SS Ch Pasadena CA 1974-1979; Dir Mision Indstrl de Puerto Rico San Juan Puerto Rico 1967-1973; Cur St Paul's Ch Bury Engl 1966-1967; Assoc P H Trin Ch Ponce Puerto Rico 1963-1966; Gr Ch Newton MA 1960-1963; Cur S Lk's And S Marg's Ch Allston MA 1960-1963. Auth, "The New Globalization," Pilgrim Press, 2005; Auth, "The Human Enterprise," Leaven Press, 1985. St. Geo Awd BSA 2012; Cert of Recognition City of Los Angeles 2007; Giant for Justice Cler and Laity Untd for Econ Justice, Los Angeles 2007; Hugh White Awd for worker justice Epis Ntwk for Econ Justice 2003; Hon Cn Cathd Cntr of St. Paul, Dio Los Angeles 2000; Proctor Fllshp EDS 1973.

GILLETTE, Howard Dennis (Pgh) 3414 Ventana Dr, Coraopolis PA 15108 B Buffalo NY 1944 s Howard & Emma. BA SUNY 1966; MS Troy U 1972; MDiv GTS 2012. D 9/13/2003 Bp Charles Edward Jenkins III P 4/11/2015 Bp Dorsey McConnell. m 4/27/1984 Mary M Gillette. Assn of Form OSI Agents 1977-2012; Assn of Profsnl Chapl 2004-2012; Assn of Ret Customs Agents 1999-2012; Intl Conf of Police Chapl 2005-2012. Bd Cert Chapl Assn of Profsnl Chapl 2004.

GILLETTE, Martha Carol (Chi) 154 Timber Ridge Ln, Lake Barrington IL 60010 **P-in-c Ch Of The H Apos Wauconda IL 2011-** B Schenectady NY 1955 d Gilbert & Dolores. Colby Coll ME 1975; BA U MN 1978; MS Old Dominion U Norfolk VA 1989; MDiv EDS 2007. D 6/9/2007 Bp John Clark

314

Buchanan P 12/15/2007 Bp Victor Alfonso Scantlebury. c 3. Wrshp Assoc S Mich's Ch Barrington IL 2007-2011; Captain Us Navy 1979-2004.

GILLIAM, John Malone (EC) 101 W Gale St, Edenton NC 27932 **S Paul's Epis Ch Edenton NC 2015-** B Alpine TX 1967 s Harvey & Helen. BA U of No Texas 1997; MDiv TESM 2007; MDiv TESM 2007. Trans 2/3/2009 as Priest Bp Mark Joseph Lawrence. m 5/25/1996 Mary S Sloan c 4. Assoc S Geo's Ch Nashville TN 2010-2015; Assoc Ch Of The H Cross Sullivans Island SC 2009-2010.

GILLIES, Bruce Nelson (WNY) 1082 Brookwood Dr, Derby NY 14047 **Dio Wstrn New York Tonawanda NY 2000-** B Buffalo NY 1940 s William & Frances. ABS Hope Coll; MS SUNY. D 6/9/1984 Bp Harold Barrett Robinson. m 11/12/1983 Clara Gillies. Chapl Collins Correctional Facility - Collins NY 1984-1996; Chapl Wmn And Chld's Hosp - Buffalo NY 1984-1989.

GILLIES, Clara (WNY) 18 N Pearl St, Buffalo NY 14202 B New York NY 1930 d Frank & Catherine. Cmnty Coll of New York NY. D 6/11/1983 Bp Harold Barrett Robinson. m 11/12/1983 Bruce Nelson Gillies c 4.

GILLILAND, Jonathon Shea 14115 Hillcrest Rd, Dallas TX 75254 B Fort Worth TX 1989 s John & Dana. BA Criswell Coll 2012; MDiv Duke DS 2017. D 6/24/2017 Bp George Robinson Sumner Jr. m 12/18/2011 Summer N Brooks c 1. sgilliland@transfiguration.net

GILLIS, Marcella R (WA) **Chr And H Trin Ch Westport CT 2016-; Yth Dir S Mk's Ch Washington DC 2011-** D 11/12/2016 P 6/17/2017 Bp Mariann Edgar Budde.

GILLISS, Columba (Md) 3200 Baker Cir Unit I209, Adamstown MD 21710 **Ret 2003-** B Washington DC 1937 d William & Ruth. BA GW 1960; MDiv GTS 1975. D 6/14/1975 Bp Paul Moore Jr P 1/30/1977 Bp James Stuart Wetmore. R Gr Ch New Mrkt MD 1990-2002; Vic S Jn's Evang Shady Slide MD 1987-1990; Ch Of St Jn The Evang Shady Side MD 1987-1989; Tri-Cnty Epis Area Mnstry Monticello NY 1985-1986; Assoc Tri-Cnty Epis Mnstry Ellenville NY 1983-1987; D-in-c S Ann's Ch For The Deaf New York NY 1977-1983. EPF 1966; EWC 1973; EWHP.

GILL-LOPEZ, John Herbert (LI) 80 La Salle St Apt 21-H, New York NY 10027 **Ret 1993-** B Washington DC 1933 s W Herbert & Dorothy. BA Ya 1954; STB EDS 1958; Patriarchal Sem Istanbul Tr 1959. D 6/14/1958 Bp Angus Dun P 8/1/1959 Bp William Foreman Creighton. m 12/14/2013 Eduardo Gill-Lopez. Assoc The Ch of S Ign of Antioch New York NY 1993-1996, Assoc 1973-1992; R The Ch Of The Epiph And S Simon Brooklyn NY 1978-1993; Assoc S Jn's Ch Huntington NY 1976-1978; Asst Ch Of The Intsn New York NY 1968-1972; P-in-c The Ch of S Edw The Mtyr New York NY 1960-1965; Cur S Columba's Ch Washington DC 1959-1960; Dir H Trin Epis Ch Inwood New York NY 1972-1973. Auth, "Gerturde Stein: Blood On The Dining Room Floor," Creative Atrs, 1982. Natl Orgnztn Of The Episcopalians For Life 1998.

GILLMAN, Paula Ruth (Minn) 520 N Pokegama Ave, Grand Rapids MN 55744 B International Falls MN 1951 d Kenneth & Margarett. D 6/21/2009 P 12/20/2009 Bp James Louis Jelinek. m 7/17/1976 Donald Gillman c 3. Reverend Chr Epis Ch Grand Rapids MN 2009-2011.

GILLOOLY, Bryan Charles (O) 19636 Scottsdale Blvd, Cleveland OH 44122 B Cleveland OH 1965 s George & Jean. BA Coll of Wooster 1987; MA Cleveland St U 1997. D 11/13/1992 Bp James Russell Moodey. m 10/7/1989 Karen E Gillooly c 2. Asst Dio Ohio Cleveland 2002-2005. NAAD.

GILMAN, Connie (SVa) 306 Boys Home Rd, Covington VA 24426 **Chr Epis Ch Smithfield VA 2016-; Chapl/Asst. Dir. of Prog All SS Chap Covington VA 2001-; Chapl and Asst. Prog Dir Boys' Hm Inc 2001-** B Radford VA 1944 d Claude & Ruth. MS Old Dominion U 1981; MDiv VTS 2001. D 6/9/2001 Bp David Conner Bane Jr P 12/15/2001 Bp Neff Powell. m 7/19/2012 Robert Ray Gilman c 1. Boys Hm Covington VA 2012-2014, 2002-2009; Dio Texas Houston TX 2011-2012; S Lk's Epis Hosp Houston TX 2009-2011; Emm Ch Covington VA 2001-2002. CWOLFE@BOYSHOMEINC.ORG

GILMAN, James Earl (SwVa) 719 Opie St, Staunton VA 24401 B Portland OR 1947 s William & Florence. BA Seattle Pacific U 1969; MDiv Denver Sem 1973; PhD Drew U 1982. D 2/15/2003 Bp Neff Powell. c 2. D Trin Ch Staunton VA 2003-2010. "Whose God What Rel: Compassion As Normative For Inter-Rel Coop," Journ Of Ecum Stds Vol 40 #3, 2003; "Fidelity Of The Heart: An Ethic Of Chr Virtue," Oxf Press, 2001.

GILMAN, Robert Ray (SwVa) 16918 Paynes Creek Dr, Cypress TX 77433 **Ch of the Gd Shpd Inc Blue Grass VA 2013-** B Carlinville IL 1943 s Ray & Ruth. BS SUNY 1965; MDiv VTS 1968. D 6/8/1968 Bp Leland Stark P 12/1/1968 Bp Charles Francis Hall. m 7/19/2012 Connie Gilman c 1. Palmer Memi Ch Houston TX 2010-2011; R The Epis Ch Of The Adv Norfolk VA 2001-2009; Off Of Bsh For ArmdF New York NY 1973-2001; Assoc To R Trin Ch Arlington VA 1970-1973; Cur S Mich's Epis Ch Arlington VA 1968-1970.

GILMER, Lyonel Wayman (NC) 2924 Wellesley Trce, Nashville TN 37215 B Rock Hill SC 1940 s George & Margaret. MDiv Columbia TS 1962; BA Cit 1962; Supvsr Acpe 1976; SWTS 1981. D 10/29/1981 Bp Quintin Ebenezer Primo Jr P 3/1/1982 Bp James Winchester Montgomery. m 7/16/1976 Mary Gilmer c 4. Chr Ch Cathd Nashville TN 2004; S Clare's Ch Matthews NC 1995-1996; Chr Ch Charlotte NC 1994, Asst R 1982-1989; S Jn's Epis Ch

Charlotte NC 1990-1993; Chapl Gd Shpd Hosp Los Angeles CA 1989-1991; Gd Samar Hosp Los Angeles CA 1989-1990; Res Chapl Georgia Mntl Hlth Inst Atlanta GA 1971-1974; Serv Presb Ch 1966-1981. Auth, "Care Of Chld In Hospitals". ACPE, Founding Mem Bioethics Resource Grp.

GILMORE, Elizabeth Lameyer (Me) 24 Fairmount St, Portland ME 04103 **Ret 2000-** B Rochester NY 1935 d William & Dorothy. BA Smith 1956; MDiv EDS 1980. D 9/16/1981 Bp Morris Fairchild Arnold P 10/27/1982 Bp John Bowen Coburn. m 10/1/1995 Roger Gilmore c 3. R Trin Epis Ch Portland ME 1990-1999; Int Trin Ch Topsfield MA 1989-1990; Int S Mk's Ch Foxborough MA 1987-1988; S Mk's Ch Southborough MA 1981-1987.

GILPIN, John Mitchell (Ct) St John's Episcopal Church, 7 Whittlesey Ave, New Milford CT 06776 **P-in-c S Jn's Ch New Milford CT 2012-** B Winchester VA 1951 s Kenneth & Lucy. BA Harv 1973; MDiv UTS 1997; Dplma Angl Stds GTS 2012. D 6/9/2012 P 12/15/2012 Bp James Elliot Curry. m 12/14/1985 Ann M Gilpin c 3.

GILPIN, Kathlyn Castiglion (SwFla) **D S Marg Of Scotland Epis Ch Sarasota FL 2006-; Asst. to the Chapl St Coll of Florida Chapl Bradenton FL 2004-** B Washington DC 1948 d Paul & Mary. BA U of So Florida 1969. D 6/18/2005 Bp John Bailey Lipscomb. m 4/6/1975 Joseph Arthur Gilpin c 1. D S Mary Magd Bradenton FL 2004-2006.

GIL RESTREPO, Silvio (Colom) Carrera 6 No 49-85, Piso 2, Bogota Colombia B 1945 Lic Universidad Santo Tomas 2000; Universidad Javeriana 2004. D 2/20/2010 Bp Francisco Jose Duque-Gomez.

GILSDORF, John Walter (EO) 1971 Sw Quinney Ave, Pendleton OR 97801 B Portland OR 1964 s John & Karen. BS Oregon Inst of Tech 1991. D 9/26/1999 P 5/24/2000 Bp Rustin Ray Kimsey. m 12/12/1992 Kimberly Conover. D Ch Of The Redeem Pendleton OR 1999-2001.

GILSON, Anne Elizabeth (WA) 5 Fernwood Cir, Harwich MA 02645 B Warren PA 1958 d Richard & Margaret. BA Chatham Coll 1982; MDiv EDS 1986; MPhil UTS 1991; PhD UTS 1993. D 6/11/2005 P 1/21/2006 Bp John Bryson Chane. m 12/30/2009 Judith Anne Davis c 1. Nativ Epis Ch Temple Hills MD 2005-2006; Chr Ch Capitol Hill Washington DC 2000-2004. Auth, "The Battle for Amer's Families: A Feminist Response to the Rel Rt," Pilgrim Press, 1999; Auth, "Eros Breaking Free: Interpreting Sexual Theo-Ethics," Pilgrim Press, 1995; Co-Ed; Co-Auth, "Revolutionary Forgiveness: Feminist Reflections of Nicaragua," Orbis Books, 1987.

GILSON, Christine (Kan) Po Box 883, El Dorado KS 67042 **R Trin Epis Ch El Dorado KS 2011-** B Denver CO 1946 d Edwin & Esther. BA Gri 1968; MS U IL 1970; MS Ft Hays St U 1994; MDiv SWTS 2002. D 8/31/2002 P 4/7/2003 Bp James Marshall Adams Jr. m 12/27/1969 Preston A Gilson c 1. Vic Trin Epis Ch Lebanon MO 2003-2010; Coun of Trst Dio Kansas Topeka KS 2013-2014; Comp in charge The Rivendell Cmnty Retreat Hse Dunnegan MO 2010-2013; Dn, Sthrn Dnry Dio W Missouri Kansas City MO 2009-2011, GC Dep 4 2009-2011, Dn, Sthrn Dnry 2008-2011. Phi Kappa Phi 1996.

GILTON, Michael R (Dal) **Ch Planter Dio Dallas Dallas TX 2016-, Ch Planter 2007-2016** B Anaheim CA 1964 BS U of Arkansas 1986; MBA U of Houston 1995; MDiv Fuller TS 2005. D 8/24/2005 P 2/25/2006 Bp David Mercer Schofield. m 5/24/1986 Kathleen Powers Gilton c 1. Vic St Pauls Epis Ch Prosper TX 2011-2016; Cur S Paul's Ch Bakersfield CA 2005-2007, Cur 2005-2007, Cur 2005-. mgilton@edod.org

GINGHER, Richard Hammond (O) 4747 Scioto #201, Toledo OH 43615 **Ret 1991-** B Columbus OH 1930 s Paul & Anna. BA Muskingum Coll 1953; ThL Bex Sem 1960; BD Bex Sem 1961. D 9/10/1961 P 6/19/1962 Bp Roger W Blanchard. Supply P Dio Ohio Cleveland 1991, Com Alcosm 1981-1990, BACAM 1979-1980, Rgnl Dioc Chapl 1975-1978; Chapl Toledo Mntl Hlth Cntr Toledo OH 1963-1991; P-in-c S Jn the Evang Swanton OH 1963-1965; Asst Min S Andr's Ch Dayton OH 1961-1963. Gingher Memi Chap Dedication Toledo Mntl Hlth Cntr 1988; Employee of the Year Toledo Mntl Hlth Cntr 1983.

GINN JR, Robert Jay (WMass) Oratory Of Saint Francis, Box 300, Templeton MA 01468 **Hermit Oratory Of S Fran Templeton MA 1999-** B IA 1946 s Robert & Bette. BA U of Nebraska 1968; MDiv Harvard DS 1972. D 6/14/1980 P 2/1/1981 Bp Alexander D Stewart. m 12/21/1974 Virginia Thomas Ginn. Vic Chr Ch So Barre MA 1994-1996; Dio Wstrn Massachusetts Springfield 1994-1995, 1988-1990, 1987-1988, 1987; Asst All SS Ch Worcester MA 1988-1991; S Thos Epis Ch Auburn MA 1987-1988; Int S Jn's Ch Worcester MA 1986-1987; Int Ch Of The Nativ Northborough MA 1985-1986; Cur S Paul's Epis Ch Gardner MA 1980-1984. Auth, "Career Coaching Your Kids," Consulting Psychologists Press, 1997; Auth, "Discovering Your Career Life-Cycle," Rad, 1994; Auth, "The Career Guide," Macmillan Pub Co, 1983; Auth, "The Coll Grad'S Career Guide," Scribner, 1981; Auth, "A Brief Intro To Vocational Testing In A Developmental Co," Harv, 1980.

GINNEVER, Richard Arthur (Md) 9259 Brush Run, Columbia MD 21045 B Mineola NY 1949 s Arthur & Mildred. AA Nassau Cmnty Coll 1969; BA U of Miami 1971; MDiv Nash 1974. D 3/25/1974 P 12/18/1974 Bp James Loughlin Duncan. m 5/24/1969 Carolyn D Ginnever c 4. R Chr Ch Columbia MD 2001-2015; R Gr Epis Ch Monroe LA 1995-2001; Dio Long Island Garden City NY 1994-1995, Chair - Missions 1985-1995, 1983-1993; R Ch Of Chr

G

The King E Meadow NY 1979-1995; Assoc R Gr Epis Ch Massapequa NY 1976-1979; Asst The Epis Ch Of The Gd Shpd Tequesta FL 1975-1976; Dio SE Florida Miami 1974.

GINOLFI, Priscilla Grant (CPa) 156 Warren Way, Lancaster PA 17601 B Elizabeth NJ 1947 d John & Constance. RN St Lukes Hosp Sch Nrsng; BS Millersville U 1976; MA Millersville U 1994; Cert Sch Chr Stds 2005. D 6/11/2005 Bp Michael Whittington Creighton. m 6/30/1973 Raymond Michael Ginolfi c 2.

GINOLFI, Sarah Catherine (Ind) 6050 N Meridian St, Indianapolis IN 46208 **S Paul's Epis Ch Indianapolis IN 2014-** B Morristown NJ 1985 d Raymond & Priscilla. BA Mssh Coll 2008; MDiv Ya Berk 2014. D 8/23/2014 Bp Robert R Gepert P 10/6/2015 Bp Cate Waynick.

GINSON, Isaias Gonzales (Haw) 1805 W.Alabama st., Houston TX 77098 **P-in-c S Marg's Ch Plainview NY 2017-** B Bacolod City, Philippines 1965 s Glicerio & Julieta. Ed.D (cand.) De la Salle U; MSPE U of the Philippines 2000; MDiv Epis TS of the SW 2010. D 6/19/2010 Bp C Andrew Doyle P 1/15/2011 Bp Claude Edward Payne. m 5/14/2000 Christie Marie Ginson. St Jn's Sch Tamuning GU 2012-2016; S Steph's Epis Ch Houston TX 2011-2012, Cur 2011-; Cur Ch Of The Gd Shpd Friendswood TX 2010-2011.

GIOVANGELO, Steven Michael (Ind) 337 North Kenyon Street, Indianapolis IN 46219 **Dio Indianapolis Indianapolis IN 2006-** B Chicago IL 1947 s Ernest & Rose. BA U of Albuquerque 1972; MDiv SWTS 1977. D 6/24/1977 P 1/7/1978 Bp James Winchester Montgomery. m 6/8/2013 Gerald J Bedard. R All SS Ch Indianapolis IN 2002-2009; R S Jn's Ch Un City NJ 1996-2002; Asst S Aug By-The-Sea Par Santa Monica CA 1995-1996; Asst S Bede's Epis Ch Los Angeles CA 1993-1996; R St Cross Epis Ch Hermosa Bch CA 1991-1993; R S Lk's Of The Mountains La Crescenta CA 1987-1991; Assoc R S Patricks Ch And Day Sch Thousand Oaks CA 1985-1987; R H Trin Ch Skokie IL 1979-1985; Cur S Mary's Ch Pk Ridge IL 1977-1979. AGO 1989; Eccl Crt 2006; Int Mnstry Ntwk 1993-1996.

GIRALDO OROZCO, Edgar (EcuL) **Litoral Dio Ecuador Guayaquil 2014-** B La Virginia Colombia 1966 s Jose & Orbilia. Lic. en Teologia Escuela Superior De Teologia 2003; Dplma Teologia Universidad Javeriana 2007; Lic. Estudios Biblicos Seminario Mayor Internacional 2014. D 6/16/2007 Bp Francisco Jose Duque-Gomez P 10/15/2014 Bp Terencio Alfredo Morante-Espana. m 12/29/2002 Luz Marleny Cifuentes Osorio c 2.

GIRARD, Jacques Andre (Nwk) 8 Shore Rd, Staten Island NY 10307 **Facilities/Chap Coordntr Intl Seafarers' Cntr 2000-** B New York NY 1945 s Georges & Simone. D 6/4/1994 Bp Richard Frank Grein. c 2. D S Matt's Ch Paramus NJ 2008-2012; Chapl Seamens Ch Inst New York NY 2001-2012; Dio New York New York NY 1994; S Andr's Epis Ch Staten Island NY 1994.

GIRARDEAU, Charles Michael (At) 1446 Edinburgh Dr, Tucker GA 30084 B Colorado Springs CO 1954 s Joseph & Olive. AA Oxford Coll of Emory U Oxford GA 1974; BA Emory U 1977; MDiv VTS 1982. D 6/12/1982 P 5/29/1983 Bp Bennett Jones Sims. m 1/5/2002 Susan Johnson c 1. Assoc R All SS Epis Ch Atlanta GA 2005-2014; R S Mary And S Martha Ch Buford GA 1995-2005; Asst for Educ H Innoc Ch Atlanta GA 1991-1995; Asst R H Trin Par Decatur GA 1987-1991; Vic S Jas Ch Cedartown GA 1983-1987; Cur Trin Epis Ch Columbus GA 1982-1983.

GIRARDEAU, Doug (Eas) 211 E Isabella St, Salisbury MD 21801 B Potosi MO 1937 s Malcolm & Mary. BA Van 1959; BD VTS 1962; DMin VTS 1987. D 6/26/1962 Bp William Evan Sanders P 5/1/1963 Bp John Vander Horst. m 11/27/1981 Ellen Girardeau c 2. Dioc Deploy Off Dio Easton Easton MD 2000-2006, 2000; R S Alb's Epis Ch Salisbury MD 1987-2000; Chr Ch S Ptr's Par Easton MD 1987; R Chr Ch Glennwood VA 1972-1986; Ch Of The Epiph Danville VA 1967-1986; Vic Chr Ch Glennwood VA 1967-1971; R Our Sav Sandston VA 1965-1967; Vic S Mary Magd Ch Fayetteville TN 1963-1965; Cur S Ptr's Ch Chattanooga TN 1962-1963. Soc of Cincinnati.

GIRARDIN, Barbara Jeanine (Colo) 2604 S Troy Ct, Aurora CO 80014 B Oakland CA 1948 d Milutin & Patricia. D 11/6/1999 Bp William Jerry Winterrowd. m 2/25/1977 Kerry Donald Girardin c 1.

GIRATA, Christopher D (Dal) St Michael & All Angels Church, 8011 Douglas Ave, Dallas TX 75225 **S Mich And All Ang Ch Dallas TX 2016-** B Lakeland FL 1980 s Daniel & Annemarie. BA Stetson U 2002; MTS Emory U 2004; MDiv VTS 2008. D 12/21/2007 P 6/29/2008 Bp J Neil Alexander. m 1/1/2005 Nicole M Girata c 3. R Calv Ch Memphis TN 2012-2016; Assoc R S Lk's Epis Ch Birmingham AL 2008-2012, 2004-2006. cgirata@saintmichael.org

GIROUX, Mark Alan (CNY) 355 Hyde St, Whitney Point NY 13862 **R S Mk's Epis Ch Binghamton NY 2002-, 1995-2001** B Watertown NY 1955 s George & Mary. Trin Evang DS; BA SUNY Potsdam 1977; MDiv SWTS 1986. D 6/14/1986 Bp James Winchester Montgomery P 12/27/1986 Bp William Augustus Jones Jr. m 5/29/1976 Paula W Warvel c 2. Dn St Paul's Syracuse Syracuse NY 2001-2002; R S Lk's Epis Ch Smethport PA 1990-1994; Trin Epis Ch Wheaton IL 1987-1990; Cur S Mart's Ch Ellisville MO 1986-1987.

GIRVIN, Calvin Shields (NwT) 4541 County Road 127, Colorado City TX 79512 B Colorado City TX 1947 s Luke & Barbara. BA U of Texas 1969; MA U of Texas 1971; MDiv Nash 1975; DMin SMU 1987. D 6/19/1975 P 12/

22/1975 Bp Archibald Donald Davies. c 4. S Lk's Epis Ch Stephenville TX 2009-2011; R S Mary's Epis Ch Texarkana TX 2000-2009; S Jn's Epis Ch Pottsboro TX 1998-2000; R S Lk's Ch Denison TX 1989-1997; Ch Of Our Sav Dallas TX 1987-1988; Bp'S Mssnr Dept Of Missions Dallas TX 1987-1988; Supply P Dio Dallas Dallas TX 1986; Assoc The Epis Ch Of The Trsfg Dallas TX 1977-1985; Chr Epis Ch Dallas TX 1975-1977; Cur The Epis Ch Of S Thos The Apos Dallas TX 1975-1977. Aamft; SocMary; Soc Of S Jn The Evang.

GITANE, Clayola Hillaker (SanD) 1020 Rose Ranch Rd, San Marcos CA 92069 **Gr Epis Ch Of The Vlly Mssn San Marcos CA 2013-; P-in-c Epis Ch in Parker Cnty 2009-** B Huntsville AL 1957 d James & Ella. MSW U of Texas Arlington 1980; MDiv SMU Perkins 2008; Cert Ang Stud CDSP 2009; Cert Ang Stud CDSP 2009. D 1/15/2009 P 12/5/2009 Bp Bavi Edna Rivera. c 3. W Dnry Cler Rep Dio Ft Worth Ft Worth TX 2011-2013; P-in-c Chr The King Epis Ch Ft Worth TX 2009-2010.

GITAU, Samson Njuguna (Ark) 243 N Mcneil St, Memphis TN 38112 **Chr Ch Sch Forrest City AR 2008-; Chapl Barth Hse Epis Cntr Memphis TN 1998-** B KE 1951 s Hezron & Gladys. BD S Pauls Untd Theol Coll Limuru Ke 1980; STM Ya Berk 1985; PhD Bos 1994. Trans 3/11/1999 Bp James Malone Coleman. m 8/14/1976 Lilian Gitau c 6. Chr Epis Ch Forrest City AR 2008-2011; Imm Epis Ch La Grange TN 2008-2010; Dio W Tennessee Memphis 1999-2008; Asst R S Jas' Epis Ch Cambridge MA 1996-1998; Prncpl Mcgregor Bible Coll 1984-1989. Auth, "Breaking the Sackles: Contemporary Perspectives in Pauls letters to the Galatians," Auth Hse, 2008; Auth, "Under the Wings: Reflections in the Bk of Ruth," Cader Pub, 2004; Auth, "One Boat One Destiny," Vintage Press, 1999; Auth, "A Comparative Study Of The Transmission," *Actualization And Stabilization Of Oral Traditions*, Umi Dissertation Serv, 1994; Auth, "Chr Freedom," Uzima Press, Nairobi, 1990.

GITHITU, James Kimari (Mass) 740 Princeton Blvd Apt 3, Lowell MA 01851 B Kiambu Kenya 1940 s John & Jane. Dplma St Paul's Untd Theol Coll 1971; BEd Nairobi U 1977; MA Cov TS MO 1993; MA Other 1993; Doctor of Pstr Counslg Andersonville TS 2010; Doctor of Pstr Counslg Other 2010; Doctor of Theol Andersonville TS 2012; Doctor of Theol Other 2012. Trans 6/26/2008 as Priest Bp M(Arvil) Thomas Shaw. m 7/31/1966 Elizabeth Mary Kimari c 5. R S Mk's Ch Dorchester MA 2011-2012; P incharge S Aug's Ch Lawr MA 2007-2009; P incharge Ch Of The Ascen S Louis MO 1992-1993; P Assoc S Lk's Epis Ch Manchester MO 1992.

GITIMU, Paul Wainaina (Pa) 1747 Church Ln, Philadelphia PA 19141 **Trin Ch Boothwyn PA 2015-** B Kiambu Kenya 1966 s Njoroge & Hannah. BDiv St Paul's U 2000; MATS EDS 2003; DMin Andersonville TS 2014. Trans 7/22/2014 as Priest Bp Clifton Daniel III. m 5/1/1993 Susan W Wainaina c 3. pgitimu2002@yahoo.com

GIVEN, Mark E (Ct) 1113 Abrams Road, #4-121, Richardson TX 75081 B Winchester MA 1954 s John & Margaret. BS U of Massachusetts 1980; MDiv Gordon-Conwell TS 1987; GTS 1988. D 6/24/1989 P 1/1/1990 Bp Charles Brinkley Morton. c 2. S Thos Ch Ennis TX 2014-2016; S Paul's Epis Ch Dallas TX 2010-2013; R Chr Epis Ch Middle Haddam CT 2001-2009; S Jn The Evang Ch Lansdowne PA 1999-2001; Chapl Epis Acad Merian PA 1999-2000; The Epis Acad Newtown Sq PA 1998-1999; Ch Of The Redeem Bryn Mawr PA 1996-1998; Asst Trin Epis Ch Redlands CA 1991-1996; Assoc Chapl U Redlands 1991-1996; S Ptr's Epis Ch Del Mar CA 1989-1991; Yth Dir S Jn's Epis Ch Gloucester MA 1986-1988. Soc of S Jn the Evang 1985-2000.

GIVLER, Gary Bruce (SO) 6215 Kenwood Rd, Madeira OH 45243 **D Calv Ch Cincinnati OH 2011-** B Springhill Nova Scotia CA 1947 s Frank & Lucy. BS Geo Wms 1970; Dio SO Diac Sch London OH 1993; MA The Athenaeum of Ohio 2001. D 12/3/1993 Bp Herbert Thompson Jr. m 3/13/1982 Susan Kay Givler c 2. Assoc Gr Ch Cincinnati OH 2006-2010; Assoc S Phil's Ch Cincinnati OH 1997-2006; Chapl Chld's Hosp Med Cntr Cincinnati OH 1993-2000; Chapl H Trin Sch Kenwood OH 1993-1997. NAAD.

GLANCEY, Bryan Eaton (Eas) 1205 Frederick Ave, Salisbury MD 21801 **S Andr's Hurlock MD 2003-** B Poughkeepsie NY 1950 s Charles & Joyce. BA Marist Coll 1972; MDiv GTS 1977. D 6/11/1977 Bp Paul Moore Jr P 12/20/1977 Bp Harold Louis Wright. m 6/6/1970 Barbara Glancey c 1. Ch Of S Paul's By The Sea Ocean City MD 1993-2003; Ch Of The H Comm Lake View NY 1989-1993; S Steph's Ch Niagara Falls NY 1987-1989; Chr Ch Albion NY 1986-1987; Vic Chr Epis Ch Danville VA 1980-1985; P-in-c Gr Epis Ch Port Jervis NY 1977-1980; Asst Min Ch Of The Gd Shpd And S Jn Milford PA 1977-1978. Auth, *Fam Plan for Ch Stwdshp*. CCN; Curs.

GLANDON, Clyde Calvin (Okla) 4223 E 84th St, Tulsa OK 74137 B Kansas City KS 1947 s Clyde & Virginia. BA U of Kansas 1969; MDiv EDS 1972; DMin Phillips TS 1994; DMin Phillips TS 1994. D 6/4/1972 Bp Edward Clark Turner P 3/1/1973 Bp Harold Barrett Robinson. m 1/25/1970 Shirley Glandon c 1. Exec Dir Cntr for Counslg And Educ 1993-2008; Assoc R Trin Ch Tulsa OK 1985-1995; R S Paul's Epis Ch Harris Hill Buffalo NY 1977-1985; Asst S Jas' Ch Batavia NY 1975-1977; Asst S Paul's Cathd Buffalo NY 1972-1974. "Pstr Counslg as a Pract of Psychoynamic Sprtlty," Journ of Pstr Care, 2000.

GLANVILLE, Polly Ann (O) 1945 26th Street, Cuyahoga Falls OH 44223 **D - Sr Mnstry S Paul's Ch Akron OH 2002-** B Salem OH 1943 d George & Susan.

BA OH SU 1965. D 11/8/1996 Bp J Clark Grew II. m 8/27/1966 Richard Harris Glanville c 2. D St. Phil's Ch Akron OH 1997-2001; S Phil's Epis Ch Akron OH 1996-2001. NAAD 1996.

GLASER, David Charles (Mich) 20500 W OLD US HIGHWAY 12, Chelsea MI 48118 **R S Barn' Ch Chelsea MI 2010-; D S Barn' Ch 2005-** B Detroit, MI 1963 s Charles & Margaret. BBA Estrn Michican U 1985. D 1/30/2010 P 11/20/2010 Bp Wendell Nathaniel Gibbs Jr. Soc of Cath Priests 2011.

GLASER, Geoffrey Scott (ECR) 3631 W Avenida Obregon, Tucson AZ 85746 B Bloomington IL 1964 s Walter & Madeline. BS U of Nthrn Colorado 1985; MA San Jose St U 1991; MDiv CDSP 1997. D 12/16/1998 P 6/16/1999 Bp Richard Lester Shimpfky. Int S Raphael In The Vlly Epis Ch Benson AZ 2008-2009; St Agnes RC Ch San Francisco CA 2003-2006; Assoc Ch Of The Adv Of Chr The King San Francisco CA 2001-2006; The Epis Sanctuary San Francisco CA 2001-2006; Vic Ch Of S Jos Milpitas CA 1999-2001.

GLASGOW, Laurette Alice (Eur) 2 Chaussee De Charleroi, Braine-I'Alleud Belgium 1420 Belgium **Asst R All SS Ch Waterloo Belgium 2008-** B Canada 1950 d Raymond & Marie-Anne. BA U of Manitoba 1971; MA Jn Hopkins 1977; Oxf GB 2007. D 10/20/2007 P 10/11/2008 Bp Pierre W Whalon. m 12/11/1982 Ross Glasgow c 2. All SS Epis Ch Braine-I'Alleud 2008-2009; Chapl - Pstr Care All SS Ch Waterloo Belgium 2006-2008; Pstr Intern The Amer Cathd of the H Trin Paris 75008 2004-2006.

GLASS, Rosalee Tyree (Me) B Key West FL 1943 BA Sthrn Connecticut St U 1966; MDiv Bangor TS 2005. D 6/18/2005 Bp Chilton Richardson Knudsen. m 6/2/1964 Christopher Glass. D Ch Of S Thos Camden ME 2005-2013.

GLASS, Vanessa (Cal) St. Francis of Assisi Episcopal Church, 967 5th Street, Novato CA 94945 **R S Fran Of Assisi Ch Novato CA 2011-; Vocational Fac Credo Inst Inc. Memphis TN 2011.** B San Francisco CA 1971 d Ralph & Thala. BA California St U 1996; MDiv CDSP 2001. D 6/2/2001 P 12/1/2001 Bp William Edwin Swing. c 2. Gr Cathd San Francisco CA 2007-2011, 2002-2003; S Paul's Epis Ch San Rafael CA 2006-2007. contributing Auth, "Lenten Meditation," *Lenten Meditations*, Epis Relief & Dvlpmt, 2013; contributing Auth, "Committees, Commissions, Agencies and Boards," *Shared Governance: The Polity of the Epis Ch*, Ch Pub, 2012. rector@stfrancisnovato.org

GLASSER, Joanne Kathleen (Eau) 111 9th St N, La Crosse WI 54601 **D Chr Ch Par La Crosse WI 2008-** B Canada 1952 d Edwin & Edith. BA U of Alberta 1973; MS USC 1979; MBA U of St Thos 1988; PhD Capella U 2005. D 5/31/2008 Bp Keith Whitmore. m 12/27/1995 James Glasser.

✠ **GLASSPOOL, The Rt Rev Mary Douglas** (NY) Episcopal Diocese of New York, 1047 Amsterdam Ave, New York NY 10025 **Dio New York New York NY 2016-; JSCN The Epis Ch New York NY 2015-** B Staten Island NY 1954 d Douglas & Ann. BA Dickinson Coll 1976; MDiv EDS 1981; Merrill Schlr Harvard DS 2006. D 6/13/1981 Bp Paul Moore Jr P 3/6/1982 Bp Lyman Cunningham Ogilby Con 5/15/2010 for Los. m 2/23/2015 Rebecca Leigh Sander. Bp Suffr of Los Angeles Dio Los Angeles Los Angeles CA 2010-2016; Cn Dio Maryland Baltimore MD 2001-2010, Dep to GC 2000-2010, Pres of Stndg Com 1995-1998; R S Marg's Ch Annapolis MD 1992-2001; R S Lk's And S Marg's Ch Allston MA 1984-1992; Asst S Paul's Ch Philadelphia PA 1981-1984; Joint Nomin Com for PBp The Epis Ch New York NY 2012-2015; SCMD The Epis Ch New York NY 2011-2015; Bd Mem Epis City Mssn Boston MA 1985-1991. Contrib, "Remembrance, Witness, and Action: Fuel for the Journey," *Wmn, Sprtlty and Transformative Ldrshp: Where Gr Meets Power*, Skylight Paths, 2011. Epis Cmnty Serv of Maryland 1993-2000; Soc of S Jn the Evang 1982. Hon Doctorate EDS 2011; Lenten Mssnr Memi Ch, Harv 2007; Bp's Awd for Outstanding Ord Mnstry Dio Maryland 1999. bpglasspool@dioceseny.org

GLAUDE, Ronald Arthur (Ct) 125 Grand View Ter, Brooklyn CT 06234 B Putnam CT 1936 s Joseph & Aurore. BA U of Connecticut 1974; MDiv EDS 1977. D 6/11/1977 Bp Joseph Warren Hutchens P 5/27/1978 Bp Morgan Porteus. m 6/28/1958 Grace C Glaude c 3. R Trin Ch Brooklyn CT 1980-2008; Cur S Jn's Ch Stamford CT 1977-1979. CHS.

GLAZIER JR, George H (SO) 10 E. Weber Rd #305, Columbus OH 43202 **P-in-c Trin Epis Ch London OH 2016-** B Huntington WV 1954 s George & Charlotte. BA Marshall U 1976; MDiv VTS 1979; DMin Sewanee: The U So, TS 2005. D 6/6/1979 P 6/4/1980 Bp Robert Poland Atkinson. m 8/1/1992 Pamela D Hootman c 2. R S Steph's Epis Ch And U Columbus OH 2001-2014; R Gr Ch Chattanooga TN 1995-2001; R Trin Ch Allnce OH 1985-1995; Assoc S Paul's Epis Ch Winston Salem NC 1982-1985; S Matt's Ch Wheeling WV 1979-1982. Soc of S Jn the Evang.

GLAZIER II, William Stuart (Ct) 30 Ice House Ln, Mystic CT 06355 **Ret 1974-** B New York NY 1925 s Philip & Clare. BA Trin Hartford CT 1948; MDiv VTS 1956; PhD Hartford Sem 1974. D 6/17/1952 P 12/1/1952 Bp Walter H Gray. m 1/1/2000 Lois Ann Glazier c 3. Vic All SS Ch Ivoryton CT 1963-1965; S Paul's Ch Westbrook CT 1963-1965; Asst Gr Epis Ch New York NY 1961-1963; P S Paul's Ch Windham CT 1956-1961; R Chr Unionville CT 1952-1955; P Trin Epis Ch Collinsville CT 1952-1955. Chapl 100th Infantry Div Assn 1994.

GLEASON, David Thomas (WA) PO Box 1617, Evergreen CO 80437 **Ret 1990-** B Rochester NY 1923 s Harold & Marion. BA U Roch 1948; LTh SWTS 1952; BD SWTS 1953. D 6/8/1952 P 12/19/1952 Bp Dudley S Stark. m 2/11/1956 Janice Clise Gleason c 3. Pstr Inter Faith Chap Leisure Wrld Silver Sprg MD 1975-1990; Assoc Inter Faith Chap Leisure Wrld Silver Sprg MD 1972-1975; Asst Pstr Inter Faith Chap Leisure Wrld Silver Sprg MD 1969-1972; Chapl/Instr S Jn's Ch Olney MD 1965-1972; R S Matt Seat Pleasant MD 1956-1965; Cur Trin Ch Geneva NY 1954-1956; Gr Ch Scottsville NY 1952-1954; Vic S Andr's Epis Ch Caledonia NY 1952-1954.

GLEASON, Dorothy Jean (SJ) Po Box 399, Ambridge PA 15003 B 1943 Cert California St U; AA Los Angeles Vlly Coll. D 4/9/2000 Bp David Mercer Schofield. SAMS Ambridge PA 2002-2003; D All SS Ch.

GLEASON, Edward Campbell (SwFla) 553 Galleon Dr, Naples FL 34102 **Sr Assoc R Trin By The Cove Naples FL 2011-, Assoc 2009-** B New Orleans LA 1974 s Harvey & Mary Frances. BA U of Texas 1996; JD Loyola U Sch of Law 2000; MDiv Nash 2008. D 12/29/2007 P 6/29/2008 Bp Charles Edward Jenkins III. m 12/4/2004 Virginia Johnson Gleason c 3. Cur & Chapl S Lk's Ch Baton Rouge LA 2008-2009. egleason@trinitybythecove.com

GLEAVES, Donna Jeanne (Mont) 5 West Olive St, Bozeman MT 59715 **Admin S Ptr's Cathd Helena MT 2015-** B Quonset Point RI 1952 d Donald & Jeanne. BS Old Dominion U 1973; n.a. Montana Sch for Deacons 2011; n.a. Other 2011. D 10/30/2011 Bp Charles Franklin Brookhart Jr. m 5/25/2002 Glen Lee Gleaves c 1. D S Jas Ch Bozeman MT 2011-2013; Admin Upper Yellowstone Epis Ch Livingston MT 2008-2011; Mem, Dioc Coun Dio Montana Helena MT 2005-2008. Assn of Epis Deacons 2008.

GLEAVES, Glen Lee (Mont) 1226 Wildflower Trl, Livingston MT 59047 **P/T R H Trin 2004-; Ret 1996-** B Fairhope AL 1951 s Donald & Leona. BA U of So Alabama 1974; MS U of Sthrn Mississippi 1982; MDiv SWTS 1988. D 6/4/1988 P 4/4/1989 Bp Charles Farmer Duvall. m 5/25/2002 Donna Jeanne Tilton c 1. Asst S Andr's Ch Livingston MT 2008-2011; p/t Asst Upper Yellowstone Epis Ch Livingston MT 2008-2011; p/t P-in-c H Trin Epis Ch Troy MT 2004-2008; S Lk's Ch Libby MT 2004-2008; p/t Asstg P S Paul's Ch Salt Lake City UT 1996-2002; Dio Utah Salt Lake City UT 1993-1996; S Paul's Epis Ch Vernal UT 1990-1992; D-In-Trng S Lk's Epis Ch Mobile AL 1988-1989.

GLEESON, Terence Patrick (ECR) All Saints Church, 555 Waverley Street, Palo Alto CA 94301 **R All SS Epis Ch Palo Alto CA 2011-** B Sydney Australia 1954 s Terence & Marie. BTh Cath Inst of Sydney 1980; MEd U of Wollongong 1987; STM GTS 2002. Rec 10/4/2003 Bp Catherine Scimeca Roskam. m 4/14/2011 Dennis L Manalo c 1. R S Steph's Ch Middlebury VT 2005-2011; Asst to R Chr And S Steph's Ch New York NY 2003-2005; Serv as RC P 1980-1993.

GLENDENNING, Audrey Geraldine (SeFla) 3322 Meridian Way N Apt A, Palm Beach Gardens FL 33410 B Centerville PA 1927 d Russell & Christine. BS Palm Bch Atlantic U 1982. D 6/20/1998 Bp Calvin Onderdonk Schofield Jr. D Gr Ch W Palm Bch FL 1998-2010.

GLENDINNING, David Cross (Me) 221 Shelburne Rd, Burlington VT 05401 **Ret 1997-; Hon Cn Cathd Ch Of S Lk Portland ME 2012-** B Lawrence MA 1936 s Geoffrey & Eve. BA Dart 1958; BD EDS 1961. D 6/25/1961 Bp Donald J Campbell P 1/6/1962 Bp Oliver L Loring. m 1/24/1982 Dorothy Glendinning c 3. P-in-c Chr Ch Biddeford ME 1994-1997; Int S Geo's Epis Ch Sanford ME 1992-1993; Int S Barth's Epis Ch Yarmouth ME 1990-1991; R S Paul's Ch Concord NH 1982-1989; R S Mk's Ch Waterville ME 1969-1982; R S Andr And S Jn Epis Ch SW Hbr ME 1963-1969; Cur Trin Epis Ch Portland ME 1961-1963.

GLENN JR, Charles Leslie (Mass) 1 Robeson St, Boston MA 02130 B Cambridge MA 1938 s Charles & Georgiana. CDSP; EDS; BA Harv; U of Tuebingen Germany; EdD Harv 1972; PhD Bos 1987. D 7/22/1963 P 6/5/1964 Bp John Melville Burgess. m 4/30/1977 Mary Glenn c 5. Asst Ch Of The H Sprt Mattapan MA 1983-1998; S Jn's Ch Jamaica Plain MA 1979-1986; Non-par 1971-1983; Epis Ch Cntr New York NY 1966-1968; Asst S Jn's S Jas Epis Ch Boston MA 1963-1965. Co-Auth w Jan De Groof, "Balancing Freedom, Autonomy, and Accountability in Educ , vol 1-3," Wolf Legal Pub (Netherlands), 2004; Auth, "The Ambiguous Embrace: Govt and Faith-based Schools and Soc Agencies," Princeton U Press, 2000; Auth, "Educating Immigrant Chld," Garland, 1996; Auth, "Educational Freedom In Estrn Europe," Cate Inst Press, 1995; Auth, "Choice Of Schools In Six Nations," US Dept of Educ, 1989; Auth, "Myth Of The Common Schlr," U of Massachusetts Press, 1988; Auth, "200 Bk chapters and arts," Var. Annual Ldrshp Awd Cntr for Publ Justice 2000; Phi Beta Kappa Harvard 1959.

GLENN, Kim B (SwVa) 200 Boston Ave, Lynchburg VA 24503 **S Jn's Ch Lynchburg VA 2015-** B Lexington VA 1957 d Irvine & Courtney. MACE Un Presb Sem 2005; MDiv Un Presb Sem 2013; MDiv Un Presb Sem 2013; MDiv Un Presb Sem 2013; Angl Stds Dplma VTS 2015. D 6/6/2015 Bp Shannon Sherwood Johnston. m 6/5/1982 Charles Erskine Buford Glenn c 3.

GLENN, Lawrance Gail (FdL) 1230 Sandpebble Dr., Rockton IL 61072 B Amboy IL 1953 s Willard & Carol. Black Hawk Coll; Moody Bible Inst; BA SUNY 1981; MDiv Bethel TS 1989; STM Nash 2001; PsyD GTF 2008. D 7/12/1998 P 1/28/1999 Bp Keith Lynn Ackerman. m 8/3/1978 Terri Glenn c 3. R Ch Of S Mary Of The Snows Eagle River WI 1999-2006; Int S Geo's Ch Macomb IL 1999; D S Ptr's Ch Canton IL 1998-1999; Chapl Illinois St Police 1994-1996; Pstr First Bapt Ch Bushnell IL 1990-1999; Chapl US Army Reserve 1987-1998.

GLENN, Michael Eugene (Okla) 106 E Crawford St, Palestine TX 75801 B Philadelphia PA 1959 s James & Ruth. BA Emory U 1981; MDiv Candler TS Emory U 1984; MA Emory U 1991. D 6/27/1992 Bp Maurice Manuel Benitez P 2/2/1993 Bp William Jackson Cox. Gd Shpd Epis Ch Sapulpa OK 2006-2007; R S Phil's Epis Ch Palestine TX 1994-2004; Asst to R Chr Epis Ch Tyler TX 1992-1994. Auth, "Uncovering Oedipus: Freud'S Choice Of The Oedipus Story In The Light Of His Personal Chld Abuse", Umi, 1991; Auth, "His Personal Chld Abuse Issues". Rotary Intl 1995. Paul Harris Fell Rotary 2002.

GLENN, Patricia Foster (Mo) 19424 Highway 54, Louisiana MO 63353 **R Calv Ch Louisiana MO 2007-; R S Jn's Ch Prairieville Eolia MO 2007-** B Cedar Rapid IA 1950 d Fred & Eileen. MercyHospital Sch of Nrsng 1971; BS MacMurray Coll 1977; Epis Sch for Mnstry 2007. D 12/20/2006 P 6/23/2007 Bp George Wayne Smith. m 4/19/1975 Edward Glenn c 5. Chapl Pike Cnty Hospice 2007-2010.

GLENNIE, Jannel (Mich) 294 Willoughby Rd, Mason MI 48854 **Sprtl Dir Lumen Hse 2008-; systems theory Instr Lumen Hse/St. Fran Retreat Cntr 2005-** B Grand Rapids MI 1947 d Harold & Virginia. BA U of Arizona 1980; MDiv SWTS 1988. D 6/25/1988 Bp Henry Irving Mayson P 4/22/1989 Bp R aymond Stewart Wood Jr. m 8/12/1967 James Glennie c 2. R S Kath's Ch Williamston MI 1996-2009; Asst All SS Ch E Lansing MI 1994-1996; Chapl M.S.U. E Lansing MI 1989-1996; S Dav's Ch Lansing MI 1989-1990; Cbury MI SU E Lansing MI 1988-1996; Stndg Com Dio Michigan Detroit MI 1997-2000. Auth, "Translations:Dance of Word and Image," *poetry and art*, Self-Pub, 2014; Auth, "Confessions Of An Ordnry Mystic," Greenleaf Bk Grp, 2000. Sprtl Dir Intl 2009. Hon Cn Dio Michigan 2014.

GLICK, Phillip Randall (EC) 184 Watersedge Drive, Kill Devil Hills NC 27948 **R S Andr's By The Sea Nags Hd NC 2010-; Spec Mobilization Spprt Plan Washington DC 2010-** B Burlington WI 1952 s W Myron & Lucinda. U of Wisconsin 1972; BA Methodist U 1982; MDiv Sewanee: The U So, TS 1986. D 6/24/1986 P 1/10/1987 Bp Brice Sidney Sanders. m 9/11/1976 Barbara Ilse Muldrow c 3. Pension Fund Mltry New York NY 2008-2010; S Dav's Epis Ch No Chesterfield VA 2001-2008; Chapl No Carolina NG 1989-2012; S Thos' Epis Ch Ahoskie NC 1989-2001; Asst S Mary's Ch Kinston NC 1987; R Ch Of The H Innoc Seven Sprg NC 1986-1989. The Bro of S Andr 2011; The Ord of the Long Leaf Pine 2012. The Dubose Awd for Serv The TS, The U So 2010.

GLIDDEN OSB, Charles Aelred (FdL) 56500 Abbey Rd, Three Rivers MI 49093 **St Greg's Abbey Three Rivers MI 2014-; Prior S Greg Abbey Three Rivers MI 1989-; Novc Mstr S Greg Abbey Three Rivers MI 1982-; Life Professed S Greg Abbey Three Rivers MI 1981-; Mem S Greg Abbey Three Rivers MI 1975-** B Zanesville OH 1952 s Charles & Beatrice. Mia 1974. D 6/18/1992 P 12/21/1992 Bp William Louis Stevens. Auth, "Var arts," *Abbey Letter*; Auth, "Abbot Primate, Benedictine," *Encyclopedia of Monasticism*; Auth, "Aelred the Hist," *Erudition in God's Serv*.

GLIDDEN, Richard Mark (Chi) 49 Larbert Rd # 6490, Southport CT 06890 B 1943 STB GTS; Cert Inst Rel & Hlth; BA Lawr. D 6/15/1968 Bp James Winchester Montgomery P 12/21/1968 Bp Gerald Francis Burrill. m 4/27/1985 Susan Campbell Glidden. Epis Mssn Soc New York NY 1984-1985; S Lk's-Roosevelt Hosp Cntr New York NY 1971-1975; The Ch Of The H Sprt Lake Forest IL 1968-1970; Hon Assoc Ch Of The Ascen. AAPC, Aamft.

GLOFF, Holly M (NC) 1520 Canterbury Rd, Raleigh NC 27608 **Asst R S Mich's Ch Raleigh NC 2006-** B Norwalk CT 1955 d Donald & Kathleen. BA Fairfield U 1977; MDiv VTS 2006. D 6/24/2006 Bp Peter J Lee. m 11/16/1996 Robert Gloff c 2. gloff@holymichael.org

GLOSSON HAMMONS, Jamesetta (Los) 1508 W 145th St, Compton CA 90220 **Asst S Barn' Par Pasadena CA 2006-** B Chicago Cook Co. IL 1945 d James & Martina. AA Compton Coll; BS U of Phoenix 1999; MA Fuller TS 2006. D 12/2/2006 Bp Joseph Jon Bruno. c 3. Dio Los Angeles Los Angeles CA 2010-2017; Episcipal Healthcare Providers Los Angeles CA 2008; Supvsr Of Governmental Billing Cnty Of Los Angeles 1974-2004. jhamo4@msn.com

✠ **GLOSTER, The Rt Rev James Gary** (NC) 2236 Fernbank Dr, Charlotte NC 28226 **Asstg Bp S Mary Of The Hills Epis Par Blowing Rock NC 2007-** B Hopkinsville KY 1936 s James & Nancy. BA Wabash Coll 1959; MDiv VTS 1962; DMin VTS 1990; VTS 1997. D 6/16/1962 P 12/1/1962 Bp John P Craine Con 7/27/1996 for NC. m 6/7/1958 Julia H Gloster. Asstg Bp Dio No Carolina Raleigh NC 2004-2007; Ret Bp Suffr of No Carolina 2004-; Suffr Bp of No Carolina 1996-2004; Vic Chap Of Chr The King Charlotte NC 1989-1996; Chr Ch Charlotte NC 1980-1989; R Chr Epis Ch Pulaski VA 1972-1980; Assoc The Ch of the Redeem Cincinnati OH 1968-1971; Prog Dir Waycross Camp & Conf Cntr IN 1966-1967; Dir Dioc Camps 1962-1971; Vic S Aug's Epis Ch Danville IN 1962-1966.

GLOVER, Beth Faulk (Nwk) 29 Village Gate Way, Nyack NY 10960 **Assoc S Aug's Epis Ch Croton Hdsn NY 2011-, 2008-2011; S Paul's Epis Ch Paterson NJ 2011-; Dir of Pstr Care and Educ New York Presb Hosp New York City NY 2007-** B Richmond VA 1966 d Bobby & Barbara. BA W&M 1988; MDiv UTS 1991; DMin NYTS 2007; STM GTS 2008. D 6/13/2002 Bp Rufus T Brome P 12/14/2002 Bp John Palmer Croneberger. Chr Hosp Jersey City NJ 2002-2007.

GLOVER, Betty Marie (Kan) Saint David's Episcopal Church, 3916 SW 17th St, Topeka KS 66604 **Dio Kansas Topeka KS 2017-, Elected Mem of Syn 2011-, Elected Dep to GC/2012 2010-, Chair, Nomin & Election Com 2009-2012, Chapl, Kansas Sch for Mnstry 2009-2012, Mem, Liturg, Arts & Mus Com 2009-2010, Elected Mem of Coun of Trst 2008-2012, Mem, COM 2008-2012** B Camp Roberts CA 1952 d Harold & Vila. BA New Mex Highlands U 1991; MSW U of Kansas 1992; M.Div VTS 2007. D 2/2/1997 Bp William Edward Smalley P 6/23/2007 Bp Dean E Wolfe. c 2. P-in-c S Dav's Epis Ch Topeka KS 2015-2017; Int S Phil's Ch Southport NC 2014-2015; Int R Ch Of The Gd Shpd Rocky Mt NC 2012-2014; Police Chapl Winfield Police Dept 2009-2012; R Gr Epis Ch Winfield KS 2007-2012; P-in-c Gr Epis and Trin Epis Winfield KS 2007-2012; Trin Ch Arkansas City KS 2007-2012; Hosp Chapl Stormont Vail Hlth Cntr 1997-2006; R Dio Cathd Topeka KS 1997-2002; Police Chapl Topeka Police Dept KS. Intl Conf of Police Chapl.

GLOVER, Hazel Smith (At) 606 Newnan St, Carrollton GA 30117 **Int S Paul's Epis Ch Newnan GA 2016-; Int Chair, COM Epis Dio Atlanta 2012-; Dn, SW Atlanta Convoc Epis Dio Atlanta 2004-** B LaGrange GA 1952 d Clarence & Martha. MPA Georgia St U 1981; BBA U of W Georgia 1981; MDiv Sewanee: The U So, TS 1993. D 6/5/1993 P 12/11/1993 Bp Frank Kellogg Allan. c 3. R S Marg's Ch Carrollton GA 2002-2016; Assoc R S Cathr's Epis Ch Marietta GA 1996-2002; Gr Ch Whiteville NC 1996; Vic Ch Of The Trsfg Rome GA 1993-1995; Vic S Jas Ch Cedartown GA 1993-1995.

GLOVER, John Frederick (Va) 14449 S Eastside Hwy, Grottoes VA 24441 **Ret 2003-** B Charleston WV 1936 s Andrew & Opal. BA Marshall U 1958; MDiv Colgate Rochester Crozer DS 1962; MDiv CRDS 1962. D 3/11/1965 P 8/6/1965 Bp Wilburn Camrock Campbell. m 5/30/1981 Susan Beth Glover c 2. R Emm Ch Harrisonburg VA 1989-2002; R Chr Ch Austin MN 1981-1989; Stndg Com Dio W Virginia Charleston WV 1976-1981, Eccl Crt 1969-1972; R Trin Ch Morgantown WV 1967-1976; R S Paul's Ch Weston WV 1965-1967; Serv Bapt Ch 1959-1964.

GLOVER, Marsha Bacon (NY) 122 Grandview Ave, White Plains NY 10605 B New York NY 1947 d Benjamin & Marguerite. BA U of Pennsylvania 1969; Col 1972; JD U of Pennsylvania 1972; MDiv Ya Berk 1994. D 6/11/1994 P 12/1/1994 Bp Richard Frank Grein. c 2. S Barth's Ch In The Highland White Plains NY 2007-2009; R S Ptr's Ch Bronx NY 2001-2007; Chr's Ch Rye NY 1997-2001; Asst S Jas Ch New York NY 1996; Asst Ch Of S Mary The Vrgn Chappaqua NY 1994-1995.

GLOVER, Mary Elizabeth (NwT) 891 Davis Dr, Abilene TX 79605 **R S Mk's Epis Ch Abilene TX 2012-, P-in-c 2011-** B Abilene TX 1956 d Billy & Bettie. BS McMurry U 1978; JD S Marys U San Antonio TX 1988; MDiv Epis TS of the SW 2001. D 12/20/2000 P 6/30/2001 Bp C Wallis Ohl. Assoc R Ch of the Heav Rest Abilene Abilene TX 2006-2010; R Trin Ch Independence MO 2003-2006; Assoc R S Andr's Epis Ch Amarillo TX 2001-2003; Dioc Educ Cmsn Dio W Missouri Kansas City MO 2004-2006. maryglover@juno.com

GLUCKOW, Kenneth Allan (NJ) 70 Mount Tabor Way, Ocean Grove NJ 07756 **Trin Epis Ch Red Bank NJ 2005-; The Ch Of S Uriel The Archangel Sea Girt NJ 2004-; Ret 2003-** B New York NY 1931 s Benjamin & Pauline. Cert RCA Inst 1957. D 4/19/1969 P 10/1/1969 Bp Alfred L Banyard. R Emer S Jas Ch Bradley Bch NJ 2003-2013, 1973-2002; The Ch of S Matt And S Tim New York NY 2003-2004; S Andr The Apos Highland Highlands NJ 1977-1978; Vic S Andr's Highlands NY 1977-1978; Asst Trin Ch Asbury Pk NJ 1969-1977. R Emer S Jas Ch 2003.

GNASSO, Enrico Mario (Los) 10961 Desert Lawn Dr Spc 252, Calimesa CA 92320 **Died 3/23/2017** B Fort Lee NJ 1928 s Enrico & Margaret. BBA Pace U 1955; BD SWTS 1964; MS U of Wisconsin 1971; CPA St of Wisconsin 1972. D 6/13/1964 Bp Leland Stark P 12/13/1964 Bp Russell T Rauscher. m 6/25/1955 Edith Marvin Gnasso c 3. Asstg Gr Mssn Moreno Vlly CA 2001-2017; Ret 1993-2017; P-in-c S Mart-In-The-Fields Mssn Twentynine Plms CA 1991-1993; P-in-c S Chris's Ch Trona CA 1987-1991; P-in-c S Geo Milwaukee WI 1974-1975; Int Dio Milwaukee Milwaukee WI 1971-1979; R S Lk's Ch Whitewater WI 1967-1971; Bursar Bexley Seabury Fed Chicago IL 1966-1967; Pastr Cmnty Ch El Portal CA 1965-1966; P-in-c Gr Ch Red Cloud NE 1964-1965; S Jn's Mssn Harvard NE 1964-1965; P-in-c S Mk's Epis Pro-Cathd Hastings NE 1964-1965.

GOBER, Patricia Derr (Mass) 17 Leroy St, Attleboro MA 02703 B Aberdeen SD 1942 d John & Nina. BA U of So Dakota 1965; MDiv Epis TS of the SW 1983. D 6/24/1983 P 1/6/1984 Bp Jackson Earle Gilliam. m 8/23/1975 Wallace Gene Gober c 3. Int Ch Of The Ascen Fall River MA 2005-2008; Mssnr Bristol Cluster No Easton MA 1994-2005; Cluster Mssnr S Jn The Evang Mansfield MA 1994-2005; S Mk's Ch No Easton MA 1994-2005; Co-Mssnr Tri-Cnty Epis Area Mnstry Monticello NY 1986-1994; Int S Andr's Ch Philipsburg MT 1985-1986; The Pintler Cluster of the Epis Ch Deer Lodge MT 1985-1986; Int S Marks Pintler Cluster Anaconda MT 1985; Cur S Jas Ch Bozeman MT 1983-1986. Dio Ma Stndg Com 2000-2001.

GOBER, Wallace Gene (Mass) 17 Leroy St, Attleboro MA 02703 B Klamath Falls OR 1939 s Clarence & Mary. BA Sthrn Oregon U 1961; DA U of Oregon 1970; MDiv Epis TS of the SW 1983; MA Iona Coll 1989. D 6/24/1983 P

1/6/1984 Bp Jackson Earle Gilliam. m 8/23/1975 Patricia Derr Gober c 2. Int St. Steph's/St. Jn's Partnership 2005-2008; S Jn's/S Steph's Ch Fall River MA 2005-2006; S Dav's Epis Ch Halifax MA 2002-2005; Chr Ch Quincy MA 2000-2002; Chr Ch Waltham MA 1999-2000; All SS Ch Chelmsford MA 1998-1999; Int Dio Massachusetts Boston MA 1996-2000, Ipc Rep Dioc Coun 1986-1995; S Andr's Ch New Bedford MA 1995-1997; S Greg's Epis Ch Woodstock NY 1993-1994; Dioc Int Consult Dio New York New York NY 1990-1995; Assoc Tri-Cnty Epis Area Clustr Mnstry 1987-1990; Tri-Cnty Epis Area Mnstry Monticello NY 1986-1993; S Jas Ch Bozeman MT 1983-1986; Asst The Pintler Cluster of the Epis Ch Deer Lodge MT 1983-1986. AAPC.

GOCHA, Teresa Payne (NH) 477 Main St, Plymouth NH 03264 **Vic Ch Of The Mssh No Woodstock NH 2003-; Vic Ch of the Mssh No Woodstock NH 2002-; Stndg Com Dio New Hampshire Concord NH 2012-, Search Com 2011-2012, Mem, COM 1995-, Chapl, AIDS Com 1989-1991** B New York NY 1959 d Edd & Mary. BA Trin 1981; MDiv GTS 1987. D 6/13/1987 Bp David Elliot Johnson P 6/9/1988 Bp Douglas Edwin Theuner. m 8/18/1990 James Gocha c 3. P-in-c S Judes Epis Ch Franklin NH 2000-2002; S Jude's Ch Franklin NH 2000-2002; Int S Steph's Ch Pittsfield NH 1999-2000; Ch Of The H Sprt Plymouth NH 1991-1999, R 1991; Chapl Plymouth St Coll Plymouth NH 1991-1999; Cur S Paul's Ch Concord NH 1988-1991.

GOCKLEY, Mary Jane (Neb) PO Box 353, Broken Bow NE 68822 **P-in-c S Jn's Ch Broken Bow NE 2010-** B Harrisburg PA 1936 d Harold & Gladys. RN Harrisburg Hosp Sch 1957; BS Albright Coll 1960. D 5/31/2010 P 12/18/2010 Bp Joe Goodwin Burnett. c 4.

GODBOLD, Richard Rives (Ind) 829 Wiltshire Dr, Evansville IN 47715 B Montgomery AL 1949 s John & Elizabeth. BA Dart 1972; MDiv EDS 1988; DMin SWTS 2001. D 8/24/1988 Bp William Davidson P 3/19/1989 Bp Terence Kelshaw. m 2/24/1979 Catherine Ann Godbold c 2. R S Paul's Epis Ch Evansville IN 2003-2015; Trin On The Hill Epis Ch Los Alamos NM 1997-2003, Assoc R 1997-2003, Cur 1988-1990; Asst To Dn S Jn's Cathd Albuquerque NM 1994-1997; R S Phil's Ch Rio Communities NM 1990-1994; Alt Dep, GC Dio Indianapolis Indianapolis IN 2010-2013, Exec Coun 2008-2012, Stndg Com 2004-2008; COM Chair Dio The Rio Grande Albuquerque 2000-2002, Co Chair 2000-, Dioc Cmsn 1999, Alt Dep, GC 1998-2001, Exec Com of Dioc Coun 1996-1998, Yth Dir 1994-1998, Dioc Coun 1993-1998, CE Cmsn 1991-1994.

GODDARD, John R (Nev) 10465 SE Waverly Ct Apt 2018, Milwaukie OR 97222 **R Dio Oregon Portland OR 2016-** B Saint Louis MO 1942 s John & Jane. BBA New Mex St U 1965; MDiv CDSP 1976; Cert Int Mnstry Ntwk 2001; Cert Other 2001; Cert Appreciative Inquiry Trng 2004; Cert Other 2004. D 8/6/1976 P 3/7/1977 Bp Richard Mitchell Trelease Jr. m 11/11/2004 Carol M Goddard c 2. Int Trin Epis Ch Ashland Ashland OR 2010-2011; Int S Jn's Epis Ch Chula Vista CA 2009-2010; Int S Marg's Ch Lawr KS 2008-2009; Int Trin Epis Ch Reno NV 2005-2008; Int All SS Epis Ch Boise ID 2002-2005; Int S Jas Pullman WA 2001-2002; R St Dav's Epis Ch Minnetonka MN 1992-1996; R Trin Ch Marshfield MA 1987-1992; R S Thos A Becket Ch Roswell NM 1980-1987; R S Fran Epis Ch Tyler TX 1978; Asst S Chris's Epis Ch Hobbs NM 1976-1978; Mem Personl Ctm 2004-2005.

GODDARD, Paul Dillon (Chi) 742 Sand Dollar Dr, Sanibel FL 33957 **Ret 1988-** B Lancaster PA 1938 s Alpheus & Margaret. BA U So 1960; STB GTS 1963; LLD S Augustines Coll Raleigh NC 1976. D 6/15/1963 P 12/19/1963 Bp James Winchester Montgomery. Ecum Off Dio Chicago Chicago IL 1975-1988, Coun Mem 1966-1972; Vic Gr Epis Ch Galena IL 1972-1988; Vic S Jude's Epis Ch Rochelle IL 1965-1972; Asst Chapl Nthrn Illinois U 1965-1968; Asst S Jn's Epis Ch Lancaster PA 1963-1965.

GODDEN, Edward Eastman (Del) 610 Lindsey Rd, Wilmington DE 19809 B Norfolk VA 1953 s Albert & Phyllis. BS Old Dominion U 1975; MDiv Sewanee: The U So, TS 1979. D 6/23/1979 P 3/19/1980 Bp Claude Charles Vache. c 3. Int R The Ch Of The Ascen Claymont DE 2010-2014; JSCN GC New York NY 2006-2009; Dio Delaware Wilmington DE 2000-2010; R Imm Ch On The Green New Castle DE 1989-2010; Dep GC 1988-2009; R Trin Ch Elkton MD 1983-1989; Cur Trin Ch Portsmouth VA 1979-1983; Dep, GC Dio Delaware Wilmington 2003-2009, Liturg Off 1996-2013; Dioc Coun Dio Easton Easton MD 1985-1989.

GODDERZ, Michael John (Mass) 209 Ashmont Street, Boston MA 02124 **R The Par Of All SS Ashmont-Dorches Boston MA 1998-** B Saint Paul MN 1952 s Hernando & Lols. BA Rutgers The St U of New Jersey 1974; MDiv Gordon-Conwell TS 1977; MA U Chi 1980. D 6/2/1984 Bp John Bowen Coburn P 6/22/1985 Bp Thomas Kreider Ray. m 6/23/1978 Ruth Martha Godderz c 1. R S Bride's Epis Ch Chesapeake VA 1991-1998; R S Barn Ch Norwich VT 1986-1991; Cur The Ch Of The Adv Boston MA 1984-1986; RurD Dio Massachusetts Boston MA 2008-2015; Chair, Archit Cmsn Dio Sthrn Virginia Newport News VA 1997-1998; Dioc Coun Dio Vermont Burlington VT 1987-1989. CCU 1998-2010; GAS 1999; SocMary 2017; SSC 1994. Phi Beta Kappa 1974.

GODFREY, Samuel Bisland (Miss) 1115 Main St., Vicksburg MS 39183 **R Chr Epis Ch Vicksburg MS 2011-** B Natchez MS 1955 s William & Irene. BS Rhodes Coll 1977; JD U of Mississippi 1983; MDiv Sewanee: The U So, TS 1997. D 6/14/1997 P 12/20/1997 Bp Alfred Marble Jr. m 12/29/1981 Patty N Godfrey c 1. Vic H Innoc' Epis Ch Como MS 1997-2011; P-in-c S Steph's Epis Ch Batesville MS 1997-2011.

GODFREY, Steven R (Ia) 339 Hickory Dr, Ames IA 50014 **Dio Iowa Des Moines IA 2015-, Dir of Cmncatn 2014-2015; S Andr's Ch Des Moines IA 2015-** B 1967 s Culver & Carolyn. BA U of Massachusetts 1993; MDiv EDS 2004. D 6/4/2005 Bp M(Arvil) Thomas Shaw P 1/7/2006 Bp Roy Frederick Cederholm Jr. m 7/2/2004 David M Martin. S Mart's Ch Perry IA 2014-2015; Gr Ch Boone IA 2014; R S Mart's Ch Des Plaines IL 2008-2013; Assoc R S Geo's Epis Ch York ME 2006-2008; Cler In Res Ch Of S Jn The Evang Boston MA 2005-2006; Mem of Congregations Cmsn Dio Chicago Chicago IL 2009-2010; Dioc Coun Dio Maine Portland ME 2006-2007. sgodfrey@iowaepiscopal.org

GODFREY, William Calvin (LI) 102 Thompson Blvd, Greenport NY 11944 **Ret 1993-** B Brooklyn NY 1927 s George & Vinetta. BA Ya 1947; MDiv Ya Berk 1950; MA LIU 1979. D 6/24/1950 P 3/10/1951 Bp James Pernette DeWolfe. m 5/31/1975 Irene Lesia Godfrey c 3. Int H Trin Epis Ch Hicksville NY 1993-1994; Vice-Pres Epis Hlth Serv Hempstead NY 1990-1993; S Johns Epis Hosp Far Rockaway NY 1985-1992; Asst Admin S Jn Hosp Smithown NY 1974-1990; Nassau Hosp Mineola NY 1973-1985; Bd Magrs Ch Charity Fndt 1954-1974; R Ch Of The Redeem Merrick NY 1954-1958; Stff Cathd Of The Incarn Garden City NY 1951-1954; Asst S Jos's Ch Queens Vlg NY 1950-1951. Auth, "Pictoral Hist Cathd Of The Incarn Garden City Ny," 1971. Amer Coll Of Hlth Care Executives 1979-1992. Theo Roosevelt Awd Nassau-Suffolk Hosp Coun 1970; DSC Dio Long Island 1962.

GODLEY, Robert James (NY) 4440 E Lady Banks Ln, Murrells Inlet SC 29565 **Ret Ret 2011-** B New York NY 1941 s Thomas & Mary. BA NYU 1971; MDiv GTS 1976. D 6/12/1976 Bp Paul Moore Jr P 12/18/1976 Bp Harold Louis Wright. m 4/14/1985 Betty Godley c 2. R S Barn Ch Ardsley NY 1977-2011; Asst Ch Of S Jas The Less Scarsdale NY 1976-1977.

GODSEY, Jeunee (SVa) 8706 Quaker Ln, North Chesterfield VA 23235 **R, Time-Certain S Mich's Ch Richmond VA 2012-** B San Gabriel CA 1963 d Jerry & Eleanor. BS Geo 1985; MDiv VTS 2000. D 6/24/2000 P 2/6/2001 Bp Peter J Lee. c 3. Cn for Congrl Dvlpmt Dio Sthrn Virginia Newport News VA 2010-2015; Campus Min Johns Memi Epis Ch Farmville VA 2010-2012; R S Anne's Ch Appomattox VA 2009-2012; Vic S Gabr's Epis Ch Leesburg VA 2003-2008; Asst S Jas' Epis Ch Leesburg VA 2000-2002. jgodsey@diosova.org

GODWIN, JD D (Oly) 2630 46th Ave SW, Seattle WA 98116 **Archv Bd The Epis Ch New York NY 2010-; Bd Archv Epis Ch Cntr New York NY 2010-, SCCM 1977-1985** B Fort Dodge IA 1944 s John & Virginia. Westmar Coll 1964; BA Drake U 1966; MDiv SWTS 1972; Coll of Preachers 1976. D 6/18/1972 P 12/20/1972 Bp Walter Cameron Righter. m 1/1/2012 David W Stinson. P-in-c S Jn The Bapt Epis Ch Seattle WA 2013-2015; R The Epis Ch Of The Trsfg Dallas TX 2000-2013, P 1982-2000; Bd Trst Bp. Mason Retreat Cntr Dallas TX 1985-1991; SCCM The Epis Ch New York NY 1977-1985; Vic S Mart's Ch Perry IA 1975-1981; Cur S Tim's Epis Ch W Des Moines IA 1972-1975; Secy Dio Conv Dio Dallas Dallas TX 1985-1989; Litur Cmsn Dio Iowa Des Moines IA 1976-1979. Associated Parishes; AAM; ADLMC; CEEP 2006; Epis Cler Assn; EPF 1998.

GOEKE, Randall Fred (Neb) 87993 482nd Ave, Atkinson NE 68713 **R S Mary's Epis Ch Bassett NE 2006-** B Atkinson NE 1962 s Roy & Patricia. BA Westmar Coll 1984; MDiv Iliff TS 1987. D 11/27/2006 P 6/6/2007 Bp Joe Goodwin Burnett. Chapl and Bereavement Counslr Hospice of Metro Denver and Hospice of St Jn 1990-1996; Serv Meth Ch 1987-1990.

GOERTZ, Linda Ruth (Ore) B Los Angeles CA 1947 d Paul & Flora. BA U of Oregon 1968; MA Roosevelt U 1970; MA Portland St U 2003. D 6/13/2015 Bp Michael Hanley. m 8/30/1980 LeRoy W Goertz.

GOETSCH, Richard William (Ida) 213 E Avenue D, Jerome ID 83338 **D Calv Epis Ch Jerome ID 1988-; supply Trin Ch Gooding ID 1999-** B Oconomowoc WI 1935 s Elmer & Sarah. D 11/6/1988 Bp David Bell Birney IV. m 7/19/1978 Aileen Amanda Goetsch c 4. NAAD.

GOETZ, Edward Craig (Ct) 504 Saybrook Road, P.O. Box 121, Higganum CT 06441 **Died 3/29/2016** B Brooklyn NY 1947 s Edward & Dorothy. BA Moravian TS 1969; MDiv VTS 1972. D 6/10/1972 Bp Joseph Warren Hutchens P 12/16/1972 Bp Morgan Porteus. m 8/4/1973 Cathleen Louise Connor. Asst H Trin Epis Ch Enfield CT 2007-2015; Chapl Narc Enforcement Off Assn 2002-2016; Chapl Fed Bureau of Investigation 2001-2016; Gr Ch Broad Brook CT 1997-2016; P S Andr's Epis Ch Enfield CT 1997-2016; Calv Ch Suffield CT 1997-2007; Asst No Cntrl Reg Mnstry Enfield CT 1997-2007; Chapl Middletown Police Dept 1993-2016; Chapl Killingworth Fire Co 1989-2016; Chapl Connecticut St Police 1986-1997; Chapl Haddam Fire Dept 1983-2010; Dio Connecticut Meriden CT 1973-1974; S Jas Epis Ch Higganum CT 1973-1974; Cur S Jn's Epis Ch Vernon Rock Vernon Rockville CT 1972-1973. Auth, *Ya Gotta Wanna: Introducing Tech into Classroom*, NSBA, 1996. Vol of Year Awd Outstanding Cmnty Serv Hartford Courant 1996.

GOFF, Nancy L (Alb) The Adirondack Mission Episcopal Churches, PO Box 119, Brant Lake NY 12815 **Assoc The Adirondack Mssn Epis Ch 2016-; Co-ordntr, Pstr Care Dept Glens Falls Hosp Glens Falls NY 2013-; Epis Chapl Glens Falls Hosp Glens Falls NY 2010-; Mem, Conv Plnng Com Dio Albany Greenwich NY 2008-** B Bethesda MD 1949 d Willard & Margaret. BS SUNY Empire St Coll Albany 2006. D 5/10/2008 Bp William Howard Love. m 8/16/1969 John Goff c 3. DOK 2005.

✠ **GOFF, The Rt Rev Susan** (Va) 110 W Franklin St, Richmond VA 23220 **Bp Suffr Dio Virginia Richmond VA 2012-, Cn to the Ordnry 2010-2012, Stndg Com 2007-2010, GC Dep 2003-2012; Mem Com on the Status of Wmn 2013-** B Paterson NJ 1953 d James & Dorothy. BA Rutgers The St U of New Jersey 1975; MDiv UTS 1980. D 6/14/1980 Bp John Shelby Spong P 5/21/1981 Bp Robert Bruce Hall Con 7/28/2012 for Va. m 1/23/1988 Charles Thomas Holliday. VTS Alexandria VA 2006, 2003, 2002; R S Chris's Ch Springfield VA 1994-2009; R Imm Ch Mechanicsvlle VA 1986-1994; Chapl S Cathr's Sch Richmond VA 1983-1986, Chapl 1983-1986; Chapl S Marg's Sch Tappahannock VA 1980-1983, Chapl 1980-1983. Auth, "arts," *Epis Tchr*; Auth, "arts," *Virginia Epis*. Epis Ch and the Visual Arts 2008. Hon DD VTS 2013; Int Dn Emer Trin Cathd, San Jose, CA 2012. sgoff@thediocese.net

GOFF, Terry Lynn (CGC) 7125 Hitt Rd, Mobile AL 36695 B Louisiana MO 1960 d Harold & Jimmie. D 2/22/2014 Bp Philip Menzie Duncan II. m 3/17/1979 John Stuart Goff c 3.

GOFORTH, Lisa A (Az) 1310 N. Sioux Ave., Claremore OK 74017 **Gr Epis Ch Lk Havasu City AZ 2012-; R S Paul's Ch Claremore OK 2009-** B York SC 1961 D 6/14/2003 Bp Peter J Lee P 12/20/2003 Bp Michael Whittington Creighton. S Andr's Ch Burke VA 2006-2008; The Memi Ch Of The Prince Of Peace Gettysburg PA 2003-2006.

GOFORTH, Thomas Robert (Chi) 1126 W Wolfram St, Chicago IL 60657 **Non-par 1976-** B Chicago IL 1942 s Robert & Violette. BA U of Wisconsin 1964; MDiv Nash 1967. D 6/17/1967 Bp James Winchester Montgomery P 12/1/1967 Bp Gerald Francis Burrill. m 2/22/1971 Donelia Goforth c 1. Dio Chicago Chicago IL 1972-1974; Chapl Cook Cnty Hse Of Correction 1968-1976; St Leonards Hse Chicago IL 1968-1972; Cur Gr Epis Ch Hinsdale IL 1967. "This Wild Life," Newtopia mag, 2005; "Shadow And Light On The Path To Partnership," Newtopia mag, 2004; "Ending The War Between The Genders," Newtopia mag, 2004.

GOGLIA, Bette Mack (CFla) 9203 Glascow Dr, Fredericksburg VA 22408 **Chapl Mary Washington Hospice 2004-** B Seattle WA 1942 d Charles & Margery. BA S Leo U 1997; MS Stetson U 2000. D 12/9/2000 Bp John Wadsworth Howe. D S Ptr The Fisherman Epis Ch New Smyrna FL 2000-2001.

GOING, Virginia Lee (NC) 400 S Boylan Ave, Raleigh NC 27603 B Roanoke VA 1942 d Robert & Virginia. Cert D Formation Prog. D 10/4/1987 Bp Robert Whitridge Estill. m 6/30/1990 Thomas R Henderson c 2. Dir Of The Triangle Aids Interfaith Ntwk 1992-1996; D S Mk's Epis Ch Raleigh NC 1990-2000; D S Johns Epis Ch Wake Forest NC 1987-1990.

GOKEY, Mary Jordheim (ND) 1742 9th St S, Fargo ND 58103 **D Geth Cathd Fargo ND 2002-** B Big Spring TX 1957 d Robert & Janet. U of Montana 1976; BS U of No Dakota 1980; MS U of Virginia 1983. D 5/10/2002 Bp Andrew Fairfield. m 6/29/1984 Franklyn Guy Gokey c 1.

GOLDACKER, Gary Wray (Mich) 225 Southwind Dr, Belleville IL 62221 **Died 10/24/2016** B Litchfield IL 1942 s Carlyle & Florence. BA Sthrn Illinois U 1966; MDiv Nash 1969; MA U IL 1972. D 5/24/1969 P 12/2/1969 Bp Albert A Chambers. m 6/24/2012 Carolyn Ann Goldacker c 2. Int Chr Ch Cathd Cincinnati OH 2013-2016; Int S Andr's Ch Burke VA 2011-2012; Int All SS Epis Ch Las Vegas NV 2010; Int Gd Shpd Epis Ch Wichita KS 2008-2009; Int Trin Ch Newport RI 2007-2008; Int Chr Ch Cathd Indianapolis IN 2005-2006; Int S Steph's Ch Richmond VA 2004-2005; Int S Paul's Epis Ch Cleveland OH 2002-2004; Int S Clare Of Assisi Epis Ch Ann Arbor MI 2001-2002; Int Chr Ch Detroit MI 1999-2001; Int Ch Of The Trsfg Evergreen CO 1996-1998; Int The Ch Of Chr The King (Epis) Arvada CO 1994-1996; R S Mk's Epis Ch Durango CO 1991-1994; R S Mich's Mssn Anaheim CA 1986-1991; Int S Steph's Epis Ch Orinda CA 1985-1986; Assoc All SS Par Beverly Hills CA 1983-1985; R Trin Ch S Chas MO 1974-1975; Assoc Chr Ch Springfield IL 1970-1974; Chapl Sangamon S U Springfield IL 1970-1974; Cur S Geo's Ch Belleville IL 1969-1970.

GOLDBERG, Mike William (CFla) 460 38th Sq Sw, Vero Beach FL 32968 **R S Aug Of Cbury Epis Ch Vero Bch FL 1997-** B Lake Forest IL 1949 s Philip & Edith. BA S Johns U 1971; MDiv PDS 1974. D 4/27/1974 P 11/2/1974 Bp Albert Wiencke Van Duzer. m 5/23/1981 Sharon L Goldberg c 2. R H Trin Epis Ch Ocean City NJ 1981-1997; R S Mths Ch Hamilton NJ 1976-1981; Cur The Ch Of S Uriel The Archangel Sea Girt NJ 1974-1976. Auth, "Preaching As Image, Story," *Idea*.

GOLDBERG, Rebecca Lee (Cal) 777 Southgate Ave, Daly City CA 94015 B San Francisco CA 1957 d Henry & Roberta. BA Notre Dame de Manor 1993; MDiv CDSP 2012. D 6/14/2014 P 12/6/2014 Bp Marc Handley Andrus.

GOLDBLOOM, Ruth Alice (Md) 52 S Broadway, PO Box 229, Frostburg MD 21532 B Frostburg MD 1953 d Edward & Emily. BA Frostburg St U 1974;

MEd Frostburg St U 1979; MS Frostburg St U 1982. D 7/6/2008 Bp John L Rabb. m 10/24/1992 Donald Scott Goldbloom. D S Jn's Ch Frostburg MD 2008-2013.

GOLDEN JR, John Anthony (Pgh) 5 Devon Ave, Lawrenceville NJ 08648 B Pittsburgh PA 1937 s John & Helen. AB U Pgh 1959; BD Drew U 1962; MPA U Pgh 1979; GTS 1989. D 11/1/1989 Bp William Davidson P 6/1/1990 Bp Alden Moinet Hathaway. m 12/17/1977 Judith Ann Golden c 1. Asstg P Trin Ch Princeton NJ 2002-2011; S Andr's Epis Ch New Kensington PA 1998-2002; S Paul's Epis Ch Kittanning PA 1996-1997; S Barth's Ch Scottdale PA 1995-1996; S Jas Epis Ch Pittsburgh PA 1993-1994; Ch Of The H Cross Pittsburgh PA 1991-1993; Asst Chr Ch No Hills PA 1989-1991.

GOLDEN, Peter Pq (LI) 2115 Albemarle Terrace, Brooklyn NY 11226 B Philadelphia PA 1944 s Lewis & Anna. BA Allen U 1965; MDiv PDS 1970. D 6/6/1970 Bp Robert Lionne DeWitt P 12/12/1970 Bp Chandler W Sterling. R S Paul's Ch-In-The-Vill Brooklyn NY 1992-2010, Int 1990-2010; Asst S Geo's Ch Brooklyn NY 1990; Int Ch of the Redeem Merrick NY 1987-1989; Int Ch Of The Redeem Merrick NY 1987-1988; Jubilee Stff Off E CC New York NY 1985-1987; Jubilee Minsitry Stff Off Epis Ch Cntr New York NY 1985-1987; Dir Archdnry of Brooklyn Brooklyn NY 1982-1989; to the Ordnry Dio Chicago Chicago IL 1982-1984; Cn to the Ordnry Dio Chicago Chicago IL 1981-1985; R S Clem's Epis Ch Inkster MI 1976-1981; R St. Clem's Ch Inkoter MI 1976-1981; S Simon Of Cyrene Epis Ch Cincinnati OH 1972-1976; R St. Simon of Cyrene Lincoln Heights OH 1972-1976; Chapl Chicago Police Dept 1982-1985; Chf Chapl Inkster Police Dept 1980-1981; Chapl Detroit Police Dept 1978-1979. Auth, *arts*. Oblates Mt Calv 1982. Sigma Rho Sigma; Phi Alpha Theta.

GOLDFARB, Ronald Allen (WTenn) 8853 Mission Hills Dr Apt 104, Memphis TN 38125 **Bd Dir- Epis Fund for Human Need Dio Indianapolis Indianapolis IN 2014-, COM- ex officio 2013-, Coun for the Diac 2013-** B Ossining NY 1946 s Irving & Clara. BA SUNY 1990. D 6/24/1997 Bp Edward Witker Jones. m 8/18/1973 Teresa Goldfarb c 3. Police Chapl Southport Police Dept Southport IN. 2012-2014; D S Thos Ch Franklin IN 2012-2013; D All SS Epis Ch Memphis TN 2007-2009; D S Tim's Ch Indianapolis IN 2001-2007; D S Mk's Ch Plainfield IN 1997-2001. NAAD 1998.

GOLDFEDER, Deborah Baker (Mo) 4520 Lucas and Hunt Rd, Saint Louis MO 63121 B Shelby NC 1949 d Thomas & Virginia. BSN U of Maryland 1980; MSN The CUA 1982; MDiv Eden TS 2004. D 11/21/2014 Bp George Wayne Smith. m 10/10/1987 Ronald David Goldfeder.

GOLDHOR, Andrew (Mass) 6 Meriam St, Lexington MA 02420 **The Ch Of Our Redeem Lexington MA 2013-** B Newton MA 1983 s Richard & Pamela. BA The U CO 2008; MDiv GTS 2013; MDiv The GTS 2013. D 6/22/2013 P 1/4/2014 Bp M(Arvil) Thomas Shaw. m 10/5/2013 Jacqueline Clark.

GOLDING, Christopher P (Haw) The Parish of St Clement, 1515 Wilder Ave, Honolulu HI 96822 **Vic The Epis Ch in Hawaii Honolulu HI 2017-** B Brisbane Australia 1983 s Douglas & Heather. Dplma of H Ord St Mk's Natl Theol Cntr 2010; Bachelor of Theol Chas Sturt U 2011. Trans 5/12/2016 as Priest Bp Robert Leroy Fitzpatrick. m 1/16/2010 Julia Frances Golding c 2. Assoc Par of St Clem Honolulu HI 2015-2016.

GOLDMAN, Norman Clifford (Ore) 94416 Langlois Mountain Rd, Langlois OR 97450 **P S Chris's Ch Port Orford OR 2001-** B Phoenix AZ 1940 BS U CO 1963; MS Arizona St U 1968. D 2/13/2001 P 10/27/2001 Bp Robert Louis Ladehoff. m 6/5/1960 Sharen Kay Earl c 3.

GOLDSBOROUGH, Neal Neal (Va) PO Box 12683, Pensacola FL 32591 B Bethesda MD 1952 s Charles & Marilyn. BA Old Dominion U 1976; MA Virginia Commonwealth U 1978; MDiv VTS 1981. D 5/31/1981 Bp David Henry Lewis Jr P 5/15/1982 Bp Robert Bruce Hall. m 1/18/1975 Carol Waple Goldsborough c 1. S Paul's Ch Charlottesville VA 2015-2017; R Chr Epis Ch Pensacola FL 2008-2015; S Jn's Ch Barrington RI 2006-2008, R 2001-2005; Navy Spec Mobilization Spprt Plan Washington DC 2005; R S Lk's Ch Alexandria VA 1991-2001; Chapl (CAPT) USNR 1986-2009; Asst Pohick Epis Ch Lorton VA 1984-1991; R S Dav's Ch Aylett VA 1982-1984; R Imm Ch Mechanicsvlle VA 1981-1984. Auth, "Where is God Amidst the Bombs? A P's Reflections from the Combat Zone," *Bk*, Forw Mvmt, 2008. Ord of St. Jn of Jerusalem Queen Eliz II 2011; DAR Medal of hon DAR 2006.

GOLDSMITH, Maurice Rusty (Tex) Saint Luke's Episcopal Church, 3736 Montrose Rd., Birmingham AL 35213 **S Steph's Epis Ch Birmingham AL 2015-; S Andrews's Epis Ch Birmingham AL 2013-; Epis Ch On W Kaua'i Eleele HI 2012-; P Affiliate S Lk's Epis Ch Birmingham AL 2007-; Fin Dept and Trst Dio Alabama Birmingham AL 2009-; Dvlpmt Com Bread for the Wrld 2007-** B Selma AL 1943 s Maurice & Sadie. BA U of Alabama 1965; MDiv Sewanee: The U So, TS 1981. D 6/6/1981 P 12/15/1981 Bp Furman Charles Stough. m 9/2/1964 Carolyn Thomas Goldsmith c 3. Int Dir Ch Of The Incarn Highlands NC 2016-2017; S Chris's Ch Pensacola FL 2014-2015; The Epis Ch of the H Apos Hoover AL 2011-2012, Int 2011-2012; S Andr's By The Sea Epis Ch Destin FL 2010-2011; Vice-R S Mart's Epis Ch Houston TX 2005; Congrl Dvlpmt Dio Texas Houston TX 2003-2004; Adj Fac Sewanee U So TS Sewanee TN 2001-2003, (Trst and) Regent 1989-1995; R S Mary's-On-

The-Highlands Epis Ch Birmingham AL 1986-2001; Sub-Dn The Cathd Ch Of The Adv Birmingham AL 1983-1986; Cur Ch Of The Nativ Epis Huntsville AL 1981-1983; Invstmt Com Mem Dom And Frgn Mssy Soc- Epis Ch Cntr New York NY 2006-2012, Invstmt Com 2005-2012; Regent U So 1989-1995. Auth, "Adios, Lash LaRue," *Sewanee Revs*, 2012; Auth, "A Trip No," *Sewanee Revs*, 2008; Auth, "Sum Saturdays," *Sewanee Revs*, 2003; Auth, "arts," *Angl Dig*; Auth, "7 Demopolis-Sermons Tapes," *SPCK*. Ord of the Hosp of St. Jn of Jerusalem 2012. D. D. The U So 1998.

GOLDSMITH III, Robert Sidney (Eas) 314 North St, Easton MD 21601 B Selma AL 1953 s Robert & Isabel. BA Hampden-Sydney Coll 1975; MDiv EDS 1980. D 9/19/1981 P 9/29/1982 Bp A(rthur) Heath Light. m 5/3/1998 Debra P Goldsmith c 2. S Steph's Ch Earleville MD 2011-2016; Assoc R Trin Ch New Orleans LA 1998-2010; S Thos Epis Christiansbrg VA 1990-1998; S Mk's Ch Fincastle VA 1985-1990; Asst Par Of The Epiph Winchester MA 1981-1985. LAND Grad; Soc of S Jn the Evang.

GOLDSMITH, Thomas Michael (Ala) 113 Brown Ave, Rainbow City AL 35906 **Ch Of The Resurr Rainbow City AL 2013-** B Montgomery AL 1970 s Maurice & Carolyn. BA U of Alabama 1994; MDiv Sewanee: The U So, TS 2013; MDiv The TS at The U So 2013. D 5/22/2013 Bp John Mckee Sloan Sr P 12/12/2013 Bp Santosh K Marray. m 11/9/1996 Kana Roess Goldsmith c 3. Camp Mcdowell Nauvoo AL 2005-2013; H Trin Epis Ch Gainesville FL 2004-2005. revmgoldsmith@gmail.com

GOLENSKI, John Donald (Cal) 1360 Montgomery St Apt 1, San Francisco CA 94133 B New Bedford MA 1947 s John & Florence. BA Boston Coll 1969; Jesuit TS 1977; EdD Harv 1978; Jesuit TS 1980. Rec 6/7/2003 Bp William Edwin Swing. Assoc S Greg Of Nyssa Ch San Francisco CA 2003-2015.

GOLLIHER, Jeffrey Mark (NY) 150 W End Ave Apt 30-M, New York NY 10023 **S Jn's Memi Ch Ellenville NY 2003-** B Elkin NC 1953 s Bobby & Evelyn. MA LSU 1975; BA Wake Forest U 1975; PhD SUNY 1989; MDiv GTS 1992. D 6/6/1992 P 1/1/1993 Bp David Charles Bowman. m 5/31/1987 Lynn Rodenberg. Dio New York New York NY 2003-2011; Cathd Of St Jn The Div New York NY 1992-2003. Auth, "Moving Through Fear," Tarcher/Penguin, 2011; Auth, "A Deeper Faith," Tarcher/Penguin, 2008.

GOLUB, Elizabeth Kress (Nwk) 18 Wittig Ter # 7470, Wayne NJ 07470 **S Agnes Ch Little Falls NJ 2016-** B Hoboken NJ 1951 BD Seton Hall U 1973; MS Seton Hall U 1977; MDiv GTS 2003. D 5/31/2003 P 1/3/2004 Bp John Palmer Croneberger. m 1/3/1981 David Golub c 3. Ch Of The Epiph Orange NJ 2014-2015; S Lk's Epis Ch Haworth NJ 2013-2015; P-in-c Ch Of The H Trin W Orange NJ 2010-2012; Assoc S Mich's Epis Ch Wayne NJ 2004-2008.

GOMAN, Jon Gifford (Ore) 2615 Nw Arnold Way, Corvallis OR 97330 B Corvallis OR 1946 s Edward & Laverne. BA U of Puget Sound 1969; U of Cambridge 1970; DMin Claremont TS 1976. D 7/31/1976 P 6/20/1977 Bp Robert Hume Cochrane. m 8/25/1979 Elizabeth Goman c 3. Dio Oregon Portland OR 2004-2012, 1982-1984; The Epis Ch Of The Gd Samar Corvallis OR 1985-2003; Chapl S Anselm Cbury Ch Corvallis OR 1982-1984; Bloy Hse Claremont CA 1980-1982; P-in-c H Nativ Par Los Angeles CA 1979-1982; S Mich And All Ang Ch Issaquah WA 1977-1978; Dio Olympia Seattle 1976-1977; Asst S Ambr Par Claremont CA 1974-1976. Auth, "A Few Comments On BCP". Instr Of The Year Linn-Benton Cmnty Coll 1989; Danforth Fellowow 1969.

GOMER JR, Richard Henry (CFla) 6400 N Socrum Loop Rd, Lakeland FL 33809 B Denver CO 1958 s Richard & Virginia. U CO 1979; BA San Jose St U 1984; MDiv TESM 1988. D 6/24/1988 Bp Charles Shannon Mallory P 12/1/1988 Bp Frank Tracy Griswold III. m 4/13/1984 Karen Kay Gomer c 3. Pstr Chr The King Ch Lakeland FL 1995-2011; Assoc Ch Of The Apos Fairfax VA 1990-1995; Asst S Mk's Epis Ch Glen Ellyn IL 1988-1990.

GOMES, Elizabeth (Kan) 912 N Amidon Ave, Wichita KS 67203 **P in Res S Chris's Epis Ch Wichita KS 2005-; Consult - Congrl Dvlpmt Dio Kansas Topeka KS 1996-, Mem Liturg Arts Cmsn 1993-2001, Mem Cler/Lay Sexual Abuse/Chld Abuse Prevention Com 1992-2001** B Pittsfield MA 1938 d Charles & Anna. RN Albany Med Cntr Sch of Nrsng 1961; BS Newton Coll of The Sacr Heart Newton MA 1971; MDiv EDS 1987; SWTS 2005. D 12/20/1990 P 6/1/1991 Bp William Edward Smalley. co-Fndr/Dir Iona Mnstry for Congrl Dvlpmt 2001-1989; co-Fndr/Dir S Columba Cntr for Congrl Dvlpmt 1995-2001; Asst S Jas Ch Wichita KS 1993-2004; Asst Gd Shpd Epis Ch Wichita KS 1991-1993. Auth, "A Manuel For Surgical Techniques". AAR; S Jn Soc; SBL; Soc Of S Jn The Evang.

GOMEZ, Edward (Tex) 2404 Marcus Abrams Blvd, Austin TX 78748 **Vic The Great Cmsn Fndt Houston TX 2015-; El Buen Samaritano Epis Mssn Austin TX 2003-** B Miami FL 1957 s Mario & Eva. BBA U of Miami 1978; MDiv Dominican Sch of Philos and Theol 1987; ThM Dominican Sch of Philos & Theol 1988. Rec 12/3/2000 Bp Claude Edward Payne. m 10/6/2012 Denise Trevino Trevino-Gomez c 2. El Buen Samaritano Epis Mssn Austin TX 2003-2010; Palmer Memi Ch Houston TX 2002-2003; S Bede Epis Ch Houston TX 2000-2002. Soc of Biblic Literture 2007.

GOMEZ, Luis Enrique (NY) 26 W 84th St, New York NY 10024 **Dio New York New York NY 2013-** B Gualaceo Ecuador 1964 s Luis & Maria. BS Empire St Coll 2009; MDiv GTS 2010. D 3/13/2010 P 9/25/2010 Bp Mark Sean Sisk. m 11/15/1996 Carmen Piedad Hajal c 1. P Ch Of The H Apos New York NY 2012-2016; R The Ch of S Matt And S Tim New York NY 2011.

GOMEZ ALMONTE, Lorenzo (DR) Calle Las Mercedes #66, Bigalindo, Hato Mayor Del Rey Dominican Republic **Dio The Dominican Republic (Iglesia Epis Dominicana) Gazcue Santo Domingo 2015-** B Dominican Republic 1962 s Felix & Mercedes. ING.AGR Pucamaima 1986; Lic Teologia Centro Estudios Teología Rep. Dominicana 2013; Lic Teologia Centro de Estodios Teologilos 2013. D 2/16/2013 P 2/15/2015 Bp Julio Cesar Holguin-Khoury. m 12/22/1990 Yoberkis Ramirez Ortiz c 3.

GOMPERTZ, Charles Bates (Cal) PO Box 713, Nicasio CA 94946 B Philadelphia PA 1935 s John & Margaret. BA U CA 1959; BA U CA, Berkeley 1959; MDiv CDSP 1962. D 6/24/1962 Bp James Albert Pike P 3/16/1963 Bp George Richard Millard. m 7/5/1985 Leslie Ross c 4. Asst St Johns Epis Ch Ross CA 1985-2007, Cur 1962-1984; Asst S Steph's Par Bel Tiburon CA 1971-1985; Vic Ch in Ignacio CA 1965-1970. Ed, "It Takes All Types! 2nd Ed," *It Takes All Types! 2nd Ed*, Baytree Pub Co, 1999; Ed, "It Takes All Types!," *It Takes All Types!*, Baytree Pub Co, 1987; Auth, *Mend a Broken Heart*, Baytree Pub Co, 1978; Auth, *Mass of the Gd Earth*, 1969; Producer, "Guaraldi Mass," *Vince Guaraldi at Gr Cathd*, Fantasy Records, 1965. S Andr's Soc of San Francisco 1987; San Francisco California Pioneers 1980. Bd Chair W Marin Sr Serv 2005; Bd Chair Nicasio Sch Bd 2000; Bd Chair Coll of Marin Fndt 1995; Natl Bd Dir Planned Parenthood 1970; Bd Chair Planned Parenthood of Marin 1967; Bd Chair Vol Bureau of Marin 1964.

GONZALES, Pat Marie (Okla) PO Box 26, Watonga OK 73772 B Anadarko OK 1950 d Joe & Clara. AARN Redland Cmnty Coll 1992; RN BSN SW Oklahoma St U 1994. D 6/20/2014 Bp Edward Joseph Konieczny. c 2.

GONZALES JR, Ricardo (Los) 859 Jessica Pl, Nipomo CA 93444 B Los Angeles CA 1943 s Ricardo & Amalia. BS California St U 1956; MS U CA 1976; MDiv Claremont TS 2001. D 6/2/2001 Bp Robert Marshall Anderson P 6/5/2002 Bp Chester Lovelle Talton. m 1/30/1965 Caryl Lee Gonzales c 2. S Ptr's Par Santa Maria CA 2007; Vic La Iglesia de Todos Los Santos Nipomo CA 2003-2005; Asst S Thos' Mssn Hacienda Hgts CA 2001-2002.

GONZALEZ, Alfredo Pedro (USC) 1115 Marion St, Columbia SC 29201 **Assoc S Mary's Ch Columbia SC 2012-** B San Jose, Costa Rica 1937 s Dagoberto & Gladys. D 7/26/2007 P 2/2/2008 Bp Dorsey Henderson. m 6/7/1969 Luisa M Gonzalez c 2. Hisp Mssnr Dio Upper So Carolina Columbia SC 2009-2013.

GONZALEZ, Betsy Carmody (WA) 1200 N Quaker Ln, Alexandria VA 22302 **Epis HS Alexandria VA 2014-** B Nashville TN 1974 d Richard & Alison. BS NWU 1997; MDiv CDSP 2010. D 6/5/2010 P 1/22/2011 Bp John Bryson Chane. m 5/11/2002 Edward Gonzalez c 1. Lower and Intermediate Sch Chapl S Andr's Epis Sch Potomac MD 2010-2014. betsygonz@gmail.com

GONZALEZ, Isabel Tapia (U) 4024 Red Hawk Rd, West Valley City UT 84119 **Property Maintenance Dio Utah Salt Lake City UT 2006-, 1996-2006** B Mexico 1963 d Enrique & Asuncion. Cmnty Coll of Salt Lake City Salt Lake City UT; San Andres Sem Mex City DF MX; U of Utah. D 6/10/2006 P 2/10/2007 Bp Carolyn Tanner Irish. m 7/3/1999 Sergio Gonzalez c 4.

GONZALEZ, Oscar (Nwk) 5711 Jefferson St Apt 214, West New York NJ 07093 **Died 10/29/2015** B Los Arabos CU 1929 s Jose & Concepcion. BA La Progresiva Sch of Cuba 1948; CPA U of Havana Cu 1952; BTh Matanzas TS 1955. Trans 9/2/1970 as Priest Bp Leland Stark. m 2/25/1956 Lilliam Ponjuan c 2. P in charge Calv Ch Bayonne NJ 2001-2010; Supply P Dio Newark Newark NJ 1995-2000, Pres Hudson Convoc 1976-1995; Ret Dio Newark 1994-2015; Rgnl Assoc ECUSA 1981-1985; Secy Natl Cmsn Hisp Mnstrs ECUSA 1978-1980; R Gr Ch Un City NJ 1970-1994; Cathd Madrid Spain 1969-1970; Serv Ch of Cuba 1955-1969.

GONZALEZ, Richard (CFla) D 6/4/2016 Bp Dabney Tyler Smith.

GONZALEZ AQUDELO, Luis Mariano (Colom) Carrera 84 North 50 A-112, Ap 301, Medellin, Antioquia Colombia B Caldas CO 1958 s Manano & Elvira. U Antioquia; BA San Javier 1977. D 5/15/1994 P 11/1/1996 Bp Bernardo Merino-Botero. m 12/15/1990 Ana Maria Hoyos Gonzalez Aqudelo. Iglesia Epis En Colombia Bogota 1995-1999.

GONZALEZ DEL SOLAR, Mario Sebastian (Va) 800 Brantley Rd, Richmond VA 23235 **Asst R S Matt's Ch Richmond VA 2004-** B Guatemala City GT 1948 s Julio & Olive. BA U of Maryland 1973; MA U of Maryland 1978; MDiv VTS 1985; DMin TESM 2005. D 6/8/1985 Bp John Thomas Walker P 5/18/1986 Bp William Hopkins Folwell. m 9/28/1974 Barbara Ann Gonzalez del Solar c 3. Int Chr Epis Ch Virginia Bch VA 2004; Int S Barth's Ch Richmond VA 2002-2004; Mem Evang Fllshp in the Angl Comm 1996-2003; R Ch Of The Gd Shpd Richmond VA 1990-2001; Assoc R Trin Ch Vero Bch FL 1985-1990; Evang Cmsn Dio Cntrl Florida Orlando FL 1988-1990. Auth, "Joy in Mnstry (Doctoral Thesis)," TESM, 2005; Auth, "Evang," *Cntrl Florida Epis*. Evang Fllshp in the Angl Comm 1996-2003.

GONZALEZ-FIGUEROA, Efrain (PR) B San Juan, PR 1944 s Manuel & Carmen. B.A U of Puerto Rico 1973; Mstr of Theol Evang Sem 1977; Mstr of Theol Evang Sem 1977; Dmin McCormick Theo. Sem 1994; Dmin McCormick Theo. Sem 1994. D 2/24/1978 P 12/3/1978 Bp Francisco Reus-Froylan. m 7/

17/1981 Janet Ruth Mourino-Lopez c 2. Dn Dio Puerto Rico Trujillo Alto PR 2004-2005, 1998-2003, 1989-1994; R Dio Michigan Detroit MI 1986-1988; Vic, Santa Margarita Our Lady of Guadalupe Fresno CA 1984; Vic, Santa Margarita Epis Mssn Epis Dio San Joaquin Modesto CA 1981-1983; Vic Mision La Santa Cruz Lares PR 1979-1981; Asst to the Dn Cathd St Jn the Bapt Santurce PR 1977-1979; Brigade Chapl (Major) Army Reserve NG 2000-2004; Brigade Chapl (Captain) Army Reserve NG 1996-2000; Chapl (First Lietenant) Army Reserve NG 1995-1996.

GONZALEZ GARAVITO, Jose Pio (PR) PO Box 902, Saint Just PR 00978 **Dio Puerto Rico Trujillo Alto PR 2011-** B Colombia 1964 s Jose & Isabel. Teologo y filosofo Juan XXIII 1990; Maestria Educacion Universida Cntrl de Bayamon 2005. Rec 10/28/2011 Bp David Andres Alvarez-Velazquez. m 8/7/2010 Mayra M Lugo Quinones.

GONZALEZ-MEJIAS, Ramon (PR) **Died 1/24/2017** B 1931 D 6/6/1968 P 3/23/1969 Bp Francisco Reus-Froylan. m 7/27/1961 Carmen Pena c 1. Dio Puerto Rico Trujillo Alto PR 1980-1993, 1970-1979.

GONZALEZ-MESA, Gustavo (Ore) 700 Se 7th St, Gresham OR 97080 B 1939 s Guillermo & Piedad. Epis TS of the SW; U Natl Mex Mx. D 6/13/1987 Bp Gordon Taliaferro Charlton P 6/1/1991 Bp Maurice Manuel Benitez. m 8/5/1989 Anne Gonzalez-Mesa. Dio Oregon Portland OR 1997-2000; Dio Oklahoma Oklahoma City OK 1994-1997; Stff Chapl S Lk's Epis Hosp Houston TX 1989-1994; S Lk's Epis Hosp Houston TX 1989-1993; Asst Vic Iglesia San Francisco de Asis Austin TX 1988-1989; The Great Cmsn Fndt Houston TX 1988-1989; Dioc Hisp Mssrn Santa Maria Mssn; Vic Santa Maria Mssn; Dir The Ch of the Gd Shpd Austin TX 1987-1989.

GONZALEZ SANTOS, Rosa Ari (PR) **Dio Puerto Rico Trujillo Alto PR 2012-** B Santurce PR 1954 d Dimas & Carmen. BA Universidad de Puerto Rico 1977; MDiv Seminario San Pedro Y San Pablo 2008. D 7/6/2008 P 5/15/2011 Bp David Andres Alvarez-Velazquez.

GOOCH, Gary Duane (Kan) 117 E Sierra Cir, San Marcos TX 78666 **Mssnr Partnr in Mnstry Kenedy TX 1997-** B Avery OK 1936 s George & Ruby. BS Oklahoma St U 1957; U of Washington 1959; MS Oklahoma St U 1967; MDiv Nash 1974; VTS 1987. D 6/22/1974 P 12/21/1974 Bp Chilton R Powell. m 7/3/1963 Donnelle Kay Gooch c 4. R All SS Epis Cluster Pittsburg KS 1988-1996; Pstr All SS Nova Cluster So E Kansas KS 1988-1996; R S Ptr's Ch Pittsburg KS 1987-1988; R St Andrews Ch Broken Arrow OK 1983-1987; Vic/R S Andr's Broken Arrow OK 1976-1987; R Dio Oklahoma Oklahoma City OK 1976-1982, Chair, Comm on Accountability and Cler Compstn 1984-1987, Chair, Const & Cn Cmsn 1981-1982, Cmsn on Accountability and Cler Compstn 1980-1987, Pres, NE Oklahoma Cler 1980-1982, COM 1977-1987, Cler Advsr, ECharF 1977-1980, Cmsn on Renwl & Evang 1976-1981; Cur Gr Ch Muskogee OK 1974-1976; Secy, Dioc Conv Dio Kansas Topeka KS 1990-1996, Dioc Coun 1987-1991. Ord of S Lk. Who's Who in Rel; Who's Who in the Midwest.

GOOD, Arthur Allen (FdL) 1068 Misty Meadow Circle, De Pere WI 54115 **D S Mk's Ch Sidney OH 2009-** B Detroit MI 1928 s Joseph & Lelia. Angl Acad. Trans 1/2/2004 Bp Herbert Thompson Jr. m 2/11/1956 Rose Mary Good c 4. D S Jas Ch Piqua OH 1996-2005. S Simeon And S Anna.

GOOD, Elizabeth (Mass) 17 Church St, Hanover MA 02339 B Glen Cove NY 1949 d John & Carol. BA Skidmore Coll 1970; MBA NEU 1979; MA St Mary of the Woods Coll 2010. D 6/22/2013 Bp M(Arvil) Thomas Shaw.

GOODALE-MIKOSZ, Desiree Ann (Chi) 20913 W Snowberry Ln, Plainfield IL 60544 **D S Ptr's Epis Ch Sycamore IL 2013-** B Joliet IL 1946 d William & Shirley. BS Elmhurst Coll 1990; MSW UIC Jane Addams Coll of Soc Wk 1994. D 1/19/2008 Bp Victor Alfonso Scantlebury. m 5/20/1989 Gerald Mikosz c 2. NAAD 2008.

GOODE, Colin (Oly) PO Box 276, Lopez Island WA 98261 **Died 2/1/2016** B Oldham Lancashire UK 1937 s George & Agnes. LTh St Johns Coll Nottingham GB 1979; BTh U of Nottingham GB 1979; DMin Fuller TS 1990. Trans 9/4/1986 Bp Alden Moinet Hathaway. m 6/29/1968 Moira Hilary Du Toit c 2. Vic Gr Ch Lopez Island WA 2002-2009; Serv Angl Ch of Can 2000-2002; R All Ang' Ch New York NY 1996-1999; Substitute Dn Trin Cathd Little Rock AR 1993-1993; Assoc Ch Of The Ascen Pittsburgh PA 1986-1989; Serv Ch of Can 1983-1986; Serv Ch of the Prov of So Afr 1979-1983. Cn Trin Cathd 1989.

GOODFELLOW, Willa Marie (EO) 1745 5th St., #8, Coralville IA 52241 B Spokane WA 1952 d Fred & Mary. BA Reed Coll 1975; Cert U of Utah 1980; MDiv Ya Berk 1981; Cert SWTS 2006. Rec 4/4/1971. m 5/1/2009 Helen Keefe c 1. Mnstry Dvlpmt Dio Iowa Des Moines IA 2003-2010, Dep, GC 1991-2007, Dio Iowa, Cler Fam Com 1990-1992; R S Lk's Ch Ft Madison IA 1997-2005; campus Min Untd Campus Mnstry Iowa City IA 1992-1998; Chapl Gri Grinnell IA 1988-1992; Vic S Paul's Epis Ch Grinnell IA 1988-1992; Int R Trin Ch Muscatine IA 1987-1988; Chr Ch Cedar Rapids IA 1986-1987; S Johns Ch Cedar Rapids IA 1986-1987; Assoc R S Lk's Ch Minneapolis MN 1981-1982; Chapl Intern S Mk Tower Salt Lake City UT 1979-1980. Auth, "The Easy Yoke," *Daughters of Sarah*, 1989. willagoodfellow@gmail.com

GOODHEART, Donald P (NC) 1303 Hwy A1A #201, Satellite Beach FL 32937 **Ret Assoc Epis Ch Of The H Apos Satellite Bch FL 2008-** B Denver CO 1947 s Donald & Allison. BA Stan 1969; MDiv Yale DS 1974. D 6/8/1974 P 2/1/1975 Bp Joseph Warren Hutchens. m 12/21/1973 Ronnie S Goodheart c 2. R S Paul's Epis Ch Winston Salem NC 1997-2007; Epiph Par of Seattle Seattle WA 1988-1997; Chapl Salt Lake City Police 1981-1988; R S Paul's Ch Salt Lake City UT 1980-1988; Chapl OSL 1978-1980; R S Andr's-In-The-Vlly Tamworth NH 1976-1980; Asst S Jas Epis Ch Farmington CT 1974-1976; Assoc S Jn's Ch New Haven CT 1973-1974; Chairman, Conv Dispatch of Bus Dio No Carolina Raleigh NC 2000-2007, Chairman, Mssy Strtgy Cmsn 2000-2003; Pres, CADO (Cler Assn) Dio Olympia Seattle 1995-1996; COM Dio Utah Salt Lake City UT 1985-1988, Dioc Coun 1983-1985.

GOODING, Ludwick E (Pa) 5910 Cobbs Creek Pkwy, Philadelphia PA 19143 B Bridgetown BB 1933 s Henry & Idalene. AIB U of Reading Gb 1976; ThD Oxf GB 1979; STM Oxf GB 2000. Trans 10/1/1989 Bp Allen Lyman Bartlett Jr. m 4/11/1956 Verna J Gooding. S Phil Memi Ch Philadelphia PA 1989-2002; R S Pat S Dav S Vinc Windward Islands 1983-1987; Serv Ch Of Engl 1979-1983.

GOODISON, Lorna Fay (SeFla) 1400 Riverside Dr, Coral Springs FL 33071 **S Mary Magd Epis Ch Pompano Bch FL 2007-** B Kingston Jamaica WI 1950 MA Florida Intl U; BSW U of The W Indies; Cert Dioc Sch for CE 2004. D 4/29/2007 Bp Leo Frade. c 2.

GOODKIND, Caroline Cox (USC) 45 Crooked Island Circle, Murrells Inlet SC 29576 B Jackson MI 1945 d Harry & Ellen. BA Duke 1965; MDiv Sewanee: The U So, TS 2001. D 6/4/2001 Bp Bob Johnson P 4/6/2002 Bp Michael B Curry. m 12/17/1985 Marcus Goodkind c 2. R S Geo Ch Anderson SC 2004-2010; Asst S Mary's Epis Ch High Point NC 2001-2004. CE Awd For Creativity And Excellence In Bib U So 2001. cgoodkind@frontier.com

GOODLETT, James Calvin (Fla) **Int S Mich And All Ang Ch Tallahassee FL 2014-; Ret Non-par 2011-** D 6/12/1977 Bp Frank S Cerveny P 12/1/1977 Bp William Henry Marmion.

GOODMAN, James Mark (RG) P.O. Box 1246, Albuquerque NM 87103 **Dn S Jn's Cathd Albuquerque NM 2007-; Pres, Stndg Com Dio The Rio Grande Albuquerque 2010-** B Oklahoma City OK 1958 s Norman & Markita. BS U of Oklahoma 1981; MS U of Iowa 1983; MDiv GTS 1991. D 10/25/1991 P 5/7/1992 Bp Don Adger Wimberly. m 8/11/1990 Dawn M Goodman c 2. R Trin Ch Myrtle Bch SC 1999-2007; R Trin Ch Hamilton OH 1994-1999; Chair Compnstn T/F Dio Sthrn Ohio Cincinnati OH 1993-1995, Dioc Coun 1992; Cn Chr Ch Cathd Cincinnati OH 1991-1994; Stndg Com So Carolina Charleston SC 2004-2007, Reg Dn 2001-2007, Dioc Coun 2000-2003. Cmnty Trsfg.

GOODMAN, Kevin M (Chi) 6033 N Sheridan Rd Apt 29g, Chicago IL 60660 **Asst S Matt's Ch Evanston IL 2004-** B New Orleans LA 1966 s Philip & Margaret. Shaaxi Teachers U 1987; BA Loyola U 1989; MDiv GTS 2004. D 6/18/2005 P 12/17/2005 Bp Bill Persell. m 10/28/2011 Antonius Puiang-Hartanto. Asstg P S Chrys's Ch Chicago IL 2012-2016; Assoc Dn Cathd Of S Jas Chicago IL 2009-2012; Cur All SS Epis Ch Chicago IL 2006-2009; Yth Outreach Min The Night Mnstry Chicago IL 2004-2006. Auth, "A Disney Monastic: a theme Pk travel guide for the God-seeker," *A Disney Monastic: a them Pk travel guide for the God-seeker*, Digital Monastics Media, 2014; "San Xia: Three Gorges and The People's Republic of China," Universal Pub, 2000. The Polly Bond Awd of Excellence ECom 2002. kevin@stmatthewsevanston.org

GOODMAN, Timothy Allen (Spr) 9267 HERRIN RD, JOHNSTON CITY IL 62951 **P-in-c S Steph's Ch Harrisburg IL 2011-, D/Asst. P 1991-2011** B Chicago IL 1938 s Frank & Fern. BS U of Evansville 1967. D 8/31/1991 Bp Donald James Parsons P 5/31/2008 Bp Peter Hess Beckwith. m 10/19/1963 Carol Michell Goodman c 3. S Jas Chap Marion Marion IL 1991-2011; Ch Of The Redeem Cairo IL 1991-2008; S Jas Epis Ch Dahlgren IL 1991-2008; S Mk's Ch W Frankfort IL 1991-2008. Ord Of S Lk.

GOODNESS, DONALD (NY) 4800 Fillmore Ave Apt 651, Alexandria VA 22311 **Ret 1997-** B Rochester NY 1932 s Alfred & Marion. BA Atlantic Un Coll 1953; BD EDS 1962. D 6/23/1962 Bp Anson Phelps Stokes Jr P 12/23/1962 Bp William A Lawrence. m 9/3/1950 Lorraine Reynolds c 1. Assoc S Jas' Epis Ch Leesburg VA 2005; Assoc St. Jas Ch Leesburg VA 2001-2011; R Ch Of The Ascen New York NY 1972-1997; Asst Chr Ch Fitchburg MA 1962-1965; Serv Seventh-Day Adventist Ch 1953-1959.

GOODPANKRATZ, Gretchen (WK) Po Box 851, Liberal KS 67905 B Liberal KS 1937 d Earl & Hortense. Cottey Gnrl 1957; BS K SU 1959. D 3/13/1989 Bp William Edwin Swing. c 4. D S Andr's Epis Ch Liberal KS 1989-2000; D SW Area Reg Cluster Ch 1989-1990. NAAD, Tertiary Of The Soc Of S Fran.

GOODRICH III, Daniel Hillman (Mich) 39 Hubbard St, Mount Clemens MI 48043 B Highland Park MI 1933 s Daniel & Harriett. MDiv CDSP; BA SU MI. D 6/29/1963 P 12/22/1994 Bp Archie H Crowley. Ed For Nwsltr Dio Michigan Detroit MI 1982-1985, Dioc Mus Cmsn 1978-1983, Dn Dioc Convoc 1978-1982; Vic S Edw The Confessor Epis Ch Clinton Twp MI 1963-2005; Chapl Prot Chld Hm Grosse Pointe Woods MI 1963-1969; Asst St Paul's Epis Romeo MI 1963-1967.

GOODRIDGE, Robert J (CFla) 4791 Longbow Drive, Titusville FL 32796 **R S Gabriels Ch Titusville FL 2009-** B Youngstown, OH 1949 s Robert & Isabel. BS U of Texas 1975; MDiv Sewanee: The U So, TS 2007. D 6/2/2007 P 12/7/2007 Bp John Wadsworth Howe. m 4/8/1989 Kathryn L Goodridge c 1. Chapl

H Trin Epis Acad Melbourne FL 2007-2009; Asst H Trin Epis Ch Melbourne FL 2007-2009; Producer 1st Bapt Ch of Orlando 2004-2005. OSL 2010.

GOODWIN, Joan Carolyn (Az) **D Dio Colorado Denver CO 1994-** B Los Angeles CA 1939 d Bascom & Velma. BA USC 1961. D 11/7/1992 Bp Joseph Thomas Heistand. m 1/26/1962 Michael Goodwin c 2. D S Columba's Flagstaff AZ 1992-1994. NAAD, Dok; Untd Epis Chars.

GOODWIN, Laura Bishop (WMass) St Andrew's Church, 53 N Main St, North Grafton MA 01536 **R S Andr's Ch No Grafton MA 2007-** B Springfield MA 1953 d Gordon & Mary. BS Fitchburg St Coll Fitchburg MA 1977; MDiv Wycliffe Coll Toronto CA 2007. D 6/2/2007 P 12/8/2007 Bp Gordon Scruton. m 8/19/1978 Todd Goodwin c 2. Chr Ch Fitchburg MA 1996-2004.

GOODWIN, Marilyn Marie (Minn) 27309 County Road 4, Naytahwaush MN 56566 B White Earth MN 1944 d John & Isabelle. D 10/29/2005 P 1/20/2007 Bp James Louis Jelinek. c 2.

GOODWIN, Sarabeth (WA) 1721 Lamont St NW, Washington DC 20010 **Transitional Latino Mssnr Dio Washington Washington DC 2014-** B Phillipi WV 1949 d Olin & Helen. BA W Virginia U 1970; MA W Virginia U 1973; MDiv VTS 2005. D 6/11/2005 P 1/21/2006 Bp John Bryson Chane. m 10/13/1984 John P Racin c 2. Latino Mssnr Ch Of S Steph And The Incarn Washington DC 2005-2014.

GOOLD, George Charles (Ore) St Stephen's Church, SW Ninth & Hurbert Sts, Newport OR 97365 **D S Steph's Ch Newport OR 2002-; D Dio Oregon Portland OR 1992-** B Portland OR 1943 s Clifford & Clara. BS Portland St U 1968. D 6/29/1992 Bp Robert Louis Ladehoff.

GOOLD, Janis Leigh (Ore) 16530 Nottingham Dr, Gladstone OR 97027 **D S Steph's Ch Newport OR 2002-** B Everett WA 1941 d Carl & Genevieve. BS Portland St U 1963; MS Portland St U 1966. D 12/27/1990 Bp Robert Louis Ladehoff. c 3. D S Ptr & S Paul.

GOOLSBEE, Arthur Leon (NwT) 602 Meander St., Abilene TX 79602 B Waco TX 1940 s William & Josephine. BA Baylor U 1967; JD U of Texas Sch of Law 1967. D 10/31/2008 Bp C Wallis Ohl. m 4/12/1963 Linda Goolsbee c 1.

GOOLSBY, Bob (Tex) 1656 Blalock Rd., Houston TX 77080 **R S Chris's Ch Houston TX 2008-** B Hollywood FL 1970 s Elmer & Rose. BA U of Cntrl Florida 2002; MDiv Epis TS of the SW 2005. D 4/17/2005 Bp Leo Frade. m 11/27/2005 Karla G Goolsby c 2. Cur Ch Of The Gd Shpd Kingwood TX 2005-2008.

GOOLTZ, Janet R (Az) 12607 W Westgate Dr, Sun City West AZ 85375 **Asstg P Ch Of The Adv Sun City W AZ 2008-** B Baltimore MD 1937 d Oscar & Garnet. BA Vas 1959; MDiv Weston Jesuit TS 1982; DMin GTF 1995. D 6/2/1984 Bp John Bowen Coburn P 5/22/1985 Bp Morris Fairchild Arnold. m 6/13/1959 Robert B Goolltz c 4. Asstg P The Ch Of Our Redeem Lexington MA 2000-2004; Dir Pstrl Care Mt Auburn Hosp Cambridge MA 1984-2007; Cathd Chapt Dio Massachusetts Boston MA 1994-1997. Assoc, Ord of Ste Anne 1994.

GOONESEKERA, Desmond Joel Peter (Tex) 2806 Belham Creek Dr, Katy TX 77494 B Sri Lanka 1946 s David & Edith. MDiv DS Colombo Sri Lanka 1968; Ldrshp Acad for New Directions 1980; BA Luth Bible Inst of Seattle 1980. Trans 6/1/1988 Bp Charles I Jones III. m 9/11/1971 Ewena Goonesekera c 2. R S Cuth's Epis Ch Houston TX 2000-2013; R Trin Epis Ch Baytown TX 1995-2000; Asst Gr And S Steph's Epis Ch Colorado Sprg CO 1991-1995; Assoc Par Evang Gr Colorado Sprg CO 1991-1995; R S Pat's Epis Ch Bigfork MT 1988-1991; Chapl Ladies Coll 1985-1987; Chapl Gnrl Hosp 1984-1987; R S Lk's Colombo Sri Lanka 1984-1987; R S Phil's Kurana Sri Lanka 1981-1985; Chapl Sri Lanka Prisons 1978-1987; Asst P S Lk's Epis Ch Seattle WA 1978-1980.

GOORAHOO, Ephraim Basant (LI) 111-16 116th St, South Ozone Park NY 11420 **Ret 1992-** B Soesdyke Demerara GY 1926 s James & Hilda. GOE Codrington Coll 1958; STM NYTS 1977; Cert Blanton-Peale Grad Inst 1984. Trans 8/1/1973 Bp Jonathan Goodhue Sherman. m 10/17/1948 Doris Goorahoo. Supply P S Ptr's Ch Rosedale NY 2006-2008; Assoc Trin-St Jn's Ch Hewlett NY 2003-2006; Int Ch Of The Resurr Kew Gardens NY 1998-2002; Int S Mary's Ch Brooklyn NY 1996-1997; Int Epis Ch of Gr and Resurr E Elmhurst NY 1995-1996; Int All Souls Ch New York NY 1993-1994; R S Barn Epis Ch Brooklyn NY 1989-1991, P-in-c 1979-1991; Dio Long Island Garden City NY 1984-1985, 1973-1978; P-in-c S Lydia's Epis Ch Brooklyn NY 1976-1980; Serv Angl Ch Of Guyana 1958-1973.

GORACZKO, Ann Kathleen Reeder (SeFla) 1801 Ludlam Drive, Miami Springs FL 33166 **S Bern De Clairvaux N Miami Bch FL 2016-; Assoc P All Ang Ch Miami FL 2013-; Chapl VITAS Innovative Hospice Care Inc. 2012-** B Miami, FL 1952 d William & Linda. MEd Florida Intl U 1993; MA Florida Intl U 2003; MDiv Florida Cntr for Theol Stds 2012. D 5/2/2010 P 5/10/2013 Bp Leo Frade. m 7/9/1978 Anthony Goraczko c 2.

GORANSON, Paul Werner (WMass) 130 Sachem Ave., Worcester MA 01606 B Worcester MA 1940 s Eric & Katri. BS Worcester Polytechnic Inst 1962; MDiv GTS 1974. D 6/14/1974 P 1/25/1975 Bp Alexander D Stewart. c 1. R Gr Ch Oxford MA 1977-2006, Vic 1974-1977. CCU 1974.

GORCHOV, Michael Ivan (Alb) 58 3rd St, Troy NY 12180 **R S Paul's Ch Troy NY 2004-** B Champange-Urbana IL 1953 s Maurice & Carol. MDiv GTS 2001;

BS SUNY 2001. D 6/9/2001 P 12/8/2001 Bp Daniel William Herzog. m 6/23/1971 Marianne C Gorchov c 3. R S Lk's Ch Catskill NY 2001-2004.

GORDAY, Peter J (WNC) 34 Lullwater Pl Ne, Atlanta GA 30307 B Fall River MA 1944 s Walter & Frances. BA Dart 1966; PhD Van 1980; MTh Columbia Presb Sem Decatur GA 1995. D 6/29/1974 Bp John Vander Horst P 5/1/1975 Bp William Evan Sanders. m 4/25/1970 Myrtle Virginia Gorday c 1. Asst Ch Of The Incarn Highlands NC 2008-2010; Assoc H Innoc Ch Atlanta GA 2001-2002; S Anne's Epis Ch Atlanta GA 1994-1999; Cn Cathd Of S Phil Atlanta GA 1987-1994; Asst S Lk's Epis Ch Atlanta GA 1980-1987; Dio Tennessee Nashville TN 1975-1980; P-in-c S Jas The Less Madison TN 1975-1980. Auth, "Fenelon: A Biography," Paraclete Press, 2012; Ed, "Ancient Chr Commentary On Scripture, NT Ix: Colossians, I-II Thessalonians, I-II Tim, Tit and Philemon," InterVarsity Press, 1999; Auth, "Principals Of Patristic Exegesis," 1983.

GORDON, Billie Mae (Mass) 290 Kingstown Way Unit 395, Duxbury MA 02332 **Chapl to Ret Cler and Surviving Spouses Dio Massachusetts Boston MA 2007-** B Washington PA 1941 d William & Ona. AS Massasoit Cmnty Coll 1978; BA Stonehill Coll 1991; MDiv Weston Jesuit TS 1997. D 12/19/1998 P 12/4/1999 Bp M(Arvil) Thomas Shaw. c 1. Sabbatical P S Andr's Ch Framingham MA 2017; Sabbatical Ch S Andr's Ch Ayer MA 2016; Sabbatical P Epis Ch Of S Thos Taunton MA 2015; Sabbatical P Trin Ch Bridgewater MA 2015; Sabbatical P Ch Of Our Sav Middleboro MA 2014; Pstr Assoc All SS Epis Ch Attleboro MA 2013-2016; Int Ch Of Our Sav Somerset MA 2009; Int Trin Epis Ch Rockland MA 2007-2009; Int Ch Of S Jn The Evang Duxbury MA 2007; Int Area Mssnr Bristol Epis Cluster Taunton/Easton/Mansfield MA 2005-2006; Int Mssnr S Jn The Evang Mansfield MA 2005-2006; Asst to the R/DRE Ch Of The Gd Shpd Waban MA 1999-2005. MA Epis Cleric Assn.

GORDON, Constance Leigh (U) 789 White Pine Dr, Tooele UT 84074 **Cur Dio Utah Salt Lake City UT 2005-** B Colorado Springs, CO 1964 d Robert & Verna. D 6/11/2005 P 4/19/2006 Bp Carolyn Tanner Irish. m 7/1/1987 James K Gordon c 2. rev.cgordon@gmail.com

GORDON, David Walter (Cal) 130 Avenida Barbera, Sonoma CA 95476 **Ret 1993-** B Oregon City OR 1927 s John & Dorothy. BS OR SU 1948; MDiv CDSP 1952. D 6/23/1951 P 12/21/1951 Bp Benjamin D Dagwell. m 12/29/1974 Ann K Gordon c 6. Stwdshp Off Dio New York New York NY 1982-1992; R Ch Of The Epiph San Carlos CA 1974-1982; R Ch Of The H Trin Richmond CA 1963-1973; Prov Secy for Coll Life 8th Prov Dio Oregon Portland OR 1960-1963; Prov Secy for Coll Wk 8th Prov PECUSA 1960-1963; Prov Secy for Coll Wk 8th Prov PECUSA Eight Prov 1960-1963; R S Jas' Epis Ch Coquille OR 1958-1960; R S Mart's Ch Lebanon OR 1953; Vic S Fran Ch Sweet Hm OR 1952-1958. Auth, *A Plan for Stwdshp Educ & Dvlpmt Through the Year*, Morehouse Pub, 1988.

GORDON JR, Harrington Manly (RI) 108 Columbia Ave, Warwick RI 02888 **Ret 1994-** B Jersey City NJ 1929 s Harrington & Ethel. BA Br 1952; BD Nash 1955; MDiv Nash 1956. D 6/24/1955 P 3/24/1956 Bp John S Higgins. m 6/27/1982 Joan Gordon. R Trin Ch Cranston RI 1988-1994; Dn - So Cntrl Dnry Dio Rhode Island Providence RI 1967-1978; R S Mk's Ch Warren RI 1957-1960; Cur All SS' Memi Ch Providence RI 1955-1957. Auth, "Dvlpmt, Money," *Plnng Process*, Dio Rhode Island, 1960. NNECA 1986. Honored - Continuous Wk For Exec Com Epis Chars Of Rhode Island; Honored - Continuous Epis Conf Cntr Dio RI.

GORDON, Jay Holland (NY) 382 Central Park W Apt 17p, New York NY 10025 **Chr And S Steph's Ch New York NY 2011-; Chairman, Bd Trst S Hilda's & S Hugh's Sch New York NY 1989-** B Glen Ridge NJ 1938 s J Holland & Dorothy. BA Br 1959; STB GTS 1962; STM 1973. D 6/9/1962 Bp Leland Stark P 12/15/1962 Bp Donald MacAdie. R The Ch of S Matt and S Tim New York NY 1973-2003; Cur Trin Par New York NY 1965-1973; Cur Gr Ch Newark NJ 1962-1965; Dioc Trst Dio New York New York NY 1998-2001, Ecum Cmsn 1996-2013, Stndg Com, Pres 1983-1984, Cathd Trst 1982-1984, Dioc Coun 1975-1977; Founding Mem and Pres The Jericho Proj NYC 1983-2001; Trst Daytop Vill 1970-1985. Soc of S Jn the Theol 1999. Cn of the Dio Bp Sisk 2003; Spec Merit Citation Mayor Jn Lindsay (NYC) 1972.

GORDON, Jim (RG) St Paul's Episcopal Church, PO Box 175, Marfa TX 79843 **Assoc Ch of the H Faith Santa Fe NM 2015-; Vic St. Paul's Epis Ch Marfa TX 2013-** B Pasadena CA 1951 s James & Mildred. California Polytechnic U - Pomona; Assoc of Arts Citrus Coll 1972; Dplma in Chr Mnstry DRG Sch for Mnstry (Trin Sch for Mnstry) 2010; Dplma in Chr Mnstry Other 2010. D 9/18/2010 Bp William Carl Frey P 12/14/2011 Bp Michael Vono. m 10/7/2005 Andrea G Shapiro. Vic S Paul's Ch Marfa TX 2013-2014.

GORDON, Rodney E (SVa) 701 S Providence Rd, North Chesterfield VA 23236 **S Ptr's Ch Oak Grove Oak Grove VA 2015-** B 1957 BMus Virginia Commonwealth U 1979; MDiv SWTS 1992; Cert Virginia Commonwealth U 2010. D 6/7/1992 P 12/12/1992 Bp Frank Harris Vest Jr. m 8/24/2007 Jennifer Gordon c 4. P-in-c Ch of the Gd Shpd Mc Kenney VA 2009-2013; S Barn Epis Ch No Chesterfield VA 2002-2007, 2002; P S Dav's Epis Ch No Chesterfield VA 2000-2001; R S Jn's Ch Hopewell VA 1994; R S Jn's Ch Petersburg VA 1992-1993.

GORDON, Walt (Minn) 834 Marshall Ave, Saint Paul MN 55104 B Montreal QC CA 1949 s Alec & Loula. BA Carleton Coll 1971; MDiv CDSP 1976. D 8/6/1976 P 10/30/1977 Bp Philip Frederick McNairy. c 2. Adv Ch Farmington MN 2006-2008; S Lk's Ch Willmar MN 2006-2008; P-in-c S Jas Epis Ch Hibbing MN 2000-2006; Cmncatn Off Dio Minnesota Minneapolis MN 1989-1997; Asst Ed, Dioc Nwspr Dio Minnesota Minneapolis MN 1988-1989; R Ascen Ch S Paul MN 1982-1985; P-in-c S Paul's Epis Le Cntr MN 1982-1984; R S Andrews Epis Ch Waterville MN 1981-1983; R S Paul's Ch Pipestone MN 1977-1978; H Trin Epis Ch Luverne MN 1976-1978; D/P-in-c S Jn Lake Benton MN 1976-1978; Hunger Mssnr Par Of The H Trin And S Anskar Minneapolis MN 1985-1988. Ed, *(Ed) A Strtgy for Growth in the Epis Ch: Joining Multiculturalism w Evang by the Rt. Rev. Mk MacDonald*, Intercultural Mnstry Dvlpmt, 1994. ECom 1991-1999; ECom 2005; ECom Bd 1997-1998; RCC Chapt Pres 1997-1998; RCC Mem 1991-1998. Fell-in-Res Sewanee 1997; Polly Bond Awards 1990-1996 ECom 1990.

GORDON, Walter Bernard (WTenn) PO Box 622, Grand Junction TN 38039 **S Jas Bolivar TN 2010-** B Memphis TN 1951 s Walter & Allene. BS Mississippi St U 1973; MS Auburn U 1984; PhD So Dakota St U 1989. D 9/1/2007 P 12/20/2008 Bp James Marshall Adams Jr.

GORDON-BARNES, Janice E (Md) 3117 Raven Croft Terrace, The Villages FL 32163 B London UK 1947 d Colin & Zena. SWTS; BA NWU 1977; MDiv U Chi 1979; DMin U Chi 1997. D 6/4/1980 Bp James Winchester Montgomery P 2/24/1981 Bp Quintin Ebenezer Primo Jr. m 11/11/2001 William Barnes. P-in-c Copley Par: The Ch Of The Resurr Joppatowne MD 2010-2012; R Ch Of The H Comf Luthvle Timon MD 1989-2009; Int S Anne's Par Annapolis MD 1984-1989; Cur S Aug's Epis Ch Wilmette IL 1980-1984.

GORE, Gina Lee (Los) 18631 Chapel Ln, Huntington Beach CA 92646 **S Wilfrid Of York Epis Ch Huntington Bch CA 2015-** B Denver CO 1965 d Michael & Sharon. U of San Diego 1984; BSM U CO@Denver 1988; Dplma of Theol Bloy Hse/Epis TS 2015; MDiv EDS 2015. D 6/6/2015 Bp Mary Douglas Glasspool P 1/16/2016 Bp Joseph Jon Bruno. m 5/30/1993 Kevin Edward Gore c 3.

GORES, Ariail Fischer (Dal) 4229 Tomberra Way, Dallas TX 75220 **D St Chris's 2004-** B New Orleans LA 1947 D 5/24/2003 Bp James Monte Stanton. c 2.

GORMAN, James Michael (Chi) 5388 W Harvey Rd, Oregon IL 61061 B Dixon IL 1937 s Leo & Ruby. D 12/26/1987 Bp Frank Tracy Griswold III. m 9/19/1959 Jeanne Carole Gorman c 3.

GORMAN, W Kenneth (NJ) 684 Sunrise Dr, Avalon NJ 08202 B Camden NJ 1944 s William & Eleanor. BA Ge 1966; MDiv PDS 1969; DMin NYTS 1990. D 4/19/1969 P 10/25/1969 Bp Alfred L Banyard. m 8/1/1992 Cheryl Lynn Gorman c 2. R H Cross Epis Ch Plainfield NJ 1997-2012; R Chr Ch So Amboy NJ 1991-1996; R S Lk the Evang Roselle NJ 1976-1991; R Chr Ch Palmyra NJ 1971-1976; Cur S Mary's Ch Haddon Heights NJ 1969-1971.

GORMLEY, Shane P (Alb) B Schenectady NY 1987 s William & Elizabeth. BA Roberts Wesleyan Coll 2009; MDiv Nash 2012; ThM PrTS 2013. D 6/2/2012 P 12/22/2012 Bp William Howard Love. Ch Of The Ascen Chicago IL 2013-2015; Dio Albany Greenwich NY 2012. sgormley@ascensionchicago.org

GORSUCH, John P (Oly) 1840 North Prospect Ave, APT 511, Milwaukee WI 53202 **Died 2/15/2017** B Denver CO 1932 s John & Freda. BA Wesl 1953; MDiv Yale DS 1956; Cert Shalem Inst for Sprtl Formation 1981. D 6/9/1956 P 12/26/1956 Bp Angus Dun. m 6/5/1955 Beverly Gorsuch c 2. 1991-2017; S Mk's Cathd Seattle WA 1987-1991, 1986; Exec Dir Cntr for Sprtl Dvlpmt Dio Olympia Seattle 1985-1990, GC 4x, Chair, Stndg Com, Chair, Exec Coun 1978-1985, GC, Stndg Com 1968-1990; R Epiph Par of Seattle Seattle WA 1968-1985; R S Tim's Epis Ch Yakima WA 1963-1968; Vic S Jn's Ch Great Bend KS 1959-1963; Assoc S Alb's Par Washington DC 1956-1959; Chair DeptCE, GC Dio Spokane Spokane WA 1965-1968; Dioc Coun, Del Angl Congr Dio Wstrn Kansas Hutchinson KS 1960-1963. Auth, "An Invitation to the Sprtl Journey," Paulist Press, 1990. jpgorsuch@gmail.com

GORTNER, David Timothy (WA) 3737 Seminary Road, Alexandria VA 22304 **Dir, Doctor of Mnstry Prog / Prof, Evang & Congrl Ldrshp VTS Alexandria VA 2008-; Strng Com Mem, Nthrn VA Cmnty Organizing VOICE Strtgy Team Alexandria VA 2015-** B Reading PA 1966 s Robert & Aileen. BA Wheaton Coll 1988; MA Wake Forest U 1994; MDiv SWTS 1997; PhD U Chi 2004. D 5/8/2003 Bp Bill Persell P 11/29/2003 Bp Victor Alfonso Scantlebury. m 10/16/1999 Heather Ann VanDeventer c 2. Meade Memi Epis Ch Alexandria VA 2016; Asst S Geo's Epis Ch Arlington VA 2009-2011; Asst S Paul's Epis Ch San Rafael CA 2007-2008; Yth & YA Mnstry Cmsn S Mk's Par Berkeley CA 2005-2006; Asst. Prof, Pstr Theol / Dir, Cntr for Angl Lrng & Ldrshp CDSP Berkeley CA 2004-2008; Lectr, Practical Theol Bexley Seabury Fed Chicago IL 2003-2004; Vic / Co-Founding Pstr Ch of Jesus Chr Reconciler Chicago 2003-2004; Natl Coordntr, Pstr Ldrshp Search Effort (PLS Fund for Theol Educ Atlanta GA 2003-2004; Pstr for YA / Young Fam Mnstrs S Mk's Ch Evanston IL 1999-2004; Resrch Dir / Lectr SWTS Evanston IL 1999-2004; Chapl Seasons Hospice Pk Ridge IL 1997-1998; Supply Chapl Evanston NW Hosp Evanston IL 1995-2000; Dio California San Francisco CA 2005-2007;

Cmsn on Campus & YA Mnstry Dio Chicago Chicago IL 1997-2004, Epis Campus Mnstry at NWU 1997-2004. Auth, "Varieties of Personal Theol: Charting the Beliefs and Values of Amer YA," *Varieties of Personal Theol: Charting the Beliefs and Values of Amer YA*, Ashgate, 2013; Auth, "Habits for Effective Ldrshp: Lessons from Beyond the Ecclesia," *ATR*, 2010; Auth, "Looking at Ldrshp Beyond Our Own Horizon," *ATR*, 2009; Auth, "Around One Table," *Around One Table*, CREDO & Coll for Bishops, 2009; Auth, "Transforming Evang," *Transforming Evang*, Ch Pub, 2008; Co-Auth, "Mentoring Cler for effective Ldrshp," *Reflective Pract*, 2007; Co-Auth, "Beyond Wish-Lists For Pstr Ldrshp: Assessing Cler Behavior & Congregat'nal Outcomes To Guide Sem. Curric," *Theol Educ*, 2005; Auth, "Varieties Of YA Personal Theologies," U Chi, 2004; Co-Auth, "The Epis Ch Welcomes You? The Challenges Of Evang w Students And YA," *Disorganized Rel (Kujawa, ed.)*, Cowley, 1997. AAR 1998; APA 1994; Ntwk of Mnstry Innovators 2007-2008; Soc for the Sci Study of Rel 2005. Conant Grant Rec Epis Ch Cntr (2005, 2010) 2010; Resrch Grant Rec Lilly Endwmt 2010; Trabert-Graebner Awd For Excellence In Biblic Languages CDSP 2008; Grant Rec EvangES (1996, 2005, 2007) 2007; Fell ECF 1998.

GOSHERT, Mary Linda (NCal) 882 Oxford Way, Benicia CA 94510 **P-in-c S Paul's Epis Ch Benicia CA 1989-, 1982-1989, R 1982-1989** B Orange CA 1944 d Richard & Velma. BA California St U 1965; MLS California St U 1973; MDiv CDSP 1979. D 6/23/1979 P 2/2/1980 Bp Robert Claflin Rusack. m 6/18/2011 Gene Ekenstam c 2. P-in-c S Lk's Mssn Calistoga CA 2013-2016; R S Ambr Par Claremont CA 2006-2011, 1998; R S Ptr's Par Santa Maria CA 2001-2006; The Par Ch Of S Lk Long Bch CA 1998-2001; R S Jn The Div Epis Ch Morgan Hill CA 1989-1997; Deploy Off The Epis Dio Nthrn California Sacramento CA 1982-1989; Cur Ch Of S Mart Davis CA 1979-1982; Chapl U Ca-Davis 1979-1982; Mem, Dioc Coun Dio Los Angeles Los Angeles CA 2004-2012, Stwdshp and Dvlpmt Cmsn 2004-2012, Disciplinary Bd 2003-2013; Stndg Com Dio El Camino Real Salinas CA 1992-1996. Auth, "Var arts Bk Revs Annuals". xtisrisen@gmail.com

GOSHGARIAN, Martin John (Mass) 85 Glenwood Rd, Somerville MA 02145 **1989-** B Boston MA 1940 s Serop & Ardemis. BA cl Harv 1962; BA Harv 1962; MDiv cl VTS 1965; MDiv VTS 1965. D 6/26/1965 P 5/19/1966 Bp John Melville Burgess. 1989-2001; R S Jas Epis Ch Teele Sq Somerville MA 1973-1989; Asst S Cyp's Ch Boston MA 1969-1972; Asst S Steph's Memi Ch Lynn MA 1965-1969; Trst Somerville (Mass.) Publ Libr 1987-1988; Exam Chapl Dio Massachusetts Boston MA 1976-1981, Libr Bd 1974-1979. 1635 Soc 1999; Fran Scott Key Soc 2002; Jn Harvard Soc 2000.

GOSHORN, Alice Elizabeth Gill (Ind) 4921 E State Road 252, Franklin IN 46131 **Archd Dio Indianapolis Indianapolis IN 2004-; Archd Dio Indianapolis Indianapolis IN 2004-** B Needham IN 1941 d Ray & Ruth. BA Franklin Coll 1963; MA Penn 1965; Chr TS 1997. D 6/24/1997 Bp Edward Witker Jones. m 7/12/1971 Robyn Kent Goshorn c 1. D S Thos Ch Franklin IN 1997-2012. Assn for Epis Deacons 1997.

GOSNELL, Linda (USC) 5 Southbridge Ct, Simpsonville SC 29680 B Spartanburg SC 1949 d Arnold & Dora. BS Winthrop U 1971; MEd U of So Carolina 1977; MDiv VTS 2005. D 6/11/2005 P 5/24/2006 Bp Dorsey Henderson. m 8/7/1971 Tandy Cleveland Gosnell c 1. Asst R H Cross Epis Ch Simpsonville SC 2006-2017; Asst S Fran Ch Greenville SC 2005-2006.

GOSS, Frank Michael (NJ) Po Box 1, Bradley Beach NJ 01/01/7720 B Montclair NJ 1947 s Frank & Theresa. BA Seton Hall U 1969; MDiv Seton Hall Univ Immac Concep Sem So Orange 1975. Rec 5/17/1997 Bp John Shelby Spong. m 7/1/1995 Roseann M Goss. R S Jas Ch Bradley Bch NJ 2004-2016; R S Lk's Ch Phillipsburg NJ 1998-2004; Asst P S Jas Ch Montclair NJ 1997-1998; Serv RC Ch 1973-1994.

GOSS III, James Paul (Cal) 792 Penny Royal Ln, San Rafael CA 94903 B Boston MA 1951 s James & Alice. BA San Francisco St U 1974; BA Epis Dio Sch for Diac 1997; MS Dominican U CA San Rafael CA 2003. D 6/7/1997 Bp William Edwin Swing. D Ch Of The Nativ San Rafael CA 1999-2001; Chr Ch Sausalito CA 1998-2000. Cherokee Soc of the Grtr Bay Area 2005; Cherokees of California 2004; Marin Amer Indn Allnce 2002; Psi Chi (Psychol hon Soc) 2000. Dr. Robert Skukraft Awd for Inspirational Ldrshp Dominican U 2003.

GOSSARD, Pamela Ann (NCal) B Torrance CA 1952 d James & Harriet. BA Humboldt St U 1978; Cert of Diac Stds The Sch for Deacons 2016. D 8/13/2016 Bp Barry Leigh Beisner. m 3/17/1973 Paul Rodney Gossard c 1.

GOSSETT JR, Earl Fowler (Ala) 1811 Cedar Crest Rd, Birmingham AL 35214 B Birmingham AL 1933 s Earl & Clara. BA Birmingham-Sthrn Coll 1954; BD Van 1957; PhD Van 1961. D 5/27/1998 Bp Robert Oran Miller P 12/1/1998 Bp Henry Nutt Parsley Jr. m 7/17/1956 Rhoda Lois Gossett c 1. Int Trin Epis Ch Bessemer AL 2001-2002; S Jn's Ch Birmingham AL 1999-2000; Prof Rel & Philos Birmingham Sthrn Coll 1965-1999; Non-Par. "Angl Essentials," Alabam Dioc Cathecism, 2005; "The Challenge Of The The Orth Theol Of Rowan Williams," The Apos, 2002; "Our Hostiric Connections - Our Common Mssn," The Apos, 2001. AAR; Soc For Chr Ethics. Phi Beta Kappa.

GOSSLING, Nancy (Mass) 25 Chapman Dr, Glastonbury CT 06033 **Dn The Cathd Ch Of S Paul Boston MA 2017-** B Boston MA 1952 d Albion & Louise.

BA Wellesley Coll 1974; MDiv Ya Berk 2000. D 6/10/2000 Bp Andrew Donnan Smith P 1/13/2001 Bp James Elliot Curry. m 6/8/1974 Paul L Gossling c 2. R S Jas Ch Glastonbury CT 2002-2012; Cur S Paul's Ch Riverside CT 2000-2002.

GOTAUTAS, Patricia Marie (USC) B Atlanta GA 1951 d John & Corinne. AA Greenville Tech Coll 1996. D 5/21/2011 Bp W illiam Andrew Waldo. c 2.

GOTCHER, Vernon Alfred (FtW) 1904 Westcliff Dr, Euless TX 76040 B Little Rock AR 1932 s Vernon & Irma. BA U of Cntrl Arkansas 1954; MDiv Sewanee: The U So, TS 1957; ThM TCU 1975; PhD Texas Womans U 1984. D 7/3/1957 P 3/19/1958 Bp Robert Raymond Brown. m 6/20/1981 Deanna D Gotcher c 3. S Alb's Epis Ch Arlington TX 1996-1998; All SS' Epis Ch Ft Worth TX 1993-1995, 1991-1993; R S Steph's Ch Huntsville TX 1988-1991, Vic 1969-1987; Non-par 1980-1988; S Steph's Epis Ch Hurst TX 1969-1979; Mssnr Dio Dallas Dallas TX 1965-1969; R S Lk's Brinkley AR 1961-1965; R S Ptr Tollville 1961-1965; R Chr Ch Mena AR 1957-1961; Trin Ch Van Buren AR 1957-1961. Auth, "Concepts Of Personality In Ta Of Berne & Harris As Related To Augustinian Doctor Of Man"; Auth, "Mar/Fam Therapists: Clincal Roles & Ther Outcome Expectations"; Auth, "Mar/Fam Therapists: Clincl Roles & Ther Outcome Expectations". Amer Assn Of Mar And Fam Therapists 1974; Tamft 1978. R Emer St Stpehens Hurst Tx 2004.

GOTKO, Raymond Morgan (At) 501 Sweet Berry Drive, Mont Eagle TN 37356 B Parris Island SC 1939 s Raymond & Kate Lee. BFA U GA 1961; MFA U GA 1963; PhD Florida St U 1972; MDiv Sewanee: The U So, TS 1990. D 6/5/1999 Bp Onell Asiselo Soto P 12/11/1999 Bp Frank Kellogg Allan. m 9/5/1964 Lynda Gotko c 2. Assoc R S Jas Epis Ch Marietta GA 2002-2009; R S Andr's Epis Ch Ft Vlly GA 1999-2002; Liturg Mus Cler Rep Dio Atlanta Atlanta GA 2005-2011, Stndg Com 2001-2003, Nomin Com IX Bp 2000-2001.

GOTT, Amanda Katherine (Ct) **R S Matt's Ch Lincoln NE 2017-** B Atlanta GA 1974 d Walter & Marcia. BA Bard Coll 1996; MDiv Iliff TS 2001; STM GTS 2005. D 6/11/2005 Bp Robert John O'Neill P 12/13/2005 Bp Vicky Gene Robinson. m 6/10/2006 Steven M Carpenter c 2. S Thos' Ch New Haven CT 2015-2016; R Gr And S Ptr's Epis Ch Hamden CT 2009-2017; Asst Ch Of The Gd Shpd Nashua NH 2005-2009. Auth, "A Bowl of Figs," *Alive Now. (March/April 2005)*, Upper Room Press, 2005.

GOTTARDI-LITTELL, Laura (Chi) Church of Our Saviour, Chicago IL 60614 **The Ch Hm At Montgomery Place Chicago IL 2017-; S Jos's And S Aid's Ch Blue Island IL 2016-** B Morristown NJ 1959 d Joseph & Eleanor. BA Antioch Coll 1982; MDiv Garrett-Evang TS 1996; Cert Theol Stud SWTS 2005. D 6/3/2006 P 12/16/2006 Bp Bill Persell. m 5/23/1986 Numa Gottardi-Littell c 2. S Phil's Epis Palatine IL 2013-2016; Asst Ch Of Our Sav Chicago IL 2009-2013; Outreach Min Imm Luth Ch Chicago 2009-2011; Co-Pstr Ch of Jesus Chr Reconciler 2007-2009. Lloyd Mentzer Awd SWTS 2005; Cert of Caring NW Cmnty Hosp 1997; Sprt Awd Luth Gnrl Hosp 1996; ABS Prize Garrett-Evang TS 1994; Hutchinson Fllshp Garrett-Evang TS 1993. numandlaura@mac.com

GOTTING, Viktoria Johanna Petra (Tex) Saint John's Church, 815 S Broadway St, La Porte TX 77571 **R S Jn's Ch La Porte TX 2015-** B New York NY 1961 d Juergen & Gisele. BA U of Houston Cntrl 2005; MDiv Harvard DS 2008; Dplma in Angl Stds Sewanee: The U So, TS 2012; Dplma in Angl Stds U So TS 2012. D 6/16/2012 P 1/20/2013 Bp C Andrew Doyle. c 2. S Chris's Ch League City TX 2012-2015; S Lk's Epis Hosp Houston TX 2012-2013; The Great Cmsn Fndt Houston TX 2012-2013. VIKTORIA@STCHRISCHURCH.ORG

GOTTLICH, Samuel Grier (WTex) 5857 Timbergate Dr Apt 1149, Apt 1149, Corpus Christi TX 78414 **Ret 1997-** B Corpus Christi TX 1929 s Samuel & Ruth. Del Mar Coll 1951; MDiv VTS 1967; VTS 1980; U So 1988. D 7/12/1967 Bp Everett H Jones P 1/1/1968 Bp Richard Earl Dicus. m 4/14/1952 Diane P Prude c 3. Dir. Dept. Psych. Guadalupe Vlly Hosp Seguin TX 1990-1996; Chapl/Dir. Dept. Psych. Guadalupe Vlly Reg Med Cntr 1989-1997; R S Barth's Ch Corpus Christi TX 1973-1989; R S Andr's Epis Ch Seguin TX 1968-1973; Vic Epiph Epis Ch Raymondville TX 1967-1968; Vic Redeem Mercedes TX 1967-1968; Asst R S Jn's Ch McAllen TX 1967-1968. Auth, "Fr It Hurts-The Subject of Pain," 1999; Auth, "I Jn," *Take You Mary*, 1969. Paul Harris Fell Rotary Intl 1992; Citizen of Year Seguin, Texas 1989.

GOUGH, Karen (WNY) 315 Oakbrook Dr, Williamsville NY 14221 **Stff Chapl Sis of Charity Hosp 1994-** B Toronto ON CA 1952 d James & Kathleen. BS U Tor 1975; MA Chr-King Sem E Aurora NY 1989; Cert Sis of Mercy Hosp Buffalo NY 1989; LSS Sis of Charity Hosp Buffalo NY 1990; Sis of Charity Hosp Buffalo NY 1992; Sloan-Kettering Memi Hosp New York NY 1992. D 6/10/1989 Bp David Charles Bowman P 1/31/2004 Bp Michael Garrison. m 6/8/1974 Kenneth Harold Gough c 2. Vic Trin Ch Lancaster NY 2006-2017; S Paul's Epis Ch Harris Hill Buffalo NY 2004-2006, D 1989-1999; Assoc St. Paul's Epis Ch Harris Hill 2004-2006; Dir Epis Ch Hm and Affiliates Buffalo NY 2000-2004; Assist. Dir of Pstr Care Epis Ch Hm Buffalo NY 1999-2000; Archd Dio Wstrn New York Tonawanda NY 1993-1996; Stff Chapl Luth Serv Soc 1989-1992. "On Guard Against Greed," *Sermons that Wk, Vol. XIV*, Morehouse Pub, 2006; "The Outcast," *Wmn Uncommon Prayers*, Morehouse Pub, 2000; "Marjorie," *Wmn Uncommon Prayers*, Morehouse Pub, 2000; "Septem-

ber Morning," *Wmn Uncommon Prayers*, Morehouse Pub, 2000. Assembly Of Epis Hlth Care Chapl 1990; ACPE.

GOUGH, Lauren A (FtW) 3733 Whitefern Dr., Fort Worth TX 76137 **Died 3/7/2016** B Peoria IL 1944 d Robert & Naomi. BA U of No Texas 1967; MDiv EDS 1983; CDSP 2001. D 6/11/1983 Bp Ned Cole P 5/28/1984 Bp O'Kelley Whitaker. m 5/30/2015 Judith Elizabeth Upham. Asstg P S Mart In The Fields Ch Keller TX 2011-2013; Called Pstr Ch of the Redeem (ELCA) Binghamton NY 2007-2010; R S Paul's Ch Endicott NY 2002-2004; R All SS Epis Ch Watsonville CA 1999-2001; R St Johns Broad Creek Ft Washington MD 1988-1997; R S Ann's Ch Afton NY 1984-1988; S Ptr's Ch Bainbridge NY 1984-1988; Cur S Jn's Ch Ithaca NY 1983-1984. Auth, "Calendar of SS," *ABS Online Devotions*, ABS, 2007. EWC 1979; WECA 1985-1997.

GOULD, Glenn Hamilton (USC) 30 Moise Dr, Sumter SC 29150 **Non-par 1996-** B Miami FL 1944 s Raymond & Leonore. Duke 1963; BA Furman U 1970; MDiv Sewanee: The U So, TS 1976. Trans 2/23/2004 Bp Michael B Curry. m 4/26/1986 Fran Carson Gould c 2. S Mk's Epis Ch Huntersville NC 1985-1996; R S Alb's Ch Lexington SC 1984-1985, Vic 1978-1983; Epis Ch Of S Simon And S Jude Irmo SC 1978; Dio Upper So Carolina Columbia SC 1976-1978; Cur S Jude's Columbia SC 1976-1978. stbarnabasusc@att.net

GOULD, Jane Soyster (Mass) 19 Nahant Pl, Lynn MA 01902 **R S Steph's Memi Ch Lynn MA 2000-** B Washington DC 1956 d Peter & Eliza. BA Stan 1978; MA Stan 1979; MDiv EDS 1986. D 6/4/1986 Bp John Bowen Coburn P 5/28/1987 Bp David Elliot Johnson. m 7/10/1982 John Allen Gould c 2. Chapl Dio Massachusetts Boston MA 1994-2001; Epis Chapl MIT 1994-2000; Int Epis City Mssn Boston MA 1993-1994; Int Co-Exec Dir Epis City Mssn 1992-1994; Assoc Gr Epis Ch Lawr MA 1991-1994; Asst Par Of The Epiph Winchester MA 1986-1990; Chapl Phillips Acad Andover MA 1985-1986. Auth, "On Engr And Evang," *Disorganized Rel*, Cowley, 1998; Auth, "Redeeming Imperialism," *Journ Of Wmn Mnstrs*, 1997; Auth, "Weaving The Wrld Together," *Epis Times*, 1996; Auth, "My Sis Struggle To Survive," *Journ Of Wmn Mnstrs*, 1995; Auth, "Cracking Walls And Opening Eyes: Remembering The Washington Four," *Wit*, 1994. ESMHE; EUC; EWC. Barbara C. Harris Awd for Soc Justice Epis City Mssn/Boston 2008; Cler Renwl Grant Lilly Fndt/Indiana 2005; Kellogg Natl Fllshp Prog WKKellogg Fndt/Michigan 1993.

GOULD, Jennie Ruth (NH) 19 Maplewood St, Watertown MA 02472 **CPE Supvsr Boston Med Cntr Boston MA 2015-; Hosp Chapl Boston Med Cntr Boston MA 2002-** B San Francisco CA 1963 d Hugh & Ruth. MDiv EDS 1996; PhD Bos 2004. D 6/11/2005 P 12/15/2005 Bp Vicky Gene Robinson. revjrgould@gmail.com

GOULD, Mary Dolores (Oly) Po Box 1193, Maple Valley WA 98038 B Brunswick GA 1946 d John & Irma. Cert Dioc TS 1990; Cert CPE 1992. D 11/12/1993 Bp Vincent Waydell Warner. m 12/11/1982 Gerald Clark Gould c 2. D S Mk's Cathd Seattle WA 2002-2003; D S Geo Epis Ch Maple Vlly WA 1999-2000; D Gd Samar Epis Ch Sammamish WA 1993-1998. NAAD.

GOULD, Robert Carwyle (NCal) 2528 Clearlake Way, Sacramento CA 95826 **Died 2/12/2016** B Vallejo CA 1919 s Jesse & Alice. BA California St U Fresno 1949; BD CDSP 1949. D 6/4/1949 P 12/17/1949 Bp Sumner Walters. m 3/17/1945 Betty Creer Gould c 4. Assoc S Geo's Ch Carmichael CA 2010-2016; Assoc S Matt's Epis Ch Sacramento CA 1982-1986; Worker P Sacramento Cnty Welf CA 1968-1985; Worker P Sacramento Vol Bureau CA 1966-1968; R S Jn The Evang Ch Chico CA 1961-1966; R S Barn Par McMinnville OR 1960-1961; R S Lk's Epis Ch Merced CA 1954-1960; Vic S Phil's Ch Coalinga CA 1949-1954; S Thos Ch Avenal CA 1949-1954.

GOWDY-JAEHNIG, Christine Annettee (Ia) D 6/6/2010 P 12/18/2010 Bp Alan Scarfe.

GOWEN, Eleanore Louise (Mass) 12 Hobart Ln, Rockland MA 02370 B 1937 d Thomas & Grace. BS Estrn Connecticut St U 1969; MA U of Connecticut 1972; PhD U of Connecticut 1980; DMin EDS 1999. D 5/14/1994 Bp Charles I Jones III. D S Lk's Epis Ch Scituate MA 1994-2003; S Fran Epis Ch Great Falls MT 1994-1998.

GOWETT, Randall James (SJ) **D & Asst To Vic Ch Of The Resurr Clovis Clovis CA 1996-** B Brawley CA 1951 s Charles & Dorothy. San Jose St U; BS U of Phoenix 1991; MDiv TESM 1995. D 6/8/1996 Bp David Mercer Schofield. m 10/27/1990 Tamberlin Rachel Spencer.

GOWING, Michael LeVern (Mich) 2696 Indian Trl, Pinckney MI 48169 **1967-** B Detroit MI 1937 s Clifford & Wanda. BA Trin 1959; STB Ya Berk 1963; MA Wayne 1969. D 6/29/1963 Bp Richard Stanley Merrill Emrich P 1/25/1964 Bp Archie H Crowley. 1964-1967; Asst S Thos Ch Trenton MI 1964-1967; Vic S Tim Flat Rock MI 1963-1967.

GOWLAND, James David (NJ) 11 N Monroe Ave, Wenonah NJ 08090 B Philadelphia PA 1946 s Edmund & Mary. D 6/9/2007 Bp George Edward Councell. m 7/2/2007 Janice Gowland c 2. officestmhh@gmail.com

GOWTY, Richard Newton (Tex) 21 Mclean Street, Brighton 4017 Australia B Melbourne VIC AU 1943 s William & Nita. Royal Melbourne Inst of Tech 1963; BTh S Fran Theol Coll 1971. Trans 6/1/1992. m 8/4/1972 Margaret Ann Gowty. Assoc R S Dav's Ch Austin TX 1992-1994; Serv Ch Of Australia 1972-1992; Non-par.

GRAB, Virginia Lee (NY) 74 Montgomery St, Tivoli NY 12583 **Asst Chapl Bard Coll Annandale NY 2000-** B Los Angeles CA 1937 d Charles & Celia. BA U CA 1962; MA Col 1965; MDiv UTS 1991. D 3/18/2000 P 9/16/2000 Bp Richard Frank Grein. c 2. Int Zion Epis Ch Wappingers Falls NY 2005; Ch Of S Jn The Evang Red Hook NY 2001-2005; The Living Pulpit Bronx NY 2001-2005.

GRABHER, Jerald (WMo) 4635 Campbell St, Kansas City MO 64110 B 1935 D 8/28/2002 Bp Barry Howe.

GRABINSKI, Kenneth Lee (Oly) 5240 46th Ave Sw, Seattle WA 98136 B 1935 D 7/14/1977 Bp Robert Hume Cochrane. m 8/24/1957 Jane Elizabeth Grabinski c 3.

GRABNER, John David (Spok) 165 SW Spruce St, Apt 1, Pullman WA 99163 B Coeur D'Alene ID 1940 s Floren & Ivy. BA U of Washington 1963; MA U of Washington 1971; MDiv PrTS 1974; MA U of Notre Dame 1978; PhD U of Notre Dame 1983. D 4/18/1998 P 10/17/1998 Bp Frank Jeffrey Terry. c 2. Supply P Dio Spokane Spokane WA 2003-2013; P Assoc S Mk's Epis Ch Moscow ID 1998-2003; Serv Meth Ch 1977-1995. Auth, "All SS' Day," *Homily Serv*, Taylor and Fran Grp, 2010; Auth, "All Souls' Day," *Homily Serv*, Taylor and Fran Grp, 2010; Auth, "There Is No Memory," *Homily Serv*, Taylor and Fran Grp, 2010; Auth, "Reign of Chr-C," *Homily Serv*, Taylor and Fran Grp, 2010; Auth, "What Kind of King?," *Homily Serv*, Taylor and Fran Grp, 2010; Auth, "The Chr Use of the Seder, The Complete Libr of Chr Wrshp," *Libr of Chr Wrshp, vol 2*, Hendrickson Pub, 1995; Auth, "Triduum: Practical Considerations," *Reformed Liturg & Mus*, 1990; Auth, "The Priesthood of the Believing Cmnty," *Sacramental Life*, Ord of S Lk, 1988; Auth, "The Touch of Blessing," *Assembly*, Notre Dame Cntr for Pstr Liturg, 1987; Auth, "A Commentary on the Rites of "An Ordinal, The Meth Ch," U Microfilms Intl , 1983; Auth, "Ord and Lay: Them-Us or We?," *Wrshp*, Liturgicql P43WW, 1980. No Amer Acad of Liturg 1975; Societas Liturgica 1975.

GRABNER-HEGG, Linnae Marie (Minn) 1619 31st Ave S, Fargo ND 58103 B St. Louis Park MN 1960 d Duwayne & Barbara. D 5/10/2002 P 5/9/2003 Bp Andrew Fairfield. m 10/17/1981 Barry Hegg c 3. D Geth Cathd Fargo ND 2002-2003.

GRACE JR, Harry Tyler (WNY) 36 Parkside Ct, Buffalo NY 14214 B Philadelphia PA 1941 s Harry & Anne. BS Penn 1963; MDiv GTS 1970. D 6/27/1970 Bp William Foreman Creighton P 1/1/1971 Bp Stephen F Bayne Jr. m 6/2/1964 Kathryn C Grace c 2. Vic S Mk's Ch Buffalo NY 2004-2006; Int St. Mich & All Ang Buffalo NY 2001-2003; S Mich And All Ang Buffalo NY 2001-2002; R Ch Of All SS Buffalo NY 1986-2000; Int S Alb Epis Ch Cleveland OH 1986; Assoc S Paul's Epis Ch Cleveland OH 1984-1986; R Calv Epis Ch Jerome ID 1979-1984; Trin Ch Buhl ID 1979-1984; Assoc Calv Epis Ch Flemington NJ 1977-1978; R Hse Of Pryr Epis Ch Newark NJ 1973-1976; Cur Gr Ch White Plains NY 1970-1973.

GRACE, Holt Buff (Minn) 215 4th St N, Stillwater MN 55082 **P Ch Of The Ascen Stillwater MN 2010-** B Waynesboro VA 1968 s Holt & Suzanne. BA U NC 1991; MDiv Sewanee: The U So, TS 2007. D 12/21/2006 P 8/11/2007 Bp J Neil Alexander. m 7/29/1995 Amy L Grace c 2. R S Teresa Acworth GA 2007-2010; Dir Of Oprtns Medshare Intl Decatur GA 2000-2004; Sch for Formation Bd Mem Dio Minnesota Minneapolis MN 2011-2013.

GRACE SR, James McKay Lykes (Tex) 2428 Swift Blvd, Houston TX 77030 **R St Andrews Epis Ch Houston TX 2014-** B Houston TX 1975 s R Randall & Jean. BA SW U Georgetown TX 1998; MDiv VTS 2005. D 6/11/2005 P 12/12/2005 Bp Don Adger Wimberly. m 1/3/2004 Marla Huseman Grace c 3. Cn Chr Ch Cathd Houston TX 2010-2014; Asst Ch Of The Epiph Houston TX 2005-2010; Yth Dir Trin Ch Houston TX 1999-2002. COM 2007.

GRACE, Patricia M. (ETenn) 4753 Scepter Way, Knoxville TN 37912 **Cn Dio E Tennessee Knoxville TN 2013-** B Trenton NJ 1955 BA Buc. D 5/29/2004 P 1/8/2005 Bp Charles Glenn VonRosenberg. S Mk's Ch Dalton GA 2011-2013; Assoc for Chr Ed. & Par Life S Lk's Epis Ch Atlanta GA 2006-2011; Cur St Jas Epis Ch at Knoxville Knoxville TN 2004-2006. pgrace@dioet.org

GRACEN, Sharon Kay (Ct) 1109 Main St, Branford CT 06405 **R Trin Ch Branford CT 2010-** B Savannah GA 1951 d Robert & Jane. BD Indiana U 1997; MDiv SWTS 2000. D 6/24/2000 P 6/23/2001 Bp Cate Waynick. m 2/2/2007 Peter Appleton Schuller c 2. Vic Faith Epis Ch Laguna Niguel CA 2004-2010; The Amer Cathd of the H Trin Paris 75008 2001-2004; Asst Chr Ch Cranbrook Bloomfield Hills MI 2000-2001. "Le Bon Dieu Aussi S'habille en Prada," Presses de la Renaissance, 2007.

GRACEY, Colin Beal (Mass) 18 Monmouth Ct, Brookline MA 02446 **Died 6/7/2016** B Newton MA 1935 s Ernest & Edna. BA Ya 1957; STB Harvard DS 1963; DMin EDS 1984. D 7/22/1963 Bp Anson Phelps Stokes Jr P 5/1/1964 Bp Donald J Campbell. m 6/10/1957 Susan Gracey c 4. Chapl NEU 1967-2016; Dio Massachusetts Boston MA 1966-2004; Cur Trin Ch Concord MA 1963-1966. Auth, "Gd Genes?: Emerging Values For Sci," *Rel & Soc*. Parson Club, ESMHE, Nacuc.

GRACIA, Kesner (Hai) **Dio Haiti Port-au-Prince HT 2002-** B 1973 D. m 11/23/2006 Anne Bedwine Darley Delica c 2.

GRACZYK, Glen Gerard (SwFla) St Marys Episcopal Church, 1010 24th Ave W, Palmetto FL 34221 **P-in-c S Mary's Epis Ch Palmetto FL 2013-** B Milwaukee WI 1953 s George & Alice. BA Cardinal Stritch Coll 1976; MDiv St Fran de Salis Sem 1981; Dplma of Angl Stds TS 2013; Dplma of Angl Stds Sewanee: The U So, TS 2013. Rec 5/19/2013 as Priest Bp Dabney Tyler Smith. frglenofstmaryspalmetto@yahoo.com

GRADY, Ann Nadine (EMich) 815 N. Grant St, Bay City MI 48708 **Eccl Trial Crt Dio Milwaukee Milwaukee WI 2006-** B Minot ND 1951 d Grover & Winifred. BA U of Wisconsin 1974; MDiv Garrett-Evang TS 1993; STM Nash 2000. D 7/22/2000 P 7/28/2001 Bp Roger John White. P-in-c Trin Epis Ch Bay City MI 2013-2016; Int Chr Ch Montpelier VT 2010-2011; Int S Lk's Luth Ch Sullivan WI 2007-2008; P-in-c S Jn In The Wilderness Elkhorn WI 2003-2007; P-in-c S Mary's Epis Ch Summit WI 2001-2003.

GRADY, Richard Charles (SwFla) 6985 Edgewater Cir, Fort Myers FL 33919 B Rochester NY 1946 s Sylvester & Lois. BA Florida Memi Coll 1970; MDiv VTS 1999. D 6/13/1999 P 12/12/1999 Bp Stephen Hays Jecko. m 8/9/1971 Ella Marie Grady c 2. Assoc R S Lk's Ch Ft Myers FL 2006-2014; Assoc R S Hilary's Ch Ft Myers FL 2002-2006; Vic S Mk's Ch Palatka FL 1999-2001; St Marys Epis Ch Palatka FL 1999-2001; COM Dio SW Florida Parrish FL 2005-2011, Eccl Crt 2002-2005; Cmsn on Yth Dio Florida Jacksonville 1999-2001. fathergrady@yahoo.com

GRAEBNER, Norman B (NC) Po Box 628, Hillsborough NC 27278 **R S Matt's Epis Ch Hillsborough NC 1990-; Historiographed Dio No Carolina Raleigh NC 2007-** B Ames IA 1951 s Norman & Laura. BA U of Virginia 1973; MDiv Duke DS 1976; PhD Duke 1984; CAS VTS 1985. D 4/21/1986 Bp Robert Whitridge Estill P 5/3/1987 Bp Frank Harris Vest Jr. m 11/24/2009 Chris A Graebner c 1. Asst to R S Ptr's Epis Ch Charlotte NC 1986-1990; Res NC Memi Hosp Chap Hill NC 1985-1986. "Epis Ch and Race in 19th c. NC," Angl and Epis Hist, 2009. Bd Mem For The HSEC 2000-2006; Secy, HSEC 2006.

GRAF, Thomas W (SeFla) St Faith's Episcopal Church, 10600 Caribbean Blvd, Cutler Bay FL 33189 **S Jas The Fisherman Islamorada FL 2013-** B New York NY 1955 s William & Joan. BA Herbert H Lehman Coll 1978; MDiv Cath Theol Un 1986. Rec 3/27/2012 as Priest Bp Leo Frade. m 2/24/1990 Isabel M Graf c 3.

GRAFF, Donald T (Pa) 1434 Alcott St, Philadelphia PA 19149 B Pasadena CA 1944 s Donald & Frances. BA California Wstrn U 1966; MDiv CDSP 1969. D 9/13/1969 P 3/21/1970 Bp Francis E I Bloy. m 11/16/1985 Elizabeth Graff c 2. Ret Dio Pennsylvania Philadelphia PA 2011, 1991-2011, 1976-1983, Cn & Mem, Cathd Chapt 1988-1995; Bd Coun ECS 1989-1999; Dn, Fairmount Dnry Fairmount Dnry 1985-1991; Vic The Free Ch Of S Jn Philadelphia PA 1984-1990; Dioc Coordntr Consult Ntwk 1980-1983; Coordntr Fairmount Team Mnstry 1976-1990; Cur The Afr Epis Ch Of S Thos Philadelphia PA 1970-1976; Cur S Jn's Par Sn Bernrdno CA 1969-1970.

GRAFF, Stephen John (SeFla) 2871 N Ocean Blvd Apt C513, Boca Raton FL 33431 B Atlantic City NJ 1945 s John & Elizabeth. BA Cath U 1970; MA Cath U 1971; PhD NYU 1976; MA St. Bernards TS and Mnstry Rochester NY 1987; MDiv St. Bernards TS and Mnstry Rochester NY 1989. Rec 5/31/2013 as Deacon Bp Leo Frade. m 5/12/2012 Sharon S Schoen.

GRAHAM III, Alexander DeWitt (Dal) 2783 Valwood Pkwy, Farmers Branch TX 75234 B Columbia South Carolina 1975 s Alexander & Debra. BA U of Tennessee 2003; MDiv Westminster TS 2008. D 1/6/2017 Bp George Robinson Sumner Jr. m 7/30/2005 Christina Oliver Graham c 3.

GRAHAM, Carolyn Jane (Kan) 1107 W 27th Ter, Lawrence KS 66046 B Kansas City MO 1934 d Robert & Ruth. BS U of Kansas 1970; MA U of Kansas 1976. D 10/27/1993 Bp William Edward Smalley. m 10/31/1975 Hillel Unz. D Trin Ch Lawr KS 1993-2015. Phi Beta Kappa.

GRAHAM, Deborah Marie Therese (Ida) 911 4th St S, Nampa ID 83651 **Supply S Jas Ch Payette ID 2011-; Supply S Lk's Ch Weiser ID 2010-; Latino Mssnr Gr Epis Ch Nampa ID 2009-** B Boise ID 1955 d Franklin & Thelma. BS U of Idaho 1978; AS Boise St U 1983; BS Boise St U 1994; MDiv CDSP 2008. D 6/29/2008 Bp Harry Brown Bainbridge III P 10/8/2009 Bp Brian James Thom. m 9/30/2005 Teresa Wood.

GRAHAM III, Earnest N (NC) 828 Kings Hwy, Suffolk VA 23432 **Cn Dio No Carolina Raleigh NC 2015-** B Westminster CA 1970 s Earnest & Jeanette. Casper Coll 1991; U of Wyoming 1998; MDiv VTS 2001. D 5/24/2001 Bp Bruce Caldwell P 12/29/2001 Bp Peter J Lee. m 8/5/2001 Shirley Elizabeth Smith c 1. Hickory Neck Ch Toano VA 2014-2015; S Matt's Epis Ch Chesterfield VA 2010-2014; S Jn's Ch Suffolk VA 2008-2010; S Fran Epis Ch Great Falls VA 2003-2007; Asst To The R/Cler Res Chr Ch Alexandria VA 2001-2003.

GRAHAM, Harry James (EMich) 534 Little Lake Dr., Ann Arbor MI 48103 **1970-** B Springfield IL 1931 s Harry & Ruth. BA Ken 1952; BD EDS 1957; MA Kent St U 1970. D 2/1/1958 P 9/17/1958 Bp Gordon V Smith. m 9/14/1957 Gail M Graham c 2. Int S Christophers Epis Ch Grand Blanc MI 1991-1992; Int Gr Epis Ch Lapeer MI 1989-1990; Instr Mott Cmnty Coll 1970-1996; P Trin Jefferson OH 1967-1970; P S Tim's Epis Ch Perrysburg OH 1963-1967; Asst Trin Ch Concord MA 1960-1963; All SS Epis Ch Storm Lake IA 1957-1960;

G

In-c S Steph's Ch Spencer IA 1957-1960; COM Dio Estrn Michigan Saginaw MI 1997-2001; COM Dio Michigan Detroit MI 1980-1984.

GRAHAM, John Kirkland (Tex) 6231 Ella Lee Ln, Houston TX 77057 **Pres and CEO Inst for Sprtlty and Hlth Houston TX 2010-** B Shreveport LA 1937 s Frank & Lasca. BS Centenary Coll 1959; MD Tul 1963; MDiv Epis TS of the SW 1994; DMin SWTS 2001. D 6/25/1994 P 1/1/1995 Bp Maurice Manuel Benitez. m 6/4/1960 Patsy Graham c 5. S Mart's Epis Ch Houston TX 1998-2009; R Trin Ch Houston TX 1996-1998; S Matt's Ch Austin TX 1994-1996; Bd Dir Epis Hlth Chars Houston TX 1998-2007. Auth, "Graham Crackers & Milk," Abringdon, 2003; Auth, "Mold Me & Shape Me," Chosen Books, 1983. AAPC 2010; AMA 2009; Amer Psych Assn 2011; Amer Soc Of Plastic & Reconstructive Surgeons 1979. jgraham@ish-tmc.org

GRAHAM, John Mark (WA) 1041 Wisconsin Ave. NW, Washington DC 20007 **R Gr Ch Washington DC 2004-** B Columbus OH 1954 s John & Doris. BA Ken 1976; MA U Chi 1977; MDiv VTS 1984. D 6/15/1984 P 12/1/1984 Bp James Winchester Montgomery. m 5/22/1982 Sakena F McWright. R Ch Of The Adv Chicago IL 1986-2004, 1984-1986; Vic La Iglesia De Nuestra Senora De Las Americas Chicago IL 1986-2004; Dio Chicago Chicago IL 1984-1986. office@gracedc.org

GRAHAM, Julie Ann (Cal) 1104 Mills Ave, Burlingame CA 94010 **Assoc R/ Chld S Paul's Epis Ch Burlingame CA 2006-** B Fort Worth TX 1961 d John & Deanna. Texas Tech U 1981; BA U of New Mex 1985; MDiv CDSP 1990. D 6/30/1990 P 6/1/1991 Bp Terence Kelshaw. m 1/4/1992 Thomas Skillings. Co-ordntr - Yth & YA Mnstrs Dio California San Francisco CA 1995-2003; Assoc S Paul's Epis Ch Walnut Creek CA 1993-1995; CDSP Berkeley CA 1992-1993; Asst S Mths Epis Ch San Ramon CA 1992-1993; Asst S Steph's Epis Ch Orinda CA 1990-1992. Auth, "Yth Mnstry Acad Manual," Diocal, 1997; Auth, "Pstr Care W/Teenagers," *Resources w Yth & YA Mnstrs*, Epis Ch Cntr.

GRAHAM III, Robert Lincoln (Alb) 153 Billings Ave, Ottawa ON K1H 5K8 Canada **Ret 2005-** B New York NY 1937 s Robert & Mary. BA Col 1960; BTh S Paul U 1989. D 5/24/1990 Bp John Baycroft P 7/1/1991 Bp David Standish Ball. m 10/1/1982 Joan E Graham. Dn S Lawr Dnry 2000-2005; R S Jn's Ch Massena NY 1995-2005; R S Phil's Ch Norwood NY 1991-1995; Trin Ch Gouverneur NY 1991-1995; S Lawr Epis Mnstry Waddington NY 1990-1995; Chapl Ottawa W End Cmnty 1989-1990; Stndg Com Dio Albany Greenwich NY 1998-2005.

GRAHAM IV, Sandy (Haw) 563 Kamoku St, Honolulu HI 96826 **Cn The Epis Ch in Hawaii Honolulu HI 2016-** B Wilmington DE 1972 s Alexander & Barbara. BMus U of Delaware 1996; MDiv GTS 2003. D 1/18/2003 P 12/4/2003 Bp Wayne Wright. m 12/23/1995 Heather Lynn Patton-Graham c 1. Assoc R S Andr's Ch Burke VA 2013-2016; P Assoc Cathd of St Ptr & St Paul Washington DC 2012-2013; R Incarn H Sacr Epis Ch Drexel Hill PA 2005-2012; Asst R The Ch Of The H Trin W Chester PA 2003-2005. acgraham@episcoopalhawaii.org

GRAHAM, Suzanne H (NY) 279 Piermont Ave, Nyack NY 10960 **Chapl Jansen Hospice and Palliative Care 2007-; Mem, Ecum and Interfaith Cmsn Dio New York New York NY 2008-** B Teaneck NJ 1943 MA Sch of Oriental and Afr Stds Lon 1974; MDiv GTS 2006. D 3/11/2006 P 9/23/2006 Bp Mark Sean Sisk. m 12/29/1999 Kelsey D Graham c 2. All SS Epis Ch Vlly Cottage NY 2009; Chapl Res Westchester Med Cntr 2005-2006.

GRAHAM, Timothy Harold (At) 1130 First Ave, Columbus GA 31901 **R Trin Epis Ch Columbus GA 2012-** B Toccoa GA 1961 s Carl & Imogene. BBA U GA 1985; MDiv GTS 1996. D 6/8/1996 P 12/14/1996 Bp Frank Kellogg Allan. m 1/30/1999 Deana Kathryn Graham c 3. R Ch Of The Gd Shpd Covington GA 2000-2012; Assoc S Mich's Ch Raleigh NC 1998-2000; Asst Emm Epis Ch Athens GA 1996-1998; Epis Chapl U of Goeorgia Athens GA 1996-1998; Stndg Com Dio Atlanta Atlanta GA 2010-2012.

GRAHAM, Wells Newell (CGC) 771 Simon Park Cir, Lawrenceville GA 30045 **Sr. Asst to the R St. Mart's in the Field Atlanta GA 2010-** B Cynthiana KY 1938 s T & Evelyn. BA Thos More Coll 1960; MDiv Nash 1963. D 6/1/1963 Bp William R Moody P 12/18/1963 Bp William Loftin Hargrave. m 12/28/1985 Mary Hair Graham c 2. Int St Pat's Atlanta GA 2009-2010; Epis Ch Of The H Sprt Cumming GA 2006-2009; Int Ch of Our Sav Atlanta GA 2005; Int S Geo's Epis Ch Griffin GA 2003-2005; Int S Lk's Epis Ch Atlanta GA 2002-2003; Int Emm Epis Ch Athens GA 1999-2000; R S Lk's Epis Ch Mobile AL 1987-1999; Dio SW Florida Parrish FL 1978-1987; Chapl Ringling Bros Barnum & Bailey Circus Venice FL 1969-1979; R S Wlfd's Epis Ch Sarasota FL 1968-1977; P S Fran Of Assisi Ch Bushnell FL 1966-1968; P S Jn's Epis Ch Brooksville FL 1964-1968; Cur S Lk's Ch Ft Myers FL 1963-1964.

GRAHAM JR, William James (Neb) 607 Toluca Ave, Alliance NE 69301 **R S Mary's Ch Rushville NE 2004-; S Mary's Ch: Holly Rushville NE 2004-; Non-par/supply 1978-** B Oriskany NY 1945 s William & Doris. BA Clarkson U 1967; MDiv EDS 1976; MS Chadron St Coll 1982. D 6/11/1977 Bp Lyman Cunningham Ogilby P 12/1/1977 Bp James Daniel Warner. m 12/23/1974 Kathryn Frances Lyon c 1. S Matt's Ch Allnce NE 1997; S Pauls Ch Merriman NE 1983-1994; Vic S Andr's Ch Seward NE 1977-1978. "Meeting of Franciscans," *Franciscan Times*, TSSF, 1992. Tertiary of the Soc of S Fran 1974.

GRAMBSCH, Mary Frances (NY) 20 Seaman Ave Apt 1k, New York NY 10034 **Zion Ch Dobbs Ferry NY 2011-; Ch Of The Gd Shpd New York NY 2009-** B New Orleans LA 1958 d Paul & Ada. BA Indiana U 1982; MDiv Ya Berk 1993. D 6/3/1995 P 12/9/1995 Bp Richard Frank Grein. m 5/15/2012 Teresa Eulalie Lucas. Port Mssnr Seamens Ch Inst New York NY 1995-2008; Pstr Team Epis Ch Of Our Sav New York NY 1995-2002; Port Mssnr / Vic SCI New York NY 1994-2008; Dioc Soc Concerns Com. Berkeley Grad Soc, No Amer Maritime Mnstrs A 1993.

GRAMLEY, Thomas S (Roch) 13 Prospect Ave, Canisteo NY 14823 B Hazleton PA 1944 s Malcolm & Edna. BA Moravian Coll 1966; STB Ya Berk 1969; MSW Tul 1972; MPA NYU 1985. D 1/28/1989 P 12/9/1989 Bp William George Burrill. m 3/14/1975 Sharon Gramley c 4. R Tri-Par Mnstry Hornell NY 2006-2010; R S Jn's Ch Clifton Spgs NY 1999-2006; Int Trin Ch Rochester NY 1998-1999; Int S Mk's And S Jn's Epis Ch Rochester NY 1997; R S Jn's Ch Sodus NY 1991-1995, R 1990-1991; Asst Zion Epis Ch Palmyra NY 1989-1990.

GRANDFIELD, Dale Terence (Be) 2747 Fairmount Blvd, Cleveland Heights OH 44106 **S Paul's Epis Ch Cleveland OH 2016-** B Aurora CO 1983 s Terence & Danese. BA Moravian Coll 2005; MDiv The TS at The U So 2016. D 6/4/2016 P 12/18/2016 Bp Sean Walter Rowe. m 5/21/2014 Bradford Paul Zuercher.

GRANFELDT SR, Robert C (Pa) 1400 Mall of Georgia Blvd Apt 1412, Buford GA 30519 B Detroit MI 1942 s Robert & Matilda. BA Wayne 1967; MDiv GTS 1971. D 6/29/1970 Bp Richard Stanley Merrill Emrich P 1/22/1972 Bp Archie H Crowley. c 3. Resurr Epis Ch Rockdale Aston PA 2000-2008; Nonpar 1991-1999; Int S Chris's Epis Ch Austin TX 1990-1991; R Emm Ch Quakertown PA 1984-1987; S Geo Mtyr Ch Tortola 1981-1984; R S Geo Sch Road Town Tortola 1981-1984; R S Geo's Ch Tortola BVI 1981-1984; P-in-c S Paul's Sea Cow Bay VI 1981-1984; Episc. Chapl, Texas Tech Univ Dio NW Texas Lubbock TX 1978-1981; Episc. Chapl, Univ of Massachusetts - Amherst Dio Wstrn Massachusetts Springfield 1975-1978; St Helenas Chap Lenox MA 1974-1975; Trin Par Lenox MA 1974-1975; Asst Min Chr Ch Detroit MI 1971-1973; Asst Min Epis Ch of The Resurr Williston Pk NY 1970-1971. ECAP 2000; ESMHE 1975-1982.

GRANGER JR, Charles Irving (Okla) 305 E Douglas Dr, Midwest City OK 73110 B Cleveland OH 1943 s Charles & Myrtis. BS Ohio U 1965; Cert Bex Sem 1971. D 6/26/1971 P 5/19/1972 Bp John Harris Burt. m 11/29/1986 Marcia L Granger c 3. R Epis Ch Of The Redeem Oklahoma City OK 2004-2006; Chapl S Fran Cmnty Serv Inc. Salina KS 2003-2004; Int All SS Ch S Louis MO 2002-2003; Chapl//Res Bapt-Luth Med. Cntr. Kansas City MO 2001-2002; S Ptr's Ch Pittsburg KS 2001-2002; Int Trin Epis Ch Kirksville MO 1999-2001; Ch of the Medtr Harbert MI 1997-1999; R S Aug Of Cbury Epis Ch Benton Harbor MI 1997-1999; R S Aug's Ch Kansas City MO 1994-1997; R Epis Ch Of The H Fam Miami FL 1991-1994; Assoc S Phil's Ch New York NY 1988-1991; Cur S Lk's Epis Ch Bronx NY 1986-1988; Vic Ch Of The Resurr Ecorse MI 1982-1986; Vic Dio Michigan Detroit MI 1980-1981; R S Thos Ch Minneapolis MN 1976-1980; R Mssh-S Barth Epis Ch Chicago IL 1972-1974.

GRANT JR, Blount (SeFla) 8500 Bluebonnet Blvd Apt 31, Baton Rouge LA 70810 **Ret 1997-** B Rome GA 1933 s Blount & Lera. U So 1953; BA U GA 1958; MDiv VTS 1962; U of Nottingham 1969. D 6/30/1962 P 6/2/1963 Bp Randolph R Claiborne. Pstr Assoc S Jas Epis Ch Baton Rouge LA 2002-2008; Trin Cathd Miami FL 1993-1996; Trst The U So 1992-1994; S Fran-In-The-Keys Episcop Big Pine Key FL 1987-1992; Dio SE Florida Miami 1980-1984; R S Columba Epis Ch Marathon FL 1976-1993; Serv Ch in Bahamas 1973-1976; R S Paul's Epis Ch Newnan GA 1969-1972; R Zion Talbottom GA 1969-1972; Assoc S Anne's Epis Ch Atlanta GA 1965-1968; Vic S Mich And All Ang Ch Stone Mtn GA 1962-1965.

GRANT, Elizabeth Wade (NC) 750 Weaver Dairy Rd Apt 176, Chapel Hill NC 27514 **Died 1/27/2017** B South Bend IN 1926 d Roderic & Florence. BA Mt Holyoke Coll 1947; U of Paris-Sorbonne Fr 1948; MA Harv 1951. D 6/17/1989 Bp Robert Whitridge Estill. c 3. Ret 2004-2017; Vision Com Dio No Carolina Raleigh NC 1997-1998, Stndg Com 1993-1996; Chapl Duke Epis Cntr Durham NC 1989-2004. Soc Of S Jn The Evang. Durham Sustained Involvement Vol Of The Year No Carolina Gvnr 1995.

GRANT, Hugh M (At) PO Box 632, Eastsound WA 98245 B Atlanta GA 1966 s Walter & Eleanor. BA Davidson Coll 1988; MSW U GA 1996; MTS Emory U 1997; MDiv GTS 2008. D 12/21/2007 P 6/29/2008 Bp J Neil Alexander. m 7/11/2009 José Roberto Gandara-Perea. Assoc The Ch Of S Lk In The Fields New York NY 2008-2013.

GRANT, Joan (WNC) 290 Old Haw Creek Rd, Asheville NC 28805 **S Jn's Ch Asheville NC 2015-** B Columbus OH 1952 d William & Beverly. AB Mia 1974; JD The OH SU Coll of Law 1978; MDiv Bex Sem 2010; MDiv Bex Sem 2010. D 10/25/2003 Bp Herbert Thompson Jr P 6/19/2010 Bp Thomas Edward Breidenthal. c 2. R Chr Epis Ch Kalispell MT 2010-2015.

GRANT, Priscilla (Percy) R (O) 2230 Euclid Ave., Cleveland OH 44115 **Cn for Mnstry Dio Ohio Cleveland 2007-** B Norwich VT 1961 d Joseph & Mary. BA Sweet Briar Coll 1983; MDiv VTS 1992. D 6/11/1992 Bp Daniel Lee Swenson P 12/16/1992 Bp Peter J Lee. m 8/9/2013 Nan Michele Hunter. Dio Virginia Richmond VA 1999-2007; St. Steph's And St. Agnes Sch Alexandria

VA 1996-1999; Chapl / Tchr St. Steph And St. Agnes Sch Alexandria VA 1995-1998; Asst S Andr's Ch Burke VA 1992-1995.

GRANT, Rebecca Ann (Me) 16 Alton Road, Apt 219, Augusta ME 04330 B Portland ME 1953 d William & Sally. BS U of Phoenix 2009; MA U of Phoenix 2011. D 6/20/2009 Bp Stephen Taylor Lane. c 1.

GRANT, Sandra Marceau (SC) B Washington DC 1944 BA Harv 1965; PhD U of Connecticut 1971; MBA Ya 1984. D 9/10/2005 Bp Edward Lloyd Salmon Jr. m 5/20/1984 Kerry Grant.

GRANTZ, Brian Glenn (NI) 117 N Lafayette Blvd, South Bend IN 46601 **Dn The Cathd Ch Of S Jas So Bend IN 2008-** B Kittanning PA 1964 s Earl & Janet. BA Penn 1986; MDiv Sewanee: The U So, TS 1997. D 12/21/1996 P 6/21/1997 Bp Francis Campbell Gray. m 11/22/1986 Tamisyn Grantz c 4. R Chr Ch Slidell LA 2006-2008; R S Anne's Epis Ch Warsaw IN 2000-2006; Cur 1997-1999. office@stjamessouthbend.org

GRATZ, Louis Paul (Vt) 208 Silver St, Bennington VT 05201 B New York NY 1946 s Louis & Jean. BA Alleg 1968; MDiv EDS 1971; MA W Virginia U 1976. D 6/25/1971 P 5/20/1972 Bp Harvey D Butterfield. m 6/7/2003 Susan Z Gratz c 2. Int S Ptr's Epis Ch Bennington VT 2010-2012; Vic S Mk's-S Lk's Epis Mssn Fair Haven VT 2009; Int Slate Vlly Mnstry Poultney VT 2003-2009; Int S Paul's Ch Steubenville OH 2001-2003; Int S Ptr's Epis Ch Butler PA 1999-2000; Assoc Gr Ch Pittsburgh PA 1994-1999; Int S Phil's Ch Coraopolis PA 1992-1994; S Andr's Epis Ch New Kensington PA 1989-1990; P S Barn Epis Ch Denton TX 1977-1978; P Dio W Virginia Charleston WV 1973-1977; St Anselms Chap 1972-1973.

GRAUER, David Ernst (Chi) 808 S Seminary Ave, Park Ridge IL 60068 **D S Mary's Ch Pk Ridge IL 1989-** B Cincinnati OH 1927 s Gerhard & Marie. BS NWU 1950; DDS U IL 1954; Chicago Deacons Sch 1989. D 12/2/1989 Bp Frank Tracy Griswold III. m 8/2/1952 Joan M Grauer c 2. Auth, *The Dentist & Temporomandibular Joint Disorders*, Clearvue, 1985; Auth, *Journ of the Acadamy of Gnrl Dentistry*, 1983; Auth, *Dental Journ*, 1980; Auth, *Dental Journ*, 1978. Amer Acadamy of Orofacial Pain 1993; Amer Acadamy of Pain Mgmt 2002; Amer Bd Orofacial Pain 1996. Mem Acad Oro-facial Pain; Omicron Kappa Upsilon; Dplma Amer Bd Orofacial Pain.

GRAUMLICH, Nancy Rice (O) 7815 Hedingham Rd, Sylvania OH 43560 **D All SS Epis Ch Toledo OH 1992-** B Toledo OH 1924 d Claude & Mabel. BS Bowling Green St U 1947. D 11/13/1992 Bp James Russell Moodey. m 6/14/1947 Albert John Graumlich c 3.

GRAUNKE, Kristine (WTex) PO Box 68, Hebbronville TX 78361 **P-in-c S Andrews by the Lake Michigan City IN 2007-** B Green Bay WI 1951 d Corbin & Eleanor. BA U of Wisconsin 1973; MDiv Chicago TS 1978; TESM 1998. D 9/21/1998 Bp Francis Campbell Gray P 3/25/1999 Bp William Walter Wiedrich. c 1. Vic S Jas Epis Ch Hebbronville TX 2009-2016; S Dav's Epis Ch San Antonio TX 2008-2009; S Andr's By The Lake Epis Ch Michigan City IN 2007; S Barn-In-The-Dunes Gary IN 2005-2007; S Paul's Epis Ch Munster IN 2000-2001; Intern S Anne's Epis Ch Warsaw IN 1999; Intern The Cathd Ch Of S Jas So Bend IN 1999. Assn of Profsnl Chapl 2006; Catechesis Gd Shpd; Epis Chapl Orgnztn 1995.

GRAVATT, Jacqueline Segar (SVa) 301 49th St, Virginia Beach VA 23451 **Assoc All SS' Epis Ch Virginia Bch VA 1999-, D 1991-1995** B Richmond VA 1949 d John & Isbell. BA Queens Coll 1971; MS U NC 1972; MDiv UTS Richmond 1984; Cert VTS 1985; DMin GTF 1997. D 5/20/1985 Bp Claude Charles Vache P 6/24/1999 Bp David Conner Bane Jr. S Aid's Ch Virginia Bch VA 2001-2002; D The Epis Ch Of The Adv Norfolk VA 1997-1999; D S Andr's Ch Norfolk VA 1995-1999; Archd Dio Sthrn Virginia Newport News VA 1990-1999; D S Paul's Ch Norfolk VA 1986-1990. AAPC 1988; ACPE 1984-2000; Assn of Profsnl Chapl 1988-2006. S Steph's Awd NAAD 1997.

GRAVES, Carol Carson (NMich) 4341 Se Satinleaf Pl, Stuart FL 34997 B Newberry MI 1951 d Joseph & Darlene. Montana St U; Dioc Sch of SE FL 2006. D 12/17/2006 Bp Leo Frade. m 11/14/1987 Fielding Graves c 2. Admin Asst St of Montana Helena Montana 1987-1992. DOK 2000.

GRAVES, Charles (SO) **Dio Sthrn Ohio Cincinnati OH 2017-** D 6/3/2017 Bp Thomas Edward Breidenthal.

GRAVES JR, Farrell Dean (Los) 5 Mill Pond Rd, Stony Brook NY 11790 **All Souls Ch Stony Brook NY 2016-** B High Point NC 1963 s Farrell & Delories. BA Duke 1986; PhD U CA 2004; MDiv GTS 2010. D 6/12/2010 Bp Mary Douglas Glasspool P 12/18/2010 Bp Lawrence C Provenzano. Assoc Caroline Ch Of Brookhaven E Setauke NY 2013-2016; S Ann's Ch Sayville NY 2010-2013.

GRAVES, Jon C (WVa) 210 S McHenry Ave, Crystal Lake IL 60014 **P Trin Ch Huntington WV 2012-** B Lansing MI 1961 s John & Suzanne. BS U of Missouri 1984; MBA Thunderbird Glendale AZ 1986; MDiv VTS 2007. D 6/2/2007 Bp Barry Howe P 12/2/2007 Bp Neff Powell. m 6/27/1992 Lisa Beyer Graves c 2. S Mary Epis Ch Crystal Lake IL 2009-2012; Asst S Jn's Ch Roanoke VA 2007-2008; Gnrl Mgr Food Merchandising Systems / Menu Maker Foods 1993-2004.

GRAVES JR, Leonard Roberts (CGC) 1302 E Avery St, Pensacola FL 32503 **P-in-c St. Dismas Mssn Sta Fountain Correctional AL 2008-; Chapl to Ret Cler and Surviving Spouses Dio the Cntrl Gulf Coast 2003-** B Norfolk

VA 1938 s Leonard & Margaret. BA VMI 1960; MDiv VTS 1963. D 6/20/1963 Bp George P Gunn P 6/27/1964 Bp David Shepherd Rose. m 1/14/1995 Jane Culwell Graves c 3. Imm Ch Bay Minette AL 2005-2006; Int St. Andr's By-The-Sea Destin FL 2003-2004; Chairman Cmsn on Wrld Mssn Dio Cntrl Gulf Coast Pensacola FL 1998-2000, chairman of Cmsn on prison Mnstry 2010-, 2000-2010, 1997-2000, 1995-1997; Assoc Chr Epis Ch Pensacola FL 1984-2003; R Trin Epis Ch Martinsburg WV 1981-1984; Assoc S Lk's Epis Ch Birmingham AL 1976-1981; Assoc S Paul's Memi Charlottesvlle VA 1972-1976; R Emm Ch Virginia Bch VA 1965-1972; Asst S Paul's Ch Petersburg VA 1963-1965.

GRAVES, Lisa Beyer (WVa) 290 Grove St., Crystal Lake IL 60014 **R S Jn's Ch Huntington WV 2012-** B Fort Stll OK 1967 d Robert & Marilyn. BA Stephens Coll 1989; MDiv VTS 2007. D 6/2/2007 Bp Barry Howe P 12/2/2007 Bp Neff Powell. m 6/27/1992 Jon C Graves c 2. R S Phil's Epis Palatine IL 2009-2012; Chapl Cbury NW Evanston IL 2009; Asst S Jn's Ch Roanoke VA 2007-2008; Mgr Ymca 2002-2004.

GRAVES, Rena B (Pa) 5421 Germantown Ave, Philadelphia PA 19144 B 1920 D 6/15/1985 Bp Lyman Cunningham Ogilby. deaconrena29@aol.com

GRAVES, Richard W (Ia) 1247 7th Ave N, Fort Dodge IA 50501 B Boston MA 1950 s Harry & Anne. BA The Coll of Idaho 1972; MDiv CDSP 1976. D 6/17/1978 P 1/1/1979 Bp Robert Claflin Rusack. c 3. R Ch Of The Gd Shpd Webster City IA 2008-2015; R S Mk's Epis Ch Ft Dodge IA 2007-2015; S Paul's Epis Ch Grinnell IA 1994-1996; R S Mk's Par Altadena CA 1985-1994; Chapl Occ Los Angeles CA 1982-1952; R S Barn' Epis Ch Los Angeles CA 1981-1985; Asst Min Trin Epis Ch Santa Barbara CA 1979-1981; The Par Ch Of S Lk Long Bch CA 1978-1979. ESMHE. stpauls50158@msn.com

GRAY, Bruce Alan (Va) 8525 Burgundy Rd, Richmond VA 23235 **Assoc S Andr's Ch Richmond VA 2008-; Chapl New York St Assn Fire Chapl 1967-** B Troy NY 1940 s C Wellington & Dorothy. Bates Coll 1960; BA Syr 1963; MDiv EDS 1966; DMin VTS 1984. D 6/11/1966 Bp Allen Webster Brown P 12/14/1966 Bp Charles Bowen Persell Jr. m 6/29/1962 Katherine A Gray c 2. P S Jn's Ch Richmond VA 1997-2007; Trin Ch Fredericksbrg VA 1996-1997; Int Ch Of The H Comf Richmond VA 1994-1996; S Paul's Epis Par Pt Of Rocks MD 1994; S Alb's Epis Ch Annandale VA 1987-1994; R S Andr's Epis Ch Albany NY 1976-1987; R S Mk's Ch Malone NY 1967-1975; Asst Min S Ptr's Ch Albany NY 1966-1967. Auth, "A Fire Chapl'S Manual," New York St Assn Of Fire Chapl.

GRAY, Bruce William (Ind) Episcopal Diocese of Indianapolis, 1100 W 42nd St, Indianapolis IN 46208 **Cn to the Ordnry Dio Indianapolis Indianapolis IN 2009-** B Sacramento CA 1960 s Wayne & Elise. BA U CA 1982; MDiv SWTS 1985. D 6/22/1985 P 12/21/1985 Bp Charles Brinkley Morton. m 9/30/2001 Cathy J Gray c 4. R S Mths' Par Whittier CA 1998-2009; R The Epis Ch Of The Gd Shpd Hemet CA 1990-1998; Vic S Jn's Ch Washington IN 1987-1990; Cur Chr Ch Coronado CA 1985-1987. gray@indydio.org

GRAY, Calvin (Colo) 1625 Larimer Street #2501, Denver CO 80202 B Flushing NY 1934 s Robert & Catherine. BA Barrington Coll 1959; STB NYTS 1963; MTh NYTS 1963; PrTS 1970; Fuller TS 1983; U of Nthrn Colorado 1990. D 6/7/1997 P 9/8/1999 Bp William Jerry Winterrowd. m 10/17/1953 Gloria L Gray c 3. R S Jas Epis Ch Wheat Ridge CO 2001-2006; Intsn Epis Ch Denver CO 1999-2001; S Paul's Epis Ch Lakewood CO 1998-1999; S Thos Epis Ch Denver CO 1997-1998.

GRAY, Cathy J (Ind) 11120 El Arco Dr, Whittier CA 90604 B Riverside CA 1952 s Louie & Barbara. BA Loma Linda U 1977; MDiv CDSP 1999. D 6/19/1999 P 1/6/2000 Bp Gethin Benwil Hughes. m 9/30/2001 Bruce William Gray c 4. Chr Ch Cathd Indianapolis IN 2009-2013; S Jas' Sch Los Angeles CA 2003-2009; Asst S Edm's Par San Marino CA 2003.

GRAY, Chris (SwFla) 8005 25th Street East, Parrish FL 34219 **Dvlpmt Off & Pstr to Ret Cler Dio SW Florida Parrish FL 2010-** B Cincinnati OH 1949 s Francis & Jane. BA U of Cntrl Florida 1976; MDiv Nash 1979. D 6/25/1979 P 1/6/1980 Bp William Hopkins Folwell. m 7/8/1978 Paula K Gray c 2. R S Mk's Epis Ch Venice FL 1991-2010; R Gr Epis Ch Inc Port Orange FL 1979-1991.

GRAY, Cindra Dee (Ore) PO Box 358, Newberg OR 97132 B Yakima WA 1956 d Harold & Nelda. The Acad for Mssn and Formation 2016. D 6/13/2015 Bp Michael Hanley. m 7/14/1978 John Munson Gray c 3.

GRAY, Douglas Alan (SVa) 3100 Shore Dr, Virginia Beach VA 23451 **Westminster-Cbury Virginia Bch VA 2013-** B Red Bank NJ 1961 s Russell & Edith. BA U of Maryland 1984; MDiv VTS 1996. D 6/15/1995 Bp Peter J Lee P 1/15/1997 Bp Edward Lloyd Salmon Jr. m 6/13/1987 Patricia Ann Gray. Chr Epis Ch Denver CO 2009-2012; Epis Ch of the Gd Shpd Summerville SC 2003-2009; Asst R S Andr's Ch Mt Pleasant SC 1996-2000.

✠ **GRAY III, The Rt Rev Duncan Montgomery** (Miss) 110 Philip Rd, Oxford MS 38655 B Canton MS 1949 s Duncan & Ruth. BA U of Mississippi 1971; MDiv VTS 1975. D 5/31/1975 P 5/27/1976 Bp Duncan Montgomery Gray Jr Con 6/17/2000 for Miss. m 8/21/1974 Kathryn Gray c 3. Bp in Res S Paul's Ch New Orleans LA 2015-2017; Bp of Mississippi Dio Mississippi Jackson MS 2000-2015; R S Ptr's Ch Oxford MS 1985-2000; Assoc Ch Of The H Comm Memphis TN 1982-1985; Chapl/Asst Headmaster Trin Epis Sch New Orleans

LA 1978-1982; Cur S Jas Ch Greenville MS 1975-1978. DD U So Sch of Theoloigical 2001; DD VTS 2001. dmgrayiii@gmail.com

✠ GRAY JR, The Rt Rev Duncan Montgomery (Miss) 3775 Old Canton Rd, Jackson MS 39216 **Died 7/15/2016** B Canton MS 1926 s Duncan & Isabel. BS Tul 1948; BD Sewanee: The U So, TS 1953. D 4/8/1953 P 10/28/1953 Bp Duncan Montgomery Gray Con 5/1/1974 for Miss. c 4. S Paul's Epis Ch Meridian MS 2002-2004, R 1965-2001; Ret Bp of Miss Dio Mississippi Jackson MS 1993-2016, Bp 1974-1993; Sewanee U So TS Sewanee TN 1991-1997, 1981-1990; Chncllr U So Sewanee TN 1991-1997; Pres Prov IV ECUSA 1984-1988; Bd Rgnts U So Sewanee TN 1981-1987; Bd Trst U So Sewanee TN 1974-1997; S Ptr's Ch Oxford MS 1957-1965; P-in-c H Innoc' Epis Ch Como MS 1957-1960; P-in-c Calv Epis Ch Cleveland MS 1953-1957; Gr Ch Rosedale MS 1953-1957; PBp's Coun of Advice Epis Ch Cntr New York NY 1984-1988. DD U So 1972. dmgrayiii@gmail.com

✠ GRAY, The Rt Rev Francis Campbell (NI) 3820 Nall Ct, South Bend IN 46614 **Ret Bp of Nthrn Indiana Dio Nthrn Indiana So Bend IN 1998-, Bp 1986-1998** B Manila PI 1940 s Francis & Jane. BA Rol 1966; BD Nash 1969; STM Nash 1979. D 6/20/1969 Bp Henry I Louttit P 12/20/1969 Bp William Loftin Hargrave Con 10/31/1986 for NI. m 2/19/1965 Karen Gray c 3. Asst Bp Dio Virginia Richmond VA 1999-2005; R Emm Ch Orlando FL 1979-1986; R S Jn's Ch Melbourne FL 1974-1979; Chapl Manatee Jr Coll Bradenton FL 1970-1974; Cur S Wlfd's Epis Ch Sarasota FL 1969-1970. Auth, "For Thou Art w Me," 2012; Auth, "Beloved," S Aug Press, 1998; Auth, "Thursday's Chld," S Aug Press, 1994; Auth, "Tithing: The Heart of the Matter," Epis Ch Cntr, 1989. Compass Rose Soc - Pres 1999-2003; PBFWR 1990-1993; PBFWR - Chair 1992-1993. Hon Cn Dio Renk, Sudan 2006.

GRAY, Giulianna C (Miss) 4600 Saint Charles Ave, New Orleans PA 70115 **S Steph's Epis Ch Indianola MS 2014-** B Glendale WV 1978 d Giulio & Anne. BSW Xavier U 2000; MSW Tul 2002; MDiv VTS 2008. D 12/29/2007 P 7/6/2008 Bp Charles Edward Jenkins III. m 5/25/2008 Peter Whittlesey Gray c 1. Dio Louisiana New Orleans LA 2009-2013; S Geo's Epis Ch New Orleans LA 2008-2009.

GRAY, Katherine Tupper (SVa) 84 Post St, Newport News VA 23601 **Hospice Chapl Riverside Hlth System Newport News VA 2002-** B Charleston SC 1945 d William & Mary. Frederick Coll Frederick MD; Sewanee: The U So, TS. D 6/6/1998 Bp Frank Harris Vest Jr. D S Mart's Epis Ch Williamsburg VA 2003-2006; R E Lee Memi Ch (Epis) Lexington VA 2000-2003; Chapl Stonewall Jackson Hosp Lexington VA 1999-2003; S Mk's Ch Hampton VA 1998-2000; Chapl Mary Immac Hosp 1997-1998. NAAD, Natl Epis Aids Cltn.

GRAY, Marie Theresa (FdL) N63W29046 Tail Band Ct, Hartland WI 53029 B Milwaukee WI 1959 d Howard & Helen. BS Marq 1981; MDiv Nash 2007; D.Min. Nash 2013. D 4/26/2008 P 11/29/2008 Bp Russell Edward Jacobus. m 5/30/1981 Michael Gray c 3. P-in-c S Paul's Ch Plymouth WI 2010-2015; Stff Chapl Agnesian Healthcare Fond du Lac WI 2008-2010; Chapl Res Aurora St. Lk's Med Cntr Milwaukee WI 2007-2008. AEHC-the Assembly of Epis Healthcare Chapl 2007.

GRAY, Melvin Kelly (Fla) 715 Sleepyvale Ln, Houston TX 77018 B Starkville MS 1948 s Malcolm & Elizabeth. BA U So 1970; MDiv Epis TS of the SW 1974. D 6/11/1974 Bp Richard Earl Dicus P 12/22/1974 Bp Harold Cornelius Gosnell. c 2. Int R S Jn's Epis Ch Tallahassee FL 2006-2008; Int R H Trin Par Epis Clemson SC 2003-2006; Int R S Steph's Ch Lubbock TX 2002-2003; Asstg Cler Hope Epis Ch Houston TX 2001-2002; R H Sprt Epis Ch Houston TX 1987-2001; R Ch Of The Gd Shpd Tomball TX 1978-1987; Assoc R Chr Epis Ch San Antonio TX 1974-1978.

GRAY, Michael Fred (Va) 712 Amanda Ct, Culpeper VA 22701 B Kalamazoo MI 1947 s James & Florence. BA Stetson U 1970; MDiv Nash 1976; MA U NC 1977. D 5/27/1976 P 5/26/1977 Bp James Loughlin Duncan. m 7/28/1990 Lynn G Gray c 3. R S Steph's Epis Ch Culpeper VA 2002-2012; R Ch Of The Resurr Miami FL 1996-2001; Asst R S Mk The Evang Ft Lauderdale FL 1993-1996; Vic S Mich's Ch SW Ranches FL 1990-1993; R Epis Ch Of The H Fam Miami FL 1980-1990; Asst Dn Trin Cathd Miami FL 1976-1980.

GRAY, Patrick Terrell (Mass) 151 Asbury St, South Hamilton MA 01982 **R Chr Ch S Hamilton MA 2009-** B Wilmington DE 1970 s Terrell & Marjorie. GTS; BA Gordon Coll 1992; MA Gordon-Conwell TS 1997; STM GTS 1998. D 6/2/2001 Bp Barbara Clementine Harris P 6/8/2002 Bp M(Arvil) Thomas Shaw. m 11/21/1992 Naomi Ruth Gray c 2. Assoc R The Ch Of The Adv Boston MA 2002-2009; Asstg D All SS Ch W Newbury MA 2001-2002. "Co-Ed of One Lord, One Faith, One Baptism: Stds in Chr Ecclesiality and Ecum in hon of J. Robert Wright," Eerdmans, 2006; "A Meaning Worthy of God: Origen and Scripture in a Pre-Constantinian Age," *One Lord, One Faith, One Baptism*, Eerdmans, 2006; "Cmnty Organizing as Lived Faith," *Why Liberal Ch are Growing*, T&T Clark, 2006; "Eliot the Enigma: An Observation of T. S. Eliot's Thought and Poetry," *ATR*, 2003; "Making Us Make Ourselves: Double Agcy and Its Christological Context in the Thought of Austin Farrer," *The Presence of Transcendence: Thinking 'Sacr' in a Postmodern Age*, Peeters, 2001. fathergray@gmail.com

GRAY, Peter Hanson (Va) 1800 Old Meadow Rd Apt 321, McLean VA 22102 B Indianapolis IN 1939 s Paul & Jane. BA Pr 1960; MDiv GTS 1966. D 6/11/1966 P 12/17/1966 Bp John P Craine. Asst S Thos Epis Ch Mclean VA 1987-2004; Mgmt Analyst Fairfax Cnty Govt 1986-2005; R H Trin Epis Ch Wyoming MI 1973-1976; Asst S Lk's Par Kalamazoo MI 1967-1973; Dir, Yth Outreach S Phil's Ch Indianapolis IN 1966-1967.

GRAY, Peter Whittlesey (Miss) Trinity Church, 1329 Jackson Ave, New Orleans LA 70130 **Ch Of The Nativ Greenwood MS 2013-** B Memphis TN 1982 s Duncan & Kathryn. BA Millsaps Coll 2004; MTS Venderbilt DS 2006; MDiv VTS 2008. D 6/7/2008 Bp Duncan Montgomery Gray Jr P 12/13/2008 Bp Duncan Montgomery Gray III. m 5/25/2008 Giulianna C Giulianna Marie Cappelletti c 2. Trin Ch New Orleans LA 2010-2013; S Anna's Ch New Orleans LA 2008-2010.

GRAY, Priscilla Grace-Gloria (Minn) 611 19th St N, Sartell MN 56377 **D S Jn's Ch S Cloud MN 2009-; D S Jn's 1987-** B Flushing NY 1946 d Nathaniel & Ilda. BS U of Maine 1968; MEd U of Maine 1972. D 10/25/1987 Bp Robert Marshall Anderson. m 7/21/1973 Warren Roscoe Gray c 4.

GRAY, Svea Blomquist (Mich) 306 N Division St, Ann Arbor MI 48104 B Harvey IL 1935 d Joseph & Sara. BA U MI 1957; PrTS 1958; Whitaker TS 1985. D 6/13/1985 Bp H Coleman Mcgehee Jr. m 12/13/1958 Whitmore Gray c 4. D S Andr's Ch Ann Arbor MI 1985-2012.

GRAY, Thomas Weddle (RG) 108 E Orchard Ln, Carlsbad NM 88220 **Corp Chapl Constructors Inc. Carlsbad NM 2008-** B Des Moines IA 1941 s Robert & Honor. BS Iowa St U 1966; MDiv SWTS 1974. D 6/15/1974 P 12/21/1974 Bp Walter Cameron Righter. m 4/28/2001 Jane Shuler c 2. R Gr Ch Carlsbad NM 1997-2007; Chapl S Lk's Epis Hosp Houston TX 1996-1997; R S Mk's Ch Austin TX 1990-1996; R S Jn's Epis Ch Alamogordo NM 1985-1990; Chapl New Mex St Penitentiary Sante Fe NM 1984-1985; R S Thos Of Cbury Epis Ch Albuquerque NM 1982-1984; R Gd Shpd Epis Ch Wichita KS 1976-1982; R S Mk Wichita KS 1976-1982; Vic Trin Ch Carroll IA 1974-1976; Cn Pstr Dio The Rio Grande Albuquerque 1999-2014, Dn, The SE Dnry 1999-2013, Dn, The SW Dnry 1987-1990. OHC 1973.

GRAY, Victoria Stephanie (Cal) B New York City NY 1939 d Victor & Emma. BS USNA 1962; MA Bos 1971; PhD U of Maryland 2002; BA Sch for Deacons 2006. D 12/2/2006 Bp Marc Handley Andrus. D S Jas Epis Ch San Francisco CA 2006-2008; Asst. Night Min San Francisco Night Mnstry San Francisco CA 2006-2008; Bk Seller Bk Passage 1999-2003.

GRAYBILL, Richard Martin (NMich) First And Canda St, Ishpeming MI 49849 B 1943 s Michael & Carol. BA Albion Coll 1965; JD Wayne 1968. D 5/2/2007 Bp James Arthur Kelsey P 11/4/2007 Bp Rustin Ray Kimsey. c 2. dick. graybill@hotmail.com

GRAYBILL, Virginia K (NMich) 301 N 1st St, Ishpeming MI 49849 B Kalamazoo MI 1943 d William & LaVerne. BA Albion Coll 1965; Grad Course Wayne St and U MI 1968. D 9/10/2013 P 5/4/2014 Bp Rayford J Ray. c 2.

GRAYDEN, Margaret Miller (NCal) **D Ch Of S Mart Davis CA 2013-; COM The Epis Dio Nthrn California Sacramento CA 2014-** B Waterloo IA 1961 d Charles & Margaret. B.A. Wellesley Coll 1983; M.A. Pr 1985; J.D. U CA at Davis Sch of Law 1993; B.D.S. The Sch for Deacons 2013. D 6/8/2013 Bp Barry Leigh Beisner. m 5/29/1987 David Ram Elias Aladjem. The Assn for Epis Deacons 2010. margaret@churchofstmartin.org

GRAY-FOW, Michael John Gregory (Mil) 120 S Ridge St, Whitewater WI 53190 B Wigan Lancashire UK 1943 s James & Eileen. Cert U of Nottingham 1967; U of Nottingham 1973; MEd U of Nottingham 1978; PhD U of Wisconsin 1985. D 8/17/1991 P 2/20/1992 Bp Roger John White. m 10/29/1983 Tiiu R Gray-Fow c 1. Vic S Lk's Epis Ch Milwaukee WI 1998-2010; Chapl SV Denis Sullivan Milwaukee 1998-2008; Vic S Jn's NW Mltry Acad Delafield WI 1995-2008; Dn and Vic NoWstrn Mltry & Naval Acad Lake Geneva WI 1992-1995; Dir Inst for Chr Stds Dioc. Milwaukee 1988-1996. Auth, "INRI," *Jnl of Latin Stds - Latomus*, Liege U., 2012; Auth, "A Problem w Evolution," *JISRS*, A.I. Cuza Univ. Rumania, 2011; Auth, "Neither Vrgn nor Mtyr," *Jnl of Latin Stds - Latomus*, Liege U., 2010; Auth, "From Proconsul to S," *Classica et Mediaevalia*, Copenhagen U., 2006.

✠ GRAY-REEVES, The Rt Rev Mary (ECR) 154 Central Ave, Salinas CA 93901 **Bp of El Camino Real Dio El Camino Real Salinas CA 2007-** B Coral Gables FL 1962 d James & Florence. AA Miami-Dade Cmnty Coll 1982; BA California St U 1987; BTh Coll S Jn Evang 1994; MDiv Coll S Jn Evang 1994. D 6/11/1994 Bp John Mc Gill Krumm P 1/14/1995 Bp Frederick Houk Borsch Con 11/10/2007 for ECR. c 2. Dio SE Florida Miami 2005-2007; R St Margarets and San Francisco de Asis Epis Ch Hialeah FL 1998-2004; Asst S Jas' Par So Pasadena CA 1997-1998; Asst Chr Ch Par Redondo Bch CA 1994-1997. Auth, "Unearthing My Rel," Morehouse, 2013; Co-Auth, "The Hosp of God," SPCK, 2011. bishopmary@edecr.org

GRAYSON, Timothy Holiday (Md) 536 Kinsale Rd, Timonium MD 21093 **Ch Of The Mssh Baltimore MD 2010-** B Wellington New Zealand 1951 s Peter & Marjorie. BA Victoria U Wellington Nz 1973; MA Victoria U Wellington Nz 1974; MDiv VTS 2007. D 6/16/2007 P 1/5/2008 Bp John L Rabb. m 1/16/1951

Kathleen Antonelli Grayson c 2. Asst S Jas' Epis Ch Baltimore MD 2007-2009; Exec Pub Lippincott Williams&Wilkins 1982-2003.

GREATHOUSE, William Matthew (WTenn) 103 S Poplar St, Paris TN 38242 B Kansas City KS 1970 s William & Janice. BA Trevecca Nazarene U 1995; MDiv Nash 2005. D 6/4/2005 P 4/29/2006 Bp Bertram Nelson Herlong. m 6/13/1992 Laureen M Greathouse c 3. R Gr Epis Ch Paris TN 2011-2014; R S Paul's Epis Ch Newnan GA 2008-2011; Assoc R/P in Charge S Paul's Epis Ch Murfreesboro TN 2005-2008.

GREATWOOD, Richard Neil (CFla) 1167 Adair Park Place, Orlando FL 32804 **Adj Prof Barry Univ Sch of Law Orlando FL 2008-** B Olean NY 1933 s Harry & Dorothy. BA Colg 1954; MDiv UTS 1957; JD U of Virginia 1960; MA Van 1970; PhD Van 1977. D 11/19/1970 P 5/1/1971 Bp William Hopkins Folwell. m 9/11/1956 Diane Greatwood. Prof Nash Nashotah WI 1975-1984.

GRECO, John Anthony (LI) 333 E 53rd St Apt 5m, New York City NY 10022 **Hon Cathd Of The Incarn Garden City NY 1998-** B Brooklyn NY 1938 s Joseph & Adeline. BA S Jn's U 1960; MA NYU 1962; MDiv GTS 1967. D 6/17/1967 P 12/23/1967 Bp Jonathan Goodhue Sherman. Dep Epis Admin Dio Long Island Garden City NY 1995-2003, Archd of Nassau Cnty 1984-2004; R Ch of S Jude Wantagh NY 1968-1994; Cur St. Anne's Brooklyn Heights 1967-1968. Bp's Cross for Distinguished Dioc Serv Dio Long Island 1992.

GREELEY, Horace (Cal) D 6/3/2006 Bp William Edwin Swing P 12/2/2006 Bp Marc Handley Andrus.

GREELEY III, Paul William (USC) 206 Kings Mountain St, York SC 29745 **P-in-c Ch Of The Gd Shpd York SC 2015-; Counslr Keystone Substance Abuse Serv 2014-; Lic Profsnl Counslr, Chapl Epis Ch Hm at York Place Inc Columbia SC 2012-** B Spartanburg SC 1952 s Paul & Mary. BA Wofford Coll 1975; MDiv SWTS 1978; DMin SWTS 2006; MA Prescott Coll 2011. D 6/24/1978 P 6/2/1979 Bp George Moyer Alexander. m 8/16/1975 Sharon S Shepherd c 2. Clincl Counslr II Ernest E. Kennedy Cntr Goose Creek SC 2011-2012; R Ch Of The Adv Spartanburg SC 2006-2009; Int Dn Trin Cathd Phoenix AZ 2005-2006; Archd Dio Arizona Phoenix AZ 1998-2006; R S Mk's Epis Ch Mesa AZ 1995-1998; Fndr/Dir The H Innoc Mnstry Chelsea AL 1989-1994; Fndr/Dir H Innoc Mnstry Chelsea AL 1988-1995; Assoc S Steph's Epis Ch Birmingham AL 1987-1988; Asst R S Lk's Epis Ch Birmingham AL 1982-1987; Vic S Lk's Ch Newberry SC 1980-1982; D-in-trng S Thad Epis Ch Aiken SC 1978-1980. Contrib, *Sundays and Seasons 2001*, Augsburg Press, 2001; Auth, "Creative Fire," *Living Ch*, 1980; Contrib, *Seabury in Memi*, 1978. pwmgreeley@icloud.com

GREEN, Andrew (SanD) 2004 East Calle Lileta, Palm Springs CA 92262 **R S Paul In The Desert Palm Sprg CA 1989-; Secy HOD Com on the St of the Ch 2012-; Mem Stndg Com - Dio San Diego 2012-; Dep GC 1995-** B Merced CA 1955 s Marvin & Marie. California St U - Stanislaus; AA Merced Cmnty Coll 1975; BA U of New Mex 1979; MDiv SWTS 1985. D 6/26/1985 Bp Richard Mitchell Trelease Jr P 1/1/1986 Bp Robert Munro Wolterstorff. m 6/18/1977 Susan Louise Croley c 3. Cur S Dunst's Epis Ch San Diego CA 1985-1988.

GREEN III, Anthony Roy (Spok) 1705 5th St, Wenatchee WA 98801 **Supply P S Jn The Bapt Epis Ch Ephrata WA 2007-; Growth and Dvlpmt Grant Revs Dio Spokane Spokane WA 2013-, Stndg Com 2005-** B Pittsburgh PA 1953 s Anthony & Dolores. BA S Meinrad Coll 1975; BTh St Augustines RC Sem of Toronto 1978; MEd Cntrl Washington U 2002. Rec 10/23/2005 Bp James E Waggoner Jr. m 5/29/1993 Jeannette C Larson c 1. Substitute Tchr Wenatchee (WA) Sch Dist 2001-2012.

GREEN, Daniel Currie (NCal) 40 5th St, Petaluma CA 94952 **R St Johns Epis Ch Petaluma CA 2010-** B Riverside CA 1965 s Alan & Ellen. BA California Inst of Integral Stds 1998; MDiv CDSP 2005. D 6/4/2005 P 12/3/2005 Bp William Edwin Swing. m 8/17/2002 Sarah Margaret Tinsley c 1. Assoc R All SS Ch Carmel CA 2005-2010. rector.episcopal.petaluma@gmail.com

GREEN, David Edward (Cal) 6103 Harwood Ave, Oakland CA 94618 B Adrian MI 1937 s Edward & Fannie. BA Harv 1960; BD CDSP 1963; Grad Theol Un 1965; MLS U CA 1969. D 6/29/1963 P 6/23/1964 Bp Richard Stanley Merrill Emrich. m 6/1/1961 Sharon Green c 3. Libr The GTS New York NY 1982-2002; Ref Libr Grad Theol Un Berkeley CA 1969-1982; Libr SFTS San Anselmo CA 1966-1969; Instr Hebr CDSP Berkeley CA 1962-1965. Transltr, *Many Theol works*. Amer Theol Libr Assn 1967-2002; Country Dance and Song Soc 1988.

GREEN, David Keith (CGC) **S Lk's Ch Marianna FL 2015-; Dio Cntrl Gulf Coast Pensacola FL 2012-** D 11/22/2014 P 6/16/2015 Bp Philip Menzie Duncan II.

GREEN, David Robert (Be) 623 Cloverfields Dr., Stevensville MD 21666 **R S Gabr's Ch Douglassville PA 2013-** B Johnstown PA 1957 s John & Nancy. BFA Clarion U of Pennsylvania 1979; MDiv TESM 1987; DMin GTF 2000. D 6/6/1987 Bp Alden Moinet Hathaway P 12/19/1987 Bp William Grant Black. m 5/2/1981 Jenifer R Green c 3. R Chr Ch Par Kent Island Stevensville MD 2004-2013; R St Chris Epis Ch Charleston WV 1989-2004; Vic S Andr's Epis Ch Wshngtn Ct Hs OH 1987-1989.

GREEN, Dru (Chi) 971 First St, Batavia IL 60510 **Ret 1999-** B Aurora IL 1936 s Drury & Christine. BA Illinois Coll 1962; BD SWTS 1965. D 6/12/1965 Bp James Winchester Montgomery P 12/18/1965 Bp Gerald Francis Burrill. m 12/9/1989 Linda Frances Green. R Calv Epis Ch Batavia IL 1998-1999, Co-R 1994-1997, R 1975-1993; Ch of the H Name Dolton IL 1967-1975; Cur Ch Of The H Comf Kenilworth IL 1965-1967. dlf971@sbcglobal.net

GREEN, Elizabeth A (WMass) 66 Highland Ave #C, Short Hills NJ 07078 **R S Jn's Epis Ch Sutton MA 2011-** B Pittsburgh PA 1961 d Charles & Therese. BA W&M 1983; MDiv Drew U 2007. D 6/7/2008 P 12/20/2008 Bp Mark M Beckwith. c 1. Ch Of The Redeem Morristown NJ 2010-2011; Asst Chr Ch Short Hills NJ 2008-2010; Interweave Summit NJ 1997-2008; Ecum/Interfaith Off Dio Newark Newark NJ 2010-2011. Auth, ""The Pract of Substituted Love,"" *Compassion: Thoughts on Cultivating a Gd Heart*, Fresh Air Books, 2008. Daniel P. Kidder Prize for Practical Theol Drew U TS 2007; Patricia Wickham Prize for Feminist/Womanist Schlrshp Drew U TS 2006; The Rev. Helen Gulick Clem Memi Schlrshp Drew U TS 2003.

GREEN, Frazier L (Ga) 1041 Fountain Lake Dr, Brunswick GA 31525 B Neptune, NJ 1958 s Frazier & Harriet. BS U of Florida 1983; Tchr Cert Armstrong Atlantic St U 1998; MDiv VTS 2007. D 2/3/2007 P 8/17/2007 Bp Henry Irving Louttit. m 8/16/1986 Victoria L Green c 4. S Athan Ch Brunswick GA 2011-2012; Assoc Pstr Ch Of The Sprt Alexandria VA 2007-2008.

GREEN, Gary (Mil) 6502 51st Ave, Kenosha WI 53142 B Pontiac IL 1949 s Harry & Louise. Illinois Cntrl Coll; Wartburg Coll 1971; LTh Nash 1986. D 6/14/1986 Bp James Winchester Montgomery P 12/20/1986 Bp William Charles Wantland. m 12/20/1969 Kathleen L Thompson c 2. P in charge S Andr's Ch Kenosha WI 1997-2015; R S Thos Of Cbury Ch Greendale WI 1991-1997; Vic Gr Ch Rice Lake WI 1986-1991; S Lukes Ch Ladysmith WI 1986-1991.

GREEN, Gretchen Hall (O) 35 Cohasset Dr, Hudson OH 44236 B Waterbury CT 1940 d Jesse & Louise. Cor; GN Mt Sinai Hosp Sch of Nrsng Cleveland OH 1963; RN Mt Sinai Hosp Sch of Nrsng Cleveland OH 1963; Dio of Ohio Diac Trng 1996. D 11/8/1996 Bp J Clark Grew II. m 6/13/1964 Robert Thomas Green c 4. D for Soc Justice Chr Ch Epis Hudson OH 2006-2008; D Chr Ch Epis Hudson OH 2002-2005; D Ch Of Our Sav Akron OH 1996-2002. Nurse of Hope Summit Cnty Amer Cancer Soc 1990.

GREEN JR, Joseph Nathaniel (SVa) 3826 Wedgefield Ave, Norfolk VA 23502 B Jenkinsville SC 1926 s Joseph & Etta. BA S Augustines Coll Raleigh NC 1949; MDiv PDS 1952; STM Sewanee: The U So, TS 1965; LLD S Augustines Coll Raleigh NC 1976. D 5/30/1953 Bp John J Gravatt P 4/17/1954 Bp Clarence Alfred Cole. m 6/17/1955 Evelyn G Green. S Mk's Ch Suffolk VA 2004-2007; Int S Jas Epis Ch Portsmouth VA 1996-2000; Dep, GC The Epis Ch 1969-1983; R Gr Ch Norfolk VA 1963-1993; Chapl S Aug's Coll Raleigh NC 1958-1963; R S Ambroses Ch Raleigh NC 1958-1959; P-in-c Epiph Ch Spartanburg SC 1955-1958; S Phil's Epis Ch Greenville SC 1955-1958; M-in-c Chruch of S Simon and S Jude Peak SC 1953-1955; M-in-c Epis Ch Of S Simon And S Jude Irmo SC 1953-1955; S Barn Ch Jenkinsville SC 1953-1955. UBE, Natl Pres 1975-1977. DD VTS 1988; Natl Conf of Christians and Jews Honoraryree 1984; DD S Paul's Coll Lawrenceville VA 1984; City Councilman & Vice Mayor Norfolk City Coun 1977.

GREEN, Kenneth William (Spok) 539 3rd Ave, Havre MT 59501 B Kingman AZ 1936 s Harold & Ruth. BS Westminster Coll 1972; MDiv VTS 1982. D 6/16/1982 Bp William Benjamin Spofford P 6/18/1983 Bp Robert Whitridge Estill. m 8/30/1967 Carol Green c 3. Vic S Mary's Bonners Ferry Bonners Ferr ID 2001-2003; R S Mk's Ch Havre MT 1996-2001; Dio Montana Helena MT 1995; Dio Utah Salt Lake City UT 1993-1994; Vic S Jn's Epis Ch Logan UT 1984-1992; Asst H Trin Epis Ch Greensboro NC 1982-1984.

GREEN, Kuulei Mobley (ETenn) 3975 E Clocktower Ln Apt 236, Meridian ID 83642 **Supply P Dio Idaho Boise ID 2009-** B Washington DC 1937 d Radford & Barbara. BA Hood Coll 1959; MDiv Sewanee: The U So, TS 1993. D 3/30/1993 Bp John Stuart Thornton P 5/1/1994 Bp Robert Gould Tharp. c 1. S Barn Nrsng Hm Chattanooga TN 2002-2008, 1994-2001; S Alb's Epis Ch Hixson TN 2001-2002; Chapl S Alphonsus Hosp 1993-1994; D S Steph's Boise ID 1993-1994.

GREEN OHC, Larry A (Chi) 1424 N Dearborn St, Chicago IL 60610 **D S Chrys's Ch Chicago IL 2005-** B Canton GA 1952 s Cornelius & Jimmie. D 2/5/2005 Bp Bill Persell. OAHC 2009. S Stephens Awd AED 2013.

GREEN, Lawrence Joseph (Minn) Saint Pauls Episcopal Church, 265 Lafayette St, Winona MN 55987 B Saint Louis MO 1941 s Lawrence & Rose. De Andreis Sem 1964; BA S Marys Sem 1964; MA S Louis U 1967; PhD S Louis U 1982. D 1/15/1994 Bp Sanford Zangwill Kaye Hampton P 12/17/1999 Bp James Louis Jelinek. m 10/7/1989 Sandra Kay Green c 6. P-in-c S Paul's Ch Winona MN 2004-2013; P-in-c Gr Memi Ch Wabasha MN 2000-2006; S Mk's Ch Lake City MN 2000-2004.

GREEN, Linda Frances (Chi) 971 First St, Batavia IL 60510 **Int S Jn The Evang Lockport IL 2016-** B New York NY 1942 d Alfred & Frances. BA Augustana Coll 1964; Rutgers The St U of New Jersey 1967; MS U IL 1968; MDiv SWTS 1991. D 6/15/1991 P 12/21/1991 Bp Frank Tracy Griswold III. m 12/9/1989 Dru Green. Chapl Bp Anderson Hse Chicago IL 2009-2015; S Ann's Ch Woodstock IL 2001-2003; Dio Chicago Chicago IL 1998-2001; Co R Calv Epis Ch Batavia IL 1994-1997; P S Paul's Ch La Salle IL 1991-1993. rector@stjohns-lockport-il.org

GREEN, Mary Emily (Tex) 4633 Tanner View Dr, Clinton WA 98236 **Chapl Iona Sch of Mnstry 2007-3012** B Shreveport LA 1944 d Robert & Beula. RN S Lk Sch of Nrsng 1966; BA Stephens Coll 1975; MS U of Missouri 1977; MDiv Epis TS of the SW 1992. D 6/27/1992 Bp Maurice Manuel Benitez P 1/19/1993 Bp William Elwood Sterling. m 9/3/1972 Robert Green c 1. Stff Chapl S Lk's Epis Hosp Houston TX 2004-2011; Stff Chapl St. Lk's Epis Hosp Houston TX 2004-2011; Vic Chr Epis Ch Cedar Pk TX 2000-2003; Chapl Epis TS Of The SW Austin TX 1997-2000; The Great Cmsn Fndt Houston TX 1992-1999; Chapl Epis Stdt Cntr TX A&M Coll Sta TX 1992-1995. Bk, "Eyes to See: The Redemptive Purpose of Icons," *Eyes to See: The Redemptive Purpose of Icons*, Ch Pub Inc., Morehouse, 2014; "Pstr Care of the Dying," *PlainViews-A Pub of Hlth Care Chapl*, 2009; "Chapl Response to Codes," *PlainViews - A Pub of Hlth Care Chapl*, 2008.

GREEN, Patricia Anne (WMich) 160 Main St, Somerset MA 02726 **Sprtl Care Coordntr Hm & Hospice Careof Rhode Island 2006-** B New York NY 1948 d James & Lily. BS U of Pennsylvania 1969; MDiv CDSP 1991. D 6/22/1991 Bp George Nelson Hunt III P 7/1/1992 Bp Rustin Ray Kimsey. m 7/29/2000 Gary Martin. R S Jn's Ch Mt Pleasant MI 2001-2005; Int Dio Nthrn Michigan Marquette MI 1999-2001; So Cntrl Reg Manistique MI 1999-2001; Mnstry Dvlpmt Spec Dio Estrn Oregon Cove OR 1992-1995.

GREEN, Patricia Lynn (RG) 1678 Tierra Del Rio NW, Albuquerque NM 87107 **Pstr St. Tim's Luth Ch Albuquerque NM 2003-** B West Point NY 1948 d Carey & Mary. BA U of New Mex 1976; MEd U of Arizona 1979; MDiv Epis TS of the SW 2000. D 6/10/2000 P 12/9/2000 Bp William Jerry Winterrowd. m 4/27/1967 Alfred L Green c 2. St Timothys Luth Ch Albuquerque NM 2003-2012; Ther Samar Counnseling Cntr Albuquerque NM 2002-2003; Samar Counslg Cntr Albuquerque NM 2002-2003; Asst S Matt's Parker CO 2000-2001.

GREEN, Randy (WNC) 343 Dogwood Knl, Boone NC 28607 **Non-par 1982-** B Atlanta GA 1944 s Daniel & Patricia. BA Georgia St U 1966; BD Sewanee: The U So, TS 1969. D 6/28/1969 Bp Milton Legrand Wood P 4/4/1970 Bp Randolph R Claiborne. m 3/30/1985 Nancy H Green c 1. S Paul's Epis Ch Wilmington NC 2010-2013; S Andr's By The Sea Nags Hd NC 2008-2010; Int S Tim's Epis Ch Winston Salem NC 2007-2008; Ch Of The Ascen Hickory NC 2005-2007; S Paul's Epis Ch Greenville NC 2004-2005; Dio Wstrn No Carolina Asheville NC 2004; Int S Mich's Ch Raleigh NC 2003-2004; Ch Of The Epiph Eden NC 2001-2003; Asst Min H Innoc Ch Atlanta GA 1969-1982.

GREEN, Richard Lee (Oly) 1645 24th Avenue, Longview WA 98632 B Angleton TX 1949 s Thurman & Jimmie. BA U of Texas 1977; MDiv CDSP 1991. D 6/8/1991 P 6/6/1992 Bp William Edwin Swing. m 4/6/1991 Kathleen Patton c 1. Int S Phil The D Epis Ch Portland OR 2011-2012; R S Steph's Epis Ch Longview WA 2000-2010; Vic S Barn Ch Mt Shasta CA 1997-2000; Int Mt. Zion Luth Ch Yreka CA 1996-1997; Chapl Siskiyou Gen Hosp Yreka CA 1996-1997; Co-R S Mk's Ch Yreka CA 1995-2000; Assoc R Chr Ch Portola Vlly CA 1992-1995; Chapl San Francisco St U San Francisco CA 1991-1992; BEC Dio Olympia Seattle 2004-2010; Bd Mem Stanford Cbury Fndt Palo Alto CA 1993-1995. Contemplative Outreach 1998.

GREEN JR, Roy Donald (EO) 275 N Main St, Providence RI 02903 B Orlando FL 1946 s Roy & Sally. BA Florida St U 1968; MDiv VTS 1971; DMin VTS 1984. D 6/29/1971 P 1/18/1972 Bp William Hopkins Folwell. m 4/28/2007 Nancy Hunnewell Sargent c 2. Int Trin Ch Bend OR 2012-2014; Theol Mentor U of Portland OR 2011-2012; Dir of Sprtl Serv Hospice of Washington Cnty Hillsboro OR 2009-2012; Sr Chapl Partnr in Care Hospice Bend OR 2002-2009; Cn For Chr Formation Dio Rhode Island Providence RI 1998-2001; R Trin Ch Newport RI 1994-1998; R Emm Epis Ch Mercer Island WA 1987-1994; R S Mk's Ch Orchard Pk NY 1978-1987; Assoc Ecum Off Dio Virginia Richmond VA 1975-1978; Asst R, P in C The Falls Ch Epis Falls Ch VA 1973-1978; Cur S Mich's Ch Orlando FL 1971-1973; Cn for Circuit Rider Mnstry Dio Estrn Oregon Cove OR 2009-2010, Cn for Circuit Rider Mnstry 2009. Auth, "A Model For Spprt Of Lay Mnstry: An Experiment In Bus Ethics," 1984. Assn fo Profsnl Chapl 2011-2012. Awd of Excellence Oregon Hospice Assn 2008. SPIRITCHASER116@AOL.COM

GREEN, Susan Louise (SanD) D 6/17/2017 Bp Jim Mathes.

GREEN, Tamara Melanie (Cal) 7211 Garden Glen Ct Apt 318, Huntington Beach CA 92648 B Butte MT 1944 d Theodore & Josephine. BA Sch for Deacons 1985. D 6/7/1986 Bp William Edwin Swing. D Ch Of The H Innoc San Francisco CA 1992-1995; D S Ptr's Epis Ch San Francisco CA 1989-1990; D S Andr's Epis Ch San Bruno CA 1986-1988. Tertiary of the Soc of S Fran.

GREENAWAY, Douglas Andrew Gordon (WA) 1116 Lamont St Nw, Washington DC 20010 **Assoc S Paul's Par Washington DC 2008-; Assoc S Paul's Rock Creek Washington DC 2008-; Natl WIC Assn Washington DC 1990-** B Bellville ON CA 1951 s Gordon & Delores. BA Carleton U 1974; MA CUA 1977; MDiv Wesley TS 2000. D 6/10/2000 P 12/10/2000 Bp Ronald Hayward Haines. c 1. Asst R S Alb's Par Washington DC 2000-2007. Auth, "W Ger-

many: Museum Without a Facade Centered on a Massive Drum," *Archit*, Amer Inst of Architects, 1985.

GREENE, Adam S (Fla) 4620 Algonquin Ave, Jacksonville FL 32210 **Jacksonville Epis HS Jacksonville FL 2016-** B Princeton NJ 1964 s Howard & Donna. BA Van 1986; Vstng Schlr Camb 2008; MDiv Ya Berk 2009. D 12/20/2008 P 6/28/2009 Bp J Neil Alexander. m 10/1/1988 Martha G Greene c 1. Epis HS Bellaire TX 2009-2016. greenea@esj.org

GREENE, Dorothy Anne (NY) 27 Willow Ave, Larchmont NY 10538 **Assoc Gr Ch 2004-; P Assoc S Jn's Ch Larchmont NY 1988-** B Mamaroneck NY 1931 d Harry & Dorothy. BS Col 1968; MA UTS 1986. D 6/13/1987 Bp Paul Moore Jr P 5/15/1988 Bp Lyman Cunningham Ogilby. m 2/3/1951 Jeffrey Greene. Asst W Dennis Cmnty Ch 2004-2006; P-in-c S Andr By The Sea Hyannis Port MA 1989-1990; S Dav's Epis Ch S Yarmouth MA 1988-1996. Phi Beta Kappa 1968.

GREENE, Edward Rideout (WVa) 19 Valley Rd, Bath ME 04530 **Ret 1998-** B Bath ME 1943 s Stanley & Ethel. BA Bow 1965; STM GTS 1968. D 6/8/1968 Bp Leland Stark P 12/21/1968 Bp Frederick Barton Wolf. c 2. P-in-c S Andr's Ch Winthrop ME 2006-2012; Nelson Cluster Of Epis Ch Rippon WV 1993-1998; Mssnr Nelson Cluster Of Epis Ch Rippon WV 1993-1998; R S Lk's Ch Worcester MA 1987-1993; Dio Wstrn Massachusetts Springfield 1981-1993; Assoc Pstr Care Chr Ch Fitchburg MA 1981-1987; Vic S Geo's Epis Ch Sanford ME 1974-1981; P-in-c Chr Ch Biddeford ME 1972-1981; Vic S Jas Ch Old Town ME 1968-1972. Soc Of S Jn The Evang 1997.

GREENE, Elinor Robinson (Pa) 6635 Mccallum St Apt B406, Philadelphia PA 19119 **D Dio Pennsylvania Philadelphia PA 1993-** B Philadelphia PA 1952 d George & Elinor. BA Hampshire Coll 1977; MA Ya Berk 1982; Pennsylvania Diac Sch 1993. D 10/30/1993 Bp Allen Lyman Bartlett Jr.

GREENE, Everett Henry (RI) 1117 Capella S, Newport RI 02840 **Asstg P S Columba's Chap Middletown RI 2001-; Ret 1994-** B Providence RI 1928 s Stephen & Flora. BA Br 1951; MDiv Colgate Rochester Crozer DS 1955; MDiv CRDS 1955; MA LIU 1974. D 6/21/1956 P 2/23/1957 Bp Dudley S Stark. c 3. Asst S Geo's Ch Newport RI 1994-2001; R Emm Ch Newport RI 1985-1994; Chapl (Col) US-Army 1965-1985; Chapl US-A 1965-1985; Vic S Aug's Ch Kingston RI 1960-1965; Chapl U RI 1960-1965; R Zion Ch Avon NY 1957-1960; Min in charge Trin Epis Ch Rockland MA 1956-1957; Chapl to the Ret Cler and Surviving Spouses Dio Rhode Island Providence RI 2006-2011, Dioc Coun 1986-1990. Mltry Chapl Assn 1977.

GREENE JR, Frank Eugene (NH) 5 Nutmeg Cir, Laconia NH 03246 **Died 3/28/2016** B Boston MA 1917 s Frank & Winifred. BA Harv 1938; STB EDS 1942. D 6/3/1942 P 12/15/1942 Bp Henry Knox Sherrill. m 6/24/1978 Edith Hathaway Greene c 3. Ret 1982-2016; Vic S Mk's Ch Ashland NH 1975-1982; Chapl Ancora St Hosp Hammonton NJ 1970-1972; R Trin Shirley Cntr MA 1967-1969; Vic S Marg Boston MA 1964-1970; R S Mich's Epis Ch Holliston MA 1962-1964; R The Par Of S Chrys's Quincy MA 1951-1962; S Mary's Epis Ch Boston MA 1947-1951; R S Jn's Epis Ch Saugus MA 1943-1947; R Our Sav Cliftondale MA 1943-1946; Cur Trin Ch Epis Boston MA 1942-1943. Auth, *News from the No Country*, 1999; Auth, *Pieces of the Rock*, 1994; Auth, *Life in the Slow Ln*, 1990; Auth, *Uncle Bob's Camp*, 1983; Auth, "Mid Canyons Deep," *Wrshp II*. Harvard Club of New Hampshire 1975; New Hampshire Soc of Mayflower Descendants 1980; New Hampshire Sons of the Amer Revolution 1982; Pilgrim Jn Howland Soc 1985.

GREENE, George Burkeholder (Alb) 53 West St, Whitesboro NY 13492 **Ret 2001-** B Mohawk NY 1929 s Arthur & Gladys. BA Indiana Cntrl U 1955; BTh PDS 1958. D 5/31/1958 P 12/6/1958 Bp Frederick Lehrle Barry. m 7/26/1958 Shirley L Greene c 3. R St Augustines Ch Ilion NY 1968-2001; R Par Of S Jas Ft Edw NY 1958-1968.

GREENE III, Joseph D (NY) 1451 Carriage Ridge Dr., Greensboro GA 30642 **R S Jn's Ch Larchmont NY 2015-** B Macon GA 1977 s Joseph & Kathryn. BA U GA 2002; MDiv GTS 2006. D 12/21/2005 P 8/3/2006 Bp J Neil Alexander. m 4/15/2010 Ashley R Greene c 3. R Ch Of The Redeem Greensboro GA 2010-2014; Cur S Columba Epis Ch Suwanee GA 2006-2010. jgreen@stjohnslarchmont.org

GREENE, Judith (Ct) 60 Bywatyr Ln, Bridgeport CT 06605 B Fairfield CT 1939 d Gavin & Grace. BA Rad 1961; MA Pur 1968; MDiv GTS 1996. D 6/24/1996 Bp Edward Witker Jones P 1/6/1997 Bp Don Adger Wimberly. c 2. R Chr Ch Trumbull CT 1999-2011; Assoc R Trin Ch Covington KY 1996-1999.

GREENE, Kim Harlene (WNY) St Paul's Cathedral, 128 Pearl St, Buffalo NY 14202 B Buffalo NY 1963 d Kenneth & Irene. D 2/13/2011 Bp Michael Garrison.

GREENE, Lynne Tuthill (SwFla) 1369 Vermeer Drive, Nokomis FL 34275 B Newburgh NY 1924 s Roswell & Dorothy. BA Syr 1945; MD Syr 1947. D 9/25/1966 Bp George E Rath. m 4/7/1945 Nora Irene Greene c 4. D S Mk's Epis Ch Venice FL 1987-2011; D S Jn's Ch Ithaca NY 1973-1987; D The Ch Of The Annunc Oradell NJ 1966-1973. AMA 1950; Amer Soc of Anesthesiologists 1963.

GREENE, Margaret C (Colo) 1300 Washington St, Denver CO 80203 **S Paul's Epis Ch Steamboat Sprngs CO 2014-; Chapl Epis Camps and Conf Cntr**

Inc 2009- B Walnut Creek CA 1972 d Marshall & Margaret. BS U CA San Diego 1994; MDiv SWTS 2002. D 6/1/2002 P 12/7/2002 Bp William Edwin Swing. m 9/12/2011 Lauren Kevin Robertson. Assoc for Faith Formation The Ch Of Chr The King (Epis) Arvada CO 2009-2011; Faith Formation Coordntr Dio Colorado Denver CO 2008-2014; P-in-c St Fran Ch-Dillon Breckenridge CO 2006-2008; Assoc R S Mk's Epis Ch Palo Alto CA 2002-2006.

GREENE, Mary Carter (Cal) 330 Ravenswood Ave, Menlo Park CA 94025 **Gr Cathd San Francisco CA 2016-** B Huntsville TX 1965 d Earl & Kathryn. BA Florida St U 1988; MA U IL 1993; MDiv CDSP 2014. D 12/6/2014 P 6/13/2015 Bp Marc Handley Andrus. m 12/19/1992 Kenneth Schatz c 2. Assoc Trin Par Menlo Pk CA 2014-2016; Other Lay Position S Mk's Epis Ch Palo Alto CA 2013-2014. mary@trinitymenlopark.org

GREENE, Michael Paul Thomas (Eau) St Luke's Episcopal Church, 221 W 3rd St, Dixon IL 61021 **Chr Ch Cathd Eau Claire WI 2011-** B Evanston IL 1974 s Richard & Gail. BA U of Pennsylvania 2004; MA Colgate Rochester Crozer DS 2006; MA CRDS 2006; MA Coll of Resurr W Yorkshire GB 2006. D 5/26/2006 P 12/21/2006 Bp Keith Lynn Ackerman. m 7/12/2003 Janet Hope Greene c 1. R S Lk's Ch Dixon IL 2007-2011; Cur Gr Epis Ch Galesburg IL 2006-2007.

GREENE, Patrick James (RI) 55 Main St, N Kingstown RI 02852 **SS Matt and Mk Barrington RI 2014-** B Providence RI 1983 s Brian & Tracy. BA U of Rhode Island 2006; MDiv VTS 2010. D 5/22/2010 P 12/18/2010 Bp Gerry Wolf. m 11/24/2012 Carmen Diane Rexroad c 1. Asst to the R S Paul's Ch N Kingstown RI 2010-2013.

GREENE, Robert B (WTex) 5151 Buffalo Speedway, Apt. 3212, Houston TX 77005 **Died 11/17/2015** B Morristown NJ 1925 s Elmer & Edythe. BA U So 1946; MDiv VTS 1949. D 8/6/1949 Bp Clinton Simon Quin P 12/1/1950 Bp John Elbridge Hines. Ret 1988-2015; Ch Of The Annunc Luling TX 1977-1988; The Resource Cntr Luling TX 1977-1988; S Jn's Epis Ch Bisbee AZ 1974-1976; Vic S Lk's Willcox AZ 1974-1976; Vic S Paul's Ch Tombstone AZ 1974-1976; R S Steph's Epis Ch Douglas AZ 1974-1976; S Andr's Epis Ch Sedona AZ 1968-1974; Vic S Thos Of The Vlly Epis Clarkdale AZ 1968-1974; Vic S Mk's Ch Tonopah NV 1966-1968; P-in-c Sisseton Reserve SD 1964-1966; P-in-c Epis Ch Uintah Ouray Reserve UT 1961-1964; Vic S Matt's Epis Ch Fairbanks AK 1959-1960; Vic S Tim's Ch Tanacross AK 1953-1959; Vic S Steph's Ch Liberty TX 1949-1953; Pres Resource Cntr for Sm Ch 2015.

GREENE, Roger Stewart (SO) 8101 Beechmont Ave, Cincinnati OH 45255 **R S Tim's Epis Ch Cincinnati OH 1993-** B Salt Lake City UT 1958 s Orrin & Joyce. BA Stan 1980; MDiv CDSP 1986. D 5/10/1986 Bp Otis Charles P 11/1/1987 Bp Morgan Porteus. m 6/13/1980 Nancy Hopkins c 2. Stff P Trin Ch Epis Boston MA 1987-1993. Soc Of S Jn The Evang.

GREENE, Timothy Patrick (NCal) 260 California Dr Section D, Yountville CA 94599 **Died 7/6/2017** B Waterport NY 1941 s George & Margaret. BA Ham 1962; MDiv EDS 1976; PsyD The Wright Inst Berkeley CA 2001. D 12/5/1992 P 12/4/1993 Bp William Edwin Swing. Dio California San Francisco CA 1992-1993; Chapl San Francisco Grnl Hosp 1985-1996.

GREENE-MCCREIGHT, Kathryn (Ct) 198 Mckinley Ave, New Haven CT 06515 B Norwalk CT 1961 d Robert & Joyce. BA Wesl 1983; MDiv Ya Berk 1988; STM Yale DS 1989; PhD Ya 1994. D 6/8/2002 P 1/25/2003 Bp Andrew Donnan Smith. m 8/4/1984 Matthew Keadle McCreight c 2. Theol-in-Res S Jn's Ch New Haven CT 2002-2008; Intern St Ptr's Epis Ch Oxford CT 2001-2002; Pstr to Yth No Haven Congrl Ch No Haven CT 1988-1989; Sum Intern Immac Concep RC Ch Hartford CT 1987; Chapiaincy Intern Wesl Memi Chap Middletown CT 1986-1987; Sum Intern Haddam Neck Congrl Ch Haddam Neck CT 1986. Auth, "Darkness Is My Only Comp: A Chr Response to Mntl Illness," Brazos Press, 2006; Auth, "Feminist Reconstructions of Chr Doctrine," Oxf Press, 2000; Auth, "Ad Litteram : How Aug, Calvin and Barth Understand the 'Plain Sense' of Genesis 1-3," Ptr Lang, 1999; Co-Ed, "Theol Exegesis: Essays in hon of Brevard Sprg Childs," Eerdmans, 1999; Auth, "Numerous arts and chapters in edited volumes," *Var Pub,* numerous from 1994 though the present, 1994. Chair, Chr Theol and the Bible, Soc of Biblic LiteratureL 2000-2010; Chair, Reformed Theol and the Bible, AAR 1994-2003; Chair, Reformed Theol and the Bible, AAR 1994-2003; Karl Barth Soc of No Amer 1995-2011; Scholarly Engagement w Angl Doctrine 1998-2005; Soc of Angl & Luth Theologians 2001-2005. Pub' Weekly Top Ten in Rel non-Fiction Darkness is my Only Comp 2006; A "Choice" Bk, 2000 Feminist Reconstructions of Chr Doctrine 2000; A "Choice" Bk, 2000 Feminist Reconstructions of Chr Doctrine 2000; Pew Evang Schlr Pew Charitable Trust 1996; Franke Fell in Hmnts Ya Grad Sch of Arts and Sciences 1989; Mstr of Div, cl Yale DS 1988; Evers Schlr Yale DS 1986; Alan MCune Schlr Wesl 1981.

GREENFIELD, Peter Alan (CPa) 122 Greenview Dr, Lancaster PA 17601 B New York NY 1933 s Harold & Judith. BA Dart 1955; STB PDS 1960. D 5/14/1960 P 12/1/1960 Bp Joseph Gillespie Armstrong. m 8/21/1954 Caroline Greenfield c 4. P-in-c S Lk's Epis Ch Mt Joy PA 2007-2011; R Bangor Ch Of Churchtown Narvon PA 2003-2007; Cn Cathd Ch Of S Steph Harrisburg PA 1998-2003; S Jn's Epis Ch Lancaster PA 1983-1995; R S Mk's Epis Ch Lewistown PA 1975-1983; R All SS' Epis Ch Hershey PA 1966-1975; Vic Gd Shpd Ch Hilltown PA 1962-1966; Cur Chr Epis Ch Pottstown PA 1960-1962; Out-

reach Dio Cntrl Pennsylvania Harrisburg PA 1973-1975. Jefferson Awd WGAL 1990; Bro Awd Roundtable of Christians and Jews 1981.

GREENLAW, William A (NY) 529 West 42nd St. Apt. 4J, New York NY 10036 **Ret 2008-; R Emer Ch Of The H Apos New York NY 2008-, R & Exec Dir, H Apos Soup Kitchen 1984-2008, Asst in Par & Proj Dir, H Apos Soup Kitchen 1983-1984** B Alhambra CA 1943 s Kenneth & Lois. BA U CA 1965; Drew U 1966; MDiv UTS 1968; PhD Duke 1971. D 6/5/1971 Bp Horace W B Donegan P 11/10/1971 Bp Paul Moore Jr. m 2/5/1977 Jane V Veitch. Assoc R Chr And S Steph's Ch New York NY 1976-1983; Asst Prof of Chr Ethics The GTS New York NY 1971-1975; full time Stdt Ord D Methodist Ch 1966-1971. The Bp's Cross Dio New York/Bp Mk Sisk 2004; Soc of St. Jn the Theol Dio New York / Bp Mk Sisk 2002.

GREENLEAF, Debra Lynn (Ida) **D S Steph's Boise ID 2015-** B Hollywood, California 1954 D 12/6/2015 Bp Brian James Thom. m 8/5/1972 James Michael Greenleaf c 2.

GREENLEAF, Richard Edward (NH) 325 Pleasant St, Concord NH 03301 **Sr Chapl S Paul's Sch Concord NH 2007-** B Winchester MA 1953 s Malcolm & Ruth. BA U of Massachusetts 1976; TS Gordon-Conwell TS 1984; MDiv Ya Berk 1988. D 2/29/1992 P 11/14/1992 Bp Douglas Edwin Theuner. m 4/19/1980 Jenny Jensen Greenleaf c 1. Dn of Chap S Paul's Sch Concord NH 1998-2007; Chapl S Paul's Sch Concord NH 1988-1998. BDS GS Pres 2005-2007; BDS GS Secy 2003-2004; Berkeley Grad Soc 2002-2007; Dio NH COM 2003-2008; Prov I Epis Sch Chapl Conf 1998. Chas D. Dickey Mstr in Rel & Ethics St. Paul's Sch 2003.

GREENLEE, Malcolm Blake (Ct) 32 Old Wagon Rd, Wilton CT 06897 B Mercedes TX 1932 s Walden & Nelle. GTS; BS Pur 1956; MBA GW 1969. D 6/12/1982 P 4/1/1983 Bp Arthur Edward Walmsley. m 12/7/1953 Dorothy Willard Richmond. Asst Gr Epis Ch Trumbull CT 1990-1998; Asst Ch Of S Thos Bethel CT 1984-1990; Asst S Steph's Ch Ridgefield CT 1982-1984. Auth, "Var arts Bus & Computers". Bd Dir Oratory Little Way.

GREENMAN, Elizabeth Travis Rees (Fla) 2959 Apalachee Parkway, Unit J6, Tallahassee FL 32301 **S Andr's Epis Ch Newport News VA 2014-** B Nashville TN 1957 d Terry & Kathleen. BBA U of No Florida 1981; MDiv VTS 1995. D 6/18/1995 P 12/1/1995 Bp Stephen Hays Jecko. m 11/26/1977 Harold A Greenman c 2. Gr Epis Ch Orange Pk FL 2003-2006; All SS Epis Ch Jacksonville FL 2001-2003, Asst To The R 2001-; Vic S Teresa Of Avila Crawfordville FL 1996-2003, 1996-2001; S Paul's Epis Ch Jacksonville FL 1995-1996, Asst R 1995-1996.

GREENSHIELDS, Kay Conner (Okla) 405 Roserock Dr, Norman OK 73026 **D S Anselm Cbury Norman OK 2001-** B Oklahoma City OK 1934 d Herald & Edna. D Formation Prog; BA U of Oklahoma 1955; Ecole De Normale De Musique 1956. D 7/1/1989 Bp James Russell Moodey. m 7/10/1955 James Bernie Greenshields c 2. Dioc Aids Cmsn 1993-1997; D S Jn's Ch Norman OK 1989-2001. Dok; NAAD; Rain Oklahoma.

GREENWELL, Gail E (SO) 318 E 4th St, Cincinnati OH 45202 **Dn Chr Ch Cathd Cincinnati OH 2013-; T/F Mem Gnrl Convnetion T/F on Mar 2013-; T/F Mem GC T/F on Mar 2013-; COM, chair Dio Kansas Topeka KS 2009-** B Portland OR 1955 d Fred & Barbara. BA U of Oregon 1977; MDiv CDSP 2001. D 5/26/2001 Bp Robert Louis Ladehoff P 12/1/2001 Bp William Edwin Swing. m 1/23/1982 James Greenwell c 2. R S Mich And All Ang Ch Mssn KS 2008-2013; R Ch Of The Epiph San Carlos CA 2004-2008; Assoc R S Steph's Par Bel Tiburon CA 2001-2004; Epis Cmnty Serv Bd Dio California San Francisco CA 2005-2008. Auth/Ed, "Cov and Blessing," S Mich and All Ang, 2011. Trailblzer Awd Cincinnati Un Bethel 2017; Natl Security Round Table The Stff Coll of the Armed Serv 2013; Pstr Ldrshp Awd Louisville Inst, KY 2008; EFM EFM 1990. ggreenwell@cccath.org

GREEN-WITT, Margaret Evelyn Ashmead (SwFla) 2499 Mapleleaf Ct, Spring Hill FL 34606 B Philadelphia PA 1920 d Robert & Anna. BS SUNY 1984. D 6/29/1991 Bp Rogers Sanders Harris. m 3/5/2000 Kenneth D Witt c 4. D S Jas Epis Ch Leesburg FL 2008-2011; D S Andr's Epis Ch Sprg Hill FL 1991-2007; Proj Dir Soup Kitchen Ch Of The H Apos New York NY 1982-1983; Asst Coordntr Capital Cmpgn The GTS New York NY 1979-1981.

GREENWOOD, April Valeria Trew (Va) 2910 Stratford Rd, Richmond VA 23225 **Westover Epis Ch Chas City VA 2013-** B Elizabeth City NC 1955 d I Frederick & Helen. BS Longwood U 1973; MEd U of Virginia 1977; MDiv VTS 1983. D 4/28/1984 P 4/1/1985 Bp David Henry Lewis Jr. m 10/13/1984 Daniel R Greenwood c 2. Varina Epis Ch Henrico VA 2009-2013; S Andr's Ch Richmond VA 2006-2007; Dio Virginia Richmond VA 2002-2006, 2001-2002; S Dav's Ch Aylett VA 1998; Chapl S Geo Sch Newport RI 1986-1995; S Andr's Epis Sch Potomac MD 1984-1985; Chapl S Andr Epis Sch Beth MD 1983-1986. Auth, "Coun For Rel In Independant Schools-How To Talk About God"; Auth, "Didache-Here I Stand: What Else Can I Do?".

GREENWOOD III, Daniel R (SVa) 2910 Stratford Rd, Richmond VA 23225 **R S Paul's Ch Petersburg VA 2009-** B Philadelphia PA 1954 s Daniel & Dorothy. Wms 1974; BA Hav 1976; MDiv VTS 1984. D 4/6/1986 P 5/1/1992 Bp George Nelson Hunt III. m 10/13/1984 April Valeria Trew Greenwood c 2. Vic Dio Virginia Richmond VA 2002-2009; R S Paul's Epis Ch Millers Tavern VA

1995-2002; Asst R S Mary's Ch Portsmouth RI 1991-1995; Chapl Washington Hosp Cntr Washington DC 1984-1985.

GREENWOOD, Don Robert (SO) 10414 Nw 13th Pl, Vancouver WA 98685 B Orange CA 1939 s Charles & Kathrine. BA U CA 1961; MDiv Sewanee: The U So, TS 1967; Cert Int Mnstry Prog 1993. D 6/27/1967 Bp William Evan Sanders P 5/1/1968 Bp William F Gates Jr. m 12/21/1962 Anna L Greenwood c 3. Int Ch of the H Sprt 2004-2005; Vic S Nich Of Myra Epis Ch Hilliard OH 1997-2001; Int Trin Ch Newark OH 1997; Int All SS Epis Ch Portsmouth OH 1996-1997; Int S Phil's Ch Columbus OH 1994-1995; Int S Ptr's Ch Gallipolis OH 1993-1994; Chapl Whetstone Care Cntr Columbus OH 1990-1992; R Ch Of The Redeem Sayre PA 1983-1990; R Gr Ch In The Mountains Waynesville NC 1978-1983; R S Fran Ch Macon GA 1972-1978; S Mary's Ch Enterprise MS 1969-1972; S Paul's Epis Ch Meridian MS 1969-1972; Asst Trin Ch Newton MS 1969-1972; Vic Chr Epis Ch Tracy City TN 1968-1969; D-in-Trng S Ptr's Ch Columbia TN 1967-1968. Auth, *S Lk Journ*; Auth, *The Rel Essence & Theol Meaning of Amer Popular Mus*; "Ord and Ret - Freedom to Choose," *Vintage Voice*. Vol of the Year Franklin Correctional Cntr 2012; Mntl Hlth Hall of Fame Reg Spprt Ntwk, Clark Cnty, WA 2007.

GREENWOOD JR, Eric Sutcliffe (Tenn) 404 Northridge Ct, Nashville TN 37221 B Memphis TN 1948 s Eric & Florence. BA LSU 1970; MDiv GTS 1973. D 6/24/1973 Bp John Vander Horst P 5/6/1974 Bp William Evan Sanders. m 9/3/1971 Sharon McCormack Greenwood c 2. R S Dav's Epis Ch Nashville TN 1988-2014; Asst to the R Gr & H Trin Epis Ch Richmond VA 1977-1988; Vic S Fran' Ch Norris TN 1974-1977; D S Jn's Epis Cathd Knoxville TN 1973-1974.

GREENWOOD, Harold Lee Hal (Okla) 2201 Nw 18th St, Oklahoma City OK 73107 **Died 2/27/2017** B Cushing OK 1949 s Harold & Doris. BS Oklahoma St U 1971; MDiv GTS 1977. D 6/18/1977 P 1/1/1978 Bp Gerald Nicholas Mcallister. m 9/6/1970 Marcia Ann Greenwood c 3. Dio Oklahoma Oklahoma City OK 1983-2013; P-in-c H Fam Oklahoma City OK 1981-1983; Ch Of The H Fam Moncks Corner SC 1981-1982; Assoc R S Jn's Epis Ch Tulsa OK 1979-1981; P-in-c All SS Ch Mcalester OK 1977-1979; Trin Ch Eufaula OK 1977-1979; Vic Trin Eutaula OK 1977-1979; Vic S Mk's 2017.

GREENWOOD, Jody (At) Christ Church Episcopal, 400 Holcomb Bridge Rd, Norcross GA 30071 **Assoc R Chr Ch Norcross GA 2013-** B Houston TX 1963 d James & Cody. BA Witt 1985; MDiv Candler TS Emory U 2013. D 12/15/2012 P 6/22/2013 Bp Robert Christopher Wright. m 5/11/2012 Alice Melott. Cross of St. Aug Awd Archbp of Cbury 2012.

GREENWOOD, Susan A (Colo) 53 Paradise Rd, Golden CO 80401 B Bartlesville OK 1947 BS U of Oklahoma 1969; MA U CO 1994; MDiv GTS 2006; MDiv GTS 2006. D 6/10/2006 P 12/9/2006 Bp Robert John O'Neill. c 2. Our Merc Sav Epis Ch Denver CO 2011, 2009-2010, 2009-2010; Assoc R S Lk's Epis Ch Ft Collins CO 2006-2008; Tchr-Title I Reading/Art Boulder Vlly Schools 1988-2003.

GREENWOOD, W(Alter) Merritt (O) 1473 Brighton Ave, Arroyo Grande CA 93420 **Epis Ch of St Jn the Bapt Aptos Aptos CA 2015-** B Fayetteville NC 1954 s Walter & Mary. BA Ken 1977; MDiv EDS 1981. D 6/27/1981 P 3/1/1982 Bp John Harris Burt. m 8/25/1979 Janette Greenwood c 2. S Barn Ch Arroyo Grande CA 2014-2015; All Souls' Epis Ch San Diego CA 2012-2013; S Steph's Ch Middlebury VT 2011-2012; S Mich's Epis Ch Brattleboro VT 2009-2011; Int S Andr's Ch Cleveland OH 2006-2009; S Paul's Epis Ch Of E Cleveland Cleveland OH 2000-2004; Assoc Chr Ch Shaker Heights OH 1998-1999; R S Mk's Ch Worcester MA 1992-1997; Dio Wstrn Massachusetts Springfield 1991-1998; S Anne's Par Scottsville VA 1986-1991; Cur S Mart's Epis Ch Charlotte NC 1981-1986. merrittgreenwood@gmail.com

GREER, Broderick Lee (WTenn) 1720 Peabody Ave, Memphis TN 38104 **Cur Gr - S Lk's Ch Memphis TN 2016-** B Fort Worth TX 1990 s Roderick & Patricia. BSSW Freed-Hardeman U; BSSW Freed¿Hardeman U; MDiv VTS 2015. D 5/30/2015 P 12/12/2015 Bp Don Edward Johnson. broderick@gracestlukes.org

GREER, David Jay (WLa) 208 Bruce Ave, Shreveport LA 71105 **Bd Visitors Kanuga Conf Cntr Hendersonville NC 1992-; Ret 1989-** B Poughkeepsie NY 1929 s Harry & Marjorie. TESM; BS Wag 1950; MDiv VTS 1955; Ldrshp Acad for New Directions 1978; VTS 1979; Coll of Preachers 1986; Sewanee: The U So, TS 1986; U So 1986; Epis TS of the SW 1987; St Petersburg Acad Russia 1992. D 6/11/1955 Bp Benjamin M Washburn P 1/7/1956 Bp Frederick D Goodwin. c 3. Int S Jn's Ch Barrington RI 2005-2006; Int Epis Ch Of The Gd Shpd Lake Chas LA 2003-2004; Int Chr Ch Grosse Pointe Grosse Pointe Farms MI 2001-2002; Int Dn Chr Ch Nacogdoches TX 2000-2011; Chr Ch Cathd Houston TX 2000; Int R S Paul's Epis Ch Alexandria VA 1998; Presiding Judge Dio Wstrn Louisiana Alexandria LA 1996-2005; Int S Jn's Epis Ch Mc Lean VA 1995-1996; Int Gr Epis Ch Monroe LA 1994-1995; Bd Live Oak Multi Faith Ret Cntr 1985-2006; R S Paul's Epis Ch Shreveport LA 1980-1989; R S Jas' Epis Ch Warrenton VA 1964-1980; R Chr Epis Ch Gordonsville VA 1958-1964; Dir Virginia Fam Conf 1957-2002; Asst S Paul's Ch Richmond VA 1955-1958. *Var arts & Revs*, 2003. Epis EvangES 1954.

GREER JR, George Holeman (NC) 301 S Circle Dr, Rocky Mount NC 27804 **R S Andr's Ch Rocky Mt NC 2005-** B Owensboro KY 1961 s George & Virginia. BA Brescia U 1984; MDiv GTS 2000. D 6/4/2000 P 1/13/2001 Bp Ted Gulick Jr. m 1/9/1988 Claire Bennett Greer c 2. R S Lk's Epis Ch Buffalo WY 2003-2005; Assoc R S Fran In The Fields Harrods Creek KY 2000-2003. rector@saint-andrews-church.org

GREER, Hilary A (Ct) 42 N Eagleville Rd, Storrs CT 06268 **Sewanee U So TS Sewanee TN 2016-; P-in-c S Mk's Chap Storrs CT 2011-** B Philadelphia PA 1974 d Robert & Anne. BA Ob 1996; MDiv EDS 2011. D 3/5/2011 P 9/10/2011 Bp Mark Sean Sisk. hgreer@stmarkschapel.org

GREER JR, James Gossett (O) 13710 Shaker Blvd Apt 404, Cleveland OH 44120 **Hon Assoc Chr Ch Shaker Heights OH 2002-** B Dallas TX 1932 s James & Lizabeth. BA U of No Texas 1955; STB GTS 1958; S Augustines Coll Cbury Gb 1959; STM Nash 1972. D 6/18/1958 P 12/20/1958 Bp John Joseph Meakin Harte. m 5/25/1984 Karen A Greer. Chapl Dept. Of Veteran Affrs Cleveland Vet. Aff. Med Cntr 1987-2002; Int S Jn's Ch Cleveland OH 1987-1996; S Ptr's Epis Ch Lakewood OH 1987; R S Jas' Epis Ch Of Albion Albion MI 1979-1983; R S Mk's Ch Newaygo MI 1976-1979; R S Thos Epis Ch Plymouth IN 1972-1976; R S Jas' Epis Ch Goshen IN 1968-1972; Vic Ch Of The H Trin So Bend IN 1963-1968; R S Barth's Ch Hempstead TX 1960-1963; Vic S Mary Mesquite TX 1958-1960; Dioc Press Ed for the D Dio Nthrn Indiana So Bend IN 1963-1976. Secy'S Awd For Excellence In Chapl Veteran Affrs 1996.

GREGG, Catherine (Nev) 2235 S. 1400 E Unit 19, Saint George UT 84790 **Dio Nevada Las Vegas 2014-; Dir of Sprtl Care Dixie Reg Med Cntr St. Geo UT 2010-; Supvsr CFDM Wstrn Reg Supvsr for Sprtl Dir 2005-; Co-Pres, Fac CFDM Sprtl Direction Prog 2004-; Adj Prof Haggard TS Azusa CA 2004-** B Rockledge FL 1954 d Charles & Iris. BA California St U Los Angeles 1975; Tchr Cred Los Angles Cnty 1976; Cert Vineyard TS 1979; TESOL Mt San Antonio Coll 1981; DMin Haggard TS 1999. D 1/31/2004 P 8/1/2004 Bp Joseph Jon Bruno. m 4/11/2000 Douglas H Gregg c 3. Dio Utah Salt Lake City UT 2007-2014, Bp Search Com 2009-2010; R Gr Epis Ch St Geo UT 2007-2014; Assoc Ch Of Our Sav Par San Gabr CA 2004-2006; Dir, D.Min. Prog Haggard TS Azusa CA 1999-2004; Chapl to Students Fuller TS Pasadena CA 1995-1999. Contributing Auth, "The Disease of Ethnocentricity," *IHC Revs*, Intermountain Hlth, 2010; Bk Reviewer, "Revs of," *Presence mag*, Sprtl Dir Intl , 2007; Auth, "Handbook for Sprtl Direction Trng," *Handbook for Sprtl Direction Trng*, CFDM, 2005; Doctoral Candidate, "The Role of Wisdom in the Cure of Souls," *HGST Archv*, HGST, 1999; Monthly Contrib, "Pryr and the Sprtl Life," *DAWN Report*, DAWN Mnstrs, 1989. Iona Cmnty 2009; SSJE 2013. Grant Rec Lilly Fndt for Cler Renwl 2012; Wmn of the Year Awd PPAU 2011; Sprt of Cmnty Awd Citizens for Dixie's Future 2010; Wmn of the Year Awd Bus and Profsnl Wmn/UT 2009; Rel Ldr of the Year Awd Washington Cnty Cltn Against Dom Violence 2009; Alum Ldrshp Memphis 1981. cgregg@episcopalnevada.org

GREGG, Jennifer E (WMass) St Stephen's Episcopal Church, 67 East St, Pittsfield MA 01201 **Dio Western Massachusetts Springfield 2007-; P Assoc S Steph's Ch Pittsfield MA 2007-** B Easton, MD 1977 d Alan. BS Elmira Coll 1999; MDiv Ya Berk 2007. D 6/9/2007 Bp Charles Ellsworth Bennison Jr P 12/15/2007 Bp Franklin Delton Turner. m 8/25/2007 Derek S Bodenstab c 3.

GREGG, Robert Clark (Cal) 659 Salvatierra St, Stanford CA 94305 B Kansas City MO 1938 s Harris & Mary. BA U So 1960; BD EDS 1963; Br 1969; PhD U of Pennsylvania 1974. D 10/28/1963 P 9/1/1964 Bp John S Higgins. m 9/8/1961 Mary Layne Gregg c 4. U Chapl Stanford Memi Ch Stanford CA 1987-1999; Assoc Chap Of The Cross Chap Hill NC 1978-1987; Co-P-in-c Trin Ch Fuquay Varina NC 1977-1987; Asst S Thos' Whitemarsh PA 1970-1971; Asst Ch Of S Mart-In-The-Fields Philadelphia PA 1969-1970; Assoc Chapl S Geo's Ch Newport RI 1963-1966. Auth, "Consolation Philos"; Auth, "Athan: The Life Of Antony & The Letter To Marcellinus"; Auth, "Jews, Pagans," & *Chr In The Golan*. Hon DD U So 1990.

✠ **GREGG, The Rt Rev William O** (NC) St. Paul's Church, 220 N. Zapapta Hwy #11, PMB 141A, Laredo TX 78043 **Epis Visitor Cmnty of the Mo of Jesus Chicago IL 2011-; Epis Visitor Angl Ord of Preachers 2010-; Asst Bp Dio No Carolina Charlotte NC 2007-** B Portsmouth VA 1951 s Otis & Geraldine. BA U Rich 1973; MDiv EDS 1977; MA Boston Coll 1980; MA U of Notre Dame 1990; PhD U of Notre Dame 1993. D 6/4/1977 Bp Robert Bruce Hall P 5/14/1978 Bp John Alfred Baden Con 9/23/2000 for EO. m 5/28/1977 Kathleen E Gregg c 1. Dio No Carolina Raleigh NC 2007-2014; GBEC 2006; Mem Intl Cmsn for Angl/Orth Dialog London 2004-2006; Bp of EO Dio Estrn Oregon Cove OR 2000-2007; HOB Theol Comm 2000-2006; R S Jas Ch New London CT 1997-2000; S Andr's Ch Paris IL 1996; S Geo Epis Ch W Terre Haute IN 1993-1996; Assoc. Prof. of Theol S Mary-of-the Woods Coll 1990-1996; Asst S Jn The Evang Ch Elkhart IN 1990-1991; Ch Of The H Trin Kokomo IN 1990; S Mich And All Ang Ch So Bend IN 1988-1989, Int R 1987-1988; R S Thos' Epis Ch Abingdon VA 1982-1987; Chapl / Tchr S Anne's-Belfield Sch Charlottesville VA 1979-1981; S Paul's Ch Charlottesville VA 1978-1979; Trin Epis Ch Highland Sprg VA 1977-1978; Exam Chapl Dio Connecticut Meriden CT

1998-2000; Stndg Com Dio Indianapolis Indianapolis IN 1993-1997. Auth, "Presence of Ch in The Cloud of Unknowing," *Amer Benedictine Revs*, 1992; Auth, "Sacramental Theol in Hooker's Laws: A Structural Perspective," *ATR*, 1991; Auth, *Benedictine Revs 92*.

GREGORIUS, Mary B (NY) 378 Bedford Rd, Pleasantville NY 10570 **R Dio New York New York NY 2012-; S Jn's Ch Pleasantville NY 2012-; Advsry Com Epis Chars of the Dio NY New York NY 2010-** B Newburgh NY 1953 d Howard & Mary. Westminster Choir Coll of Rider U 1983; D Formation Prog 1998; BA SUNY 2001; MDiv GTS 2009. D 5/16/1998 Bp Richard Frank Grein P 9/12/2009 Bp Mark Sean Sisk. m 11/6/1983 Harold S Gregorius c 2. Chapl Westchester Med Cntr 2010-2011; Assoc P S Marg's Ch Staatsburg NY 2009-2011; D Chr Ch Poughkeepsie NY 1998-2005. mbgregor@optonline.net

GREGORY, Brian Joseph Yth Dir S Thos Epis Ch Medina WA 2011- D 7/6/2017 Bp Gregory Harold Rickel.

GREGORY, Emma Jean (Nev) 4201 W Washington Ave, Las Vegas NV 89107 B Collinsville AL 1941 d Samuel & Edgie. BS Tuskegee Inst 1962; MBA Kent St U 1969; MS Ed Pepperdine U 1975; M.Div Epis TS of the SW 2011. D 6/10/2007 Bp Jerry Alban Lamb. c 1.

GREGORY, Leslie Burtner (NwT) 822 Keeler Ave, Dalhart TX 79022 **Died 9/24/2016** B Buffalo NY 1948 d Orville & Mildred. BA U of Kansas 1970; MDiv Epis TS of the SW 1991. D 9/14/1991 Bp William Edward Smalley P 5/1/1992 Bp Sam Byron Hulsey. m 7/31/1988 Alan Bryant Gregory c 1. Chapl for Prison Mnstrs Dio NW Texas Lubbock TX 1999, Chapl for Prison Mnstrs 1997-1998, Supply P 1991-2016, Chair, Priestly Titles Com 1995, Chair, Sprtl Dvlpmt Com 1994-1996, Missions Com 1992-1994.

GREGORY, Pamela S (RI) 251 Danielson Pike, North Scituate RI 02857 B Des Moines IA 1951 d David & Berdean. BA Coe Coll 1973; MS Drake U 1978; MDiv SWTS 1986; DMin SWTS 1990. D 5/31/1986 P 12/17/1986 Bp Walter Cameron Righter. c 4. R Trin Ch N Scituate RI 1998-2016; Vic S Chad Epis Ch Loves Pk IL 1990-1998; P-in-c Trin Ch Carroll IA 1986-1990. Alb Inst 1997.

GREGORY, Phillip Richard (Chi) 2612 Gateshead Dr, Naperville IL 60564 B Aurora IL 1948 D 2/7/2004 Bp Victor Alfonso Scantlebury. m 12/22/1996 Deborah Gregory.

GREGORY, Rachael Anne (Chi) 410 Grand Ave, Waukegan IL 60085 B Paoli IN 1966 d Norman & Lois. AA Oxford Coll of Emory U 1987; BA Berry Coll 1989; MDiv Sewanee: The U So, TS 2010. D 6/5/2010 P 2/12/2011 Bp John Wadsworth Howe. R Ch Of The H Fam Pk Forest IL 2013-2015; Non-Stipendiary Other Cler Chr Ch Waukegan IL 2010-2013; CPE Res Iowa Methodist Hosp Des Moines Iowa 2010-2011. revrachael@gmail.com

✠ GREIN, The Rt Rev Richard Frank (NY) 150 West End Avenue, Apt. 9H, New York NY 10013 **Ret Bp Dio New York New York NY 2001-, Bp 1994-2001, Bp Coadj 1989-1994** B Bemidji MN 1932 s Lester & Lavina. BA Carleton Coll 1955; BA Carleton Coll 1955; MDiv Nash 1959; STM Nash 1971; Nash 1981; DD Nash 1981; GTS 1989; DD GTS 1989. D 6/20/1959 Bp Hamilton Hyde Kellogg P 12/21/1959 Bp Philip Frederick McNairy Con 5/22/1981 for Kan. m 5/28/2004 Anne Frances Connor. Trst GTS New York NY 1989-2001; Chair, Cmsn on Pstr Letters Com Pstr Letter 1987-1992; Bp Dio Kansas Topeka KS 1981-1988, Dep, GC 1976-1980; R S Mich And All Ang Ch Mssn KS 1974-1981; Prof, Pstr Theol Nash Nashotah WI 1973-1974; R St Dav's Epis Ch Minnetonka MN 1969-1973; Dept of Missions Dio Minnesota Minneapolis MN 1968-1971, Dept of CSR 1964-1971, 1959-1963; R S Matt's Epis Ch Minneapolis MN 1964-1969; St Michaels All Ang Ch Minneapolis MN 1962-1963; Mem of Bp's Counsel H Trin Epis Ch Elk River MN 1959-1963; St Johns Ch Waseca MN 1959-1963; Trin Ch Becker MN 1959-1963; HOB Cmsn on Theol and Pstr Dvlp ECUSA New York NY; Trst, CO WDC Ecusa / Mssn Personl New York NY 1985-1991. Contrib, "On Being A Bp (Contrib)," Ch Hymnal Corp, 1992; Auth, "Angl Theol & Pstr Care (Contrib)," Morehouse Pub, 1985. Bp Visitor, Cmnty of S Mary 1994-2000; Bp Visitor, CHS 1990-2001; Coun, Associated Parishes 1970-1981; OHC 1989-2003; OHC 1957-2005. Hon Metropltn of the Ecum Throne Ecum Patriarch 1994; Prelate in Priory in USA Ord of S Jn of Jerusalem 1989.

GREINER, Robert Charles (Mass) 138 Tremont St, Boston MA 02111 B Atlantic City NJ 1944 s Robert & Katharine. None Amer U 1965; BA Hunter Coll 1980. D 6/4/2016 Bp Alan Gates. m 8/25/2013 Baoxin Zhang. Admin The Cathd Ch Of S Paul Boston MA 2016, Other Lay Position 2013-2016; Other Lay Position Dio Massachusetts Boston MA 2012-2013.

GREISER, Ronald Edmond (WNC) 5601 Oak Ridge Ave, New Port Richey FL 34652 **Ret 1997-** B Cincinnati OH 1934 s Melvin & Ada. BA U Cinc 1957; MDiv Sewanee: The U So, TS 1977. D 6/18/1977 Bp William F Gates Jr P 12/19/1977 Bp William Evan Sanders. m 1/28/1986 Rita Greiser c 4. S Paul's Ch Edneyville NC 2004-2009; S Fran' Epis Ch Rutherfordton NC 2003-2004; Int Ch of the Redeem Epis Ch Greenville SC 2002-2003; Int St. Simons-On-the-Sound Epis Ch Ft. Walton Bch FL 1999-2000; Trin Epis Ch Columbus GA 1991-1994; R S Andr's Epis Ch Panama City FL 1990-1997; R S Jn The Apos Ch Belle Glade FL 1986-1990; Asst H Trin Epis Ch W Palm Bch FL 1981-1986; R S Matt's Epis Ch Mcminnville TN 1979-1981; Dio Tennessee

Nashville TN 1978-1981; Otey Memi Par Ch Sewanee TN 1977-1978. Ord of S Lk 1982; SocMary 1975.

GREMILLION, Dorothy (Tex) 2708 Butler National Dr, Pflugerville TX 78660 B Algiers LA 1942 d Donald & Marie. MA Loyola U 1991; MA McNeese St U 1994; MDiv Epis TS of the SW 2000. D 6/3/2000 P 12/9/2000 Bp Robert Jefferson Hargrove Jr. c 3. R S Lk's Ch Livingston TX 2005-2009; Assoc S Andr's Ch Roswell NM 2001-2004; R Chr Memi Ch Mansfield LA 2000-2001.

GRENNEN, Thomas Kyle (Alb) Grace Church, 32 Montgomery St, Cherry Valley NY 13320 **R Gr Ch Cherry Vlly NY 2011-; R S Mary's Ch Springfld Ct NY 2011-** B New Brunswick NJ 1955 s Raymond & Anna. BS Montana St U 1977; MDiv EDS 1988. D 6/11/1988 Bp George Phelps Mellick Belshaw P 2/11/1989 Bp Vincent King Pettit. m 2/11/1983 Vita Grennen c 1. S Jn's Ch Johnstown NY 2009-2010; S Paul's W Middleburgh NY 2008-2012; R Ch Of The Gd Shpd Rangeley ME 2002-2007; R Chr Ch Greenville NY 1990-2002; Trin Ch Rensselaerville Rensselaerville NY 1990-2002; Cur S Ptr's Ch Medford NJ 1988-1990. Contrib, "A Formation Prog for New Monastics," *Visio Divina, A Rdr in Faith and Visual Arts*, LeaderResources, 2009. Anamchairde Celtic Ntwk; Ord Of S Aid.

GRENZ, Linda L (RI) 275 N Main St, Providence RI 02903 **Dio Rhode Island Providence RI 2012-** B Eureka SD 1950 d Milbert & Frieda. BA Westmar Coll 1972; MTS Harvard DS 1974; MDiv EDS 1977. D 6/9/1976 P 4/25/1977 Bp Morris Fairchild Arnold. m 12/27/1992 Delbert C Glover. Pub & CEO Ldr Resources Leeds MA 2010-2012, 2008, Pub & CEO 1994-2008; R Gd Shpd Epis Ch Silver Sprg MD 2008-2009; Adult Ed, Lay Min, Ldrshp Dev Stff Epis Ch Cntr New York NY 1991-1994, Adult Ed, Lay Min, Ldrshp Dev Stff 1991-1994; Cler Team Ldr S Matt's Ch Jersey City NJ 1989-1991; Assoc Imm Ch On The Green New Castle DE 1984-1987; R S Paul's Ch Camden Wyoming DE 1977-1983. Auth, "Guide to New Ch's Tchg Series," Cowley, 2000; Auth, "Doubleday Pocket Bible Guide," Doubleday, 1997; Auth, "The Mar Journey," Cowley, 1996; Ed, "I Love to Tell the Story," Cntr for Chr Formation, 1994; Auth, "A Cov of Trust," Forw Mvmt, 1994; Ed, "The Bible's Authority in Today's Wrld," Trin Press, 1993; Ed, Contrib, "In Dialogue w Scripture," Epis Ch Cntr, 1992; Contrib, "Homilies for Chr People," Pueblo Press, 1989. linda@episcopalri.org

GRESSLE, Richard (NY) 130 1st Ave, Nyack NY 10960 B Pittsburgh PA 1945 s Lloyd & Marguerite. BA Hobart and Wm Smith Colleges 1967; MDiv EDS 1971. D 6/10/1971 Bp Lloyd Edward Gressle P 6/1/1972 Bp William Henry Mead. m 4/19/2008 Amy Lehman. R Gr Epis Ch Nyack NY 1995-2011; R Ch Of The Gd Shpd Ft Lee NJ 1980-1995; The Germaine Lawr Sch Arlington MA 1978-1980; Asst Calv Ch Pittsburgh PA 1973-1978. Proctor Fell 1992.

GREVE, John Haven (Ia) New Song Episcopal Church, 912 20th Ave, Coralville IA 52241 B East Lansing MI 1957 s John & Sally. Dioc Mutual Mnstry Curric. D 7/26/2009 P 1/31/2010 Bp Alan Scarfe. m 5/11/1985 Joanna Kay Turner-Greve c 2.

GREVE JR, Paul Andrew (NI) 611 W Berry St, Fort Wayne IN 46802 B Cleveland OH 1951 s Paul & Muriel. BA Ohio Wesbyan U 1973; Capital U 1982; JD Capital U 1982; Cert Nthrn Indiana TS 2015. D 7/10/2015 P 2/20/2016 Bp Edward Stuart Little II. m 9/17/1988 Lynn Grashaw Greve c 1.

✠ GREW II, The Rt Rev J Clark (O) One Huntington Avenue, # 304, Boston MA 02116 **Bd Maine Sea Coast Mssn 2009-; Bd St. Mk's Sch Southborough MA 2006-; Ret Bp of Ohio Dio Ohio Cleveland 2005-, Bp of OH 1994-2004** B New York NY 1939 s Henry & Selina. EDS; BA Harv 1962; MDiv EDS 1978; DD EDS 1997. D 6/18/1978 P 12/20/1978 Bp Morris Fairchild Arnold Con 3/5/1994 for O. m 12/27/1972 Sarah L Grew c 3. Chair of the Bd EDS Cambridge MA 2005-2009; Com on Pstr Dvlpmt HOB 2001-2003; Presding Bp's Coun of Advice 1997-2003; Pres Prov V. 1997-2003; Bd EUC 1995-2000; Bd Ken Gambier OH 1994-2004; R The Ch Of The H Sprt Lake Forest IL 1982-1993; R S Jn's Epis Ch Westwood MA 1978-1982. Soc of S Jn the Evang 1985.

GREWELL, Genevieve Michael (Oly) 1551 Tenth Ave. E, Seattle WA 98102 **D S Mary's Ch Lakewood WA 2014-; Bd Mem Assn of Epis Deacons 2015-; Archd Dio Olympia Seattle 2009-** B Seattle WA 1946 d John & Geraldine. D 6/24/2000 Bp Sanford Zangwill Kaye Hampton. m 1/7/1983 Gary Eugene Grewell c 2. D Ch Of The Gd Shpd Vancouver WA 2013-2014; S Jn's Epis Ch Olympia WA 2009-2013, D 2000-2013; D S Ben Epis Ch Lacey WA 2003-2009.

GRIBBLE, Robert Leslie (Tex) 301 E 8th St, Austin TX 78701 **Assoc P S Dav's Ch Austin TX 2013-** B Houston TX 1954 s Joseph & Lorraine. BBA U of Texas 1976; MDiv VTS 1979. D 11/27/1979 Bp John Elbridge Hines P 12/1/1980 Bp Maurice Manuel Benitez. m 1/20/2001 Gretchen Gribble c 2. The Great Cmsn Fndt Houston TX 2010; R S Mary's Ch Bellvile TX 1999-2010; Cleric Trin Ch Galveston TX 1996-1999; R Ch Of The Epiph Houston TX 1989-1996; R S Ptr's Epis Ch Brenham TX 1985-1989; Assoc R S Mart's Epis Ch Houston TX 1979-1985.

GRIBBON, Robert T (Eas) PO Box 1493, Salisbury MD 21802 **Consultat Dio Delaware Wilmington DE 2012-** B Plainfield NJ 1943 s Robert & Ruth. BA U of Maryland 1964; STB GTS 1967; DMin Wesley TS 1999. D 5/20/1967 P 12/17/1967 Bp George Alfred Taylor. m 8/28/1965 Nancy Insley c 2. R Old Trin

Ch Ch Creek MD 2007-2012; Bp's Asst for Mnstry Dio Delaware Wilmington 2001-2006; Deploy Off Dio Easton Easton MD 2000-2001; Int S Paul's Ch Georgetown DE 1999-2001; Int Ch Of The Epiph Washington DC 1998-1999; Crdntr Prov III 1991-1998; R S Paul's Ch Centreville MD 1987-1998; Consult The Alb Inst Beth MD 1981-1987; Campus Min Untd Coll Mnstrs In Nthrn Va Mc Lean VA 1980; R ADDISON Chap Seat Pleasant MD 1976-1979; Vic St Matthews Ch Bowie MD 1976-1979; Chapl Ecum Coll Maryland and Nthrn Virginia 1971-1980; Campus Minster Dio Washington Washington DC 1969-1980; Chapl U of Maryland Coll Pk MD 1969-1975; Vic Dio Easton Easton MD 1967-1969. Auth, "Developing Faith in YA," The Alb Inst; Auth, "Let's Put YP in Their Place," ECUSA; Co-Auth, "Peacemaking Without Div," The Alb Inst.

GRIEB, Anne Katherine (WA) 3737 Seminary Rd, Alexandria VA 22304 **Prof VTS Alexandria VA 2007-; Prof VTS Alexandria VA 1994-** B Chestertown MD 1949 d Henry & Lillian. BA Hollins U 1971; JD CUA 1975; MDiv VTS 1983; PhD Yale DS 1997. D 6/11/1983 P 12/10/1983 Bp John Thomas Walker. Assoc Ch Of S Steph And The Incarn Washington DC 1996; Assoc Prof VTS Alexandria VA 1994-2007; Asst Trin Epis Ch Portland ME 1984-1989. Auth, "The Story of Romans: A Narrative Defense of God's Righteousness," Westminster Jn Knox, 2002.

GRIEB, Ray Kline (Wyo) 487 Goodrich Rd, Wheatland WY 82201 **Serv ELCA 1999-** B Pueblo CO 1934 s George & Lucille. BA U CO 1957; MDiv Nash 1960. D 6/21/1960 P 12/21/1960 Bp Joseph Summerville Minnis. c 3. Vic S Christophers Ch Cozad NE 1995-2003; R Chr Ch Sidney NE 1987-1992; R S Paul's Epis Ch Dixon WY 1984-1987; Epis Mssn of the San Luis Vlly Alamosa CO 1976-1981; S Thos The Apos Epis Ch Alamosa CO 1975-1980; Ch Of The H Sprt Colorado Spg CO 1974-1976; S Paul's Epis Ch Lakewood CO 1973-1974; S Ptr's By-The-Lake Ch Montague MI 1970-1973; Chapl Starr Commonwealth for Boys Albion MI 1968-1970; Vic Cathd Ch Of S Paul Detroit MI 1962-1968; S Ptr's Ch Clearfield UT 1962-1965; Vic S Andr's Ch Cripple Creek CO 1960-1962.

GRIESBACH, Sigrid Jane (WMass) 921 Pleasant St, Worcester MA 01602 B 1947 d Herbert & Marjorie. Art Hist Queens Coll 1974. D 12/13/2008 Bp Gordon Scruton.

GRIESER, Jonathan (Mil) 116 W Washington Ave, Madison WI 53703 **R Gr Ch Madison WI 2009-** B Wauseon OH 1958 s Dale & Dorothy. BA Goshen Coll 1981; MDiv Harvard DS 1985; ThD Harvard DS 1993. D 6/11/2005 P 5/10/2006 Bp Dorsey Henderson. m 6/13/1987 Corrie Ellen Grieser. Assoc R S Jas Epis Ch Greenville SC 2005-2009.

GRIESHEIMER, James Cade (Ia) 506 W Broadway St, Decorah IA 52101 B Chillicothe OH 1942 s James & Emaline. BS/BM OH SU 1965; MM Arizona St U 1967; PhD Indiana U 1990. D 6/6/2010 P 12/18/2010 Bp Alan Scarfe. m 8/20/1989 Martha Lenore Keiger c 3.

GRIESMANN, Donald Andre (NJ) Po Box 7, Pago Pago AS 96799 B Washington DC 1932 s Otto & Muriel. BA Ge 1954; STB PDS 1957; JD Rutgers Sch of Law Camden NJ 1973. D 4/2/1957 P 11/1/1957 Bp Alfred L Banyard. m 5/13/1989 Barbara Ann Griesman. Cn Dio New Jersey Trenton NJ 1967-1970; Nonpar Camden Epis Cmnty Cntr (Camden NJ) 1962-1971; R S Jn's Camden NJ 1959-1971; R S Aug's Ch Camden NJ 1959-1967; Cur Gr Epis Ch Plainfield NJ 1957-1959. Auth, "An Urban Par As Mssn".

GRIESMEYER, Walter Jimmy (Chi) 1468 Elizabeth St, Crete IL 60417 **Died 2/3/2017** B Plainfield NJ 1940 s Walter & Elizabeth. BA Chapman U 1969; BA Chapman U 1970; MDiv SWTS 1974. D 6/15/1974 P 1/4/1975 Bp Robert Claflin Rusack. m 8/3/1974 Cathy Jill Griesmeyer. Ch Of The Gd Shpd Momence IL 2001-2005; St Cyprians Ch Chicago IL 1998-2000; All Souls Ch Kaycee WY 1986-1988; S Lk's Ch Cleveland OH 1982-1984; 1980-1982; S Paul Epis Ch Conneaut OH 1978-1979; Cur S Andr's Ch Longmeadow MA 1976-1978; Cur Trin Epis Ch Orange CA 1974-1975. Natl Assn for the Self-Supporting Active Mnstry; RACA.

GRIEVES, Brian (Haw) 7007 Hawaii Kai Drive Apt A21, Honolulu HI 96825 **Namibia Afr 1994-** B London UK 1946 s Philip & Meron. BA U of Hawaii 1968; MDiv CDSP 1972. D 7/29/1972 P 5/6/1973 Bp Edwin Lani Hanchett. m 7/5/2016 Young Jin Kim. Sr Dir for Mssn Centers and Dir, Advocacy C Epis Ch Cntr New York NY 2008-2010; Dir / Peace and Justice Mnstrs Epis Ch Cntr New York NY 1988-2008; Camp Mokule'Ia Waialua HI 1977-1987; Dir, Camps and Conferences The Epis Ch in Hawaii Honolulu HI 1977-1987; S Andr's Cathd Honolulu HI 1977-1978; Ch Of The H Nativ Honolulu HI 1973-1977; Assoc S Steph's Ch Wahiawa HI 1972-1973. Ed, "No Outcasts: The Publ Wit of Edmond L Browning," FMP. Hon Doctorate CDSP 2004.

GRIFFIN, Barry Quentin (At) Po Box 169, Morrow GA 30260 **R S Aug Of Cbury Morrow GA 1994-** B Brunswick GA 1955 s Pleasant & Eva. BA Valdosta St U 1977; MA Georgia St U 1982; MDiv GTS 1988. D 6/11/1988 Bp Charles Judson Child Jr P 4/21/1989 Bp Frank Kellogg Allan. Asst R Emm Epis Ch Athens GA 1990-1994; D S Marg's Ch Carrollton GA 1988-1990; Epis Chars Bd Dio Atlanta Atlanta GA 1994-1997. Lilly Fndt Grant 2008; Lilly Fndt Grant 2008; Fullbright Schlrshp For Mus 1977.

GRIFFIN, Calvin Russell (USC) 200 Tyborne Cir, Columbia SC 29210 B Baltimore MD 1951 s Russell & Elizabeth. BA Morgan St U 1973; MDiv Palmer (Estrn) TS 1976; S Chas Borromeo Sem 1976. D 10/18/1977 P 2/1/1978 Bp Hunley Agee Elebash. m 9/2/1972 Regina R Griffin c 2. R S Lk's Epis Ch Columbia SC 1994-2017; R Ch Of The Gd Shpd Mobile AL 1988-1994; R S Tit Epis Ch Durham NC 1980-1987; R S Mk's Ch Wilmington NC 1977-1980. Cmnty Faith-Mobile Cmnty Orgnztn. Outstndng Young Men Amer 1979; Serv Awd Hd Start 79; Serv Awd 94 Wilmer Hall Chld Hm.

GRIFFIN, Christopher E (Chi) 1356 W Jarvis Ave # 1, Chicago IL 60626 **S Mart's Ch Chicago IL 2010-** B Gary IN 1961 BS MIT 1983; EdM Harv 1993; MA U Chi 1997; MDiv U Chi DS 1997; CAS SWTS 2002. D 6/15/2002 P 12/21/2002 Bp Bill Persell. S Matt's Ch Evanston IL 2002-2010. ECF Fell ECF 2005.

GRIFFIN, Donald J (Dal) **Ch Of The Annunc Lewisville TX 2016-** B Dallas, TX 1991 s David & Mary. BA U of Oklahoma 2013; MDiv Nash 2016. D 4/30/2016 Bp Paul Emil Lambert P 2/11/2017 Bp George Robinson Sumner Jr. m 6/10/2016 Sarah A Mock. dgriffin@annunciationlewisville.org

G

GRIFFIN, Emily A (WA) St. Alban's Episcopal Church, 3001 Wisconsin Ave Nw, Washington DC 20016 **S Alb's Par Washington DC 2015-** B Syracuse NY 1974 MDiv PrTS 2001; MSW Rutgers The St U of New Jersey 2002; STM GTS 2003. D 6/7/2003 Bp David Bruce Joslin P 12/13/2003 Bp George Edward Councell. m 9/5/2009 Michael C Zito. Assoc S Jn's Epis Ch Mc Lean VA 2013-2015; Assoc R S Matt's Ch Pennington NJ 2003-2013. emilyg@stalbansdc.org

GRIFFIN, Horace Leeolphus (Cal) **P All Souls Par In Berkeley Berkeley CA 2009-** B Starke FL 1961 BA Morehouse Coll 1983; MDiv Bos TS 1988; PhD Van 1995. D 6/18/2005 P 12/17/2005 Bp Bill Persell. The GTS New York NY 2005-2009; Bexley Seabury Fed Chicago IL 2005.

GRIFFIN, Janet (Spok) 803 Symons St, Richland WA 99354 **Cong Dvlp Dio Spokane 2011-** B Margaretville NY 1942 d Arnold & Elizabeth. BS Syr 1963; MDiv CDSP 1983. D 6/25/1983 P 6/9/1984 Bp William Edwin Swing. R All SS Ch Richland WA 2000-2009; Assoc The Epis Ch Of S Mary The Vrgn San Francisco CA 1986-2000; Asst Pstr Gr Cathd San Francisco CA 1983-1986.

GRIFFIN, Jeremiah (RG) PO Box 175, Marfa TX 79843 **S Chad's Epis Ch Albuquerque NM 2017-** B Houston TX 1979 s James & Renee. MDiv Epis TS Of The SW; MDiv Epis TS of the SW; BS Steph F. Austin St U 2002; MA Texas St U 2006. D 6/15/2013 Bp C Andrew Doyle. m 6/8/2008 Meredith Marie Imken c 2. S Paul's Ch Marfa TX 2015-2016; D Trin Ch Galveston TX 2013-2015.

GRIFFIN, Jon Edward (Spr) 449 State Highway 37, West Frankfort IL 62896 B Herron IL 1949 s John & Georgia. BA Sthrn Illinois U 1971; BS Sthrn Illinois U 1992. D 10/5/2001 P 8/24/2002 Bp Peter Hess Beckwith. m 5/1/1999 Sara Beth Griffin. S Mk's Ch W Frankfort IL 2011-2013, 2002-2005; Dio Springfield Springfield IL 2005-2006.

GRIFFIN, Mary-Carol Ann (Me) 862 Eagle Lake Rd, Bar Harbor ME 04609 B Albuquerque NM 1950 d Karl & Ramona. D Formation Prog 1998; EFM 1998. D 3/20/1999 Bp Chilton Richardson Knudsen. m 4/30/1968 Karl Russell Griffin. Ch Of Our Fr Hulls Cove ME 1999-2001, D 1999-.

GRIFFIN, Patrick Corrigan (Colo) 127 W Archer Pl, Denver CO 80223 B Dallas TX 1947 s James & Marjorie. MDiv EDS; BBA TCU. D 8/23/1973 P 2/1/1993 Bp William Harvey Wolfrum. Yth Min S Jn's Epis Ch Boulder CO 1993-1994; Chapl Chart Hosp 1992-1993; Non-par. AAPC.

GRIFFIN, Pauline Ruth (EC) 25 S 3rd St, Wilmington NC 28401 B Suffolk VA 1966 d Joe & Betty. BA Furman U 1988; MEd Converse Coll 1991; MDiv Sthrn Bapt Sem 1994; MDiv Sthrn Bapt Sem 1994; MDiv Sthrn Bapt TS 1994; Post-Grad Cert in Angl Stds VTS 2015. D 6/20/2015 Bp Robert Stuart Skirving. m 6/26/2004 Ashton Thomas Griffin. S Jas Par Wilmington NC 2015-2017; Other Lay Position S Steph's Ch Goldsboro NC 2008-2010.

GRIFFIN, P Joshua (Cal) St David Of Wales, 2800 SE Harrison St, Portland OR 97214 **Ldrshp Team Epis Ecological Ntwk 2012-; Assoc S Dav's Epis Ch Portland OR 2011-** B Providence RI 1981 BA Dart 2004; MDiv Harvard DS 2009; M.A. Other 2013; M.A. U of Washington 2013. D 6/5/2010 P 12/4/2010 Bp Marc Handley Andrus. m 7/12/2008 Elizabeth K Harrington. Assoc Ch Of The H Innoc San Francisco CA 2010-2011; Environ Justice Mssnr Dio California San Francisco CA 2009-2011. Acad Fell ECF 2013; PIX Sustainability Serv Awd Prov IX Syn 2011.

GRIFFIN, Ronald Wayne (ECR) 1007 Persimmon Ave, Sunnyvale CA 94087 **Founding Dir Hse w the Red Door 2001-** B Frankfort KY 1953 s Orville & Lois. Cumberland U 1975; MTS Iliff TS 2006. D 1/22/2000 P 8/5/2000 Bp William Jerry Winterrowd. m 7/18/1974 Charlotte T Griffin c 2. P S Tim's Epis Ch Mtn View CA 2012-2016; P Chr Ch Eureka CA 2008-2012; P S Mart In The Fields Aurora CO 2006-2007; P Epis Ch Of S Jn The Bapt Breckenridge CO 2000-2006.

GRIFFIN, Russell Agnew (NJ) 219 Philadelphia Blvd, Sea Girt NJ 08750 **Chapl Sea Girt Fire Dept Sea Girt New Jersey 2013-; R The Ch Of S Uriel The Archangel Sea Girt NJ 2004-** B Neptune NJ 1953 s Charles & Gertrude. BS Norwich U 1976; MDiv Nash 1979; STM Nash 1998. D 6/2/1979 P 12/21/1979 Bp Albert Wiencke Van Duzer. m 4/25/1981 Cynthia Griffin c 2. Dio

Cntrl Florida Orlando FL 2000-2004, COM 2000-2003; R S Anne's Ch Crystal River FL 1993-2004; Vic S Mk's At The Crossing Ch Williamstown NJ 1979-1993; Com to elct Bp Dio New Jersey Trenton NJ 1992-1993, Dioc Fndt 1986-1989, Cathd Chapt 1985-1988, Trial Crt 1985, 1980-1991. OSL 1981; SocMary 2005; SSC 1983.

GRIFFIN, Timothy Lee (Pa) 2730 Cranston Rd, Philadelphia PA 19131 **R Memi Ch Of S Lk Philadelphia PA 2004-** B Keokuk IA 1957 s Timothy & Sandra. BA Wstrn Illinois U 1981; PhD U IL 1995; MA Providence Coll 2002; MDiv EDS 2004. D 10/10/2004 P 4/9/2005 Bp Gerry Wolf. m 11/29/2005 Harriet Kollin c 1. P-in-c S Andr's In The Field Ch Philadelphia PA 2010-2012; Asst All SS Crescentville Philadelphia PA 2004-2005.

GRIFFIN JR, William Leonard (Ark) 40 Cliffdale Dr, Little Rock AR 72223 **D S Mk's Epis Ch Little Rock AR 1998-** B Little Rock AR 1948 s William & Rita. BS U of Arkansas 1970; MS U of Arkansas 1971; Cert Theol Stud Nash 1983. D 4/7/1984 Bp Charles Thomas Gaskell. m 6/13/1970 Beverly Griffin. D S Jn's Ch Fremont MI 1992-1998; D H Cross Epis Ch Wisconsis Dells WI 1983-1992.

GRIFFIS SR, Terrell Hathorn (La) 316 Driftwood Dr, Meridian MS 39305 **Assoc The Epis Ch Of The Medtr Meridian MS 2007-** B Sturgis MS 1932 s Sam & Pauline. BS Delta St U 1957; MDiv Candler TS Emory U 1970. D 6/1/1974 Bp John Maury Allin P 5/1/1975 Bp Duncan Montgomery Gray Jr. m 11/29/1957 Marcia W Griffis c 2. Vic All SS Epis Ch Ponchatoula LA 1989-1999; S Tim's Ch La Place LA 1987-1999; S Andr's Paradis Luling LA 1987-1989; S Nath's Ch Alexandria LA 1981-1987; R S Steph's Ch Innis LA 1979-1987; Ch Of The Creator Clinton MS 1979; Vic S Mary's Epis Ch Bolton MS 1975-1978; Serv Methodist Ch 1970-1974.

GRIFFITH, Bernard Macfarren (SeFla) 15100 Sw 141st Ter, Miami FL 33196 B BB 1942 s Elric & Norma. Cert Erdiston Teachers Coll 1970; BA Codrington Coll 1976; ThM Columbia TS 1985; MTh Columbia TS 1985; Ford 1986. Trans 9/1/1988 Bp Walter Decoster Dennis Jr. m 7/2/1966 Nadine Rosetta Griffith c 3. R Chr Epis Ch Miami FL 1994-2011; R Ch Of S Simon The Cyrenian New Rochelle NY 1988-1994; Serv Ch of Barbados 1976-1988.

GRIFFITH, Bruce Derby (LI) Po Box 145, Pultneyville NY 14538 **Actg Dn Cathd Of The Incarn Garden City NY 2013-** B Braham MN 1944 s Melvin & Clela. BA Hamline U 1965; STB U Tor 1968; STM GTS 1969; ThD U Tor 1979. D 6/24/1968 Bp Hamilton Hyde Kellogg P 3/22/1969 Bp Kenneth Daniel Wilson Anand. c 2. Int Chr Ch Rochester NY 2006-2009; Int S Ptr's Ch Morristown NJ 2004-2006; Int Gr Ch Brooklyn NY 2002-2004; Prof Geo Mercer TS Garden City NY 1994-2000; R Chr Ch Oyster Bay NY 1987-2002; P-in-c Epis Tri-Par Mnstry Dansville NY 1981-1987; Int Chr Epis Ch Hornell NY 1979-1981; R S Mich And All Ang Buffalo NY 1974-1976; R S Clem Buffalo NY 1972-1974; Stff P Cathd Ch Of S Mk Minneapolis MN 1969-1971; Cur S Mk's Ch Mendham NJ 1968-1969. Auth, "Yearning: Greg Of Nyssa & The Vision Of God," *Sewanee Theol Revs*, 2000. Angl-RC Natl Consult 1984-1989; Dir Consortium Endowed Epis Parishes 1995-2001; No Amer Reg Comittee 2001-2014; Past Pres Trin Div Assn (Toronto) 1985-1991. Hon Cn Cathd of the Incarn 2013; R Emer Chr Ch, Oyster Bay 2004.

GRIFFITH, Charles (WK) 8631 Beulah Land Dr, Ozark AR 72949 **Non-par 1973-** B Little Rock AR 1937 s Charles & Margaret. BS U of Arkansas 1959; MDiv VTS 1963; MS Ft Hays St U 1973; CFP Coll for Fin Plnng 1984; BA Arkansas Tech U 2007. D 6/25/1963 P 1/1/1964 Bp Robert Raymond Brown. m 11/3/1989 Renee Griffith c 3. Int P Epis Ch Of S Jn The Bapt Breckenridge CO 1976-1977; Trin Epis Ch Norton KS 1966-1973; Vic S Lk's Ch Phillipsburg NJ 1966-1967; Chr Ch Mena AR 1964-1965; Vic S Barn Ch Foreman AR 1964-1965. Auth, "A Shelton Lineage: Five Generations," self, 1993; Auth, "The Descendants Of Lafayette F Griffith & Cynthia Bradley," self, 1991; Auth, "A Dysart Lineage: Seven Generations," self, 1986.

GRIFFITH, David M (Los) 821 Valley Crest St, La Canada CA 91011 B Los Angeles CA 1946 s George & Leona. BA Claremont TS; BS USC. D 9/15/1973 P 3/1/1974 Bp Robert Claflin Rusack. m 2/1/1968 Donna G Griffith c 1. Asst to R S Andr's Par Fullerton CA 1986-1989; Vic Imm Mssn El Monte CA 1982-1986; Vic S Paul's Mssn Barstow CA 1980-1982; Serv St Columbas Epis Ch Big Bear City CA 1978-1980; S Mths' Par Whittier CA 1973-1977.

GRIFFITH, David W (NY) 1209 Proust Rd, Virginia Beach VA 23454 B Georgetown GY 1931 s Charles & Lucille. BA Bishops Coll 1965. Trans 12/31/1988 Bp Paul Moore Jr. m 6/2/1956 Mary Ann Griffith. Assoc S Andr's Ch Bronx NY 1991-1998; Assoc Trin Ch Of Morrisania Bronx NY 1980-1991; Asst P S Lk's Epis Ch Bronx NY 1979-1980; Serv Ch Of W Indies 1965-1979.

GRIFFITH, Gregory Erwin (O) 705 Main St, Coshocton OH 43812 B Akron OH 1946 s Howard & Florence. BA Hiram Coll 1968; MDiv Andover Newton TS 1976; Shalem Inst Washington DC 1984; DMin Columbia TS 2000. D 6/19/1976 Bp John Harris Burt P 6/26/1977 Bp Philip Alan Smith. R Trin Ch Coshocton OH 2000-2009; Hoosac Sch Hoosick NY 1995-2000; S Ptr's Ch Rome GA 1992-1995; R S Steph's Boise ID 1990-1991; Stwdshp Cmsn Dio Delaware Wilmington 1984-1985, Chair 1988-1990, Dioc Coun 1983-1987; Trin Par Wilmington DE 1981-1990, Assoc R 1981-1990; Cur S Jn's Ch Portsmouth NH 1976-1981. Soc of S Marg. Mart Luther King, Jr. Awd Delaware Mart Luther King, Jr. Memi Fndt 1990.

GRIFFITH, Nickolas C (Los) **Chr Ch Par Redondo Bch CA 2016-; Int St Gregorys Epis Ch Long Bch CA 2015-** Trans 4/14/2016 Bp Joseph Jon Bruno.

GRIFFITH JR, Norman Early (WTex) 1601 E 19th St, Georgetown TX 78626 **Ret 1992-** B Charlotte NC 1926 s Norman & Pearl. BS Duke 1947; BD VTS 1968. D 7/30/1968 Bp Everett H Jones P 2/1/1969 Bp Harold Cornelius Gosnell. m 10/4/2014 Jane Elizabeth Van Horn. S Bon Ch Comfort TX 1991-1992; Vic S Chris's Ch Bandera TX 1991-1992; Assoc R S Jn's Ch McAllen TX 1990-1991; Int Trin Epis Ch Pharr TX 1989-1990; R Emm Epis Ch Lockhart TX 1984-1989; R Emm Epis Ch San Angelo TX 1974-1984; Assoc S Mk's Ch Beaumont TX 1970-1974; D S Jn's Epis Ch Sonora TX 1968-1970.

GRIFFITH JR, Robert L (LI) 199 Carroll St, Brooklyn NY 11213 **Assoc Bus Analyst The CPG New York NY 2012-, Data Analyst 2005-2010; Asstg P S Paul's Ch Brooklyn NY 2011-, Cur 2005-2010** B Lorain OH 1961 s Robert & Judith. BS Bowling Green St U 1984; MEd Kent St U 1994; MDiv GTS 2005. D 6/4/2005 Bp Mark Hollingsworth Jr P 6/3/2006 Bp Arthur Williams Jr. Bp's Mssnr Dio Long Island Garden City NY 2010-2011; Webmaster Dio Ohio Cleveland OH 1998-2001; Campus Chapl Studenten fur Christus Munich Germany 1990; Campus Chapl Chi Alpha Chr Fllshp Kent OH 1987-1992; Campus Chapl Chi Alpha Chr Fllshp Bowling Green OH 1984-1987; Chair, Dioc Coll Wk Com Dio Ohio Cleveland 1998-1999, Mem, Dioc Coll Wk Com 1997; Epis Ch Rep to the Bd Dir Prot Campus Mnstry at Kent St Univ. Kent OH 1997-1999. Contributer, "Authenticity, YA, and the Ch," *Yearning: Authentic Transformation, YA, and the Ch*, Ch Pub, Inc., 2013. Intl Soc for Performance Improvement 2015; Soc of Cath Priests 2010. rgriffith@cpg.org

GRIFFITH, Shawn Lynn (WNC) 3658 Gaston Day School Rd, Gastonia NC 28056 **R S Mk's Ch Gastonia NC 2005-** B Huntington 1952 s Thomas & Betty. MA Ball St U; MBA Golden Gate U; MDiv VTS. D 6/10/2000 Bp David Conner Bane Jr P 12/9/2000 Bp Donald Purple Hart. m 12/6/1974 Nellie Roseanne Griffith. R All SS Ch So Hill VA 2000-2005.

GRIFFITHS, Robert Stephen (Fla) 2613 Vista Cove Rd, Saint Augustine FL 32084 **Int Off of the Bp of Florida Jacksonville FL 2008-** B Neptune NJ 1938 s Harold & Lois. BA Monmouth U 1960; STB GTS 1963. Trans 10/1/1967 Bp Walter H Gray. m 6/26/1965 Diane Griffiths c 2. Cn Dio Florida Jacksonville 2008-2015; Int San Jose Epis Ch Jacksonville FL 2005-2007; Int Ch Of The Gd Shpd Jacksonville FL 1999-2003; Int All SS' Epis Ch Scotch Plains NJ 1997-1999; Int S Lk's Epis Ch Montclair NJ 1996-1997; Trin Educ Fund New York NY 1978-1990; Chapl Kent Girls Sch Kent CT 1971-1976; Kent Sch Kent CT 1971-1976; R S Andr's Ch Kent CT 1967-1971; Serv Ch Of SW Afr 1963-1967; Dir Trin Par New York NY 1976-1994.

GRIFO, Lynne (Ct) **S Lk's Epis Ch New Haven CT 2017-** D 6/22/1990 Bp Orris George Walker Jr P 4/11/1991 Bp Franklin Delton Turner.

GRIGG, Joel Thomas (Alb) 145 Main Street, Massena NY 13662 B Coldwater MI 1959 s Frederick & Allie. BS U of Sthrn Mississippi 1987; MPA Auburn U at Montgomery 1993; MDiv TESM 2001. D 12/9/2000 Bp Keith Lynn Ackerman P 6/23/2001 Bp Daniel William Herzog. m 7/29/1978 Carolyn Jean Grigg c 2. R S Jn's Ch Massena NY 2005-2012; S Matt's Ch Unadilla NY 2001-2005.

GRIGGS, Linda Mackie (RI) 50 Orchard Avenue, Providence RI 02906 **S Mart's Ch Providence RI 2015-** B 1959 AB UNC-Chap Hill 1982; MSLS UNC-Chap Hill Sch of Libr and Info Sci 1984; MDiv Ya Berk 2014. D 10/7/2015 P 5/7/2016 Bp W Nicholas Knisely Jr. m 5/23/1981 Malcolm David Griggs c 2. lgriggs@stmartinsprov.org

GRIM, Leland Howard (Minn) 2636 County Road 94, International Falls MN 56649 B 1943 s Howard & Adella. Other; Total Mnstry Trng in Minnesota; BA No Dakota St U 1965; MS No Dakota St U 1969. D 7/8/2006 Bp James Louis Jelinek. m 9/3/1966 Donna Carol Cann Grim c 2.

GRIMES, Charles Gus (Tenn) 510 W Main St, Franklin TN 37064 B Memphis TN 1948 s Edward & Willa. AS SW Tennessee Cmnty Coll 1975; BS U of Memphis 1977; Cert St Mary's at Sewanee Diac Stds 2011. D 1/25/2014 Bp John Bauerschmidt. m 6/13/1969 Rebecca Viar Grimes c 2.

GRIMES, Daphne B (Wyo) 16 Thomas The Apostle Rd, Cody WY 82414 **Mem, Bd Dir Thos the Apos Retreat Cntr Cody WY 1990-** B Tulsa OK 1929 d George & Dorothy. BFA U of Houston 1952; MA Col 1954; MA Epis TS of the SW 1985. D 8/11/1982 P 11/1/1986 Bp Bob Gordon Jones. m 11/6/1964 Thomas Grimes. Assoc Chr Ch Cody WY 1995-2004, D 1982-1994; Sprtl Advsr Cmnty of Celebration Aliquippa PA 1990-2008; Dir, Thos-Apos Retreat Cntr Dio Wyoming Casper 1990-2000; Vic S Andr's Ch Meeteetse WY 1987-1990; Non-par Chapl 1985-1986. "Journeys in Time and Space," Wordsworth Press, 2006; "Journeys in the Sprt," Wordsworth Press, 2005; Auth, "Though I Walk Through the Vlly," The Print Shop, 1989; Auth, "Journeyings," Wyndham Hall Pr, 1984. Cmnty Celebration - Comp 1987; CHS 2002; Compass Rose Soc - Bd 1998-2006; ECW 1978; EPF; EWC; No Amer Reg Consultants for S Geo's Coll, 2000-2007; Ord of Julian of Norwich - Assoc 1988-2002; Publ Plcy Ntwk.

GRIMES, Eve Lyn (Colo) 624 W 19th St, Pueblo CO 81003 **D Dio Colorado Denver CO 1992-** B Worthington MN 1941 d Ralph & Mildred. AD U of Sthrn Colorado 1975; Bishops Inst for Diac Formation 1992. D 10/24/1992 Bp William Jerry Winterrowd. c 2. NAAD.

GRIMM, Susan (SVa) 1104 Lakepoint Dr, Clarksville VA 23927 **R Trin Epis Ch So Boston VA 2013-; R S Tim's Epis Ch Clarksville VA 2008-; Stndg Com Dio Sthrn Virginia Newport News VA 2017-, Sprtl Dir, Curs Sec 2016-, Dn, Convoc IX 2013-, Pres, Stndg Com 2012-2013, Stndg Com 2010-2013, COM, Dioc Formation 2008-2012, Eccl Crt 2007-2010, Exec Bd 2007-2010, Bp Search Com 2007-2008, Bp Search Com 1987-1988, Curs Sec, Lay Dir 1985-1991** B Richmond VA 1953 d Rexdel & Margaret. BA U Rich 1976; JD U Rich 1978; MDiv Sewanee: The U So, TS 2006; DMin TS 2014; DMin Sewanee: The U So, TS 2014. D 6/3/2006 Bp Bob Johnson P 12/16/2006 Bp John Clark Buchanan. Cntrl Mecklenburg Cure Chase City VA 2006-2008. Auth, "Emancipation to Jim Crow: Wk Among the Afr-Amer Population of the Epis Ch in the Dio of VA 1865-1892," U So, 2014. Comm. of St. Mary (Sthrn) Assoc 2006; Phi Beta Kappa 1976. susan@susangrimm.com

GRIMSHAW, Gretchen Sanders (Mass) 28 Robbins Rd, Watertown MA 02472 **R Par Of S Paul Newton Highlands MA 2008-** B Cincinnati Ohio 1959 d James & Cynthia. BA Smith 1983; MDiv EDS 2004; ALM Harv 2004. D 6/3/2006 Bp M(Arvil) Thomas Shaw P 1/6/2007 Bp Gayle Harris. m 5/31/2009 Thalia Meehan. Assoc S Jn's Ch Jamaica Plain MA 2007-2008; Intern St. Jn's Epis Ch Jamaica Plain MA 2005-2007. "Big Bug Creek," Renaissance Works, 1998.

GRINDON, Carri Patterson (Los) 1014 E. Altadena Dr., Altadena CA 91001 **R S Mk's Par Altadena CA 2009-** B Orange CA 1960 d Charles & Martha Priscilla. BA Occ 1982; MDiv Ya Berk 1992. D 6/24/1995 Bp Chester Lovelle Talton P 1/1/1996 Bp Frederick Houk Borsch. m 10/9/1993 Alfred P Grindon c 2. Asst S Anne's Epis Ch Atlanta GA 2006-2009; Asst S Edw's Epis Ch Lawrenceville GA 2000-2006; Assoc S Columba's Par Camarillo CA 1996-1999; Ch Of Our Sav Par San Gabr CA 1995-1996. carripg@att.net

GRINER, Robert (Nwk) 115 Cedar Dr, Newton NJ 07860 **Chr Ch Newton NJ 2003-** B Houston TX 1958 s Ray & Joanne. BA Drew U 1981; MDiv Yale DS 1985. D 2/19/1986 Bp Arthur Edward Walmsley P 10/4/1986 Bp John Shelby Spong. m 1/11/1997 Erika Danielle Maresca c 2. R Gr Epis Ch Plainfield NJ 1993-1999; Assoc R S Geo's-By-The-River Rumson NJ 1988-1993; Asst R All SS Ch Millington NJ 1986-1988. Soc Of S Jn The Evang.

GRINNELL, Janice Louise (RI) 263 Orchard Woods Drive, Saunderstown RI 02874 **Archd S Aug's Ch Kingston RI 2012-** B Harrisburg PA 1947 d Paul & Jean. BS Shippensburg U 1969; MBA FD 1973; Rhode Island Sch for Deacons 1991. D 3/16/1991 Bp George Nelson Hunt III. m 7/1/2007 Ann Hamm c 2. D S Paul's Ch N Kingstown RI 2010-2012; D Trin Ch Newport RI 2008-2010; D S Mich's Ch Bristol RI 1991-2010; Strng Com for Cntr for Recon Dio Rhode Island Providence RI 2015-2016, Archd 2013-, COM 2009-. Auth, "In Response to the Steps," *In Response to the Steps*, Xlibris, 2009. Assn for Epis Deacons 1991. Steph Awd Assn for Epis Deacons 1916.

GRINNELL, Lynn Dean (SwFla) 15102 Amberly Dr, Tampa FL 33647 B Ft Belvoir VA 1952 d Joseph & Jean. BA SMU 1973; MS U of Laverne 1984; PhD U of So Florida 2003. D 12/7/2013 Bp Dabney Tyler Smith. m 10/23/1990 Richard S Grinnell.

GRISCOM, Donald Wayne (SwFla) 3324 Chicago Ave, Bradenton FL 34207 B Sellersville PA 1944 s Russel & Helen. D 1/18/2002 Bp John Bailey Lipscomb. m 1/1/1983 Shirley A Griscom.

GRISHAM JR, Lowell Edward (Ark) Po Box 1190, Fayetteville AR 72702 **S Paul's Ch Fayetteville AR 1997-** B Portland OR 1952 s Lowell & Jo. BA U of Mississippi 1972; MDiv GTS 1980. D 6/11/1980 P 2/24/1981 Bp Duncan Montgomery Gray Jr. m 6/7/1975 Kathryn Grisham c 1. R S Jn's Epis Ch Ft Smith AR 1992-1997; Curs Com Epis Ch Cntr New York NY 1990-1992; R S Columb's Ch Ridgeland MS 1982-1992; Trin Ch Natchez MS 1980-1982. Presiding Off 1997-2002; Professed OA 1994.

GRISWOLD, Edwin A (O) 9629 W Campana Dr, Sun City AZ 85351 **Died 9/28/2015** B Defiance OH 1928 s Rollie & Millicent. BA Heidelberg U 1956; MDiv Untd TS 1959. D 11/21/1960 Bp Robert Lionne DeWitt P 6/29/1961 Bp Richard Stanley Merrill Emrich. m 10/31/1948 Naarah T Corl c 2. R Gr Ch Defiance OH 1984-1990; R S Martha's Ch Detroit MI 1969-1984; R Epiph Detroit MI 1963-1969; Vic S Jn's Ch Clinton MI 1959-1963. Alum Hon Schlrshp Awd Untd TS 1962.

✠ GRISWOLD III, The Rt Rev Frank Tracy (Chi) **Bp Visitor Soc of St Jn the Evang Cambridge MA 1985-** B Bryn Mawr PA 1937 s Frank & Louisa. AB Harv 1959; GTS 1960; BA Oxf GB 1962; MA Oxf GB 1966. D 12/15/1962 Bp Andrew Y Tsu P 6/23/1963 Bp Joseph Gillespie Armstrong Con 3/2/1985 for Chi. m 11/27/1965 Phoebe Griswold c 2. Co-Chair Angl RC Intl Cmsn 1999-2004; PBp of the Epis Ch Epis Ch Cntr New York NY 1998-2006; Co-Chair ARC-USA 1992-1997; Chair Stndg Lit Com 1992-1997; Bp Dio Chicago Chicago IL 1987-1997, Bp Coadj 1985-1987; R Ch Of S Mart-In-The-Fields Philadelphia PA 1974-1985; R S Andr's Ch Yardley PA 1967-1974; Cur Ch Of The Redeem Bryn Mawr PA 1963-1967. Auth, "Praying Our Days," Morehouse, 2009; Auth, "Opening Remarks and Closing Reflections," *Waging Recon*, CPC, 2002; Auth, "Called to Another Way," *Where was God on Sept 11?*, Herald Press, 2002; Auth, "Going Hm: An Invitation to Jubilee," Cowley, 2000; Auth, "Chr: The Sovereign Word," *A New Conversation*, CPC, 1999; Auth,

"Listening w the Ear of the Heart," *Crosscurrents*, 1998; Auth, "Experiencing Catholicity," *Amer*, 1997; Auth, "The Bp as Presider, Tchr and Person of Pryr," *ATR*, 1995; Auth, "Preaching and the Mnstry of Bishops," *Breaking the Word*, CHC, 1994; Auth, "Towards Catholicity: Naming & Living the Mystery," *Living the Mystery*, DTL, 1993; Auth, "The Mid-day Demon," *Phos*, Trin Inst, 1984; Auth, "Wrshp," *Being God's Fam*, 1982. DD CDSP 2007; DD Bex 2006; DD EDS 2006; Doctor of Hmnts Rikkyo U, Tokyo 2005; DHL Epis TS of the SW 2004; DD Berkeley TS 2002; DD Nashotah TS 2001; DD U So 2001; DD VTS 1999; DD GTS 1985; DD SWTS 1985.

GRISWOLD-KUHN, Karl E (Alb) 6 Silvester St, Kinderhook NY 12106 **The Ch Of The Mssh Glens Falls NY 2014-** B Albany NY 1976 s Ulrich & Kathleen. BA SUNY at Albany 2007; MDiv Ya Berk 2011; MDiv Ya Berk 2011. D 6/4/2011 P 12/8/2011 Bp William Howard Love. m 1/26/2008 Jennifer C Griswold-Kuhn. S Paul's Ch Kinderhook NY 2011-2014. fatherkarl@gmail.com

GRITTER, Joshua Michael (CFla) **Trin Ch Vero Bch FL 2017-** B Altamonte Springs Florida 1987 s Jack & Elizabeth. D 1/30/2017 Bp Gregory Orrin Brewer. m 11/16/2013 Amy L Gritter c 1. Yth Dir S Ptr's Epis Ch Lake Mary FL 2013-2016.

GRIZZLE, Anne Fletcher (SwVa) 123 W Washington St, Lexington VA 24450 B Staunton VA 1955 d Forest & Helen. BS Harv 1977; MS Col 1979. D 5/12/2017 Bp Mark Bourlakas. m 7/29/1978 James David Grizzle c 3.

GROB, Bruce Russell (Fla) 151 Nc Highway 9 Pmb 227, Black Mountain NC 28711 B Camden NJ 1951 BA Drew U 1973; MDiv Yale DS 1976; PhD Drew U 1984. D 12/8/2002 P 6/8/2003 Bp Stephen Hays Jecko. m 5/20/1978 Banta Whitner c 1. Exec Dir No Florida Susan G. Komen For the Cure 2011-2013; Dvlpmt Consult One Jax Jacksonville FL 2010-2013; Exec Dir Siyafundisa 2004-2010; Fresh Mnstrs Jacksonville FL 1994-2010; Vice Chair Fresh Mnstrs Jacksonville FL 1994-2010. Co-Auth, "This Congruent Life," Outskirts Press, 2009.

GROFF, Addison Keiper (Nwk) 6415 Lowry Rd, Los Angeles CA 90027 B Rochester NY 1919 s Addison & Rebecca. BA Franklin & Marshall Coll 1941; BD Lancaster TS 1944; GTS 1949. D 7/20/1949 P 6/29/1950 Bp Harold E Sawyer. c 2. Chr Ch Milford DE 1989-1997; Dio Easton Easton MD 1989-1997; S Jn The Bapt Epis Ch Milton DE 1989-1997; S Mary's Ch Bridgeville DE 1989-1997; S Steph's Ch Harrington DE 1989-1997; Team Mnstry Dio Delaware Wilmington 1989; S Ptr's Ch Rochelle Pk NJ 1971-1989; R Satin Ptr's Ch Rochelle Pk NJ 1971-1989; Chapl Hse H Comf W Orange NJ 1964-1989; S Agnes And S Paul's Ch E Orange NJ 1953-1971; St Agnes Ch E Orange NJ 1953-1971; Vic S Andr New Castle PA 1950-1953; Cur Trin Ch New Castle PA 1950-1953; Vic Chr Ch Punxsutawney PA 1949-1950. Angl Soc.

GROFF JR, John Weldon (Ala) 12656 N Shoreland Pkwy, Mequon WI 53092 **Ret 2000-** B Atlantic City NJ 1939 s John & Tillie. LTh Sewanee: The U So, TS 1974; Coll of Preachers 1979; U of Notre Dame 1982; U of Notre Dame 1984; Naropa U 1985; U of Notre Dame 1990. D 5/28/1974 P 12/19/1974 Bp Furman Charles Stough. c 2. Int S Fran Ch Menomonee Falls WI 2002-2004; Dir The Mystic Journey Retreat Cntr 1989-2002; R S Mary's Epis Ch Childersburg AL 1983-1987; Dio TEE Coordntr Dio Alabama Birmingham 1978-1981, Dept of CE 1975-1977; Adj Lectr Mystical Lit Univ of AL 1977-1978; R Ch Of The Epiph Guntersville AL 1976-1983; Vic S Tim's Epis Ch Athens AL 1974-1976; Vstng Lectr Psychol of Rel Amer Bapt TS Nashville TN 1973-1974. Auth, "Sebastian," Authorhouse, 2000; Auth, "The Smell of Incense, Sound of Silence," Forw Mvmt Press, 1988; Auth, "The Mystic Journey," Forw Mvmt Press, 1979; Auth, "arts," *Chr New Age Quarterly*; Auth, "arts," *Gnosis*; Auth, "arts," *Inner Directions Journ*; Auth, "arts," *Intuitive Explorations*; Auth, "arts," *LivCh*.

GROFF, Mary Elizabeth (Ala) 6141 Sherry Dr, Guntersville AL 35976 **Chapl Mssn Trip to Haiti 2011-; Psych/Pstr Counslr Mtn Crest Counslg Guntersville AL 1998-; Mem AAPC 1985-** B Atlantic City NJ 1939 d John & Dorothy. EFM Sewanee: The U So, TS 1980; MSW U of Alabama 1985; ALA Deacons Sch 2004; Nash 2009. D 10/30/2004 Bp Marc Handley Andrus. c 2. Assoc for Pstr Care Ch Of The Nativ Epis Huntsville AL 2012-2013, 2004-2011; D Chr Ch Albertville AL 2011-2012. Amer. Assoc. of Pstr Counselors 1986; Natl Assn Soc Worker 1980; No Amer Assoc. for the Diac 2004. +4000 hours of Serv 2011; +4000 hours of Serv 2011; Presidential Lifetime Vol Awd RSVP 2011.

GROFF JR, Sanford (SeFla) 3395 Burns Rd, Palm Beach Gardens FL 33410 **S Mk's Ch Palm Bch Garden FL 2014-** B Singapore 1980 s Sanford & Nancy. DMin VTS; BA Grove City Coll 2003; MDiv Duke DS 2007. D 6/2/2012 Bp Joe Goodwin Burnett P 1/26/2013 Bp Eugene Taylor Sutton. Chapl S Paul's Sch Brooklandville MD 2012-2014.

GROH, Clifford Herbert (Mich) B Windsor Ontario Canada 1933 Trans 11/30/1967. m 5/12/1956 Mavis Groh.

GRONEK, Marianna L (Az) Church of the Epiphany, 423 N Beaver St, Flagstaff AZ 86001 **Ch Of The Epiph Flagstaff AZ 2016-** B Fort Huron MI 1959 d William & Wanda. BFA Rocky Mtn Coll of Art And Design Denver CO 1994; MDiv SWTS 2006. D 6/10/2006 Bp Robert John O'Neill P 12/9/2006 Bp Wendell Nathaniel Gibbs Jr. S Mich's Ch Grosse Pointe MI 2008-2016; Assoc R

S Clare Of Assisi Epis Ch Ann Arbor MI 2006-2008; Chapl NW Cmnty Hosp 2004-2006. reverendmarianna@gmail.com

GRONEMAN, Leslie Joyce (Alb) D 5/31/2014 Bp William Howard Love.

GROSCHNER, Peter Kingston (Mich) 19759 Holiday Rd, Grosse Pointe Woods MI 48236 **Ret 2007-** B Detroit MI 1938 s Robert & Margaret. BA Hillsdale Coll 1960; MDiv PDS 1964. D 6/29/1964 Bp Richard Stanley Merrill Emrich P 2/23/1965 Bp Chauncie Kilmer Myers. m 12/6/1980 Kathleen Ann Groschner. P Assoc S Mich's Ch Grosse Pointe MI 1993-2007, Asst 1964-1966; Non-par 1980-1989; R S Tim's Ch Detroit MI 1975-1980; Asst S Steph's Ch Troy MI 1966-1975. Auth, "Pstr'S Referral Guide".

GROSE, Fayette Powers (O) 310 E Lincoln Way, Lisbon OH 44432 **Ret 1998-** B Youngstown OH 1933 s James & Arminda. BA Duke 1955; BD Bex Sem 1964. D 6/13/1964 P 12/1/1964 Bp Nelson Marigold Burroughs. m 8/8/1980 Phyllis Elaine Grose. H Trin Ch Lisbon OH 1988-1998; R Ch Of Our Sav Salem OH 1980-1987; Ch Of The Redeem Lorain OH 1971-1980; R S Paul's Epis Ch Smithfield NC 1969-1971; Chapl (Cmdr) Untd States Naval Reserve 1966-1969; M-in-c Trin Jefferson OH 1964-1966.

GROSH, Christine Marie (Neb) 7921 N Hazelwood Dr, Lincoln NE 68510 B North Platte NE 1953 d George & Patricia. BA U of Nebraska 1977; EFM 1984; MA Fuller TS 1991. D 5/7/1988 Bp James Daniel Warner. m 4/28/1990 David Ryder Pitts c 2. P S Bede's Epis Ch Los Angeles CA 1989-1991. Amer Assn of Chr Counselors; NAAD.

GROSHART, Nancy Louise (U) 1051 Allen Peak Cir, Ogden UT 84404 **D Ch Of The Gd Shpd Ogden UT 1992-** B Moline IL 1947 d Joseph & Margaret. U of Iowa 1967; BS U of Wyoming 1976. D 11/5/1992 Bp George Edmonds Bates. m 10/5/1977 Jerry Groshart c 2.

GROSJEAN, Lyle Wood (ECR) 3255 Amber Dr, Paso Robles CA 93446 B Omaha NE 1933 s Milton & Leora. BA San Francisco St U 1962; MDiv CDSP 1965. D 6/20/1965 Bp James Albert Pike P 2/1/1966 Bp George Richard Millard. c 2. R S Andr's Epis Ch San Bruno CA 1986-1998; Assoc R S Tim's Ch Danville CA 1983-1986; Vic S Lk's Ch Atascadero CA 1979-1983; Vic S Alb's Epis Ch Brentwood CA 1975-1979; Vic S Dav's Ch Pittsburg CA 1975-1979; Exec Dir Ecum Mnstry in The Haight - Ashbury 1967-1974; Cur All Souls Par In Berkeley Berkeley CA 1965-1967.

GROSKOPH, Elizabeth May (Roch) PO Box 541, Hancock NY 13783 **P S Jas Ch Callicoon NY 2012-; Vic Gr Epis Ch Whitney Point NY 2002-; S Jn's Ch Marathon NY 2002-** B White Plains NY 1938 d Frederic & Lillian. BA Wells Coll 1959; MA NYU 1967; Cert GTS 1988; Cert Mercer Hosp Sch of Nrsng 1988. D 5/21/1988 Bp Jose Antonio Ramos P 12/1/1988 Bp William George Burrill. m 7/18/1959 Ralph Gordon Groskoph c 3. Dir, CE Chr Ch Cuba NY 1998-2002; S Andr's Ch Friendship NY 1998-2002; Convenor New Directions NE Hancock NY 1994-1995; Assoc Allegany Cnty Epis Mnstry Belmont NY 1988-2002; Our Sav Bolivar NY 1988-2002; Dir, CE S Jn's Ch Wellsville NY 1988-2002; S Paul's Ch Angelica NY 1988-2002; S Phil's Ch Belmont NY 1988-2002; Allegany Cnty Epis Mnstry Belfast NY 1988-2001; Bp Search, Nomination Com Dio Rochester Henrietta 1998-1999, COM 1997-.

GROSKOPH, Ralph Gordon (Roch) PO Box 541, 211 Somerset Lake Rd, Hancock NY 13783 **P S Jas Ch Callicoon NY 2012-** B Brooklyn NY 1936 s Ralph & Dorothy. BA Cor 1958; MBA NYU 1965; Cert GTS 1988; Cert Mercer TS 1988. D 5/21/1988 Bp Jose Antonio Ramos P 12/17/1988 Bp William George Burrill. m 7/18/1959 Elizabeth May Groskoph c 3. Int R S Paul's Ch Endicott NY 2004-2006; Treas New Directions Mnstrs Inc NY 2003-2005; Int Rectpr All SS Epis Ch Johnson City NY 2002-2004; Admin Allegany Cnty Epis Mnstrs Belmont NY 1998-2002; Stndg Com Doicese of Rochester 1998-2002; Trst Diocese of Rochester Rochester NY 1995-1997; COM Dio Rochester 1994-2000; New Directions NE NY 1991-2004; Admin Allegany Cnty Epis Mnstry Belfast NY 1988-2001; Stndg Com Dio Rochester Henrietta 1998-2002.

GROSS, Brian K (Wyo) 2625 Main St, Torrington WY 82240 **R All SS Epis Ch Torrington WY 2015-, D 2014-2015** B Casper WY 1965 s William & Helen. BS Phillips U 1999; MDiv EDS 2015. D 9/9/2013 Bp James Monte Stanton P 8/6/2014 Bp John Smylie. m 9/9/1995 Julie E Gross c 3. revbriangross@gmail.com

GROSS, Daniel La Rue (NY) 76 Saint Albans Pl, Staten Island NY 10312 **S Alb's Epis Ch Staten Island NY 2015-** B Denver CO 1958 s Harvey & Anna. BA Col 1980; Dplma Ya Berk 2004; MDiv Yale DS 2004. D 6/12/2004 Bp John Bryson Chane P 1/4/2005 Bp Catherine Scimeca Roskam. R Emm Epis Ch Chestertown MD 2007-2015; Cur Chr's Ch Rye NY 2004-2007; Chair, COM Dio Easton Easton MD 2011-2015, Mem, COM 2008-2011; Trst Ya Berk New Haven CT 2011-2013. dlrgross@gmail.com

GROSS, Donald William (CFla) 800 Lake Port Blvd Apt D402, Leesburg FL 34748 **Corpus Christi Epis Ch Okahumpka FL 2008-** B Takoma Park MD 1936 s William & Pauline. BS Towson U 1958; STB Pos 1963; U of Birmingham Birmingham GB 1968; DMin S Marys Sem and U 1981. D 7/20/1963 Bp Noble C Powell P 6/1/1964 Bp Harry Lee Doll. H Trin Epis Ch Fruitland Pk FL 2001-2010; Stff P Old Donation Ch 1994-2000; Old Donation Ch Virginia Bch VA 1993-1998; Co-R Ch Of H Apos Virginia Bch VA 1979-1990; Dio Sthrn

Virginia Newport News VA 1977-1978; R Chr Ch Columbia MD 1970-1977; R Gr Memi Darlington MD 1964-1970; Cur Our Sav Baltimore MD 1963-1964.

GROSS, Robert Arthur (FtW) 1009 Bedford Ct W, Hurst TX 76053 B Detroit MI 1942 s Alan & Elizabeth. BA Mus Educ New Mex St U 1965; MA Mus Educ New Mex St U 1971; MDiv Laud Hall Sem 2004. D 6/7/2008 P 12/6/2008 Bp William Carl Frey. m 8/17/1987 Jessie Louise Harris c 2. P-in-c S Steph's Epis Ch Hurst TX 2015-2017, Int 2014-2015; R H Sprt Epis Ch El Paso TX 2008-2014; Admin All SS Epis Ch El Paso TX 2008. bob.gross@edfw.org

GROSSMAN, Stacey (Cal) St. Timothy's Episcopal Church, 1550 Diablo Rd, Danville CA 94526 **S Tim's Ch Danville CA 2015-** B San Jose CA 1958 4 units completed, Bd Certification eligible CPE; BA Pomona Coll 1980; MBA NYU 1983; MDiv CDSP 1996. D 6/1/1996 P 6/7/1997 Bp William Edwin Swing. Int Fac Mem, Pstr Theol CDSP Berkeley CA 2009; Dio California San Francisco CA 2007-2008, Stndg Com 2005-2009, Receiver, Cler Sexual Misconduct Complaints 2004-2008, 2001-2007, Chair, Personl Practices Cmsn 2001-2003, GC Dep 2010-2013; R Ch Of The Nativ San Rafael CA 1999-2014; S Fran' Epis Ch San Francisco CA 1996-1999; Chapl San Francisco St U 1996-1998. Cnvnr and Primary Auth, "Called To Rt Relatns," *Dioc Safe Ch Guidelines*, Dio California, 2008. OHC - Assoc 2002. Pres Stndg Com, Dio California 2008. sgrossman@sainttimothysdanville.org

GROSSO, Andrew (Kan) 2777 Mission Rd, Nashotah WI 53058 **P Nash Nashotah WI 2014-** B Royal Oak MI 1967 s Thomas & Sharon. BA Calvin Coll 1989; MA Wheaton Coll 1996; PhD Marq 2004; MDiv Sewanee: The U So, TS 2004. D 6/5/2004 Bp Steven Andrew Miller P 1/22/2005 Bp Dean E Wolfe. m 10/17/1998 Diana M P Bauson. Mssnr for Theol Formation Dio Kansas Topeka KS 2011-2014, Cn Theol 2009-2014; R Trin Ch Atchison KS 2008-2014; Cn Res Gr Cathd Topeka KS 2004-2008. "Personal Being: Polanyi, Ontology, and Chr Theol," Ptr Lang, 2007; "Trin and Wrshp: the Reception of the Basilian Liturg in BCP (1979)," *Sewanee Theol Revs 47, no. 3*, 2004. agrosso@nashotah.edu

GROSSOEHME, Daniel Huck (SO) Pulmonary Medicine Mlc2021, Cchmc, Cincinnati OH 45229 **Stff Chapl III Cincinnati Chld's Hosp Med Cntr 2009-; Assoc Prof (Resrch) Cincinnati Childrens Hosp Med Ctr 2008-; Asst Prof Cincinnati Chld's Hosp Med Cntr 2008-; Stff Chapl II Cincinnati Childrens Hosp Med Ctr Cincinnati OH 2003-; P S Thos Epis Ch Terrace Pk OH 2003-** B Cincinnati OH 1963 s Floyd & Joann. BS Indiana U 1985; Cert U Cinc 1989; MDiv VTS 1992; DMin Louisiana Presb TS 2006; MS U Cinc Coll of Med 2012. D 7/25/1992 Bp Herbert Thompson Jr P 6/1/1993 Bp Arthur Williams Jr. m 5/23/1992 Henrietta H Haigh c 1. Stff Chapl II Cincinnati Chld's Hosp Med Cntr Cincinnati OH 2003-2009; Assoc Chr Ch Epis Hudson OH 2000-2001; P S Phil's Epis Ch Akron OH 2000; Dir of Chapl Serv Akron Chiildrens Hosp Akron OH 1993-2003; Dir Pstr Care Cincinnati Chld's Hosp Med Cntr Akron OH 1993-2003; Chapl Cleveland Clnc Fndt Hosp Cleveland OH 1992-1993. Auth, "Parental use of faith related to treatment adherence," *Journ of Hlth Care Chapl*, 2013; Auth, "Use and sanctification of complementary/alternative Med by parents of Chld w cystic fibrosis," *Journ of Hlth Care Chapl*, 2013; Auth, "Chapl and Narrative Theory: A Response to Risk's Case Study," *Journ of Hlth Care Chapl*, 2013; Auth, "Is adolescents' Rel coping w cystic fibrosis associated w the rate of decline in pulmonary function?," *Journ of Hlth Care Chapl*, 2013; Auth, "Testing the validity of a protocol to screen for Sprtl risk among parents of Chld w cystic fibrosis," *Resrch in the Soc Sci Study of Rel*, 2013; Auth, "Resrch as a Chapl intervention," *Journ of Hlth Care Chapl*, 2012; Auth, "Using Sprtlty after an adult CF diagnosis: cognitive reframing and adherence motivation," *Journ of Hlth Care Chapl*, 2012; Auth, "Relatns of adherence determinants and parental Sprtlty in cystic fibrosis," *Pediatric Pulmonology*, 2012; Auth, "We were chosen as a Fam: Parents' evolving use of Rel when their Chld has cystic fibrosis.," *Journ of Hlth Care Chapl*, 2011; Auth, "Written prayers and Rel coping in a paediatric Hosp setting," *Mntl Hlth, Rel & Culture*, 2011; Auth, "We can handle this: Parents' use of Rel in the first year following their Chld's diagnosis w cystic fibrosis," *Journ of Hlth Care Chapl*, 2010; Auth, "Written prayers in a pediatric Hosp: linguistic analysis," *Psychol of Rel & Sprtlty*, 2010; Auth, "Sprtlty's role in chronic disease self-Mgmt: Sanctification of the body," *Journ of Hlth Care Chapl*, 2009; Auth, "Dvlpmt of a Sprtl screening tool for Chld and adolescents," *Journ of Pstr Care and Counslg*, 2009; Auth, "Sprtl and Rel experiences of adolescent Psych inpatients versus healthy peers," *Journ of Pstr Care and Counslg*, 2007; Auth, *Pstr Care of Chld*, Haworth Press, 1999. Assembly of Epis Hlth Care Chapl, Pres Elect 1999-2000; Assembly of Epis Hlth Care Chapl, Secy 1977-1999; Assn of Profsnl Chapl 1997; Soc of S Jn the Evang 1998-2006. Outstanding Clincl Resrch Profsnl CCHMC Clincl Resrch Professionals 2012; Bd Cert Chapl Assn of Profsnl Chapl 1997.

GROSSOEHME, Henrietta H (Ind) 111 S Grant St, Bloomington IN 47408 **Trin Epis Ch Bloomington IN 2013-** B Toledo OH 1959 d Lawrence & Ellen. BA Indiana U 1982; MDiv VTS 1991. Trans 12/5/2003 Bp J Clark Grew II. m 5/23/1992 Daniel Huck Grossoehme c 1. Assoc Chr Ch Cathd Cincinnati OH 2011-2013; Vic Gr Epis Ch Florence KY 2008-2011; Chapl Epis Ret Hm Inc. Cincinnati 2006-2008; Chapl Bethany Sch 2004-2006; Chapl Hospice of

Cincinnati 2003-2004; Chapl Res The Cleveland Clnc Fndt Hosp 2002-2003; R S Ptr's Ch Akron OH 1996-2002; Asst Chr Ch Shaker Heights OH 1991-1996. EvangES.

GROTZINGER, Terri (Mont) 130 S 6th St E, Missoula MT 59801 **P-in-c Ch Of The H Sprt Missoula MT 2011-** B Palo Alto CA 1957 d Hudson & Nancy. BS Colorado St U 1980; MDiv CDSP 1993. D 6/5/1993 P 6/1/1994 Bp William Edwin Swing. Vic Gd Shpd Epis Ch Belmont CA 2008-2011; Ch Of The H Fam Fresno CA 2000-2011; S Mk's Par Berkeley CA 1994-2000; Transitional D Trin Par Menlo Pk CA 1993-1994.

GROUBERT, Gerri Helen (Nev) 3665 Largo Verde Way, Las Vegas NV 89121 B Canton OH 1949 d Gerald & Dorothy. Kent St U; La Salle U 1976. D 11/8/1998 Bp Stewart Clark Zabriskie.

GROUT III, Earl Leroy (Oly) 6801 30th Ave Ne, Seattle WA 98115 B Minneapolis MN 1944 BA Macalester Coll 1966; PhD U of Washington 1974. D 6/28/2003 Bp Vincent Waydell Warner. m 1/25/1967 Nancy Elizabeth Austin c 2. D S Mk's Cathd Seattle WA 2009-2013; D S Steph's Epis Ch Seattle WA 2003-2009.

GROVER III, Charles Lowell (Roch) 4006 Brick Kiln Dr, Chittenango NY 13037 B Philadelphia PA 1937 s Charles & Norma. BS Webb Inst 1958; MDiv GTS 1963. D 6/7/1963 Bp Walter M Higley P 6/27/1964 Bp Ned Cole. m 7/19/1958 Joan S Grover c 4. P Assoc Chr Ch Pittsford Pittsford NY 2000-2004; Int S Steph's Ch Rochester NY 1998-1999; Int S Steph's Ch Niagara Falls NY 1997-1998; Int S Jas Ch Hyde Pk NY 1995-1997; Int S Paul's Ch Rochester NY 1994-1995; Int Ch Of The H Comm S Louis MO 1993-1994; Int S Lk's Ch Scranton PA 1991-1993; Cn to the Ordnry Dio W Virginia Charleston WV 1990-1991; Archdn & Admnstrtr Dio Cntrl New York Liverpool NY 1988-1990, Dpty for Prog 1971-1986; Mssnry S Matt's Epis Ch Liverpool NY 1968-1971; Mssnry S Andr's Ch Evans Mills NY 1963-1964.

GROVES, Barbara T (CNY) 141 Main St, Whitesboro NY 13492 B Rome NY 1942 d William & Lucille. BS Empire St Coll 1994; Loc Formation Prog Syracuse NY 2005. D 11/19/2005 Bp Gladstone Bailey Adams III. m 8/7/1965 Thomas Groves c 3. Quality Mgmt St. Eliz Hosp.

GRUBB, Daniel Studd (WMich) 4770 W Park Rd, New Era MI 49446 B London UK 1928 s Norman & Pauline. BA Wheaton Coll 1953; MAT Duke 1957; MA U MI 1963; PhD U MI 1967. D 6/6/1984 P 12/19/1984 Bp Alden Moinet Hathaway. m 6/4/1960 Rosemary Grubb c 1. Supply P Dio Wstrn Michigan Kalamazoo MI 1998-2003; Asst S Ptr's By-The-Lake Ch Montague MI 1995-1998; Vic S Mary Epis Ch Red Bank Templeton PA 1990-1995; 1986-1990; Vic S Ptr's Epis Ch Blairsville PA 1984-1986. Auth, *Another Gulliver*; Auth, *Cause & Effect: Deductive & Inductive Methods of Argument*.

GRUBB, Sarah Ann (Neb) 8800 Holdrege St, Lincoln NE 68505 B Omaha NE 1949 d Dean & Edna. D 4/29/2010 Bp Joe Goodwin Burnett. m 1/16/1974 John Grubb c 4.

GRUBBS, Lucas Michael (Colo) 630 Gilpin St, Denver CO 80218 **The Ch Of The Ascen Denver CO 2012-** B Brawley CA 1979 s Michael & Dee. BA U of Idaho 2001; MDiv Ya Berk 2005; STM Yale DS 2007. D 6/11/2005 Bp James E Waggoner Jr P 3/11/2006 Bp James Elliot Curry. m 8/6/2005 Meredith Farmer Grubbs. Cn Pstr S Mich's Cathd Boise ID 2007-2012; Cur Chr Ch New Haven CT 2005-2007. The Soc of Cath Priests 2009. The Hands and Heart of Jesus Awd Dio Idaho 2009.

GRUBE, David Quinn (Nev) 777 Sage St., Elko NV 89801 **D S Paul's Epis Ch Elko NV 2008-** B Ashton ID 1958 s Rulon & Doris. BA Idaho St U 1981. D 10/24/2008 P 5/9/2009 Bp Dan Thomas Edwards.

GRUBERTH, Cole (CNY) **P S Thos Epis Ch Slaterville Sprg NY 2013-** B Pompton Plains NJ 1967 s Frederick & Lynn. SB MIT 1989; MA Cor 1997; MDiv GTS 2007. D 6/9/2007 Bp Gladstone Bailey Adams III P 12/15/2007 Bp Jim Mathes. m 6/7/1989 Corie L Gochicoa c 1. Dio Rochester Henrietta 2012; P-in-c Allegany Cnty Mnstry Belmont NY 2011-2013, 2010; P-in-c Tri-Par Mnstry Hornell NY 2011; Assoc R S Barth's Epis Ch Poway CA 2007-2010.

GRUMAN, Stephen Cowles (Ala) 131 Silver Lake Cir, Madison AL 35758 **Suffr Chapl Porter Cup Ft. Gaines GA 1995-** B Birmingham AL 1949 s Shelton & Edna. BA U of Alabama 1987; MDiv Epis TS of the SW 1990. D 4/17/1991 P 10/23/1991 Bp Robert Oran Miller. m 4/20/2006 Gertrude F Gruman c 4. R St. Matt's Epis Ch Madison AL 2000-2016; R Trin Ch Wetumpka AL 1991-2000. Golf Whisperer, "The Art of The Whisper," *The Golf Whisper*, Self Pub, 2010. Cranmer Cup 2010; Cranmer Cup 2006; Cranmer Cup 2004.

GRUMBINE, Eugene Edmund (Va) 506 Danray Dr, Richmond VA 23227 **Died 5/22/2017** B Chicago IL 1925 s Eugene & Mable. Cert Theol Stud Bex Sem 1960. D 6/28/1960 Bp Frederick D Goodwin P 7/8/1961 Bp Robert Fisher Gibson Jr. m 3/16/1974 Gaynelle Grumbine c 3. Ret 1986-2017; 1974-1986; Vic Ch of the Incarn Mineral VA 1973-1974; R Our Sav Sandston VA 1971-1973; P-in-c S Mart's Epis Ch Richmond VA 1963-1971; Asst St Jas Ch Richmond VA 1961-1963; Assoc Ch Of The H Comf Vienna VA 1960-1961.

GRUMHAUS, Jennifer Wood (Mass) 23 Loew Cir, Milton MA 02186 **Assoc S Mich's Ch Milton MA 1994-; Dir S Aug's Camp 1990-** B Chicago IL 1962 d David. BS Boston Coll 1984; MDiv EDS 1990. D 6/16/1990 Bp Frank Tracy Griswold III. Camp S Aug Inc Boston MA 1990-1993.

GRUNDY, Elizabeth A (Mass) 421 Wianno Ave, Osterville MA 02655 **S Ptr's Ch Osterville MA 2016-** B Norwood MA 1959 d John & Amy. BA Simmons Coll 1981; MA Sarah Lawr Coll 1991; MDiv Andover Newton TS 1996; CAS GTS 1997. D 6/7/1997 P 5/30/1998 Bp M(Arvil) Thomas Shaw. Gr Cathd San Francisco CA 2014-2016; S Jn's Ch Sandwich MA 2013-2014; Chr Ch Swansea MA 2003-2013; P-in-c S Andr's Ch New Bedford MA 1997-2003. rector@stpeters-capecod.org

GRUNDY, Sandra A (Colo) 9345 Carr St, Westminster CO 80021 B Allentown PA 1951 d Stephen & Helen. BS U of Missouri 1973; MA VTS 1980; MA U of Nthrn Colorado 2007. D 6/14/1985 P 12/22/1985 Bp William Carl Frey. m 6/14/1986 Jimmy Wayne Grundy c 1. The Epis Ch of the Resurr Boulder CO 1999-2008; Int S Jas Epis Ch Wheat Ridge CO 1994-1995, 1993; S Jn's Epis Ch Boulder CO 1993-1999; Int S Martha's Epis Ch Westminster CO 1993. Sprtl Dir Intl .

GRUNFELD, Matthew Theodore (SwFla) Episcopal Church of Annunciation, 4408 Gulf Dr, Holmes Beach FL 34217 **P-in-c Ch Of The Annunc Holmes Bch FL 2015-; Fac, Sch for Mnstry Dvlpmt Dio SW Florida Parrish FL 2017-** B Columbus GA 1981 s David & Carol. BA Emory U 2003; MDiv GTS 2008. D 12/21/2006 P 11/2/2008 Bp J Neil Alexander. P-in-c All SS Ch Montgomery AL 2011-2015; R Emm Epis Ch Opelika AL 2008-2011; Assoc S Mk's Epis Ch Lagrange GA 2007-2008; D Sem Ch Of The H Trin New York NY 2006-2007; Chapl Res St. Fran Hosp Columbus GA 2003-2004; Alt Dep, 78th GC Dio Alabama Birmingham 2015, Dioc Coun 2011-2014. One Montgomery 2011. mtggts@gmail.com

GRUSELL, Katrina L (Md) 5057 Stone Hill Dr, Ellicott City MD 21043 **S Jn's Ch Ellicott City MD 2016-; Epis Chapl UMBC 2012-** B Worcester MA 1963 d Frank & Sandra. AS Anna Maria Coll 1984; BS Worcester St Coll 1993; MDiv VTS 1999; DMin Drew U 2010. D 6/12/1999 Bp John L Rabb P 1/8/2000 Bp Robert Wilkes Ihloff. m 10/20/1984 David C Grusell c 2. R The Ch Of The H Apos Halethorpe MD 2001-2015; Asst R St Martins-In-The-Field Ch Severna Pk MD 1999-2001. kgrusell@umbc.edu

GRUSENDORF, William Connor (WTex) 401 W Dry St, San Saba TX 76877 **Vic S Lk's Epis Ch San Saba TX 1981-** B Waco TX 1931 s Monroe & Della. BA TCU 1954; MA U of Texas 1967; Sewanee: The U So, TS 1981. D 6/30/1981 Bp Stanley Fillmore Hauser P 6/23/1982 Bp Scott Field Bailey. m 2/16/1952 Patricia Kay c 2. stlukessansaba@centex.net

GRYGIEL, Janet Carol (Chi) 1415 Temple Cir, Rockford IL 61108 B Woosung IL 1942 d John & Sadie. D 2/1/2003 Bp Bill Persell.

GUAILLAS CARANGUI, Raul (DR) Cafetos Oe-3-76 Y Nazareth, Quito 00593 Ecuador **Dio The Dominican Republic (Iglesia Epis Dominicana) Gazcue Santo Domingo 2013-; Iglesia Cristo Liberador Quito 2006-, Vicario 2006-** B Molleturo Cuenca Azuay 1966 Programa De Educacion; Grad Universidad Del Azuay 1992; Grad Tecnica Particular De Loja 1997; Politecnica Salesiana 2000. D 10/15/2000 Bp Jose Neptali Larrea-Moreno P 2/11/2006 Bp Orlando Jesus Guerrero. m 1/7/2002 Amada Del Rocio Recalde c 2. Iglesia Epis Del Ecuador Quito 2004-2013.

GUAMAN AYALA, Francisco (EcuC) Brasilia Y Buenos Aires, Ambato Ecuador **Vic Tungurahua Prov 1988-** B Sangolqui EC 1957 s Augusto & Maria. BA S Vinc De Paul 1976; U Cntrl 1984. D 12/18/1988 Bp Adrian Delio Caceres-Villavicencio. m 5/28/1987 Maria Villegas.

GUBACK, Thomas Henry (WMich) 6300 North ManitouTrail, Northport MI 49670 B Passaic NJ 1937 s Stephen & Margaret. BA Rutgers The St U of New Jersey 1958; MS U IL 1959; PhD U IL 1964; MDiv Nash 2000. D 5/27/2000 P 11/25/2000 Bp Edward Lewis Lee Jr. m 6/18/1988 Sylvia Linde c 1. R S Christophers Ch Northport MI 2000-2007. Phi Beta Kappa 1958.

GUCK, Sarah St John (RG) PO Box 2795, Silver City NM 88062 B Albany NY 1966 d Alan & Charlotte. BA NYU 1998; MSW NYU 1999. D 9/14/2013 P 5/14/2016 Bp Michael Vono. m 11/19/1994 Anthony Guck c 2. Ch Of The Gd Shpd Silver City NM 2013-2015.

GUDGER JR, Gordon B (Tex) **Died 12/3/2016** B 1931 D 6/21/1960 Bp James Parker Clements P 5/25/1961 Bp Frederick P Goddard. m 3/19/1994 Sharon Gudger. All SS Epis Ch Hitchcock TX 1985-1993; Chr The King Epis Ch Humble TX 1979; S Steph's Ch Liberty TX 1972-1985.

GUENTHER, John Howard (WNY) 88 Cedar Terrace, Hilton NY 14468 **Ret 1995-** B Atlantic City NJ 1919 s William & Anna. BS Drexel U 1942. D 12/14/1968 Bp George West Barrett P 11/18/1972 Bp Robert Rae Spears Jr. m 6/24/1988 Nancy Louise Guenther. R S Paul's Ch Holley NY 1989-1995; Chapl Epis Ch Hm Rochester NY 1974-1987; Assoc All SS Angl Ch Rochester NY 1973-1974; D S Mk's And S Jn's Epis Ch Rochester NY 1968-1972.

GUENTHER, Margaret (WA) 4101 Albemarle St NW Apt 651, Washington DC 20016 **Died 12/11/2016** B Kansas City MO 1929 d Otto & Adah. BA U of Kansas 1950; U of Zurich 1950; MA U of Kansas 1953; PhD Harv 1958; MDiv GTS 1983. D 12/5/1983 Bp Paul Moore Jr P 6/24/1984 Bp Walter Decoster Dennis Jr. m 6/11/1956 Jack Guenther c 3. Assoc S Columba's Ch Washington DC 1998-2016; Prof The GTS New York NY 1985-1997; Assoc Ch Of The H Trin New York NY 1983-1997. Auth, "Walking Hm: From Eden to Emmaus," Ch Pub, 2010; Auth, "At Hm in the Wrld," Ch Pub, 2006; Auth, "Just Passing Through," Ch Pub, 2002; Auth, "Notes From A Sojourner," Ch Pub, 2002; Auth, "My Soul In Silence Waits," Cowley Press, 2000; Auth, "H Listening"; Auth, "Toward H Ground"; Auth, "The Pract Of Pryr". Phi Beta Kappa 1949.

GUENTHER, Nancy Louise (WNY) 200 East Center St., Medina NY 14103 **Vic S Jn's Ch Medina NY 2010-** B Framingham, MA 1939 d Charles & Louisa. BS SUNY at Brockport 1983; MDiv Colgate Rochester Crozer DS 1989; MDiv CRDS 1989. D 4/9/2005 P 10/22/2005 Bp Michael Garrison. m 6/24/1988 John Howard Guenther c 3.

GUERNSEY, Jacqueline Louise (CFla) 25510 Belle Alliance, Leesburg FL 34748 B Flint MI 1932 d Warren & Thelma. BS Estrn Michigan U 1964; MA Estrn Michigan U 1969; Diac Stds Whitaker TS 1989. D 11/25/1989 Bp Henry Irving Mayson. m 12/30/1950 Floyd J Guernsey. D H Trin Epis Ch Fruitland Pk FL 1999-2009; D S Fran Epis Ch Grayling MI 1990-2000. NAAD.

GUERNSEY, Justine Marie (Alb) 563 Kenwood Ave, Delmar NY 12054 **D S Steph's Ch Delmar NY 2014-** B Albany NY 1955 d Gerald & Mary. AS Albany Bus Coll Albany NY 1977; BS SUNY 2000; BBA Sage Coll of Albany 2008. D 3/25/2000 Bp Daniel William Herzog. m 12/28/1979 William Leon Guernsey c 3. D S Matt's Ch Latham NY 2010-2013; D Cathd Of All SS Albany NY 2000-2010; D Formation Sch, Asst. Dir Dio Albany Greenwich NY 2010-2017, D Formation Fac, Fac Mem 2007-2010.

GUERRA, Carrie L (WTex) **Dio W Texas San Antonio TX 2017-; Other Lay Position S Jn's Ch McAllen TX 2003-** D 5/31/2017 Bp David Mitchell Reed.

GUERRA, Norma Yanira (Los) **Other Lay Position All SS Ch Pasadena CA 2013-** D 6/4/2016 P 1/14/2017 Bp Joseph Jon Bruno.

GUERRA-DIAZ, Juan Antonio (Ore) Po Box 1731, Hillsboro OR 97123 **Int Vic S Mich's/San Miguel Newberg OR 2007-** B Santiago Chile 1943 s Francisco & Lidia. Inacap Santiago Cl 1975; Locutres De Chile Santiago Cl 1980; Latino Radio Broadcasting Portland OR 1998. D 9/30/2000 P 6/9/2001 Bp Robert Louis Ladehoff. m 6/12/1989 Rilda Oliva de Guerra. Vic Todos Los Santos Hillsboro OR 2001-2013. Appreciation Kbvm-Fm 88.3 1996; Appreciation Kbvm-Fm 88.3 1994; Appreciation Washington Cnty Cmnty Action Orgnztn 1983.

✠ GUERRERO, The Rt Rev Orlando Jesus (Ve) Centro Diocesano, Avenue Caroni No. 100, Colinas de Bello Monte, Caracas Venezuela B 1945 D P Con 1/1/1995 for Ve. Bp of Venezuela Dio Venezuela Caracas 2004-2017.

GUERRERO-STAMP, Carmen Bruni (Az) 114 W Roosevelt, Phoenix AZ 85003 **Vic Santa Maria Epis Ch Phoenix AZ 2014-; Dio Arizona Phoenix AZ 2008-, 2005-2006; Cn For Peace And Justice Dio Arizona 2005-** B Corpus ChristiTX 1941 d Louis & Priscilla. BA Our Lady of the Lake U 1972; MS Our Lady of the Lake U 1980; MDiv Sewanee: The U So, TS 1984; CDSP 1994. D 6/21/1984 Bp Scott Field Bailey P 1/25/1985 Bp Leo Frade. m 4/6/2004 Paul S Stamp c 1. Jubilee Natl Off Epis Ch Cntr New York NY 1999-2006; St Mary's Cnvnt Los Angeles CA 1994; Archd Multicultural Dio Los Angeles Los Angeles CA 1990-1999; Santa Fe Epis Mssn San Antonio TX 1989-1990; Dio W Texas San Antonio TX 1984-1990.

GUERRIER, Michel Marguy (Hai) **Dio Haiti Port-au-Prince HT 2012-** B 1969 s Borgella & Rene. D 7/29/2012 P 3/13/2014 Bp Jean Zache Duracin.

GUERRIER, Panel Marc (SwFla) 3901 Davis Blvd, Naples FL 34104 **P-in-c The Ch Of The Gd Shpd Labelle FL 2016-; S Paul's Ch Naples FL 2013-** B Arcahaie HT 1957 s Pierre & Solange. BA 1989; Ceeteh 1989. D 7/30/1989 P 2/14/1990 Bp Luc Anatole Jacques Garnier. m 12/16/1993 Magareth Guerrier c 3. P-in-c St Andre Cazale 2003-2004; P-in-c St Esprit Cap-Haitien 1998-2003; P-in-c Sts Innoc Port-de-Paix 1993-1998; P-in-c Annonciation -Darbonne Haiti 1990-1993; Dio Haiti Port-au-Prince HT 1989-2004.

GUEVARA RODRIGUEZ, Carlos Eduardo (Colom) Calle 30 No 17-08, Barrio Armenia, Teusaquillo, Bogota Colombia **Iglesia Epis En Colombia Bogota 2016-; P Mision El Divino Salvador Bogota 2014-, P-in-c 2014-; D Mision del Espiritu Santo Soacha 2006-, D 2006-** B Pasca cundinamarca 1968 s Juan & Rosa. Universidad Santo Tomás 1974. D 9/9/2006 Bp Francisco Jose Duque-Gomez. m 4/23/2004 Blanca Janeth Guacheta Sanchez c 3.

GUFFEY, Andrew Ryan (Va) **Chapl Cbury NW Evanston IL 2015-** D 6/7/2014 P 12/6/2014 Bp Shannon Sherwood Johnston.

GUFFEY, Emily Williams (Va) 4550 N Hermitage Ave, Chicago IL 60640 **All SS Epis Ch Chicago IL 2015-** B Pontiac MI 1981 d Gregory & Mary. BA NWU 2003; MA Garrett - Evang TS 2008; MDiv VTS 2015. D 6/6/2015 Bp Shannon Sherwood Johnston P 12/12/2015 Bp Jeff Lee. m 7/18/2009 Andrew Ryan Guffey c 2. emily@allsaintschicago.org

GUGLIERMETTO, Gian Luigi (Los) B Torino Italy 1965 s Giuseppe & Ester. Universita Torino 1937; Laurea Universita Torino 1937; PhD Claremont Grad U 2008. D 10/31/2015 P 5/5/2016 Bp Joseph Jon Bruno.

GUIBORD, Gwynne Marlyn (Los) 146 S Beachwood Dr, Los Angeles CA 90004 **Nonstipendiary Asstg St Johns Pro-Cathd Los Angeles CA 2007-** B Flint MI 1944 D 1/6/2004 Bp Sergio Carranza-Gomez P 1/22/2005 Bp Joseph Jon Bruno. m 8/6/2001 Lois M Sprague. Dio Los Angeles Los Angeles CA 2004-2009; S Thos The Apos Hollywood Los Angeles CA 2004-2005.

GUIDA, Angela G (Az) 2480 Virginia St Apt 4, Berkeley CA 94709 **Asst S Aid's Ch San Francisco CA 2011-** B Tampa, FL 1950 d Angelo & Violet. BS

Amer U 1985; MSW CUA 1988; MTS CDSP 2010. D 11/30/2009 P 6/12/2010 Bp Kirk Stevan Smith. m 12/20/2012 Nancy G Eswein c 2. Sojourn Multifaith Chapl San Francisco CA 2013-2015; San Francisco Ntwk Mnstrs San Francisco CA 2012-2013; Ch Of The Redeem San Rafael CA 2011-2012.

GUIDRY, Robert Turner (WNC) 869 Daylily Dr, Hayesville NC 28904 B Baton Rouge LA 1947 s Robert & Gwendolyn. BA Centenary Coll 1969; MA Steph F Austin St U 1973. D 9/6/1997 Bp Bob Johnson. m 4/25/1987 Georgia Skelton.

GUILE, Frederic Corwith (Alb) 1680 Liebig Rd., Granville NY 12832 **Died 1/15/2016** B Albany NY 1927 s George & Gertrude. BA RPI 1949; BD Ya 1954. D 6/6/1954 P 12/1/1954 Bp Frederick Lehrle Barry. c 3. Chapl Emer Integrity Albany 1981-2016; Ret 1979-2016; Chapl Integrity Albany 1979-1980; R S Dav's Epis Ch Castleton NY 1969-1979; Asst S Geo's Ch Clifton Pk NY 1968-1969; R Ch Of The Nativ Star Lake NY 1963-1968; R S Mary's Epis Ch Rockport MA 1962-1963; R S Jn's Ch Johnstown NY 1956-1961; Vic S Lk's Troy NY 1954-1956. Chapl Emer Integrity, Albany 1979; R Emer Ch of the Nativ, Star Lake-- Hermon 1968.

GUILFOYLE, David Martin (Ind) D 7/16/2016 Bp Cate Waynick.

GUILLAUME-SAM, Sully (LI) 1405 Bushwick Ave, Brooklyn NY 11207 **R Ch Of S Thos Brooklyn NY 2013-** B Haiti 1968 s Jacksius & Rose. BA Grand Seminaire ND 1998; BA Universite D'Etat D'Haiti 1999; MA Fordham Unvserity 2006; Dip Ang Stud GTS 2010. Rec 6/26/2010 Bp Lawrence C Provenzano. m 9/2/2011 Marie Jirlande Fenelon Guillaume-Sam c 1. Cur S Gabr's Ch Brooklyn NY 2010-2013; Epis Cmnty Serv Long Island 1927 Bay Shore NY 2007-2010.

GUILLEN, Anthony Anthony (Los) 198 Via Baja, Ventura CA 93003 **Dom And Frgn Mssy Soc- Epis Ch Cntr New York NY 2005-; Mssnr, Latino/Hisp Mnstrs Epis Ch Cntr 2005-; Mssnr for Latino/Hisp Mnstry Epis Ch Cntr New York NY 2005-** B Richmond TX 1953 s Jesus & Simona. CTh Epis TS of the SW 1990; MA Epis TS of the SW 2000; BS U of Phoenix 2000. D 9/21/1984 P 4/14/1985 Bp Samuel Espinoza-Venegas. m 7/6/1991 Guadalupe M Guillen c 3. R All SS Epis Ch Oxnard CA 1993-2005; Assoc R S Clem's-By-The-Sea Par San Clemente CA 1990-1992; Vic Dio Wstrn Mex Zapopan Jalisco 1989-1990; Vic San Miguel Ciudad Guzman Mex 1986-1987; Vic Templo De Cristo Guadalajara Mex 1984-1987; Exec Coun Mem Dio Los Angeles Los Angeles CA 2000-2006; Liaison from Exec Coun Stndg Cmsn on Liturg & Mus 2000-2003. Auth, "Cnfrmtn and Sacraments in Latino Mnstry," *Signed, Sealed, Delievered*, Morehouse Pub, 2014; Auth, "Lift High the Cross," *Praises Abound: Hymns & Meditations for Lent & Easter*, Ch Pub, 2012; Auth, "The Epis Ch's Strategic Vision for Reaching Latinos/Hispanics," Off of Latino/Hisp Mnstrs, 2009; Auth, "Crossing the Cultural Divide," *Doing H Bus*, Ch Pub, 2006. Hon Cn Dio Ecuador Cntrl 2007; Hon Cn Dio Puerto Rico 2006. aguillen@episcopalchurch.org

GUINN, Patricia J (WNY) 2753 Eastwood Rd, East Aurora NY 14052 **D S Matt's Ch Buffalo NY 2012-; Chapl to Ret Cler and Cler Widows Dio Wstrn New York Tonawanda NY 2012-, Dioc Coun Chautauqua Dnry 2011-2012** B Buffalo NY 1944 d Rudolph & G. BA SUNY at Buffalo 1966; MLS SUNY at Geneseo 1967; MSW St Univeristy of New York at Buffalo 1996. D 9/12/1998 Bp David Charles Bowman. c 3. Chapl Beechwood Hm Amherst NY 2013-2015; D S Ptr's Ch Westfield NY 2011-2012; D S Aid's Ch Alden NY 2007-2011; Chapl Cbury Woods Williamsville NY 2006-2009; Chapl Epis Ch Hm Buffalo NY 2005-2006; D S Simon's Ch Buffalo NY 2002-2007; Chapl Erie Cnty Hm Alden NY 2001-2006; D Trin Ch Lancaster NY 1999-2001; D S Jude's Ch Buffalo NY 1999. NAAD 1998-2000.

GUINTA, Denise Gray (SwVa) 5011 McGregor Blvd, Fort Myers FL 33901 **Dio SW Virginia Roanoke VA 2017-** B Graet Falls Va 1962 MA S Mary-Of-The-Woods Coll. D 5/26/2002 P 6/14/2003 Bp Mark Lawrence Macdonald. m 3/15/1988 Ronald Guinta c 2. Chr Epis Ch Roanoke VA 2014-2015; S Mk's Epis Ch Of Tampa Tampa FL 2013-2014; S Hilary's Ch Ft Myers FL 2012-2013; Chr Epis Ch Luray VA 2010-2011; Chapl @ Univ. of So Florida Dio SW Florida Parrish FL 2008-2009, 2007-2009; H Innoc Epis Ch Valrico FL 2006-2007; H Trin Epis Ch In Countryside Clearwater FL 2004-2005; Int S Alfred's Epis Ch Palm Harbor FL 2003-2004.

GUISTOLISE, Kathryn Jean Mazzenga (Chi) 5555 N Sheridan Rd #608, Chicago IL 60640 **Coordntr Of Pstr Care Bethany Terrace Nrsng Cntr In Morton Grove 1994-** B Chicago IL 1948 d Frank & Betty Helene Livick. Cert SWTS 1995. D 2/3/1996 Bp Frank Tracy Griswold III P 1/6/2005 Bp Bill Persell. m 6/9/1985 Philip Guistolise. H Trin Ch Skokie IL 2006-2011; Par Ministers Coordntr/D S Mk's Ch Evanston IL 1996-2000; Chapl Methodist Hosp Chicago IL 1993-1994. Auth, "Var arts". ESMA Chicago; Soc Of S Jn The Evang. The Rev Rbt Dahl Schlrshp.

✠ GULICK JR, The Rt Rev Ted (Va) 425 S 2nd St, Louisville KY 40202 **Asst Bp Dio Virginia Richmond VA 2011-; Ret Bp of Kentucky Dio Kentucky Louisville KY 2010-, Bp Of Kentucky 1994-2010** B Washington DC 1948 s Edwin & Nelle. Shalem Inst Washington DC; VTS; BA Lynchburg Coll 1970; MDiv VTS 1973; Sewanee: The U So, TS 1995. D 6/5/1973 Bp William Henry Marmion P 2/9/1974 Bp David Keller Leighton Sr Con 4/17/1994 for Ky. m 8/15/1970 Barbara Gulick c 1. R S Steph's Ch Newport News VA 1982-1994; R

Gr Ch Elkridge MD 1976-1982; Asst Trin Ch Towson MD 1973-1976. Intl Angl RC Cmsn For Unity And Mssn (Aircum); Scer Angl / RC Dialogue. Hon DD Stuso 1995; Hon DD VTS 1994. tgulick@thediocese.net

GULLETT, John Manford (CFla) **R St Alb's of Auburndale Inc Auburndale FL 2015-** D 3/10/2015 P 9/13/2015 Bp Gregory Orrin Brewer.

GUMBS, Delores Elvida (VI) PO Box 6454, Christiansted, St Croix VI 00823 B St Kitts VI 1940 d Hubert & Evangeline. RFN The Royal Coll of Nrsng 1963; RN The Royal Coll of Nrsng 1966; NM The Royal Coll of Nrsng 1968. D 6/21/2008 Bp Edward Gumbs. c 1.

✠ GUMBS, The Rt Rev Edward (VI) P.O. Box 7488, St Thomas VI 00801 **Bp of the Vrgn Islands Dio Vrgn Islands Charlotte Amalie St Thom VI 2005-, 1987** B Stoney Ground Anguilla 1949 s Edward & Drucilla. U of Maryland 1980; BA U of the Vrgn Islands 1984; MDiv VTS 1987. D 6/14/1987 P 6/12/1988 Bp Egbert Don Taylor Con 6/11/2005 for VI. m 8/7/1999 Phillis Berdean Gumbs c 2. R S Andr's Ch St Thos VI 1988-2005. DD VTS 2006. bpambrose@edotvi.org

GUNDERSON, David John (Mont) 313 S Yellowstone St, Livingston MT 59047 B Seattle WA 1952 s John & Ellen. BA U of Washington 1974; MDiv EDS 1980; MEd U of Puget Sound 1990. D 7/25/1980 Bp Robert Hume Cochrane P 5/4/1981 Bp Paul Moore Jr. m 1/24/2009 Kory M Gunderson c 1. R Upper Yellowstone Epis Ch Livingston MT 2004-2017; R S Andr's Ch Livingston MT 2004-2015; Mssn to Seafarers Seattle WA 2002-2004; Int Ch Of The Ascen Seattle WA 2001-2002; S Hilda's - S Pat's Epis Ch Edmonds WA 1999-2000; S Mary's Ch Lakewood WA 1987-1990; Vic Ch Of Our Sav Monroe WA 1983-1987; Seamens Ch Inst New York NY 1980-1983. Auth, "Earth & Sprt". admin@ecuy.net

GUNDERSON, Gretchen Anne (Oly) 629 Taft Ave, Raymond WA 98577 **Pstr First Luth Ch 2015-; P S Jn's Epis Ch So Bend WA 1992-** B Los Angeles CA 1943 d Robert & Grace. U CA; U of Washington; WA SU; BA U CA 1964. D 8/29/1992 P 3/1/1993 Bp Vincent Waydell Warner. m 4/9/1976 Karl Gunderson c 2.

GUNN, **Daniel Cube** (Be) 201 Crestview Rd, Bridgewater NJ 08807 **Chr Ch Ridgewood NJ 2015-** B Union MS 1973 s David & Bobbie. Doctorate Drew U; BS Lee U 1997; MDiv Ch of God TS 1999; MA W Chester U of Pennsylvania 2001; CAS Ya Berk 2002; STM Yale DS 2003. D 4/6/2002 P 10/6/2002 Bp Paul Victor Marshall. S Ptr's Ch Clarksboro NJ 2014-2015; R S Steph's Epis Ch Wilkes Barre PA 2006-2013; Asst to R Chr Ch Bronxville NY 2002-2006; Chapl S Lk's Hosp Bethlehem PA 1999-2001.

GUNN, Kevin Paul (Los) All Saints Parish, 5619 Monte Vista St, Los Angeles CA 90042 B Omaha NE 1955 s Gerald & Joan. BA St. Olaf Coll 1977; BA St. Olaf Coll 1977; Dplma ETSBH 2009. D 12/20/2015 Bp Joseph Jon Bruno.

GUNN, Reginald Richard (Ga) 688 Covecrest Dr, Tiger GA 30576 **Died 9/24/2016** B Tifton GA 1940 s John & Helen. BA U GA 1962; MDiv SWTS 1965. D 5/29/1965 P 3/25/1966 Bp Albert R Stuart. m 6/5/1965 Mary Luise Ackerman Gunn c 2. R Calv Ch Americus GA 1992-2006; Assoc S Jas Epis Ch Baton Rouge LA 1990-1992; Chapl St. Andr's Soc of Savannah GA 1979-2016; R S Thos Ch Savannah GA 1977-1990; Chapl Clan Gunn Soc of No Amer 1975-2016; R S Patricks Ch Albany GA 1971-1977; R S Andr's Epis Ch Douglas GA 1969-1971; Vic S Lk's Epis Hawkinsville GA 1965-1969; Vic St Peters EAstman GA 1965-1969; Trin Ch Cochran GA 1965-1969; Pres, Stndg Com Dio Georgia Savannah GA 1980-1990, Dep Gnrl Conventions 1972-1981. OHC 1962.

GUNN, Sally Watkins Pope (Va) D 4/16/2016 Bp Shannon Sherwood Johnston.

GUNN, Scott Alan (SO) Forward Movement, 412 Sycamore St, Cincinnati OH 45202 **Exec Dir Forw Mvmt of the Epis Ch Cincinnati OH 2011-** B Gardner KS 1967 s Ronald & Nancy. BA Luther Coll 1994; MA Ya Berk 1992; MDiv Ya Berk 1996; CAS Ya Berk 1996; MA Br 1997. D 2/5/2005 P 9/10/2005 Bp Gerry Wolf. m 12/5/1992 Sherilyn Pearce. R Chr Ch In Lonsdale Lincoln RI 2007-2011; Ch of the Epiph Rumford RI 2006-2007; Asst St Mich & Gr Ch Rumford RI 2006-2007; Cmncatn Off Dio Rhode Island Providence RI 2006.

GUNNESS, Margaret B (Mass) 641 Pleasant St, Belmont MA 02478 B Shreveport LA 1937 d James & Margaret. BA Connecticut Coll 1959; LUniversite de Caen - France/Fulbright Schlr 1960; MDiv EDS 1980. D 6/7/1980 Bp John Bowen Coburn P 2/18/1981 Bp Morris Fairchild Arnold. m 8/17/1962 Peter Gunness c 3. S Mary's Cathd Memphis TN 2001-2002; Calv Ch Memphis TN 1999-2001; R Chr Ch Ridgewood NJ 1991-1999; Stff P Trin Ch Epis Boston MA 1987-1990; Chr Ch Cambridge Cambridge MA 1980-1987.

✠ GUNTER, The Rt Rev Matthew A (FdL) 22w400 Hackberry Dr, Glen Ellyn IL 60137 **Bp Dio Fond du Lac Appleton WI 2014-** B Warsaw IN 1957 s Doyle & Sue. BA Indiana U 1980; Gordon-Conwell TS 1981; MDiv VTS 1996. D 6/8/1996 Bp David Mercer Schofield P 12/21/1996 Bp Frank Tracy Griswold III Con 4/26/2014 for FdL. m 5/30/1981 Leslie R Gunter c 3. R S Barn' Epis Ch Glen Ellyn IL 2000-2014; Asst S Dav's Ch Glenview IL 1996-1999. Auth, "The Wildness Of God," *Prism mag*, 2001. Jn Hines Preaching Awd Jn Hines Preaching Awd 2001. mgunter@diofdl.org

GUNTHORPES, Alexander (LI) 2666 E 22nd St, Brooklyn NY 11235 **R Emm Epis Ch of Sheepshead Bay Brooklyn NY 1999-** B 1948 s Charles & Sarah.

LTh Codrington Coll 1975; MS NYTS 1987; DMin Andersonville Bapt Sem 2001. Trans 2/1/1987 Bp Robert Campbell Witcher Sr. m 6/30/1973 Kathleen Girlette Adassa Parker c 4. Emm Epis Ch Of Sheepshead Bay Brooklyn NY 1990-2015; Dio Long Island Garden City NY 1987-1990; Asst Ch Of S Thos Brooklyn NY 1984-1987.

GURNIAK, David Fyodor (Ct) 610a Heritage Villiage, Southbury CT 06488 **Died 4/4/2016** B Philadelphia PA 1934 s John & Anna. BS U of Pennsylvania 1956; STB Ya Berk 1959; MTh Yale DS 1959. D 5/16/1959 P 12/1/1959 Bp William P Roberts. m 7/9/1960 Janet G Grayshon. Ret 1998-2016; Int S Jn's Ch No Haven CT 1996-1998; S Ptr's Ch Fernandina Bch FL 1991-1996; Chr Epis Ch Dayton OH 1989-1991; Trin Ch Ft Wayne IN 1988-1989; R S Mk's Ch Evanston IL 1984-1988; S Mich's Ch Litchfield CT 1961-1984; Asst H Apos And Medtr Philadelphia PA 1959-1961.

GURRY, Jane Todd (NC) 817 Rosemont Ave, Raleigh NC 27607 **Non-stip assoc. S Mich's Ch Raleigh NC 2007-** B Philadelphia MS 1932 d Lindsay & Sarah. BA U of Mississippi 1953; MEd U NC 1972; MDiv VTS 1980. D 6/21/1980 Bp Thomas Augustus Fraser Jr P 3/1/1981 Bp Roger W Blanchard. m 7/1/1956 Ellis T Gurry c 3. P For Liturg And Tchg S Ambroses Ch Raleigh NC 2002-2003; R S Mk's Epis Ch Raleigh NC 1989-1997; R Ch Of Our Sav Cincinnati OH 1985-1988.

GUSTAFSON, Elyse Marie (Chi) 4901 N Mesa St Apt 4206, El Paso TX 79912 **Off Of Bsh For ArmdF New York NY 2013-; Yth Dir S Ptr's Epis Ch Arlington VA 2010-** B Arlington Heights IL 1984 d Wesley & Therese. BA Wheaton Coll 2007; MDiv Duke DS 2010. D 7/21/2012 P 2/3/2013 Bp James Beattie Magness.

GUSTAFSON II, Karl Edmund (Az) 3949 W Alexander Rd Unit 1268, Norht Las Vegas NV 89032 **Died 6/28/2016** B Denver CO 1935 s Karl & Ruth. BA U Denv 1969; Wstrn St Coll of Colorado 1971; Epis TS in Kentucky 1975; Epis TS in Kentucky 1976. D 3/14/1975 P 11/18/1975 Bp Addison Hosea. m 7/30/1955 Nancie A Mitchell c 7. S Andrews Crippled Childrens Clnc Inc Nogales AZ 1994-2000; S Andr's Chld's Clnc Nogales AZ 1993-2016; Epis Ch Of S Fran-In-The-Vlly Green Vlly AZ 1993-2001; S Andr's Epis Ch Nogales AZ 1988-1994; R Ch Of The H Comm Rock Sprg WY 1981-1988; R Gr Ch Ishpeming MI 1979-1981; Vic Adv Ch Cynthiana KY 1975-1979. ECF; RACA.

GUSTAFSON III, Karl Edmund (Nev) 4201 W Washington Ave, Las Vegas NV 89107 B Denver CO 1957 s Karl & Nancie. BA U of Wyoming 1991; MA Lesley Coll 1996. D 9/8/1996 Bp Stewart Clark Zabriskie. m 5/31/1990 Margaret Ellen Gustafson c 4.

GUSTAFSON, Mary (WMass) 1840 University Ave W Apt 201, Saint Paul MN 55104 **Chapl CPC 2009-** B Bethlehem PA 1946 d Robert & Nancy. BA Coll of Wooster 1968; MM U of Kentucky 1972; MFA U of Iowa 1976; MDiv TESM 2000; DMin Luther TS 2007. D 6/9/2001 P 12/17/2001 Bp Robert William Duncan. m 8/17/1974 Ray Everett Gustafson c 4. Int P Mssh Epis Ch St. Paul MN 2015-2016; R H Trin Epis Ch Southbridge MA 2004-2012; St Johns Luth Ch Pittsburgh PA 2002-2004; P-in-c S Matt's Epis Ch Homestead PA 2001-2004. Scholarly Achievement Awd ABS 2000; Scholarly Achievement Awd ABS 1997.

GUSTIN, Pete (Va) 301 W Broad St Apt 762, Falls Church VA 22046 **S Steph's Ch Catlett VA 2016-; Prog Analyst, Emergency Oprtns L-3 Cmncatn Chantilly VA 2002-** B Long Beach CA 1953 s Albert & Muriel. BA Coppin St Coll 1979; MDiv VTS 1987; DMin SWTS 2001. D 6/13/1987 P 3/19/1988 Bp Peter J Lee. m 10/22/1977 Debra Gustin c 2. Ch Of The Gd Shpd Burke VA 2013; Vic Chr Epis Ch Lucketts Leesburg VA 2002-2010; Ed Untd States Pharmacopoea Rockville MD 2001-2002; R Cunningham Chap Par Millwood VA 1990-2002; Vic Calv Ch Hanover VA 1987-1990; Asst to R Ch Of S Jas The Less Ashland VA 1987-1990. Auth, "Virginia Sem Journ"; Auth, "Virginia Sem Journ". CERT 2005; ESBVM 1986-1989; VGEC 1998; VOAD 2003. ststephencatlett@yahoo.com

GUTGSELL, Jessie Katherine (Mich) **S Clare Of Assisi Epis Ch Ann Arbor MI 2016-** B 1989 d Terence & Katherine. Bachelors of Mus Indiana U 2011; Masters of Div Ya Berk 2016. D 12/19/2015 P 6/21/2016 Bp Cate Waynick. m 7/7/2016 Joseph R Dodson. Auth, "The Gift of Tears: Weeping in the Rel Imagination of Wstrn Medieval Christainity," ATR, 2015.

GUTHRIE, Donald Angus (Mont) 1801 Selway Dr., Missoula MT 59808 **Ret 1993-** B Dundee Scotland GB 1931 s Frederick & Alison. Westcott Hse Cambridge; BA Oxf GB 1954; MA Oxf GB 1958. Trans 10/1/1989. c 3. Stndg Com Dio Montana Helena MT 1989-1991, RurD 1985-1989, Ecum Off 1984-1990, 1977-1979; R Ch Of The H Sprt Missoula MT 1979-1993; Serv Ch in Scotland & Engl 1958-1977.

GUTHRIE, Emily (WA) 7215 Arthur Dr, Falls Church VA 22046 B Bridgeport CT 1964 d Hugh & Elizabeth. BA Pr 1985; MDiv Yale DS 1995. D 6/12/1999 Bp Ronald Hayward Haines P 1/16/2010 Bp John Bryson Chane. m 10/29/2006 Michael J Lindner. S Marg's Ch Washington DC 2010-2014; Exec Dir Capitol Hill Grp Mnstry 2001-2008; D Assoc Chr Ch Capitol Hill Washington DC 1998-2000; Yth Dir S Mk's Ch Washington DC 1989-1992. Cmnty Achievement Awd Capitol Hill Cmnty Fndt 2008. emily@ccpk.org

G

GUTHRIE JR, Harvey Henry (Mich) 1486 Old Telegraph Rd, Fillmore CA 93015 **Ret 1995-** B Santa Paula CA 1924 s Harvey & Emma. BA Missouri Vlly Coll 1944; UTS 1946; STB GTS 1949; STM GTS 1953; ThD GTS 1958. D 6/21/1947 P 11/27/1948 Bp Charles K Gilbert. m 12/29/1945 Doris Mignonette Guthrie c 4. R S Andr's Ch Ann Arbor MI 1985-1995; R St. Andr's Ch Ann Arbor MI 1985-1995; Prof/Dn EDS 1985-1995; Prof/Dn EDS Cambridge MA 1958-1985; Tutor/Instr GTS New York NY 1950-1958; Tutor/Instr The GTS New York NY 1950-1958, Fell and Tutor, Instr 1950-1958; Vic S Fran Assisi And S Martha White Plains NY 1947-1950; Vic St. Martha's Ch White Plains NY 1947-1950; Stndg Com Dio Michigan Detroit MI 1989-1995; Dep GC Dio Massachusetts Boston MA 1973-1982. Auth, "Theol as Thanksgiving," *Theol as Thanksgiving*, Seabury Press, 1981; Auth, "Israel's Sacr Songs," *Israel's Sacr Songs*, Seabury Press, 1966; Auth, "God & Hist in the OT," *God & Hist in the OT*, Seabury Press, 1961. Assn of Theol Schools in the US and Can - Presi 1980-1982. Hon Cn Dio Los Angeles 2013; DD EDS 1985.

GUTHRIE, Suzanne Elizabeth (NCal) 31 Oriole Drive, 105 Federal Hill Road, Woodstock NY 12498 B Hempstead NY 1951 d James & Lois. BA GW 1973; MTS Oblate TS 1979. Trans 10/22/2003 Bp Mark Sean Sisk. m 10/16/1995 William C Consiglio c 4. S Jn's Epis Ch Kingston NY 2015; Res P CHS 2007-2013; Chapl Epis Ch At Cornell Ithaca NY 2003-2007; CE Mssnr Ch Of The H Cross Kingston NY 1998-2000; Dio New York New York NY 1997-1998; Pstr S Anne's Ch Washingtonville NY 1993-1998; Pstr Hudson Vlly Mnstrs New Windsor NY 1993-1996; Pstr Assoc Tri-Cnty Epis Area Mnstry 1992-1993; Guesthouse Admin Asst H Cross Monastary W Pk NY 1990-1991; Asst Ch Of S Mart Davis CA 1984-1986. Auth, "Gr's Window: Entering the Seasons of Pryr," Ch Pub, 2008; Auth, "Praying the Hours," Cowley, 2000. Ord of S Ben, Camaldolese Oblate 1983; Res Comp, CHS 2007.

GUTHRIE, William Anthony (Nwk) 2812 Sequoyah Drive, Haines City FL 33844 B Bartica GY 1949 s Charles & Latchmin. LTh U of The W Indies 1972; DIT Codrington Coll 1974; BA U of The W Indies 1974; DMin VTS 1986. Trans 2/1/1980 Bp Robert Bruce Hall. m 6/24/1977 Elizabeth Guthrie c 3. Ret Chr Epis Ch E Orange NJ 1993-2011; R S Cyp's Ch San Francisco CA 1989-1990; Vic Trin Epis Ch Charlottesvlle VA 1980-1988; Serv Ch of W Indies 1974-1980. Auth, "Transformed and Renewed," *Pub*, Outskirts Press, Inc., 2012; Auth, "Bartica–Gateway to the Interior of Guyana," *Pub*, Outskirts Press, Inc., 2008; Auth, "Stwdshp in the Loc Ch," *Unpublished*, Unpub. Diss., VTS, 1986. NAACP 1985; Natl Geographic Soc 1980; NOEL 1987; UBE 1995. Fllshp Lily Endwmt Grant 2003; Arthur Lichtenberger Awd Trin & St. Phil's Cathd 2001; Bp Allin Fllshp PBp's Off 1987.

✠ **GUTIERREZ, The Rt Rev Daniel** (Pa) 601 Montano Rd. N.W., Albuquerque NM 87107 **Dio Pennsylvania Philadelphia PA 2016-** B Albuquerque NM 1964 s George & Ramona. MTS S Norberts Coll; BA U of New Mex 1987; MPA U of New Mex 1993. D 6/7/2008 Bp William Carl Frey P 12/12/2008 Bp Jim Mathes Con 7/16/2016 for Pa. m 2/12/1997 Suzanne F Gutierrez c 1. Cn Dio The Rio Grande Albuquerque 2011-2016; S Mich And All Ang Ch Albuquerque NM 2010-2011. dgutierrez@diopa.org

GUTIERREZ, Hayr (PR) Villas De Castro, Calle 25 Ee-19, Caguas PR 00726 Puerto Rico **Asst Cristo Rey Caguas PR 2000-** B Buga CO 1952 s Delfin & Herlyna. AA Pontificia Borivariana U 1977; BA U of Javeriana 1978; Lic U of La Salle 1979; MA U of Javeriana 1980; MA U of La Salle 1980; GTF 2005. Rec 10/27/1992 as Priest Bp Orris George Walker Jr. m 4/7/1984 Iris N Padin. Vicario San Judas Tadeo Ch Aibonito Puerto Rico 2000-2001; Vic San Juda Tadeo Aibonito PR 1998-1999; Dio Puerto Rico Trujillo Alto PR 1998; Int S Cecilia's 1997-1998; Assistnat San Bartolome Lares PR 1995-1996; Asst San Andres Mayaguez PR 1994-1995; Ch Of The Redeem Astoria NY 1992-1993; Asst 1992-1993. Charman Cath Epis Sch Inc. 2004.

GUTIERREZ, Janssen J (Tex) 895 Palm Valley Rd, Ponte Vedra FL 32081 **Iglesia San Mateo Houston TX 2016-** B Valencia Venezuela 1972 s Claudio & Maria Petrona. Logos Chr Coll; Tecnologico de Musica 1995; Universidad Tecnológica del Centro 1998; BTh Logos Chr Coll 2003; MA Logos Chr Coll 2007. D 8/9/2009 P 8/9/2009 Bp Samuel Johnson Howard. m 10/20/1995 Mariely J Coronel c 2. P-in-c San Francisco Del Campo Jacksonville FL 2010-2016.

GUTIERREZ, Jorge Martin (Roch) 48 Whitcomb Road, Boxborough MA 01719 B Habana CU 1947 s Francisco & Rissett. BA W Virginia U 1969; VTS 1971; MDiv GTS 1973. D 6/7/1973 P 2/25/1974 Bp Wilburn Camrock Campbell. m 7/6/1974 Carolyn T Taylor c 1. Stndg Com on Nomin Epis Ch USA Untd States 2006-2008; Ch Deploy Bd Mem Epis Ch USA Untd States 1998-2003; Stndg Cmsn Mnstry Dvlpmt Epis Ch USA Untd States 1998-2000; Coun Dvlpmt Mnstry Epis Ch USA Untd States 1996-1997; R Chr Ch Corning NY 1991-2009; Stewart Pk Hsng Corp Corning NY 1991-2008; Fndr S Ptr's Haven Hmless Fams Shltr Clifton NJ 1986-1991; R S Ptr's Ch Clifton NJ 1981-1991; Vic Gr Epis Ch Elkins WV 1975-1981; Ch Of The Gd Shpd Elkins WV 1975-1976; Cur The Ch of S Edw The Mtyr New York NY 1973-1975; Dio Newark, Stndg Com Dio Newark Newark NJ 1990-1991. Bp's Cert of Merit for Outstanding Serv Dio Newark 1987.

GUTIERREZ, Jorge Pablo (SeFla) 1003 Allendale Rd, West Palm Beach FL 33405 **Chapl JFK Med Cntr Atlantis Fl. 2013-** B Jovellanos Cuba 1951 s Pablo & Catalina. Electronics Palm Bch St Coll 1972; Bus Barry U 1991; Dioc Sch of Chr Stds 2012. D 11/23/2013 Bp Leo Frade. m 5/14/2005 Martha C Delgado c 2.

GUTIERREZ-DUARTE, Edgar A (Mass) 32 Franklin Ave, Chelsea MA 02150 **Vic S Lk's/San Lucas Epis Ch Chelsea MA 2007-** B Bogotá, Colombia 1953 BA Dominican Coll 1986; MA Antioch U 1988; MS Rutgers The St U of New Jersey 1999; MDiv GTS 2003. D 6/7/2003 P 12/14/2003 Bp John Palmer Croneberger. Assoc R S Paul's Epis Ch Paterson NJ 2003-2007.

GUTWEIN, Martin (NJ) 527 N 2nd St, Camden NJ 08102 B San Diego CA 1945 s Martin & Martha. BA Hobart and Wm Smith Colleges 1967; MA EDS 1969; MDiv EDS 1972. D 6/24/1972 Bp Robert Rae Spears Jr P 12/24/1972 Bp Albert Wiencke Van Duzer. m 5/27/1978 Toni Gutwein c 3. Dio New Jersey Trenton NJ 1984-1994; S Wilfrid's Ch Camden NJ 1983-1993; Ch Of Our Sav Camden NJ 1983; R S Paul's Ch Camden NJ 1980-2015; Asst Chr Ch New Brunswick NJ 1972-1978.

GUY, Kenneth Gordon (FdL) N11052 Norway Ln, Tomahawk WI 54487 B Auburn NY 1943 s Kenneth & Ann. BA Coll of Wooster 1966; Harvard DS 1969; JD U of Wisconsin 1969; MDiv Nash 1988. D 5/6/1988 P 11/1/1988 Bp Roger John White. m 12/26/1964 Barbara R Guy c 3. R S Ptr's Ch (S Mary's Chap) Ripon WI 2001-2007; R S Mary's Chap Wautoma WI 2001; R S Mart's Ch Milwaukee WI 1990-2001; Asst Trin Ch Milwaukee WI 1988-1990.

GUZMAN, Pedro S (NJ) 7709 Piersanti Ct, Pennsauken NJ 08109 **Ch Of S Andr The Apos Camden NJ 2004-, 1998-2003** B DO 1954 s Pedro & Luz. Rec 11/1/1996 as Priest Bp David Andres Alvarez-Velazquez. m 8/9/1996 Odeida D Dalmasi c 3. Santa Teresa de avila Chicago IL 2003-2004; Vic Aibonito In Puerto Rico 1997-1998; Serv RC Ch 1979-1996.

GUZMAN VELEZ, Francisco Inocencio (PR) PO Box 902, Saint Just PR 00978 Puerto Rico **Dio Puerto Rico Trujillo Alto PR 2012-** B Santo Domingo DR 1972 s Porfirio & Altagracia. Bachiller Filosofia Letra Universidad Cntrl de Bayamon 2001; Maestria en Divinidad Universidad Cntrl de Bayamon 2004. Rec 10/29/2011 as Priest Bp David Andres Alvarez-Velazquez. m 6/30/2011 Yahaira De Leon Abreu.

GWIN, Connor Brindley (SwVa) 1002 1st St SW, Roanoke VA 24016 **Dio SW Virginia Roanoke VA 2015-** B Charlottesville VA 1990 s John & Pamela. BA Jas Madison U 2012; MDiv VTS 2015. D 6/6/2015 Bp Shannon Sherwood Johnston P 12/5/2015 Bp Mark Bourlakas. m 4/4/2014 Emma Leigh Cobb. cgwin@dioswva.org

GWIN JR, Lawrence Prestidge (Tex) Po Box 404, Bay City TX 77404 **Chr Ch Matagorda TX 2004-** B Houston TX 1959 s Lawrence & Rebekah. BA U of Texas 1982; JD U of Mississippi 1985. D 2/3/2002 Bp Leopoldo Jesus Alard P 12/21/2002 Bp Don Adger Wimberly. m 10/2/2004 Roseanne Ritchie-Fusaro. S Thos Ch Wharton TX 2002-2003.

GWINN, Thomas Wallace (Alb) PO Box 286, North Stratford NH 03590 B Sioux City IA 1941 s Ira & Hope. BA Morningside Coll 1963; U of Wisconsin 1964; STB Ya Berk 1968. D 6/22/1968 P 12/20/1968 Bp Gordon V Smith. m 8/12/1967 Edith T Gwinn c 5. Dn Dio Albany Greenwich NY 1991-1997; Dio Albany Albany NY 1989-1993; R S Mk's Ch Malone NY 1986-2005; Gr Epis Ch Chas City IA 1975-1986; P-in-c S Andr's Epis Ch Waverly IA 1975-1986; Other Cler Positions Dio Iowa DesMoines IA 1970-1986; Ch Of S Thos Algona IA 1968-1975; P-in-c Trin Ch Emmetsburg IA 1968-1975; Secy Dioc Coun Dio Iowa Des Moines IA 1983-1986.

GWYN III, Lewis R. (CFla) 5855 39th Ln, Vero Beach FL 32966 **Chapl Indn River Vol Ambulance Squad 2004-** B Bronxville NY 1942 s Lewis & Priscilla. BA U So 1969. D 12/14/2002 Bp John Wadsworth Howe. m 9/1/1968 Clare Gwyn c 2. D Trin Epis Ch 2012; D Trin Ch Vero Bch FL 2008-2012; D S Aug Of Cbury Epis Ch Vero Bch FL 2003-2008.

GWYN, Roxane S (NC) 115 Sherman Pines Drive, Fuquay-Varina NC 27526 **Vic Trin Ch Fuquay Varina NC 2011-** B Griffin GA 1953 d Louis & Sybil. BA U NC 1974; MDiv Duke DS 2007; STM GTS 2010. D 6/19/2010 P 3/8/2011 Bp Michael B Curry. m 6/12/1976 Owen Gwyn c 2. rox6@mac.com

GWYNN, Caron A. (WA) St. Timothy's Episcopal Church, 3601 Alabama Avenue, S.E., Washington DC 20020 B Washington DC 1954 d Alverse & Dorothy. BS Towson St U 1977; BS Towson U 1977; MDiv VTS 2006. D 6/10/2006 P 1/20/2007 Bp John Bryson Chane. R S Tim's Epis Ch Washington DC 2011-2017; The Ch Of The Ascen Lexingtn Pk MD 2010-2011; Asst S Marg's Ch Washington DC 2006-2009.

GWYNNE, Geoff Carrington (Tex) 1104 Peregrine Dr, Friendswood TX 77546 **R Ch Of The Gd Shpd Friendswood TX 2012-** B Burlingame CA 1960 s Samuel & Nancy. BA Mia 1982; Cert TESM 1984; U So 1986; U So 1986; MDiv Ya Berk 1988. D 6/11/1988 Bp James Russell Moodey P 4/15/1989 Bp Arthur Williams Jr. m 2/10/1990 Karen N Gwynne c 3. Vic Chr the King Epis Ch Harrisonburg VA 2009-2012; Dio Virginia Richmond VA 2004-2009; P-in-c Chr Epis Ch Aspen CO 2003; Vic H Apos Epis Ch Englewood CO 1995-2002; Assoc Chr Epis Ch Denver CO 1989-2002; D-In-Trng Chr Ch Epis Hudson OH 1988-1989; Chapl The U So 1984-1986; Yth Min St. Barn Epis Ch 1982-1983.

H

HAACK, Christopher Allyn (Minn) 877 Jessie St, Saint Paul MN 55130 B Rochester MN 1968 s Kenneth & Theld Ann. D 12/11/2008 Bp James Louis Jelinek.

HAACK, Marcus John (Ia) **Deacn Trin Ch Iowa City IA 2015-** B Cedar Rapids, IA 1951 s Richard & Dorothy. D 12/19/2015 Bp Alan Scarfe. m 6/26/1999 Barbara Ann Custis c 3. mhaack@trinityic.org

HAAS, Kirk Bayard (WVa) 112 South Walnut St., Morgantown WV 26501 B Bethlehem PA 1944 s Harold & Adele. BA Leh 1966; BS Leh 1967; Gordon-Conwell TS 1976; MDiv EDS 1978; DMin Pittsburgh TS 1996. D 6/10/1978 Bp Morris Fairchild Arnold P 6/7/1979 Bp John Bowen Coburn. m 8/31/1968 Charlotte Haas c 3. R Trin Ch Morgantown WV 1991-2008; R Ch Of The H Sprt Erie PA 1981-1991; Asst All SS' Epis Ch Belmont MA 1978-1981; Chapl Mclean (Ma) Hosp Belmont MA 1978-1981; Area Dir Young Life Cmpgn Boston MA 1968-1972.

HAAS, Margaret Ann (Mich) 2923 Roundtree Blvd Apt A2, Ypsilanti MI 48197 **Dio Michigan Detroit MI 2006-** B Rochester NY 1943 d John & Marie. Estrn Michigan U; S Johns Prov Sem; SWTS; Whitaker TS; BA Skidmore Coll 1965. D 6/28/1986 Bp Henry Irving Mayson P 9/22/1990 Bp R aymond Stewart Wood Jr. Asst Chr Ch Dearborn MI 2003-2006; Supply P Dio Michigan Detroit MI 1996-2003; Asst Ch Of The H Sprt Livonia MI 1991-1996; Par Growth Pstr S Mart Ch Detroit MI 1989-1991; Asst Trin Epis Ch Farmington MI 1986-1989.

HAAS, Michael James (NI) 2006 E Broadway, Logansport IN 46947 **Prof of Philisophy & Relgigion (P-t) Franklin Pierve U|Rindge NH 2004-** B Kalamazoo MI 1942 s Terrence & Jane. BA H Cross Sem 1965; MA S Johns Sem 1969; MS U MI 1972; MDiv SWTS 1992. Rec 3/1/1992 as Priest Bp Francis Campbell Gray. m 5/28/1971 Mary F Haas c 6. Trin Epis Ch Logansport IN 1992-2003.

HAASE, Sylvia Anne (Oly) Po Box 208, Vaughn WA 98394 **D - Vol S Hugh Of Lincoln Allyn WA 2002-** B Tacoma WA 1939 d Henry & Minna. BA Whittier Coll 1962; MA U CO 1966; Universitat Hamburg Hamburg DE 1972. D 11/30/2002 Bp Sanford Zangwill Kaye Hampton.

HABECKER, Elizabeth A (Los) Po Box 743, Bristol RI 02809 B Montclair NJ 1941 d Alfred & Elizabeth. BA Ohio Nthrn U 1965; MDiv GTS 1977. D 6/11/1977 Bp George E Rath P 12/16/1977 Bp Frederick Barton Wolf. m 4/22/1976 John Christian Habecker c 3. R S Mk's Par Downey CA 2000-2013; S Columba's Par Camarillo CA 1999-2000; Congrl Dvlpmt Dio Los Angeles Los Angeles CA 1998-2000; Dio Los Angeles Los Angeles CA 1997-1999; Vic S Clare Of Assisi Rancho Cucamonga CA 1990-1998; Assoc S Aug By-The-Sea Par Santa Monica CA 1989; R S Paul's Epis Ch Santa Paula CA 1984-1988; Asst S Jn's Memi Ch Ramsey NJ 1983-1984; Assoc Chr Ch Ridgewood NJ 1982-1984; Vic Ch Of The Incarn W Milford NJ 1980-1983; Vic S Ann's Epis Ch Windham Windham ME 1977-1980.

HABECKER, John Christian (Nwk) 47 Av Sur #723 Colonia Flor Blanca, Apartado (01) 274, San Salvador CA 000 **P-in-c S Jn's Ch Dover NJ 2008-; Non-par 1988-** B Ancon EC 1943 s John & Ann. BA U of Maryland 1975; MDiv GTS 1978. D 10/23/1977 Bp Robert Claflin Rusack P 5/1/1978 Bp Frederick Barton Wolf. m 4/22/1976 Elizabeth A Habecker. Exec Coun Appointees New York NY 2005-2008; S Raphaels Ch San Rafael CA 1996; R S Paul's Epis Ch Santa Paula CA 1984-1987; Int S Lk's Ch Hope NJ 1984; Vic Ch Of The Incarn W Milford NJ 1980-1984; Vic S Ann's Epis Ch Windham Windham ME 1977-1980.

HABERKORN, Violet M(arie) (Ind) 5045 W 15th Street, Speedway IN 46224 **Hospice Vol Vstng Nurse Serv Indianapolis IN 2007-** B Peoria IL 1954 d Paul & Emma. BSW Illinois St U 1976; MDiv SWTS 1984. D 6/17/1989 Bp Frank Tracy Griswold III P 4/6/1991 Bp Arthur Williams Jr. Chapl Wishard Memi Hosp 2005-2006; R S Johns Ch Indianapolis IN 2000-2004; Pstrl Assoc S Paul's Ch Akron OH 1992-2000; R S Mk's Epis Ch Wadsworth OH 1991-1997.

HABERSANG, Paul Matthew (Vt) 605 Getz Rd, Williamstown VT 05679 **Chr Ch Montpelier VT 2011-** B Meriden CT 1961 s Ralph & Susan. BS Quinnipiac U 1984; MDiv GTS 2008. D 6/14/2008 P 12/20/2008 Bp Andrew Donnan Smith. c 2. S Jas Ch Glastonbury CT 2008-2011. Brookhaven Treatment Cntr, Bd Trst 2016.

HABIBY, Samir Jamil (Ga) 24 Sawyers Crossing Rd, Swanzey NH 03446 **Spec Asst to Angl Bp in Jerusalem Dio Jerusalem Jerusalem 2007-** B Haifa IL 1933 s Judge Jamil & Mary. Epis TS in Kentucky; Ibrahim U Eg 1953; BA Phillips U 1955; MDiv CDSP 1958. D 6/29/1958 Bp Henry H Shires P 1/1/1959 Bp James Albert Pike. m 4/8/1972 Kathryn S Habiby c 5. Assoc Epis Cmnty Ft Stewart US-A Post 1995-2000; S Phil's Ch Hinesville Hinesville GA 1995-1998; P-in-c Trin-S Mich's Ch Fairfield CT 1993-1995; Int S Paul's Ch Riverside CT 1991-1992; Int S Andr's Ch Meriden CT 1990-1991; S Ptr's Epis Ch Monroe CT 1988-1989; Int Trin Ch Branford CT 1988; Int Rep Un Angl Consult Coun 1985-1988; Spec Envoy Archbp Of Cbury on Hostage Hmntrn Issues 1984-1988; Epis Ch Cntr New York NY 1978-1988; R S Anselm Of Cbury Par Garden Grove CA 1970-1978; Chapl (Cmdr) USN 1966-1992; R S

Marg's Epis Ch So Gate CA 1964-1966; Asst Chapl UCLA 1961-1962; Assoc H Faith Par Inglewood CA 1960-1961; S Lk's Epis Ch Jolon CA 1958-1960; Vic S Matt's Ch San Ardo CA 1958-1960; Bd Mgrs All SS Ch Ivoryton CT 1992-1995; Chair Prog Grp Cmncatns Dio Los Angeles Los Angeles CA 1973-1976; Fndr/Dir S Anselm's Cross-Cultural Cmnty Ctr Garden Grove CA 1970-1978. Auth, "Patient Care Coordntng Team," *An Adj To Htlh Serv*; Auth, "Middle E, Lebanon, Uganda," *Jerusalem For Spec Affrs Updates Dps & Hostage Issues*, Pbfwr/Pub; Auth, "Vol Grp Stds Mnstry To Yth: 4 Part Prog, Mssy Wk Of Dio Jerusalem," *Lebanon & Syria*. Bro Of S Andr; Chapl Ord S Jn Jerusalem. LHD ETSKy 1986; Cn Cesarea Cathd S Geo.

HACKBARTH, Michael George (FdL) **D St Paul's Epis Cathd Fond Du Lac WI 2005-** B Fond du Lac WI 1949 s George & Beverly. BA Marian Coll of Fond Du Lac 1990. D 8/27/2005 Bp Russell Edward Jacobus. m 6/17/1972 Debra Lynn Hackbarth c 2.

HACKER, Craig A (Me) Po Box 775, Waddington NY 13694 **S Ptr's Epis Ch Bridgton ME 2011-** B Albany NY 1951 MDiv Oblate TS. D 9/7/2002 Bp Daniel William Herzog P 3/23/2003 Bp David John Bena. m 4/6/1975 Linda Louise Hacker c 2. Vic S Paul's Ch Waddington NY 2002-2008.

HACKER, David (Spok) PO Box 356, Zillah WA 98953 **S Mich's Epis Ch Yakima WA 2016-** B Swickely 1958 s Willis & Grace. BS U Denv 1982; MDiv CDSP 1987. D 10/16/2011 P 6/10/2012 Bp James E Waggoner Jr. c 3. Chr Epis Ch Zillah WA 2012-2016.

HACKETT, Ann Riley (At) Po Box 169, Morrow GA 30260 B Paris TN 1933 d James & Wilna. AA Chr Coll For Wmn 1953. D 11/14/1992 Bp Sanford Zangwill Kaye Hampton. c 4. D S Aug Of Cbury Morrow GA 1999-2002; D S Mary's Ch S Paul MN 1993-1997.

HACKETT JR, Charles Dudleigh (At) 10298 Big Cnoe, Big Canoe GA 30143 **Epis Ch Of The H Fam Jasper GA 2001-; Prof Emory U 1973-** B Binghamton NY 1937 s Charles & Mildred. BA Br 1958; STB Ya Berk 1964; PhD Emory U 1975. D 6/20/1964 P 1/1/1965 Bp Lauriston L Scaife. m 1/4/1987 Deborah Freudenthal c 2. Dir of Angl Stds Emory U 1973-2006; S Barth's Epis Ch Atlanta GA 1971-1974, 1967-1971, R 1967-1971; Cur S Jas' Ch Batavia NY 1964-1966. Co-Auth, "Preaching the Revised Common Lectionary," Abingdon Press, 2007; Auth, "Entrance Rites, Confessions of Sin, and Identity in the 16th Century," *Angl and Epis Hist*, 2004; Co-Auth, "The Lord Be w You," OSL Pub, 1990; Ed, "Wmn of the Word," Susan Hunter Press, 1983. Amer Assn Of Mar And Fam Therapists 1971.

HACKETT, Christopher James (ETenn) 413 Cumberland Ave, Knoxville TN 37902 **P S Jn's Epis Cathd Knoxville TN 2012-** B Kingsport TN 1974 s David & Doris. BA The U of Tennessee at Chattanooga 2000; MDiv Sewanee: The U So, TS 2012; MDiv The TS at The U So 2012. D 5/20/2012 P 12/1/2012 Bp George Young III. m 7/21/2001 Jennifer Nell Hackett c 3. chackett@stjohnscathedral.org

HACKETT, David Robert (ETenn) 7994 Prince Dr., Ooltewah TN 37363 B New Madrid MO 1941 s James & Ella. BS U of Tennessee 1967; MDiv Sewanee: The U So, TS 1970. D 6/28/1970 Bp William Evan Sanders P 5/1/1971 Bp William F Gates Jr. m 9/3/1961 Doris Kay Hackett c 4. Int Chr Ch Epis S Pittsburg TN 2010-2011; Int St Jas Epis Ch at Knoxville Knoxville TN 2008-2009; S Jn's Epis Ch Charleston WV 2007-2008; Int Chr and St. Lk's Ch Nofolk VA 2005-2007; Chr Ch Epis Hudson OH 2003-2005; Int St Jas Epis Ch and Sch Alexandria LA 2002-2003; R S Tim's Ch Signal Mtn TN 1989-2001; R S Steph's Epis Ch Oak Ridge TN 1985-1989; R H Trin Ch Memphis TN 1978-1985; P-in-c S Chris's Ch Kingsport TN 1974-1978; Dio Tennessee Nashville TN 1971-1978; P-in-c H Innoc' Trenton TN 1971-1974; S Lk's Epis Ch Jackson TN 1971-1974; S Thos The Apos Humboldt TN 1971-1974; D Calv Ch Memphis TN 1970-1971. Auth, *Selected Sermons*. Cmnty Cross of Nails.

HACKETT, Michael George (La) **D S Augustines Ch Metairie LA 2002-; Volenteer Chapl Louisiana St Penit 1992-** B Decatur IL 1939 s George & Bessie. BA NE Louisiana U 1961. D 2/23/2002 Bp Charles Edward Jenkins III. m 1/1/2001 Janice Ann Dugas Hackett c 2.

HACKLER WSHS, Wendy Kaye Douglas (Az) 10486 N. Autumn Hill Lane, Tucson AZ 85737 B Excelsior Sprgs MO 1952 d Kenneth & Betty. CPE 1986; W Missouri Sch of Mnstry 1992. D 1/18/1992 Bp John Clark Buchanan. m 9/16/1972 Frederick R Hackler c 1. Chapl Carondelet St. Jos's Hosp Tucson AZ 2008-2017; Chapl Casa de la Luz Hospice 2006-2008; Chapl Carondelet St. Jos's Hosp Tucson AZ 1998-2006; Chapl Chld Mercy Hosp KS City MO 1992-1993; Ch Of The Gd Shpd Kansas City MO 1992-1993. Arizona Chapl Assn; AEHC; ACPE; NAAD.

HACKLEY, Staley Paxton (Lex) 106 S Maxwell St, Ulysses KS 67880 **Died 11/7/2015** B Amarillo TX 1933 s Frank & Abbie. BS W Texas A&M U 1954; MTh SMU 1959. D 3/17/1964 P 7/19/1964 Bp Russell T Rauscher. m 5/1/2011 Joan Farnsley Farnsley Tribble c 1. Mssnr S Jn's Ch Ulysses KS 2003-2015; R Chr Epis Ch Harlan KY 1995-2003; Trin Ch Quanah TX 1988-1995; Vic Gr Ch Vernon TX 1988-1994; Non-par 1967-1987; Asst Trin Cathd Omaha NE 1963-1965. Oblate Ord Julian Of Norwich.

HACKNEY, Lisa E (Chi) 2954 Essex Rd, Cleveland Heights OH 44118 **Sub-Dn Cathd Of S Jas Chicago IL 2015-; Exec Com Grtr Cleveland Congregations Cleveland OH 2011-; Chair, Cmsn for Racial Understanding Dio Ohio 2007-; Epis Cmnty Serv Dvlpmt Coun Mem Dio Ohio 2007-; Vice-Pres , Bd Trst InterAct Cleveland Cleveland OH 2007-; Epis Cmnty Serv, Dvlpmt Coun Mem Dio Ohio Cleveland 2007-, Mem, Mssn Strtgy T/F 2006-2007** B Omaha NE 1963 d William & Erna. Wayne 1985; BA NE Illinois U 2000; MDiv SWTS 2003. D 6/21/2003 P 12/20/2003 Bp Bill Persell. m 5/16/2009 Alan C James c 4. Assoc R S Paul's Epis Ch Cleveland OH 2006-2014; Mem, Dioc Coun Dio Chicago 2004-2006; Cur The Ch Of The H Sprt Lake Forest IL 2003-2006; Chair, Dioc Coun Unity Cmsn Dio Chicago Chicago IL 2005-2006. Cantor's Awd Seabury-Wstrn Theol Sem 2003.

HADAWAY, Elizabeth Leigh (WVa) 913 Briarwood Ct, Morgantown WV 26505 B Harrisonburg VA 1968 d Walter & Ruth. BA U of Virginia 1990; MFA U NC--Greensboro 1993; MA U of Virginia 1995; MTS VTS 2000; Angl Stds Cert. VTS 2015. D 12/5/2015 P 6/4/2016 Bp William Michie Klusmeyer. m 5/20/2000 Michael Miller Hadaway. D in charge Chr Ch Fairmont WV 2016, P-in-c 2016-. Auth, "Fire Baton," U of Arkansas Press, 2006. hadawayelizabeth@gmail.com

HADAWAY JR, Michael Miller (WVa) PO Box 205, Kingsville MD 21087 **R Trin Ch Morgantown WV 2010-; Mem Liturg & Mus Com Dio Maryland MD 2007-** B Washington DC 1970 s Michael & Vivian. BA Salisbury U 1993; MDiv VTS 2000. D 9/9/1999 Bp John Henry Smith P 6/10/2000 Bp Claude Charles Vache. m 5/20/2000 Elizabeth Leigh Palmer. R S Jn's Ch Kingsville MD 2005-2010; Mem Exec Bd Dio Virginia VA 2002-2004; R Varina Epis Ch Henrico VA 2001-2005; Cur Trin Ch Parkersburg WV 2000-2001.

HADDAD, Mary E (Eur) 4 Rue Henri Duchene, Paris 75015 France **The Amer Cathd of the H Trin Paris 75008 2015-** B Windsor ON Canada 1953 d Nicholas & Adele. BA U of Windsor 1974; MDiv GTS 2000. D 6/10/2000 P 1/28/2001 Bp Frederick Houk Borsch. Convoc of Epis Ch in Europe Paris 2015; S Jas Epis Ch Kamuela HI 2014; H Innoc' Epis Ch Lahaina HI 2013; Dio Los Angeles Los Angeles CA 2011; All SS Par Beverly Hills CA 2010-2011, 1993-1997; Cn Gr Cathd San Francisco CA 2007-2009; Sr Assoc R S Barth's Ch New York NY 2000-2007; Assoc St. Barth Ch New York NY 2000-2007.

HADDIX JR, Theodore Ray (Va) 3825 Indianview Ave, Cincinnati OH 45227 B Parkersburg WV 1948 s Theodore & Mary. BA W Virginia U 1974; MDiv VTS 1977; ThM UTS Richmond 1979. D 6/8/1977 P 6/1/1978 Bp Robert Poland Atkinson. m 8/14/1976 Cecelia Haddix c 2. Abingdon Epis Ch White Marsh VA 1997-2000; Indn Hill Ch Cincinnati OH 1990-1997; R Indn Hill Epis Presb Ch White Marsh VA 1990-1997; Vic Ch Of The Creator Mechanicsvlle VA 1979-1986; S Thos Epis Ch Wht Sphr Spgs WV 1977-1978; Vic S Thos' Ch Richmond VA 1977-1978. AAPC.

HADDOCK, Gene Moore (La) 1122 W. Chestnut St, Denison TX 75020 **Died 9/6/2016** B Denison TX 1938 s Olvis & Mary. BS Texas Wesl 1961; MDiv Nash 1964; S Georges Coll Jerusalem IL 1982. D 6/21/1964 P 12/21/1964 Bp Chandler W Sterling. R S Aug's Ch Baton Rouge LA 1990-1993; Vic Ascen And S Mk Bridgeport TX 1986-1990; Vic S Thos Ch Jacksboro TX 1986-1988; Dio Ft Worth Ft Worth TX 1970-1990; S Simon Of Cyrene Epis Ch Ft Worth TX 1969-1988; Vic S Anth's Ch Alvarado TX 1969-1970; S Alb's Epis Ch Vicksburg MS 1967-1969; Vic S Mary's Ch Vicksburg MS 1967-1969; Vic S Eliz's Mssn Collins MS 1966-1968; S Steph's Ch Columbia MS 1966-1968; Cur S Jn's Ch Butte MT 1964-1966.

HADDOX, Jason M (Okla) 1512 Vine St, Norman OK 73072 **R S Mich's Epis Ch Norman OK 2016-** B Baytown TX 1969 s Ronald & Anna. BA Rice U 1992; MDiv Epis TS of the SW 2000; MA Drew U 2007. D 6/17/2000 Bp Claude Edward Payne P 6/26/2001 Bp Don Adger Wimberly. m 6/4/1994 Shannon L Haddox. R S Aug Of Cbury Ch Augusta GA 2010-2016; S Ptr's Ch Mt Arlington NJ 2009-2010; Assoc R S Ptr's Ch Morristown NJ 2005-2009; Asst R S Paul's Ch Waco TX 2000-2003; Chapl Waco Coll Mnstry (Cbury) 2000-2003. rector@stmichaelsnorman.org

HADE, Lynn Augustine (Pa) Church of the Advent, 12 Byberry Rd, Hatboro PA 19040 **Ch Of The Adv Hatboro PA 2014-** B Ames IA 1954 d Robert & Pauline. BS Iowa St U 1981; MDiv GTS 2007. D 6/7/2008 P 2/18/2009 Bp Nathan Dwight Baxter. c 2. Assoc R Chr Ch St Michaels Par S Mich MD 2012-2014; Assoc S Jas Ch Lancaster PA 2008-2012. rectoradvent4@gmail.com

HADEN JR, Robert Lee (NC) 798 Evans Rd., Hendersonville NC 28739 B Greenville SC 1938 s Robert & Mary. BA U So 1960; MDiv VTS 1964; STM GTS 1988. D 6/18/1964 P 6/1/1965 Bp Matthew George Henry. m 6/4/1963 Mary Anne Barnes Easterling c 3. Ch Of The Ascen Hickory NC 1995-1996; Pres The Haden Inst Flat Rock NC 1994-2011; R S Jn's Epis Ch Charlotte NC 1973-1994; P-in-c S Andr's Ch Bessemer City NC 1965-1968; P-in-c Trin Ch Kings Mtn NC 1964-1968; Assoc R Trin Cathd Columbia SC 1968-1973. Auth, "Unopened Letters From God," Haden Inst, 2010; Auth, "Souls Labyrinth," Haden Inst, 1994. bobhadenconsulting@gmail.com

HADLER JR, Jacques Bauer (WA) 1736 Columbia Rd NW Apt 201, Washington DC 20009 B Washington DC 1943 s Jacques & Caryl. BA U of Wisconsin 1967; MDiv EDS 1972. D 6/17/1972 P 3/17/1973 Bp William Foreman Creighton. m 6/6/1967 Susan J Hadler c 2. Dir, Field Educ VTS Alexandria VA 1993-2010; Dir, Field Educ VTS Alexandria VA 1993-2010; P-in-c S Phil's Epis Ch Laurel MD 1992-1993; P-in-c All Souls Memi Epis Ch Washington DC 1991-1992; R S Paul's Epis Ch Piney Waldorf MD 1979-1991; P-in-c Trin Ch Manassas VA 1979; Dio Sthrn Highlands New York NY 1975-1979; Lectr S Phil Coll Kongwa Tanzania 1975-1978; Asst S Matt's Epis Ch Hyattsville MD 1972-1975; Co-Chair, Com on Racial Recon Dio Washington Washington DC 2002-2008, Chair, COM 1996-2000, 1989-2002. Auth, "Two-way Bridge: Tae Cross - Cultural Collancy at Virginia Sem," *Tchg Theol and Rel Vol. 4 No. 2,* Blackwell Pub., 2001; Auth, "Genogram of Cong," *Proceedings of the 24th Biennral Consult of rthe Asseration for Theol Field Edneaton,* 1997. Assn for Theol Field Educ 1995-2009; WECA 1972. Phi Beta Kappa 1966.

HADLEY, Arthur Clayton (SO) 1500 Shasta, McAllen TX 78504 B Rochester IN 1938 s Noah & Mary. BA Pur 1960; MDiv Bex Sem 1963; PMD Harv 1970; MA Ball St U 1973; EdD Ball St U 1974. D 6/11/1963 P 12/21/1963 Bp John P Craine. m 6/18/1960 Jane Ellen Hadley c 2. Int S Ptr & St Paul Ch Mssn TX 2011; Int Ch Of The Epiph Kingsville TX 2008-2009; Int S Ptr's Epis Ch Rockport TX 2007-2008; Int S Jas' Epis Ch Goshen IN 2006; S Jn's Ch Worthington OH 1994-2006; Dio Michigan Detroit MI 1993; Dio Missouri S Louis MO 1984-1994; S Mary's Ch Erie PA 1984; Cn To Ordnry Dio NW Pennsylvania Erie PA 1979-1984; Assoc St Johns Epis Ch Lafayette IN 1973-1979; Assoc Trin Ch Ft Wayne IN 1970-1972; P-in-c S Jas Ch New Castle IN 1969-1970; Cur Trin Ch Indianapolis IN 1968-1969; R S Steph's Epis Ch New Harmony IN 1963-1968. Auth, "Resource for Faith-Based Gardens," Alabama Coop.Ext, 2007; Auth, "Yth Wk And Cmnty Dvlpmt".

HADLEY, Douglas J (Ore) 2261 Hidden Valley Ln, Charlevoix MI 49720 B Seattle WA 1943 s Wayne & Eleanore. BA U of Washington 1965; NYU 1968; PrTS 1968; MDiv GTS 1970; ThM St Vladimirs Sem 2006. D 8/6/1970 P 5/22/1971 Bp Ivol I Curtis. m 3/28/1987 Karen Kassiani Hadley c 2. Int S Lk's Epis Ch Seattle WA 2000; R S Jas Epis Ch Portland OR 1994-2000; R S Paul's Epis Ch St Jos MI 1988-1994; R S Matt Ch Tacoma WA 1982-1988; R Emm Ch Hailey ID 1975-1982; S Thos Epis Ch Sun Vlly ID 1975-1982; Assoc Epiph Par of Seattle Seattle WA 1972-1974; Cur S Eliz's Ch Seattle WA 1970-1971; Mssy Iran 1968-1969; Mssy Iran 1965-1966.

HAENKE, Roger Alan (SanD) Rec 5/26/2017 as Priest Bp Jim Mathes.

HAFER, Joel Gilbert (WNC) 776 N. Main St., Hendersonville NC 28792 **R S Jas Epis Ch Hendersonvlle NC 2004-; Com Mem/Pres Pardee Hosp Med Ethics Com Hendersonville NC 2006-** B Kalamazoo MI 1957 s Jack & Phyllis. BA Albion Coll 1980; MDiv Sewanee: The U So, TS 1986; DMin VTS 2013. D 6/7/1986 P 2/13/1987 Bp Harry Woolston Shipps. m 4/27/2002 Anne Jackson c 4. R All SS Ch Florence SC 1996-2004; R Chr Epis Ch Dublin GA 1989-1996; Asst S Paul's Ch Albany GA 1986-1989; 1st Alt Dep to GC Dio Wstrn No Carolina Asheville NC 2015, Dn, Hendersonville Dnry 2013-2015, Dep to GC 2012-2013, Dep to GC 2012, Pres, Stndg Com 2010-2011, Stndg Com 2007-2011; Bd Mem Four Seasons Hospice Hendersonville NC 2004-2011; Bd Mem/Exec Com Florence Fam YMCA Florence SC 1998-2003; Stndg Com So Carolina Charleston SC 1998-2002; Bd Mem/Fam Selection Com Florence Area HabHum Florence SC 1996-2002; Pres, Stndg Com Dio Georgia Savannah GA 1994-1996, 1st Alt to GC 1994, Mssn Dvlpmt Cmsn 1991-1996, Stndg Com 1991-1995, Dioc Coun 1990-1996, Dn, Dublin Convoc 1989-1996; Bd Mem HabHum Dublin GA 1993-1996; Mem Rotary 1990-2013. OHC 1984.

HAGAN JR, John Ronald (WVa) 1001 Loudon Heights Rd, Charleston WV 25314 B Columbia MO 1951 s John & Dorothy. BA U of Kansas 1973; MDiv SWTS 1980. D 6/14/1980 Bp Quintin Ebenezer Primo Jr P 12/13/1980 Bp James Winchester Montgomery. m 5/29/1982 Deborah A Ballard c 1. S Matt's Ch Charleston WV 2012-2016; R Trin Ch Belleville MI 1986-2012; Dio Nthrn Michigan Marquette MI 1983-1986; S Jn's Ch Iron River MI 1983-1986; S Mk's Ch Crystal Falls MI 1983-1986; Vic S Mary-Pines Ralph 1983-1986; Cur Trin Epis Ch Wheaton IL 1980-1983.

HAGANS, Michele Victoria (WA) 1645 Myrtle St Nw, Washington DC 20012 **Cn Dio Washington Washington DC 2012-, 2010-2012** B Washignton DC 1949 d Theodore & Delores. MBA GW; BS How; M Eng How; M Div How Sch of Div; D Min How Sch of Div. D 6/9/2007 P 1/19/2008 Bp John Bryson Chane. c 3. Assoc Gr Epis Ch Silver Sprg MD 2010-2015; Ch Of The H Comf Washington DC 2007-2012. mhagans@edow.org

HAGBERG, Joe (CGC) 9101 Panama City Beach Parkway, Panama City Beach FL 32407 **R Gr Epis Ch Panama City Bch FL 2007-; Dn Reg VI Dio Cntrl Gulf Coast Pensacola FL 2014-, Ecum Off for Florida 2010-, Chairman Stwdshp and Planned Giving Cmsn 2007-2010** B Chicago IL 1951 s Joseph & Ann. S Ign Coll Prep 1969; BS Loyola U 1973; MDiv GTS 1976. D 5/27/1976 P 11/27/1976 Bp James Winchester Montgomery. R S Jas' Epis Ch Port St Joe FL 2002-2007; Int S Mary's Epis Ch Dyersburg TN 2001-2002; Int Ch Of The H Comf Montgomery AL 1999-2001; Int S Steph's Epis Ch Sherman TX 1998-1999; R Ch Of The H Cross Dallas TX 1996-1998; R Ch Of S Mich And All Ang Berwyn IL 1983-1996; Chapl German Amer Police Assn Chicago 1982-1996; Asst ReVive Cntr for Hsng and Healing Chicago IL 1981-1983; Cur Ch Of The H Fam Pk Forest IL 1978-1980; Cur S Simons Ch Arlington Hts IL 1976-1978. CCU 1976; Panama City Beaches ChmbrCom 2007; SSC 1981. gracerector@knology.net

HAGE, Raymond Joseph (WVa) 2105 Wiltshire Blvd, Huntington WV 25701 **Chr Ch Point Pleasat WV 2004-; P-in-c and Mssnr Riverbend Epis Mnstrs Point Pleasant WV 2003-** B Huntington WV 1943 s Raymond & Cathleen. U of Kentucky 1963; BBA Marshall U 1966; MA 1967; U of Virginia 1971; MA Wheeling Jesuit U 1997. D 6/14/1997 Bp John Henry Smith P 12/20/2003 Bp William Michie Klusmeyer. m 6/27/1964 Susan Lee Hage c 3. River Bend Cluster Pt Pleasant WV 2004-2015; S Jn's Ch Huntington WV 1997-2004.

HAGEN, Amelia (Me) 39 Highland Ave, Millinocket ME 04462 **Dio Maine Portland ME 2000-** B Winthrop MA 1939 d Augustine & Cecile. BA Bos 1964; MA U CA 1968; MDiv CDSP 2000. D 6/3/2000 P 12/2/2000 Bp William Edwin Swing. c 2. Ch Of The Gd Shpd Rangeley ME 2007-2009; S Andr's Ch Millinocket ME 2006-2007; Chr Ch Sausalito CA 2004-2005; Int H Trin Epis Ch Gillette WY 2002-2004; Int Trin Epis Ch Alpena MI 2001-2002; D All SS' Ch San Francisco CA 2000-2001. Int Mnstry Ntwk; Natl Assn Of Epis Int Mnstry Specialists.

HAGEN, Jim (NY) 21-15 34th Ave apt 14C, Astoria NY 11106 **P-in-c Holyrood Ch New York NY 2010-; Ret 1998-; Hon Assoc Chr And S Steph's Ch New York NY 1998-** B Akron OH 1940 s John & Wilda. BA Mt Un Coll 1962; STM EDS 1965. D 6/12/1965 Bp Beverley D Tucker P 12/21/1965 Bp Nelson Marigold Burroughs. m 8/26/1967 June Steffensen Hagen c 2. R Ch Of The Redeem Astoria NY 1982-1997; Vic S Andr's Ch Brooklyn NY 1968-1982; Asst S Ptr's Ch New York NY 1967-1968; Cur S Paul's Ch Canton OH 1965-1967. TSSF 2013.

HAGEN, Maureen (Ore) 3030 Se Bybee Blvd, Portland OR 97202 **Dio Oregon Portland OR 2011-** B Rochester NY 1956 d William & Kathleen. BA S Lawr Canton NY 1978; MIA Col 1983; Col 1985. D 9/18/2004 Bp Johncy Itty. m 6/22/1985 Robie Willard Greene. S Paul's Epis Ch Salem OR 2006-2009; Outreach Coordntr Trin Epis Cathd Portland OR 2005-2006.

HAGENBUCH, Chris Barrett (Spok) 311 South Hall St, Grangeville ID 83530 **Vic H Trin Epis Ch Grangeville ID 2011-, 2006-2008, D 2004-2005, Vic 2004-2005; Chapl (Vol) Syringa Gnrl Hosp 2005-; Epis Relief & Dvlpmt Dio Spokane Spokane WA 2012-, Co- Chair of Anti-Racism T/F 2010-, COM 2007-2010, Anti- Racism Trng Co-Chair 2007-** B Washington DC 1963 s Richard & Joan. DECO of Spokane. D 10/31/2004 P 9/1/2005 Bp James E Waggoner Jr. m 10/31/1986 Marcia Kay Hagenbuch c 2. cbhholytrinity@hotmail.com

HAGER, Marty Monroe (Va) St Thomas Episcopal Church, 8991 Brook Rd, McLean VA 22102 B Bryan TX 1953 s Roy & Gladys. BA Averett Coll 1981; MDiv SE Sem 1984; Cert Diac Formation Inst 2010. D 2/5/2011 Bp Shannon Sherwood Johnston. m 5/8/2005 Kim P Hager c 4.

HAGERMAN, Steven William (Colo) 1110 Saint Stephens Church Rd, Crownsville MD 21032 B Saint Louis MO 1951 s Morris & Mary. Cert Boston Theol Inst; BS Sthrn Illinois U 1975; MDiv CDSP 1982. D 6/19/1982 Bp Quintin Ebenezer Primo Jr P 12/18/1982 Bp James Winchester Montgomery. m 12/29/1973 Bernadette M Jaroch-Hagerman c 4. R S Steph's Ch Severn Par Crownsville MD 2004-2016; R S Mk's Epis Ch Riverside RI 1995-2004; R S Ptr's Ch Harrisonville MO 1992-1995; Assoc S Barn On The Desert Scottsdale AZ 1991-1992; R S Jas Memi Epis Ch Titusville PA 1986-1991; Chr Epis Ch Hornell NY 1985-1986; Assoc Epis Tri-Par Mnstry Dansville NY 1985-1986; Vic S Ann's Ch For The Deaf New York NY 1983-1984; Cur Ch Of The Adv Chicago IL 1982-1983. Epis Conf of the Deaf 1983; Faith and Sci Exch 2001.

HAGERTY, Stephen Pierre (NY) 84 Ehrhardt Rd, Pearl River NY 10965 **S Steph's Ch Pearl River NY 2015-** B Portland ME 1974 s Thomas & Yvonne. BA U of New Hampshire 1996; MA The New Sch for Soc Resrch 2001; MDiv Yale DS 2015; Dplma Angl Stds Yale DS 2015. D 3/7/2015 P 9/19/2015 Bp Andrew Marion Lenow Dietsche. m 7/6/2009 Frederick Nuguid.

HAGGENJOS, Babette Florence (NCal) **D St Johns Epis Ch Roseville CA 2016-** B 1955 d Lewis & Lois. Degree DeVry U; Cert Epis Sch for Deacons 2016. D 8/13/2016 Bp Barry Leigh Beisner. m 3/14/1997 Clifford R Haggenjos c 6.

HAGGENJOS JR, Clifford R (NCal) 1905 Third Street, Napa CA 94559 **R St Johns Epis Ch Roseville CA 2010-** B Evanston IL 1959 s Clifford & Elizabeth. BS Marq 1981; JD Marq 1984; MDiv SWTS 2006. D 12/17/2005 P 6/24/2006 Bp Russell Edward Jacobus. m 3/14/1997 Babette Florence Oliver c 1. Asst S Mary's Epis Ch Napa CA 2006-2010; D S Aug's Epis Ch Wilmette IL 2005-2006.

HAGLER, James Robert (ETenn) 933 S. 17th St., Newark NJ 07108 **S Andr's Ch Newark NJ 2014-, Int Vic 2005-; Monastic OHC 1977-** B Knox TN 1946 s John & Martha. MLS Geo Peabody Coll for Teachers; BA U So; SWTS 1969; MDiv Trin 1984; MDiv Trin U Tor 1984. D 10/10/1982 Bp William Evan Sanders P 5/14/1983 Bp Lewis Samuel Garnsworthy. P-in-c Angl Ch of Can Toronto ON 1978-1981.

HAGNER, Nancy (NJ) **Trin Ch Princeton NJ 2014-** D 6/4/2014 P 12/12/2014 Bp William H Stokes.

HAGOOD II, Monroe Johnson (CFla) 7745 Indian Oaks Dr Apt H114, Vero Beach FL 32966 **Asst S Aug Of Cbury Epis Ch Vero Bch FL 2009-** B Durham NC 1936 s Monroe & Ann. BA Cit 1958; MDiv VTS 1963; MS LIU 1972; MA Pepperdine U 1977. D 7/10/1963 P 2/1/1964 Bp Thomas H Wright. m 9/15/1962 Betty Hagood c 3. Int H Faith Epis Ch Port St Lucie FL 2005-2008; R S Ptr's By-The-Sea Swansboro NC 1981-2003; Off Of Bsh For ArmdF New York NY 1964-1982; Chapl US-Army (Maj) 1964-1981; S Thos' Epis Ch Bath NC 1963-1964; P Zion Epis Ch Washington NC 1963-1964.

HAGUE, Betsy (WA) 4507 Leland St, Chevy Chase MD 20815 B Cleveland OH 1944 d Joseph & Virginia. BSN Geo 1971; MSN U of Maryland 1974; CAS GTS 1993; MDiv Wesley TS 1994. D 6/11/1994 P 12/9/1995 Bp Ronald Hayward Haines. c 4. Pstr N St Vill Washington DC 2000-2001; Pstr Luther Place Memi Ch Washington DC 1996-1999; Asst Pstr Luther Place Memi Ch Washington DC 1995-2001; Prog Dir N St. Vill a Lg Shltr for homeless Wmn 1995-2001; Asst Chr Ch Prince Geo's Par Rockville MD 1994-1995.

HAGUE, Jane Milliken (WA) **S Marg's Ch Annapolis MD 2013-** B Houston TX 1955 d Walter & Anne. BS Geo 1977; MTS VTS 1984. D 6/4/2011 Bp John Bryson Chane P 1/21/2012 Bp Mariann Edgar Budde. m 5/30/1981 William Hague c 2. Ch of Our Sav Silver Sprg MD 2012-2013; S Lk's Ch Brighton Brookeville MD 2011-2012.

HAGUE, Leslie Janette (Va) 1132 N Ivanhoe St, Arlington VA 22205 **All SS Prot Epis Ch Ft Lauderdale FL 2016-** B Richmond VA 1967 d Wayne & Janet. BA W&M 1989; MDiv GTS 1998. D 6/13/1998 Bp Peter J Lee P 4/17/1999 Bp Henry Irving Louttit. m 11/23/2012 Catherine Juanita Casteel. R S Mich's Epis Ch Arlington VA 2002-2016; S Ptr's Epis Ch Savannah GA 1998-2002. leslie@allsaintsfl.org

HAGUE, Sarah Anne (NH) 23 Alice Peck Day Dr Unit 247, Lebanon NH 03766 B Troy NY 1938 d Howard & Grace. BA U of Oregon 1968; MEd U of Oregon 1977; MA U of Oregon 1987; MDiv GTS 1991. D 5/29/1991 Bp Robert Louis Ladehoff P 3/8/1992 Bp Douglas Edwin Theuner. c 4. Int Trin Ch Claremont NH 2002-2004; Assoc R Gr Ch New Bedford MA 1996-2001; Chapl Dart NH 1992-1996; Asst R S Thos Ch Hanover NH 1992-1996.

HAGUE, William (WA) 4001 Franklin St, Kensington MD 20895 B Honolulu HI 1952 s James & Henriette. DMin Hartford Sem; BA U of Virginia 1974; MDiv VTS 1980. D 6/28/1980 Bp William Edwin Swing P 7/1/1981 Bp William Benjamin Spofford. m 5/30/1981 Jane Milliken c 2. VTS Alexandria VA 2001; R Chr Ch Par Kensington MD 1988-2013; Asst Chr Ch Georgetown Washington DC 1983-1988; Dio Connecticut Meriden CT 1982-1983; Asst S Jn's Epis Ch Vernon Rock Vernon Rockville CT 1982-1983; Asst S Mk's Chap U Of Connecticut-Storrs 1982-1983; Asst S Marg's Ch Washington DC 1980-1982.

HAHN, Dorothee Elisabeth (Eur) 815 2nd Ave, New York NY 10017 **Exec Coun Appointees New York NY 2012-** B Kiel DE 1966 d Ferdinand & Elfriede. Law St Exam Ludwig-Maximilians-Universitat Munich 1991; Law St Exam Ludwig-Maximilians-Universitat Munich 1994; MTS VTS 2005. D 5/7/2005 P 11/26/2005 Bp Pierre W Whalon. Asst R, Vic of St. Bon, Augsburg and St. Ja Ch of the Ascen Munich 2006-2011.

✠ HAHN, The Rt Rev Doug (Lex) 2134 Wells Dr, Columbus GA 31906 B Lumberton NC 1952 s William & Martha. BA U GA 1974; MDiv Sthrn Bapt TS 1977; Candler TS Emory U 1980; DAS GTS 1996; The Pstr Inst 2005; DMin Sewanee: The U So, TS 2010. D 6/8/1996 P 12/14/1996 Bp Frank Kellogg Allan Con 12/15/2012 for Lex. m 8/1/1998 Kaye H Hahn c 3. Bp of Lexington Dio Lexington Lexington 2012-2016; R S Thos Epis Ch Columbus GA 1999-2012; S Clem's Epis Ch Canton GA 1996-2015; S Geo's Epis Ch Griffin GA 1996-1999; Serv Sthrn Bapt Ch 1979-1996; GC Alt Dio Atlanta Atlanta GA 2012, Convoc Dn 2003-2012. dhahn@diolex.org

HAHNE, Ruth Olive (CFla) 9260-C Sw 61st Way, Boca Raton FL 33428 **D S Mary Magd Epis Ch Pompano Bch FL 1998-** B Maplewood NJ 1933 d Richard & Eddie. Dio Sch SE Florida FL; U of Delaware 1954; BS Med Coll of Virginia 1956. D 9/11/1998 Bp John Lewis Said.

HAHNEMAN, Geoffrey (Ct) 180 Battery Park Dr, Bridgeport CT 06605 **R S Jn's Ch Bridgeport CT 2005-** B Houston TX 1954 s Kenneth & Gloria. BA Baylor U 1977; MDiv VTS 1980; PhD Oxf GB 1987. D 6/16/1980 Bp Roger Howard Cilley P 12/19/1980 Bp Frederic Cunningham Lawrence. m 2/14/2003 Lisa Dinunno c 4. Int R S Columba's Chap Middletown RI 2004-2005; Int R Ch Of The H Trin Tiverton RI 2004; Int R S Andr's Ch New London NH 2001-2003; R Trin Ch Portsmouth VA 1995-2000; Cn Cathd Ch Of S Mk Minneapolis MN 1990-1994; R All SS Epis Ch Braine-l'Alleud 1987-1990; Pro-Cathd Of The H Trin Brussels 1987-1990; Cur St. Mary Magd Oxford Engl Untd Kingdom 1984-1987; Cur The Ch Of The Adv Boston MA 1980-1984. Auth, "The Muratorian Fragment and the Origins of the NT Cn," *The Cn Debate*, Hendrickson Pub, 2002; Auth, "The Muratorian Fragment & The Dvlpmt of the Cn," Oxford Press, 1992; Auth, "More on Redating The Muratorian Fragment," *Studia Patristica*, 1988. Minneapolis Awd Mayor of Minneapolis 1994.

HAHNEMAN, Lisa (Ct) 154 Jackman Ave, Fairfield CT 06825 **R Ch of the H Sprt W Haven CT 2009-** B Washington DC 1956 d Joseph & Mary. BA CUA

1977; MEd U of Virginia 1978; PhD U of Virginia 1982; MDiv VTS 1999. D 6/10/1999 Bp David Conner Bane Jr P 12/16/1999 Bp Donald Purple Hart. m 2/14/2003 Geoffrey Hahneman. Vic S Ptr's Epis Ch Oxford CT 2005-2009; Assoc S Barn Ch Falmouth MA 2001-2005; Assoc Trin Ch Portsmouth VA 1999-2000.

HAIG, David William (Alb) PO Box 1834, Orleans MA 02653 **S Lk's Ch Mechanicville NY 2014-; R Cmnty of Jesus Orleans MA 2007-; Prncpl Contractor HHI Coporation Orleans MA 1989-** B Groton MA 1960 s John & Mary. BA Queens U 1982; MDiv EDS 2004; MDiv EDS 2004. D 6/10/2006 P 12/17/2006 Bp Daniel William Herzog. m 7/17/1982 Catherine Anne Haig c 3. Cmnty of Jesus 1983. dave.hhi@verizon.net

HAIG, Martha Karen (Oly) 4685 Taylor Ave NE, Bainbridge Island WA 98110 **Assoc S Thos Epis Ch Medina WA 2010-** B Killeen TX 1954 d Arthur & Martha. BA U of Washington 1977; MDiv CDSP 2010. D 4/17/2010 P 11/2/2010 Bp Gregory Harold Rickel. m 5/21/2005 James Louis Friedrich c 1.

HAILEY, Victor (Md) 1110 Saint Stephens Church Rd, Crownsville MD 21032 **S Steph's Ch Severn Par Crownsville MD 2016-** B Lynchburg VA 1981 s Mark & Vicki. BA S Andrews Presb Coll 2003; MDiv Sewanee: The U So, TS 2009. D 6/11/2009 P 12/11/2009 Bp Neff Powell. m 1/4/2014 Abby Lynn Thornton c 1. Asst R S Jas Ch Monkton MD 2009-2016.

HAIN, John Walter (NJ) 13 Madison Ave, Flemington NJ 08822 **D Calv Epis Ch Flemington NJ 2006-; Chapl Hunterdon Med Cntr Flemington NJ 2006-** B Woodbury NJ 1950 s Walter & Margaret. AAS Gloucester Coll 1976. D 10/31/1998 Bp Joe Doss. m 11/4/1972 Hope Ann Meiler. D Ch Of S Jn-In-The-Wilderness Gibbsboro NJ 1998-2005.

HAINES, Harry Jeffrey (WNY) 24 Cobb Ter, Rochester NY 14620 B Philadelphia PA 1940 s Harry & Ruth. AAS Monroe Cmnty Coll 1969; BA S Jn Fisher Coll 1979; MDiv Colgate Rochester Crozer DS 1988; MDiv CRDS 1988. D 6/22/1988 P 1/1/1989 Bp William George Burrill. m 4/17/1976 Katherine Anne Haines c 2. Int Gr Ch Lyons NY 2002; R Chr Ch Albion NY 1989-2002; S Geo's Ch Hilton NY 1989; Cur S Geo's Rochester NY 1988-1989. gracescottsville@frontiernet.net

HAINES, Marlene (Pa) 31 Kleyona Ave, Phoenixville PA 19460 B Troy NY 1945 d Marvin & Gloria. BA SUNY-Albany 1970; MS U of Wisconsin-Milwaukee 1973; MDiv(cl) GTS 1997. D 6/21/1997 Bp Allen Lyman Bartlett Jr P 6/6/1998 Bp Franklin Delton Turner. m 10/8/1977 Thomas C Wand c 2. Asst Ch Of S Lk And Epiph Philadelphia PA 1997-2011; Dir S Lk's Hosp Cntr Philadelphia PA 1997-2011.

HAINES III, Ralph Edward (SVa) 42 Park Ave, Newport News VA 23607 B San Francisco CA 1944 s John & Winifred. BA U Rich 1967; MDiv Crozer TS 1970. D 12/18/1971 Bp David Shepherd Rose P 12/1/1972 Bp John B Bentley. c 2. Secy of the Dio Dio Sthrn Virginia Newport News VA 1979-2010; R S Aug's Epis Ch Newport News VA 1972-2011, D-in-c 1971-1972. Man Of The Year Omega Psi Phi 1984; Outstanding Serv Awd 85 Naacp.

HAINES-MURDOCCO, Sandra (RI) 109 Old Post Rd, Wakefield RI 02879 **Assoc Chr Ch Westerly RI 2014-; COM Dio Rhode Island Providence RI 2013-, Stndg Com 2004-2012, COM 1995-2003** B Washington DC 1950 d Samuel & Toni. BS Towson U 1972; BS Towson U 1976; MA Loyola Coll 1981; MDiv GTS 1988. D 6/18/1988 P 5/20/1989 Bp Albert Theodore Eastman. m 10/18/1997 James Murdocco. Assoc S Lk's Epis Ch E Greenwich RI 2009-2010; R Ch Of The Ascen Wakefield RI 1994-2008; Chapl Garrison Forest Sch Owings Mills MD 1989-1994; Assoc S Thos' Ch Garrison Forest Owings Mills MD 1989-1994, D 1988-1989; Stndg Com Dio Maryland Baltimore MD 1992-1994.

HAIRSTON, Raleigh Daniel (EC) 3183 Kings Bay Cir, Decatur GA 30034 B Amonate VA 1934 s Samuel & Elsie. BS Bluefield St Coll Bluefield WV 1959; MSW Atlanta U Atlanta GA 1962; MA Bex Sem 1969; MA Case Wstrn Reserve U 1975; DMin Colgate Rochester Crozer DS 1978; DMin CRDS 1978. D 6/24/1970 Bp Thomas Augustus Fraser Jr P 5/9/1971 Bp John Melville Burgess. c 2. R S Mk's Ch Wilmington NC 2001-2004; Our Sav & St. Monica's Washington DC 1998-2000; Chapl S Aug's Coll Raleigh NC 1995-1998; Asst Calv Ch Washington DC 1989-1991; Vic Crummell Memi Highland Pk MI 1985-1988; Vic Dio Michigan Detroit MI 1985-1986; Asst Ch Of The Trsfg Cleveland OH 1981-1982; R Dio Sthrn Ohio Cincinnati OH 1979-1981; S Simon Of Cyrene Epis Ch Cincinnati OH 1978-1981; Asst Incarn Cleveland OH 1971-1972. Assoc Ed, "The Trial Sermon" in "Coal Camps and Castor Oil," *A Living Hist of Sthrn W Virginia*, Hometown Memories Pub Co, 2009; Assoc Ed, "The Trial Sermon in Coal Camps and Castor Oil," *A Living Hist of Sthrn W Virginia*, Hometown Memories Pub Co, 2009; Stdt, "Blacks and the Epis Ch in the Dio Ohio," *Doctor's Dissertation*, Colgate Rochester DS, 1978; Stdt, "A study of Trng,employment and Jobs for Negro HS Grads in Tampa, Florida," *Mstr's Thesis*, (Clark) Atlanta U, 1962. Interdenom Mnstr Assn; Lic Indep Clincl Soc Worker; Prtr Ecum; UBE. DSA S Aug Coll 1998; Who's Who Among Afr Americans Gale Resrch Inc 1996; Who's Who Among Black Americans Gale Resrch Inc 1994.

HAKIEL, Nicholas Edward (Ida) 1014 Wildwood St, Sultan WA 98294 B Leeds UK 1953 s Zbigniew & Olga. BA U of Lancaster Gb 1975; MA U of Durham

Gb 1976; MA Idaho St U 1991; EdS Idaho St U 1994. D 6/14/1997 P 8/13/1998 Bp John Stuart Thornton. m 11/3/1991 Barbara Robinson. Asst Ch Of Our Sav Monroe WA 1999-2009.

HALAPUA, Sione (Los) 8614 Foothill Blvd Apt 223, Sunland CA 91040 **Died 2/29/2016** B Nukualofa To Ga 1940 d Fine & Lesieli. LTh S Jn Coll Nz; CTh S Johns Bapt Coll Fj; BA Claremont Coll 1973. D 9/9/1972 P 3/17/1973 Bp Francis E I Bloy. c 2. S Simon's Par San Fernando CA 1989-1990; S Mk's Par Altadena CA 1975-2000; Ch Of The Ascen Tujunga CA 1975-1987; Cur The Ch Of The Ascen Sierra Madre CA 1974-1975.

HALBROOK, Thomas Robert (Oly) 1805 Graves Ave, Aberdeen WA 98520 **Died 7/18/2016** B Wauwautosa WI 1935 s Thomas & Rose. BD U of Missouri-Rolla 1960; MS MI SU 1962; Olympia TS 1980; MDiv CDSP 1986. D 8/3/1982 P 7/22/1986 Bp Robert Hume Cochrane. m 5/7/1960 Ramona Rose c 2. Supply P St Peters Epis Ch Seaview WA 2009-2016; R Emer St Andrews Epis Ch Aberdeen WA 2006-2016; R S Andr's Epis Ch Aberdeen WA 1986-2000; Asst S Marg's Epis Ch Bellevue WA 1982-1985. Auth, "The Viscoelastic Response Of Open Celled Foams," The Boeing Co., 1965. Amer Soc of Civil Engr 1958; Chairman Aberdeen WA Civil Serv Comm. 2000; Chapl For Grp Harbor Com 1988-1992; Chapl Harbors Hm and Hospice 2002; Civil Serv Cmsn 1999; Evergreen Couseling Bd Dir 2000-2003; RWF Bd Dir 1990-1994.

HALE, Douglas J (Ore) 2785 Elysium Ave, Eugene OR 97401 **Dio Oregon Portland OR 2013-; Int Chapl Epis Campus Mnstry Eugene OR 2013-; S Anselm Cbury Ch Corvallis OR 2013-; S Mary's Epis Ch Eugene OR 2013-** B Portland OR 1955 s Herbert & Elizabeth. BS U of Oregon 1978; MDiv SFTS 1986; MTS Garrett-Evang TS 1995. D 2/25/2002 P 8/3/2002 Bp William O Gregg. m 8/11/1990 Patricia Ann Benson c 1. Chapl Evercare Hospice and Palliative Care Waltham MA 2007-2011; Vic S Dav's Epis Ch Halifax MA 2005-2008; Co-R All SS Par Whitman MA 2003-2007; Cn Mssnr Dio Estrn Oregon Cove OR 2002-2003; Sprtl Care Coordntr Grande Ronde Hospice La Grande OR 2000-2002; Pstr Meth Ch 1986-1999. Auth, "Sprtlty IN THE Ch OF H SERGIUS AT TEL NESSANA," Garret-Evang TS, 1995; Auth, "Prepared After All," *Mustard-Seed Ch*, Fortress Press, 1990. uochaplain@comcast.net

HALE, Jane Currie Linnard (Ct) Trinity Episcopal Church, Po Box 276, Brooklyn CT 06234 **Dio Connecticut Meriden CT 2016-; Trin Ch Brooklyn CT 2016-** B Minneapolis MN 1974 d David & Barbara. MDiv Andover Newton TS; Ed.M Harv; BA Hobart and Wm Smith Colleges. D 6/14/2016 Bp Ian Theodore Douglas P 12/21/2016 Bp Laura Ahrens. m 6/20/1998 Laurence Newton Hale c 3.

HALE, Linda Mosier (Spok) PO Box 456, Sunnyside WA 98944 B Pendleton OR 1941 d Ernest & E Virginia. BS U of Oregon 1963; MEd WA SU 1994. D 11/1/2009 Bp James E Waggoner Jr. m 7/13/2006 Jack Hale c 1.

HALE, Patricia Ann (Ore) 2785 Elysium Avenue, Eugene OR 97401 **R S Matt's Epis Ch Eugene OR 2011-** B Portland OR 1970 d Willis & Virginia. BA U of Oregon 1992; MDiv Garrett-Evang TS 1996; DMin Aquinas Inst of Theol 2014; DMin Other 2014; DMin Other 2014. D 2/25/2002 P 8/3/2002 Bp William O Gregg. m 8/11/1990 Douglas J Hale c 1. Vic S Dav's Epis Ch Halifax MA 2005-2007; R All SS Par Whitman MA 2003-2011; Cn S Matt's Epis Ch Ontario OR 2003; Cn Dio Estrn Oregon Cove OR 2002-2003; Serv Meth Ch 1992-2001.

HALE, William Charles (Mich) 1067 Hubbard St, Detroit MI 48209 **Chapl Cbury On The Lake Waterford MI 2009-; P-in-c Chr The King Epis Ch Taylor MI 2003-; Dream Cluster Allen Pk MI 2003-; S Lk's Epis Ch Allen Pk MI 2003-** B Pottstown PA 1951 s William & Margaret. BA Indiana U 1973; MA U of Pennsylvania 1975; PhD U of Pennsylvania 1978; MDiv GTS 1989. D 6/24/1989 P 1/1/1990 Bp H Coleman Mcgehee Jr. m 2/18/1982 Lori Alyson Hale. Vic Trin Ch Detroit MI 1989-1992; Dioc Of Liturg Wrshp And Mus Com. Natl Conf Of Christians & Jews 1987.

HALEY-RAY, Judith (Pa) 163 Colket Ln, Devon PA 19333 **D S Mary's Ch 2002-** B Chattanooga TN 1944 d James & Corinne. MWC 1964; U NC 1965; BA Villanova U 1988; Sch of Diac Philadelphia PA 1992; CSD Neumann Coll Aston PA 1996. D 10/17/1992 Bp Franklin Delton Turner. m 6/19/1965 William Allen Ray c 1. Non-par 2000-2002; D S Gabr's Epis Ch Philadelphia PA 1992-1999. Sprtl Dir Intl 1997.

HALFORD, Cathrine Nance (Miss) 147 Daniel Lake Blvd, Jackson MS 39212 B Cleveland MS 1948 d John & Mary. BS Georgia St U 1975; MEd Georgia St U 1976; EdS Delta St U 1991. D 5/29/2008 Bp Duncan Montgomery Gray III. c 2.

HALKETT, Thomas Richmond (Me) PO Box 564, Machias ME 04654 B Bangor ME 1951 s James & Geraldine. BA Hampden-Sydney Coll 1973; MDiv Yale DS 1979. D 6/15/1979 P 1/1/1980 Bp Frederick Barton Wolf. m 8/12/2006 Diane Helder c 5. Dio Maine Portland ME 2000-2004; Epis Cmnty Serv Washington Cnty Cherryfield ME 1987-1990; Chr Epis Ch Eastport ME 1986-1987; S Aidans Ch Machias ME 1985-2004; P-in-c Chr Ch New Haven CT 1982-1985; Asst Ch Of The Redeem Bryn Mawr PA 1980-1982.

HALL, Addison Curtis (Mass) 79 Denton Rd, Wellesley MA 02482 B Northampton MA 1947 s Richard & Mary. BA Mid 1969; MDiv EDS 1974. D 6/8/1974 Bp Harvey D Butterfield P 12/8/1974 Bp Robert Shaw Kerr. m 12/27/1970

Joanna Hall c 2. R S Andr's Ch Wellesley MA 1990-2012; R S Steph's Ch Middlebury VT 1978-1990; Cur Cathd Ch Of S Paul Burlington VT 1974-1978.

HALL, Albert Benjamin (WMass) 775 Columbia Northwest, Port Charlotte FL 33952 **Non-par 1971-** B Boston MA 1939 s Raymond & Mary. BA Br 1961; MDiv EDS 1964; MLS Wesl 1973. D 6/13/1964 P 12/1/1964 Bp Oliver L Loring. m 11/6/1965 Faith Hall c 2. Asst S Paul's Ch Holyoke MA 1964-1966. Auth, "arts Math".

HALL, Allen Keith (Colo) 3950 W 12th St Nr 10, Greeley CO 80634 **Ret 1990-** B Milwaukee WI 1924 s Forrest & Crystal. BA Ripon Coll Ripon WI 1949; MA Middle Tennessee St U 1963; MDiv Nash 1985. D 6/14/1985 P 12/22/1985 Bp William Carl Frey. m 7/5/1947 Mary Lou Ida Becker c 3. Int Trin Ch Greeley CO 1996-1997; Int S Mk's Epis Ch Durango CO 1994-1995, Int 1990-1993, Int 1990-1991; Vic Glenmark-Waikari Par New Zealand 1988-1999; Serv Ch in New Zealand 1988-1989; Vic S Andr's Epis Ch Ft Lupton CO 1985-1990; Vic S Eliz's Epis Ch Brighton CO 1985-1990. Soc of S Fran - Tertiary 1985.

HALL, Caroline J A (ECR) Po Box 6359, Los Osos CA 93412 **P-in-c S Ben's Par Los Osos CA 2008-, 2006-2008, 2005** B Woking Surrey England 1955 d Francis & Kathleen. ETSBH; BA U of Bradford Bradford UK 1977; MBA Herriott Watt U 1997; MDiv CDSP 2003; PhD U of Leeds Gb 2009. D 6/28/2003 P 2/21/2004 Bp Richard Lester Shimpfky. m 6/17/2008 Jill Victoria Denton. S Steph's Epis Ch Sn Luis Obispo CA 2016; Lectr Bloy Hse Claremont CA 2008-2009; Assoc S Lk's Ch Atascadero CA 2003-2006; Dnry Yth Min Dio El Camino Real Salinas CA 2003-2006, Multi-Dioc Disciplinary Bd 2011-, Conf Educ Resource Team 2009-2011, Dioc Revs Com, Chair 2009-2011, T/F on Theol of Mar 2009-2010, Supply 2004-2009, Dioc Coun 2004-2006. Ph D, "Homosexuality as a Site of Angl Identity and Dissent," Leeds U, UK, 2009; Auth, "H and Cath," *LivCh*, 2004; Auth, "For the Love of God," *New Times San Luis Obispo*, 2003. Integrity 1997; Integrity, Pres 2011. Promising Schlr ECF 2005.

HALL, Charlotte Melissa (Nwk) 11 S Kingman Rd, South Orange NJ 07079 **P S Jas Ch Montclair NJ 2014-** B New York NY 1953 MS NYU; BA SUNY; MDiv UTS 2003. D 5/31/2003 P 12/7/2003 Bp John Palmer Croneberger. m 12/9/2011 Frances C Lapinski c 1. Asst S Ptr's Ch Morristown NJ 2010-2013; Asst Ch Of The Redeem Morristown NJ 2007-2010; All SS Epis Par Hoboken NJ 2004-2007; D S Steph's Ch.

HALL, Daniel Charles (NJ) 114 Willow Dr, North Cape May NJ 08204 **D Ch Of The Adv Cape May NJ 2007-** B Atlantic City NJ 1936 s Floyd & Mildred. Dplma Philadelphia Coll of Bible 1961; BA Thos Edison St Coll 1981; MTh New Brunswick TS 1995. D 4/13/1985 Bp George Phelps Mellick Belshaw. m 5/4/1963 Barbara Elaine Hall c 2. D S Barn By The Bay Villas NJ 1985-2007. Assoc, OHC.

HALL, Daniel Emerson (Pgh) 412 Locust St, Pittsburgh PA 15218 **Asst. Prof of Surgery U Pgh Pittsburgh PA 2007-; Epis P in Res First Luth Ch Pittsburgh PA 2005-; Bd Mem Pilgrim Afr Seattle WA 2013-** B Hastings NE 1969 s David & Elizabeth. BA Ya 1991; MDiv Ya Berk 1996; MD Ya 1999; MA Duke 2005. D 6/12/1999 Bp Clarence Nicholas Coleridge P 10/7/2001 Bp Robert William Duncan. c 1. Assoc Ch Of The H Fam Chap Hill NC 2003-2005; Fell In Rel & Med Duke Med. Cntr-Cntr For Relig.& Med. 2002-2005; Cn Mssnr For YA Trin Cathd Pittsburgh PA 2001-2002; Surgical Res Hosp 1999-2007.

HALL, David A (Ala) 2753 11th Ave S, Birmingham AL 35205 **S Mths Epis Ch Tuscaloosa AL 2015-; Dvlpmt Dept Dio Alabama Birmingham 2016-, COM 2014-, Epis Place Bd Dir 2011-2014** B Seattle WA 1957 s Ernest & Reba. Dplma in Fin Plnng Bos; BA Louisiana Coll 1980; MDiv Sewanee: The U So, TS 1992. D 6/6/1992 P 5/15/1993 Bp Alex Dockery Dickson. m 11/25/2008 Phyllis Turnham c 1. SVP/Chf Dvlpmt Off YMCA of Grtr Birmingham 2014-2017; Assoc R Epis Ch Of The Ascen Birmingham AL 2008-2015; VP Untd Way of Cntrl Alabama Birmingham AL 2007-2014; R Ch Of The Resurr Rainbow City AL 2002-2007; Assoc R St Thos Epis Ch Huntsville AL 2000-2002; Headmaster H Comf Epis Day Sch Gadsden AL 1999-2000; Chapl St. Geo's Schools Germantown TN 1996-1999; Asst to the R S Geo's Ch Germantown TN 1994-1996; Asst Dio W Tennessee Memphis 1992-1994; S Andr's Epis Ch Collierville TN 1992-1994. Fin Plnng Assn 2012; Rotary Intl 2007. Cert Fundraising Exec (CFRE) CFRE Intl 2015; Cert Fin Planner TM CFP Bd Standards Inc. 2012.

HALL, David Moreland (WMass) 20 Winchester Ave, Auburn MA 01501 B Cincinnati OH 1949 s Harold & Vivian. OH SU 1970; BA Thos More Coll 1976; MDiv EDS 1977. D 6/4/1977 P 3/2/1978 Bp John Mc Gill Krumm. m 8/17/2008 Lisle M Hall c 6. R S Thos Epis Ch Auburn MA 2009-2015; R Chr Ch Montpelier VT 1989-2009; R Chr Epis Ch Clinton MD 1982-1989; R Trin Ch Coshocton OH 1979-1982; Asst S Paul's Epis Ch Dayton OH 1977-1979.

HALL, Dianne Costner (Ga) 212 N Jefferson St, Albany GA 31701 **D Calv Ch Americus GA 2012-** B Raleigh NC 1947 d Robert & Ruth. BA Mars Hill Coll 1969. D 3/25/2009 Bp Henry Irving Louttit. c 3.

HALL, Donna (SeFla) 941 Allendale Rd, West Palm Beach FL 33405 **P H Sprt Epis Ch W Palm Bch FL 2004-; Nrsng Hm Chapl No Palm Bch Dnry 2004-** B Fayetteville TN 1954 d Donald & Betty. BA Middle Tennessee St U 1975;

MEd U GA 1982; MDiv Epis TS of the SW 2004. D 4/17/2004 P 11/9/2004 Bp Leo Frade. m 5/28/1977 James H Hall c 2.

HALL, Ernest Eugene (Spr) 1808 Lakeside Dr Unit A, Champaign IL 61821 B Mansfield LA 1932 s Alvin & Rose. BA Louisiana Coll 1953; BD Sthrn Bapt TS 1956; MA LSU 1959; PhD LSU 1963. D 11/14/1997 Bp Calvin Onderdonk Schofield Jr P 6/13/1998 Bp John Lewis Said. m 12/27/1955 Reba Frances Hall c 3. P Assoc Emm Memi Epis Ch Champaign IL 2000-2011; S Mk's Ch Palm Bch Garden FL 1998-1999. *Proclaim the Word: the Bases of Preaching*, Broadman Press, 1983; *Remember to Live*, Broadman Press, 1980.

HALL, Everett (Ore) 11939 NE Davis St Apt 343, Portland OR 97220 **Died 10/29/2015** B Duluth MN 1928 s Charles & Elva. BA U MN 1951; MDiv Bex Sem 1954. D 6/20/1954 P 3/1/1955 Bp Stephen E Keeler. Assoc Chr Ch Las Vegas NV 1998-2008; R S Matt's Epis Ch Portland OR 1974-1992; R S Mary's Ch Woodburn OR 1959-1974; Chapl Veteran's Hosp Dallas Dallas TX 1957-1959; Texas Chapt Amer Gld of Org Dallas TX 1957-1958; Stndg Com Dio Oregon Portland OR 1984-1986, Dioc Liturg Com 1982-1986, Dept of Missions 1980-1990. ESMA 1977-1982.

HALL, Gary (Los) Cathedral of St Peter & St Paul, 3101 Wisconsin Ave NW, Washington DC 20016 B Los Angeles CA 1949 s Huntz & Leslie. Ya 1968; BA U CA 1972; MDiv EDS 1976; MA U CA 1984; PhD U CA 1989. D 6/19/1976 P 1/15/1977 Bp Robert Claflin Rusack. m 4/17/1978 Kathleen M Hall c 1. Cathd of St Ptr & St Paul Washington DC 2012-2015; Chr Ch Cranbrook Bloomfield Hills MI 2010-2012, 1978-1981, Asst 1978-1979; Dn & Pres Bexley Seabury Fed Chicago IL 2005-2010; Ch Of The Redeem Bryn Mawr PA 2001-2004; Cathd Cntr Of S Paul Cong Los Angeles CA 2001; Bloy Hse Claremont CA 1999, 1995; All SS Ch Pasadena CA 1992-2001; R S Geo's Par La Can CA 1989-1990; Vic S Aid's Epis Ch Malibu CA 1983-1989; Ch Of The Epiph Oak Pk CA 1981-1983; Vic Epiph Westlake Vill CA 1981-1983; Chapl Cranbrook Schools 1979-1981; Int S Jn The Evang Mansfield MA 1977-1978; D Intern Dio Los Angeles Los Angeles CA 1976-1977. Auth, "From Heresy to Sex," *ATR*, 2003. Phi Beta Kappa 1972. Hon Cn Cathd Cntr of St. Paul 2001; ECF Fell 1983.

HALL, George (Ct) 496 F Heritage Vlg, Southbury CT 06488 B Riverton NJ 1930 s George & Kathryn. BA U So 1954; GTS 1957; MS Cntrl Connecticut St U 1976. D 4/26/1957 P 11/2/1957 Bp Alfred L Banyard. m 7/7/1987 Beverly D Barras c 3. P-i-charge Epihany Ch Southbury CT 2010-2011; All SS Ch Wolcott CT 2006-2009; Ret 2003-2006; P-in-c S Mk's Ch Bridgewater CT 1995-2000; Dir Oratory of the Little Way Gaylordsville Dio Connecticut Meriden CT 1992-1995; R S Lk's Ch So Glastonbury CT 1969-1992; R Calv Epis Ch Flemington NJ 1961-1969; R S Jas Ch Bradley Bch NJ 1957-1961. OHC.

HALL, James Harold (SVa) 3628 Applewood Ln, Antioch TN 37013 **Died 2/14/2016** B Brunswick GA 1928 s James & Clara. Talladega Coll 1947; BA S Augustines Coll Raleigh NC 1950; MDiv Nash 1953; MA U of Montana 1971. D P 12/21/1953 Bp Martin J Bram. m 4/26/1987 Pauline M. Ret 1996-2016; R S Cyp's Epis Ch Hampton VA 1987-1996; R Ch Of The H Trin Nashville TN 1982-1987; Ch Of The Redeem Kenmore WA 1982; Vic S Mich And All Ang Ch Tallahassee FL 1974-1979; Vic S Andr's Epis Ch Polson MT 1964-1974; Vic Trin Thompson Falls MT 1964-1974; Asst Ch Of The H Sprt Missoula MT 1963-1964; Vic S Tim's Epis Ch Daytona Bch FL 1958-1963; Vic Ch Of S Chris Ft Lauderdale FL 1954-1958; S Andr's Epis Ch Of Hollywood Hollywood FL 1954-1958; S Phil's Ch Pompano Bch FL 1954-1958; Vic Ch Of S Jn Lake Worth FL 1953-1958; S Cuth's Ch Boynton Bch FL 1953-1958; S Mary's Epis Ch Of Deerfield Deerfield Bch FL 1953-1958; S Matt's Epis Ch Delray Bch FL 1953-1958.

HALL, John (At) 265 Mail Rd., Exeter RI 02822 B Newport RI 1936 s Richard & Marguerite. BA Trin Hartford CT 1957; STB Ya Berk 1960; EDS 1977. D 6/18/1960 P 12/19/1960 Bp John S Higgins. m 10/2/1965 Mary B Hall c 4. Dio Atlanta Atlanta GA 1998-2001; R All SS Ch Warwick RI 1990-1998; Co-Dir Epis Conf Cntr RI 1980-1998; S Aug's Ch Kingston RI 1978-1989; Dio Rhode Island Providence RI 1966-1997; Chapl U Rhode Island-Kingston 1966-1989; Cur S Jn's Ch Barrington RI 1960-1965. Ed, "Rhode Island Epis News," 1998. Hon Cn S Jn's Cathd 1986.

HALL, John C (Va) 124 Quietwalk Ln, Herndon VA 20170 **S Anne's Epis Ch Reston VA 2016-** B New York NY 1958 s Harry & Marietta. BA U of Arizona 1981; MDiv VTS 1989; DMin SWTS 2005. D 6/11/1989 Bp Joseph Thomas Heistand P 12/14/1989 Bp Calvin Onderdonk Schofield Jr. m 5/28/1983 Jean Ellen Hall c 4. R S Bon Ch Sarasota FL 2013-2015; R S Matt's Ch Chandler AZ 1998-2012; Assoc R S Barn On The Desert Scottsdale AZ 1994-1998; Assoc R S Mich And All Ang Ch Mssn KS 1992-1994; Asst R S Mary Magd Epis Ch Pompano Bch FL 1989-1992; Yth Min S Phil's In The Hills Tucson AZ 1984-1986. Auth, "What I Would Have Told You," *LivCh*, LivCh Fndt, 2007; Auth, "Strangers and Aliens, Citizens and SS: Multicultural Challenges for Hisp/Latino Mnstry in the Ch," *Doctoral Thesis*, SWTS, 2005; Auth, "Simply Invisible," *LivCh*, LivCh Fndt, 2004; Auth, "When the Ch Lacks Vision," *LivCh*, LivCh Fndt, 2002. jhall@bonifacechurch.org

HALL, John Liston (Ia) 20 Mcclellan Blvd, Davenport IA 52803 B Elmwood NE 1937 s Ted & Margaret. BS U of Nebraska 1958; BD SWTS 1963; MA U of

Nebraska 1968; PhD U of Nebraska 1971. D 6/8/1963 P 12/1/1963 Bp Russell T Rauscher. m 8/6/1966 Kay M Hall c 3. Dn Trin Cathd Davenport IA 1989-2005; S Jn's Epis Ch Decatur IL 1979-1989; P-in-c S Jos's Clinton IL 1972-1980; P-in-c S Andr's Ch Seward NE 1971-1972, P-in-c 1966-1970; H Trin Ch York NE 1966-1967; Asst Chapl S Mk's On The Campus Lincoln NE 1965-1970; Vic S Jos's Ch Mullen NE 1963-1965.

HALL, Jon William (Mo) 15764 Clayton Rd, Ellisville MO 63011 **R S Mart's Ch Ellisville MO 2010-** B Shreveport Louisiana 1963 Centenary Coll 1986; Asbury TS 2003; Cert Ang Stud GTS 2005. D 6/18/2005 P 12/23/2005 Bp Stacy F Sauls. m 12/27/1987 Colleen Eastman Hall c 1. R S Phil's Ch Harrodsburg KY 2005-2010.

HALL, Karen Elizabeth (SD) 302 S.Maple, Watertown SD 57201 B Cut Bank MT 1942 d Carl & Helen. Nash; So Dakota St U; BA U CO 1966; MDiv Sewanee: The U So, TS 1991. D 4/15/1986 P 11/16/1986 Bp Craig Barry Anderson. c 4. R Trin Ch Ennis MT 2007-2011; Cn to the Ordnry Dio So Dakota Sioux Falls SD 2006-2007; Supply H Trin Epis Ch Luverne MN 2001; Cn Dio So Dakota Pierre SD 2000-2007, 1987-1999, Cn to the Ordnry/Congrl Dvlpmt 2000-2007; R Trin Epis Ch Watertown SD 1991-2000; Chr Ch Alto Decherd TN 1990-1991; Gr Epis Ch Madison SD 1986. Sis of Mary (Assoc). cl U So 1991. kehall42@gmail.com

HALL, Kathleen (WMo) 100 E Red Bridge Rd, Kansas City MO 64114 **Bp Spencer Place Inc Kansas City MO 2013-; P St Ptr & All SS Epis Ch Kansas City MO 2011-** B Midland MI 1952 d John & Frances. BA Cntrl Michigan U 1974; JD Marshall-Wythe Sch of Law 1989; MISLT U of Missouri 2005; Angl Stds Geo Herbert Inst of Pstr Stds 2010; Mstr of Div Other 2013; Mstr of Div S Paul TS 2013. D 6/4/2011 P 12/3/2011 Bp Martin Scott Field. m 8/9/1997 James Anthony Rynard. khall@saint-lukes.org

HALL, Laurens Allen (Tex) 3725 Chevy Chase Dr, Houston TX 77019 B San Antonio TX 1942 s Wilton & Ada. BBA U of Texas 1965; MDiv CDSP 1968; CDSP 1995. D 7/24/1968 Bp Everett H Jones P 1/28/1969 Bp Richard Earl Dicus. m 12/30/1968 Bennie Hall c 3. R S Jn The Div Houston TX 1981-2014; R S Dav's Ch Austin TX 1975-1981; Asst R Chr Epis Ch San Antonio TX 1968-1971. DD CDSP 1995.

HALL, Leigh E (Ga) P.O. Box 74, Swainsboro GA 30401 **S Paul's Ch Albany GA 2015-** B Statesboro GA 1980 d Thomas. AA E Georgia Coll 2000; BA U GA 2003; MDiv VTS 2009. D 2/7/2009 P 8/27/2009 Bp Henry Irving Louttit. Assoc Chr Ch Frederica St Simons Is GA 2012-2015; Dio Georgia Savannah GA 2009-2012.

HALL, Lisbeth Jordan (Mass) 1239 Peterkin Hl, South Woodstock VT 05071 B Philadelphia PA 1933 d Claus & Charlotte. BA Mt Holyoke Coll 1954; MDiv EDS 1995. D 12/19/1998 P 12/4/1999 Bp M(Arvil) Thomas Shaw. c 6. Dio Wstrn Massachusetts Springfield 2003; Assoc All SS Par Brookline MA 2002-2003; P-in-c Ch Of S Jn The Evang Boston MA 1999-2002.

HALL JR, Lyle Gillis (Mass) 1239 Peterkin Hill Road, South Woodstock VT 05071 **Died 9/26/2016** B Ridgway PA 1929 s Lyle & Jane. Ya 1952; BS Bos 1975; MDiv EDS 1978. D 6/10/1978 P 12/10/1978 Bp Donald James Davis. m 11/5/1955 Lisbeth Jordan Hall c 6. Ret Vermont 2002-2016; P-in-c Ch Of S Jn The Evang Boston MA 1999-2002; R S Dunstans Epis Ch Dover MA 1993-1999, 1983-1989; Assoc All SS Par Brookline MA 1992-1999, 1981-1982; Chair - Trst EDS Cambridge MA 1987-2000; Chapl Dana Hall Sch Wellesley MA 1980-1981; Asst The Ch Of The Adv Boston MA 1979-1980; V-Chair Stackpole Corp 1976-1983. OHC.

HALL, Mark (SJ) 2212 River Dr, Stockton CA 95204 **Chapl Epis Dio San Joaquin Modesto CA 2011-, Chapl 2011-, 2008-2011, Cn to the Ordnry 2008-2011, Cn to Bp 1981-1982, Chair DeptCE 1988-1992** B Los Angeles CA 1946 s Kempton & Emily. BA U of Hawaii 1969; MDiv EDS 1973; MA U of Maine 1986. D 9/16/1975 P 3/16/1976 Bp Frederick Barton Wolf. m 11/18/1990 Susan Hall c 2. Epis Ch Cntr New York NY 2008; R Epis Ch Of S Anne Stockton CA 2002-2008, 2000-2001; H Trin Epis Ch Madera CA 1991-1995; S Alb's Ch Los Banos CA 1987-1990, Vic 1987-1990, Vic 1987-1990, 1982; Asst S Jas Epis Ch Kent WA 1987; Int S Andr's Ch Millinocket ME 1984-1985; Int S Pat's Ch Brewer ME 1983-1984; S Johns Epis Ch Brownville ME 1982-1983; Int S Jos's/St. Jn's ME 1982-1983; Int St Josephs Ch Sebec ME 1982-1983; St Anth Ch Patterson CA 1982; Chapl Chapl USAFR 1980-1995; Serv St Nich Epis Ch Atwater CA 1980-1982; Serv S Lk's Ch Caribou ME 1976-1978. Auth, "Bp McIlvain, The Reluctant Frontiersman," *Ch Hist mag.*

HALL, Mark Robert (Dal) 5100 Ross Ave, Dallas TX 75206 B Des Moines IA 1957 s George & Marilyn Ann. BA Drake U 1978; JD Geo Law Cntr 1981; Dplma n Mnstry The Stanton Cntr for Mnstry Formation 2014. D 6/14/2014 Bp Paul Emil Lambert. m 5/12/1990 Perilynn Fran Willis.

HALL, Mavis Ann (Neb) 3214 Davy Jones Dr, Plattsmouth NE 68048 **S Lk's Ch Plattsmouth NE 2003-** B Sioux City IA 1951 D 5/31/2003 P 11/30/2003 Bp James Edward Krotz. m 7/3/1971 Michael Clifford Hall c 2. stlukeschurchplattsmouth@gmail.com

HALL, Melinda (NwPa) Holy Trinity Church, 62 Pickering St, Brookville PA 15825 **Vic Ch Of Our Sav Dubois PA 2012-** B Dayton OH 1984 d Rickey & Velda. BA Georgetown Coll 2006; MDiv PrTS 2010; Angl Stds GTS 2012. D 6/16/2012 Bp George Edward Councell P 1/12/2013 Bp Sean Walter Rowe. m 8/21/2010 Nathaniel Wade Royster. vicarmelinda@gmail.com

HALL, Michael Gregory (CFla) Shepherd of the Hills, 2540 W Norvell Bryant Hwy, Lecanto FL 34461 **D Shpd Of The Hills Epis Ch Lecanto FL 2008-** B Heidleberg Germany 1958 s Charles & Margaret. BBA Fonthonne Coll 1996; MBA U of Mary 2002. D 6/22/2007 Bp Michael Smith. m 5/9/1987 Linda Ann Liebert-Hall.

HALL, Patrick Mckenzie (Tex) 915 Saulnier St # B, Houston TX 77019 **Dio Texas Houston TX 2014-; H Sprt Epis Sch Houston TX 2007-** B 1982 s James & Rosine. BA U of Texas 2003; MDiv VTS 2007. D 6/23/2007 Bp Don Adger Wimberly. Assoc H Sprt Epis Ch Houston TX 2007-2012; Virginia Sem 2004-2007.

HALL, Paula Claire (WLa) 361 Cypress Loop, Farmerville LA 71241 B El Dorado AR 1945 BS Louisiana Tech U 1967; MBA U of Hawaii 1970; JD UALR Sch of Law 1977; U of Memphis 1989; MDiv Nash 2003. D 6/7/2003 P 3/4/2004 Bp D Avid Bruce Macpherson. S Jas Ch Magnolia AR 2012-2013; Int S Andr's Epis Ch Mer Rouge LA 2011-2012; Int S Alb's Epis Ch Monroe LA 2010-2011; Int Chr Memi Ch Mansfield LA 2009-2010; Dio Wstrn Louisiana Alexandria LA 2009; Int Ch Of The Redeem Ruston LA 2008-2009; P-in-c Gr Ch Lk Providence LA 2005-2007; Int S Thos' Ch Monroe LA 2003-2005; Stndg Com, Pres Dio Wstrn Louisiana Alexandria LA 2009-2011, Stndg Com 2008-2011, Chair, Comm on Sprtl Formation 2003-. "Sprtl Formation column," *Alive*, Dio Wstrn Louisiana. AFP, US Exec Coun 2005; Benedictine Oblate, Subiaco Abbey 1997.

HALL, Richard Charles (Los) 1310 E Orange Grove Blvd, Unit 107, Pasadena CA 91104 **Died 3/5/2017** B Syracuse NY 1935 s Richard & Elizabeth. BA Ham 1957; MDiv GTS 1961; PhD Claremont Coll 1970. D 6/1/1961 Bp Allen Webster Brown P 2/14/1962 Bp Lyman Cunningham Ogilby. c 3. Ret 2000-2017; Asst S Paul's Pomona Pomona CA 1985-1991; S Barn Sr Serv Los Angeles CA 1975-2000; Asst S Mk's Epis Ch Upland CA 1975-1983; R S Jn The Bapt Par Corona CA 1970-1975; Prof St Andrews TS Quezon City Phili 1962-1967; Chapl Easter Sch Epiph Mssn Baguio City Pi 1961-1962.

HALL, Richard Hastings (Me) 29 Tarratine Dr, Brunswick ME 04011 **Ret 2001-** B Holyoke MA 1942 s John & Emma. BA U of Massachusetts 1968; MDiv Ya Berk 1971; STM NYTS 1975; DMin Andover Newton TS 1986. D 6/20/1971 Bp Alexander D Stewart P 1/7/1972 Bp Frederick Barton Wolf. m 1/21/1967 Elizabeth Ellen Hall c 3. R S Phil's Ch Wiscasset ME 1974-2001; Asst S Jn's Ch Bangor ME 1971-1974.

HALL, Rosalind Katherine (SwFla) Episcopal Church of Nativity, 5900 N Lockwood Ridge Rd, Sarasota FL 34243 B Tampa FL 1959 d Peter & Elizabeth. D 6/13/2015 Bp Dabney Tyler Smith. m 2/27/1990 Dennis S Hall c 1.

HALL, Ryan Ashley (SD) St. Paul's Episcopal Church, 726 6th St, Brookings SD 57006 B Luttrell TN 1980 s Randy & Donna. U of Nebraska; BA Carson-Newman Coll 2002; MDiv SWTS 2007. D 6/11/2007 P 5/1/2008 Bp Joe Goodwin Burnett. m 1/12/2008 Mary Kyle Hall. R S Paul's Ch Brookings SD 2009-2013; Cur S Mk's On The Campus Lincoln NE 2007-2009. Friend (Oblate) of the SS-JE 2007; SocMary 2008.

HALL, Samuel Leslie (RG) 1023 Acequia Trl Nw, Albuquerque NM 87107 **Ret 1999-** B San Francisco CA 1928 s John & Iris. BA U CA 1951; MDiv VTS 1956; S Augustines Coll Cbury Gb 1966. D 6/25/1956 P 2/7/1957 Bp Francis E I Bloy. m 12/23/1976 Leila Hall c 4. R S Mk's On The Mesa Epis Ch Albuquerque NM 1987-1988; Chapl Gd Samar Hosp 1974-1987; Gd Samar Hosp Los Angeles CA 1974-1987; R The Par Ch Of S Lk Long Bch CA 1967-1974; R S Steph's Par Whittier CA 1962-1967, Vic 1959-1961; Cur S Edm's Par San Marino CA 1956-1959; Chair Archit Cmsn Dio Los Angeles Los Angeles CA 1975-1980.

HALL, Sidney J (SVa) 218 Grove Dr, Clemson SC 29631 **Died 6/5/2016** B Hartsville SC 1930 s James & Lola. UTS; VTS; BA Baylor U 1955; BD SW Bapt TS 1959. D 11/5/1988 P 3/1/1989 Bp Claude Charles Vache. c 2. Ret 1996-2016; Chr Ch Amelia Ct Hs VA 1990-1996; R Emm Epis Ch Powhatan VA 1990-1996; R S Jas Ch Cartersville VA 1990-1996; Asst R Manakin Ch Huguenot Sprg VA 1989-1990; Manakin Epis Ch Midlothian VA 1989-1990; Asst R S Lk's Ch Powhatan VA 1989-1990; Serv Sthrn Bapt Ch 1959-1987.

HALL, Stephen Monteith (Ga) PO Box 69, Clayton GA 30525 B Milaukee WI 1942 s Robert & Jay. BA Lawr 1964; MDiv Nash 1981. D 4/28/1981 Bp William Harvey Wolfrum P 11/1/1981 Bp William Carl Frey. m 8/2/1992 Roxanne L Hall c 5. R S Jas Epis Ch Clayton GA 2006-2017; Ch Of The Gd Shpd Webster City IA 1993-1998; R S Mk's Epis Ch Ft Dodge IA 1990-2006; Cn Theol Calv Cathd Sioux Falls SD 1987-1990; R S Paul's Ch Brookings SD 1981-1987. shall17@me.com

HALL, Tod Latham (NH) 140 Muzzy Hill Rd, Milan NH 03588 B Winchester MA 1941 s Charles & Constance. Lon GB 1963; BA Dart 1964; S Jn Coll GB 1967; BD EDS 1968. D 6/15/1968 P 12/1/1968 Bp Charles Francis Hall. m 1/30/1976 Patricia Louise Hall c 3. Dio New Hampshire Concord NH 1996, 1991-1993; S Barn Ch Berlin NH 1994-1999; S Lk's Ch Woodsville NH 1986-1991; Vic Ch Of The Epiph Lisbon Lisbon NH 1985-1996; Trin Ch Epis

Boston MA 1972-1985; Chapl Ethel Walker Sch Simsbury CT 1971-1972; Asst S Geo's Epis Ch Dayton OH 1968-1971.

HALL, Vernon Donald (O) 2432 Romar Dr, Hermitage PA 16148 **R S Lk's Epis Ch Niles OH 2009-** B Connellsville PA 1947 s Vernon & Rita. BA S Vinc Coll Latrobe PA 1969; MA Mt St Marys Sem 1977; MS U Pgh 1982; MPA U Pgh 1983. Rec 5/1/1998 as Priest Bp Paul Victor Marshall. m 8/10/1996 Mary Theresa Hall. S Andr Ch Canfield OH 2003-2008; Int Trin Ch New Castle PA 1999-2000; Assoc S Gabr's Ch Douglassville PA 1997-1999; Serv RC Ch 1990-1995. NASW.

HALL, Virginia B (Ind) 3436 E. Longview, Bloomington IN 47408 B Summit NJ 1942 d Harold & Virginia. Wells Coll; BA U of New Hampshire 1965; MDiv CDSP 1969; MA Grad Theol Un 1985; Cert Jn F Kennedy U 1987. D 7/14/1979 P 9/20/1980 Bp Philip Alan Smith. c 2. Assoc R Trin Epis Ch Bloomington IN 2007-2013; Vic S Lk's Epis Ch Shelbyville IN 2003-2007; St Paul's/San Pablo Epis Ch Salinas CA 2003; Int S Mk's-In-The-Vlly Epis Los Olivos CA 2002; Exec Coun Appointees New York NY 1997-2001; Dio Guatemala New York NY 1997; Mssy Tchr, Dn of Sem Serv Epis Dio Guatemala Guatemala - Var lo 1993-2000; Pstr Assoc Ch Of The Resurr Pleasant Hil CA 1992-1996; Pstr Counslr S Anselm's Epis Ch Lafayette CA 1988-1991; Pstr Counslr S Paul's Epis Ch Walnut Creek CA 1986-1987; Asst S Thos Ch Dover NH 1979-1980. AAPC, Epis Wmn 1985-1990; Benedictine Oblate 2012; DOK 2001. Human Rts Awd City of Bloomington Human Rts. Cmsn 2012; Fllshp The Epis Ch Fundation 2007.

HALLADAY, Richard Allen (Ind) 448 Freeman Ridge Rd, Nashville IN 47448 **Ret 2002-** B Langdon NH 1932 s Ralph & Belle. BA Natl Coll Kansas City MO 1964; MDiv Epis TS in Kentucky 1967; DMin GTF 1990. D 12/16/1966 P 5/26/1967 Bp William R Moody. m 8/26/1972 Janice R Halladay c 3. Cn to the Ordnry Dio Indianapolis Indianapolis IN 1997-2001; S Thos Ch Franklin IN 1982-1997; Vic S Lk's Epis Ch Shelbyville IN 1982-1986; R Trin Ch Anderson IN 1970-1972; Lectr ETSKy (Epis. Theo. Sem. in Ky.) Lexington KY 1968-1970; Assoc R Trin Ch Covington KY 1968-1970; Vic S Pat Ch Somerset KY 1966-1968. Auth, "Formation, Instrn," *Reflection*; Auth, *Sm Congregations - Sm Communities*.

HALLAHAN, T Mark (Los) **R S Paul's Pomona Pomona CA 2007-, R 2006-** B Youngstown OH 1952 s George & Elizabeth. D 6/11/2005 Bp Chester Lovelle Talton P 1/14/2006 Bp Joseph Jon Bruno. m 8/2/2008 James Anthony Kenny. Dio Los Angeles Los Angeles CA 2005-2006; All SS Par Beverly Hills CA 2003-2005. Soc of Cath Priests 2010; SocMary 2006.

HALLANAN, Sunny (Eur) Chaussee de Charleroi 2, 1420 Braine-l'Alleud Belgium **All SS Epis Ch Braine-l'Alleud 2012-, R 2012-; Angl Rep Interfaith Com of Brussels Belgium 2013-** B Watertown NY 1958 d George & Alice. BA Cor 1979; MDiv Ya Berk 1987. D 6/20/1987 Bp O'Kelley Whitaker P 2/27/1988 Bp William George Burrill. c 2. Trst Epis Cmnty Serv 2007-2011; Del Ecum Working Grp on Mid-E Peace 2001-2011; Bd SABEEL Philadelphia 2001-2011; Dn Vlly Forge Dnry 2000-2005; Cnvnr Middle E Study Grp 1999-2008; R S Jas Ch Collegeville PA 1995-2011; Evang Consult Dio Rochester Henrietta 1988-1995; Trst Finger Lakes Conf 1988-1991; Assoc R S Thos Epis Ch Rochester NY 1987-1995; Yth Coordntr Dio Massachusetts Boston MA 1980-1983; Asst Chapl Epis Chap at MIT Cambridge MA 1979-1983; Pres of the Bp's Coun of Advice Convoc of Epis Ch in Europe Paris 2014, Dep to GC 2014-, Yth Cmsn 2012-2014; Pres, Dio of Pennsylvania Assn Natl Ntwk Of Epis Cler Assn Lynnwood WA 2007-2011. ESMHE.

HALLAS, Cynthia Johnston (Chi) 3025 Walters Ave, Northbrook IL 60062 **R S Giles' Ch Northbrook IL 2004-** B Lakewood OH 1954 d Hugh & Patricia. BA Adrian Coll 1976; MA OH SU 1979; MDiv SWTS 2000. D 6/9/2000 Bp Michael Whittington Creighton P 1/30/2001 Bp Bill Persell. m 9/11/1982 Alvin Jon Hallas c 2. Assoc S Lawr Epis Ch Libertyville IL 2000-2004.

HALLE, Michael Addenbrooke (Az) 241 S.Beverly Street, Chandler AZ 85225 **D S Matt's Ch Chandler AZ 2011-** B Tucson AZ 1964 s Michael & Nancy. BS U of Arizona 1988; MAOM U of Phoenix Tucson AZ 1994. D 1/24/2009 Bp Kirk Stevan Smith. D S Alb's Epis Ch Tucson AZ 2010.

HALLENBECK, Edwin F (RI) 101 Larchmont Rd, Warwick RI 02886 **Epis Chars, Bd Advisors Dio Rhode Island Providence RI 2007-, Dioc Coun 2002-2016, Cmsn on Fin, Secy 2001-2007** B Oakland CA 1926 s Wilbur & Elizabeth. BA Occ 1951; MA Col 1954; Rhode Island Sch For Deacons 1985. D 7/13/1985 Bp George Nelson Hunt III. m 6/25/1950 Patricia Jean Hallenbeck c 3. Pres Fund for the Diac New York NY 2011-2015; D S Lk's Epis Ch E Greenwich RI 1997-2001; D S Barn Ch Warwick RI 1992-1997; Exec Dir N Amer Assoc for the Diac Providence RI 1989-2006; Dir Fund for the Diac New York NY 1987-2015; S Eliz's Ch Hope Vlly RI 1987-1991; D S Thos' Alton Wood River Jct RI 1987-1991; D All SS Ch Warwick RI 1985-1987; Bd Mem, Treas Steere Hse Providence RI 1997-2014. Auth, "Diakonia-Prophetic Praxis-Agir," Naad, 2002; Auth, "Working Paper Trial Liturg For Celebration Of D Mnstry," Naad, 1996; Auth, "The Ord Of Mnstry-Reflections On Direct Ord," Naad, 1996; Auth, "Personal Mnstry Plnng," Plnng Lab, 1990. The Bp Geo C. Harris Awd In Recognition Of Outstanding Serv To Deacons NAAD 2003.

HALLER, Robert Bennett (NJ) Trinity Episcopal Church, Vincentown NJ 08088 **P-in-c Trin Epis Ch Vincentown NJ 2013-** B Clarksburg WV 1940 s Robert & Clara. PhL Aquinas Inst 1966; STB Immac Concep Coll 1968; PhD CUA 1986. Rec 6/23/2012 as Priest Bp George Edward Councell.

HALLER BSG, Tobias Stanislas (NY) 305 West Lafayette Avenue, Baltimore MD 21217 **Assoc Ch Of The Adv Baltimore MD 2016-** B Baltimore MD 1949 s William & Mary. BA scl Towson St Coll 1971; MDiv cl GTS 1997. D 6/14/1997 P 12/13/1997 Bp Richard Frank Grein. m 7/29/2011 James Teets. Mem and Secy T/F on Study of Mar 2013-2015; Rel and Culture Bk Revs Ed ATR 2012-2016; Chair HOD Study Cttee Ch Gov and Polity 2009-2012; Vic S Jas Epis Ch Fordham Bronx NY 1999-2015; Asst Secy of Conv Dio New York New York NY 1997-1999; Pstr S Paul's Ch Yonkers NY 1997-1999; Asst Pub Dir Epis Ch Cntr New York NY 1983-1991. Auth, "What About Sex?," Ch Pub, Inc., 2017; Auth, "Preparing for a Wedding in the Epis Ch," Ch Pub, Inc., 2016; Ed, "The Epis Handbook Revised Ed," Morehouse Pub, 2015; Ed, "Shared Governance," Ch Pub, 2012; Auth, "Reasonable and H," Seabury Books, 2009; Auth, "Defender of His Faith / Henry VII," *Fllshp Papers*, CFEC, 1996; Auth, "St of the Rel Life," BSG, 1991; Auth, "God First: A Tithing Catechism," BSG/TEC, 1990; Ed, "Sermons," *Selected Sermons*, TEC, 1986; Ed, "Var arts," *The Servnt*, BSG, 1983. BSG 1980; Convenor NAECC 2005-2007; Ord of St Jn 2005; Pres CFEC 1988-1994. Bp's Cross Bp of New York 2014; Off Ord of St Jn 2009; Clem J Whipple, Bp of Newark and J Wilson Sutton Prizes GTS 1997; Polly Bond Awd Epis Cmnctr 1991.

HALLETT, Timothy Jerome (Spr) 3007 N Ramble Rd W, Bloomington IN 47408 **Mem, Bd Dir Waycross Epis C&C Morgantown IN 2012-** B Fergus Falls MN 1940 s Leslie & Rosa. BA U So 1962; Amer Inst H Land Stds IL 1964; MDiv SWTS 1965; MA U Chi 1973. D 6/24/1965 Bp Hamilton Hyde Kellogg P 3/28/1966 Bp Philip Frederick McNairy. m 8/19/1967 Mary Hallett c 2. R Chap Of S Jn The Div Champaign IL 1976-2011; Asst Gr Epis Ch Hinsdale IL 1974-1976; Epis Chapl Minnesota St U Mankato MN 1968-1971; Cur S Jn's Epis Ch Mankato MN 1965-1968; Pres ESMHE 1986-1988; Trst Bexley Seabury Fed Chicago IL 1983-1998. Transltr, "Symbolism Of The Biblic Wrld"; Transltr, "Paul The Apos". ESMHE Pres 1976-2003; Interfaith Com for Worker Justice 2001-2005; Ord of St Jn 2010. Off Ord of St. Jn 2013; Distinguished Ldrshp Awd Off of Campus Mnstrs, The Epis Ch 2006.

HALLEY, Marcus George (WMo) 6401 Wornall Ter, Kansas City MO 64113 B Leominster MA 1986 s Milton & Kelly. BA Johnson C. Smith U; MDiv The Interdenominational Theo. Cntr; Mstr of Sacr Theol The TS. D 12/15/2012 Bp Robert Christopher Wright. P S Andr's Ch Kansas City MO 2013-2017.

HALLISEY, L Ann (NCal) 1711 Westshore St, Davis CA 95616 **Ch Of S Mart Davis CA 2017-; Owner Hallisey Consulting 2005-** B Los Angeles CA 1949 d William & Leah. Cert Profsnl Co-Active Coach Coach Trng Intl ; BA U CA 1971; MDiv Yale DS 1975; MS California St U 1987; DMin CDSP 2005; DMin CDSP 2005. D 5/1/1983 P 1/6/1984 Bp John Lester Thompson III. m 5/2/1998 Barry Leigh Beisner c 3. Dn of Students CDSP Berkeley CA 2011-2017, Field Educ Supvsr 1993-2000, Adj Fac 1993-1999; Int Asst S Jn's Epis Ch Oakland CA 2010-2011; Int Vic The Epis Ch Of The Gd Shpd Berkeley CA 2007-2010; Natl Coordntr, Fresh Start Epis Ch Cntr New York NY 2006; Dir, Cornerstone ECF Inc New York NY 2001-2005; R Ascen Epis Ch Vallejo CA 1992-2001; Asst R S Paul's Epis Ch Benicia CA 1989-1991, Asst to the R 1987-1988; Int Trin Ch Sonoma CA 1986-1987; Int Epiph Epis Ch Vacaville CA 1985-1986, Asst to the R 1983-1984; Sprtl Dir Bread of Life Cntr Sacramento CA 2008-2011; Alum Coun Yale DS New Haven CT 2007-2011; Chair, Stndg Com The Epis Dio Nthrn California Sacramento CA 2000-2002, Stndg Com 1999-2002, GC Dep 1997-2000, Victim Advoc, Com on Sexual Misconduct 1995-2002, Chair, COM 1992-2000, COM 1989-2001. California Assn of Mar & Fam Therapists 1987.

HALLMARK, Charlotte Anne (Va) PO Box 306, Middleburg VA 20118 B Chicago IL 1945 d John & Mildred. BA CUA 1970; MDiv SWTS 1987. D 6/1/1987 Bp James Winchester Montgomery P 12/12/1987 Bp Frank Tracy Griswold III. m 5/21/1977 Nelson Stephen Hallmark c 1. R Emm Ch Middleburg VA 2008-2017; Int S Jn's Ch Roanoke VA 2005-2007; Int Ch Of Our Sav Charlottesvlle VA 2004-2005; Int S Mart In The Fields Ch Atlanta GA 2003-2004; Int S Mary's-On-The-Highlands Epis Ch Birmingham AL 2001-2002; Int S Ptr's Epis Ch Charlotte NC 1999-2001; Int S Jn's Epis Ch Columbia SC 1998-1999; Int S Mk's Epis Ch Raleigh NC 1997-1998; Asst S Jas Ch Potomac MD 1996-1997; Int Chr Ch Capitol Hill Washington DC 1995-1996; P in Charge S Thos Ch Pawhuska OK 1991-1995; Int Chr The King Ch Lansing IL 1990-1991; Int S Lk's Ch Dixon IL 1989-1990; Chapl Cntrl Dupage Alco & Drug Treatment Cntr 1988-1989; Cur S Bede's Epis Ch Bensenville IL 1987-1989.

HALLOCK JR, Harold H (Va) 920 Flordon Dr, Charlottesville VA 22901 B Greenport,NY 1938 s Harold & Katharine. BA U of Virginia 1959; MDiv Sewanee: The U So, TS 1977. D 6/26/1977 Bp William Evan Sanders P 4/30/1978 Bp William F Gates Jr. m 5/13/1961 Virginia S Somerville c 2. R Ch Of Our Sav Charlottesvlle VA 1981-2004; Asst Ch Of The Gd Shpd Lookout Mtn TN 1977-1981.

HALLY SSAP, Jane Eloise (At) 18 Lenox Pointe NE Ste A, Atlanta GA 30324 **Psych/Pstr Counslr Priv Pract 2010-** B Boston MA 1943 d James & Pauline. AB Vas 1964; MDiv Candler TS Emory U 1982; MSW U GA 2000. D 6/12/1982 P 5/4/1983 Bp Bennett Jones Sims. c 1. Pstr Counslr Cathd Counslg Cntr Atlanta GA 2005-2010; Pstr Counslr Wieuca Counslg Cntr Atlanta GA 1995-2005; Pstr Counslr S Barth's Epis Ch Atlanta GA 1986-1995; Chapl GBMC Atlanta GA 1984-1986; D Ch Of The Atone Sandy Sprg GA 1982-1984; Bursar Soc of S Anna the Prophet 2007-2012. Auth, "sermons," *Wmn of the Word*, Susan Smith Pub, 1984. The Soc of S Anna the Prophet 2005. jehally@gmail.com

HALSTEAD, Jan (Tex) Christ Episcopal Church, 3520 Whitestone Blvd, Cedar Park TX 78613 B Piggott AR 1953 d Ralph & Lue. MEd Midwestern St U 1970; Educ Midwestern St U 1975; Counslg Texas St 2003. D 6/15/2013 Bp C Andrew Doyle. m 6/3/1972 Gerald Bay Halstead c 2.

HALT, David Jason Andrew (Spr) 2153 Crest Rd, Cincinnati OH 45240 **S Matt's Epis Ch Bloomington IL 2010-** B Toledo OH 1973 s David & Phyllis. BA Sprg Arbor U 1995; MATS Untd TS 2002; MDiv Bex Sem 2003. D 10/25/2003 Bp Herbert Thompson Jr P 6/19/2004 Bp Kenneth Lester Price. m 5/22/1993 Amy D Halt c 2. R S Jas Epis Ch Cincinnati OH 2006-2009; P-in-c H Sprt Epis Ch Cincinnati OH 2004-2006. Congregations of the Comp of the H Sav 2006.

HALTER, Karl Stuttgart (WA) 2059 Huntington Ave Apt 1203, Alexandria VA 22303 **Ret 1992-** B Freiburg Germany 1926 s Karl & Rosa. Bapt TS at Hamburg 1949; Berkeley Bapt TS 1958; Sem of Old Cathd Ch Bonn DE 1969; VTS 1987. D. Asst The Ch Of The Redeem Beth MD 1982-1992, Asst 1973-1981; Serv Mssn In Korea 1981-1982; Asst S Mich And All Ang Anniston AL 1971-1972; Serv Mssn In Germany 1967-1971; Serv Ch In Vietnam 1966-1967; Serv Mssn In Germany 1964-1965. Bronze Star Us Army 1975.

HALVERSON-RIGATUSO, Kathryn (Ia) D 1/23/2010 P 7/21/2010 Bp Alan Scarfe.

HALVERSTADT JR, Albert Nast (Colo) 1244 Detroit St, Denver CO 80206 B Cincinnati OH 1935 s Albert & Jane. BA Ken 1957; MDiv EDS 1975. D 6/14/1975 P 12/1/1977 Bp Lyman Cunningham Ogilby. m 7/8/1988 Susan Weeks c 4. R S Barn Epis Ch Denver CO 1990-2000; R Epiph Ch Dulaney Vlly Luthvle Timon MD 1977-1986; Asst To R S Thos' Whitemarsh PA 1975-1977; S Thos' Ch Whitemarsh Ft Washington PA 1975-1977.

HALVORSEN, Douglas Carl (NJ) 28 Oakhurst Ln, Mount Laurel NJ 08054 **Evergreens Chap Moorestown NJ 1999-; The Evergreens Moorestown NJ 1999-; Asst Trin Ch Moorestown NJ 1999-** B Lexington KY 1949 s Carl & Marcella. BA Asbury U 1970; MSW Rutgers The St U of New Jersey 1975; MS Rutgers The St U of New Jersey 1975; MDiv PrTS 1976. D 4/5/1986 Bp George Phelps Mellick Belshaw P 11/16/1986 Bp Vincent King Pettit. m 8/21/1970 Cheryl Grace Halvorsen c 2. Assoc Chr Ch New Brunswick NJ 1995-1998; Non-par 1976-1998. Auth, "Top Twenty Ways To Beat A Dead Horse," *Open Minds*, 1999; Auth, "From My Perspective, Wall St Journ," *Natl Bus Employment Weekly*, 1998.

HAMBLETON, Coralie Voce (NMich) St Paul's Episcopal Church, 201 E Ridge St, Marquette MI 49855 **D S Paul's Ch Marquette MI 2007-** B Marquette MI 1954 d George & Lottie. BSW Nthrn Michigan U 1977. D 5/27/2007 Bp James Arthur Kelsey. m 10/27/1990 Patrick Hambleton c 3.

HAMBLIN, Fr Jeffrey L. (LI) 423 West 46th Street, New York NY 10036 **S Clem's Ch New York NY 2015-; Dio Long Island 2004-; Dio New York 1994-** B Batesville IN 1953 s David & Opal. BS Indiana U 1975; MDiv Nash 1980; MS AUC 1990; MD AUC 1992. D 6/11/1980 P 12/20/1980 Bp William Cockburn Russell Sheridan. Chr Ch Bay Ridge Brooklyn NY 2009-2014; S Phil's Ch Brooklyn NY 2003-2004; Permanent Supply St Phil's Decatur St 2003-2004; Ch Of S Mary The Vrgn New York NY 1993-1994; St Philips Epis Ch Waukesha WI 1993-1994; S Jn Ch/Mision San Juan Milwaukee WI 1991-1993; Dio NW Pennsylvania Erie PA 1987-1995, 1982-1986; S Mary's Ch Erie PA 1984, 1981-1983; S Mk's Ch Erie PA 1981-1989; Chr Ch Gary IN 1980-1981. AACAP 1999; AMA 1999; Amer Psych Assn 1999; Bd Trst, Amer U of the Caribbean 1993; Soc of S Barn 1979-1981. Attending Physcian of the Year Kings Cnty Hosp, Brooklyn 2008; Soc WorkerCitizen of the Year Dio NW Pennsylvania. jlh@jeffreyhamblin-md.com

HAMBLIN, Sheldon Neilson (LI) 4301 Avenue D, Brooklyn NY 11203 **R S Paul's Ch-In-The-Vill Brooklyn NY 2013-** B Barbados 1971 MDiv SWTS. D 6/24/2003 P 3/25/2004 Bp Orris George Walker Jr. m 7/10/2004 Lisa Maria Hamblin c 1. Ch Of The Nativ Brooklyn NY 2007-2012; S Aug's Epis Ch Brooklyn NY 2006-2007; Dio Long Island Garden City NY 2003-2005.

HAMBY, Daniell C (Pa) 10 Lorile Cir, Eufaula AL 36027 B Atlanta GA 1950 s Joseph & Helen. BA Presb Coll 1973; DMin Columbia TS 1977; MA U of Notre Dame 1990; Cert Ecumenical Inst 1993; Nash 1994; SWTS 1994. D 6/14/1994 P 12/15/1994 Bp Francis Campbell Gray. m 6/16/1973 Virginia S Sonnen c 2. R S Andr's Ch Yardley PA 1998-2016, Asst 1996-1997; P-in-c Ch Of The Redeem Bensalem PA 1997-1998; P-in-c All SS Epis Ch Levittown PA 1995-1996; Gnrl Secy The COCU Princeton NJ 1994-1998; Serv Presb Ch 1977-1992; Chair, Cler Salaries and Pensions Dio Pennsylvania Philadelphia PA 2008-2011, Ecum Off 1999-. Pres Epis Dioc Ecum and Interriligious Off 2009-2016; Pres of the Philadelphia Theol Inst 1995. Sabbatical Grant EJ Lily Co 2010. daniellhamby@gmail.com

HAMBY, Timothy Christopher (Lex) 25 S 3rd St, Wilmington NC 28401 **S Jas Par Wilmington NC 2016-; Tech Off Missional Voices 2015-** B Lexington KY 1986 s Timothy & Iva. BA Transylvania U 2008; MDiv VTS 2015. D 3/7/2015 P 10/3/2015 Bp Doug Hahn. m 7/16/2011 Amanda K Todd c 1. Chr Ch Alexandria VA 2015-2016. chris@stjamesp.org

HAMER, Donald (Ct) 240 Kenyon St, Hartford CT 06105 **R Trin Epis Ch Hartford CT 2004-; Bd Vice Chair Trin Episcpal Day Sch on Asylum HIll 2013-; Bd Chair Farming Asylum Bus Dist 2011-; Bd Chair Grtr Hartford Conf of Ch 2010-; Prog and Bdgt Com Dio Connecticut Meriden CT 2006-** B Hartford CT 1950 s Frank & Marjorie. AB Geo 1972; JD Geo 1977; DAS Ya Berk 2000; MDiv Yale DS 2000. D 6/10/2000 Bp Andrew Donnan Smith P 12/16/2000 Bp James Elliot Curry. m 4/30/1977 Deborah Ann Hamer c 2. Asst S Mary's Epis Ch Manchester CT 2000-2003.

HAMERSLEY, Andrew C (NJ) 414 East Broad Street, Westfield NJ 07090 **R S Paul's Epis Ch Westfield NJ 2000-** B New York NY 1953 s Louis & Elsey. U Pac 1973; BA Bos 1975; MS Bos 1979; MDiv EDS 1984. D 3/25/1985 Bp Roger W Blanchard P 4/2/1986 Bp John Bowen Coburn. m 9/26/1981 Rosamond Hooper-Hamersley c 2. R S Andr's Epis Ch Albany NY 1988-2000; Par Of Chr Ch Andover MA 1985-1988; Dn Nthrn Convoc Dio New Jersey Trenton NJ 2004-2007; Stndg Com Dio Albany Greenwich NY 1995-1997. Soc of S Jn the Evang 1981. Winner of the Best Sermon Competition Epis Evang Fndt 1995.

HAMES, Patricia Margaret (Ct) 21 N Main St, Niantic CT 06357 **S Ann's Epis Ch Old Lyme CT 2016-** B Eynesbury Cambs UK 1945 d Allan & Daisy. BA U of Maryland 1984; MDiv Ya Berk 1988. D 6/10/1989 Bp Arthur Edward Walmsley P 5/26/1990 Bp Jeffery William Rowthorn. c 2. R S Mk's Ch New Britain CT 1995-2015; Chr And Epiph Ch E Haven CT 1994-1995; Int Chr and the Epiph E Haven CT 1994-1995; Dn - Danbury Dnry Dio Connecticut Meriden CT 1992-1994; Trin Ch Newtown CT 1989-1994.

HAMILL, Allardyce Armstrong (CFla) Church of our Saviour, 200 NW 3rd St, Okeechobee FL 34972 B Plainfield NJ 1931 d John & Myrtle. BS Agnes Scott Coll 1953; MLS Florida St U 1978. D 12/1/2007 Bp John Wadsworth Howe. c 2.

HAMILL, Charles Brent Wagner (Pgh) Christ Episcopal Church North Hills, 5910 Babcock Blvd, Pittsburgh PA 15237 **Chr Epis Ch No Hills Pittsburgh PA 2012-** B Sewickley PA 1976 s John & Jane. BS U of Missouri 1998; MDiv Pittsburgh TS 2012. D 6/2/2012 Bp Kenneth Lester Price P 12/15/2012 Bp Dorsey McConnell.

HAMILL, Jan Elizabeth (Md) 703 Peppard Dr, Bel Air MD 21014 **Assoc for Formation Resources Ch of the H Comf Lutherville MD 2013-; Dir Epis Serv Corps-MD 2011-; Dir Epis Serv Corps-Maryland 2011-** B Ann Arbor MI 1953 d Peter & Margot. St Johns Coll Annapolis MD 1973; Cert Universite de Poitiers Tours FR 1973; BA Marlboro Coll 1976; MDiv Ya Berk 1980. D 4/26/1980 P 11/22/1980 Bp David Keller Leighton Sr. m 9/5/1981 Mark Francis Gatza c 2. Chapl Copper Ridge Sykesville MD 2011-2013; Cn for Chr Formation Cathd Of The Incarn Baltimore MD 2001-2010; Catechist S Jas Ch Monkton MD 1995-2001; H Cross Ch St MD 1990-2001; R Chr Ch Forest Hill MD 1990-1993; Asst St Martins-In-The-Field Ch Severna Pk MD 1984-1990; P-in-c S Jas Ch Irvington Baltimore MD 1983-1984; Chapl S Tim's Sch Stevenson MD 1982-1983; Asst Epiph Ch Dulaney Vlly Luthvle Timon MD 1980-1982; Com on Liturg Dio Maryland Baltimore MD 1999-2010, Stndg Com 1994-1999, Chair, COM 1988-1993. Soc of Comp of H Cross 1980. Par of H Cross Bp's Awd Outstanding Cong Dio Maryland 1999. escmaryland@gmail.com

HAMILTON, Abigail W (Nwk) 681 Prospect Ave # 7052, West Orange NJ 07052 B Orange NJ 1941 d John & Ruth. BA Bryn 1962; MDiv UTS 1974. D 6/8/1974 P 1/5/1977 Bp George E Rath. c 2. R Ch Of The H Innoc W Orange NJ 1990-2006; Vic S Andr's Ch Newark NJ 1984-1990; P-in-c Newark Epis Coop For Min & Miss Newark NJ 1979-1983; Cur S Paul's Epis Ch Morris Plains NJ 1974-1979.

HAMILTON, David George (Vt) 129 Cumberland Rd, Burlington VT 05408 **R All SS' Epis Ch S Burlington VT 2009-; Dir, Sprtl Resources Dept. Fletcher Allen Healthcare Burlington VT 1996-** B Fitchburg MA 1942 s James & Ruth. BA Clark U 1964; MDiv EDS 1968; STM Andover Newton TS 1970; DMin Andover Newton TS 1973. D 6/27/1968 Bp Robert McConnell Hatch P 2/2/1969 Bp Charles Francis Hall. m 8/24/1963 Alida Jane Hamilton c 1. Fletcher Allen Healthcare Burlington VT 1996-2009; Ch Of S Jn The Evang Dunbarton NH 1994-1996; Pstr Counslr Cornerstone Cntr Concord NH 1982-1995; Adj Prof ANTS Newton Cntre MA 1980-1995; Dn Cntrl Convoc Dio New Hampshire Concord NH 1972-1976; R S Paul's Ch Concord NH 1970-1981, Cur 1968-1969.

HAMILTON, David Hendry (Nwk) 75 Summerhill Dr, Manahawkin NJ 08050 B Newark NJ 1941 s David & Mildred. BA Bloomfield Coll 1966; MDiv Ya Berk 1970; DMin Drew U 1975. D 6/13/1970 Bp Leland Stark P 12/19/1970 Bp George E Rath. c 2. R S Paul's Ch In Bergen Jersey City NJ 2000-2007;

Trin And S Phil's Cathd Newark NJ 1998-2000; Int Chr Ch Glen Ridge NJ 1995-1997; Chapl S Jn the Bapt Sch Mendham NJ 1971-1972; S Paul's Epis Ch Morris Plains NJ 1970-1996. Hon Cn Trin & S Phil Cathd.

HAMILTON, Gordon William (USC) 101 Woodside Dr, Gaffney SC 29340 **Chr Epis Ch Lancaster SC 2010-** B Montreal QC CA 1946 s Robert & Grace. Edison Jr Coll Asheville-Biltmore Coll; BS U of Lethbridge 1974; MDiv U of Wstrn Ontario CA 1983. Trans 10/1/1995 Bp Dorsey Henderson. m 5/16/1987 Carol-Lynn R Hamilton c 3. Chr Ch Greenville SC 2008-2009; R Ch Of The Incarn Gaffney SC 1995-2007; R Par Of Westfield Westfield New Brunswick 1987-1995; Asst Cur Trin Ch S Thos Ontario 1983-1987.

HAMILTON SR, James Edward (Tex) 13618 Brighton Park Drive, Houston TX 77044 B Toledo OH 1949 s Edward & Patricia. BA U of Texas 1974; MDiv Epis TS in Kentucky 1979. D 5/13/1979 Bp Addison Hosea P 2/3/1980 Bp Calvin Onderdonk Schofield Jr. m 7/31/1976 Jan S Hamilton c 2. R S Tim's Epis Ch Houston TX 2004-2012; Chapl S Lk's Epis Hosp Houston TX 2004; R H Trin Epis Ch Dickinson TX 1985-2003; R S Jn's Epis Ch Marlin TX 1980-1985; Asst S Mk The Evang Ft Lauderdale FL 1979-1980; Chapl S Mk's Epis Sch Ft Lauderd FL 1979-1980; Pres, Sch Bd H Trin Epis Sch 2004-2011; TCC Bd Mem Const Com 2001; Crop Bd Pres Ch Wrld Serv 1990-2002; Ecum Off Dio Texas Houston TX 1990-2002; Chair of Del Texas Conf of Ch 1990-2002. Auth, "The Liturg Coordntr," *The Liturg Coordntr*, Hymnary Press, 1984. BroSA 1977; CROP 1988; Mnstrl Soc 1985; TCC 1985. Distinguished Alum Bos TS 2007; Proclamation Day Dickinson Mayor 2004; Roothbert Fell Roothbert Fund 2002; Pioneer Awd Ch Wrld Serv 2000; Houston Cmpgn for Homeless Interfaith Mnstrs 1998; Citizen of the Year NASW 1979.

HAMILTON, James G (Md) Canton/Fells Point Church Plant, 1025 S Potomac St, Baltimore MD 21224 **Dio Maryland Baltimore MD 2014-** B 1977 s Robert & Patricia. BA Hope Coll 1999; MDiv SWTS 2008. D 3/7/2009 Bp Mark Sean Sisk P 9/24/2009 Bp Wendell Nathaniel Gibbs Jr. m 7/27/2002 Elizabeth Rogers c 1. Chr Ch Cranbrook Bloomfield Hills MI 2011-2014; R Trin Epis Ch Farmington MI 2010-2014; Assoc S Jn's Ch Royal Oak MI 2009.

HAMILTON, Jamie L (NH) 20 Main St, Exeter NH 03833 **P All SS Ch Peterborough NH 2014-; Tchr of Rel Phillips Exeter Acad Exeter NH 1995-** B San Rafael CA 1955 d James & Frankie. BA Cntrl Washington U 1977; MDiv UTS 1985. D 6/8/1991 P 12/14/1991 Bp Richard Frank Grein. c 2. Emm Ch Dublin NH 2006, 2005, 2004, 2003, 2002; Ch Of The Heav Rest New York NY 1992-1995.

HAMILTON, John M (NY) 1 Hudson St., Yonkers NY 10701 **R S Eliz's Epis Ch Dahlonega GA 2017-** B Meridan MS 1962 s Joseph & Mary. BA Rhodes Coll 1984; BA Oxf GB 1989; MPA Georgia St U 1997; MDiv GTS 2004. D 6/5/2004 P 2/5/2005 Bp J Neil Alexander. Trin Ch Natchez MS 2016-2017; The Epis Ch Of The Medtr Meridian MS 2016; P-in-c S Jn's Ch Getty Sq Yonkers NY 2007-2016; Int Ch Of The Redeem Astoria NY 2006-2007; Cur Gr Ch Newark NJ 2004-2006.

HAMILTON, Lucy B (SwFla) 626 Hibiscus Dr, Venice FL 34285 **Chapl Venice Theatre 2015-; Vol Loveland Cntr for Developmentally Disabled Adults 2014-; Fac CREDO 2011-** B Bloomington IN 1959 d William & Edna. Harlaxton Coll 1978; BA DePauw U 1980; MA Indiana U 1983; MA Indiana U 1987; MDiv Ya Berk 1995; STM Ya Berk 1996; DMin SWTS 2018. D 12/11/1999 Bp Robert William Duncan P 3/17/2001 Bp Andrew Donnan Smith. m 10/13/2007 James Lee Grubbs c 1. P-in-c S Edm's Epis Ch Arcadia FL 2015-2017; Assoc R S Thos' Epis Ch St Petersburg FL 2012-2014; Guardian Hospice Venice FL 2009-2011; Ed, Epis Life Media Epis Ch Cntr 2008-2009; Epis Ch Cntr New York NY 2008-2009, 2005; Chr Ch Norwalk CT 2007; Consult Trin Wall St New York NY 2006-2008; Trin Par New York NY 2006, 1999-2000; Consult Epis Migration Mnstrs 2005-2006; Consult GC of the Epis Ch 2001-2003; Asst to R Chr Ch Greenwich CT 2000-2004; Video Producer Trin Wall St New York NY 1995-2000; Publ Relatns & Prod Mister Rogers' Nbrhd 1986-1991. Auth, "The Times, Are They Changing?," *The Sewanee Theol Revs*, U So, 2016; Auth, "Online w Darkwood Brew," *Faith and Ldrshp*, Duke, 2014; Auth, "Prayers for Times of Grief," Paraclete Press, 2012; Auth, "arts for Chld," *Cobblestone, Cricket, Faces, Humpty Dumpty*, Carus, 2012; Auth, "Wisdom from the Middle Ages for Middle-aged Wmn," Morehouse, 2007; Auth, "Prayers to the God of My Life: Psalms for Morning and Evening," Morehouse, 2003; Auth, "For Those We Love and See No Longer: Daily Off for Times of Grief," Paraclete Press, 2001; Auth, "The Gospel According to Fred: A Visit w Mister Rogers," *Chr Century*, 1996; Auth, "One of the Five-Thousand," *Journ of Biblic Storytelling*, 1995; Auth, "Feeding the Five Thousand," *Journ of Narrative Homil*, 1994. Pres, Alum Assoc., Berkeley Div. Sch. at Yale 2002-2011; Soc of S Marg 1997. Rel and the Arts Awd Yale DS 1995; Preaching Excellence Conf Preaching Excellence Prog 1994. lisa@lisabhamilton.com

HAMILTON, Michael Pollock (WA) 3111 44th St Nw, Washington DC 20016 **S Mary's Epis Ch Foggy Bottom Washington DC 2004-; Ret 1993-** B Belfast Northern Ireland 1927 s Hugh & Blanche. BA U Tor 1951; MDiv VTS 1955. D 6/3/1955 Bp Frederick D Goodwin P 12/1/1955 Bp Henry W Hobson. m 6/13/1981 Eleanoré Hamilton c 2. Int S Jas Ch Potomac MD 1998-1999; Serv Ch in the Netherlands 1995-1997; Serv Coun on Frgn Relatns 1980-2002; Cn

Cathd of St Ptr & St Paul Washington DC 1964-1993; Chapl Fac & Stdts Dio Los Angeles Los Angeles CA 1958-1964; Cur Ch Of The Adv Cincinnati OH 1955-1958. Ed, *A Hospice Handbk-New Way to Care for Dying*, Eerdhams, 1986; Ed, *Amer Character & Frgn Plcy*, Eerdhams, 1986; Ed, *To Avoid Catastrophe: A Study in Future Nuclear Plcy*, Eerdhams, 1978; Ed, *Ord of Wmn-Pro & Con*, Morehouse Pub, 1975; Ed, *Chrsmtc Mvmt-Confusion or Blessing?*, Eerdhams, 1974; Ed, *New Genetics & Future of Man*, Eerdhams, 1972; Ed, *This Little Planet*, Scribner's, 1967; Ed, *Vietnam War: Ch Perspective*, Eerdhams, 1967.

HAMILTON, Paul Edward Connell (LI) 176 Davis Ln, Hamden NY 13782 **Pstr First Presb Ch Unadilla New York 2014-; Adj Prof (Human Serv/ Amer Urban Stds) Metropltn Coll of New York 2002-** B Sharon PA 1945 s Russell & Alice. BA Youngstown St U 1967; Kings Coll London - Lon 1968; MDiv GTS 1971; DD Chr TS 1978; MSW Yeshiva U 1992; CASAC LIU 1996. D 7/11/1971 P 3/25/1972 Bp William Crittenden. c 1. R S Paul's Ch Coll Point NY 1999-2009; Headmaster S Paul's Sch NY 1999-2002; R S Mary's Ch Brooklyn NY 1985-1996; Dio Long Island Garden City NY 1983-1985; P-in-c Emm Epis Ch Of Sheepshead Bay Brooklyn NY 1983; Asst S Mart's Ch New York NY 1980-1981; Assoc Ch Of The Intsn New York NY 1976-1979; Asst S Phil's Ch New York NY 1973-1976; Asst All Ang' Ch New York NY 1971-1973. NASW 1993. DD Chr Sem 1989; Hon Kentucky Colonel Govenor of Kentucky 1974.

HAMILTON, Reid Henry (Mich) 4657 Dexter Ann Arbor Road, Ann Arbor MI 48103 **Chapl Epis Stdt Fndt Ann Arbor MI 2004-** B Joplin MO 1956 s Eugene & Mary. BA Westminster Coll 1978; JD Van 1981; MDiv Candler TS Emory U 1998. D 6/6/1998 Bp Frank Kellogg Allan P 12/7/1998 Bp John Clark Buchanan. m 6/11/1987 Debra K Garner c 2. S Phil's Epis Ch Akron OH 2004; R Chr Epis Ch Kent OH 2001-2004; Secy Dio W Missouri Kansas City MO 1999-2001; Asst R S Paul's Ch Kansas City MO 1998-2001. Auth, "Better Get It In Your Soul: What Liturgists Can Learn from Jazz," Ch Pub, 2008. Sam Portaro Awd for creative expression in campus Mnstry Off for YA and Campus Mnstrs 2011; DD Nash, Nashotah 2009.

HAMILTON, Robert Earl (NC) 1200 N Elm St, Greensboro NC 27401 **Asst S Andr's Ch Greensboro NC 1989-; Dir, Pstr Care Moses Cone Hlth System 1979-** B Olean NY 1945 s Howard & Jane. BA High Point U 1967; BD VTS 1970; CPE Duke 1976; CPE Delaware St Hosp DE 1977. D 6/29/1970 P 5/1/1971 Bp David Shepherd Rose. m 7/26/1981 Lynn Hamilton c 3. P-in-c Ch Of The Mssh Mayodan NC 1981-1989; Trin Par Wilmington DE 1977; P-in-c Old Swedes Ch Wilmington DE 1976-1977; Dio No Carolina Raleigh NC 1975-1976; S Mk's Epis Ch Roxboro NC 1975-1976; R S Barn Chesterfield Cnty VA 1973-1975; S Barn Epis Ch No Chesterfield VA 1973-1975; Asst S Jn's Ch Hampton VA 1970-1973. AEHC 1978; ACPE 1979; Assn for Psychol Type 1989; Cert Chapl Assn Prof Chapl; No Carolina Chapl Assn 1980. Outstanding St Ldr Awd Assn of Profsnl Chapl 1993.

HAMILTON, Roger John (CFla) 4018 Shorecrest Drive, Orlando FL 32804 B Trenton NJ 1949 s Horace & Marie. BA Trenton St Coll 1971; MDiv PDS 1974. D 4/27/1974 P 11/23/1974 Bp Albert Wiencke Van Duzer. m 4/25/1970 Karen Hoover c 2. R S Mich's Ch Orlando FL 1998-2014; R Chr Ch Somers Point NJ 1980-1998; Cur Chr Ch In Woodbury Woodbury NJ 1975-1980; Cur S Ptr's Ch Freehold NJ 1974-1975. OHC, Assoc 1983. Divemaster Profsnl Assn of Diving Instructors 1987.

HAMILTON, Terrell Eugene (SJ) 401 N Marilyn Ave, Wenatchee WA 98801 B Santa Ana CA 1945 s Terrell & Mabel. BA California St U 1976; MDiv Fuller TS 1979. D 12/16/1979 P 12/1/1980 Bp Victor Manuel Rivera. m 12/30/1967 Claudia Hamilton. Int S Fran Epis Ch Fair Oaks CA 2002-2004; Chapl Chapl USAF 1985-2001; Chapl Off Of Bsh For ArmdF New York NY 1985-2001; Vic Chr Ch Lemoore CA 1980-1985; Cur S Paul's Epis Ch Visalia CA 1979-1980.

HAMILTON, William Edward (SeFla) 1728 13th Ave N, Lake Worth FL 33460 B Philadelphia PA 1940 s Frederick & Mildred. LTh Epis TS in Kentucky 1976; VTS 1999. D 5/16/1976 P 12/1/1977 Bp Addison Hosea. m 9/16/1960 Charlotte Hamilton c 4. Vic Ch Of S Jn Lake Worth FL 1988-1991; R S Andr's Ch Lake Worth FL 1986-2005; S Mart's Epis Ch Pompano Bch FL 1984-1986; All SS Ch Newport KY 1982-1984; Vic All SS' Cold Sprg KY 1982-1983; S Davids Ch Pikeville KY 1978-1982; Vic S Dav's Ch Pikeville KY 1978-1982; Asst Ch S Mich The Archangel Lexington KY 1976-1977; Curs Dio SE Florida Miami 2001-2002, Dn, So Palm Bch Dnry 1991-1994. Mssn Cleric of the Year Dio Lexington 1983.

HAMILTON, W Michael (Mass) 19 Bradford Rd, Natick MA 01760 **Sr Pharmacist Lahey Clnc Med Cntr 2002-** B Boston MA 1960 s Walter & Margaret. AS Nthrn Essex Cmnty Coll Haverill MA 1981; BS U of Rhode Island 1991. D 6/2/2007 Bp M(Arvil) Thomas Shaw. m 7/30/2004 Daniel R Collier c 2.

HAMLIN, Richard Lee (Roch) 6258 County Road 31a, Friendship NY 14739 **Ret The Epis Ch 2006-; Stndg Com Dio Rochester Henrietta 2015-** B Rochester NY 1948 s Roy & Florence. BA SUNY 1970; MA SUNY 1972; MDiv EDS 1975. D 6/29/1975 P 4/10/1976 Bp Robert Rae Spears Jr. m 8/21/1976 Stephanie P Pentecost c 2. Tchr Miami-Dade Cnty Publ Schools

2006-2012; R S Andr's Epis Ch Miami FL 1999-2006; R Ch Of The Resurr Oswego NY 1988-1999; R S Paul's Ch Troy NY 1982-1988; Asst Min S Ptr's Ch Albany NY 1980-1982; P-in-c Allegany Cnty Mnstry Belmont NY 1975-1980.

HAMLIN, W Richard (Mich) 1016 Poxson Ave, Lansing MI 48910 **P in Res Trin Epis Ch Grand Ledge MI 2015-; Stwdshp Com Dio Wstrn Michigan Kalamazoo MI 2015-; Secy of Dioc Conv Dio Michigan Detroit MI 2013-, Bp's Advsry Com for Total Mnstry 2011-2013, Stndg Com 2011-, Alt Dep to GC 2010-2016, Dn, Capital Dnry 2010-2013, Whitaker Institue Advsry Coun 2009-2015, Stndg Com 2005-2011, Stndg Com 2005-2009** B Syracuse NY 1946 s Walter & Eleanor. BA Hobart and Wm Smith Colleges 1968; MA U Roch 1971; PhD U Roch 1981; MDiv Bex Sem 1992. D 8/10/1991 P 4/8/1992 Bp William George Burrill. m 6/27/1970 Claudia Lois Hamlin c 3. R S Mich's Epis Ch Lansing MI 2004-2012; Chapl Dio Cntrl New York Liverpool NY 2004, Dep to GC for Total Mnstry 1998-2004; R Trin Epis Ch Canastota NY 1999-2004; R S Jn's Epis Ch Oneida NY 1999-2003; Bd Dir Bex Seabury Wstrn Sem Fed; Chicago IL 2013-2016; Bd Trst Bex Sem Columbus OH 2010-2013; Co-Chair, 2003--2006 SCSD 2001-2006; Participant Epis/Polish Natl Cath Dialogue 1995-2003. Assoc SSM 1998; Associated Parishes 1992; TENS 2000. Outstanding Adult Eductr Elmira Coll, Elmira NY 1991; Phi Beta Kappa Hob 1968.

HAMLYN, Robert Cornelius (NY) 127 Fulton Ave Apt J1, Poughkeepsie NY 12603 **Assoc S Ptr's Epis Ch Peekskill NY 1991-; Ret St. Ptr's Peekskill NY P Assoc 1991-** B Palmer NE 1929 s Robert & Helen. BA Laf 1950; STB GTS 1953; MDiv GTS 1968. D 6/13/1953 P 12/19/1953 Bp Benjamin M Washburn. m 1/16/1954 Klara V Hamlyn c 3. Dir Pstr Care Westchester Cnty Med Cntr 1983-1991; Ret Rel & Mntil Hlth Inc.Pasoral Councillor 1968-1991; Pres Rel & Mntl Hlth Inc 1968-1983; Dir Educ Rel & Mntl Hlth Inc 1968-1978; Fdn For Rel & Mntl Hlth Briarcliff NY 1964-1980; Asst to R Gr Epis Ch New York NY 1959-1961; Vic S Steph Coytesville NJ 1953-1959. Auth, "Fact Finders Journey to Europe," *Journ of Rel & Hlth*. Dplma AAPC 1968-2006.

HAMMATT JR, Edward Augustus (SeFla) 16330 Sw 80th Ave, Miami FL 33157 **D Dio SE Florida Miami 1993-** B Baton Rouge LA 1939 s Edward & Ida. BS LSU 1963. D 12/20/1993 Bp Calvin Onderdonk Schofield Jr. m 9/6/1975 Judith Drake Hammatt c 2.

HAMMETT, Robert Lee (Mass) P.O. Box 224, Oak Bluff MA 02557 **Ret 1993-** B Brooklyn NY 1929 s John & Margaret. BA Wesl 1951; MDiv VTS 1954. D 6/9/1954 P 1/1/1955 Bp Walter H Gray. m 9/28/1957 Sarah V Hammett c 3. R S Jn's Ch Newtonville MA 1981-1993; S Geo's Ch Middlebury CT 1975-1981; Chapl Emma Willard Sch Troy NY 1966-1975; R Chr Ch Sharon CT 1957-1966; Cur S Lk Noroton CT 1954-1957.

HAMMON, LeRoy R (Ore) 820 Berwick Ct, Lake Oswego OR 97034 B 1937 s LeRoy. MDiv Epis TS of the SW 2003. D 6/25/2003 Bp Robert Louis Ladehoff P 1/11/2004 Bp Johncy Itty. m 1/16/1995 Ina L Hammon c 2. Int CBO Dio Oregon Portland OR 2008; Asst P Chr Ch Par Lake Oswego OR 2004-2008.

HAMMOND, Blaine Randol (ECR) PO Box 293, Ben Lomond CA 95005 **S Andr's Ch Ben Lomond CA 2009-** B Lincoln NE 1946 s Blaine & Mary. BA U of Washington 1979; MDiv Iliff TS 1982; CAS CDSP 1988. D 6/11/1988 P 1/28/1989 Bp William Carl Frey. m 9/18/1965 Elizabeth Dianne Hammond c 3. Vic S Ptr's Ch Seaview WA 1996-2008; Cur Chr's Epis Ch Castle Rock CO 1989-1991; Vic S Irenaeus Lyons CO 1988-1989. Auth, "Donatism For Today," *LivCh*, 2000; Auth, "Peninsula Ch Cntr Celebrates 25 Years Of Joint Mnstry," *The Epis Voice*, 1999; Auth, "Is God Truly Loving?," *The Chr Mnstry*, 1998; Auth, "The Psychol Of Rel In Mnstry (By H Newton Malony)," *The Chr Mnstry*, 1997; Auth, "Hiding In Plain Sight," *The Chr Mnstry*, 1997.

HAMMOND, Constance Ann (Ore) 4045 S.E. Pine St., Portland OR 97214 B Salem OR 1937 d William & Constance. BS U of Oregon 1959; MEd U of Oregon 1962; CAS Harv 1980; MDiv Harvard DS 1985; DMin SFTS 2005. D 6/4/1986 Bp John Bowen Coburn P 5/1/1987 Bp David Elliot Johnson. Asst All SS Ch Portland OR 2002-2013; Int S Andr's Epis Ch Aberdeen WA 2000-2002; Int S Paul's Ch Walla Walla WA 1999-2000; S Steph's Epis Par Portland OR 1990-1998; The Ch Of The Gd Shpd Acton MA 1989-1990; Old No Chr Ch Boston MA 1987-1989; Gr Ch Newton MA 1986-1987; Chapl U Hosp Boston MA 1985-1987. Auth, "Shalom/Salaaw/Peace A Liberation Theol of Hope," 2008. Soc Of S Jn The Evang 1984. Refugee Immigration Mnstry Constance Hammond Awd Refuge Immigration Mnstry, EDS 1996; Billings Prize Harvard DS 1985; Potter Fllshp U Hosp 1985.

HAMMOND, David Murray (Cal) 11 Mesa Ave, Mill Valley CA 94941 **Ch Of The Nativ San Rafael CA 1999-; Ret 1989-** B Brandon MT CA 1923 s Stephen & Hattie. BA U CA 1949; BD EDS 1952. D 6/23/1952 P 2/19/1953 Bp Francis E I Bloy. m 8/3/1947 Muriel Hammond c 3. Elctn Process Com Dio California San Francisco CA 1978-1979, Chair Com Resolutns 1975-1989; R Ch Of Our Sav Mill Vlly CA 1957-1989; Vic S Barth's Mssn Pico Rivera CA 1952-1957.

HAMMOND, Henry L (Md) 6705 Maxalea Rd, Baltimore MD 21239 B Baltimore MD 1941 s W Hollyday & Emma. BA Br 1963; MDiv EDS 1967; MA Emory U 1968. D 10/27/1968 P 12/1/1969 Bp Horace W B Donegan. m 10/9/1995 Leigh Price Hammond c 2. Asst Memi Ch Baltimore MD 1985-1993;

Asst S Mich And All Ang Ch Baltimore MD 1980-1985; Assoc H Evang Baltimore MD 1978-1980; Asst Ch Of The H Nativ Baltimore MD 1977-1978; S Barn Epis Ch Sykesville MD 1974-1977; R S Barn' Skyesville MD 1974-1977; R Gr Epis Ch Port Jervis NY 1970-1974; Asst S Mich's Ch New York NY 1969-1970; Vic Stras Memi Tazewell VA 1968-1969; Vic Trin Ch Richlands VA 1968-1969.

HAMMOND, James Allen (Va) 102 Cottage Drive, Winchester VA 22603 B Baltimore MD 1944 s William & Emma. BA U of Maryland 1968; MDiv SWTS 1972. D 6/6/1972 P 2/2/1973 Bp David Keller Leighton Sr. m 5/8/1982 Gina B Hammond c 1. P-in-c Chr Epis Ch Brandy Sta VA 1995-2008; S Lk's Ch Remington VA 1995-2008, R 1993-1995; R S Paul's Par Kent Chestertown MD 1995; Assoc Epiph Epis Ch Odenton MD 1992-1993; Assoc Epiph Ch Dulaney Vlly Luthvle Timon MD 1989-1992; Dn Dio Maryland Baltimore MD 1988-1992; R S Dav's Epis Ch Topeka KS 1986-1988; R H Trin Ch Churchville MD 1981-1986; Assoc Calv Epis Ch Williamsville NY 1978-1981; Chapl Garrison Forest Sch Garrison MD 1973-1978; Asst Ch Of The Mssh Baltimore MD 1972-1973. Auth, "Sine Nomine," *Leaven*, 1993; Auth, "No Longer Immune: A Counslr's Guide to AIDS, Chapt 12," *Amer Assn of Counslg and Dvlpmt*, 1989; Auth, "Strive to Thrive," *LivCh*, 1986; Auth, "Dissolution: Theol, Pragmatism & Morality," *Leaven*, 1983; Auth, "Rel Manifestations," *Hse*, 1978; Auth, "Who Says You Can Teach Ethics," *CRIS Nwsltr*, 1977; Auth, "Early Amer Evang," *Hse*, 1975. Cramer Awd SWTS 1969; Anderson Awd SWTS 1969. hammond.jim@gmail.com

HAMMOND, Jeffrey Benjamin (WTex) 14526 Spaulding Dr, Corpus Christi TX 78410 **P S Barn Epis Ch Fredricksburg TX 2009-** B Chattanooga TN 1960 BA U CA; MA Epis TS of the SW 1994; MDiv Sewanee: The U So, TS 2003. D 6/5/2003 Bp Robert Boyd Hibbs P 1/6/2004 Bp James Edward Folts. m 10/18/1997 Barclay Livingston Hammond c 2. Vic S Andr's Epis Ch Corpus Christi TX 2003-2009.

HAMMOND, Marion Junior (Colo) 9 Chusco Rd, Santa Fe NM 87508 **Ret 1989-** B Gardner KS 1927 s Marion & Rose. BA U Denv 1948; MDiv Ya Berk 1951. D 4/7/1951 Bp Austin Pardue P 10/7/1951 Bp Harold L Bowen. m 8/25/1950 Opal Hammond c 5. Sch Bd Dio Colorado Denver CO 1977-1983; R S Thos Epis Ch Denver CO 1963-1988; R S Barn Of The Vlly Cortez CO 1951-1963; Vic S Paul's Ch Mancos CO 1951-1963.

HAMMONDS, Joanie (Ala) 755 Plantation Dr, Selma AL 36701 B Mobile AL 1957 d Frederick & Vivian. D 10/30/2004 Bp Henry Nutt Parsley Jr. m 1/1/1981 James Hammonds c 2.

HAMNER IV, James Edward (At) 3110-A Ashford Dunwoody Rd Ne, Atlanta GA 30319 **Fin Com Dio Atlanta 2005-** B Norfolk VA 1957 s James & Joan. BA W&L 1980; MDiv Sewanee: The U So, TS 1984; MPhil Oxf GB 1989; PhD Oxf GB 1991. D 6/9/1984 Bp John Thomas Walker P 3/1/1985 Bp James Barrow Brown. m 10/15/2011 Cynthia Diane Williamson c 3. Headmaster S Mart's Epis Sch Atlanta GA 2000-2017; Asst. Headmaster Epis HS Baton Rouge Baton Rouge LA 1992-2000; Assoc R S Paul's Ch New Orleans LA 1991-1992; P-in-c S Mich-Northgate Oxford Engl 1988-1989; Asstg P S Mich-Northgate Oxford Engl 1987-1991; Asst R S Jas Epis Ch Baton Rouge LA 1984-1987. AAR 1992; CAT 1992; SAES Exec Bd 1992-2000; SBL 1992. Presidential Schlr Distinguished Tchr White Hse Cmsn on Presidential Scholars 1997.

HAMP, Gary (WMich) 245 Rose Bud Ct, Traverse City MI 49696 **P-in-c S Andr's Ch Big Rapids MI 2013-** B Lansing MI 1943 s Charles & Genevieve. BS Ferris St U 1970; MDiv GTS 1984; STM GTS 1985; PhD SFTU 2003. D 6/30/1984 Bp Henry Irving Mayson P 2/2/1985 Bp Henry Boyd Hucles III. m 12/14/1979 Patricia Hamp. Int S Lk's Par Kalamazoo MI 2008-2009; Int S Mk The Evang Ft Lauderdale FL 2005-2008; S Alfred's Epis Ch Palm Harbor FL 2003-2004; Int Emm Epis Ch S Louis MO 2001-2003; Int S Jas Epis Ch Birmingham MI 2000-2001; Int S Mich & S Geo S Louis MO 1997-2000; Int Gr Epis Ch Port Huron MI 1996-1997; Int Trin Epis Ch Bay City MI 1994-1996; R S Jn's Epis Ch Odessa TX 1990-1994; R Chr Epis Ch Owosso MI 1985-1990; S Lk's Ch Forest Hills NY 1984-1985.

HAMPTON, Carol McDonald (Okla) 1414 N Hudson Ave, Oklahoma City OK 73103 B Oklahoma City OK 1935 d Denzil & Mildred. BA U of Oklahoma 1957; MA U of Oklahoma 1973; PhD U of Oklahoma 1984; CTh Epis TS of the SW 1998; MDiv Phillips TS 1999. D 6/26/1999 P 12/19/1999 Bp Robert Manning Moody. m 2/22/1958 James Wilburn Hampton c 4. Cur S Paul's Cathd Oklahoma City OK 1999-2001; Off Multicultural Mnstry (PB Stff) 1994-1998; Field Off Native Amer Mnstry (PB Stff) 1986-1994. Ed, *First Peoples Theol Journ*. AltGld (Natl) 2007; Indigenous Theol Trng Inst Bd 1999.

HAMPTON, Cynthia Marie (SO) 410 Torrence Ct, Cincinnati OH 45202 **Dir of Sprtl Serv Hyde Pk Hlth Cntr Cincinnati OH 2007-** B Louisville KY 1958 d Donald & Mary. BA Agnes Scott Coll 1980; PhD NWU 1984; MDiv Ya Berk 1996. D 6/29/1996 Bp Herbert Thompson Jr P 4/12/1997 Bp Kenneth Lester Price. Hyde Pk Hlth Cntr Cincinnati OH 2007-2009; Dir of Sprtl Serv Epis Ret Hm: Deupree Cmnty Cincinnati OH 2000-2007; Epis Ret Serv Cincinnati OH 2000-2007; Dio Sthrn Ohio Cincinnati OH 1999; Chapl Anna Louise Inn Cincinnati OH 1998-2000; Supply Chap Of The Nativ Cincinnati OH 1998-2000; Asst and Chapl Ch Of The Adv Cincinnati OH 1997-1998; Asst S

Jn's Epis Ch Lancaster OH 1996-1997. Auth, "Pleasure Knowledge & Being: Analysis Of Plato'S Philebus," SUNY Press, 1990.

HAMPTON, Roger Keith (Los) Po Box 260304, Corpus Christi TX 78426 **Vic S Mk's Holtville CA 1982-** B Los Angeles CA 1947 s Gordon & Ruth. Emory U 1967; BA Stan 1970; PSR 1973; Tubingen U Tubingen DE 1973; MDiv CD-SP 1975. D 6/21/1975 P 2/1/1976 Bp Robert Claflin Rusack. m 1/25/1981 Nohemi Hampton c 1. St Dunstans Epis Ch Moreno Vlly CA 1986; S Lk's Mssn Fontana CA 1984-1986; All SS Epis Ch Brawley CA 1982-1983; St Marks Mssn Holtville CA 1982-1983; Epis Chapl USC 1980-1982; Vic Ch Of The H Comm Gardena CA 1979-1982; Ch Of Our Sav Par San Gabr CA 1975-1978; Cur Our Sav Alhambra CA 1975-1978. Auth, "A Pilgrims Progress". Phi Beta Kappa.

✠ **HAMPTON, The Rt Rev Sanford Zangwill Kaye** (Oly) La Vida Real, 11588 Via Rancho San Diego Apt D 3049, El Cajon CA 92019 **Asstg Bp Dio Olympia Seattle 2010-, Chapl to the Ret 2001-, Asstg Bp 1996-2004, 1996-2000; Chaplin to the Ret Dio Olympia 2001-** B Passaic NJ 1935 s Sanford & Renee. BS NWU 1956; MDiv SWTS 1966; DD Honorus Causa SWTS 1990. D 6/11/1966 Bp James Winchester Montgomery P 12/17/1966 Bp Gerald Francis Burrill Con 4/5/1989 for Minn. m 12/18/1953 Marilynn Prage c 4. Cleric in Charge St Steph's Epis Ch Oak Harbor WA 2011-2012; Asstg Bp Dio Oregon Portland OR 2008-2010; PBp Nomin Com ECUSA New York NY 1994-1997; Com on PB & Liturg, GC ECUSA New York NY 1991-1997; Bp Suffr Dio Minnesota Minneapolis MN 1989-1996; Chair, Dioc Cmsn on Liturg & Mus Dio Washington Washington DC 1985-1988, Initiatory Rites T/F 1984-1985, Cler Assn Bd 1982-1985, Stndg Com 1986-1988, Adj Fac 1984-1985, Long-R Plnng Com 1983, Cler Assn Bd 1982; VTS Alexandria VA 1984-1988; R S Barn Epis Ch Temple Hills MD 1980-1989; R S Ptr's Ch La Grande OR 1977-1980; Vic S Fran Ch Moab UT 1972-1977; R S Jas Epis Ch Midvale UT 1967-1972; Cur The Ch Of S Jn The Evang Flossmoor IL 1966-1967. EPF 2000. DD SWTS 1990.

HAN, Heewoo Daniel (Va) 4060 Championship Dr, Annandale VA 22003 **St Andr's Ch-Shatin Shatin NT 2011-** B Sangjoo S.Korea 1979 s Valentine & Theresa. Wheaton Coll 2002; Yale DS 2007. D 6/16/2007 Bp Peter J Lee P 12/17/2007 Bp David Colin Jones.

HAN, Valentine S (Va) 4060 Championship Dr, Annandale VA 22003 B Sachun KR 1951 s Yee-Sun & U-Shun. BA Pusan Natl U Pusan Kr 1976; MDiv S Michaels Sem 1979. Trans 2/1/2000 Bp D L Joseph. m 5/26/1979 Theresa K Han c 2. Doctor of Mnstry Regent U Virginia Bch Virginia 2004-2007; H Cross Korean Epis Ch Fairfax VA 2000-2017, Vic 2000-2017; Dio Virginia Richmond VA 1999-2000; COM Dio Virginia 2013-2014. valentinehan1951@gmail.com

HANAHAN, Gwin Hunter (At) 2744 Peachtree Rd NW, Atlanta GA 30305 B Hartsville SC 1948 d William & Jane. BA Clemson U 1971; MA Clemson U 1975; MDiv Luth Theol Sthrn Sem - Lenoir-Rhyne Univ. 2012. D 6/9/2012 Bp J Neil Alexander P 4/6/2013 Bp Robert Christopher Wright. m 2/11/1978 James Ross Hanahan c 4.

HANBACK, Holly (Va) 14 Cornwall St NW, Leesburg VA 20176 B La Crosse WI 1973 d Richard & Lynn. D 2/23/2013 Bp Shannon Sherwood Johnston. m 9/21/1996 Clinton Hanback c 4. S Dav's Ch Ashburn VA 2013-2014.

HANCHEY, Howard (SVa) 3003 Larkspur Run, Williamsburg VA 23185 B Richmond VA 1941 s Daniel & Anne. VPI 1961; BA U NC 1963; BD VTS 1967; DMin UTS Virginia 1974; Cert S Georges Coll Jerusalem IL 1991. D 7/10/1967 P 7/10/1968 Bp Robert Fisher Gibson Jr. m 8/17/1963 Anne Summers Hanchey c 2. Int R Wicomico Par Ch Wicomico Ch VA 2011-2012; Int R Trin Ch Portsmouth VA 2007-2009; Int R Gr Ch Kilmarnock VA 2005-2006; Int R Old Donation Ch Virginia Bch VA 2003-2004; Arthur Lee Kinsolving Prof Pstr Theol VTS Alexandria VA 1978-2001; R S Andr's Ch Meriden CT 1976-1978; Field Ed Supvsr Yale Univ New Haven CT 1976-1978; Clincl Fac UTS Richmond VA 1975-1976; Assoc R Estrn Shore Chap Virginia Bch VA 1972-1976; Asst to Jack Spong S Paul's Ch Richmond VA 1970-1972; Chapl Supvsr Med Coll Of Virginia Richmond VA 1969-1972; R Emm Epis Ch Delaplane Delaplane VA 1967-1969. Auth, "From Survival To Celebration: Ldrshp," for the Confident Ch, Cowley, 1992; Auth, "Ch Growth and the Power of Evang," Cowley, 1990; Auth, "CE Made Easy," Morehouse, 1989; Auth, "Creative CE," Morehouse, 1985; Contrib, "Par Based CPE: A Sampling Of Prog (Homer Bain," Texas Med Cntr, 1974. AAPC - Mem 1972-2000; ACPE - Supvsr 1969; Assn Of Profsnl Chapl - Fell 1972-2000; EvangES 1977.

HANCKEL, Ellen Jervey (SwVa) 1013 Oakwood Ct, Martinsville VA 24112 B CharlestonSC 1949 d Richard & Ruth. BA Tul 1971; MEd Clemson U 1974; MA U of So Carolina 1982; MDiv Sewanee: The U So, TS 1995; DMin Sewanee: The U So, TS 2003. D 6/10/1995 P 5/25/1996 Bp Dorsey Henderson. m 1/25/1997 Robert Allan Scott Derks c 3. Exec Coun Appointees New York NY 2012-2015; Chr Ch Martinsville VA 2004-2011; Dio No Carolina Raleigh NC 2004; Assoc S Jn's Epis Ch Charlotte NC 2002-2004; Assoc S Mary's Ch Columbia SC 1997-2002; S Dav's Epis Ch Columbia SC 1995-1997. Auth, "For Whom The Bell Tolls," Sewanee Theol Revs, 1998. Sis Of S Mary 1997.

HANCOCK, Art (Eau) 13705 Perry Lake Road, Cable WI 54821 **R Ch Of The Ascen Hayward WI 2005-** B Nashville TN 1961 s Arthur & Charlotte. MA U So 1984; MDiv VTS 1990. D 7/14/1990 P 5/5/1991 Bp George Lazenby Reynolds Jr. m 8/23/1995 Katherine Leigh Hancock. S Andr's Ch Ashland WI 2010-2011; S Clem's Epis Ch Clemmons NC 1993; S Paul's Ch Franklin TN 1990-1993.

HANCOCK, Bayard (NH) 96 Hogback Rd, Campton NH 03223 **Died 12/3/2015** B Nutley NJ 1924 s John & Margery. BA Hobart and Wm Smith Colleges 1949; STM Ya Berk 1952; U of Rhode Island 1960; Coll of Preachers 1969. D 6/15/1952 P 12/20/1952 Bp Benjamin M Washburn. c 4. Ret 1990-2015; Dep Gc Dio New Hampshire Concord NH 1979-1985, Dioc Coun 1963-1988, Chair Dioc Cmncatns Cmsn 1982-1988, Dn Lakes Reg Convoc 1974-1981, Chair Dept Csr 1963-1973; R Ch Of The H Sprt Plymouth NH 1960-1990; Chapl Plymouth St Coll Plymouth NH 1960-1990; R S Mk's Ch Ashland NH 1960-1964; Vic S Jn The Div Ch Saunderstown RI 1956-1960; Vic Trin Epis Ch of Bergen Cnty Allendale NJ 1952-1956. Fllshp Coll Of Preachers 1969; Phi Beta Kappa.

HANCOCK, Carol Jean (Va) 10730 Scott Dr, Fairfax VA 22030 **S Jn's Ch Centreville VA 2014-** B Ridgewood NJ 1954 d Bayard & Phyllis. BA Keene St Coll 1976; MDiv VTS 1985. D 9/28/1985 Bp Philip Alan Smith P 5/10/1986 Bp William Arthur Beckham. c 2. The Ch Of The Epiph Oak Hill VA 2013; Int Ch Of The Resurr Alexandria VA 2011-2013; Int S Chris's Ch Springfield VA 2009-2011; Int Ch Of The H Comf Vienna VA 2008-2009; Int S Jn's Epis Ch Mc Lean VA 2007-2008; Int S Mk's Ch Alexandria VA 2005-2007; Int S Dunst's Ch Mc Lean VA 2004-2005; Assoc All SS' Epis Ch Chevy Chase MD 1997-2003; Trin Cathd Columbia SC 1989-1996; Asst S Martins-In-The-Field Columbia SC 1989-1995; Dio Upper So Carolina Columbia SC 1988-1996; Int S Phil's Epis Ch Greenville SC 1988; D Epis Ch Of The Redeem Greenville SC 1985-1986. stjohnscvpriest@gmail.com

HANCOCK, Paul B (Ga) 1317 Gordon Ave, Thomasville GA 31792 **R All SS Epis Ch Thomasville GA 2012-; Long Term Supply P Gr Epis Ch Wheatland CA 2006-** B London England 1951 s Ronald & Vera. BA U of Bristol Gb 1971; MA U of Bristol Gb 1973; Oxf GB 1975; Ripon Coll Cuddesdon Oxford Gb 1975. Trans 1/1/1980 Bp Scott Field Bailey. m 7/12/1975 Cynthia E Hancock c 2. Headmaster S Johns Epis Sch Roseville CA 2006-2011; Headmaster St Johns Epis Sch Roseville CA 2005-2010; Assoc P H Trin 2004-2006; Vic S Paul's/H Trin New Roads LA 1999-2004; Epis HS Baton Rouge Baton Rouge LA 1983-2003; Headmaster Epis HS Baton Rouge LA 1983-2003; Lectr Trin U San Antonio TX 1981-1983; Chapl Texas Mltry Inst San Antonio TX 1980-1983; Asst S Lk's Epis Ch San Antonio TX 1979-1983; Chapl / Dn Of Fac Texas Mltry Inst San Antonio TX 1978-1983; Cur/Dioc Yth Off Croydon Par Ch Croydon 1975-1978.

HAND, Gary Dean (Los) 69/659 Moo Ban Far Rangsit, Bungyeetho, Thanyaburi, Pathum Thani Thailand 12130 Thailand B Inglewood CA 1942 s Lawrence & Billie. Near E Sch Archlgy 1962; BA Orlinda Childs Pierce Memi TS 1964; BA Wheaton Coll 1964; MDiv GTS 1967; Irish Sch of Ecumenics 1994. D 9/9/1967 P 3/1/1968 Bp Francis E I Bloy. m 7/2/1995 Prasert Tieonieo c 2. R St Marks Epis Ch Van Nuys CA 1988-1995; S Ptr's Par Rialto CA 1976-1988; R Gr Epis Ch Glendora CA 1972-1975; S Aug By-The-Sea Par Santa Monica CA 1970-1972; Asst S Aug's Sea Santa Monica CA 1969-1972; Asst S Jn's Par Sn Bernrdno CA 1967-1969. "Go Forth: The Ch Moves Into the 21st Century," Pub privately, 1995. OHC, Rialto Mnstry Assn.

HANDLOSS, Patricia Diane (Mass) 115 Bayridge Lane, Duxbury MA 02332 B Oakland CA 1944 d Paul & Audrey. California St U 1965; BA U CA 1967; S Louis U 1970; MDiv EDS 1976; EDS 1993. D 5/22/1977 P 12/1/1978 Bp George Leslie Cadigan. c 3. Assoc Old No Chr Ch Boston MA 2005-2009; Int S Thos Ch Winn ME 2001-2002; R S Paul's Epis Ch Bedford MA 1993-1995; R S Augustines Ch S Louis MO 1990-1993; Asst S Ptr's Epis Ch S Louis MO 1980-1982; Assoc S Ptr's Ladue MO 1980-1982; Assoc R S Dunstans Epis Ch Dover MA 1978-1979; Asst S Mk's Ch Foxborough MA 1977-1978. Auth, "Var arts". EvangES.

HANDS, Donald Raymond (Mil) 6 Becks Retreat, Savannah GA 31411 B New York NY 1943 s Richard & Mary. BA Loyola Jesuit Sem 1967; MA Col 1970; PhD SUNY 1973; Cert U of Wisconsin 2011. D 8/20/1977 Bp Harold Barrett Robinson P 6/17/1979 Bp Robert Bracewell Appleyard. m 6/1/2002 Lydia Bishop c 2. Chapl St. Johns on the Lake Milwaukee WI 2007-2011; Asst S Chris's Ch Milwaukee WI 2003-2007; Clincl Psych Corrections Dept- Psychol Dir 1993-2009; Other Dio Milwaukee Milwaukee WI 1993; Dir St. Barn Cler Treatment Cntr 1987-1993; Chapl Pittsburgh Pstr Inst Pittsburgh PA 1977-1980. Auth, Sprtl Wholeness for Cler/Alb Inst, 1993; Auth, 20 Pub arts. AAMFT 1988; ATSA 1998; APA 1993; CCHP 2001. 1st Prize Cath Poetry Soc of Amer 1964.

HANDSCHY, Daniel John (Mo) 9373 Garber Rd, Saint Louis MO 63126 **Epis Sch for Mnstry Dio Missouri S Louis MO 2012-; Adj Fac, Chr Ethics Eden TS Webster Groves MO 2011-; R Ch Of The Adv S Louis MO 1992-** B Walnut Creek CA 1958 s John & Pauline. BA U CO 1980; MDiv Harvard DS 1985; PhD S Louis U 2012. D 6/11/1986 P 1/17/1987 Bp Robert Shaw Kerr. m 6/2/1984 Shelley Palumbo c 2. Ch Of The Redeem Providence RI 1992, Int

1991-1992; Asst All SS Epis Ch Attleboro MA 1986-1991. Phi Beta Kappa 1976.

HANDWERK, Larry Wayne (Chi) 9517 Springfield Ave, Evanston IL 60203 **Asst S Simons Ch Arlington Hts IL 2015-; Asst S Elis's Ch Glencoe IL 2009-** B Chambersburg PA 1941 s Wayne & Dorothy. BS Penn 1963; BA Amer Conservatory of Mus 1965; MDiv Nash 1969; STM 1986; DMin SWTS 1998. D 6/24/1969 Bp Gerald Francis Burrill P 12/21/1969 Bp James Winchester Montgomery. m 4/3/1970 Victoria Handwerk c 2. Int Chr Ch Elizabethtown KY 2005-2007; Exec Dir All SS Epis Cntr Leitchfield KY 2002-2009; Dioc Stff Dio Kentucky Louisville KY 2001-2002; R S Lk's Ch Evanston IL 1983-2002; R Trin Ch Buckingham PA 1981-1983; Dioc Stff Dio Maryland Baltimore MD 1975-1980; R S Ptr's Epis Ch Ellicott City MD 1973-1981; Asst S Barn Epis Ch Temple Hills MD 1971-1973; Cur Ch Of The H Comf Kenilworth IL 1969-1971. Assoc All SS Sis of the Poor 1975; Assoc of the OHC 1975.

HANEN, Patricia Lida (O) 3785 W 33rd St, Cleveland OH 44109 B Seattle WA 1947 d Willis & Grace. BA Reed Coll 1967; MA Cor 1968; PhD Cor 1974; MDiv EDS 1986. D 6/14/1986 Bp John Thomas Walker P 12/20/1986 Bp William George Burrill. m 8/20/2008 Elaine K McCoy. R New Life Epis Ch Uniontown OH 2009-2013; Congrl Dvlpmt Off Dio Ohio Cleveland 1998-2009, Bp Dep 1996-1998, 1994-1996, Dio Oh Mssnr 1994-1996; R S Mk's Epis Ch Penn Yan NY 1986-1993; Intrn Peace Cmsn Dio Washington Washington DC 1982-1983. Assn For Death Educ And Counslg. Wilson Fellowow; Phi Beta Kappa; Awd For Meritorious Civilian Serv Secy Of Defense.

HANEY, Jack Howard (NH) 2 Leeward Way, Fairhaven MA 02719 B Camden NJ 1938 s John & Beulah. BA W Virginia Wesleyan Coll 1962; MDiv Drew U 1966. D 6/10/1989 Bp Paul Moore Jr P 2/24/1990 Bp Frederick Barton Wolf. c 2. Int Epis Ch Of S Mary The Vrgn Falmouth ME 2004-2005; Int Chr Ch Biddeford ME 2002-2003; Ch of theTransfiguration Bretton Woods NH 1992-2002; R Chr Ch No Conway NH 1992-2001; Assoc The Ch Of The H Trin Rittenhouse Philadelphia PA 1989-1991; Adj Prof The GTS New York NY 1987-1989; Serv Untd Ch of Chr 1966-1989. Ord of H Cross 1995.

HANEY V, James Paul (NwT) St. Paul's-on-the-Plains, 1510 Avenue X, Lubbock TX 79401 **R S Paul's On The Plains Epis Ch Lubbock TX 2008-; Mentor, Sch of Mnstry Dio NW Texas Lubbock TX 2013-, COM 2009-2012** B Cambridge MA 1963 s James & Nancy. BA Texas Tech U 1985; MDiv SWTS 1995. D 6/10/1995 P 12/13/1995 Bp Sam Byron Hulsey. m 11/17/1984 Cynthia R Plummer c 2. R Gd Shpd Epis Ch Wichita KS 1998-2008; Gr Ch Vernon TX 1995-1998; S Lk's Ch Childress TX 1995-1998; Vic Trin Ch Quanah TX 1995-1998; Chair, Exam Chapl Dio Kansas Topeka KS 2004-2008, Coun of Trst 2004-2008, Dn, SW Convoc 1999-2004, Chair, Liturg and Mus Cmsn 1998-2002; Transition Com for PBp Ecusa / Mssn Personl New York NY 2004-2006, Joint Nomin Com PBp 2000-2003. The Chas T. Mason Awd SWTS 1995; The Seabury-Wstrn Prize SWTS 1995; The Alum Awd In Engl Bible SWTS 1993. frjim@stpaulslubbock.org

HANEY, James Paul (NwT) 4904 14th Street, Lubbock TX 79416 **P-in-c The Epis Ch Of The Gd Shpd Brownfield TX 2005-, P-in-c 2005-** B Pittsburgh PA 1939 s James & Helen. BS U Pgh 1961; MDiv EDS 1965; MA W Texas A&M U 1978. D 6/13/1965 Bp Donald J Campbell P 12/17/1965 Bp George Henry Quarterman. m 3/14/1993 Janis Haney c 3. R S Chris's Epis Ch Lubbock TX 1979-2005; Chapl Dio NW Texas Lubbock TX 1975-1979; P-in-c Epis Ch Of S Geo Canyon TX 1975-1979; Assoc S Jn's Epis Ch Odessa TX 1971-1974; Chapl US Navy 1968-1971; Vic S Mk's Epis Ch Coleman TX 1965-1968.

HANISIAN, James Andrew (SO) 1409 W Gantry Ct, Leland NC 28451 **Vice-Pres Epis Ret Hm Cincinnati OH 2005-; P in Charge S Phil's Ch Southport NC 2017-** B Queens NY 1947 s John & Jane. BA Hobart and Wm Smith Colleges 1969; MDiv GTS 1972; DMin Untd Sem Dayton OH 1997. D 6/17/1972 P 12/1/1972 Bp Jonathan Goodhue Sherman. m 12/12/2006 Kathleen A Chesson c 3. Prof Bex Sem Columbus OH 2006-2009; Archd Dio Sthrn Ohio Cincinnati OH 2001-2005; R The Ch of the Redeem Cincinnati OH 1979-2001; Vic S Marg's Ch Plainview NY 1977-1978; Dio Long Island Garden City NY 1975-1976; Asst S Mk's Ch Islip NY 1972-1975. "The Cross is the Way of Life," Forw Mvmt, 2000; Auth, "Mnstry of Encouragement," 1996; Auth, "The People of His Pasture," 1984; Auth, "More Than Fine Gold," CDO, 1978. jim. hanisian@gmail.com

HANISIAN, Matthew R (Md) St Martins-in-the-Field, 375 Benfield Rd, Severna Park MD 21146 **St Martins-In-The-Field Ch Severna Pk MD 2016-** B W Islip NY 1974 s James & Lauren. BA Indiana U 1996; MDiv VTS 2010. D 6/13/2009 P 6/11/2011 Bp Thomas Edward Breidenthal. m 7/13/2013 Kathryn A Glover c 2. S Alb's Par Washington DC 2011-2016; S Paul's Epis Ch Alexandria VA 2010-2011.

HANK, Daniel Hayman (USC) 1151 Elm Savannah Rd, Hopkins SC 29061 **S Jn's Epis Ch Congaree Hopkins SC 2013-** B Charleston SC 1949 s Francis & Alice. BA U NC 1971; MA NYU 1976; PhD NYU 1978; Cert of Angl Stds Nash 2008. D 12/1/2008 P 6/9/2009 Bp Mark Joseph Lawrence. m 3/22/1986 Allyson Way Hank c 1. Ch Of The H Apos Barnwell SC 2010-2013.

HANKINS, Samuel Scott (Az) 2501 W. Zia Road, #8205, Santa Fe NM 87505 B Salina KS 1951 s Samuel & Vera. BMus Ob Conservatory 1973; MM Ya Sch of Mus 1975; MDiv GTS 1984. D 6/9/1984 Bp Arthur Edward Walmsley P 3/23/1985 Bp William Bradford Hastings. m 4/19/2015 Randall Joseph Hayden. Vic S Paul's Epis Ch Winslow AZ 2010-2011; Admin Asst Hopi Mssn Sch 2009-2010; R Chr Epis Ch Norwich CT 2000-2009; P-in-c S Alb's Ch Danielson CT 1998-1999; Vic Ch Of The Resurr Norwich CT 1993-1999; Cur S Jas Ch New London CT 1984-1993. Pi Kappa Lamda 1973.

HANKINSON JR, Benjamin D (Spr) **P Trin Ch Mt Vernon IL 2014-** B Florence SC 1986 s Benjamin & Barbara. BA U of So Carolina 2009; MDiv Nash 2014; MDiv Nash TS 2014. D 1/30/2014 P 8/1/2014 Bp Daniel Hayden Martins. frbenhankinson@gmail.com

HANKS JR, Alexander Hamilton (WNC) Po Box 8893, Asheville NC 28814 **R Ch Of The Redeem Asheville NC 2000-** B Asheville NC 1946 s Alexander & Frances. BA U NC 1982. D 12/18/1999 P 6/21/2000 Bp Bob Johnson. m 4/4/1971 Linda Susan Keys Hanks c 2.

HANLEY, Elise Ashley (NY) 860 Orange St, New Haven CT 06511 **Trin Ch On The Green New Haven CT 2017-** B NY 1982 d William & Judith. MDiv - Trans GTS; BFA NYU 2004; MDiv - Trans GTS 2014; MDiv UTS 2016. D 3/5/2016 Bp Allen Shin P 10/15/2016 Bp Andrew Marion Lenow Dietsche. m 6/20/2015 Christopher J Ashley. ehanley@trinitynewhaven.org

HANLEY, Ian David (Los) 59131 Wilcox Ln, Yucca Valley CA 92284 B Isleworth UK 1946 s Patrick & Joan. ThM U of Oxford Oxford Uk 1998. Trans 12/7/2006 Bp Joseph Jon Bruno. m 3/23/1968 Gwenda Joyce Hanley c 2. Dio Los Angeles Los Angeles CA 2006-2008; Very Reverend Ch Of St Peters New Zealand 2002-2006.

✠ HANLEY, The Rt Rev Michael (Ore) Episcopal Diocese of Oregon, 11800 SW Military Ln, Portland OR 97219 **Bp of Oregon Dio Oregon Portland OR 2010-** B Tulsa OK 1954 s Eugene & Frances. BA U of Oklahoma 1976; MDiv SWTS 1981; DMin SWTS 2005. D 6/6/1981 Bp Gerald Nicholas Mcallister P 4/15/1982 Bp William Jackson Cox Con 4/10/2010 for Ore. m 12/27/1975 Marla M Hanley c 2. Stndg Committe Chair Dio Minnestoa 2004-2005; R S Chris's Epis Ch S Paul MN 1998-2010; R S Lk's Epis Ch Hastings MN 1990-1998; Assoc R S Tim's Epis Ch S Louis MO 1987-1990; Asst R S Lk's Epis Ch Bartlesville OK 1983-1987; Cur Epis Ch Of The Resurr Oklahoma City OK 1981-1983. Auth, "6 Tips On Sizing Up A Boss," *Epis*, 1988. bishop@episcopaldioceseoregon.org

HANNA, Daniel Bassett (Chi) 760 Magazine Street #205, New Orleans LA 70130 **Non-par 1964-** B Mishawaka IN 1935 s Russell & Jane. BA Aurora U 1957; MDiv SWTS 1960; MA NWU 1966; MS Loyola U Chicago 1983. D 6/24/1960 P 1/6/1961 Bp Lauriston L Scaife. R Our Sav Lackawanna NY 1960-1964; R S Matt's Ch Buffalo NY 1960-1964.

HANNA, Gerald Benson (Oly) 11527 9th Ave Ne, Seattle WA 98125 B San Antonio TX 1938 s Harvey & Anna. BA U CO 1960; MFA U MN 1971; MDiv Nash 1986. D 6/14/1986 P 12/1/1986 Bp William Carl Frey. m 12/20/1981 Kay Lynn Kessel-Hanna c 2. S Dav Emm Epis Ch Shoreline WA 1999-2003; Supply P S Geo Epis Ch Maple Vlly WA 1995-1998; The Cntr For Sprtl Dvlpmt Seattle WA 1991-2003; R S Paul's Epis Ch Steamboat Sprngs CO 1988-1991; Dio Colorado Denver CO 1987-1988; S Mk's Ch Craig CO 1986-1987.

HANNA, Nancy Wadsworth (NY) 100 Edward Bentley Rd., Lawrence NY 11559 B Washington DC 1946 d Arthur & Betty. BA Harv 1973; EdM Lesley U 1974; MDiv UTS 1985. D 11/17/1985 Bp Paul Moore Jr P 6/1/1986 Bp Walter Decoster Dennis Jr. m 8/24/1974 Alistair Hanna c 1. Assoc Calv and St Geo New York NY 2004-2010; Assoc St. Barth Ch New York NY 1996-2004; Assoc Chr's Ch Rye NY 1990-1996; Asst S Mary's Ch Of Scarborough Briarcliff NY 1985-1989.

HANNA, Raymond J (EC) Po Box 1043, Mount Airy NC 27030 **S Steph's Ch Goldsboro NC 2016-** B Philadelphia PA 1959 s Raymond & Joan. BA U So 1984; MDiv SWTS 1991. D 6/15/1991 P 4/5/1992 Bp Allen Lyman Bartlett Jr. c 2. R Trin Ch Mt Airy NC 2003-2016; S Andr's Ch Mt Holly NJ 1999-2002; R Westover Epis Ch Chas City VA 1995-1999; Asst R S Paul's Ch Richmond VA 1993-1995; Cur S Paul's Ch Doylestown PA 1991-1993.

HANNA, William James (Miss) 783 Rosewood Pointe, Madison MS 39110 **Ch Of The Creator Clinton MS 2010-** B Natchez MS 1952 s Hugh & Nona. BA Millsaps Coll 1974; MA Mississippi St U 1985. D 1/4/2003 Bp Alfred Marble Jr. m 11/26/1977 Jacquelyn Therese Logue c 2. All SS Ch Jackson MS 2003-2010.

HANNABASS, Katherine Tootle (NMich) **Died 11/12/2016** B St. Joseph MO 1929 d William & Mildred. Hollins U 1950; MA E Tennessee St U 1980. D 8/12/2001 Bp James Arthur Kelsey. c 5.

HANNIBAL, Preston Belfield (WA) Washington National cathedral, Mount St. Alban, Washington DC 20016 **Gvrng Bd NAES 2011-; Gvrng Bd Bp Jn T. Walker Sch For Boys 2006-; RTD Com TEC Off of Black Mnstrs 2003-** B New York NY 1948 s Hamilcar & Netha. BA Westmont Coll 1971; Ridley Hall Cambridge 1972; U of Cambridge 1972; MDiv Bex Sem 1974; St Edmunds Coll U of Cambridge 1983. D 6/15/1974 P 1/4/1975 Bp Robert Claflin Rusack. m 5/15/1976 La Sandra Cook c 3. Cathd of St Ptr & St Paul Washington DC 2014-2016; Cn for Acad and Transition Mnstrs Dio Washington Washington DC 2003-2013; Sr Chapl and Chair of the Rel Dept. Belmont Chap at S Mk's Sch Southborough MA 1995-2003; Assoc Min Memi Ch Harv Cambridge 1986-1995; Vic Ch Of S Jn The Evang Dunbarton NH 1984-1985, Vic 1981-1984; Assist Chapl & Rel Tchr Dickey Mstr in Rel S Paul's Sch Concord NH 1974-1986; Asst Chapl and Rel Tchr S Paul's Sch Concord NH 1974-1986. Phi Beta Kappa Alpha of Massachusetts at Harv 1989; Chas D. Dickey Mstr of Rel and Ethics St. Paul's Sch, NH 1980. phannibal@cathedral.org

HANNON, Timothy Robert (Ore) D 6/10/2017 Bp Michael Hanley.

HANNUM, Christopher Cary Lee (At) 2148 Winding Creek Ln Sw, Marietta GA 30064 **Middle Sch Chapl H Innoc Epis Sch Atlanta GA 2002-** B Utica NY 1949 s Ellwood & Lillian. BA U So 1971; MDiv SWTS 1976. D 6/22/1976 Bp Archibald Donald Davies P 11/1/1977 Bp James Winchester Montgomery. m 8/14/1976 Kathleen Ann Hannum c 2. Chapl Dio Atlanta Atlanta GA 2006-2015; H Innoc' Epis Sch Atlanta GA 2000-2005; Int Chapl H Innoc Ch Atlanta GA 2000-2001, 1996-1998; S Alfred's Epis Ch Palm Harbor FL 1998-2000; S Mary's Par Tampa FL 1995-1996, 1986-1995; St Marys Epis Day Sch Tampa FL 1984-1996; Int S Phil's Ch Easthampton MA 1983-1984; R Chr Memi Ch No Brookfield MA 1979-1983; Cur S Aug's Epis Ch Wilmette IL 1977-1979; Cur The Epis Ch Of The H Nativ Plano TX 1976-1977. NAES; Ref.

HANSCOM, John David (Ak) St. Christopher's Episcopal, 7208 Duben Ave., ANCHORAGE AK 99504 **Died 12/26/2016** B Indianapolis, IN 1946 s Howard & Mary. U of Oklahoma 1977; U So EFM 1984. D 7/25/2007 Bp Mark Lawrence Macdonald. m 8/26/1967 Roberta Lee Hanscom c 2.

HANSEL, Robert Raymond (SO) PO Box 217, Little Switzerland NC 28749 **Vic Ch Of The Resurr Little Switzerland NC 2011-** B Cincinnati OH 1936 s Virgil & Christina. BA U Cinc 1958; MDiv EDS 1961; DMin SWTS 1979. D 6/12/1961 P 12/24/1961 Bp Roger W Blanchard. m 3/15/1983 Dale Blue Hansel c 6. P All SS Ch Hilton Hd Island SC 2008-2011; Chap Min Chap By-the-Sea Captiva Island FL 2004-2010; Int Calv Ch Memphis TN 2002-2004; P-in-c Indn Hill Ch Cincinnati OH 1997-1999; Cn Dio Indianapolis Indianapolis IN 1991-1997; P S Brigid's Mssn Batesville IN 1991-1996; Prog Dir Roslyn Conf Cntr Richmond VA 1988-1991; Roslyn Managers Corp Richmond VA 1988-1991; Dn & Prog Asst to Bp Dio Sthrn Ohio Cincinnati OH 1978-1988; Hdmstr S Mk Sch Southborough MA 1974-1978; St. Mk's Sch of Southborough Inc. Southborough MA 1974-1978; Chapl S Geo Sch Newport RI 1969-1974; Chapl S Geo's Sch Middletown RI 1969-1974; Yth and YA Mnstrs Exec Coun New York City NY 1965-1969; R S Lk's Epis Ch Fall River MA 1964-1965; Asst Trin Ch Columbus OH 1961-1964. "All Shall Be Well," *Chapt Contrib*, Ch Pub Inc., 2009; "Free To Be," *Adult/Yth Dialogue*, Seabury; Auth, "Study Guide for," *Faith of the Ch (Ch Tchg Series)*, Seabury; Auth, *Henry Wise Hobson*, Forw Mvmt; Auth, "The Life of St. Aug," *Life of S Aug*, Crowell/Collier; Auth, "Like Fr, Like Son---Like Hell!," *Like Fathter,Like Son---Like Hell!*, Seabury; "Showdown in Seattle," *Showdown in Seattle*, Seabury; Auth, *Vestries in the Epis Ch*, Forw Mvmt. Conf Dio Exec; Credo Proj/Conf Ldr; Deploy Off Ntwk.

HANSELL, Susan Weir (CFla) 2048 Ryan Way, Winter Haven FL 33884 **D S Paul's Ch Winter Haven FL 2001-** B Troy NY 1943 d George & Ruth. BS Tufts U 1965; MEd U of Virginia 1972; Cert Inst for Chr Stds Florida 2000. D 12/8/2001 Bp John Wadsworth Howe. c 1. Secy - St of the Ch Com - GC Epis Ch Cntr New York NY 2000-2003; Dio Cntrl Florida Orlando FL 1997-2000.

HANSELMAN, David (CNY) PO Box 88, Greene NY 13778 **R S Paul's Ch Oxford NY 2011-; D Zion Epis Ch Greene NY 2011-** B Newark NY 1969 s David & Jean. BA SUNY at Albany 1995; U GA - Athens 2003; MDiv S Bernards TS and Mnstry 2010. D 5/7/2011 P 11/12/2011 Bp Gladstone Bailey Adams III. m 6/26/1993 Sonja L Hanselman c 2.

HANSEN, Carl R (ECR) 959 Vista Cerro Dr., Paso Robles CA 93446 B Watsonville CA 1943 s Raymond & Lillian. BS Santa Clara U 1965; MDiv CDSP 1978; DMin CDSP 2002. D 6/24/1978 Bp William Foreman Creighton P 6/1/1979 Bp John Raymond Wyatt. m 1/31/1987 Susan K Hansen c 2. All SS Ch Carmel CA 1988-2005; R Santa Lucia Chap Big Sur Carmel CA 1988-2005; Prison Mnstrs Coordntr Dio El Camino Real 1986-1988; Dio El Camino Real Salinas CA 1986-1988; R S Jas Ch Paso Robles CA 1980-1986; Asst S Giles Ch Moraga CA 1978-1980. Auth, *Inclusive Evang (thesis)*, CDSP, 2002; Auth, *Friends in Faith*, Sunflower Ink, 1998; Auth, "Friends in Faith," *Monterey Cnty Herald & Scripps-Howard News Serv*.

HANSEN, Janis Lee Harney (Mont) 2430 Sw Crestdale Dr, Portland OR 97225 **D Chr Ch Sheridan MT 2010-; D S Barth's Ch Beaverton OR 1997-** B Elko NV 1942 d Howard & June. BA U of SW Louisiana 1964; DA U of Oregon 1978; Oregon Sch of The Diac 1997; Cert of Trng Sprtl Dvlpmt, Cntr Trin Cathd, Portland 2006. D 10/18/1997 Bp Robert Louis Ladehoff P 7/25/2015 Bp Charles Franklin Brookhart Jr. m 9/27/1969 David Jen Hansen. Enrons Chairman Awd 1999.

HANSEN, Jessica V (Cal) 1532 Burlingame Ave, Burlingame CA 94010 B Stanford CA 1957 d Heber & Barbara. BA U CA 1979; MA San Francisco St U 1989; MDiv CDSP 1990. D 6/3/2000 P 12/2/2000 Bp William Edwin Swing. m 9/27/1980 Robert M Fellows c 1. Assoc R S Matt's Epis Ch San Mateo CA 2000-2002.

HANSEN, Karen Sue (Okla) 310 E. Noble Ave., Guthrie OK 73044 B Oklahoma City OK 1953 d Marvin & Henrietta. BBA U of Cntrl Oklahoma 1993. D 6/21/2003 Bp Robert Manning Moody. m 1/1/2006 Harris Lynn Hansen c 2.

HANSEN, Knute Coates (Ct) **D S Paul's Epis Ch Shelton CT 2011-** B New Haven CT 1939 s Knud & Emily. BS U MI 1957; MS U of Bridgeport 1964. D 9/17/2005 Bp Andrew Donnan Smith. m 7/6/1957 Jane Hansen c 3. D Trin Epis Ch Trumbull CT 2008-2011; D Trin Ch Branford CT 2005-2008; Bp/ Dioc Exec Coun and Evang Comm. Dio Connecticut Meriden CT 1990-2003.

HANSEN, Michael (Cal) 1055 Taylor St, San Francisco CA 94108 **Died 3/18/2017** B Saint Paul MN 1945 s Kenneth & Lorraine. BA U of St Thos 1968; MDiv Untd TS 1979. D 6/25/1979 P 12/1/1979 Bp Robert Marshall Anderson. m 5/30/2014 Linnette Caprice Jones. P Dio California San Francisco CA 1988-2017, 1985-2007, Cn Mssnr 1985-1988; Chapl Breck Sch Minneapolis MN 1981-1985; S Mart's By The Lake Epis Minnetonka Bch MN 1981-1983; Asst S Jn The Evang S Paul MN 1979-1981. Auth, "Doing A Needs Assessment".

HANSEN, Michelle H (Ct) 125 Parklawn Dr, Waterbury CT 06708 **P All SS' Epis Ch E Hartford CT 2012-; St Mich's Naugatuck Ct 1983-** B Oakland CA 1945 d Estle & Evelyn. BA U of Rhode Island 1967; MDiv Ya Berk 1970; MDiv Ya Berk 1970; STM Ya Berk 1971. D 6/27/1970 Bp John S Higgins P 5/1/1971 Bp Joseph Warren Hutchens. c 3. Middlesex Area Cluster Mnstry Higganum CT 1998-2006; P-t Mssnr Middlesex Area Cluster Minixtry Durham CT 1998-2006; Part time Mssnr Waterbury Cluster Waterbury CT 1988-1998; S Mich's Ch Naugatuck CT 1983-1984; Dio Connecticut Meriden CT 1978-1983; S Ptr's Ch Hamden CT 1978-1983; Vic S Ptr's-Hill Epis Ch Hamden CT 1978-1983; Dio Kansas Topeka KS 1974-1978; Chapl U of Kansas Lawr KS 1974-1978; Asst S Jas's Ch W Hartford CT 1972-1974; Asst S Paul's Ch Southington CT 1970-1972. shelhnsn@yahoo.com

HANSEN JR, Robert F (ECR) 16 Salisbury Dr Apt 7217, Asheville NC 28803 **Ret 1994-** B Tulsa OK 1934 s Robert & Betty. BS U of Oklahoma 1956; MS U of Oklahoma 1958; MDiv Nash 1966. D 6/17/1966 P 12/1/1966 Bp Chilton R Powell. m 8/27/1955 Mary C Hansen c 1. Ch of Our Sav Campbell CA 1991-1994; Assoc Our Sav Campbell CA 1991-1994; R S Steph's Ch Gilroy CA 1979-1991; Co-R S Lk's Epis Ch Akron OH 1975-1979; Assoc Ch Of The Redeem Houston TX 1970-1975; Assoc R S Lk's Epis Ch Bartlesville OK 1967-1970; Cur S Andr's Epis Ch Lawton OK 1966-1967; Dioc Coun Dio El Camino Real Salinas CA 1980-1985; Evang Cmsn Dio Ohio Cleveland 1977-1979.

HANSEN, Thomas Parker (NI) 3717 N Washington Rd, Fort Wayne IN 46802 B Goshen NY 1951 s Edgar & Kathryne. AA Orange Cnty Cmnty Coll 1973; BA SUNY 1975; MDiv Nash 1978; DMin Fuller TS 2000. D 6/3/1978 Bp Paul Moore Jr P 12/1/1978 Bp William Carl Frey. m 8/2/1981 Nancy Mccammon Hansen c 1. R Trin Ch Ft Wayne IN 2006-2016; R S Lk's Ch Kearney NE 2001-2006; Pstr Dvlp S Martha's Epis Ch Papillion NE 2001; Cn Mssnr Dio Nebraska 1991-2001; Cn Mssnr Dio Nebraska Omaha NE 1991-2001; R S Jn's Ch Broken Bow NE 1986-1991; Vic Shpd-Hills Dunning 1986-1990; Chapl U Of No Colorado Greeley 1984-1985; R S Steph's Ch Casper WY 1981-1984; Cur S Lk's Epis Ch Ft Collins CO 1978-1981.

HANSKNECHT, Jeanne Marie (CNY) 10 Mill St, Cazenovia NY 13035 **S Jn's Ch Plymouth MI 2014-, 2013-2014; S Ptr's Epis Ch Cazenovia NY 2014-** B Tawas City MI 1967 d Harold & Alberta. BA MI SU 1990; MA Estrn Michigan U 1994; MDiv Ecum TS 2010. D 12/12/2009 P 7/17/2010 Bp Wendell Nathaniel Gibbs Jr. m 3/17/1990 Blane Hansknecht c 4. Cur/Asst R S Andr's Ch Ann Arbor MI 2010-2013.

HANSLEY, Mary Belfry (SVa) 6219 Chelsea Crescent, Williamsburg VA 23188 B Minneapolis MN 1944 d Albert & Marsena. Mt Holyoke Coll 1964; BA NWU 1967; MDiv VTS 1975. D 8/15/1975 P 1/16/1977 Bp Philip Frederick McNairy. Int R S Matt's Epis Ch Chesterfield VA 2015-2017; Int Sunday Supply Brandon Epis Ch Disputanta VA 2011-2013; Int S Mart's Epis Ch Williamsburg VA 2004-2005; Assoc S Mich's Ch Barrington IL 1998-2003; Int Chr Ch S Paul MN 1997; P-in-c S Pat Minneapolis MN 1994-1996; Int Trin Ch Excelsior MN 1994; Int S Mk's Ch Fairland Silver Sprg MD 1990-1992; Chapl Seabury Resources Washington DC 1988-1990; Assoc Ch Of Our Redeem Aldie VA 1987-1988; Assoc Emm Ch Middleburg VA 1987-1988; Assoc Chapl and Dir of Alum/ae Affrs VTS Alexandria VA 1981-1987; Cn Cathd Ch Of S Mk Minneapolis MN 1977-1981, D 1975-1977.

HANSON III, Aquilla B (Fla) 406 Glenridge Rd, Perry FL 32348 **R S Jas Epis Ch Perry FL 2007-** B Columbia SC 1947 s Earnault & Dorothy. BA Cit 1969; MA Oral Robers U, TS 1992; MDiv VTS 1993. D 6/2/1993 P 12/1/1993 Bp Edward Lloyd Salmon Jr. m 12/30/1994 Dorothy Hanson c 1. Int R S Mk's Epis Ch Jacksonville FL 2005-2006; Int R Trin Epis Ch Baton Rouge LA 2004-2005; R All SS Ch Jackson MS 1999-2004; Chapl Hermon Hosp Houston TX 1998-1999; R Ch Of The Adv Sumner MS 1996-1997; Vic Chr Our Lord Epis Ch St Helena Island SC 1994-1996; Vic S Chris's Ch Sumter SC 1993; Bd Dir Doctor's Memi Hosp 2006-2013. Masters Thesis, "The Euch, An OT Rite Perfected," *Oral Roberts Grad TS*. stjameschurch@fairpoint.net

HANSON, Deborah Ann (Miss) 5400 Old Canton Rd, Jackson MS 39211 B Canada 1954 d Frederick & Shirley Anne. D 1/15/2011 Bp Duncan Montgomery Gray III. m 9/21/1974 Peter Allen Hanson c 3.

HANSON, Jay D (Minn) 1201 Yale Pl, Apt 1007, Minneapolis MN 55403 **1995-** B Saint James MN 1937 s Lloyd & Margaret. BA U MN 1959; MDiv VTS 1962; U of No Dakota 1970. D 6/29/1962 Bp Hamilton Hyde Kellogg P 6/1/1963 Bp Philip Frederick McNairy. m 8/26/1961 Madge N Hanson c 4. Int Ch Of The Mssh Rhinebeck NY 2009-2010; Int S Jn In The Wilderness S Paul MN 2002-2003; S Edw The Confessor Wayzata MN 1988-1996; Dio Minnesota Minneapolis MN 1986-2003; 1970-1985; Chapl U No Dakota 1964-1970; P-in-c S Lk's Walshville ND 1964-1968; P-in-c Chr Ch Crookston MN 1964-1965; Cur St Dav's Epis Ch Minnetonka MN 1962-1964.

HANSON, Norma Halmagyi (Del) 405 Lady Huntingdon Ln, Asheville NC 28803 **P-in-c S Fran of Assisi Cherokee NC 2012-** B Welch WV 1937 d Anthony & Mildred. BA Randolph-Macon Wmn's Coll 1958; MS U of Virginia 1960; MDiv Lancaster TS 1994; Cert VTS 1994; DMin Luth TS 2004. D 10/8/1994 P 10/14/1995 Bp Cabell Tennis. c 4. Vic Ch Of The Trsfg Saluda NC 2009-2011; R Chr Ch Delaware City DE 2002-2004; D Chr Ch Christiana Hundred Wilmington DE 1995; Chapl Christiana Care 1994-1998; Chapl Ldr Nrsng Hm 1994-1995. APC 1997-1999; Ord of S Lk 1971-1982. Phi Sigma Univ. of Virginia 1960.

HANSON-FOSS, Patricia Jean (Alb) PO Box 237, Au Sable Forks NY 12912 B Canton NY 1964 D 6/29/2003 Bp David John Bena. c 2.

HANSTINE, Barbara Ann (Alb) 287 Leonard St, Hancock NY 13783 B Middletown NY 1940 d John & E Belle. BS SUNY 1979; MS SUNY 1982. D 5/27/1989 Bp David Standish Ball. m 10/3/1975 William Hanstine c 3. D St Chris's Epis Ch Cobleskill NY 2002-2009; Fac Dio Albany Greenwich NY 2000-2002; Fam Mnstry Coordntr - Susquehanna Dnry 1985-1999; D Chr Ch Deposit NY 1989-2002. NAAD; Ord Of S Lk.

HANTEN, Helen Bailey (Minn) 66 E. St. Marie St. #205, Duluth MN 55803 B Caspian MI 1927 d Carlton & Katherine. U of Wisconsin 1948; BS U MN 1966; MS U MN 1975. D 10/25/1987 Bp Robert Marshall Anderson. m 8/20/1949 Paul Thomas Hanten c 3. D S Andr's By The Lake Duluth MN 1987-2001.

HANWAY JR, Donald Grant (Neb) 128 N 13th St Apt #1009, Lincoln NE 68508 B Lincoln NE 1943 s Donald & Blanche. BA U of Nebraska 1965; MA U of Nebraska 1967; MDiv VTS 1971; DMin VTS 1997. D 6/17/1971 Bp Robert Patrick Varley P 12/20/1971 Bp Russell T Rauscher. m 5/28/1966 Nadine K Hanway c 3. Secy Dio Nebraska Omaha NE 1998-2004, Exec Cmsn 1989-1997, COM 1983-1988, 1979-1982, Ed, The Nebraska Churchman 1972-1978, Chmn. Dept of CE 1979-1981; Chart Mem Instnl Revs Bd U of Nebraska-Lincoln Lincoln NE 1993-1995; R S Mk's On The Campus Lincoln NE 1981-2003; Engaged Encounter Team Natl EEE 1980-1983; R Chr Ch Epis Beatrice NE 1977-1981; Dio Michigan Detroit MI 1975-1977; Cur S Lk's Par Kalamazoo MI 1975-1977; Vic S Eliz's Ch Holdrege NE 1971-1975; 1st Lt US-A 1966-1968; Chmn. Dept of CE Dio Wstrn Michigan Kalamazoo MI 1975-1977. Auth, "Words of Life," *Selected Sermons,* iUniverse Bloomington, 2009; Auth, "Her Appearing: A Love Story," iUniverse Bloomington, IN, 2008; Auth, "Theol of Gay and Lesbian Inclusion: Love Letters to the Ch," *Love Letters to the Ch,* Haworth Pstr Press Binghamton NY, 2006. Lincoln Torch Club 1995. Knight Cmdr Ord of St. Mich the Archangel Grand Duchess Maria of Russia 2012; Silver Torch Awd Int'l. Assoc. of Torch Clubs 2009; Chancellors Awd U of Nebraska-Lincoln 2007; Geo Peek Memi Awd St. Mk's on the Campus 2002; Phi Beta Kappa U of Nebraska- Lincoln 1965.

HANYZEWSKI, Andrew J (Mil) 303 Merchants Ave, Fort Atkinson WI 53538 **R S Peters Epis Ch Ft Atkinson WI 2011-; Dn of the Cntrl Convoc Dio Milwaukee Milwaukee WI 2014-, Cler Day Com 2013-; Chapl for the 2013 Wood Badge Course Chgo. Area Coun BSA 2013-** B Melrose Park IL 1963 s Daniel & Ann. MDiv Nash 2009. D 8/23/2008 P 8/16/2009 Bp Keith Whitmore. m 5/28/2006 Aimee J Hanyzewski. S Andr's By The Lake Epis Ch Michigan City IN 2009-2011; S Fran Ch Chesterton IN 2009-2011; Assoc Ed Misssioner a Pub of the Sem Nash Sem - Nashotah WI 2012-2014; Mnstry Models Task Grp Dio Nthrn Indiana So Bend IN 2010-2011.

HAPTONSTAHL, Stephen R (Minn) 807 Louisiana Ave, Cumberland MD 21502 **Mnstry Mentor Emm Ch Moorefield WV 2011-** B Independence IA 1943 s Omer & Helen. Knox Coll 1964; Bachelor's U of Nebraska at Omaha 1969; MDiv EDS 1973. D 6/16/1973 Bp John Harris Burt P 3/16/1974 Bp Robert Claflin Rusack. m 12/31/1977 Thomasina D Dennis c 4. P in Res Emm Ch Keyser WV 2012-2013; Int S Paul's Ch Brainerd MN 2006-2008; 1997-1998; Int S Phil's Ch S Paul MN 2004-2005; Mnstry Mentor Ch Of The Gd Samar Sauk Cntr MN 2003-2009; Int H Trin Intl Falls MN 2001-2002; Mentor Trin Epis Ch Hinckley MN 2000-2009; P-in-c S Jas Epis Ch Hibbing MN 1998-1999; Mentor S Andr's Ch Cloquet MN 1994-1997; R S Edw's Ch Duluth MN 1991-1996; Skilled metal worker Artistic Metal Spinning Cleveland OH 1988-1991; Supply P Dio Ohio Cleveland 1985-1991; Asst. Dir. of Personl Cuyahoga Cnty Hsng Authority 1985-1988; Int S Paul's Ch Of E Cleveland Cleveland OH 1984-1985; Int Gr Ch Cleveland OH 1982-1983; P-

in-c S Lk's Ch Cleveland OH 1978-1981; R S Thos' Epis Ch Port Clinton OH 1975-1978; Asst R Trin Epis Ch Redlands CA 1973-1975. Auth, 1981.

HARBIN, J Derek (SVa) 424 Washington St, Portsmouth VA 23704 **Reg Aquatics Com Sthrn Reg BSA 2012-; R S Jn's Ch Portsmouth VA 2011-; Natl Camp Inspctr Sthrn Reg BSA 2011-; Chair, Dioc Liturg Cmsn Dio Sthrn Virginia Newport News VA 2013-; Natl Camp Inspctr BSA 2011-; Aquatics Instr BSA 1980-** B Winston-Salem NC 1961 s Edgar & Sally. BS Davidson Coll 1983; MDiv Nash 1988; DMin SWTS 1999. D 5/20/1988 P 11/30/1988 Bp William Gillette Weinhauer. m 9/3/1989 Clifford King Harbin c 3. P-in-c S Andr's Ch Bessemer City NC 2008-2011; Founding P / Ch Planter Ch Of The Beloved Charlotte NC 2005-2008; Adj Fac, Presenter, Thesis Rdr SWTS 2000-2010; Dio No Carolina Raleigh NC 1999-2004; R S Andr Epis Ch Kokomo IN 1992-1999; Asst Gr Ch Asheville NC 1988-1992; Dioc Coun Dio Nthrn Indiana So Bend IN 1997-1999, Congrl Revitalization & Dvlpmt Com 1994-1999, 71st GC Host Com 1994-1996, Alt Dep to the 71st GC 1994, Dioc Liturg Emcee Team 1993-1999, Dioc Curs Sprtl Advsr 1993-1995; Dioc Liturg/Emcee of Robert H. Johnson Consecration in 1989 Dio Wstrn No Carolina Asheville NC 1989-1992, Established & Serv on Dioc Catechumenal Process Com 1989-1992; Sthrn Reg Aquatics Com BSA. Auth, "It'S Not About Us," *Searching For Sacr Space,* Ch Pub, 2002; Auth, "Assuming The Nature Of A Liturg Servent," *Open (The Of Associated Parishes),* 2000; Auth, "No Mtn Too Steep," S Fran Ch, 1993. Chapl Gnrl 3rd Ord of Cubs Fans in Canaan God, Ultimately 2013; 1st Year Outstanding Tchr of the Year Cmnty Hse Middle Sch 2009; St. Geo Epis Awd BSA 1988; Natl DSA Ord of the Arrow, BSA 1983; Vigil hon Ord of the Arrow, BSA 1978; Eagle Scout BSA 1976; Phi Kappa Phi UNH 1949.

HARBOLD, Sally (NC) 221 Union St, Cary NC 27511 B Columbus OH 1952 d Charles & Mary. AA Valencia Cmnty Coll 1988; BA U of Cntrl Florida 1989; MDiv Ya Berk 1992; DMin GTF 2005. D 6/20/1992 Bp John Wadsworth Howe P 12/1/1992 Bp William Hopkins Folwell. m 9/2/2012 Marion Francis Thullbery. Assoc R S Paul's Epis Ch Cary NC 2000-2013; Yth & CE Dio No Carolina Raleigh NC 1995-2014; Int Gr Ch Whiteville NC 1995; Asst to the R The Epis Ch Of The Gd Shpd Lake Wales FL 1992-1994.

HARBORT, Raymond Louis (Be) 1841 Millard St, Bethlehem PA 18017 B Tarrytown NY 1944 s Herbert & Edna. BA Rutgers The St U of New Jersey 1965; STB GTS 1968. D 6/8/1968 P 12/21/1968 Bp Horace W B Donegan. m 12/16/2013 Henry Spalding Baird. R S Geo's Epis Ch Hellertown PA 2005-2009; Trin Par Menlo Pk CA 2002-2003; Int S Paul's Epis Ch Burlingame CA 2001-2002; Ch Of The Adv Of Chr The King San Francisco CA 1999-2001; Int Ch of the Adv of Chr the King San Francisco CA 1999-2001; S Ptr's Epis Ch Redwood City CA 1999; S Mary's Ch Haledon NJ 1991-1998; 1990-1991; R S Anth Of Padua Ch Hackensack NJ 1988-1989; P-in-c S Paul's Ch Chester NY 1975-1977; R Chr Ch Warwick NY 1971-1987; Cur S Ptr's Epis Ch Peekskill NY 1968-1971.

HARDAWAY IV, John Benjamin (USC) 795 Wilson St, Anderson SC 29621 **R Gr Epis Ch Anderson SC 2004-** B Ames IA 1968 s John & Mary Lynne. BA Furman U 1990; MDiv VTS 1995. D 6/10/1995 P 5/26/1996 Bp Dorsey Henderson. m 6/6/1992 Susan Hardaway c 3. R S Paul's Epis Ch Ft Mill SC 1997-2004; Asst S Ptr's Epis Ch Greenville SC 1995-1997.

HARDAWAY, Ripp Barton (WTex) 312 S Guenther Ave, New Braunfels TX 78130 **Vic S Jn's Ch New Braunfels TX 2015-, Vic 2009-2014** B Midland TX 1970 s Ron & Susan. BA Texas A&M U 1992; MA Hardin-Simmons U 1998; MDiv Sewanee: The U So, TS 2003. D 6/10/2003 P 1/6/2004 Bp James Edward Folts. m 8/13/1985 Susan R Hardaway c 2. R S Chris's By The Sea Portland TX 2005-2009; Cur The Ch Of The H Sprt Dripping Spgs TX 2003-2005.

HARDAWAY, Susan (USC) 404 North St, Anderson SC 29621 **P-in-c S Andr's Ch Hartwell GA 2015-; Yth Dir H Cross Epis Ch Simpsonville SC 2012-** B Valdosta GA 1967 d Henry & Jayne. BA U So 1989; MDiv VTS 1993. D 5/29/1993 Bp Harry Woolston Shipps P 12/1/1993 Bp Peter J Lee. m 6/6/1992 John Benjamin Hardaway c 3. S Ptr's Epis Ch Greenville SC 2013-2014; P-in-c Ch Of The Epiph Laurens SC 2009-2015; Asst H Trin Par Epis Clemson SC 2005-2009; P-in-c S Mk's Ch Chester SC 2003-2004; Chapl York Place Epis Cluster York SC 2003-2004; Vic S Jas Ch Mooresville NC 1999-2003; Cbury Chapl Furman U Greenville SC 1995-1997; Asst S Jas Epis Ch Greenville SC 1995-1997; Asst Trin Ch Manassas VA 1993-1995.

HARDEN, Rosa Lee (Cal) 15 Riparian Way, Asheville NC 28778 **Cn for Money & Meaning The Cathd Of All Souls Asheville NC 2011-; Exec Producer SOCAP San Francisco CA 2008-; Exec Dir Everyvoice Ntwk San Francisco CA 2003-** B Fulton MS 1952 d Delmus & Rubye. BS Mississippi Coll 1974; MDiv CDSP 1999. D 5/27/1999 P 3/4/2000 Bp Alfred Marble Jr. m 12/28/1974 Kevin Jones. Ch Of The H Innoc San Francisco CA 2000-2010.

HARDENSTINE, Autumn Hecker (Pa) 126 Grist Mill Rd, Schuylkill Haven PA 17963 B Erie PA 1948 d Joseph & Lodeme. BS Edinboro U 1970; MEd Edinboro U 1976; MDiv Luth TS 1985; STM Luth TS 1992; DMin Luth TS 1995. D 6/15/1985 P 6/11/1986 Bp Lyman Cunningham Ogilby. m 7/1/2007 James Hardenstine c 1. R S Phil in the Fields Oreland PA 1994-2004; Chapl Inglis Hse: A Wheelchair Cmnty 1987-1994; Asst S Anne's Ch Abington PA

1987-1990; Asst to R S Paul Ch Exton PA 1985-1987. Auth, "Gifts Of Heart: The Challenge Of Enrichment For The Physically Disabled"; Auth, "Rachel Weeping For Her Chld"; Auth, "Images Of God"; Auth, "The Legacy," *Journ Of Wmn Mnstry*; Auth, "Bk Revs Of Clincl Handbook Of Pstr Counslg," *Journ Of Wmn Mnstry*. Fell Coll Of Chapl 1987; Profsnl Mem Of Assn Of Chapl 1986; Soc Of S Marg 1986.

HARDER, Cheryl Anne (Minn) 10 E Penton Blvd, Duluth MN 55808 **P Trin Epis Ch Hermantown MN 2005-** B 1956 d Arthur & Joyce. BS U MN 1986; MEd U of Wisconsin 1994. D 10/17/2004 P 7/23/2005 Bp James Louis Jelinek. m 1/12/1985 Edward Harder c 1.

HARDIE JR, John Ford (WTex) 6709 Pharaoh Dr, Corpus Christi TX 78412 **R S Mk's Ch Crp Christi TX 1999-** B San Antonio TX 1960 s John & Hazel. BA Tul 1983; MDiv VTS 1987. D 6/14/1987 P 12/17/1987 Bp John Herbert MacNaughton. m 5/27/1989 Melanie Hardie c 3. R S Phil's Ch Uvalde TX 1995-1999; Assoc R All SS Par Beverly Hills CA 1990-1995; S Barth's Ch Corpus Christi TX 1987-1990. johnh@stmarkscc.com

HARDIN, Glennda Cecile (Tex) PO Box 10357, Liberty TX 77575 **D S Steph's Ch Liberty TX 2012-** B Nacogdoches TX 1949 d Glenn & MaryLouise. Baylor U 1971; BS Lamar U 1973; MEd Sam Houston St U 1994; Cert Iona Sch for Mnstry 2011; Cert Iona Sch for Mnstry 2012. D 6/18/2011 Bp C Andrew Doyle. m 4/17/2004 William Eugene Stubblefield c 3. Assn of Epis Deacons 2011.

HARDING, Kerith (Haw) **P-in-c S Jn's Epis Ch Kula HI 2012-; Stndg Com The Epis Ch in Hawaii Honolulu HI 2014-, Compstn Revs Com 2013-** D 5/30/2009 Bp Sanford Zangwill Kaye Hampton P 1/9/2010 Bp Andrew Donnan Smith.

HARDING, Leander Samuel (Alb) Trinity School For Ministry, 311 Eleventh Street, Ambridge PA 15003 **R S Lk's Ch Catskill NY 2013-** B New York NY 1949 s Leander & Blanche. BA New Coll 1970; MDiv Andover Newton TS 1978; PhD Boston Coll 1989. D 12/3/1980 P 5/7/1981 Bp Frederick Barton Wolf. m 7/3/1971 Claudia Bolin Harding c 3. Fox Chap Epis Ch Pittsburgh PA 2008-2009; Asst. Prof of Pstr Theol TESM Ambridge PA 2005-2013; R S Jn's Ch Stamford CT 1989-2005; R Ch Of Our Sav Arlington MA 1984-1989; Int Ch Of The Gd Shpd Houlton ME 1982-1983; Vic S Anne Mars Hill ME 1981-1984; S Anne's Ch Blaine ME 1981-1984. Auth, "In the Breaking of the Bread," WipfandStock, 2010; Auth, "Reverence for the Heart of the Chld," YTC Press, 2008; Auth, "Why Is Dialogue So Difficult," *Trin Journ*, Trin Sch for Mnstry, 2008; Auth, "Flying Saucers and Christmas," IUinverese Press, 2006; Auth, "What The Ang Say," *Sermons That Wk*, 2002; Auth, "Christmas And Flying Saucers," *Sermons That Wk*, 2001; Auth, "Power And Dignity Of Priesthood," *Sewanee Theol Revs*, 2000; Auth, "What Have We Been Telling Ourselves About The Priesthood," *Sewanee Theol Revs*, 2000; Auth, "Atone And Fam Ther," *ATR*, 1984. ECF Fell 1985-1988; Soc For Ecum Doctrine 1991-2002; VP Mass Epis Cler Assn 1988-1989.

HARDING, Leslie Frank (Mich) 15178 Murray Woods Ct, Byron MI 48418 **Died 8/18/2015** B Pittsburgh ON CA 1931 s Charles & Ethel. BA 1959. Trans 12/16/1966 as Priest Bp Richard Stanley Merrill Emrich. m 5/8/1960 Judith A Rodie c 4. Int S Andr's Ch Waterford MI 2009-2015; Ret 2001-2015; Ret 2001-2015; Chapl (LTC) MI Wing CAP 1983-2001; Vic S Anne's Epis Ch Walled Lake MI 1972-2001; Chapl Novi Police Dept 1970-2001; Vic Ch Of The H Cross Novi MI 1969-2001; Nativ Cmnty Epis Ch Holly MI 1966-1969; Serv Ch of Can 1956-1966. Soc of S Jn the Evang (Can) 1956-1966.

HARDING, Rona (WA) 22968 Esperanza Drive, Lexington Park MD 20653 B Cleveland OH 1948 d Talbot & Cecilia. Muskingum Coll 1970; MTh U of S Andrews Fife Scotland 1973. D 5/7/1977 P 11/18/1977 Bp John Mc Gill Krumm. Int S Mk's Epis Ch Durango CO 2011-2012; Int Trin Epis Par Hughesville MD 2009-2011; R The Ch Of The Ascen Lexingtn Pk MD 1988-2009; Cn Cathd Ch Of S Mk Minneapolis MN 1982-1988; Chapl Bos Boston MA 1980-1982; Chapl Untd Campus Mnstrs Oxford OH 1979.

HARDING, Sahra Megananda (O) 3004 Belvedere Blvd, Omaha NE 68111 **Prog Dir Epis Serv Corps - Trin Cleveland 2012-** B Fairfield CA 1979 d Richard & Deni. AA Solano Cmnty Coll 1999; BA U CA Santa Cruz 2001; MDiv GTS 2010. D 6/2/2010 P 12/2/2010 Bp Joe Goodwin Burnett. m 6/3/2013 Aaron Michael Humphreys. Cur Trin Cathd Cleveland OH 2011-2014; Reverend Dio Nebraska Omaha NE 2010-2011. The Beatitudes Soc 2009.

HARDING, Scott Mitchell (At) 25 Bonner Dr, Queensbury NY 12804 **R S Jos's Epis Ch Mcdonough GA 2013-; R The Ch of the Mssh Glens Falls NY 2004-** B Rochester NY 1971 s Jonathan & Sandra. BS U Pgh 1992; MDiv TESM 1997; DMin Gordon-Conwell TS 2012; DMin Other 2012; DMin Other 2012. D 4/25/1998 P 10/31/1998 Bp Robert William Duncan. c 4. R The Ch Of The Mssh Glens Falls NY 2004-2013; R Chr Ch Gilbertsville NY 2001-2003; Assoc S Thos Memi Epis Ch Oakmont PA 1998-2001. fatherscott@me.com

HARDING, Stephen Riker (NY) 1047 Amsterdam Ave, New York NY 10025 **S Ptr's Ch New York NY 2013-; Dir, Pstr Care NYU Med Cntr New York NY 2005-; Prot Chapl Fire Dept New York NY 2003-** B FR 1957 s John & Margaret. BA Colby Coll 1980; MDiv GTS 1993; STM GTS 1994; Cert Assn of Profsnl Chapl 1997. D 6/23/1995 Bp Orris George Walker Jr P 5/8/1999 Bp Rodney Rae Michel. m 9/18/2004 Storm Swain c 1. The Ch of S Matt And

S Tim New York NY 2011-2013; Dio New York New York NY 2010-2011; Assoc The Ch of S Ign of Antioch New York NY 2007-2009; The Ch Of The Epiph New York NY 2000-2004; P S Paul's Ch Brooklyn NY 1999-2000; Chapl Beth Israel Med Cntr New York NY 1997-2005; Chapl Jacob Perlow Hospice Bklyn NY 1996-2002.

HARDMAN, J(ohn) (Chi) 222 Kenilworth Ave., Kenilworth IL 60043 **Assoc R Ch Of The H Comf Kenilworth IL 2008-** B Little Rock AR 1948 s Louis & Florence. BS U of Arkansas 1981; MDiv VTS 1986. D 6/28/1986 P 5/1/1987 Bp Herbert Alcorn Donovan Jr. m 1/24/1970 Elizabeth McCulloch Hardman c 2. R S Tim's Ch Wilson NC 2002-2008; R S Thos Epis Ch Eustis FL 1992-2002; Vic S Steph's Epis Ch Jacksonville AR 1987-1992; D-in-Trng S Mk's Epis Ch Little Rock AR 1986-1987.

HARDMAN, Louise O'Kelley (Fla) 256 E Church St, Jacksonville FL 32202 B Tallahassee FL 1941 d Artemas & Louise. BA U NC 1961. D 5/23/2010 Bp Samuel Johnson Howard. c 2.

HARDMAN, Richard Joseph (NJ) 3902 Se Fairway W, Stuart FL 34997 **Died 1/28/2016** B Pittsburgh PA 1922 s Joseph & Violet. BA U Pgh 1947. D 9/16/1949 P 3/18/1950 Bp Austin Pardue. m 6/15/1950 Patricia Gillespie. Ret 1982-2016; St Pauls Trust Westfield NJ 1971-1982; R S Paul's Epis Ch Westfield NJ 1957-1982; Asst Secy Urbn Industrl Ch Wk Ecec Dio Pittsburgh Pittsburgh PA 1956-1957; R S Steph's Epis Ch Mckeesport PA 1950-1956; Asst Calv Ch Pittsburgh PA 1949-1950. Hon Cn Trin Cathd 1967.

HARDMAN, Robert Rankin (Minn) 2338 Como Ave, Saint Paul MN 55108 B Framingham MA 1939 s George & Vera. BA Hobart and Wm Smith Colleges 1962; MDiv VTS 1969; Johnson Inst 1973. D 6/11/1969 Bp John Henry Esquirol P 1/1/1970 Bp Joseph Warren Hutchens. m 8/23/1969 Susan Dukehart Hardman c 3. P Assoc S Mart's By The Lake Epis Minnetonka Bch MN 2000-2013, 1972-1976; Epis Ch Hm S Paul MN 1989-1999; Dio Oregon Portland OR 1988-1989; R The Epis Ch Of The Gd Samar Corvallis OR 1982-1988; R The Par of St Paul's Epis Ch Duluth MN 1976-1982; Asst R S Mart's Lake Wayzata MN 1972-1976; Cur Chr Ch Greenwich CT 1969-1972.

HARDWICK, Dana (Lex) 7620 Summerglen Dr, Raleigh NC 27615 B Akron OH 1942 d Lewis & Mary. BS U of Wisconsin 1967; MDiv Lexington TS 1990; Cert Colorado Cntr For Healing 2000. D 6/17/1990 P 12/22/1990 Bp Don Adger Wimberly. R S Pat Ch Somerset KY 2003-2009; Chapl S Eliz Med Cntr 1996-2002; P Chap Of The Nativ Cincinnati OH 1996-1998; Cbury Crt Dayton OH 1995-1996; Trin Ch Covington KY 1992-1995; Chapl Duke Med Cntr Durham NC 1991-1992. Auth, "Oh Thou Wmn That Bringest Gd Tidings"; Auth, "Men'S Prattle, Wmn Word: The Biblic Mssn Of Kath Bushnell," *Sprtl & Soc Responsibility: Vocational Vision Of Wmn In The Methodist.* Assn Of Epis Healthcare Chapl 1997; Hti 1999; Sdi 1995; Tertiary Of The Soc Of S Fran 1997.

HARDWICK, Lada Eldredge (Colo) 4490 Hanover Ave, Boulder CO 80305 B Chattanooga TN 1941 d Harold & Marinell. BA E Tennessee St U 1964; MDiv Sewanee: The U So, TS 1990. D 6/17/1990 Bp William Evan Sanders P 1/9/1993 Bp Robert Gould Tharp. m 9/3/1964 David Hardwick c 2. Primary Pstr All SS Ch Hamlet NC 2002-2004; Sandhills Cluster Carthage NC 2000-2004; Cn Sandhills Epis Cluster of Ch Rockingham NC 2000-2004; Greenbrier Monroe Epis Mnstry Wht Sphr Spgs WV 1996-2000; Mssnr Greenbrier River Cluster White Sulphur Sprg WV 1996-2000; Vic S Jn's Ch Marlinton WV 1993-1995; D Cbury Grp Dio Cyprus and the Gulf 1990-1992.

HARDWICK, Linda C (Mo) 1001 Pheasant Hill Drive, Rolla MO 65401 **Chapl Phelps Cnty Reg Med Cntr 2011-; Hospice Chapl Phelps Reg Homecare 2009-** B Saint Louis MO 1959 d Lewis & Mary. BA DePauw U 1981; MDiv Ya Berk 1986. D 11/22/1986 P 10/1/1987 Bp William Grant Black. m 6/16/1990 Michael Eugene Hardwick c 2. Trin Ch S Jas MO 2003-2007; S Mich's Epis Ch O Fallon IL 1996-1999; The Epis Ch Of The Ascen Middletown OH 1991-1996; Int Calv Ch Cincinnati OH 1989-1990; Chap of the H Chld at Chld's Hosp Cincinnati OH 1988-1989; Dio Sthrn Ohio Cincinnati OH 1988; Assoc Min Indn Hill Ch Cincinnati OH 1986-1988.

HARDWICK, William (Ct) 19 1/2 Murray St, Norwalk CT 06851 B New York NY 1945 s Henry & Josephine. BA Iona Coll 1962; MA U of Notre Dame 1968; CDSP 1992; DMin SWTS 1999. D 6/13/1992 Bp Chester Lovelle Talton P 12/12/1992 Bp George Richard Millard. m 5/25/1991 Marian Stinson c 2. Pstr S Geo's Ch Middlebury CT 2006-2012; R Gr Epis Ch Norwalk CT 2000-2006; Vic S Richard's Epis Ch Skyforest CA 1995-2000; Asst S Matt's Epis Ch San Mateo CA 1992-1995.

HARDY, Cameron Reynolds (NY) 696 Deep Hollow Rd., Millbrook NY 12545 **Asst S Ptr's Ch Millbrook NY 2009-** B Newport RI 1960 d David & Cecily. AB Bow 1983; MDiv Ya Berk 2009. D 3/7/2009 P 9/12/2009 Bp Mark Sean Sisk. m 7/11/1987 William Hardy c 2.

HARDY JR, Jerry Edward (Mass) 51 John Ward Ave, Haverhill MA 01830 B 1939 m 8/20/1983 Judith Marie Gentle. S Steph's Memi Ch Lynn MA 1992-2000; The Epis Ch Of S Ptr And S Paul Marietta GA 1990-1992; H Innoc Ch Atlanta GA 1986-1990.

HARDY, Karen (WNY) 200 Cazenovia St, Buffalo NY 14210 B N Adams MA 1947 d Albert & M Eloise. BS Buffalo St Coll 1977; MDiv Bex Sem 2005. D

5/28/2005 Bp Michael Garrison P. c 2. S Simon's Ch Buffalo NY 2010-2015; Ch Of All SS Buffalo NY 2007-2009.

HARDY, Kim (Mass) 138 W. Plain St., Wayland MA 01778 **S Jas Epis Ch Essex Jct VT 2016**- B Elmira NY 1958 d Donald & Lois. BMus Ob 1981; MM Ithaca Coll 1983; DAS Ya Berk 1989; MDiv Yale DS 1989; Cler Ldrshp Proj 2005; Cert Cler Ldrshp Inst 2009; Cert Int Mnstry Ntwk 2011. D 6/17/1989 Bp O'Kelley Whitaker P 12/17/1989 Bp William George Burrill. m 5/28/1988 Frederick Perkins Moser c 2. Int S Paul's Ch Dedham MA 2014-2015; P-in-c S Mk's Ch Foxborough MA 2011-2014; Int S Ptr's Epis Ch Cambridge MA 2010-2011; Celtic Liturg Coordntr All SS Par Brookline MA 2006-2016; Dir of Admin & Liturg, Cler Ldrshp Proj Trin Par New York NY 2006-2010; R All SS Ch Stoneham MA 1996-2007; Coordntr of the Chld's Choir Emm Ch Boston MA 1994-1995; P-in-c S Lk's Ch Branchport NY 1989-1994; Dioc Coun Dio Massachusetts Boston MA 2006-2007, Dio Liturg Com Co-Chair 2004-, Dioc Conv Strng Com 2001-2011, Dioc Liturg and Mus Com 1999-2007; Dioc Coun Dio Rochester Henrietta 1992-1993. Auth, "Inclusive Lang Hymnal Supplement for the Epis Ch," Self-Pub, 1995.

HARDY, Mary Elizabeth Holsberry (La) Po Box 3654, Durango CO 81302 **Asst S Mary Magd Ch Boulder CO 2009-; Ret 2001**- B Pensacola FL 1938 d John & Ethel. Van 1958; Tul 1959; BA Wesleyan Coll 1960; MEd Tul 1971; MDiv CDSP 1992. D 6/13/1992 Bp James Barrow Brown P 12/6/1992 Bp William Edwin Swing. c 3. Asst R S Mk's Epis Ch Durango CO 2001; Assoc R Trin Ch New Orleans LA 1993-2001; P-in-c S Mk's Epis Ch Palo Alto CA 1992-1993. Auth, "Preaching Excellence," Cdsp, 1991. Graduated w dist CDSP 1992; Prching Excellence CDSP 1991.

HARDY, (Patricia) Joyce (Ark) 2114 Center St, Little Rock AR 72206 B Pryor OK 1951 d Omer & Reba. BD U of Arkansas 1973; MEd NE St U 1978. D 8/24/1985 Bp William Jackson Cox. Arkansas Dth Penalty Moratorium Cmpgn Little Rock AR 2008-2010; D Chr Epis Ch Little Rock AR 2005-2011, D 2005-2011; Dio Arkansas Little Rock AR 2001-2007; D Trin Cathd Little Rock AR 2000-2005; S Fran Hse Little Rock AR 1997-1999; Celebration Mnstrs Little Rock AR 1996-2000; S Marg's Epis Ch Little Rock AR 1992-1996; Asst S Paul's Ch Fayetteville AR 1989-1991; Asst S Matt's Ch Sand Sprg OK 1986-1989; Chapl Holland Hall Sch Tulsa OK 1985-1989; Asst S Andr's Ch Grove OK 1985-1986; D/Outreach Coordntr Chr Ch Little Rock AR; Cler Rep for Prov VII Exec Coun Appointees New York NY 2006-2012. EPF Bd; EWC; Episcopalians for Global Recon; Exec Coun; NAAD.

HARDY, Stanley P (Mass) Po Box 657, Humarock MA 02047 B Gloucester MA 1929 s Ralph & Viola. BA Bos 1956; STB Ya Berk 1959; MS Emerson Coll 1991. D 6/20/1959 Bp Anson Phelps Stokes Jr P 12/1/1959 Bp William A Lawrence. m 2/3/1973 Jane L Hardy. Assoc P Ch Of S Jn The Evang Hingham MA 1993-2000; Trin Ch Marshfield MA 1993-2000; Supplement Accounts Boston MA 1975-1976; R S Mk's Epis Ch Fall River MA 1974-1978; 1970-1974; Assoc The Ch Of S Mary Of The Harbor Provincetown MA 1964-1970; S Andr's Ch Kansas City MO 1964-1968; Cur S Steph's Memi Ch Lynn MA 1959-1964.

HARDY, Velinda Elaine (NC) P.O. Box 86, 4880 Highway 561 East, Tillery NC 27887 B Tarboro NC 1948 d Edwin & Ethel. BA S Augustines Coll Raleigh NC 1970; MA Clark Atlanta U 1972. D 5/19/2001 Bp James Gary Gloster. D S Lk's Ch Tarboro NC 2010-2012; D Calv Ch Tarboro NC 2001-2016.

HARE, Ann DuBuisson (NY) 255 Huguenot St Apt 1712, New Rochelle NY 10801 **Chapl Dept Of Corrections New York NY 1996**- B New York NY 1933 d Elijah & Eileyne. BA CUNY 1954; MA NYU 1965; MA GTS 1991. D 5/30/1992 Bp Richard Frank Grein. m 2/6/1970 Norman B Hare c 4. Chapl Dept Of Corrections New York NY 1994-1995; D Ch Of The Gd Shpd Wakefield Bronx NY 1992-1998. Auth, "Jewish & Black Dialogue Over The Past 30 Years," 1991. Afr Mnstry Com 2001; Alt Del Prov Syn 1998-2000; Coun Adv Prison Mnstry Natl Ch; Del Prov Syn 2001-2003; Del Prov Syn 1995-1997; E Bronx IPC Chairperson 2008; E Bronx IPC Vice Chair 2004-2008. Lights Awd Bronx Epis Aids Mnstry.

HARE, Delmas (At) 104 Sequoyah Hills Drive, Fletcher NC 28732 B Baileyton AL 1934 s Herbert & Clifford. BA Berea Coll 1955; BD Sewanee: The U So, TS 1961; PhD Emory U 1982. D 6/17/1961 P 12/23/1961 Bp Matthew George Henry. m 6/16/1956 Mabel C Herren c 3. P Assoc Ret Calv Epis Ch Fletcher NC 2002-2003; R Gd Shpd Epis Ch Austell GA 1993-1999; 1991-1993; Mssnr St Fran Epis Ch Acworth GA 1990; 1989-1990; R Ch Of The Resurr Atlanta GA 1987-1989; R Emm Ch Staunton VA 1983-1986; Asst Chr Ch Macon GA 1982; 1979-1981; R S Jn's Epis Ch Marion NC 1966-1979; Vic S Steph's Epis Ch Morganton NC 1961-1966; Vic St Mary's and St Steph's Epis Ch Morganton NC 1961-1966.

HARER, Mark P (CPa) 251 S Derr Dr, Lewisburg PA 17837 B Williamsport PA 1950 s Mark & Mary. BA Lycoming Coll 1972; MDiv UTS 1976; DIT Oxf GB 1977; JD PSU/Dickinson Sch of Law 1992. D 6/29/1980 Bp Dean Theodore Stevenson P 2/8/1981 Bp Charlie Fuller Mcnutt Jr. m 5/18/1985 Mary E Harer c 1. R S Andr's Epis Ch Lewisburg PA 2007-2015; R Prince Of Peace Epis Ch Dallas PA 2006-2007; Epis Mnstry of Unity All SS Epis Ch Lehighton PA 1997-2005; R S Jn's Epis Ch Palmerton PA 1997-2005; Asst St Andrews in the City Epis Ch Harrisburg PA 1992-1997; R Nrthrn Tier Epis Cluster 1985-1989; Vic S Jas Ch Mansfield PA 1985-1989; Vic S Andr's Ch Tioga PA 1981-1985; S Jn's Ch Westfield PA 1981-1985; Dio Cntrl Pennsylvania Harrisburg PA 1980-1981, Pres, Disciplinary Bd 2011-.

HARGIS, James Frederick (NCal) 742 El Granada Blvd, Half Moon Bay CA 94019 B Carthage MO 1946 s Frederick & Mary. BA Drury U 1968; MDiv CD-SP 1974; MA Grad Theol Un 1975; PhD U CA 1976. D 2/14/1982 Bp George Richard Millard P 2/14/1982 Bp William Edwin Swing. m 6/25/1988 Masumi Ann Hargis c 2. R Gr Epis Ch Fairfield CA 2002-2003; All SS Ch Kapaa HI 1998-2002; P-in-c True Sunshine Par San Francisco CA 1996-1998; Int S Steph's Epis Ch Longview WA 1993-1994; S Steph's Epis Ch Seattle WA 1991-1993; Chapl US-A All SS' Cmnty Heidelberg Germany 1988-1991; Chapl Off Of Bsh For ArmdF New York NY 1985-1991; Chapl US-A S Jn's Cmnty Ft Knox KY 1985-1987; R S Andr's Epis Ch Prineville OR 1983-1985; Vic S Alb's Epis Ch Redmond OR 1982-1985; Asst S Tim's Ch Danville CA 1980-1982; Asst S Steph's Epis Ch Orinda CA 1976-1977; Chapl San Francisco Gnrl Hosp 1975-1980; The Epis Ch Of S Mary The Vrgn San Francisco CA 1973-1976; S Jn's Epis Ch Oakland CA 1972-1973; St Johns Epis Ch Petaluma CA 1971-1972; Dioc Coun The Epis Ch in Hawaii Honolulu HI 1998-2002. "Sleeping w Zeus: Why Cats are better than Men"; Auth, "Visions, Reflections, Wanderings, Thrills of Taneycomo".

HARGIS, Kathleen A (WK) PO Box 1414, Dodge City KS 67801 **S Corn Epis Ch Dodge City KS 2015**- B Oklahoma City OK 1987 d David & Kathleen. BA U of Oklahoma 2009; MDiv The TS at The U So 2015. D 11/1/2014 P 8/15/2015 Bp Mike Milliken. Other Lay Position Chr Cathd Salina KS 2012. revkatiehargis@gmail.com

HARGREAVES, Helen (Ark) 10 Camp Mitchell Rd, Morrilton AR 72110 **Camp Mitchell Morrilton AR 2003**- B San Luis Obispo CA 1952 d William & Nina. El Ed Arkansas Tech U 1990. D 6/21/2003 Bp Larry Maze. m 9/23/1972 Richard Hargreaves c 1.

HARGREAVES, Mark Kingston (SanD) St James Episcopal Church, 743 Prospect St, La Jolla CA 92037 **S Jas By The Sea La Jolla CA 2016**- B Manchester UK 1963 s Ronald & Rosemary. BA Oxford 1985; BA The U of Oxford 1985; PhD Ridley Hall, Cambridge 1991; MA Kings Coll 2013. Trans 3/8/2016 as Priest Bp Jim Mathes. m 6/21/1991 Laura L Pirok c 2.

HARGREAVES, Robert Alan (Me) Po Box 96, Nobleboro ME 04555 **Instr & Counslr Two Bridges Reg Jail Wiscasset ME 2007-; Non-par 1994**- B Providence RI 1937 s Alan & Virginia. BA GW 1959; MDiv VTS 1962; TESM 1990; U of Maine 1996. D 6/9/1962 P 6/1/1963 Bp Robert Fisher Gibson Jr. m 7/31/1965 Frances M Hargreaves c 2. Chapl Lincoln Cnty Jail Wiscasset ME 2003-2007; R S Mk's Ch Augusta ME 1983-1993; R Emm Epis Ch Cumberland RI 1973-1983; Vic S Mths Ch Coventry RI 1969-1973; Ch of the Incarn Mineral VA 1964-1969; R S Jas Epis Ch Louisa VA 1964-1969; Asst Chr Epis Ch Winchester VA 1962-1963; Chapl Shenandoah Coll & Consrvatory Mus 1962-1963; Dioc Coun Dio Rhode Island Providence RI 1973-1976. Auth, "From A Parson'S Desk (Weekly Column)," Cntrl Virginian, 1964.

HARGROVE, Thomas J (Pa) 1628 Prospect St, Ewing NJ 08638 **Chapl Vitas Innovative Hospice 2010**- B Fitzgerlad GA 1951 s Gordon & Virginia. BBA California St U 1989; MDiv Nash 1992. D 11/14/1992 P 3/1/1994 Bp George Nelson Hunt III. m 2/25/2013 Dirk Christian Reinken. P-in-c S Phil Memi Ch Philadelphia PA 2009-2010; S Simon The Cyrenian Ch Philadelphia PA 2002-2009; S Mary's Ch E Providence RI 1994-1999; Cur S Steph's Ch Providence RI 1992-1993. OHC (Assoc) 1989.

HARIG, Richard Oliver (O) 3583 Sparrow Pond Cir., Akron OH 44333 **Died 5/6/2016** B Akron OH 1924 s William & Mary. BA Bowling Green St U 1947; BD Bex Sem 1950; S Augustines Coll Cbury GB 1963. D 6/13/1950 P 5/19/1951 Bp Beverley D Tucker. m 6/26/1965 Ruth Murray c 2. Int S Phil's In The Hills Tucson AZ 2001; Int S Dav's Ch Wayne PA 1996; Int S Jn's Of Lattingtown Locust Vlly NY 1995-1996; Int The Ch Of The Redeem Baltimore MD 1993-1995; S Alb's Epis Ch Tucson AZ 1992-1993; Int S Barn On The Desert Scottsdale AZ 1991-1992; Int Chr Ch Cathd Cincinnati OH 1990-1991; R Ch Of Our Sav Akron OH 1964-1990; P-in-c S Mk's Ch Canton OH 1956-1962; Assoc S Paul's Epis Ch Cleveland OH 1952-1956; P-in-c S Jn The Evang Ch Napoleon OH 1951-1952; D-in-c S Jn's Epis Ch Bowling Green OH 1950-1951; ExCoun Dio Ohio Cleveland 1966-1976, Chair Yth Div 1960-1965.

HARING, Charlotte (Az) 3942 E Monte Vista Dr, Tucson AZ 85712 B New Milford NJ 1928 d John & Jenny. D 10/21/1989 Bp Joseph Thomas Heistand. c 3. Wmn & Infant Frensdorff Mnstry 1995-2002; Asstg D S Andr's Epis Ch Tucson AZ 1993-2011; Dir Frensdorff Hse Aids Facility 1993-1995; Asstg D/Dir Outreach Mnstrs Gr St Pauls Epis Ch Tucson AZ 1990-1993.

HARKER, Margaret Ann Griggs (NI) 1364 N Pinebluff Dr, Marion IN 46952 B Dunkirk NY 1942 d Robert & Margaret. BA MWC 1964; MDiv SWTS 1993. D 4/30/1993 P 11/1/1993 Bp Francis Campbell Gray. m 8/15/1964 Albert C Harker c 4. S Paul's Epis Ch Gas City IN 2008-2011; Chr The King Epis Ch Huntington IN 1993-2004.

HARKINS, James Robert (NY) 235 Walker Street, Apt. 43, Lenox MA 01240 **Ch Of The Resurr New York NY 2002-; Chapl S Jn's Ch 1999-** B Watertown SD 1927 s James & Mae. BA U MN 1949; LTh SWTS 1952; BD SWTS 1953; U Madrid Madrid Es 1964. D 6/21/1952 P 12/21/1952 Bp Stephen E Keeler. c 1. Chapl Chr Ch Trieste 1993-1999; Vic French Ch De S Espirit New York NY 1991-1993; French Ch Of S Esprit New York NY 1991-1993; Dn S Mary's Cathd Caracas Venezuela 1985-1991; Exec Coun Appointees New York NY 1979-1991; Vic Epiph Pstr Un Ch Santo Domingo 1979-1985; Chapl Cmnty Trsfg & S Mary's Hm Glendale OH 1974-1979; The Soc of the Trsfg Cincinnati OH 1974-1979; R S Jas Epis Ch Prospect Pk PA 1972-1974; Vic S Ptr's & S Paul's Bayamon PR 1966-1970; Chapl S Mich's Hse & Trsfg Cnvnt 1960-1966; Vic S Mich's Ponce PR 1960-1966; Chapl S Lk's Hosp & Nrsng Sch Ponce PR 1960-1963; Vic S Alb's Ch Brooklyn NY 1958-1960; Vic Trsfg Brooklyn NY 1956-1958; Assoc S Andr's Ch Denver CO 1954-1955; Cur Geth Ch Minneapolis MN 1952-1954. SSC, Conf Of The Blessed Sacrame. Hon Cn S Mary Cathd.

HARKINS III, J William (At) 1703 Grace Ct SE, Smyrna GA 30082 **Cn Assoc. Cathd Of S Phil Atlanta GA 2004-** B Atlanta GA 1955 s John & Myrium. BA Rhodes Coll 1977; MDiv Van 1986; PhD Van 2001. D 6/9/2001 Bp Robert Gould Tharp P 11/12/2002 Bp J Neil Alexander. m 9/12/1981 Victoria Joanne Harkins c 2. Asst To The P Epis Ch Of The H Fam Jasper GA 2002-2004; D / Asst R S Jas Epis Ch Marietta GA 2001-2002. Auth, "Psycho Pathology, Sin, and Evil," *A Case Study of the Disconnected Man*, Jounral of Sprtlty and Mntl Hlth, 2008; Auth, "Monday, Tuesday, Wednesday H Week," *Pstr Perspectives on Lectionary*, Feasting on the Word, 2008; Auth, "My Continental Divide," *An Experiental Journey*, Journ for Preachers, 2006. AAMFT Clincl Mem 1997; AAPC Fell 1998.

HARLACHER, Richard Charles (CPa) 486 Fencepost Ln, Palmyra PA 17078 B Harrisburg PA 1940 s William & Florence. Pontifical Coll Josephinum 1967. Rec 5/27/1976 as Priest Bp Dean Theodore Stevenson. m 12/14/1974 Carol Lynn Harlacher. Chapl Country Meadows Ret Cmnty PA 1998-2000; R S Paul's Ch Columbia PA 1981-1998; S Andr's Ch Tioga PA 1976-1981; S Jn's Ch Westfield PA 1976-1981; Dio Cntrl Pennsylvania Harrisburg PA 1976-1977; Serv RC Ch 1967-1974.

HARLAN, Barry Stephen (WVa) 3887 Carriage Ln SW, Conyers GA 30094 B Newport RI 1948 s Marvin & Geraldine. BA Leh 1970; MDiv VTS 1973; MLS U Pgh 1977. D 6/8/1973 P 3/1/1974 Bp Dean Theodore Stevenson. m 4/7/2006 Richard F Harlan. Assoc Chr Ch Norcross GA 1985-1997; R S Pauls Epis Ch Williamson WV 1981-1985; Int S Mk's Epis Ch St Albans WV 1977-1978; Assoc Ch Of The Gd Shpd Pittsburgh PA 1976-1977; D Dio Cntrl Pennsylvania Harrisburg PA 1976, 1973-1974; Vic S Andr's Ch Tioga PA 1974-1976; S Jn's Ch Westfield PA 1974-1976.

HARLAN, James Robert (SeFla) 141 S County Rd, Palm Beach FL 33480 **R The Epis Ch Of Beth-By-The-Sea Palm Bch FL 2011-; Bd Mem Forw Mvmt of the Epis Ch Cincinnati OH 2015-** B Denver CO 1966 s Donald & Kay. BS U CO 1988; MDiv SWTS 1994. D 6/11/1994 P 12/10/1994 Bp William Jerry Winterrowd. m 5/10/1997 Elizabeth June Harlan c 1. Adj Fac Iliff TS 2003-2011; R The Ch Of The Ascen Denver CO 2002-2011; Command Chapl, US Naval Mobile Construction Battalion ONE Off Of Bsh For ArmdF New York NY 1999-2003; R Epis Ch Of S Jn The Bapt Breckenridge CO 1997-1999; Chapl US Naval Reserve 1995-2002; Asst to the R Ch Of S Mich The Archangel Colorado Spg CO 1994-1997; Yth Dir S Jn's Cathd Denver CO 1988-1991; Dn, No Palm Bch Dnry Dio SE Florida Miami 2014-2017; Pres, Epis Camp and Conf Mnstrs of Colorado, Inc. Dio Colorado Denver CO 2010-2011, Mem, Stndg Com 2009-2011, Chair, COM 2004-2008, 2002-2011, Mem, Dioc BEC 1995-1999; Rdr for the Gnrl Ord Exam Dom And Frgn Mssy Soc- Epis Ch Cntr New York NY 2008-2015. Ord of St. Jn 2013.

HARLAND, Mary Frances (Spok) Po Box 1510, Medical Lake WA 99022 **Chapl Correction Cntr Dio Spokane Spokane WA 1995-, Chapl 1984-1994** B Lakin KS 1931 d Everett & Helen. BS Idaho St U 1953; Dioc TS Seattle WA 1978; Pacific Luth U 1982. D 3/10/1979 Bp Robert Hume Cochrane P 5/8/1986 Bp Leigh Allen Wallace Jr. m 8/20/1955 Delmar C Harland. Chapl Correction Cntr Dio Olympia Seattle WA 1994-1995. Cert Med Hlth Counslr. WA St Employee of the Year St of WA 1982.

HARMAN, Torrence M (Va) 1927 Stuart Ave, Richmond VA 23220 B Richmond VA 1943 BS Virginia Commonwealth U. D 1/14/2004 P 7/17/2004 Bp Peter J Lee. m 7/27/1985 Julian Weir Harman c 3. S Mary's Whitechapel Epis Lancaster VA 2007-2015; Asst St Jas Ch Richmond VA 2004-2007.

HARMON, Elsa Wittmack (Ia) 3131 Fleur Dr Apt 901, Des Moines IA 50321 **D S Paul's Cathd Des Moines IA 2002-; Chr Ch Bayfield WI 1998-** B Des Moines IA 1941 d Charles & Elsa. BS U of Wisconsin 1963. D 1/10/1999 Bp Chris Christopher Epting. m 6/18/1966 Henry Andrew Harmon. S Lk's Ch Des Moines IA 2001-2002; D The Cathd Ch Of S Paul Des Moines IA 1998-1999.

HARMON, John Robert (Md) 10128 Camshire Ct Apt B, Saint Ann MO 63074 **Died 4/27/2017** B Saint Louis MO 1943 s Robert & Dorothy. U of Missouri 1963; BA Drury U 1966; BD CDSP 1969. D 6/24/1969 P 12/1/1969 Bp George Leslie Cadigan. c 4. Dio Maryland Baltimore MD 1996; All Hallows Par So

River Edgewater MD 1992-1996; Chr Epis Ch Bensalem PA 1985-1992; Ch Of Our Sav Jenkintown PA 1984; Non-par 1983-2017; R Ch Of The Mssh Lower Gwynedd PA 1979-1982; R S Andr's Epis Ch Lewisburg PA 1977-1979; Asst S Paul's Ch Philadelphia PA 1975-1977; S Barn Ch Moberly MO 1969-1975; Vic S Matthews Epis Ch Mex MO 1969-1975.

HARMON, John TW (WA) 7005 Piney Branch Rd NW, Washington DC 20012 **Pres Trin Dvlpmt Corporation 2001-; Trin Ch Washington DC 2000-** B Cape Palmas LR 1964 s Henry & Annie. BA S Pauls Coll 1988; Lancaster TS 1989; MDiv VTS 1991; ThM UTS 1998. D 6/8/1991 Bp Claude Charles Vache P 2/1/1992 Bp Frank Harris Vest Jr. m 10/17/1992 Keeva P Harmon c 3. Sprtl Fac CREDO Inst Inc 2001-2011; S Steph's Ch Petersburg VA 1993-2000; Epis Chapl Virginia St U Petersburt VA 1993-1997; Asst R Gr Ch Norfolk VA 1991-1993; Epis Chapl Norfolk St U Norfolk VA 1991-1993; Pres of Stndg Com Dio Sthrn Virginia Newport News VA 1997-2000.

HARMON, Joseph Albion (Nwk) 8 Rosemont Ct, West Orange NJ 07052 **R Chr Epis Ch E Orange NJ 2011-; Stndg Com Dio Newark Dio Newark Newark NJ 2016-, GC Dep 2015-, Cathd Chapt 2014-2017, COM 2014-2016, Disciplinary Bd 2012-, Anti-Racism Cmsn 2008-2013, Eccl Crt 2008-2012, Dioc Coun 2007-2013, Com on Const and Cn 2006-2017** B Philadelphia PA 1953 s Joseph & Althea. BA Cor 1975; MDiv GTS 1978; JD Widener U Sch of Law 2001. D 2/18/1978 Bp Robert Bracewell Appleyard P 8/19/1978 Bp Philip Edward Randolph Elder. c 2. Cbury Bd Mem Chr Hosp Jersey City NJ 2009-2013; P-in-c Ch Of The Incarn Jersey City NJ 2006-2011; Assoc St Andrews in the City Epis Ch Harrisburg PA 1999-2006; Vic Ch Of The Epiph Chicago IL 1997-1999; R Gr Ch White Plains NY 1994-1997; R S Matt's And S Jos's Detroit MI 1989-1994; R S Cyp's Epis Ch Detroit MI 1988-1989; Cn Mssnr Cathd Of All SS Albany NY 1986-1988; Chapl Kent Sch Kent CT 1985-1986; P Assoc Gr Ch Newark NJ 1982-1985; P-in-c Gr Epis Ch Eliz NJ 1980-1982; R Ch of the Resurr Eliz NJ 1979-1982; S Eliz's Ch Eliz NJ 1978-1982; S Phil's Ch Brooklyn NY 1978; Cbury Bd Mem Chr Hosp Jersey City NJ 2009-2013. Assoc OHC 2006.

HARMON, Jude Aaron (Cal) Grace Cathedral, 1100 California St, San Francisco CA 94108 **P Gr Cathd San Francisco CA 2012-** B New Haven CT 1981 s James & Dyann. BA Hav 2003; MDiv Harvard DS 2006; MDiv Harvard DS 2006; MDiv VTS 2012. D 6/2/2012 Bp Gayle Harris P 12/1/2012 Bp Marc Handley Andrus. judeh@gracecathedral.org

HARMON, Judith Lynn (Mich) 8874 Northern Ave, Plymouth MI 48170 **S Aid's Ch Ann Arbor MI 2012-** B Ypsilanti MI 1954 AA Schoolcraft Cmnty Livonia MI 1997; BS Estrn Michigan U 1999; DMin SWTS 2005. D 7/2/2005 P 2/8/2006 Bp Wendell Nathaniel Gibbs Jr. m 12/6/2008 George Harmon c 2. Trin Ch St Clair Shrs MI 2008-2012; Cur Ch Of The Incarn Pittsfield Twp Ann Arbor MI 2005-2007. trinity-scs@juno.com

HARMON, Robert Dale (Spr) 1119 Oakland Ave, 1119 Oakland Ave, Mount Vernon IL 62864 B Alton IL 1941 s Dale & Evelyn. BA U of Evansville 1968; MDiv SWTS 1971. D 6/19/1971 Bp Gerald Francis Burrill P 12/17/1971 Bp Albert A Chambers. m 9/6/1969 Kitty Ann Schmidt c 2. R Trin Ch Mt Vernon IL 1974-2002; P-in-c S Jn's Epis Ch Decatur IL 1973-1974.

HARMON, Zachary Charles (Ore) 1444 Liberty St SE, Salem OR 97302 **Dio Oregon Portland OR 2015-** B Newport VT 1983 s Douglas & Judith. BA Willamette U 2005; MDiv VTS 2015. D 6/13/2015 P 12/12/2015 Bp Michael Hanley. m 6/7/2016 Katherine Harmon Katherine Mary Siberine. S Paul's Epis Ch Salem OR 2015-2016.

HARMS, Richard Benjamin (Los) 2731 Jody Pl, Escondido CA 92027 B Pasadena CA 1932 s Herman & Gertrude. BA U of Redlands 1955; MDiv CDSP 1958; DMin Fuller TS 1999. D 6/16/1958 Bp Donald J Campbell P 2/1/1959 Bp Francis E I Bloy. c 4. Actg Headmaster S Jn Chrys Rancho Santa Margarita CA 1994-1996; S Jn Chrys Ch Rcho Sta Marg CA 1989-1995; Vic S Jn Chrys Rancho Santa Margarita CA 1989-1994; Archd Dio San Diego San Diego CA 1984-1989; Cn Mssnr Dio San Diego San Diego CA 1978-1984, 1977-1989; All SS Epis Ch Brawley CA 1978; St Marks Mssn Holtville CA 1978; Vic S Mk's Holtville CA 1976-1978; InterFaith Hsng Corp Los Angeles CA 1972-1974; S Mk's Par Altadena CA 1969-1972, Cur 1958-1968; Ch Of The Redeem Eagle Pass TX 1966-1968; P-in-c H Trin Carrizo Sprg TX 1966-1968; Cn Cathd S Jn the Bapt Santurce PR 1963-1966; Assoc H Trin Ponce PR 1960-1963; Chapl Inter Amer U San German PR 1960-1963. "Paradigms from Lk-Acts for Multicultural Communities," Ptr Lang, 2001.

HARMUTH, Karl Michael (Dal) 9021 Church Rd, Dallas TX 75231 **Ret 1998-; Chapl Chapl Epis Sch of Dallas 1998-** B Pittsburgh PA 1937 s Joseph & Lucille. BA S Vinc Coll Latrobe 1959; MDiv S Vinc Sem Latrobe 1963; STM SMU 1974. Rec 10/1/1967 Bp Charles A Mason. m 7/15/1965 Marianne Mudrick c 3. Chapl Chapl F.B.I. 1991-2007; Chapl Chapl to Dallas Police Dept. 1989-2007; R Epis Ch Of The Ascen Dallas TX 1986-1998; R S Andr's Epis Ch Arlington VA 1979-1986; Archd Dio NW Pennsylvania Erie PA 1976-1979; P-in-c H Trin Ch Rockwall TX 1975-1976; Cn To Ordnry Dio Dallas Dallas TX 1973-1976; R All SS Epis Ch Dallas TX 1970-1973, Cur 1967-1970; Serv RC Ch 1963-1965. Cmnty Serv Awd Mha 1986; Awd For Outstanding Serv Untd Way 1986.

HARNEY, Margaret Ferris (At) 4393 Garmon Rd Nw, Atlanta GA 30327 **Exec Dir Mary and Martha's Place Atlanta GA 1994-; Assoc S Dunst's Epis Ch Atlanta GA 1994-, Int 1990-1992** B Panama PA 1947 d Raymond & Mary. BA Randolph-Macon Coll 1969; Cert U CA 1971; MDiv Candler TS Emory U 1988. D 6/11/1988 Bp Charles Judson Child Jr P 4/8/1989 Bp Frank Kellogg Allan. m 9/20/1969 Thomas C Harney c 2. Rel Tchr / Chapl H Innoc Epis Sch Atlanta GA 1992-1994; Chapl H Innoc' Epis Sch Atlanta GA 1992-1994; Asst The Ch Of S Matt Snellville GA 1988-1989. Theta Phi Candler TS 1987.

HARPER, Anna Katherine (CFla) St Mary's Church, 5750 SE 115th St, Belleview FL 34420 B Sanford NC 1949 d Monter & Mary. D 12/10/2011 Bp John Wadsworth Howe. c 1.

HARPER, Barbara Anne (ETenn) 1155 Woodlawn Rd, Lenoir City TN 37771 **Trin Epis Ch Gatlinburg TN 2007-** B Memphis TN 1941 d Paul & Pollyanna. BD U of Florida 1963; EFM 1992; Dio E Tennessee Diac Prog 1994. D 9/18/1994 Bp Robert Gould Tharp. m 9/29/1967 Kenneth Allen Harper c 4. Ch Of The Ascen Knoxville TN 2002-2004; Dio E Tennessee Knoxville TN 1997-1998. Ch Denominational Leaders Assn; EFM Mentor; NAAD; Ord of S Lk.

HARPER, Catherine Ann (Mass) 124 Front St, Marion MA 02738 **D S Gabr's Epis Ch Marion MA 2013-** B Holyoke MA 1954 d George & Shirley Ann. D 6/22/2013 Bp M(Arvil) Thomas Shaw. m 10/6/1972 Douglas James Harper c 1.

HARPER, David Scott (CPa) 5598 Arminda St, Harrisburg PA 17109 B Harrisburg PA 1946 s Walter & Ruth. Bos TS; BA McDaniel Coll 1968; MDiv Gettysburg TS 1972; DMin Gettysburg TS 1984. D 11/9/1996 P 6/14/1997 Bp Michael Whittington Creighton. m 1/11/1997 Donna L Harper c 3. R Olivet Epis Ch Alexandria VA 2002-2013; R S Tim's Ch Bp CA 1999-2002; R H Trin Epis Ch Shamokin PA 1997-1999; R S Steph's Ch Mt Carmel PA 1996-1999; Dir Reli Affrs S Jn's Epis Ch Carlisle PA 1990-1996; Rep - Luth-Epis Coordntng Com Dio Virginia Richmond VA 2008-2013, Com on Ecum and Interfaith Relationships 2002-2013.

HARPER, Fletcher (Nwk) 241A Johnson Ave Apt M1, Hackensack NJ 07601 **GreenFaith Highland Pk NJ 2002-** B New York NY 1963 s Fletcher & Prudence. BA Pr 1985; MDiv UTS 1991. D 6/13/1991 Bp Richard Frank Grein P 12/21/1992 Bp John Shelby Spong. c 2. R S Lk's Epis Ch Haworth NJ 1997-2002, R 1994-1996, Asst R 1992-1993; R All SS Ch Bergenfield NJ 1994-1996, Asst R 1992-1993. "Sprt, Stwdshp, Justice and the Earth," *Diversity in the Environ Mvmt*, Yale, 2007; "Ground for Hope," *Eco-Sprt*, Fordham, 2007.

HARPER, Harry Taylor (WA) 36303 Notley Manor Ln, Chaptico MD 20621 **Int S Paul's Epis Ch Baden MD 2007-; Int S Paul's Par Prince Geo's Cnty Brandywine MD 2007-; P-in-c All SS' Epis Ch Oakley MD 2006-; P-in-c H Trin Epis Ch St. Mary's City MD 2005-; S Alb's Epis Ch Of Bexley Columbus OH 2002-; The Ch Of The Ascen Lexingtn Pk MD 2002-** B Sydney NSW AU 1926 s Charles & Lilias. Moore Theol Coll Sydney 1956. Trans 3/22/1964 Bp Randolph R Claiborne. c 3. Int S Alb's Epis Ch Bexley OH 2002-2005; Int S Thos Par Croom Uppr Marlboro MD 2001-2002; Middleham & S Ptr's Par Lusby MD 2000-2002; Int S Paul's Epis Ch Piney Waldorf MD 2000-2002; R The Ch Of The Redeem Beth MD 1974-1992; R S Geo's Ch Glenn Dale MD 1971-1974; R All SS Ch Oakley Av MD 1968-1971; S Andr's Ch Leonardtown California MD 1968-1971; R Ch Of The Incarn Atlanta GA 1963-1968; Serv Ch of New Zealand 1956-1963. stpaulsbaden@aol.com

HARPER, Helen Othelia (Haw) 210 Drummond Ave, Ridgecrest CA 93555 **St Michaels Epis Ch Ridgecrest CA 2015-; Vic St Jn the Bapt Epis Ch Waianae HI 2013-, Supply P 2012** B Manhattan NY 1949 d Evermond & Blanch. Mstr of Div Vancouver TS, Vancouver, BC, Can 1993. D 6/1/2002 Bp Rufus T Brome P 5/17/2003 Bp John Palmer Croneberger. m 6/19/2009 Barry Alan Johnson. S Nich Epis Ch Aiea HI 2013-2014; Prog Mgr Compass Hsng Allnce Seattle WA 2009-2012; Asstg P S Mk's Cathd Seattle WA 2009-2012; Int R H Apos And Medtr Philadelphia PA 2007-2008; P-in-c Chr Epis Ch Bensalem PA 2004-2007; Cur S Paul's Ch Englewood NJ 2002-2004; Dir of Prog (Haven for Families) S Ptr's Ch Clifton NJ 2002-2004. Amer Mntl Hlth Counselors Assn 2009; The UBE 2008. urbanpriest@gmail.com

HARPER, John Brammer (Ia) 1310 Bristol Dr, Iowa City IA 52245 B Des Moines IA 1941 s John & Mary. BA Stan 1962; MBA U of Iowa 1966; U of Iowa 1974. D 9/16/1995 Bp Chris Christopher Epting. COM Dio Iowa Des Moines IA 2004-2006, Dep GC 2003, 2002-2004, Dir - Mnstrs Retreat Prog 2001-2007; D New Song Epis Ch Coralville IA 1995-2014.

HARPER, John Harris (Ala) 2600 Arlington Ave S Apt 62, Birmingham AL 35205 B Florence AL 1938 s Harry & Mabel. BA Emory U 1960; JD Emory U Sch of Law 1962; MDiv Ya Berk 1980. D 4/26/1982 P 6/18/1983 Bp George Paul Reeves. m 12/5/1964 Margaret McCall c 2. Vice Dn The Cathd Ch Of The Adv Birmingham AL 2005-2010, Int Dn 2004-2005, Vice Dn 2000-2010; Int S Andr's Ch Darien GA 1998-1999; Int S Cyp's Ch Darien GA 1998-1999; Int S Andr's Epis Ch Douglas GA 1993-1994; Int Pstr Amelia Island Chap Amelia Island FL 1991-1992; Sum Asst All SS Epis Chap Linville NC 1984-1990; Vic Chr Ch S Marys GA 1984-1988; S Mk's Ch Brunswick GA 1984-1985, Asst 1982-1983. Auth, "Witnesses to the Light," *Witnesses to the Light*, EBESCO,

2013; Auth, "Sermons and Words 2000-2010," *Sermons and Words 2000-2010*, 2011. Who's Who in Amer Law 1991; Who's Who in Rel 1984; Exceptional Serv Awd Dept of the Treasury 1976; Distinguished Serv Awd 1968.

HARPER, Katherine Stuart (Ala) **St Thos Epis Ch Huntsville AL 2017-** D 6/2/2017 Bp John Mckee Sloan Sr.

HARPER JR, William Rhoderick (SVa) 6829 Cape View Avenue, Norfolk VA 23518 **Died 7/20/2016** B Birmingham AL 1931 s William & Sara. BA Birmingham-Sthrn Coll 1958; MDiv TESM 1981. D 12/27/1981 Bp Furman Charles Stough P 6/29/1982 Bp George Edward Haynsworth. Chr Ascen Ch Richmond VA 1997-1998; R Brandon Par Burrowville VA 1989-1994; R Chr Ch Waverly VA 1989-1994; Brandon Ch Hopewell VA 1989-1993; Vic S Mich's Wayne Township PA 1985-1989; S Paul's Epis Ch Kittanning PA 1984-1989; S Matt's Ch (Ft Motte) St Matthews SC 1982-1984; P-in-c S Matt's Ft Motte SC 1982-1984. Auth, "Calhoun Times". Compassionate Friends; EvangES; Curs; BSA.

HARPER, William Roland (Oly) 5836 Packard Lane, Bainbridge Island WA 98110 B Seattle WA 1958 s Roland & Carol. BA U of Washington 1980; PrTS 1983; MDiv GTS 1984. D 6/30/1984 Bp Robert Hume Cochrane P 2/11/1985 Bp James Stuart Wetmore. m 12/29/1979 Carolyn Harper c 2. R Gr Ch Bainbridge Island WA 1994-2015; R Ch Of S Mary The Vrgn Chappaqua NY 1987-1994; Chapl SUNY Purchase NY 1985-1986; Cur S Jn's Ch Larchmont NY 1984-1987.

HARPFER, Nancy Jean Fuller (EMich) St Andrews Episcopal Church, PO Box 52, Harrisville MI 48740 **P S Andrews-By-The-Lake Epis Ch Harrisville MI 2012-** B Ann Arbor MI 1933 d Richard & Elsie. BA U MI 1954; MA Cntrl Michigan U 1980. D 10/23/2011 P 4/28/2012 Bp Steven Todd Ousley. m 6/13/1953 Harold Evans Harpfer c 3.

HARPSTER, Chris (ETenn) St Paul's Episcopal Church, 161 E Ravine Rd, Kingsport TN 37660 **Chapl Dio E Tennessee Knoxville TN 2009-; S Paul's Epis Ch Kingsport TN 2009-** B Lewistown PA 1966 s Wilbur & Barbara. E Tennessee St U 2002. D 12/8/2007 Bp Charles Glenn VonRosenberg. m 11/20/1993 Deborah L Harpster c 3. Gld Of St. Vinc 2008.

HARRELL, Linda J (Ore) 99 Brattle St, Cambridge MA 02138 **Non-par 1995-** B Omaha NE 1946 d Kyle & Jane. EDS; BA California St U 1973; MDiv VTS 1978. D 6/17/1978 P 1/1/1979 Bp Robert Claflin Rusack. c 1. Dio Oregon Portland OR 1988-1994, 1980-1984; Vic S Fran Sweet Hm OR 1986-1994; S Fran Ch Sweet Hm OR 1986-1987; Chapl Sacr Heart Hosp Eugene OR 1985-1993; Assoc S Mary's Epis Ch Eugene OR 1979-1980; Chapl U Of Oregon-Eugene 1979-1980; Chapl Wmn Mnstrs 1978-1979; Liturg Asst S Matt's Epis Ch Eugene OR 1985-1993; CE S Aug By-The-Sea Par Santa Monica CA 1978-1979. ESMHE, EWC, EPF.

HARRELSON JR, Ernest S (Spok) 915 S 22nd Ave, Yakima WA 98902 B Trenton NJ 1945 s Ernest & Isabel. BA Coll of Wooster 1968; MDiv Bex Sem 1971. D 6/26/1971 P 5/20/1972 Bp John Harris Burt. m 11/20/1976 Dorothy M Harrelson c 4. R S Mich's Epis Ch Yakima WA 2001-2015; R S Paul's Ch Winona MN 1998-2001; S Jn Minneapolis MN 1995-1998; R Trin Ch Litchfield MN 1994-1998; Supply P Dio El Camino Real Salinas CA 1989-1994; S Mk's Ch Candor NY 1983-1989; Calv Epis Ch Mc Donough NY 1976-1980; Chr Ch Guilford CT 1976-1980; R S Paul's Ch Oxford NY 1976-1980; R Gr Ch Ravenna OH 1973-1976; Asst S Paul's Ch Maumee OH 1971-1973.

HARRELSON, Larry Eugene (Ida) 3095 W. Ravenhurst St., Meridian ID 83646 **Exam Chapl Dio Idaho Boise ID 2010-, COM 2007-2010** B McLeansboro IL 1944 s Willis & Verla. B.S. Drury U 1969; M.A. U of Missouri 1970; M.A. U of Oklahoma 1973; Theol Stds Epis TS in Kentucky 1976; Cert U S Army Chapl Basic Course 1981; Doctor of Mnstry Phillips U Grad Sem 1982; Cert U S Army Chapl Advncd Course 1984; Cert U. S. Army Command and Gnrl Stff Coll 1989; Licensure St of Idaho 1991; Cert Shalem Inst for Sprtl Formation 2001. D 6/19/1976 P 12/18/1976 Bp Chilton R Powell. m 6/6/1970 Willa R Sommer c 3. Assoc Ch Of H Nativ Meridian ID 2009-2012; Assoc S Steph's Boise ID 2004-2008; R Epis Ch Of The Trsfg Sis OR 1995-2004; Clinician Idaho Mntl Hlth & Adult Serv Lewiston ID 1991-1995; R Epis Ch of the Nativ Lewiston ID 1984-1991; Battalion, Brigade, and St Chapl Idaho Army NG Lewiston & Boise ID 1980-2003; Vic H Trin Epis Ch Wallace ID 1979-1984; Vic Dio Oklahoma Oklahoma City OK 1978-1979; S Jn's Epis Ch Woodward OK 1978-1979; Cur S Matt's Ch Enid OK 1976-1977; Chair, COM Dio Estrn Oregon Cove OR 1998-2000, Stndg Com 1996-2000; COM Dio Spokane Spokane WA 1988-1992, Dioc Coun 1986-1992. Auth, "arts," *Rel & Mltry Periodicals, Newspapers*, Var. Third Ord, SSF 2001. Paul Harris Fell Rotary Club 2004; Legion of Merit U. S. Army 2003; Meritorious Serv Medallion The Epis Ch 2002; Unit Mnstry Team of the Year U.S. Army 1988; Grad Fllshp U of Missouri 1969; Illinois St Schlrshp St of Illinois 1962.

HARRES, Elisa P (At) 13479 Spring View Dr, Alpharetta GA 30004 **The Epis Ch Of S Ptr And S Paul Marietta GA 2008-; Chapl Dept Of Veteran's Affrs 2004-** B Philadephia PA 1957 d William & Martha. Radford Coll; BSW Virginia Commonwealth 1979; MDiv TESM 2003. D 12/14/2002 P 8/9/2003 Bp Robert William Duncan. c 3. Ch Of The Annunc Marietta GA 2009, P-in-c

2008-2009; Chapl S Jos's Hosp Altanta GA 2004-2007; D Chr The King Epis Ch Beaver Falls PA 2003.

HARRIES, Susan Gratia (NMich) 1111 Bingham Ave, Sault Sainte Marie MI 49783 **P S Jas Ch Of Sault S Marie Sault Sainte Marie MI 2006-** B Santa Fe NM 1953 d Harvey & Gratia. BS U of Arizona 1975. D 11/28/2005 P 5/28/2006 Bp James Arthur Kelsey. m 6/9/1979 Richard Grant Harries c 2. Mem, Epis Mnstry Discernment Team Dio Nthrn Michigan Marquette MI 2008-2009.

HARRIES, Thomas (Minn) 10520 Beard Ave S, Bloomington MN 55431 **R Ch Of The H Comm S Ptr MN 2005-** B Saint Paul MN 1955 s Gilbert & Beverly. BA S Olaf Coll 1978; MDiv Ya Berk 1983; DMin Untd TS of the Twin Cities 2009. D 12/29/1983 P 7/1/1984 Bp Robert Marshall Anderson. m 6/24/1989 Diannah Robertson c 1. S Jas Ch Marshall MN 2008-2011; S Paul's Epis Le Cntr MN 2008; R S Nich Ch Minneapolis MN 2004-2005; Asst R S Jn The Evang S Paul MN 1984-1988; Dio Minnesota Minneapolis MN 1984. Auth, "Faith and Environ Impace: Congregations Learn About, Celebrate, and Care for Creation," *Congregations*, The Alb Inst, 2011; Auth, "Sprtl Checkins," Action Info; Auth, "The Cell Wall: A Metaphor For Healthy Boundaries," *Congregations*, The Alb Inst.

HARRIGAN, Kate (CPa) 1105 Old Quaker Rd, Etters PA 17319 **S Paul's Epis Ch Harrisburg PA 2009-; Cn for Formation Dio Cntrl Pennsylvania Harrisburg PA 2007-; Chapl S Steph's Epis Sch Harrisburg PA 2000-** B New York NY 1950 d John & Ann. Amer U 1970; BS U GA 1972; MA MI SU 1976; MDiv Ya Berk 1989. D 6/10/1989 Bp Paul Moore Jr P 6/10/1990 Bp Jeffery William Rowthorn. m 3/19/2005 William T Alford c 3. Dio Cntrl Pennsylvania Harrisburg PA 2004-2013, Dn, Sch of Chr Stds 2002-, Eccl Crt 2000-, Dept of Cong Develpmnt 1999-, Dep GC, chair of deputation 1997-, 1996-2000, VP Cler Assn 1996-2000, COM 1995-, Com Ecum Affrs 1995-, Dioc Coun 1993-1996, Com Litur & Ch Mus, Chair 1993-, Bp Com for Chld Advocacy & Fam Life 1992-1998; R S Mich And All Ang Ch Middletown PA 1992-2007; Asst Gr And S Ptr's Epis Ch Hamden CT 1989-1991. Ord of S Helena 1984. Kappa Delta Pi U GA 1972; Phi Kappa Phi U GA 1972.

HARRIGFELD, Chris Louis (Cal) 8872 Bronson Dr., Granite Bay CA 95746 **Died 6/12/2017** B Squirrel ID 1928 s William & Freda. BS U of Idaho 1950; MD U of Oregon 1960. D 6/3/2000 Bp William Edwin Swing. m 6/24/1968 Bridget Harney c 1. S Matt's Epis Ch San Mateo CA 2000-2004.

HARRIMAN, Barbara June (Nwk) **Chapl The Vlly Hosp. Ridgewood NJ 2003-; Chapl Essex Cnty Correctional Facility Newark NJ 1999-** B Philadelphia PA 1941 d Archie & Jessie. Orange Coast Coll 1986; Newark TS 2004. D 5/21/2005 Bp John Palmer Croneberger. m 9/26/1959 Allan W Harriman c 3. Treas Dioc AltGld Dio Newark Newark NJ 1999-2007.

HARRINGTON, Debra Lynn (Chi) 1250 Averill Dr, Batavia IL 60510 B Rogers City MI 1956 d Harold & Mary. Estrn Michigan U. D 2/3/2007 Bp Bill Persell. m 4/16/1983 John Harrington c 2.

HARRINGTON, Lynn Beth (NY) 203 Salem Rd, Pound Ridge NY 10576 B White Plains NY 1943 d Peter & Elizabeth. BA SUNY 1979; MDiv Yale DS 1983; ThM Maryknoll TS 1991. D 6/4/1983 P 2/5/1984 Bp Paul Moore Jr. m 7/30/1970 Denis Harrington c 3. Rgnl Advsr Wmn Advoc Mnstry Wmn Advoc Mnstry New York NY 1996-2005; R S Jn's Ch So Salem NY 1988-2011; Asst S Jas' Ch No Salem NY 1985-1988; Asst S Fran Ch Stamford CT 1983-1985; Conv Plnng Com Dio New York New York NY 2002-2005, Exec Commit 1996-2001, Conv Credntls Com 1993-1995. The Soc of S Jn the Theol Bp of New York 1999.

HARRINGTON, Thomas Anthony (Okla) 2961 N 23rd St W, Muskogee OK 74401 **D Gr Ch Muskogee OK 1995-** B Racine WI 1948 s Gordon & Mary. BS Tri-St U 1970. D 6/24/1995 Bp Robert Manning Moody. m 9/12/1970 Sheila Kay Harrington c 1.

HARRIOT, Cameron (Los) 5672 Castle Dr, Huntington Beach CA 92649 **Died 5/23/2017** B Mamaroneck NY 1925 s Wesley & Helen. BA Occ 1948; CDSP 1951; MS Natl U 1988. D 2/19/1951 P 11/1/1951 Bp Francis E I Bloy. m 11/22/1978 Deborah L Lee c 2. Int S Steph's Par Beaumont CA 2001-2004; Int St Jas the Great Epis Ch Newport Bch CA 1998-1999; S Barth's Mssn Pico Rivera CA 1989-1998; Serv S Wilfrid Of York Epis Ch Huntington Bch CA 1989-1996; Serv S Lk's Epis Ch Monrovia CA 1965-1978; 1964-1965; Vic S Patricks Santa Rosa CA 1962-1964; P-in-c S Eliz's Ketchikan AK 1956-1962; P-in-c S Mk's Ch Nenana AK 1952-1956; Cur S Lk's Of The Mountains La Crescenta CA 1951-1952.

HARRIS, Anne (Miss) 705 Rayburn Ave, Ocean Springs MS 39564 **R S Paul's Ch Columbus MS 2011-; Asst Chap Of S Andr Boca Raton FL 2008-** B Inglewood New Zealand 1953 d Eric & Eileen. BA Massey U 1973; MA Massey U 1975; Cert Dio SE Florida Dioc Sch 2004; MDiv VTS 2008. D 12/22/2007 P 6/22/2008 Bp Leo Frade. m 9/4/1976 Marc L Harris c 2. S Jn's Epis Ch Ocean Sprg MS 2009-2011. revanneharris@gmail.com

✠ HARRIS, The Rt Rev Barbara Clementine (Mass) 11 Atherton Rd., Foxboro MA 02035 **Ret Bp Suffr of Massachusetts Dio Massachusetts Boston MA 2003-, Suffr Bp Of Mass 1989-2002** B Philadelphia PA 1930 d Walter & Beatrice. D 9/29/1979 P 10/18/1980 Bp Lyman Cunningham Ogilby Con 2/11/1989 for Mass. Dio Washington Washington DC 2003-2007; Int Geo W So Ch of Advoc

Philadelphia PA 1988, D-Intrn 1979-1980; Epis Ch Publ CO 1984-1988; The Epis Ch Pub Co Scranton PA 1982-1989; P-in-c S Aug Of Hippo Norristown PA 1980-1984. Auth, "Monthly Column," *Wit*, 1988. Hon DD GTS 1990; Hon DD Ya 1990; Hon DD Amherst 1989; Hon DD EDS 1989; Hon DD Trin 1989; Hon STD Hobart and Wm Smith Colleges 1981.

HARRIS, Carl Berlinger (Md) 1506 Eton Way, Crofton MD 21114 B Baltimore MD 1929 s Alfred & Helen. BA Muhlenberg Coll 1952; GTS 1956. D 9/29/1956 Bp Harry Lee Doll P 7/1/1957 Bp Noble C Powell. m 10/5/1967 Tomolyn T Harris c 2. Asst P Ch Of The Ascen Westminster MD 1998-1999; R S Steph's Ch Severn Par Crownsville MD 1971-1996; Asst S Anne's Par Annapolis MD 1968-1971, Cur 1956-1967; Vic S Andr The Fisherman Epis Mayo MD 1958-1967.

HARRIS, Carl Burton (Va) 2727 Fairview Ave E Apt 3b, Seattle WA 98102 **Non-par 1967-** B Cleveland OH 1932 s Carle & Myra. BA Ohio Wesl 1956; MDiv VTS 1961. D 3/3/1962 P 10/1/1962 Bp William Foreman Creighton. m 12/31/1988 Judy M Harris. R S Alb's Epis Ch Annandale VA 1964-1967; R Redeem Washington DC 1962-1964.

HARRIS, Cheryl Jeanne (Neb) 820 Weat 9th Street, Alliance NE 69301 **D S Matt's Ch Allnce NE 1999-** B Alliance NE 1943 d Richard & Yvonne. D 12/10/1999 Bp James Edward Krotz. m 12/16/1961 S Todd Harris c 3.

HARRIS, Christopher Ross (SanD) D 6/11/2016 Bp Jim Mathes.

HARRIS, Donald Bell (SVa) 121 Jordans Journey, Williamsburg VA 23185 B Boston MA 1936 s Robert & Ruth. BA W&M 1957; U of Iowa 1958; Claremont Coll 1960; MDiv CDSP 1964; U CA 1966; U CA 1969. D 1/10/1964 Bp George Richard Millard P 7/11/1964 Bp Robert B Gooden. m 11/28/1964 Faye Ruth Harris c 3. Assoc S Mart's Epis Ch Williamsburg VA 1990-2003; Epis Chapl Wm and Mary Bruton Par Williamsburg VA 1988-1990; Assoc Trin Par New York NY 1986-1988; Sr Chapl US Coast Guard Gvnr I. NY 1986-1988; Assoc Ch Of The H Comm Charleston SC 1984-1986; Chapl USN Hosp Charleston SC 1984-1986; Off Of Bsh For ArmdF New York NY 1979-1988, 1964-1978; Cur S Lk's Epis Ch Ft Collins CO 1977-1978; Chapl Ship Chapl USS SAIPAN (LHA2). Auth, *That's How the Light Gets In: A Credo of Friendship*, Credo Inst, 1994; Auth, *CREDO: Ministering in the Twilight of the 20th Century*; Auth, *The Chapl as Fisherman & Shpd*. Bd Inst of Clincal Theologicy, Regent U 1992-1993; Bd, Regent U Sch of Counslg 1994-2001. Graduated w hon CDSP 1964.

HARRIS, Edmund Immanuel (Oly) 1336 Pawtucket Ave, Rumford RI 02916 **St Ptr's Epis Par Seattle WA 2015-** B Virginia Beach VA 1981 s Robert & Laura. BA U of Virginia 2004; MDiv U Chi DS 2008; MDiv U Chi DS 2008; STM Ya Berk 2010. D 6/5/2010 Bp Jeff Lee P 12/11/2010 Bp David Bruce Joslin. m 6/22/2013 Michael P Jaycox. Asst to the R Ch of the Epiph Rumford RI 2010-2014.

HARRIS, Edward Ridgway (Minn) 2225 Crest Ln Sw, Rochester MN 55902 B Rochester NY 1928 s Edward & Anne. Trin Hartford CT 1950; BS Col 1956. D 1/17/1977 Bp Philip Frederick McNairy. m 3/7/1964 Emily Van Voorhis Harris c 4. D Calv Ch Rochester MN 1977-1990.

HARRIS, Gareth Scott (At) Po Box 191708, Atlanta GA 31119 B Athens GA 1941 s George & Hazel. BS Georgia Inst of Tech 1965; BD Epis TS of the SW 1970. D 6/28/1970 Bp R aymond Stewart Wood Jr P 1/1/1971 Bp Randolph R Claiborne. c 2. Vic S Jas Ch Cedartown GA 1987-1992; Non-par 1971-1987; Cur H Trin Par Decatur GA 1970-1971.

✠ HARRIS, The Rt Rev Gayle (Mass) 138 Tremont St, Boston MA 02111 **Bp Suffr of Massachusetts Dio Massachusetts Boston MA 2002-** B Cleveland OH 1951 d Nelson & Dorothy. BA L&C 1978; MDiv CDSP 1981; CDSP 2001. D 6/19/1981 Bp James Winchester Montgomery P 2/11/1982 Bp John Shelby Spong Con 1/18/2003 for Mass. R S Lk And S Simon Cyrene Rochester NY 1992-2002; P-in-c Ch Of The H Comm Washington DC 1984-1992; Asst To Vic S Phil The Evang Washington DC 1982-1984; Dir Of Pstr Mnstrs Gr Ch Van Vorst Jersey City NJ 1981-1982.

HARRIS, Gerald Joaquin (NwPa) 2604 Toucan Ave., McAllen TX 78504 B Torreon Coahuila Mexico 1939 s Leslie & Rachel. BBA U of Texas 1963; MDiv Bex Sem 1991. D 6/8/1991 P 1/1/1992 Bp David Charles Bowman. m 5/4/1963 Mary R Harris c 2. Int St Ptr & St Paul Ch Mssn TX 2011; Int All SS Epis Ch San Benito TX 2008-2009; Supply Preist Dio W Texas San Antonio TX 2005-2011; Pres Ridgway Cler Assn 2004; Treas Elk & Cameron Counties Red Cross 2003-2005; Chapl Helpmate Hospice of Ridgway 2003-2005; Dep to GC Dio NW Pennsylvania Erie PA 2002-2003, Alt Dep to Gnrl Convntion 1997-1998, Dioc Ecum Com 2002-2005, Dn of SE Dnry 1996-2005, Spanish Partnership Mssn Com 1996-2005, Dioc Bdgt Com 1993-2002, COM 1993-1998; 911 Wrld Trade Cntr Fam Serv Elk & Cameron Counties Red Cross 2001; R S Agnes' Epis Ch S Marys PA 2000-2005; Chairman of the Bd Elk & Cameron Counties Red Cross 2000-2003; Treas Elk & Cameron Counties Red Cross 1999; Chair of Golf Tournament Elk & Cameron Counties Red Cross 1998-2005; Chairman of the Bd Elk & Cameron Counties Red Cross 1997-1998; Disaster Com Elk & Cameron Counties Red Cross 1996-2005; Ethics Com Elk Cnty Reg Med Cntr 1996-1999; Pres Ridgway Cler Assn 1996; Bd Dir Elk & Cameron Counties Red Cross 1995-2005; Pres Ridgway Rotary

Club 1995; Ridgway Cler Assn Rep Elk Cnty FEMA Coun 1993-1999; Mem Salvation Army Serv Unit of Ridgway 1992-1997; Gr Epis Ch Ridgway PA 1991-2005; Chapl Ridgway Vol Fire Departmment 1991-2005.

HARRIS, Henry G (O) 735 Woodrich St SW, Massillon OH 44646 B Toledo OH 1945 s Henry & Janet. BBA U of Toledo 1967; JD U of Toledo 1970; MDiv VTS 1985. D 6/15/1985 Bp James Russell Moodey P 3/7/1986 Bp John Thomas Walker. m 8/12/1967 Constance Diane Kolby c 2. R S Tim's Epis Ch Massillon OH 1989-2015; Assoc All SS' Epis Ch Chevy Chase MD 1985-1989.

HARRIS, Herman (USC) 633 Swallow Rd, Elgin SC 29045 B North Haven CT 1948 s Gilmore & Elizabeth. BS New Hampshire Coll 1983. D 12/1/1990 Bp Arthur Edward Walmsley. m 10/13/1977 Delmonte Doris Harris c 4. D S Steph's Epis Ch Ridgeway SC 1994-1996; D Dio Connecticut Meriden CT 1990-1994.

HARRIS JR, James Wesley (Dal) 1700 N Westmoreland Rd, Desoto TX 75115 **S Anne's Epis Ch Desoto TX 2014-** B TN 1962 s James & Talca. BA Sthrn Illinois U 1995; MDiv Aquinas Inst of Theol 1998; Cert SWTS 1998; DMin SWTS 2011. Trans 3/16/2004 Bp Peter Hess Beckwith. m 12/17/1983 Laural L Harris c 2. S Jas Epis Ch Ormond Bch FL 2009-2014; Dn Trin Cathd Davenport IA 2006-2009; R Ch Of The Gd Shpd Jacksonville FL 2004-2006; Vic St. Thos Epis Ch Glen Carbon IL 1999-2004; S Thos Epis Ch Glen Carbon IL 1999-2002; Cur S Geo's Ch Belleville IL 1998-1999.

HARRIS, John Carlyle (WA) 3050 Military Rd NW #2104, Washington DC 20015 B Boston MA 1930 s Charles & Janet. BA Wms 1952; MDiv VTS 1955; MS CUA 1978. D 6/18/1955 P 12/22/1955 Bp Wallace E Conkling. m 6/29/1962 Ruth T Ayers Harris c 3. 1978-1996; Bd Trst Dio Washington Washington DC 1973-1976, Asst to Bp 1970-1976; Asst Dio Washington & Maryland Washington DC 1965-1970; R S Jn's Oxon Hill MD 1958-1965; Assoc R S Alb's Par Washington DC 1955-1958; VTS Alexandria VA 1973-1974. Auth, "Cler & Their Wk," Alb Inst, 1977; Auth, "Pract of Supervision," Dio Washington, 1970; Auth, "Stress, Power & Mnstry," Alb Inst; Auth, *Pstr Care of Pastors*, Journ of Pstr Care; Auth, *Planned Self Appraisal for Ch.*

HARRIS, John E (Ga) 30 Anderson Ave., Holden MA 01520 B Sarasota FL 1935 s John & Rebecca. AB Amh 1956; MDiv VTS 1959; ThM Duke 1969; DMin GTF 1989. D 6/29/1959 Bp William Francis Moses P 1/10/1960 Bp Richard Henry Baker. m 5/3/2003 Deborah Johansen Harris c 2. Int The Epis Ch Of S Jn The Bapt Sanbornville NH 2000-2001; R S Andr's Ch Darien GA 1994-1997; R S Cyp's Ch Darien GA 1994-1997; Int Calv Epis Ch Ashland KY 1992-1994; Cmnty Med Cntr Toms River NJ 1990-1992; S Elis's Epis Ch Memphis TN 1989-1990; The Epis Counslg Cntr Memphis TN 1989; Non-par 1983-1992; Memphis Inst Of Med & Rel Memphis TN 1983-1988; Assoc Chr and S Lk's Epis Ch Norfolk VA 1976-1983; R S Lk's Epis Ch Durham NC 1967-1974; Assoc Chr Epis Ch Raleigh NC 1965-1967; Vic S Andr's Ch Rocky Mt NC 1961-1965; Asst S Ptr's Epis Ch Charlotte NC 1959-1961; Ret; Vic S Cyp. Auth, "Cumberland Sem Journ," 1989; Auth, "Supervision Biblic Model," *Journ Of Supervision Mnstry*, 1979; Auth, "b Again: Emancipation From The Mo Complex," *from the Negatice Mo Complex*. Amer Assoc. of Pstr Counselors 1986; ACPE 1976; Coll of Pstr Supervision and Psych 1980. Supervisory Certification ACPE 1981; Dplma Aapc 1977.

HARRIS, John T. (NCal) P.O. Box 1291, Gridley CA 95948 **Vic S Tim's Ch Gridley CA 2011-, Assoc 2004-2011; Living Stones Coordntr The Epis Dio Nthrn California Sacramento CA 2010-** B Oroville CA 1941 s Glen & Dixie. BA U CA 1962; JD U CA 1965. D 9/10/2004 P 3/19/2005 Bp Jerry Alban Lamb. m 9/4/1965 Marny Helen Harris c 3.

HARRIS, Jonathan (SwVa) 3286 Avenham Ave Sw, Roanoke VA 24014 **Dio SW Virginia Roanoke VA 2013-** B Rochester MN 1970 s Edward & Emily. BA S Olaf Coll 1993; MDiv Van 2000; Cert SWTS 2004. D 5/8/2004 P 12/4/2004 Bp Neff Powell. m 10/14/2000 Darla Yvonne Harris c 1. S Eliz's Ch Roanoke VA 2014-2017; P-in-c Trin Ch Buchanan VA 2004-2014.

HARRIS, Julie Nan (WVa) 200 W King St, Martinsburg WV 25401 **R Trin Epis Ch Martinsburg WV 2006-** B Portland OR 1951 d Edward & Nancy. BFA Pacific Luth U 1973; Portland St U 1974; MDiv GTS 1996. D 6/29/1996 Bp Robert Louis Ladehoff P 1/18/1997 Bp J Clark Grew II. Int R S Paul's Ch Canton OH 2004-2006; Int P-in-c S Andr's Ch Akron OH 2000-2004; Int P-in Charge S Phil's Epis Ch Akron OH 2000-2004; Dioc Coun Chr Ch Epis Hudson OH 1999-2000; Assitant to the R S Ptr's Epis Ch Lakewood OH 1996-1998; COM Dio W Virginia Charleston WV 2009-2014, T/F on Congrl Vitality 2009-2012, BEC 2009-, Stwdshp Cmsn 2008-2015; Dio Ohio Cleveland 1999-2001. Int Mnstry Ntwk 2000; Shalem Soc 2011.

HARRIS, Ladd Keith (WMich) 5527 N Sierra Ter, Beverly Hills FL 34465 B Scranton PA 1941 s Chester & Dorothy. BD Mansfield U of Pennsylvania 1963; BD VTS 1966. D 6/18/1966 P 3/11/1967 Bp Frederick Warnecke. m 6/21/1969 Judith S Harris c 2. P-in-c Shpd Of The Hills Epis Ch Lecanto FL 2004-2010; R S Mk's Ch Grand Rapids MI 1995-2003; Dio Cntrl New York Liverpool NY 1986-1991; R Gr Ch Baldwinsville NY 1977-1995; Trin Ch Lowville NY 1970-1977; Cur Chr Ch Reading PA 1966-1970. Curs.

HARRIS JR, Lawrence (WA) 10450 Lottsford Road, #1218, Mitchellville MD 20721 B Baltimore MD 1940 s Lawrence & Sarah. BA Trin Hartford CT 1962;

MDiv VTS 1965. D 6/22/1965 P 6/20/1966 Bp Harry Lee Doll. m 6/29/1968 Susan Harris c 1. R S Barn' Ch Leeland Uppr Marlboro MD 1976-2011; R S Matt's Epis Ch Hyattsville MD 1966-1976; Asst H Trin Epis Ch Essex MD 1965-1966.

HARRIS, Lee Marshall (Los) 330 E 16th St, Upland CA 91784 **S Mk's Epis Sch Upland CA 2015-; Chapl-Rel Tchr S Mk's Epis Ch Upland CA 2003-** B Altadena CA 1948 s E Marshall & Madaly. BS U CA 1969; Cert Diac Stud ETSC/Bloy Hse 2010. D 2/4/2010 Bp Chester Lovelle Talton. c 2.

HARRIS, Lorraine Denise (NJ) PO Box 1551, Camden NJ 08101 B Camden NJ 1953 d Wilbur & Phyllis. BS Rutgers U 2008; MDiv UTS 2012; Cert in Angl Stds Luth TS 2016. D 12/16/2015 P 6/17/2016 Bp William H Stokes. c 2. S Paul's Ch Camden NJ 2016-2017.

HARRIS, Margaret Stilwell (Ia) 1120 45th St, Des Moines IA 50311 B Hollywood CA 1938 d Leland & Elizabeth. BA Drake U 1971. D 4/13/1996 Bp Chris Christopher Epting. m 4/4/1959 John R Harris.

HARRIS, Mark (Del) 207 E Market St, Lewes DE 19958 **Asst S Ptr's Ch Lewes DE 2003-** B Mobile AL 1940 s Edward & Anne. BA Tul 1961; U of Alberta 1964; MDiv EDS 1967; DMin EDS 1995. D 6/10/1967 Bp Leland Stark P 3/6/1968 Bp Francisco Reus-Froylan. c 2. Global Epis Mssn Ntwk Newark 2000-2002; R S Jas Ch Wilmington DE 1995-2000; Partnership Offcr E Asia Pacific & Middle E Epis Ch Cntr New York NY 1991-1994, Coordntr Mnstry Higher Ed. 1982-1987; Coordntr Ovrs Missionaries Dio Delaware Wilmington 1987-1991, 1979-1982, 1972-1978; U MI Dio Michigan Detroit MI 1969-1972; Fajardo Dio Puerto Rico Trujillo Alto PR 1967-1969. Auth, "Challange Of Change," *Angl Comm In Post Mod Era*, Ch Pub Inc, 1998; Ed, "Epis Ch & Its MHE," *Plumbline*, FMP, 1982; Ed, "Plumbline," *Plumbline*, Epis Soc Mnstry Higher Ed., 1978. ESMHE 1972-1990; Epis Urban Caucaus 1996-2000; Global Epis Mssn Ntwk 2000-2006; Integrity 2005; The Consult 2008. Doctor of Hmnts Trin U of Asia 2008.

HARRIS, Mark Hugh (Ore) 385 Doral Place, Pinehurst NC 28374 B Union SC 1932 s William & Iris. BS U CA 1959; DIT Oxf GB 1964; MDiv Mt Ang Abbey 1976. Trans 12/1/1968 Bp Chauncie Kilmer Myers. m 12/6/1969 Marilyn M Harris c 3. Chapl Arlington Hosp VA 1979-2004; Chapl Gd Samar Hosp Corvallis OR 1973-1979; The Epis Ch Of The Gd Samar Corvallis OR 1973-1979; 1970-1973; Asst All SS Ch Carmel CA 1968-1970; Asst Ch of So Afr Kimberley So Afr 1964-1967. Fllshp Assn of Profsnl Chapl 1976-2004.

HARRIS, Marsue (RI) 99 Main St, North Kingstown RI 02852 B Rochester PA 1940 d John & Jeanette. BS Penn 1961; MDiv CDSP 1981. D 6/28/1980 Bp William Edwin Swing P 8/20/1981 Bp George Nelson Hunt III. m 5/19/1985 Ralph C Porter c 2. P in Charge Trin Pawtuxet Vill 2010-2014; P-in-c S Geo's Ch Newport RI 2002-2010; Int S Paul's Ch Pawtucket RI 2000-2002; Int S Aug's Ch Kingston RI 1998-2000; S Barn Ch Warwick RI 1995-1997; S Ptr's By The Sea Narragansett RI 1986-1988; Assoc S Steph's Par Bel Tiburon CA 1980-1982; Dioc Coun Dio Rhode Island Providence RI 1993-1995, Stndg Com 1986-1992, COM 1983-1985. Auth, "Var 1988-2004," *Rel Columnist*, Providence Journ Bulletin, 2004.

HARRIS, Martha Caldwell (CGC) 79 6th St., Apalachicola FL 32320 **R Trin Ch Apalachicola FL 2005-** B Portsmouth VA 1952 d Ralph & Mildred. BA U GA 1976; MDiv Candler TS Emory U 1993. D 6/8/1996 P 12/1/1996 Bp Frank Kellogg Allan. m 7/23/2013 Edward Mitchell c 4. Asst R S Chris's Ch Pensacola FL 2003-2005; Assoc R S Simon's On The Sound Ft Walton Bch FL 2000-2003; Asst S Edw's Epis Ch Lawrenceville GA 1997-2000; S Mk's Ch Dalton GA 1997.

HARRIS, Melissa Anderson (Okla) **D S Andr's Ch Grove OK 2007-** B Stroud OK 1933 d William & Harriett. D 6/16/2007 Bp Robert Manning Moody. c 2. NAAD 2008.

HARRIS, Michael William Henry (SwFla) 24311 Narwhal Lane, Port Charlotte FL 33983 B GY 1942 s William & Ethel. LTh Codrington Coll 1969; STM NYTS 1977. D 6/1/1970 P 7/1/1970 Bp The Bishop Of Guyana. m 4/3/1972 Beatrice Celestine Harris c 2. S Geo's Epis Ch Bradenton FL 2001-2003; The Epis Ch Of The Gd Shpd Venice FL 2000-2001; Dio Long Island Garden City NY 1998-1999; Chr Ch Cobble Hill Brooklyn NY 1994-1998; R Ch Of S Thos Brooklyn NY 1976-1994; Serv Ch In Guyana 1970-1975. OHC.

HARRIS, Neal Joseph (WMo) 1636 E Grand St, Springfield MO 65804 **Died 1/4/2017** B Slick OK 1923 s Neal & Vivian. BA NE St U 1952; Bex Sem 1955. D 6/26/1955 P 12/1/1955 Bp Chilton R Powell. m 10/8/1988 Cecilia Jane Harris c 1. R S Jn's Ch Springfield MO 1979-1985, Assoc 1972-1978; P Ch Of The Trsfg Mtn Grove MO 1978-1985; Chapl Ng 1972-1976; Chapl (Maj) US-Army 1966-1972; S Jn's Ch Durant OK 1964-1965; Vic S Ptr's Ch Coalgate OK 1964-1965; Vic S Barn Ch Poteau OK 1962-1964; Vic S Fran Assisi Wilburton OK 1961-1964; R All SS Ch Mcalester OK 1960-1964; Asst S Jn's Epis Ch Tulsa OK 1958-1959; Vic S Ptr's Ch Tulsa OK 1956-1958; Vic S Jas Claremont OK 1955-1958; S Jas Epis Ch Wagoner OK 1955-1956; Vic St Mart of Tours Epis Ch Pryor OK 1955-1956.

HARRIS, Paula (Mil) St. Luke's Episcopal Church, 4011 Major Ave, Madison WI 53716 B Dallas TX 1964 d Joseph & Shelby. BA Wheaton Coll 1986; MTS SWTS 2006; DMin Luth TS at Chicago 2012; DMin Other 2012. D 6/3/2006

P 12/14/2006 Bp Steven Andrew Miller. m 4/24/2004 Dragutin Cvetkovic c 2. R S Lk's Ch Madison WI 2009-2016; D S Dunst's Ch Madison WI 2006; Assoc Dir Urbana Stdt Mssn Conv Madison WI 1989-2005. Auth, "Being White," *Being White*, InterVarsity Press, 2004; Auth, "Postmodernity is not the Antichrist.," *Postmission*, Paternoster Press, 2002; Auth, "Calling YP to a Mssy Vocation in a Yahoo Wrld.," *Missiology Journ*, Amer Soc of Missiology, 2001; Auth, "Nestorians: Listening to Mssn that Arises from Cmnty and Sprtlty," *Global Missiology for the 21st Century: Reflections from the Iguassu Dialogue*, Wrld Evang Fllshp, 2000. Sprtl Dir Intl 2009. Moss Awd for Acad Achievement SWTS 2006. stlukesmadisonrector@gmail.com

HARRIS JR, Paul Sherwood (Pa) 810 Pine St, Philadelphia PA 19107 **Non-par 1983-** B Baltimore MD 1939 s Paul & Grace. U of Pennsylvania; BA JHU 1961; MDiv PDS 1965. D 6/22/1965 P 6/1/1966 Bp Harry Lee Doll. Int St. Phil-In-The-Fields 2004-2005; Int Ch Of The Gd Shpd 2003-2004; Assoc S Ptr's Ch Philadelphia PA 1978-1983; Non-par 1967-1975.

HARRIS, Phillip Jay (SO) Po Box 484, Circleville OH 43113 **S Jas Epis Ch Columbus OH 2013-** B Point Pleasant WV 1967 BS U of Rio Grande 1991; MDiv VTS 2003. D 4/16/2003 Bp Herbert Thompson Jr P 11/1/2003 Bp Kenneth Lester Price. R S Phil's Ch Circleville OH 2003-2013.

HARRIS, Randall Sellers (Ct) 129 Oil Mill Rd, Waterford CT 06385 **Died 6/2/2017** B Hamilton OH 1934 s Guy & Ruth. AB Harv 1956; STB Ya Berk 1961. D 6/13/1961 P 3/17/1962 Bp Walter H Gray. c 3. Ret 1996-2017; Hartford Dnry Manchester CT 1982-1985; Hartford Archdnry All Ang Nrsng Hm Mnstry 1982-1984; Rel Consult Shirley Frank Fndt New Haven CT 1981-1987; Counslr Epis Soc Serv Old Baybrook CT 1975-1980; Instr Mt Hermon Sch Mt Hermon MA 1967-1971; Chapl (Lieutenant) Untd States Naval Reserve 1963-1966; Asst S Jas Ch New London CT 1961-1963.

HARRIS, Robert Carradine (WTex) 512 Belknap Pl, San Antonio TX 78212 **Chr Epis Ch San Antonio TX 2014-** B Houston TX 1973 s James & Janet. BCM Wayland Bapt U 2008; MDiv Epis TS Of The SW 2014; MDiv Epis TS of the SW 2014. D 1/10/2014 Bp David Mitchell Reed P 7/11/2014 Bp Gary Richard Lillibridge. m 9/8/2001 Kelly Ann Harris c 3. S Barn Epis Ch Fredricksburg TX 2001-2003. robh@cecsa.org

HARRIS, Robert Charles (Kan) 6649 Nall Dr, Mission KS 66202 **P in Res Gr Epis Ch Ottawa KS 2011-; Stff Chapl Truman Med Centers Kansas City Missouri 2006-** B Kansas City MO 1952 s Clifford & Lucille. BBA U of Houston 1975; MBA U of Missouri 1977; MDiv SWTS 2005. D 6/11/2005 P 1/21/2006 Bp Dean E Wolfe. m 11/17/1984 Debra Louise Harris c 5. graceottawaks@wordpress.com

✠ HARRIS, The Rt Rev Rogers Sanders (SwFla) 5502 Exum Drive, West Columbia SC 29169 B Anderson SC 1930 s Wilmot & Sarah. BA U So 1952; BD Sewanee: The U So, TS 1957; STM Sewanee: The U So, TS 1969; DMin VTS 1977. D 8/6/1957 P 4/5/1958 Bp Clarence Alfred Cole Con 3/9/1985 for USC. m 3/28/1953 Anne Harris. HOB Pstr Response Team 1996-1997; Bp Coun of Advice to PBp 1994-1997; Drafting Com HOB Pstr Tchng on Human Sxlty 1991-1994; SLC 1991-1994; Dio SW Florida Parrish FL 1989-1997, Bp of SW Florida 1989-1997; Suffr Bp of USC Dio Upper So Carolina Columbia SC 1985-1989, Dn Spartanburg Deanry 1974-1977, Bd Dioc Fndt 1973-1977, Dn Spartanburg Deanry 1974-1977, Bd Dioc Fndt 1973-1977, Chair Div Evang 1973-1976; VTS Alexandria VA 1974-1977; R S Chris's Ch Spartanburg SC 1969-1985; R Ch Of The Gd Shpd Greer SC 1965-1969, P-in-c 1959-1964; Ch Of The Ridge Trenton SC 1957-1959; P-in-c S Paul's Ch Batesburg SC 1957-1959. Auth, *The Commitment of Cnfrmtn*, VTS, 1977. OHC Comp 1989. DD U So 1986; DD VTS 1986.

HARRIS, Rory Hb (CFla) 827 Tomlinson Ter, Lake Mary FL 32746 **Vic Ch of the Incarn Oviedo FL 2014-** B Boise ID 1953 s Thomas & Margaret. Ya Berk; BA Syr 1977; MDiv Melodyland TS 1982; STM Ya Berk 1984. D 1/19/1985 P 7/31/1985 Bp Charles Shannon Mallory. m 4/21/1990 Stacie L Harris c 4. R H Cross Epis Ch Sanford FL 2005-2013; R S Jas Epis Ch Prospect Pk PA 1997-2005; Bd Pres Gr Place 1992-1995; Com on Aging Dio Maryland Baltimore MD 1990-1992, Chair Evang Com 1992-1993, Com on Aging 1988-1991; R S Jn's Ch Hvre De Gr MD 1988-1997; Yth Dir/ Dir Rel Educ St Jas the Great Epis Ch Newport Bch CA 1985-1988, Yth Dir/DCE 1979-1984; S Clem's-By-The-Sea Par San Clemente CA 1985-1987; Cur S Jn's Ch New Haven CT 1983-1985; DE Dnry Exec Com Dio Pennsylvania Philadelphia PA 1998-2001; Yth Min Epis Ch Of The Gd Shpd Salinas CA 1982-1983. Auth, *Sex & Chr Dating*, S Jas Press, 1980. AFP, Fllshp of Wit, Epis Ren. Outstanding Young Men in Amer 1986; Intl Yth in Achievement Awd 1981.

HARRIS, Stephen Dirk (CPa) 1138 Boyds School Rd, Gettysburg PA 17325 B Cambridge,MA 1938 s Samuel & Bernice. BS NEU 1963; MDiv VTS 1969; DMin Sewanee: The U So, TS 1987. D 6/21/1969 Bp Anson Phelps Stokes Jr P 6/21/1970 Bp William Foreman Creighton. m 2/24/1968 Rebecca B Harris c 2. Int R Calv Chap Beartown PA 2014-2015; Int R Ch Of The Trsfg Blue Ridge Summit PA 2014-2015, Int 1990-1991; Int The Memi Ch Of The Prince Of Peace Gettysburg PA 2012-2013; Serv Evang Luth Ch in Amer 2006-2007; Calv Chap Beartown Blue Ridge Summit PA 1990-1991; R S Mary's Epis Ch Waynesboro PA 1987-2005; Chr Ch Binghamton NY 1984-1987; Assoc Ch Of

The Gd Shpd Raleigh NC 1974-1984; Chapl Natl Institutes of Hlth Beth MD 1973-1974; Intern St. Eliz's Hosp Washington DC 1972-1973; Asst S Matt's Epis Ch Hyattsville MD 1969-1972. Epis Cler Assn Of Cntrl PA 1993; EPF; HSEC 1970; NNECA 1970.

HARRIS, Suzanne Love (NJ) Box 864, Wilson WY 83014 **1992-** B Brooklyn NY 1942 d Hamilton & Cynthia. Col; Drew U; BA Caldwell Coll 1981; MDiv GTS 1985. D 6/8/1985 P 12/14/1985 Bp John Shelby Spong. m 7/9/1966 George Harris c 3. Assoc Ch of S Jn on the Mtn Bernardsville NJ 1987-1991; Res Chapl Columbia Presb Hosp New York NY 1986-1987; S Lk's Epis Ch Montclair NJ 1985-1986. Auth, "Lasting," Ariadne Press, 2000. Ariadne Prize Ariadne Press 2000; Carl Michalson Schlrshp Drew TS 1982.

HARRIS, Thomas G (Chi) 5749 N Kenmore Ave, Chicago IL 60660 B Hammond IN 1937 s Henry & Ethel. BA NWU; MA SWTS. D 4/15/1973 Bp James Winchester Montgomery.

HARRIS, Vincent Powell (WA) 3917 Peppertree Ln, Silver Spring MD 20906 B Houston TX 1952 s Toussaint & Edna. BA Morehouse Coll 1975; MDiv VTS 1979. D 6/5/1979 P 12/18/1979 Bp Frank S Cerveny. m 12/23/1986 Joyce B Harris c 3. VTS Alexandria VA 2004, 2001, 1998; Ret S Geo's Ch Washington DC 1991-2012; Chapl Dio Washington Washington DC 1989-1991; Epis Chapl How Washington D.C. 1989-1991; Chapl Dir Cbury Cntr Atlanta GA 1983-1989; Chapl Dio Atlanta Atlanta GA 1983-1988; R S Mich And All Ang Ch Tallahassee FL 1980-1983; Asst H Trin Epis Ch Gainesville FL 1979-1980. Conf of S Ben 1979.

HARRIS, William Henry (NwPa) 940 Route 46, Emporium PA 15834 B Bakerton PA 1926 s William & Mary. BD EDS. D 6/13/1969 Bp Earl M Honaman P 12/1/1969 Bp Dean Theodore Stevenson. m 12/31/1961 Margaret H Harris c 1. Supply P S Andr's Ch Clearfield PA 2003-2005; Emm Epis Ch Emporium PA 1974-1992; S Agnes' Epis Ch S Marys PA 1974-1992; P-in-c S Andr's Ch Tioga PA 1969-1976; S Jn's Ch Westfield PA 1969-1976.

HARRIS-BAYFIELD, Maeva Hair (Tex) 300 Westmnstr Cantrbry Dr, Apt 405, Winchester VA 22603 **Ret 1998-** B Maui HI 1934 d Edward & Christine. Mills Coll 1956; Trin Theol Coll Singapore 1983; MRE S Thos U Houston Texas 1988; Penn CPE Residency 1989. D 6/15/1990 Bp Charlie Fuller Mcnutt Jr P 7/15/1992 Bp William Elwood Sterling. m 8/20/2005 Ralph Wesley Bayfield c 2. Chapl S Fran Epis Day Sch Houston TX 2000-2005; S Lk's Epis Hosp Houston TX 1995-1996; Assoc R Trin Ch Galveston TX 1992-1995; D Trin Ch Houston TX 1991-1992; D S Andr's Epis Ch York PA 1990-1991. Auth, "Journ Of Pstr Care". Coll Of Chapl, So Texas Assn Of Chapl, Eva 1990-1998; Epis Hospitalital Chapl Assn 1995-1998.

✠ **HARRISON, The Rt Rev Dena Arnall** (Tex) 3402 Windsor Rd, Austin TX 78703 **Chair, Bd Trst Epis TS of the SW 2009-; Bp Suffr Dio Texas Houston TX 2006-, Archd 2003-2006, Cn to the Ordnry 2000-2003** B Lufkin TX 1947 d Lloyd & Edith. BBA U of Texas 1967; MDiv Epis TS of the SW 1987. D 6/6/1987 Bp Gordon Taliaferro Charlton P 1/8/1988 Bp Anselmo Carral-Solar Con 10/7/2006 for Tex. m 6/10/1967 Larry N Harrison c 2. Chair, Bd Trst Epis Hlth Chars Houston TX 2007-2009; Trst Epis TS of the SW 2004-2009; Trst S Lk Epis Hlth System Houston TX 2000-2009; Trst Epis Hlth Chars 1998-2007; R S Jas The Apos Epis Ch Conroe TX 1997-2000; Trst Bp. Quin Fndt Houston TX 1993-2000; R S Jas' Epis Ch La Grange TX 1991-1997; Asst All SS Epis Ch Austin TX 1987-1992. DD Sem of the SW 2008. dharrison@epicenter.org

HARRISON JR, Edward H (SanD) 1114 9th St., Coronado CA 92118 B Jacksonville FL 1951 s Edward & Laura. BA U So 1975; MDiv Yale DS 1981. D 7/19/1981 P 6/29/1982 Bp Charles Farmer Duvall. m 8/23/1975 Teresa S Sanderson c 2. R Chr Ch Coronado CA 2009-2014; Dn S Jn's Cathd Jacksonville FL 2001-2008; S Chris's Ch Pensacola FL 1992-2001; R S Paul's By-The-Sea Epis Ch Jaxville Bch FL 1986-1992; Assoc R Trin Ch Concord MA 1984-1986; Vic S Paul Irvington AL 1982-1984; Cur S Lk's Epis Ch Mobile AL 1981-1984; Trst Sewanee U So TS Sewanee TN 2002-2008, Trst 1996-2001, Trst 1990-1995. ehh2009@gmail.com

HARRISON, Elizabeth Arendt (CFla) 215 S Lake Florence Dr, Winter Haven FL 33884 **H Cross Ch Winter Haven FL 2003-** B Orlando FL 1935 d George & Elizabeth. BA U of So Florida 1966; MA U of So Florida 1978; PhD U of So Florida 1990. D 12/8/2001 Bp John Wadsworth Howe. c 2. D St Alb's of Auburndale Inc Auburndale FL 2000-2007.

HARRISON JR, Frederick Clarence (SwFla) 140 Bilbao Dr, Saint Augustine FL 32086 **Died 12/12/2016** B South Bend IN 1922 s Frederick & Lora. VTS 1956; BS Florida Intl U 1975; MDiv VTS 1975; PhD Walden U Minneapolis MN 1979; DD VTS 1993. D 6/24/1956 Bp Richard Henry Baker P 1/12/1957 Bp Edwin A Penick. m 8/15/1973 Lucille Harrison c 6. Assoc S Anne's Ch Crystal River FL 2003-2008; Exec Dir Ch Counslg Cntr Naples FL 1989-1993; Ret 1984-2016; Int S Andr's Epis Ch Charlotte NC 1983-1986, R 1958-1982; Ch Counslg Cntr Naples FL 1979-1984; Fndr & Exec Dir Ch Counslg Cntr Naples FL 1979-1984; Fndr, Exec Dir Unity Hse Auburn NY 1974-1978; Fndr, Exec Dir Spectrum Prog Miami FL 1968-1974; Chapl Illinois St Penit System IL 1960-1968; M-in-c S Jas' Ch Kannapolis NC 1956-1958; Chair, Dept of Yth Dio No Carolina Raleigh NC 1957-1960. Auth, "Responsibility: The Moral Substance of Existance"; Auth, "Theory of Dependant Behavior"; Auth,

H

363

"Dependency-Responsibility-Moralty: A Metapsychological Synthesis"; Auth, "A Metapsychology for Soc Psychol"; Auth, "A Metapsychology for Dynamic Psychol'". NY Acad of Sciences 1986. Colonel, U S Army Chapl Dept of Defense 1995; hon Natl Inst of Hlth & U of Miami 1972.

HARRISON JR, G Hendree (ETenn) Po Box 326, Athens TN 37371 **P S Paul's Ch Athens TN 2006-; R St. Paul's Churcha Athens TN 2006-** B Atlanta GA 1975 s George & Carol. BA U So 1997; MDiv Sewanee: The U So, TS 2003. D 6/7/2003 P 12/18/2003 Bp J Neil Alexander. m 6/26/1999 Kristin Harrison c 2. S Mk's Ch Dalton GA 2003-2006.

HARRISON, Harold Donald (At) 3823 Cherokee Frd, Gainesville GA 30506 **Vic S Anth's Epis Ch Winder GA 2009-; U Chapl Brenau U Gainesville GA 2006-** B Atlanta GA 1935 s Harold & Hazel. BA Emory U 1957; BD Sewanee: The U So, TS 1960; MA Georgia St U 1974. D 6/13/1960 P 12/21/1960 Bp Randolph R Claiborne. m 9/15/1984 Barbara Harrison c 2. Asst Gr-Calv Clarkesville GA 2006-2009; Assoc Epis Ch Of The H Sprt Cumming GA 2005-2006; Assoc R and Int R Gr Epis Ch Gainesville GA 1998-2003; Dn Dio Atlanta Atlanta GA 1998-2000; R S Jos's Epis Ch Mcdonough GA 1988-1998; Asst Ch Of The Atone Sandy Sprg GA 1985-1986, Assoc 1973-1984; Assoc S Bede's Ch Atlanta GA 1978-1985; R S Dunst's Epis Ch Atlanta GA 1965-1969; Vic; R S Marg's Ch Carrollton GA 1960-1965; Chapl W GA Coll 1960-1965. Omicron Delta Kappa.

HARRISON, James E (FdL) All Saints Episcopal Church, 100 N Drew St, Appleton WI 54911 **R All SS Epis Ch Appleton WI 2016-** B Greensburg, PA 1958 s William & Nellie. MDiv SWTS 2010. D 12/20/2009 P 6/12/2010 Bp Steven Todd Ousley. m 11/24/1979 Melissa D Moore c 2. R Trsfg Epis Ch Indn River MI 2012-2016; Cur Chr Ch Winnetka IL 2010-2012. allsaintsfatherjim@tds.net

HARRISON, Merle Marie (Colo) 816 Harrison Ave, Canon City CO 81212 B El Dorado KS 1932 d August & Agnes. BA U CO 1953; MLS U of Maryland 1974. D 11/17/2007 Bp Robert John O'Neill. c 3.

HARRISON, Merritt Raymond (Mass) 12 Remington St Apt 105, Cambridge MA 02138 B Fort Wayne IN 1933 s Carlos & Helen. BA Dart 1957; MDiv McCormick TS 1960. D 12/20/1962 Bp Chandler W Sterling P 4/27/1963 Bp James Winchester Montgomery. m 6/21/1992 Kathleen M MacDonald c 3. R S Matt And The Redeem Epis Ch Boston MA 1999-2002; Int Trin Epis Ch Stoughton MA 1996-1998; Int Chr Ch Somerville MA 1995-1996; R S Jn's Memi Ch Ellenville NY 1966-1968; Asst S Jn's Ch New York NY 1964-1966; Cur Ch Of The H Sprt Missoula MT 1962-1963; Serv Presb Ch 1960-1962.

HARRISON JR, Robert (WA) Churchillplein 6, The Hague 2517 JW Netherlands **Global Issues Mgr Intl Baccalaureate 2011-** B Cadiz KY 1962 s Claude & Zelma. BA Wstrn Kentucky U 1983; MDiv Sthrn Bapt TS 1986; PhD Duke 1991; Cert VTS 1992. D 5/30/1992 Bp Huntington Williams Jr P 6/1/1993 Bp Jane Hart Holmes Dixon. m 12/20/1987 Ellen Louise Lyons c 3. Tchr/ Admin Fairfax Cnty Publ Schools 2001-2010; Adj Fac VTS Alexandria VA 2001, 1994, 1993; Asst R S Jn's Ch Chevy Chase MD 1992-1995; Serv Sthrn Bapt Ch 1983-1986. Auth, "Jn Walker: A Man for the Twenty-First Century," Forw Mvmt, 2004; Auth, *ATR*; Auth, *Biblic Archeol*. Cathd Biblic Assn Soc of Biblicalal Lit. Phi Beta Kappa 1991.

HARRISON, Ronald Edward (Alb) 24 Summit Ave, Latham NY 12110 B Los Angeles CA 1946 s William & Glady. BA Biola U 1972; California St U 1975; Cert ETSBH 1977; MDiv CDSP 1979. D 6/23/1979 P 1/13/1980 Bp Robert Claflin Rusack. m 9/14/1968 Pamela Harrison c 7. R S Matt's Ch Latham NY 1991-2009; R Calv Ch Underhill VT 1984-1991; Asst R The Par Of All SS Ashmont-Dorches Boston MA 1982-1984; Headmaster S Tim's Epis Ch Apple Vlly CA 1980-1982; Asst Ch Of Our Sav Par San Gabr CA 1979-1980. CBS, NOEL. Phi Alpha Theta; Delta Epsilon Chi.

HARRISON, Sherridan (WTex) 2431 Michele Jean Way, Santa Clara CA 95050 B Neosho MO 1945 d Lawrence & Eleanor. BA Pittsburg St U 1965; MA Pittsburg St U Kasas 1968; Cert Theol Stud Epis TS of the SW 1984. D 5/31/1994 Bp John Herbert MacNaughton P 12/8/1994 Bp James Edward Folts. m 6/20/2003 Lawrence J Harrison c 2. Int Ch Of S Jude The Apos Cupertino CA 2011-2012; Int All SS Epis Ch Palo Alto CA 2009-2011; Int All SS Epis Ch Corpus Christi TX 2007-2009; Asst S Mk's Epis Ch San Antonio TX 2004-2007; R Chr Ch Epis Laredo TX 1999-2003; Asst R S Barth's Ch Corpus Christi TX 1994-1999; Cbury Chapl Dio W Texas Corpus Christi TX 1994-1996.

HARRISS, Mary L (Chi) 2338 Country Knolls Ln, Elgin IL 60123 **D Ch Of The Redeem Elgin IL 1991-** B Elgin IL 1935 d Edward & Evelyn. Cert Chicago Deacons Sch 1991. D 12/7/1991 Bp Frank Tracy Griswold III. m 11/5/1955 Lucas Edward Harriss c 2.

HARRISS, Susan Carol (NY) 2 Rectory St, Rye NY 10580 **Bd NAES 2012-** B Norfolk VA 1952 d Ernest & Evangeline. BA Denison U 1973; MDiv UTS 1977. D 6/2/1979 P 6/9/1980 Bp Paul Moore Jr. m 8/13/1977 Kenneth Ruge c 3. R Chr's Ch Rye NY 2000-2016; Cathd Of St Jn The Div New York NY 1998-2000, 1992-1995; Vic Cong Of S Sav New York NY 1996-1998; Theol-In-Res S Mich's Ch New York NY 1989-1991, Asst 1983-1984; Assoc R S Jas Ch New York NY 1984-1989; Dio New York New York NY 1980-1983,

Co-Chair, Assessment Adjustment Bd 2011-2013, Trst 2011-, Co-Chair, Assessment Adjustment Bd 2009-2013, Co-chair, Spec Com on the Assessment 2009-2012. Auth, "Jamies Way: Stories For Wrshp & Fam Devotion," Cowley Press, 1991. Phi Beta Kappa 1972. rectorina@gmail.com

HARRITY, Alison (CFla) 5151 Lake Howell Rd, Winter Park FL 32792 **R S Richard's Ch Winter Pk FL 2011-** B Watertown NY 1973 d David & Diana. BA Hobart and Wm Smith Colleges 1995; MDiv CDSP 2000. D 6/14/2000 Bp Calvin Onderdonk Schofield Jr P 12/16/2000 Bp John Lewis Said. c 2. Assoc P S Dav's Ch Wayne PA 2004-2011; Asst to R S Greg's Ch Boca Raton FL 2000-2004.

HARRON II, Frank Martin (WA) 10708 Brewer House Rd, North Bethesda MD 20852 B 1945 BA JHU 1969; MDiv EDS 1973; MEd JHU 1973. D 4/23/1973 P 1/25/1974 Bp David Keller Leighton Sr. m 5/28/2013 Thomas Y Wadsworth. S Barn Ch Wilmington DE 2000-2001; Prog Stff Trin Ch Wall St New York NY 2000-2001; Cn Vic Cathd of St Ptr & St Paul Washington DC 1997-2000; Trin Par New York NY 1997-2000; R S Ptr's Ch In The Great Vlly Malvern PA 1983-1997; Prog Dir Untd Mnstrs in Educ PA 1980-1983; Untd Mnstrs In Higher Ed S Louis MO 1980-1982; P-in-c S Jn's Ch Ellicott City MD 1979; Asst Chapl Jn Hopkins U Baltimore MD 1977-1978; Chapl U of Maryland Coll Pk MD 1973-1976. Auth, *Hlth & Human Values: Making your Own Decisions*, Ya Press, 1992.

HARROP, Stephen (Tai) 16 W 3rd St, Essington PA 19029 B Sheffield UK 1948 s Douglas & Joan. Cert S Johns Coll of Educ Gb 1974; Edinburgh Theol Coll 1979; U of Manchester 1985; 1990. Trans 10/1/1997. P-in-c Ch Of S Jn The Evang Essington PA 1999-2003; S Jn's Ch Bala Cynwyd PA 1998-1999; Chapl Eng Lang Mnstry S Jas Taichung Taiwan 1997-1998; Serv Ch Of Engl 1979-1998. Auth, "arts," *Friendship*; Auth, "arts," *S Jn'S Revs*. Indstrl Missions Assn.

HART, Alan Reed (Alb) 120 Waters Rd, Scotia NY 12302 **D S Ann's Ch Amsterdam NY 2012-** B Schenectady NY 1946 BA SUNY 1969; MA SUNY 1996. D 6/10/2006 Bp Daniel William Herzog. m 5/22/1994 Mary Carol Hart c 4. Sports Writer, Ed Albany Times Un 1968-2003.

HART, Benjamin James (Ky) Grace Episcopal Church, 216 E 6th St, Hopkinsville KY 42240 **S Matt's Epis Ch Louisville KY 2016-** B Murray KY 1988 s John & Sharon Elizabeth. BFA Murray St U 2010; MDiv VTS 2014. D 11/8/2013 P 5/30/2014 Bp Terry Allen White. Asst Gr Ch Hopkinsville KY 2014-2016.

HART, Curtis Webb (NY) 132 N Broadway 1NW, Tarrytown NY 10591 B New York NY 1946 s Frank & Dorothy. BA Harv 1968; Cert Rutgers The St U of New Jersey 1972; MDiv UTS 1972. D 6/10/1972 P 1/27/1973 Bp Leland Stark. m 5/16/2009 Stephanie Suzanne St Pierre c 2. Ed in Chf Journ of Rel and Hlth 2011; P-in-c S Matt's Ch Paramus NJ 2004-2005; Dio New York New York NY 2002, 1997; P-in-c Ch Of The Gd Shpd - Roosevelt Island Roosevelt Island NY 1999-2001; P-in-c S Geo's Epis Ch Maplewood NJ 1999; P-in-c S Jn's Ch Pleasantville NY 1999; Lectr Weill Cornell Med Coll 1998-2011; Int S Mary's Ch Haledon NJ 1998; Int S Paul's Ch Sprg Vlly NY 1996; Int S Ptr's Ch Rochelle Pk NJ 1995-1996; Int Ch Of The H Comm Norwood NJ 1994-1995; Dir Pstr Care New York Presb Hosp 1985-2009; The Healthcare Chapl Inc New York NY 1985-2003; Chapl Dir Toledo Mntl Hlth Cntr 1978-1985; Asst S Mk's Ch Brooklyn NY 1973-1975. Auth, "Var," *Profsnl Journ*. Soc for values in Higher Educ 2010-2011. Excellence in Tchg Awd Weill Cornell Med Coll 2005.

✠ HART, The Rt Rev Donald Purple (Haw) P.O. Box 461, Peterborough NH 03458 B New York NY 1937 s Donald & Ann. BA Wms 1959; BD EDS 1962. D 6/20/1962 Bp Robert McConnell Hatch P 6/2/1963 Bp William A Lawrence Con 11/30/1986 for The Episcopal Church in Haw. m 9/8/1962 Elizabeth A Howard c 2. Asst Bp of SVa Dio Sthrn Virginia Newport News VA 1998-2001; Asst Bp of Md Dio Maryland Baltimore MD 1997-1998; Int S Mary's Epis Ch Manchester CT 1996-1997; Asst Bp of Ct Dio Connecticut Meriden CT 1995-1996; Ret Bp of Hawaii The Epis Ch in Hawaii Honolulu HI 1995, Bp 1986-1995; R Par Of S Jas Ch Keene NH 1983-1986; R S Matt's Epis Ch Fairbanks AK 1973-1983; P-in-c Gd Shpd Huslia AK 1964-1969; Cur Ch Of The Redeem Chestnut Hill MA 1962-1964; Chair Fairbanks Chld Protection T/F Dio Alaska Fairbanks AK 1981-1983, Stndg Com 1978-1980, Stff 1969-1977. Auth/Compiler, "The Making of A Bp," Dio New Hampshire, 2013.

HART, Donnalee (NCal) St Francis in the Redwoods, 66 E Commercial St, Willits CA 95490 **D S Fran In The Redwoods Mssn Willits CA 2012-** B Omaha NE 1948 d Jess & Esther. BA U of Hawaii 1977; ND Bastyr U 2002. D 11/24/2012 Bp Barry Leigh Beisner. c 1. Third Ord of the SSF 2010. donnalee@saber.net

HART, Frederick Morgan (WTenn) 78 Ottaray Ct, Brevard NC 28712 **Ret 2004-** B Pittsburgh PA 1938 s William & Margaret. BS W Virginia Wesleyan Coll 1960; Cert Theol Stud Mercer TS 1985; Cert Eger Luth Hm Staten Island NY 1987. D 6/8/1987 P 11/30/1989 Bp Robert Campbell Witcher Sr. m 2/22/1963 Roberta G Hart c 6. Dioc Coun Mem Dio W Tennessee Memphis 2001-2004; R S Jas Epis Ch Un City TN 2000-2004; Hd Sprtl Advsr Curs Dio Long Island Garden City NY 1996-1997; R Gr Ch Riverhead NY 1994-2000; Chapl Ord of

S Lk 1990-2000; Chapl Bro of S Andr 1988-2000; Asst S Thos Ch Farmingdale NY 1987-1994. Bro of S Andr 1987-2000; Ord of S Lk 1990-2000. Walter Wiley Jones Mem AwD BroSA, Prov II 2000.

HART JR, George Barrow (Ark) 3802 Hwy 82 W, Crossett AR 71635 B Memphis TN 1941 s George & Sarah. BA U So 1963; MDiv Sewanee: The U So, TS 1972. D 6/25/1972 Bp William F Gates Jr P 5/1/1973 Bp John Vander Horst. m 1/1/1985 Carolyn Hart c 5. Vic Emm Ch Lake Vill AR 1997-2005, 1988-1989; S Mk's Ch Crossett AR 1991-2004; S Mich's Epis Ch Little Rock AR 1988-1991; 1984-1991; R S Ptr Tollville AR 1979-1984; St Ptr's Epis Ch Devalls Bluff AR 1979-1984; Vic Chr Ch Brownsville TN 1974-1978; Dio Tennessee Nashville TN 1973-1978; Vic Imm Ch Ripley TN 1973-1978.

HART, J. Joseph (Md) 6701 N Charles St, Towson MD 21204 B Baltimore MD 1956 s John & Kathleen. Salisbury U 1979; STB,MDiv St Mary Sem and U 1983. Rec 9/12/2015 as Priest Bp Eugene Taylor Sutton.

HART, Lois Ann (Me) 1100 Washington St, Bath ME 04530 B Lewiston ME 1931 d Gilbert & Anna Marie. D 6/28/2008 Bp Chilton Richardson Knudsen. c 4. D Gr Epis Ch Bath ME 2008-2011.

HART, Mary Carol (Alb) 120 Waters Rd, Scotia NY 12302 **D S Ann's Ch Amsterdam NY 2014-; Sr Spprt Investigator, Chld Spprt Worker Cnty Of Schenectady 1979-** B 1956 D 6/10/2006 Bp Daniel William Herzog. m 5/22/1994 Alan Reed Hart c 4.

HART, Robert Lee (Colo) 1471 Bennaville Ave, Birmingham MI 48009 **Int S Jn's Ch Royal Oak MI 2012-** B Athens TN 1944 s Frederick & Mary. BA Maryville Coll 1967; BD PrTS 1970; Cert Coll of the Resurr, Mirfield 1971; Cert GTS 1971; Cert Other 1971. D 6/12/1971 Bp Leland Stark P 6/25/1972 Bp The Bishop Of Reading. m 6/10/1978 Rebecca Hart c 2. Int S Jas Epis Ch Birmingham MI 2011-2012, Int 2011-; Int Chr Ch Dearborn MI 2009-2011; P-in-c Chr Ch Detroit MI 2008-2009; R All SS Epis Ch Pontiac MI 1999-2007; Int S Paul's Epis Ch Lansing MI 1997-1999; Int S Andr's Ch Ann Arbor MI 1995-1997; Int S Jn's Epis Ch Saginaw MI 1993-1995; R S Benedicts Ch Ft Lauderdale FL 1991-1993; Cn Gr And H Trin Cathd Kansas City MO 1983-1991, Cn 1973-1983; R Trin Ch Independence MO 1978-1983; Cur S Ptr Oxford Engl 1971-1973; COM Dio SE Florida Miami 1992-1993; COM, Exam Chapl Dio W Missouri Kansas City MO 1990-1991, Dn Metro Deanry 1987-1989, Dn Cntrl Deanry 1977-1986. Soc of Cath Priests 2010.

HART, Stephen Anthony (Alb) 2849 Laurel Park Hwy, Hendersonville NC 28739 B Lubbock TX 1954 s Bill & Beverly. BA U of Texas 1976; MPA Baylor U 1979; MDiv Nash 1997. D 6/21/1997 P 12/21/1997 Bp Jack Leo Iker. m 12/22/2012 Lorraine M Hart c 4. R S Mich's Albany NY 2002-2017; Vic Our Lady Of The Lake Clifton TX 1999-2002; Cur The Epis Ch Of S Ptr And S Paul Arlington TX 1997-1999. Auth, "Article," Living Ch.

HART, Valerie Ann (ECR) 8 Daytona Dr, Laguna Niguel CA 92677 **Asst S Paul's Epis Ch Tustin CA 2015-** B Lakewood OH 1948 d Ralph & Lorna. BA Carnegie Mellon U 1970; MS U Pgh 1973; PhD U Pgh 1974; MDiv CDSP 1991. D 6/8/1991 P 6/7/1992 Bp William Edwin Swing. c 3. Dio El Camino Real Salinas CA 2006-2014; R S Barn Ch Arroyo Grande CA 2006-2014; Vic S Alb's Epis Ch Brentwood CA 1994-2006; S Anne's Ch Fremont CA 1991-1992. Auth, "Removing Dirt - Reversing Direction," Preaching Through the Year of Mk: Sermons That Wk VIII, Morehouse Pub, 1999; Auth, "Var arts".

HART, Virginia Frances (Nev) 451 N. Broadway St. Apt. E., Fallon NV 89406 **Died 5/26/2017** B Colusa CA 1923 d Alvah & Ivy. Butte-Glenn Cmnty Coll; California St U. D 7/19/1986 Bp William Benjamin Spofford. c 5. D H Trin Epis Ch Fallon NV 1996-2017; D S Jn's 1986-1996. Ord Of S Lk 1991.

HART, William Gardner (NY) 414 Haines Rd # 4, Mount Kisco NY 10549 **D S Mk's 1987-** B Madera CA 1921 s Lucas & Evelyn. BS U CA 1943. D 10/17/1967 Bp Archie H Crowley. m 4/2/1949 Mavis Thomas Davis c 3. D Ch Of S Mary The Vrgn Chappaqua NY 1982-1983, D 1972-1981; D S Paul's Ch Greenville MI 1980-1981; D Saw Mill Inter-Par Coun 1970-1972; Asst S Jn's Epis Ch Alma MI 1967-1970.

HARTE, Barry Jay (Pa) 27 Conshohocken State Rd, Bala Cynwyd PA 19004 **Ch Of S Asaph Bala Cynwyd PA 2009-** B Bethlehem PA 1960 s Robert & Eleanor. BA W&M 1982; MDiv Luth TS 1986. Rec 5/12/2011 Bp Charles Ellsworth Bennison Jr. c 2.

HARTE JR, John Joseph Meakin (Az) 1000 E. Ponderosa Parkway, Flagstaff AZ 86001 **Assoc Gd Shpd Of The Hills Cave Creek AZ 2013-** B Austin TX 1945 s John Joseph & Alice. BA SMU 1967; MDiv GTS 1970. D 6/18/1970 P 12/21/1970 Bp John Joseph Meakin Harte. m 11/5/2005 Susan Brainard Harte c 2. R Ch Of The Epiph Flagstaff AZ 1992-2002; R S Jas Ch Riverton WY 1980-1992; Cur Ch Of The H Cross Dallas TX 1978-1980; R S Andr Botswana Afr 1975-1977; Vic S Aug Dallas TX 1972-1975; P Dio Dallas Dallas TX 1970-1977; Asst S Phil Dallas TX 1970-1972; Bd Trst The GTS New York NY 1988-1992; Bd Natl Ntwk Of Epis Cler Assn Lynnwood WA 1987-1990. Soc of S Jn the Evang Fllshp 1985.

HARTE, Kathleen Audrey (LI) D 11/19/2011 Bp Lawrence C Provenzano.

HARTE, Susan Brainard (Az) 1000 E. Ponderosa Parkway, Flagstaff AZ 86001 **D Gd Shpd Of The Hills Cave Creek AZ 2013-** B Tucson AZ 1942 d Hollis & June. Wheaton Coll at Norton Mass 1961; BA U of Arizona 1964. D 10/

14/2000 Bp Robert Reed Shahan. m 11/5/2005 John Joseph Meakin Harte c 2. D Ch Of The Epiph Flagstaff AZ 2000-2005; Jail Chapl Coconino Cnty Sheriff's Off 1995-2014. DOK 1992; Fllshp of S Jn 2000; Intl Conf of Police Chapl 2010; Intl Critical Incident Stress Fndt 2003. Nominee: Chapl of the Year Natl Sheriff's Assn 2010; Nominee: Chapl of the Year Natl Sheriff's Assn 2010; Natl Publ Serv Recognition Awd Coconino Cnty Bd Supervisors 2009.

HARTER, Ralph Millard Peter (Roch) 98 Canfield Rd, Pittsford NY 14534 **Gr Ch Willowdale Geneva NY 2010-** B Auburn NY 1946 s Donald & Ruth. BA Hobart and Wm Smith Colleges 1968; JD The Cornell Law Sch Ithaca NY 1972; MDiv Bex Sem 2007. D 6/20/2007 P 4/10/2008 Bp Jack Marston Mckelvey. m 9/13/1997 Leslie Jt Teage c 2. Assoc S Ptr's Epis Ch Henrietta NY 2007-2008.

HART GARNER, Eleanor E (Be) 125 Mount Joy St, Mount Joy PA 17552 **P-in-c S Lk's Epis Ch Mt Joy PA 2011-; P-in-c St. Lk's Epis Mt Joy PA 2011-** B Coatsville PA 1942 d Henry & Miriam. MA Kutztown U; BS Keene St Coll 1966. D 4/22/1989 P 10/1/1994 Bp James Michael Mark Dyer. m 12/27/2014 Daniel Garner c 1. P-in-c S Thos Epis Ch Morgantown PA 2002-2011; S Barn Ch Kutztown PA 2001-2002; Assoc S Alb's Epis Ch Reading PA 1998-2008; Int S Anne's Epis Ch Trexlertown PA 1996-1998; P Chr Ch Reading PA 1994-1996; D S Mich's Epis Ch Birdsboro PA 1989-1994.

HARTJEN JR, Raymond Clifton (Kan) 1015 S. 5th St., Leavenworth KS 66048 **P-in-c Ch Of St Thos Holton KS 2008-** B Syracuse NY 1940 s Raymond & Bertha. BA Furman U 1963; MS No Dakota St U 1977; EdD Ball St U 1985; MDiv Epis TS in Kentucky 1989; CTh Epis TS of the SW 1989. D 6/23/1989 P 3/7/1990 Bp Edward Witker Jones. m 5/5/2015 Helen Farley Hartjen c 2. P-in-c Ch Of St Thos Holton KS 2008-2014; R Trin Ch Atchison KS 1996-2006; Dn SW Dnry 1995-1996; Pres Vincennes Ministrial Assn 1993-1996; R S Jas Ch Vincennes IN 1991-1996; Asst R S Chris's Epis Ch Carmel IN 1989-1991. Auth, Ethics in Orgnztn Ldrshp, 1984; Auth, Human Relatns in the Mltry Enviroment, 1979. Bro of S Andr.

HARTL, Palmer (Va) 240 South 3rd Street, Philadelphia PA 19106 B Saint Louis MO 1943 s Konrad & Myrtle. BA Gri 1965; MDiv VTS 1968. D 6/22/1968 Bp George Leslie Cadigan P 6/1/1969 Bp Robert Fisher Gibson Jr. m 8/28/1965 Judith E Hartl c 2. Chr Ch Philadelphia Philadelphia PA 2005-2007, 2000-2004; Assoc S Chris's Ch Gladwyne PA 1986-1997; 1973-2002; Co-R S Anne's Epis Ch Reston VA 1971-1973; Asst Min S Steph's Ch Richmond VA 1968-1971. Auth, "The Ten Commandments of Mgmt," Bk, Koehler books Pub, 2014; Auth, "The Optioned Wk Force," Advance mag, 1996.

HARTLEY, Chris (Ala) 1000 W 18th St, Anniston AL 36201 **S Mich And All Ang Anniston AL 2014-** B Birmingham AL 1969 s Felix & Wynonna. BA Sanford U 1991; MDiv Sewanee: The U So, TS 2014; MDiv The TS at The U So 2014. D 5/21/2014 Bp Santosh K Marray P 1/14/2015 Bp John Mckee Sloan Sr. m 4/30/2005 Allison M Mcfarlin c 1. chartley@stmichaelsanniston.org

HARTLEY, Harold Aitken (Mich) 1106 Riverview St, Rogers City MI 49779 B 1921 s Herbert & Ethyl. Whitaker TS. D 6/30/1984 Bp Henry Irving Mayson P 11/1/1985 Bp William Jones Gordon Jr. m 12/16/1950 Marvella Josephine Gook. Int R S Paul's Fed Point E Palatka FL 2002-2003; Asst Trin Ch St Clair Shrs MI 1984-1985. Ord Of S Ben.

HARTLEY, James Peyton (USC) **S Dav's Epis Ch Columbia SC 2016-** B Charlotte, NC 1978 s Robert & Nancy. Bachelor of Arts U of So Carolina 2001; Mstr of Div VTS 2016. D 6/3/2016 P 2/2/2017 Bp W illiam Andrew Waldo. m 6/3/2006 Caroline Goldston c 3.

HARTLEY, Loyde Hobart (CPa) St James Church, 119 N Duke St, Lancaster PA 17602 B Parkersburg WV 1940 s Hobart & Mildred. BA Otterbein U 1962; MDiv Untd TS 1965; PhD Emory U 1968. D 10/29/2011 Bp Nathan Dwight Baxter. m 6/23/1962 Carol B Hartley c 3.

HARTLEY, Melissa M (At) 735 University Ave, Sewanee TN 37383 **Assoc Chapl Sewanee U So TS Sewanee TN 2012-** B Atlanta GA 1971 d Charles & Bonnie. BA U So 1993; MDiv GTS 1998; STM GTS 2005; MPhil Drew U 2010; PhD Drew U 2012. D 6/6/1998 P 2/20/1999 Bp Frank Kellogg Allan. Supply P S Ptr's Ch Washington NJ 2012; Int Ch of S Jn on the Mtn Bernardsville NJ 2009-2011, Assoc R 2007-2009; Asst R S Ptr's Ch Morristown NJ 2006-2007; Assoc R H Trin Par Decatur GA 2001-2004; Asst R Gr Epis Ch Gainesville GA 1998-2001. No Amer Acad of Liturg 2008. mmhartle@sewanee.edu

HARTLEY, Robert Henry (NCal) 14530 N Line Post Ln, Tucson AZ 85755 B Seattle WA 1922 s Charles & Marion. BS U CA 1943. D 8/28/1969 Bp John Joseph Meakin Harte. m 7/6/1946 Lucille Mae Meyer c 1. D S Barn Ch Mt Shasta CA 1986-1990; Asst Cathd Of S Jn The Evang Spokane WA 1980-1986; Asst All SS Ch Phoenix AZ 1979-1980, D 1969-1978; Asst Epiph Epis Ch Denver CO 1976-1979. Ord Of S Lk.

HARTLEY, Sherry L (EO) 31535 Union, Box 146, Bonanza OR 97623 **Died 10/22/2015** B Klamath Falls OR 1956 d Robert & Virginia. BS Sthrn Oregon U 1978. D 7/10/1993 Bp Rustin Ray Kimsey. Dio Estrn Oregon Cove OR 2000-2009. shartley@eoni.com

HARTLING, David Charles (CFla) 1606 Fort Smith Blvd, Deltona FL 32725 B Northampton MA 1940 s George & Madeline. BS Emerson Coll 1965; MDiv

Sewanee: The U So, TS 1974. D 6/14/1974 P 6/14/1975 Bp William Hopkins Folwell. m 5/8/1976 Diana B Hartling. R Ch Of The Epiph Kirkwood S Louis MO 1998-2000; Vic S Jude's Ch Orange City FL 1989-1994; Asst Ch Of The Gd Shpd Maitland FL 1987-1988, Asst 1979-1986, Asst 1974-1978; Serv Ch in Bahamas 1979-1980; Chapl Intern Georgia Reg Hosp Augusta GA 1978-1979; Vic S Nath Ch No Port FL 1977-1978; Asst S Andr's Epis Ch Tampa FL 1976.

HARTLING, Gardner J (Lex) 1013 Marshall Park Dr, Georgetown KY 40324 **Adv Ch Cynthiana KY 1989-** B Middleboro MA 1948 s Rennels & Pearl. AS Daytona Bch Cmnty Coll 1976; Lic Epis TS in Kentucky 1988. D 2/5/1989 Bp Don Adger Wimberly. m 10/16/1971 Janet Lee Hartling c 1.

HARTMAN, Anthony Eden (EMich) 3458 E Mckinley Rd, Midland MI 48640 B Lakeland FL 1961 s Paul & Anne. BS USMMA 1983; MDiv TESM 1994. D 6/18/1994 Bp John Wadsworth Howe P 1/28/1995 Bp H Coleman Mcgehee Jr. m 9/29/1990 Sarah Mckoly Hartman c 1. D S Jn's Epis Ch Midland MI 1994-1996.

HARTMAN, Holly H (Mass) PO Box 920372, Needham MA 02492 B Nashua NH 1959 d Vernan & Colleen. BS U of New Hampshire 1981; MA Andover Newton TS 2009. D 6/16/2012 Bp M(Arvil) Thomas Shaw. m 10/8/1988 Lester James Hartman c 2. hhartman@diomass.org

HARTMAN, John Franklin (Be) 30 Butler St, Kingston PA 18704 **R Gr Epis Ch Kingston PA 2009-; Incorporated Trst Dio Bethlehem Bethlehem PA 2012-** B Lebanon PA 1948 s John & Geraldine. Empire St Coll SUNY; Geo Washington U; New Sch U; York Coll of Pennsylvania; MDiv SWTS 2008. D 6/7/2008 Bp George Edward Councell P 9/29/2009 Bp Paul Victor Marshall. D S Andr's Epis Ch New Providence NJ 2009; Dir of Ch Relatns Seamens Ch Inst New York NY 2008-2009. Chas T. Mason Awd/Liturg SWTS 2008.

HARTMAN, Kathleen Thomas (Vt) PO Box 383, Bethel VT 05032 B Louisville KY 1952 d Jerome & Joanne. BA Merc 1975; MEd U GA 1985. D 1/22/2017 Bp Thomas C Ely. c 1.

HARTMAN, Phyllis Colleen (Tex) 1803 Highland Hollow Dr, Conroe TX 77304 **D S Jas The Apos Epis Ch Conroe TX 2009-** B Harrisonburg VA 1942 d Leroy & Margaret. BAS Sam Houston U 1995; Iona Sch of Mnstry 2009. D 2/22/2009 Bp Don Adger Wimberly. c 3.

HARTMAN, Samuel Henry (Eas) 5 School House Lane, North East MD 21901 B Chester PA 1944 s Adolph & Eleanor. BA Bow 1966; STB GTS 1969; DMin Lancaster TS 2003. D 6/28/1969 P 12/28/1969 Bp Frederick Barton Wolf. m 11/26/1977 Judith B Hartman c 2. R S Mary Anne's Epis Ch No E MD 1990-2013; Serv Ch In Italy 1983-1990; R St Jas Ch 1983-1990; R S Andr's Ch Newcastle ME 1978-1983; Ch Of St Jn Bapt Sebec ME 1972-1978; St Josephs Ch Sebec ME 1972-1978; S Jas Ch Old Town ME 1972-1974; Non-par 1971-1972; Gr Epis Ch Bath ME 1969-1970.

HARTMANS, Robert Gerrit (ETenn) 5008 14th Ave, Chattanooga TN 37407 **Dio E Tennessee Knoxville TN 2015-** B Knoxville TN 1980 s James & Ava. U of Tennessee 2007; MDiv VTS 2013. D 6/15/2013 P 12/15/2013 Bp George Young III. P S Tim's Ch Signal Mtn TN 2013-2015. rhartmans@sttimsignal.com

HARTNETT, John Godfrey (Nwk) 169 Fairmount Rd, Ridgewood NJ 07450 **R S Eliz's Ch Ridgewood NJ 1993-** B Saint Louis MO 1951 s Godfrey & Thelma. BA Harv 1973; MDiv UTS 1987. D 6/13/1987 Bp Paul Moore Jr P 4/23/1988 Bp Desmond Mpilo Tutu. m 7/1/2000 Susan B Hartnett. Asst S Jas Ch New York NY 1991-1992, Dir of Cmncatn 1979-1981; Chair Admin Dio New York New York NY 1988-1992; Asst Ch Of The Heav Rest New York NY 1987-1991; Cathd Chapt Dio Newark Newark NJ 1994-1997.

HARTNETT, John L (SwFla) 5441 9th Ave N, St Petersburg FL 33710 **Died 8/15/2015** B Carroll IA 1950 BA U of Iowa 1973; MDiv Nash 1986. D 6/14/1986 Bp James Winchester Montgomery P 12/27/1986 Bp Charles Brinkley Morton. m 8/25/1973 Wendy MacInnes c 2. R S Vinc's Epis Ch St Petersburg FL 2008-2015; Chapl City of Pinellas Pk Fire Dept 2005-2008; Pres Pinellas Pk Mnstrl Assn 2003-2008; Exec Com Tampa Bay Billy Graham Crusade 1996-1998; VP St. Giles Manor I & II Bd Dir 1992-2010; R S Giles Ch Pinellas Pk FL 1990-2008; All SS Ch San Diego CA 1986-1990; Sprtl Dir Curs Sec 2012-2015; St. Petersburg Dnry Dn Dio SW Florida Parrish FL 2003-2010, COM 1998-2004, Dioc Coun 1993-1998.

HARTNEY, Michael Elton (Roch) 210 Reading Rd, Watkins Glen NY 14891 **Ret Dio Rochester 2016-; Dep / Alt GC 1994-; Stndg Com/Secy Dio Rochester Henrietta 2014-** B Gardner MA 1948 s Michael & Juliet. U So 1968; U of New Hampshire 1970; Ya Berk 1974; MDiv Yale DS 1974; S Georges Coll Jerusalem IL 1996. D 5/31/1974 P 6/11/1975 Bp Philip Alan Smith. m 10/14/1978 Susan Bradley c 2. S Jas' Ch Watkins Glen NY 2006-2016; R S Jn's Epis Ch Odessa NY 2006-2016; S Paul's Ch Montour Falls NY 2006-2016; R S Columba Epis Ch Marathon FL 2002-2004; R S Mths Epis Ch E Aurora NY 1983-2001; R Ch of the H Cross Ft Plain NY 1978-1983; R The Ch Of The Gd Shpd Canajoharie NY 1978-1983; Asst Min S Ptr's Ch Albany NY 1976-1978; Asst Min S Thos Ch Hanover NH 1974-1976; Dn, Keys Dnry Dio SE Florida Miami 2003-2006. Cmnty Dispute Resolution Cntr, Bd Pres 2008-2017; Corp for the Relief of Widows and Chld of New York, VP 2013. Cmnty Sprt Awd Watkins Glen Area ChmbrCom 2013; Bp's Awd Dio Wstrn New York 1997.

HARTSFIELD, Paula Kindrick (Mo) **D Gr Ch Jefferson City MO 2013-; Bd Mem Epis Sch for Mnstry - Dio Missouri 2012-** B Springfield MO 1954 d Clarence & Hilda. Bachelor of Sci in Ed. Missouri St U 1976; MS K SU 1978; PhD U of Missouri 1991; Three-Year Theol Cert Epis Sch for Mnstry 2012. D 11/16/2012 Bp George Wayne Smith. m 5/1/1982 George Thomas Hartsfield.

HARTSUFF, Jadon (WA) Saint John's Cathedral, 1350 Washington St, Denver CO 80203 **All Souls Memi Epis Ch Washington DC 2016-** B Jackson MI 1977 s Thomas & Sally. BA Albion Coll 1999; MDiv GTS 2012; MDiv The GTS 2012. D 6/16/2012 Bp Diane Jardine Bruce P 1/31/2013 Bp Nathan Dwight Baxter. Cn S Jn's Cathd Denver CO 2013-2016; Cur S Jas Ch Lancaster PA 2012-2013. Fllshp of S Jn 2013. jadon@sjcathedral.org

HARTT, Paul Jonathan (Alb) 8 Loudon Hts S, Loudonville NY 12211 **R S Ptr's Ch Albany NY 2004-** B Philadelphia PA 1959 s Walter & Marilyn. S Jn Coll Annapolis; U of Pennsylvania; BA NYU 1989; MA S Jn Coll Annapolis 1990; MDiv Ya Berk 1995. D 6/23/1995 Bp Orris George Walker Jr P 2/1/1996 Bp Clarence Nicholas Coleridge. m 3/7/1993 C Jeffrey Hartt c 1. S Jn's Ch Delhi NY 1998-2004; R S Ptr's Ch Stamford NY 1998-2004; Cur S Mk's Ch Mystic CT 1995-1998.

HARTT, Walter Fred (NJ) 408 Kingfisher Rd, Tuckerton NJ 08087 **Supple Dio New Jersey Trenton NJ 2017-** B East Orange NJ 1936 s Walter & Loretta. BD Reformed Epis Sem 1960; BA U of Pennsylvania 1963; PDS 1964; MA U of Pennsylvania 1967; ThD GTS 1969; PhD U of Lancaster Lancaster Engl UK 1972. D 6/20/1964 Bp Andrew Y Tsu P 12/1/1964 Bp Allen J Miller. m 8/27/1957 Marilyn Ruth Hartt c 2. Supply Trin Ch Delran New Jersey 2015-2016; Supply S Mart-In-The-Fields Lumberton NJ 2013-2015; Int Ch Of The H Sprt Tuckerton NJ 2008-2009; S Mary's Epis Ch Pleasantville NJ 2001; R Chr Ch Toms River Toms River NJ 1985-2001; Ch Of The Atone Laurel Sprg NJ 1982-1985; R Ch of the Atone Laurel Sprg NJ 1982-1985; Trin Ch Princeton NJ 1982-1983; The GTS New York NY 1976-1982; R S Mk's Epis Ch Perryville MD 1972-1974; Assoc S Ptr's Ch Salisbury MD 1964-1967; Serv Reformed Epis Ch Phildelphia PA 1960-1963. "Complete Idiot's Guide to Grandparenting," MacMillian CO, 1998. Cmnty of S Mary; Sprtl Life Cntr. Fell ECF 1969; Fell GTS 1967.

HARTWELL, Edward Mussey (Tex) 5502-B Buffalo Pass, Austin TX 78745 **Ret 1988-** B Houston TX 1926 s Arthur & Clare. BA SW U Georgetown TX 1950; MDiv VTS 1953; MA U of Texas 1970. D 6/29/1953 Bp Clinton Simon Quin P 7/1/1954 Bp John Elbridge Hines. m 6/14/1998 Karen Hartwell c 7. The Great Cmsn Fndt Houston TX 1985-1988; P-in-c S Geo's Epis Ch Gatesville TX 1983-1988; Chr Ch Sch Temple TX 1979-1981; Hd of Sch Chr Ch Beaumont TX 1979-1981; Asst Chr Epis Ch Temple TX 1979-1981; P-in-c S Jas' Epis Ch La Grange TX 1968-1975; R S Geo's Ch Austin TX 1960-1968; Hd of Sch All S's Epis Sch Beaumont TX 1956-1960; Dce S Mk's Ch Beaumont TX 1956-1960; Vic S Paul's Epis Ch Woodville TX 1955-1957; Chr Ch San Aug TX 1953-1956; Vic Trin Epis Ch Jasper TX 1953-1956. Natl Epis Sch Assn 1957-1961.

HARTWELL, Michael (Mass) 620 Flick Cir., Thomasville NC 27360 **Non-par 1987-** B Norwood MA 1938 s John & Shirley. BBA GW 1962; Cert Geo Mercer TS Dio of LI 1979. D 1/6/1979 P 8/11/1979 Bp Albert Wiencke Van Duzer. m 6/27/1964 Sandra M Hartwell c 3. R S Ptr's Ch On The Canal Buzzards Bay MA 1985-1986; Vic S Ann's Epis Ch Windham Windham ME 1982-1984; Assoc The Ch Of The H Sprt Orleans MA 1979-1982.

HARTZELL, Susan (Va) 5911 Fairview Woods Dr, Fairfax Station VA 22039 **S Peters-In-The-Woods Epis Ch Fairfax Sta VA 2013-** B Boston MA 1963 d Albert & Cathleen. BS Emerson Coll 1985; JD Suffolk U Law Sch 1993; MDiv VTS 2013. D 3/2/2013 P 9/7/2013 Bp Andrew Marion Lenow Dietsche. m 9/11/1993 Peter M Hartzell c 2.

HARTZOG, Dorothy Chatham (Tenn) 211 Chip N Dale Dr., Clarksville TN 37043 B Fort Worth TX 1947 d Edward & Josephine. BA Carson-Newman Coll 1969; MA So Carolina St U 1979; Luth Theol Sthrn Sem 1992; MDiv VTS 1994. D 6/3/1994 P 1/25/1995 Bp Edward Lloyd Salmon Jr. c 1. Assoc R Gr Chap Rossview Clarksville TN 2003-2015; Trin Ch Clarksville TN 2003-2015; Prncpl Pstr / Vic S Martha's Epis Ch Bethany Bch DE 1998-2002; P-in-c H Cross Faith Memi Epis Ch Pawleys Island SC 1997-1998; Mgr, St. Eliz Place Camp Baskerville Pawleys Island SC 1996-1998; Org French Hugenot Ch Charleston SC 1995-1996; D S Steph's Epis Ch Charleston SC 1994-1995; Mem Dioc Coun Dio Tennessee Nashville TN 2006-2010, Supply P 2002-2005; Mem, Dioc Coun Dio Delaware Wilmington 2001-2002.

HARTZOG, Howard Gallemore (WTex) 2229 Aiken Way, El Dorado Hills CA 95762 B Marlin TX 1945 s Howard & Anna. AA Victoria Coll Victoria TX. D 4/14/2002 P 2/28/2003 Bp James Edward Folts. m 7/3/1971 Frances Wedig c 2. interum Epis Ch Of The Gd Shepard Geo W TX 2009; Vic S Jas Epis Ch Hebbronville TX 2005-2009; Mssnr Partnr In Mnstry Estrn Convoc Kenedy TX 2003-2005; Mssnr Partnr In Mnstry Lavaca TX 2003-2005.

HARVALA, Eileen Gay (Minn) Trinity Episcopal Church, 345 Main St, Portland CT 06480 B Fargo ND 1956 d Edward & Marjorie. BA Moorhead St U; MPA

Humphrey Sch of Publ Affrs 2010. D 6/27/2013 Bp Brian N Prior. m 7/1/1978 Steven Wester Harvala c 2.

HARVEY, Edwin Edward (WTex) 868 Porter Rd, Cochran GA 31014 **Ret 1995-** B Dodge City KS 1930 s John & Edna. BA Rhodes Coll 1952; Drew U 1956; MDiv VTS 1958; STM VTS 1959; ThD Heidelberg U 1965. D 6/20/1958 P 6/1/1959 Bp Edward Hamilton West. c 3. Assoc S Mk's Epis Ch San Antonio TX 1990-1995; R All SS Epis Ch Corpus Christi TX 1981-1990; Assoc S Dav's Ch Austin TX 1976-1981; Asst S Mk's Epis Ch Jacksonville FL 1974-1976; Cn H Trin Cathd Suva Fiji 1965-1974; Chapl Jacksonville U FL 1960-1962; Asst S Paul's Epis Ch Jacksonville FL 1959-1960.

HARVEY, Errol Allen (NY) 800 North Miami Ave., Apt. 302, Miami FL 33136 **Part time Int P in charge The Ch of the Incarn Miami FL 2012-** B Grand Rapids MI 1943 s Fred & Elizabeth. BA Aquinas Coll 1965; BD SWTS 1969; MPA NYU 1977; Commonwealth U TS 1991. D 6/9/1968 Bp Charles Bennison Sr P 5/25/1969 Bp George E Rath. R S Aug's Ch New York NY 1983-2008; R S Andr's Ch Bronx NY 1977-1983; Dio New York New York NY 1972-1976; R S Mk's Ch Dorchester MA 1970-1972; Cur Trin And S Phil's Cathd Newark NJ 1968-1970; Part time Asst Trin Cathd Miami FL 2011-2012. DD Commonwealth Univertsity TS 1991. eahnyc@yahoo.com

HARVEY, Rick E (Ida) 2080 Bodine Ct, Boise ID 83705 **D S Mich's Cathd Boise ID 1997-; D Dio Idaho Boise ID 1983-** B Boise ID 1949 s Roy & June. BFA Boise St U 1973. D 10/6/1988 Bp David Bell Birney IV. m 8/7/1971 Connie Sue Harvey c 2. Idaho Assn For Pstr Care, NAAD.

HARVEY, Robert William (WA) Episcopal Church of Our Saviour, 1700 Powder Mill Road, Silver Spring MD 20903 **R Ch Of Our Sav Silver Sprg MD 2006-** B Pittsburgh PA 1964 s Roberta. BA Clearwater Chr Coll 1986; MDiv Reformed TS 1989; STM Sewanee: The U So, TS 1998; DMin VTS 2013; DMin VTS 2014. D 12/17/1994 Bp Robert Oran Miller P 7/1/1995 Bp Charles Lovett Keyser. m 6/16/1990 Anne Harvey. Chapl Griffin Hosp Derby CT 2001-2006; R Chr Ch Ansonia CT 1999-2006; Int Ch Of The Mssh Lower Gwynedd PA 1998-1999; Assoc S Jas Ch Oneonta NY 1997-1998; Cur / Asst Washington Memi Chap Vlly Forge PA 1995-1997. Choral Arts Soc of Washington 2012; OHC - Assoc 1996.

HARVEY, Robert William (Az) 9901 Penn Ave S Apt 336, Bloomington MN 55431 B Toronto ON CA 1930 s Francis & Virginia. Cert U MN 1978; Cert Theol Stud Toronto Dioc Trng Sch 1995. D 6/24/1965 Bp Hamilton Hyde Kellogg P 4/2/1966 Bp Philip Frederick McNairy. c 7. Ch Of The Apos Oro Vlly AZ 2007-2013; EfM Coordntr Epis Dio Arizona 2004-2013; R Gd Shpd Epis Ch Wichita KS 1989-1995; Dn Sw Convoc Dio Kansas Topeka KS 1987-1991; R S Mk Wichita KS 1983-1989; Exec Dir First Step Minneapolis MN 1979-1982; R S Jn The Bapt Epis Ch Minneapolis MN 1970-1982; Vic Emm Epis Ch Alexandria MN 1965-1970.

HARWOOD, John Thomas (CPa) 137 3rd St, Renovo PA 17764 **P-in-c Trin Ch Renovo PA 2011-; Pstr Zion's Evang Luth Ch Renovo PA 2011-** B Ottumwa IA 1947 s Arthur & Nyta. BA Wartburg Coll 1968; PhD U of Nebraska 1977; Cert of Angl Stds CDSP 2013. D 10/31/2010 P 10/19/2011 Bp Nathan Dwight Baxter. m 2/26/1983 Kathryn Grossman c 2. Auth, "Theologizing the Wrld: A Reflection on the Theol of Sallie McFague," *ATR*, 2015.

HARY, Barbara A (CPa) 20 Heatherland Rd, Middletown PA 17057 **D S Mich And All Ang Ch Middletown PA 1996-** B Bronxville NY 1931 d Malcolm & Dorothy. Harrisburg Area Cmnty Coll; Cert Pennsylvania Diac Sch 1991; S Johns Carlisle PA 1996; S Mich & Alll Ang Middletown PA 2000. D 6/14/1991 Bp Charlie Fuller Mcnutt Jr. m 1/3/1954 Charles Philip Hary. Dio Cntrl Pennsylvania Harrisburg PA 1983-1996. NAAD; Tertiary Of The Soc Of S Fran.

HASEN, Elizabeth Sorchan (Spok) 409 W 22nd Ave, Spokane WA 99203 B New York NY 1955 d George & Charlotte. Bryn 1975; BA Amh 1977; MDiv VTS 1991. D 6/11/1991 P 12/14/1991 Bp Daniel Lee Swenson. Ch Of The Resurr Veradale WA 2010-2011; S Alb's Epis Ch Louisville KY 1994-2004; Cathd Ch Of S Paul Burlington VT 1991-1994.

HASKELL, Robert Finch (Alb) 9 Long Creek Dr, Burnt Hills NY 12027 **Cn to the Ordnry Dio Albany Greenwich NY 2007-** B Washington,DC 1942 s Francis & Mary. BS Cor 1965; BS Cor 1965; MBA NYU 1972; MDiv EDS 1973. D 6/9/1973 Bp Paul Moore Jr P 2/1/1974 Bp Ned Cole. m 7/5/1980 Margaret J Joggerst c 2. P-in-c S Jas Ch Oneonta NY 2001-2003; R Ch Of The Redemp Southampton PA 1989-2001; R S Andr's Epis Ch Syracuse NY 1975-1988; Cur Trin Memi Ch Binghamton NY 1973-1975. rhaskell@albanydiocese.org

HASLETT III, William Warner (Pgh) 418 Jerad Ln., Windber PA 15963 B Johnstown PA 1968 s William & Louise. BA U Pgh 1990; MDiv TESM 1993. D 6/26/1993 P 6/1/1994 Bp Alden Moinet Hathaway. m 8/21/1993 Tammy Haslett c 2. S Fran In The Fields Somerset PA 1995-1997; Vic S Ptr's Epis Ch Blairsville PA 1994; Cur S Barn Ch Wilmington DE 1993; Chrmstr S Mk's Ch Johnstown PA 1983-1990.

HASS, Caroline Vada (WNY) Po Box 161, Alexander NY 14005 **Secy and Mem of Bd My Bro's Hse (Ecum) Warsaw NY 2005-; Chapl,Mem of Cmsn Wyoming Cnty Jail Chapl Cmsn Warsaw 2005-; Chapl NY St Veteran's Hm Batavia NY 2000-** B Dalton NY 1933 d Alfred & Frances. New Engl Coll 1956; BS Liberty U 1986; EFM Brent Sch E Aurora NY 1996; CPE U Roch

1996; Cont edu Masters Intl Sch of Div 2005. D 8/7/1999 Bp Michael Garrison. D for Cler supply The Ch Of The H Apos - Epis Perry NY 2005-2011; D S Lk's Epis Ch Attica NY 1999-2005; Chapl Ben Hse Buffalo NY. 1994-2000; Pstr Cmnty Ch (ABA Affiliated) Varysburg NY. 1973-1983; Mssy Onondaga Indn Reserve Mssn Nedrow (Syracuse) NY. Asse 1959-1965. Auth, "Encounter (poetry)," *Colors of Life*, Intl Libr of Poetry Watermark Press, 2003; Auth, "Beside Still Waters," *Sharing*, Int'l OSL, 2001; Auth, "From the Vlly of The Shadow," *Sharing*, Int'l OSL, 2001. Amer Soc of Clincl Pathologists (Assoc) 1982-1994; Natl Soc for Histotechnology 1973-1994.

HASSAN, Rose Cohen (Nwk) 954 Ave C, Bayonne NJ 07002 **Epis Ch of St Lk and St Mary Belvidere NJ 2017-** B New York NY 1953 d Saul & Bonita. SUNY 1973; BA Molloy Coll 1977; CUNY 1989; MDiv GTS 1993; Cert GTS 1994; STM GTS 1997; Cert Coaches Trng Inst 2009. D 4/24/1993 P 11/18/1993 Bp Orris George Walker Jr. m 4/27/2012 Judy A Piscerchia c 1. S Mary's Ch Belvidere NJ 2015-2016; Trin Ch Asbury Pk NJ 2014-2015; Gr Epis Ch Plainfield NJ 2014; Mgr of Soc Serv Windmill Allnce Inc. Bayonne NJ 2011-2014; Trin Ch Bayonne NJ 2011-2013; Assoc P for Pstr Care and Educ Calv Ch Bayonne NJ 2011-2012; Int Prog Dir Ch Of The Gd Shpd Ft Lee NJ 2007; Int Dir of Oasis Dio Newark Newark NJ 2002, Dist 7 Co-Cnvnr 2009-2011, Dist 7 Cnvnr 2009-2011, Hisp Mnstry T/F 2007, Liturg and Mus Cmsn 2005-2007, Hisp Mnstry T/F 2004-2007, Dioc Sprtl Dir for Vocare 2002-2011, Dist 7 Cnvnr 2001-2003, Wmn Cmsn 2001-2003, Liturg and Mus Cmsn 2000-2003, Camp Com 1999-2001, T/F on Minority Vendors 1999-2001, Camp Com 1999-2000, Ward Herbert Bd 1998-2000, Wmn Cmsn 1996-2000, Dioc Coun 1996-1998, Dioc Coun Rep 1996-1998; Pstr Counslr at AIDS Resource Cntr S Barn Ch Newark NJ 1997-2001; Pstr Counslr The Aids Resource Cntr At St. Barn Ch Newark NJ 1997-2001; Vic Trin Epis Ch Kearny NJ 1995-2011; Chapl Vill Nrsng Hm 1995-1997; Assoc S Ptr's Ch New York NY 1993-1995; Sprtl Dir for Intl Exec. Com Epis Vocare Inc 2007-2009; Dio Newark Sprtl Dir Epis Vocare Inc 2002-2011; The Oasis Newark NJ 1996-2000, Bd Mem 1996-2000. Tertiary Ord Of S Helena 1992.

HASSE III, Edward Max (Nwk) 4 Woodland Rd, Montvale NJ 07645 **R S Paul's Ch Montvale NJ 1996-** B Englewood NJ 1963 s Edward & Barabara. BS Ithaca Coll 1985; MDiv VTS 1989. D 6/3/1989 P 12/9/1989 Bp John Shelby Spong. m 8/22/1987 Melissa Hasse c 2. Mem, Stndg Com Dio Newark Newark NJ 2000-2012, Dep to GC 2000-, Alt Dep. to GC 1994-2000, Chair, T/F on Yth 1994-1996, Mem, Yth Mnstry Bd 1991-1999; R Ch Of The H Sprt Verona NJ 1991-1996; Assoc R S Jas Ch Montclair NJ 1989-1991. Integrity; RACA. Cbury Schlr Awd Dio Newark 2000; Bp's Outstanding Serv Awd Dio Newark 1997.

HASSELBROOK, Audrey Caroline (Nwk) 18 Shepard Pl, Nutley NJ 07110 **Asst S Jas Ch Montclair NJ 2007-; Asst R The Episcoapl Ch of St. Jas Upper Montclair NJ 2006-; Assoc Gr Ch in Nutley Nutley NJ 2005-** B Kearny NJ 1957 d Roy & Patricia. BS Montclair St U 1979; MAT Montclair St U 2001; MDiv GTS 2005. D 6/11/2005 Bp John Palmer Croneberger P 2/25/2006 Bp Carol J Gallagher. m 6/9/1979 James Hasselbrook c 3. Trin And S Phil's Cathd Newark NJ 2005-2006; Cur Trin and St. Phil's Cathd Newark NJ 2005-2006.

HASSELL, Mariann Barbara (Tenn) 1204 Jackson Dr, Pulaski TN 38478 **P-in-c S Bede's Epis Ch Manchester TN 2012-** B Dayton OH 1941 d Robert & Nellie. MA Franciscan TS 1989. D 1/25/1992 Bp David Mercer Schofield P 2/26/2006 Bp Bertram Nelson Herlong. c 4. Assoc The Epis Ch Of The Mssh Pulaski TN 2007-2009; S Mk's Epis Ch Tracy CA 1993-1994; CE & Yth Min S Paul's Epis Ch Modesto CA 1989-1990; Cleric Our Sav.

HASSEMER, Donald William (RG) Po Box 747, Medanales NM 87548 B St Louis MO 1944 s Clarence & Virginia. D 1/5/1981 P 1/8/1982 Bp Richard Mitchell Trelease Jr. m 10/3/1970 Wendy Hassemer c 3.

HASSERIES, Robert Alan (Spok) East 360 Springview Drive, Coeur D'Alene ID 83814 **P S Jas Epis Ch Cashmere WA 2003-, 1981-1990** B Evansville IN 1940 s Robert & Ruth. BA U of Arizona 1962; BD CDSP 1964. D 7/3/1965 P 1/1/1966 Bp John Joseph Meakin Harte. m 8/28/1964 Kitty Kay Hasseries c 3. R S Lk's Ch Coeur D Alene ID 1990-2000; Dio Spokane Spokane WA 1984-1990; S Lk's Epis Ch Wenatchee WA 1981-1983; Vic S Cuth's Epis Ch Oakland CA 1975-1981; R Epis Ch Of Our Sav Placerville CA 1969-1975; Cur S Steph's Ch Phoenix AZ 1967-1969; S Paul's Ch Tombstone AZ 1965-1967; Vic S Raphael In The Vlly Epis Ch Benson AZ 1965-1967. Tertiary Of The Soc Of S Fran.

HASSETT, Miranda Katherine (Mil) 6325 Shoreham Dr, Madison WI 53711 **R S Dunst's Ch Madison WI 2011-** B Boston MA 1975 d Eliot & Pamela. BA Indiana U 1997; PhD U NC 2004; MDiv EDS 2008. D 6/28/2008 Bp Alfred Marble Jr P 2/6/2009 Bp Michael B Curry. m 12/8/2001 Philip A Hassett c 2. Asst S Andr's Epis Ch Contoocook NH 2008-2010; Sem/Lay Asst for Fam Mnstrs Chr Epis Ch Needham MA 2006-2008. Auth, "Angl Comm in Crisis," *Angl Comm in Crisis*, Pr Press, 2006.

HASSETT, Steve (Cal) **R S Steph's Epis Ch Orinda CA 2014-** B 1971 MDiv CDSP; DMin CDSP; BFA SUNY 1994. D 6/3/2006 Bp William Edwin Swing P 12/2/2006 Bp Marc Handley Andrus. m 4/27/2002 Clancy C Drake c 2. Asst CDSP Berkeley CA 2014; St Johns Epis Ch Ross CA 2008-2014; Ch

367

Of The Redeem San Rafael CA 2007-2008; Dio California San Francisco CA 2006-2007. steve@ststephensorinda.org

HASTIE, Cornelius Dewitt (Mass) 24 Castleton St, Jamaica Plain MA 02130 **Died 6/15/2016** B Spring Lake NJ 1931 s Frank & Cecile. ABS Harv 1952; MDiv EDS 1956. D 6/9/1956 Bp Angus Dun P 12/7/1956 Bp Anson Phelps Stokes Jr. m 4/18/1981 Linda M Hastie c 2. R S Jn's S Jas Epis Ch Boston MA 1996, Serv 1988-1995, 1956-1987; S Jas Educ Cntr Boston MA 1987-1996; R S Jn's Ch Charlestown (Boston) Charlestown MA 1973-1981; Chapl Deer Island Correctional Boston MA 1969-1992; S Jas Pre-Kindergarten Sch Boston MA 1965-1987; R/Vic S Jas Epis Ch Boston MA 1956-1965; Dioc Coun Dio Massachusetts Boston MA 1984-1988, Bd, Epis City Mssn 1976-1983.

HASTINGS, Brian J (Chi) 857 W. Margate Terrace, #1-W, Chicago IL 60640 **R Ch Of Our Sav Chicago IL 1998-; Cur Ascen 1985-** B Brantford ON CA 1954 s James & Gertrude. BA U of Wstrn Ontario CA 1977; MDiv Hur CA 1980. Trans 3/23/1989 as Priest. m 5/20/2014 Roger Gumm. Ch Of The Ascen Chicago IL 1988-1991; Serv Ch Of Can 1980-1985.

HASTINGS, K(Empton) (Pa) 2119 Old Welsh Rd, Abington PA 19001 **Died 10/27/2016** B Princeton NJ 1961 s Howard & Lucia. BA Hobart and Wm Smith Colleges 1984; MDiv UTS 1989; DMin Nash 2015; DMin Nash 2017. D 6/10/1989 P 3/31/1990 Bp George Phelps Mellick Belshaw. m 5/6/2000 Pamela A Hastings c 2. R S Anne's Ch Abington PA 1994-2016; Int All SS Epis Ch Lakewood NJ 1993-1994; Asst Chr Ch Toms River Toms River NJ 1990-1993; Cur S Jn's Ch Salem NJ 1989-1990. Auth, "A Certain Kind of Affection," Friesen Press, 2014; Auth, "The Only Way Out for Henry Clatt," Westbow Press, 2013. Abington Hosp Pstr Care Com 1994; Bd Emergency Food Bank Dio NJ 1990-1994; Chr Soc Relation Dio NJ 1990-1994; Discovery Bible Study Trainers 2014; Econ Justice Com Dio PA 1994-1999; Pastors Untd in Pryr, Abington, PA 1999; Resolutns Com Dio NJ 1990-1994; Soc for the Advancement of Chr Faith in Pennsylvania 2004-2010. Alum Awd Chapin Sch 1998; Phi Beta Kappa 1984.

HASTINGS, Mark Wayne (Mich) PO Box 287, Onsted MI 49265 **P S Mich And All Ang Brooklyn MI 2011-** B Ann Arbor MI 1944 s William & Alma. BA Siena Heights U 2002. D 10/27/2010 P 5/24/2011 Bp Wendell Nathaniel Gibbs Jr. m 6/11/1966 Susan Hastings c 3. Julian of Norwich 2007; Soc of Cath P 2012.

HATCH, Albert H (SO) 3108 Fort St, Edisto Island SC 29438 **Ret 1991-** B Augusta GA 1931 s James & Ann. U GA 1953; BD Sewanee: The U So, TS 1956. D 6/17/1956 P 3/1/1957 Bp Albert R Stuart. m 4/10/2007 Anne Goldthwaite Hatch c 2. R H Trin Epis Ch Charleston SC 1991-1993; R S Tim's Epis Ch Cincinnati OH 1981-1991; S Clem's Epis Ch Canton GA 1980-1981; Dioc Nwspr Atlanta GA 1978-1981; R S Mk's Ch Dalton GA 1975-1978; R S Tim's Ch Signal Mtn TN 1966-1968; R S Jas Epis Ch Marietta GA 1962-1966; Vic S Fran Ch Menomonee Falls WI 1960-1962; Vic H Apos' Savannah GA 1958-1960; Vic S Mich And All Ang Savannah GA 1958-1960; Vic Chr/S Mary's Woodbine GA 1956-1958; Vic S Mk's Ch Brunswick GA 1956-1958. Auth, "Forw Day By Day".

HATCH, Jessica Ann (U) 2586 Elizabeth St Apt 6, Salt Lake City UT 84106 B New York NY 1946 d Gilbert & Virginia. BA Seattle U 1968; MDiv GTS 1989. D 6/10/1989 P 1/13/1990 Bp Frederick Houk Borsch. m 4/24/2004 Steven B Kiger. Stndg Com Dio Utah 2009-2011; P-in-c S Mary's Ch Provo UT 2009-2011; Int Ascen St. Matt's Price UT 2007-2009; Educ & Resource Off Dio Utah Salt Lake City UT 2006-2009; Dir Epis Cmnty Serv Inc Salt Lake City UT 2002-2006; Dir Epis Cmnty Serv Inc. Salt Lake City 2002-2006; Int All SS Ch Salt Lake City UT 2001-2002; Assoc Dn The GTS New York NY 1999-2001, Pstr Assoc 1996-1998; Sr Consult Ch Of The Incarn New York NY 1998-2001; Dio New York New York NY 1998-2001; Deploy Mntsry NE Deploy Mnstry Conf NE 1996-1998; The Ch Of S Lk In The Fields New York NY 1996-1998; Dio Arizona Phoenix AZ 1994-1996, Co Cnvnr Rgnl Par 1993-1995, Dioc Coun 1993-1995; Dn Trin Cathd Phoenix AZ 1994-1995; Assoc Gr St Pauls Epis Ch Tucson AZ 1991-2014; Assoc Gr St. Paul's Tucson AZ 1991-1994; Asst R S Mich And All Ang Par Corona Dl Mar CA 1989-1991. "Living Boldly," *an eNewsletter*, Epis Dio Utah, 2007; Auth, "Where Do Wmn Find Themselves," *The Epis New Yorker*, Epis Dio NY, 1999. Polly Bond Awd of Excellence ECom 1998.

HATCH, Mark (WMass) 267 Locust Street, Apt 2K, Florence MA 01062 B Boston MA 1958 s John & Mary. BA Dart 1980; BA Dart 1980; MA U of Massachusetts 1987; MDiv Harvard DS 1989. D 3/6/1991 P 11/24/1991 Bp Bob Johnson. m 6/10/2014 Annelise Martin c 2. Int S Matt's Ch Lincoln NE 2015-2016; Dio Wstrn Massachusetts Springfield 2015, 2005-2009, 1999-2003, 1998-1999, 1993-1996; Trin Ch S Louis MO 2014; Int Cathd Ch Of S Paul Burlington VT 2012-2013; Therapeutic Cmnty Prog The Austen Riggs Cntr Stockbridge MA 2010-2012; P-in-c S Phil's Ch Easthampton MA 2009-2010; Int Ch Of The Atone Westfield MA 2007-2009; Int Gr Ch Great Barrington MA 2006-2007; Int S Paul's Epis Ch Stockbridge MA 2005-2006; Int Cathd Ch Of S Steph Harrisburg PA 2004-2005; Int Dio Caledonia Prince Rupert BC 2003-2004; P-in-c Chr Ch So Barre MA 2003; Assoc S Fran Ch Holden MA

1999-2003; S Andr's Ch No Grafton MA 1993-1996; R Ch Of The H Fam Mills River NC 1991-1992.

HATCH, Rebekah (Ct) 2852 Kimmeridge Dr, Atlanta GA 30344 **S Alb's Ch Simsbury CT 2015-** B Decatur GA 1976 BA Salem Coll Winston-Salem NC; MDiv VTS 2004. D 6/5/2004 P 1/25/2005 Bp J Neil Alexander. m 2/17/2001 Anthony R Hatch c 1. Chapl St Benedicts Epis Day Sch Smyrna GA 2012-2015; St Ben's Epis Ch Smyrna GA 2012-2015; Int US Chapl H Innoc' Epis Sch Atlanta GA 2011-2012; Asst to the R S Aid's Epis Ch Milton GA 2010-2012; Assoc R Ch Of The Gd Shpd Towson MD 2006-2009; Asst Chapl S Paul's Sch Brooklandville MD 2004-2006.

HATCH, Victoria Theresa (Los) 1095 Dysar, Banning CA 92220 B Tacoma Park MD 1947 d William & Nancy. FD 1967; U of Maryland U Coll Europe 1967; BA Amer U 1969; VTS 1975. D 6/5/1975 Bp Robert Bruce Hall P 1/15/1977 Bp Robert Claflin Rusack. Dio Los Angeles Los Angeles CA 2006, 1976-1977, Dep Gc 1982-1985; S Geo's Ch Riverside CA 2003-2006; P-in-c S Steph's Par Beaumont CA 2000-2001; S Alb's Epis Ch Yucaipa CA 1983-1986; S Agnes Mssn Banning CA 1978-2003; Asst Chapl Vet A Hosp Lomalinda CA 1978-1980; St Cross Epis Ch Hermosa Bch CA 1977, Asst 1976-1977. Auth, "Our Call"; Auth, "Living Ch".

HATCHER JR, John Harris (Va) Apdo 632- 1250, Escazu, San Jose 10201 Costa Rica **Ret 1998-** B Castalian Sprgs TN 1935 s John & Fayola. BA Van 1956; MDiv VTS 1963; MA U of Tennessee 1974. D 6/21/1963 Bp George P Gunn P 5/19/1964 Bp David Shepherd Rose. c 2. R S Anne's Epis Ch Reston VA 1987-1998; Epis Chapl, Vanderbilt Univ S Aug's Chap Nashville TN 1971-1987; R Ch Of The Gd Samar Knoxville TN 1969-1970; Asst Calv Epis Ch Williamsville NY 1967-1968; Cur Bruton Par Williamsburg VA 1963-1967. Auth, "Santayanas Naturalization Of Catholicsm". john21012@gmail.com

HATCHER, Spencer Elizabeth (Md) **Epiph Ch Dulaney Vlly Luthvle Timon MD 2016-** D 1/16/2016 Bp Chilton Richardson Knudsen P 9/3/2016 Bp Eugene Taylor Sutton.

HATCHETT JR, Jefferson Bryan (Ala) Po Box 596, Heflin AL 36264 **Died 9/26/2015** B Greenville GA 1929 s Jefferson & Louise. BA Emory U 1950; BD UTS 1953. D 2/1/1964 P 6/22/1964 Bp William Henry Marmion. m 4/17/1982 Meredith Brewer c 3. R Ch Of The Mssh Heflin AL 1996-2001; S Jas Ch Macon GA 1990-1992; Int S Tim's Decatur GA 1989-1990; Cur The Ch Of Our Sav Atlanta GA 1987-1989; Non-par 1973-1986; R S Paul's Pomona Pomona CA 1970-1972; R Emm Ch Harrisonburg VA 1966-1970; Cur/Asst/Assoc Chr Epis Ch Roanoke VA 1963-1966; Serv Presb Ch Serv Presb Ch 1953-1963. Auth, "Stwdshp: A Basic Statement". jbhatchett@bellsouth.net

HATFIELD, Adele Dees (Nwk) 221 Boulevard, Mountain Lakes NJ 07046 **Co-R S Ptr's Ch Mtn Lks NJ 2009-** B Coral Gables FL 1950 d James & Mary. BS Barton Coll 1972; MDiv VTS 2005. D 6/25/2005 P 1/6/2006 Bp Clifton Daniel III. m 11/11/2006 Charles J Hatfield c 3. Assoc Iona Hope Epis Ch Ft Myers FL 2006-2008; Asst R S Jas Par Wilmington NC 2005-2006.

HATFIELD JR, Charles J (Nwk) 221 Boulevard, Mountain Lakes NJ 07046 **Co-R S Ptr's Ch Mtn Lks NJ 2009-** B Baltimore MD 1952 s Charles & Doris. VPI 1982; MDiv VTS 2005. D 6/29/2005 P 4/28/2006 Bp Neff Powell. m 11/11/2006 Adele Dees Miller c 2. Assoc R S Monica's Epis Ch Naples FL 2005-2009.

HATFIELD, Russ (SwVa) 101 Logan St, Bluefield VA 24605 **R The Tazewell Cnty Cluster Of Epis Parishes Tazewell VA 2001-, P-in-c 1999-2001, Asst 1998-1999** B Matewan WV 1944 s Major & Mildred. BA Catawba Coll 1966; Towson U 1971; MS Radford U 1976; Sewanee: The U So, TS 2000. D 10/25/1997 P 5/17/1998 Bp Neff Powell. m 9/5/1975 Debra Joan Billips c 1. Pres of Stndg Com Dio SW Virginia Roanoke VA 2008-2009, Dn of Abingdon Convoc 2006-2012.

✠ **HATHAWAY, The Rt Rev Alden Moinet** (SC) 107 Laurens St., Beaufort SC 29902 **Par Ch of St. Helena Beaufort SC 2007-** B Saint Louis MO 1933 s Earl & Margaret. BS Cor 1955; BD EDS 1962. D 6/9/1962 P 12/19/1962 Bp Nelson Marigold Burroughs Con 6/27/1981 for Pgh. m 11/24/2007 Barbara Nesbitt Hathaway c 3. Bp-In-Res S Jn's Epis Ch Tallahassee FL 1999-2007; Ret Bp of Pittsburgh Dio Pittsburgh Pittsburgh PA 1998-2011, Bp of Pittsburgh 1983-1997, Bp of Pittsburgh 1983-1997, Bp Coadj of Pittsburgh 1981-1982; R S Chris's Ch Springfield VA 1972-1981; Assoc Chr Ch Cranbrook Bloomfield Hills MI 1965-1971; Min in charge Ch Of The H Trin Epis Bellefontaine OH 1962-1965. AAC 1988; Angl Ldrshp Inst 2015; Irenaeus Grp 1988; Solar Light for Afr 1978. None: Save that of knowing Jesus Chr and Him crucified. 1974.

HATHAWAY, Dale Caldwell (Haw) 1863 Rock Glen DR Apt 103, Rock Hill SC 29732 **Lectr Chaminade U 2012-** B Ray AZ 1950 s Dale & Helen. BA Colorado Coll 1972; MDiv Nash 1981; MA U of Notre Dame 1986. D 6/2/1982 Bp William Carl Frey P 12/8/1982 Bp Charles Thomas Gaskell. m 12/9/2012 Mary Pat Sjostrom c 5. R S Mary's Epis Ch Honolulu HI 2001-2012; R S Andr's By The Lake Epis Ch Michigan City IN 1991-2001; Vic S Ptr's Ch Rensselaer IN 1987-1990; Asst The Cathd Ch Of S Jas So Bend IN 1984-1988; Asst Trin Ch Milwaukee WI 1982-1984; Pres Stndg Com The Epis Ch in Hawaii Honolulu HI 2010-2011.

HATZENBUEHLER, Robin Ritter (WTenn) 1544 Carr Ave, Memphis TN 38104 **Chapl Trezevant Epis Hm Memphis TN 2007-; Chapl / Dir of Pstr Care and Rel Serv Trezevant Epis Ret Cmnty Memphis TN 2007-** B Memphis TN 1949 d Louis & Gloria. BA Rhodes Coll 1971; MA U of Memphis 1977; MDiv Memphis TS 2004. D 6/18/2005 P 1/7/2006 Bp Don Edward Johnson. m 7/1/1972 Daniel Bruce Hatzenbuehler c 2. Cur Gr - S Lk's Ch Memphis TN 2005-2007; Cur Gr-St. Lk's Epis Memphis TN 2005-2007. robin@ trezevantmanor.org

HAUCK, Barbara Horsley (Minn) 32 W College St, Duluth MN 55812 **Outreach Coordntr S Paul's Epis Ch Duluth MN 2004-** B Midland MI 1950 d Lee & Fern. D 6/17/2001 Bp James Louis Jelinek. m 12/28/1971 Steven Arthur Hauck. D The Par of St Paul's Epis Ch Duluth MN 2001-2013. NAAD 2000.

HAUCK, Mary Rockett (NCal) 11489 Phoebe Ct, Penn Valley CA 95946 **Sierra Dnry The Epis Dio Nthrn California Sacramento CA 2013-, Pres of Stndg Com 2004-2006, Chair of Chr Formation Com 1998-2000** B Kansas City MO 1950 d Edward & Billie. BA U CA 1972; Tchg Cred U CA 1972; MA U CA 1985; MDiv CDSP 1995. D 5/24/1995 P 11/30/1995 Bp Jerry Alban Lamb. m 3/21/1971 Paul D Hauck c 3. R S Mich's Epis Ch Carmichael CA 2004-2012, Asst 1996-2000, Chapl 1996-2000; R S Clem's Ch Rancho Cordova CA 2000-2004; S Mich's Epis Day Sch Carmichael CA 1996-1997; P-in-c S Lk's Ch Galt CA 1995-1997. Contrib, "Preaching to the Chld of God," *Preaching as Pstr Caring*, Morehouse, 2005. canonhauck@gmail.com

HAUERT, Robert Harold (Los) 1419 Jorn Ct, Ann Arbor MI 48104 **Ret 1993-** B San Gabriel CA 1928 s Emil & Maria. BA Occ 1953; BD EDS 1959. D 6/22/1959 Bp Francis E I Bloy P 1/16/1960 Bp Donald J Campbell. Dir Off Ethics & Rel U MI Ann Arbor MI 1964-1993; Chapl U MI Ann Arbor MI 1959-1964.

HAUFF, Bradley S (Pa) 9601 Frankford Ave, Philadelphia PA 19114 **Epis Ch Cntr New York NY 2017-; BEC Dio Pennsylvania Philadelphia PA 2012-** B Sioux Falls SD 1963 s Sylvan & Margaret. BA Augustana Coll 1985; MEd So Dakota St U 1987; MDiv SWTS 1990; PsyD Minnesota Sch of Profsnl Psychol 2005. D 7/23/1990 Bp Craig Barry Anderson P 10/23/1991 Bp Sanford Zangwill Kaye Hampton. m 4/11/1999 Ruth E Hauff. R All SS Ch Philadelphia PA 2012-2017; R S Thos Flagler Cnty Palm Coast FL 2008-2012; Assoc R Ch Of The Epiph Epis Minneapolis MN 2004-2007; Dio Minnesota Minneapolis MN 2001-2003, 1996-1998; Asst S Jn In The Wilderness S Paul MN 1998-2001; Asst Ch Of The Epiph Richardson TX 1994-1995; Assoc S Jn The Evang S Paul MN 1991-1994; Vic Dio So Dakota Pierre SD 1990-1991; BEC Dio Florida Jacksonville 2010-2012; Bd Dir Fam Life Cntr Bunnell Florida 2008-2012; Bd Trst Bexley Seabury Fed Chicago IL 2006-2009. Auth, "Vine DeLoria's Influence on Native Amer Identity," *First People's Journ of Theol*, Indigenous Theol Trng Inst, 2010; Auth, "Congruence as a Pre-Rogerian Sprtl Construct," *Doctoral dissertation*, Minnesota Sch of Profsnl Psychol, 2005. Oglala Sioux Tribe 1985. Lilly Endwmt Sabbatical Schlr Eli Lilly Corp 2007; Markovitz Schlr Amer Schools of Profsnl Psychol 1996.

HAUG, Phillip Russell (Lex) 100 Daisey Dr, Richmond KY 40475 B Merced CA 1938 s Russell & Evelyn. BS U of Nevada at Reno 1960; SMM MIT 1976; MDiv VTS 1990. D 6/2/1990 P 12/1/1990 Bp Peter J Lee. m 5/27/1959 Anna V Haug c 4. Int Trintiy Ch Danville KY 2010-2011; Int Chr Epis Ch Harlan KY 2008-2010; S Ptr's Ch Paris KY 2006-2007; Int S Jn's Ch Versailles KY 2002-2004; Vic Epis Ch of Our Sav Richmond KY 1994-2002; R S Ptr's Port Royal Port Royal VA 1990-1994; Vauters Ch Loretto VA 1990-1994. SAMS 1977-2000. prhaug@aol.com

HAUGAARD, Jeffrey James (CNY) 101 E Williams St, Waterloo NY 13165 **S Paul's Ch Waterloo NY 2016-** B San Jose, California 1951 s Viggo & Mary-Lois. BA U CA at Santa Cruz 1973; MA U of Santa Clara 1984; PhD U of Virginia 1990; Cert of Angl Stds CDSP 2014. D 5/9/2015 P 11/21/2015 Bp Gladstone Bailey Adams III.

HAUGAARD, William P (Chi) 1365 Twin Rivers Blvd, Oviedo FL 32766 **Died 7/30/2016** B Brooklyn NY 1929 s William & Bess. BA Pr 1951; STB GTS 1954; ThD GTS 1962. D 5/8/1954 Bp Wallace J Gardner P 11/1/1954 Bp Russell S Hubbard. m 5/24/1976 Luisa Collazo. Ret 1995-2016; Vice-Pres/Assoc Dn Bexley Seabury Fed Chicago IL 1984-1994; Epis Sem Of The Caribbean Carolina PR 1963-1977; Serv Ch In Puerto Rico 1962-1976; Vic S Jas Epis Ch Brewster WA 1954-1958; Vic Trsfg Twisp WA 1954-1958; Fell & Tutor The GTS New York NY 1958-1962. Auth, "Reformation In Engl," *Tudor Engl: An Encyclopedia*, 2001; Auth, "arts On Miles Coverdale And Richard Hooker," *Hist Handbook Of Major Biblic Interpreters*, 1998; Auth, "Introductions And Commentaries To The Preface And Books Ii, Iii,, The Folger Libr Ed Of The Works Of Richard Hooker," *Vi*, 1993; Auth, "The [Hooker-Travers] Controversy," *The Folger Libr Ed Of The Works Of Richard Hooker*, 1990; Auth, "The Scriptural Hermeneutics Of Richard Hooker: Hist Conte," *This Sacr Hist: Angl Reflections For Jn Booty*, 1990; Auth, "The Bible In The Angl Reformation," *Anglicanism And The Bible*, 1984; Auth, "The Continental Reformation," *A Faithful Ch: Issues In The Hist Of Catechesis*, 1981; Auth, "Eliz & The Engl Reformation," Cambridge Univesity Press, 1968. HSEC 1962. The Powel Mills Dawley Memi Lecture GTS 1990; ECF Fllshp ECF 1966; Rockefeller Fndt Rockefeller Doctoral Fllshp In Rel 1960; Phi Beta Kappa Pr 1951; The Daily Princetonian Awd Pr Sudent Govt 1950.

HAUGEN, Alice Bordwell Fulton (Ia) 1483 Grand Ave, Iowa City IA 52246 **P-in-c S Paul's Ch Durant IA 2011-; Assoc P Trin Ch Iowa City IA 2005-** B Nyack NY 1952 d Paul & Charlotte. BS Br 1973; PhD Br 1977. D 4/30/2005 P 1/14/2006 Bp Alan Scarfe. m 12/26/2002 Thomas Haugen c 2. Asst Gr Ch Cedar Rapids IA 2006-2014. alice.haugen@gmail.com

HAUGH, William Walter (Okla) 10126 S Kraft Dr, Vail AZ 85641 **Died 1/21/2016** B Bethlehem PA 1934 s John & Emilie. BA U of Arizona 1958; BFT Amer Inst Frgn Trade 1960; MDiv Epis TS of the SW 1981. D 6/13/1981 Bp William Jackson Cox P 5/1/1982 Bp Gerald Nicholas Mcallister. m 6/4/1959 Nancy Jane Haugh c 2. Chr The King Ch Tucson AZ 2002-2003; R S Lk's Ch Chickasha OK 1985-1992; Cn S Paul's Cathd Oklahoma City OK 1981-1985.

HAUGHN, Terry Lee (WMich) 111 W Brighton St, Plainwell MI 49080 **Assoc P St. Tim Epis Ch Richland MI 2016-; R S Steph's Epis Ch Plainwell MI 2004-, 2001-2013** B Jackson MI 1946 s Charles & Anna. AA Jackson Cmnty Coll Jackson MI 1972; Cert Whitaker TS 1987; LTh VTS 1991. D 6/27/1987 Bp H Coleman Mcgehee Jr P 5/18/1991 Bp R aymond Stewart Wood Jr. m 1/29/1966 Karen Aileen Goller c 2. R Epis Ch Of The Gd Shpd Allegan MI 1992-2000; Asst R Trin Ch Manassas VA 1991-1992; Asst S Chris's Ch Springfield VA 1988-1991; Asst S Ptr's Ch Tecumseh MI 1987-1988.

HAUSER, NancyTayler (Pa) Episcopal Church of the Advent, 201 Crestline Dr, Kennett Square PA 19348 **R The Epis Ch Of The Adv Kennet Sq PA 2017-, D 2005-2017** B Syracuse NY 1956 d Bruce & Janet. BS SUNY 1979; MS SUNY 1981; MDiv Luth TS 2005. D 6/4/2005 Bp Charles Ellsworth Bennison Jr P 6/15/2013 Bp Clifton Daniel III. m 8/4/1979 Edwin Paul Hauser c 4.

HAUTTECOEUR, Mario Alberto (ECR) 95 Stillbreeze Ln, Watsonville CA 95076 **St Paul's/San Pablo Epis Ch Salinas CA 2014-; Dio El Camino Real Salinas CA 2004-** B Cuba 1951 Rec 9/17/2003 Bp Richard Lester Shimpfky. El Cristo Rey Seaside CA 2004-2013.

HAVENS, Helen Markley Morris (Tex) 2401 Dryden Rd, Houston TX 77030 B Oak Bluffs MA 1935 d Walter & Grace. BA Rice U 1957; MA Indiana U 1960; MDiv EDS 1975. D 4/28/1976 P 4/1/1977 Bp Richard Mitchell Trelease Jr. m 6/1/1957 Adrian Havens. R S Steph's Epis Ch Houston TX 1981-2004; Asst S Fran Ch Houston TX 1976-1981. Cntr For Progressive Chr; EWC, Associated Parishes, Sw Ntwk, Womens Ministers, EWHP, Girls Club Of Houston; Integrity Inc Tx Faith Ntwk Claremont Consult. Outstanding Wmn In Rel; Natl Fell Amer Ldrshp Forum.

HAVERKAMP, Heidi R (Chi) 365 Rolfe Rd, Dekalb IL 60115 B Chicago IL 1976 d Larry & Wenche. B.A. The Coll of Wooster; MDiv U Chi DS 2006; Cert Ang Stud SWTS 2007. D 6/2/2007 Bp Bill Persell P 12/15/2007 Bp Victor Alfonso Scantlebury. m 8/30/2008 Adam Michael Frieberg. Assoc S Chrys's Ch Chicago IL 2016-2017; Vic Ch Of S Ben Bolingbrook IL 2007-2016; Mem, COM Dio Chicago Chicago IL 2011-2015, Mem, Bp Search Com 2006-2010. Auth, "Take and eat? When Ch members prefer just a blessing," *The Chr Century*, The Chr Century, 2016; Auth, "The Mosque Next Door: Getting to know our Muslim neighbors," *The Chr Century*, The Chr Century, 2015; Auth, "Living By The Word," *The Chr Century*, The Chr Century, 2014. Benedictine Oblates of H Wisdom Monstry 2014. revhhaverkamp@gmail.com

HAVERLY, Tom P. (NJ) Saint Andrew's Episcopal Church, 419 South St, New Providence NJ 07974 **P-in-c S Andr's Epis Ch New Providence NJ 2013-; Adj Prof Luth TS at Chicago 2009-; Vstng Prof of Bible S Paul TS Kansas City MO 2005-** B Chicago IL 1953 s Charles & Ruth. BA Olivet Nazarene U 1974; MDiv Nazarene TS 1978; PhD U of Edinburgh Gb 1983; MLS Syr 1993. D 6/17/1995 P 1/22/1996 Bp David Bruce Joslin. m 8/8/2001 Christine Wenderoth c 2. Int R Trin Epis Ch Oshkosh WI 2011-2013; Int R Ch Of Our Sav Elmhurst IL 2009-2011; Long-term supply Mssh-S Barth Epis Ch Chicago IL 2008-2009; Adj Prof Loyola U Chi Chicago IL 2006-2009; Sr Lectr Meadville Lombard TS Chicago IL 2006-2008; P in Charge S Paul's Epis Ch Stafford NY 1998-2004; Par Assoc S Lk And S Simon Cyrene Rochester NY 1996-1999; Libr & Adj Fac In NT Colgate-Rochester Crozier DS 1994-2005; Assoc Prof Of Rel Estrn Nazarene Coll Quincy MA 1983-1992. Auth, "You Will Know Them by Their Fruits," *Currents in Theol and Mssn*, Luth TS at Chicago, 2008; Auth, "Info Overloaded: Info Literacy, the Libr and the Sem Curric," *A.T.L.A. Proceedings*, Amer Theol Libr Assn, 2005; Auth, "Cataloging Q(s): a Critical Revs of the Quest for Q and Its Literary Hist," *A.T.L.A. Proceedings*, Amer Theol Libr Assn, 1996. Amer Theol Libr Assn 1992-2008; SBL 1980.

HAWES III, Charles M (NC) 6 Fountain View Cir Apt C, Greensboro NC 27405 B Chicago IL 1938 s Charles & Minnie. BA Trin Hartford CT 1961; MDiv EDS 1964. D 6/6/1964 P 12/1/1964 Bp Horace W B Donegan. m 5/6/2006 Faith Steverman c 1. Dio No Carolina Raleigh NC 1984-2006; Chapl S Mary's Hse Epis/Angl Campus Greensboro NC 1984-2006; R S Paul's Epis Ch Smithfield NC 1975-1978; Assoc Gr Ch Grand Rapids MI 1973-1975; Vic S Paul's Ch Canaan VT 1971-1973; S Steph's Epis Mssn Colebrook NH 1971-1973; Serv Ch In Can 1970-1973; Headmaster S Dunst's Sch St Croix VI 1966-1969; Cur S Paul's Ch Rochester NY 1964-1966. Eugene Rogers, "Mar & Idolatry," *Theol & Sxlty*, Blackwell, 2002; Ellis Gladwin, "As One P Sees

St. Croix Today," *Living in the Changing Caribbean*, MacMillan, 1970. St. Jn's Soc, E.D.S. 2006.

HAWES, Peter Wortham (USC) 32 Locust Ln, Tryon NC 28782 B Chicago IL 1941 s Charles & Mimi. BA U NC 1963; MDiv Sewanee: The U So, TS 1978. D 6/17/1978 Bp Thomas Augustus Fraser Jr P 5/6/1979 Bp George Mosley Murray. m 6/4/1966 Anna Henry c 3. R Ch Of The Resurr Greenwood SC 2001-2006; R S Geo's Ch Germantown TN 1986-2001; R S Paul's Ch Selma AL 1981-1986; Asst Chr Epis Ch Pensacola FL 1978-1981. R Emer St. Geo's Ch Germantown TN 2011; Faithful Alum Awd TS Sewanee 2000.

HAWKES, Daphne (NJ) 50 Patton Ave, Princeton NJ 08540 B Paris FR 1938 d Robert & Lorraine. BS Penn 1960; MDiv PrTS 1975; Bryn-Sch of Soc Wk 1985. D 4/26/1975 P 1/29/1977 Bp Albert Wiencke Van Duzer. c 4. Assoc Trin Ch Princeton NJ 2000, Asst 1977-1980, D 1975-1977; Vic S Andr's Ch Trenton NJ 1998-2001; P-in-c S Mich's Ch Trenton NJ 1995-1996, Assoc 1981-1994; Chapl Groton Sch Groton MA 1990-1993; Mem Sccm 1988-1990; Assoc S Matt's Ch Pennington NJ 1983-1986. Auth, "Wmn In The Pastorate"; Auth, "Theol Today".

HAWKINS, Charles Thomas (Miss) 3003 Curran Rd, Louisville KY 40205 **Dio Mississippi Jackson MS 2015-; S Jn's Epis Ch Ocean Sprg MS 2013-** B Guntersville AL 1965 s Billy & Charlene. BA Samford U 1987; MDiv Sthrn Bapt TS 1990; ThM Duke 1991; PhD Sthrn Bapt TS 1995. D 5/31/1998 P 1/9/1999 Bp Ted Gulick Jr. m 8/7/1987 Katherine A Kingren c 2. R S Mk's Epis Ch Louisville KY 2000-2013; Cur S Matt's Epis Ch Louisville KY 1998-2000. Auth, "Beyond Anarchy & Tyranny In Rel Epistemology".

HAWKINS, Deborah (Cal) 280 Country Club Dr., South San Francisco CA 94080 **Vic S Eliz's Epis Ch S San Fran CA 2014-, P-in-c 2010-2014** B San Mateo CA 1954 d Robert & Maureen. BS U CA 1976; MDiv CDSP 2009. D 6/13/2009 P 1/12/2010 Bp Barry Leigh Beisner. m 4/15/1978 Daniel W Hawkins c 1. P-in-c S Andr's Epis Ch San Bruno CA 2012-2016; Asst S Matt's Epis Ch Sacramento CA 2009-2010. steandarev@gmail.com

HAWKINS JR, Frank Jay (Tex) 1827 Green Gate Dr, Rosenberg TX 77471 **Chapl Amer Hospice Houston TX 2001-** B Washington DC 1945 s Frank & Phyllis. BA S Marys U San Antonio TX 1968; MA S Marys U San Antonio TX 1972; MDiv VTS 1982; DMin SWTS 2001. D 7/4/1982 P 1/20/1983 Bp Joseph Thomas Heistand. m 9/14/1984 Susan Jean Hawkins c 1. All SS Epis Ch Stafford TX 2002-2003; S Mk's Epis Ch Richmond TX 1994-2002; Chapl S Lk's Epis Hosp 1993-1994; S Lk's Epis Hosp Houston TX 1993-1994; R Iglesia San Mateo Houston TX 1991-1992; Chapl Arizona St Prison 1989-1990; Vic Iglesia Epis De San Pablo Phoenix AZ 1982-1989.

HAWKINS, Gary Altus (WVa) 1803 New Windsor Road, New Windsor MD 21776 B Pauls Valley OK 1943 s Altus & Olive. BA U of Oklahoma 1969; MDiv MidWestern Bapt TS 1973. D 6/21/1994 P 1/18/1995 Bp Martin Gough Townsend. c 2. R Chr Ch Fairmont WV 1999-2003; Vic S Phil's Ch Quantico MD 1997-1999; Vic All SS Epis Ch Delmar DE 1995-1999.

HAWKINS IV, J(Ames) Barney (Md) 3737 Seminary Rd, Alexandria VA 22304 **VP for Instnl Advancement and the Associa VTS Alexandria VA 2000-** B Greenville SC 1949 s James & Jertie. BA Furman U 1970; U of Edinburgh Gb 1972; MDiv Duke DS 1974; PhD Duke 1981. D 6/30/1979 P 5/3/1980 Bp William Gillette Weinhauer. m 5/24/1975 Linda Wofford Hawkins c 1. Imm Ch-On-The-Hill Alexandria VA 2006-2008; R The Ch Of The Redeem Baltimore MD 1995-2000; R Ch Of The Ascen Hickory NC 1981-1995; Trin Epis Ch Asheville NC 1979-1981.

HAWKINS, Jodene (Haw) 203 Kulipuu St, Kihei HI 96753 B Ellensburg WA 1945 d Joseph & Virginia. BA U of Washington 1985; MDiv VTS 1990. D 6/12/1990 P 6/2/1991 Bp Vincent Waydell Warner. m 8/29/1965 Kittredge E Hawkins. R S Eliz's Ch Honolulu HI 2004-2009; Seabury Hall Makawao HI 2002-2003; Non-par Sacr Sojourns for Wmn in H Lands 2001-2004; R St Ptr's Epis Par Seattle WA 1995-2001; Chapl S Geo Of Jerusalem Coll Jerusalem Israel 1994-1996; Int S Nich Ch Tahuya WA 1994-1995; Asst R S Paul's Epis Ch Bremerton WA 1991-1994. Polly Bond Awd ECom 1994.

HAWKINS, Linda Wofford (Va) 4801 Ravensworth Rd, Annandale VA 22003 B Florence SC 1950 d Walter & Ruby. Salem Coll Winston-Salem NC 1970; BA Duke 1972; MDiv Duke DS 1976; ThM Duke 1979. D 10/28/1984 P 11/1/1986 Bp William Gillette Weinhauer. m 5/24/1975 J(Ames) Barney Hawkins c 2. VTS Alexandria VA 2002; R S Barn Ch Annandale VA 2001-2017; Assoc R Ch Of The Gd Shpd Towson MD 1997-2001; Assoc Memi Ch Baltimore MD 1995-1997; P-in-c S Steph's Epis Ch Morganton NC 1992-1995; Ch Of The Epiph Newton NC 1991-1992; Chapl Gr Hosp Morganton NC 1988-1993; The Patterson Sch Lenoir NC 1986-1988.

HAWKINS, Mary Alice (Spok) 560-F Spengler Road Unit F, Richland WA 99354 B Hamilton OH 1931 d Ezekiel & Mary. BS Un Coll Barbourville KY 1952; MA U of Nthrn Colorado 1960. D 11/13/1999 Bp Leigh Allen Wallace Jr. m 11/8/1958 James Harrison Hawkins c 1. D All SS Ch Richland WA 1999-2014. NAAD.

HAWKINS, Penelope Elizabeth (Vt) Po Box 492, North Bennington VT 05257 **D S Ptr's Epis Ch Bennington VT 1992-** B Bennington VT 1941 d Arthur & Ruby. Bennington Coll. D 6/22/1988 Bp Daniel Lee Swenson. m 9/10/1989 Richard Farrara c 2.

HAWKINS, Richard Thurber (Pa) W396 n5918 Meadow Ln, Oconomowoc WI 53066 **P-in-c S Alb's Epis Ch Sussex WI 2004-; Ret 1998-; Chapl NG 1976-** B Walpole MA 1933 s Edward & Harriet. BS USMA 1955; BD EDS 1961. D 6/24/1961 Bp Anson Phelps Stokes Jr P 1/6/1962 Bp Henry W Hobson. m 6/17/1989 Nansi Hawkins c 4. S Clare of Assisi Epis Ch Snoqualmie WA 2001-2004, P-in-c 2001-2004; S Geo Epis Ch Maple Vlly WA 1999-2001, P in charge 1999-2001; Emm Ch Philadelphia PA 1996-1997, Int R; Cathd Ch Of The Nativ Bethlehem PA 1996; Int R H Apos & Medtr 1993-1996; H Apos And Medtr Philadelphia PA 1993-1996, Int R 1993-1996; Chair Bd Chr Memi Mssy 1989-1991; Bd Fam Serv Philadelphia PA 1982-1992; Chair All SS Hosp Springfield PA 1982-1984; Bd Coun Epis Cmnty Serv 1974-1984; S Thos' Ch Whitemarsh Ft Washington PA 1968-1995; R S Thos' Whitemarsh PA 1968-1993; S Mk's Epis Ch Fall River MA 1963-1968, R 1963-1968; The Ch of the Redeem Cincinnati OH 1961-1963, Asst 1961-1963. Auth, "mag arts," 2003. Int Mnstry Ntwk.

HAWKINS, Tom (O) 14900 Mark Twain St, Detroit MI 48227 **Ch Of The Resurr Ecorse MI 2016-** B Kansas City KS 1960 s George & Shirley. BA U of Kansas 1982; MDiv S Meinrad TS 1986; Cert Int Int Mnstry Ntwk 2008. Rec 9/27/1987 as Deacon Bp Richard Frank Grein. m 5/25/2003 Sianee Hawkins c 1. S Geo's Ch Milford MI 2011-2016; R S Mk's Ch Canton OH 2009-2010; S Andr's Epis Ch Livonia MI 2008-2009; S Tim's Ch Detroit MI 1999-2008; Fam Preservation Stafford 1996-1999; Ch of the Ascen Kansas City KS 1989-1999; Serv RC Ch 1982-1986; Dn Dn of Detriot 2007-2009; Dn Dn of McCoskry Area Coun 2003-2006; Mem Dioc Strategic Plnng 2002-2003; Mem Dioc Coun Del 2001-2003; Bd Mem Interdiocesan on Anti-Racism Dioceses W. Missourii/Kansas 1997-1999; Bd Mem Epis Soc Serv Inc. Wichita KS 1989-1996. Ch & City 1990-1996; UBE 2005-2008. Cn Dio Kansas 2008; Chapl Legislature of the St of Kansas 1998.

HAWKINS, William Mills (Ark) D 4/1/2017 Bp Larry Benfield.

HAWLEY, Carter Ricks (Ore) St Thomas Episcopal Church, 1465 Coburg Rd, Eugene OR 97401 B Evanston IL 1964 d James & Patricia. AA MacMurray Coll 1984; BS MacMurray Coll 1985; MA Sthrn Illinois U 1986. D 10/21/2011 Bp Gregory Harold Rickel. m 9/16/1989 John Kent Hawley c 3.

HAWLEY, Christian N (Tex) 800 S Northshore Dr, Knoxville TN 37919 **S Matt's Ch Austin TX 2014-** B Danbury CT 1978 s James & Vanessa. BS U of Notre Dame 2001; MDiv Van 2011; MDiv Van 2011; MAR Epis TS Of The SW 2013; MAR Epis TS of the SW 2013. D 6/15/2013 P 12/22/2013 Bp George Young III. m 11/15/2014 Madeline Shelton Hawley. D Ch Of The Ascen Knoxville TN 2013-2014. chawley@stmattsaustin.org

HAWLEY, Frank Martin (WTex) 4518 Winlock Dr, San Antonio TX 78228 B San Antonio TX 1953 s Alfred & Eva. BS Texas A&M U 1976; MDiv VTS 1984. D 6/30/1984 Bp Scott Field Bailey. m 12/21/1978 Patricia Hawley c 2. Chr Ch Shoshone ID 1984-1985; Epis Ch Of The Gd Shepard Geo W TX 1984-1985; S Mich's Ch Lake Corpus Christi TX 1984-1985.

HAWLEY, Kristen (WA) Christ Church, 3116 O St NW, Washington DC 20007 **Chr Ch Georgetown Washington DC 2013-** B New Hartford NY 1974 d Steven & Virginia. BA Ham 1996; MDiv VTS 2013. D 1/26/2013 P 7/27/2013 Bp Mariann Edgar Budde. m 7/3/1999 Rollin James Hawley c 4.

HAWLEY, Madeline Shelton (Tex) B 1986 BSPH Tul 2009; MDiv Epis TS Of The SW 2015. D 6/20/2015 Bp C Andrew Doyle P 1/6/2016 Bp Dena Arnall Harrison. m 11/15/2014 Christian N Hawley. S Jas Ch Austin TX 2015-2017.

HAWLEY, Oral Robers (Ak) B Kotzebue 1964 s Amos & Louise. D 2/5/2002 Bp Mark Lawrence Macdonald.

HAWS, Howard Eugene (ETenn) 1418 Lonas Dr, Maryville TN 37803 **Ret 1996-** B Knoxville TN 1931 s Henry & Rudy. BS U of Tennessee 1953; BD Candler TS Emory U 1960; U So 1966. D 6/29/1966 Bp William Evan Sanders P 1/25/1967 Bp John Vander Horst. m 10/26/1956 Andra T Haws. S Andr's Ch Maryville TN 1975-1996; R H Trin Ch Memphis TN 1969-1976; P S Thos The Apos Humboldt TN 1966-1969; Serv Methodist Ch 1961-1965.

HAWS, Molly Elizabeth (Cal) Episcopal Church of the Redeemer, 123 Knight Dr, San Rafael CA 94901 **P-in-c Ch Of The Redeem San Rafael CA 2012-** B Norwalk CT 1964 d Ray & Eleen. BA U of Texas 1986; MDiv CDSP 2006; MDiv CDSP 2006. D 6/5/2010 P 12/4/2010 Bp Marc Handley Andrus. Vol Coordntr & Trng Asst Sojourn Chapl at San Francisco Gnrl Hosp 2011-2013. Auth, "'Put Your Finger Here': Resurr and the Construction of the Body," *Theol & Sxlty*, SAGE Pub, 2007. vicar.redeemer@gmail.com

HAWTHORNE, Nanese Arnold (Eas) All Hallows Episcopal Church, 109 W Market St, Snow Hill MD 21863 **EFM Coordntr Dio Delaware Wilmington 2011-** B Newport News VA 1945 d Samuel & Elsie. BS Missouri Vlly Coll 1968; MDiv VTS 2003; Cert Shalem Inst 2014. D 1/18/2003 P 12/4/2003 Bp Wayne Wright. c 2. R All Hallow's Ch Snow Hill MD 2013-2017; R St Lk's Par Ch Hill MD 2006-2012; P-in-c Ch Of Our Sav Jenkintown PA 2003-2006; Mem Stndg Com 2012-2015; Angl Cov Com Dio Easton Easton MD 2011-2012, EFM Coordntr 2011-, COM 2010-2013, Dioc Coun 2009-2012. EPF 2002; Shalem Inst 2012.

HAY, Audrey Leona (NMich) 4955 12th Rd, Escanaba MI 49829 B Escanaba MI 1929 d Edwin & Leona. D 2/21/1993 Bp Thomas Kreider Ray. m 4/19/1952 William Howard Hay c 4.

HAY, Charles (Ga) 1014 Shore Acres Dr, Leesburg FL 34748 **Ret Assoc St Jas Leesburg FL 1999-** B Portland ME 1934 s Roger & Evelyn. BA U of Florida 1956; MDiv Sewanee: The U So, TS 1959; MA Rol 1970. D 6/28/1959 Bp William Francis Moses P 12/28/1959 Bp Henry I Louttit. m 6/6/1964 Dorothy Herlong c 3. Dir Honey Creek Epis Camp & Conf Cntr Waverly G 1990-1998; Conf Cntr Dir Dio Georgia Savannah GA 1990-1997; R S Paul's Epis Ch Jesup GA 1985-1990; R S Thos Epis Ch Thomasville GA 1977-1985; R Calv Ch Americus GA 1970-1977; Asst All SS Ch Of Winter Pk Winter Pk FL 1964-1970; Vic S Edw The Confessor Mt Dora FL 1961-1964; Cur S Paul's Ch Winter Haven FL 1959-1961.

HAY, Daryl (Tex) 2917 Fairfax Dr, Tyler TX 75701 **S Andr's Ch Bryan TX 2013-** B San Antonio TX 1971 s Michael & Annanelle. BA U of Texas 1995; MDiv Epis TS of the SW 2003. D 6/21/2003 Bp Don Adger Wimberly P 12/22/2003 Bp Rayford Baines High Jr. m 12/27/1997 Terri R Hay c 3. R S Jas' Epis Ch La Grange TX 2005-2013; Asst R Chr Epis Ch Tyler TX 2003-2005. rector@standrewsbcs.org

HAY, John Gardner (Spok) 2411 E 35th Ave, Spokane WA 99223 **Assoc Cathd Of S Jn The Evang Spokane WA 2005-; Ret 1991-** B Altoona PA 1925 s Thomas & Jane. BA Wms 1948; Col 1950; UTS 1951; STB EDS 1954. D 6/17/1954 Bp Joseph Thomas Heistand P 12/1/1954 Bp Henry Hean Daniels. m 6/9/1958 Marcella M Hay c 4. Int P S Andr's Ch Spokane WA 2002-2004; Int Minster (6 Parishes) Dio Spokane Spokane WA 1992-2001; Pres - COM Dio Spokane 1985-1988; S Steph's Epis Ch Spokane WA 1968-1990; Pres - Stndg Com Dio Montana 1963-1966; R St Jas Epis Ch Dillon MT 1959-1967; Chr Ch Sheridan MT 1954-1959; S Paul's Ch Virginia City MT 1954-1959; Vic Trin Ch Ennis MT 1954-1959. Auth, *In The W of Ireland 94, 95, 96*; Auth, *Poetry Anthologies: Emily Dickinson Edgar Allan Poe, Edna S Vinc Millay*. Natl Ch - Supervision and Ldrshp Trng (SALT) 1962-1966; Natl Ch - Town and Country Cmsn 1958-1964. johnnhay@home.com

HAY, Lesley J H (Cal) 1100 California St, San Francisco CA 94108 B Cardiff UK 1948 d William & Mary. Yale DS 2006; Westcott Hse Cambridge 2007. Trans 1/19/2010 Bp Andrew Donnan Smith. Gr Ch Madison NJ 2015-2016; Gr Cathd San Francisco CA 2013-2015; Chr Ch Stratford CT 2012-2013; R S Jos's On-The-Mtn Mentone AL 2010-2012; Int Gr And S Ptr's Epis Ch Hamden CT 2008-2010; Asst Chr Ch Bethany CT 2008.

HAYASHI, Koji (Ida) 2282 S Southshore Way, Boise ID 83706 B Engaru cho Hokkaido JP 1935 s Shinzaburo & Sue. BD Tokyo Cntrl TS 1964; Toronto Gnrl Hosp Toronto Can 1967; Queens Mntl Hospita Toronto Can 1968; Wycliffe Coll Can 1968; Zions Reformed Ch Greenville PA 1970; Appalachian Reg Hosp Harlan KY 1972; Menninger Clnc 1976. m 8/4/1963 Marilee Ann Hayashi c 3. Cmsn of Mnstry S Mich's Cathd Boise ID 1974-1992; Dir, Pstr Care Dept S Lk's Reg Med Cntr Boise ID 1973-1992; St Lukes Med Cntr Boise ID 1973-1992; Chapl / Assoc Dir Appalachia Reg Hosp Harlan KY 1972-1973; Serv Angl Comm in Japan 1964-1970; Dio Idaho Boise ID 1974-1977. Auth, "Dvlpmt of a Pstr Care Assn in a Sparsely Populated Area, Coll of Chapl Bulletin," *Spec Ediction on Pstr Care*, Amer Prot Hosp Assn, 1983. ACPE inc. 1973; Collage of Pstr Supervision and Psych Inc. 1998-2008; Coll of Chapl 1972-1992. Diplomate Coll of Pstr Supervision and Psych. Inc 1998; Fell : Coll of Chapl Amer Hosp Chapl's Orgnztn 1983; ACPE Supvsr ACPE. Inc 1982; Actg CPE Supvsr ACPE. Inc 1972; WCC Ecum Schlr WCC 1967; WCC Ecum Schlr WCC 1967.

✠ HAYASHI, The Rt Rev Scott Byron (U) 2649 E. Chalet Circle, Cottonwood Heights UT 84093 **Bp of Utah Dio Utah Salt Lake City UT 2010-** B Tacoma WA 1953 s Mitsuru & Flora. BSW U of Washington 1977; MDiv Harvard DS 1981; Cert CDSP 1984. D 6/2/1984 P 10/16/1984 Bp Leigh Allen Wallace Jr Con 11/6/2010 for U. m 6/6/1981 Amy P O'Donnell c 3. Cn Dio Chicago Chicago IL 2005-2010; R Chr Ch Portola Vlly CA 1998-2005; R Ch Of The Gd Shpd Ogden UT 1989-1998; Vic S Dunst's Epis Ch Grand Coulee WA 1984-1989; S Jn The Bapt Epis Ch Ephrata WA 1984-1989; St Dunstans Ch Electric City WA 1984-1989. shayashi@episcopal-ut.org

HAYCOCK, Randall Hilton (Chi) 935 Dorchester Pl Apt 301, Charlottesville VA 22911 **S Anne's Par Scottsville VA 2013-** B Chicago IL 1953 s George & Ann. MDiv Nash 1982; BA NE Illinois U 1982. D 6/19/1982 Bp Quintin Ebenezer Primo Jr P 12/18/1982 Bp James Winchester Montgomery. m 5/14/1977 Terry Haycock c 1. Int R Gr Ch Keswick VA 2012-2013; Sunday Asst Ch Of The Ascen And S Agnes Washington DC 2008-2012; Chapl Clinician, Walter Reed Army Med Cntr, Washington, DC Pension Fund Mltry New York NY 2008-2011, Site Spprt Chapl, Ft McCoy, WI 2007-2011, Site Spprt Chapl, Ft McCoy, WI 2007-2008, Dep Installation Chapl for Mobilization, Ft MCCoy, WI 2003-2007; Int All SS Ch Wstrn Sprgs IL 2000-2002; R Ch Of The Redeem Elgin IL 1986-2000; Cur Ch Of The H Comf Kenilworth IL 1982-1986. Guest Auth, "The Human Cost of War," *VTS Journ*, VTS, 2011. Assn of Profsnl Chapl 2008. rhhaycock@aol.com

HAYDE, Ronald Edward (SeFla) St Mark the Evangelist, 1750 E Oakland Park Blvd, Oakland Park FL 33334 **S Mk The Evang Ft Lauderdale FL 2012-** B Oceanside NY 1955 s Francis & Julia. MDiv Sem of the Immac Concep 1981; MA U of Notre Dame 1991. Rec 3/21/2012 as Priest Bp Leo Frade.

HAYDEN, Andrea Rose-Marie (NJ) 1002 4th Ave, Asbury Park NJ 07712 **S Nath Ch No Port FL 2016-** B Saint Andrew Jama CA 1958 d George & Icill. Illinois Inst of Tech; BS Chicago St U 1987; MDiv SWTS 1998. D 9/19/1998 Bp Herbert Alcorn Donovan Jr P 7/3/1999 Bp Bill Persell. S Aug's Epis Ch Asbury Pk NJ 2005-2012; S Gabr's Ch Brooklyn NY 2003-2005; Dio Washington Washington DC 2002-2003; S Lk's Ch Washington DC 2002; All Souls Memi Epis Ch Washington DC 1999-2001; Ch Of The H Comf Washington DC 1999; D S Mart's Ch Chicago IL 1998-1999. UBE, EWC.

HAYDEN JR, Daniel Frank (Mass) B 1935 D 6/23/1962 Bp Anson Phelps Stokes Jr P 5/23/1963 Bp William A Lawrence. m 9/19/1959 Leslyn Anderson.

HAYDEN, John Carleton (WA) 3710 26th St Ne, Washington DC 20018 **Angl Chapl S Geo's Ch Washington DC 1994-, Asst 1973-1982** B Bowling Green KY 1933 s Otis & Gladys. BA Wayne 1955; MA U of Detroit Mercy 1962; LTh S Chad Coll Regina SK 1963; PhD How 1972; MDiv The Coll of Emm and S Chad CA 1992. Trans 8/1/1971 as Priest Bp William Foreman Creighton. m 4/8/1972 Jacqueline Hayden c 2. P-in-c S Lk's Ch Washington DC 2010-2011; P-in-c Calv Ch Washington DC 2007; Epis/Angl Mnstry Washington DC 1994-2002; P-in-c S Mich And All Ang Hyattsville MD 1992-1994; Assoc Dn Sewanee U So TS Sewanee TN 1987-1992; Prlmntrn/ Bd Mem UBE 1986-1993; R Ch Of The H Comf Washington DC 1982-1986; Dioc Chapl Bro of S Andr 1979-1980; Adj Prof Ch Hist VTS Alexandria VA 1978-1987; Ed Com, Ch in Hist Ch's Tchg Series 1976-1977; Bd Mem HSEC 1973-1986; P-in-c S Monica's Epis Ch Washington DC 1972-1973; Asst Ch Of The Atone Washington DC 1971-1972; Dioc Coun Mem Dio Washington Washington DC 2004-2010, Interracial T/F 1977-2003, Eccl Appeals Crt 1977-1979, Com on Records and Archv 1974-1979; Bd Mem Kanuga Confererences Inc Hendersonvlle NC 2000-2006; Bd Mem Washington Epis Sch Beth MD 1998-2003; Bd Advisors S Andr's-Sewanee Sch Sewanee TN 1990-1999; Bd Secy S Mary's Sewanee Sewanee TN 1988-1992; Bd Mem Natl Coun Of Ch New York NY 1987-1995; Bd Mem S Pat's Epis Day Sch Washington DC 1982-1986; Serv Angl Ch of Can Toronto ON 1963-1968. -, "Absalom Jones, Mart Luther King Jr, Alexander Crummell," Ch Pub, 2006; "The Ch and the Civil Rts Mvmt: Freedom's Matrix," *Afr Amer and Civil Rts: A Reappraisal*, Associated Pub, 1997; Auth, "The Black Ch And The Civil Rts Mvmt|Amer And Civil Rts:The Black Ch And The Civil Rts Mvmt," *Amer And Civil Rts: A R*, Associated, 1997; -, "From Holly to Turner: Black Bishops in the Amer Succession," *Linkage - DFMS*, 1988; "Afro-Angl Linkages, 1700-1900: Ethiopia Shall Soon Stretch Out her Hands to God," *Journ of Rel Thought*, 1987; "The Co of Wmn Who Bore the Tidings: Black Epis Mssy Teachers, 1865-1877," *Linkage*, 1984; "Jas Theo Holly (1829-1911) First Afro Amer Epis Bp," *Black Apos: Afro-Amer Cler Confron the Twentieth Century*, GK Hall, 1978; -, "Forw Mvmt," *Struggle, Strife and Salvation: The Role of Blacks in the Epis Ch*, 1976; "After the War: The Mssn of the Epis Ch to Blacks, 1865-1877," *Hist mag of the Prot Epis Ch*, 1971. Cmnty of S Mary, Assoc 1992; CBS 1967; GAS 1982; Ord of S Ben, Confracter 1953; Sis of S Jn the Div, P Assoc 1978; UBE 1968. Man of the Year St Geo's Ch 2011; Doctor of Cn Law Emm/S Chad's Coll Saskatoon SK CA 2004; Sesquicentennial Celebration Appreciation H Trin Nashville TN 2002; Distinguished Serv Kanuga Conferences 1992; Absalom Jones Awd UBE 1987.

HAYDEN, John Hart (O) 206 S Oval Dr, Chardon OH 44024 **Assoc S Hubert's Epis Ch Mentor OH 2013-** B Detroit MI 1940 s Carl & Florence. BA U MI 1962; MDiv Ya Berk 1965; STM Yale DS 1974. D 6/29/1965 Bp Richard Stanley Merrill Emrich P 2/1/1966 Bp Chauncie Kilmer Myers. Int S Andr Epis Ch Mentor OH 2006-2007; R S Lk's Epis Ch Chardon OH 1990-2004; R H Fam Epis Ch Midland MI 1984-1990; Assoc Chr Ch Cranbrook Bloomfield Hills MI 1980-1984; Asst S Mich's Ch Grosse Pointe MI 1976-1980; R Ch Of The H Sprt Livonia MI 1973-1976; Vic H Sprt Westland MI 1973-1976; Asst S Lk's Par Darien CT 1969-1973; Asst S Jas Epis Ch Birmingham MI 1965-1969.

HAYDEN JR, Louis Harold (FtW) 7193 Neshoba Cir, Germantown TN 38138 B Memphis TN 1935 s Louis & Clara. BS U of Memphis 1957; MDiv VTS 1964; STM Sewanee: The U So, TS 1976. D 6/22/1964 P 3/18/1965 Bp Thomas H Wright. m 2/15/1957 Marie Lemee Bargas c 2. Int Headmaster St. Nich Epis Sch Chattanooga TN 2004-2005; Int Headmaster St. Fran Epis Sch Houston Texas 2000-2001; Int Headmaster The Hutchison Sch Memphis TN 1999-2000; Int Headmaster St. Nich Epis Sch Chattanooga TN 1998-1999; Headmaster All SS Epis Sch Dio Ft Worth Ft Worth TX 1988-1998; Headmaster Cbury Sch of Florida Cathd Ch Of S Ptr St. Petersburg FL 1976-1988; Headmaster St Steph's Epis Sch Bradenton FL 1971-1976; Chapl S Andr's Sch S Andrews TN 1967-1971; Chapl Marg Hall Sch 1965-1967; Vic S Jn's Ch Versailles KY 1965-1967; P-in-c S Thos' Epis Ch Bath NC 1964-1965; P-in-c Zion Beaufort Cnty NC 1964-1965.

HAYDEN, Robert Stoddard (SVa) 1101 Sixth Ave, Farmville VA 23901 **Ret 1993-** B Camden ME 1928 s Ralph & Ethel. BA Bishops U QC CA 1951; MDiv

H

GTS 1954; MA U NC 1975; PhD U GA 1979. D 4/22/1954 P 11/27/1954 Bp Oliver L Loring. m 6/26/1954 Jean M Hayden c 2. S Andr's Ch Baskerville VA 2001-2007; Int S Jas Ch Boydton VA 2001-2007; Int Manakin Epis Ch Midlothian VA 1998-2000; Int Epis Ch Of S Paul And S Andr Kenbridge VA 1996-1998; Gibson Memi Crewe VA 1996-1998; R S Jn's Epis Ch Charlotte NC 1967-1973; R S Barth's Ch Nashville TN 1961-1967; Cn Pstr Gr And H Trin Cathd Kansas City MO 1958-1961; All SS Epis Ch Skowhegan ME 1955-1958; Vic S Lk's Ch Farmington ME 1955-1958; Cur Ch Of The Incarn New York NY 1954-1955; Bp Coun Dio Tennessee Nashville TN 1964-1967. Auth, *arts Var Geographic Journ*; Auth, *Geographic Journ*. S.Va. Epis Cler Assn. 1990. NASA-ASEE Fac Fllshp 1986; Warren Nystrom Awd Assn of Amer Geographers 1977.

HAYEK, Hal T (Md) 4 East University Parkway, Baltimore MD 21218 **S Tim's Sch Stevenson MD 2015-** B Cedar Rapids IA 1962 BA Clarke Coll Dubuque IA 1984; MDiv Aquinas Inst of Theol 1991; STM Nash 2000. Rec 6/7/2000 Bp Roger John White. m 5/24/1996 Marianne E Ley c 3. Dn Cathd Of The Incarn Baltimore MD 2009-2015; R S Anne's Ch Winston Salem NC 2002-2009; Asst S Dav's Ch Glenview IL 2000-2001. hayek.mandhal@gmail.com

HAYES III, Christopher Thomas (Va) 1131 Oaklawn Dr, Culpeper VA 22701 B Warrenton VA 1936 s Christopher & Elizabeth. BA VPI 1979; MDiv TESM 1982. D 6/9/1982 Bp David Henry Lewis Jr P 6/4/1983 Bp Robert Bruce Hall. m 12/26/1964 Julie A Hayes c 3. P-in-c Little Fork Epis Ch Rixeyville VA 2003-2007; Bp Comsn On Alcosm 1982-1984; Dn Dio Cntrl New York Liverpool NY 1992-1995, 1991; R S Andr's Epis Ch Syracuse NY 1990-2003; R Ch of the H Sprt Wylie TX 1987-1990; Supply P Dio Dallas Dallas TX 1986-1987; Asst The Epis Ch Of The Resurr Dallas TX 1984-1986; Int S Mk Par Culpeper VA 1983-1984; Asst S Steph's Epis Ch Culpeper VA 1982-1984; Dio Virginia Richmond VA 1982-1984. BroSA 2008; NOEL 1986. ct3njhayes@yahoo.com

HAYES, E Perren (NY) 33165 W Chesapeake St, Lewes DE 19958 **Ret 2002-** B Albany NY 1930 s E Perren & Gladys. BA Un Coll New York NY 1952; STB GTS 1955; Securities Prncpl NASD 1983. D 5/29/1955 P 12/3/1955 Bp David Emrys Richards. m 11/10/2009 Geraldine T Hayes. Dio New York New York NY 2001-2002, Dept of CE 1956-1971; R Ch Of The Incarn Uppr Marlboro MD 1998-2001; R S Thos Par Croom Uppr Marlboro MD 1997-2001; Asst Par of St Monica & St Jas Washington DC 1996; Assoc S Paul's Par Washington DC 1991-1995; Int S Chris's Ch Spartanburg SC 1985-1986, Asst 1983-1988; Securities Prncpl Edw D. Jones ; Co./ Integrated Resources 1982-1989; Int Ch Of The Resurr Norwich CT 1980; Spec Rep US ChmbrCom 1977-1982; P-in-c Emm Ch Killingworth CT 1973-1979; Non-par 1971-1974; R S Ptr 1965-1971; R S Steph's Ch Woodlawn NY 1960-1965; Asst S Ptr 1958-1960; Asst Ch Of S Jas The Less Scarsdale NY 1956-1958; Cur Trin Ch Albany NY 1955-1956; Int, St. Matt, H Cross and St. Chris Dio Upper So Carolina 1984-1989. Auth, "Our Fr in Heaven"; Auth, "Notes on BCP"; Auth, "Making the People of God"; Auth, "The s God is Incarnate"; Auth, "Making the People of God"; Auth, "The s God is Incarnate"; Auth, "Our Fr in Heaven"; Auth, "Notes on BCP"; Auth, "A Sprtlty For Now"; Auth, "Three Retreats"; Auth, "The Old Way". CCU, NY Metro Branch 1956-1971; OHC 1946. The Hoyt L. Hickman Awd Bangor TS 2010; Pres Cath Cler UnionNYMetro Branch 1964.

HAYES, John Michael (Md) 217 N Carey St, Baltimore MD 21223 B Brooklyn NY 1949 s John & Rosemary. BA Cath U 1971; MA Cath U 1972; PhD Cath U 1977; Angl Stds Nash 2014; MA St Mary's Sem 2014. D 1/10/2015 P 6/14/2015 Bp Eugene Taylor Sutton. m 2/15/2009 Karen R Jones c 3.

HAYES, Margaret Leigh (CFla) B Eglin AFB FL 1962 d Jerry & Virginia. D 12/10/2011 Bp John Wadsworth Howe. c 2.

HAYES, Pamela T. (EC) 1004 Bonner Bussells Dr, Southport NC 28461 B 1956 d Craig & Joanne. D 5/22/2016 Bp Robert Stuart Skirving. m 4/29/1995 Robert Elliott Hayes. pam@southport-realty.com

HAYES, Valerie Jean (Va) 543 Beulah Rd NE, Vienna VA 22180 **Ch Of The H Comf Vienna VA 2013-; D Assoc. All SS Ch Alexandria VA 2009-; Chapl Res Geo Hosp 2009-** B Madison WI 1965 d Richard & Judith. BBA U GA 1987; MEd U GA 1989; MDiv VTS 2009. D 6/13/2009 Bp Herman Hollerith IV P 12/11/2010 Bp Shannon Sherwood Johnston. m 7/3/2014 James W Wolfe c 2.

HAYES JR, Walter LeRoy (SanD) 3663 Princeton Ave, San Diego CA 92117 **Died 12/27/2016** B Swainsboro GA 1936 s Walter & Margaret. BS U GA 1960; MDiv GTS 1971. D 9/11/1971 P 3/18/1972 Bp Francis E I Bloy. Asst S Alb's Epis Ch El Cajon CA 1990; Non-par 1987-1990; S Eliz's Epis Ch San Diego CA 1973-1985; Cur Chr Ch Coronado CA 1971-1973; Ret 2016.

HAYES-MARTIN, Gianetta Marie (Cal) 2650 Sand Hill Rd, Menlo Park CA 94025 **R S Bede's Epis Ch Menlo Pk CA 2013-** B Charlotte NC 1977 d James & Claire. BA Xavier U 1999; MA Van 2001; PhD Van 2004; MDiv CDSP 2010. D 6/5/2010 Bp Mark Hollingsworth Jr P 4/9/2011 Bp Marc Handley Andrus. m 8/3/2007 Melville Knox Martin. Assoc R S Matt's Epis Ch San Mateo CA 2010-2013; Cmncatn Dir S Paul's Epis Ch Cleveland OH 2004-2007. gia@stbedesmenlopark.org

HAYMAN, Robert Fleming (Oly) 1102 E Boston St, Seattle WA 98102 **Ret Ret 1992-; Cn of hon St Jn's Cathd Sligo Ireland 1989-** B Kittanning PA 1931 s Firman & Catharine. BA Pr 1953; MDiv GTS 1956. D 4/28/1956 P 10/27/1956 Bp Alfred L Banyard. m 9/8/1962 Sarah P Hayman c 2. Asst S Thos Epis Ch Medina WA 2000-2003; Serv Ch of Ireland 1988-1992; R Drumcliffe Par Cnty Sligo Ireland 1988-1992; R S Lk's Ch San Francisco CA 1983-1988; Archd Dio Olympia Seattle 1977-1983; R S Jn's Ch Kirkland WA 1958-1977; Asst Min S Geo's-By-The-River Rumson NJ 1956-1958. Auth, "Var arts," *Living Ch*. Fell Coll of Preachers 1982; A.A. (Hon) Bellevue Cmnty Coll, Bellevue, WA 1973.

HAYNES, Alice (USC) 3136 Cimarron Trl, West Columbia SC 29170 B Boston MA 1948 d Winfield & Lois. AA St Marys Coll Raleigh NC 1968; BA U of So Carolina 1970; Luth Theol Sthrn Sem 1993; MDiv Sewanee: The U So, TS 1995. D 8/21/2004 P 2/26/2005 Bp Neff Powell. c 3. Chapl York Place York SC 2011-2013; Vic S Mths Ch Rock Hill SC 2006-2011; Int Assoc R Ch Of The Adv Spartanburg SC 2005-2006; P S Jn's Ch Lynchburg VA 2005, D 2004-2005; Campus Mssnr for Cbury Randolph Macon Wmn's Coll Lynchburg VA 2001-2005; Res Chapl SC Dept of Mntl Hlth Columbia SC 1998-2000; Dir of Chr Ed and Yth Mnstrs Ch Of The Adv Nashville TN 1997-1998. SCHC - Soc of Comp of the H Cross 2005.

HAYNES, Argola Electa (Los) 1979 Newport Ave, Pasadena CA 91103 B San Bernardino CA 1940 d T A & Ruth. BA Pasadena Coll 1962; MEd USI U 1989; MDiv CDSP 1998. D 6/15/1998 Bp Chester Lovelle Talton P 5/13/1999 Bp Frederick Houk Borsch. c 1. P-in-c Chr The Gd Shpd Par Los Angeles CA 2008-2010; D Epis Ch Of The Adv Los Angeles CA 2000-2001; Asst S Bede's Epis Ch Los Angeles CA 1998-2007. Auth, "Pryr," *Wmn Uncommon Prayers*, Morehouse Pub, 2000. Delta Kappa Gamma 1980; Delta Sigma Theta Sorority 1973; Phi Delta Kappa 1975-1999.

HAYNES, Elizabeth Stephenson (Be) 621 Prices Dr, Cresco PA 18326 B Catavi BO 1939 d Thoris & Marjorie. Our Lady of Lourds BO 1962; Gr Downs 1963; Cert GTS 1991. D 6/14/1997 P 12/12/1997 Bp Paul Victor Marshall. m 12/14/1963 William Haynes c 3. Trin Epis Ch Mt Pocono PA 2011; R Chr Ch Stroudsburg PA 2001-2010; Int Gr Epis Ch Allentown PA 1999-2000; Trin Ch Easton PA 1999.

HAYNES, Frank James (EMich) 2518 Woodstock Dr, Port Huron MI 48060 **R Chr Ch Port Huron MI 1966-** B Ann Arbor MI 1935 s Frank & Effie. BA U of Wstrn Ontario CA 1958; BTh Hur CA 1961. D 6/29/1961 Bp Archie H Crowley P 3/1/1962 Bp Robert Lionne DeWitt. m 6/18/1960 Yolanda Mary Haynes c 2. Asst Min Chr Ch Detroit MI 1963-1966; Vic Our Sav Detroit MI 1961-1963; Asst S Matt's And S Jos's Detroit MI 1961-1963.

HAYNES, John Connor (NJ) 45 W Broad St, Burlington NJ 08016 **R S Mary's Ch Burlington NJ 1996-** B Decatur IL 1959 s Harrington & Janet. BA Illinois Coll 1980; MDiv Nash 1986. D 6/14/1986 P 12/1/1986 Bp Donald Maynard Hultstrand. m 4/18/2015 Christy Lynn Haynes c 2. R All SS Ch Morton IL 1986-1995. SSC. frchaynes@gmail.com

HAYNES, Kendall Thomas (Oly) PO Box 6906, Tacoma WA 98417 **P-in-c S Matt Ch Tacoma WA 2012-** B Portland OR 1975 s Thomas & Elisabeth. BA Willamette U 1998; MDiv GTS 2005. D 6/18/2005 Bp Bill Persell P 12/21/2005 Bp Johncy Itty. m 5/22/2014 Elizabeth Ann Haynes c 3. Assoc S Andr's Epis Ch Tacoma WA 2011-2013; R S Mary's Ch Lakewood WA 2008-2011; Assoc Ch Of The H Comf Kenilworth IL 2005-2008; Dioc Coun Mem Dio Olympia Seattle 2013-2016, Rainier Reg Mnstry Co-Cnvnr 2009-2011; Anti-Racism Cmsn Co-Chair Dio Chicago Chicago IL 2007-2011. Fllshp of St. Alb and St. Sergius 2005.

HAYNES SR, Larry Lee (NY) 34 Point St, New Hamburg NY 12590 B Greenfield OH 1947 s David & Lucy. D 5/30/1992 Bp Richard Frank Grein. m 1/20/1967 Michele Elizabeth Haynes. D Ch Of S Nich On The Hudson New Hamburg NY 1992-2004.

HAYNES, Peter Davis (Los) 4300 Park Newport, Newport Beach CA 92660 B Evanston IL 1946 s Donald & Margaret. BA U CA 1968; STM EDS 1971; MSW U CA 1973. D 3/8/1972 Bp Francis E I Bloy P 7/11/1973 Bp CE Crowther. m 6/30/1985 Frances B Haynes c 1. R S Mich And All Ang Par Corona Dl Mar CA 1988-2017; All Souls Par In Berkeley Berkeley CA 1982-1988; Assoc R S Mk's Par Berkeley CA 1982-1988; URC ESMHE Berkeley Area Interfaith Coun 1975-1988; Berkeley Cbury Fndt Berkeley CA 1973-1988; Chapl Univeristy of California Berkeley 1973-1988; Serv Free Ch 1971-1973; Trst CDSP Berkeley CA 2010-1988; Dn of Orange Cnty Coastal Dnry Dio Los Angeles Los Angeles CA 2002-2017, Wrld Mssn Grp 1992-2008, Prog for Mnstry w Higher Educ 1990-2006. Auth, "Plumbline," *Plumbline*, 1978. ESMHE 1973; GEM 1996. Ph.D. KN 2002. phaynes@stmikescdm.org

HAYNES, Rachel Fowler (NC) Po Box 504, Davidson NC 28036 B Atlanta GA 1939 d Samuel & Wilhelmina. BA Agnes Scott Coll 1961; MDiv Candler TS Emory U 1979; DMin Columbia TS 1996. D 9/22/1979 Bp Charles Judson Child Jr P 6/27/1980 Bp Bennett Jones Sims. c 2. Assoc R S Alb's Ch Davidson NC 1998-2002; Int Chr Ch Charlotte NC 1995-1998; S Mart's Epis Ch Charlotte NC 1989-1995; S Jn's Epis Ch Charlotte NC 1987-1989; Ch Of The Cov Atlanta GA 1984; Asst S Barth's Epis Ch Atlanta GA 1980-1981; Dio Atlanta Atlanta GA 1979-1980; D-In-Trng S Lk's Epis Ch Atlanta GA 1979-1980.

Auth, "In The Image Of God? Wmn In The Newtestament Period & Beyond"; Auth, "Black & Feminist Perspectives". ACPE 1984-1990.

HAYNES, Susan B (NI) 616 Lincolnway East, Mishawaka IN 46544 **R S Paul's Ch Mishawaka IN 2008-; CDI Trnr Dio Nthrn Indiana So Bend IN 2010-, Dep, GC 2012 2010-, Dioc Coun 2008-, Dioc Liturg 2005-, Chair, Ethics Com 2004-** B Tampa FL 1959 d Randolph & Karen. BA U So 1981; MA Middle Tennessee St U 1989; MDiv Van 1993. D 12/21/2004 P 6/24/2005 Bp Edward Stuart Little II. m 6/12/1982 Thomas E Haynes c 2. P-in-c The Cathd Ch of S Jas So Bend IN 2007-2008; P-in-c The Cathd Ch Of S Jas So Bend IN 2006-2008, Assoc 2005-2008.

HAYNES, Thomas E (NI) St. Thomas Episcopal Church, PO Box 421, Plymouth IN 46563 **P-in-c S Thos Epis Ch Plymouth IN 2013-; Chapl The Culver Academies 2000-; Fin Com Dio Nthrn Indiana So Bend IN 2011-** B Cedar Key FL 1960 s John & Ann. BA U So 1981; MST Middle Tennessee St U 1992; Nthrn Indiana TS 2010; DMin VTS 2013. D 6/15/2010 P 1/14/2011 Bp Edward Stuart Little II. m 6/12/1982 Susan B Haynes c 2. Pstr S Eliz's Epis Ch Culver IN 2010-2013.

HAYNES, Warren Edward (LI) 429 E 52nd St Apt 27h, New York NY 10022 **Ret 1998-; Mem Ecum Cmsn Dio New York New York NY 2005-** B Pensacola FL 1932 s James & Mary. BA Birmingham-Sthrn Coll 1952; STM Van 1955; Coll of Preachers 1966. D 6/29/1955 Bp Theodore N Barth P 3/26/1956 Bp John Vander Horst. m 6/28/1979 Mary Haynes. Assoc P Calv - St. Geo's New York NY 2006-2008; Asst Ch Of The Trsfg New York NY 2000-2006; R S Mary's Ch Hampton Bays NY 1986-1998; Ch Of The Incarn New York NY 1983-1984; Supply Wk Dio New York 1981-1985; S Ptr's Ch Morristown NJ 1981-1982; Dn Chr Ch Cathd Houston TX 1977-1980; R Calv Ch Memphis TN 1973-1977; R Chr Ch Epis Savannah GA 1967-1973; R S Andr's Ch Maryville TN 1959-1967; R S Mary's Epis Ch Dyersburg TN 1956-1959; Cur S Steph's Epis Ch Oak Ridge TN 1955-1956.

HAYNIE, Amy Peden (FtW) 771 Lakewood Ct, Highland Village TX 75077 **Trin Epis Ch Ft Worth TX 2016-; P-in-c All SS Ch Wichita Falls TX 2014-; P-in-c Ch Of The Gd Shpd Wichita Falls TX 2014-; P-in-c The Epis Ch of Wichita Falls Wichita Falls TX 2014-; InReach / Recon Coordntr Dio Ft Worth Ft Worth TX 2011-, Yth Coordntr to Prov VII 2010-2013** B Clovis NM 1967 d Gary & Laura. BS Midwestern St U 1991; MDiv SMU Perkins 2009. D 5/25/2011 P 12/10/2011 Bp C Wallis Ohl. m 9/26/1992 David Haynie c 2. S Mart In The Fields Ch Keller TX 2011-2014. amy.haynie@edfw.org

HAYS, Bret (Mass) 48 Middle St, Gloucester MA 01930 **R S Jn's Epis Ch Gloucester MA 2011-** B Washington DC 1981 s Louis & Maude. BA U of Pennsylvania 2004; MDiv VTS 2008. D 6/14/2008 Bp Andrew Donnan Smith P 1/10/2009 Bp Robert John O'Neill. Int The Ch Of Chr The King (Epis) Arvada CO 2011; Cur S Jn's Cathd Denver CO 2008-2011. Auth, "Dual-Use Tech In the Context of the Non-Proliferation Regime," *Hist and Tech*, Taylor & Fran, 2006.

HAYS, Donald Lewis (O) 322 Wendy Ln, Waverly OH 45690 **Died 12/16/2016** B Malcolm NE 1928 s Hobart & Allegra. BA U of Nebraska 1950; STM PDS 1966. D 5/28/1966 Bp William S Thomas P 12/1/1966 Bp Austin Pardue. m 7/3/1951 Barbara Hays c 2. Supply S Ptr's Ch Gallipolis OH 2000-2001, Supply 1997-1999; Ret 1993-2016; R S Paul's Epis Ch Put In Bay OH 1988-1993; Bd Nbrhd Hse Mke 1981-1987; R S Chris's Ch Milwaukee WI 1980-1988; No Hills Yth Mnstry Cmncatns Cmsn 1969-1973; Pgh Dept Csr 1968-1979; Chr Epis Ch No Hills Pittsburgh PA 1966-1980; Rep Intra Ch Broadcasting Cmsn W PA 1966-1971.

HAYS, Joseph Spurgeon (At) 666 E College St, Griffin GA 30224 B Gorden GA 1936 s Joseph & Jewell. BA Merc 1960; BD SE Bapt TS 1963; MDiv SE Bapt TS 1968; DMin VTS 1982. D 10/23/1988 P 2/1/1989 Bp Don Adger Wimberly. c 2. Ch Of The Epiph Atlanta GA 2000-2003; R S Geo's Epis Ch Griffin GA 1992-2003; Ch Of The Gd Shpd Lexington KY 1989-1991; Dio Lexington Lexington 1988-1989; Serv Sthrn Bapt Ch 1963-1976.

HAYS, Lloyd Philip Whistler (Pgh) Po Box 43, Ambridge PA 15003 B Oklahoma City OK 1950 s Miller & Barbara. BFA SMU 1972; MDiv Fuller TS 1977. D 6/11/1983 Bp Arthur Edward Walmsley P 6/14/1984 Bp William Bradford Hastings. m 9/7/1974 Mary Maggard Hays c 2. P-in-c S Dav's Epis Ch Peters Township PA 2008; Assoc Prof TESM Ambridge PA 1991-2006; Exec Dir Rock The Wrld Yth Mssn Allnce Ambridge PA 1989-2010; Assoc R All SS Epis Ch Woodbridge VA 1985-1989; Cur Trin Ch Tariffville CT 1983-1985. Auth, "(Video) Many Crowns: Wrshp In The Loc Ch," *ERM*, 1988; Auth, "(Video) Jesus, Hd Of The Ch," *Epis Radio-Tv Fndt*, 1980.

HAYS, Louis B (Pgh) 505 Kingsberry Cir, Pittsburgh PA 15234 **Pres, Dioc Coun Dio Pittsburgh Pittsburgh PA 2014-, VP, Dioc Coun 2013, Mem, Com on Const and Cn 2008-2014, Chairperson, COM 2008-** B Burbank CA 1945 s Marion & Carolyn. BA U of Redlands 1966; JD U CA 1969; MPH JHU 1994; MDiv VTS 1999. D 6/12/1999 Bp John L Rabb P 12/11/1999 Bp Robert Wilkes Ihloff. c 2. P-in-c S Dav's Epis Ch Peters Township PA 2012-2013; R S Paul's Epis Ch Pittsburgh PA 2007-2017; R S Andr's Ch Madison CT 2001-2007; Asst R S Jas' Par Lothian MD 1999-2001. Auth, "Mssn and Mnstry: Responding to Schism and Econ Downturn," *ATR*, ATR, 2010.

HAYS, Miriam Peggy Wall (Ark) 16 Birchwood Dr., Conway AR 72034 **Died 8/14/2016** B Little Rock AR 1937 d Harry & Verna. BA U of Arkansas 1959; MS U of Arkansas 1976; MDiv Ya Berk 1990; CAS Ya Berk 1990. D 6/23/1990 P 1/18/1991 Bp Herbert Alcorn Donovan Jr. c 3. Ret 2001-2016; P S Ptr's Ch Conway AR 1999-2000, Vic 1990-1998; Dio Arkansas Little Rock AR 1999; P-in-c S Matt's Epis Ch Benton AR 2016.

HAYS-SMITH, Melissa B (SwVa) Christ Episcopal Church, 1101 Franklin Rd SW, Roanoke VA 24016 **Dio SW Virginia Roanoke VA 2017-; Chr Epis Ch Roanoke VA 2007-** B Parkersburg WV 1955 d Samuel & Mary. BS VPI 1977; MSW Virginia Commonwealth U 1982; D Formation Prog-- Dio No Carolina 2007. D 10/20/2007 Bp A(rthur) Heath Light. m 5/25/2017 Howard J Smith c 2.

HAYWARD, Dennis Earl (Vt) 511 Rankinville Rd, Mabou NS B0E1X0 Canada B Newport NH 1944 s Earl & Eleanor. BA Nath Hawthorne Coll 1978; MDiv EDS 1981; Dip U of Wales 2006. D 5/23/1981 Bp Philip Alan Smith P 1/25/1982 Bp Harold Barrett Robinson. m 6/20/2004 Deborah Hayward c 2. Cathd Ch Of S Paul Burlington VT 2005-2007; Dioc Coun Mem of Exec Committe Dio Vermont 2004-2006; Dioc Coun Mem Dio Vermont 2002-2006; R S Lk's Ch S Albans VT 1990-2007; R Ch Of The Ascen Buffalo NY 1984-1990; Cur S Lk's Epis Ch Jamestown NY 1981-1984; Cler Compstn Com Dio Vermont Burlington VT 2002-2005. Auth, "Encounter the 80's," *Radio Programing*, WJTN, 1982. Soc of S Jn the Evang 1981.

HAYWARD, Stephen H (WA) Stephen H Hayward, 154 Mills Point Rd, Brooksville ME 04617 **Cler supply Maine Parishes 2010-** B Cleveland OH 1949 s Joseph & Rosemary. BA Van 1971; MDiv CDSP 1974. D 6/22/1974 P 12/14/1974 Bp George Leslie Cadigan. m 6/29/1974 Kathleen B Blackwood c 3. Int S Jn's Ch Chevy Chase MD 2008-2010; Int Ch Of The Ascen Gaithersburg MD 2007; R S Ptr's Ch Poolesville MD 1982-2006; Vic Trin Epis Ch Kirksville MO 1978-1982; Asst Calv Ch Columbia MO 1975-1978; Cur Emm Epis Ch S Louis MO 1974-1975. WECA 1982.

HAYWORTH, Joseph Allison (NC) 910 Croyden St, High Point NC 27262 B High Point NC 1926 s Charles & Myrtle. BA Duke 1948; BD VTS 1954; MA Col 1964. D 7/15/1954 Bp Richard Henry Baker P 2/1/1955 Bp Edwin A Penick. c 1. Non-par 1997-2003; Int S Matt's Epis Ch Kernersville NC 1996-1997; Int All SS Ch Greensboro NC 1994-1995; Int Chr Ch Albemarle NC 1991-1992; P-in-c S Eliz Epis Ch King NC 1984-1995; Non-par 1968-1984; Asst S Barn Ch Irvington NY 1962-1964; Asst R S Jas Ch Hyde Pk NY 1958-1960; M-in-c S Thos Epis Ch Sanford NC 1954-1958.

HAZEL, Dorothy Massey (USC) 546 Woodland Hills West, Columbia SC 29210 **Cn Dio Upper So Carolina Columbia SC 2005-; Asst to Cn to the Ordnry Epis Dio Upper So Carolina SC 2005-** B Greenville SC 1960 d John & Caroline. Luth Theol Sthrn Sem; BS Winthrop U 1982. D 12/14/2002 Bp Dorsey Henderson. m 2/5/1983 Tony C Hazel c 3. Dn Dioc Sch for Mnstry - Upper So Carolina SC 2004-2005; S Mary's Ch Columbia SC 2002-2005. dhazel@edusc.org

HAZEL, Jim (FtW) 6828 Woodstock Road, Fort Worth TX 76116 **1987-; Pres, Corp of the Dio Dio Ft Worth Ft Worth TX 2009-** B Jennings LA 1948 s Robert & Betty. BS LSU 1970; MDiv Epis TS of the SW 1973; Advncd CPE 1979. D 6/24/1973 P 3/1/1974 Bp Iveson Batchelor Noland. m 8/8/1968 Marileen Hazel c 3. Asst Trin Epis Ch Ft Worth TX 1987, Asst 1974-1978, Asst 1974-1978; Samar Hlth Serv Corvallis OR 1986-1987; Chapl Baylor All SS Med Cntr Ft Worth TX 1979-1986; Chapl All SS Hosp 1979-1985; P Dio Louisiana New Orleans LA 1973-1974.

HAZELETT, Jackson Reiser (Ore) 18989 Ne Marine Dr Slip 4, Portland OR 97230 **Died 6/18/2016** B Salt Lake City UT 1926 s Jackson & Blanche. BA Willamette U 1949; MDiv CDSP 1965. D 6/29/1965 P 1/6/1966 Bp James Walmsley Frederic Carman. m 8/29/2009 Elizabeth Patterson Hazelett c 7. Assoc S Ptr's Ch Litchfield Pk AZ 1996-2010; Assoc S Ptr And Paul Epis Ch Portland OR 1993-1996; Chair Stwdshp Consult Dio Oregon Portland OR 1982-1988, 1981-1984, Stwdshp Consult 1976-1981, 1970-1980; Dn Sunset Convoc 1979-1982; Bd Trst Legacy Gd Samar Hosp Portland OR 1973-1979; Conf Site Dvlpmt Com 1969-1977; Tchr Ce Ore Epis Schs 1969-1977; R S Jas Epis Ch Portland OR 1967-1992; Advsr Dnry Yth Dept C&C 1966-1976; Cur S Mich And All Ang Ch Portland OR 1965-1967. Biblic Archeological Soc, Assn Of S Jn The B. R Emer St. Jas Epis Ch 2006.

HAZELETT, William Howard (CFla) 1666 Parkgate Dr., Kissimmee FL 34746 **Ret 1998-** B Abington PA 1935 s William & Clarissa. BS Tem 1957; MDiv PDS 1960. D 5/14/1960 Bp Joseph Gillespie Armstrong P 11/24/1960 Bp Benjamin M Washburn. P-in-c Chr Ch Ft Meade FL 1998-2010; R Ch of Our Sav Palm Bay FL 1990-1997; R S Mk's Epis Ch Haines City FL 1987-1990; H Nativ Day Sch Panama City FL 1986-1987; H Nativ Epis Ch Panama City FL 1986-1987; Vic Ch Of The Epiph Crestview FL 1985-1986; Vic S Agatha's Epis Ch Defuniak Spgs FL 1985-1986; Cur S Andr's By The Sea Epis Ch Destin FL 1982-1983; R Ch Of The Epiph Newport NH 1970-1982; Asst St Marks Epis Ch Van Nuys CA 1967-1968; Vic Par Of S Jas Ch Keene NH 1963-1966; S Jn's Ch Walpole NH 1963-1966; P-in-c S Ptr Drewsville NH 1963-1966; Cur

S Geo's Par Flushing NY 1961-1963; Cur Cathd Ch Of S Paul Burlington VT 1960-1961.

HAZEN, Albie (Ore) 5944 SE Glen Eagle Way, Stuart FL 34997 B Hancock NY 1951 s Alba & Eva. LTh VTS 2001. D 4/21/2001 P 9/29/2001 Bp Paul Victor Marshall. m 7/31/1997 Susan Marcotte Hazen c 4. Vic S Jas' Epis Ch Coquille OR 2009-2017; Int S Lk's Ch Kearney NE 2006-2007; Int St Georges Ch Leonardtown MD 2004-2006; Int Assoc S Dav's Par Washington DC 2003-2004; Int S Lk's Ch Trin Par Beth MD 2001-2003; Dn Dio Oregon Portland OR 2013-2015.

HAZEN, Susan Marcotte (Be) St John's Episcopal Church, PO Box 246, Bandon OR 97411 B Omaha NE 1950 d Robert & Barbara. BA Cedar Crest Coll 1996; MDiv VTS 2000. D 4/29/2000 Bp Paul Victor Marshall P 11/12/2000 Bp Peter J Lee. m 7/31/1997 Albie Hazen c 2. Int S Jn-By-The-Sea Epis Ch Bandon OR 2009-2012; Dio Oregon Portland OR 2007-2009; Assoc St Georges Ch Leonardtown MD 2005-2006; Assoc Chr Ch Columbia MD 2002-2004; Asst Pohick Epis Ch Lorton VA 2000-2002.

HAZLETT, Brant Vincent (Spr) 600 N Mulberry St # 674, Mount Carmel IL 62863 **R Ch Of S Jn The Bapt Mt Carmel IL 1997-** B Latrobe PA 1951 s Paul & Ethel. Indiana U of Pennsylvania 1971; BA S Marys Sem & U Baltimore 1974; MDiv S Vinc Sem 1978; Cert TESM 1990. Rec 5/29/1990 as Priest Bp Alden Moinet Hathaway. m 7/31/1982 Stephanie Hazlett c 5. R Chr Ch Cape Girardeau MO 1992-1997; R The Ch Of The Adv Jeannette PA 1990-1992; Serv RC Ch 1977-1982. sjtb600@netzero.net

HEACOCK, Donald Dee (WLa) 3218 Line Ave # 101, Shreveport LA 77104 **Ret 1996-; Dir, H Cross Chld Placement Agcy, Inc Ch Of The H Cross Shreveport LA 1983-** B Anthony KS 1934 s Carl & Thelma. ThD Slidell Bapt Sem; BA Washburn U 1956; BD UTS 1959; MSW Barry U 1971; MS Barry U 1971; ThD Slidell Bapt Sem 1995. D 6/29/1964 Bp Richard Stanley Merrill Emrich P 1/6/1965 Bp Chauncie Kilmer Myers. m 9/4/1953 Margaret Ann Heacock c 2. 1969-1973; R Santa Maria Margarita Panama 1966-1969; Vic S Jn's Ch Clinton MI 1963-1966; Serv Evang Untd Bretheran Ch 1954-1963; COM Dio Wstrn Louisiana Alexandria LA 1980-1990; COM Dio Louisiana New Orleans LA 1978-1979.

HEAD JR, Edward Marvin (WLa) 407 Tulane St, Bastrop LA 71220 **P-in-c Chr Ch Bastrop LA 2007-** B Bastrop LA 1942 s Edward & Johnnie. BS NE Louisiana U 1966; MDiv Sewanee: The U So, TS 1986. D 5/31/1986 P 11/30/1986 Bp Willis Ryan Henton. m 9/5/1964 Mary Head c 2. R Ch Of The Redeem Ruston LA 1996-2007; R Ch Of The Ascen Lafayette LA 1988-1996; R S Alb's Epis Ch Monroe LA 1986-1988. Ord Of S Mary.

HEAD, Janice (Colo) D 6/10/2017 Bp Robert John O'Neill.

HEAD, Paul Anthony (CFla) 656 Avenue L, NW, Winter Haven FL 33881 **R S Paul's Ch Winter Haven FL 2011-** B Miami FL 1964 s George & Alice. BS U of No Florida 2003; MDiv Sewanee: The U So, TS 2006. D 6/4/2006 Bp Samuel Johnson Howard P 1/13/2007 Bp Clifton Daniel III. m 7/30/1988 Callie L Head c 2. Assoc R S Paul's Ch Beaufort NC 2006-2011.

HEALD, David Stanley (Me) 8 Pine Ln, Cumberland Foreside ME 04110 **Chapl Hospice of Sthrn Maine 2014-; S Nich Epis Ch Scarborough ME 2011-** B Weymouth MA 1955 s John & Elizabeth. BA Amh 1978; MDiv Harvard DS 1982; CAS GTS 1983. D 5/28/1983 P 12/3/1983 Bp Frederick Barton Wolf. m 12/12/1987 Susan Bradbury Curtis c 2. R S Barth's Epis Ch Yarmouth ME 1991-2006; Vic S Dav's Epis Mssn Pepperell MA 1988-1991; Assoc S Andr's Ch Wellesley MA 1983-1988. Soc For Buddhist Chr Stds; Soc Of S Jn The Evang. stnicksrev@gmail.com

HEALEY, Joseph Patrick (NY) 1045 Cook Rd, Grosse Pointe MI 48236 B Scranton PA 1943 s John & Margaret. BA Pontificia U Gregoriana Rome IT 1965; PHL Pontificia U Gregoriana Rome IT 1966; STB CUA 1970; MA CUA 1971; PhD Harv 1981. Rec 10/1/1983 as Priest Bp Claude Charles Vache. m 9/14/1974 Kathleen Ellen Elizabeth Scaldini c 4. Asst to R S Ptr's Memi Geneva NY 1983-1986; Cur S Agnes' Reading MA 1972-1973; Cur Our Lady Concord MA 1971-1972. Auth/Contrib, "7 arts," *Anchor Bible Dictionary*; Auth, "Kition Tariffs," *Basor*; Auth, "Macabean Revolt," *New Perspectives in Ancient Judaism*; Auth/Contrib, "Sublimation of the Goddess," *Semeia*; Auth, "Bible and Hist," *Wm & Mary Bulletin*. AAR 1980; Cath Biblic Assn 1973; SBL 1975.

HEALY, Catherine Elizabeth (Ore) 79 Denton Rd, Wellesley MA 02482 **S Andr's Ch Wellesley MA 2015-** B Chicago IL 1985 d Michael & Cathy. BA Swarthmore Coll 2007; MDiv Harvard DS 2015. D 6/13/2015 Bp Michael Hanley P 2/27/2016 Bp Alan Gates. m 12/9/2012 Heather Marie Canapary. Yth Dir S Paul's Ch Brookline MA 2012-2016; Other Lay Position Dio Oregon Portland OR 2009.

HEALY, Denise Catherine (SwFla) 1502 Paddock Dr, Plant City FL 33566 **H Innoc Epis Ch Valrico FL 2011-** B Baltimore MD 1954 d Carmen & Mary. Cert Essex Cmnty Coll 1980; BA Goucher Coll 1983; MSW U of Hawaii 1988; Dio Haw Ministers Trng Prog 1989. D 6/29/1991 Bp Rogers Sanders Harris. D St Cathr of Alexandria Epis Ch Temple Terrace FL 2007-2008; D S Ptr's Ch Plant City FL 1991-1993.

HEALY, Linda (Miss) D 6/4/2016 Bp Brian Seage.

HEALY, Ruth Tenney (At) 1403 Oakridge Cir, Decatur GA 30033 **Asst Ch Of The Gd Shpd Covington GA 2009-** B London UK 1929 d Kent & Ruth. BA Smith 1951; MA Col 1958; MDiv Candler TS Emory U 1988; GTS 1991. D 6/8/1991 P 1/1/1992 Bp Frank Kellogg Allan. Asscoiate S Jn's Atlanta GA 2002-2005; Int S Eliz's Epis Ch Dahlonega GA 2000-2002; Ch Of The Epiph Atlanta GA 1997-2001; Chapl Grady Memi Hosp 1991-2000; P H Innoc Ch Atlanta GA 1991-1995. ACPE; SSAP 2006.

HEANEY, David Lloyd (SanD) 690 Oxford St, Chula Vista CA 91911 B Chicago IL 1951 s Lloyd & Mary. Monmouth Coll 1971; BA SUNY 1973; MDiv Yale DS 1976; MA U of San Diego 1993. D 6/19/1976 P 1/1/1977 Bp Robert Claflin Rusack. m 12/19/1998 Lynda M Heaney c 4. Epis Cmnty Serv Natl City CA 1995-1998; R All Souls' Epis Ch San Diego CA 1988-1995; R S Barn Epis Ch Bainbridge Island WA 1983-1987; S Andr's By The Sea Epis Par San Diego CA 1979-1983; Cur S Paul's Epis Ch Tustin CA 1976-1979. Aamft; Ca Assn Mar And Fam Therapists; Natl Soc Fund Raising Exec.

HEARD, Fred (Ore) 1239 Wigh St SE, Salem OR 97302 B Prineville OR 1940 s Darrell & Wilma. BS Sthrn Oregon U 1963; MS Sthrn Oregon U 1968; MDiv CDSP 2003. D 6/21/2003 Bp Robert Louis Ladehoff P 12/6/2003 Bp Johncy Itty. m 6/11/1966 Adair E Flann c 3. R S Paul's Ch Cambria CA 2009-2012; Assoc R Trin Par Menlo Pk CA 2003-2008.

HEARD, Thomas (CGC) **R S Jn's Epis Ch Mobile AL 2007-; Strng Com Mem Sprg Hill Coll/Trialogue of Mobile 2013-; COM Dio Cntrl Gulf Coast Pensacola FL 2012-, D Sch Coordntr 2012-, Ecum Offier for Alabama 2012-, Interfaith Off for Alabama 2012-, COM 2011-, Instr, Sch for Deacons 2009-, Bd Dir of Murray Hse 2008-2012, Fin Cmsn 2008-2011** B Saint Louis MO 1953 s John & Edith. U of Kansas; Cert Dio Missouri/Sch for Mnstry 2003; MDiv GTS 2007. D 12/20/2006 P 6/29/2007 Bp George Wayne Smith. m 12/11/1983 Cheryl L Wierenga c 1. Asst Chr Ch Cathd S Louis MO 2007; D Ch Of S Mary The Vrgn New York NY 2006-2007. Soc of Cath Priests 2011. rector@stjohnsmobile.org

HEARD, Victoria R.T. (Dal) 1630 N Garrett Ave, Diocese of Dallas, Dallas TX 75206 **Epis Ch Of The Redeem Irving TX 2016-** B Washington DC 1956 d Ralph & Rose. BA U of Virginia 1978; MDiv VTS 1982. D 4/16/1983 P David Henry Lewis Jr P 3/17/1984 Bp Robert Bruce Hall. m 7/15/1978 David Ridgely c 3. P-in-c The Epis Ch Of The Resurr Dallas TX 2007-2008; Cn for Ch Planting Dio Dallas Dallas TX 2006-2016; VTS Alexandria VA 2006, 2004, 2003, 2001; Mssnr For Ch Planting Dio Virginia Richmond VA 1997-2006; P-in-res S Andr's Epis Ch Arlington VA 1997-2000; Int S Geo's Epis Ch Arlington VA 1995-1997; Cn Asst To Bp ArmdF Europe 1990-1993; P-in-c Epis Cong Vincenza Italy 1990-1992; Mssnr S Dav's Ch Ashburn VA 1989-1990; Asst R Pohick Epis Ch Lorton VA 1988-1989; Assoc R S Jas' Epis Ch Leesburg VA 1987-1988, Asst to R 1983-1986. Auth, "Ch Planting In The Of Dio Va," 1998. vheard@edod.org

HEARD, William (WTex) 415 E Beach St Apt 302, Galveston TX 77550 **Died 6/3/2017** B Dallas TX 1935 s Charles & Nell. BA Texas A&M U 1957; BD Epis TS of the SW 1964. D 6/10/1964 Bp Frederick P Goddard P 6/1/1965 Bp James Milton Richardson. m 9/1/1962 Margot T Heard. Non-par 1980-2017; R Gr Ch Weslaco TX 1975-1980; Vic Ch Of The Gd Samar Dallas TX 1968-1972; Chr Ch Jefferson TX 1965-1968; Vic S Paul's Ch Marshall TX 1965-1968; Asst R S Thos Ch Houston TX 1964-1965. Auth, "Mao'S Legacy-Marxism As A Political Rel".

HEARN, Arnold Withrow (Ark) 232 Pearl St., Marianna AR 72360 **Ret Supply in Arkansas for numerous Cong 1994-** B Suzhou Jiangsu China 1926 s Walter & Olive. BA U of Missouri 1946; MDiv UTS 1949; PhD Col 1961. D 6/12/1965 Bp Oliver L Loring P 3/4/1966 Bp James Milton Richardson. m 3/31/1975 Mary Patricia Hearn. Mssn Chapl S Andr's Epis Ch Cherokee Vill AR 1994-2003; R S Andr's Ch Marianna AR 1987-1993; Dn Cntrl Convoc Dio Arkansas Little Rock AR 1982-1986; Vic S Fran Ch Heber Sprg AR 1979-1987; Non-par USDA Forest Serv Blanchard Sprg Caverns 1974-1979; Assoc Prof Epis TS Of The SW Austin TX 1965-1974; Pstr Methodist Ch 1949-1962. "arts & Revs," 2003. AAR 1970; Soc Of Chr Ethics 1962. Phi Beta Kappa 1946.

HEARN, Roger Daniel (Va) 2201 Foresthill Rd, Alexandria VA 22307 **Chapl S Steph & S Agnes Sch 1989-** B Washington DC 1955 s Roger & Marie. BS Babson Coll 1978; MDiv VTS 1988. D 6/18/1988 P 5/10/1989 Bp Elliott Lorenz Sorge. m 10/7/1989 Deirdre Anne Hearn c 1. St. Steph's And St. Agnes Sch Alexandria VA 1992-2004; St Steph Sch Alexandria VA 1990-1992; Cur S Fran Ch Potomac MD 1988-1989.

HEARNSBERGER, Keith (Ark) D 6/15/2017 Bp Larry Benfield.

HEATH, Claudia H (U) 326 Fairfax Dr, Little Rock AR 72205 **S Mich's Epis Ch Little Rock AR 2001-** B Memphis TN 1944 d James & Chole. BA U of Arkansas 1966; MS U of Arkansas 1990. D 11/3/2001 Bp Larry Maze. m 2/2/2002 Jack Hollis. Dir Soc Mnstry S Dav's Epis Page AZ 2003-2006.

HEATH, Glendon Edward (Mich) 19751 Northbrook Dr, Southfield MI 48076 B San Jose CA 1929 s William & Gladys. BD SFTS 1961; BA San Jose St U 1961; Cert GTS 1962. D 9/23/1962 P 4/1/1963 Bp John S Higgins. m 11/10/1984 Barbara S Heath c 2. S Matt's And S Jos's Detroit MI 1995-1997;

S Steph's Ch Troy MI 1990-1991; S Mich And All Ang Epis Ch Lincoln Pk MI 1988-1990; Dio Michigan Detroit MI 1986-1988; Dio Michigan Detroit MI 1984-1986; S Geo's Epis Ch Warren MI 1982-1983; R Gr Ch Detroit MI 1979-1981; Dio Rhode Island Providence RI 1975-1978; R S Jas Ch The Par Of N Providence RI 1974-1982; R S Mary's Ch Warwick RI 1968-1974; Vic S Mich's Epis Ch Holliston MA 1964-1968; Cur S Mart's Ch Providence RI 1962-1964; Serv Presb Ch 1955-1961. ESCRU 1962-1964.

HEATH, Susan Blackburn (USC) 1115 Marion Street, Columbia SC 29201 B Birmingham AL 1956 d Henry & Gladys. BA Randolph-Macon Coll 1979; BA Randolph-Macon Wmn's Coll 1979; MDiv VTS 1983. D 12/18/1983 P 12/1/1984 Bp William Arthur Beckham. m 11/28/1992 Benjamin R Smith c 1. Dio Upper So Carolina Columbia SC 2016, 2016-; Trin Cathd Columbia SC 2011-2014, Cn 1984-2004; Dir of Vol S Mk's Ch Washington DC 1983-1984. sheath@edusc.org

HEATHCOCK, Deborah Beth (WLa) 404 Ansley Blvd Apt B, Alexandria LA 71303 **St Jas Epis Ch and Sch Alexandria LA 2015-** B Birmingham AL 1953 d James & Genevieve. BA U NC Wilmington 1992; MDiv CDSP 1999. D 6/12/1999 Bp Clifton Daniel III P 6/24/2000 Bp Vincent Waydell Warner. Int R S Mich And All Ang Lake Chas LA 2014-2015; Int Ch Of Our Sav Lakeside AZ 2013-2014; P-in-c S Jn's Epis Ch Gig Harbor WA 2010-2011; Int Gr St Pauls Epis Ch Tucson AZ 2009-2014; Chapl Providence St. Ptr's Med Cntr Olympia WA 2009; Int S Geo Epis Ch Maple Vlly WA 2009; P-in-c S Andr's Epis Ch Tacoma WA 2005-2007; Cluster P Komo Kulshan Cluster Mt Vernon WA 2003-2005; Assoc R S Jn's Epis Ch Olympia WA 1999-2003. rector@ saintjamesonline.org

HEATHCOCK, J Edwin (Mo) 14485 Brittania Dr, Chesterfield MO 63017 B Detroit MI 1937 s James & Laurel. BS Cntrl Michigan U 1966; MDiv Duke DS 1970; ThM Duke 1971; PhD Intl Coll Los Angeles CA 1980. D 1/18/1984 P 5/25/1984 Bp Sam Byron Hulsey. m 12/12/1978 Elizabeth A Porter c 3. S Lk's Hosp Chesterfield MO 1986-2006; Dir of Pstr Care S Lk's Hosp Chesterfield MO 1986-2006; Asst P S Andr's Epis Ch Amarillo TX 1984-1986. Auth, "A Parallel Process Seminar for Use in CPE," *The Journ of Pstr Care & Counslg*, v58, no 3, 2004; Auth, "A Supervisory Effort to Be Unpredictable," *Journ of Supervivion and Trng in Mnstry*, v7, 1996; Auth, "Rel Lang & Pstr Care," *Bulletin of APHA 75*. Amer Assn for Mar and Fam Ther 1975; ACPE 1970; Assn of Profsnl Chapl 1971-2006. Who's Who in the Midwest; Who's Who in Rel.

HEATHMAN, Sharron Gae (WMo) PO Box 307, Lexington MO 64067 B Lexington MO 1939 d John & Ellen. Cntrl Missouri St U; Cntrl Missouri St U; Wenthworth Adult Educ; W Missouri Sch of Mnstry. D 2/7/2009 Bp Barry Howe. m 8/13/1965 Dawson H Heathman c 3.

HEBERT, Francis Noel (NJ) 33 Throckmorton St., Freehold NJ 07728 B New Milford CT 1955 s Jean-Serge & Frances. BA Buc 1977; MLS Wesl 1981; MDiv CDSP 1987. D 6/13/1987 P 12/19/1987 Bp Charles Brinkley Morton. c 2. R S Ptr's Ch Freehold NJ 1995-2012; Vic H Trin Epis Ch Wenonah NJ 1988-1995; Cur Chr Ch Coronado CA 1987-1988.

HECK, John Hathaway (SwVa) 65 Rock Ridge Rd, Callaway VA 24067 **Exec Dir Dio SW Virginia Roanoke VA 1999-, Stndg Com 2015-2018, COM 2013-2017** B Hamilton OH 1959 s David & Ann. BA U So 1981; MDiv VTS 1989. D 1/26/1991 Bp Girault M Jones P 7/25/1991 Bp Robert Poland Atkinson. m 4/26/1997 Delia Rosenblatt Heck c 2. R S Ptr's Epis Ch Callaway VA 1998, R 1998-; Assoc Chr Ch Of The Ascen Paradise Vlly AZ 1991-1998.

HECKEL, Deborah Lee (FdL) Church of the Holy Apostles, 2937 Freedom Rd, Oneida WI 54155 **D Ch Of The H Apos Oneida WI 2005-** B Green Bay, WI 1950 d Leland & Leatrice. NE WI Tech Coll 2001. D 8/27/2005 Bp Russell Edward Jacobus. m 5/19/1984 Charles Heckel c 2.

HECOCK, Georgia Ingalis (Minn) St. Luke's Episcopal Church, P.O. Box 868, Detroit Lakes MN 56502 B Upland CA 1941 d John & Margaret. BA Gri 1964; MA Estrn Michigan U 1968. D 12/8/2007 Bp Daniel Lee Swenson P 9/13/2008 Bp James Louis Jelinek. m 12/23/1967 Richard Douglas Hecock c 2. Loc P S Lk's Ch Detroit Lakes MN 2008-2013.

HECTOR JR, John Robert (WMich) 348 Waltonia Road, Drake CO 80515 **Ret 2006-** B Berkeley CA 1943 s John & Elelya. BA Claremont Mens Coll 1965; ACPE Cov Hosp Chicago IL 1972; MDiv SWTS 1973; DMin SWTS 2003. D 5/12/1973 Bp Quintin Ebenezer Primo Jr P 12/8/1973 Bp James Winchester Montgomery. m 8/24/1974 Barbara J Ashby c 3. P-in-c Trin Epis Ch Mineral Point WI 2006-2015, P-in-c 2006-, Vic 1977-1987; R Gr Epis Ch Of Ludington Ludington MI 1987-2006; S Jas' Epis Ch Of Pentwater Pentwater MI 1987-2006; Dio Milwaukee Milwaukee WI 1986; Trin Epis Ch Platteville WI 1977-1986; Cur Trin Epis Ch Rock Island IL 1975-1976; Cur S Andr's Ch Downers Grove IL 1972-1974. Rural Mnstrs Ntwk 1980. Silver Beaver G.R.Ford Coun, B.S.A. 2001; Paul Harris Awd Rotary Intl 2001. frbobandbarbara@gmail.com

HEDEN, Eileen May (WK) 311 N 4th St, Sterling KS 67579 B Willits CA 1941 d Edwin & Alberta. BA California St U 1975; MS California St U 1983; MDiv CDSP 2001. D 6/30/2001 Bp Robert Louis Ladehoff P 1/20/2002 Bp William Edwin Swing. c 1. DCE Dio Wstrn Kansas Salina KS 2007-2008; Vic H Apos Ch Ellsworth KS 2007; Vic S Mk's Ch Lyons KS 2007; Vic S Thos Ch Gar-

den City KS 2007; Gd Shpd Luth Ch Liberal KS 2004-2007; Pstr Gd Shpd Luth Ch Liberal KS 2004-2007; R S Andr's Epis Ch Liberal KS 2004-2006; Assoc R S Fran Of Assisi Ch Novato CA 2001-2004; Bdgt/Fin Com Mem Dio Wstrn Kansas Hutchinson KS 2005-2008.

HEDGER, John Spencer (Me) 524 Lake Louise Cir Apt 501, Naples FL 34110 **Ret 1993-** B Bay Shore NY 1931 s F Howard & Nathalie. BA U of Delaware 1955; STB Ya Berk 1958. D 4/25/1958 P 10/31/1958 Bp Gordon V Smith. m 8/28/1954 Islay Hedger. Vic St Fran By The Sea Epis Ch Blue Hill ME 1990-1993; Int S Dunst's Ch Ellsworth ME 1988-1989; Chr Epis Ch Eastport ME 1982-1985; Vic S Aidans Ch Machias ME 1981-1985; 1975-1980; R Chr Epis Ch Clinton IA 1968-1975; Chapl Grinnell U Grinnell IA 1965-1968; Vic S Paul's Epis Ch Grinnell IA 1965-1968; Chapl Drake U Des Moines IA 1963-1965; Vic S Mart's Ch Perry IA 1962-1965; Vic S Andr's Ch Clear Lake IA 1958-1962; Exec Coun Dio Iowa Des Moines IA 1964-1968. AAMFT.

HEDGES BSG, David Benedict (Az) 602 N Wilmot Rd, Tucson AZ 85711 **Epis Par Of S Mich And All Ang Tucson AZ 2016-** B Modesto CA 1975 s Tom & Ida. BA San Francisco St U 2002; MDiv SWTS 2005. D 6/4/2005 Bp William Edwin Swing P 12/17/2005 Bp Bill Persell. m 12/17/2010 Carly Flagg c 1. R S Ptr's Epis Ch Sycamore IL 2007-2016; Cur S Mary Epis Ch Crystal Lake IL 2005-2007; Cler Dep to GC Dio Chicago Chicago IL 2015, Bp and Trst 2011-2014; Bd Dir Gr Place Campus Mnstry Dekalb IL 2010-2015.

HEDGES, Merry Helen (Ark) 8201 Hood Rd, Roland AR 72135 **Ret 2003-** B Little Rock AR 1932 d Samuel & Ola. AA Mt Vernon Jr Coll 1953; BD U of Arkansas 1955; Memphis TS 1990; Epis TS of the SW 1992. D 1/22/1993 Bp Herbert Alcorn Donovan Jr. m 7/23/1955 Harold Herbert Hedges. D Chr Epis Ch Little Rock AR 1998-2003; D Trin Cathd Little Rock AR 1994-1998; D S Mich's Epis Ch Little Rock AR 1993-1994. NAAD.

HEDGIS, Sarah Emily (Pa) 5421 Germantown Ave, Philadelphia PA 19144 **Cathd Ch of Our Sav Philadelphia PA 2016-** B Augusta GA 1987 d Nicholas & Deborah. BA Merc 2009; MDiv Emory U 2012; Angl Dplma GTS 2015. D 6/13/2015 P 1/16/2016 Bp Clifton Daniel III. Other Lay Position Dio Pennsylvania Philadelphia PA 2015.

HEDGPETH, Martha Holton (NC) 1412 Providence Rd, Charlotte NC 28207 **Assoc R Chr Ch Charlotte NC 1996-** B Greensboro NC 1953 d James & Martha. BA Smith 1975; MDiv Yale DS 1982. D 6/5/1982 Bp Paul Moore Jr P 2/10/1983 Bp John Bowen Coburn. R Gr Ch Newington CT 1989-1996; Assoc R S Andr's Ch Wellesley MA 1984-1989; Asst Calv and St Geo New York NY 1982-1984; Trst Ya Berk New Haven CT 1990-1996.

HEDIN, Joanne Christine (SD) 104 E Saint Patrick St, Rapid City SD 57701 B Danville PA 1953 d George & Anna. D 4/5/2002 Bp Creighton Leland Robertson. m 4/30/2005 Nyle Eames Hedin. Emm Epis Par Rapid City SD 2002-2005.

HEDLUND, Arnold Melvin (ECR) PO Box 2131, Salinas CA 93902 **P St Paul's/San Pablo Epis Ch Salinas CA 1992-** B Glendale CA 1936 s John & Helga. AA Los Angeles City Coll 1953; BA Bethany Coll 1957; MDiv Luth TS 1962; MA San Jose St U 1971. D 12/7/1992 P 4/28/1993 Bp Richard Lester Shimpfky. m 8/4/1957 Janet Eidem Hibbard. stpaulssalinas@att.net

HEDMAN, James Edward (SwFla) 9719 33rd Ave E, Palmetto FL 34221 **Vic S Mary Magd Bradenton FL 2006-** B St Petersburg FL 1966 BS U of So Florida 1994; MDiv Epis TS of the SW 2004. D 6/12/2004 Bp Rogers Sanders Harris P 12/21/2004 Bp John Bailey Lipscomb. m 7/3/1993 Amanda Baskerville Hedman c 3. Asst P Ch Of The Redeem Sarasota FL 2004-2006.

HEDQUIST, Ann Whitney (Kan) 3205 Sw 33rd Ct, Topeka KS 66614 **D S Phil's Epis Ch Topeka KS 1995-** B Kansas City MO 1938 d John & Georganna. Cert Bereavement FAC; EFM Sewanee: The U So, TS 1990; BA Washburn U 1990. D 5/17/1995 Bp William Edward Smalley. m 1/30/1959 Glenn Hedquist c 3. Dio Kansas Topeka KS 1981-1996. Ord of S Lk.

HEE, Malcolm Keleawe (Haw) 229 Queen Emma Sq, Honolulu HI 96813 B Honolulu HI 1962 s Harvey & Rania. MEd U of Hawaii at Manoa 1987; MEd U of Hawaii at Manoa 1990; PhD U of Hawaii at Manoa 2007; Cert Waiolaihui'ia Dioc P Formation Prog 2015; Cert Waiolaihui'ia P Formation Prog 2015. D 10/23/2015 P 6/25/2016 Bp Robert Leroy Fitzpatrick. m 10/17/1987 Faye Fumi Sato c 2.

HEFFNER, John H (Be) 129 Fairfax Rd, Bryn Mawr PA 19010 B Lebanon PA 1947 s W Howard & Marian. BS Lebanon Vlly Coll 1968; MA Bos 1971; PhD Bos 1976; BA Lebanon Vlly Coll 1987; DAS GTS 2001; MA Lancaster TS 2002. D 10/23/2001 P 10/6/2002 Bp Paul Victor Marshall. c 2. R S Jas Ch Shuykl Haven PA 2001-2012.

HEFFNER, Meredith Tobin (WA) 11815 Seven Locks Rd, Potomac MD 20854 **S Jas Ch Potomac MD 2017-** B Bermuda 1963 d Byron & Sarah. BA Smith 1985; MDiv VTS 2008. D 6/24/2008 P 12/14/2008 Bp Peter J Lee. m 9/13/1987 Douglas Heffner c 3. Assoc R S Mk's Ch Alexandria VA 2008-2017.

HEFFRON, Judith Ann Williams (Los) 4959 Ridgeview St, La Verne CA 91750 B Burbank CA 1941 d Sherrell & Jeanne. BA Westmont Coll 1963; California St U 1968; MDiv Fuller TS 1989. D 6/10/1989 P 1/13/1990 Bp Frederick Houk Borsch. c 1. R H Trin Epis Ch Covina CA 1995-2013, Int 1993-1994; Assoc S Geo's Par La Can CA 1992-1993; Asst St Cross Epis Ch Hermosa Bch CA

1990-1992; Asst To P-in-c S Lk's Epis Ch Monrovia CA 1989-1990; Dir S Mk's Par Glendale CA 1981-1987.

HEFLIN, Tim (Va) St Andrew's Episcopal Church, 6509 Sydenstricker Rd, Burke VA 22015 **R S Andr's Ch Burke VA 2012-** B Jackson MS 1968 s Barney & Marjorie. BA Mississippi Coll 1991; MDiv PrTS 1994; Cert Ang Stud Nash 2008. D 5/31/2008 Bp Charles Edward Jenkins III P 12/6/2008 Bp Michael Smith. m 6/4/2011 Alexis L Heflin. Assoc R Trin Epis Ch Baton Rouge LA 2008-2012.

HEFLING JR, Charles (Mass) 1619 Massachusetts Ave, Cambridge MA 02138 B Dennison OH 1949 s Charles & Martha. BA Harv 1971; BD Harvard DS 1974; ThD Harvard DS 1981; PhD Boston Coll 1982. D 6/8/1974 Bp John Melville Burgess P 12/8/1974 Bp Morris Fairchild Arnold. Ed-In-Chf ATR 2002-2006; Assoc Prof, Systamic Theol Boston Coll Chestnut Hill MA 1988-2013; Asst Prof, SystematicTheology Boston Coll Chestnut Hill MA 1982-1988; Ch Sch Dir Memi Ch Harv 1977-1988; Grad Fell ECF 1977-1980; Assoc Trin Ch Topsfield MA 1976-1977; Cur S Steph's Memi Ch Lynn MA 1974-1976. Ed, "Oxford Guide to BCP," Oxf Press, 2006; Ed, "Sic Et Non: Encountering 'Dominus Iesus,'" Orbis Press, 2002; Auth, "Why Doctrines?," Boston Coll, 2000; Ed, "Our Selves Our Souls & Bodies: Sxlty & Household Of God," Cowley Press, 1996. AAR; Amer Theol Soc; Fllshp S Jn; Soc Of Angl & Luth Theologians. Grad Fllshp ECF 1978.

HEFLING, David (Roch) St. John's Episcopal Church, 183 North Main Street, Canandaigua NY 14424 **Dn Dio Rochester Henrietta 2014-, COM - Peer Mentor co-chair 2012-, Conv Chair 2011-2012, COM 2011-; Trst Wood-lawn Cemetery Canandaigua NY 2013-; R S Jn's Ch Canandaigua NY 2010-; Trst Woodlawn Cemetery Canandaigua NY 2012-; Mem & Schlr-shp subcommittee MLK Jr. Celebration Com Canandaigua 2011-** B Erie PA 1955 s Charles & Martha. BS Kent St U 1980; MA U of Akron 1986; EdS Kent St U 1998; MDiv SWTS 2003. D 6/14/2003 P 1/6/2004 Bp J Clark Grew II. m 2/14/2006 Michael Devere Dudley. R The Par Of S Chrys's Quincy MA 2006-2010; P S Andr's Ch Akron OH 2005; P S Phil's Epis Ch Akron OH 2004-2005; D, P Assoc New Life Epis Ch Uniontown OH 2003-2004; Bd Mem - Barbara C. Harris Camp & Conf Cntr Dio Massachusetts Boston MA 2008-2010. S Julian of Norwich (Oblate) 1994. rector@rochester.rr.com

HEFNER, Judith Ann (WNY) 1307 Ransom Rd, Grand Island NY 14072 **Chr Ch Albion NY 2016-; Dio Wstrn New York Tonawanda NY 2000-** B Buffalo NY 1947 d Francis & Mary. BA SUNY 1969; MS U of Maryland 1971; MDiv VTS 1996. D 6/8/1996 P 9/6/1997 Bp David Charles Bowman. Vic S Matt's Ch Buffalo NY 1999-2016; Dio Cntrl New York Liverpool NY 1997. DOK.

HEFTI, William Joseph (NCal) 24300 Green Valley Rd, Auburn CA 95602 B Minneapolis MN 1942 s Joseph & Dolores. AS Rca Inst of Tech 1970. D 4/13/1985 Bp George Phelps Mellick Belshaw. m 5/30/1970 Linda Joan Holland c 2.

HEGE, Andrew Joseph (Lex) **Ch Of The Gd Shpd Lexington KY 2014-** D 6/21/2014 Bp Anne Hodges-Copple P 1/17/2015 Bp Doug Hahn.

HEGEDUS, Frank M (Los) 12340 Seal Beach Blvd Ste B, Seal Beach CA 90740 **Chapl S Marg's Angl Ch Budapest Hungary 2011-** B Muskegon MI 1948 s Frank & Jennie. BA S Louis U 1971; U of Munich 1973; MA MI SU 1976; DMin Colgate Rochester Crozer DS 1980; DMin CRDS 1980; MBA U of S Thos S Paul MN 1984. Rec 2/1/1987 as Priest Bp Robert Marshall Anderson. Int Epis Ch in Almaden San Jose CA 2009-2010; Int Sts Ptr And Paul Epis Ch El Centro CA 2009; Int S Ptr's Epis Ch Del Mar CA 2008-2009; P-in-c S Alb's Epis Ch El Cajon CA 2005-2007; Int S Jn's Ch Plymouth MI 2004-2005; Int Trin Epis Ch Redlands CA 2002-2003; Asstg P S Wilfrid Of York Epis Ch Huntington Bch CA 2001-2002; P-in-c S Fran Mssn Norwalk CA 1998-1999; Asstg P Trin Epis Ch Orange CA 1997-1998; R Adv Ch Farmington MN 1988-1996; Int Ch Of The H Cross Dundas MN 1988-1990; All SS Ch Northfield MN 1988-1989; R S Paul's On-The-Hill Epis Ch Minneapolis MN 1987-1988; Asst Retreat Dir RC Franciscan Retreat Cntr Prior Lake MN 1979-1980; Asst Pstr H Cross RC Ch Lansing MI 1974-1978; Trst Dio Minnesota Minneapolis MN 1989-1990, Stndg Com 1988-1989. Writer, "Sermons That Wk," Var Sermons, Epis Ch, 2013; Reviewer, "Bk Revs," LivCh, LivCh Fndt, 2008; Writer, "One Prchr's Modest Proposal," Sunday Stwdshp Insert, The Ecum Stwdshp Cntr, 2006; Reviewer, "Bk Revs," LivCh, LivCh Fndt, 2005; Writer, "Stwdshp During Transition," ReVisions, Int Mnstry Ntwk, 2004; Presenter, "The Ret Pstr: An Issue in Int Mnstry," Annual Conf, Int Mnstry Ntwk, 2003; Auth, "Coping w Chronic Pain," Coping w Chronic Pain, Sis Kenny Inst, 1984; Auth, "Beginning Experience Manual," Beginning Experience Manual, Beginning Experience Prog, 1980. Cert Employee Assistance Profsnl 2002; Profsnl Transition Spec 2005; Profsnl in HR 2002. Fulbright Stdt Fulbright Orgnztn 1973; Phi Beta Kappa S Louis U 1973.

HEGG, Camille Sessions (At) 753 College St, Macon GA 31201 B Anniston AL 1945 d Lewe & Diana. BA Auburn U 1967; MDiv Candler TS Emory U 1978. D 6/10/1978 Bp Charles Judson Child Jr P 6/1/1979 Bp Bennett Jones Sims. S Paul's Ch Macon GA 2004-2010; R The Ch Of The Redeem Mobile AL 1996-2004; Assoc R S S Jas Epis Ch Marietta GA 1980-1996; S Dunst's Epis Ch Atlanta GA 1979-1980; Dio Atlanta Atlanta GA 1978-1979. Auth, "Wmn Of The Word". Netwk Of Biblic Storytellers; Sthrn Ord Of Storytellers.

HEGLUND, Janice N (Cal) 84 San Gabriel Dr, Fairfax CA 94930 **D Chr Ch Sausalito CA 2007-** B Portland OR 1936 d Robert & Thelma. OR SU 1957; BA Sch for Deacons 1994. D 6/4/1994 Bp William Edwin Swing. m 1/20/1978 Richard Lee Heglund c 3. D Chr Ch Sausalito CA 2006-2012; D Ch Of Our Sav Mill Vlly CA 1994-2005; Diac Field Ed Ch Of The Nativ San Rafael CA 1992-1994; Sr Wrdn St Johns Epis Ch Ross CA 1980-1992. Auth, "Helping First Responders Withstand Traumatic Experiences," FBI Law Enforcement Bulletin, U.S. Dept. of Justice, 2009; InterviewedAuthor, "Cops Best Friend," Marin Indep Journ, Marin Indep Journ, 2008; Interviewed, "Jan Heglund Story: Police Chapl," Wmn in Ldrshp inm Faith, Roberta Swan, 2003; Auth, "Marin Police Chapl's Time at Ground Zero," Marin Indep Journ, Marin IJ, 2002; Auth, "I am a D and Police Chapl," Mod Profiles of an Ancient Faith, Epis Dio Calif., 2001; Auth, "What You Do And Think Does Matter," Marin Indep Journ, Marin IJ, 1999; Auth, "She Takes Pryr on Patrol," Marin Indep Journ, Marin IJ, 1998. Critical Incident Stress Mgmt 1995; Intl Conf of Police Chapl 1995; Marin Cnty Chapl Assn 1995; Marin THETA Alum 2011; Narin Soroptimist 2011; NAAD 1995; W Coast Post Trauma Retreat 2001. Cler of the Year NAMI 2010; Making A Difference for Wmn Awd Soroptimist Intl 2008; Sr Level Rating Intl Conf of Police Chapl 2006.

HEGNEY, Georgina (CNY) 210 Twin Hills Dr, Syracuse NY 13207 **Gr Epis Ch Utica NY 2016-; Stndg Com Dio Cntrl New York Liverpool NY 2013-, Intake Off 2011-, GC Dep 2010-, Fresh Start Fac 2009-, Dioc Conv Resolutns Com 2008-, COM Mem 2007-** B New York NY 1951 d George & Phyllis. BS SUNY 1973; MDiv Bex Sem 2007. D 6/9/2007 P 12/13/2007 Bp Gladstone Bailey Adams III. m 8/30/2014 Steven R Prievo c 2. St Paul's Syracuse Syracuse NY 2014-2016; R S Jn's Ch Marcellus NY 2007-2014.

HEHR, Randall Keith (SwFla) 3200 McMullen Booth Road, Clearwater FL 33761 **R H Trin Epis Ch In Countryside Clearwater FL 2013-** B Saint Petersburg FL 1952 s Gordon & Mae. BMus Indiana U 1976; MM Other 1980; MAR Yale DS 1980; MM Yale Mus Sch 1980; DMIN VTS 2012. D 6/14/1986 P 5/30/1987 Bp Arthur Edward Walmsley. m 7/30/1977 Pamela J Rogers-Hehr c 2. Vic St Johns Epis Ch Tampa FL 2003-2013; Dn Cathd Ch Of S Ptr St. Petersburg FL 1998-2003, Asst Org/Chrmstr 1970-1973; R Ch Of The Gd Shpd Dunedin FL 1991-1998; Chapl S Paul Epis Sch 1991-1998; Asst R Ch Of The Ascen Clearwater FL 1988-1991; Asst R S Mk's Ch New Canaan CT 1986-1988; Org/Chrmstr & Asst To The R S Matt's Epis Ch Wilton CT 1978-1986; Congrl Dvlpmt Com Dio SW Florida Parrish FL 2011-2012, Dn of Tampa Dnry 2008-2011, Evang Com 1989-2008. rhehr@holytrinityclw.org

HEICHLER, Katherine (WA) Saint Columba's Church, 4201 Albemarle St NW, Washington DC 20016 **S Columba's Ch Washington DC 2016-** B 1958 BFA NYU. D 6/21/2003 P 2/7/2004 Bp Andrew Donnan Smith. P-in-c Epis Ch of Chr the Healer Stamford CT 2007-2016; Cur Chr Ch Bethany CT 2003-2007. kheichler@columba.org

HEIDECKER, Eric Vaughn (Nev) 14645 Rim Rock Dr, Reno NV 89521 B Erie PA 1957 s Jack & Dorothy. BA Geneva Coll 1979; MDiv CDSP 1987. D 10/16/1988 P 5/13/1989 Bp Stewart Clark Zabriskie. P-in-c S Pat's Ch Incline Vlg NV 2012-2016; Navajoland Area Mssn Farmington NM 2010-2011; Dio Nevada Las Vegas 1988-2003.

HEIDEL, Jerry (SwVa) PO Box 779, Hot Springs VA 24445 **S Lk's Ch Hot Sprg VA 2015-** B St Louis MO 1951 s Raymond & Orienjo. BSN Lunchburg Coll 1991; MSN Old Dominion U 1995; MDiv EDS 2003. Trans 2/13/2008 as Priest Bp Thomas C Ely. m 5/26/2001 Marcie Lynn Nicholas c 2. Dio Colorado Denver CO 2013-2015; R S Barn Ch Glenwood Spgs CO 2009-2015; R Calv Ch Underhill VT 2007-2009; Coop Chr Mnstry Burlington VT 2007-2009. Columnist (Bi-weekly), "The View From The Cntr," Mtn Gazette, Brenda Bountin, Mtn Gazette. SSJE 2003.

HEIDMANN, Tina Jeanine (ECR) 98 Kip Dr, Salinas CA 93906 B Maywood CA 1949 d Edmond & Daisy. AA Cabrillo Coll 1971; BS U CA 1990; BA Sch for Deacons 2013. D 10/26/2013 Bp Mary Gray-Reeves. m 6/28/2003 David Donald Heidmann c 2.

HEIDT, James Kevin (CNY) St John's Church, 341 Main St, Oneida NY 13421 **Trin Epis Ch Canastota NY 2013-; Zion Ch Rome NY 2013-; Asst Publ Defender Cnty Of Oneida 1999-** B Suffern NY 1953 s Herbert & Dorothy. BA SUNY 1975; JD Ohio Nthrn U Ada OH 1978. D 7/9/2007 P 12/15/2007 Bp Gladstone Bailey Adams III. m 1/23/1995 Suzanne Heidt c 2. S Jn's Epis Ch Oneida NY 2009-2012; D Gr Epis Ch Utica NY 2007-2010.

HEIGHAM JR, Llewellyn Maitland (Mo) 182 Ameren Way Apt 462, Ballwin MO 63021 B Washington DC 1933 s Llewellyn & Naomi. BA U of Maryland 1956; MDiv S Paul Sem 1963; STM Drew U 1968; ThM PrTS 1971; DMin Sewanee: The U So, TS 1983. D 6/24/1974 P 12/1/1974 Bp Arthur Anton Vogel. m 6/12/1961 Ella Jean Dixon c 3. Dio Missouri S Louis MO 1995-1998, Mem, Stndg Com 1988-1992; Gr Ch S Louis MO 1986-1999; Vic S Barn Moberly MO 1980-1987; S Barn Ch Moberly MO 1980-1986; P-in-c S Mich's Epis Ch Independence MO 1979-1980; Asst Ch Of The Resurr Blue Sprg MO 1974-1979; Serv Methodist Ch 1961-1973; Mem, Bd Trst Sewanee U So TS Sewanee TN 1994-2012. Lichtenberger Soc 1986-2010. Distinguished Grad Awd St Paul TS 1986.

HEIJMEN, Rutger-Jan Spencer (Tex) St Martin's Episcopal Church, 717 Sage Rd, Houston TX 77056 **S Mart's Epis Ch Houston TX 2012**- B Amsterdam NL 1976 s Ton & Hilary. BA UC-Berkeley 1998; MDiv TESM 2009. Trans 7/14/2012 as Priest Bp C Andrew Doyle. m 6/26/1999 Jaime Heijmen c 3.

HEILIGMAN, Sara (Sally) (CNY) 187 Brookside Ave., Amsterdam NY 12010 **P S Jn's Ch Whitesboro NY 2013**- B Muskogee OK 1943 d Robert & Dorothy. BA The Coll of S Rose 1965; MDiv Bex Sem 1999. D 6/5/1999 Bp William George Burrill P 6/24/2000 Bp Jack Marston Mckelvey. m 2/6/1982 Edmund Heiligman c 3. Dio Cntrl New York Liverpool NY 2005-2007; R Gr Epis Ch Cortland NY 2004-2009; R S Jas Ch Pulaski NY 2001-2004; Dio Rochester Henrietta 1999-2001; Epis Tri-Par Mnstry Dansville NY 1999-2001; Cur Trin Par Mnstry 1999-2001. galsal187@gmail.com

HEIN, Charles Gregory (CGC) 533 Woodleaf Ct, Saint Louis MO 63122 **S Jude's Epis Ch Niceville FL 2006-; Beckwith C&C Fairhope AL 1996**- B Huntington WV 1955 s Charles & Mary. BA Marshall U 1977; MDiv Sewanee: The U So, TS 1982. D 6/2/1982 P 6/1/1983 Bp Robert Poland Atkinson. m 7/23/2006 Cindy Anne Hein c 3. Gr Ch S Louis MO 2000-2006; Beckwith C&C Fairhope AL 1996-2000; R S Ptr's Epis Ch Bon Secour AL 1992-1996; H Cross Stateburg Sumter SC 1984-1992; R H Cross Statesburg SC 1984-1992; Asst S Steph's Epis Ch Beckley WV 1982-1984.

HEINE, Mary Anne Rose (La) 15249 Brandon Dr, Ponchatoula LA 70454 **P-in-c S Paul's Ch Woodville MS 2009**- B New Orleans LA 1946 d Harold & Althea. Mallinckrodt Coll 1964; BA U of Dallas 1972; MRE Notre Dame Sem Grad TS 1977; MDiv VTS 1992; DMin SWTS 2005. D 6/13/1992 P 2/2/1993 Bp Charles Farmer Duvall. P-in-c S Mich's Ch Baton Rouge LA 2003-2004; R Par Of The Medtr-Redeem Mccomb MS 2000-2002; Asst R S Ptr's By The Lake Brandon MS 1998-2000; S Jn's Epis Ch Bainbridge GA 1994-1998; S Paul's Epis Ch Daphne AL 1992-1994. Auth, "Var Serv - Pstr Liturg Aids," 1984; Auth, "Var Pieces On Chld'S Liturg," 1977; Auth, "Var Pieces On Chld'S Liturg," 1974.

HEINE JR, William AJ (La) 436 Jefferson Ave., Metaire LA 70005 **R S Augustines Ch Metairie LA 2006**- B New Orleans LA 1964 s William & Linda. BA Rhodes Coll 1986; MDiv SWTS 2003. D 12/28/2002 P 7/5/2003 Bp Charles Edward Jenkins III. m 5/29/2016 Shannon Michelle Payne c 2. Assoc R S Jas Epis Ch Baton Rouge LA 2003-2006.

HEINEMANN, Ann E (Ga) 539 N Westover Blvd Apt 103, Albany GA 31707 **S Fran Ch Camilla GA 2010-; Ret 2009**- B Albany GA 1945 d Charles & Eloise. Dplma All SS Epis Sch 1963; BS Valdosta St U 1968; MEd Georgia St U 1976; MDiv TESM 1983. D 6/2/1984 P 1/8/1985 Bp Alden Moinet Hathaway. Int The Epis Ch Of S Jn And S Mk Albany GA 2008-2009; Int Calv Ch Americus GA 2006-2007; R S Steph's Epis Ch Indianola MS 1997-2005; Asst S Thad Epis Ch Aiken SC 1989-1996; Vic S Mk Pittsburgh PA 1986-1988; Dio Pittsburgh Pittsburgh PA 1984-1986.

HEINRICH, Judith Capstaff (Chi) 853 Oak Hill Rd, Barrington IL 60010 **D S Mich's Ch Barrington IL 2003**- B Van Nuys CA 1939 d Albert & Genevieve. D 2/1/2003 Bp Bill Persell. m 4/25/1958 William Heinrich c 3.

HEISCHMAN, Daniel R (Ct) 20 Park Ave, #9A, New York NY 10016 **Tchr VTS Alexandria VA 2010-; NAES New York NY 2007-; Natl Assoc Of Epis Schools- Epis Ch New York NY 2007**- B Columbus OH 1951 s Robert & Mary. BA Coll of Wooster 1973; BA U of Cambridge 1975; STM Yale DS 1976; MA U of Cambridge 1979; DMin PrTS 1987; Ya Berk 2011. D 5/29/1976 P 11/30/1976 Bp John Mc Gill Krumm. Chapl Trin Chap Hartford CT 2003-2007; Cathd of St Ptr & St Paul Washington DC 1994-2003; Asst S Alb's Par Washington DC 1994-2003; Councill For Rel In Indep Schools 1987-1994; Ch Of The Incarn New York NY 1986-1987; S Ann And The H Trin Brooklyn NY 1982-1984; Chr's Ch Rye NY 1980-1981; Trin Preschool New York NY 1979-1987; Chapl Trin Sch New York NY 1979-1987; S Paul's Ch Englewood NJ 1976-1979. "Gd Influence," *Tchg the Wisdom of Adulthood*, Ch Pub, 2009. NAES, Bd Directorss, 1994-2000; Rea Treas 1992-1996. Phi Beta Kappa. drh@episcopalschools.org

HEISTAND, Virginia (RI) Saint Paul's Church, 55 Main St, North Kingstown RI 02852 **S Paul's Ch N Kingstown RI 2012**- B Richmond VA 1962 d Joseph & Roberta. BA U of Arizona 1983; MDiv VTS 1991. D 6/15/1991 P 12/18/1991 Bp Joseph Thomas Heistand. m 12/10/2004 James S Wilson c 4. R Westover Epis Ch Chas City VA 2000-2012; Chr Ascen Ch Richmond VA 1996-1997; All SS Ch Richmond VA 1993-1996; Asst Ch Of The Gd Shpd Corpus Christi TX 1991-1993.

HEKEL, Dean (Mil) 7017 Colony Dr, Madison WI 53717 B Rowley IA 1938 s Raymond & Hazel. DD/DMIN Chr Bible Coll and Sem; Iowa St U; USNA 1959; BSEE Pur 1964; MSEE Pur 1964; U of Hawaii 1972; U of Wisconsin 1991; MDiv SWTS 1993; CCC Advncd CPE(CPE) 1994. D 4/17/1993 P 5/24/1994 Bp Roger John White. m 11/3/1977 Barbara Ruth English c 3. Chapl Wm S. Middleton VA Hosp Madison WI 2004-2015; Vic Ch Of The Gd Shpd Sun Prairie WI 1999-2004; R S Jn The Div Epis Ch Burlington WI 1994-1998; Chapl Veteran's Admin Hosp Madison WI 1993-2004; Chapl /Meriter Hosp Madison WI 1993-1994; Chr Ch Epis Madison WI 1993-1994. Auth/Ed, *Natl Emergency Procedures & Mltry Cmncatn& Navigational Procedures*, 1978.

HELFERTY, Scott Hanson (Mass) 57 Hillside Ave, Salt Lake City UT 84103 B Minneapolis MN 1947 s John & Iryne. BA S Olaf Coll 1969; MDiv GTS 1973; Westcott Hse Cambridge 1989; Harvard DS/EDS 2000. D 6/2/1973 Bp Hanford Langdon King Jr P 12/8/1973 Bp James Winchester Montgomery. Int S Mary's Ch Provo UT 2004-2006; Bd Incorporators Barbara C Harris Cntr 2002-2003; Co-Chair Suffragen Bp Search Com 2001-2002; Dn Mt Hope/Buzzards Bay Dnry 1996-2003; R Gr Ch New Bedford MA 1994-2003; R S Ptr And Paul Epis Ch Portland OR 1984-1994; Chapl Untd States Naval Reserve 1983-1992; Sr Asst Trin Epis Cathd Portland OR 1979-1984; Asst R S Chrys's Ch Chicago IL 1976-1979; Cur Ch Of The Ascen Chicago IL 1973-1976; Dioc Coun Dio Oregon Portland OR 1981-1984, Chair Radio-TV Com 1980-1983. Consulting Ed, "Early Chrsnty," *Calliope*, 2003.

HELGESON, Gail Michele (Oly) 2909 7th St, Port Townsend WA 98368 B Albany CA 1949 d Willis & Dorothy. BA U CA 1973; VTS 1983; MDiv Ya Berk 1987. D 6/13/1987 Bp Charles Brinkley Morton P 4/29/1988 Bp David Keller Leighton Sr. m 6/19/1971 Marc Helgeson c 2. Vic S Jos And S Jn Ch Lakewood WA 2006-2010; Dio Olympia Seattle 2004-2005; R S Paul's Epis Ch Port Townsend WA 1998-2004; Assoc R S Andr's Ch Jacksonville FL 1994-1996; Contract Chapl US Naval Base - Naples Italy Italy 1993-1994; Assoc R Trin Ch Newport RI 1991-1992; Int S Ptr's By The Sea Narragansett RI 1991; Prot Chapl Bryant Coll Smithfield RI 1989-1992; P-in-c Ch Of The H Trin Tiverton RI 1989-1991; Chapl Res H Cross Hosp Silver Silver Sprg MD 1987-1988; D S Andr's Ch Burke VA 1987-1988.

HELLER, Amy Groves (Dal) 6119 Black Berry Ln, Dallas TX 75248 B Roanoke VA 1967 d Donald & Barbara. BA Colg 1989; MDiv Ya Berk 1994; MDiv Yale DS 1994. D 1/31/2004 P 10/10/2004 Bp James Monte Stanton. m 11/20/1993 Roy Heller c 2. Assoc R The Epis Ch Of The Trsfg Dallas TX 2011-2014; Chapl to the Sch The Par Epis Sch Dallas TX 2005-2011; Assoc R For Adult Educ S Mich And All Ang Ch Dallas TX 2004-2005.

HELLER, Jan C (Oly) 1663 Bungalow Way NE, Poulsbo WA 98370 **Int P S Barn Epis Ch Bainbridge Island WA 2016**- B Altoona PA 1954 s George & Helen. AB The Kings Coll Briarcliff 1977; MDiv PrTS 1981; CAS SWTS 1982; PhD Emory U 1995. D 6/5/1982 P 12/11/1982 Bp Charlie Fuller Mcnutt Jr. m 6/7/1980 Linda Sue Shaffer c 1. Asst S Barn Epis Ch Bainbridge Island WA 1998-2010; S Anne's Epis Ch Atlanta GA 1993-1999; R S Paul's Ch Manheim PA 1985-1988; Cn Cathd Ch Of S Steph Harrisburg PA 1984-1985; Int S Mk's Epis Ch Lewistown PA 1983-1984; Dio Cntrl Pennsylvania Harrisburg PA 1982-1983; Asst Chapl Penn St Coll PA 1982-1983. Ed, "Guide to Profsnl Dvlpmt in Compliance," Aspen Pub Inc., 2001; Auth, "Faithful Living, Faithful Dying," Morehouse Pub, 2000; Ed, "Contingent Future Persons," Kluwer Acad Pub, 1997; Auth, "Human Genome Resrch and the Challenge of Contingent Future Persons," Creighton U Press, 1996.

HELLER, Richard C (WVa) 266 Paw Paw Ln, Saint Marys WV 26170 **Chr Memi Ch Williamstown WV 2010-; P-in-c Gr Ch St Marys WV 2010-; Hospice Chapl Marietta Memi Hosp Marietta OH 2010-; S Ann's Ch N Martinsvlle WV 2010**- B Akron OH 1948 s Newton & Mary. BA Mar 1975; MA Wheeling Jesuit U 1996; MDiv Bex Sem 2003. D 10/26/2002 P 6/21/2003 Bp Herbert Thompson Jr. m 4/5/1986 Lisa Ann Davis-Heller c 2. Ohio Vlly Epis Cluster Williamstown WV 2003-2008; Chapl S Jos's Hosp Parkersburg WV 1996-2010.

HELLMAN, Gary L (NY) 224 W 11th St Apt 2, New York NY 10014 B Miami FL 1944 s Stewart & Gussie. BA U of Texas 1967; MDiv GTS 1973; Cert Blanton-Peale Grad Inst 1978. D 6/10/1973 Bp Archibald Donald Davies P 12/1/1973 Bp Paul Moore Jr. m 6/28/1966 Rebecca Hellman c 1. Asst S Jn's Ch New York NY 1976-1978; Ch Of The H Apos New York NY 1973-1974. AAPC.

HELMAN, Peter Alan (Lex) 131 Edgewood Rd, Middlesboro KY 40965 **S Phil's In The Hills Tucson AZ 2016**- B Knoxville TN 1984 s Rowland & Mary-Alice. BA Jn Br 2008; BA Jn Br 2008; MDiv PrTS 2011; STM Yale DS 2013; STM Yale DS 2013; STM Yale DS 2013. D 6/8/2013 Bp George Edward Councell P 12/7/2013 Bp Doug Hahn. S Mary's Epis Ch Middlesboro KY 2013-2016. Soc of Cath Priests 2010. st.marys.mboro@gmail.com

HELMER, Ben Edward (Ark) 28 Prospect Ave, Eureka Springs AR 72632 B SanduskyOH 1947 s Ben & Marian. BA MI SU 1969; MDiv GTS 1973. D 3/19/1973 P 9/21/1973 Bp Samuel Joseph Wylie. m 6/9/1973 Margaret Jane Coleman c 2. P-in-c S Jas Ch Eureka Spgs AR 2009-2014; Epis Ch Cntr New York NY 1999-2005; Chr Ch Epis Boonville MO 1993-1999; Chr Ch Lexington MO 1993-1999; NE Reg Mnstry Lexington MO 1993-1999; S Mary's Ch Fayette MO 1993-1999; Cn Mssnr S Phil's Ch Trenton MO 1993-1999; Trin Epis Ch Marshall MO 1993-1999; Epis Ch Of The Incarn Salina KS 1989-1991, Vic 1982-1986; New Directions For Ch In Sm Communities Cape Coral FL 1987-1989; Ecec 1986-1991; Vic S Anne's Ch Mcpherson KS 1982-1993; Ascen-On-The-Prairie Epis Ch Colby KS 1981; Dio Wstrn Kansas Hutchinson KS 1980-1993; Secy C-14 1980-1982; R S Paul's Epis Ch Goodland KS 1975-1981; P-in-c Gr Epis Ch Menominee MI 1973-1975. "When the Environ Changes, Ch Changes," *not dertmined*, CPG, March, 2009.

HELMER BSG, Richard Edward (Cal) Church of Our Saviour, 10 Old Mill St, Mill Valley CA 94941 **R Ch Of Our Sav Mill Vlly CA 2006-; Alt Dep to GC Dio California 2016-2018; Secy of HOD Resolutns Revs Com GC 2015-2018** B Marinette WI 1974 s Ben & Margaret. Bradley U 1994; BMus U NC 1997; NWU 1998; MDiv CDSP 2002. D 6/8/2002 Bp Barry Howe P 12/7/2002 Bp William Edwin Swing. m 6/18/2000 Hiroko Fujita c 2. R (Long-term Int) Ch of Our Sav Mill Vlly CA 2006-2007; Vic Chr Epis Ch Sei Ko Kai San Francisco CA 2002-2006; Stndg Com Pres Dio California San Francisco CA 2014-2015, Dep to GC 2013-2016, Stndg Com Secy 2012-2014, Marin Dnry Pres 2010-2011, Alt Dep to GC 2007-2013. BSG 2010; OHC - Assoc 2000. Knights Templar Mnstry Schlrshp Knights Templar 2001; Excellence in Mnstry Schlrshp CDSP 1999. rector@oursaviourmillvalley.org

HELMS III, David Clarke (SO) 1 Marlborough Avenue, Bromsgrove B6O 2PG Great Britain (UK) **Indstrl Chapl Dio Worcester 1988-** B Wilmington DE 1950 s David & Jeane. BA Bos 1972; MDiv Yale DS 1977. D 6/18/1977 Bp William Hawley Clark P 12/18/1977 Bp John S Higgins. m 7/22/1998 Eleanor Mary Bowen. All SS Ch Cincinnati OH 1986-1988; Dio Delaware Wilmington 1983-1986; S Lk's Epis Ch E Greenwich RI 1979-1980; Chr Ch Westerly RI 1977-1978.

HELMUTH, Bradley Mathew (NCal) Holy Trinity Church, 202 High St, Nevada City CA 95959 **H Trin Ch Nevada City CA 2012-** B Lynwood CA 1969 s Gerald & Brenda. BA California St U 1991; MDiv Denver Sem 1998. D 10/13/2012 P 5/18/2013 Bp Barry Leigh Beisner. m 8/6/1994 Amanda Prentice Helmuth c 3.

HELT, Dwight Neil (Okla) 130 Rue de Montserrat, Norman OK 73071 **R S Jn's Ch Norman OK 2003-** B Oklahoma City OK 1953 s Bobby & Lovene. BA Oklahoma St U 1975; MS Oklahoma St U 1983; MDiv Epis TS of the SW 1988. D 6/18/1988 Bp Gerald Nicholas Mcallister P 4/22/1989 Bp Robert Manning Moody. m 5/17/1975 Mary Martha Helt c 2. Instr Cameron U Lawton Oklahoma 2000; R All SS' Epis Ch Duncan OK 1992-2003; Chapl S Steph Epis Sch Austin TX 1989-1992; Chapl S Steph's Epis Sch Austin TX 1989-1992; Cur S Jn's Epis Ch Tulsa OK 1988-1989; Instr Tulsa Jr Coll 1983; Chapl Holland Hall Sch Tulsa Oklahoma 1981-1985; Dir St. Crisp's Sum Camp Seminole Oklahoma 1980-1985; Campus Chapl St. Andr's Epis Ch Stillwater Oklahoma 1979-1981; Rep Oklahoma St U Stillwater Oklahoma 1972-1978; Stndg Com Dio Oklahoma Oklahoma City OK 2010-2013.

HEMENWAY, Henry Jack (Me) 80 Lyme Rd, Apt 250, Hanover NH 03755 **Died 3/3/2016** B Clarence NY 1926 s Frank & Amalia. BA Colg 1950; BD Yale DS 1956. D 6/24/1965 P 10/1/1965 Bp Harvey D Butterfield. m 7/23/1970 Harriet Corning Rawle. Non-par 1968-2016; Asst Cathd Ch Of S Paul Burlington VT 1965-1968; Serv Congrl Ch 1956-1964.

HEMINGSON, Celeste A (NH) 340 Main St # 3229, Hopkinton NH 03229 B Chicago IL 1942 BA Smith 1963; MDiv EDS 2002. D 7/27/2003 Bp Douglas Edwin Theuner P 2/7/2004 Bp Vicky Gene Robinson. All SS Ch Peterborough NH 2013-2014; S Andr's Ch New London NH 2011-2013; S Mk's Ch Ashland NH 2009-2011; Int S Paul's Ch Concord NH 2007-2009; Cur S Thos Ch Hanover NH 2003-2006.

HEMINGWAY, George Thomson (Ore) PO Box 192, Nehalem OR 97131 **Died 11/8/2015** B Corvallis OR 1940 s George & Margaret. BS San Diego St U 1966; MS San Diego St U 1973; DIT ETSBH 1983; DMin Geo Fox Evang Sem 2005; DMin Geo Fox Evang Sem 2005. D 7/16/1984 P 3/25/1985 Bp Charles Brinkley Morton. m 5/25/1968 Jean Ann Hemingway c 1. Acad Advsr, DMin Prog Geo Fox Evang Sem Portland OR 2009-2015; P S Cathr Of Alexandria Epis Ch Nehalem OR 2006-2015; P-in-res St Cathr/Santa Catalina Nehalem OR 2006-2015; Mssnr Dio Oregon Portland OR 2001-2006; P-in-c S Mich's/San Miguel Newberg OR 2001-2006; Int All SS Ch Vista CA 2000-2001; Cn Dio San Diego San Diego CA 1996-2000; Vic La Iglesia Del Espiritu Santo Mssn Lake Elsinore CA 1989-1995; Asst S Dav's Epis Ch San Diego CA 1984-1985; Asst S Matt's Ch Natl City CA 1983-1986. Auth, *Var arts in Sci Journ (Engl and Spanish)*, 1975. Natl Assn for the Self- Supporting Active Mnstry 1985; Oregon Cler Assn 2001; Var Sci societies 1975. Var Sci hon in US and Mex 1984.

HEMMERS, Louis Emanuel (Los) 1634 Crestview Rd, Redlands CA 92374 **Ret 2002-** B Jackson MI 1932 s Louis & Hollis. BA U MI 1958; MDiv SWTS 1962. D 6/18/1962 P 12/1/1962 Bp Edward Clark Turner. m 8/23/1958 Joan S Hemmers c 3. R Trin Epis Ch Redlands CA 1981-2002; R Calv Ch Louisville KY 1974-1981; R S Geo's Ch Belleville IL 1965-1974; Vic Gr Ch Washington KS 1962-1965; S Mk's Ch Blue Rapids KS 1962-1965; Vic S Paul's Ch Marysville KS 1962-1965. Auth, "Seabury Quarterly". R Emer Trin, Redlands, CA 2002; Hon Cn (Cathedrdal Cntr) Dio Los Angeles 1995; Hon Archd (Alton) Dio Springfield (Illinois) 1968.

HEMPHILL, Margaret Ayars (Chi) 53 Loveland Rd, Norwich VT 05055 B San Francisco CA 1931 d David & Margaret. BA NWU 1979; MDiv SWTS 1986. D 6/14/1986 Bp James Winchester Montgomery P 12/13/1986 Bp Frank Tracy Griswold III. Asst R S Thos Ch Hanover NH 2001-2003; Assoc P The Epis Ch Of S Jas The Less Northfield IL 1997-1998. Who'S Who In Amer 2001.

HEMPSTEAD, James Breese (Ind) 512 Woodland Ave, Petoskey MI 49770 **Ret 1998-** B Saginaw MI 1936 s James & Helen. BA Alma Coll 1958; MDiv VTS 1962; Hurley Med Cntr Flint MI 1976; Ldrshp Acad for New Directions 1985. D 6/29/1962 Bp Robert Lionne DeWitt P 2/8/1963 Bp Richard Stanley Merrill Emrich. m 12/26/1959 Susanne Beth Pomeroy c 2. Chapl Chapl to the Ret Westin MI 2007-2008; Sunday Supply P Dio Estrn Michigan Saginaw MI 1999-2014; Sunday Supply P Dio Nthrn Michigan Marquette MI 1999-2014; Sunday Supply P Dio Wstrn Michigan Kalamazoo MI 1999-2014; Dn Grand Traverse Deanry 1979-1984; R S Paul's Epis Ch Evansville IN 1990-1998; Int Gr Ch Holland MI 1990; Dn The Cathd Ch of Chr the King Portage MI 1986-1989; Dn The Par Ch Of Chr The King Kalamazoo MI 1986-1989; P-in-c Ch Of The Nativ Boyne City MI 1985-1986; R Emm Ch Petoskey MI 1976-1986; Vic S Barth's Ch Swartz Creek MI 1966-1976; Par Mssn Stff S Paul's Epis Ch Flint MI 1966-1976; Vic St. Bartholemew's Epis Ch Swartz Creek MI 1966-1976; Vic Chr The King Epis Ch Taylor MI 1964-1966; Cur S Mich And All Ang Epis Ch Lincoln Pk MI 1962-1966; Mssn Com Dio Indianapolis Indianapolis IN 1995-1997, Stndg Com 1991-1997. Auth, "sev arts," *Anthology: Voices From The Boyne*, 2012; Auth, "Come, Journey To Bethlehem," *Self-Pub - Printed by Lulu*, 2012; Auth, "sev arts," *Voices From The Boyne*, 2012; Auth, "A Cong of Otters," *SPITBALL*, 2007; Auth, "Jim, It's What I Want That Matters!," *Sharing*, 1995. Ord of S Lk. Liberty Bell Awd Emmet Cnty Bar Assn 1981.

HENAULT JR, Armand Joseph (Vt) 374 Spring Street, St Johnsbury VT 05819 B Worcester MA 1953 s Armand & Amelia. MEd Harv 1975; MA Norwich U 1996; CAS Dioc Study Prog 1999; Cert Dio VT Dioc Study Prog 1999. D 1/6/2009 Bp Thomas C Ely. m 6/8/1975 Linda Henault c 2.

HENAULT, Rita Laverne (At) **R The Epis Ch Of The Nativ Fayetteville GA 2007-** B Houston MO 1955 D 11/30/2002 P 7/24/2003 Bp William Edward Smalley. m 7/21/1975 David Mark Henault c 2. Assoc S Mary's Ch Edmond OK 2003-2007.

HENDERSON, Catherine Ann Graves (Ga) St Francis of the Islands, 590 Walthour Rd, Savannah GA 31410 B Hampton VA 1949 d George & Mary Ann. BS Emory U 1971; MSW U of So Carolina 2008. D 6/30/2012 Bp Scott Anson Benhase. c 1.

HENDERSON III, Charles (CNY) 39 E Church St, Adams NY 13605 **R Zion Ch Pierrepont Manor NY 1995-** B Lawrence MA 1946 s Charles & Ethel. BA U NC 1971; MDiv Gordon-Conwell TS 1989. Trans 9/1/1995 Bp David Bruce Joslin. m 4/10/2010 Elise Dennis c 2. R Emm Ch Adams NY 1995-2011; Serv Angl Ch of Can 1991-1995.

HENDERSON, Don Keith (Colo) 40 Cougar Trl, Ridgway CO 81432 B Amarillo TX 1939 s William & Mable. Colorado Sch of Mines 1961; MS Colorado Sch of Mines 1963; MDiv Sewanee: The U So, TS 1991. D 6/15/1991 Bp William Jerry Winterrowd P 12/22/1991 Bp William Harvey Wolfrum. m 6/23/1990 Patricia Jennings c 3. Prog Dir Epis Mnstrs To Colorado U At Boulder 1998-2001; Chair Com Dio Colorado Denver CO 1992-1994, Chair Coll & YA Mnstry Cmsn 1994-1996; S Aid's Epis Ch Boulder CO 1991-2004.

✠ **HENDERSON, The Rt Rev Dorsey** (USC) 1115 Marion St, Columbia SC 29201 B Bainbridge GA 1939 s Dorsey & Murlean. BA Stetson U 1961; JD U of Florida Coll of Law 1967; MDiv VTS 1977. D 4/17/1977 P 11/1/1977 Bp James Loughlin Duncan Con 2/3/1995 for USC. Ret Bp of Upper So Carolina Dio Upper So Carolina Columbia SC 2010, Bp of USC 1995-2009; Dn St Paul's Epis Cathd Fond Du Lac WI 1990-1994; Curs Sprtl Dir Dio SE Florida Miami 1986-1987; R S Benedicts Ch Ft Lauderdale FL 1981-1989, R 1981-1989, P-in-c 1980-1981, P-in-c 1980, Cur 1977-1979; Dep GC Dio Fond du Lac Appleton WI 1991-1994. Sis of the H Nativ (Assoc) 1990. DD VTS 1996; DD U So at Sewanee 1995; Phi Delta Phi U Coll of Law 1965; US-AR Cmmndtn Medal U.S. Army 1964; Walter C Hayes Awd Stetson U 1960.

HENDERSON, Dumont Biglar (Me) 65 Eustis Pkwy., Waterville ME 04901 B Bakersville NC 1935 s Robert & Doris. AB U of Maine 1958. D 6/20/2009 Bp Stephen Taylor Lane. m 9/22/1990 Roxanne Henderson c 4.

HENDERSON JR, George Raymond (Fla) 1516 Marsh Inlet Ct, Jacksonville Beach FL 32250 B Atlanta GA 1957 s George & Betty. BS Auburn U 1981; MDiv Sewanee: The U So, TS 1988. D 6/6/1988 Bp Furman Charles Stough P 12/1/1988 Bp Robert Oran Miller. m 6/1/1985 Rebecca Jane Henderson c 1. S Geo Epis Ch Jacksonville FL 2014, R 2014-; R S Cathr's Ch Jacksonville FL 1992-1997; Cur S Jn's Ch Decatur AL 1988-1992.

HENDERSON, Harvey George (ND) 801 2nd St N, Wahpeton ND 58075 B Winnipeg MT CA 1952 s James & Lillian. McMaster U; BS U of Manitoba 1974; MDiv U of Wstrn Ontario CA 1982. Trans 8/20/1995. c 2. Dio No Dakota Fargo ND 1998-2001; Geth Cathd Fargo ND 1998, 1997; Trin Ch Wahpeton ND 1995-2002; Serv Ch of Can 1982-1995.

HENDERSON, Jane Pataky (Chi) 624 Colfax St, Evanston IL 60201 B Bridgeport CT 1942 d Francis & Charlotte. BA Mia 1964; UTS 1984. D 2/28/1982 Bp Paul Moore Jr P 10/1/1982 Bp Walter Decoster Dennis Jr. m 11/4/1989 Eugene Yerby Lowe c 1. S Matt's Ch Evanston IL 1997-2011; Dio New Jersey Trenton NJ 1994-1997; R S Ptr's Ch Freehold NJ 1991-1994; Ch Of The Heav Rest New

York NY 1984-1991; The Healthcare Chapl Inc New York NY 1982-1984; Asst Calv and St Geo New York NY 1980-1984.

HENDERSON, Luther Owen (WMo) 288 Cedar Glen Dr Unit 4B, Camdenton MO 65020 B Quincy FL 1949 s Dorsey & Murlean. AA Brevard Cmnty Coll 1970; BA Florida St U 1972; MDiv SW Bapt TS 1976; CAS Nash 1994. D 6/20/1994 P 12/29/1994 Bp Jack Leo Iker. m 10/20/1990 Courtney B Henderson. R S Geo Epis Ch Camdenton MO 2005-2016; Dir of Pstr Care All S's Epis Hosp Ft Worth TX 2000-2002; R All SS Epis Ch Weatherford TX 1996-2000; Cur All SS' Epis Ch Ft Worth TX 1994-1996.

HENDERSON, Mark William (Cal) 795 Buena Vista Ave W Apt 6, San Francisco CA 94117 **Assoc D S Aid's Ch San Francisco CA 2010-** B Laurens IA 1951 s Lloyd & Margaret. BA Wayne St Coll 1973; MA Iowa St U 1979; MA U of Iowa 1981; BA Sch for Deacons 2000. D 6/3/2000 Bp William Edwin Swing. c 1. D S Cyp's Ch San Francisco CA 2002-2008; Fac Sch For Deacons Berkeley CA 2001-2012; D Ch Of The Adv Of Chr The King San Francisco CA 2000-2002.

HENDERSON, Michael Brant (Lex) 381 Bon Haven Rd, Maysville KY 41056 **R Ch of the Nativ Maysville KY US 2006-** B Baton Rouge LA 1951 s Joseph & Nina. BA Loyola U 1974; Weston Jesuit TS 1979; Cert Ang Stud Yale DS 2005. D 10/8/2005 Bp Johncy Itty P 5/6/2006 Bp Stacy F Sauls. m 5/20/1984 Emily Henderson c 1. R Ch Of The Nativ Maysville KY 2006-2016. Oblate of the H Cross 2005.

HENDERSON, Michael Jack (Fla) 1746 Hillgate Ct, Tallahassee FL 32308 B Canton GA 1942 s James & Evelyn. BBA Georgia St U 1976; MBA Merc 1986; Bishops Sch For Mnstry 1999. D 12/11/1999 P 6/18/2000 Bp Stephen Hays Jecko. m 6/15/1973 Sterling Archibald Henderson c 2. Gr Mssn Ch Tallahassee FL 2000-2007.

HENDERSON, Patricia Ann (Tex) St. Francis Episcopal Church, 432 Forest Hill Rd, Macon GA 31210 B San Francisco CA 1944 d Charles & Virginia. BA Thos Edison St Coll 1990; Cert Iona Sch for Mnstry 2013. D 6/15/2013 Bp C Andrew Doyle. pat@stfrancismacon.org

HENDERSON, Robert Bobo (Ala) 5375 US Highway 231, Wetumpka AL 36092 **Trin Ch Wetumpka AL 2011-** B Memphis TN 1950 s J W & Elizabeth. BBA U of Mississippi 1972; JD U of Mississippi 1974; MDiv Epis TS of the SW 1986. D 6/11/1986 P 5/1/1987 Bp Duncan Montgomery Gray Jr. m 8/29/1970 Charlotte Henderson c 3. R S Jas Ch Eufaula AL 1989-2011; Assoc S Paul's Ch Columbus MS 1986-1988. Auth, "The Epis Tchr"; Auth, "Ch Eductr"; Auth, "Living Ch". bob@trinitywetumpka.org

HENDERSON III, Samuel G (Me) 134 Park St, Portland ME 04101 B Portland ME 1941 s Samuel & Winnifred. STB GTS; BA Ricker; Maine Cntrl Inst 1960. D 6/8/1968 Bp Leland Stark P 12/1/1968 Bp Frederick Barton Wolf. P-in-c S Dav's Epis Ch Kennebunk ME 2015-2016; S Ptr's Ch Portland ME 2006; Trin Ch Saco ME 2002-2006; S Alb's Ch Cape Eliz ME 1983-1990; S Pat's Ch Brewer ME 1982-1983; R Chr Ch Norway ME 1971-1979; Asst S Jn's Ch Bangor ME 1968-1971.

HENDERSON, Sterling Archibald (Fla) 1746 Hillgate Ct, Tallahassee FL 32308 B Jacksonville FL 1947 d Millard & Julia. Bishops Sch For Mnstry 1999. D 12/11/1999 P 6/18/2000 Bp Stephen Hays Jecko. m 6/15/1973 Michael Jack Henderson c 2. P-in-c Epis Ch Of The H Sprt Tallahassee FL 2004-2005; Gr Mssn Ch Tallahassee FL 2000-2009.

HENDERSON, Stuart Hanford (Va) 55 Sunfield Dr, Carolina Shores NC 28467 **Died 5/6/2016** B Orange NJ 1934 s Frederick & Marjorie. BA U of Virginia 1956; MDiv VTS 1964; Coll of Preachers 1975. D 6/13/1964 Bp Leland Stark P 12/16/1964 Bp Lane W Barton. m 8/15/1956 Beverly Ann Brown c 4. Ret 1995-2016; Int R S Steph's Epis Ch Culpeper VA 1993-1994; Dn Reg 15 1981-1985; R Gr Ch Keswick VA 1976-1993; R S Jn's Epis Ch Randolph VT 1970-1976; Assoc R S Lk's Ch Alexandria VA 1966-1970; Ch of Our Sav Sum Lake OR 1964-1966; Vic S Lk's Ch Lakeview OR 1964-1966.

HENDERSON, Susan (SwFla) 12630 Panasoffkee Dr, North Fort Myers FL 33903 **D, TLC Mnstrs of Dio SWFL St. Jn's Epis Ch Pine Island FL 2009-; Ch Of The Epiph Cape Coral FL 2003-; Tchr, New Directions Class for Female Inmates Lee Cnty Sheriff's Dept Prog Div 1999-** B Jacksonville 1950 d Calvin & June. BA U of Florida 1999. D 6/12/1999 Bp John Bailey Lipscomb. m 8/17/1973 Robert Page Henderson c 2. D S Hilary's Ch Ft Myers FL 1999-2003.

HENDERSON JR, Theodore Herbert (Pa) 236 Glen Pl, Elkins Park PA 19027 **P-in-c Chr Ch Bridgeport PA 2001-** B Providence RI 1938 s Theodore & Millicent. BS U of Pennsylvania 1960; MDiv PDS 1964; Tem 1970. D 5/23/1964 Bp William S Thomas P 12/19/1964 Bp Austin Pardue. m 9/14/1963 Barbara Ann Henderson c 1. The Afr Epis Ch Of S Thos Philadelphia PA 1983-1991; Locten S Paul Memi Philadelphia PA 1983-1987; Trin Epis Ch Ambler PA 1978-1981; Seamens Ch Inst Philadelphia PA 1976-1978; Dio Pennsylvania Philadelphia PA 1975-1976; P-in-c S Lk Kensington Philadelphia PA 1970-1977; St Lukes Ch Philadelphia PA 1970-1977; Dce Ch Of Our Sav Jenkintown PA 1967-1968; Gnrl Mssy Dio Pittsburgh Pittsburgh PA 1964-1967. Csss. Exceptional Persons Citation Pa Jvnl Crt Judges Cmsn.

HENDRICK, Elizabeth (At) 1520 Oak Rd, Snellville GA 30078 **R The Ch Of S Matt Snellville GA 2014-** B Biloxi MS 1950 d Robert & Elizabeth. BS U of Florida 1976; MBA Rol 1990; MDiv Epis TS of the SW 2008. D 6/7/2008 P 1/10/2009 Bp Joseph Jon Bruno. m 7/9/2009 Robert Keith Riley. Cn Pstr The Amer Cathd of the H Trin Paris 75008 2011-2014; Assoc R All SS-By-The-Sea Par Santa Barbara CA 2008-2011.

HENDRICKS III, Frisby (SeFla) 2303 N.E. Seaview Drive, Jensen Beach FL 34957 **Ecum Off Dio SE Florida Miami 2007-, Exec Bd 2009-2012, Ecum Off 2007-** B Malone NY 1945 s Walter & Ruth. BA E Carolina U 1971; MDiv SWTS 1974. D 6/29/1974 P 2/1/1975 Bp David Shepherd Rose. m 6/28/1980 Jean A Hendricks c 3. R Elect All SS Epis Ch Jensen Bch FL 2005-2017; Alum Assn VP Bexley Seabury Fed Chicago IL 2004-2008; Bd Trst 1988-2003; Bd Trst 1979-1987; R H Trin Epis Ch W Palm Bch FL 2001-2005; St Paul's Syracuse Syracuse NY 1992-1996; R Chr Ch Binghamton NY 1989-2001; R S Mart's Epis Ch Richmond VA 1982-1989, Vic 1978-1981; Int Trin Ch Portsmouth VA 1974-1978; Stndg Com Dio Cntrl New York Liverpool NY 1996-2001; Liturg Com Dio 1990-1995, Ex Bd 1987-1989; Nomntns Com-Bp Coadj Dio Virginia Richmond VA 1983-1984. fatherfrisby@yahoo.com

HENDRICKS, Mary D (Colo) **S Paul's Epis Ch Lamar CO 2013-** B South Haven MI 1946 d Ernest & Mary. BA Hastings Coll 1969; MS U of Nebraska at Kearney 1975; EdS U of Nebraska at Kearney 1977; PhD U of Sthrn Mississippi 1989; Dip Ang Stud Ya Berk 2006; MDiv Yale DS 2006. D 3/11/2006 P 11/10/2006 Bp Larry Maze. Vic St Andr Epis & H Cross Luth Ch La Junta CO 2013-2017; R S Alb's Epis Ch Mc Cook NE 2008-2013; Asst Trin Cathd Little Rock AR 2006-2007.

HENDRICKS, Rebecca Lanham (EO) Po Box 293, Milton Freewater OR 97862 **R S Jas Epis Ch Milton-Freewater OR 2007-; S Jas Ch Milton Frwtr OR 2006-** B Pendleton Oregon 1951 BA Whitman Coll 1973. D 6/10/2006 Bp William O Gregg P 7/11/2007 Bp James E Waggoner Jr. m 6/9/1973 Scott A Hendricks c 2.

HENDRICKSON, Patricia Dee (Los) 265 W Sidlee St, Thousand Oaks CA 91360 **Bd Mem ECW 2005-** B New York NY 1942 BA Thos Edison St Coll 2001; CTh CDSP 2002; BA Sch for Deacons 2003. D 9/8/2002 Bp Chester Lovelle Talton. m 7/9/2008 Kate Lewis c 2. S Aug By-The-Sea Par Santa Monica CA 2002-2007.

HENDRICKSON III, Robert J (Az) Saint John's Cathedral, 1350 Washington St Fl 3, Denver CO 80203 **S Phil's In The Hills Tucson AZ 2016-** B Chicago IL 1976 s Robert & Rene. Cor 2001; Beijing Frgn Stds U 2003; BA U of Mississippi 2004; MDiv GTS 2009. D 6/12/2010 Bp Ian Theodore Douglas P 1/15/2011 Bp Laura Ahrens. m 9/8/2001 Karrie C Hendrickson c 2. Cn S Jn's Cathd Denver CO 2013-2016; Chr Ch New Haven CT 2010-2013.

HENDRICKSON, Thomas Samuel (Va) 3845 Village Views Pl, Glen Allen VA 23059 **Vic Gr Ch Bremo Bluff VA 2008-** B Rochester NY 1942 s Samuel & Kathleen. BS Ottawa U 1965; MDiv GTS 1969; MBA UB 1981; PhD CPU 1992. D 6/21/1969 P 12/1/1969 Bp George West Barrett. m 6/17/1966 Catherine Hendrickson. Int Chr Ch Par Epis Watertown CT 1995-1996; S Ptr's Epis Ch Oxford CT 1993; Int S Paul's Huntington CT 1987-1988; Int Epis Ch of Chr the Healer Stamford CT 1985-1986; Exec Coun Appointees New York NY 1981-1984; Asst S Paul's Ch Darien CT 1975; Vic St Marys Mssn Spencerport NY 1971; Vic S Mary's Spencerport NY 1969-1972. Who's Who 1994; Psych Fell 68-68 Gnrl Theolgical Sem.

HENERY, Charles Robert (Mil) 20 Oakwood Dr, Delafield WI 53018 B Kansas City MO 1947 s James & Morene. BA U of Kansas 1969; STM GTS 1973; ThD GTS 1996. D 5/24/1973 P 11/30/1973 Bp Philip Alan Smith. m 11/27/1999 Jennifer Lynne Henery c 4. S Jn's Mltry Acad Delafield WI 2008-2013; Ch Of S Jn Chrys Delafield WI 1990-2013; Prof Nash Nashotah WI 1983-2008; The GTS New York NY 1979-1982; Assoc S Geo's Epis Ch Schenectady NY 1975-1979; Cur S Paul's Ch Concord NH 1973-1975; Exam Chapl Dio Milwaukee Milwaukee WI 2005-2014. Auth, "Yankee Bishops: Apos in the New Republic, 1783 to 1873," Ptr Lang, 2015; Co-Ed, "Sprtl Counsel in the Angl Tradition," Wipf and Stock, 2010; Ed, "A Spkng Life: The Legacy of Jn Keble," Gracewing, 1995; Ed, "Beyond the Horizon: Frontiers for Mssn," Forw Press, 1986. HSEC 2007; LivCh Fndt 2007-2014. Prof Emer of Ch Hist Nash TS 2016.

HENKING, Patricia Ellen (NH) 2 Lavender Ct, Merrimack NH 03054 **Adj, Hmnts St. Anselm Coll Manchester NH 2011-; Vic Faith Epis Ch Merrimack NH 1988-** B Darby PA 1954 d George & Betty. BS RPI 1976; MDiv GTS 1979; STM GTS 1997; STM Bos 2004. D 6/2/1979 Bp Wilbur Emory Hogg Jr P 12/1/1980 Bp Frederick Barton Wolf. Asst & Chapl S Thos Ch Hanover NH 1986-1988; Asst Epis Ch Of S Mary The Vrgn Falmouth ME 1980-1986.

HENLEY, Carol Eileen (Pgh) 1212 Trevanion Ave, Pittsburgh PA 15218 **Asst Calv Ch Pittsburgh PA 2009-; Chapl U Pgh Med Cntr Pittsburgh PA 2005-** B Kentfield CA 1945 d Edward & Eileen. BA Valparaiso U 1968; MDiv GTS 1982. D 6/5/1982 P 3/18/1983 Bp Albert Wiencke Van Duzer. St Andrews Epis Ch Pittsburgh PA 2005-2007; All SS Epis Ch Verona PA 2000-2003, 1997-1998; Int S Thos Ch In The Fields Gibsonia PA 1998-1999; Assoc R S Paul's Epis Ch Winston Salem NC 1991-1994; Vic S Anne's Ch Win-

H

ston Salem NC 1988-1990; Assoc R Gr Ch Madison NJ 1987-1988, Asst R 1985-1986; Assoc R All SS Par Beverly Hills CA 1983-1985.

HENLEY, Charles Wilbert (ND) PO Box 524, Valley City ND 58072 B Devils Lake ND 1928 s Wilbert & Maude. BD Bex Sem 1957; BA U of No Dakota 1957; Grad Stdt Vlly City St Coll 1969. D 6/11/1957 P 3/1/1958 Bp Richard R Emery. m 7/2/1955 Odella O Henley c 2. All SS Ch Vlly City ND 1977-1995, R 1964-1969; Cn Geth Cathd Fargo ND 1960-1963; M-in-c S Ptr And S Jas Ch Grafton ND 1957-1960; M-in-c S Ptr's Pk River ND 1957-1960.

HENLEY JR, Edward Joseph (SwFla) 404 Park Ridge Ave, Temple Terrace FL 33617 **Fac Bowen Cntr for the Study of the Fam 2017-** B East Chicago IN 1949 s Edward & Eileen. BA New Coll of Florida 1972; MDiv GTS 1978. D 6/12/1978 P 3/19/1979 Bp Emerson Paul Haynes. m 11/3/1984 Sheryl M Henley c 3. Int R All SS Ch Tarpon Spgs FL 2016-2017; Int R S Alfred's Epis Ch Palm Harbor FL 2013-2015; R S Mk's Epis Ch Of Tampa Tampa FL 2000-2013, Vic 1997-2013; Int S Jas Hse Of Pryr Tampa FL 1995-1996, 1989-1990; Int St Cathr of Alexandria Epis Ch Temple Terrace FL 1993-1994; Int S Chad's Ch Tampa FL 1989; USF, Tampa Dio SW Florida Parrish FL 1981-1987, Dioc Fin Com 2012-, Dn, Tampa Dnry 2011-, Dioc Coun 2010-; Asst S Mary's Par Tampa FL 1978-1981.

HENLEY, Robert P (ETenn) 351 Hardin Ln, Sevierville TN 37862 B Winchester TN 1946 BS Mars Hill Coll 1971; MDiv Sewanee: The U So, TS 1978; CPE Charlotte Memi Hosp Charlotte NC 1989. D 6/24/1978 Bp William Gillette Weinhauer P 11/2/1979 Bp William Jones Gordon Jr. m 2/15/1969 Ann Henley c 2. Dio E Tennessee Knoxville TN 2002-2011; R S Jos The Carpenter Sevierville TN 2001; Vic S Barth's Epis Ch Mio MI 1996-2001; Vic S Fran Epis Ch Grayling MI 1996-2001; P-in-c S Andr Ch Mt Holly NC 1992-1996; S Thos Ch Dubois WY 1982-1984; Vic S Helen's Epis Ch Crowheart WY 1981-1985; M-in-c S Paul's Epis Ch Gladwin MI 1978-1981. ALMACA 1989-1996; Comp Dio Relatns; Dioc Pstr Response Team 2005; EPF 1978; Native Amer Mnstrs 1982. Cler of the Year Crawford Cnty 2001.

HENNAGIN, Bob (Ala) Church Of The Holy Comforter, 2911 Woodley Rd, Montgomery AL 36111 **R Ch Of The H Comf Montgomery AL 2012-** B Detroit MI 1957 s Robert & Loretta. BA Albion Coll 1979; MDiv Epis TS of the SW 1992. D 6/20/1992 Bp Donis Dean Patterson P 4/3/1993 Bp James Monte Stanton. m 11/15/1986 Kari G Hennagin c 4. S Andr's Epis Ch Sprg Hill FL 2012; R S Hilary's Ch Ft Myers FL 1998-2012; Vic All SS Ch Atlanta TX 1994-1998; The Randy Smas Shltr for the Homeless Texarkana TX 1994-1998; Cur S Barn Ch Garland TX 1992-1994. "I am a P," Living Ch, Living Ch, 2003.

HENNE, Bruce Charles (Minn) 1270 118th Ave NW, Coon Rapids MN 55448 **Vic SS Martha And Mary Epis Ch S Paul MN 2008-** B Jackson MI 1941 s Charles & Ruth. BA MI SU 1964; MA U of W Georgia 1972; MDiv VTS 1985. D 6/24/1985 P 1/1/1986 Bp Robert Marshall Anderson. m 11/17/1961 Penny K Henne c 2. R S Lk's Epis Ch Idaho Falls ID 2002-2007; R All SS Epis Ch Boise ID 1999-2002; R S Jn's Ch S Cloud MN 1989-1999; Cathd Ch Of S Mk Minneapolis MN 1985-1989.

HENNESSEY, Nancy H (Md) 66 Highland Ave, Short Hills NJ 07078 **Sherwood Epis Ch Cockeysville MD 2016-** B Wilmington DE 1961 d Herbert & Susanne. BA Hood Coll 1983; MDiv The GTS 2016. D 1/16/2016 Bp Chilton Richardson Knudsen P 7/20/2016 Bp Eugene Taylor Sutton. m 1/26/1985 Frederick Kevin Hennessey c 3. Dio Newark Newark NJ 2016. sherwoodrector@ gmail.com

HENNESSY, F(rank) Scott (SVa) 132 Blue Ridge Dr, Orange VA 22960 **S Paul's Ch Norfolk VA 2006-** B Pittsburgh PA 1955 s George & Kathleen. BA U of Virginia 1978; MDiv VTS 1986. D 6/11/1986 P 3/19/1987 Bp Peter J Lee. m 8/25/1985 Patricia H Hennessy. R S Thos Epis Ch Orange VA 1994-2006; Asst Ch Of Our Sav Charlottesvlle VA 1988-1993; Asst Emm Ch At Brook Hill Richmond VA 1986-1988.

HENNESSY, Jeanne Katherine (Minn) 13946 Echo Park Cir, Burnsville MN 55337 **Psychol Healing Connectons 2011-; CPE Intern St. Fran Reg Med Cntr Shakopee MN 2011-** B Dubuque IA 1952 d Ambrose & Ethel. BA Mt Mercy Coll; MEd Universit of MN; PsyD U of St Thos. D 3/12/2006 P 9/16/2006 Bp Daniel Lee Swenson. P S Jas Ch Marshall MN 2006-2011.

HENNING, Joel Peter (HB) 2607 Grant St, Berkeley CA 94703 **Non-par 1972-** B East Orange NJ 1939 s Joseph & Patricia. VTS 1963; LTh SWTS 1966. D 6/11/1966 Bp James Winchester Montgomery P 12/1/1966 Bp Gerald Francis Burrill. m 6/8/1963 Jean Louise Henning c 2. Cur S Simons Ch Arlington Hts IL 1966-1972.

HENNING, Kristina Louise (FdL) 6426 S. 35th Street, Franklin WI 53132 B Milwaukee WI 1950 d Roy & Genevieve. TS; BS U of Wisconsin 1973; MDiv SWTS 2004. D 7/24/2004 P 5/21/2005 Bp Russell Edward Jacobus. c 2. Vic Ch Of The H Apos Oneida WI 2008-2012; Vic Ascen/St. Ambr Epis Ch Merrill & Antigo WI 2005-2008; Vic Ch of the Ascen Merrill WI 2005-2008. DOK 2002.

HENNINGER, Annie (SD) 105 E 12th St, Gregory SD 57533 **Rosebud E Epis Mssn Dio So Dakota Pierre SD 2010-, Secy, Niobrara Coun 2016-, Liturg Off 2014-, Stndg Com Mem 2014-** B Cleveland OH 1948 d Joseph & Maryanne. BA Ursuline Coll 1971; MA St Jn Sem/TS 1991. D 7/20/2008 P 2/19/2009 Bp James Louis Jelinek. m 5/26/1973 Jay Edgar Henninger c 6.

HENRICHSEN, Robert Anton (Neb) B Harlan IA 1939 s Karl & Lettie. D 8/15/2004 Bp Joe Goodwin Burnett. m 6/27/1980 Sula Grace Henrichsen c 3.

HENRICK, Mother Joan (Ala) 5789 Tydan Ln, Gadsden AL 35907 **Calv Ch Oneonta AL 2015-; EFM Mentor Sewanee U So TS Sewanee TN 2010-** B Lee County 1955 d Burmon & Opal. RN Sylacauga Hosp Sch of Nrsng Sylacauga AL 1979; BSN Auburn U 1992; MS Troy St U Phenix City AL 2000; MDiv Sewanee: The U So, TS 2007. D 6/9/2007 P 12/11/2007 Bp Henry Nutt Parsley Jr. m 4/21/2007 Richard Henrick c 1. S Columba-In-The-Cove Owens X Rds AL 2012-2014; R H Comf Ch Gadsden AL 2009-2012; H Cross-St Chris's Huntsville AL 2007-2009; Intern Pstr Inst Columbus GA 1999-2000; Sr Wrdn, Eucharistic Min, Yth Min, Pastora Emm Epis Ch Opelika AL 1985-2004; Cmsn on Sprtlty Dio Alabama Birmingham 2000-2003. DOK 2003. Inducted as Mem Chi Sigma Iota Counslg and Profsnl hon Soc Intl 2000; Inducted as Mem Sigma Theta Tau hon Soc of Nrsng 1992; Awd Awd for Acad Excellence 1979.

HENRICKSON, Mark (Los) 32A Wingate Street, Avondale, Auckland 0600 New Zealand (Aotearoa) **Serv Angl Ch of the Prov of New Zealand 2001-; Assoc Prof Massey U Auckland New Zealand 2003-** B Wilmington DE 1955 s Bruce & Elaine. BA Trin Hartford CT 1977; MDiv EDS 1980; MSW U of Connecticut 1990; PhD U CA Los Angeles 1996. D 6/14/1980 P 2/13/1981 Bp Morgan Porteus. S Andr's Epis Ch Ojai CA 1995; 1986-2004; 1986-1996; S Monica's Ch Hartford CT 1983-1986; Cur Trin Ch Torrington CT 1980-1982; Dioc Counc Dio Los Angeles Los Angeles CA 1996-1999. Co-Auth, "Vulnerability and Marginality in Human Serv," Routledge, 2017; Ed in Chf, "Getting to Zero: Global Soc Wk Responds to HIV," UNAIDS and Intl Assn of Schools of Soc Wk, 2017; Auth, "Queer Meaning," *Routledge Handbook of Rel, Sprtlty and Soc Wk*, Routledge, 2017; Co-Auth, "¿Treating Africans differently¿: Using skin colour as proxy for HIV risk," *Journ of Clincl Nrsng*, 2016; Co-Auth, "What Do Afr New Settlers 'Know' About HIV?," *New Zealand Med Journ*, 2016; Co-Auth, "Stigma, Lack of Knowledge, and Prevalence Maintain HIV Risk Among Black Africans in New Zealand," *Australia New Zealand Journ of Publ Hlth*, 2015; Auth, "A Queer Kind of Faith: Rel and Sprtlty in Lesbian, Gay and Bisexual New Zealanders," *Rel and LGBTQ Sexualities*, Ashgate, 2015; Lead Auth, "'Just talking about it opens your heart': Meaning-making in Black Afr migrants and refugees living w HIV," *Culture, Hlth andSexuality*, 2013; Co-Auth, "'They don't even greet you': HIV stigma... experienced by Afr immigrants and refugees in NZ," *Journ of HIV and Soc Serv, 12(1), 44-65,* 2013; Auth, Co-Ed, "Soc Wk Educ and sexual minorities," *Soc Wk Educ: Voices from the Asia Pacific (2nd ed.),* U of Sydney Press, 2013; Lead Auth, "Living the dream: Rel in the construction of sexual identity," *Fieldwork in Rel 7(2), 117-133,* 2012; Co-Auth, "AfricaNZ Count: An estimate of currently Res and HIV positive Africans in New Zealand," *Tech report*, Hlth Resrch Coun of New Zealand, 2012; Co-Ed, "Soc Wk Field Educ and Supervision across Asia-Pacific," U of Sydney Press, 2011; Co-Auth, "'Stndg in the fire': Experiences of HIV positive Black Afr migrants and refugees to New Zealand," *Tech Report,* U of Auckland, 2011; Auth, "Civilized unions, civlized Rts: Same-sex relationships in Aotearoa New Zealand," *Journ of Gay and Lesbian Soc Serv 22(1/2), 40-55,* 2010; Auth, "Sxlty, Rel and authority: Towards reframing estrangement," *Journ of Rel and Sxlty in Soc Wk 28(1/2), 48-62,* 2009; Co-Auth, "HIV disease," *Chronic Illness & Disabil: Principles for Nrsng Pract*, Elsevier, 2008; Co-Auth, "The Const of lavender families: A LGB perspective," *Journ of Clincal Nrsng 18, 849-856,* 2008; Lead Auth, "Lavender Islands: The New Zealand study," *Journ of Homosexuality 53(4), 223-248,* 2007; Auth, "Lavender faith: Rel and Sprtlty in lesbian, gay and bisexual New Zealanders," *Journ of Rel and Sprtlty in Soc Wk 26(3), 63-80,* 2007; Auth, "Ko wai ratou? Mng multiple identities in lesbian, gay and bisexual New Zealand Maori," *New Zealand Sociol 21(2), 251-273,* 2006. Eileen Younghusband Awd Intl Assn. of Schools of Soc Wk 2016.

HENRY, Barbara Dearborn (WA) 5333 N Sheridan Rd Apt.8H, Chicago, Chicago IL 60640 **Assoc Epis Ch Of The Atone Chicago IL 2007-** B Bangor ME 1934 d Lloyd & Marion. BA Bos 1956; MA Bos 1962; MLS U Pgh 1964; MDiv GTS 1983. D 6/2/1983 P 12/11/1983 Bp John Thomas Walker. Assoc All Souls Memi Epis Ch Washington DC 2004-2007; Non-par 1995-1999; Par of St Monica & St Jas Washington DC 1991-1994; S Jas Epis Ch Scarborough ME 1991-1994; Asst R S Jn's Ch Georgetown Par Washington DC 1985-1988; Asst R/Urban Res Ch Of S Steph And The Incarn Washington DC 1983-1985.

HENRY, David Winston (VI) Po Box 6119, Christiansted VI 00823 **Ret 2000-** B Antigua 1932 s William & Matilda. London GCE GD. MDiv ETSC 1966. D 6/4/1966 P 6/1/1967 Bp Cedric Earl Mills. m 8/6/1995 Sonia Dolores Henry c 2. P in Residened S Geo's Par Tortola VI 2000-2002; R Epis Ch of the H Cross Kingshill St Croix VI 1991-2000; Vic H Cross S Croix VI 1987-1991; 1980-1987; Vic St Peters Epis Ch St Croix VI 1972-1980; Dio Vrgn Islands Charlotte Amalie St Thom VI 1971-1977; Cur S Paul's S Croix VI 1968-1972; Asst S Geo's Par Tortola VI 1967-1968; P-in-c S Paul's Tortola VI 1967-1968; Asst S Barth's Ch Baltimore MD 1966-1967.

HENRY, Dean (NJ) 14 Winding Lane, Southwest Harbor ME 04679 B Louisville KY 1948 s Robert & Ethelene. BS Pur 1970; MBA Claremont Grad Sch 1984;

MDiv GTS 1988. D 6/25/1988 Bp Frederick Houk Borsch P 3/4/1989 Bp George Phelps Mellick Belshaw. m 10/1/1988 Alice Lacey Downs c 2. R Chr Ch Middletown NJ 1990-2010; Asst S Ptr's Ch Perth Amboy NJ 1988-1990. OHC, Assoc 1989.

HENRY, Earl Fitzgerald (SeFla) 4401 W Oakland Park Blvd, Fort Lauderdale FL 33313 **R Ch Of The Atone Ft Lauderdale FL 1998-** B Belize CA BZ 1951 s Ezekiel & Catherine. DIT Codrington Coll 1978; BA Coll of New Rochelle 1991; Blanton-Peale Grad Inst 1995; MA Audrey Cohen Sch of The Metropltn Coll of New York 1997. Trans 11/15/1988 Bp Robert Campbell Witcher Sr. m 7/19/1980 Carmen Higging c 1. R S Barn Epis Ch Brooklyn NY 1992-1998; Supply P Dio Long Island Garden City NY 1990-1992; S Aug's Epis Ch Brooklyn NY 1989-1990; Serv Angl Ch of Belize 1978-1986.

HENRY, George Kenneth Grant (NC) 34 Red Fox Lane, Brevard NC 28712 B Tarboro NC 1942 s Matthew & Cornelia. BA U So 1964; MDiv VTS 1971. D 6/6/1971 Bp Matthew George Henry P 2/19/1972 Bp Randolph R Claiborne. c 3. R S Mich's Ch Raleigh NC 1997-2002; Dio No Carolina Raleigh NC 1992-2002, Stndg Com 1983-1997, Liturg Cmsn 1977-1991; R Ch Of The H Comf Charlotte NC 1980-1997; R Trin Epis Ch Statesville NC 1975-1980; R Epis Ch of the Gd Shpd Charleston SC 1973-1975; Cur Emm Epis Ch Athens GA 1971-1973.

HENRY, James Russell (SwVa) 4647 Prince Trevor Dr, Williamsburg VA 23185 **Ret 1998-** B Athens GA 1940 s Jones & Elizabeth. BA U GA 1962; MDiv VTS 1965; DMin VTS 1987; MEd Lynchburg Coll 1997. D 6/26/1965 P 3/17/1966 Bp Randolph R Claiborne. m 6/21/1969 Nancy Ann Henry c 1. Supply P St.Thos Epis Ch 2004-2006; S Jn's Ch Bedford VA 1997-1998, 1981-1991, R 1981-1991; P-in-c S Jn's Epis Ch Glasgow VA 1996-1998; Assoc R Chr Epis Ch Roanoke VA 1993-1996, P Assoc 1991-1993; Pstr Counslg Cntr Of Roanoke Vlly Inc Roanoke VA 1991-1993; Counslr Roanoke Vlly Pstr Counslg Cntr 1991-1993; Asst S Paul's Epis Ch Alexandria VA 1971-1981; R Ch of the Incarn Mineral VA 1969-1979; Emm Epis Ch Athens GA 1967-1969; R S Jas Epis Ch Louisa VA 1967-1969; Vic Calv Ch Cornelia GA 1965-1967; Gr-Calv Epis Ch Clarkesville GA 1965-1967; Vic S Jas Epis Ch Clayton GA 1965-1967. Auth, *Death Educ: The Tip of the Iceberg*, 1987; Auth, *Alexandria: a Town in Transition 1800-1900*; Auth, *Ch.* AAPC 1997; Chi Sigma Iota 1997. Lic Profsnl Counslr St of Virginia 2001; Fell AAPC 1998; Natrional Certied Counslr Natl Bd Cert Counselors 1997.

HENRY, John Reeves (Spr) 415 S Broad St, Carlinville IL 62626 **R S Paul's Epis Ch Carlinville IL 2010-** B Decatur IL 1949 s Richard & Mildred. BS U IL 1971; MS Estrn Illinois U 1980; MDiv Nash 2010. D 11/30/2010 Bp Donald James Parsons P 6/29/2011 Bp Daniel Hayden Martins. m 4/14/1973 Sheila Henry c 6. Vic S Ptr's Ch Chesterfield IL 2010-2012.

HENRY II, John W (Alb) P.O. Box 175, Clifton Park NY 12065 B Bay Shore NY 1955 s John & Florence. BA Indiana U 1978; MDiv Sewanee: The U So, TS 1983. D 6/13/1983 P 1/21/1984 Bp Robert Campbell Witcher Sr. m 6/30/1984 Karen E J Wood c 4. S Geo's Ch Clifton Pk NY 2008-2015; S Andr's Epis Ch Livonia MI 2006-2008; Asst P Ch Of The H Cross Novi MI 2004-2006; Ch Of The Ascen Bradford PA 1998; Dioc Mssnr Dio NW Pennsylvania Erie PA 1996-2002; Vic S Margeret Mt Jewett PA 1996-2002; Fndng Pstr San Marcos Mssn Tarrytown Ny 1993 1995 1993-1995; R Chr Epis Ch Tarrytown NY 1991-1995; Dio New York New York NY 1991-1995; S Jas Ch Brookhaven NY 1988-1991; Chapl Brookhaven Fire Dept & Ambulance CO 1985-1991; Dio Long Island Garden City NY 1985-1987; Cur S Jn's Ch Huntington NY 1983-1985.

HENRY, Karen E J (NY) St John's Church, 365 Strawtown Rd, New City NY 10956 **P-in-c S Jn's Ch New City NY 2014-** B New York NY 1950 d John & Eleanor. BA SUNY 1981; MDiv UTS 1985; GTS 1991. D 6/15/1991 Bp Orris George Walker Jr P 2/2/1992 Bp Walter Decoster Dennis Jr. m 6/30/1984 John W Henry c 4. P Adirondack Mssn Pottersville NY 2011-2013; Assoc S Geo's Ch Clifton Pk NY 2009-2015; Dn Trin Dnry Dio Michigan 2006-2008; Instr Whitaker TS Detroit MI 2005-2008; P-in-c Ch Of The H Cross Novi MI 2002-2008; R S Lk's Epis Ch Smethport PA 1996-2002; Asst S Barth's Ch In The Highland White Plains NY 1994-1995; Dn Cntrl Westchester Dio NY 1993-1995; P Chr Ch Bronxville NY 1991-1994; Coordntr for Hurricane Relief Dio Michigan Detroit MI 2005-2006. Auth, "Change Agt," *Living Ch*, 2001; Auth, "Cathd," *Angl Dig*, 1991. The Ord of S Lk, Chapl 2000.

HENRY, Lloyd I (LI) 4607 Avenue H, Brooklyn NY 11234 B Belize HN 1947 s Gerald & Hortense. Untd Theol Coll of The W Indies Kingston Jm; MDiv NYTS 1988; NYTS 1991. Trans 10/21/1982 Bp Robert Campbell Witcher Sr. c 3. All SS Ch Woodhaven NY 2010-2013; S Mk's Ch Brooklyn NY 2005-2008, Asst P 1978-1981; R S Aug's Epis Ch Brooklyn NY 1981-1998.

HENRY, Richard Arlen (SJ) 1155 Leavell Park Cir, Lincoln CA 95648 **Assoc S Jas Epis Par Lincoln CA 2005-** B Cleveland OH 1930 s Clifford & Ada. BA U CA 1952; MDiv CDSP 1961; DMin Jesuit TS 1978. D 6/12/1961 P 12/16/1961 Bp Sumner Walters. m 5/3/1957 Allene M Henry c 3. Assoc Chr Ch Eureka CA 2000-2004; Assoc S Columba Ch Fresno CA 1993-2000; R S Mary's Epis Ch Fresno CA 1965-1993; R S Mths Ch Oakdale CA 1961-1965. OHC, Assoc 1965.

HENRY, Richard Lynn (Nev) 228 Hillcrest Dr, Henderson NV 89015 B Berkeley CA 1953 s Robert & Frankie. AGS Clark Cnty Cmnty Coll 1985; CDSP 1989. D 6/27/1988 P 6/11/1989 Bp Stewart Clark Zabriskie. c 3. Dio Nevada Las Vegas 2012-2013, 1989-2003; Vic S Lk's Epis Ch Las Vegas NV 1990.

HENRY JR, Wayman Wright (USC) 116 Sedgewood Ct, Easley SC 29642 B Greenville SC 1937 s Wayman & Helen. BA Clemson U 1966; MDiv Erskine Coll 1979; VTS 1981. D 1/27/1981 P 12/1/1981 Bp William Arthur Beckham. m 9/21/1965 Carol Terry Henry c 2. S Geo Ch Anderson SC 2002-2003; All SS Ch Cayce SC 1994-1996; Ch Of The H Comf Sumter SC 1994; All SS Epis Hosp Ft Worth TX 1993-1994; R The Ch Of The Epiph Eutawville SC 1992-1993; S Jn's Ch Charleston SC 1992; Chr/St Paul's Epis Par Hollywood SC 1991-1992; R S Paul's Yonges Island SC 1991-1992; R Ch Of The Redeem Orangeburg SC 1991; R Ch Of The Incarn Gaffney SC 1982-1991; S Fran Ch Greenville SC 1982; Cur Ch Of The Gd Shpd Greer SC 1981.

HENSARLING JR, Larry Reid (CFla) 146 Oak Sq S, Lakeland FL 33813 B Shreveport LA 1956 s Larry & Joan. BS LSU 1978; MA U of Texas 1981; MDiv TESM 1992; DMin Reformed TS Orlando 2010. D 6/6/1992 P 12/5/1992 Bp Robert Jefferson Hargrove Jr. m 6/28/1980 Mary D Hensarling c 2. P-in-c All SS Epis Ch Lakeland FL 2016, R 2016-, Assoc R 2003-2016; R Ch Of The Redeem Germantown TN 1999-2003; R S Paul's Ch Bennettsville SC 1994-1999; Cur S Mths Epis Ch Shreveport LA 1992-1994; Chair Dept Yth Mnstrs So Carolina Charleston SC 1996-1999. Bk, "The Biblic Gospel: Its Significance and Impact in Sprtl Renwl," WestBow Press, 2013.

HENSEL, Charles Howard (Chi) 2625 TEchny Rd Apt 620, Northbrook IL 60062 **Ret 1998-** B Bridgeton NJ 1933 s Howard & Grace. BA Trin Hartford CT 1954; MDiv Nash 1957. D 12/22/1956 P 2/1/1958 Bp Alfred L Banyard. m 6/4/1960 Sarah Anne Hensel. Int S Tim's Ch Griffith IN 1996-1998; Int Geth Epis Ch Marion IN 1994-1996; Vic S Nich w the H Innoc Ch Elk Grove Vlg IL 1982-1993; Chr Plnnr Ceta Gary IN 1980-1982; Employee Counslr Foundry Cntr Oak Brook IL 1980-1982; Int Chr Ch W River MD 1979-1980; R S Jn's Epis Ch Decatur IL 1974-1979; R S Barn-In-The-Dunes Gary IN 1971-1974; Vic H Trin Epis Ch Geneseo IL 1960-1964; S Jn's Epis Ch Preemption IL 1960-1964; Cur S Andr Ch Grayslake IL 1959-1960; Cur The Ch Of The Epiph And S Simon Brooklyn NY 1958-1959.

HENSHAW, Richard Aurel (Roch) 199 Crosman Terr., Rochester NY 14620 B San Francisco CA 1921 s Aurelius & Ruth. BS U CA 1943; BD CDSP 1953; PhD Hebr Un Coll 1966. D 6/28/1953 Bp Henry H Shires P 1/6/1954 Bp Henry W Hobson. m 6/8/1943 Marjorie Henshaw c 2. Int Chapl Epis Ch Hm Rochester NY 2003-2005; The Chap of the Gd Shpd Rochester NY 2003; Vstng Prof Theol Chung Chi Coll Chinese Univ Of Hong Kong 1985-2006; Bex Sem Columbus OH 1968-1993; R Ch Of Our Sav Cincinnati OH 1958-1960; Cur Chr Ch Cathd Cincinnati OH 1953-1958. Auth, "Priesthood," *Eerdmans Bible Dictionary*, 2000; Auth, "Wmn In Israel Cult," *Eerdmans Bible Dictionary*, 2000; Auth, "Female & Male - The Cultic Personl," Pickwick Press, 1994; Auth, "Which Bible," *Forw Mvmt*, 1991; Auth, "Neo Assyrian Offcl," *Journ Of Amer Oriental Soc*, 1967. Amer Oriental Soc 1943; Astronomical Soc Of The Pacific 1953; SBL 1943-2006.

HENSLEY, Erin S (Tex) PO Box 368, Austin TX 78767 **S Alb's Epis Ch Austin Austin TX 2015-** B Henderson KY 1977 d David & Mary. BS Guilford Coll 1999; MDiv VTS 2007. D 11/15/2007 P 6/29/2008 Bp Michael B Curry. m 7/10/2004 Samuel E Hensley c 1. Assoc S Jn's Ch Roanoke VA 2009-2015; Asst S Alb's Par Washington DC 2007-2009.

HENSLEY JR, Joseph H (Va) 905 Princess Anne St, Fredericksbrg VA 22401 **R S Geo's Ch Fredericksburg VA 2015-; Dioc Coun Dio No Carolina Raleigh NC 2010-** B Winfield IL 1973 s Joseph & Linda. BA U NC 1996; MDiv VTS 2007. D 5/19/2007 P 12/19/2007 Bp Michael B Curry. m 4/24/1999 Sarah S White c 4. Asst To The R S Lk's Epis Ch Durham NC 2007-2014.

HENSLEY, Lane Goodwin (SanD) 47535 State Highway 74, Palm Desert CA 92260 **R S Marg's Epis Ch Palm Desert CA 2010-; Disciplinary Bd Dio San Diego San Diego CA 2010-** B Shreveport LA 1965 s Edward & Dorothy. AB Duke 1987; MDiv SWTS 2001. D 6/16/2001 P 12/15/2001 Bp Bill Persell. m 4/24/1993 Rebecca Ruth Hensley c 2. Chapl Palos Pk Police Dept 2009-2010; R Ch Of The Trsfg Palos Pk IL 2003-2010; Cur Chr Ch Winnetka IL 2001-2003; Bd Trst Bexley Seabury Fed Chicago IL 1999-2011. lhensley@stmargarets.org

HENSLEY-ECHOLS, Beth Marie (WA) Brooke Army Medical Center, 3851 Roger Brooke Dr, San Antonio TX 78234 **CPE Supvsr Brooke Army Med Cntr 2009-** B Cambridge MD 1961 BA U of Maryland 1985; MDiv VTS 1989. D 6/10/1989 Bp John Thomas Walker P 9/1/1990 Bp Ronald Hayward Haines. m 11/20/1990 Karl William Echols. CE Asst S Barn' Ch Leeland Uppr Marlboro MD 1990-1995; Chapl Queen Anne Sch Upper Marlboro 1989-1995; Asst to R Ch Of Our Sav Silver Sprg MD 1989-1990.

HENSON, David R (WNC) 471 W Martintown Rd, North Augusta SC 29841 **Trin Epis Ch Asheville NC 2016-** B Siler City NC 1981 s Harold & India. BA Samford U 2003; MA Grad Theol Un 2009. D 6/29/2013 Bp Barry Leigh Beisner P 2/1/2014 Bp W illiam Andrew Waldo. m 11/1/2003 Amber Stanley Henson c 2. S Barth's Ch No Augusta SC 2011-2013.

HENSON, Paula (NAM) Good Shepherd Mission, PO Box 618, Fort Defiance AZ 86504 **Admin Ch Of The Gd Shpd Ft Defiance AZ 2011-; Navajoland Area Mssn Farmington NM 2011-** B Gallup NM 1955 d Henry & Alice. Deacons Formation Acad 2010. D 10/15/2011 Bp David Earle Bailey. m 11/22/1997 Hank Henson c 2. officegoodshepherdmission@gmail.com

HENSON, Tula (USC) 253 Bridleridge Rd, Lexington SC 29073 **R S Tim's Ch Columbia SC 2007-** B Piraeus Greece 1953 ADN Bristol Cmnty Coll; BSN Med Coll of Georgia; BSHCA U IL -Carbondale; MDiv Sewanee: The U So, TS 2005. D 2/5/2005 P 8/8/2006 Bp Henry Irving Louttit. m 4/2/2005 Walter H Henson c 4. Assoc S Mk's Ch Brunswick GA 2005-2007.

HENWOOD, Karen Lee (Colo) 5604 E Nichols Pl, Centennial CO 80112 **S Tim's Epis Ch Littleton CO 2005-** B Colorado Springs CO 1937 d Joseph & Alice. BA U of Nthrn Colorado 1960; MA U CO 1972. D 11/10/2001 Bp William Jerry Winterrowd. m 9/21/2002 William Arthur Henwood c 2. D All SS Epis Ch Denver CO 2001-2005.

HENWOOD, William Arthur (Colo) 5604 E Nichols Pl, Centennial CO 80112 **Gd Shpd Epis Ch Centennial CO 1995-** B Kingston JM 1931 s Charles & Myrtle. BS Queens U 1963. D 10/21/1989 Bp Joseph Thomas Heistand. m 9/21/2002 Joan Clements c 3. Dio Indianapolis Indianapolis IN 1993-1995; D S Mk's Ch Plainfield IN 1993-1995; Gr St Pauls Epis Ch Tucson AZ 1989-1993.

HERALD, Erin Carol (NwPa) St Jude's Episc Church, PO Box 1714, Hermitage PA 16148 B Brookville PA 1981 d Dennis & Nancy. Inst for Mnstry 2012. D 5/20/2012 Bp Sean Walter Rowe. m 5/28/2005 Joshua Lee Herald c 1. erin@stjudesepiscopal.org

HERBST, Gary (Dal) 8320 Jack Finney Blvd., Greenville TX 75402 B Alexandria VA 1951 s Grant & Lila. BA U of Texas 1973; MDiv VTS 1976. D 6/16/1976 P 6/1/1977 Bp Roger Howard Cilley. m 1/11/1986 Sandra J Herbst c 3. R S Paul's Epis Ch Greenville TX 2002-2017; R S Jn's Ch Ketchikan AK 1986-2002; Trin Epis Ch Jasper TX 1980-1986; The Great Cmsn Fndt Houston TX 1980-1982; Assoc R Ch Of The Epiph Houston TX 1976-1979. "Formation for Vestries: Where Equipping the SS Begins," *Vstry Papers*, ECF, 2007.

HERGENRATHER, Lynda May Stevenson (Va) 5904 Mount Eagle Dr Apt 318, Alexandria VA 22303 B Newark NJ 1948 d Leonard & Adelaide. BA Eckerd Coll 1970; MA U of So Florida 1972; MDiv UTS Richmond 1979. D 6/23/1979 Bp Robert Bruce Hall P 5/1/1980 Bp David Henry Lewis Jr. Assoc S Lk's Ch Alexandria VA 1989-2004, P-in-c 1981-1983, Asst 1979-1981; Nonpar 1983-1989; Adj Fac VTS In Alexandria 1980-1983; Chapl Mt Vernon Hosp 1979-1981. church@saintlukeschurch.net

HERKNER JR, Robert Thomas (O) 328 Windsor Ct, Huron OH 44839 B Detroit,MI 1945 s Robert & Vivian. Amer U of Beirut 1966; BA Hope Coll 1967; MA U MI 1969; MDiv EDS 1973. D 6/30/1973 Bp H Coleman Mcgehee Jr P 2/17/1974 Bp Frederick Hesley Belden. m 8/8/1987 Kay Ellen Herkner c 2. Int Mnstry 2002-2004; S Paul's Ch Fremont OH 2002-2004; Int Ch Of The Ascen Lakewood OH 2001-2002; R Calv Ch Sandusky OH 1975-2000; Asst Trin Ch Newport RI 1973-1975. Auth, "Paper The Un Mnstry Of Epis Ch".

HERLIHY, Phyllis Cleo (SwFla) 514 50th St W, Bradenton FL 34209 B Waverly NY 1927 d Ellsworth & Esther. D 6/29/1991 Bp Rogers Sanders Harris. c 3. D Chr Ch Bradenton FL 1991-1999. Alfa 2001; Disciples Of Chr Cmnty; Fa Lead Lab I, Ii Supvsr & Coordntr.

HERLOCKER SR, John Robert (Ida) 3700 NW Orchard Dr, Terrebonne OR 97760 **Ret Ret 1996-** B Greenville TX 1935 s James & Doyle. U So 1952; BBA U of Texas 1956; MDiv Sewanee: The U So, TS 1967; Boise St U 1985; CREDO 2003; CREDO 2009. D 7/26/1967 P 4/21/1968 Bp William Jones Gordon Jr. m 2/28/1959 Peggy Felmet c 5. Cn to Ordnry for Dioc Adm Dio Idaho Boise ID 1990-1996, Archd 1982-1990, Dioc Admin 1979-1989; Dioc Fiscal Off Dio Estrn Oregon Cove OR 1975-1979; Epis Ch Of The Trsfg Sis OR 1974-1978; Vic S Alb's Epis Ch Redmond OR 1974-1978; R H Trin Epis Ch Ukiah CA 1972-1974; Vic S Mary's Ch Winnemucca NV 1969-1972; Vic St Anne's Ch Ft McDermitt Indn Res McDermitt 1969-1972; Chapl, Admin St Jn's Cathd Boys Sch Angl Ch of Can 1968-1969; Vic All SS' Epis Ch Anchorage AK 1967-1968. bobnpeg2@gmail.com

HERLOCKER, Thomas Dean (Kan) 1704 E 10th Ave, Winfield KS 67156 **D Gr Epis Ch Winfield KS 1988-** B Winfield KS 1938 s John & Carolan. Stan 1957; BA U of Kansas 1960; JD U of Kansas 1963. D 10/28/1988 Bp Richard Frank Grein. m 6/8/1960 Judith Ann Herlocker c 3. Dio Kansas Topeka KS 1994-2000. NAAD 1987.

HERMAN, Alice McWreath (SO) 345 Ridgedale Dr N, Worthington OH 43085 **S Jn's Ch Worthington OH 2003-** B McDonald PA 1937 d Guy & Mary. BA Thiel Coll 1959; MDiv Methodist TS in Ohio 1989. D 11/9/1990 Bp Herbert Thompson Jr. m 4/22/1961 Fred W Herman c 2. D S Andr's Ch Pickerington OH 1990-1992. Coll of Chapl.

HERMAN, Elizabeth Frances (Minn) 615 Vermillion St, Hastings MN 55033 **D S Lk's Epis Ch Hastings MN 2010-** B Monticello MN 1942 d Emil & Elizabeth. D 1/9/2010 Bp James Louis Jelinek. c 1.

HERMANSON, David Harold (NJ) 56 Grace Drive, Old Bridge NJ 08857 B Ransomville NY 1956 s Clair & Gayle. Loyola U 1984; BA Hav 1986; MDiv GTS 1990; S.T.M. GTS 2003; S.T.M. GTS 2004; Post-Bacc. Stds Drew U 2005; Post-Bacc. Stds Drew U 2007. D 6/16/1990 P 1/30/1993 Bp Allen Lyman Bartlett Jr. m 5/29/1982 Lynn Hermanson. Vic S Thos Ch Lyndhurst NJ 2003-2005; R Trin Ch Asbury Pk NJ 1993-2003, Chapl, Interfaith Zendo 1998-2003; Mssnr Dio Pennsylvania Philadelphia PA 1990-1993; Sem in Charge Ch Of S Jn The Evang Philadelphia PA 1989; Coun and Co-chair of Pub Associated Parishes Inc. Ft Worth TX 2001-2009; Chair, Bp's Com on Liturg & Mus Dio New Jersey Trenton NJ 1999-2001, Bp's Com on Liturg & Mus 1998-2003, Exam Chapl for Theol and Liturg 1998-2003, Chair, Com on Theol 1996-2002, Chapl, Integrity - NJ 1995-2003, Bp's Com on Theol 1994-2002; Workshop Ldr All SS Co San Francisco CA 1998-2003; Co-Chair Gvnr's T/F for Urban Dvlpmt / Asbury Pk 1995-2001; Co-Chair Asbury Pk Consult on Hunger 1994-2003; Chair Asbury Pk Progressive Mnstry T/F 1994-1998.

HERMERDING, Joseph R (Dal) Church Of The Incarnation, 3966 Mckinney Ave, Dallas TX 75204 **Assoc R Ch Of The Incarn Dallas TX 2012-** B Fridley MN 1983 s Gregg & Constance. BA Wheaton Coll 2006; Gordon-Conwell TS 2007; MDiv Nash 2009. D 10/23/2008 P 5/16/2009 Bp Keith Lynn Ackerman. m 6/3/2006 Ellora L Hermerding c 4. Cur/Chapl S Lk's Ch Baton Rouge LA 2009-2012. jhermerding@incarnation.org

HERMES, Jonathan Robert (ETenn) B Kingsport TN 1975 s Alfred & Sharon. D 2/11/2017 Bp George Young III.

HERN, George Neal (Dal) 4329 Irvin Simmons Dr, Dallas TX 75229 **Died 3/8/2017** B Saint Louis MO 1939 s George & Helen. BA Westminster Coll 1961; MDiv EDS 1964. D 6/21/1964 P 12/1/1964 Bp George Leslie Cadigan. c 2. Asst S Mich And All Ang Ch Dallas TX 2000-2012; S Thos Ch Ennis TX 1998-2000; P Dio Dallas Dallas TX 1998-1999, P 1981-1997; S Mths' Epis Ch Athens TX 1989-1998; Ch Of The Gd Shpd Dallas TX 1984-1986; Assoc S Lk's Epis Ch Dallas TX 1977-1980; R Ch Of S Mths Dallas TX 1974-1976; Cur Gr Ch S Louis MO 1964-1966.

HERNANDEZ, Alejandro Felix (SeFla) 9460 Fontainebleau Blvd Apt 334, Miami FL 33172 **R Iglesia Epis De Todos Los Santos Miami FL 2002-, 1996-1997** B CU 1959 s Emilio & Edivia. BS U of Havana Cu 1983; BA Theol Sem of Matantas 1992. Trans 12/11/1995 Bp Calvin Onderdonk Schofield Jr. m 3/19/1983 Vilma Gonzalez Pasos c 3. Santa Cruz-Resurr Epis Ch Biscayne Pk FL 1998-2002; S Faith's Epis Ch Miami FL 1997-1998.

HERNANDEZ, Gustavo (Los) Po Box 893, Downey CA 90241 B Cisneros CO 1934 s Eleazar & Eva. BA Xaverian U 1958; MS Gregorian U 1963; BA Xaverian HS 1963; DMin U of Notre Dame 1988. Rec 3/1/1984 as Priest Bp Quintin Ebenezer Primo Jr. c 3. R S Clem's Mssn Huntington Pk CA 1989-1999; Dio Chicago Chicago IL 1985-1988; Asst R Our Lady Annunc Waukegan IL 1984-1988; The Annunc Of Our Lady Gurnee IL 1984-1985; Vic Cristo Rey Chicago IL 1982-1984; Serv RC Ch 1963-1981.

HERNANDEZ, Jorge A (Nev) 2000 S Maryland Pkwy, Las Vegas NV 89104 B Mexico 1963 s Jesus & Iongcia. Tchr Universidad de Gro, Chilpancingo Guerrero Mex 1983; St Fran of Assisi 1998; Rel Art U of So Los Angeles 2000. Rec 12/12/2012 Bp Dan Thomas Edwards. m 5/8/1997 Ana Lorena Hernandez c 3. Dio Nevada Las Vegas 2013-2014.

HERNANDEZ, Luis Alfonso (Hond) B 1952 m 4/30/1992 Dulce Venice Cuellar c 3. Dio Honduras San Pedro Sula 1998-2014.

HERNANDEZ, Miguel Angel (Nwk) **Ch Of The H Trin W Orange NJ 2014-** B El Salvador 1957 s Miguel & Maria. BT The City Coll of New York 1982; MSEE Polytechnic U of New York 1992; MDiv GTS 2013; MDiv The GTS 2013. D 9/28/2013 P 3/29/2014 Bp Mark M Beckwith. m 1/3/2007 Maria Leonor Molina-Hernandez c 1.

HERNANDEZ JR, Nicolas (Alb) Trinity Episcopal Church, 1336 1st Ave, Watervliet NY 12189 **D, Latino/Hisp Mssnr Trin Ch Watervliet NY 2013-; EMT-Basic NY St Bureau of Emergency Med Serv 2011-; Hisp/Latino Mssnr Dio Albany Greenwich NY 2013-** B Havana Cuba 1953 s N Nicolas & Olga. BA Iona Coll 1973; MA Cor 1977; PhD Cor 1982; MA Theol St Bern's TS 2003; AAS Hudson Vlly Cmnty Coll 2012. D 10/12/2011 Bp William Howard Love. m 6/3/1978 Edmee Palen-Hernandez c 1. Latino/Hisp Mssnr S Andr's Epis Ch Albany NY 2012-2013; D S Ptr's Ch Albany NY 2011-2012; On-Call Chapl Samar Hosp Troy NY 1999-2011. Auth, "arts on Chrsnty, Index of Prohibited Books, Mystics, and Reformation," *Greenwood Encyclopedia of Love, Courtship & Sxlty thru Hist, v.3, Early Mod Period. Ed V Mondelli & C Gottsleben*, Greenwood Press, 2008; Co-Auth w KM Seaburg, "Spanish for the Hlth Allied Professions: A Revs of the Lit, Resources, Materials and Techniques," *Proceedings of the 16th Annual Conf of the Natl Assn of Hisp and Latino Stds. Ed. L. Berry*, Univ of Maine, 2008; Auth, "Quilombo & El otro Francisco: Post Modernist Attempt to Rewrite Contempor'y Hist & Colonial Slavery in Brazil & Cuba," *Chasqui, Spec Issue No. 1. Ed. Lúcia Costigan*, 2005; Auth, "Quilombo and El otro Francisco: Post Modernist Attempt to Rewrite Contempor'y Hist and Colonial Slavery in Brazil and Cuba," *Chasqui, Spec Issue No. 1. Ed. Lúcia Costigan*, 2005; Auth, "Critical essays on Lady Anne Barnard, Harriet Lee, the Honourable Emily Lawless, and Lisa St. Aubin de Terán," *An Encyclopedia of British Wmn Writers. Eds. Paul & June Schlueter*, Rutgers Univ Press, 1999; Auth, "Critical essays on Lady Anne Barnard, Harriet Lee, the Honourable Emily Lawless, and Lisa St. Aubin de

Terán," *An Encyclopedia of British Wmn Writers. Eds. Paul and June Schlueter*, Rutgers Univ Press, 1999; Auth, "El caso del Steppenwolf criollo," *Narrativa y Libertad: Cuentos de la diáspora cubana, vol. II. Ed. Julio Hernández-Miyares*, Ediciones Universal, 1996; Auth, "El caso del Steppenwolf criollo," *Narrativa y Libertad: Cuentos de la diáspora cubana, vol. II. Ed. Julio Hernández-Miyares*, Ediciones Universal, 1996; Auth, "Latin Amer Databases: Tech Resources for Scholars in the Nineties," *Proceedings of the CALICO 1993 Symposium on "Assessment." Ed. Frank Borchardt*, Duke Univ, 1993; Auth, "Revs: Pinstripe Presenter," *Computers and the Hmnts*, 1991; Auth, "An Intro to ISAAC: IBM's Info System for Advncd Acad Computing at the U of Washington-Seattle," *CALICO Journ*, 1988; Co-Auth, "Biobibliographies on Pilar Valderrama and Angeles Villarta," *Wmn Writers of Spain*, Greenwood Press, 1986; Co-Auth w E Palen-Hernandez, "Biobibliographies on Pilar Valderrama and Angeles Villarta," *Wmn Writers of Spain. Ed. Carolyn Galerstein.*, Greenwood Press, 1986; Auth, Univ of Nebraska-Kearney, 1981; Auth, "Emma, Ana and Rel: A Comparative Study of Madame Bovary and La Regenta," *Platte Vlly Revs*, U of Nebraska-Kearney, 1981. Bro of St Andr 2012; Coalición de Episcopales Latinos 2012.

HERNANDEZ ROJAS, Martin Antonio (Colom) Carrera 6 No 49-85, Piso 2, Bogota Colombia B Convencion NdeS Colombia 1958 s Luciano & Mana. Seminario Reg Barranguilla 1979; Theol Seminario Reg 1984; Lic Universidad Sto Tomas 1995; Universidad Sto Tomas 1999. Rec 3/22/2009 Bp Francisco Jose Duque-Gomez. m 12/8/1998 Magda Yasmin Gil Delgado c 2.

HERNDON, James C (Ida) 1055 Riverton Rd, Blackfoot ID 83221 **D Dio Idaho Boise ID 1988-** B Oklahoma City OK 1941 s John & Lucile. BS U of Idaho 1963; JD U of Idaho 1966. D 4/30/1988 Bp David Bell Birney IV. m 4/19/1974 Tommye Rae Low.

HERON, James (NY) 54 Angela Ct, Beacon NY 12508 B Plainfield NJ 1941 s Robert & Helen. BA Norwich U 1963; STB PDS 1966; DMin Drew U 1978. D 4/23/1966 P 10/29/1966 Bp Alfred L Banyard. c 2. Dir Diac Formation Prog Dio New York New York NY 1994-1998; R Trin Ch Fishkill NY 1981-2003; Chapl, Chairman of Dept of Rel Trin Pawling Sch Pawling New York 1968-1980; Trin-Pawling Sch Pawling NY 1968-1980; Cur S Mary's Ch Burlington NJ 1966-1968. "Denning's Point," *A Hudson River Hist*, Black Dome Press, 2006; Auth, *Tchg Death & Dying to Late Adolescents*, 1978.

HERON, Marsha S (U) 4447 E Lake Cir S, Centennial CO 80121 B Eureka KS 1947 D 12/7/2002 Bp William Edwin Swing. m 4/10/1982 Michael R Carney. S Anselm's Epis Ch Lafayette CA 2003-2006.

HERRERA, Lourdes del Carmen (Hond) IMS SAP Dept 215. PO Box 523900, Miami FL 33152 Honduras B 1972 d Basidio & Dolores. D 10/22/2009 P 8/28/2010 Bp Lloyd Emmanuel Allen. m 6/11/1993 Heriberto Santos Urrutia c 3.

HERRERA, Maria I (Pa) B 1949 MDiv Ya Berk; MDiv Ya Berk; ABS U CA. D 6/3/1989 P 6/9/1990 Bp John Shelby Spong. S Paul's Ch Elkins Pk PA 1999-2011; The Ch Of The H Trin Rittenhouse Philadelphia PA 1997-1999; Dio Pennsylvania Philadelphia PA 1995-1997; S Dav's Ch Philadelphia PA 1995-1997; S Ptr's Ch Morristown NJ 1990-1993.

HERRERA CHAGNA, Raul (EcuC) Avenue Amazonas #4430, Igl Epis Del Ecuador, Quito Ecuador **Vic Iglesia San Lucas Pilahuin Ambato 1996-** B Otavalo EC 1957 s Samuel & Maria. ETSBH; Epis TS; Pontifical Cath U of Ecuador 1987; Pontifical Cath U of Ecuador 1989; ETSBH 1995; Epis TS 1995. D 4/17/1994 P 5/1/1997 Bp Jose Neptali Larrea-Moreno. m 8/16/1991 Zoila Chacon c 5. Iglesia Epis Del Ecuador Quito 1996-2016.

HERRICK, Robert Frank (NY) 159-00 Riverside Drive West, Apt 6K-70, New York NY 10032 B Bethlehem PA 1942 s Robert & Elizabeth. BA Pr 1964; STB GTS 1967; MBA Col 1981. D 6/17/1967 P 3/30/1968 Bp Frederick Warnecke. Int The Ch Of The Ascen Rockville Ct NY 2010-2012; Int The Ch of the Ascen Rockville Cntr NY 2010-2012; Supply P Chr Epis Ch Lynbrook NY 1999-2007; P-in-c S Jn's Ch New Rochelle NY 1985-1987; P-in-c S Andr's Epis Ch Hartsdale NY 1983-1984; Cur Trin Par New York NY 1969-1974; P-in-c S Dav's Scranton PA 1967-1969.

HERRING, Dianne Lerae (Wyo) PO Box 12, Kaycee WY 82639 B Laramie WY 1947 d Vernon & Virginia. D 8/18/2007 Bp Vernon Edward Strickland. m 8/12/1972 Gordon Herring c 2.

HERRING, John Foster (At) 634 W Peachtree St NW, Atlanta GA 30308 **R S Ptr's Ch Rome GA 2012-** B Livingston NJ 1969 s Joseph & Bonita. BA Washington Coll 1991; MDiv Sewanee: The U So, TS 2008. D 12/21/2007 P 10/19/2008 Bp J Neil Alexander. m 9/22/2001 Keri Lynne Herring c 3. Assoc R All SS Epis Ch Atlanta GA 2008-2012.

HERRING, Joseph Dahlet (At) 5575 N Hillbrooke Trce, Johns Creek GA 30005 B Englewood NJ 1934 s Joseph & Alice. AB Dart 1955; STB GTS 1960; STM GTS 1971. D 6/11/1960 P 12/17/1960 Bp Leland Stark. m 1/26/1963 Bonita Lynn Herring c 3. Asst , Anglo and Hisp Chr Epis Ch Norcross GA 2005-2007; Int S Steph's Ch Ridgefield CT 2003-2005; Int Emm Ch Middleburg VA 2002-2003; Int S Barth's Ch Cherry Hill NJ 2000-2002; Int S Steph's Ch Goldsboro NC 1999-2000; Int S Mich's Ch Bristol RI 1996-1999; Int Gr Ch Madison NJ 1995-1996; R Chr Ch Newton NJ 1983-1995; R S Steph's Ch Millburn NJ 1968-1983; Vic Ch Of The Trsfg Towaco NJ 1963-1968; Asst S

Paul's Epis Ch Paterson NJ 1960-1963; VOICE Ed Bd Dio Newark Newark NJ 1977-1996, COM 1971-1983, BEC 1965-1971; Com on Election, Bp Coadj Dio Newark 1975-1976. Soc of Jn the Bapt 1972. Bp's Outstanding Serv Awd Dio Newark 1987; Polly Bond Awd for Ed Writing ECom 1987; Polly Bond Awd for Ed Writing ECom 1985; Fell 83 Coll of Preachers 1983; Polly Bond Awd for Ed Writing ECom 1983; Americanism Awd Millburn/Short Hills 1983.

HERRING, Virginia (NC) 428 S Shore Dr, Osprey FL 34229 **P-in-c S Wlfd's Epis Ch Sarasota FL 2013-** B Norfolk VA 1945 d Joseph & Mildred. BA U NC 1985; MDiv Duke DS 1988; Sewanee: The U So, TS 1988; ThM Duke DS 1999. D 5/28/1988 Bp Frank Harris Vest Jr P 6/1/1989 Bp Robert Whitridge Estill. c 6. H Trin Epis Ch Greensboro NC 1999-2013; R S Anne's Ch Winston Salem NC 1992-1999; Asst to R S Lk's Ch Salisbury NC 1988-1992. va. herring413@gmail.com

HERRINGTON III, Willet Jeremiah (Mich) 30420 Rush St, Garden City MI 48135 B Bad Axe MI 1927 s Willet & Margaret. BA U MI 1950; MA U MI 1952; Whitaker TS 1970. D 3/18/1967 Bp Archie H Crowley P 4/30/1970 Bp Richard Stanley Merrill Emrich. m 12/21/1957 Joan Elizabeth Olsen. Asst S Andr's Epis Ch Livonia MI 1988-1999; Asst Journey of Faith Epis Ch Dearborn MI 1967-1987. Soc Of S Paul.

HERRMANN, H W (Dal) 623 Ector St, Denton TX 76201 **Alum Wrdn Nash Nashotah Wisconsin 2010-; R S Dav's Ch Denton TX 2006-** B Flushing NY 1951 s Herbert & Gloria. BS U of Texas Arlington 1974; MDiv Nash 1989. D 12/28/1988 P 10/23/1989 Bp Clarence Cullam Pope Jr. m 5/21/1977 Ginger A Till c 2. R St Johns Ch Quincy IL 1995-2006; Gr Epis Ch Monroe LA 1993-1995; S Fran Of Assisi Epis Ch Aledo TX 1990-1993; Cur S Mk's Ch Arlington TX 1989-1990. Bro of S Andr 1995; CBS 2002; SocMary 1992; SSC 1991.

HERRON, Daniel Peter (Az) St Mark's Church, 322 N Horne, Mesa AZ 85203 B Philadelphia PA 1946 s Edward & Catherine. Rec 9/7/2007 as Deacon Bp Carolyn Tanner Irish. m 6/20/1970 Elizabeth A Herron c 3. D S Mk's Epis Ch Mesa AZ 2010-2015.

HERRON-PIAZZA, Katherine Ann (Ct) 22 Coulter Ave, Pawling NY 12564 **The Par Of Emm Ch Weston CT 2015-** B Panama CZ 1972 d Philip & Ann. BA Ohio Wesl 1994; MPA Cleveland St U 1997; MDiv GTS 2006. D 6/3/2006 Bp Mark Hollingsworth Jr P 1/6/2007 Bp J Clark Grew II. m 5/27/2006 Jerome Mario Piazza c 2. Ch Of The H Trin Pawling NY 2013-2015; Cur S Jn's Ch Larchmont NY 2006-2011. htcoffice@gmail.com

HERSHBELL, Jackson Paul (SwVa) 274 Still House Dr, Lexington VA 24450 B Northampton PA 1935 s Paul & Elizabeth. BA Laf 1955; MA U of Pennsylvania 1956; STB GTS 1963; PhD Harv 1964. D 6/22/1963 P 6/6/1964 Bp Anson Phelps Stokes Jr. m 9/1/1984 Anne Snyder c 2. P Chr Epis Ch Buena Vista VA 2007-2012; Assoc R E Lee Memi Ch (Epis) Lexington VA 2004-2006; S Jn's Epis Ch Waynesboro VA 2002-2003; S Ptr's Ch Altavista VA 2002-2003; P-in-c Ascen Ch S Paul MN 1985-2000; Asst P S Chris's Epis Ch S Paul MN 1984-2000; P-in-c H Trin Epis Ch Elk River MN 1972-1980; 1967-1972; Cur Ch Of S Jn The Evang Hingham MA 1963-1966. Auth, *Iamblichus on the Mysteries*, Scholars Press, 2003; Auth, *Iamblichus on the Pythagorean Way of Life*, Scholars Press, 1991; Auth, "Numerous Pub in," *Hermes*, Classical Journ, Ancient Soc, Gk and Roman Stds. Amer Philological Assn 1969; Amer Philos Assn 1969. U of Durham 1993; Fllshp Alexander von Humboldt U of Munich 1977; Inst for Resrch in the Hmnts U of of Wisco 1969.

HERTH, Daniel Edwin (Cal) 32 Mallorie Park Drive, The Garden House, Ripon North Yorkshire HG42QF Great Britain (UK) **Serving Ch of Engl 1998-** B Cincinnati OH 1936 s Edwin & Alva. BS Xavier U 1958; MDiv CDSP 1983. D 6/25/1983 P 6/1/1984 Bp William Edwin Swing. m 5/18/2002 Sheila Margaret Farnell c 5. R Chr Ch Alameda CA 1986-1998; Asst S Paul's Ch Oakland CA 1983-1986. "Memories and Reflections: Hiroshima and the Trsfg," *The Friends Quarterly*, 'The Friend' Pub Ltd., 2005; "How do we know Jesus?," *The Friends Quarterly*, 'The Friend' Pub Ltd., 2003.

HERTLEIN, Chris (Ore) 2490 NE Highway 101, Lincoln City OR 97367 **S Jas Ch Lincoln City OR 2014-** B Seattle WA 1949 d Gordon & Florence. not completed U of Puget Sound; MDiv Epis TS Of The SW 2012; MDiv Epis TS of the SW 2012. D 1/17/2012 P 9/12/2012 Bp Gregory Harold Rickel. c 2. Mssnr for Hisp Mnstrs in So King and Pierce Counties Dio Olympia Seattle 2012-2013.

HERVEY JR, Theodore E (Tex) 933 N Fm 1174, Bertram TX 78605 B Frankfurt, Germany 1951 s Theodore & Cornelia. U of Montana 1970; BS VPI 1973; MDiv VTS 1976. D 6/7/1976 Bp Harold Cornelius Gosnell P 12/12/1976 Bp Scott Field Bailey. m 4/20/1990 Carol Jane Hervey c 1. R Epis Ch Of The Epiph Burnet Burnet TX 1994-2013; Int S Steph's Epis Ch Wimberley TX 1988; R Gr Ch Weslaco TX 1981-1987; Asst S Thos Epis Ch And Sch San Antonio TX 1978-1981; Asst All SS Epis Ch Corpus Christi TX 1976-1979; Hisp Mnstry Chair - Dio W Tx Dio W Texas San Antonio TX 1982-1986.

HERZOG, Carole Regina (Los) 1471 Cloister Dr, La Habra Heights CA 90631 **Com 1987-** B Montclair NJ 1943 d Joseph & Stephanie. BS Seton Hall U 1965; MA ETSBH 1983. D 6/18/1983 Bp Albert Wiencke Van Duzer P 1/1/1984 Bp Robert Claflin Rusack. m 4/6/1988 William A Herzog. S Steph's Par Whittier CA 1986-1996; Asst S Andr's Par Fullerton CA 1983-1986, 1980-1983.

✠ HERZOG, The Rt Rev Daniel William (Alb) 612 S Shore Rd, Delanson NY 12053 **Dir of Healing and Sprtl Formation Mnstry Chr the King Sprtl Life Cntr Greenwich NY 2014-; Ret Bp of Albany Dio Albany Greenwich NY 2007-, Bp of Albany 1998-2007, Bp Coadj of Albany 1997-1998, Stndg Com 1995-1997, Stndg Com 1995-1997, Com 1990-1996** B Ogdensburg NY 1941 s William & Mary. BA S Bonaventure U 1964; Nash 1970; MEd S Lawr Canton NY 1971; Nash 1998. D 5/12/1971 Bp Allen Webster Brown P 11/13/1971 Bp Charles Bowen Persell Jr Con 11/29/1997 for Alb. m 2/27/1965 Carol Herzog c 5. Alpha Course 1995-2002; R Chr Ch Schenectady NY 1995-1997; Pres Morristown Area Cler Assn 1990-1991; Theol Reflector Wadhams Hall Sem Coll 1982-1994; R Chr Ch Morristown NY 1976-1995; Cur S Jn's Ch Ogdensburg NY 1971-1976; Personl Dir St Lawr Psych Cntr Ogdensburg NY 1967-1995. Assn Of The Cmnty Of S Mk - Greenwich, Ny 2001; Benedictine Oblate 1964.

HERZOG, Kenneth Bernard (Fla) 3545 Olympic Dr, Green Cove Springs FL 32043 **Asst Trin Epis Ch St Aug FL 2009-** B Erlanger KY 1951 s Bernard & Rita. MA S Vinc de Paul Sem 1990; MDiv Sewanee: The U So, TS 1995. D 7/29/1995 Bp John Lewis Said P 1/1/1996 Bp Calvin Onderdonk Schofield Jr. m 5/24/1985 Elizabeth A Herzog c 1. S Marg's-Hibernia Epis Ch Fleming Island FL 1998-2009; S Mary's Epis Ch Stuart FL 1995-1998.

HESCHLE, John Henry (Chi) 7100 North Ashland Blvd, Chicago IL 60626 **R S Paul's By The Lake Chicago IL 1993-** B Hackensack NJ 1953 s John & Dorothy. BA Hope Coll 1975; MDiv SWTS 1978. D 12/20/1978 P 6/29/1979 Bp James Winchester Montgomery. Chair, Pstr Care Morrison Cmnty Hosp Morrison IL 1980-1993; The Ch Of S Anne Morrison IL 1979-1993; Gr Ch Sterling IL 1979-1982.

HESS, George Robert (HB) **Non-par 1969-** B Gilmer TX 1941 s Robert & Alice. STB Ya Berk; BA Baylor U 1963; Oxf GB 1964. D 6/13/1967 Bp Walter H Gray P 12/1/1967 Bp Charles A Mason. m 6/3/1967 Martha Hess. Cur S Lk's Epis Ch Dallas TX 1967-1969.

HESS, Howard (ETenn) 8500 Cambridge Woods Ln, Knoxville TN 37923 B Atlantic City NJ 1944 s Howard & Alice. MA U Chi 1970; DSW U of Alabama 1981; MDiv Ya Berk 2000. Trans 2/3/2004 Bp Charles Glenn VonRosenberg. m 10/17/1970 Mary Hess c 2. R Ch Of The Ascen Knoxville TN 2007-2015; S Chris's Ch Kingsport TN 2003-2007; Assoc R S Thad Epis Ch Aiken SC 2000-2003.

HESS III, Raymond Leonard (NCal) 9001 Crowley Way, Elk Grove CA 95624 **Assoc S Fran Epis Ch Fair Oaks CA 2013-; P-in-c S Geo's Ch Carmichael CA 2013-** B Sewickley PA 1947 s Raymond & Ruth. BA Stan 1969; MDiv CDSP 1972; DMin Fuller TS 2000. D 6/29/1974 Bp Chauncie Kilmer Myers P 2/27/1975 Bp Jackson Earle Gilliam. m 4/1/1978 Deborah Lee Hess c 3. St Marys Ch Elk Grove Sacramento CA 2011-2012, R 2007-2009; Ch of the Gd Shpd Colorado Spg CO 2001-2007; R S Mk's Epis Ch Santa Clara CA 1994-2001; Vic S Mths Epis Ch San Ramon CA 1984-1994; R Chr Ch Cedar Rapids IA 1980-1984; Assoc All SS Ch Carmel CA 1977-1980; Cur Ch Of The H Sprt Missoula MT 1974-1977; Dn The Epis Dio Nthrn California Sacramento CA 2012-2015.

HESS, Richard Walton (Cal) 601 Torre Malibu, 325 Calle Amapas, Puerto Vallarta Mexico B Stewartstown PA 1932 s Walton & Alice. BA U of Pennsylvania 1955; BD Drew U 1958; VTS 1960. D 11/27/1960 Bp Oliver J Hart P 6/1/1961 Bp Joseph Gillespie Armstrong. c 3. Int The Ch Of S Jn The Evang Flossmoor IL 1994-1995; Gr Cathd San Francisco CA 1988-1993; Actg Dn Trin Cathd Miami FL 1987-1988; Non-par 1986-1987; The Epis Ch Of Beth-By-The-Sea Palm Bch FL 1985-1987; R S Dav's Ch Wayne PA 1967-1983, Asst Min 1963-1966; Vic S Christophers Epis Ch Oxford PA 1960-1963.

HESSE, Alan Roger (Mass) 409 Common St, Walpole MA 02081 **Chr Ch Swansea MA 2015-; Barbara C Harris Camp & Conf Ctr Boardmember Dio Massachusetts Boston MA 2011-, Dioc Coun 2010-, Dioc. Liturg Com 2006-** B Sioux City IA 1963 s Marvin & Elizabeth. BA Morningside Coll 1986; MDiv EDS 2001. D 5/25/2001 Bp Steven Charleston P 1/18/2002 Bp Thomas Kreider Ray. m 5/21/2004 Timothy Orwig c 1. R Epiph Par Walpole MA 2005-2015; Asst All SS Ch Worcester MA 2001-2005. Auth, "How Do You See God," *The Angl Dig*, 2002. alhesse@verizon.net

HESSE JR, Rayner Wilson (NY) 415 Collins St, Bethany Beach DE 19930 B Baltimore MD 1955 s Rayner & Dorothy. BA U of Maryland 1976; MDiv UTS 1982; STM GTS 1989; DMin NYTS 2005. D 6/5/1982 P 12/12/1982 Bp Paul Moore Jr. m 1/1/2012 Anthony Frank Chiffolo. Pstr S Jn's Ch New Rochelle NY 1994-2013; R S Andr's Epis Ch Hartsdale NY 1984-1994; Asst S Jn's Ch Getty Sq Yonkers NY 1982-1984. Co-Auth, "Cooking w the Movies: Meals on Reels," ABC-Clio, 2010; Auth, "Jewelry Making Through Hist: An Encyclopedia," Greenwood, 2007; Co-Auth, "Cooking w the Bible: Biblic Foods, Feasts & Love," Greenwood, 2006; Co-Auth, "We Thank You God For These: Blessings & Prayers for Fam Pets," Paulist, 2004.

HESSE, Vicki K (Mich) Episcopal Diocese of Michigan, 4800 Woodward Ave, Detroit MI 48201 **Assoc Chr Ch Grosse Pointe Grosse Pointe Farms MI 2015-** B Redondo Beach CA 1959 d Frederick & Wylma. BS California St U 1982; BS California St U 1982; MDiv Iliff TS 2007; Post Grad Dplma Angl Stds VTS 2012. D 6/2/2012 Bp Porter Taylor P 12/8/2012 Bp Kirk Stevan

Smith. m 10/17/2014 Leah Michelle Mccullough. S Phil's In The Hills Tucson AZ 2012-2015. vhesse@edomi.org

HESSE, William Arthur (Okla) 1805 N Canary Dr, Edmond OK 73034 **Chapl Fountains at Cbury Ret Cntr 2001-; D S Mary's Ch Edmond OK 1993-** B Deadwood SD 1938 s Arthur & Thelma. AA El Camino Coll 1964; BA UCLA 1966. D 6/26/1993 Bp Robert Manning Moody. m 7/7/1962 Diane B Hesse.

HETHCOCK, William Hoover (Tenn) Po Box 3310, Sewanee TN 37375 B Thomasville NC 1932 s Hugh & Emma. BA U NC 1954; MDiv GTS 1959; DMin Sewanee: The U So, TS 1984. D 9/18/1959 P 3/19/1960 Bp Richard Henry Baker. m 7/29/1972 Phebe Anne Hethcock c 3. Vstng Prof VTS Alexandria VA 2002-2004; Int Bruton Par Williamsburg VA 1999-2000; Prof Homil Emer Sewanee U So TS Sewanee TN 1997, Assoc Prof Homil 1985-1996; S Lk's Epis Ch N Little Rock AR 1992; Asst Chr Ch Cathd Cincinnati OH 1974-1979; Dir Prog Dio No Carolina Raleigh NC 1967-1974, Dir Prog 1967-1974; R S Lk's Epis Ch Durham NC 1960-1966; Cur S Andr's Ch Greensboro NC 1959-1960. Acad of Homilitics 1985-1987. Jess Trotter Vstng Fell VTS 2000.

HETHERINGTON, Robert Gunn (Va) 1500 Westbrook Ct Apt 2133, Richmond VA 23227 B Buffalo NY 1941 s Arthur & Betty. BA Ya 1963; MDiv EDS 1966. D 6/11/1966 Bp William S Thomas P 12/17/1966 Bp Austin Pardue. m 8/28/1965 Elizabeth B Hetherington. c 3. R S Paul's Ch Richmond VA 1984-2006; R Trin Epis Ch Buffalo NY 1973-1984, Assoc 1969-1972; Asst S Steph's Ch Sewickley PA 1966-1969. Hon Cn Dio Wstrn New York 1982.

HETLER, Gwendolyn Kay (NMich) 3135 County Road 456, Skandia MI 49885 B 1939 BA Albion Coll 1961; MS Wayne 1973. D 12/17/2000 P 7/1/2001 Bp James Arthur Kelsey. m 6/21/1986 James Leo Livingston. *Beginning Algebra: Once and For All*, Kendall/Hunt, 2000.

HETRICK JR, Budd Albert (Ida) 7470 Sundance Dr, Boise ID 83709 B Nampa ID 1949 s Budd & Sylvia. D 1/29/1994 Bp John Stuart Thornton. m 7/14/1967 Sharlene Fields. D S Mich's Cathd Boise ID 1998-2001; P Trin Epis Ch Pocatello ID 1994-1995, Yth & Acolyte Coordntr 1994-1995; Acolyte Coordntr & Cmnty Outreach Ch Of H Nativ Meridian ID 2001-2002; Liturg & Adult Educ S Dav's Epis Ch Caldwell ID 1995-1998.

HETZEL, Alan Dorn (WNC) Po Box 442, Highlands NC 28741 B Charleston SC 1933 s Harry & Geraldine. U So 1954; BA U of Florida 1955. D 12/18/1999 Bp Bob Johnson. m 11/17/1972 Hazel Crawford. D Trin Epis Ch Asheville NC 2000-2002; D Ch Of The Incarn Highlands NC 1999-2004.

HEUSS, William Beresford (Mass) 15 Thimbleberry Rd, South Yarmouth MA 02664 B Evanston IL 1941 s John & Elizabeth. BA Wag 1964; MDiv Sewanee: The U So, TS 1968; DMin Bos 1976. D 6/16/1968 P 12/21/1968 Bp Chilton R Powell. m 11/21/2009 Margaret Anne Huess. R S Dav's Epis Ch S Yarmouth MA 1996-2008; R The Ch Of The Gd Shpd Acton MA 1983-1996; Epis Cler Assoc Dio Massachusetts Boston MA 1974-2008; S Andr's Ch Wellesley MA 1974-1983; Assoc Trin Ch Tulsa OK 1968-1974. Auth, "The Sermon'S Over - Hit The Offertory!," *New Par New Cure*. Assn Of Psychol Type 1988; Enneagram Personality Types Assn 1993. Winner For Best Cartoons Associated Rel Press 1985; Winner For Best Cartoons Associated Rel Press 1984.

HEVERLY, Craig Brian (Ore) 925 Se Center St, Portland OR 97202 B Buffalo NY 1938 s Samuel & Ruth. BA Colg 1960; MA Colg 1967; Lon GB 1976; MDiv Chicago TS 1983. D 6/8/1985 P 5/1/1986 Bp O'Kelley Whitaker. m 6/30/1962 Judy Jo Heverly c 2. Seven Rivers Cluster Payette ID 1988-1995; Paris Cluster Chadwicks NY 1986-1988; R S Mk's Ch Clark Mills NY 1986-1988; Assoc S Jas' Ch Clinton NY 1985-1988; Dio Cntrl New York Liverpool NY 1985-1986; Epis Chapl Syr Syracuse NY 1985-1986. Synagogy.

HEWETSON, Richard Walton (Cal) B Harvey, Ill. 1930 s Reginald & Clara. BA U MN 1954; MDiv SWTS 1957. D 6/24/1957 Bp Hamilton Hyde Kellogg P 2/18/1958 Bp Philip Frederick McNairy.

HEWETT, Clayton Kennedy (Pa) 510 Augusta Rd, Winslow ME 04901 **Died 8/1/2015** B Providence RI 1927 s William & Phylis. VTS 1958; Urban Trng Cntr 1964. D 6/21/1958 Bp Oliver J Hart P 12/20/1958 Bp William Blair Roberts. c 1. R Ch Of S Jas The Less Philadelphia PA 1971-1976; R Calv Epis Ch Hillcrest Wilmington DE 1967-1971; Urban Mssnr Dio Pennsylvania Philadelphia PA 1965-1967; R The Ch Of The Atone Morton PA 1958-1965. OHC 1963-1980; S Richard's Gld - Fndr & Dir 1979. Cn to the Ordnry Dio the Resurr 1978.

HEWIS, Clara Mae (CGC) 7979 N 9th Ave, Pensacola FL 32514 B Winchester MA 1940 d Arthur & Louise. MEd Cambridge Coll; EFM-Cert Sewanee: The U So, TS 2003; EFM-Cert The TS at The U So 2003; Cert of Ord Other 2011; Cert of Ord Sch for the Diac, Dio Cntrl Gulf Coast 2011. D 2/10/2011 Bp Philip Menzie Duncan II. c 1. Par Admin St. Fran of Assisi Epis Ch Gulf Breeze FL 1999-2010.

HEWITT, Emily Clark (NY) 1848 Commonwealth Ave Apt 56, Boston MA 02135 **Non-par 1975-** B Baltimore MD 1944 d John & Margaret. BA Cor; MA UTS 1975; JD Harv 1978. D 6/3/1972 Bp Paul Moore Jr P 7/29/1974 Bp Robert Lionne DeWitt. Auth, "Wmn P: Yes Or No?"; Auth, "arts Revs".

HEYBOER, Bobbi Jo (WMich) 30 Justice St, Newaygo MI 49337 **S Mk's Ch Newaygo MI 2016-** B Grand Rapids MI 1970 d Jerry & Trudy. BA Calvin Coll 1992; MDiv The U So TS 2016. D 6/11/2016 Bp Whayne Miller Hougland Jr.

HEYD, Matthew F (NY) 74 Trinity Pl, New York NY 10006 **Ch Of The Heav Rest New York NY 2013-** B Greenville NC 1969 s Peter & Delores. BA U NC 1992; MAR Yale DS 1995; STM GTS 2009. D 3/7/2009 P 9/12/2009 Bp Mark Sean Sisk. m 6/1/1996 Ann Duggan Thornton c 1. Dir of Faith in Action Trin Par New York NY 2011-2013, 2009-2013; Stndg Com Dio New York New York NY 2010-2014.

HEYDT, Charles Read (SwFla) 523 S Palm Ave Apt 7, Sarasota FL 34236 B Cleveland OH 1937 s Richard. BA Dart 1959; MS NWU 1968; MDiv VTS 1979. D 6/30/1979 P 1/10/1980 Bp William Gillette Weinhauer. m 10/9/2014 Diane Parker Heydt c 2. R S Andr's Ch Boca Grande FL 2005-2012; Int S Paul's Ch Albany GA 2003-2005; Int S Jn's Epis Ch Clearwater FL 2001-2003; Int S Mk's Epis Ch Jacksonville FL 1999-2000; Assoc Trin By The Cove Naples FL 1995-1999; Stndg Com Dio Ohio Cleveland 1992-1994; R Chr Ch Epis Hudson OH 1984-1995; Asst Trin Ch Toledo OH 1979-1984. Int Mnstry Ntwk 1999. readheydt3@comcast.net

HEYDUK, Terri (U) St James Episcopal Church, 7486 S Union Park Ave, Midvale UT 84047 **S Jas Epis Ch Midvale UT 2015-; Cler Coach/Consult Samar Counslg Cntr Naperville IL 2010-** B Philadelphia PA 1952 d Walter & Marie. BA Marymount Coll 1981; MDiv GTS 1996. D 6/1/1996 P 12/7/1996 Bp Richard Frank Grein. m 9/3/2012 Pamela J Holliman. Int S Paul's Ch Salt Lake City UT 2013-2014; Int S Chrys's Ch Chicago IL 2012-2013; Int Pstr S Jn The Evang Lockport IL 2010-2011; R S Andr's Ch Brewster NY 2000-2009; Int S Steph's Ch Pearl River NY 1999-2000; Asst R Trin-St Jn's Ch Hewlett NY 1996-1999. mheyduk@gmail.com

HEYES, Andrew Robin (SwFla) 706 W 113th Ave, Tampa FL 33612 **R S Clem Epis Ch Tampa FL 2006-** B United Kingdom 1961 s George & Joan. Trans 12/7/2006 Bp John Bailey Lipscomb.

HEYING, R Christopher (WLa) 3301 Saint Matthias Dr, Shreveport LA 71119 **Vic S Mths Epis Ch Shreveport LA 2017-** B Socorro NM 1964 s Robert & Doris. BA, hon U of No Texas 1986; MDiv, hon Nash 1998. D 6/27/1998 P 12/28/1998 Bp Jack Leo Iker. m 9/1/1990 Cindy P Perkins c 3. S Paul's Ch Abbeville LA 2015-2017; P-in-c Emm Epis Ch Chatham VA 2012-2015; R S Steph's Epis Ch Forest VA 2004-2012; Ch Of S Jn The Div Burkburnett TX 2001-2004; Dio Ft Worth Ft Worth TX 2001-2004; Vic The Epis Ch of Wichita Falls Wichita Falls TX 2001-2004; Cur Ch Of The Trsfg New York NY 2001; Asst S Paul's Epis Ch Murfreesboro TN 1999-2001; Cur S Jn's Ch Ft Worth TX 1998-1999.

HEYVAERT, Bruce T (Ark) Saint James Church, PO Box 846, Magnolia AR 71754 **S Thos Epis Ch Sanford NC 2016-; Vic S Jas Ch Magnolia AR 2013-** B Torrington CT 1955 s John & Ruth. S Mary Coll Winona Minnesota 1975; Iowa St U Ames Iowa 1977; BA S Thos Sem 1979; MDiv S Thos Sem 1983. Rec 9/29/1994 as Priest Bp Bob Gordon Jones. m 4/30/2016 Deborah Baker. Assoc S Anth On The Desert Scottsdale AZ 2011-2013; Assoc R S Ptr's Epis Ch 1994-1998; Assoc Pstr St Pat's Cath Ch 1982-1985. Aircraft Owners and Pilots Associaton 1985.

HEYWARD, Isabel Carter (Mass) PO Box 449, Cedar Mountain NC 28718 B Charlotte NC 1945 d Robert & Mary. BA Randolph-Macon Coll 1967; MA Col 1971; MDiv UTS 1973; PhD UTS 1980. D 6/9/1973 Bp Paul Moore Jr P 7/29/1974 Bp Robert Lionne DeWitt. Prof Theol EDS Cambridge MA 1975-2005. Auth, "Keep Your Courage: A Radical Chr Speaks," 2010; Auth, "The Redemp of God, 2nd Ed," w Preface by Janet L. Surrey, Ph.D., 2010; Auth, "Flying Changes: Horses as Sprtl Teachers," 2005; Auth, "God In The Balance: Chr Sprtlty In Timeo Of Terror," 2002; Auth, "Saving Jesus From Those Who Are Rt," 1999; Auth, "Staying Power," 1995; Auth, "When Boundaries Betray Us," 1993; Auth, "Spkng Of Chr," 1989; Auth, "Teachng Our Strength: Erotic As Power & The Love Of God," 1989; Auth, "Revolutionary Forgiveness," 1986; Auth, "God'S Fierce Whimsey," 1985; Auth, "Our Passion For Justice," 1984; Auth, "Redemp Of God: Theol Of Mutual Relatns," 1982; Auth, "A P Forever: Formation of a Wmn and a a Pries," 1975. Distinguished Alum Awd Randolph-Macon Wmn'S Coll 2001; Distinguished Alum Awd UTS, NYC 1998; Danforth Fllshp 1977.

HIATT, Anthony Ray (FtW) PO Box 22, Decatur TX 76234 B Indianapolis IN 1958 s Lloyd & Treva. BS Pur 1982; MA Brite DS 2014. D 10/7/2014 P 4/11/2015 Bp Rayford Baines High Jr. m 10/1/1983 Lydia Campbell Hiatt c 3. tony. hiatt@edfw.org

HIATT, Kathleen Mary (Nev) Po Box 146, Pioche NV 89043 B Pioche NV 1950 d John & Kathleen. Cosmetology Sch. D 12/7/1995 Bp Stewart Clark Zabriskie. m 11/10/1972 Melvin Lee Hiatt c 3.

✠ HIBBS, The Rt Rev Robert Boyd (WTex) 1 Towers Park Ln Apt 1807, San Antonio TX 78209 **Died 4/17/2017** B Philadelphia PA 1932 s Robert & Hazel. BA Trin Hartford CT 1954; STB GTS 1957; MA U Tor 1959. D 6/1/1957 Bp William P Roberts P 12/21/1957 Bp Oliver J Hart Con 1/6/1996 for WTex. m 8/24/1957 Nancy Hibbs c 2. Ret Bp Suffr of W Texas Dio W Texas San Antonio TX 2004-2017, Bp Suffr Of W Texas 1996-2003; Sr Asst Ch Of The Gd Shpd Corpus Christi TX 1988-1996; R S Barn Epis Ch Fredricksburg TX 1983-1988; Prof Epis TS Of The SW Austin TX 1980-1983, Fac 1972-1975; Dn St. Andrews Sem Manila the Philippines 1976-1979; Fac St. Andrews Sem Manila the Philippines 1961-1972; Serv Ch In Can 1957-1961. Sem Rep Epis Preaching Fndt Seminar 2011; Vic Emer St. Jn the Evang Epis Ch 2011; D.D. Epis TS of the SW 1996; D.D. GTS 1996; Phi Beta Kappa Trin, Hartford, CN 1954.

HICKENLOOPER, Andrew Morgan (CGC) Po Box 27120, Panama City FL 32411 B Cincinnati OH 1946 s Smith & Virginia. BS Buc 1968; MBA Syr 1970; JD U of Missouri 1980; MDiv Epis TS of the SW 1993. D 6/5/1993 Bp John Clark Buchanan P 12/18/1993 Bp John Forsythe Ashby. m 5/16/1998 Mary Kennedy c 3. R Gr Epis Ch Panama City Bch FL 2001-2006; Cn To the Ordnry & Deploy Off Dio Michigan Detroit MI 1995-2001; Dio Wstrn Kansas Hutchinson KS 1993-1995; Vic S Anne's Ch Mcpherson KS 1993-1995. Beta Gamma Sigma (Bus) 1970; Law Sch hon Soc 1980; Missouri Bar Assn 1980; Trst ETSSw 1996-2000.

HICKEY, John D (Mil) 7845 N River Rd, River Hills WI 53217 **Exec Dir Seedling Mnstrs Milwaukee WI 2010-** B South Bend IN 1951 s Austin & Rosemary. BA Marq 1973; JD Marq 1991; MDiv SWTS 2005; MDiv SWTS 2005; MDiv SWTS 2005. D 6/4/2005 P 6/13/2007 Bp Steven Andrew Miller. c 2. S Lk's Epis Ch Milwaukee WI 2012-2013; S Bon Ch Thiensville WI 2007-2010; Asstg P S Chris's Ch Milwaukee WI 2007.

HICKEY-TIERNAN, Joseph J (Oly) 3415 S 45th St Apt G, Tacoma WA 98409 **Vstng Prof of Rel Pacific Luth U 2006-** B Philadelphia PA 1944 s Arnold & Catherine. BA S Marys Sem & U Baltimore 1966; STB S Marys Sem and U 1968; STL CUA 1971. P 2/7/1971 Bp Robert Hume Cochrane. m 12/29/2001 Deborah L Hickey-Tiernan c 2. S Jas Epis Ch Kent WA 2014-2015; St Paul's Seattle Dio Olympia Seattle 2010-2013, St Paul's Seattle 2004-2005, Stndg Com Pres 1995-1998, Const & Cns Com 1994-1995, Draft Com Profsnl Standards 1992-1995, Com 1984-1987; Vstng Prof.of Rel Pacific Luth U Tacoma WA 2006-2015; R S Barn Epis Ch Bainbridge Island WA 1988-2004; Dn Cntr For Diac Dio Oregon Portland OR 1984-1988, Cmsn Mssn 1979-1983, Wa Assn Chs T/F On Theol Educ 1978; R All SS Ch Portland OR 1981-1988; Vic S Hilda's - S Pat's Epis Ch Edmonds WA 1977-1981; S Jn's Epis Ch Olympia WA 1976-1977. Auth, "Coping w A Dissolution Struggle: Survival," Leaven, 1995.

HICKMAN, Clare L (Mich) 851 Reagan St, Canton MI 48188 **R S Lk's Ch Ferndale MI 2008-** B Wembury UK 1967 d John & Dorothy. BA Macalester Coll 1989; M.T.S. Harvard DS 1992; MDiv SWTS 1998. D 6/27/1998 P 2/10/1999 Bp R aymond Stewart Wood Jr. m 6/28/2014 Brian Wallman. Asst Chr Ch Dearborn MI 1998-2008. rector@stlukesferndale.org

HICKMAN, Donald Royce (Dal) 183 Rainbow Dr # 8309, Livingston TX 77399 **Died 10/31/2016** B Tulsa OK 1940 s Hugh & Nola. BA U of Tulsa 1969; MDiv VTS 1973. D 6/16/1973 P 12/9/1973 Bp Chilton R Powell. m 4/3/1959 Lorena Nell Hickman c 2. R S Mths' Epis Ch Athens TX 1999-2005; Asst P Ch Of The Epiph Flagstaff AZ 1998-1999; Grand Canyon Cmnty Ch Grand Canyon AZ 1997-1998; Chapl Grand Canyon Natl Pk AZ 1997-1998; R Ch Of The Ascen Salida CO 1986-1997; Vic Little Shpd Of The Hills Chap Alamosa CO 1986-1997; Ch of the H Sprt Rifle CO 1983-1986; S Jn's Cathd Denver CO 1983-1986; Vic S Jn's Epis Ch New Castle CO 1983-1986; R S Paul's Epis Ch Dixon WY 1982-1983; Vic Our Fr's Hse Lander WY 1979-1982; St Michaels Ch - Ethete Lander WY 1979-1982; R All SS Epis Ch Miami WY 1975-1979; Cur Trin Ch Tulsa OK 1974-1975; S Jn's Epis Ch Vinita OK 1973-1974; Cur St Mart of Tours Epis Ch Pryor OK 1973-1974. Fed Of Fire Chapl 1994-1997. donandlorena@yahoo.com

HICKS, Catherine D (Va) PO Box 399, Port Royal VA 22535 **VTS Alexandria VA 2014-, 2013, 2012; Coordntr of Chap Wrshp VTS 2012-; Sprtl Dir VTS 2011-; R S Ptr's Port Royal Port Royal VA 2010-** B Columbus GA 1954 d Matthew & Lola. BA Salem Coll 1976; Cert Med Coll of Virginia/VCU 2001; MSW Virginia Commonwealth U 2001; MDiv VTS 2010; Cert Washington Theol Un 2011. D 6/5/2010 P 12/11/2010 Bp Shannon Sherwood Johnston. m 4/23/1977 Ben Hicks c 3. Com on the Stwdshp of Creation Dio Virginia Richmond VA 2009-2012. The hon Soc of Phi Kappa Phi 2001. Jn Hines Preaching Awd VTS 2013.

HICKS, John Wellborn (CGC) 502 La Rose Dr, Mobile AL 36609 B Mobile AL 1947 s Wellborn & Dorothy. BA S Mary 1968; MTh Mt S Marys Sem 1973. Rec 7/1/1980 as Deacon Bp James Winchester Montgomery. m 9/7/1974 Patricia R Hicks c 1. S Andr's Ch Mobile AL 2004-2012; Ch Of S Marys-By-The-Sea Coden AL 1996-2012; Non-par 1989-1991; Int S Ptr's Ch Jackson AL 1984-1985; S Mich's Ch Mobile AL 1981-1982; Asst Dir Dioc Chld Hm Wilmer Hall Mobile AL 1981-1982; Asst S Paul's By The Lake Chicago IL 1976-1980. stmaryscoden@gmail.com

HICKS, Mary Kohn (WMass) 88 Masonic Home Rd, #R404, Charlton MA 01507 B Newberry SC 1923 d Hal & Verna. BA Winthrop U 1944. D 10/9/1982 Bp Alexander D Stewart. m 2/10/1945 John Hick c 5. D H Trin Epis Ch Southbridge MA 1998-2011, D 1982-1997; D Ch Of The Recon Webster MA 1990-1996.

HICKS, Paul L (WVa) 430 Juliana St., Parkersburg WV 26101 B Roswell NM 1963 s Paul & Vivian. BS W Virginia U 1985; JD W Virginia U Coll of Law 1997; Cert Bex Sem 2007. D 5/1/2008 P 12/13/2008 Bp William Michie

H

Klusmeyer. m 4/9/1994 Beverly Meares. Pstr Assoc Trin Ch Parkersburg WV 2008-2015, Pastorial Assoc 2008-. frpaulhicks@trinity-church.org

HICKS, Richard William (La) 2507 Portola Ave Apt 20, Livermore CA 94551 B San Francisco CA 1938 s Richard & Phyllis. Nash; BA San Francisco St U 1972; MDiv CDSP 1975. D 6/28/1975 Bp George Richard Millard P 1/1/1976 Bp Clarence Rupert Haden Jr. c 2. S Tim's Epis Ch Chehalis WA 2001-2002; Emm Ch Coos Bay OR 2000-2001; Trin Epis Ch Ashland Ashland OR 1999-2000; Int S Barth's Ch Beaverton OR 1998-1999; S Paul's/H Trin New Roads LA 1995-1998; Dio Wstrn Kansas Hutchinson KS 1993-1995; Trin Epis Ch Norton KS 1990-1991; Vic S Paul's Epis Ch Beloit WI 1989-1995; Ch Of The Epiph Concordia KS 1989-1993; Beloit First Chr Beloit KS 1989; Assoc S Jude's Chld's Ranch Boulder City Nv 1988-1989; Chapl Eskaton Hlth Corp 1986-1987; Trin Ch Ennis MT 1983-1986; R H Trin Ennis Mtn CA 1983-1985; R S Lk's Ch Auburn CA 1977-1983; Vic Ch Of The Gd Shpd Orland CA 1975-1977; Vic H Trin Epis Ch Willows CA 1975-1977.

HICKS, Sally Sue (Colo) Po Box 1590, Granby CO 80446 B Glenrock WY 1934 d Ira & Julia. BA Regis U 1992. D 11/4/1995 Bp William Jerry Winterrowd. c 2. D St. Jn the Bapt Epis Ch Granby CO 1996-2003; S Ambr Epis Ch Boulder CO 1995-1996. NAAD 1995. Bp's Cross Sprtl Direction Mnstry Bp W.interrowd 2001.

HICKS, Warren Earl (WMass) 921 Pleasant St, Worcester MA 01602 **Dn of Cntrl & Wstrn Worcester Dnry Dio Wstrn Massachusetts Springfield 2008-** B Ft Sill OK 1960 s Donovan & Sally. AOS Culinary Inst of Amer 1987; BA Metropltn St Coll of Denver 2000; MDiv Epis TS of the SW 2003. D 6/14/2003 P 12/13/2003 Bp William Jerry Winterrowd. m 4/4/1986 Mary Cecilia Hutchinson c 2. R S Lk's Ch Worcester MA 2006-2015; S Mk's Ch Worcester MA 2006-2014; Vic Epis Mssn of the San Luis Vlly Alamosa CO 2003-2006; Vic Epis Mssn In The San Luis Vlly Monte Vista CO 2003-2006.

HIEBERT, Cornelius A (Dal) 8105 Fair Oaks Xing, Dallas TX 75231 B Wichita KS 1952 s Franklin & Elma. BD Wichita St U 1976; MDiv Nash 1981. D 7/9/1981 Bp Richard Frank Grein P 1/3/1982 Bp Robert Elwin Terwilliger. c 1. The Epis Ch Of The Resurr Dallas TX 1981-1982. Auth, "Living The Gd News," *Sunday Sch Curric*, 1976.

HIERS JR, John Douglas (SwFla) 1004 Woodcrest Ave, Clearwater FL 33756 **R Ch Of The Ascen Clearwater FL 2000-** B 1953 s John & Mary. BA U of So Florida 1975; MDiv VTS 1978. D 6/14/1978 P 3/17/1979 Bp Emerson Paul Haynes. m 6/21/1975 Brenda D Hiers c 3. Asst Chr Ch Bradenton FL 1983-2000; Asst S Mk's Epis Ch Venice FL 1978-1983.

HIERS, Sharon Leigh (At) 2089 Ponce de Leon Ave NE, Atlanta GA 30307 **Assoc Ch Of The Epiph Atlanta GA 2015-** B Hampton SC 1971 d James & Lucyle. BS Coastal Carolina U 1996; MDiv TS 2007; MDiv Sewanee: The U So, TS 2007; MDiv Sewanee The U So, TS 2007; DMin TS 2015; DMin Sewanee: The U So, TS 2015. D 2/21/2009 P 9/13/2009 Bp J Neil Alexander. m 9/9/2011 Lisa Ann Newton. Assoc R for Yth & YA Formation S Barth's Epis Ch Atlanta GA 2009-2015. sharon@epiphany.org

HIGGINBOTHAM, John E (RI) 99 Pierce St, East Greenwich RI 02818 **Ch Of The H Trin Tiverton RI 2012-; Ecum Off Dio Rhode Island Providence RI 2014-; Cler Compstn & Benefits Com Dio Rhode Island 2014-** B Providence RI 1954 s Robert & Dorothy. BA S Meinrad Coll 1982; MDiv EDS 2010. D 1/8/2011 P 10/18/2011 Bp Gerry Wolf. c 4. D S Lk's Epis Ch E Greenwich RI 2011, P 2011-.

HIGGINBOTHAM, Richard Cann (Chi) 3800 N Lake Shore Dr # 1j, Chicago IL 60613 **Int R S Thos Ch Morris IL 2016-** B Saint Louis MO 1950 s Richard & Jocelyn. BA Macalester Coll 1972; MA U MN 1973; MA U IL 1978; MDiv SWTS 1994. D 6/18/1994 P 12/17/1994 Bp Frank Tracy Griswold III. Asst Ch Of The Ascen Chicago IL 1996-2008; Epis Campus Mssnr Neiu Chicago IL 1994-2003; Asst S Chris's Epis Ch Oak Pk IL 1994-1996.

HIGGINBOTHAM, Stuart Craig (At) 2900 Paces Ferry Rd SE Bldg D, Atlanta GA 30339 **R Gr Epis Ch Gainesville GA 2015-, 2014-2015; Cur St Ben's Epis Ch 2008-** B 1979 s Marion & Teresa. BS Lyon Coll 2001; MDiv Columbia TS 2005; Dip Ang Stud Sewanee: The U So, TS 2008. D 12/21/2007 P 6/29/2008 Bp J Neil Alexander. m 5/31/2003 Lisa R S Stiles c 1. P St Ben's Epis Ch Smyrna GA 2010-2013; Dio Atlanta Atlanta GA 2008-2009. stuart@gracechurchgainesville.org

HIGGINS, Kent (WVa) St Matthews Episcopal Church, 36 Norwood Rd, Charleston WV 25314 B Oak Hill WV 1944 s Stanley & Jean. Cert Dioc Trng Prog; BS W Virginia U 1972. D 12/16/2006 P 6/16/2007 Bp William Michie Klusmeyer. m 1/27/1972 Gail Higgins c 2. P in Res S Matt's Ch Charleston WV 2011-2012; P-in-c Ascen Epis Ch Hinton WV 2009.

HIGGINS, Pam (Cal) 272 W I St, Benicia CA 94510 B Bakersfield CA 1950 d James & Delores. BA U CA 1972; MLS U CA 1974; JD U of San Francisco 1978; MDiv CDSP 1991. D 6/8/1991 P 6/1/1992 Bp William Edwin Swing. Vic Ch Of The H Trin Richmond CA 2005-2009; Int S Barth's Epis Ch Livermore CA 1995-1996; Assoc Gr Cathd San Francisco CA 1992-1995. M.Div. w dist CDSP 1991.

HIGGINS, Rock (Va) **S Paul's Ch Richmond VA 2017-** B Newport News VA 1969 s William & Doris. BA U Rich 1991; MDiv Bapt TS 1995; MS Geo Ma-

son U 2002. D 7/27/2013 Bp Susan Goff P 2/8/2014 Bp Shannon Sherwood Johnston. m 12/19/1992 Stephanie Gurnsey c 2. P S Thos' Ch Richmond VA 2013-2016; Anna Julia Cooper Epis Sch Richmond VA 2013-2014. rhiggins@stthomasrichmond.org

HIGGINS, Teddy John (USC) **Vic S Paul's Ch Batesburg SC 2005-** B Biloxi MS 1952 s Preston & Barbara. BS Clemson U 1983; MA Embry-Riddle Aeronautical U Daytona FL 1987; Doctorate of Mnstry GTF 2008; Doctorate of Mnstry Other 2008. D 6/11/2005 P 3/26/2006 Bp Dorsey Henderson. m 6/16/1972 Kimberley Higgins c 5.

HIGGINS, Timothy John (Me) 25 Twilight Ln, Gorham ME 04038 **R S Ann's Epis Ch Windham Windham ME 2007-; Dio Maine Portland ME 2004-** B Lewiston ME 1959 s Gene & Claudette. BS S Michaels Coll Vermont 1981; S Marys Sem & U Baltimore 1987; MDiv S Marys Sem and U 1987. Rec 10/22/2004 Bp Chilton Richardson Knudsen. m 5/26/2006 Maureen Higgins c 3. Chapl Long Creek Yth Dvlpmt Cntr So Portland ME 2001-2007.

HIGGINS, William Harrison (Va) 8000 Hermitage Rd, Richmond VA 23228 B Richmond VA 1949 s William & Emily. BA Davidson Coll 1971. D 2/23/2013 Bp Shannon Sherwood Johnston. m 6/2/2002 Susan G Higgins.

HIGGINSON, Paul Howard (NH) 472 Swazey La, Bethlehem NH 03574 **D All SS Epis Ch Littleton NH 2005-; Chapl The White Mtn Sch Bethlehem NH 2005-** B Waterbury CT 1945 s Howard & Edna. BS Cntrl Connecticut St U 1977. D 12/7/1991 Bp Arthur Edward Walmsley. m 10/28/1995 Sheelagh Mary Higginson c 2. D S Jn's Ch New Milford CT 1999-2004; D S Paul's Ch Woodbury CT 1994-1999; D Grtr Waterbury Area Ch 1992-1994; D S Mk's Chap Storrs CT 1991-1992. NAAD.

HIGGINS-SHAFFER, Diane Hazel (Ore) 503 N Holladay Dr, Seaside OR 97138 B San Francisco CA 1946 d Leonard & Hazel. BS Wstrn Washington U 1968; BA Wstrn Washington U 1970; MS Wstrn Oregon U 1990. D 6/13/2015 Bp Michael Hanley. c 1.

HIGGITT, Noel (ECR) 1325 San Mateo Dr, Menlo Park CA 94025 B Liverpool UK 1938 s Charles & Emma. BS Liverpool Coll of Commerce Gb 1963; BA Sch for Deacons 1989; MDiv CDSP 1994. D 6/9/1990 Bp William Edwin Swing P 6/1/1996 Bp Richard Lester Shimpfky. m 5/14/1988 Anne Higgitt c 2. S Mk's Par Berkeley CA 1994-1995; D S Jas Epis Ch San Francisco CA 1990-1995.

✠ **HIGH JR, The Rt Rev Rayford Baines** (Tex) 4709 Marbella Cir, Fort Worth TX 76126 **Exec Bd Angl Hlth Ntwk Geneva Switzerland 2009-** B Houston TX 1941 s Rayford & Helen. BA U So 1963; MDiv ETSBH 1966; D.D. U So 2014. D 6/28/1966 Bp Everett H Jones P 1/6/1967 Bp Richard Earl Dicus Con 10/4/2003 for Tex. c 3. Provsnl Bp of Ft Worth Dio Ft Worth Ft Worth TX 2012-2015; Dir St. Lk's Hosp Houston Tx 2011-2013; Chair, Bd St. Jas Hse Baytown Tx 2009-2011; Bd All SS Epis Sch Tyler Tx 2003-2011; Bp Suffr of Texas Dio Texas Houston TX 2003-2011; Cn 1998-2003; Dir St. Lk's Hlth System Houston Tx 2000-2011; PB Nomin Com GC 2000-2003; R S Paul's Ch Waco TX 1981-1998; Dep, Dio Texas GC 1979-2003; R S Jn's Ch McAllen TX 1977-1981; Dir Citizens Hosp Victoria Tx 1972-1977; Dir Reg Coun Alcosm Victoria Tx 1972-1977; R S Fran Epis Ch Victoria TX 1969-1977; Asst S Mk's Epis Ch San Antonio TX 1966-1969. Humanitarian of the Year Waco Conf of Christians and Jews 1997. rayford.high@edfw.org

HIGHLAND, Terrence Irving (Pa) B Chicago IL 1941 s Irving & Julia. BA S Olaf Coll 1963; MDiv Sewanee: The U So, TS 1989. D 6/11/1989 Bp Arthur Anton Vogel P 12/16/1989 Bp John Wadsworth Howe. m 6/10/1995 Mary Susan Highland c 4. R Chr Epis Ch Pottstown PA 2007-2013; Assoc Hope Epis Ch Melbourne FL 2006-2007; R Chr the Redeem Merritt Island Fl 1994-2006; Asst Chr Wrshp Cntr Cocoa FL 1993-1994; R Gloria Dei Epis Ch Cocoa FL 1991-1993; Asst R S Jn's Ch Melbourne FL 1989-1991; Curs Sprtl Dir Dio Pennsylvania Philadelphia PA 2008-2012; Sprtl Dir Via De Cristo Cocoa Fl 1995-2006.

HIGHSMITH, Jennifer Lynn (Ga) 102 Borrell Blvd, Saint Marys GA 31558 B Pawtucket RI 1958 d Layton & Jeanne. Dio Georgnia; EFM U So. D 9/6/2006 Bp Henry Irving Louttit. c 1. Camden Cnty Mntl Hlth Crisis Counslr Gateway Cmnty Serv 1996.

HILDEBRAND, Nancy Steakley (WA) St Nicholas Episcopal Church, 14100 Darnestown Rd Ste B, Germantown MD 20874 B Denver CO 1947 d Joe & Margaret. U IL; BA U Chi 1969; U CO 2007; VTS 2007; MDiv Wesley TS 2007. D 6/9/2007 P 1/19/2008 Bp John Bryson Chane. m 6/17/1967 Peter Henry Hildebrand c 3. S Jas' Ch Indn Hd MD 2015-2017; Assoc S Dav's Par Washington DC 2013-2015; Ch Of The Ascen Gaithersburg MD 2012-2013; Asst S Nich Epis Ch Germantown MD 2007-2009; Washington Liaison Adapt 2000-2004. nancyhildebrand@verizon.net

HILDEBRANDT, Lise (NH) 1400 1st Avenue, Longmont CO 80501 B Columbus OH 1959 d Theodore & Mary. BA U NC 1980; MDiv Ya Berk 1986; MPH Bos 2004. D 11/14/1986 Bp Robert Whitridge Estill P 1/30/1988 Bp Alden Moinet Hathaway. c 2. Vic H Cross Epis Ch Weare NH 2011-2014; Int Ch Of The Gd Shpd Wareham MA 2010; Int S Dunstans Epis Ch Dover MA 2009; Consult Massachusetts Coun of Ch 2007-2008; P-in-c S Jn's Ch Worcester MA 2005-2009; Int Dio Wstrn Massachusetts Springfield 2002-2009, 1997-2001;

Chr Memi Ch No Brookfield MA 2002-2004; Chr Ch Rochdale MA 1997-2001; Asst/Assoc R Chr Epis Ch No Hills Pittsburgh PA 1987-1992; D Ch Of The Servnt Wilmington NC 1986-1987; Chapl Lower Cape Fear Hospice 1986-1987.

HILDESLEY, Christopher Hugh (NY) 570 Park Ave Apt 6-D, New York NY 10021 **Non-par 1994-** B Cambridge UK 1941 s Paul & Mary. Oxf GB. D 6/12/1976 Bp Paul Moore Jr P 12/1/1976 Bp Harold Louis Wright. m 1/17/1964 Constance Hildesley c 3. Ch Of The Heav Rest New York NY 1983-1995, Asst 1977-1983; Asst The Ch Of The Epiph New York NY 1976-1977. Auth, "Journeying w Julian". Osjj.

HILE, Jeanette Theresa (Nwk) 16 Day Rd, Landing NJ 07850 **Hse Of The Gd Shpd Hackettstown NJ 2008-; Prof Of Mus Seton Hall U 1980-** B Morristown NJ 1949 d James & Carolyn. Immac Concep Sem; BA Montclair St U 1971; MA Montclair St U 1977. D 12/9/2006 Bp Carol J Gallagher.

HILEMAN, Mary E sther (Okla) 2809 W 28th Ave, Stillwater OK 74074 B Detroit MI 1945 d William & Esther. BS U MI 1967; MS U MI 1969; PhD U MI 1973; MDiv VTS 1989. D 6/17/1989 P 12/16/1989 Bp Robert Manning Moody. Vic S Mk's Ch Perry OK 2009-2013; Chair - Dio. Cmsn on Min in Higher Ed Dio Oklahoma Oklahoma City OK 2005-2011, First Alt Dep Gen. Conv. 2000-2004, Reg Dn 1991-1999, half-time (OK St U) 1989-2011, Reg Dn 2011-2014, Pres. Stndg Comm 2010-2011, Dep Gen Conv 2009-2012, Pres. Stndg Comm 2007-2008, Dep Gen Conv 2006-2009, Dep Gen Conv. 2003-2006, Pres. Stndg Comm 2001-2002, Dep. Gen. Conv. 1997-2000; Stg Comm Dom Mssn & Evangel HOD of The Epis Ch 2003-2006; Full-time (OK St U) S Aug Cbury Cntr Stillwater OK 1991-2011; S Andr's Ch Stillwater OK 1989-2011; Ch Of The Ascen Pawnee OK 1989-1990; Coordntr-Min in Higher Ed Prov VII Fairfax VA 1997-2004. Epis Soc for Mnstry in Higher Eucation 1991-2005.

HILFIKER, Gerald Milton (WNY) 10085 Pfarner Road, Boston NY 14025 **Archd Dio Wstrn New York Tonawanda NY 2011-; D S Paul's Epis Ch Springville NY 2002-** B Rochester NY 1942 s Milton & Florence. BS SUNY 1964; MS Alfred Adler Inst of Chicago 1986. D 9/14/2001 Bp Michael Garrison. m 8/14/1971 Karen Anne Hilfiker c 4.

HILGARTNER, Elizabeth (Vt) Po Box 6, Orford NH 03777 **P Dio Vermont Burlington VT 2011-** B Baltimore MD 1957 d Charles & Carol. BA Harv 1979; MDiv EDS 1986. D 6/11/1979 P 12/1/1986 Bp Robert Shaw Kerr. m 9/16/1979 Ernest Alfred Drown. S Barn Ch Norwich VT 2004-2014; S Lk's Ch Woodsville NH 2001-2004; Int S Jas Ch Woodstock VT 1999-2000; Int S Thos Ch Hanover NH 1996-1997; The Holderness Sch Plymouth NH 1993-1996; Chapl Holderness Sch Plymouth NH 1993-1995; R S Lk's Ch Charlestown NH 1989-1993; Un-St. Lk's Epis Ch Claremont NH 1989-1993; Cur Chr Ch Montpelier VT 1986-1989. Auth, "Cats In Cyberspace," Meisha Merlin Pub, 2000; Auth, "A Necklace Of Fallen Stars"; Auth, "Colors In The Dreamweaver'S Loom"; Auth, "The Feast Of The Trickster"; Auth, "A Murder For Her Majesty". beth@cameoarts.org

HILL, C(harleen) Diane (Ala) 1806 Meadows Dr, Birmingham AL 35235 B Macon GA 1954 d Willie & Annie. Savannah St Coll 1976; BA Ft Vlly St U 1988; MDiv Lexington TS 1994; Sewanee: The U So, TS 1994. D 6/11/1994 P 5/1/1995 Bp Don Adger Wimberly. H Cross-St Chris's Huntsville AL 2014-2016; All SS Ch So Hill VA 2012-2013; S Mk's Ch Birmingham AL 2006-2008; Asst to R S Paul's Ch Henderson KY 1999-2000; Ch Of Our Merc Sav Louisville KY 1996-1999; Ch S Mich The Archangel Lexington KY 1994-1996.

HILL, David Ernest (Minn) 103 West Oxford Street, Duluth MN 55803 **D The Par of St Paul's Epis Ch Duluth MN 2006-; D Trin Epis Ch Hermantown MN 2001-** B Bay City TX 1942 s Ernest & Ebba. BA Texas Tech U 1972. D 6/17/2001 Bp James Louis Jelinek. m 11/21/1964 Diana Van Dyke Hill c 2.

HILL, Deborah (Ala) Cathedral Church of the Advent, 2017 6th Ave N, Birmingham AL 35203 **Cn The Cathd Ch Of The Adv Birmingham AL 2012-** B Pittsburgh PA 1979 d Christopher & Janet. BA Wheaton Coll 2001; MDiv TESM 2008. Trans 11/9/2012 as Priest Bp John Mckee Sloan Sr. m 2/29/2016 Scott A Hill c 1. deborah@cathedraladvent.com

HILL, Derrick C (ETenn) 626 Mississippi Ave, Signal Mountain TN 37377 **R S Tim's Ch Signal Mtn TN 2015-** B Birmingham AL 1966 s Steve & JoAnn. BS Auburn U 1990; MPPM Birmingham Sthrn Coll 1995; MDiv Sewanee: The U So, TS 2011. D 5/18/2011 Bp Henry Nutt Parsley Jr P 12/13/2011 Bp John Mckee Sloan Sr. m 9/26/1998 Beverly H Hill c 2. Asst S Mary's-On-The-Highlands Epis Ch Birmingham AL 2011-2015. dhill@sttimsignal.com

HILL, Donald B (Roch) 321 E Market St, Jeffersonville IN 47130 **Co-Pstr-in-Charge S Paul's Epis Ch Jeffersonvlle IN 2011-** B Buffalo NY 1945 s Donald & Phyllis. BA SUNY 1967; MDiv Bex Sem 1970; Cert Assn of Profsnl Chapl 1998; Cert Cler Ldrshp Inst 2010. D 6/29/1970 P 1/25/1971 Bp Harold Barrett Robinson. m 10/12/1991 Nancy Woodworth c 1. Asst S Mk's Ch Newark NY 2009-2011; P-in-c S Geo's Ch Hilton NY 2006-2009; R Trin Ch Rochester NY 2000-2009; Dir Pstrl Care Epis Ch Hm Buffalo NY 1995-2000; R Ch Of The Ascen Buffalo NY 1991-1995; Ch Of The Trsfg Buffalo NY 1991-1995; Ed Dio Wstrn New York Tonawanda NY 1984-1996; R S Mk's Ch Buffalo NY 1982-1991; Dioc Cmncatn Off Ch of Can Toronto ON 1980-1982; Dio Toron-

to Toronto ON 1980-1982; R All SS Ch Round Lake NY 1979-1980; Asst Dio Albany Greenwich NY 1976-1980, Asst Dir Ecum Cmncatns Off 1976-1980; Assoc Chr Epis Ch Ballston Spa NY 1976-1979; Assoc Ch Of Beth Saratoga Spg NY 1974-1976; Chapl Doane Stuart Sch Albany NY 1972-1974; Chapl S Agnes Sch Loudonville NY 1972-1974; Cn Sacrist Cathd Of All SS Albany NY 1970-1972. Assn of Profsnl Chapl 1997-2010; ECom 1978-2010. Serv to Mankind Awd SERTOMA, Buffao NY 1987; Citizen of the Year Buffalo News 1984.

HILL, Ellen R. (Los) 5066 Berean Ln, Irvine CA 92603 B Akron,OH 1938 d Milo & Alice. BA Ohio Wesl 1960; MDiv Claremont TS 1988; DMin Claremont TS 1997. D 6/25/1988 P 1/21/1989 Bp Frederick Houk Borsch. m 8/27/1960 Lamar M Hill c 2. R S Mich and All Ang Epis Ch Studio City CA 1993-2003; Assoc Ch Of The Mssh Santa Ana CA 1988-1992. Auth, "A Prog for Congrl Stwdshp Dvlpmt"; Auth, "Resurr: Renwl & Rebirth in Congregations Experienced Betrayal Pstr Trust".

HILL, Gary Hill (Tex) 9541 Highland View Dr., Dallas TX 75238 **Supply St Mths Ch Athens TX 2011-** B Norfolk VA 1948 s Woodrow & Beatrice. BGS U of SW Louisiana 1982; MDiv Nash 1985. D 6/1/1985 P 11/30/1985 Bp Willis Ryan Henton. m 8/19/1972 Nancy Hill c 3. R Chr Ch Nacogdoches TX 1997-2010; R Trin Epis Ch Jasper TX 1991-1997; Ch Of The Ascen Epis Springfield MO 1988-1991; Vic Dio W Missouri Kansas City MO 1988-1991; Asst S Paul's Epis Ch Shreveport LA 1985-1987.

HILL III, George Aldrich (SO) 22 Vintage Walk, Cincinnati OH 45249 **Chapl Fed Bureau of Investigation 1991-** B Boston MA 1946 s George & Marguerite. BA Indiana U 1971; MDiv Methodist TS 1974; DMin Methodist TS 1987; STM Bos 1998. D 2/12/1978 P 6/1/1978 Bp John Mc Gill Krumm. m 9/1/1974 Amy Edgeworth c 2. R S Barn Epis Ch Cincinnati OH 1982-2011; Cur S Thos Epis Ch Terrace Pk OH 1978-1982; Pstr Meth Ch 1972-1978. Intl Conf of Police Chapl; Intl Ord of S Lk the Physcn.

HILL, Gordon Carman (Az) 2257 E Becker Ln, Phoenix AZ 85028 B Parishville NY 1932 s Reuben & Dorothy. BS SUNY 1959; MA Arizona St U 1963. D 1/19/1992 Bp Joseph Thomas Heistand. m 9/9/1956 Nazaly D Hill. SocMary.

HILL III, Harry Hargrove (Dal) Church Of The Incarnation, 3966 McKinney Ave, Dallas TX 75204 **P Ch Of The Incarn Dallas TX 2011-** B Lexington VA 1947 s Harry & Ellen. BA W&L 1970; JD W&L 1974; MDiv VTS 1992. Trans 1/9/2004 Bp David Conner Bane Jr. Sr Assoc Chr Epis Ch Pensacola FL 2004-2011; Chr Epis Ch Virginia Bch VA 2003; R S Bride's Epis Ch Chesapeake VA 2000-2003; Gr Epis Ch Goochland VA 1994-2000; Asst S Fran In The Fields Harrods Creek KY 1992-1993. Soc of S Jn the Evang.

HILL IV, Harvey (WMass) 19 Ward Avenue, Northampton MA 01060 **Assoc S Andr's Ch Longmeadow MA 2013-; P-in-c S Dav's Ch Feeding Hills MA 2011-** B Atlanta GA 1965 s Harvey & Sarah. BA Ya 1987; MTS Candler TS Emory U 1991; PhD Emory U 1996; EDS 2008. D 12/20/2008 P 6/28/2009 Bp J Neil Alexander. m 8/1/1992 Carrie Baker c 2. Vic S Jas Ch Cedartown GA 2009-2011. co-Auth, "Modernists Left, Rt, and Cntr," CUA Press, 2008; Auth, "The Politics of Modernism: Alfred Loisy and the Sci Study of Rel," CUA Press, 2002; co-Ed, "Personal Faith and Instnl Commitment: RC Modernist and Anti-Modernist Autobiography," U of Scranton Press, 2002. Fac Mem of the year Berry Coll 2011; Carden Awd Berry Coll 2004; Fac Mem of the year Berry Coll 2000.

HILL, Heather L (O) 8911 W Ridgewood Dr, Parma OH 44130 **R All SS Ch Cleveland OH 2009-** B Hong Kong 1978 BA Buc 2000; MDiv Harvard DS 2003. D 12/20/2003 P 6/26/2004 Bp Wendell Nathaniel Gibbs Jr. m 1/30/2010 Dustin David Berg c 2. R S Phil in the Fields Oreland PA 2006-2009; Asst S Jn's Ch Plymouth MI 2003-2006.

HILL, H Michael (CGC) 2255 Valle Escondido Dr, Pensacola FL 32526 B Mobile AL 1954 s Henry & Larcena. MDiv Notre Dame Sem Grad TS 1988; U So 2000. Rec 6/3/2000 Bp Charles Farmer Duvall. m 6/18/1994 Geneva Hill. Dio of Cntrl Gulf Coast (Epis Day Sch) Pensacola FL 2006-2015, Chapl 2000-2002; Vic S Cyp's Epis Ch Pensacola FL 2001-2016, Vic 2000-; Day Sch Chapl Chr Epis Ch Pensacola FL 2000-2002; Dio Cntrl Gulf Coast Pensacola FL 2000.

HILL, Jerry Echols (Dal) 281 Becky Ln, Waxahachie TX 75165 B Texarkana TX 1937 s Harry & Malva. BS Sthrn Arkansas U Magnolia 1969; MDiv SWTS 1972; DMin McCormick TS 1978. D 4/10/1972 Bp Theodore H McCrea P 10/18/1972 Bp Quintin Ebenezer Primo Jr. m 4/29/1960 Gloria Hill c 2. Ch Planter S Paul's Epis Ch Waxahachie TX 2000-2004, P-in-c 1989-1999; Ex. Dir Shltr Mnstrs Of Dallas Dallas TX 1998-1999; Ch Planter Ch Of The Gd Shpd Cedar Hill TX 1981-1989; Urban Mnstrs (Dir.) Dio Dallas Dallas TX 1977-1998; Dir S Phil Cmnty Cntr & Mssn Dallas TX 1975-1977; St Philips Ch Dallas TX 1975-1977; Chapl Cathd Shltr Chicago IL 1972-1975.

HILL, John Spencer (WTex) St Margaret's Episcopal Church, 5310 Stahl Rd, San Antonio TX 78247 **S Marg's Epis Ch San Antonio TX 2013-** B San Antonio TX 1965 s Herbert & Josephine. BBA SW U Georgetown TX 1987; MDiv VTS 1998. D 2/20/1998 Bp James Edward Folts P 10/22/1998 Bp Robert Boyd Hibbs. m 7/17/1993 Holly Baker Hill c 2. Asst S Mk's Epis Ch San Antonio TX 2001; Yth Min Dio W Texas San Antonio TX 2000-2004; Asst R S Alb's Ch Harlingen TX 1998-2000. jhill@stmargs.org

HILL, Joshua Ashton (ETenn) 950 Episcopal School Way, Knoxville TN 37932 **The Epis Sch Of Knoxville Knoxville TN 2013-** B Knoxville TN 1981 s Julian & Vickie. BA Emory & Henry Coll 2003; MDiv Ya Berk 2009. D 1/31/2013 Bp Ian Theodore Douglas P 8/27/2013 Bp George Young III. m 6/5/2004 Hannah S Hill c 2. S Mk's Ch New Canaan CT 2009-2012.

HILL SSF, Jude (Cal) 573 Dolores St, San Francisco CA 94110 **Franciscans San Francisco CA 2015-; P Ch Of The Adv Of Chr The King San Francisco CA 2006-; Min Prov Soc of St Fran 2005-; Soc Of S Fran - San Damiano Friary San Francisco CA 1998-; Bro SSF San Francisco CA 1979-** B Lancaster England 1957 s Leonard & Renee. BA Sul 1993; MA Sul 1995; PhD Uil 2002. D 6/3/2006 Bp William Edwin Swing P 12/2/2006 Bp Marc Handley Andrus. AAPC 2000; Intl Assn for Analytical Psychol 2013.

HILL, Mary Ann (Okla) 5635 E. 71st. St., Tulsa OK 74136 **Dn Tulsa Reg Dio Oklahoma 2012-; S Dunst's Ch Tulsa OK 2008-** B Alton IL 1965 d James & Katharina. BA U IL 1987; MDiv Sewanee: The U So, TS 2001. D 6/17/2001 P 5/31/2002 Bp Edward Stuart Little II. Dn Rockford Dnry Dio Chicago IL 2006-2008; R Gr Epis Ch Freeport IL 2002-2008; Cur S Mich And All Ang Ch So Bend IN 2001-2002. Shettle Prize for Liturg Reading Sewanee 2001.

HILL, Nicholas Thomas (Minn) 4 Saint Paul Ave, Duluth MN 55803 B Saint Paul MN 1938 s Samuel & Jean. No Dakota St U 1960; BA Dickinson St U 1961; U of Texas 1962; MDiv Epis TS of the SW 1965; Coll of Preachers 1969. D 7/1/1965 P 2/1/1966 Bp George T Masuda. m 11/11/1989 Sharyn Hill c 2. Supply P S Andr's Ch Moose Lake MN 2001-2004; H Trin Intl Falls MN 1990; R Ch Of The Gd Shpd Windom MN 1987-1990; R H Trin Epis Ch Luverne MN 1987-1990; S Jn Worthington MN 1987-1990; Dio No Dakota Fargo ND 1985-1986; Dio Minnesota Minneapolis MN 1984-1997; R Stndg Rock Epis Indn Mnstry 1984-1986; R White Earth Epis Indn Mnstry 1983-1984; R S Edw's Ch Duluth MN 1978-1983; Asst To R S Jas Ch Wichita KS 1973-1978; Cur S Jn's Epis Ch Tulsa OK 1971-1973; Ch Of Our Sav Langdon ND 1965-1971; Vic S Jas' Grafton ND 1965-1971; Vic S Ptr's Ch Walhalla ND 1965-1971. Auth, "3 Went In A Boat The New Indn".

HILL, Ralph Julian (SD) 1224 Junction Ave, Sturgis SD 57785 B Greensboro NC 1945 s Ralph & Mary. GTS; BS No Carolina St U 1967; JD Amer U 1973; GTS 1984; MDiv VTS 1986. D 6/11/1986 P 3/1/1987 Bp Peter J Lee. m 8/29/1998 Jane T Trowbridge c 3. R Ch Of All Ang Spearfish SD 1991-2015; Asst to R S Aid's Ch Alexandria VA 1986-1991.

HILL, Renee Leslie (NY) 575 Grand St Apt 1801, New York NY 10002 **Non-par 2003-** B Washington DC 1962 d William & Betty. BA Bryn 1985; MDiv UTS 1990; PhD UTS 1996. D 6/13/1992 P 12/1/1992 Bp Richard Frank Grein. m 10/12/1991 Mary Lova Foulke c 2. Sr Assoc All SS Ch Pasadena CA 1998-2002; Fac EDS Cambridge MA 1996-1998; Asst P S Mary's Manhattanville Epis Ch New York NY 1993-1996; Asst P Cathd Of St Jn The Div New York NY 1992-1993. Auth, "Beyond Colonial Anglicanism," 1999; Auth, "Who Are We For Each Other? Sex, Sexism & Womanist Theol," *Black Theol: A Documentary Hist Volume 2*, 1995; Auth, "Black Faith And Publ Talk". AAR; UBE. Lace Awd For Sprtl Ldrshp Los Angeles Gay And Lesbian Cntr 2000.

HILL, Robert Samuel (Lex) **S Jas Ch Piqua OH 2017-** D 1/9/2016 Bp Doug Hahn P 9/17/2016 Bp Bruce Caldwell.

HILL, Susan Diane (Ga) 3101 Waters Ave, Savannah GA 31404 B Marietta GA 1956 d Joseph & Ella. MDiv EDS; BGS Georgia Sthrn U. D 5/31/2014 Bp Scott Anson Benhase. m 5/22/1976 Daniel Hill c 2.

HILL, Susan Elizabeth (NY) 225 W 99th St., New York NY 10025 **Asstg P Ch Of The H Apos New York NY 2013-** B Fort Lee VA 1965 d Robert & Mary. BS Hav 1987; MBA Columbia Bus Sch 1992; MDiv UTS 2008; STM GTS 2009; Cert - Sprtl Direction GTS 2012. D 3/7/2009 P 9/12/2009 Bp Mark Sean Sisk. Assoc P S Mich's Ch New York NY 2009-2013. Maxwell Fllshp Auburn Sem 2009.

HILL, Vernon Willard (SJ) PO Box 153, Bakersfield CA 93302 **Asst St Paul's Epis Ch Bakersfield CA 2008-** B San Diego CA 1944 s Vernon & Cynthia. AB San Diego St U 1965; RelD TS Claremont CA 1969. D 11/15/2008 P 5/30/2009 Bp Jerry Alban Lamb. m 6/11/1993 Melinda Hill c 4.

HILLEBRAND, Walter V (LI) 23 Cedar Shore Dr, Massapequa NY 11758 **P-in-c Gr Epis Ch Massapequa NY 2014-, P-in-c 2013-2014** B Italy 1965 s Richard & Gertrud. MBM Coll of Bavaria 2004; MIM U of Salzburg 2006; MDiv NYTS 2011. D 11/19/2011 P 6/9/2012 Bp Lawrence C Provenzano. m 4/28/2007 Aissa Hillebrand c 4. Asst P-in-c Chr Epis Ch Lynbrook NY 2012-2013; Asst R Trin-St Jn's Ch Hewlett NY 2012-2013, D 2011-2013.

HILLEGAS, Eric (Mass) Parish of St. Chrysostom, 1 Linden Street, Quincy MA 02170 **R The Par Of S Chrys's Quincy MA 2016-, P-in-c 2010-2016; Pres InterChurch Coun Quincy MA 2015-** B Downy CA 1973 s Roger & Elaine. BA U of Notre Dame 1995; MDiv Gordon-Conwell TS 2005; Cert Ang Stud EDS 2008. D 6/7/2008 Bp M(Arvil) Thomas Shaw P 1/10/2009 Bp Roy Frederick Cederholm Jr. m 8/19/2006 Kendyll Hillegas c 1. Assoc S Mary's Epis Ch Boston MA 2008-2010; Chairperson Mayor's Pryr Breakfast Quincy MA 2012-2015; Epis City Mssn Boston MA 2011-2014. reveric@stcquincy.org

HILLENBRAND, Pamela M (Chi) 412 North Church St, Rockford IL 61103 B Duluth MN 1948 d John & Althea. Augsburg Coll 1967; U MN 1969; BA Metropltn St U 1988; MA Luther TS 1991. D P 5/21/1989 Bp Francisco Reus-Froylan. m 1/17/2009 Robert A Hillenbrand. R Emm Epis Ch Rockford IL 2007-2013; Stndg Comm Pres Dio Wstrn Michigan Kalamazoo MI 1999-2003, 1999; S Andr's Ch Big Rapids MI 1994-2007; R S Chris's Ch Havelock NC 1991-1994; Serv Ch Of Pr PR 1988-1991.

HILLER, Michael T. (Cal) 278 Hester Ave, San Francisco CA 94134 **Bexley Seabury Fed Chicago IL 2017-** B Los Angeles CA 1945 s Carl & Ruth. BA Concordia Sr Coll 1967; M.Div. Concordia Sem 1971; M.Div. Other 1971. Rec 12/6/2008 Bp Marc Handley Andrus. m 8/8/2013 Arthur Morris c 1. S Mk's Epis Ch Santa Clara CA 2014-2016; Ch Of Our Sav Mill Vlly CA 2013; S Anne's Ch Fremont CA 2013; Int R S Mk's Par Berkeley CA 2010-2017; Vic Trin Ch San Francisco CA 2008-2010. Soc of Cath Priests 2011. rector@stmarksberkeley.org

HILLGER, Cindy Lou (Minn) 2801 Westwood Rd, Minnetonka Beach MN 55361 B Minneapolis MN 1958 d William & Elynor. BA Hamline U 1980. D 6/26/2014 Bp Brian N Prior. m 8/24/1985 John Culliton c 2.

HILLIARD-YNTEMA, Katharine Arnold (At) 737 Woodland Ave SE, Atlanta GA 30316 **D Ch Of The H Comf Atlanta GA 2011-** B Atlanta GA 1949 d Joseph & Marie. BS U GA 1971; MD Med Coll of Georgia 1979; EFM U of So Sewanee 2002. D 8/6/2011 Bp J Neil Alexander. m 9/20/1986 John Richard Yntema c 1. Soc of S Anna the Prophet 2008.

HILLIN JR, Harvey Henderson (WK) **Vic S Andr's Ch Hays Hays KS 2014-; S Eliz's Ch Russell KS 2014-; Vic S Mich's Ch Hays KS 2014-** B Houston TX 1946 s Harvey & Edna. BA U So 1968; VTS 1969; MSW U of Kansas 1974; MS K SU 1978; PhD K SU 1983; Cert Bp Kemper Sch for Mnstry 2014. D 6/8/2014 P 5/24/2015 Bp Mike Milliken. m 6/6/1970 Mary Rita Hillin c 2. h_hillin@yahoo.com

HILLMAN, George Evans (FdL) P O Box 215, Sturgeon Bay WI 54235 **Vic Ch Of The H Nativ Jacksonport Sturgeon Bay WI 2007-** B Philadelphia PA 1952 s Evans & Peggy. BA Lycoming Coll 1974; MDiv Nash 1977. D 6/4/1977 P 12/17/1977 Bp Albert Wiencke Van Duzer. m 4/6/2002 Deborah Hillman. Vic Chr the King/H Nativ (Sturgeon Bay) Sturgeon Bay WI 2007-2015; Dn All SS' Cathd Milwaukee WI 1998-2007; R S Jas Epis Ch Milwaukee WI 1988-1998; R S Helena's Ch Burr Ridge IL 1982-1988; The Par Of All SS Ashmont-Dorches Boston MA 1979-1982; S Mary's Ch Haddon Heights NJ 1977-1978; Dio New Jersey Trenton NJ 1977.

HILLMAN, Harry Randall (Ak) PO Box 870995, Wasilla AK 99687 B Monroe LA 1951 s Harry & Kathryn. BBA Amber U 1990; U of Pacific 2009; EFM U of So 2011. D 10/23/2011 P 5/11/2014 Bp Mark A Lattime. m 1/18/1975 Susan Gardner Hillman c 1.

HILLQUIST, Catherine Rinker (Mo) same, same MO 63124 **P-in-c All SS Epis Ch Farmington MO 2009-** B Washington DC 1944 d St John & Esther. BS Jas Madison U 1966; CPA California St U 1989; MDiv ETSBH 2000. D 6/24/2000 Bp Chester Lovelle Talton P 1/6/2001 Bp Frederick Houk Borsch. m 12/18/1965 David K Hillquist c 1. Vic S Pauls Epis Ch Ironton MO 2001-2016.

HILLS, Frances Ann (WMass) 2 Amy Ct, Pittsfield MA 01201 **Chapl to Berkshire Ret Cler Dio Wstrn Massachusetts Springfield 2017-, Epis Search Com 2011-2012, COM 2008-2015, Const and Cn Com 2008-2013** B Oklahoma City OK 1948 d Cecil & Athalee. BS Oklahoma St U 1971; MDiv Epis TS of the SW 1991. D 3/17/1992 P 3/4/1993 Bp Sam Byron Hulsey. m 10/12/2013 Marc Lawrence Britt. R Gr Ch Great Barrington MA 2013; Vic St Geo's Ch Lee MA 2011-2012; R S Jas Ch Great Barrington MA 2007-2012; Chapl Cler Ldrshp Proj W Cornwall CT 2002-2011; R S Andr's Epis Ch Elyria OH 1996-2007; Asst R S Paul's Ch Maumee OH 1993-1996; Int Sch Chapl S Andr's Epis Ch Amarillo TX 1992-1993; Chapl NW Texas Hosp Amarillo TX 1992; Commissionon Mnstry Dio Ohio Cleveland 2004-2007, Cmsn to End Racism, Chair 2003-2006, Epis Transition Com 2003-2004.

HILLS, John Bigelow (WMich) 1450 S Ferry St Apt 104, Grand Haven MI 49417 B Providence RI 1928 s Henry & Florence. BA Ya 1949; MA Ya 1950; MDiv Nash 1959. D 6/14/1958 Bp Charles L Street P 12/22/1958 Bp Horace W B Donegan. c 2. Asst Gr Ch Grand Rapids MI 2002-2004; Int The Epis Ch Of S Jas The Less Northfield IL 1992-1993; Int Chr Ch Winnetka IL 1991-1992; Assoc R S Lk's Par Kalamazoo MI 1989-1991; Deploy Off Dio Wstrn Michigan Kalamazoo MI 1986-1991; R S Jn's Epis Ch Grand Haven MI 1971-1986; R H Trin Epis Ch Manistee MI 1965-1971; Vic S Alb's Epis Ch Ft Wayne IN 1962-1965; DCE Trin Ch Ft Wayne IN 1959-1961.

HILLS, Julian Victor (Mil) 3046 N Cambridge Ave, Milwaukee WI 53211 **P-in-c S Simon The Fisherman Epis Ch Port Washington WI 2000-** B London UK 1953 s Victor & Audrey. BA U of Durham Gb 1975; Ripon Coll Cuddesdon Oxford Gb 1976; STM McCormick TS 1977; Southward 1984; ThD Harvard DS 1985. D 9/1/1984 Bp George E Rath P 6/1/1985 Bp John Bowen Coburn. m 2/25/1995 Nancy Hays c 1. S Mk's Ch Milwaukee WI 1999-2000; Asst Emm Ch Boston MA 1984-1985. Auth, "Common Life In The Early Ch," Trin Press, 1998; Auth, "Tradition And Composition In The Epistula Apostolorum," Fortress Press, 1990. Cath Biblic Assn; SBL.

HILLS, Lindsay Marie (Cal) 1 S El Camino Real, San Mateo CA 94401 **S Matt's Epis Ch San Mateo CA 2013-** B California 1982 d Barry & Maria. BA

H

Bryn 2004; MDiv CDSP 2011. D 6/11/2011 P 1/14/2012 Bp Charles Ellsworth Bennison Jr. m 2/27/2016 Michelle M Johnson c 1. All SS Ch Worcester MA 2011-2013.

HILLS, Nancy Hays (Mil) D 6/11/2016 Bp Steven Andrew Miller.

HILLS, Wes (Chi) 221 W 3rd St, Dixon IL 61021 **S Lk's Ch Dixon IL 2017-** B Key West FL 1944 s Kenneth & Zola. M.Div. CDSP; BA San Diego St U 1967; JD U CA Hastings Coll of the Law 1971; MDiv CDSP 1990. D 6/9/1990 P 6/1/1991 Bp William Edwin Swing. m 10/13/1985 Terri A Newhouse c 4. P-in-c Ch Of The Gd Shpd Athens OH 2012-2014; R The Epis Ch Of S Andr Encinitas CA 1995-2012; R Ch Of The Redeem Hermitage PA 1991-1995; Asst S Paul's Ch Oakland CA 1990-1991; Pres of Stndg Com Dio San Diego San Diego CA 2008-2010, Chair of Resolutns Comittee 2007-2012, Bp Search Com 2004-2005, Eccl Trial Crt 1998-2004, Corp 1998-2001.

HILLS JR, William Leroy (SC) 727 Atlantic St, Mt Pleasant SC 29454 B Charleston SC 1943 s William & Anna. BA U of So Carolina 1966; MS Florida St U 1967; PhD Florida St U 1972; MDiv Sewanee: The U So, TS 1990. D 6/30/1990 P 6/1/1991 Bp Edward Lloyd Salmon Jr. m 10/14/1967 Elizabeth S Hills. Ch Of The Adv Spartanburg SC 2004-2005; S Marys Epis Ch Goose Creek SC 2000-2004; Trin Epis Ch Pinopolis SC 2000; S Matt's Ch (Ft Motte) St Matthews SC 1996-1999; St Anne's Epis Ch Conway SC 1993-1996; Asst S Jn's Ch Florence SC 1990-1993; R S Paul's.

HILSABECK, Polly H (NC) 184 Grey Elm Trl, Durham NC 27713 **Instr Duke DS Durham NC 2006-** B Cedar Rapids IA 1949 d James & Wava. BS U CA,LosAngeles&Irvine 1971; MDiv CDSP 1985; ACPE 1995. D 6/15/1985 P 12/21/1985 Bp Robert Claflin Rusack. m 3/21/1970 David Hilsabeck c 2. P-in-c S Tit Epis Ch Durham NC 2010-2011; Int Chr Epis Ch Halifax VA 2007-2009; Int S Phil'sEpiscopalChurch Maile HI 2001-2002; Seabury Hall Makawao HI 1997-2001; Chapl Seabury Hall Sch Makawao HI 1997-2000; Dir, Pstr Care Childrens Hosp Los Angeles 1995-1996; Vic S Edm's Epis Ch Pacifica CA 1989-1991; Assoc S Paul's Ch Oakland CA 1986-1989.

HILTON, Duncan Lindsley (Mass) 16 Bradley Ave, Brattleboro VT 05301 B Dover NH 1980 s George & Karen. AB Harvard Colleg 2002; MDiv Harvard DS 2008. D 6/3/2017 Bp Gayle Harris.

HILTON, Elizabeth Grant (At) PO Box 169, Morrow GA 30260 B Kalamazoo MI 1956 d Thomas & Jacquelyn. BA Clayton St U 1995. D 8/6/2011 Bp J Neil Alexander. m 9/4/1976 Phyl Eugene Hilton c 4.

HILTON, Olivia Parsons Lillich (WA) B Syracuse NY 1961 d Richard & Meredith. BA Wellesley Coll 1983; MA U of Hawaii 1988; MDiv Wesley TS 2005. D 6/11/2005 P 1/21/2006 Bp John Bryson Chane. m 4/10/1990 Robert Hilton c 2. Serv Angl Ch of Sweden (St. Ptr and St. Sigfrid's) 2006-2009; S Dav's Par Washington DC 2006, D 2005-2006.

HILYARD, Jack (Ore) 311 NW 20th Ave, Portland OR 97209 **Ret 1996-** B La Grande OR 1933 s George & Gladys. BA U of Nthrn Colorado 1954; BD CDSP 1959. D 6/17/1959 P 12/18/1959 Bp James Walmsley Frederic Carman. c 2. DRE Dio Oregon Portland OR 1973-1995; Chapl MI SU E Lansing MI 1970-1973; Chapl U of Oregon Eugene OR 1964-1970; S Jas Ch Lincoln City OR 1961-1964; Vic S Steph's Ch Newport OR 1961-1964; Cur S Mich And All Ang Ch Portland OR 1959-1961. Auth, "Becoming Fam," St. Mary's Press. Hon Doctorate CDSP 2008.

HIMES, John Martin (Tex) 106 N Grove St, Marshall TX 75670 **Min-Gnrl The Francsican Ord of the Div Compassion Marshall TX 2008-; R Trin Ch Marshall TX 2005-; Bd Dir Forw in Faith No Amer 2013-; Min-Gnrl Franciscan Ord of the Div Compassion 2004-** B Eglin AFB FL 1952 s David & Merle. AA Cntrl Texas Coll Killeen TX 1991; BS U of Cntrl Texas 1993; Mstr of Div Epis TS of the SW 2002; Doctor of Mnstry Nash 2013. D 6/22/2002 Bp Claude Edward Payne P 7/24/2003 Bp Don Adger Wimberly. m 6/16/1973 Megan Y Himes. Vic-Gnrl The Franciscan Ord of the Div Compassion Houston TX 2002-2008; Cur Ch Of The Ascen Houston TX 2002-2005; Intern Chr Epis Ch Temple TX 2000-2002; Secy-Gnrl The Francsican Ord of the Div Compassion Austin TX 2000-2002; Dist Chair, Caddo Dist BSA 2012-2014; Strategic Mssn Grant Com Dio Texas Houston TX 2011-2017, Quin Fndt Bd 2010-2017, Greenfields Cmsn 2010-2015; Vic-Gnrl Franciscan Ord of the Div Compassion 2002-2004. Auth, "Common Pryr and the Dvlpmt of Cmnty," *Common Pryr and the Dvlpmt of Cmnty*, Nash, 2013; Auth, "The Fallacy of Conversation," *Nevertheless: A Texas Ch Revs*, 2005; Ed, "The Serv Bk of Common Prayers and Devotions for Use in Cmnty," *The Serv Bk of Common Prayers and Devotions for Use in Cmnty*, The Franciscan Ord of the Div Compassion, 2004. Amer Angl Coun 1997; AmL 2005; Comm Partnr Rectors 2008; CBS 2006; Forw in Faith - Wrld (Amer) 1997; The Franciscan Ord of the Div Compassion 1996; VFW 1991; Warrant Off Assn 1989. Assoc P Shrine of Our Lady of Walsingsham 2007; Assoc CBS 2006; Assoc Shrine of Our Lady of Walsingham 2004; Ord of S Barbara US-A Field Artillery Assn 1988.

HIMMERICH, Maurice Fred (Mil) 107 Fairview St, Watertown WI 53094 **Ret 1995-** B Grand Forks ND 1930 s Fred & Florence. BA Macalester Coll 1956; MA U MN 1960; MDiv Nash 1962; PhD Marq 1985. D 3/16/1962 P 9/15/1962 Bp Donald H V Hallock. c 5. Int Dn All SS' Cathd Milwaukee WI 2007-2008; Int S Alb's Ch Sussex WI 2000, 1999; R S Paul's Ch Watertown

WI 1965-1995; Cur S Paul's Epis Ch Beloit WI 1962-1965. Auth, "Entries," *An Epis Dictionary of the Ch*, Ch Pub Inc, 2002; Auth, "arts & Bk Revs," *Living Ch mag*, 1970. Masons. Hon Cn Dio Milwaukee 1998.

HINCAPIE LOAIZA, David Hernan (Colom) Manzana 26 Barrio Simon Bolivar, Armenia-Quindio Columbia Colombia B 1969 s Nestor & Nory. Juan de Castellanos; Lic Universidad del Quindio; Nuestra Senora del Rosario 1989. D 10/14/2006 P 6/6/2007 Bp Francisco Jose Duque-Gomez. m 1/18/1992 Dolly Mariem Guzman Lozano c 2.

HINCHLIFFE, George Lewis (Fla) PO Box 1238, Live Oak FL 32064 **R S Lk's Epis Ch Live Oak FL 2015-, Asst 2012-2015, 2011-2012; Chairman, Dioc Common Mnstry Bdgt Dio Florida Jacksonville 2015-, Mem - Dioc Disciplinary Bd 2012-, Mem, Dioc Outreach Cmsn 2011-2012** B Tallahassee FL 1952 s Lewis & Waunitta. BS Florida St U 1973; MDiv VTS 2011. D 12/5/2010 P 6/19/2011 Bp Samuel Johnson Howard. m 6/10/1972 Mary Ellen Hinchliffe c 2.

HINDS, Eric (Cal) 1 S El Camino Real, San Mateo CA 94401 **R S Matt's Epis Ch San Mateo CA 2007-** B New York NY 1958 s Howard & Patricia. BS SUNY 1981; MS Syr 1983; MDiv GTS 1994. D 6/11/1994 Bp Richard Frank Grein P 1/1/1995 Bp William Jerry Winterrowd. m 6/23/1984 Anne Read Hinds c 3. R S Ptr's Ch Mtn Lks NJ 1998-2007; Asst R S Paul's Epis Ch Westfield NJ 1996-1998; Asst R S Barn Ch Irvington NY 1994-1996; Dir. of Chr Ed. Ch Of S Jas The Less Scarsdale NY 1989-1992.

HINDS, Gilberto Antonio (LI) 9707 Horace Harding Expy Apt 8L, Corona NY 11368 **P-in-c Epis Ch of Gr and Resurr E Elmhurst NY 2015-** B Panama R of Panama 1946 s Evelyn & Olive. BS CUNY 1977; MPH CUNY 1989; MDiv Ya Berk 2001. D 6/24/2003 P 8/6/2004 Bp Orris George Walker Jr. c 1. P-in-c Ch Of The Resurr Kew Gardens NY 2008-2015; Asst Ch Of The Redeem Astoria NY 2004-2008; Ch Of S Jas The Less Jamaica NY 2003-2004; D St. Jas the Less Jamaica NY 2003-2004.

HINES, Caroline V (NH) 2 Wentworth St, Exeter NH 03833 **S Andr's-In-The-Vlly Tamworth NH 2016-** B Hazard KY 1953 d James & Virginia. BA U of Sthrn Mississippi 1975; MA Illinois St U 1977; MDiv GTS 2000. D 6/10/2000 Bp Bob Johnson P 12/16/2000 Bp Douglas Edwin Theuner. Par Of S Jas Ch Keene NH 2015-2016; S Michaels In The Hills Toledo OH 2014-2015; The Par Of S Mary And S Jude NE Harbor ME 2013-2014; Asst Chr Ch Exeter NH 2011-2013, 2000-2009; Gr Ch New Mrkt MD 2011; S Geo's Epis Ch York ME 2009-2010.

HINES JR, Chester (Mo) 1210 Locust St, St. Louis MO 63103 B Macon MS 1946 s Chester & Lola. Epis Sch For Mnstry. D 11/21/2014 Bp George Wayne Smith. m 6/26/1972 Elizabeth E Hines c 2.

HINES, John C (Tex) 4603 Pro Ct, College Station TX 77845 B Augusta GA 1940 s John & Helen. BA Coll of Wooster 1962; BD CDSP 1968. D 12/29/1968 Bp James Milton Richardson P 12/1/1969 Bp John Elbridge Hines. m 10/25/2006 Lisa Stolley Lisa Kathryn Stolley c 2. Chapl Hospice Austin TX 1995-2006; Chapl S Dav's Hosp 1989-1994; S Jas' Epis Ch La Grange TX 1989; S Steph's Epis Sch Austin TX 1984-1989; Chapl S Steph's Epis Sch Austin TX 1984-1989; Chapl U Of Texas 1976-1984; Asst Chapl U Of Texas-Austin 1972-1976; The Great Cmsn Fndt Houston TX 1970-1984; Chapl Steph F Austin St U 1970-1972; Asst Chr Epis Ch Tyler TX 1968-1970.

HINES, John Moore (Ky) 5722 Coach Gate Wynde, Louisville KY 40207 **P S Ptr's Epis Ch Louisville KY 2012-, P 2001-2012** B Houston TX 1945 s John & Helen. BA Duke 1967; MDiv VTS 1970. D 6/17/1970 P 12/20/1970 Bp John Elbridge Hines. m 4/16/1988 Maria G Partlow c 2. P S Paul's Ch Henderson KY 2011-2012; P S Thos Epis Ch Louisville KY 2009-2010; P Calv Ch Louisville KY 2007-2009; P Ch Of The Adv Louisville KY 2004-2006; P S Alb's Epis Ch Louisville KY 2002-2004; P S Lk's Ch Louisville KY 2000-2002; P S Andr's Ch Louisville KY 1977-2000; P S Fran HS Louisville KY 1977-1984; P S Fran Sch (K-8) Goshen KY 1972-1996; P Trin Ch Columbus OH 1970-1972. Auth, *Dull Dinners Into Sacr Feasts*, Forw Mvmt Press, 1984; Auth, *By Water & the H Sprt*, Seabury Press, 1972.

HINES, John S (WNC) 219 Chunns Cove Rd, Asheville NC 28805 B Austin TX 1949 s John & Helen. BA Hobart and Wm Smith Colleges 1971; MDiv Epis TS of the SW 1976. D 6/16/1976 P 6/1/1979 Bp John Elbridge Hines. Ch Of The Gd Shpd Cashiers NC 2007, 1982-1990; Trin Epis Ch Danville KY 2006-2007; Trin Ch Hattiesburg MS 2004-2006; Ch Of The Incarn Highlands NC 2003-2004; Int S Lk's Epis Ch Asheville NC 1991-2003; Mssy Haiti 1990-1991; Asst S Mart's Epis Ch Houston TX 1978-1982; S Steph's Epis Sch Austin TX 1976-1978; Asst Chapl S Steph's Sch Austin TX 1976-1978. Auth, "Life Of Chr".

HINES, Lisa Stolley (Tex) Calvary Episcopal Church, PO Box 721, Bastrop TX 78602 **R Calv Epis Ch Bastrop TX 2010-; Ethics Cmsn City of Bastrop Texas 2012-** B New Orleans 1959 d Carl & Marcia. BA U So 1981; JD U of Texas 1984; MDiv Epis TS of the SW 2007. D 6/23/2007 Bp Don Adger Wimberly P 1/30/2008 Bp Dena Arnall Harrison. m 10/25/2006 John C Hines c 3. Asst S Thos Epis Ch Coll Sta TX 2007-2010; Admin, Asst.Tchr Gd Shpd Epis Sch Austin TX 1997-2005; Transition T/F, St. Lk's Hosp System Dio Texas Houston TX 2013, Exec Bd 2011-, Pres, Disciplinary Bd 2010-, Bd Trst, El

389

Buen Samaritano 2009-2012. Contrib of hymn lyrics, "In Winter's Grip," *Praises Abound*, Ch Pub, 2012.

HINES, Travis S (Tenn) 4800 Belmont Park Ter, Nashville TN 37215 **Dir, Cntr fro Distance Lrng TESM Ambridge PA 2001-** B Dallas TX 1970 s Hul & June. BA U of Texas 1995; MDiv TESM 2005. D 6/7/2008 Bp Robert William Duncan. m 7/11/2008 Leslie F Hines c 4. Assoc S Barth's Ch Nashville TN 2015, 2015-. thines@stbs.net

HINKLE, Daniel Wayne (Be) 234 High St, Atglen PA 19310 **S Thos' Epis Ch Glassboro NJ 2016-; Int St Paul's Untd Ch of Chr Robesonia PA 2009-; Int First Unioted Ch of Chr Royersford PA 2006-** B Trenton NJ 1953 s George & Lois. BA Trenton St Coll 1977; MDiv Sewanee: The U So, TS 1981. D 6/6/1981 P 12/1/1981 Bp Albert Wiencke Van Duzer. m 10/30/2004 Barbara Peirce c 4. Int S Jn's Ch Kingsville MD 2014-2016; P-in-c S Jas' Epis Ch Parkton MD 2012-2014; Int Ch Of The Trsfg Braddock Heights MD 2011-2012; 1st UCC E Vinc Charge Cov Sprg City PA 2006-2008; Int S Jn The Evang Ch Blackwood NJ 2005-2006; Int St. Jn's Epis Ch Chews Landing NJ 2003-2006; Pleasantville Untd Ch Of Chr Chalfont PA 2003-2004; Int Bethany Evang Luth Ch Reading PA 2002-2003; Int St Peters Luth Ch New Tripoli PA 2000-2002; Int St. Ptr's Un Ch Lynville - New Tripoli PA 2000-2002; R S Barn Ch Kutztown PA 1998-2001; R Trin Ch Uppr Marlboro MD 1991-1998; Asst S Ptr's Ch In The Great Vlly Malvern PA 1988-1991; R S Paul's Berlin MD 1983-1988; Cur S Mary's Ch Haddon Heights NJ 1981-1983. Int Mnstry Ntwk 2002. office@stthomasglassboro.comcastbiz.net

HINMAN, Allen (Nwk) 149 Pennington Ave, Passaic NJ 07055 **Ret Ret 2004-** B Louisville KY 1942 s Charles & Alice. BA Cor 1964; BD UTS 1970; GTS 1971. D 7/5/1970 P 6/1/1971 Bp Leland Stark. m 8/31/1969 Marion v G van Gelder. R S Jn's Ch Passaic NJ 1985-2004; P in Charge S Phil's Ch New York NY 1983-1985, Asst Min 1975-1982; P in Charge All Souls Ch New York NY 1974-1975, Asst Min 1970-1973; No Manhattan IPC New York NY 1974-1975. Purple Heart 1967. Bronze Star for Valor US Army 1967; Combat Medic Badge US Army 1967.

HINO, Moki (Haw) Church of the Holy Apostles, 1407 Kapiolani Street, Hilo HI 96727 **Cn S Andr's Cathd Honolulu HI 2007-** B Guam 1965 s Graham & Leilani. BA U of Hawaii 1988; U of Hawaii 1989; MDiv SWTS 2005. D 7/3/2005 P 2/4/2006 Bp Richard Sui On Chang. R Ch Of The H Apos Hilo HI 2011-2016; Chapl S Andr's Priory Sch Honolulu HI 2010-2011; Chapl Seabury Hall Makawao HI 2005-2007.

HINRICHS, William Roger (Alb) 1201 Vineyard St., Cohoes NY 12047 **R S Jn's Ch Cohoes NY 2016-** B Mexico DF MX 1951 s Guillermo & Eileen. BSBA U Denv 1974; MDiv Nash 1978; DMin Drew U 1999. D 6/29/1978 P 4/25/1979 Bp William Carl Frey. m 1/20/1979 Barbara J Black c 2. R S Geo's Ch Clifton Pk NY 1991-2008; R S Jn's Ch Massena NY 1987-1991; R S Barn Of The Vlly Cortez CO 1980-1986; Cur Ch Of The Ascen Pueblo CO 1979-1980; D to Bp Dio Colorado Denver CO 1978-1979; P in Charge Chr's Ch Duanesburg NY 2009-2016. Cmnty of S Mary; Fllshp of Merry Christians.

HINSE, Mary N (Cal) 2230 Huron Dr., Concord CA 94519 **D Ch Of The H Trin Richmond CA 2013-; Dir of Prog Dvlpmt Trin Cntr Walnut Creek CA 2012-; Fac D Sacr Space Oakland CA 2011-** B Portland OR 1952 d Nels & Janet. BA Augustana Coll 1973; U IL 1984; Cert Merritt Coll Oakland CA 1996; Cert Ang Stud Epis Sch for Deacons 2008. D 12/6/2008 Bp Marc Handley Andrus. c 3. D S Geo's Epis Ch Antioch CA 2011-2013.

HINSON, Bryan T (At) 582 Walnut St, Macon GA 31201 **S Paul's Ch Macon GA 2016-** B Macon GA 1968 s Thomas & Mary. BS Georgia Inst of Tech 1989; MA U GA 1991; MDiv Candler TS Emory U 2015. D 12/20/2014 P 6/20/2015 Bp Robert Christopher Wright. m 7/29/1989 Stacy Timbrook c 1. Chr Ch Macon GA 2015-2016.

HINSON, Jerome Andrew (WMo) 5 Averil Ct, Fredericksburg VA 22406 **Off Of Bsh For ArmdF New York NY 1994-** B Sikeston MO 1963 s Elvis & Janet. BA Knox Coll 1985; MS U of Missouri 1987; MDiv SWTS 1991; STM Bos 2004. D 6/8/1991 Bp William Augustus Jones Jr P 12/15/1991 Bp John Clark Buchanan. m 5/27/1989 Ruth Ann Hinson c 3. Asst R Chr Epis Ch Springfield MO 1991-1994. Mltry Chapl Assn 1996-2003.

HINSON, Michael Bruce (Va) 6033 Queenston St, Springfield VA 22152 **Assoc The Falls Ch Epis Falls Ch VA 2012-; St. Steph's And St. Agnes Sch Alexandria VA 2006-; Chapl / Tchr St. Steph's & St. Agnes Sch Alexandria VA 1990-** B Albany Georgia 1963 s William & Nancy. BBA U GA 1987; MA UTS Richmond 1990; VTS 2005. D 6/24/2006 P 2/3/2007 Bp Peter J Lee. m 6/26/1993 Jane Steiner Hinson c 2. S Chris's Ch Springfield VA 2007-2012. Marshall Garrett Grant St. Steph's & St. Agnes Sch 1995; Marshall Garrett Grant St. Steph's & St. Agnes Sch 1992.

HINTON, Brad (Del) 2320 Grubb Road, Wilmington DE 19810 **S Dav's Epis Ch Wilmington DE 2007-; Chair, GC Deputation Dio Delaware Wilmington 2017-, Chairman, GC Deputation 2015, Disciplinary Bd 2015, Dep to GC 2012, Dep to GC 2009; Chapl S Dav's Epis Day Sch Wilmington DE 2007-** B Mobile AL 1966 s Robert & Irmgard. BS U of Montevallo 1990; MDiv GTS 2000. D 5/20/2000 P 12/5/2000 Bp Henry Nutt Parsley Jr. m 7/4/2015

Thomas Nathaniel Wood. Assoc R Trin Par Wilmington DE 2002-2007; R S Mich's Epis Ch Fayette AL 2000-2002; VP Dioc Coun Inc Wilmington DE 2004-2007. Ord of St. Jn 2001-2006.

HINTON, Gregory (CPa) PO Box 701, Wellsboro PA 16901 **Cn R S Paul's Ch Wellsboro PA 1994-; Mem, Stndg Com Dio Cntrl Pennsylvania Harrisburg PA 2011-, Chair, Anti-Racism Cmsn 2010-2014, Judge, Ecclesiatical Trial Crt 2008-2011, Pres, Stndg Com 2005-2008, Stndg Com Pres 2005-2008, Exam Chapl in Scripture 2000-, Exam Chapl in Scripture 2000-, Cnvnr of Nthrn Tier Convoc 1994-2000, Cnvnr of Nthrn Tier Convoc 1994-2000** B Yukon FL 1954 s Stanley & Lorraine. BA Blackburn Coll 1976; MDiv Nash 1979. D 6/9/1979 Bp Quintin Ebenezer Primo Jr P 12/8/1979 Bp James Winchester Montgomery. m 12/27/1992 Susan Oldberg c 3. One In Chr Ch Prospect Heights IL 1981-1994; Cur S Paul's Ch Kankakee IL 1979-1981. "Christmas Hope," Wellsboro Gazette, 2008; "Caveat Emptor-The Da Vinci Code," Wellsboro Gazette, 2006; "Maybe Come Easter," Wellsboro Gazette, 2003. Confraterinity of the Blessed Sacr; Soc of S Jn the Evang ,Conf of the Bles. Hon Cn Dio Cntrl PA 2008. frgreg@ptd.net

HINTON, Michael (VI) Box 199, Cruz Bay, Saint John VI 00831 **P Counslr S Ursula's Cntr 1989-** B London UK 1933 s Ernest & Ena. Kings Coll London - Lon 1956; GOE S Bon Coll/Sem 1957. Trans 6/1/1989 Bp Egbert Don Taylor. m 11/12/1986 Frances Eleanor Hinton. Dio Vrgn Islands Charlotte Amalie St Thom VI 1989-1991; Serv Ch Of Engl 1957-1989.

HINTON, Wesley Walker (SO) 5907 Castlewood Xing, Milford OH 45150 **Const and Cn Com Dio Sthrn Virginia Newport News VA 1987-, Strtgy and Plnng Com 1986-, Exec Bd 1985-, Dn of So Richmond Convoc 1984-** B Orange NJ 1944 s Walker & Lucy. BA Kean U 1971; MDiv Sewanee: The U So, TS 1983. D 9/20/1983 Bp Robert Bruce Hall P 6/9/1984 Bp Claude Charles Vache. m 7/26/1969 Lee Snyder Hinton c 3. Int Assoc S Thos Epis Ch Terrace Pk OH 2009-2010, Assoc R 1996-2004; Int Pstr Assoc. Chr Ch Cathd Cincinnati OH 2008, Int Pstr Assoc. 2004-2006; Int Epiph Epis Ch Richmond VA 1995-1996; R Ch Of S Jas The Less Ashland VA 1989-1995; Assoc R S Mich's Ch Richmond VA 1983-1989. Auth, "Sermons That Wk," Morehouse Pub, 2000; Auth, "How Much Is Enough," *Preaching Through The Year Of Lk*, Morehouse Pub, 2000. Caso/ NNECA; Int Mnstry Ntwk; Ord of S Lk.

HINTZ, Mary Louise (Cal) 623 28th Street, Richmond CA 94804 **Bd Mem Grtr Richmond Interfaith Prog Richmond CA 2007-** B Saint Louis MO 1946 d Walter & Louise. BA California Sch for Deacons 1994; AA Contra Costa Coll 1994. D 6/3/1995 Bp William Edwin Swing. m 9/24/1966 Gregory Alan Hintz c 1. D (non-stipendiary) All Souls Par In Berkeley Berkeley CA 2006-2013; Epis Sch For Deacons Berkeley CA 2003-2017; D Ch Of The H Trin Richmond CA 1995-2005; Dioc Coun Mem Dio California San Francisco CA 2005-2008.

HINXMAN, Frederic William (Lex) 5639 Highway #1, Granville Ferry NS B0S 1K0 Canada **Ret 1995-** B Portland ME 1932 s Leroy & Rachel. Acadia Div Coll; Fell New Engl Insitute; Portland Jr Coll; U of Maine; LTh Epis TS in Kentucky 1973. D 6/1/1974 Bp Addison Hosea P 12/1/1974 Bp Morris Fairchild Arnold. m 8/6/1960 Joanna G Tschamler c 4. Serv Ch of Can 1974-1995. Soc of S Jn the Evang, P Assoc 1975. RCMP H Div Chapl Royal Can Mounted Police 2007; Hon Padre Ortona Branch 1994.

HIPP JR, Thomas Allison (USC) 910 Hudson Rd, Greenville SC 29615 B Washington DC 1961 s Thomas & Langhorne. Coll of Charleston 1983. D 9/24/2011 Bp W illiam Andrew Waldo. m 8/10/1991 Karen Bruning Hipp c 3.

HIPPLE, Judy Kay (Chi) 4511 Newcastle Rd, Rockford IL 61108 **Rockford Dnry 2005-** B Dekalb IL 1943 d Edgar & Florence. MDiv SWTS 1994. D 5/1/1995 P 12/1/1995 Bp Frank Tracy Griswold III. Vic S Chad Epis Ch Loves Pk IL 1999-2003; Asst The Epis Ch Of The H Trin Belvidere IL 1995-2000.

HIPPLE, Maureen AtLee (Be) 298 Country View Drive, Towanda PA 18848 **R Chr Ch Towanda PA 1998-** B New Orleans LA 1953 d Frank & Ruth. Miami-Dade Cmnty Coll. D 1/6/1994 P 7/6/1994 Bp James Michael Mark Dyer. c 2. Exch P Dio Meath & Kildare Ireland 1996-1997; Asst S Ptr's Epis Ch Tunkhannock PA 1994-1995; Vic S Jn Monastervan Kildare Ireland.

✠ HIRSCHFELD, The Rt Rev A Robert (NH) 103 Hedgerose Ln, Hopkinton NH 03229 **Bp of New Hampshire Dio New Hampshire Concord NH 2012-** B Red Wing MN 1961 s Robert & Marie. BA Dart 1983; GTS 1986; MDiv Ya Berk 1991; D.D. Ya Berk 2013. D 6/8/1991 P 1/18/1992 Bp Arthur Edward Walmsley Con 8/4/2012 for NH. m 9/15/1990 Polly M Ingraham c 2. R Gr Ch Amherst MA 2001-2012; Vic-Chapl S Mk's Chap Storrs CT 1993-2001; Asst Chr Ch New Haven CT 1991-1993; Dio Wstrn Massachusetts Springfield 2007-2011; Ya Berk New Haven CT 2006-2010. Auth, "Without Shame or Fear: From Adam to Chr," Ch Pub, 2017; Auth, "Preparing A Mansion For God," Untd Mnstrs, 1998. Soc Of S Jn The Evang 1993. arh@nhepiscopal.org

HIRSCHMAN, Portia Royall Conn (Md) 11860 Weller Hill Dr, Monrovia MD 21770 B Plandone NY 1947 d Robert & Virginia. AAS Pur 1974; BS Pur 1974; MDiv SWTS 1993. D 6/24/1993 P 3/24/1994 Bp Edward Witker Jones. m 6/26/1976 Richard Hirschman c 1. R S Jas Epis Ch Mt Airy MD 2002-2014; Vic H Fam Epis Ch Fishers IN 1994-2002; Assoc R Ch Of The Nativ Indianapolis IN 1993-1994.

HIRST, Dale Eugene (SVa) 4127 Columbus Ave, Norfolk VA 23504 **S Steph's Ch Norfolk VA 2015-** B Cheyenne WY 1952 s Ronald & Onita. BS USMA 1974; MDiv VTS 1984; MEd Old Dominion U 1994. D 6/13/1984 Bp Roger Howard Cilley P 2/1/1985 Bp Gordon Taliaferro Charlton. c 2. Asst to R Galilee Epis Ch Virginia Bch VA 1986-1993; Asst to R Ch Of The Gd Shpd Friendswood TX 1985; Asst to R Trin Epis Ch Baytown TX 1984; . *Whos Who in Amer Educ*, 2004; *Whos Who in Amer Educ*, 2003; *Whos Who in Amer Educ*, 2002.

HIRST, Robert Lynn (Kan) Po Box 1859, Wichita KS 67201 **D Gd Shpd Epis Ch Wichita KS 2004-** B Boulder CO 1947 s LeRoy & Betttyjo. Guam Cmnty Coll 1966; BA SW Coll Winfield KS 1969; Wichita St U 1985; Kansas Sch of Mnstry 1999. D 8/15/1999 Bp William Edward Smalley. Epis Soc Serv Inc. Wichita KS 2003-2005; On-site Coordntr/innkeeper Bp Kemper Sch of Mnstry Topeka KS 1999-2007; D S Stephens Epis Churchrch Wichita KS 1999-2004.

HITCH, Catherine Elizabeth (Colo) 1320 Arapahoe Street, Golden CO 80401 **Pstr for Adult Formation & Wmn Mnstrs Calv Ch Golden CO 2006-, 2001-2003** B Denver CO 1970 d William & Nancy. BA Stan 1993; MA U CO 1996; MDiv TESM 2001. D 6/9/2001 P 12/23/2001 Bp William Jerry Winterrowd. m 1/13/2007 Bradley Hitch.

HITCH, Kenneth R (EMich) 405 N Saginaw Rd, Midland MI 48640 **R S Jn's Epis Ch Midland MI 2015-** B Columbus OH 1977 s Thomas & Ellen. BS OH SU 1999; MDiv GTS 2002. D 10/20/2001 P 6/1/2002 Bp Herbert Thompson Jr. m 7/23/2015 Wendy Catherine Powers c 2. P S Jas Epis Ch Essex Jct VT 2007-2015; P All SS Ch Cincinnati OH 2002-2007. ken@sjec-midland.org

HITCHCOCK JR, H(Orace) Gaylord (Haw) 1030 Aoloa Place, Apt 206A, Kailua HI 96734 **Asst Ch Of The Resurr New York NY 2009-, Cur 1971-1976; Ret 2006-** B New York NY 1944 s Horace & Elinor. BA Dart 1966; MDiv GTS 1971; STM GTS 1975. D 6/26/1971 P 1/4/1972 Bp John Melville Burgess. m 5/24/2014 John Merrill Whitlock. Int Pstr S Mk's Ch Honolulu HI 2007-2008; Alt Dep GC 2004-2007; R The Ch of S Ign of Antioch New York NY 1996-2006; Dio Newark Newark NJ 1991-1996, Dept Mssn 1984-1991, Stndg Com 1991-1996; Dep GC 1991-1996; R Gr Epis Ch Westwood NJ 1979-1996; Cur S Jn's Ch Norristown PA 1976-1979; Chair, Cler Critical Needs Com Dio New York New York NY 2000-2007, Ecum and Interfaith Cmsn 1999-2011. Soc of Cath Priests 2009. Bp of Newark, Cbury Schlr Dio Newark 1990; Phi Beta Kappa 1966.

HITCHCOCK, Jessica (WA) 5225 Pooks Hill Rd Apt 1208 South, Bethesda MD 20814 **Asst R S Lk's Ch Trin Par Beth MD 2010-** B Atlanta GA 1979 d Gene & Kathrine. BA Oglethorpe U 2001; MDiv VTS 2005. D 12/21/2004 P 6/16/2005 Bp J Neil Alexander. Yth Mssnr Dio Washington Washington DC 2009-2012; Int Asst for CE and Pstr Care S Jn's Ch Lafayette Sq Washington DC 2009; Asst To The R For Yth, YA & Evang Ch Of The Ascen Gaithersburg MD 2005-2009.

HITE, Jean (SwFla) St Nathaniel's Episcopal Church, 4200 S Biscayne Dr, North Port FL 34287 **Trin By The Cove Naples FL 2015-** B Logan OH 1954 d Charles & Mabel. BM Capital U 1976; MM The OH SU 1977; MDiv GTS 2012; MDiv The GTS 2012. D 12/10/2011 P 8/26/2012 Bp Dabney Tyler Smith. P S Mary's Epis Ch Bonita Sprg FL 2014-2015; P-in-c S Nath Ch No Port FL 2012-2014. jhite@stmarysbonita.org

HITE SPECK, Nancy J (NJ) 201 Meadow Ave, Point Pleasant NJ 08742 **P-in-c S Raphael The Archangel Brick NJ 2012-** B Detroit MI 1942 d Robert & Margaret. AA Bennett Coll 1962; BD Pace U 1983; MDiv PrTS 2002; DAS GTS 2003. D 6/12/2004 P 1/23/2005 Bp George Edward Councell. m 8/20/1986 Richard Theophilus Speck c 2. Int S Mths Ch Hamilton NJ 2010-2011; Int The Epis Ch Of The H Comm Fair Haven NJ 2008-2009; Supply P Dio New Jersey Trenton NJ 2007-2008; Asst S Mk's Ch Basking Ridge NJ 2004-2007.

HITT, Mary (RI) 11 Beaufort St, Providence RI 02908 **Died 11/8/2016** B Garfield UT 1924 d Arthur & Marion. BA MacMurray Coll 1945; MA U IL 1946; BS K SU 1954. D 4/13/1995 Bp Donald Purple Hart. c 4. D S Jn's Ch Ashton RI 2002-2006; D St Mich & Gr Ch Rumford RI 1999-2002; Jpic Prov I 1996-2016; D Ch Of The Gd Shpd Pawtucket RI 1995-1999; Environ T/F Prov I 1994-2016; Chair, Environ Mnstry Dio Rhode Island Providence RI 1991-2008. Auth, "Column, E-Column," *Rhode Island Source For Epis News*. NAAD 1992.

HIXON, Beth (Pa) 1201 Lower State Rd, North Wales PA 19454 **P-in-c Ch Of The Epiph Royersford PA 2014-** B Joliet IL 1952 d William & Phyllis. BD U of Florida 1974; MA U of Florida 1980; MDiv GTS 1997. D 6/8/1997 P 1/10/1998 Bp Stephen Hays Jecko. c 1. Assoc Ch Of The Redeem Bryn Mawr PA 2010-2014; Asst R Ch Of S Mart-In-The-Fields Philadelphia PA 2002-2010; Asst R S Matt's Ch Maple Glen PA 1997-2001. Phi Kappa Phi Scholastic hon Soc 1974; Sigma Theta Tau Nrsng hon Soc 1974. bhixon52@gmail.com

HIXSON, Mary Louise (WK) 19 Deer Creek Tr, Anthony KS 67003 **D Gr Ch Anth KS 2001-** B Anthony KS 1956 d John & Mary. BS SW Oklahoma St U 1978; MEd SW Oklahoma St U 1979. D 11/30/2001 Bp Vernon Edward Strickland P 12/13/2002 Bp James Marshall Adams Jr.

HIYAMA, Paul Shoichi (Mich) 734 Peninsula Ct, Ann Arbor MI 48105 **Ret 1990-** B Mukilteo WA 1924 s Koju & Hisa. BA Kalamazoo Coll 1949; New

Sch U 1952; BD U Chi 1956; SWTS 1957. D 6/15/1957 Bp Charles L Street P 12/21/1957 Bp Gerald Francis Burrill. c 3. Int S Jn's Ch Westland MI 1995-1996; R S Andr's Ch Clawson MI 1993-1995, R 1959-1992; R S Lk's Ch Utica MI 1977-1990; Asst R Chr Ch Grosse Pointe Grosse Pointe Farms MI 1974-1977; Cur Ch Of S Paul And The Redeem Chicago IL 1957-1959; ExCoun Dio Michigan Detroit MI 1981-1984, Trst 1975-1980, Ecum Cmsn 1971-1974, BEC 1966-1970, Cathd Chapt 1965, Dn Woodward Convoc 1963-1964.

HIZA, Douglas William (Minn) 10 Meynal Crescent, South Hackney, London E97AS Great Britain (UK) **Hon P S Giles' Cripplegate 1995-** B Newport News VA 1938 s Martin & Reubena. BA U Rich 1960; BD VTS 1963; BS Minnesota St U Mankato 1972. D 6/22/1963 Bp George P Gunn P 6/1/1964 Bp Conrad H Gesner. m 6/9/1979 Joan Hiza c 2. Chapl Homerton/Hackney Hosp 1980-1996; Dio Minnesota Minneapolis MN 1975-1980; Chapl Mankato St U MN 1974-1980; R S Ptr's Ch New Ulm MN 1971-1980; Ch Of The H Comm S Ptr MN 1971-1979; Non-par 1969-1971; Ch Of Our Most Merc Sav Santee NE 1965-1969; Vic Ch Of The Gd Shpd Sioux Falls SD 1965-1966; Cur Calv Cathd Sioux Falls SD 1963-1965. Auth, "Sprtl Pain: Our Own And Others,'" 1997; Auth, "Hospice: A New Way To Care"; Auth, "Death & Sxlty". Ellison Nash Awd S Barth'S Hosp 1984.

HIZER SSAP, Cynthia A (At) 550 Jenkins Rd, Covington GA 30014 **Vic Ch Of The Gd Shpd Ft Defiance AZ 2015-; Navajoland Area Mssn Farmington NM 2015-; Writer Self-Employed 1980-; Cmsn on Sprtl Formation Dio Atlanta Atlanta GA 2013-, Cmsn on Environ Stwdshp 2008-2013** B Logansport IN 1950 d Frederick & Miriam. BS Indiana U 1972; MS Indiana U 1975; MDiv Candler TS Emory U 2006; MDiv Candler TS Emory U 2006; CAS GTS 2007; CAS GTS 2007. D 12/21/2006 P 7/8/2007 Bp J Neil Alexander. m 8/27/2014 Margaret Mary Putnam c 1. The Epis Ch In Navajoland Coun Farmington NM 2015; Sr Assoc Ch Of The Epiph Atlanta GA 2007-2015.

HLASS, Lisa (Ark) 2606 Beach Head Ct, Richmond CA 94804 **S Mich's Epis Ch Little Rock AR 2010-; Dir, Mentoring Prog Multicultural Inst Berkeley CA 2006-** B Wilmington NC 1957 d Joseph & Wanda. BS Arkansas St U 1983; MS Oklahoma St U 1995; MDiv CDSP 2006. D 1/15/2006 P 7/23/2006 Bp Larry Maze. S Alb's Ch Albany CA 2009; The Epis Ch Of The Gd Shpd Berkeley CA 2006-2010.

HLAVACEK, Frances (Be) 110 W Catherine St, Milford PA 18337 B Passaic NJ 1967 d Joseph & Judith. D 11/1/2011 Bp Paul Victor Marshall. m 9/13/1986 Glen Douglas Hlavacek c 1.

HO, Edward HC (Mass) 24 Greenleaf St, Malden MA 02148 **Ret 1996-** B HK 1924 s Wing & Lin. LTh Untd Theol Coll of The W Indies Kingston Jm 1953. D 11/27/1988 P 6/1/1989 Bp Don Edward Johnson. m 1/25/1964 Yat Yeung. Cn Asiamerica Mnstry 1995-1996; Vic Boston Chinese Mnstry 1989-1996.

HO, Jeng-Long Philip (Tai) #200 Ziqiang 1st Rd, Samin Dist, Kaohsiung Taiwan **Dio Taiwan Taipei 2010-** B Taiwan 1954 MA Fu Jen Cath U; BA Natl Changhwa U of Educ; MA Natl Taiwan Normal U; PhD U of Idaho. D 12/18/2010 P 1/6/2012 Bp Jung-Hsin Lai. m 11/12/1979 Hsiao Lan Liao c 3.

HO, Jui-En (Tai) **Dio Taiwan Taipei 2013-** B Taipei 1981 s Jeng-Long & Hsiao Lan. BA Natl Chung Hsing U 2004; MDiv Tainan Theol Coll and Sem 2011. D 1/4/2013 Bp Jung-Hsin Lai. m 6/26/2010 Pei-Yin Wen.

HOAG, David Stewart (NY) 503 North Causeway #102, New Smyrna Beach FL 32169 **Assoc S Paul's Epis Ch New Smyrna Bch FL 2009-; Ret 1998-** B Newark NJ 1934 s Robert & Frances. BA Trin Hartford CT 1955; MDiv EDS 1963; Cert AASECT 1974; Cert AASECT 1977. D 6/8/1963 P 12/14/1963 Bp Oliver L Loring. m 4/24/2004 Susan Morris Hoag. Gr Epis Ch Inc Port Orange FL 1998-2011; Assoc S Ptr The Fisherman Epis Ch New Smyrna FL 1998-2002; Chapl NY St Fed Police 1984-1998; Vic S Jos's Ch Bronx NY 1984-1986, Vic 1972-1983; R Ch of the Redeem Pelham NY 1971-1974; The GTS New York NY 1967-1978; R Par of Chr the Redeem Pelham NY 1966-1998; Chapl Pelham & Pelham Manor Fire and Police Departments 1966-1998; R Chr Ch Pelham Manor NY 1966-1974; Cur Chr's Ch Rye NY 1963-1966. Auth, *arts*.

HOARE, Geoffrey Michael St John (WA) **S Alb's Par Washington DC 2017-; Adj Instr Candler TS at Emory U Atlanta GA 2007-** D 4/29/1983 P 4/29/1984 Bp Robert Whitridge Estill.

HOBART, Terri Lynn (NCal) 967 5th St, Novato CA 94945 **The CPG New York NY 2017-; R S Lk's Ch Woodland CA 2015-** B Waco TX 1965 d John & Sue. BBA Baylor U 1987; MDiv CDSP 2014; MDiv CDSP 2014. D 6/29/2013 Bp Barry Leigh Beisner. c 2. Assoc All Souls Par In Berkeley Berkeley CA 2015; S Tim's Ch Danville CA 2014-2015.

HOBBS, Bryan Arthur (SeFla) 751 Sw 98th Ter, Pembroke Pines FL 33025 B Connellsville PA 1946 s Kenneth & Fay. BS Marshall U 1968; MDiv Sewanee: The U So, TS 1975; DMin Fuller TS 1997. D 6/1/1975 P 12/11/1975 Bp James Loughlin Duncan. m 6/1/1968 Annabel Hobbs c 2. Archd For Congrl Mnstry Dio SE Florida Miami 2003-2016; R H Sacr Hollywood FL 1978-2003; R S Ptr's Epis Ch Key W FL 1975-1978; Assoc S Paul's Ch Key W FL 1975-1976. the Dubose Awd for Serv The TS 2008.

HOBBS, Edward Craig (Cal) 32 Upson Road, Wellesley MA 02482 B Richmond IN 1926 s Vernon & Benona. BA U Chi 1946; PhD U Chi 1952. D 11/27/1959 P 5/1/1960 Bp James Albert Pike. m 6/17/1950 Violet V Hobbs c 1. Assoc R S Eliz's Ch Sudbury MA 1982-1988; CDSP Berkeley CA 1959-1981; S Mk's Ch No Easton MA 1994. Auth, "Hermeneutical Cartography," Univ. of California Press, 1990; "Gospel Stds," Angl Theol Rev. Press, 1976; Auth, "Wesley Ord of Common Pryr," Abingdon Press, 1957; "A Stubborn Faith," Sthrn Methodist Univ. Press, 1956; Auth, "Bk of the Judges of Israel," Univ. of Chicago Press, 1950.

HOBBS, Mercy Gardiner (SD) 405 N Madison Ave, Pierre SD 57501 **R Trin Epis Ch Pierre SD 2010-** B Teaneck NJ 1959 d Field & Mary. BA Concordia Coll 1982; MDiv SWTS 1995. D 6/9/1995 P 4/14/1996 Bp Creighton Leland Robertson. m 7/1/1995 David Payne Hussey c 1. Asst S Paul's Epis Ch Vermillion SD 2002-2010, Vic 1997-2002; P-in-c Ch Of Our Most Merc Sav Santee NE 1997-2002; Asst Dio So Dakota Pierre SD 1995-2010, Niobrara Sch for Mnstry,co-chair 2007-, Stndg Com Pres 2005-, COM Liaison 2004-, Dn of Estrn Dnry 2003-2005, Stndg Com Mem 1999-; Ch Of The Blessed Redeem Niobrara NE 1995-2002; S Mk's Ch Creighton NE 1995-1998; P-in-c S Ptr's Ch Neligh NE 1995-1998. trinity.dakota2k@midconetwork.com

HOBBS, William Battersby (WMass) 45 Park Ave., Athol MA 01331 **Dio Wstrn Massachusetts Springfield 1999-; R S Mk's Ch Worcester MA 1999-** B Abington PA 1952 s Wayne & Kathryn. BA Nthrn Arizona U 1977; MDiv Bex Sem 1982; VTS 1983. D 5/27/1984 P 12/22/1984 Bp Donald James Davis. m 6/19/1998 Shirley Hobbs c 1. R H Trin Epis Ch Southbridge MA 1989-1998; S Jn's Ch Athol MA 1989-1997; R S Jn's Ch Kane PA 1986-1989; Ch Of The Ascen Bradford PA 1984-1986; S Jos's Ch Port Allegan PA 1984-1986; S Matt's Epis Ch Eldred PA 1984-1986; Dio NW Pennsylvania Erie PA 1984.

HOBBS, William Ebert (O) 18 Donlea Dr, Toronto ON M4G 2M2 Canada **Ret 1984-** B Ashton ON Canada 1924 s Robert & Blanche. BA Bishops U QC CA; BD S Jn Coll. Trans 2/1/1974 Bp John Harris Burt. c 5. Dio Ohio Cleveland 1972-1980; Serv Ch of Can 1951-1971. Auth, "Jesus," *Dollars & Sense*; Auth, *The Cov Plan.* Royal Can Legion 1982; Royal Can Mltry Inst 1966; Royal Commonwealth Soc 1980. Can Forces Decoration Dept of Defense 1980.

HOBBY, Kim A (ETenn) Christ Church Episcopal, P.O. Box 347, South Pittsburg TN 37380 **R Chr Ch Epis S Pittsburg TN 2011-** B Fayetteville AR 1965 d Thomas & Diane. BS U of Arkansas 1988; MDiv Sewanee: The U So, TS 2008. D 6/7/2008 Bp Larry Benfield P 1/31/2009 Bp Charles Glenn VonRosenberg. m 1/21/1995 Richard B Hobby c 2. Asst to the R All SS' Epis Ch Morristown TN 2008-2011.

HOBDEN, Brian Charles (RG) 3160 Executive Hills Rd, Las Cruces NM 88011 **Chair, Discernment Com Dio The Rio Grande Albuquerque 2004-, Pres, Stndg Com 2004-, Cn Liturg 2003-, Status of Pars and Missns 1988-1998, Exec Bd 1984-1987, Com Sprtlty & Lay Mnstry 1981-1989, Evang Comm 1980-1988, VIM Comm 1978-1980, Dept. Missn 1977-1981** B Battle Sussex UK 1938 s Cyril & Winifred. Oak Hill Theol Coll 1966. Trans 5/1/1977. m 4/3/1961 Mary Hobden c 3. Dio Rio Grande Albuquerque 2001-2005; R S Jas' Epis Ch Las Cruces NM 1998-2007; R S Jn's Ch Portsmouth VA 1987-1998; DN Petersburg Convoc 1984-1987; Bd Jackson-Field Girls Hm 1981-1982; Brandon Epis Ch Disputanta VA 1976-1987; R Chr Ch w Brandon Par Ch Waverly VA 1976-1987; Chr Ch Waverly VA 1976-1987; Serv Ch of Engl 1966-1976.

HOBGOOD, **Bob** (EC) 1870 Holly St SW, Ocean Isle Beach NC 28469 B Jacksonville FL 1943 s Robert & Doris. BA U of Florida 1965; MDiv VTS 1968. D 6/26/1968 P 6/24/1969 Bp Edward Hamilton West. m 7/31/1965 Nancy P Packard c 4. R S Tim's Epis Ch Greenville NC 1990-2006; Vic, then R S Fran Of Assisi Epis Ch Tallahassee FL 1980-1990; Vic, then R S Jn's Epis Ch Tallahassee FL 1977-1979; P-in-c Tallahassee Mssn Area Tallahassee FL 1976-1990; Dio Florida Jacksonville 1975-1978, Chair, Congrl Dvlp. 1981-1987, Area Mssnr 1976-1990; Vic S Jas Epis Ch Perry FL 1973-1977; S Mary's Epis Ch Madison FL 1973-1977; Chapl/Tchr S Mary's Chap Sch Raleigh NC 1970-1973; Assoc. R S Mk's Epis Ch Jacksonville FL 1968-1970; Chair,COM Dio E Carolina Kinston NC 2005-2007, Chair, Stndg Com 1996-2004.

HOBGOOD JR, **Walter P** (Ga) 1036 Cherry Creek Dr, Valdosta GA 31605 **Dio Georgia Savannah GA 2015-; Dir, Ldrshp Mnstrs Dio Georgia 2014-** B New Roads LA 1948 s Walter & Velma. Sewanee: The U So, TS; Sewanee: The U So, TS; BS LSU 1971; MS LSU 1973; Standford U 1990. D 2/11/2011 P 9/24/2011 Bp Scott Anson Benhase. m 1/30/1971 Gail Riedie c 3. P-in-c S Marg Of Scotland Epis Ch Moultrie GA 2012-2016. wphobg@gmail.com

HOBSON, Carol Gordon (Dal) B Sweet Water TX 1946 d Hershel & Charlsa. Cathd Cntr for Cont Educ Dallas TX; U of Dallas; BA Pacific Luth U 1968. D 11/10/2007 Bp James Monte Stanton. c 4.

HOBSON JR, George Hull (Eur) 119 Blvd. Du Montparnasse, Paris 75006 France **Cn ot the Bp for Theol Educ Convoc of Epis Ch in Europe Paris 2008-** B New York NY 1940 s George & Felice. BA Harv 1962; DIT Oxf GB 1980; MA Oxf GB 1982; CTh Oxf GB 1984; PhD Oxf GB 1989. D 12/10/1988 Bp Matthew Paul Bigliardi P 6/2/1996 Bp Jeffery William Rowthorn. m 6/13/1971 Victoria Lewis. Cn Theol/ Cannon Pstr The Amer Cathd of the H

Trin Paris 75008 1995-1997. "Forgotten Genocides of the 20th Century," Garod Books, UK, 2005; "Rumours of Hope," Piquant Editions, UK, 2004; Auth, "La Guerison Interieure En Rapport Avec La Doctrine Chretienne," 1979. Bp'S Awd For Distinguished Serv Bp Of Convoc Of Amer Ch In Europe 2004; 2nd Prize The Bridport Intl Poetry Competition, UK 1995.

HOBSON III, **Jennings Wise** (Va) Po Box 247, Washington VA 22747 B Fairbanks AK 1948 s Jennings & Isobel. BA Trin Hartford CT 1970; MDiv VTS 1973. D 5/26/1973 Bp Robert Bruce Hall P 6/1/1974 Bp John Alfred Baden. m 6/12/1970 Mary H Hobson c 2. R Trin Epis Ch Washington VA 1974-2015, Vic 1973-1974; Reg Dn Dio Virginia Richmond VA 2006-2010, Com on Congrl Missions 1997-2006, Reg Dn 1984-1988. Loc Citizen Of The Year Rappahannock News 2014; Loc Citizen Of The Year Rappahannock News 1993.

HOBSON, Patricia Shackelford (SO) 2955 Thrushfield Terrace, Cincinnati OH 45238 **Ret 1995-** B Middletown OH 1952 d James & Lois. BS U of New Engl 1978; MDiv Bex Sem 1986. D 6/14/1986 P 6/1/1988 Bp William Grant Black. c 1. Vic Chap Of The Nativ Cincinnati OH 1989-1994; Dio Sthrn Ohio Cincinnati OH 1989-1994; Our Sav Ch Mechanicsburg OH 1987-1989; Vic Our Sav 1986-1989; Asst Chr Epis Ch Of Springfield Springfield OH 1986-1987. Ord S Eliz Of Hungary.

HOBSON, Thomas Prunty (Colo) 1236 S High St, Denver CO 80210 B Paducah TX 1928 s Benjamin & Dietta. BA U of No Texas 1955; BD Nash 1959. D 6/20/1959 Bp Charles A Mason P 12/21/1959 Bp John Joseph Meakin Harte. m 9/18/1976 Sally R Hobson c 4. St Catherines Epis Ch Aurora CO 1987-1988; Vic St. Cath's Mssn Aurora CO 1986-1988; S Thos Epis Ch Denver CO 1981-1988; Asst S Thos' Epis Ch Denver CO 1974-1988; S Martha's Epis Ch Westminster CO 1969-1974; LocTen S Jn's Epis Ch Bisbee AZ 1966-1967; Vic S Steph's Ch Sierra Vista AZ 1963-1969; Mssnr San Juan Mssn Farmington NM 1962-1963; Cur All SS' Epis Ch Ft Worth TX 1960-1962; Vic S Barn Ch Garland TX 1959-1960.

HOCH, Helen Elizabeth (Kan) 314 N 3rd St, Burlington KS 66839 **P Calv Ch Yates Cntr KS 2001-; Cn Ix P H Trin Reg Mnstry - KS 2001-** B Kansas City MO 1950 d Murray & Pauline. BS Ft Hays St U 1972; MS Emporia St U 1975. D 8/16/2000 P 2/17/2001 Bp William Edward Smalley. m 12/20/1974 Stephen Ernest Hoch. P Gr Ch Chanute KS 2001-2011.

HOCHE-MONG, Raymond (Cal) Box 937, Montara CA 94037 **Chapl Gr Cathd San Francisco CA 1993-** B Cairo EG 1932 s William & Marie. BA U of Tennessee 1961; MDiv CDSP 1964; Joint Grad Camb 1977; ThD Grad Theol Un 1977. D 6/26/1964 Bp William Evan Sanders P 5/1/1965 Bp John Vander Horst. m 11/6/1983 Emily Hoche-Mong c 2. Assoc S Eliz's Epis Ch S San Fran CA 1995-1997; S Edm's Epis Ch Pacifica CA 1974-1976; Chair Cmsn of Liturg Dio California San Francisco CA 1972-1978; Vic S Clem's Ch Rancho Cordova CA 1968-1971; Assoc Dir S Mk's Appalachia So Inc 1965-1969; Vic S Mk's Cooperhill TN 1965-1969; D-In-Trng S Mary's Cathd Memphis TN 1964-1965. Auth, "Adventures of Nimo," *Autobiography*, Amazon, 2015; Auth, "Into the Frozen," *Bk Novel*, Amazon, 2014; Auth, "Encounters w Early Art," Achette, 1985; Auth, "The Dynamic City," *Bk*, Bechtel, 1985; Auth, "The Drama of the Euch," *Bk*, GTU, 1977; Auth, "Love, Bribes," *Principles Things Like That*, Self, 1970; Auth, "The Ch In Politics," U of the So, 1968. Amer Inst of Aeronautics 1977; No Amer Acad of Liturg.

HOCKENSMITH, David Albert (Pa) PO Box 90, Morgan VT 05853 B Indianapolis IN 1941 s Harold & Dorothy. BA Wabash Coll 1963; BD EDS 1966; MA Butler U 1974. D 6/11/1966 P 12/11/1966 Bp John P Craine. m 7/9/1966 Stephanie C Hockensmith. Dn Pennypack Deanry Dio Pennsylvania Philadelphia PA 1986-1992; R S Mk's Ch Philadelphia PA 1981-1999; R S Ptr's Epis Ch Hazleton PA 1975-1981; R S Ptr's Ch Smyrna DE 1971-1975; Asst S Lk's Ch Scranton PA 1968-1971; Cur S Paul's Epis Ch Indianapolis IN 1966-1968.

HOCKER, William (Cal) 6135 Laird Ave, Oakland CA 94605 **Pediatric Stff Chapl UCSF Med Cntr/Benioff Chld's Hosp SF CA 2012-** B Detroit MI 1956 s Wilbur & Mary. BA U MI 1978; MS Wayne 1982; MDiv CDSP 2006. D 6/3/2006 Bp William Edwin Swing P 12/2/2006 Bp Marc Handley Andrus. Per Diem Pediatric Chapl UCSF Med Cntr SF CA 2011-2012; Pediatric Chapl Res UCSF Med Cntr SF CA 2010-2011; Assoc S Greg Of Nyssa Ch San Francisco CA 2007-2014; Exec Dir Sojourn Multifaith Chapl San Francisco CA 2006-2010. Co-Auth, "Coping w the threat of AIDS: An approach to psychosocial assessment," *Amer Psychol, Vol 39(11), Nov 1984, 1297-1302.*, APA, 1984. Mildred Bennett Awd Nebraska Cntr for the Bk 2011; Sprt Awd Sojourn Chapl at SFGH 2011; DSA SE Missouri Hosp 2009; Outstanding Donor EDS 2006; Evang for the 21st Century Grant Epis EvangES 2004; Sem Consult on Mssn Grant Sem Consult on Mssn 2004; Regent's Awd Amer Coll of Healthcare Executives 2002; Henry Hallam Tweedy Prize - Pstr Ldrshp Yale DS 2001; Human First Awd Horizons Cmnty Serv 1996; Young Publ Hlth Worker of the Year Illinois Publ Hlth Assn 1988; Outstanding Tchr Awd Washington U Sch of Med 1985; Profsnl Merit ScholarshipWayne St U Wayne Sch of Soc Wk 1982.

HOCKING, Charles Edward (NC) 632 Hughes Rd, Hampstead NC 28443 **Ret 1997-** B Meriden CT 1930 s Scovill & Alma. BS U of Connecticut 1953; STB GTS 1964. D 6/11/1964 Bp Walter H Gray P 3/27/1965 Bp John Henry Esquirol. m 5/24/1997 Gail Shirley Hocking c 3. R S Paul's Epis Ch Cary NC

1981-1996; R S Ptr's Epis Ch Cheshire CT 1972-1979; R Ch Of The Resurr Norwich CT 1966-1972; Cur Chr Ch Greenwich CT 1964-1966. OHC 1965.

HOCKRIDGE, Ann Elizabeth (Pa) Po Box 716, Lyndonville VT 05851 B Norristown PA 1965 d Ralph & Doris. BA Duke 1987; MDiv EDS 1994. D 6/4/1994 P 6/1/1995 Bp Allen Lyman Bartlett Jr. The Ch Of The H Trin Rittenhouse Philadelphia PA 1994-1997.

HODAPP, Tim Leo (Ct) 1335 Asylum Ave, Hartford CT 06105 **Cn for Mssn Ldrshp Dio Connecticut Meriden CT 2013-** B Albert Lea MN 1958 s Philip & Kathleen. BA S Mary U Winona MN 1981; MDiv Mt S Marys Sem Emmitsburg MD 1984; MDiv Mt S Marys Sem Emmitsburg MD 1984; MA Mt S Marys Sem Emmitsburg MD 1985. Rec 1/7/2010 as Priest Bp James Louis Jelinek. m 10/30/2008 Gerard C Sullivan. Mssnr for Mssn Dio Minnesota Minneapolis MN 2011-2012; R S Chris's Epis Ch S Paul MN 2010. thodapp@ctdiocese.org

HODGE, Reginald Roy (VI) B Anguilla 1950 s Herbert & Esther. D 4/7/2013 Bp Edward Gumbs. m 7/21/1973 Bernice Eulalie Hodge c 1.

HODGE SR, Vincent Stafford (Va) Po Box 767, West Point VA 23181 B Little Dix Anguilla BW Indies 1941 s Herbert & Esther. Commonwealth Universityf; W&M 1964; ECA Trng Cntr Brooklyn NY 1965; W&M 1970; UTS 1971; Sch of CPE 1972. D 5/26/1973 Bp Robert Bruce Hall P 5/18/1974 Bp John Alfred Baden. c 5. Dio Virginia Richmond VA 1994-2008; Calv Ch Hanover VA 1973-2008; Vic Gr Ch Millers Tavern VA 1973-2008; Vic S Paul's Epis Ch W Point VA 1973-1994. Auth, "Apathy in Black Cmnty," *Major Causes & What Ch Ought to Do About It.* Captain ECA 1966; Ch Army.

HODGE SR, Wayne Carlton (SVa) 114 Cross Ter, Suffolk VA 23434 B Martinsville VA 1946 s Ernest & Rebecca. BS Virginia St U 1970; MA Hollins U 1980; MDiv VTS 1989. D 7/25/1989 Bp A(rthur) Heath Light P 6/1/1990 Bp Claude Charles Vache. m 5/17/1970 Shirley Hodge c 3. Vic S Mk's Ch Suffolk VA 1989-1999. Bread For The Wrld.

HODGES, Corinne (NI) St. Anne's Episcopal Church, 424 W. Market St., Warsaw IN 46580 **R S Anne's Epis Ch Warsaw IN 2011-; Stndg Com Dio Nthrn Indiana So Bend IN 2012-, COM 2009-2012** B Flushing NY 1965 d Chuck & Heidi. BA Indiana U 1987; MDiv SWTS 2006. D 6/2/2007 Bp Bill Persell P 12/15/2007 Bp Victor Alfonso Scantlebury. m 6/24/1989 Michael Hodges. P-in-c S Jn Of The Cross Bristol IN 2008-2011; Presb Hm Evanston IL 2007-2008; Asstg P S Elis's Ch Glencoe IL 2006-2008; Chapl Presb Hm Evanston IL 2002-2008.

HODGES, David Burton (NC) 520 Summit St., Winston Salem NC 27101 **Chr Cathd Salina KS 2017-; S Fran Cmnty Serv Inc. Salina KS 2015-** B Gastonia NC 1959 s Ruford & Jo. BS Samford U 1982; MS U of Alabama 1987; MDiv Epis TS of the SW 1996. D 1/13/1996 P 7/20/1996 Bp Robert Oran Miller. m 11/24/2009 Lisa Paul Hodges c 4. R S Paul's Epis Ch Winston Salem NC 2009-2013; R Ch Of The H Comf Charlotte NC 1999-2009; Assoc The Ch of the Gd Shpd Austin TX 1997-1999; Assoc Chr Ch Tuscaloosa AL 1996-1997. tmcdowell@stpauls-ws.org

HODGES, Michael John (Mass) 29 Central St, Andover MA 01810 **P Par Of Chr Ch Andover MA 2014-** B Waterville ME 1966 s Terry & Mary. BA Gordon Coll 1988; MDiv PrTS 1992. D 6/2/2001 Bp Barbara Clementine Harris P 6/8/2002 Bp M(Arvil) Thomas Shaw. m 6/20/1987 Laurie Jean Hodges c 2. R S Paul's Ch Dedham MA 2005-2014; Vic S Paul's Ch Brockton MA 2001-2005.

⚓ HODGES-COPPLE, The Rt Rev Anne (NC) 1104 Watts St, Durham NC 27701 **Bp Suffr of No Carolina Dio No Carolina Raleigh NC 2013-, 1992-2005** B Austin TX 1957 d Richard & Joan. BA Duke 1979; MDiv PSR 1984. D 9/14/1987 Bp Robert Whitridge Estill P 9/24/1988 Bp Frank Harris Vest Jr Con 6/15/2013 for NC. m 10/15/1983 John Norval Hodges Copple c 3. S Lk's Epis Ch Durham NC 2005-2013, R 2005-2013, Asst to R 1987-1992; Chapl Duke Epis Cntr Durham NC 1992-2005. bishopanne@episdionc.org

HODGKINS, Lewis (Spok) 1000 Vey Way Apt 264, The Dalles OR 97058 **Assoc S Pauls Epis Ch The Dalles OR 1991-; Ret 1990-** B Bangor ME 1927 s Norris & Gladys. BA Duke 1949; BD Sewanee: The U So, TS 1952. D 6/24/1952 Bp Edwin A Penick P 4/12/1953 Bp William Jones Gordon Jr. m 6/24/1955 Barbee F Hodgkins c 1. Int S Matt's Epis Ch Fairbanks AK 1989-1990; Gr Ch Dayton WA 1976-1989; Vic S Ptr's Ch Pomeroy WA 1976-1989; S Anne's Ch Omak WA 1971-1976; Vic S Paul's Omak WA 1971-1976; Vic S Jn's Okanogan WA 1967-1976; Vic Trsfg Twisp WA 1967-1971; Assoc All SS' Epis Ch Anchorage AK 1959-1967; Vic S Geo's Ch Cordova AK 1956-1959; Vic S Eliz's Ketchikan AK 1952-1956.

HODGKINS, Margaret S R (Ct) Trinity Episcopal Church, PO Box 400, Southport CT 06890 **R Trin Epis Ch Southport CT 2015-; Epis Election Com Dio New Jersey Trenton NJ 2012-, Com on Priesthood 2007-** B Fort Campbell KY 1957 d David & Alice. BA Mid 1979; MDiv UTS 1996. D 6/1/1996 Bp John Shelby Spong P 12/7/1996 Bp Jack Marston Mckelvey. m 8/20/1983 Robin C L Hodgkins c 3. Int S Matt's Ch Pennington NJ 2013-2015; R S Andr's Epis Ch New Providence NJ 2005-2011; Assoc Chapl Epis Ch at Pr Princeton NJ 2001-2005; Assoc R Trin Ch Princeton NJ 2001-2005; Assoc R Calv Epis Ch Summit NJ 1996-2001. Fell Wilson Coll, Pr 2003; Highest hon Russian Dept, Mid 1979.

HODGKINS, Nelson Bainbridge (NC) 874 Simmons Grove Church Rd, Pilot Mountain NC 27041 **Supply P S Phillips Ch 2013-; Ret Pilot Mtn 1995-; Int P Dio No Carolina Raleigh NC 2008-, Int 1988-2007** B Lewiston ME 1932 s Franklin & Inez. AAS Rochester Inst of Tech 1952; BS U of Houston 1953; MDiv VTS 1960; MS No Carolina A&T St U 1980. D 6/13/1960 P 1/23/1961 Bp Thomas H Wright. c 2. Part Time Vic S Paul's Ch Salisbury NC 2004-2008; Trin Ch Mt Airy NC 2000-2003; Int S Thos Epis Ch Reidsville NC 2000-2002; Int S Lk's Ch Eden NC 1995-1998, Int P 1983-1994; S Paul's Epis Ch Thomasville NC 1994-1995; Int S Chris's Epis Ch High Point NC 1992-1995, Int 1985-1988; Int S Anne's Ch Winston Salem NC 1991-1992; S Andr's Ch Greensboro NC 1977; Indstrl Counslg Serv Greensboro NC 1969-1984; S Thos' Epis Ch Bath NC 1965-1967; P-in-c Zion Epis Ch Washington NC 1965-1967; Gr Ch Whiteville NC 1960-1965; Min in charge S Jas The Fisherman Epis Ch Shallotte NC 1960-1964. Auth, *Influence Mozarabic Rite Liturg Ch of Spain,* 1959. RACA 1967. Paul Harris Fllshp Rotary Intl 1980.

HODGSON, Gregory Scott (SVa) 11940 Fairlington Lane, Midlothian VA 23113 **Dn Dio Sthrn Virginia Norfolk VA 2007-** B New York NY 1959 s Lawrence & Diane. BA SUNY 1981; MDiv Sewanee: The U So, TS 1984. D 6/23/1984 Bp Henry Boyd Hucles III P 1/19/1985 Bp Robert Campbell Witcher Sr. m 2/17/2001 Sherrill Lynn McKay c 2. R S Mich's Ch Richmond VA 2006-2014; Assoc Gr Ch Cathd Charleston SC 2002-2006; Dn Dio Massachusetts Boston MA 1996-2002; R Trin Epis Ch Wrentham MA 1990-2002; Cur S Mk's Ch Islip NY 1984-1990.

HODSDON, Douglas Graham (Fla) 1439 N Market St, Jacksonville FL 32206 **Int S Jas' Epis Ch Lake City FL 2012-** B Boston MA 1949 s George & Evelyn. BA U NC 1972; MDiv VTS 1984. D 6/15/1984 Bp Claude Charles Vache P 6/1/1985 Bp Robert Whitridge Estill. m 7/7/1973 Mary Gallen c 3. R Ch Of The Gd Shpd Jacksonville FL 2007-2011; R S Thos Epis Ch Sanford NC 1991-2007; R S Jn's Ch Winnsboro SC 1988-1991; Cur Ch Of The H Comf Charlotte NC 1984-1988.

HOEBERMANN, Christine Marie (Oly) 123 L St NE, Auburn WA 98002 B Arlington, WA 1958 d Gary & Rae. AA Everett Cmnty Coll. D 6/28/2003 Bp Wendell Nathaniel Gibbs. m 8/20/1994 Jay Robert Hoebermann c 2.

HOECKER, Maria Janine (Me) 32 Emery Ln, Boothbay Harbor ME 04538 **P in Charge S Columba's Epis Ch E Boothbay ME 2012-, R 2012-** B Wichita KS 1962 d Robert & Janice. BS SW Coll Winfield KS 1984; MDiv Sewanee: The U So, TS 2005. D 6/29/2005 Bp Dean E Wolfe P 2/4/2006 Bp Porter Taylor. c 2. Assoc R S Phil's Ch Brevard NC 2005-2010. Guest Ed, "Chld and the Kingdom: Educ and Formation," *Sewanee Theol Revs,* Univ. of the So, Sewanee TN, 2005; Auth, "Expectation ~a poem and article.," *Sewanee Theol Revs,* Univ. of the So, Sewanee TN, 2004; Guest Ed, "Chld and the Kingdom: The Theol of Childhood," *Sewanee Theol Revs,* Univ. of So, Sewanee TN, 2004.

HOECKER, Marsha Hogg (Mass) 188 Center Road, Shirley MA 01464 **The Cathd Ch Of S Paul Boston MA 2014-; R Trin Chap Shirley MA 2014-, 2006-2009; S Dav's Epis Mssn Pepperell MA 2009-** B Portsmouth VA 1950 d Frank & Catherine. Carleton Coll; BS Windham Coll 1978; MDiv EDS 1995. D 4/1/1995 P 10/16/1995 Bp Mary Adelia Rosamond Mcleod. m 12/29/1990 Henry T Hoecker c 2. P-in-c Shirley Pepperell Epis Partnership Pepperell MA 2009-2013; Mssnr Middlesex Area Cluster Mnstry Higganum CT 2002-2006; Yth Mnstry Dio Vermont Burlington VT 1998-2002, Cn for Yth Mnstry 1998-2002; P-in-c H Trin Epis Ch Swanton VT 1998-2001; Asst S Barn Ch Falmouth MA 1995-1998.

HOEDEL, Barbara Anne (Ak) PO Box 1661, Kodiak AK 99615 B Kodiak AK 1949 d Norman & Margaret. D 8/17/2015 Bp Mark A Lattime. m 9/10/2005 Robert John Hoedel.

HOEKSTRA, Robert Bruce (Eau) 909 Summit Ave, Chippewa Falls WI 54729 **Hospice Chapl St. Jos's Hosp CHippewa Falls WI 1995-; Dir of Pstr Care Chippewa Manor Ret Cmnty Chippewa Falls WI 1985-** B South Holland IL 1957 s Thomas & Gay. BA Trin Bible Coll 1981; Trin Evang DS 1983; MA Multnomah Bible Coll and Biblic Sem 1997; Cert Coll of Preachers 2002; STM Nash 2010. D 11/7/2002 P 5/8/2003 Bp Keith Whitmore. m 9/26/1981 Heidi Nohr c 4. P-in-c S Simeon's Ch Chippewa Falls WI 2009-2015; COM Dio Eau Claire 2004-2007; P-in-c S Lk's Ch Altoona WI 2004-2006; Stndg Com Dio Eau Claire Eau Claire WI 2007-2009, Chapl To Dioc Exec Coun 2005-2006.

HOELTZEL, George Anthony (NY) 721 Warburton Ave, Yonkers NY 10701 **The Sharing Comunity 1988-** B Kansas City MO 1948 s Orval & Marjorie. BA U of So Alabama 1969; MDiv GTS 1973. D 6/9/1973 Bp Leland Stark P 12/15/1973 Bp Paul Moore Jr. m 9/15/1969 Susan Hoeltzel c 2. P H Cross Yonkers NY 2009-2014; Assoc S Jn's Ch Getty Sq Yonkers NY 1985-1995; Proj Coordntr The Sharing Comunity 1985-1988; R All SS Ch Harrison NY 1977-1985; Chapl SUNY-Purchase 1977-1985; Asst Gr Epis Ch Nyack NY 1975-1976; Cur S Barth's Ch In The Highland White Plains NY 1973-1975. Fllshp Recon.

HOELZEL III, William Nold (Chi) 3257 Anika Dr, Fort Collins CO 80525 B Chicago IL 1942 s William & Celeste. BA NWU 1964; BD Nash 1968. D 6/15/1968 Bp James Winchester Montgomery P 12/21/1968 Bp Gerald Francis Burrill. c 3. R S Mary Epis Ch Crystal Lake IL 1976-2007; Vic Gr Epis Ch New Lenox IL 1971-1976; Cur S Matt's Ch Evanston IL 1968-1971.

HOEY, Anne Knight (Tex) 5608-A Jim Hogg Ave., Austin TX 78756 B Austin TX 1938 d Fred & Elizabeth. Wellesley Coll 1958; BA U of Texas 1960; MDiv Epis TS of the SW 1988. D 6/24/1988 Bp Anselmo Carral-Solar P 5/26/1989 Bp Maurice Manuel Benitez. c 3. Assoc R S Mich's Ch Austin TX 2001-2005; R S Jas' Epis Ch La Grange TX 1997-2000; The Ch of the Gd Shpd Austin TX 1990-1997.

HOEY, Lori Jean (CFla) 901 Clearmont St, Sebastian FL 32958 B W Islip NY 1965 d Walter & Patricia. Cert Istitute for Chr Stds 2009; BA Grand Canyon U 2010. D 12/12/2009 Bp John Wadsworth Howe. m 8/15/1987 Thomas Hoey c 2. D S Eliz's Epis Ch Sebastian FL 2009-2011.

HOFER, Christopher David (LI) 1400 Poulson St, Wantagh NY 11793 **Dep GC 2009 2009-; Pres Wantagh Cler Coun Wantagh NY 2009-; R Ch of S Jude Wantagh NY 2004-; Secy of Conv Epis Dio Long Island 2003-** B Jasper IN 1971 s David & Katherine. BA Walsh U 1993; MDiv GTS 2002. D 6/8/2002 Bp Arthur Williams Jr P 12/11/2002 Bp J Clark Grew II. m 8/12/2011 Kerry Michael Brady. Assoc Mssnr Epis W Side Shared Mnstry Cleveland OH 2002-2004. Blogger, "Vital Post Blog," *Epis Ch Vital Practices Blog*, ECF, 2011; Featured, "Transforming Ch," *Transforming Ch (Wantagh) Documentary*, Epis Ch Cntr, 2011. EUC 2003.

HOFER, Larry John (CPa) 32801 Ocean Reach Dr, Lewes DE 19958 **Assoc S Ptr's Ch Lewes DE 2014-** B Toledo OH 1939 s Harry & Mary. BA Ken 1961; MDiv Trin Luth Sem 1964; GTS 1987. D 6/12/1987 Bp Charlie Fuller Mcnutt Jr P 10/21/1987 Bp Dean Theodore Stevenson. m 4/25/1970 Susan Hofer c 2. Dir of Diac Dio Delaware 2011-2012; R S Andr's Ch St Coll PA 1994-2008; R S Alb's Epis Ch Reading PA 1990-1994; Asst to R St Andrews in the City Epis Ch Harrisburg PA 1987-1990; Dir of the Diac Dio Delaware Wilmington 2011-2012. SSJE 2000.

HOFF, Timothy Joseph (Ala) 2601 Lakewood Cir, Tuscaloosa AL 35405 B Freeport IL 1941 s Howard & Zillah. BA Tul 1963; JD Tul 1966; LLM Harv 1970. D 7/31/1983 P 2/22/1984 Bp Furman Charles Stough. m 3/21/1987 Virginia Nevill Hoff c 4. R S Mich's Epis Ch Fayette AL 2003-2010, R 1988-1996; Int Epis Black Belt Mnstry Greensboro AL 2002-2003; Trin Ch Demopolis AL 2002-2003; Assoc Cbury Chap Tuscaloosa AL 1996-2000; Assoc Cbury Chap Tuscaloosa AL 1985-1988; Int Ch Of The H Comf Montgomery AL 1984-1985; Asst S Paul's Ch Greensboro AL 1983-1984; Secy of the Dio Dio Alabama Birmingham 2006-2009. Auth, "Rel's Accommodation to Amer Law and Culture," *Legal Responses to Rel Practices in the Untd States*, Camb Press, 2012; Auth, "The Interpretative Process," *Merc Judgments*, Camb Press, 2011; Auth, "Harper Lee," *Yale Biographical Dictionary of Amer Law*, Ya Press, 2009; Auth, "Anatomy of a Murder," *Legal Stds Forum*, 2000; Auth, "Marketing Law & Lit," *Journ of the Legal Profession*, 1999; Auth, "Lawyers in the Subjunctive Mood," *Legal Stds Forum*, 1999; Auth, "Amer Monarchists & the Cult of Chas I," *Legal Stds Forum*, 1998; Auth, "Influences on Harper Lee," *Alabama Law Revs*, 1994; Auth, "Jn Tyler Morgan & Sthrn Autonomy," *Gulf Coast Hist Revs*, 1994; Auth, "Limitation of Actions, 2nd ed.," Harrison Pub Co, 1992; Auth, "Commencement Invocation," *Journ of the Legal Profession*, 1986; Auth, "Theol Influences on Wstrn Law," *Alabama Law Revs*, 1985; Auth, "Eleventh Circuit Survey Intro," *Mercer Law Revs*, 1982; Auth, "Error in the Formation of Contracts," *Tulane Law Revs*, 1979; Auth, "Joinder of Parties & Claims:," *Alabama Law Revs*, 1973. CBS 1977; GAS 1977; Sectn on Law & Rel, Assn Am Law Schools 1970; Soc of King Chas the Mtyr 1977. Who's Who in Amer 1992; Phi Beta Kappa 1963.

HOFFACKER, Charles (WA) 9A Parkway #202, Greenbelt MD 20770 B Philadelphia PA 1953 s Carl & Anne. BA St Johns Coll Annapolis MD 1975; MDiv Nash 1982; Coll of Preachers 1992; CDI Sewanee: The U So, TS 1996. D 6/2/1982 Bp William Carl Frey P 12/18/1982 Bp James Winchester Montgomery. m 8/3/2013 Jelena Mirtova c 1. R S Paul's Par Prince Geo's Cnty Brandywine MD 2014-2017; Int R Par of St Monica & St Jas Washington DC 2012-2014; P-in-c Chris's Ch New Carrollton MD 2010-2012; Int R S Andr's Ch St Coll PA 2008-2009; Int Pstr S Ptr's Ch Poolesville MD 2006-2008; Rdr GBEC W Hartford CT 1998-2014; Adj Fac St. Clair Cnty Cmnty Coll Port Huron MI 1998-2005; Dn Blue Water Convoc Dio Michigan Detroit MI 1993-1994; R S Paul's Epis Ch Port Huron MI 1992-2006; R S Ptr's Ch Akron OH 1986-1992; Lectr Theol Loyola U Chicago IL 1985-1986; Int P in Charge S Jude's Epis Ch Rochelle IL 1985-1986; Epis Chapl Epis Coun At Nthrn Illinois U Sycamore IL 1984-1986; Assisant S Paul's Ch Dekalb IL 1982-1983. Auth, *A Matter of Life and Death: Preaching at Funerals*, Cowley, 2003; Auth, "numerous arts, sermons, Revs. columns". Blue Water Peace Awd A Season for Nonviolence 2006; Excellence in Mnstry Awd Dio Estrn Michigan 2005.

HOFFACKER, Michael Paul Niblett (Pa) PO Box 765, Devon PA 19333 **Nonpar 1973-** B Washington DC 1942 s Carl & Anne. BA U of Pennyslvania 1964; STB PDS 1967; MS Drexel U 1976. D 6/10/1967 P 2/1/1968 Bp Robert Lionne DeWitt. m 12/2/1967 Antoinette Eugenie Hoffacker. Asst Nevil Memi Ch Of S Geo Ardmore PA 1970-1973; Cur Gr Ch Mt Airy 1967-1970; Gr Epiph Ch Philadelphia PA 1967-1970.

HOFFER, Jack Lee (CPa) 830 Washington Avenue, Tyrone PA 16686 **D Trin Epis Ch Tyrone PA 2011-; Instr Mt Aloysius Coll Cresson PA 2007-** B Windber PA 1945 s Maurice & Mary Ellen. BS Penn 1973; Cert EFM/Sewanee 2006; Cert Dioc Sch of Chriatian Stds 2007. D 6/9/2007 Bp Nathan Dwight Baxter.

HOFFER, Wilma Marie (EO) 64849 Casa Ct, Bend OR 97701 B Rockford IL 1937 d Ronald & Lola. Cert CDSP 1991. D 6/20/1991 Bp George Edmonds Bates. m 2/2/1958 Richard Ernest Hoffer c 2. D Trin Ch Bend OR 1998; Dio Utah Salt Lake City UT 1997-1998, Pstrl Vis 1992-1998; D All SS Ch Salt Lake City UT 1994-1998; Epis Cmnty Serv Inc Salt Lake City UT 1992-1996; D S Lk's Ch Pk City UT 1991-1994; Dir Campus Chr Cntr U Ut-Salt Lake City 1986-1988.

HOFFMAN, Arnold R (Spr) 1226 Olive St Unit 505, Saint Louis MO 63103 **Pstr Care St. Andr's Epis Ch Edwardsville IL 2014-** B Stillwater MN 1938 s Milton & Lena. BA U of Kansas 1963; MA U of Kansas 1965; PhD MI SU 1970; MDiv Nash 1978; Sewanee: The U So, TS 1996. D 6/9/1976 Bp Archie H Crowley P 6/8/1978 Bp William Cockburn Russell Sheridan. m 8/29/1982 Sharon Hoffman c 2. Supply Cler S Paul's Epis Ch Sikeston MO 2005-2011; Chair - Bec Dio Springfield Springfield IL 1996-2003, Cn Mssnr 1995-2004, COM, Chair 1997-1998; S Marys Ch Columbia MO 1991-1995; R H Trin Ch Skokie IL 1986-1990; R S Jn's Epis Ch Kewanee IL 1981-1986; Actg Vic Chr The King Epis Ch Huntington IN 1980-1981; R S Paul's Epis Ch Gas City IN 1978-1981. Auth, "Var arts," *Poetry*. Som 1991.

HOFFMAN, Charles Lance (Ct) 8 Sharon Ln, Old Saybrook CT 06475 **Int R St Paul's Epis Ch Darien CT 2014-** B Chicago IL 1941 s Peter & Jayne. BA Trin 1962; BD EDS 1968; DMin Andover Newton TS 1979. D 6/15/1968 Bp James Winchester Montgomery P 4/10/1969 Bp Gerald Francis Burrill. m 11/27/1976 Ellendale Mccollam c 4. Pstr Assoc St Paul's Epis Ch Darien CT 2013-2014; Ret Gr Ch Old Saybrook CT 1988-2013; R Ch Of The Mssh Woods Hole MA 1971-1988; Asst Par Of The Epiph Winchester MA 1969-1971; Cur The Par Of S Chrys's Quincy MA 1968-1969; Dir Shoreline Chr Counslg Serv 2001-2010; Chairman Dioc Cmsn on Evang 2000-2003; Mem Dioc Exec Coun 1995-2000; Dir Woods Hole Cmnty Dvlpmt Fndt 1981-1986; Mem Dioc Cmsn on Wmn and Mnstry 1978-1980; Dir Samaritans Suicide Prevention 1977-1980; Mem Study Com on Mltry Chapl 1974-1976; Alt Dep GC 1973; Mem Town Human Serv Com 1972-1988; Mem Joint Cmsn on Human Affrs 1971-1976; Agenda Com GC 1970; Mem Joint Cmsn on Renwl 1968-1970. Ord of S Lk 1993.

HOFFMAN JR, Edgar Henry Hap (Ark) 7 Rubra Ct, Little Rock AR 72223 B Cheyenne WY 1934 s Edgar & Pearl. BS U Denv 1956; Cert Epis TS of the SW 1994. D 6/15/1995 P 1/19/1996 Bp Larry Maze. m 5/8/1965 Barbara J Hoffman. Vic S Alb's Ch Stuttgart AR 2002-2006, Chapl 1997-2000; R Gr Ch Pine Bluff AR 2000-2002; Cur S Steph's Epis Ch Jacksonville AR 1995-1997.

HOFFMAN, Ellendale Mccollam (Ct) 8 Sharon Ln, Old Saybrook CT 06475 **P-in-c Gr Ch Old Saybrook CT 2013-, Assoc 1992-2013; Mar and Fam Ther Priv Pract Old Saybrook CT 1988-; Hon Cn, Chr Ch Cathd Dio Connecticut Meriden CT 2014-, Cler and Fam Enrichment Com 1991-1995; Jvnl Diversion Bd Town of Old Saybrook Connecticut 2011-; Healthy Cmnty/Yth Advsry Bd Yth and Fam Serv Old Saybrook CT 2007-** B Alexandria LA 1951 d William & Hope. AA Briarcliffe Coll 1971; BA Manhattanville Coll 1973; MDiv EDS 1976; DMin Andover Newton TS 1978. D 6/19/1976 Bp James Barrow Brown P 7/1/1977 Bp John Bowen Coburn. m 11/27/1976 Charles Lance Hoffman c 2. Psychol Priv Pract Falmouth MA 1981-1988; Clincl Dir Cntr for Alco Problems Hyannis MA 1979-1981; Supvsr Pstrl Inst TrngAlco Problems EDS Cambridge MA 1976-1978; Prog Dir Marion Cntr for Human Serv Marion MA 1976-1977. CT LMFT 1988; Clincl Mem, Amer Assn for Marital and Fam Ther 1982; Fell, AAPC 1982; MA Lic Clincl Psychol 1979. gracechurcholdsaybrook@gmail.com

HOFFMAN, Jeffrey Paul (CNY) B Rochester NY 1954 s Nels & Ruthe. MDiv Sewanee: The U So, TS 2007. D 6/9/2007 P 12/11/2007 Bp Gladstone Bailey Adams III. m 8/1/1998 Margaret Hoffman c 7. Cler-in-Charge S Matt's Epis Ch Horseheads NY 2007-2010.

HOFFMAN, Lisa A (NJ) St. Barnabas by the Bay Church, 13 W. Bates Avenue, Villas NJ 08251 **Vic S Barn By The Bay Villas NJ 2011-** B Neptune NJ 1962 d William & Sheila. BS Kutztown U 1984; MDiv VTS 2011. D 12/4/2010 P 6/30/2011 Bp George Edward Councell. m 7/27/1985 Jeffrey L Hoffman c 3. S Mary's Epis Ch Stone Harbor NJ 2011-2013.

HOFFMAN, Mary E (Ia) 2704 E garfield, Davenport IA 52803 B Oklahoma City OK 1933 d Henry & Vera. BD Drake U 1954; MS U of Iowa 1985. D 8/15/1995 Bp Chris Christopher Epting. m 6/6/1953 Larry Gene Hoffman c 2. D Trin Cathd Davenport IA 1995-2007. Cmnty of S Mary.

HOFFMAN, Michael Patrick (CGC) Christ Episcopal Church, 18 W Wright St, Pensacola FL 32501 **R Chr Chr Epis Ch Pensacola FL 2016-** B Biloxi, MS 1978 s John & Barbara. BA U So 2000; MDiv Sewanee: The U So, TS 2005. D 6/28/2005 P 1/5/2006 Bp James Edward Folts. m 7/5/2005 Amy Black Hoffman c 2. R S Ptr's Ch Mc Kinney TX 2011-2016; St Ptr & St Paul Ch Mssn TX 2007-2011; S Helena's Epis Ch Boerne TX 2005-2011; S Andr's Epis Ch Seguin TX 2005-2007. michael@christ-church.net

HOFFMAN, Roy Everett (SVa) 2 BL Jackson Road, Newport RI 02840 **Chapl US Navy 2002-** B Alexandria VA 1957 s Charles & Doreen. BS Auburn U

1979; JD U GA 1983; MDiv SWTS 1994; DMin GTF 2008. D 9/24/1994 P 5/12/1995 Bp Robert Gould Tharp. c 1. Vic Ch Of S Ben Bolingbrook IL 1996-2002; Asst Ch Of The Gd Samar Knoxville TN 1994-1996. Auth, "Jn Wesley's Reflection on the Lord's Pryr," *Fndt Theol*, Victoria Press, 2009.

HOFFMAN, William Charles (SVa) 4101 Mingo Trl, Chesapeake VA 23325 **Died 5/20/2017** B Columbus OH 1923 s William & Mildred. BA W&M 1948; VTS 1951. D 6/12/1951 P 6/1/1952 Bp George P Gunn. c 1. R S Bride's Epis Ch Chesapeake VA 1954-1988; P-in-c Pruden Par Gretna VA 1951-1954.

HOFFMANN, Beth Borah (Ore) 2409 Crescent Rd, Navarre FL 32566 **Vic S Jn-By-The-Sea Epis Ch Bandon OR 2012-** B Evansville IN 1943 d Frank & Barbara. AA Stephens Coll 1963; BS U of Bridgeport 1990; Col 1992; Pittsburgh TS 1997; MDiv GTS 2000. D 6/10/2000 Bp Robert William Duncan P 12/27/2000 Bp Andrew Donnan Smith. m 12/19/1963 Lewis Edward Hoffmann c 1. Vic Ch Of The Epiph Durham CT 2008-2011; Asst S Mary's Epis Ch Manchester CT 2002-2005; Chapl Incarn Cntr Deep River CT 2000-2001; Dir EAP Norwalk Hosp 1988-1993.

HOFF NOLAN, Daryce D 6/17/2017 Bp Jeff Lee.

HOFMANN, Therese Marie (Mass) 108 Stratford St, West Roxbury MA 02132 **Dir, Sprtl Life Curry Coll 2010-** B Buffalo NY 1952 d Robert & Jean. BA U of Massachusetts 1974; MA U of Massachusetts 1978; MBA Simmons Coll 1987; MDiv EDS 2009. D 6/16/2012 Bp M(Arvil) Thomas Shaw. D S Jn's Ch Jamaica Plain MA 2012-2015.

HOGAN, Claudia S M (Eau) **D S Simeon's Ch Chippewa Falls WI 2010-** B Quincy IL 1943 d Claude & Maxine. BS Eureka Coll 1965; Dio Milwaukee Inst of Chr Stds WI 1990; AAS Madison Area Tech Coll 2001. D 9/8/1990 Bp Roger John White. m 6/28/2008 Patrick M Hogan. D S Andr's Epis Ch Monroe WI 1990-2008. NAAD 1990.

HOGAN, Faye (Los) 1237 Laguna Ln, San Luis Obispo CA 93035 **Pstr Assoc S Ptr's Par Santa Maria CA 2009-** B Baton Rouge LA 1932 d Oauthor & Frances. BS Texas Womans U 1953; MA Texas Womans U 1956; EdD USC 1983; MDiv ETSBH 1997. D 6/1/1996 P 1/18/1997 Bp Chester Lovelle Talton. Asst S Ben's Par Los Osos CA 2006-2008; Int St. Aid's Epis Ch 2004-2005; S Paul's Epis Ch Ventura CA 2002-2004, 1996-1999; Trin Epis Ch Santa Barbara CA 2000-2004; Chapl S Johns Reg Med Cntr Oxnard CA 1993-2004. Assn Of Profsnl Chapl - Bd-Cert Chaplai; OHC.

HOGAN, Lucy Lind (WA) 4500 Massachusetts Ave Nw, Washington DC 20016 **Prof Prchng & Wrshp Wesley TS Washington DC 1987-** B Minneapolis MN 1951 d Wilfred & Margaret. BA Macalester Coll 1973; MDiv VTS 1981; DMin Wesley TS 1987; PhD U of Maryland 1995. D 6/29/1981 P 1/25/1982 Bp Robert Marshall Anderson. m 5/26/1973 Kevin Patrick Hogan c 2. Asst S Lk's Ch Trin Par Beth MD 1989-1995, Asst 1983-1984; VTS Alexandria VA 1989-1990; Asst S Fran Ch Potomac MD 1981-1982. Auth, "The Six Deadly Sins of Preaching," Abingdon Press, 2012; Auth, "Lenten Serv," Abingdon Press, 2009; Ed, "Preaching As A Lang of Hope," Protea Bk Hse, 2007; Auth, "Graceful Speech An Invitatn to Preaching," Westminster Jn Knox Press, 2006; Auth, "Connecting w The Cong: Rhetoric And The Art Of Preaching," Abingdon Press, 1999. Acad Of Homil, Pres 1994; Societas Homiletica, Past Pres 1998; WECA 1981.

HOGG, Douglas (EC) 347 South Creek Drive, Osprey FL 34229 **1968-** B Charleston WV 1936 s Francis & Kathleen. BA Randolph-Macon Coll 1958; BD Epis TS of the SW 1963; U of Tennessee 1968; HGC 1980. D 6/27/1963 P 6/1/1964 Bp David Shepherd Rose. m 10/10/2016 John Post Powers. R S Chris's Ch Havelock NC 1965-1967; Asst R Chr And Gr Ch Petersburg VA 1963-1965.

HOGG JR, Paul (SVa) 7858 Sunset Dr, Hayes VA 23072 B Newport News VA 1946 s Paul & Dorothy. BA Randolph-Macon Coll 1969; MDiv VTS 1974; DMin VTS 1991. D 6/6/1974 P 12/10/1974 Bp David Shepherd Rose. m 8/10/1968 Toni C Hogg c 2. Int R S Jn's Ch Hampton VA 2011-2013; Int R Gr Ch The Plains VA 2010-2011; Int R Chr Epis Ch Raleigh NC 2009-2010; Int R Trin Ch Portsmouth VA 2008-2009; Int R S Paul's Ch Richmond VA 2007-2008; Int R S Mart's Epis Ch Williamsburg VA 2005-2007; R S Aid's Ch Virginia Bch VA 1979-2005; Vic S Dav's Epis Ch No Chesterfield VA 1974-1979; Epis Ch Of Our Sav Midlothian VA 1974-1978; Vic Dio Sthrn Virginia Newport News VA 1974-1976. Auth, *Empowerment for Mnstry: Developing Lay Pstr Caregivers*, VTS, 1991.

HOGIN, Christopher W (ETenn) Church Of The Ascension, 800 S Northshore Dr, Knoxville TN 37919 **Ch Of The Ascen Knoxville TN 2016-** B Knoxville TN 1972 s John & Beverly. BA U of Tennessee; JD U of Tennessee Coll of Law 1999; MDiv Duke DS 2013. D 6/8/2013 Bp Shannon Sherwood Johnston P 1/5/2014 Bp Anne Hodges-Copple. c 1. S Mich's Ch Raleigh NC 2013-2016.

HOGUE, Kelsey Graham (Colo) 9 W 35th St, Scottsbluff NE 69361 B Bedford IN 1950 s James & Ethel. BS U CO 1972; MDiv CDSP 1992. D 6/20/1992 P 12/15/1992 Bp William Jerry Winterrowd. m 7/11/1970 Deborah Lyn Hogue c 2. R S Fran Epis Ch Scottsbluff NE 2006-2013; Int S Ptr's Ch Basalt CO 2005-2006; Wstrn Coloorado Dio Colorado Denver CO 2000-2005, Cn Mssnr - Mtn Reg 1998-2000, Stndg Com-ex oficio 2000-2005, mutual Mnstry Coordntr 1996-1999, COM 1993-1996; Cranmer Memi Chap Granby CO 1992-2000;

Vic Epis Ch Of S Jn The Bapt Granby CO 1992-2000; Trin Ch Kremmling CO 1992-1998; Bp Search Com Dio Nebraska Omaha NE 2010-2011. Fell Coll of Preachers 2000.

HOGUE, Marlene Christine Harshfield (Eau) PO Box 637, Hayward WI 54843 B Joliet IL 1959 d Keith & Charlotte. Deacons' Acad, Eau Claire, WI; BS U IL Urbana-Champaign 1981; MS Nthrn Illinois U 1990. D 8/8/2015 Bp William Jay Lambert III. m 12/21/1985 Richard Raye Hogue c 2.

HOGUE JR, Richard R (Nwk) 575 Kearny Ave, Kearny NJ 07032 **Dio Newark Newark NJ 2016-** B Olympia Fields IL 1987 s Richard & Marlene. BA Wabash Coll 2009; MDiv CDSP 2016. D 12/19/2015 P 9/24/2016 Bp Mark M Beckwith. m 11/11/2016 Maura H Schmitz.

HOHENFELDT, Robert John (Mil) 1310 Rawson Ave, South Milwaukee WI 53172 **Asst S Mk's 1965-** B Marinette WI 1924 D 8/3/1963 Bp Donald H V Hallock. m 4/19/1952 Dolores Ruth Aubinger c 2.

HOHLT, Allan Hunter (Del) 94 Oak Ridge Rd, Plymouth NH 03264 **Ret 1994-** B Brenham TX 1932 s Ernest & Sarah. BBA Texas A&M U 1954; BD CDSP 1966; DHL S Augustines Coll Raleigh NC 1989. D 6/22/1966 Bp James Milton Richardson P 5/30/1967 Bp Scott Field Bailey. m 8/8/1964 Winifred L Hohlt c 2. Cathd Ch Of S Jn Wilmington DE 1970-1994; R S Paul's Epis Ch Freeport TX 1970-1976; Vic H Cross Epis Ch Sugar Land TX 1966-1967.

HOIDRA, Carol (Ct) 245 East 72nd Street, Apt. 2D, New York NY 10021 B Warren OH 1952 d Peter & Anna. BA Arcadia U 1974; MDiv Ya Berk 2003. D 6/10/2006 P 1/20/2007 Bp Andrew Donnan Smith. Assoc Dir, Mssn Funding Epis Ch Cntr New York NY 2008-2012; Asst to the R (Int) S Mk's Ch New Canaan CT 2007-2008; Cur S Mary's Epis Ch Manchester CT 2006-2007; Dvlpmt Assoc St. Barth Ch New York NY 2004-2006.

HOKE, Stuart Hubbard (NY) 536 Fearrington Post, Pittsboro NC 27312 B Memphis TN 1946 s Wallace & Mildred. BA SMU 1968; MDiv EDS 1972; STM GTS 1996; ThD GTS 2000. D 7/1/1972 P 12/16/1972 Bp Chilton R Powell. c 2. Chapl Trin Par New York NY 2000-2008; The Ch of S Ign of Antioch New York NY 1999-2000; Int Ch Of The Gd Shpd Ft Lee NJ 1995-1996; R S Fran Ch Houston TX 1991-1995; R S Andr's Epis Ch Amarillo TX 1981-1991; R S Jn's Ch Harrison AR 1976-1981; Asst S Mk's Epis Ch Little Rock AR 1974-1976; Cur S Dunst's Ch Tulsa OK 1972-1974. Auth, "A Generally Obscure Calling: Character Sketch Of Isabel Hapgood," *S Vladimir'S Quarterly*, 2001; Auth, "Broken Fragments: Wm Reed Huntington'S Quest For Unity," *Journ Of Angl/Epis Hist*, 2000.

HOLBEN, Lawrence Robert (NCal) 701 Lassen Ln, Mount Shasta CA 96067 **Dn, Superior Dnry The Epis Dio Nthrn California Sacramento CA 2013-; P-in-c S Barn Ch Mt Shasta CA 2010-** B Los Angeles CA 1945 s Gordon & Margaret. D 6/12/2010 P 12/12/2010 Bp Barry Leigh Beisner.

HOLBERT, John Russell (La) 1645 Carol Sue Ave, Terrytown LA 70056 B Charleston SC 1945 s John & Alice. D 10/23/2005 Bp Charles Edward Jenkins III. c 2. Patrolman Iv Class New Orleans Police Dept 1983-1991.

HOLBROOK JR, Paul Evans (Lex) 308 Madison Pl, Lexington KY 40508 B Ashland KY 1949 s Paul & Frances. BA Denison U 1971; MDiv Harvard DS 1974; ThM Harvard DS 1976; MA U of Kentucky 1983; PhD U of Kentucky 1988. D 8/15/1975 Bp Addison Hosea. D S Aug's Chap Lexington KY 1996-2003, Asst Chapl 1979-1995; D Ch S Mich The Archangel Lexington KY 1980-1982; D Calv Epis Ch Ashland KY 1977-1979. Auth, "Victor Hammer," *Printer & Typographer*, The Anvil Press, 1981; Auth, "Notes for," *Phenomena of Aratus Soliensus*, King Libr Press, 1975. Comp to The Solitary Of Dekoven 1996; Sr Chapl Mltry and Hospitaller, Ord of S Laz 1992; Tertiary of the Soc of S Fran 1978. Paul Harris Fell Rotary Club 2007; Diac Cn The Collgt Chap of St. Jn, The DeKoven Cntr 2007; Off The Most Venerable Ord of the Hosp of St. Jn of Jerusalem 2003; Knight Grand Cross Sovereign Mltry Ord of Temple of Jerusalem 1992.

HOLCOMB, Justin S (CFla) 100 W Jefferson St, Charlottesville VA 22902 **Cn Dio Cntrl Florida Orlando FL 2013-** B Sarasota FL 1973 BA SE U 1994; MA Reformed TS 1997; MA Reformed TS 1997; PhD Emory U 2003. Trans 6/25/2008 as Priest Bp Peter J Lee. m 12/1/2006 Lindsey A Holcomb c 2. Cathd Ch Of S Lk Orlando FL 2014-2015; Assoc R Chr Epis Ch Charlottesvlle VA 2008-2009. Co-Auth, "God Made All of Me: A Bk to Help Chld Protect Their Bodies," New Growth Press, 2015; Auth, "What Do You Do for a Living?," New Growth Press, 2015; Co-Auth, "Rid of My Disgrace: Sm Grp Discussion Guide," New Growth Press, 2015; Co-Auth, "Is It My Fault?: Hope and Healing for Those Suffering Dom Violence," Moody, 2014; Auth, "Know the Heretics," Zondervan, 2014; Auth, "Know the Creeds and Councils," Zondervan, 2014; Auth, "Acts: A 12-Week Study," Crossway, 2014; Ed, "For the Wrld: Essays in hon of Richard L. Pratt Jr.," P&R Pub, 2014; Auth, "On the Gr of God," Crossway, 2013; Co-Auth, "Rid of My Disgrace: Hope and Healing for Victims of Sexual Assault," Crossway, 2011; Ed, "Chr Theologies of Scripture," NYU Press, 2006. jholcomb@cfdiocese.org

HOLCOMB, Steve A-Retired (WNC) 1500 Maltby Rd, Marble NC 28905 **P & Pstr Gr Mountainside Luth/Epis Ch Robbinsville NC 2004-; M-in-c Gr Mountainside Luth/Epis Ch Robbinsville NC 2002-; D Gr Mountainside Luth/Epis Ch Robbinsville NC 1984-** B Brunswick GA 1949 s Henry &

Amelia. BA Stetson U 1971; MA Wstrn Carolina U 1992. D 6/29/1983 Bp William Gillette Weinhauer P 7/14/2004 Bp Bob Johnson. m 9/10/1972 Linda Laine c 2. Ret Pstr & P-in-c Gr Ch Robbinsville NC 2004-2014, D 1984-2004; D Ch Of The Mssh Murphy NC 1983-2000.

HOLCOMBE, Matthew P (Pa) 1412 Providence Road, Charlotte NC 28207 **P Chr Ch Charlotte NC 2014-** B Tucson AZ 1981 s Scott & La Nora. BA Shpd U 2002; MDiv GTS 2011. D 6/11/2011 P 1/14/2012 Bp Charles Ellsworth Bennison Jr. m 8/31/2002 Alicia A Brabitz c 2. Assoc R S Dav's Ch Wayne PA 2011-2014; VP Hotwire Cmncatn 2002-2008. holcombem@ christchurchcharlotte.org

HOLCOMBE, Scott T (CFla) 4146 Millstone Dr, Melbourne FL 32940 **P Ch Of S Dav's By The Sea Cocoa Bch FL 2010-** B Lakeland FL 1954 s Paul & Marilyn. BA U of So Florida 1975; MDiv Sewanee: The U So, TS 1978. D 6/18/1978 Bp Emerson Paul Haynes P 6/16/1979 Bp Thomas Augustus Fraser Jr. m 3/16/1974 La Nora Holcombe c 4. R Chr Ch Short Hills NJ 2008-2010; R S Steph's Ch Lakeland FL 2001-2008; R Chr Ch Clarksburg WV 1993-2001; R All Souls' Epis Ch Miami Bch FL 1992-1993; R Chr Epis Ch Kennesaw GA 1985-1992; Asst S Phil's In The Hills Tucson AZ 1981-1985; Asst S Andr's Ch Greensboro NC 1978-1981.

HOLDBROOKE, Charles Henry (LI) Calvary & St. Cyprian's Church, Brooklyn NY 11221 **P-in-c Ch Of Calv And S Cyp Brooklyn NY 2013-, R 2014-** B 1957 s John & Christina. LTh St Nich TS 1988; MA SWTS 2002. Trans 11/25/2008 Bp Orris George Walker Jr. m 11/30/1991 Rachel M Holdbrooke c 2. Dir of Pstr Care Epis Hlth Serv 2008-2012; Chapl Epis Hlth Serv Far Rockaway NY 2008-2012; Chapl S Jn's Epis Chap Brooklyn NY 2008-2012; Par P/Dio Treas Dio Sekondi (Ghana) 1989-2000.

HOLDEN, Elizabeth G (Tex) 4709 Laurel St, Bellaire TX 77401 **Epis HS Bellaire TX 2008-; Chapl St. Thos Epis HS Houston TX 2008-** B Kansas City MO 1961 d Edward & Susan. BA Wesl 1984; MDiv VTS 1990. D 6/17/1990 P 3/4/1991 Bp Maurice Manuel Benitez. m 6/27/1992 Samuel O Holden c 2. Cn Chr Ch Cathd Houston TX 1995-2001; Asst R S Jn The Div Houston TX 1990-1995.

HOLDER, Anthony Brian (SeFla) 2801 N University Dr, Pembroke Pines FL 33024 **R H Sacr Hollywood FL 2011-** B Christ Church BB 1965 s Anthony & Audrey. AA Barbados Cmnty Coll 1982; U of the W Indies 1993; MDiv U of the W Indies 1993; DMin TESM 2009. Trans 3/1/2001 Bp Peter Hess Beckwith. m 8/31/1996 Judith De-Ann Holder c 2. Vic S Mich's Epis Ch O Fallon IL 2001-2010; Mem, Bd Dir, Priv Elem Sch Angl Dio Barbados 2000-2001; Chair, Bd Mgmt, Publ Elem Schools Angl Dio Barbados 1995-1998; Chapl, Publ & Priv Elem Schools Angl Dio Barbados 1993-2001; Pres Pro Tem, Dioc Coun Dio Springfield Springfield IL 2010, Pres, Stndg Com 2009-2010, Pres, Stndg Com 2005-2006, Mem, Stndg Com 2003-2010, Web Mgr 2002-2010, Mem, Dioc Coun 2001-2010, Sprtl Dir, Happ 2001-2005. frtony@holysacrament.org

HOLDER, Arthur Glenn (Cal) 2400 Ridge Rd, Berkeley CA 94709 **Prof of Chr Sprtlty Grad Theol Un Berkeley CA 2016-; Assoc P S Paul's Epis Ch Benicia CA 2011-** B Atlanta GA 1952 s Charles & Mary. BA Duke 1973; MDiv GTS 1976; PhD Duke 1987. D 3/12/1977 P 12/17/1977 Bp William Gillette Weinhauer. m 10/21/1978 Sarah Noble Henry c 1. Dn & VP of Acad Affrs Grad Theol Un Berkeley CA 2002-2016; Assoc P S Mk's Par Berkeley CA 1987-2010; Prof CDSP Berkeley CA 1986-2007; R Ch Of The H Cross Valle Crucis NC 1978-1985; Asst S Jas Epis Ch Hendersonvlle NC 1977-1978. Transltr, "The Venerable Bede: On the Song of Songs and Selected Writings," Paulist Press, 2011; Ed, "Chr Sprtlty: The Classics," Routledge, 2009; Ed, "Blackwell Comp to Chr Sprtlty," Blackwell, 2005; Transltr, "Bede: Biblic Miscellany," Liverpool U Press, 1998; Transltr, "Bede: On The Tabernacle," Liverpool U Press, 1994. AAR 1989; Amer Soc Of Ch Hist 1981; Medieval Acad Of Amer 1981; No Amer Patristics Soc 1985; Soc For The Study Of Chr Sprtlty 1996. Assoc OHC 1978; Phi Beta Kappa 1973. aholder@gtu.edu

HOLDER, Charles Richard (Md) PO Box A, Rohrersville MD 21779 B Hagerstown MD 1943 s Charles & Helen. BA Frostburg St U 1965; MEd Frostburg St U 1969; Sewanee: The U So, TS 1979. D 7/7/1978 Bp William Jackson Cox P 5/6/1979 Bp David Keller Leighton Sr. m 6/10/1967 Trudie Holder c 2. Vic S Lk's Ch Brownsville MD 1987-2015, Vic 1979-1987; S Andr's Ch Clear Sprg MD 1986. Auth, "Stdt Oriented Clasroom- Engl and Soc Stds," WCPS, 1969. CBS 1978; SocMary 1978. Nancy S. Grasmick Execllence for Minority Achievement Awd Maryland St Dept of Educ 1999.

HOLDER, Jennifer Sutton (NwT) 1318 Amarilla St, Abilene TX 79602 **R S Chris's Epis Ch Lubbock TX 2017-, P-in-c 2016-2017; Chapl Cbury Epis Campus Mnstry at Texas Tech Lubbock TX 2014-** B Greensboro NC 1952 d Worthe & Helen. BA U of Texas 1973; MA U NC 1991. D 6/8/2002 Bp James Monte Stanton P 1/16/2010 Bp James Scott Mayer. c 3. Chapl Dio NW Texas Lubbock TX 2014-2017; S Anne's Epis Ch Desoto TX 2007-2008. mtrjennifer@stchristophers.org

HOLDER, Lauren R (At) 435 Peachtree St Ne, Atlanta GA 30308 **S Lk's Epis Ch Atlanta GA 2015-** B Lubbock TX 1980 d Stephen & Kristy. BA W&L 2003; MALA St Jn's Coll 2007; MDiv GTS 2014; MDiv The GTS 2014. D 6/21/2014 Bp Anne Hodges-Copple P 1/17/2015 Bp Michael B Curry. m 9/3/

2011 Jason G Holder c 2. Trin Par New York NY 2014-2015; Chr Ch Charlotte NC 2008-2012. lauren@stlukesatlanta.org

HOLDER, Michael Rawle (SVa) 926 Thomasson Lane, South Hill VA 23970 **Vic So Mecklenburg-Brunswick Cure 1987-** B 1944 s Eustace & Edith. ThD Codrington Coll 1975. Trans 9/1/1987 Bp Claude Charles Vache. So Mecklenburg-Brunswick Cure So Hill VA 1986-1997; Serv Ch Of Barbados 1975-1985. OHC.

HOLDER, Timothy (ETenn) 142 Lovers Ln, Elizabethton TN 37643 **P-in-c St. Thos Epis Ch Elizabethton Tennessee USA 2015-** B Elizabethton TN 1955 s John & Ruth. BA The U So 1977; MPA Middle Tennessee St U 1979; MDiv Harvard DS 1997. Trans 10/1/2003 Bp Henry Nutt Parsley Jr. Assoc Chr Ch Toms River Toms River NJ 2013-2015, 2010-2012; R Historic Ch of Ascen Atlantic City NJ 2007-2009; R Trin Ch Of Morrisania Bronx NY 2002-2007; R Gr Ch Birmingham AL 1998-2002; Gr Epis Ch Dio Alabama Birmingham 1997; Dir of Dvlpmt PBFWR 1990-1994. Auth, "I Ain't Got No Hope, Hip Hop Recon," *Ambassadors for God: Envisioning Recon Rites for the 21st Century, Liturg Stds Five*, Ch Pub, Inc., 2010; Ed and Contrib, "The Hip Hop PB, 2nd ed.: The Remix," *The Hip Hop PB, 2nd ed.: The Remix*, Ch Pub, Inc., 2009; Creator, Writer and Artist, "And the Word Was Hip Hop, a cd," *And the Word Was Hip Hop, a cd*, Ch Pub, Inc., 2007; Ed and Contrib, "The Hip Hop PB, 1st Ed," *The Hip Hop PB*, Ch Pub, Inc., 2006. The Amer Soc of the Most Venerable Ord of The Hosp of St. Jn of Jerusalem 2000-2011. Mart Luther King, Jr., Awd Sthrn Chr Ldrshp Conf 2006; First Decade Awd Harvard DS 2005; Human Rts Awd Equality Alabama 2002; Fell, TS The U So, Sewanee 2002. tholdertn@gmail.com

HOLDER-JOFFRION, Kerry Elizabeth (Ala) 3009 Barcody Rd Se, Huntsville AL 35802 B Cleveland OH 1964 d Douglas & Judith. BA Furman U 1986; MDiv PrTS 1990. D 11/14/1991 P 6/1/1992 Bp Charles I Jones III. m 7/24/1999 Ronald Guy Sibold c 1. Assoc Ch Of The Nativ Epis Huntsville AL 1997-2006; R S Jas Ch Lewistown MT 1995-1997; Dio Montana Helena MT 1993-1995; Ch Of The Incarn Great Falls MT 1991-1992. Auth, "Rediscovering Lost Traditions: A Pstr Guide To The New"; Auth, "Supplemental Texts 89". S Aid. Pbf Dom Initiative Proj 1996.

HOLDING, Megan (Mass) 15 Saint Paul St, Brookline MA 02446 B Toledo OH 1971 d James & Eileen. BA Amh 1993; JD Geo Law Cntr 1997; Dplma in Angl Stds Berk 2014; Dplma in Angl Stds Ya Berk 2014; MDiv Yale DS 2014. D 6/7/2014 Bp M(Arvil) Thomas Shaw P 1/10/2015 Bp Alan Gates. m 8/22/1998 Christopher Todd Holding c 2. S Paul's Ch Brookline MA 2014-2016.

HOLDING, Suzann (Chi) 2728 6th Ave, San Diego CA 92103 **Admin Bexley Seabury Fed Chicago IL 2015-, 2014-2015** B Huntington WV 1955 d Albert & Zeda. BA DePauw U 1976; MA Amer Grad Sch of Intl Mgmt Glendal 1977; MDiv SWTS 1999. D 6/19/1999 P 12/18/1999 Bp Bill Persell. c 2. Cn to the Ordnry Dio San Diego San Diego CA 2009-2013; Stndg Com (Pres.2009) Dio Chicago Chicago IL 2006-2009; R Ch Of Our Sav Elmhurst IL 2003-2009; Assoc R Trin Epis Ch Wheaton IL 1999-2002. sholding@bexleyseabury.org

HOLDORPH, Jedediah D (EO) 2203 Dollarhide Way, Ashland OR 97520 **P Trin Ch Bend OR 2014-; R S Mk's Epis Par Medford OR 2005-** B Saginaw MI 1958 s John & Edith. BA U of Arizona 1980; MDiv EDS 1988. D 6/2/1988 Bp Joseph Thomas Heistand P 1/6/1989 Bp William Davidson. m 7/19/1980 Barbara Estes Price c 2. R S Lawr Epis Ch Libertyville IL 1993-2005; R Chr Ch Lexington MO 1991-1993; Dio W Missouri Kansas City MO 1990; Int S Mk's On The Mesa Epis Ch Albuquerque NM 1988-1990. Auth, "Plnng A Funeral Serv," Morehouse, 1998. jed@trinitybend.org

HOLE, Jeremy G (Fla) 4141 Nw 18th Dr, Gainesville FL 32605 **Asstg P H Trin Epis Ch Gainesville FL 1984-** B Detroit MI 1937 s Harrison & Estelle. BA U of Florida 1959; STB EDS 1965. D 9/18/1965 P 4/1/1966 Bp George West Barrett. m 5/3/1986 Myra S Brown. Int S Mich's Ch Gainesville FL 1983-1984; Int Chapl Epis U Cntr Gainesville FL 1982-1983; 1970-1982; Chapl S Dunst's Sch Christiansted VI 1967-1970; Cur Chr Ch Pittsford Pittsford NY 1965-1967.

✠ HOLGUIN-KHOURY, The Rt Rev Julio Cesar (DR) Agape Flights Dms 13602, 100 Airport Ave E, Venice FL 34285 **Hon Pres Rel for Peace 2008-; Bp of the Dominican Republic Dio The Dominican Republic (Iglesia Epis Dominicana) Gazcue Santo Domingo 1991-, Vic, Iglesia Epis San Marcos, Haina 1976-; TRC Priesident Prov IX New York NY 2015-** B San Francisco de Macoris DO 1948 s Julio & Consuelo. Universidad Autonoma De Santo Domingo Santo Domingo Do 1973; Lic Sacr Theol S Andrews TS MX 1976. D 7/11/1976 P 7/1/1977 Bp Telesforo A Isaac Con 8/16/1991 for DR (DomRep). m 4/17/1977 Milagros Hernandez c 3. Mem Exec Coun 2003-2009; Bd Dir, Pres Consejo Latinoamericano Iglesias 2001-2007; PBp Caribbean Reg 1993-1997; Theol Educ Cmsn for Latin Amer and the C 1988-1995; Vic Iglesia Epis San Andres Santo Domingo Di 1987-1991; Vic Iglesia Epis Jesus Nazareno San Francisco de Macoris 1979-1987; Iglesia Epis San Marcos Haitiana Ft Lauderdale FL 1976-1979; Pres Theol Educ Cmsn for Latin Amer and the C 2013-2015.

HOLLAND, Albert L (Del) 4858 Smick St, Philadelphia PA 19127 B Baltimore MD 1950 s Albert & Estelle. BS Nthrn Illinois U 1972; MDiv SWTS 1979; U of Texas 1995. D 6/9/1979 Bp Quintin Ebenezer Primo Jr P 12/1/1979 Bp James Winchester Montgomery. m 5/19/2011 James Boaldin c 2. Dioc Coun Dio

H

Delaware Wilmington 2008-2010, Chair Cmsn on Slavery Slavery 2006-2009; R The Ch Of The Ascen Claymont DE 2006-2010; Int Ch Of Our Sav Silver Sprg MD 2004-2006; Int Ch of Our Sav Silver Sprg MO 2004-2006; Dio Arizona Stndg Com 2002-2004; Stndg Com Dio Arizona Phoenix AZ 2002-2004; R S Andr's Ch Glendale AZ 1999-2004; Assoc S Mk's Epis Ch Mesa AZ 1996-1998; R H Sprt Epis Ch El Paso TX 1990-1995; Fin Cmsn Dio The Rio Grande Albuquerque 1990-1994, Sprtl Advsr 1989-1991; Chapl Rio Grande DOK 1987-1991; Assoc R S Fran On The Hill El Paso TX 1986-1990; R S Greg's Epis Ch Deerfield IL 1979-1986; Strtgy Com Dio Chicago Chicago IL 1980-1986. Phi Sigma Kappa.

HOLLAND, Carol L (Va) P.O. Box 1626, Kilmarnock VA 22482 B Norfolk VA 1959 d Edwin & Enid. BA Hood Coll 1981; JD U Rich 1984; MDiv VTS 2007. D 6/16/2007 Bp Peter J Lee P 12/16/2007 Bp Shannon Sherwood Johnston. S Ptr's Ch Oak Grove Oak Grove VA 2014; S Mary's Fleeton Reedville VA 2010-2012; Kingston Par Epis Ch Mathews VA 2007-2009.

HOLLAND, Clayton Theodore (Dal) 517 W Hull St, Denison TX 75020 B Brooklyn MI 1930 s Claude & Lillian. BA Estrn Michigan U 1957; MDiv Epis TS in Kentucky 1962. D 6/9/1962 P 12/1/1962 Bp William R Moody. Chf Chapl Veterans' Admin Med Cntr Bonham TX 1981-1996; ArmdF and Fed Ministires New York NY 1980-1996; Chapl Veterans' Admin Med Cntr Ft Meade SD 1975-1981; R S Thos Epis Ch Sturgis SD 1975-1980; R Gr Ch Cuero TX 1973-1975; P-in-c S Jas Epis Ch Hebbronville TX 1971-1973; P-in-c S Lk's El Campo TX 1969-1971; P-in-c Trin Epis Ch Edna TX 1969-1971; Cur S Jos's Epis Ch Boynton Bch FL 1967-1969; Cur S Mk's Ch Cocoa FL 1966-1967; Vic Ch Of The H Fam Mc Kinney TX 1963-1966; D S Andr's Ch Lexington KY 1962-1963.

HOLLAND, David Wesley (Dal) Po Box 292365, Lewisville TX 75029 B Denver CO 1946 s Charles & Mary. BS Missouri St U 1968; MDiv GTS 1971. D 5/25/1971 Bp Stephen F Bayne Jr P 11/28/1971 Bp Theodore H McCrea. m 5/3/2014 Marina Djinis c 1. Cmsn On Archit Dio Dallas Dallas TX 2005-2009, Exec Coun 1995-1998; R Ch Of The Annunc Lewisville TX 1990-2011; Bd Trst Bp Mason Retreat & Conf Cntr 1990-1996; R S Chris's Ch Houston TX 1989-1990; Ch Of The H Comf Angleton TX 1982-1989; Vic S Philips Epis Ch Sulphur Spgs TX 1979-1982; R S Jas' Epis Ch Fremont NE 1978-1979; Asst Trin Cathd Omaha NE 1973-1978; Cur S Chris's Ch And Sch Ft Worth TX 1971-1973. Tertiary Of The Soc Of S Fran. Hon Cn Trin Cathd 1978.

HOLLAND, Donald Keith (Ga) D 5/14/2016 P 11/16/2016 Bp Scott Anson Benhase.

HOLLAND, Eleanor Lois (Md) 3204 Bayonne Ave, Baltimore MD 21214 B Atlanta GA 1948 d Dolphus & Musette. BS Georgia Sthrn U 1971; MDiv VTS 2001. D 6/9/2001 P 2/7/2002 Bp Jane Hart Holmes Dixon. m 8/18/2012 Helen S Langa. R S Mths' Epis Ch Baltimore MD 2004-2012; S Paul's Epis Ch Prnc Frederck MD 2003-2004; S Jas' Epis Ch Baltimore MD 2001-2003.

HOLLAND, Janet M (Cal) 1042 Dead Indian Memorial Road, Ashland OR 97520 B Avalon CA 1940 d Robert & Zoe. BA California St U 1975; Cert California St U 1976; MDiv ETSBH 1992. D 6/13/1992 Bp Chester Lovelle Talton P 1/9/1993 Bp Frederick Houk Borsch. m 7/1/1995 Lawrence Scott Hunter c 3. Assoc S Steph's Epis Ch Orinda CA 2006-2011; Assoc S Steph's Ch 2005-2006; Int S Tim's Epis Ch Apple Vlly CA 2004; Assoc S Jn's Mssn La Verne CA 1998-2004; Asst S Martha's Epis Ch W Covina CA 1997-1998; Int Gr Epis Ch Glendora CA 1995-1997; Asst S Paul's Epis Ch Tustin CA 1992-1995. jan@hollandhunter.com

HOLLAND, J Mark (ETenn) 601 W Main St, Morristown TN 37814 **All SS' Epis Ch Morristown TN 2017-; Exec Bd Together Baton Rouge 2009-; Bd Trst Epis High of Baton Rouge 2003-** B Altus AFB OK 1958 s William & Donna. BS Louisiana Tech U 1981; MDiv SWTS 1994. D 6/18/1994 P 12/17/1994 Bp Robert Jefferson Hargrove Jr. m 3/6/1982 Elizabeth L Langhorst c 3. S Fran Ch Denham Spgs LA 2016-2017; R S Jas Epis Ch Baton Rouge LA 2003-2017; Dioc Exec Com Dio Wstrn Louisiana Alexandria LA 2001-2003, Stndg Com 1997-2000, Cmsn Mnstry 2000-2003, Cmsn Mnstry 2000-, Dn Lake Chas Convoc 1999-2003, Dn Lake Chas Convoc 1999, Sprtl Dir Happenning 1998, Stndg Com 1996-1998, Stndg Com 1996-1997, Ch Hist Instr Bp Sch For Mnstry 1995-2001, Ch Hist Instr Bp Sch For Mnstry 1995; P-in-c Epis Ch Of The Gd Shpd Lake Chas LA 1995-1996, R 1994-2003, Assoc 1994-1995. Auth, "A Defense For The Theol Of Dioc Giving," *Alive*, Dio Wstrn Louisiana, 2001. Cler Ldrshp Proj Class XIII 1999-2003. mholland@stjamesbr.org

HOLLAND, John Stewart (HB) **Mssy Dio Guatemala 1965-** B Oakland CA 1934 s Francis & Alice. BS California Inst of Tech 1956; MTh Dallas TS 1961; STB GTS 1962. D 12/22/1963 Bp William G Wright. m 6/23/1962 Karen Andrea Holland. Vic S Geo's Reno Nv 1963-1964; Asst S Tim's Seagoville TX 1960-1961.

HOLLAND III, Jule Carr (Nwk) 7404 Halifax Rd, Youngsville NC 27596 **Sum Min Siasconset Un Chap 2014-; Advsr, Conf panel Dio No carolina 2013-** B Raleigh NC 1949 s Jule & Winifred. BA U NC 1972; MDiv GTS 1976. D 6/19/1976 P 5/29/1977 Bp William Gillette Weinhauer. c 1. Assoc S Paul's Epis Ch Cary NC 2015-2016; Pstr Responce Team Dio No Carolina Raleigh NC 2013-2017; S Ambroses Ch Raleigh NC 2012; R Gr Ch Newark NJ

1995-2010, Cur 1977-1994; R S Mk's Ch Mendham NJ 1986-1995; R S Clem's Ch Hawthorne NJ 1981-1986; S Ptr's Epis Ch Livingston NJ 1980-1981; Asst Gr Ch Asheville NC 1976-1977; Trst Apos Hse Newark NJ 2006-2011; Stndg Com Dio Newark Newark NJ 2006-2011, Chair, COM 2004-2006, Cmsn on Ministery 1997-2006, Isaiah Team, Cong. Dev. 1991-1998, Dep to Prov Syn 1988-1996, Stwdshp Cmsn, Consult 1983-1994. Assoc, Cmnty of St. Jn Bapt 1985; Soc of Cath Priests 2009.

HOLLAND, Katharine Grace (Ore) 13265 Nw Northrup St, Portland OR 97229 B Pasadena CA 1950 d Kenneth & Catherine. U of Redlands; BA California St U 1976. D 10/1/1994 Bp Robert Louis Ladehoff. m 11/26/1977 Darryl Gene Holland.

HOLLAND, Meghan C (Tenn) Trinity Episcopal Church, 317 Franklin St, Clarksville TN 37040 **R Trin Ch Clarksville TN 2015-; P-in-c S Ptr's of the Lakes Gilbertsville KY 2012-** B York PA 1984 d James & Barbara. BS Murray St U 2007; MDiv VTS 2011. D 12/18/2010 P 6/17/2011 Bp Terry Allen White. m 7/26/2008 Tyler W Holland c 1. Asst Gr Ch Paducah KY 2011-2015. meghan@trinityparish.com

HOLLAND JR, Melford Elias (Pa) 121 Penns Grant Dr, Morrisville PA 19067 B Montgomery WV 1942 s Melford & Hilda. BA Wake Forest U 1965; MDiv GTS 1968; U CO 1971; ThM PrTS 1985; DMin PrTS 1993. D 6/11/1968 P 12/18/1968 Bp Wilburn Camrock Campbell. m 9/2/1967 Ann H Holland c 3. Coordntr, Off of Min. Dev. Epis Ch Cntr New York NY 1998-2009; Bp's Asst for Mnstry and Deploy Off Dio Pennsylvania Philadelphia PA 1994-1998; R S Jas Ch Collegeville PA 1982-1993; Coordntr of Prog Dio Wstrn No Carolina Asheville NC 1976-1981; Assoc Trin Epis Ch Asheville NC 1974-1982; Asst S Thos Epis Ch Denver CO 1971-1973; Grant Admin St of Colorado 1970-1973; Vic S Barn Bridgeport WV 1968-1970.

HOLLAND, Nancy R (SanD) B Boston, MA 1946 d Hunter & Jean. Completion Sch for Mnstry, Dio San Diego 2016. D 6/11/2016 Bp Jim Mathes. c 2. nholland@edsd.org

HOLLAND-SHUEY, Marilyn Basye (Ala) 3740 Meridian St N, Huntsville AL 35811 B Lexington KY 1947 d James & Dorothy. BA Scarritt Coll 1968; MA Van/Geo Peabody Coll 1972; DMin Sewanee: The U So, TS 2010; MDiv Van 2011. D 5/16/2011 Bp Henry Nutt Parsley Jr P 12/13/2011 Bp John Mckee Sloan Sr. m 5/14/1988 Ralph Allen Shuey. H Cross-St Chris's Huntsville AL 2011-2013. Producer, "H Hosp," *Interfaith Dialogue as Sprtl Pract*, DVD & Prog Guide, 2010.

HOLLAR, Sarah Darnell (NC) 19107 Southport Drive, Cornelius NC 28031 **R S Mk's Epis Ch Huntersville NC 2005-; GC Dep Dio No Carolina Raleigh NC 2011-** B Oklahoma City OK 1955 d Donald & Janella. BA U NC 1983; MDiv VTS 2003. D 6/14/2003 P 1/18/2004 Bp Michael B Curry. m 4/4/2011 G Peter Macon c 2. Asst S Lk's Ch Salisbury NC 2003-2005.

HOLLEMAN, Virginia Falconer (Dal) 5518 Merrimac Ave, Dallas TX 75206 B Montgomery AL 1943 d Bradley & Mary. BA U of Connecticut 1964; MDiv SMU Perkins 2001. D 6/9/2001 Bp D Avid Bruce Macpherson P 5/13/2002 Bp James Monte Stanton. m 2/15/2003 William Thomas Holleman c 2. Asst to R The Epis Ch Of The Trsfg Dallas TX 2005-2011; Cur/P Assoc S Ptr's Ch Mc Kinney TX 2001-2005.

HOLLENBECK, Jon Nelson (Dal) 2215 Tracey Ann Ln, Killeen TX 76543 B Watertown NY 1951 s Howard & Annabelle. BD U of Texas 1975; MDiv Epis TS of the SW 1989. D 6/17/1989 Bp Donis Dean Patterson P 5/1/1990 Bp Scott Field Bailey. m 6/10/2000 Cynthia Jane Hollenbeck c 2. Off Of Bsh For ArmdF New York NY 1996-2013; S Lk's Epis Ch Dallas TX 1994-1995; Chr Epis Ch Plano TX 1993-1994; S Andr's Epis Ch Corpus Christi TX 1991-1993; Vic S Andr's Dallas TX 1991-1993; Cur S Chris's Ch Dallas TX 1989-1991.

HOLLENBECK, Scott Warren (Colo) 820 2nd Street, Meeker CO 81641 **Dio Colorado Denver CO 2015-, NW Reg Mssnr 2015-; R S Jas' Epis Ch Meeker CO 2007-** B Chilton WI 1957 s Warren & Patricia. BA Lakeland Coll 1979; MDiv Epis TS of the SW 2005. D 6/10/2006 P 12/18/2006 Bp Robert John O'Neill. m 8/9/1980 Dawn Zacher c 1. hollenbecktx@yahoo.com

✠ HOLLERITH IV, The Rt Rev Herman (SVa) 600 Talbot Road, Norfolk VA 23505 **Bp of Sthrn Virginia Dio Sthrn Virginia Newport News VA 2008-** B Baltimore MD 1955 s Herman & Agnes. BS Denison U 1978; MDiv Ya Berk 1981. D 6/11/1983 Bp Robert Bruce Hall P 12/10/1983 Bp A(rthur) Heath Light Con 2/13/2009 for SVa. m 10/27/1984 Elizabeth S Hollerith c 3. R Bruton Par Williamsburg VA 1999-2008; Prince Geo Winyah Epis Preschool Georgetown SC 1990-1999; Prince Geo Winyah Epis Ch Georgetown SC 1990-1999; Assoc R S Jn's Ch Lynchburg VA 1985-1990; P-in-c Chr Epis Ch Roanoke VA 1983-1985; Dept S Eliz's Hosp Washington DC 1982-1983. AAPC; ACPE. BISHOP@DIOSOVA.ORG

HOLLERITH, Melissa Kaye Zuber (Va) 5503 Toddsbury Rd, Richmond VA 23226 **Chapl S Chris's Sch Richmond VA 2003-; 1994-** B Baton Rouge LA 1962 d B Rivers & Nancy. BA Tul 1984; Cert Ya Berk 1990; MDiv Yale DS 1990. D 12/12/1991 P 10/14/1992 Bp Peter J Lee. m 12/31/1988 Randolph M Hollerith c 1. S Albans Sch Washington DC 2017; S Chris's Sch Richmond VA 2003-2016; Chapl S Chris's Sch Richmond VA 1990-1994.

HOLLERITH, Randolph M (WA) 1205 W Franklin St, Richmond VA 23220 **Cathd of St Ptr & St Paul Washington DC 2016-** B Washington DC 1963 s Herman & Agnes. BA Denison U 1986; MDiv Ya Berk 1990. D 6/2/1990 P 4/16/1991 Bp Peter J Lee. m 12/31/1988 Melissa Kaye Zuber Hollerith c 2. R St Jas Ch Richmond VA 2000-2016; R S Ptr's Epis Ch Savannah GA 1995-2000; Asst R S Steph's Ch Richmond VA 1990-1995. Auth, "A Connection Between Rudolf Bultmann & Leo Tolstoy," *Ch Divinty 89-90*, 1990.

HOLLETT, Robert Titus (LI) 220 Valley Rd, Chestertown MD 21620 **Died 5/3/2016** B Rockville Center NY 1923 s Norman & Elizabeth. BA Hofstra U 1949; MDiv PDS 1954. D 4/24/1954 P 11/13/1954 Bp James Pernette De-Wolfe. m 8/29/1953 Patricia Gray c 2. Int Shrewsbury Par Ch Kennedyville MD 1994-1995; P-in-c Chr Ch Worton MD 1992-1999; Int S Steph's Ch Earleville MD 1990-1992; Int Ch Of The H Trin Oxford MD 1989-1990; Mem, Dioc Mus & Liturg Comm. 1988-2016; Ret 1988-2016; Int Aug Par Chesapeake City MD 1988-1989; Mem of the Bd Ch Chars Fndt 1980-1986; Dn, Nassau Dnry Dio Long Island 1980-1985; Secy, Cathd Chapt Dio Long Island Garden City NY 1979-1987, Mem, Cathd Chapt 1974-1987, Mem, Liturg Cmsn 1973-1979; R Chr Ch Oyster Bay NY 1968-1987; R Emm Epis Ch Chestertown MD 1963-1968; Assoc Imm Ch Highlands Wilmington DE 1961-1963; Vic Gr Ch Mt Vernon MD 1957-1961; R S Andr's Ch Princess Anne 1957-1961; S Lukes Ch Bohemia NY 1954-1957; P-in-c S Mary's Ch Lake Ronkonkoma 1954-1957; Mem, Exec Coun Dio Easton Easton MD 1964-1968. Hon Cn Cathd of the Incarn 1985.

HOLLEY, James Paul (Okla) 7609 Nw Stonegate Dr, Lawton OK 73505 B Washington DC 1931 s James & Constance. MDiv Trin TS; BS VMI 1953; MS Shippensburg St Coll 1975. D 6/19/1988 Bp Gerald Nicholas Mcallister. m 7/3/1960 Sonja Myrie Holley c 3. Hospice Chapl S Andr's Epis Ch Lawton OK 1988-1995. NAAD 1988; Oblate Ord Of S Ben 1998; Oklahoma Assn For Helathcare Ethics 1998.

HOLLEY, Richard Hedge (SVa) 202 Devils Den Road, Hampton VA 23669 B Fort Sill OK 1936 s James & Constance. BBA U of Oklahoma 1961; MDiv VTS 1964. D 6/20/1964 Bp Chilton R Powell P 12/21/1964 Bp Frederick Warren Putnam. m 11/26/1959 Lois Holley c 3. Asst S Andr's Epis Ch Newport News VA 1999-2017; Emm Epis Ch Portsmouth VA 1995; Off Of Bsh For ArmdF New York NY 1986-1994; Chapl (Colonel) US-A 1968-1994; Cur S Jn's Ch Norman OK 1964-1968.

HOLLIDAY, Charles Thomas (Va) 3001 Stonewall Avenue, Richmond VA 23225 B Rocky Mount NC 1944 s Wilton & Jessie. BS Jas Madison U 1971; MEd Jas Madison U 1976; MDiv VTS 1979. D 6/23/1979 P 5/1/1980 Bp Robert Bruce Hall. m 1/23/1988 Susan Goff. Int S Paul's Ch Bailey's Crossroads Falls Ch VA 2008-2009, 1995-1996; S Jas' Epis Ch Warrenton VA 2005-2007; Cunningham Chap Par Millwood VA 2002-2005; S Ptr's Epis Ch Purcellville VA 2000-2002; S Anne's Epis Ch Reston VA 1998-1999; Old Donation Ch Virginia Bch VA 1997-1998; Chr Epis Ch Christchurch VA 1994-1995; S Thos' Ch Richmond VA 1991; Int S Dav's Epis Ch No Chesterfield VA 1990; Vic Ch of Our Sav Epis Sandston 1986-1989; Vic Our Sav Sandston VA 1986-1989; Trin Epis Ch Highland Sprg VA 1986-1989; Cur S Aid's Ch Alexandria VA 1978-1986.

HOLLIDAY, Fran (Chi) 5057 W. Devon Ave, Chicago IL 60646 **R S Mary Epis Ch Crystal Lake IL 2014-** B Chicago IL 1960 d Robert & Stella. BA U IL 1989; MDiv SWTS 2003. D 6/21/2003 P 12/20/2003 Bp Bill Persell. m 10/11/2014 Eileen M Flynn. All SS Epis Ch Chicago IL 2009-2014; R S Richard's Ch Chicago IL 2005-2009; Cur Chr Ch Waukegan IL 2003-2005. fran@saintmaryepiscopal.org

HOLLIGER, John Charles (O) 70 Welshire Court, Delaware OH 43015 B Sandusky OH 1946 s Herbert & Ardis. EDS; BA Ob; MDiv Yale DS. D 6/8/1974 Bp Joseph Warren Hutchens P 5/1/1975 Bp Morgan Porteus. m 4/27/1976 Carol Holliger c 2. R S Paul's Ch Marion OH 1997-2004; S Jas Epis Ch Wooster OH 1990-1997; S Geo's Ch Bolton CT 1977-1990; Dio Connecticut Meriden CT 1977-1981; Cur Chr Ch Stratford CT 1974-1977.

✠ HOLLINGSWORTH JR, The Rt Rev Mark (O) 2230 Euclid Ave, Cleveland OH 44115 **Bp of Ohio Dio Ohio Cleveland 2004-** B Boston MA 1954 s Mark & Caroline. BA Trin Hartford CT 1976; MDiv CDSP 1981. D 6/27/1981 P 5/27/1982 Bp William Edwin Swing Con 4/17/2004 for O. m 7/30/1988 Susan H Hollingsworth c 4. Archd Dio Massachusetts Boston MA 1994-2004; R S Anne's In The Fields Epis Ch Lincoln MA 1986-1994; Assoc R S Fran In The Fields Harrods Creek KY 1983-1986; Chapl Cathd Sch For Boys San Francisco CA 1981-1983. mh@dohio.org

HOLLINGSWORTH-GRAVES, Judy Lynn (SD) 1508 S Rock Creek Dr # 168, Sioux Falls SD 57103 B Tracy MN 1949 d Leonard & Helen. D 12/21/2006 Bp Creighton Leland Robertson c 4. D Calv Cathd Sioux Falls SD 2006-2010.

HOLLIS, Anthony Wolcott Linsley (Md) 712 Murdock Rd, Baltimore MD 21212 **Assoc The Ch Of The Nativ Cedarcroft Baltimore MD 2007-; Ret 2002-** B Bermuda 1940 s Francis & Elisabeth. BA McGill U 1961; MDiv GTS 1964; BA CPE 1970; MA LIU 1976. D 6/22/1964 P 5/17/1965 Bp Harry Lee Doll. m 6/16/1965 Linda L B Hollis c 3. P-in-c S Geo's 2004-2007; St. Ptr's Angl Ch St Georges 1997-2001; R S Ptr's Ch 1992-2002; Sherwood Epis Ch Cockeysville

MD 1980-1992; Chapl US-AR 1979-1993; Off Of Bsh For ArmdF New York NY 1967-1979; Chapl US-A 1967-1979; Assoc Ch Of The H Nativ Baltimore MD 1967; Vic S Ptr's Ch Lonaconing MD 1966-1967.

HOLLIS, Joanna Pauline (NJ) 5 Paterson St, New Brunswick NJ 08901 **R Chr Ch New Brunswick NJ 2013-** B Atlantic City NJ 1975 d Arnold & Janice. BA Connecticut Coll 1997; MATFL Monterey Inst of Intl Stds 2001; MDiv CDSP 2009. D 6/6/2009 P 12/10/2009 Bp Mary Gray-Reeves. m 9/15/2013 Karen B Walsh c 1. Assoc R Trin Epis Ch Santa Barbara CA 2009-2013.

HOLLIS, Robin Buckholtz (Az) St James the Apostle Episcopal Church, 975 E Warner Rd, Tempe AZ 85284 **Dir, D Formation Acad Dio Arizona Phoenix AZ 2015-, D's Coun 2013-, Anti-Racism Com Mem 2012-; Bd Mem Arizona Career Pathways Form of Vlly Interfaith Proj. 2013-; Bd Mem Ahwatukee-Foothills Fam YMCA 1992-** B Washington DC 1954 d David & Audrey. BA Occ 1976; MBA USC 1981; D Formation Acad Dio Arizona 2012; Ed.D U of Pennsylvania 2012. D 5/5/2012 Bp Kirk Stevan Smith. m 9/20/1975 Roy Stone Hollis c 2. Auth, "A Study of Generation Y in the Workplace: Values, Ldrshp, and Workplace Ldrshp Decision-Making," *U of Pennsylvania, Pub dissertation*, U of Pennsylvania, 2012; Auth, "Banner Hlth: Keeping the Promise in Challenging Times," *Trng and Dvlpmt (T&D)mag*, ASTD -T & D mag, 2009; Auth, "Ldr-as-Tchr: A Model for Exec Dvlpmt Success," *Orgnztn Dvlpmt Journ*, MediaTec, 2007. ATD 2004; Delta Phi Epsilon-Frgn Serv Fraternity 1973; SHRM 2008. Schlr Geo F. Baker Trust Schlr 1973.

HOLLOWAY, Eric Andre Cole (Tex) **Dio Texas Houston TX 2016-; Mssy Bdgt Dot 2014-** D 6/21/2014 Bp Dena Arnall Harrison P 1/22/2015 Bp C Andrew Doyle.

HOLLOWELL II, James Rhoads (Colo) 11675 Flatiron Dr, Lafayette CO 80026 **Chapl Assoc Avista Hosp Louisville CO 1995-; GC Coordntr Epis Ch Cntr New York NY 2006-** B Charleston SC 1961 s Samuel & Joyce. BS Pr 1983. D 11/7/1998 Bp William Jerry Winterrowd. m 7/7/1984 Kim Susan Mavor. D S Mary Magd Ch Boulder CO 1998-2011.

HOLLY, Francis Eugene (Nev) 2481 Anderson Lake Rd # 417, Chimacum WA 98325 **S Paul's Epis Ch Port Townsend WA 2006-, 2004-2005** B Farmington NM 1935 s Charles & Jessie. BS New Mex St U 1957; MS Van 1960; PhD U CA 1970. D 4/1/2000 Bp John Stuart Thornton P 9/30/2000 Bp George Nelson Hunt III. m 5/11/1974 Lois Elaine Holly c 4. Supply St Steph's Epis Ch Oak Harbor WA 2008-2011; S Mk's Ch Tonopah NV 2005-2006; P Gr In The Desert Epis Ch Las Vegas NV 2002-2006; S Lk's Epis Ch Las Vegas NV 2002-2003. *99 papers, abstracts, etc.*. Fell Amer Coll of Med Physics 1990; Fell Amer Assoc of Physicists in Med 1988; Commendation Medal US AF 1961.

HOLLY, William David (Okla) **Chapl S Simeons Epis Hm Tulsa OK 2005-; P S Aid's Epis Ch Tulsa OK 2003-** B Houston TX 1955 s Earl & Nancy. BA Oklahoma St U 1980; MDiv Epis TS of the SW 1983. D 6/25/1983 P 5/19/1984 Bp Gerald Nicholas Mcallister. m 1/24/1997 Marlo Louise Stewart. Dio Oklahoma Oklahoma City OK 2003-2012, 1991-1996, Vic, St. Columba Mssn, Tulsa, OK 1991-1995; Vic S Pat's Epis Ch Broken Arrow OK 1995-1996; Cur S Dunst's Ch Tulsa OK 1983-1990. bholly@saintsimeons.org

HOLLYWOOD, Trula Louise (Be) 701 S Main St, Athens PA 18810 B Coudersport PA 1959 d Samuel & Kathryn. D 8/15/2005 P 8/15/2006 Bp Paul Victor Marshall. c 3.

HOLM, Marjorie H (NC) 635 Hamilton St., Roanoke Rapids NC 27870 B Rochester MN 1954 d William & Marjorie. D 6/1/1996 Bp Frank Harris Vest Jr P 1/29/2004 Bp Carol J Gallagher. m 12/19/1976 Richard P Holm. R All SS Ch Roanoke Rapids NC 2007-2015; Chapl Chapl Serv of the Ch of Virginia 1992-2007. *Report from Virginia*, St Update Nwsltr of Prison Fllshp Mnstrs, 2003; *Plcy and Procedures Manual*, Chapl Serv of the Ch of Virginia, 1998. VA Coll of Chapl.

HOLMAN, Emily Clark (NJ) 96 Fairacres Dr, Toms River NJ 08753 **D Chr Ch Toms River Toms River NJ 2000-; Bd Mem Nthrn Ocean HabHum 2010-; Com on the Diac Dio New Jersey Trenton NJ 2008-** B Deposit NY 1944 d Yerby & Emily. BA Ge 1966; MLS U NC 1971; Cert NJ D Formation Prog 2000. D 10/21/2000 Bp David Bruce Joslin. Auth, "Gospel Journeys: Travels of a D," *collection of sermons and arts*, AuthorHouse, 2011. NAAD 2000.

HOLMAN, John Earl (Tex) 2400 Spring Raindrive, #1018, Spring TX 77379 **Ret 1989-** B Joplin MO 1923 s Jack & Stella. BA Subiaco 1949; MA U of San Francisco 1965. Rec 8/1/1971 as Priest Bp Philip Frederick McNairy. m 11/27/1954 June Elaine Holman c 3. Assoc Ch Of The Gd Shpd Tomball TX 2007-2009; R S Chad's S Paul MN 1978-1989; R Chr Ch Albert Lea MN 1972-1975; Asst Trin Ch Excelsior MN 1971-1972; Serv RC Ch 1951-1952. Auth, "Hist Of The Old Cath Ch In Amer".

HOLMAN, J(oseph) Lawrence (Be) RR 1 Box 125A, Towanda PA 18848 **D Chr Ch Towanda PA 2005-; D Dio Bethlehem Bethlehem PA 1989-** B Moberly MO 1931 s Lawrence & Amy. BS U of Missouri 1953; MS U IL 1954. D 5/20/1989 Bp James Michael Mark Dyer. m 6/22/1957 Sharon Davis Holman c 2. D Ch Of The Redeem Sayre PA 1989-2005. NAAD 1989. Ord of S Steph NAAD 1995.

HOLMAN, Kathryn Daneke (At) 1883 Clinton Dr, Marietta GA 30062 B Bartlesville OK 1953 BA U GA 1975. D 8/6/2006 Bp J Neil Alexander. m 7/12/1975 William Holman c 2.

HOLMBERG, Sandra A (Minn) 14266 E Fox Lake Rd, Detroit Lakes MN 56501 B Beach ND 1953 d Wilbur & Malah. BA Concordia Coll 1974; MDiv Van 1979; MS Minnesota St U Mankato 1990; DMin Sewanee: The U So, TS 1998. D 2/25/1980 P 8/17/1980 Bp Robert Marshall Anderson. m 6/26/1976 G Bruce Holmberg. Dio Minnesota Minneapolis MN 2000-2013, Epis Chapl at Mankato St U 1980-1983; Dio No Dakota Fargo ND 2000, Asst to Bp of No Dakota 1990-2000, Asst 1985-1989; R S Steph's Ch Fargo ND 1985-2000; R S Jn's Ch Moorhead MN 1985-1990; Chapl in Res Abbot NW Hosp Minneapolis MN 1979-1980.

HOLMES, Anna Rilla (USC) 205 Meadowlark Ln, Fountain Inn SC 29644 Cbury Chapl Furman U Greenville SC 2012- B Birmingham AL 1963 d Harold & Alice. Auburn U 1986; BA Iowa St U 1988; CDSP 1996; MDiv Ya Berk 1998. D 6/5/1999 Bp William Edwin Swing P 12/4/1999 Bp Catherine Scimeca Roskam. m 6/28/1986 Akil Abbas Rangwalla. S Ptr's Epis Ch Greenville SC 2013-2014; H Cross Epis Ch Simpsonville SC 2008; P-in-c Trin Ch Abbeville SC 2002-2008; Cur S Mk's Ch Mystic CT 1999-2002. Pi Kappa Phi hon Soc 1988. Distinguished Alum Awd Iowa St U 2008.

HOLMES, Douglas (USC) PO Box 446, Camden SC 29020 Died 10/15/2015 B Los Angeles CA 1953 s Harry & Alice. BS USC 1979; MDiv GTS 1985. D 6/15/1985 P 12/20/1985 Bp Robert Claflin Rusack. m 10/15/2015 Francine Reynolds Holmes c 2. R Gr Epis Ch Camden SC 2005-2011; Int S Lk's Ch Salisbury NC 2004-2005; Assoc R S Marg's Epis Ch Waxhaw NC 2002-2004; R S Jn's Ch Cornwall NY 1993-2002; Assoc All SS-By-The-Sea Par Santa Barbara CA 1991-1993; Ch Of The Epiph Oak Pk CA 1985-1991; Vic Epiph Westlake Vill CA 1985-1991. Auth, *Video Let My People In: Realizing Dream of Inclusive Wrshp.*

HOLMES, Forrest Milton (Ida) 1100 Burnett Dr Unit 416, Nampa ID 83651 Ret 1997- B Wapato WA 1932 s Forrest & Cordelia. D 12/13/1968 P 12/1/1969 Bp Norman L Foote. m 3/21/1954 Oudean Holmes. Int S Dav's Epis Ch Caldwell ID 1997-1998; R Gr Epis Ch Nampa ID 1988-1997; Vic S Thos Of Cbury Mammoth Lakes CA 1986-1988; Assoc Trin Epis Ch Pocatello ID 1974-1986; P-in-c S Jn's Epis Ch Amer Fls ID 1969-1974.

HOLMES, Francine Reynolds (NY) 944 Thistlegate Rd, Oak Park CA 91377 Non-par 1989- B Elmira NY 1953 d Joseph & Veronica. BA Barnard Coll of Col 1976; GTS 1985; MDiv UTS 1985. D 3/26/1987 Bp Walter Decoster Dennis Jr P 5/1/1988 Bp Reginald Heber Gooden. c 1. Asst All SS Par Beverly Hills CA 1987-1988.

HOLMES, James Colomb (WA) 10450 Lottsford Rd Apt 5005, Mitchellville MD 20721 Ret 2003- B Baton Rouge,LA 1946 s William & Halcyon. BA Van 1968; BD EDS 1971; MBA GW 1983. D 6/21/1971 P 2/10/1972 Bp Iveson Batchelor Noland. m 8/15/2011 Timothy Sabin. S Thos' Par Washington DC 1992-2003; Dio Washington Washington DC 1979-1999; Assoc S Jn's Ch Lafayette Sq Washington DC 1978-1992; 1977-1978; Asst The Ch Of The Adv Boston MA 1973-1976; Cur S Mk's Ch Foxborough MA 1971-1973. Associated Parishes 1992. timandjim@me.com

HOLMES, Jane Victoria Frances (NC) 2540 Bricker Drive, Charlotte NC 28273 Trin Jubilee Cntr Lewiston ME 2004- B Bedfont England 1941 d Ivan & Honor. U of Connecticut; AA Broward Cmnty Coll 1990; Sewanee: The U So, TS 2003. D 6/5/2004 Bp Chilton Richardson Knudsen. m 8/10/2002 Hartley La Duke c 2. D S Mk's Epis Ch Huntersville NC 2007-2009.

HOLMES, John Arthur (Haw) Died 2/11/2016 D 11/11/1983 Bp Edmond Lee Browning.

HOLMES, Joyce Ann Woolever (Kan) Grace Episcopal Church, 209 South Lincoln, Chanute KS 66720 R Gr Ch Chanute KS 2011- B Detroit MI 1949 d John & Patricia. BA Florida St U 1971; Florida St U 1972; MDiv Sewanee: The U So, TS 1991. D 6/8/1991 Bp Joseph Thomas Heistand P 1/18/1992 Bp William Edward Smalley. c 2. Vic The Epis Ch Of The Redeem Avon Pk FL 2001-2010; R S Matt's Epis Ch Newton KS 1994-2001; Asst S Stephens Epis Churchrch Wichita KS 1991-1994; Dioc Coun Dio Kansas Topeka KS 1993-1997. Garnet Key Hon Ldrship-FSU FSU 1971; Pres, Univ. Rel. Coun FSU FSU Rel Comm. 1971; Pres Cbury Club-FSU FSU Epis Chap 1970.

HOLMES, Kristine Marie (Mass) 91 Main St, Bridgewater MA 02324 B Beloit WI 1953 d Oren & Geraldine. BSE U of Wisconsin-Whitewater. D 6/4/2016 Bp Alan Gates.

HOLMES, Marsha Evans (Fla) 400 San Juan Dr, Ponte Vedra Beach FL 32082 D Chr Epis Ch Ponte Vedra FL 2014- B Baltimore MD 1949 d Meredith & Thelma. BA Morgan St U 1971. D 2/4/2014 Bp Samuel Johnson Howard. c 1. mholmes@christepiscopalchurch.org

HOLMES, Martha Hixson (Ala) 5712 1st Ave N, Birmingham AL 35212 Dio Alabama Birmingham 2015-; D Gr Ch Birmingham AL 2011- B St Joseph MO 1951 d Clarence & Mary Cecelia. BS U of Missouri 1973; MS U of Missouri 1978. D 10/1/2011 Bp John Mckee Sloan Sr. m 6/12/1981 Horace Franklin Holmes c 3.

HOLMES, Phillip Wilson (WNY) 418 Virginia St, Buffalo NY 14201 Supply P Dio Wstrn New York Tonawanda NY 1969- B Jamestown NY 1937 s Louis & Sara. BA Hobart and Wm Smith Colleges 1961; STB GTS 1964. D 6/20/1964 Bp Lauriston L Scaife P 1/30/1965 Bp Dudley B McNeil. Cur Gr Ch Lockport NY 1964-1969.

HOLMES, Rebecca Elizabeth (NC) 237 N Canterbury Rd, Charlotte NC 28211 Hospice and Palliative Care Chapl Dio No Carolina Raleigh NC 2004- B Des Moines IA 1941 d William & Anne. BA U of San Francisco 1978; MDiv CDSP 1983. D 12/10/1983 Bp William Edwin Swing P 12/9/1984 Bp Charles Shannon Mallory. Dir, Pstr Care for Ret Cmnty Dio No Carolina Raleigh NC 1991-2004, Dioc Com on Aging 1994-1996, 1991-1993; Assoc S Phil's In The Hills Tucson AZ 1986-1991; Yth Min S Andr's Ch Saratoga CA 1983-1986.

HOLMES, Stanley W (WVa) Po Box 79, Hansford WV 25103 The New River Epis Mnstry Pratt WV 2007-; Pstr Calv Ch Montgomery WV 1998- B Montgomery WV 1952 s Jack & Mildred. P 6/1/1998 Bp John Henry Smith. m 1/10/1970 Joan Holmes. Pstr New River Cluster Mnstry.

HOLMGREN, Stephen Carl (WMich) 2200 Thornapple River Dr Se, Grand Rapids MI 49546 R Gr Ch Grand Rapids MI 2007- B Minneapolis MN 1956 s Carl & Dorothy. BA Pacific Luth U 1980; BA Oxf GB 1982; MDiv Nash 1983; MA Oxf GB 1988; PhD Oxf GB 1995. D 5/21/1983 Bp William Louis Stevens P 4/1/1984 Bp Alex Dockery Dickson. m 6/21/1980 Martha Ellen Holmgren c 3. Gr Ch Of W Feliciana St Francisvlle LA 2000-2007; S Simon The Fisherman Epis Ch Port Washington WI 1997-2000; Assoc Prof Nash Nashotah WI 1992-2000; Asst S Mary's Cathd Memphis TN 1991-1992; Asst Chapl Keble Coll Oxford 1988-1991; R Gr Epis Ch Paris TN 1985-1988; Cur Calv Ch Memphis TN 1983-1985. Auth, "Ethics After Easter - A Volume In The New Ch'S Tchg Series," Cowley Press, 2000. Grad Fllshp ECF 1989; Cleaver & Liddon Scholarships Keble Coll 1988; Dorothy Given Fell. stephenholmgren@me.com

HOLMQUIST, David Wendell (Neb) St Augustine of Canterbury, 285 S 208th St, Elkhorn NE 68022 B Elmhurst IL 1946 s Wendell & Jane. BA Parsons Coll 1968; MA U of Nebraska 1996; Cert U So 2002. D 10/21/2012 Bp Scott Scott Barker. c 2.

HOLROYD, David D (Me) 3 Elizabeth Rd, South Berwick ME 03908 Assoc Chr Ch Exeter NH 2009- B Fitchburg MA 1941 s Franklyn & Ruth. BA Trin Hartford CT 1963; MDiv CDSP 1967; DMin Andover Newton TS 1976. D 6/24/1967 Bp Chauncie Kilmer Myers P 6/24/1968 Bp Joseph Summerville Minnis. m 1/24/1970 Lucille Holroyd c 2. Int S Anne's In The Fields Epis Ch Lincoln MA 2008-2009; Int Jas' Ch Greenfield MA 2006-2008; Int Trin Epis Ch Portland ME 2000-2001; R S Geo's Epis Ch York ME 1973-1999; Assoc Chr Ch Gardiner ME 1968-1973; Co-chair Bp Nomntns Com Dio Maine Portland ME 1996-1997, GC Dep 1985-2000, Dep GC 1985-1995, Pres of Stndg Com 1984-1990, Stndg Com Pres 1983-1990, Dioc Coun 1976-1984. Outstanding Young Men Amer 1971.

HOLSAPPLE, Kevin G (Me) 7208 W Milwe Lane, Crystal Rivet FL 34429 S Aug's Epis Ch Dovr Foxcroft ME 2015-; S Johns Epis Ch Brownville ME 2015- B Valley Stream NY 1956 s Donald & Betty. AS U of Maine 1977; BA U of Maine 1979; LTh Montreal TS CA 1989; MA Bangor TS 2001. Trans 2/12/1998 as Priest. m 3/14/1975 Bobbi J Holsapple c 4. R S Anne's Ch Crystal River FL 2005-2015; R S Jn's Ch Bangor ME 1997-2005.

HOLSTON III, George Wilson (Fla) 804 Doubles Ct, Harker Heights TX 76548 Asst H Trin Epis Ch Gainesville FL 2015-; Chapl US-A 2006- B Chattanooga TN 1954 s George & Ethel. BA Florida Sthrn Coll 1976; MDiv Candler TS Emory U 1978; MS Columbus St U 1994. D 6/22/1980 P 1/11/1981 Bp William Hopkins Folwell. c 3. Dio Florida Jacksonville 1999-2006; Vic S Alb's Epis Ch Chiefland FL 1999-2006; Chapl US-A 1991-1999; Off Of Bsh For ArmdF New York NY 1987-1990; Non-par 1986-1987; P-in-c Cov Atlanta 1985-1986; Dio Minnesota Minneapolis MN 1984-1985; P-in-c Trin Epis Ch Pk Rapids MN 1984-1985; Vic S Chrys Douglasville GA 1983-1984; S Julian's Epis Ch Douglasville GA 1983-1984; Intrn Chapl Grady Memi Hosp 1982-1983; The Epis Ch Of The Gd Shpd Lake Wales FL 1980-1982. ACPE.

HOLSTROM, Susan Ann (Chi) 737 N Randall Rd, Aurora IL 60506 B Chicago IL 1947 d Edwin & Fern. BS Nthrn Illinois U 1969; Cert EFM 1991; MDiv SWTS 1995. D 5/7/1995 P 11/25/1995 Bp Roger John White. m 6/25/1994 Richard Lambert c 1. R S Dav's Epis Ch Aurora IL 1999-2012; Ch Of The Gd Shpd Momence IL 1995-1999; Asst S Paul's Ch Kankakee IL 1995-1998; COM Dio Chicago Chicago IL 2000-2006, Bdgt Com 1996-1999.

HOLT, Ann Case (NJ) 60 Main St, Clinton NJ 08809 Assoc Calv Epis Ch Flemington NJ 2007- B Rahway NJ 1934 d Clifford & Ruth. BA Mid 1956; MDiv PrTS 1980. D 6/6/1981 Bp Albert Wiencke Van Duzer P 1/9/1982 Bp George Phelps Mellick Belshaw. m 6/29/1957 John C Holt c 3. Assoc S Lk's Ch Gladstone NJ 2002-2006; Chapl Nj Womens Prison Dio New Jersey Trenton NJ 1994-1997, Com 1986-2000, Stndg Com 2000-2003, Dioc Coun 1997-2000, 1994-1996, 1992-1993; S Thos Ch Alexandria Pittstown NJ 1982-1999; Asst Ch Of The H Sprt Lebanon NJ 1981-1982. ESMA 1981. Winner Epis Best Sermon Competition 1994.

HOLT, Charles L (CFla) 700 Rinehart Road, Lake Mary FL 32746 **Pres and CEO Bible Study Media Inc. 2014-; Cert Chr Conciliator Inst of Chr Conciliation 2011-; Collaborative Partnr Pathways to Hm Seminole Cnty FL 2011-; R S Ptr's Epis Ch Lake Mary FL 2001-** B Gainesville FL 1971 s Charles & Sue. BS U of Florida 1993; Reformed TS 1996; MDiv SWTS 1997. D 9/6/1997 Bp John Wadsworth Howe P 3/28/1998 Bp James Gary Gloster. m 8/12/1995 Brooke E Holt c 3. Bd Mem Chr Peacemaking Resources Inc. Orlando 2010-2014; Asst R S Jn's Epis Ch Charlotte NC 1997-2001; Dep to GC Dio Cntrl Florida Orlando FL 2010-2013. Auth, "The Sprt-Filled Life: All the Fullness of God," *The Chr Life Trilogy*, Bible Study Media, 2015; Auth, "The Resurrected Life: All Things New," *The Chr Life Trilogy*, Bible Study Media, 2015; Auth, "The Crucified Life: Seven Words from the Cross," *The Chr Life Trilogy*, Bible Study Media, 2014; Auth, "Skeptical of the Skeptics: A Critique of the Jesus Seminar," *Cntrl Florida Epis*, 2011; Auth, "SCLM's Rite in Progress: 'The Outline of Mar'?," *LivCh*, 2011; Auth, "Foreword," *Out of the Vlly*, Creation Hse, 2008; Auth, "The Slippery Slope of Conflict," *www.revcharlieholt.com*, 2007; Auth, "A Journey Through The Bible," *Journey Through The Word*, 1999; Auth, "Psalms: A Pilgrim Journey," *Journey Through The Word*, 1996; Auth, "Early Hist: Joshua, Judges & Ruth," *Journey Through The Word*, 1996. revholt@stpeterslakemary.org

HOLT, David Lewis (Mass) 81a Cockle Bay Road, Cockle Bay, Auckland 2014 New Zealand (Aotearoa) **Died 10/22/2015** B Auckland, NZ 1938 s Alan & Leila. ScD MIT 1967; MDiv EDS 1978. D 6/10/1978 Bp Morris Fairchild Arnold P 6/1/1979 Bp John Bowen Coburn. m 7/4/1967 Judith G Greene c 3. P Angl Cathd Auckland 2002-2006; Vic H Trin Ch Otahuhu New Zealand 1987-1998; Cur Chr Ch Papakura New Zealand 1985-1987; P S Steph's Epis Ch Boston MA 1982-1983; R Gr Ch Fed Boston MA 1978-1984; Dioc Coun Mem Dio Massachusetts Boston MA 1981-1984. Post-Ord Schlrshp S Jn Coll, Auckland 1996.

HOLT, Jane L (Bonnie) (Minn) 224 2nd St N, Cannon Falls MN 55009 **The Epis Cathd Of Our Merc Sav Faribault MN 1999-** B Cannon Falls MN 1935 d Carl & Louise. D 10/17/1992 Bp Sanford Zangwill Kaye Hampton. m 2/7/1959 Lavern Holt c 3. D Adv Ch Farmington MN 1992-1999. mcholt@frontiernet. net

HOLT, Joseph (Cal) 2237 Fulton #103, San Francisco CA 94117 **Assoc Ch Of The Incarn San Francisco CA 2009-** B Seagraves TX 1948 s Joseph & Imogene. BA Texas Tech U 1973; MA Texas Tech U 1978; MA U of Dallas 1986; MDiv CDSP 1992. D 6/20/1992 Bp Donis Dean Patterson P 6/6/1993 Bp William Edwin Swing. m 11/23/2009 Paula B Holt. Ch Of The Epiph San Carlos CA 2004; Asst S Steph's Epis Ch Orinda CA 1998-2003; R Incarn San Fran CA 1997-1998; The Epis Ch Of S Mary The Vrgn San Francisco CA 1997; Int S Cyp's Ch San Francisco CA 1996-1997; D The Epis Ch Of S Jn The Evang San Francisco CA 1992-1996. Auth, "The Communal Aspect Of Scriptural Auth," *Ch Div*, 1990; Auth, "Story-Telling In The Weedy Garden," *Ch Div*, 1988.

HOLT, **William Mayes** (Tenn) 202 Kimberly Dr, Dickson TN 37055 B Nashville TN 1939 s JP & Grace. Evangel U 1957; Van 1958; Tennessee Tech U 1959; LTh Sewanee: The U So, TS 1973. D 7/1/1973 Bp William Evan Sanders P 5/25/1974 Bp William F Gates Jr. m 12/31/1966 Patricia Harper c 3. Vic S Jas Ch Dickson TN 1989-2008; Vic 1983-1989; Vic S Columba's Epis Ch Bristol TN 1976-1983; Asst Ch Of The Gd Shpd Lookout Mtn TN 1973-1976; Sem-In-Charge S Bern's Ch Sewanee TN 1972-1973; CE Com Dio Tennessee Nashville TN 1990-2004, Vacancy Consult 1988-1991, Steph Mnstry Trnr/Supvsr 1986-1991, Bp and Coun 1986-1989, Liturg Cmsn 1983-1986.

HOLT III, William Therrel (Az) 854 E Florida Saddle Dr, Green Valley AZ 85614 B San Francisco CA 1941 s William & Ellen. BA U of Tennessee 1965; MDiv Sewanee: The U So, TS 1968. D 6/14/1968 Bp William F Gates Jr P 4/25/1969 Bp John Vander Horst. m 6/2/1979 Diane P Pettigrew c 3. S Phil's In The Hills Tucson AZ 2015-2016; Int R Chr Ch Clermont-Ferrand France Royat 63130 2011-2012; Int Vic S Mich's Ch Coolidge AZ 2008-2009; R Epis Ch Of S Fran-In-The-Vlly Green Vlly AZ 1993-2007; Assoc R The Epis Ch Of Beth-By-The-Sea Palm Bch FL 1981-1993; Chapl Cmnty Mntl Hlth Cntr W Palm Bch FL 1979-1981; Chapl Georgia Mntl Hlth Inst Atlanta GA 1974-1976; Assoc R H Trin Epis Ch W Palm Bch FL 1972-1974; P-in-c Ch Of The Redeem Shelbyville TN 1969-1972; Int R S Alb's Epis Ch Tucson AZ 1968-2008. Ord of St. Jn of Jerusalem 2000. Hon Cn Dio Dar es Salaam, Tanzania 2007. wthiii@juno.com

HOLTHUS, Jessica Trout Knowles (Md) 106 W Church St, Frederick MD 21701 **Asst to the R All SS Ch Frederick MD 2010-** B Baltimore MD 1984 d Douglas & Sarah. BS Towson U 2006; MDiv VTS 2010. D 6/19/2010 Bp John L Rabb P 1/15/2011 Bp Eugene Taylor Sutton. m 10/21/2013 Nicholaus Holthus c 1.

HOLTKAMP, Patrick John (LI) 7712 35th Ave Apt A64, Jackson Heights NY 11372 B Saint Louis MO 1948 s Ferdinand & Lorene. BA S Fran Coll 1971; MDiv Crosier Hse of Stds 1975; MA Ford 1986. Rec 4/1/1988 as Priest Bp Walter Decoster Dennis Jr. m 6/26/1982 Elisabeth Holtkamp c 2. R Zion Ch Douglaston NY 1992-2011; Asst Ch Of The H Trin New York NY 1988-1992;

ECBF New York NY 1988-1992; Vice-Pres ECBF New York NY 1988-1992; R RC Ch 1975-1982. Auth, *Ch*. No Amer Acad of Liturg 1988.

HOLTMAN, Kimberly Erica (Nwk) 655 W Briar Pl, Apt 1, Chicago IL 60657 B New Brunswick NJ 1966 d John & Diane. BA U of Virginia 1988; MA SUNY 1992; MDiv GTS 1998. D 6/6/1998 Bp David Charles Bowman P 12/12/1998 Bp Franklin Delton Turner. m 5/30/2004 Eric Holtman. R The Ch Of The Annunc Oradell NJ 2000-2003; Cur Trin-St Jn's Ch Hewlett NY 1999-2000; Cur S Dav's Ch Wayne PA 1998-1999. HP Mongomery Prize; H Land Travel Prize; J Wilson Sutton Prize; Psi Chi; SUNY Presidential Fell; Wm C Winslow Prize.

HOLTON, Edie H (NCal) 120 E J St, Benicia CA 94510 **Fairhaven Sykesville MD 2015-** B Takoma Park MD 1960 d Elwin & Betty Jo. BSW Loma Linda U 1984; MDiv Fuller TS 1998. D 6/29/2013 P 1/13/2014 Bp Barry Leigh Beisner. Asst S Mary's Epis Ch Napa CA 2015.

HOLTON, Stephen C (Ct) Christ Episcopal Church, 84 Broadway, New Haven CT 06511 **R Chr Ch New Haven CT 2016-, 2011-2012, Cur 2011-2012** B Dublin GA 1973 s Tommy & Jacqueline. BA Emory U 1995; Dplma, Angl Stds Ya Berk 2011; MDiv Yale DS 2011. D 4/30/2011 P 12/7/2011 Bp Keith Whitmore. Assoc Gr Epis Ch New York NY 2012-2016. sholton@christchurchnh. org

HOLTON, Stephen Cathcart (NY) 91 Greenwood Lane, White Plains NY 10607 **Fndr & Dir Neighborhool Embrace New York NY 2013-; Fndr & Chair Epis Muslim Relatns Comm. New York 1991-** B Washington DC 1960 s David & Dorothy. BA Hav 1982; MDiv GTS 1988; Cler Ldrshp Proj 2002; STM GTS 2013. D 6/25/1988 Bp Frederick Houk Borsch P 5/1/1989 Bp Richard Frank Grein. m 6/3/1989 Charlotte B Bacon c 2. Chr Ch New Haven CT 2016; Int S Jn's Ch Cornwall NY 2011-2012; Envoy to Afghanistan Dio New York New York NY 2002-2003; R S Pauls On The Hill Epis Ch Ossining NY 1992-2011; Cur All SS Ch New York NY 1989-1992; Fndr & Chair Dioc Environ Comm. New York 2008-2011. STM hon GTS 2013; Harris Awd for Acad Excellence and Ldrshp VTS 2012.

HOLTZ, Frank John (Kan) 106 Naroma Ct, Abilene KS 67410 **Died 12/17/2015** B Minneapolis KS 1940 s Harold & Olive. DDS U of Missouri 1965; BA Washburn U 1985. D 3/17/1996 P 11/24/1996 Bp William Edward Smalley. D S Jn's Ch Abilene KS 1996-2015.

HOLTZEN, Thomas Lee (Mil) 2777 Mission Rd, Nashotah WI 53058 **Prof Nash Nashotah WI 2003-; P-in-c S Paul's Ch Ashippun Oconomowoc WI 2003-** B Aurora NE 1968 BA U of Nebraska--Lincoln 1992; MA Gordon-Conwell TS 1996; PhD Marq 2002; PhD Nash 2002. D 5/10/2003 Bp Russell Edward Jacobus P 11/13/2003 Bp Steven Andrew Miller. m 12/28/1991 Candace Kay Holtzen c 4. tholtzen@nashotah.edu

HOLZ JR, John Clifford (Ak) **S Jude's Epis Ch No Pole AK 2016-; Chapl Alaska St Troopers Fairbanks AK 2001-** B New London CT 1952 s John. MDiv Estrn Bapt TS; BA San Diego St U; AA SW Cmnty Coll Chula Vista CA. D 3/28/2004 P 10/18/2004 Bp Mark Lawrence Macdonald. m 8/2/1975 Carol Mary Holz c 2. P S Matt's Epis Ch Fairbanks AK 2004-2016, D 2004; Chapl US-A 1980-2001.

HOLZHALB, Leon (La) 100 Christwood Blvd, Covington LA 70433 B New Orleans LA 1940 s Leon & Irene. BA U So 1962; STB GTS 1967; DMin PrTS 1997. D 10/7/1967 Bp Iveson Batchelor Noland P 10/1/1968 Bp Girault M Jones. m 10/27/2005 Julie Anne Hopkins c 2. R, Adv Hse Chr Ch Cathd New Orleans LA 1996-2003; R Chr Ch Covington LA 1976-1996; Vic S Alb's Epis Ch Monroe LA 1970-1976; Vic S Pat's Epis Ch W Monroe LA 1970-1974; Cur Ch Of The Ascen Lafayette LA 1968-1970; Chapl SW Louisiana U 1968-1970; Chapl/Intern Cntrl St Hosp Milledgeville GA 1967-1968.

HOMEYER, Charles Frederick (WMich) 3539 Quiggle Ave Se, Ada MI 49301 **Ret 2009-** B Saint Louis MO 1944 s August & Ruth. BA Br 1966; MAT Wesl 1968; MDiv CDSP 1974. D 6/22/1974 P 12/21/1974 Bp George Leslie Cadigan. m 2/17/1968 Sara Homeyer c 2. COM Dio Wstrn Michigan 2005-2008; Ch Of The H Cross Kentwood MI 1978-2009; Cur Gr Ch S Louis MO 1974-1978.

HONAKER, Martha Anne (Ind) 111 Ivy Lane, Sparta NC 28675 B Asheville NC 1946 d Ernest & Selma. MDiv 1983. D 6/2/1984 P 12/18/1984 Bp Alden Moinet Hathaway. R S Steph's Epis Ch New Harmony IN 2002-2010; S Jn's Cathd Albuquerque NM 2001-2002; Assoc H Trin Epis Ch Fayetteville NC 1993-2000; R S Jas Epis Ch Pittsburgh PA 1985-1990; Asst All SS Ch Aliquippa PA 1983-1985.

HONDERICH, Thomas E (Ind) 3941 N Delaware St, Indianapolis IN 46205 B Detroit MI 1944 s Merrill & Helen. BA Albion Coll 1966; BD SWTS 1970. D 5/19/1970 Bp Charles Ellsworth Bennison Jr P 12/1/1970 Bp John P Craine. m 10/18/2011 Gordon Lee Chastain. Affilliate All SS Ch Indianapolis IN 1979; Cur S Paul's Epis Ch Indianapolis IN 1976-1978; S Steph's Elwood IN 1973-1976; Cur Gd Samar Epis Ch Clearwater FL 1971-1972; Trin Ch Indianapolis IN 1970-1972.

HONEA, Janice Bailey (CFla) 6246 Tremayne Dr, Mount Dora FL 32757 B Memphis TN 1952 BA U of Memphis 1974. D 1/31/2004 Bp Joe Goodwin Burnett. m 5/19/1973 James Edward Honea c 3. S Andr's Ch Omaha NE 2004-2008.

HONEYCHURCH, John Robert (Los) 1000 Concha St, Altadena CA 91001 B Butte MT 1957 s Fred & Dorothy. BS Montana St U 1979; MDiv SWTS 1984; DMin SWTS 1999. D 6/12/1984 P 12/13/1984 Bp Jackson Earle Gilliam. m 3/10/1985 Sylvia A Sweeney c 1. Int R All SS-By-The-Sea Par Santa Barbara CA 2012-2014; Prof of Ch Ldrshp Bloy Hse Claremont CA 2009-2014; Mssnr for Congrl Vitality Epis Ch Cntr New York NY 2008-2012; Adj Fac CDSP Berkeley CA 2002-2007; R S Jas Ch Fremont CA 2001-2008; Dio Idaho Boise ID 2001, 1999-2000; Co-R S Lk's Epis Ch Idaho Falls ID 1992-2001; Pstr Assoc H Trin Epis Ch Troy MT 1988-1992; Vic S Lk's Ch Libby MT 1984-1992.

HONNOLD, Sandra Elizabeth (NCal) PO Box 7063, PMB 295, Ocean View HI 96737 B Oakland CA 1944 d Ronald & Edna. Cosumes River Comm Coll Placerville CA 1993; BTh Sch for Deacons 1996. D 10/16/1996 Bp Jerry Alban Lamb. m 10/12/1963 Frederic Kelly Honnold c 3. D Chr Ch Kealakekua HI 2011-2013; D S Jude's Hawaiian Ocean View Ocean View HI 2009-2011; Supply Cler St. Jude Epis Mssn Ocean View) HI 2006-2008; D Ch Of The H Apos Hilo HI 2005-2009; Pstr Asst Trin Ch Sutter Creek CA 1996-2005. Auth, "Creative Pilgrim Walks," Bk, iUniverse, 2011. No. Amer Assn for the Diac 1993-1996.

HONODEL, Jill (Cal) 285 Kaanapali Dr, Napa CA 94558 **S Geo's Epis Ch Antioch CA 2017-** B Vallejo,CA 1966 d Nicholas & Carolyn. BA U CA 1989; MDiv Fuller TS 1995; MA CDSP 1996. D 12/4/1998 P 9/25/1999 Bp Jerry Alban Lamb. Vic Dio California San Francisco CA 2016; Gr Ch Martinez CA 2004-2015; Asst S Paul's Epis Ch Benicia CA 1998-2002. st.georgesandst. albans@gmail.com

HONSE, Robert Wayne (Kan) B 1943 D 6/11/2005 Bp Dean E Wolfe. c 1.

HOOD, Nancy E (Dal) 6883 Lagoon Dr, Grand Prairie TX 75054 **Suppy S Mart's Ch Lancaster TX 2009-; Non-par 1980-** B Washington DC 1941 d James & Elizabeth. Longwood U 1960; Dioc TS 1973; TCU 1979; BA U of Texas 1980; MEd Ntsu 1983; PhD Texas Womans U 1994. D 6/25/1978 Bp Robert Elwin Terwilliger P 5/22/1996 Bp James Monte Stanton. m 4/15/1981 Charles V Smith c 3. Assoc Ch Of The Apos Coppell TX 2004-2009; Ch Of The Gd Shpd Dallas TX 2001-2003; S Paul's Epis Ch Dallas TX 1997-2001; S Jas Ch Dallas TX 1997, Asst 1978-1980. Dok, Assn Of Wmn In Mnstry 1980-1984. Kappa Delta Pi.

HOOD, Stephen Dale (Ala) 3648 Dabney Drive, Vesatvia Hills AL 35243 **R Epis Ch Of The Ascen Birmingham AL 2007-; R Epis Ch of the Ascen Vestavia Hills AL 2007-** B La Marque TX 1967 s Charles & Martha. BA Texas St U San Marcos 1995; MDiv Sewanee: The U So, TS 2002. D 12/27/2001 P 7/7/2002 Bp Charles Edward Jenkins III. m 3/26/2016 Tracy A Hood c 2. Assoc R S Jas Epis Ch Baton Rouge LA 2004-2007; R S Jn's Epis Ch Thibodaux LA 2002-2004; Intern S Fran Of Assisi Epis Ch Ooltewah TN 2001-2002; Chair, Dept of Camp McDowell Dio Alabama Birmingham 2010-2013, Dioc Coun 2008-2012. Sabbath Lv Grant Cntr for Pstr Excellence, Samford U 2012.

HOOD, William Rienks (La) 1808 Prospect St, Houston TX 77004 **Chapl (Captain) Untd States Naval Reserve TX 1986-** B Austin TX 1956 s Charles & Antoinette. BA S Edwards U Austin TX 1979; MDiv Epis TS of the SW 1983; MTh SMU 1994. D 6/28/1983 P 1/1/1984 Bp Gordon Taliaferro Charlton. m 11/17/2007 Martha Parker c 3. Spec Mobilization Spprt Plan Washington DC 2008-2010; Pension Fund Mltry New York NY 2008-2009; S Paul's Ch New Orleans LA 2006-2008; The Great Cmsn Fndt Houston TX 2003; S Steph's Ch Beaumont TX 2002; R S Jn's Ch La Porte TX 1998-2002; Off Of Bsh For ArmdF New York NY 1986-1998; Cur S Chris's Ch League City TX 1983-1986.

HOOGERHYDE, Scott Matthew (Nwk) 7 E Main St, Mendham NJ 07945 B Midland MI 1962 s James & Karen. BA Estrn Michigan U 1985; UTS 1992; MDiv GTS 1993. D 6/19/1993 P 1/15/1994 Bp R aymond Stewart Wood Jr. m 10/10/1993 Lynne Cheryl Hoogerhyde. R S Mk's Ch Mendham NJ 1996-2010; Cur S Paul's Ch Doylestown PA 1993-1996.

HOOK, Andrew S (Spr) Cathedral Church of Saint Paul the Apostle, 815 South Second Street, Springfield IL 62704 **The Cathd Ch Of S Paul Springfield IL 2015-** B Newton KS 1980 s Steven & Lavonne. BA Estrn Mennonite U 2003; ThM Newman U 2012. D 5/25/2013 P 11/30/2013 Bp Mike Milliken. Gr Epis Ch Hutchinson KS 2013-2015; Yth Dir 2010-2013. frandyhook@gmail.com

HOOK, Edward Lindsten (Colo) PO Box 1388, Green Valley AZ 85622 B Oak Park IL 1933 s Joseph & Esther. BA NWU 1956; MDiv VTS 1963. D 6/22/1963 Bp Robert McConnell Hatch P 1/24/1964 Bp William A Lawrence. m 8/20/1955 Barbara B Hook c 3. P Epis Ch Of S Fran-In-The-Vlly Green Vlly AZ 2001-2002; R S Dav Of The Hills Epis Ch Woodland Pk CO 1991-1999; Assoc R Gr And S Steph's Epis Ch Colorado Sprg CO 1988-1991, Int 1986-1987; Supply P Epis Ch Of S Jn The Bapt Breckenridge CO 1971-1975; R All SS Ch Worcester MA 1966-1971, Asst 1963-1965. Auth, Case Hist of Tentmakers. NASSAM 1971.

HOOKE, Ruthanna Brinton (WMass) 3737 Seminary Rd, Alexandria VA 22304 **Adj Cler S Thos Par 2004-; Asst Prof VTS Alexandria VA 2003-** B Boston MA 1963 d Richard & Ruth. BA Harv 1986; MA Emerson Coll 1993; MDiv Ya Berk 1996; PhD Ya 2007. D 5/16/1998 P 1/30/1999 Bp Arthur Edward Walmsley. c 1. S Paul's Ch Wallingford CT 2000-2003; Presb Ch Of The

Epiph Durham CT 1999-2000; Emm Ch Killingworth CT 1999-2000; Middlesex Area Cluster Mnstry Higganum CT 1998-2000; S Andr's Ch Northford CT 1998-1999; S Jas Epis Ch Higganum CT 1998-1999; D S Paul's Ch Westbrook CT 1998-1999. Auth, "I Am Here In This Room," Homil, 2002. Acad Of Homil 1998; Amer Acad of Relgion 1997; SBL 2007. rhooke@vts.edu

HOOKER, Alan Bruce (Va) 6645 Northumberland Hwy, Heathsville VA 22473 **R S Jas Ch Montross VA 2013-, R 2013-, Int 2011-2012** B Norwalk CT 1950 s Alexander & Alice. W&L 1969; BA W&M 1972; MDiv VTS 1976; MA U of Connecticut 1986. D 6/12/1976 Bp Joseph Warren Hutchens P 4/2/1977 Bp Morgan Porteus. m 6/1/1974 Cathy S Hooker c 3. R S Geo's Ch Pungoteague Pungoteague VA 2000-2008; R S Jas' Ch Accomac VA 2000-2008; R S Steph's Epis Ch Culpeper VA 1995-2000; R Cople Par Hague VA 1986-1995; R S Paul's Epis Ch Willimantic CT 1983-1984; R Chr Ch Canaan CT 1978-1983; Cur Chr Ch Cathd Hartford CT 1976-1978. BroSA 1995. Melvin Jones Fell Lions Clubs Intl 2007; AOC Hall of Fame Inductee Accociation of Old Crows 2003. abhook143@hotmail.com

HOOKER, Hannah G (Ark) St Marks Episcopal Church, 531 W College Ave, Jonesboro AR 72401 **Cur S Mk's Epis Ch Jonesboro AR 2016-** B 1988 d John & Melba. Bachelor of Arts Hendrix Coll 2010; Masters of Div VTS 2016. D 3/19/2016 P 10/1/2016 Bp Larry Benfield. S Ptr's Ch Conway AR 2011-2012; Chapl Intern UAMS Little Rock Arkansas 2012-2013.

HOOKER, John L (WMass) 22c Castle Hill Rd, Agawam MA 01001 B Leesville LA 1944 s Roy & Laura. BA Centenary Coll 1966; MA SMU 1968; Cert Fulbright Schlr Staatliche Fuer Mus 1969; DMA U of Memphis 1978; MDiv EDS 1992. D 6/13/1992 Bp Joseph Thomas Heistand P 3/6/1993 Bp Otis Charles. m 6/7/2004 David Bucchiere. Missional P Gr Ch Broad Brook CT 2014-2015; Ascen Memi Ch Ipswich MA 2000-2004; Assoc S Phil's In The Hills Tucson AZ 1998-2000; Min of Mus 1984-1989; EDS Cambridge MA 1992-1998; Par Of The Mssh Auburndale MA 1992-1993; Min of Mus Calv Ch Memphis TN 1976-1984; Min of Mus S Paul's Epis Ch Chattanooga TN 1971-1976. Auth, "Ldr's Guide to Wonder, Love," & Praise; Auth, "Hymn Tunes and Harmonies," Gather; Ed, In The Shadows of H Week: Tenebrae; Auth, "Hymn Tunes and Harmonies, Wonder," Love and Praise, Ch Pub Inc; Auth, "Hymn Tunes and Harmonies," The Hymnal 1982, Ch Pub Inc; Auth, "Hymn Tunes and Harmonies," The Presb Hymnal. AGO; Assn of Angl Mus; ADLMC. revdrhooker@comcast.net

HOOP, Kimberly Ann (WMich) 4155 S Norway St Se, Grand Rapids MI 49546 B Grand Rapids MI 1955 d Raymond & Dorothy. BD Amer U 1977; Grand Vlly St U 1996. D 11/16/1996 Bp Edward Lewis Lee Jr. D Ch Of The H Cross Kentwood MI 1996-2010. 3rd Ord Francisan; NAAD.

HOOPER, Elizabeth E (Los) 1014 E. Altadena Drive, Altadena CA 91001 **Assoc P/Chapl S Mk's Par Altadena CA 1999-; Dio Los Angeles Los Angeles CA 2009-** B CA 1961 d R & F. BA Pitzer Coll 1983; MDiv GTS 1987. D 6/27/1987 P 1/16/1988 Bp Oliver Bailey Garver Jr. m 2/29/1992 Thomas Alan Hooper-Rosebrook c 2. Vic S Thos' Mssn Hacienda Hgts CA 1993-1999; Assoc R S Columba's Par Camarillo CA 1990-1993; S Lk's Epis Ch Monrovia CA 1987-1990.

HOOPER, John Kontz (Mich) 42 Cottage Circle, West Lebanon NH 03784 **Ret 1998-** B Cincinnati OH 1933 s William & Elizabeth. ACSW Acad of Cert Soc Workers; U of Detroit Mercy; U MN; BS U GA 1955; Cert St of Michigan 1981; MSW U MI 1981; Dip 1983; Lic St of Michigan 2004. D 6/25/1958 Bp Archie H Crowley P 3/1/1959 Bp Richard Stanley Merrill Emrich. m 8/27/1955 Carolyn Jane Hooper c 4. Environ Justice Coordntr Dio Michigan Detroit MI 2001-2005, Environ Justice Coordntr 2001-2005; 1981-1998; R Trin Epis Ch Farmington MI 1970-1981; R S Jn's Ch Howell MI 1965-1970; Vic S Dunst's Epis Ch Davison MI 1960-1965; S Edw The Confessor Epis Ch Clinton Twp MI 1958-1960; Asst Trin Ch St Clair Shrs MI 1958-1960. DSA Mich. Alco & Addictions Assoc 1986.

HOOPER, Larry Donald (SeFla) 401 Duval St, Key West FL 33040 **S Paul's Ch Key W FL 2009-** B Birmingham AL 1952 s Donald & Katie. AS Palm Bch Jr Coll 1974; BA Florida St U 1986; MDiv VTS 1989. D 6/12/1989 Bp Calvin Onderdonk Schofield Jr P 12/21/1989 Bp Rogers Sanders Harris. m 12/17/1983 Katherine M Hooper c 3. Int Chr Ch Rolla MO 2007-2009; S Mart's Ch Ellisville MO 2000-2007; Gr Ch Tampa FL 1996-2000; Dio SW Florida Parrish FL 1993-1995; Asst R Trin By The Cove Naples FL 1989-1992.

HOOPER III, Robert Channing (Ct) 10 Cumberland Rd, West Hartford CT 06119 **R S Jas's Ch W Hartford CT 2002-** B Albany NY 1963 s Robert & Janet. BA New Engl Coll 1987; MDiv VTS 1995. D 6/10/1995 Bp Clarence Nicholas Coleridge P 1/10/1996 Bp Peter J Lee. m 1/2/1988 Priscilla Hooper c 3. R Ch Of The Adv Medfield MA 1997-2002; Asst S Fran Epis Ch Great Falls VA 1995-1997.

HOOPER, Ruth Isabelle (Az) 1710 W. Dalehaven Cir, Tucson AZ 85704 B Stambaugh MI 1950 d Lloyd & Brenda. D 1/29/2011 Bp Kirk Stevan Smith.

HOOPES OHC, David Bryan (LI) Church of St Edward the Martyr, 14 E 109th St, New York NY 10029 B San Antonio TX 1943 s Harry & Genevieve. BA Findlay Coll 1966; MDiv Andover Newton TS 1970. Trans 2/4/1988 as Priest Bp Robert Campbell Witcher Sr. Int The Ch of S Edw The Mtyr New York

NY 2008-2010; Dep to GC Dio Long Island Garden City NY 2000-2003, Mem, Stndg Com 1997-2000, Chapl, Dioc AltGld 1995-2005, Secy, Cathd Chapt 1995-1999, Dn, St. Mk's Dnry, Archdnry of Brooklyn 1994-1999, Reg Dn, Archdnry of Brooklyn 1989-1993, Pgr. Dir., Archdnry of Brooklyn 1985-1987; Dn, Cntrl Nassau Dnry, Archdnry of Brooklyn Dio Long Island 1995-1999; R S Thos Ch Farmingdale NY 1993-1999; Secy Epis Chars 1988-1997; Assoc Gr Ch Brooklyn NY 1987-1993; Serv Angl Ch of Nassau & The Bahamas 1975-1981. Chapl Ord of S Lk 1997-1999; EDEIO 2008; Ecum Off- CAROA 2008; Life Professed Ord of H Cross 1977; Pres CAROA 2000-2008.

HOOVER, Greg T (Ark) 107 Walnut Ln, Branson MO 65616 **S Jn's Ch Harrison AR 2014-** B Independence MO 1968 s Fred & Bernice. Missouri Sthrn St U 1992; Geo Herbert Inst of Pstr Stds 2009; MDiv Providence TS 2010. D 6/5/2010 P 12/8/2010 Bp Barry Howe. m 10/28/2000 Kristen Hoover c 3. R Shpd Of The Hills Branson MO 2010-2015.

HOOVER, John Frain (CPa) 99 Willowbrook Blvd, Lewisburg PA 17837 B Philadelphia PA 1942 s Creighton & Marjorie. BS Tem 1963; MDiv GTS 1966; DMin GTF 1995; Cert PSU 1995. D 6/11/1966 P 1/28/1967 Bp Robert Lionne DeWitt. m 9/3/1966 Margaret B Hoover c 2. Consult Dio Cntrl Pennsylvania Harrisburg PA 2009-2011, Sr Consult for Sm Ch Mnstry 2008-2011; Assoc Mssnr Gleam Williamsport PA 2004-2008; P-in-c S Jas Ch Muncy PA 2000-2004; P-in-c S Paul's Ch Lock Haven PA 1988-2000; R Chap Of The Gd Shpd Hawk Run PA 1987-1998; R S Paul's Ch Philipsburg PA 1987-1998; R S Andr's In The Field Ch Philadelphia PA 1966-1987.

HOOVER, Joshua Aaron (Mich) 355 W Maple Rd, Birmingham MI 48009 **P-in-c S Jas Epis Ch Birmingham MI 2015-** B Wilmington DE 1972 BA Alfred U. D 6/1/2002 P 1/11/2003 Bp Jack Marston Mckelvey. m 11/23/2009 Allison C Hoover c 3. R S Jude's Epis Ch Fenton MI 2005-2014; Asst Chr Ch Pittsford Pittsford NY 2002-2005.

HOOVER, Judy Verne Hanlon (Minn) 2020 Orkla Dr, Golden Valley MN 55427 **Supply Trin Litchfield Minnesota 2013-; Asstg P Ch of Epiph 2009-** B Minneapolis MN 1933 d Vernon & Bertha. BS U MN 1955; MBA U of St Thos 1983; Cert SWTS 1991; MDiv Untd TS of the Twin Cities 1991. D 6/24/1991 P 1/6/1992 Bp Robert Marshall Anderson. m 10/18/2008 Raymond Edward Jorgensen c 4. R S Edw The Confessor Wayzata MN 1996-1998; Asst Ch Of The Epiph Epis Minneapolis MN 1991-1996; Yth Dir Dio Minnesota Minneapolis MN 1982-1989, Stndg Com 1985-1989, Yth Coordntr 1982-1989, Trst 1981-1985; Prov Yth Coordntr Dom And Frgn Mssy Soc- Epis Ch Cntr New York NY 1985-1989; Mem Exec Coun Appointees New York NY 1985-1987. "Flames and Faith," *Doing H Bus*, Ch Pub, 2006. Associated Parishes for Liturg and Mnstry 1996; Int Mnstry Ntwk Associated Parishes 1993-1996; Minnesota Epis Cleric Assn 1992. Paul Harris Fell Rotary Inst 2001.

HOOVER, Melvin Aubrey (SO) 1870 Commonwealth Ave., Auburndale MA 02466 B Columbus OH 1944 s Alfred & Felicia. BS OH SU 1968; Colgate Rochester Crozer DS 1972; CRDS 1972; U Assoc Intrnshp 1976. D 7/3/1971 Bp John Mc Gill Krumm. m 12/18/1970 Rosemary Edington. Coun Of Ch And Synagogues Sw Fairfield Cnty MA 1978-1987; Asst Calv & S Andr's 1968-1970. Auth, "Living Ecum". Outstanding Ldr Rochester Cmnty 1976.

HOOVER, Richard A (CFla) 209 S Iowa Ave, Lakeland FL 33801 B MO 1950 s Mario & Ruth. BA SW Missouri St U 1971. D 12/1/2007 Bp John Wadsworth Howe. m 6/1/1974 Melanie Hoover. D All SS Epis Ch Lakeland FL 2011-2014, Dir of Cmncatn 2011-.

HOOVER, Todd Jay (SeFla) 952 SW 7th St, Ft Lauderdale FL 33315 **Supply P St Jas-in-the-Hills Hollywood FL 2016-; Adj All SS Epis Ch Ft Lauderdale FL 2012-; S Mary Magd Epis Ch Pompano Bch FL 2011-** B Clearwater FL 1962 s John & Emily. BS U of the Redlands 1986; MAT Webster U 1987; MBA Brenau U 1992; MDiv GTS 2011. D 6/22/2011 P 2/25/2012 Bp Leo Frade. m 5/16/2011 Ronald Ralph Michel c 1. toddjhoover@bellsouth.net

HOOVER-DEMPSEY, Randy (Tenn) 1829 Hudson Rd, Madison TN 37115 B Greensboro NC 1947 s Luther & Merrimon. BA U NC 1969; MDiv Columbia TS 1976; BS Middle Tennessee St U 1982. D 6/10/2006 P 12/16/2006 Bp Bertram Nelson Herlong. m 5/23/1982 Kathleen V Hoover-Dempsey c 4. Cur Dio Tennessee Nashville TN 2010-2016; Cur S Mary Magd Ch Fayetteville TN 2009-2010; Asst S Barth's Ch Nashville TN 2006-2009; Tchr U Sch Of Nashville 1984-2004.

HOPEWELL, Gloria Grayson (Chi) 939 Hinman Ave, Evanston IL 60202 **Gr Epis Ch Galena IL 2012-; D.Min. Core Grp Fac Seabury Wstrn TS Evanston IL 2011-; P Assoc S Lk's Ch Evanston IL 2010-** B Sandwich IL 1945 d Raymond & Patricia. BS Nthrn Illinois U 1968; MBA Loyola U 1979; MDiv Chicago TS 1996; DMin Garrett-Evang 2007; DMin Garrett-Evang TS 2007. D 6/5/2010 P 12/11/2010 Bp Jeff Lee. c 2.

HOPKINS, Christine Carroll (Spr) 102 E Mchenry St, Urbana IL 61801 **D Emm Memi Epis Ch Champaign IL 2000-** B Mayfield KY 1950 d Conrad & Martha. Bachelors U IL 1972; Masters U IL 1973. D 6/11/2000 Bp Peter Hess Beckwith. m 6/13/1971 Robert Michael Hopkins c 3.

HOPKINS, Daniel W (Colo) 7127 S. Quemoy St., Aurora CO 80016 **D S Thos Epis Ch Denver CO 2002-** B Nuremburg Germany 1954 s Willie & Lula. BA U of Oklahoma 1977; MDiv GTS 1985. D 6/14/1985 P 12/22/1985 Bp

William Carl Frey. m 12/23/2001 Sheila Hopkins. Assoc S Lk's Ch Hot Sprg AR 2001-2006; Non-par 1992-1993; Dio Colorado Denver CO 1992-1993; R Ch Of The H Redeem Denver CO 1985-1992. Ne Denver Mnstrl Allnce.

✠ HOPKINS JR, The Rt Rev Harold Anthony (ND) 15 Piper Rd Apt K211, Scarborough ME 04074 B Philadelphia PA 1930 s Harold & Ellen. BA U of Pennsylvania 1952; MDiv GTS 1955; GTS 1980. D 5/7/1955 Bp Joseph Gillespie Armstrong P 11/21/1955 Bp Oliver J Hart Con 2/18/1980 for ND. m 6/11/1955 Nancy Hopkins. Dir - Pstr Dvlpmt Epis Ch Cntr New York NY 1988-1998; Presdng Bp Com Indn Affrs 1986-1989; Sccsc 1986-1988; Pres Prov VI 1986-1988; C-14 1983-1986; Bp Of Nd Dio No Dakota Fargo ND 1980-1988; Archd Dio Maine Portland ME 1978-1979, Asst to the Bp 1969-1978; Exec Secy Prov I 1974-1980; Vic S Barth's Epis Ch Yarmouth ME 1974-1978; R S Sav's Par Bar Harbor ME 1963-1969; R S Andr's Ch Millinocket ME 1957-1963; Cur Par of Chr the Redeem Pelham NY 1955-1957. Contrib, "Restoring The Soul Of A Ch," Liturg Press, 1995; Auth, "The Interval Between Election And Consecration," 1992; Auth, "Nominees In An Epis Process," 1989.

HOPKINS, John Leonard (Alb) 34 Velina Dr, Burnt Hills NY 12027 B Glens Falls NY 1946 s John & Ruth. MA SUNY; BA SUNY 1968; MA SUNY 1982; MA S Bernards TS and Mnstry Albany 2001. D 6/2/2002 Bp Daniel William Herzog P 11/30/2002 Bp David John Bena. m 7/30/1977 Cynthia Hopkins c 2. S Lk's Ch Mechanicville NY 2010-2014; S Lk's Ch Cambridge NY 2008-2009; Asst S Geo's Ch Clifton Pk NY 2002-2007.

HOPKINS, Lydia Elliott (La) B 1949 D 10/23/2005 Bp Charles Edward Jenkins III.

HOPKINS, Michael Warren (Roch) 67 E Main St, Hornell NY 14843 **Treas Finger Lakes SPCA Bath NY 2016-; Secy Trin-CASA Geneseo NY 2015-** B Avoca NY 1961 s William & Patricia. BS SUNY at Plattsburgh 1983; Nash 1985; MDiv SWTS 1988; CUA 1992. D 6/17/1989 Bp Frank Tracy Griswold III P 1/10/1990 Bp Ronald Hayward Haines. m 7/22/2010 John C Bradley. P S Mich's Ch Geneseo NY 2014-2015; P-in-c Ch Of The Ascen Rochester NY 2013-2014; Dn Dio Rochester Henrietta 2011-2014, Stndg Com 2012-2014, GC Dep 2012-, Com on Const & Cn 2011-, Dioc Coun 2006-2010, Bp Search Com 2006-2008, Dioc Cmsn on Liturg& Mus 2005-2007; P-in-c S Steph's Ch Rochester NY 2007-2008; R S Lk And S Simon Cyrene Rochester NY 2004-2014; R S Geo's Ch Glenn Dale MD 2002-2004, 1990-1995, Vic 1990-1995; Assoc Par of St Monica & St Jas Washington DC 1989-1990; Bd Mem AIDS Care Rochester NY 2011-2014; Bd Mem (VP 12-) Interfaith Allnce of Rochester 2010-2014; SCLM T/F on C056 Dom And Frgn Mssy Soc- Epis Ch Cntr New York NY 2010-2011; Bp Search Com Dio Washington Washington DC 2001-2002, Dioc Coun (Moderator 98-00) 1994-2000, Cmsn on Liturg & Mus 1989-1996. Auth, "Paying the Price: A No Amer Perspective," *Rebuilding Comm: Who Pays the Price?*, Monad Press, 2008; Auth, "Reaffirmation of Ord Vows," *Baptism & Mnstry*, Ch Pub, 1994. Associated Parishes 1989-2006; ECom 1997-1999; Epis Ntwk for Econ Justice 2010; EPF 1997; EUC (BD 09-13) 2002; EWC 1998; Fllshp of the SSJE 2006; Integrity (Pres 98-03; Dir Com 96-98) 1985; OA 1994-2002. Pres's Awd Integrity 2006; Polly Bond Awd ECom 1998.

HOPKINS, Terry Robert (Minn) P.O. Box 402, Monticello MN 55362 B Bradford PA 1947 s Robert & Virginia. BA Estrn U 1969; MA U of Vermont 1976. D 11/14/1992 Bp Sanford Zangwill Kaye Hampton. m 6/19/1971 Janice Ruth Hopkins c 2. D S Jn's Ch Of Hassan Rogers MN 1996-1999; D S Mich & All Ang Ch Monticello MN 1994-1996; D S Chris's Epis Ch S Paul MN 1992-1994.

HOPKINS, Vivian Louise (Oly) 32820 20th Ave S #61, Federal Way WA 98003 **D The Ch of the Gd Shpd Fed Way WA 2006-; Dir of Outreach Ministies Chr Epis Ch Miami FL 2001-; Coordntr of Epis Relief and Dvlpmt Dio SE Florida Miami 2002-** B Miami FL 1937 d Joseph & Iva. BS USC 1960; MA California St Polytechnic U 1977; Cert Dio SE Florida Sch for CE 2001. D 9/1/2001 Bp Leo Frade. c 1. D St. Lk the Physcn Miami FL 2003-2006.

HOPKINS-GREENE, Nancy (SO) 6255 Stirrup Rd, Cincinnati OH 45244 **Asst The Ch of the Redeem Cincinnati OH 2004-** B Philadelphia PA 1957 d Robert & Louise. BA Stan 1980; MDiv EDS 1992. D 6/5/1993 Bp David Elliot Johnson P 12/3/1994 Bp Herbert Thompson Jr. m 6/13/1980 Roger Stewart Greene c 2. Asst Ed Forw Mvmt of the Epis Ch Cincinnati OH 2009-2016; S Anne Epis Ch W Chester OH 2004; S Tim's Epis Ch Cincinnati OH 1994-2003.

HOPLAMAZIAN, Julie M (LI) The Church of St. Luke and St. Matthew, 520 Clinton Ave, Brooklyn NY 11238 **The Ch Of S Lk and S Matt Brooklyn NY 2017-; Asst Gr Ch Corona NY 2012-** B Philadelphia PA 1979 d Joseph & Sona. BS Ge 2000; MDiv PrTS 2006. D 6/2/2012 P 12/8/2012 Bp Lawrence C Provenzano. m 1/4/2014 Jeremy Warren Kerr. Assoc Gr Ch Brooklyn NY 2015-2017. revjuliehop@gmail.com

HOPNER, Kathryn Ann (Nev) St Paul's Episcopal Church, PO Box 737, Sparks NV 89432 **CE Dir Trin Epis Cathd Sacramento CA 2013-** B Denver CO 1953 d Franklin & Marilyn. BA San Jose St U 1987; MEd Chapman U 2000; MDiv CDSP 2007. D 6/2/2007 Bp Barry Leigh Beisner P 12/8/2007 Bp Jerry Alban Lamb. m 9/29/1972 Victor Hopner c 2. Assoc Trin Epis Ch Reno NV

2007-2013; Assoc P S Paul's Epis Ch Sparks NV 2007-2011. kathrynhopner@gmail.com

HOPPE, Robert Donald (FdL) 806 4th St, Algoma WI 54201 **Ch Of S Agnes By The Lake Algoma WI 1992-; Ch of the Precious Blood Gardner WI 1992-** B Mankato MN 1961 s Robert & Judith. BS Minnesota St U Mankato 1983; BS Minnesota St U Mankato 1985. D 8/15/1992 Bp William Louis Stevens P 9/6/1997 Bp Russell Edward Jacobus. Vic Dio Fond du Lac Appleton WI 1992-1995. SocMary 1999.

HOPPER, Edgar Wilson (NY) St Augustines, 333 Madison St, New York NY 10002 B 1929 D 5/20/2000 Bp Richard Frank Grein.

HOPWOOD, Alfred Joseph (Minn) 1417 Blue Flag Ct, Northfield MN 55057 **P SS Martha & Mary Epis Ch Eagan MN 2010-; Asst SS Martha And Mary Epis Ch S Paul MN 2010-, Vic 2002-2010** B New York NY 1933 s Alexander & Winifred. BS Colorado St U 1956; PhD Colorado St U 1967; MA S Johns U Collegeville MN 1987. D 6/24/1986 P 12/30/1986 Bp Robert Marshall Anderson. m 6/22/1955 Lillian Barbara Hopwood c 4. Assoc SS Martha & Mary Epis Ch Eagan MN 2002-2004; Int Chr Epis Ch Grand Rapids MN 2000-2001; R All SS Ch Northfield MN 1993-1999; Assoc S Jn's Ch S Cloud MN 1986-1993. "Nine Meditations," *Soundings: The mag of the Dio Minnesota*, 1979.

HORD, Christine D (CGC) **S Jn's Ch Pensacola FL 2017-** D 11/22/2014 P 7/7/2015 Bp Philip Menzie Duncan II.

HOREN, Anna Lynn (Cal) 4529 Lakewood St, Pleasanton CA 94588 **S Jas Ch Fremont CA 2017-** B Bronx NY 1955 d Fortunato & Vittoria. BA Ford 1976; MA U CA Davis 1978; MS U CA Davis 1981; MA Grad Theol Un 1997; Cert CDSP 2015. D 6/11/2016 Bp Marc Handley Andrus. m 6/27/1981 Robert Sydney Horen c 2. revanna.horen@comcast.net

HORGAN, Daniel E (Mass) 204 Monument Rd, Orleans MA 02653 B Quincy MA 1962 s Thomas & Anne. BA Wstrn New Engl Coll 1996. D 6/25/2011 Bp M(Arvil) Thomas Shaw. m 1/5/1985 Cynthia Ann Horgan c 5.

HORLE, Garrison Locke (Colo) 720 Downing St, Denver CO 80218 B Bronxville NY 1940 s Ariel & Elizabeth. BA U CO 1962; MBA U Denv 1976; MDiv Iliff TS 1996. D 6/7/1997 P 12/6/1997 Bp William Jerry Winterrowd. m 7/8/1966 Carol Horle c 2. Int The Ch Of Chr The King (Epis) Arvada CO 2011; Int Ch Of Our Sav Colorado Sprg CO 2009-2011; Int S Matt's Ch Grand Jct CO 2007-2009; Int S Paul's Epis Ch Lakewood CO 2006-2007; Int S Tim's Epis Ch Littleton CO 2004-2006; R All SS Epis Ch Denver CO 1999-2004; P-in-c S Andr's Ch Cripple Creek CO 1997-1999.

HORN, John C (Ia) Trinity Episcopal Cathedral, 121 W. 12th St., Davenport IA 52803 **Dn Trin Cathd Davenport IA 2012-** B Philadelphia PA 1952 s William & Ruth. BA Ob 1974; PhD Duke 1981; MDiv SWTS 2007. D 12/16/2006 P 6/16/2007 Bp Alan Scarfe. m 8/1/1975 Raisin Gaiz c 1. R Chr Epis Ch Burlington IA 2009-2012; Asst S Ptr's Ch Bettendorf IA 2008-2009; Prof of Biology St Ambr U 1982-2009. john@qctrinity.org

HORN, Mike (ND) 15757 N 90th Pl Apt 2053, Scottsdale AZ 85260 B Mobridge SD 1951 s Robert & Dorothy. BS So Dakota Sch Mines & Tech 1973; MDiv Nash 1977. D 6/30/1977 P 1/18/1978 Bp Walter H Jones. R S Geo's Epis Ch Bismarck ND 1998-2014; Vic S Barth's Epis Ch Bemidji MN 1991-1998; Dio Minnesota Minneapolis MN 1984-1991; P S Antipas Ch Redby MN 1984-1991; S Jn-In-The-Wilderness Red Lake MN 1984-1991; Vic All SS Epis Ch Herrick SD 1977-1983; Dio So Dakota Pierre SD 1977-1983; Ch Of The Incarn Greg SD 1977-1980; S Andr's Ch Bonesteel SD 1977-1980. Land 1987.

HORN, Peter Moya (Ala) **Died 6/16/2016** B Bessemer AL 1933 s Joseph & Mildred. BA U So 1956; MDiv VTS 1961. D 6/24/1961 P 5/1/1962 Bp Charles C J Carpenter. m 9/13/1956 Patricia F Forrester c 4. Assoc R S Steph's Epis Ch Birmingham AL 1988-2004; Assoc R Ch Of The Nativ Epis Huntsville AL 1986-1988; R Trin Epis Ch Bessemer AL 1976-1986; R The Epis Ch of The Redeem Jacksonville FL 1968-1976; Vic Emm Epis Ch Opelika AL 1962-1968; S Matthews In The Pines Seale AL 1962-1968; Cur S Paul's Ch Mobile AL 1961-1962. peterhorn@att.net

HORN, Raisin (Ia) Trinity Church, 320 E College St, Iowa City IA 52240 **R Chr Epis Ch Clinton IA 2017-; U Of Iowa Chapl Iowa City IA 2007-** B Chicago IL 1953 d Vincent & Delores. BA Ob 1975; MA Hollins U 1978; MDiv SWTS 2007. D 12/16/2006 P 6/16/2007 Bp Alan Scarfe. m 8/1/1975 John C Horn c 1. Asst R Trin Ch Iowa City IA 2008-2016; Chapl Dio Iowa Des Moines IA 2007-2015, Dep to Prov Syn 2011-, GC Dep 2003-; S Ptr's Ch Bettendorf IA 1999-2004. christepiscopal2@qwestoffice.net

HORN, S Huston (Los) 334 S Parkwood Ave, Pasadena CA 91107 B Nashville TN 1930 s Claude & Lillian. BA Van 1956; Mercer TS 1966; BD EDS 1969. D 6/28/1969 Bp Chauncie Kilmer Myers P 1/20/1970 Bp Robert Claflin Rusack. c 4. Dio Los Angeles Los Angeles CA 1987-1988; Non-par: Dir of Caltech Y California Inst of Tech Pasadena CA 1982-1986; The Caltech Y Pasadena CA 1982-1984; Dir Pstr Mnstrs All SS Ch Pasadena CA 1969-1981. Auth, "The Pioneers," Time/Life Old W Series, 1972.

HORNADAY, Evelyn (WMo) St. Peter & All Saints Episcopal Church, 100 E. Red Bridge Rd., Kansas City MO 64114 B Muskogee OK 1941 d Fredrick & Evelyn. BMus U of Tulsa 1963; U of Texas 1964; MDiv Epis TS of the SW 2000. D 6/3/2000 P 12/9/2000 Bp Barry Howe. c 1. Cn S Jn's Cathd Denver CO

2017; St Ptr & All SS Epis Ch Kansas City MO 2014-2016; Gr Ch Pine Bluff AR 2012-2013; P Assoc Trin Cathd Little Rock AR 2011-2013; P All SS Epis Ch Paragould AR 2011-2012, P 2011-; Int R S Marg's Epis Ch Little Rock AR 2009-2011; Int R All SS Epis Ch Stafford TX 2008-2009; H Cross Epis Ch Sugar Land TX 2007-2008; All SS Epis Ch Russellville AR 2005-2007; S Jn's Epis Ch Helena AR 2003-2005; Ch Of The Ascen Epis Springfield MO 2000-2003. "Death and Dying Done Well," *Reflection on Bioethics and Chr Theol*, U of Texas SW Med Cntr, 2008. Dn Metro-Niorthern Dnry, Dio W Missouri 2013; Dn Sthrn Dnry, Dio W Missouri 2001. evelyn@sjcathedral.org

HORNBECK, Jennifer (NCal) PO Box 274, Kenwood CA 95452 **S Patricks Ch Kenwood CA 2013-** B Berkeley CA 1976 d Parker & Janel. MDiv Ya Berk; California St U 1998. D 6/2/2001 P 12/1/2001 Bp William Edwin Swing. S Bede's Epis Ch Menlo Pk CA 2013; The Epis Ch Of S Mary The Vrgn San Francisco CA 2006-2012; Asst Trsfg Epis Ch San Mateo CA 2001-2005; Assoc Epis Ch of St. Mary the Vrgn.

HORNE, Lance Cameron (Fla) 3275 Tallavana Trl, Havana FL 32333 B Gulfport Mississippi 1945 s Roger & Helen. BS USNA 1968; MS Untd States Naval Postgraduate Sch 1972; MDiv VTS 2001. D 6/10/2001 P 3/17/2002 Bp Richard Sui On Chang. m 8/19/1989 Elizabeth Horne c 1. S Barth's Ch High Sprg FL 2011; S Paul's Epis Ch Jacksonville FL 2007-2011; S Paul's Epis Ch Quincy FL 2004-2007; D S Geo's Epis Ch Honolulu HI 2001-2004.

HORNE, Martha (Va) 3809 Fort Worth Ave, Alexandria VA 22304 **Dn, presidential Ldrshp Prog Assn of Theol Schools 2007-** B Durham NC 1948 d Robert & Martha. BA Duke 1970; MDiv VTS 1983. D 6/11/1983 P 5/1/1984 Bp Robert Bruce Hall. m 3/30/1969 McDonald Horne c 2. Dn & Pres VTS Alexandria VA 1994-2008; Assoc R Chr Ch Alexandria VA 1985-1986; Asst To Vic S Andr's Ch Burke VA 1983-1985. DD Sem of the SW 2012; R Emer Epis Ch of St Jn the Evang 2008; DD Berk 2007; Dio Los Angeles Hon Cn 2003; DD U So 2001; DD EDS 1998; Maestria en Divinidad mcl Seminario Evangelico de Puerto Rico 1997; Meritissimus U of S Thos 1972.

HORNER, John Scott (O) 813 West Main St, Elizabeth City NC 27909 **P Assoc Chr Ch Eliz City NC 2011-; Ret Eliz City 2009-** B Richmond VA 1944 s Charlie & Mildred. BS VMI 1967; MDiv Duke DS 1971; CPE Virginia Commonwealth U 1976. D 6/28/1977 P 10/18/1978 Bp Robert Bruce Hall. m 4/13/1974 Annette Maddra Horner c 2. Fndr, Chairman of Bd Wick Neighbors Inc/Smoky Hollow Dvlpmt Youngstown 2002-2007; R S Jn's Ch Youngstown OH 2000-2009; Fndr, Chairman of Bd Ardmore Affordable Hsng Ardmore PA 1992-1999; R S Mary's Epis Ch Ardmore PA 1987-2000; Fndr, Bd Secy Grtr Berks Food Bank Reading PA 1982-1987; Assoc Chr Ch Reading PA 1981-1987; Asst Ch Of The H Comf Richmond VA 1977-1980.

HORNER, Robert William (Tex) 8 Coralvine Ct, The Woodlands TX 77380 **D Trin Epis Ch The Woodlands TX 1987-, D/Asst 1979-1986** B Trenton NJ 1929 s Lafayette & Edith. BS Rider U 1957; MBA U Pgh 1971; D Formation Prog 1974. D 12/15/1974 Bp James Winchester Montgomery. m 3/5/1951 Jane Lee Horner c 3. D/Asst H Comf Epis Ch Sprg TX 1985-1986; D/Asst S Tim's Epis Ch S Louis MO 1978-1979; D/Asst S Simons Ch Arlington Hts IL 1975-1978.

HORNER, William McKinley (Miss) 14981 W Verde Ln, Goodyear AZ 85338 **D Dio Mississippi Jackson MS 1997-** B Chicago IL 1924 s William & Margaret. ICS S Jos/Coll Troy St U; Mississippi TS 1997. D 1/4/1997 Bp Alfred Marble Jr. m 2/21/1947 Elvira De Angelis.

HORNING, David J (Mich) 104 Mount Homestake Dr., Leadville CO 80461 B Detroit MI 1951 s Walter & Dorothy. Michigan TS; Wayne; MA Colgate Rochester Crozer DS 1989; MA CRDS 1989. D 10/18/1979 Bp Henry Irving Mayson P 8/6/1982 Bp H Coleman Mcgehee Jr. m 10/12/1974 Jane Ann Woodward c 4. Co-Dn Dio Michigan Detroit MI 1996-1999, BEC 1994-2001, Econ Justice Com 1988-1995; Nat'L Rep - Mnstry To Burned Ch Ecusa 1996-1998; S Jas' Epis Ch Dexter MI 1993-2004, 1992; S Andr's Epis Ch Flint MI 1993; Ch Of The Mssh Detroit MI 1986-1989, 1982-1984.

HORNSBY, James Harmon (Mass) 260 Lake Ave, Fall River MA 02721 **R Emer S Lk's Epis Ch Fall River MA 2003-, 1967-1999** B Cambridge MA USA 1939 s Robert & Gladys. BA Harv 1961; MDiv ETSC 1965; MS Ricssw 1982. D 6/26/1965 Bp Anson Phelps Stokes Jr P 12/26/1965 Bp Francisco Reus-Froylan. c 3. Serv Ch In Puerto Rico 1965-1967.

HORST, Diane Elizabeth (NMich) 12769 W Lakeshore Dr, Brimley MI 49715 **D S Jas Ch Of Sault S Marie Sault Sainte Marie MI 2006-** B Detroit MI 1949 d Duane & Shirley. I; BS Indiana U 1971. D 5/28/2006 Bp James Arthur Kelsey. c 2.

HORTON, Carol J (NJ) 3 Plumstead Ct, Annandale NJ 08801 **R S Thos Ch Alexandria Pittstown NJ 2006-** B Morristown NJ 1949 d William & Jean. Kean U; BA Westminster Choir Coll of Rider U 1971; MDiv Drew U 1992; CAS GTS 1995. D 6/17/1995 P 12/16/1995 Bp James Michael Mark Dyer. R Susquehanna Country Mnstry Hallstead PA 1995-2006. Cmnty of S Jn Bapt, Assoc. rector@stthomaspc.org

HORTON, Cathy Bosworth (O) 411 Chagrin Blvd, Chagrin Falls OH 44022 B Columbus OH 1962 JD Coll of Law OH SU at Columbus; ThM U of Kent; BA

403

U MI. Trans 1/22/2004 Bp J Clark Grew II. c 2. Chr Ch Shaker Heights OH 2004-2009.

HORTON, Edward Robert (Cal) 6618 Taylor Dr., Woodridge IL 60517 **S Mary Of The Ang Epis Ch Orlando FL 2000-** B Crawfordsville IN 1931 s George & Leah. BA Illinois Coll 1953; MS USN Sch 1960. D 2/25/1969 Bp Chauncie Kilmer Myers. m 1/6/2001 Mary Potter Horton c 2. Asst S Andr's Ch Downers Grove IL 2000-2012; Asst Cur Aiyura Kainantu Ehp Papua New Guinen 1977-1999; Asst S Fran' Goroka Ehd Papua New Guinea 1973-1977; Asst S Jn's Cathd Albuquerque NM 1971-1973; Asst S Barth's Epis Ch Livermore CA 1969-1971. Wycliffe Bible Transltr.

HORTON, Fred Lane (NC) 2622 Weymoth Rd, Winston Salem NC 27103 B Alexandria VA 1944 s Fred & Loetta. BA U NC 1964; BD UTS 1967; PhD Duke 1971; CAS VTS 1985. D 6/11/1985 P 6/1/1986 Bp Frank Harris Vest Jr. m 8/29/1964 Patricia Horton c 2. S Paul's Epis Ch Winston Salem NC 1996-1998; Asst R 1985-1991; Int S Clem's Epis Ch Clemmons NC 1993-1994; Non-par Dept of Rel Wake Forest U 1970-2011. Auth, "The Melchizedek Tradition," Camb Press, 1976. AAR 1970-1990; Amer Schools Of Oriental Resrch 1976; Egypt Exploration Soc 1969; Ord Of S Lk 1987; Phi Beta Kappa 1971; SBL 1968. Prof Emer Wake Forest U 2011; Jn Thos Albritton Prof of Rel Wake Forest U 1991.

HORTON, James Roy (EC) 1060 Dixie Trl, Williamston NC 27892 B Baltimore MD 1942 s Leslie & Marie. BA W&L 1964; MDiv VTS 1967. D 6/20/1967 P 6/6/1968 Bp Harry Lee Doll. m 6/4/1966 Lucy D Horton c 2. R Ch Of The Adv Williamston NC 1972-2012; Asst Chr Ch New Bern NC 1968-1972; Asst S Thos' Ch Garrison Forest Owings Mills MD 1967-1968; Pres-Stndg Com Dio E Carolina Kinston NC 2011-2012. Ord of the Long Leaf Pine Gvnr of No Carolina 2013; Cn Dio Arkansas 1995; Rec DSA Jaycees 1975.

HORTON JR, James Taylor (FtW) 7413 Hillstone Dr, Benbrook TX 76126 B Fort Worth TX 1941 s James & Eleanor. BA Louisiana Coll 1963; MA Van 1966; MDiv Epis TS of the SW 1972; DMin Sewanee: The U So, TS 1982. D 6/11/1972 P 5/1/1973 Bp John Maury Allin. m 8/15/1969 Anne B Horton. S Elis Ch Ft Worth TX 2002-2007; S Steph's Epis Ch Erwin NC 1991-1992; Dn S Mary's Cathd Memphis TN 1989-1990; R Emm Epis Ch San Angelo TX 1985-1989; R S Lk's In The Meadow Epis Ch Ft Worth TX 1978-1985; R S Mich's Ch La Marque TX 1975-1978; Cur S Andr's Cathd Jackson MS 1972-1974.

HORTON, Sarah (Vt) 17 Mack Ave, West Lebanon NH 03784 B Bristol UK 1943 d John & Olwen. BA Oxf GB 1965; PhD Col 1980. D 6/11/1991 P 12/18/1991 Bp Daniel Lee Swenson. m 6/21/1971 Gunnar Urang c 2. R S Barn Ch Norwich VT 1992-2003; Asst St Mary's in The Mountains Epis Wilmington VT 1991-1992. Auth, "Kindled In The Flame," 1983.

HORTON-SMITH, Sandra (Kan) St Paul's Episcopal Church, 601 Poyntz Ave, Manhattan KS 66502 B Akron OH 1967 d Robert & Mary. None K SU; BSN Washburn U 2007; Cert Kansas Sch for Mnstry 2012. D 6/2/2012 Bp Dean E Wolfe. m 6/30/1990 Glenn Arthur Horton-Smith c 2.

HORTUM, John (Va) 1407 N Gaillard St, Alexandria VA 22304 B Arlington VA 1948 s Ernest & Eileen. VTS; BA JHU 1971; STB Gregorian U 1975. P 9/8/1996 Bp Peter J Lee. m 11/30/1985 Leslie Anne Hortum c 2. R The Ch of S Clem Alexandria VA 2000-2016, Asst to R 1996-1998; Goodwin Hse Incorporated Alexandria VA 1998-2000.

HORVATH, Leslie Ferguson (USC) 400 Dupre Dr., Spartanburg SC 29307 **Chapl Spartanburg Cnty Sheriff's Off Spartanburg SC 2011-; D S Chris's Ch Spartanburg SC 2009-; Convoc D Dio Upper So Carolina Columbia SC 2009-, Matt 25 Com Mem 2009-** B Latta SC 1960 d William & Mary. BS U of Tennessee 1983; MM U of Kentucky 1988; Cert Dioc Sch For Mnstry 2007; Cert Dioc Sch For Mnstry 2007. D 1/31/2009 Bp Dorsey Henderson. m 10/22/1983 Gary Horvath c 1.

HORVATH, Michael J (NY) B Sangley Point Philippines 1970 s James & Edna. BA Virginia Commonwealth U 1995; Juris Doctor U Rich Sch of Law 1998; MDiv The GTS 2017. D 3/4/2017 Bp Mary Douglas Glasspool. m 3/18/2017 Charles C Calhoun.

HORVATH, Victor John (Vt) 6 South St, Bellows Falls VT 05101 B Buffalo NY 1949 s Victor & Adelaide. U of Bridgeport; BS Manhattan Coll 1971. D 11/19/2002 P 6/7/2003 Bp Thomas C Ely. m 9/23/2000 Arne Andersen. R Imm Ch Bellows Falls VT 2003-2012.

HOSEA, Beverly Ann (Oly) 215 14th Ave E Apt 401, Seattle WA 98112 **Assoc R for Pstr Care and Sprtl Formation Emm Epis Ch Mercer Island WA 2007-; The Cmnty of the Lamb Seattle WA 2002-** B Spokane WA 1946 d Noel & Margaret. BA U of Washington 1968; MDiv CDSP 1983. D 6/8/1985 Bp William Edwin Swing P 3/6/1986 Bp Robert Marshall Anderson. c 2. Int Ch Of Our Sav Monroe WA 2006-2007; Int S Eliz's Ch Seattle WA 2003-2005; Exec Dir The Cmnty Of The Lamb Mercer Island WA 2002-2003; Int S Matt Ch Tacoma WA 2002; Reg Mssnr Chr Epis Ch Zillah WA 1994-1999; S Matt's Ch Prosser WA 1994-1999; Chr Ch Duluth MN 1990-1994; H Apos Ch Duluth MN 1990-1994; Vic for Total Mnstry S Andr's Ch Cloquet MN 1990-1994; Dir Pk Rapids Area Hospice Pk Rapids MN 1985-1989; R Trin Epis Ch Pk Rapids MN 1985-1989; D S Mk's Ch Houston TX 1985; Chapl Hermann Hosp Houston TX 1983-1985. Auth, "Var postings," *The Pryr of the Lamb Blog*, http://prayerofthelambmeditation.blogspot.com, 2007; "Var arts," *Dawn Pie*, Cntr for Sprtl Dvlpmt, 2001; Auth, "A People Gathered Around a Mnstry," *Crossroads*, RWF, 1994; "Total Mnstry," *Soundings*, Dio Minnesota, 1990; "Total Mnstry models...in Minnesota," *Crossroads*, RWF, 1989. Curs Sec, Dio Olympia 2007-2009; MN Epis Cler Assn 1985-1994; RWF 1986-1999; Sindicators 1991-1999; Third Ord, Soc of S Fran 1981. bhosea@mac.com

HOSEA, Janice Forney (RG) 7171 Tennyson St NE, Albuquerque NM 87122 **Assoc S Chad's Epis Ch Albuquerque NM 2010-** B Tulsa OK 1948 d Jene & Dorothy. BS U of Tulsa 1971; MA S Mary U 1997. D 9/19/2009 P 9/25/2010 Bp William Carl Frey. m 6/25/1983 Bruce James Hosea. S Jn's Cathd Albuquerque NM 2010-2011.

HOSKINS, Charles L (Ga) 4629 Sylvan Dr, Savannah GA 31405 **Ret 1996-** B 1931 s Clement & Florencia. Mt S Ben Abbey Trinidad 1961; Lic S Thos U, Rome, Italy 1964; Sc. Soc. D S Thos U, Rome, Italy 1966. Rec 5/1/1970 as Deacon Bp George E Rath. m 4/1/1991 Evalena M Hoskins. S Matt's Ch Savannah GA 1975-1996; R Trin Ch Montclair NJ 1970-1975; Serv RC Ch 1961-1970. Auth, "Back savannahians," *W. W. Law and His People: a Timeline and Biographies*, Chas L. Hoskins, 2013; Auth, "black savannahians," *W. W. Law and His People: a Timeline and Biographies*, Chas L. Hoskins, 2013; Auth, "Black episcopalians," *SS stepher, Aug, and Matt; 150 years of struggle, hardship and success*, chartles l. hoskins, 2005; Auth, "Black savannah," *Out of Yamacraw and beyond; discovering black savannah*, Chas l. hoskins, 2002; Auth, "Black savannahians," *Yet w a sready beat; biographies of early black savannah*, Chas l. hoskins, 2001; Auth, "Black savannahians," *The Trouble They Seen: Profiles in the Life of Jn H. Deveaux1846-1909*, Chas l.hoskins, 1989; Auth, "Black Episcopalians," *Black Episcopalians in Savannah*, Chas L. Hoskins, 1983; Auth, "Black Episcopalians," *Black Episcopalians in Georgia: strife, struggle and salvation*, Chas L. Hoskins, 1980.

HOSKINS, Jo Ann Smith (Fla) 4241 Duval Dr, Jacksonville Beach FL 32250 B Atlanta GA 1944 AA Florida Cmnty Coll at Jacksonville. D 9/21/2003 Bp Stephen Hays Jecko. m 3/24/1963 Charles Ross Hoskins c 2. D/Dir Of Lay Mnstrs And Newcomers Chr Epis Ch Ponte Vedra FL 1998-2009.

HOSLER, Carol Smith (Az) PO Box 171, 408 Jamestown Road, Kearny AZ 85137 **Dio Arizona Phoenix AZ 2016-, GC Dep 2009-, GC Dep 2006-, GC Dep 2003-, GC Dep 2000-, GC Dep 1997-; P-t Vic S Mich's Ch Coolidge AZ 2012-; GC Dep Dio Nthrn Michigan Marquette MI 1991-, Co-Ed of Dioc Nwspr 1989-1994, Ed of Dioc Nwspr 1988-1994, GC Dep 1988-; GC Dep Dio Idaho Boise ID 1985-, GC Dep 1982-, Ed of Dioc Nwspr 1979-1995, GC Dep 1979-, Ed of Dioc Nwspr 1978-1986, COM 1977-, COM 1976-1986; GOE Rdr Dio Bethlehem Bethlehem PA 1973-, COM 1972-** B Portland OR 1945 d Harold & Dorothy. BA Linfield Coll 1968; MA Colgate Rochester Crozer DS 1970; MA CRDS 1970. D 8/4/1991 P 2/29/1992 Bp Thomas Kreider Ray. m 12/19/1969 Samuel Odyth Hosler c 2. Pstr Meth Ch of the Gd Shpd 2008-2011; Int Ch Of Our Sav Lakeside AZ 2007-2008; S Geo's Epis Ch Holbrook AZ 1994-2005; Co-Vic S Paul's Epis Ch Winslow AZ 1994-2005; Chapl RTA Hospice 1994-1996; P/Mnstry Spprt Team Ch Of The Gd Shpd S Ignace MI 1991-1994. ECom 1977-1994; Synagogy 1994-1999. Bp's Awd of Appreciation Dio Idaho 1984.

HOSLER, Joshua Luke (Oly) 2117 Walnut St, Bellingham WA 98225 **S Paul Epis Ch Bellingham WA 2014-** B Scranton PA 1972 s Samuel & Carol. BA Olivet Coll 1994; MDiv VTS 2014. D 12/21/2013 P 7/22/2014 Bp Gregory Harold Rickel. m 8/28/1999 Christine U Hosler c 1. S Thos Epis Ch Medina WA 2006-2011.

HOSLER, Samuel Odyth (Az) 408 Jamestown Road, Kearny AZ 85137 **Ecum Assoc Ch of the Gd Shpd Kearny Arizona 2007-** B Seligman AZ 1945 s Odyth & Ada. BA U of Arizona 1967; BD Bex Sem 1970. D 6/28/1970 P 6/13/1971 Bp John Joseph Meakin Harte. m 12/19/1969 Carol Smith c 2. Reg Mssnr S Paul's Epis Ch Winslow AZ 1995-2006; Reg Mssnr S Geo's Epis Ch Holbrook AZ 1994-2006; Reg Missioneer Dio Arizona Phoenix AZ 1994-2005; Cn Dio Nthrn Michigan Marquette MI 1986-1993; Estrn Upper Peninsula Epis Convoc Moran MI 1986-1991; S Jas Ch Burley ID 1976-1986; R St Matthews Epis Ch Rupert ID 1976-1986; Assoc Chr Ch Delaware City DE 1975-1976; Imm Ch On The Green New Castle DE 1975-1976; Asst S Lk's Ch Scranton PA 1972-1975; Asst Trin Cathd Phoenix AZ 1970-1971. Associated Parishes; ECom; EPF 1969; Land Viii; RWF; Sindicators; Synagogy.

HOSPADOR, Dorothea Cecelia (NJ) 247 Carr Ave, Keansburg NJ 07734 B Perth Amboy NJ 1945 d Chester & Dorothea. D 5/9/2015 Bp William H Stokes. c 2.

HOSTER JR, David William (Tex) 30003 Edgewood Drive, Georgetown TX 78628 **Int S Andr's Ch Bryan TX 2012-** B Philadelphia PA 1947 s David & Marilyn. BA Ken 1969; MDiv Yale DS 1973. D 6/11/1973 Bp Scott Field Bailey P 6/1/1974 Bp James Milton Richardson. m 4/8/1973 Terrie C Hoster c 4. P-in-c S Chris's Ch Killeen TX 2017, Int 2012; Int S Jas Ch Austin TX 2015-2017; Int S Jas' Epis Ch La Grange TX 2013-2014; Int S Mary's Ch Bellville TX 2010-2012; R S Geo's Ch Austin TX 1989-2010; R S Thos Ch Wharton TX 1983-1989; Chapl S Steph's Sch Austin TX 1981-1983; S Steph's Epis Sch Austin TX 1980-1983; Asst Chapl S Steph's Sch Austin TX 1980-1981;

Asst Trin Ch Longview TX 1977-1980; H Comf Epis Ch Sprg TX 1974-1977; The Great Cmsn Fndt Houston TX 1974-1977. "Sermons at St. Geo's 2007," Lulu, 2008; "Sermons at St. Geo's 2006," Lulu, 2007; "Continuous Creation," Lulu, 2007.

HOSTER, Elizabeth M (O) Trinity Episcopal Church, 316 Adams Street, Toledo OH 43604 **R Trin Ch Toledo OH 2007-; COM Dio Ohio Cleveland 2009-** B Columbus OH 1965 d George & Nancy. BA Ohio U 1987; MDiv Sewanee: The U So, TS 2003. D 9/19/2002 P 6/7/2003 Bp William Michie Klusmeyer. m 11/23/2009 Barbara E Clarke. S Jn's Epis Ch Charleston WV 2003-2007.

HOSTETLER, Hugh Steiner (WMich) 313B 15th Ave S, Surfside Bch SC 29575 **Ret 1987-** B Sugarcreek OH 1922 s Lester & Charity. BD UTS 1950; Cert Amer Fndt of Rel & Psych 1957; BA Bethel U 2043. D 9/18/1971 P 6/1/1972 Bp Walter C Klein. m 6/7/1952 Harriet Hostetler. Supply P Trin Ch Three Rivers MI 1999-2001; Supply P S Steph's Epis Ch Plainwell MI 1989-1996; R S Paul's Epis Ch Dowagiac MI 1981-1987; Supply P S Paul's Epis Ch Grand Rapids MI 1980; Cn The Cathd Ch Of S Jas So Bend IN 1972-1979; Pstr Counslr Amer Fndt Rel & Psych NY NY 1955-1957; Grp Mnstry E Harlem Prot Par 1948-1955; Mem of Exec Coun Dio Wstrn Michigan Kalamazoo MI 1985-1987. Diplomate Amer Psych Assn; No Amer Angl Soc.

HOSTETTER, Jane (USC) 2303 NE Seaview Dr, Jensen Beach FL 34957 B NJ 1952 d Frederick & Blanche. D 12/15/2007 Bp Leo Frade. Candidate for H Ord All SS Epis Ch Jensen Bch FL 2007-2010.

HOTCHKISS, Thomas S (Dal) 11122 Midway Rd, Dallas TX 75229 **Ch Of The Gd Shpd Dallas TX 2014-** B Washington DC 1960 s George & Mary. BA Van 1982; MA Fuller TS 1990; MDiv VTS 1993. D 6/22/1993 P 5/14/1994 Bp Alex Dockery Dickson. m 5/10/1986 Marcia W Wheat c 2. Vice-R S Mart's Epis Ch Houston TX 2012-2014; R Ch Of The Adv Nashville TN 2001-2012; Chapl Adv Day Sch Birmingham AL 1995-2001; Cn The Cathd Ch Of The Adv Birmingham AL 1995-2001; Asst to R S Lk's Epis Ch Jackson TN 1993-1995; Yth Dir S Jn's Epis Ch Memphis TN 1987-1991; Min to Yth and YA Sait Jn's Epis Ch Memphis TN 1987-1991.

HOTRA, Nancy Louise (WMich) 9733 Sterling, Richland MI 49083 **Ecum Relatns Off Dio Wstrn Michigan Kalamazoo MI 2011-** B Bay City MI 1946 d Robert & Doris. BS U MI 1969; PharmD U MI 1971; MDiv SWTS 1997. D 6/21/1997 P 1/17/1998 Bp Edward Lewis Lee Jr. m 8/26/1972 Nicholas J Hotra c 2. R Ch Of The Resurr Battle Creek MI 1997-2007.

HOTZE, Janice A (Ak) Po Box 91, Haines AK 99827 **Vic S Mich And All Ang Ch Haines AK 1992-** B Berwyn IL 1948 d Wilfred & Elaine. BA Blackburn Coll 1970; MDiv SWTS 1974; Cert U of Alaska 1994; MA U of Alaska 2004. D 9/15/1980 P 5/1/1981 Bp William Augustus Jones Jr. S Phil's Ch Wrangell AK 1987-1988; Dio Alaska Fairbanks AK 1983-1986; Stephens Coll Columbia MO 1981-1982; Chapl Stephens Coll Columbia MO 1980-1983; Calv Ch Columbia MO 1980-1981; Trin Ch S Louis MO 1975-1979; Dir Emm Epis Ch La Grange IL 1975-1976. SocMary 1996.

HOUCK III, Ira Chauncey (USC) 120 Norse Dr, Columbia SC 29229 **Trin Cathd Columbia SC 2015-; P Assoc Gr Ch Pittsburgh PA 2001-; Off Of Bsh For ArmdF New York NY 1992-** B Pittsburgh PA 1953 s Ira & Jeannine. BA U of So Carolina 1975; MDiv VTS 1980; DMin Pittsburgh TS 1991. D 6/14/1980 P 12/15/1980 Bp Robert Bracewell Appleyard. m 5/26/1979 Margaret Houck c 1. Cn For Mnstrs Cathd Ch Of The Nativ Bethlehem PA 1991-1992; R S Ptr's Brentwood PA 1983-1991; S Ptr's Epis Ch Brentwood Pittsburgh PA 1983-1990; Cur Ch Of The Ascen Pittsburgh PA 1981-1983; Chapl S Eliz's Hosp Washington DC 1980-1981. ira.houck11@gmail.com

HOUCK, John Bunn (Chi) 5236 S Cornell Ave, Chicago IL 60615 B Little Rock AR 1936 s Jesse & Jane. BS Mississippi St U 1958; TCU 1961; MDiv SWTS 1964; Kirchliche Hochschule Wuppertal DE 1965; MA U Chi 1968; PhD Illinois Inst of Tech 1974. D 6/18/1964 Bp Theodore H McCrea P 2/12/1965 Bp Roderic Norman Coote. m 3/18/2014 Thelma Torres Houck c 2. Vic S Geo/S Mths Ch Chicago IL 2004-2011, P-in-c 2001-2004; Asst Ch Of S Paul And The Redeem Chicago IL 1988-1991; Pstr Counslg Serv Of Grtr Chicago IL 1976-1996; Pstr So Cmnty Ch Chicago IL 1975-1976; Campus Min Illinois Inst Of Tech Chicago IL 1968-1976; Campus Min Untd Campus Mnstry Chicago IL 1968-1976; Int Ch Of The Gd Shpd Momence IL 1967-1968; P LocTen Emm Epis Ch La Grange IL 1965-1966; Serv Ch In Germany 1964-1965. Auth, "Leiblichkeit Und Grenzen In Praktischer Theologie," *Leiblichkeit Als Hauptthema Der Praktische Theologie*, 1997; Auth, "Pstr Psychol -- The Fee For Serv Model & Profsnl Identity, Journ Of Rel And Hlth, Vol. 16, No. 3," *1977*, 1977. AAPC, Fell 1973; APA 1975; Chicago Psychol Assn 1990-1994; Illinois Psychol Assn 1995; Intl Transactional Analysis Assn 1974.

HOUCK, Kay M (EMich) **P-in-c Trin Epis Ch Lexington MI 2015-** B Virginia Beach VA 1984 d Theodore & Margaret. BS Florida Sthrn Coll 2006; M.Div SWTS 2009. D 8/3/2011 P 3/28/2012 Bp Gladstone Bailey Adams III. m 6/20/2015 Matthew Alan Neddo. Chr Ch Binghamton NY 2013-2015; P-in-c Zion Epis Ch Windsor NY 2012-2015. revkaymhouck@gmail.com

HOUGH III, Charles (Dal) 2900 Alemeda St, Fort Worth TX 76108 B Findlay OH 1954 s Charles & Alice. BA U of Texas 1976; MDiv Nash 1979. D 6/10/1979 Bp Archibald Donald Davies P 5/31/1980 Bp Robert Elwin Terwilliger. m

8/10/1973 Marilyn Hough c 2. Cn Dio Ft Worth Ft Worth TX 1994-2008; R S Andr's Ch Grand Prairie TX 1989-1993; R Gd Shpd Granbury TX 1982-1989; Ch Of The Redeem Sarasota FL 1981-1982; Ch Of The Epiph Richardson TX 1979-1981. Soc of H Cross 1983. S Geo Awd BSA 1981.

HOUGH, George Willard (NwPa) 904 Holiday Hills Dr, Hollidaysburg PA 16648 B Williamsport PA 1938 s Eben & Marian. BA Leh 1960; STB PDS 1963; MA S Fran Coll Loretto PA 1989. D 6/17/1963 Bp Joseph Thomas Heistand P 3/1/1964 Bp William Crittenden. m 8/19/1961 Elizabeth P Hough c 5. R S Jas' Memi Titusville PA 1992-1998; S Jas Memi Epis Ch Titusville PA 1992-1997; Ch Of The H Cross No E PA 1989-1992; R Gr Ch Waverly NY 1989-1992; R H Trin Epis Ch Hollidaysburg PA 1975-1989; Vic S Mich And All Ang Ch Middletown PA 1973-1975; Asst S Jn's Epis Ch Lancaster PA 1972-1973; Chr Ch Milton PA 1966-1972; Vic S Jas Epis Ch Exch PA 1966-1972; St Jas Epis Ch Exch PA 1966-1972; Vic Ch Of The H Trin Houtzdale PA 1963-1966; Vic S Lawr's Osceola Mills PA 1963-1966. Theta Kappa Alpha.

HOUGH, Johnnie Lynne (Miss) 2501 Gulf Ave Apt 2, Gulfport MS 39501 **Died 12/22/2015** B Louisville MS 1938 d John & Lena. Gulf Coast Jr Coll; Phillips Coll; Wm Carey U; 1985. D 2/18/1996 Bp Alfred Marble Jr. c 2. Chapl Mem Hosp Gulfport MS 1996-2015; D S Patricks Epis Ch Long Bch MS 1996-2015; D S Ptr's By The Sea Gulfport MS 1996-1999. "D As Hosp Chapl," Many Servnt/Cowley, 2004. AEHC. St Steph Awd Naad 2005.

HOUGHTON, Alanson Bigelow (Mass) 43 Blockade Dr, Pawleys Island SC 29585 **Died 1/24/2016** B Corning NY 1930 s Amory & Laura. MBA Harv 1959; GTS 1966; LLD Emerson Coll 1970. D 6/4/1966 P 12/1/1966 Bp Horace W B Donegan. Ret 1993-2016; S Steph's Epis Ch Charleston SC 1985-1993; Ch Of The Heav Rest New York NY 1974-1983; R Chr Ch Shaker Heights OH 1969-1974; Cur The Ch Of The Epiph New York NY 1966-1969. Auth, *Be Not Afraid-Words of Hope & Promise*; Auth, *Epis*; Auth, *Living Ch*; Auth, *Partnr in Love-Ingredients For A Deep & Lovely Mar*; Auth, *Priv Choices-Publ Consequences*; Auth, *Readers Dig*.

HOUGHTON, Frederick Lord (EMich) 4138 N Francis Shores Ave, Sanford MI 48657 B Ionia MI 1941 s Edwin & Katharine. BA Ken 1963; MA MI SU 1967; STB GTS 1969. D 6/11/1969 Bp Charles Ellsworth Bennison Jr P 7/1/1970 Bp The Bishop Of Damaraland. c 2. Dn of Formation Stds Dio Estrn Michigan Saginaw MI 1999-2001; R, Tri Par Cluster Dio Estrn Michigan Saginaw MI 1996-2005; Epis Tri Par Cluster Gladwin MI 1996-1999; H Fam Epis Ch Midland MI 1991-1996; Cathd Ch Of S Paul Detroit MI 1989-1991; S Phil And S Steph Epis Ch Detroit MI 1982-1989; R S Paul's Epis Ch Brighton MI 1977-1981; Vic S Ptr's Ch New York NY 1974-1977; Dir S Mary's Mssn (Namibia) Oshikango 1969-1970. LAND.

HOUGHTON, John William (NI) 609 Houghton St., Culver IN 46511 **Assoc Chr Epis Ch Pottstown PA 2008-; Chapl & Chair, Dept. of Rel Stds The Hill Sch Pottstown PA 2007-** B South Bend Indiana 1953 s Forrest & Leta. AB Harv 1975; MA Indiana U 1977; Dplma Ya Berk 1989; MA Yale DS 1989; MMS U of Notre Dame 1991; PhD U of Notre Dame 1994. D 10/16/2006 P 5/25/2007 Bp Edward Stuart Little II. Co-Auth, "Tolkien, King Alfred and Boethius: Platonist Views of Evil in The Lord of the Rings," *Tolkien Stds*, W Viriginia U, 2005; Auth, "Aug in the Cottage of Lost Play: The Ainulindalë as Asterisk Cosmogony," *Tolkien the Medievalist*, Routledge, 2002; Auth, "St. Bede among the Controversialists: A Survey," *Amer Benedictine Revs*, 1999; Auth, "No Bp, No Queen: Queens Regnant and the Ord of Wmn," *Angl and Epis Hist*, 1998; Auth, "The Augustinian Tradition: A Different Voice," *Rel Educ*, 1984. Nelson Burr Prize HSEC 1998; Dorothy A. Given Fllshp ECF 1990; Lansing Hicks Serv Prize Ya Berk 1989. jhoughton@thehill.org

HOUGHTON, Phil (WNY) 105 S. Clinton St., Olean NY 14760 **Died 1/9/2017** B Joliet IL 1942 s Francis & Marguerite. BA W Chester U of Pennsylvania 1965; BD Westminster TS 1971; MDiv Westminster TS 1997. D 11/17/1971 P 5/1/1972 Bp Alexander D Stewart. m 4/20/1968 Ann Houghton c 3. R S Steph's Ch Olean NY 2008-2011; S Jas Bedford PA 2001-2007; The Ch Of The H Sprt Ocean City MD 2000; R S Paul's Ch Weston WV 1997-2000; R Memi Ch Of The H Nativ Jenkintown PA 1989-1997; Asst To R All SS Ch Wynnewood PA 1986-1989; S Geo's Ch Waynesburg PA 1984-1986; S Geo's Epis Ch Sanford ME 1982-1983; Nevil Memi Ch Of S Geo Ardmore PA 1978-1981; S Ptr's Epis Ch Uniontown PA 1977-1978; S Barth's Ch Nashville TN 1975-1977; Chapl Greene Cnty Jail 2017. Auth, "Bk Revs," *Eternity mag*, 1972. Ch Soc 1981; EFAC 1981.

HOUGHTON, William Clokey (NwT) 27 Painted Canyon Place, The Woodlands TX 77381 B Pasadena CA 1930 s William & Carolyn. BA U CA Los Angeles 1955; MDiv CDSP 1958. D 6/2/1958 Bp Francis E I Bloy P 3/15/1959 Bp Lyman Cunningham Ogilby. m 5/14/1966 Candida B Baguyos c 1. Int S Barn Epis Ch Houston TX 1999-2009; Pres Stndg Com Dio NW Texas Lubbock TX 1990, Stndg Com 1987-1990, Dioc Rgstr 1983-1996, Rgstr 1983-1996, COM and Mssn 1980, Exec Coun 1976-1980; Mem Stndg Com Dio NW Texs 1987-1990; Mem Exec Coun Dio NW Texas 1983-1987; Vic All SS Epis Mssn Perryton TX 1980-1996; Mem Rgstr Dio NW Texas 1980-1983; Mem Exec Coun Dio NW Texas 1976-1980; Vic/R S Ptr's Epis Ch Borger TX 1975-1996;

S Paul's Epis Ch Dumas TX 1975-1981; Serv Schools and Ch in the Philippines 1958-1975. whoughclok@aol.com

HOUGLAND, Erin Elizabeth (Ind) **D Dio Indianapolis Indianapolis IN 2017-** D 6/1/2017 Bp Jennifer Baskerville-Burrows.

✠ HOUGLAND JR, The Rt Rev Whayne Miller (WMich) Episcopal Diocese of Western Michigan, 535 S Burdick St, Kalamazoo MI 49007 **Bp Dio Wstrn Michigan Kalamazoo MI 2013-** B Owensboro KY 1962 s Whayne & Elaine. BA U of Kentucky 1986; MDiv Sewanee: The U So, TS 1998. D 6/13/1998 P 12/19/1998 Bp Don Adger Wimberly Con 9/28/2013 for WMich. m 8/4/1984 Dana L Hougland c 3. R S Lk's Ch Salisbury NC 2005-2013; Cn Evang Chr Ch Cathd Lexington KY 1998-2004. wmhougland@edwm.org

HOUI-LEE, Samuel Sroun (Oly) 34608 8th Ave Sw, Federal Way WA 98023 **Dio Olympia Seattle 2005-** B Phnom Penh KH 1955 s Ock & Lim. D 6/28/1997 Bp Vincent Waydell Warner P 3/1/1998 Bp Sanford Zangwill Kaye Hampton. m 5/24/1992 Phet Von Gvanith. D H Fam of Jesus Epis Ch Tacoma WA 1997-1998.

HOUK, David Stangebye (Dal) 848 Harter Road, Dallas TX 75218 **R S Jn's Epis Ch Dallas TX 2006-** B Ludington MI 1970 s Charles & Vicki. BA Wheaton Coll 1992; Wheaton Coll 1998; MDiv TESM 2000. D 6/9/2001 P 12/15/2001 Bp Robert William Duncan. m 9/16/1995 Meghan S Houk c 4. Cur/Assoc R Ch Of S Mths Dallas TX 2001-2006; Asst in Mnstry St Andrews Epis Ch Pittsburgh PA 2000-2001.

HOUK, Vickie Lynn (SwVa) 739 Prospect Ave., Pulaski VA 24301 B Rapid City SD 1948 d Rodney & Lois. BS So Dakota St U 1970; MDiv Sewanee: The U So, TS 1989. D 7/2/1989 Bp Craig Barry Anderson P 4/19/1990 Bp James Russell Moodey. R Chr Epis Ch Pulaski VA 1996-2014; Int Trin Ch Allnce OH 1995-1996; Int S Paul's Ch Medina OH 1994-1995; P-in-c Zion Ch Monroeville OH 1993-1994; Cur Gr Epis Ch Sandusky OH 1990-1992; Cur S Michaels In The Hills Toledo OH 1989-1990. vlhouk@comcast.net

HOULE, Michael Anthony (EMich) 4525 Birch Run Rd, Birch Run MI 48415 B Detroit MI 1935 s Jack & Thelma. BA Sacr Heart Sem 1958; MDiv S Johns Prov Sem 1980; MS Wayne 1980. Rec 2/27/1998 as Priest Bp Edwin Max Leidel Jr. m 1/17/1986 Elaine Barbara Houle. R S Mk's Epis Ch Bridgeport MI 1998-2006; Serv RC Ch 1962-1981.

HOULIK, Michael Andrew (Colo) 2712 Geneva Place, Longmont CO 80503 B Wichita KS 1951 s Anton & Barbara. BA U of Kansas 1973; MDiv Nash 1978. D 4/25/1978 P 11/1/1978 Bp Edward Clark Turner. m 5/29/1976 Barbara Ann Houlik c 2. Mssnr Dio Colorado Denver CO 2005-2010; R S Mary Magd Ch Boulder CO 2004-2013; R S Mary Magd Ch Boulder CO 1991-2013; R Ch Of The Gd Samar Gunnison CO 1980-1991; Cur S Jas Ch Wichita KS 1978-1980.

HOUPT, Cameron Wheeler (Colo) 10222 W Ida Ave Unit 238, Littleton CO 80127 B Rochester NY 1943 d Harold & Jean. BS Syr 1965; MS Mia 1967. D 11/15/2008 Bp Robert John O'Neill. c 3.

HOUSE, Karen Ellen (CFla) 1120 Sunshine Ave, Leesburg FL 34748 **D S Fran Of Assisi Ch Bushnell FL 2013-** B Pittsburgh PA 1950 d Carnot & Cleone. BSEd Ohio U 1972. D 12/13/2008 Bp John Wadsworth Howe. c 2. D Corpus Christi Epis Ch Okahumpka FL 2008-2012. OSL 2007.

HOUSER, Lucy Anne Latham (Ore) 11476 SW Riverwoods Rd., Portland OR 97219 **Bd Epis Sr Living Serv 2002-; Co-Convenor- Bd, EPM Mentor Epis Prison Mnstry OR 1997-; D Gr Memi Portland OR 1995-** B Durham NC 1939 d Ector & Grace. U of Virginia 1959; BA Whitman Coll 1960; S Georges Coll Jerusalem IL 1990. D 3/13/1989 Bp Robert Louis Ladehoff. m 9/1/1961 Douglas Guy Houser c 3. Natl Cler Rep - W Curs 1999-2002; Bd Epis Schools 1996-1999; Coordntr Dio Oregon Portland OR 1989-2005, Pres - Dioc Ecw 2002-2005, Dioc Coun 1998-2001; D All SS Ch Portland OR 1989-1995.

HOUSER III, Richard Truett (Tex) 13131 Fry Rd, Cypress TX 77433 **Trin Ch Houston TX 2014-** B Corpus Christi TX 1978 s Richard & Melinda Ann. BA Texas A&M U 2001; MDiv Sewanee: The U So, TS 2009. D 6/20/2009 Bp C Andrew Doyle P 1/12/2010 Bp Rayford Baines High Jr. m 10/28/2006 Patricia Muras c 1. Dio Texas Houston TX 2013-2014, 2011-2012; S Aid's Ch Cypress TX 2009-2011.

HOUSER, Teresa (Neb) D 6/17/2017 Bp Scott Scott Barker.

HOUSNER-RITTER, Jenny Lee (Mich) **Yth Dir S Jas' Epis Ch Dexter MI 2011-; CE Dir S Paul's Epis Ch Brighton MI 2008-** B Howell 1970 d Gerald & Doris. D Formation Whitaker Inst 2013. D 6/22/2013 Bp Wendell Nathaniel Gibbs Jr. c 1.

HOUSTON, Barbara Pearce (EC) 206 North Fairlane Drive, Box 939, Grifton NC 28530 B Louisville KY 1940 d Edward & Sue. Dio Ec Sch For Mnstry; U of Kentucky Spencerian Coll Murray St Colle. D 8/17/1996 Bp Brice Sidney Sanders. m 12/20/1961 Russell Houston. D S Mary's Ch Kinston NC 1996-2015. Ord Julian Of Norwich.

HOUZE, Jared Foster (NwT) **Vic All SS Ch Colorado City TX 2015-; S Steph's Ch Sweetwater TX 2015-** B Dallas TX 1981 s Daniel & Kimberly. BBS Hardin-Simmons U 2004; MA Hardin-Simmons U 2007; MDiv Epis TS Of The SW 2013; MDiv Epis TS of the SW 2013. D 1/19/2013 Bp James Scott Mayer. m 8/7/2004 Ericka M Colon c 3. Emm Epis Ch San Angelo TX 2013-2015.

HOVENCAMP, Otis (WNY) 85 Wide Beach Rd, Irving NY 14081 B Bath PA 1937 s Otis & Lillian. BA Kent St U 1959; MDiv SWTS 1971; DMin Chr TS 1972. D 8/28/1971 P 3/1/1972 Bp John P Craine. m 5/31/1970 Maxine C Hovencamp c 3. Ch Of The Adv Buffalo NY 1999-2001; St Mk Epis Ch No Tonawanda NY 1998-1999; S Pat's Ch Buffalo NY 1990-1998; R S Jn's Ch Medina NY 1987-1990; Vic Trin Ch Bryan OH 1977-1987; R All Faith Epis Ch Charlotte Hall MD 1974-1977; Stff Chr Ch Cathd Indianapolis IN 1971-1972. Theta Phi.

HOVERSTOCK, Rolland William (Colo) 1419 Pine St, Boulder CO 80302 **Died 10/2/2015** B Buffalo NY 1942 s Gerald & Margueritte. BS U CO 1970; Cert Sewanee: The U So, TS 1980. D 4/25/1983 P 12/1/1983 Bp William Harvey Wolfrum. m 8/19/1967 Beatrice Black c 3. R S Jn's Epis Ch Boulder CO 2004-2011, Asst 1983-2004; R Ch Of The Gd Shpd Sioux Falls SD 1987-1991. Ord Of S Jn.

HOVEY JR, Frederick Franklin (WNC) 724 Cobblestone Dr, Ormond Beach FL 32174 **Ret 1979-** B Jacksonville FL 1930 s Frederick & Margery. LTh SWTS 1965. D 6/24/1965 Bp James Loughlin Duncan P 12/27/1965 Bp Henry I Louttit. m 6/6/1953 Velva LaVonia Hovey c 2. Int S Jas Epis Ch Ormond Bch FL 2008-2010; Dn Wstrn Deanry Dio Wstrn No Carolina Asheville NC 1973-1978; R Ch Of The Incarn Highlands NC 1972-1978; Asst Ch Of The Redeem Sarasota FL 1968-1972; Vic Gloria Dei Epis Ch Cocoa FL 1965-1968; ExCoun Dio SW Florida Parrish FL 1970-1972, Chair Dnry Coll Chapl Prog 1969.

HOWANSTINE JR, John Edwin (Md) 3090 Broomes Island Road, Port Republic MD 20676 B Carlisle PA 1949 s John & Gloria. BA Florida Presb Coll 1971; MDiv Wstrn TS 1979; Cert SWTS 1980. D 6/14/1980 Bp Quintin Ebenezer Primo Jr P 12/13/1980 Bp James Winchester Montgomery. m 12/30/1977 Catherine Johnson Howanstine c 2. R Chr Ch Port Republic MD 1985-2014; Assoc R All SS' Epis Ch Chevy Chase MD 1982-1985; Asst to the R S Mk's Ch Evanston IL 1980-1981. Bro Of S Andr.

HOWARD, Anne Sutherland (Los) 950 Dena Way, Santa Barbara CA 93111 **Exec Dir The Beatitudes Soc Santa Barbara CA 2006-** B Red Wing MN 1952 d Carl & Jean. BA U CA 1975; MA EDS 1985. D 6/25/1988 P 1/21/1989 Bp Frederick Houk Borsch. m 8/9/1975 Randall Hugh Howard c 1. Exec Dir The Beatitudes Soc 2006-2015; Assoc R Trin Epis Ch Santa Barbara CA 1998-2006, Prchr-in-Res 2006-; Prog Dir Mt. Calv Retreat Hse Santa Barbara CA 1996-1999; Mt Calv Monstry Santa Barbara CA 1996-1998; Cn Dio Los Angeles Los Angeles CA 1993-1995; All SS-By-The-Sea Par Santa Barbara CA 1988-1993. Auth, "Claiming the Beatitudes: Nine Stories for a New Generation," Alb, 2009. Core Curric in Preaching Coll of Preachers 1999.

HOWARD, Coleen Gayle (Ore) PO Box 1319, Gresham OR 97030 B Westwood CA 1939 d Eric & Ruby. Diac Acad for the Formation of Mnstry 2013. D 6/29/2013 Bp Michael Hanley. m 12/20/1993 Charles Fredrick Howard c 2.

HOWARD, Cynthia A (CGC) 2005 Boxwood Ave, Andalusia AL 36421 **R S Mary's Epis Ch Andalusia AL 2011-** B Carthage MO 1954 d Charles & Gloria. BS Missouri Sthrn St U 1976; MA U of Missouri 1978; PhD Cor 1984; MDiv Epis TS of the SW 2007. D 6/2/2007 P 12/1/2007 Bp Barry Howe. c 1. R S Anne's Ch Lees Summit MO 2007-2011; Prof And Chair U of Kansas Med Cntr 2000-2004; Assoc Prof/Prg Dir U of Alabama at Birmingham 1998-2000; Assoc Prof/Prg Dir U of Alabama at Birmingham 1988-2000; Asst Prof S Louis U 1984-1988.

HOWARD, David Z (SO) B 1940 MDiv Pittsburgh TS 1967; MEd U Pgh 1968; Cert Childrens Med Cntr 1994. Trans 12/1/1992 Bp William Grant Black. m 2/20/1971 Albertha Howard c 4. P H Sprt Epis Ch Cincinnati OH 2007-2009, 1997-2004; Dio Sthrn Ohio Cincinnati OH 2004-2005, 1992-1994; Trin Ch Lawrenceburg IN 1995-1996; P Ch Of S Mich And All Ang Cincinnati OH 1991-1993; P Dio Liberia Monrovia 1979-1982, Asst R/ Mem of Stndg commitee/ Chairman of Com on Educ 1981-1989.

HOWARD, Francis Curzon (Ct) 116 Terry's Plain Road, Box 423, Simsbury CT 06070 **Assoc S Andr's Ch Longmeadow MA 2000-** B Bedford UK 1927 s Harry & Eleanor. Lon GB; S Aidans TS GB 1957. Trans 9/1/1971 Bp Alexander D Stewart. m 9/1/1973 Joyce Howard c 2. Trin Sum Chap Kennebunk Bch ME 2000-2010; R Trin Ch Tariffville CT 1976-1998; Ch Of The Atone Westfield MA 1972-1976; Serv Ch of Bermuda 1965-1971; Serv Ch of Engl 1957-1965; Wrdn of New Engl OSL 1973-1977. *arts Ch mag*, 2003. Chapl Ord of S Lk 1972-1985. Cn Dio Sokato 1986.

HOWARD III, George Williams (Spr) 1811 Highland Vw, Mount Vernon IL 62864 **Vic S Jn's Epis Ch Albion IL 2011-** B Mount Vernon IL 1935 s George & Mabel. BS U IL 1956; JD U IL 1959. D 6/29/2004 Bp Peter Hess Beckwith P 12/8/2012 Bp Daniel Hayden Martins. m 12/21/1957 Sylvia Lord c 2. Asstg D S Jas Epis Ch Dahlgren IL 2004-2010. gwh@mvn.net

HOWARD, Harry Lee (ETenn) 2668 Karenwood Dr, Maryville TN 37804 B Dubuque IA 1945 s Hillard & Johanna. BA Tennessee Wesleyan Coll 1967; MTh SMU Perkins 1970; MA SMU 1971; PhD U of Tennessee 1980. D 6/18/2005 P 1/21/2006 Bp Charles Glenn VonRosenberg. m 6/24/1966 Nancy Ellen Howard c 1. S Andr's Ch Maryville TN 2006.

HOWARD II, Joseph B (Tenn) 2458 Center Point Rd, Hendersonville TN 37075 **P-in-c S Jos Of Arimathaea Ch Hendersonvlle TN 2010-, R** B Asheville NC 1980 s Joseph & Mamie Lee. BA U NC Asheville 2003; MDiv Sewanee: The U So, TS 2006. D 6/10/2006 P 12/17/2006 Bp Bertram Nelson Herlong. m 6/3/2006 Anna A Howard c 2. Vic S Fran Ch Goodlettsvlle TN 2007-2009; Dio Tennessee Nashville TN 2006-2007, Chr Formation Cmsn 2012-, Cathd Chapt 2010-, Ecum Off 2008-2013; Bp & Coun Trin Ch Winchester TN 2006-2007. Auth, "Emerging Questions," *LivCh*, LivCh Fndt, 2011; Auth, "Reviving the Quadrilateral," *LivCh*, LivCh Fndt, 2009; Co-Auth, "Approaches to Ch, Cmnty and Age: Discussing the Ideas of Stanley Hauerwas," *Aging & Sprtlty*, The Amer Soc on Aging, 2003.

HOWARD, Karin D (SwVa) 4461 S Main St Apt 111, Acworth GA 30101 **Chapl Sthrn Care Hospice Roanoke VA 2007-** B Chicago IL 1937 d John & Margaret. Watts Sch of Nrsng 1978; Lic VTS 1990. D 6/2/1990 Bp Peter J Lee P 3/1/1991 Bp A(rthur) Heath Light. m 1/2/1988 William A Lindsay c 4. Asst S Jn's Ch Roanoke VA 2004-2007; S Phil's In The Hills Tucson AZ 2000-2001; All SS Epis Ch Atlanta GA 1998-2000; Trin Epis Ch Rocky Mt VA 1993-1998; Asst R S Paul's Epis Ch Lynchburg VA 1990-1993. Comp H Cross.

HOWARD, Kenneth W(ayne) (WA) 9 Liberty Heights Court, Germantown MD 20874 **Auth-Presenter-Consult-Coach PracticingParadoxy.com Germantown MD 2010-; Prncpl Consult Sprtl Formation Cntr Darnestown MD 2010-; Chair - Rel Land Use Working Grp Faith Cmnty Advsry Coun 2013-** B Lubbock TX 1952 s Kenneth & Ann. BS Old Dominion U 1979; MEd Virginia Commonwealth U 1989; MDiv VTS 1993; MDiv VTS 1993; Glastonbury Abbey 2004; Camb - Westcott Hse 2005; Yale DS 2007. D 6/5/1993 P 12/12/1993 Bp Frank Harris Vest Jr. m 2/14/1976 Rhee M Howard c 2. Founding Vic S Nich Epis Ch Germantown MD 1995-2017; Asst Ch OF The Ascen Gaithersburg MD 1993-1995; Eccl Trial Crt Dio Washington Washington DC 2007-2012, GC Alt Del (74th Conv) 2003-2006, T/F on Human Sxlty Dialogue (Cnvnr) 2003-2005, Bp's Rep for Epis-Jewish Dialogue 2002-2003, Bp's Pstr Rep to Chr Ch, Accokeek 2001-2002, Dioc Coun (Exec Com) 2000-2003, GC Alt Del (73rd Conv) 2000-2003, GC Alt Del (72nd Conv) 1997-2000, Dioc Coun (Mem) 1996-2003. Auth, "Excommunicating the Faithful: Jewish Chrsnty in the Early Ch," KDP, 2014; Auth, "Paradoxy: Creating Chr Cmnty Beyond Us & Them," Paraclete Press, 2010; Auth, "A New Middle Way: Surviving and Thriving in the Coming Rel Realignment," *ATR*, The Epis Ch, 2010; Auth, "Jewish Chrsnty in the Early Ch," VTS, 1993; Auth, "Power Meetings: Working Effectively in Groups," Ken Howard Assoc, Inc., 1990; Auth, "A Comprehensive Theory of Adult Educ Motivation," *Adult Educ Quarterly*, Sage Pub, 1989; Co-Auth, "Strategic Plnng," *The Bd Effectiveness Trng Series*, Commonwealth of Virginia, 1988; Co-Auth, "Ldrshp," *The Bd Effectiveness Trng Series*, Commonwealth of Virginia, 1987; Co-Auth, "Decision Making," *The Bd Effectiveness Trng Series*, Commonwealth of Virginia, 1987; Co-Auth, "Mgmt Skills," *The Trnr Effectiveness Series*, Commonwealth of Virginia, 1986; Co-Auth, "Presentation Skills," *The Trnr Effectiveness Series*, Commonwealth of Virginia, 1985; Co-Auth, "Design Skills," *The Trnr Effectiveness Series*, Commonwealth of Virginia, 1984; Co-Auth, "Adolescence: Intervention Strategies," Commonwealth of Virginia, 1983. Amer Soc for Trng & Dvlpmt 1981-1991; Washington Epis Cler Assn 1993. hon in Ch Hist VTS 1990. rector@saintnicks.com

HOWARD, Leonard Rice (Haw) 98-1128 Malualua St, Aiea HI 96701 B Detroit MI 1933 s Wilkie & Carolyn. BA Albion Coll 1954; MD U MI 1957. D 11/7/1993 Bp Donald Purple Hart. m 6/18/1955 Marilyn Joanne Howard. D S Tim's 1993-1996. Ord Of S Lk.

HOWARD, Lois Waser (Lex) 713 Dicksonia Ct, Lexington KY 40517 B Pottstown PA 1937 d John & Agnes. BS U of Nebraska 1959; MA U MI 1963; MRE PrTS 1968; MRE PrTS 1968; BA Estrn Kentucky U 1987. D 6/26/1999 Bp Don Adger Wimberly. m 2/3/1968 Scott Howard c 2. D Ch Of The Resurr Nicholasville KY 2008-2012; Min of Chr Formation S Raphael's Ch Lexington KY 2006-2007; Min Of Chr Formation Emm Epis Ch Winchester KY 2003-2005; Serv Presb Ch 2000-2003; Min of Chr Formation Presb Ch Of Danville Danville KY 2000; Min of Chr Formation Ch Of The Gd Shpd Lexington KY 1999-2000, Min of Chr Formation 1999-2000; Min Of Chr Formation Chr Ch Cathd Lexington KY 1988-1994, Asst Org 1987-1988. Writer, "Using Godly Play w Alzheimers," *The Diakonia*, No Amer Assn of Deacons, 2010; Writer, "Using Godly Play w Alzheimers," *The Advoc*, The Epis Dio Lexington, 2009; Writer, "Godly Play w Adults The Advoc," *The Advoc*, The Epis Dio Lexington, 2002. AGO 1986; NAAD 1999.

HOWARD, Mary Merle (SeFla) **Mem Dio SE Florida Bdgt Com 2005-; Chair Dio SE Florida Environ Cmsn 2003-; Instr SE Florida Dioc Sch for Chr Stds 2003-** B Columbus MS 1942 d Merle & Eugenia. BA U GA 1964; MA U GA 1968; Cert Dioc Sch of Chr Stds 2003. D 7/26/2003 Bp Leo Frade. c 1. Admin The Epis Ch Of The Gd Shpd Tequesta FL 2004-2014, 2001-2004; Mem Dio SE Florida COM 2004-2007; D Dio SE Florida Miami 2003-2013.

HOWARD, Noah B (NC) 206 Maryland Ave, Tarboro NC 27886 B Tarboro NC 1931 s Henry & Ella. Read Under Bp. D 6/12/1976 P 6/18/1977 Bp Thomas

Augustus Fraser Jr. m 10/15/1949 Evelyn Ruth Howard. Cluster Mssnr To Yadkin Vlly Cluseter Ch Of The Gd Shpd Cooleemee NC 2001-2004.

HOWARD, Norman (SwFla) 766 Lake Forest Rd, Clearwater FL 33765 **Ret 1992-** B Fence Houses Durham UK 1926 s George & Florence. AKC Kings Coll London U 1957; St Bon Coll Warminster GB 1958; St Bon College-Warminster GB 1958. Trans 2/1/1969. m 7/28/1959 Sybil Irene Howard. Ch Of The H Cross St Petersburg FL 1995-1997, Int Vic 1993-1994; Int S Cecilia's Ch Tampa FL 1994-1996; Int S Anne Of Gr Epis Ch Seminole FL 1992-1993; Gd Samar Epis Ch Clearwater FL 1975-1992; Trst Bp Gray Inn Dio SW Florida Parrish FL 1972-1992; Vic S Jn The Div Epis Ch Sun City Cntr FL 1969-1973; Serv Jamaica Ch 1962-1969; Serv Ch Of Engl 1958-1962.

HOWARD, Sally Anne (Los) 132 N Euclid Ave, Pasadena CA 91101 **D All SS Ch Pasadena CA 2013-** B Columbia City IN 1957 d Bruce & Charlotte. BA Wheaton Coll 1980; MA Fuller Sem 1983; PhD Fuller Sem 1987; PSyD Inst of Contemporary Psychoanalysts 1997. D 6/8/2013 Bp Mary Douglas Glasspool P 1/11/2014 Bp Diane Jardine Bruce. m 5/24/1997 Peter Abelin Schou c 1.

✠ HOWARD, The Rt Rev Samuel Johnson (Fla) 325 N Market St, Jacksonville FL 32202 **Dio Florida Fndt Jacksonville FL 2012-; Bp of Florida Dio Florida Jacksonville 2003-** B Lumberton NC 1951 s Samuel & Helen. BA Wms 1973; JD Wake Forest U 1976; MDiv VTS 1989. D 6/1/1989 Bp Robert Whitridge Estill P 6/8/1990 Bp Huntington Williams Jr Con 11/1/2003 for Fla. m 6/1/1974 Marie Howard c 2. Trin Educ Fund New York NY 1998-2003; Vic Trin Par New York NY 1997-2003; R S Jas Ch Charleston SC 1992-1997; Asst R Ch OF The H Comf Charlotte NC 1989-1992. DD U So 2004; DD VTS 2004. jhoward@diocesefl.org

HOWARD, Sylvia Lord (Spr) 1811 Highland Vw, Mount Vernon IL 62864 **D S Jn's Ch Centralia IL 2006-** B Wichita Falls TX 1936 BS U IL 1958; MS Sthrn Illinois U 1977. D 6/29/2004 Bp Peter Hess Beckwith. m 12/21/1957 George Williams Howard c 2. D Trin Ch Mt Vernon IL 2004-2006.

HOWARD, Theodore B (Colo) 1419 Pine St., Boulder CO 80302 **Assoc R S Jn's Epis Ch Boulder CO 2014-, 2007-2014; Mem, Bd Examing Chapl Dio Colorado Denver CO 2011-, Mem, Front Range Exec Com 2009-** B Chicago IL 1942 s John & Dorothy. BA Dart 1964; MPA U Pgh 1968; PhD Col 1972; MDiv VTS 2007. D 6/9/2007 P 12/8/2007 Bp Robert John O'Neill. m 6/27/1992 Sallye Howard c 5.

HOWARD, William Alexander (Colo) 7168 Burnt Mill Rd, Beulah CO 81023 **Vic Ch Of S Ptr The Apos Pueblo CO 2015-, Pstr 2003-2009, 1993; S Ben Epis Ch La Veta CO 2010-** B Chattanooga TN 1939 s William & Alma. BA Trin U San Antonio 1966; MDiv Sewanee: The U So, TS 1969; MS U of Tennessee 1979; DMin Sewanee: The U So, TS 2008. D 6/10/1969 P 12/10/1969 Bp Harold Cornelius Gosnell. m 12/22/1992 Carla Jean Jackson-Howard c 4. Int Vic S Thos The Apos Epis Ch Alamosa CO 2010-2015; Dn - Sangre De Cristo Dio Colorado Denver CO 1993-1998; Chapl Parkview Epis Med Cntr Pueblo CO 1982-2003; Parkview Hosp Pueblo CO 1982-2003; Asst P St Andr Epis & H Cross Luth Ch La Junta CO 1979-1982; Asst P S Thaddaeus' Epis Ch Chattanooga TN 1976-1979; R Ch of the Redeem Mercedes TX 1969-1971; Vic Epiph Epis Ch Raymondville TX 1969-1971. OHC 1990.

HOWCOTT, Jeffernell Ophelia Green (Mich) 19320 Santa Rosa Dr, Detroit MI 48221 **D S Jn's Ch Royal Oak MI 2001-** B Dayton OH 1934 d Samuel & Mary. BS OH SU 1956; MA U of Detroit Mercy 1975; Whitaker TS 1982. D 6/20/1982 Bp H Coleman Mcgehee Jr. m 5/14/1956 James Fredrick Howcott c 2. Gvrng Bd Whitaker TS 1998-2003; Asst to Bp for Faith & Wrshp Dio Michigan Detroit MI 1983-2008; Asst All SS Ch Detroit MI 1982-2001. Auth, "Simple Abundance," *Diakoneo*, NAAD, 1999. DOK 2003; Delta Sigma Theta Sorority, Inc. 1953; NAAD 1985; Untd Black Episcopalians 1978; Whitaker TS, Bd Dir 1997-2003. St.Stephens Awd NAAD; Hall of Fame Whitaker TS.

✠ HOWE, The Rt Rev Barry (WMo) PO Box 413227, Kansas City MO 64141 **Asstg Bp of SW Florida Dio SW Florida Parrish FL 2011-, Dn St Petersburg Deanry 1988-2011** B Norristown PA 1942 s Nathan & Sarah. BA Ge 1964; MDiv PDS 1967; DMin Sewanee: The U So, TS 1989; Sewanee: The U So, TS 2001. D 6/10/1967 P 1/13/1968 Bp Robert Lionne DeWitt Con 3/14/1998 for WMo. m 6/26/1965 Mary Howe c 2. Bp of W Missouri Dio W Missouri Kansas City MO 1998-2011; Dn Cathd Ch Of S Ptr St. Petersburg FL 1987-1998; R Chr Ch S Hamilton MA 1983-1987; Par Cmsn Dio Cntrl Florida Orlando FL 1981-1983, Bd Dio 1977-1980; R S Richard's Ch Winter Pk FL 1978-1983; Cn Cathd Ch Of S Lk Orlando FL 1973-1978; Assoc S Bon Ch Sarasota FL 1971-1973; Cur S Dav Devon PA 1967-1971. DD STUSo 2001.

HOWE, Garth (Chi) 637 S Dearborn St, Chicago IL 60605 **The CPG New York NY 2017-** B San Diego CA 1955 s Guy & Mildred. D 6/17/2017 Bp Jeff Lee. m 6/20/2008 Michael Chris Terry c 1. Other Lay Position S Jas By The Sea La Jolla CA 2003-2009.

HOWE, Gregory Michael (Del) 7 Conway St, Provincetown MA 02657 **Ret Chr Ch Dover 1998-** B New York NY 1939 s James & Dorothy. BA Col 1961; STB GTS 1964; Cert S Georges Coll Jerusalem IL 1980. D 6/6/1964 Bp Horace W B Donegan P 6/5/1965 Bp John Brooke Mosley. Custodian Bk of Common Pryr 2000-2015; Dep GC Dio Delaware Wilmington 1973-1997, Off Liturg Cmsn 1971-1973; R Chr Ch Dover DE 1964-1998. Auth, "On Becoming a Confessor," *Liturg Stds, Vol. 5*, 2010; Auth, "Blessing of a Betrothal," *Changes*, 2007; Auth, "PB Translations," *LivCh*, 2006; Auth, "Expansive Lang in Cyberspace," *Gleanings*, 2001; Auth, "H Name," *H Land*, 1996; Auth, "Death, Appearance, and Reality," *Liturg Stds, Vol. 3*, 1996; Auth, "Theol Reflections on the Biotechnical Revolution," *Delaware Lawyer, Vol. 5*, 1987.

HOWE, Heath (Chi) 1229 Hinman Ave, Evanston IL 60202 **Assoc Ch Of The H Comf Kenilworth IL 2010-** B Helena AK 1968 d John & Claudia. Boston Coll 1991; MDiv CDSP 2000. D 6/17/2000 P 1/4/2001 Bp Bill Persell. m 10/6/2007 David P Jones c 2. Chapl St. Paul's Sch Concord NH 2005-2007; S Paul's Ch Concord NH 2004-2005; Asst Trin Memi Ch Binghamton NY 2000-2003.

HOWE, Jeffrey Newman (Lex) 201 Price Rd Apt 216, Lexington KY 40511 **Ldrshp Team Dio Lexington 2011-** B Maysville KY 1960 s William & Betty. BA Morehead St U 1982; MA Estrn Kentucky St U 1983. D 8/22/2009 Bp Stacy F Sauls. D Ch Of The Gd Shpd Lexington KY 2011-2016; S Mk's Ch Hazard KY 2010-2013; Exec Coun Dio Lexington Lexington 2010-2013. AED 2009.

✠ HOWE, The Rt Rev John Wadsworth (CFla) 5583 Jessamine Lane, Orlando FL 32830 **Cn Tanzania 1981-** B Chicago IL 1942 s John & Shirley. BA U of Connecticut 1964; MDiv Yale DS 1967; DD Ya 1989; DD Sewanee: The U So, TS 1990; DD Nash 1991; PhD GTF 2011. D 6/6/1967 Bp Charles Francis Hall P 6/22/1968 Bp John Henry Esquirol Con 4/15/1989 for CFla. m 9/1/1962 Karen Elvgren Howe c 3. Bp of Cntrl Florida Dio Cntrl Florida Orlando FL 1989-2012; R Truro Epis Ch Fairfax VA 1976-1989; Assoc S Steph's Ch Sewickley PA 1972-1976; Chapl Miss Porter Sch Farmington CT 1969-1972; Chapl Loomis Sch Windson CT 1967-1969. Auth, "Anointed by the Sprt," Creation Hse, 2012; Auth, "Our Angl Heritage," Cascade, 2010; Auth, "Who Swallows Jonah Today?," Bible Reading Fllshp, 1993; Auth, "Sex: Should We Change the Rules?," Creation Hse, 1991; Auth, "Which Way? A Guide for New Christians," Morehouse-Barlow, 1973. Acts 29 Mnstrs 1977; Fllshp of Witness 1973; NOEL, Pres 1985; Sharing of Ministers Abroad 1978. bcf3@aol.com

HOWE, Karen Elvgren (CFla) 5583 Jessamine Ln, Orlando FL 32839 B Evanston IL 1938 d Gillette & Janet. BA Ohio Wesl 1961; MA U of Connecticut 1964; Cert Inst for Chr Stds, Dio Cntrl Florida 2004; Cert Other 2004. D 12/18/2004 Bp John Wadsworth Howe. m 9/1/1962 John Wadsworth Howe c 3. D S Mary Of The Ang Epis Ch Orlando FL 2005-2010; Dir Cathd Media 1989-2012; COM Dio Cntrl Florida Orlando FL 2009-2012. Auth, *Which Way? A Guide for New Christians*, Morehouse-Barlow, 1973.

HOWE JR, Ralph (La) 8965 Bayside Ave, Baton Rouge LA 70806 **Assoc S Jas Epis Ch Baton Rouge LA 2014-; Sr Chapl Epis HS Baton Rouge LA 2005-** B Baton Rouge LA 1956 s Ralph & Anne. BA U So 1978; MDiv GTS 1983. D 6/9/1983 Bp James Barrow Brown P 5/24/1984 Bp Robert Campbell Witcher Sr. m 8/14/1981 Suzette F Howe c 4. Epis HS Baton Rouge Baton Rouge LA 2004-2014; Trin Epis Ch Baton Rouge LA 1991-2004; R Trin Ch Crowley LA 1986-1991; Cur St Jas Epis Ch and Sch Alexandria LA 1984-1986; D Trin Ch New Orleans LA 1983-1984. rhowe@stjamesbr.org

HOWE, Raymond Jordan (Be) 833 Gillinder Place, Cary NC 27519 B Boston MA 1939 s Norman & Rosaleen. BA Bates Coll 1961; MDiv VTS 1965; DMin VTS 1987. D 6/26/1965 Bp Anson Phelps Stokes Jr P 6/4/1966 Bp John Melville Burgess. m 8/13/1966 Beverly Ann Howe c 2. R S Phil's Ch Easthampton MA 2000-2009; R S Ptr's Epis Ch Tunkhannock PA 1978-2000; R Ch Of Our Sav Arlington MA 1967-1978; Cur Chr Ch Quincy MA 1965-1967. The Fllshp of The Way of The Cross (Vice Superior 2007-2009) 2002.

HOWE, Wendy Salisbury (ECR) 203 Lighthouse Ave, Pacific Grove CA 93950 **COM Dio El Camino Real Salinas CA 2010-, Bp Transition Com 2006-2007, Bd, El Camino Cler Orgnztn 2005-2008, COM 2003-2007, 2000-2009** B Phoenix AZ 1944 d Grant & Phyllis. Cert Allnce Française 1965; BA MI SU 1967; MDiv CDSP 1997. D 5/18/1997 P 11/20/1997 Bp Richard Lester Shimpfky. m 2/1/1969 Kevin Howe c 4. Int S Geo's Ch Salinas CA 2010-2011; Int Epis Ch Of The Gd Shpd Salinas CA 2009; Int S Lk's Ch Hollister CA 2008-2011; Chapl Epis Sr Communities Lafayette CA 2007-2009; Chapl All SS' Epis Day Sch Carmel CA 2001-2007; Asst S Dunst's Epis Ch Carmel CA 1997-2000.

HOWELL, David Silva (NCal) Po Box 52008, Toa Baja PR 00950 B Sacramento CA 1958 s Joseph & Gilda. AA Amer River Coll 1978; BS California St U Sacramento 1980; Cert Sonoma St U 1984; CDSP 1993; MDiv TESM 1993. D 6/10/1993 Bp Jerry Alban Lamb P 12/20/1993 Bp David Charles Bowman. m 10/23/1982 Linda Gail Howell c 1. P-in-c St Marys Ch Elk Grove Sacramento CA 2013-2014; Dio Puerto Rico Trujillo Alto PR 2004-2010, 1996-2003; Cathd St Jn the Bapt Santurce PR 1995; Cur H Apos Epis Ch Tonawanda NY 1993-1995. EUC 2003.

HOWELL, Edward Allen (NCal) 1953 Terry Rd, Santa Rosa CA 95403 **P-in-c Ch Of The Gd Shpd Cloverdale CA 2008-; Ret 2000-** B Brookings SD 1938 s Edward & Wilda. BA U of Oklahoma 1965; MS Bos 1971; MDiv SWTS 1990. D 3/2/1981 P 5/8/1982 Bp Walter H Jones. m 12/28/1963 Terry J Howell c 4. P-in-c Ascen Epis Ch Vallejo CA 2004-2007; Int Ch Of The Incarn Santa Rosa CA 2001-2003; Assoc S Patricks Ch Kenwood CA 2000-2007; R S Edw The Mtyr and Chr Epis Ch Joliet IL 1991-2000; Vic St. Andrews Pentecost Epis Ch Evanston IL 1988-1991; R S Thos Epis Ch Sturgis SD 1983-1987; Asst Ch Of

The H Apos Sioux Falls SD 1981-1983; Devlpmt Off Dio So Dakota Pierre SD 1981-1983; Emm Epis Par Rapid City SD 1981-1982; Epis Dioc Fndt The Epis Dio Nthrn California Sacramento CA 2004-2007; Chair Comp Dio 2001-; Chair Cong Dvlpmt Com Dio Chicago Chicago IL 1996-2000, Dioc Coun 1991-1995. Bro of S Andr, 1976-2000; Chapl Chicago Assembly 1990-1997.

HOWELL, Laura (Be) 44 E Market St, Bethlehem PA 18018 **Trin Ch Bethlehem PA 2001-** B Johnson City NY 1951 BA SUNY 1972; MA SUNY 1975; CPE Lehigh Vlly Hosp 1993; Cert Oasis Mnstrs 2000. Rec 5/6/2001 Bp Paul Victor Marshall. m 8/3/1996 David Howell.

HOWELL, Margery E (SVa) 3316 Hyde Cir, Norfolk VA 23513 **Chapl Beacon Shores Nrsng & Rehab Virginia Bch VA 2011-** B Pulaski VA 1949 d Asher & Frances. D Formation Prog; BS Oklahoma St U 1972. D 6/9/2007 Bp John Clark Buchanan. D S Chris's Epis Ch Portsmouth VA 2009-2015; D S Fran Ch Virginia Bch VA 2007-2009.

HOWELL, Miguelina (Ct) Christ Church Cathedral, 45 Church St, Hartford CT 06103 **Chr Ch Cathd Hartford CT 2013-** B Santo Domingo 1976 d Saturnino & Rosa. Bachelor Theol Centro de Estudios Teologicos 2002; Bachelor Psychol Universidad Nacional Pedro Henriquez Urena 2002. D 9/7/2001 Bp Julio Cesar Holguin-Khoury P 9/13/2002 Bp William Jones Skilton. m 9/3/2010 Daniel M Howell. Epis Ch Cntr New York NY 2008-2009; S Paul's Epis Ch Paterson NJ 2008-2009; Mem Epis Ch Exec Coun 2005-2007; Dio The Dominican Republic (Iglesia Epis Dominicana) Gazcue Santo Domingo 2003-2008. lina.howell@cccathedral.org

HOWELL, Peggy Ann (Mass) Po Box 134, North Billerica MA 01862 B Hartford CT 1947 d Salvino & Lora. BA U MI 1969; MDiv Andover Newton TS 1991. D 8/15/1992 P 4/3/1993 Bp Douglas Edwin Theuner. m 11/23/1968 John P Howell c 2. R S Anne's Ch No Billerica MA 1996-2014; Assoc R S Mart's Ch Providence RI 1992-1996.

HOWELL, Robert M (SO) 69081 Mount Herman Rd, Cambridge OH 43725 **D S Jn's Epis Ch Cambridge OH 2012-** B Sumter SC 1940 s Alfred & Mildred. DDS Med Coll of Virginia 1965; MS Indiana U 1967; BS U of Nebraska 1990; Dioc Trng Prog 2004. D 12/10/2005 Bp William Michie Klusmeyer. m 11/7/1991 Joan Carol Gibson-Howell c 2. D S Jas Epis Ch Zanesville OH 2007-2012; Trin Ch Morgantown WV 2005-2007; Coun of Deacons Dio Sthrn Ohio Cincinnati OH 2010-2011. NAAD 2006-2014; OSL 2008.

HOWELL, Sydney C (Va) 495 Melrose Dr, Monticello FL 32344 B Blakely GA 1941 d Sidney & Jane. BS Brenau U 1977; MDiv EDS 1984. D 6/23/1984 Bp Peter J Lee P 3/1/1985 Bp Edward Cole Chalfant. c 2. S Fran Ch Macon GA 2008-2009; R S Paul's Epis Ch Millers Tavern VA 2002-2006; Gr & H Trin Epis Ch Richmond VA 2001-2002; Ch Of The Gd Shpd Rangeley ME 2001; Counslg/Sprtl direction 1987-2000; Downeast Epis Cluster Deer Isle ME 1985-1986; Vic Missions E Penobscot ME 1985-1986; Pstr care Calv Epis Ch Bridgeport CT 1984-1985; Asst to R S Paul's Epis Ch Willimantic CT 1984.

HOWELL, Terry Robert (At) 2135 Zelda Dr Ne, Atlanta GA 30345 **Atty Fields Howell Athens 2004-** B Warner Robins GA 1961 s Garneff & Linda. ABS U GA 1983; JD U GA 1986. D 8/6/2006 Bp J Neil Alexander. m 8/6/1983 Paige Howell c 2.

HOWELL-BURKE, Undine Jean (Neb) 7425 Stevens Ridge Rd, Lincoln NE 68516 **Non-par 1980-** B New Orleans LA 1947 d Roy & Yvonne. BA OH SU 1970; MA U of Massachusetts 1972; MDiv CDSP 1976; MD U of Nebraska 1985. P 9/1/1978 Bp Chauncie Kilmer Myers. m 6/28/1975 James T Howell-Burke c 2. Ch Of The H Trin Lincoln NE 1992-1993; Ch Of The H Trin Richmond CA 1978-1979.

HOWELLS, Donald Arthur (Be) 1936 Chestnut Hill Road, Mohnton PA 19540 **S Thos Epis Ch Morgantown PA 2003-** B Robertsdale PA 1934 s Arthur & Florean. Diac Traning Prog 1970. D 12/19/1970 Bp Frederick Warnecke. m 2/14/1959 Florence Patricia Howells c 4. S Gabr's Ch Douglassville PA 1971-2006; Assoc S Mary's Epis Ch Reading PA 1971-1973.

HOWLETT, Louise (NH) 131 E Harrisville Rd, Dublin NH 03444 **Celebrant, Rite Now All SS Ch Peterborough NH 2016-; Couple and Fam Ther Maps Counslg Cntr 2016-; Bd Dir VISIONS-Inc 2010-** B Washington DC 1961 d William & Virginia. BA Pr 1983; Cert of Angl Stds Ya Berk 1988; MDiv Yale DS 1988; MFT Drexel U Coll of Hlth Professions 2013. D 4/25/1990 Bp Arthur Edward Walmsley P 12/5/1990 Bp Cabell Tennis. m 6/15/1990 Gordon Lindsay Brown. P Assoc S Jas Ch Wilmington DE 2013-2016; Asst St Annes Epis Ch Middletown DE 2005-2009, Asst 2002-2003; Chapl S Anne's Epis Sch Middletown DE 2002-2011; S Andrews Sch Of Delaware Inc Middletown DE 1990-2002; Assoc Chapl S Andr's Sch Chap Middletown DE 1988-2002; Co-Ldr of PACT, Inclusion and diversity Mssn Dio Delaware Wilmington 2014-2016, Intake Off 2012-2016, Co-Coordntr of Par Life Day 2003-2016. lhowlett@mapsnh.org

HOWSER, Carol Louise Jordan (Ore) 192 Harrison St, Ashland OR 97520 B Burns OR 1939 d Daniel & Emma. Cntr for Diac Mnstry; BD U of Oregon 1961. D 1/18/1996 Bp Robert Louis Ladehoff.

HOWZE, Lynn Corpening (CFla) 215 West Park, Lakeland FL 33803 **Asst All SS Epis Ch Lakeland FL 2002-** B Asheville NC 1946 d Jessie & Vera. LTh VTS 1978; BA Eckerd Coll 1989; MDiv VTS 1989. D 6/3/1978 Bp John Alfred Baden P 6/1/1979 Bp Robert Bruce Hall. Dio Cntrl Florida Orlando FL 1997-1999; S Jn's Epis Ch Charleston WV 1981-1982; Ch Of The H Comf Charlotte NC 1978-1980.

HOY, Lois (Cal) 36 Dos Posos, Orinda CA 94563 **Ret 2000-** B Seattle WA 1935 d Gale & Lois. Stan 1955; BS U of Washington 1957; CDSP 1976. D 6/26/1976 Bp Chauncie Kilmer Myers P 6/24/1977 Bp CE Crowther. c 2. R S Giles Ch Moraga CA 1980-1999; P-in-c S Mich And All Ang Concord CA 1979-1980; Assoc S Paul's Ch Oakland CA 1978-1979; Chapl Los Gatos Meadows CA 1977-1978; Asst S Andr's Ch Saratoga CA 1976-1977; Epiph Par of Seattle Seattle WA 1970-1971; S Mk's Cathd Seattle WA 1962-1970. Auth, "Pastoring Wmn in Crises"; Auth, "The Forgotten Faithful"; Auth, "Understanding Islam"; Auth, "Truth," *Justice & Peace.*

HOY, Mary Ann (Me) 6 Old Mast Landing Rd, Freeport ME 04032 B Clifton Forge VA 1940 d Edward & Helen. BS Syr 1962; MDiv Bangor TS 1999. D 5/22/1999 P 3/25/2000 Bp Chilton Richardson Knudsen. m 8/9/1969 Robert Hoy c 2. S Andr's Ch Newcastle ME 2001-2010; Dio Maine Portland ME 1999-2001.

HOYT, Calvin Van Kirk (CPa) 1418 Walnut St, Camp Hill PA 17011 **Supply P S Andrews in the City Epis Ch Harrisburg PA 2013-; Hon Cn of the Cathd Cathd Ch Of S Steph Harrisburg PA 1985-** B Reading PA 1938 s Ralph & Josephine. BA Albright Coll 1961; mDiv Sewanee: The U So, TS 1964. D 6/20/1964 P 3/27/1965 Bp Frederick Warnecke. m 12/22/1956 Judith Hoyt c 1. R Mt Calv Camp Hill PA 1970-2009; R Chr Ch Susquehanna PA 1964-1970; S Mk's New Milford PA 1964-1970.

HOYT, Tim (WNC) 479 Whispering Woods Dr, Saluda NC 28773 B Dobbs Ferry NY 1942 s Richard & Mary. BA Hanover Coll 1964; BD EDS 1969. D 6/14/1969 P 12/20/1969 Bp Dudley S Stark. Mssnr for Latino Mnstry Dio Wstrn No Carolina Asheville NC 1994-2007; Vic H Cross Epis Ch Boring OR 1988-2007; Mssnr for Latino Mnstry Dio Oregon Portland OR 1980-1994; R S Paul's Ch Holley NY 1974-1980; Genesee Orleans Mnstry Of Concern Albion NY 1969-1973.

HROSTOWSKI, Susan (Miss) 1861 Tryon Dr Unit 3, Fayetteville NC 28303 **S Eliz's Mssn Collins MS 2013-** B 1958 d Michael & Mary. Mississippi U For Wmn 1976; Jefferson Davis Jr Coll 1977; BA U of Sthrn Mississippi 1979; MDiv VTS 1987. D 5/27/1987 P 5/1/1988 Bp Duncan Montgomery Gray Jr. Assoc R H Trin Epis Ch Fayetteville NC 1989-1990; Cur S Paul's Epis Ch Meridian MS 1987-1989; Int Supply P. Golden Rule Awd Outstanding Vol Serv Jc Penney.

HSIEH, Nathaniel (Eur) 44 Rue Docteur Robert, Chatillon Sur Seine 21400 France B 1940 s Wen-Hwa & Yen-Yu. BTh Chung Tai Theol Coll TW 1968; Birmingham Bible Inst Gb 1977; S Jn Coll Nottingham Gb 1978. P 9/1/1994 Bp Jeffery William Rowthorn. m 7/22/1968 Eunice Su-Yen Wu c 2. The Amer Cathd of the H Trin Paris 75008 1996-2005; Dio Taiwan Taipei 1995-1996; R Gd sheperd Ch Taipei Taiwan Epis Ch 1994-1996; Mem of Coun Advice Convoc of Epis Ch in Europe Paris 1998-2003. Auth, "Film Voice Of Hope For Question Of Chinese Refugees In Paris"; Auth, "Cassettes Daily Devotions In Mandarin".

HU, Kuo-Hua (Tai) Chieh Shou Road 5, Kangshan 82018 Taiwan **Cur Gd Shpd 1970-** B Anhwei CN 1934 s Chi-Ching & Ting. Tainan Theol Coll and Sem TW 1969. D 6/29/1968 P 6/1/1970 Bp James Chang L Wong. m 3/15/1959 Yuen Mei Hu. Dio Taiwan Taipei 1969-1999; D S Paul's Kaohsiung Taiwan 1969-1970.

HUACANI, Amy J (NC) PO Box 2263, Durham NC 27702 B Souderton PA 1972 d Nicolas & Joanna. BA U of Kentucky 1995; MDiv Sthrn Bapt TS 1996; MDiv Bapt Theol Semianry 2000; MDiv Bapt TS 2000; MA U of Tennessee 2000; Luth TS 2005. Rec 10/23/2011 as Priest Bp Michael B Curry. Ch Of The Gd Shpd Rocky Mt NC 2013-2014; Assoc R Emm Par Epis Ch Sthrn Pines NC 2011-2013.

HUAL, Jeffrey Charles (CGC) 2430 K St NW, Washington DC 20037 **S Jn's Ch Huntingdon Baltimore MD 2016-** B Pensacola FL 1969 s Charles & Donna. B.A Acctg U of W Florida 1991; M.A U of W Florida 1994; MDiv VTS 2015. D 11/22/2014 P 5/24/2015 Bp Philip Menzie Duncan II. m 5/20/1995 Kerry Dawn Smith c 1. S Paul's Par Washington DC 2015-2016.

HUANG, Peter P (Los) 2200 Via Rosa, Palos Verdes Estates CA 90274 **S Fran' Par Palos Verdes Estates CA 2015-** B Taipei Taiwan 1970 s James & Reiko. BS MIT 1992; MDiv Fuller TS 1996; MS, MFT Fuller TS 2004; Cert in Angl Stds Bloy Hse, ETS 2015. D 6/6/2015 Bp Diane Jardine Bruce P 1/16/2016 Bp Joseph Jon Bruno. m 7/26/2014 Christine Ma. peter.huang@stfrancispalosverdes.org

HUBBARD, Carol Murphy (WNC) 211 Montford Ave, Asheville NC 28801 **Chairman of Cmsn on Mnstrs Dio Wstrn No Carolina Asheville NC 2011-** B Ann Arbor MI 1951 d Ralph & Mary. BA Smith 1973; MDiv Duke DS 1977; STM GTS 2001. D 6/16/2001 Bp Dorsey Henderson P 3/3/2002 Bp Catherine Scimeca Roskam. m 5/27/1978 Stanley B Hubbard c 2. Assoc Trin Epis Ch Asheville NC 2005-2016; P-in-c Chr Epis Ch Sparkill NY 2003-2004; Dio New York New York NY 2003-2004; Asst The Ch Of The Epiph New York NY 2001-2003.

HUBBARD JR, Charles Clark (Ga) 227 McDuffie Drive, Richmond Hill GA 31324 **R S Eliz's Epis Ch Richmond Hill GA 2005-; Assoc S Barth's Tonawanda NY 2001-** B Montgomery AL 1952 s Charles & Henrietta. BA JHU 1974; MS Auburn U Montgomery 1984; MDiv TESM 2001; DMin TESM 2011. D 12/9/2000 P 6/24/2001 Bp Keith Lynn Ackerman. m 11/6/1992 Emily C Hubbard c 5. Auth, "Integrating the Chrsmtc Experience into Par Wrshp and Mnstry," *DMin Thesis,* self, 2011.

HUBBARD, Colenzo James (WTenn) 604 Saint Paul Ave, Memphis TN 38126 **Memphis Ldrshp Fndt Memphis TN 2013-; Emm Ch Memphis TN 2011-** B Brighton AL 1955 s Dudley & Cynthia. BS U of Alabama 1977. D 9/30/1986 Bp Robert Oran Miller P 10/1/1987 Bp Furman Charles Stough. m 11/3/2007 LaVerne K Comerie-Hubbard c 2. Ch Of The Redeem Germantown TN 2004-2010; S Paul's Ch Memphis TN 2004-2005; Emm Cntr Inc Memphis TN 1998-2013; Dio W Tennessee Memphis 1989-1997; Chr Ch Fairfield AL 1988-1989. Cook Halle Cmnty Ldrshp Awd Carnival Memphis; Cmncatn Ldrshp Awd Toastmaster Intl .

HUBBARD, Cynthia Plumb (Mass) 45 White Trellis, Plymouth MA 02360 **Gr Ch Vineyard Haven MA 2017-** B Springfield MA 1951 d David & Faith. BA Smith 1973; EDS 1976; STM McGill U 1978. D 7/30/1977 Bp William Augustus Jones Jr P 2/3/1979 Bp Alexander D Stewart. m 5/15/1976 Theodore L Hubbard c 2. Int S Dav's Epis Ch S Yarmouth MA 2014-2016; P-in-c Trin Ch Marshfield MA 2012-2014; Cn for Transition and Deploy Dio Massachusetts Boston MA 2006-2012; Int Ascen Memi Ch Ipswich MA 2004-2006; Int Par Of The Epiph Winchester MA 2003-2004, 2000-2001, Int Asst 2000-2001; Int S Mk's Ch Westford MA 2001-2003; Dir of Dvlpmt Cmnty Day Chart Sch Lawr MA 1999-2000; P-in-c S Lk's Epis Ch Malden MA 1998-2000; Dir of Cmnty Serv Pingree Sch S. Hamilton MA 1989-1999; Assoc Trin Ch Topsfield MA 1978-1989. Auth, "The Gift of the Butterfly Weed," *Faith at Wk Journ,* 2000; Auth, "Risk Mgmt," *Crit Iss in K-12 Serv-Lrng,* 1996; Auth, "The Lesson from the Oyster," *Natl Inst for Campus Mnstry Journ.* HAWC Cmnty Awd Help for Abused Wmn and Chld Shltr 1998.

HUBBARD, Francis Appleton (NJ) 5 North Rd, Berkeley Heights NJ 07922 **Asstg P S Andr's Epis Ch New Providence NJ 2016-; Mem Int Mnstry Ntwk 2010-** B Boston MA 1951 s Charles & Nathalie. BA Ob 1974; MDiv EDS 1981; DMin SWTS 2010. D 5/30/1981 P 5/27/1982 Bp John Bowen Coburn. m 6/24/2000 Elda G Balbona c 1. S Mk's Ch Plainfield NJ 2013-2015; Int Chr Ch New Brunswick NJ 2011-2013; Int S Steph's Ch Riverside NJ 2010-2011; Chapl So Brunswick NJ Police Dept 2007-2010; Chapl Kendall Pk NJ First Aid Squad 2005-2010; Pres So Brunswick NJ Cler Assn 1990-2003; R S Barn Epis Ch Monmouth Jct NJ 1984-2009; Asst All SS' Epis Ch Belmont MA 1981-1984; Chapl Prot Chapl Mclean Hosp Belmont MA 1981-1984; Chapl, Accountability and Fair Share T/F Dio New Jersey Trenton NJ 2012-2013, Alt Dep, 2012 GC 2011-, Cmsn on Cler Compstn 2010-2013, Chair, Property T/F 2010-, Fin and Bdgt Com 2005-2008, Coun 2002-2005, Chair, Loan and Grant Com 2001-. Auth, "four Liturg dramas," *(included in) Skiturgies,* Ch Pub, 2011. Chapl Ord Of S Lk 2001.

HUBBARD, James Alan (SwVa) 384 Waughs Ferry Rd, Amherst VA 24521 B Erie PA 1942 s Vernon & Lucile. BA Lee U 1963; BD Fuller TS 1966; MA California St U 1970; PhD U of Tennessee 1976; Cert GTS 1981. D 9/6/1981 Bp William Evan Sanders P 4/25/1982 Bp William F Gates Jr. m 5/20/2000 Mary J Hubbard c 3. R S Mk's Ch Amherst VA 2006-2016; Int Gr And H Trin Cathd Kansas City MO 2003-2004; Dio Virginia Richmond VA 2002; Int S Jn's Ch Roanoke VA 2000-2002; S Geo's-By-The-River Rumson NJ 2000, Int R 1999-2000; S Lk's Epis Ch Jamestown NY 1999-2000; Int S Paul's Epis Ch Cary NC 1997-1998; Int S Paul's Epis Ch Lynchburg VA 1995-1997; R Trin Epis Ch Pottsville PA 1993-1995; R Trin Ch Easton PA 1991-1993; R S Jn's Ch Canandaigua NY 1986-1991; Dio Tennessee Nashville TN 1981-1986; Vic S Matt's Epis Ch Mcminnville TN 1981-1986. Auth, *arts Psychol Behavior.*

HUBBARD, Lani Marie (Oly) 225 Mar Vista Way, Port Angeles WA 98362 B Los Angeles CA 1944 d Frank & Marjorie. AS Brigham Young U 1965. D 12/9/2006 Bp Charles Glenn VonRosenberg. D Ch Of The Gd Shpd Knoxville TN 2010-2015.

HUBBARD, Martha L (Mass) St. Paul's Church, 166 High St., Newburyport MA 01950 **R S Paul's Ch Newburyport MA 2007-** B Poughkeepsie NY 1964 d William & Norma. BA SUNY 1986; MDiv Ya Berk 1993. D 6/12/1993 Bp Richard Frank Grein P 2/12/1994 Bp Robert Scott Denig. m 8/6/1994 Markus Brucher c 2. R Ch of S Aug of Cbury 65189 Wiesbaden 2003-2007; R S Mk's Epis Ch Penn Yan NY 1995-2003; Cur Ch Of The Atone Westfield MA 1993-1995; Dio Wstrn Massachusetts Springfield 1993-1995. Muehl Preaching Prize Ya- Berk DS; Mersick Preaching Prize Ya- Berk DS.

HUBBARD, Mavourneen Ann (NY) 17 South Ave, 855 Wolcott Ave, Beacon NY 12508 B Buffalo NY 1952 d Edward & Loretta. BS SUNY at Plattsburgh 1975. D 5/1/2010 Bp Mark Sean Sisk. m 3/5/1971 James T Hubbard c 2.

HUBBARD, Philip R (LI) 20309 W 219th Ter, Spring Hill KS 66083 **R S Mary's Ch Hampton Bays NY 2014-; 2008-07-01 St Clares Ch Sprg Hill KS 2008-** B Kansas City MO 1961 s Robert & Nadine. BA U of Missouri Kansas City 1983; MA PrTS 1987; MBA U of Connecticut 1992; MDiv CDSP 2008.

D 6/7/2008 P 12/6/2008 Bp Dean E Wolfe. m 12/21/1999 Sonya S Hubbard c 1. 2008-07-01 Dio Kansas Topeka KS 2008-2014, Mem Congrl Dvlpmt Cmsn 2010-.

HUBBARD, Thomas Beckwith (Los) 621 Mayflower Rd 104, Claremont CA 91711 **Adj Assoc Pstr Care and Sprtl Growth All SS Ch Pasadena CA 1979-** B Cleveland OH 1938 s Harold & Janet. BA Hiram Coll 1960; MDiv EDS 1964. D 6/13/1964 P 12/18/1964 Bp Nelson Marigold Burroughs. m 5/10/1997 Mary P Hubbard c 2. LocTen S Tim's Epis Ch Apple Vlly CA 1982-1983; Chapl CA St U Bakersfield CA 1974-1977; Epis Dio San Joaquin Modesto CA 1974-1977; Assoc/R S Paul's Ch Bakersfield CA 1974-1977; Consult Par Rnwl Dio Cntrl New York Liverpool NY 1971-1974, Chair Childrens Cmsn 1967-1970; R Geth Ch Sherrill NY 1966-1974; Cur Trin Ch Elmira NY 1964-1966. Auth, "Hm Sweet Tax Break," *Hm Sweet Tax Break*, 1982; Contrib, "Celebration," *Celebration*, 1973. Epis Cleric Assn 1970-1974; Fiduciary Round Table 2000-2004; Fin Plnng Assn 1984-2004.

HUBBELL, Gilbert Leonard (O) 1094 Clifton Ave # 2, Akron OH 44310 B 1936 s Leonard & Mae. BA Bex Sem 1958; BA U of Toledo 1958. D 6/19/1968 P 1/1/1969 Bp John Harris Burt. m 1/21/1999 Diana Lynn Sollberger c 2. Asst S Lk's Epis Ch Akron OH 1982-1984; Brunswick Epis Ch Brunswick OH 1977-1981; Vic H Cross Brunswick OH 1977-1981; Int S Paul's Ch Canton OH 1976; R Trin Ch Coshocton OH 1970-1974; Cur S Ptr's Epis Ch Lakewood OH 1968-1970.

HUBBELL, Sally Hanes (NCal) 209 Matheson St, Healdsburg CA 95448 **P-in-c S Paul's Ch Healdsburg CA 2013-** B Charlotte NC 1968 d Andrew & Letitia. BA Hampshire Coll 1990; MDiv Duke DS 1999; Cert Ang Stud Iliff TS 2009. D 6/6/2009 P 1/9/2010 Bp Robert John O'Neill. m 5/23/1992 David Hubbell c 3. Asst Ch Of S Mich The Archangel Colorado Spg CO 2009-2012. sally@stpauls-healdsburg.org

HUBBY III, Turner Erath (Tex) 329 Meadowbrook Dr, San Antonio TX 78232 B Waco TX 1936 s Turner & Helen. Texas Tech U 1955; Texas A&M U 1956; BBA Midwestern U 1961; MDiv Epis TS of the SW 1987. D 6/23/1987 Bp Anselmo Carral-Solar P 2/1/1988 Bp Maurice Manuel Benitez. m 11/4/1956 Martha H Harris c 4. S Jn's Epis Ch Marlin TX 1987-2002.

HUBER, Amy Whitcombe (Eau) 234 Avon St, La Crosse WI 54603 B Madison WI 1951 d Edward & Marie. BS U of Wisconsin 1989. D 6/17/2001 Bp James Louis Jelinek. m 8/18/1990 Steven Huber c 4.

HUBER, Donald Marvin (Neb) 10807 Scott Peddler Rd, Cattaraugus NY 14719 **Bp and Trst Dio Nebraska Omaha NE 2009-** B Buffalo New York 1948 BS SUNY at Buffalo 1970; MDiv Nash 1978. D 6/3/1978 P 3/31/1979 Bp Harold Barrett Robinson. m 6/6/2003 Beth A Lucht c 3. Cn Vic S Paul's Cathd Buffalo NY 2012-2014; R Calv Ch Hyannis NE 2006-2012; R S Matt's Ch Allnce NE 2006-2012; Var Int Pastorates Untd Ch of Chr 1987-2002; Chapl NYS Dept of Corrections 1980-1987; R S Mary's Epis Ch Gowanda NY 1980-1983; Cur S Ptr's Ch Niagara Falls NY 1978-1980.

HUBER, Ellen (Ct) 171 Old Tannery Rd # 6468, Monroe CT 06468 **R Chr Ch Easton CT 2004-** B Coatesville PA 1969 BA Mills Coll. D 6/9/2001 P 12/15/2001 Bp Andrew Donnan Smith. m 8/9/1997 Kurt J Huber c 3. S Lk's Epis Ch New Haven CT 2002-2004. revellen@att.net

HUBER, E Wendy (Colo) 76 Spring Ridge Ct, Glenwood Springs CO 81601 **S Barn Ch Glenwood Spgs CO 2016-** B Cambridge MA 1958 d Frederick & Penelope. IONA Sch of Mnstry; Doctor of Jurisprudence U of Houston. D 6/16/2012 Bp C Andrew Doyle P 12/22/2012 Bp Jeff Fisher. m 8/11/1990 Stephen Kurt Huber c 2. Vic S Jn's Epis Ch New Castle CO 2017, Vic 2017-; R S Barth's Ch Hempstead TX 2015-2016; R S Jn's Epis Ch Marlin TX 2011-2015. Co-Auth (Name Trachte-Huber), "Mediation and Negotiation: Reaching Agreement in Law & Bus (2nd Ed)," *Mediation and Negotiation: Reaching Agreement in Law & Bus (2nd Ed)*, Lexis-Nexis, 2007; Co-Auth (Name Trachte-Huber), "Mediation and Negotiation: Reaching Agreement in Law and Bus," *Mediation & Negotiation: Reaching Agreement in Law & Bus*, Anderson, 1998. revwend@gmail.com

HUBER, Frank A (Colo) 12295 West Applewood Drive, Lakewood CO 80215 B Erie PA 1942 s Frank & Jean. BA Colg 1964; DVM U of Pennsylvania 1967; MDiv Sewanee: The U So, TS 1990. D 6/10/1990 P 12/19/1990 Bp David Reed. m 9/7/1969 Lynn Huber. R S Jos's Ch Lakewood CO 2000-2007; R Gr Ch Pine Bluff AR 1994-2000; Chr Epis Ch Bowling Green KY 1990-1994; Chapl Wstrn KY U-Bowling Green 1990-1992.

HUBER, Glenna J (WA) 1820 Greenberry Rd, Baltimore MD 21209 **S Andr's Epis Ch Coll Pk MD 2016-** B Tulsa OK 1975 d Lawrence & Jayne. BA Spelman Coll 1997; MDiv GTS 2001. D 6/9/2001 Bp Robert Gould Tharp P. m 10/1/2011 Richard J Huber c 2. Vic Dio Maryland Baltimore MD 2009-2015, Stndg Com 2011-2015; S Paul's Epis Ch Atlanta GA 2006-2008; H Innoc Ch Atlanta GA 2003-2006; S Mart In The Fields Ch Atlanta GA 2001-2003; S Mart's Epis Sch Atlanta GA 2001-2003.

HUBER, Kurt J (Ct) 171 Old Tannery Rd, Monroe CT 06468 **R S Ptr's Epis Ch Monroe CT 2002-** B Royal Oak MI 1971 s Edwin & Shirley. BGS U MI 1993; MDiv CDSP 1998. D 6/27/1998 P 1/20/1999 Bp R aymond Stewart Wood Jr.

m 8/9/1997 Ellen Huber c 5. Asst R Trin Ch Newtown CT 1998-2002. rector@stpetersonthegreen.com

HUBER, Stephen A (Los) 506 N. Camden Drive, Beverly Hills CA 90210 **All SS Par Beverly Hills CA 2010-; Vic Washington Natl Cathd Washington DC 2006-; Trst Ya Berk 2014-** B Dayton OH 1951 s Arthur & Helen. BA Duns Scotus Coll 1973; MDiv Yale DS 1998. D 6/13/1998 Bp Ronald Hayward Haines P 4/10/1999 Bp Jane Hart Holmes Dixon. Cathd of St Ptr & St Paul Washington DC 2006-2010; P-in-c St. Columba's Ch Washington DC 2004-2006; S Columba's Ch Washington DC 2000-2006; Calv St Geo's Epis Ch Bridgeport CT 2000; Ya Berk New Haven CT 1998-2000; Dioc Coun Dio Washington Washington DC 2004-2010.

HUBERT, Deven Ann (Roch) 66 Little Briggins Circle, Fairport NY 14450 **Bp's Transition Com Dio Rochester 2007-; Dio Rochester Rochester 2006-; R S Lk's Ch Fairport NY 2004-** B Tomah WI 1957 d Richard & Joyce. BA Stetson U 1978; MDiv Yale DS 1982. D 12/8/1985 P 12/21/1986 Bp Robert Poland Atkinson. m 7/21/2012 Frederick Paul Koehler c 2. Assoc R Ch Of The H Comf Burlington NC 1999-2004; Cbury Sch Greensboro NC 1996-1999; Chapl Cbury Sch Greensboro NC 1996-1999; Renwl and Evang Com Dio Bethlehem Bethlehem PA 1992-1995, COM 1994-1995; Assoc P Cathd Ch Of The Nativ Bethlehem PA 1989-1995; Vic S Lk's Ch Wheeling WV 1986-1989. NAES.

HUBERT, Lawrence William (Alb) 970 State St, Schenectady NY 12307 **D Chr Ch Schenectady NY 2009-** B Schenectady NY 1947 s Lawrence & Marion. D 5/30/2009 Bp William Howard Love. m 7/18/1981 Jerusha Hubert c 4.

HUCK, Beverly (Nwk) 155 Rainbow Dr # 5549, Livingston TX 77399 B Dumont NJ 1952 d Kenneth & Rose. BS Montclair St U 1981; MDiv VTS 1984; Isaiah Team 1995; Cler Ldrshp Inst 2005; Credo 2008. D 6/9/1984 P 12/18/1984 Bp John Shelby Spong. m 6/10/1989 William V Magnus c 1. Vic S Alb's Ch Littleton NC 2011-2016; R The Ch Of The Sav Denville NJ 1992-2009; R Trin Epis Ch Kearny NJ 1986-1992; Cur Calv Epis Ch Summit NJ 1984-1986; Stndg Com Dio Newark Newark NJ 2004-2009, Dioc Coun 1987-1992.

HUCKABAY JR, Harry Hunter (ETenn) 1706 Glenroy Ave., Chattanooga TN 37405 B Shreveport LA 1934 s Harry & Katherine. BS LSU 1956; MDiv Sewanee: The U So, TS 1969; DMin Sewanee: The U So, TS 1984; Sewanee: The U So, TS 2000. D 6/28/1969 Bp Girault M Jones P 5/1/1970 Bp Iveson Batchelor Noland. m 2/9/1957 Prestine Huckabay c 3. R S Paul's Epis Ch Chattanooga TN 1986-2006; Ch Of The Ascen Lafayette LA 1972-1986; Epis Sch Of Acadiana Inc. Cade LA 1972-1977; Asst R Trin Ch New Orleans LA 1969-1972; Chapl Trin Sch 1969-1972; COM, Chair Dio Wstrn Louisiana Alexandria LA 1980-1986. thesis, "Lord to Whom Shall We Go?," Univerity of the So, 1984; optime merens, "How the NT speaks to Issues and questions in the Bk of Ecclesiastes," U So, 1969. DD U So 2000; Distinguished Alum STUSo 1995.

HUDAK, Bob (EC) St Paul's Church, 401 E. 4th St, Greenville NC 27858 **R S Paul's Epis Ch Greenville NC 2005-** B Passaic NJ 1948 s Robert & Anne. BA CUA 1971; MDiv Washington Theol Un 1983. Rec 4/1/1998 as Priest Bp Frank Kellogg Allan. m 11/3/1991 Louise M Hudak c 2. R S Tim's Epis Ch Greenville NC 2005-2006; R The Epis Ch Of The Nativ Fayetteville GA 2003-2005, Vic 1998-2002.

HUDAK, Mary L. (NCal) 1240 Mission Ave., Sacramento CA 95608 **P S Mich's Epis Ch Carmichael CA 2013-; Dn of the Capital Dnry The Epis Dio Nthrn California Sacramento CA 2015-; Bd Mem River City Food Bank 2014-** B Detroit MI 1962 d Charles & Bernice. BA U MN 2004; MDiv CDSP 2008. D 7/26/2007 P 7/8/2008 Bp James Louis Jelinek. m 10/21/1989 James Hudak c 5. P S Steph's Epis Ch Orinda CA 2008-2013. revmary@stmichaelcarmichael.org

HUDDLESTON, Kevin (Kan) 6417 W 65th Ter, Overland Park KS 66202 **S Mich And All Ang Ch Mssn KS 2014-** B Rockford IL 1956 s Jack & Dorothy. BA Milligan Coll 1977; MDiv Van 1982; DMin SWTS 2005. D 3/8/1988 P 7/18/1988 Bp Maurice Manuel Benitez. m 9/1/1984 Gayle Lynn Sharp c 3. Assoc for Mssn and Outreach S Mich And All Ang Ch Dallas TX 2007-2014, Assoc 1989-1994; Chapl St. Mk's School of Texas Dallas TX 2003-2008; R S Barn Epis Ch Fredricksburg TX 1999-2003; Asst Ch Of The H Comm Memphis TN 1996-1999; R Ch Of The Gd Shpd Cedar Hill TX 1994-1996; Yth Min S Dav's Ch Austin TX 1988-1989; Exec Com Coll Cler Dio W Tennessee Memphis 1997-1999. Auth, "Resources Mnstrs w Yth & YA".

HUDDLESTON, Nathan (Nwk) **Calv Epis Ch Summit NJ 2016-** B Nashville,TN 1980 s Kevin & Celeste. B.A. Oklahoma St U 2003; M.A. Middle Tennessee St U 2007; M. Div Sewanee: The U So, TS 2016. D 12/6/2015 Bp Samuel Johnson Howard P 10/29/2016 Bp Mark M Beckwith. m 11/14/2009 Katherine Louise O'Quinn. Other Lay Position Chr Epis Ch Ponte Vedra FL 2013. nhuddleston@calvarysummit.org

HUDLOW, A Kelley (Ala) 521 20th St N, Birmingham AL 35203 **Dio Alabama Birmingham 2015-** B Mobile AL 1979 d Charles & Melrose. BA U of So Alabama 2002; JD U of Alabama Sch of Law 2005. D 10/1/2011 Bp John Mckee Sloan Sr. m 1/14/2017 Shanti Renee Weiland. khudlow@dioala.org

HUDSON, Aaron (Ia) St. Paul's Episcopal Church, 22 Dillman Drive, Council Bluffs IA 51503 **S Andr's Epis Ch Staten Island NY 2016-; S Paul's Ch Coun Blfs IA 2014-; COM Dio Iowa Des Moines IA 2014-** B Leon IA 1981 s Daniel & Linda. ASN Mercy Coll 2005; MDiv Epis TS Of The SW 2013; MDiv

Epis TS of the SW 2013. D 12/15/2012 P 6/15/2013 Bp Alan Scarfe. m 10/3/2014 Brian E Levels. The Epis Ch Of The Trsfg Dallas TX 2013-2014; The Par Epis Sch Dallas TX 2013-2014. csarector@gmail.com

HUDSON, Andrew (SeFla) 7538 Granville Dr, Tamarac FL 33321 **Dir Of Evang S Ambr Epis Ch Ft Lauderdale FL 2010-** B Flint MI 1931 s Edward & Helen. BS Wstrn Michigan U 1952. D 10/14/1986 Bp Calvin Onderdonk Schofield Jr. m 6/25/1954 Bobsie Lou Popilek c 2.

HUDSON, Andrew George (SeFla) 2250 SW 31st Ave, Fort Lauderdale FL 33312 B Athens Greece 1966 s Peter & Tatiana. BA S Thos U 1992. D 6/5/2010 Bp Leo Frade. m 3/31/2001 Laura Hudson c 1.

HUDSON, Betty Brownfield (SVa) 120 John Bratton, Williamsburg VA 23185 B Fort Worth TX 1948 d Jack & Elizabeth Mackey. BA Tul 1970; MBA Simmons Coll 1976; MDiv GTS 1986. D 6/7/1986 Bp Paul Moore Jr P 6/24/1987 Bp Walter Decoster Dennis Jr. m 6/9/1984 John F Hudson c 2. Asst S Andr's Epis Ch Newport News VA 2009-2013; Transition R Trin Ch Portsmouth VA 2009; R Gr Ch Hastings Hds NY 1991-2007; Int R S Steph's Ch Pearl River NY 1987-1991.

HUDSON, Daniel Mark (La) 1329 Jackson Ave, New Orleans LA 70130 **D Trin Epis Sch New Orleans LA 2013-** B New Orleans LA 1957 s Daniel & Susan. BA SE Louisiana U 1979; MBA Tul 1996. D 12/1/2007 Bp Charles Edward Jenkins III. m 3/26/1983 Debra Hudson c 1.

HUDSON, Henry Lee (Ala) 1424 4th St, New Orleans LA 70130 B Birmingham AL 1951 s William & Lois. BA Tul 1974; MDiv Nash 1977. D 5/26/1977 P 12/15/1977 Bp Furman Charles Stough. m 5/22/1976 Mary Hudson c 2. R Trin Ch New Orleans LA 2007-2016; Dn and R Trin Cathd Little Rock AR 1996-2007; R S Paul's Epis Ch Meridian MS 1984-1996; R Ch Of The Adv Sumner MS 1980-1984; Cur Ch Of The Nativ Epis Huntsville AL 1977-1980. EPF; Itfs.

HUDSON, Joel Pinkney (At) 1225 N Shore Dr, Roswell GA 30076 **Ret 2003-** B Atlanta GA 1931 s James & Lois. BD Clemson U 1953; MDiv VTS 1963. D 6/15/1963 P 12/1/1963 Bp Nelson Marigold Burroughs. m 6/12/1953 Shirley Ann Hudson c 4. Chr Ch Norcross GA 1988-2003; Assoc Ch Of The Atone Sandy Sprg GA 1973-1978; 1971-1973; Assoc S Eliz's Ch Ridgewood NJ 1969-1971; Assoc H Trin Epis Ch Bowie MD 1967-1969; Asst Min Chr Ch Shaker Heights OH 1963-1967.

HUDSON, John Richard Keith (Del) 1300 Morris Ave, Villanova PA 19085 **Died 5/8/2016** B London UK 1935 s John & Nora. BA Oxf GB 1960; GOE Lincoln Theol Inst 1962; MA Oxf GB 1964; PhD SUNY 1983. Trans 4/1/1984. m 5/11/2002 Sandra R Hudson. P-in-c S Paul's Ch Chester PA 2011-2016; Int Calv Epis Ch Hillcrest Wilmington DE 2003-2006; Chapl De Hospice 1992-1996; P-in-c S Paul's Ch Camden Wyoming DE 1985-2002; Asst R St Jas Epis Ch and Sch Alexandria LA 1984-1985. Auth, "Free To Share Books I And Ii," Ch Info Off Of London, 1973.

HUDSON, Kimberly Karen (WA) 11403 Trillum St, Bowie MD 20721 B Ft Bragg NC 1964 d Willie & Betty. BA U NC 1986; JD The Dickinson Sch of Law 1990. D 6/29/2002 Bp Michael B Curry. kimberly.hudson@ssa.gov

HUDSON, Linda Ann (Wyo) 860 S 3rd St, Lander WY 82520 B Denver CO 1950 d John & Garnet. BA U of Nthrn Colorado 1971; MA U of Wyoming 1978. D 8/25/2007 Bp Bruce Caldwell. c 1.

HUDSON, Mary Bowen (CFla) 4345 Indian River Dr, Cocoa FL 32927 B Atlanta GA 1925 d Sylvester & Roberta. BA Georgia St U 1960. D 2/20/1988 Bp William Hopkins Folwell. m 5/11/1990 Joseph A Hudson. Dok.

HUDSON, Mary Jo (EMich) **P-in-c S Matt's Epis Ch Saginaw MI 2017-** D 5/8/2016 P 11/5/2016 Bp Steven Todd Ousley.

HUDSON, Michael Vincent (WNC) Po Box 152, Cullowhee NC 28723 **R S Dav's Ch Cullowhee NC 1992-** B Greenville SC 1950 s Heyward & Ruth. BA Furman U 1973; MDiv TESM 1989. D 6/23/1989 Bp Claude Charles Vache P 3/1/1990 Bp Frank Harris Vest Jr. m 5/29/1976 Barbara Jane Hardie c 1. Asst R Ch Of The Gd Shpd Norfolk VA 1989-1992. "Songs for the Cycle," Ch Pub Corp, 2004; Auth, "Lrng to Trust," 1990; Auth, "Enter His Gates," 1985. Dove Awd for Song of the Year CMA 1980.

HUDSON, Thomas James (Md) **S Lk's Ch Brownsville MD 2015-; P-in-c S Ptr's Ch Lonaconing MD 2012-** D 12/21/2007 Bp John L Rabb P 6/29/2008 Bp Katharine Jefferts Schori.

HUDSON-LOUIS, Holly (ECR) 65 Highway 1, Carmel CA 93923 **Chapl All SS' Epis Day Sch Carmel CA 2006-** B San Rafael CA 1957 d David & Sabra. BS U CA 1981; MDiv CDSP 1991. D 6/29/1991 P 3/25/1992 Bp Richard Lester Shimpfky. m 5/23/1981 August James Louis c 2. Asst All SS Ch Carmel CA 2000-2005; Assoc Trin Cathd San Jose CA 1997-1999; Cur S Phil's Ch San Jose CA 1991-1995; Yth Dir S Fran Epis Ch San Jose CA 1985-1987. Citation of Excellence-Chld's Mnstry, Trin Cathd Dio El Camino Real 1999. hhudson-louis@asds.org

HUDSPETH, Denise (SeFla) 208 Nw Avenue H, Belle Glade FL 33430 B Bronx NY 1953 d Arnold & Lillian. Cert Diac Sch For Mnstry 1985; AS Palm Bch Cmnty Coll 1986; Bachlor Arts in Mnstry Palm Bch Atlantic Univ. 2002; M.DIV. TS 2002; M.DIV. Sewanee: The U So, TS 2002. D 6/29/1989 Bp Calvin Onderdonk Schofield Jr P 6/1/2002 Bp John Lewis Said. m 1/22/1973 William Broughton Hudspeth c 3. St Margarets and San Francisco de Asis Epis Ch Hialeah FL 2006-2008; S Jn The Apos Ch Belle Glade FL 2002-2006; D H Sprt Epis Ch W Palm Bch FL 1989-2002. Yth Mnstry, CE Mnstry To Elderly, Mnstry In 12 Step Recovery Prog.

HUERTA, Efrain (FtW) 12607 Banchester Ct, Houston TX 77070 **Dir Comp Pension Relatns The CPG New York NY 2002-** B San Martin de las Flores MX 1937 s Crescencio & Praxedis. CTh S Andrews Sem Mex City MX 1964; U Mariano Galvez Guatemala City GT 1964; MDiv Epis TS of the SW 1981; Epis TS of the SW 2002. D 9/13/1964 P 4/1/1965 Bp Jose Guadalupe Saucedo. m 4/24/1965 Silvia Huerta. Dir Cntr for Hisp Mnstrs 1993-2001; The Cntr For Hisp Mnstrs Austin TX 1993-2001; Dio Ft Worth Ft Worth TX 1983-1993; R San Juan Apostol Ft Worth TX 1982-1993; Dio Dallas Dallas TX 1982; Serv Ch in Mex 1981-1982; Dio Guatemala New York NY 1968-1980; Serv Ch in Guatemala 1968-1979; Serv Ch in Mex 1965-1968. Auth, *Meditaciones Diarias*, Centro Para Ministerios Hispanos, 1998; Auth, *Coments Biblicos*, Centro Para Ministerios Hispanos, 1996; Auth, *Quince Anos*, Centro Para Ministerios Hispanos, 1995; Auth, *Necesidad de un Proceso Administrativo*, Universidad Mariano Galvez, 1978. Amnesty Prog 1987-1993; Hogar Taller de Guatemala 1970-1979. Necesidad de Un Proceso Administrativo Guatemalteco.

HUERTA GARCIA, Huerta (Tex) Chamela 33 A, Tlaquepaque Jalisco 45589 Mexico **Vic The Great Cmsn Fndt Houston TX 2000-; D San Esteban Martir San Sebastian El Grande 1989-** B 1961 s Daniel & Antonia. S Andrews TS MX 1988. D 1/22/1989 P 11/12/1989 Bp Samuel Espinoza-Venegas. m 10/30/1981 Maria Del Rosario Huerta c 5. Dio Wstrn Mex Zapopan Jalisco 1989-2000.

HUFF, Carolyn Tuttle (Pa) 1121 N Trooper Rd, Eagleville PA 19403 **Assoc Ch Of The Gd Samar Paoli PA 2011-** B Iowa City IA 1965 d Roger & Barbara. BS Truman St U 1988; MDiv VTS 1998. D 6/6/1998 P 12/19/1998 Bp William Jerry Winterrowd. m 1/25/2003 David Huff c 1. Assoc Trin Luth Ch Fairview Vill PA 2008-2011; Asst St. Thos' Ch Whitemarsh PA 2005-2008; Assoc S Dav's Ch Wayne PA 1999-2004; Asst S Steph's Ch Longmont CO 1998-1999.

HUFF, Christopher Mercer (SC) 1612 Dryden Ln, Charleston SC 29407 **Asst S Geo's Epis Ch Summerville SC 2012-** B Charleston SC 1956 s William & Dorothy. BA Coll of Charleston 1978; MDiv TESM 1988. D 6/23/1988 P 5/31/1989 Bp Christopher FitzSimons Allison. m 8/19/1978 Kim Huff c 2. W Shore Epis Charleston SC 1998-2008; Epis Ch of the Gd Shpd Charleston SC 1993-1998; S Paul's Ch Bennettsville SC 1988-1993.

HUFF, Clark Kern (Tex) 2252 Garden Court, San Marcos TX 78666 B New Orleans LA 1936 s Joe & Ethyl. BS U of Texas 1958; MDiv Epis TS of the SW 1994. D 6/17/2000 P 4/18/2001 Bp Claude Edward Payne. m 3/25/1978 Rebecca Huff c 2. Partnr In Mnstry Estrn Convoc Kenedy TX 2005-2006; Vstng P Partnr in Mnstry San Antonio TX 2005-2006; P-in-c of Trin Cntr Mnstrs S Dav's Ch Austin TX 2002-2005; S Aug's Epis Ch Galveston TX 2000-2008; The Great Cmsn Fndt Houston TX 2000-2002.

HUFF, Susan Ellen (At) 1031 Eagles Ridge Ct, Lawrenceville GA 30043 B Providence RI 1949 d Edward & Margaret. D 8/6/2006 Bp J Neil Alexander.

HUFFMAN, Charles Howard (Tex) 8124 Greenslope Dr, Austin TX 78759 B Houston TX 1926 s Ben & Lattie. BS U of Texas 1949; MDiv Epis TS of the SW 1966; STM Epis TS of the SW 1968. D 6/24/1966 Bp James Milton Richardson P 6/6/1967 Bp Scott Field Bailey. m 3/10/1951 Carolyn Barlow c 3. Int S Mk's Ch New Canaan CT 1995-1996; Int Trin Ch Newtown CT 1994-1995; Int Chr Ch Greenwich CT 1993; R S Matt's Ch Austin TX 1973-1991; Assoc Dir The Pittsburgh Experiment 1971-1973; Asst S Dav's Ch Austin TX 1966-1971.

HUFFMAN, Robert Nelson (SVa) 2212 Lynnwood drive, Wilmington NC 28403 **Ret 1994-** B Chicago IL 1931 s Troy & Mary. BA U of Florida 1953; MDiv SWTS 1958; STM Sewanee: The U So, TS 1976. D 6/29/1958 Bp William Francis Moses P 12/30/1958 Bp Henry I Louttit. c 1. Exec Bd Dio Sthrn Virginia Newport News VA 1981-1985, Dn Convoc IV 1981-1984, Exec Bd 1981-1985; R Trin Ch Portsmouth VA 1977-1993; Stndg Com Dio Cntrl Florida Orlando FL 1976-1977, Chair Lakeland Dnry 1970-1973, Secy of the Conv 1969-1977, Stndg Com Mem 1976-1977, Chairman, Lakeland Dnry 1970-1973; R H Trin Epis Ch Bartow FL 1964-1977; Asst S Mary's Epis Ch Daytona Bch FL 1961-1964; H Nativ Pahokee FL 1958-1961; P-in-c S Jn The Apos Ch Belle Glade FL 1958-1961.

HUFFORD, Robert Arthur (SO) 52 Bishopsgate Dr Apt 703, Cincinnati OH 45246 **Chapl S Mary's Meml Hm Cincinnati OH 1992-** B Chicago IL 1944 s Harold & Barbara. BA Br 1966; McGill U 1966; MDiv Nash 1972. D 6/17/1972 P 12/16/1972 Bp James Winchester Montgomery. The Soc of the Trsfg Cincinnati OH 1992-2014; Epis Chapl Nthrn Kentucky 1983-1992; R S Steph's Epis Ch Latonia KY 1983-1992; Chapl Cbury Hse Richmond KY 1982-1983; R S Alb's Ch Chicago IL 1974-1981; Cur Chr Ch Waukegan IL 1972-1974. CT, Assoc 1989; Csss 2001.

HUFFSTETLER, Joel W (ETenn) 3920 Clairmont Dr Ne, Cleveland TN 37312 **R S Lk's Ch Cleveland TN 2003-** B Charlotte NC 1962 s Joe & Pansy. BA Elon U 1985; Emory U 1987; MDiv Sewanee: The U So, TS 1990. D 5/24/1990 P 3/1/1991 Bp Bob Johnson. m 11/22/1998 Deborah Ann Williams. Asst R S Paul's Epis Ch Chattanooga TN 1995-2003; S Andr's Epis Ch Canton NC

1990-1995. Auth, "Henry Lee & Banastre Tarleton How Historians Use Their Memoirs"; Auth, "Sthrn Hist".

HUFT, Jerry Ray (CGC) Po Box 595, Wewahitchka FL 32465 **Ret 2001-** B Beckley WV 1938 s John & Lyda. BA SE U 1977; MDiv TESM 1980. D 6/22/1980 Bp William Hopkins Folwell P 2/14/1981 Bp Calvin Onderdonk Schofield Jr. m 3/17/1963 Jacqueline Huft. S Jas' Epis Ch Port St Joe FL 1984-2000; S Jn The Bapt Epis Ch Wewahitchka FL 1984-2000; Cur S Paul's Ch Delray Bch FL 1980-1983. Bro Of S Andr. st.john.wewahitchka@aol.com

HUGGARD, Linda (SJ) 4300 Keith Way, Bakersfield CA 93309 **Int Emm Luth Ch Bakersfield CA 2011-; Assoc Open Door Mnstrs Frazier Pk Ca. 2010-; Chap St Brigid Epicopal Cmnty Bakersfield Ca. 2010-** B Berkeley CA 1950 d Dewey & Allison. BA Sonoma St U 1995; MDiv CDSP 2005. D 6/2/2007 Bp Marc Handley Andrus P 12/21/2007 Bp Barry Leigh Beisner. c 1. S Jn's Epis Ch Stockton CA 2015-2017; P-in-c St Michaels Epis Ch Ridgecrest CA 2013-2015; Int Emm Luth Ch Bakersfield CA 2010; Dioc Coun Epis Dio San Joaquin Modesto CA 2008-2013, VP of So Dnry 2011-, Co Chair/ Cmsn on Equality 2009-; D S Tim's Ch Gridley CA 2007-2008.

HUGGINS, Arthur Hoskins (VI) P.O. Box 748, St. Vincent Saint Vincent & the Grenadines **Died 10/28/2016** B 1928 s William & Annie. Codrington Coll. Trans 5/1/1984 Bp Edward Mason Turner. m 7/4/1972 Patricia A Huggins c 3. R S Paul's Epis Angl Ch Frederiksted St Croix VI 1986-1999; S Geo Mtyr Ch Tortola 1984-1985; R S Geo The Mtyr Frederiksted S Croix VI 1984-1985; Archd Grenada S Geo's 1973-1984; Vic Gnrl Dio Windward Island 1972-1984; Dn S Geo's Cathd Kingstown S Vinc 1970-1973.

HUGHES, Alan (Pa) 1408 Sw 20th Ct, Gresham OR 97080 B Llanelli Dyfed South Wales GB 1934 s Daniel & Beatrice. BA U of Wales 1954; LTh S Michaels TS 1960; DMin Lancaster TS 1979. Trans 3/15/1976 Bp Lloyd Edward Gressle. Ch Of The H Cross Cumberland MD 1989-1991; R Ch Of The Redeem Springfield PA 1981-1989; R S Mich's Epis Ch Birdsboro PA 1976-1980; Serv Ch Of Engl 1960-1976. Auth, "Pstr Care Adult Pre-Operative Cardiac Patient," 1979. Ord Of S Lk.

HUGHES, Carlye J (FtW) Trinity Episcopal Church, 3401 Bellaire Drive South, Fort Worth TX 76109 **R Trin Epis Ch Ft Worth TX 2012-** B Tulsa OK 1958 d Robert & Jackie. BA U of Texas 1998; MDiv VTS 2005. D 3/19/2005 P 9/17/2005 Bp Mark Sean Sisk. m 10/18/2008 David R Smedley. R S Ptr's Epis Ch Peekskill NY 2007-2012; P S Jas Ch New York NY 2005-2007.

HUGHES, Frank Witt (WLa) 1107 Broadway St, Minden LA 71055 **R S Jn's Epis Ch Minden LA 2013-** B Texarkana TX 1954 s William & Mary. BA Hendrix Coll 1975; MDiv SWTS 1979; MA U Chi 1981; PhD NWU 1984. D 1/19/1981 Bp James Winchester Montgomery P 12/5/1981 Bp Quintin Ebenezer Primo Jr. Gr Epis Ch Monroe LA 2012-2013; Int Trin Epis Ch Columbus GA 2011-2012; Int S Tim's Ch Alexandria LA 2009-2011; Int S Paul's Ch New Orleans LA 2009; Int Ch Of The H Cross Shreveport LA 2008-2009; Int S Jn's Epis Ch Decatur IL 2006-2008; Supply P S Jas Ch Magnolia AR 2005-2006; Appointed Mssy ECUSA 2000-2004; Appointed Mssy Exec Coun Appointees New York NY 2000-2004; Sr Lectr in NT Codrington Coll Barbados 1998-2004; Sr Lectr Codrington Coll 1998-2000; R S Mk's Epis Ch Lewistown PA 1991-1997; Int S Jas Ch Greenridge Aston PA 1990-1991; Asst S Lk's Ch Philadelphia PA 1987-1990; Asst S Fran Ch Greensboro NC 1985-1986; Asst Ch Of The Epiph Chicago IL 1981-1985. Auth, "The Soc Situations Implied by Rhetoric," *The Thessalonians Debate*, Eerdmans, 2000; Auth, "Thessalonians, First and Second Letters to the," *Dictionary of Biblic Interp*, Abingdon Press, 1999; Auth, "Rhetorical Criticism," *HarperCollins Bible Dictionary*, HarperCollins, 1996; Auth, "Diakonos and Diakonia in Pauline Traditions," *Diac Mnstry: Past, Present, and Future*, NAAD, 1994; Auth, "The Parable of the Rich Man and Lazarus," *Rhetoric and the NT*, Sheffield Acad Press, 1993; Auth, "The Rhetoric of 1 Thessalonians," *The Thessalonian Correspondence*, Peeters, 1990; Auth, "Early Chr Rhetoric and 2 Thessalonians," *JSNTSup 30*, Sheffield Acad Press, 1989; Auth, "Feminism and Early Chr Hist," *ATR*, 1987. Angl Assn of Biblic Scholars, Secy Treas 1994; SBL 1977; Studiorum Novi Testamenti Societas 1996. Fulbright Schlr, U of Göttingen Fulbright-Kommission, Germany 1986.

✠ HUGHES, The Rt Rev Gethin Benwil (SanD) 461 Quail Run Rd, Buellton CA 93427 **Ret Bp of San Diego Dio San Diego San Diego CA 2005-, Bp Of San Diego 1992-2005; ECBF 1997-** B Lampeter Cardiganshire GB 1942 s Hubert & Sarah. BA Exeter U - Engl; MDiv SWTS 1967; Oxf GB 1968. Trans 2/1/1972 as Priest Bp Francis E I Bloy Con 6/20/1992 for SanD. m 6/22/1968 Arame Lenore Hughes c 1. R All SS-By-The-Sea Par Santa Barbara CA 1980-1992; Mssnr Dio Los Angeles Los Angeles CA 1975-1980, Stndg Com 1986-1989; Vic Prince of Peace Epis Ch Woodland Hls CA 1973-1975; Asst Cathd Cong Los Angeles CA 1969-1972; Epis Chap Of S Fran Los Angeles CA 1969-1972; Serv Ch Of Wales 1967-1969; Trst Bexley Seabury Fed Chicago IL 1986-2002. DD Seabury Wstrn 1993.

HUGHES, James Anthony (Va) 9320 West St, Manassas VA 20110 B Philadelphia PA 1949 s Anthony & Elizabeth. MDiv Mt St. Mary's Sem 1981; MA Cath U 1982. Rec 12/10/2016 as Priest Bp Ted Gulick Jr. m 12/9/2016 Frank E Walworth.

HUGHES, Jennifer Scheper (Mass) 1147 Walnut St, Berkeley CA 94707 B Berkeley CA 1969 BA U CA. D 6/7/2003 P 6/5/2004 Bp M(Arvil) Thomas Shaw. m 2/3/1995 Santos Roman c 1. Bloy Hse Claremont CA 2012-2016, 2010; Ch Of The Mssh Santa Ana CA 2012-2013; All SS Epis Ch Riverside CA 2007-2010; Chr Ch Hyde Pk MA 2006; Iglesia De San Juan Hyde Pk MA 2006.

HUGHES, John Richard (Lex) 2449 Larkin Rd, Lexington KY 40503 B Milwaukee WI 1957 s John & Mary. BA U of Wisconsin 1979; MDiv Gordon-Conwell TS 1984; CAS Nash 1991. D 6/9/1991 P 1/4/1992 Bp Roger John White. c 2. Ch S Mich The Archangel Lexington KY 1993-1998; Ch Of The Ascen Frankfort KY 1992-1993.

HUGHES, Laura K (WMo) St. George Episcopal Church, 423 N Highway 5, Camdenton MO 65020 **S Geo Epis Ch Camdenton MO 2017-** B Grand Rapids MI 1960 d Willis & Ruth. AA Mssn Coll 1986; BA San Jose St U 1989. D 5/3/2014 P 11/7/2014 Bp Martin Scott Field. m 9/4/1993 Howard Howard Hughes. P Dio W Missouri Kansas City MO 2014-2016. rector.saint.george@gmail.com

HUGHES, Linda M (Ia) 103 Melissa St, Elizabethtown KY 42701 B Fort Wayne IN 1943 d Willard & Mary. AGS Indiana U 1985; BGS Indiana U 1989; MDiv SWTS 1995. D 3/25/1995 P 10/5/1995 Bp Francis Campbell Gray. c 8. Chapl Hospice of Perry Iowa 2003-2006; R S Mart's Ch Perry IA 1999-2008; Vic All SS Ch Syracuse IN 1995-1999; Multicultural Cmsn Mem Dio Iowa Des Moines IA 2007-2008, Bd Dir Mem 2006-2008, One Wrld-One Ch Cmsn Mem 2003-2008. Ord of S Lk 1992-1995; Ord of S Lk 2005.

HUGHES, Malcolm Albert (FdL) Saint John's Episcopal Church, 139 South Smalley, Shawano WI 54166 **Ret 1998-** B Liverpool UK 1933 s William & Fredericka. BA Bishops U QC CA 1958; Lic Sacr Theol Bishops U QC CA 1960. Trans 9/1/1985 as Priest Bp Frederick Barton Wolf. m 11/14/2008 Lydia Barnes c 3. Dir, The Clarion - dio. Nwspr Dio Fond du Lac Fond du Lac WI 2004-2008; S Jn's Ch Shawano WI 2004-2008; R S Sav's Par Bar Harbor ME 1985-1998; Serv Angl Ch of Can Montreal 1971-1985; Chapl Can Legion 1971-1985; Serv Dio Nassau & The Bahamas 1966-1969; Serv Ch of Engl 1961-1970; Presiding Judge, Eccl Trial Crt Dio Fond du Lac Appleton WI 2006-2008. Auth, "A Handbook for Ch Wardens," 1982; Auth, "Hiding Behind a Teacup," 1981. Off, Ord of S Jn of Jerusalem HM Eliz II, Queen of Engl 1982.

HUGHES, Mary London Carswell (ECR) 902 California Ave, San Jose CA 95125 **R S Fran Epis Ch San Jose CA 2013-; Dep to GC Dio El Camino Real Salinas CA 2014-, Bp's Coun of Advice 2013-, Stndg Com 2013-, Secy of Conv 2009-, Alt Dep to GC 2008-2014, COM Vocations Secy 2008-, Bp's Search Com 2006-2007** B Atlanta GA 1959 d Matthew & Mary London. BA Brenau U 1981; MDiv CDSP 1996. D 11/18/1996 P 6/3/1997 Bp Richard Lester Shimpfky. m 7/1/2006 Allan Charles Hughes c 3. Assoc R Ch Of S Jude The Apos Cupertino CA 2010-2012; P Exec S Tim's Epis Ch Mtn View CA 2000-2010; Asst R S Mk's-In-The-Vlly Epis Los Olivos CA 1997-2000; Yth Dir Chr Epis Ch Los Altos CA 1997; Yth Min Trin Cathd San Jose CA 1997. DOK 1999. Bp's Cross Awd Dio El Camino Real 2014. maly@stfranciswillowglen.org

HUGHES III, Robert Davis (SO) 335 Tennessee Ave, Sewanee TN 37383 B Boston MA 1943 s Robert & Nancy. BA Ya 1966; BD EDS 1969; MA U of St Michaels Coll 1974; PhD U of St Michaels Coll 1980. D 6/28/1969 P 1/11/1970 Bp Roger W Blanchard. m 6/12/1965 Barbara B Hughes c 1. Sewanee U So TS Sewanee TN 2006-2009, Norma and Olan Mills Prof of Div 2001-, Prof Syst Theol 1992-2005, Asst Prof 1980-1991; Asst S Steph-Field Toronto ON 1975-1976; Cur S Anne Toronto ON 1972-1975; Ch Of The Epiph Nelsonville OH 1969-1972; Asst Ch Of The Gd Shpd Athens OH 1969-1972; GBEC Secy HOB 2000-2009. Auth, "Beloved Dust," Continuum, 2008; Auth, "S," *Var arts*. AAR 1999; Assoc, C.S.M. 1980; Soc for the Study of Anglicanism 2003; Soc for the Study of Chr Sprtlty 1999; Soc of Angl and Luth Theologians 1978. Shortlisted, Mich Ramsey Prize Archbp of Cbury 2011; Shortlisted, Mich Ramsey Prize Archbp of Cbury 2011; des Places-Libermann Awd in Pneumatology Duquesne U 2010; Fellowowship ECF 1972; Phi Beta Kappa 1966.

HUGHES, Rosalind Claire (O) **Ch Of The Epiph Euclid OH 2012-** B Wells UK 1968 d Alan & Ann. BA Oxf GB 1989; MDiv Bex Sem 2011. D 6/4/2011 P 1/24/2012 Bp Mark Hollingsworth Jr. m 9/7/1991 Gareth David Hughes c 3. Assoc S Andr's Epis Ch Elyria OH 2011-2012. rosalindchughes@oh.rr.com

HUGHES II, Theron Rex (WK) 1825 Spring St, Quincy IL 62301 **Died 10/9/2015** B Casper WY 1924 s Theron & DeEtte. BA Knox Coll 1950; MDiv Nash 1953. D 4/27/1953 P 11/4/1953 Bp William L Essex. m 8/30/1954 Anne Agee c 4. Ret 1989-2015; P-in-c S Jas Epis Ch Griggsville IL 1989-1992; Beloit First Chr Beloit KS 1984-1989; R Ch Of The Epiph Concordia KS 1982-1989; R S Andr's Ch Kenosha WI 1975-1982; NI Dio Quincy Peoria IL 1971-1974, Dep GC 1961-1967, Chair Cmsn 1959-1968, Div C&C 1958-1970; Vic S Tim's Ch Griffith IN 1968-1975; S Andr's Ch Peoria IL 1954-1968; S Steph's Ch Harrisburg IL 1954-1959; Vic St Johns Ch Quincy IL 1954-1959; Vic S Mich Mendon IL 1953-1954; Vic S Steph's Ch Peoria IL 2015; Dioc Coun Dio Nthrn Indiana So Bend IN 1972-1974. SSC 1973. DD Nash 1992.

HUGHES, Thomas Downs (WNC) 16 Salisbury Dr Apt 7206, Asheville NC 28803 B Shamokin PA 1933 s Franklin & Ora. Maryville Coll 1951; BA Ohio U 1954; BD Ken 1958; MDiv Bex Sem 1972. D 6/1/1958 Bp Henry W Hobson

P 12/10/1958 Bp Harry Sherbourne Kennedy. m 6/12/1961 Margaret A Masters c 2. Asst Trin Epis Ch Asheville NC 1998-2007; P-in-c Ch Of S Mths Asheville NC 1992-1996; VP Mssn Healthcare Fndt Asheville NC 1991-1998; VP S Lk's Healthcare Fndt Cedar Rapids IA 1981-1991; Int Chr Ch Cedar Rapids IA 1980; R S Paul's Ch Minneapolis MN 1974-1979; Dn The Epis Cathd Of Our Merc Sav Faribault MN 1970-1974; Asst S Lk's Ch Minneapolis MN 1964-1970; Chr Ch Frontenac MN 1962-1964; Vic S Mk's Ch Lake City MN 1962-1964; Cn S Andr's Cathd Honolulu HI 1960-1962; Vic Chr Memi Ch Kilauea HI 1958-1960; In-c Conf Cntr Kauai HI 1958-1960; St Thos Ch Hanalei HI 1958-1960. Auth, "Estate Plnng," *Older Americans Almanac*, Gale Resrch Inc., 1994.

HUGHES JR, Thomas Roddy (Eas) 852 Spring Valley Dr, Fredericksburg VA 22405 **Int S Mary's Ch Colonial Bch VA 2013-** B Chattanooga TN 1944 s Thomas & Leta. BA U of Tennessee 1968; MDiv Sewanee: The U So, TS 1975. D 6/15/1975 Bp John Vander Horst P 5/10/1976 Bp William Evan Sanders. m 12/21/1993 Janet E Elmore c 3. Assoc S Geo's Ch Fredericksburg VA 2011-2013; R Shrewsbury Par Ch Kennedyville MD 1995-2010; St Mary the Vrgn Ch Vrgn Gorda VG 1150 1992-1994; Asst Chr Epis Ch Charlottesvlle VA 1987-1990; R Ch Of The Nativ Ft Oglethorp GA 1980-1985; Trin Epis Ch Fulton KY 1980; Dio Tennessee Nashville TN 1976-1980; S Jn's Ch Mart TN 1976-1980; Chapl U of Tennessee-Mart Mart TN 1976-1980; D-in-Trng S Jn's Epis Cathd Knoxville TN 1975-1976. Harriet Tubman Awd Dio Easton 1998.

HUGHES-EMPKE, Sheryl Ann (Ia) PO Box 486, Perry IA 50220 **S Mart's Ch Perry IA 2014-** B Davenport IA 1950 d John & Lillian. Epis Stds Seabury Wstrn; BA Clarke Coll 1972; MA U of Nthrn Iowa 1975; MA Mundelein Coll 1981. D 12/7/2013 P 6/29/2014 Bp Alan Scarfe. c 3. Gr Ch Boone IA 2015. revhughesempke@gmail.com

HUGHES-HABEL, Deborah Jean (U) 4615 S 3200 W, West Valley City UT 84119 **Asst All SS Ch Salt Lake City UT 2011-** B Iowa City IA 1951 d William & Wilma. AS U of Nebraska 1974; BSA Weber St U 1991; MDiv Epis TS of the SW 2010. D 6/12/2010 Bp Carolyn Tanner Irish P 5/21/2011 Bp Scott Byron Hayashi. m 6/15/1991 Ronald William Habel c 7. Cur S Steph's Ch W Vlly City UT 2010-2012.

HUGHS, Leslie Curtis (LI) 16 Birch Road, Danbury CT 06811 **Assoc S Steph's Ch Ridgefield CT 2009-** B Watertown NY 1941 s Richard & Margaret. BS SUNY 1963; MDiv PDS 1971. D 6/5/1971 Bp Allen Webster Brown P 12/11/1971 Bp Charles Bowen Persell Jr. m 6/17/1967 Linda Hughs c 3. P S Jn's Ch Cohoes NY 2006-2008; Int S Paul's Epis Ch Albany NY 2004-2007, 1980-1988; Int S Paul's Ch Troy NY 2003-2004; R Chr Ch Manhasset NY 1988-2002; R S Mk's Ch Malone NY 1976-1980; The Epis Ch Of The Cross Ticonderoga NY 1972-1976; Untd Putnam Ch Putnam Sta NY 1972-1976; Cur Chr Ch Schenectady NY 1971-1972. R Emer S Paul's Ch, Albany, NY 2005.

HUGUENIN, Robert (Fla) 4224 Coastal Hwy, Crawfordville FL 32327 B New York NY 1943 D 12/22/2002 P 6/29/2003 Bp Stephen Hays Jecko. m 9/11/1965 Sandra Abbott c 3. Epis Prison Mnstry Clarksdale MS.

HUINER, Peter Bruce (Del) 500 Woodlawn Rd, Wilmington DE 19803 **Assoc SS Andr & Matt 2004-** B Oak Park IL 1935 s Bernard & Edith. BA Calvin Coll 1957; BD Calvin TS 1962; CAS SWTS 1970. D 5/19/1970 Bp Charles Ellsworth Bennison Jr P 9/29/1970 Bp Gerald Francis Burrill. m 8/13/1960 Tona L Kenbeek c 5. Vic S Barn Ch Wilmington DE 2009-2011; Cn Cathd Ch Of S Jn Wilmington DE 2000-2005; R Gr Epis Ch Wilmington DE 1987-1997; R S Alb's Ch Silver Creek NY 1985-1987; R Ch Of S Jn The Bapt Dunkirk NY 1983-1987; Assoc S Paul's Cathd Buffalo NY 1979-1982; Archd Dio Wstrn New York Tonawanda NY 1975-1982; Dn Bexley Seabury Fed Chicago IL 1973-1975; Chapl Nthrn Illinois U 1970-1973; Assoc S Paul's Ch Dekalb IL 1970-1973; Serv Chr Reformed Ch 1961-1969.

HULBERT, Edward R (Los) St Richard of Chichester Church, PO Box 1317, Lake Arrowhead CA 92352 B Dover NJ 1940 s Edward & Agnes. STB CUA TS 1966; MA CUA 1968; PhD CUA 1969. Rec 6/7/2012 as Priest Bp Joseph Jon Bruno. m 10/10/2008 Terry Clark Cook. erhulbert72@gmail.com

HULBERT, James Edward (NJ) 1620 Mayflower Ct Apt A405, Winter Park FL 32792 **Ret 1988-** B New York NY 1926 s Jason & Anna. BA Hobart and Wm Smith Colleges 1949; MDiv GTS 1952. D 6/15/1952 P 12/20/1952 Bp Benjamin M Washburn. Serv Dio New Jersey Trenton NJ 1985-1988, Serv 1970-1984; R The Ch Of S Uriel The Archangel Sea Girt NJ 1971-1988; R H Trin Ch So River NJ 1965-1971; Urban Deptartment Dio Newark Newark NJ 1959-1961, DRE 1956-1958; R S Mk's Ch W Orange NJ 1957-1965; Vic S Lk's Epis Ch Haworth NJ 1952-1957. Ord of H Redeem. DD Nash 1982; Hon Cn Trin Cathd 1970.

HULEN, Jennifer L (Ind) St Christopher's Episcopal Church, 1402 W. Main, Carmel IN 46032 **S Chris's Epis Ch Carmel IN 2013-** B Park Ridge IL 1965 d Thomas & Judith. BA U of Tulsa 1986; MDiv SW Bapt TS 1990; Cert in Mandarin Beijing Second Frgn Lang Inst 1992; Dplma in Angl Stds Seabury Wstrn 2012. D 6/9/2012 P 2/3/2013 Bp Cate Waynick. m 5/17/1986 Peter L Hulen c 2.

HULET, Jefferson R (NJ) 14 Saint Remy Ct, Newport Coast CA 92657 **Mem/Chapl Bd Rgnts Harris Manchester Coll Oxford 2010-** B Champaign Illinois

1951 s Richard & Kathleen. BS U of San Francisco 1981; CTh Oxf GB 2002; STM Oxf GB 2003; MDiv GTS 2006. D 6/3/2006 P 12/9/2006 Bp George Edward Councell. m 3/21/1987 Deborah Hulet c 1. Asst S Mich And All Ang Par Corona Dl Mar CA 2010-2011; R Steph's Ch Riverside NJ 2007-2009; R Chr Ch Palmyra NJ 2006-2007; P-in-c Riverfront Epis Team Mnstry Riverside NJ 2006-2007; Pstr Response Team Dio New Jersey Trenton NJ 2007-2009.

HULL, Carol Wharton (SO) 14590 Wilmot Way, Lake Oswego OR 97035 B Providence RI 1943 d Willard & Mildred. BA U of Texas 1963; MS Elmira Coll 1969; MDiv Bex Sem 1984. D 6/16/1984 Bp Robert Rae Spears Jr P 12/17/1984 Bp William George Burrill. m 8/10/1963 Tommy A Hull c 2. Bex Sem Columbus OH 1997-2008; R S Geo's Epis Ch Dayton OH 1991-2008; R S Jas Ch Hammondsport NY 1987-1991; P Ch of the Redeem Addison NY 1987; Dn SE Distr Dio Rochester Henrietta 1986-1991; Vic Ch Of The Gd Shpd Savona NY 1984-1991.

HULL, George Andrew (Chi) 509 Brier St, Kenilworth IL 60043 **Pstr Assoc Ch Of The H Comf Kenilworth IL 2007-; Chapl to Ret Cler & Surviving Spouses Dio Chicago Chicago IL 2011-** B Elmore MN 1939 s Andrew & Naomi. BA Roa 1962; MDiv VTS 1981. D 5/28/1981 Bp A(rthur) Heath Light P 11/29/1981 Bp James Winchester Montgomery. m 8/27/1966 Jean L Hull. R S Mk's Barrington IL 1993-2007; Assoc R S Chrys's Ch Chicago IL 1981-1993; Stdt VTS Alexandria VA 1978-1981; Trst Epis Chars And Cmnty Serv (Eccs) Chicago IL 2001-2007; Bd Dir ReVive Cntr for Hsng and Healing Chicago IL 1983-1994.

HULL, Nicholas Andrew (At) PO Box 1146, Columbus GA 31902 **Chr Ch Martinsville VA 2016-; Cur Trin Epis Ch Columbus GA 2014-** B Lima OH 1986 s Andrew & Deborah. BA Sewanee 2009; MDiv VTS 2014. D 12/21/2013 P 6/21/2014 Bp Robert Christopher Wright. rev.nickhull@gmail.com

HULL, S (Los) 13025 Bloomfield St., Studio City CA 91604 **Campbell Hall Vlly Vlg CA 2010-** B New Orleans LA 1963 s Frank & Katherine. BA Claremont Coll 1985; MDiv CDSP 1995. D 6/10/1995 Bp Chester Lovelle Talton P 1/1/1996 Bp Frederick Houk Borsch. m 6/17/1989 Susan Elizabeth Hull c 1. R St Marks Epis Ch Van Nuys CA 1997-2010; S Mich and All Ang Epis Ch Studio City CA 1995-1997.

HULL IV, William Franklin (Fla) 630 S Sapodilla Ave Apt 214, West Palm Beach FL 33401 **1978-** B Pittsburgh PA 1941 s William & Elva. MDiv UTS; U of Ghana Legon GH Afr; BA Westminster Coll; DEd Penn 1970; NYU 1986. D 1/19/1974 P 11/1/1975 Bp John Harris Burt. c 2. S Thos Flagler Cnty Palm Coast FL 2012-2013; S Mk's Epis Ch Jacksonville FL 2005-2006; Dio Eau Claire Eau Claire WI 2003-2004; Asst All SS-By-The-Sea Par Santa Barbara CA 1977-1978; 1974-1977. Auth, *Innovations & Tchg Todays Undergraduates*; Auth, *The Chrisitan Coll*. amra227@yahoo.com

HULLAR, Leonard Earl (Ct) 115 W Main St, Plainville CT 06062 **Ch of our Sav Plainville CT 2016-; R S Lk's Ch Livingston TX 2012-** B Birmingham AL 1954 s Joseph & Barbara. BA U of Alabama 1975; MA U of Alabama 1976; Cert Iona Sch for Mnstry 2009. D 6/20/2009 Bp C Andrew Doyle P 1/9/2010 Bp Rayford Baines High Jr. m 6/7/1975 Sharon Hullar c 2. Vic S Barn Epis Ch Houston TX 2008-2010.

HULLINGER, Jon M (Kan) 3750 E Douglas Ave, Wichita KS 67208 **Trin Ch Atchison KS 2015-** B ████████ 1955 s Jasper & Joyce. Rec 6/8/2014 as Priest Bp Dean E Wolfe. S Ja█████████ on ██ KS 2014-2015. office@trinityepiscopal.church

HULL-RYDE, Norman Arthur (wNC) 2535 Sheffield Dr, Gastonia NC 28054 B New York NY 1930 s Arthur & Kathleen. Kent Sch; BA U NC 1952. D 12/5/1982 Bp William Gillette Weinhauer. m 9/9/1952 Anne Dewsnap Bergh c 3. D S Mk's Ch Gastonia NC 1983-2005.

HULME, Steven Edward (Ct) 26 Colony Road, East Lyme CT 06333 **Ret 1998-** B Iowa City IA 1934 s Edward & Helen. BA U of Iowa 1956; MDiv GTS 1959. D 6/10/1959 P 12/16/1959 Bp Gordon V Smith. m 12/31/1960 Mary S Sergeant c 3. R S Jn's Epis Ch Niantic CT 1971-1998; Chapl Kent Girls Sch kent CT 1963-1971; Vic S Alb's Ch Davenport IA 1960-1963; Cur Trin Cathd Davenport IA 1959-1960. auther, "You've Got to Start Young," iUniverse, 2013. Distinguished Alum Awd GTS 2017; R Emer St. Jn's, Niantic 2015.

HULME, Thomas Stanford (Ia) 1617 W Benton St, Iowa City IA 52246 **Ret 1991-; Assoc P Trin Ch Iowa City IA 1991-, DCE' 1968-1990** B Burlington IA 1930 s Edward & Helen. BA U of Iowa 1952; STB GTS 1955; MSW U of Iowa 1970. D 6/15/1955 P 12/16/1955 Bp Gordon V Smith. m 6/16/1978 Jean M Hulme c 5. Convenor Epis Clerics Fam Life Proj 1992-1998; S Lk's Ch Ft Madison IA 1989; S Paul's Epis Ch Grinnell IA 1988; Trin Epis Par Waterloo IA 1988; Trin Ch Muscatine IA 1987; S Paul's Ch Durant IA 1986-1987; Asst Dir St Serv for Crippled Chld U of Iowa 1973-1991; Psych Soc Worker Dept of Psych U of Iowa Hospitals 1970-1973; R Gr Ch Cedar Rapids IA 1959-1968; P-in-c St. Martins Perry IA 1956-1959; P-in-c Gr Ch Boone IA 1955-1959. Auth, *Mntl Hlth Consult w Rel Leaders*; Auth, *Networking Through Reg Chld's Hlth Centers*; Auth, *Plnng Fam Enrichment Weekends - A Manual*. Cn Dio Iowa, St. Paul's Cathd, Des Moines, Iowa 2005.

HULS II, Frederick Eugene (Az) 2812 N 69th Pl, Scottsdale AZ 85257 **D S Jas The Apos Epis Ch Tempe AZ 2011-; Chapl Arizona Dept Of Corrections**

Phoenix AZ 1999- B Columbus OH 1941 s Frederick & Alice. BD Nthrn Arizona U 1990. D 6/5/1993 Bp Robert Reed Shahan. m 12/15/1962 Patricia Taylor Huls c 2. Chapl Arizona Dept of Corrections - Chapl 1999-2012; Chapl Ecum Chapl for the Homeless 1995-1997; Chapl Ecum Chapl For The Homeless Phoenix AZ 1995-1996; D S Steph's Ch Phoenix AZ 1993-2011; Admin Trin Cathd Phoenix AZ 1991-1996. NAAD 1993. Phi Kappa Phi Nthrn Arizona U 1990.

HULS, Patricia Taylor (Az) 2310 N 56th St, Phoenix AZ 85008 B Lakewood OH 1941 d Clyde & Helen. BS OH SU 1963; BSN Arizona St U 1980. D 1/26/2008 Bp Kirk Stevan Smith. m 12/15/1962 Frederick Eugene Huls c 2. D S Steph's Ch Phoenix AZ 2008-2010.

HULSE JR, Granvyl G (NH) 57 Pleasant St, Colebrook NH 03576 B Seattle WA 1929 s Granvyl & Mae. D 6/21/1986 P 1/31/1987 Bp Douglas Edwin Theuner. c 4. P S Paul's Ch Canaan VT 1998-2011; Vic S Steph's Epis Mssn Colebrook NH 1986-1998. Auth, "The News & Sentinel," *Hist Resrch*, N&S Pub, 2012; Auth, "Colebrook, New Hampshire. The First 100 Years," *Hist Resrch*, N&S Pub, 2010; Auth, "From Paddy Acre to the Stevens Store," *Hist Resrch*, N&S Pub, 2008; Auth, "From Pleasant to Parsons," *Hist Resrch*, N&S Pub, 2008; Auth, "Let's Eat Out," *Hist Resrch*, N&S Pub, 2002; Auth, "A Hist of St. Steph's Epis Ch, Colebrook," *Hist*, N&S Pub, 2000.

✠ HULSEY, The Rt Rev Sam Byron (NwT) 801 Hillcrest St, Fort Worth TX 76107 **Bd NAES 2002-; Ret Bp of NW Texas Dio NW Texas Lubbock TX 1997-, Exec Coun 1991-1997, Bp 1980-1997** B Fort Worth TX 1932 s Simeon & Ruth. BA W&L 1953; MDiv VTS 1958; VTS 1981; Sewanee: The U So, TS 1985; Epis TS of the SW 1998. D 6/18/1958 P 1/25/1959 Bp John Joseph Meakin Harte Con 12/13/1980 for NwT. m 9/21/2002 Isabelle Brown Newberry. HOB Plnng Com 1991-1997; Pres Prov VII 1990-1993; R Ch Of The H Trin Midland TX 1978-1980; R S Dav's Epis Ch Nashville TN 1973-1978; P-in-c All SS Epis Mssn Perryton TX 1966-1973; S Matt's Ch Pampa TX 1966-1973; Asst S Mich And All Ang Ch Dallas TX 1963-1966; Cur/Asst S Jn's Epis Ch Corsicana TX 1958-1960. DD TS U So 1985; DD VTS 1981.

HULTMAN, Eugene Bradlee (Mass) 255 N Central Ave, Quincy MA 02170 B Quincy MA 1949 s Eugene & Marion. BA U of Massachusetts 1977; MDiv GTS 1985. D 6/1/1985 Bp John Bowen Coburn P 5/9/1986 Bp O'Kelley Whitaker. c 4. Dio Massachusetts Boston MA 2002-2006; S Andr's Ch Hanover MA 2000-2006; R Trin Ch Bridgewater MA 1996-2000; Ch Of The Gd Shpd Fairhaven MA 1991-1996; S Steph's Ch Providence RI 1989-1991; Dio Cntrl New York Liverpool NY 1988-1989; Vic Emm Ch E Syracuse NY 1988-1989; Int Gr Epis Ch Utica NY 1987-1988; Cn St Paul's Syracuse Syracuse NY 1985-1987.

✠ HULTSTRAND, The Rt Rev Donald Maynard (Spr) 1706 Parkins Mill Rd, Greenville SC 29607 **Bp-in-Res Chr Ch Greenville SC 2005-** B Parkers Prairie MN 1927 s Aaron & Selma. BA Macalester Coll 1950; BD Bex Sem 1953; MDiv Bex Sem 1972; DD Nash 1986; Nash 1986; DD Bex Sem 2004; Bex Sem 2004. D 6/14/1953 Bp Hamilton Hyde Kellogg P 12/19/1953 Bp Stephen E Keeler Con 2/6/1982 for Spr. m 2/18/2006 Lenora Hultstrand c 2. Ret Bp of Springfield Dio Springfield Springfield IL 1991-1992, Ch Deploy Bd 1985-1991, Joint Cmsn on Evang & Renwl 1985-1988, Joint Cmsn Prog Bdgt & Fin 1983-1989, Bp 1982-1991, Joint C███ ██vang & Renwl 1985-1988; Epis Radio/TV Fndt 1983-1987; R Trin C████████ley CO 1979-1981; The AFP Lancaster PA 1975-1979; R The Par of St Paul's Epis Ch Duluth MN 1969-1975; Assoc S Andr's Ch Kansas City MO 1968-1969; R S Mk's Ch Canton OH 1962-1968; Instr Breck Sch 1961-1962; R Gr Memi Ch Wabasha MN 1957-1961; H Trin Epis Ch Luverne MN 1953-1957; S Jn Worthington MN 1953-1957; Vic S Jn's By the Lake Luverne MN 1953-1957. Auth, "Life in the Sprt"; Auth, "H Living Today"; Auth, *And God Shall Wipe Away All Tears*; Auth, *The Praying Ch*. AFP, Exec Dir 1975-1979; Living Ch, Pres 1991-2001. Hon Cn Trin Cathd 1966.

HUMBER, Michael R (Colo) 2201 Dexter St, Denver CO 80207 B Memphis TN 1979 s Michael & Teresa. BA Wake Forest U 2001; MA Mid 2002; MDiv CDSP 2013; MDiv CDSP 2013. D 6/13/2015 Bp Marc Handley Andrus P 12/5/2015 Bp Chester Lovelle Talton. m 1/19/2015 Brian M Sanderson. S Thos Epis Ch Denver CO 2015-2016.

HUMKE, Richard Herbert (Ky) 200 S Galt Ave, Louisville KY 40206 **Ret 1996-; ExCoun Dio Kentucky Louisville KY 1963-** B Dubuque IA 1931 s Frederick & Martha. BA U of Iowa 1955; BD VTS 1956. D 6/21/1956 P 12/21/1956 Bp Gordon V Smith. m 8/20/1960 Joan Humke c 2. R S Matt's Epis Ch Louisville KY 1973-1996; Assoc S Fran In The Fields Harrods Creek KY 1968-1973; R Gr Ch Hopkinsville KY 1961-1968; Chapl Cbury Hse Honolulu HI 1958-1961; P-in-c Gd Samar Epis Ch Honolulu HI 1958-1961; Cur Trin Cathd Davenport IA 1956-1958.

HUMM, Richard (Md) St Paul's Church, 25 Church St, Prince Frederick MD 20678 B Akron OH 1979 s Richard & Carolyn. BA SE U 2002; MDiv VTS 2008; MDiv VTS 2008. D 6/13/2009 P 12/19/2009 Bp Mark Hollingsworth Jr. m 12/15/2001 Charity A Humm c 3. Vic S Jn The Evang Lockport IL 2011-2016; Cler-in-Charge S Alb Epis Ch Cleveland OH 2009-2011; Yth Min S Paul's Epis Ch Cleveland OH 2009-2011, Yth Min 2009-2011; Intern St. Jas

Epis Ch Wooster OH 2008-2009. Rosary Soc (VTS Chapt) 2007; Soc of Cath Priests 2010.

HUMMEL, Gini (Ct) 30 Woodland Street, #6D, Hartford CT 06105 B York PA 1936 d Richard & Thelma. BA U of Delaware 1958; MDiv GTS 1994. D 6/4/1994 Bp Jack Marston Mckelvey P 12/17/1994 Bp Joe Doss. c 2. P-in-c S Andr's Ch Milford CT 2006-2009; R S Lk's Ch So Glastonbury CT 1999-2006; Cur S Lk's Epis Ch Metuchen NJ 1994-1999.

HUMMEL, Thomas Charles (Va) 1200 N Quaker Ln, Alexandria VA 22302 **Chair, Dept. of Theol, Asst Chapl Epis HS Alexandria VA 1987-** B Middletown CT 1947 s Reginald & Beatrice. BA Ups 1969; MDiv Yale DS 1972; Fell Oxf GB 1976; MA Van 1976; PhD Van 1981. D 9/10/1972 P 7/25/1973 Bp George E Rath. m 12/28/1968 Ruth Hummel. VTS Alexandria VA 2006, 1991; Chapl, Tchr Moravian Acad Bethlehem PA 1981-1987; Instr in Ch Hist U So St. Lk's Sem Sewanee 1980-1981; Chapl, Tchr St. Jn Bapt Sch Mendham NJ 1978-1980; Grad Chapl Pusey Hse Oxford Great Britain (UK) 1976-1978; P-in-c S Anselm's Epis Ch Nashville TN 1974-1975. "Lord Who May Dwell in Your Sanctuary, Who May Abide on your H Hill: A Palestinian Pilgrimage," *They Came and They Saw*, Melisende, London, 2000; "Patterns of the Past Prospects for the Future: The Chr Heritage in the H Land," Melisende, London, 1999; Auth, "Patterns of The Sacr," Scorpion Cavendish, London, 1995; Auth, "Engl Prot Pilgrims of the 19th Century," *The Chr Heritage in the H Land*, Scorpion Cavendish, London, 1995; "The Sacramentality of the H Land," *The Sense of the Sacramential*, SPCK, London, 1995. Conf of Angl Theologicans. Natl Endwmt Fell 1989; Fulbright Fell 1987; Jarvis Fellowshp Yale DS 1972; Fellowshp 76-78 Epis Ch Fndtn.

HUMMELL, Mark William (NY) 160 Cabrini Blvd Apt 36, New York NY 10033 **Gr Ch Sch New York New York NY 2014-** B Cincinnati OH 1965 s Mitchell & Virginia. BA U of Notre Dame 1987; MS Arizona St U 1999; MDiv Yale DS 2002. D 6/21/2003 P 6/9/2004 Bp Andrew Donnan Smith. m 12/29/2012 Peter Lars Christensen. Counslr NYU 2010-2014; Asst St. Andr's Angl Ch-Abu Dhabi 2010-2014; Assoc R Ch Of The Ascen New York NY 2007-2010; Dio New York New York NY 2003-2007, Chair, Soc Concerns Cmsn 2008-2010; Assoc Dir Epis Chars Of The Dio New York 2003-2007; Cathd Of St Jn The Div New York NY 2003. Auth, "Designed for Well-Being," *Connections Quarterly*, The Cntr for Sprtl and Ethical Educ, 2017; Auth, "The Growing Presence of Muslim Students At St. Fran Xavier U," *Linking Theory to Pract: Case Stds For Working w Coll Students*, Routledge, 2012. NASW 1988. R. Wm Muehl Awd For Preaching Berkeley Div. At Yale 2002. mhummell@gcschool.org

HUMPHREY, Christine Ann (Mich) 544 W Iroquois Rd, Pontiac MI 48341 B Lansing MI 1946 d Harold & Dorothea. BA Albion Coll 1968; Bex Sem 1989; S Cyril Methodist Sem 1989. D 12/2/1989 Bp H Coleman Mcgehee Jr P 4/1/1991 Bp R aymond Stewart Wood Jr. R S Mary's-In-The-Hills Ch Lake Orion MI 1995-2011; Assoc Trin Epis Ch Farmington MI 1993-1994; All SS Epis Ch Pontiac MI 1991-1993.

HUMPHREY, Georgia Lehman (Ia) 15064 Sheridan Ave, Clive IA 50325 **Chapl St Louis U Med Cntr 1996-** B Lancaster PA 1941 d Joseph & Georgiana. BS Millersville U 1963; MEd Arcadia Coll 1983; MDiv SWTS 1993; DMin SWTS 2003. D 6/19/1993 P 4/27/1994 Bp Hays H. Rockwell. m 6/12/2009 Janet M Nelson c 3. Dir of Congrl Dvlpmt and Tchr Bexley Seabury Fed Chicago IL 2006-2007; S Barn Epis Ch Denver CO 1996-2006; Min For Mssn & Dir Chr Ch Cathd S Louis MO 1993-1995. Richard Hooker Forum; SCHC 1987.

HUMPHREY JR, Howard MacKenzie (O) 6295 Chagrin River Rd, Chagrin Falls OH 44022 B Edenton NC 1949 s Howard & Emma. BS U of Texas 1972; MS U of Texas 1974; MDiv Epis TS of the SW 1983. D 6/25/1983 P 4/1/1984 Bp Gerald Nicholas Mcallister. m 6/13/1987 Sharon A Humphrey. R S Mart's Ch Chagrin Fall OH 2001-2014; R S Mich's Epis Ch Arlington VA 1996-2001; R S Dav's Ch Oklahoma City OK 1988-1995; Cur S Jn's Ch Oklahoma City OK 1983-1987. SHN 1990.

HUMPHREY, Marian Teresa (WA) 9801 Livingston Rd, Fort Washington MD 20744 **All Faith Epis Ch Charlotte Hall MD 2016-** B Hartford CT 1954 d Patrick & Joan. BA S Jos Coll 1976; MSW Virginia Commonwealth U 1988; MDiv Wesley TS 2007; Dip VTS 2010. D 6/4/2011 Bp John Bryson Chane P 1/21/2012 Bp Mariann Edgar Budde. Int S Patricks Ch Falls Ch VA 2014-2015; The Falls Ch Epis Falls Ch VA 2013-2014; Chr Ch Wm And Mary Newburg MD 2013; Ch Of The Gd Shpd Burke VA 2012; Asst St Johns Broad Creek Ft Washington MD 2011-2012.

HUMPHREY, M(ary) Beth (WA) St Albans School, Mount St Albans, Washington DC 20016 **Cathd of St Ptr & St Paul Washington DC 2003-; Lower Sch Chapl S Albans Sch Washington DC 2003-** B Hartselle AL 1956 d Wayne & Sue. BS U of Alabama 1977; PhD U NC 1982; MDiv Sewanee: The U So, TS 2003. D 5/20/2003 Bp Marc Handley Andrus P 1/26/2004 Bp Albert Theodore Eastman. m 12/31/2003 Jonathan Hemenway Glazier c 5. S Jn's Chap Groton MA 2010-2016; Groton Sch Groton MA 2010-2015; S Geo's Epis Ch Arlington VA 2005.

HUMPHREY, Nathan J A (RI) The Zabriskie Memorial Church of Saint John the Evangelist, 61 Poplar St, Newport RI 02840 **Rel Stds Tchr St. Geo's Sch**

Middletown RI 2016-; S Jn The Evang Ch Newport RI 2013-; Dioc Coun Dio Rhode Island Providence RI 2013- B Anaheim CA 1973 s David & Lois. BA St Johns Coll Annapolis MD 1994; DAS Ya Berk 1997; MDiv Yale DS 1997; Cert JHU 1999; Westcott Hse Cambridge 2006. D 11/1/2001 Bp John L Rabb P 5/9/2002 Bp Robert Wilkes Ihloff. m 9/4/2004 Anne McCabe Stone c 2. Vic S Paul's Par Washington DC 2005-2013; Catechist S Jas Acad Monkton MD 2001-2005; Cur S Jas Ch Monkton MD 2001-2005; Chapl Washington Epis Sch Beth MD 1999-2001. Auth, "A Sense of the Tragic," *LivCh mag*, TLC Fndt, 2010; Auth, "Dual Citizenship?," *LivCh mag*, TLC Fndt, 2009; Auth, *Gathering The NeXt Generation: Essays on the Formation and Mnstry of GenX Priests*, Morehouse Pub, 2000; Auth, "The Still, Sm Multiple Choice," *Re:Generation Quarterly*, 2000; Auth, "A Bapt Benediction," *Re:Generation Quarterly*, 2000. Gathering The NeXt Generation Core Team 2002; Grad Soc Coun, Ya Berk 2001-2002; Trst, Ya Berk 1995-1997. Thos Phillips Awd for Liturg Excellence Ya Berk 1997; Resrch Fell Yale DS 1997; Harriet Jackson Ely Prize in Theol Ya 1996; Hooker Fllshp in Theol Stds Ya 1996; Palmer Schlrshp for Serv to Berkeley Ya Berk 1995. rector@saintjohns-newport.org

HUMPHREYS, Eugene L (NC) 425 E 17th St, Charlotte NC 28206 **Ch Of The H Comf Charlotte NC 2017-** B Rome GA 1955 s William & Alice. Diac Stds Duke; BA Queens U 1984. D 6/20/2009 Bp Michael B Curry.

HUMPHREYS, Walter Lee (ETenn) 7113 Hampshire Dr, Knoxville TN 37909 B Long Beach CA 1939 s Cecil & Alberta. BA U Roch 1961; STB Ya Berk 1964; PhD UTS 1970. D 6/16/1964 P 1/1/1965 Bp George West Barrett. m 6/22/1963 Laurel Kristine Humphreys c 1. Cur Chr Epis Ch Hornell NY 1964-1966. Auth, "Crisis & Story: Intro To OT"; Auth, "Tragedy & Hebr Tradition The Jos Story In Genesis".

HUMPHRIES, Charles Emerson (SeFla) **Chapl Memi Hosp Hollywood Florida 2012-; D All Souls' Epis Ch Miami Bch FL 2010-; Treas NEAC Washington DC 2009-; Chapl AGO/Miami 2008-** B Newark NJ 1937 s Charles & Mary. Cert Dioc Sch for Chr Stds 2003. D 12/16/2005 Bp James Hamilton Ottley. Conf of Blessed Sacr 1979.

HUMPHRIES JR, John Curtis (CNY) 405 Euclid Avenue, Elmira NY 14905 **Ret 1997-** B Alexandria VA 1932 s John & Kathleen. BA U of Lynchburg (Va) 1957; MDiv VTS 1960. D 6/28/1960 Bp Frederick D Goodwin P 1/14/1961 Bp Nelson Marigold Burroughs. c 4. R Trin Ch Elmira NY 1975-1997; Asst S Mk's Ch Mt Kisco NY 1968-1975; Min in charge S Mk's Epis Ch Wadsworth OH 1960-1968.

HUNDLEY, Brooks (WA) **P Cathd of St Ptr & St Paul Washington DC 2005-; S Albans Sch Washington DC 2005-** B New York NY 1970 s Jay & Isabel. BA Skidmore Coll 1992; MDiv UTS 2002. D 6/11/2005 P 1/21/2006 Bp John Bryson Chane. m 6/20/1998 Courtney Hundley c 2.

HUNGATE, Carla Valinda (At) 4318 Windmill Trce, Douglasville GA 30135 B Montgomery AL 1954 d Obie & Lavada. EFM Sewanee: The U So, TS; U of W Georgia. D 10/28/1995 Bp Frank Kellogg Allan. m 4/2/1973 Robert Benjamin Hungate c 3.

HUNGERFORD, Eric Paul (Tex) 3901 S Panther Creek Dr, The Woodlands TX 77381 **S Jas' Epis Ch La Grange TX 2014-** B Austin TX 1984 s Donald & Michelle. BA Austin Coll 2006; MDiv Epis TS of the SW 2010. D 6/19/2010 Bp C Andrew Doyle. m 8/5/2006 Shyla C Ray c 2. Assoc S Mk's Ch Houston TX 2012-2014; Cur Trin Epis Ch The Woodlands TX 2010-2012.

HUNGERFORD, Roger (Chi) 2805 32nd Avenue Dr, Moline IL 61265 **Vic All SS Epis Ch Moline IL 2013-** B Iowa City IA 1955 s Mahlon & Georgia. BA Iowa St U 1978; MDiv Epis TS Of The SW 2012; MDiv Epis TS of the SW 2012. D 6/9/2012 P 12/15/2012 Bp Herman Hollerith IV. m 2/4/1991 Elizabeth Ann Hungerford. rog.hungerford@gmail.com

HUNKINS, Claire (SVa) PO Box 186, Oak Hall VA 23416 **Vic Emm Ch Temperanceville VA 2008-** B New Brunswick NJ 1950 d Edwin & Margaret. BS U of Kentucky 1973; MDiv Bex Sem 2006. D 5/14/2005 Bp Herbert Thompson Jr P 6/24/2006 Bp Kenneth Lester Price. m 2/25/2017 Robert Beckwith c 7. P-in-c Trin Epis Ch London OH 2006-2008.

HUNKINS, Orin James (Okla) 3724 Bonaire Pl, Edmond OK 73013 B Lincoln NE 1935 s Orin & Mary. BA U of Nebraska 1961; MDiv SWTS 1962; MS U of Missouri 1982. D 6/20/1962 P 12/21/1962 Bp Russell T Rauscher. m 5/29/1959 Carol Hunkins c 4. Int S Paul's Ch Altus OK 2006-2008; Int S Mary's Ch Edmond OK 2001-2002; Emm Epis Ch San Angelo TX 2000-2005; R S Andr's Epis Ch Lawton OK 1994-2000; R Trin Ch Arkansas City KS 1986-1993; Asst S Paul's Ch Kansas City KS 1981-1986; Dio Missouri S Louis MO 1979-1980; R S Alb's Epis Ch Fulton MO 1977-1979; S Lk's Ch Kearney NE 1971-1977; R S Thos' Epis Ch Falls City NE 1967-1971; S Mk's Ch Creighton NE 1962-1967; R S Ptr's Ch Neligh NE 1962-1967. ECom 1991-1994.

HUNLEY, Deborah Hentz (SwVa) 2042 Lee HI Rd SW, Roanoke VA 24018 B Minneapolis MN 1952 d Robert & Zelda. BA Hollins U 1974; MDiv Yale DS 1977. D 5/29/1977 P 12/3/1977 Bp William Henry Marmion. m 4/20/1985 William Johnson Hunley c 1. R Chr Epis Ch Roanoke VA 1991-2014, Assoc R 1985-1990; 1982-1985; Dio SW Virginia Roanoke VA 1980-1981, Stndg Com 2012-2015, COM 2003-2013, GC Dep 1997, 2000, 2003, 2006, 2009, 2012

1996-2014; Epis Chapl Hollins Coll Roanoke VA 1978-1982; Asst S Jas Ch Roanoke VA 1977-1979. greatoaktradingco@gmail.com

HUNN, Meg Buerkel (NC) 412 N East Street, Raleigh NC 27604 **Assoc R Chr Epis Ch Raleigh NC 2010-** B Tupelo MS 1973 d Jay & Susan. BA Mary Baldwin Coll 1996; MDiv GTS 2004. D 6/24/2004 P 1/6/2005 Bp Neff Powell. m 6/27/2009 Michael CB Hunn. Ch Of The Nativ Raleigh NC 2010; Dio No Carolina Raleigh NC 2007-2009; Assoc R S Alb's Ch Davidson NC 2007-2009; Asst P The Ch Of The H Trin Rittenhouse Philadelphia PA 2004-2007. mhunn@christchurchraleigh.org

HUNN, Michael CB (NC) 412 N East St, Raleigh NC 27604 **Dom And Frgn Mssy Soc- Epis Ch Cntr New York NY 2015-; Epis Ch Cntr New York NY 2015-** B Palo Alto CA 1970 s Bruce & Thera. BA Mid 1994; MA U of Cambridge 1996; Cert SWTS 1997. D 5/17/1997 P 11/22/1997 Bp Mary Adelia Rosamond Mcleod. m 6/27/2009 Meg Buerkel c 3. Cn to the Ordnry Dio No Carolina Raleigh NC 2006-2015, Pstr Response Team 2006-, Transition Off 2006-; Chapl to Davidson Coll and Assoc R S Alb's Ch Davidson NC 2004-2006; Sr. Assoc R Ch Of The H Comf Kenilworth IL 2001-2004; Chapl Kent Sch Kent CT 1997-2001; Pres Transition Mnstry Conf 2010-2013. "Al's Garage and Soul Repair Shop," *Middlebury mag*, Mid, 2010; "Al's Garage and Soul Repair Shop," *Middlebury mag*, Mid, 2010. michael.hunn@episdionc.org

HUNSINGER, Jimmie Ruth Coffey (Fla) 350 Sw Stallion Gln, Lake City FL 32024 **D Dio SW Florida Parrish FL 1990-** B Birmingham AL 1935 d Houston & Frances. BSN U of Vermont 1953; MEd Rhode Island Coll 1973. D 6/30/1990 Bp Rogers Sanders Harris. m 4/15/1994 Vern Richard Hunsinger. S Jas' Epis Ch Lake City FL 2000-2011. NAAD 1990.

HUNT, Ashley Stephen (EC) 1 Palmerston Road, Melton Mowbray Great Britain (UK) **Team Vic Melton-Mowbray Team Mnstry 1991-** B London UK 1950 s Frederick & Margaret. GOE St Johns Coll Nottingham Gb 1983. Trans 2/3/1988 as Priest Bp Calvin Onderdonk Schofield Jr. m 7/13/2013 Jan Zaidan c 2. R S Thos' Ch Windsor NC 1988-1991; S Mk The Evang Ft Lauderdale FL 1988, Assoc R 1987-1988; Serv Ch Of Engl 1983-1987.

HUNT SSP, Barnabas John William (SanD) PO Box 34548, San Diego CA 92163 **Serving Off The Ord of the Hosp of St. Jn of Jerusalem 2008-; Bd Mem Dorcas Hse San Diego CA 2006-; R Soc of S Paul San Diego CA 1989-; Archv Conf. of Angl Rel. Ord of Amer. 1982-** B Sayre PA 1937 s Clarence & Margarite. BS Penn 1958; Elmira Coll 1959; Portland St U 1963; Mt Hood Cmnty Coll Gresham OR 1970. D 11/3/1983 P 5/5/1984 Bp Charles Brinkley Morton. Bd Pres Dorcas Hse San Diego CA 2008-2009; Mutual Mnstry Revs Team Dio San Diego San Diego CA 2002-2003; Mem Chapt of St. Paul's Cathd San Diego CA 2000-2012; Bd Mem S Paul's Sr Hm & Serv San Diego CA 2000-2012; VP Conf. of Angl Rel. Ord of Am. 1992-1997; Int S Jn's Ch Indio CA 1988-1989, Int 1984-1985; Lectr & Clrgy Consult Betty Ford Cntr Rancho Mirage CA 1984-1989; Pres Natl Gld Chmn San Diego CA 1982-2011; Novc Dir / Assoc R Soc of S Paul San Diego CA 1975-1989; Pres / VP & Admin./ Admin. S Jude's Hm Inc. OR 1964-2010; Headmaster S Lk's Par Day Sch Gresham OR 1962-1964. Amer Coll of Hlth Care Admin 1975; Conf of Angl Rel Ord of Amer 1972; NECAD 1982; Recovery Ministers 1982; Soc of S Paul 1961; The Most Venerable Ord of the Hosp of St. Jn of Jerusal 2008. Hon Cn S Paul's Cathd 2000; Fell Amer Coll Healthcare Admin 1978.

HUNT, Donald Aldrich (Mass) 221 Atlantic Ave, Marblehead MA 01945 **Ret Ret 1992-** B Pawtucket RI 1930 s Gordon & Helen. BA Bos 1954; MDiv Ya Berk 1960. D 6/18/1960 P 12/21/1960 Bp Anson Phelps Stokes Jr. m 8/21/1971 Louise A Hunt c 4. Chapl, ACPE Supvsr Beverly Hosp Beverly MA 1969-1992; Chapl City Hosp Boston MA 1968-1969; R Ch Of Our Sav Middleboro MA 1967-1968; Asst Chapl Correctional Inst Norfolk MA 1964-1967; R S Jn's Epis Ch Franklin MA 1962-1967; Cur S Ptr's Ch Beverly MA 1960-1962.

HUNT, Edward Walter (Ala) 1024 12th St. S., Birmingham AL 35205 **S Mich's Ch Grosse Pointe MI 2016-** B West Orange NJ 1959 s Edward & Lorraine. BA SUNY 1981; MA U of Delaware 1984; MDiv GTS 2002. D 6/1/2002 P 12/6/2002 Bp Jack Marston Mckelvey. m 3/15/1986 Mary Coleman Hunt c 2. R H Comf Ch Gadsden AL 2015-2016; Ch Of The H Comf Montgomery AL 2015; Dio Alabama Birmingham 2013; S Andrews' Epis Ch Birmingham AL 2011-2012; R Zion Ch Rome NY 2004-2011; Cur S Paul's Ch Rochester NY 2002-2004.

HUNT III, Ernest Edward (Eur) 3310 Fairmount St Apt 9b, Dallas TX 75201 B Oakland CA 1934 s Ernest & Maselia. BA Stan 1956; MDiv Epis TS of the SW 1959; MA Stan 1965; Coll of Preachers 1974; Epis TS of the SW 1976; DMin PrTS 1980; DD Epis TS of the SW 1997; Emer Ch of the Epiph, nyc 2004. D 6/21/1959 Bp James Albert Pike P 3/1/1960 Bp George Richard Millard. m 8/23/1958 Elsie Hunt c 2. Dn The Amer Cathd of the H Trin Paris 75008 1992-2002; Dn S Matt's Cathd Dallas TX 1988-1992; R The Ch Of The Epiph New York NY 1972-1988; R S Tim's Creve Coeur S Louis MO 1966-1972; Assoc St Paul's/San Pablo Epis Ch Salinas CA 1963-1966; Chapl US-AR 1961-1971; Vic H Sprt Salinas CA 1959-1964; Chapl Soledad St Prison Gonzales CA 1959-1963; Vic Trin Ch Gonzales CA 1959-1963. Auth, "Aristocrats of the Sprt," 2015; Auth, "Terror in the City of Lighhts," Chelsea Sq Press, 2013; Auth, "Terror on the Border," Unrivaled, 2011; Auth, "Terror on E 7nd.

St," Publish Amer, 2009; Auth, "Paris On Fire," Publish Amer, 2008; Auth, "A Death in Dallas," Publish Amer, 2007; Auth, "Paris Under Siege," Publish Amer, 2006; Auth, "Sermon Struggles," Seabury Press, 1982. Cmnty of Cross & Nails 1978; Ord of S Jn of Jerusalem 2000. Par hall named in hon. H Trin, Paris, France 2003; DD Epis TS SW 1997.

✠ **HUNT III, The Rt Rev George Nelson** (RI) 1401 Fountain Grove Pkwy #107, Santa Rosa CA 95403 **Asstg Bp S Patricks Ch Kenwood CA 1998-; Ret Bp of Rhode Island Dio Rhode Island Providence RI 1994-, Prog Bdgt & Fin 1983-1994, Bp 1980-1982, Ret Bp of RI 1995-** B Louisville KY 1931 s George & Jessie. BA U So 1953; MDiv VTS 1956; DD Ya Berk 1980; MDiv/DD VTS 1981; DD Br 1991; LHD U of Rhode Island 1996. D 6/13/1956 Bp Charles Gresham Marmion P 12/13/1956 Bp James W Hunter Con 5/3/1980 for RI. m 6/18/1955 Barbara P Plamp c 3. Asst Bp Dio New Jersey Trenton NJ 1997-1998; Int Bp The Epis Ch in Hawaii Honolulu HI 1995-1996; Bp Protector SSF 1989-1994; Human Affrs Com 1988-1991; Human Affrs & Hlth Com 1986-1988; R St Paul's/San Pablo Epis Ch Salinas CA 1970-1975; Vic S Anselm's Epis Ch Lafayette CA 1965-1970; R S Alb's Ch Worland WY 1962-1965; Asst S Paul's Ch Oakland CA 1960-1962; P-in-c S Fran Chap Reno Jct WY 1959-1960; P-in-c S Jn Upton WY 1957-1960; Vic H Trin Epis Ch Gillette WY 1956-1960; Exec Off Dio California San Francisco CA 1975-1980, Chair COM 1971-1975. Never Again Awd Ri Jewish Fed 1985; Civil Libertarian Of The Year ACLU 1984.

HUNT, Hazel Bailey (Be) Po Box 86, Towanda PA 18848 B PA 1943 d Thomas & Hazel. D 10/23/2001 Bp Paul Victor Marshall P 9/24/2016 Bp Sean Walter Rowe. m 5/9/1964 Ronald Leroy Hunt c 1. Dn Chr Ch Towanda PA 2001-2005.

HUNT, John C (O) 44267 Route 511 East, Oberlin OH 44074 **Non-par 1966-** B Louisville KY 1936 s George & Jessie. BA U of Louisiana 1959; BD VTS 1964. D 1/6/1965 Bp Charles Gresham Marmion. m 5/11/1963 Louise Martin c 1. Vic S Ptr's Vlly Vlly Sta KY 1964-1966.

HUNT, J Patrick (NJ) 57 Putters Pl, Savannah GA 31419 B Pasadena CA 1946 s John & Virginia. BA Otterbein U 1969; MDiv UTS 1980; Cert Blanton-Peale Grad Inst 1992. D 6/21/1980 Bp John Harris Burt P 6/6/1981 Bp Robert Campbell Witcher Sr. R S Jas Ch Bovina NY 2006-2015; Int S Simeon's By The Sea Wildwood NJ 2004-2006; S Jn The Evang Ch Blackwood NJ 2001-2004; R Historic Ch of Ascen Atlantic City NJ 1996-2000; Assoc Admin S Geo's Par Flushing NY 1990-1991; R S Phil And S Jas Ch New Hyde Pk NY 1985-1990; S Ptr's Ch Rosedale NY 1984-1985; P H Trin Epis Ch Vlly Stream NY 1982-1983; Cur Ch Of The Trsfg Freeport NY 1980-1982. SSC 1990.

HUNT, Katherine Ann (Ak) 2006 W 31st Ave, Anchorage AK 99517 **Chr Ch Anchorage AK 2006-** B Bellington WA 1963 d Arthur & Jean. BA U of Alaska. D 12/16/2000 P 6/18/2001 Bp Mark Lawrence Macdonald. m 6/25/1994 Arthur Franklin Bell c 3. S Mary's Ch Anchorage AK 2001-2004.

HUNT, Lisa (Tex) 419 Woodland St, Nashville TN 37206 **R S Steph's Epis Ch Houston TX 2006-** B Pikeville TN 1959 d Howard & Frona. BA U of Toledo 1982; MDiv Van 1986; CAS GTS 1987. D 9/19/1987 P 4/16/1988 Bp George Lazenby Reynolds Jr. m 11/18/1989 Bruce S Farrar c 2. S Ann's Ch Nashville TN 1989-2006; Sewanee U So TS Sewanee TN 1988-1989; Dio Tennessee Nashville TN 1987-1988; Int S Andr's Epis Ch New Johnsonville TN 1987-1988.

HUNT, Marshall William (Mass) Po Box 1205, East Harwich MA 02645 **Chapl to Ret Cler Dio Massachusetts 2007-; Dio Massachusetts 2001-** B Bristol CT 1931 s Henry & Ardena. BA U of New Hampshire 1953; EDS 1956; MEd MI SU 1964. D 6/16/1956 P 4/15/1957 Bp Charles Francis Hall. m 11/24/2001 Victoria Wells Hunt c 1. Co-R S Dav's Epis Ch S Yarmouth MA 2008-2010; Int S Chris's Ch Chatham MA 2001-2003; Int S Anne's In The Fields Epis Ch Lincoln MA 1998-2001, Int 1994-1997; Int Gr Ch Vineyard Haven MA 1996-1998; Int The Ch Of The Epiph Washington DC 1992-1994; Chair, HOD Stwdshp Comm. The GC 1991-1994; Mem, Coun of Advice to Pres., HOD The GC 1991-1994; Mem, HOD St of the Ch Comm. The GC 1985-1994; Dep to GC The Epis Ch 1982-1994; Stwdshp Off Dio Massachusetts Boston MA 1981-1987, Mem, Stndg Com 1990-1992, Chair, SLC 1984-1986, Mem, Stndg Com 1977-1980; R S Anne's Ch Lowell MA 1969-1992; Assoc R Gr Ch Detroit MI 1967-1969; S Jn's Ch Royal Oak MI 1961-1967; Assoc R S Pat's Epis Ch Madison Hts MI 1961-1967; R S Ptr's Epis Ch Hillsdale MI 1958-1961; Cur Par Of S Jas Ch Keene NH 1956-1958; Mem, Cathd Chapt Dio Michigan Detroit MI 1966-1969, Exam Chapl 1961-1965. Int Mnstry Ntwk 1988; Mem, Marg Coffin PB Soc 2004; Phillips Brooks Cler 1976-1992; Pres, Marg Coffin PB Soc 2005.

HUNT, Meredith (WMich) 4708 State Park Hwy, Interlochen MI 49643 **Mssnr and Presenter Var Healing Missions OSL 1992-; Presenter Var Alcosm and Addiction Conferences 1978-; Dioc Addiction Recovery Cmsn Dio Wstrn Michigan Kalamazoo MI 2014-, Epis Curs Weekend Sprtl Advsr 2006-, Trst, Whittemore Fndt 2006-** B Philadelphia PA 1948 d Harry & Edythe. BA Swarthmore Coll 1970; MDiv EDS 1974. D 6/8/1974 Bp John Melville Burgess P 6/18/1977 Bp H Coleman Mcgehee Jr. m 9/19/1970 David Matthew Lillvis c 2. R St Jn's Epis Ch of Sturgis Sturgis MI 2004-2013; Cn Evang Cathd Ch Of S Paul Detroit MI 1992-2004; Assoc P S Lk's Epis Ch Allen Pk MI

1989-1992; ArmdF and Fed Ministires New York NY 1984-1992; Prot Chapl (fulltime) VA Med Cntr (USA) Allen Pk MI 1983-1992; Asst Chr Ch Dearborn MI 1979-1980; Assoc Emm Ch Detroit MI 1977-1978; Consult Var parishes Detroit Metropltn Area MI 1976-2004; EDS Cambridge MA 1975-1976; Adj to Fac and Alcosm Instr EDS Cambridge MA 1975-1976; New Ch Plnng Consult Dio Massachusetts Boston MA 1974-1975; Cmsn on Alcosm and Chairperson Dio Michigan Detroit MI 1982-1988. Auth, "Healing at Tenebrae," *Sharing mag*, OSL, 2011; Auth, "A Moment w Mary Chester," *Guideposts*, Guideposts mag, 2005. Assn of Profsnl Chapl - Bd Cert 1984; Intl OSL the Physcn 1992; Michigan Assn of Alco and Drug Abuse Counselors - Cert 1984. Acad Fell Epis Sem of the SW 1997.

HUNT, Paul Stuart (Pa) 212 S High St, West Chester PA 19382 **The Ch Of The H Trin W Chester PA 2008-** B Gilette WY 1958 s George & Barbara. BA Providence Coll 1983; MDiv CDSP 1988. D 6/25/1988 P 1/28/1989 Bp George Nelson Hunt III. m 8/6/1983 Jennifer L Hunt c 3. S Dunst's Epis Ch Succasunna NJ 2006-2008; S Jas Ch Montclair NJ 2005-2006; Cn Dio Newark Newark NJ 1999-2005; R S Andr's Epis Ch Lincoln Pk NJ 1991-1999; Asst S Chris's Ch Chatham MA 1988-1991.

HUNT, Teresa Gioia (Pgh) 1335 Berryman Avenue, Bethel Park PA 15102 **P-in-c S Paul's Ch Monongahela PA 2012-** B New York NY 1946 d Joseph & Concetta. BA Manhattanville Coll 1968; MA U MI 1972; MDiv TESM 1988; PhD Duquesne U 2009. D 6/4/1988 Bp Alden Moinet Hathaway P 12/17/1988 Bp Jose Antonio Ramos. m 5/12/2012 Laurita Ann Stebler c 2. Celebrant and Mentor for Total Mnstry S Pat's Epis Ch Madison Hts MI 2004-2010; Bd Cert Chapl (APC) Van Elslander Cancer Cntr Grosse Pinte MI 2004-2008; Bd Cert Chapl (APC) St. Jn No Shores Rehab Hosp 2001-2008; Long Term Supply S Mich And All Ang Epis Ch Lincoln Pk MI 2001-2002; R Gr Ch Mt Clemens MI 1997-1999; R S Andr's Epis Ch New Kensington PA 1991-1997; Assoc S Thos Ch Mamaroneck NY 1988-1990; Cler Assn Pres Dio Pittsburgh Pittsburgh PA 2013-2014, Cler Assn Treas 2012-2013. Assn of Profsnl Chapl 2004; Bd Salvation Army Mt. Clemens. MI 1997-1999; Epis Natl Cleric Assn 1988; Intl Assn of Wmn Ministers 2012; P.E.O. Intl 1976; SE Michigan Hosp Chapl Assn 2001-2009. Grant Doctoral Resrch Ford Fndt 1973; Fulbright Fllshp Untd States Govt 1968.

HUNT, Terry Lynn (Nev) 79 Northwood Commons Pl, Chico CA 95973 B Holt MI 1937 s Ernest & Virgilene. BA Alma Coll 1959; BD VTS 1967. D 6/15/1967 Bp Charles Ellsworth Bennison Jr P 7/1/1968 Bp Charles Bennison Sr. m 11/9/1975 Carol J Hunt c 4. R S Steph's Epis Ch Reno NV 1987-1989; Stff Trin Ch Toledo OH 1976-1987; Assoc S Michaels In The Hills Toledo OH 1969-1976; Asst S Mk's Ch Grand Rapids MI 1967-1969; Caplain U of Nevada, Reno Dio Nevada Las Vegas 1989-1990. Jefferson Awd Amer Inst for Publ Serv 1985.

HUNT, Victoria Wells (Mass) Po Box 1205, East Harwich MA 02645 **Supply P Ch Of The Gd Shpd Fairhaven MA 2012-; Chapl to Ret Cler Dio Massachusetts Boston MA 2007-, Supply P 2002-** B Cleveland OH 1938 d Reginald & Vera. BA Wellesley Coll 1960; MA Andover Newton TS 1970. D 11/26/1977 Bp Morris Fairchild Arnold P 5/5/1979 Bp John Bowen Coburn. m 11/24/2001 Marshall William Hunt. Co-Int P S Dav's Epis Ch S Yarmouth MA 2008-2010; R Trin Epis Ch Weymouth MA 1983-2001; Asst Ch Of S Jn The Evang Duxbury MA 1980-1982; D Gr Ch Newton MA 1977-1979; Prog Coordntr SCHC Adelynrood Byfield MA 1976-1979; Lay Asst S Ptr's Ch Weston MA 1973-1976; Chapl/Tchr Priv schools 1960-1973. P Assoc SSM (SSM) 1968; SCHC (SCHC) 1977.

HUNT, William Gilbert (Miss) 510 Godsey Rd., Apt. 183, Bristol TN 37620 **Ret 1994-** B Norfolk VA 1934 s Gilbert & Mildred. AA Miami-Dade Cmnty Coll 1966; LTh Nash 1969. D 6/24/1969 P 12/29/1969 Bp James Loughlin Duncan. m 2/23/1952 Myra Hunt c 3. Vic Calv Epis Ch Cleveland MS 1990-1994; Chapl Delta S U Cleveland MS 1990-1994; Gr Ch Rosedale MS 1990-1994; Asst H Cross Epis Ch Sanford FL 1987-1990; Vic S Jude's Ch Orange City FL 1984-1986; Asst All SS Epis Ch Kansas City MO 1980-1984; Dio W Missouri Kansas City MO 1978-1980; Vic S Geo Epis Ch Camdenton MO 1978-1980; Trin Epis Ch Lebanon MO 1978-1980; R H Sacr Hollywood FL 1974-1978; Cn Trin Cathd Miami FL 1972-1974; Cur S Mart's Epis Ch Pompano Bch FL 1969-1972.

HUNTER, Christina M (Alb) 2331 15th St, Troy NY 12180 **Dio Albany Greenwich NY 2012-; Pstr Oaks of Righteousness 2010-** B Athens OH 1978 d Lowell & Margaret. BS Ohio U 1999; MDiv TESM 2010. D 6/5/2010 P 12/18/2010 Bp William Howard Love. c 1.

HUNTER, Colenthia (SO) 8387 Vicksburg Dr, Cincinnati OH 45249 **D S Simon Of Cyrene Epis Ch Cincinnati OH 2007-** B Madison Wisconsin 1938 BS Cntrl St U 1960; MEd Xavier U 1968; PhD U Cinc 1983. D 5/13/2006 Bp Kenneth Lester Price. m 5/23/1959 Thomas Hunter c 2. D Ch Of Our Sav Cincinnati OH 2006-2007.

HUNTER, Elizabeth Lane (Miss) 327 N First St, Rolling Fork MS 39159 **D Ch of the H Trin Vicksburg MS 2005-** B Greenville MS 1955 d Afred & Mary. Mississippi St U 1978; Mississippi Sch For Deacons Jackson MS 2004. D 1/15/

2005 Bp Duncan Montgomery Gray III. c 1. Chap Of The Cross Rolling Fork MS 2005-2006.

HUNTER, Elizabeth Sue (U) 231 E 100 S, Salt Lake City UT 84111 **D Cathd Ch Of S Mk Salt Lake City UT 2001-** B Berlin NH 1945 d George & Jane. BEd Plymouth St U 1967; MEd Brigham Young U 1971; EFM U So 1993; EFM Universitynof the So 1993. D 6/14/2001 Bp Carolyn Tanner Irish. Dio Utah Salt Lake City UT 2014-2015, D 1999-2003; Epis Cmnty Serv Inc Salt Lake City UT 1999-2003. lhunter@episcopal-ut.org

HUNTER JR, Herschel Miller (Va) Po Box 37, Ivy VA 22945 B Gallatin TN 1954 s Herschel & Virginia. BA U So 1976; MA U of Alabama 1979; MDiv GTS 1988. D 5/24/1988 P 12/14/1988 Bp Robert Oran Miller. m 8/26/1978 Carol Frances Richardson c 3. Vic Chr Epis Ch Raleigh NC 2010-2015; R S Paul's Ch Charlottesville VA 1994-2010; Chapl The Cathd Ch Of The Adv Birmingham AL 1990-1994; Cur Ch Of The H Comf Montgomery AL 1988-1989.

HUNTER II, James Nathaniel (Ak) 322 Cross Way, North Pole AK 99705 B Glasgow VA 1943 s James & Helen. BA S Pauls Coll Lawrenceville 1966; BD Bex Sem 1969; MS SUNY 1970. D 6/21/1969 P 12/1/1969 Bp George West Barrett. m 7/22/1972 Sharron Hunter. Vic S Jude's Epis Ch No Pole AK 1988-2003, Assoc R 1983-1985; Asst S Simon's Epis Ch Rochester NY 1969-1972. Mart Luther King Cmnty Awd NAACP 2002; Man of the Year ChmbrCom 2000; Golden Rule Awd JC Penney 1995; Cmnty Serv Awd ML King Jr 1985.

HUNTER, James Wallace (RG) St Mary's Church, 1500 Chelwood Park Blvd NE, Albuquerque NM 87112 **P S Mary's Epis Ch Albuquerque NM 2008-; Disciplinary Bd Dio The Rio Grande Albuquerque 2014-, NW Dnry Pstr 2011-** B Central Islip NY 1954 s Harold & Nadene. BA Tul 1976; MDiv VTS 1984. D 2/9/1985 Bp James Russell Moodey P 8/24/1985 Bp Rogers Sanders Harris. m 12/5/2007 Jeannine Hunter. P-in-c All Faith Epis Ch Charlotte Hall MD 2003-2007; Chapl Gd Nws Jail & Prsn Mnstry La Plata MD 2000-2007; R S Fran Ch Virginia Bch VA 1997-2000; P S Steph's Epis Ch Morganton NC 1996-1997; R Ch Of The Epiph Newton NC 1992-1996; Chapl Off Of Bsh For ArmdF New York NY 1989-1999; Chapl - US Naval Reserve Dio Upper So Carolina Columbia SC 1989-1992; Cur H Trin Par Epis Clemson SC 1985-1989; Cur S Ptr's Ch Mtn Lks NJ 1984-1985; Pres of Stndg Com Dio Wstrn No Carolina Asheville NC 1995-1996. Auth, *The Battle Hymn of the Republic*, 1991. Polly Bond Awd of Excellence 1992.

HUNTER, Karen (Ida) 204 Courthouse Dr, Salmon ID 83467 **Assoc Gr Epis Ch Nampa ID 2007-** B 1952 BA Concordia Coll; MA U of San Francisco. D 10/19/1997 P 4/10/1998 Bp John Stuart Thornton. m 10/24/2012 Randall L Hunter. P Dio Idaho Boise ID 2007-2009; First Presb Ch Salmon ID 1999-2004; Ch Of The Redeem Salmon ID 1997-2007; Ch Of The H Sprt Missoula MT 1988-1993. ESMHE.

HUNTER, Kay Smith (WLa) 401 Washington Ave, Mansfield LA 71052 B Shreveport LA 1947 d Boardman & Mary Alice. BA Louisiana Tech U 1968; MA Louisiana NW St U Natchitoches 1986. D 6/7/2008 Bp D Avid Bruce Macpherson. c 2.

HUNTER, Kenneth Eugene (Alb) 29 Walnut St., Oneonta NY 13820 **R S Jas Ch Oneonta NY 2003-** B Kansas City MO 1952 s Clarence & Della. BA Rgnts U Albany NY 1984; MDiv GTS 1989. Trans 11/14/2003 Bp Russell Edward Jacobus. m 3/16/1980 Mary Veronica Hunter c 5. Ch of St Jn the Evang Wisconsin Rapids WI 1997-2003; S Andr's Ch Dallas TX 1996-1997; R S Mk's Ch Irving TX 1995-1996; St Jas the Great Epis Ch Newport Bch CA 1990-1995; Assoc R The Ch Of The Ascen And H Trin Cincinnati OH 1989-1990. Auth, "First Things;" Auth, "Chr Challenge;" Auth, "The Evang Cath".

HUNTER, Lawrence Scott (Cal) 1042 Dead Indian Memorial Road, Ashland OR 97520 B Everett WA 1947 s William & Doris. BA U of Washington 1974; MDiv CDSP 1992; DMin CDSP 2004. D 6/13/1992 Bp Chester Lovelle Talton P 1/9/1993 Bp Frederick Houk Borsch. m 7/1/1995 Janet M Chalmers. R S Steph's Epis Ch Orinda CA 2004-2014; R S Jn's Mssn La Verne CA 1995-2004; Asst S Wilfrid Of York Epis Ch Huntington Bch CA 1994-1995.

HUNTER, Marcia G (Lex) 104 Dellwood Dr, Berea KY 40403 **S Pat Ch Somerset KY 2014-; Chapl Hospice Care Plus Berea KY 2008-** B Saint Paul MN 1940 d Robin & Doris. BS U MN 1962; MDiv Untd TS of the Twin Cities 1992; Nash 1994. D 6/29/1994 Bp James Louis Jelinek P 6/28/1995 Bp Sanford Zangwill Kaye Hampton. c 2. Chr Ch Lexington MO 2005-2008; Cn Chr Ch Cathd Lexington KY 2005-2007; R S Paul's Ch Brookings SD 1997-2004; Cur Ch Of Our Sav Colorado Sprg CO 1994-1997.

HUNTER, Mary Veronica (Alb) 305 Main St, Oneonta NY 13820 B Pennsylvania 1956 D 5/30/2009 Bp William Howard Love. m 3/16/1980 Kenneth Eugene Hunter c 5.

HUNTER, Paul A (Alb) Christ Episcopal Church, 69 Fair St, Cooperstown NY 13326 **Dio Albany Greenwich NY 2017-; Cathd Of All SS Albany NY 2014-** B New York NY 1986 s Kenneth & Mary. BA Thos Aquivas 2008; MDiv TESM 2012; MDiv Trin Sch for Mnstry 2012. D 1/19/2013 Bp William Howard Love. Cur Chr Ch Cooperstown NY 2013-2014.

HUNTER SR, Robert Fulton Boyd (WA) 12213 Rolling Hill Ln, Bowie MD 20715 B Sheffield AL 1935 s Robert & Ella. BA Fisk U 1956; LTh SWTS 1959. D 7/1/1959 Bp Theodore N Barth P 7/1/1960 Bp John Vander Horst. m 5/16/1959 Dorothea V Gregg c 3. R Ch Of The Atone Washington DC 1975-2003; R S Paul's Epis Ch Atlanta GA 1964-1975; S Mary's Ch Chattanooga TN 1960-1964; Asst Emm Ch Memphis TN 1959-1960. UBE 1961.

HUNTER, S Scott (Mich) The Cathedral Church of St. Paul, 4800 Woodward Ave, Detroit MI 48201 **Bd Mem Karmanos Cancer Cntr Detroit MI 2009-; Dn Cathd Ch Of S Paul Detroit MI 2007-; Bd Mem Midtown Detroit Inc. 2007-; Mem No Amer Conf of Deans 2007-; Dioc Trst/V.P. Dio Michigan Detroit MI 2012-, Comm on Constitutions & Cn 2010-, Stndg Com 2010-, Stndg Com 2010-, Dioc Trst/ V.P. 2007-2010, Cn to Ordnry 2000-2007, Dioc Coun Off 2000-2007** B Greenville SC 1959 s James & Lulie. BS Wofford Coll 1981; MDiv SWTS 1988; Cert Coll of Preachers 1995; DMin GTF 2012. D 6/11/1988 P 5/20/1989 Bp William Arthur Beckham. m 8/10/1985 Tina Campbell Hunter c 1. Mem/Bd Off Nathan Ntwk 2001-2009; Bd Mem/Off Mariners Inn Detroit MI 2001-2008; Mem/Bd Off CODE (CODE) 2001-2007; R Trin Ch Parkersburg WV 1997-2000; Mem Barrington Area Yth Coun Barrington IL 1992-1997; Assoc S Mich's Ch Barrington IL 1991-1997; Bd Mem/Pres. Mnstrl Allnce Recycling Mnstry Asheville NC 1990-1991; Asst Calv Epis Ch Fletcher NC 1989-1991; Bd Mem Kershaw Cnty SC Guardian Ad Litem 1989; D Ch Of The Ascen (Hagood) Rembert SC 1988-1989; Gr Epis Ch Camden SC 1988-1989; COM Dio W Virginia Charleston WV 1998-2000, Dioc Coun 1998-2000, Peterkin Camp & Conf Bd 1998-2000; Dn of Dnry Dio Wstrn No Carolina Asheville NC 1990-1991. Anamchara Fllshp (Comp) 2010. shunter@detroitcathedral.org

HUNTER JR, Victor Edward (Dal) 1115 S. Bryan St., Mesquite TX 75149 **Vol KAIROS TDCJ TX 2005-** B Dallas TX 1935 s Victor & Irene. BBA U of No Texas 1958; SMU 1961; VTS 1963; MDiv GTS 1964; Cathd Cntr for Cont Educ Dallas TX 1976. D 8/28/1975 P 10/13/1976 Bp Archibald Donald Davies. m 12/21/1968 Barbara Lee Smith c 1. S Andr's Ch Dallas TX 2000-2005; Chapl Dallas Cnty Jail 1996-1998; Dept Of Missions Dallas TX 1984-1990; Chapl BSA Lancaster TX 1980-1985; S Mart's Ch Lancaster TX 1977-2001; Vic S Mary Mesquite TX 1975-1977; St Marys Ch Mesquite TX 1975-1977; Exec Coun Dio Dallas Dallas TX 1995-1996. SocMary; Travel Seminars.

HUNTER, Walcott Wallace (SwFla) Po Box 646, Kinderhook NY 12106 **S Steph's Ch New Prt Rchy FL 2010-** B Central Islip NY 1959 s Harold & Nadene. BA Wag 1982; MDiv Nash 1985. D 5/11/1985 P 6/7/1986 Bp William Louis Stevens. m 5/25/1985 Teri-Lea Hunter c 3. P-in-c S Mart's Epis Ch Hudson FL 2010-2013; R S Paul's Ch Kinderhook NY 1998-2010; Ch of the Ascen Merrill WI 1987-1998; S Barn Epis Ch Tomahawk WI 1987-1998; St Jas Epis Ch Mosinee WI 1987-1998; Dio Fond du Lac Appleton WI 1987-1995; Cur S Thos Epis Ch Medina WA 1985-1987. CBS, Soc Of The H Cro.

HUNTER-SPENCER, Dorothy Elaine (CFla) D 9/10/2016 Bp Gregory Orrin Brewer.

HUNTINGTON, Carol L (Me) 121 Bowery St, Bath ME 04530 **Clincl Soc Worker Mid Coast Parkview Med Cntr Addictions Resource Cente 2015-; Chapl Mid Coast Parkview Hosp 2008-** B Natick MA 1946 d Jonathan & Joan. BA Hood Coll 1968; MSW Bos Sch of Soc Wk 1973; MDiv Drew U 1991. D 4/6/2002 Bp Paul Victor Marshall. m 2/14/1993 Albert R Ferguson. D S Andr's Ch Winthrop ME 2007-2010; Mentor, EfM Sewanee U So TS Sewanee TN 2006-2014; Chapl Parkview Hosp Adventist Ch Brunswick ME 2005-2007; D S Jn's Epis Ch Hamlin PA 2002-2003; Chapl -per diem St Lk's Roosevelt Med Cntr NYC 1991-1994; Serv as LLPastor Meth Ch Nthrn NJ Conf Paterson 1991-1994; Assoc Pstr, Dir St Ptr's Haven S Ptr's Ch Clifton NJ 1987-1988; Assoc Min S Jn's Epis Ch Westwood MA 1986-1987; Mssnr Ch Of The H Sprt Mattapan MA 1984-1986; Soc Worker Trin Ch Epis Boston MA 1981-1983; Com on Indn Relatns Dio Maine Portland ME 2006-2011. authored and presented, "AIDS and Spiruality: Seeking Life in the Midst of Death," *5th Internation AIDS Conf, Montreal Can*, same in abstracts 5th Intl Conf, 1989; co authored, "The Way We Go to Sch the Exclusion of Chld in Boston," Beacon Press, 1970. EUC 1980-1990; Natl Assn of Lay Professionals in the Epis Ch 1990-2002.

HUNTINGTON, Francis Cleaveland (NY) 11 Rassapeague, Saint James NY 11780 B New York NY 1931 s Prescott & Sarah. BA Harv 1953; STB GTS 1957; MTh PrTS 1961. P 12/1/1957 Bp James Pernette DeWolfe. m 1/8/1966 Patricia Florence Huntington c 2. Seamens Ch Inst New York NY 1978-1985; Dir Wall St Mnstry New York NY 1966-1972; Trin Par New York NY 1964-1966; Asst Trin Ch Princeton NJ 1957-1964. Trst, Halo USA 2002.

HUNTINGTON, Frederic DuBois (Va) 219 Wolfe St, Alexandria VA 22314 **Pstr San Marcos Cong Alexandria VA 1999-** B Washington DC 1946 s E C & Catherine. BA Colg 1969; MA U of Arizona 1973; MDiv VTS 1979; Lic Dio Ely GB 1989. D 12/27/1979 P 6/28/1980 Bp Anselmo Carral-Solar. m 11/25/1971 Linda B Budinger c 3. P-in-c Iglesia Epis San Marcos Alexandria VA 1999-2011; Mssnr Gr Epis Ch Alexandria VA 1998-2008; R Ch Of The H Comf Miami FL 1983-1987; P-in-c S Jas Guatemala 1980-1982; Mssy Exec Coun

Appointees New York NY 1979-1983; D-in-c S Jas Guatemala 1979-1980; Asst Gr Chap Tucson AZ 1971-1976.

HUNTLEY, Stuart Michael (LI) 9 Carlton Ave, Port Washington NY 11050 B Folkstone UK 1973 s Denis & Jennifer. BENG Southampton U 1994; BA Trin Theol Coll 2008. Trans 11/1/2011 Bp Lawrence C Provenzano. m 12/14/2002 Louise Huntley c 2. R S Steph's Ch Prt Washington NY 2011-2014; Chapl Victoria Coll Jersey Combined Cadet Force 2010-2011; Cur St Helier Par Ch Jersey UK 2008-2011. STUART@STSTEPHENSPW.ORG

HUPF, Jeffrey Lee (RG) 2801 Westwood Rd S, Minnetonka Beach MN 55361 B Wichita KS 1970 s Gary & Deborah. BBA U of Wisconsin 1992; MDiv Regent Coll Vancouver CA 2002. D 9/7/2002 Bp David John Bena P 3/21/2003 Bp Daniel William Herzog. m 1/22/2005 Carmen R Hupf c 1. Assoc S Mart's By The Lake Epis Minnetonka Bch MN 2009-2013; R St Fran on the Hill Ch El Paso TX 2004-2008; S Fran On The Hill El Paso TX 2003-2008; Asst. R St Fran on the Hill Ch El Paso TX 2003-2004; St Marys Cnvnt Greenwich NY 2003; D Zion Ch Morris NY 2002-2003.

HUR, Won-Jae (Cal) 206 Arborway Apt 3, Boston MA 02130 B Seoul Korea 1975 BA Ob 1996; MDiv EDS 2000; STM Bos 2001; STM Bos 2001. D 7/31/1999 Bp Arthur Williams Jr P 12/16/2000 Bp Barbara Clementine Harris. m 4/9/2011 Hanna Eun Kyong Bae. Dio California San Francisco CA 2009-2010; Int S Jas Epis Ch San Francisco CA 2009-2010; Dio Los Angeles Los Angeles CA 2007-2009.

HURD JR, Austin Avery (Pgh) 102 Fountain Cv, 160 Marwood Rd Apt 3314, Cabot PA 16023 B Sewickley PA 1931 s Austin & Hannah. LTh Epis TS in Kentucky 1967. D 6/3/1967 Bp William S Thomas P 12/16/1967 Bp Austin Pardue. m 9/1/1953 Mary Nell J Johnstone c 2. Ret Assoc S Jas Epis Ch Leesburg FL 1998-2013; Chapl St. Marg Memi Hosp Pittsburg PA 1993-1995; R S Thos Memi Epis Ch Oakmont PA 1972-1993; Vic S Fran In The Fields Somerset PA 1967-1972. Cnvnt of Trsfg (P Assoc) 1991.

HURLBURT, Martha Cornue (EO) 801 Jefferson St, Klamath Falls OR 97601 **P S Barn Ch Bonanza OR 2013-; Vic S Paul's Ch Klamath Fall OR 2011-** B Bellingham WA 1944 d Frank & Hazel. BA Whitman Coll 1966; Tchr Cred Chico St U 1995. D 6/24/2006 Bp William O Gregg P 11/28/2007 Bp Barry Leigh Beisner. c 3.

HURLBUT, Terence James (WMass) 7 Woodbridge St, South Hadley MA 01075 B North Adams MA 1957 s James & Catherine. D 11/16/2013 Bp Doug Fisher. m 10/7/1978 Elaine Marie Hurlbut c 2.

HURLEY, Hal Owen (SeFla) 418 N Sapodilla Ave, West Palm Beach FL 33401 B Barbados WI 1954 s Wycliffe & Adelaide. BBA Baruck Coll 1977; MPS NYTS 2003. D 12/9/2006 Bp John Palmer Croneberger. m 8/20/1977 Pamela Patricia Gilkes c 2.

HURLEY, Janet (Los) St John the Evangelist Episcoapl Church, PO Box 183, Needles CA 92363 **Vic S Jn The Evang Mssn Needles CA 2002-** B Wakefield UK 1938 D 6/7/2002 P 12/19/2002 Bp Joseph Jon Bruno.

HURLEY, Thomas James (Neb) 113 N 18th St, Omaha NE 68102 B Pigeon MI 1946 s Grover & Lois. BS Cntrl Michigan U 1969; MDiv Yale DS 1972. D 6/26/1972 Bp Richard Stanley Merrill Emrich P 9/1/1973 Bp H Coleman Mcgehee Jr. m 8/9/1969 Doris Diane Hurley c 1. Ch Of The Resurr Omaha NE 1997; Dn Trin Cathd Omaha NE 1995-2012, Dn 1995-; R Chr Epis Ch Yankton SD 1988-1995; Chr Epis Ch Lead SD 1985-1988; R S Jn's Ch Deadwood SD 1985-1988; P-in-c S Andr's Ch Philipsburg MT 1981-1985; R S Marks Pintler Cluster Anaconda MT 1981-1985; The Pintler Cluster of the Epis Ch Deer Lodge MT 1981-1985; S Jn's Chap Monterey CA 1981; S Matt's Epis Ch Saginaw MI 1978-1979; R Hope - S Jn's Epis Ch Oscoda MI 1976-1978; Cur S Mich's Ch Grosse Pointe MI 1974-1976; Cur S Phil's Epis Ch Rochester MI 1972-1974.

HURST, Hassell J (Ga) PO Box 50555, Nashville TN 37205 **Vic Chr Ch Cathd Nashville TN 2012-; Ret 2007-** B Middleboro KY 1946 s Oliver & Jewell. MDiv EDS 1972. D 12/21/1971 P 6/1/1972 Bp Addison Hosea. R S Anne's Ch Tifton GA 1982-2006; S Mk's Ch Brunswick GA 1979; Chr Ch Cathd Lexington KY 1975-1976; Vic S Alb's Ch Morehead KY 1972-1976; Chapl Untd Campus Mnstry Morehead St U 1972-1976. jhurst@christcathedral.org

HURST, Michael W (Dal) 400 S Church St, Paris TX 75460 **P Ch Of The Sav Allen TX 2014-** B Nashville TN 1961 s Robert & Bettye. BA Middle Tennessee St U 2005; MDiv Sewanee: The U So, TS 2009. D 6/6/2009 P 1/9/2010 Bp John Bauerschmidt. m 11/29/1980 Gilda H Hurst c 3. Ch Of The H Cross Paris TX 2011-2014; Assoc Ch Of The Adv Nashville TN 2009-2011.

HURST, Rodney Shane (RG) 508 W Fox St, Carlsbad NM 88220 **R Gr Ch Carlsbad NM 2009-; COM Dio The Rio Grande Albuquerque 2011-** B Vancouver Washington 1970 s John & Shirley. BA NW U 1992; MDiv Nash 2009. D 10/23/2008 P 5/16/2009 Bp Keith Lynn Ackerman. m 4/29/2006 Carolyn M Hurst c 2. Third Ord Carmelites (T.OCarm.) 2009.

HURST, William George (NH) 108 Wecuwa Dr, Fort Myers FL 33912 B Butte MT 1921 s Percy & Dora. BD EDS 1969; DMin Andover Newton TS 1979. D 6/10/1969 P 12/13/1969 Bp Charles Francis Hall. m 11/16/2007 Mary Lou Morrison c 5. Asst Iona Hope Epis Ch Ft Myers FL 1998-2011; Asstg P S Hilary's Ch Ft Myers FL 1988-1998; Int Ch Of The Trsfg Derry NH 1981-1982;

Nevil Memi Ch Of S Geo Ardmore PA 1981-1982; Dir/Counslr Durham Pstr Counslg Cntr Durham NH 1979-1986; Chapl Tewksbury MA 1978-1980; R S Andr's Ch Manchester NH 1969-1977. Auth, "One Soldier'S Love Story," Rit Amelia Press, 2004. AAPC 1977-1987; ACPE 1977-1981. Distinguished Grad USAF Command & Stff Coll 1961; Distinguished Grad USAF Command & Stff Coll 1961.

HURTADO, Homero (EcuC) Guallabamba 214, Cuenca Ecuador B Cuenca EC 1938 s Julio & Clementina. LTh Sem Mayor De Quito 1967. Rec 6/1/1981 as Priest Bp Adrian Delio Caceres-Villavicencio. m 12/23/1979 Nelly Fabiola Hurtado c 2. Iglesia de la Reconciliacion Quito 1981-1995; Iglesia Epis Del Ecuador Quito 1980-2004; Iglesia Huaquilias Huaquillas 1980-2004; Iglesia Machala El Oro 1980-2004; Vic Iglesia Sagrada Familia Cuenca 1980-2004.

HURTT, Annie Lawrie (Pa) 659 W Johnson St, Philadelphia PA 19144 **Int H Trin Rittenhouse Sq 1996-** B Boston MA 1955 d Spencer & Anne. BA Ob 1980; MDiv EDS 1988. D 12/2/1989 P 6/24/1990 Bp Daniel Lee Swenson. The Ch Of The H Trin Rittenhouse Philadelphia PA 1996-1998; Cn Cathd Ch Of Our Sav Philadelphia PA 1993-1996; Cathd Ch of Our Sav Philadelphia PA 1993-1996; Epis Cmnty Serv Philadelphia PA 1991-1993; The Epis Com Univ Of Pa Philadelphia PA 1989-1991.

HURWITZ, Ellen Sara (Md) 12147 Pleasant Walk Rd, Myersville MD 21773 B Baltimore MD 1951 d William & Marilyn. BA Reed Coll 1976; MDiv EDS 1982. D 6/28/1986 Bp Henry Irving Mayson P 10/1/1987 Bp H Coleman Mcgehee Jr. Assoc Ch Of The Trsfg Braddock Heights MD 2000-2004; Pres Washington Cnty Homelessness Taskforce 1995-1996; S Johns Shltr For The Homeless Hagerstown MD 1995; Case Mgr S Jn's Homeless Shltr Hagerstown MD 1993-1997; Vic S Anne's Epis Ch Smithsburg MD 1992-1995.

HUSBAND, John Frederick (Minn) 16533 Long Beach Dr, Detroit Lakes MN 56501 **Bd Mem Detroit Lakes Libr Bd 100th Centennial Com 2013-; Mem Wadena Recovery Com 2009-; Mem Rotary Intl 2008-; Bd Mem Wadena Renwl 2008-** B Rochester MN 1941 s Ross & Frances. BA U MN 1963; BD SWTS 1966. D 6/29/1966 P 3/19/1967 Bp Philip Frederick McNairy. m 6/2/1990 JoAnn Lois Husband c 2. S Helen's Ch Wadena MN 2004-2007; S Barth's Epis Ch Bemidji MN 2004, 1999-2003; S Lk's Ch Detroit Lakes MN 1990-1998; S Andr's By The Lake Duluth MN 1985-1988; Dio Minnesota Minneapolis MN 1974-1990; Chapl U MN Duluth MN 1966-1990.

HUSBY, Mary Eloise Brown (SD) 1504 S Park Ave, Sioux Falls SD 57105 **Ret 2000-** B Sioux Falls SD 1927 d Roger & Agnes. BA Augustana Coll 1951. D 8/23/1984 Bp Craig Barry Anderson. m 12/22/1950 Earl Milton Husby c 2. D Calv Cathd Sioux Falls SD 1986-2011. ESMA.

HUSHION, Timothy V (NC) 328 6th St, Pittsburgh PA 15215 **Vic All Souls Ch Ansonville NC 2016-; Calv Ch Wadesboro NC 2016-** B Amityville NY 1952 s Timothy & Muriel. BA Cit 1973; ADN Trident Tech Coll 1995; MDiv Trin Epis Sch 2011; MDiv TESM 2011. D 10/5/2011 P 2/25/2012 Bp Kenneth Lester Price. m 1/6/1993 Marcella W Hushion c 3. P-in-c Trin Cathd Pittsburg PA 2012-2015; S Chris's Epis Ch Mars PA 2011-2013.

HUSSEY OSB, David Payne (SD) 405 N Madison Ave, Pierre SD 57501 **Cn to the Ordnry Dio So Dakota Pierre SD 2001-** B Chicago IL 1945 s Charles & Marjorie. BA Geo Wms 1975; MA Webster U 1983; MDiv SWTS 1995. D 12/21/1998 P 10/18/2000 Bp Creighton Leland Robertson. m 7/1/1995 Mercy Gardiner Hobbs c 2. Chapl U of So Dakota Vermillion SD 1999-2005; Assoc Ch Of Our Most Merc Sav Santee NE 1998-2010; Ch Of The Blessed Redeem Niobrara NE 1998-2010; S Paul's Epis Ch Vermillion SD 1998-2010. canondavid. diocese@midconetwork.com

HUSSEY-SMITH, Teddra R (EC) 5071 Voorhees Rd, Denmark SC 29042 B Kinston NC 1954 d Theodore & Beulah. BS Hampton U 1977; MDiv Duke DS 2000; CAS VTS 2001. D 1/19/2002 Bp Michael B Curry P 2/22/2003 Bp James Gary Gloster. c 2. S Jos's Epis Ch Fayetteville NC 2013-2015; Chr Epis Ch Bensalem PA 2009-2010; S Cyp's Ch Oxford NC 2002-2007; D S Steph's Ch Oxford NC 2002-2007; S Phil's Chap Denmark SC 2002-2006; Voorhees Coll Charleston SC 2002-2006; D Voorhees Coll - S Phil's Ch Denmark SC 2002-2003; The Epis Ch of Oxford Oxford NC 2002.

HUSSON, Brenda G (NY) 865 Madison Ave, New York NY 10021 **R S Jas Ch New York NY 1996-, Assoc R 1988-1992; Epis Chars Trst Dio New York New York NY 2000-, 1999-** B Syracuse NY 1954 d George & Patricia. BA Beloit Coll 1976; MDiv UTS 1983. D 12/17/1983 Bp O'Kelley Whitaker P 7/15/1984 Bp Ned Cole. m 7/29/1995 Tom Faulkner c 1. Trst UTS 2002-2011; Int Pstr S Jn's Ch New City NY 1994-1996; Exec Dir Epis EvangES Arlington VA 1993-1996; EvangES 1993-1996; Int Pstr Gr Ch White Plains NY 1992-1994; Assoc R All Ang' Ch New York NY 1983-1987. "Lost Sheep Lost Coins," Restoring Faith; Walker and Co., 2001. DD Berk 1998; Phi Beta Kappa Beloit Coll 1975.

HUSTAD, Siri Hauge (Minn) 519 Oak Grove St, Minneapolis MN 55403 **Cathd Ch Of S Mk Minneapolis MN 2015-** B Minneapolis MN 1959 d Bjorn & Betty. BA Coll of St Scholastica 1982. D 1/24/2013 P 6/23/2013 Bp Brian N Prior. m 9/17/1988 Todd Arthur Hustad c 2.

HUSTON, Jeffrey Clayton (Okla) **Chapl S Andr's Ch Stillwater OK 2013-; Chapl S Aug Cbury Cntr Stillwater OK 2009-; Cur Dio Oklahoma Okla-**

homa City OK 2005-; S Jas Epis Ch Oklahoma City OK 2005- B Tulsa Ok 1978 s Paul & Virginia. BA Drury U 2000; MDiv VTS 2005. D 6/25/2005 P 12/21/2005 Bp Robert Manning Moody. m 10/13/2007 Elisa Huston c 1.

HUSTON, Julie Winn (At) 2950 Mt. Wilkinson Pkwy, Unit 817, Atlanta GA 30339 **Ret 2002-** B Atlanta GA 1942 d Robert & Mae. BA Emory U 1963; MDiv Candler TS Emory U 1989. D 6/10/1989 P 3/26/1990 Bp Frank Kellogg Allan. c 2. Dn No Atlanta Convoc Dio Atlanta Atlanta GA 1991-1999; S Anne's Epis Ch Atlanta GA 1989-2002. Theta Phi 1989.

HUSTON, Mary Ann (Tex) 3816 Bellaire Blvd, Houston TX 77025 **Cur S Mk's Ch Houston TX 2013-** B Fort Worth TX 1956 d James & Margaret. BA Gri 1978; MA U of Washington 1981; MDiv Epis TS Of The SW 2010; MDiv Epis TS of the SW 2010. D 6/15/2013 P 1/15/2014 Bp C Andrew Doyle. m 10/20/1984 Michael Alan Huston c 2.

HUSTON, Nancy Williams (Neb) 923 S 33rd St, Omaha NE 68105 B Johnson City TN 1932 d Charles & Julia. BS Carson-Newman Coll 1954; MEd U NC 1976. D 11/8/1985 Bp James Daniel Warner. D S Aug's Barbes Honduras 1987-1988; D Ch Of The H Sprt Bellevue NE 1985-1993. NAAD.

HUTCHENS, Holly Blair (WMo) St Ninians Cottage, Melton, Drumnadrochit SCOTLAND IV63 6UA Great Britain (UK) **Serving The Scottish Epis Ch 2005-** B Petersburg VA 1942 d Edward & Charlotte. BA U MI 1964; MA U Chi 1969; MDiv SWTS 1988. D 6/18/1988 P 12/17/1988 Bp Frank Tracy Griswold III. S Aid's Ch Olathe KS 2004; R Ch Of The Resurr Blue Sprg MO 1996-2004; S Mich And All Ang Ch Mssn KS 1995-1996, Int Pstr 1993-1995; Int Trin Ch Lawr KS 1993-1995; S Chris's Epis Ch Wichita KS 1993; Int S Matt's Epis Ch Newton KS 1991-1992; Cur S Jas Ch Wichita KS 1989-1991.

HUTCHENS, Marquita L (WVa) St. John's Episcopal Churh, 1105 Quarrier Street, Charleston WV 25301 **R S Jn's Epis Ch Charleston WV 2015-, P-in-c 2014-2015; Compstn and Benefits Com Dio E Carolina Kinston NC 2011-** B Purcell OK 1947 d Gilbert & Helen. MA U of Oklahoma 1972; MA Adler Sch of Profsnl Psychol 1979; MDiv Brite DS 2002; MDiv Brite DS 2002; STM Sewanee: The U So, TS 2007. D 6/2/2007 Bp C Wallis Ohl P 12/16/2007 Bp Charles Glenn VonRosenberg. Assoc R Chr Ch New Bern NC 2009-2014; Asst S Paul's Epis Ch Kingsport TN 2007-2009; Resolutns Com Dio E Tennessee Knoxville TN 2008-2009.

HUTCHERSON, Anne V (WMo) 624 W 61st Ter, Kansas City MO 64113 B Englewood NJ 1941 d Konrad & Phyllis. BFA Wesleyan Coll 1963; MA U of So Dakota Vermillion SD 1964; MDiv S Paul TS 2006. D 6/2/2007 P 12/1/2007 Bp Barry Howe. m 4/8/1989 Robert M Hutcherson. Assoc R S Andr's Ch Kansas City MO 2007-2013; Mng Dir-Oprtns Short's Travel Mgmt 2002-2007. Biblic Stds S Paul TS 2006; Excellence: Theol and.

HUTCHERSON, Brian (Va) 74 Peterson Pl, Fishersville VA 22939 **D S Lk's Simeon Charlottesville VA 2016-** B Charlottesville VA 1976 s James & Bettie. Bachelor of Arts Jas Madison U; Mstr Jas Madison U. D 4/16/2016 Bp Shannon Sherwood Johnston. m 12/28/2013 Amy Johnson c 2.

HUTCHERSON, Robert M (WMo) 624 West 64th Terrace, Kansas City MO 64113 B Marshall MO 1944 s Willis & Hattie. BS U of Missouri 1966; MS Pur 1969; MDiv GTS 1971. D 6/12/1971 Bp John P Craine P 12/18/1971 Bp Albert A Chambers. m 4/8/1989 Anne V Valentin c 1. Ch Growth Dio W Missouri Kansas City MO 1989-1990, Dioc Coun 1988-1989, Pres 1988-1989, Bec 1985-1992, Chair Liturg Cmsn 1984-1993, Dept Mssns 1980-1982, 1976-1978, Stndg Com 1995-1998, Dioc Coun 1991-1993, Dioc Coun 1984-1985, Dioc Coun 1980-1982; R S Matt's Ch Kansas City MO 1983-2008; R S Mary's Epis Ch Kansas City MO 1978-1983; Ch Of The Resurr Blue Sprg MO 1976-1978; Vic S Mich's Epis Ch Independence MO 1976-1978; P-in-c Chap Of S Jn The Div Champaign IL 1975-1976; The ECF Champaign IL 1971-1976; Asst Chapl U IL 1971-1975. Assn Of Dioc Liturg & Mus Com; ESMHE.

HUTCHINGS, Douglas Wayne (LI) 4102 S New Braunfels Ave Ste 110s, San Antonio TX 78223 **Died 11/16/2016** B San Antonio 1935 s Horace & Mable. BA JHU 1957; BD VTS 1960; Coll of Preachers 1968. D 6/24/1960 Bp Noble C Powell P 6/1/1961 Bp Harry Lee Doll. Ret 2006-2016; S Jas Epis Ch Del Rio TX 2000-2011; R S Paul's Ch Glen Cove NY 1998-2005; Int Gr Epis Ch Massapequa NY 1997-1998; R S Jn's Ch New Milford CT 1995-1997; P-in-c S Mk's Ch S Milwaukee WI 1994-1995; Assoc S Barn On The Desert Scottsdale AZ 1990-1993; Non-par 1979-1987; Vic S Dunst's Epis Ch Houston TX 1969-1971; Vic Ch Of The Gd Shpd Tomball TX 1966-1969; Vic Gd Shpd Humble TX 1966-1969; Asst S Jn's Par Hagerstown MD 1963-1966; Asst S Thos' Baltimore MD 1961-1963; Vic Epiph Ch Dulaney Vlly Luthvle Timon MD 1960-1961. Bro Of S Andr.

HUTCHINS, Margaret Smith (EC) 7909 Blue Heron Dr W Apt 2, Wilmington NC 28411 **Ret 1994-** B Flushing NY 1932 d Matthew & Laurie. BS NWU 1953; MDiv EDS 1981. D 6/13/1981 Bp Arthur Edward Walmsley P 2/27/1982 Bp Clarence Nicholas Coleridge. m 6/16/1953 Walter James Hutchins c 4. Int Ch Of The Gd Shpd Hartford CT 1993-1994; S Alb's Ch Danielson CT 1992-1993; Int S Andr The Apos Rocky Hill CT 1990-1991; Int S Ptr's Epis Ch Cheshire CT 1989-1990; Int Trin Ch Seymour CT 1988-1989; Int S Paul's Ch Wallingford CT 1987-1988; Int S Paul And S Jas New Haven CT 1985-1987; Int S Ptr's Ch So Windsor CT 1984-1985; Int S Mk's Chap Storrs

CT 1983-1984; Vic Chr Ch Par Epis Watertown CT 1981-1984; Chr Ch Harwinton CT 1981-1983. Soc For The Increase Of The Mnstry.

HUTCHINS, M(aurice) Gene (RG) Po Box 223, Tyrone NM 88065 **Died 8/17/2016** B Cody WY 1927 s John & Emma. U of Wyoming 1946; BS U CO 1955; BD Nash 1970. D 12/29/1969 P 6/29/1970 Bp Edwin B Thayer. c 2. Ret 1994-2016; R Pecos Team Mnstry Pecos TX 1991-1994; S Mk's Epis Ch Pecos TX 1991-1994; Asst Ch Of The Gd Shpd Silver City NM 1990-2016; Dio The Rio Grande Albuquerque 1988-1991; Vic Urban Indn Mnstry Albuquerque NM 1988-1990; S Paul's Epis Ch Vernal UT 1983-1988; Vic Ch Of The H Sprt Randlett UT 1982-1988; 1979-1982; S Mk's Ch Craig CO 1976-1978; Vic S Jn's Epis Ch New Castle CO 1975-1976; S Barn Ch Glenwood Spgs CO 1972-1976; Cur Chr Epis Ch Denver CO 1970-1972.

HUTCHINS, Susan Ellen (RG) St Luke's Episcopal Church, Po Box 1258, Deming NM 88031 **S Lk's Epis Ch Deming NM 2016-** B Ridgewood, NJ 1952 d William & Helen. Mstr of Div Luth TS Philadelphia 2009. D 10/10/2015 P 10/15/2016 Bp Michael Vono. c 2.

HUTCHINSON, Anthony Alonzo (Ore) Trinity Episcopal Church, 44 N 2nd St, Ashland OR 97520 **Trin Epis Ch Ashland Ashland OR 2012-; Dioc Coun Dio Oregon Portland OR 2013-** B Berkeley CA 1953 s Abraham & Grace. BA Brigham Young U 1976; MA Brigham Young U 1978; MA CUA 1980; PhD CUA 2001; Certificates Ming Hua TS 2008. Trans 4/2/2012 as Priest Bp Michael Hanley. m 12/28/1974 Elena Beth Fails Hutchinson c 4. Assoicate Pstr Cong of the Gd Shpd Beijing China 2009-2011; Chapl St. Jn's Angl Cathd. Hong Kong 2008-2011; Lectr Ming Hua TS Hong Kong 2007-2011. Soc of Cath Priests 2012.

HUTCHINSON, Barbara (CPa) 9 Carlton Ave, Port Washington NY 11050 **S Andr's Epis Ch Shippensburg PA 2012-** B Westchester PA 1954 d James & Joyce. BA Millersville U; MDiv GTS 2008. D 6/7/2008 P 2/18/2009 Bp Nathan Dwight Baxter. m 1/1/1983 William Hutchinson c 2. Asst R S Steph's Ch Prt Washington NY 2008-2011; Dir of Stwdshp & Congrl Dvlpmt S Jas Ch Lancaster PA 1999-2004.

HUTCHINSON JR, John Fuller (Del) 350 Noxontown Rd, Middletown DE 19709 **Chapl S Andr's Sch Chap Middletown DE 2010-; S Andrews Sch Of Delaware Inc Middletown DE 2002-; Tchr, Cmnty Serv Dir St. Andr's Sch Delaware 2000-** B Monterey CA 1962 s John & Donna. BA Amh 1984; MDiv Harvard DS 2000. D 6/15/2002 P 5/31/2003 Bp M(Arvil) Thomas Shaw. m 8/11/1984 Elizabeth Ann Mather c 1. S Paul's Ch Lancaster NH 2015. jhutchinson@standrews-de.org

HUTCHINSON, Ninon N (CNY) 7029 Texas Road, Croghan NY 13327 **P-in-c S Jn's Ch Black River NY 2013-; Chapl S Aug Foxboro MA (Sum) 1986-** B Princeton NJ 1952 d Charles & Pauline. BA Trenton St Coll 1979; MDiv EDS 1984; MSW Yeshiva U 1994; MSW Yeshiva U Wurzweiler Sch of Soc Wk 1994. D 6/2/1984 P 6/25/1986 Bp George Phelps Mellick Belshaw. m 4/24/2010 Boman B Bushor. Dio New York New York NY 1997-2013; S Jn's Epis Ch Monticello NY 1997-2013, 1995-1996; Tri-Cnty Epis Area Mnstry Monticello NY 1995, 1989-1990; CPE Res Methodist Hosp Brooklyn NY 1988-1989; Asst Prog Dir S Jn's Chap Cambridge MA 1987-2014; Asst Prog Dir Emery Hse SSJE 1987-1988; Soc-St Jn The Evang Cambridge MA 1987-1988; Stff S Hilda & S Hugh Sch New York NY 1986-1987; Asst Gr Epis Ch Eliz NJ 1985-1986; Int Asst S Andr's Epis Ch New Providence NJ 1984-1985; Assoc H Trin Glendale Glendale Sprg NC 1984. NASW 1992; Samoyed Club Of Amer 1997; Soc of S Jn the Evang 1984; Ther Dogs Intl 1997. Trin Transformational Fell Trin Ch NY, NY 2007.

HUTCHISON, Hal (ETenn) 309 Quail Dr., Johnson City TN 37601 **R S Jn's Epis Ch Johnson City TN 2007-** B Orange TX 1950 s Horace & Alice. BA U Denv 1972; MDiv Nash 1980; DMin Sewanee: The U So, TS 2003. D 6/16/1980 Bp Willis Ryan Henton P 3/18/1981 Bp James Barrow Brown. m 9/1/1984 Sandy Hutchison c 3. R H Trin Epis Ch Sulphur LA 1997-2006; Chapl Epis Sch Acadiana Lafayette LA 1995-1997; Chapl Epis Sch Of Acadiana Inc. Cade LA 1995-1997; R S Paul's Ch Edneyville NC 1989-1994; Asst S Ptr's Ch Oxford MS 1987-1989; Chapl U of Mississippi Oxford MS 1987-1989; R Chr Memi Ch Mansfield LA 1985-1987; Vic S Pat's Epis Ch W Monroe LA 1983-1985; Asst S Paul's Ch New Orleans LA 1983-1984.

HUTCHISON, Jonathan Schofield (Ind) Hc 81 Box 6009, Questa NM 87556 B Danville PA 1951 s Schofield & Edith. BA Ham 1974; MDiv Ya Berk 1981. D 8/6/1981 P 5/19/1982 Bp Richard Mitchell Trelease Jr. m 9/14/1974 Deborah P Pender. Chapl Hospice Of So Cntrl Indiana 1993-1998; Vic S Dav's Ch Beanblossom Beanblossom IN 1991-2009; Coordntr Of Yth Mnstry Dio Indianapolis Indianapolis IN 1986-1993; Asst S Jas Epis Ch Taos NM 1982-1986; Dio The Rio Grande Albuquerque 1981-1982. EPF.

HUTCHISON, Sheldon Butt (ECR) 921 Eton Way, Sunnyvale CA 94087 **Asst S Thos Epis Ch Sunnyvale CA 2007-** B Alton IL 1950 BA U IL 1971; MS U IL 1977; PhD U IL 1980; MDiv CDSP 2003. D 6/28/2003 P 1/31/2004 Bp Richard Lester Shimpfky. m 4/19/1997 Eileen Patricia Hutchison c 1. Mssnr Trin Cathd San Jose CA 2003-2007. Cn Mssnr To Silicon Vlly El Camino Real 2003.

HUTCHSON, Lee Allen (Va) 18256 Oxshire Ct, Montpelier VA 23192 **R S Mart's Epis Ch Richmond VA 2004-** B Creighton NE 1963 s Richard & Ann.

U of So Dakota; BA Iowa St U 1987; MDiv Nash 1991. D 12/19/1990 P 7/1/1991 Bp James Edward Krotz. m 9/1/1990 Ursula Michele Magyar-Hutchson c 1. S Paul's Epis Ch Quincy FL 2000-2004; Non-par Ch of the Gd Shpd Thomasville Georgia 1994-1999; S Matt's Ch Lincoln NE 1991-1994.

HUTH, Harvey Checketts (Alb) St Stephen's Church, 16 Elsmere Ave, Delmar NY 12054 **Archd S Steph's Ch Delmar NY 2009-** B New Berlin NY 1943 s Harry & Betty. MA Colg 1966; EdD SUNY - Albany 1978. D 6/14/2003 Bp David John Bena. m 6/11/1965 Nancy Huth c 1.

HUTJENS, Dale Henry (FdL) 123 Nob Hill Ln, De Pere WI 54115 **D S Anne's Epis Ch De Pere WI 2003-** B Green Bay WI 1952 BA S Norbert Coll 1976. D 8/30/2003 Bp Russell Edward Jacobus. m 5/16/1981 Winifred Elaine Hutjens c 2.

HUTSON, Blake Robert (Ala) Church Of The Holy Apostles, 424 Emery Dr, Hoover AL 35244 **R The Epis Ch of the H Apos Hoover AL 2012-** B 1979 s Carl & Carol. BA Lipscomb U 2001; MDiv PrTS 2004; STM Sewanee: The U So, TS 2005. D 6/11/2005 P 1/14/2006 Bp George Edward Councell. m 5/17/2003 Christina L Hutson c 1. Asst to the R S Phil's In The Hills Tucson AZ 2007-2012; Asst to the R Trin Ch Moorestown NJ 2005-2007. bhutson@holyapostleshoover.org

HUTSON, Linda Darlene (Az) 12111 N La Cholla Blvd, Oro Valley AZ 85755 B Battle Creek MI 1948 d Elmer & Geraldine. The Epis Dio Arizona D Formation Acad; The Epis Dio Arizona D Acad 2012. D 6/7/2014 Bp Kirk Stevan Smith. m 8/29/1987 Robert Erwin Hutson c 1.

HUTSON, Thomas Milton (ETenn) 3502 Wood Bridge Dr, Nashville TN 37217 B Chattanooga TN 1929 s William & Thelma. BS U of Chattanooga 1955; STM Ya Berk 1958. D 6/24/1958 Bp John Vander Horst P 3/4/1959 Bp Theodore N Barth. m 8/30/1958 Shirley Crooks c 4. Asst R S Paul's Epis Ch Chattanooga TN 1988-1994; R Ch Of The Adv Nashville TN 1979-1987; Asst R Ch Of The Ascen Knoxville TN 1974-1979; R S Paul's Ch Memphis TN 1964-1974; Vic Ch Of The Redeem Shelbyville TN 1960-1964; Vic S Thos The Apos Humboldt TN 1959-1960; P-in-c H Innoc Trenton TN 1958-1960.

HUTTAR BAILEY, Julia Ruth (Mich) **Trin Epis Ch Farmington MI 2014-** B Beverly MA 1961 d Charles & Joy. BA Hope Coll 1983; MMus U MI 1987; MDiv Ecum TS 2011. D 12/11/2010 P 6/11/2011 Bp Wendell Nathaniel Gibbs Jr. m 6/22/2014 Kenneth J Wilson c 1. P-in-c S Mich And All Ang Epis Ch Lincoln Pk MI 2011-2013; S Clare Of Assisi Epis Ch Ann Arbor MI 1984-2007.

HUTTO, Kelsey (Ind) 422 N 13th Ave, Beech Grove IN 46107 **S Dav's Ch Beanblossom Beanblossom IN 2015-** B Daytona Beach FL 1986 d James & Jamie. BSK Georgia Sthrn U 2010; MDiv Sewanee: The U So, TS 2012; MDiv The TS at The U So 2012. D 6/30/2012 Bp Scott Anson Benhase P 1/5/2013 Bp Dabney Tyler Smith. m 5/15/2010 Reginald Alan Hutto. Asst S Paul's Ch Augusta GA 2013-2015; S Hilary's Ch Ft Myers FL 2012-2013. clergy1.stdavidsbb@gmail.com

HUTTON, Linda Arzelia (Tenn) Box 3167, Sewanee TN 37375 **Designated Supply P Chr Epis Ch Tracy City TN 2006-; Prov IV CE Consult 2004-; P-in-c St Jas Epis Ch Sewanee TN 2001-** B Eugene OR 1948 d Arthur & Gladys. Estrn Oregon U 1982; BA Kensington U 1990; MBA GTF 1995; DIT Sewanee: The U So, TS 1995; DMin VTS 2005. D 3/16/1986 Bp Robert Louis Ladehoff P 9/15/1997 Bp Chris Christopher Epting. m 3/29/1981 Peter Michael Hutton. Chr Epis Ch Tracy City TN 2008-2013; Trin Ch Winchester TN 2001, Int 1999-2000; Prog Dir Sewanee U So TS Sewanee TN 1996-2006; Dio Iowa Des Moines IA 1987-1996; CE Consult Epis Ch Cntr New York NY 1990-1996. "DMin," *Praise is What We Do - Initiating Change in the Culture of a Congregation from Scarcity to Abundance*, VTS, 2005; Auth, "Docc 16/20," *Curric*, 1999; Auth, *Ang Unaware*, GTF, 1995; Auth, *The Mnstry of Hosp*, GTF, 1995; Auth, "Outdoor Mnstrs," *Plnng Guide*, 1994. DOK 2002.

HUTTON, Linda Vaught (Va) **R S Thos Epis Ch Orange VA 2007-** B Oakland CA 1951 d William & Marion. Cert VTS; BS Florida St U 1973; MA Geo 1982; MDiv Sewanee: The U So, TS 2004; DMin Sewanee: The U So, TS 2010. D 6/26/2004 Bp Peter J Lee P 1/25/2005 Bp Edward Stuart Little II. P-in-c S Anne's Epis Ch Warsaw IN 2004-2007; Pres of the Stndg Com Dio Virginia Richmond VA 2015-2016, Stndg Com 2013-2016, Dio Exec Bd, Bdgt Com Chair 2012-2013, Dio Exec Bd 2011-2013. rectorstt@verizon.net

HUTTON III, Skip (SVa) 3429 Boyce Court, Norfolk VA 23509 **Assoc S Jn's Ch Hampton VA 2006-; Dir Cntr for Psych and Healing Norfolk VA 1994-** B Raleigh NC 1952 s James & Elizabeth. BA U NC 1974; MDiv Duke DS 1978; Cert VTS 1979. D 6/30/1979 P 6/1/1980 Bp William Gillette Weinhauer. m 7/7/1979 Cindy H Hutton c 1. Int S Paul's Ch Norfolk VA 2004-2007; Ctr. For Sprtl Formation Norfolk VA 1988-2009; Dir Cntr For Sprtl Formation 1988-1994; R S Steph's Ch Norfolk VA 1982-1988; Assoc S Mich's Ch Raleigh NC 1979-1982.

HUXLEY, Dave (NwT) Saint Luke's Church, 146 S Church St, Whitewater WI 53190 **P S Nich' Epis Ch Midland TX 2013-** B Detroit MI 1951 s Frank & Anne. MDiv Nash 2004. D 6/5/2004 P 12/6/2004 Bp Steven Andrew Miller. m 8/8/1992 Lois N Huxley c 2. P S Lk's Ch Whitewater WI 2009-2013; S Jn's Epis Ch Vinita OK 2007-2009; P-in-c S Jn The Bapt Portage WI 2004-2007.

HUYCK, Jonathan Taylor (RI) 175 Mathewson St, Providence RI 02903 **R Gr Ch In Providence Providence RI 2010-** B New York City 1969 BA Br 1991; MDiv U Chi DS 1995; STM GTS 2003. D 3/13/2004 P 9/18/2004 Bp Mark Sean Sisk. m 8/23/2004 Ann D Huyck c 2. Cn The Amer Cathd of the H Trin Paris 75008 2004-2010.

HUYNH, Tinh Trang (Va) 64 Horseshoe Ln N, Columbus NJ 08022 **R S Patricks Ch Falls Ch VA 2012-, Vic 1997-2014** B Hai-Phong VN 1948 s Luyen & Thien. BA Dalat U 1971; MDiv VTS 1994. D 6/11/1994 P 12/14/1994 Bp Peter J Lee. m 10/13/1971 Kim-Anh Huynh c 2. Assoc Vic S Pat's Ch An Anglo-Vietnamese Epis 1994-1998; P Dio Virginia Richmond VA 1994-1997.

HYATT, David (Pa) 404 Donna Ln, Phoenixville PA 19460 **Non-par 1981-** B Owego NY 1933 s Howard & Ruth. BA McKendree U 1955; MDiv Tem 1958. D 6/13/1964 Bp Robert Lionne DeWitt P 12/1/1964 Bp Angus Dun. m 8/28/1955 Susan R Rohde c 3. R Trin Ch Gulph Mills Kng Of Prussia PA 1974-1981; Asst H Apos And Medtr Philadelphia PA 1964-1967; Serv Methodist Ch 1958-1963. "Rules On Trial Not The Pstr," Philadelphia Inquirer/Knight Ridder, 2004. Legion Of hon Chap Of The Four Chapl 1967.

HYBL, Andrew David (Ark) 925 Mitchell St, Conway AR 72034 **CDSP Berkeley CA 2014-** B Omaha NE 1980 s Larry & Linda. BA U of Arkansas 2002; MDiv PSR 2011; MDiv PSR 2011; Cert of Angl Stds CDSP 2012. D 3/24/2012 P 9/29/2012 Bp Larry Benfield. m 10/8/2011 Julie Wilkinson Hybl c 1. Cur S Ptr's Ch Conway AR 2012-2014. ahybl@cdsp.edu

HYCHE, Jerald (Tex) 1803 Highland Hollow Drive, Conroe TX 77304 **R S Jas The Apos Epis Ch Conroe TX 2010-; St. Lk's The Woodlands Hosp Bd S Lk's Epis Hosp Houston TX 2012-** B Gadsden AL 1960 s Jesse & Wanda. BA U of Alabama 1982; MDiv VTS 2004. D 6/12/2004 P 4/16/2005 Bp Philip Menzie Duncan II. m 4/26/1985 Colleen M Hyche c 3. Assoc R S Mart's Epis Ch Houston TX 2006-2010; Cur S Jas Ch Fairhope AL 2004-2006; Sprtl Formation Bd Mem Dio Texas Houston TX 2007-2010; Cmncatn Bd chair Dio Cntrl Gulf Coast Pensacola FL 2005-2006. Writer, "Daily reflections," *Finding God Day by Day*, Forw Mvmt, 2010; Reporter, "News and feature arts," *GC Daily*, Epis News Serv, 2009; Writer, "Daily reflections," *Praying Day by Day*, Forw Mvmt, 2009; Writer, "Dioc Nwspr," *The Texas Epis*, Dio Texas, 2008; Ed, "Dioc Nwspr," *The Coastline*, Dio Cntrl Gulf Coast, 2006.

HYDE, John Ernest Authur (SwFla) 4650 Cove Cir Apt 407, Madeira Beach FL 33708 **Assoc S Anne Of Gr Epis Ch Seminole FL 2009-** B Montreal QC CA 1941 s William & Barbara. BTh S Paul U Ottawa CA 1986. Trans 6/20/2000 Bp John Bailey Lipscomb. m 2/2/1963 Katherine Frances Hyde c 3. Assoc S Dunst's Epis Ch Largo FL 2001-2009; R Ch Of The Annunc Holmes Bch FL 2000-2001; Int Gd Samar Epis Ch Clearwater FL 1998-1999; Int Gr Epis Ch Camden SC 1997-1998; Int S Mary's Epis Ch Bonita Sprg FL 1995-1996.

HYDE, Lillian (Tex) Po Box 580117, Houston TX 77258 **Chapl Iona Sch for Mnstry 2012-; T/F Texas Epis Disaster Relief & Dvlpmt 2011-** B Greenville MS 1950 d George & Betty. BA Mississippi St U 1972; MDiv Epis TS of the SW 2004. D 5/29/2004 Bp Duncan Montgomery Gray III P 11/30/2004 Bp Don Adger Wimberly. m 12/26/1978 Robert Willis Hyde c 1. Chapl Dio Texas Houston TX 2011-2015; R S Geo's Epis Ch Texas City TX 2008-2011; Assoc R Trin Ch Galveston TX 2004-2008; Bd Pres S Vincents Hse Galveston TX 2011-2012, Bd Dir 2008-2012; Bd Dir S Lk's Epis Hosp Houston TX 2010-2012; Bd Dir S Jas Hse Of Baytown Baytown TX 2009-2012; Bd Dir Wm Temple Epis Ctr Galveston TX 2008-2011.

HYDE, Pamela Wilson (Az) 75 Church Ln, Westport CT 06880 **Epis Ch Of S Fran-In-The-Vlly Green Vlly AZ 2016-** B Cleveland OH 1963 d Alan & Charlotte. BA Amh 1985; JD and AM Duke 1989; Grad Cert U of Arizona 2011. D 6/6/2015 P 6/4/2016 Bp Kirk Stevan Smith. m 10/11/2008 Douglas S Brozovsky.

HYDE III, Robert Willis (Tex) 208 Seawall Blvd, Galveston TX 77550 B Jackson MS 1947 s Robert & Rufie. BD U of Mississippi 1970; MDiv Epis TS of the SW 1994. D 6/24/1994 P 12/21/1994 Bp Alfred Marble Jr. m 12/26/1978 Lillian Hyde c 3. R S Thos The Apos Epis Ch Houston TX 2004-2014; Gr Epis Ch Georgetown TX 2004; All SS Epis Ch Austin TX 2002-2004; Ch Of The Creator Clinton MS 1998-2002; S Lk's Ch Brandon MS 1994-1998.

HYER, Darin Stant (CGC) St Simon's on the Sound Episcopal Church, 28 Miracle Strip Pkwy SW, Fort Walton Beach FL 32548 B Long Branch NJ 1962 s Raymond & Louise. BA Millsaps Coll 1984; MTS Candler TS Emory U 1998; MTS Emory U Candler TS 1998; MDiv Candler TS Emory U 2003; MDiv Emory U Candler TS 2003; Sewanee: The U So, TS 2012; U So TS 2012. D 12/21/2011 P 6/20/2012 Bp Philip Menzie Duncan II. m 11/12/2007 Rachael L Hyer c 3. S Simon's On The Sound Ft Walton Bch FL 2012.

HYLDEN, Emily R (USC) 448 Cami Forest Ln, Columbia SC 29209 **St Aug of Hippo Epis Ch Dallas TX 2016-** B St Paul MN 1986 d Pierre & Terri. AB Duke 2008; Masters of Div Duke DS 2012. D 6/2/2012 P 12/5/2012 Bp William Howard Love. m 5/29/2011 Jordan L Hylden. Cn for YA Mnstrs Trin Cathd Columbia SC 2013-2015; Cur S Mich & S Geo S Louis MO 2012-2013.

HYLDEN, Jordan L (Dal) 6345 Wydown Blvd, Saint Louis MO 63105 **Dio Dallas Dallas TX 2016-** B Grand Forks ND 1983 s Mark & Esther. AB Harvard Coll 2006; MDiv Duke DS 2010; MDiv Duke DS 2010. D 12/21/2012 Bp

George Wayne Smith P 7/6/2013 Bp Michael Smith. m 5/29/2011 Emily R Hylden. Cur S Mary's Ch Columbia SC 2013-2015. jhylden@edod.org

HYNDMAN, David Lee (NI) 8981 E 5th Ave Apt 101, Gary IN 46403 B Gary IN 1939 s William & Mary. BA Shimer Coll 1961; BD SWTS 1964. D 5/30/1964 P 12/1/1964 Bp Walter C Klein. R S Augustines Ch Gary IN 1991-2006; Vic All SS Ch Syracuse IN 1966-1991; Cur Chr Ch Gary IN 1964-1966. stauggary@att.net

I

IALONGO, Donna Marie (Chi) 2s697 Parkview Dr, Glen Ellyn IL 60137 **Ch Of S Ben Bolingbrook IL 2016**- B Evergreen Park IL 1947 d Arthur & Jane. B.A. U IL 1973; M.A. U IL 1975; PhD Nthrn Illinois U 1979; M.Div. SWTS 2009. D 6/6/2009 P 12/5/2009 Bp Jeff Lee. c 1. S Barn' Epis Ch Glen Ellyn IL 2014-2015, 2011; S Jn's Epis Ch Chicago IL 2013; Dir of Assessment Bexley Seabury Fed Chicago IL 2009-2011. donnarnold@rocketmail.com

IBE, Morgan Kelechi (Okla) 2424 Pinon Pl, Edmond OK 73013 **R Epis Ch Of The Redeem Oklahoma City OK 2010**- B Nigeria 1968 s Justice & Janet. BA Trin Theol Coll NG 1991; BS Imo St U Nigeria 1997; CPE ST LOUIS U Hosp ST LOUIS MO 2008. Trans 5/15/2007 as Priest Bp George Wayne Smith. m 2/16/1999 Charity C Ibe c 3. R Trin Ch Hannibal MO 2007-2010; R S Paul's Ch Palmyra MO 2005-2011; R Trin/St Paul Partnership 2005-2011. Auth, "LORD TEACH US TO PRAY," *GUIDE TO EFFECTIVE Pryr*, SKILL Mk, 2003.

IDEMA III, Henry (WMich) 13562 Redbird Ln, Grand Haven MI 49417 **Asst Gr Ch Holland MI 2008**- B Grand Rapids MI 1947 s Henry & Jane. BA U MI 1969; MDiv EDS 1975; MA U MI 1981; PhD U Chi 1987. D 6/2/1975 Bp Charles Ellsworth Bennison Jr P 6/1/1976 Bp Charles Bennison Sr. m 12/27/1986 Karen Fennel c 2. S Jn's Epis Ch Grand Haven MI 1987-2008; Assoc R The Ch Of The H Sprt Lake Forest IL 1984-1987; Asst S Mary's Ch Pk Ridge IL 1981-1984; Ch of the H Sprt Belmont MI 1977-1980; Dio Wstrn Michigan Kalamazoo MI 1977-1978, 1975-1976; 1975-1977. Auth, "Before Our Time, A Theory of the Sixties From a Rel, Soc and Psychoanalytic Perspective," U Press of Amer, 1996; Auth, "Freud, Rel and the Roaring Twenties," Rowman & Littlefield, 1990.

IDICULA, Mathew (Chi) The Church of St Columba of Iona, 1800 Irving Park Rd, Hanover Park IL 60133 B Kodukulanji India 1950 s P & Mariamma. BA Bp Moore Coll 1971; MA Luth TS at Chicago 2004; DMin Luth TS at Chicago 2009; CPE The Ch Hm at Montgomery Place 2009. Trans 11/1/2007 Bp Bill Persell. m 7/9/1977 Elizabeth P Mathew c 3. R Ch Of S Columba Of Iona Hanover Pk IL 2007-2017, Vic 2007-; Inventory Analyst Motion Industries 1972-2003. Auth, "A Travelogue," *In the Land of Jesus*, ISPCK, Delhi, 2011; Auth, "Bk," *Captive of Culture*, ISPCK, Delhi, 2010.

IFILL, Angela Sylvia S (O) 64 Bayley Ave, Yonkers NY 10705 B TrinidadWI 1944 d Henry & Esther. Ford; BA SUNY 1992; MDiv VTS 1995. D 6/23/1995 Bp Orris George Walker Jr P 7/11/1996 Bp Charles Lovett Keyser. c 3. Epis Ch Cntr New York NY 2004-2016; Assoc R S Paul's Epis Ch Cleveland OH 1998-2004; Cn Pstr Trin And S Phil's Cathd Newark NJ 1996-1998; D Trin-St Jn's Ch Hewlett NY 1995-1996. Ord of S Helena 1989-1998.

IGARASHI, Peter Hiroshi (Pa) 600 E Cathedral Rd # D202, Philadelphia PA 19128 **Died 4/15/2016** B Sacramento CA 1923 s Kensaburo & Toshi. BA Colby Coll 1944; BD Crozer TS 1946; ThD Harvard DS 1950; Cert VTS 1960. D 6/28/1960 Bp Frederick D Goodwin P 12/1/1960 Bp Frederick Warnecke. m 6/26/1949 Kimiko K Kato. Ret 1988-2016; R S Mk's Ch Waterville ME 1983-1988; Ch Of The Redeem Sayre PA 1983; Trin Ch Bethlehem PA 1983; Ch Of S Jn The Div Hasbrouck Hts NJ 1981-1983; Vic S Cyp's Epis Ch Hackensack NJ 1981-1983; Sewanee U So TS Sewanee TN 1966-1981; Vic S Jas-S Geo Epis Ch Jermyn PA 1964-1966; Asst Cathd Ch Of The Nativ Bethlehem PA 1960-1964.

IGO, Nancy Elle (NwT) Episcopal Diocese of Northwest Texas, 1802 Broadway, Lubbock TX 79401 **Admin Dio NW Texas Lubbock TX 2008**- B Lubbock TX 1956 d George & Elizabeth. none Amarillo Coll; NW Texas Sch for Deacons; Elem.Ed Cert W Texas A & M U; Bachelor of Sci Texas Tech U 1978. D 11/17/2012 Bp James Scott Mayer. m 10/8/2006 Russell Mark Igo c 1. nigo@nwtdiocese.org

IHIASOTA, Isaac Iheanyichukwu (WNY) 8283 Effie Drive, Niagara Falls NY 14304 **Adj Prof Niagara U Niagara Falls New York 2007-; Cler Dep Dio Wstrn New York Tonawanda NY 2009-, Mem of Dicesan Coun 2006-2008** B Atta-Owerri NG 1950 s Michael & Angelinah. DIT Trin Theol Coll NG 1976; DIT Lon GB 1977; BA MI SU 1986; MA MI SU 1988; PhD MI SU 1994. Trans 8/11/1997 Bp Edward Lewis Lee Jr. m 12/11/1982 Agatha C Ihiasota c 6. S Steph's Ch Niagara Falls NY 2006-2014; S Dunst's Epis Ch Succasunna NJ 2004-2006; Adj Prof Caldwell Coll Caldwell New Jersey 2004; Adj Prof Centenary Coll Hackettstown New Jersey 2004; Gr Epis Ch Ft Wayne IN 2001-2003; Adj Prof Sthrn Illinois U Carbondale Illinois 1999-2000; Adj Prof Jn A. Logan Coll Carterville Illinois 1998-2004; R S Andr's Ch Carbondale IL 1997-2001;

Adj Prof Kellogg Cmnty Coll Battle Creek Michigan 1996; Adjuct Prof Davenport Coll of Bus Lansing Michigan 1992-1994; Int R Trin Epis Ch Grand Ledge MI 1991-1997; Int R S Mich's Epis Ch Lansing MI 1989-1991; Grad Asst MI SU E Lansing Michigan 1988-1991; Asstg R S Dav's Ch Lansing MI 1986-1989; Asst Chapl All SS Ch E Lansing MI 1984-1986; Stwdshp Com Dio Newark Newark NJ 2005; First Alt Cler Dep Dio Nthrn Indiana So Bend IN 2001-2002; Stndg Com Dio Springfield Springfield IL 2000-2001, Cler Dep 1999-2001. Auth, "Mass Media Changing Partisanship & British," 1994; Auth, "Electoral Behavior". Electoral Behavior 1994; Mass Media Changing Partisanship And British; Phd Dissertation MI SU.

✠ IHLOFF, The Rt Rev Robert Wilkes (Md) 1200 Steuart St Unit 1020, Baltimore MD 21230 B New Britain CT 1941 s Ernest & Mildred. BA Ursinus Coll 1964; MDiv EDS 1967; MA Cntrl Connecticut St U 1971; Boston Gestal And Inst 1978; DMin EDS 1985; U of Cambridge 1992; EDS 1996. D 6/13/1967 P 3/30/1968 Bp Walter H Gray Con 10/21/1995 for Md. m 6/11/1966 Nancy V Ihloff c 2. Workshop Ldr Listening Hearts Mnstrs 2012-2013; Bp Dio Maryland Baltimore MD 1995-2007, Bp 1995-2007; Bd Inst For Chr & Jewish Stds 1995-1997; Adj Fac Drew TS Madison NJ 1992-1995; R Gr Ch Madison NJ 1987-1995; R S Paul's Ch Natick MA 1976-1987; P-in-c Trin Epis Ch Southport CT 1972-1976; Vic S Geo's Ch Bolton CT 1969-1972; Cur S Mk's Ch New Britain CT 1967-1969; Epis Visitor Epis Carmel of St. Teresa 2007-2013. Auth, "Sharing Resources To Bared A Cmnty-Based Ch," *Wit*, 2002; Auth, "Contributions In One Minute Stwdshp Sermens," Morehouse, 1997; Auth, "The Journey Toward Wholeness w S Theresa Of Avila," *Word & Sprt*, 1988; Auth, "Suffering To Grow," *Journ Rel & Hlth*, 1976. Assoc Of The OHC 1976; Fell Coll Of Preachers 1985. Guja MemorialScholarship ETS Claremont 2012; DD Ursinus Coll 2008; DD Virginia TS 1996; Doctor Of Divinny Epis Divinty Sch 1995.

IJAMS, Carl Phillip (Mass) 38295 S Bogie Ct, Tucson AZ 85739 **Ret 1993**- B Tombstone AZ 1928 s Sheldon & Jessie. BA U of Arizona 1951; MDiv Ya Berk 1958. D 6/11/1958 Bp Walter H Gray P 12/20/1958 Bp Reginald Heber Gooden. Assoc Chr The King Ch Tucson AZ 1994-2011; R Ch Of The H Nativ S Weymouth MA 1970-1972; R Trin Epis Ch Stoughton MA 1963-1970; Cler Dio Panama 1958-1961. Phillips Brooks Cler Club 1965-1993.

IKENYE, Ndungu John Brown (Chi) 1930 Darrow Ave, Evanston IL 60201 B Gakoe-Thika KE 1954 s Ikenye & Wanjiku. BA Pan Afr Chr Coll Nairobi Ke 1984; MA Intl TS 1986; MA Garrett-Evang TS 1989; DMin Garrett-Evang TS 1993; PhD NWU 1996. Trans 6/1/1997 Bp Frank Tracy Griswold III. m 5/9/1981 N Rose Ikenye c 3. Exec Coun Appointees New York NY 2006-2016; Vic St. Andrews Pentecost Epis Ch Evanston IL 1998-2006; Prof Bexley Seabury Fed Chicago IL 1997-1999; Assoc Ch Of The Epiph Chicago IL 1990-1993; Serv Ch In Kenya 1978-1988. Auth, "Decolonization Of The Soul," Envoy Graphic @ Print Systems, 2003; Auth, "Afr Chr Counslg," Envoy Graphic @ Print Systems, 2002; Auth, "Bi-Cultural Personality For Mnstrs," *ATR*, 2001; Auth, "Ritual In Cross Cultural Pstr Care & Counsritual In Cross Cultural Pstr Care & Counslg," *Journ Of Supervision*, 1998; Auth, "Trng & Supervision For Mnstry In Kenya," *Journ Of Supervision*, 1992. AAMFC 1996; AAPC 1994; AEHC 1993.

ILLAS, Antonio (WTex) PO Box 1948, San Benito TX 78586 **S Matthews Auburn WA 2016**- B Aguadilla PR 1966 s Adolfo & Carmen. BA Cntrl Connecticut St U 1988; MDiv Seminario Evangelico de Puerto Rico 2005. D 6/3/2012 P 1/20/2013 Bp David Andres Alvarez-Velazquez. m 11/24/1989 Cela T Tecamachaltzi Campos c 1. All SS Epis Ch San Benito TX 2015-2016.

ILLES, Joseph Paul (NI) 56869 Sundown Rd, South Bend IN 46619 **D The Cathd Ch Of S Jas So Bend IN 1992**- B South Bend IN 1926 s Joseph & Theresa. Diac Sch For Faith & Mnstry 1991. D 10/9/1991 Bp Francis Campbell Gray. m 9/3/1949 Lillian Marie Illes c 3. Ord Of S Lk, OHC.

ILLINGWORTH, David Paul (Me) 28 Wayne St, Portland ME 04102 B Waterville ME 1948 s Paul & Phyllis. AB Harv 1971; Harvard DS 1973; MDiv GTS 1980. D 5/17/1975 P 11/21/1975 Bp Frederick Barton Wolf. Dio Maine Portland ME 2010-2011; Epis Ch Of S Mary The Vrgn Falmouth ME 2010-2011; Cathd Ch Of S Lk Portland ME 2010, 2003-2005; Int S Ann's Epis Ch Windham Windham 2005-2006; S Ann's Epis Ch Windham Windham ME 2005-2006; Int Cathd Ch of S Lk Portland ME 2003-2005; Asst 1994-2002; Int 1991-1992; S Jn's Ch Jamaica Plain MA 1991-1992, 1986-1988; The Par Of S Chrys's Quincy MA 1988; Int 1986-1988; 1981-1985; Vic S Hugh Ch Lincoln ME 1975-1980; Vic S Hugh of Lincoln Ch ME 1975-1980; Vic S Thos Ch Winn ME 1975-1980.

ILOGU, Edmund Christopher Onyedum (WA) 2355 Weymouth Ln, Crofton MD 21114 **Died 12/6/2015** B Ihiala NG 1920 s Ilogu & Agnes. Prog Advncd Rel Stds; ALCD Lon GB 1953; STM UTS 1958; MA Col 1959; PhD U Leiden Nl 1974. Trans 8/1/1988 Bp John Thomas Walker. m 4/25/1946 Elizabeth Chineze Obiago c 3. Int Chapl How Washington DC 1988-1989; Int Calv Ch Washington DC 1986-1988; Serv Ch Of Nigeria 1949-1986. Auth, "Coping w Three Cultures: an Autobiography," Sungai Books, 1999; Auth, "Chrsnty and Igbo Culture," E.J. Brill, 1974; Auth, "W Meets E," C.M.S. London, 1954.

IMARA, Mwalimu (Ind) 4550 Orkney Ln Sw, Atlanta GA 30331 **Died 10/6/2015** B Halifax NS CA 1930 s William & Blanche. BA Case Wstrn Reserve U 1964; DMin Meadville Lombard TS 1968. P 9/18/1982 Bp Edward Witker Jones. m 5/14/1960 Saburi Imara c 3. Ret 1998-2015; S Tim's Decatur GA 1994; S Steph's Ch Griffin GA 1984-1991; Chapl, Assoc Prof of Ethics, Chair, Dept of Counseli Morehouse Sch of Med Atlanta GA 1983-1998; 1982-1984; Prot Min 1968-1982. Auth, "Growing Through Grief," *Hospice Care: Principles and Pract*, Springer, 1983; Auth, "A Theol of Hospice From Encounters w Howard Thurman," *Debate & Understanding*, Bos, 1982; Auth, "Coping w Death," *Encyclopedia Americana*, 1979; Auth, *Dying as the Last Stage of Growth*, Prentice Hall, 1975. AAPC Dplma 1970; Sigma Pi Phi Fraternity 1979. Schlr in Res Fetzer Inst 1997; Tchg Execellence Awd Morehouse Sch of Med Dept of Publich Hlth: Resi 1994; Tchg Exellence Awd Morehouse Sch of Med 1988; Recognition Natl Hospice Orgnztn 1988; Recognition Natl Hospice Orgnztn 1983.

IMBODEN, Stanley Franklin (CPa) 315 Dead End Rd, Lititz PA 17543 B Reading PA 1932 s Livingstone & Margaret. BA Lebanon Vlly Coll 1955; STB Tem 1958; STM Tem 1971; Lebanon Vlly Coll 1988. D 6/14/1959 P 12/15/1959 Bp John Thomas Heistand. m 2/11/2006 Sandra Imboden c 2. P-in-c Bangor Ch Of Churchtown Narvon PA 1996-2003; Planned Giving Off Dio Cntrl Pennsylvania Harrisburg PA 1995-1996; S Jas Ch Lancaster PA 1978-1994; R S Andr's Epis Ch York PA 1972-1978; Ch Of The Redemp Southampton PA 1964-1967; S Paul's Epis Ch Harrisburg PA 1964-1967; S Mary's Epis Ch Waynesboro PA 1962-1964; Vic Hope Epis Ch Manheim PA 1959-1962; S Paul's Ch Manheim PA 1959-1962. Auth, "War and Peace," *Tidings (Dioc news)*, 1991; Auth, "arts & Poems in Collgt & Ch Pub," *Sunday Sch Times*, 1952. EUC; ood of S AndrewBrotherh 1959-1990. Hon Cn Cathd of St. Steph, Harrisburg PA 1982; Hon Alum PDS 1959.

IMMEL, Otto Wigaart (NJ) Po Box 2379, Tybee Island GA 31328 B Reading PA 1937 s Amos & Loretta. BA Leh 1959. D 4/22/1972 P 10/1/1972 Bp Alfred L Banyard. c 2. R S Thos' Epis Ch Glassboro NJ 1979-1999; Evergreens Chap Moorestown NJ 1974-1979; The Evergreens Moorestown NJ 1974-1979; Cur Trin Cathd Trenton NJ 1972-1974.

IMPICCICHE, Frank S (Ind) **S Matt's Ch Indianapolis IN 2016-** B Crawfordsville IN 1962 s Albert & Juana. Dplma Angl Stds Seabury-Wstrn; BA St Meinrad Sem 1985; MA U of Dayton 1995. D 6/9/2012 P 2/3/2013 Bp Cate Waynick. m 4/29/2012 Susan Laura Wolf c 1. Vic Dio Indianapolis Indianapolis IN 2013-2016. frfrank@stmattsindy.org

INAPANTA PAEZ, Lourdes Esther (EcuC) **Iglesia Epis Del Ecuador Quito 2012-, 2000-2009** B Quito 1964 d Miguel. Programa De Educacion Teologica. D 10/14/2000 Bp Jose Neptali Larrea-Moreno P 2/11/2006 Bp Orlando Jesus Guerrero. m 8/24/1982 Jose Flores Suarez c 2.

INCE JR, Edgar Elmer (WTenn) 3749 Kimball Ave, Memphis TN 38111 **Died 8/23/2016** B Memphis TN 1927 s Edgar & Camilla. D 12/21/1962 Bp John Vander Horst P 1/27/2001 Bp James Malone Coleman. m 8/29/1947 Flora Marie Young c 1. D H Trin Ch Memphis TN 1962-1990.

INCORVATI, Rick (SO) **D Chr Epis Ch Of Springfield Springfield OH 2016-** B Akron 1964 s Lou & Willretta. BSBA JCU 1987; MA U NC at Chap Hill 1992; PhD U NC at Chap Hill 2001. D 6/11/2016 Bp Thomas Edward Breidenthal. m 6/15/2013 Kent Ross Brooks. rincorvati@wittenberg.edu

INESON JR, John Henry (Me) 53 High St., Damariscotta ME 04543 **Assoc S Mk's Ch Marco Island FL 2007-** B Rochester NH 1939 s John & Mary. BA U of New Hampshire 1961; STB Ya Berk 1964. D 6/4/1964 P 12/16/1964 Bp Charles Francis Hall. m 12/24/1975 Hannah Christine Ineson c 1. Vic S Barn Ch Augusta Augusta ME 1997-2008; R S Andr's Ch Newcastle ME 1984-1995; Chapl Colby Coll Waterville ME 1981-1984; Non-par 1972-1984; R Trin Epis Ch Fayetteville NY 1970-1972; R Trin Ch Lowville NY 1967-1970; Cur Chr Ch Binghamton NY 1964-1967. Auth, "The Way Of Life," Japan Pub, 1986.

INFANTE PINZON, John Edwin (WMich) 524 Washington Ave, Grand Haven MI 49417 **S Jn's Epis Ch Grand Haven MI 2017-** B Bogota Colombia 1965 s Mario & Rosalba. D 6/30/2012 Bp Francisco Jose Duque-Gomez. deaconjohn@stjohnsepiscopal.com

INGALLS JR, Arthur B (Md) PO Box 25, Churchville MD 21028 **R H Trin Ch Churchville MD 2006-** B San Angelo TX 1951 s Arthur & Bementa. BA Steph F Austin St U 1973; MPA Lamar U 1984; MDiv VTS 2004. D 5/22/2004 P 1/22/2005 Bp John Wadsworth Howe. m 1/1/1972 Margaret Eileen Fowler Ingalls c 2. Asst H Trin Epis Ch Fruitland Pk FL 2005-2006.

INGALLS, Clayton Dean (Tenn) 5501 Franklin Pike, Nashville TN 37220 B Atlanta GA 1979 s Clyde & Betty. BA Belmont U 2002; MDiv TESM 2007. D 6/10/2006 P 12/16/2006 Bp Bertram Nelson Herlong. m 12/15/2001 Teresa L Ingalls c 2. Asst Chr Ch Of The Ascen Paradise Vlly AZ 2012-2015; P-in-c Calv Epis Ch Kaneohe HI 2011; Emm Epis Ch Kailua HI 2011; Vic S Geo's Epis Ch Honolulu HI 2009-2011; D Ch Of The Adv Nashville TN 2006-2008.

INGALLS, Jason T (Tex) 1100 N. 15th St., Waco TX 76707 **R Epis Ch Of The H Sprt Waco TX 2014-; Dvlpmt Asst Ridley Hall Cambridge Engl 2012-** B Marshall TX 1981 s Ricki & Terri. BA Jn Br 2003; MDiv PrTS 2006; ThM Wycliffe Coll U Tor 2010. D 6/5/2010 P 1/8/2011 Bp John Bauerschmidt. m 5/19/2001 Monique M Ingalls c 1. Dvlpmt Assoc Ridley Hall Cambridge Engl 2011; St. Matt's Riverdale Angl Ch of Can Toronto ON 2010-2011. The Soc of Schlr-Priests 2012. Can Bible Soc Awd for Excellence in the Publ Reading of Scripture Can Bible Soc 2011; The Leonard Griffith Prize for Expository Preaching Wycliffe Coll, U Tor 2010. jingalls@holyspiritwaco.com

INGALLS, Margaret Eileen Fowler (WA) Transfiguration Church, 13925 New Hampshire Ave, Silver Spring MD 20904 **R Ch Of The Trsfg Silver Sprg MD 2008-; Reg 4 Convenor Dio Washington Washington DC 2012-, Prov Rep 2011-, Multi-Cultural Consortium, Inc. Convenor 2009-** B Macon GA 1951 d Waller & Geneva. BA Steph F Austin St U 1973; MA Auburn U 1979; MDiv VTS 1989. D 6/10/1989 P 3/17/1990 Bp Peter J Lee. m 1/1/1972 Arthur B Ingalls c 2. R H Trin Epis Ch Fruitland Pk FL 1993-2008; Asst Ch Of The H Comf Richmond VA 1989-1993; D Ch Of The H Comf Vienna VA 1989. Amer Friends of Jerusalem 1992; Via Media USA 2004.

INGEMAN, Peter Lyle (Ga) 3128 Huntington Ridge Circle, Valdosta GA 31602 B Chicago IL 1939 s Milton & Ellen. BA Rutgers The St U of New Jersey 1960; MA Baylor U 1975; MDiv Nash 1987. D 7/22/1982 Bp George Paul Reeves P 6/6/1987 Bp Harry Woolston Shipps. m 6/17/1961 Harriet Ingeman c 2. R Chr Ch Valdosta GA 2000-2011, 1987-1989; R S Fran Of The Islands Epis Ch Savannah GA 1989-2000; Dio Georgia Savannah GA 1987-1989; Chapl Valdosta St Coll 1987-1989; Chapl S Jn Mtry Acad Delafield WI 1984-1987; D S Anskar's Epis Ch Hartland WI 1984-1987; D S Aug Of Cbury Ch Augusta GA 1982-1984. OHC.

INGERSOLL, Russ (WNC) 52 Sturbridge Lane, Greensboro NC 27408 B Saint Paul MN 1938 s Russell & Jeanette. MDiv VTS; BA Dart 1960; MDiv VTS 1965. D 6/24/1965 P 1/1/1966 Bp Hamilton Hyde Kellogg. m 12/21/1960 Patricia An Podas c 3. Calv Epis Ch Fletcher NC 2002-2004; Chr Sch Arden NC 1993-2004; Headmaster Chr Sch Chap Arden NC 1993-2003; Chapl S Mk Sch Dallas TX 1989-1993; S Marks Sch Of Texas Dallas TX 1989-1993; Hdmstr S Greg Hs Tuscon AZ 1979-1989; S Greg HS Tucson AZ 1979-1988; R Chatam Hall Chatam VA 1976-1979; Chatham Hall Chatham VA 1975-1979; Hdmstr Kemper Hall Kenosha WI 1974-1976; Instr Rel S Paul Sch Concord NH 1967-1974; Chapl Breck Sch Minneapolis MN 1965-1967. Auth, "Role Of Ch Sch"; Ed, "Role Of Chapl In Epis Schools & Coll". Jn Verdery Awd For Serv To Epis Schools Natl Assoc Of Epis Schools 2002.

INGRAHAM, Doris Williams (SeFla) 15955 Nw 27th Ave, Opa Locka FL 33054 **D S Agnes Ch Miami FL 2005-** B Hawkinsville GA 1937 d Albert & Maggie. BD Barry U 1995. D 9/1/2001 Bp Leo Frade. m 4/30/1983 Tellis Clyde Ingraham.

INIESTA-AVILA, Bernardo (Nev) 4201 W Washington Ave, Las Vegas NV 89107 **Dio Nevada Las Vegas 2010-** B 1971 s Victor & Esperanza. BA Seminario Conciliar Mex DF; MDiv Pontifical Coll Josephinum 2001. Rec 12/7/2008 Bp Dan Thomas Edwards. m 12/7/2007 Delores Iniesta.

INMAN, John Wesley (WMich) 135 Old York Road, New Hope PA 18938 B Michigan City IN 1932 s John & Alice. BA Denison U 1954; MDiv EDS 1964. D 6/12/1965 P 12/1/1965 Bp Horace W B Donegan. Int S Jn's Ch Norristown PA 2003-2004, Asst 1998-2003; Int S Tim's Ch Roxborough Philadelphia PA 2002-2003; Asst S Paul's Ch Doylestown PA 1996-1997; Int S Paul's Epis Ch Grand Rapids MI 1995-1996; Asst Gr Ch Grand Rapids MI 1995; Int S Mk's Ch Grand Rapids MI 1994-1995; R Ch of the H Sprt Belmont MI 1992-1994; Nonpar/Sabbatical 1988-1991; R S Lk's Epis Ch Smethport PA 1983-1988; Stff Ch Of The Ascen Chicago IL 1981-1983; Stff Ch Of The Resurr Norwich CT 1980-1981; Stff Chr Ch Cathd Hartford CT 1977-1979; Stff Trin Ch Ft Wayne IN 1972-1977; Cmnty of Chr the King Mt Vernon NY 1969-1971; R H Trin Epis Ch Inwood New York NY 1968-1969; Cur S Alb's Epis Ch Of Bexley Columbus OH 1965-1967. The Ord of Julian of Norwich 1994-1994.

INMAN, Virginia Bain (NC) 607 N Greene St, Greensboro NC 27401 **Bd Trst Cbury Epis Sch 2015-; Chair, Const and Cn Dio No Carolina Raleigh NC 2014-, Pstr Response Team 2006-, Mssn Implementation Team 2005-; Chair of Endowed Conferences Kanuga 2008-** B Lakeland FL 1972 BS Randolph-Macon Coll 1994; MDiv Van 1999; JD Van 1999; CAS VTS 2004. D 6/19/2004 P 1/29/2005 Bp Michael B Curry. m 4/26/2003 Stephen Thomas Inman. H Trin Epis Ch Greensboro NC 2011, Assoc 2011-; The Ch Of The Gd Shpd Augusta GA 2011; Assoc R S Paul's Epis Ch Winston Salem NC 2004-2009. ginny@holy-trinity.com

INNES, Neil Fraser (WTex) 1702 S Medio River Cir, Sugar Land TX 77478 **P Calv Epis Ch Richmond TX 2012-** B New York NY 1930 s Walter & Doris. BA U of Texas Pan Amer 1976; MDiv Epis TS of the SW 1979. D 6/13/1979 P 12/14/1979 Bp Scott Field Bailey. m 11/7/1953 Mary Ann Innes c 3. R S Geo Ch San Antonio TX 1990-1995; R S Mk's Ch Austin TX 1984-1990; R Gr Ch Cuero TX 1981-1984; Asst R All SS Epis Ch Corpus Christi TX 1979-1981.

INSCOE, Laura D (Va) 2319 E. Broad Street, Richmond VA 23223 B Richmond VA 1954 d Ernest & Anne. BA U of Virginia 1977; JD U Rich 1980; MDiv UTS Richmond 2001; VTS 2001. D 6/15/2002 P 12/16/2002 Bp Peter J Lee. m 5/1/1993 Walter R Inscoe. R S Jn's Ch Richmond VA 2009-2017; Assoc R S Mary's Epis Ch Richmond VA 2002-2009; Resolutns Com Dio Virginia Richmond VA 2010-2012, Dn of Reg XII 2009, Clerk, Eccl Trial Crt 2008-2009, Bdgt Com 2005-2008, Exec Bd 2005-2008. linscoe@gmail.com

INSERRA, John Michael (Wyo) Saint Peter's Episcopal Church, 1 S Tschirgi St, Sheridan WY 82801 **R S Ptr's Epis Ch Sheridan WY 2012-** B Jamestown, NY 1979 s Richard & Dolores. AA Niagara Cnty Comunity Coll 2003; BA Canisius Coll 2006; MDiv Nash 2010. D 6/5/2010 P 12/7/2010 Bp William Howard Love. m 5/27/2006 Sarah E Inserra c 1. Assoc S Paul's Ch New Orleans LA 2010-2012. jminserra@gmail.com

IRELAND, Clyde Lambert (USC) 2517 Duncan St, Columbia SC 29205 B Columbia SC 1929 s Clyde & Hallie. BA U of So Carolina 1951; MDiv VTS 1954. D 6/10/1954 P 6/6/1955 Bp Clarence Alfred Cole. m 8/1/1955 Betty Jean Ireland c 4. P in charge S Thos Ch Eastover SC 1999-2010; Bp Gravatt Cntr Aiken SC 1993-1996; Lectr U of SC Aiken SC 1990-2006; Dio Upper So Carolina Columbia SC 1981-1992, Consult - Chr. Ed. Dir-Camp Gravatt, Youthj 1957-1961; Vic S Jn's Ch No August SC 1981-1987; R Calv Epis Ch Richmond TX 1978-1981; Dir - Ch Relatns Sewanee U So TS Sewanee TN 1976-1978; Assoc S Lk's Epis Ch Birmingham AL 1970-1976; Dir Camp Kanuga Hendersonville NC 1966-1968; R Epis Ch Of The Redeem Greenville SC 1961-1970; Vic H Cross Epis Ch Simpsonville SC 1956-1957; So Carolina Charleston SC 1954-1961; All SS Epis Ch Clinton SC 1954-1957; Ch Of The Epiph Laurens SC 1954-1957; D-in-c S Lk's Ch Newberry SC 1954-1955.

IRELAND, Joel T (LI) 532 E 1st St, Tucson AZ 85705 **Int Chr Ch Bay Ridge Brooklyn NY 2014-; Chapl Gnrl OTCG Tucson AZ 2003-** B Tucson AZ 1953 s Alfred & Ann. MA OH SU 1977; MDiv GTS 1981; JD U of Arizona 1990. D 6/11/1981 P 12/8/1981 Bp Joseph Thomas Heistand. c 2. R S Mary's Epis Ch Shltr Island NY 2012-2014; S Paul's Ch Tombstone AZ 2010-2012; Tuller Sch Tucson AZ 2008-2010; Asst Epis Par Of S Mich And All Ang Tucson AZ 1981-1987. Auth, "The Trsfg of the Lemon Test: Ch & St Reign Supreme in Bowen vs Kendrick," *Arizona Law Revs*, 1990; Auth, "Bowen vs Kendrick," *Arizona Law Revs*, 1990. St Bar of Arizona,St Bar of Arizona 1990.

✠ IRISH, The Rt Rev Carolyn Tanner (U) 1930 South State, Salt Lake City UT 84115 B Salt Lake City UT 1940 d Obert & Grace. BA U MI 1962; MLitt Oxf GB 1968; MDiv VTS 1983. D 6/11/1983 P 1/7/1984 Bp John Thomas Walker Con 5/31/1996 for U. m 6/16/2001 Eugene Frederick Quinn c 4. Ret Bp of Utah Dio Utah Salt Lake City UT 2010, Bp of Utah 1996-2010; Assoc for Sprtl Dvlpmt Cathd of St Ptr & St Paul Washington DC 1988-1995; Assoc Fac Coll of Preachers Washington DC 1988-1995; Prog Stff Shalem Inst for Sprtl Formation 1988-1995; Archd Dio Michigan Detroit MI 1986-1988; H Faith Ch Saline MI 1986-1988; Vic H Faith Ch Saline MI 1985-1988; Asst Ch Of The Gd Shpd Burke VA 1984-1985; Asst Min The Ch Of The Epiph Washington DC 1983-1984. Auth, "Love Thy Neighbor: Par Resouces for Faithfulness in Creation". Hon Doctoral Degree VTS 2002; Hon Doctoral Degree CDSP 1999.

IRISH, Charles Manning (O) 6015 Steeple Chase Way, Medina OH 44256 **Died 10/12/2015** B Lorain OH 1929 s Warren & Marie. BA Ohio Wesl 1957; BD Bex Sem 1966. D 6/11/1966 P 12/10/1966 Bp Nelson Marigold Burroughs. m 7/20/2007 Dorothy A Irish c 1. Ret 1994-2015; Assoc S Lk Bath OH 1992-1994; Acts 29 Mnstrs Thomasville GA 1986-1992; Natl Coordntr ERM 1985-1992; S Lk's Epis Ch Akron OH 1969-1994; R S Lk Bath OH 1969-1985; Vic Trin Ch Bryan OH 1966-1969. Auth, *Back to the Upper Room*; Auth, *By My Sprt*; Auth, *Gospel Conspiracy Workbook*.

IRIZARRY, J E (Ct) 200 exeter st, Hartford CT 06106 **P-in-c Ch Of The Gd Shpd Hartford CT 2013-** B 1940 M.Div. Seminario Epis del Caribe 1965; M.A. U of Waterloo 1973; D.Min. Estrn U 1992. m 8/2/1986 Ivelin A Irizarry c 4. Dio Connecticut Meriden CT 1996-2003; Exec Coun Appointees New York NY 1992-1996; Holyrood Ch New York NY 1986-1990.

IRONSIDE, Susan R (NJ) 414 E Broad St, Westfield NJ 07090 **R Ch of S Jn on the Mtn Bernardsville NJ 2011-** B Philadelphia PA 1971 d Kenneth & Valerie. Kean U 2000; MDiv GTS 2010. D 11/14/2009 P 6/19/2010 Bp George Edward Councell. m 1/9/1993 Andrew P Moore c 2. Cur S Paul's Epis Ch Westfield NJ 2010-2011.

IRSCH, Leona M (WNY) 108 S Thomas Ave, Edwardsville PA 18704 B Tulsa OK 1939 d Charles & Medora. BA Valparaiso U 1962; MS U of Maryland 1968; MDiv Bex Sem 1983; DMin Luth TS at Gettysburg 2007. D 9/17/1983 P 5/12/1984 Bp Robert Rae Spears Jr. Int S Mk's Ch Buffalo NY 1997-1999; Dn Dio Rochester Henrietta 1988-1990; R Zion Ch Avon NY 1984-1990; Asst Chr Ch Rochester NY 1983-1984. Auth, "A Subject Misunderstood," *LivCh*, 2000.

IRVIN, Cynthia Diane (Colo) 546 N Elm St # 1496, Cortez CO 81321 **Dir Gd Samar Cntr CO 1981-; D S Barn Of The Vlly Cortez CO 1981-** B Massillon OH 1943 d Leroy & Beulah. Prchr Lewis Sch of Mnstry 1987. D 6/12/1988 Bp William Carl Frey. m 2/7/1970 Vernon Lee Irvin c 4. SHN 1985. Citizens Police Acad Montezuma Police Dept 1998; Cmnty Serice Awd Seventh-Day Adventist Ch 1993; Bellringer Awd Salvation Army 1989.

IRVIN, Henry Stuart (WA) 425 Crowfields Dr, Asheville NC 28803 **Died 6/24/2017** B Augusta GA 1932 s Willis & Willye. No Carolina St U; U of Pennsylvania; BA U NC 1952; MDiv Candler TS Emory U 1955; CWA VTS 1957; MA Amer U 1972; DMin SFTS 1978. D 12/22/1956 P 6/22/1957 Bp Angus Dun. m 12/28/1957 Georgia K Irvin c 2. R All SS' Epis Ch Chevy Chase MD 1981-1997, Assoc 1964-1979; R S Mary's Chap of Ease Ridge MD 1957-1964; St Georges Ch Leonardtown MD 1956-1957; St Marys Par St Marys City MD

1956-1957. Mem Emer, Hon. Gen. Coun of Ch Untd for Globa Crystal Cathd Mnstrs 2007; Hon Gnrl Coun of Ch Untd for Global Mssn Crystal Cathd Mnstrs 1978.

IRVINE OJN, Peter Bennington (NI) 1140 Blaine Ave, Janesville WI 53545 B Chattanooga TN 1951 s James & Susan. BA U of Tennessee 1974; JD U of Tennessee 1979; MDiv GTS 2002. D 6/3/2006 Bp Mark Hollingsworth Jr P 12/3/2006 Bp Steven Andrew Miller. m 10/25/2008 Janet M Collins. Chapl Harbor Light Hospice 2011-2015; The Ch Of S Jn The Evang Flossmoor IL 2010-2012; Dekoven Fndt for Ch Wk Racine WI 2008; Precentor Chr Ch Waukegan IL 2007-2010; S Lk's Ch Racine WI 2006-2007; S Lk's Hosp Racine WI 2006-2007; Chapl Mayview Hosp Bridgeville PA 2003-2006; Assoc The Ch Of The Redeem Pittsburgh PA 2003-2006. Auth-Compsr, "Hymns & Spirituals, New & Old," 2017; Ed, "The Inner Voice: a Hymnic Tribute to Julian of Norwich," Ord of Julian of Norwich, 2008. AGO 2007-2012; Assn of Ch Musicians 2016; The Hymn Soc 2005.

IRVING, Anthony Tuttle (Oly) 5445 Donnelly Dr Se, Olympia WA 98501 **D S Ben Epis Ch Lacey WA 1999-** B Butte MT 1936 s Irving & Kathryn. BA U of Washington 1963. D 6/26/1999 Bp Vincent Waydell Warner. m 1/8/1982 Leona Rackleff. Auth, "The Road To Self Understanding And Ord," *Diakoneo*, Michaelmass, 2000.

IRVING, Hannah Jocelyn (WA) 9713 Summit Cir Apt 1B, Upper Marlboro MD 20774 **R Ch Of The Atone Washington DC 2005-** B Paterson NJ 1951 d Vian & Ceceilyn. BA Wm Paterson U 1973; MDiv Drew U 1999. D 6/21/2000 P 2/24/2001 Bp John Palmer Croneberger. c 4. Assoc S Lk's Epis Ch Montclair NJ 2000-2005.

IRVING, Stanley Herbert (Vt) 5205 Georgia Shore Rd, Saint Albans VT 05478 **Ret 1989-** B Brome QC CA 1924 s Joseph & Marjorie. BA Concordia U 1949; BD McGill U 1953; LTh Montreal Dioc Theol Coll 1953. Trans 3/1/1961 as Priest Bp The Bishop Of Montreal. c 2. Trin Milton VT 1971-1976; R S Lk's Ch S Albans VT 1961-1989; Dept Mssn S Barn Ch Norwich VT 1961-1971; Serv P Ch of Can 1952-1961; Chair Stndg Com Dio Vermont Burlington VT 1976-1977, Chair Dnry Grants Com 1974-1975, Secy Convoc 1965-1973, Secy Dioc Coun 1963-1964.

IRWIN, Margaret Bertha (Mil) 6989 Apprentice Pl, Middleton WI 53562 **Asstg P Gr Ch Madison WI 2007-** B Madison WI 1942 d Fred & Lena. BA U of Wisconsin 1964; MA U of Wisconsin 1968; MDiv CDSP 1986. D 6/29/1986 P 6/6/1987 Bp Charles Shannon Mallory. m 8/29/1964 Joseph Paul Irwin c 3. R All SS Epis Ch Palo Alto CA 1994-2004; Int Epis Ch of St Jn the Bapt Aptos Aptos CA 1993-1994; Int Asst S Thos Epis Ch Sunnyvale CA 1993; Int Trin Cathd San Jose CA 1991-1992; Assoc S Andr's Ch Saratoga CA 1986-1991. AFP 1986-2003; Associated Parishes 1986-2004; EWC 1986; NNECA 2002-2006. Phi Beta Kappa U of Wisconsin-Madison 1964.

IRWIN, Sara (Pgh) B Erie PA 1978 d Zachary & Monica. BA New Coll of Florida 2000; MDiv GTS 2004. D 6/12/2004 P 1/8/2005 Bp M(Arvil) Thomas Shaw. m 2/15/2003 Noah H Evans c 2. R Chr Ch Waltham MA 2005-2017; Asst R Emm Ch Boston MA 2004-2005. Auth, "Ashes/What Remains," *Ashes/What Remains*, Back Pages Books, 2013; Auth, "The religiophoneme: Liturg and some uses of deconstruction," *the Journ Wrshp*, Liturg Press, 2006; Auth, "My Red Couch," *My Red Couch*, Pilgrim Press, 2005.

IRWIN, Zachary Tracy (NwPa) 4216 E South Shore Dr, Erie PA 16511 **D S Mary's Ch Erie PA 2000-** B Port Jervis NY 1947 s William & Margaret. ABS Ham 1968; MA JHU 1973; PhD Penn 1978. D 6/10/2000 Bp Robert Deane Rowley Jr. m 6/4/1968 Monica Irwin c 1.

ISAAC, Donald Tileston (Mass) 99 Centre Avenue, Rockland MA 02370 **Died 4/13/2017** B Brockton MA 1932 s Melville & Doris. BA Bos 1954; STB Ya Berk 1957; MA Bos 1974. D 6/22/1957 P 12/21/1957 Bp Anson Phelps Stokes Jr. c 5. Ret 1998-2017; Emer Trin Epis Ch Rockland MA 1997-2017, 1960-1996; Cur S Mk's Ch Westford MA 1957-1960.

ISAAC III, Frank Reid (O) 2181 Ambleside Drive, Apartment 412, Cleveland OH 44106 **Ret 2000-** B Baltimore MD 1925 s Frank & Majorie. BA Drew U 1946; BD Yale DS 1949; Coll of Preachers 1982. D 6/15/1955 P 12/17/1955 Bp Angus Dun. S Paul's Epis Ch Cleveland OH 1984-1990; Ch Of The H Trin New York NY 1975-1984; Ed Seabury Press New York NY 1973-1975; Reg Off Dio New York New York NY 1971-1973; R S Barn Ch Irvington NY 1968-1971; Chapl Ch Sch of S Jas New York NY 1965-1966; Ed/Coordntr Exec Coun Dept. of Educ NY 1960-1968; Cur S Columba's Ch Washington DC 1955-1956. Auth, *Fleshing the Word*, St. Paul's Press, 1996; Auth, *Conversations w the Crucified*, Seabury, 1982; Auth, *What is God Doing Today*, Seabury, 1967.

✠ ISAAC, The Rt Rev Telesforo A (SwFla) JP 8600, PO Box 02-5284, Miami FL 33102 **Prof Centro de Estudios Teologicos (CET) - Santo Domingo 2000-; Ret Bp of the Dominican Republic Dio The Dominican Republic (Iglesia Epis Dominicana) Gazcue Santo Domingo 1991-, Bp 1972-1986** B DO 1929 s Simon & Violet. ETSBH 1958; Epis TS 1958; U Antonoma de Santo Domingo Santo Domingo DO 1970; MDiv ETSC 1971; Universidad Pontificia de Salamanca España 1988. D 6/11/1958 P 12/14/1958 Bp Charles Alfred Voegeli Con 3/9/1972 for DR (DomRep). m 8/30/1961 Juana Maria Zorilla c 3. Int Bp of

VI Dio Vrgn Islands Charlotte Amalie St Thom VI 2004-2005, Int 1996-2003; Dio SW Florida Parrish FL 1991-1996; Exec Coun Appointees New York NY 1987-1991; Vic San Esteban San Pedro de Macoris in the Dominican Republic 1971-1972; Vic Iglesia Epis San Andres Santo Domingo Di 1965-1971; Vic Jesus Nazareno San Francisco de Macoris Dominican Republic 1961-1965; Cur San Esteban San Pedro de Macoris in the Dominican Republic 1958-1961. Auth, "Bk," *Presencia Anglicana en República Dominicana*, IGLEPIDOM, 2013; Auth, "Bk," *Presencia Anglicana en República Dominicana*, IGLEPIDOM, 2013; Auth, "Bk," *Comentarios en Domingos de Cuaresma*, CETALC, 2010; Auth, "Bk," *Fe y Práctica de la Espiritualidad Cristiana*, Promociones y Publicidad, Inc., 2002; Auth, "Bk," *La Labor Educativa Iglesia Epis*, Eligio Delgado, Inc., 1972; Auth, "Monografia," *Pautas para el diálogo cristiano-marxista*, EL NACIONAL, 1971; Auth, "Monografia," *Pautas para el diálogo cristiano-marxista*, EL NACIONAL, 1971. Asociación Desarrollo Provincia Duarte 1964-1965; Centro de Rehabilitación 1973-1991; Comité de Derechos Humanos 1990-1991; Dialogo Dominica - Haitiano 2006-2012; Fundación ZILE 2009-2013. Hijo Adoptivo Municipio de San Francisco de Macoris 2003; Macorisano Ejemplar Ayuntamiento San Pedro Macoris 1999; Cert of Merit as Distinguished Citizen Ayuntamiento San Pedro de Macoris 1983.

ISAACS, James Steele (WA) St James Church, 11815 Seven Locks Rd, Potomac MD 20854 **Asst S Jas Ch Potomac MD 2011-** B 1976 s James & Amy. BA Sarah Lawr Coll 1999; MDiv VTS 2002; MA Estrn Mennonite U 2010. D 5/18/2002 Bp Charles Lindsay Longest P 11/23/2002 Bp John Bailey Lipscomb. m 9/4/2010 Margaret Mary Brewinski. R S Andr The Fisherman Epis Mayo MD 2005-2009; Assoc R S Paul's Ch Naples FL 2002-2005.

ISADORE, Daniel Joseph (Pgh) 5801 Hampton St, Pittsburgh PA 15206 **Dio Pittsburgh Pittsburgh PA 2015-** B Pittsburgh PA 1984 s Dennis & Karen. BA Grove City Coll 2006; MDiv Pittsburgh TS 2013. D 7/22/2015 P 6/5/2016 Bp Dorsey McConnell. m 7/29/2006 Hallie Marissa Young.

ISHIZAKI, Norman Yukio (Los) 580 Hilgard Ave, Los Angeles CA 90024 B Sacramento CA 1939 s Yazo & Esther. BA U CA 1962; BD SWTS 1967. D 9/9/1967 P 3/9/1968 Bp Francis E I Bloy. m 9/7/1953 Velda Marie Ishizaki c 2. S Alb's Epis Ch Los Angeles CA 1967-2003.

ISHMAN, Martha S. (NwPa) 245 Valley Trails Ln, Franklin PA 16323 **Vic S Jas Memi Epis Ch Titusville PA 2011-; Cn to the Ordnry Dio NW Pennsylvania Erie PA 2007-** B Columbia PA 1955 d Burton & Marjorie. BS Penn 1977; MDiv VTS 1998. D 5/23/1998 P 11/22/1998 Bp Robert Deane Rowley Jr. c 2. R S Clem's Epis Ch Greenville PA 1998-2007. mishman@dionwpa.org

ISLEY, Carolyn W (ETenn) 118 Oak Grove Rd, Greeneville TN 37745 B Buckingham County VA 1944 BA U of Louisville; MDiv Sthrn Bapt TS 1984; Cert Ang Stud U So Sewanee TN 2003. D 10/29/2003 P 5/14/2005 Bp Charles Glenn VonRosenberg. c 2. R S Jas Epis Ch of Greeneville Greeneville TN 2005-2016; D Dio E Tennessee Knoxville TN 2003-2005, Bp Search Com 2010-2011.

ISRAEL, Carver Washington (LI) 322 Clearbrook Ave, Lansdowne PA 19050 **S Phil's Ch Brooklyn NY 2007-** B Kingstown VC 1956 s Claude. Codrington Coll 1983; BTh U of The W Indies 1983. Trans 6/11/1991 as Priest Bp George Phelps Mellick Belshaw. m 7/8/1987 Suzette A Israel c 3. R H Apos And Medtr Philadelphia PA 1997-2007; Emm Ch Memphis TN 1993-1996; Assoc Ch Of Our Sav Camden NJ 1991-1993; S Wilfrid's Ch Camden NJ 1991-1993; Assoc S Paul's Ch Camden NJ 1991-1992; Serv Angl Ch Of Windward Islands 1983-1991. stphilipschurch@optonline.net

ISRAEL JR, Fielder (Md) 4720 Winterberry Ct, Williamsburg VA 23188 **Ret 2004-** B Washington DC 1937 s Fielder & Margaret. BA W&L 1964; MDiv VTS 1975; CPE 1983; Cert VTS 1990. D 6/7/1975 Bp William Foreman Creighton P 5/27/1978 Bp Gray Temple. m 8/21/1971 Gretchen Scherer Israel c 2. S Mart's Epis Ch Williamsburg VA 2005-2007; Asst Chapl Fairhaven Inc Sykesville MD 1994-2004; Fairhaven Sykesville MD 1994-2004; R S Lk's Ch Eden NC 1986-1994; Ch Of The Gd Shpd Columbia SC 1982-1986; Vic Ch Of The Adv Marion SC 1978-1982; Asst Min S Jas Ch Charleston SC 1977-1978; Asst Min S Jn's Ch Chevy Chase MD 1975-1977.

ISWARIAH, James Chandran (Va) 465 Walnut Ln, King William VA 23086 B Madras India 1950 s David & Sarojini. BCA U of Madras 1975; MDiv Serampore U IN 1979. Trans 3/1/2000 Bp Peter J Lee. m 9/14/1981 Sheila M Iswariah c 2. S Dav's Ch Aylett VA 2002-2012; R Ch in Australia Perth Wstrn Australia 1994-1999; R Ch in India Madras TN 1980-1992.

✠ ITTY, The Rt Rev Dr Johncy (Ore) 10 Avalon Road, Garden City NY 11530 **Dio Long Island Garden City NY 2017-, Mssnr 2013-2014; S Ptr's by-the-Sea Epis Ch Bay Shore NY 2014-** B Bhopal Madhya Pradesh IN 1963 s John & Annakutty. BA CUNY 1985; MA CUNY 1985; MA Col 1986; MPhil CUNY 1994; PhD CUNY 1994; MDiv NYTS 1994. Trans 12/29/1995 Bp Orris George Walker Jr Con 9/20/2003 for Ore. m 1/10/1990 Jolly Itty c 2. P Ch Of Calv And S Cyp Brooklyn NY 2009-2012; Geo Mercer TS Garden City NY 2009-2010; Bp Dio Oregon Portland OR 2003-2008; Cathd Of The Incarn Garden City NY 1998-2003; Soc Justice Epis Ch Cntr New York NY 1998-2000; Int Ch Of The Nativ Mineola NY 1998; Int S Gabr's Ch Hollis NY 1997-1998; Int S Matt's Ch Woodhaven NY 1996-1998, Assoc P 1993-1995. "Bishops Column," *Oregon Epis Ch News*, OECN, 2008; "Lectionary Reflections," *Wit*, Wit mag, 2005;

"The Global Debt Crisis," *Angl Wrld*, Angl Comm Sec, 1996; Johncy Itty, "The Role Of Political Ldrshp In Political Dvlpmt Of India: A Comparative Case Study," *Political Ldrshp*, CUNY, 1994; "The Fin Crisis in Perspective," *Sec News*, Untd Nations Sec, 1986; "Operation Bluestar," *Queens Coll, CUNY*, Queens Coll, CUNY, 1985. Pi Sigma Alpha; Whos Who Among Amer Colleges & Universities 1985. dist in Mnstry Awd NYTS 2008; DD GTS 2006; Phi Beta Kappa; Phi Beta Kappa Schlr; PhD Merit Fllshp Schlr; Phi Beta Kappa.

IVATTS, Justin Anthony (Va) **S Jn's Epis Ch Mc Lean VA 2015-** B London UK 1976 s Stanley & Sarah. BTh Westminster Coll 1998; Dplma on Mus Open U 2002; MDiv VTS 2005. D 6/6/2015 Bp Shannon Sherwood Johnston P 12/12/2015 Bp Susan Goff. m 8/30/2003 Katrina Rose-Ingold Glynn c 1. S Thos Epis Ch Mclean VA 2015.

IVES, Joel (Mass) 23 Monmouth St., Brookline MA 02446 **R Ch Of Our Sav Brookline MA 2007-** B Gloucester MA 1961 s Frederick & Nancy. BA U of Hartford 1983; MDiv GTS 1996. D 9/8/1996 P 5/17/1997 Bp M(Arvil) Thomas Shaw. m 8/22/1998 Florence S Ives c 3. CPE Chapl Beth Israel Hosp Boston MA 2011; Hospice Chapl Nantucket Cottage Hosp Nantucket MA 2004-2006; R S Paul's Ch In Nantucket Nantucket MA 1999-2006; Cox Fell The Cathd Ch Of S Paul Boston MA 1996-1999; CPE Chapl Bellevue Hosp Cntr NYC NY 1994-1998; COM Dio Massachusetts Boston MA 2003-2009. Fllshp Of The Soc Of S Jn The Evang 2002.

IVES, Nathan Warren (Ct) **Gr Ch Stafford Sprg CT 2016-** B Gloucester MA 1965 s Frederick & Nancy. BA U of Hartford; BA U of Hartford 1987; MA Hartford Sem 2014; MAR Hartford Sem 2014. D 7/18/2015 P 2/9/2016 Bp Laura Ahrens. m 6/4/1989 Mary Anne Anne Connolly c 2. Middlesex Area Cluster Mnstry Higganum CT 2015-2016.

IVEY, Betsy (Pa) 1401 S 22nd St, Philadelphia PA 19146 **Dio Pennsylvania Philadelphia PA 2017-; St Jas Sch Philadelphia PA 2016-** B Harrisburg PA 1951 d Sidney & Betty. BA U of Pennsylvania 1987; MDiv Lancaster TS 2012; STM GTS 2013. D 6/2/2013 P 3/1/2014 Bp Nathan Dwight Baxter. c 2. S Simon The Cyrenian Ch Philadelphia PA 2015-2017; S Andr's Epis Ch Shippensburg PA 2013-2015. curate.standrew@comcast.net

IVEY, Valerie Ann (Ore) 15240 Nw Courting Hill Dr, Banks OR 97106 **D Trin Epis Cathd Portland OR 1992-** B Kingston Surrey UK 1934 d William & Elsie. BA Lon GB 1955; AMIA Lon GB 1957; MS Bryn 1962; MS Portland St U 1982. D 6/23/1992 Bp Robert Louis Ladehoff. m 10/10/1964 Dean Ivey c 2. NAAD.

IWICK, Richard Edward (Mich) 25755 Kilreigh Ct, Farmington Hills MI 48336 **Supply P S Eliz's Ch Redford Chart Township MI 2011-** B Oshkosh WI 1936 s Edward & Theresa. BA Lawr 1958; STM GTS 1961; MS Iowa St U 1976. D 6/18/1961 P 12/22/1961 Bp William Hampton Brady. m 12/15/1996 Diana Rowe Iwick c 1. Supply P S Mart Ch Detroit MI 2001-2015; Dn So Oakland Area Coun 1996-1998; Archd Dio Michigan Detroit MI 1992-1994; Bd Pres Samar Counslg Cntr 1991-1993; Convenor Farmington Mnstrl Assn 1987-1988; Dn So Oakland Convoc 1985-1987; R Trin Epis Ch Farmington MI 1983-1999; Assoc R Trin Ch Anderson IN 1980-1983; Supply P Dio Iowa Des Moines IA 1974-1976; R S Alb's Ch Superior WI 1968-1972; Asst S Mk's Ch Milwaukee WI 1965-1968; Vic Chr the King/H Nativ (Sturgeon Bay) Sturgeon Bay WI 1961-1965; P-in-c H Nativ Jacksonport WI 1961-1965. Auth, "An Evaltn Of The Ottumwa Yth Dvlpmt Bureau"; Auth, "An Evaltn Of Dubuque Yth Serv".

IX, Victoria Shippee (WMass) Other Lay Position Dio Wstrn Massachusetts Springfield 2014- D 6/10/2017 Bp Doug Fisher.

IZADI, Samira (Dal) 6941 kingdom estates drive, Dallas TX 75236 B Shiraz Iran 1970 MDiv SMU Perkins; MA U of Shiraz. D 6/26/2010 Bp Paul Emil Lambert P 5/12/2011 Bp James Monte Stanton. c 2. St Pauls Epis Ch Prosper TX 2010-2012; Fndr and Exec Dir Gateway of Gr Mnstrs. samira@gatewayofgrace.org

IZUTSU, Margaret W (Mich) 18 Fairview Ave, Arlington MA 02474 B Pontiac MI 1955 d Charles & Margaret. MDiv Harvard DS 1995. D 6/18/1994 Bp R aymond Stewart Wood Jr P 6/1/1995 Bp Arthur Edward Walmsley. m 2/6/1983 Meguru Izutsu. Asst - Pstr Care Par Of The Epiph Winchester MA 1995-1996; Chapl Untd Staes And Japan 1991-1994. Auth, "Ao-Tung". Japanese Cntr For The Quality Of Life Stds. Natl Media Awd Mntl Hlth Assn 1980; Marg Augur Schlrshp Awd 73.

IZZO, Joanne (NY) 8411 13th Ave # 2nd Floor, Brooklyn NY 11228 B Brooklyn NY 1956 d Joseph & Lucille. BA Ford 1979; MSW NYU Grad Sch of Soc Wk 1990; MA Immac Concep 1996; MDiv St Jn's U 2000; MDiv St Jn's U 2000; DAS GTS 2013; DAS The GTS 2013; STM GTS 2014; STM The GTS 2014. D 3/15/2014 P 9/27/2014 Bp Andrew Marion Lenow Dietsche. Asst Chr Epis Ch Tarrytown NY 2014-2016. revjoanneizzo@gmail.com

J

JABLONSKI, Carol J (WA) 4512 College Ave, College Park MD 20740 B Milwaukee WI 1951 d George & Eleanor. BA Alleg 1973; MA Pur 1975; PhD Pur 1979; MDiv VTS 2006. D 6/10/2006 Bp John Bailey Lipscomb P 2/4/2007 Bp Michael B Curry. m 3/14/1987 John Tyler Jones. R S Andr's Epis Ch Coll Pk MD 2009-2016; Assoc S Steph's Ch Durham NC 2006-2009; Chapl Intern Duke Med Cntr Pstr Care Svcs Durham 2004. Harris Prize VTS 2006.

JACKSON, Brad Lee (Va) Po Box 305, Madison VA 22727 **P-in-c Little Fork Epis Ch Rixeyville VA 2014-** B Pratt KS 1953 s Claude & Ilya. BM and BMEd Phillips U 1976; BA Phillips U 1976; MMEd Wichita St U 1983; MA Wichita St U 1983; MDiv VTS 1989. D 6/21/1989 Bp John Forsythe Ashby P 1/25/1990 Bp William Edward Smalley. m 2/25/1984 Jayne E Jackson c 2. R Piedmont Ch Madison VA 1995-2014; R Imm Ch King and Queen Courthouse VA 1992-1995; S Jn's Ch W Point VA 1992-1995; Asst R S Paul's Ch Leavenworth KS 1989-1992.

JACKSON, Bruce A (Az) 7719 W Bluefield Ave, Glendale AZ 85308 **R S Jn The Bapt Epis Ch Glendale AZ 2011-** B New London CT 1947 s Chester & Elizabeth. BA U of Connecticut 1971; JD St Jn's U 1976. D 9/8/2012 Bp Kirk Stevan Smith. m 11/27/2002 Barbara J Nation c 2. bjackson@stjohnsaz.org

JACKSON, Carl Thomas (Va) 2940 Corries Way, Conneaut OH 44030 B Painesville OH 1938 s Carl & Pearl. BSME Case Wstrn Reserve U 1961; MDiv VTS 1995; DMin Austin Presb TS 1999. D 11/4/1973 Bp William Crittenden P 12/23/1989 Bp Donald James Davis. m 8/5/1961 Carol Jackson c 2. Dn Dio Virginia Richmond VA 2006-2008; Cmsn Cong Dev Dio Virginia 2004-2008; R S Paul's Ch Bailey's Crossroads Falls Ch VA 1996-2009, Adj 1992-1995; R Epis Ch Of The Mssh Gonzales TX 1995-1996; Int Ch Of The H Sprt Erie PA 1991-1992; Int S Mary's Ch Erie PA 1989-1990; Stff Cathd Of S Paul Erie PA 1987-1991; D Gr Ch Lake City PA 1977-1987; D S Steph's Ch Fairview PA 1973-1977; Com Mssn Strtgy Dio NW Pennsylvania Erie PA 1981-1984, Liturg Cmsn 1976-1980. Auth, "Behold," *I Make All Things New: Mssn As Catalyst For Revitalization,* Austin Pres Theo Sem, 1999. Ord Of S Lk 1991.

JACKSON, David (SwFla) All Souls Episcopal Church, 14640 N Cleveland Ave, North Fort Myers FL 33903 **Vic All Souls Epis Ch No Ft Myers FL 2013-** B Leicester 1946 s David & Gertrude. MBChB U of Glasgow GB 1970; MBCB U of Glasgow GB 1970; MRCGP Royal Coll of Gnrl Practitioners 1975; MA Min Nash 2013. D 6/6/2009 P 3/17/2013 Bp Dabney Tyler Smith. m 12/14/1968 Yvette Jackson c 3. Vic The Ch Of The Gd Shpd Labelle FL 2013-2015.

JACKSON, David G (Chi) 203 S Kensington Ave, La Grange IL 60525 **Emm Epis Ch La Grange IL 2017-** B Southampton England 1977 s David & Yvette. Dplma in Angl Stds Bexley-Seabury; Mstr of Sci JHU; Bachelor of Arts JHU; Mstr of Div Nthrn Sem. D 12/17/2016 P 6/29/2017 Bp Jeff Lee. m 4/22/2006 Stacy Lynn Jackson. assistant@eeclg.org

JACKSON, David Hilton (USC) 245 Cavalier Drive, Greenville SC 29650 **Chr Ch Epis Sch Greenville SC 2015-** B Leicester GB 1962 s Dennis & Georgiana. MS Oxf GB; MDiv PrTS; BA Stan 1984. Trans 10/23/2002 as Priest Bp Joseph Jon Bruno. m 6/21/2015 Muriel Jayne Allen c 1. Seabury Hall Makawao HI 2013-2015; Ch Of The Epiph Honolulu HI 2009-2013; Bloy Hse Claremont CA 2006-2009; Chapl Epis-Luth Campus Mnstry Stanford Univ 2006; Stanford Cbury Fndt Palo Alto CA 2006; Int S Jn's Mssn La Verne CA 2004-2005; Sr Assoc for Par Life All SS Ch Pasadena CA 2003-2004; S Mk's Epis Ch Upland CA 2002-2003.

JACKSON, Deborah Mitchell (Fla) 4849 Hampshire Pl, Hixson TN 37343 **Sewanee U So TS Sewanee TN 2013-** B Gainesville FL 1958 d Jerry & Mary. BA Rol 1979; MBA Jacksonville U 1983; MDiv Sewanee: The U So, TS 2007; DMin Colgate Rochester Crozer DS 2013; DMin CRDS 2013. D 5/27/2007 P 12/9/2007 Bp Samuel Johnson Howard. m 9/4/1982 James B Jackson c 3. Int Assoc R S Mk's Epis Ch Jacksonville FL 2012-2013; Asst R S Paul's By-The-Sea Epis Ch Jaxville Bch FL 2010-2012; Cn S Jn's Cathd Jacksonville FL 2007-2010.

JACKSON, Eric Michael Colin (Oly) 26291 Pennsylvania Ave NE APT 105, Kingston WA 98346 B Grand Prairie Alberta CA 1933 s Eric & Ivy. LST Bishops U QC CA 1965; MTh McGill U Can 1966. Trans 6/1/1966 Bp Clarence Rupert Haden Jr. m 8/25/1988 June Eloise Fryer Jackson c 4. Asstg P S Mk's Cathd Seattle WA 2001-2013; Dio Olympia Seattle 1974-1987; TACS Sr Trnr Epiph Par of Seattle Seattle WA 1974-1986; Asstg P Cathd Of S Jn The Evang Spokane WA 1974; Dio Spokane Spokane WA 1972-1974; LTD Trnr S Jas Pullman WA 1972-1974; R S Ptr's Epis Ch Red Bluff CA 1969-1972; Vic Gr Epis Ch Wheatland CA 1968-1969; S Tim's Ch Gridley CA 1968-1969; Vic S Andr's Of The Redwoods Redway CA 1966-1968; Vic S Fran In The Redwoods Mssn Willits CA 1966-1968; P Serv Angl Ch of Can 1964-1966. Awd, Mem of the British Empire HM Queen Eliz II 1962; Hon Mem, Natl Press Club of Can Natl Press Club, Ottawa, Can 1962.

JACKSON, Gary Jon (Ga) St Mark's Episcopal Church, 900 Gloucester St, Brunswick GA 31520 **Asst S Mk's Ch Brunswick GA 2013-** B Hartford CT 1944 s John & Mary. BA La Salette Sem 1968. D 6/30/2012 P 4/19/2013 Bp Scott Anson Benhase. m 4/18/1970 Dolores Marie Jackson c 5. D S Mk's Epis Ch Woodbine GA 2012-2013.

JACKSON JR, Gary Leon (CFla) 500 W Stuart St, Bartow FL 33830 **S Mk's Ch Cocoa FL 2016-** B Arkadelphia AR 1970 s Gary & Verda. BS Henderson St U 1993; MDiv Nash 2011. D 6/11/2011 Bp Hugo Luis Pina-Lopez P 12/18/2011 Bp John Wadsworth Howe. m 1/26/1991 Christina Lee Jackson c 2. R H Trin Epis Ch Bartow FL 2011-2016.

JACKSON JR, Hillyer Barnett (Okla) 3149 NW 24th St, Oklahoma City OK 73107 **Died 5/2/2016** B Oklahoma City OK 1934 s Hillyer & Roberta. BA U of Oklahoma 1956; MDiv Epis TS of the SW 1959; Jas Mills Fllshp Cambridge GB 1968. D 5/23/1959 P 11/30/1959 Bp Chilton R Powell. Supply Chr Memi Epis Ch El Reno OK 1999-2016, 1987-1998; Ret 1996-2016; Alt Dep GC Dio Oklahoma Oklahoma City OK 1991-1997, Chrmn Div of Mnstry Dvlpmt 1991-1996, Chair - Dioc Liturg 1987-1996, Rgnl Dn OK City OK 1987-1992, Stndg Com 1976-1997, Chrmn BEC 1972-1997; R S Jn's Ch Oklahoma City OK 1980-1987; R S Matt's Ch Enid OK 1968-1980, Assoc 1966-1968; Vic Ch Of The Ascen Pawnee OK 1964-1966; S Mk's Ch Perry OK 1964-1966; Vic S Jas Ch Antlers OK 1959-1964; S Mk's Ch Hugo OK 1959-1964; Bd Trst Epis TS Of The SW Austin TX 1977-1982. Angl/RC Cmsn OK 1981. The Bp's Cross The Bp, Dioc. of Oklahoma 2012; The Bp's Awd The Bp, Dioc. of Oklahoma 1997; Cn Dio LA 1996.

JACKSON, Hugo T (At) 4246 Glenforest Way Ne, Roswell GA 30075 B Toronto Ontario 1953 MDiv Vancouver TS CA. m 10/15/1982 Ann Margaret Jackson c 1. Ch Of The Annunc Marietta GA 2011-2015; S Teresa Acworth GA 2003-2005.

JACKSON, Ira Leverne (Ga) Grace Episcopal Church, PO Box 617, Sandersville GA 31082 B 1930 D 2/7/2009 P 8/8/2009 Bp Henry Irving Louttit. m 12/9/1995 Mildred Jackson c 2.

JACKSON, Jared Judd (Pgh) 903 Orchard Park Dr., Gibsonia PA 15044 **Prof Of The OT Pittsburgh TS PA 1985-** B New Haven CT 1930 s William & Dorothy. BA Harv 1952; BD EDS 1958; ThD UTS 1962. D 6/21/1958 Bp Frederic Cunningham Lawrence P 12/1/1958 Bp Anson Phelps Stokes Jr. m 7/21/1984 Cynthia Irene Bonnett c 4. Asst The Ch Of The Redeem Pittsburgh PA 1997-2002; Dn Of The Trng Prog For Mnstry Dio Pittsburgh Pittsburgh PA 1978-1981, Chair Of The BEC 1970-1977; Assoc Prof Of The OT Pittsburgh TS PA 1969-1985; Asst Prof Of The OT Pittsburgh TS PA 1965-1969; Asst Prof In The Dept Of Rel Wms Williamstown MA 1964-1965; Prof Hur In London Ontario Can 1962-1964; Asst Gr Epis Ch Westwood NJ 1961-1962; Asst S Matt's Ch Bedford NY 1958-1961. Auth, "Rhetorical Criticism".

JACKSON, Jeffery R (At) 69 Mobley Road, PO Box 752, Hamilton GA 31811 **R S Nich Epis Ch Hamilton GA 2008-** B Memphis TN 1978 s Albert & Glenda. BA Berry Coll 2000; MDiv VTS 2003. D 2/8/2003 P 8/1/2003 Bp Henry Irving Louttit. m 8/18/2001 Molly Elizabeth Jackson c 4. S Ptr's Epis Ch Savannah GA 2004-2008.

JACKSON, Jimmy (Kan) Saint Matthew's Episcopal Church, 2001 Windsor Dr, Newton KS 67114 **S Matt's Epis Ch Newton KS 2016-; R S Jn's Epis Ch Odessa TX 2011-** B Lubbock TX 1956 s Jimmy & Lucille. BSW Texas Tech U 1989; Dip Ang Stud Epis TS of the SW 2011. D 10/29/1999 Bp C Wallis Ohl P 8/13/2011 Bp James Scott Mayer. m 5/22/1983 Valinda Joan Bradshaw-Jackson c 2. D S Chris's Epis Ch Lubbock TX 1999-2010. stmattsrector@ kscoxmail.com

JACKSON, Judy Ann (Chi) B 1949 BA Iowa Wesleyan Coll 1971; MSEd Nthrn Illinois U 1981. D 6/28/2014 Bp John Clark Buchanan.

JACKSON, Julius (Pa) 803 Macdade Blvd, Collingdale PA 19023 **Died 10/17/2016** B Freetown SL 1949 s Taiwo & Isabella. AA Spartanburg Jr Coll 1974; BA Wofford Coll 1976; AA Spartanburg Tech Coll 1982; MDiv VTS 1988; Cert Int Mnstry Ntwk 2012. D 6/11/1988 P 5/1/1989 Bp William Arthur Beckham. m 8/22/1998 Kanku Jackson c 1. Vic S Dismas Epis Mssn At Graterford Philadelphia PA 1995-2011; S Mary's Epis Ch Philadelphia PA 1995-2010; R S Phil's Ch Buffalo NY 1989-1995; D-In-Trng S Lk's Epis Ch Columbia SC 1988-1989.

JACKSON, Kimberly (At) 3737 Seminary Rd, Alexandria VA 22304 **All SS Epis Ch Atlanta GA 2016-** B Elkins WVA 1984 d Timothy & Brenda. BA Furman Univeristy 2006; MDiv Candler TS Emory U 2009; MDiv Candler TS Emory U 2009; Cert Ang Stud VTS 2010. D 12/19/2009 Bp J Neil Alexander. m 4/12/2011 La Trina Pauline Jackson. P Emmaus Hse Epis Ch Atlanta GA 2014-2016; Chapl Dio Atlanta Atlanta GA 2010-2016.

JACKSON, Larry Dean (WVa) 2004 Maxwell Ave, Parkersburg WV 26101 B Parkersburg WV 1948 s Donald & Mildred. BA Glenville St Coll 1970; MDiv TESM 1982. D 6/5/1982 Bp Robert Bracewell Appleyard P 5/17/1983 Bp Alden Moinet Hathaway. m 6/26/1971 Ruby J Jackson c 2. R Trin Ch Parkersburg WV 2004-2015; Mssnr Chr Ch Wellsburg WV 1998-2004; Mssnr Olde S Jn's Ch Colliers WV 1998-2004; Mssnr S Matt's Ch Chester WV 1998-2004; Mssnr S Thos' Epis Ch Weirton WV 1998-2004, 1990-1997; Brooke-Hancock Cluster Weirton WV 1997-2004; R Gr Epis Ch Drakes Branch VA 1983-1990; S Jn's Epis Ch Chase City VA 1983-1990; S Tim's Epis Ch Clarksville VA 1983-1990; Cur S Thos Ch In The Fields Gibsonia PA 1982-1983; Hstgr/Archv

Dio W Virginia 2000-2014. "I Started a Joke...," *Hstgr (NEHA)*, 2003. S Meinrad's Archabbey - Oblate 2003. Who's Who in Amer Ch Ldrshp 1989; Chase City Citizen of the Year ChmbrCom 1986.

JACKSON, Margaret Ruth Brosz (Ia) B Parkston SD 1937 d Oscar & Ruth. BA Yankton Coll 1958; BA Augustana Coll 1968; MA U of St Thos 1990; Untd TS of the Twin Cities 2003. D 6/12/2004 P 1/15/2005 Bp Alan Scarfe. m 1/23/1958 John Philip Jackson c 2. P-in-res Trin Ch Emmetsburg IA 2008-2015; P Assoc Ch Of The Gd Shpd Webster City IA 2005-2008; S Mk's Epis Ch Ft Dodge IA 2005-2008.

JACKSON, Micah T (Tex) 501 E 32nd St, Austin TX 78705 **Assoc Prof of Preaching Epis TS Of The SW Austin TX 2008-** B Cleveland Heights OH 1969 s James & Donna. MDiv Meadville Lombard TS 2002; MTS SWTS 2004; PhD Grad Theol Un 2012. D 6/3/2006 Bp Bill Persell P 12/2/2006 Bp Marc Handley Andrus. m 5/19/2002 Laura W Jackson c 1. S Dav's Ch Austin TX 2012; S Mk's Par Berkeley CA 2008; Associated P St. Mk's Epis Ch Berkeley CA 2006-2008; Assoc Dn of Acad Affrs and Rgstr SWTS Evanston IL 2004-2005.

JACKSON, Patricia Gladys (Ct) 120 Sigourney St, Hartford CT 06105 B Jamaica WI 1937 d Ivan & Ethel. BS Empire St Coll 1991. D 9/15/2007 Bp Andrew Donnan Smith. c 2.

JACKSON, Paula Marie (SO) 65 E Hollister St, Cincinnati OH 45219 **R Ch Of Our Sav Cincinnati OH 1990-** B Springfield MO 1952 d Herman & Frances. BA U of Missouri 1974; MDiv Sthrn Bapt TS 1979; CAS GTS 1985; PhD Sthrn Bapt TS 1985. D 6/30/1985 P 6/30/1986 Bp David Reed. m 8/16/1975 Daniel Marshall Watson c 2. Assoc Chr Ch Cathd Cincinnati OH 1987-1990; Int S Geo's Epis Ch Louisville KY 1986-1987; D Calv Ch Louisville KY 1985-1986. Integrity.

JACKSON, Paul Phillip (CFla) 1620 Mayflower Ct. A-211, Winter Park FL 32789 B Atlanta GA 1921 s Paul & Dora. BA Emory U 1949. D 6/15/1975 Bp William Hopkins Folwell. m 2/5/1955 Mary Jean Atwood c 2. D All SS Ch Of Winter Pk Winter Pk FL 1976-2011; Asst Chr The King Epis Ch Orlando FL 1975-1976. Chapl Ord of S Lk, Chapl DOK 1986. Chap OSL 1988; Chap DOK 1986.

JACKSON, Peter (Nwk) 130 Bessida St, Bloomfield NJ 07003 **Chf Ed Untd Nations 1992-** B Georgetown Guyana 1947 PhD U of Bordeaux FR; BA U of Guyana. D 6/3/2006 Bp John Palmer Croneberger. m 1/11/1991 Lorita Jackson c 2.

JACKSON, Peter Jonathan Edward (WA) 1 The Green, London N14 7EG Great Britain (UK) **Vic Chr Ch Southgate London UK 2003-** B Swansea Wales 1953 s Edward & Madge. BA Oxf GB 1974; MA Oxf GB 1978; PGCE Oxf GB 1978; Cert Theol Stud St Stephens Hse Oxf 1980. Trans 12/31/2002 Bp John Bryson Chane. Assoc R and Dir of Educ S Pat's Ch Washington DC 2001-2003; Chapl & Hd of Rel Stds Harrow Sch London UK 1990-2001; Chapl Aldenham Sch Herts. UK 1982-1989; Cur Malvern Link Worcs. UK 1980-1982; Cur St Mich at the No Gate Oxford UK 1979-1980. Auth, "Ethics," SPCK, 2011; Auth, "Faith Confirmed," SPCK, 1997; Auth, "The People of God," Herga Press, 1991; Auth, "The Ways of God," Herga Press, 1990; Auth, "The Ch of God," Herga Press, 1990.

JACKSON, Phillip A (NY) 50 Pine St, New York NY 10005 **Vic Trin Par New York NY 2015-** B Chicago IL 1963 s Albert & Margaret. BA Amh 1985; JD Ya 1989; MDiv CDSP 1994. D 6/24/1994 Bp Donald Purple Hart P 1/25/1995 Bp Claude Edward Payne. m 4/27/1996 Page Y Underwood. R Chr Ch Of The Ascen Paradise Vlly AZ 2007-2014; Dio Arizona Phoenix AZ 2007; R Chr Ch Detroit MI 2001-2007; Cn Educ Cathd Ch Of S Paul Detroit MI 1998-2001; Vic Ch Of The Incarn Houston TX 1994-1998; The Great Cmsn Fndt Houston TX 1994-1998. pjackson@trinitywallstreet.com

JACKSON, Reginald Fitzroy (LI) 1695 E 55th St, Brooklyn NY 11234 **Airline Mgr TAP Portugal Newark NJ 1979-** B Antigua WI 1949 s Herbert & Ruth. BBA CUNY 1985; MBA CUNY 1988; Mercer Hosp Sch of Nrsng 2005. D 2/24/2006 Bp Rodney Rae Michel. m 4/13/1987 Sadie C Jackson c 2.

JACKSON, Rhea E (Ark) PO Box 36, Roland AR 72135 B Little Rock AR 1941 s Rhea & Arline. BA U of Arkansas at Little Rock 1963; BD Epis TS of the SW 1966. D 6/29/1966 P 3/1/1967 Bp Robert Raymond Brown. m 9/1/1964 Virginia Nelson c 3. Int Dn & R Trin Cathd Little Rock AR 2008-2009; Int Dn & R 1994-1995; Vic S Fran Ch Heber Sprg AR 2003-2007; Int R S Mk's Epis Ch Little Rock AR 2001-2003; R S Jn's Epis Ch Helena AR 1972-1974; Asst S Geo's Ch Nashville TN 1969-1972; Vic Emm Ch Lake Vill AR 1966-1969; S Clem's Ch Arkansas City AR 1966-1969; S Paul's Ch Mc Gehee AR 1966-1969; Chapl Jones Collegiate Sch Little Rock AR 2003-2004. Cn Dio Arkansas 1995; Highest hon Russian Dept, Mid 1979.

JACKSON, Robert Sumner (Mass) 339 S Madison St, Woodstock IL 60098 **Non-par 1961-** B New York NY 1926 s Sumner & Jean. BA Beloit Coll 1949; Oxf GB 1954; STB Harvard DS 1956; PhD U MI 1958. D 11/23/1958 P 12/1/1959 Bp Anson Phelps Stokes Jr. m 1/1/1974 Jacqueline Jackson c 4. Chapl H Sprt New Haven CT 1959-1961. Robert S. Jackson, "Breakthrough In Econ Well Being For All People," *Journ For Global Transformation*, Landmark Educ Corp., 2001; Robert S. Jackson, "No Amer Gold Stocks," Probus Pub,

1988; Robert S. Jackson, "Gold As Barbaric Relic: Modernist Myth," *Nomos mag*, Nomos mag, 1985; Robert S. Jackson & Sarah Cook, "The Bailly Area," *Porter Cnty Indiana*, Robert Jackson & Assoc, 1974; Robert S. Jackson, "Jn Donne's Chr Vocation," NWU Press, 1970. Non-Stipendiary Priests Assn Of Chicago 1966. Hon Grad Berk. Date? 1962.

JACKSON, Rosemary Herrick (WNC) 145 Old Mt Olivet Rd, Zirconia NC 28790 B New York NY 1947 d Richard & Helene. BFA New Sch Parsons Sch of Desnan 1970; MDiv Epis TS of the SW 2001. D 9/14/2003 Bp Rayford Baines High Jr P 5/27/2004 Bp Don Adger Wimberly. The Wm Temple Fndt Galveston TX 2004-2005; Asst Gr Ch Galveston TX 2002-2007; Exec Dir Epis Ch Cntr New York NY 2001-2007.

JACKSON, Terry Allan (NY) 600 W 246th St Apt 1515, Bronx NY 10471 **S Andr's Ch New York NY 2001-** B Birmingham AL 1957 s Terry & Lucy. BA U of Alabama 1979; MDiv GTS 1986. D 5/24/1986 Bp Furman Charles Stough P 11/18/1987 Bp Frank Tracy Griswold III. Supply S Ambr Epis Ch New York NY 1998-1999; Wooster Sch Danbury CT 1994-1997; Asst Ch Of S Mary The Vrgn New York NY 1987-1994; S Hilda's And S Hugh's Sch New York NY 1987-1994; Chapl S Hilda's And Sainthugh's Sch - 1987-1994. Nasd 1997; Nfa 1997. standrewsharlem@live.com

JACKSON, Terry Wightman (CFla) 728 Lake Dora Dr, Tavares FL 32778 **Died 12/26/2015** B Palestine TX 1939 s Chester & Vera. BA U of Kansas 1961; MDiv SWTS 1964; MS Florida Inst of Tech 1972; DMin PrTS 1982; Cert Oxf GB 1985. D 6/11/1964 Bp Edward Randolph Welles II P 12/21/1964 Bp James Loughlin Duncan. m 8/8/1959 Donna Knutson c 4. Dn Leesburg Deanry Dio Cntrl Florida Orlando FL 1995-1999, 1984-1994, 1976-1983, Chair Prog Com 1974-1978, Chair - COM 1974-1975, 1973, Dn Melbourne Deanry 1972-1973, Plnng Com 1972, Com Coll Wk 1971, Del GC 1997-2015, Pres Stndg Com 1970-1978; R S Jas Epis Ch Leesburg FL 1973-2004; R S Jn's Ch Melbourne FL 1968-1973; Asst R H Trin Epis Ch Melbourne FL 1964-1968. Auth, *Intro to Philos*. Who's Who in Rel 1976.

JACKSON, Thomas C (Cal) Christ Episcopal Church, 1700 Santa Clara Avenue, Alameda CA 94501 **S Cyp's Ch San Francisco CA 2013-; Chapl Epis Chapl at Stanford Hosp & Clinics 2011-; Epis Chapl at Stanford Hosp & Clinics San Francisco CA 2011-; Chapl Los Gatos Hosp 2011-; Pres Oasis California 2005-** B Ayer MA 1949 s Wallace & Helen. U of Maryland 1969; U of Connecticut 1971; MBA U of New Haven 1987; MDiv CDSP 2008. D 6/5/2010 P 12/4/2010 Bp Marc Handley Andrus. m 6/26/2005 Alexander Jonghee Han c 2. Asstg Preist Chr Ch Alameda CA 2011-2013; Int Admin Ch Of The Epiph San Carlos CA 2011; D S Bede's Epis Ch Menlo Pk CA 2010; CPE Res CPE Prog Stanford Hosp 2008-2009; On Call Chapl Stanford Hosp & Clinics Stanford CA 2006-2011. Ed, "So the People May Know: A Guide to Water Utility Publ Info Practices," *Bk*, Amer Water Works Assn, Denver, CO, 1993; Ed, "Nuclear Waste Mgmt: The Ocean Alternative," *Bk*, Pergamon Press, New York, NY, 1983; Ed, "Coast Alert: Scientists Speak Out," *Bk*, Friends of the Earth Books, San Francisco, CA, 1981. tcjackson@gmail.com

JACKSON, Thomas Lee (Ala) Po Box 4155, Tyler TX 75712 **Abbot Ord of Chr Workers Tyler TX 1993-** B Detroit MI 1942 s Clifford & Mary. BA Washington U 1964; MDiv VTS 1967; PhD Amer Inst 1988. D 6/29/1967 Bp Richard Stanley Merrill Emrich P 1/6/1968 Bp Archie H Crowley. m 8/2/1997 Patricia Elaine Jackson c 3. Dioc Counslr Dio Alabama Birmingham 1985-1988; Dir Untd Campus Mnstry At Ohio U Athens OH 1969-1972; Assoc R S Paul's Ch Englewood NJ 1968-1969; Cur Ch Of The Mssh Detroit MI 1967-1968. Auth, "Me & Us: A Journey Of Self-Discovery," Xlibris, 2003; Auth, "Moments Of Clarity," Xlibris, 2002; Auth, "In Any Given Moment," Xlibris, 2002; Auth, "Moments Of Clarity," *Vol. II*, Xlibris, 2002; Auth, "Life'S Secrets (Parts 1&2)," Ad Hoc Press, 1984; Auth, "Go Back, You Didn't Say May I," Seabury Press & Xlibris, 1974.

JACKSON-MCKINNEY, Statha Frances (SwFla) 484 E Shade Dr, Venice FL 34293 B Hopewell VA 1935 D 6/14/2003 Bp John Bailey Lipscomb. m 11/3/1956 Curtis McKinney. D S Mk's Epis Ch Venice FL 2003-2012.

JACOB, James Neithelloor (RI) B Kallooppara Kerala India 1949 s Neithelloor & Aleyamma. BSc Kerala U 1969; MSc Aligarh Muslim U 1971; PhD Indn Inst of Sci 1976; MDiv Andover Newton TS 2005. Trans 11/16/2015 as Priest Bp W Nicholas Knisely Jr. m 9/2/1976 Ninni Sarah Jacob c 2.

JACOB, Jerry Elias (Ala) 305 Arnold St NE, Cullman AL 35055 **D Dio Alabama Birmingham 2011-** B New Orlean LA 1945 s Jack & Julie. MA U of Alabama 1972. D 10/1/2011 Bp John Mckee Sloan Sr. m 9/1/1966 Marcia Palfrey Jacob.

JACOBS, Allston Alexander (Md) 2019 Division St, Baltimore MD 21217 **R Ch Of S Kath Of Alexandria Baltimore MD 2009-** B Antigua 1948 s Alexander & Daisy. Dip Theol Stud Codrington Coll 1976; BA Somerset U 1986; MA St Marys Sem & U 1990. Trans 1/7/2010 as Priest Bp Eugene Taylor Sutton. m 8/19/1978 Margo E Jacobs c 2.

JACOBS, Connie Hartquist (SJ) 2635 2nd Ave Apt 730, San Diego CA 92103 **Ret 1991-** B Austin MN 1943 d Richard & Margaret. BA U CA 1966; Tchr Cert California St U 1968; Cert Dioc Sch for Mnstrs 1979; Bachelor of Theol Stds Sch for Deacons 1985. D 6/25/1979 Bp George West Barrett. m 5/18/2002 Thomas Jacobs. D S Cuth's Epis Ch Oakland CA 2003-2004; Dio California San Francisco CA 1986-1990; Dir, Epis Chapl San Francisco Gnrl Hosp 1985-1991; D S Aid's Ch San Francisco CA 1981-1983; S Lukes Hosp San Francisco CA 1980-1984; Chapl S Lk's Hosp San Francisco CA 1978-1985. Auth, *Franciscan*. NAAD.

JACOBS, Gregory Alexander (Nwk) 31 Mulberry St., Newark NJ 07102 **Cn to the Ordnry Dio Newark Newark NJ 2008-, Cathd Properties Com 2017-, Cler Wellness Com 2014-2016, Dignity in the Workplace Taskforce 2014-2016, Liturg & Wrshp Com 2014-, Bp's Bd for Soc Justice 2012-2015, NEWARK ACTS Bd 2010-2013, Anti-Racism Committe (NAMASTE) 2009-; Taskforce on Cler Ldrshp in Sm Congregations Dom And Frgn Mssy Soc- Epis Ch Cntr New York NY 2015-, Exec Coun Com on Econ Loan Justice 2012-2015, Bd For Transition Mnstry 2006-2012, Evang GC Cognate Com 2003, Stndg Com on Const & Cn 2000-2006** B Bilwaskarma NG 1952 s Solomon & Lynette. BA Pr 1974; JD Col 1977; MDiv Bex Sem 1995. D 6/17/1995 Bp J Clark Grew II P 12/17/1995 Bp Arthur Williams Jr. c 2. Asst to Bp for Urban Mnstry Dio Massachusetts Boston MA 2006-2008, Anti-Racism Com 2006-2008; Cn for Mssn & Mnstry Trin Cathd Cleveland OH 2001-2005; Asst to Bp for Urban Congregations & Yth Dio Ohio Cleveland 1999-2001, D 1995; Vic S Phil's Epis Ch Akron OH 1995-1999; Cur S Paul's Ch Akron OH 1995-1998; Const & Cn Epis Ch Cntr New York NY 2000-2006. Epis Ntwk for Econ Justice 2008; EPF 2001; EUC 2000; UBE 1991. gjacobs@dioceseofnewark.org

JACOBS, John Ray (CFla) 21 Riviera Dr, Pinehurst NC 28374 B Fort Smith AR 1955 s Joyce. BA U So 1978; JD U of Memphis 1981; MDiv Sewanee: The U So, TS 2000; DMin Sewanee: The U So, TS 2006. D 5/27/2000 P 12/9/2000 Bp John Wadsworth Howe. m 5/16/1981 Elizabeth P Jacobs c 2. Trin Ch Vero Bch FL 2010-2012; R S Thos Epis Ch Eustis FL 2003-2009; Asst S Barn Ch Deland FL 2000-2003.

JACOBS, Marlene M (Oly) 1917 Logan Ave S, Minneapolis MN 55403 **S Lk's Ch Tacoma WA 2015-** B Harlan IA 1962 d Gerald & Marietta. BA U of St Thos 1987; MS U of Wisconsin 1995; MDiv VTS 2005. D 6/15/2005 Bp James Louis Jelinek P 12/18/2005 Bp Robert R Gepert. R S Paul's Ch Minneapolis MN 2007-2015; Asst to the R S Lk's Par Kalamazoo MI 2005-2007.

JACOBS III, Philip (Mass) 203 Chapman St, Canton MA 02021 B Newton MA 1944 s Philip & Lillian. BS U of Maine 1966; MDiv Ya Berk 1971; STM Yale DS 1972; ThM Weston Jesuit TS 1982; Boston Coll 1983; S Deiniols Libr Hawarden GB 1985; Bos 2012. D 11/7/1970 Bp John Melville Burgess P 5/29/1971 Bp Joseph Warren Hutchens. m 8/3/1968 Phebe Elizabeth Jacobs c 3. Del Prov I 2009-2011; Dioc Coun Dio Massachusetts Boston MA 2002-2009, Archv & Libr Bd 1988-2011, Peace & Justice Cmsn 1987-, Dioc Coun 2002-2009, GC Alt Dep 1997-2001, GC Dep 1994, Anti-Racism T/F 1992-1996, GC Alt Dep 1991, Archv & Libr Bd 1988-, Dioc Coun 1987-1990, Peace & Justice Com 1987-; Chair, Natl Exec Coun EPF 1993-1997; R Trin Ch Canton MA 1990-2016; Mem EPF 1987-1997; R Ch Of The Gd Shpd Fairhaven MA 1982-1990; R S Ptr's Ch On The Canal Buzzards Bay MA 1974-1982; Asst All SS' Epis Ch Belmont MA 1972-1974; Chapl McLean Hosp Belmont MA 1972-1974; Asst Imm S Jas Par Derby CT 1971-1972; Asst Chr Ch New Haven CT 1970-1971. Assoc, Soc of S Jn the Evang 1975; Comp, Oratory of Gd Shpd 2007; Conf of Blessed Sacr 1967; EPF 1967; EUC 1993; GAS 1975; Interfaith Worker Justice Massachusetts Chapt 2010; P Assn OWL 2002. Cmnty Sprt Awd Watkins Glen Area ChmbrCom 2013; Kappa Delta Pi hon Soc 1966.

JACOBS, Robert Alexander (NY) 20 Trestle Way, Dayton NJ 08810 **D Ch Of The H Apos New York NY 2010-, D 2010-** B New York NY 1943 s Randolph & Iona. Cert Amer Inst of Banking New York NY 1965; BS Manhattan Coll 1972. D 5/30/1992 Bp Richard Frank Grein. m 10/4/1975 Miriam Mary Jacobs c 3. D Cathd Ch of St Jn the Div New York NY 1997-2010; D Cathd Of St Jn The Div New York NY 1997-2010; Chapl S Lk's / Roosevelt Hosp New York NY 1994-2002; D S Phil's Ch New York NY 1992-1997; Mem Exec Coun Appointees New York NY 1993-1995.

JACOBSON, Harold Knute (Mo) 123 S. Ninth Street, Columbia MO 65201 **Calv Ch Columbia MO 2010-** B New Haven CT 1954 s Harold & Merelyn. BD U MI 1976; MDiv Yale DS 1980; ThM PrTS 1981. D 6/20/1982 P 10/1/1986 Bp H Coleman Mcgehee Jr. m 12/28/1985 Rosemary E Jacobson c 4. R S Tim Ch Richland MI 2000-2010; R S Matt's Ch Charleston WV 1996-2000; Int S Paul's Epis Ch Shreveport LA 1995-1996; R S Steph's Ch Beaumont TX 1991-1995; Assoc S Jn's Epis Ch Saginaw MI 1986-1991; 1982-1986.

JACOBSON, Jeanne (CPa) 616 Spruce St., Hollidaysburg PA 16648 **H Trin Epis Ch Hollidaysburg PA 2005-** B Tulsa OK 1954 BA LSU 1975; MDiv SWTS 2004; MDiv SWTS 2004. D 6/12/2004 P 7/23/2005 Bp Andrew Donnan Smith. Trin Epis Ch Tyrone PA 2005-2009; Exec Asst Obs 1996-2001.

JACOBSON, Marc R (Pgh) 4604 Crew Hall Ln, Quezon City, Waxhaw NC 28173 **Mssy P, Philippines Dio Pittsburgh Manila Philippines 2005-** B Palo Alto CA 1951 s Ray & Patricia. BA Gordon Coll 1976; MA TESM 2004. D 6/12/2004 Bp Robert William Duncan P 12/14/2004 Bp Henry W Scriven. m 5/25/1975 Suzanne M Jacobson c 3. Dio Pittsburgh Pittsburgh PA 2004-2016; Trin Cathd Pittsburgh PA 2004. marc_jacobson@sil.org

JACOBSON, Matthew Daniel (NY) 145 W 46th St, New York NY 10036 B Bologna Italy 1975 s Richard & Janet. D 3/4/2017 Bp Mary Douglas Glasspool. m 10/1/2005 Meredith Bree Linn.

JACOBSON, Mr. Jacobson (NH) 9 Esty Way, Groveland MA 01834 B Erie PA 1935 s Earl & Mary. BA Ken 1956; LTh SWTS 1959; Coll of Preachers 1988. D 6/29/1959 P 3/12/1960 Bp Lauriston L Scaife. m 6/18/1966 Gayle D Jacobson c 3. S Paul's Ch Concord NH 2006-2009; P-in-c St Andr's Ch Hopkinton NH 2005-2006; P-in-c All SS' Ch Petersborough NH 2001-2004; Int Gr Ch Manchester NH 2000-2001; Int S Jn's Ch Beverly MA 1998-1999; R S Jn's Ch Bala Cynwyd PA 1990-1998; R Ch Of The Redeem Bryn Mawr PA 1989; Dn Cathd Ch Of S Paul Burlington VT 1982-1989; R S Paul's Ch Pawtucket RI 1973-1982; R S Paul's Epis Ch Mayville NY 1963-1973; Ch Of The Gd Shpd Irving NY 1960-1963; Vic S Ptr's Ch Forestville NY 1960-1963; Cur Trin Epis Ch Buffalo NY 1959-1969; Stndg Com Dio Rhode Island Providence RI 1979-1982. Auth, *Cathedrals Are More Than Just Buildings*; Auth, *Epis*.

JACOBSON, Steve (Pa) 155 Bayside Drive, Eastham MA 02642 B Melrose MA 1938 s Carl & Alice. BA Tufts U 1960; MDiv EDS 1966; DMin Estrn Bapt TS 1993. D 6/25/1966 P 2/18/1968 Bp Anson Phelps Stokes Jr. m 3/18/1960 Denise Elizabeth Jacobson c 3. Int S Gabr's Epis Ch Marion MA 2008-2009; Int S Mary's Epis Ch Bonita Sprg FL 2003-2004; Int S Jas Epis Ch Pt Charlotte FL 2002-2003; Int Chr Ch Milwaukee WI 1999-2000; Int Trin By The Cove Naples FL 1999; Int Chr Ch Exeter NH 1998-1999; Int Chr Ch Grosse Pointe Grosse Pointe Farms MI 1997; Asst S Matt's Ch Maple Glen PA 1996-1997; R S Dav's Ch Wayne PA 1984-1997; R S Mary's Epis Ch Manchester CT 1974-1984; Vic S Geo's Ch Middlebury CT 1970-1974; Asst Trin Ch Topsfield MA 1967-1969; Cur S Mk's Ch Foxborough MA 1966-1967. Auth, "SPERANZA," *A Novel*, Self, 2011; Auth, "The Novation," *Epis Life*, 1976; Auth, "Ulster's Bitter Fruit: The Troubles in Ulster," *The Epis*, 1976; Auth, "The Great Manuscript Hoax," *Yankee mag*, 1972. stephenkentjacobson@gmail.com

✠ **JACOBUS, The Rt Rev Russell Edward** (FdL) 17786 Valley View Rd, Townsend WI 54175 B Milwaukee WI 1944 s Lester & Sarah. BA U of Wisconsin-Milwaukee 1967; MDiv Nash 1970. D 2/21/1970 P 8/22/1970 Bp Donald H V Hallock Con 5/24/1994 for FdL. m 5/25/1968 Jerrie E Evrard c 3. Dio Eau Claire Eau Claire WI 2009; Bp Of Fond du Lac Dio Fond du Lac Appleton WI 1994-2013; Stndg Com Dio Milwaukee Milwaukee WI 1991-1994, Sprtl Dir Curs 1984-1990, Stndg Com 1983, Dep Gc 1982, Exec Bd 1977-1981, Com 1982-1986; Equal Opportunity Cmsn City Of Waukesha WI 1985-1988; R St Mths Epis Ch Waukesha WI 1980-1994; Vic S Ptr's Ch Northlake WI 1977-1979; R S Anskar's Epis Ch Hartland WI 1974-1980; Asst Trin Ch Milwaukee WI 1970-1973; Trst Nash Nashotah WI 2008-2014, Trst 1990-2007. Sis Of The H Nativ -- Assoc 1994-2017. DD Nash Sem 1994; P of the Year Dio Milwaukee 1984. rjacobus@att.net

JACOBY, Lisa Anne (Los) St George Episcopal Church, 23802 Avenida De La Carlota, Laguna Hills CA 92653 B Madison WI 1958 d James & Carolynn. BA U of Alabama; MEd U Cinc; EdS Natl Louis U 1995; MDiv ETS at Claremon 2016. D 5/22/2016 Bp Joseph Jon Bruno. c 2.

JACQUES, Mary Martha (Mont) 13100 Highway 41 North, Dillon MT 59725 **R 1997-** B Tampa FL 1940 d Adolphus & Lillian. U of Tampa 1962; BS U of Missouri 1963; MS Washington U 1967; PhD Washington U 1971; MDiv CDSP 1984. D 6/9/1984 Bp William Edwin Swing P 12/17/1984 Bp Jackson Earle Gilliam. m 4/25/1987 Justin Knox Burgin. Chr Ch Sheridan MT 1993-1997, Vic 1984-1992; Dio Montana Helena MT 1993-1995; The Majestic Mountains Mnstry Dillon MT 1991-1992; Int St Jas Epis Ch Dillon MT 1985-1986. Auth, "Pathways, Kdbm Dillon," *Montana*, 1998; Auth, "Reflections, Kdbm Dillon," *Montana*, 1998; Auth, "Outpourings Of Love Images Of Stwdshp," *Natl Ch Video*, 1989. Land.

JAEGER, Nick (Ky) 2502 Jefferson St., Paducah KY 42001 B Washington DC 1940 s George & Eleanor. BA U of Maryland 1966; MDiv PDS 1968. D 6/29/1968 Bp William Foreman Creighton P 12/29/1968 Bp Leland Stark. m 8/17/1968 Julie T Teeple c 5. Assoc S Ptr's of the Lakes Gilbertsville KY 2005-2012; Dio Kentucky Louisville KY 1995-2004, 1991-1994, 1990, 1989, 1987-1988; Gr Ch Paducah KY 1987-2003; Dio Wstrn Michigan Kalamazoo MI 1979-1986; Dn The Par Ch Of Chr The King Kalamazoo MI 1979-1986; Dio New Jersey Trenton NJ 1974-1979; R Trin Ch Matawan NJ 1972-1979; Cur S Paul's Epis Ch Chatham NJ 1968-1972.

JAEKLE, Charles Roth (WA) 7446 Spring Village Dr Apt 307, Springfield VA 22150 **Ret 1992-** B Bayonne NJ 1922 s Charles & Martha. BA Doane Coll; Grad U Texas U Pennsylvania; STM Luth TS; BD UTS. D 6/21/1958 Bp James Parker Clements P 3/1/1959 Bp John Elbridge Hines. m 11/24/1945 Ann Murden c 2. Non-par 1966-1992; Pstr Counslg Cntr Oakton VA 1964-1987; Assoc Prof Of Care Epis TS Of The SW Austin TX 1958-1966; Chapl St Hosp Austin TX 1954-1958; Chapl Riverside Hosp In New York City 1952-1954; Serv Luth Ch 1950-1952. Auth w Wm Clebsch, "Pstr Care In Hist Perspective," Prentice-Hall New Jersey, 1964; Auth, "Ang: Their Mssn & Message," *Pstr Care in Histocal Perspective*, Jason Aronson New York, 1964; Auth, "Pilgrimage: Journ Pstr Psychol".

J

JAENKE, Karen Ann (NJ) 24 Woodland Road, Fairfax CA 94930 **Dir, Ecotherapy Prog Jn F. Kennedy U 2011-** B Arlington VA 1957 d Edwin & Claire. BA Wake Forest U 1980; MDiv PrTS 1986; CAS GTS 1989; PhD California Inst of Integral Stds 2000. D 6/9/1990 Bp George Phelps Mellick Belshaw. Dissertation Dir Inst of Imaginal Stds 2001-2008; Adj Fac Jn F. Kennedy U 2000-2011; Asst to Bp Chr Ch Trenton NJ 1990-1991; Dio New Jersey Trenton NJ 1990-1991; Chapl to AIDS Population NJ Dept of Corrections 1987-1988. Ed, "Earth Dreaming," *Revs: Journ of Consciousness & Transformation*, ReVisionpublishing.org, 2011; Auth, "Dreaming w the Earth," *Revs: Journ of Consciousness & Transformation*, ReVisionpublishing.org, 2011; Ed, "Shamanism and the Wounded W," *Revs: Journ of Consciousness & Transformation*, Re-Visionpublishing.org, 2010; Auth, "Ed's Essay: Shamanism & the Wounded W," *Revs: Journ of Consciousness & Transformation*, ReVisionpublishing.org, 2010; Auth, "Earth Dreaming," *Rebearths: Conversations w a Wrld Ensouled*, Wrld Soul Books, 2010; Auth, "Soul & Soullessness," *Revs: Journ of Consciousness & Transformation*, ReVisionpublishing.org, 2009; Auth, "Earth, Dreams, Body," *Revs: Journ of Consciousness & Transformation*, ReVisionpublishing.org, 2008; Auth, "Dreaming the Ritual Onward," *Revs: Journ of Consciousness & Transformation*, Heldref, 2006; Auth, "Dreaming w the Ancestors," *Revs: Journ of Consciousness & Transformation*, Heldref, 2006; Auth, "The Participatory Turn," *Revs: Journ of Consciousness & Transformation*, Heldref, 2004; Auth, "Ode to the Intelligence of Dreams," *Revs: Journ of Consciousness & Transformation*, Heldref, 2004; Auth, "Personal Dreamscape as Ancestral Landscape," *Dissertation*, UMI, 2000; Auth, "Water & Stone: All of Nature Participates in Our Remembering," *Revs: Journ of Consciousness & Transformation*, Heldref, 1998. Assn for the Study of Dreams 1996. Phi Beta Kappa Phi Beta Kappa 1979.

JAIKES, Donald William (Mass) 1095 Pinellas Pt Dr So Unit 327, Saint Petersburg FL 33705 **Ret 1995-** B Wilkes Barre PA 1930 s William & Margaret. BS Wilkes Coll 1957; MDiv Bex Sem 1967. D 6/24/1967 P 5/18/1968 Bp Anson Phelps Stokes Jr. m 4/26/1958 Joan Jaikes c 2. S Andr's Epis Ch Sprg Hill FL 1997-2003; R Ch Of The Ascen Fall River MA 1972-1995; S Lk's Epis Ch Malden MA 1967-1972; Min in charge S Paul's Ch Malden MA 1967-1971.

JAKOBSEN, Wilma Terry (ECR) St Jude the Apostle Church, 20920 McClellan Rd, Cupertino CA 95014 **Ch Of S Jude The Apos Cupertino CA 2012-** B Cape Town South Africa 1959 d Kjeld & Gwendolyn. BS U of Cape Town Cape Town Za 1979; MDiv Fuller TS 1987; STM UTS 1997. Trans 6/19/2003. Sr Assoc For Liturg Peace And Justice All SS Ch Pasadena CA 2003-2012. "Lang Matters: Towards And Inclusive Cmnty," Journ For The Study Of Rel, 2001; "Like Water In A Desert: Wmn Ch In So Afr," Dissident Daughters: Feminist Liturgies In Global Context, 2001; "Ethics In Feminist Theol," Doing Ethics In Context Orbis Books, 1994; "Wmn And Vocation: The 'If' Question," Wmn Hold Up Half The Sky; Cluster Pub Sa, 1991.

JALLOUF, Georges (Okla) 5850 E 78th Pl, Tulsa OK 74136 **R S Lk's Ch Tulsa OK 2010-** B Damascus Syria 1964 s Moussa & Jeanette. MPhil Oriental Franciscan Sem 1987; MTh Studium Theologicum Franciscanum 1992; Lic Lateranese U Rome Italy 1995; Cert Ang Stud Sewanee: The U So, TS 2007. Rec 4/25/2003 as Priest Bp Pierre W Whalon. m 4/27/2012 Maha George Saidawi. Asst S Lk's Epis Ch Jacksonville FL 2007-2010; Chapl Chr Ch Cedar Key FL 2007; Asst In Admssns Off U So TS At Sewanee 2006-2007.

JAMBOR, Christopher Noel (FtW) 1805 Malibar Rd, Fort Worth TX 76116 **Par Assoc All SS' Epis Ch Ft Worth TX 1995-** B Cincinnati OH 1951 s James & Louise. BS Trin U San Antonio 1974; MD U of Kansas 1978; MDiv Nash 1995. D 11/30/1994 P 6/1/1995 Bp Keith Lynn Ackerman. m 4/23/1978 Patricia Ann Jambor c 2. SocMary, CBS.

JAMES, Alan C (Chi) 400 E Westminster, Lake Forest IL 60045 **Mssh-S Barth Epis Ch Chicago IL 2017-; R The Ch Of The H Sprt Lake Forest IL 2014-** B Chula Vista CA 1967 s Frederick & Nyla. BSFS Geo 1989; MDiv VTS 1996. D 6/8/1996 P 12/15/1996 Bp Gethin Benwil Hughes. m 5/16/2009 Lisa E Hackney c 8. Cn to the Ordnry Dio Ohio Cleveland 2005-2014; R S Matt's Epis Ch Brecksville OH 1999-2005; Cur S Dunst's Epis Ch San Diego CA 1996-1999. ajames@chslf.org

JAMES, Charles (CGC) Po Box 29, Bon Secour AL 36511 B Memphis TN 1938 s Spencer & Mary. BS U of So Carolina 1961; BD VTS 1968. D 6/21/1968 P 1/1/1969 Bp Gray Temple. m 8/12/1967 Sylvia James c 2. R S Ptr's Epis Ch Bon Secour AL 1996-2006; R Trin Ch Winchester TN 1982-1996; R S Phil's Ch Nashville TN 1980-1982; Vic H Cross Epis Ch Simpsonville SC 1974-1980; Asst All SS Ch Florence SC 1972-1974; R S Paul's Ch Bennettsville SC 1969-1972; Cur Epis Ch of the Gd Shpd Summerville SC 1968-1969. Chapl Asst, Ord of S Lk.

JAMES, Claudia Jan (Az) 423 N. Beaver St., Flagstaff AZ 86001 B Waco TX 1948 d Thomas & Martha. BA U of Texas 1988; MDiv Brite DS 1997. D 6/19/1999 P 6/7/2000 Bp James Monte Stanton. m 9/18/1971 Robert Cullum James c 3. R Ch Of The Epiph Flagstaff AZ 2006-2014; Trin Epis Ch The Woodlands TX 2002-2006; S Jas Ch Dallas TX 1999-2002. Auth, "Journ Of Pstr Care," 1999; Auth, "Power Of Valuing In Brief Pstr Counslg". Intl Soc Theta Phi.

JAMES, Darryl Farrar (LI) 3312 S Indiana Ave, Chicago IL 60616 **R Gr Ch Jamaica NY 2007-** B Bridgeport CT 1954 s Anthony & Laurayne. BA How 1976; MDiv Yale DS 1979. D 6/30/1984 Bp Henry Irving Mayson P 2/2/1985 Bp John Melville Burgess. R Mssh-S Barth Epis Ch Chicago IL 1985-2007; S Matt's And S Jos's Detroit MI 1984-1985; Asst To R S Matt/S Jos Chicago IL 1981-1985.

JAMES, Edmund Ludwig (Okla) 104 W Hanover St, Hoyt OK 74472 **Supply P S Jas Epis Ch Wagoner OK 2011-** B Leutershausen, Germany 1956 s Edward & Tilli. BA NE St U 1980; MDiv Phillips TS 2008. D 6/22/2002 Bp Robert Manning Moody P 5/14/2011 Bp Edward Joseph Konieczny. m 8/3/1979 Diana Ruth James c 2. D Trin Ch Eufaula OK 2002-2011.

JAMES, Jay Carleton (NC) 4523 Six Forks Road, Raleigh NC 27609 **Chapl S Tim's Sch Raleigh NC 1997-; R S Tim's Ch Raleigh NC 1993-; Bd Mem St Timothys Sch 1993-** B Houlton ME 1956 s Carleton & Josephine. BS U of Maine 1978; MDiv GTS 1985. D 6/8/1985 P 12/14/1985 Bp Frederick Barton Wolf. m 10/22/1988 Elizabeth M James c 2. Cur The Par Of All SS Ashmont-Dorches Boston MA 1985-1993. SocMary 2015. jjames@sttimothys.org

JAMES, John Hugh Alexander (Ct) Christ Episc Church, 78 Washington St, Norwich CT 06360 **R Chr Epis Ch Norwich CT 2012-** B Cardiff Wales UK 1956 s Richard & Barbara. BA U of Durham 1978; DipTh St Mich's TS 1981; MPhil U of Wales 2002. Trans 7/18/2012 as Priest Bp Ian Theodore Douglas. m 4/13/1985 Susan Jane Alexander James. Auth, "A Fitting End," *A Fitting End: making the most of a funeral*, Cbury Press, 2004; Auth, "Chld & H Comm," *Chld & H Comm: Info for Parents*, Ch in Wales Pub, 1991; Auth, "Chld & H Comm," *Chld & H Comm: Some considerations of the issue from the perspective of the Ch in Wales*, Ch in Wales Pub, 1991; Auth, "Chld and H Comm," *Chld and H Comm: Some considerations of teh issue from the perspective of the Ch in Wales*, Ch in Wales Pub, 1991; Contrib, "Chld & H Comm," *Chld & H Comm: an Ecum consideration amongst Ch in Britain and Ireland*, British Coun of Ch, 1989; Ed, "A Guide to Par Yth Wk," *A Guide to Par Yth Wk*, Ch in Wales Pub, 1987.

JAMES, Marcus Gilbert (Roch) B 1920 Trans 1/2/1946 Bp Bartel H Reinheimer.

JAMES, Molly F (Ct) 37 Griswold Dr, West Hartford CT 06119 **Dn of Formation Epis Ch in CT 2013-; Adj Prof U of St. Jos 2012-; Adj Prof Hartford Sem 2011-** B New Haven CT 1980 d Eliot & Catherine. BA Tufts U 2002; MDiv Ya Berk 2005; PhD U of Exeter 2011. D 6/11/2005 P 12/16/2005 Bp Chilton Richardson Knudsen. m 6/4/2005 Reade W James c 2. Formation Consult Dio Connecticut Meriden CT 2012-2013, Secy of the Dio 2011-2014, Stndg Com 2010-2012, Prog and Bdgt Com 2007-2012, Fin Com 2012-2013; Presb Middlesex Area Cluster Mnstry Higganum CT 2012-2013; S Jn's Epis Ch Essex CT 2006-2011; Chapl Yale-New Hosp New Haven CT 2005-2006; Asst Secy of GC Com on Governance and Structure GC- Epis Ch Cntr New York NY 2015, Secy of Stndg Cmsn on Structure, Governance, Const and Cn 2015-; Personal Rep of the HOD SCMD 2012-2015. Auth, "w Joyful Acceptance, Maybe," *w Joyful Acceptance, Maybe*, Wipf & Stock, 2012. AAR 2011; Soc of Schlr Priests 2012.

JAMES, Nancy Carol (WA) 713 E St Ne, Washington DC 20002 B Laredo TX 1954 d Franklin & Eve. BA California St U 1981; MDiv VTS 1984; PhD U of Virginia 1997. D 6/22/1985 P 5/10/1986 Bp Peter J Lee. m 1/31/2005 Roger James Nebel c 2. R Trin Epis Par Hughesville MD 2011-2014; Gr Ch Washington DC 2008-2011; Int S Thos Par Croom Uppr Marlboro MD 2007-2008; Assoc S Jn's Ch Lafayette Sq Washington DC 2000-2009; Prof of Rel Amer U 1999-2005; Emm Ch Rapidan VA 1991-1997; Chr Epis Ch Brandy Sta VA 1986-1995; D The Falls Ch Epis Falls Ch VA 1985-1986. Auth, "The Complete Madame Guyon," Paraclete Press, 2011; Auth, "Bastille Witness: The Prison Autobiography of Madame Guyon," U Press, 2011; Auth, "In Your Mercy, Lord, You Called Me," Edwin Mellen Press, 2010; Auth, "The Developing Schism Within the Epis Ch 1960-2010," Edwin Mellen Press, 2010; Auth, "Chas Phil Price," *Blackwell Comp to the Theologians*, Wiley-Blackwell, 2009; Auth, "The Conflict Over the Heresy of," Edwin Mellen Press, 2008; Auth, "The Pure Love of Madame Guyon: The Great Conflict in the Crt of Louis XIV," U Press, 2007; Auth, "Stndg in the Whirlwind," Pilgrim Press, 2005. AAR 1999; Auth's Gld 2005.

JAMES JR, Ralph Matthew (WVa) PO Box 145, Union WV 24983 B Charleston WV 1946 s Ralph & LaRene. BA Concord Coll 1968; MS GW 1971. D 12/15/2007 P 6/14/2008 Bp William Michie Klusmeyer. m 6/8/1968 Renda James c 1. Vic All SS Ch Un WV 2008-2014.

JAMES, Robert Arthur (LI) 5 Fig Ct E, Homosassa FL 34446 **Assoc S Andr's 2004-; Ret 1998-** B Chicago IL 1935 s William & Martha. BA Knox Coll 1957; STB GTS 1960; MA Villanova U 1970; MS U of Pennsylvania 1975; EdD U of Pennsylvania 1978. D 6/18/1960 P 12/21/1960 Bp Gerald Francis Burrill P 12/21/1960 Bp Oliver L Loring. c 2. S Andr's Epis Ch Sprg Hill FL 2001-2005; Int S Steph's Epis Ch Ocala FL 2000-2001; Chapl Prov II BroSA 1997-1998; Dioc AIDS Cmsn Dio Long Island Garden City NY 1993-1998; R Chr Ch Bay Ridge Brooklyn NY 1991-1998; Chair Human Sxlty Cmsn Dio Pennsylvania Philadelphia PA 1990-1991, CEC 1988-1991; S Mary's Ch Wayne PA 1983-1991, 1981-1982; H Trin Ch Lansdale PA 1982-1983, 1975-1976;

S Clements Ch Philadelphia PA 1978-1979; Int Trin Ch Gulph Mills Kng Of Prussia PA 1969-1970; Vic S Columba Epis Ch Marathon FL 1964-1968; R H Trin Epis Ch Bartow FL 1963-1964; Gr Epis Ch Of Ocala Ocala FL 1962-1963; Cathd Ch Of S Lk Portland ME 1960-1962; Chapl Brooklyn Assembly BroSA. Auth, *Model for a Long-R Developmental Plan*, U Microfilms, 1978. Bro of S Andr 1994. Ford Fellowowship Admin Ldrshp U of Pennsylvania 1972.

JAMES, Robin L (NY) 660 S 500 E, Salt Lake City UT 84102 **S Andr's Epis Ch New Paltz NY 2014-** B Ottawa KS 1964 Bachelor of Arts U of Kansas; Mstr of Sci in Educ U of Kansas 1992; Mstr of Div CDSP 2003. D 6/19/2003 P 5/29/2004 Bp Carolyn Tanner Irish. m 6/2/2010 Susan Jean Roberts. Cn Precentor Cathd Ch Of S Mk Salt Lake City UT 2003-2013; COM Dio Utah Salt Lake City UT 2006-2010, Dioc Liturg Com 2005-2008.

JAMES, Sally Patricia (NMich) 402 W Fleshiem St, Iron Mountain MI 49801 **D H Trin 1998-** B Houghton MI 1937 d Dante & Arthenia. Coll S Scholastica Nrsng Duluth MN 1957. D 3/1/1998 Bp Thomas Kreider Ray.

JAMES, William Evans (CGC) 1530 University Dr NE Apt 15, Atlanta GA 30306 B Atlanta GA 1939 s Herman & Sarah. BA Georgia St U 1961; BD Sewanee: The U So, TS 1965. D 6/26/1965 P 3/19/1966 Bp Randolph R Claiborne. Vic S Mk's Epis Ch Troy AL 1988-1990; R S Mich's Ch Mobile AL 1979-1988; S Paul's Ch Greensboro AL 1970-1977; Cur S Barth's Epis Ch Atlanta GA 1965-1967.

JAMESON, Elizabeth Butler (Chi) 232 S. Dwyer, Arlington Heights IL 60005 **R S Simons Ch Arlington Hts IL 2013-** B Michigan 1968 d Samuel & Katherine. Cntr for Action and Contemplation; BA Harv 1990; MDiv SWTS 1997. D 6/26/1997 P 1/24/1998 Bp Richard Sui On Chang. m 9/4/2010 James Jameson c 2. P-in-c S Elis's Ch Glencoe IL 2012-2013; VP and COO Bexley Seabury Fed Chicago IL 2005-2013; Assoc Ch Of The H Comf Kenilworth IL 1997-2005; Fac for Ldrshp Credo Inst Inc. Memphis TN 2012-2016. elizabeth@saintsimons.org

JAMESON, J Parker (Tex) 8 Troon Dr, Lakeway TX 78738 B Abilene TX 1953 s Jay & Mary. AB Harv 1975; MDiv Epis TS of the SW 1981; DMin SWTS 2006. D 6/11/1981 P 6/29/1982 Bp Sam Byron Hulsey. m 1/17/1981 Paula W Whitfield c 2. Adj Fac Epis TS Of The SW Austin TX 2015-2016, 2014, 2014; Assoc R S Lk's On The Lake Epis Ch Austin TX 1998-2016; R S Tim's Ch Alexandria LA 1988-1998; Asst R S Lk's Epis Ch San Antonio TX 1983-1988; S Paul's Epis Ch Dumas TX 1981-1983; Cur S Ptr's Epis Ch Amarillo TX 1981-1983.

JAMIESON, Sandra Swift Cornett (SwFla) 301 Jasmine Way, Clearwater FL 33756 **D H Trin Epis Ch In Countryside Clearwater FL 2010-** B Warham MA 1946 d Walter & Eloise. AS St Petersburg Jr Coll St Petersburg FL 1967. D 1/18/2002 Bp John Bailey Lipscomb. m 6/3/1967 Harry Bruce Jamieson. D Gd Samar Epis Ch Clearwater FL 2001-2010.

JAMIESON JR, William Stukey (WNC) 15 Macon Ave, Asheville NC 28801 B Jacksonville FL 1943 s William & Suzannne. BA U of Arizona 1965; MS Georgia St U 1976. D 10/21/1989 Bp Joseph Thomas Heistand. m 9/6/1969 Kennon Barksdale c 2. Chruch of the Advoc Dio Wstrn No Carolina Asheville NC 1997-2001; D The Cathd Of All Souls Asheville NC 1996-1997; D Epis Ch Of The H Sprt Mars Hill NC 1995-1996; Archd Dio Arizona Phoenix AZ 1993-1995. Achievement Awd, Citizen Awd (Both w dist) Arizona St U; Alumnini Awd, w Distiction Georgia St U; Citizen Awd, w Distiction Phoenix Un HS Dist.

JAMIESON-DRAKE, Victoria Kapp (NC) 304 E Franklin St, Chapel Hill NC 27514 **Assoc for Pstr Mnstry Chap Of The Cross Chap Hill NC 1995-** B 1957 d John & Ruth. Ya Berk; BA Wellesley Coll 1978; MDiv Duke DS 1985. D 6/24/1986 Bp Frank Harris Vest Jr P 7/2/1987 Bp Robert Whitridge Estill. m 8/8/1981 David Jamieson-Drake c 3. Int S Andrews Ch Durham NC 1995; Vic Ch Of The H Sprt Greensboro NC 1990-1994; Asst to R S Phil's Ch Durham NC 1986-1989; Hisp Mssn Dvlpmt Com; Com Dio No Carolina Raleigh NC 1988-1992.

JAMISON, Dale Martin (NMich) 901 Dakota Ave, Gladstone MI 49837 **D Trin Ch Gladstone MI 2010-** B Detroit MI 1948 s Robert & Dolores. BS Nthrn Michigan U 1971; MA Ferris St U 1988. D 9/12/2010 Bp Thomas Kreider Ray. m 9/5/1970 Susan Jamison c 3.

JAMISON, Dorothy Lockwood (Cal) 501 Portola Rd Apt 12J, Portola Valley CA 94028 **D Chr Ch Portola Vlly CA 2006-, D 1990-2005** B Philadelphia PA 1939 d John & Dorothy. BA DePauw U 1960; BA California Sch for Deacons 1989; Bex Sem 1990; MDiv CDSP 1992. D 6/9/1990 Bp William Edwin Swing. m 3/3/1962 Rex Lindsay Jamison c 2. D Chr Epis Ch Los Altos CA 1998-2003; Epis Chapl Stan Hosp Stanford CA 1993-2000. Auth, "New PB, New Mnstrs," *Mod Profiles of an Ancient Faith*, The Epis Dio CA, 2001. Assn of Epis Hosp Chapl 1994-2002. Dn & Trst' Awd The Sch for Deacons, Dio California 2003; Pres's Awd NAAD 1997.

JANDA, Mary Sheridan (U) **Anti-Racism Com Dio Utah Salt Lake City UT 2014-, Dioc Coun 2013-, COM 2010-2013, Anti-Racism Com 2007-; Supply P The Dio Utah 2013-** B Plymouth IN 1951 d William & Rudith. St Marys Coll 1971; BA Indiana U 1976; Dio Utah - Formation for Mnstry 2007. D 6/9/2007 P 1/26/2008 Bp Carolyn Tanner Irish. m 2/25/1978 James F Janda c 2. Int S Jn's

Epis Ch Logan UT 2013; All SS Ch Salt Lake City UT 2009-2012; Assoc R S Jas Epis Ch Midvale UT 2009-2010. Auth, "Out of the Storm," Outskirts Press, 2006.

JANELLE, Nicole (Los) St. Michael's University Church, 6586 Picasso Rd., Isla Vista CA 93117 B Augusta ME 1978 d Andre & Suzanne. BA NWU 2000; MDiv UTS 2004; Universidad Biblica Latinoamericana San Jose Costa Rica 2004. D 6/13/2004 P 12/18/2004 Bp Chilton Richardson Knudsen. c 1. Vic and Chapl S Mich's U Mssn Isla Vista CA 2006-2015; S Mary's Epis Ch Los Angeles CA 2004-2006. nsjanelle@gmail.com

JANE REDDICK, Mary (Tex) 2525 Seagler Rd, Houston TX 77042 B Maryville MO 1947 d Emmett & Helen. D 6/20/2015 Bp C Andrew Doyle. m 5/23/1970 Max E Reddick c 3.

JANESS, Nancy Kingswood (Nev) B Englewood NJ 1941 d George & Thelma. BA U of Nevada at Reno 1999. D 6/28/2003 Bp Katharine Jefferts Schori. m 4/18/1959 William King Janess c 4.

JANG, Teduan Vincent (Cal) 5072 Diamond Heights Blvd, San Francisco CA 94131 B San Francisco CA 1948 s Yok & Christine. AA City Coll of San Francisco 1969; BA San Francisco St U 1980; BTS Sch for Deacons 2001. D 12/4/2004 Bp William Edwin Swing. D S Jas Epis Ch San Francisco CA 2011-2017; D Emer True Sunshine Epis Ch San Francisco CA 2011-2017; Bishops Liaison San Francisco San Mateo Curs Sec 2007-2013; Sub Comm Mem SC Liturg and Mus New York NY 2007; D True Sunshine Par San Francisco CA 2004-2011, Lay Assoc 2000-2004; Convenor Asian Cmsn San Francisco CA 2004-2009; Rel OHC W Pk NY 1970-1973.

JANIEC, Thomas Daniel (Chi) 342 E Wood St, Palatine IL 60067 B Chicago IL 1941 s Stephen & Lorraine. AA Elgin Cmnty Coll 1978; BS Natl Coll of Educ 1984; MDiv SWTS 1998; Cert Inst of Sprtl Comp 2000. D 6/18/1988 P 12/17/1988 Bp Frank Tracy Griswold III. m 7/26/1996 Anne Marie Janiec c 2. R S Phil's Epis Palatine IL 1996-2008; R Annunc Bridgeview IL 1988-1996; Ch Of The Annunc Bridgeview IL 1988-1996. SocMary 1996; Soc of S Fran 2000-2006. Spec Serv Awd M.E.B.T.C. 2003; Cert of Sprtl Dir 2000; Cert in Advncd Pstr Psychol Stds 1993; Cert of CPE Elmhurst Meml Hosp 1986; Phi Theta Kappa 1977.

JANKOWSKI, John A (Minn) 10174 Bald Eagle Trl, Woodbury MN 55129 B Virginia MN 1963 s Victor & Irene. BA Gustavus Adolphus Coll 1985; MDiv Untd TS of the Twin Cities 2007. D 6/14/2007 P 12/20/2007 Bp James Louis Jelinek. m 7/19/1963 Jennifer L Jankowski c 2. R S Jn's Ch S Cloud MN 2009-2014; The Rev S Mk's Ch Lake City MN 2007-2009; Consult Cpc Inc 2005.

JARA, Francisco Gonzalo (EcuC) B 1970 s Manuel & Rosario. Egresado San Leon Magno 1998; Licenciado en Teologia Universidad del Azuay 2007. Rec 6/29/2012 as Priest Bp Victor Alfonso Scantlebury. m 6/2/2008 Eulalia Alejandrina Piedra c 2. Iglesia Epis Del Ecuador Quito 2013-2014.

JARRELL, Robin Campbell (CPa) 229 Alana Ln, Lewisburg PA 17837 **P S Matt's Epis Ch Sunbury PA 2008-** B Augusta GA 1959 d Robert. BA Wellesley Coll 1991; MA Claremont TS 1994; MDiv VTS 2002. D 6/8/2002 P 1/19/2003 Bp Michael Whittington Creighton. m 8/22/1992 Chris James Boyatzis c 1. Chr Ch Milton PA 2002-2008. stmatthewsunbury@gmail.com

JARRETT III, John J (SeFla) 1052 Nw 65th St, Miami FL 33150 **Assoc Ch Of The Incarn Miami FL 2008-** B Miami FL 1952 s John & Altermeas. BA Florida Intl U 1976; MDiv VTS 1985. D 7/19/1986 P 6/24/1987 Bp Calvin Onderdonk Schofield Jr. S Andr's Epis Ch Of Hollywood Hollywood FL 2003-2008; P-in-c S Anne's Epis Ch Hallandale Bch FL 2003-2007; P-In-Chrge St. Anne Epis Ch 2003-2007; R S Phil's Epis Ch Grand Rapids MI 1998-2002; Asst S Lk's Ch Washington DC 1987-1997; Dio SE Florida Miami 1986-1987; D S Lk's Epis Ch Atlanta GA 1986-1987.

JARRETT-SCHELL, Peter (WA) 1700 Powder Mill Rd, Silver Spring MD 20903 **Calv Ch Washington DC 2012-** B San Francisco 1980 s Donald & Ellen. MDiv Yale DS 2002; MDiv CDSP 2006. D 6/3/2006 Bp William Edwin Swing P 12/2/2006 Bp Marc Handley Andrus. m 7/26/2006 Rondesia Jarrett-Schell c 1. Assoc Ch Of Our Sav Silver Sprg MD 2007-2012.

JARRETT-SCHELL, Rondesia (WA) 13925 New Hampshire Ave, Silver Spring MD 20904 **Ch Of The H Comm Washington DC 2012-** B Germany 1978 BA Gonzaga U 2000; MDiv CDSP 2005. D 6/11/2005 P 6/9/2007 Bp James E Waggoner Jr. m 7/26/2006 Peter Jarrett-Schell. The Bp Jn T Walker Sch for Boys Washington DC 2012-2014; Asst Ch Of The Trsfg Silver Sprg MD 2008-2012; Asst Meml Ch Baltimore MD 2007-2008; Records Coordntr Luteran Fam Serv 2006-2007.

JARVIS III, Frank Washington (Mass) 1241 Adams St Apt 511, Dorchester MA 02124 **Dir, Educational Ldrshp and Mnstry Prog Ya Berk New Haven CT 2008-; Headmaster Emer The Roxbury Latin Sch 2004-; Assoc The Par Of All SS Ashmont-Dorches Boston MA 1976-** B Pittsburgh PA 1939 s Frank & Prudence. BA Harv 1961; BD EDS 1964; MA U of Cambridge 1967. D 6/13/1964 Bp Beverley D Tucker P 1/24/1965 Bp Nelson Marigold Burroughs. Headmaster Roxbury Latin Sch Boston MA 1974-2004; Cur S Paul's Epis Ch Cleveland OH 1964-1971. Auth, "w Love and Prayers," Godine, 2000; Auth, "Var arts," *Schola Illustris*, Godine, 1995; Auth, "And Still is Ours Today,"

Seabury, 1980; Auth, "Prophets, Poets," *Priests Kings*, Seabury, 1974; Auth, "Come & Follow," Seabury, 1972. Doctor of Letters (Litt.D.) Mid 2004; Pres Country Day Sch Headmaster's Assn 2001; Doctor of Humane Letters (L.H.D.) Bow 1998; Pres Headmaster's Assn of the U.S. 1993; Chairman Cmsn on Indep Schools NEAS&C 1991.

JARVIS, Leon Gerald (NMich) 1300 West Ave, Marquette MI 49855 B Detroit MI 1958 s Darcey & Dolores. Nthrn Michigan U 1991. D 7/27/2004 P 1/30/2005 Bp James Arthur Kelsey. m 12/24/1988 Lesa Ann Bozek c 2. Monk, Bon Jn Osb Sylvestrine Cong. O.S.B. Oxford MA 1978-1986.

JASMER, Gerald Bruce (Mont) 36 30th St W, Billings MT 59102 **Asst S Steph's Ch Billings MT 2010-** B Miles City MT 1940 s Paul & Florence. BS Montana St U 1966. D 8/15/1990 P 11/15/1997 Bp Charles I Jones III. Part Time S Lk's Ch Billings MT 2004-2010, 1990-2004.

JASPER SR, John Weaver (CFla) 1151 Sw Del Rio Blvd, Port Saint Lucie FL 34953 **D Epis Ch Of The Nativ Port St Lucie FL 1998-; D Dio SE Florida Miami 1990-** B Lewiston ME 1933 s Charles & Jennette. BS Barry U 1983. D 2/14/1990 Bp Calvin Onderdonk Schofield Jr. m 11/18/1976 Joan Marie Jasper.

JASPER, Michael Angelo (Okla) 13112 N Rockwell Ave, Oklahoma City OK 73142 B Kansas City MO 1951 s William & Anna. BA U of Missouri 1975; MDiv Nash 1989. D 5/9/1989 Bp Arthur Anton Vogel P 11/10/1989 Bp John Clark Buchanan. c 2. R Epis Ch Of The Resurr Oklahoma City OK 2001-2015; S Barn' Epis Ch Of Odessa Odessa TX 1996-2001; S Lk's Epis Hosp Houston TX 1995-1996; Chapl S Lk's Hosp Houston TX 1995-1996; R Gr Epis Ch Houston TX 1990-1995; Dio W Missouri Kansas City MO 1989-1990; Vic S Lk's Epis Ch Excelsior Sprg MO 1989-1990. ecotr@att.net

JAVIER, Nazareno C (Pa) **Gr Epiph Ch Philadelphia PA 2015-; Supply Cler Gr Epiph Ch Philadelphia PA 2014-** B Pasay City Philippines 1972 s Renato & Victoria. BA St Johns U 1993; MA Sem of the Immac Concep 1997; MDiv Sem of the Immac Concep 1998; MDiv Sem of the Immac Concep 1998; MSW Ford 2004; MSW Ford 2004. Rec 6/14/2014 as Priest Bp Clifton Daniel III. nazjavier@verizon.net

JAY, Lynn (Los) 26084 Viento Ct, Valencia CA 91355 **Adj Cler All SS' Epis Ch Pasadena CA 2013-** B Santa Monica CA 1941 d Rex & Virginia. California St U; ETSBH; BA California St U 1976; MDiv Claremont TS 1982. D 6/19/1982 P 1/22/1983 Bp Robert Claflin Rusack. m 6/22/1963 Herman Jay c 3. Vic S Steph's Epis Ch Santa Clara CA 1985-2008; R S Steph's Epis Ch Valencia CA 1984-2011; Asst Epis Ch Of S Andr And S Chas Granada Hills CA 1982-1984. Assn of Wmn Clerics 1983; Camp Wrightwood Advsry Bd 2000; Los Angeles Cler Assn Bd 2006. Cn Dio Los Angeles 1997.

JAYAWARDENE, Thomas Devashri (Los) 1141 Westmont Rd, Santa Barbara CA 93108 **Asst Trin Epis Ch Santa Barbara CA 2000-** B Dalugama Kelaniya LK 1946 s John & Cecilia. DSS U Internazionale Rome It 1972; Lic Sacr Theol U Pontifical Rome IT 1972; PhD U of Surrey Guildford Gb 1978. Rec 8/25/1986 as Priest Bp William Cockburn Russell Sheridan. m 11/14/1980 Jasmine Fernando.

JAYNES, Ronald P (Pa) 431 Atkins Ave, Lancaster PA 17603 B Geneva NY 1941 s Paul & Doris. BA IL Wesl 1963; MDiv Nash 1966. D 6/11/1966 Bp James Winchester Montgomery P 12/1/1966 Bp Gerald Francis Burrill. m 1/21/1983 Colleen E Jaynes c 4. Int Bruton Par Williamsburg VA 2009-2011; Int Chr Ch Coronado CA 2006-2009; Int S Jas By The Sea La Jolla CA 2003-2006; Int Ch Of The Gd Shpd Philadelphia PA 2002-2003; Int S Mary's Epis Ch Ardmore PA 2000-2002; Asst S Paul's Ch Philadelphia PA 1998-2000; R St Cathr of Alexandria Epis Ch Temple Terrace FL 1994-1998; R S Dav's Epis Ch Wilmington DE 1986-1994; R S Jn's Epis Ch Little Silver NJ 1972-1986; R Prince of Peace Epis Ch Sterling CO 1969-1972; Cur S Lk's Epis Ch Ft Collins CO 1967-1969; Cur Gr Ch Sterling IL 1966-1967. Int Mnstry Ntwk 1997; Int Mnstry in the Epis Ch (IMEC) 2000.

JAYNES, Ruth Louise McKinney (Neb) 1322 S 52nd St, Omaha NE 68106 **P-in-c S Mary's Epis Ch Blair NE 2016-** B Topeka KS 1951 d Eugene & Leone. MA Epis TS of the SW; BA U of Wyoming. D 5/31/2002 P 12/1/2002 Bp James Edward Krotz. S Martha's Epis Ch Papillion NE 2010-2012; Ch Of The H Sprt Bellevue NE 2008; Dio Nebraska Omaha NE 2004-2010; Mssnr S Jn's Ch Broken Bow NE 2002-2006; On Track Mnstry Lexington NE 2002-2004.

JEAN, Macdonald (Hai) Box 1309, Port-Au-Prince Haiti **R Redemp In Gonaives 1979-** B Latortuo PR 1941 s Thomas & Parlera. BA Coll S Pierre PR 1965; STB ETSC 1969; Institut Catholique De Paris 1979; U of Paris-Sorbonne Fr 1979. D 11/30/1968 Bp Charles Alfred Voegeli P 12/1/1969 Bp John Brooke Mosley. m 12/19/1970 Marie Gisele Jean c 1. Dio Haiti Port-au-Prince HT 1999-2006, 1968-1995; Dir ETSC Puerto Rico 1973-1976; P-in-c S Esprit Cap-Haitien 1970-1976; Asst S Esprit Cap-Haitien 1969-1970. Auth, "Theol Reflection On Pryr For Ord Of Bp"; Auth, "Theol Reflection On Voodoo Initiation In Haiti"; Auth, "Procession & Creation In Plato'S Philos," *Prot & Dvlpmnt In Haiti*.

JEANES III, Paul (NJ) 33 Mercer St, Princeton NJ 08540 **R Trin Ch Princeton NJ 2008-** B Louisville KY 1965 s Paul & Betty. BA Wake Forest U 1987; DAS GTS 1997; MDiv Louisville Presb TS 1997; MAMFT Louisville Presb TS 1997; MA Louisville Presb TS 1997. D 6/28/1997 P 1/18/1998 Bp Ted Gulick

Jr. m 7/8/1995 Christina B Jeanes c 3. R S Jas Ch Pewee Vlly KY 1999-2008; Asst Chr Ch Cathd Louisville KY 1997-1999. jeanesp@trinityprinceton.org

JEAN-JACQUES, Harry Musset (Hai) Boite Postale 1309, Port-Au-Prince Haiti **Ch Of The H Sprt Mattapan MA 2015-; P-in-c L'Eglise Episcopale A La Conave 1986-** B Hinche HT 1953 D 12/15/1985 P 10/12/1986 Bp Luc Anatole Jacques Garnier. m 12/30/1980 Martha Rosier.

JEAN-PHILIPPE, Jean-Alphonse (Hai) PO Box 407139, C/O Lynx Air, Fort Lauderdale FL 33340 **Dio Haiti Port-au-Prince HT 1999-** B 1961 D 4/25/1999 P 12/26/1999 Bp Jean Zache Duracin. m 7/12/2001 Marie Marjorie Merisier Jean-Philippe c 1.

JEFFERS, Mary Elisabeth (USC) 711 S McDuffie St, Anderson SC 29624 B Newport RI 1957 d Frederick & Joan. BS U of Rhode Island 1982. D 1/15/2014 Bp W illiam Andrew Waldo. m 9/6/1982 Steven Nye Jeffers c 4.

JEFFERSON, Alyce Lee (La) 1329 Jackson Ave, New Orleans LA 70130 B New Orleans LA 1949 d Stockton & Vilma. BA U of New Orleans 1971. D 12/27/2008 Bp Charles Edward Jenkins III. c 2.

✠ JEFFERTS SCHORI, The Rt Rev Katharine (Nev) Episcopal Diocese of San Diego, 2083 Sunset Cliffs Blvd, San Diego CA 92107 **DELS Bd Natl Acad of Sciences 2009-; Primate Mem Angl Comm Stndg Com 2007-** B Pensacola FL 1954 d Keith & Elaine. BS Stan 1974; MS OR SU 1977; PhD OR SU 1983; MDiv CDSP 1994. D 5/26/1994 P 11/30/1994 Bp Robert Louis Ladehoff Con 2/24/2001 for Nev. m 9/1/1979 Richard M Schori c 1. PBp of The Epis Ch Dom And Frgn Mssy Soc- Epis Ch Cntr New York NY 2006-2015, Mem, Spec Cmsn on ECUSA & Angl Comm 2005-2006, Bd for Ch Deploy 2003-2006, GBEC 2003-2006; PBp Epis Ch Cntr New York NY 2006-2015; Bp of Nevada Dio Nevada Las Vegas 2001-2006; Hospice Chapl Benton Hospice Svc. Corvallis OR 1995-2000; The Epis Ch Of The Gd Samar Corvallis OR 1994-2001; Dept CE Dio Oregon Portland OR 1994-2000; Mem Pres's Advsry Cncl on Faith-Based Nbrhd Partnr 2011-2014; Bd Trst CDSP Berkeley CA 2004-2006. Auth, "Creation and the Effective Word," *ATR*, 2017; Auth, "Gathering at God's Table: The Meaning of Mssn in the Feast of Faith," Skylight Paths, 2012; Auth, "The Heartbeat of God: Finding the Sacr in the Middle of Everything," Skylight Paths, 2010; Auth, "Gospel in the Global Vill: Seeking God's Dream of Shalom," Morehouse, 2009; Auth, "A Wing and a Pryr: A Message of Faith and Hope," Morehouse Pub, 2007; Auth, "Bldg Bridges/Widening Circles sermon in Preaching Through H Days and Holidays," *Sermons that Wk XI*, Morehouse Pub, 2003; Auth, "Multicultural Issues in Preaching sermon in Preaching Through the Year of Matt," *Sermons that Wk X*, Morehouse Pub, 2001; Auth, "The Nag sermon in Preaching Through the Year of Lk," *Sermons that Wk IX*, Morehouse Pub, 2000; Auth, "Maundy Thursday sermon," *What Makes this Day Different?*, Cowley, 1998; Auth, "Sermon: Preaching as the Art of Sacr Conversation," *Sermons that Wk VI*, Morehouse Pub, 1997; Auth, "Article," *LivCh (March 3, 1996)*, LivCh Fndt, 1996. CHS 1991. DD Oxf 2014; DD Huron U 2011; DD Bexley 2010; DD GTS 2009; DD Bex 2008; DD U So 2008; DD VTS 2008; Doctor of Humane Letters Coe Coll 2007; DD ETSS 2007; DD Seabury-Wstrn 2007; DD CDSP 2001; The Preaching Excellence Conf 1993. kjefferts@edsd.org

JEFFERY, Anne-Marie (NJ) St Peters Episcopal Church, 183 Rector St, Perth Amboy NJ 08861 **R S Ptr's Ch Perth Amboy NJ 2011-** B NYC 1967 d Alfred & Agnes. BS SUNY 1988; MS U of Connecticut 1990; PhD U of Connecticut 1993; MDiv VTS 2004. D 6/12/2004 P 1/22/2005 Bp John Bryson Chane. m 12/31/2014 Lisa Alexis Jones. Int S Marg's Ch Washington DC 2010-2011; Dio Washington Washington DC 2007-2010; Bowie St Unversity Chapl S Jas Epis Ch Bowie MD 2007-2009; Urban Mssnr The Ch Of The Epiph Washington DC 2004-2007.

JEFFERY, David Luce (Fla) 1843 Seminole Rd, Atlantic Beach FL 32233 **Ret 1998-** B Lansing MI 1936 s Donald & Constance. BA Syr 1958; MTh SMU 1973; DMin VTS 1990. D 6/10/1973 P 12/13/1973 Bp Archibald Donald Davies. m 10/4/1980 Priscilla Jeffery c 4. P-in-c S Lk's Epis Ch Jacksonville FL 2005-2007; P-in-c S Paul's By-The-Sea Epis Ch Jaxville Bch FL 2001-2002, P-in-c 1992; R S Geo Epis Ch Jacksonville FL 1995-1998; Assoc All SS Epis Ch Jacksonville FL 1988-1992; R S Paul's Epis Ch Lees Summit MO 1986-1988; 1984-1986; Dn Of Convoc Dio Arkansas Little Rock AR 1982-1995, 1982-1986, Dn NW Convoc 1982-1983; R S Thos Ch Springdale AR 1982-1986; Gr Ch Vernon TX 1980-1982; Trin Ch Quanah TX 1980-1982; Dio NW Texas Lubbock TX 1980-1981; R S Jos's Epis Ch Grand Prairie TX 1977-1980; Vic S Pat's Ch Bowie TX 1974-1977; Vic Trin Ch Henrietta TX 1974-1977; Assoc Trin Epis Ch Ft Worth TX 1973-1974; Natl Ch Field Off For Stwdshp; Mentor EFM; Chair Stwdshp Dio Florida Jacksonville 1989-1991, Exec Coun 1989-1990; Chair -Yth Div; Exec Coun Dio Dallas Dallas TX 1976-1980. Dav L. Jeffery, "Effective Lay Hosp Visitation," *Same*, DMin VTS, 1990. OHC, Ord Of S Lk; Ord of Julian of Norwich 2003.

JEFFERY, Vincent James (Nev) 1500 Mount Rose St, Reno NV 89509 B Elgin IL 1933 s Stanley & Helen. BA Ohio Nthrn U 1954; STM Bos 1957; MA OH SU 1961. D 12/21/1965 P 5/9/1972 Bp Nelson Marigold Burroughs. m 4/15/1972 Leslie Jeffery c 1. R Trin Epis Ch Reno NV 1973-2005; M-In C Gr Mssn To Deaf Akron OH 1967-1971; Cur S Paul's Ch Akron OH 1965-1972; Pstr

Methodist Ch Columbus Toledo 1957-1965. Vision Awd Nevada Cler Assn 2010; R Emer Trin Epis Ch, Reno 2005; Humanitarian Of The Year Awd Conf Of Christians & Jews 1990.

JEFFREY, Kathryn G (Spr) 29 Nord Circle Rd, North Oaks MN 55127 **S Andr's Ch Carbondale IL 2013**- B Hadley MA 1956 d Edward & Mary. BA Br 1977; JD Geo 1980; MDiv Ya Berk 1985; STM Ya Berk 1987. D 6/29/1985 P 3/1/1986 Bp A(rthur) Heath Light. c 2. Dio Minnesota Minneapolis MN 2001-2003; R S Jn The Evang S Paul MN 2000-2001; Int H Cross-St Chris's Huntsville AL 1999-2000; Organizer Unidad Cooperataive Huitzitzilingo Mex 1996-1998; Int Ch Of The Ascen Cranston RI 1991-1992; S Geo's Ch Newport RI 1988-1991; Lead R Dio Cntrl New York Liverpool NY 1987-1988; Utica Area Coop Mnstry Whitesboro NY 1987-1988; Assoc Chr Ch Poughkeepsie NY 1986-1987; Asst S Jn's Epis Ch Niantic CT 1985-1986; Dir Dio Massachusetts Boston MA 1993-1995. "A Mighty Flood," *Epis News*, 1993. Phi Beta Kappa. kgjeffrey@msn.com

JEFFREY, Peter Leigh (Mass) 8 Kirk St, Lowell MA 01852 B Frankfurt Germany 1946 s Edmund & Hilda. AS NEU 1974; BS NEU 1976. D 6/16/2012 Bp M(Arvil) Thomas Shaw. m 4/28/1966 Kathy Ann Jeffrey c 1.

JEKABSONS, Wendie Susan Scudds (ETenn) 334 Sourwood Hill Rd, Bristol TN 37620 B Hamilton ON CA 1942 d Harold & Helen. BA E Tennessee St U 1982; MA U of Tennessee 1990; Cert Sewanee: The U So, TS 2001. D 6/30/1985 Bp William Evan Sanders P 6/20/2001 Bp Charles Glenn VonRosenberg. c 3. P-in-c Emm Epis Ch Bristol VA 2007-2008; P-in-c The Sav Epis Ch Newland NC 2001-2003; Chapl Epis U Mnstry Johnson City TN 1993-2000; D S Columba's Epis Ch Bristol TN 1985; Mem of Episcopate Com Dio E Tennessee Knoxville TN 1997-1998, Mem of COM 1993-1998, Int 1992-1993, Mem of Bp and Coun 1991-1995. "Called to be a D," *Diakoneo, vol.17 #1*, No Amer Assoc. for the Diac, 1995; "Called to be a D," *E Tennessee Epis*, Dio E Tennessee, 1994. NAAD.

✠ JELINEK, The Rt Rev James Louis (Minn) 957 25th St NW, Washington DC 20037 **Int S Paul's Par Washington DC 2013**- B Milwaukee WI 1942 s James & Ruth. Cert Universite Laval 1963; BA Carthage Coll 1964; Van 1967; STB GTS 1970. D 6/28/1970 Bp John Vander Horst P 1/14/1971 Bp James Milton Richardson Con 10/29/1993 for Minn. m 6/18/1988 Marilyn Kay Wall c 1. Ret Bp of Minnesota Dio Minnesota Minneapolis MN 2010, Bp of Minnesota 1993-2010; R S Aid's Ch San Francisco CA 1985-1993; R Ch Of S Mich And All Ang Cincinnati OH 1977-1984; Assoc Ch Of The H Comm Memphis TN 1972-1977; Cur S Barth's Ch Nashville TN 1971-1972; Chapl S Lk's Hosp Houston TX 1970-1971. DD GTS 1994.

JELLEMA, Alice (Md) 1401 Carrollton Ave, Ruxton MD 21204 **R Ch Of The Guardian Ang Baltimore MD 1997**- B Buffalo NY 1956 d Lyman & Alice. BA Colby Coll 1978; MDiv GTS 1992. D 6/6/1992 Bp David Charles Bowman P 12/1/1992 Bp Frank Harris Vest Jr. Ch Of The Gd Shpd Towson MD 1994-1997; Asst to R Emm Epis Ch Hampton VA 1992-1994. guardianangelremington@gmail.com

JELLISON, Mary Lavon (Wyo) 3129 Pinewood Ave, Bellingham WA 98225 B Portland OR 1940 d Howard & Emily. BA L&C 1963; Wstrn Washington U 1969; Olympia TS 1991; MDiv EDS 2001. D 4/22/1993 Bp Vincent Waydell Warner P 5/26/2001 Bp Robert Wilkes Ihloff. c 3. R All SS Epis Ch Torrington WY 2003-2012; Asst R S Ptr's Epis Ch Ellicott City MD 2001-2003; D Emm Ch Cumberland MD 1996-2001; D S Paul Epis Ch Bellingham WA 1994-1996. DOK 1986.

JEMMOTT, Brian Anthony Lester (NJ) 2005 South Columbia Place, Decatur GA 30032 **Dio New Jersey Trenton NJ 2016**- B Trinidad W.I. 1955 s Lester & Ena. BA Tougaloo Coll 1982; MDiv SWTS 1993; DMin EDS 2009. Trans 5/25/1996 Bp Frank Tracy Griswold III. m 9/5/1987 Michelle C Jemmott c 2. R Ch Of The H Cross Decatur GA 2006-2016; S Tim's Decatur GA 2004-2006; S Andr's Epis Ch Cincinnati OH 2001-2002; Absalom Jones Stdt Cntr & Chap Atlanta GA 1997-2003; Dio Atlanta Atlanta GA 1997-2001; S Geo/S Mths Ch Chicago IL 1996-1997; Vic SS Geo & Mths Chicago IL 1996-1997; Cur Cathd of the H Trin Port of Spain Trinidad 1993-1996. Soc Of S Jn The Evang 1992. BJemmott@dioceseofnj.org

JENCKS, Jeffrey A (CGC) 7979 N 9th Ave, Pensacola FL 32514 **Chapl U.S. Army Reserves 2008**- B Warwick RI 1951 s Leo & Blanche. BA Our Lady of Providence 1974; MDiv S Marys Sem and U 1978. Rec 4/1/1986 as Priest Bp George Nelson Hunt III. m 1/6/1996 Eileen J McCarten c 1. R H Cross Ch Pensacola FL 2008-2013; S Jn's Ch Ashton RI 2007-2008, 2004-2005, 1988-2003; Spec Mobilization Spprt Plan Washington DC 2005-2006; Pension Fund Mltry New York NY 2003-2004; R S Jn In Ashton 1988-2008; Serv RC Ch 1977-1982.

JENKINS, Al W (CFla) 103 W Christina Blvd, Lakeland FL 33813 **Dioc Stwdshp Consult Parishes/Missions/Retreats 2009**- B Milan TN 1946 s Paul & Allie. AA Sandhills Cmnty Coll 1969; BS Lambuth U 1976; MDiv Sewanee: The U So, TS 1979; DMin Sewanee: The U So, TS 1983. D 6/24/1979 Bp William F Gates Jr P 9/22/1980 Bp Emerson Paul Haynes. m 10/22/1966 Vivian R Rogers c 1. Mem Dioc Exec Com 2009-2011; Mem Dioc Stndg Com 2008-2012; Mem Dioc Honduras Cmsn 2006-2008; Judge Dioc Eccl Trial Crt 2005-2009; Dioc

Stwdshp Consult Parishes/Missions/Retreats 2002; Stwdshp Instr Inst for Chr Stds 2001-2002; Mem Dioc Exec Com 2001; Mem Dioc Capital Cmpgn Strng Com 2000-2001; Chairman Dioc Stwdshp Cmsn 2000-2001; Bd Mem Dioc Bd (2nd Term) 1999-2001; Dn SW Dnry 1999-2001; Dioc Chapl BroSA 1998; Pres Lakeland (Florida) Mnstrl Assn 1994; Dioc Chapl Daughter's of the King 1992-1993; Bd Mem Anchor Hse Hm for Boys 1991; Mem Bp¿s Advsry Com of Sexual Misconduct Among 1991; Pres Lakeland (Florida) Mnstrl Assn 1991; Founding Mem Lakeland (Florida) Police Chapl's Bd 1991; R All SS Epis Ch Lakeland FL 1989-2015; Chairman Bp's Consecration Strng Com 1989; Mem Dioc Evang Strng Com 1989; Bd Dir Cbury Conf Cntr 1988-1989; Mem Dioc Transition Com for a New Bp 1988-1989; Mem Citrus Cnty (Florida) Correctional Plnng Cmsn 1988; Mem Dioc Cler Life Cmsn 1988; Chairman Inverness (Florida) Downtown Dvlpmt Assn 1987-1988; Alt Citrus Cnty (Florida) Plnng Cmsn 1987; Mem Citrus Cnty Hospice Bd 1987; R S Marg's Ch Inverness FL 1986-1989; Assoc S Dunst's Epis Ch Largo FL 1982-1986; R S Jas Epis Ch Pt Charlotte FL 1981-1982; Asst Chr Ch Bradenton FL 1980-1981; Sewanee U So TS Sewanee TN 1979-1980; Chairman of the 4th Bp Election Dio Cntrl Florida Orlando FL 2010-2012, Pres of the Stndg Com 2009-2011, Const & Cn Com 2002-2009, Pres of the Stndg Com 2002-2009; Founding Mem All SS' Acad Winter Haven FL 1997-1998; Founding Mem Lakeland (Florida) Hab-Hum 1994; Mem Lambda Chi Alpha Fraternity - Un U 1975. Contrib and Ed, "The Hist of All SS' Epis Ch, 1884-1947, 2nd Ed," 2010; Auth, "Hist Of Epis Churchwomen In The Dio Tennessee," 1981.

✠ **JENKINS III, The Rt Rev Charles Edward** (La) P.O. Box 3000, St. Francisville LA 70775 **Ret Bp of Louisiana Dio Louisiana New Orleans LA 2010-, Bp of La 1998-2010, Chair Stndg Com 1992-1993, Stndg Com 1989-1993, Chair Div Yth 1978-1979** B Shreveport LA 1951 s Don & Helen. BA Louisiana Tech U 1973; MDiv Nash 1976. D 6/17/1976 P 4/13/1977 Bp James Barrow Brown Con 1/31/1998 for La. m 6/28/1975 Charlotte L Jenkins c 2. R S Lk's Ch Baton Rouge LA 1985-1997; R S Mk's Ch Arlington TX 1979-1985; Asst Gr Epis Ch Monroe LA 1977-1979; Asst Chapl S Alb's Chap & Epis U Cntr Baton Rouge LA 1976-1977; PBp's Coun of Advice The Epis Ch New York NY 2006-2008; BEC Dio Ft Worth Ft Worth TX 1982-1985; Bd Trst Nash Nashotah WI 1981-1991. CBS 2000. DD The GTS 2011; DD TS U So 1999; DD Nash 1992.

JENKINS, David P (Alb) 517 Lakeside Circle, Pompano Beach FL 33060 B South Weymouth MA 1935 s Alexander & Eva. BA Br 1958; MDiv GTS 1961; MA U of Rhode Island 1970; EdD SUNY 1976. D 6/17/1961 P 12/23/1961 Bp John S Higgins. Int Ch Prov W Indies Dio Windward Is 1997-2002; P-in-c S Jas Layou & S Mary Buccament S Vinc Is 1996-1997; P-in-c Ch King Carriacon Grenada W Indies 1995-1996; P-in-c S Mathias S Columbas Epiph Trinidad W Indies 1994-1995; Var Int Mnstrys Dio Albany Greenwich NY 1988-1991; Int S Steph's Ch Delmar NY 1987-1988; Chr Ch Greenville NY 1982-1986; R Trin Ch Rensselaerville Rensselaerville NY 1982-1985; P-in-c S Paul's Ch Bloomville NY 1970-1982; P-in-c S Ptr's Ch Stamford NY 1970-1982; R S Paul's Ch Portsmouth RI 1962-1969; Stdt Personl SUNY Albany Albany NY 1970-1991. Auth, "Drugs A-Z," 1972. OHC.

JENKINS, George Washburn (Ct) 567 S Farms Ct, Southington CT 06489 **Ret 2001**- B Ridgewood NJ 1936 s George & Harriet. BA Rutgers The St U of New Jersey 1962; MDiv VTS 1965. D 6/12/1965 Bp Leland Stark P 6/18/1966 Bp Gray Temple. m 5/3/1971 Loreli Jenkins c 4. R S Jas Ch Glastonbury CT 1986-2001; Dioc Fndt Dio New Jersey Trenton NJ 1985-1986, Bd Missions 1979-1984; R H Trin Ch So River NJ 1977-1986; Non-par 1969-1977; Asst Min Ch Of The Redeem Orangeburg SC 1968-1969; Epis Chapl SC St Coll 1968-1969; S Paul's Epis Ch Orangeburg SC 1968-1969; P-in-c Ch of Our Sav Goose Creek SC 1966-1968; D-in-c Ch of the H Sprt Hanahan SC 1965-1966.

JENKINS JR, Harry (La) 1534 7th St, Slidell LA 70458 **Chr Ch Slidell LA 2011**- B Savannah GA 1952 s Harry & Marion. BA Armstrong Atlantic St U 1974; EdS Georgia Sthrn U 1987; MDiv Sewanee: The U So, TS 2011. D 5/21/2011 Bp Scott Anson Benhase P 12/6/2011 Bp Morris King Thompson Jr. m 7/6/2011 Regina Brewster-Jenkins c 2.

JENKINS, James Leonard (Minn) 5250 Vernon Ave S Apt 232, Edina MN 55436 **Ret 1992**- B 1931 s Jasper & Ethel. BA Macalester Coll 1952; BD SWTS 1955. D 6/29/1955 Bp Hamilton Hyde Kellogg P 12/21/1955 Bp Stephen E Keeler. c 2. R Trin Ch Excelsior MN 1982-1992; 1975-1982; R St Geo's Epis Ch Minneapolis MN 1969-1975; R S Jas On The Pkwy Minneapolis MN 1964-1969; Chapl Breck Sch MN 1962-1963; R S Paul's Ch Virginia MN 1957-1962; Min in charge S Ptr's Epis Ch Kasson MN 1955-1957.

JENKINS, James Morgan (CPa) St. Paul's Episcopal Church, 101 E Main St, Bloomsburg PA 17815 **D S Paul's Ch Bloomsburg PA 2017**- B Wichita Falls TX 1954 s James & Bessie. BS U of Nebraska 1977; MBA U of So Dakota 1985. D 6/13/2015 Bp Michael Hanley. m 8/6/1977 Karen Elaine Allison c 3. D S Matt's Epis Ch Eugene OR 2015-2016. jim-jenkins@comcast.net

JENKINS, John Stone (La) 708 Forest Point Dr, Brandon MS 39047 **Ret 1984**- B Shreveport LA 1924 s Robert & Glena. BA LSU 1947; MA U Chi 1948; BD SWTS 1951; SWTS 1973. D 7/15/1951 P 9/1/1952 Bp Girault M Jones. m 1/25/1985 Lynn B Jenkins c 2. R Trin Ch New Orleans LA 1971-1984; Dn S Andr's Cathd Jackson MS 1967-1971; R All SS Vicksburg MS 1962-1968; Asst Hdmstr S Mart's Epis Ch Metairie LA 1954-1962; Chapl Leake & Watts Chld Hm Yonkers NY 1951-1953. Auth, "What Think Ye Of Jesus".

JENKINS, John William Andrew (Ga) **S Paul's Ch Augusta GA 2015-** D 5/21/2015 Bp John Mckee Sloan Sr P 11/24/2015 Bp Scott Anson Benhase.

JENKINS, Judith Ann (RG) 601 Montano Rd. N.W., Albuquerque NM 87107 **S Mich And All Ang Ch Albuquerque NM 2011-** B Albuquerque NM 1942 d CF Ted & Dorothy. BS Colorado St U 1967; Tchr Cert Boise St 1980; MAR Denver U 1993; MAR Iliff TS 1993. D 6/7/2008 Bp William Carl Frey. c 2.

JENKINS, Kathryn E (Va) 3507 Pond Chase Dr, Midlothian VA 23113 B Rochester NY 1963 d Richard & Susanne. BA Mt Holyoke Coll 1986; MEd U of Virginia 1991; MDiv VTS 2002. D 6/15/2002 Bp David Conner Bane Jr P 12/18/2002 Bp Carol J Gallagher. m 6/24/1989 Stephen G Jenkins c 3. Assoc S Paul's Ch Richmond VA 2007-2014; Ch Of The Redeem Midlothian VA 2002-2007; Assoc Epis Ch Of The Redeem Midlothian VA 2002-2007.

JENKINS, Kit Reid (WVa) D 6/5/2017 Bp William Michie Klusmeyer.

JENKINS, Mark A (NH) 20260 Williamsville Rd, Gregory MI 48137 B Greeneville TN 1958 s Paul & Mary. Ohio Wesl 1976; BA Wayne 1982; MDiv Sewanee: The U So, TS 1985. D 6/29/1985 Bp H Coleman Mcgehee Jr P 1/1/1986 Bp William Jones Gordon Jr. m 5/14/1977 Leigh H Jenkins c 2. R Par Of S Jas Ch Keene NH 2010-2015; P-in-c S Andr's Ch Clawson MI 2009-2010; Fac Wayne 1996-2007; Chf Fin Off Dio Michigan Detroit MI 1994-1995, Dioc Coun 2005-2007, GC Dep / Alt 1997-2009, Dioc Coun 1990-1993; Chapl Epis/Luth Chapl at Wayne Grosse Pointe MI 1992-1994; R Journey of Faith Epis Ch Dearborn MI 1990-2009; S Jn's Epis Ch Sand Point MI 1985-1990; S Jn's Epis Ch Sandusky MI 1985-1990; P-in-c S Paul's Epis Ch Bad Axe MI 1985-1990; P-in-c The Epis Ch In Huron Cnty Bad Axe MI 1985-1990. Chelsea Writer's Workshop 2015.

JENKINS, Martha L (SVa) 120 Reykin Dr, Richmond VA 23236 B Rutherfordton NC 1935 d Carl & Gladys. BA U NC 1956; MDiv VTS 1997. D 6/14/1997 Bp Frank Harris Vest Jr P 12/13/1997 Bp David Conner Bane Jr. c 3. S Matt's Epis Ch Chesterfield VA 1997-2010; Dio Sthrn Virginia Newport News VA 1997-2001; Chapl VA St U 1997-2001.

JENKINS, Michael Lemon (WNC) 5165 Hayes Waters Rd, Morganton NC 28655 **D Gr Ch Morganton NC 2011-; Dir Towel Mnstry 1993-** B Asheville NC 1951 s Grover & Anne. U NC 1972. D 12/18/1999 Bp Bob Johnson. m 8/12/1979 Linda Kay Mitchell. D S Jn's Epis Ch Marion NC 2007-2010; D St Mary's and St Steph's Epis Ch Morganton NC 1999-2007. Cert of Merit City of Morganton 2013; Blue Water Peace Awd A Season for Nonviolence 2006.

JENKINS, Stephanie (Kan) 835 SW Polk St, Topeka KS 66612 **Bp Seabury Acad Lawr KS 2016-** B Texarkana TX 1977 d Alan & Helen. BA U of Oklahoma 1999; MDiv EDS 2010; EDS 2010; EDS 2010. D 1/16/2010 P 7/31/2010 P Edward Joseph Konieczny. m 6/24/2006 Richard A Jenkins c 2. Dio Kansas Topeka KS 2013-2015; Asst S Ptr's Ch Weston MA 2012-2013; Dio Oklahoma Oklahoma City OK 2010-2012; Asst S Lk's Epis Ch Bartlesville OK 2010-2012. sjenkins@episcopal-ks.org

JENKINS, William David (Kan) 314 N Adams St, Junction City KS 66441 **Ch Of The Cov Jct City KS 2012-** B Fredonia KS 1955 s Ernest & Ann Paulina. MDiv Phillips TS 1984; MDiv The Menninger Fndt 1984; MDiv The Menninger Fndt 1984; MA US Army War Coll 2012. D 6/2/2012 P 1/5/2013 Bp Dean E Wolfe. m 6/4/1988 Mary Anna Nelson c 2. william.david.jenkins@us.army.mil

JENKS, Alan W (WVa) 450 Elm St, Morgantown WV 26501 **Restored [see comments] 1984-** B Las Vegas NM 1934 s William & Mildred. BA U of New Mex 1956; MDiv CDSP 1959; ThD Harvard DS 1965. D 6/26/1959 Bp C J Kinsolving III P 4/14/1960 Bp Donald J Campbell. m 8/29/1959 Denda Jenks c 3. Vic S Mich's Ch Kingwood WV 1984; Released from H Ord 1975-1984; Prof W Virginia U Morgantown WV 1974-1995; Prof Duke Durham NC 1967-1974; P-in-c S Jos's Ch Durham NC 1966-1968; Prof Wellesley Coll Wellesley MA 1961-1965. Auth, "Eating and Drinking in the OT," *Anchor Bible Dictionary*, 1992; Auth, "The Elohist," *Anchor Bible Dictionary*, 1992; Auth, "Theol Presuppositions of Israel's Wisdom Lit," *Horizons in Biblic Theol*, 1985; Auth, *The Elohist and No Israelite Traditions*, Scholars Press, 1977; Auth, *Tchg the OT in Engl Classes*, Indiana U Press, 1973. Cath Biblic Assn 1973-2003. Fulbright Fllshp in Semitic Linguistics Israel and US Governments 1965; B.D. w dist CDSP, Berkeley, CA 1956.

JENKS, Glenn B (Az) 5417 E Milton Dr, Cave Creek AZ 85331 **Assoc Gd Shpd Of The Hills Cave Creek AZ 2013-, 2002-2009; Non-par 1984-** B Wilkinsburg PA 1944 s Glenn & Dorothy. BA Muskingum Coll 1966; MDiv PDS 1969; JD U of Arizona 1985. D 5/24/1969 Bp William S Thomas P 12/20/1969 Bp Robert Bracewell Appleyard. c 2. S Jn The Bapt Epis Ch Glendale AZ 1996-1998; Vic Ch Of The Resurr Tucson AZ 1979-1984; Epis Par Of S Mich And All Ang Tucson AZ 1979-1984; Asst Gr St Pauls Epis Ch Tucson AZ 1974-1979; R All SS Ch Aliquippa PA 1970-1974.

JENKS, Peter Q (Me) 200 Main St, Thomaston ME 04861 **Dio Maine Portland ME 2000-; R The Epis Ch Of S Jn Bapt Thomaston ME 1992-** B Chicago IL 1956 s Bruce & Susan. BA U So 1979; MDiv GTS 1985. D 6/24/1985 Bp

Robert Marshall Anderson P 3/22/1986 Bp Claude Charles Vache. m 7/18/2004 Emily Jenks c 5. Assoc R S Andr's Epis Ch Newport News VA 1985-1992. stjohnsinthomaston@gmail.com

JENNEKER, Bruce William Bailey (WA) St George's Cathedral, 5 Wale St, Cape Town 8001 South Africa **Cn Precentor & Cathd Admin S Geo's Cathd Cape Town So Afr 2005-** B 1948 s Gordon & Helen. CUA; BA U Coll Wstrn Cape 1969; MDiv EDS 1984. D 1/1/1985 Bp Roger W Blanchard P 6/1/1985 Bp John Thomas Walker. Assoc Trin Ch Epis Boston MA 1996-2005; Cn Precentor Cathd of St Ptr & St Paul Washington DC 1992-1996; VTS Alexandria VA 1991; Assoc S Alb's 1985-1995.

JENNER, Helen McLeroy (NC) 1079 Ridge Dr, Clayton NC 27520 B Savannah GA 1933 d Hugh & Lillian. BA Wesl 1954; MA NWU 1957; MDiv Sewanee: The U So, TS 1996. D 6/29/1996 Bp Robert Carroll Johnson Jr. c 3. Dio No Carolina Raleigh NC 1998, 1997; S Barth's Ch Pittsboro NC 1997; S Paul's Epis Ch Smithfield NC 1996-1997.

JENNEY, Joe Allen (EMich) **S Andrews-By-The-Lake Epis Ch Harrisville MI 2012-** B Marshall MI 1939 s Olin & Evelyn. BS Michigan Tech U 1960; PhD U MI 1966. D 10/23/2011 P 4/28/2012 Bp Steven Todd Ousley. m 6/25/1960 Ann H Jenney c 2.

JENNINGS, Albert Arthur (O) 8667 Shepard Rd # 204, Macedonia OH 44056 **R S Tim's Ch Macedonia OH 1988-** B Richmond VA 1951 s George & Betty. BS Virginia Commonwealth U 1973; MDiv EDS 1977. D 6/4/1977 Bp Robert Bruce Hall P 5/20/1978 Bp John Alfred Baden. m 8/14/1976 Gay Clark c 2. R Ch Of The Redeem Lorain OH 1980-1988; Asst Trin Ch Arlington VA 1977-1980; COM Dio Ohio Cleveland 2008-2011, Stndg Commitee 2001-2005, Congrl Developpment Comm. 1987-2002, Int Consult 1987-.

JENNINGS, Debora (Okla) 814 N Vinita Ave, Tahlequah OK 74464 **Vic S Basil's Epis Ch Tahlequah OK 2009-** B Morris IL 1954 d Kenneth & Helen. Shalem Inst; BS Arizona St U 1990; MDiv CDSP 1993; SWTS 1995. D 6/5/1993 P 12/18/1993 Bp Robert Reed Shahan. c 1. R H Trin Epis Ch Sunnyside WA 2006-2009; Dio Utah Salt Lake City UT 1998-2006; Vic S Jude's Ch Cedar City UT 1998; S Lk's Ch Prescott AZ 1994-1998; Dio Arizona Phoenix AZ 1993-1994. Auth, "poems/prayers," *Lifting Wmn Voices*, Ch Pub, 2009; Auth, "Aquinas & Eckhart S & Sinner?". Delta Kappa Gamms 1995; Kiwanis 1994; PEO 2009. Wmn Of Excellence Awd Aauw.

JENNINGS, Gay Clark (O) 168 Hiram College Dr, Sagamore Hills OH 44067 **Pres of HOD Dom And Frgn Mssy Soc- Epis Ch Cntr New York NY 2012-, VP 2012-; Pres of the HOD The Epis Ch 2012-; Assoc Dir CREDO Inst Inc. Memphis 2003-; TEC Cler Rep Angl Consultative Coun 2012-** B Syracuse NY 1951 d Robert & Nancy. BA Colg 1974; MDiv EDS 1977; D.D. EDS 2014; D.D. Colg 2015. D 4/22/1978 P 5/1/1979 Bp Ned Cole. m 8/14/1976 Albert Arthur Jennings c 2. Assoc Dir Credo Inst Inc. Memphis TN 2003-2012; Cn to the Ordnry Dio Ohio Cleveland 1986-1993; GC Dep 1986-2003; Int Cn Pstr Trin Cathd Cleveland OH 1986-1987; Int R S Ptr's Epis Ch Lakewood OH 1985-1986, Asst R 1980-1986; Stff Chapl Chld's Hosp Natl Med Ctr Washington DC 1978-1980; P Assoc The Ch of S Clem Alexandria VA 1978-1980; Mem of Exec Coun Exec Coun Appointees New York NY 2006-2012; Trst EDS Cambridge MA 2003-2008.

JENNINGS, James Courtney (HB) 5701 Snead Rd, Richmond VA 23224 **Nonpar 1970-** B 1940 D 6/24/1970 Bp William Foreman Creighton.

JENNINGS, Kelly Kathleen (Tex) **Mcilhany Par Charlottesville VA 2004-** B Evanston IL 1968 d Kirk & Kendall. BA U of Kansas 1991; MA Oxf GB 1994; MDiv Ya Berk 2001. D 1/14/2004 P 7/17/2004 Bp Peter J Lee. m 8/12/2000 Nathan Grady Woodruff. S Jas' Ch Taylor TX 2006-2012.

JENNINGS, Mary Kay (RG) Yankton Mission Cluster, 126 N Park NE, Wagner SD 57380 **Vic Loc Congregations Yankton Mssn Cluster SD 2007-** B Sioux Falls SD 1942 d Gordon & Genevieve. BS DSU 1974; MA U CO 1989; MDiv Sewanee: The U So, TS 2007. D 4/27/2007 P 12/21/2007 Bp Creighton Leland Robertson. c 1. R S Thos Epis Ch Sturgis SD 2010-2014; Vic Ch of the H Sprt Wagner SD 2007-2009; Dio So Dakota Pierre SD 2007-2009.

JENNINGS, Nathan Grady (Tex) PO Box 2247, Austin TX 78768 **Assoc Prof of Liturg and Angl Stds Epis TS Of The SW Austin TX 2009-** B Austin TX 1974 s Lloyd & Marsha. BA U of Texas 1997; MDiv Ya Berk 2001; PhD U of Virginia 2007. D 6/20/2009 P 2/9/2010 Bp C Andrew Doyle. m 8/12/2000 Kelly Kathleen Jennings c 2. Auth, "Theol as Ascetic Act," Ptr Lang, 2010.

JENNINGS, Richard Paul (NMich) 1015 Parnell St, Sault Sainte Marie MI 49783 **Died 10/7/2016** B Flint MI 1926 s Richard & Maybelle. BA U MI 1950; MDiv VTS 1953; MA Cntrl Michigan U 1970. D 6/27/1953 Bp Russell S Hubbard P 1/25/1954 Bp Richard Stanley Merrill Emrich. m 9/18/1948 Lillian Gill c 3. R S Paul's Epis Ch S Clair MI 1962-1969; P S Andr's Ch New Berlin NY 1960-1962; S Matt's Ch So New Berlin NY 1960-1962; Chapl USAF 1957-1960; D & R Chr Epis Ch E Tawas MI 1953-1957; Asst S Jn Au Sable MI 1953-1954.

JENNINGS, Robert Tallmadge (Ky) 2002 High Ridge Rd, Louisville KY 40207 B Evanston IL 1949 s William & Beverly. BA Cntr Coll 1971; MDiv VTS 1974. D 6/29/1975 Bp William Evan Sanders P 5/1/1976 Bp William F Gates

Jr. m 7/15/1972 Mary Jennings. R S Fran In The Fields Harrods Creek KY 1983-2014, Assoc 1978-1982; Asst S Mary's Cathd Memphis TN 1975-1978.

JENNINGS III, William Worth (NC) 702 Hillandale Ln, Garner NC 27529 B Wellsboro PA 1941 s Edwin & Ruth. MDiv PDS; BA U Pgh. D 5/26/1973 P 12/1/1973 Bp Robert Bracewell Appleyard. m 7/31/1976 Gaynell D Jennings. Vic S Chris's Epis Ch Garner NC 1986-2008; S Jas Epis Ch Pittsburgh PA 1985; Vic S Geo Pittsbuurgh PA 1973-1983; St Georges Ch Pittsburgh PA 1973-1983.

JENNINGS TODD, Margaret Herring (USC) 301 W Liberty St, Winnsboro SC 29180 **S Mich And All Ang' Columbia SC 2015-** B Greenwood SC 1949 d Walter & Wilmer. BA Col 1971; MEd Clemson U 1976; Cert Sch for Mnstry - EDUSC 2007. D 1/31/2009 Bp Dorsey Henderson. m 12/27/2007 William Lane Todd c 1. childelc@saintmichaelepiscopal.org

JENSEN, Anne Hislop (Cal) 865 Walavista Ave., Oakland CA 94610 B Fort Sill OK 1945 d George & Virginia. BA Stan 1967; MA Stan 1968; Untd TS 1985; MDiv Ya Berk 1988. D 6/23/1988 Bp Robert Marshall Anderson P 4/8/1989 Bp Clarence Nicholas Coleridge. m 6/22/1968 Douglas O Jensen c 3. Chr Ch Alameda CA 2012-2013, 2009-2010; S Paul's Ch Oakland CA 2007-2009; Int Trin Par Menlo Pk CA 2005-2007; Int Chr Ch Redding CT 2003-2005; S Andr's Ch New Haven CT 2003; Int S Andr's Ch Meriden CT 2001-2003; Int S Tim's Ch Fairfield CT 2000-2001; Int Trin Ch Portland CT 1999-2000; Epis Ch At Yale New Haven CT 1998-1999; Int Chapl Epis Ch Ya New Haven CT 1998-1999; P-in-c Ch Of The Gd Shpd Shelton CT 1997; Asst S Jn's Ch Bridgeport CT 1990-1996; Asst S Fran Ch Stamford CT 1989-1990; Asst Chr And H Trin Ch Westport CT 1988-1989.

JENSEN, Barbara Ann (NJ) 238 Main St, South River NJ 08882 **Chapl Cave Alternatives Cranford NJ 2004-** B York PA 1944 d Stowell & Olive. BA U of So Florida 1967; MPA Kean U 1991; D Formation Prog 2002. D 9/21/2002 Bp David Bruce Joslin. m 6/10/1972 Robert R Jensen c 2.

JENSEN, Jan D (Tex) 11 Sherwood St, Dayton TX 77535 B Salt Lake City UT 1953 s Darrel & Florence. Hochschule fuer Musik Vienna 1975; Ohr Somayach 1975; BA U of Utah 1976; MDiv Epis TS of the SW 2002. D 6/22/2002 Bp Claude Edward Payne P 7/16/2004 Bp Don Adger Wimberly. m 1/2/2013 Margaret Kasisi Gichanga c 2. Intercontinental Ch Soc Warwick 2010-2011; S Lk's Epis Hosp Houston TX 2008-2009; R S Steph's Ch Liberty TX 2004-2008; D/Assoc P Ch Of The Epiph Houston TX 2002-2004. "Lost Legions of Rome," Greystone Productions, 1996. Amer Soc of Composers, Authors, and Pub 1995.

JENSEN, Jonathon W (Pgh) 315 Shady Avenue, Pittsburgh PA 15206 **P Calv Ch Pittsburgh PA 2014-; Cn Theol Dio Kansas 2004-** B Greenville KY 1971 s Charles & Linda. BA Transylvania U 1993; MDiv VTS 1996. D 6/8/1996 Bp Don Adger Wimberly P 1/11/1997 Bp Ronald Hayward Haines. m 9/14/1996 Natalia V Jensen. Trin Cathd Little Rock AR 2009-2014; R Trin Ch Lawr KS 2002-2009; Cn Chr Ch Cathd New Orleans LA 1998-2002; Asst S Fran Ch Potomac MD 1996-1998. Ed, "The Catalyst". jjensen@trinitylittlerock.org

JENSEN, Julia Kooser (Ore) 2020 SW Knollcrest Dr., Portland OR 97225 **Dioc Coun Mem Dio Oregon Portland OR 2013-; D Epis Par Of S Jn The Bapt Portland OR 2007-** B Kansas City MO 1937 d Parke & Ruth. BA Colorado Coll 1959; BA Sch for Deacons 2002. D 6/1/2002 Bp William Edwin Swing. m 7/3/1965 William Charles Jensen c 3. D S Steph's Par Bel Tiburon CA 2005-2006; Dioc Coun Mem Dio California San Francisco CA 2004-2006; D Ch Of The Redeem San Rafael CA 2002-2005. Phi Beta Kappa 1959.

JENSEN, Patricia Ann (CFla) 9301 Hunters Park Way, Tampa FL 33647 **Nonpar 1998-** B Tampa FL 1948 d George & Betty. BS Florida St U 1971; Inst For Chr Stds 1977. D 6/9/1979 Bp William Hopkins Folwell. m 8/5/1972 Dan Jensen. D St Alb's of Auburndale Inc Auburndale FL 1991-1998; Asst S Jn Sarasota FL 1980-1986; D S Wlfd's Epis Ch Sarasota FL 1979-1980.

JENSON, Constance (WA) 17413 Audrey Road, Cobb Island MD 20625 B Evanston IL 1945 d Urban & Mary. BA U of La Verne 1978; MDiv VTS 2001. D 6/9/2001 P 12/14/2001 Bp Jane Hart Holmes Dixon. R Chr Ch Wm And Mary Newburg MD 2001-2011. charmolly@aol.com

JERAULD, Philip Eldredge (Mass) 1 Concord Coach Ln, Litchfield NH 03052 **Ret 1991-** B Barnstable MA 1926 s Bruce & Jenny. BA Bos 1949; MDiv CDSP 1954; STM Yale DS 1968; Naval Chapl Sch 1974. D 6/18/1954 P 1/9/1955 Bp William Jones Gordon Jr. m 6/19/1982 Nancy Jerauld c 2. S Andr's Ch Framingham MA 1985-1991; Int All SS' Epis Ch Belmont MA 1984-1985; Int Gr Epis Ch Medford MA 1983-1984; Int Msntry Haw 1981-1982; Off Of Bsh For ArmdF New York NY 1958-1981; Chapl USN 1958-1981; Vic S Mary's Ch Anchorage AK 1956-1958; Asst All SS' Epis Ch Anchorage AK 1954-1956. Navy Achvmnt Medal USN; Meritorious Serv Medal USN.

JERGENS, Andrew MacAoidh (SO) 2374 Madison Rd, Cincinnati OH 45208 **Ret 1996-** B Omaha NE 1935 s Alfred & Edna. BS Ya 1957; MBA U of Pennsylvania 1962. D 6/2/1973 P 12/22/1973 Bp John Mc Gill Krumm. m 2/21/1977 Linda Busken Jergens c 2. Int Chap Of The Nativ Cincinnati OH 1995-1996; Secy of Conv Dio Sthrn Ohio Cincinnati OH 1994-1995; S Thos Epis Ch Terrace Pk OH 1994; 1993-1995; Int S Andr's Epis Ch Cincinnati OH 1992-1993; Int Chr Ch - Glendale Cincinnati OH 1990-1991; Assoc The Ch of the Redeem Cincinnati OH 1979-1990, Serv 1973-1978. Assoc, OHC 1980. Spec Recognition Ohio St Senate 2007; Trst Emer Cincinnati Playhouse in the Pk 1975.

JERNAGAN III, Luke (Mo) 110 N Warson Rd, Saint Louis MO 63124 **R S Ptr's Epis Ch S Louis MO 2013-** B Pensacola FL 1980 s Louis & Betty. BS U of Alabama 2003; MDiv GTS 2006; STM GTS 2008. D 6/3/2006 P 5/12/2007 Bp Philip Menzie Duncan II. m 1/18/2008 Hope Virginia Welles c 3. Assoc R Chr Epis Ch Ponte Vedra FL 2008-2013; Asst Chr Ch Bronxville NY 2007-2008; Asst S Paul's Epis Ch Daphne AL 2006-2007. lukej@stpetersepiscopal.org

JEROME, Douglas Darrel (EO) 1332 SW 33rd St, Pendleton OR 97801 B Blackduck MN 1939 s Frederick & Phyllis. Sewanee: The U So, TS 1998. D 6/16/1999 Bp Rustin Ray Kimsey P 4/3/2002 Bp William O Gregg. m 9/30/1967 Phyllis J Jerome c 2. D Ch Of The Redeem Pendleton OR 1999-2002.

JEROME, Joseph (LI) 3956 44th St, Sunnyside NY 11104 **Vic Dio Long Island Garden City NY 2016-, 1991-1993** B Cazale HT 1957 s Thelamon & Maria. BS LIU 1987; MDiv SWTS 1991. D 6/15/1991 P 6/6/1992 Bp Orris George Walker Jr. R All SS' Epis Ch Long Island City NY 1997-2016; Int S Gabr's Ch Hollis NY 1996-1997; Int S Bon Epis Ch Lindenhurst NY 1995-1996; S Phil's Ch Brooklyn NY 1994-1995; Cur The Ch Of S Lk and S Matt Brooklyn NY 1991-1993. Alb Inst; Cmnty Bd Two; Kiwanis Intl Sunnyside; Sunnyside ChmbrCom.

JERSEY, Jean Staffeld (Vt) 32 Liberty St, Montpelier VT 05602 **P Assoc S Mich's Epis Ch Brattleboro VT 2004-, 1999-2000** B Detroit MI 1931 d John & Muriel. Bos 1951; BA Goddard Coll 1984; MDiv EDS 1987. D 6/11/1987 P 12/1/1987 Bp Daniel Lee Swenson. c 4. R Chr Ch Bethel VT 1987-1997. "Her Daughters Shall Rise Up: the Wmn Witnessing Cmnty at Lambeth 1988," Off of Wmn in Mssn & Mnstry, 1989.

JESION, Lawrence Michael (Ga) Christ Episcopal Church, 1904 Greene St, Augusta GA 30904 B Detroit MI 1962 s Kenneth & Mary. D 6/22/2013 P 5/13/2017 Bp Scott Anson Benhase. m 5/24/2003 Pamela Jesion c 2.

JESKE, Mark William (WMo) 4401 Wornall Rd, Kansas City MO 64111 **Chapl St Lk's Chap Kansas City MO 2016-** B Kansas City MO 1971 s Richard & Emily. Rec 11/4/2016 as Priest Bp Martin Scott Field. mjeske@saint-lukes.org

JESSE JR, Henry (Colo) 7787 E Gunnison Pl, Denver CO 80231 **Ret 1984-** B Mill Valley CA 1924 s Henry & Maria. BA U CA 1953; MDiv CDSP 1958; MEd WA SU 1971. D 9/20/1958 Bp Henry H Shires P 3/1/1959 Bp James Albert Pike. m 8/22/1988 Ann Loomis c 5. Assoc S Jn's Cathd Denver CO 1989-2001; Int Chap Of The H Comf New Orleans LA 1987-1988, Assoc R 1983-1986; Int Chr Ch Bay S Louis MS 1985-1986; P-in-c S Andr's Paradis Luling LA 1982-1983; Dioc Coun Dio Olympia Seattle 1974-1977, Chair - Coll Wk 1972-1975; R Chr Ch Seattle WA 1971-1979; R S Jas Pullman WA 1969-1971; Secy of the Convoc Dio Nevada Las Vegas 1964-1969; Vic S Steph's Epis Ch Reno NV 1962-1964; Assoc Vic S Andr's Ch Saratoga CA 1960-1962; Vic S Phil El Sobrante CA 1958-1960. Cmnty of Cross of Nails 1993-2001. Bd Dir Cmnty of the Cross of Nails 2002.

JESSETT, Frederick Edwin (Oly) 5309 S. Myrtle Lane, Spokane WA 99223 **Ret Dio Olympia 1998-** B Wenatchee WA 1934 s Thomas & Louise. BA U of Washington 1956; BD CDSP 1961; MS Montana St U 1968. D 6/7/1961 P 12/11/1961 Bp Conrad H Gesner. m 6/25/1960 Kristen Ann Olson c 4. Vic And Overlake Mssnr Gd Samar Epis Ch Sammamish WA 1989-1998; Vic S Paul's Ch Cheney WA 1984-1985; Archd for Prog and Mnstry Dio Spokane Spokane WA 1980-1989, Dep to GC 1981-1984; Vic S Tim Med Lake WA 1974-1985; Assoc P Rosebud Epis Mssn Mssn SD 1969-1973, Assoc 1963-1969; Chapl to Montana St U Dio Montana Helena MT 1965-1969; Assoc P Rosebud Epis Mssn Mssn SD US 1963-1965; Vic Trin Epis Ch Mssn SD 1961-1963; Dep to GC Dio So Dakota Pierre SD 1973. Auth, "Mountains Melt Away," Smashwords, 2014; Auth, "That's Gr?," Networking, Epis Ntwk for Stwdshp, 2010; Auth, "The Prchr's Gift," Ancient Paths, Skyler H. Burris, 2007; Auth, "(Three short stories)," On The Hm Front - So Dakota Stories, So Dakota Hmnts Coun, 2007; Auth, "Remembering Gr," Remembering Gr, FMP, 2006; Auth, "Gr Happens: Who's Rich," Networking, Epis Ntwk for Stwdshp, 2003; Auth, "(Three short stories)," Country Congregations: So Dakota Stories, So Dakota Humanties Coun, 2002; Auth, "Drummer Loves Dancer," New Voices III, Goodfellow Press, 2000; Auth, "Recalling A Long Ago Prank," Seattle Times, Seattle Times Inc, 2000; Auth, "Gr Happens monthly column," Epis Voice, So Dakota Epis ChurchNews and Inland Epis, Var Dioc Newspapers, 1999; Auth, "The Par Mnstry Of Priests And Deacons," Liturg Volume 21 #6, Liturg Conf, 1976; Co-Auth w/ Kristen Jessett, "12 Rules For Marital Fighting," 12 Rules for Marital Fighting, FMP, 1974; Auth, "Chanukah," Simple Gifts Volume 2, Liturg Conf, 1974; Auth, "Chanukah," Liturg Volume 17 #8, Liturg Conf, 1972; Co-Auth w/ Kristen Jessett, "Sioux Farming Today," The Indn Hist, The Amer Indn Hist Soc, 1970. ACLU 2002; Amnesty Intl 1981; Cler Assn Of The Dio Olympia 1991; Fllshp Of Merry Christians 1996; Kiwanis Intl 1993; Museum of Hist and Industry 2000; Pacific NW Writers Assn 1998; The Interfaith Allnce 2000. fredjessett@comcast.net

JESSUP, Dorothy Margaret Paul (Pa) 278 Friendship Dr, Paoli PA 19301 B Philadelphia PA 1929 d Samuel & Dorothy. Luth TS 1987. D 6/20/1987 Bp Allen Lyman Bartlett Jr. c 3. D Ch Of The Gd Samar Paoli PA 1987-1993; Liturg & Mus Com. Bd Trst Dss Ret Fund Soc.

JESSUP, Elaine Anderson (SeFla) 464 NE 16th St, Miami FL 33132 **D Trin Cathd Miami FL 2008-** B Miami FL 1945 d Perry & Ethelyn. BS Indiana U 1982; MS Nova SE U 1989; EdS Nova SE U 1994. D 12/22/2007 Bp Leo Frade. c 3.

JESTER, Pamela Jean (Cal) 911 Dowling Blvd, San Leandro CA 94577 **All SS Epis Ch San Leandro CA 2015-** B Eugene OR 1949 d Curtis & Jean. BS U of Oregon 1971; MPA Syr 1972; JD/MBA Golden Gate U 1978; BDS Epis Sch for Deacons 2014. D 6/13/2015 Bp Marc Handley Andrus. m 10/18/2013 Hilary Dreyfuss.

JETT, Charles D (SC) 107 Sea Lavender Ln, Summerville SC 29486 **D S Thos Epis Ch N Charleston SC 2013-** B Milledgeville GA 1938 s William & Estelle. Coll of Charleston; BA U of So Carolina 1961; BA Sch for Deacons 1994. D 6/3/1995 Bp William Edwin Swing. m 8/15/1959 Margaret Jane Adams c 2. D S Steph's Epis Ch Spokane WA 1999-2014; D S Steph's Epis Ch Charleston SC 1997-1999; Emm Ch Kellogg ID 1996-1999; D H Trin Epis Ch Wallace ID 1996-1999; D S Mich And All Ang Concord CA 1995-1996; Dioc Coun Dio Spokane Spokane WA 2002-2006.

JETT, Mary J (NY) Church of St Mary the Virgin, 145 W 46th St, New York NY 10036 **Cathd Of St Jn The Div New York NY 2016-** B Urbana IL 1981 PhD UTS; MDiv GTS 2013; STM GTS 2013. D 2/6/2012 P 10/3/2012 Bp Charles Franklin Brookhart Jr. Dio New York New York NY 2015-2016; Ch Of The Trsfg New York NY 2015; Ch Of S Mary The Vrgn New York NY 2013-2014; S Jas Ch Bozeman MT 2007-2010.

JEULAND, Eric Vincent (Ct) 25 Church St, Shelton CT 06484 B Chicago IL 1981 s Abel & Maretta. BA U Chi 2003; Dip Ang Stud Ya Berk 2008; MDiv Yale DS 2008. D 6/12/2010 Bp Ian Theodore Douglas P 6/11/2011 Bp James Elliot Curry. m 6/17/2006 Jane Catherine Eppley Jeuland. Dio Connecticut Meriden CT 2010-2011; S Paul's Epis Ch Shelton CT 2010.

JEULAND, Jane Catherine Eppley (Ct) 300 Main St, Wethersfield CT 06109 B New York NY 1979 d Richard & Carole. BA Harv 2003; MDiv Ya Berk 2009. D 6/12/2010 P 12/18/2010 Bp Ian Theodore Douglas. m 6/17/2006 Eric Vincent Jeuland. Trin Ch Wethersfield CT 2010-2011.

JEVNE, Lucretia Ann (NCal) 120 Loraine Ct, Vacaville CA 95688 **Bd Pres Epis Cmnty Serv of Nthrn California 2013-; P S Brigid's Epis Ch Rio Vista CA 2013-; Bd Mem and Secy Interfaith Coun of Solano Cnty Fairfield CA 2006-; Chair, Millennium Dvlpmt Goals Com The Epis Dio Nthrn California Sacramento CA 2010-, Mem, Dioc Coun 2008-, Pres, Bd Epis Cmnty Serv 2006-2009** B Norwalk CT 1946 d Henry & Helen. BA Hobart and Wm Smith Colleges 1968; MDiv CDSP 1996. D 8/24/1996 Bp Jeffery William Rowthorn P 6/20/1997 Bp Robert Louis Ladehoff. m 11/20/1996 Walter E Phelps. Bd Mem St. Lk's Preschool Calistoga CA 2007-2012; P-in-c S Lk's Mssn Calistoga CA 2007-2011; Int Trin Ch Sonoma CA 2005-2007; Int S Clem's Ch Rancho Cordova CA 2004-2005; Int Gr Epis Ch Fairfield CA 2003-2004; Asst Epiph Epis Ch Vacaville CA 2000-2002; R S Alb's Epis Ch Tillamook OR 1996-1999. Assoc Of The Ord Of S Lk 2002; Cler Assn Of Nthrn California 2001-2004; Oregon Cler Assosciation 1997-1998.

JEW, Cynthia Lynne (Los) Trinity Episcopal Church, 600 Saratoga, Fillmore CA 93016 **S Paul's Epis Ch Santa Paula CA 2016-; Trin Par Fillmore CA 2011-; Prof California Luth U 2000-** B Denver CO 1960 d James & Dorie. ETSBH; MA U CO 1986; PhD U Denv 1991. D 7/9/2010 P 2/12/2011 Bp Joseph Jon Bruno. c 2. S Steph's Epis Ch Valencia CA 2010-2011. stpaulschurchsp@aol.com

JEWELL, Kenneth Arthur (Nev) 732 Aesop Dr, Spring Creek NV 89815 B Flint MI 1950 s Kenneth & Elizabeth. BS U of Wisconsin 1973. D 7/3/2009 Bp Dan Thomas Edwards. m 12/31/2005 Donna Selleck c 3. Vocational D S Paul's Epis Ch Elko NV 2009-2016.

JEWETT, Ethan A (Chi) 2013 Appletree St, Philadelphia PA 19103 **Gr Ch Chicago IL 2015-** B Kalamazoo MI 1971 s Ronald & Helen. BA Kalamazoo Coll 1993; MA U Chi 1995; MDiv Chicago TS 2012; Dplma in Angl Stds SWTS 2012. D 2/4/2012 Bp Jeff Lee P 8/4/2012 Bp Rodney Rae Michel. S Clements Ch Philadelphia PA 2012-2013. ethanajewett@gmail.com

JEWISS, Anthony Harrison (Los) 1290 Kent Street, Brooklyn NY 11222 B Dorking UK 1939 s Stanley & Patricia. UE Sacr Heart Coll Auckland Nz 1957; ETSBH 1990; BA Pacific Wstrn U 1992; MDiv VTS 1992. D 6/13/1992 Bp Chester Lovelle Talton P 1/9/1993 Bp Frederick Houk Borsch. Epis Ch Cntr New York NY 1999-2007; Chapl To Bp Of Los Dio Los Angeles Los Angeles CA 1992-1999.

JEWSON, Alfred Joseph (WMo) 7511 Rannells Ave, Saint Louis MO 63143 **Cert in Int Mnstry Cler Ldrshp Inst 2010-** B Saint Louis MO 1943 s Alfred & Lillian. BA Cardinal Glennon Coll 1965; Kenrick-Glennon Sem 1967; MA S Louis U DS S Louis MO 1970. Rec 12/3/1994 Bp John Clark Buchanan. m 3/25/1988 Dayna Jewson c 1. Int R Chr Ch Cape Girardeau MO 2013-2014; R Chr Ch Warrensburg MO 2001-2010; Vic Ch Of The Gd Shpd Springfield MO 1998-2001; Assoc R S Andr's Ch Kansas City MO 1996-1998; Assoc Prof St. Mary's Jr Coll O'Fallon Missouri 1970-1972; P RC Ch 1968-1974; Mem of COM Dio W Missouri Kansas City MO 2008-2012, Dn of Sthrn Dnry 2000-2008. padreal@charter.net

JEWSON, Dayna (Mo) 7511 Rannells Ave, Saint Louis MO 63143 **D All SS Epis Ch Kansas City MO 2012-** B Los Angeles CA 1953 d Roderic & Nancy. RN S Lukes Hosp Sch of Nrsng Webster U 1983; W Missouri Sch for Mnstry 2003. D 2/7/2004 Bp Barry Howe. m 3/25/1988 Alfred Joseph Jewson c 2. D Chr Ch Warrensburg MO 2004-2010. NAAD 2004.

JILLARD, Christina Liggitt (Oly) Saint Margaret's Episcopal Church, 4228 Factoria Blvd SE, Bellevue WA 98006 **R S Marg's Epis Ch Bellevue WA 2008-** B Grove City PA 1952 d Oliver & Mary. BA Grove City Coll 1974; MA Ohio U 1976; MLS U Pgh 1977; MDiv GTS 2001. D 6/8/2001 P 12/8/2001 Bp Michael Whittington Creighton. m 6/2/1989 William Richard Jillard c 2. Chapl, on-call Altoona Reg Med Cntr Altoona PA 2004-2008; R S Lk's Epis Ch Altoona PA 2001-2008. cjillard@saintmargarets.org

JIM, Rosella A (NAM) Po Box 5854, Farmington NM 87499 **All SS Farmington NM 2005-** B Farmington NM 1951 d Allen & Elizabeth. AA San Juan Coll 1980; San Juan Coll 1981. D 6/12/2005 Bp Mark Lawrence Macdonald P 12/13/2005 Bp Rustin Ray Kimsey. m 7/1/1971 Tommy Jim c 4. San Juan Mssn Farmington NM 2005-2014; Navajoland Area Mssn Farmington NM 1981-2005.

JIMENEZ, Darla Sue (NwT) B Pontiac MI 1960 d Carl & Treva. D 12/3/2005 P 7/1/2006 Bp C Wallis Ohl. m 3/23/1996 Jose Jimenez.

JIMENEZ, Juan (Los) 311 W South St, Anaheim CA 92805 B Camaguey CU 1945 s Juan & Mirta. BA K SU 1970; MDiv Epis TS of the SW 1988. D 3/14/1987 Bp James Daniel Warner P 3/25/1988 Bp Anselmo Carral-Solar. m 11/20/1983 Janice K Jimenez c 3. R Iglesia Epis De Todos Los Santos Miami FL 1997-2001; S Matt's Cathd Dallas TX 1990-1997; El Buen Samaritano Austin TX 1988-1990; Vic Iglesia San Francisco de Asis Austin TX 1988-1990; The Great Cmsn Fndt Houston TX 1988-1990. padrejuan@gmail.com

JIMENEZ-IRIZARRY, Edwin (Ct) Urb. El Vedado, Calle 12 de Octubre #428-A, San Juan PR 00918 **Serv St. Mary Magd Adv Epis Ch Puerta Rico 1989-** B 1946 s Heriberto & Gladys. BA Universidad Interamericana De Puerto Rico 1968; MDiv ETSC 1971; MS Psychol Inst PR 1976. Trans 5/11/1981 Bp Clarence Nicholas Coleridge. m 2/16/1980 Celida Jimenez c 4. Dio Puerto Rico Trujillo Alto PR 2004-2008, 1990-2003; Hisp Hartford Mssnr 1981-1988; Dio Connecticut Meriden CT 1981-1987.

JIMENEZ-MESENBRING, Maria Jesus (Oly) 2020 E. Terrace St., Seattle WA 98122 **Spanish Tchr, Dioc TS Dio Olympia Seattle 2008-** B Burgos Castilla Spain 1954 d Rafael & Carmen. BA U of Madrid; MDiv NYTS 1992. D 2/20/1999 Bp Calvin Onderdonk Schofield Jr. m 6/1/1991 David Gary Mesenbring c 2. All SS Prot Epis Ch Ft Lauderdale FL 2004-2006; D S Steph's Ch Coconut Grove Miami FL 2000-2004; Port Chapl SCI Ft Lauderdale FL 1988-2006.

JINETE, Alvaro E (Chi) 3241 Calwagner St, Franklin Park IL 60131 B Manati CO 1951 s Alfredo & Ramona. MA McCormick TS 1987. Rec 4/1/1987 as Deacon Bp James Winchester Montgomery. m 2/23/1985 Erlina Jinete c 2. Dio Chicago Chicago IL 1989-1999; San Pedro Mssn Franklin Pk IL 1987-2006.

JIZMAGIAN, Mary Gibson (Cal) 2570 Chestnut St, San Francisco CA 94123 **The Epis Ch Of S Mary The Vrgn San Francisco CA 1987-** B Kingston Jamaica West Indies 1949 d James & Myrtis. BA Austin Coll 1970; MDiv CDSP 1985. D 6/8/1985 P 6/1/1986 Bp William Edwin Swing. m 1/15/1983 George J Jizmagian c 2. Chapl Presidio Gates Apartments 1986-2001; Asst S Jas Epis Ch San Francisco CA 1985-1987.

JOBES, Amy Louise Carle (WTenn) 2 Beverly Commons Dr, Beverly MA 01915 **Died 8/23/2015** B Birmingham AL 1936 d Howard & Louise. BA St Johns Coll Annapolis MD 1959; MS U of Memphis 1984; Sewanee: The U So, TS 1992. D 11/19/1995 P 6/1/1996 Bp Larry Maze. m 6/3/1961 James W Jobes Jr c 2. Asst (Ret.) Vol S Ptr's Ch Beverly MA 2004-2015; Ch Of The H Comm Memphis TN 2001-2002; S Mary's Epis Ch Monticello AR 2000-2002; Mssnr Chapl Ch Of The Gd Shpd Little Rock AR 2000-2001; Dioc Mssnr S Lk's Epis Ch N Little Rock AR 1998-2000, Cur 1996-1997; Ch Of The H Cross W Memphis AR 1996; S Paul's Ch Mc Gehee AR 2000-2002.

JODKO, Juliusz Siegmond (Ct) St. Michael's Parish, 210 Church St, Naugatuck CT 06770 **P-in-c S Mich's Ch Naugatuck CT 2012-** B Heerlen Netherlands 1951 s Piotr & Genevieve. BA Leh 1973; MBA U of Scranton 1990; MDiv GTS 2010. D 6/11/2011 Bp Laura Ahrens P 12/17/2011 Bp Ian Theodore Douglas. m 6/15/1974 Anne Frost Wiegand c 2. Asst to the R S Barn Epis Ch Greenwich CT 2011-2012; Assoc Par of St Paul's Ch Norwalk Norwalk CT 2010-2011. julesjodko@hotmail.com

JOFFRION JR, Felix Hughes (Ala) 1180 11th Ave S, Birmingham AL 35205 **Dio Pstr Counslg Ctr Birmingham AL 1993-** B Vicksburg MS 1938 s Felix & Kathleen. BA U of Alabama 1961; MDiv VTS 1967; ThM Duke 1971; ThD Candler TS Emory U 1982. D 6/10/1967 P 5/1/1968 Bp George Mosley Murray. m 7/13/1968 Isabelle Joffrion c 2. Dio Alabama Birmingham 1978-2010, Pstr Counslr 1967-1968; 1974-1978; Cur All SS Epis Ch Birmingham AL 1969-1971; Asst S Mk's Ch Washington DC 1968-1969. Diplomate AAPC; Lic Profsnl Counslr.

JOHANNS, Karen (Mich) 1651 Maplewood St, Sylvan Lake MI 48320 **Died 8/31/2015** B Jersey City NJ 1959 d Henry & Blanche. BA Mt Holyoke Coll 2003; MDiv CDSP 2006. D 6/3/2006 Bp William Edwin Swing P 1/26/2007 Bp Jerry Alban Lamb. R All SS Epis Ch Pontiac MI 2008-2014; Assoc Trin Epis Ch

Reno NV 2006-2008; COM Dio Michigan Detroit MI 2009-2012. Soc of Cath Priests 2009.

JOHANNSEN, Carole (NY) 8 Pine Road, Bedford Hills NY 10507 **Hosp Chapl Phelps Memi Hosp Cntr Sleepy Hollow NY 2002**- B New York NY 1942 d Christian & Mary. Doctor of Mnstry NYTS; AA Dn Coll 1961; BA Wstrn Connecticut St U 1983; MDiv Yale DS 1986. D 6/9/1990 Bp Arthur Edward Walmsley P 4/14/1991 Bp Jeffery William Rowthorn. c 2. R S Lk's Ch Katonah NY 1998-2001; Int Trin Epis Ch Hartford CT 1997-1998; Prince Of Peace Luth Ch Brookfield CT 1996-1997; Int Prince-Peace Luth 1996-1997; Int S Ptr's Epis Ch Monroe CT 1995-1996; S Matt's Epis Ch Wilton CT 1994; Trin Ch Newtown CT 1993; Asst for CE Chr And H Trin Ch Westport CT 1991-1993; Asst S Barn Epis Ch Greenwich CT 1990-1991; Chair, Nwspr Ed Advsry Comm. Dio New York New York NY 1999-2002; Exam Chap Dio Connecticut Meriden CT 1992-1997. Auth, "Epiphanies of Sr Sprtlty," *Reflections*, Yale DS, 2013. Assn for Psychol Type 1998-2010; Assn of Profsnl Chapl 2002; Ord of S Helena (Assoc) 1991. Awd of Recognition Amer Muslim Wmn Assn 2011.

JOHANNSON, Johanna-Karen (NY) PO Box 1412, Bucksport ME 04416 **P-in-c S Dunst's Ch Ellsworth ME 2013**- B Augusta ME 1950 d Albert & Millicent. BS SUNY 1984; MDiv GTS 1987. D 6/13/1987 Bp Paul Moore Jr P 1/10/1988 Bp Alexander D Stewart. Dio New York New York NY 1997-2011; H Trin Epis Ch Inwood New York NY 1997-2011, Vic 1991-1996; The Ch Of The Epiph New York NY 1987-1990. Wmn Helping Wmn Soroptomists's Intl 2002; Cmnty Action Hero Awd Upper Manhattan Fresh Yth Initiatives 2000. abishag51@yahoo.com

JOHANSEN, Paul Charles (SwFla) 504 3rd St Nw, New Philadelphia OH 44663 **Ret 1996**- B Cambridge MA 1933 s Martin & Beth. BEd U of Miami 1961; STB Ya Berk 1964; Command and Gnrl Stff Coll 1979; US Army Chapl Cntr and Sch 1989. D 6/24/1964 Bp William Loftin Hargrave P 12/28/1964 Bp James Loughlin Duncan. m 9/7/1991 Barbara J Johansen c 3. P-in-c Trin Ch New Phila OH 2001-2014; P-in-c S Ptr's Ch Gallipolis OH 1998-2001; Serv (Dio Limerick and Killawe) Ch of Ireland 1996-1998; R S Steph's Ch New Prt Rchy FL 1985-1995; R S Mary's Ch Dade City FL 1982-1985; R S Bede's Ch St. Petersburg FL 1969-1982; Vic St Cathr of Alexandria Epis Ch Temple Terrace FL 1966-1969; Chapl Florida Army NG 1965-2013; Cur Cathd Ch Of S Ptr St. Petersburg FL 1964-1966; Dioc Coun Dio SW Florida Parrish FL 1975-1980. Auth, "The Gift of Ought to Be," *Tampa Bay mag*, 1966.

JOHANSON, Norman Lee (Neb) 116 S Sunset Pl, Monrovia CA 91016 B Colusa CA 1944 s Earl & Anna. D 11/8/1985 Bp James Daniel Warner. m 7/15/1967 Patricia Carol Johanson c 3. Non-par.

JOHANSSEN, John (SO) 9429 Lighthouse Cut, Thornville OH 43076 **Adj Fac Bex Sem 2005-; R St. Alb's Epis Ch OH 2004**- B Lafayette IN 1946 s John & Ruth. BS OH SU 1970; MA OH SU 1971; JD U of Toledo 1975; MDiv VTS 1990. D 6/9/1990 P 2/23/1991 Bp James Russell Moodey. m 5/12/1984 Pamela Knowlton c 2. Cn Dio Sthrn Ohio Cincinnati OH 2008-2011; R S Alb's Epis Ch Of Bexley Columbus OH 2004-2008; Treas Bex Sem 2004-2006; Dio Colorado Denver CO 2001-2003; R Gd Shpd Epis Ch Centennial CO 1996-2003; R Gr Epis Ch Menomonie WI 1991-1996; Asst S Paul's Ch Akron OH 1990-1991; Ecum Cmsn Dio Eau Claire Eau Claire WI 1991-1996.

JOHN, James Howard (Kan) 7603 E Morris St, Wichita KS 67207 **Asst S Alb 1982**- B Chanute KS 1944 s James & Doris. BBA Wichita St U 1973. D 4/30/1982 Bp Richard Frank Grein. m 4/14/1966 Marilyn Kay Miller c 2.

JOHN, Rene (NJ) 16 Fanning Way, Pennington NJ 08534 **Dn Trin Cathd Trenton NJ 2007**- B San Fernando TT 1960 s George & Phyllis. STM GTS; LTh Codrington Coll 1984. Trans 1/1/1991 Bp Orris George Walker Jr. m 6/16/1984 Andrea John c 3. R Ch Of S Thos Brooklyn NY 1994-2006; Assoc R S Paul's Ch Brooklyn NY 1990-1994; S Paul's Ch-In-The-Vill Brooklyn NY 1990-1994; Dio Long Island NY; Bdgt Dept Dio Long Island Garden City NY, Dioc Revs Com. Bro of S Andr 1997. Cler Renwl Sabbatical Lily Endwmt 2005; Pstr of the Year CWU 1999.

JOHNS, Ernest William (SwFla) 20024 Behan Ct, Port Charlotte FL 33952 **Ret 1996-; Ret 1995**- B Sault Saint Marie MI 1932 s Ernest & Jean. BA Wag 1953; STM Drew U 1956; GTS 1960; Coll of Preachers 1966; Coll of Preachers 1971; Coll of Preachers 1987. D 1/15/1960 P 10/12/1960 Bp Charles Francis Boynton. m 6/24/1956 Beverly Johns c 2. S Edm's Epis Ch Arcadia FL 1993-1995; R S Steph's Epis Ch Forest VA 1989-1993; R The Memi Ch Of The Prince Of Peace Gettysburg PA 1982-1989; R S Jas' Ch Springfield MO 1979-1982; Chr Ch Of Ramapo Suffern NY 1968-1979; R S Andr's Ch Brewster NY 1961-1968; Evang Com Dio SW Virginia Roanoke VA 1989-1993; BEC Dio Virginia Richmond VA 1987-1989; Bd Sch Chr Stds Dio Cntrl Pennsylvania Harrisburg PA 1983-1987; COM Dio W Missouri Kansas City MO 1980-1982; Trst Cathd Of St Jn The Div New York NY 1971-1976; Dioc Coun Dio New York New York NY 1968-1971. Auth, *Intro to the Epis Ch: Pstr Perspective*. Int Minstry Ntwk 1997-2004.

JOHNS, Leila Margaret (NMich) 416 S 28th St, Escanaba MI 49829 **Died 3/18/2016** B Sale VIC AU 1919 d Henry & Mary. Cert Melbourne Teachers Coll 1939. D 2/21/1993 Bp Thomas Kreider Ray. m 7/6/1944 Benjamin Hartley Johns. ECW 2016.

JOHNS, Martha (Los) 30382 Via Con Dios, Rancho Santa Margarita CA 92688 **Trin Cathd Phoenix AZ 2016-; Bd Mem The Gooden Cntr Pasadena CA 2013**- B Des Moines IA 1947 d Dale & Ruth. BA U of Wisconsin 1969; MBA U Chi 1973; MDiv Fuller TS 2014. D 6/7/2014 P 1/17/2015 Bp Joseph Jon Bruno. c 2. martha@trinitycathedral.com

JOHNS III, Norman S (Oly) 5787 Lenea Dr Nw, Bremerton WA 98312 **1983**- B Philadelphia PA 1944 s Norman & Marianne. BA U of Maryland 1974; MDiv GTS 1977. D 5/13/1978 Bp William Foreman Creighton P 5/13/1978 Bp John Thomas Walker. m 1/17/1964 Eileen E B Johns c 2. Dio Olympia Seattle 2006; Epis Ch Of The Trsfg Mesa AZ 2002-2006; Vic S Jos And S Jn Ch Lakewood WA 1998-2006; S Dav Emm Epis Ch Shoreline WA 1993-1994; S Paul's Ch Seattle WA 1992-1993; St Steph's Epis Ch Oak Harbor WA 1991-1992; St Bede Epis Ch Port Orchard WA 1988-1989; S Paul's Epis Ch Bremerton WA 1981-1987; R Epis Ch Of King Geo VA 1980-1981; The Epis Ch-King Geo Co King Geo VA 1980-1981; Chair - Dioc Hunger Ctte 1979-1982; Asst R Ch Of The H Comf Vienna VA 1977-1980. Auth, "Lord Of Morning," *Lord Of Light*. Ord Of S Lk.

JOHNS, Richard Gray (Los) 1199 Marinaside Crescent, Apt. 1701, Vancouver BC V6Z 2Y2 Canada **Ret 1996**- B Seattle WA 1928 s Ernest & Mary. BA Whitman Coll 1949; PhD U CA 1952; MDiv CDSP 1955. D 6/12/1955 P 12/17/1955 Bp Karl M Block. c 4. Gnrl Secy Conf on the Rel Life 1991-1996; Cmnty Of The Sis Of The Ch Oakville ON 1991-1995; Serv Ch of Can 1972-1991; R San Jorge in Guatemala 1961-1964; R Todos los Santos in Managua Nicaragua 1958-1961; R Gr Ch S Helena CA 1956-1958; Vic S Barth's Epis Ch Livermore CA 1955-1956. Auth, *The Amer's: How Many Worlds?*.

JOHNSON, Alston Boyd (WLa) 140 Devereaux Dr, Madison MS 39110 **P S Mk's Cathd Shreveport LA 2012**- B Memphis TN 1968 s Cleveland & Fay. BA U of Vermont 1991; MDiv Sewanee: The U So, TS 1998. D 5/27/1998 P 1/1/1999 Bp Alfred Marble Jr. m 4/9/1994 Elizabeth J Johnson c 3. The Chap Of The Cross Madison MS 2005-2012; S Andr's Cathd Jackson MS 2003-2005; Calv Epis Ch Cleveland MS 2002-2003; Cur Ch Of the Nativ Greenwood MS 1999-2002.

JOHNSON JR, Alvin Carl (Chi) 212 Biltmore Dr, N Barrington IL 60010 **Cn Dio NW Pennsylvania Erie PA 2014-; Adj Fac Seabury Wstrn TS 2003-; Assoc Seabury Inst 1994**- B Chicago IL 1953 s Eileen. BS U of Tulsa 1975; MDiv SWTS 1979; DMin SWTS 1998. D 6/9/1979 Bp Quintin Ebenezer Primo Jr P 12/1/1979 Bp James Winchester Montgomery. m 1/3/1976 Victoria Johnson c 4. VTS Alexandria VA 2010; R S Mich's Ch Barrington IL 1990-2010; Field Assoc Natl Off of Cong Dvlpmt 1984-1994; Ch Of The Incarn Bloomingdale IL 1984-1990; Dio Chicago Chicago IL 1981-1984; Cur S Dav's Ch Glenview IL 1979-1981. Auth, *Ldrshp mag*. ajohnson@dionwpa.org

JOHNSON, Andrew (Roch) 1957 Five Mile Line Rd., Penfield NY 14526 B Rochester NY 1938 s Byron & Charlotte. BA U Roch 1962; Diac Stds Bexley Inst 2008. D 5/2/2009 Bp Prince Grenville Singh. m 11/2/1984 Linda D Johnson c 4.

JOHNSON, Andy (Dal) Saint John's Episcopal Church, 848 Harter Rd, Dallas TX 75218 **S Jn's Epis Ch Dallas TX 2016**- B Louisville, KY 1975 s Ewell & Linda. Bachelor Georgia Inst of Tech 1999; Mstr of Theol Dallas TS 2013. D 4/30/2016 Bp Paul Emil Lambert P 12/3/2016 Bp George Robinson Sumner Jr. m 8/7/2004 Kristyn Elizabeth Spearman. Chapl Res UT SW Med Cntr Dallas TX 2015-2016. Evang Theol Soc 2013. ajohnson@stjohnsepiscopal.org

JOHNSON, Ann Elizabeth Simmons (Az) PO Box 40, 13803 North Watts Lane, Fort Thomas AZ 85536 B Decatur GA 1939 d Jesse & Sara. BS Auburn U 1962; Florida St U 1965; MA Cntrl Michigan U 1984. D 10/5/2002 Bp Robert Reed Shahan. m 8/25/1962 James Donaldson Johnson c 2. R All SS Epis Ch Safford AZ 2002-2014. Amer Soc For Clincl Laboratory Scientists 1976.

JOHNSON, Ann L (Ct) 1105 Quarrier St, Charleston WV 25301 **S Mary's Epis Ch Manchester CT 2017-; R Trin Ch Torrington CT 2013**- B Cambridge MA 1963 BS U of Rhode Island. D 12/22/2001 Bp Wendell Nathaniel Gibbs Jr P 3/21/2003 Bp Chilton Richardson Knudsen. c 2. S Mk's Epis Ch St Albans WV 2012-2013; Assoc S Jn's Epis Ch Charleston WV 2009-2012; R S Phil's Ch Wiscasset ME 2003-2009.

JOHNSON, Ann Ruth (Az) 701 North Apollo Way, Flagstaff AZ 86001 B Corsicana TX 1942 d James & Eliza. BS U of Texas 1965; MA Texas A&M U 1979; Angl TS 1996; Cert Theol Stud Epis TS of the SW 2006. D 7/29/2006 P 2/3/2007 Bp Kirk Stevan Smith. c 3. Vic Dio Arizona Phoenix AZ 2006-2014; Vic St Johns Epis-Luth Ch Williams AZ 2006-2011.

JOHNSON, Arthur Everitt (Miss) 1052 Deer Dr, Bay Saint Louis MS 39520 **P S Paul's Epis Ch Picayune MS 2012**- B San Antonio TX 1943 s Woodrow & Hattie. BS Trin U San Antonio 1966; MDiv Sewanee: The U So, TS 1972; DMin Sewanee: The U So, TS 1989. D 6/11/1972 Bp Harold Cornelius Gosnell P 12/21/1972 Bp Richard Earl Dicus. m 6/1/1985 Gail H Johnson c 2. Chr Ch Bay S Louis MS 1985-2003; Dio Atlanta 1982-1985; Dn Convoc Dio Atlanta 1982-1985; S Greg The Great Athens GA 1981-1985; Emm Epis Ch Athens GA 1975-1981; Asst The Ch Of The Gd Shpd Augusta GA 1973-1975; Chapl Georgia Reg Hosp 1972-1973. Auth, "Why Bother w Adv," *Angl Dig*, Adv, 1992; Auth, "January Eagerness (poem)," Journ of Sch Theol, 1981; Auth, "Greening

435

J

of Dr Mart Luther & the Conversion of Chas A Reich," Journ of Sch Theol, 1972.

✠ **JOHNSON, The Rt Rev Bob** (WNC) 21 Lincolnshire Loop, Asheville NC 28803 **Ret Bp of WNC Dio Wstrn No Carolina Asheville NC 2005-, Bp 1989-2004** B Jacksonville FL 1934 s William & Edith. BSBA U of Florida 1956; MDiv VTS 1963. D 6/24/1963 P 3/26/1964 Bp Edward Hamilton West Con 3/11/1989 for WNC. m 8/25/1962 Julie McMaster c 2. R H Innoc Ch Atlanta GA 1972-1989; Cn Pstr S Jn's Cathd Jacksonville FL 1968-1972; P-in-c S Mart's-in-the-Highlands Jacksonville FL 1963-1968; P-in-c Ch Of Our Sav Jacksonville FL 1963-1965; S Geo Epis Ch Jacksonville FL 1963-1965; Chair, Ch Deploy Bd Dom And Frgn Mssy Soc- Epis Ch Cntr New York NY 1994-1997, HOB Pstr Dvlpmt Com 1991-2005, GBEC 1988-1991; Stndg Cmsn on Structure of the Ch Epis Ch Cntr New York NY 1994-1997; Bd Rgnts Sewanee U So TS Sewanee TN 1993-1999; Pres, Alum Coun VTS Alexandria VA 1981-1988; GC Dep Dio Atlanta Atlanta GA 1976-1988, Chair COM Cler Dvlpmt 1976-1983, Chair Stwdshp Dept 1973-1975; Pres Northside Suburban Mnstrl Associ Atlanta GA 1975-1976. DD U So TS 1990; DD VTS 1990.

JOHNSON, Brian David (Los) 1836 N Mira Loma Way, Palm Springs CA 92262 B Albany NY 1960 s Robert & Mary. RN Memi Sch Nrsng 1980; BS Emml 1984; PhD California Sch of Profsnl Psychol 1989; MDiv CDSP 1992. D 6/27/1992 P 12/20/1992 Bp Gethin Benwil Hughes. Int H Nativ Epis Ch Westchester CA 2003-2004; P-in-c S Mart's Epis Ch Compton CA 1997-2000; P H Faith Par Inglewood CA 1995-1996; D Gr Cathd San Francisco CA 1992-1993.

JOHNSON, Broaddus (NY) 2336 Meadow Rdg, Redding CT 06896 **Died 1/26/2016** B Springfield MA 1922 s Andrew & Mildred. BA Ya 1948. D 5/30/1992 Bp Richard Frank Grein. m 8/20/1949 Kate deForest Johnson c 3. D S Matt's Ch Bedford NY 1992-2016.

JOHNSON, Candine E (Va) **S Jn's Epis Ch Richmond VA 2015-; Chapl S Marg's Sch 2004-** B Brooklyn NY 1953 BS CUNY 1976; MEd U of Virginia 1978; PhD U of Virginia 1983; MDiv GTS 2004. D 6/26/2004 P 1/18/2005 Bp Peter J Lee. Vauters Ch Loretto VA 2011-2015; S Marg's Sch Tappahannock VA 2004-2012. candinejohnson@gmail.com

JOHNSON, Carolynn Elayne (Mich) D 12/10/2016 Bp Wendell Nathaniel Gibbs Jr.

JOHNSON, Charlie (Va) 132 Lancaster Dr Apt 626, Irvington VA 22480 **To Ret Cler Cmnty Dio Virginia Richmond VA 2005-, Asst to Bp for Mnstry & Cong Dvlpmt 1980-1989, Transition Comm. -Election of Bp Coadj 2006-2008, Chapl To Ret Cler Cmnty 2005-, Bp's Chapl to Ret Cler and Families 2004-, Dioc Mssy Soc 1999-2008, Stndg Com 1995-1998; Ret Kingston Par Mathews Va. 1999-** B Four Oaks NC 1937 s Ira & Cartha. BA Roa 1962; Cert VTS 1965; Cert VTS 1980. D 6/12/1965 P 6/18/1966 Bp Robert Fisher Gibson Jr. m 7/29/1961 Virginia S Johnson c 2. Int S Mich's Ch Richmond VA 2004-2006; Int All SS Ch Richmond VA 2000-2001; R Kingston Par Epis Ch Mathews VA 1993-1999; R Chr Ch Gardiner ME 1989-1993; R S Barn Epis Ch No Chesterfield VA 1976-1980; Asst S Matt's Ch Richmond VA 1970-1976; R S Paul's Ch Haymarket VA 1967-1970; Asst, & P-in-c S Thos' Ch Richmond VA 1965-1967. EvangES 1989.

JOHNSON, Christopher Allen (Colo) 45 Woodland Ave, Glen Ridge NJ 07028 **R S Raphael Epis Ch Colorado Sprg CO 2013-** B Maracaibo VE 1958 s Robert & Cynthia. AS Onondaga Cmnty Coll 1978; BS Franciscan U of Steubenville 1980; MDiv Epis TS of the SW 2000. D 6/10/2000 P 12/23/2000 Bp William Jerry Winterrowd. m 5/8/1980 Debra Eyler Johnson c 3. Epis Ch Cntr New York NY 2008-2012; Vic Our Merc Sav Epis Ch Denver CO 2006-2008; Our Merc Sav Mnstrs Denver CO 2002-2007; 32nd Av Jubilee Cntr Denver CO 2001-2008; Cur Ch Of S Jn Chrys Golden CO 2000-2001.

JOHNSON, David (Miss) 116 Cedar Pointe, Fairhope AL 36532 B Columbia MS 1952 s Wilton & Frances. BA U of Mississippi 1975; MDiv Sewanee: The U So, TS 1987. D 5/30/1987 P 12/3/1987 Bp Duncan Montgomery Gray Jr. m 7/13/1974 Nora K Johnson c 2. Cn to the Ordnry Dio Mississippi Jackson MS 2001-2017; R Ch Of The Resurr Starkville MS 1993-2001; Assoc R S Geo's Ch Nashville TN 1992-1993; Vic S Patricks Epis Ch Long Bch MS 1987-1992; Cur Trin Ch Epis Pass Chr MS 1987-1990. Fell Coll of Preachers 1999.

JOHNSON, David Allen (Ga) 1700 Ashwood Blvd, Charlottesville VA 22911 **Chr Ch Valdosta GA 2014-** B Newport RI 1968 s Darold & Judy. BA Oral Roberts U 1991; MDiv Gordon-Conwell TS 2001; STM Nash 2002; DMin TESM 2010. D 9/12/2001 Bp Edward Lloyd Salmon Jr. m 7/21/1990 Stephanie J Johnson c 5. Assoc Chr Epis Ch Charlottesvlle VA 2007-2014; Vic St Andrews Epis Ch Charlottesvlle VA 2003-2007; Asst S Andr's Ch Mt Pleasant SC 2001-2003; Yth Dir Dio Wyoming Casper 1995-1996. dave@christchurchvaldosta.org

JOHNSON, David George (NMich) 1021 E E St, Iron Mountain MI 49801 B 1942 D 8/13/2003 P 2/29/2004 Bp James Arthur Kelsey. m 8/15/1964 Mary Richardson Johnson c 1.

JOHNSON, Dennis Lee (Wyo) Po Box 3485, Jackson WY 83001 B Chula Vista CA 1946 s Herbert & Elsie. AA Palomar Coll. D 2/3/2000 Bp Bruce Caldwell. m 7/25/1986 Vicki Smith c 2. COM Dio Wyoming Casper 1996-2006.

JOHNSON, Deon K (Mich) 200 W Saint Paul St, Brighton MI 48116 **R S Paul's Epis Ch Brighton MI 2006-** B Bridgetown Barbados 1977 s Henderson & Verna. BA Case Wstrn Reserve U 2000; BA Case Wstrn Reserve U 2000; MDiv GTS 2003. D 6/15/2003 Bp J Clark Grew II. Assoc R Chr Ch Shaker Heights OH 2003-2006. rector@saintpaulsbrighton.org

JOHNSON, Diana P (U) 1854 Kensington Avenue, Salt Lake City UT 84108 B Syracuse NY 1943 d William & Lucille. BS Utah St U 1975; MDiv CDSP 1994. D 4/30/1994 P 12/8/1994 Bp Stewart Clark Zabriskie. m 4/1/1978 Gerald T Johnson c 1. Cn Pstr Cathd Ch Of S Mk Salt Lake City UT 2003-2009; R S Steph's Ch W Vlly City UT 2000-2003; Int Ch Of The Gd Shpd Ogden UT 1998-2000; Int Ch Of The Gd Shpd Rocky Mt NC 1998; Int S Mich's Ch Raleigh NC 1998; Int S Paul's Ch Louisburg NC 1996-1997; Chapl Duke Epis Cntr Durham NC 1996; Int S Mths Ch Louisburg NC 1995-1996; Gr Ch Whiteville NC 1995.

JOHNSON, Donald Keith (Dal) 2026 Cherrywood Ln, Denton TX 76209 **R S Barn Epis Ch Denton TX 1995-** B Greenville TX 1957 s Cecil & Mary. BS Texas A&M U 1978; BS Texas A&M U-Commerce 1978; MS Texas A&M U 1984; MS Texas A&M U-Commerce 1984; MDiv Sewanee: The U So, TS 1988. D 6/18/1988 P 6/18/1989 Bp Donis Dean Patterson. m 4/20/1991 Emanda R Johnson. Ch Of The Epiph Commerce TX 1991-1995; Vic S Philips Epis Ch Sulphur Spgs TX 1991-1995; Vic All SS Ch Atlanta TX 1990-1991; Cur S Matt's Cathd Dallas TX 1988-1990; Trst Sewanee U So TS Sewanee TN 1991-1994. rector.stbarn@verizon.net

✠ JOHNSON, The Rt Rev Don Edward (WTenn) 692 Poplar Ave, Memphis TN 38105 **Bp of W Tennessee Dio W Tennessee Memphis 2001-** B Nashville TN 1949 s Eldridge & Fonda. BA Van 1972; MDiv SWTS 1976; DMin Grad Theol Un 1988. D 6/20/1976 Bp John Vander Horst P 5/1/1977 Bp William Evan Sanders Con 6/30/2001 for WTenn. m 5/31/1975 Jean Johnson c 2. R The Epis Ch Of The Resurr Franklin TN 1996-2001; R S Jn's Epis Ch Johnson City TN 1986-1996; R Chr Ch - Epis Chattanooga TN 1978-1986; Chapl U of Tennessee in Chattanooga 1978-1986; P-in-c Calv Ch Memphis TN 1977-1978; D S Paul's Ch Memphis TN 1976-1977; S Paul's Epis Ch Chattanooga TN 1976-1977. DD S Lk's Sem 2002; DD Seabury Wstrn TS 2002. bishopjohnson@episwtn.org

JOHNSON, Doris Buchanan (Ga) 3 Westridge Rd, Savannah GA 31411 **S Ptr's Epis Ch Savannah GA 2016-** B Miami Beach FL 1946 d Frank & Miriam. BA U of Florida 1968; MA U of So Florida 1986; MDiv VTS 1999; D. Min. VTS 2013. D 6/12/1999 P 12/16/1999 Bp John Bailey Lipscomb. c 2. R St Martins-In-The-Field Ch Severna Pk MD 2007-2014; Assoc R S Jn's Ch Ellicott City MD 2000-2007; Asst P H Trin Epis Ch In Countryside Clearwater FL 1999-2000; COM Mem Dio Maryland Baltimore MD 2001-2007. Auth, "Where is God?," Preaching Through the H Days and Holidays: Sermons that Wk, Morehouse, 2003. Mem Phi Kappa Phi Hon 1985. djohnson@stpeterssavannh.org

JOHNSON, Douglas Peter (WMo) 9905 N Hawthorne Ave, Kansas City MO 64157 B Sidney NE 1951 s Wright & Mary. BA Indiana U 1973; MHA Indiana U 1975; MDiv Nash 1982; DMin SWTS 1998. D 4/30/1982 Bp William Cockburn Russell Sheridan P 12/10/1982 Bp William Hopkins Folwell. m 4/27/1991 M Suzanne Blaco c 2. Int S Matt's Ch Enid OK 2013-2015; Int Gr Epis Ch Ponca City OK 2012-2013; R S Ptr's Ch Harrisonville MO 2000-2011; Chapl S Lk's Epis Hosp Kansas City MO 1999-2000; Chapl St Lk's Chap Kansas City MO 1999-2000; St Lk's So Chap Overland Pk KS 1999-2000; R S Tim's Ch Indianapolis IN 1993-1998; Cn to the Ordnry Dio W Missouri 1989-1993; Vic Chr Ch Lexington MO 1984-1989; Lakeland Dnry Exec Comm Dio Cntrl Florida Orlando FL 1983-1984; Cur The Epis Ch Of The Gd Shpd Lake Wales FL 1982-1984; Chair, Epis Transition Comm Dio W Missouri Kansas City MO 2009-2011; throughout the years Numerous Positions 1982-2013. Auth, A Time of Transition, Seabury-Wstrn, 1998. Alb Inst 1982; AFP 1982; AP 1994; RWF 1985. Bp's Shield Awd Dio W Missouri 1992; Bp's Shield Awd Dio W Missouri 1988.

JOHNSON, Edwin Daniel (Mass) 14 Cushing Ave, Dorchester MA 02125 **P-in-c S Mary's Epis Ch Boston MA 2013-; COM - Mem Dio Massachusetts Boston MA 2011-** B Boston MA 1982 s Walter & Vilma. BA Tufts U 2004; MDiv CDSP 2010. D 6/5/2010 Bp Gayle Harris P 1/8/2011 Bp M(Arvil) Thomas Shaw. m 8/25/2012 Susan M Johnson. Asst R S Jas' Epis Ch Cambridge MA 2010-2013. Outstanding Fac Mem California Cmsn on Peace Off Standards and Trng 2013; Fran Toy Price For Multicultural Mnstry In Field Educ CDSP 2010; Trabert-Graebner Awd For Excellence In Biblic Languages CDSP 2008; Jn Hines Preaching Awd Virginia Theologial Sem 2006. padreedwinj@gmail.com

JOHNSON, Emmanuel W (SC) 20268 Macglashan Ter, Ashburn VA 20147 **S Dav's Ch Ashburn VA 2003-** B Fishtown LR 1924 s Sie & Helena. BS Langston U 1958; MA Roosevelt U 1959; Dip Seth C Edw Theo Inst Monrovia RL 1967. Trans 5/18/1998 Bp Edward Lloyd Salmon Jr. m 11/6/1965 Henrietta Beatrice Johnson c 4. Chapl/Vic S Phil's Chap Denmark SC 1991-2003; Dn Trin Cathd Monrovia Liberia 1982-1990; P-in-c S Johns Irving Robertsport Liberia 1981-1982; R S Stephens Monrovia Liberia 1973-1974; Dio Liberia Monrovia 1970-1982. H Cross 1988; The Intl Ord of St Lk The Physcn 2005.

DSA Cuttington U 2011; Lifetime Educ Awd Liberian Awards 2010; DD (Honoris Causa) Cuttington U Coll 1984; LLD (Honoris Causa) S Aug's Coll 1973.

JOHNSON, Eric N (Oly) Christ Episcopal Anacortes, 1216 7th St, Anacortes WA 98221 **D Chr Epis Ch Anacortes WA 2013-; COM Dio Olympia Seattle 2015-** B Franklin IN 1947 s Denzil & Ines. BA U CO 1971; MPS Auburn U 1983. D 4/11/2013 Bp Gregory Harold Rickel. m 6/11/1969 Lynette Lea Rosenberg c 2.

JOHNSON, Erin Minta (Va) **Cur Ch Of The Gd Shpd Cashiers NC 2017-** D 6/10/2017 Bp Shannon Sherwood Johnston.

JOHNSON, Frances Kay Carter (Haw) 959 W 41st Street, Houston TX 77018 B Fort Worth TX 1953 d James & Rubye. Trng Candidate C. G. Jung Inst Zurich; BS TCU 1975; MDiv Bex Sem 1989; PhD Pacifica Grad Inst 2007. D 6/4/1989 Bp William Augustus Jones Jr P 12/18/1989 Bp William George Burrill. m 10/20/1979 Robert Allen Johnson c 2. Vol Assoc St. Mk's Ch Houston Texas 2009-2012; S Lk's Epis Ch Honolulu HI 2001-2002; Cn Pstr S Andr's Cathd Honolulu HI 1997-2001; Cn Pstr Cathd Of S Paul Erie PA 1994-1997; Com Dio NW Pennsylvania Erie PA 1992-1995, Dioc Coun 1991-1997; Vic S Mary's Ch Erie PA 1990-1997; Chapl Brevillier Vill Erie PA 1990-1993.

JOHNSON, Franklin Orr (Mont) 355 Francis Way, Jackson WY 83001 **Ret 2003-** B Buffalo NY 1938 s Philip & Clare. BS Mar 1960; MS U of Wyoming 1963; MDiv VTS 1966. D 6/3/1966 P 12/15/1966 Bp Wilburn Camrock Campbell. m 8/4/1973 Sally Johnson. Int S Fran Of The Tetons Alta WY 2007-2008; R All SS Epis Ch Columbia Falls MT 2001; R S Jn's Epis Ch Jackson WY 1981-2001; Ch Of The Trsfg Jackson WY 1981-2000; Assoc S Lk's Epis Ch Birmingham AL 1977-1981; Asst Chr Ch Cathd Lexington KY 1971-1977; R S Ptr's Ch Huntington WV 1966-1971.

JOHNSON, Frank T (SanD) 651 Eucalyptus Ave, Vista CA 92084 B Nampa ID 1939 s Jay & Olive. BA Pepperdine U 1976; MDiv Nash 1980. D 6/10/1980 P 12/1/1980 Bp Robert Munro Wolterstorff. c 3. Gr Epis Ch Of The Vlly Mssn San Marcos CA 1982-1991; All SS Ch Vista CA 1980-1982, Cur 1980-1982; Dio San Diego San Diego CA 1980-1982.

JOHNSON JR, Fred Hoyer (NY) 118 Lake Emerald Drive - #409, Oakland Park FL 33309 B Columbus GA 1943 s Fred & Viola. Ohio Wesl 1962; BA Ya 1965; U of Paris 1966; MDiv Yale DS 1970; M.Div. Ya DS 1970. D 6/26/1971 Bp John Harris Burt P 2/1/1973 Bp Joseph Warren Hutchens. Supply P, De facto Pstr Ch of the Intsn Ft Lauderdale FL 2011-2014; Chapl Trin Sch New York NY 1993-2004; Assoc Ch Of The Intsn New York NY 1980-1983, Assoc 1977-2009, Assoc 1977-1980; Chap Coordntr Packer Collgt Inst 1973-1980; Tchr & Asst to Chapl Choate Sch Wallingford CT 1968-1973. Transltr, "No Souvenirs," *No Souvenirs*, Harper & Row, 1977; Auth, "When the Wrld Is No Longer Flat," *Packer Collgt Alum mag*, Packer Collgt Inst; Auth, "(Article)," *Reflections*, CSEE. Phi Beta Kappa 1965. Vic Emer Ch of the Intsn/New York City 2008; Macquarrie Fell GTF at Oxf 2002. halfsquarehead@yahoo.com

JOHNSON, Gregory Mervin (Haw) PO Box 893788, Mililani HI 96789 **S Mary's Epis Ch Honolulu HI 2014-** B Stillwater MN 1951 s Mervin & Delores. BA U of Hawaii 1973; MTS Sewanee: The U So, TS 1976; MTS Sewanee: The U So, TS 1976; DMin S Thos Cath Sem 1981; DMin S Thos Cath Sem 1981; Dplma USAF Chapl Sch 1981; Dplma Acad Instr Sch 1982; Dplma Acad Instr Sch 1982; Cert St. Steph's Hse Oxford 1994. D 3/23/1993 P 9/14/1993 Bp Donald Purple Hart. m 6/10/1973 Rebecca Gwynn Boardman Johnson c 4. Int Vic S Lk's Epis Ch Honolulu HI 2011-2013; Int Vic S Steph's Ch Wahiawa HI 2011-2013; P-in-c S Tim's Ch Aiea HI 2008-2010; P-in-c Gd Samar Epis Ch Honolulu HI 2005-2008; Int Vic H Cross Kahuku HI 2004-2005; Supply P The Epis Ch in Hawaii Honolulu HI 2003-2004, Supply P 2000-2001, Dioc Coun 1997-2003, Cathd Chapt 2006-2009, Dioc Coun 1996-1999, COM 1995-1996, Eccl Crt 1994-1999; P-in-c Ch Of The Epiph Honolulu HI 2001-2002; Assoc R S Mk's Ch Honolulu HI 1996-2000; Int R Par of St Clem Honolulu HI 1994-1995; Prof Rel Stds HI Pacific U Honolulu HI 1986-2007; Cur S Geo's Epis Ch Honolulu HI 1986-1994; Base Chapl USAF Chapl 1980-1986. santamariahawaii@yahoo.com

JOHNSON JR, Harold Vance (WA) 12194 Cathedral Dr, Lake Ridge VA 22192 **Asstg the R S Anne's Epis Ch Reston VA 2013-** B Niles MI 1938 s Harold & Shirlee. BA U MI 1960; MDiv EDS 1963; MBA Drexel U 1972. D 6/11/1963 Bp Charles Bennison Sr P 12/14/1963 Bp William Foreman Creighton. m 8/7/1975 Mary Gaunt Johnson c 3. Pres (Non-par) Inst for Orgnztn Resrch & Dvlpmt Inc. 1975-2003; Asstg P Ch Of The Resurr Alexandria VA 1972-2010; R S Chris's Ch New Carrollton MD 1966-1970; Asst Min S Jn's Ch Georgetown Par Washington DC 1963-1966; Asst Min S Jn's Ch Lafayette Sq Washington 1963-1966. iordinc@aol.com

JOHNSON JR, Harrel Brown (NC) 210 South Chestnut Street, Henderson NC 27536 **D The Ch Of The H Innoc Henderson NC 2011-** B Brunswick GA 1947 s Harrel & Doris. BS U GA 1970. D 6/20/2009 Bp Michael B Curry. m 2/16/1974 Amy Johnson c 2.

JOHNSON, Herbert Alan (WNC) 245 Laurel Falls Rd, Franklin NC 28734 **Ret 2007-; Ch Of The Cross Columbia SC 1999-** B Jersey City NJ 1934 s Harry & Magdalena. BA Col 1955; LLB New York Law Sch 1960; MA Col 1961; PhD Col 1965; Luth Theol Sthrn Sem 1984. D 9/28/1991 Bp William Arthur

Beckham. m 6/4/1983 Jane Johnson c 2. D All SS Epis Cmnty Franklin NC 2005-2007; D St. Cyp's Franklin NC 2002-2005; Chapl Ang Med Cntr Hospice Franklin NC 2002-2004; Select Cmsn on Const & Cn Dio Upper So Carolina Columbia SC 1995-1999, Cmsn on Daic 1996-2000; D St. Jn's (Shandon) Columbia SC 1991-1998; Chapl Assoc Bapt Med Cntr Columbia SC 1983-2002. Ed, *Amer Legal & Const Hist, 2nd Ed*, 2001; Auth, *Wingless Eagle: U.S. Army Aviation through Wrld War I*, 2001; Auth, *Chf Justiceship of Jn Marshall*, 1997. Assembly of Epis Hospitals & Chapl 2000; Coll of Chapl 1989-2008.

JOHNSON, Horace S (Ct) 3404 Castlebar Cir, Ormond Beach FL 32174 **Asstg P S Thos Flagler Cnty Palm Coast FL 2006-** B Jamaica WI 1941 s David & Agatha. Andover Newton TS; Ya Berk; MBA U of Hartford 1979. D 6/9/2001 Bp Andrew Donnan Smith P 12/15/2001 Bp James Elliot Curry. m 5/6/1967 Fay Johnson. Assoc R Trin Epis Ch Hartford CT 2001-2006.

JOHNSON, Ida Louise (Cal) 535 Joaquin Ave #D, San Leandro CA 94577 **Non-par San Francisco CA 2004-** B Miami FL 1948 d Samuel & Dorothy. S Augustines Coll Raleigh NC 1968; BA San Francisco St U 1991; MDiv CDSP 1994. D 6/4/1994 P 6/3/1995 Bp William Edwin Swing. c 1. R S Barth's Ch Pittsboro NC 2001-2004; Vic S Mich And All Ang Epis Ch Charlotte NC 1997-2001; Chapl Dio No Carolina Raleigh NC 1996-1997; Yth Dir Dio Massachusetts Boston MA 1995-1996; Dio California San Francisco CA 1994-1995; S Cyp's Ch San Francisco CA 1994-1995; Afr Amer Mssnr San Francisco CA 1994-1995. UBE.

JOHNSON, Ira Joseph (WTenn) 4150 Boeingshire Dr, Memphis TN 38116 B Gastonia NC 1949 s Ira & Lydia. BA Belmont Abbey Coll 1974; MDiv GTS 1977. D 6/25/1977 P 3/1/1978 Bp William Gillette Weinhauer. m 4/25/1993 Linda Johnson c 5. Voorhees Coll Charleston SC 2006-2011; Emm Ch Memphis TN 1999-2004; S Paul's Epis Ch Orangeburg SC 1992-1999; Ch Of The H Cov Baltimore MD 1988-1992; S Steph's Epis Ch Winston Salem NC 1985-1988; S Thos Ch Minneapolis MN 1982-1985; R S Aug's Ch Kansas City MO 1978-1982; S Andr's Ch Dayton OH 1977-1978.

JOHNSON, James Arthur (WNC) 525 Urquhart Dr, Sandersville GA 31082 **Died 8/8/2015** B Washington DC 1947 s Herbert & Lily. BA Shorter Coll 1968; MDiv VTS 1975; DMin Drew U 1991; MA Georgia Sch of Profsnl Psychol Atlanta GA 1999. D 5/24/1975 P 4/25/1976 Bp Robert Poland Atkinson. m 8/17/1968 Betty Jean Smith c 2. R Ch Of The Mssh Murphy NC 2005-2012; Assoc The Ch Of S Matt Snellville GA 1998-2005; Int The Epis Ch Of The Adv Madison GA 1995-1996; R S Andr's Epis Ch Douglas GA 1991-1993; R All SS Ch Bergenfield NJ 1988-1991; P S Clem's Ch Hawthorne NJ 1987-1988; Asst S Paul's Ch Englewood NJ 1986-1987; Vic S Gabr's Ch Oak Ridge NJ 1981-1985; Vic St Josephs Ch Newark NJ 1981-1983; Vic S Matt's Ch Chester WV 1979-1981; R S Thos' Epis Ch Weirton WV 1977-1981; Dio W Virginia Charleston WV 1975-1977; Cur S Mk's Epis Ch St Albans WV 1975-1977. Auth, *Dissertation Developing An Outreach Mnstry in Bergenfield New Jersey*, 1991; Auth, *Mnstry From A Minefield*, 1986. AAMFT (Amer Assn for Mar and Fam Ther)(Cl 1998; AAPC (AAPC) (Fell) 1995; Natl Conf of Viet Nam Veterans Ministers 1988; Soc for Post Traumatic Stress Stds 1988. Cross of Gallantry Republic of So Vietnam 1970; Commendation Medal, Viet Nam Cmpgn USAF 1970.

JOHNSON, James Baxter (Colo) 1715 Holly Way, Fort Collins CO 80526 **Asst S Mich And All Ang' Ch Denver CO 2001-; Ret 1998-** B Minneapolis MN 1936 s Harold & Kathryn. BA U CO 1959; MDiv Nash 1962; MS Adams St Coll 1973. D 6/18/1962 P 12/21/1962 Bp Joseph Summerville Minnis. m 10/9/1976 Anne Elizabeth Moorhead c 4. Ch Of The H Nativ Kinsley KS 1999-2000; Chapl Hospice of the Prairie Dodge City KS 1992-1998; R S Corn Epis Ch Dodge City KS 1989-1998; R S Jas' Epis Ch Meeker CO 1986-1989; Cur S Thos Epis Ch Denver CO 1965-1967; Epis Ch Of S Jn The Bapt Granby CO 1963-1965; Vic Trin Ch Kremmling CO 1963-1965; Vic S Andr's Ch Cripple Creek CO 1962-1963; Dioc Coun Dio Wstrn Kansas Hutchinson KS 1993-1997; CDO Dio Colorado Denver CO 1984-1989, Chairman, Coll Dept 1969-1975. FIFNA 1989; SSC 2002.

JOHNSON, Jane Margaret (FdL) 1316 Ellis St., Stevens Point WI 54481 **R Intsn Epis Ch Stevens Point WI 2011-; Chair of COM Dio Fond du Lac Appleton WI 2012-** B Shenandoah IA 1966 d Paul & Carol. BA U of Wisconsin Eau Claire 1989; MDiv Sewanee: The U So, TS 2011. D 12/18/2010 P 7/9/2011 Bp Russell Edward Jacobus. m 8/5/1989 Murray D Johnson c 4. rector@intercessionsp.org

JOHNSON, Janet H. (NJ) 538 Epping Forest Road, Annapolis MD 21401 **Died 2/10/2016** B Orange NJ 1939 d Ernest & Jean. BA Cor 1961; Cert Harvard-Radcliffe Prog In Bus Admin 1962; MBA Harv 1967; MDiv UTS 1997; CSD GTS 1999. D 6/22/2002 P 12/21/2002 Bp David Bruce Joslin. S Geo's Ch Perryman MD 2006-2008; Stff Liaison Dio New Jersey Trenton NJ 2002-2005; Vic Trin Ch Rocky Hill NJ 2002-2005.

JOHNSON, Janis Lynn (Oly) 1541 Vista Loop SW #33-101, Tumwater WA 98512 B Raymond, WA 1952 d Harold & Virginia. BA Seattle Pacific U 1974; Fuller TS 2004; MDiv GTS 2006. D 6/24/2006 Bp Vincent Waydell Warner P 1/6/2007 Bp William O Gregg. P All SS Memi Epis Ch Heppner OR 2006-2009.

J

437

JOHNSON, Jay Brooks (NC) 2690 Fairlawn Dr, Winston Salem NC 27106 B Port Jefferson NY 1970 s Robert & Myrta. BS Campbell U 1992; MDiv Ware Forest U 2009; MDiv Ware Forest U 2009; Angl Stds VTS 2011. D 1/24/2015 Bp Anne Hodges-Copple. m 6/7/2009 Catherine H Johnson c 2.

JOHNSON, Jay Emerson (Cal) 632 38th St, Richmond CA 94805 **Prof PSR Berkeley CA 2005-; Assoc The Epis Ch Of The Gd Shpd Berkeley CA 1992-** B Ann Arbor MI 1961 s James & Rosemary. BA Wheaton Coll 1983; MDiv Nash 1988; PhD Grad Theol Un 1998. D 6/18/1988 P 12/17/1988 Bp Frank Tracy Griswold III. Prof CDSP Berkeley CA 1997-1998; Cur S Simons Ch Arlington Hts IL 1988-1991. Auth, "Peculiar Faith: Queer Theol for Chr Witness," Seabury Books, 2014; Auth, "Div Comm: A Eucharistic Theol of Sexual Intimacy," Seabury Books, 2013; "Dancing w God: Angl Chrsnty And The Pract Of Hope," Morehouse Pub, 2005. Newhall Resrch Fllshp Grad Theol Un 1996; Bogard Tchg Fllshp CDSP 1995; Ecf Grad Fllshp 1992.

JOHNSON, Joan Cottrell (Mass) 4833 Europa Dr, Naples FL 34105 B Darby PA 1927 d William & Helen. BA Penn 1948; MDiv CDSP 1984. D 12/8/1984 P 12/1/1985 Bp William Edwin Swing. c 2. S Paul's Epis Ch Hopkinton MA 1992-1999; Assoc S Andr's Ch Edgartown MA 1988-1991; Assoc R S Thos Epis Ch Sunnyvale CA 1985-1988.

JOHNSON, Johan (NY) 521 W 126th St, New York NY 10027 **Peddie Sch Hightstown NJ 2015-; S Mart's Ch New York NY 2008-, 2006, 1999-2005** B 1963 s John & Faith. BA Clark U 1985; MDiv UTS 1989. D 9/9/1990 P 5/1/1991 Bp Edward Harding MacBurney. m 7/28/2011 Gabriela Johnson c 2. Trin Epis Day Sch Hartford CT 2011-2013; S Andr's Epis Sch Ridgeland MS 2006-2008; Chapl S Mary Cntr.

JOHNSON, John Brent (Tex) St. John's Episcopal Church, 1305 Roosevelt, Silsbee TX 77656 B Houston TX 1961 s Robert & Shirley. BA Lamar U 1993; MPA Lamar U 1993; JD So Texas Coll of Law 1998; JD St of Texas Coll of Law 1998; MPA Lamar U 2003; Dip Iona Sch for Mnstry Dio TX 2007. D 6/23/2007 Bp Don Adger Wimberly P 1/19/2008 Bp Rayford Baines High Jr. c 2.

JOHNSON JR, John Romig (NY) 1020 Tyron Cir, Charleston SC 29414 **Sr Assoc S Steph's Epis Ch Charleston SC 2009-** B Augusta GA 1935 s John & Harriet. BA Furman U 1957; MDiv GTS 1960; PhD UTS 1966; CG Jung Inst 1977. D 6/13/1960 P 5/27/1961 Bp Clarence Alfred Cole. m 8/3/1995 Nicole watts c 3. Assoc S Andr's Mssn Charleston SC 2005-2009; R S Jn's Ch Staten Island NY 1999-2005; Assoc Chr Ch Riverdale Bronx NY 1995-1999; Assoc The Ch Of The Epiph New York NY 1980-1995; Pstr Theol The GTS New York NY 1970-1982; Assoc Prof Of Pstr Theol Ya Berk New Haven CT 1965-1970; Chapl S Jas' Ch Sch Madison Av New York NY 1963-1965; P-in-c S Ptr's Ch Great Falls SC 1960-1962. Auth, "Shaping The Mnstry For The 70'S," Ats, 1971; Auth, "Stdt Changes In Pstr Role Perception," *Journ Of Pstr Care*, 1967. AAPC, Diplomate 1977; Intl Assn For Analytical Psychol 1977; New York Assn For Analytical Psychol 1977.

JOHNSON, Juanita Hanger (Neb) 10761 Izard St, Omaha NE 68114 **D Ch Of The Resurr Omaha NE 1999-** B 1929 d Saybert & Ione. D 2/22/2004 Bp Joe Goodwin Burnett. m 8/2/1958 George Warren Johnson c 2.

JOHNSON, Julie Anna (Tenn) St Mary Magdalene Church, PO Box 150, Fayetteville TN 37334 B Vallejo CA 1961 d Norman & Geraldine. BA Humboldt St U 1984; MDiv Sewanee: The U So, TS 2008. D 12/17/2007 P 6/30/2008 Bp Edward Stuart Little II. m 4/27/2008 Thomas D Johnson c 3. R S Mary Magd Ch Fayetteville TN 2011-2013; R S Alb's Epis Ch Hixson TN 2009-2010; Fam and Yth Asst St Andr's Epis Ch 2002-2005.

JOHNSON, June (Ga) 519 Parker Ave, Decatur GA 30032 B Albany GA 1946 d Willard & Eunice. BMusEd U GA 1968; MDiv Candler TS Emory U 2009. D 2/7/2009 P 8/20/2009 Bp Henry Irving Louttit. m 5/26/1990 Richard K Failing. D Ch Of The H Nativ St Simons Is GA 2013-2017; Int S Jn's Epis Ch Bainbridge GA 2010-2012.

JOHNSON, June B (Oly) 114 20th Ave SE, Olympia WA 98501 B Chehalis WA 1947 d Frank & Dorothy. AA Centralia Coll 1991; BA Evergreen St Coll 2002; MDiv CDSP 2007. D 6/28/2008 Bp Bavi Edna Rivera. m 8/12/1978 David Johnson c 2. P Assoc S Jn's Epis Ch Olympia WA 2008-2016.

JOHNSON, Karen Brown (WA) 18404 Tea Rose Pl, Gaithersburg MD 20879 B Worcester 1943 d Chester & Dorothy. BA Bates Coll 1965; MDiv Yale DS 1980. D 5/28/1980 Bp Frederick Barton Wolf P 1/11/1981 Bp Charles Francis Hall. c 3. Assoc Chr Ch Prince Geo's Par Rockville MD 2003-2007, 1996-2000; Chapl Chr Epis Sch Rockville MD 2000-2007; Chapl Chr Epis Sch Rockville MD 1995-2007; Cmnty Mnstrs Of Rockville Rockville MD 1994-1995; Int Chapl Bates Coll Lewiston ME 1993-1994; R S Anne's Ch Damascus MD 1985-1993; Asst R Ch Of The Ascen Gaithersburg MD 1983-1985; Chapl S Cath Sch Richmond VA 1980-1983; Chapl S Cath's Sch Richmond VA 1980-1983; Pres, WECA Dio Washington Washington DC 1990-1992. Winner, Best Sermon Contest 1992.

JOHNSON, Katherine Bradley (NC) 2504 Englewood Ave, Durham NC 27705 B Durham NC 1950 d David & Gail. BA Ob 1971; U of Texas 1975; JD U NC 1979; MDiv VTS 1982. D 5/31/1992 Bp Robert Whitridge Estill. m 8/21/1981 Jeffrey Hirst Johnson. Dio No Carolina Raleigh NC 1998-2000; Admin Asst Duke Epis Cntr Durham NC 1998-2000; D S Matt's Epis Ch Hillsborough NC 1994-1998; D S Phil's Ch Durham NC 1992-1994; Cler Alt Dep Dio No Carolina 2006-2009. Auth, "The Wide Appeal Of Harry Potter, Novelist," *An On-Line Pub Of Ebsco Pub*, 2000; Auth, "Going For The Gold, Novelist," *An On-Line Pub Of Ebsco Pub*, 2000; Auth, "Reading Sum, Novelist," *An On-Line Pub Of Ebsco Pub*, 2000. EPF 1989; NAAD 1991.

JOHNSON, Kellaura Beth Jones (Tex) 235, Royal Oaks, Huntsville TX 77320 **S Steph's Ch Huntsville TX 2016-; S Mary's Epis Ch Cypress TX 2000-** B Syracuse NY 1978 d Steven & Lucinda. BA The U So 2000; MDiv Epis TS of the SW 2014. D 6/21/2014 P 1/9/2015 Bp Dena Arnall Harrison. m 5/1/2004 Nicholas Stewart Johnson. Calv Epis Ch Richmond TX 2014-2016.

JOHNSON, Kenneth William (Mass) 11699 Bennington Woods Rd, Reston VA 20194 **D 1970-** B Omaha NE 1941 s Philip & Wilma. BA DePauw U 1963; BD EDS 1969. D 6/21/1969 Bp Anson Phelps Stokes Jr. Cur S Paul's Ch Holyoke MA 1969-1970.

JOHNSON, Kent William (LI) 6626 52nd Rd, #1, Maspeth NY 11378 B Washington DC 1949 s Reuben & Bernice. BA Bow 1971; PhD Br 1976; MDiv GTS 1984. D 1/28/1984 Bp Alexander D Stewart P 8/6/1984 Bp Andrew Frederick Wissemann. m 8/21/1982 Rita Johnson c 2. P-t Asst Chr Ch Manhasset NY 2008-2009; Dio Long Island Garden City NY 2003-2004; R All SS Ch Bayside NY 2002-2003; R S Mich's Ch Marblehead MA 1998-2002; Vic S Chris's Ch Hampstead NH 1986-1998; Asst S Mich's-On-The-Heights Worcester MA 1984-1986. Colloquium On Violence And Rel 1998-2004; FVC 1988-2002; Soc Of Ord Scientists 1999-2009.

JOHNSON, Kevin Allen (FtW) St. Alban's Episcopal Church, 316 W Main St, Arlington TX 76010 **S Alb's Epis Ch Arlington TX 2015-** B Amarillo TX 1963 BA U of Texas 1986; MDiv VTS 2003. D 6/17/2003 Bp Robert Boyd Hibbs P 1/6/2004 Bp James Edward Folts. m 12/30/1987 Sandra Lynne Johnson c 2. R S Ptr's Epis Ch Washington NC 2007-2015; Asst St Fran Epis Ch San Antonio TX 2003-2007. Auth, "Scattered Gifts: Along the Way to Santiago". kevin.saintalbans.episcopal@gmail.com

JOHNSON, Kristine Ann (Va) 6715 Georgetown Pike, Mclean VA 22101 **S Jn's Epis Ch Mc Lean VA 2016-** B San Jose CA 1965 d Jon & Elizabeth. BA U CO 1986; MA The GW 1988; MDiv VTS 2016. D 6/11/2016 P 12/10/2016 Bp Shannon Sherwood Johnston. m 6/3/1989 Melvin Glen Dubee c 2.

JOHNSON, Lee (SJ) 310 Audubon Dr, Lodi CA 95240 B Saint Louis MO 1945 d Charles & Patricia. BA Florida Bible Coll 1987; Cert Ang Stud San Joaquin Schools For Mnstry 2006; Cert Ang Stud San Joaquin Schools For Mnstry 2006. D 12/16/2006 Bp David Mercer Schofield. m 4/20/1996 Robert George Johnson. Bereavement Coordntr Hospice Of San Joaquin 1998-2008.

JOHNSON, Linda Catherine (Ind) IU Episcopal Campus Ministry, PO Box 127, Bloomington IN 47402 **Indiana U Dio Indianapolis Indianapolis IN 2007-, Dn of NW Dnry 2012-, Dn of NW Dnry 2011-, Stndg Com 1997-2005, COM 1997-1998, Eccl Trial Crt 1995-1998, COM in Higher Educ 1994-; Mem of Instnl Revs Bd Indiana U Bloomington IN 1998-** B Thomas WV 1949 d Theodore & Wilma. BA Berea Coll 1971; MA Ohio U 1973; MDiv GTS 1994; CSD Ben Inn/Mnstry Indianapolis IN 2002; PhD Indiana U 2010. D 7/29/1994 P 2/24/1995 Bp A(rthur) Heath Light. Pres Indiana Unversity Campus Rel Leaders Assn 2009-2013; Assoc R & Chapl Trin Epis Ch Bloomington IN 1994-2006; Dir Gr Hse On The Mtn S Paul VA 1994. "Integrating Indiana's Latino Newcomers: Levinson, Everitt, and Johnson, A Study of St and Cmnty Responses to the New Im," *Cntr for Educ and Soc, Working Paper #1*, Cntr for Educ and Soc, Indidan U, 2007; Auth, *Colonialism in Mod Amer: The Appalachian*; Auth, *The Chr Century*; Auth, *The Mnstry Dvlpmt Journ*; Auth, *Wit*. ESMHE 1995-2003; Pi Lambda Theta 2006; Sprtl Dir Intl 2002. Discipline Based Schlrshp in Educ Assoc Indiana U 2005; Cler Renwl Grant Lilly Endwmt 2000; Ch and Soc Prize for M.Div. Thesis GTS 1994.

JOHNSON, Linda Marie (Oly) Po Box 354, Westport WA 98595 B Seattle WA 1944 d Walter & Marjorie. AA Clackamas Cmnty Coll 1991; Total Mnstry Trng Westport WA 1997. D 11/19/1997 Bp Sanford Zangwill Kaye Hampton P 6/27/1998 Bp Vincent Waydell Warner. D S Christophers Epis Ch Westport WA 1997-1998.

JOHNSON, Lori Elaine (EMich) 315 1/2 N Maple St, Flushing MI 48433 B La Mesa, CA 1967 d Theodore & Joanne. BA California St U 1992; MDiv Epis TS of the SW 2006; MDiv Epis TS of the SW 2006. D 6/4/2006 Bp Jim Mathes P 1/5/2007 Bp Gary Richard Lillibridge. R Trin Epis Ch Flushing MI 2008-2013; Asst S Dav's Epis Ch San Antonio TX 2006-2008.

JOHNSON JR, Lucius Curtis (Ga) 552 Hunterdale Rd, Evans GA 30809 **P Ch Of The Gd Shpd Swainsboro GA 2011-; P Ch of the Gd Shpd Detroit MI 2009-; D The Ch Of The Gd Shpd Augusta GA 2000-** B Cuthbert GA 1947 s Lucius & Mary. D 2/15/1999 P 11/20/2009 Bp Henry Irving Louttit. m 2/15/1991 Martha Ann Kobs.

JOHNSON, Lynn H (NJ) 3 Azalea Dr, Lumberton NJ 08048 **Exec Dir Trin Cathd Acad Trenton NJ 08618 2006-; Serv S Barth's Ch Cherry Hill NJ 2002-; Archd for Diac Discernmnt Dio New Jersey 2014-** B Camden NJ 1945 d Charles & Mollye. Ed.D Rutgers The St U of New Jersey; BA Fisk U 1969; BA Fisk U 1969; MA Rowan U 1979; Ed.D Rutgers The St U of New Jersey 1989. D 10/21/2000 Bp David Bruce Joslin. m 2/15/1969 Vernon Johnson c 2. Supt Fairfield Township Publ Sch Dist 2000-2004; Serv S Jn's Epis Ch Maple Shade NJ 2000-2002; Prncpl Camden City Publ Schools 1984-1997; Mem, Audit Com Dio New Jersey Trenton NJ 2006-2007, Com on the Diac, Chair 2004-, Mem, Epis Election Com 2002-2003. Auth, "Getting to Know You," *A manual for Members - New & Old*, lhjpublications, 2001; Auth, "ABCDeacon," lhjpublications, 1998; Auth, "So . . . You're On The Vstry," Ihj, 1998; Auth, "When The Mstr Calls," Ihj, 1998; Auth, "Presenting The Alt-Gld," Ihj Pub, 1997. Alpha Kappa Alpha Sorority 1991; The Links, Incorporated 1987. Barbara C. Harris Awd A Wmn Committed to Soc Transformation 2013; Outstanding Wmn Awd Jack & Jill Incorporated 2012; Upstream Navigator Cmnty Serv Awd Geo Elliot Heardy Memi Fndt 1997; Dedicated Serv Awd Chr The King Ch 1995; Wrld Class Serv Awd Zeta Phi Beta Sorority 1995.

JOHNSON, Maeve Maud Vincent (Az) 114 W Roosevelt St., Phoenix AZ 85003 B Phoenix AZ 1951 d Thomas & Frances. BA U of Arizona 1972; MEd Arizona St U 1981; Cert Untd States Green Build Coun USGBC 2010. D 10/14/2006 Bp Kirk Stevan Smith. m 2/19/1993 Richardson Stater Studer c 2.

JOHNSON, Malinda Margaret Eichner (Ct) 9 Arrow Head Rd, Westport CT 06880 B Stamford CT 1963 d Lambert & Joann. BA Connecticut Coll 1985; MA Harvard DS 1989. D 6/8/2002 P 12/14/2002 Bp Andrew Donnan Smith. m 6/17/1993 Krister Frederick Johnson c 2. Calv St Geo's Epis Ch Bridgeport CT 2010-2011; Cur S Jn's Epis Par Waterbury CT 2002-2007.

JOHNSON, Marietta (Mont) Po Box 78, Red Lodge MT 59068 B Shreveport LA 1939 d Thurston & Martha. Tchr Cert Montana St U 1961; Mnstry Formation Prog 2001. D 10/31/2001 P 4/13/2002 Bp Charles Lovett Keyser. m 12/22/1962 Joseph E Johnson c 2. Spec Educ Tchr.

JOHNSON, Marta D. V. (Md) 4603 Rocks Road, PO Box 103, Street MD 21154 **P H Cross Ch St MD 2011-** B New York NY 1951 d Pedro & Genoveva. BS Pace U 1974; MA S Marys Sem & U Baltimore 1998; MSc Loyola Coll Baltimore MD 2005; MDiv VTS 2008. D 6/14/2008 P 1/10/2009 Bp John L Rabb. m 6/4/1977 Alfred D Johnson c 4.

JOHNSON, Mary Peterson (ND) All Saints' Church, 301 Main St S, Minot ND 58701 **P-in-c All SS Ch Minot ND 2011-** B Montreal QC CA 1955 d David & Grace. Wheaton Coll; BA U IL 1976; MA U IL 1977; MDiv PrTS 1983; STM GTS 1986. D 6/14/1986 P 1/14/1987 Bp George Phelps Mellick Belshaw. m 6/19/1976 Wayne Paul Johnson c 5. Dio No Dakota Fargo ND 2011-2013, Dioc Ecum Off 2014-, Dep to GC 2013-; R Epis Ch Of The H Fam Jasper GA 2004-2011; Assoc for Chr Nurture Trin Ch Columbus OH 1999-2001; S Jn's Ch Worthington OH 1998-1999; Org S Nich Mssn Galloway OH 1995-1998; S Nich Of Myra Epis Ch Hilliard OH 1995-1997; Chapl Epis Campus Mnstry at OH SU 1992-1993; Chapl OSU Hospitals Columbus OH 1991-1993; Assoc S Mk's Epis Ch Columbus OH 1991-1993, Int 1989-1990; Chr Ch Cranbrook Bloomfield Hills MI 1988-1989; DCE S Bern's Ch Bernardsville NJ 1986-1987. office@allsaintsminot.org

JOHNSON, Mary Richardson (NMich) 1021 E E St, Iron Mountain MI 49801 B 1943 D 2/29/2004 Bp James Arthur Kelsey. m 8/15/1964 David George Johnson c 1.

JOHNSON, Matt (NC) 231 N Church St, Rocky Mount NC 27804 **Ch Of The Gd Shpd Rocky Mt NC 2014-** B Atlanta GA 1978 s William & Candis. AB W&M 2000; MDiv GTS 2008. D 5/24/2008 P 12/6/2008 Bp Peter J Lee. m 1/5/2008 Katharina P Johnson c 2. Assoc R S Steph's Ch Richmond VA 2011-2014; Assoc R Gr Ch The Plains VA 2008-2011. mjohnson@goodshepherdrmt.org

JOHNSON, Michaela (Kay) (RI) 1214 Noyes Dr, Silver Spring MD 20910 B New York NY 1937 d Erwin & Ilse. BA Swarthmore Coll 1958; MDiv Ya Berk 1987; MS U of Connecticut 1987. D 8/22/1987 P 2/27/1988 Bp Andrew Frederick Wissemann. m 8/20/1960 Richard August Johnson c 4. S Thos' Par Washington DC 2005-2007; The Ch Of The Epiph Washington DC 2002; R Ch Of The Mssh Providence RI 1992-2000; Dio Wstrn Massachusetts Springfield 1987-1992; Asst Gr Ch Amherst MA 1987-1992. "No One is Ever Alone," *Sermons that Wk IV*, Forw Mvmt, 1994. Polly Bond Awd ECom 1999.

JOHNSON, Michael R (SD) PO Box 434, Deadwood SD 57732 **R S Jn's Ch Deadwood SD 2012-** B Ada MN 1948 s Ralph & Pearl. BA Minnesota St U Moorhead 1970; Ecole Internationale De Mime Marcel Marceau Paris France 1971; PCIM Mableton GA 1987. D 6/15/2005 P 12/17/2005 Bp Michael Smith. c 1. Dio No Dakota Fargo ND 2011-2012; Assoc for Pstr Care Geth Cathd Fargo ND 2011-2012, 2006-2007; P-in-c S Jn's Ch Moorhead MN 2008. Ord of S Lk the Physcn 1990.

JOHNSON, Mildred Jane (U) 147 N 875 E, Logan UT 84321 **D S Jn 1991-** B Indianapolis IN 1921 d Harry & Jessie. BA Ob 1944; MA Westminster Choir Coll of Rider U 1948; PhD Indiana U 1955. D 5/21/1991 Bp George Edmonds Bates.

JOHNSON, Neil Edward (NwPa) 18 Harrogate Square, Williamsville NY 14221 **Int St.Jn's Epis 2004-; Assoc Cler S Paul's Epis Ch Lewiston NY 1997-** B Corning NY 1942 s Hans & Wilma. Syr; AS Corning Cmnty Coll 1964; BS Elmira Coll 1974. D 1/6/1996 P 12/21/1996 Bp Robert Deane Rowley Jr. m 6/28/1980 Dianne Jean Gradl. P-in-c Ch Of The Epiph Niagara Falls NY 1998-2000.

JOHNSON, Patricia A (Ia) 2222 McDonald St, Sioux City IA 51104 **Dir Morrell Transition Cntr 2010-; D S Thos' Epis Ch Sioux City IA 1999-** B Sioux City IA 1953 d Donald & Leona. BA Briar Cliff U 1986; Cert Sewanee: The U So, TS 1998. D 4/24/1999 Bp Chris Christopher Epting. c 2. Fair Hsng Investigator Sioux City Human Rts Cmsn 2002-2010; Probation Parole Off Dept. of Adult Corrections Third Judicial Dist 2001; Mgr Woodbury Cnty Atty's Off 1989-2001. Auth, "Comp on the Way," *Diakeno*, Michaelmas, 2000; Auth, "The Activist Decade, Essays in Hist," *E.C. Barksdale Lectures*, 1988. Phi Alpha Theta. Hist Schlrshp 1985.

JOHNSON, Paul Andrew (Tex) 17706 Linkview Dr, Dripping Springs TX 78620 **Vic The Great Cmsn Fndt Houston TX 2013-** B Hinsdale IL 1961 s Alvin & Eileen. BA Duke 1983; MDiv Ya Berk 1990. D 6/2/1990 P 4/23/1991 Bp Peter J Lee. m 8/23/1986 Bernadette D Johnson c 3. Chr Ch Glen Allen VA 1995-2013; S Paul's Ch Richmond VA 1990-1994.

JOHNSON, Ralph Foley (SeFla) 88181 Old Highway, #G41, Islamorada FL 33036 **Died 10/6/2016** B Aiken SC 1929 s William & Mae. BS Newberry Coll 1952; BD Sewanee: The U So, TS 1958; MEd U of Miami 1967; EdD U of Miami 1971. D 6/11/1958 P 3/21/1959 Bp Clarence Alfred Cole. m 12/2/1961 Louise Johnson c 1. S Jas The Fisherman Islamorada FL 1995-1996; Ret 1991-2016; Non-par 1970-1995; Vic S Adrian Islamorada FL 1968-1974; S Paul's Ch Delray Bch FL 1966-1970; Assoc All Souls' Epis Ch Miami Bch FL 1966-1968; Vic Incarn Caffney FL 1961-1966.

JOHNSON, Randy Wayne (Minn) 2175 1st St, White Bear Lake MN 55110 **S Jn In The Wilderness S Paul MN 2015-** B St Paul MN 1956 s Donald & Dorothy. BS U MN 1978. D 6/26/2014 P 6/20/2015 Bp Brian N Prior. m 3/17/1979 Kimberly Sue Johnson c 2.

JOHNSON, R Dean (At) 1480 Pineview Ln Nw, Conyers GA 30012 B Amery WI 1928 s James & Helene. BA Gustavus Adolphus Coll 1950; STM GTS 1956. D 6/18/1956 Bp Charles L Street P 12/21/1956 Bp Gerald Francis Burrill. S Simon's Epis Ch Conyers GA 1984-1987; R S Mich's Ch Gainesville FL 1979-1983; R S Ptr's Epis Ch Sycamore IL 1963-1973; Bd Ext 1960-1963; Vic Annunc Waukegan IL 1957-1963; Cur S Ptr's Epis Ch Chicago IL 1956-1957. 1st Place Awd For Rel Journalism Georgia Press Assn.

JOHNSON SR, Richard E (Me) PO Box 688, Castine ME 04421 **Died 1/25/2017** B Mount Pleasant TX 1935 s Ernest & Martha. MDiv SMU Perkins 1961; PhD Wright Inst 1978. D 4/17/1978 Bp Frederick Barton Wolf P 11/1/1978 Bp Harvey D Butterfield. m 5/24/2000 Christine R Talbott c 4. P-in-c S Jas Ch Old Town ME 2014-2017; Aroostook Epis Cluster Caribou ME 1997-2000; Ch Of The Adv Limestone ME 1997-2000; S Anne's Ch Blaine ME 1997-2000; S Jn's Ch Presque Isle ME 1997-2000; P S Lk's Ch Caribou ME 1997-2000; S Paul's Ch Ft Fairfield ME 1997-2000; R S Mary's Epis Ch Inc Lampasas TX 1981-1987; Vic Chr Ch Gardiner ME 1979-1981; Asst S Matt's Epis Ch Hallowell ME 1978-1981. Auth, *A Beautiful Way to Make a Living*; Auth, *Wisdom as Viewed by Older Adults*. Amer Assn of Mar and Fam Ther 1974-2004; AAPC 1973-2004.

JOHNSON, Richard E (Mont) 902 Logan St, Helena MT 59601 **S Ptr's Cathd Helena MT 2014-, 2011-2013, 2008-2010, 1990-1994; Dioc D 1990-; Dioc Yth Coordntr Circuit Rider Big Sky Dnry 1983-** B Deer Lodge MT 1950 s Wilbur & Frances. BA Carroll Coll 1973. D 7/20/1990 Bp Charles I Jones III. Dio Montana Helena MT 1995-1996; Yth Coordntr Of Prov Vi 1988-1992. bookkeeper@stpeterscathedral.net

JOHNSON, Robert Gaines (SVa) 1411 25th St, Galveston TX 77550 **R Chr Epis Ch Eastville VA 2044-** B Corsicana TX 1951 s Clyde & Ann. MDiv Epis TS of the SW; JD So Texas Coll of Law Houston TX; BA U of Texas 1975. D 6/17/2000 Bp Claude Edward Payne. m 3/14/1982 Joanie Milligan. Hungars Par Machipongo VA 2004-2012; S Jn's Ch La Porte TX 2001-2003; D Trin Ch Galveston TX 2000-2001.

JOHNSON III, Roberts Poinsett (Ala) 3620 Belle Meade Way, Birmingham AL 35223 **Int Gr Ch Birmingham AL 2006-** B Winnfield LA 1940 s Roberts & Dee. BA LSU 1962; MDiv GTS 1965. D 6/29/1965 Bp Iveson Batchelor Noland P 5/26/1966 Bp Girault M Jones. m 1/4/1970 Barbara B Johnson c 2. Dio Alabama Birmingham 1993-2006; R S Alb's Ch Hoover AL 1987-2006; Asst R S Mary's-On-The-Highlands Epis Ch Birmingham AL 1985-1987; Asst R S Lk's Epis Ch Birmingham AL 1983-1985; S Matt's Epis Sch Houma LA 1978-1983; Non-par 1974-1983; Cur S Mart's Epis Ch Metairie LA 1971-1978; Yth Dir Dio Louisiana New Orleans LA 1971-1974; Vic S Tim's Ch La Place LA 1967-1971; Vic All SS Epis Ch Ponchatoula LA 1966-1971; Asst Chapl S Mart Sch Metairie LA 1965-1967.

JOHNSON, Robert Wallace (CFla) D 9/10/2016 Bp Gregory Orrin Brewer.

JOHNSON, Ronald A (SwFla) 4030 Manatee Ave W, Bradenton FL 34205 **Chr Ch Bradenton FL 2017-** B Longmont CO 1971 BA Oral Roberts U 1994; MDiv Nash 1998. D 11/7/2002 P 4/15/2003 Bp Keith Whitmore. m 6/22/2002 Lisa J Le Barron c 2. R Adv Epis Ch Westlake OH 2010-2017; R H Trin Prot Epis Ch Onancock VA 2004-2010; P-in-c S Lk's Ch Altoona WI 2003-2004.

JOHNSON, Ronald Norman (SeFla) 320 Dudley Creek Rd, Hardy VA 24101 B Tampa FL 1942 s Norman & Mildred. Cit 1962; BA Stetson U 1964; MBA W&M 1971; MDiv Sewanee: The U So, TS 1977; ThM PrTS 1991. D 6/

11/1977 P 12/17/1977 Bp Emerson Paul Haynes. m 8/21/1967 Johnnie Grace Hevener. R S Jas The Fisherman Islamorada FL 2001-2008; S Fran Cmnty Serv Inc. Salina KS 1999-2001; Sr VP The S Fran Acad Inc. Salina KS 1999-2001; Chapl Off Of Bsh For ArmdF New York NY 1981-1999; Chapl (Ltc) US-Army 1981-1999; R H Innoc Key W FL 1978-1980; R S Ptr's Epis Ch Key W FL 1978-1980; Cur S Hilary's Ch Ft Myers FL 1977-1978. Clincl Mem, Amer Assn For Mar And Fam Ther 1996; Fell, Amer Assn Of Pastorlal Counselors 1993; Mem, Amer Coll Of Healthcare Executives 1999-2002.

JOHNSON, Russell L (SwFla) 13555 Heron Cir, Clearwater FL 33762 B Jamestown NY 1944 s E Milton & Gladys. BS USNA 1967; MDiv Sewanee: The U So, TS 1982; DMin Sewanee: The U So, TS 2001. D 6/7/1982 P 12/1/1982 Bp Hunley Agee Elebash. m 8/5/1983 Judith A Johnson c 5. Cathd Ch Of S Ptr St. Petersburg FL 2004-2008; Dn and R St. Ptr's Cathd St. Petersburg FL 2004-2008; Cn Chr Ch Cathd Lexington KY 1999-2004; R Chr Ch Detroit MI 1997-1999; R S Paul's Epis Ch Edenton NC 1991-1997; R Trin Ch Lumberton NC 1988-1991; R Trin Epis Ch Pinopolis SC 1984-1988; Asst to R S Jn's Epis Ch Wilmington NC 1982-1984. "Call, Response, Restoration," *Disciples of Chr in Cmnty*, Sewanee, 2001.

JOHNSON, Russell Michael (Haw) 296 Nikolau Pl, Hilo HI 96720 B Chicago IL 1950 s James & Lucille. SW Cmnty Coll Chula Vista CA 1982; BA Natl U 1984; MDiv Sewanee: The U So, TS 1987; Cert SWTS 2002. D 6/6/1987 P 12/21/1987 Bp Donald James Davis. m 11/25/1975 Margo Johnson c 3. Ch Of The H Apos Hilo HI 2004-2010; S Jn's Ch Green River WY 1996-2004; Ch Of The H Comm Rock Sprg WY 1995-2004; Vic S Jos's Ch Port Allegan PA 1987-1995; S Marg's Epis Ch Kane PA 1987-1995; S Matt's Epis Ch Eldred PA 1987-1995; Tri-Mssn Mnstry Port Allegan PA 1987-1995; Congrl Hlth and Growth Com The Epis Ch in Hawaii Honolulu HI 2005-2010; Dio Coun Dio Wyoming Casper 2000-2003; COM Dio NW Pennsylvania Erie PA 1992-1995.

JOHNSON JR, Russell Woodrow (WMo) 409 E Liberty, Independence MO 64050 **P-in-c Trin Ch Independence MO 2016-; Participant Red Bridge Mnstrl Allnce - So Kansas City 1997-** B Olivia MN 1951 s Russell & Dorothy. BA Gustavus Adolphus Coll 1973; Untd TS of the Twin Cities 1981; MDiv SWTS 1982; DMin SWTS 2007. D 6/24/1982 P 12/30/1982 Bp Robert Marshall Anderson. m 12/30/1978 Susan L Johnson c 2. Preaching, Pstr care, Admin, outreach, Educ St Ptr & All SS Epis Ch Kansas City MO 1997-2013; Chapl Rotary Intl - Leawood KS 1997-2004; Preaching, Pstr care, Admin, outreach, Educ S Mary's Ch S Paul MN 1986-1997; Supply P Dio Minnesota Minneapolis MN 1986; Pstr Care, preaching, Admin Chr Ch Albert Lea MN 1985-1986; Yth Mnstry, Pstr care, Yth Educ Chr Ch S Paul MN 1982-1985; Chairman - Search/Transition/Consecration Com for a new Bp Dio W Missouri Kansas City MO 2009-2011, Pres of Stndg Com 2007-2011, Dn - Metro Dnry 2000-2004, Cnvnr - Wrshp and Sprtlty Cmsn 1998-2008. Auth, "The Search Process for a new Bp," *The Sprt*, Epis Dio W Missouri, 2009; Auth, "Sm Groups: How they change the life of the Par Cmnty," *Thesis*, Seabury-Wstrn Sem, 2007. Angl-Luth Conf 1988-1997; Associated Parishes 1982-2000; Assn Of Dioc Liturg & Mus Com 1985-2000; Epis Cler Assoc. 1988-1997; Rotary Intl 1982-2004; Rotary Intl 2013. rtrinitychurch@gmail.com

JOHNSON, Ryder Channing (WNY) 19013 N 74th Dr, Glendale AZ 85308 **Died 3/17/2016** B Ithaca NY 1928 s Elmer & Amelia. BA Cor 1950; MDiv Ya Berk 1953; STM Sewanee: The U So, TS 1971; PhD SUNY 1973. D 6/29/1953 Bp Walter M Higley P 6/6/1954 Bp Lauriston L Scaife. m 5/25/1977 Joyce V Dashiell c 4. Non-Stipen S Lk's At The Mtn Phoenix AZ 2007-2014; Assoc R S Andr's Ch Glendale AZ 1996-2005, Asst 1995; P-in-c All Ss Williamsville NY 1969-1974; Asst Calv Epis Ch Williamsville NY 1967-1968; Chapl Hob Geneva NY 1962-1966; Vic S Lk's Epis Ch Attica NY 1956-1962; Cur S Jas' Ch Batavia NY 1953-1956. R Channing Johnson, Amazon, 2013; RC Johnson, Amazon, 2012; Auth, "Cercla Site Assessment Workbook," USDOE, 1994; Auth, "Chemicals From Wood: Plcy Implications Of Fed Subsidy," The MITRE Corp, 1983; Auth, "Workshop," *Workshop Psychol Stress Associated w The Proposed Restart Of 3 Mile Island*, The MITRECorp, 1982; Auth, "Spprt Documents For The Natl Priorities List," USEPA. Amer Chem Soc 1976-1990; Human Factors Soc 1973-1990. Prog Achievement Awd The MITRE Corp 1987.

JOHNSON, Sandra Parnell (SwFla) 14640 N Cleveland Ave, N Ft Myers FL 33903 **D All Souls Epis Ch No Ft Myers FL 2009-** B Norfolk VA 1943 d Troy & Martha. D 10/10/2009 Bp Dabney Tyler Smith. m 8/21/1962 Emery Johnson c 3. D S Hilary's Ch Ft Myers FL 2009.

JOHNSON, Sanford Ralph (WMass) 50 Shaker Farm Rd N, Marlborough NH 03455 B Geneva NY 1949 s Kenneth & Elva. U of Massachusetts 1969; BA U of Maine 1972; MDiv Andover Newton TS 1975. D 9/18/1975 P 4/9/1976 Bp Alexander D Stewart. m 6/13/1970 Barbara Bragg c 1. Assoc S Lk's Ch Chester VT 2008-2015, Assoc 2008; Par Of S Jas Ch Keene NH 2005, 1999-2000, Int 1999-2000, Assoc 1996-2007; P-in-c Ch Of The Epiph Newport NH 2000-2001; Assoc Gr Ch Amherst MA 1983-1985; Vic S Jn's Ch Ashfield MA 1977-1983; Cur Chr Ch Fitchburg MA 1975-1977; Chair of Fin Com Dio New Hampshire Concord NH 2004-2007, Dioc Coun 2004-2007, Fin Com 2002-2007; Camp Bd Dir Dio Wstrn Massachusetts Springfield 1979-1983,

Mem of Dioc Coun 1979-1983, Liturg Cmsn 1978-1983, Ecum Coun Cmsn 1977-1978.

JOHNSON, Simeon O (NY) 165 Saint Marks Pl Apt 10H, Staten Island NY 10301 **S Jos's Ch Bronx NY 2016-; Supply P Dio New York New York NY 2006-, Chapl 1995-2005** B Freetown 1956 s Simeon & Olive. HTC U of Sierra Leone MMTC 1982; Sierra Leone Theol Hall 1987; AA Coll of Staten Island 2005; BA Coll of Staten Island 2006; MDiv GTS 2008. Trans 3/1/1996 Bp Walter Decoster Dennis Jr. m 8/29/1993 Renate Celiana Denise Johnson c 2. P S Mary's Castleton Staten Island NY 2013-2015; S Simon's Ch Staten Island NY 2012-2013; S Edm's Ch Bronx NY 2009-2011; Asst All SS Ch Staten Island NY 1996-2001; Assoc Chapl Chr Hosp Jersey City NJ 1996-1997.

JOHNSON, Stephanie McDyre (Ct) 37 Avon Street, New Haven CT 06511 **S Paul's Ch Riverside CT 2016-** B Brooklyn, NY 1964 d Robert & Patricia. BA Ford 1988; Dip U of Stockholm 1990; MDiv Ya Berk 2010; STM Yale DS 2013. D 3/13/2010 P 9/25/2010 Bp Mark Sean Sisk. m 12/29/1990 Gordon G Hinshalwood c 2. CE Dir S Paul's Ch Fairfield CT 2013-2016; Epis Ch Cntr New York NY 2013, 2012; Dio Vermont Burlington VT 2012; Epis Prov Of New Engl Portland ME 2011-2014; Yth Dir S Ann's Epis Ch Old Lyme CT 2010-2012.

JOHNSON, Susan Elaine (Eur) Schiesstaettberg 44, Eichstatt AL 49842 Germany **D Ch of the Ascen Munich 2003-** B Bedford UK 1944 BA Lon GB 1966; E Angl Mnstrs Trng Course Cambridge Gb 2001. D 5/31/2003 P 11/30/2003 Bp Pierre W Whalon.

JOHNSON, Susan Heckel (At) 571 Holt Road, Marietta GA 30068 B Camp Atterbury IN 1946 d Charles & Jacqueline. BA U of So Carolina 1968; MM Florida St U 1971; MS Florida St U 1990; MDiv Sewanee: The U So, TS 1997. D 6/8/1997 Bp Stephen Hays Jecko P 12/1/1997 Bp Frank Kellogg Allan. c 3. Assoc S Cathr's Epis Ch Marietta GA 2008-2017; R S Clare's Epis Ch Blairsville GA 2000-2008; Asst H Innoc Ch Atlanta GA 1997-2000. ammasusan97@gmail.com

JOHNSON, Thalia Felice (Mich) 8261 Cypress Way, Dexter MI 48130 **1st Cler Alt. Gen Conv 2012 Dio Michigan Detroit MI 2012-, 1st Cler Alt. Gen. Conv 2009 2009-2012, 1st Cler Alt. Gen. Conv 2012 2012-, 1st Cler Alt. Gen. Conv 2009 2009-, Cler Alt 1, Gen. Conv 2012 2009-, Cler Alt 4, Gen. Conv 2006 2004-; D Ch Of The Incarn Pittsfield Twp Ann Arbor MI 2008-** B Flint MI 1946 d Donald & Shirley. BS MI SU 1968; MA MI SU 1976; Cert Whitaker TS 1987. D 9/10/1987 Bp H Coleman Mcgehee Jr. D S Mich And All Ang Brooklyn MI 1991-2005; D Chr Ch Adrian MI 1987-1991. Cambios Inc 1997-2002; NAACP; NAAD. Awd of St. Steph NAAD 2007.

JOHNSON, Theodore Arthur (Nev) P.O. Box 4551, South Lake Tahoe CA 95729 B Madera CA 1922 s Jordon & Theodora. AA Ventura Cnty Cmnty Coll 1966. D 1/6/1985 P 7/1/1985 Bp Wesley Frensdorff. m 2/14/1945 Betty Jean Price.

JOHNSON, Theodore William (WA) PO Box 386, Basye VA 22810 B Worcester MA 1944 s Theodore & Carol. BA Franklin & Marshall Coll 1966; UTS 1969; MDiv VTS 1986; DMin SWTS 2000. D 6/11/1986 P 4/11/1987 Bp Peter J Lee. Int Emm Epis Ch Chestertown MD 2006; Supply P Var congregations 2004-2011; Int Ch Of The Ascen Silver Sprg MD 2003-2004; P-in-c All Faith Epis Ch Charlotte Hall MD 2000-2002; Int S Dav's Epis Ch No Chesterfield VA 1996-2000; Int S Mk's Ch Alexandria VA 1996; Consult and coach Var congregations 1994-2011; Int Emm Ch Middleburg VA 1994-1996; Int Ch Of S Paul's By The Sea Ocean City MD 1992-1993; Int Meade Memi Epis Ch Alexandria VA 1991-1992; R Emm Epis Ch Delaplane Delaplane VA 1988-1991; Int S Paul's Epis Ch Prnc Frederck MD 1987-1988; Asst Emm Epis Ch Alexandria VA 1986-1987.

JOHNSON, Thomas Stanley (NCal) 214 Leafwood Way, Folsom CA 95630 **Assoc Trin Ch Folsom CA 2013-** B Minneapolis MN 1940 s Stanley & Muriel. No Pk U; BA U CA Los Angeles 1965; BD Fuller TS 1968; ETSBH 1997. D 12/14/1997 P 6/1/1998 Bp Gethin Benwil Hughes. m 12/12/1986 Susan Noel Johnson c 2. P-in-c S Mich Ch Alturas CA 2011-2013; R S Jn's Ch Indio CA 2002-2006; Vic Santa Rosa Del Mar Desert Shores CA 2002-2006; Dio San Diego San Diego CA 2002-2005; Vic Santa Rosa del mar Mssn Desert Shores CA 2002-2005; Vic S Hugh Of Lincoln Mssn Idyllwild CA 1998-2002. Min Prov, Third Ord SSF 2014; Professed, 3rd Ord, Soc of S Fran 1996.

JOHNSON, Tim (WA) Washington Episcopal School, 5600 Little Falls Parkway, Bethesda MD 20816 **Chr Ch Port Tobacco Paris La Plata MD 2014-; Cler Assoc The Ch Of The Epiph Washington DC 2013-** B Charlottesville VA 1975 s Roy & Janice. BA Jas Madison U 1996; MDiv Un Presb Sem 2000; MPP Geo Mason U 2008. D 1/26/2013 P 7/27/2013 Bp Mariann Edgar Budde. Chapl Washington Epis Sch Beth MD 2013-2014.

JOHNSON, Vicki Lynn (Spok) 1322 Kimball Ave, Richland WA 99354 B Ft Scott KS 1951 d Kenneth & Mary. AA Oakland Cmnty Coll 1971; BS Cntrl Michigan U 1973. D 10/19/2014 Bp James E Waggoner Jr. m 2/15/1986 Allen Johnson. deacon@allsaintsrichland.org

JOHNSON OHC, Walter (Los) 1264 N Kings Rd Apt 17, West Hollywood CA 90069 **D S Thos The Apos Hollywood Los Angeles CA 2007-; Dio Los Angeles Los Angeles CA 2002-** B Wilmington DE 1938 s Walter & Mary. D 12/2/2006 Bp Chester Lovelle Talton. c 1. Soc Cath P 2010.

JOHNSON, Ward Kendall (ND) 1003 Crescent Ln, Bismarck ND 58501 B Fargo ND 1931 s Ward & Peggy. BS U of No Dakota 1960; The Coll of Emm and S Chad CA 1993. D 6/6/1986 P 10/2/1988 Bp Harold Anthony Hopkins Jr. m 6/23/1956 Anne Whittemore Short. Assoc R S Geo's Epis Ch Bismarck ND 1988-2008.

JOHNSON, William Alexander (NY) 27 Fox Meadow Rd, Scarsdale NY 10583 B Brooklyn NY 1931 s Charles & Ruth. BA CUNY 1953; BD Drew U 1956; MA NYU 1957; PhD Col 1959; ThD Lund U 1962. D 12/2/1967 P 3/30/1968 Bp John P Craine. m 6/11/1955 Carol Genevieve Lundquist c 3. Cathd Of St Jn The Div New York NY 1985-2001; P-in-c S Paul's Within the Walls Rome 1975-1976; Ch Of S Jas The Less Scarsdale NY 1970-1974; San Andres Ch Yonkers NY 1967-1970; Asst S Andr's Ch Yonkers NY 1965-1968. Auth, *Search for Transcendence*, 1975; Auth, *Philos & The Gospel*, 1971; Auth, *Invitation to Theol*, 1970; Auth, *On Rel*, 1965; Auth, *Nature & the Supernatural*, 1960; Auth, *Philos of Rel of Anders Nygren*, 1960. AAR 1960; Amer Philos Soc 1960. Who's Who in Amer 1976; Phi Beta Kappa 1960.

JOHNSON, William Curtis (Oly) 19303 Fremont Ave N, Shoreline WA 98133 **Died 3/20/2016** B Asbury Park NJ 1913 s William & Laura. Ch Army Trng Coll 1948. D 11/11/1952 P 5/1/1953 Bp Frank A Rhea. c 3. Asst P Ch Of The Ascen Seattle WA 1980-2001; Ret 1978-2016; R S Andr's Ch Seattle WA 1968-1978; Archd Dio Idaho Boise ID 1958-1967; R All SS Epis Ch Boise ID 1954-1958; Vic S Jas Ch Burley ID 1952-1954; St Matthews Epis Ch Rupert ID 1952-1954.

JOHNSON, William Francis (Chi) 5749 N Kenmore Ave, Chicago IL 60660 B Schaffer MI 1935 s Carl & Cecile. BA Elmhurst Coll 1961; MDiv SWTS 1964. D 6/13/1964 Bp James Winchester Montgomery P 12/1/1964 Bp Gerald Francis Burrill. Epis Ch Of The Atone Chicago IL 1964-2004.

JOHNSON, William Gerald (Az) 11,000 east Calle Vaqueros, Tucson AZ 85749 B Putnam CT 1939 s William & Phyllis. AA Bos 1960; BA Bos 1962; STM Ya Berk 1965; MPA U of Arizona 1969. D 6/19/1965 P 2/12/1966 Bp John S Higgins. m 10/23/1988 Barbara Johnson. Vic S Raphael In The Vlly Epis Ch Benson AZ 1998-2007; Vic S Paul's Ch Tombstone AZ 1989-1998; R All Faith Epis Ch Charlotte Hall MD 1968-1970; Chapl to Cadets Charlotte Hall Mltry Acad 1968-1970; Asst Ch Of S Matt Tucson AZ 1967-1980; Asst Gr St Pauls Epis Ch Tucson AZ 1967-1968; Cur S Paul's Ch N Kingstown RI 1965-1967.

JOHNSON, William Joseph (Roch) 1378 Lakeland Ave, Lakewood OH 44107 **Non-par 1982-** B Brantford ON CA 1922 MA Col; BA McGill U. D 6/15/1974 P 5/1/1975 Bp John Harris Burt.

JOHNSON III, William Pegram (WA) 2004 Floyd Ave, Richmond VA 23220 **Ret 1998-** B Petersburg VA 1939 s William & Nolie. BA W&M 1960; BD VTS 1965; STM Sewanee: The U So, TS 1970; PhD Emory U 1978. D 9/19/1965 Bp David Shepherd Rose P 6/10/1966 Bp George P Gunn. c 1. S Asaph's Par Ch Bowling Green VA 2004-2010; R Chr Ch S Jn's Par Accokeek MD 1985-1998; Cbury Sch Accokeek MD 1978-1985; Non-par 1972-1985; Chapl S Marg Sch Tappahannock VA 1969-1972; Asst So Farnham Par Tappahannock VA 1969-1971; Asst S Jas Par Wilmington NC 1967-1969; Chapl Chris Newport Coll 1965-1967; Cur S Steph's Ch Newport News VA 1965-1967. Auth, "The Roads From Bethlehem," 1993. Sewanee Fllshp STUSo 1998; Woods Fllshp VTS 1996; Fell Coll Of Preachers 1989; Fell For Hist Resrch Mellon.

JOHNSON-TAYLOR, Allan B (WA) 4211 Enterprise Rd, Bowie MD 20720 **R S Paul's Rock Creek Washington DC 2012-, 2011; R Epiph Ch 2005-** B Bluefields NI 1961 s Artemus & Alice. BA U of Maryland 1989; MDiv VTS 1993; ThM PrTS 1999. D 6/12/1993 P 12/16/1993 Bp Peter J Lee. m 5/24/2003 Donna J J Bailey c 1. R Ch Of The Epiph Washington DC 2004-2011; Assoc S Mich And All Ang Ch Baltimore MD 2002-2004; Int S Phil Memi Ch Philadelphia PA 2002; R S Mich's Ch Lansdowne PA 1995-2001; Asst Vic Trin Epis Ch Charlottesvlle VA 1993-1995.

JOHNSON-TOTH, Louise M (Roch) 243 Genesee Park Blvd, Rochester NY 14619 B Buffalo NY 1946 d Theodore & Betty. BA U Roch 1969; MA U Roch 1970; MSW Syr 1978; MDiv Bex Sem 1993. D 6/5/1999 Bp William George Burrill P 5/27/2000 Bp Jack Marston Mckelvey. m 5/4/1985 Gregory Martin Toth. R Gr Ch Scottsville NY 2001-2007; R S Andr's Epis Ch Caledonia NY 2001-2007; Int Assoc S Mk's & S Jn's Epis Ch Rochester NY 1999-2000.

JOHNSTON, Cathy Lynn (ETenn) 2152 Hawthorne St, Kingsport TN 37664 B Kingsport TN 1959 d William & Clara. BS Bristol U 1983; Theol Formation Prog Epis Sch for Mnstry 2012. D 11/16/2012 Bp George Wayne Smith.

JOHNSTON, Clifford A (CPa) 3147 Grahamton Rd, Morrisdale PA 16858 **Long-term supply P St. Andr's Epis Ch Clearfield PA 2015-; P-in-c Chap Of The Gd Shpd Hawk Run PA 2008-; Mem, Bd Stevenson Sch for Mnstry Dio Cntrl Pennsylvania Harrisburg PA 2015-, Mem Stndg Com 2010-2012** B Philipsburg PA 1956 s Clifford & Mabel. BA Franklin & Marshall Coll 1979; N/A Dioc Sch of Chr Stds 2007; N/A Pennsylvania St Univerdity 2007. D 6/9/2007 P 12/22/2007 Bp Nathan Dwight Baxter. m 1/31/1987 Rebecca Susan Alberth. EPF 2006; Integrity 2006. Serv Playing Cert AGO 2000. clijo77@gmail.com

JOHNSTON, David Knight (Mass) 78 Bishop Dr, Framingham MA 01702 **Chapl to the Ret Cler Ret Cler of the Dio Massachusetts 2007-; Ret . 2006-** B New York NY 1934 s John & Lucile. CPE Advncd CPE; Dplma Deerfield Acad 1952; BA Colg 1956; MDiv VTS 1961; Coll of Preachers 1973. D 7/6/1961 P 6/29/1962 Bp Noble C Powell. m 4/20/1963 Valerie S Johnston c 2. Int Trin Chap Shirley MA 2004-2006; Int Ch Of The H Trin Marlborough MA 2000-2004, Int 1988-1999, Int 1988-1989; Asst S Andr's Ch Framingham MA 1999-2000; Int S Andr's Ch Methuen MA 1998-1999; Int S Paul's Ch Peabody MA 1997-1998; Int S Ptr's Ch Salem MA 1995-1997; Int R Trin Par of Newton Cntr Newton Cntr MA 1993-1995; Int S Steph's Ch Westborough MA 1991-1992; Int S Jn's Ch Winthrop MA 1989-1991; Int Trin Epis Ch Shrewsbury MA 1986-1987; Int Gr Ch Fed Boston MA 1985-1986; Int S Lk's And S Marg's Ch Allston MA 1983-1984; Int Trin Ch Canton MA 1983; Int S Anne's Ch No Billerica MA 1981-1982; Int S Geo's Ch Maynard MA 1976-1977; S Paul's Ch Natick MA 1975-1976, Int 1975-1976; R Ch Of The H Sprt Wayland MA 1969-1975; Asst The Ch Of The Nativ Cedarcroft Baltimore MD 1965-1969; Vic S Ptr's Ch Lonaconing MD 1963-1965; Asst R Ch of Our Sav Baltimore MD 1962-1963; Asst S Jn's Ch Ellicott City MD 1961-1962; Mus Cmsn Dio Massachusetts Boston MA 1970-1973. Fell, AAPC 1979; Int Ntwk 1983.

JOHNSTON, Duncan Howard (CPa) 125 N 25th St, Camp Hill PA 17011 B Matlock ENGLAND 1963 s Alan & Edna. BA U of Hull Hull Gb 1985; MA S Johns Coll Nottingham GB 1993. Trans 8/31/2004 Bp Robert R Gepert. m 7/21/2005 Cindy Lou Johnston c 3. Mt Calv Camp Hill PA 2004-2016; S Jn's Ch Fremont MI 2004-2010.

JOHNSTON, Edward (NY) 1215 5th Ave Apt 12d, New York NY 10029 **Ret Ret 1997-; Trst Emer Cathd Of St Jn The Div New York NY 1984-** B Clinton IA 1938 s Edward & Dorothy. BA Gri 1960; GTS 1962; STB EDS 1963; MA Col 1964. D 6/19/1963 P 6/19/1964 Bp Gordon V Smith. m 6/3/1962 Sally Eileen Edgar c 2. S Ptr's Ch Millbrook NY 1998-2013, Vic 1997-1998; R Emer Chr's Ch Rye NY 1979-1997; R S Dav's Ch Kinnelon NJ 1967-1979; Cur S Mk's Ch Mt Kisco NY 1964-1967; Asst S Mich's Ch New York NY 1963-1964; Trst Dio New York New York NY 1991-1993, Secy Cathd Bd Trst 1989-1998, Chair - Fin Com 1986-1990, Chair Funding Cmsn 1981-1984, Fin Com 1979-1985; Chair Cler Cont Educ Com Dio Newark Newark NJ 1978-1979, Chair Com Elctn Bp Coadj 1975-1977; Trst Emer Cathd of St. Jn the Div, New York 1998; R Emer Chr's Ch, Rye, New York 1998.

JOHNSTON, Frank Norman (LI) PO Box 566, Onset MA 02558 **Ret 1987-** B New York NY 1929 s Frank & Edith. BA S Lawr Canton NY 1952; MDiv S Lawr Canton NY 1955. D 6/25/1955 P 6/1/1956 Bp Norman B Nash. c 5. Int Cathd Ch of All SS St Thos VI 1989-1991; Chr Ch Manhasset NY 1988-1989, 1967-1987, R 1967-1986; Assoc Prof Mercer TS Garden City NY 1984-1987; R S Mk's Ch Foxborough MA 1957-1967; Cur Trin Par of Newton Cntr Newton Cntr MA 1955-1957.

JOHNSTON, Hewitt Vinnedge (NJ) 41087 Calla Lily St, Indian Land SC 29707 B Milwaukee WI 1939 s Milton & Katherine. BA Hope Coll 1961; LTh SWTS 1964. D 7/26/1964 P 7/25/1965 Bp Charles Bennison Sr. m 8/20/1964 Cynthia Jo Johnston c 1. Exec Dir Philharmonic Orchestra of NJ 2000-2007; S Paul's Epis Ch Bound Brook NJ 1999-2000; Int Ch of S Jn on the Mtn Bernardsville NJ 1998-1999; Int S Lk's Ch Gladstone NJ 1997-1998; Int Ch Of The Ascen Clearwater FL 1996; Int S Anselm Epis Ch Lehigh Acres FL 1995-1996; Dio SW Florida Parrish FL 1988-1993; R S Mary's Par Tampa FL 1983-1994; R S Geo's Ch Belleville IL 1976-1983; Vic S Paul's Epis Ch Elk Rapids MI 1970-1976; Chr Epis Ch Charlevoix MI 1967-1976; Dio Wstrn Michigan Kalamazoo MI 1967-1976; Asst S Lk's Par Kalamazoo MI 1964-1967.

JOHNSTON, Laurel (ECR) 2767 Delpha Court, Thousand Oaks CA 91362 **Trin Epis Ch Santa Barbara CA 2017-** B Milton MA 1964 d Thomas & Margaret. BA U CA, Davis 1987; MDiv CDSP 2006; MDiv CDSP 2006. D 6/24/2006 P 4/21/2007 Bp Sylvestre Donato Romero. CDSP Berkeley CA 2014-2016; Stwdshp Off Epis Ch Cntr New York NY 2008-2014; Epis Ch of St Jn the Bapt Aptos Aptos CA 2006-2008; Account Mgr Microsoft 2000-2002.

JOHNSTON, Lewis Tyra (WMo) 2105 Quail Creek Dr, Lawrence KS 66047 **Ret 1990-; Mid-Amer Reg Coun 1972-** B Minneapolis MN 1930 s Raymond & Ruth. BA U MN 1953; MDiv SWTS 1957; MPA U of Missouri 1982. D 6/24/1957 P 2/1/1958 Bp Hamilton Hyde Kellogg. m 12/27/1952 Virginia Johnston c 3. R St Ptr & All SS Epis Ch Kansas City MO 1989, Vic 1964-1969; Cmnty Advsr S Jos's Hosp Kansas City MO 1973-1976; Headmaster S Ptr Day Sch Kansas City MO 1969-1989; S Andr's Ch Kansas City MO 1964-1969; Vic S Edw's Ch Duluth MN 1959-1964; P-in-c S Paul Two Harbors MN 1959-1960; D & P-in-c Geth Ch Appleton MN 1957-1959; D & P-in-c Gr Montevideo MN 1957-1959; Chair - Com on Aging Dio W Missouri Kansas City MO 1982-1990, COM 1978-1981, Eccl Crt 1976-1977, Bp's Coun 1966-1975; Bp's Coun Dio Minnesota Minneapolis MN 1958-1964. Deer Lke Assn 1990; Endacott Soc 1992; ESMA 1979-1989. Citizen of the Year Jackson Cnty 1975.

JOHNSTON, Madelynn (RG) Po Box 8716, Santa Fe NM 87504 **S Paul's Peace Ch Las Vegas NM 2015-; Non-par 1977-** B Chicago IL 1945 d James & Madelynn. D 9/23/1977 Bp Richard Mitchell Trelease Jr P 9/6/2001 Bp Terence Kelshaw. m 10/20/2004 Charles Johnston c 2. S Jerome's Epis Ch Chama NM 2012-2013; S Bede's Epis Ch Santa Fe NM 2004-2013.

J

JOHNSTON, Mark Wylie (Ala) 105 Delong Rd, Nauvoo AL 35578 **Exec Dir Chap Of The Ascen Nauvoo AL 1990-** B Nashville TN 1950 s Archie & Martha. BA U So 1973; MDiv S Lk TS 1980; MDiv Sewanee: The U So, TS 1980. D 6/12/1980 P 12/1/1980 Bp Furman Charles Stough. m 8/14/2004 Margaret Johnston. P Dio Alabama Birmingham 1991-2017, 1988-1989; S Mths Epis Ch Tuscaloosa AL 1984-1987; R S Mich's Fosters AL 1980-1990; S Mich's Epis Ch Fayette AL 1980-1984; Dioc Yth Coordntr. Outstanding Young Al Rel Ldr Jaycees. mark@campmcdowell.com

JOHNSTON, Martha Suzanne (Tenn) 1216 Sneed Rd W, Franklin TN 37069 B Paducah KY 1954 d Earl & Jerry. BA Rhodes Coll 1976; MLIS LSU 1987; None VTS 2012. D 6/1/2013 Bp Morris King Thompson Jr. m 8/25/2001 George V Silbernagel c 2.

JOHNSTON, Michael Adair (WMo) 3726 W/ 75th Street, Prairie Village KS 66208 **Died 12/3/2015** B Kansas City MO 1946 s Ellis & Lucille. BA Colorado Coll 1968; MS U of Glasgow Glasgow GB 1971; MA Ya 1973; PhD Ya 1974; MDiv GTS 1991. D 6/15/1991 Bp Frank Tracy Griswold III P 1/18/1992 Bp William Walter Wiedrich. Schlr-in-Res (part time) Gr and H Trin Cathd Kansas City MO 2007-2015; Gr And H Trin Cathd Kansas City MO 2007-2013; R Gr Ch Oak Pk IL 1997-2005; Vic Ch Of The Epiph Chicago IL 1996-1997; Assoc S Matt's Ch Evanston IL 1991-1996. Auth, "Praying w Icons," *ATR*, 2000; Auth, "Engaging the Word," *New Ch's Tchg Series*, Cowley Press, 1998; Auth, "Renaissance Sacr Arti," *Angl Theol Art*, 1993.

JOHNSTON, Nature N (Colo) **R Ch Of The Nativ Grand Jct CO 2007-** B Miami FL 1954 d Bovard & Elizabeth. AA Florida St U 1974; BS Florida A&M U 1980; MDiv Ya Berk 2001. D 6/11/2005 P 12/17/2005 Bp Robert John O'Neill. Assoc P All SS Epis Ch Denver CO 2006-2007.

JOHNSTON, Philip Gilchrist (Va) 4773 Thornbury Dr, Fairfax VA 22030 **Assoc Ch Of The Gd Shpd Burke VA 2002-, Int 1977-1978, Int 1977-1978** B Buhl MN 1929 s Kenneth & Arlyn. BS U of Kentucky 1952; MDiv Epis TS in Kentucky 1958; Grad Stds LIU 1969; Grad Stds VTS 1979. D 6/14/1958 P 9/19/1958 Bp William R Moody. m 5/23/1987 Carol Lawton Johnston c 2. Int S Matt's Epis Ch Sterling VA 1999-2001; Vic Piedmont Ch Madison VA 1983-1995; Int S Andr's Epis Ch Arlington VA 1978-1979; Asst Pohick Epis Ch Lorton VA 1978; Nave Chapl (Mltry) Cathd of St Ptr & St Paul Washington DC 1970-1972; Chapl Dept of Defense - US Army 1960-1977; R Chr Epis Ch Harlan KY 1958-1960; Infantry Off Dept of Defense - US Army 1952-1955. Auth, *Var arts*. Coll of Commerce Stdt Pres 1951-1952. Milton Hamolsky Outstanding Physcn of the Year RI Hosp Med Stff Assn 2013; Coll Bus Fraternity Delta Sigma Pi 1951.

JOHNSTON III, Robert Hugh (Dal) 5311 Ridgedale Dr, Dallas TX 75206 **S Mich And All Ang Ch Dallas TX 2016-** B Wharton TX 1966 s Robert. BS Baylor U; MTS SMU Perkins 2005. D 11/15/2003 P 6/3/2004 Bp James Monte Stanton. m 7/15/1989 Robin Lynn Johnston c 2. Assting Ch Of The Incarn Dallas TX 2004-2015.

JOHNSTON JR, Robert Hugh (WTex) 102 E. Live Oak St., Cuero TX 77954 **Partnr in Mnstry 2009-** B Houston TX 1930 s Robert & Meddie. MD Baylor Coll Med; BS Baylor U. D 6/8/2009 P 12/9/2009 Bp Gary Richard Lillibridge. m 8/20/1955 Sara Stuart Johnston c 4.

JOHNSTON, Robert Owen (SVa) 207 Marshall St, Petersburg VA 23803 B Uniontown PA 1919 s Walter & Edna. Indiana U of Pennsylvania 1946; MA U Chi 1949; Command and Gnrl Stff Coll 1951; Penn 1951; MDiv VTS 1970. D 6/29/1970 P 4/9/1971 Bp David Shepherd Rose. c 6. Vstng :Mnstrs to the Caribbean 1990-1995; P in Charge Dominica Belize 1990-1995; R Bath Par Dinwiddie Cnty VA 1979-1985; Calv Ch Bath Par Mc Kenney VA 1979-1984; R Ch of the Gd Shpd Mc Kenney VA 1979-1984; R Jackson Field Hm Jarratt VA 1975-1979; R Bath Par Dinwiddie Cnty VA 1970-1975.

JOHNSTON, Roy Wayne (WLa) 243 Whippoorwill Ln SW, Rome GA 30165 B Lexington KY 1936 s Roy & Elsie. BBA U of Miami 1959; BD Lexington TS 1962; MDiv Lexington TS 1969; Cont Educ Sewanee: St. Lk's TS 1969. D 12/27/1969 P 5/1/1970 Bp George Leslie Cadigan. m 10/27/1978 Mary C Johnston c 1. Assoc Chr Epis Ch Tyler TX 1999-2001; R Ch Of The Redeem Oak Ridge LA 1990-1999; R S Andr's Epis Ch Mer Rouge LA 1990-1999; R S Thos' Ch Monroe LA 1988-1990; R S Steph's Ch Heathsville VA 1986-1989; R Emm Ch Cumberland MD 1974-1978; Chapl/Prof. of Rel Hampden Sydney/ Longwood Colleges 1971-1974; P-in-c S Alb's Epis Ch Fulton MO 1970-1972; Chapl/Prof. of Rel Wm Woods Coll Fulton Missouri 1964-1971; Bp's Coun Dio Maryland Baltimore MD 1976-1978.

JOHNSTON, Sally (USC) 392 Stonemarker Rd, Mooresville NC 28117 B Charlotte NC 1950 d William & Virginia. BA U NC 1972; MPA California St U 1979; MDiv GTS 2004. D 6/19/2004 P 1/15/2005 Bp Michael B Curry. m 1/28/1980 Harold L Newfield c 2. R S Martins-In-The-Field Columbia SC 2009-2016; Assoc Ch Of The H Comf Charlotte NC 2004-2009; SVP HR Wachovia Charlotte NC 1980-2001. revsallyjohnston@gmail.com

✠ JOHNSTON, The Rt Rev Shannon Sherwood (Va) 110 W Franklin St, Richmond VA 23220 **Bp of Virginia Dio Virginia Richmond VA 2007-** B Florence AL 1958 s Albert & Nancy. BA U So 1981; MDiv SWTS 1988. D 6/11/1988 P 12/14/1988 Bp Robert Oran Miller Con 5/26/2007 for Va. m 5/20/1995 Ellen G

Johnston. R All SS' Epis Ch Tupelo MS 1994-2007; R Ch Of The Adv Sumner MS 1990-1994; Cur S Paul's Ch Selma AL 1988-1990; Dep Gen Conv Dio Mississippi Jackson MS 2000-2006, Dn Dioc Conv 1998-2006. Omicron Delta Kappa; Phi Beta Kappa; Vstng Stdt Schlr Westcott Hse Theol Coll. sjohnston@ thediocese.net

JOHNSTON, Suzanne Elaine (Roch) 1245 Culver Rd., Rochester NY 14609 **Ephphatha Mssn For The Deaf Gates NY 2009-** B Canada 1959 d William & Jean. BA SUNY at Geneseo 1981; MA SUNY at Buffalo 1983. D 5/2/2009 Bp Prince Grenville Singh. m 6/4/1983 William Johnston c 3. S Mk's And S Jn's Epis Ch Rochester NY 2009.

JOHNSTON, William Merrill (FdL) 1010 Congress St, Neenah WI 54956 **Chapl Chapl to Ret Cler Dio Fond du Lac 1997-; Ret Dio Fond Du Lac 1997-; Com Dio Fond Du Lac 1977-; Dn - Minneapolis Metropltn Reg Dio Minnesota 1971-; Dept Of CSR Dio Minnesota 1964-** B Beloit WI 1935 s Wallace & Evelyn. BA Macalester Coll 1957; LTh SWTS 1960; Cert Minneapolis Mha Minneapolis MN 1971; MDiv SWTS 1976. D 6/18/1960 Bp Hamilton Hyde Kellogg P 5/22/1961 Bp Philip Frederick McNairy. m 12/20/ 1958 Beverly Hogan c 4. Cmsn For Cong Dvlpmt Dio Fond Du Lac 1992-1993; Stndg Com Pres Dio Fond Du Lac 1985-1987; Stndg Com Secy Dio Fond Du Lac 1977-1985; R S Thos Ch Menasha WI 1976-1997; R S Thos Neenah WI 1976-1997; R S Jas On The Pkwy Minneapolis MN 1969-1976; P-in-c S Mich & All Ang No S Paul MN 1962-1969; Vic S Jn Silver Bay MN 1960-1962; Cler Deploy Off Dio Fond du Lac Appleton WI 1997-2010, Cn to the Ret Cler 1997-.

JOHNSTON, Zula J (Oly) 8527 46th Ct Ne, Olympia WA 98516 **D S Jos And S Jn Ch Lakewood WA 2009-; D S Ben Epis Ch Lacey WA 2005-; Stndg Com Mem Dio Olympia Seattle 2006-** B Pittsburgh PA 1939 BS No Carolina Cntrl U 1972; MS U CO 1976. D 6/18/2003 Bp Sanford Zangwill Kaye Hampton. D S Ben Epis Ch Lacey WA 2003-2005. Ord of S Lk 1992.

JOHNSTONE, Elise (Lex) **Cn Dio Lexington Lexington 2014-, GC Dep 2011-, Liturg and Mus Co-Chair 2007-, Mem, Exec Coun 2006-2009, Mem, Commisson on Mnstry 2006-** B 1975 d John & Sandra. BA U GA 1997; MDiv GTS 2005. D 6/18/2005 P 1/5/2006 Bp Stacy F Sauls. m 2/10/2007 Ryan Douglas Shrauner c 1. Ch Of The Gd Shpd Lexington KY 2011-2014; Assitant To The R Ch Of The H Trin Georgetown KY 2005-2011. elise@diolex.org

JOHNSTONE, Mary Boardman McAvoy (RI) 39 Washington St, Newport RI 02840 **Sprtl Dir Bethany Hse of Pryr at St. Anne-Bethany Arlington MA 2004-; Ret 2003-** B New York NY 1935 d Clifford & Frances. Smith 1956; BA NWU 1970; Rhode Island Sch for Deacons 1985; MA Ya Berk 1989; Dio So Carolina SC 2000. D 7/13/1985 P 6/24/1989 Bp George Nelson Hunt III. m 6/ 16/1956 Robert L Johnstone c 4. Assoc Gr Ch Cathd Charleston SC 1998-2003; Vic S Columba's Epis Ch E Boothbay ME 1994-1996; Emm Ch Newport RI 1994; Chapl Newport Hosp Newport RI 1986-1987; Trin Ch Newport RI 1985-1989, D 1985-1989; Chapl Kent Cnty Hosp Warwick RI 1985-1986; Eccl Crt Dio Maine Portland ME 1994-1996; Eccl Crt Dio Rhode Island Providence RI 1989-1994.

JOINER, James (Ore) St David Of Wales Epis Ch, 2800 SE Harrison St, Portland OR 97214 **S Dav's Epis Ch Portland OR 2013-; D S Mich And All Ang Ch Portland OR 2013-** B Raleigh NC 1982 s Robert & Kathy. MDiv GTS 2012; MDiv The GTS 2012. D 6/29/2013 Bp Michael B Curry P 1/4/2014 Bp Michael Hanley. m 4/4/2013 Nathanael D LeRud. Dio Oregon Portland OR 2013, 2013-.

JOLLY, Anne B (Chi) 3201 Windsor Rd, Austin TX 78703 **S Greg's Epis Ch Deerfield IL 2016-** B North Carolina 1970 d Rhett & Patricia. BA Furman U 1992; MDiv Sewanee: The U So, TS 2013; MDiv The TS at The U So 2013. D 6/1/2013 Bp William Andrew Waldo P 1/18/2014 Bp Dena Arnall Harrison. m 9/5/1992 David T Jolly c 3. Cur The Ch of the Gd Shpd Austin TX 2013-2016; Chr Ch Greenville SC 2004-2010. austinjollys@gmail.com

JOLLY, Marshall A (WNC) Grace Episcopal Church, 303 S King St, Morganton NC 28655 **Gr Ch Morganton NC 2015-** B Lexington KY 1987 s William & Bonnie. BA Transylvania U 2009; MDiv Candler TS Emory U 2012. D 1/22/2012 P 8/11/2012 Bp Chilton Richardson Knudsen. m 5/23/2015 Elizabeth Stewart Anderson. P-in-c Gr Epis Ch Florence KY 2012-2015. rector@ gracemorganton.org

JONES, Adrea (Okla) 1901 Skyline Place, Bartlesville OK 74006 **Vic S Thos Ch Pawhuska OK 2010-; Prov Syn Dio Oklahoma Oklahoma City OK 2010-** B Saint Cloud MN 1945 d William & Mary. U of Cntrl Missouri 1963; U of Iowa 1966; AA Kirkwood Cmnty Coll 1990; MDiv Sewanee: The U So, TS 1997. D 6/12/2000 Bp Chris Christopher Epting P 5/1/2001 Bp Robert Manning Moody. m 8/16/1967 William Jones c 3. Assoc S Lk's Epis Ch Bartlesville OK 2009-2010, Asst 2000-2003; R S Matt's Ch Sand Sprg OK 2006-2009; R All SS Epis Ch Miami OK 2005-2006; R S Jas' Epis Ch Fremont NE 2003-2005; Bp's Com Dio Nebraska Omaha NE 2004-2005. OSL 1985-1987.

JONES, Alan (Cal) 1100 California St, San Francisco CA 94108 B London UK 1940 s Edward & Blanche. BA U of Nottingham 1963; STB GTS 1965; STM GTS 1968; GTS 1968; PhD U of Nottingham 1971; DLitt U of San Francisco 2008. Trans 3/15/1967 as Priest Bp Horace W B Donegan. m 4/18/1999 Virginia F Jones c 3. Dn Gr Cathd San Francisco CA 1985-2009; Ascetical

Theol The GTS New York NY 1975-1985; Assoc Dir Dio New York New York NY 1971-1974; Asst Dir Trin Par New York NY 1971-1972; Tutor Lincoln Theol Coll UK 1968-1971; Asst The Ch of S Ign of Antioch New York NY 1967-1968. Auth, "Common Pryr on Common Ground," *Common Pryr on Common Ground*, Morehouse, 2006; Auth, "Reimagining Chrsnty," *Reimagining Chrsnty*, Wiley, 2005; Auth, "Seasons of Gr," *Seasons of Gr*, Wiley, 2003; Auth, "Living the Truth," *Living the Truth*, Cowley, 2001; Auth, "The Soul's Journrey," *The Soul's Journey*, Cowley, 2001; Auth, "Exploring Sprtl Direction," *Exploring Sprtl Direction*, Cowley, 1992; Auth, "Sacrifice and Delight," *Sacrifice & Delight*, Harper Collins, 1992; Auth, "Passion for Pilgrimage," *Passion for Pilgrimage*, Harper and Row, 1989; Auth, "Soul Making," *Soul Making*, HarperSanFrancsico, 1985; Auth, "Living in the Sprt," *Living in the Sprt*, Seabury, 1982; Auth, "Journey Into Chr," *Journey into Chr*, Cowley, 1977. OBE(Ord of the British Empire) Queen of Engl 2003; Hon Cn-Chartres Cathd Chartres Cathd 2001; Chapl The Venerable Ord of St. Jn 1985.

JONES, Andrew Lovell (Ct) Po Box 1083, Norwalk CT 06856 B Huntington WV 1949 s Franklin & Ruth. BA Marshall U 1971; MDiv VTS 1974; Cert Mid-Atlantic Trng & Consulting 1977; Cert Mid-Atlantic Trng & Consulting 1978; MBA U of Bridgeport 1990. D 6/10/1974 Bp Robert Poland Atkinson P 2/22/1975 Bp Wilburn Camrock Campbell. m 6/14/2003 Kathleen Crist Jones c 2. Supply P Calv Epis Ch Bridgeport CT 1997-1999, Supply P 1986-1996; Supply P S Lk's/S Paul's Ch Bridgeport CT 1986-1987; P in Charge Trin Epis Ch 1983; Assoc R Trin Epis Ch 1981-1984; Trin Epis Ch Southport CT 1981-1984; Vic S Dav's Cross Lanes WV 1976-1981; St Davids Ch 1974-1981; Cur The Memi Ch Of The Gd Shpd Parkersburg WV 1974-1976; Asst R The Memi Ch of the Gd Shpd 1974-1976. Ord of S Vinc 1975-1981.

JONES, Andy (Mil) 2920 Pelham Rd, Madison WI 53713 **R S Andr's Ch Madison WI 2006-; GC Dep Dio Milwaukee Milwaukee WI 2010-, Dn, W Convoc 2009-, Exec Coun 2009-** B Baltimore MD 1960 s Stanley & Linda. BA Juniata Coll 1982; MDiv VTS 2002. D 6/8/2002 Bp John L Rabb P 1/4/2003 Bp Robert Wilkes Ihloff. m 8/13/1983 Suzanne Eileen Brown c 2. Asst R All SS Ch Frederick MD 2002-2006. Bp's Shield Awd Dio Milwaukee 2011. rector@standrews-madison.org

JONES, Angela Louise (Neb) 1555 14Th St, Mitchell NE 69357 **Mus Tchr St Agnes Cath Sch Scottsbluff NE 2005-** B Falls City NE 1949 d Roy & Deila. D 12/9/2006 Bp Joe Goodwin Burnett. c 2.

JONES, Anthony Edward (LI) St Jone's Episcopal Church, 12 Prospect St, Huntington NY 11743 B Abilene TX 1970 s Edward & Norma. BS Lamar U 1992; JD So Texas Coll of Law 1995; Diac Stds Mercer TS 2013. D 10/5/2013 Bp Lawrence C Provenzano.

JONES II, Bennett Green (WMass) 569 Main Street, Fitchburg MA 01420 **R Chr Ch Fitchburg MA 2012-, P-in-c 2010-2012; Dio Wstrn Massachusetts Springfield 2010-** B Cleveland OH 1959 s Wayne & Shirley. BA Bowling Green St U 1982; MDiv VTS 1986. D 6/28/1986 Bp James Russell Moodey P 1/12/1987 Bp Furman Charles Stough. m 5/1/1993 Carolyn G Gibson c 2. R S Paul's Epis Ch Munster IN 2000-2010; Int Chr Ch Cape Girardeau MO 1999-2000; All SS Epis Ch Farmington MO 1998-1999; Int S Pauls Epis Ch Ironton MO 1998-1999; Dio Maryland Baltimore MD 1997-1998; Supply P Dio Missouri S Louis MO 1997-1998; Supply P Dio Los Angeles Los Angeles CA 1994-1997; Vic Ch Of The Trsfg Lake S Louis MO 1988-1994; Asst R S Paul's Ch Selma AL 1986-1988.

JONES, Beverly Jean (Alb) 7460 Se Concord Pl, Hobe Sound FL 33455 B Norwalk OH 1950 d Donald & Miriam. Florida Atlantic U; AA Palm Bch Cmnty Coll 1970; BA Barry U 1999. D 12/21/1991 Bp Calvin Onderdonk Schofield Jr. m 8/11/2004 Michael Stephen Jones. S Mary's Epis Ch Stuart FL 2000-2002; Assoc For Cmncatns The Epis Ch Of Beth-By-The-Sea Palm Bch FL 1993-1995; D S Dav's-In-The-Pines Epis Ch W Palm Bch FL 1991-1995.

✠ JONES, The Rt Rev Bob Gordon (Wyo) 900 Cottonwood Dr, Fort Collins CO 80524 **Cn St. Geo's Cathd Jerusalem 1996-** B Paragould AR 1932 s F H & Helen. BBA U of Mississippi 1956; MDiv Epis TS of the SW 1959; DD Epis TS of the SW 1978. D 6/29/1959 P 4/25/1960 Bp Robert Raymond Brown Con 10/31/1977 for Wyo. m 5/22/1993 Mary Page Jones c 4. Int Chr Epis Ch Pensacola FL 2007-2008; Int Emm Epis Ch Geneva 1201 2006; Int S Eliz's Ch Honolulu HI 2004-2005; Assoc Bp (Ret) Chr Ch Cody WY 2002-2011; Asst Bp of Cyprus Dio Cyprus 2000-2004; Ret Bp of Wyoming Dio Wyoming Casper 1997-1998, Bp of Wyoming 1977-1996, C14 Exec Comm 1981-1987; Dn S Geo's Coll Jerusalem 1996-2000; Exec Coun Appointees New York NY 1996; No Amer Rgnl Com S Geo's Coll Jerusalem 1987-1996; PBFWR 1985-1991; R S Christophers Ch Anchorage AK 1975-1977, Vic 1967-1974; Vic S Ptr's Ch Seward AK 1974-1975; Vic S Barth's Ch Palmer AK 1967-1971; Chapl Native Hosp Anchorage AK 1967-1969; P-in-c S Geo In The Arctic Kotzebue AK 1962-1967; Asst Trin Cathd Little Rock AR 1959-1962; Pres Wyoming Coun of Ch Casper WY 1985-1986; Chair, Bd Laramie Yth Crisis Ctr Laramie WY 1981-1996. Newcomin Soc 1978-1996. Hon DD Epis TS of the SW 1978.

JONES, Bonnie Quantrell (Lex) 1801 Glenhill Dr, Lexington KY 40502 **All SS Epis Ch Lexington KY 2006-** B Detroit MI 1944 d Arthur & Eleanor. BA U MN 1966; MDiv Lexington TS 1996. D 11/30/1996 P 5/31/1997 Bp Don Adger

Wimberly. m 7/21/1984 William Jones c 2. R St Martha's Epis Ch Lexington KY 2007-2009; Vic St. Martha's Ch Lexington KY 2006-2007; Dio Lexington Lexington 2006; S Ptr's Ch Paris KY 1996-2005. Philanthropist of the Year Assoc. of Fundraising Professionals 2007; Bluegrass Bus Hall of Fame JA of the Bluegrass 1999; YWCA Wmn of the Year YWCA of the Bluegrass 1995.

JONES, Bryan William (Los) 5306 Arbor Road, Long Beach CA 90808 B Salt Lake City UT 1953 s Felton & Rose. BA U of Utah 1976; MDiv EDS 1979. D 11/6/1978 P 6/1/1979 Bp Otis Charles. m 11/11/2005 Amy Fay Pringle. S Lk's Of The Mountains La Crescenta CA 2009-2014; S Thos Of Cbury Par Long Bch CA 2002-2009; S Aid's Epis Ch Malibu CA 2000-2002; MHA Long Bch CA 1987-1995; R Ch Of The Epiph Los Angeles CA 1982-1987; Int S Steph's Epis Ch Boston MA 1981-1982; Int Chr Ch Swansea MA 1980-1981; Dio Utah Salt Lake City UT 1979-1980; P-in-c S Jn's Epis Ch Logan UT 1979-1980.

JONES, Carolyn G (WMass) 4 Carousel Ln, Lunenburg MA 01462 **Chr Ch Fitchburg MA 2011-; Yth Min Dio Wstrn Massachusetts Springfield 2011-** B Philadelphia PA 1949 d Mark & Bernice. Weston Jesuit TS; BA Arcadia U 1971; MDiv EDS 1985. D 6/8/1985 Bp Paul Moore Jr P 6/9/1986 Bp Robert Rae Spears Jr. m 5/1/1993 Bennett Green Jones. Wrshp Min S Paul's Epis Ch Munster IN 2008-2010; Vstng Prof Pur Calumet Hammond IN 2004-2010; Cmnty Mem Rush U Med Cntr Instnl Revs Bd 2002-2010; VP for Mssn & Ethics St. Jn's Mercy Hlth Care St. Louis MO 1999-2001; Dir St Andr Epis Fdn 1997-1999; Assoc For Fam Mnstrs All SS Par Beverly Hills CA 1994-1997; Cn For Educ And Admin Chr Ch Cathd S Louis MO 1991-1994; VP for Analysts and Assoc Merrill Lynch Invstmt Banking New York NY 1987-1991; Asstg P Trin Par New York NY 1987-1991; Asst Ch Of The H Trin New York NY 1986-1987; Dir of Chr Ed St. Jas' Ch New York NY 1979-1982; Cler Alt Dep Dio Nthrn Indiana So Bend IN 2009, Examing Chapl 2007-2010. Keynoter ECW, Arkansas 2001; Keynoter ECW, Cntrl Gulf Coast 2001; Keynoter ECW, W Texas 2001; Chapl Ecw Trien, Denver 2000; Keynoter Aspiring Wmn Conf, Pgh 1998; Prchr Twa Flight 800 Memi Serv, LA 1996. associaterector@gmail.com

JONES JR, Cecil Baron (Miss) 117 Demontluzin Ave Apt 25, Bay St Louis MS 39520 **Ret 2001-** B Meridian MS 1941 s Cecil & Margaret. BA U of Mississippi 1963; MDiv Sewanee: The U So, TS 1966. D 5/28/1966 P 5/1/1967 Bp John Maury Allin. c 3. R All SS' Epis Ch Tupelo MS 1980-1993; Gr Epis Ch Canton MS 1970-1980; R The Chap Of The Cross Madison MS 1970-1977; S Eliz's Mssn Collins MS 1968-1970; Vic S Steph's Ch Columbia MS 1968-1970; Ch Of The Redeem Greenville MS 1966-1968; Cur S Jas Ch Greenville MS 1966-1968; Non-par.

✠ JONES III, The Rt Rev Charles I (Mont) PO Box 86, Gulf Shores AL 36547 B El Paso TX 1943 s Charles & Helen. BS Cit 1965; MBA U NC 1966; S Geo Coll 1976; MDiv Sewanee: The U So, TS 1977; Ldrshp Acad for New Directions 1982; DD Sewanee: The U So, TS 1989. D 6/2/1977 Bp David Shepherd Rose P 12/10/1977 Bp David Reed Con 2/8/1986 for Mont. m 6/18/1966 Ashby M Jones c 4. Bp Of Montana Dio Montana Helena MT 1986-2001; Archd Dio Kentucky Louisville KY 1982-1985, Coll Chapl 1977-1981; Barren River Area Coun Louisville KY 1977-1985; Vic Trin Ch Russellville KY 1977-1985. Auth, "Total Mnstry: A Practical Approach," *Bk*, Archegos, 1991; Auth, "Mssn Strtgy In The 21st Century," *Bklet*, Self, 1988. DD TS U So 1989.

JONES, Charles James (CNY) 9 Jutland Road, Binghamton NY 13903 **Assoc Chr Ch Binghamton NY 2012-; Ret Dio Cntrl New York Liverpool NY 1999-, Dn 1982-2000, Dn 1982-1999, 1982-1991, Chair Educ Mnstry Dept 1977-1981, 1974-1982, Chapl to Ret Cler & Surviving Spouse 2005-** B Niagara Falls NY 1934 s Theodore & Dorothy. BS SUNY 1962; MDiv VTS 1967. D 6/17/1967 P 3/9/1968 Bp Lauriston L Scaife. m 8/27/1960 Joan Margaret Coleman c 2. Vic Zion Epis Ch Windsor NY 2000-2011; Coll Chapl Broome Cnty Coun of Ch Binghamton NY 1978-1989; R The Ch Of The Gd Shpd Binghamton NY 1974-1999; Asst Gr Epis Ch Elmira NY 1969-1974; Mssyin-c S Jn's Epis Ch Elmira NY 1967-1969; P-in-c S Mk Epis Ch Millport NY 1967-1969.

JONES, Christine Ann (NY) **S Lk's Ch Somers NY 2016-** B Milwaukee WI 1957 d Robert & Dorothy. BS U of Wisconsin 1980; MFA Wayne 1985; MDiv GTS 2014; MDiv The GTS 2014. D 3/15/2014 P 9/27/2014 Bp Andrew Marion Lenow Dietsche. m 8/28/2010 Julie A Vincent.

JONES, Chuck (RG) B 1955 Mstr of Arts GTS 1983. D 6/4/2016 Bp Michael Vono. c 2.

JONES, Connie (SVa) 6214 Monroe Pl, Norfolk VA 23508 **Assoc Gr Ch Yorktown Yorktown VA 2006-** B Plainfield NJ 1947 d Hugh & Patricia. BA Mt Holyoke Coll 1968; MA Duke 1970; PhD Duke 1974; Cert UTS 2002; Cert VTS 2003. D 6/14/2003 P 12/14/2003 Bp Carol J Gallagher. c 2. Assoc Chr and S Lk's Epis Ch Norfolk VA 2003-2007. Auth, "She's Leaving Hm: Letting Go as My Daughter Goes to Coll," Andrews McMeel, 2002; co-Auth, "A Goodly Heritage:The Dio Sthrn Virginia 1892-1992," Pictorial Heritage, 1992. Phi Beta Kappa 1974. Prof Emer Tidewater Cmnty Coll 2004; Mem Phi Beta Kappa 1974.

JONES, Corey Matthew (Ala) D 6/2/2017 Bp John Mckee Sloan Sr.

JONES, Curtis Carl (Ark) 20900 Chenal Pkwy, Little Rock AR 72223 **Int Gr Ch Pine Bluff AR 2014-** B Little Rock AR 1950 s Tracy & Leone. Henderson St Coll; U of Arkansas Little Rock. D 10/28/2000 Bp Larry Maze P 10/9/2010 Bp Larry Benfield. m 9/28/1996 Mary Price Jones c 2. S Marg's Epis Ch Little Rock AR 2011.

JONES, Dale Jackson (Ga) **D Trin Ch Cochran GA 2015-** B 1951 BSE Educ Georgia SW St U 1974; MED Educ Georgia SW St U 1981; Sewanee: The U So, TS 2015. D 11/6/2015 P 5/21/2016 Bp Scott Anson Benhase. m 3/19/1975 Kathy Marie Floyd c 2.

JONES, Daniel Gwilym (Be) 315 Calvin St, Dunmore PA 18512 **COM Dio Bethlehem Bethlehem PA 2007-, Dioc Coun 1999-2006** B Scranton PA 1932 s Thomas & Sarah. BS U of Scranton 1963; MBA Wilkes Coll 1969; EFM Sewanee: The U So, TS 1996. D 6/14/1997 P 12/13/1997 Bp Paul Victor Marshall. m 6/20/1959 Laura Dovaston Jones c 1. R H Cross Epis Ch Wilkes Barre PA 1998-2010; D Gr Epis Ch Kingston PA 1996-1998.

JONES SR, Daniel L (Alb) 15 Center St, Deposit NY 13754 **Chr Ch Deposit NY 2013-** B Memphis TN 1955 s Robert & Maudie. BM U of Memphis 1980; MA Nash 2014; MA Nash 2014. D 6/1/2013 P 12/8/2013 Bp William Howard Love. m 11/8/1980 Deborah K Jones c 9.

JONES, David Alexander (Md) Po Box 121, Highland MD 20777 **Died 1/17/2017** B Huntington,NY 1931 s J Denovan & Jessie. BA MI SU 1953; BD EDS 1957. D 6/30/1957 Bp Richard Stanley Merrill Emrich P 2/1/1958 Bp Archie H Crowley. m 2/27/1960 Rose Jones c 4. Non-par 1968-2017; Dir Of Coll Wk Dio Maryland Baltimore MD 1964-1968; R S Andr's Ch Manchester NH 1961-1964; Min Chr Ch Cranbrook Bloomfield Hills MI 1957-1958.

✠ JONES, The Rt Rev David Colin (Va) 6043 Burnside Landing Drive, Burke VA 22015 B Youngstown OH 1943 s John & Jean. BA W Virginia U 1965; MDiv VTS 1968; Coll of Preachers 1980; DMin VTS 1991; VTS 1996. D 6/11/1968 P 12/18/1968 Bp Wilburn Camrock Campbell Con 6/24/1995 for Va. m 6/5/1965 Mary B Jones c 2. SCSD 1998-2000; Bp Suffr Of VA Dio Virginia Richmond VA 1995-2012, Bp Suffr Of VA 1995-2012, Cmsn On Ch Planting 1991-1994, Dioc Bdgt Com 1987-1991, Bd Theol Educ 1995-1997, Chair, Comm on Cong Missions 1990-1993, Chair, Dioc Bdgt Comm 1990-1991, Exec Bd 1988-1991, Chair, E Afr Mnstry Comm 1985-1988, Stndg Com 1985-1988, Chair, Evang Comm 1983-1986; R Ch Of The Gd Shpd Burke VA 1978-1995; R S Steph's Epis Ch Beckley WV 1972-1977; Greenbrier Monroe Epis Mnstry Wht Sphr Spgs WV 1972; Vic S Jas' Epis Ch Lewisburg WV 1968-1972; SCSD Dom And Frgn Mssy Soc- Epis Ch Cntr New York NY 1998-2000; Field Ed Mentor VTS Alexandria VA 1980-1995.

JONES, David G (ECR) 1061 Garcia Rd, Santa Barbara CA 93103 **Ret 1996-** B Nashville TN 1931 s George & Elizabeth. PhD Columbia Pacific U; BA U So 1953; BD Sewanee: The U So, TS 1957. D 6/24/1957 Bp John Vander Horst P 12/1/1957 Bp Theodore N Barth. m 9/8/1996 Sandra E Tripp-Jones. Asst Trin Cathd San Jose CA 1991; Asst Epis Ch of St Jn the Bapt Aptos Aptos CA 1972-1990; Serv S Steph The Mtyr Ch Minneapolis MN 1967-1971; Chair - Yth Div 1959-1961; R Chr Whitehaven TN 1957-1961. Auth, "The Kit For Ch Renwl"; Auth, "Beyond Bravery," *The Courage To Lead.* Presidential Round Table 1990.

JONES, David James (ECR) Le Bourg, 47120 Loubes-Bernac, Duras 47120 France B Palo Alto CA 1945 s James & Annette. BA San Francisco St U 1967; BD EDS 1970; S Georges Coll Jerusalem IL 1986. D 6/27/1970 Bp Chauncie Kilmer Myers P 5/1/1971 Bp George Richard Millard. m 10/3/1970 Martha Jones. R Calv Epis Ch Santa Cruz CA 1981-2001; Vic S Lk's Ch Hollister CA 1974-1981; Asst Chapl H Trin Brussels Belgium 1972-1974; Cur All SS Epis Ch Palo Alto CA 1970-1972; Secy Conv Dio El Camino Real Salinas CA 1987-1997, Stndg Com 1985-1986, Chair Dept Yth Mnstrs 1975-1984.

JONES, David P (Chi) 1229 Hinman Avenue, Evanston IL 60202 **Chapl Evanston Fire/Police Dept 2010-** B Saint Louis MO 1949 s Howard & Frances. Loyola U 1970; BA Hobart and Wm Smith Colleges 1971; MDiv PDS 1974; S Georges Coll Jerusalem 1978; DMin Fuller TS 1986. D 6/22/1974 P 12/14/1974 Bp Robert Bracewell Appleyard. m 10/6/2007 Doris Heath Howe c 2. S Mary's Ch Pk Ridge IL 2013-2014; Dvlpmt and PR Off Bexley Seabury Fed Chicago IL 2007-2008; Cler Connections for the Homeless 2006-2011; Chapl NH Senate 1992-2006; R S Paul's Ch Concord NH 1991-2006; Archd Dio Pittsburgh Pittsburgh PA 1985-1991; R S Jas Epis Ch Pittsburgh PA 1979-1984; Asst Chr Epis Ch No Hills Pittsburgh PA 1974-1979. Soc of S Jn the Evang - Assoc 2001. davidinnh@hotmail.com

JONES, Derek Leslie (Cal) 786 Tunbridge Rd, Danville CA 94526 B London UK 1939 s Frederick & Lucy. D 10/23/1978 Bp Robert Marshall Anderson. m 4/16/1966 Selena-Jane Lees Verral c 3. Asst St Dav's Epis Ch Minnetonka MN 1978-1991.

JONES, Donald Avery (Ind) 2652 E Windermere Woods Dr, Bloomington IN 47401 B Oak Park IL 1938 s Avery & Margaret. BA Beloit Coll 1960; MD CDSP 1963. D 6/15/1963 Bp James Winchester Montgomery P 12/21/1963 Bp Gerald Francis Burrill. m 5/26/1963 Margaret S Jones c 2. R Trin Epis Ch Bloomington IN 2000-2006; R Ch Of The Nativ Indianapolis IN 1987-2000;

Cn Res St Paul's Epis Ch Peoria IL 1979-1987; R Ch Of The H Comm Lake Geneva WI 1971-1979; Cur Emm Epis Ch Rockford IL 1963-1966.

JONES, Dorothy Kovacs (Cal) Po Box 768, Tiburon CA 94920 **Pres, Bd of Trst Epis Sch For Deacons Berkeley CA 2010-** B Lorain OH 1931 d Louis & Sophia. BA Kent St U 1955; BA Sch for Deacons 1990. D 12/8/1990 Bp William Edwin Swing. Archd Dio California San Francisco CA 1999-2007, Vocations Secy 1996-2006, Bd Trsts Dioc Sch 1991-1995, Archd Emerita 2007-; Bd Trst Epis Sch for Deacons 1990-1996; D S Andr's Epis Ch San Bruno CA 1990-1993; S Steph's Par Bel Tiburon CA 1975-1986. NAAD 1990.

JONES, Duncan Haywood (NC) 102 E Calhoun St, Jackson NC 27845 B Fayetteville NC 1932 s Duncan & Mary. BS USNA 1957; MS Untd States Naval Postgraduate Sch 1969. D 5/28/2000 Bp Bob Johnson. m 5/10/2003 Frances Jones c 3.

JONES JR, Eddie Ellsworth (Fla) 160 Bear Pen Rd, Ponte Vedra Beach FL 32082 B MobileAL 1947 s Eddie & Mattie. BS U of W Alabama 1969; MDiv Candler TS Emory U 1972. D 6/11/1989 P 12/1/1989 Bp Frank S Cerveny. m 7/6/1967 Janine Jones c 1. Vic S Gabriels Epis Ch Jacksonville FL 2005-2008; Int St Fran in the Field Ponte Vedra FL 2004-2005; Int St. Fran In-The-Field 2004-2005; R Chr Ch Monticello FL 1996-2004; Chapl (Ltc) Florida NG 1991-1998; Chapl Off Of Bsh For ArmdF New York NY 1989-1997; Chapl (Maj.) US-AR 1979-1991; Chapl Fed Bureau Prisons 1975-1997; Min Methodist Ch 1973-1989.

JONES, Edward Wilson (Va) Diocese Of Virginia, 110 W Franklin St, Richmond VA 23220 **D Dio Virginia Richmond VA 2013-** B Richmond VA 1948 s Arthur & Virginia. BA Harvard Coll 1970; JD U of Virginia Sch of Law 1973. D 2/23/2013 Bp Shannon Sherwood Johnston. m 10/9/1982 Peggy Rae Marshall. ejones@thediocese.net

JONES, Elizabeth Claiborne (At) 5668 Stillwater Court, Stone Mountain GA 30087 Virgin Islands (U.S.) **Int R St. Mich and All Ang Epis Ch 2015-** B Durham NC 1950 d Claiborne & Annie. Mt Holyoke Coll 1969; BA U NC 1972; MDiv Candler TS Emory U 1978. D 6/10/1978 Bp Charles Judson Child Jr P 6/12/1979 Bp Bennett Jones Sims. Dir/Vic Dio Atlanta Atlanta GA 2005-2014, 1978-1979, Chair Com 1985-1988, Pres Cler Assn 1981-1983; R Ch Of The Epiph Atlanta GA 1985-2004; Chapl/Asst Ch Of The H Comf Atlanta GA 1979-1985; H Innoc Ch Atlanta GA 1979-1985; H Innoc' Epis Sch Atlanta GA 1979-1985; D Epis Ch Of The H Sprt Cumming GA 1978-1979. Auth, "Wmn Of The Word". Centennial Alum Awd Candler TS 2014; Ldrshp Atlanta Ldrshp Atlanta 1988; Sr Preaching Awd Candler TS 1978. cjones@stmichael.cc

JONES, Elizabeth Goodyear (Miss) 621 Briarwood Dr, Long Beach MS 39560 **Sprtl Fac Credo Inst Inc. Memphis TN 2009-** B Key West FL 1946 d William & Sarah. BA U of Mississippi 1968; MDiv CDSP 1986. D 6/7/1986 P 6/6/1987 Bp William Edwin Swing. m 2/14/1981 David B Jones c 1. Chapl/Hd of Sch Coast Epis Sch 2015-2017; Int P Trin Epis Ch 2014; Hd of Sch Coast Epis Sch 2010-2013; Chapl CoastEpiscopal Sch 2010-2013; Int R S Ptr's By The Sea Gulfport MS 2008-2009; Forum Ldr Landmark Educ Corp 2007-2008; R S Jas Ch Greenville MS 2001-2007; Vic S Paul's Epis Ch Corinth MS 1995-2001; Int R S Phil's Ch Jackson MS 1994-1995; S Andr's Epis Sch Ridgeland MS 1992-1993; Chapl S Andr's Cathd Jackson MS 1991-1993; Vic S Matt's Epis Ch Forest MS 1989-1991; Yth/Assoc S Paul's Epis Ch Walnut Creek CA 1986-1988; Stndg Com Dio Mississippi Jackson MS 2006-2007, Exec Com 2004-2006, Dn Delta Convoc 2002-2007, Non-par 1993-2002. Rotary Intl 2001-2007. Hon Fellowowship Sem of the SW 1996; Millsaps Leadship Millsaps Coll 1995.

JONES, Eustan Ulric (LI) 721 E 96th St Apt 2, Brooklyn NY 11236 B Calliaqua St. Vincent 1941 s Wilfred & Gertrude. Dip Theol Stud Codrington Theol Coll, Barbados 1977. Trans 11/1/1993 Bp Orris George Walker Jr. m 10/20/1965 Marilyn S Jones c 3. R Ch Of S Jas The Less Jamaica NY 1994-2007; Asst Gr Ch Jamaica NY 1993-1994; Serv Ch in the Dio Nassau & the Bahamas 1988-1991; Serv Ch in the Dio the Winward Islands 1976-1988; Stndg Com Dio Long Island Garden City NY 2001-2007, DCOM; Merc Bd Thel 1998-2000.

JONES, Frederick Lamar (At) 901 Stewart Lake Rd, Kent OH 44240 B Winston-Salem NC 1947 s Lamar & Anne. MDiv SWTS 1973; BA U So 1973. D 6/25/1973 P 2/9/1974 Bp Christoph Keller Jr. m 12/5/2003 Christine A Jones c 3. Assoc Cathd Of S Phil Atlanta GA 2001-2004; Gr Epis Ch Gainesville GA 1988-2001; R S Paul's Ch Fayetteville AR 1979-1988; Dio Arkansas Little Rock AR 1976-1979; Chapl S Mart's U Cntr Fayetteville AR 1976-1979; Asst Trin Ch Pine Bluff AR 1975-1976; R S Steph's Ch Blytheville AR 1973-1975.

JONES, Gary Durward (Va) 412 Maple Ave, Richmond VA 23226 **R S Steph's Ch Richmond VA 2005-** B Chapel Hill NC 1958 s Durward & Nancy. BA U NC 1980; MDiv Ya Berk 1985. D 6/23/1985 P 4/1/1986 Bp William Evan Sanders. m 6/6/1981 Cherry H Jones c 3. R Ch Of The H Comm Memphis TN 2001-2005; S Andr's Epis Ch Charlotte NC 2001; Epis. Urban Mnstry Charlotte NC 2000-2001; R Ch Of The Redeem Bryn Mawr PA 1999-2000; R S Ptr's Epis Ch Charlotte NC 1991-1999; R S Eliz's Epis Ch Knoxville TN 1990-1991;

Dio E Tennessee Knoxville TN 1987-1989, Cn For Soc Mnstry 1987-1988; S Jn's Epis Cathd Knoxville TN 1985-1987. Soc of S Jn The Evang.

JONES, Gary H (Tex) 3806 Kiamesha Dr, Missouri City TX 77459 B Bellingham WA 1947 s Howard & Ellen. BS Pacific Luth U 1970; MDiv CDSP 1975. D 1/6/1979 Bp Chauncie Kilmer Myers P 1/12/1980 Bp William Edwin Swing. m 4/30/1992 Lyn Jones. Dir of Chapl Dio Texas Houston TX 2011-2014; S Lk's Epis Hosp Houston TX 2007-2011; Chapl Samar Hlth Serv Corvallis OR 1997-2007; Int Chr The King Ch Houston TX 1997; The Great Cmsn Fndt Houston TX 1996-1997; Int S Steph's Ch Beaumont TX 1995-1996; Chapl Casa Hosp & Md Anderson Cancer Cntr 1990-1995; Int Gr Ch Galveston TX 1989-1990; Assoc S Chris's Ch Houston TX 1986-1989; Vic S Andr's Ch Chelan WA 1980-1986; S Jas Epis Ch Brewster WA 1980-1985; Assoc Chr Ch Portola Vlly CA 1979-1980. Auth, "Proficient Pstr Care," Goodsam Pub, 2000. Assoc of Epis Healthcare Chapl 2006-2010; Assn Of Clincl Pstr Educators 1997.

JONES, Greg (NC) 1520 Canterbury Rd, Raleigh NC 27608 **Trst The GTS New York NY 2007-; R S Mich's Ch Raleigh NC 2004-; Dn of Raleigh Convoc Dio No Carolina Raleigh NC 2011-** B Charlottesville VA 1969 s Samuel & Helen. BA U NC 1991; MDiv GTS 1999. D 4/14/1998 P 6/20/1999 Bp Leo Frade. m 5/23/1998 Melanie Bartol Jones c 3. Assoc R St Jas Ch Richmond VA 1999-2004; Chapl Catedral Epis El Buen Pstr San Pedro Sula 1994-1996. Auth, "On the Priesthood," *ATR*, ATR, 2009; Auth, "Beyond Da Vinci," Seabury, 2004; Auth, "Baxter to Cummins: The Baptismal Regeneration Controversy (1662-1873)," *GTS Thesis*, 1999. Fac Hist Prize GTS 1999; Sutton Prize for Best Grad Thesis GTS 1999; hon GTS 1999.

JONES, Helen Hammon (Ky) 30 River Hill Rd, Louisville KY 40207 **Bd Com Ch ; Hlth Mnstrs Norton Healthcare 2002-; Pstr Assoc S Matt's Epis Ch Louisville KY 2001-; Sprtl Dir St. Matt's Epis Ch 2001-; Bd Com Ch & Hlth Mnstrs Norton Healthcare Louisville KY 1998-** B Lexington KY 1934 d Stratton & Helen. AB Vas 1955; MDiv Louisville Presb TS 1980; Claremont TS 1982; DMin Louisville Presb TS 1994; MFA in Writing Spalding U 2008. D 10/19/1987 Bp David Reed P 10/27/2007 Bp Ted Gulick Jr. m 5/24/1987 Thomas Howell Pike c 3. Dio Kentucky Louisville KY 2005-2008; Dio Kentucky Louisville KY 2003-2005; Sr Chapl Norton Hosp Louisville KY 1989-2001; Dir of Pstr Care Jas Graham Brown Cancer Cntr Louisville KY 1982-1989; Stndg Com Dio Kentucky Louisville KY 1996-2002, Com for Nomntns of Bp 1993-1995, Stndg Com 1990-1992. Essayist, "On Waiting," *Waiting and Being*, Fons Vitae, Louisville, 2010. APC (Fell) 1989-2003; AEHC 1983-2003; Soc of S Jn the Evang 1984; Sprtl Dir Intl 1999-2002. The Wayne Oates Awd for Lifetime Achievement in Pstr Care Wayne Oates Inst 2011; Distinguished Alum Awd Louisville Collgt Sch 2006.

JONES, Herbert H (Va) **R Ch Of Our Sav Montpelier VA 2011-** B Richmond VA 1955 s John & Elizabeth. JD W&M - Law 1988; MDiv UTS Richmond 2011; MDiv UTS Richmond 2011; Cert Ang Stud VTS 2011. D 6/4/2011 P 12/10/2011 Bp Shannon Sherwood Johnston. herbert.jones57@gmail.com

JONES JR, Hugh Burnett (ETenn) PO Box 1408, Ridgeland MS 39158 B Paterson NJ 1948 s Hugh & May. BA Millsaps Coll 1970; MA Middle Tennessee St U 1975; MDiv Sewanee: The U So, TS 1976; EdD Mississippi St U 1990. D 5/29/1976 P 5/19/1977 Bp Duncan Montgomery Gray Jr. m 4/13/1985 Debra Jones c 3. Int S Mich And All Ang Anniston AL 2011-2014; Int S Thaddaeus' Epis Ch Chattanooga TN 2007-2011; R S Alb's Epis Ch Hixson TN 1994-2007; R S Mk's Ch Bay City TX 1987-1994; Asst S Mk's Ch Houston TX 1985-1986; Vic S Bernards Ch Okolona MS 1982-1985; Ch Of The Ascen Brooksville MS 1978-1985; Vic Ch Of The Nativ Macon MS 1978-1985; Epis Chapl Mississippi St U Starkville MS 1978-1985; Cur S Jn's Ch Laurel MS 1976-1978.

JONES, Jack Monte (WTex) 1615 S Monroe St, San Angelo TX 76901 **Ret 1998-** B San Angelo TX 1936 s Arvid & Christine. BA Sul Ross St U 1961; MA Sul Ross St U 1967; MDiv Sewanee: The U So, TS 1977. D 6/14/1977 P 6/9/1978 Bp Willis Ryan Henton. m 2/3/1962 Eira Virginia Jones c 2. Calv Ch Menard TX 2001-2004; Trin Ch Jct TX 2001-2004; S Mk's Epis Ch Abilene TX 1999-2000; Vic S Jas Epis Ch Ft McKavett TX 1987-1998; R S Jn's Epis Ch Sonora TX 1984-1988; All SS Ch Colorado City TX 1977-1984; S Jn's Ch Snyder TX 1977-1984; St Johns Ch Lubbock TX 1977-1984; Dio NW Texas Lubbock TX 1977-1981. "Biscuits O'Bryan, Texas Storyteller," *Statehouse Press*, 2005; Auth, "More Bull From Biscuits," *Record Stockman Press*, 1992; Auth, "Biscuits O'Bryan's Bk of Beans, Bread & Bull," *Rercord Stockman Press*, 1989. Acad Of Wstrn Artists. Best Cowboy Humorist Acad of Wstrn Artists 2003; Listed in "Who's Who in SW" 1995; VP, Texas Cowboy Poets Assn 1994; Sul Ross St U Distinguished Alum 1994.

JONES, Jacqueline Sydney (Alb) **D Asst Trin Ch Gloversville NY 2007-; Asst Dir Comm. For Phsician Hlth 2003-** B Amsterdam NY 1956 d Richard & Madelyn. BA SUNY Potsdam 1978; MS Coll of St Rose Albany NY 1981; Cert Pstr Stud S Bernards TS and Mnstry 2007. D 6/9/2007 P 12/2/2007 Bp William Howard Love. m 8/10/1985 Kevin Stewart Jones c 1.

JONES, James (NJ) Oceanview Towers 30, 510 Ocean Ave, Long Branch NJ 07740 **Assoc S Geo's-By-The-River Rumson NJ 2009-; Prof of Rel Rutgers U 1971-** B Detroit MI 1943 s James & Betty. BA Earlham Coll 1964; MDiv

EDS 1967; PhD Br 1970; PsyD Rutgers The St U of New Jersey 1985. D 6/29/1967 Bp Richard Stanley Merrill Emrich P 3/25/1968 Bp John S Higgins. m 6/3/2006 Kathleen Gayle Bishop. Auth, *,The Blood That Cries Out From the Earth*, Oxford U Press, 2008; Auth, *,The Mirror of God*, Palgrave, 2003; Auth, *,Rel & Psychol in Transition*, Yale U Press, 1996; Auth, *,The Sprt & The Wrld*, Hawthorn Press, 1975; Auth, *,Shattered Synthesis*, Yale U Press, 1973. AAR.

JONES, James Place (SeFla) 9013 SW 62nd Ter, Miami FL 33173 **R S Matt the Apos Epis Ch Miami FL 2007-** B Morristown NJ 1950 s Joseph & Grace. BA Amer U 1972; MDiv EDS 1976; PhD Bos 1981. D 6/5/1976 P 3/5/1977 Bp George E Rath. m 9/6/1975 Karen H Jones c 2. R S Paul's Epis Ch Laporte IN 2002-2007; R S Ptr's Ch Albany NY 2000-2002; R S Marg's Ch Inverness FL 1993-2000; Int S Thos Epis Ch Eustis FL 1991-1993; Dir - Epis Coun Cntr Dio Cntrl Florida Orlando FL 1990-1993; Asst R Truro Epis Ch Fairfax VA 1988-1990; Int Gr Ch Everett MA 1987-1988; Assoc S Ptr's Ch Beverly MA 1985-1987. Auth, "A Lifecycle Approach to Mnstry w The Aging," *Journ of Pstr Care*, 1999; Auth, "Psychol Hm Vstng Serv," *Emergency Psychol*, 1984.

JONES, James Walter (Mont) D 6/26/2016 Bp Charles Franklin Brookhart Jr.

JONES, Jane Denton (Los) 457 W 39th St, San Pedro CA 90731 B Columbus OH 1943 d Sterling & Mary Jane. BS Otterbein U 1966; Cert U CA 1985; EFM U So 2002; ETSBH 2006. D 12/2/2006 Bp Chester Lovelle Talton. m 8/16/2008 John Jones c 5. D St Gregorys Epis Ch Long Bch CA 2010-2015; D S Andr's Par Torrance CA 2006-2008. LA ECW Bd Dir- D 2008; N. Amer Assn of the Diac 2006.

JONES, Janice Lynn (Tex) 1314 E University Ave, Georgetown TX 78626 **S Chris's Ch Killeen TX 2012-** B Bridgeport CT 1953 d Edward & Heste. BS Sthrn Connecticut St U 1971; MS Sthrn Connecticut St U 1974; MDiv Epis TS of the SW 2008. D 6/28/2008 Bp Don Adger Wimberly P 1/10/2009 Bp C Andrew Doyle. m 8/23/1986 Richard B Jones c 3. Asst R Gr Epis Ch Georgetown TX 2008-2012.

JONES, Jerry Steven (WK) 1113 Pinehurst St, Hays KS 67601 B Omaha NE 1939 s Beecher & Margaret. BA Dana Coll 1962; LTh SWTS 1965. D 6/6/1965 P 12/1/1965 Bp Russell T Rauscher. m 6/1/1990 Susan Andrea Jones c 2. Dn Chr Cathd Salina KS 2006-2010; S Mich's Ch Hays KS 1996-2002; R S Steph's Ch Casper WY 1993-1996; S Pauls Epis Ch Arapahoe NE 1990-1993; S Eliz's Ch Holdrege NE 1989-1993; Vic S Eliz's Ch Russell KS 1989-1993; All SS' Epis Ch Ft Worth TX 1979-1982; Cur S Stephens Epis Churchrch Wichita KS 1977-1979; R S Matt's Epis Ch Newton KS 1974-1977; R S Mk's Omaha NE 1970-1974; S Mk's Ch Gordon NE 1968-1970; Vic S Mary Holly NE 1968-1970; S Pauls Ch Merriman NE 1968-1970; Cur All SS Epis Ch Omaha NE 1965-1968.

JONES, JoAnn B (Pa) D 6/17/2017 Bp Daniel Gutierrez.

JONES, John Tyler (WA) 11040 Baltimore Ave, Beltsville MD 20705 B Franklin PA 1951 s Thomas & Opal. BA JCU 1973; MBA Gannon U 1986; MTS VTS 2006. D 9/22/2012 Bp Mariann Edgar Budde. m 3/14/1987 Carol J Jablonski.

JONES, Judith Anne (Ore) 316 3rd St Ne, Waverly IA 50677 **Dio Oregon Portland OR 2017-; Assoc Prof Of Rel Wartburg Coll 2000-** B Wasim Maharashtra India 1961 d Donald & Willa. BA Point Loma Coll 1982; MDiv PrTS 1986; Cert Ang Stud Sewanee: The U So, TS 1990; PhD Emory U 1999. D 12/18/2004 P 6/18/2005 Bp Alan Scarfe. m 7/26/1980 Brian Jones c 2. P-in-c S Andr's Epis Ch Waverly IA 2010-2017, 2005-2007; P-in-c Gr Epis Ch Chas City IA 2005-2009. coauthor w/ Edmond F. Desueza, "Conversations w Scripture: Daniel," Ch Pub, 2011. Angl Assn of Biblic Scholars 1998; SBL 1983; The Ch in Metropltn Areas 2005. brian.jones@wartburg.edu

JONES, Judith Gay (Tex) PO Box 28, Pflugerville TX 78691 B Austin TX 1947 d John & Wilma. certification Other 2008; certification The Iona Sch for Mnstry 2008. D 6/28/2008 Bp Don Adger Wimberly P 1/24/2009 Bp Dena Arnall Harrison. m 12/14/1985 Lewis Jones c 1. Vic S Paul's Epis Ch Pflugerville TX 2005-2013.

JONES, Kenneth Leon (Mass) 62 Hopetown Road, Mt.Pleasant SC 29464 **1976-** B Charleston SC 1941 s Leon & Estelle. BS Coll of Charleston 1963; CTh U of Cambridge 1967; MDiv VTS 1970. D 7/12/1970 Bp Robert Bruce Hall P 6/1/1971 Bp Robert Fisher Gibson Jr. m 6/12/1960 Sandra H Harley c 2. R S Paul's Epis Ch Alexandria VA 1972-1975; Asst Imm Ch-On-The-Hill Alexandria VA 1970-1972.

JONES, Kent Trevor (Chi) 3706 W Saint Paul Ave, McHenry IL 60050 B Lansing MI 1969 s Thomas & J Kaye. D 5/23/2009 Bp Victor Alfonso Scantlebury. m 6/13/1992 Alice Jones c 4.

JONES, Leland Bryant (SanD) 1118 W Country Club Ln, Escondido CA 92026 **Int S Jn's Ch Fallbrook CA 2011-** B Yuma AZ 1947 s Bryant & Helen. BA U Pac 1969; MDiv CDSP 1973. D 4/1/1973 P 5/5/1974 Bp John Joseph Meakin Harte. m 10/3/1969 Sheila Jones c 4. Int S Andr's By The Sea Epis Par San Diego CA 2009-2010; Dir, Ramona Fire Recovery Cntr Salvation Army 2008-2009; Vic S Mary's In The Vlly Ch Ramona CA 2006-2008; Vic of St. Mary's Dio San Diego San Diego CA 2000-2005, First Vice-Pres, Dioc Coun 2003-2005; Chapl Irvine Police Dept Irvine CA 1997-2000; Vic St Andr Epis Ch Irvine CA 1989-2000; R The Epis Ch Of The Gd Shpd Hemet CA 1980-1989; R S Steph's Ch Phoenix AZ 1976-1980; Cur Chr Ch Of The Ascen

445

Paradise Vlly AZ 1973-1976; Dir, Ramona Fire Recovery Cntr Salvation Army San Diego CA 2008-2009; Instr for Courts for Anger Mgmt San Diego Cnty Ramona CA 2005-2007; Chapl Irvine Police Dept Irvine CA 1997-2000; Counslr for Abusive Parents Maricopa Cnty Phoenix AZ 1978-1980. Fndr Comps In Mnstry, Chapl Ord Of S Lk. lelandbjones47@yahoo.com

JONES, Lynne Elizabeth (SeFla) 206 Pendleton Ave, Palm Beach FL 33480 **S Mary's Epis Ch Of Deerfield Deerfield Bch FL 2012-** B Boynton Bch FL 1955 d Howard & Ella. AA Palm Bch Jr Coll 1975; BA Florida St U 1977; JD U of Florida 1980; MDiv GTS 1993. D 6/2/1993 P 12/21/1993 Bp Calvin Onderdonk Schofield Jr. The Epis Ch Of Beth-By-The-Sea Palm Bch FL 2004-2010; R Epis Ch Of S Simon And S Jude Irmo SC 2000-2004; R S Columba Epis Ch Marathon FL 1995-2000; R S Fran-In-The-Keys Episcop Big Pine Key FL 1995-2000; Asst All SS Prot Epis Ch Ft Lauderdale FL 1993-1995. pastorlynnejones@comcast.net

JONES, Margaret W (WTenn) 4757 Walnut Grove Rd, Memphis TN 38117 B Saint Louis MO 1937 d Claude & Highland. Memphis TS; BA Hollins U 1959. D 1/22/1994 Bp Alex Dockery Dickson. m 4/21/1979 Frank Aubrey Jones c 2. Calv Ch Memphis TN 1994-1999. Auth, *The Christmas Invitation.*

JONES BSG, Mark Andrew (SeFla) 2707 NW 37th St, Boca Raton FL 33434 **P Ch Of S Nich Pompano Bch FL 2011-** B Indianapolis IN 1957 s Norman & Edith. BA Indiana U 1979; MPA Indiana U 1981; JD U Chi Law Sch 1989; MDiv Florida Cntr for Theol Stds 2010; Dip Ang Stud Sewanee: The U So, TS 2010. D 6/5/2010 P 12/4/2010 Bp Leo Frade. m 6/6/1981 Diane D Jones c 2. D S Greg's Ch Boca Raton FL 2010-2011.

JONES, Mark Stephen (Ga) 212 N Jefferson St, Albany GA 31701 B Atlanta GA 1976 s Eddie. BS Florida St U 1999; MDiv VTS 2003. D 6/8/2003 P 12/7/2003 Bp Stephen Hays Jecko. m 2/26/2000 Emily J Jones c 2. R S Paul's Ch Albany GA 2005-2011; Asst. R Ch Of Our Sav Jacksonville FL 2003-2005.

JONES, Mary Alice (Mont) D 6/26/2016 Bp Charles Franklin Brookhart Jr.

JONES, Mary-Frances (Minn) 911 - 8th Avenue Northwest, Austin MN 55912 B Melrose Park IL 1931 d James & Alice. The Coll of Emm and S Chad CA; BA U MN 1977; D Formation Prog 1981. D 6/29/1982 Bp Robert Marshall Anderson. D Chr Ch Austin MN 1996-2006. RWF.

JONES, Michael Stephen (Alb) 785 Forest Ridge Dr, Youngstown OH 44512 B Indianapolis IN 1947 s James & Alice. BA NE Illinois U 1971; MDiv Nash 1976. D 8/6/1976 P 6/1/1977 Bp James Loughlin Duncan. m 8/11/2004 Beverly Jean Jones c 3. S Eustace Ch Lake Placid NY 2005-2008; R S Steph's Epis Ch Steubenville OH 1996-2003; S Jas Epis Ch Boardman OH 1982-1996; Asst Chr Epis Ch Warren OH 1980-1982; Asst All SS Prot Epis Ch Ft Lauderdale FL 1979-1980; S Dav's-In-The-Pines Epis Ch W Palm Bch FL 1978-1979; P-in-c S Dav's W Palm Bch FL 1977-1979; Asst Ch Of The H Redeem Lake Worth FL 1977; Dio SE Florida Miami 1976; Prov Syn; Pres Boardman Mnstrl Assn.

JONES, Nelson Bradley (Alb) 970 State St, Schenectady NY 12307 **R Chr Ch Schenectady NY 1998-** B New Orleans LA 1957 s Nelson & Martha. BA U So 1979; MDiv VTS 1991. D 6/9/1991 P 12/18/1991 Bp James Barrow Brown. m 9/29/1984 Mary Helen Jones c 7. Assoc S Andr's By The Sea Epis Ch Destin FL 1994-1998; Cur Ch Of The Ascen Montgomery AL 1991-1993. Amer Angl Coun; NOEL.

JONES, Nikki Lou (NwT) 1514 Neff St, Sweetwater TX 79556 **D S Steph's Ch Sweetwater TX 2000-** B Stamford TX 1943 d Thaddeus & Letha. BA Hardin-Simmons U 1965. D 10/29/2000 Bp C Wallis Ohl. m 8/1/1988 Bernard Wayne Jones.

JONES, Patricia Loraine (Alb) 1295 Myron St, Schenectady NY 12309 **D S Steph's Ch Schenectady NY 1982-** B Rochester NY 1936 d Arthur & Blanche. BA Hobart and Wm Smith Colleges 1957; MDiv Bex Sem 1990. D 12/1/1982 Bp Wilbur Emory Hogg Jr. m 6/12/1958 Christopher Curtiss Jones c 2.

JONES, Patricia Wayne (WNC) 260 21st Ave Nw, Hickory NC 28601 B Camp Lejeune NC 1947 D 12/18/1999 Bp Bob Johnson. m 6/14/1969 David Scott Jones c 3.

JONES, Patsy Ann (Spok) 323 Catherine St, Walla Walla WA 99362 B Wichita Falls TX 1934 d Andrew & Mary. D 6/18/2011 Bp James E Waggoner Jr. m 6/6/1953 Morris Coburn Jones c 2.

JONES, Peter Hoyt (HB) 7571 Greenlake Way #B, Lantana FL 33462 **Non-par 1970-** B Cleveland OH 1937 s Eben & Alfreda. BA Ya 1959; STB GTS 1962. D 6/9/1962 Bp Nelson Marigold Burroughs P 12/1/1962 Bp Richard S Watson. m 7/7/1959 Susan Robin Jones. Vic S Geo Kennewick WA 1966-1970; Vic S Jas Salt Lake City UT 1963-1966; Cur All SS Ch Salt Lake City UT 1962-1966.

JONES, Rebecca (Colo) 8235 W. 44th Ave, Wheat Ridge CO 80033 **S Jas Epis Ch Wheat Ridge CO 2016-** B Cleveland TN 1958 d Paul & Viola. **BS** E Tennessee St U 1980; MA OH SU 1984; MDiv Iliff TS 2007. D 11/15/2008 P 6/13/2015 Bp Robert John O'Neill. S Thos Epis Ch Denver CO 2015-2017; Dioc Jubilee Off Dio Colorado Denver CO 2014-2015, Dioc Jubilee Off 2008-2016; D S Fran Cntr Denver CO 2009-2015. becky@sjwr.org

JONES, Rich (SwVa) 2455 N Stevens St, Alexandria VA 22311 B Washington DC 1943 s Homer & Alice. BA Ob 1964; MA JHU 1966; MDiv VTS 1972; PhD U Tor 1988. D 6/17/1972 Bp William Foreman Creighton P 12/17/1972 Bp Adrian Delio Caceres-Villavicencio. m 11/30/2013 Christine Cheevers Jones c

2. Serv-Prof. of Muslim-Chr Stds Washington Theol Consortium Washington DC 2009-2014; Prof VTS Alexandria VA 1988-2009; Serv Angl Ch of Can 1984-1988; Asst S Jn's Ch Lynchburg VA 1980-1984; Vic S Mary's Epis Ch Andalusia AL 1978-1980; Cur Ch Of The Epiph Enterprise AL 1975-1980; The Epis Ch Of The Nativ Dothan AL 1975-1978; Vic Chr King Ch Guayaquil Ecu 1972-1975. Auth, "Mssn Is What?," 2015; Auth, "Nairobi Muslims' Concept of Prophethood," *Journ of Muslim Minority Affrs*, 2002; Auth, "How To Talk To Your Muslim Neighbor," *Forw Mvmt*, 1996; Auth, "Wlfd Cantwell Smith & Kenneth Cragg on Islam as a Way of Salvation," *Intl Bulletin of Mssy Resrch*, 1992. Amer Friends of the Epis Ch of Sudan 2005; Amer Soc of Missiology 1985.

JONES, Richmond A (At) 432 Forest Hill Rd, Macon GA 31210 B Atlanta GA 1986 s Steven & Marjorie. BA Jacksonville U 2014; MDiv Sewanee TS 2015; MDiv Sewanee: The U So, TS 2015. D 12/20/2014 P 6/20/2015 Bp Robert Christopher Wright. m 5/24/2014 Perry Hodgkins Jones. S Fran Ch Macon GA 2015-2017.

JONES, Robert Michael (WNC) PO Box 729, Highlands NC 28741 B Eufala AL 1942 s William & Margaret. BA U So 1965; MDiv VTS 1969; STM Sewanee: The U So, TS 1977; DMin Van 1988. D 6/20/1969 P 1/1/1970 Bp Gray Temple. m 6/20/1970 Agnes Elizabeth Jones c 4. R Ch Of The Incarn Highlands NC 1995-2003; R S Dav's Epis Ch Columbia SC 1987-1995; R S Paul's Ch Bennettsville SC 1985-1987; R Angl Par Cow Hd Newfoundland Can 1982-1985; R Ch Of The H Comf Sumter SC 1974-1982; R S Jude's Epis Ch Walterboro SC 1971-1974. Auth, "One Eye Squinted Flannery O'Connor'S Vision Of Judgement & Gr".

JONES, Roland Manning (NC) 501 Parkmont Dr, Greensboro NC 27408 **Died 10/6/2016** B Washington DC 1932 s Roland & Rachael. BS U of Maryland 1953; MDiv VTS 1958. D 6/14/1958 P 12/1/1958 Bp Angus Dun. m 12/26/1953 Marcia Jones c 3. Ret 1995-2016; Field Wk Supvsr Ya Berk New Haven CT 1991-1995, Par Supvsr 1985-1990; R S Mk's Ch New Canaan CT 1984-1995; R S Fran Ch Greensboro NC 1974-1984; Pres Epis Clerics Assn 1970-1971; R Ch Of The Ascen Silver Sprg MD 1967-1974; Field Wk Supvsr VTS Alexandria VA 1959-1973; R Chr Ch S Jn's Par Accokeek MD 1958-1967; Prog Com Dio Connecticut Meriden CT 1986-1989. Auth, *Know Your Par*; Auth, *The Unfreezing of Ascenension*.

JONES, Ross (Okla) 385 Racquet Club Rd., Asheville NC 28803 B Woodville MS 1940 s Ben & Frances. BA Tul 1962; MDiv Sewanee: The U So, TS 1965; DMin Sewanee: The U So, TS 1998. D 5/29/1965 Bp Duncan Montgomery Gray P 5/1/1966 Bp John Maury Allin. m 8/31/1963 Gwin S Jones c 3. Dn St. Geo's Coll Jerusalem 2000-2004; R Trin Ch Tulsa OK 1992-2000; R St Jas Epis Ch and Sch Alexandria LA 1981-1992; R S Paul's Epis Ch Jacksonville FL 1978-1981; Chapl Epis U Cntr Tallahassee FL 1971-1978; R S Steph's Epis Ch Indianola MS 1968-1971; Cur S Andr's Cathd Jackson MS 1965-1968. Citizen Of The Year La 1988.

JONES, Ruth Elise (NwT) 3010 - 60th, Lubbock TX 79413 B Newellton LA 1936 d Robert & Josephine. LSU 1955; AAS Clarendon Jr Coll 1981; BA Texas Tech U 1982; MEd Texas Tech U 1986. D 10/25/1985 Bp Sam Byron Hulsey. m 11/27/1955 Louis Clinton Jones c 5. D S Paul's On The Plains Epis Ch Lubbock TX 1993-2007; Sewanee U So TS Sewanee TN 1986-1995; D S Chris's Epis Ch Lubbock TX 1985-1993. AEHC; No Amer Assn of Deacons; OHC.

JONES, Sandra Lee Spoar (U) PO Box 981208, Park City UT 84098 B Syracuse NY 1952 d George & Betty. AD Bay Path Jr Coll 1980; BA San Francisco St U 1982. D 6/29/2013 Bp Scott Byron Hayashi. m 12/28/1977 Robert E Jones c 2.

JONES, Scott Daniel (Az) 10716 E Medina Ave, Mesa AZ 85209 **Dio Arizona Phoenix AZ 2014-** B Melbourne FL 1960 s John & Constance. BS U of Florida 1982; MDiv Epis TS of the SW 2007. D 1/6/2007 P 7/14/2007 Bp Leo Frade. m 1/12/1985 Yolanda Irizarry c 2. R S Mk's Epis Ch Mesa AZ 2009-2014; Assoc R Gd Shpd Of The Hills Cave Creek AZ 2007-2009. frscott@resurrectiongilbert.org

JONES, Stanley Boyd (WVa) 53 Windward Lane, Box 1848, Shepherdstown WV 25443 **Died 12/23/2016** B Baltimore MD 1938 s Arthur & Lillian. BA Dart 1960; Yale DS 1963. D 6/11/1991 P 6/13/1992 Bp John Henry Smith. m 1/22/2017 Judith Miller Jones c 1. Assoc Trin Ch Shepherdstown WV 1992-2000. Auth, "What'S Driving The Hlth System Change," *Hlth Affrs*, 1997; Auth, "Why Not The Best For The Chronically Ill," *GW Resrch Brief*, 1996; Auth, "Many Will Be Hurt," *Bulletin Of New York Acad Of Med*, 1990; Auth, "Competition Or Conscience," *Inquiry*, 1987. Fllshp Of Contemplative Pryr 1995. Elected Mem Natl Acad Of Soc Ins 1990; Elected Mem Inst Of Med / Natl Acad Of Sciences 1980; Elected Fell Inst Of Soc, Ethics, & The Life Sciences 1978.

JONES, Stephen Bradley (ETenn) **S Andr's Ch Harriman TN 2015-; P Dio E Tennessee Knoxville TN 2012-** B Atlanta GA 1970 s Robert & Catherine. MDiv GTS; BA Jacksonville St U. D 12/17/2011 P 6/24/2012 Bp J Neil Alexander. m 6/8/2006 Gale E Jones c 2.

JONES, Stephen Chad (Tenn) 1216 Sneed Rd W, Franklin TN 37069 **Cn The Epis Ch Of The Resurr Franklin TN 2016-** B Milton FL 1976 BA LSU 1999; MDiv Nash 2003. D 2/1/2003 Bp Clarence Cullam Pope Jr P 8/20/2003 Bp Charles Edward Jenkins III. m 12/12/1998 Kimberly L Smith c 3. R S Pat's

Ch Zachary LA 2008-2016; Assoc Trin Epis Ch Baton Rouge LA 2006-2008; Cn Dio Louisiana New Orleans LA 2005-2006, Exec Bd 2013-2016, Chair of Stndg Com 2013-2014, GC, Com on Evang 2012-, Stndg Com 2010-2014, GC Dep 2008-, COM 2006-2010, Chair of Discpatch of Bus 2004-2014, Com on Liturg and Mus 2003-2008, Com on Missions, Chair 2003-2005; R S Matt's Ch Bogalusa LA 2003-2005. fatherchad@resurrectionfranklin.org

JONES JR, Stewart H (Colo) 2421 S Krameria St, Denver CO 80222 **Assoc St. Jn's Cathd Denver Colorado 2002-** B Bethlehem PA 1940 s Stewart & Elizabeth. BA NWU 1962; GTS 1963; BD SWTS 1965. D 5/29/1965 Bp William S Thomas P 12/21/1965 Bp Joseph Summerville Minnis. m 8/3/1963 Jean Correy Jones c 2. Non-par 1980-1992; S Ambr Epis Ch Boulder CO 1974-1980; Non-par 1969-1974; Asst Chr Epis Ch Denver CO 1968-1969; Cur Ch Of S Phil And S Jas Denver CO 1965-1968.

JONES, Tammy Lynn (Ida) PO Box 324, Rupert ID 83350 **D St Matthews Epis Ch Rupert ID 2006-** B Nampa ID 1961 d Claude & Geraldine. D 10/22/2006 Bp Harry Brown Bainbridge III. m 2/28/1985 Ronald Jones c 2.

JONES, Teresa Crawford (NY) 5 Christopher Ave, Highland NY 12528 **D Ch Of The Ascen And H Trin W Pk NY 1999-** B Bend OR 1949 d Ralph & Mary. BA Arizona St U 1971. D 5/15/1999 Bp Richard Frank Grein. m 10/28/1988 Geoffrey Albert Jones.

JONES, Theodore Grant (Md) 2604 Halcyon Avenue, Baltimore MD 21214 **Ret 2003-** B Utica NY 1940 s Emerson & Inza. BArch Cor 1963; MFA Pr 1965; MDiv EDS 1970. D 6/14/1970 P 5/25/1971 Bp Ned Cole. c 1. Int Ch Of The Mssh Baltimore MD 2001-2002; Int The Ch Of The H Apos Halethorpe MD 2001; R Ch Of S Kath Of Alexandria Baltimore MD 1999-2001; Int Chr Ch S Ptr's Par Easton MD 1998-1999; Int S Ptr's Ch Clifton NJ 1997-1998; Int Chr Ch Waukegan IL 1996-1997; R S Barn Epis Ch Portage MI 1995-1996; 1994-1995; Int Ch Of The H Comm Washington DC 1993-1994; R S Chris's Ch Springfield VA 1982-1993; R S Steph's Ch New Hartford NY 1975-1982; Asst S Jn's Ch Ithaca NY 1970-1975; Chapl Ithaca Coll Ithaca NY 1970-1973. Soc of S Marg 1977. Fulbright Schlr Amer Acad 1966.

JONES, Thomas A (Neb) **R Ch Of The H Sprt Bellevue NE 2008-** B Chicago IL 1955 s Arthur & Alma. BS Sthrn Illinois U 1979; MS Embry Riddle Aeronautical U 1989; MDiv Sewanee: The U So, TS 2006. D 9/26/2006 P 3/27/2007 Bp Joe Goodwin Burnett. m 11/22/1975 Sharon Jones c 2. Cur/Assoc S Andr's Ch Omaha NE 2006-2008; Pilot U.S.A.F. 1975-2003.

JONES, Thomas Glyndwr (At) 4425 Colchester Ct, Columbus GA 31907 B Caersws Wales GB 1941 s John & Hilda. Clifton Theol Coll GB 1965. P 9/1/1966 Bp The Bishop Of London. m 7/24/1965 Nan R Fager c 2. R Trin Epis Ch Columbus GA 1987-2004; R Gr Ch Anniston AL 1973-1987; R Chr Ch Fairfield AL 1969-1973; Serv Ch of Engl 1965-1969.

JONES, Timothy Dale (WNC) 290 Old Haw Creek Rd, Asheville NC 28805 **D S Jas Epis Ch Hendersonvlle NC 2010-** B Hendersonville NC 1969 s Charles & Sharon. BA Bob Jones U 1991. D 1/23/2010 Bp Porter Taylor. m 6/29/1991 Kerry Jones c 2.

JONES, Timothy Kent (USC) St Georges Church, 4715 Harding Pike, Nashville TN 37205 **Trin Cathd Columbia SC 2012-** B Phoenix AZ 1955 s Francis & Susan. MDiv PrTS; STM Sewanee: The U So, TS; BA Pepperdine U 1976. D 6/23/2001 P 4/21/2002 Bp Bertram Nelson Herlong. m 5/27/1978 Jill Zook c 3. Sr Assoc R S Geo's Ch Nashville TN 2005-2012; S Paul's Epis Ch Murfreesboro TN 2002-2005, 2001; Dio Tennessee Nashville TN 2002. Auth, "The Art of Pryr," WaterBrook Press, 2005; Auth, "Workday Prayers," Loyola Press, 2000; Auth, "Awake My Soul," Doubleday Image, 1999.

JONES, Tyler (NY) 161 Mansion St., Poughkeepsie NY 12601 **Vic Dio New York New York NY 2006-; Vic S Paul's Ch Poughkeepsie NY 2006-** B Seattle WA 1948 s Bradley & Phyllis. BA Alaska Pacific U 1990; MDiv GTS 2004. D 4/17/2004 P 10/31/2004 Bp Leo Frade. m 12/12/1972 Mary L Jones c 2. Cur Ch of the Ascen Munich 2004-2006.

JONES OHC, Vern Edward (Cal) 3814 Jefferson Ave, Emerald Hills CA 94062 **Chapl (for Ret Cler and spouses) Dio California 1992-; NAVE Chapl Gr Cathd San Francisco CA 1992-; Ret Ret 1992-; Bd Mem Cantebury Stan 1992-; Chapl Cortelius Mntl Hosp Redwood City CA 1977-** B Enid OK 1927 s Cary & Agnes. BA Phillips U 1949; STB STS 1952; S Augustines Coll Cbury Gb 1960; S Augustines Coll Cbury Gb 1963; GTS 1964; Phillips U 1977. D 6/16/1952 P 12/17/1952 Bp Chilton R Powell. P Chr Ch Mandarin Chinese Cong Los Altos CA 2003-2012; Actg Cbury Chapl Stan Stanford CA 2002-2003; Mandarin Chinese Cong Chr Epis Ch Los Altos CA 1999-2008; R S Ptr's Epis Ch Redwood City CA 1977-1992; Dio Oklahoma Oklahoma City OK 1976-1977, Dep to GC 1970-1976; Bd Trst The GTS New York NY 1974-1980; Bd Trst GTS NYC 1973-1979; Vic S Jos Shattuck OK 1967-1973; Vic King Chas of the Mtyr Buffalo OK 1965-1975; Vic/Fndr St Chas Par Laverne OK 1963-1977; Fndr and P H Fam Watonga OK 1961-1969; Vic/Fndr Ch of S Chas Buffalo OK 1960-1977; Vic S Jn's Epis Ch Woodward OK 1957-1977; Chapl Wstrn St Mntl Hosp Ft Supply OK 1957-1977; Vic S Steph's Ch Guymon OK 1957-1960; Cbury Chapl Oklahoma City U 1955-1957; Chrmstr S Jn's Ch Oklahoma City OK 1955-1957, Cur 1955-1957; Vic S Jas Ch Antlers OK 1952-1955; Vic S Lk The Beloved Physcn Idabel OK 1952-1955; Vic S

Mk's Ch Hugo OK 1952-1955; Dept Of Missions Dio California San Francisco CA 1983-1987. Auth, "O Come, Let Us Adore Him," *The Vintage Voice*, CPF, 2005; Auth, "A Goodly Heritage," *The Vintage Voice*, CPF, 2003. Assoc OHC 1951; Soc Of King Chas The Mtyr 1951. Ord of St. Laud of Cbury Soc of King Chas the Mtyr 2011.

JONES JR, Vernon A. (Ala) 6312 Willow Glen Dr, Montgomery AL 36117 **Died 11/14/2015** B Brunswick County VA 1924 s Vernon & Harriet. BA Virginia Un U 1945; BD VTS 1948; MDiv VTS 1970. D 4/7/1948 Bp William A Brown P 6/2/1949 Bp George P Gunn. c 3. Ret 1990-2015; S Andr's Ch Tuskegee Inst AL 1957-1990; R S Steph's Ch Petersburg VA 1953-1957; P-in-c S Jas Ch Emporia VA 1949-1953; S Thos Ch Freeman VA 1949-1953; Vic Chr Epis Ch Halifax VA 1948-1949.

JONES, Walton (Miss) 308 South Commerce St., Natchez MS 39120 **Ch Of The Resurr Starkville MS 2016-** B Grenada MS 1978 s Girault & Sandra. BS Mississippi St U 2003; MDiv Sewanee: The U So, TS 2007. D 6/2/2007 P 1/23/2008 Bp Duncan Montgomery Gray III. m 10/19/2002 Keri D Jones c 2. R Trin Ch Natchez MS 2011-2016; Assoc S Paul's Epis Ch Meridian MS 2007-2010.

✠ JONES JR, The Rt Rev William Augustus (Mo) 58 Kendal Dr, Kennett Square PA 19348 B Memphis TN 1927 s William & Martha. BA Rhodes Coll 1948; BD Yale DS 1951. D 1/1/1952 P 7/25/1952 Bp Edmund P Dandridge Con 5/3/1975 for Mo. m 8/26/1949 Margaret Jones c 4. Ret Bp of Missouri Dio Missouri S Louis MO 1993, Bp of Missouri 1975-1993; R S Jn's Epis Ch Johnson City TN 1972-1975; Dir Resrch/Exec Dir Sthrn Rgnl Assn Chr Trng and Serv 1966-1972; Assoc S Lk's Epis Ch Birmingham AL 1965-1966; R S Mk's Epis Ch Lagrange GA 1958-1965; Cur Chr Ch Cathd Nashville TN 1957-1958; P-in-c The Epis Ch Of The Mssh Pulaski TN 1952-1957. DD Rhodes Coll 1986; DD Ya Berk 1975; DD U So TS 1975.

JONES, William Henry (O) 2651 Cheltenham Rd, Toledo OH 43606 **Directory (Trin Cnslng Cntr) Addiction Treatment Serv-Addicti 1986-** B Tarpon Sprgs FL 1929 s Holton & Lotta. BA Ohio Wesl 1951; MA U Chi 1955; VTS 1956; Lic LPCC/SC 1992; Lic Chem Dependency Counslr Supvsr/ US 1997; DMin Ecum TS 1997; Cert CSAT/SC Intl 2002; Cert CMAT/SC 2008. D 6/1/1956 Bp Frederick D Goodwin P 6/1/1957 Bp Robert Fisher Gibson Jr. c 4. Toledo Metroplitn Mssn Toledo OH 1986-1989; Toledo Reg Coun Perrysburg OH 1985; P-t Stff Toledo Area Mnstry (TMM) Toledo OH 1982-2007; Asst Dio Ohio Cleveland 1964-1984; Imm Ch King and Queen Courthouse VA 1959-1964; R S Jn's Ch W Point VA 1959-1964; Cur S Thos' Ch Richmond VA 1956-1959. Auth, *Exploring the Fam Map*, ETS, 1997; Auth, "The Impact of Multiple Counsultants in the Treatment of Addictions," *Please Help Me w This Fam*, Brunner/Mazel, 1994; "Agony Called Unemployment," *Journ of Meth Wmn*, 1988.

JONES, William Ogden (SVa) 8137 Brown Rd, Bon Air VA 23235 **Bd Fund for the Diac 1997-; Archd Dio Sthrn Virginia Newport News VA 2008-** B Atlanta GA 1937 s Benjamin & Elizabeth. Hendrix Coll; Loc Formation Prog; U of Arkansas; CLU The Amer Coll 1987. D 6/15/1989 Bp Claude Charles Vache. m 5/15/1957 Gaye Jones c 3. D Ch Of The Redeem Midlothian VA 2002-2007, D 1989-2001; D Trin Ch Milwaukee WI 1999-2002; Pres NAAD 1997-1999; D S Dav's Epis Ch No Chesterfield VA 1993-1996; Trst; COM Angl TS Dallas TX; Dio Sthrn Virginia Norfolk VA. "Diokonia," 1991.

JOO, Indon Paul (Chi) 1300 Hallberg Ln, Park Ridge IL 60068 **One In Chr Ch Prospect Heights IL 2000-** B Republic of Korea 1962 s Kyunghoon & Aein. BA Yonsei U 1985; MDiv S Mich Sem Seoul KR 1989. Trans 5/29/2001 Bp Bill Persell. m 4/8/1989 Youngsook Deborah Joo c 2. P-in-c Serv Angl Ch Of Can Toronto Onatario 1994-1997; Assistance P, Cathd and Stff of Dio Seoul Serv Angl Ch Of Korea Seoul Seoul 1989-1994; Dioc Stff Serv Angl Ch of Korea Seoul Seoul 1989-1991. "The Lord Shall Reign Forever and Ever," *Exodus Bible Study in Korean*, Maleunoolleem(Korean), 2004.

JOOS, Heidi L (Minn) 3105 W 40th St, Minneapolis MN 55410 B Columbus WI 1945 d Loyal & Ethel. BS U of Maryland 1967; MD U MI 1971; MDiv Ya Berk 1980. D 12/11/1993 P 12/11/1993 Bp Charlie Fuller Mcnutt Jr. m 12/28/2013 Ivy Bunting Booth. S Jn The Bapt Epis Ch Minneapolis MN 1998-2014; S Paul's Epis Ch Harrisburg PA 1993-1996; Serv Methodist Ch 1987-1993.

JOPLIN, Susan Colley (Okla) 2513 Sw 123rd St, Oklahoma City OK 73170 **P S Paul's Cathd Oklahoma City OK 1993-** B Austin TX 1951 d Thomas & Margaret. BFA U of Oklahoma 1978; MA U of Oklahoma 1982; MDiv Epis TS of the SW 1991. D 6/22/1991 P 1/25/1992 Bp Robert Manning Moody. m 4/28/1996 Larry Ercell Joplin. Dio Oklahoma Oklahoma City OK 2006-2009, 1991-1993.

JOPLING, Wallace Malcolm (Fla) B Lake City FL 1948 BS Wofford Coll 1970; MDiv Sewanee: The U So, TS 2005. D 6/5/2005 P 12/11/2005 Bp Samuel Johnson Howard. m 11/24/1973 Marsha Lynn Jopling c 2. R The Epis Ch of The Redeem Jacksonville FL 2010-2015; R Chr Ch Monticello FL 2005-2010.

JORDAN, Elizabeth Joy (Mass) B Erie PA 1951 d Roger & Lois. Cert D Formation Prog - Dio Massachusetts; PhD The Un Inst; BSN Villa Maria Coll. D 6/4/2016 Bp Alan Gates. m 7/25/2009 Barbara L Barbara Jean Ligget.

JORDAN SR, John E (Nev) 7560 Splashing Rock Dr., Las Vegas NV 89131 **D S Tim's Epis Ch Henderson NV 2003-** B Dallas TX 1945 s Ralph & Ethel.

Estrn New Mex U 1964; Riverside City Coll 1965; Rio Grande Sch For Mnstry 1997. D 2/21/1998 Bp Terence Kelshaw. m 8/5/1965 Carol Marie Hennings c 3. DCE All SS Epis Ch Las Vegas NV 2001-2002; D Chr Ch Las Vegas NV 2000-2001; D H Sprt Epis Ch El Paso TX 1998-2000.

JORDAN, Katherine H (WA) 3156 Gracefield Rd. Apt. 501, Silver Spring MD 20904 **Ret Silver Sprg 2013-; Vol Chaplin Washington Natl Cathd 2008-** B Cleveland OH 1939 d Lewis & Gwendolyn. BA Wells Coll 1961; MLS U Pgh 1964; MDiv VTS 1992. D 6/13/1992 Bp Robert Poland Atkinson P 12/16/1992 Bp Peter J Lee. c 1. R S Jn's Epis Ch Zion Par Beltsville MD 1997-2007; Assoc R S Phil's Epis Ch Laurel MD 1994-1997; Asst S Jn's Epis Ch Arlington VA 1992. EWC 1989-2015; WECA 1996.

JOSE, Nancy (WA) 8213 Bald Eagle Ln, Wilmington NC 28411 B Washington DC 1949 d William & Harriett. BS Jas Madison U 1971; MS Towson U 1976; PhD Sthrn Illinois U 1979; MDiv Candler TS Emory U 1991; MA VTS 1998. D 6/20/1998 Bp Calvin Onderdonk Schofield Jr P 1/9/1999 Bp Michael Whittington Creighton. m 7/12/2003 Wayne Floyd. R S Thos' Par Washington DC 2004-2016; Int R S Jn's Ch Suffolk VA 2003-2004; Assoc R S Paul's Ch Norfolk VA 2001-2003; VTS Alexandria VA 2001; Cn Pstr Cathd Ch Of S Steph Harrisburg PA 1998-2001. Auth, "Silent Gift Proj; A Method For Sprtl Hlth," *Joy Of Sch Hlth*, 1987; Auth, "Sprtl Hlth, A look At Barriers To its Inclusion In Hlth Educ Curric," *Eta Sigma Gamma*, 1986; Auth, "Death: Fam Adjustment to Loss," *Stress and the Fam Vol 2: Coping w Catastrophe*, Brunner-Mazel Inc., 1983; Auth, "Sexism and Ageism," *Educ in the 80s*, NEA, 1981. Jn Owen Smith Preaching Awd Candler TS 1991; Patillo Fndt Middle E Schlrshp Candler TS 1989; Dn Schlr Awd Candler TS 1988; Elmer T Clark Schlr Awd Sthrn Illinois Univeristy 1979.

JOSEPH, Annette Beth (Mo) 420 N Main St, Poplar Bluff MO 63901 **R H Cross Epis Ch Poplar Bluff MO 2011-; Chapl Poplar Bluff Reg Med Cntr 2011-** B Portland ME 1966 d Frank & Catherine. BA U of ME Farmington 2006; MDiv Bangor TS 2010. D 6/19/2010 Bp Stephen Taylor Lane P 1/20/2011 Bp George Wayne Smith. m 10/11/1998 Richard M Joseph c 5. Reflection, "A Geth Reflection," *Journ of Pstr Care & Counslg*, 2009; Prayers, "Seeing," *Lifting Wmn Voices*, Morehouse Pub, 2009; Prayers, "Come," *Lifting Wmn Voices*, Morehouse Pub, 2009; Prayers, "Walls," *Lifting Wmn Voices*, Morehouse Pub, 2009; Sermon, "The Light of the Wrld," *Journ of Rel & Abuse*, The Haworth Press, 2008. The Hoyt L. Hickman Awd Bangor TS 2010; Young Publ Hlth Worker of the Year Illinois Publ Hlth Assn 1988.

JOSEPH, Arthur E (NY) 450 Convent Ave, New York NY 10031 B 1940 s John & Grace. DIT Codrington Coll 1974. Trans 10/1/1987 Bp Paul Moore Jr. m 6/21/1967 Omah Joseph c 3. Cmsn of Mnstry Dio New York New York NY 1990-1997; R Ch Of The Crucif New York NY 1987-2012.

JOSEPH, Augustine (EC) 509 Ramsey St, Fayetteville NC 28301 B 1942 s Lucien & Adriana. LTh Codrington Coll 1972; BA U of The W Indies 1974. D 6/1/1973 P 6/1/1974 Bp The Bishop Of Trinidad. m 12/22/1966 Barbara Joseph c 1. R S Jos's Epis Ch Fayetteville NC 1991-2007; Chapl Voorhees Coll Denmark SC 1988-1992; Voorhees Coll Charleston SC 1988-1991; Serv Ch Of Trinidad & Tabago 1982-1987; Serv Ch Of Barbados 1980-1982; Serv Ch Of Trinidad & Tabago 1973-1980. augustinebban6@aol.com

JOSEPH, Jean Jeannot (Hai) P.O. Box 1390, Port-Au-Prince Haiti **Dio Haiti Port-au-Prince HT 1991-** B 1959 s Alfred & Lorene. Cert TS 1991. D 9/15/1991 P 4/1/1992 Bp Luc Anatole Jacques Garnier. m 5/22/1997 Aline Ceus Joseph c 1.

JOSEPH, Joseph Hyvenson (SeFla) **P-in-c S Phil's Ch Pompano Bch FL 2011-** B Port-Au-Prince Haiti 1971 s Jean & Ema. Bachelor of Sci Florida Atlantic U 2001; Mstr of Div Other 2004; Mstr of Div Sewanee TS 2004; Mstr of Div Sewanee: The U So, TS 2004; PhD Other 2009; PhD Universite Laval 2009; Mstr Sacr Theol Other 2010; Mstr Sacr Theol Sewanee TS 2010; Mstr Sacr Theol Sewanee: The U So, TS 2010; MBA Nova SE U 2011. D 4/17/2004 P 10/23/2004 Bp Leo Frade. P-in-c S Ptr's Epis Ch Key W FL 2004-2007. Who's Who in Amer Marquis 2013; Fllshp The Epis Ch Fundation 2007.

JOSEPH, Pierre Jean (Ve) Calle Tiuna y Callejon, Sta Elena Venezuela Venezuela **Dio Venezuela Caracas 2007-** B Cabaret Haiti 1953 s Alias & Teremise. D 3/30/2007 Bp Orlando Jesus Guerrero. m 2/5/1985 Marie Mimose De Joseph c 2.

JOSEPH, Winston B (SeFla) **R S Patricks Ch W Palm Bch FL 2000-** B 1947 Trans 10/4/2000 Bp Leo Frade. m 8/24/1974 Moilan Joseph c 1.

✠ JOSLIN, The Rt Rev Dr David Bruce (CNY) 10 Meadow Ridge Rd, Westerly RI 02891 **Asstg Bp Dio Rhode Island Providence RI 2004-, 1979-2004, 1978, 1975-1977; Assoc Chr Ch Westerly RI 1987-, R 1974-1986** B Collingswood NJ 1936 s Sheppard & Elizabeth. BA Drew U 1958; MDiv Drew U 1961; Cert EDS 1965. D 3/31/1965 Bp Leland Stark P 8/8/1965 Bp George E Rath Con 11/9/1991 for CNY. c 2. Asstg Bp Dio New Jersey Trenton NJ 2000-2003; Bp of Cntrl New York Dio Cntrl New York Liverpool NY 1991-2000; R S Steph The Mtyr Ch Minneapolis MN 1987-1991; R S Dav's Epis Ch Wilmington DE 1967-1974; Asst S Paul's Ch Montvale NJ 1965-1967. Angl Soc 1982. DD VTS 2004.

JOSLIN, Roger (Ark) 20 Pease Dr, Bella Vista AR 72715 **Ch Of The Redeem Mattituck NY 2017-** B Cleburne TX 1951 s Hollis & Lillian. BA U of Texas 1973; MA U of Texas 1976; MDiv Epis TS of the SW 2005. D 5/13/2006 P 12/2/2006 Bp Larry Maze. c 2. Vic All SS Ch Bentonville AR 2010-2017; Ch Planter S Paul's Ch Fayetteville AR 2006-2009. Auth, "Sch of Love: Planting a Ch in the Shadow of Empire," Morehouse Pub, 2015; Auth, "Running the Sprtl Path," St. Mart's Press, 2003.

JOSLYN-SIEMIATKOSKI, Daniel Edmond Duncalf-Villavaso Prof of Ch Hist Epis TS Of The SW Austin TX 2014- D 6/10/2017 Bp Marc Handley Andrus.

JOY, Charles Austin (SVa) 1009 W Princess Anne Rd, Norfolk VA 23507 B Bangor ME 1944 s Nathan & Jessie. BA W&M TS 1969; Coll of Preachers 2006. D 6/14/1969 P 5/23/1970 Bp Robert Bruce Hall. m 8/20/1966 Marilyn Joy c 1. R S Andr's Ch Norfolk VA 1982-2007; Assoc St Jas Ch Richmond VA 1980-1982; D-in-c, R S Mart's Ch Doswell VA 1969-1980; St Martins Par Ruther Glen VA 1969-1980. Auth, "Poems," *Living Ch*; Auth, "Poems," *New Fire*. Soc of S Marg 1988.

JOYCE, Thomas Joseph (Chi) 214 Hillside Dr., East Berlin PA 17316 **Assoc S Lk's Epis Ch Mechanicsburg PA 2009-** B Boston MA 1933 s Martin & Mary. BA Boston Coll 1955; MA Boston Coll 1959; Lic Sacr Theol Weston Jesuit TS 1966; PhD Geo 1980. Rec 7/1/1987 as Priest Bp Peter J Lee. m 10/7/1989 Margaret Wise. P in Res Hope Epis Ch Manheim PA 2004-2008; R S Jn's Epis Ch Chicago IL 1996-2004; Asst Chr Epis Ch Winchester VA 1989-1995; S Patricks Ch Falls Ch VA 1988-1989; P RC Ch 1965-1972; Select Com. for Ord Dio Cntrl Pennsylvania Harrisburg PA 2010-2011; Dn Chicago W Dio Chicago Chicago IL 1998-2002, Select Com. for Ord 1997-2003. Pdk Tchr Of The Year Awd 1982.

JOYNER, Thomas Roland (Ala) 1170 11th Ave S, Birmingham AL 35205 **Chapl Birmingham Epis Campus Mnstrs Birmingham AL 2015-; Dio Alabama Birmingham 2014-** B Birmingham AL 1971 s Frank & Myra. BA U of Alabama 1995; MA U of Mississippi 2000; MDiv GTS 2008. D 5/20/2008 P 12/16/2008 Bp Henry Nutt Parsley Jr. S Lk's Epis Ch Jacksonville AL 2014; Assoc R H Trin Epis Ch Auburn AL 2010-2014; Cur Ch Of The H Comf Montgomery AL 2008-2010; Yth Dir S Steph's Epis Ch Huntsville AL 2001-2005. thomas@trinitycommons.org

JOYNER JR, William Henry (NC) 309 N Boundary St, Chapel Hill NC 27514 **D S Cyp's Ch Oxford NC 2017-; Archd Dio No Carolina Raleigh NC 2006-, Bp's Com on the Diac 1999-2005** B Washington DC 1946 s William & Nancy. BS U of Virginia 1968; PhD Harv 1973. D 5/30/1992 Bp Richard Frank Grein. m 12/21/1968 Mary Brenda Payne c 2. D Chap Of The Cross Chap Hill NC 1998-2016; D S Ann's Ch Of Morrisania Bronx NY 1997-1998; S Mk's Ch Mt Kisco NY 1997-1998; D S Lk's Ch Katonah NY 1992-1996; COM Dio New York New York NY 1995-1998, Com on the Diac 1993-1998. Assn for Epis Deacons 1992.

JOYNER-GIFFIN, Sally B (Md) 13736 Catoctin Furnace Rd, Thurmont MD 21788 **R Harriet Chap Catoctin Epis Par Thurmont MD 2006-** B Richmond VA 1954 d Edward & Carol. BA Lyndon St Coll 1977; MEd Jas Madison U 1979; MDiv Sewanee: The U So, TS 2005. D 6/11/2005 P 1/25/2006 Bp John L Rabb. m 10/31/1981 John Ellis Giffin c 3. Asst St Jas Epis Ch Sewanee 2005-2006.

JUAREZ, Jose Martin (ECR) 113 Morcroft Ln, Durham NC 27705 **La Iglesia De San Pablo Seaside CA 2014-; P To The Latino Cmnty S Andr's Epis Ch 2004-** B San Luis Potosi Mexico 1964 Sem Guadalupano Josefino San Luis Potosi Slp 1982; Sem Guadalupano Josefino San Luis Potosi Slp 1990. Rec 12/6/2003 as Priest Bp William Edwin Swing. m 1/9/2013 Esperanza Juarez c 3. Vic Dio El Camino Real Salinas CA 2012-2014; Iglesia El Buen Pstr Durham NC 2009-2012; Dio California San Francisco CA 2006-2009.

JUAREZ VILLAMAR, Betty Marlene (EcuL) Coop Esperanza Mz.1 Sl.7, Canton Catarama Ecuador **Litoral Dio Ecuador Guayaquil 2007-** B Canton Catarama Ecuador 1951 d Galo & Amada. DIT Litoral Sem Guayaquil Ec. D 7/14/2002 P 4/13/2008 Bp Terencio Alfredo Morante-Espana. m 5/14/1997 Pedro Andaluz c 2. D San Eduardo Canton Ventanas Ecuador 2002-2004.

JUBINSKI, Christopher David (WA) Christ Episcopal Church, PO Box 8, Chaptico MD 20621 **Chr Ch Chaptico MD 2015-** B Silver City NM 1964 s James & Gretchen. BA S Basil Coll 1986; CUA 1989; MDiv GTS 1998. D 6/20/1998 P 5/29/1999 Bp Charles Ellsworth Bennison Jr. m 8/24/1991 Carol Jones c 3. R S Paul's Ch Centreville MD 2006-2014; S Paul's Epis Ch Santa Paula CA 2001-2006; Assoc Chr Ch Alexandria VA 2000-2001; Asst R Chr Ch Epis Ridley Pk PA 1998-2000.

JUCHTER, Mark Russell (NwPa) 5007 Lions Gate Lane, Killeen TX 76549 **Chapl USAF Ft Hood TX 2014-** B Erie PA 1972 s John & Annabelle. BS Gannon U 1994; Commissioned Off Trng 2002; MDiv SWTS 2003. D 6/15/2003 P 12/20/2003 Bp Robert Deane Rowley Jr. Chapl USAF Nellis AFB NV 2011-2014; Chapl USAF Tinker AFB OK 2008-2011; Int Par of St Clem Honolulu HI 2007-2008; Chapl USAF Hickam AFB HI 2006-2008; Vic S Geo's Epis Ch Honolulu HI 2005-2007; Cur S Jn's Epis Ch Sharon PA 2003-2005.

JUDD, Steven William (Minn) 460 Willow Creek Dr, Owatonna MN 55060 **D S Paul's Epis Ch Owatonna MN 1999-** B Saint Paul MN 1950 s Allen & Elizabeth. BA S Olaf Coll 1972. D 1/15/1994 Bp Sanford Zangwill Kaye Hampton. m 1/29/1972 Barbara C Judd c 2. D S Ptr's Epis Ch Kasson MN 1994-1999.

JUDSON, Donald Irving (Chi) 425 E May St, Elmhurst IL 60126 **Asst Ch of Our Sav Elmhurst IL 2003-** B Newark NJ 1930 s Lemuel & Helen. BA Amh 1952; BD EDS 1956; MA U Chi 1977; MA U Chi 1989. D 6/21/1956 Bp William A Lawrence P 12/21/1956 Bp Frederick Lehrle Barry. m 7/29/1978 Jean Judson c 2. Chr Ch River Forest IL 1989-2000; Chapl Epis Ch Coun U Chi Chicago IL 1975-1978; Min Untd Campus Mnstry Oxford OH 1967-1974; R S Paul's Ch Fremont OH 1959-1967; P-in-c S Paul's Epis Ch Albany NY 1956-1958. Auth, "Importance of Awe & Mystery," *LivCh*, 2008; Auth, "Branches of the Vine," *LivCh*, 2002; Auth, "Ch in the Wrld," *The L:iving Ch*; Auth, "Lay Mnstry," *LivCh*; Auth, "Scenario for Ch," *LivCh*.

JUDSON, Horace Douglas (Los) 1065 Lomita Blvd Spc 197, Harbor City CA 90710 **Ret 1994-** B Glendale CA 1935 s Horace & Blanche. ETSBH; BA U CA 1961. D 9/12/1970 P 3/1/1971 Bp Francis E I Bloy. m 5/28/1966 Kathryn L Judson. Int S Mich The Archangel Par El Segundo CA 1993-1994; 1989-1992; S Tim's Par Compton CA 1982-1989; Asst S Fran' Par Palos Verdes Estates CA 1978-1981; Assoc S Jn's Epis Ch Marysville CA 1977-1978; Vic S Mk's Epis Ch Tracy CA 1975-1977; Epis Dio San Joaquin Modesto CA 1972-1977; Vic S Jn's Epis Ch Tulare CA 1972-1975; Asst Ch Of The H Trin and S Ben Alhambra CA 1970-1972. OHC.

JUDSON, Marguerite D All Souls Par In Berkeley Berkeley CA 2017- B New London Conn. 1951 BA St. Jn's Coll, Annapolis MD; MTS VTS 1977; Cert in Angl Stds CDSP 2017. D 6/10/2017 Bp Marc Handley Andrus.

JULIAN, Mercedes I (RI) Ascension Church, 390 Pontiac Ave, Cranston RI 02910 Panama **P Ch Of The Ascen Cranston RI 2010-; Iglesia Epis de San Juan Johns Island SC 2005-** B Higuey Dominican Republic 1949 d Napoleon & Ludis. Universidad Republica Dominicana 1978; Centro de Estudios Teologicos 1982. D 11/30/1988 P 5/1/1990 Bp James Hamilton Ottley. c 2. Dio Rhode Island Providence RI 2010-2014; S Jn's Epis Par Johns Island SC 2005-2010; Gr Ch New Orleans LA 2004-2005; Centro Buen Pstr San Pedro de Macoris 1997-2003; Vic Iglesia Epis San Esteban San Pedro de Macoris 1997-2003; Vic Iglesia Epis San Juan El Bautista Bonao 1994-1997; Dio The Dominican Republic (Iglesia Epis Dominicana) Gazcue Santo Domingo 1993-2004, 1981-1987; Dio Panama 1988-1993.

JULNES-DEHNER, Noel (SO) 3491 Forestoak Court, Cincinnati OH 45208 **Asstg P Chr Ch Cathd Cincinnati OH 2014-; Asstg P S Thos Epis Ch Terrace Pk OH 1996-, Int 1995-1996** B Seattle WA 1951 d Norval & Marilyn. BA Eckerd Coll 1973; VTS 1974; MDiv CDSP 1978. D 5/26/1978 P 6/24/1979 Bp John Mc Gill Krumm. m 11/19/1983 Joseph Julnes Dehner c 2. Asst Ed Forw Mvmt of the Epis Ch Cincinnati OH 2009-2012; Par Asst St. Thos Epis Ch Terrace Pk OH 2009-2010; Par Asst Indn Hill Epis Presb Ch 1999-2000; Par Asst The Ch of the Redeem Cincinnati OH 1986-1987; Asst The Ch Of Ascen And H Trin Cincinnati OH 1980-1982; Cler Spouse Partnr Chapl Dio Sthrn Ohio Cincinnati OH 2007-2011. Dir, writer, producer, "The Rt Track"; Co-writer, "The Body of Chr"; Dir, writer, producer, "The Rt Track"; Co-writer, "The Body of Chr"; Producer/Writer/Dir, "The Rt Track: Stories of Justice & Redemp"; Producer/Writer/Dir, "Ukraintsi"; Producer/Writer, "Y a-t-il une vie?"; Producer/Writer, "The Kharkov Connection"; Producer/Writer, "Under Fire: Soviet Wmn Combat Veterans, WWII".

JUMP, Douglas Brian (CFla) **D S Steph's Ch Lakeland FL 2015-** D 9/12/2015 Bp Gregory Orrin Brewer.

JUNK, Dixie (Kan) 2701 W 51st Ter, Westwood KS 66205 **P-in-c S Paul's Ch Kansas City KS 2010-; Dioc Jubilee Off Dio Kansas Topeka KS 2010-, Capital Cmpgn Bldg Com 2008-, Cmsn on Archit & Allied Arts 2000-** B Hutchinson, KS 1957 d Dick & Patsy. AA Hutchinson Cmnty Coll 1977; BA K SU 1981; MDiv S Paul TS 2008. D 6/5/2010 P 1/8/2011 Bp Dean E Wolfe. m 8/9/1980 Robert P Junk c 1. Accreditation Self-Study Com S Paul TS Kansas City MO 2009-2011.

JUNKIN, Hays Maclean (NH) Church of Our Saviour, P.O. Box 237, Milford NH 03055 **Int Ch Of Our Sav Milford NH 2011-** B Pittsburgh PA 1952 s John & Margaret. BA Washington and Jefferson U 1975; MDiv VTS 1978. D 6/9/1978 P 12/13/1978 Bp Dean Theodore Stevenson. m 4/20/2009 Sarah Rockwell c 2. Int R Ch Of The H Sprt Plymouth NH 2010-2011; P-in-c S Jas Epis Ch Laconia NH 2005-2008; R S Andr's Epis Ch Contoocook NH 1987-2005; R S Dav's Epis Ch Buffalo NH 1980-1987; Cur S Jas Ch Lancaster PA 1978-1980.

JUPIN, J Michael (SO) 70 S Remington Rd, Columbus OH 43209 **Chapl to the Ret Dio Sthrn Ohio 2014-; Supvsr Wellstrams Spir. Dir. Formation Prog Columbus OH 2011-; Fac, Ldrshp Seminar Healthy Congregations Inc. Trin Luth Sem 2009-; Chapl to the Ret Cler, Spouses/Partnr & Surviving Sopuses/Partnr Dio Sthrn Ohio Cincinnati OH 2014-** B Indianapolis IN 1942 s John & Maxine. BA Br 1964; BD EDS 1967; STM GTS 1986. D 6/24/1967 P 6/15/1968 Bp John P Craine. m 8/24/1982 Barbara E Jupin c 1. Int R S Jn's Epis Ch Charleston WV 2012-2013; Transitional R S Alb's Epis Ch Of Bexley Columbus OH 2008-2011; Int Chr Ch Clarksburg WV 2006-2007; CRE-

DO II Vocational Fac Credo Inst Inc. Memphis TN 2005-2011; Int Ch Of The Gd Shpd Athens OH 2003-2006; Ch Of The Epiph Nelsonville OH 1999-2003; P-in-c S Paul's Epis Ch Logan OH 1999-2003; R S Mk's Epis Ch Columbus OH 1990-1998; R Chr Ch Corning NY 1984-1990; Cn Trin Cathd Cleveland OH 1974-1984; Asst Gr Ch In Providence Providence RI 1973-1974; Dir Main Line Peace Cntr Haverford PA 1972-1974; Asst S Chris's Ch Gladwyne PA 1969-1971; Asst Par Of The Epiph Winchester MA 1967-1969. Healthy Congregations, Inc. Bd Dir 2005; Voyagers - The Ed Friedman Mem. Soc 2001; Wellstreams Prog - Advsry Coun 2016. jmjupin7@gmail.com

JURADO, Ruben Dario (Nwk) 326 Westervelt Pl, Lodi NJ 07644 **S Mart's Ch Maywood NJ 2014-; Cmsn on Hisp/Latino Mnstry Newark NJ 2007-** B Manizales Colombia 1961 s Dario & Blanca. MDiv Our Lady of the Rosary 1987. Rec 9/16/2006 Bp John Palmer Croneberger. m 6/15/1996 Maria Jurado c 2. Hisp Min Trin Epis Ch Kearny NJ 2006-2011.

JURKOVICH-HUGHES, Jocelynn Lena (NCal) 216 A Street, Davis CA 95616 **Campus Chapl Belfry: Luth Epis Campus Mininstry Davis CA 2008-** B Sacramento CA 1976 d David & Jacquelynn. BA Goucher Coll 1998; MA U of So Florida 2000; Cert U of So Florida 2001; MDiv Ya Berk 2004. D 6/25/2004 P 12/19/2004 Bp Jerry Alban Lamb. m 7/27/2002 Christopher A Hughes c 3. Assoc R The Epis Ch Of S Andr Encinitas CA 2004-2008; Prov Coordntr for Campus Mnstry Prov VIII San Diego CA 2012-2014. pastor@thebelfry.org

JUSTICE, Simon Charles (Ore) 445 NW Elizabeth Drive, Corvallis OR 97330 **R The Epis Ch Of The Gd Samar Corvallis OR 2006-** B Cheslyn Hay Staffordshire UK 1966 s Keith & Norma. BD S Davids Coll Lampeter UK 1988; MTh U of Edinburgh Edinburgh GB 1990; Cranmer Hall U of Durham UK 1992. Trans 1/1/1995 Bp David Standish Ball. m 9/3/1992 Michele Justice c 3. R Epis Ch of Scotland 2004-2006; R S Jas Epis Ch Portland OR 2001-2004; R S Paul's Ch Troy NY 1995-2001; Cur Ch of Engl 1992-1995; Stndg Com Dio Oregon Portland OR 2007-2011, Dn of Sunset Convoc 2004-2007; Cn Capitular Cathd Of All SS Albany NY 1998-2001.

JUSTIN, Daniel (Los) 14311 Dickens St Apt 111, Sherman Oaks CA 91423 **R S Mich and All Ang Epis Ch Studio City CA 2012-** B Harvey IL 1972 s Larned & Kathleen. DMin Luther Sem; BS Missouri Bapt U 1995; MA Lindenwood U 2001; MDiv SFTS 2008. D 6/6/2009 Bp Sergio Carranza-Gomez P 12/11/2009 Bp Jeff Lee. Asst R S Mary's Ch Pk Ridge IL 2009-2012. rector@stmikessc.org

K

KADEL, Andrew (NY) 1 Alexander Street, Yonkers NY 10701 **Trin Epis Ch Roslyn NY 2017-; Dir of St. Mk's Libr Ch Of The H Apos New York NY 2003-** B Nampa ID 1954 s Donald & Bernice. BA Ob 1976; MDiv CDSP 1981; MLS Rutgers The St U of New Jersey 1989. D 7/15/1981 Bp Hanford Langdon King Jr P 2/26/1982 Bp James Daniel Warner. m 5/22/1999 Paula Schaap c 3. S Jas Epis Par Lincoln CA 2016-2017; Assoc Trin Ch Of Morrisania Bronx NY 2014-2016; The GTS New York NY 2014-2015, Dir of the Christoph Keller, Jr. Libr 2011-2015, Dir of St. Mk's Libr 2003-2014; Dir of the Libr Wesley TS Washington DC 2000-2003; Assoc S Ptr's Ch Port Chester NY 1995-1998; Ref & Collection Libr UTS New York NY 1990-2000; Cur S Mk's Epis Ch Yonkers NY 1989-1995; Asst S Lk's Ch Trenton NJ 1985-1989; Vic Trin Epis Ch Kirksville MO 1983-1985; Asst S Matt's Ch Lincoln NE 1981-1983; Chapl S Monica Hm Lincoln NE 1981-1982. Auth, ""Christoph Keller, Jr. Libr, GTS, New York" in a Forum on Bldg/renovation projects," *Theol Librarianship 4:2, 2011*, 2012; Auth, ""Healey Willan and Liturg Song at the Ch of St. Mary Magd,"" *Never Enough Singing: Essays in hon of Seth Kasten*, Amer Theol Libr Assn, 2011; Auth, ""A better adaption of ancient formularies to present wants": W. R. Huntington's notes ... BCP.," *The Angl*, 2011; Auth, "A better adaption of ancient formularies to present wants: W. R. Huntington's notes … BCP," *The Angl*, 2011; Auth, "Mart Niemöller: transformation of an oral text," *Journ of Rel and Theol Info*, 1996; Auth, *Matrology: Bibliography of Writings by Chr Wmn from the 1st to the 15th Centuries*, Continuum, 1995.

KAEHR, Michael G (SanD) 9503 La Jolla Farms Rd, La Jolla CA 92037 B Decatur IN 1942 s Lores & La Vera. BA Heidelberg U 1964; MA U of Wisconsin 1970; MDiv Nash 1983. D 4/16/1983 P 10/15/1983 Bp William Louis Stevens. m 1/25/1997 Nancy Kaehr. Hon Cathd Ch Of S Paul San Diego CA 2009-2015; R S Jn's Epis Ch Chula Vista CA 1988-1997; Asst R S Jas By The Sea La Jolla CA 1985-1988; Asst to Dn St Paul's Epis Cathd Fond Du Lac WI 1983-1985. SHN.

KAETON, Elizabeth (Nwk) 35647 Joann Dr, Millsboro DE 19966 **P All SS and St Georges Ch Rehoboth Bch DE 2011-; Dept Of Missions 1991-** B Fall River MA 1949 d John & Lydia. BS Lesley U 1983; MDiv EDS 1986; U of Sheffield Gb 1999; DMin Drew U 2008. D 4/12/1986 P 10/1/1986 Bp Frederick Barton Wolf. m 8/9/2013 Barbara R Vigeant c 1. R S Paul's Epis Ch Chatham NJ 2002-2011; Assoc Ch Of The Redeem Morristown NJ 1998-2002; The Oasis

Newark NJ 1996-2002; Chapl Newark Police Dept 1995-2002; Hse Of Pryr Epis Ch Newark NJ 1995-1996; P-in-c Hse Of Pryr Newark NJ 1995-1996; Dir Of Pstr Care Vnsny Hospice 1995-1996; Dio Newark Newark NJ 1995; Adj Fac Drew U TS 1994-1998; Bd Chr Hosp 1992-1996; Vic S Barn Ch Newark NJ 1991-1995; Non-par 1988-1991; Founding Exec Dir Chase Brexton Clnc Baltimore MD 1988-1991; Memi Ch Baltimore MD 1987-1989; P-in-c S Dav's Ch Salem NH 1986-1987; Chapl U Of Massachusetts-Lowell Campus Mnstry 1986-1987. Auth, "Two Grooms Revisited," *A Sea Of Stories: The Shaping Power Of Narrative*, Harrington Pk, 2000; Auth, "To Have And To Hold," *Journ Of Lcgm*, 2000; Auth, "The Power Of Pryr," *The Voice*, 2000; Auth, "The Adv Of Desire, Sermons That Wk Vii," *Adv Iii*, Morehouse, 1999; Auth, "Called To Full Humanity: Letters To Lambeth Bishops," *Journ Of Lgcm*, 1998; Auth, "Pstr Care At The End Of Life," *Journ Of Palliative Med*, 1998; Auth, "Lambeth," *The Voice*, 1998; Auth, "Dealing w Grief," *Wit*, 1998; Auth, "Beyond Inclusion Report," *Wit*, 1998; Auth, "Maria'S Chld," *Wit*, 1997. Beyond Inclusion: Just Commitments Natl Coordntng Grp 1998; Coun Of Wmn Mnstrs 2000; Dir Of Prog-Integrity Usa 1999; EWC 2000-2012; Integrity 1976-2012; New Commandment T/F On Recon 2000; Nj Rel Cltn On Reproductive Rts 2000; No Jersey Epis City Mssn Bd 1996-2000; Oasis-Pres, Bd 1996-2002; The Consult 1999; Voice Ed Bd 1992-2000. Awd Of Merit For Spec Achievement In Ch Cmncatn ECom 1999; Resolution Of Gratitude, Lambeth Oasis Bd Dir 1998; 3 Awards Of Excellence In Rel Journalism ECom 1997; Wmn Of Influence Ywca 1995; Awd Of Gratitude Latino/A People Living w Aids 1992.

KAHL JR SSJE, Robert Mathew (NJ) 107 E Tampa Ave, Villas NJ 08251 B Brigham City UT 1945 s Robert & Anna. STB GTS; STM UTS; AA Amer Coll of Switzerland 1966; BA U of Pennsylvania 1968; MPhil U of St Andrews 1997. D 6/29/1971 P 7/2/1972 Bp Chilton R Powell. Adj. Prof. Wrld Rel Atlantic Cape Cmnty Coll May Landing NJ 1999-2005; Chr Ch Bridgeport PA 1998-2001; Dioc Dept Of Cmncatn 1986-1994; Ed Asst Of Dioc News 1986-1994; Dn Of The Atlantic Convoc 1986-1989; Dioc Cmsn On Drug & Alco Abuse 1985-1994; Dioc Dept Of CE 1982-1994; Dir Of The Dioceasan Epishon Soc 1982-1994; R Adv Fife Engl 1979-1994; Ch Of The Adv Cape May NJ 1979-1994; Chair - Dept Of CE Moorestown Cmnty Ch 1976-1979; Asst Trin Ch Moorestown NJ 1973-1979; Asst Ch Of The Resurr New York NY 1972-1973; Asst Chapl SS Hilda & Hugh Sch In New York City 1972-1973; Asst S Mary The Vrgn Kuala Lumpur W Malaysia 1971-1972. Auth, "Chr & Hisp Communities," Ed. Bibliography, 1990; Auth, "Living Ch"; Ed and Auth, "Chr and Chrsnty," *Intro*; "Numerous Revs," *TLC and ATheology Journ*. Soc Of S Jn The Evang 1974.

KAHLE, George Frank (SVa) 16711 Holly Trail Dr, Houston TX 77058 **Asst S Thos Nassao Bay TX 1996-; Ret 1988-** B Pensacola FL 1919 s George & Blanche. BD U of Alabama 1947. D 6/6/1979 P 6/1/1980 Bp Robert Poland Atkinson. m 1/4/1947 Jeanne Burcher. Asst Gr Ch Galveston TX 1989-1996; Wm Temple Epis Ctr Galveston TX 1988-1989; Vic Emm Ch Temperanceville VA 1984-1988; Cur S Matt's Ch Charleston WV 1980-1984.

KAHLER, Jerome Evans (Los) 9061 Santa Margarita Rd, Ventura CA 93004 B Los Angeles CA 1944 s James & Rosemary. BA Whittier Coll 1966; MDiv Nash 1970. D 8/17/1969 P 7/26/1970 Bp Robert Claflin Rusack. m 6/1/1968 Elizabeth H Henderson c 1. R S Paul's Epis Ch Ventura CA 1988-2010; Deploy Off Dio Los Angeles CA 1986-1988; Exec. Dir. VIM Dio Los Angeles CA 1984-1986; Cn Dio Los Angeles Los Angeles CA 1983-1988, Cmsn on Sch 1996-2000, Stndg Com 1991-1994; Stwdshp Off Dio Los Angeles CA 1983-1988; R S Paul's Epis Ch Santa Paula CA 1979-1984; Asst to the R S Geo Sch La Can CA 1971-1979; Headmaster S Geo Sch La Can CA 1971-1979; Asst S Geo's Par La Can CA 1971-1979; Asst S Mich's Mssn Anaheim CA 1970-1971; Dn Dnry 1 Dio Los Angeles 2000-2012. Cn Dio Los Angeles 2009.

KAHN, Paul Stewart (NY) 552 West End Avenue, New York NY 10024 **D The Ch of S Ign of Antioch New York NY 2008-** B Bethpage NY 1957 s Sam & Hazel. BA Ob 1979; MBA NYU 1985. D 5/5/2007 Bp Mark Sean Sisk. D Ch Of The Gd Shpd New York NY 2007-2008.

KAIGHN, Reuel Stewart (Be) 145 The Hideout, Lake Ariel PA 18436 **Shared Supply Chr Ch Indn Orchard 2006-; Ret 2000-** B Hartford CT 1936 s Reuel & Sarah. BA U of Pennsylvania 1958; MDiv EDS 1964. Trans 12/6/2003 Bp Robert William Duncan. m 1/22/2000 Barbara B Kaighn c 3. Assoc S Jn's Epis Ch Hamlin PA 2002-2004; Chapl S Marg Memi Hosp Verona PA 1996-1997; R All SS Epis Ch Verona PA 1992-2000; R Trin Epis Ch Beaver PA 1984-1991; R S Jn's Epis Ch Montclair NJ 1970-1984; Asst Trin Ch Princeton NJ 1967-1970; Cur S Mk's Ch New Britain CT 1964-1967.

KAISCH, Kenneth Burton (Los) 2112 Camino Del Sol, Fullerton CA 92833 **Non-par 1984-** B Detroit MI 1948 s Kenneth & Marjorie. Ken 1969; BA San Francisco St U 1972; MDiv CDSP 1976; MS Utah St U 1982; PhD Utah St U 1986. D 8/15/1976 P 3/1/1977 Bp Otis Charles. P-in-c S Jn's Epis Ch Logan UT 1980-1984; Vic S Fran Ch Moab UT 1977-1980; Ordinand'S Trng Prog Dio Utah Salt Lake City UT 1976-1977. Auth, "Finding God: A Handbook Of Chr Meditation". Phi Kappa Phi 82.

KALAS, Steven Curtis (Nev) 3607 Blue Dawn Dr, North Las Vegas NV 89032 **Chapl Nathan Adelson Hospice 1997-** B Phoenix AZ 1957 s William & Shirley. BS Nthrn Arizona U 1979; MA SMU 1983. D 11/30/1997 P 5/1/1998 Bp Stewart Clark Zabriskie. m 3/30/1991 Jennifer Diane Kalas c 2. Chr Ch Las Vegas NV 2001-2006; Dio Nevada Las Vegas 1999-2001.

KALEMKERIAN, Louise Knar (Ct) 5030 Main St, Trumbull CT 06611 **Assoc St. Paul's on the Green Norwalk CT 2005-** B Detroit MI 1945 d Arshavir & Bettye. BA Wayne 1968; MA SWTS 1970; CAS GTS 1994; STM GTS 1998. D 6/3/1995 Bp John Shelby Spong P 12/2/1995 Bp Jack Marston Mckelvey. m 8/7/1971 Joseph Kalemkerian c 3. S Jn's Ch No Haven CT 2015-2017; Gr Epis Ch Trumbull CT 2014-2015; Assoc Par of St Paul's Ch Norwalk Norwalk CT 2014-2015, 2004; Chr Ch Trumbull CT 2012-2014; Int S Ptr's-Trin Ch Thomaston CT 2009-2011; Asst to the R Chr And H Trin Ch Westport CT 2009; Int S Andr's Ch Madison CT 2007-2009; Int S Mary's Ch Of Scarborough Briarcliff NY 2004-2005; Int St. Mary's Ch Scarborough 2004-2005; S Lukes Cmnty Serv Inc. Stamford CT 2003-2007; R Emm Ch Stamford 1999-2003; R Emm Epis Ch Stamford CT 1999-2003; Int S Mary's Ch Sparta NJ 1997-1998; Int S Paul's Epis Ch Morris Plains NJ 1996-1997; Asst hd S Phil Acad Newark NJ 1995-1996; Asst for Educ Trin And S Phil's Cathd Newark NJ 1995-1996.

KALLENBERG, Richard Arthur (NI) 55805 Oak Manor Pl, Elkhart IN 46514 B Anderson IN 1944 s Herbert & Helen. BA Hanover Coll 1966; BD Nash 1969. D 6/11/1969 Bp John P Craine P 11/11/1969 Bp Albert Ervine Swift. m 3/31/1970 Kathryn Kallenberg. Int S Mich And All Ang Ch So Bend IN 2008-2012; Dn Elkhart Dnry 1990-1993; R S Jn The Evang Ch Elkhart IN 1987-2008; Dn Wi River Dnry 1985-1987; Cmsn Indo-Chinese Mnstry 1982-1984; R Intsn Epis Ch Stevens Point WI 1977-1987; P Chr the King/H Nativ (Sturgeon Bay) Sturgeon Bay WI 1970-1977; Ch Of The H Nativ Jacksonport Sturgeon Bay WI 1970-1977; Dio Fond du Lac Appleton WI 1970-1977; Cur S Mk's Ch Cocoa FL 1969-1970. SHN. Hon Cn The Cathd Ch Of St. Jas 2004.

KALLIO, Craig (ETenn) 119 Newell Lane, Oak Ridge TN 37830 B Painesville OH 1949 s Melvin & Maxine. BA Adrian Coll 1971; MDiv Iliff TS 1983; DMin SWTS 1998. D 6/6/1988 P 10/14/1988 Bp Francis Campbell Gray. m 5/2/1987 Pamela K Kallio. R S Steph's Epis Ch Oak Ridge TN 2000-2016; R All SS Ch Wstrn Sprgs IL 1991-2000; Cur Trin Ch Ft Wayne IN 1988-1991; CPE Chapl So Bend Memi Hosp IN 1987-1988; Serv Methodist Ch 1983-1987. Auth, "Unity in Chr," *The Angl Dig*, Sprg, 2013; Auth, "Trust God in All Things," *The Angl Dig*, Winter, 2012; Auth, "A Chr Way of Hearing," *The Angl Dig*, Sum, 2010; Auth, "The Anatomy of Emptiness," *The Angl Dig*, Winter, 2009; Auth, "The Poor," *The Angl Dig*, Pentecost, 2008; Auth, "Greet the Unepected," *The Angl Dig*, Adv, 2008; Auth, "Baptismal Identity," *The Angl Dig*, Easter, 2008. Ord of S Lk 1991.

KALOM, Judith Christine Lilly (At) B Sturgis MI 1939 d Harold & Grace. D 12/19/1990 Bp Don Adger Wimberly. m 8/26/1961 Peter Grant Kalom c 2.

KALUNIAN, Peter John (Spok) 5506 W. 19th Ave., Kennewick WA 99338 **P-in-c H Trin Epis Ch Sunnyside WA 2012-, P-in-c 2011-; Chapl Kennewick Fire Dept. 1995-** B Waltham MA 1942 s John & Rose. BA Parsons Coll 1967; MEd Boston St Coll 1969; EdD Bos 1974; MDiv CDSP 1990. D 6/2/1990 Bp Joseph Thomas Heistand P 12/1/1990 Bp Frank Jeffrey Terry. m 5/9/1991 Kathryn A Bonacci c 2. Ch Of The Resurr Bellevue WA 2004-2008; Dioc Ecum Off Dio Spokane Spokane WA 1998-2001, Dioc Ecum Off 1998-2001, Stndg Com 1997, COM 1993-1996, Stndg Com 1997-2002, Dn - Snake River Dnry 1997-; R S Paul's Epis Mssn Kennewick WA 1994-2004; Vic Gr Ch Dayton WA 1990-1994; S Ptr's Ch Pomeroy WA 1990-1994.

KAMANO, Charles Lansana (Ct) 28 Church St, West Haven CT 06516 B Guinea 1972 s Bobor & Finda. Rec 3/16/2017 as Priest Bp Ian Theodore Douglas. c 1.

KAMINSKAS, Karen A (Pa) **S Mary's Epis Ch Ardmore PA 2017-; D's Coun Mem Dio Pennsylvania Philadelphia PA 2015-; Mem of Bd Com on Res care and compliance barclay friends W chester pa 2014-** D 6/14/2014 Bp Clifton Daniel III.

KAMINSKI, Neil (Ark) 188 Elcano Dr, Hot Springs Village AR 71909 **R H Trin Epis Ch Hot Sprg AR 2013-** B Montreal QC CA 1959 s Mitchell & Alice. BA Asbury U 1982; MTS Sprg Hill Coll 1988; MDiv Sewanee: The U So, TS 1995. D 5/27/1995 P 1/23/1996 Bp Charles Farmer Duvall. m 8/28/1986 Gwendolyn Rose Smith c 1. R The Epis Ch Of S Fran Of Assisi Pelham AL 2007-2013; Vic St Aug of Cbury Navarre FL 1998-2007; Cur Trin Epis Ch Mobile AL 1995-1998.

KAMM, Wayne Kenneth (Ia) 1451 Salem Rd., Salem IA 52649 B Dubuque Iowa 1936 s Kenneth & Sadie. BA U of Dubuque 1958; MDiv Garrett-Evang TS 1963. D 4/9/1985 P 10/23/1985 Bp Walter Cameron Righter. m 6/2/1990 Mary Louise Kamm c 2. Assoc Chr Epis Ch Burlington IA 2000; R S Mich's Ch Mt Pleasant IA 1985-1999; Vic Ch of the Gd Shpd Detroit MI 1984-1985; Chapl Hospice of Henry Cnty Iowa 1973-1999; Serv Meth Ch 1961-1984; Dioc Search Com Dio Iowa Des Moines IA 1987-1988, Bd Dir 1986-1994, Chair - Com 1986-1990, COM 1986-1990. Land 1989.

KANE, Dennis Edward (Ct) 679 Farmington Ave, West Hartford CT 06119 B Colon Republic of Panama 1944 s Donald & Elizabeth. BS DePaul U 1971; MA

NWU 1982. D 9/10/2011 Bp Laura Ahrens. m 10/1/2010 Russell C Eckhart c 1. St Johns Ch W Hartford CT 2010-2013.

KANE, E Ross (Va) 3737 Seminary Rd, Alexandria VA 22304 **Prof VTS Alexandria VA 2017-, 2014** B 1979 s Robert & Anne. BA U of Virginia 2002; MDiv Duke DS 2009; PhD U of Virginia 2016. D 11/14/2009 Bp Shannon Sherwood Johnston P 5/15/2010 Bp David Colin Jones. m 8/25/2006 Elizabeth MD Kane c 2. Assoc S Paul's Epis Ch Alexandria VA 2009-2017. rkane@vts.edu

KANE, Maria A (WA) 4535 Piney Church Rd, Waldorf MD 20602 **S Paul's Epis Ch Piney Waldorf MD 2014-; Com on Human Sxlty Dio Sthrn Virginia Newport News VA 2011-** B Dallas TX 1980 d Samuel & Patricia Anne. BA How 2003; MDiv Duke DS 2006; MA W&M 2008. D 6/19/2010 Bp Michael B Curry P 5/4/2011 Bp Herman Hollerith IV. Cur Hickory Neck Ch Toano VA 2011. Auth, "That Darn Collar," *Fidelia's Sis*, Young Wmn Cler Proj, 2011; Contributing Auth, "Prayers for Chld," *Forty Days of Pryr in hon of 9/11*, Meth Ch, 2011. pineyrector@gmail.com

KANE, Paul (SeFla) St James In The Hills Episcopal, 3329 Wilson St, Hollywood FL 33021 **R S Paul's Ch Delray Bch FL 2015-; Exec Bd Mem Dio SE Florida Miami 2015-; Vice-Chairperson of the Bd Dir The Jubilee Cntr of So Broward Inc. 2015-** B Des Plaines IL 1965 s William & Mary. BA La Salle U 1987; MA St Vinc de Paul Reg Sem 1995; MDiv St Vinc de Paul Reg Sem 1996. Rec 6/14/2013 as Priest Bp Leo Frade. m 1/7/2012 Irene Tello c 1. P S Jas-In-The-Hills Epis Ch Hollywood FL 2013-2015. revpaul@stpaulsdelray.org

KANELLAKIS, Theodore (NY) 10 Rawson Ave, Camden ME 04843 B Brooklyn NY 1943 s Louis & Pauline. Inst of Theol New York NY 1981; BA SUNY 1981. D 6/13/1981 Bp Paul Moore Jr P 1/23/1982 Bp James Stuart Wetmore. m 6/28/1974 Susan Kanellakis c 3. Int P S Ptr's Ch Rockland ME 2007-2008; P in Charge S Paul's And Trin Par Tivoli NY 1989-2005; Ch Of The Regeneration Pine Plains NY 1989-1998; Assoc Ch Of The H Trin New York NY 1982-1989; Cler Day Com Dio Maine Portland ME 2006-2009; Dioc Coun Dio New York New York NY 1992-1996.

KANESTROM, Glenn Walter (SJ) 6443 Estelle Ave, Riverbank CA 95367 **R S Paul's Ch Marinette WI 2017-** B Seattle WA 1961 s Gilbert & Priscilla. Syr; BA Seattle Pacific U 1983; MDiv SWTS 1991. D 6/22/1991 Bp O'Kelley Whitaker P 5/12/1992 Bp David Bruce Joslin. m 6/14/1986 Jane Ellen Kanestrom c 2. S Paul's Epis Ch Modesto CA 2015-2016; R Chr The King Ch Riverbank CA 2002-2014; S Paul's Epis Ch Laporte IN 1997-2002; Asst To The R Trin Epis Ch Hartford CT 1993-1997; Dio Cntrl New York Liverpool NY 1991-1993; Dioc Intern Trin Memi Ch Binghamton NY 1991-1993.

KANG, Hi-Jae Peter (La) PO Box 28, St Francisvle LA 70775 **D Gr Ch Of W Feliciana St Francisvlle LA 2014-** B Fairfax VA 1983 s Han & Winnifred. BA U of Virginia 2006; MA U of Virginia 2013; PhD U of Virginia 2013; MDiv Bexley-Seabury 2014. D 8/23/2014 P 2/27/2015 Bp Morris King Thompson Jr. m 9/10/2016 Samantha L Copping Kang.

KANGAS, John Gilbert (NMich) 302 E Arch St, Ironwood MI 49938 **P Ch Of The Trsfg Ironwood MI 1999-** B New York NY 1930 s John & Tyyne. Beloit Coll; Nthrn Michigan U. D 11/12/1997 P 5/1/1998 Bp Thomas Kreider Ray. m 8/16/1953 Maj-Britt Nyberg.

KANNENBERG, James Gordon (Ia) 605 Avenue E, Fort Madison IA 52627 B Fond du lac WI 1952 s Vernon & Carol. BS U of Wisconsin 1975; MD U of Wisconsin 1979. D 10/25/2009 P 5/9/2010 Bp Alan Scarfe. m 7/7/1978 Kathy Anderson.

KANOUR, Marion Elizabeth (SwVa) 732 S Chestnut Ave, Arlington Heights IL 60005 **Gr Epis Ch Massies Mill VA 2013-** B Norfolk VA 1953 d Marion & Mildred. BS OR SU 1982; MDiv Ya Berk 1985; CAS VTS 1992. D 6/7/1992 Bp Frank Harris Vest Jr P 12/1/1992 Bp Frank Kellogg Allan. m 9/9/2011 Barbara Heyl. R Trin Epis Ch Lynchburg VA 2009-2013; R S Barn Ch Lynchburg VA 2003-2009; Vic The Ch Of The H Innoc Hoffman Schaumburg IL 2001-2003; Asst S Barth's Epis Ch Atlanta GA 1997-2001; Int Emmaus Hse Epis Ch Atlanta GA 1997, Int 1996-1997, D 1992-1993; Dio Atlanta Atlanta GA 1996; Assoc All SS Epis Ch Atlanta GA 1993-1997; Chapl Grady Hospice Prog Atlanta GA 1993-1996; Hosp Chapl Scottish Rite Chld's Med Cntr 1992-1993. Pi Sigma Alpha.

KANYI, Peter (ETenn) 630 Mississippi Ave, Signal Mtn TN 37377 B Londiani 1946 s Muraya & Wangui. BS Dallas Chr Coll 2000; MAR Emmanual Sch of Rel Johnson City TN 2004; MDiv VTS 2008. D 5/31/2008 P 1/24/2009 Bp Charles Glenn VonRosenberg. m 10/29/2008 Anne Kanyi c 3. P Dio E Tennessee Knoxville TN 2011-2015; S Tim's Ch Signal Mtn TN 2009-2011, D 2008-2013.

KANZLER JR, Jay Lee (Mo) 20 Southmoor Dr, Clayton MO 63105 B Washington DC 1961 s Jay & Gail. BS Maryville U 1988; JD S Louis U 1991; MTh S Louis U 2005. D 12/22/2004 P 9/11/2005 Bp George Wayne Smith. m 6/10/1989 Karen Kanzler c 2. S Ptr's Epis Ch S Louis MO 2004-2013.

KAOMA, Kapya John (Mass) Christ Church, Po Box 366202, Hyde Park MA 02136 B Mwense Zambia 1970 s Misheck & Jessy. Trans 9/27/2016 as Priest Bp Alan Gates. m 6/20/2004 Phillipa Kaoma c 5.

KAPP, Charl Ann (NwPa) 1731 Warren Rd, Oil City PA 16301 **D Chr Epis Ch Oil City PA 1996-** B Oil City PA 1936 d William & Elizabeth. Dioc Sch for Mnstry Titusville PA 1995. D 1/28/1996 Bp Robert Deane Rowley Jr. c 3.

KAPP, John Deane (Az) 2800 W Ina Rd, Tucson AZ 85741 B Phoenix AZ 1945 s George & Louise. BFA Arizona St U 1973; MFA U of Arizona 1977. D 1/23/2010 Bp Kirk Stevan Smith. m 6/16/1973 Martha Kapp c 2.

KAPPEL, Roger D (EC) 1313 Deer Creek Dr, Denison TX 75020 B Clinton OK 1947 s Roy & Ruby. BA Sthrn Nazarene U 1969; MDiv S Paul TS 1972. D 12/14/1996 P 6/11/1997 Bp Robert Manning Moody. m 9/14/1990 Dollie M Kappel c 2. Trin Ch Lumberton NC 2003-2013; Command Chapl 1st Corps Spprt Command Airborne Ft Bragg NC 2001-2004; Stff Chapl 104th Area Spt Grp Hanau Germany 1998-2001; Off Of Bsh For ArmdF New York NY 1997-2004; Installation Chapl Off of the Installation Chapl Ft Sill OK 1996-1998; Chapl US-Army 1975-2004; Serv Meth Ch 1970-1996. Our Lady of Walsingham 2009; The Angl Soc 2007.

KAPURCH, Linda Marie (Pa) 343 Elizabeth Dr, Kennett Square PA 19348 **P-in-c Ch Of The Ascen Parkesburg PA 2016-; Chapl YMCA of Grtr Brandywine W Chester PA 2013-** B Worcester MA 1950 d Joseph & Rita. BA Coll of New Rochelle 1972; MS SUNY 1976; MDiv VTS 2002. D 6/15/2002 P 12/18/2002 Bp Peter J Lee. Asst The Epis Ch Of The Adv Kennet Sq PA 2013-2016, Assoc 2011; P-in-c Trin Ch Gulph Mills Kng Of Prussia PA 2011-2013; Assoc S Matt's Ch Maple Glen PA 2006-2011; Int Assoc S Geo's Epis Ch Arlington VA 2005-2006; Asst S Jas' Epis Ch Leesburg VA 2002-2005. Friends of Cbury Cathd US 2008; Friends of St. Ben 2002; Shalem Contemplative Soc 2010. Ursula Laurus Coll of New Rochelle 2017; Cbury Schlr Cbury- Cathd Intl Study Canter 2001; Fulbright Awd Fulbright Cmsn 1973. ascensionpriest@gmail.com

KARANJA, Daniel Njoroge (Spr) PO BOX 534, BLYTHEWOOD SC 29016 **Off Of Bsh For ArmdF New York NY 1998-** B 1965 s Joseph & Saraphina. BA E Afr TS 1989; MDiv Bos TS 1994; DMin Andover Newton TS 1999. D 12/1/1988 P 12/1/1990 Bp The Bishop Of Nairobi. m 7/10/1993 Joyce Muthoni Karanja c 3. Chapl USAF. "Female Genital Mutilation In Afr," Xulon Press, 2003. Jonathan Daniels Fllshp EDS Cambridge Ma 1993.

KARCHER, David Pirritte (SeFla) 5374 Sw 80th St, Miami FL 33143 **D S Phil's Ch Coral Gables FL 1999-** B Chicago IL 1933 s Leo & Lida. Dioc Sch For Mnstry; BA U Chi 1953; JD U of Miami 1961. D 9/29/1986 Bp Calvin Onderdonk Schofield Jr. m 3/4/1955 Joanne Leona Karcher c 3. Assoc Trin Cathd Miami FL 1986-2000.

KARCHER, Steven Michael (SJ) D 11/22/2014 Bp David C Rice.

KARDA, Margaret R (Nwk) 6095 Summerlake Dr, Port Orange FL 32127 B Grand Rapids MN 1953 d Richard & Mitzi. BS Van 1975; MA CUNY 1978; MA GTS 1983; STM GTS 1991. D 6/15/1991 P 1/1/1992 Bp Orris George Walker Jr. m 10/11/1997 William J Karda c 1. Ch Of The Gd Shpd Ringwood NJ 2000-2006; Ch Of The Incarn W Milford NJ 1995-2006; Vic Ch of the Incarn W Milford NJ 1995-2000; Asst S Lk's Ch Forest Hills NY 1991-1995.

KARDALEFF, Patricia Payne (Okla) 777 Chosin, Lawton OK 73507 **D S Andr's Epis Ch Lawton OK 2005-** B Tulsa OK 1940 d Charlie & Lavone. BA Cameron U 1980; BS Cameron U 1981; MLIS U of Oklahoma 1987. D 6/19/2004 Bp Robert Manning Moody. m 6/7/1961 Steven T Kardaleff c 3. Tchr/Sch Libr Lawton Publ Schools 1981-2003.

KAREFA-SMART, Rena Joyce Weller (WA) 4601 N Park Ave Apt 1202, Chevy Chase MD 20815 B Bridgeport CT 1921 d Sailsman & Rosa. BEd Cntrl Connecticut St U 1940; MA Drew U 1942; BD Ya Berk 1945; ThD Harvard DS 1976. D 6/11/1988 P 2/1/1989 Bp John Thomas Walker. m 3/27/1948 John Albert Mussulman Karefa-Smart. Assoc Ascen 1994-1995; EDEO 1991-1996; SCER 1991-1996; Asst to R S Aug's Epis Ch Washington DC 1989-1990; Serv Afr Methodist Epis Ch 1983-1988; Cntrl Com WCC 1983-1988; Ecum & Interfaith Off Dio Washington Washington DC 1991-1996. Auth, "The Halting Kingdom"; Auth, "Homily Serv"; Auth, "Ecum Encounters". Cntr For Theol And Publ Plcy Coun, Chuches Of Grtr Washington Dc 1983-1996; Metro Washington Dc 85-96 Intl Div Exec Amer Friends Serv Com 92-95.

KARELIUS, Bradford Lyle (Los) 29602 Via Cebolla, Laguna Niguel CA 92677 B Pasadena CA 1945 s Lyle & Linnea. USC 1966; BA Baldwin-Wallace Coll 1967; MDiv PSR 1970. D 5/16/1971 P 12/15/1971 Bp Robert Claflin Rusack. m 11/27/1971 Janice E Karelius c 2. Int The Epis Ch Of The Blessed Sacr Placentia CA 2013-2014; Dn Orange Cnty Congregations Los Angeles CA 1997-1999; Judge Eccl Trial Crt Dio Los Angeles CA 1996-1998; Pres Stndg Com Dio Los Angeles CA 1994-1996; Cmsn on Camping Los Angeles CA 1990-1995; GC Wrshp Com ECUSA NY 1982-1985; R Ch Of The Mssh Santa Ana CA 1981-2011; Cmsn on Liturg and Ch Mus Dio Los Angele 1980-1988; Assoc S Mary's Par Laguna Bch CA 1972-1981; Asst S Mary Laguna Bch CA 1970-1981. Auth, "The Sprt in the Desert: Pilgrimages to Sacr Sites in the Owns Vlly, CA," Bk Surge, 2009; Auth, "Light and Hope in the Nbrhd," *Amer*, 1999. AAR 2009; AAUP 2009; Amer Philos Assn 2001; Assn of Cath Priests in USA and Can 2009; Assn of Cath Pub 2011; California Cattlemen's Assn 2000; Nevada Archeol Assn 1999; Wstrn Lit Assn 2010; Wstrn Writers of Amer 2008. Hon Cn Cathd Cntr of St. Paul, Los Angeles 2006.

K

KARKER, Arthur Lee (Me) Po Box 277, West Rockport ME 04865 **Methodist Conf Hm Inc. 1994-** B Leavittsburg OH 1947 s Oliver & Louise. BA Estrn Nazarene Coll 1968; MA Bos 1971; MDiv Yale DS 1980. D 10/22/2006 P 5/23/2007 Bp Chilton Richardson Knudsen. c 2. Assoc S Ptr's Ch Rockland ME 2006-2010.

KARL JR, John Charles (Roch) 995 Park Ave, Rochester NY 14610 **Non-par 1974-** B Milwaukee WI 1942 s John & Edna. BA NWU 1964; BD Colgate Rochester Crozer DS 1967; BD CRDS 1967; EDS 1968; STM Bos 1969; MA Sch Pstr Care 1969; DMin Colgate Rochester Crozer DS 1974; DMin CRDS 1974. D 6/22/1968 P 12/1/1969 Bp George West Barrett. m 8/6/1966 Sharon Leith Karl. Samar Pstr Couns Ctr Rochester NY 1974-2003; Asst Ch Of The Ascen Rochester NY 1969-1974. Auth, "Conversations In Many Tongues A Model Of Pstr Consult"; Auth, "Faith & Mnstry: In Light Of The Double Brain"; Auth, "The Presence Of Care In Nrsng". AAPC, Aamft.

KARL, Sharon Leith (Roch) 995 Park Ave, Rochester NY 14610 B Washington DC 1942 d Robert & Frances. BA U Rich 1964; MA Colgate Rochester Crozer DS 1966; MA CRDS 1966; MDiv Bex Sem 1986. D 6/13/1987 P 6/1/1988 Bp William George Burrill. m 8/6/1966 John Charles Karl. R S Ptr's Epis Ch Henrietta NY 1990-2006; Ch Of The Gd Shpd Webster NY 1987-1990.

KARNEY JR, George James (Del) 2812 Faulkland Rd, Wilmington DE 19808 **Assoc Chr Ch Christiana Hundred Wilmington DE 2012-; Ret 2000-** B Chicago IL 1934 s George & Ella. BA NWU 1955; MDiv Yale DS 1958. D 6/11/1959 P 3/15/1960 Bp Walter H Gray. m 2/24/1979 Carolyn Karney. P-in-c S Paul's Ch Chester PA 2002-2007; Chapl Epis Ch Hm 1991-2000; R S Barn Ch Wilmington DE 1990-2000; Int S Mich's Ch Barrington IL 1988-1990; Int S Anskar's Ch Rockford IL 1985-1986; Cur Chr Ch Waukegan IL 1982-1997; 1982-1985; 1971-1977; Vic S Gabr's Ch E Berlin CT 1969-1971; R Gr Ch Newington CT 1966-1971; Vic S Jn's Epis Ch Bristol CT 1963-1966; Asst Ch Of The Gd Shpd Hartford CT 1959-1963; Stndg Com Dio Delaware Wilmington 1995-1999.

KARPF, Ted (WA) PO Box 6654, Santa Fe NM 87502 B Peekskill NY 1948 s William & Joan. MTh Bos 1970; BA Texas Wsleyan U 1974; Cert Gestalt Inst-Washington 2000. D 6/11/1982 Bp Theodore H McCrea P 10/18/1982 Bp Archibald Donald Davies. c 2. Asstg P Trin Ch Epis Boston MA 2012-2013; Dir of Dvlpmt/Fac Dos TS 2011-2013; Dio Washington Washington DC 2004-2013, Dvlpmt and Deploy 1999-2001, Cn for Life 1999-2001; Supply Convoc of Epis Ch in Europe Paris 2004-2010; Sr Resrch Fell Duke Univ-Sanford Inst Durham NC 2003-2011; Partnerships Off Wrld Hlth Orgnztn Geneva Switzerland 2003-2010; Prov Cn Missionr for HIV/AIDS Angl Ch Prov of Sthrn Afr Cape Town SA 2001-2003; Cn Mssnr for HIV/AIDS Exec Coun Appointees New York NY 2001-2003; Cathd of St Ptr & St Paul Washington DC 1999-2003; R S Lk's Ch Washington DC 1998-1999; NEAC Washington DC 1993-1998; Exec Dir NEAC Washington DC 1993-1998; Asst Ch Of The Ascen Gaithersburg MD 1993; US PHS Dallas TX 1989-1993; Dir of Mnstry The Epis Ch Of S Thos The Apos Dallas TX 1984-1988; Pstr Care and Dvlpmt Chr The King Epis Ch Ft Worth TX 1983-1984; Cur S Andr's Ch Grand Prairie TX 1982; Ed of the Dioc PaperNewspaper Dio Ft Worth Ft Worth TX 1981-1983; Texas Cmsn on Campus Mnstry Denton TX 1979-1982; Dir U Mnstry Cntr - UNT Denton TX 1976-1982; Prof of Rel U of No Texas Denton TX 1976-1982; Tchr of Rel-Chapl City of Bath Tech Coll Bath Untd Kingdom 1974-1975. Prncpl Ed, "Restoring Hope: Decent Care in the Midst of HIV/AIDS," *Restoring Hope: Decent Care in the Midst of HIV/AIDS*, Palgrave Macmillan, 2008; Auth, "Foreword," *Sound Sprt: Pathway to Faith*, Hay Hse, Inc., 2008; Auth, "Restoring Hope," *Restoring Hope: Decent Care in the Midst of HIV/AIDS*, WHO EURO Pub, 2007; Auth, "Confessions of an AIDS Activist," *In Times Like These: How We Pray*, Seabury, 2006; Auth, "Soul Care and HIV," *AIDS & The Cure Of Souls*, NEAC, 1997; Auth, "AIDS and Pstr Care," *AIDS: The Caregivers Handbook*, St Mart's Press, 1991; Auth, "AIDS and Death," *Gospel Imperative in the Midst of AIDS*, Morehouse, 1989. Claflin Soc - Bos 2011. Secy Gnrl's Awd of Achievement Untd Nations/WHO 2009; Distinguished Alum Bos TS 2007; Chancellors Awd U of Nebraska-Lincoln 2007; Red Ribbon Awd Natl AIDS Partnership 2005; Distrinuished Alum Texas Wesl 2003; Minority Achievement Awd USDptHealth&Human Serv 1991; PHS Awd USDptHealth&Human Serv 1990; Citizen of the Year NASW 1979.

KARSHNER, Donald Lee (Del) 250 S 13th St Apt 2d, Philadelphia PA 19107 **Died 12/2/2015** B Columbus OH 1926 s Glenn & Louise. BS OH SU 1950; MA OH SU 1954; MDiv UTS 1957. D 12/22/1960 P 6/24/1961 Bp Roger W Blanchard. c 2. Ret 1987-2015; R Ch of St Andrews & St Matthews Wilmington DE 1968-1987; S Matt's Ch Wilmington DE 1968-1987; Assoc R Chr Ch Cathd Cincinnati OH 1964-1968; Vic S Andr Addyston OH 1960-1961.

KASEY, Philip Howerton (NJ) 4326 Teall Beach Rd, Geneva NY 14456 **P-in-c S Lk's Ch Branchport NY 2012-** B Philadelphia PA 1950 s Virginius & Virginia. BA U NC 1972; MDiv SWTS 1979. D 6/2/1979 Bp Albert Wiencke Van Duzer P 12/7/1979 Bp George Phelps Mellick Belshaw. m 5/26/1979 Polly Mcwilliams c 2. R H Trin Ch So River NJ 2004-2011; R S Elis's Ch Glencoe IL 1990-2004; Asst Chr Ch Short Hills NJ 1986-1990; Chapl Kent Sch Kent CT 1981-1986; Chapl So Kent Sch So Kent CT 1981-1982; Cur S Lk's Ch Gladstone NJ 1979-1981.

KASEY, Polly Mcwilliams (NJ) 4326 Teall Beach Rd, Geneva NY 14456 **Trin Epis Ch Seneca Falls NY 2011-** B Shreveport LA 1946 d Martin & Lucia. BA U CO 1968; MDiv GTS 1981. D 6/6/1981 Bp Albert Wiencke Van Duzer P 1/21/1982 Bp Arthur Edward Walmsley. m 5/26/1979 Philip Howerton Kasey c 2. Pstr Assoc H Trin Ch So River NJ 2008-2010; Asst S Lk's Ch Gladstone NJ 2007-2008; Gr Ch Pemberton NJ 2006-2007; Int Gr Epis Ch Pemberton NJ 2005-2007; H Comf Ch Rahway NJ 2005-2006; Dio New York New York NY 2005; R S Elis's Ch Glencoe IL 1990-2004; Asst Chr Ch Short Hills NJ 1986-1990; Kent Sch Kent CT 1981-1986; Chapl S Jos's Chap at the Kent Sch Kent CT 1981-1986.

KASIO, Joseph Lelit (Nev) B Kenya 1941 s Mayiane & Wamoui. Cert Ch Army Trng Coll; MDiv Trin; MDiv Trin; LTh Wycliffe Coll Can. Trans 2/19/1997 Bp Stewart Clark Zabriskie. m 1/1/1970 Naomi Wanjiru Kasio. S Tim's Epis Ch Henderson NV 2004-2010; Afr Chr Fllshp Henderson NV 2004-2007; Asst Pstr St. Jude 1997-2000.

KASSABIAN, Robin Lynn (Los) 25 E Laurel Ave, Sierra Madre CA 91024 B Whiteplains NY 1966 d David & Diane. BA UCSD 1988; MDiv Bloy Hse/ETSC 2017; MDiv Claremont TS 2017. D 6/3/2017 Bp Diane Jardine Bruce. m 3/12/2005 Paul Richard Kassabian c 3.

KASSEBAUM, John Albert (NY) 53 S Clinton Ave, Hastings On Hudson NY 10706 B New York NY 1937 s Robert & Ruth. D 5/16/1998 Bp Richard Frank Grein. m 3/3/1962 Joan Carol Kassebaum c 1. D Gr Ch Hastings Hds NY 1998-2007. No. Amer Assn for the Diac 1995.

KASWARRA, George (NY) 23 N Willow St, Montclair NJ 07042 B Fort Portal UG 1948 s Enock & Evelyn. Makerere U 1983; BD Bp Tucker Theol Coll Mukono Ug 1993; MA PrTS 1996. Trans 12/19/2002 as Priest Bp John Palmer Croneberger. m 1/21/1985 Maude Kaswarra c 4. Dio New York New York NY 2007-2011; S Fran Assisi And S Martha White Plains NY 2007-2011; P-in-c Trin Ch Montclair NJ 2001-2007.

KATER JR, John (Cal) 2116 Tice Creek Drive #2, Walnut Creek CA 94595 **Mem Cmsn for Theol Educ in Latin Amer 2013-** B Winchester VA 1941 s John & Mary. BA Col 1962; MDiv GTS 1966; PhD McGill U 1973. D 6/4/1966 P 12/17/1966 Bp Horace W B Donegan. Fac Emer CDSP Berkeley CA 1990-2005; Dio Panama Dio Panama 1984-1990; R Chr Ch Poughkeepsie NY 1974-1984, Asst R 1966-1970; Exec Coun Appointees New York NY 1984-1990. Auth, "Jesus My Mentor," Chalice, 2004; Auth, "Finding Our Way," Cowley, 1991; Auth, "Making Sense of Life," Cowley, 1987; "Christians on the Rt," Seabury, 1982. Hon Cn S Lk's Cathd, Panama 1989.

KATHMANN, Charmaine M (La) St. John's Episcopal Church, 2109 17th Street, Kenner LA 70062 **Outreach; Chld's Art Mnstry; Disaster Mgmt S Jn's Ch Kenner LA 2010-; D Epis Dio Louisiana 2007-** B New Orleans LA 1955 d Salvador & Gloria. Loyola U Inst for Mnstry - New Orleans LA; BS U of New Orleans 1996; BS LSU 2000; Cert Dio Louisiana Sch for Mnstry 2004. D 12/1/2007 Bp Charles Edward Jenkins III. m 5/23/1976 Richard Kathmann c 2. Chld's Art Mnstry; Disaster Recovery Gr Ch New Orleans LA 2007-2010.

KATNER, Kirk Vaughan Chris (WNY) 88 Main St S, Perry NY 14530 **Died 8/19/2015** B Bath NY 1949 s Theodore & Eileen. BA SUNY at Geneseo 1970; MA SUNY at Geneseo 1971. D 4/25/2009 P 5/2/2010 Bp Michael Garrison. m 6/20/1970 Anne Elizabeth Nye c 2. Vic The Ch Of The H Apos - Epis Perry NY 2010-2015.

KATON, Joanne Catherine (SeFla) 1800 Southwest 92nd Place, Miami FL 33165 B Glendale NY 1943 d Frank & Josephine. AA Barry U 1961; Miami-Dade Cmnty Coll 1970; Dio SE Florida 1991. D 4/5/1992 Bp Calvin Onderdonk Schofield Jr. m 7/30/1971 Robert William Katon c 3. S Kevin's Epis Ch Opa Locka FL 2006-2010; S Andr's Epis Ch Miami FL 1996-2006; D S Philips Epis Ch Coral Gables 1992-1995; Chapl Vistas Hospice Miami FL 1986-1993. NACED 1999; NAMI 2000; NAAD 1995; Soc of S Jn's the Div 1995.

KATONA, Kenneth J (Az) **P-in-c S Ptr's Ch Casa Grande AZ 2015-** B Hampton VA 1978 s Kenneth & Jeanne. Philos California U of PA 2007; MDiv VTS 2014. D 6/22/2013 P 4/19/2015 Bp Kirk Stevan Smith. m 2/9/2016 Theresa Poulson. Chr The King Ch Tucson AZ 2014-2015.

KATZ, Nathaniel Peter (Los) 514 W Adams Blvd, Los Angeles CA 90007 **All SS Par Beverly Hills CA 2016-** B Summit NJ 1980 s Michael & Marcia. BA USC 2002; MDiv Harvard DS 2010; MDiv Harvard DS 2010. D 6/7/2014 P 1/17/2015 Bp Joseph Jon Bruno.

KAUFFMAN, Bette Jo (WLa) 79 Quail Ridge Dr, Monroe LA 71203 B Washington County IA 1945 d Henry & Isabelle. BA U of Iowa 1980; MA U of Pennsylvania 1982; PhD U of Pennsylvania 1992; Cert Dioc TS 2008. D 6/7/2008 Bp D Avid Bruce Macpherson. Cbury Min S Thos' Ch Monroe LA 2011-2017, D 2011-2017; D S Alb's Epis Ch Monroe LA 2008-2017; Prof U of Louisiana at Monroe 1997-2017; Cmsn on Cbury Mnstry Dio Wstrn Louisiana Alexandria LA 2014-2015, Dismantling Racism Cmsn 2013-, Ed Bd 2012-2015, Cmsn on the Diac 2012-2013. Auth, "A Rock w a Heart: Finding Heaven on Earth," *Bk of Sermons*, Parson's Porch Books, 2016; Auth, "Deacons in Scripture," *Alive!*, Dio Wstrn LA, 2013; Auth, "Deacons in Hist," *Alive!*, Dio Wstrn LA, 2013;

K

Auth, "Deacons in Hist, cont'd," *Alive!*, Dio Wstrn LA, 2013; Auth, "Deacons in Liturg," *Alive!*, Dio Wstrn LA, 2013. Assn for Epis Deacons 2007.

KAUFMAN, Linda Margaret (WA) 701 S Wayne St, Arlington VA 22204 **Natl Mvmt Mgr Cmnty Solutions Washington DC 2014-; Ch Of S Steph And The Incarn Washington DC 1998-** B Seattle WA 1951 d Jerome & Margaret. Gordon-Conwell TS; NWU; BS Geo Mason U 1975; MDiv VTS 1986. D 6/11/1986 P 4/11/1987 Bp Peter J Lee. m 4/9/2010 Liane Gay Rozzell c 2. Estrn US Field Organizer 100 000 Hm Cmpgn of Cmnty Solutions 2011-2014; Exec Dir Var positions in homeless Serv 1993-2011; Ch Of The H Comf Vienna VA 1989-1993; Chapl S Marg's Sch Tappahannock VA 1986-1988. NAES, Soc Of Biblic. Soroptomist: Helping Wmn Awd; Hero Of The Week, Fox Tv.

KAUTZ, Richard Arden (Ind) 913 Brentwood Ct, New Albany IN 47150 **R S Paul's Epis Ch New Albany IN 2012-** B Casper WY 1953 s William & Dorothy. BA U of Nthrn Colorado 1978; MDiv Nash 1984. D 6/16/1984 P 12/21/1984 Bp William Carl Frey. m 6/15/2013 William P Strauss c 3. R S Paul's Ch Richmond IN 2008-2012; R Ch Of The H Redeem Denver CO 2005-2008; Asst The Ch Of Chr The King (Epis) Arvada CO 2004-2005; R Trin Ch Greeley CO 1997-2003; R S Mart In The Fields Aurora CO 1992-1997; Assoc St Johns Epis Ch Tampa FL 1990-1992; Asst S Thos Epis Ch Terrace Pk OH 1986-1990; Cur S Aid's Epis Ch Boulder CO 1984-1986. Auth, "A Labyrinth Year; Walking the Seasons of the Ch," Morehouse, 2006. rkautz@stpaulna.org

KAVAL, Lura M (Md) 8522 Light Moon Way, Laurel MD 20723 **Ch of the Incarn Mineral VA 2016-; R St Chris Epis Ch Linthicum 2004-** B Erie PA 1962 d Gerald & Lura. BS Ohio U 1983; Cert Amer U 1985; MDiv VTS 1998. D 6/13/1998 P 12/19/1998 Bp Robert Wilkes Ihloff. m 3/17/2012 Richard S Harlow. Exec Coun Appointees New York NY 2012-2014; Chr Ch Columbia MD 2011-2012, 1999-2001; R - Full Time S Chris Epis Ch Linthicum Hts MD 2002-2011; Prov III Baltimore MD 2002-2004; Assoc R S Jas Ch Jackson MS 1998-1999. Md. Epis Cler Asso. (MECA) 2004.

KAVROS, Peregrine Murphy (NY) 4 West 109th Street Apt 2D, New York NY 10025 B Fowler CA 1954 d Elbert & Patricia. BA California St U 1979; MS California St U 1980; MBA Notre Dame Coll 1982; MBA Notre Dame du Namur 1982; MDiv GTS 1990; PhD CUNY 2002; CUNY 2005; NYU Sch of Med 2011. D 6/8/1991 Bp George Phelps Mellick Belshaw P 12/14/1991 Bp Richard Frank Grein. m 10/6/2007 Harry Emanuel Kavros. S Steph's Ch Armonk NY 2005-2006; Dio New York New York NY 2001-2005, 1991-1995; P-in-c San Andres Ch Yonkers NY 2001-2005; Int S Mary's Ch Mohegan Lake NY 1998-2001; Asst S Mk's Ch Mt Kisco NY 1996-1998; Asst Ch Of The Incarn New York NY 1995-1996; Asst Cathd Of St Jn The Div New York NY 1991-1995; Chairperson, Yonkers Allnce for Latino Immigrant Serv City of Yonkers New York 2003-2005; Mem, Hisp Latino Cmsn Epis Dio New York 2002-2005; Mem, Justice Cltn of SW Yonkers Dist Atty's Off Westchester Cnty 2002-2003; Co-Chair, Cler Wholeness Com Epis Dio New York 1998-2003; Mem, COM Epis Dio New York 1996-2002. Auth, "Rel, Religiousness, Religiosity," *Encyclopedia of Psychol & Rel*, Springer, 2010; Auth, "Impact of Sprtlty & Religiousness on Outcomes in Patients w ALS," *Neurology*, The Amer Acad of Neurology, 2000; Auth, "Sophia - Div Bearer of Wisdom," *The Living Pulpit*, The Living Pulpit, Inc., 2000.

KAY, Frances Creveling (WLa) 2914 W Prien Lake Rd, Lake Charles LA 70605 **D Epis Ch Of The Gd Shpd Lake Chas LA 2003-, Hd of Sch 2000-; Bp Noland Epis Day Sch Lake Chas LA 2000-** B Lake Charles LA 1948 d Donald & Ellanora. BS LSU 1970; BS LSU 1970; MEd McNeese St U 1986; MEd McNeese St U 1986; EdS McNeese St U 1990; Bp Sch 2000; Sewanee: The U So, TS 2014. D 3/25/2000 Bp Robert Jefferson Hargrove Jr P 6/28/2014 Bp Jacob W Owensby. c 3. The Gnrl Soc of Mayflower Descendents 2013. Sustainer of the Year Jr League of Lake Chas, Inc. 2015; A. Dn Calcote Awd The SW Assn of Epis Schools 2006; Jn D. Verdery Awd NAES 2004; Pres of the Exec Bd SW Associaion of Epis Schools 1996.

KAYE, Robert Pleaman Skarpmoen (EO) 365 SE Highland Park Dr, College Place WA 99324 **Ret Coll Place WA 2002-; P Assoc S Paul's Ch Walla Walla WA 2002-** B Milwaukee WI 1937 s Harold & Ruby. Miami Bible Inst 1960; BS Florida Intl U 1974; MPA Nova SE U 1977; MDiv Sewanee: The U So, TS 1988. D 9/17/1988 P 3/1/1989 Bp Calvin Onderdonk Schofield Jr. c 2. Grand Chapl Masonic Grand Lodge OR 1994-1995; Vic S Jas Ch Milton Frwtr OR 1991-2002; Asst to R S Greg's Ch Boca Raton FL 1988-1991. "The Fascist Pig Cookbook"; Auth, "Safe Streets Unit vol. 1-3," Law Enforcement Assistance Admin.

KAYIGWA, Beatrice Mbatudoe (WMass) 209 Union St, Clinton MA 01510 B Uganda 1952 d Yekosotati & May. D 11/16/2013 Bp Doug Fisher. m 5/24/1980 David Kayigwa.

KAYNOR, Robert Kirk (NC) 82 Kimberly Dr, Durham NC 27707 **R S Steph's Ch Durham NC 2005-** B Springfield MA 1948 s Kenneth & Doris. BA Trin Hartford CT 1972; MDiv EDS 1976; EdM Harv 1982; CAS Harv 1986. D 6/9/1979 Bp John Bowen Coburn P 5/1/1980 Bp Morris Fairchild Arnold. R Chr Ch Hyde Pk MA 2001-2005, 1983-1985, Cur 1979-1982; Assoc S Paul's Epis Ch Bedford MA 1997-1999; Assoc S Dunstans Epis Ch Dover MA 1993-2001; Assoc S Mich's Ch Milton MA 1986-1992; Chapl Morgan Memi Goodwill In-

dustries Boston MA 1977-1979. Auth, "Mapping The Anatomy Of Ethical Arguments In The Divestment Debate," Harvard Grad Sch Of Ed., 1986; Auth, "Ch Case Stds," Harvard Grad Sch Of Ed., 1981; Auth, "Plnng & Decisionmaking Suny-Albany," Harvard Bus Sch, 1980. bob.kaynor@ssecdurham.org

KAZANJIAN, Rosanna Case (Mass) Po Box 1215, Sonoita AZ 85637 B Topeka KS 1934 d Harold & Phyllis. BA Bos 1956; MEd Bos 1971; MDiv EDS 1985. D 6/1/1985 Bp John Bowen Coburn P 4/1/1986 Bp Donis Dean Patterson. c 3. Int S Andr's Epis Ch Nogales AZ 2003-2004; Affiliate S Phil's In The Hills Tucson AZ 2002-2007; Non-par 1999-2001; Pres Greenfire Retreat Hse & Cmnty ME 1991-1999; R S Jn's Ch Jamaica Plain MA 1988-1991; R S Jn's Epis Ch Westwood MA 1988-1991; Assoc R Ch Of The Epiph Richardson TX 1985-1988; Dir Psychol Counslg Dana Hall Sch 1971-1981.

KAZANJIAN JR, Victor Hanford (Mass) Wellesley College, 106 Central St, Wellesley MA 02481 **Untd Rel Initiative San Francisco CA 2013-; Dn Wellesley Coll 1993-** B Boston MA 1959 s Victor & Rosanna. BA Harv 1981; MDiv EDS 1986. D 6/4/1986 Bp John Bowen Coburn P 5/1/1987 Bp Don Edward Johnson. m 7/6/2003 Michelle Marie Lepore. Epis City Mssn Boston MA 1991-1993; Prog Dir Epis City Mssn Boston MA 1991-1993; Asst to R S Mich's Ch Milton MA 1986-1991; Sem Asst S Ann's Ch Of Morrisania Bronx NY 1984-1985. vkazanjian@uri.org

KE, Jason Chau-sheng (Tai) 37 Jen-Chih St., Nanton City Taiwan **Vic S Ptr 1973-** B Amoy Fukien CN 1935 s Fu-liang & Juei-lan. BTh Tainan TS TW 1965. D 9/17/1970 Bp Edmond Lee Browning P 6/1/1971 Bp James T M Pong. c 2. Dio Taiwan Taipei 1970-2000; Chapl to Bp Dio Taiwan 1970-1973; Vic Epiph Taipei Taiwan 1970-1973.

KEARLEY, David Arthur (Ala) 154 Morgans Steep Rd, Sewanee TN 37375 **Ret 1994-** B Mobile AL 1929 s Frank & Josephine. BA U of Alabama 1951; MA U of Alabama 1956; MDiv GTS 1958; MLS Peabody Coll 1969. D 6/22/1958 P 6/11/1959 Bp George Mosley Murray. m 8/11/1962 Marion Kearley. Sewanee U So TS Sewanee TN 1982-1994; Dir, Jesse Ball du Pont Libr U So Sewanee TN 1982-1994; Asst S Paul's Ch Franklin TN 1973-1982; Vic S Mich's Epis Ch Fayette AL 1969-1973; Pres Mnstry Assn Florence AL 1965-1966; Vic S Barth's Epis Ch Florence AL 1963-1968; Cur Trin Epis Ch Florence AL 1960-1963; Emm Epis Ch Opelika AL 1958-1960; Vic S Steph's Epis Ch Smiths Sta AL 1958-1960; ExCoun Dio Alabama Birmingham 1967-1968. "Article," *Apos (Dio ALA)*; Auth, "Article," *Hist mag.* Cmnty of S Mary, Assoc 1985.

KEARNEY, James A (NY) **D Ch Of The Redeem Houston TX 1982-, Asst Bus Admin 1974-1981** B Staten Island NY 1947 s Alton & Janet. Ya Berk; BBA Pace U; MDiv PDS. D 6/3/1972 Bp Paul Moore Jr.

KEARNS, Jada Dart (CFla) 1601 Alafaya Trl, Oviedo FL 32765 B Fort Myers FL 1964 d Russell & Linda. BS U of Cntrl Florida 1990; PhD U of Cntrl Florida 1995; MS Troy St U 1998; MA Nashotah TS 2014. D 5/24/2014 Bp Gregory Orrin Brewer. m 2/2/1991 Kevin Kearns c 3.

KEATOR, Marnie Knowles (Haw) PO Box 2037, 1 Carley Lane, South Londonderry VT 05155 B Greenwich CT 1941 d James & Phoebe. AAS Bennett Coll 1961; BD U of Connecticut 1989; MDiv EDS 2000. D 5/20/2000 Bp Mary Adelia Rosamond Mcleod P 12/2/2000 Bp Arthur Edward Walmsley. m 8/25/1962 Gerrit Keator c 3. R S Andr's Ch Turners Fall MA 2005-2013; Bd Mem Alpha New Engl MA 2003-2008; Chapl DOK VT 2003-2007; Curs Sec Dio Vermont Burlington VT 2002-2004, Dioc Coun 1998-2001, FA Bd Mem 1996-1997; Assoc Zion Ch Manchestr Ctr VT 2000-2002.

KEBBA, Elaine Marguerite Bailey (NC) 6003 Quail Ridge Dr, Greensboro NC 27455 B Albuquerque NM 1944 d Lawrence & Betty. BS U of Maryland 1970; MS U NC 1972; MDiv VTS 1979. D 6/23/1979 Bp John Thomas Walker P 1/5/1980 Bp Lyman Cunningham Ogilby. m 10/12/1974 Thomas Kebba. Servnt Ldrshp Stff H Trin Epis Ch Greensboro NC 2003-2009; R S Dav's Ch Kinnelon NJ 1990-2002; R S Mary's Ch Haledon NJ 1985-1990; Asst Trin Ch Swarthmore PA 1979-1985. Hon Cn Trin & S Phil Cathd 1993.

KEBLESH JR, Joe (O) 4617 Crestview Dr, Sylvania OH 43560 B Akron OH 1945 s Joseph & Mary. BS U of Akron 1978; MBA U of Akron 1980; MDiv VTS 1985. D 6/15/1985 Bp James Russell Moodey P 3/1/1986 Bp William Grant Black. m 9/28/2013 Laurel Ann Keblesh c 4. Metroplltn Toledo Ch Untd 1995-1999; Curs Sec Dio Ohio 1993-1998; R S Matt's Epis Ch Toledo OH 1992-2017; R Emm Epis Ch Winchester KY 1987-1991; Asst Chr Ch Xenia OH 1985-1987; S Andr's Epis Ch Wshngtn Ct Hs OH 1985-1987; Exec Coun Dio Lexington Lexington 1988-1991. Beta Gamma Sigma 1978.

KECK, Carolyn (Tenn) Church of the Messiah, 114 N 3rd St, Pulaski TN 38478 **R The Epis Ch Of The Mssh Pulaski TN 2012-** B Maquoketa IA 1951 d Allen & Phoebe. AA Cottey Coll 1972; BS Phillips U 1974; MSW U of Kentucky 1990; MDiv SWTS 2005. D 5/22/2004 P 6/25/2005 Bp Herbert Thompson Jr. Vic Ch Of S Edw Columbus OH 2005-2010.

KEEBLE, George McCullough (WTex) 4201 Adina Way, Corpus Christi TX 78413 **P-in-c Epis Ch Of The Gd Shepard Geo W TX 2007-** B Corpus Christi TX 1941 s Walter & Louise. BS Texas A&M U 1966; DDS U of Texas 1973; MDiv Epis TS of the SW 1985. D 1/23/1985 Bp Stanley Fillmore Hauser P 8/9/1985 Bp Scott Field Bailey. m 5/19/1962 Gay C Cotrell c 2. R S Ptr's Epis

Ch Rockport TX 2003-2007; R S Steph's Epis Ch Wimberley TX 1989-2003; Calv Ch Menard TX 1986-1989; Vic Trin Ch Jct TX 1986-1989; Cur Trin Ch Victoria TX 1985-1986.

KEECH, April Irene (NY) B 1954 Trans 10/1/1991 as Deacon Bp Richard Frank Grein. Chr And S Steph's Ch New York NY 1992-1995.

KEEDY, Susan Shipman (SeFla) 1200 Heron Ave, Miami Springs FL 33166 **Hd of Sch All Ang Epsicopal Acad Miami Sprg FL 2001-** B Jackson MS 1946 d William & Juliet. BA California St U 1970; MS Florida Intl U 1997; MDiv Yale DS 2001. D 6/16/2001 Bp John Lewis Said P 12/16/2001 Bp Leo Frade. c 2. All Ang Ch Miami FL 2002-2016; Chap of the Venerable Bede Coral Gables FL 2001-2002.

KEEFER, John S (Pa) 124 High St, Sharon Hill PA 19079 B Danville PA 1946 s Bruce & Anna. BA NEU 1969; MDiv Epis TS in Kentucky 1972; ThM Westminster TS 1979; ThD U of Bern Bern CH 1990. D 6/22/1972 Bp Addison Hosea P 6/16/1973 Bp Chandler W Sterling. The Ch Of The Gd Shpd Rosemont PA 2011-2012, Int R 2011-2012, Asst P 1992-2011, Int/Asstg P 1978-1979; P-in-c Emm Ch Philadelphia PA 2003-2009; P-in-c Ch Of The Redeem Bensalem PA 2000-2003; Int Ch Of Our Sav Jenkintown PA 1998, P 1994; P-in-c Ch of Engl Dio Gibralter Bucharest-So 1984-1986; P Ch of Engl Dio Gibralter Gibralter 1984-1986; Asst Trin Epis Ch Ambler PA 1975-1978; Asst S Steph's Ch Philadelphia PA 1974-1975; Cur S Tim's Ch Roxborough Philadelphia PA 1972-1974. Auth, "European Ch - E and W," *Crossroads*, 1993; Auth, "Sin," *Crossroads*, 1993; Auth, "Natl Thanksgiving," *Congressional Record*, 1983; Auth, "Capital Punnishment: A Priestly View," *S Dismas Drummer*, 1979. CCU, Philadelphia Chapt 1972. Notable Americans 1978; Listed in "Cmnty Leaders and Noteworthy Americans," 10th an.

KEEHN, Randy P (ND) B Des Moines IA 1952 s Robert & Jeannette. BA Luther Coll 1974. D 1/30/1999 P 10/1/1999 Bp Andrew Fairfield. m 4/5/1986 Jo Ann Keehn c 2.

KEEL, Ronald David (WMo) B Kansas City MO 1944 s Charles & Betty. BS U of Missouri 1966; MA Cntrl Michigan U 1980; MDiv Epis TS of the SW 2005. D 6/4/2005 P 12/3/2005 Bp Barry Howe. m 12/30/1995 Victoria H Erickson c 2. R Ch Of The Resurr Blue Sprg MO 2005-2015.

KEELER, Charles Bobo (Miss) 925 Stiles St, Clarksdale MS 38614 **S Geo's Epis Ch Clarksdale MS 2000-** B Clarksdale MS 1936 BS Mississippi St U 1963. D 1/15/2000 Bp Alfred Marble Jr. m 12/21/1960 Margaret Rice c 3.

KEELER, Donald Franklin (Ia) 121 W Marina Rd, Storm Lake IA 50588 B 1943 BS Truman Coll Chicago IL 1967; MA U of Kansas 1973. D 12/17/2006 P 10/24/2010 Bp Alan Scarfe. m 9/27/2007 Paula Keeler. ms4updq-@q.com

KEELER, Elizabeth Franklin (Va) 3116 O St NW, Washington DC 20007 **Asst to the R Chr Ch Georgetown Washington DC 2014-** B Greenwich CT 1967 d Kenneth & Elizabeth. BA Davidson Coll 1989; MDiv VTS 2014. D 6/7/2014 P 12/6/2014 Bp Shannon Sherwood Johnston. m 6/1/1996 Michael John Keeler c 3. elizabeth@christchurchgeorgetown.org

KEELER, John Dowling (At) 225 Brookhaven Cir, Elberton GA 30635 B Bedford VA 1945 s Peter & Mary. BA Wstrn Carolina U 1975; MA W Carolina U 1976; CTh U So 2006. D 8/6/2006 P 7/1/2007 Bp J Neil Alexander. m 12/15/1976 Robyn Keeler c 1. S Alb's Ch Elberton GA 2012-2017; All Ang Epis Ch Eatonton GA 2007-2012; Ged Tchr Cmnty Partnership 2004-2005.

KEEN JR, Charles Ford (Dal) 206 Mansfield Blvd., Sunnyvale TX 75182 B Pueblo CO 1938 s Charles & Dorothy. BA U CO 1961; BD Nash 1967. D 6/5/1967 P 12/1/1967 Bp Joseph Summerville Minnis. Resurr Gr Epis Ch Dallas TX 2003-2007; Dio Dallas Dallas TX 1999-2002; Cur H Trin Epis Ch Garland TX 1998-2002; Ch Of The Gd Shpd Cedar Hill TX 1996-1998; S Dav's Ch Garland TX 1995-1996; S Mary's Epis Ch And Sch Irving TX 1993-1995; Vic Ch Of Our Sav Dallas TX 1986-1992; Dept Of Missions Dallas TX 1986; Asst-In-Charge Of Lay Ministers The Epis Ch Of The Resurr Dallas TX 1982-1986; All SS Ch Loveland CO 1970-1981; Vic Chap Of The Resurr Limon CO 1967-1970; Vic S Paul Byers CO 1967-1970; Chair - Dept Yth Dio Colorado Denver CO 1968-1982. Assn Chr Therapists.

KEEN, George Comforted (CFla) 1225 W Granada Blvd, Ormond Beach FL 32174 **Natl Chapl Alpha Tau Omega Coll Fraternity 1998-** B Tampa FL 1945 s Clarence & Joni. AA Seminole Cmnty Coll 1970; BA U of Cntrl Florida 1972; MDiv SWTS 1979. D 6/25/1979 P 1/6/1980 Bp William Hopkins Folwell. m 2/17/1968 Judy Dee Keen. R Ch Of The H Chld Ormond Bch FL 1998-2013; Asst Pstr Epis Ch Of The H Sprt Tallahassee FL 1995-1998; Chapl Police Chapl 1990-1994; R St Alb's of Auburndale Inc Auburndale FL 1984-1995; Asst H Trin Epis Ch Melbourne FL 1980-1984; Cur S Mk's Ch Cocoa FL 1979-1980; Yth Min All SS Ch Of Winter Pk Winter Pk FL 1974-1976. Alpha Tau Omega Coll Fraternity - Natl Chapl 1988.

KEEN, Lois (Ct) 20 Hudson St, Norwalk CT 06851 **Trin Ch Wethersfield CT 2014-** B Wendover UT 1945 d William & Louisa. BA U of Delaware 1968; MDiv SWTS 1997. D 5/26/1998 P 1/21/1999 Bp Martin Gough Townsend. m 1/31/1981 Walter Keen. Dio Connecticut Meriden CT 2012-2013; P-in-c Gr Epis Ch Norwalk CT 2006-2013; P-in-c S Mart's Epis Ch Upper Chichester PA 2005-2006; Int. Asst. to Int. R S Steph's Ch Ridgefield CT 2003-2005; R Chr Ch Milford DE 2000-2003; Cur Cathd Ch Of S Jn Wilmington DE 1998-2000.

KEENAN, John P (Vt) 73 Oak St, Newport VT 05855 B Philadelphia PA 1940 s John & Mary. BA S Chas Borromeo Sem 1962; STM S Chas Borromeo Sem 1966; MA U of Pennsylvania 1976; PhD U of Wisconsin 1980. Rec 10/21/1988 as Priest Bp Daniel Lee Swenson. m 5/20/1972 Linda K Keenan c 2. S Mk's Epis Ch Newport VT 2008-2009, R 2007, P-in-c 2004-2007; Vic S Nich Epis Ch Scarborough ME 2002-2003; Assoc S Steph's Ch Middlebury VT 1994-1997; Bp's Vic Calv Ch Underhill VT 1991-1993. Auth, "I Am / No Self: A Chr Commentary on the Heart Sutra," Eerdmans/Peeters, 2011; Auth, "Grounding Our Faith in a Pluralist Wrld---w a little help from Nagarjuna," Wipf & Stock, 2009; Auth, "The Wisdom of Jas: Parallels w Mahayana Buddhism," Newman (Paulist), 2005; Co-Ed, "Beside Still Waters: Jews, Christians, & the Way of the Buddha," Wisdom, 2003; Auth, "Gospel of Mk: A Mahayana Reading," Orbis Books, 1995; Auth, "How Mstr Mou Removes our Doubts," SUNY Press, 1994; Auth, "The Meaning of Chr: A Mahayana Theol," Orbis Books, 1989. Soc for Buddhist-Chr Stds 1985. Frederick J. Streng Bk of the Year Awd Soc for Buddhist-Chr Stds 2004; Frederick J. Streng Bk of the Year Awd Soc for Buddhist-Chr Stds 1995.

KEENE, Christopher Paul (Del) Immanuel Church, 100 Harmony St, New Castle DE 19720 **R Imm Ch On The Green New Castle DE 2012-; Mem - Dioc Coun Dio Delaware Wilmington 2014-, Mem - Priestly Formation Com 2012-** B Pinckneyville IL 1966 s Daniel & Donna. BA U of Baltimore 1993; MDiv GTS 2003. D 6/14/2003 Bp Robert Wilkes Ihloff P 11/30/2003 Bp John L Rabb. R Ch Of The Adv Baltimore MD 2003-2012; Chair - Appeals Com Dio Maryland Baltimore MD 2010-2012, Mem - COM 2009-2012, Pres - Harbor Reg 2009-2012, Mem - Liturg and Mus Com 2007-2012, Mem - Baltimore Urban Cler 2006-2012. P Assoc of the Shrine of Our Lady of Walsingham 2005; Soc of Cath Priests 2009. Best Publ Reading of the Liturg GTS 2003.

KEENE, Katheryn C (Ct) 92 Bryn Mawr Ave, Auburn MA 01501 **Consult Consult Consult Consult MA 2002-** B Boston MA 1954 d John & Abigail. BA Smith 1976; MDiv Yale DS 1980; Advncd CPE 1983. D 6/13/1981 Bp Arthur Edward Walmsley P 2/1/1982 Bp William Bradford Hastings. c 3. Pstr Bethel Luth Ch 2011-2013; All SS Epis Ch Attleboro MA 2007-2008; Transitional Pstr Gd Shpd Luth Ch Westboro MA 2006-2007; Chr Epis Ch Marion VA 2003-2006; Trin Ecum Ch Moneta VA 2001-2002; Assoc R S Jn's Ch Lynchburg VA 1998-2000; S Paul's Epis Ch Salem VA 1998-1999; St Johns Ch W Hartford CT 1997; St Gabr's Ch E Berlin CT 1995-1996; Chapl Curtis Hm Meriden CT 1993-1998; Int S Ptr's Ch So Windsor CT 1991-1992; Mssnr Middlesex Area Cluster Durham CT 1987-1991; Int Ch Of The Resurr Norwich CT 1987-1988; Int Dio Connecticut Meriden CT 1986-1987; Int Chr Ch Stratford CT 1985-1986; Int Gr And S Ptr's Epis Ch Hamden CT 1983-1984; S Ptr's Ch Hamden CT 1983-1984; Assoc S Andr's Ch Madison CT 1981-1983.

KEENE, R Claire (ETenn) 4000 Shaw Ferry Rd, Lenoir City TN 37772 B Memphis TN 1950 d Richard & Betty. BA Carson-Newman Coll 1972; MA U CA 1973; MDiv Sewanee: The U So, TS 2002. D 5/25/2002 P 1/11/2003 Bp Charles Glenn VonRosenberg. m 12/27/1990 Michael Lawrence Keene c 2. R Ch Of The Resurr Loudon TN 2007-2016, P-in-c 2005-2007; Mem, Chr Formation Com Dio E Tennessee Knoxville TN 2004-2009, Mem, COM 2011-, 2009-2011, 2004-2009; Asst S Steph's Epis Ch Oak Ridge TN 2002-2005. optime merens STUSo 2002; Urban T. Holmes III Prize for Excellence in Preaching STUSo 2002.

KEENER, E Michaella (Pa) P.O. Box 594, 36 Bayview Avenue, Stonington ME 04681 **Assoc Ch Without Walls Gwynedd PA 2003-; 1994-** B Hartford CT 1934 d Ashley & Esther. BD Wayne 1979; MDiv EDS 1982. D 6/20/1982 P 5/8/1983 Bp H Coleman Mcgehee Jr. m 8/4/2000 Leland M Dewoody. Dir The Shpd's Kitchen 1988-1994; Dioc Coun Dio Pennsylvania Philadelphia PA 1988-1989, Com for Sexual Inclusiveness 1986-1990, Race Rela Com 1986-1990, Congreg Spprt Com 1986-1989, Hisp Com 1986-1988; S Giles Ch Upper Darby PA 1986-1994; R S Giles Upper Darby PA 1986-1994; Trin Ch Detroit MI 1985; Asst Chr Ch Detroit MI 1982-1984; Hisp Com Dio Michigan Detroit MI 1983-1985. Soc of S Jn the Evang 1987. Wm Dietrich Jr Awd for Urban Mssn in Ch EDS 1982.

KEENER JR, Ross Fulton (SVa) 117 Cove Road, Newport News VA 23608 **R Glebe Ch Suffolk VA 1998-** B Birmingham AL 1932 s Ross & Beulah. BA U of Alabama 1963; MDiv Sewanee: The U So, TS 1981. D 9/20/1981 P 4/21/1982 Bp Claude Charles Vache. m 10/10/2008 Janet Farson c 3. R S Geo's Epis Ch Newport News VA 1986-1997; Trin Ch Gretna VA 1982-1986; R Emm Epis Ch Chatham VA 1981-1986.

KEENEY, Albert J (Roch) 2901 Capen Dr, Bloomington IL 61704 B Chicago Heights IL 1945 s George & Jane. BA Loyola U 1968; MA S Louis U 1970; MDiv Drew U 1990. D 6/2/1990 Bp John Shelby Spong P 12/8/1990 Bp Walter Cameron Righter. m 7/17/2016 Teresa Dulyea-Parker c 2. Int S Mich's Ch Geneseo NY 2010-2011; Int Trin Ch Rochester NY 2009-2010; Cn Dio Rochester Henrietta 2008-2009, 2000-2002; R S Jn's Ch Canandaigua NY 1994-2008; R S Matt's Ch Paramus NJ 1990-1994. H Cross Mnstry OHC 1990.

KEENEY, Randall James (NC) Po Box 1547, Clemmons NC 27012 **Vic S Barn' Ch Greensboro NC 2006-** B Columbus GA 1959 s James & Myrtle. ABS Middle Georgia Coll 1978; BBA Georgia Sthrn U 1982; MDiv Nash 1988. D 6/11/

1988 P 5/1/1989 Bp Harry Woolston Shipps. m 7/17/2004 Wanda M Keeney c 2. Dio No Carolina Raleigh NC 2003; R S Clem's Epis Ch Clemmons NC 1994-2003; Vic Ch Of The Atone Hephzibah GA 1992-1994; S Paul's Ch Albany GA 1989-1992; Assoc S Paul's Epis Ch Albany NY 1989-1992; D S Fran Of The Islands Epis Ch Savannah GA 1988-1989.

KEENEY-MULLIGAN, Gail Donnell (Ct) 12928 N. May Ave Apt 147, Oklahoma City OK 73120 **Chapl Seabury Sr Living Cmnty Bloomfield CT 2009-** B Laramie WY 1956 d Allen & Jean. BSW U of Wyoming 1978; MDiv Bex Sem 1984; DMin NYTS 1994. D 5/6/1984 Bp Robert Rae Spears Jr P 11/19/1984 Bp William George Burrill. c 2. Seabury Ret Cmnty Bloomfield CT 2009-2011; R S Jn's Ch New Milford CT 2002-2009; Vic S Aid's Epis Ch Tulsa OK 1995-2002; Dio Oklahoma Oklahoma City OK 1994-2002; P-in-c Chr Ch by the Sea Colon Panama 1991-1994; Dio Panama 1991-1994; Asst Chr Ch Poughkeepsie NY 1988-1992; Chair, Legis Concerns Comm New York St Coun of Ch 1988-1991; Mid Hudson Catskill Rural and Migrant Min Poughkeepsie NY 1987-1991; Dir Mid-Hudson Rural & Migrant Mnstry 1987-1991; Int S Marg's Ch Staatsburg NY 1987-1988; Assoc S Thos Epis Ch Rochester NY 1984-1986. Auth, "Healing Life's Hurts," 2009. EUC 1980. Outstanding Ldrshp New York St Coun of Ch 1987; Wmn of the Year Wmn Day mag 1986.

KEE-REES, James Louis (WTex) 1501 N Glass St, Victoria TX 77901 **Trin Ch Victoria TX 2014-; Mssnr H Fam Watonga OK 2007-** B Ada OK 1966 s James & Barbara. BA Oklahoma Bapt U 1990; MDiv Sthrn Bapt TS 1994; CPE Emory Cntr for Pstr Serv Atlanta GA 1995; CPE Emory Cntr for Pstr Serv Atlanta GA 1996; STM GTS 2001. D 6/9/2001 Bp Robert Gould Tharp P 1/20/2002 Bp J Neil Alexander. m 10/11/1997 Josephine Elizabeth Kee-Rees c 2. Native Amer Mssnr Dio Oklahoma Oklahoma City OK 2007-2014; Ch Of The Epiph Atlanta GA 2001-2006; Pstr Care & Yth S Jas Epis Ch Marietta GA 1996-2000.

KEESE, Peter Gaines (ETenn) 905 Chateaugay Rd., Knoxville TN 37923 **Vic Chr Ch Rugby TN 2002-** B Chattanooga TN 1936 s William & Elsie. BA Harv 1958; STB GTS 1961; MTh Duke 1977. D 6/25/1961 P 5/5/1962 Bp John Vander Horst. m 5/3/1963 Helen V Keese c 2. Chapl & Dir Cpe U Tn Med Cntr 1987-2002; Dir CPE U of Tennessee Med Cntr Knoxville TN 1987-2001; Chapl Supvsr Duke Med Cntr Durham NC 1973-1986; Epis. Chapl & CPE Supvsr Duke Med Cntr Durham NC 1973-1986; CPE Chapl Res Cntrl St Hosp Milledgeville GA 1972-1973; Chapl Res Cntrl St Hosp Milledgeville GA 1972-1973; Chapl Intern Cpe Prog Van Hosp Nashville TN 1971-1972; CPE Chapl Intern Van Hosp Nashville TN 1971-1972; Chair Div Yth Deptce S Jas The Less Madison TN 1966-1971; P-in-c S Anne's Ch Millington TN 1962-1966; Asst S Jn's Epis Cathd Knoxville TN 1961-1962; Bp Coun Dio E Tennessee Knoxville TN 1999-2001, Bp Coun 1992-1998; Dio Tennessee Nashville TN 1966-1970. Auth, "Jesus Has Left the Bldg," WipfandStock, 2014. AAPC 1979; ACPE 1976. Helen Flanders Dunbar Awd ACPE 2009; Obert Kempson Awd SE Reg Assn for Clibical Pstr Educ 2003; No Carolina Ptr G Keese Awd Hospice of No Carolina 1986; No Carolina Med Soc Jn Huske Anderson Awd No Carolina Med Soc 1986.

KEESHIN, Joyce Jenkins (SO) St James Episcopal Church, 3207 Montana Ave, Cincinnati OH 45211 **The Ch of the Redeem Cincinnati OH 2016-** B Cincinnati OH 1947 d Hugh & Jean. BA Wstrn Coll for Wmn 1969; MA The Athenaeum of Ohio 1991; MDiv Bex Sem 2013. D 6/29/2013 P 6/14/2014 Bp Thomas Edward Breidenthal. c 1. S Jas Epis Ch Cincinnati OH 2013-2015. joyce.hpredeemer@gmail.com

KEESTER, John Carl (Los) 627 Leyden Ln, Claremont CA 91711 **Ret 1991-** B Kane PA 1929 s Carl & Alice. BA U CA 1952; BD CDSP 1955. D 6/13/1955 P 12/12/1955 Bp Sumner Walters. m 8/16/2014 Betty Powell Dennison. Asst S Clare of Assisi Rancho Cucamonga CA 1997-2002; R S Tim's Ch Catonsville MD 1985-1991; R All SS Ch Bakersfield CA 1980-1985; Coun Of Dvlpmt Mnstry 1980-1984; R Exch S Cuth's Derbyshire Engl 1976-1977; Bloy Hse Claremont CA 1974-1980; Actg Wrdn ETS Bloy Hse Claremont CA 1972-1974; Prof Of Homil ETS Bloy Hse Claremont CA 1969-1980; R S Ambr Par Claremont CA 1966-1980; Assoc Chapl U CA Los Angeles CA 1965-1966; Vic S Mich's U Mssn Isla Vista CA 1961-1965; Chapl U CA Santa Barbara CA 1961-1965; Cur S Jude's Epis Par Burbank CA 1958-1961; In-Charge S Ptr Arvin CA 1955-1958; Ret.

KEGGI, J John (Me) 62 Crest Rd, Wellesley MA 02482 B Riga LV 1932 s Janis & Ruta. BS CUNY 1954; MS Ya 1958; PhD Ya 1962. D 2/24/1984 P 8/26/1984 Bp Samuel Espinoza-Venegas. m 8/26/1995 Jeanne D Schork c 3. R S Mk's Ch Augusta ME 1995-2004; Int Trin Ch Bridgewater MA 1994-1995; Int Ch Of The H Sprt Wayland MA 1992-1994; Int All SS Par Brookline MA 1989-1992; Serv Ch in Mex 1986-1988; Dio Maine Portland ME 1984-2007; Dio Mex Mex City MOR 1984-1989. Auth, "As the Vic of Wakefield would have it," *Festschrift for Arthur Peacocke*, 1990; Auth, "Serratamolide, A Metabolite Of Serratia Marcescens|Journ Of Ameriserratamolide, A Metabolite Of Serratia Marcescens," *Journ Of Amer Chem Soc*, 1962. Soc of Ord Scientists 1988. Genesis Awd for Sci and Rel Episcoapl Ntwk for Sci, Tech, & Faith 2005.

KEHRER, William Francis (HB) 3574 Miller Rd, Ann Arbor MI 48103 **Non-par 1971-** B Detroit MI 1923 s Charles & Gertrude. LTh VTS 1965. D 6/29/1965

P 1/1/1966 Bp Richard Stanley Merrill Emrich. m 4/11/1942 Lillian Kehrer. R Gd Shpd Lexington MI 1966-1971; D Gd Shpd Lexington MI 1965-1966.

KEILL, David (Va) 8212 Pilgrim Ter, Richmond VA 23227 **Vic Chr Ascen Ch Richmond VA 1999-** B Ridgewood NJ 1965 s James & Judith. BA Ob 1987; MDiv Yale DS 1993. D 6/5/1993 Bp James Russell Moodey P 6/4/1994 Bp Arthur Williams Jr. m 4/21/2001 Cynthia Keill. R S Geo's Ch Pennsville NJ 1995-1999; Asst S Barn Ch Wilmington DE 1994-1995; Ch Of S Jas The Apos New Haven CT 1993-1994; Asst S Jas' Ch New Haven CT 1993-1994. Auth, "The Epis Sun Lectionary Computer Prog". Co-Winner Wm A Muehl Purchasing Prize Berk 1993.

KEIM, Robert Lincoln (ECR) 301 Trinity Ave, Arroyo Grande CA 93420 **S Barn Ch Arroyo Grande CA 2015-; Fin Contrllr Cisco Systems 2008-; Pres Stanford Cbury Fndt Palo Alto CA 2009-** B Camp Lejune NC 1964 s Robert & Suzanne. BA NWU 1986; MBA Duke 1991; MDiv Fuller TS 2007; Cert Ang Stud CDSP 2008. D 6/6/2009 P 12/5/2009 Bp Marc Handley Andrus. m 6/21/2014 Jeffrey L Diehl c 1. Int S Thos Epis Ch Sunnyvale CA 2013-2015; Asstg P Calv Epis Ch Santa Cruz CA 2012-2013; Asstg P S Mk's Epis Ch Palo Alto CA 2009-2012; Dir of D Mnstrs Menlo Pk Presb Ch Menlo Pk CA 2004-2005; Fin Dir Hewlett-Packard 1997-2003; Chair, Dioc Nomin Com Dio California San Francisco CA 2011-2013, 2008-2010. rob.stbarnabas@gmail.com

KEITH, Briggett J (Nwk) 3004 Overton Rd, Henrico VA 23228 B Hammond IN 1950 d Willis & Jayne. BA Sweet Briar Coll 1972; MDiv VTS 1991. D 6/15/1991 Bp Peter J Lee P 2/15/1992 Bp Arthur Williams Jr. R H Trin Epis Ch Hillsdale NJ 2007-2016; R Trin Epis Ch of Bergen Cnty Allendale NJ 1996-2006; Asst S Chris's By-The River Gates Mills OH 1991-1996.

KEITH, George Arthur (SanD) 4424 44th St Apt 305, San Diego CA 92115 B San Antonio TX 1942 s Ray & Mary. BS Texas St U San Marcos 1964; MPS NYTS 1990. D 6/10/1990 P 12/10/1990 Bp Richard Frank Grein. m 12/21/1996 Joan M Keith c 1. R S Jn's Epis Ch Chula Vista CA 1993-2009; Hdmstr S Jn Sch 1993-1997; Vic Calv and St Geo New York NY 1990-1993; The CPG New York NY 1990-1991. Auth, "Shksp, Gk classics, Mod classics," *Adaptation of Classics for Secondary Sch Theatre*; Playwright, "To Be Remembered," *Off Broadway Prod.* Chapl- Ord of the H Temple of Jerusalem; Chula Vista Arts Coun; NAES.

KEITH JR, John Matthew (Ala) 15001 Searstone Dr Apt 111, Cary NC 27513 **Ret 2000-** B Canton GA 1937 s John & Mildred. BA Duke 1960; STB Harvard DS 1963. D 10/12/1969 P 2/15/1970 Bp George Edward Haynsworth. m 6/6/1969 Rilla Carter Keith c 1. Assoc Chap Of The Cross Chap Hill NC 2011-2016; Int R Trin Ch Wetumpka AL 2004-2005; R S Paul's Epis Ch Lowndesboro AL 2001-2003; R Gr Epis Ch Pike Road AL 1984-2000; St Marys Epis Ch Dadeville AL 1983; R Emm Epis Ch Opelika AL 1977-1982; Dept. of MHE AL 1974-1977; Vic H Cross Ch Uniontown AL 1972-1977; S Wilfrid's Ch Marion AL 1972-1977; St Michaels/H Cross Uniontown AL 1972-1977; P-in-c H Sprt Nice France 1971-1972; Pstr S Fran Managua Nic 1969-1971; Min Un Ch Managua Nic 1966-1971; Serv Bapt Ch 1961-1966; Pres Stndg Com Dio Alabama Birmingham 1999-2000, Chair, Dioc Peace Cmsn 1988-1990. Auth, "Nicaraguan Gringa," New So Books, 2014; Auth, "Canebrake Bch," New So Books, 2012; Auth, "True Div in Chr w Four Short Stories," New So Books, 2010; Auth, "Complete Humanity in Jesus," *A Theol Memoir*, New So Books, 2009. EPF 1980.

KEITH, Judith Ann (Ga) PO Box 33, 216 Remington Avenue, Thomasville GA 31799 **R S Thos Epis Ch Thomasville GA 2007-** B Chicago IL 1943 d Jerome & Rose. U of Tennessee; BA S Mary of the Woods Coll 1984; MDiv SWTS 1997. D 6/14/1997 P 2/11/1998 Bp Henry Irving Louttit. m 11/30/2012 Nathan Reed Keith c 4. R S Dav's Barneveld NY 2002-2007; S Steph's Ch New Hartford NY 2002-2007; R Gr Ch Sterling IL 2000-2002; Assoc R Emm Epis Ch Rockford IL 1997-2000. Producer/Dir, "Chld and Stwdshp," *Video*, St. Lk's - Atlanta, 1991.

KEITH III, Stuart Brooks (Colo) Po Box 1591, Edwards CO 81632 **R Epis Ch Of The Trsfg Vail CO 1998-, Asst 1995-1996** B Tampa FL 1964 s Stuart & Kay. BA U of So Florida 1985; MDiv VTS 1992. D 6/20/1992 Bp John Wadsworth Howe P 1/1/1993 Bp William Jerry Winterrowd. m 5/16/1992 Julie Papa Keith c 2. Ch Of S Jn Chrys Golden CO 1992-1995; Cur S Jn Chrys Edwards CO 1992-1995. Auth, "Who Do You Say That I Am? Facilitating YP'S Encounters w The Gospel," *Resource Bk For Mnstrs w Yth & YA In The Episcop*, Dfms, 1995.

KEITH, Thomas Aaron (NwT) B Wichita Falls, Texas 1983 s David & Carlotta. D 12/12/2015 Bp James Scott Mayer. m 7/6/2015 Steve Burton Hennessee.

KEITH, Thomas Frederick (WK) 406 Champions Dr, Rockport TX 78382 **Vic Ch Of Our Sav Aransas Pass TX 2002-; Vic Epis Ch of Our Sav Aransas Pass TX 2002-** B Alger OH 1935 s Frederick & Virginia. BA U of So Florida 1965; BD Epis TS of the SW 1968; MEd U of Texas 1977; PhD U of Texas 1987. D 6/12/1968 Bp Frederick P Goddard P 5/1/1969 Bp James Milton Richardson. m 10/19/1985 Adelaide K Keith c 2. SS Mary And Martha Of Bethany Larned KS 1995-2000; Dio Wstrn Kansas Hutchinson KS 1992-2000; H Apos Ch Ellsworth KS 1990-1995; S Jn's Ch Great Bend KS 1990-1995; Sterling Coll Sterling KS 1987-2000; S Mk's Ch Lyons KS 1985-1990; R S Jn's

K

Ch New Braunfels TX 1978-1984; R S Paul Burnet TX 1974-1978; Trin Epis Ch Marble Falls TX 1968-1978; Vic Epis Ch Of The Epiph Burnet Burnet TX 1968-1974; The Great Cmsn Fndt Houston TX 1968-1973.

KEITH, William (SC) PO Box 145, Lookout Mountain TN 37350 **R H Cross Faith Memi Epis Ch Pawleys Island SC 2012-** B Asheville NC 1978 s William & Lynda. BA Appalachian St U 2001; MDiv Sewanee: The U So, TS 2009. D 5/30/2009 Bp Porter Taylor P 1/16/2010 Bp Charles Glenn VonRosenberg. m 5/29/2004 Amanda T Keith c 2. Asst R Ch Of The Gd Shpd Lookout Mtn TN 2009-2012; Assoc Proctor S Andr's-Sewanee Sch 2006-2009.

KEITH-LUCAS, Diane Dorothea (Mass) **Dio Massachusetts Boston MA 2013-; Chapl Epis Chap at MIT Cambridge MA 2013-** B Sewanee TN 1976 BA Swarthmore Coll 1997; MA Harvard DS 2000; MDiv EDS 2004. D 6/4/2005 P 1/7/2006 Bp M(Arvil) Thomas Shaw. m 8/7/1999 Jacob M Montwieler c 2. R All SS Epis Ch of the No Shore Inc Danvers MA 2007-2013; Coordntr Of CE Trin Ch Randolph MA 2005-2007.

KEITHLY JR, Thomas Graves (Dal) 1612 Kiltartan Dr, Dallas TX 75228 B Saint Louis MO 1931 s Thomas & Amy. BA W&M 1953; BA Oxf GB 1955; GTS 1956; MA Oxf GB 1959. D 6/21/1956 P 12/21/1956 Bp Edward Randolph Welles II. m 8/13/1955 Virginia Keithly c 3. Seniors Min Ch Of The Incarn Dallas TX 1995-1999; Int Ch Of The Gd Shpd Terrell TX 1993-1995; Dept Of Dioc Ministers Dio Ft Worth Ft Worth TX 1986-1989, Exec Coun 1986-1989, 1984-1985, Fin Com 1974-1976, Dn Of The SW Dnry 1972-1976, Dept Of Mssn 1971-1983, Exec Coun 1971-1976; Ch Of The H Cross Paris TX 1985-1994; R S Jn's Epis Ch Brownwood TX 1967-1985; Asst To Dn S Matt's Cathd Dallas TX 1959-1967; Vic S Chris's Ch And Sch Ft Worth TX 1958-1959; Vic Shpd Of The Hills Branson MO 1956-1958; Chair - Cntrl Convoc Dio Dallas Dallas TX 1995-1997. Cmnty Of S Mary 1961.

KEIZER, Garret John (Vt) 770 King George Farm Rd, Sutton VT 05867 B Paterson NJ 1953 s John & Joan. BA Montclair St U 1975; MA U of Vermont 1978. D 6/16/1992 P 12/19/1992 Bp Daniel Lee Swenson. m 7/19/1975 Kathleen Van Haste c 1. Vic Chr Ch Island Pond VT 1992-2003; Lay Vic Chr Ch Island Pond VT 1983-1992. Auth, "Help: The Original Human Dilemma," Harper Collins, 2004; Auth, "The Enigma of Anger," Jossey-Bass, 2002; Auth, "Dresser of Sycamore Trees," Viking, 1991; Auth, "No Place But Here," Viking, 1988.

KELAHER, Edward Thomas (WA) 3 Chevy Chase Cir, Chevy Chase MD 20815 **All SS' Epis Ch Chevy Chase MD 2011-; Dn, Georgetown Dnry So Carolina Charleston SC 2007-** B Bayonne NJ 1954 s Jerome & Norma. Drew U 1973; BS Buc 1976; JD New York Law Sch 1980. D 9/14/1997 P 3/31/2001 Bp Edward Lloyd Salmon Jr. m 7/16/1977 Patricia A Kelaher c 2. Chr the King Pawleys Island SC 2007-2011; D The Epis Ch Of The Resurr Myrtle Bch SC 1997-2001. Bucknell Univ. Humanitarian Awd Buc 1995; Natl Pro Bono Lawyer Awd ABA 1993; S. C. Pro Bono Lawyer Of The Year So Carolina Bar 1992; Cnty Vol Of The Year Sun News (Nwspr) 1992; Citizen Of The Year Surfside Bch, Sc 1992.

KELB, Sarah (Mass) Church of the Holy Spirit, 204 Monument Rd, Orleans MA 02653 **S Paul's Epis Ch No Andover MA 2014-** B Toledo OH 1975 d Roger & Susan. BA Capital U 2000; MDiv Sewanee: The U So, TS 2011; MDiv The TS at The U So 2011; STM Sewanee: The U So, TS 2014; STM The TS at The U So 2014. D 6/22/2013 P 1/4/2014 Bp M(Arvil) Thomas Shaw. The Ch Of The H Sprt Orleans MA 2013-2014.

KELDERMAN, Kate E (Ct) Kent School, 1 Macedonia Rd, Kent CT 06757 **Kent Sch Kent CT 2014-** B Roanoke VA 1963 d Joseph & Jane. BS U So 1985; MT U of Virginia 1994; MDiv VTS 2004. D 6/26/2004 Bp Peter J Lee P 1/6/2005 Bp James Louis Jelinek. m 5/12/1990 Theo Kelderman c 2. Assoc The Epis Ch Of Beth-By-The-Sea Palm Bch FL 2012-2014; R The Memi Ch Of The Prince Of Peace Gettysburg PA 2007-2012; Assoc R St Dav's Epis Ch Minnetonka MN 2004-2007.

KELLAM, Patricia Marie (SVa) Po Box 468, Amelia Court House VA 23002 B Nassawadox VA 1942 d Harry & Nannie. BS Virginia Commonwealth U 1979; BS Virginia Commonwealth U 1979; MEd Virginia Commonwealth U 1983; MEd Virginia Commonwealth U 1983; UTS Richmond 1985; MDiv Sewanee: The U So, TS 1991. D 6/1/1991 P 2/2/1992 Bp Charles Farmer Duvall. c 2. Chr Ch Amelia Ct Hs VA 2012-2014; Emm Ch Cape Chas VA 2010-2011; Coordntr of Chapl Hospice of the Estrn Shore Onancock VA 2010-2011; Dir of Pstr Care Shove Memi Hosp Nassawadox VA 2000-2008; S Phil's Ch Quantico MD 2000; Assoc H Trin Prot Epis Ch Onancock VA 1999-2005; S Paul's Ch Vienna MD 1999-2000; Chapl Med Coll Va Hosp Richmond VA 1998-1999; Chapl Mercy Med Mobile Hm Hospice Mobile AL 1993-1996; Vic Imm Ch Bay Minette AL 1991-1995; D H Nativ Epis Ch Panama City FL 1991; Chapls Coordntr Hca Gulf Coast Hosp Panama City FL 1986-1989; Coordntr S Andr's Epis Ch Panama City FL 1986-1989. Hampton Roads Chapl Assn 2000-2008; Virginia Chapl Assn 2000-2008.

KELLAWAY, James L (Ct) 123 Babbitt Hill Road, Pomfret Center CT 06259 B Amityville NY 1950 s James & Helen. BA Colg 1972; MDiv EDS 1977. D 6/11/1977 Bp Jonathan Goodhue Sherman P 4/1/1978 Bp Robert Campbell Witcher Sr. m 11/24/1979 Genevieve D Kellaway c 3. P-in-c Trin Ch Brooklyn CT 2008-2011; R S Jn's Epis Ch Vernon Rock Vernon Rockville CT

1989-2008; R Chr Ch Fairmont WV 1983-1989; Asst Chr Ch Greenwich CT 1977-1983; Dioc Disaster Relief Com Dio Connecticut Meriden CT 2011, Dn, Hartford Dnry 2004-2011, Stwdshp Com 1995-2011, Stwdshp Consult 1995-2003, Fin Com 1991-1994; Stwdshp Com & Chair Dio W Virginia Charleston WV 1984-1986. Poet, "The Moonlight Mowers," *Stars In Our Hearts,* Wrld Poetry Mvmt; Mus & Lyrics, "A Habitat for All Humanity," *The Habitat Songbook,* HabHum; Auth, "The Mystical Mangers," *Unpublished.* Epis Ntwk for Stwdshp 2000-2005.

KELLER, Anthony (Los) 808 Foothill Blvd, La Canada CA 91011 **D S Geo's Par La Can CA 2007-; Dio Los Angeles Los Angeles CA 2013-** B Cleveland OH 1954 s Frank & Helen. Diac Stds Epis TS 2010. D 2/6/2010 Bp Chester Lovelle Talton. m 10/14/2016 Felix Yamaguchi Djie. Compsr, "Introit," *Make A Joyful Noise,* Harrock Hall Mus, 2004; Compsr, "Instrumental," *Pelude for Two Trumpets and Organ,* Harrock Hall Mus, 2004.

KELLER JR, Charles Edward (Nwk) 711 S Custer Ave, Miles City MT 59301 B Orange NJ 1932 s Charles & Dorothy. BA Dart 1954; UTS 1959; MA FD 1976. D 5/23/1959 Bp Donald MacAdie P 12/1/1959 Bp Leland Stark. m 3/12/1955 Barbara F Keller c 2. Pres of the Passaic Convoc 1984-1989; 1979-1983; Bp Anand Resource Cntr 1978-1982; Dept of Missions 1975-1980; S Agnes Ch Little Falls NJ 1962-1996; Cur Chr Ch Glen Ridge NJ 1959-1962.

KELLER III, Christoph (Ark) 5224 Country Club Blvd, Little Rock AR 72207 **Trin Cathd Little Rock AR 2014-; Dir Inst for Theol Stds at St. Marg's 2004-; Theol-in-Res S Marg's Little Rock Arkansas 2004-; Dir Epis Collgt Sch Little Rock AR 2010-; Dir The GTS New York NY 2010-** B El Dorado AR 1955 s Christoph & Caroline. BA Amh 1977; Harv 1979; MDiv EDS 1982; ThD GTS 2009. D 6/26/1982 Bp Herbert Alcorn Donovan Jr P 5/28/1983 Bp Christoph Keller Jr. m 4/15/1978 Julie Keller c 2. S Marg's Epis Ch Little Rock AR 1993-1998; Dio Arkansas Little Rock AR 1990-1992, 1982-1983; Trin Van Buren AR 1983-1990; Vic S Aug's Ch Ft Smith AR 1983-1986; Intern Cur Trin Ch Pine Bluff AR 1982-1983; Trst ECBF No Chesterfield VA 2001-2004. HSEC 2004. Fell ECF 2003; Hon Cn Dio Arkansas 1998.

KELLER JR, David Gardiner Ross (WNC) 31 Alexander Farms Lane, Alexander NC 28701 **Co-Steward Inst for Contemplative Stds Pract and Living 2009-; Dir Contemplative Mnstry Proj 2006-** B New York NY 1937 s David & Elizabeth. BA Hobart and Wm Smith Colleges 1958; MDiv GTS 1961; EdD NYU 1985. D 6/29/1961 Bp Alfred L Banyard P 1/4/1962 Bp William Jones Gordon Jr. m 1/4/2003 Emily Wilmer c 4. Steward, Epis Hse of Pryr Dio Minnesota Minneapolis MN 1994-2002; Steward Epis Hse Of Pryr Collegeville MN 1994-2002; Cn Trin Cathd Phoenix AZ 1991-1994; Dir Dept Of Mnstry Dvlpmt Dio Arizona Phoenix AZ 1982-1994, Cn of Trin Cathd 1991-; Cook Chr Trng Sch Tempe AZ 1981-1982; Coordntr Ak Tee Dio Alaska Fairbanks AK 1974-1981; P-in-c S Jas Ch Tanana AK 1969-1972; P-in-c S Geo's Ch Cordova AK 1968-1969; P-in-c S Lk's Ch Shageluk AK 1961-1968. Auth, "Desert Banquet:Wisdom from the Desert Fathers and Mothers," *Trade Bk,* Liturg Press, 2011; Auth, "Come and See: The Transformation of Personal Pryr," *Trade Bk,* Morehouse Pub, 2009; Auth, "Oasis of Wisdom: The Worlds of the Desert Fr and Mothers," *Trade Bk,* Liturg Press, 2005; Auth, "Tchg Life of Jesus," *TEE Course,* Chas Cook TS, 1982; Auth, "Gods Living Word: A Biblic Survey," *TEE Course,* Dio Alaska, 1975.

KELLER, John Speake (O) 20508 Hilliard Blvd, Rocky River OH 44116 B Washington DC 1950 s Howard & Ann. BA U Rich 1972; MDiv VTS 1975; MA Presb Sch CE 1976. D 7/27/1975 Bp Samuel B Chilton P 6/5/1976 Bp Charles Francis Hall. m 7/17/2003 Donald J Jackson. Ch Of The Epiph Euclid OH 2012; Int Ch Of The Ascen Lakewood OH 2008-2011; Int The Memi Ch Of The Prince of Peace Gettysburg PA 2005-2007; Int S Jn's Epis Ch Lancaster PA 2004-2005; Assoc R S Ptr's Epis Ch Lakewood OH 2000-2004; Int The Ch Of The Nativ Cedarcroft Baltimore MD 1999-2000; Int S Dav's Ch Baltimore MD 1997-1999; Int Trin Ch Towson MD 1996-1997; Int All SS Ch E Lansing MI 1994-1996; Int Sherwood Epis Ch Cockeysville MD 1993-1994; Assoc S Thos' Par Washington DC 1989-1992; Non-par St. Thos Par Washington DC 1986-1987; Assoc S Lk's Ch Gladstone NJ 1984-1986; LocTen Ch Of The H Comm S Louis MO 1981-1984; Asst Gr Ch S Louis MO 1979-1981; Cur Chr Epis Ch Little Rock AR 1977-1979; Cur S Thos' Ch Richmond VA 1975-1977. Auth, "Weca Nwsltr".

KELLER SR, Patterson (Oly) Po Box 1808, Cody WY 82414 **Ret 1995-** B Highland Park IL 1930 s Christoph & Kathryn. BA Trin Hartford CT 1953; MDiv VTS 1956. D 6/21/1956 Bp Allen J Miller P 2/25/1957 Bp William Jones Gordon Jr. m 6/10/1958 Cornelia Keller c 4. R Emm Ch Orcas Island Eastsound WA 1988-1995; R Chr Ch Cody WY 1971-1988; Vic S Andr's Ch Meeteetse WY 1971-1978; Vic Ch Of The Gd Shpd Sundance WY 1963-1971; P-in-c Gd Shpd Huslia AK 1956-1963.

KELLER, Susan (Md) Trinity And Saint Philip's Cathedral, 24 Rector St, Newark NJ 07102 **S Paul's Epis Ch Mt Airy MD 2012-** B Detroit MI 1955 d Thomas & Freddie. BA How 1976; MDiv How 1991; CAS VTS 1992. D 6/13/1992 Bp Ronald Hayward Haines P 1/9/1993 Bp Jane Hart Holmes Dixon. m 7/3/1976 Paul F Keller c 1. Dn Trin And S Phil's Cathd Newark NJ 2009-2012; R S Mary Magd Ch Silver Sprg MD 2003-2008; S Fran Ch Virginia Bch VA

2000-2003; Dir Prog Dio Sthrn Virginia Newport News VA 1996-2000; Asst Ch Of Our Sav Silver Sprg MD 1992-1996; Jubilee Intern For The Epis Campus Mssn U Of Maryland In Coll Pk 1991-1992. EPF, UBE. stpaulschurch-mtairy@verizon.net

KELLERMANN, Alan Seth (NCal) 245 S Church St, Grass Valley CA 95945 **R Emm Epis Ch Grass Vlly CA 2009-** B New Orleans LA 1976 s Alan & Carol. BA W&L 1999; MDiv TESM 2006. D 8/19/2006 P 3/24/2007 Bp James Monte Stanton. m 8/8/1998 Tara Dorothy Kellermann c 4. Chf of Stff S Phil's Epis Ch Frisco TX 2008-2009; Cur Ch Of The Epiph Richardson TX 2006-2008. frsethk@gmail.com

KELLETT, James William (SVa) 11233 Tierrasanta Blvd, #40, San Diego CA 92124 B Ely NV 1933 s Ernest & Mary. BA Bos 1955; MDiv Bex Sem 1959. D 6/20/1959 P 12/20/1959 Bp Anson Phelps Stokes Jr. m 4/13/1980 Anne Kellett c 4. Asst S Barth's Epis Ch Poway CA 2007-2014; Int S Andr's Ch La Mesa CA 2004-2006; Bruton Par Williamsburg VA 2000; Hickory Neck Ch Toano VA 1987-2000; S Paul's Ch Windsor VT 1983-1987; Salisbury Sch Salisbury CT 1975-1983; Chapl Salisbury Sch CT 1975-1983; R S Andr's-In-The-Vlly Tamworth NH 1970-1975; R S Matt's Ch Goffstown NH 1966-1970; P-in-c Redeem Wind River WY 1963-1966; P-in-c S Dav's Epis Ch Ft Bridger WY 1963-1966; Vic All SS Epis Ch Wolfeboro NH 1961-1963; Cur S Paul's Ch Brockton MA 1959-1961; Chapl Hospice Spprt Care Of Williamsburg VA.

KELLEY, Barbara A (Pa) 159 Windsor Ave, Southampton PA 18966 **R S Jas Ch Langhorne PA 2008-, Int 2004-2006** B New York NY 1954 d Arthur & Dorothy. BA Lawr 1976; MS U of Wisconsin 1978; MDiv GTS 1980. D 6/7/1980 Bp Robert Campbell Witcher Sr P 12/16/1981 Bp Lyman Cunningham Ogilby. Int Ch Of The H Nativ Wrightstown PA 2006-2008; Int Trin Ch Buckingham PA 2006; Ch Of The H Sprt Harleysville PA 2001-2004, Int 2001; Int Gd Shpd Ch Hilltown PA 1999-2000; Int Ch Of The Mssh Lower Gwynedd PA 1998-1999; Int Gr Epiph Ch Philadelphia PA 1995-1998; Int S Jas Ch Collegeville PA 1994-1995; Int Ch Of The Incarn Morrisville PA 1992-1993; Int Trin Ch Solebury PA 1991-1992; Int Trin Ch Gulph Mills Kng Of Prussia PA 1991; Int S Paul's Ch Elkins Pk PA 1990-1991; Int S Mary Anne's Epis Ch No E MD 1989-1990; Int S Nathanaels Ch Philadelphia PA 1989; Int Ch Of The Redemp Southampton PA 1987-1989; Asst Min The Epis Ch Of The Adv Kennet Sq PA 1981-1987; Cur All SS Ch Great Neck NY 1980-1981.

KELLEY, Brian Scott (Mass) 47 Concord Sq, Boston MA 02118 **Ret 1995-** B Quebec City QC CA 1928 s Arthur & Mary. BA Bishops U QC CA 1949; BEd McGill U 1953; MDiv EDS 1957; Cert Harvard DS 1972; EdD Harv 1976. Trans 5/15/1963 as Priest Bp Anson Phelps Stokes Jr. m 9/8/1956 Sara Avery Kelley c 3. R S Lk's And S Marg's Ch Allston MA 1979-1983; Int Ch Of The Trsfg Derry NH 1977-1978; The Cathd Ch Of S Paul Boston MA 1970-1995; Assoc St. Paul's Cathd Boston MA 1966-1995; Asst Gr Ch Everett MA 1963-1966; R S Jn's Ch Charlestown (Boston) Charlestown MA 1960-1966; Serv Ch of Can 1957-1960. Auth, "Poems," *Peacework*, 1999; Auth, "Poems," *The Boston Poet*, 1997. Clipper Ship Fndt 1985. Mary B Newman Awd Untd Way of Mass Bay 2000; Establishment of the Cn Brian Scott Kelley Awd Soc Action Mnstrs 1993; Citizen of the Year Awd Boston Downtown Crossing Assn 1988.

KELLEY, Carlton F (WMich) 57607 M-51 South, Dowagiac MI 49047 **Gr Epis Ch Traverse City MI 2016-** B Fort Pierce FL 1949 s Otis & Lydia. BSN U of Maryland 1978; MDiv GTS 1982; Int Mnstry Prog 2000. D 6/29/1982 Bp David Keller Leighton Sr P 2/24/1983 Bp Charlie Fuller Mcnutt Jr. Trin Ch Three Rivers MI 2015; R S Paul's Epis Ch Dowagiac MI 2012-2015; P-in-c S Paul's Ch Richmond IN 2001-2004; Supply S Wlfd's Epis Ch Sarasota FL 1998-2006; 1991-1998; Int All SS Mssn Venice FL 1990-1991; Dio SW Florida Parrish FL 1990-1991; Int R S Ptr's Epis Ch Ellicott City MD 1984-1989; Vic S Andr's Epis Ch Glenwood MD 1984-1985; Cur S Jas Ch Lancaster PA 1982-1984. Natl Epis Hlth Mnstrs 2001; Ord of Julian of Norwich 2008; Recovered Alchoholic Cler Assn 2007; Recovery Mnstrs of the Epis Ch 2009.

KELLEY, James Thomas (Mont) St John's Episcopal Church, 15 N Idaho St, Butte MT 59701 **D S Paul's Ch Wheeling WV 2007-; D S Lk's Ch Wheeling WV 2000-** B Wheeling WV 1945 s William & Frieda. D 9/21/2000 Bp Claude Charles Vache. m 6/16/1990 Theresa M Robson.

KELLEY, Theresa M (Mont) 3350 Keokuk St, Butte MT 59701 **P S Marks Pintler Cluster Anaconda MT 2014-; P-in-c S Paul's Ch Wheeling WV 2006-; P-in-c S Lk's Ch Wheeling WV 2001-** B Spokane WA 1957 d Richard & Helen. BA W Liberty St Coll 2004. D 9/21/2000 P 6/9/2001 Bp Claude Charles Vache. m 6/16/1990 James Thomas Kelley c 2. tmkelley57@gmail.com

KELLIHER, James William (RI) B Providence 1964 s Daniel & Lois. D 6/11/2016 Bp W Nicholas Knisely Jr. m 9/12/2015 Paul Andrew Mayben c 3. revjwkelliher@gmail.com

KELLINGTON, Brian T (Spr) 17085 SE 93rd Yondel Cir, The Villages FL 32162 B Medford OR 1949 s George & Mary. BA U of Oregon 1971; MDiv CDSP 1984. D 6/29/1984 Bp Robert Hume Cochrane P 6/1/1985 Bp Matthew Paul Bigliardi. m 7/24/1976 Laurie R Dugnolle. P-in-c All SS Ch Morton IL 2009-2015; R S Paul's Epis Ch Pekin IL 2005-2015; Vic S Phil's Ch Norwood NY 2001-2005; Pres Herkimer Interfaith Cler Coun 1993-1998; R Chr Ch Herkimer NY 1988-2001; Int Calv Ch Seaside OR 1988; S Andr's Ch Cottage Grove OR 1984-1988; Vic S Dav's Ch Drain OR 1984-1988; Evang and Spritual Enrichment Chair Dio Springfield Springfield IL 2010-2014, Dn-Nthrn Dnry 2009-2014, Stwdshp Chair 2006-2010; Sprtl Advsr Curs Sec Dio Albany Greenwich NY 1994-1998. Chapl Intl Ord of S Lk 2013; Natl Epis Curs Com 2001-2003.

KELLINGTON, Laurie R (Spr) 17085 SE 93rd Yondel Cir, The Villages FL 32162 **D All SS Ch Morton IL 2009-; D S Paul's Epis Ch Pekin IL 2005-** B Englewood CA 1955 d Charles & Barbara. BA Utica Coll 1993; MA S Josephs Coll Maine 2006. D 6/9/2001 Bp Daniel William Herzog. m 7/24/1976 Brian T Kellington. D S Phil's Ch Norwood NY 2001-2005; D Chr Ch Herkimer NY 2001; COM Dio Springfield Springfield IL 2014-2015. Chapl Intl Ord of S Lk 2013.

KELLNER, Andrew Locke (Pa) **S Chris's Ch Gladwyne PA 2017-; St Jas Sch Philadelphia PA 2016-; Other Lay Position Dio Pennsylvania Philadelphia PA 2013-; Bd Mem Epis Serv Corps Chicago IL 2014-** B 1982 s Karl & Michelle. BA MI SU 2004; MA Chld, Yth & Fam Mnstrs Luther Sem, St. Paul, MN 2012; STM Sewanee: The U So, TS 2016. D 1/16/2016 P 6/11/2016 Bp Clifton Daniel III. m 10/30/2009 David John Kasievich. S Simon The Cyrenian Ch Philadelphia PA 2016-2017; Bd Mem Forma Hammond LA 2011-2015.

KELLO, Rebecca Ruth (NwT) D 6/14/2017 Bp James Scott Mayer.

KELLOGG, Alicia Sue (Me) 27 Forest Ave, Winthrop ME 04364 **Dir Of Hr St Of Maine 1984-** B Marion OH 1947 d Charles & Doris. BA OH SU 1969. D 6/23/2007 Bp Chilton Richardson Knudsen. c 1. D S Matt's Epis Ch Hallowell ME 2007-2010.

KELLOGG III, Edward Samuel (SanD) 3407 Larga Cir, San Diego CA 92110 B Pasadena CA 1933 s Edward & Dorothy. BS USNA 1954; BA Sch for Deacons 1984. D 8/5/1984 P 12/1/1990 Bp Charles Brinkley Morton. m 6/26/1954 Margaret Anne Kellogg c 3. S Andr's By The Lake Lake Elsinore CA 1991; S Barth's Epis Ch Poway CA 1990; D Ch Of The Gd Samar San Diego CA 1987-1989; D Cathd Ch Of S Paul San Diego CA 1984-1986; Sem Asst Ascen Epis Ch Vallejo CA 1981-1984.

KELLOGG, John A (La) 7215 Zimpel St, New Orleans LA 70118 **Dio Louisiana New Orleans LA 2014-; P-in-c S Mk's Epis Ch Harvey LA 2014-** B Shreveport LA 1986 s John & Martha. BS Millsaps Coll 2008; MDiv GTS 2012. D 6/9/2012 P 12/12/2012 Bp Duncan Montgomery Gray III. m 7/16/2011 Brittany Tait Kellogg. R Epis Ch Of The Incarn W Point MS 2012-2014. jkellogg@edola.org

KELLUM, Rose Edna (Miss) B Vicksburg MS 1957 d Thomas & Jennie. Hinds Cmnty Coll 1981; Cpe Res GV Sonny Montogmer Va Med Cntr 2002. D 1/6/2001 Bp Alfred Marble Jr. c 3. D Chr Ch St Jos LA 2004-2012.

KELLY, Arthur James (Pa) 1171 Sandy Ridge Rd, Doylestown PA 18901 **Non-par 1999-; Acad Sub Com of COM Dio Pennsylvania Philadelphia PA 1988-, Dioc Relatnshp Com 1986-1991, Cmsn Racism 1986-1990, Chr Ed. Comm. 1985-1990, Dioc Coun 1985-1990, Soc Concerns Com 1984-1990, Chair Black Cler 1983-1990** B Colon Panama 1931 s Arthur & Dorcas. BA CUNY Hunter Coll 1962; MDiv GTS 1966; STM NYTS 1972; PhD NYU 1981. D 6/4/1966 P 12/17/1966 Bp Horace W B Donegan. m 4/20/1996 Imogene Carol Kelly c 4. Adj Prof NY Area 1983-1998; R S Aug's Philadelphia PA 1978-1999; Prof Higher Ed. Metro. NY 1976-1978; Prot Chapl St. Jn's R.C. Boys Hm Dio Long Island Garden City NY 1973-1978, Mssn 1972-1978, Eccl. Crt 1972-1974, Counsellor Queens Pstr Couns. Serv- Jamaica Fam Co 1970-1975; Chair Advsry Com. Queens 1971-1978; Chapl Gd Samar Hse Jamaica NY 1971-1974; R S Steph's Epis Ch Jamaica NY 1969-1978; Yth Min Ch Of The Intsn New York NY 1966-1969. Auth, "The Response Of The Epis Ch To Soc Change And Soc Issues 1960-1978," *PHD Dissertation*, 1981. Phi Delta Kappa. Phi Delta Kappa.

KELLY, Christopher Douglas (SeFla) 110 Selfridge Rd, Gansevoort NY 12831 B Sydney NSW AU 1941 s Fred & Maude. BA Pr 1963; MA Ya 1966; PhD Ya 1968; MDiv EDS 1972; DMin Sewanee: The U So, TS 1990. D 6/17/1972 Bp Jonathan Goodhue Sherman P 12/21/1972 Bp James Loughlin Duncan. m 5/29/1971 Pamela Kelly c 2. S Mary's Ch Lake Luzerne NY 2006-2007; R S Christophers Ch W Palm Bch FL 1978-2002; Cur S Mart's Epis Ch Pompano Bch FL 1972-1978.

KELLY III, Colin Purdie (RG) 4 Inca Ln, Los Alamos NM 87544 B March AFB Riverside CA 1940 s Colin & Marion. BS USMA 1963; MDiv PDS 1970; MEd LIU 1977; DMin SWTS 2001. D 6/6/1970 P 12/1/1970 Bp Robert Lionne DeWitt. m 6/6/1985 Sue Hutchens. Cn Mssnr Dio The Rio Grande Albuquerque 2008-2010; Trin On The Hill Epis Ch Los Alamos NM 1985-2012; R Ch Of S Mich The Archangel Colorado Spg CO 1983-1985; Off Of Bsh For ArmdF New York NY 1973-1983; P-in-c Gr Ch Dalton MA 1971-1973; Asst to R Trin Ch Moorestown NJ 1970-1972.

KELLY, Francis J (CFla) 1250 Paige Pl, The Villages FL 32159 **S Geo Epis Ch The Villages FL 2014-** B Syracuse NY 1955 s Francis & Wilda. BA Houghton Coll 1977; MDiv VTS 1986. D 6/21/1986 P 5/21/1987 Bp O'Kelley Whitaker. m 8/20/1978 Letitia M Kelly c 4. Trin Ch Lansingburgh Troy NY 2004-2014; S Jn's Epis Ch Troy NY 2001-2004; R Ch Of The Epiph Glenburn Clarks Sum-

K

mit PA 1994-2001; R S Mk's Ch Newark NY 1989-1994; Vic Chr Ch Sackets Hbr NY 1986-1989; Cur Trin Epis Ch Watertown NY 1986-1989. EvangES. fjkelly55@gmail.com

KELLY, James Lester (Nev) 1075 Oxen Rd, Incline Village NV 89451 B Granite Falls MN 1931 s Lester & Barbara. CDSP; TESM; BS U CA 1954; MBA Harv 1958. D 1/9/2005 P 7/25/2005 Bp Katharine Jefferts Schori. m 1/31/1953 Lora Kelly c 2. D S Pat's Ch Incline Vlg NV 2005-2012; Stndg Com Mem Dio Nevada Las Vegas 2005-2011. OSL 1996.

KELLY, Jane Young (SwFla) The Church of the Good Shepherd, 401 W. Henry St., Punta Gorda FL 33950 **D Ch Of The Gd Shpd Punta Gorda FL 2010-** B Youngstown OH 1946 d Earl & Gladys. D 6/6/2009 Bp Dabney Tyler Smith. D S Jas Epis Ch Pt Charlotte FL 2009-2010.

KELLY, Joan Hickey (Md) D 6/10/2017 Bp Chilton Richardson Knudsen.

KELLY, Karen Joy (WMich) **Chapl Westminster-Cbury Of Lynchburg Lynchburg VA 2003-** B Highland Park MI 1938 d William & Agnes. BA MI SU 1960; CAS Sewanee: The U So, TS 2003; MDiv Wstrn TS 2003. D 12/18/2003 Bp Robert R Gepert P 6/29/2004 Bp Neff Powell. c 2. Int R S Jn's Epis Ch Glasgow VA 2014-2016; Int Trin Epis Ch Lynchburg VA 2013-2014; Vic All SS' Epis Fllshp 2010-2012; R S Ptr's Ch Altavista VA 2003-2010; Stndg Com Pres Dio SW Virginia Roanoke VA 2010-2011.

KELLY, Kathleen M (SanD) 308 E Acacia Ave, Hemet CA 92543 B Alhambra CA 1951 d Richard & Mary. BA Ya 1973; JD U CA 1976; MDiv CDSP 2005. D 6/29/2005 P 1/29/2006 Bp Jerry Alban Lamb. R The Epis Ch Of The Gd Shpd Hemet CA 2010-2016; Cn Trin Epis Cathd Sacramento CA 2005-2010.

KELLY, Linda Louise (NwT) 218 Oak Hill Dr, Kerrville TX 78028 B Eads CO 1953 d William & Margaret. BA Nebraska Wesl 1976; MTh SMU 1983; Epis TS of the SW 1986; MEd Texas Tech U 1999. D 9/21/1987 Bp Maurice Manuel Benitez P 1/25/1988 Bp Gordon Taliaferro Charlton. R S Matt's Ch Pampa TX 2005-2014; Asst R S Ptr's Epis Ch Kerrville TX 1998-2011; Assoc R S Paul's On The Plains Epis Ch Lubbock TX 1995-1998; R S Paul's Epis Ch Orange TX 1991-1995; Chapl Baylor U Waco TX 1987-1991; Assoc R S Paul's Ch Waco TX 1987-1991; Serv Meth Ch 1983-1986. jmtthor@sbcglobal.net

KELLY, Margaret I (Ida) 1800 N Cole Rd Apt E204, Boise ID 83704 **Non-par 1995-** B Wendell ID 1945 d Ray & Margaret. Csi 1991. D 1/28/1995 Bp John Stuart Thornton. m 3/7/1966 Earl Kelly c 1. Happ For Id; NAAD.

KELLY, Roger K (Ga) 3101 Waters Ave, Savannah GA 31404 **S Mich And All Ang Savannah GA 2014-** B Valdosta GA 1967 s Roger & Bonnie. BA Valdosta St U 1991; MDiv VTS 1994. D 5/25/1994 P 12/9/1994 Bp Harry Woolston Shipps. m 12/28/1993 Christine S Kelly c 3. Trin Epis Ch Baton Rouge LA 2012-2013; R Trin Ch Huntington WV 2001-2011; S Dav's Ch Roswell GA 1998-2001; Assoc S Mart-In-The-Fields 1996-1998; S Mart In The Fields Ch Atlanta GA 1995-1997; Chapl Sch 1995-1996; Vic S Lk's Epis Hawkinsville GA 1994-1995; Vic Trin Ch Cochran GA 1994-1995.

KELLY, Sarah Elizabeth (O) 9160 Putnam Rd, Pandora OH 45877 **Sprtl Care Coordntr & Mgr of Soc Wk Blanchard Vlly Hosp Findlay Ohio 2012-** B Crestview FL 1957 d Homer & Margaret. BA U So 1978; MDiv Duke DS 1990; MSW The OH SU 2011. D 9/23/1990 Bp Arthur Edward Walmsley P 10/30/1991 Bp Huntington Williams Jr. m 6/12/1988 Raymond Franklin Person c 2. Sprtl Care Coordntr Blanchard Vlly Hosp Findlay Ohio 2000-2012; Co-Dir of Prog for Sprtlty in Med Ketterin Med Cntr Kettering Ohio 1999-2001; CPE Res Kettering Med Cntr Kettering Ohio 1997-1999; R S Paul's Ch Bellevue OH 1994-1996; Assoc Chap Of The Cross Chap Hill NC 1993; Asst S Barth's Ch Pittsboro NC 1990-1993. Jn Templeton Fndt Awd For Sprtlty And Med Cirriculum In Primary Care (Med Residencies, $15,000).

KELLY, Shannon (Mil) 37 Grandwood Dr, Forestdale MA 02644 **Dom And Frgn Mssy Soc- Epis Ch Cntr New York NY 2014-** B Gooding ID 1973 d Earl & Margaret. Pacific U; BA U of Idaho 1995; MDiv CDSP 1999. D 11/8/1998 Bp John Stuart Thornton P 10/31/1999 Bp Harry Brown Bainbridge III. m 9/4/1999 Thomas C Ferguson c 1. Samar Fam Wellness Glendale WI 2014-2015; Epis Ch Cntr New York NY 2011-2012, Prov V Yth Mnstrs Liaison 2012-2014; Chr Formation Consult and Writer Epis Ch Cntr 2011; Chapl St Fran Hse Madison WI 2006-2009; Sr Assoc for Chld, Yth & Families All SS Ch Pasadena CA 2003-2006; Asst R Par of Chr the Redeem Pelham NY 2001-2003; Asst R for Chld and Yth S Mk's Epis Ch Palo Alto CA 1998-2001; COM Pres Dio Milwaukee Milwaukee WI 2009-2011, Chr Formation T/F Chair 2008-2009, COM Pres 2006-2009. Writer/Ed, "God of My Heart," *God of My Heart*, Ch Pub, 2012; Writer, "Lesson Plans that Wk," *Lesson Plans that Wk*, Epis Ch Cntr, 2011; Contrib, "Act Out! Yth Formation," *Water Camping Module*, Epis Relief and Dvlpmt, 2010. Epis Cams and Conf Centers 2009; Forma 2009. skelly@episcopalchurch.org

KELLY, Steven Joseph Patrick (Mich) 791 Westchester Rd, Grosse Pointe Park MI 48230 **R S Jn's Ch Detroit MI 2001-** B Brooklyn NY 1966 s Joseph & Sharon. U of Pennsylvania 1988; BA Tem 1991; MDiv Nash 1994. D 5/27/1994 Bp Edward Harding MacBurney P 11/26/1994 Bp Keith Lynn Ackerman. m 11/5/1994 Jennifer C Kelly c 4. Chapl Detroit Police Dept Chapl Corps 2004-2009; R S Mary's Ch Charleroi PA 1996-2001; Cur The Ch Of The Gd Shpd Rosemont PA 1994-1996. Angl P's Eucharistic League 1996; Conf of the

Blessed 1993; Forw in Faith No Amer 1995; Franciscan Ord of the Div Compassion 1995; GAS 1993; SocMary 1993; SocOLW 1997; SSC 1995. Wrdn Angl Priests Eucharistic League 2002.

KELLY, Tracey Elizabeth (Va) 9220 Georgetown Pike, Great Falls VA 22066 **S Fran Epis Ch Great Falls VA 2015-** B Baltimore MD 1965 BA GW 1987; MA VPI 1997; MDiv VTS 2011. D 6/4/2011 P 12/10/2011 Bp Shannon Sherwood Johnston. m 10/20/1990 David Graham Kelly c 3. Ch Of The H Comf Vienna VA 2013; Chr Ch Georgetown Washington DC 2012-2013; S Jn's Epis Ch Mc Lean VA 2012; St. Steph's And St. Agnes Sch Alexandria VA 2011-2015. tkelly@stfrancisgreatfalls.org

KELLY, Verneda Joan (Neb) 1014 N 6th St, Seward NE 68434 B Beatrice NE 1953 d Virgil & Alma. Cetificate of Presbyteral Stds Bp Kemper Sch for Mnstry 2015. D 1/31/2015 P 8/5/2015 Bp Scott Scott Barker. m 8/22/1998 Richard Owen Kelly c 3. D S Andr's Ch Seward NE 2015-2016.

KELM, Mark William (Minn) 109 Lawn Terrace, Golden Valley MN 55416 **Chapl U.S. Secret Serv- Minneapolis Dist 2009-; Chapl Intl Conf of Police Chapl 2000-; Conv Prlmntrn Dio Minnesota Minneapolis MN 2010-** B Red Wing MN 1970 s William & Judith. AAS Inver Hills Cmnty Coll 1992; BS Winona St U 1993; MDiv GTS 1999. D 5/27/1999 P 12/17/1999 Bp James Louis Jelinek. m 12/30/2000 Elizabeth Jane Hyduke-Kelm c 3. R S Jn In The Wilderness S Paul MN 2003-2016; Cn Liturg & Fam Pstr Cathd Ch Of S Mk Minneapolis MN 2000-2003; Asst R S Mart's By The Lake Epis Minnetonka Bch MN 1999-2000. Afr Friends in Need Ntwk 2004; Cmnty of the Cross of Nails 2002; Intl Conf of Police Chapl 2000. rector@stjohnwilderness.org

KELM, William Ernest (Minn) 1914 Launa Ave, Red Wing MN 55066 B Goodhue County MN 1941 s E H & Adeline. Hamline U; Winona St U. D 4/3/1986 Bp Robert Marshall Anderson. m 6/5/1965 Judith Annette Kelm c 2. Asst R S Mart's By The Lake Epis Minnetonka Bch MN 2000-2001.

KELMEREIT, Alan Henry (SwFla) 4554 Springview Cir, Labelle FL 33935 **Ch Of S Mich And All Ang Sanibel FL 2015-** B Paterson NJ 1942 s Henry & Margaret. BA Estrn U 1964; MPA Auburn U Montgomery 1973; MDiv TESM 1996. D 6/22/1996 P 12/22/1996 Bp Alden Moinet Hathaway. m 11/17/1967 Deborah E Spaeth c 2. Vic All Souls Epis Ch No Ft Myers FL 2010-2012; Vic The Ch Of The Gd Shpd Labelle FL 2003-2010; R Chr The King Epis Ch Beaver Falls PA 1996-2003; Dn, Ft Myers Dnry Dio SW Florida Parrish FL 2009-2012.

KELSEY, Anne Hunter (Mo) Po Box 4740, Saint Louis MO 63108 B Cleveland OH 1947 d Raymond & Barbara. U of Oregon; BA Mills Coll 1971; MDiv CDSP 1989. D 6/22/1989 Bp Robert Louis Ladehoff P 2/14/1990 Bp William Edwin Swing. m 9/30/1995 Brooke Myers c 3. R Trin Ch S Louis MO 2001-2013; Assoc S Jas Ch Fremont CA 1994-2001; Int S Anne's Ch Fremont CA 1993-1994; Asst All Souls Par In Berkeley Berkeley CA 1989-1993.

KELSEY, Julie Vietor (Ct) 38 Brocketts Point Rd, Branford CT 06405 **Asst Dn of Students Yale DS New Haven CT 2008-; Chapl to Chap on the Green Associated Cler Trin Ch on the Green New Haven 2013-** B New York NY 1942 d Thomas & Carolyn. BA Smith 1963; MS U of Bridgeport 1980; MDiv Ya Berk 1984; MDiv Yale DS 1984. D 6/8/1996 P 1/18/1997 Bp Clarence Nicholas Coleridge. m 5/9/1987 David Hugh Kelsey c 2. R Gr And S Ptr's Epis Ch Hamden CT 2001-2008; Calv Epis Ch Bridgeport CT 2001; Assoc R Trin Epis Ch Southport CT 1996-2000.

KELSEY II, Preston Telford (Ct) Kendal @ Hanover #213, 80 Lyme Rd., Hanover NH 03755 **Ret 1998-** B Montclair NJ 1936 s Preston & Suzanne. BA Dart 1958; BD CDSP 1961. D 6/25/1961 P 5/7/1962 Bp James Albert Pike. m 5/21/1966 Virginia Kelsey c 4. Asst to PB Dom And Frgn Mssy Soc- Epis Ch Cntr New York NY 1996-1998; Trst Fndt for Theol Educ 1991-1999; Executive Dir BTE Epis Ch Cntr New York NY 1984-1998; R Trsfg Epis Ch San Mateo CA 1973-1984, R 1973-1984; Cur 1961-1962; R S Alb's Ch Albany CA 1966-1973; Cur S Thos Ch Hanover NH 1963-1966; Cur S Ptr Redcar Yorks Engl (C of E) 1962-1963. DD VTS 2013; DD CDSP 1990; DD St. Paul's Coll, VA 1986.

KELSEY, Stephen (Az) 138 N White Willow Pl, Tucson AZ 85710 **P Assoc Gr St Pauls Epis Ch Tucson AZ 2014-; Mssnr/Supt Grtr Hartford Reg Mnstry 2004-** B Baltimore MD 1952 s Arthur & Louise. BA Colby Coll 1974; MDiv GTS 1979. D 6/1/1979 Bp Robert Shaw Kerr P 11/30/1979 Bp David Rea Cochran. m 1/14/1984 Kathleen M Barrett c 3. Mnstry Dvlp Navajoland Area Mssn Farmington NM 2010-2012; Mssnr Supt Grtr Hartford Reg Mnstry E Hartford CT 2004-2009; Int S Ptr's Epis Ch Hebron CT 2003-2004; Dir Harvesters Partnership New Haven CT 2003; EDS Cambridge MA 2002; Coordntr Harvesters Partnership Of New Engl 2001-2003; Mssnr Ch Of The Epiph Durham CT 1995-2001; Mssnr Emm S Ch Killingworth CT 1995-2001; Mssnr S Andr's Ch Northford CT 1995-2001; Mssnr S Jas Epis Ch Higganum CT 1995-2001; Mssnr S Paul's Ch Westbrook CT 1995-2001; Mssnr Middlesex Area Cluster Mnstry Higganum CT 1994-2001; Mssnr Dio Nthrn Michigan Marquette MI 1993-1994; Estrn Upper Peninsula Epis Convoc Moran MI 1992-1994; R Chr Ch Warwick NY 1988-1992; Mssnr Tri-Cnty Epis Area Mnstry Monticello NY 1982-1988; Dio Alaska Fairbanks AK 1979-1982; S Andr's Epis Ch Petersburg AK 1979-1982; Co-R S Phil's Ch Wrangell AK

1979-1982; Outreach Worker S Jn The Bapt Epis Hardwick VT 1974-1976. Design Team, "Lifecycles: Chr Transformation In Cmnty," 2003; Auth, "Celebrating The Mnstry Of All The Baptized At The Welcoming Of," *A PB For The 21st Century: Lit Stds 3*, 1996; Auth, "Mnstry Or Discipleship?," *Mnstry In Daily Life*, 1996; Auth, "Celebrating Baptismal Mnstry At The Welcoming Of New Min," *Baptism & Mnstry*, 1994; Ed Team, "Re-Shaping Mnstry," Jethro, 1990. Leaveners 1997-2004; New Directions/New Directions NE 1976-2004; Roland Allen Forum Of The NE 1996-2003; Sindicators 1985-2003.

KELSON, Laura Jayne (CGC) 1 Saint Francis Dr, Gulf Breeze FL 32561 B Pensacola FL 1962 d Charles & Elanor Laura. BS Troy St U; AS Troy St U; Vocational D D Sch - Dio the Cntrl Gulf Coast 2014. D 2/22/2014 Bp Philip Menzie Duncan II.

KELTON, Barbara Smoot (Dal) 719 Pampa Street, Sulphur Springs TX 75482 **Vic S Philips Epis Ch Sulphur Spgs TX 2007-** B Dallas TX 1946 d Lloyd & Fay. BA Baylor U 1968; MS Baylor U 1973; Lic Sacr Theol Angl TS 1986. D 6/14/1986 P 7/8/1987 Bp Donis Dean Patterson. m 4/19/1969 Edward F Kelton c 2. S Fran Ch Winnsboro TX 2007-2008; Mssnr to Campus Mnstry Epis Dio Dallas 1996-2005; Chapl S Alb's Collgt Chap -SMU Dallas TX 1996-2005; Bp Mason Retreat & Conf Cntr 1992-1995; Bd Trst Angl TS 1991-1994; Fac Angl TS 1991-1994; Asst The Epis Ch Of The Trsfg Dallas TX 1986-1996. CHS.

KEM, Robert Andrew (Ia) 538 NW Scott St, Ankeny IA 50023 B Des Moines IA 1953 s Robert & Roselyn. BS Simpson Coll 1975; MS Wstrn Illinois U 1980; MDiv SWTS 1985. D 5/17/1985 Bp Walter Cameron Righter P 2/2/1986 Bp Wesley Frensdorff. m 8/9/1975 Debra Kem c 2. S Anne's By The Fields Ankeny IA 2002-2016; R S Andr's Ch Omaha NE 1990-2002; Assoc S Barn On The Desert Scottsdale AZ 1985-1990; Pres Stndg Com Dio Nebraska Omaha NE 1998-2001, Chair of Nomin Com 1994-1997, Chair of Nomin Commitee 1990-1993. Pres Ankeny Mnstrl Assn 2003-2015; Rotary Intl 2002-2009; Screen Actors Gld About Schmidt 2002-2002. Cmnty Eductr of the Year Ankeny Cmnty Educ 2014; Opened US Senate in Pryr Senator Chuck Hagel 1998; Thos Arkle Clark Awd ATO Nationals 1975; Pres of ATO Fraternity Beta Alpha Chapt 1974. rector@saechurch.org

KEM SR, Robert William (Ia) 3013 - 34th Street Place, Des Moines IA 50310 **Died 6/25/2017** B Davenport IA 1921 s Daniel & Birdie. BS S Ambr U 1942; STM EDS 1949; MRE Drake U 1957; Coll of Preachers 1962; ETSBH 1963. D 6/29/1949 Bp Elwood L Haines P 5/1/1950 Bp Gordon V Smith. c 1. Ret 1988-2017; Vic S Jn's Lincoln Engl 1965-1966; S Andr's Ch Des Moines IA 1961-1987; Cur The Cathd Ch Of S Paul Des Moines IA 1949-1951. Des Moines Rotary Club 1984; Emer Club S Ambr U 1992. Hon Cn (Lifetime) S Paul'S Cathd 2000; Hon Cn Trinty Cathd 1974.

KEMEZA, Maureen Dallison (Mass) 17 Munroe Pl., Concord MA 01742 B Scranton PA 1948 d Donald & Marie. BA Rutgers The St U of New Jersey 1970; MDiv EDS 1977; PhD Boston Coll 1993. D 6/1/1991 Bp David Elliot Johnson P 5/15/1992 Bp Barbara Clementine Harris. m 9/24/1971 William J Kemeza c 2. Assoc Trin Ch Concord MA 2010-2013, Assoc 1991-1993, P-in-c Emm Ch Boston MA 2005-2007; R Par Of S Paul Newton Highlands MA 1996-2005; Int Gr Ch Salem MA 1995-1996.

KEMMERER, Stanley Courtright (Ct) Po Box 2025, Burlington CT 06013 B Brooklyn NY 1943 s Lorenzo & Edna. AB Mid 1965; Hartford Sem 1967; MDiv CDSP 1969. D 6/24/1969 Bp Harvey D Butterfield P 12/28/1969 Bp Gordon V Smith. m 6/3/2000 Nancy Harwood Kemmerer. P-in-c Chr Ch Par Epis Watertown CT 2009-2010; P-in-c Trin Epis Ch Bristol CT 2007-2009; Assoc Chr Ch Cathd Hartford CT 2006-2007; Assoc Trin Epis Ch Collinsville CT 2002-2006; Supply P Dio Connecticut Meriden CT 1998-2002; P Assoc S Andr's Ch Wellesley MA 1996-1997; Assoc Trin Ch Concord MA 1988-1996; P-in-c Chr And Epiph Ch E Haven CT 1969-2013; P S Paul's Ch Durant IA 1969-1978; Evan Com Dio Iowa Des Moines IA 1972-1978. Assoc Of H Cross 1962-2015. stankemmerer@challengergray.com

KEMMLER, Richard Sigmund (NY) 1420 Pine Bay Dr, Sarasota FL 34231 **Asst S Marg Of Scotland Epis Ch Sarasota FL 2009-** B Chattanooga TN 1937 s Richard & Viola. BS U of Chattanooga 1965; MA Portland St U 1968; PhD NYU 1972; MDiv GTS 1990. D 1/23/1991 P 9/21/1991 Bp Walter Decoster Dennis Jr. Int Ch Of The Gd Shpd Granite Spgs NY 2003-2004; Int Ch Of The Ascen Staten Island NY 2000-2001, 1993-1994; Int S Lk's Ch Forest Hills NY 1998-1999; S Ptr's Ch New York NY 1996-1997; Int Chr Ch New Brighton Staten Island NY 1994-1995; Asst Chr Ch Riverdale Bronx NY 1991-1992.

KEMP, Drusilla Rawlings (Ky) Church Of The Advent, 901 Baxter Ave, Louisville KY 40204 **D Ch Of The Adv Louisville KY 2012-** B Manchester 1943 d William & Jane. BSW U of Kentucky 1965; MSSW U of Louisville 1967; PhD U of Louisville 2006; Cert Coll of Mnstry/Dio Kentucky 2011. D 12/4/2012 Bp Terry Allen White. m 12/1/1979 William L Kemp c 1.

KEMP, Matthew Benjamin (WK) 138 S 8th St, Salina KS 67401 **S Paul's By The Lake Chicago IL 2015-** B Columbus OH 1985 s Raymond & Karen. BA No Pk U 2009; MDiv Nash 2013. D 11/1/2014 P 5/10/2015 Bp Mike Milliken. m 5/29/2010 Alethea Anna Savoy c 2. Chr Cathd Salina KS 2014-2015, Cur 2013-2014. Soc of Schlr Priests 2014.

KEMP, Rowena Jessica (Ct) 55 New Park Ave, Hartford CT 06106 **Gr Epis Ch Hartford CT 2016-; Asst Trin Ch On The Green New Haven CT 2014-** B Nassau Bahamas 1966 d Audley & Diane. BS Coll of Mt St Vinc 1991; MS/MPH Sch of Publ Hlth - NY Med Coll 2003; MDiv Ya Berk 2013; MDiv Ya Berk 2013. D 6/8/2013 P 12/14/2013 Bp Ian Theodore Douglas. Middlesex Area Cluster Mnstry Higganum CT 2013-2014. revrowenagrace@frontier.com

KEMPF, Barbara Anne (Ind) St Christopher's Episcopal Church, 1402 W Main St, Carmel IN 46032 **P S Paul's Epis Ch Indianapolis IN 2013-** B Connersville IN 1959 d Fred & Ruth. BSN Indiana U 1982; JD Indiana U 1987; MDiv SWTS 2007. D 6/23/2007 P 6/1/2008 Bp Cate Waynick. m 9/5/1987 Richard Allen Kempf c 3. S Chris's Epis Ch Carmel IN 2009-2012; Assoc Dio Indianapolis Indianapolis IN 2007-2009; Cur S Matt's Ch Indianapolis IN 2007-2009. kempfbarbara@hotmail.com

KEMPF, Victoria Nystrom (Colo) 2220 Katahdin Dr, Fort Collins CO 80525 B Pittsburgh PA 1946 d George & Lillian. BA Barrington Coll 1969; MDiv SWTS 1986; DMin GTF 2006. D 6/14/1986 Bp James Winchester Montgomery P 12/13/1986 Bp Frank Tracy Griswold III. m 6/6/1987 Joseph Kempf c 2. Int S Paul's Epis Ch Ft Collins CO 2002-2004; Int S Matt's Ch Grand Jct CO 2001-2002; Dio SW Florida Parrish FL 1997-2001, Cn for Mnstry Dev 1999-2001, Dep for Cmncatn 1997-1999; Assoc Ch Of The Gd Shpd Punta Gorda FL 1995-1997; Int S Nich w the H Innoc Ch Elk Grove Vlg IL 1994-1995; Int S Lawr Epis Ch Libertyville IL 1991-1993; S Edw The Mtyr and Chr Epis Ch Joliet IL 1990-1991; Int Ch Of The H Fam Lake Villa IL 1989-1990; Dio Chicago Chicago IL 1988; Ch Of Our Sav Elmhurst IL 1987-1988; Cur S Richard's Ch Chicago IL 1986-1987. Hon Cn Cathd Ch of St. Ptr 1999.

KEMPSELL JR, Howard Frederic (Va) Post Office Box 2360, Centreville VA 20122 **S Andr's Ch Burke VA 2016-; S Ptr's Epis Ch Arlington VA 2014-; P & Yth Min Fairfax Chinese Chr Ch Centreville VA 2002-; VTS Alexandria VA 2007-** B Morristown NJ 1954 s Howard & Jane. Emory U 1974; BA U Rich 1976; MDiv VTS 1980; DMin GTF 1992. D 6/14/1980 Bp John Shelby Spong P 2/15/1981 Bp George Paul Reeves. m 6/28/1980 Ann Gore Kempsell c 2. S Andr's Epis Ch Arlington VA 2015; Design Team & Fac - The Art of Sprtl Comp Cathd of St Ptr & St Paul Washington DC 2007-2009; Cler Ldrshp Proj - Class XV Trin Par New York NY 2002-2006; R S Jn's Ch Centreville VA 1994-2013; R Chr Ch Par Plymouth MA 1990-1994; Dio Upper So Carolina Columbia SC 1985-1990; Trin Ch Statesboro GA 1982-1985; S Paul's Ch Albany GA 1980-1982; Cmsn on Congrl Dvlpmt (Percept) Dio Massachusetts Boston MA 1992-1994. Auth, "The Changing Context of Sprtl Direction:S D in an Age of Mobility w Var Means of Rapid Cmncatn," *The Fellows Yearbook*, GTF, 1992. Assoc, Sis of S Marg 1994. Coordntr for Visits of His Gr, the Archbp of Canterbu Dio Upper SC 1987.

KEMPSON-THOMPSON, Deborah (Nev) 1776 US Highway 50, Glenbrook NV 89413 B Pensacola FL 1947 d Burnehe & Eliz. BA U of W Florida 1972; MA U of W Florida 1990; MDiv CDSP 2008; MDiv CDSP 2008. D 11/9/2014 P 5/2/2015 Bp Dan Thomas Edwards. c 1.

KEMPSTER, Jane (WNC) 10450 Lottsford Rd Apt 355, Mitchellville MD 20721 B Chico CA 1937 d James & Flora. BA California St U 1959; MA Wesley TS 1993; DAS VTS 1995. D 10/31/1995 P 6/15/1996 Bp John Henry Smith. m 6/30/1957 Norman Roy Kempster c 2. Chapl Washington Natl Cathd 2007-2015; R S Lk's Epis Ch Lincolnton NC 2002-2006; Asst P Nelson Cluster Of Epis Ch Rippon WV 1996-2002.

KEMPSTER, Patricia Sue (NCal) 2098 Tracy Court, Folsom CA 95630 **Assoc R Trin Ch Folsom CA 2005-, Assoc R 2001-2005** B Albany CA 1935 d Robert & Majorie. BS Geo Mason U 1994; VTS 1996; MDiv CDSP 1997. D 3/26/2000 P 10/28/2000 Bp Jerry Alban Lamb. m 5/22/1982 Thomas Kempster. Asst R Epis Ch Of Our Sav Placerville CA 2000-2001; VTS Alexandria VA 1991-1993; Ch Of The Gd Shpd Burke VA 1988-1991. Natl Cler Assn 2000; Nthrn California Cler Assn 2000.

KENDALL, Michael Jonah (NC) 403 E Main St, Durham NC 27701 **S Phil's Ch Durham NC 2008-** B Waterbury CT 1974 s Michael & Janet. BA S Lawr Canton NY 1996; MDiv VTS 2001. D 3/10/2001 P Richard Frank Grein P 9/16/2001 Bp Mark Sean Sisk. m 9/21/2002 Catherine Kendall c 2. All SS Ch Harrison NY 2003-2007; Asst To The R Ch Of The H Trin New York NY 2001-2003.

KENDALL, Michael Samuel (NY) 9 1/2 Church St, Bristol RI 02809 B Cincinnati OH 1940 s Harry & Blanche. BA Earlham Coll 1962; Oxf GB 1962; Ya 1965; MDiv GTS 1966. D 6/11/1966 Bp Walter H Gray P 12/17/1966 Bp John Henry Esquirol. m 5/25/1985 Anne Kendall c 3. Pres Epis Ntwk for Econ Justice 2002-2005; Chair Natl Jubilee Grants Prog 2000-2003; Chair Publ Plcy Com New York St Coun of Ch 1999-2008; Pres Fndt for St Mart-in-the-Fields London 1998-2015; Pres Coun of Ch of New York City 1997-2000; Secy Advsry Coun to the Angl Observer to the UN 1995-2005; Pres Global Epis Mssn 1994-2000; Archd Dio New York New York NY 1984-2008; Jubilee Off Dio New York 1984-2008; Co-Chair EUC 1980; Chair Stndg Cmsn Ch in Metropltn Areas 1979-1982; R Ch Of S Jas The Less Scarsdale NY 1978-1984; Pres Ch and City Conf 1977-1980; Pres Coun of Ch of Waterbury Connecticut

459

1974-1978; Dep GC 1973-2000; R S Jn's Epis Par Waterbury CT 1968-1978; Cur S Jn's Ch Stamford CT 1966-1968. Auth, "Jub Report To Stndg Com Of GC"; Auth, "Trial Baptism Liturg," *Chr Initiation*. Archd Emer Dio New York 2008; EAAM' Cross Epis Asiamerica Minisrties 2003; Bp'S Cross Dio New York 2000.

KENDALL-SPERRY, David (O) St Paul Episcopal Church, 100 E High St, Mount Vernon OH 43050 **Treas Global Epis Mssn Ntwk Dublin Ohio 2015-; Cmsn Mem Cmsn for Global & Dom Mssn 2013-; R S Paul's Ch Mt Vernon OH 2012-; Mem Natl & Wrld Mssn Cmsn 2009-; Dioc Disciplinary Bd Dio Ohio Cleveland 2016-, Chair, Cmsn for Global and Dom Mssn 2014-2015, Bd Mem, Cmsn for Global and Dom Mssn 2013-2016** B Iowa 1955 s George & Patricia. BA Simpson Coll 1977; MDiv Bex Sem 2008. D 6/23/2007 P 6/28/2008 Bp Thomas Edward Breidenthal. m 8/27/1977 Karen Kendall-Sperry c 3. Bd Dir Mem Global Epis Mssn Ntwk Dublin Ohio 2014-2017; Pres Epis Cmnty Serv Fndt 2010-2011; Trst Epis Cmnty Serv Fndt 2008-2011; Asst to R S Jn's Ch Worthington OH 2008-2011; D S Matt's Epis Ch Westerville OH 2007-2008, D 2007; Pres, Epis Cmnty Serv Fndt Dio Sthrn Ohio Cincinnati OH 2009-2011, Trst, Epis Cmnty Serv Fndt 2007-2011. BroSA 1989; Sigma Chi Fraternity 1974.

KENDRICK, David (WMo) St Johnh's Church, 515 E Division St, Springfield MO 65803 **P S Jn's Ch Springfield MO 2013-** B Vero Beach FL 1961 s Robert & Bobbye. BA Wofford Coll 1983; MDiv VTS 2007. D 6/16/2007 Bp Peter J Lee P 12/17/2007 Bp David Colin Jones. m 6/27/1987 Laura M Moore c 1. Chr Epis Ch Albertville AL 2009-2013; The Ch Of The Epiph Oak Hill VA 2008; S Dav's Ch Ashburn VA 2007-2008.

⨯ **KENDRICK, The Rt Rev Russell** (CGC) 3557 Hampshire Drive, Birmingham AL 35223 **Dio Cntrl Gulf Coast Pensacola FL 2015-** B Fort Walton Bch FL 1960 s Claude & Helen. BS Auburn U 1984; BA Auburn U 1984; MDiv VTS 1995. D 5/27/1995 P 1/28/1996 Bp Charles Farmer Duvall Con 7/25/2015 for CGC. m 7/11/1987 Robin Kendrick c 2. R S Steph's Epis Ch Birmingham AL 2007-2015; R S Paul's Epis Ch Newnan GA 1998-2006; Cur The Epis Ch Of The Nativ Dothan AL 1995-1998. russell@diocgc.org

KENDRICK, William Barton (NCal) 19 Five Iron Ct, Chico CA 95928 **Ret 1997-** B Saint Louis MO 1932 s Warren & Gertrude. BS U of Arizona 1954; BD CDSP 1957. D 8/3/1957 P 2/1/1958 Bp William F Lewis. c 3. R S Mich And All Ang Ch Ft Bragg CA 1991-1997; The Epis Dio Nthrn California Sacramento CA 1987-1993; H Trin Epis Ch Willows CA 1978-1991; Ch Of The Gd Shpd Orland CA 1978-1983; Ch Of The Incarn Santa Rosa CA 1973-1978; R S Steph's Epis Ch Colusa CA 1965-1973; Vic S Fran Ch Fortuna CA 1960-1965; S Mary's Mssn Ferndale CA 1960-1965; Vic S Barn In Dunsmuir & S Jn In Mccloud 1959-1960; Cur Trin Epis Ch Reno NV 1957-1959.

KENNA, Jennifer Anne (CNY) 235 John St, Clayton NY 13624 **Chr Ch Clayton NY 2017-** B Pawtucket, RI 1947 d Henry & Mildred. BA Syr 1969; Cert Dioc Formation Prog 2010. D 5/1/2010 P 6/18/2011 Bp Gladstone Bailey Adams III. c 3. Asst Trin Epis Ch Watertown NY 2012-2016.

KENNARD, Susan Johnson (Tex) 3000 Ave L, Bay City TX 77414 **R Trin Ch Galveston TX 2012-** B Houston TX 1955 d Joseph & Joyce. BSN U of Texas 1976; MDiv VTS 2004. D 6/12/2004 P 12/12/2004 Bp Don Adger Wimberly. m 11/18/1977 William Walker Kennard c 1. R S Mk's Ch Bay City TX 2006-2012; Asst R S Mk's Ch Beaumont TX 2004-2006.

KENNEDY, Arthur Thomas (Ida) 261 Los Lagos, Twin Falls ID 83301 **Ret 1990-** B Los Angeles 1926 s Raymond & Elizabeth. BA U CA 1950; MDiv CDSP 1970. D 6/27/1970 P 2/6/1971 Bp Chauncie Kilmer Myers. Dn of Formation For Mnstry Dio Idaho Boise ID 1991-1997, 1988-1989, Pres Mstrl Assn 1981-1985; Mtn Rivers Epis Cmnty Idaho Falls ID 1989-1991; S Jn's Ch Amer Fls ID 1982; S Paul's Ch Blackfoot ID 1980-1988; Vic S Aug Fairfax CA 1976-1980; St Augustines Ch Fairfax CA 1976-1980; Asst Min Chr Epis Ch Los Altos CA 1970-1973.

KENNEDY, David Crichton (SeFla) 7231 Hearth Stone Ave, Boynton Beach FL 33437 **P-in-c The Ch Of The Guardian Ang Lake Worth FL 2007-, 1966-2003** B Floral Park NY 1937 s Albert & Emma. BA U of Miami 1959; MDiv Nash 1963. D 6/15/1963 Bp James Loughlin Duncan P 12/21/1963 Bp Henry I Louttit. m 5/23/1967 Beverly J Kennedy c 2. Nash Nashotah WI 1985-1993; Alum Trst Dio SE Florida Miami 1985-1987; R S Cuth's Ch Boynton Bch FL 1969-2003; Chapl Florida NG 1966-1992; Cur All SS Epis Ch Lakeland FL 1963-1966. All SS Sis of the Poor P Assoc; CBS; Fllshp of Concerned Churchmen; Forw in Faith; GAS; PB Soc; Shrine of Our Lady of Walsingham; Soc of King Chas the Mtyr; SSC, SocMary. DD Nash Nashotah WI 2002.

KENNEDY, David Kittle (Haw) 1 Keahole Pl Apt 3409, Honolulu HI 96825 **Mentor Dioc Post Educ Prog 2013-** B Alamosa CO 1932 s Harry & Katharine. BA Trin Hartford CT 1954; MDiv CDSP 1963. D 7/7/1963 P 1/12/1964 Bp Harry Sherbourne Kennedy. m 11/1/1956 Anna Marie Kennedy c 4. Int R H Nativ Ch Honolulu HI 2012-2013; Int R St. Chris's Ch Kailua HI 2011-2012; R Trin Ch By The Sea Kihei HI 2007-2008; Asstg P S Andr's Cathd Honolulu HI 2000-2005; R S Ptr's Ch Honolulu HI 1998-2000, Comm. on Dioc. Status, Chair 1968-1997; Int R S Chris's Epis Ch Honolulu HI 1996-1998; Headmaster S Andr's Priory Sch Honolulu HI 1981-1996; R S Tim's Ch Aiea HI 1973-1981; Reserve Chapl U.S. AF 1969-2000; Vstng P Ch of the Ascen Kwajalein Atoll Marshall Islands 1969-1972; Vic S Barn' Epis Ch Honolulu HI 1963-1968; Dep to Gen'l Conv, '70,'73,'76,'79,'82,'85,'91 The Epis Ch in Hawaii Honolulu HI 2004-2009, Chair, Int Mgmt Comm. 1994-1995, Stndg Com, Pres. 1991-1995, Dep, GC 1991, Chair, Int Mgmt Comm. 1985-1986, Dioc Coun, Pres. 1983-1986, Co-chair, VIM 1980, Stndg Com, Pres. 1978-1981, Chair, Int Mgmt Comm. 1975-1976, Trst, St. Andr's Priory 1973-2004, Fin Com 1973-1976, Dioc Coun, VP and Pres 1971-1978, Dep, GC 1970-1985, Dn, Honolulu Dnry 1970-1973, Comm on Dioc Status 1968-1969, Comm on Dioc Status, Chair 1968-1969. DSC Dio Hawaii 1971.

KENNEDY, Dennis (Colo) **Supply P Ch of Colorado Epis Dio 2016-; Formation Team Epis Serv Corps Colorado 2014-** B 1946 M. Div. DeAndreis Sem 1973; M.A. U of Notre Dame 1973; Doctorate in Mnstry CUA 1985. Rec 6/18/ 2016 as Priest Bp Robert John O'Neill. m 4/30/1994 Mary Kennedy.

KENNEDY, Ellen Kathleen (Ct) 243 Harbor St, Branford CT 06405 B Staten Island NY 1949 D 6/8/2002 P 4/12/2003 Bp Andrew Donnan Smith. c 2. Vic Trin Epis Ch Trumbull CT 2006-2016; Asst Calv Epis Ch Bridgeport CT 2003-2006.

KENNEDY, Gary Grant (Kan) 1900 E Front St, Galena KS 66739 **P S Mary's Epis Ch Galena KS 1999-; Assoc S Steph's Ch Columbus KS 1999-** B Joplin MO 1940 s Claude & Catherine. BS Pittsburg St U 1964; MS Pittsburg St U 2003. D 7/20/1999 P 2/15/2000 Bp William Edward Smalley. m 8/6/1960 Carol Rae Means. stmarysgalena@wordpress.com

KENNEDY, Hilda L (WVa) Po Box 665, Northfork WV 24868 **D S Lk/Sthrn Cluster Northfork WV 2000-** B Wyoming County WV 1945 d Ray & Eugenia. BA Concord U 1966; BSW Concord U 1987. D 6/10/2000 Bp Claude Charles Vache. Dio W Virginia Charleston WV 2000-2008; Mc Dowell Reg Mnstrs Welch WV 2000-2008.

KENNEDY, John Ira (Ala) **S Paul's Ch Greensboro AL 2016-** D 5/14/2016 P 11/12/2016 Bp John Mckee Sloan Sr.

KENNEDY, Karen (Oly) D 10/13/2015 Bp Gregory Harold Rickel.

KENNEDY, Nan N (At) 790 Bellhaven Chase Ct, Mableton GA 30126 B Taylor TX 1953 d William & Virginia. BS U of Texas 1977; MDiv Epis TS of the SW 1992. D 6/13/1992 P 1/16/1993 Bp Robert Manning Moody. m 11/20/ 1993 Stephen Glen Kennedy. Ch Of The Redeem Greensboro GA 2015; Assoc S Lk's Epis Ch Atlanta GA 2003-2008; All SS Epis Sch Beaumont TX 1998-2002; Assoc R S Steph's Ch Beaumont TX 1998-2001; Holland Hall Sch Tulsa OK 1997-1998; Chapl Holland Hall Sch Tulsa OK 1997-1998; Trin Ch Tulsa OK 1996-1997, 1992-1995.

KENNEDY, Thomas B (Mass) 46 Glen Road, Brookline MA 02445 B New Milford CT 1942 s Robert & Roberta. BA Claremont McKenna Coll 1964; BD EDS 1968. D 6/22/1968 Bp Anson Phelps Stokes Jr P 5/15/1969 Bp John Melville Burgess. m 8/29/1964 Joanna W Kennedy c 3. Bay Bank/Bank-Boston/Sovereign Bank Boston MA 1989-2008; P S Paul's Ch Brookline MA 1989-1991; Dn The Cathd Ch Of S Paul Boston MA 1983-1989; Trin Ch Epis Boston MA 1968-1983, Outreach 1968-1983, Min to Stdts 1968-1970. Auth, "Article," *Jesus Dollars & Sense*. Morris F Arnold Awd, Epis City Mssn.

KENNEDY, Zelda (Los) 2194 Cooley Pl, Pasadena CA 91104 **Assoc All SS Ch Pasadena CA 2003-** B Nassau BS 1947 d Cyril & Mildred. D 6/4/2000 Bp Robert Carroll Johnson Jr P 4/28/2001 Bp Michael B Curry. S Pat's Epis Ch Mooresville NC 2000-2003.

KENNELLY, Margery (Mass) 379 Hammond St, Chestnut Hill MA 02467 B Baltimore MD 1965 d William & Barbara. AB Harvard Coll 1987; MDiv Gordon-Conwell TS 2010; Advnced Theol study EDS 2011. D 6/2/2012 Bp Gayle Harris P 1/13/2013 Bp M(Arvil) Thomas Shaw. m 10/29/1988 Richard B Kennelly c 2. Ch Of The Redeem Chestnut Hill MA 2012-2017. MKENNELLY@REDEEMERCHESNUTHILL.ORG

KENNEY, Christine Swarts (Okla) 505 Fieldstone Dr, Georgetown TX 78633 B Rushville IN 1944 BS Butler U 1967; MDiv Epis TS of the SW 2002. D 6/29/ 2002 P 2/8/2003 Bp Robert Manning Moody. m 6/17/1967 Joseph Kenney c 2.

KENNEY, Marguerite Shirley (SVa) 800 Little John Ct, Virginia Beach VA 23455 **Died 5/13/2017** B Cincinnati OH 1924 d Harvey & Helen. BA U Cinc 1946; MDiv VTS 1977. D 6/25/1977 Bp William Foreman Creighton P 2/27/ 1978 Bp John Thomas Walker. c 7. Ret 1988-2017; Gd Samar Epis Ch Virginia Bch VA 1983-1988; Chr Ch Chaptico MD 1982; S Marg's Ch Woodbridge VA 1980-1981; St Johns Broad Creek Ft Washington MD 1977-1980. Chapl Ord Of S Lk; Curs.

KENNINGTON, Curtis A (CGC) **S Mk's Epis Ch Troy AL 2017-; The GTS New York NY 2014-** D 12/3/2016 Bp Russell Kendrick.

KENNINGTON, Spergeon Albert (CGC) 212 Margaret Dr, Fairhope AL 36532 **Assoc S Paul's Epis Ch Daphne AL 2008-; Chapl to Ret Cler/Spouses Dio Cntrl Gulf Coast 2013-; Secy of Dio Dio the Cntrl Gulf Coast 2013-; Mem, Prog Chair Mobile Chr-Jewish Dialogue Bd Dir 2008-; Dep GC 2006-; Dep GC 2000-; Dep GC 1997-; Dep GC 1994-; Dep GC 1991-; Dep GC 1988-; Dep GC 1985-; Dep GC 1982-** B Butler AL 1942 s Spergeon & Florence. BS Troy U 1964; MA U of Alabama 1967; MDiv Sewanee: The U So, TS 1974. D 6/20/1974 P 5/17/1975 Bp George Mosley Murray. m 12/20/1969 Nancy Butler Kennington c 3. R Trin Epis Ch Mobile AL 1985-2007, 1983-2007, Cur 1983-1985, 1974-1977; R S Mary's Epis Ch Milton FL 1977-1983; Vic S Monica's Cantonment FL 1977-1978; Secy of Dio Dio the Cntrl Gulf Coast 2004-2009; Mem SCER 1994-2000; Secy of Dio Dio the Cntrl Gulf Coast 1986-1991; Mem, Stndg Com Dio the Cntrl Gulf Coast 1983-1986; Mem, Stndg Com Dio the Cntrl Gulf Coast 1978-1981; Secy of Dio Dio the Cntrl Gulf Coast 1977-1981. Auth, "arts," *Forw Day by Day*, Forw Mvmt, 2011; Auth, "Hearing God through the Noise," Forw Mvmt, 2008; Auth, "From The Day Of Sm Things," Factor Press, 1996; Auth, "The Epis Ch: A Primer For Inquirers," Self; Auth, "arts," *Angl Dig*; Auth, "arts," *Living Ch.* revsak@gmail.com

KENNY JR, John Roy (Md) 9106 River Crescent Dr, Annapolis MD 21401 B Portland OR 1922 s John & Flora. BS U CA 1944; SWTS 1972; EFM Sewanee: The U So, TS 1983. D 9/16/1972 Bp James Winchester Montgomery. c 4. Assoc S Andr's Ch Pasadena MD 1998-2016; Asst S Anne's Par Annapolis MD 1998-2016; Asst S Paul's Epis Ch Bantam CT 1986-1997; Asst S Ann's Epis Ch Old Lyme CT 1978-1986; Asst S Jas' Epis Ch Of Pentwater Pentwater MI 1976-1978; Asst Trin Ch Long Green MD 1973-1976; Asst The Epis Ch Of S Jas The Less Northfield IL 1972-1973.

KENNY, Susie Fowler (Los) 1020 N. Brand Blvd., Glendale CA 91202 **D S Mk's Par** Glendale CA 2008- B Inglewood CA 1956 d Luther & Gwendolyn. D 5/25/2008 Bp Chester Lovelle Talton. c 3. susie@saintmarks.la

KENT, Clifford Eugene (NCal) 5555 Montgomery Dr # 62, Santa Rosa CA 95409 **Died 11/26/2016** B Butler County KS 1920 s Oris & Lucy. BD Pur 1942; Cert Dioc Sch/Mnstrs CA 1980; BS Pur 2042. D 3/25/1982 P 3/19/1984 Bp Charles Shannon Mallory. m 6/24/2006 Virginia Canfield-Kent c 3. Assoc S Patricks Ch Kenwood CA 1990-2016; Asst P Trin Ch Sonoma CA 1987-1989; Assoc S Andr's Ch Saratoga CA 1982-1986; Supply P The Epis Dio Nthrn California Sacramento CA 1987-2016. Auth, "Environ Aspects of Nuclear Power Stations," *ASME Journal*, Int'l Atomic Energy Agcy, 1971; Auth, "Environ Aspects of Nuclear Power Stations," *Intl Atomic Energy Agcy*, 1970. Amer Chem Soc 1943; Amer Inst of Chem Engr 2043-1982. Three USA Patents in High Energy Batteries US Patent Off (1966-1968) 1966.

KENT, David Williamson (Kan) 1900 Spyglass Court, Lawrence KS 66047 **P-in-c S Tim's Ch Iola KS 2015-; Ret 2002-; Consult CODE (CODE) 2002-** B Montclair,NJ 1938 s Frederick & Helen. BA U of Wisconsin 1960; MDiv Nash 1963; MEd Bos 1972; MA LIU 1974; Command and Gnrl Stff Coll 1978; US-A War Coll 1984. D 3/9/1963 Bp Robert E Campbell P 9/21/1963 Bp Donald H V Hallock. m 5/8/1965 Orean H Kent c 1. Mem Ch Deploymnt Bd 2000-2006; Cn Ordnry Dio Kansas Topeka KS 1992-2002; Asst S Mich And All Ang Ch Mssn KS 1987-1992; Chapl (COL) USA Off Of Bsh For ArmdF New York NY 1966-1987; Cur Ch Milwaukee WI 1963-1966. Mltry Chapl Assn 1970. Legion of Merit US-A 1987; Phi Beta Kappa 1960.

KENT, Stuart Matthews (Dal) PO Box 429, North Stonington CT 06359 B Westerly RI 1944 BA U of Connecticut 1966; STB Ya Berk 1969. D 6/21/1969 P 6/1/1970 Bp John S Higgins. m 6/8/1968 Paula S McNutt. S Dav's Ch Garland TX 2001-2008; S Anne's Epis Ch Desoto TX 1991-1992; St Gabriels Ch Desoto TX 1987-1991; Dio Rhode Island Providence RI 1976, 1971-1974; P-in-c S Ptr's And S Andr's Epis Providence RI 1971-1972; Cur S Mary's Ch Portsmouth RI 1969-1971.

KENWORTHY, Stuart A (WA) 2801 Mexico Avenue NW, Apt 711, Washington DC DC 20007 B Toledo OH 1951 s Stuart & Alice. BD Ohio U 1973; MDiv Bos TS 1976; DMin Andover Newton TS 1980; GTS 1984. D 6/16/1984 Bp Lyman Cunningham Ogilby P 12/7/1984 Bp Walter Decoster Dennis Jr. m 9/27/1980 Frances P Kenworthy c 3. Int Vic S Dav's Par Washington DC 2016-2017; Cathd of St Ptr & St Paul Washington DC 2015; Chapl US ARNG 1994-2007; R Chr Ch Georgetown Washington DC 1991-2014; Cur S Thos Ch New York NY 1986-1991; Asst Ch Of The Heav Rest New York NY 1984-1986. The Bishops Awd Dio Washington 2007; Iraq Cmpgn Medal US Army 2006; Global War on Terrorism Serv Medal US Army 2006; Iraqi Freedom Medal US Army 2006; The Bronze Star Medal US Army 2006.

KENYI, Alex Lodu (ND) 3725 30th St, San Diego CA 92104 B Juba 1953 s Ezekiel & Sarah. BA S Paul Untd Theol Coll Limuru Ke 1989; MDiv Nairobi Intl TS KE 1995. Trans 5/1/1998 Bp Andrew Fairfield. m 10/3/1981 Hellen Lodu c 4. R S Jn's Ch Moorhead MN 2000-2011; Dio No Dakota Fargo ND 2000-2010, 1998; Cur S Lk's Ch San Diego CA 1998-2000. Ord Of S Lk.

KENYON, James Howard Benjamin (Alb) 1606 5th St, Rensselaer NY 12144 **Asst S Dav's Ch Schodack NY 2007-; Trin Ch Whitehall NY 2001-; Ret 1989-; Dioc Refugee Coordntr Dio Albany Greenwich NY 2004-, Dioc Refugee Coordntr 1998-2003, Dioc Refugee Coordntr 1989-1997, 1981-1988** B Lake Placid NY 1925 s Raymond & Hariot. BA Hobart and Wm Smith Colleges 1947; LTh GTS 1950. D 5/21/1950 P 11/26/1950 Bp Vedder Van Dyck. m 9/28/1957 Grace Kenyon. Asst St Fran Mssn Albany NY 2002-2005; Chr & S Barn Troy NY 1998-2002; P-in-c Chr and S Barn Ch Troy NY 1998-2002; Dioc Refugee Coordntr Dio Long Island 1983-1989; R S Barth's Ch Brooklyn NY 1980-1988; R S Alb's Ch Superior WI 1979-1980; Chap Of Chr The King Charlotte NC 1977-1979; Dir Chr the King Cntr 1968-1979; P-in-c S Mich And All Ang Epis Ch Charlotte NC 1968-1979;

Dio No Carolina Raleigh NC 1968-1976; Vic S Ptr's Ch Mt Arlington NJ 1966-1968; Pres S Tim Hse 1960-1966; Chapl Essex Cnty Yth Hse 1958-1966; P-in-c Chr Epis Ch E Orange NJ 1954-1966; Tchr Stevens Acad 1952-1954; S Jn The Bapt Epis Hardwick VT 1951-1952; S Jn's In The Mountains Stowe VT 1951-1952; Chr Ch Montpelier VT 1950-1951; Dioc Supvsr for Legalization Dio Long Island Garden City NY 1987-1988. "(autobiography)," *The Time of My Life*, Troy Bookmakers. DeWitt Clinton Masonic Awd 1995.

KEOUGH, Christopher John (Mil) 313 Lakeview Drive Apt 2, Hartland WI 53029 **Vic Gd Shpd 2004-** B Fort Wayne IN 1962 s Robert & Sarah. AA U of Wisconsin 1988; BA U of Wisconsin 1990; MDiv Nash 1993; DMin SWTS 2002. D 5/29/1993 P 11/27/1993 Bp Roger John White. m 10/6/1984 Dawn Marie Keough c 1. Dio Milwaukee Milwaukee WI 2004-2007, 1993-1995; R S Barth's Ch Pewaukee WI 1995-2003; Assoc R S Jn Ch/Mision San Juan Milwaukee WI 1993-1995; St Mths Epis Ch Waukesha WI 1993-1995, 1993-1995. "A Theol Of Evang For The Epis Ch," Dio Milwaukee, 2002. Franciscan 3rd Ord Div Compassion.

KEPLINGER, Stephen James (Az) 2331 E Adams St, Tucson AZ 85719 **R S Dav's Epis Page AZ 2004-** B Baltimore MD 1953 s William & Elizabeth. MDiv CDSP 2001. D 1/18/2001 P 8/4/2001 Bp Carolyn Tanner Irish. Gr St Pauls Epis Ch Tucson AZ 2010-2014; Dio Utah Salt Lake City UT 2001-2010; R S Dav's Epis Page AZ 2001-2010. "TheComeback Kids," *Bk*, Pub's Place, 1989. Polly Bond Awd ECom 2004. rector@grace-stpauls.org

KEPPELER, Lisa Leialoha (Pa) 124 S Main Street, Coopersburg PA 18036 **R Ch Of The H Nativ Wrightstown PA 2016-, 2014-2016** B Hoolehua HI 1956 d Richard & Gail. BA L&C 1978; MDiv GTS 1989; Cert Dio NY Int Mnstry Trng 2001; Cert Other 2001. D 5/6/1989 P 11/10/1989 Bp David Bell Birney IV. c 2. R Emm Ch Quakertown PA 2007-2013; Gr Epis Ch Monroe NY 2006-2007; P-in-c S Lk's Ch Katonah NY 2001-2004; Sabbatical Pstr S Pauls On The Hill Epis Ch Ossining NY 2001; EFM Coordntr Dio New York New York NY 1999-2000, Diac Formation Bd Mem 1994-1999, Com to Elect a Bp 1994-1996; P-in-c Ch Of The H Comm Mahopac NY 1994-1998; Asst S Mary's Ch Mohegan Lake NY 1992-1994; Asst S Mk's Ch Mt Kisco NY 1989-1992.

KEPPY, Susan C (WNY) 419 Cherry Ln, Lewiston NY 14092 **Chapl Lewiston Police Dept Lewiston NY 2000-** B Toledo OH 1953 d Clyde & Helen. BS U Cinc 1976; MDiv GTS 1981. D 6/27/1981 Bp John Harris Burt P 2/4/1982 Bp William Davidson. m 1/27/1996 John Keppy. R S Paul's Epis Ch Lewiston NY 1993-2011; Assoc R Trin Epis Ch Buffalo NY 1986-1993; Cur S Dav's Ch Wayne PA 1981-1986. Intl Critical Incident Stress Fndt 2002; Intl Dio Police Chapl 2000.

KERBEL, Carol Ann (NJ) 232 Camino De La Sierra, Santa Fe NM 87501 B Waco TX 1940 d Dee & Anna. BA Texas Tech U 1963; MDiv GTS 1981. D 9/13/1980 Bp Albert Wiencke Van Duzer. m 6/8/1962 Waldemar Kerbel c 3. Asst Trin Ch Princeton NJ 1992-2001; Nassau Presb Ch Princeton NJ 1983-1992; D New Brunswick Epis Wk Com 1983-1992; New Brunswick Episurban Wk Com No Brunswick NJ 1981-1983; Chr Ch New Brunswick NJ 1980-1981; Dio New Jersey Trenton NJ 1980; Non-par; Admin Dir Crisis Ministers In Princeton & Trenton NJ. NAAD (Past Pres).

KERBEL, Walter Jarrett (Pa) 1418 E 57th St, Chicago IL 60637 **R Ch Of S Mart-In-The-Fields Philadelphia PA 2011-** B Fort Worth TX 1966 s Waldemar & Carol. BA NWU 1989; U Chi 1990; MDiv UTS 1992; GTS 1994. D 6/11/1994 Bp Richard Frank Grein P 2/1/1995 Bp Charlie Fuller Mcnutt Jr. m 10/9/1993 Alison Leslie Kerbel c 2. The Crisis Mnstry of Princeton and Trenton Trenton NJ 2008-2011; S Mary's Ch Pk Ridge IL 2003-2007; Assoc R Ch Of S Paul And The Redeem Chicago IL 1999-2003; Assoc R The Ch Of S Jn The Evang Flossmoor IL 1995-1999; S Edm's Epis Ch Chicago IL 1995-1996; Chapl S Edw's Acad Chicago IL 1995-1996; D Intern Chr Memi Epis Ch Danville PA 1994-2002. OHC.

KERN, David Paul (Nwk) Po Box 1703, North Eastham MA 02651 B Brooklyn NY 1928 s Samuel & Sabina. BS NYU 1952; MDiv Ya Berk 1956; MA NYU 1966. D 6/3/1956 P 12/1/1956 Bp Horace W B Donegan. m 12/20/1954 Elenor M Kern c 4. Meadowlands Mnstrs Rutherford NJ 1983-1992; Ch Of Our Sav Secaucus NJ 1980-1992; The Gunnery Washington CT 1969-1980; P-in-c S Ann Morrisiana NY 1961-1964; R Ch Of The Div Love Montrose NY 1957-1961; Asst Min S Andr's Ch Beacon NY 1956-1957. Auth, "The Indep Sch Bulletin". Phi Delta Kappa U Ct Chapt.

KERN, Karl Lee (Be) 182 Gable Dr/, Myerstown PA 17067 B Lebanon PA 1949 s Lester & Doris. FBI Natl Acad 1978; AA Harrisburg Cmnty Coll 1978; BS York Coll 1989; MDiv GTS 1994. D 4/23/1994 P 11/27/1994 Bp James Michael Mark Dyer. c 1. R S Alb's Epis Ch Reading PA 2001-2016; Commonwealth Of Pennsylvania Lebanon PA 1997-2001; R S Jas Ch Shuykl Haven PA 1997-2001; Chr Ch Reading PA 1994-1997.

KERN, Roy Allen (CPa) 613 Eschol Ridge Rd, Elliottsburg PA 17024 B Carlisle PA 1958 D 6/8/2002 Bp Michael Whittington Creighton. m 6/24/1989 Karen Ann Lightner c 2. D S Jn's Epis Ch Carlisle PA 2003-2013.

KERNER, Sandra Barbary (SVa) 2755 Buckstone Dr, Powhatan VA 23139 **R S Lk's Ch Powhatan VA 2011-** B Pittsburgh PA 1956 d Austin & Aurletta. BS Penn 1978; MDiv UTS Richmond 2005; CAS VTS 2005. D 6/4/2005 P 12/

461

3/2005 Bp David Conner Bane Jr. Dir of Healing Pryr Mnstry Richmond Hill Retreat Cntr Richmond VA 2008-2011; Supply P Trin Ch So Hill VA 2007, D 2005-2006; R S Lk's Ch Blackstone VA 2005-2011; Chair, COM: Dioc Formation Dio Sthrn Virginia Newport News VA 2008-2010, Dn of Reg 2007-2010. Fllshp of Chr the Healer USA; Co-Fndr and Mem 2004; OSL the Physcn 1998.

KERR, Catherine D (Pa) Good Shepherd Church, P.O. Box 132, Hilltown PA 18927 **Gd Shpd Ch Hilltown PA 2014-** B Baltimore MD 1951 d Spencer & Catherine. AB Bryn 1973; Cert GTS 2012; MDiv The GTS 2012. D 6/9/2012 Bp Charles Ellsworth Bennison Jr P 1/12/2013 Bp Edward Lewis Lee Jr. m 10/28/1978 Christopher John Kerr c 2. Ch Of The H Sprt Harleysville PA 2012-2014. revckerr@gmail.com

KERR, Denniston Rupert (SwFla) 5609 N Albany Ave, Tampa FL 33603 B Hanover JM 1939 s Hartford & Sarah. Coll Arts Sci & Tech 1960; Wilson Carlyle Trng Coll 1965; Untd Theol Coll of The W Indies Kingston Jm 1979. Trans 10/1/1992 Bp Rogers Sanders Harris. m 7/23/1966 Clarissa Kerr c 1. S Jas Hse Of Pryr Tampa FL 1995-1997; St Jas Ch Tampa FL 1992-2008; Serv Ch Of Jamaica 1978-1992.

KERR, Kyra Anne (RG) P.O. Box 188, Tesuque NM 87574 B Houston TX 1939 D 6/21/2003 Bp Terence Kelshaw.

KERR, Lauri Ann (CPa) 1435 Scott St, Williamsport PA 17701 **P Chr Soc Mnstry Montoursville PA 2009-; Assoc Gleam Williamsport PA 2009-** B Wellsboro PA 1970 d Thomas & Deborah. MDiv VTS; BS Mansfield U of Pennsylvania 1995. D 6/8/2001 P 12/12/2001 Bp Michael Whittington Creighton. P S Paul's Ch Manheim PA 2001-2004.

KERR, Linda (Pa) 1603 Yardley Commons, Yardley PA 19067 B Bryn Mawr PA 1950 d David & Ruth. BA Hobart and Wm Smith Colleges 1972; MA Wheaton Coll 1978; MDiv Yale DS 1985. D 6/21/1986 Bp Lyman Cunningham Ogilby P 5/9/1987 Bp Allen Lyman Bartlett Jr. P-in-c Ch Of The Incarn Morrisville PA 2011-2016; Chapl CFS The Sch At Ch Farm Exton PA 2011; R S Mart's Ch Wayne PA 2006-2011; Assoc The Ch Of The Redeem Baltimore MD 2000-2005; Chapl S Andew's Sch Boca Raton FL 1991-2000; Chapl S Andr's Sch Boca Raton FL 1991-2000; Asst Chapl Epis Acad Merion PA 1987-1991; The Epis Acad Newtown Sq PA 1987-1991; Asst S Fran-In-The-Fields Malvern PA 1986-1987; Chapl S Paul Sch Concord NH 1985-1986; Ovrs Mssy in Rwanda Afr Sem Tchr 1979-1983. Auth, *A Mod Mssy.*

KERR, Richard S (Cal) 442 34th Ave, San Francisco CA 94121 **1985-** B Denver CO 1938 s John & Katherine. BA Ken 1960; STB GTS 1963. D 6/20/1963 P 2/1/1964 Bp Chandler W Sterling. m 1/1/2001 Jane Nadene Kerr c 2. Dir of Homeless Prog Trin Ch San Francisco CA 1981-1982; Spalding Rehab Cntr Denver CO 1979; Secy 1977-1978; 1973-1978; R Ch Of The H Redeem Denver CO 1970-1979; Cur S Thos Epis Ch Denver CO 1968-1970; Cur S Paul Denver CO 1966-1968; R The Pintler Cluster of the Epis Ch Deer Lodge MT 1964-1966; Cur Ch Of The H Sprt Missoula MT 1963-1964.

KERR, Robert Anthony (Mich) 23851 Goddard Rd, Taylor MI 48180 **Instr The Whitaker Inst Detroit Michigan 2009-; Psych Priv Pract Psych Southfield Michigan 1990-** B Belleville MI 1963 s Robert & Helen. BA Concordia U 1987; MA Estrn Michigan U 1990; PsyS The Cntr for Humanistic Stds 1992; PhD The U on Inst and U 1997; MA Ashland TS 2002. D 11/18/2004 P 3/18/2005 Bp Wendell Nathaniel Gibbs Jr. R S Jn's Ch Westland MI 2009-2015; Dir of Pstr Care Cbury On The Lake Waterford MI 2007-2009; P S Martha's Ch Detroit MI 2005-2007; Profsnl Fell Ashland TS Detroit Michigan 2002-2010; Chapl Hospice of Michigan Detroit Michigan 2000-2005; P Our Lady of Walsingham Orth Mssn Taylor Michigan 1998-2004; P Incarn Orth Ch Detroit Michigan 1998; Psych Lincoln Behavioral Serv Dearborn Michigan 1997-2000; D Incarn Orth Ch Detroit Michigan 1997-1998; Commision on Mnstry Dio Michigan Detroit MI 2005-2011. Auth, "A Psychodynamic Revs of "Stranger at the Gate,"" *Journ of Psychol and Chrsnty*, Chr Assn of Psychol Stds, 1996. GAS 1995; SocMary 1995. Bd Cert Diplomate in Psych Amer Psych Assn 2009.

KERR JR, Thomas Albert (Del) 111 Canterbury Dr, Wilmington DE 19803 B New York NY 1938 s Thomas & Jean. AB Pr 1959; STB GTS 1962. D 4/28/1962 P 10/27/1962 Bp Alfred L Banyard. m 7/24/1965 Janet S Kerr c 3. Cn for Deploy Dio New Jersey Trenton NJ 2004-2006, Cn to the Ordnry 2002-2003, Vic, Ch of our Sav, Cheesequake, NJ 1965-1968; Ret Dio Delaware Wilmington 2002; Bd EUC 1997-2000; R Imm Ch Highlands Wilmington DE 1995-2002; Dep GC Dio Delaware 1994-2000; Bd NNECA 1992-1997; Cn Pstr Cathd Ch Of S Jn Wilmington DE 1985-1995; R Gr Epis Ch Plainfield NJ 1982-1985; Dir, Trng Prog for Deacons Dio New Jersey NJ 1979-1985; Epis Chapl, Rutgers U The Wm Alexander Procter Fndt Trenton NJ 1972-1982; R S Jn's Epis Ch Little Silver NJ 1968-1972; Cur Gr Ch Merchantville NJ 1962-1965. Fell Coll of Preachers 1971.

KERR, Verdery (NC) Po Box 6124, Charlotte NC 28207 B Fayetteville NC 1949 s Douglas & Stuart. BA U NC 1972; MDiv VTS 1976. D 6/26/1976 Bp Hunley Agee Elebash P 1/27/1977 Bp Arthur Anton Vogel. m 8/4/1973 Mary Ann O Kerr c 2. Sr Assoc Chr Ch Charlotte NC 1999-2014; R S Thos' Epis Ch Sioux City IA 1992-1999; Chair Stwdshp Com Dio No Carolina Raleigh NC 1990-1991, Chair Hunger Com 1986-1990; R S Thos Epis Ch Reidsville NC

1983-1991; Asst S Steph's Ch Durham NC 1979-1983; Assoc S Paul's Ch Kansas City MO 1976-1979.

KERRICK, Michael W (NCal) 2612 Colin Rd, Placerville CA 95667 B Santa Cruz CA 1948 s William & Irma. AA Amer River Coll 1972; BA California St U Sacramento 1974; Cert Csus Sacramento 1982; MDiv CDSP 2007. D 6/2/2007 P 1/26/2008 Bp Barry Leigh Beisner. m 6/9/1968 Judy S Kerrick c 1. Int S Mich's Epis Ch Carmichael CA 2013; Int Trin Ch Folsom CA 2011-2012; Int Pstr St. paul's Luth Ch Sacramento Calif. 2009-2010; Asst R Trin Ch Sutter Creek CA 2007-2008.

KERSCHEN, Charles Thomas (WK) 520 East Ave S, Lyons KS 67554 **Chr Ch Kingman KS 2012-** B Modesto CA 1957 s James & Mary. BA Dominican Sch of Philos & Theol 1997; MA Franciscan TS 1999. D 9/1/2007 P 3/15/2008 Bp James Marshall Adams Jr. m 12/28/1999 Karen J Kerschen c 2. S Mk's Ch Lyons KS 2008-2013.

KERTLAND, Gail Ellen (LI) 36 Cathedral Ave, Garden City NY 11530 **Asst Dio Long Island Garden City NY 2012-** B North Kingstown RI 1951 d Floyd & Anna. ADSN New Hampshire Tech Inst 1974; BTS Other 1998; BTS Sch for Deacons 1998. D 12/5/1998 Bp William Edwin Swing. m 6/15/1973 Alan Keith Kertland c 1.

KESHGEGIAN, Flora A (Pa) 601 Montgomery Ave Apt 308, Bryn Mawr PA 19010 B Brooklyn NY 1950 d Charles & Asdghig. BA U of Pennsylvania 1969; MDiv PDS 1974; EDS 1978; PhD Boston Coll 1992. D 6/15/1974 P 1/29/1977 Bp Lyman Cunningham Ogilby. Assoc S Fran' Epis Ch San Francisco CA 2012-2016; Assoc Fac Grad Theol Un 2012-2014; Assoc Prof of Pstr Theol and Wmn in Mnstry CDSP Berkeley CA 2010-2014; Fac Ombudsperson Br Providence RI 2006-2009; Asst Prof Systematic Theol Epis TS Of The SW Austin TX 1999-2005; Assoc Chapl Br Providence RI 1984-1998; Int Par Of S Paul Newton Highlands MA 1982; Asst All SS Epis Ch of the No Shore Inc Danvers MA 1981; Epis Campus Min, Tem Dio Pennsylvania Philadelphia PA 1974-1978. Auth, "Voices of Anguish: Listening to Victims of Violence," *Ambassadors For God: Recon Rites for the 21st Century*, Ch Pub, 2011; Auth, "God Reflected: Metaphors for Life," Fortress Press, 2008; Auth, "Time for Hope: Practices for Living in Today's Wrld," Continuum Pub Grp, 2006; Auth, "Finding a Place Past NIght: Armenian Genocidal Memory in Diaspora," *Rel, Violence, Memory, and Place*, Indiana U Press, 2006; Auth, "Coming to Terms: Exploring the Dynamics of Our Differences," *ATR. Vol. 86*, 2004; Auth, "Witnessing Trauma: Dorothee Soelle's Theol of Suffering in a Wrld of Victimization," *The Theol of Dorothee Soelle*, Trin Press Intl , 2003; Auth, "Defining Testimoies: Narrative Remembrances by Armenian Survivors of Genocide," *Proteus: A Journ of Ideas, Vol, 19*, 2002; Auth, "Redeeming Memories: A Theol of Healing and Transformation," Abingdon Press, 2000; Auth, "The Scandal of the Cross: Anselm and His Feminist Critics," *Angl Theol Revs, Vol. 82*, 2000; Auth, "Power to Wound, Power to Mend: Toward a Non-Abusing Theol," *Journ of Rel and Abuse*, 1999. AAR 1985; Authors Gld 2006. Trin Prize Trin Press Intl Fndt 2005; Fllshp Roothbert Fund 1983; Fllshp ECF 1980.

KESLER, Walter Wilson (FtW) 3937 Anewby Way, Fort Worth TX 76133 **Ret 2004-; Ret 2004-** B Exeter NH 1942 s Robert & Ellen. BS USNA 1964; MDiv VTS 1979. D 5/24/1979 P 12/5/1979 Bp Philip Alan Smith. m 5/30/1998 Maria Zelia Brandon c 2. Int S Alb's Epis Ch Arlington TX 2009-2010; Assoc Trin Epis Ch Ft Worth TX 2000-2004; Headmaster Trin Vlly Sch Ft Worth TX 1994-2000; Hdmstr Trin Vlly Sch Ft Worth TX 1994-1999; Chapl Holderness Sch Plymouth NH 1979-1994; Asst. Headmaster The Holderness Sch Plymouth NH 1979-1994; Vic Trin Ch Meredith NH 1979-1994.

KESSEL-HANNA, Kay Lynn (Oly) 11527 9th Ave NE, Seattle WA 98125 **D S Andr's Ch Seattle WA 2009-** B Blue Earth, MN 1953 d Ray & Doris. BS U of Wisconsin 1978; MA Bastyr U 1996; MA Seattle U 2010. D 10/17/2009 Bp Gregory Harold Rickel. m 12/20/1981 Gerald Benson Hanna c 2.

KESSELUS, Kenneth William (Tex) 1301 Church St., Bastrop TX 78602 **R Emer Calv Epis Ch Bastrop TX 2012-, R 1981-2000; Ret 2003-** B Bastrop TX 1947 s William & Kathryn. BA U of Texas 1969; MDiv Epis TS of the SW 1972; Coll of Preachers 1979; Epis TS of the SW 1991. D 6/25/1972 Bp Scott Field Bailey P 6/21/1973 Bp James Milton Richardson. m 6/14/1969 Antoinette Bonelli c 2. Exec Boafd Dio Texas 2013; Stndg Com Dio Texas 2013; P-in-c S Chris's Epis Ch Austin TX 2003-2006; Exec Coun Natl Ch 2000-2006; R S Paul's Ch Waco TX 2000-2003; Stndg Com Dio Texas 1998-2001; Secy Providence VII 1997-1999; Exec Boafd Dio Texas 1995-1998; GC Dep Natl Ch 1994-2003; Chair Sm Ch Prov VII 1994-1996; Del Prov VII 1987-1993; Vic/R S Andr's Epis Ch Pearland TX 1972-1981; Dept Evang Dio Texas Houston TX 1987-1990, chair - Dispatch of Bus 1986-2003, Sum Camp Dir 1973-1992; Alum Strng Com Epis TS Of The SW Austin TX 1983-1985. Auth, "Jn E Hines: Granite On Fire," Sem of the SW, 1995. Distinguish Alum Sem of the SW 1997; Texas Rural Min Of The Year TX A & M Ext Serv 1991.

KESSLER, Edward Scharps (Pa) 44 Hinde Street, Sheffield S4 8HJ Great Britain (UK) **Lectr Of Urban Theol U Of Sheffield 1974-** B Newark NJ 1926 s Samuel & Hortense. BA Pr 1947; MA Chicago Chicago IL 1951; DIT S Chad Coll Gb 1966. D 9/1/1966 Bp The Bishop Of Jarrow P. m 2/17/1955 Elizabeth Allen Goldsmith. P-in-c Kimblesworth Par 1974-1980; Plnng Off Dio Durham

1970-1975; Cur S Ign Sunderland Engl 1968-1970; Cur S Lk Sunderland Engl 1966-1968. Auth, "Practical Chr Radicalism"; Auth, "A Jubilee & Disciples".

KESSLER, Judith Maier (CNY) 17 Elizabeth St, Binghamton NY 13901 B Syracuse NY 1939 d Frederick & Charlotte. BA Buc 1961; Bex Sem 1993. D 6/8/1985 P 5/1/1986 Bp O'Kelley Whitaker. m 8/5/1961 Brian Richard Kessler c 2. Asstg Cler S Mk's Epis Ch Binghamton NY 2000-2014, Asst 1985-1999; Supply P Zion Epis Ch Windsor NY 1989-1994.

KESSLER, Rachel Cheryl (O) Harcourt Parish, Po Box 377, Gambier OH 43022 **Harcourt Par Gambier OH 2016-** B Thomaston GA 1981 d Charles & Patricia. AB Ken 2004; AB Ken 2008; AB Ken 2008; PhD U Tor 2008; MDiv Wycliffe Collge, U Tor 2011. Trans 8/26/2016 as Priest Bp Mark Hollingsworth Jr. m 7/28/2006 Leeman Leeman Tarpley c 1.

KESTER, Martha Ruth (Ia) 1916 Merklin Way, Des Moines IA 50310 **R S Lk's Ch Des Moines IA 2011-, Asst 2006-2010; Chapl Iowa Army NG Johnston Iowa 2009-** B Englewood NJ 1967 d Lee & Patricia. BA Franklin & Marshall Coll 1990; MDiv TESM 2006. D 5/27/2006 Bp John Wadsworth Howe P 12/2/2006 Bp Alan Scarfe. Pension Fund Mltry New York NY 2010-2011; Spec Mobilization Spprt Plan Washington DC 2010-2011; Chapl Candidate Iowa Army NG Johnston Iowa 2006-2009; Dioc Conv Registration Chair Dio Iowa Des Moines IA 2012, Dioc Conv Registration Chair 2011, Commissiom on Mnstry 2009-.

KETNER, Thomas Howard (Wyo) 411 E Center St, Douglas WY 82633 B Flint MI 1955 s Howard & Anna. BS U MI 1978; MA Black Hills St Coll 1986. D 6/6/2015 P 12/19/2015 Bp John Smylie. m 2/11/1977 Virginia Lynn Bond c 4.

KETTLEWELL, Charles G (Ark) 13456 Victory Gallop Way, Gainesville VA 20155 **Died 8/29/2016** B Muskingum County OH 1939 s Samuel & Emma. CDSP; BA Muskingum Coll 1961; MDiv VTS 1970. D 6/29/1970 P 4/1/1971 Bp David Shepherd Rose. m 9/9/1960 Gail B Kettlewell c 3. P-in-c Meade Memi Par White Post VA 2008-2016; Int S Ptr's Epis Ch Washington NC 2006-2007; Int St Lk's Par Ch Hill MD 2005-2006; Int Chr Epis Ch Great Choptank Par Cambridge MD 2003-2005; Int S Phil's Epis Ch Rochester MI 2001-2003; Int S Paul's Ch Naples FL 2000-2001; Int Trsfg Epis Ch Indn River MI 1998-2000; P-in-c Ch Of The Gd Shpd Bluemont VA 1991-1998; R S Jn's Ch Camden AR 1983-1990; Vic S Jas Epis Ch Portsmouth VA 1981-1983; Vic S Mk's Ch Suffolk VA 1978-1980; Dio Sthrn Virginia Newport News VA 1978; Vic Emm Epis Ch Portsmouth VA 1970-1983.

KETTLEWELL, John Michael (Alb) 110 Monument Dr, Schuylerville NY 12871 B Chicago IL 1930 s John & Audrey. BA Harv 1952; STB GTS 1955; MA U of Virginia 1969. D 6/18/1955 Bp Charles L Street P 12/15/1955 Bp Horace W B Donegan. m 5/23/1992 Susan Anne Kane-Kettlewell c 2. S Steph's Ch Schuylerville NY 2004-2015; Gr Ch Stanardsville VA 1969-1990; Blue Ridge Sch Dyke VA 1965-1990; Chapl Fac Blue Ridge Sch Dyke VA 1965-1990; R S Mk's Ch Geneva IL 1960-1965; Chapl Skidmore Coll 1959-1960; Asst Ch Of Beth Saratoga Spg NY 1957-1960; Cur Trin Par New York NY 1956-1957. Auth, *Issues In Philos and Rel*, 1999; Auth, "Truth, Beauty," *Goodness & Committment*, 1983.

KETTLEWELL, Paula Swaebe (Va) 705 Wilder Dr, Charlottesville VA 22901 B Boston MA 1934 d Henry & Pauline. U of Virginia; Wheaton Coll; Ya; BA NWU 1956. D 6/14/1980 Bp Arnold M Lewis P 5/1/1981 Bp Robert Bruce Hall. c 2. Assoc R S Paul's Memi Charlottesvlle VA 1986-2003, Assoc R 1982-1985; Chapl Blue Ridge Sch Dyke VA 1980-1982. Auth, "Hist Of S Paul Memi Ch".

KEUCHER, Gerald Werner (LI) 1 Pendleton Pl, Staten Island NY 10301 **P-in-c S Mary's Ch Brooklyn NY 2012-, P-in-c 2010-2012** B New Haven CT 1952 s Werner & Martha. BA Indiana U 1973; MA Indiana U 1975; MDiv PrTS 1993; STM Yale DS 1994. D 1/15/1994 Bp Walter Decoster Dennis Jr P 7/30/1994 Bp Egbert Don Taylor. Vic Ch Of The Intsn New York NY 2006-2009; Chf of Fin & Oprtns Dio New York New York NY 2006-2008; Dep to GC Dio New York New York NY 2003-2009, 1995-2002, Dep to GC 2003-2010; Cur S Jn's Ch Getty Sq Yonkers NY 1994-1995. Auth, "Back from the Dead," Ch Pub Grp, 2012; Auth, "Humble and Strong," Ch Pub Grp, 2010; Auth, "Remember the Future," Ch Pub Grp, 2006. Phi Beta Kappa Indiana U 1972.

KEVERN, John R (WVa) C/O Trinity Epis Church, PO Box P, Moundsville WV 26041 **Oriental Orth Dialogue 1993-** B Dixon IL 1953 s Walter & Esther. U of Paris IV 1974; BA U IL 1975; MDiv GTS 1980; PhD U Chi 1996. D 6/14/1980 Bp Quintin Ebenezer Primo Jr P 12/1/1980 Bp James Winchester Montgomery. S Paul's Within the Walls Rome 2011-2012; Trin Ch Moundsville WV 2010-2011; Prof Bex Sem Columbus OH 1992-2010; S Bon Ch Tinley Pk IL 1990-1992; S Raphael The Archangel Oak Lawn IL 1989; S Fran Epis Ch Chicago IL 1988-1989, Vic 1986-1988; Cathd Of S Jas Chicago IL 1985; Dio Chicago Chicago IL 1983-1984; Luth-Epis Dialogue III 1982-1990; Cur S Chris's Epis Ch Oak Pk IL 1980-1982. Auth, "The Trin and Soc Justice," *ATR*, 1997; Auth, "Ecclesiology of the Concordat," *The Angl*, 1996; Auth, "A Future for Angl Cath Theol," *Angl Theoligical Revs*, 1994; Auth, "Form inTragedy: Balthasar as Correlational Theol," *Communio*, 1994. Affirming Catholicism 1998; AAR 1988; ATR 2001. DD The GTS 2004; Fell ECF.

KEW, William Richard (Tenn) 2272 Lewisburg Pike, Franklin TN 37064 **Assoc S Geo's Ch Nashville TN 2015-; Dvlpmt Dir Ridley Hall Cambridge UK 2007-; Mem, Bp and Coun Dio Tennessee Nashville TN 2016-, Mem, Bp and Coun 2004-2007, Mem, Episcopate Com 2004-2006, Mem, COM 1997-2004; Cn Mssnr Cathd of the Trsfg Owerri Nigeria 2012-** B Luton Bedfordshire England 1945 s William & Brenda. LTh London Coll Div Gb 1968; BD Lon GB 1969. Trans 10/1/1977 Bp John Bowen Coburn. m 7/20/1968 Rosemary A Kew c 2. Ridley Hall Cambridge 2009-2013; The Epis Ch Of The Resurr Franklin TN 2006-2007; Ch Of The Apos Thompsons Sta TN 2003-2006; Us Angilcan Congr Nashville TN 2000-2002; Cnvnr Us Angl Congr 2000-2002; Dir Angl Forum For The Future 1997-2000; Dir Of Mnstry AFP 1997-1999; AFP Orlando FL 1996-1998; Coordntr Russian Mnstry Ntwk 1995-2000; Russian Mnstry Ntwk Murfreesboro TN 1995-1999; SPCK USA 1985-1995; Spck/Usa Sewanee TN 1985-1995; R All SS Angl Ch Rochester NY 1979-1985; Chr Ch S Hamilton MA 1977-1979; Serv Ch Of Engl 1969-1976; Mem, 20/20 Taskforce Dom And Frgn Mssy Soc- Epis Ch Cntr New York NY 2000-2001; Chair and Trst SAMS Ambridge PA 1976-1985. Auth, "Brave New Ch," Morehouse, 2001; Auth, "Toward 2015: A Ch Odyssey," Cowley, 1997; Auth, "Vision Bearers," Morehouse, 1996; Auth, "Venturing Into The New Millennium," Latimer, 1994; Auth, "Starting Over," Abingdon, 1994; Auth, "New Millennium, New Ch," *New Ch*, Cowley, 1992; Auth, "No Foothold in the Swamp," Zondervan, 1988. Cmnty Of Mary 1986. Lifetime Trst SAMS 1996. richard.kew@stgeorgesnashville.org

KEY, Nancy Anne (SJ) PO Box 7446, Visalia CA 93290 B Loma Linda CA 1948 d Lawrence & Jacqueline. BA California St Unversity 1972; Standard Tchg Credit California St U 1973; Bach.Diac Stds Epis Sch for Deacons 2015. D 8/15/2015 Bp David C Rice. c 2.

KEY, Sanford Allen (NY) St. Luke's Church, POB 94, Somers NY 10589 **Assoc Chr's Ch Rye NY 2015-** B Beaufort SC 1968 s Jimmy & Cheryl. BA Cit 1990; MDiv Sewanee: The U So, TS 1997. D 6/21/1997 P 6/20/1998 Bp Robert Carroll Johnson Jr. m 1/9/1993 Laura Lynn Key c 2. R S Lk's Ch Somers NY 2007-2015; Coll Chapl Bruton Par Williamsburg VA 2001-2007; Cur & Chapl Cathd Of S Lk And S Paul Charleston SC 1998-2001; D Chr Ch Charlotte NC 1997-1998. Auth, "DOCC 16/20," *DOCC 16/20*, Sewanee, Univ. of the So, 1999.

KEYDEL JR, John F (Mich) 6981 Lindsay Ln, Easton MD 21601 **Chr Ch St Michaels Par S Mich MD 2016-** B Detroit MI 1954 s John & Jane. BA Hampshire Coll 1976; MEd Bos 1977; MBA U of Connecticut 1985; MDiv Ya Berk 1995; CAGS SWTS 2003; ABT Adizes Grad Sch 2010. D 6/10/1995 Bp Clarence Nicholas Coleridge P 2/3/1996 Bp R aymond Stewart Wood Jr. m 7/24/1976 Margaret Jean Keydel c 2. Int Chr Ch - Glendale Cincinnati OH 2014-2016; S Barn Epis Ch Cincinnati OH 2012-2014; Int R Ch Of The Trsfg Palos Pk IL 2010-2011; Int R S Jas Ch Skaneateles NY 2009-2010; Dio Michigan Detroit MI 1998-2009; Treas Dio Michigan 1998-2000; R Nativ Epis Ch Bloomfield Township MI 1998-2000; Asst to R S Jas Epis Ch Birmingham MI 1995-1998. Int Mnstry Ntwk 2002.

KEYES, Charles Don (NY) 5801 Hampton St, Pittsburgh PA 15206 B Wewoka OK 1937 s Robert & Ruth. BA U of Oklahoma 1958; BD SWTS 1961; STM SWTS 1964; MA U Tor 1966; ThD U Tor 1966; PhD Duquesne U 1968. D 6/17/1961 P 12/1/1961 Bp Chilton R Powell. m 8/20/1966 Aileen May Keyes. Assoc The Ch of S Ign of Antioch New York NY 2000-2009; St Andrews Epis Ch Pittsburgh PA 1996-1997; Non-par 1969-1996; Asst Prof The GTS New York NY 1967-1969; Fell ECF 1964-1967; Vic S Steph's Ch Guymon OK 1961-1963; Hon Asst Ch Of The Trsfg New York NY 1997-2000. Auth, "Brain Mystery Light And Dark," London: Routledge, 1999. Fndr Julian Casserley Resrch Cntr. Phi Beta Kappa U Of Oklahoma 1958.

KEYES, John Irvin (SD) 513 Douglas Ave, Yankton SD 57078 B Sommers Point NJ 1948 s John & Ruth. BS U of So Dakota 1977. D 12/4/2010 Bp John Tarrant. m 2/6/1993 Jo Neubauer c 4.

KEYES, Samuel N (Ala) Saint Paul's Church, 905 Church St, Greensboro AL 36744 **St Jas Sch Hagerstown MD 2015-** B Gulfport MS 1981 s Samuel & Ruth. BA U Rich 2004; MDiv Duke DS 2009; Cert Angl Stds Nash 2010; PhD Boston Coll 2015. Trans 3/21/2012 as Priest Bp James Monte Stanton. m 8/13/2011 Gretchen G Keyes c 2. S Paul's Ch Greensboro AL 2013-2015; Cur The Ch Of The Adv Boston MA 2012-2013. skeyes@stjames.edu

KEYS, Joel Thompson (Tenn) PO Box 24183, Saint Simons Island GA 31522 **Ret 1993-** B Seneca SC 1947 s Theodore & Margery. BA Davidson Coll 1969; MDiv VTS 1973. D 6/14/1973 P 4/27/1974 Bp Gray Temple. m 10/3/1969 Mary Elizabeth Taylor c 2. Asst Chr Ch Frederica St Simons Is GA 2005; Int S Thos Epis Ch Diamondhead MS 1997-1998; R S Geo's Ch Nashville TN 1991-1993; Pres, Stndg Com Dio SW Virginia Roanoke VA 1990-1991, Long-R Plnng 1985-1990; Trst VTS Alexandria VA 1988-1991, Trst 1988-1991; R S Jn's Ch Lynchburg VA 1984-1991; Long Range Plnng Com Dio No Carolina Raleigh NC 1983-1984, Deploy Off 1981-1984, COM Co-Chair 1980-1981, COM 1979-1981, Dept Mssn 1976-1984, CDO 1980-1984; R Trin Epis Ch Statesville NC 1980-1984; Assoc Chr Ch Charlotte NC 1976-1980; COM So Carolina Charleston SC 1974-1975, Dept of Missions 1974-1975; Chr Ch Den-

K

mark SC 1973-1975; Asst Ch Of The Redeem Orangeburg SC 1973-1975. Auth, *Letters to the Newly Baptized*, Forw Mvmt, 1995; Auth, "Columns," *GC Daily*, Epis Ch, 1988; Auth, *Our Older Friends*, Fortress Press, 1983.

KEYSE, Andrew Carl (Ala) 262 Creekside Dr, Florence AL 35630 **R Trin Epis Ch Florence AL 2007-** B Rochester NY 1969 s Howard & Mary. BA U So 1992; MDiv Sewanee: The U So, TS 2002. D 6/15/2002 P 12/21/2002 Bp Bill Persell. m 10/22/1994 Elizabeth JS Keyse c 2. Chair, Liturg and Dioc. Events Dio Chicago Chicago IL 2005-2007, Dioc Conv Wrshp Comm. 2003-2004, Chair, Liturg and Dioc Events 2005-2007, Dioc Conv Wrshp Com 2004-2006; Assoc R Gr Epis Ch Hinsdale IL 2002-2007; Dept of Camp McDowell Dio Alabama Birmingham 2009-2012, Dept of Par Dvlpmt and Evang 2008-.

✠ KEYSER, The Rt Rev Charles Lovett (Fla) 4719 Ivanhoe Rd, Jacksonville FL 32210 **Ret Bp Suffr of ArmdF Off Of Bsh For ArmdF New York NY 2000-, 1960-2000** B Greenville SC 1930 s Lovett & Catherine. BA U So 1951; MDiv Sewanee: The U So, TS 1954. D 6/24/1954 P 2/15/1955 Bp Frank A Juhan Con 3/24/1990 for Armed Forces and Federal Ministires. m 8/6/1955 Christine Keyser. Asstg Bp of Florida Dio Florida Jacksonville 2007-2015; Bp Asstg Dio Georgia Savannah GA 2004-2005; Bp Asstg Chr Ch Cathd New Orleans LA 2001-2003; Dio Montana Helena MT 2001-2003; Bp for the ArmdF, VA Hospitals and Fed Prison Epis Ch Cntr New York NY 1990-2000; S Jas Ch Montross VA 1986-1990; R S Ptr's Ch Oak Grove Oak Grove VA 1986-1989; Chapl USN 1960-1986; Chapl S Lk Hosp Jacksonville FL 1954-1959; P-in-c S Tim's Epis Ch Jacksonville FL 1954-1959. DD TS U So 1993.

KEYWORTH, Gill (Tex) 1215 Ripple Creek Dr, Houston TX 77057 **D S Paul's Ch Katy TX 2013-** B Thornton Heath UK 1947 d Ronald & Joan. BS Bradford U Bradford Yorkshire Uk 1969; Iona Texas 2007. D 2/9/2007 Bp Don Adger Wimberly. m 9/4/1971 John Keyworth c 2. deacon@stpaulskaty.org

KEZAR, Dennis Dean (SwFla) 4030 Manatee Ave W, Bradenton FL 34205 B Webster City IA 1946 s Roger & Donna. BA New Coll of Florida 1967; Oxf GB 1968; MDiv Sewanee: The U So, TS 1971; PhD Oxf GB 1974. D 6/29/1971 P 2/1/1972 Bp William Loftin Hargrave. c 3. R S Mary's Par Tampa FL 2005-2011; Chr Ch Bradenton FL 1980-2004; Cathd Ch Of S Ptr St. Petersburg FL 1976-1979; Chapl Cbury Sch S Petersburg FL 1974-1975; Asst Ch Of The Redeem Sarasota FL 1971-1974.

KHALIL, Adeeb Mikhail (WVa) 127 Brookwood Ln, Beckley WV 25801 B Jerusalem 1937 s Mikhail & Nagla. BTh Evang TS Cairo 1971. D 7/1/1970 P 8/1/1972 Bp The Bishop Of Jerusalem. m 7/2/1982 Marcia B Khalil c 2. Asst R S Steph's Epis Ch Beckley WV 2010-2012, Asst R 1974-; Dn New Sthrn Dnry WV 2000-2002; Ch Of The Redeem Ansted WV 1979-1987; Vic S Andr's Ch Oak Hill WV 1979-1984; S Andr's Ch Beckley WV 1977-2003; Vic All SS Ch Un WV 1975-1979; Vic S Mich's Salt Sulpher Sprg WV 1975-1979; Vic Ascen Epis Ch Hinton WV 1975-1977.

KHAMIN, Alexei (Nwk) All Saints Episcopal Church, 230 E. 60th St., New York NY 10022 **Ch Of S Jn The Div Hasbrouck Hts NJ 2012-; Exec Coun Appointees New York NY 2007-** B Yaroslavl Russia 1970 s Sergey & Lioudmila. MDiv S Vladimirs Orth TS 1998; MPhil Drew U 2001; PhD Drew U 2007. D 6/2/2007 P 12/15/2007 Bp Mark M Beckwith. m 11/3/2008 Ronald Wei. Chr Ch Teaneck NJ 2011-2012; S Mary's Ch Sparta NJ 2010-2011; Asst All SS Ch New York NY 2007-2009.

KHOO, Oon-Chor (Tex) 3203 W Alabama St, Houston TX 77098 B Penang MY 1931 s Cheng-Hoe & Chin-Poh. BS U of Singapore SG 1955; AMLS U MI 1971; MA Gordon-Conwell TS 1973; MA Bos 1974; CTh Epis TS of the SW 1985; DMin Sewanee: The U So, TS 1993. D 5/1/1986 Bp William Jackson Cox P 9/1/1988 Bp Gerald Nicholas Mcallister. m 12/27/1958 Peck-Lim Khoo. P-in-c Ch Of The Ascen Houston TX 2000-2002; The Great Cmsn Fndt Houston TX 1998-2002; Asian Mssnr Chr The King Ch Houston TX 1998-2000; Chr The Redeem Luth Ch Tulsa OK 1998; Org Redeem Luth Tulsa OK 1997-1998; Ascen Luth Ch Tulsa OK 1995-1997; Org Ascen Luth Tulsa OK 1995-1997; Org/Choir S Lk Tulso OK 1991-1994; S Lk's Ch Tulsa OK 1990-1994; Dio Oklahoma Oklahoma City OK 1988-1990; Cur S Elis Nowata OK 1987-1990; Ch Of The H Sprt - Epis Tulsa OK 1986-1987. Ord of S Lk.

KIBLER SR, Bryant C (Lex) 607 HWY 1746, 607 Highway 1746, Irvine KY 40336 **Chr Epis Ch Harlan KY 2015-; P-in-c S Thos Ch Beattyville KY 2013-; Archd Dio Lexington Lexington 2004-, 1983-1997; P-in-c S Tim's Barnes Mtn Irvine KY 1994-** B Stuttgart DE 1953 s Nelson & Emilie. BA Cit 1976; MAT Cit 1978; MDiv Epis TS in Kentucky 1983. D 6/4/1983 P 12/10/1983 Bp Addison Hosea. m 4/6/2002 Connie Gayle Kibler c 1. P-in-c S Mk's Ch Hazard KY 2013-2015, Supply 1997-2013; Vic S Jn's Ch Corbin KY 1983-1994; P-in-c S Jos Mssn Sta Ravenna KY 1982-1984.

KIBLINGER, Charles Edward (Va) 651 Rivendell Blvd, Osprey FL 34229 **1992-** B Independence KS 1939 s Cleo & Maxine. BA U So 1961; MDiv VTS 1966; MA CUA 1973; Oxf GB 1980; Sewanee: The U So, TS 1996. D 6/18/1966 P 12/18/1966 Bp Edward Clark Turner. m 6/9/1962 Janet P Kiblinger c 1. Dir Of Ldrshp / Mnstry Dvlpmt VTS Alexandria VA 2000-2003; S Jn's Cathd Denver CO 1991-2000; S Jas Ch Jackson MS 1981-1991; Assoc S Alb's Epis Ch Annandale VA 1967-1973; Cur S Lk's Epis Ch Shawnee KS 1966-1967; Com; Dep fo GC Dio Colorado Denver CO 1994-1997; Stndg Com 1992-1996; COM

Dio Mississippi Jackson MS 1983-1991. Auth, "Preaching From Cathd". Comp Ccn, Fell Shalem Inst; CEEP.

KIDD, Paul David (At) 10952 NW 32nd Ave, Gainesville FL 32606 B Fisher IL 1936 s Shirley & Mable. BS U of Florida 1959; MDiv SWTS 1976. D 6/6/1976 P 12/12/1976 Bp Frank S Cerveny. m 4/17/1960 Margaret A Kidd c 2. Vic S Barth's Ch High Sprg FL 2005-2011; Int/Vic St Barth's Ch 2005-2011; Ch Of The Trsfg Rome GA 1996-2002; Coun For Mnstry Cedartown GA 1996-2002; Vic S Jas Ch Cedartown GA 1996-2002; Vic Ch Of The Nativ Jacksonville FL 1991-1996; Vic S Barn Epis Ch Williston FL 1985-1987; Vic S Alb's Epis Ch Chiefland FL 1978-1987; Chr Ch Cedar Key FL 1978-1984; Dio Florida Jacksonville 1976-1991; S Cathr's Ch Jacksonville FL 1976-1978; S Jas Ch Macclenny FL 1976-1978; Ret. Bp's Cross Dio Florida 2011.

KIDD, Reggie M (CFla) **Cathd Ch Of S Lk Orlando FL 2014-** D 6/8/2013 P 1/5/2014 Bp Gregory Orrin Brewer.

KIDD, Sandra (SO) D 6/11/2016 Bp Thomas Edward Breidenthal.

KIDD, Saundra Kay (Fla) D 5/1/2016 Bp Samuel Johnson Howard.

KIDD, Scott Austin (At) 20 Whisperwood Way, Cleveland GA 30528 **R Ch of the Resurr Sautee Nacoochee GA 2007-** B Marietta GA 1959 s Michael & Betty. EFM Sewanee: The U So, TS 1996; BS Excelsior Coll 2001; MDiv Candler TS Emory U 2005. D 10/18/1998 Bp Onell Asiselo Soto P 1/21/2006 Bp J Neil Alexander. m 9/15/1984 Patricia Bridges Kidd c 4. Assoc R Chr Ch Macon GA 2006-2007; D S Teresa Acworth GA 1998-2006. NAAD 1998.

KIDD, Stephen Willis (Miss) 11322 E Taylor Rd, Gulfport MS 39503 **P-in-c S Mk's Ch Gulfport MS 2013-** B Monroe LA 1976 s Willis & Mary. BA Nthrn Arizona U 2002; MDiv Epis TS of the SW 2010. D 6/5/2010 P 5/27/2011 Bp James Monte Stanton. m 10/9/1999 Melanie L Kidd c 2. Cn Trin Cathd Little Rock AR 2011-2013, D-Transitional 2010-2013; Yth Dir The Epis Ch Of The Trsfg Dallas TX 2003-2007. stephenw.kidd@gmail.com

KIDDER, Ann (O) PO Box 519, Gates Mills OH 44040 **S Chris's By-The River Gates Mills OH 2014-** B Plymouth NH 1955 d Kent & Lurlyne. BA U of New Hampshire 1977; MDiv GTS 1993. D 7/22/1993 P 1/27/1994 Bp Douglas Edwin Theuner. m 9/18/1993 Theodore G Fletcher c 2. S Pat's Ch Brewer ME 2011-2014; S Jas Ch Old Town ME 2011-2013; S Marg's Ch Belfast ME 2008-2009; R S Andr And S Jn Epis Ch SW Hbr ME 1998-2004; Vic Gr Epis Ch Concord NH 1996-1998; Cur Epis Ch Of S Mary The Vrgn Falmouth ME 1993-1995.

KIDDER, Frederick Elwyn (PR) B 1919 D 12/12/1976 P 5/28/1977 Bp Francisco Reus-Froylan. m 8/10/1957 Georgina Garrett.

KIEFER, Lee Roy (EO) 428 King St, Wenatchee WA 98801 **Mssnr S Alb's Epis Ch Redmond OR 2003-** B Syracuse KS 1949 s Lee & Neva. K SU 1969; BA Wichita St U 1971; MDiv Sewanee: The U So, TS 1990. D 5/26/1990 Bp William Edward Smalley P 12/14/1990 Bp Donald Purple Hart. m 1/1/2005 Marcia L Kiefer. S Lk's Epis Ch Wenatchee WA 2011-2014; Cn Dio Estrn Oregon Cove OR 2007-2011, 2002-2006; R Ch Of The Epiph Honolulu HI 1992-2002; Inst For Human Serv Inc Honolulu HI 1990-1992; S Matt's Epis Ch Waimanalo HI 1990-1992.

KIENZLE, Edward Charles (Mass) 165 Pleasant St Apt 303, Cambridge MA 02139 B Flushing NY 1946 s Edward & Ethel. BS U of Maryland 1970; PhD Boston Coll 1976; MDiv Harvard DS 1995. D 6/5/1996 Bp M(Arvil) Thomas Shaw P 2/1/1997 Bp Roger W Blanchard. m 6/14/1969 Beverly M Kienzle c 1. P Assoc S Ptr's Epis Ch Cambridge MA 2009-2016; Int S Steph's Ch Cohasset MA 2007-2008; Int Ch Of Our Sav Brookline MA 2005-2006; Int S Andr's Ch Ayer MA 2005; R S Geo's Par Flushing NY 2002-2004; R Ch Of The Gd Shpd Dedham MA 1999-2002, P-in-c 1997-1999; Asst Emm Ch W Roxbury MA 1997, D 1996-1997; Mem, Audit Com Dio Long Island Garden City NY 2003-2004; Mem, Bd Dir, Epis Chars of Long Island 2002-2004; Chair, Jubilee Debt Forgiveness Com, Dioc Coun Dio Massachusetts Boston MA 2000-2002. Auth, "Study Guide w Readings for Stiglitz's Econ of the Publ Sector," W.W. Norton & Co, 1989; Auth, "Post-Fisc Distributions of Income: Measuring Progressivity w Application to the Untd States," *Publ Fin Quarterly*, Sage Pub, 1982; Auth, "Measurement of the Progressivity of Publ Expenditures and Net Fiscal Incidence," *Sthrn Econ Journ*, Sthrn Econ Assn, 1981; Auth, "Measurement of Tax Progressivity: Comment," *Amer Econ Revs*, Amer Econ Assn, 1980; Auth, "The Cyclical Response of U.S. Income Inequality: Some New Empirical Results," *Publ Fin Quarterly*, Sage Pub, 1980. Epis Ntwk For Econ Justice 1995-2000.

KIESCHNICK, Frannie (Cal) 134 La Goma St, Mill Valley CA 94941 B Santa Barbara CA 1953 d George & Sarah. BA Ya 1975; MDiv EDS 1982. D 6/19/1982 P 1/1/1983 Bp Robert Claflin Rusack. m 6/29/1985 Michael Hall-Kieschnick c 1. Assoc Trin Par Menlo Pk CA 2008-2012, 1994-1995, 1989-1994; Asst The Epis Ch Of S Mary The Vrgn San Francisco CA 1998-2003; Asst R H Trin Menlo Pk 1989-1998; Asst R S Bede's Epis Ch Menlo Pk CA 1986-1989; All SS Ch Pasadena CA 1982-1986.

KIESSLING, Donna Jean (Del) 22 N. Union Street, Smyrna DE 19977 **R S Ptr's Ch Smyrna DE 2012-** B Neptune City NJ 1963 d David & Claudia. ABA Ursinus Coll 1987; BBA Ursinus Coll 1993; MDiv Luth TS 2006; MDiv Other 2006; MDiv Other 2006. D 5/17/2006 P 9/9/2007 Bp Paul Victor Mar-

464

shall. Assoc S Alb's Epis Ch Reading PA 2011-2012; Assoc S Gabr's Ch Douglassville PA 2007-2011; Stwdshp Cmsn Chairperson Dio Bethlehem Bethlehem PA 2010-2012. Rotary Intl 2013.

KIKER, Norman Wesley (Okla) 5705 Earl Dr, Shawnee OK 74804 B Shawnee OK 1947 s James & Kathleen. D 7/1/1989 Bp Robert Manning Moody. m 7/20/1968 Claudia Bea Henderson. D Dio Oklahoma Oklahoma City OK 1989-2002.

KILBOURN, Lauren Michelle (NC) 221Union St, Cary NC 27511 B Decatur GA 1982 d Lawrence & Deidre. BA Florida Sthrn Coll 2004; MDiv Duke DS 2007; Cert Ang Stud VTS 2010. D 6/19/2010 P 11/9/2011 Bp Michael B Curry. m 10/13/2007 Holly Gaudette. Assoc S Paul's Epis Ch Cary NC 2011-2013; Cur S Andr And H Comm Ch So Orange NJ 2010-2011.

KILBOURN, Thomas Lewis (Ct) 51 Paddy Hollow Rd, Bethlehem CT 06751 B Torrington CT 1941 s Norton & Helen. BA Norwich U 1964; BD Ya Berk 1967; MA Fairfield U 1970. D 6/13/1967 Bp Walter H Gray P 3/1/1968 Bp John Henry Esquirol. m 12/22/1973 Maureen Kilbourn. S Paul's Epis Ch Bantam CT 1991-2006; Int S Paul's Ch Woodbury CT 1986-1987; Non-par 1983-1986; All SS Ch Wolcott CT 1980-1981; Non-par 1967-1979. Tchr Of Year Finalist 1991.

KILBOURN-HUEY, Mary Esther (Lex) 310 Edgemont Rd, Maysville KY 41056 D S Fran' Epis Ch Flemingsburg KY 2013-; D S Andr's Ch Lexington KY 2011- B Saint Clair Shores MI 1949 d Robert & Mary. BD U of Kentucky 1981; MS Nthrn Kentucky U 2007. D 7/10/1999 Bp Don Adger Wimberly P 4/16/2016 Bp William Michie Klusmeyer. m 10/4/1997 Howard Terry Huey c 4. Ch Of The Nativ Maysville KY 2005-2009, Montessori Sch Bd Dir 2008-2011; Dio Lexington Lexington 1999-2002; D Mgr S Marg's Chap Lexington KY 1999-2002; Res Mgr S Agnes Hse Lexington KY 1996-2002. NAAD 1999. S Steph Recognition NAAD 2001. mekh1949@yahoo.com

KILBY, John Irvine (Ia) 4903 California St Apt 5, Omaha NE 68132 Ret 1994- B Pittsylvania County VA 1931 s Virginus & Willie. BA Hampden-Sydney Coll 1953; BD VTS 1959; Cert Creighton U 1997. D 6/27/1959 P 7/2/1960 Bp Clarence Alfred Cole. COM Dio Iowa Des Moines IA 1978-1980, Stndg Com 1986-1989, Dioc Coun 1980-1985; R Chr Epis Ch Clinton IA 1976-1994; Chr Ch (Limestone) Hanna City IL 1974-1976; Chair Dept Mnstry Dio Quincy Peoria IL 1971-1976, 1970-1972, Secy Dioc Conv 1970-1971; Cn Pstr St Paul's Epis Ch Peoria IL 1969-1976; P-in-c S Andr's Epis Ch Greenville SC 1962-1969; P-in-c Ch of the H Comf Columbia SC 1959-1962.

KILFOYLE, J Richard (WMass) 240 Belmont St Apt 103, Worcester MA 01604 Ret 1994- B Cambridge MA 1933 s John & Doris. BA Emerson Coll 1959; MDiv Ya Berk 1962. D 6/23/1962 P 4/20/1963 Bp Anson Phelps Stokes Jr. R S Jn's Epis Ch Sutton MA 1993-1994; 1990-1993; Dio Wstrn Massachusetts Springfield 1985-1994; R S Mk's Ch Worcester MA 1985-1990; The Ch Of The Adv Boston MA 1983; R 1973-1979; S Jn's Ch Jamaica Plain MA 1973-1978; Assoc Old No Chr Ch Boston MA 1972; Ltrgcs Com Dio Massachusetts Boston MA 1965-1972; R S Jn's Epis Ch Lowell MA 1964-1972; Cur Gr Ch New Bedford MA 1962-1964. Soc of S Marg, Soc of S Jn the Evang.

KILGORE, John W (Mo) 320 Union Blvd, Saint Louis MO 63108 B Joplin MO 1953 BA U of Missouri 1975; MD U of Missouri 1980; Cert GTS 2004. D 3/28/2003 P 3/25/2004 Bp George Wayne Smith. Chr Ch Cathd S Louis MO 2004-2005; S Mich & S Geo S Louis MO 2003-2004.

KILIAN, Joan M (Ga) 9003 Oakfield Dr, Statesboro GA 30461 R Trin Ch Statesboro GA 2002- B El Paso TX 1958 d Joseph & Jeune. BS Penn 1980; MFA Savannah Coll of Art & Design 1989; MDiv Sewanee: The U So, TS 1997. D 5/16/1997 P 12/13/1997 Bp Henry Irving Louttit. Stdg. Comm. Pres Dio Georgia 2005-2007; Dioc Coun Mem Dio Georgia 1999-2002; Ch Of Our Sav Augusta GA 1997-2002. Woods Ldrshp Awd U So 1995.

KILLEEN, David Charles (Fla) St. John's Episcopal Church, 211 North Monroe St., Tallahassee FL 32301 R S Jn's Epis Ch Tallahassee FL 2010-; Trst Amer Friends of the Angl Cntr in Rome 2014-; Stndg Com Dio Florida Jacksonville 2013-; Cmncatn and Engagement Com Epis Relief and Dvlpmt 2013- B Red Bank NJ 1973 s Charles & Nancy. BA Muhlenberg Coll 1995; MDiv GTS 2004. D 3/13/2004 P 9/18/2004 Bp Mark Sean Sisk. m 12/12/1998 Carol Ann Killeen c 4. Assoc R S Mk's Epis Ch Jacksonville FL 2007-2010; Cur/Int S Mary's-In-Tuxedo Tuxedo Pk NY 2004-2007; Dir of Cmncatn St. Barth Ch New York NY 1999-2001.

KILLIAN, David Allen (Mass) 882 Watertown St, West Newton MA 02465 Gr Ch Newton MA 2015-; Pres Coop Metropltn Mnstrs 2014-; Chapl, COM Dio Massachusetts Boston MA 2013-, Stndg Com 1995-1999 B Mondovi WI 1940 s Alphonse & Helen. Marq 1959; S Ptr's Coll Baltimore MD 1959; BA S Paul's Coll Washington DC 1964; MA New Sch U 1984; DMin Andover Newton TS 1990. Rec 12/17/1988 Bp David Elliot Johnson. m 6/23/1984 Barbara A O'Neil c 2. R All SS Par Brookline MA 1992-2012; Int Ch Of The Gd Shpd Watertown MA 1991; Int S Mich's Ch Marblehead MA 1990; Assoc R and Int S Dunstans Epis Ch Dover MA 1989-1990; Exec Dir Interfaith Counslng Serv Inc Newton MA 1985-1992; P RC Ch 1967-1988. Auth, "Developing the Sm Groups Your Cong Needs," PACE, 1982; Auth, "Paulist PB," Mssy SSP, 1981. Alb Inst 1989; EPF 1989; Ma Epis Cler Assn 1989. Ruah Sprt Awd Coop Metropltn Mnstrs 2013.

KILLIAN, Kathleen Erin (Me) S Sav's Par Bar Harbor ME 2015- D 12/20/2014 P 5/30/2015 Bp Leo Frade.

KILLINGSTAD, Mary Louise (Spok) 502 Hillside Dr, Yakima WA 98903 Hisp Cmsn Chairman 1990- B Parsons KS 1933 d Forrest & Mary. Yakima Vlly Coll 1980; Heritage Coll Toppenish WA 1987; Cemanahuac Spanish Lang Sch 1990. D 11/1/1980 Bp Leigh Allen Wallace P 7/13/2003 Bp James E Waggoner Jr. m 12/31/1952 John Killingstad. Com 1988-1994; Asst S Mich's Epis Ch Yakima WA 1984-1992; 1983-1989; Chapl Intern Kadlec Hosp Richland WA 1981-1982; Asst H Trin Epis Ch Sunnyside WA 1980-1983.

KIM, Andrew (Los) 13091 Galway St, Garden Grove CA 92844 B 1961 MS Philadelphia Biblic U; DMin Regent U Norfolk; CAS Sewanee: The U So, TS. D 12/13/2004 P 6/18/2005 Bp Leo Frade. m 11/17/1990 Esther Sum Kim. P-in-c Ch Of The Resurr Anaheim CA 2008-2013; The Rev The U So Sewannee TN 2001-2005.

KIM, John D (Los) St James Episcopal Church, 3903 Wilshire Blvd, Los Angeles CA 90010 Assoc S Jas Par Los Angeles CA 2015-, 2012-2015 B Seoul Korea 1956 s Young & Sam. St Mich's Theol Coll 1988. Trans 3/9/2012 as Priest Bp Joseph Jon Bruno. m 1/23/1993 Eun Ju Kim c 1.

KIM, John Jong-Kun (Pa) 3204 Ashy Way, Drexel Hill PA 19026 Chapl Seamens Ch Inst New York NY 2008- B Kea-san KR 1944 s Moon Bae & Alma. LLB Chung Angl U Kr 1971; Vancouver TS CA 1994; SFTS 1997. D 4/5/1988 Bp Donald Purple Hart P 2/28/1998 Bp Charles Ellsworth Bennison Jr. m 1/11/1975 Sue Kim c 1. Assoc Cathd Ch of Our Sav Philadelphia PA 2000-2007; Vic S Mart's Korean Ch Philadelphia PA 1998-2007; Dio Pennsylvania Philadelphia PA 1997-2007; D 1988-1998.

KIM, Jonathan Jang-Ho (WNY) Kumi Box 1039, Kumi Kyungbuk 730-600 Korea (South) B Kwang Ju KR 1932 s Jae & Soon-Sam. BS Seoul Natl U Seoul Kr 1955; MS Carnegie Mellon U 1961; PhD U of Oklahoma 1965; U Tor 1993. D 6/5/1993 P 5/1/1994 Bp David Charles Bowman. m 10/28/1957 Kun Ai Chu. Assoc S Andr's Ch Buffalo NY 1993-2011.

KIM, Richard (Mich) 19983 E Doyle Pl, Grosse Pointe MI 48236 B 1927 s Cs & Cs. Command and Gnrl Stff Coll; Dickinson Coll; U So. D 11/2/1973 P 5/1/1974 Bp Furman Charles Stough. m 10/19/1985 Helen Ann Kim c 4. S Jn's Ch Detroit MI 1987-1997; R Trin Epis Ch Lexington MI 1981-1987; Pres/Fndr Blue Water Hospice Port Huron MI 1981-1985; Dn Of The Blue Water Convoc 1981-1983; R Gd Shpd Maui HI 1977-1981; The Par Of Gd Shpd Epis Ch Wailuku HI 1977-1980; Prov Iv Hunger Taskforce & Conf Dio Alabama Birmingham 1975-1976, Prov Iv Hunger Taskforce & Conf 1975-1976; R Gr Ch Sheffield AL 1974-1977. Ord Of S Lk.

KIM, Stephen Yongchul (Los) 45267 Sancroft Ave, Lancaster CA 93535 B Inchon KR 1947 s Myung & Kyung. BA Yonsei U KR 1970; S Nich Sem Seoul KR 1972; Presb TS Seoul KR 1986. Trans 2/1/1997 Bp Frederick Houk Borsch. m 1/28/1974 Kyung Ja Yuk c 2. Chapl Gd Samar Hosp Los Angeles CA 2004-2014; Assoc Cathd Cntr Los Angeles CA 2002-2014; Assoc Dio Los Angeles Los Angeles CA 2002-2014; Vic S Nich Korean Mssn Los Angeles CA 1991-2001; Vic Serv Angl Ch of Korea 1973-1990. EAM. Cn of the Cathd in the Dio LA The Dio Los Angeles 2014.

KIM, Yein Esther (Los) 840 Echo Park Ave, Los Angeles CA 90026 Dio Los Angeles Los Angeles CA 2016- B Seoul Korea 1980 d Keun Sang & Jung Hee. BA Korea U 2004; MDiv EDS 2014. Trans 12/10/2014 as Deacon Bp Joseph Jon Bruno.

KIM, Yong Gul Ninian (LI) 2235 36th St, Astoria NY 11105 B 1939 s Shin-Duk & Yang-Soon. Trin Sem; BS In-Ha U 1968; S Michaels Sem 1970. D 3/1/1971 P 9/1/1979 Bp The Bishop Of Seoul. m 9/28/1974 Chung Martha Kim. P-in-c St Josephs Epis Korean Ch Great Neck NY 1990-2005, P-in-c 1981-1983; Dio Long Island Garden City NY 1983-1989; Serv Ch Of Korea 1971-1979.

KIMBALL, Anne Bogardus (Ct) 14890 David Drive, Fort Myers FL 33908 B New Rochelle NY 1934 d Paul & Elizabeth. BA Vas 1956; MDiv Ya Berk 1986. D 6/14/1986 P 2/7/1987 Bp Arthur Edward Walmsley. m 6/21/1958 Richard A Kimball c 3. Assoc Calv Ch Stonington CT 2002-2008; Assoc S Mk's Ch New Canaan CT 1997-2000; Chapl Ya Berk New Haven CT 1995-2000; Assoc S Lk's Par Darien CT 1986-1994. Doctor of Cn Law Ya Berk 1999.

KIMBALL JR, George Allen (Mil) 320 E Pleasant St Unit 301, Oconomowoc WI 53066 Ret 2000- B Monroe LA 1938 s George & Stephen. BA Pr 1960; LLB LSU 1965; MDiv Nash 1980; MA Marq 1990. D 6/11/1980 P 3/1/1981 Bp James Barrow Brown. m 8/26/1962 Doris D Kimball c 2. Chair - Human Affrs & Hlth Nash Nashotah WI 1990-1992, Acad Sub-Dn & Rgstr 1987-1989, Instr 1983-1990, Tchg Asst 1980-1983; Vic S Mary's Epis Ch Summit WI 1989-2000; P-in-c S Aidans Ch Hartford WI 1981-1982; Mem- Ecclelsiastical Crt Dio Milwaukee Milwaukee WI 1996-2000, 1990-2000. Grad Fell ECF 1981.

KIMBALL, Jennifer Warfel (Va) 125 Beverly Rd, Ashland VA 23005 S Andr's Epis Ch Newport News VA 2016- B Urbana IL 1967 d Linden & Constance. BA Wheaton Coll 1989; MA CUA 1993; MDiv VTS 2004. D 6/26/2004 P 1/18/2005 Bp Peter J Lee. m 8/3/1991 Sven Layne Vanbaars. Chapl Christchurch Sch Christchurch VA 2014-2015; S Jn's Ch W Point VA 2012-2014; Chanco on

465

the Jas Surry VA 2010; Dio Sthrn Virginia Newport News VA 2009; Epis HS Alexandria VA 2007-2008; Cur Ch Of S Jas The Less Ashland VA 2004-2007.

KIMBALL, John Charles (Pa) 202 Park Ave, Collegeville PA 19426 **Ret 1996-** B New London CT 1929 s Charles & Georgiana. BA Daniel Baker Coll 1951; STB Ya Berk 1954. D 6/2/1954 P 6/14/1955 Bp Walter H Gray. m 7/15/1972 Barbara N Kimball c 2. Int Emm Ch Philadelphia PA 1997-1999; P-in-c Ch Of S Jn The Evang Philadelphia PA 1989-1996; Assoc S Jas Ch Collegeville PA 1988-1989; 1980-1988; Vic S Mary Warwick PA 1977-1980; 1971-1977; Chapl All SS Hosp Epis Cmnty Servs Philadelphia PA 1967-1971; Chr Ch Cuba NY 1961-1965; P-in-c Our Sav Bolivar NY 1961-1965; Vic Gd Shpd Ft Hall ID 1958-1961; Vic Gr Epis Ch Glenns Ferry ID 1955-1958; S Jas Ch Mtn Hm ID 1955-1958; Vic S Jn Bruneau ID 1955-1958; Cur Ch Of The H Trin Middletown CT 1954-1955; Dept Mssns Dio Albany Greenwich NY 1962-1964; BEC Dio Idaho Boise ID 1957-1961.

KIMBALL, Melodie Irene (Ore) 257 E Milton St, Lebanon OR 97355 **Dio Oregon Portland OR 2016-; S Mart's Ch Lebanon OR 2016-** B Seattle WA 1949 d Bert & Helen. AAS Shoreline Cmnty Coll 1981; Grad Dioc TS Dio Olympia Mnstry Dev 1995; BA City U of Seattle 2003. Trans 1/20/2017 as Priest Bp Michael Hanley. c 2.

KIMBLE, Shell Teyssier (WA) 5316 Taylor Rd, Riverdale MD 20737 **S Barn Epis Ch Temple Hills MD 2010-** B Hollywood, FL 1970 d Wynn & Sophie. MS Florida St U; BA Florida St U; MDiv VTS 2009. D 6/13/2009 P 1/16/2010 Bp John Bryson Chane.

KIMBROUGH, Brendan Lee 200 Oyster Creek Dr, Lake Jackson TX 77566 **S Tim's Epis Ch Lake Jackson TX 2017-** B Dallas TX 1964 s Richard & Nancy. BBA U of Mississippi 1991; MDiv Westminster TS 2009. D 6/5/2010 P 5/19/2011 Bp James Monte Stanton. m 4/24/1999 Stephanie Kimbrough c 1. Vic, St. Timothys Epis Ch Dio Dallas Dallas TX 2012-2017; Cur S Jas Ch Dallas TX 2010-2012. bkimbrough@stimothy.org

KIMBROUGH, Timothy Edward (Tenn) 435 Patina Circle, Nashville TN 37209 **Dn Chr Ch Cathd Nashville TN 2010-, 2009-2010** B Birmingham AL 1957 s S T & Sarah. BA Duke 1979; MDiv Duke DS 1983; CAS GTS 1984. D 5/31/1984 P 6/1/1985 Bp Robert Whitridge Estill. m 1/9/1982 Darlene J Mary Kathleen Detomo c 4. R Ch Of The H Fam Chap Hill NC 1989-2009; Vic S Dav's Epis Ch Laurinburg NC 1984-1989; Hd Counslr S Phil's Cmnty Kitchen Durham NC 1981-1982; Joint Com on the Philippine Cov Exec Coun Appointees New York NY 2004-2009; Liturg Off Dio No Carolina Raleigh NC 1998-2001, Liturg Cmsn 1984-1997. "We Will Be God's People," *Kids' Praise*, GBGMusik, 2007; "Canticle H," *Global Praise III*, GBGMusik, 2004; "Jesus, your light again I view," *Songs of Love and Praise*, GBGMusik, 2003; Auth, "Whither Should Our Full Souls Aspire," *A Song for the Wrld*, GBGMusik, 2002; Auth, "Violence," *Preaching Through the Year of Matt*, Morehouse Pub, 2001; Auth, "10, 22, 43, 45, 46," *Global Praise II*, GBGMusik, 2000; Auth, "Peace is My Last Gift," *Global Praise I Resource Bk*, GBGMusik, 1997; Auth, "37, 54, 55," *Global Praise I*, GBGMusik, 1996; Auth, *Theol in Hymns? (translation)*, Kingswood Books: Abingdon Press, 1995; Mus Ed, *A Song for the Poor*, GBGMusik, 1990; Auth, "74, 652, 799, 821, 844," *The Meth Hymnal*, Abingdon Press, 1989. AAM 1989; Chas Wesley Soc 1988; Hymn Soc of the U.S. and Can 1990. tkimbrough@christcathedral.org

KIMES, Nicki Sagendorf (Ct) 134 East Ave, New Canaan CT 06840 **Assoc Chr Ch Redding CT 2011-** B New York NY 1944 d Forrest & Nadia. BA Chart Oak St Coll 2006; MDiv GTS 2006. D 6/10/2006 P 12/16/2006 Bp Andrew Donnan Smith. m 1/28/1967 Russell Astfalk Kimes c 2. Asst S Paul's Ch Fairfield CT 2006-2010. Ntwk of Biblic Stotytellers, Intl. 2010.

KIMMELMAN, Sandra Sue (Miss) **S Timothys Epis Ch Southaven MS 2010-, Other Lay Position 2007-2009; Vol Chapl Bapt Hosp 2016-; Hse Parent CPG Spec Sessions 2010-** B Jennings, LA 1949 d Louis & Inez. D 6/4/2016 Bp Brian Seage. m 7/23/1999 James Kimmelman c 2. Vol Chapl Methodist Hosp 2013-2016.

KIMMEY, Jimmye Elizabeth (NY) 928 W Hickory St, Denton TX 76201 **Cn Mssnr Dio New York New York NY 1995-, Cn to Ordnry, Mnstry Dvlpmt 1983-1995, Cn Mssnr 1995-, Cn to the Ordnry, Mnstry Dvlpmt 1991-1995, Exec for Mnstry 1983-1991** B Houston TX 1925 d John & Mary. BA U of Texas 1948; MA Col 1954; PhM Col 1973; MDiv UTS 1980. D 6/7/1980 Bp Paul Moore Jr P 12/14/1980 Bp Walter Decoster Dennis Jr. Assoc S Barn Epis Ch Denton TX 1995-2013; Assoc The Ch Of The Epiph New York NY 1980-1982. Graduated cl NYU 2007; Cn Mssnr Bp RIchard Grein 1995.

KIMMICK, Donald William (Nwk) 9625 Miranda Dr, Raleigh NC 27617 **Ret 1993-** B Teaneck NJ 1932 s William & Marie. BA Trin Hartford CT 1954; STB Ya Berk 1957; MA Col 1968; EdD Col 1975. D 6/15/1957 P 12/21/1957 Bp Benjamin M Washburn. m 6/23/1956 Genevieve Kimmick c 2. Sr Chapl Seamens Ch Inst New York NY 1986-1993; R Ch Of The Gd Shpd Midland Pk NJ 1957-1986; Dioc Coun Dio Newark Newark NJ 1984-1986, Stndg Com 1978-1983, COM 1970-1978, Bdgt Com 1963-1977. Auth, "Role Playing & Lecture-Discussion Parent Educ"; Auth, "Statement On Ch Mem"; Auth, "Lit Of Evang". AAMFT 1993-2009.

KIMURA, Gregory W (Los) 9900 Toakee Cir, Eagle River AK 99577 **S Andr's Epis Ch Ojai CA 2017-** B Saint Paul MN 1968 s Kerry & Betty. BA Marq 1990; MDiv Harvard DS 1993. D 8/21/1993 P 4/1/1994 Bp Steven Charleston. m 7/27/1991 Joy N Atrops-Kimura. H Sprt Epis Ch Eagle River AK 1994-1999. Auth, "Anchorage Daily News". Theta Alpha Kappa; Alpha Sigma Nu. standrews.office@sbcglobal.net

KIN, Nancy Elizabeth (Alb) 1249 3rd St, Rensselaer NY 12144 **Ch Of The Redeem Rensselaer NY 2014-** B Kankakee IL 1950 d John & Betty. BA Gvnr' St U 1975; MBA U Chi 1989; MMA Nash 2014. D 5/31/2014 P 12/13/2014 Bp William Howard Love.

KINARD III, George Oscar (SeFla) **Chaplin Mart Correctional Inst 2002-** B West Palm Beach FL 1939 s George & Sidney. Dioc Sch For Chr Stds; AA Palm Bch Jr Coll 1959. D 3/24/2007 Bp Leo Frade. m 12/30/1989 Judith Kinard c 3.

KINCAID III, S Thomas (Dal) 708 Harrison St, La Porte IN 46350 **Asst R Ch Of The Incarn Dallas TX 2009-** B Dallas TX 1982 s Samuel & Barbara. BA SMU 2005; MDiv Duke DS 2009; MDiv Duke DS 2009. D 6/6/2009 P 12/5/2009 Bp James Monte Stanton. m 7/9/2011 Elisabeth R Kincaid c 2. S Eliz's Epis Ch Culver IN 2013-2015; P-in-c S Fran Ch Chesterton IN 2012-2015; P-in-c S Paul's Epis Ch Laporte IN 2012-2015. tkincaid@incarnation.org

KINDEL JR, William H (Colo) 802 Navajo Avenue, Fort Morgan CO 80701 **S Eliz's Epis Ch Brighton CO 2016-; Vol P St. Clare's Mnstrs Denver CO 2009-** B Denver CO 1948 s William & Jane. SB MIT 1970; MS OH SU 1971; MDiv Epis TS of the SW 2007. D 6/9/2007 P 12/8/2007 Bp Robert John O'Neill. m 1/2/2010 Cynthia Elizabeth Kindel c 3. P-in-c Par Ch Of S Chas The Mtyr Ft Morgan CO 2008-2011; Secy of Conv Dio Colorado Denver CO 2007-2008; Lay Rep, Dioc Coun Dio Massachusetts Boston MA 1991-1997.

KINDERGAN, Walter Bradford (CGC) **R S Chris's Ch Pensacola FL 2015-** D 12/14/2013 P 7/12/2014 Bp Philip Menzie Duncan II.

KING, Allan Brewster (Mass) 222 Sayre Drive, Princeton NJ 08540 **Ret 1999-** B Boston MA 1936 s Allan & Carolyn. BA Harv 1957; JD Harv 1960; MDiv EDS 1967. D 6/24/1967 Bp Anson Phelps Stokes Jr P 10/6/1968 Bp Frederic Cunningham Lawrence. m 12/30/1978 Helen King c 1. Asst P Trin Ch Princeton NJ 2008-2009; Vic S Alb's Ch Lynn MA 1975-1999; LocTen S Jas Epis Ch Teele Sq Somerville MA 1971-1972; Cur The Ch Of Our Redeem Lexington MA 1968-1969; Dioc Coun Dio Massachusetts Boston MA 1978-1980.

KING, Benjamin John (Mass) School of Theology University of the South, 335 Tennessee Ave., Sewanee TN 37383 **Dir of the Advncd Degrees Prog Sewanee U So TS Sewanee TN 2010-, Assoc Prof of Ch Hist 2009-** B Brighton East Sussex UK 1974 s Roger & Carolyn. BA U of Cambridge 1996; BA Westcott Hse Cambridge 1999; MA U of Cambridge 2000; MTh Harvard DS 2003; PhD Dur 2007. Trans 1/28/2003 Bp M(Arvil) Thomas Shaw. m 8/1/2009 Leyla King c 2. Chapl Harvard Radcliffe Ch Cambridge MA 2005-2009; Cur The Ch Of The Adv Boston MA 2002-2005. Co-Ed, "Receptions of Newman," Oxf Press, 2015; Auth, "'Jn Henry Newman and the Ch Fathers: Writing Hist in the First Person,'" *Irish Theol Stds 78:2*, 2013; Auth, "'The Consent of the Faithful' from 1 Clem to the Angl Cov,'" *Journ of Angl Stds*, 2013; Auth, "'Seeking consensus within the Angl tradition: the example of Chas Gore,'" *The Open Body: Essays on Angl Ecclesiology , ed. Chas M. Stang and Zachary Guiliano*, Ptr Lang, 2012; Auth, "Newman and the Alexandrian Fathers: Shaping Doctrine in Nineteenth-Century Engl," Oxf Press, 2009; Auth, "'In Whose Name I Write': Newman's Two Translations of Athan,'" *Journ for the Hist of Mod Theol 15:1*, 2008. HSEC 2012. Awd for Theol Promise Jn Templeton Fndt/FIIT, Heidelberg 2011.

KING JR, Charles Baldwin (Alb) 5 Jodiro Ln Apt 100, Colonie NY 12205 B Schenectady NY 1943 s Charles & Alma. BA SUNY 1966; MDiv SWTS 1969. D 6/15/1969 Bp Charles Bowen Persell Jr P 12/15/1969 Bp Allen Webster Brown. m 6/12/1965 Alice King c 4. Ret and Vic S Jas Ch Ft Edw 2008-2013; Ret and Vic Gr and H Innoc Albany NY 2006-2008; Cn Cathd Of All SS Albany NY 1999-2006; Dio Albany Greenwich NY 1996-1999, Chair Cler Compstn Com 1986-1993; R Ch Of The H Cross Warrensburg NY 1994-2006; R Chr Ch Deposit NY 1980-1994; R Trin Ch Gouverneur NY 1975-1980; Calv Epis Ch Cairo NY 1970-1975; Gloria Dei Epis Ch Palenville NY 1970-1975; Vic Trin Ch Ashland Ashland NY 1970-1975; All SS Ch N Granville NY 1969-1970; Vic Trin Ch Whitehall NY 1969-1970. Forw in Faith 1997; GAS 2011; NOEL; SocMary; SSC 2003. Hon Cn Cathd of All SS, Albany 2001; Bp's Awd Dio Albany 1995.

KING, Charles Malcolm (SD) 15A Church St, New Milford CT 06776 B New York NY 1943 s Charles & Margaret. BA Queens Coll 1965; MA Col 1967; MDiv EDS 2003. D 12/21/2006 P 5/17/2008 Bp Creighton Leland Robertson. m 10/18/1997 Carolyn King c 1. Calv Cathd Sioux Falls SD 2008-2010; Vic Dio So Dakota Pierre SD 2008-2010; Chapl (on call) Sioux Vlly Hosp (now Sanford Medcal) 2005-2006.

KING, Chester W (RG) 10033 Cork Dr, El Paso TX 79925 **R All SS Epis Ch El Paso TX 1982-, 1981-2008** B Conway AR 1939 s Chester & Clara. BS U of Cntrl Arkansas 1965; MDiv Epis TS in Kentucky 1975. D 5/18/1975 P 11/18/1975 Bp Addison Hosea. m 11/4/2007 Karen D Brandan c 2. Vic S

K

Phil's Ch Harrodsburg KY 1975-1982, 1975-1981; S Barn Ch Nicholasville KY 1975-1977; St Barn Ch Nicholasville KY 1975-1977; S Tim's Barnes Mtn Irvine KY 1975-1976.

KING, Christopher (ECR) 220 W Penn St, Long Beach NY 11561 **Vic Par Of S Jas Of Jerusalem By The Sea Long Bch NY 2008-** B Columbus MS 1965 s John & Wanda. BA Baylor U 1987; MA CDSP 1991; DPhil Oxf GB 2000. D 6/26/1999 Bp Richard Lester Shimpfky P 1/28/2000 Bp Catherine Scimeca Roskam. Hon Non-Stip Assoc The Ch Of S Lk In The Fields New York NY 2006-2007; Assoc St. Barth Ch New York NY 2004; Dioc Yth Cdntr Dio New York New York NY 1999-2004. Auth, "Origen on the Song of Songs as the Sprt of Scripture: The Bridegroom's Perfect Mar-Song," Oxf Press, 2005; Auth, "A Love As Fierce As Death: Reclaiming The Song Of Songs For Gay Men and Lesbians," *Take Back the Word*, Pilgrim Press, 2000; Auth, "A Commentary On The Catechism Or Outline Of Faith," *A Faith for Living*, Enoptika Productions, 1994. Fell ECF 1993; Phi Beta Kappa 1987.

KING, Darlene Dawn (EMich) 3201 Gratiot Ave, Port Huron MI 48060 B Midland MI 1936 d Richard & Reva. D 12/13/2008 Bp Steven Todd Ousley. m 6/13/1953 Robert John King c 4.

KING JR, Earle Cochran (WNY) 2595 Baseline Rd, Grand Island NY 14072 **R S Mart In The Fields Grand Island NY 1987-; GC Dep Dio Wstrn New York Tonawanda NY 2015-2018, Stndg Com 2015-2017, GC Dep 2012-2015, GC Dep 2009-2012, Stndg Com 2008-2012, GC Dep 2006-2009, Stndg Com 2003-2007, GC Dep 2003-2006, GC Dep 2000-2003** B Ellwood City PA 1950 s Earle & Margaret. BA Eastman Sch of Mus 1972; MA U of Oklahoma 1974; MDiv SWTS 1985. D 6/25/1985 Bp Richard Mitchell Trelease Jr P 1/6/1986 Bp Harold Barrett Robinson. m 7/15/1972 Paula J King c 2. Asst S Jas' Ch Batavia NY 1985-1987; Mem, St of the Ch HOD 2012-2015.

KING, Ed (WMass) 4571 Lakeshore Rd, Lexington MI 48450 **Dio Estrn Michigan Saginaw MI 2013-** B Cochrane ON CA 1940 s Albert & Dorothy. BA Ryerson U 1962; Michigan TS 1973; MA S Johns Prov Sem 1988. D 6/30/1979 Bp William Jones Gordon Jr P 6/28/1985 Bp Henry Irving Mayson. m 5/7/2017 Ann Elizabeth Barkley c 2. R All S's Ch of the Berkshires No Adams MA 2003-2012; R S Jn's Ch No Adams MA 2003-2012; R H Trin Epis Ch Southbridge MA 1999-2003; P-in-c Dio Michigan Detroit MI 1996-1999; P-in-c Dream Cluster Allen Pk MI 1996-1999; P S Lk's Epis Ch Allen Pk MI 1985-1996; Asst S Andr's Epis Ch Livonia MI 1979-1985.

KING, Francis Marion Covington (WNC) 140 Saint Marys Church Rd, Morganton NC 28655 B Tulledega AL 1950 s Johnsey & Marie. BA Mississippi Coll; JD U of Mississippi 1984; MDiv Sewanee: The U So, TS 2000. D 2/12/2006 P 8/20/2006 Bp Charles Edward Jenkins III. m 8/30/1997 Peggy Walker c 1. St Mary's and St Steph's Epis Ch Morganton NC 2009-2015; Ch Of The H Sprt New Orleans LA 2006-2008.

KING JR, Frank Hiram (NI) 904 N Fenton Rd, Marion IN 46952 B Marion IN 1933 s Frank & Freda. BA Franklin Coll 1955. D 9/12/1987 P 3/25/1988 Bp Francis Campbell Gray. m 8/8/1969 Marilyn Jo King c 1. S Andr Epis Ch Kokomo IN 2003-2005; S Paul's Ch Naples FL 2003-2005; S Paul's Epis Ch Gas City IN 1993-1997; Asstg P Geth Epis Ch Marion IN 1987-1993. CBS. Pstr Emer St Andr / Kokomo 2007.

KING, Frank Walter (WNC) 4425 Huntington Dr, Gastonia NC 28056 B Wilmington NC 1958 s John & Mary. BA U NC 1980; MDiv VTS 1985; DMin SWTS 2001. D 5/1/1985 P 11/1/1985 Bp Brice Sidney Sanders. m 6/13/1981 Jocelyn Ann King. S Mk's Ch Gastonia NC 2001-2004; R The Epis Ch Of The Epiph So Haven MI 1996-2001; R Chr Epis Ch Hope Mills NC 1986-1994; R S Mk Fayetteville NC 1986-1989; St Marks Ch Hope Mills NC 1986-1988; Int S Jn's Epis Ch Fayetteville NC 1985-1986.

KING, Gayle (Colo) 1347 Allen Ave, Erie CO 80516 **Ret 1998-** B Denver CO 1932 d Harold & Jeanette. K SU 1953; Sarah Lawr Coll 1972; MDiv SWTS 1987. D 6/12/1987 P 6/1/1988 Bp Arthur Anton Vogel. m 2/22/1969 William R King c 5. Assoc S Jn's Epis Ch Boulder CO 2001-2010; Assoc S Bon Ch Sarasota FL 1992-1998; Assoc S Matt's Ch Evanston IL 1987-1992.

KING, Giovan Venable (Haw) 93 N Kainalu Dr, Kailua HI 96734 **R S Chris's Ch Kailua HI 2011-** B Winston Salem NC 1956 d Joel & Joann. AB Dart 1979; MDiv Harvard DS 1983; JD Stanford Law Sch Palo Alto CA 1988; DMin VTS 2005. D 5/26/2007 P 1/12/2008 Bp Joseph Jon Bruno. m 1/26/1998 Thomas King c 1. Faith Epis Ch Laguna Niguel CA 2010-2011; S Edm's Par San Marino CA 2010; Assoc R S Jas Par Los Angeles CA 2007-2009; Fac, Sum Collegium VTS Alexandria VA 2006-2010; Sr Min Hyde Pk Congrl Ch Los Angeles CA 2001-2006; Chapl Washington Med Cntr Culver City CA 1998-1999; Sr Min Ch of the Mssh Los Angeles CA 1992-1994; Assoc/Chapl/Int First Congrl Ch Of Los Angeles 1983-2007. Auth, "Psalms in the Key of Life," *Intl Congrl Journ*, ICF, 2006; Auth, "Preaching: Our Hope for Years to Come," *The Congrl*, NACCC, 2003; Auth, "Courts and Congregationalism," *Stanford Law Revs*, Stanford Law Sch, 1989. Cmsn on Ecum and Interreligious Concerns 2007; Eccl Crt Judge 2008; Friends of Jerusalem 2009. JJ Russell Sermon Awd Natl Assn 2006; La Rochelle Schlr Huguenot Soc for VTS 2004; Natl Playwriting Awd Natl Assn 2003; Billings Preaching Prize Harvard 1983; Phi Beta Kappa Dartmouth 1979.

KING, Janet Gay Felland (Ida) 678 E 400 N, Rupert ID 83350 **D Dio Idaho Boise ID 1986-** B Ann Arbor MI 1947 d Robert & Marjorie. BSN Ball St U 1972; MNSc U of Arkansas 1976. D 12/20/1986 Bp David Bell Birney IV. m 10/26/1974 Robert Allen King c 1.

KING, Jonathan LeRoy (NY) 340 Godwin Ave, Ridgewood NJ 07450 **Ret 1997-** B New York NY 1929 s Frederic & Edith. BA Harv 1951; EDS 1953; MDiv GTS 1956; STM NYTS 1975. D 10/18/1956 Bp Horace W B Donegan P 5/9/1957 Bp Charles Francis Boynton. m 5/10/1958 Jacqueline King c 4. S Barth's Ch In The Highland White Plains NY 1995-1997; Gr Epis Ch Nyack NY 1993-1995; The Ch Of S Jos Of Arimathea White Plains NY 1993; All Ang' Ch New York NY 1991-1993; S Mich's Epis Ch Wayne NJ 1990-1991; All SS' Epis Ch Glen Rock NJ 1988-1990; Trin Ch Irvington NJ 1988; All SS Ch Bergenfield NJ 1986-1988; Cathd Of St Jn The Div New York NY 1974-1986; Chapl Veterans' Admin Hosp Lyons NJ 1973-1974. Angl Soc 1955; Retreat Hse Redeem Nyc 1992.

KING, Joseph Willet (Az) 7735 N Via Laguna Niguel, Tucson AZ 85743 **D Chr The King Ch Tucson AZ 2006-** B Springfield MO 1934 s Charles & Evelyn. BA SMU 1956; MD U of Texas 1962; EFM Sewanee: The U So, TS 1996. D 6/22/1996 Bp Robert Manning Moody. m 7/2/1972 Doris Ann Toby c 4. D S Andr's Epis Ch Lawton OK 1998-2000; Lic D S Phil's In The Hills Tucson AZ 1997-2004; Vocational D S Dunst's Ch Tulsa OK 1996-1998. NAAD 2001.

KING SSJE, Kale Francis (Wyo) 3107 Summit Hills Trl, Mount Airy NC 27030 **Ret 1989-** B Eaton CO 1924 s Francis & Charlotte. BA Colorado Coll 1950; LTh Bex Sem 1953; Cert Ldrshp Acad for New Directions 1975. D 6/16/1953 P 12/15/1953 Bp James W Hunter. m 10/8/1961 Amory M King c 2. All SS Ch Wheatland WY 1985-1989, R 1985-1989, Vic 1953-1957; Ch Of Our Sav Hartville WY 1985-1989, Vic 1985-1989, 1953-1984, Vic 1953-1957; H Sprt Epis Ch Dover ID 1979-1985, Vic 1979-1985; S Mary's Bonners Ferry Bonners Ferr ID 1979-1985, Vic 1979-1985; All SS Ch 1973-1979; Vic All SS Scobey MT 1973-1979; S Mary's Ch Helena MT 1973-1979; S Matt's Ch Glasgow MT 1973-1979, R 1973-1979; Cn Pstr H Trin Monrovia Liberia 1972-1973; Dio Idaho Boise ID 1971-1972, Archd 1971-1972; St Matthews Epis Ch Rupert ID 1959-1963, Vic 1959-1963; S Mich's Cathd Boise ID 1957-1959, Cn 1957-1959; S Matt's Epis Cathd Laramie WY 1954-1955; S Jn The Bapt Ch Glendo WY 1953-1957, Vic 1953-1957. Tertiary of the Soc of S Fran 1967. Hon Cn H Trin Cathd, Monrovia, Liberia 1973.

KING, Karen (Chi) 125 E 26th St, Chicago IL 60616 **Exec Coun Appointees New York NY 2016-** B Chicago IL 1955 d Edward & Evelyn. BOG Chicago St U 2007; MDiv SWTS 2010. D 6/4/2011 P 1/24/2013 Bp Jeff Lee. c 3. Emm Epis Ch Rockford IL 2012-2013.

KING, Karen Gail (Mont) P.O. Box 158, Troy MT 59935 **Assoc S Patricks Ch Kenwood CA 2014-** B Lake Charles LA 1947 d Jean & Alice. BS LSU 1970; MEd LSU 1976; MDiv GTS 2010. D 12/10/2009 P 5/1/2011 Bp Charles Franklin Brookhart Jr. c 2. R Dio Montana Helena MT 2011. DOK 2000.

KING, Karen L (Ind) 3401 Lindel Ln, Indianapolis IN 46268 **Assoc R for Outreach and Pstr Care Trin Ch Indianapolis IN 2010-, Assoc R for Mssn and Outreach 2002-** B Springfield MA 1953 d Samuel & Frances. BA Knoxville Coll 1975; MS U of Tennessee 1977; MDiv Chr TS 2002. D 6/29/2002 P 6/8/2003 Bp Cate Waynick. c 2. Dep to GC 2012 Dio Indianapolis Indianapolis IN 2011-2012, COM 2008-2011, Stndg Com 2002-2005.

KING, Kathryn Louise (Nwk) 28 Ralph St, Bergenfield NJ 07621 **Gr Epis Ch Traverse City MI 2011-; S Alb's Ch Oakland NJ 2009-** B Monroe LA 1961 d W(Illiam) & Audrey. BS Elizabethtown Coll 1984; MDiv CDSP 1995. D 6/3/1995 Bp John Shelby Spong P 12/1/1995 Bp Jack Marston Mckelvey. c 1. Vic All SS Ch Bergenfield NJ 2003-2009; S Tim's Ch Danville CA 1998-2003; Asst Chr Epis Ch Los Altos CA 1996-1998; Asst S Ptr's Ch Mtn Lks NJ 1995-1996.

KING JR, Kenneth Vernon (EO) 702 Grant Street, Summit MS 39666 B Lexington MS 1950 s Kenneth & Louise. BS U of Mississippi 1973; Cert Theol Stud CDSP 2000; MDiv CDSP 2003; CPE Med Cntr of San Francisco Mofit/Long Hosp 2005; Cert Pstr Stud PSR 2005. D 6/4/2005 Bp William Edwin Swing P 11/30/2005 Bp Julio Ernesto Murray Thompson. m 12/17/2009 Barbara Ann King. R Ch Of The Redeem Pendleton OR 2010-2011; Supply P Dio Mississippi Jackson MS 2008-2009; Mssy P Exec Coun Appointees 2005-2008; Prov of Bocas del Toro Exec Coun Appointees New York NY 2005-2008; Chapl Mnstry At Sea Oakland CA 2003-2005; Mssy P Dom And Frgn Mssy Soc- Epis Ch Cntr New York NY 2005-2008. Supply Cler Dio Mississippi 2009; Mssy P Angl Global Relatns 2005.

KING, Leslie Anne (NCal) 55 Maria Dr Ste 837, Petaluma CA 94954 **Non-stipendiary Assoc S Patricks Ch Kenwood CA 2008-** B Baltimore MD 1956 d William & Virginia. BA Colby Coll 1978; MA Bos 1986; PhD Bos 1996. D 6/29/1993 P 7/29/1994 Bp Edward Cole Chalfant. St Johns Epis Ch Petaluma CA 2009-2010; S Tim's Epis Ch W Des Moines IA 2003-2004; Vic S Paul's Epis Ch Grinnell IA 1997-2002; Cur Ch Of The H Sprt Sfty Harbor FL 1994-1995. Auth, "Surditas:The Understandings of the Deaf and Deafness in the Writings of Aug, Jerome, and Bede," *Dissertation*, Bos, 1996.

K

KING, Leyla (ETenn) 1607 W 43rd St, Chattanooga TN 37409 **R Thankful Memi Ch Chattanooga TN 2010-** B Houston TX 1981 d Joseph & May. BA Dart 2002; Cert Mid 2004; MDiv Harvard DS 2009. D 10/26/2008 P 9/5/2009 Bp Michael Garrison. m 8/1/2009 Benjamin John King c 1. Asst Dio Massachusetts Boston MA 2008-2009.

KING, Margaret Creed (Fla) 704 Vauxhall Dr, Nashville TN 37221 **S Jn's Epis Sch Ocean Sprg MS 2004-; Asst R St. Jn's Epis Ch 2004-** B Knoxville TN 1952 d Albert & Merrillyn. D 5/30/2004 Bp Samuel Johnson Howard P 1/6/2005 Bp Duncan Montgomery Gray III. m 10/17/1986 John C King c 1. S Geo's Ch Nashville TN 2007-2012; S Jn's Epis Ch Ocean Sprg MS 2004-2007. marciacking@gmail.com

KING, Robert Andrew (Ky) 3935 Sunnyside Dr, Harrisonburg VA 22801 **Ret 1995-; Ret 1995-** B Homestead PA 1932 s John & Mary. BA Ken 1954; BD Bex Sem 1966. D 6/11/1966 P 10/12/1966 Bp Nelson Marigold Burroughs. m 12/28/1957 Regina King c 2. Vol Chapl Mahr Cancer Cntr 1995-2007; Calv Ch Louisville KY 1995; R S Mary's Ch Madisonville KY 1979-1995; R S Barth Mayfield Vill OH 1971-1979; S Barth's Ch Cleveland OH 1971-1979; P-in-c S Barn Dennison OH 1966-1971; R Trin Ch New Phila OH 1966-1971. marybeth.showalter@gmail.com

KING, Steven (Kan) 12251 Antioch Rd, Overland Park KS 66213 **Assoc Trin Cathd Omaha NE 2017-** B Shawnee KS 1986 s Dennis & Teresa. BGS The U of Kansas 2009; MDiv VTS 2014. D 6/7/2014 Bp Dean E Wolfe. m 7/28/2012 Ellen V King c 1. S Thos The Apos Ch Overland Pk KS 2014-2017.

KING, Tom Earl (NC) 2725 SE 39th ST, MOORE OK 73160 B Waco TX 1948 s Hershel & Virgie. BA Baylor U 1970; MDiv Sthrn Bapt TS 1973; ThM Sthrn Bapt TS 1978; PhD Sthrn Bapt TS 1982; Cert Epis TS of the SW 1995. D 7/5/1995 Bp Sam Byron Hulsey P 1/1/1996 Bp William Elwood Sterling. m 3/6/1993 Judy Ann Gibson c 4. Int S Mich's Epis Ch Norman OK 2014-2016; R Gr Epis Ch Lexington NC 2004-2014; Int S Paul's Epis Ch Pflugerville TX 2001-2004; Int S Jas' Epis Ch La Grange TX 2001; Vic S Thos' Epis Ch Rockdale TX 1996-1997. Amer Assn for Mar and Fam Ther 1977-2004; AAPC, AAMFT 1975-2004.

KING, William Michael (Ala) 905 Castlemaine Drive, Birmingham AL 35226 **Pat-time Cler Transition Off Dio Cntrl Gulf Coast Pensacola FL 2009-** B Birmingham AL 1941 s Richard & Mary. BA S Mary Coll Lebanon KY 1963; MA Notre Dame Sem Grad TS 1966; Univ of San Francisco 1968; MSW Tul 1971; Sewanee: The U So, TS 1987. Rec 6/1/1987 as Priest Bp Furman Charles Stough. m 6/7/1969 Patricia A King c 3. R Trin Epis Ch Clanton AL 2006-2007; Dio Alabama Birmingham 1998-2007, Dep to GC 2002-2005, Diac Formation Dir 2000-2011, Pres of the Stndg Com 1994-1995; R All SS Epis Ch Birmingham AL 1990-1998; Assoc R S Mary's-On-The-Highlands Epis Ch Birmingham AL 1987-1990. Auth, "Places of Secret Pryr: Pilgrimage In Alabama," Samford U Press, 2004.

KINGDON, Arthur M (Vt) 334 Oak Grove Rd, Vassalboro ME 04989 B Wisconsin Rapids WI 1943 s Robert & Anna. BA Ob 1965; MTh U Chi 1967; MA U Chi 1970. D 11/6/1980 P 7/16/1981 Bp Frederick Barton Wolf. m 6/14/1966 Linda B Kingdon c 2. R S Ptr's Epis Ch Bennington VT 1992-2003; R All SS Ch So Hadley MA 1985-1992; Dio Wstrn Massachusetts Springfield 1985-1992; 1980-1985.

KINGMAN, Donna Watkins (WMass) 3 Newington Ln, Worcester MA 01609 B West Point GA 1943 d William & Florence. BS Jacksonville St U 1964; MDiv EDS 1967; MA Assumption Coll 2000. D 10/18/1977 Bp George T Masuda. m 10/14/1967 Perry Alden Kingman c 2. D Trin Epis Ch Milford MA 2014-2016; D Ch Of The Gd Shpd Clinton MA 2007-2014; D Ch Of The Recon Webster MA 1996-2006; D Aroostook Epis Cluster Caribou ME 1990-1996; D Chr Ch No Conway NH 1985-1990; D H Trin Intl Falls MN 1977-1985; COM Dio Wstrn Massachusetts Springfield 1997-2001; Lay Mnstry Com Dio New Hampshire Concord NH 1988-1990. Assn of Epis Deacons 1980; Intl OSL the Physcn 2008.

KINGMAN, Perry Alden (WMass) 3 Newington Ln, Worcester MA 01609 **Ret Dio Wstrn Massachusetts Worcester MA 2006-** B Orange NJ 1941 s Barclay & Eleanora. BA Wms 1963; MDiv EDS 1966. D 6/11/1966 Bp Leland Stark P 12/16/1966 Bp George E Rath. m 10/14/1967 Donna Watkins c 2. R Ch Of The Recon Webster MA 1996-2006; Sr P Aroostook Epis Cluster Caribou ME 1990-1996; Chr Ch No Conway NH 1985-1990; P Ch of theTransfiguration Bretton Woods NH 1985-1990; R H Trin Intl Falls MN 1976-1985; P S Ptr's Ch Warroad MN 1976-1977; Instr Rel Vlly City St Coll Vlly City ND 1972-1976; All SS Ch Vlly City ND 1969-1976; P Ch Of The H Trin 1969-1976; P Gr Ch Madison NJ 1966-1969; Dioc Coun Dio Wstrn Massachusetts Springfield 1998-2003; Dioc Coun Dio Maine Portland ME 1992-1996; Dioc Coun Dio New Hampshire Concord NH 1987-1989; Dioc Coun Dio No Dakota Fargo ND 1974-1976. AAM 2006; RWF 1980-1996.

KINGSLEY, Josh (Ore) 11229 NE Prescott St, Portland OR 97220 **S Matt's Epis Ch Portland OR 2014-** B Lansing MI 1983 s Stephen & Paula. MM Portland St U; BM U of Idaho; MDiv Geo Fox Evang Sem 2014. D 7/16/2014 P 2/7/2015 Bp Michael Hanley. m 2/19/2000 Macie Larea Kingsley c 1. Dio Oregon Portland OR 2014-2017.

KINGSLEY, Myra Jessica (Az) 100 W Roosevelt St, Phoenix AZ 85003 **D Trin Cathd Phoenix AZ 2009-** B New Jersey NJ 1948 d Judd & Mina. BSN Arizona St U 1987; MS Arizona St U 1993. D 1/24/2009 Bp Kirk Stevan Smith. m 6/15/1968 Donald Kingsley c 3.

KINGSLEY, Timothy Miles (Minn) D 6/27/2017 Bp Brian N Prior.

KINGSLEY MURRAY, Miguel (DR) Dr Zafra# 3, Puerto Plata Dominican Republic **Dio The Dominican Republic (Iglesia Epis Dominicana) Gazcue Santo Domingo 2010-; D Iglesia Epis Cristo el Rey Puerto Plata 2010-; Vic Iglesia Santa Maria Llena de Gracia Mao Valverde 2010-** B 1946 s Gregorio & Elena. Centro de Estudios Teologicos Santo Domingo 2010. D 2/14/2010 Bp Julio Cesar Holguin-Khoury. c 2.

KINGSLIGHT, Kathleen Anne (Oly) 700 Callahan Dr, Bremerton WA 98310 **R S Paul's Epis Ch Bremerton WA 2010-** B Owosso MI 1952 d Robert & Therese. Cert Coll of Congrl Dvlpmt; MI SU 1972; BA Concordia Luth U 1993; MDiv Epis TS of the SW 1993; Cert Marywood Dominican Cntr Grand Rapids MI 1995; Cert Cler Ldrshp Proj 2005; Cert CISM InterCritical Incident Stress 2006; Cert Spanish Lang Immersion 2007; Cert SWTS 2009. D 8/24/1993 Bp Bob Gordon Jones P 3/17/1994 Bp Edward Lewis Lee Jr. m 7/11/1976 John Victor Koenigsknecht c 2. Dep to GC Dio Wstrn Michigan 2009; Dep To GC Dio Wstrn Michigan 2006; Alt to GC Dio Wstrn Michigan 2003; Mem of Exec Coun Dio Wstrn Michigan 1998-2003; R S Barn Epis Ch Portage MI 1997-2010; Chapl to the DOK Dio Wstrn Michigan 1997-2007; Assoc S Tim Ch Richland MI 1993-1997; Chapl to Curs Sec Dio Olympia 2012-2013; Trnr for Safeguarding God's Adults Dio Wstrn Michigan Kalamazoo MI 2000-2009, Trnr for Safeguarding God's Chld 2000-2009. Performer/Compsr, "Heart of Love," Audio Rcrdng, Self Pub, 1989; Compsr/Performer, "De Colores," Audio Rcrdng, Self Pub, 1989; Compsr/Performer, "The Light of Christmas," Audio Rcrdng, Self Pub, 1988; Compsr/Performer, "He's Shinin,'" Audio Rcrdng, Self Pub, 1986; Compsr/Performer, "Let Light Stream Forth," Audio Rcrdng, Self Pub, 1979. Oblate Ord Of S Ben 1998. Lily Fndt Grant for Ongoing Renwl of Cler in Active Mnstry Lily Fndt 2006; Mk Jorjorian Preaching Excellence Awd Epis Theo. Sem. of SW 1992; Natl Merit Scholarships St of Michigan 1970.

KINGSTON, Louise Lauck (NJ) 85 Westcott Rd, Princeton NJ 08540 **Asst Trin Ch Princeton NJ 1978-** B Bryn Mawr PA 1941 d Peter & Annette. BA Vas 1963; MDiv PrTS 1977. D 6/4/1977 Bp Albert Wiencke Van Duzer P 1/14/1978 Bp George Phelps Mellick Belshaw. m 6/22/1963 Michael Kingston c 3. Chapl Dept Rel Mnstrs Princeton Med Ctr Princeton NJ 2000-2002; Trin Ch Princeton NJ 1993-2003; Comm On Rel Mnstry Of Princeton Princeton NJ 1978-2001; Dir and Chapl Dept Rel Mnstrs Princeton Med Ctr Princeton NJ 1978-2000. AEHC 1979-2009; Bd Cert Chapl Assn of Profsnl Chapl 1979-2009.

KINMAN, Mike (Los) 6209 Pershing Ave, Saint Louis MO 63130 **All SS Ch Pasadena CA 2016-** B Santa Clara CA 1968 s Thomas & Jacqueline. BA U of Missouri 1990; MDiv Ya Berk 1996. D 7/27/1996 P 6/24/1997 Bp Hays H. Rockwell. m 6/27/1992 Robin L Kinman c 2. Dn Chr Ch Cathd S Louis MO 2009-2016; Exec Dir Episcopalians for Global Recon 2006-2009; Epis Campus Mssnr - Washington U in St. Louis Dio Missouri S Louis MO 1999-2005; Assoc S Mich & S Geo S Louis MO 1996-1999. Auth, "Sermon for Wrld Mssn Sunday, Matt 17:1-9," Sermons That Wk, Epis Ch, 2005; Auth, "An Army of One, A Palm Sunday Sermon," Get Up Off Your Knees: Preaching the U2 Catalog, Cowley, 2003; Auth, "A Bp For The 21st Century Ch," The Catalyst/Gathering The Next Generation, 2001; Auth, "Who Owns The Ch, A Sermon on Romans 7:13-25 and Jn 2:13-22," Sermons That Wk VIII, Morehouse, 1999. Jn Hines Preaching Awd VTS 2008. mkinman@allsts-pas.org

KINMAN, Thomas David (Az) PO Box 40126, Tucson AZ 85717 **D Epis Par Of S Mich And All Ang Tucson AZ 2007-** B Rugby UK 1928 s Thomas & Ella. MA Oxf GB 1954; PhD Oxf GB 1954. D 2/8/1997 Bp Robert Reed Shahan. m 1/19/1963 Jacqueline Louise Schroedter c 2.

KINNER, Heidi Ellen (Mont) St. Peters Episcopal Cathedral, 511 N. Park Avenue, Helena MT 59601 B Alamosa CO 1970 BA Colorado St U 1993; MDiv Nash 2004. D 6/19/2004 Bp Chester Lovelle Talton P 1/22/2005 Bp Joseph Jon Bruno. m 7/21/1994 Scott John Kinner. Dn S Ptr's Cathd Helena MT 2011-2017; Cn The Cathd Ch Of The Adv Birmingham AL 2005-2011; Vic S Mart-In-The-Fields Mssn Twentynine Plms CA 2004-2005. dean@stpeterscathedral.net

KINNETT, Kenneth (WNC) 57 Half Timber Ln, Flat Rock NC 28731 **Died 9/26/2015** B Atlanta GA 1934 s Frank & Joyce. BA U So 1956; MDiv Sewanee: The U So, TS 1969. D 6/21/1969 Bp Milton Legrand Wood P 4/8/1970 Bp Randolph R Claiborne. m 7/7/1956 Loyd N Nichols c 3. Ret 1994-2015; Ch Of The Cov Atlanta GA 1982-1985; P-in-c Cov Atlanta GA 1980-1985; Dio Atlanta Atlanta GA 1980-1981, 1970-1979; R S Greg The Great Athens GA 1973-1980; Sewanee U So TS Sewanee TN 1971-1974; Univesity of the So TS Sewanee TN 1971-1974; Ch Of The H Comf Atlanta GA 1970-1973; Chapl Intern Georgia Mntl Hlth Cntr Atlanta GA 1970-1971; Vic S Simon's Epis Ch Conyers GA 1970-1971; Cur S Bede's Ch Atlanta GA 1969-1970. AAPC 1988-1990.

KINNEY, Elise (Mass) 193 Clifton St, Malden MA 02148 B New York NY 1944 d John & Alice. BA Transylvania U 1965; MDiv EDS 1981. D 6/4/1983

Bp Paul Moore Jr P 5/12/1984 Bp Vincent King Pettit. m 1/6/1983 J Woods. Emm Ch W Roxbury MA 1995-1996; S Andr's Ch Of The Deaf Brookline MA 1994-1995; Mnstry Of Healing S Aug & S Mart Roxbury MA 1988-1989; Supply P Dio Massachusetts Boston MA 1984-1989; Dre S Jn's Ch Arlington MA 1983-1984.

KINNEY, Genie (Cal) 1746 29th Ave, San Francisco CA 94122 B Mount Vernon IL 1938 d Eugene & Virginia. BA U of Wyoming 1965; MDiv Iliff TS 1982; CAS CDSP 1990. D 6/16/1984 Bp William Carl Frey P 11/25/1990 Bp William Harvey Wolfrum. Ch Of The Incarn San Francisco CA 1992-2005; S Jas Epis Ch San Francisco CA 1988-1989.

KINNEY, Kathleen (Oly) 610-906-9690, Eastsound WA 98245 **Co-R Emm Ch Orcas Island Eastsound WA 2013-** B East Cleveland OH 1944 d Edwin & Marcelline. BD S Jn Coll 1967; MA U of Notre Dame 1976; MS Pace U 1984; MDiv NYTS 1992. D 6/11/1994 P 12/1/1994 Bp Richard Frank Grein. Co-R All SS Epis Ch Seattle WA 2003-2010; Cn S Mk's Cathd Seattle WA 1995-2001; Assoc S Ptr's Ch New York NY 1994-1995.

KINNEY, Robert Paul (SwFla) **Fin Admin All SS Ch Tarpon Spgs FL 2003-** D 12/3/2016 Bp Dabney Tyler Smith.

KINNEY, Robert Sturgis (Okla) 5231 Wedgefield Rd, Granbury TX 76049 B Endicott NY 1933 s John & Louise. BBA U of Texas 1955; MBA U of Texas 1961; MDiv CDSP 1962; STM Sewanee: The U So, TS 1969; DMin Sewanee: The U So, TS 1977. D 6/28/1962 Bp Everett H Jones P 12/1/1962 Bp William Jones Gordon Jr. m 4/26/1958 Emily Kinney c 2. Dioc Mssnr Dio Oklahoma Oklahoma City OK 1986-1997; R S Barn Epis Ch Saratoga WY 1980-1985; R S Andr's Epis Ch Amarillo TX 1975-1980; R Ch Of The Epiph Kingsville TX 1968-1975; Ch Of Our Sav Aransas Pass TX 1965-1968; Vic Trin-By-The-Sea Port Aransas TX 1965-1968; Vic S Jn's Ch Allakaket AK 1962-1965.

KINNEY, Stephen W (Tex) 2306 Cypress Pt W, Austin TX 78746 B Houston TX 1955 s William & Patricia. BA U of Texas 1979; MDiv Epis TS of the SW 1984; MA U of Texas 2009; PhD U of Texas 2011. D 6/7/1984 Bp Maurice Manuel Benitez P 1/29/1985 Bp Gordon Taliaferro Charlton. m 6/8/1985 Gwendolyn Carlisle Kinney c 3. Epis TS Of The SW Austin TX 2014, Adj Fac 2002-2010; Exec Dir Front Porch Proj 2009-2011; P-in-c of Bethell Serv S Dav's Ch Austin TX 2002-2008; Int S Chris's Ch Killeen TX 2000-2002; R S Barn Epis Ch Fredricksburg TX 1992-1998; Asst S Jn The Div Houston TX 1989-1992; Chapl Epis HS Bellaire TX 1984-1988. Auth, "Sustaining Mar in a Post-Traditional, Postmodern Wrld," *Dissertation*, U of Texas, 2011. swk. kinney@gmail.com

KINSER, Dixon (NC) St Paul's Episcopal Church, 520 Summit St, Winston Salem NC 27101 **S Paul's Epis Ch Winston Salem NC 2014-** B Memphis TN 1974 s William & Caroline. BA U of So Carolina 1996; MDiv TESM 2007. D 6/2/2007 P 3/30/2008 Bp John Bauerschmidt. m 1/2/1999 Kristin Erin Kinser c 2. Asst S Barth's Ch Nashville TN 2007-2014, 1999-2003; Yth Dir S Dav's Epis Ch Peters Township PA 1999-2003.

KINSEY, Douglas Andrew (Pgh) D 12/11/2016 P 6/18/2017 Bp Dorsey McConnell.

KINSEY, Kevin Lee (Me) 650 Main St Ste A, Caribou ME 04736 **Aroostook Epis Cluster Caribou ME 2012-** B Plainwell MI 1962 s Kenneth & Donna. BA Witt 1984. D 6/23/2012 P 1/26/2013 Bp Stephen Taylor Lane. m 7/13/1985 Pamela Hancock Kinsey c 2.

KINSEY, Theron Harvey (Cal) 917 Avis Dr, El Cerrito CA 94530 **Non-par 1973-** B Albany CA 1942 s Raymond & Alice. BA California St U Sacramento 1964; BD CDSP 1969; MA U of Wyoming 1973. D 12/28/1969 P 8/1/1970 Bp George Richard Millard. m 8/29/1964 Kathryn Lee Chandler.

KINSEY, Thomas Burton (SO) 5004 Upton Ave S, Minneapolis MN 55410 B Cleveland OH 1942 s Harold & Gladys. BA Heidelberg U 1965; MDiv EDS 1972. D 6/17/1972 Bp John Harris Burt P 12/1/1972 Bp John Mc Gill Krumm. m 6/19/1999 Nancy Slifer. Assoc S Steph's Epis Ch And U Columbus OH 1983-1988; R Chr Ch Xenia OH 1980-1983; R S Paul's Ch Bellevue OH 1975-1980; Asst Trin Ch Columbus OH 1972-1976.

KINSOLVING, John Armistead (RG) 107 Washington Ave, Santa Fe NM 87501 B Santa Fe NM 1936 s Charles & Mary. BA U of New Mex 1958; MA U of New Mex 1963; BD CDSP 1964. D 6/7/1965 Bp C J Kinsolving III P 12/7/1965 Bp James W Hunter. m 1/30/1959 Patricia Kinsolving c 1. S Bede's Epis Ch Santa Fe NM 1969-1977; Chair - Dept Chr Soc Rel 1966-1969; R S Paul's Epis Ch Evanston WY 1965-1969; Stff Of The Yth Div & Chapl Wy St Hosp 1965-1969.

KINYON, Brice Wayne (USC) 1900 Woodvalley Drive, Columbia SC 29212 **Stff Mem Lexington Med Cntr W Colombia SC 2017-; Stff Mem Trin Cathd Colombia SC 2016-; Chapl Bd Lexington Med Cntr 2011-; Chapl, Ret Cler, etc. Dio Upper So Carolina Columbia SC 2007-** B Camden NJ 1936 s Brice & Zilla. BA Duke 1958; MDiv Sewanee: The U So, TS 1961. D 7/15/1961 P 2/11/1962 Bp John Vander Horst. m 11/23/1984 Carolyn Jean Templeton c 4. P-in-c S Thos Ch Eastover SC 2010-2016; P-in-c Ch Of The Epiph Laurens SC 2006-2009; Chapl Still Hopes Epis Ret Cmnty W Columbia SC 1999-2006; Chapl Cbury Ret Commnity OK City 1990-1999; Chapl S Anth Hosp Oklahoma City 1989-1999; P-in-c S Paul's Ch Clinton OK 1989-1994;

Judge Eccl Crt Dio Oklahoma Oklahoma City OK 1982-1999; Chapl Hospitals & Nrsng Hm Tulsa OK 1981-1989; Chapl Epis Ch Coun Tulsa OK 1981; S Jn's Ch Kenner LA 1973-1981; R S Tim's Ch La Place LA 1973-1978; Chapl Epis HS Baton Rouge 1972-1973; Assoc Vic Casady Sch Oklahoma City 1970-1972; P-in-c S Mary's Ch Chattanooga TN 1969-1970; Vic Ch Of The Nativ Ft Oglethorp GA 1967-1969; P-in-c Chr Ch Brownsville TN 1963-1967; Imm Ch Ripley TN 1963-1966; Cur S Paul's Epis Ch Chattanooga TN 1962; Asst Ch Of The Ascen Knoxville TN 1961-1962; Chapl E Tennessee Chld's Hosp Knoxville 1961-1962; Bd Trst Epis Ch Hm at York Place Inc Columbia SC 2007-2012; Bd Trst Finlay Hse Columbia SC 2004-2016. Assembly of Epis Healthcare Chapl 1982; Assembly of Epis Healthcare Chapl, Pres 1999-2001; Bd Cert Chapl of Assn of Profsnl Chapl 1992; Lexington Med Cntr Assoc Chapl 2005-2016; Pres Oklahoma Chapl Assn 1986-1987; S.C. Soc of Chapl 1999. DSA Coll of Chapl 1998. wkinyon@att.net

KIRBY, Elisa Mabley (EC) 320 Pollock St, New Bern NC 28560 B Huntington WV 1945 d Carlton & Virginia. BA Salem Coll 1968; MMin Providence TS 2015. D 6/20/2015 Bp Robert Stuart Skirving. c 1.

KIRBY, Erin C (FdL) PO Box 936, Minocqua WI 54548 **R S Mths Minocqua WI 2015-** B Boone NC 1958 d Jack & Eva. MA Appalachian St U 1995; EdD Appalachian St U 2004; MDiv CDSP 2011. D 12/18/2010 Bp Porter Taylor P 9/8/2012 Bp Gordon Scruton. c 1. S Jas Par Wilmington NC 2014-2015; R Trin Epis Ch Shrewsbury MA 2012-2014; Jr Dn Ripon Coll Cuddesdon Cuddesdon Oxford 2011-2012; Cur (NSM) Berinsfield Baldons Drayton St Leonard 2011-2012. Fllshp of the Way of the Cross 2014; Soc of Cath Priests 2012. reverinstmatthias@gmail.com

KIRBY, Harry Scott (Eau) 1712 Lehman St., Eau Claire WI 54701 **Co-chair w Spouce Chapl to Ret Cler and Spouses 2013-; P-in-c Gr Ch Rice Lake WI 2005-** B Richmond VA 1938 s William & Lucille. BA U Rich 1960; MDiv GTS 1963. D 6/15/1963 Bp Robert Fisher Gibson Jr P 12/20/1963 Bp Lauriston L Scaife. m 6/22/1963 Heather Roberts c 2. Vice Pesident HOD 2012; Pres Stndg Com Dio Eau Claire Eau Claire WI 1991-2002, Dep Gc 1991-, Chair, COM 2002-, Chair, CoM 1996-2010, Exam Chapl 1994-2010, Exam Chapl 1994-, Liturg Off 1992-; Dep GC Chr Ch Cathd Eau Claire WI 1989-2005; Dio Wstrn Kansas Hutchinson KS 1989-2005, Ecum Off 1983-1988, Liturg Off 1981-1988; P-in-c Epis Ch Of The Incarn Salina KS 1980-1981; Cn Chr Cathd Salina KS 1979-2005; Res Dir - VP S Fran Cmnty Serv Inc. Salina KS 1979-1989; Pres Morristown Hosp Chapl Morristown NJ 1975-1978; R Ch of S Jn on the Mtn Bernardsville NJ 1973-1979; Pres's Coun of Advice HOD. Auth, "arts, Appeal Letters, etc.," *Developmental & Estate Plnng*, St. Fran Acad. Angl Soc 1973; Cmnty of S Jn The Bapt 1973. VP - Nomination - HOD 2011; VP - Nomination - HOD 2011; CAP (Chapl Capt.) USAF 2003; Finalist for Bp - Utah 1996; Finalist for Bp - Utah 1996; Finalist for Bp = Rio Grand 1989; Finalist for Bp = Rio Grand 1989; Bp's Serv Awd Dio Wstrn Kansas 1980.

KIRBY, Jacquelyn Walsh (RI) PO Box 317, Jamestown RI 02835 **S Geo's Sch Middletown RI 2014-** B Baltimore MD 1966 d Semmes & Annette. BA Ya 1989; PhD NYU 2001; MDiv Ya Berk 2008; MDiv Berkeley at Yale 2008. D 6/21/2014 P 1/22/2015 Bp W Nicholas Knisely Jr. m 5/21/2005 Edward Gerard Kirby c 1. jackie_kirby@stgeorges.edu

KIRBY, Kelly Ellen (Ky) 330 N Hubbards Ln, Louisville KY 40207 **S Matt's Epis Ch Louisville KY 2014-** B Royal Oak MI 1977 d Thomas & Jeannie. BS MI SU 1998; MDiv CDSP 2002. D 12/22/2001 P 7/17/2002 Bp Wendell Nathaniel Gibbs Jr. m 1/10/2003 Brian S Kirby c 2. R S Andr Epis Ch Mentor OH 2007-2014; R Trin Ch Claremont NH 2004-2007; Asst All SS Epis Ch Pontiac MI 2002-2004. kkirby@stmatthewsepiscopallouisville.org

KIRBY, Richard Allen (Neb) B 1929 D 2/24/1955 Bp Howard R Brinker.

KIRBY, Whitney B (Az) 100 W. Roosevelt, Phoenix AZ 85003 **S Andrews Epis Sch Austin TX 2016-** B San Antonio TX 1984 d Patrick & Sharon. BA The U of Texas at Austin 2007; BA The U of Texas at Austin 2007; MDiv VTS 2012. D 6/7/2014 Bp Shannon Sherwood Johnston P 12/13/2014 Bp Kirk Stevan Smith. Trin Cathd Phoenix AZ 2014-2016; Ch Of The H Comf Vienna VA 2012-2014. wkirby@holycomforter.com

KIRCHER, Kathleen L (SwFla) 1741 Winding Oaks Way, Naples FL 34109 B Rochester NY 1943 d Joseph & Ruth. BA Nazareth Coll 1968; MS Boston Coll 1974; PhD U Roch 1992. D 10/17/2001 P 4/19/2002 Bp John Bailey Lipscomb. S Paul's Epis Ch Elk Rapids MI 2004-2011; Assoc R S Monica's Epis Ch Naples FL 2002-2011.

KIRCHHOFFER, James Hawley (Cal) 922 Valle Vista Ave, Vallejo CA 94590 **1967-** B Mobile AL 1933 s Richard & Arlene. BA Wabash Coll 1955; BD VTS 1958; CFP VTS 1980. D 6/21/1958 P 12/1/1958 Bp Richard Ainslie Kirchhoffer. m 9/16/1978 Elaine Marie Kirchhoffer c 3. Vic S Giles Ch Moraga CA 1963-1967; Asst R S Jn's Ch Youngstown OH 1960-1963; Vic Trin Ch Lawrenceburg IN 1958-1960.

KIRCHMIER, Anne Ruth (SVa) 45 Main Street, Newport News VA 23601 **S Andr's Epis Ch Newport News VA 2017-** B Pittsburgh PA 1965 d Thomas & Ruth. BS Westfield St Coll 1987; MDiv SWTS 2001. D 6/16/2001 Bp Gordon Scruton P 12/29/2001 Bp Peter J Lee. m 9/7/2013 John William Herbst. R S Geo's Epis Ch Newport News VA 2012-2016; R The Fork Ch Doswell VA

2005-2012; Asst R Chr Epis Ch Winchester VA 2003-2005; Asst to the R / Cler Res Chr Ch Alexandria VA 2001-2003; Dn of Reg XI Dio Virginia Richmond VA 2010-2012. annekirchmier.saec@gmail.com

KIRK, Deborah (WA) 14300 Saint Thomas Church Rd, Upper Marlboro MD 20772 **S Alb's Par Washington DC 2015-** B Wilmington DE 1950 d Clifford & Ellinore. BA W&M 1972; MA GW 1976; JD GW 1979; MDiv Wesley TS 2015. D 11/8/2014 P 6/13/2015 Bp Mariann Edgar Budde. c 3. Cathd of St Ptr & St Paul Washington DC 2014-2015.

KIRK, Jeffrey Malcolm (NJ) 102 Pearlcroft Rd, Cherry Hill NJ 08034 **R Gr Ch Merchantville NJ 2010-** B Astoria NY 1946 s Francis & Hazel. BS Leh 1968; MBA Kent St U 1971; MDiv EDS 1975; DMin Colgate Rochester Crozer DS 1982; DMin CRDS 1982. D 6/21/1975 Bp John Harris Burt P 12/27/1975 Bp David Shepherd Rose. m 8/29/1981 Betsey L Kirk c 2. R Ch Of The Atone Laurel Sprg NJ 2000-2010; R S Mary's Ch Haddon Heights NJ 1990-1995; R Epis Ch Of S Mary The Vrgn Falmouth ME 1987-1990; R Ch Of The Ascen Rochester NY 1982-1987; Asst S Paul's Ch Rochester NY 1978-1982; Asst S Jn's Ch Hampton VA 1975-1978. "Intelligent Design," LivCh, 2005; "Baptism," *First Act of Stwdshp*, LivCh, 1985. Beta Gamma Sigma Kent St U 1971; Chi Epsilon Leh 1968.

KIRK, Patricia Lanier (USC) 501 S La Posada Cir Apt 118, Green Valley AZ 85614 **D Epis Ch Of S Fran-In-The-Vlly Green Vlly AZ 2000-** B Decatur AL 1933 d Charner & Pearl. U of No Alabama. D 10/14/2000 Bp Robert Reed Shahan. m 5/24/1953 William Leroy Kirk c 3.

KIRK, Richard Joseph (Pa) 189 Kendal Dr, Kennett Square PA 19348 **Ret 1996-** B Trenton NJ 1931 s Richard & Jane. BSE Pr 1953; MDiv GTS 1956; STM Tem 1960; U of Missouri 1965; New Sch U 1967; DMin Eden TS 1976; Neumann Coll 1993. D 4/28/1956 P 10/28/1956 Bp Alfred L Banyard. m 4/17/1993 Janice M Kirk c 6. Ldrshp Dn Cler Ldrshp Proj 1997-2001; Dn Brandywine Deanry Dio Pennsylvania Philadelphia PA 1994-2000; Consult Orgnztn Ch Consult 1981-2009; R The Epis Ch Of The Adv Kennet Sq PA 1979-1996; Dio Missouri S Louis MO 1976-1979; Assoc Alb Inst 1974-1998; Assoc S Ptr's Epis Ch S Louis MO 1968-1976; Assoc Dce Dio New York New York NY 1963-1968; R S Mk's Epis Ch Yonkers NY 1958-1963; Vic S Jn's Epis Ch Maple Shade NJ 1956-1958. Auth, "Love Anew," *Love Anew*, Self-Pub, 1996; Auth, "On The Calling And Care Of Pastors; Orgnztn And Function Of The Bp'S Off - A Behavioral Sci View," *Patterns For Par Dvlpmt*, Crossroads, 1974; Auth, "On Calling & Care Pastors".

KIRK, Virginia Adele (Pa) 354 Heathcliffe Rd, Huntingdon Valley PA 19006 **Died 1/10/2016** B Philadelphia PA 1942 d John & Muriel. Sewanee: The U So, TS 1986; NOD La Salle U 1987. D 12/12/1987 Bp Allen Lyman Bartlett Jr. D Ch Of The Resurr Philadelphia PA 2000-2016; Assoc Chapl Epis Hosp Philadelphia PA 1987-1999; D The Free Ch Of S Jn Philadelphia PA 1987-1999. NAAD 1987; OA 1985-1995.

KIRKALDY, David (Tex) 612 Duroux Rd, La Marque TX 77568 B Northumberland UK 1935 s David & Lilian. BD U of Nottingham 1956; PhD U of Nottingham 1959. D 6/11/2005 Bp Don Adger Wimberly P 12/15/2005 Bp Rayford Baines High Jr. m 8/22/1959 Doris Kirkaldy c 4. Sr Chem Rohm & Haas Deer Pk TX 1968-1997.

KIRKHAM II, Hall (Mass) 112 Randolph Avenue, Milton MA 02186 **R S Mich's Ch Milton MA 2012-** B Cleveland OH 1964 s Walter & Jane. BA Amh 1987; MSc U of Edinburgh 1988; MBA U of Pennsylvania 1994; MDiv EDS 2008. D 6/7/2008 Bp M(Arvil) Thomas Shaw. m 9/13/2003 Marjorie Marie Rose Susan Asfour-Kirkham c 4. Asst R S Ptr's Ch Weston MA 2008-2012. Jn Robbins Hart Memi Prize for Excellence in Preaching EDS 2008. hall. kirkham@gmail.com

KIRKING, Kerry Clifton (Spok) 6533 Seaview Ave. NW, 505A, Seattle WA 98117 **P Assoc S Paul's Ch Seattle WA 2009-** B Coeur d'Alene ID 1946 s Hilbert & Mary. BA Pacific Luth U 1968; MA Yale DS 1972. D 10/15/1994 Bp Frank Jeffrey Terry P 6/2/2001 Bp James E Waggoner Jr. m 7/12/1975 Judith Marie Kirking c 2. P Assoc Cathd Of S Jn The Evang Spokane WA 2001-2011, D 1996-2000, D 1994-1995; D-in-c W Cntrl Epis Mssn Spokane WA 1995-1996. Affirming Angl Catholicism 1994; CBS 1999. Wolcott Calkins Prize for Preaching Yale DS 1974.

KIRKLAND, Patricia Ann (Ia) D 1/8/2012 Bp Alan Scarfe.

KIRKLEY, John Lawrence (Cal) 4616 California St, San Francisco CA 94118 **R S Jas Epis Ch San Francisco CA 2010-** B Gary IN 1967 s John & Joan. BA Indiana U 1989; MDiv Chicago TS 1993; Cert CDSP 2002. D 6/1/2002 P 12/7/2002 Bp William Edwin Swing. m 9/14/2008 Andrew Russell Aldrich c 1. Resolutns Com Dio California 2005-2008; Oasis/CA Bd Pres Dio California 2005-2006; R The Epis Ch Of S Jn The Evang San Francisco CA 2004-2010; Mar & Blessing TF Co-Chair Dio California 2004-2005; Every Voice Ntwk San Francisco CA 2004; Strng Com Claiming the Blessing 2002-2006; Assoc Ch Of The H Innoc San Francisco CA 2002-2004; Alt Dep GC2006 Dio California. "Struggling for Sacramental Equality," Witness mag, 2005; "A Contest Between the Normalcy of Civilization and the Reign of God," Do Justice Series/Louie Crew's Angl Pages, 2005; "Why I Believe In Gay Mar," Pacific Ch News, 2004; "Mod Demoniacs," Do Justice Series/Louie Crew's Angl Pages, 2004. Integrity 2000.

KIRKMAN, John Raymond (WMich) 4713 Rockvalley Dr NE, Grand Rapids MI 49525 B Adrian MI 1942 s Ernest & Kathryn. BS Wstrn Michigan U 1965; MDiv Bex Sem 1968. D 6/29/1968 Bp Charles Bennison Sr P 12/30/1968 Bp Frederick Barton Wolf. m 7/11/1991 Sherry L Kirkman c 2. S Paul's Ch Greenville MI 1994-2007; S Andr's Ch Grand Rapids MI 1985-1990, Assoc 1983-1985; R Emm Ch Petoskey MI 1973-1975; R S Jn's Epis Ch Saugus MA 1970-1973; Vic Chr Ch Norway ME 1969-1970; Cur Epis Ch Of S Mary The Vrgn Falmouth ME 1968-1969.

KIRK-NORRIS, Barbara H (NwT) PO Box 2949, Big Spring TX 79721 **Assoc Ch Of The H Trin Midland TX 2015-, 2013-2015; Chapl Emergency Chapl Serv Big Sprg & Howard Co. TX 2011-** B Knoxville TN 1967 d Joseph & Helen. BS Middle Tennessee St U 1990; MS U of Tennessee 1993; MDiv VTS 2004. D 5/29/2004 Bp Charles Glenn VonRosenberg P 1/22/2005 Bp Ted Gulick Jr. m 11/22/1997 William Christopher Norris. R The Epis Ch Of S Mary The Vrgn Big Sprg TX 2009-2013; Chapl Flaget Memi Hosp Bardstown KY 2006-2008; R Ch Of The Ascen Bardstown KY 2004-2008; judicial Crt Dio Kentucky Louisville KY 2006-2007. Pres (two years) Bardstown Mnstrl Assn 2008. revbarbara@holytrinity.org

KIRKPATRICK, Daisy (CNY) 741 West Second St, Elmira NY 14905 B Northampton MA 1944 d John & Hope. BS Cor 1989; MDiv Bex Sem 2003. D 8/21/2003 Bp Gladstone Bailey Adams III. c 2. Par D Gr Epis Ch Elmira NY 2008-2011; Intern Chemung Vlly Cluster Elmira NY 2007-2008; Cur Zion Epis Ch Greene NY 2004-2005; D in Charge Shared Epis Mnstry E Lowville NY 2003-2004. Cmnty of the Gospel 2006-2010; Comp of St. Lk 2003-2006.

KIRKPATRICK, Frank Gloyd (Ct) 154 Clearfield, Wethersfield CT 06109 **Prof of Rel Trin Hartford CT 1986-; P Assoc Trin Epis Ch Hartford CT 1980-** B Washington DC 1942 s George & Amy. BA Trin Hartford CT 1964; MA UTS 1966; PhD Br 1970. D 6/9/1973 P 5/1/1974 Bp Morgan Porteus. m 6/11/1966 Elizabeth Kirkpatrick c 2. Exam Chapl GBEC BEC Hartford CT 2006-2010; Assoc Prof of Rel Trin Hartford CT 1969-1986; Chair - COM Dio Connecticut Meriden CT 1982-1994. authohr, "The Epis Ch in Crisis," *The Epis Ch in Crisis*, Praeger, 2009; Auth, "The Ethics of Cmnty," *The Ethics of Cmnty*, Blackwells, 2001; Auth, "A Moral Ontology for A Theistic Ethics," *Moral Ontology for a Theistic Ethic*, Ashgate, 1996; Auth, "Together Bound," *Together Bound*, Oxford, 1993; Auth, "Cmnty: A Trin of Models," *Cmnty: A Trin of Models*, Georgetown, 1986. AAR 1972; Soc for Philos of Rel 1996. Brownell Prize for Tchg Excellence Trin 2011; Bp's Awd for Distinguished Serv Dio Connecticut 1999; Chas A Dana Resrch Prof Trin 1993; Ellsworth M Tracy Lectureship Trin 1981; Phi Beta Kappa Trin 1963.

KIRKPATRICK, Martha G (Del) St Barnabas Church, 2800 Duncan Rd, Wilmington DE 19808 **S Barn Ch Wilmington DE 2014-** B Portland ME 1956 d William & Priscilla. BA Skidmore Coll 1978; JD GW 1981; MDiv Harvard DS 2007. D 6/9/2007 P 12/15/2007 Bp Chilton Richardson Knudsen. S Marg's Ch Belfast ME 2009-2014; Dio Maine Portland ME 2007-2009; Asst Gr Epis Ch Bath ME 2007-2008.

KIRKPATRICK, Nathan Elliott (NC) 8410 Merin Rd, Chapel Hill NC 27516 B New Orleans LA 1978 s Rickey & Kathy. BA Wake Forest U 2000; MDiv Duke DS 2003; PhD Dur 2017. D 6/20/2015 Bp Michael B Curry P 12/20/2015 Bp Anne Hodges-Copple.

KIRKPATRICK, Rebecca Blair (Oly) 111 NE 80th St, Seattle WA 98115 **S Phil Ch Marysville WA 2017-; S Matthews Auburn WA 2016-** B Fort Collins CO 1977 d John & Susan. BA Mt Holyoke Coll 2001; MDiv Yale DS 2004. D 6/28/2008 Bp Bavi Edna Rivera P 1/17/2009 Bp Gregory Harold Rickel. m 8/15/2015 Cara Eileen Lanctot. Dio Olympia Seattle 2012-2017; Dir Chld & Yth Mnstrs S Andr's Ch Seattle WA 2008-2012. rector@saint-philips.org

KIRKPATRICK JR, Robert Jr Frederick (Lex) 9801 Germantown Pike, Apt 115, Lafayette Hill PA 19444 B Montgomery AL 1940 s Robert & Margaret. BA U So 1962; MDiv VTS 1971; DMin Sewanee: The U So, TS 1981. D 6/11/1971 Bp Furman Charles Stough P 12/5/1971 Bp George Mosley Murray. c 2. R Trin Epis Ch Danville KY 1990-2006; R Ch Of The Gd Shpd Covington GA 1979-1990; Asst Ch Of The Ascen Clearwater FL 1976-1979; Non-par Dyson & Co Pensacola FL 1973-1976; S Jn The Evang Robertsdale AL 1971-1973; Vic S Paul's Ch Foley AL 1971-1973.

KISNER, Mary Elizabeth (CPa) 712 E 16th St, Berwick PA 18603 **R Chr Ch Berwick PA 2010-** B Detroit MI 1950 d Walter & Alexandria. BS Drexel U 1972; MA U of Scranton 2003. D 11/3/1994 P 7/12/1995 Bp James Michael Mark Dyer. m 8/3/1974 Francis C Kisner. R S Paul's Ch Troy PA 2000-2010, R 1995-1999; D Ch Of The Redeem Sayre PA 1994-1995. mekisner@gmail.com

KISS, Margaret Mary (Mil) 3775 S 27th St Apt 210, Milwaukee WI 53221 **D S Thos Of Cbury Ch Greendale WI 2013-; Exec Secy Dio Milwaukee 2015-; COM Dio Milwaukee Milwaukee WI 2010-** B Milwaukee WI 1944 d Louis & Regina. BA Alverno Coll 1966; MEd Dayton U 1991. D 6/5/2010 Bp Steven Andrew Miller. D All SS' Cathd Milwaukee WI 2011-2013.

KISSAM, Todd William (Eas) 105 Church Lane, Church Hill MD 21623 **Dio Easton Easton MD 2017-** B Glens Falls NY 1966 s William & Diane. MDiv

Washington Theol Un 1996. Rec 12/19/2001 as Priest Bp William Jerry Winterrowd. m 5/28/2004 Heather K Calloway Kissam c 1. St Lk's Par Ch Hill MD 2013-2017; R S Ptr's Ch Salisbury MD 2009-2012; R Ch Of Our Sav Washington DC 2005-2009; Asst Chr's Epis Ch Castle Rock CO 2002-2004.

KISSINGER, Debra Jean (Ind) 1100 W. 42nd St., Indianapolis IN 46208 **Cn for Transition Mnstrs & Ldrshp Dvlpmt Dio Indianapolis Indianapolis IN 2008-, Dioc Deploy/Transition Off 2009-, Liaison to COM 2008-** B Pottsville PA 1961 d Kenward & Anna. AS Penn 1981; BA La Salle U 1988; MDiv Ya Berk 1992; Cert The Ch Dvlpmt Inst 1996; Cert The Ch Dvlpmt Inst 1997; Cert Cler Ldrshp Proj 2007; Cert Fresh Start Trainers 2008; Cert Off of Transition Mnstrs 2010; Cert Cler Ldrshp Inst 2012; Cert Int Mnstry Ntwk 2013; Cert Kellogg Ldrshp - Seabury/Bexley 2015. D 6/13/1992 Bp Allen Lyman Bartlett Jr P 12/12/1992 Bp Richard Frank Grein. m 12/20/2014 John V Oaks c 1. Adj Faculy Moravian TS 2011; Dio Bethlehem Bethlehem PA 2001-2008, Lifelong Formation 2001-2008; R Gr Epis Ch Willoughby OH 1997-2001; Vic S Ptr's Epis Ch Oxford CT 1993-1997; Sum Camp Chapl Dio Connecticut Meriden CT 1993; Asst S Barn Ch Irvington NY 1992-1993; Publ Educ & Literacy Natl Coun of Ch Cleveland OH 2004-2008; Epis Coun for CE Epis Ch Cntr New York NY 2001-2008; Congrl Dvlpmt Cmsn Dio Ohio Cleveland 1997-2001. Auth, "Var arts," *Go Forth*, Dio Indianapolis, 2010; Auth, "Var arts," *Dioc Website*, www.indydio.org, 2008; Auth, "Var arts," *Dioc Life*, Dio Bethlehem, 2003; Auth, "Var arts," *Epis Tchr*, Virginia Sem, 2002; Auth, "Var arts," *AWE: Chld's Mnstrs*, www.diobethkids.org, 2001; Auth, "Var arts," *The Windows of St. Ptr's*, St. Ptr's Ch, Oxford, CT, 1994; Auth, "Var arts," *Epis Life*, ECUSA, 1990. kissinger@indydio.org

KITAGAWA, Chisato (WMass) 5 Hickory Ln, Amherst MA 01002 **Non-par 1973-** B Tokyo Japan 1932 s Chiaki & Sumi. BA Rikkyo U Jp 1958; BD EDS 1964; PhD U MI 1972. D 6/20/1964 P 1/1/1965 Bp Robert McConnell Hatch. m 6/17/1961 Mary Joan Kitagawa c 2. Serv H Faith Ch Saline MI 1970-1972; Non-par 1968-1969; Cur Gr Ch Amherst MA 1964-1967. Auth, "Typological variations of Hd-internal relatives in Japanese," *Lingua 115.1243-1276*, 2005; Auth, "Jodoshi," Aratake Shuppan, 1988; Auth, Heinemann, 1987.

KITAGAWA, John Elliott (Az) 1700 E Chula Vista Rd, Tucson AZ 85718 B Minneapolis MN 1950 s Daisuke & Fujiko. BA Hobart and Wm Smith Colleges 1972; Inter/Met Sem 1977; CPE St Elizabeths Hosp Washington DC 1977; MDiv UTS 1978; DMin SWTS 2005. D 6/3/1978 P 12/3/1978 Bp Paul Moore Jr. m 7/10/1982 Kathleen A Kitagawa. R S Phil's In The Hills Tucson AZ 2001-2015; Com Mem Exec Coun Anti-Racism Com New York NY 1999-2009; Dio Maryland Baltimore MD 1998-2001, Cn Ordnry 1997-2001, Exec Offcr 1991-1997, 1984-1990, Cn For Mssn Dvlpmt 1984-1988; Bd Mem Archv of the Epis Ch Austin TX 1996-2009; Vice Chair and Chair Stndg Cmsn on Structure of the Ch 1994-2000; Gvrng Bd Natl Coun Ch 1990-1999; Com Mem SCWM 1988-1991; Interfaith Coop Mnstrs New Haven CT 1980-1984; Asst Calv and St Geo New York NY 1978-1980; Com Mem SCER 1976-1985; Excoun Dio Connecticut Meriden CT 1981-1984. Cn, Trin Cathd, Phoenix, AZ Bp Kirk S. Smith 2012.

KITAYAMA, Scott D (WTex) **Assoc Chr Epis Ch San Antonio TX 2008-** B 1962 s Neho & Kay. MDiv Fuller TS 2003; MDiv Fuller TS 2003; Cert Ang Stud VTS 2006; Cert Ang Stud VTS 2006. D 6/24/2006 Bp Don Adger Wimberly P 1/10/2007 Bp Rayford Baines High Jr. m 9/7/2002 Susanna Kitayama c 3. S Cyp's Ch Lufkin TX 2006-2008; S Jn The Div Houston TX 2002-2005.

KITCH, Anne E (Be) 333 Wyandotte St, Bethlehem PA 18015 **Cn for Formation in the Chr Faith Dio Bethlehem Bethlehem PA 2008-, GC Deputation 2013-, GC Deputation, chair 2010-2013, Cmsn for Lifelong Chr Formation. chair 2009-, GC Deputation, chair 2007-2010, Stndg Com 2004-2013, Liturg and Mus Cmsn 2001-** B 1962 d John & Betsy. BA Carleton Coll 1984; MA U of St Thos 1993; MDiv GTS 1995. D 6/3/1995 P 12/9/1995 Bp Richard Frank Grein. m 8/6/1988 James H Peck c 2. Cn for Chr Formation Cathd Ch Of The Nativ Bethlehem PA 1999-2008; Asst to R S Ptr's Epis Ch Peekskill NY 1995-1999; Chapl Res New York Methodist Hosp Brooklyn NY 1993-1994. Auth, "Preparing for Baptism in the Epis Ch," Ch Pub, 2015; Auth, "Water of Baptism, Water of Life," Ch Pub, 2012; Auth, "Stumbling Into the Sacr: Meditations for Lent," Ldr Resources, 2011; Auth, "Adv Morning," *Wisdom Found: Stories of Wmn Transfigured by Faith*, Forw Mvmt, 2011; Auth, "In the Dark Night," *Lifting Wmn Voices: Prayers to Change the Wrld*, Morehouse Pub., 2009; Auth, "What We Do in Lent," Morehouse Pub, 2007; Auth, "Taking The Plunge: Baptism and Parenting," Morehouse Pub., 2006; Auth, "What We Do in Adv," Morehouse Pub., 2006; Auth, "Tending The Hm Fires," *Doing H Bus: The Best of Vstry Papers*, Ch Pub, 2006; Auth, "What We Do in Ch," Morehouse Pub, 2004; Auth, "The Angl Fam PB," Morehouse Pub., 2004; Auth, "Bless This Way," Morehouse Pub, 2003; Auth, "One Little Ch Mouse," Morehouse Pub, 2002; Auth, "Bless This Day," Morehouse Pub, 2000. ECom 2010-2016; Forma 2008. anne@diobeth.org

KITCH, Sarah Underhill (Los) 280 Royal Ave, Simi Valley CA 93065 **Chapl/ Tchr S Patricks Ch And Day Sch Thousand Oaks CA 2014-; P S Fran Of Assisi Epis Ch Simi Vlly CA 2015-** B White Plains New York 1956 d Charles & Julie. Syr 1976; Cert Sprtl Dir Stillpoint Cntr for Sprtl Direction 2006; Diac

Stds Cert Bloy Hse/ETSC 2010; Masters of Div EDS 2015. D 5/23/2010 Bp Chester Lovelle Talton P 4/25/2015 Bp Joseph Jon Bruno. m 6/21/1980 David John Kitch. Fam Spprt/Sprtl Care Buena Vista Hospice Thousand Oaks CA 2012-2014. stfrancis.simi@gmail.com

KITT, Michael (Chi) 523 Courtland Ave, Park Ridge IL 60068 **Dir/Treas Assn for Epis Deacons (NAAD) 2013-; Pres Neighbors Together Fndt NFP 2012-; Chf Fin Off The Delves Grp LLC 2006-; D S Mary's Ch Pk Ridge IL 2002-** B Phoenix AZ 1950 s Carl & Barbara. BS Roosevelt U 1975. D 2/2/2002 Bp Bill Persell. m 10/9/1982 Stephanie Lucille Kitt. Int Chapl Cbury NW Evanston IL 2012-2015. Dir'S Serv Awd Cmnty Counslg Centers Of Chicago 1994. mkittskitt@cs.com

KITTELSON, Alan Leslie (Vt) 6 Park St, Vergennes VT 05491 **R S Paul's Epis Ch On The Green Vergennes VT 2008-** B Montevideo MN 1950 s Leslie & Rudell. BA S Olaf Coll 1972; U of Oslo Oslo NO 1973; U MN 1975; MDiv EDS 1986. D 6/24/1987 Bp Robert Marshall Anderson P 7/22/1989 Bp Edward Cole Chalfant. Int Ch of the Epiph Wilbraham MA 2005-2006; Gr Ch Amherst MA 2001-2008, Asst 1998-2000; Epis Ch Of The Epiph Wilbraham MA 1998-2006; S Andr's Ch Newcastle ME 1990-1997; S Paul's Epis Ch Waxahachie TX 1987-2015; Stff Assoc Pax Christi Cntr on Conscience & War Charlestown MA 1987-1988.

KITTREDGE, Cynthia Briggs (Tex) Seminary of the Southwest, 501 East 32nd Street, Austin TX 78705 **Dn and Pres Epis TS Of The SW Austin TX 2013-, Prof of New Testaament 1999-2013; The Ch of the Gd Shpd Austin TX 2000-** B New York NY 1957 d Taylor & Jane. BA Wms 1979; MDiv Harvard DS 1984; ThM Harvard DS 1989; ThD Harvard DS 1996. D 6/2/1984 Bp John Bowen Coburn P 4/1/1985 Bp Christoph Keller Jr. m 7/12/1981 Frank D Kittredge c 3. Emm Chap Manchester MA 1997-1999; Vstng Instr H Cross Coll Worcester MA 1994-1998; Chapl Beverly Hosp Beverly MA 1987-1992; Asst to R S Jn Manchester MA 1984-1986; S Jn's Ch Beverly MA 1984-1986. Auth, "A Lot of the Way Trees Were Walking," Wipf and Stock, 2015; Ed, "Fortress Commentary on the NT," Fortress Press, 2014; Ed, "The Bible in the Publ Sq," Fortress Press, 2008; Auth, "Conversations w Scripture: The Gospel of Jn," *Angl Assn of Biblic Scholars*, Ch Pub, 2007; Auth, "Intro and Annotation - Hebrews," *New Oxford Annotated Bible*, Oxf Press, 2000; Auth, "Cmnty & Authority," *Cmnty & Authority*, Trin Press, 1999; Auth, "Pauline Texts," *Dictionary of Feminist Theologies*, Westminster/Jn Knox, 1996; Ed, "Hebrews," *Searching the Scriptures*, Crossroad/Continuum, 1994. AAR; Angl Assn Biblic Scholars; ECF; EvangES; Soc of Biblicalal Lit. Chr Faith and Life Grant Louisville Inst 2007; Grant EvangES 2005; Conant Fund Incentive Grant Conant Fund 2004; Conant Fund Sabbatical Grant Conant Fund 2003; Eugene M. Stetson Fllshp ECF 1990.

KITTS, Joseph (Eur) Windyridge, Cottage Lane, Saint Martins, Oswestry, Shropshire SY11 3BL Great Britain (UK) B Saint Helens Lancashire UK 1927 s Richard & Catherine. Brasted Kent; Tyndale Hall Bristol Gb. D 5/1/1960 P 5/1/1961 Bp The Bishop Of Liverpool. m 3/26/1949 Freda Jones. Asst Truro Epis Ch Fairfax VA 1976-1994; Gr Ch Henryetta OK 1975-1976; R Ch Of The Redeem Okmulgee OK 1974-1976; Serv Ch Of Engl 1960-1974.

KIVEL, Virginia McDermott (Dal) D 6/4/2016 Bp George Robinson Sumner Jr.

KLAAS III, Anthony Rudolph (La) 4 Yacht Club Apt 36, Daphne AL 36526 B Mobile AL 1933 s Anthony & Marietta. BA Georgia Inst of Tech 1956; MBA Pace U 1978; MDiv TESM 1983; MA SE Bapt TS 1999. D 6/11/1983 Bp William Grant Black P 1/1/1984 Bp James Russell Moodey. m 4/22/1957 Beverly Klaas c 4. S Phil's Ch New Orleans LA 1993-1996; S Mary's Ch Franklin LA 1989-1993; St Georges Ch Pittsburgh PA 1985-1988; S Geo's Ch Waynesburg PA 1984-1988; Assoc S Lk's Epis Ch Akron OH 1983-1985.

KLAM, Warren Peter (Va) 4200 Harbor Blvd., Oxnard CA 93035 B Cambridge MA 1946 s Najeeb & Louise. Tul 1967; MD LSU 1971; MS U of Texas in Dallas 2004. D 6/16/1978 Bp John Alfred Baden P 6/29/1979 Bp Robert Bruce Hall. m 8/24/1968 Caroline Daspit. Chapl Hope USN Base Yokosuka Japan 1997-2000; Non-par 1987-1996; Assoc Ch Of The H Cross Dunn Loring VA 1984-1986; Asst S Paul's Rock Creek Washington DC 1980-1984; D S Lk Wellington MD 1978-1979.

KLEE, George Martin (Ark) 1516 Willow St., Blytheville AR 72315 **1993-** B Memphis TN 1947 s George & Carolyn. BA U of Memphis 1969; MDiv Sthrn Bapt TS 1972; Cert SWTS 1983; STM GTS 1995; ThD GTS 2004. D 2/4/1984 P 10/1/1984 Bp Alex Dockery Dickson. m 5/18/1991 Martha Klee. P-in-c S Steph's Ch Blytheville AR 2006-2010; Assoc St. Geo's Epis Ch Germantown TN 2000-2005; S Geo's Ch Germantown TN 2000-2004; Vic S Paul's Ch Mason TN 1987-1992; Trin Ch Mason TN 1987-1992; Dio W Tennessee Memphis 1985-1992; P-intern Chr Ch Brownsville TN 1985-1986; Imm Ch Ripley TN 1985-1986; Asst S Mary's Cathd Memphis TN 1984. "Celtic Sprtlty," *The Angl*, 1995; Auth, *Lauderdale Cnty Voice*.

KLEFFMAN, Todd Aaron (Ind) 5757 Rosslyn Ave, Indianapolis IN 46220 B Indianapolis IN 1963 s Herschell & Doris. BA Ball St U 1987; MDiv SWTS 2001. D 6/30/2001 P 1/6/2002 Bp Cate Waynick. m 5/23/2012 Michael S Scime. S Jn's Epis Ch Crawfordsvlle IN 2005-2011; S Fran In The Fields Zionsville IN 2001-2005.

K

KLEIN, Craig Alan (Kan) 67 SW Pepper Tree Ln, Topeka KS 66611 **D S Mary's Ch Provo UT 2012-** B Kansas City MO 1955 s Ralph & Nancy. Cert The U So; BS U of Kansas 1978; MA Indiana U 1985; EdD U of Florida 1992. D 2/4/2006 Bp Jerry Alban Lamb. m 12/24/1989 Marybeth Fitzpatrick.

KLEIN, Everett H (WMich) 7521 Anthony St, Whitehall MI 49461 B New York New York 1942 s Henry & Cecelia. BS U of Maryland U Coll Europe 1979; MDiv SWTS 2001. D 12/1/2001 Bp Edward Lewis Lee Jr P 9/14/2002 Bp Robert R Gepert. m 2/27/1968 Barbara Carol Klein c 1. R S Alb's Mssn N. Muskegon MI 2008-2014; R S Ptr's By-The-Lake Ch Montague MI 2002-2014; H Trin Epis Ch Wyoming MI 2001-2002.

KLEIN, John Conrad (Mich) 231 E Grand Blvd, Detroit MI 48207 B Philadelphia PA 1942 s Walter & Helene. D 12/16/2001 P 6/29/2002 Bp Wendell Nathaniel Gibbs Jr. m 9/9/1978 Jean Mildred Klein c 3.

KLEIN, John Harvey (SeFla) 3586 Woods Walk Blvd, Lake Worth FL 33467 **Chapl US-A 1980-; Chapl US-AR 1967-** B Tampa FL 1933 s Frank & Helen. BA U of Florida 1955; MDiv GTS 1962. D 7/3/1962 Bp Henry I Louttit P 1/1/1963 Bp William Loftin Hargrave. m 3/15/1958 Sylvia J Klein. Pstr Asst S Dav's-In-The-Pines Epis Ch W Palm Bch FL 2005-2009; R St Margarets and San Francisco de Asis Epis Ch Hialeah FL 1984-1987; R Trin Epis Ch Natchitoches LA 1974-1980; Vic S Pat's Ch Ocala FL 1969-1974; Asst All SS Prot Epis Ch Ft Lauderdale FL 1964-1969; M-in-c S Lk The Evang Ch Mulberry FL 1962-1964.

KLEIN, Susan Webster (Los) 9606 Oakmore Rd, Los Angeles CA 90035 **R S Alb's Epis Ch Los Angeles CA 2004-** B Saint Louis MO 1951 d Louis & Crockett. BA Wheaton Coll at Norton 1973; MDiv Ya Berk 1977. D 7/30/1977 P 2/5/1978 Bp William Augustus Jones Jr. c 1. Min in Res Eden Sem 2014; S Aid's Epis Ch Malibu CA 1990-2004; Assoc St Andr Epis Ch Irvine CA 1984-1989; Chapl U CA Irvine Irvine 1984-1989; Cn Chr Ch Cathd S Louis MO 1977-1984; Epis Chapl U CA irvine 1984-1989. Auth, "Preaching Through The Year," *Sermons That Wk, Volumes VIII, IX and X*, Morehouse Pub. ES-MHE 1984-1989. Bachelor of Arts (Philos) - mcl Wheaton Coll 1973.

KLEIN-LARSEN, Martha Susan (Ct) 117 Oenoke Ridge, New Canaa CT 06840 **S Mk's Ch New Canaan CT 2015-** B 1955 d John & Margaret. BA Concordia U 1976; MDiv Luth TS at Chicago 1981; PhD Chicago TS 2005. Rec 1/24/2009 Bp Andrew Donnan Smith. m 7/31/2010 Joachim Pengel c 2. P-in-c S Jn's Epis Ch Bristol CT 2009-2014; Int S Jas Epis Ch Danbury CT 2009; P-in-c Ch Of The Epiph Southbury CT 2004-2007; Int Gr Ch Newington CT 2002-2004; Int Gloria Dei Luth Ch Forestville CT 2001-2002; Int Gloria Dei Luth Forestville CT 2001-2002; Workshop Ldr: Safe Ch Yale DS New Haven CT 2000; Workshop Ldr: Safe Ch Yale DS New Haven CT 1999; Pstr Concordia Luth Ch Mancester CT 1998-2000; Adj Fac Trin Hartford CT 1998; Int First Luth Southington CT 1997-1998; Adj Fac Hartford Sem Hartford CT 1994-2000; Assoc Pstr Emanuel Luth Manchester CT 1994-1997; Asst P (during Int Comm) St. Jas' Epis Danbury CT 1990-1991; Hired by Off of Mayor Overflow Shltr Coordntr Danbury CT 1988-1989; Co-Pstr St. Paul's Luth Danbury CT 1982-1988; CPE Luth Gnrl Hosp Pk Ridge IL 1981; Appointed Bd Mem Assn of Rel Communities 2007-2009; Vol Parent Mem Cmnty of Concern W Hartford CT 2002-2007; Appointed Vol Bd Mem W Hartford Substance Abuse Cmsn W Hartford CT 2002-2007; Co-Fndr and Admin Dir Co-Fndr of Ecum Choir GodSong Manchester 2001-2007; Appointed Area Cler Bd Mem Manchester Area Ntwk on AIDS (MANA) Manchester CT 2000-2003; Appointed by the New Engl Syn Bp, ELCA Prov I Safe Ch Liason New Engl Syn ELCA 1998-2006; Appointed by Bp Chair Cmsn for Wmn New Engl Syn-ELCA 1996-2002; Elected Pres of Bd Assn of Rel Communities Danbury CT 1984-1996. Article, "Voices from the Margins: Using a Fndt Analysis of Power in Cases of Cler Sexual Misconduct," *Mod Believing: Ch and Soc*, Mod Churchpeople's Un, 2007; Chapt, "A Feminist Perspective on Aging," *Aging, Sprtlty, and Rel*, Fortress Press, Minneapolis, 1995. AAR 1992-1998; Int Mnstry Ntwk 1997-2006. mkleinlarsen@stmarksnewcanaan.org

KLEMMT, Pierce (Va) 1208 N Pitt St, Alexandria VA 22314 B Cincinnati OH 1949 s Raymond & Jane. BA Wabash Coll 1972; MDiv Ya Berk 1976. D 6/9/1976 P 12/12/1976 Bp John Mc Gill Krumm. m 12/29/1976 Mary T Klemmt c 2. R Chr Ch Alexandria VA 1994-2014; Chr Epis Ch Springfield MO 1986-1993; Trin Epis Ch Troy OH 1980-1986; Asst S Mk's Ch Evanston IL 1976-1980; Chairman of the Bd Alb Institue 2005-2017; Bd Mem Alexandria Cmnty Trust 2005-2017; Bd Mem Alexandria Seaport Fndt 2000-2017.

KLENZMANN, Joseph G. (Va) **D Ch Of The H Comf Richmond VA 2016-** B Perth Amboy, NJ 1961 D 4/16/2016 Bp Shannon Sherwood Johnston. m 10/27/2001 Darlene Michele Grebow.

KLEVEN, Terence J (Ia) 1334 N. Prairie St., Pella IA 50219 **S Jas Epis Ch Oskaloosa IA 2012-, 2003-2010** B British Columbia Canada 1955 BA U of Calgary Ab CA. Trans 7/17/2003 Bp Alan Scarfe. m 7/5/1986 Kathryn Kleven. Trin Ch Ottumwa IA 2003-2008. Auth, "Trsfg Of Chr In Lk 9:22-36," *Princeton Theol Revs*, 2001; Auth, "Bk Revs: Wrld Of Ibn Tufayl," *Bulletin Of Middle E Medievalists*, 2000; Auth, "Bk Revs: Alcinous: Handbook Of Platonism," *Mind*, 1999; Auth, "Tam Fontaine'S Account Of Ibn Daud'S The Exalted Faith," *Interpretaion*, 1998; Auth, "Inquiry Into The Fndt Of Law," *Jewish Political Stds Revs*, 1997; Auth, "Bk Revs: Allegory And Philos," *Intl Journ Of Middle Estrn Stds*, 1996; Auth, "Use Of Snr In Agaritic And 2 Samuel V8," *Vetus Testamentum*, 1994. stjamesosky@live.com

KLICKMAN OHC, John Michael (Dal) 4017 Hedgerow Dr, Plano TX 75024 **Non-par 1987-** B Saint Louis MO 1944 s John & Marianne. AB Wm Jewell Coll 1965; MDiv VTS 1969; MBA U of Dallas 1988. D 6/24/1969 Bp George Leslie Cadigan P 1/6/1970 Bp C J Kinsolving III. m 7/22/1986 Jody Klickman c 1. Archd Dio Panama 1986; R Ch Of The Epiph Richardson TX 1981-1985; R S Tim's Epis Ch Lake Jackson TX 1974-1981; Assoc Pro Cathd Epis Ch Of S Clem El Paso TX 1969-1974. Contrib, "Aicpa Item Dvlpmt Workshop," 2009; Reviewer, "Cost Acctg," Prentice Hall, 2002; Reviewer, "Cost Acctg," McGraw-Hill; Auth, "Gnrl Motors Schlr"; Auth, "Album," *Today You Shall Be w Me*. Hugs, Inc 2012-2015; Make A Wish-Audit Com 2009-2011; Ord Of H Cross 1974-2011; SAMS, Bd Trst 1976-1986; St Phil's Epis Sch Bd-Dallas 1981-1986.

KLIMAS, Marcella Louise (CPa) 4355 Georgetown Square Apt 141, Atlanta GA 30338 B Plainfield NJ 1948 d Joseph & Helen. Oxf GB 1969; BA Douglass Coll 1970; MDiv EDS 1981; DMin Columbia TS 1994. D 6/13/1981 Bp William Foreman Creighton P 3/6/1982 Bp Lloyd Edward Gressle. R Ch Of The Trsfg Blue Ridge Summit PA 1986-1990; Assoc R Ch Of The Redemp Southampton PA 1983-1986; Dioc Intern S Lk's Ch Scranton PA 1981-1983. Auth, "Journey Toward The Promised Land". Jonathan Daniels Memi Fllshp 1980.

KLINE, Andy (Colo) 5 Brookside Dr, Greenwood Village CO 80121 B Cheyenne WY 1956 s Duane & Joanna. BA Dart 1979; MDiv Ya Berk 1983. D 6/29/1983 Bp Bob Gordon Jones P 2/2/1984 Bp William Bradford Hastings. m 4/28/1984 Kathleen A Kovener Kline c 4. Inst of Amer Values New York NY 2012-2014; S Aug Of Hippo Norristown PA 2010-2014; R Chr Epis Ch Denver CO 2003-2009; S Thos Ch Hanover NH 1994-2003; S Steph's Ch E Haddam CT 1986-1994; S Jas' Ch New Haven CT 1983-1985.

KLINE, John William (NwPa) 825 Matilda Dr, Plano TX 75025 **Assoc The Epis Ch Of The H Nativ Plano TX 1999-** B Ridley Park PA 1933 s John & Christine. BS W Chester U of Pennsylvania 1955; Drew U 1957; MDiv Luth TS at Gettysburg 1959; CTh PDS 1965; STM Luth TS at Gettysburg 1971. D 4/24/1965 Bp Oliver J Hart P 8/24/1965 Bp Harvey D Butterfield. m 6/24/1955 Jane Kline c 4. Int Epis Ch Of The Ascen Dallas TX 1998-1999; Prov Coordntr Prov III EDEO 1993-1997; R Ch Of The Ascen Bradford PA 1983-1997; Dn Dio NW Pennsylvania Erie PA 1983-1997; Pres.,Stndg Com. Dio NW Pennsylvania Erie PA 1979-1997; Archd Dio NW Pennsylvania Erie PA 1979-1983; Dn 1983-1997; Dep GC 1976-1997; R S Jn's Epis Ch Sharon PA 1975-1979; R S Matt's Epis Ch Sunbury PA 1968-1974; R S Mary's Ch Williamsport PA 1967-1968; Chr Ch Bethel VT 1965-1967; R S Jn's Epis Ch Randolph VT 1965-1967; Pstr Adv Luth Ch Lancaster PA 1960-1964; Pstr Bittinger Luth Par Bittinger MD 1959-1960. Assoc.,OHC 1965; Chapl, Ord of S Lk 1973.

KLINE, Nancy Wade (CFla) St. Barnabas Episcopal Church, 319 W. Wisconsin Ave., Deland FL 32720 **D S Barn Ch Deland FL 2004-; Substitute Tchr Volusia Cnty Sch System Deland FL 1995-** B LaFayette GA 1947 d Thomas & Anna. BA U of Cntrl Florida 1972; Inst for Chr Stds Sch of Diac Trng 2004. D 12/18/2004 Bp John Wadsworth Howe. m 11/17/1973 Sims Dubose Kline c 2.

KLINE, Timothy Eads (WK) 50 Oyster Bay Dr, Graford TX 76449 B Cincinnati OH 1942 s Edward & Reva. BS USAF Acad 1964; MA LSU 1972; MDiv VTS 1991. D 12/10/1991 Bp Peter J Lee P 6/1/1992 Bp John Forsythe Ashby. m 6/7/1964 Bonnie Louise Kline c 3. Pres Dio Wstrn Kansas Hutchinson KS 2002-2004; Stndg Com 2002-2004, Dep, GC 2005-2006, Chair, Cio. Com Dep, GC 1998-, MBR-Dio Coun 2002-2005, Chair - COM 1993-2006; Dn Chr Cathd Salina KS 1999-2006; Dio Oklahoma Oklahoma City OK 1992-1999; S Steph's Ch Guymon OK 1992-1999; Reg Mssnr S Tim's Epis Ch Hugoton KS 1992-1999; S Jn's Ch Ulysses KS 1991-1999; D/Asst for Mnstry S Aid's Ch Alexandria VA 1991-1992. Phi Kappa Phi LSU 1972.

KLINE-MORTIMER, Sandra L (Md) Po Box 3298, Shepherdstown WV 25443 **S Anne's Epis Ch Smithsburg MD 2005-** B Santa Ana CA 1957 d George & Leslie. BS W Virginia U; MDiv VTS 1989; MS Loyola U 1995. D 7/19/1989 P 6/1/1990 Bp John Henry Smith. Asst R Trin Epis Ch Martinsburg WV 1990-1992; D S Steph's Epis Ch Beckley WV 1989-1990. asksaintannes@outlook.com

KLINGELHOFER, Stephan Ernest (Eas) 545 Fey Rd # 21620-, Chestertown MD 21620 **Trst Landon Sch Beth MD 2011-; Assoc Shrewsbury Par Ch Kennedyville MD 2000-; Stndg Com Dio Easton Easton MD 2017-, Dioc Coun 2015-2017** B Fond du Lac WI 1943 s Herbert & Mary. BA Ya 1964; JD Duke 1967; MDiv VTS 1979. D 6/23/1979 P 1/6/1980 Bp John Thomas Walker. m 6/19/1965 Diane D Dundas c 1. Dir Cmnty Mediation Upper Shore 2012-2014; VP- Pres Intl Cntr for Not-for-Profit Law 1994-2015; R S Lk's Par Kalamazoo MI 1988-1992; Adj Fac VTS Alexandria VA 1985-1988; R Gr Ch Washington DC 1982-1988; Assoc The Ch Of The Epiph Washington DC 1979-1982; Del to GC Dio Wstrn Michigan Kalamazoo MI 1991; Stndg Com Dio Washington Washington DC 1984-1988, Dioc Coun 1982-1983.

KLINGENBERG, Ralph Gerard (SeFla) 1400 Riverside Dr, Coral Springs FL 33071 **S Ambr Epis Ch Ft Lauderdale FL 2017-; Admin S Mart's Epis Ch Pompano Bch FL 2004-** B Cincinnati 1955 s Ralph & Mary. BA U of Dayton 1978; MDiv Epis TS of the SW 2013. D 1/18/2013 Bp Calvin Onderdonk Schofield Jr P 12/3/2013 Bp Mary Gray-Reeves. m 11/22/2013 Lawrence A Grishaber. S Andr's Epis Ch Of Hollywood Hollywood FL 2014; Ch Of S Nich Pompano Bch FL 2013-2016.

KLINGENSMITH, Roxanne Elizabeth Pearson (Mont) 1715 South Black, Bozeman MT 59715 **Archd Dio Montana 2004-; D S Jas Ch 2001-** B Duluth MN 1940 d Vernon & Maxine. BS U MN 1962. D 5/8/1999 Bp Charles I Jones III. m 11/5/2014 Constance Campbell-Pearson c 1. S Jas Ch Bozeman MT 2011-2012, 2005-2009; D S Jas Ch 2001.

KLITZKE, Dale E (USC) 1816 Crestwood Ln, Menomonie WI 54751 **Vic S Aug Of Cbury Aiken SC 2012-** B Mauston WI 1947 s Kenneth & Lucille. D 9/29/1985 P 8/16/1992 Bp William Charles Wantland. m 7/16/1966 Linda Marion Klitzke c 3. P-in-c Dio Upper So Carolina Columbia SC 2013-2015; R Gr Epis Ch Menomonie WI 2003-2012; S Mary's Epis Ch Tomah WI 1998-2001, 1992-1996; D S Jn's Epis Ch Mauston WI 1985-1992.

KLITZKE, Paul Kenneth (Dal) 8787 Greenville Avenue, Dallas TX 75243 **R Epis Ch Of The Ascen Dallas TX 2015-** B Tomah WI 1979 s Dale & Linda. BAF Viterbo U 2002; MDiv Sewanee: The U So, TS 2005. D 2/27/2005 Bp Mark Lawrence Macdonald. m 8/10/2001 Sarah E Holley c 2. P S Nich Epis Ch Aiea HI 2010-2015; S Mary's Ch Anchorage AK 2006-2010; R S Dav's Epis Ch Wasilla AK 2005-2010. paul.klitzke@ascensiondallas.org

KLOPFENSTEIN, Timothy David (CGC) 106 Galaxy Ave, Bonaire GA 31005 B Hartsville IN 1940 s Clarence & Bernice. BS Auburn U 1964; MS Untd States Naval Postgraduate Sch 1973; MDiv Sewanee: The U So, TS 1984; DMin GTF 2000. D 6/4/1984 P 4/1/1985 Bp Charles Farmer Duvall. m 12/18/2007 Hannah McKinley Klopfenstein. Wilmer Hall Mobile AL 2005; R S Jn's Epis Ch Mobile AL 1991-2005; Vic S Anna's Ch Atmore AL 1986-1991; R Trin Epsicopal Ch Atmore AL 1986-1991; H Nativ Day Sch Panama City FL 1985-1986; Headmaster Dio Cntrl Gulf Coast Pensacola FL 1984-1986; Cur H Nativ Epis Ch Panama City FL 1984-1986.

KLOTS, Stephen Barrett (Ct) 40 Bulls Bridge Rd, South Kent CT 06785 **Trst Bishops' Fund for Chld Epis Ch in Connecticut 2015-; Chapl S Mich's Chap So Kent CT 1999-; So Kent Sch So Kent CT 1999-** B Tallahassee FL 1962 s Cornelius & Mary. BA Trin Hartford CT 1984; MDiv Harvard DS 1989; STM Ya Berk 1999. D 6/5/1999 P 6/3/2000 Bp M(Arvil) Thomas Shaw. Auth, *Native Americans & Chrsnty*, 1997; Auth, *Carl Lewis*, 1995; Auth, *Ida Wells-Barnett*, 1994; Auth, *Richard Allen*, 1991.

KLOZA, Wanda Margaret (CPa) 101 Pine St, Harrisburg PA 17101 B London England 1953 d Sergiousz & Sylvia. D 4/22/2012 Bp Nathan Dwight Baxter. m 3/20/1979 Joseph Dennis Saint Martin Kloza.

✠ KLUSMEYER, The Rt Rev William Michie (WVa) 1 Roller Rd, Charleston WV 25314 **Trst GTS 2009-; Bd Bex Sem 2007-; Bp of WVa Dio W Virginia Charleston WV 2001-; Bd WV Coun of Ch 2001-; Trst The GTS New York NY 2010-; Bd Bex Sem Columbus OH 2007-; Trst VTS Alexandria VA 2001-** B Glen Cove NY 1955 s William & Mary. BA Illinois Coll 1977; MDiv GTS 1980; DD GTS 2001; DD VTS 2002. D 6/14/1980 Bp Quintin Ebenezer Primo Jr P 12/13/1980 Bp James Winchester Montgomery Con 10/13/2001 for WVa. m 8/13/1977 Marsha H Klusmeyer c 2. R Trin Epis Ch Wheaton IL 1990-2001; Campus Mnstry Highland Cmnty Coll 1981-1990; Gr Epis Ch Freeport IL 1980-1990; Mem, Prog Bdgt & Fin Com Dom And Frgn Mssy Soc-Epis Ch Cntr New York NY 2003-2012; Bd - Peoples Resource Cntr Dio Chicago Chicago IL 1998-2001, Stndg Com 1994-1997, Bd, Cathdral Shltr 1990-1993, Chair Dioc T/F on Cnfrmtn 1985-1989. Sis of Charity - Epis Visitors 2002-2008. mklusmeyer@wvdiocese.org

KLUTTERMAN, David Lee (FdL) 330 McClellan, Wausau WI 54401 **R Ch Of S Jn The Bapt Wausau WI 1996-** B Watertown WI 1955 s Gerald & Kathleen. BA U of Wisconsin 1977; MDiv GTS 1980. D 4/12/1980 Bp William Hampton Brady P 11/15/1980 Bp William Louis Stevens. m 11/8/2013 Marilyn Julie Klutterman c 3. P St Jas Epis Ch Mosinee WI 2009-2015; Dep GC 1992-2000; S Jas Ch Manitowoc WI 1984-1996; Dio Fond du Lac Appleton WI 1980-1984; S Mths Minocqua WI 1980-1984; Ch Of S Mary Of The Snows Eagle River WI 1980-1981. Auth, "Bringing Chr Hm," Self Pub, 2007; Auth, "A Catechism Curric," LeaderResources, 1995.

KNAPICK, Veronica Helene (Ak) 6816 E. Riverwood Cir, Palmer AK 99645 B Johnson City NY 1945 d Joseph & Veronica. BS SUNY 1967; MEd U of Montana 1971; MDiv CDSP 1985; Int Mnstry Prog 1993. D 6/30/1985 P 4/29/1986 Bp George Clinton Harris. R S Phil's Ch Wrangell AK 1997-1998; R S Steph's Epis Ch Douglas AZ 1995-1996; Int S Dunst's Ch Tulsa OK 1994-1995; Ch Of The Gd Shpd Houlton ME 1993-1994; Non-par 1992-1993; R S Giles Ch Jefferson ME 1989-1992; Non-par 1988-1989; R S Jude's Epis Ch No Pole AK 1986-1987; D S Mary's Ch Anchorage AK 1985-1986.

KNAPP, Carl Jude (Pa) 584 Fairway Ter, Philadelphia PA 19128 **Ret PA 2012-** B Philadelphia PA 1939 s Carlyle & Anne. BS W Chester U of Pennsylvania 1961; MS U of Pennsylvania 1968; MA La Salle U 1984. D 6/12/1982 Bp Ly-

man Cunningham Ogilby. m 7/11/1964 Josephine Ann Knapp c 1. D S Tim's Ch Roxborough Philadelphia PA 1982-2012. Phi Delta Kappa 1976.

KNAPP, Clayton L (WMass) 3003 Dick Wilson Dr., Sarasota FL 34240 B Albany NY 1940 s Alden & Harriette. BS Siena Coll 1967; MDiv PDS 1971; DMin Andover Newton TS 1993. D 6/5/1971 P 12/14/1971 Bp Allen Webster Brown. m 8/4/1990 Judith A Bolam c 2. Dio Wstrn Massachusetts Springfield 1990-2001; Vic S Chris's Ch Fairview Chicopee MA 1990-2001; Pstr Counslr Worcester Pstr Counslg Cntr 1988-1994; Cn Chr Ch Cathd Springfield MA 1979-1988; Legis Liason N Y St Coun Of Ch Syracuse NY 1978; R The Ch Of The Mssh Glens Falls NY 1974-1977; R Chr's Ch Duanesburg NY 1971-1974. Fell - AAPC 1989-1998. Cum Honoribus PDS 1971; Coll hon Soc Mem Delta Epsilon Sigma 1967.

KNAPP, Cynthia Clark (At) 43 Twin Oak Ln, Wilton CT 06897 **Chr Ch Macon GA 2016-; P S Ptr's Epis Ch Milford CT 2012-** B Columbia MO 1963 d Ralph & Carolyn. BS Duke 1985; MDiv VTS 1989. D 6/9/1990 Bp Arthur Edward Walmsley P 6/15/1991 Bp Clarence Nicholas Coleridge. m 6/4/1988 Cheston D Knapp c 3. S Barn Epis Ch Greenwich CT 2005-2011; Trin Epis Ch Southport CT 2002-2004; Supply P Dio Connecticut Meriden CT 1998-2004; Asst to R Trin Ch Branford CT 1996-1998; Asst S Sav's Epis Ch Old Greenwich CT 1993-1996; Chr Ch Greenwich CT 1990-1993.

KNAPP, Donald Hubert (Be) 162 Springhouse Rd, Allentown PA 18104 B Kent OH 1928 s John & Florence. BA S Mary Coll KY 1953; Final degree - Ord The Athenaeum of Ohio (St.Mary's of the W) 1957; MDiv PDS 1968. Rec 3/1/1968 Bp Robert Lionne DeWitt. m 8/6/1965 Virginia Mary Knapp c 3. Mem, Liturg Cmsn Dio Bethlehem Bethlehem PA 2006-2009, Mem, Dioc Peace Cmsn 2008-, Justice and Advocacy Cmsn/ Jubillee Com 1980-2007; Int R S Barn Ch Kutztown PA 2004-2005; Int S Lk's Ch Lebanon PA 2000-2002; Int S Geo's Epis Ch Hellertown PA 1996-2000; Int S Alb's Epis Ch Reading PA 1995-1996; R Gr Epis Ch Allentown PA 1969-1993; R H Sacr Ch Upper Darby PA 1968-1969. Lehigh Cnty Conf of Ch - Secy 1971-1973; Lehigh Cnty Prison Soc - Fndr and Pres 1970-2006; Pennsylvania Prison Soc 1976-2006. Human Relatns Awd Human Relatns Cmsn 1978.

KNAPP, Gretchen Bower (Mont) Po Box 794, Hilger MT 59451 B Worland WY 1941 d Vernon & Mary. BA U of Wyoming 1964; Montana Mnstry Formation Prog 1996. D 8/10/1996 Bp Charles I Jones III. m 10/19/1974 Franklin Theodore Knapp. D S Jas Ch Lewistown MT 1996-2013.

KNAPP, Kate S (Miss) 1316 N Jefferson St, Jackson MS 39202 **Died 9/16/2015** B Waltham MA 1913 d William & Elinor. Wells Coll 1933; BA Barnard Coll of Col 1935; MA SWTS 1970. D 8/6/1970 Bp William Hopkins Folwell. m 10/10/1936 Walter Howard Knapp. Outreach D S Andr's Cathd 1994-2015; D Ch Of The H Cross Decatur GA 1993-1994; D S Tim's Ch Aiea HI 1990-1992; Serv S Jn's By The Sea Kaneohe HI 1985-1986; Serv H Trin-By-The-Sea Daytona Bch FL 1982-1984; Post OHF 1978-1980; Serv S Andr's Ch Denver CO 1977-1979; Epis Ch Of S Ptr And S Mary Denver CO 1976-1977; Serv H Trin-By-The-Sea Daytona Bch FL 1975-1976; Pryr Mnstry Dio Cntrl Florida Orlando FL 1972-1974, Stff On The Renwl Taskforce 1970-1974; Asst The Epis Ch Of S Jn The Bapt Orlando FL 1972-1974; Com Dio Colorado Denver CO 1976-1979. Soc Of S Marg. Seabury Convoc Cross 1970.

KNAPP, Ron (Eas) 11240 Gail Dr, Princess Anne MD 21853 **Mem personel comm Mem Bd Managers for \the Corp\ 2010-; S Paul's Epis Ch Hebron MD 2008-** B Batavia NY 1942 s Charles & Virginia. BS SUNY 1964; MDiv Ya Berk 1969. D 6/21/1969 P 1/10/1970 Bp Lauriston L Scaife. c 2. Pres. of Stndg Com Dio Easton 2003-2004; Chapl Penninsula Reg Med. Cntr 1997-2006; R S Andr's Epis Ch Princess Anne MD 1996-2005; P-in-c S Aid's Ch Alden NY 1994-1996; Int S Mk's Epis Ch Le Roy NY 1992-1994; Int S Jn's Ch Medina NY 1990-1992; Pres of the Stndg Com 1987-1988; 1985-1988; Urban Mnstry Com 1985-1988; Vic Ch Of The Redeem Niagara Falls NY 1982-1988; Bd Trst for the Coun of Ch 1977-1978; Chapl Memi Hosp 1974-1990; Pres of the Niagara Coun of Ch 1974-1977; R Ch Of The Epiph Niagara Falls NY 1972-1990; Asst to R Trin Epis Ch Hamburg NY 1969-1972.

KNAUFF, Elizabeth Ann (Ct) 155 Wyllys St, Hartford CT 06106 B New London CT 1943 d James & Helen. D 9/15/2007 Bp Andrew Donnan Smith. c 3.

KNAUP JR, Daniel Joseph (O) 2341 Ardleigh Drive, Cleveland Heights OH 44106 **Chapl Off Of Bsh For ArmdF New York NY 2009-; Chapl US-AR 1998-** B Inglewood CA 1958 s Daniel & Blanche. MA S Paul Sem Sch of Div; MDiv S Paul Sem Sch of Div; BA California Polytechnic St U San Luis Obispo 1982. Rec 6/13/2009 as Priest Bp Mark Hollingsworth Jr. m 7/7/2000 Vicky Stouffer. Command Chapl Intl Security and Assistance Force - Afghanistan 2010-2011; Grp Chapl 10th Spec Forces Grp (A) - Ft Carson CO (Army) 2004-2006. Soc of Cath Priests 2011; SocMary 2010. djknaup@gmail.com

KNEE, Jacob S (Mont) St Stephen's Episcopal Ch, 1241 Crawford Dr, Billings MT 59102 B Blackburn UK 1966 s Anthony & Gillian. BS London Sch of Econ 1987; MSc London Sch of Econ 1988; BA Ripon Coll Cuddesdon 1993; MA Ripon Coll Cuddesdon 1997. Trans 10/19/2007 Bp Charles Franklin Brookhart Jr. m 5/23/1993 Susan M Knee c 3. R S Steph's Ch Billings MT 2007-2017; Vic St Geo Engl 2000-2007.

KNEIPP, Lee Benson (WTenn) Po Box 3874, Pineville LA 71361 B Shreveport LA 1956 s Leonard & Patricia. BA Centenary Coll 1978; MDiv Sewanee: The U So, TS 1982; MA McNeese St U 1988; PhD ETSBH 1991; PhD Epis TS 1991. D 6/12/1982 P 2/1/1983 Bp Willis Ryan Henton. m 10/18/2003 Melinda Kneipp c 2. Gr - S Lk's Ch Memphis TN 2003-2004; S Alb's Epis Ch Monroe LA 1998-2003; St Mich's Epis Ch Pineville LA 1992-1997; Assoc Ch Of The H Cross Shreveport LA 1990-1992; Gr Epis Ch Monroe LA 1986-1988; S Andr's Ch Lake Chas LA 1986; Dio Wstrn Louisiana Alexandria LA 1982-1985; Ch Of The Ascen Lafayette LA 1982-1983. Auth, "Differences In Comprehension Processes As A Function Of Hemisphericity"; Auth, "Perceptual & Motor Skills"; Auth, "Texan Psychol". Cmnty Of Intsn. Alexander Awd For Resrch In Bio-Psychol Tx Psychol Assn 1991.

KNIGHT, Arthur James (NJ) 3 Blueberry Rd, Shamong NJ 08088 **Dio New Jersey Trenton NJ 2016-, 2016-, Mem Bd Missions 2016-; D The Bro Of S Andr Inc. Ambridge PA 2010-; D S Barth's Ch Cherry Hill NJ 2009-** B Detroit MI 1942 s Arthur & Eleanore. BA U of Texas 1971. D 10/21/2000 Bp David Bruce Joslin. m 5/26/1979 Margaret Elizabeth Whitehurst c 1. D Trin Epis Ch Vineland NJ 2004-2009; D Timber Creek Epis Area Mnstry Gloucester City NJ 2000-2004. Assn for Epis Deacons 2000; BroSA 2010.

KNIGHT, David Hathaway (Va) 6005 S Crestwood Ave, Richmond VA 23226 **Com To Elect Bp Suffr 1992-; Dep - Prov Syn 1990-; Com 1986-; Com - Consecration Bp 1984-; Westminster/Cbury 1984-; Lutharan-Epis Dialogue Com 1983-; Next Step In Mssn Com 1983-; R Frederick Par Chr & S Paul-On-The-Hill 1978-** B Salem MA 1945 s Edward & Lois. BA U of Massachusetts 1968; VTS 1971. D 6/20/1971 P 12/1/1971 Bp Alexander D Stewart. m 7/4/1970 Jean L Knight. S Mich And All Ang Ch Dallas TX 2005-2007; Assoc R S Steph's Ch Richmond VA 1995-2005; Bd - Va Cler Assn 1988-1990; Fin Com 1988-1990; Dioc Mssn Soc 1986-1990; Virginia Hm Dio Virginia Richmond VA 1984-2007; Com To Plan Dioc Conventions 1981-1984; Exec Bd 1980-1983; Chair - Area VIM 1979-1980; Chr Epis Ch Winchester VA 1978-1994; Chapl Thornton Nrsng Hm 1976-1978; Stwdshp Advsry Serv Dio Wstrn Massachusetts Springfield 1976-1977, Bd Admin & Fin 1975-1978, Ed Bd 1973-1975, Evang Cmsn 1974-1977; S Steph's Ch Westborough MA 1972-1978; Cur S Paul's Ch Holyoke MA 1971-1972.

KNIGHT, Frank Lauchlan (NY) 3859 Dogwood Trl, Allentown PA 18103 B New York NY 1938 s Frank & Grace. BA City Coll of New York 1959; STB PDS 1962. D 6/9/1962 P 12/22/1962 Bp Horace W B Donegan. m 9/16/1967 Noel Berkel c 2. R Ch Of The Medtr Bronx NY 1974-2003; R S Lk Beloved Physcn New York NY 1967-1974; Asst All Souls Ch New York NY 1965-1967; Asst The Ch of S Edw The Mtyr New York NY 1962-1963.

KNIGHT IV, Frank Michael (Pa) 803 Montbard Dr, West Chester PA 19382 B Saratoga Sprgs NY 1945 s Frank & Elizabeth. BS Un Coll Schenectady NY 1967; MDiv PDS 1974; Cert Estrn Bapt TS 1981. D 6/15/1974 P 12/21/1974 Bp Jonathan Goodhue Sherman. P-in-c S Steph's Epis Ch Norwood PA 2007-2017; Vic Ch Of The Trsfg W Chester PA 1992-2007; Vic S Mary Epis Ch Chester PA 1976-1985; Asst S Giles Ch Upper Darby PA 1975-1976. michaelknight@sstephen.org

KNIGHT, Harold Stanley (Az) 145 N Fraser Dr, Mesa AZ 85203 **Ret 1977-** B Rochester NY 1912 s Merton & Elizabeth. BA U Roch 1934; MDiv Colgate Rochester Crozer DS 1937; MDiv CRDS 1937. D 1/6/1949 P 7/6/1949 Bp Malcolm E Peabody. m 10/30/1971 Edithanne Davis Ball c 2. Hon Cn Dio Arizona Phoenix AZ 1977-1978; R S Mk's Epis Ch Mesa AZ 1957-1977; R The Ch Of The Epiph Gates NY 1950-1957; P-in-c S Mk's Ch Clark Mills NY 1948-1950; S Ptr's Ch Oriskany NY 1948-1950; Serv Bapt Ch 1937-1948. Man of Year Awd City of Mesa 1977.

KNIGHT, Hollinshead T (Cal) 485 Bridgeway Apt 1, Sausalito CA 94965 B Philadelphia PA 1934 s R Barclay & Mary. BA Ya 1956; MDiv EDS 1962. D 6/16/1962 Bp Oliver J Hart P 12/19/1962 Bp Norman L Foote. m 7/19/1974 Ann Bishop c 3. Int The Epis Ch Of S Mary The Vrgn San Francisco CA 2011-2012, Int 2011-; Mssnr S Matt's Epis Ch Portland OR 2010-2011; Deploy Off Dio Oregon Portland OR 2008-2010, Secy of Conv 2008-2010; Int S Steph's Epis Par Portland OR 2006-2008; Int S Paul's Epis Ch Salem OR 2004-2005; Int S Jn's Epis Ch Jackson WY 2000-2003; Int Gd Shpd Epis Ch Belmont CA 1999-2000; Int S Matt's Epis Ch San Mateo CA 1997-1999; Int H Chld At S Mart Epis Ch Daly City CA 1996-1997; Dir Ring Lake Ranch Dubois WY 1994-1998; Dn S Andr's Cathd Honolulu HI 1984-1994; R S Aid's Ch San Francisco CA 1973-1984; Assoc S Lk's Ch San Francisco CA 1964-1973; Gr Epis Ch Glenns Ferry ID 1962-1964; Vic S Barn Wendell ID 1962-1964; Vic Trin Ch Gooding ID 1962-1964; Pres of Stndg Com The Epis Ch in Hawaii Honolulu HI 1989-1990; Stndg Com Dio California San Francisco CA 1981-1984.

KNIGHT, J David (CGC) Saint Simon's On The Sound, 28 Miracle Strip Pkwy SW, Fort Walton Beach FL 32548 **S Simon's On The Sound Ft Walton Bch FL 2016-** B Meridian MS 1958 s Harold & Elizabeth. BS U of Sthrn Mississippi 1981; MDiv SWTS 2002. D 5/26/2002 P 12/14/2002 Bp Duncan Montgomery Gray III. m 9/24/1983 Jennifer F Forrester c 3. Int Chr Epis Ch Pensacola FL 2015-2016; S Paul's Ch Delray Bch FL 2013-2015; S Jas Ch Jackson MS 2012-2013; R S Patricks Epis Ch Long Bch MS 2004-2012; Cur S Jas Ch Greenville MS 2002-2004. Preaching Awd Seabury Wstrn 2002. rector@stsimons-fwb.org

KNIGHT, Joseph Sturdevant (CGC) 436 Lapsley Street, Selma AL 36701 **S Paul's Ch Selma AL 2004-; S Paul's Epis Ch Lowndesboro AL 2004-** B Selma,AL 1932 s Claude & Clara. U of Tampa; BS Samford U 1960; BD New Orleans Bapt TS 1964; MPA Auburn U 1980. D 8/21/1988 Bp Furman Charles Stough P 5/1/1989 Bp Robert Oran Miller. m 5/5/1973 Anne Falkenber Knight c 3. Vic Trin Ch Apalachicola FL 2000-2004; R Epis Ch Of The Epiph Leeds AL 1990-2000; D S Steph's Epis Ch Birmingham AL 1988-1990. hazenone@bellsouth.net

KNIGHT, Kimberly Adonna (La) 200 Chapel Crk Apt 116, Mandeville LA 70471 **S Chris's By-The-Sea Epis Ch Key Biscayne FL 2017-; Chr Epis Sch Covington LA 2015-** B Coral Gables FL 1972 d Donald & Barbara. BA Florida St U 1994; MS U of Miami 1996; MDiv VTS 2000. D 6/14/2000 P 11/17/2001 Bp Calvin Onderdonk Schofield Jr. c 2. Chapl The Soc of the Trsfg Cincinnati OH 2008-2015; Assoc Chapl Epis HS Bellaire TX 2004-2008; Asst R / Sch Chapl S Mk The Evang Ft Lauderdale FL 2001-2004; Asst R S Matt's Ch Chandler AZ 2000-2001; S Thos Epis Par Miami FL 1996-1997. "Ash Wednesday, Psalm 131, Time Out," *Preaching from psalms, oracles, & parables*, Moorhouse Pub, 2004.

KNIGHT, Patricia Cullum (NwT) 1601 S Georgia St, Amarillo TX 79102 **Died 5/20/2016** B Holdenville OK 1936 d Clifford & Dorris. BA Texas Tech U 1958; MA Texas Tech U 1968. D 8/28/2010 Bp James Scott Mayer. D S Andr's Epis Ch Amarillo TX 2010-2016.

KNIGHT, Samuel Theodore (Mich) 28725 Sunset Boulevard West, Lathrup Village MI 48076 **1992-** B AG 1939 s Gershom & Patience. GOE Codrington Coll 1964; BA U of Wstrn Ontario CA 1971; MA Marygrove Coll 1990; MA Wayne 2009. D 12/1/1963 P 12/1/1964 Bp The Bishop Of Antigua. c 2. P-in-c S Martha's Ch Detroit MI 1999-2002; S Andr's Ch Clawson MI 1998-1999; Tchg Mnstry Detroit Bd Educ 1992-2011; R Gr Ch Detroit MI 1985-1991; Asst to R S Jas' Epis Ch Baltimore MD 1983-1984; P-in-c S Matt in Barbados W Indies 1974-1982; P-in-c S Geo in Antigua W Indies 1972-1973; Asst Cur S Jn's Cathd in Antigua W Indies 1971-1972; Asst to R H Sav in Waterloo Ontario Can 1968-1971; P-in-c S Paul S Kitts 1965-1968; Asst to R S Anth's Montserrat 1964-1965; D-in-Trng Barbadis & Antigua in the W Indies 1963-1964.

KNIGHT, Skully (La) 3200 Woodland Ridge Blvd, Baton Rouge LA 70816 **Chapl Epis HS Baton Rouge Baton Rouge LA 2007-** B Baton Rouge LA 1969 s William & Johnelle. BA LSU 1991; MDiv Sewanee: The U So, TS 2004. D 6/5/2004 P 5/25/2005 Bp D Avid Bruce Macpherson. m 1/8/1994 Mary Sue S Knight c 2. Chapl All SS Epis Sch Tyler TX 2007-2011; Cur S Mk's Cathd Shreveport LA 2004-2007.

KNIGHT II, Stephen Herrick (SanD) 403 Shalimar Drive, Prescott AZ 86303 **Chapl The 5th Chapt Prescott AZ 2002-; Ret 1994-** B Detroit MI 1933 s Hale & Mary. BS NWU 1955; STB EDS 1961; Cert Rutgers The St U of New Jersey 1965. D 6/29/1961 Bp Archie H Crowley P 6/1/1962 Bp Robert Lionne DeWitt. m 9/3/1961 Joanna V Knight c 2. Tchr Teijin-Seki Ogaki JAPAN 1996-1998; Chapl Navy Alco Rehab Cntr Miramar CA 1985-1994; Counslr/ Chapl Navy Alco Rehab Cntr San Diego CA 1977-1985; Vic S Aug Fairfax CA 1970-1977; Serv Fairfax Cmnty Ch 1970-1974; Stff Dio California San Francisco CA 1968-1970; Chapl Detroit Hse Of Correction Plymouth MI 1965-1968; Asst S Jn's Ch Plymouth MI 1965-1968; P-in-c Mariners Ch Detroit MI 1964-1965; Asst S Jn's Ch Detroit MI 1963-1964; R S Jn's Ausable MI 1962-1963; P-in-c S Jn's Ausable MI 1961-1962; Chapl Corps (Capt Ret) US Naval Reserve USA 1951-1993. Founding Mem RACA 1968. Navy Commendation Medal (2) U.S. Navy 1993; Meritorious Serv Medal U.S. Navy 1992; Navy Commendation Medal U.S. Navy 1991.

KNIGHT, Theolinda Lenore Johnson (Cal) 806 Jones St, Berkeley CA 94710 B New Britain CT 1936 d Theodore & Virginia. BTh Sch for Deacons 1986. D 6/8/1991 Bp William Edwin Swing. m 1/1/1960 Warren Knight c 2. D The Epis Ch Of The Gd Shpd Berkeley CA 1998-2000; D S Aug's Ch Oakland CA 1992-1997; D S Paul's Epis Ch Walnut Creek CA 1991-1992.

KNIGHT, W Allan (Md) 58 Hanson Rd, Chester NH 03036 **Gr Ch Manchester NH 2003-** B Meaford ON CA 1937 s Charles & Olive. BA McMaster U 1959; BD McMaster Div Coll 1962; STM Andover Newton TS 1969. D 1/30/1982 Bp Morris Fairchild Arnold P 3/13/1983 Bp George E Rath. m 9/19/1987 Jane Whitbeck Van Zandt c 6. Int The Epis Ch Of S Andr And S Phil Coventry RI 2002-2003; Int S Andr's By The Sea Little Compton RI 2001-2002; Int Ch Of Our Sav Milford NH 1999-2000; Int S Barn Epis Ch Sykesville MD 1998-1999; Vic H Trin Epis Ch Essex MD 1991-1998; R S Steph's Ch Fall River MA 1985-1991; Int All SS Par Brookline MA 1983-1984; Dio Massachusetts Boston MA 1983, 1982-1983; D The Par Of All SS Ashmont-Dorches Boston MA 1982; Pstr Bapt and UCC Ch 1962-1974. EPF 1985; HabHum 1992; NEAC 1985.

KNISELY, Harry Lee (Ct) 365 Hickory Rd, Carlisle PA 17015 **Assoc P S Paul's Epis Ch Harrisburg PA 2009-; Mem of the Cmsn on Anti Racism Dio Cntrl Pennsylvania Harrisburg PA 2001-, Mem of the Cmsn on Anti Racism**

2001- B Hopewell Township PA 1940 s Harry & Ada. BA Juniata Coll 1963; MEd Shippensburg St Teachers Coll 1965; STB Ya Berk 1969. D 6/4/1969 Bp Dean Theodore Stevenson P 12/7/1969 Bp Earl M Honaman. m 5/27/1967 Gail Marie Knisely c 4. S Jn's Ch New Milford CT 1999-2000; S Jn's Ch Bridgeport CT 1997-1998; Int Trin Epis Ch Trumbull CT 1996-1997; Chr And Epiph Ch E Haven CT 1995-1996; Chr Epis Ch Burlington IA 1989-1995; R Chr Epis Ch Oil City PA 1981-1989; Chapl Oil City Theo's Chapt 1981-1989; Vic All SS Williamsville NY 1974-1981; Ch Of All SS Buffalo NY 1974-1981; Coordntr Of Prog Dio Estrn Oregon Cove OR 1972-1974; R S Mary's Ch Williamsport PA 1969-1972. Auth, "Reverend Doctor Edw R Hardy Jr: P, Tchr, Schlr," *Friend*, 1969. Int Mnstry Ntwk 1995.

✠ **KNISELY JR, The Rt Rev W Nicholas** (RI) Episcopal Diocese of Rhode Island, 275 N Main St, Providence RI 02903 **Bp of Rhode Island Dio Rhode Island Providence RI 2012-** B Harrisburg PA 1960 s William & Joan. BA Franklin & Marshall Coll 1982; MS U of Delaware 1986; MDiv Ya Berk 1991. D 6/8/1991 P 6/13/1992 Bp Cabell Tennis Con 11/17/2012 for RI. m 8/28/1982 Karen M McTigue c 1. Dn Trin Cathd Phoenix AZ 2010-2012; R Trin Ch Bethlehem PA 1998-2006; R S Barn Ch Brackenridge PA 1993-1998; Cur S Barn Ch Wilmington DE 1991-1993; GC Dep Dio Arizona Phoenix AZ 2009-2012, COM 2006-2012; Chair, Stndg Cmsn on Cmncatn and Tech Dom And Frgn Mssy Soc- Epis Ch Cntr New York NY 2006-2012, Mem, Moravian Epis Dialog 2003-2009; GC Dep Dio Bethlehem Bethlehem PA 2003-2006, VP of Dioc Coun 2003-2006; Pres of Dioc Coun Dio Pittsburgh Pittsburgh PA 1996-1998. Soc of Ord Scientists 2012. DD Ya Berk 2013; Sub Chapl The Most Venerable Ord of St. Jn of Jerusalem 1995. nicholas@episcopalri.org

KNOCKEL, Wayne J (WNY) Saint Peter's Episcopal Church, 205 Longmeadow Rd, Eggertsville NY 14226 **S Ptr's Epis Ch Buffalo NY 2016-** B Dubuque IA 1964 s Walter & Celine. BA Luther Coll 1987; MA U of Nthrn Iowa 1995; MDiv Trin Luth Sem 2000. Rec 12/20/2006 as Priest Bp Wendell Nathaniel Gibbs Jr. Ch Of The H Sprt Livonia MI 2010-2011; S Aug Of Cbury Mason MI 2008-2010.

KNOLL LENON, Katherine Genevieve (Kan) D 6/17/2017 Bp George Wayne Smith.

KNOLL-SWEENEY, Sarah Jacqueline (Tex) 4120 Clinton Pkwy, Lawrence KS 66047 **St Ben's Workshop San Antonio TX 2017-** B Topeka KS 1981 d Steven & Marlene. BA U of Kansas 2003; MDiv CDSP 2008. D 6/7/2008 P 12/6/2008 Bp Dean E Wolfe. m 9/6/2013 James Shay Sweeney c 1. Epis TS Of The SW Austin TX 2014; Chapl Dio Texas Houston TX 2013-2015; Bp Seabury Acad Lawr KS 2008-2010.

KNOTT, Joseph Lee (Ala) 5528 - 11th Court South, Birmingham AL 35222 **P Assoc Gr Ch Birmingham AL 1989-** B Birmingham AL 1928 s Joseph & Lillian. BA Birmingham-Sthrn Coll 1953; MDiv Van 1955; Sewanee: The U So, TS 1962; MEd U of Montevallo 1988. D 6/1/1962 P 1/1/1963 Bp George Mosley Murray. c 3. Epis Chapl U of Montevallo AL 1982-1989; R S Andr's Ch Montevallo AL 1982-1988; Dir of Pstr Care Bryce Hosp Tuscaloosa AL 1978-1982; Assoc S Mths Epis Ch Tuscaloosa AL 1977-1982; Chapl Bryce Hosp Tuscaloosa AL 1972-1978; Chapl/Intern Bapt Med Cntr Birmingham AL 1971-1972; R S Jn's Ch Birmingham AL 1965-1972; Vic Ch of the Epiph Enterprise AL 1962-1965; Vic S Mich's Ch Ozark AL 1962-1965; Serv Methodist Ch 1955-1961. Auth, *Bible Lessons for Yth*.

KNOTTS, Harold Wayne (Mich) 26431 W Chicago, Redford MI 48239 B Fort Worth TX 1939 s R A & Nettie. BA Oklahoma City U 1966; MDiv Nash 1975; Command and Gnrl Stff Coll 1987. D 6/28/1975 Bp Frederick Warren Putnam P 1/1/1976 Bp Chilton R Powell. m 12/30/1972 Katherine Eve Knotts. S Eliz's Ch Redford Chart Township MI 1994-2002; S Alb's Epis Ch Marshfield WI 1993-1995; S Jn's Mltry Acad Delafield WI 1991-1993; Vic Of Cong H Trin Louisville WI 1989-1991; Ch Of The Gd Shpd Swainsboro GA 1989-1990; Off Of Bsh For ArmdF New York NY 1983-1989; R S Jn's Ch Durant OK 1979-1982; Vic S Paul's Ch Clinton OK 1977-1979; Dio Oklahoma Oklahoma City OK 1976-1979; S Jas Epis Ch Oklahoma City OK 1975-1976.

KNOUSE, Amanda Rue (Va) 9668 Maidstone Rd, Delaplane VA 20144 **Emm Epis Ch Delaplane Delaplane VA 2012-; Asst S Mk's Chap Deale Deale MD 2008-** B Carlisle PA 1982 d Wilmer & Robin. BA Juniata Colllege 2004; MDiv VTS 2008. D 6/7/2008 Bp Nathan Dwight Baxter P 2/21/2009 Bp Eugene Taylor Sutton. m 5/9/2012 John Robert Knouse c 2. Asst R S Jas' Par Lothian MD 2008-2012.

KNOWLES II, Harold Frank (Los) 623 El Centro St, South Pasadena CA 91030 B Chicago IL 1937 s Harold & Maxine. BA U CA 1958; MDiv CDSP 1961. D 9/7/1961 P 3/1/1962 Bp Francis E I Bloy. S Jas' Par So Pasadena CA 1969-1989; Assoc R S Mk's Par Glendale CA 1967-1969; Cur St Cross Epis Ch Hermosa Bch CA 1961-1967; Dioc Cmsn Of Ecum. Chapl Soc Mayflower Descendants; Ord S Lazarus, Ord S Jn Bapt, Ord S Jn Jerusalem. Who'S Who In Rel; Zeta Psi; Chi Delta Pi.

KNOWLES, Melody D (Chi) 3737 Seminary Rd, Alexandria VA 22304 **Prof VTS Alexandria VA 2013-; Asst Chapl Brent Hse 2004-** B Surrey BC Canada 1969 BA Trin Wstrn U Langley BC CA 1991; MDiv PrTS 1994; PhD PrTS 2001. D 2/7/2004 Bp Victor Alfonso Scantlebury P 12/18/2004 Bp Bill Persell.

m 6/10/2001 John Allan Knight c 2. "COntesting Texts: Jews and Christians in Conversation about the Bible," Fortress Press, 2007; "Jerusalem Practiced: Jerusalem in the Rel Practices of Yehud and the Diaspora in the Persian Period," Scholars Press, 2006; "The Flexible Rhetoric of Retelling: The Choice of Dav in the Texts of the Psalms," *Cath Biblic Quarterly*, 2005; "The Returns in Ezra as Pilgrimage:," *Journ of Biblic Lit*, 2004. Assn of Angl Biblic Scholars 2002.

KNOWLES, Roberta Gertrude (Tex) 2704 Rossedale Street, Houston TX 77004 **R Hope Epis Ch Houston TX 2011-** B Nassau Bahamas 1956 d Arthur & Louise. BS Bethune-Cookman Coll 1978; MDiv TESM 2005. D 5/28/2005 Bp John Wadsworth Howe P 2/2/2006 Bp Don Adger Wimberly. c 1. The Great Cmsn Fndt Houston TX 2009-2010; Vic S Phil The Joy Giver Austin TX 2007-2009; Reverend S Jas Epis Ch Houston TX 2005-2007.

KNOWLES, Walter Roy (Oly) 11020 Ne 64th St, Kirkland WA 98033 B Seattle WA 1951 s Harold & Joy. BA Westmont Coll 1972; MDiv U Tor Can 1977; PhD Grad Theol Un 2009. Trans 7/1/1980 Bp Robert Hume Cochrane. m 12/18/1971 Lorelette Meryl Knowles c 1. Min of Mus All SS' Ch San Francisco CA 2008-2011; Assoc R for Liturg and Mus Ch Of The Redeem Kenmore WA 1985-2005; Vic S Lk's Epis Ch Elma WA 1984; Vic Estrn Grays Harbor Mssn Montesano WA 1980-1984; Vic S Mk's Epis Ch Montesano WA 1980-1984; Serv Ch Of Can 1977-1980. Ed, "Drenched in Gr," Pickwick Books, 2013; Auth, "Incorporated into the Soc of the Sprt: Baptismal Pract and Ecclesiology in Aug's No Afr," *Drenched in Gr*, Pickwick Books, 2013; Auth, "H Week in Hippo: The Weeks Surrounding Easter in a No Aftican Par," *Studia Liturgica*, 2010; Auth, ""Numbering" Liturg: An Augustinian Aesthetic of Liturg," *Proceedings of the No Amer Acad of Liturg*, 2009. No Amer Acad of Liturg 2008; Societas Liturgica 2009.

KNOWLTON, Beth (WTex) 315 E Pecan St, San Antonio TX 78205 **R S Mk's Epis Ch San Antonio TX 2014-** B Atlanta GA 1968 d Richard & Susan. BA Albion Coll 1990; MPP U MI 1991; MDiv Candler TS 2004; MDiv Candler TS Emory U 2004. D 6/5/2004 P 1/9/2005 Bp J Neil Alexander. c 2. Cathd Of S Phil Atlanta GA 2006-2014; The Epis Ch Of S Ptr And S Paul Marietta GA 2004-2006. bknowlton@stmarks-sa.org

KNOX, David Paul (CFla) 216 Sheridan Ave, Longwood FL 32750 B Sydney NSW AU 1959 s David & Alisa. MDiv Regent Coll Vancouver CA 1990; ThM Moore Theol Coll Sydney 2000. Trans 9/1/1999. m 8/23/1997 Susan E Knox c 1. R Chr Ch Longwood FL 1999-2013; Asst The Falls Ch Epis Falls Ch VA 1996-1999; Asst S Matthews Kensington So Australia 1994-1995; Asiistant Gd Shpd Cairns Queensland Australia 1992-1993.

KNOX, Floyd L (La) 10587 Birchwood Dr, Baton Rouge LA 70807 **Ret 1999-** B Oak Ridge LA 1928 s Foster & Celia. BS Sthrn U Baton Rouge LA 1948; MA Col 1951; Profsnl Dplma Col 1955; Col 1955; Boston Coll 1964; Cert Theol Stud Nash 1987. D 12/19/1984 P 6/27/1987 Bp James Barrow Brown. P-in-c S Mich's Ch Baton Rouge LA 1997-1999, Asst 1987-1997.

KNOX, Jannet Marie (Mont) 59 Mill Creek Rd # 463, Sheridan MT 59749 B Alpena MI 1930 d Guy & Gertrude. No Cntrl Coll 1949. D 11/19/1994 Bp Charles I Jones III. m 9/20/1953 Bruce Edward Knox c 2.

KNOX, Jeffrey Donald (CNY) 1755 State Route 48, Fulton NY 13069 **Chapl to the Ret Cler and Spouses Dio Cntrl New York Liverpool NY 2001-** B Seneca Falls NY 1941 s Donald & Norma. BA U of Tampa 1963; Ya Berk 1966. D 6/4/1966 Bp Walter M Higley P 10/4/1967 Bp Ned Cole. c 2. R All SS Ch Fulton NY 1974-2001; Emm Ch Adams NY 1968-1974; P-in-c Zion Ch Pierrepont Manor NY 1968-1974; Asst Headwaters Epis Mssn Boonville NY 1966-1968. Soc of S Marg 1981.

KNOX, John Michael (WK) 16019 W 80th St, Lenexa KS 66219 B Whittier CA 1954 s Albert & Grace. BA U of Kansas 1978; MDiv Nash 1981. D 6/11/1981 P 12/1/1981 Bp Richard Frank Grein. m 12/18/1976 Carole Denis Knox c 1. Off Of Bsh For ArmdF New York NY 1987-1990; R S Lk's Epis Ch Scott City KS 1985-1987; S Andr's Epis Ch Emporia KS 1984-1985; S Jas Ch Wichita KS 1981-1984; Non-par. SSC.

KNOX, Regina Gilmartin (Me) 143 State St, Portland ME 04101 B Philadelphia PA 1950 d Eugene & Marguerite. BA Villanova U 1980; MA EDS 2004. D 6/19/2010 P 6/25/2011 Bp Stephen Taylor Lane. m 4/28/1984 John B Knox c 1. P-in-c S Phil's Ch Wiscasset ME 2012-2013; Dio Maine Portland ME 2011-2014.

✠ **KNUDSEN, The Rt Rev Chilton Richardson** (Me) Diocese of Maryland, 4 E University Pkwy, Baltimore MD 21218 **Dio Maryland Baltimore MD 2015-; Conflict Medtr 1994-** B Washington DC 1946 d William & Anne. BA Chatham Coll 1968; MDiv SWTS 1980; DD SWTS 1999. D 6/9/1980 Bp James Winchester Montgomery P 2/24/1981 Bp Quintin Ebenezer Primo Jr Con 3/28/1998 for Me. m 5/29/1971 Michael J Knudsen c 1. Asst Dio Long Island Garden City NY 2014-2015; Asst Bp Dio New York New York NY 2013-2014; Int Bp of Lexington Dio Lexington Lexington 2011-2012; Pres Prov I (New Engl) 2003-2006; Dioc Bp Dio Maine Portland ME 1998-2008; Trst CPF NY 1994-2006; Instr Theol Diac Prog Dio Chicago Chicago IL 1987-1998; P Asst Ch Of Our Sav Elmhurst IL 1986-1987; Vic Ch Of S Ben Bolingbrook IL 1982-1986; Trst Berk 2009-2012. Platt and Knudsen, "Depend-

475

ing on the Gr of God," Forw Mvmt, 2014; Platt and Knudsen, "So You Think You Don't Know One," Morehouse, 2011; Knudsen, "After-Pastoring," Dio Chicago, 1996. EWC 1978; OHC 1979; Recovery Mnstrs 1986. Maine Wmn Hall of Fame Maine W Hall of Fame 2006; Rel Ldrshp Awd Maine Coun of Ch 1999; Outstanding Wmn Ldr YWCA 1991.

KNUDSON, James Clarence (Mass) 85 Grozier Rd, Cambridge MA 02138 **Ret 2000-** B Denver CO 1933 s Clarence & Frank. BA U Denv 1956; MDiv EDS 1962; DMin EDS 1992. D 6/23/1962 P 6/1/1963 Bp Anson Phelps Stokes Jr. m 7/11/1964 Esther Louise Knudson c 2. P-in-c Gr Epis Ch Medford MA 1997-2000; Int S Anne's Ch No Billerica MA 1995-1996; Int All SS Epis Ch of the No Shore Inc Danvers MA 1993-1995; Supply Dio Massachusetts Boston MA 1991-1993; Int Ch Of The Gd Shpd Waban MA 1990-1991; Cmssnr Mnstry Dvlpmt Dio Rhode Island Providence RI 1982-1986, Dir Intern in Mnstry Prog 1981-1989, EFM Mentor 1981-1987, Rdr GOEs 1977-1987, Com Lay Mnstry 1976-1982, Com Cont Educ Mnstry 1971-1974, Sprtl Dir 1986-1989, Curs Secy 1982-1985, Dioc Coun 1975-1981, COM 1973-1974, DeptCE 1971-1972; R All SS Ch Warwick RI 1973-1989; Asst S Lk's Epis Ch E Greenwich RI 1967-1973; Asst S Jn the Bapt Crawley Sussex Engl 1965-1967; Asst Chr Ch Waltham MA 1963-1965. Auth, *Var arts & Revs.* Bp Atwood Prize in Hist Epis TS.

KNUDSON, Kay Francis (Neb) 1304 Wade St, Lexington NE 68850 **R On Track Mnstry Lexington NE 2005-; P S Ptr's In The Vlly Lexington NE 2005-** B Knox County NE 1935 s Francis & Grace. BS U of Nebraska 1957. D 12/13/2004 P 6/13/2005 Bp Joe Goodwin Burnett. m 8/11/1957 Shirley Mae Knudson c 3.

KNUDSON, Richard Lewis (Alb) 9 Saint James Pl Apt 207, Oneonta NY 13820 **Vic Ch Of The H Sprt Schenevus NY 2001-** B Newton MA 1930 s Henry & Magda. BS U of Sthrn Maine 1957; MS U of Maine 1960; DEd Bos 1970. D 6/9/2001 Bp Daniel William Herzog P 7/31/2004 Bp David John Bena. m 6/23/1957 Ann Knudson c 2.

KNUTH, Charles H (U) **Trin Ch Folsom CA 2016-** B Salt Lake City, UT 1986 s Ricky Lee & Sherrie. M.Div. Ya Berk 2016. D 6/16/2016 P 1/25/2017 Bp Scott Byron Hayashi. cknuth@trinityfolsom.org

KNUTSEN, James Kenyon (NCal) P.O. Box 3601, Santa Rosa CA 95402 **Assoc Shpd by the Sea Epis/Luth Mssn Gualala CA 2011-** B San Rafael CA 1960 s Martin & Elaine. BA Stan 1983; MA EDS 1985; Cert No Chas Inst for the Addictions 1985; MDiv EDS 1990. D 6/27/1990 Bp John Lester Thompson III P 4/27/1991 Bp David Bell Birney IV. Ch Of The Incarn Santa Rosa CA 2009, Int Assoc R 2007-2008, Asstg Cler 2007-, Asst 1994-1996; S Jn's Chap Cambridge MA 2004-2014; Post/Novc Soc of S Jn the Evang Cambridge MA 2004-2006; Soc-St Jn The Evang Cambridge MA 2004-2006; R S Mich And All Ang Ch Ft Bragg CA 1998-2003; Assoc Trin Ch Sonoma CA 1998; Assoc Gr Ch S Helena CA 1997-1998; Int S Lk's Mssn Calistoga CA 1993-1994; Cur Ch Of S Jn The Evang Hingham MA 1990-1993.

KNUTSON, Randy A (NCal) 201 E. Fir St. (P.O. Box 124), Fort Bragg CA 95437 **P-in-c S Mich And All Ang Ch Ft Bragg CA 2015-** B Coeur d'Alene ID 1957 s Edward & Patricia. BA Pacific Luth U 1980; MA California St U 1992; MDiv CDSP 2011. D 6/28/2014 P 4/25/2015 Bp Barry Leigh Beisner. m 5/30/1981 Robin A Johnson c 2. D S Jn The Bapt Lodi CA 2014-2015; Mus Dir Ch of St Jn The Bapt Lodi Ca 2000-2015. randyknutson@sbcglobal.net

KOCH, Adrienne Marie **Chapl Dio No Carolina Raleigh NC 2017-** D 6/17/2017 Bp Anne Hodges-Copple.

KOCH, Eunice Jane (Minn) PO Box 513, Ely MN 55731 B Duluth MN 1935 d Arthur & Grace. BA Metropltn St 1983. D 6/20/2015 Bp Brian N Prior. c 3.

KOCH JR, John Dunbar (Ky) Saint Francis In The Fields, PO Box 225, Harrods Creek KY 40027 **S Fran In The Fields Harrods Creek KY 2012-** B Baton Rouge LA 1977 s John & Sally. BA W&L; MDiv TESM 2007. D 6/2/2007 Bp John Wadsworth Howe P. m 9/7/2004 Elizabeth Tucker Koch c 1. F.O.C.U.S. Vero Bch FL 2001-2004. jadyk@stfrancisinthefields.org

KOCH, William Christian (RG) P.O. Box 1614, Blue Hill ME 04614 B Santa Fe NM 1933 s Ferdinand & Anna. BA Knox Coll 1955; MDiv CDSP 1958. D 6/28/1958 P 4/7/1959 Bp C J Kinsolving III. m 8/3/1985 Jean Alice Uehlinger Koch c 1. NSM Ch of Engl Dio Gloucester Bisley 1993-1999; NSM Ch of Engl Beaminster Team Mnstry 1985-1990; Fllshp Of The Ascen Hse Wellesley Hl MA 1984; Dir Hse Of The Ascen 1983-1985; Chair Of The Liturg Cmsn 1978-1983; Ch Hm Soc 1978-1982; R All SS Par Brookline MA 1973-1983; Vic Ch Of The Ascen Parkesburg PA 1967-1969; Chapl U Denv CO 1963-1967; Novc Soc Of S Fran 1960-1963; Asst Chapl Tulane & Newcomb Coll New Orleans LA 1959-1960; Cur Pro Cathd Epis Ch Of S Clem El Paso TX 1958-1959; Dir Santa Fe Cmnty Partnership 1991-1992; Dir Amer Red Cross Santa Fe NM Chapt 1990-1991; Dn of Students Shipley Sch Bryn Mawr PA 1971-1973. Chapl SCHC 1977-1984.

KOCHENBURGER, Philip A (Tex) 24011 Sunset Sky, Katy TX 77494 **Epis HS Bellaire TX 2016-; Off Of Bsh For ArmdF New York NY 1999-** B Bergen County NJ 1962 s John & Patricia. Assemblies of God TS; BA SE U 1989; MDiv Gordon-Conwell TS 1993. D 12/3/1995 Bp John Wadsworth Howe P 6/2/1996 Bp Hugo Luis Pina-Lopez. m 7/4/2011 Ilona E Kochenburg-

er. S Agnes Ch Sebring FL 1997-1999; Assoc R Gr Epis Ch Of Ocala Ocala FL 1996-1997. Auth, "arts Var Pub"; Auth, "The Blood"; Auth, "The Sound Of His Voice". pkochenburger@ehshouston.org

KOCHTITZKY, Rodney Morse (Tenn) The Pastoral Center for Healing, 1024 Noelton Ave, Nashville TN 37204 **Couples Ther The Pstr Cntr for Healing 2009-** B Nashville TN 1953 s Otto & Marjorie. BA U So 1975; MDiv GTS 1982; Cert Inst of Imago Relatns Ther 1991; Cert Blanton-Peale Grad Inst 1995; Cert Imago Relationships Intl 1995; Cert Imago Relationships Intl 1996; Cert Imago Relationships Intl 2009. D 6/20/1982 P 4/10/1983 Bp William Evan Sanders. c 2. Pstr Counslr S Dav's Epis Ch Nashville TN 2002-2009; P-in-c Dio New York New York NY 1988-1991; Epis Ch Of SS Jn Paul And S Clem Mt Vernon NY 1988-1991; P-in-c S Paul & Clem Mt Vernon NY 1988-1991; Asst Ch Of S Jas The Less Scarsdale NY 1986-1988; Vic Dio Tennessee Nashville TN 1983-1986, D-In-Trng 1982-1983; D Gr Ch Chattanooga TN 1982-1983. Cmnty Of S Mary 1997; Fell Amer Assn Pstr Counselors 1987. Serv Recognition Awd Assoc. of Imago Ther 2002.

KODERA, T James (Mass) 212 Old Lancaster Rd, Sudbury MA 01776 **Prof of Rel Wellesley Coll 1976-** B JP 1945 s Haruo & Utae. BA Carleton Coll 1969; Yale DS 1970; MA Col 1972; MPhil Col 1974; PhD Col 1976; EDS 1983. D 6/1/1985 Bp John Bowen Coburn P 5/6/1986 Bp Roger W Blanchard. m 3/27/1995 Nancy S Kodera c 2. Pres Epis Asiamerica Mnstry Coun 2009-2011; VP Epis Asiamerica Mnstry Coun 2007-2011; S Lk's Ch Hudson MA 2003-2017, P-in-c 2000-2002; Co-Chair Racial Ethnic Mnstrs Com 1995-1997; Asst S Eliz's Ch Sudbury MA 1992-2000; Pres Epis Asiamerica Mnstry Advocates 1991-1997; Fndr & Assoc P Boston Japanese Mnstry 1991-1995; Assoc S Mk's Ch Southborough MA 1988-1991; Asst All SS Par Brookline MA 1985-1988. Auth, "Why Asian Amer Stds Matter: challenges and pPromises in the Undergraduate Curric," *ASIANETWORK Journ*, ASIANetwork, 2008; Auth, "Asian Americans: Where Do They Belong?," *Wit*, The Ch Pub Co., 2004; Auth, "Asians In Amer Soc & Ch: Their Struggles & Calling," *THE JAPAN Chr Revs*, The Chr Lit Soc of Japan, 1996; Auth, "Reshaping of Consceience: Challenges and Promises of Multiculturalism in Amer Educ," *THE JAPAN Chr Revs*, The Chr Lit Soc of Japan, 1994; Auth, "Am I My Sis's Keeper?," *PLUMBLINE: A Journ OF Mnstry IN HIGHER EDUCAITON*, ECUSA, 1992; Auth, "Paradoxes of Being Rel: A Case of Mod Japan," *REKISHI KENKYU*, The Hist Sudy Grp of the Angl Ch of Japan, 1990; Transltr, "The 1979 Bk of Common Pryr," *into Japanese*, ECUSA, 1988; Co-Ed, "DIALOGUE & Allnce: ENCOUNTERS BETWEEN ASIAN & Wstrn CONCEPTIONS OF THE ULTIMATE," Paragon, 1987; Auth, "What Are We To Do?," *PLUMBLINE: A Journ OF MHE*, ECUSA, 1987; Auth, "Uchimura Kanzo & His 'No Ch Chrsnty: Its Origin & Significance in Early Mod Japan," *Rel SUDIES*, Cambridge U Press, 1987; Auth, "Continuity Of Change And Change In Continuity," *THE DHARMA Wrld*, The Kosei Pub Co., 1984; Auth, "A Vortex Of E & W: Probelems Of Contextualization," *THE Ecum Revs*, WCC, Geneva, 1983; Auth, "The Study Of Rel At Wellesley Coll: Tradition & Change, The Coun On The Study Of Rel Bulletin," *THE Coun O THE STUDY OF Rel BULLETIN*, AAR, 1982; Auth, "Toward And Asianization Of Chrsnty:Demise Or Metamorphosis, Ten Theologians Respond To The Unificaiton Ch," *TEN THEOLOGIANS RESPOND TO THE UNIFICAITON Ch*, The Rose of Sharon Press, 1981; Auth, "DOGEN'S FORMATIVE YEARS IN CHINA," Routledge & Kegan Paul, London, 1980; Auth, "Nichiren And His Nationalistic Eschatology," *Rel Stds*, Cambridge U Press, 1979; Auth, "Images Of The Ideal: Islamic, Buddhist And Confucian," *Sekai Gakusei Shimbun*, 1979. AAR; Assn For Asian Stds; Buddhist-Chr Dialogue; Coun For Asian And Pacific Theol; Intl Assn Buddhist Stds; Soc Of S Jn The Evang.

KOEHLER, Anne E (Nwk) PO Box 611, East Orleans MA 02643 B Pensacola FL 1951 BA Duke 1973; MBA NWU 1974; MDiv PrTS 2002; DAS GTS 2003. D 5/31/2003 P 12/13/2003 Bp John Palmer Croneberger. m 6/22/1974 Steven H Koehler. Int Chr Ch Glen Ridge NJ 2006-2013; S Thos Ch Alexandria Pittstown NJ 2005-2006; Cur S Lk's Ch Gladstone NJ 2003-2005.

KOEHLER, Michael Alban Collins (WTex) 6000 FM 3237 Unit A, Wimberley TX 78676 **S Lk's Epis Ch San Antonio TX 2017-** B Rockford IL 1980 s Robert & Terry. BA Baylor U 2005; MDiv Sewanee: The U So, TS 2012; MDiv The TS at The U So 2012. D 5/31/2012 Bp Gary Richard Lillibridge P 12/5/2012 Bp David Mitchell Reed. m 4/14/2007 Erin Elizabeth Koehler c 3. Texas Mltry Inst San Antonio TX 2014-2016; S Steph's Epis Ch Wimberley TX 2012-2014. mkoehler@tml-sa.org

KOEHLER III, Norman Elias (Pgh) 408 Forest Highlands Dr, Pittsburgh PA 15238 B Washington PA 1934 s Norman & Elizabeth. BA Grove City Coll 1956; Linguist 4/5 Defense Lang Inst 1965; MS USC 1969; PhD U Pgh 1973; MA Pittsburgh TS 2002. D 6/15/2002 P 12/13/2006 Bp Robert William Duncan. m 10/13/1956 Virginia Ann Schadt c 3. Epis P in Res Gd Shpd Luth Ch 2014-2015; P S Thos Memi Epis Ch Oakmont PA 2008-2013; Int S Paul's Epis Ch Kittanning PA 2008-2009; Int St Mary's Ch Red Bank PA 2007; Int St. Barnbas Ch Brakenridge PA 2006-2007; D S Andr's Epis Ch New Kensington PA 2004-2008; D The Ch Of The Redeem Pittsburgh PA 2002-2004; Chapl (1/2 time) Presb Sr Care Oakmont PA 2001-2011; Chapl Asst Presb Sr Care Oakmont PA 2000-2015. Auth, "F.D. Maurice and Soc Trin," *Mstr's Thesis*, Pittsburgh TS, 2002. OSL the Physcn 2009. Kennedy Lifetime Achievement Awd Grove City Coll 2011.

KOEHLER, Robert Brien (Spr) 19206 Boca del Mar, San Antonio TX 78258 **Assoc R Chr Epis Ch San Antonio TX 2012-; Chapl Nash Nashotah WI 2012-, Trst 1994-** B Hastings NE 1950 s Robert & Melba. BA U of Dallas 1972; U of Wisconsin 1973; MDiv Nash 1976. D 5/1/1976 P 11/1/1976 Bp Charles Thomas Gaskell. m 8/5/1972 Terry Koehler c 3. R S Lk's Ch Baton Rouge LA 2001-2011; R S Lk's Ch Ft Myers FL 1993-2001; ESA Admin The Esa Mssy Soc Inc. Ft Worth TX 1991-1993; Cn to the Ordnry Dio Ft Worth Ft Worth TX 1989-1991, Exec Secy To The Bp 1987-1989; Vic Ch Of The H Cross Burleson TX 1984-1987; R S Raphael's Ch Ft Myers Bch FL 1981-1984; Cur Emm Epis Ch Rockford IL 1978-1981; Dekoven Fndt for Ch Wk Racine WI 1976-1978; Chapl to Sis of St Mary S Lk's Ch Racine WI 1976-1978. Ancient & Honorable Artillery Co Of Massachusetts 1984; CCU 1976; CBS 1997; Ecm/ESA/Forw In Faith 1977; GAS 1986; Soc Of Colonial Wars 1985; SSC 1978; Sons Of The Amer Revolution 1982. brienkoehler@gmail.com

KOELLIKER, Karulynn Travis (Ga) B Charlottesville VA 1946 Old Dominion U 1967; BA Georgia St U 1969. D. c 2.

KOELLN, Theodore Frank (CFla) 505 Ne 1st Ave, Mulberry FL 33860 **P-in-c H Trin Epis Ch Fruitland Pk FL 2010-; Chapl All SS Acad 1999-** B Boston MA 1944 s Theodore & Geneva. BS Dakota St U 1967; MDiv Sewanee: The U So, TS 1988. D 6/10/1988 P 1/1/1989 Bp Craig Barry Anderson. m 6/19/1999 Patricia N Koelln. R Gd Shpd Decatur AL 2004-2009; S Lk The Evang Ch Mulberry FL 1996-2004; S Paul's Ch Brookings SD 1991-1996; D Chr Epis Ch Milbank SD 1988-1998; S Mary's Epis Ch Webster SD 1988-1998; Dio So Dakota Pierre SD 1988-1991.

KOENIG, Diane L (Chi) 86 Pomeroy Ave # 2, Crystal Lake IL 60014 **D/Pstr S Mary Epis Ch Crystal Lake IL 1998-** B Michigan City IN 1940 d Lewis & Ann. MA Amer Conservatory of Mus 1964. D 2/7/1998 Bp Herbert Alcorn Donovan Jr. m 5/20/1967 Peter Frederick Koenig. NAAD.

KOENIG, John Thomas (NJ) 17546 Drayton Hall Way, San Diego CA 92128 B Fort Wayne IN 1938 s Melvin & Doris. BA Concordia Sr Coll 1961; BD Concordia TS 1965; ThD UTS 1971. D 6/12/1993 P 12/14/1993 Bp George Phelps Mellick Belshaw. m 6/5/1976 Kathleen J Koenig. Prof The GTS New York NY 1993-2007; Assoc Prof, NT UTS 1976-1978; Instr/Asst Prof, NT PrTS Princeton NJ 1971-1976; Sub-Dn for Acad Affrs The Gnrl Sem NYC 1992-2001; Sub-Dn GTS 1991-2000. Auth, "Soul Banquets," Morehouse Pub, 2007; Auth, "The Feast of the Wrld's Redemp," Trin Press Intl , 2000; Auth, "Rediscovering NT Pryr," HarperCollins; Wipf & Stock, 1992; Auth, "Hosp," *Encyclopedia of Rel*, Macmillan, 1990; Auth, "NT Hosp," Fortress Press; Wipf & Stock, 1985; Auth, "Philippians, Philemon," *Augsburg Commentary on the NT*, Augsburg, 1985; Auth, "Jews & Christians in Dialogue: NT Foundations," Westminster, 1979; Auth, "Charismata: God's Gifts," Westminster, 1978. Angl Assn of Biblic Scholars; Soc for Values in Higher Educ; SBL.

KOENIGER, Margaret Smithers (Nwk) 574 Ridgewood Rd, Maplewood NJ 07040 B Rhinebeck NY 1949 d John & Margaret. AA Pine Manor Jr Coll 1970; BFA U of New Mex 1973; MDiv Drew U 1995. D 6/3/1995 Bp Jack Marston Mckelvey P 12/9/1995 Bp John Shelby Spong. m 5/29/1976 John Crawford Koeniger c 3. Chapl Atlantic Hlth & Hospice Millburn NJ 2005-2009; Serv Dio Newark Newark NJ 2005-2009, Int 2002-2004; Dvlpmt St Philips Acad Newark NJ 2004-2005; S Paul's Epis Ch Chatham NJ 1996-2002, 1995-1996. Alb Inst.

KOEPKE, Jack (SO) 412 Sycamore Street, Cincinnati OH 45202 **Cn to the Ordnry Dio Sthrn Ohio Cincinnati OH 2011-, Chair - Com 2011-, 2001-2010** B Cannonsburg PA 1953 s John & Catherine. BA Hobart and Wm Smith Colleges 1975; MDiv Yale DS 1979. D 6/9/1979 P 12/8/1979 Bp Robert Bracewell Appleyard. m 6/4/1977 Nanci Ann Koepke c 2. R S Paul's Epis Ch Dayton OH 1997-2011; R Ch Of Our Sav Silver Sprg MD 1986-1997; Cn For Pstr Dvlpmt Dio Wstrn Michigan Kalamazoo MI 1982-1986; Vic S Steph's Epis Ch Plainwell MI 1982-1985; Asst R Fox Chap Epis Ch Pittsburgh PA 1979-1982; Ch Dedploy Bd Epis Ch Cntr New York NY 1998-2006. Auth, "Var arts". jkoepke@diosohio.org

KOERNER, Travers 314 Lincoln Ave, Rockville MD 20850 B New Orleans LA 1944 s John & Katherine. BS Tul 1973; Cert Oxf GB 1974; MEd Tul 1974; MDiv GTS 1977. D 6/11/1977 Bp Paul Moore Jr P 12/10/1977 Bp Harold Louis Wright. Assoc Chr Ch Cathd New Orleans LA 2012-2016; S Barth's Ch Gaithersburg MD 1999-2000; Trin Ch Epis Pass Chr MS 1982-2000, Assoc 1982-2000; P-in-c S Steph's Ch Armonk NY 1979-1980, 1977, Cur 1976-1978; Ch Of The Gd Shpd New York NY 1978; Fac Cathd Of St Jn The Div New York NY 1977-1980; Non-par. Soc Of S Jn The Evang.

KOFFRON-EISEN, Elizabeth Mary (Ia) 945 Applewood Ct #1, Coralville IA 52241 **D Trin Ch Iowa City IA 1996-** B Cedar Rapids IA 1952 d Marvin & Esther. Mt Mercy Coll 1973; BA Coe Coll 1975; EFM 1994. D 1/7/1996 Bp Chris Christopher Epting. m 6/8/1985 Thomas Jay Eisen. D Gr Ch Cedar Rapids IA 1996-1999. Animal Cmncatn Spec; NAAD, ESMA, Steph Mnstry Ldr.

KOH, Aidan Y (Los) 4344 Lemp Ave, Studio City CA 91604 **S Jas' Sch Los Angeles CA 2006-; Chapl St. Jas Sch Los Angeles CA 2006-** B 1953 s Basil

& Ruth. BA Hankook Theol Coll 1981; MDiv Hankook TS 1987; CDSP 1991. D 6/15/1991 P 1/1/1992 Bp Frederick Houk Borsch. m 9/10/1983 Christina Eunkyung Koh c 1. Asst S Jas Par Los Angeles CA 1991-2006.

KOHL, Stacey (Ct) D 6/10/2017 Bp Ian Theodore Douglas.

KOHLBECKER, Eugene Edmund (NI) 12 Clearview Ave, Hilton NY 14468 B Urbana IL 1954 s Eugene & Billie. BS MacMurray Coll 1975; MS U IL 1977; PhD Indiana U 1986; MDiv Sewanee: The U So, TS 1992. D 6/20/1992 Bp George Nelson Hunt III P 2/6/1993 Bp Alfred Marble Jr. Examing Chapl Dio Nthrn Indiana 2004-2006; R Trin Ch Michigan City IN 2000-2006; Assoc Epis Ch Of The Gd Shpd Lake Chas LA 1996-1999; Vic All SS Ch Dequincy LA 1994-1995; S Andr's Ch Lake Chas LA 1994-1995; D-in-c Chr Ch St Jos LA 1993-1994; Gr Ch S Jos LA 1993-1994; Asst Trin Ch Natchez MS 1992-1994; Chapl Trin Epis Day Sch Natchez MS 1992-1993.

KOHLMEIER, Susan (Roch) 1017 Silvercrest Dr, Webster NY 14580 **Zion Epis Ch Palmyra NY 2008-; Joint Pastorate Trin Evang Luth Ch 2002-** B Clifton Springs NY 1956 d John & Ramona. BA S Jn Fisher Coll 1978; MA S Bernards TS and Mnstry 1988; MDiv S Bernards TS and Mnstry 1992. D 3/13/1993 P 2/11/1994 Bp William George Burrill. m 10/17/1981 Charles P Kohlmeier c 2. S Mths Epis Ch Rochester NY 2005-2008, 1995-2002; Dio Rochester Henrietta 2002-2005; Asst The Ch Of The Epiph Gates NY 1994-1995; Asst Ch Of The Gd Shpd Webster NY 1993-1994; Chapl S Jn's Nrsng Hm Rochester NY 1993-1994. zionoffice@rochester.rr.com

KOHN, George Frederick (ECR) 980 W Franklin St, Monterey CA 93940 **R S Jas' Ch Monterey CA 2001-** B Evanston IL 1949 s Clyde & Doris. BA U of Iowa 1971; MDiv GTS 1975; MA U of Iowa 1989; MA Pacifica Grad Inst 2008; PhD Pacifica Grad Inst 2012. D 6/11/1975 P 12/13/1975 Bp Walter Cameron Righter. m 5/18/2002 Molly Jean Lewis c 2. R Epis Ch Of The Gd Shpd Salinas CA 1985-1994; R Trin Ch Muscatine IA 1978-1985; Cur Trin Cathd Davenport IA 1975-1978; Fin Cmsn Dio El Camino Real Salinas CA 1989-1994, COM 1986-1994; Alcosm Cmsn Dio Iowa Des Moines IA 1980-1985. Auth, "Hunukul: Archetypal Reflections on the Soul of a Place," Proquest UMI, 2013; Contrib, "Rebearths: Conversations w a Wrld Ensouled," Wrld Soul Books, 2010; Auth, "Toward a Bi-Model Model of Sprtlty and Alcosm," *Journ of Rel and Hlth*, Human Sciences Press, 1984.

KOHN-PERRY, Ellen Marie (Nwk) **P-in-c Chr Ch Budd Lake NJ 2015-** B Morris Town NY 1962 d George & Maryanne. BA Hollins U 2001; MDiv Drew TS 2012; MDiv Drew U 2012. D 5/18/2013 P 12/14/2013 Bp Mark M Beckwith. m 12/15/2001 Duane Joseph Perry c 1. Chr Ch Short Hills NJ 2013-2014.

KOLANOWSKI, Ronald James (Ct) St. James Episcopal Church, 95 Route 2A, Preston CT 06365 **Vic S Jas Ch Preston CT 2010-** B Manistee MI 1957 s Arthur & Helen. BA CUA 1979; MA Washington Theol Un 2002; MDiv EDS 2006; MDiv EDS 2006. D 6/9/2007 P 12/15/2007 Bp Andrew Donnan Smith. m 4/12/2009 Arthur Engler c 3. Cur Trin Epis Ch Hartford CT 2007-2010; Min of Aging and Sprtlty St. Paul and St. Jas Epis Ch New Haven CT 2002-2004; Res Chapl Asbury Methodist Vill 1999-2001.

KOLB, Jerry Warren (WMo) 8256 Outlook Lane, Prairie Village KS 66208 **Coordntr, Provinces V, VI & VII, Chapl to Ret Cle The CPG New York NY 2002-; Chapl to Ret Cler and Surviving Spouses Dio W Missouri Kansas City MO 2000-; Chapl Emer S Lk's Hosp Kansas City 1999-** B Denver CO 1936 s Lewis & Jean. BS U CO 1958; MDiv SWTS 1968. D 6/11/1968 Bp Joseph Summerville Minnis P 12/4/1968 Bp Edwin B Thayer. m 2/8/1964 Brenda M Morgan c 2. Chapl St. Lk's Hosp of Kansas City Kansas City MO 1987-1999; Chapl St Lk's Chap Kansas City MO 1986; Assoc Chapl St. Lk's Hosp of Kansas City Kansas City MO 1972-1987; Asst R Epiph Epis Ch Denver CO 1971-1972; CPE Res Presb Med Cntr Denver CO 1970-1971; Cur S Tim's Epis Ch Littleton CO 1968-1970. Auth, "A Randomized, Controlled Trial of the Effects of Remote, Intercessory Pryr on Outcomes in Patients Admitted to the Coronary C," *Archv of Internal Med*, 1999. ACPE 1970; Assn of Profsnl Chapl 1976; Comp Worker Sis of the H Sprt 1979-2008. Bp's Shield Dio W Missouri 1999; Chapl Emer S Lk's Hosp of KC 1999.

KOLB, William Albert (WTenn) 531 S. Prescott St, Memphis TN 38111 **Chapl to families of Ret Cler Dio W Tennessee Memphis 2015-** B New York NY 1937 s Bernard & Alice. U of Florida 1958; LTh (full course for MDiv) VTS 1973; VTS 1986; Epis TS of the SW 1990; Cert Int Mnstry Prog 2000; U of Memphis 2007; U of Memphis 2008; U of Memphis 2009. D 6/5/1973 Bp William Henry Marmion P 12/15/1973 Bp George Leslie Cadigan. m 12/26/2003 Melinda S Shoaf c 2. Regular Supply P Emm Ch Memphis TN 2007-2010; Int R Estrn Shore Chap Virginia Bch VA 2004-2005; Int R S Jas Ch Jackson MS 2001-2002; Int R Gr - S Lk's Ch Memphis TN 2000-2001; Assoc R Calv Ch Memphis TN 1992-2004; R S Thos Ch Mamaroneck NY 1978-1992; Ch Of The H Apos Barnwell SC 1976-1978; Vic Chr Ch Denmark SC 1976-1977; Vic S Alb's Ch Blackville SC 1976-1977; Cn Chr Ch Cathd S Louis MO 1973-1976.

KOLBET, Paul Robert (Oly) 8 Ivy Cir., Wellesley MA 02482 **Lectr Yale DS New Haven CT 2013-** B Reno NV 1968 s Robert & Diana. BA Oral Roberts U 1990; MDiv Ya Berk 1994; STM Yale DS 1995; MA U of Notre Dame 1999; PhD U of Notre Dame 2003. D 6/24/1995 Bp Vincent Waydell Warner P 5/

K

18/1996 Bp Francis Campbell Gray. m 5/24/2003 Amy C Egloff c 1. Assoc R S Paul's Ch Natick MA 2010-2016; Asst P S Andr's Ch Wellesley MA 2006; Asst Prof Boston Coll - Dept of Theol Chestnut Hill MA 2003-2010; Asst P S Mich And All Ang Ch So Bend IN 1999, Cur 1996-1998. Auth, "Rhetoric, Redemp, and the Practices of the Self: A Neglected Mode of Aug¿s Thinking," *Praedicatio Patrum: Stds on Preaching in Late Antique No Afr*, Brepols, pp. 351-377, 2017; Co-Ed, "The Harp of Prophecy: Early Chr Interp of the Psalms," *The Harp of Prophecy: Early Chr Interp of the Psalms*, U of Notre Dame Press, 2015; Auth, "Aug Among The Ancient Therapists: Ch.," *Aug and Psychol*, Lexington Books, pp. 91-114, 2013; Auth, "Rethinking the Rationales for Origen's Use of Allegory," *Studia Patristica*, Vol. 56 pp. 41-50, 2013; Auth, "Aug and the Cure of Souls: Revising a Classical Ideal," *Aug and the Cure of Souls: Revising a Classical Ideal*, U of Notre Dame Press, 2010; Auth, "Rethinking the Christological Foundations of Reinhold Niebuhrs Chr Realism," *Mod Theol*, Vol. 26 pp 437-65, 2010; Auth, "Rethinking Mnstrl Ideals in Light of the Cler Crisis," *Ecclesiology*, Vol. 5 pp 192-211, 2009; Auth, "Torture and Origen's Hermeneutics of Nonviolence," *Journ of the AAR*, Vol. 76 pp. 545-72, 2008; Auth, "Athan, the Psalms, and the Reformation of the Self," *Harvard Theol Revs*, Vol. 99 pp. 85-101, 2006; Auth, "Formal Continuities Between Aug's Early Philos Tchg and Late Homiletical Pract," *Studia Patristica*, Vol. 43 pp. 149-54, 2006. AAR 1995; Massachusetts Epis Cler Assn 2010; No Amer Patristic Soc 1995; SBL 1995.

KOLLIN, Harriet (Pa) 3738 W Country Club Rd, Philadelphia PA 19131 **Ch Of The Incarn Morrisville PA 2016-; H Innoc S Paul's Ch Philadelphia PA 2014-; Mem of Anti-racism team Dio Pennsylvania Philadelphia PA 2009-** B Philippines 1952 BD Trin of Quezon City Ph 1974; MS U of Pennsylvania 1993; MDiv EDS 2004. D 6/19/2004 P 6/4/2005 Bp Charles Ellsworth Bennison Jr. m 11/29/2005 Timothy Lee Griffin. Assoc Ch Of S Mart-In-The-Fields Philadelphia PA 2011-2014; P-in-c Ch Of S Jn The Evang Philadelphia PA 2004-2011; D Ch Of S Asaph Bala Cynwyd PA 2004.

KOLLIN JR, James T (NJ) 120 Sussex St Apt 1b, Hackensack NJ 07601 **Chapl Seamen's Ch Cntr 2011-; Chapl Seamens Ch Inst New York NY 2001-; P S Lk And All SS' Ch Un NJ 2000-** B 1963 s James & Maria. m 11/28/1992 Jet O Kollin c 3. Dio No Cntrl Philippines Baguio City 1990-1993.

KOMSTEDT JR, William A (FtW) 1625 Hermosa Ave Unit 33, Grand Junction CO 81506 **Died 9/24/2016** B New York NY 1928 s William & Estelle. DIT Nyack Coll 1948; BA U of Sthrn Mississippi 1958; Joint Forces Stff Coll 1964; MS U of Sthrn Mississippi 1965; DMin TCU 1984; PhD NW Intl U Ballerup DK 2002. D 12/31/1972 Bp Clarence Edward Hobgood P 9/21/1973 Bp Wilburn Camrock Campbell. m 8/21/1948 Martha Komstedt. Assoc S Geo Epis Ch The Vill FL 2003-2016; Assoc Epis Ch Of S Mary Belleview FL 2003-2008; P-in-c S Fran Of Assisi Ch Bushnell FL 2000-2003; S Geo Epis Ch The Villages FL 1998-1999; Chr Ch Cathd Louisville KY 1997-1999; S Raphael's Ch Lexington KY 1997-1999; Ret 1992-2016; R Emeritis S Fran of Assisi Epis Ch Willow Pk TX 1992-2016; S Fran Of Assisi Epis Ch Aledo TX 1987-1990; Dio Ft Worth Ft Worth TX 1984-1987, ExCoun 1989-1991; Vic/R S Fran of Assisi Epis Ch Willow Pk TX 1982-1991; The Epis Ch Of The Resurr Dallas TX 1980-1982; Chr The King Epis Ch Ft Worth TX 1980; Chapl/Clincl Trng Baylor U Med Cntr Dallas Dallas TX 1978-1979; Cur/Day Sch Chapl All SS' Epis Ch Ft Worth TX 1977-1978; Dio Oklahoma Oklahoma City OK 1976-1977; Serv in US AF Chapels Worldwide 1972-1977. Auth, *Redemptive Side of Anger*, (self-Pub), 1995. Assn for CPE 1981; Assn of Profsnl Chapl 1982; Assy of Epis Hospitals and Chapl 1981; ComT 1981; CBS 1977. Fell Fell of NW Intl U 2002; Bd Cert Chapl Assn of Profsnl Chapl 1981; Listed in "Who's Who in Rel" Marquis Who's Who Pub Bd 1977; Legion of Merit US Govt 1977; Legion of Merit US Govt 1972.

KONDRATH, William Michael (Mass) 25 Richards Ave, Sharon MA 02067 **Consult VISIONS-Inc Boston MA 2003-; Ed Journ of Rel Ldrshp 2015-** B Glendale CA 1948 s Joseph & June. S Johns Sem Coll Camarillo CA 1969; BA CUA 1971; MDiv U Tor CA 1974; MA U Tor 1977; EdM Harv 1983; DMin Andover Newton TS 1987. Rec 2/1/1986 as Priest Bp Morris Fairchild Arnold. m 9/11/1982 Christina Emma Robb c 2. Field Educ Dir & Prof Pstr Theol EDS Cambridge MA 1995-2014; R S Mk's Ch Foxborough MA 1989-1995; Asst All SS' Epis Ch Belmont MA 1985-1988. Auth, "Bk/e-Bk," *Congrl Resources for Facing Feelings*, Alb Inst, 2013; Auth, "Bk/e-Bk," *Facing Feelings in Faith Communities*, Alb Inst, 2013; Auth, "Bk/e-Bk," *God's Tapestry: Understanding & Celebrating Differences*, Alb Inst, 2008. Acad of Rel Ldrshp, Pres 2013-2014; VISIONS-Inc., Consult 2003.

✠ **KONIECZNY, The Rt Rev Dr Edward Joseph** (Okla) Episcopal Diocese Of Oklahoma, 924 N Robinson Ave, Oklahoma City OK 73102 **Bp of Oklahoma Dio Oklahoma Oklahoma City OK 2007-** B Spokane WA 1954 s Edwin & Johanna. AA Long Bch City Coll 1976; BA California St U 1987; MDiv CDSP 1994; DMin SWTS 2001; DD SWTS 2007; DD CDSP 2014. D 5/28/1994 Bp John Mc Gill Krumm P 11/30/1994 Bp Claude Edward Payne Con 9/15/2007 for Okla. m 8/17/1978 Debra Lynn Konieczny c 2. R S Matt's Ch Grand Jct CO 2002-2007; R Epis Ch Of The H Sprt Waco TX 1996-2002; Asst S Mk's Ch Beaumont TX 1994-1996; Alt GC Dep Dio Colorado Denver CO 2006, Ch &

Congrl Growth Com 2005-2007, Stndg Com Pres 2005-2007, Fin Com 2003-2011; Chair Supervisors and Tellers Dio Texas Houston TX 1996-2002. DD CDSP 2014; DD SWTS 2008. bishoped@epiok.org

KONYHA, Dorothy (NwPa) D 5/7/2017 Bp Sean Walter Rowe.

KOONCE, Kelly Montgomery (Tex) 6625 Whitemarsh Valley Walk, Austin TX 78746 **P-in-c S Paul's Epis Ch Pflugerville TX 2013-** B Houston TX 1969 s Kenneth & Beverly. BA Drew U 1993; MA Austin Presb TS 1996; MDiv Epis TS of the SW 2002. D 6/22/2002 Bp Claude Edward Payne P 7/6/2003 Bp Don Adger Wimberly. m 1/20/1996 Kimberley C Koonce c 1. St Julian of Norwich Epis Ch Round Rock TX 2015-2016; Asst The Great Cmsn Fndt Houston TX 2015, 2013-2014; The Front Porch Austin TX 2012-2013; The Ch of the Gd Shpd Austin TX 2007-2012, 2002-2004; Asstg P S Steph's Epis Ch Orinda CA 2005-2007.

KOONS, Zachary Gunnar (Tex) 1420 E Palm Valley Blvd, Round Rock TX 78664 **S Richard's Of Round Rock Round Rock TX 2015-** B Muncie IN 1987 s Kelly & Wendy. BA Wheaton Coll 2009; MDiv Duke DS 2012. D 5/6/2015 Bp Dena Arnall Harrison P 10/22/2015 Bp C Andrew Doyle. m 5/14/2011 Anna Lindsay Both.

KOOPERKAMP, Sarah Jennifer (LI) 612 Greenwood Ave, Brooklyn NY 11218 **P-in-c Ch Of The H Apos Brooklyn NY 2014-** B New York NY 1983 d William & Elizabeth. BA Amh 2005; MDiv UTS 2008; Dplma GTS 2011. D 3/3/2012 P 9/29/2012 Bp Mark Sean Sisk. m 6/7/2008 William Charles Lopez c 2. S Ann And The H Trin Brooklyn NY 2012-2014.

KOOPERKAMP, William Earl (Vt) Church Of The Good Shepherd, 39 Washington St, Barre VT 05641 **P-in-c Ch Of The Gd Shpd Barre VT 2012-** B Louisville KY 1956 s Wayne & Eileen. BA Hampshire Coll 1979; LUCB U Coll Buckingham Gb 1980; MDiv UTS 1983; PhD UTS 2002. D 6/10/1984 P 6/18/1988 Bp David Reed. m 6/27/1980 Elizabeth B Kooperkamp c 3. Asst Organier E Brooklyn Congregations 2013; Asst Min Ch Of The Intsn New York NY 1991-2000; Int S Ann's Ch Of Morrisania Bronx NY 1991; S Mary's Manhattanville Epis Ch New York NY 1985-1991, D 1985-1991.

KOOR, Margaret Platt (SwFla) 4017 Heaton Ter, North Port FL 34286 **D S Nath Ch No Port FL 2003-, Par nurse 2003-; Par Nurse Natl Epis Hlth Mnstry SW FL 2001-; Disciplinary Bd Dio SW Florida Parrish FL 2011-** B Westerly RI 1944 d Thomas & Mildred. Jos Lawr Sch of Nrsng 1965. D 6/13/1992 Bp Rogers Sanders Harris. c 3. Par nurse S Bon Ch Sarasota FL 1995-2002; D Ch of the Nativ Sarasota FL 1992-1995. Ord of Julian of Norwich - Oblate 1998.

KOOSER, Robert Lee (Pgh) 221 S Prospect St, Connellsville PA 15425 **Died 8/3/2015** B Connellsville PA 1929 s Harry & Della. BA Waynesburg Coll 1952; MDiv Bos TS 1957; DAS EDS 1962. D 6/23/1962 Bp Anson Phelps Stokes Jr P 5/25/1963 Bp Roger W Blanchard. Ret 1993-2015; Vic Trin Ch Connellsville PA 1980-1992; Non-par 1976-1979; R S Ptr's Epis Ch Brentwood Pittsburgh PA 1973-1975; Non-par 1965-1972; Cur Trin Par of Newton Cntr Newton Cntr MA 1963-1964; Asst All SS Ch Cincinnati OH 1962-1963.

KOPERA, Dorothy Jean (NMich) 214 E Avenue A, Newberry MI 49868 B Croswell MI 1950 d Arthur & Vera. Nthrn Michigan U 1969. D 7/15/1993 P 1/1/1994 Bp Thomas Kreider Ray. m 8/14/1971 Paul Kopera. Non-par.

KOPPEL, Mary E (Okla) PO Box 5176, Austin TX 78763 **R All SS Epis Ch Miami OK 2015-** B New Orleans LA 1977 d Harwood & Evelyn. BA U So 1999; MDiv SWTS 2002. D 12/27/2001 P 7/3/2002 Bp Charles Edward Jenkins III. m 10/10/2004 Mark A Vicknair c 1. P The Ch of the Gd Shpd Austin TX 2012-2015; Dio Louisiana New Orleans LA 2011-2012; Cn for Yth & YA Mnstry Chr Ch Cathd New Orleans LA 2007-2011; R All SS Ch Kapaa HI 2005-2007; Asst R S Mart's Epis Ch Metairie LA 2002-2005. mary@gsaustin.org

KOPREN, Kristin Corinne (NY) 1055 Route 6, Mahopac NY 10541 **Ch Of The H Comm Mahopac NY 2017-; S Jn's Ch Tuckahoe Yonkers NY 2012-** B Santa Ana CA 1964 d Wayne & Barbara. BA Appalachian St U 1986; MDiv GTS 1997. D 6/14/1997 P 12/13/1997 Bp Richard Frank Grein. m 6/6/1994 Thomas Masterson c 2. S Hilda's And S Hugh's Sch New York NY 2003-2014; Asst The Ch of S Matt And S Tim New York NY 1997-2003. kckopren@aol.com

KORATHU, Anna Maria (Oly) 19229 65th Place Northeast, Seattle WA 98155 B Seattle WA 1946 d John & Clarise. BA Wstrn Washington U 1991; MDiv CDSP 1997. D 6/28/1997 Bp Vincent Waydell Warner P 12/19/1998 Bp Sanford Zangwill Kaye Hampton. R S Geo's Ch Seattle WA 1999-2011, Asst 1997-1999.

KORIENEK, Martha (Cal) 802 Broadway, New York NY 10003 **Gr Epis Ch New York NY 2016-; Sprtl Dir Camp Chicago: Dio Chicago Sum Camp 2013-** B Elgin Illinois 1979 d John & Jane. BA U IL 2001; Cert Ya Berk 2006; MDiv Yale DS 2006. D 6/3/2006 P 1/6/2007 Bp Joseph Jon Bruno. S Paul's Epis Ch Burlingame CA 2013-2016; S Jn's Ch Chevy Chase MD 2013, 2013; Chld's Chap Min The Ch Of The Ascen Lexingtn Pk MD 2013; Asst R Ch Of Our Sav Chicago IL 2011-2012; Campus Min Cbury: Campus Mnstry at UC-Irvine Irvine CA 2006-2011; Mem Prog Grp on MHE Dio Los 2006-2011; Asst R S Mich And All Ang Par Corona Dl Mar CA 2006-2011; Mem COM Dio Los Angeles CA 2006-2007. mkorienek@gracechurchnyc.org

KORN, Elizabeth Louise (NMich) N2809 River Dr, Wallace MI 49893 B Marinette WI 1939 d Clifford & Barbara. D 6/4/2006 Bp James Arthur Kelsey. m 9/20/1997 Paul Herman Korn c 5. Inspctn/Shipping Mgr Winsert 1978-1998.

KORTE, Mary (Kan) Saint Stephen's Church, 7404 E Killarney Pl, Wichita KS 67206 **S Stephens Epis Churchrch Wichita KS 2014-; Consult Dio Rhode Island Providence RI 2008-** B Newport RI 1956 d James & Abbie. DMin Colgate Rochester Crozer DS; DMin CRDS; BS K SU 1984; MDiv EDS 1991; CTh EDS 1992. D 1/27/1996 Bp Morgan Porteus P 1/11/1997 Bp Gerry Wolf. m 6/5/1976 Timothy Korte c 2. Int Ch Of The Trsfg Providence RI 2010-2013; Int S Jn The Div Ch Saunderstown RI 2008-2009; Chr Formation S Lk's Epis Ch E Greenwich RI 2007; Suppy Epis Dio Rhode Island Providence RI 2005-2007; R Ch Of The Mssh Woods Hole MA 2002-2006; R (After Pstr) The Par Of Emm Ch Weston CT 2000-2002; Assoc Trin Ch On The Green New Haven CT 1997-2000. Wm Dietrich Memi Prize for Urban Mnstry 1990; Geo F Mercer Memi Schlrshp Awd 1989. mary@sbcglobal.net

KOSHNICK, Loxley Jean (Minn) PO Box 868, Detroit Lakes MN 56502 **Total Mnstry D S Lk's Ch Detroit Lakes MN 2008-** B Fond Du Lac WI 1946 d Arthur & Jean. BS Iowa St U 1968. D 9/13/2008 Bp James Louis Jelinek. m 7/5/1969 Robert Arthur Koshnick c 2.

KOSKELA, David Michael (Colo) 5433 South Buckskin Pass, Colorado Springs CO 80917 B Worcester MA 1947 s Arne & Virginia. Worcester St Coll 1968; BA U of Texas 1974; Cert Epis TS of the SW 1977; MS Our Lady of the Lake U 1979. D 1/24/1987 Bp Brice Sidney Sanders P 12/27/1997 Bp William Jerry Winterrowd. m 6/9/1972 Jane Koskela c 3. R S Raphael Epis Ch Colorado Sprg CO 2000-2012; Asst to R Ch Of S Mich The Archangel Colorado Spg CO 1998-2000; D H Trin Epis Ch Fayetteville NC 1987-1989. ACPE 2006.

KOSKELA, Robert N (Mil) 1260 Deming Way Apt 310, Madison WI 53717 B Evanston IL 1942 s Elmer & Ina. BA Trin Deerfield IL 1964; MA U of Wisconsin 1967; PhD U of Wisconsin 1973; MS Edgewood Coll 2001. D 7/20/2002 Bp Roger John White P 3/25/2003 Bp Chilton Richardson Knudsen. m 8/8/1964 Ruth Alma Koskela. Gr Ch Madison WI 2003-2004; S Lk's Ch Madison WI 2003.

KOSKELA, Ruth Alma (Mil) 1260 Deming Way Apt 310, Madison WI 53717 B Madison WI 1942 d Leif & Doris. BA Trin Deerfield IL 1964; MS U of Wisconsin 1975; PhD U of Wisconsin 1985; MS Edgewood Coll 2001. D 7/20/2002 Bp Roger John White P 3/25/2003 Bp Chilton Richardson Knudsen. m 8/8/1964 Robert N Koskela. S Lk's Ch Madison WI 2003.

KOSKI, Hope Gwendlyn Phillips (LI) 4526 Nw 34th Dr, Gainesville FL 32605 **Died 11/30/2016** B New Haven CT 1939 d Robert & Hope. BA U of Connecticut 1961; SMM UTS 1963; STM Nash 1980. D 5/31/1981 Bp H Coleman Mcgehee Jr P 3/12/1982 Bp Henry Irving Mayson. m 8/15/2015 Sharon Virginia Tolley c 3. S Jos's Ch Newberry FL 2009-2015; P-in-c S Alb's Epis Ch Chiefland FL 2007-2016; Eucumenical Cmsn Dio Long Island Garden City NY 2005-2006, 1997-2006, Trst 1993-1995, Cmsn on Liturg & Mus 1991-1995, COM 1989-1996, ECW Chapl 1991-1997; R S Lawr Of Cbury Ch Dix Hills NY 1989-2006; Cn Trin Cathd Cleveland OH 1985-1987; Assoc S Matt's And S Jos's Detroit MI 1983-1985; Ch Of The Gd Shpd Dearborn MI 1982-1983; Vic Gd Shpd in Dearborn Heights MI 1982-1983; St Paul's Epis Romeo MI 1981-1982. AGO 1958; Associated Parishes 1981; Liturg Conf 1981; Long Island Coun of Ch (Pres since 2000) 1989-2006. Dn, Atlantic Dnry Dio Long Island 1999.

KOSKI, John Arthur (FdL) B 1952 B.S. No Cntrl U 1985; M.A. Wheaton Coll 1986; CPE (2 units) Vill at Manor Pk 2011. D 6/4/2011 Bp Steven Andrew Miller. m 6/27/1987 Mary Helen Johnson. D S Jn The Div Epis Ch Burlington WI 2014-2016; D Epis Ch Of The Resurr Mukwonago WI 2011-2014. koski@wi.rr.com

KOSSLER, Robert Joseph (Cal) **S Fran' Epis Ch San Francisco CA 2003-** B Glendale CA 1958 s Robert & Carolann. BS Harvey Mudd Coll 1980; MS Stan 1983; MDiv CDSP 2004. D 12/6/2003 P 6/5/2004 Bp William Edwin Swing. m 9/10/1983 Carol Theorin c 1. Ch Of The Adv Of Chr The King San Francisco CA 2003-2013.

KOSTAS, George Agapios (WVa) 133 Riverside Dr, Logan WV 25601 **P H Trin Ch Logan WV 2001-** B Dorothy WV 1930 s Agapios & Irene. BS U of Maryland 1952. D 6/9/2001 Bp Claude Charles Vache P 6/8/2002 Bp William Michie Klusmeyer. m 5/13/1959 Elizabeth Savas Kostas. Hon Degree of Doctor of Hmnts Sthrn W Virginia Comminity and Tech Coll 1998.

KOSTIC, Elizabeth M (Pa) 2523 E Madison St, Philadelphia PA 19134 B Philadelphia PA 1949 d John & Sara. D 10/23/1999 Bp Charles Ellsworth Bennison Jr. m 10/10/1981 John A Kostic c 2. D Gr Ch And The Incarn King of Prussia PA 2008-2010, D 2002-2004; D Trin Ch Oxford Philadelphia PA 2004-2008; D Chr Epis Ch Bensalem PA 1999-2002.

KOTRC, Ronald Fred (Ak) 5129 N. Tongass Hy, Ketchikan AK 99901 **S Jn's Ch Ketchikan AK 2010-, 2004-2010** B Loup City NE 1938 s Carl & Nora. BA U of Nebraska 1960; MA U of Washington 1963; PhD U of Washington 1970; MDiv Sewanee: The U So, TS 1996. D 6/8/1996 Bp Robert Reed Shahan P 12/8/1996 Bp Don Adger Wimberly. m 12/17/2006 Christa Kotrc. Trin Cathd Davenport IA 1999-2004; Assoc R S Andr's Ch Ft Thos KY 1996-1999.

KOTUBY, Janice (NY) 860 Wolcott Ave, Beacon NY 12508 **Ch Of The Resurr Hopewell Jct NY 2016-** B Rahway NJ 1960 d George & Dorothy. BS Muhlenberg Coll 1982; MS Penn 1984; PhD LSU 1989; MDiv CDSP 2010. D 6/12/2010 Bp Carolyn Tanner Irish P 12/18/2010 Bp Scott Byron Hayashi. m 11/6/2014 John F Williams. Cur S Jas Epis Ch Midvale UT 2010-2014; COM Dio Utah Salt Lake City UT 2011-2014. resurrectionrev@gmail.com

KOULOURIS, Beulah (Mass) 12 Sunrise Ave, Plymouth MA 02360 B Plymouth NC 1937 d Cleveland & Beulah. BA Lynchburg Coll 1960; Westminster Choir Coll of Rider U 1968; MA Col 1971; MDiv EDS 1989. D 6/3/1989 P 5/1/1990 Bp Don Edward Johnson. m 4/24/1965 Constantine Koulouris. Chr Ch Epis Harwich Port MA 2006-2007; Wyman Memi Ch of St Andr Marblehead MA 2005-2006; Ch Of Our Sav Somerset MA 2004-2005; Int S Jn's Ch Newtonville MA 2002-2003; Int Ch Of The Gd Shpd Wareham MA 2001-2002; P-in-c S Mk's Epis Ch Fall River MA 1999-2001; Int S Mk's Epis Ch Burlington MA 1997-1999; Gr Ch Salem MA 1996-1997, Int P 1993-1996; Int Gr Ch Newton MA 1995-1996; S Ptr's Ch Osterville MA 1993-1995; Asst R S Gabr's Epis Ch Marion MA 1990-1993; Chr Ch Par Plymouth MA 1989-2009; Int S Andr's Ch Wellesley MA 1989-1990; Org/Chrmstr S Mk's Ch Foxborough MA 1988-1989. Sr hon Soc Lynvhburg Coll 1960; Who'S Who Among Amer. Un. Col. constantinekoulouris@gmail.com

KOUMRIAN, Paul Sprower (RI) PO Box 294, Tiverton RI 02878 **Trin Ch Newport RI 2005-** B Jamaica NY 1938 s Moses & Dorothy. BA Mid 1959; Amer Theatre Wing 1961; MDiv GTS 1967; Institue of Hlth & Rel 1972; DMin EDS 1984. D 6/17/1967 P 12/21/1967 Bp Jonathan Goodhue Sherman. c 1. R Ch Of The H Trin Tiverton RI 1991-2003; Int S Mary's Ch Newton Lower Falls MA 1991; Chapl Perkiomen Sch Pennsburg RI 1990-1991; R S Andr's Ch Harvard MA 1976-1990; S Andr's Ch Ayer MA 1976-1989; Asst S Geo's-By-The-River Rumson NJ 1972-1976; R Chr Ch Roxbury CT 1969-1972; Cur S Lk's Ch Forest Hills NY 1967-1969. Contrib, *Homily Serv*, 1986. Soc of S Jn the Evang (Fllshp Mem) 1997.

KOUNTZ, Peter James (Pa) B Toledo OH 1944 s Frederick & Emma. BA S Meinrad Coll 1967; MA The U Chi 1969; Reading for H Ord VTS 2015. D 1/17/2015 P 6/13/2015 Bp Clifton Daniel III. m 11/7/1981 Nanci Nowicki Kountz c 3.

KOUNTZE, Louise Priscilla (WMich) 255 Ivanhoe Street, Denver CO 80220 **Gr Epis Ch Traverse City MI 2000-, 1995-1999, Asst R 1986-; Chapl Munson Med Cntr Traverse City MI 1988-** B Denver CO 1950 d Harold & Pricilla. Wheaton Coll at Norton 1971; BA U Denv 1980; MDiv SWTS 1985. D 6/14/1986 Bp James Winchester Montgomery P 12/18/1986 Bp Howard Samuel Meeks. m 10/12/1983 Barton W DeMerchant c 4.

KOVACH, Gary David (WNC) 19 Old Youngs Cove Rd, Candler NC 28715 **D S Mary's Ch Asheville NC 2002-** B Pittsburgh PA 1943 s Gasper & Marion. D 11/23/2002 Bp Bob Johnson. m 12/28/1965 Geraldine Valarie Kovach c 2.

KOVIC, Fenton Hubert (Tex) 821 Pam Dr, Tyler TX 75703 **Ret P S Fran Epis Ch Tyler TX 2002-** B Pittsburgh PA 1937 s Raymond & Olive. BS U of No Texas 1960; STM Epis TS in Kentucky 1964. D 6/20/1964 P 12/1/1964 Bp John Joseph Meakin Harte. m 12/16/1959 Judith Ann Kovic c 2. S Fran Ch Winnsboro TX 1999-2001; S Matt's Ch Henderson TX 1998; Vic-in-charge S Lk's Epis Ch Lindale TX 1994-1999; Owner D'Col Aviation 1979-2002; Var Sm Ch in Dio of Texas and Dio of Dallas 1971-1994; Reg Dir Yth for Understanding 1970-1979; R Chr Epis Ch Lead SD 1968-1971; Asst Gr St Pauls Epis Ch Tucson AZ 1965-1968; Vic White Mountains Mssn Snowflake AZ 1964-1965.

KOVITCH, Joseph Gerard (SO) PO Box 176, Westerville OH 43086 **R S Matt's Epis Ch Westerville OH 2014-** B Euclid OH 1964 s Joseph & Angela. BA Cleveland St U 1989; MDiv Trin Luth Sem 1993; MDiv Trin Luth Sem 1993; DMin St Mary Sem Cntr for Pstr Ldrshp 2005; DMin St Mary Sem Cntr for Pstr Ldrshp 2005. Rec 1/16/2014 as Priest Bp Thomas Edward Breidenthal. m 4/5/1986 Marie Rosenberg Kovitch c 2.

KOVOOR, George Iype (Ct) 400 Humphrey St, New Haven CT 06511 B Chennai India 1957 s Iype & Anne. BA Delhi U; BDL Un Biblic Sem 1982. Trans 6/18/2015 as Priest Bp Ian Theodore Douglas. m 6/24/1984 Chitra Lydia Kovoor c 3. Other Lay Position S Jn's Ch New Haven CT 2013-2016.

KOWALEWSKI, Mark Robert (Los) 841 Kodak Dr., Los Angeles CA 90026 **Dn St. Jn's Cathd Los Angeles CA 2008-; Dn And R St Johns Pro-Cathd Los Angeles CA 2006-** B Buffalo NY 1957 s Eugene & Evelyn. SUNY; BA Franciscan U of Steubenville 1981; PhD USC 1990; Cert Ang Stud CDSP 1995. D 6/10/1995 Bp John Mc Gill Krumm P 1/13/1996 Bp Chester Lovelle Talton. Dio Los Angeles Los Angeles CA 1999-2005; Asst S Wilfrid Of York Epis Ch Huntington Bch CA 1995-1999. Auth, "Gays, Lesbians and Fam Values," The Pilgrim Press, 1998; Auth, "All Things To All People: The Cath Ch Confronts The Aids Crisis" Assn Of The Sociol Of Rel; Rel Resrch Assn. Cn of the Cathd Cntr of St. Paul Dio Los Angeles 2005.

KOWALEWSKI, Paul James (Los) 54280 Avenida Montezuma, La Quinta CA 92253 B Buffalo NY 1947 s Eugene & Evelyn. BA Chr the King Sem 1969; MDiv Chr the King Sem 1972; PhD SUNY 1982. Rec 6/1/1990 as Priest Bp James Michael Mark Dyer. m 11/4/1978 Karen Marie Kowalewski. R S Jas Par Los Angeles CA 2005-2013; Cn Visionary Dio Cntrl New York Liverpool

NY 2002-2005, 1999-2005; R S Dav's Ch Fayetteville NY 1993-2001; R S Mk's Epis Ch Binghamton NY 1990-1993; Prot Chapl Syr NY 1987-1990; Serv Methodist Ch 1984-1987; Prof St U Of Ny In Fredonia 1982-1985; Grad Asst St U Of Ny In Buffalo 1978-1981; Serv RC Ch 1973-1978.

KOWALSKI, James August (NY) The Cathedral Church of Saint John the Divine, 1047 Amsterdam Ave, New York NY 10025 **Dn Cathd Of St Jn The Div New York NY 2002-** B Willimantic CT 1951 s Thaddeus & Sophie. BA Trin Hartford CT 1973; MDiv EDS 1978; DMin Hartford Sem 1991. D 6/10/1978 P 3/24/1979 Bp Morgan Porteus. m 9/4/1976 Anne Kowalski c 2. R S Lk's Par Darien CT 1993-2002; R Ch Of The Gd Shpd Hartford CT 1982-1993; Asst Trin Ch Newtown CT 1978-1982. Chapt Auth, "Committees of Discernment: A Strtgy for a Shared Vision of Philanthropy," *Mapping the New Wrld of Amer Philanthropy*, Wiley, 2007. Amer Ldrshp Forum - Fell 1990-1992; Aspen Inst - Crown Fell 1997-1999; OHC - Assoc 1982; Ord of the Hosp of S Jn of Jerusalem 2002. DD Berk 2003; Pi Gamma Mu Trin 1973; Phi Beta Kappa Trin 1973.

KOWALSKI, Mark Joseph (Chi) Diocese of Nebraska, 109 N 18th St, Omaha NE 68102 B Chicago IL 1960 s Joseph & Geraldine. D 1/30/2013 Bp Jeff Lee.

KOWALSKI, Ronald Chester (SwFla) 7349 Ulmerton Rd, Lot# 1398 Balboa St., Largo FL 33771 **P-in-c S Mart's Epis Ch Hudson FL 2015-** B Chicago IL 1946 s Chester & Helen. MDiv Sacr Heart TS Hales Corners 1980. Rec 6/6/2009 as Priest Bp Dabney Tyler Smith. R Gd Samar Epis Ch Clearwater FL 2009-2014. frk701@gmail.com

KOWALSKI, Vesta Marie (Me) Po Box 598, Mount Desert ME 04660 B Malad City ID 1939 d Charles & Lelia. BA San Diego St U 1961; MDiv GTS 1981; STM GTS 1983; PhD Jewish TS 1996. D 6/9/1984 P 12/20/1984 Bp John Shelby Spong. c 1. S Andr And S Jn Epis Ch SW Hbr ME 2004-2006, Int Pstr 2004-2006, Int 1996-2004; Int St Fran By The Sea Epis Ch Blue Hill ME 1999-2001; Int S Sav's Par Bar Harbor ME 1998-1999; R Par Of S Jas Ch Keene NH 1992-1994; Asst The Ch Of S Lk In The Fields New York NY 1987-1992; Int S Jn's Ch New York NY 1986-1987. SBL 1981-2009.

KOZAK, Jan (EO) PO Box 214, Madras OR 97741 B Oakland CA 1947 d Homer & Patricia. BA U CA 1969. D 5/1/2002 P 4/24/2003 Bp William O Gregg. m 9/8/1979 Albert Allen Kozak. Vic S Mk's Epis and Gd Shpd Luth Madras OR 2004-2013.

KOZIELEC, Mark A (Mo) Saint Mark's Church, 4714 Clifton Ave, Saint Louis MO 63109 **R S Mk's Ch S Louis MO 2012-** B NJ 1958 BA U of New Hampshire 2002; MDiv EDS 2005. D 6/11/2005 P 12/17/2005 Bp Vicky Gene Robinson. m 4/10/2005 Charles J Doyle. P-in-c Trin Epis Ch Tilton NH 2007-2012; Asst P S Andr's Ch Yardley PA 2005-2007. mark@saintmarks-stl.org

KOZIKOWSKI, Mary Carol (NMich) 922 10th Ave, Menominee MI 49858 B Menominee MI 1949 d Daniel & Edna. D 11/23/2014 Bp Rayford J Ray.

KOZLOWSKI, Joseph Felix (WNY) **Supply Dio Wstrn New York Tonawanda NY 2011-** B North Tonawanda NY 1947 s Felix & Mary. BA S Jn Vianney Sem 1969; MDiv S Jn Vianney Sem 1973; MDiv S Jn Vianney Sem 1973; MS St U at Buffalo 1973. Rec 3/12/2011 Bp Michael Garrison. m 11/6/2010 Robin E Kozlowski. jfkozlowski@roadrunner.com

KOZLOWSKI, Matthew William (SeFla) 623 SE Ocean Blvd, Stuart FL 34994 **Admin VTS Alexandria VA 2014-; Sprtl Dir for Mens Curs Dio SE Florida Miami 2013-, Strng Com for Nehemiah Process 2013-** B Boston MA 1983 s John & Lynne. BA Trin 2005; MDiv VTS 2011. D 12/21/2010 P 6/21/2011 Bp Leo Frade. m 6/17/2006 Danielle M Kozlowski c 2. Asst S Mary's Epis Ch Stuart FL 2011-2013. Phi Beta Kappa 2005. St Georges Coll Jerusalem Awd VTS 2011.

KOZUSZEK, Jeffrey Frank (Spr) 512 W Main St, Salem IL 62881 **Trin Epis Ch Mattoon IL 2014-** B Pickneyville IL 1965 s Eugene & Margaret. D 11/30/2010 Bp Donald James Parsons P 6/10/2011 Bp Daniel Hayden Martins. m 12/29/1994 Bonnie Kozuszek c 2. S Thos Ch Salem IL 2010-2012.

KRADEL, Adam (Pa) 311 S Orange St, Media PA 19063 **S Jn's Epis Ch Carlisle PA 2017-; GOE Rdr BEC 2013-** B New Martinsville WV 1973 s Paul & Susan. Candler TS Emory U; VTS; BA Bethany Coll 1995; MA U of Wisconsin 2003; PhD U of Wisconsin 2008. D 9/24/1998 P 6/12/1999 Bp John Henry Smith. m 7/28/2001 Melissa Quincy Wilcox c 3. R Chr Ch Media PA 2009-2017; S Fran Hse U Epis Ctr Madison WI 2005-2006; St Fran Hse Madison WI 2005-2006; Asst R S Dav's Ch Glenview IL 2002; Asst R S Jn's Epis Ch Charleston WV 1999-2001; D S Mk's Epis Ch Berkeley Spg WV 1998-1999; Pstr Asst The Amer Cathd of the H Trin Paris 75008 1997-1998. Amer Political Sci Assn.

KRAEMER, C Jeff (Dal) 760 Burchart Dr, ., Prosper TX 75078 **Ret 2009-** B Lake Charles LA 1946 s Carl & Hazel. BA McNeese St U 1969; MDiv Epis TS of the SW 1974. D 7/7/1974 P 7/22/1975 Bp Willis Ryan Henton. m 5/29/1969 Mary Kraemer. R S Dunst's Epis Ch Carmel CA 1999-2009; Headmaster S Geo's Epis Ch Laguna Hills CA 1993-1999; Assoc R Gr Epis Ch Monroe LA 1989-1993; R S Lk's Ch Mineral Wells TX 1987-1989; Cbury Hse Dallas TX 1982-1983; Chapl/Dir S Alb's Collgt Chap -SMU Dallas TX 1982-1983; Assoc S Lk's Epis Ch San Antonio TX 1976-1981; Ch Of The H Trin Midland

TX 1974-1976; Dio NW Texas Lubbock TX 1974-1976. CHS 1984; St. Jn of Jerusalem 2004. La St Bd Educ Louisiana.

KRAFT, Carol Joyce (Chi) 124 West Prairie Street, Wheaton IL 60187 **D S Barn' Epis Ch Glen Ellyn IL 1989-** B Jackson MI 1935 d Lester & Grace. Mid; BA Wheaton Coll 1957; MA Col 1958; MA U MI 1960; Goethe Inst Munich DE 1978. D 12/2/1989 Bp Frank Tracy Griswold III. "Birthed by the Sprt," Image Pub, 2005. Friend of SSJE 1992; NAAD.

KRAFT, Harry Bishop (LI) 17117 108th Ave, Jamaica NY 11433 **Ret 1994-** B New York NY 1931 s Harry & Margaret. BS SUNY 1953; MDiv CDSP 1970. D 12/28/1969 Bp Edwin B Thayer P 6/28/1970 Bp William Hampton Brady. R Ch Of S Jas The Less Jamaica NY 1986-1994; Dio Long Island Garden City NY 1985-1986; S Barth's Ch Brooklyn NY 1985-1986; Ch Of The Resurr Warwick RI 1980-1984; R S Mich Clarks Town Jamaica W Indies 1978-1980; Vic Calv Epis Ch Roundup MT 1976-1977; R H Trin Epis Ch Madera CA 1973-1975; R S Paul's Epis Ch Winslow AZ 1971-1973; Asst To Dn St Paul's Epis Cathd Fond Du Lac WI 1970-1971. Curs 1983; OHC.

KRAKOWSKY, Lisa Posey (NY) 12 W 11th St, New York NY 10011 **Ch Of The Ascen New York NY 2017-; guest Lectr UTS 2013-** B Atlanta GA 1962 d Robert & Deanna. HS Phillips Acad 1980; BA Harv 1984; MDiv UTS 2012; STM GTS 2015. D 3/7/2015 P 9/19/2015 Bp Andrew Marion Lenow Dietsche. m 1/19/1991 Philippe E Krakowsky c 2. The Ch Of S Lk In The Fields New York NY 2015-2017. Writer, "PB Ecclesiology," *Angl and Epis Hist*, HSEC, 2014.

KRAMER, Caroline Anne (SwVa) **Assoc Chr Epis Ch Ponte Vedra FL 2014-** B UK 1970 d Gerald & Barbara. BTh Oxf GB 1998. Trans 8/29/2003 Bp Neff Powell. m 10/8/1994 Beaman Kristopher Kramer c 4. Gr Epis Ch Alexandria VA 2007-2009; Chr Ch Pearisburg VA 2006-2007, R 2006-.

KRAMER, Charles Edward (NY) 4536 Albany Post Rd, Hyde Park NY 12538 **R S Jas Ch Hyde Pk NY 1997-** B Decatur IL 1961 s James & Susan. Ripon Coll Ripon WI; BA Indiana U 1984; MAT Indiana U 1987; MDiv GTS 1990. D 6/9/1990 P 12/15/1990 Bp Richard Frank Grein. m 2/8/1992 Elizabeth Granados c 3. R St Mary's and St Steph's Epis Ch Morganton NC 1995-1997; Asst S Ptr's Epis Ch Peekskill NY 1990-1995; Chapl Westledge Nrsng Hm Peekskill NY 1990-1995.

KRAMER, Esther Ann (Mil) 1111 Genesee St, Delafield WI 53018 **Dir of Instnl Resrch and Effectiveness Nash Nashotah WI 2016-; Profsnl Consult Com Mem VMP Healthcare and Cmnty Living 2016-** B Princeton IL 1961 d Cletus & Eileen. B.F.A. U of Wisconsin - Milwaukee 1984; M.S. U of Wisconsin - Whitewater 1988; Ph. D. Wayne 1995; D Formation Prog Dio Milwaukee 2016; D Formation Prog The Epis Ch Dio Milwaukee 2016. D 6/11/2016 Bp Steven Andrew Miller. m 8/30/1986 Thomas John Schlaefer. ekramer@nashotah.edu

KRAMER, Frederick Ferdinand (Ia) 1304 S 4th Ave W, Newton IA 50208 **Ret 1998-** B El Paso TX 1926 s Paul & Gay. BA NWU 1950; MDiv Ya Berk 1953. D 6/13/1953 P 2/20/1954 Bp Stephen E Keeler. m 6/21/1956 Carol A Kramer c 2. Chapl Skiff Med Cntr Newton IA 1989-1999; S Paul's Ch Marshalltown IA 1988-1989; R S Steph's Ch Newton IA 1966-1989; Dn NoWstrn Deanry Dio Minnesota Minneapolis MN 1960-1966, Archd for Indn Wk 1956-1966, Bps Vic for Indn Wk 1955-1959, V.P. Epis Cmnty Serv. 1960-1966, Del to Prov. VI 1956-1966, Dioc Coun 1955-1965; S Phil Rice Lake MN 1953-1960; Vic Samuel Memi Naytahwaush MN 1953-1960; Exec Com Prov VI Dio Iowa Des Moines IA 1984-1987, Dioc Coun 1975-1983; Cmssnr Human Rts Cmsn St of Minnesota 1958-1966. Rotary 1960. DD Sem of the SW 2013; Hon Cn St Paul's Cathd Des Moines IA 2005; Hon Cn St. Mk's Cathd, Mpls.,MN 1960.

KRAMER, Linda Jean (SD) 23120 S Rochford Rd, Hill City SD 57745 **Fndr and Dir Borderlands Educ & Sprtl Cntr Hill City SD 1997-** B Washington DC 1946 d Harry & Beverly. BA Colorado Womens Coll 1968; MDiv VTS 1987. D 6/11/1988 P 12/20/1988 Bp John Thomas Walker. c 3. Asst Emm Epis Par Rapid City SD 2005-2006, Pstr Asst 2002-2005, 2002-2004; J2A Grant Position Ch Of Our Sav Silver Sprg MD 2002-2003, 2001-2002; Int / Grant Gr Epis Ch Silver Sprg MD 1999-2001, 1998-2001, Asst 1998; Int Ch Of All Ang Spearfish SD 1999, Int 1998; Cn Dio So Dakota Pierre SD 1992-1997; Asst to the R for CE S Jn's Ch Chevy Chase MD 1988-1992. Green Faith Fell GreenFaith.org 2008; Pstr Ldr Study Grant Louisville Inst 2000.

KRANTZ, Jeffrey Hoyt (LI) 43 Cedar Shore Dr, Massapequa NY 11758 B Columbus OH 1955 s Albert & Barbara. BA E Carolina U 1978; MDiv GTS 1993. D 7/16/1993 Bp Brice Sidney Sanders P 2/1/1994 Bp Charles Lovett Keyser. m 4/28/1979 Saralouise Camlin c 1. Geo Mercer TS Garden City NY 1999-2000; Ch Of The Adv Westbury NY 1996-2015; S Jn's Of Lattingtown Locust Vlly NY 1994-1996.

KRANTZ, Kristin (Md) 1307 N Main St, Mount Airy MD 21771 **S Jas Epis Ch Mt Airy MD 2015-** B Louisville KY 1973 d Michael & Phyllis. BA Indiana U 1996; MDiv EDS 2006. D 6/3/2006 Bp Bill Persell P 12/2/2006 Bp Marc Handley Andrus. m 7/29/2000 Bryan Krantz c 2. Memi Ch Baltimore MD 2014-2015; Assoc R All Souls Par In Berkeley Berkeley CA 2006-2014. office@stjamesmtairy.org

KRANTZ, Saralouise Camlin (LI) 555Advent Street, Westbury NY 11590 **Mem Bd Epis Mnstrs(Chars) 2011-** B Hamlet NC 1944 d Mervin & Sarah. BSN

U NC 1966; MDiv GTS 1990. D 6/16/1990 Bp Brice Sidney Sanders P 1/12/1991 Bp Richard Frank Grein. m 4/28/1979 Jeffrey Hoyt Krantz c 3. Del-Prov Ii Dio Long Island Garden City NY 2003-2006, Bdgt 1996-2002; R Gr Epis Ch Massapequa NY 1999-2007; R S Bede's Epis Ch Syosset NY 1994-1998; S Andr's Ch Oceanside NY 1993-1994; Asst Ch Of The H Trin New York NY 1990-1993; R, Mem Sch Bd Gr Epis Day Sch 1999-2007; Bd Mem, Bdgt Com Epis Cmnty Serv Dio Long Island 1998-2004; Secy, Chair of Bdgt Dept Dioc Coun Dio Long Island 1996-2003; Dn Dn No Shore Dio Long Island 1995-1998.

KRAPF, Richard David (Roch) 15 Granger Street, Canandaigua NY 14424 **Fndr & Dir Hands of Hope Kitchen Bloomfield NY 2015-; D S Ptr's Epis Ch Bloomfield NY 2013-** B Dunmore PA 1963 s Richard & Sarah. BArch Tem 1990; Diac Stds Bex Sem 2007. D 3/29/2008 Bp Jack Marston Mckelvey. m 8/20/1988 Lisa Browning c 2. D S Jn's Ch Canandaigua NY 2009-2013.

KRASINSKI, Joseph Alexander (Ct) 2 Cannondale Dr, Danbury CT 06810 **R S Jas Epis Ch Danbury CT 2009-** B Brooklyn NY 1954 s Thomas & Katherine. BS S Fran Coll Brooklyn NY 1977; MDiv GTS 1983; DMin Hartford Sem 1989; MS RPI 1993. D 6/5/1982 Bp Paul Moore Jr P 1/1/1983 Bp Arthur Edward Walmsley. m 6/27/2009 James Hughes c 2. Consult Dio Connecticut Meriden CT 1996-2009; R S Ptr's-Trin Ch Thomaston CT 1995-2009; Dir of Pstr Care Noble Horizons Salisbury CT 1986-1996; R Chr Ch Canaan CT 1984-1992; Cur Chr And H Trin Ch Westport CT 1982-1984. joseph@saintjamesdanbury.org

KRATOVIL, Mildred Elsie Ida Johanna (Md) 204 West St Apt A4, Williamsburg IA 52361 B Cleveland OH 1925 d Carl & Elsie. BA Cleveland Inst of Mus 1951. D 6/17/1989 Bp Albert Theodore Eastman. c 2. D Trin Ch Waterloo Elkridge MD 1991-1995; D Epiph Epis Ch Odenton MD 1989-1990. Cnvnt Of Trsfg Cincinnati; NAAD.

KRAUS, Susan (Me) 65 Eddy Rd, Edgecomb ME 04556 **P-in-c S Giles Ch Jefferson ME 2009-** B Trenton NJ 1950 d William. BA Cedar Crest Coll 1972; BA Coll of New Rochelle 1985; MS Coll of New Rochelle 1987; PhD Pace U 1993; MDiv GTS 2005. D 3/19/2005 P 9/17/2005 Bp Mark Sean Sisk. m 8/2/1972 Donald C Kraus. Asst Cler Par of St Paul's Ch Norwalk Norwalk CT 2006-2008; Asst Cler Gr Ch Millbrook NY 2005-2006.

KRAUSE, David (Dal) 12109 Mossygate Trl, Manor TX 78653 **Adj Fac Strayer U Dallas TX 2013-** B Maryville MO 1958 s Robert & Lois. ThD Other; ThD Providence TS; BA U of Iowa 1981; MDiv VTS 1990; MA Texas Tech U 1998. D 6/23/1990 Bp Robert Manning Moody P 12/23/1990 Bp John Forsythe Ashby. m 5/12/2012 Janice Krause c 1. P-in-c S Dav's Ch Garland TX 2010-2017; P-in-c Ch Of The H Trin Bonham TX 2009-2012; Instr U of Phoenix 2009-2012; R S Ptr's Ch Mc Kinney TX 2006-2009; Adj Fac Texas Tech U Lubbock TX 1998-2005; Adj Fac Texas Tech U Lubbock TX 1998-2005; Mentor EFM Lubbock TX 1994-2006; Chapl Cbury at Texas Tech U Lubbock TX 1993-2006; Adj Fac Garden City Cmnty Coll Garden City KS 1992-1993; Adj Fac Garden City Cmnty Coll Garden City KS 1992-1993; Adj Fac St. Mary of the Plains Coll Dodge City KS 1992; Adj Fac St. Mary of the Plains Coll Dodge City KS 1991; S Lk's Epis Ch Scott City KS 1990-1993; Vic S Fran Epis Ch Russell Sprg KS 1990-1991; Coun for the Diac Dio NW Texas Lubbock TX 2004-2006, Ecum Relatns Com (chair) 2002-2005, Comp Dio Com 2001-2004, Prov Treas for Mnstrs in Higher Educ 2000-3006, COM Mem, chair, and cont. ed. Off 1998-2006, Bp Nomin Com 1996-1997, Curs Sec 1995-2007, Prov Coordntr of Mnstrs in Higher Educ 1995-1999, Convenor of T/F on Sexual Misconduct 1995-1998, Eccl Trial Crt 1995-1997, Yth Com (chair) 1994-2005; Bd Mem ESMHE 2001-2003; COM Dio Wstrn Kansas Hutchinson KS 1990-1993, Curs Sec 1990-1993, Exec Coun 1990-1993, Yth Com 1990-1993. Auth, "A Few Things I Have Learned About Love and Mar," *Plumbline*, ESMHE, 2003. HSEC 1990. frdavidkrause@gmail.com

KRAUSE, Janice (Tex) 10043 Boyton Canyon Rd, Frisco TX 75035 **S Jas Ch Austin TX 2017-** B Cleavand, OH 1959 d Frederick & Patricia. BS Pur 1981; MDiv Brite DS 2007. D 12/13/2008 P 5/22/2010 Bp James Monte Stanton. m 5/12/2012 David Krause. Exec Pstr S Phil's Epis Ch Frisco TX 2010-2016; Yth and Outreach S Ptr's Ch Mc Kinney TX 2008-2009. Cmnty of St. Benedicct 2000. janicekrause@stphilipsfrisco.org

KRAUSS, Harry Edward (NY) 2 West 90th St Apt 5B, New York NY 10024 **Dn Emer Cathd Of S Jn Providence RI 2011-, Dn 2005-2011** B Philadephia PA 1945 s Harry & Josephine. AB W&M 1967; MDiv VTS 1977. D 5/21/1977 Bp Robert Bruce Hall P 3/4/1978 Bp Lyman Cunnington Ogilby. Vic S Thos Ch New York NY 1997-2005; R All SS Ch Wynnewood PA 1979-1997, Cur 1977-1978. Ord of S Jn of Jerusalem - Chapl 1994; Royal Soc for the Advancement of the Arts- Fell 2000; SocMary - Natl Bd 1983-2005; The Burgon Soc - Fell; Uff Savoy Ord of Merit-Cmdr 1999. Hon Cn S Andr Cathd 1988.

KREAMER, Martha Hutchison (CGC) Po Box 57, Lillian AL 36549 B Quantico VA 1944 d Byron & Mary. BA Van 1966; MDiv Sewanee: The U So, TS 2001. D 6/2/2001 P 2/24/2002 Bp Philip Menzie Duncan II. m 9/17/1966 Paul Stoddard Kreamer c 1. Vic Ch Of The Adv Lillian AL 2004-2014; Vic S Mich's Ch Ozark AL 2001-2004; Stndg Com Dio Cntrl Gulf Coast Pensacola

FL 2008-2010. Intl OSL The Physcn 1992. Optime Merens TS, Univ. Of The So 2001.

KREFT, Armand John (Mass) 1717 E. Vista Chino, #A7-266, Palm Springs CA 92262 B San Mateo CA 1948 s Edwin & Wynifred. BA New Coll of California 1986; CS CDSP 1987. D 6/3/1989 P 6/9/1990 Bp William Edwin Swing. S Dav's Epis Ch S Yarmouth MA 2010-2014; R Ch Of The Ascen Buffalo NY 2007-2010; P-in-c Epiph Par of Seattle Seattle WA 2005-2007; Assoc S Paul In The Desert Palm Sprg CA 2002-2004; Asst S Jas Epis Ch San Francisco CA 2001-2002; Dn Trin Cathd San Jose CA 2000-2001; Vic Ch Of The H Innoc San Francisco CA 1993-1999. nqocd@earthlink.net

KREITLER, Peter Gwillim (Los) 16492 El Hito Ct, Pacific Palisades CA 90272 **Min for the Environ Dio Los Angeles Los Angeles CA 1992-** B Middletown CT 1942 s John & Muriel. BA Br 1966; MDiv VTS 1969. D 6/14/1969 Bp Leland Stark P 4/27/1970 Bp Robert Rae Spears Jr. m 4/20/1985 Catharine Bates Kreitler c 3. The Par Of S Matt Pacific Plsds CA 1974-1991; Assoc S Andr's Ch Kansas City MO 1969-1974. "Untd We Stand," Chronicle Books, 2001; Auth, "The Earth's Killer C's," Morning Sun Press, 1995; "Flatiron," AIA Press, 1991; Auth, "Affair Prevention," Macmillan, 1981.

KREJCI, Richard Scott (Va) 346 Laurel Farms Ln, Urbanna VA 23175 B Cleveland OH 1941 s Richard & Doris. BA Adrian Coll 1964; BD Bex Sem 1967. D 6/29/1967 Bp Archie H Crowley P 4/10/1968 Bp Richard Stanley Merrill Emrich. c 2. Chr Epis Ch Christchurch VA 1995-2004; S Steph's Ch Newport News VA 1994-1995; Int R 1993-1994; R S Jas Ch Grosse Ile MI 1982-1993; Assoc S Andr's Epis Ch Livonia MI 1977-1982; P-in-c The Ch Of The Gd Shpd Canajoharie NY 1970-1977; Vic S Pat's Epis Ch Madison Hts MI 1967-1970. Bro Of S Andr.

KRELL, Thomas William (Mich) 16200 W 12 Mile Rd, Southfield MI 48076 B Detroit MI 1943 s Ernest & Adelaide. BA Sacr Heart Sem Coll 1965; MA St Jn Prov Sem 1969; BSN Wayne 1993. Rec 5/22/2013 as Priest Bp Wendell Nathaniel Gibbs Jr. m 9/26/1987 Sandra I Krell.

KRELLER, Daniel Ward (Nwk) 161 W Prospect St, Waldwick NJ 07463 B Dallas TX 1951 s Bert & Martha. BA Houghton Coll 1972; PrTS 1975; MDiv GTS 1977. D 6/4/1977 Bp Albert Wiencke Van Duzer P 1/28/1978 Bp George Phelps Mellick Belshaw. m 6/30/1973 Janet Kreller c 2. R S Barth's Epis Ch Ho Ho Kus NJ 1984-2017; R S Jn the Bapt Epis Ch Linden NJ 1979-1984; Assoc S Andr Murray Hill NJ 1977-1979; S Andr's Epis Ch New Providence NJ 1977-1979.

KRESS, Raymond Paul (SwFla) 6530 Manila Palm Way, Apollo Beach FL 33572 **Died 8/30/2016** B Newark NJ 1935 s John & Rose. BA Laf 1959; MDiv GTS 1962; MEd Florida Atlantic U 1968. D 6/9/1962 Bp Leland Stark P 12/1/1962 Bp Benjamin M Washburn. c 6. Int S Giles Ch Pinellas Pk FL 2009; Int S Geo's Epis Ch Bradenton FL 2005-2006; Chapl Westminster Sun Coast Manor St Petersburg FL 2004-2007; Res Chapl Kent Sch Westminster CT 2004; P-in-c Dio SW Florida Parrish FL 1998-2002; S Edm's Epis Ch Arcadia FL 1998-2002; R S Raphael's Ch Ft Myers Bch FL 1984-1998; Asst All SS Ch Tarpon Spgs FL 1982-1984; Chapl, Headmaster Adm Farragut Acad St Petersburg FL 1970-1984; The Headmaster St Petersburg FL 1970-1977; Chapl, Hd Dept Theol S Andr's Sch Boca Raton FA 1965-1970; Chapl Trin Pawling Sch Pawling NY 1962-1965.

KREUTZER, Michael Alan (SO) 7 Lonsdale Avenue, Dayton OH 45419 **Mem Dayton Publ Schools Fam and Cmnty Engagement Panel 2012-; Trnr, Safe Ch Prog Dio Sthrn Ohio Cincinnati OH 2010-, Insructor, Sch for Mnstry 2001-2011, Profsnl Dvlpmt Com 2000-, COM 1997-2000; Bd Mem Sch-Ch Partnership Bd 2010-; Civilian Chapl Wright-Patterson AFB 2009-; Co-Chair The St. Mk Biblic Forum 2004-; R S Mk's Epis Ch Dayton OH 1996-** B Cincinnati OH 1949 s Stanley & Helen. SBL; MA The Athenaeum of Ohio 1975; MA The Athenaeum of Ohio 1976; U of San Francisco 1979; Sinclair Cmnty Coll 1983; SWTS 2001; U of Dayton 2004. Rec 6/9/1991 as Priest Bp Herbert Thompson Jr. m 1/14/1983 Judith Ann Kreutzer c 4. Temporary Supply S Paul's Epis Ch Dayton OH 2012-2015; Chr Epis Ch Dayton OH 1982-1991; D / Par P RC Ch Archdiocese of Cincinnati OH 1974-1982. SBL 2005.

KREYMER, Donald Neal (FtW) 423 East Calle Bonita, Santa Maria CA 93455 **Ret 1988-** B Sigourney IA 1922 s Allen & Nina. BA U of Iowa 1947; U of Iowa 1948; MDiv SWTS 1950; Ya 1956; USN Reserves Chapl Advancement Sch 1978. D 7/21/1950 Bp Gordon V Smith P 3/1/1951 Bp Wallace E Conkling. c 3. Int S Ptr's By-The-Sea Epis Ch Morro Bay CA 1994-1995; Ch Of The H Sprt Graham TX 1982-1988; Vic Ch Of The Gd Samar Dallas TX 1981-1982; Dio Los Angeles Los Angeles CA 1980; S Mk's Par Glendale CA 1980; Vic S Fran Of Assisi Epis Ch Simi Vlly CA 1970-1980; LocTen S Paul's Epis Ch Bremerton WA 1969-1970; Chapl Untd Statee Navy Reserve 1963-1969; R Chr Ch Epis Beatrice NE 1959-1963; R S Andr's Epis Ch Emporia KS 1953-1959; Cur S Matt's Ch Evanston IL 1950-1953. Auth, "The Ch Teaches Us". CBS; Pahh Assn SocOLW.

KRICKBAUM, Donald (SeFla) 1008 Skyline Trail, Harpers Ferry WV 25425 **Died 5/30/2017** B Tampa FL 1938 s Ralph & Mary. BA U So 1960; STB GTS 1963. D 6/29/1963 Bp William Foreman Creighton P 2/16/1964 Bp David Emrys Richards. m 8/27/1966 Gail Krickbaum. Adj Stff Shalem Inst For Sprtl Formation 2003-2017; Assoc Shalem Inst For Sprtl Formation 1990-1992; Dn Trin Cathd Miami FL 1988-2003; Instr Dio SE Florida Miami 1987-1990, Chair-Com 1986, Exec Bd 1981-1985, Com 1977-1980; R The Epis Ch Of The Gd Shpd Tequesta FL 1976-1988; R S Paul's Ch Key W FL 1970-1976; Fell For Pstr Care & Counslg Menninger Fndt 1969-1970; R Dio Costa Rica St. Mk's Puerto Limon 1963-1969.

KRIEGER, Frederick Gordon (SO) 5538 Sebastian Place, Halifax B3K 2K6 Canada B Saint Louis MO 1938 s John & Virginia. BA Hobart and Wm Smith Colleges 1960; BD EDS 1963; U Tor 1970. D 6/15/1963 Bp George Leslie Cadigan P 12/1/1963 Bp Roger W Blanchard. m 7/8/1960 Janet Cleghorn Kelley c 3. Assoc Prof of Theol Atlantic TS Halifax Can 1971-2001; Asst Prof of Theol U of Kings Coll Halifax Can 1970-1971; Cur Gr Ch Cincinnati OH 1963-1966. DD Atlantic TS 2002; Hon Cn All SS Cathd 1991; Phi Beta Kappa Hob 1960.

KRIEGER, Walter Lowell (Be) Fifth & Court, Reading PA 19603 **Assoc S Alb's Epis Ch Reading PA 2010-; Vice-Pres Of The Acad Of Preachers 1995-** B Shamokin PA 1939 s Walter & Ethel. BA Wheaton Coll 1961; MA JHU 1962; MDiv PDS 1965; U of Pennsylvania 1970. D 5/1/1965 P 11/6/1965 Bp Alfred L Banyard. m 6/17/1961 Judith L Krieger c 2. Assoc The Epis Ch Of The Medtr Allentown PA 2006-2010; Pres Of The Stndg Com Dio Bethlehem Bethlehem PA 1987-1990, Dep Gc 1982-1997; R Chr Ch Reading PA 1979-2003; R S Jas Epis Ch Wooster OH 1973-1979; Min Of Educ Trin Ch Moorestown NJ 1970-1973; Vstng Lectr Philadelpia DS PA 1968-1971; Cur Gr Ch Merchantville NJ 1965-1967. Auth, "Var Bk Revs & arts"; Auth, "Acad Of Preachers".

KRISS, Gary W (Alb) PO Box 26, Cambridge NY 12816 **Vic S Paul's Ch Salem NY 2003-** B Baltimore MD 1946 s Warren & Margaret. AB Dart 1968; MDiv Yale DS 1972. D 5/28/1972 P 12/29/1972 Bp Harvey D Butterfield. Int Dn S Jn's Cathd Albuquerque NM 2006-2007; Int R S Paul's Ch Troy NY 2001-2002; Dn and Pres Nash Nashotah WI 1992-2002; Dn Cathd Of All SS Albany NY 1984-1991, Cn Precentor 1978-1984; Chapl SUNY Albany Albany NY 1980-1984; Vic S Mk's-S Lk's Epis Mssn Fair Haven VT 1974-1978; Dir Rock Point Sum Conferences Burlington VT 1973-1977; Chapl Cathd Ch Of S Paul Burlington VT 1972-1974. *Var arts.* Cmnty of the Cross of Nails; Soc-Mary. DD Nash 2001. gkriss@nycap.rr.com

KROH, Timothy Edward (Md) **Ch Of The Adv Baltimore MD 2014-; P-in-c Mision San Pablo Chester PA 2007-** B DuBois PA 1979 s Edward & Patricia. BA Penn 2002; MDiv VTS 2005. D 7/2/2005 Bp John L Rabb P 1/6/2006 Bp Robert Wilkes Ihloff. S Jn's Ch Kingsville MD 2013-2014; Gr Ch New Mrkt MD 2011-2013; S Thos' Ch Garrison Forest Owings Mills MD 2011; Dio Maryland Baltimore MD 2010-2013; P-in-c S Paul's Ch Chester PA 2007-2010; Assoc R Emm Ch Baltimore MD 2005-2007. Assoc, Epis Carmel of St. Teresa 2006; P Assoc, Shrine of Our Lady of Walsingham 2006. advent. baltimore@gmail.com

KROLL, Brenda M (Ark) 1402 Pagosa Trl, Carrollton TX 75007 **D Ch Of The Epiph Richardson TX 2009-** B Louisville KY 1953 d Milton & Gertrude. Epis Sch for Mnstry. D 10/26/1986 Bp Sam Byron Hulsey. m 1/1/1981 J F Carpenter c 1. D Ch Of The Annunc Lewisville TX 1998-2009; D S Lk's Epis Ch N Little Rock AR 1995-1997; D S Nich' Epis Ch Midland TX 1986-1995. Cleric Of Year Awd Kiwanis.

KROM, Judith Sue (NJ) 410 S Atlantic Ave, Beach Haven NJ 08008 **D The Ch Of The H Innoc Bch Haven NJ 2009-, D 2009-** B Hartford, CN 1942 d Benson & June. BA Gordon Coll 1963; MA Syr 1965; PhD SUNY-Buffalo 1979. D 5/16/2009 Bp Sylvestre Donato Romero. m 5/14/1976 Bernard Braen c 4.

KROMHOUT, Linda Adams (CFla) 2104 Golden Arm Rd, Deltona FL 32738 **D All SS Epis Ch Deltona FL 1992-** B South Bend IN 1938 d Robert & Linda. Pur. D 11/7/1992 Bp John Wadsworth Howe. m 6/7/1958 Ysbrand Kromhout c 2. Pi Beta Phi.

KROOHS, Kenneth (NC) 700 Sunset Drive, High Point NC 27262 B New York City 1949 s William & Celilia. BS NEU 1972; MRP Cor 1974; MDiv Duke DS 1995; Cert VTS 1995. D 6/10/1995 P 6/29/1996 Bp Robert Carroll Johnson Jr. m 6/18/2005 Shirley Ann Lawrence c 3. All SS Ch Greensboro NC 2015-2016; R S Chris's Epis Ch High Point NC 1995-2015; Vic S Chris's Epis Ch 1995-2002; R S Paul's Epis Ch Thomasville NC 1995-2002. Auth, "The Barely Ch," *NetResults*, Net Results Inc, 2011.

KROOHS, Mary (NC) 1700 Queen St, Winston Salem NC 27103 **D S Tim's Epis Ch Winston Salem NC 2009-, D 1991-2009** B El Paso TX 1950 d Thomas & Jeanne. BS NEU 1972; No Carolina Diac Prog 1991. D 5/25/1991 Bp Huntington Williams Jr. c 3.

✠ KROTZ, The Rt Rev James Edward (Neb) 3484 520th Road, Rushville NE 69360 B Rushville NE 1948 s Anton & Naomi. BA Chadron St Coll 1970; MDiv SWTS 1973. D 6/13/1973 P 12/7/1973 Bp Robert Patrick Varley Con 9/30/1989 for Neb. m 6/13/1970 Phyllis Christine Krotz c 2. Ret Bp of Nebraska Dio Nebraska Omaha NE 1990-2003, Ret Bp of Nebraska 1989-2003; R S Matt's Ch Lincoln NE 1986-1989, Asst 1973-1977; R Ch of Our Sav No Platte NE 1977-1986; Vic H Trin Ch York NE 1973-1977; Vic S Andr's Ch Seward NE 1973-1976; Chair Stwdshp Cmsn; ExCoun; Stndg Com.

KRUEGER, Albert Peter (Ore) 1926 W Burnside St Unit 909, Portland OR 97209 **First Nations Mssnr Dio Oregon Portland OR 2011-** B McAllen TX 1948 s Harold & Esther. BA U of Arizona 1976; MDiv CDSP 1980. D 7/22/1980 Bp Chauncie Kilmer Myers P 12/1/1981 Bp Leigh Allen Wallace Jr. m 2/9/2013 Diana Lynn Krueger. S Andr's Ch Portland OR 1999-2013; All SS Ch Hillsboro OR 1988-1995; Assoc S Paul's Epis Ch Salem OR 1984-1988; Assoc S Paul's Ch Walla Walla WA 1980-1984.

KRUEGER, James Gordon (Alb) 55 Lake Delaware Dr, Delhi NY 13753 **S Jas Ch Bovina NY 2014-** B Orange NJ 1970 s Harold & Janet. BA Burlington Coll 1995; MA Naropa U 2000; MTS Nash 2014. D 12/9/2013 P 6/14/2014 Bp William Howard Love. m 6/9/2013 Maureen Krueger. info@monsnubifer.org

KRUGER, Ann Dufford (CFla) 167 Clear Lake Cir, Sanford FL 32773 **Asst H Cross Epis Ch Sanford FL 2009-** B Sewickley PA 1936 d Clair & Margaret. U of Paris Fr 1957; BA Thiel Coll 1958; MDiv TESM 1967. D 12/7/1997 P 6/1/1998 Bp Stephen Hays Jecko. c 1. R S Mk's Ch Fincastle VA 1999-2006; S Andr's Ch Interlachen FL 1998; St Marys Epis Ch Palatka FL 1998; Assoc S Jn River Reg. OSL 1990.

KRUGER, Diane Renee (Kan) D 6/17/2017 Bp George Wayne Smith.

KRUGER, Matthew Carl (Mass) 81 Elm St, Concord MA 01742 B Concord MA 1984 s Paul & Karen. BA Tufts U 2006; MDiv Harvard DS 2009; MDiv Harvard DS 2009; PhD Boston Coll 2014. D 6/6/2009 Bp M(Arvil) Thomas Shaw P 1/9/2010 Bp Roy Frederick Cederholm Jr. Old No Chr Ch Boston MA 2011-2013; Cur Trin Ch Concord MA 2009-2012.

KRUGER, Susan Marie (Minn) 1711 Stanford Ave, Saint Paul MN 55105 B Cedar Rapids IA 1954 d Amos & Lola. BA Cor 1977; MDiv Ya Berk 1981. D 11/3/1985 P 7/10/1986 Bp Robert Marshall Anderson. D S Mary's Ch S Paul MN 1985-1986.

KRULAK JR, Victor Harold (SanD) 3118 Canon St Apt 4, San Diego CA 92106 **Asst All SS Ch San Diego CA 2003-, Asst 1990-1994** B Manila PH 1937 s Victor & Amy. AB W&M 1960; MDiv CDSP 1963. D 5/17/1963 P 11/28/1963 Bp Harry Sherbourne Kennedy. Asst H Trin 1994-2003; Headmaster All SS Sch San Diego CA 1990-1994; Chapl U. S. Navy Off Of Bsh For ArmdF New York NY 1966-1990; Chapl (Cmdr) USN 1966-1990; Assoc S Ptr's Ch Honolulu HI 1964-1966; Vic H Cross Malaekahana HI 1963-1964.

KRULAK, William Morris (Md) 113 W Hughes St, Baltimore MD 21230 **Chair of Bd St. Mary's Outreach Cntr Baltimore MD 2003-** B Quantico VA 1940 s Victor & Amy. BS USNA 1962; MS U Roch 1972; MDiv Ya Berk 1991. D 6/15/1991 Bp Peter J Lee P 12/16/1991 Bp Robert Poland Atkinson. m 7/23/2009 Sharon D Krulak c 2. Bd Mbr Hampton Fam Cntr Baltimore MD 2002-2005; R S Dav's Ch Baltimore MD 1999-2007; R S Jn's Epis Ch Richmond VA 1993-1998; Vic Gr Ch Stanardsville VA 1991-1993; Dioc Coun Dio Maryland Baltimore MD 2000-2002; Exec Bd Dio Virginia Richmond VA 1994-1998.

KRUMBHAAR, Andrew Ramsay (CFla) 144 Carretera Chapala-Ajijic Pmb 108, San Antonio Tlaycapan Mexico B New York NY 1934 s George & Catherine. BA Harv 1956; BD Epis TS of the SW 1961. D 4/6/1961 Bp Richard Earl Dicus P 10/9/1961 Bp Everett H Jones. c 4. Asst S Barn Ch Deland FL 1985-1997; Dio Cntrl Florida Orlando FL 1985; R Chr Ch Longwood FL 1976-1984; Asst Ch Of The Gd Shpd Maitland FL 1973-1976; Cur Emm Epis Ch San Angelo TX 1966-1973; R H Comm Epis Ch Yoakum TX 1962-1966; Resurr Gr Epis Ch Dallas TX 1962-1966; Vic S Matt's Epis Ch Kenedy TX 1961-1962. Phi Alpha Theta Stetson Uninversity 1992.

KRUMENACKER JR, Gerald Walter (Dal) 5720 Forest Park Rd, No. 2-406, Dallas TX 75235 B Trenton NJ 1970 s Gerald & Penelope. BA So Dakota St U 1992; MDiv SWTS 1996; MBA U of Dallas 2008. D 6/7/1996 P 12/14/1996 Bp James Louis Jelinek. m 6/6/1992 Amy Marie Krumenacker c 2. R Chr Epis Ch Dallas TX 2009; Cn Mssnr for Hisp Mnstry S Matt's Cathd Dallas TX 2001-2002; Asst R Ch Of The Ascen Stillwater MN 1999-2001; P-in-c Trin Ch Waseca-Janesville Waseca MN 1996-1999; P-in-c Chr Ch Albert Lea MN 1996-1998.

KRUMLAUF, Dennis Skyler (Eur) **Transitional D Cathd Ch Of S Lk Orlando FL 2011-** B Port Huron MI 1949 s Edward & Arlene. BA Olivet Nazarene U 1973; MDiv Nazarene TS 1979. D 6/11/2011 Bp Hugo Luis Pina-Lopez P 3/25/2012 Bp Pierre W Whalon. m 5/22/1971 Jane Mosshart Krumlauf c 3.

KRUMME, Judith Sterner (Mass) 349 Simon Willard Rd, Concord MA 01742 B Pittsburgh PA 1938 d William & Dorothy. BS Mills New York NY 1967; MA Ya Berk 1988. D 6/10/1989 Bp Paul Moore Jr P 3/1/1990 Bp Richard Frank Grein. m 12/27/1963 Robert Darrel Krumme c 4. Ret, P Assoc. and Sprtl Dir Trin Ch Concord MA 2005-2012, 1993-2000, Assoc 1993-2000, Pstr Asst 1990-1992; R Emm Ch Braintree MA 2000-2004; Dir Of Pstr Care And Chapl Sherrill Hse Inc. Boston MA 1993-2000; Chapl Hospice W Waltham MA 1992-1993; Prot Chapl Norwood Hosp Norwood MA 1991-1992; Assoc S Jn's Ch Larchmont NY 1983-1990; Chapl and Dir of Pstr Care Sherrill Hse Inc. Boston MA 1992-2004. ACPE; Braintree Interfaith Cler Assn; CHS; Ma Chapl Assn; Match-Up Vol Bd.; Meca; Natl Hospice Assn; Sherrill Hse Bd Mem; Sprtl Dir Intl .

KRUSE, William G (Chi) 1413 Potomac Ct, Geneva IL 60134 **Asst R S Mk's Ch Geneva IL 1997-** B Chicago IL 1926 s Theodore & Margaret. BA U IL

1975; MA SWTS 1976. D 6/14/1975 Bp Quintin Ebenezer Primo Jr P 12/1/1975 Bp James Winchester Montgomery. m 6/26/1982 Becky Kondiles Morris c 4. S Bede's Epis Ch Bensenville IL 1977-1992; Assoc R S Elis's Ch Glencoe IL 1975-1976; Chair Dio Chicago Chicago IL 1981-1985. Bro Of S Andr 1997; EPF 2002; Ord Of S Lk 1999.

KRUTZ, Charles (La) 527 North Boulevard, Fourth Floor, Baton Rouge LA 70802 B Blytheville AR 1946 s Charles & Lillian. BA SMU 1968; MDiv Ya Berk 1971; DMin VTS 1995. D 6/18/1971 Bp Theodore H McCrea P 12/1/1971 Bp William Paul Barnds. m 11/24/1973 Julie Krutz c 2. P-in-c S Fran Ch Denham Spgs LA 2007-2014; Int S Geo's Epis Ch New Orleans LA 2006-2007; Int Chr Ch Slidell LA 2004-2006; Int S Matt's Epis Ch Houma LA 2003-2004; S Mary's Ch Morganza LA 2000; S Greg's Ch Prairieville LA 1999-2003; Louisiana Interchurch Conf Baton Rouge LA 1992-2014; R S Jas Epis Ch Shreveport LA 1981-1992; Cur S Andr's Epis Ch New Orleans LA 1976-1981; Epis Coll Cntr Hammond LA 1975-1976; Chr Epis Ch Dallas TX 1974-2013; All SS Epis Ch Ponchatoula LA 1974-1976; Ch Of The Incarn Amite LA 1974-1976; Asst Dio Louisiana New Orleans LA 1974-1975. Natl Assn Ecum Stff.

KRYDER-REID, Thomas Marshall (Ind) 5354 Olympia Dr, Indianapolis IN 46228 R Trin Ch Indianapolis IN 2000- B 1952 s Edward & R. BA Syr 1974; MA U Chi 1983; MDiv VTS 1986. D 5/31/1986 P 12/1/1986 Bp Harold Barrett Robinson. m 8/27/1988 Elizabeth B Kryder-Reid c 2. H Trin Epis Ch Oxford OH 2014-2016; P-in-c S Tim's Ch Indianapolis IN 1999-2000; R S Barth's Ch Baltimore MD 1991-1998; Asst S Columba's Ch Washington DC 1986-1991.

KUBBE, AnnaLeigh (EMich) Diocese of Eastern Michigan, 924 N Niagara St, Saginaw MI 48602 B Detroit MI 1943 d Leighton & Leora. BA Estrn Michigan U 1980; MA Estrn Michigan U 1988. D 4/18/1998 Bp Edwin Max Leidel Jr. m 8/20/1979 Myron Kubbe c 3. Trin Epis Ch Bay City MI 2012; Dio Estrn Michigan Saginaw MI 2007-2015.

KUBICEK, Kirk Alan (Md) 8400 Greenspring Ave, Stevenson MD 21153 Chapl/Tchr S Tim's Sch Stevenson MD 2009-; Wrshp That Works sermons 1998- B Oak Park IL 1949 s Robert & Patricia. BA Trin Hartford CT 1972; MDiv GTS 1983. D 6/18/1983 Bp George Nelson Hunt III P 12/17/1983 Bp James Winchester Montgomery. m 11/1/1975 Mallory M H Kubicek c 3. Dio Maryland Reparations T/F 2005-2006; GC Budgetary Funding T/F 2003; Dio MD Appeals Comm - Chr Relatns Baltimore MD 2002-2011; Bd Mem Mnstry of Money 1998-2008; R S Ptr's Epis Ch Ellicott City MD 1994-2012; Bishops Advsry Com on Jewish-Chr Relatns MD 1994-1998; Stwdshp Consult Off of Stwdshp and TENS 1993-2011; R S Ptr's Epis Ch Monroe CT 1989-1994; Bishops Advsry Com on Jewish-Chr Relatns MD 1986-1989; Stwdshp Cmsn Dio Maryland 1986-1989; Asst Ch Of The Gd Shpd Towson MD 1985-1989; Asst R Gd Shpd Ruxton MD 1985-1989; Cur Chr Ch Winnetka IL 1983-1985. "Living w Money," Epis Media; Auth, Cler & Money TENS Nwsltr. Mnstry of Money 1985; TENS 1995.

KUBLER, Barry P(Aul) (EC) 340 Shade Tree Circle, Woodstock GA 30188 Ret/Supply Cler Lic in Dio Atlanta 2014- B SuffernNY 1947 s Jack & Barbara. BS U of So Florida 1976; MDiv VTS 1997. D 6/29/1991 Bp Rogers Sanders Harris P 6/14/1997 Bp John Bailey Lipscomb. m 2/15/1969 Vonceal Arlene Kubler c 2. R S Phil's Ch Southport NC 2004-2013; R S Mart's Epis Ch Hudson FL 2004-2006; Virginia Sem Alexandria VA 1994-1997; D S Ptr's Ch Plant City FL 1991-1994.

KUEHL JR, H August (RI) 40 Bagy Wrinkle Cv, Warren RI 02885 Ret 1989- B Dennison OH 1923 s Henry & Della. BA Moravian TS 1944; MDiv PrTS 1946; Coll of Preachers 1960. D 6/11/1948 P 12/18/1948 Bp Frank W Sterrett. c 4. Cmsn Apportnmnt & Rev Chair Dio Rhode Island Providence RI 1988-1990, Cmsn Apportnmnt & Rev 1985-1988, Comp Dioc ExCoun 1983-1990, Dept Stwdshp 1977-1983, Dept Prom & Publ Chair 1977-1982, Conv Prog 1974-1977, Chair - Scholarshp Fund 1993-1999, Scholarshp Fund 1988-1992, ExCoun 1983-1987, Dioc Coun 1982, Dn E Bay Deanry 1980-1981, Chair Com Trans Epispcy 1979, Com on Deferred Giving 1978, ExCoun 1977-1980, Dept Prom & Publ 1974-1977; R S Jn's Ch Barrington RI 1973-1988; P-in-c S Lk And S Simon Cyrene Rochester NY 1972-1973; R S Paul's Ch Rochester NY 1964-1969; ExCoun Dio Rochester Henrietta 1962-1964, Dioc Coun 1961-1964; R S Barn Ch Irvington NY 1955-1964; R Ch Of Our Merc Sav Penns Grove NJ 1951-1955; R S Mary's Epis Ch Reading PA 1949-1951; Cur S Lk's Ch Scranton PA 1948-1949; Chapl Coll 1946-1947; Chapl USNR 1944-1946; Del Prov II Syn Dio Bethlehem Bethlehem PA 1954-1955, Dir Yth Div DeptCE 1950-1953. Coll of Preachers 1960; EvangES 1964. R Emer St Jn's Epis Ch, Barrington, RI 1992.

KUEHN, Craig (NCal) 2821 Bronzecrest St, Placerville CA 95667 B Salt Lake City UT 1951 s Charles & Louise. U of Arizona 1970; U of Utah 1972; BA Westminster Coll 1986; MDiv CDSP 1993. D 12/26/1985 P 9/19/1986 Bp Otis Charles. m 10/7/1972 Suzanne Ileen Kuehn c 2. Sprtl Care Provider Snowline Hospice Diamond Sprg CA 2013-2017; Dn The Epis Dio Nthrn California Sacramento CA 2005-2011, Reg Mssnr 1993-1999, Pres, Stndg Com 2012-2013, RurD 2006-2012; R Epis Ch Of Our Sav Placerville CA 1999-2014; Reg Mssnr S Paul's Epis Ch Oroville CA 1997-1999; S Steph's Epis Ch Colusa CA 1997-1999; H Trin Epis Ch Willows CA 1993-1999; S Tim's Ch Gridley CA 1993-1999; P S Steph's Ch W Vlly City UT 1986-1990. therev@c-skuehn.net

KUEHN, Jerome Frederick (FdL) 806 4th St, Algoma WI 54201 D Chr the King/H Nativ (Sturgeon Bay) Sturgeon Bay WI 2009- B Chicago IL 1947 s William & Grace. D 7/25/1992 Bp William Charles Wantland. m 8/4/1969 Vicki Florence Kuehn. Asst S Jn's Epis Ch Sparta WI 1992-1999.

KUENKLER, Richard Frederick (CNY) 1 W Church St, Elmira NY 14901 B Milwuakee WI 1935 s Arthur & Grace. BA JHU 1956; Cert Peabody Conservatory of Mus 1958; MDiv UTS 1963. D 6/14/1978 P 11/1/1978 Bp Ned Cole. m 11/7/1992 Natalie B Kuenkler c 1. R Gr Epis Ch Elmira NY 1986-1996; Chapl Wells Coll Aurora NY 1976-1986; R S Paul's Aurora NY 1970-1986; Pstr Presb Ch Aurora NY 1968-1970; Assoc 1st Presb Auburn NY 1963-1968; Chair - Cmsn Of Ord Mnstry.

KUENNETH, John (Tenn) 538 Hickory Trail Drive, Nashville TN 37209 Ret 1998- B Litchfield IL 1932 s Harold & Grace. BA U Denv 1954; MDiv Nash 1957; CPE Wesley Med Cntr, Wichita, KS 1984. D 6/24/1957 P 1/6/1958 Bp Joseph Summerville Minnis. m 8/20/1966 Loralee Kay Kuenneth c 3. Chapl S Thos' Med Cntr Nashville TN 1992-1997; Dir, Instnl Mnstrs Dio Tennessee Nashville TN 1987-1993; Chapl HCA Wesley Med Cntr Wichita KS 1984-1987; R S Jas Ch Wichita KS 1971-1984; R S Jas Epis Ch Wheat Ridge CO 1968-1971; R Prince of Peace Epis Ch Sterling CO 1964-1968; R All SS' Ch Sterling CO 1963-1968; Cur S Mary Denver CO 1961-1963; Vic Clear Creek Vlly Missions Idaho Sprg CO 1957-1961; Gr Epis Ch Georgetown CO 1957-1961. ACPE 1984-1987. Phi Beta Kappa Gamma of Coloado 1954. beadseye32@icloud.com

KUHLMANN, Frederick Jennings (Ct) 35A Heritage Village, Southbury CT 06488 P Assoc S Paul's Ch Woodbury CT 1993-; Ret 1992- B St. Paul MN 1923 s Frederick & Ruth. BEE U MN 1944; MDiv VTS 1967; Ya 1974. D 6/13/1967 Bp Walter H Gray P 12/16/1967 Bp John Henry Esquirol. c 2. Vic S Ptr's Epis Ch Oxford CT 1975-1992; Int S Mk's Chap Storrs CT 1973-1974; Vic Chr Ch Trumbull CT 1967-1973; Prog and Bdgt Com Dio Connecticut Meriden CT 1983-1992, Fin Com 1981-1992, Exec Counsel 1980-1992.

KUHLMANN, Martha Chandler (Cal) 107 Franciscan Dr, Danville CA 94526 H Cross Epis Ch Castro Vlly CA 2008-; Assoc H Cross Epis Ch Castro Vlly CA 2005- B Boston MA 1948 d Alan & Harriette. BA Bates Coll 1970; MDiv CDSP 2002. D 6/1/2002 P 12/7/2002 Bp William Edwin Swing. m 5/27/1977 Ronald Kuhlman c 2. Assoc P S Geo's Epis Ch Antioch CA 2002-2005.

KUHN, Darlene (WMich) R S Jas' Epis Ch Of Albion Albion MI 2015-, P-in-c 2012-2014 B Owen Sound Canada 1957 d Kenneth & Mae. BMath U of Waterloo 1980; MDiv Huron U Coll 2012; MDiv Huron U Coll 2012. D 6/16/2012 P 12/22/2012 Bp Robert R Gepert. m 5/22/1982 Jonathan Richard Dixon Kuhn. Stff Chapl Memi Hosp So Bend IN 2012.

KUHN, Michael Cray (La) Trinity Episcopal School, 1315 Jackson Ave, New Orleans LA 70130 Chapl S Mart's Epis Sch Metairie LA 2014-; Headmaster Trin Epis Sch New Orleans LA 2001- B Philadelphia PA 1956 s William & Marion. BA U So 1979; MDiv GTS 1982; DMin EDS 1998. Trans 2/26/2004 Bp M(Arvil) Thomas Shaw. m 9/24/1988 Maria Elliott c 2. Trin Ch New Orleans LA 1994-2014; Chapl Trin Epis Sch New Orleans LA 1994-2001; Emm Ch Boston MA 1990-1994; The Cathd Sch New York NY 1989-1990; Cathd Of St Jn The Div New York NY 1983-1989; The Ch of S Matt And S Tim New York NY 1982-1983. Auth, "Bk Revs," Books & Rel.

KUHN, Philip James (Mass) 25 Wood lane, Maynard MA 01754 Trin Ch Randolph MA 2013- B Columbus OH 1968 s Bernard & Geraldine. BA/BS Providence Coll 1990; MDiv Epis TS of the SW 1995. D 12/16/1995 P 6/15/1996 Bp John Stuart Thornton. m 6/22/1991 Marilyn Anne Kuhn c 3. Chr Ch Hyde Pk MA 2011-2012; R S Lk's Ch Branchport NY 2006-2011; R Tri-Par Mnstry Hornell NY 1998-2005; Vic Chr Ch Shoshone ID 1996-1998; Trin Ch Gooding ID 1996-1998. trinity.randolph@verizon.net

KUHN, Thomas Randall (EC) 328 Kelly Ave, Oak Hill WV 25901 Non-par 1987- B Welch WV 1939 s James & Beatrice. BA Wofford Coll 1964; BD Epis TS in Kentucky 1967. D 6/12/1967 P 2/1/1968 Bp Wilburn Camrock Campbell. m 8/12/1966 Mary Helen Kuhn. Asst S Ptr Louisburg NC 1981-1987; S Ptr's Epis Ch Washington NC 1981-1983; R H Trin Ch Logan WV 1976-1981; R Chr Ch Point Pleasat WV 1972-1976; Vic Epis Ch of the Trsfg Buckhannon WV 1969-1972; Mt Zion Epis Ch Hedgesville WV 1967-1969; Vic S Mk's Epis Ch Berkeley Spg WV 1967-1969.

KUHR, Carolyn S. (Mont) 2409 West Irene Street, Boise ID 83702 Chapl Kalispell Reg Med Cntr Kalispell MT 2007- B Yakima WA 1946 d James & Phyllis. BA Cntrl Washington U 1969. D 9/14/1984 Bp Jackson Earle Gilliam P 1/6/1987 Bp Charles I Jones III. c 2. Stff Chapl Kalispell Reg Med Cntr Kalispell Montana 2007-2013; Asst Ch Of The H Sprt Missoula MT 2005-2007; S Pat's Epis Ch Bigfork MT 1998-2005; S Mich And All Ang Eureka MT 1998-2002; R Dio Montana Helena MT 1993-1996; H Trin Epis Ch Troy MT 1993-1996; S Lk's Ch Libby MT 1993-1996; R S Mk's Ch Havre MT 1987-1992; Ch Of The Incarn Great Falls MT 1985-1987.

KUHR, Elisabeth Schader (Spok) 2490 Thompson Rd, Cowiche WA 98923 **P Chr Epis Ch Zillah WA 1999-** B Jamaica NY 1941 d Fredrich & Frances. BS California St Polytechnic U 1964; BA California St U Stanislaus 1969. D 4/14/1999 Bp Cabell Tennis P 10/16/1999 Bp John Stuart Thornton. c 2.

KUJAWA-HOLBROOK, Sheryl Anne (Los) Claremont School of Theology, 1325 N College Avenue, Claremont CA 91711 **VP for Acad Affrs and Dn of the Fac Claremont TS Wichita KS 2013-, Prof 2009-; Prof of Angl Stds Bloy Hse Claremont CA 2009-; Prof Claremont Grad U 2009-; Joint Com on Philippine Cov JCPC 2013-** B Milwaukee WI 1956 d Alexis & Elaine. BA Marq 1977; MATS Harvard DS 1979; MA Sarah Lawr Coll 1979; MDiv EDS 1983; PhD Boston Coll 1993; EdD Col 1993; EdD UTS 1993. D 6/1/1985 P 6/25/1986 Bp John Bowen Coburn. m 11/17/2001 Paul Holbrook c 1. Prof Claremont Linc 2011-2013; Acad Dn EDS Cambridge MA 2004-2009, Prof 1998-2009; Prog Dir, Mnstrs w YP Epis Ch Cntr New York NY 1995-1998, Yth Dir 1988-1998; Asst Ch Of The Incarn New York NY 1991-1998; Yth Dir Dio Massachusetts Boston MA 1985-1988; Asst Epis Prov Of New Engl Portland ME 1985-1988; The Cathd Ch Of S Paul Boston MA 1985-1988. Auth, "Hildegard of Bingen: Annotated and Explained," SkyLight Paths, 2015; Auth, "God Beyond Borders," Cascade, 2013; Auth, "Pilgrimage: A Sacr Art," Sky-Light Paths, 2013; Co-Auth, "b of Water, b of Sprt," Alb Inst, 2010; Auth, "The Heart of A Pstr," Forw Mvmt, 2010; Co-Auth, "Injustice and the Care of Souls," Augsburg Fortress, 2009; Ed, "Seeing God in Each Other," Morehouse, 2006; Co-Ed, "Deeper Joy: Lay Wmn And Vocation in the 20th Century Epis Ch," Ch Pub, 2005; Auth, "By Gr Came the Incarn," Books Just Books, 2004; Auth, "A Hse of Pryr for All Peoples," Alb Inst, 2003; Auth, "Freedom is a Dream," Ch Pub, 2002; Ed, "Disorganized Rel," Cowley, 1998; Auth, "God Works," Morehouse Pub, 1997; Auth, "Handbook For Mnstrs w Younger Adolescents," Epis Ch Cntr, 1996; Auth, "Handbook For Mnstrs w Older Adolescents," Epis Ch Cntr, 1996; Ed, "Resource Bk for Ministeries w Yth and YA," Epis Ch Cntr, 1995. Amer Academiy of Rel 2000; EPF 1998; EUC 1990; EWC 1990; EWHP 1998; HSEC 1993; Soc of S Jn the Evang 1981; Sprtl Dir Intl 2005. Morehouse Coll Distinguished Scholars Morehouse Coll Chap 2012; Chr Ldrshp Fllshp Amer Jewish Com and the Shalom Hartman Inst, Jeruslaem, 2010- 2011; Fisher Fac Tchg Awd Claremont TS 2011; Fisher Fac Mentoring Awd Claremont TS 2010; Bogert Grant for the Study of Chr Mysticism Soc of Friends 2010; Conant Grant Epis Ch, 2000, 2003, 2005 2008; Adelaide Teague Case Awd EWHP 2006; Jn W. Withers Awd NYU 2005; Resolution Cambridge City Coun 2004; Evang for the 21st Century Grant Epis EvangES, 2000, 2003; Hist Resrch Grant HSEC 2003; Alb Inst Grant 2002; EWHP Travel Grant EWHP 2002; Fllshp Boston Coll, 1981-1984 1984; BTI Urban Educ Grant Boston Theol Inst 1982; Bradley Fisk Fllshp Harvard DS 1979; Ford Fndt Fllshp Sarah Lawr Coll 1978; Alum Educ Grant Marq 1977. skujawa-holbrook@cst.edu

KUKOWSKI, Rich (WA) 412 Colesville Manor Dr, Silver Spring MD 20904 **Prov III Coordntr, Chapl to the Ret The CPG New York NY 2017-; Chapl Cathd of St Ptr & St Paul Washington DC 2006-; Ret Ch of the Trsfg Silver Sprg MD 2006-; Exec Bd Corp for the Relief of Widows and Chld Baltimore MD 2006-** B Winona MN 1943 s George & Helen. BA S Marys U MN 1965; STB CUA 1968; MA CUA 1969; CAS GTS 1976. Rec 12/21/1975 as Priest Bp George E Rath. m 12/27/1975 Elaine Klein. Pres Corp for the Relief of Widows and Chld Baltimore MD 2014-2016; Vice-Pres Corp for the Relief of Widows and Chld Baltimore MD 2010-2014; Washington Epis Cler Assn Treas Dio Washington Washington DC 2009-2015, Wrdn of Fllshp of St. Jn 2008-2015, Sthrn Afr Partnership Chair 2006-2012, Chapl to the Ret Cler/Spouses 2007-; Alum/ae Exec Com GTS New York City NY 2004-2010; Supvsr VTS Alexandria VA 1981-2006; R Ch Of The Trsfg Silver Sprg MD 1979-2006; S Andr's Ch Turners Fall MA 1977-1979; Vic S Jas' Ch Greenfield MA 1977-1979; Pres Coun Ch Greenfield MA 1976-1979; P-in-c Gr Ch Madison NJ 1976-1977; Yth Dir S Ptr's Ch Morristown NJ 1975-1976; Serv RC Ch MN 1969-1974. Action In Montgomery 1999-2014; Action In Montgomery, Treas 2005-2014; Fllshp of St Jn 2006-2015; WECA 1979.

KULP, John Eugene (SwFla) 17 W Vernon Ave Unit 301, Phoenix AZ 85003 B New York NY 1944 s John & Mary. BA Sthrn Illinois U 1968; MDiv Nash 1971; MS California Coast U 2006. D 6/12/1971 P 12/1/1971 Bp Jonathan Goodhue Sherman. m 6/26/1971 Dianne L Kulp.

KUNDINGER, Hazel Doris (CFla) 2404 Fairway Dr, Melbourne FL 32901 **Epis Ch of the Blessed Redeem 2008-** B Hackensack NJ 1943 d Salvatore & Hazel. Asbury TS; MDiv Sewanee: The U So, TS; Inst for Chr Stds Florida 1995; AA Brevard Cmnty Coll 1997. D 12/13/1997 P 2/6/2005 Bp John Wadsworth Howe. m 6/3/1976 Robert Kundinger. Vic Epis Ch of the Blessed Redeem Palm Bay FL 2005-2015; Vic Ch of Our Sav Palm Bay FL 2005-2012; D H Trin Epis Ch Melbourne FL 1997-2003. DOK; Ord Of S Lk The Physcn - Wrdn, Reg IIII (Pres. 1980.

KUNHARDT, Daniel Bradish (WMass) 25 Thornton Way Apt 110, Brunswick ME 04011 **Ret 1991-** B Lawrence MA 1926 s George & Joan. BA Bow 1949; MDiv GTS 1952; Cert Springfield Coll 1978. D 6/8/1952 Bp David Emrys Richards P 4/29/1953 Bp Stephen F Bayne Jr. Non-par 1973-1991; Asst Chr Ch Cathd Springfield MA 1967-1973; Vic Epis Ch Of The Epiph Wilbraham

MA 1958-1966; S Mary's Epis Ch Thorndike MA 1958-1959; Chapl Us AF 1955-1958; Vic S Matt Ch Tacoma WA 1954-1955; Cur Chr Ch Tacoma WA 1952-1954.

KUNHARDT III, Philip B (NY) Po Box 33, Waccabuc NY 10597 B Morristown NJ 1951 s Philip & Katharine. BA Coll of the Atlantic 1977; MDiv EDS 1980. D 6/13/1981 Bp Paul Moore Jr P 4/3/1982 Bp Lyman Cunningham Ogilby. m 10/1/1984 Margaret Kunhardt c 4. Asst S Mk's Ch Mt Kisco NY 1997-2012; Asst S Barth's Ch In The Highland White Plains NY 1991-1997; R S Pauls On The Hill Epis Ch Ossining NY 1984-1991; Asst Ch Of Our Sav Jenkintown PA 1981-1984; Ch Of S Asaph Bala Cynwyd PA 1981-1984. Auth, "Looking for Lincoln," Knopf, 2008; Auth, "Pbs-Tv Miniseries," *The Amer Pres*, 2000; Auth, "The Amer Pres," Riverhead, 1999; Auth, "P.T. Barnum: Amer's Greatest Showman," Knopf, 1995; Auth, "Lincoln: An Illustrated Biography," Knopf, 1992; Auth, "Abc-Tv Miniseries," *Lincoln*, 1992. The Century Club 2001.

KUNKLE, George Owen (RG) 1914 Tijeras Rd, Santa Fe NM 87505 **D S Bede's Epis Ch Santa Fe NM 1985-** B Leavenworth KS 1940 s George & Elizabeth. Harvard DS; BA S Johns Coll 1962; MA Emory U 1966; LPN NMMCC 1984. D 1/15/1985 Bp Richard Mitchell Trelease Jr. m 10/8/1977 Gail Margaret Kunkle c 5.

KUNZ JR, Andrew George (Va) 1006 Greenway Ln, Richmond VA 23226 **Ret 1998-** B Rome NY 1936 s Andrew & Leonora. BA Colg 1957; Drew U 1959; Drew U 1959; BD EDS 1961. D 6/10/1961 P 12/21/1961 Bp Leland Stark. m 11/27/1992 Claire H Kunz. Vic S Ptr's Epis Ch Richmond VA 1981-1998; Chapl Integrity Richmond VA 1981-1993; Vic Prince of Peace S Louis MO 1980-1981; Stndg Com Mem Dio Missouri S Louis MO 1975-1980, 1974-1981; Vic Ch Of The Ascen S Louis MO 1971-1980; Gr Epis Ch Rutherford NJ 1968-1974; Cur 1961-1967; Assoc R Trin Ch S Louis MO 1964-1965; Exec Bd Mem Dio Virginia Richmond VA 1990-1993; Dn of Richmond Reg 1984-1989.

KUNZ JR, Carl (Del) Po Box 5856, Wilmington DE 19808 B Philadelphia PA 1937 s Carl & Ethel. BA Hav 1958; MDiv EDS 1961. D 6/17/1961 P 3/1/1962 Bp Oliver J Hart. m 11/25/1961 Carol H Kunz c 2. Sr Chapl S Andr's Sch Chap Middletown DE 2000-2004; S Andrews Sch Of Delaware Inc Middletown DE 1993-2004; Dio Delaware Wilmington 1972-1993, Dioc Del 1972-1992, Exec Off 1972-1987; R St Annes Epis Ch Middletown DE 1967-1972; Asst S Paul's Ch Newburyport MA 1963-1964; Cur S Dav's Ch Wayne PA 1961-1963.

KUNZ, Phyllis Ann (Minn) 67982 260th Ave, Kasson MN 55944 B Winona MN 1955 d Thomas & Lela. LPN Rochester Sch of Practical Nrsng Rochester MN 1974. D 6/18/2005 Bp James Louis Jelinek. m 7/7/1979 Thomas Leo Kunz c 3. D S Lk's Epis Ch Rochester MN 2005-2010.

KUNZ, Richard Andrew (NY) Grace Church, 33 Church St, White Plains NY 10601 **R Gr Ch White Plains NY 2010-** B Philadelphia PA 1951 s William & Eleanor. BS NWU 1972; MDiv PrTS 1979; GTS 1980. D 6/14/1980 P 12/13/1980 Bp Robert Bracewell Appleyard. m 10/17/2009 Barbra Ann McCune c 2. Exec Dirrector, El Hogar Projects, Honduras Exec Coun Appointees New York NY 2004-2010; R All SS Ch Princeton NJ 1993-2004; Vic Emm Ch Pittsburgh PA 1986-1993; Cn Trin Cathd Pittsburgh PA 1981-1986; S Mk Pittsburgh PA 1980-1982.

KUOL, Daniel Kuch (Ky) 8701 Shepherdsville Rd, Louisville KY 40219 B Sudan 1978 s Kuol & Aluel. Cert Sch of Mnstry. D 7/8/2010 Bp Ted Gulick Jr. m 3/14/2013 Deborah Ajoh Malith c 1.

KURATKO, Lauren (At) 3110 Ashford Dunwoody Rd NE, Atlanta GA 30319 **Asst S Mart In The Fields Ch Atlanta GA 2012-** B Montgomery AL 1980 d Larry & Catherine. BA Rhodes Coll 2002; MDiv VTS 2005. D 5/25/2005 Bp Marc Handley Andrus P 12/13/2005 Bp Henry Nutt Parsley Jr. m 9/14/2007 Ryan Patrick Kuratko c 2. Gr & H Trin Epis Ch Richmond VA 2008-2012; Cbury Epis Campus Mnstry at Texas Tech Lubbock TX 2006-2008; Dio NW Texas Lubbock TX 2006-2008; S Jn's Ch Decatur AL 2005-2006; S Jn's Ch Montgomery AL 2005-2006.

KURATKO, Ryan Patrick (Va) P.O. Box 788, Mechanicsville VA 23111 B Odessa TX 1981 s Charles & Connye. BA NWU 2003; MDiv VTS 2006. D 12/14/2005 P 7/23/2006 Bp C Wallis Ohl. m 9/14/2007 Lauren Kuratko. R Imm Ch Mechanicsvlle VA 2009-2012; Assoc R S Paul's On The Plains Epis Ch Lubbock TX 2006-2008; Quarterman Ranch Lubbock TX 2006.

KURTZ, James Edward (CFla) 1352 Seburn Rd, Apopka FL 32703 B Mechanicsburg PA 1941 s Kenneth & Margaret. U Pgh 1969; AA Valencia Cmnty Coll 1973; BS Florida Sthrn Coll 1976; Cert Inst for Chr Stds 1991; MDiv TESM 2000. D 11/7/1992 P 7/30/2000 Bp John Wadsworth Howe. c 7. R S Agnes Ch Sebring FL 2000-2012; Ch Of The Ascen Pittsburgh PA 1997-2000; Epis Ch Of The Ascen Orlando FL 1992-1997.

KURTZ, Kelli Grace (Los) 408 Greenfield Ct, Glendora CA 91740 **Vic S Jn's Mssn La Verne CA 2007-; Dn of Dnry Six Dio Los Angeles Los Angeles CA 2013-, Cn for Mssn Congregations 2009-, 2008-, Prog Grp on Mssn Congregations 2008-; Bd Trst Bloy Hse Claremont CA 2007-** B Fresno CA 1964 d Martin & Margaret. BA California St U 1986; MA Claremont TS 1996. D 11/22/1997 Bp Chester Lovelle Talton P 10/21/2006 Bp Robert Marshall

Anderson. m 7/7/1985 Mark S Kurtz c 4. Asst All SS Epis Ch Riverside CA 1999-2007; Cur S Mary's Par Laguna Bch CA 1998-1999. Ord Julian Of Norwich 1996-1999. vicar@stjohnslaverne.org

KURTZ, Margaret Eileen (Ida) 3185 E Rivernest Dr, Boise ID 83706 **Assoc S Mich's Cathd Boise ID 1996-** B La Crosse WI 1942 d William & Marie. BD U of Iowa 1976; MA U of Iowa 1979. D 12/22/1996 P 6/29/1997 Bp John Stuart Thornton. m 5/15/1993 Karl Bunning Kurtz c 2.

KURTZ, Robert Guy (Eas) 1 Meadow St, Apt. 120, Berlin MD 21811 **Died 11/24/2015** B Fort Collins CO 1920 s Guy & Harriette. BS USMA 1943; Epis TS in Kentucky 1966. D 12/16/1966 Bp William R Moody P 11/1/1967 Bp Egbert Don Taylor. c 2. Ret 1985-2015; Dn Of The Sthrn Convoc 1979-2015; R S Andr's Epis Ch Princess Anne MD 1975-1984; Const & Cn Strategic Plnng Com 1974-2015; R Emm Epis Ch Chestertown MD 1972-1975; 1971-1973; Dn Of The Sthrn Convoc 1970-1972; R All Hallow's Ch Snow Hill MD 1967-1972.

KUSCHEL, Catherine Mary (Eau) 3774 Goodwin Ave N, Oakdale MN 55128 **P-in-c Ch Of S Thos And S Jn New Richmond WI 2017-; Counslr Yth Rehab & Treatment Cntr Geneva NE 2010-** B Milwaukee WI 1951 d Richard & Dolores. BS U of Wisconsin 1973; MS U of Wisconsin 1980; MDiv SWTS 1990; Cert Int Mnstry Prog 1992; Cert Racine Dominican Sprtl Gdnc Trng Prog 2004; MA Doane Coll 2010. D 4/29/1990 P 12/1/1990 Bp Roger John White. m 7/21/1973 Joseph Kuschel c 1. Bereavemen Counslr Asera Care Hospice Keaney NE 2009-2010; Chapl Asera Care Hospice Kearney NE 2009-2010; R S Steph's Ch Grand Island NE 2005-2009; Int S Anskar's Ch Rockford IL 2003-2005; Int Our Saviors Luth Ch Milwaukee WI 2002-2003; Int Chr Ch Milwaukee WI 2000-2002; Int Chr Ch Epis Madison WI 1998-2000; Int S Dav Of Wales Ch New Berlin WI 1996-1998; P-in-c Trin Epis Ch Mineral Point WI 1994-1996; Int S Chris's Ch Milwaukee WI 1992-1994; Cur S Lk's Ch Madison WI 1991-1992; Stndg Com Dio Milwaukee Milwaukee WI 1992-1996. CSM 2004; Ord of Julian of Norwich 1991-1995. Outstanding Stdt Awd Doane Coll 2010; Helen Ledyard Field Prize in Homil SWTS 1990; Henry Benjamin Whipple Schlr SWTS 1990; Chas Palmerson Anderson Schlr SWTS 1989.

KUSKY, Donna Lee Stewart (EMich) 13685 Block Rd, Birch Run MI 48415 **D S Mk's Epis Ch Bridgeport MI 1992-** B Flint MI 1942 d Vernon & Olga. Whitaker TS 1992; AA Mott Cmnty Coll 1993. D 6/13/1992 Bp R aymond Stewart Wood Jr. m 2/13/1965 William Paul Kusky c 4.

KWAN, Franco C (Cal) 425 Swallowtail Ct, Brisbane CA 94005 **The SCSD Cmsn of GC Ch Cntr CA 2006-; Natl Cnvnr of Chinese Convoc Epis Asiamerica Mnstry Ch Cntr NY 2004-** B Canton CN 1950 s Lok & Kwok. LLB Chinese Culture U Taipei TW 1976; BD Chung Chi Sem Chinese U of Hong Kong CN 1979; MSW CUNY 1990; DMin NYTS 1993. D 7/25/1979 Bp James T M Pong P 9/21/1980 Bp Poi-Yeung Cheung. c 3. R True Sunshine Par San Francisco CA 1999-2017; S Geo's Par Flushing NY 1992-1999; Racial Justice Cmsn Dio Long Island Garden City NY 1991-1998, Rep Ecum Wrkng Grp Asian Pacific Amers 1989-1996, 1988-1991, Chair Asian Com on Aging 1987-1996, Dioc Coun 1993-1994, Cler Advsry Com Chld Abuse & Neglect NY St 1985-1987; Vic Epis Ch Of Our Sav New York NY 1984-1987; Dio Taiwan Taipei 1979-1984; Serv Dio Taiwan Taipei 1979-1983; Dept of Mssn Dio California San Francisco CA 2001-2006, Vice Chair of China Friendship Com 2000-, Asian Cmsn of the Dio California 1999-. "A Mssy from the E," *Mod Profiles of An Ancient Faith*, Epis Dio California, 2001; Auth, "The Needs of the Chinese Elderly -- Who Should Care for Them," *ACA*, 1990. Citation of Outstanding Contributions to the Flushing Cmnty Lunar New Year Fest Com 1999; Citation of hon Pres of Manhattan, New York 1999; Citation of hon Pres of Queens Borough, New York 1999; Proclamation The City Coun of New York 1999; Citation of hon The Mayor of New York New York City 1999; Who's Who among Asian Americans Gale Resrch Inc., 1994.

KWIATKOWSKI, Janet J (Mil) 9333 W Goodrich Ave, Milwaukee WI 53224 **P--Dir of Pstr Care S Jn's On The Lake Milwaukee WI 2004-** B Milwaukee WI 1955 d Jerome & Helen. BA Alverno Coll 1977; MS Capella U 2003; SWTS 2006. D 12/7/2002 Bp Roger John White P 9/14/2006 Bp Steven Andrew Miller. m 12/15/1979 Dennis A Kwiatkowski c 4. Asstg P S Chris's Ch Milwaukee WI 2007-2009, 2003-2005, D 2002-2004; S Jn's on The Lake Milwaukee WI 2005-2007.

KYGER JR, Paul Scholl (Chi) 2304 Finwick Ct, Kissimmee FL 34743 **Ret 1993-** B Glen Ridge NJ 1930 s Paul & Lola. BA Wesl 1952; BD SWTS 1955. D 6/18/1955 Bp Charles L Street P 12/21/1955 Bp Gerald Francis Burrill. c 4. P-in-c S Ambr Ch Chicago Hts IL 1976-1992; R S Richard's Ch Chicago IL 1971-1976; Chair Dio Chicago Urban Div Dept Ch Ext 1960-1963; Vic St Cyprians Ch Chicago IL 1956-1963; Cur Gr Ch Oak Pk IL 1955-1956; Dn, Joliet Dnry Dio Chicago Chicago IL 1990-1992, Cn for Chr Soc Relatns 1963-1989, Dn, Chicago W Dnry 1962-1963.

KYLE, Anne Meredith (WMo) Calvary Episcopal Church, 713 S Ohio Ave, Sedalia MO 65301 **Calv Epis Ch Sedalia MO 2016-** B Evanston IL 1962 d Andrew & Thelma. Cert of Presbyteral Stds Bp Kemper Sch for Mnstry; BS U of Missouri 1984. D 11/6/2015 P 6/18/2016 Bp Martin Scott Field. m 6/14/2008 Michael Raymond Kyle c 1.

KYLE, Michael Raymond (Mo) 3932 Oxford Rd, Jefferson City MO 65109 **Trin Ch Hannibal MO 1995-** B Hamilton OH 1949 s Franklin & Patricia. BA Kent St U 1972; MDiv Bex Sem 1975. D 6/2/1976 P 3/1/1977 Bp John Mc Gill Krumm. m 6/14/2008 Anne Meredith Kyle c 2. All SS Ch W Plains MO 2011-2015, P-in-c 2011-2015, 2011, 2008-2011; Dio W Missouri Kansas City MO 2004-2010; No Convoc Palmyra MO 1995-2004; S Paul's Ch Palmyra MO 1995-2004; Calv Ch Louisiana MO 1995-2000; Mssnr Gr Ch Clarksville MO 1995-2000; S Jn's Ch Prairieville Eolia MO 1995-2000; Mssnr Epis Ch 1995-1986; P-in-c S Ptr's Epis Ch Bonne Terre MO 1989-1995; Trin Ch De Soto MO 1989-1995; R Emm Epis Ch Alexandria MN 1987-1989; S Andr's-In-The-Vlly Tamworth NH 1981-1985; Emm Epis Ch S Louis MO 1976-1981, Intern 1975-1976.

L

LABARRE, Barbara L Root (Okla) 10901 S Yale Ave, Tulsa OK 74137 **D Ch Of The H Sprt - Epis Tulsa OK 1984-** B Newton KS 1935 d Vincent & Frieda. U of Oregon; BS K SU 1957; EFM Sewanee: The U So, TS 1986. D 6/28/1984 Bp William Jackson Cox. m 12/27/1956 Gary C LaBarre c 3. CHS.

LABATT, Walter Bruce (Mo) 520 Coventry Cir, Dexter MI 48130 **Asst S Andr's Ch Ann Arbor MI 2013-** B Petoskey MI 1940 s Dee & Mary. BA U MI 1962; MDiv SWTS 1991. D 6/23/1990 P 4/1/1991 Bp R aymond Stewart Wood Jr. m 9/19/1981 Judith La Batt. Int S Steph's Ch Troy MI 2011-2012; Asst Gr Epis Ch Mansfield OH 2004-2006; Int S Simon's On The Sound Ft Walton Bch FL 2003-2004; Int The Epis Ch Of The Nativ Dothan AL 2002-2003; Int Peace Evang Luth Ch 2001-2002; Int Untd Evang Luth Ch Of Peace Steeleville IL 2001-2002; Int No Convoc Palmyra MO 2001; Int S Gabr's Epis Ch Eastpointe MI 1999-2001; R S Paul's Ch S Louis MO 1994-1999; Vic S Mich's Epis Ch O Fallon IL 1991-1994; D S Dav's Ch Southfield MI 1990-1991.

LABELLE, Philip N (Mass) 27 Main St, Southborough MA 01772 **P S Mk's Ch Southborough MA 2011-** B Mount Clemens MI 1970 s Russell & Betty. BA Gordon Coll 1992; MA NEU 1998; MDiv Ya Berk 2004. D 6/19/2004 P 1/23/2005 Bp Gordon Scruton. m 12/29/1995 Melissa T LaBelle c 2. R The Ch Of Chr The King (Epis) Arvada CO 2007-2011; Assoc R S Lk's Par Darien CT 2004-2007.

LABORDA HARRIS, Christy Elisa (NCal) St. Stephen's Episcopal Church, PO Box 98, Sebastopol CA 95472 **R S Steph's Epis Ch Sebastopol CA 2011-** B Wynnwood PA 1981 d Oscar & Suzanne. BA Bryn 2003; MDiv VTS 2007. D 6/9/2007 Bp Charles Ellsworth Bennison Jr P 12/9/2007 Bp Michael B Curry. m 9/24/2011 Kai Harris. Vic Dio El Camino Real Salinas CA 2009-2011; Vic Iglesia El Buen Pstr Durham NC 2007-2009. christy@ststephenssebastopol.org

LABUD, Richard John (CFla) 28097 Se Highway 42, Umatilla FL 32784 **D S Thos Epis Ch Eustis FL 1995-** B Pasadena CA 1959 s William & Lillian. Inst for Chr Stds; AA Lake-Sumter Cmnty Coll 1979. D 11/11/1995 Bp John Wadsworth Howe. m 8/4/1979 Lisa Patricia Labud c 2.

LACEY, John Howard (SwFla) 851 Moonlight Ln, Brooksville FL 34601 **Ret 1988-** B London UK 1923 s Horace & Dorothy. MDiv Sewanee: The U So, TS 1975. D 6/11/1975 Bp William Loftin Hargrave P 12/22/1975 Bp Emerson Paul Haynes. c 2. Vic S Jn's Epis Ch Brooksville FL 1979-1988; Vic S Aug's Epis Ch St Petersburg FL 1975-1979.

LACEY, Maryanne (SanD) 3208 Old Heather Rd, San Diego CA 92111 B Brooklyn NY 1943 d Milton & Anne. AA Mesa Cmnty Coll 1986; BA Natl U 1988; DIT ETSBH 1991; MA Stc 1993. D 6/15/1991 Bp Joseph Thomas Heistand P 6/1/1994 Bp Gethin Benwil Hughes. Ch Of The Gd Samar San Diego CA 2005-2006; S Tim's Ch San Diego CA 2003-2004, D 1991-1992; R S Phil The Apos Epis Ch Lemon Grove CA 1999-2006; Chr Ch Cranbrook Bloomfield Hills MI 1996-1998; All SS Ch Wheatland WY 1995-1996; Cathd Ch Of S Paul San Diego CA 1994-1995, D 1992-1994; Chapl To Bp Dio San Diego San Diego CA 1992-1994; Epis Cmnty Serv Natl City CA 1991-2003.

LACOMBE, Edgar A (Alb) 5708 State Highway 812, Ogdensburg NY 13669 **R Chr Ch Morristown NY 2012-** B Ogdensburg NY 1951 s Edgar & Winifred. Potsdam St U; AAS Mater Dei Coll Ogdensburg NY 1975; BS Clarkson U 1977; LTh McGill U 1986. D 6/7/1986 P 12/1/1986 Bp David Standish Ball. m 6/20/1974 Carolyn B LaCombe c 4. Dn - Nthrn Adirondack Dnry Albany Epis Dio Albany NY 2005-2011; P-in-c Chr & St. Jn's Ch Champlain NY 2003-2012; P-in-c Chr/St Jn's Par Champlain NY 2003-2012; Sr Chapl New York St OMRDD Tupper Lake NY 1989-2005; P-in-c S Thos Ch Tupper Lake NY 1989-2003; Asst Sprtl Dir Albany Curs 1988-2004; Int Gr Epis Ch Canton NY 1988-1989; Asst P S Jn's Ch Ogdensburg NY 1986-1989.

LACRONE, Frederick Palmer (SeFla) 3059 Casa Rio Ct, Palm Beach Gardens FL 33418 **Ret 1999-** B Kalamazoo MI 1936 s Fred & Margaret. BA MI SU 1958; MDiv GTS 1961; DMin So Florida Cntr of Theol Miami FL 1992; MA Florida Atlantic U 2001. D 6/20/1961 P 12/21/1961 Bp Charles Bennison Sr. c 4. Pres Mnstrl Fllshp Palm Beaches 1995-1997; Dioc Liturg Com 1990-1992; R Gr Ch W Palm Bch FL 1981-1998; Rgnl Assoc Evang & Renwl Dio Sthrn Ohio

Cincinnati OH 1978-1981; Evang Com Chair 1977-1980; R S Steph's Epis Ch Cincinnati OH 1975-1981; Assoc S Thos Epis Ch Terrace Pk OH 1969-1975; Dn Lakeshore Dnry 1966-1969; R Gr Epis Ch Of Ludington Ludington MI 1963-1969; Cur Trin Ch Niles MI 1961-1963; Bd Comprehensive Alco Proj W Palm Bch; ExCoun Dio Wstrn Michigan Kalamazoo MI 1965-1969. CT 1980. Faith and Rel Awd Bus & Profsnl Wmn 1996.

LACROSSE, Diana Parsons (Dal) 2700 Warren Cir, Irving TX 75062 B Del Rio TX 1939 d Chester & Audrey. BS U of Texas 1961; MS U of Nebraska 1975. D 6/3/2001 Bp James Edward Krotz. m 4/6/2008 Julian Terry LaCrosse c 2.

LACY, Mimi (SVa) 107 Louis St, Greenville NC 27858 **Emm Ch Virginia Bch VA 2015-; Dn Dio E Carolina Kinston NC 2007-, Dn of the Pamlico Dnry 2011-, Dep to GC 2011-, Vice-Chair of Exec Coun 2010-, Fin Com 2009-, Mssn Dvlpmt 2008-2011, Fin Com 2008-, Stwdshp Cmsn 2008-** B Johnstown PA 1956 d John & Gertrude. BS Indiana U of Pennsylvania 1978; MDiv SWTS 2001. D 6/16/2001 P 12/15/2001 Bp Bill Persell. m 2/18/1984 Thomas S Lacy c 3. R S Tim's Epis Ch Greenville NC 2007-2015; Assoc R S Andr's Ch Downers Grove IL 2001-2007; Chair, Conv Plnng Com Dio Chicago Chicago IL 2005-2007, COM 2003-2007, COM 2002-2007, Sprtl Dir Chicago Epis Curs 2002-2007.

LACY II, Thomas Alonzo (Ga) St. Anne's Episcopal Church, P.O. Box 889, Tifton GA 31793 **Mem of Bd Trst S Anne's Ch Tifton GA 2009-; Dep to GC 2012 Dio Georgia Savannah GA 2011-, Mem of COM 2010-** B Valdosta GA 1980 s James & Anne. BA Reinhardt Coll Waleska GA 2002; MDiv VTS 2006. D 2/4/2006 P 8/10/2006 Bp Henry Irving Louttit. m 8/7/2004 Jessica Whitmire Lacy c 2. Epis Chapl Epis Campus Mnstry at Georgia Sthrn U 2006-2009; Asst R Trin Ch Statesboro GA 2006-2009; VTS Alexandria VA 2009-2011.

✠ LADEHOFF, The Rt Rev Robert Louis (Ore) 1330 SW 3rd Ave., Apt. P8, Portland OR 97201 **Ret Bp of Oregon Ascen Par Portland OR 2008-; Ret Bp of Oregon Dio Oregon Portland OR 2003-, Bp 1985-2003** B Ridgway PA 1932 s Henry & Bertha. BA Duke 1954; STB GTS 1957; DMin VTS 1980. D 6/15/1957 Bp Edwin A Penick P 12/18/1957 Bp Richard Henry Baker Con 11/30/1985 for Ore. c 1. R S Jn's Epis Ch Fayetteville NC 1974-1985; R St. Chris's Ch 1960-1974; S Paul's Epis Ch Thomasville NC 1957-1960; Min in charge Chr Ch Walnut Cove NC 1957-1959; Min in Charge S Phil's Ch Germantown NC 1957-1959; Chair C&C Cntr Plnng Com Dio E Carolina Kinston NC 1982-1985; BEC Dio No Carolina Raleigh NC 1962-1974.

LAEDLEIN, George Robert (CNY) 201 Granite Rd Apt 340, Guilford CT 06437 **Ret 1985-** B Philadelphia PA 1924 s Hepburn & Florence. BA Trin Hartford CT 1947; ThB PDS 1950; MA Trin Hartford CT 1951; MDiv PDS 1959. D 6/3/1950 Bp William P Remington P 12/21/1950 Bp Noble C Powell. c 5. Int S Geo's Ch Middlebury CT 1989-1991; Int & Supply P Dio Connecticut Hartford CT 1985-1998; Pstr Asst Gr Epis Ch Trumbull CT 1985-1997; R S Paul's Ch Owego NY 1978-1984; R Emm Par Epis Ch Sthrn Pines NC 1976-1978; R The Par Of Emm Ch Weston CT 1966-1976; Evang Dio Maryland Baltimore MD 1961-1966, Ldrshp Trng Div DeptCE 1958-1966, Dir Sr HS Conf 1954-1960; Vic S Chris Epis Ch Linthicum Hts MD 1952-1966; Chapl Montrose - Rosewood Trng Schs 1951-1952; Cur S Dav's Ch Baltimore MD 1950-1952; Bd Epis Soc Serv Dio Connecticut Meriden CT 1969-1975.

LAFFLER, Brian H (Nwk) 72 Lodi St, Hackensack NJ 07601 **R S Anth Of Padua Ch Hackensack NJ 1990-** B Passaic NJ 1957 s Howard & Mary. BA Montclair St U 1980; MDiv GTS 1987. D 6/8/1987 Bp Robert Campbell Witcher Sr P 6/1/1988 Bp David Standish Ball. m 8/12/1979 Patricia Catherine Augenti. Cur S Geo's Epis Ch Schenectady NY 1987-1990. CBS, GAS, SSC.

LAFLER, Mark Alan (CFla) 414 Pine St, Titusville FL 32796 **S Edw The Confessor Mt Dora FL 2016-** B Hollywood FL 1975 s Donald & Diane. DAS Trin Sch for Mnstry; BA Global U 2001; MATS Regent Coll 2010. D 5/23/2015 P 11/28/2015 Bp Gregory Orrin Brewer. m 6/20/1995 Tera M Carlson c 4. Asst S Gabriels Ch Titusville FL 2015-2016, 2014-2015.

LAFON, Alvin Paul (Los) 2691 Foxglove Loop Se, Albany OR 97322 **Ret 1995-** B Cambridge MA 1927 s Louis & Sophorina. BA Bos 1951; MDiv CDSP 1954; DIT S Augustines Coll Cbury GB 1965; Cert Coll of Preachers 1969. D 6/14/1954 P 12/21/1954 Bp Richard S Watson. m 12/11/1993 Dorothy Lafon c 3. Asst S Geo's Epis Ch Laguna Hills CA 1987-1998; The Cbury Pasadena CA 1985-1986; Kensington Epis Hm Alhambra CA 1976-1978; Assoc All SS Ch Pasadena CA 1973-1975; R S Mich's-On-The-Heights Worcester MA 1966-1973; R S Mk's Ch Leominster MA 1960-1966; Cur S Steph's Ch Pittsfield MA 1956-1960; Vic S Jn's Epis Ch Logan UT 1954-1956. Auth, *COP Fllshp Paper*; Auth, *Clergical Placement & Career Dvlpmt*; Auth, "Reordering a Ch for a More Meaningful Liturg Wrshp," *The Angl*.

LAFON, Kirk David (Miss) 950 Episcopal School Way, Knoxville TN 37932 **S Andr's Epis Sch Ridgeland MS 2012-** B Staunton VA 1972 s James & Shirley. BA U of Virginia 1994; MTS VTS 1998; MDiv Sewanee: The U So, TS 2010. D 5/29/2010 P 4/30/2011 Bp Charles Glenn VonRosenberg. m 6/17/1995 Kristan Irene LaFon. Assoc St Jas Epis Ch at Knoxville Knoxville TN 2011-2012, Assoc 2011-; The Epis Sch Of Knoxville Knoxville TN 2010-2012.

LAFOND II, Charles Drummond (Colo) 1023 Pleasant Street, Webster NH 03303 **Cn S Jn's Cathd Denver CO 2013-; Cn for Stwdshp The Dio New**

Hampshire Concord NH 2006- B Washington DC 1963 s Charles & Anne. BA U So 1986; MDiv VTS 2001. D 6/23/2001 P 12/29/2001 Bp Peter J Lee. Dio New Hampshire Concord NH 2008-2013; Ch Of The Gd Shpd Nashua NH 2006-2008; Monk The Soc of St. Jn The Evengelist Cambridge MA 2003-2006; Cur Ch Of Our Sav Charlottesvlle VA 2001-2003. charles@sjcathedral.org

LAFONTANT, Fritz Raoul (Hai) Eglise Street Pierre, Mirebalais Haiti **R S Ptr 1956-** B 1925 s Bores & Elizabeth. D 7/10/1949 P 2/1/1950 Bp Charles Alfred Voegeli. m 1/31/1951 Yolande Lafontant. Dio Haiti Port-au-Prince HT 1949-1990; Vic S Thos In Arcahaie Haiti 1949-1956.

LAFOREST, Charlotte Henning (Ct) PO Box 422, Essex CT 06426 **S Jn's Epis Ch Essex CT 2015-** B Mineola NY 1983 d Douglas. AB Geo 2006; MA,MSW Boston Coll 2009; MDiv, Dplma in Angl Stds Ya Berk 2015. D 6/6/2015 Bp Gayle Harris P 12/15/2015 Bp Ian Theodore Douglas. m 7/7/2007 Eric John LaForest c 1.

LAFORTUNE, Patrick 74 S Common St, Lynn MA 01902 B Haiti 1978 s Marie. D 6/3/2017 Bp Gayle Harris. c 3.

LAGANA, Gaye Lynn (Nev) PO Box 18917, Spokane WA 99228 B Pittsburgh PA 1943 d Leroy & Marie. BA Penn 1965; MA Immac Heart Coll 1980. D 6/7/2008 Bp James E Waggoner Jr. m 2/18/1995 Stephen Lagana c 4.

LAGER, Michael Alan (Ark) 16816 Summit Vista Way, Louisville KY 40245 **R S Jn's Epis Ch Ft Smith AR 2010-** B Saint Paul MN 1964 s Dennis & Judith. BA Cntrl Bible Coll Springfield MO 1986; MA Assemblies of God TS 1987; MDiv Sthrn Bapt TS 1994; CAS GTS 1996. D 6/22/1996 P 1/18/1997 Bp Ted Gulick Jr. m 6/22/1990 Kimberly Dawn Lager c 2. Stndg Com Dio Kentucky Louisville KY 2005-2006, Com 2001-2006; R S Thos Epis Ch Louisville KY 2000-2010; Asst R S Matt's Epis Ch Louisville KY 1996-2000.

LAGO, Ana Mercedes (PR) B 1935 Dio Puerto Rico Trujillo Alto PR 2004-2007, 2001-2003, 1994-1998.

LAHEY, Stephen Edmund (Neb) 1935 Sewell St, Lincoln NE 68502 **Assoc S Matt's Ch Lincoln NE 2006-, P Assoc 2004-** B Philadelphia PA 1960 s Allen & Barbara. BA W Chester U of Pennsylvania 1986; MA U of Kansas 1990; PhD U of Connecticut 1997; Cert Ang Stud SWTS 2002. D 12/13/2003 Bp Gladstone Bailey Adams III P 9/21/2004 Bp Joe Goodwin Burnett. m 7/2/1994 Julia McQuillan c 1. P-in-c St. Aug Of Cantebury 2004-2007; Auth, "Philos And Politics In The Thought Of Jn Wyclif," Cambridge Univ. Press, 2003; Auth, "Wyclif And Lollardy," The Medieval Theologians/Blackwell, 2001; Auth, "Wm Ockham And Trope Nominalism," Franciscan Stds Vol.55, 1998; Auth, "Wyclif On Rts," Journ Of The Hist Of Ideas Vol.58, 1997. Mem Phi Beta Kappa 2010.

✠ LAI, The Rt Rev Jung-Hsin (Tai) 7, Lane 105, Hangchow S. Road Sec. 1, Taipei 10060 Taiwan **Bp Dio Taiwan Taiwan 2000-; Dio Taiwan Taipei 1976-, Vice-Chair on the Stndg Com** B Cha-Yi TW 1948 s Bee-Yi & Chou. MDiv Tainan Theol Coll and Sem TW 1975; ThM SE Asia TS 1993. D 3/23/1975 P 4/11/1976 Bp James T M Pong Con 11/25/2000 for Tai. m 9/2/1974 Shu-Ying Lai Lin c 2. Vic Gr Ch Taiwan 1987-2000; Vic St. Tim's Ch Taiwan 1985-1987; Vic St. Mk's Ch Taiwan 1984-1985; Vic St. Mths' Ch Taiwan 1983-1984; Vic St Andr's Ch Taiwan 1976-1982. Auth, *Video Tape Land of Bible & Jesus*.

LAI, Paul C (LI) 1321 College Point Blvd, College Point NY 11356 **Dio Long Island Garden City NY 2012-** B Taiwan 1976 s Jung-Hsin & Shu-Ying. BS Polytechnic U 1998; MDiv GTS 2010. D 6/26/2010 P 6/4/2011 Bp Lawrence C Provenzano. m 3/12/2006 Lichia Yang c 2. Asst S Jas Ch Elmhust NY 2011-2015; S Paul's Ch Coll Point NY 2011-2012; S Lk's Ch Forest Hills NY 2010-2011. PLAI01@YAHOO.COM

LAI, Peter Pui-Tak (LI) 1000 Washington Ave, Plainview NY 11803 B HK 1956 s Nelson & Pauline. BA U Sask CA 1980; MA U Tor 1986; Off Trng Sch 1995. D 1/15/1984 P 9/1/1985 Bp Poi-Yeung Cheung. c 2. S Mary's Ch Carle Place NY 2014-2016; S Bon Epis Ch Lindenhurst NY 2013-2016; S Mich And All Ang Seaford NY 2013-2014; Dio Long Island Garden City NY 2009-2013; S Marg's Ch Plainview NY 2004-2010; Chr Ch Worton MD 2001-2004; Off Of Bsh For ArmdF New York NY 1995-1998; Dio Olympia Seattle 1994; Epiph Par of Seattle Seattle WA 1994; Ch Of The H Apos Seattle WA 1988-1994; Dio Taiwan Taipei 1986-1987; Asst S Jn's Cathd In Taipei Taiwan 1986-1987; Vic Asiamer Mnstry In Boston MA 1984-1986; Dio Massachusetts Boston MA 1984-1986.

LAINE, Jeanty (SeFla) 404 SW 3rd St, Delray Beach FL 33444 **The Blessed Jas T Holly Epis Mssn Delray Bch FL 2014-** B Limonade Haiti 1955 s Philome & Anela. BA Grand Seminaire Notre-Dame 1985; Lic CDSP 2013; Lic CDSP 2013. Rec 10/2/2013 as Priest Bp Leo Frade. m 8/18/2008 Flore Laine c 2. jeanlaine85@yahoo.com

LAING, Christopher A (Ore) 8275 Sw Canyon Ln, Portland OR 97225 B Minneapolis MN 1944 s George & Kathryn. Carleton Coll 1963; BA U MN 1966; MA U of Oregon 1968; MDiv Nash 1977. D 6/24/1977 P 2/24/1978 Bp Philip Frederick McNairy. m 9/13/1969 Judy T Laing c 3. Chapl Portland St U Portland Oregon 1998-2007; Portland Metro Epis Campus Mnstry Portland OR 1998-2006; S Gabr Ch Portland OR 1997-1999; R Ch Of The H Apos S Paul MN 1992-1997; H Trin Intl Falls MN 1991-1992; R S Phil's Ch S Paul MN 1987-1990; Chapl Shattuck-St Mary's Sch Faribault MN 1985-1987; R Ch

Of The H Comm S Ptr MN 1980-1984; S Andrews Epis Ch Waterville MN 1977-1980; Vic So Cntrl Area Mnstry Waseca MN 1977-1980. *Revs & arts*, 2003. Conf Ord of S Ben 1977; Epis Ntwk Econ of Justice 1994-2000; EUC 1989-2000. Alumnni of Notable Achievement U MN 1994.

LAINSON, Vinnie Van (Va) 9325 West Street, Manassas VA 20110 **Assoc R Trin Ch Manassas VA 2000-** B Hastings NE 1953 d John & Phyllis. BA Hastings Coll 1976; St Georges Coll Jerusalem 1999; MDiv VTS 2000. D 12/7/2000 Bp David Colin Jones P 6/10/2001 Bp Peter J Lee. c 3. Adj VTS 2011-2012; Sum R St. Jas Prouts Neck ME 2004-2010; Sem Supvsr VTS 2003-2010; Cmsn Wmn/Mssn/Mnstry Dio Virginia Richmond VA 2002-2006.

LAIRD, Daniel Dale (NC) 1737 Hillandale Rd, Durham NC 27705 **D S Lk's Epis Ch Durham NC 2015-** B Erie PA 1955 s Robert & Mildred. B.S Penn 1978. D 1/24/2015 Bp Anne Hodges-Copple. m 7/10/2014 Timothy Wayne Laird Truelove.

LAIRD, I Bruce (Colo) 606 Newnan St, Carrollton GA 30117 B Wichita KS 1945 s David & Mary. BS K SU 1968; MDiv Epis TS of the SW 1987. D 6/9/1987 Bp Anselmo Carral-Solar P 2/1/1988 Bp Maurice Manuel Benitez. m 6/6/1964 Sherrie Lou Laird c 3. S Marg's Ch Carrollton GA 2016; Fac St. Steph's Epis Sch Bradenton FL 2007-2008; Mssnr - Wstrn Retion Dio Colorado Denver CO 1998-2002, Dn - San Juan Convoc 1996-1998; R S Jn's Epis Ch Ouray CO 1994-2006; P-in-c S Mich's Ch Telluride CO 1994-2000; Chr Epis Ch Mexia Mexia TX 1993-1994; The Great Cmsn Fndt Houston TX 1993-1994; S Ptr's Epis Ch Brenham TX 1989-1993; Asst R S Jas The Apos Epis Ch Conroe TX 1987-1989.

LAIRD, Lucinda Rawlings (Eur) 330 N Hubbards Ln, Louisville KY 40207 **Dn The Amer Cathd of the H Trin Paris 75008 2013-; Com Dio Kentucky Louisville KY 1998-** B New York NY 1952 d Carroll & Barbara. BA Barnard Coll of Col 1979; MDiv GTS 1982. D 6/5/1982 P 12/1/1982 Bp Paul Moore Jr. R S Matt's Epis Ch Louisville KY 1997-2013; Dep Gc Dio Newark Newark NJ 1994-1997, Com 1991-1995, Stndg Com 1996-1997, Dioc Coun 1989-1993; S Mk's Ch Teaneck NJ 1986-1997; R S Mk's Ch W Orange NJ 1986-1997; Asst Coll Min Cathd Of St Jn The Div New York NY 1984-1986; Asst Par of Chr the Redeem Pelham NY 1982-1984; Stndg Com On Ecum Relatns Epis Ch Cntr New York NY 1995-2000. Auth, "Television Show Point Of View," 1991; Auth, "Chld'S Video Tell Me Why God". Ord Of S Helena, Assoc 1982. Bp Outstanding Serv Awd Dio Newark 1996; Hon Lifetime Cn Trin & S Phil'S Cathd.

LAIRD, Robert C (Oly) 316 E 88th St, New York NY 10128 **S Jn's Epis Ch Olympia WA 2015-** B Glenwood MN 1978 s Robert & Elizabeth. BA Hamline U 2005; MDiv GTS 2010. D 7/23/2009 Bp James Louis Jelinek P 7/29/2010 Bp Brian N Prior. m 5/24/2008 Angela B Merrill c 2. Dio Olympia Seattle 2012-2014; Lilly Fell Ch Of The H Trin New York NY 2010-2012.

LAITE JR, Robert Emerson (Me) 200 Main St, Thomaston ME 04861 B Camden ME 1957 s Robert & Eugenia. Assoc of Bus U of Maine; Assoc of Bus U of Maine 1978; Assoc Degree New Engl Inst of Applied Arts & Sciences 1979; D Formation Prog Bangor TS 2005. D 6/18/2005 Bp Chilton Richardson Knudsen.

LAKE, Mark William (RG) 2602 S 2nd St, Tucumcari NM 88401 **S Mich's Ch Tucumcari NM 2012-** B Sac City IA 1949 s William & Anna. BA U of Nthrn Iowa 1971; MDiv Dubuque TS 1980. D 9/18/2010 Bp William Carl Frey P 12/3/2011 Bp Michael Vono. m 12/27/1969 Beverly Lake c 3.

LAKE JR, Orloff Levin (Chi) 7706 Blue Heron Dr W Apt 1, Wilmington NC 28411 **Ret 1990-** B Chattanooga TN 1927 s Orloff & Hallie. BA SMU 1949; MDiv SWTS 1952. D 6/20/1952 Bp Charles A Mason P 12/22/1952 Bp Gerald Francis Burrill. m 9/19/2009 Jean Marie Ulrick c 3. Dn Joliet Deanry Dio Chicago Chicago IL 1988-1990, Search Com 1983-1987, Nmntns Com 1980-1982, Com Ecum Affrs 1970-1979; R S Edw The Mtyr and Chr Epis Ch Joliet IL 1965-1990; Vic Ch Of The H Nativ Clarendon Hls IL 1955-1965; Vic Chr The King Epis Ch Ft Worth TX 1953-1955; Cur All SS' Epis Ch Ft Worth TX 1952-1953.

LAKEMAN, Thomas Edmund (CGC) 127 Oak Bend Ct, Fairhope AL 36532 B Clanton AL 1928 s Edmund & Pauline. BA Birmingham-Sthrn Coll 1951; ABT U of Alabama 1954; MDiv Epis TS of the SW 1959. D 6/11/1959 P 2/7/1960 Bp Albert R Stuart. m 8/18/1984 Linda C Lakeman c 6. Consult Baldwin Cnty Mntl Hlth Cntr Fairhope Alabama 1997-2009; Vic Imm Ch Bay Minette AL 1978-1980; R S Mich's Ch Mobile AL 1976-1978; Exec Dir Mobile Mntl Hlth Cntr Mobile Alabama 1972-1997; Vic S Ptr's Ch Jackson AL 1972-1983; R All SS Epis Ch Mobile AL 1968-1976; Vic S Geo's Epis Ch Savannah GA 1961-1964; Vic Chr Epis Ch Cordele GA 1959-1961. Stff Sociol, "Resrch," *How a Cmnty Took Action to Dvlp a Comprehensive Hlth and Rehab Facility*, US Hlth and Rehab, 1972.

LALONDE, Kathryn Nan (Pgh) 100 Great Pl Ne, Albuquerque NM 87113 B 1946 D 12/19/1992 P 10/19/1993 Bp Alden Moinet Hathaway. m 9/5/2004 Walter Joseph LaLonde. Hope in the Desert Eps Ch 2001-2004; S Mk's On The Mesa Epis Ch Albuquerque NM 1993-2000.

LALONDE, Walter Joseph (Pgh) 139 N Jefferson Ave, Canonsburg PA 15317 **S Andr's Epis Ch Las Cruces NM 2015-** B Syracuse NY 1961 s James & Phyl-

lis. AAS Cmnty Coll of New Mex 1996; MDiv TESM 2014; MDiv Trin Sch for Mnstry 2014. D 1/10/2015 P 7/25/2015 Bp Dorsey McConnell. m 9/5/2004 Kathryn Nan LaLonde. S Thos' Epis Ch Canonsburg PA 2015.

LALOR, Donald Jene (Minn) B 1932 D 5/16/1978 Bp Robert Marshall Anderson.

LAM, Connie M. Ng (Mass) 138 Trement Street, Boston MA 02111 **Chinese Min Dio Massachusetts Boston MA 2013-, Cn for Asian Amer Mnstrs 2013-** B Canton China 1955 d Yuet & Lai. AS Contra Costa Coll 2002; AS Contra Costa Coll 2003; BA Sch for Deacons 2005; CAS CDSP 2012; CAS CDSP 2013. D 6/3/2006 Bp William Edwin Swing P 6/2/2007 Bp Marc Handley Andrus. m 12/13/1981 Santos Lam c 1. Assoc P Chr Epis Ch Sei Ko Kai San Francisco CA 2011-2013; Assoc P True Sunshine Par San Francisco CA 2007-2010; Asst Cler S Jas Epis Ch San Francisco CA 2006-2007; Mem of COM Dio California San Francisco CA 2011-2013, Pres of Asian Cmsn 2009-2013. connienglam@diomass.org

LAM, Peter (LI) 33 Howard Pl, Waldwick NJ 07463 B HK 1942 s Chap & Sheh. BA U of Hong Kong HK 1965; LTh UTS Hk 1971; MDiv Queens Coll 1976; MDiv GTS 1983. Trans 8/9/1996 Bp Orris George Walker Jr. m 11/11/1972 Nancy Wai Ling Lam c 2. Dio Long Island Garden City NY 1992-2014; Serv Ch Of Hong Kong 1972-1989; Port Chapl SCI. Auth, "The Ord Of H Comm w Explanation"; Auth, "Mus For The Morning," *Evening Prayers & H Comm*.

LAM, Vivian P (LI) 500 S Country Rd, Bay Shore NY 11706 B Hong Kong 1977 d Peter & Nancy. BA NYU 1998; MDiv CDSP 2009. D 6/22/2009 Bp James Hamilton Ottley P 1/16/2010 Bp Lawrence C Provenzano. m 12/15/2011 Matthew Bascom Guffin. S Ptr's by-the-Sea Epis Ch Bay Shore NY 2009-2011.

LA MACCHIA, James R (Mass) 32 Mountain Ash Dr, Kingston MA 02364 **Trin Par of Newton Cntr Newton Cntr MA 2016-** B Brookline MA 1952 s Robert & Elizabeth. BA U of Massachusetts 1973; MA U of Massachusetts 1976; MA EDS 1990. D 10/15/1994 P 5/25/1995 Bp Douglas Edwin Theuner. R Par Of The Mssh Auburndale MA 2012-2015; Chapl St. Mk's Sch of Southborough Inc. Southborough MA 2008-2012; Angl Chapl Andover Newton TS 1996-1998; Assoc S Chris's Ch Hampstead NH 1995-1998; Cur S Dav's Ch Salem NH 1994-1995. Auth, "The Riches of the Word of God," Polygraphia Ltd., 2001. Contemplative Outreach 1999; Fllshp of S Jn 1989; NAES 1998-2012; Newton Cler Assn 2012. cl Soc S Mk's Sch 1998; Phi Beta Kappa U of Mass at Amherst 1973; Commonwealth Schlr St of Massachusetts 1969.

LAMAZARES, Gabriel (NY) 4312 46th St, Sunnyside NY 11104 **Vic All SS' Epis Ch Long Island City NY 2016-** B San Juan PR 1971 s Avelino & Sara. BA Boston Coll 1992; MDiv GTS 2010. D 6/19/2010 Bp Michael B Curry P 1/8/2011 Bp Michael Hanley. m 10/26/2009 Robert T Milner. Assoc The Ch Of S Lk In The Fields New York NY 2013-2016; P St Lukes Chap New York NY 2013; Asst S Mich And All Ang Ch Portland OR 2010-2013. vicar@allsaintssunnyside.org

LAMB, Jan M (NC) 3064 Colony Rd Apt D, Durham NC 27705 **Tchr The Hill Cntr Durham NC 1985-** B Hattiesburg MS 1951 BA Millsaps Coll 1973; MEd U of Texas 1976. D 6/3/2006 Bp Michael B Curry. c 2.

✠ **LAMB, The Rt Rev Jerry Alban** (NCal) 1065 Villita Loop, Las Cruces NM 88007 **Ret Bp of Nthrn California The Epis Dio Nthrn California Sacramento CA 2007-, Bp of Nthrn California 1991-2006** B Denver CO 1940 s Dale & Mary. BA S Thos Sem 1964; MA S Thos Sem 1966; MA U of Oregon 1973; CDSP 1992. Rec 3/1/1977 as Deacon Bp Matthew Paul Bigliardi Con 6/9/1991 for The Episcopal NCal. m 8/7/1971 Jane M Lamb c 1. Provsnl Bp of San Joaquin Epis Dio San Joaquin Modesto CA 2008-2011; Asst Dio Oregon Portland OR 1988-1991, Dn Sthrn Conv 1982-1988, Dioc Coun 1979-1981; R Trin Epis Ch Ashland Ashland OR 1980-1988; Asst Emm Ch Coos Bay OR 1978-1980; Asst S Mary's Epis Ch Eugene OR 1977-1978; Serv RC Ch 1966-1971.

LAMB, Ridenour Newcomb (Ga) 2425 Cherry Laurel Ln., Albany GA 31705 **D The Epis Ch Of S Jn And S Mk Albany GA 2009-** B Albany GA 1949 d Robert & Muriel. AD U of Nevada at Reno 1979; EFM U So 2007. D 6/13/2009 Bp Henry Irving Louttit. m 9/20/1969 Donald Lamb c 3.

LAMB, Thomas Jennings (Chi) 503 Macon Dr, Rockford IL 61109 B Norwalk CT 1937 s Roger & Dorothy. BTh Queens Coll 1984. Trans 10/19/1990 Bp Frank Tracy Griswold III. Vic S Bride's Epis Ch Oregon IL 1990-2008; Serv Ch Of Can 1984-1990; Dn Of The Rockford Dnry.

LAMB, Trevor Vanderveer (CFla) 316 Ocean Dunes Rd, Daytona Beach FL 32118 **D S Jas In Ormond Bch 1988-** B Bayshore NY 1947 s Trevor & June. BA Colg 1968; JD U of Florida 1971. D 2/4/1976 Bp William Hopkins Folwell. m 2/7/1975 Cynthia Stiles. D Gr Epis Ch Inc Port Orange FL 1979-1988; D S Mary's Epis Ch Daytona Bch FL 1976-1979.

LAMB, Watson (La) 10701 Saint Francis Dr, Philadelphia MS 39350 **Ch Of The H Sprt New Orleans LA 2017-** B Greenwood MS 1985 s Henry & Rebecca. BA Mississippi St U 2007; MDiv Sewanee: The U So, TS 2011. D 6/4/2011 P 12/4/2011 Bp Duncan Montgomery Gray III. m 5/3/2008 Maria Katherine Isay Lamb c 3. Cur S Lk's Ch Baton Rouge LA 2015-2017, 2013-2015; D S Fran Of Assisi Ch Philadelphia MS 2011-2013.

L

LAMBERT, Bob (Mil) 6303 Partridge Hills Dr, Mount Pleasant WI 53406 **P-in-c S Lk's Ch Racine WI 2013-; Int S Dav's Epis Ch Aurora IL 2012-** B Los Angeles CA 1949 s Fred & Rita. AA Pasadena City Coll 1971; BA California St U 1973; MDiv Nash 1977; MS So Dakota St U 1991. D 11/4/1979 P 2/1/1981 Bp Walter H Jones. m 6/14/1986 Jan M Harvey. Int S Lk's Epis Ch Milwaukee WI 2011-2012; Int S Dunst's Ch Madison WI 2008-2010; Int S Lk's Ch Whitewater WI 2005-2008; Int S Andr's Ch Milwaukee WI 2004-2005; Int S Alb's Ch Sussex WI 2002-2004; R S Dav Of Wales Ch New Berlin WI 2000-2002; On Track Mnstry Lexington NE 1999-2000; S Pauls Epis Ch Arapahoe NE 1995-1999; P-in-c S Ptr's In The Vlly Lexington NE 1995-1999; Non-par 1983-1995; P-in-c Chr Ch Chamberlain SD 1979-1983. priestofstlukes@gmail.com

LAMBERT, Dave (Ala) Episcopal Church of the Epiphany, 1338 Montevallo Rd, Leeds AL 35094 B Montgomery AL 1955 s James & Eva. EFM Sewanee: The U So, TS; BS Chem Engr U Of Florida. D 10/1/2016 Bp John Mckee Sloan Sr. m 9/12/1975 Janet L Hood c 2. DeaconDave2016@gmail.com

LAMBERT, Gary (Mil) 205 Nichols Rd, Monona WI 53716 B Stevens Pt WI 1948 s Donald & Aune. BA MI SU 1976; MDiv SWTS 1986. D 6/14/1986 Bp James Winchester Montgomery P 12/13/1986 Bp Frank Tracy Griswold III. m 9/22/1973 Jeri S Lambert c 3. S Matt's Ch Kenosha WI 2011-2012; S Edmunds Ch Milwaukee WI 2009-2011; S Ptr's Ch Milwaukee WI 2009-2011; S Aidans Ch Hartford WI 2008-2009; R S Lk's Ch Madison WI 1995-2008; Vic Gr Epis Ch Galena IL 1989-1995; Vic S Paul's Ch Savanna IL 1989-1995; Asst P S Ptr's Epis Ch Sycamore IL 1986-1990; Dio Chicago Chicago IL 1986-1988. 3rd OHC.

LAMBERT, George A (Me) 259 Essex St. Apt. 3, Bansor ME 04401 B Springfield MA 1947 s Arthur & Evelyn. MDiv EDS 1992; RA NYU 1997. D 5/30/1992 P 5/1/1993 Bp David Elliot Johnson. c 2. Gr Epis Ch Bath ME 2014-2015; P Chr Ch Gardiner ME 2012-2014; Int R S Jas Ch Old Town ME 2008-2011; Int S Geo's Epis Ch Sanford ME 2007-2008; Assoc S Lk/San Lucas Chelsea MA 1998-2000; Int Chr Ch Hyde Pk MA 1994-1997; Dio Massachusetts Boston MA 1992-1995; The Cathd Ch Of S Paul Boston MA 1992-1994.

LAMBERT, John Peck (Oly) 26621 128th Ave South East, Kent WA 98030 B Oklahoma City OK 1945 s Robinson & Page. BA U of Oklahoma 1967; MA U of Oklahoma 1968; MDiv VTS 1971. D 6/29/1971 P 12/18/1971 Bp Chilton R Powell. m 1/25/1964 Jean Bates Lambert c 3. R S Jas Epis Ch Kent WA 1996-2003; Int Emm Epis Ch Mercer Island WA 1994-1996; R Ch Of The Resurr Bellevue WA 1980-1993; Assoc All SS Epis Ch Kansas City MO 1976-1980; Asst Chr Epis Ch S Jos MO 1973-1976; Cur S Marg's Ch Lawton OK 1971-1973. Ord of S Helena - P Assoc. 1981; Ord of S Lk 1973; WBHS 1976.

✠ LAMBERT, The Rt Rev Paul Emil (Dal) 1439 Tranquilla Dr., Dallas TX 75218 B Reno NV 1950 s Paul & Norma. BA San Francisco St U 1972; MDiv Nash 1975. D 6/24/1975 P 6/9/1976 Bp Victor Manuel Rivera Con 7/12/2008 for Dal. m 5/24/1975 Sally Lynne Lambert c 3. Bp Suffr of Dallas Dio Dallas Dallas TX 2008-2016, Cn 2002-2008; R S Jas Epis Ch Texarkana TX 1987-2002; Assoc The Epis Ch Of The H Nativ Plano TX 1984-1987; R S Jn's Ch Great Bend KS 1981-1984; Asst The Epis Ch Of The Trsfg Dallas TX 1978-1981; Epis Dio San Joaquin Modesto CA 1977-1978; S Andr's Ch Taft CA 1977-1978; S Mths Ch Oakdale CA 1975-1977; S Paul's Epis Ch Modesto CA 1975-1977. Hon DD Nash TS 2009. lambert.paul59@gmail.com

LAMBERT, Sally Anne (Ore) 8265 Sw Canyon Ln, Portland OR 97225 **Died 10/11/2016** B Parsons KS 1938 d Dale & Sarah. EFM Sewanee: The U So, TS; BA Washburn U 1960; MA Geo Fox U 1965; MA Geo Fox U 1965; EFM Sewanee: The U So, TS 1969. D 6/18/1983 Bp John Forsythe Ashby. c 2. Adj Fac, Grad Sch Geo Fox U 2003-2016; D S Phil The D Epis Ch Portland OR 2002-2012; D S Jas Epis Ch Portland OR 1987-2002; D Chr Cathd Salina KS 1983-1987.

✠ LAMBERT III, The Rt Rev William Jay (Eau) 510 S Farwell St, Eau Claire WI 54701 **Bp of Eau Claire Dio Eau Claire Eau Claire WI 2013-** B Detroit MI 1948 s William & Louise. BA Rol 1970; MA U GA 1976; MDiv Nash 1981. D 6/29/1981 P 5/1/1982 Bp Emerson Paul Haynes Con 3/16/2013 for Eau. m 8/23/1969 May Ruth B Lambert c 3. R S Jas Epis Ch Leesburg FL 2007-2013; R S Bon Ch Thiensville WI 1990-2007; Chapl USNR 1986-2008; R S Ptr's Ch Milwaukee WI 1983-1990; Asst Calv Ch Indn Rk Bc FL 1981-1983; Pres Stndg Com Dio Milwaukee Milwaukee WI 1996-1997; Cler Ldrshp Proj 1995-1996, Fin Com 1995. administrator@dioec.net

LAMBORN, Amy B (Tenn) The General Theological Seminary, 440 West 21st Street, New York NY 10011 **P-in-c Dio Tennessee Nashville TN 2016-; The GTS New York NY 2014-, Fac 2011-2014; Epis Partnr For Catechesit 1996-** B Dyersburg TN 1969 d Gordon & Carolyn. BA Un U Jackson TN 1991; MDiv Sewanee: The U So, TS 1996; PhD UTS NYC 2009. D 6/24/1997 Bp Edward Witker Jones. m 5/28/1994 Robert C Lamborn c 1. S Lk's Ch Somers NY 2015; Theol in Res Chr Ch Bronxville NY 2009-2011; R S Mk's Ch Plainfield IN 2000-2004; Cur Chr Ch Cathd Indianapolis IN 1998-2000; Asst For Educ And Sprtl Formation 1997-1998; Asst Dio Indianapolis Indianapolis IN 1997-1998; Asst S Andr's Epis Ch Greencastle IN 1997-1998. amy.lamborn@gmail.com

LAMBORN, Robert C (Tenn) Otey Memorial Parish, Po Box 267, Sewanee TN 37375 **R Otey Memi Par Ch Sewanee TN 2016-; R Chr Ch Riverdale Bronx NY 2004-** B Fort Oglethorpe GA 1965 s Robert & Elinor. BMus U GA 1987; BA U GA 1987; MM Indiana U 1989; MA Indiana U 1989; MDiv Sewanee: The U So, TS 1994; DMin VTS 2007. D 6/24/1994 P 3/29/1995 Bp Edward Witker Jones. m 5/28/1994 Amy B Bentley c 1. Ch Of S Jas The Less Scarsdale NY 2015; Int S Lk's Ch Katonah NY 2012-2015; R Chr Ch Riverdale Bronx NY 2004-2012; R S Jn's Epis Ch Crawfordsvlle IN 1996-2004; Mem, Stewadship Cmsn Dio Indianapolis Indianapolis IN 1995-2000, Mem, Wrshp & Mus Cmsn 1995-1997, Mem, Stndg Com 1997-1999; Precentor Chr Ch Cathd Indianapolis IN 1994-1996. oteyparishrector@gmail.com

LAMKIN, Melissa Warren (Ct) 139 W 91st St, NY NY 10024 **Trin Sch New York NY 2016-** B New Rochelle NY 1962 d Robert & Caroline. BA Br 1984; MDiv UTS 2015. D 10/3/2015 P 4/14/2016 Bp Laura Ahrens. c 3.

LAMMING, Sarah Rebecca (Md) 1601 Pleasant Plains Road, Annapolis MD 21409 **S Mary Magd Ch Silver Sprg MD 2016-; S Andr's Epis Ch Coll Pk MD 2015-** B Lincoln England 1977 d John & Sheila. BA Middlesex U 2002; CTM Westcott Hse Cambridge GB 2004; CTM Westcott Hse Cambridge GB 2004. Trans 2/10/2011 Bp Charles Ellsworth Bennison Jr. m 1/4/2013 Diana E Carroll. Yth Formation S Marg's Ch Annapolis MD 2011-2015; Dio Pennsylvania Philadelphia PA 2011; Asst to the Vic Geo W So Ch of Advoc Philadelphia PA 2010-2011.

LAMONTAGNE, Allen Allen (Eas) 2019 Featherwood Dr W, Jacksonville FL 32233 **Assoc S Jn's Cathd Jacksonville FL 2017-** B Springfield MA 1950 s Robert & Elizabeth. BA Barrington Coll 1975; MDiv Ya Berk 1994. D 6/10/1995 Bp Clarence Nicholas Coleridge P 1/20/1996 Bp Donald Purple Hart. c 2. The Ch Of The H Sprt Ocean City MD 2014-2016; R S Paul's Par Kent Chestertown MD 2006-2014; R S Paul's Epis Ch Put In Bay OH 1998-2006; Cur Trin Ch Torrington CT 1995-1998. Berk's Grad Soc 1994.

LAMPE, Christine Kay (WK) 710 N Main St, Garden City KS 67846 B Hanover KS 1951 d Alvin & Virginia. BA Marymount Coll 1982; MA K SU 1991. D 9/1/2007 Bp James Marshall Adams Jr. c 1.

LAMPERT, Richard B (SwFla) 826 Hampton Wood Ct, Sarasota FL 34232 **P Assoc for Pstr Care Ch of the Redeem Sarasota 2017-** B Washington DC 1941 s James & Margery. BA Lawr 1964; MSW Boston Coll 1969; BD EDS 1970; DMin VTS 2000. D 6/14/1970 P 6/1/1971 Bp Ned Cole. m 11/21/1973 Molly Ann Lampert c 3. Hisp Mssnr S Mary's Epis Ch Palmetto FL 2013-2015; Asst Ch Of The Redeem Sarasota FL 2009-2010; Hisp Mssnr/P Assist. Ch of the Redeem Sarasota FL 2006-2012; R The Epis Ch Of The Gd Shpd Venice FL 2001-2006; Gr Ch Un City NJ 1996-2001; R S Jn The Evang S Paul MN 1988-1996; Urban Mssn Com Dio Massachusetts Boston MA 1985-1988; Vic S Steph's Epis Ch Boston MA 1983-1988; R Chr Ch Binghamton NY 1978-1983; Dio Nthrn Mex Nuevo Leon 1975-1978; Serv Angl Ch of Mex 1975-1977; Evang Cmsn Dio Minnesota Minneapolis MN 1990-1994. Soc of S Jn the Evang 1985.

LAMPHERE, Mary Kathryn (Spok) 15319 E 8th Ave, Spokane Valley WA 99037 B Pueblo CO 1945 d Jobie & Ada. BSN U of Utah 1980; MN Estrn WA U 1994; Teem Prog CDSP 2014. D 10/19/2014 P 6/6/2015 Bp James E Waggoner Jr. m 3/30/1963 Dale Alan Lamphere c 3.

LANCASTER, James Mansell (Miss) 2721 Brumbaugh Rd, Ocean Springs MS 39564 B Greenville MS 1940 s Archie & Irma. BS Delta St U 1964; MS U of Sthrn Mississippi 1974. D 1/4/2003 Bp Alfred Marble Jr. m 8/5/1977 Emily Williams Lancaster.

LANCASTER, Robert Vaughan (WNY) 537 Cortez St., Sante Fe NM 87501 **Died 5/25/2016** B Wilmington DE 1921 s Vaughan & Ida. BA U of Delaware 1946; MA U of Delaware 1949; BTh PDS 1955; PhD Syr 1974. D 7/23/1955 Bp John Brooke Mosley P 11/1/1955 Bp Russell S Hubbard. m 6/25/1943 Serene Lancaster. Ret 1987-2016; R Trin Ch Lancaster NY 1960-1965; Vic S Ptr's Ch Pomeroy WA 1955-1960; Exec Coun Dio Wstrn New York Tonawanda NY 1963-1965; Bec Dio Spokane Spokane WA 1958-1960. Auth, "Ella Middleton Tybout:De Writer". Ord Of S Ben.

LANCE, Philip J (Los) 6464 Sunset Blvd., Suite 845, Los Angeles CA 90028 B Redlands CA 1959 s Wayne & Jessie. BA Wheaton Coll 1981; MDiv GTS 1987; Ph.D. Pacifica Grad Inst 2013. D 6/20/1987 P 1/1/1988 Bp Oliver Bailey Garver Jr. m 12/13/2013 Raul Santos Garcia. Pueblo Nuevo Epis Ch Los Angeles CA 1993-2001; Dio Los Angeles Los Angeles CA 1987-1992; Dioc Jubilee Off 1987-1990; Bishops Assoc Dioc Urban Mnstry 1987-1989.

LANCTOT, Mervyn John (Me) 832 Wicklow St., Winnipeg MB R3T 0H7 Canada **Serv Angl Ch of Can 2005-** B Melfort Sask Canada 1954 BA Can Nazarene Coll 1991; BTh S Paul U Ottawa CA 1995. Trans 8/9/2003 Bp Chilton Richardson Knudsen. m 4/26/1974 Susan E Lanctot c 2. S Matt's Epis Ch Lisbon Falls ME 2003-2005; R S Matt's Epis Ch Lisbon Falls ME 2003-2005; Serv Angl Ch of Can Can 1995-2003.

LANDER, Barbara Temple (ND) 319 S 5th St, Grand Forks ND 58201 B Denver CO 1928 d Wesley & Ethel. DSW Stephens Coll 1948; U Denv 1956. D 10/8/1999 Bp Andrew Fairfield. c 1.

LANDER III, James Rollin (Los) 1101 E Terrace St. #202, Seattle WA 98122 B Minneapolis MN 1976 s James & Donna. BA Emory U 1998; MDiv GTS 2003; MPA U of Washington 2009. D 8/17/2003 P 3/13/2004 Bp J Neil Alexander. S Fran' Par Palos Verdes Estates CA 2015-2016; Vic Faith Epis Ch Laguna Niguel CA 2015; Vic S Columba's Epis Ch Kent WA 2010-2014; Assoc R for Chr Formation S Augustines In-The-Woods Epis Par Freeland WA 2007-2009; Epis Plse Coordntr The Fund For Theol Educ 2004-2005; Assoc R S Alb's Epis Ch Los Angeles CA 2003-2004.

LANDER, Stephen King (Minn) 5029 Girard Ave S, Minneapolis MN 55419 **Sprtl Dir Sprtl Direction 2009-; Adj Prof S Mary's U 1998-** B Grand Forks ND 1951 s Edward & Barbara. MA Antioch/W 1983; PhD Cntr For Psychol Study Albane CA 1993; MDiv SWTS 2002. D 6/15/2002 P 12/17/2002 Bp James Louis Jelinek. m 8/27/2008 Benjamin Dann Lander c 2. S Jn The Bapt Epis Ch Minneapolis MN 2007; Int S Clem's Ch S Paul MN 2005-2006; Int S Matt's Ch S Paul MN 2004, 2002-2003; Int S Jn In The Wilderness S Paul MN 2002-2003.

LANDERS, Davidson Texada (Ala) 5220 Midway Cir, Tuscaloosa AL 35406 **Ret 2001-** B New Orleans LA 1943 s Edward & Mary. BA Louisiana Coll 1966; MDiv Sewanee: The U So, TS 1970. D 6/22/1970 P 5/1/1971 Bp Iveson Batchelor Noland. c 3. Int Ch Of The Ascen Montgomery AL 2007; Int Chr Ch Tuscaloosa AL 2004-2005; Int S Barth's Epis Ch Florence AL 2002-2003; R S Lk's Ch Scottsboro AL 1998-2001; R Ch Of The Adv Nashville TN 1988-1997; R S Andr's Epis Ch Collierville TN 1979-1988; Assoc Gr - S Lk's Ch Memphis TN 1975-1979; R S Phil's Ch New Orleans LA 1973-1975; Cur S Andr's Epis Ch New Orleans LA 1971-1973; Chapl NW St U in Natchitoches LA 1970-1971; Vic S Paul's Ch Winnfield LA 1970-1971. DD EDS 2013; Alum Ldrshp Memphis 1981; Pres St. Lk's Soc, U So, TS 1970; Pres St. Lk's Soc, U So, TS 1969.

LANDERS JR, Edward Leslie (Tenn) 6536 Jocelyn Hollow Rd, Nashville TN 37205 B Alexandria LA 1935 s Edward & Mary. BA Louisiana Coll 1958; MDiv Sewanee: The U So, TS 1965; Van 1969. D 6/24/1965 Bp Iveson Batchelor Noland P 5/1/1966 Bp Girault M Jones. m 6/18/1958 Carolyn Landers c 2. Cov Assn Inc Nashville TN 1994-1995; Chf Admin Dio Tennessee Nashville TN 1991-1993, 1986-1993, Asst To Bp 1985-1991; Urban & Reg Mnstry Nashville TN 1977-1985; Chr Ch Cathd Nashville TN 1975-1977; Assoc Chr In Tn TN 1975-1977; Vic Bp Polk Memi Mssn Leesville LA 1965-1968; Exec Vice-Pres Cov Assn Inc; Secy-Treas Epis Fam Ntwk; Secy ESMA. Auth, "Plnng Skills For Profsnl Ministers". ESMA, Epis Fam Netwk. Outstanding Cmnty Proj Ford Fndt.

LANDERS, Gail Joan (Md) 12400 Manor Road, PO Box 4001, Glen Arm MD 21057 B Baltimore MD 1958 d James & Myrtle. AA Essex Cmnty Coll 1977. D 6/6/2009 Bp John L Rabb. m 8/9/1997 Michael Landers c 4.

LANDERS, Greg Leroy (NY) 2150 Baileys Corner Rd, Wall Township NJ 07719 **Non-par 1985-** B Cayonville OR 1953 s Marvin & Pauline. BA Portland St U 1980; MDiv GTS 1983; MS CUNY 1985. D 10/24/1984 Bp Paul Moore Jr P 11/23/1985 Bp Walter Decoster Dennis Jr.

LANDERS, Kay Marie (Los) 1136 Scenic View St, Upland CA 91784 **Mgr Of Pstr Care Alameda Cnty Med Cntr Fairmont CA 1997-** B Oakland CA 1935 d Edward & Leah. BA San Francisco St U 1979; MA Wheaton Coll 1979; BTh Sch for Deacons 1997. D 6/7/1997 Bp William Edwin Swing. m 6/17/1956 David Leonard Landers c 3. D All SS Epis Ch San Leandro CA 1997-2001. Auth, "Clutched From Cler Reserves," Chapl Today, 2002; Auth, "God'S Fuel," Mavian Holdings Ltd., 1998; Auth, "A Heart For God," Sekand Printing Co, 1994; Auth, "I Wonder What'S Going To Happen?," Wrld Radio Mssy Fllshp, 1991; Auth, "Landscape Of The Poor," Wrld Radio Mssy Fllshp, 1988; Auth, "Catch A Wild Pony," Wrld Radio Mssy Fllshp, 1986; Auth, "Antenna Country," Moody Press, 1972. Assn Profsnl Chapl 1997. Caregiver Of The Year Alameda Cnty Med Cntr 2002.

LANDERS, Sylvia C (Neb) 206 Westridge Drive, Norfolk NE 68701 **D Trin Epis Ch Norfolk NE 1989-** B Minden NE 1935 d Clarence & Hildur. Nebraska St Coll 1955; EFM Sewanee: The U So, TS 1987. D 8/25/1989 Bp James Daniel Warner. m 9/17/1987 Larry Ray Jones c 3. Liturg Cmsn Dio Nebraska Omaha NE 1996-2006, Exec Cmsn 1990-1994, Bp Search Com 1989-1990, EFM Mentor 1987-1996. NAAD 1989.

LANDRETH, Robert Dean (Mass) 7 Mechanic Sq, Marblehead MA 01945 **Ret 1998-** B Modesto CA 1926 s Clifton & Zala. BA San Jose St U 1950; MA San Jose St U 1957. D 6/19/1966 Bp James Albert Pike P 5/28/1981 Bp Charles Shannon Mallory. m 7/8/1950 Jean Emerson Miller. Assoc Wyman Memi Ch of St Andr Marblehead MA 1999-2007; Vic Ch Of The H Sprt Campbell CA 1994-1998; Assoc S Fran Epis Ch San Jose CA 1981-1998; COM Dio El Camino Real Salinas CA 1984-1998. The Bp's Cross Bp Richard Shimpfy 1995.

LANDRITH, Richard Stanley (EO) 123 S G St, Lakeview OR 97630 **Stated Supply Pstr First Presb Ch Lakeview OR 2005-; P-in-c S Lk's Ch Lakeview OR 2005-** B 1949 s Richard & Margaret. Arizona St U; BA U of Idaho 1974. D 2/2/1991 Bp James Edward Krotz P 7/12/2005 Bp William O Gregg. m 5/31/1998 Marsha Landrith.

LANDRY, Brad (WTex) St Paul's Episcopal Church, 1018 E Grayson St, San Antonio TX 78208 **S Paul's Epis Ch San Antonio TX 2013-** B Columbia, MO 1981 s Larry & Janine. BA Samford U 2003; MDiv Sewanee: The U So, TS 2010; MDiv The TS at The U So 2010. D 5/19/2010 Bp Henry Nutt Parsley Jr P 12/7/2010 Bp John Mckee Sloan Sr. m 5/25/2002 Rebecca Elizabeth Landry c 3. Asst Ch Of The Nativ Epis Huntsville AL 2010-2013. rector@stpauls-satx.org

LANDRY, Robert Wayne (Me) **D S Andr's Ch Millinocket ME 2005-** B Bangor ME 1954 s Edgar & Mary. BD U of Maine 2004; Bangor TS 2005. D 5/22/2005 Bp Chilton Richardson Knudsen. m 5/14/1977 Catherine Landry c 3.

LANDWER, Virginia Bess (SeFla) 401 66th Street Ocean, Marathon FL 33050 **S Columba Epis Ch Marathon FL 2000-** B Platterville WI 1929 D 10/17/2000 Bp Leo Frade.

LANE III, Calvin (SO) St George's Episcopal Church, 5520 Far Hills Ave, Dayton OH 45429 **S Geo's Epis Ch Dayton OH 2014-; Prof Nash Nashotah WI 2012-** B Rocky Mount NC 1980 s Lewis & Ann. BA U NC 2002; PhD U of Iowa 2010; MTS Nash 2011. D 6/11/2011 Bp Hugo Luis Pina-Lopez P 12/13/2011 Bp Morris King Thompson Jr. m 7/24/2010 Denise D Kettering-Lane c 2. P-in-c S Mary's Ch Franklin LA 2011-2014. Monograph, "The Laudians and the Elizabethan Ch," *Rel Cultures in the Early Mod Wrld*, Pickering & Chatto, 2013.

LANE III, Edward Jacob (Ky) D 4/17/2010 Bp Ted Gulick Jr.

LANE, John Charles (Oly) 311 Ridge Dr, Port Townsend WA 98368 B Nampa ID 1938 s Irvin & Priscilla. U of Washington 1958; BA The Coll of Idaho 1961. D 5/14/1972 Bp John Raymond Wyatt. m 12/26/1958 Jacqueline K Gleason c 4. Dir Dio Corp- Docese of Spokane 1973-1976; Dir Diocc Corp Dio Spokane Spokane WA 1972-1975, Stdng Com 1971-1973; Dir Dio Corp- Dio Spokane 1973-1976. Auth, "Forum For Contemporary Hist"; Auth, "Bank Admin".

LANE, John David (SwVa) 307 Rainbow Dr, Staunton VA 24401 **Trin Ch Staunton VA 2009-, Ret 1987-2007** B Princeton NJ 1944 s Howard & Doris. BA Amh 1966; MDiv GTS 1972; DMin Drew U 1991. D 6/3/1972 Bp Paul Moore Jr P 12/9/1972 Bp Horace W B Donegan. m 9/4/1971 Elizabeth Bartelink c 3. Structure Cmsn ECUSA 2000-2006; Exec Coun Dom And Frgn Mssy Soc- Epis Ch Cntr New York NY 1994-2000, GBEC 1982-1988, Stndg Cmsn on Structure 2000-2006, Epis Life-Bd of Gvnr 1997-2000, Stndg Cmsn on Peace w Justice 1994-1997; Exec Coun ECUSA 1994-2000; Ed The Epis Profsnl Pages 1983-1990; GBEC ECUSA 1982-1988; Auth Forw Day by Day 1982-1983; Dio Louisiana New Orleans LA 1978-1982; Ed Leaven 1978-1981; R Chap Of The H Comf New Orleans LA 1975-1987; Cur Ch Of The H Comf Charlotte NC 1972-1975; Tchr Peace Corps Baitadi Nepal 1966-1968. Auth, "Two - Five - Oh," Heritage, 1996; Auth, "Plain Preaching," Heritage, 1996; Ed, "Trin Ch as an Instrument of Serv in the Staunton Area," U of Michigan, 1991.

LANE, Johnny (Ga) Route #4, Leslie Road, Box 1455, Americus GA 31709 **D Calv Ch Americus GA 2012-** B Clay Sink FL 1933 s John & Pearl. BS U of Florida 1960. D 11/11/1990 Bp Harry Woolston Shipps. m 12/16/1978 Elizabeth H Lane c 4. D The Epis Ch Of S Jn And S Mk Albany GA 1999-2007.

LANE, Joseph Andrew (Cal) 527 E Woodbury Rd, Altadena CA 91001 **Asstg P S Mk's Par Altadena CA 2015-; Ret Ret 2012-** B Pine Bluff AR 1954 s Ethiel & Maxine. BA U of Arkansas 1976; MDiv CDSP 1995; DMin SWTS 2011. D 6/3/1995 P 6/1/1996 Bp William Edwin Swing. m 11/4/2008 Jay Framson. Vic Ch Of The Redeem San Rafael CA 2010-2012; P Assoc S Bede's Epis Ch Menlo Pk CA 2008-2010, Assoc R 1997-2000; R Gd Shpd Epis Ch Belmont CA 2000-2008; Cur/Asst R S Matt's Epis Ch San Mateo CA 1995-1997.

LANE, Keith Cecil (NY) 487 Hudson St, New York NY 10014 B The Bronx NY 1948 s Cecil & Zelphia. MDiv GTS; BA New Sch U 2008. D 3/5/2011 P 9/10/2011 Bp Mark Sean Sisk. m 5/7/1968 Marion Lane c 1. Ch Of S Simon The Cyrenian New Rochelle NY 2012-2014.

LANE, Nancy Upson (CNY) **Fndr/ A Healing Mnstry Elmira NY 1993-** D 6/11/1983 Bp Ned Cole P 4/10/1984 Bp O'Kelley Whitaker.

LANE, Peter Austin (RI) 200 Meshanticut Valley Pkwy, Cranston RI 02920 **P S Dav's On The Hill Epis Ch Cranston RI 2011-** B East Providence RI 1957 s Howard & Elinor. BA U of New Hampshire 1982; Cert Kennedy Sch of Ethics at Georgetown U 1997; MDiv VTS 1998. D 6/13/1998 Bp Philip Alan Smith P 2/27/1999 Bp Douglas Edwin Theuner. m 9/25/1993 Kate Austin Reed c 2. Vic Ch Of Our Sav Monroe WA 2009-2011; Vic Trin Ch Hampton NH 2000-2008; Cur Trin Ch Newport RI 1998-2000; COM Dio New Hampshire Concord NH 2002-2007. "Reaching Out: Pstr Care w The Elderly," Self-Pub, 1997.

LANE, Peter Carlson (Chi) 4945 S Dorchester Ave, Chicago IL 60615 **R Ch Of S Paul And The Redeem Chicago IL 2010-, R 2010-, Asst 2007-2010** B Oak Park IL 1977 s Robert & Patricia. BA U Chi 1999; MDiv PrTS 2003; STM GTS 2007. D 6/9/2007 Bp Charles Ellsworth Bennison Jr P 12/15/2007 Bp Victor Alfonso Scantlebury. m 7/3/1999 Erin Pfautz Lane c 2. Tchr Nveva Esperanza Acad 2003-2006. pcl@sp-r.org

LANE, Stephen Edward (WNY) 371 Delaware Ave, Buffalo NY 14202 **Bexley Seabury Fed Chicago IL 2017-; Pres Epis Partnership For Mssn and Outreach Dio WNY 2012-; D Trin Epis Ch Buffalo NY 2009-, D 2009-** B Whittier 1958 s Warren & Virginia. BS U of Arizona 1985. D 6/29/2008 Bp Michael Garrison. m 5/21/1985 Ellyn Lane c 3.

✠ **LANE, The Rt Rev Stephen Taylor** (Me) 84 Parsons Rd., Portland ME 04103 **Bp of Maine Dio Maine Portland ME 2008-** B Batavia NY 1949 s William & Elizabeth. BA U Roch 1971; MDiv Colgate Rochester Crozer DS 1978; MDiv CRDS 1978. D 10/28/1978 P 5/1/1979 Bp Robert Rae Spears Jr Con 5/3/2008 for Me. m 7/10/1976 Gretchen J Farnum c 3. Cn Dio Rochester Henrietta 2000-2008; R Zion Epis Ch Palmyra NY 1985-2000; Assoc Chr Ch Corning NY 1984-1985, Asst 1978-1983; Ch of the Redeem Addison NY 1979-1983. DD Bex 2008; Cler Ldrshp Proj 1995; Rossiter Schlr Bex 1983. slane@episcopalmaine.org

LANE, Wendy DeFoe (Chi) 1775 W Newport Ct, Lake Forest IL 60045 B Norwalk CT 1941 d Warner & Patricia. BA Barat Coll 1997; MDiv SWTS 2000. D 12/21/2000 P 6/26/2001 Bp Bill Persell. m 7/14/1962 Charles A Lane c 2. Assoc R The Ch Of The H Sprt Lake Forest IL 2004-2010; Assoc R S Simons Ch Arlington Hts IL 2001-2004.

LANE, William Benjamin (Del) 614 Loveville Rd., B-1-I, Hockessin DE 19707 **Ret 2006-** B Baltimore MD 1938 s William & Bessie. BA U of Maryland 1960; MDiv VTS 1963. D 7/26/1963 Bp Noble C Powell P 6/11/1964 Bp Harry Lee Doll. m 8/5/1967 Beverly G B Lane c 1. Int Cathd Ch Of S Jn Wilmington DE 2006-2012; Eccl Crt Dio Bethlehem Bethlehem PA 1998-2006; Dn Cathd Ch Of The Nativ Bethlehem PA 1997-2005; Assoc Chr Ch Christiana Hundred Wilmington DE 1986-1997; Dio Delaware Wilmington 1980-1985; Vic S Nich' Epis Ch Newark DE 1975-1980; Vic S Jas' Epis Ch Parkton MD 1968-1975; Asst Ch Of The Mssh Baltimore MD 1963-1967; Pres Interfaith Hsng Corp.

LANG, Anne Adele (FdL) B Milwaukee WI 1949 d John & Dorothy. BS U of Wisconsin 1981; MS U of Wisconsin 1983. D 11/6/2004 Bp Russell Edward Jacobus. c 3. D All SS Epis Ch Appleton WI 2004-2015.

LANG, Ellen Davis (SD) 3504 E. Woodsedge St., Sioux Falls SD 57108 B Norfolk VA 1939 d Fredrick & Ellen. BS Jas Madison U 1961; MDiv Ya Berk 1988. D 6/9/1990 P 10/7/1991 Bp Arthur Edward Walmsley. c 2. Vic S Paul's Ch Plainfield CT 1991-2005; Cur Chr Ch Ansonia CT 1990-1991.

LANG, Mark William (NwT) 727 W Browning Ave, Pampa TX 79065 **R S Matt's Ch Pampa TX 2014-** B Pampa TX 1952 s Carl & Henny. D 6/8/2013 P 12/18/2013 Bp James Scott Mayer. m 6/26/1976 Karen Cortner Lang c 2.

LANG, Martha Ellen (Ia) 2101 Nettle Ave, Muscatine IA 52761 **Healthcare Chapl U of Iowa Hospitals and Clinics 2011-; D Trin Ch Muscatine IA 2009-, D 1999-2009** B Bloomfield IA 1954 d Crayton Creighton & Zoe. MEd Sthrn Illinois U -Carbondale 1980; MDiv Wartburg TS 2011. D 11/22/1999 Bp Chris Christopher Epting P 1/14/2017 Bp Alan Scarfe. D New Song Epis Ch Coralville IA 2004-2009.

LANG, Nicholas Gerard (Ct) 14 France St, Norwalk CT 06851 **R Par of St Paul's Ch Norwalk Norwalk CT 2003-, 1993-1999** B Orange NJ 1948 s Eugene & Josephine. Seton Hall U 1970; S Andrews TS Jamaica NY 1973; BS U of Bridgeport 1988; MS U of Bridgeport 1989; PhD Cpu San Raphael CA 1997. Rec 1/13/1993 as Priest Bp Arthur Edward Walmsley. Serv Ukranian Orth Ch Of Amer 1973-1993.

LANG, Thomas Andrew (Ore) 2812 Ne Kaster Dr, Hillsboro OR 97124 **D S Gabr Ch Portland OR 2004-** B Patuyent NAS 1958 s William & Mary. D 9/18/2004 Bp Johncy Itty. m 6/20/1981 Kathy Lynn Lang c 2.

LANGDON, Clarence Merle (Chi) 1249 Hedgerow Dr, Grayslake IL 60030 **Mnstry Dvlpmt Dio Chicago Chicago IL 2001-, Dn Elgin Deanry 1990-2001** B Fowler CO 1936 s Ronald & Adadah. BA Colorado St U 1959; STB GTS 1962; U Chi 1968; DMin McCormick TS 1985. D 6/18/1962 P 12/1/1962 Bp Joseph Summerville Minnis. m 5/23/2005 Dewann C Drout c 3. S Mary's Ch Pk Ridge IL 1976-2001; R Gr Epis Ch Freeport IL 1970-1976; R S Geo/S Mths Ch Chicago IL 1965-1970; Cur Ch Of The Ascen Pueblo CO 1962-1965; Cur H Trin Ch Pueblo CO 1962-1965.

LANGDON, David Stetson (Miss) PO Box 40, Parchman MS 38738 **Chapl Parchman Prison 1980-; Long-term Supply Ch Of The Redeem Greenville MS 2011-** B Norfolk NY 1939 s Walter & Ada. STB GTS 1965; DMin Drew U 1977; Cert Assn of Prot Chapl 1985; Cert ACPE 1987; Cert ACPE 1987; Cert Coll of Chapl 1987; STM Sewanee: The U So, TS 1999; MTS Sprg Hill Coll Moblie 2006; non delta St U 2013. D 6/12/1965 P 12/18/1965 Bp Charles Bowen Persell Jr. m 5/26/1990 Louise M Langdon c 4. Int Vic of St. Vincents Dio Mississippi Jackson MS 2011-2017, 2004-2007; All Sts. Grenada, Ms All SS Epis Ch Grenada MS 2010; Parchman Prison Ch Of The Nativ Greenwood MS 1999-2003; Parchman Prison S Geo's Epis Ch Clarksdale MS 1996-1998; S Paul's Ch Leland MS 1994-2008; Asst All SS Epis Ch Lakeland FL 1993-1994; Int S Fran Of Assisi Epis Ch Lake Placid FL 1991-1992; Chapl Bp Gray Inns Davenport Fl. 1987-1994; Dir. of Sprtl Care Wm Crane Gray Inn For Old People Davenport FL 1987-1990; R S Mk's Ch Malone NY 1981-1986; Beaver Cross Dir Dio Albany Greenwich NY 1976-1978; Chapl & Adj. Fac Plattsburgh St U Coll Plattsburgh NY 1973-1979; R Ch Of The Gd Shpd Elizabethtown NY 1966-1981; S Jn's Ch Essex NY 1966-1981; Cur S Steph's Ch Schenectady NY 1965-1967. Auth, "The Episcopate of Theo DuBose Bratton," *Third Bp of Mississippi*, U So, 1999; Auth, *Quality Assurance in Gerontological Chapl*,

APC, 1990; Auth, "Sailing & Gerontology," *BGI News*, 1987; Auth, *Cnfrmtn in a Rural Par*, U. Microfilms, 1973. Assn of Profsnl Chapl 1985; Epis Chapl 1993; OHC 1959. Cmssnr's Coin Cmssnr of Prisons, St of Mississippi 2012; Wm Wiseman Awd Interfaith Allnce of Tulsa, OK 2004.

LANGENFELD, Robert Joseph (Minn) 615 Vermillion St, Hastings MN 55033 **P S Lk's Epis Ch Hastings MN 2010-** B Hastings MN 1951 s Frank & Leona. D 6/24/2009 P 1/9/2010 Bp James Louis Jelinek.

LANGE-SOTO, Anna Beatriz (Cal) 1503 E Campbell Ave, Campbell CA 95008 **Secy Cltn of Epis Latinos 2009-; Chair Migration & Immigration T/F Dio California 2007-; Vic Dio California San Francisco CA 1998-; Mem Latino Cmsn Dio California 1998-** B Douglas AZ 1952 d Harry & Beatriz. BA Stan 1974; MBA Santa Clara U 1989; BTh Dio El Camino Real Sch for Deacons 1995. D 11/20/1993 P 11/18/1997 Bp Richard Lester Shimpfky. m 11/23/2009 Russell L Briggs. Mem Search Com Dio California 2005-2006; Mem Anti-Racism Cmsn Dio California 2004-2007; Mem Anti-Racism Com Exec Coun of TEC 2003-2006; Mem Stndg Com Dio California 2003-2005; Dio Arizona Phoenix AZ 1998; Mem Dioc Coun Dio El Camino Real 1996-1998; Trin Cathd San Jose CA 1996-1998; Treas Centro Latino Dio El Camino Real 1994-1998. Cltn of Epis Latinos 2010; Integrity 1998. St. Steph's Cross Dio of CA Sch for Deacons 1995.

LANGEVIN, Ann Elizabeth (Nev) St Thomas Episcopal Church, 5383 E Owens Ave, Las Vegas NV 89110 B Kansas City MO 1944 d Oliver & Mary. BA U of Missouri 1966; MLA U Denv 1969; Spec U of Wisconsin 1972. D 12/17/2011 Bp Dan Thomas Edwards. m 8/1/1980 Robert Gerard Langevin c 2.

LANGFELDT, John Addington (EO) 1000 Vey Way Apt 361, The Dalles OR 97058 **Ret 1999-** B Cedar Rapids IA 1936 s Lawrence & Mary. BA U of Washington 1960; MDiv CDSP 1964. D 6/29/1964 Bp William F Lewis P 3/9/1965 Bp Ivol I Curtis. S Philips Epis Ch Sulphur Spgs TX 1990-1998; R S Pauls Epis Ch The Dalles OR 1988-1998; Exec Coun Appointees New York NY 1983-1988; Ovrs Mssy Saudi Arabia 1983-1987; Vic S Pat's Ch Incline Vlg NV 1972-1983; Vic S Jn's In The Wilderness Ch Glenbrook NV 1972-1980; Chapl S Mk's Chap Salt Lake City UT 1971-1972; Vic Ch Of The Resurr Centerville UT 1967-1971; Cur S Mk's Cathd Seattle WA 1964-1967. Auth, "Arabian Archeol & Epigraphy," 1994; Auth, "Recently Discovered Early Chr Monuments In NE Arabia," *Arabian Archeol & Epigraphy*. ASOR; SBL.

LANGFORD, Thomas William (Spr) 873 S Park Ave, Springfield IL 62704 **D Trin Ch Jacksonville IL 1996-** B Pittsburgh PA 1937 s Thomas & Anna. Carnegie Inst of Tech 1957; BS U of Pennsylvania 1962; MBA U of Pennsylvania 1964; PhD U of Pennsylvania 1976. D 11/22/1988 Bp Donald Maynard Hultstrand. m 7/24/1980 Elisabeth Lenore Langford c 3. COM, Chairman Dio Springfield Springfield IL 2009-2013, Springfield Sch for Mnstry 2008-, Mssn & Wrshp, Chairman 2005-2008, Admin & Fin, Chairman 2002-2005; D S Lk's Ch Springfield IL 1993-1996; D Chr Ch Springfield IL 1990-1993; D The Cathd Ch Of S Paul Springfield IL 1988-1990.

LANGI, Viliami (Haw) 720 N King St, Honolulu HI 96817 B Tonga 1936 s Mosese & Anahiwa. D 6/14/2015 Bp Robert Leroy Fitzpatrick. m 12/31/2005 Anapesi Langi.

LANGILLE, David (Minn) Messiah Episcopal Church, 1631 Ford Pkwy, Saint Paul MN 55116 **R S Mart's By The Lake Epis Minnetonka Bch MN 2011-; Assoc Min Mssh Epis Ch 1999-** B Halifax Canada 1960 s Arnold & Shirley. BA Nova Scotia Coll of Art and Design 1983; MCS Regent Coll Vancouver CA 1992; Atlantic TS 2005. D 6/14/2007 P 12/20/2007 Bp James Louis Jelinek. m 3/4/1995 Diane Marie Langille c 3. Mssh Epis Ch S Paul MN 2007-2011.

LANGLE, Susan (NH) Unit 6, 26 Myrtle St, Claremont NH 03743 B N Kingstown RI 1956 d John & Jean. AB Assumption Coll 1978; JD U of Connecticut 1981; MDiv EDS 2007. D 6/28/2007 P 2/15/2008 Bp Vicky Gene Robinson. m 6/2/2013 Sara Joan Groesch. P-in-c Trin Ch Claremont NH 2008-2015; Chapl Res Yale New Haven Hosp New Haven CT 2007-2008.

LANGLOIS, Donald Harold (Spr) 916 W Loughlin Dr, Chandler AZ 85225 B Rochester NY 1940 s Harold & Eleanor. BA Ken 1962; MDiv GTS 1966; MLS CUNY Queens Coll 1973. D 6/11/1966 P 1/7/1967 Bp George West Barrett. m 8/28/1965 Ullrike Langlois c 2. S Aug's Epis Ch Tempe AZ 1991-1992; R Ch Of The H Trin Danville IL 1985-1987; Vic S Lukes Ch Ladysmith WI 1983-1985; R Gr Ch Rice Lake WI 1976-1985; Vic S Mk's Barron WI 1976-1982; P-T Asst S Geo's Par Flushing NY 1973-1976; Vic Ch of the Redeem Addison NY 1967-1972; Asst Chr Epis Ch Hornell NY 1966-1967; P-T Chapl SUNY Alfred NY 1966-1967. CBS; GAS; SHN (P Assoc); Soc of King Chas the Mtyr; SocMary. Beta Phi Mu Queens Coll, Flushing NY 1973.

LANGSTON, Michael Griffith (NC) 203 Denim Dr, Erwin NC 28339 B Philadelphia PA 1965 s Randall & Glee. PhD Case Wstrn Reserve U; AA Florida St U 1984; BA U of W Florida 1986; MA U of W Florida 1989; MDiv Ya Berk 1990. D 8/6/1991 P 2/1/1992 Bp Rogers Sanders Harris. m 7/1/2008 Jessica Kaplan Langston. S Steph's Epis Ch Erwin NC 1999-2002; H Trin Epis Ch W Palm Bch FL 1996-1999; S Paul's Ch Naples FL 1991-1996. Auth, "Mntl Hlth Values Of Ministers".

LANIER, Justin (Vt) 200 Pleasant St, Bennington VT 05201 **R S Ptr's Epis Ch Bennington VT 2012-** B Alexandria LA 1978 s Ray & Jennifer. BA U of

490

Delaware 2001; MDiv CDSP 2010. D 6/12/2010 P 6/11/2011 Bp Thomas Edward Breidenthal. m 3/20/2010 Heather Lanier c 2. S Pat's Epis Ch Lebanon OH 2010-2012. fr.justin@stpetersvt.org

LANIER, Stanley Lin (At) PO Box 637, Waycross GA 31502 B Waycross GA 1952 s Sidney & Willie. Grad Theol Un; BA S Andrews Presb Coll 1974; Andover Newton TS 1976; MA Wesley TS 1979; U of Virginia 1985; MDiv GTS 1993. D 6/5/1993 P 12/1/1993 Bp Frank Kellogg Allan. Asst To Bp Dio Atlanta Atlanta GA 1993-1994; Non-par.

LANIGAN, Sean Robert (Vt) 525 E 7th St, Long Beach CA 90813 **S Ptr's Ch Philadelphia PA 2015-** B North Olmstead OH 1982 s John & Karen. BA Br 2005; MDiv Vale Div 2009; MDiv Yale DS 2009; Dplma Angl Stds GTS 2013; Dplma Angl Stds The GTS 2013. D 11/10/2013 P 7/2/2014 Bp Thomas C Ely. The Par Ch Of S Lk Long Bch CA 2013.

LANNING JR, James Clair (Chi) 1315 W. Roosevelt Rd., Wheaton IL 60187 **D Trin Epis Ch Wheaton IL 1986-; Dioc Coun Dio Chicago Chicago IL 2012-, D Formation Com 1992-** B Grand Island NE 1948 s James & Marian. BA U of Nebraska 1971; JD U of Nebraska 1973; LLM Geo 1976. D 1/25/1984 Bp Robert Marshall Anderson. m 6/7/1969 Nancy Lanning c 2. D S Mths Ch St Paul Pk MN 1985-1986.

LANNON, Nicholas Jewett (Nwk) Grace Church Van Vorst, 39 Erie St., Jersey City NJ 07302 **S Fran In The Fields Harrods Creek KY 2015-** B Alexandria VA 1978 s Paul & Susan. BA U of Arizona 2000; MDiv TESM 2007. D 6/9/2007 Bp Jim Mathes. m 5/22/2004 Ayala Masayo Solis Lannon c 2. The Ch Of The Sav Denville NJ 2011-2013; Asst R Gr Ch Van Vorst Jersey City NJ 2007-2011.

LANPHERE, Lynette (Ala) 8132 Becker Ln, Leeds AL 35094 **Mem Dept of Chr Formation Dioces of Alabama AL 2004-** B Marshalltown IA 1947 d Guy & Helen. BA Briar Cliff U 1969; MS Creighton U 1978; MA Loras Coll 1990; MDiv Sewanee: The U So, TS 2002. D 6/20/2002 Bp Thomas Kreider Ray P 12/17/2002 Bp Marc Handley Andrus. Mem Dept of Par Dvlpmt Dio Alabama AL 2005-2009; R Epis Ch Of The Epiph Leeds AL 2004-2014; Int St. Steph's Epis Ch Huntsville AL 2003-2004; S Steph's Epis Ch Huntsville AL 2002-2004; Assoc St. Steph's Epis Ch Huntsville AL 2002-2003.

LANSFORD, Theron George (NI) 10225 Calverton Pass, Fort Wayne IN 46825 **Died 9/10/2015** B Denton TX 1931 s Marcus & Lucille. BA U of Texas 1957; MA U of Texas 1959; PhD S Johns 1998. D 10/9/1971 P 4/22/1972 Bp Walter C Klein. m 9/1/1959 Mary Elizabeth Lansford. P-in-c H Fam Ch Angola IN 2005-2006, P-in-c 1974-2005; Asst Gr Epis Ch Ft Wayne IN 1995-2005. Auth, "Var Sci Pub". Who'S Who Among Amer Tchrs; Who'S Who In Amer Sci,; Who'S Who In Amer Rel.

LANTER, James Joseph (WVa) HC 69 Box 88, Slatyfork WV 26291 **Chap on the Mt Snowshoe WV 2008-; Cler in Charge S Jn's Ch Marlinton WV 2008-** B Marion IL 1936 s Joseph & Kathryn. BS Pur 1964; MA DePaul U 1968; PhD CUA 1971; Cert VTS 2008. D 9/30/2008 P 6/15/2009 Bp William Michie Klusmeyer. m 1/1/1982 Joyce Carolina Lanter c 6.

LANTZ, Frederick William (Nwk) 1115 Black Rush Cir, Mt Pleasant SC 29466 **Died 6/1/2016** B Quantico VA 1940 s William & Catharine. BS VPI 1963; MDiv GTS 1968. D 6/29/1968 Bp William Foreman Creighton P 6/1/1969 Bp Paul Moore Jr. c 2. Pstr Assoc Chr Epis Ch Mt Pleasant SC 2002-2016; R S Dunst's Epis Ch Succasunna NJ 1997-2001; Chapl Hamptons Aentara Hosp Hampton VA 1997-1998; Asst Estrn Shore Chap Virginia Bch VA 1996-1997; R Chr Epis Ch Smithfield VA 1990-1996; R S Chris's Ch Charlotte NC 1975-1990; Vic S Davids Ch Brunswick GA 1970-1975; Asst S Aug's Epis Ch Washington DC 1968-1969; Chairman Dept of Stwdshp Dio Sthrn Virginia Newport News VA 1993-1996.

LANTZ, John Daron (SC) 1150 E Montague Ave, North Charleston SC 29405 **Died 2/7/2016** B Carlisle PA 1922 s Samuel & Florence. BS Millersville U 1946; MS U of Bridgeport 1962; MS U of Bridgeport 1975. D 12/3/1988 Bp Arthur Edward Walmsley. m 4/22/1957 Sidnea Jane Lantz c 3. D S Mk's Epis Ch Charleston SC 2007-2016; Chapl Epis Cbury Hse Charleston SC 1999-2016; D S Thos Epis Ch N Charleston SC 1995-2006; D Chr Ch Trumbull CT 1988-1994; Instr U Of Bridgeport Bridgeport CT 2016.

LAPENTA-H, Sarah (ECR) 4775 Cambridge St, Boulder CO 80301 **Ch Of S Jude The Apos Cupertino CA 2016-** B Detroit MI 1974 d Joe & Cecelia. BS Pur 1997; MDiv Fuller TS 2008. D 6/12/2010 Bp Diane Jardine Bruce P 1/8/2011 Bp Mary Douglas Glasspool. m 8/11/1996 Paul A Hebblethwaite. R S Mary Magd Ch Boulder CO 2014-2016; S Jn's Ch Chevy Chase MD 2011-2014; St Johns Pro-Cathd Los Angeles CA 2010-2011; Chapl Providence Hlth and Systems Sthrn California 2008-2011. Auth, "Sexism," *Global Dictionary of Theol: A Resource for the Worldwide Ch*, Intervarsity Press, 2008. sarah@saintjudes.org

LAPRE, Alfred Charles (Ct) 616 Shamrock Dr, Fredericksburg VA 22407 B Norwich CT 1932 s Alfred & Victoria. CEU Sewanee: The U So, TS 1989. D 12/3/1988 Bp Arthur Edward Walmsley. m 5/21/1955 Mary C Boller.

LAQUINTANO, David Lloyd (NJ) 2998 Bay Ave, Ocean City NJ 08226 B Stroudsburg PA 1950 s David & Irene. BA Estrn Bapt Coll 1972; MDiv Estrn Bapt TS 1975; U of Wales 1976. D 6/20/1987 P 11/7/1987 Bp Allen Lyman Bartlett Jr. m 6/3/1972 Christine Margaret Laquintano c 3. R H Trin Epis Ch Ocean City NJ 1999-2013; R Gr Epis Ch Kingston PA 1989-1999; Asst Chr Ch Philadelphia Philadelphia PA 1987-1989; Serv Amer Bapt Ch 1976-1985. frdavidoc@live.com

LARA, Juana (Dal) St Barnabas Episcopal Church, 1200 N Shiloh Rd, Garland TX 75042 B Ixmiquilpan Hidalgo MX 1971 d Jesus & Balvina. 2 years E Field Coll; 3 years Instituto Teologio de San Mateo. D 6/11/2011 Bp James Monte Stanton. m 6/12/1996 Lino Lara c 3. D S Barn Ch Garland TX 2011-2012.

LARA, Lino (Dal) 5923 Royal Lane, Dallas TX 75230 **Vic Dio Dallas Dallas TX 2012-** B Hidalgo Mexico 1965 s Pedro & Silvia. Instituto Teologio de San Mateo 1998. D 6/26/2010 Bp Paul Emil Lambert P 5/28/2011 Bp James Monte Stanton. m 6/12/1996 Juana Lara c 3. Cur S Lk's Epis Ch Dallas TX 2010-2012. linoalara@gmail.com

LARA, Pedro D (Dal) **Dio Dallas Dallas TX 2017-** D 6/24/2017 Bp George Robinson Sumner Jr.

LARCOMBE, David John (Vt) 37 Premo Rd, Roxbury VT 05669 B Exeter UK 1951 s Raymond & Patricia. BS U Natal Gb 1972; DIT S Paul Sem 1974; BTh U Safr 1978. Trans 8/28/1984 Bp John Bowen Coburn. m 1/17/2003 Sandra Carrillo c 2. Ch Of The Gd Shpd Barre VT 2004-2007; S Paul's Ch Peabody MA 1996-1997; Int Ch Of Our Sav Arlington MA 1989-1992; R Emm Epis Ch Wakefield MA 1984-1989; Int Trin Par Melrose MA 1981-1982; Assoc R Ascen Memi Ch Ipswich MA 1979-1980.

LAREMORE, Darrell Lee (SeFla) 6003 Back Bay Ln, Austin TX 78739 B New Castle IN 1942 MA Florida Atlantic U 1971; Florida Atlantic U 1973; MDiv Epis TS of the SW 2003. D 12/16/2003 Bp James Hamilton Ottley P 3/13/2005 Bp Leo Frade. m 12/15/1989 Karyn Laremore c 1. S Jn's Epis Ch Austin TX 2004-2005.

LAREMORE, Richard Thomas (RI) 147 Bay Spring Ave Apt 227, Barrington RI 02806 **Ret 1996-** B Albany NY 1925 s Thomas & Ellen. BA Br 1951; STM EDS 1954; U of Rhode Island 1980. D 6/20/1954 P 3/5/1955 Bp John S Higgins. c 3. Int Emm Ch Newport RI 1994-1995; Int S Jn The Div Ch Saunderstown RI 1992-1994; Int Ch Of The Mssh Providence RI 1991-1992; Int Trin Epis Ch Whitinsville MA 1990-1991; Int S Alb's Ch N Providence RI 1988-1990; Chapl VetA Hosp Providence RI 1986-1991; Int S Jn's Ch Ashton RI 1986-1988; Ch Of The Ascen Cranston RI 1986; Asst S Dav's On The Hill Epis Ch Cranston RI 1984-1985; S Andr's Ch Turners Fall MA 1982-1983; S Jas' Ch Greenfield MA 1982-1983; Int Gr Ch Dalton MA 1981-1982; Ch of the Epiph Rumford RI 1980-1981; St Mich & Gr Ch Rumford RI 1980-1981; R SS Matt and Mk Barrington RI 1959-1979, Min in charge 1954-1958; Chapl (LTC) US-Army 1954-1978; S Mk's Epis Ch Riverside RI 1954-1956. Freedom Fndt Awd 1978.

LARGE, Alexander R (Tex) 717 Sage Rd, Houston TX 77056 **S Mart's Epis Ch Houston TX 2013-** B Grosse Point MI 1979 s James & Nancy. BA W&L 2002; MDiv TESM 2006. D 5/27/2006 Bp John Wadsworth Howe P 12/9/2006 Bp Robert John O'Neill. m 8/13/2005 Emily A Large c 3. Asst R All SS' Epis Ch Chevy Chase MD 2008-2013; Cur Epis Ch Of The Trsfg Vail CO 2006-2008. alarge@stmartinsepiscopoal.org

LARGENT, Lacy (Tex) Po Box 10603, Houston TX 77206 **Ch Of The Redeem Houston TX 2015-; Port Chapl Houston Int'l Seafarers' Cntr Houston TX 2002-; Chapl The Great Cmsn Fndt Houston TX 2002-; Camp Allen Navasota TX 2001-, 1996-2000, Bd Secy 2005-; Sprtl Dir Camp Allen Navasota TX 2000-; Sprtl Dir of Dioc AltGld Dio Texas Houston TX 2007-, Dn of Cntrl Convoc 2002-2006, Exec Bd 1996-1999, Sprtl Dir of Happ 1996-1998, Chair of Dioc Single Adults 1991-1998** B Fort Smith AR 1960 d Larry & Anne. BA U of Arkansas 1982; MSW Washington U 1983; MDiv Epis TS of the SW 1990. D 6/16/1990 Bp Maurice Manuel Benitez P 1/13/1991 Bp Anselmo Carral-Solar. R S Paul's Ch Navasota TX 1994-2002; Asst R Ch Of The Gd Shpd Kingwood TX 1991-1994; Stff Chapl Cullen Memi Chap Houston TX 1990-1991; S Lk's Epis Hosp Houston TX 1990-1991. Hal Brook Perry Distinguished Alum Awd Sem of the SW 2009; Five Outstanding Young Texans Awd Texas Jaycees 2000.

LARIBEE JR, Richard (CNY) 20 Masonic Ave Apt A4, Camden NY 13316 **Asst Prof Amer U of Iraq - Sulaimani Iraq 2010-** B Rome NY 1952 s Richard & Eileen. BA The Kings Coll Briarcliff Manor NY 1974; Wheaton Coll 1974; ThM Dallas TS 1981; CITS Epis TS of the SW 1997; DMin Fuller TS 1998. D 6/7/1997 P 12/21/1997 Bp William Jerry Winterrowd. c 3. R Trin Epis Ch Watertown NY 2012-2017; R S Mk's Ch Highland MD 2002-2010; R S Andr The Fisherman Epis Mayo MD 1998-2002; Asst The Ch Of Chr The King (Epis) Arvada CO 1997-1998; Sr Pstr Non-Epis Congregations 1980-1993. "From Generation to Generation: Intergenerational Wrshp," *Ch Mus Workshop*, 2006.

LARIVE, Armand Edward (Spok) 4812 Fremont Ave, Bellingham WA 98229 B Winner SD 1936 s Armand & Martha. BA Whitman Coll 1958; BD Bex Sem 1961; MA U of Missouri 1970; PhD Claremont Grad U 1976. D 7/11/1961 P 3/1/1962 Bp Lane W Barton. m 8/30/1959 Ruby D Larive c 2. S Jas Pullman WA 1975-2001; P-in-c H Trin Vale OR 1963-1968; P-in-c S Paul's Epis Ch Nyssa OR 1961-1968. Auth, "After Sunday: A Theol Of Wk," Continuum, 2004.

LARKIN, Gregory Bruce (Los) 1251 Las Posas Rd, Camarillo CA 93010 **R S Columba's Par Camarillo CA 2000-** B Los Angles CA 1955 s Robert & Catherine. BA U of Redlands 1977; MDiv GTS 1982. D 6/19/1982 P 2/5/1983 Bp Robert Claflin Rusack. m 5/31/1986 Nancy L Larkin c 2. R S Thos Of Cbury Par Long Bch CA 1987-2000; S Lk's Of The Mountains La Crescenta CA 1984-1987; Cur & Asst S Mich's Mssn Anaheim CA 1982-1984. Cn Cathd Cntr Of St. Paul Dio Los Angeles 1999. canonbaseball@verizon.net

LARKIN, Lauren Renee Ellis (CFla) B Englewood NJ 1975 d Harold & Katherine. BA Davidson Coll 1997; MDiv Trin Sch for Mnstry 2007; STM Trin Sch for Mnstry 2011. D 1/30/2017 Bp Gregory Orrin Brewer. m 10/14/2005 Daniel Joseph Larkin c 3.

LARKIN, Patrick (ETenn) B 1933 D 6/27/1971 Bp William F Gates Jr P 2/26/1972 Bp John Vander Horst. m 4/13/1957 Jean Adams. S Jas Epis Ch of Greeneville Greeneville TN 1983-1986; Ch Of Our Sav Gallatin TN 1982-1983; Dio Tennessee Nashville TN 1971-1981.

LAROCCA, Lucy D(riscoll) (Ct) 1109 Main St, Branford CT 06405 **R Zion Epis Ch N Branford CT 2011-** B Bristol CT 1959 d Arthur & Lucy. AA Albertus Magnus Coll 1979; BFA Paier Coll of Art 1983; MS Sthrn Connecticut St U 1996; MDiv Ya Berk 2008. D 6/4/2008 P 12/20/2008 Bp Andrew Donnan Smith. m 5/30/1987 David LaRocca c 2. Trin Ch On The Green New Haven CT 2010-2011; Cur Trin Ch Branford CT 2008-2010.

LAROCHE WILSON, Jill Monica (Pa) 246 Fox Rd, Media PA 19063 **S Jn's Ch Glen Mills PA 2012-** B Gardner MA 1975 d James & Diane. BA Bos 1997; MDiv EDS 2002. D 6/22/2002 P 5/31/2003 Bp Charles Ellsworth Bennison Jr. Asst R S Ptr's Ch In The Great Vlly Malvern PA 2002-2005.

LAROM JR, Richard U (NY) Po Box 577, Ivoryton CT 06442 **Incarn Cntr 2004-; Allnce of Epis Maritime Mnstrs 2003-** B Bay Shore NY 1946 s Richard & Pauline. CUNY; BA Cor; STB GTS. D 6/17/1972 P 12/14/1972 Bp Jonathan Goodhue Sherman. m 2/5/1977 Margaret Smith Larom c 2. Exec Dir Seamens Ch Inst New York NY 1992-2002; Gr Ch White Plains NY 1985-1992; Mssy Uganda 1981-1984; Exec Coun Appointees New York NY 1980-1985; Cathd Of St Jn The Div New York NY 1977-1978; R S Geo's Ch Astoria NY 1975-1980; Cur Chr Epis Ch Tarrytown NY 1974-1975. Auth, *Seafarer's Handbook*, 1995; Auth, *Commentary on St. Mk*, 1984; Auth, *Pstr*, 1984; Auth, *Practical Guide for Ch Leaders*, 1984. Century Assn; Marine Soc; Pilgrims. Dn's Medal, GTS 2002; Paul Harris Rotary Fellowowship 1991; Ethical Culture Soc Humanitarian Awd 1991; Westchester Human Rts Awd 1991; Hon Cn Ch of Uganda 1991.

LARRIMORE, Chip Barker (Cal) 61 Santa Rosa Ave., Sausalito CA 94965 **R Chr Ch Sausalito CA 2012-** B Miami Beach FL 1963 s Sloane & Donna. BA U of Oregon 1985; MDiv CDSP 1995. D 6/3/1995 P 6/1/1996 Bp William Edwin Swing. m 7/27/2013 David Frederick Houghton c 2. R S Ptr's Epis Ch Redwood City CA 1999-2012; Assoc Pstr Gr Cathd San Francisco CA 1995-1999. email@christchurchsausalito.com

LARSEN, Erik W (RI) Saint Columba's Chapel, 55 Vaucluse Ave, Middletown RI 02842 **S Columba's Chap Middletown RI 2012-; Cn for Transition Mnstry Dio Connecticut Hartford CT 2007-; Cmsn on Fin Dio Rhode Island 2013-** B Hartford CT 1953 s Erik & Margaret. BA Trin Hartford CT 1975; MDiv EDS 1980. D 6/14/1980 P 12/15/1980 Bp Morgan Porteus. m 10/13/1984 Karin Bengtson c 2. Dio Connecticut Meriden CT 2007-2011; Stndg Com 1998-2003; Dn, D Formation Prog Epis Dio CT 2006-2012; R S Alb's Ch Simsbury CT 1994-2006; St Johns Cathd Hong Kong 1990-1995; Chapl/Precentor S Jn's Cathd Hong Kong China 1990-1994; R S Andr's Epis Ch Marble Dale CT 1983-1990; Cur Ch Of The H Trin Middletown CT 1980-1983; Congrl Dvlpmt Com Dio Rhode Island 2013-2016. Soc of S Jn the Evang 1980. Hon Cn Chr Ch Cathd 2007.

LARSEN, Gilbert Steward (Ct) 9160 Sw 193rd Cir, Dunnellon FL 34432 B New York NY 1943 s Lawrence & Astrid. BA Hamline U 1965; MDiv GTS 1968. D 6/8/1968 P 12/21/1968 Bp Horace W B Donegan. m 6/22/1968 Judith B Larsen c 2. P-in-c S Anne's Ch Crystal River FL 2015-2016, P-in-c 2005-2006, Assoc P 2000-2005; Sum Chapl St. Barth's Angl Ch Dinard France 1989; R Chr Ch Sharon CT 1983-2000; R Ch Of The H Comm Mahopac NY 1980-1983; Dn Of SW Nassau Dio Long Island Garden City NY 1979-1980, Liturg Cmsn 1972-1978; Rep For Long Island Epis Camp & Conf Cntr Ivoryton CT 1978-1980; R Chr Epis Ch Lynbrook NY 1972-1980; Chapl Lynbrook Fire Dept 1972-1980; Cur Trin Epis Ch Roslyn NY 1968-1971; Cler & Fam Enrichment Com Dio Connecticut Meriden CT 1991-1993. SSC 1992-2011.

LARSEN, Matthew David (Dal) 3966 McKinney Ave, Dallas TX 75204 **Cur Chr Ch New Haven CT 2013-; Ch Of The Incarn Dallas TX 2009-** B Oklahoma City OK 1982 s David & Victoria. BA Texas A&M U 2006; ThM Dallas TS 2011. D 12/10/2011 Bp Paul Emil Lambert P 5/10/2013 Bp James Monte Stanton. m 6/4/2005 Lauren Alayne Carter c 2.

LARSEN, Peter Michael (LI) 515 Eastlake Dr, Muscle Shoals AL 35661 **P-in-c S Andr's Dune Chap Southampton NY 1989-** B Hackensack NJ 1948 s Knud & Mary. BA Wofford Coll 1970; MDiv VTS 1974; Naval Chapl Sch 1984. D 6/5/1974 Bp William Hopkins Folwell P 12/19/1974 Bp Frederick Hesley Belden. m 6/28/1986 Nancy B Slater c 3. R S Jn's Epis Ch Southampton NY 1989-2014; CAPT Naval Reserve Chapl Corps 1983-2003; R S Jn The Div Ch Saunderstown RI 1983-1989; Atone Ch Walterboro SC 1978-1983; P-in-c S Jude's Epis Ch Walterboro SC 1978-1983; Asst S Jn's Ch Lafayette Sq Washington DC 1975-1978; Cur S Jn's Ch Barrington RI 1974-1975. arts in LivCh. Distinguished Trst Awd Untd Hosp Fund of NY 2013; Gd Samar Awd Hospice 2002; Outstanding Achievement Awd Mltry Chapl Assn 2001; Reserve Chapl of the Year Awd Reserve Off Assn 1998; Cmnty Serv Awd So Carolina 1980.

LARSEN JR, Richard James (Pa) PO Box 341490, Dayton OH 45434 **P-in-c S Paul's Epis Ch Greenville OH 2011-, P-in-c 2011-** B Iowa City IA 1942 s Richard & Isabel. BA U of Iowa 1964; STB Ya Berk 1968; MS U of Wisconsin 1982. D 6/20/1968 P 12/21/1968 Bp Gordon V Smith. m 4/19/1974 Donna K Larsen c 2. Int S Geo's Epis Ch Dayton OH 2008-2010; R Washington Memi Chap Vlly Forge PA 2001-2007; R S Mary's Epis Ch Bonita Sprg FL 1997-2001; R H Trin Ch Cincinnati OH 1986-1997; R S Ambr Epis Ch Ft Lauderdale FL 1982-1986; Vic S Mich's Ch SW Ranches FL 1981-1982; Vic Trin Ch River Falls WI 1978-1979; Chr Ch Cathd Eau Claire WI 1973-1978; Vic S Lk's Ch Altoona WI 1973-1978; P-in-c Trin Ch Winterset IA 1970-1974; P-in-c S Paul Epis Ch Creston IA 1968-1974; P-in-c H Trin Atlantic IA 1968-1970. Kappa Delta Pi; Phi Delta Kappa.

LARSON, Donna J (WMass) 19 Pleasant St, Chicopee MA 01013 B Panama City FL 1944 d Arthur & Alice. BS SUNY 1972; MEd Leh 1976; MDiv GTS 2004. D 4/17/2004 P 10/31/2004 Bp Paul Victor Marshall. c 3. P-in-c Gr Ch Chicopee MA 2011-2016; R S Lk's Ch Lanesboro MA 2011-2015; R S Geo's Ch Lee MA 2006-2013; Cur Trin Ch Easton PA 2004-2006; Dicocesan Coun Dio Wstrn Massachusetts Springfield 2007-2010, Bement/Waterfield Schlrshp Comm. 2007-. St. Matt's Soc 1998.

LARSON, Frances Jean (Minn) 1010 1st Ave N, Wheaton MN 56296 B Windom MN 1938 d Edward & Gladys. S Barn Hosp Minneapolis MN; LPN Miller Hosp Sch Nrsng S Paul MN 1960; BSW Bemidji St U 1996. D 10/25/1987 Bp Robert Marshall Anderson. m 7/28/1962 Louis I Larson c 2. D Emm. Oustanding Soc Wk Stdt Bemidi St U 1995; Who'S Who Amer Coll Stdt 96; S Geo Epis Awd 82 Emm Epis Ch.

LARSON, John Milton (Los) 2665 Tallant Rd Apt W307, Santa Barbara CA 93105 **Ret 2002-** B Chicago IL 1935 s John & Lillian. BMus NWU 1956; MDiv SWTS 1959. D 6/20/1959 P 12/19/1959 Bp Charles L Street. m 11/27/1970 Barbara Schulz. Asst The Ch Of The Ascen Sierra Madre CA 2002-2013; R S Barn' Par Pasadena CA 1996-2002; Int Chr The Gd Shpd Par Los Angeles CA 1995, Asst 1977-1984; Asst S Mk's Par Downey CA 1985-1989; Asst Chr Ch Las Vegas NV 1974-1975; Serv Dio Nassau & the Bahamas 1970-1974; Asst S Simons Ch Arlington Hts IL 1968-1969; R St Ambr Epis Ch Antigo WI 1966-1968; Vic Chr-the-King Nassau 1965-1966; R Our Lady & S Steph Bimini1963 1963-1965; Asst S Barn Nassau 1962-1963; Monk St. Greg's Priory. Three Rivers MI 1962-1963; St Greg's Abbey Three Rivers MI 1961-1962; Cur Emm Epis Ch Rockford IL 1959-1961. OHC 1957.

LARSON, Laurence (Chi) 2424 41st St Apt 48, Moline IL 61265 **Co Pstr All SS Mssn Moline IL 2009-; Ret Epis Ch 2001-** B East Chicago IN 1936 s Roy & Agnes. BA Illinois Coll 1960; MDiv Nash 1963; DMin GTF 1988. D 6/15/1963 Bp James Winchester Montgomery P 12/21/1963 Bp Gerald Francis Burrill. m 12/30/1961 Betty L Larson c 3. Asst R Trin Epis Ch Rock Island IL 1977-2001; Ch Of S Jn The Bapt Elkhart IL 1971-1977; Trin Ch Lincoln IL 1971-1977; Epis Chapl Indiana U Bloomington 1967-1971; R Trin Par Bloomingdale IN 1967-1971; Asst. Chapl. Chap of St. Thos. Cbury Orono ME 1965-2001; Asst S Jas Ch Old Town ME 1965-1967; Epis Chapl Nthrn illinois U Dekalb IL 1963-1965; Epis Chapl S Jude's Epis Ch Rochelle IL 1963-1965; Chapl to the Ret Cler and Surviving Spouses Dio Quincy Peoria IL 2001-2014. CBS 1984. Cn Theol Dio Quincy 1998; Ord of St. Paul Awd Dio Quincy 1995; Phi Beta Kappa ILL Coll 1960.

LARSON, Lawrence Andrew Adolph (NY) 1 Bayview Ter, New Fairfield CT 06812 **Died 1/16/2016** B Chicago IL 1934 s Adolph & Beverley. BS Indiana U 1957; Drew U 1959; MDiv Bos TS 1962; MS Bos 1967. D 12/24/1967 P 4/1/1968 Bp Robert McConnell Hatch. m 11/26/1983 Patricia J B Belcher c 2. R S Andr's Ch Brewster NY 1981-1999; 1975-1978; R Chr Ch Ansonia CT 1969-1981; Asst Gr Ch Great Barrington MA 1967-1969. Auth, "Chr Symbolism & The Tragic Point Of View"; Auth, "The Cinematic & The Biblic Points Of View: A New Correlation". Alb Inst Assn Rel & Intellectual Life; Angl Soc, Gld S Raphael.

LARSON JR, L(awrence) John (Cal) 1835 NW Lantana Dr., Corvallis OR 97330 **Ret 1998-** B Arcadia FL 1935 s Lawrence & Kathryn. BA U of Florida 1957; Ya 1958; BD SMU 1960. D 1/26/1963 Bp George Richard Millard P 6/10/1963 Bp James Albert Pike. m 2/3/1978 Ellen Gay Larson. Assoc S Lk's Ch Sequim WA 1999; S Lk's Ch San Francisco CA 1997; Clerics Assn 1994-1995; R Ch Of The Nativ San Rafael CA 1990-1997; R Ch Of The Epiph Flagstaff AZ 1984-1990; R The Ch Of The H Trin Juneau AK 1977-1984; R S Lk's Ch Coeur D Alene ID 1970-1977; Vic S Lawr Campbell CA 1968-1970; Vic S Anne's Ch Fremont CA 1962-1968; Serv Methodist Ch 1960-1962; Com on Environ Dio California San Francisco CA 1992-1997; ExCoun 1969-1991; Stndg Com

Dio Alaska Fairbanks AK 1981-1984; Dioc Coun Dio Spokane Spokane WA 1972-1977.

LARSON, Robert Anton (Colo) P.O. Box 563, Ouray CO 81427 B Greeley CO 1945 s Ralph & Hallie. Colorado Sch of Mines 1968. D 11/14/2009 Bp Robert John O'Neill. m 4/12/1969 Pamela Larson c 2.

LARSON, Steven Shaw (Ga) PO Box 74, Swainsboro GA 30401 B Westberry NY 1952 s Glen & Nancy. BA U So 1974; MS U of So Carolina 1977; Angl Stds Prog Sewanee: The U So, TS 2011; Angl Stds Prog U So TS 2011. D 6/30/2012 P 2/21/2014 Bp Scott Anson Benhase. m 3/22/1986 Nancy Dianne Davis Larson.

LARSON, Wayne (Md) 15 East Bishop's Road, Baltimore MD 21218 **Dir of Chapl Serv Fairhaven Sykesville MD 2005-** B Buffalo Center IA 1954 s Jerome & Maxine. BS Minnesota St U Mankato 1978; Ch Army Trng Coll 1987; MDiv Hur CA 2003. D 6/29/2003 P 1/25/2004 Bp Edwin Max Leidel Jr. P-in-c S Jn's Epis Ch S Johns MI 2003-2005; On-Call Team Chapl McLaren Reg Hosp 1999-2001; Dir of Chr Cntr S Paul's Epis Ch Flint MI 1988-2001; Jubilee Cntr Visitor Dom And Frgn Mssy Soc- Epis Ch Cntr New York NY 1994-1997; New Ch Planting Com Dio Michigan Detroit MI 1991-1994; Bd Mem The Ch Army Usa Beaver Falls PA 1987-1990. Ch Army 1987. Vol of Year Escape Mnstrs 2009; Azell Cromwell Awd Chr Cntr 2008; Bp's Awd Dio Estrn Michigan 1998.

LARSON-MILLER, Lizette (Cal) 926 Santa Fe Ave, Albany CA 94706 **CDSP Berkeley CA 2010-, 2003; Assoc S Mk's Par Berkeley CA 2010-** B Los Angeles CA 1958 d Robert & Billie. BA USC 1978; MA S Johns U 1982; PhD Grad Theol Un 1992. D 1/18/2003 Bp Joseph Jon Bruno P 9/6/2003 Bp Chester Lovelle Talton. m 4/10/1983 Steven Miller c 2. Assoc Ch Of The Adv Of Chr The King San Francisco CA 2003-2010. Auth, "Anointing the Sick," Liturg Press, 2005; Auth, "Medieval Liturg: A Bk of Essays," Garland, 1997. Affirming Catholicism 2005; Intl Angl Liturg Consult 2000; Soc of Cath Priests 2009. Lilly Fac Resrch Grant Eli Lilly 2005; Bp Garner Cler Awd Garner Fund, Dio of LA 2004; SCOM Grant SCOM 2004; Luce Fell Luce 2002.

LA RUE, Howard Arlen (Va) PO Box 72, Searsport ME 04974 **Ret 1996-** B Maud OK 1930 s William & Veloura. VTS 1967. D 6/22/1967 Bp George P Gunn P 5/1/1968 Bp David Shepherd Rose. R Emm Epis Ch Greenwood VA 1969-1995; R H Cross Ch Afton VA 1969-1995; Epis Ch Of S Paul And S Andr Kenbridge VA 1967-1969; R Gibson Memi Crewe VA 1967-1969; USN 1948-1964.

LA RUE, Michael Dreyer (FtW) **S Barn Epis Ch Houston TX 2017-** B 1964 D 12/28/1988 P 11/18/1989 Bp Clarence Cullam Pope Jr. S Jn's Ch Ft Worth TX 1989-1991.

LASCH, Ian (Mo) 8605 Spoon Dr, Saint Louis MO 63132 **S Ptr's Epis Ch S Louis MO 2016-** B Charlotte NC 1983 s Steven & Connie. BS Excelsior Coll 2010; MDiv VTS 2016. D 5/14/2016 Bp Scott Anson Benhase P 1/6/2017 Bp George Wayne Smith. m 10/21/2011 Loren V Hague c 2. ilasch@stpetersepiscopal.org

LASCH, Loren V (Mo) Diocese Of Missouri, 1210 Locust St # 3, Saint Louis MO 63103 **Yth Dir Dio Missouri S Louis MO 2016-** B Charlottesville VA 1981 d Wayne & Janet. BA U GA 2003; MDiv VTS 2008. D 2/9/2008 P 8/28/2008 Bp Henry Irving Louttit. m 10/21/2011 Ian Lasch c 1. S Pat's Ch Washington DC 2013-2016; Asst R The Ch Of The Gd Shpd Augusta GA 2008-2013; Stdt Host VTS 2006-2008. llasch@diocesemo.org

LASH, Rebecca Henry (NwPa) 870 Diamond Park, Meadville PA 16335 **P Chr Epis Ch Meadville PA 2014-** B Greenville SC 1949 d Daniel & Eloise. NW-PA Dioc Sch for Mnstry; ADN Villa Maria Coll 1983; BASS Edinboro U of Pennsylvania Edinboro PA 1988; BS Edinboro U of Pennsylvania Edinboro PA 1988. D 11/1/2008 P 6/6/2010 Bp Sean Walter Rowe. m 7/1/2000 David Lash c 4. Vic Ch Of The H Sprt Erie PA 2010-2013.

LASITER JR, Douglas Norman (La) 302 Greenwood St, Morgan City LA 70380 **R Trin Epis Ch Morgan City LA 2014-** B Houston TX 1962 s Douglas & Jony. U of Houston 2005; MDiv Epis TS of the SW 2009. D 6/20/2009 Bp C Andrew Doyle P 1/5/2010 Bp Rayford Baines High Jr. m 7/16/1988 Robi J Lasiter c 2. Emm Ch Miles City MT 2012-2014; S Mich's Ch La Marque TX 2011; Assoc/Cur Ch Of The Ascen Houston TX 2009-2011. dnlasiter@comcast.net

LASKE, Holger (Los) Riehler Strasse 7, Koeln 50668 Germany **Non-par 1999-** B Hagen DE 1965 s Heinz & Gisela. Kirchliche Hochschule Wuppertal DE; U of Bochum Ruhr DE; MDiv Georgeaugust U De 1991; MDiv Old Cath Sem Bonn 1996. P 9/24/1998 Bp Frederick Houk Borsch. S Bede's Epis Ch Los Angeles CA 1998-1999.

LASLEY, Jerry Drew (NC) **S Chris's Epis Ch High Point NC 2017-** Rec 2/19/2015 as Priest Bp Michael B Curry.

LASSALLE, David Fredric (SVa) 1336 Bolling Ave, Norfolk VA 23508 B Greenville PA 1941 s Fredric & Elizabeth. BA Thiel Coll 1963; STM PDS 1966. D 6/18/1966 P 6/1/1967 Bp William Crittenden. m 8/28/2016 Sally Keyte Lassalle c 4. Ch of H Apos Virginia Bch VA 1997-2009; S Ptr's Epis Ch Norfolk VA 1996-1997; Dio Sthrn Virginia Newport News VA 1978-2011; Chapl Old Dominion U Norfolk VA 1978-2011; Vic Ch Of The Epiph Grove City PA

1969-1978; Vic S Jn's Ch Kane PA 1966-1969; S Marg's Epis Ch Kane PA 1966-1969.

LASSEN, Coryl Judith (Cal) 409 Topa Topa Dr, Ojai CA 93023 B San Antonio TX 1955 d Carl & Carol. BA U of Pennsylvania 1977; MDiv EDS 1982. D 4/8/1983 Bp Lyman Cunningham Ogilby P 5/1/1984 Bp George Nelson Hunt III. S Mk's Par Berkeley CA 2012-2016; S Mk's Epis Ch Palo Alto CA 2010-2011, 2007; Trsfg Epis Ch San Mateo CA 2009-2010; Trin Par Menlo Pk CA 2008-2009; Stanford Cbury Fndt Palo Alto CA 2007-2009; R S Andr's Epis Ch Ojai CA 1995-2005; Pres Of The Stndg Com Dio Rhode Island Providence RI 1993-1994, Stndg Com 1990-1994, Intrnshp Mnstry Prog 1989-1995; S Ptr's And S Andr's Epis Providence RI 1989-1995; Vic Calv Ch Pascoag RI 1985-1995; Prot Chapl Bryant Coll No Smithfield RI 1985-1989; Epis Chapl Zambarano St Hosp Pascoag RI 1985-1987; S Jn's Ch Barrington RI 1983-1985. Auth, "Report On The Condition Of The Cler Cmnty Of The Dio Ri". SCHC. coryllassen@gmail.com

LASSITER, Richard Bruce (Nev) 1311 Ramona Ln, Boulder City NV 89005 B Lebanon NH 1946 s Jerry & Bertha. AGS CCSN/UNLV 2000; AGS Ccsn 2000. D 8/28/1996 P 3/1/1997 Bp Stewart Clark Zabriskie. m 7/28/1990 Eleanor Lassiter. P S Chris's Epis Ch Boulder City NV 1997-2000.

LATHAM, Betty Craft (ETenn) 628 Magnolia Vale Dr, Chattanooga TN 37419 B Memphis TN 1953 d Henry & Norma. BS Van 1975; MS U of Tennessee 1978; MDiv VTS 1995. D 6/24/1995 P 1/1/1996 Bp Robert Gould Tharp. m 6/7/1975 Luther Cleveland Latham c 1. R Ch Of The Nativ Ft Oglethorp GA 1998-2013; Epis. Comm. Of Se Tennessee Signal Mtn TN 1995-1998; Asst Chr Ch; Campus Min Univ Of Tennessee & Chattanooga St Chattanooga TN. Dok.

LATHAM, Donald Conway (LI) 75 Meadow Rue Pl, Ballston Spa NY 12020 **Died 3/5/2016** B Rockville Centre NY 1933 s Walter & Agnes. BA Hobart and Wm Smith Colleges 1955; MDiv Ya Berk 1958; Adel 1961. D 4/12/1958 P 10/25/1958 Bp James Pernette DeWolfe. m 10/10/1959 Margaret A Thomas c 1. Vic All SS Ch Round Lake NY 2005-2013; Ret 1994-2016; Chapl Nassau Police Dept 1991-1994; R The Ch Of The Ascen Rockville Ct NY 1972-1994; Cn to Bp Dio Long Island Garden City NY 1967-1972; Chapl (Lt) US Navy 1966-1967; Vic All Souls Ch Stony Brook NY 1958-1966. Who's Who Rel 1977; Dictionary Intl Biographies 1970.

LATHROP, Brian Albert (NY) 63 Downing St Apt 4-A, New York NY 10014 **Pstr Psychoanalyst Psych & Sprtlty Inst 1993-** B Buffalo NY 1957 s Calvin & Wilma. BA Canisius Coll 1979; MDiv GTS 1983; PsyD Westchester Inst 1992. D 6/11/1983 P 3/1/1984 Bp Harold Barrett Robinson. m 10/26/2013 John Eugene Verzi. Sr Asst Gr Epis Ch New York NY 1987-1993; Tutor The GTS New York NY 1986-1988; S Geo's-By-The-River Rumson NJ 1985-1987; Cur St Geo By-The- River 1985-1987; Cur Gr Epis Ch Utica NY 1983-1985. AAPC 1993; Amer Grp Psych Assoc 2000; Natl Assn Advancement Of Psychoanalysis 1993.

LATHROP, John (Me) 101 Paseo Encantado Ne, Santa Fe NM 87506 **Team Mnstry Chili Line Mnstry Espanola & Chama NM 2003-** B Norwalk CT 1947 s Alvin & Dorothea. BFA Denison U 1969; MDiv Yale DS 1972; ADN U of Maine 1986. D 6/16/1972 P 12/20/1972 Bp John Mc Gill Krumm. m 9/4/2004 Ann Dilworth. Int S Paul's Ch Brunswick ME 1986-1988; The Hunger Ntwk Columbus OH 1980-1984; Dio Sthrn Ohio Cincinnati OH 1979-1980; R Our Sav Ch Mechanicsburg OH 1977-1984; Trin Ch Columbus OH 1972-1976; Pres / CEO Cmnty Hsng Serv Pasadena CA 1979-1995.

LATHROP, John Campbell (Los) 1447 Kentwood Lane, Pisgah Forest NC 28768 **Died 12/9/2015** B Detroit MI 1931 s Henry & Thelma. BA U CA 1955; MDiv Epis TS of the SW 1958; PhD California Grad TS 1974; PhD Grad Theol Un 1974; Command and Gnrl Stff Coll 1975. D 6/16/1958 P 2/1/1959 Bp Donald J Campbell. m 11/29/1981 Leslie Slagle. Ret 2000-2015; Ch Commissioners, Ex. Sec. Angl Ch of Uganda Kampala Uganda 1992-1994; R S Tim's Par Compton CA 1991-2000, R 1991-2000, R 1960-1966; P-in-c S Dav's Par N Hollywood CA 1990-1991; P-in-c S Jas' Par So Pasadena CA 1989; Ch Of Our Sav Par San Gabr CA 1979-1980; Assoc Ch of Our Sav San Gabr CA 1978-1980; R S Geo's Par La Can CA 1966-1978, Vic / R 1966-1978; S Paul's Pomona Pomona CA 1958-1959; Pres / CEO Cmnty Hsng Serv Pasadena CA 1979-1995; Vic St Pauls Ch San Jacinto CA 1958-1959. Assn of CA Inst of Tech; Sons of the Amer Revolution. R Emer S Tim's Par, Compton CA 2000; Prov Cn All SS Cathd, Kampala, Uganda (Angl) 1993; Legion of Merit and 27 Decorations and Awards U.S. Army 1991; Colonel U.S. Army 1984.

LATIMER, Susan (SwFla) 502 Druid Hills Road, Temple Terrace FL 33617 **R St Cathr of Alexandria Epis Ch Temple Terrace FL 2011-** B Escondido CA 1960 d James & Jane. BA Ya 1982; MA USC 1984; MDiv Candler TS Emory U 1992. D 6/6/1992 P 12/12/1992 Bp Frank Kellogg Allan. m 5/9/1992 John B Roberts c 2. R S Jn's Epis Ch Charleston WV 2008-2011; R S Mk's Ch Waterville ME 2001-2008; Asst S Barth's Epis Ch Atlanta GA 1998-2001; Chapl Agnes Scott Coll 1996-1998; Assoc H Trin Par Decatur GA 1994-1998; Asst Emm Epis Ch Athens GA 1992-1993; Chapl Res Ga Bapt Med Cntr Atlanta GA 1990-1992. ACPE; Compass Rose Soc. Theta Pi.

LATTA, Dennis James (Ind) 2742 S Hickory Corner Rd, Vincennes IN 47591 **Vic S Jas Ch Vincennes IN 2015-, 2014-2015; Dn SW Dnry Dio Indianapo-**

lis 2014-; **Vic S Jn's Ch Washington IN 1994-** B Terre Haute IN 1948 s Dennis & Marjorie. BA Indiana St U 1970; MS Indiana St U 1972; MS Indiana St U 1976. D 6/24/1994 P 2/25/1995 Bp Edward Witker Jones. m 6/20/1976 Mary Kathryn Barekman c 3.

✠ **LATTIME, The Rt Rev Mark A** (Ak) 1205 Denali Way, Fairbanks AK 99701 **Bp of Alaska Dio Alaska Fairbanks AK 2010-** B Puerto Rico 1966 s Roy & Deborah. BA Dickinson Coll 1988; MDiv Bex Sem 1997. D 5/31/1997 P 12/13/1997 Bp William George Burrill Con 9/4/2010 for Ak. c 3. R S Mich's Ch Geneseo NY 2000-2010; Asst R E Lee Memi Ch (Epis) Lexington VA 1997-2000; Pres Livingston Cnty Cltn of Ch 2006-2010; Stwdshp Consult Dio Rochester Henrietta 2004-2010, GC Dep 2003-2010, Dist Dn 2001-2010. mlattime@gci.net

LAU, Gordon K (Cal) 1003 Azalea Dr, Alameda CA 94502 **Died 11/9/2016** B Canton Kwangtung CN 1942 s Baldwin & Yi-So. BS California Bapt U 1973; MDiv CDSP 1976; DMin CDSP 2000; CDSP 2007. Trans 3/18/1980 as Priest Bp Robert Hume Cochrane. m 10/22/1977 Yvonne Man c 2. R Epis Ch Of Our Sav Oakland CA 1985-2008; Vic Ch Of The H Apos Seattle WA 1980-1984; Vic S Jas of Jerusalem Seattle WA 1979-1984; Dio Olympia Seattle 1979; Serv Hong Kong Angl Ch 1976-1979. "Chinese Bk of Common Pryr (Translation)," Ch Pub, Inc., New York, 2004. DD CDSP 2007.

LAU, Ronald Taylor Christensen (LI) 326 Clinton St, Brooklyn NY 11231 **R Chr Ch Cobble Hill Brooklyn NY 1999-** B Los Angeles CA 1947 s Edward & Robley. BA U CA 1970; MDiv GTS 1973; STM GTS 1975; Harv 1982; Cert Col-Bus Sch 1996. D 6/9/1973 Bp Paul Moore Jr P 12/16/1973 Bp Horace W B Donegan. m 3/12/2013 Haigo H Salow. Dio Long Island Garden City NY 2004-2007; P-in-c Ch Of The Nativ Brooklyn NY 1998-1999; Dio New York New York NY 1997-1998; Vic S Jas Epis Ch Fordham Bronx NY 1996; Int S Jas' Epis Ch Hackettstown NJ 1995-1996; Int All SS Epis Par Hoboken NJ 1995; R Epis Par Of S Mich And All Ang Tucson AZ 1988-1994; R Ch Of The H Nativ Bronx NY 1983-1988; Asst S Jn's Ch Norristown PA 1979-1981; Asst S Jos's Ch Queens Vlg NY 1976-1977; Asst Ch Of S Mary The Vrgn New York NY 1974; Treas Geo Mercer TS Garden City NY 2000-2002. Ed, "The 1979 Bk of Common Pryr and the New Revised Standard Version Bible w the Apocrypha," Oxf Press, 1993; Ed, "The Cath Study Bible," Oxf Press, 1990; Ed, "1981 Epis Ch Annual," Morehouse-Barlow, 1981; Ed, "1980 Epis Ch Annual," Morehouse-Barlow, 1980; Ed, "New Scofied Reference Bibleof Common Pryr," Oxf Press, 1980; Ed, "1979 Epis Ch Annual," Morehouse-Barlow, 1979; Ed, "1978 Epis Ch Annual," Morehouse-Barlow, 1978; Ed, "New Revised Standard Version Study Bible," Oxf Press, 1977; Ed, "1977 Epis Ch Annual," Morehouse-Barlow, 1977; Ed, "1976 Epis Ch Annual," Morehouse-Barlow, 1976; Ed, "1975 Epis Ch Annual," Morehouse-Barlow, 1975; Ed, "1974 Epis Ch Annual," Morehouse-Barlow, 1974. Affirming Catholicism 1999; Angl Soc 1972.

LAUCHER, Bill (Tex) 417 Avenue Of Oaks St, Houston TX 77009 **Vic S Alb's Ch Houston TX 2001-; Vic The Great Cmsn Fndt Houston TX 2001-** B Saint Louis MO 1950 s Richard & Jean. TCU 1969; BA U of Houston 1973; MDiv VTS 1994. D 6/25/1994 Bp Maurice Manuel Benitez P 1/3/1995 Bp William Elwood Sterling. m 4/5/1974 Cheryl E Laucher c 2. Asst Calv Epis Ch Richmond TX 1994-2001; Mssy SAMS Ambridge PA 1982-1989; Chair Sprtl Dir Sch Dio Texas Houston TX 2004-2011; Hisp Cmsn 2002-. Bro Of S Andr; Ord Of S Lk. St. Geo Epis Awd Epis Ch And Bsa 2000; 6-Year Serv Recognition SAMS 1989.

LAUDISIO, Patricia Devin (Colo) 3328 Sentinel Dr, Boulder CO 80301 B Sarasota FL 1943 d Fletcher & Mary. Hollins U; Iliff TS; Loyola U; BS Metropltn St Coll of Denver; OH SU; S Thos Sem; U of Florida. D 6/18/1994 Bp William Jerry Winterrowd. m 5/26/1969 Antonio L Laudisio c 2. D S Jn's Epis Ch Boulder CO 1994-2008. Colorado Haiti Proj; Contemplative Outreach.

LAUER, Daniel Donald (WTex) B Duluth MN 1967 s Donald & Mary. MDiv Epis TS of the SW 2002. D 6/4/2002 Bp Robert Boyd Hibbs P 2/28/2003 Bp James Edward Folts. m 11/12/1988 Renae Ann Lauer c 4. Cur Chr Epis Ch San Antonio TX 2002-2007.

LAUGHLIN III, Ledlie I (WA) 4201 Albemarle St NW, Washington DC 20016 **R S Columba's Ch Washington DC 2015-; Pres, Stndg Com Dio Pennsylvania Philadelphia PA 2010-** B New York NY 1959 s Ledlie & Roxana. BA Ob 1982; Cert Urasenke Chanoyu Gakuen TS Kyoto JP 1984; MDiv Ya Berk 1987. D 10/9/1988 Bp Paul Moore Jr P 5/6/1989 Bp John Shelby Spong. m 11/7/1987 Sarah C Clifford c 2. R S Ptr's Ch Philadelphia PA 1999-2015; R Gr Epis Ch Norwalk CT 1993-1999; R S Paul's Ch In Bergen Jersey City NJ 1991-1993; Asst R S Pat's Ch Washington DC 1989-1991; Par Mssnr S Paul's Epis Ch Paterson NJ 1988-1989.

LAUGHLIN JR, Ledlie Irwin (Eur) 63 Ford Hill Rd, West Cornwall CT 06796 **Ret 1995-** B Princeton NJ 1930 s Ledlie & Roberta. BA Pr 1952; STB GTS 1955. D 6/19/1955 P 1/1/1956 Bp Benjamin M Washburn. m 4/19/1958 Roxana Dodd Laughlin c 3. Int Cathd Ch Of S Paul Burlington VT 1996-1997; S Jas Epis Ch Firenze 50123 1992-1995; St Jas Ch 1992-1995; Hon Cn The Amer Cathd of the H Trin Paris 75008 1992-1995; Joint Cmsn on AIDS Dio New York New York NY 1988-1991, Chair, COM 1988-1990, Educ Off 1971-1987,

Adult Educ Div DeptCE ECEC 1969-1970; The Ch Of S Lk In The Fields New York NY 1976-1992; Trin Par New York NY 1972-1976; Dn Trin And S Phil's Cathd Newark NJ 1963-1969; Assoc Gr Ch Van Vorst Jersey City NJ 1955-1963.

LAUGHLIN, Ophelia (NJ) Waterman Avenue, Rumson NJ 07760 **R S Geo's-By-The-River Rumson NJ 2000-, Cur 1993-1997** B Princeton NJ 1959 d James & Julia. BA Pr 1981; MS Pace U 1983; MDiv GTS 1993. D 6/12/1993 Bp George Phelps Mellick Belshaw. m 5/3/1996 Eric Pearl c 2. R S Paul's Ch Southington CT 1997-2000.

LAUGHMAN JR, Richard (NCal) St. James of Jerusalem Episcopal Church, 556 N George Washington Blvd, Yuba City CA 95993 B Elkhart IN 1952 s Richard & Patricia. AB Coll of Wm & Mary; MS Indiana U at So Bend. D 3/23/2013 P 11/1/2013 Bp Barry Leigh Beisner. m 4/16/1983 Chowkeaw Laughman.

LAUK, Candice Ruth (NMich) 1003 Wickman Dr, Iron Mountain MI 49801 **P H Trin Ch Iron Mtn MI 2004-** B 1956 D 3/1/1998 Bp Thomas Kreider Ray P 2/29/2004 Bp James Arthur Kelsey. m 5/12/1984 Vincent C Lauk c 3.

LAURA, Ronald Samuel (Vt) 158 Concord Rd Apt K9, Billerica MA 01821 B Boston MA 1945 D 8/29/1970 Bp Harvey D Butterfield.

LAURINEC, Jennene Ellen (Tex) 308 Cottage Rd., Carthage TX 75633 **Vic S Jn's Epis Ch Carthage TX 2008-; Bus Mgr and Chapl Trin Epis Sch 2001-** B Craig CO 1954 d Dean & Viola. BBA LeTourneau U 2001. D 6/28/2008 Bp Don Adger Wimberly P 1/10/2009 Bp Rayford Baines High Jr. m 1/29/1977 Steven Laurinec c 3.

LAURITZEN, Ruth (Wyo) D 6/25/2016 P 6/16/2017 Bp John Smylie.

LAUTENSCHLAGER, Paul John (Colo) 11 W. Madison Street, Colorado Springs CO 80907 B Kitchener ON CA 1946 s Kenneth & Lucile. BA Mssh Coll 1969; MDiv PDS 1972. D 5/27/1972 P 3/14/1973 Bp Dean Theodore Stevenson. m 12/28/1989 Nancy J Harp-Lautenschlager c 1. Reg Mssnr Dio Colorado Denver CO 2006-2009; Reg Mssnr Dio Colorado Denver CO 2003-2004; R Ch Of S Mich The Archangel Colorado Spg CO 2001-2011; R Ch Of The Trsfg Palos Pk IL 1992-2001; R S Mk's Ch S Louis MO 1985-1992; Asst R S Tim's Epis Ch S Louis MO 1978-1984; R S Paul's Ch Philipsburg PA 1975-1978; Asst R Cathd Ch Of S Steph Harrisburg PA 1972-1975; Dio Cntrl Pennsylvania Harrisburg PA 1972-1973; Mssnr, Sangre de Cristo Reg Dio Colorado Denver CO 2006-2009, Mssnr, Sangre de Cristo Reg 2003-2005; COM Dio Missouri S Louis MO 1986-1987.

LAUZON, Marcia (Mont) D 5/18/2014 Bp Charles Franklin Brookhart Jr.

LAVALLEE, Armand Aime (Ct) 5523 Birchhill Rd, Charlotte NC 28227 **P Assoc S Mart's Epis Ch Charlotte NC 2000-, Asst 1998; Mentor, EFM Sewanee U So TS Sewanee TN 1983-** B Pawtucket RI 1934 s Alphonse & Stacia. BA Ken 1956; MDiv EDS 1959; PhD Harv 1967. D 6/20/1959 P 12/19/1959 Bp John S Higgins. m 4/7/2005 Alison Hadley LaVallee c 2. Asst S Jas Epis Ch Danbury CT 1982-1998; Fac Dio Rhode Island Providence RI 1982-1987, Dep GC 1973-1981; R S Mk's Epis Ch Riverside RI 1971-1982, Asst 1960-1962; R S Thos Ch Greenville RI 1962-1970; Cur S Barn Ch Warwick RI 1959-1960.

LAVALLEE, Donald Alphonse (RI) 1665 Broad St, Cranston RI 02905 B Central Falls RI 1940 s Alphonse & Stacia. BA Br 1962; BD EDS 1965; DMin Sewanee: The U So, TS 1982; MBA U of Rhode Island 1990. D 6/19/1965 P 2/1/1966 Bp John S Higgins. m 6/30/1991 Terri Idskou c 1. Ch Of The Trsfg Providence RI 1965-1999.

LAVANN, Jason Gary (Mil) 216 E Chandler Blvd, Burlington WI 53105 **S Lk's Epis Ch Milwaukee WI 2016-** B West Allis WI 1978 s Gary & Barbara. BA Marq 2001; MDiv St Fran Sem 2006. Rec 9/3/2013 Bp Steven Andrew Miller. m 8/24/2012 Kristy Lynn Lavann. S Jn The Div Epis Ch Burlington WI 2013-2016. jason.lavann@gmail.com

LAVENGOOD, Henrietta Louise (NJ) 211 Falls Ct, Medford NJ 08055 **Pstr Counslg/Rx Henrietta L. Lavengood D.Min. LLC 2011-; Asstg P/Pstr Counslr Trin Ch Moorestown NJ 2010-** B Mount Holly NJ 1954 d Henry & Francis. BA Drew U 1976; MDiv UTS 1982; Cert Blanton-Peale Grad Inst 1985; DMin NYTS 2002; Cert Trauma Cntr Boston MA 2004. D 6/7/1986 P 12/11/1986 Bp Paul Moore Jr. m 1/3/1997 Martin Brownlee Lavengood. Stff Ther Coun for Relationships Philadelphia PA 2004-2011; Vic S Mary's Ch Clementon NJ 2004-2008; Trin Ch Ft Wayne IN 2000-2001; Stff Ther Samar Counslg Cntr Elkhart IN 1997-1998; Int S Jn Of The Cross Bristol IN 1997; Assoc P Par of Chr the Redeem Pelham NY 1995-1997; S Mk's Ch Mt Kisco NY 1994-1995; Dir Mid Westchester Pstr Counslg Ctr. Tarrytown NY 1992-1996; Stff Ther Blanton Peale Counslg Cntr New York NY 1982-1991. AAPC 1988.

LAVENGOOD, Martin Brownlee (NJ) 211 Falls Ct, Medford NJ 08055 **P The Evergreens Moorestown NJ 2009-** B New York NY 1953 s Russell & Roberta. BA Eisenhower Coll 1976; MA Col 1983; MDiv GTS 1991. D 6/8/1991 P 12/1/1991 Bp Richard Frank Grein. m 1/3/1997 Henrietta Louise Brandt. All SS Ch Syracuse IN 2000-2003; R S Alb's Epis Ch Ft Wayne IN 1998-2000; R S Jas' Epis Ch Goshen IN 1994-1998. Roberta C Rudin Dioc Schlr.

LAVER, Michael (Roch) D 6/3/2017 Bp Prince Grenville Singh.

LAVERONI, Alfred Frank (Md) 312 Cigar Loop, Hvre De Grace MD 21078 B New York NY 1938 s Walter & Annette. BA Hofstra U 1960; MDiv GTS 1963; MS Amer Tech U 1974; DMin Drew U 1983. D 6/15/1963 Bp James Per-

L

nette DeWolfe P 12/1/1963 Bp Jonathan Goodhue Sherman. m 8/30/1973 Jean Mohr c 1. Alt - Dioc Coun 1996-1999; Pres Harford Cnty Reg Coun Of Epis Ch 1995-1996; Vice-Pres Harford Cnty Reg Coun Of Epis Ch 1994-1995; Pres Harford Cnty Reg Coun Of Epis Ch 1991-1992; Vice-Pres Harford Cnty Reg Coun Of Epis Ch 1990-1991; Mssn Cltn Taskforce Dio Maryland Baltimore MD 1989-1993; Assoc S Mary's Ch Abingdon MD 1986-2000; LocTen Gr Memi Ch Darlington MD 1985-1986; Assoc Gr Ch Pemberton NJ 1982-1983; R S Barth Arlington TX 1975-1977; Off Of Bsh For ArmdF New York NY 1967-1987; Chapl (Major) US-A 1967-1987; R Atone Brooklyn NY 1964-1967. Auth/Ed, "The Seder: Serv Bklet"; Auth, "Personl Effectiveness Trng Manual"; Auth, "Soc Alienation In Jr Enlisted Ranks"; Auth, "Ldrshp In Pluralistic Setting".

LAVERY, Patricia Anne (NwPa) PO Box 287, Grove City PA 16127 **D Ch Of Our Fr Foxburg PA 2013-; D Ch Of The Epiph Grove City PA 2013-** B Pittsburgh PA 1950 d Charles & Irene. BS Ohio U 1972; MA Carlow U 2002. D 12/4/2010 Bp Sean Walter Rowe. c 2.

LAVETTY, Denise Jean (NY) 224 Waverly Pl, New York NY 10014 **Dio New York New York NY 2013-; Assoc Dir Ecclesia Mnstrs of New York 2012-; D S Jn's Ch New York NY 2011-** B Flushing NY 1951 d Eugene & Margaret. AS LaGuardia Cmnty Coll 1986; BA Baruch Coll 1992; MA GTS 2013. D 5/7/2011 Bp Mark Sean Sisk. c 1.

LAVINE, Patricia Iva (Alb) 323 Lakeshore Dr, Norwood NY 13668 B Potsdam NY 1942 d Clarence & Harriett. D 6/30/2002 Bp Daniel William Herzog. m 6/1/1963 Richard Douglas LaVine c 2. D Zion Ch Colton NY 2004-2005; D S Phil's Ch Norwood NY 2002-2004.

LAVOE, John F (CNY) 210 Yoxall Ln, Oriskany NY 13424 **arts & Bk Revs Acad of Par Cler 2011-; Ret Var: Wrshp supply; educational & Sprtl Prog 2009-** B Brooklyn NY 1946 s George & Josephine. S Josephs Novitiate Valatie NY 1965; S Edwards U Austin TX 1967; BA Rockhurst U 1969; MDiv PDS 1972; Lic FCC-Ham & Gnrl Radiotelephone 1985; Cert Par Dvlpmt Inst 1987; DMin Ecum TS 1999. D 5/15/1972 Bp Ned Cole P 6/20/1973 Bp Lloyd Edward Gressle. m 10/4/1986 Susan L Lavoe c 2. Dir of Dioc Formation Dio Cntrl New York Liverpool NY 2005-2008, 1986-1991; S Jn's Ch Whitesboro NY 2000-2009, In-charge; then R 1987-1994; R S Geo's Epis Ch Chadwicks NY 1995-2000; R All SS Ch Utica NY 1990-2008, R 1981-1990; Utica Area Coop Mnstry Whitesboro NY 1990-2008; Lead R Utica NY Area Coop Mnstry 1987-1990; R Emm Ch Adams NY 1975-1981; Sum only Chapl St. Lk's by the Lake Henderson Harbor NY 1975-1981; Zion Ch Pierrepont Manor NY 1975-1981; Cur Chr Ch Reading PA 1972-1975. Auth, "Multiple Rel Bk Revs; 1992-2014," *Sharing the Pract*, APC Journ, 2014; Auth, "Var arts on Mnstry; 1992-2014," *Sharing the Pract*, APC Journ, 2014; Auth, "Acrostic Offertory," *LivCh*, 1993; Auth, "6 Selected Sermons; 1978 -1984," *LayR Sermons*, Seabury, 1984; Auth, "New Beatitudes," *Wit*, 1984; Auth, "Bk Revs," *Angl Theol Rev.*, 1974. Acad of Par Cler 1984; Cbury Way 1991-2013.

LAW, Eric Hung-Fat (Los) 351 Sandpiper St, Palm Desert CA 92260 **P Kaleidoscope Inst Los Angeles CA 2006-** B HK 1957 s Kwok-Nam & Un-Oi. BS Cor 1978; MDiv EDS 1984. D 6/23/1984 Bp O'Kelley Whitaker P 6/2/1985 Bp Robert Claflin Rusack. m 7/10/2013 Steve Rutberg. Dio Los Angeles Los Angeles CA 2002-2005, Mssnr for Congrl Dvlpmt 2000-2006, 1984-1991; Congrl Dvlpmt Off Serv the Angl Ch of Can 1996-2000; Diversity and Cong Consult 1991-1996. "El Labo Habitara con el Cardero," Cathd Cntr Press, LA; Auth, "Finding Intimacy in a Wrld of Fear," Chalice Press, St Louis; Auth, "The Wolf Shall Dwell w The Lamb," Chalice Press, St Louis; Auth, "Inclusion," Chalice Press, St Louis; Auth, "The Bush Was Blazing But Not Consumed:," Chalice Press, St Louis; Auth, "Sacr Acts, H Change," Chalice Press, St Louis; Auth, "The Word at the Crossings," Chalice Press, St Louis.

LAWBAUGH, William M (CPa) 813 Franklin Avenue, Aliquippa PA 15001 **open Dio Cntrl Pennsylvania 2012-** B St Marys MO 1942 s Emmanuel & Halita. PhD U of Missour Columbia MO 1972; MA Mt St Marys Sem Emmitsburg MD 1995; MTS VTS 2007. D 6/9/2007 P 12/22/2007 Bp Nathan Dwight Baxter. c 7. Dio Cntrl Pennsylvania Harrisburg PA 2012; R S Paul's Ch Lock Haven PA 2007-2012. Cmnty of Celebration (Comp) 2004.

LAWLER, Gary Elwyn Andrew (Chi) 6033 North Sheridan Road - 27J, Chicago IL 60660 B Monroe WI 1944 s Elwyn & Shirlah. BA Elmhurst Coll 1966; MDiv Nash 1989. D 6/17/1989 Bp Frank Tracy Griswold III P 12/17/1989 Bp James Winchester Montgomery. R The Ch Of S Anne Morrison IL 1997-2015; S Greg's Ch Prairieville LA 1991-1997; S Mich's Ch Baton Rouge LA 1991-1997; Cur Ch Of S Mary The Vrgn New York NY 1989-1991. SocMary, La Epis Cleric Assn, Ord Of S Ben.

LAWLER, Rick (WNC) Po Box 2680, Blowing Rock NC 28605 **R S Mary Of The Hills Epis Par Blowing Rock NC 1995-** B Chicago IL 1957 s Joseph & Helen. BA Indiana U 1979; MDiv Nash 1985. D 6/14/1985 P 12/1/1985 Bp William Carl Frey. m 12/22/1984 Elizabeth Lawler c 2. R S Raphael Epis Ch Colorado Sprg CO 1987-1995; S Tim's Epis Ch Littleton CO 1987; Cur S Jos's Ch Lakewood CO 1985-1987. Soc Of S Jn The Evang.

LAWLER, Steven William (Mo) 33 N Clay Ave, Saint louis MO 63135 **Mng Dir Opinions Incorporated 2004-; Fac and Coordntr Bus Stds Washington U in**

St Louis - U Coll 2004-; Int R S Steph's Ch S Louis MO 2001- B Woodstock IL 1954 s James & Helen. BS Rockford Coll 1981; MDiv SWTS 1984; STM Ya Berk 1988; MBA Washington U 1997; PhD Tilburg U Tilburg Nl 2014. D 6/16/1984 Bp Quintin Ebenezer Primo Jr P 12/15/1984 Bp James Winchester Montgomery. m 11/2/2006 Lynda Anne Morrison c 1. Int S Matt's Epis Ch Warson Woods Kirkwood MO 1998-1999; Prncpl The Lawler Orgnztn 1997-2001; Dir Of Rel Stds Holland Hall Sch 1995-1998; Assoc for Educ and Formation S Mich & S Geo S Louis MO 1988-1998; Dir of Rel Stds Holland Hall Sch Tulsa OK 1986-1988. Auth, "Chrsnty & Crisis"; Auth, "The Angl Dig"; Auth, "Thesquare.Com"; Auth, "The St Louis Post-Dispatch"; Auth, "LivCh"; Auth, "The Ch Times"; Auth, "Sprtlty And Hlth". Amer Chapl Ord Of S Jn Of Beverley 1990.

LAWLOR, Jay R (WMich) Diocese of Western Michigan, 535 S. Burdick Street, Suite 1, Kalamazoo MI 49007 B Exeter NH 1970 s Joseph & Lois. BA Stonehill Coll 1993; MA U of Connecticut 1995; MDiv EDS 2002. D 6/15/2002 P 5/31/2003 Bp M(Arvil) Thomas Shaw. m 7/20/2002 Angela Kay Lawlor c 1. Dio Wstrn Michigan Kalamazoo MI 2012-2014; R S Lk's Par Kalamazoo MI 2009-2012; Assoc Ch Of The Nativ Raleigh NC 2008-2009; R S Paul Ch Exton PA 2005-2007; Assoc S Mary's Epis Ch Ardmore PA 2003-2005; Asst Gr Ch New Bedford MA 2002-2003. Auth, "Faithful Action: How Each Chr Can End Pvrty," Gold Lion, 2008; Contrib, "Reconcilers in a Violent Wrld," *Get Up Off Your Knees: Preaching the U2 Catalog*, Cowley, 2003; Auth, "The Ch and Intl Dvlpmt: Seeking Justice and Peace in Mssn to the Wrld's poor," Universal Pub, 1999.

LAWRENCE JR, Albert Sumner (Tex) 14 Sedgewick Pl, The Woodlands TX 77382 **Ret 2000-** B Medford MA 1936 s Albert & Gladys. BA U of Maryland 1958; BD EDS 1961; DMin Luther TS 1979. D 9/10/1961 P 12/30/1962 Bp Frederic Cunningham Lawrence. m 4/20/1968 Dawn Lawrence c 4. R Ch Of The Ascen Houston TX 1979-2000; R S Paul's Ch Winona MN 1971-1979; Assoc S Jas Ch Lancaster PA 1966-1970; Asst Chr Ch Cambridge Cambridge MA 1961-1966. Auth, "The Contentment You Long For," *Winepress Grp*, 2009; Auth, "The Original Christmas Gift," *Selah*, Selah, 2001. EvangES 1971-1979; FOW 1971-1979; Ord Of S Lk 1971-1979.

LAWRENCE, Amy (Cal) 2711 Harkness St, Sacramento CA 95818 B Walnut Creek CA 1964 d Gary & Joan. BA U Pac 1986; MDiv UTS 1991. D 6/4/1994 P 6/3/1995 Bp William Edwin Swing. All Souls Par In Berkeley Berkeley CA 2004; Asst S Ptr's Epis Ch Redwood City CA 1995-1998.

LAWRENCE, Bruce Bennett (NC) C/O Department Of Religion, Duke University, Durham NC 27706 **Prof Of Rel Duke 1979-** B Newton NJ 1941 s Joseph & Emma. BA Pr 1962; BD EDS 1967; PhD Ya 1972. D 6/13/1967 P 12/1/1967 Bp Walter H Gray. m 4/20/1983 Miriam Lawrence c 2. Non-par 1974-1979; Cur S Barth's Ch Pittsboro NC 1972-1974; Cur Ascen Ch New Haven CT 1967-1971. Auth, "Notes From A Distant Flute"; Auth, "Ibn Khaldun & Islamic Ideology".

LAWRENCE, Catherine Abbott (NY) 1415 Pelhamdale Ave, Christ Church, Pelham NY 10803 **Assoc D Chr's Ch Rye NY 2012-** B San Francisco CA 1939 d Louis & Shirley. D 5/1/2010 Bp Mark Sean Sisk. c 3.

LAWRENCE, Charles Kane Cobb (Lex) 101 S. Hanover Ave, Apt 7M, Lexington KY 40502 **Ret 1982-; Ret 1981-** B Lynn MA 1917 s William & Hannah. BA Harv 1938; BD VTS 1941; GTS 1952; STM UTS 1952. D 6/13/1941 Bp William A Lawrence P 5/28/1942 Bp Edwin A Penick. m 6/14/1980 Mildred Terrell Lawrence c 4. Epis TS Lexington KY 1971-1981; Prof of Systematic & Moral Theol Epis TS Lexington KY 1958-1982; Chapl (U of K) S Aug's Chap Lexington KY 1958-1962; Chapl U of Pennsylvania Philadelphia PA 1953-1958; Vic Chr Ch Biddeford ME 1944-1949; Cur Trin Epis Ch Columbus GA 1942-1943; Cur Calv Ch Tarboro NC 1941-1942; ExCoun Dio Lexington Lexington 1959-1965; Coll Wk Cmsn Dio Pennsylvania Philadelphia PA 1953-1958. Hon DD ETSKy 1970.

LAWRENCE, Dean (Tex) 1101 Rock Prairie Road, College Station TX 77845 **P-in-c S Fran Epis Ch Coll Sta TX 2013-** B Houston TX 1970 s James & Mary. BS Texas A&M U 1993; MDiv VTS 2009. D 6/20/2009 P 1/28/2010 Bp C Andrew Doyle. m 11/1/1997 Sarah B Lawrence c 1. Assoc R S Chris's Ch League City TX 2009-2013.

LAWRENCE, Eric John (Nev) 2306 Paradise Dr Apt 222, Reno NV 89512 B Buffalo WY 1967 BA U of Nevada at Reno. D 6/21/2003 P 12/24/2003 Bp Katharine Jefferts Schori. m 10/18/2002 Robyn Opoka.

LAWRENCE, Gerard Martin (Mass) 22874 NE 127th Way, Redmond WA 98053 B Long Beach CA 1936 s Joseph & Tillie. California Inst of Tech 1958; BA U of Washington 1960. D 9/29/1975 Bp Ivol I Curtis P 6/13/1980 Bp Robert Hume Cochrane. m 4/3/1982 Karen Lawrence c 8. P-in-c Trin Epis Ch Rockland MA 1999-2007; Assoc S Lk's Epis Ch Scituate MA 1997-1998; Assoc S Wilfrid Of York Epis Ch Huntington Bch CA 1986-1996; Assoc Emm Epis Ch Mercer Island WA 1982-1984; Assoc S Marg's Epis Ch Bellevue WA 1975-1982.

LAWRENCE JR, Harry Martin (ETenn) 1800 Lula Lake Rd, Lookout Mountain GA 30750 **Asstg P Chr Ch - Epis Chattanooga TN 1979-** B Chattanooga TN 1931 s Harry & Mildred. BS W&L 1953; MD U of Tennessee 1956; MS Mayo Clnc 1967. D 6/25/1978 Bp William F Gates Jr P 6/1/1979 Bp William Evan

L

Sanders. m 12/29/1957 Martha Sue Rice. P-in-c S Mary The Vrgn Chattanooga TN 1981-1983; S Mart Of Tours Epis Ch Chattanooga TN 1979-1980. Auth, "Effect Of Corneal Contact Lenses In Rabbits".

LAWRENCE, John Arthur (Chi) 712 Mockingbird Lane, Kerrville TX 78028 **Ret 1999-** B Fort Worth TX 1935 s Kelley & Hazel. BA Sewanee U So 1957; MDiv SWTS 1971. D 6/16/1971 P 12/21/1971 Bp Iveson Batchelor Noland. m 1/9/1987 Waynoka Lee Lawrence. R Gr Epis Ch Hinsdale IL 1989-1999; R S Augustines Ch Metairie LA 1979-1989; EFM Mentor Sewanee U So TS Sewanee TN 1976-1999; Chapl NE LA U Monroe LA 1972-1979; R S Thos' Ch Monroe LA 1972-1979; Cur Gr Memi Hammond LA 1971-1972; HOB - Ligislative Secy GC 2000-2013.

LAWRENCE, John Elson (WA) 4336 Wordsworth Way, Venice FL 34293 **Asstg P S Mk's Epis Ch Venice FL 2013-** B Brooklyn NY 1945 s Edward & Gladys. Capital U; BA GW 1967; MDiv GTS 1970. D 6/13/1970 P 12/19/1970 Bp Jonathan Goodhue Sherman. m 5/10/1986 Jeramy Lawrence c 3. Int R The Epis Ch Of The Gd Shpd Venice FL 2012; Int R S Alb's Par Washington DC 2010-2011; Int R S Pat's Ch Washington DC 2008-2010; Int R Calv Ch Columbia MO 2006-2008; Chf Judge, Trial Crt Dio Rhode Island 2001-2006; R Trin Ch Newport RI 2000-2006; Cn to the Ordnry Dio Sthrn Ohio Cincinnati OH 1991-2000; R S Chris's Ch Fairborn OH 1987-1991; Ed, LEAVEN NNECA 1981-1988; Dn Great So Bay Dnry 1981-1985; R S Ann's Ch Sayville NY 1980-1985; Secy of Dio Dio Long Island 1978-1985; R All SS Ch Bayside NY 1975-1980; Asst R Gr Epis Ch Nyack NY 1971-1975; Cur All SS Ch Great Neck NY 1970-1971; Chair, Cler Compstn Com Dio Rhode Island Providence RI 2001-2006. Auth, *Leaven (Ed) (1981-1988)*, NNECA. Hon Cn Chr Ch Cathd, Cincinnati, Ohio 1993.

LAWRENCE, Matthew Richard (NCal) 18 Foremast Cv, Corte Madera CA 94925 B Missoula MT 1956 s Van & Dulcie. BA Reed Coll 1980; UTS 1981; MDiv U Chi DS 1986; MA U Chi 1987; DMin SWTS 2011. D 6/3/1989 Bp David Elliot Johnson P 6/17/1990 Bp Barbara Clementine Harris. c 1. R Ch Of The Incarn Santa Rosa CA 2003-2015; Sr Chapl Epis Stdt Fndt Ann Arbor MI 1996-2003; Dir Par Mssn S Geo's Ch Milford MI 1995-1996; Int Epis City Mssn Boston MA 1993-1994; R Ch Of Our Sav Arlington MA 1992-1995; D The Cathd Ch Of S Paul Boston MA 1989-1990; Epis Chapl Tufts U Medford MA 1989-1990; Dep GC The Epis Dio Nthrn California Sacramento CA 2008-2011, Stndg Com 2007-2011, First Alt Dep GC 2005-2008; COM Dio Michigan Detroit MI 1999-2003; Chair, Peace and Justice Cmsn Dio Massachusetts Boston MA 1992-1994. Auth, "Letter to an Alpha Friend," *Living Ch*, 2002; Auth, "It's Time for a New Kind of Reformation," *Living Ch*, 2001; Auth, "How to Create a Successful Cmnty-Based Proj," *Congregations*, 2000; Auth, "Bad Preaching 101," *Living Ch*, 1999; Auth, "Foolish Beatitudes," *Chr Century*, 1993; Auth, "Helping the H Sprt Elect a Bp," *Chr Century*, 1989; Auth, "Urban Job Creation Strategies: An Evaltn," *Cntr for Urban Resrch and Plcy Stds*, U Chi, 1986. Natl hon Soc 1974. Urban Scholars Fllshp U Chi 1987. matt. lawrence.in.sr@gmail.com

LAWRENCE, Novella E (NY) 20 Laguardia Ave Apt 4f, Staten Island NY 10314 **D S Paul's Ch Darien CT 2000-; Chapl S Vinc's Cath Med Syatems Staten Island NY 1997-** B Brooklyn NY 1937 d Herbert & Pauline. BS SUNY 1995. D 4/26/1997 Bp Richard Frank Grein. Amer Angl Coun 2002; Evang Fllshp Of Angl Comm 1998.

LAWRENCE, Phil (Okla) 32251 S 616 Rd, Grove OK 74344 **Vic S Andr's Ch Grove OK 2011-** B Tulsa OK 1940 s Philip & Evelyn. BA U of Kansas 1964. D 12/21/2001 P 7/20/2002 Bp Robert Manning Moody. m 3/10/1984 Donna Annis Lawrence. Dio Oklahoma Oklahoma City OK 2006-2012.

LAWRENCE JR, Raymond Johnson (SwVa) 913 Ash Tree Ln., Niskayuna NY 12309 **Gnrl Secy Coll of Pstr Supervision and Psych 1990-** B Portsmouth VA 1934 s Raymond & Gertrude. Randolph-Macon Coll 1954; AB Bos 1956; U of St Andrews 1957; Oxf GB 1958; STM Sewanee: The U So, TS 1966; Chicago Urban Trng Cntr 1967; DMin NYTS 2000. D 6/22/1962 P 6/1/1963 Bp George P Gunn. m 10/30/1993 Ruth Kuo c 4. Dir Of Pstr Care Presb Hosp New York 1991-2007; Pstr Consult Blue Ridge Mntl Hlth Roanoke VA 1988-1991; Chapl Supvsr Goldwater Memi Hosp In New York City 1986-1988; Epis Mssn Soc New York NY 1986-1987; Chapl Supvsr Methodist Hosp Brooklyn NY 1983-1988; Lectr In Pstr Theol U Of S Thos Houston TX 1979-1981; Dir Of Chapl Harris Cnty Jail 1975-1979; Fac Inst Of Rel 1973-1975; Dir Of Chapl Serv S Lk's Hosp Houston TX 1969-1975; Chapl In Res Cntrl St Hosp Milledgeville GA 1968-1969; Asst Ch Of The Ascen Knoxville TN 1964-1966; Cur S Andr's Epis Ch Newport News VA 1962-1964; Serv Methodist Ch 1958-1961. Auth, "Sexual Liberation: The Scandal of Christendom," Praeger, 2007; Auth, "The Poisoning Of Eros," Aug Moore Press, 1989; Auth, "Dav The Bubble Boy & The Boundries Of The Human," *Journ Of The AMA*, 1985. AK Rice 1993; Coll of Pstr Supervision and Psych 1990.

LAWRENCE, Wade William (Pgh) 6911 Prospect Ave, Pittsburgh PA 15202 **D Chr Epis Ch No Hills Pittsburgh PA 2004-; Trin Cathd Pittsburgh PA 1992-** B Almont MI 1947 s Wade & Amelia. BS Wayne 1975; Cert Whitaker TS 1984. D 6/30/1984 Bp Henry Irving Mayson. m 12/23/1967 Ann Alice Lawrence c 3. D Trin Epis Cathd Pittsburgh PA 1992-2004; D S Brendan's

Epis Ch Franklin Pk PA 1990-1992; D S Dav's Ch Southfield MI 1989-1990, D 1986-1988; D S Chris-S Paul Epis Ch Detroit MI 1987-1988; D S Tim's Epis Ch Winston Salem NC 1985-1986. Ord of S Lk 1956-2002.

LAWS III, Robert J (Eas) 30513 Washington St, Princess Anne MD 21853 **S Andr's Epis Ch Princess Anne MD 2013-** B Burlington NC 1968 s Robert & Evelyn. BS E Coast Bible Coll Charlotte NC 1990; MRE Duke DS 1994; MDiv TESM 2000. D 6/10/2000 Bp Robert William Duncan P 12/12/2000 Bp Henry Irving Louttit. m 6/6/1992 Kimiko Laws c 1. Ch Of The Adv Baltimore MD 2012-2013; S Andr The Fisherman Epis Mayo MD 2010-2012; Asst R/ Cbury Chapl Trin Ch Fredericksbrg VA 2007-2010; Int S Paul's Ch Bennettsville SC 2004-2005; Vic S Mary Magd Ch Troy NC 2002-2004; Asst S Thos Ch Savannah GA 2000-2002. SocMary 1998.

LAWS, Thomas Richard (Nwk) 11 Harvard St, Montclair NJ 07042 B Burlington KS 1939 s Floyd & Vesta. BA U of Kansas 1960; MDiv UTS 1964. D 6/3/1967 P 12/1/1967 Bp Horace W B Donegan. c 3. S Gabr's Ch Oak Ridge NJ 2000-2011; All SS' Epis Ch Scotch Plains NJ 1999-2000; Chr Ch Belleville NJ 1997-1999; Chr Ch Newton NJ 1997; Ch Of The H Sprt Verona NJ 1997; R San Andres Ch Yonkers NY 1972-1974; Asst Min Ch Of S Mary The Vrgn New York NY 1967-1971. Auth, "The New Professionals".

LAWSON, Daniel Matthew Custance (Mich) **St Paul's Epis Romeo MI 2016-** B 1976 BA Kalamazoo Coll 1999; MA U of Notre Dame 2003; PhD U of Notre Dame 2005. D 12/12/2015 P 6/11/2016 Bp Wendell Nathaniel Gibbs Jr. m 10/16/1999 Lisa Marie Denton c 3.

LAWSON, Frederick Quinney (U) 4294 Adonis Dr, Salt Lake City UT 84124 **Dn Emer Cathd Ch Of S Mk Salt Lake City UT 2010-, Dn 2002-2010, Cn 1984-2002** B Dayton OH 1945 s Frederick & Janet. Hobart and Wm Smith Colleges 1965; BA U of Leicester 1972; GOE Oxf GB 1975; GOE Oxf GB 1979. Trans 6/1/1989 Bp George Edmonds Bates. Serv Ch of Engl 1983-1989; Stndg Com - Secy Dio Utah Salt Lake City UT 2002-2005. Auth, "Through the Eyes of Many Faiths," *Through the Eyes of Many Faiths 2nd Ed*, Utah Hist Soc, 1992. Fell of Edw King Soc St. Stephens Hse, Oxf Engl 2008; DD Utah St U, Logan, Utah 2007; Doctor of Publ Serv Westminster Coll, Salt Lake City, Utah 2005.

LAWSON, Neil-St Barnabas J (SJ) P.O. Box 7606, Stockton CA 95267 **S Paul's Epis Ch Visalia CA 2009-; R S Ptr's Epis Ch Talladega AL 2002-** B Chicago IL 1951 s Charles & Natalie. BA California St U 1974; MDiv CDSP 1990. D 6/3/1990 P 6/14/1991 Bp David Mercer Schofield. m 2/15/1981 Cynthia S Zepeda c 4. St Pauls Epis Fllshp Visalia CA 2009-2010; S Ptr's Epis Ch Talladega AL 2006-2008; R Ch Of The Redemp Southampton PA 2002-2006; Chr Ch Lemoore CA 1993-2002; Epis Ch Of The Sav Hanford CA 1991-1992.

LAWSON, Paul David (Los) 567 Mayflower Rd, Claremont CA 91711 B Davenport IA 1946 s David & Winifred. BA S Mary Coll Moraga CA 1968; MDiv Epis TS of the SW 1979; DMin Claremont TS 1998. D 8/24/1979 P 2/24/1981 Bp Lemuel Barnett Shirley. m 8/8/1970 Cristina W Lawson c 1. St Cross Epis Ch Hermosa Bch CA 1994-2009; Cathd Cntr Of S Paul Cong Los Angeles CA 1993; Cn for Soc Mnstry Dio Los Angeles Los Angeles CA 1989-1993; R S Thos of Cbury Dio Rio Grande NM 1985-1988; S Thos Of Cbury Epis Ch Albuquerque NM 1984-1989; Asst S Mk's On The Mesa Epis Ch Albuquerque NM 1983-1984; Serv Dio Cyprus and the Gulf 1982-1983; Exec Coun Appointees New York NY 1982-1983; Dio Panama 1979-1982; Serv Ch in Panama 1979-1981; GC Coordntr Epis Ch Cntr New York NY 1985-2005. Auth, "Pryr and the Wk of Cler," *Sprtlty,Contemplation & Transformation*, Lantern Books, 2008; Auth, "Old Wine in New Skins," Lantern Books, 2001; Auth, "Change & Contemplation," *The Div Indwelling*, Continuum, 2001; Auth, "Ldrshp & Change Through Contemplation," *The Sewanee Theol Revs Volume 43:3 Pent*, 2000; Auth, "Breaking Free: Freedom and Self-differentiation," *Leaven Volume 28 no 11 June/July*, 1999; Auth, "Systems Theory and Centering Pryr," *Centering Pryr in Daily Life and Minisry*, Continuum, 1998; Auth, "Pstr & Ch Anxiety," *Leaven*, 1997; Auth, "Losing the W a Second Time," *Evang Outlook*, 1991. Miata Club of Sthrn California 1995; No Amer Patristic Soc 1993-2005. Cn Dio Los Angeles 2002; hon Pub Claremont Theol 1998.

LAWSON, Peter Raymond (Cal) 805 North Webster Street, Petaluma CA 94952 B New Britain CT 1929 s Raymond & Alice. BA Br 1950; STB Ya Berk 1956; Hartford Sem Fndt 1958. D 8/30/1956 P 6/14/1957 Bp Walter H Gray. m 2/14/1981 Danielle Durham c 5. Self-employed Writer/Auth 2002-2015; R S Jas Epis Ch San Francisco CA 1985-1997; Mssnr Dio California San Francisco CA 1982-1985; Int Epis Ch Of Our Sav Oakland CA 1980-1984; Self-employed Consult and Supply P 1971-1980; Dn Chr Ch Cathd Indianapolis IN 1964-1971, Dir of Downtown Mnstry 1962-1963; Cn Trin And S Phil's Cathd Newark NJ 1960-1962; Vic Gr Ch Broad Brook CT 1957-1960; Cur Trin Epis Ch Southport CT 1956-1957; Stndg Com Dio Indianapolis Indianapolis IN 1965-1971. Auth, "Lifeline for the Endtimes: Creating a New Humanity During the Apocalypse and Beyond," *Bk*, W Cnty Press, 2015; Auth, "JESUS CIRCLES, A Way to Heal Our Wounds, Subvert the Domination System, and Build an Abundant Future," *Bk*, XLIBRIS, 2004.

LAWSON, Richard (WTenn) 1720 Peabody Ave, 1602 Vinton Ave, Memphis TN 38104 **Dn S Jn's Cathd Denver CO 2017-** B Guntersville AL 1974 s

Richard & Mary. BA Auburn U 1997; MDiv GTS 2001; STM Sewanee: The U So, TS 2009. D 6/3/2001 Bp Onell Asiselo Soto P 12/4/2001 Bp Henry Nutt Parsley Jr. m 11/30/2009 Katherine Evans Lawson c 2. R Gr - S Lk's Ch Memphis TN 2010-2017; Cur S Jn's Ch Decatur AL 2001-2010. Richard Lawson, "Where In Hell? Greg of Nyssa's Map of the Soul's Journey," *Sewanee Theol Revs*, 2015; Auth, "Greg of Nyssa's Homilies on the Song of Songs: Is the Erotic Left Behind?," *Sewanee Theol Revs*, 2010. richard@sjcathedral.org

LAWSON, Rolfe Adrian (Vt) B Albany NY 1936 D 1/26/1964 Bp Allen Webster Brown P 12/10/1964 Bp Charles Bowen Persell Jr. m 8/23/1958 Patricia Ruth Lawson c 1.

LAWSON, Victor Freeman (WVa) 64 Barley Lane, Charles Town WV 25414 B Washington DC 1943 s Victor & Isabell. BA S Aug 1964. D 6/27/1970 P 3/7/1971 Bp William Foreman Creighton. m 9/27/1999 Ruby N Nesbitt c 1. Gr Epis Ch Kearneysville WV 1999-2007; Mssnr Nelson Cluster Of Epis Ch Rippon WV 1999-2007; S Andr's-On-The-Mt Harpers Ferry WV 1999-2007; Mssnr S Barth's Leetown Kearneysville WV 1999-2007; S Phil's Ch Chas Town WV 1999-2007; St Johns Epis Ch Harpers Ferry WV 1999-2007; R Ch Of Our Sav Washington DC 1976-1999; Res II Chapl St Eliz's Hosp 1974-1976; Cur S Geo's Ch Washington DC 1970-1972.

LAWSON-BECK, David Roswell (NJ) 143 W Milton Ave, Apt 4, Rahway NJ 07065 B Hartford CT 1944 s James & Florence. D 5/16/2009 Bp Sylvestre Donato Romero. c 3.

LAWTON, John Keith (Ak) Po Box 530, Palmer AK 99645 Non-par 1978- B Watertown NY 1930 s John & Edrienne. BA Hobart and Wm Smith Colleges 1953; BD EDS 1956; MDiv EDS 1967. D 6/29/1956 Bp Walter M Higley P 6/1/1957 Bp Malcolm E Peabody. m 8/23/1952 Jacqueline Joan Lawton c 4. Dio Alaska Fairbanks AK 1976-1978; Asst S Barn' Ch Leeland Uppr Marlboro MD 1967-1969; Asst R Par Of The Epiph Winchester MA 1965-1966; P-in-c S Thos Ch Point Hope AK 1959-1965; Asst Seneca/Tompkins Mssn Field Romulus NY 1956-1959.

LAWYER, Evelyn Virden (Minn) 4539 Keithson Dr, Arden Hills MN 55112 B Shanghai CN 1939 d Frank & Katherine. EDS; BA Wellesley Coll 1962; D Formation Prog 1984. D 11/4/1984 Bp Robert Marshall Anderson. m 2/1/1964 John Elder Lawyer c 4. Asst Chapl Epis Ch Hm S Paul MN 1993-1999; Refugee Resettlement Coordntr Dio Minnesota Minneapolis MN 1990-1991; D S Matt's Ch S Paul MN 1985-2004; D S Jn's Ch S Cloud MN 1984-1985. NAAD 1985. St. Steph Awd NAAD 2004.

LAYCOCK, John (Mich) 7112 Kauffman Blvd., Presque Isle MI 49777 **Gr Epis Ch Lachine MI 2010-** B Orlando FL 1945 s Ralph & Constance. BA Denison U 1969; MDiv GTS 1984. D 6/30/1984 Bp Henry Irving Mayson P 4/1/1985 Bp H Coleman Mcgehee Jr. Int S Jn's Epis Ch Grand Haven MI 2008-2010; Int S Mich's Ch Grosse Pointe MI 2006-2008; Int S Thos Ch Trenton MI 2005-2006; Int St Paul's Epis Romeo MI 2001-2005; Int S Jas Ch Grosse Ile MI 1999-2001; Int Gr Epis Ch Southgate MI 1997-1999; Int S Geo's Ch Milford MI 1996-1997; R S Columba Ch Detroit MI 1986-1996; Assoc R Chr Ch Detroit MI 1984-1986.

LAYCOCK JR, Ralph Bradley (SwVa) 2725 Wilshire Ave SW, Roanoke VA 24015 **Int R S Steph's Epis Ch Forest VA 2013-** B Rockledge FL 1943 s Ralph & Constance. BA Dart 1966; MBA Bowling Green St U 1968; MDiv Colgate Rochester Crozer DS 1996; MDiv CRDS 1996; CTh Epis TS of the SW 1999. D 6/7/1999 P 12/18/1999 Bp Robert Jefferson Hargrove Jr. m 3/22/1994 Letitia Lee Smith c 2. Int R S Paul's Epis Ch Salem VA 2006-2011; Int R H Trin Ch Churchville MD 2005-2006; R Aug Par Chesapeake City MD 2000-2005; Asst to the R Ch Of The Mssh Lower Gwynedd PA 1999-2000.

LAYDEN, Daniel Keith (NI) 11009 Brandy Oak Run, Fort Wayne IN 46845 **R S Alb's Epis Ch Ft Wayne IN 2007-** B . 1971 BS OH SU; MDiv VTS; MDiv VTS. D 10/20/2001 P 6/1/2002 Bp Herbert Thompson Jr. c 1. S Paul's Epis Ch Greenville OH 2002-2007; S Mk's Epis Ch Columbus OH 1996-1999; P-in-c S Paul's Epis Ch.

LAYNE, Najah Suzanne (Kan) 631 E. Marlin St., McPherson KS 67460 **Ret 1998-** B Elmira NY 1935 d Ernest & Beatrice. Potsdam St Teachers Coll 1956; Wichita St U 1976. D 12/19/1993 Bp William Edward Smalley. m 5/23/1979 Robert Patterson Layne. D S Matt's Epis Ch Newton KS 2006-2008; D Gr Epis Ch Winfield KS 2003-2006; Trin Ch Arkansas City KS 2000-2003; Serv./ D Epis Ch Of S Fran-In-The-Vlly Green Vlly AZ 1998-2000; Pstr Care/ D S Dav Topeka KS 1994-1998; Serv./ D S Dav's Epis Ch Topeka KS 1993-1997; Hosp Chapl S Fran Med Cntr Topeka KS 1990-1993; Choir Dir S Bath Witchita KS 1987-1989. Mus Hon Soc.

LAYNE, Robert Patterson (Kan) The Cedars, 807 N Maxwell St, Mc Pherson KS 67460 **Ret 1998-** B Louisville KY 1933 s Herman & Mary. BA Bellarmine U 1959; MDiv VTS 1968. D 6/18/1968 P 5/20/1969 Bp Charles Gresham Marmion. m 5/23/1979 Najah Suzanne Layne. P-in-c S Matt's Epis Ch Newton KS 2006-2008; R S Dav's Epis Ch Topeka KS 1989-1997; R S Barth's Ch Wichita KS 1981-1989; 1980-1982; S Stephens Epis Churchrch Wichita KS 1970-1979; Vic Trin Epis Ch Fulton KY 1968-1970. Cmnty Columnist, Bi-Weekly, "The Hutchinson News, Hutchinson Kansas," 2011.

LAZARD, Amirold (Hai) **Dio Haiti Port-au-Prince HT 2002-** B 1970 D. m 12/15/2005 Marie Yvelande P Lazard c 1.

LEA, Gail Ann (U) PO Box 96, Moab UT 84532 B Missoula MT 1949 d Walter & Kathryn. BA Utah St U 1973. D 6/7/2003 P 5/30/2004 Bp Carolyn Tanner Irish.

LEA, William Howard (Ga) 1 Fair Hope Ln, Savannah GA 31411 **P-in-c S Ptr's Epis Ch Savannah GA 2015-** B Greenville MS 1941 s J C & Winona. BS Colorado St U 1963; MDiv Nash 1979. D 6/29/1979 P 1/24/1980 Bp William Carl Frey. m 6/29/1989 Ellen Lea c 4. P-in-c S Phil's Ch Hinesville Hinesville GA 2010-2015; Assoc S Fran Of The Islands Epis Ch Savannah GA 2006-2009; Int Emm Epis Ch Winchester KY 2004-2006; Int Trin Ch Milwaukee WI 2002-2004; Int Ch Of The Nativ Epis Huntsville AL 2001-2002; R Ch Of The Redeem Brookhaven MS 1995-2001; Vic S Jn's Ch Leland MS 1992-1995; Vic Ch Of The Redeem Greenville MS 1992-1994; Vic S Paul's Ch Leland MS 1992-1994; Int H Innoc' Epis Ch Como MS 1991-1992; Int S Jn's Ch Barrington RI 1988-1990; Int All SS Ch Stoneham MA 1987-1988, Int R 1986-1987; R S Fran Of Assisi Colorado Spg CO 1983-1985; Vic Ch of the H Sprt Rifle CO 1979-1982; S Jn's Cathd Denver CO 1979-1982; Vic S Jn's Epis Ch New Castle CO 1979-1982. Intl Coaching Fed 2014.

LEACH, Duane Lamar (Haw) 57-077 Eleku Kuilima Pl Apt 97, Kahuku HI 96731 B Michigan City IN 1943 s Wendell & Dorothy. BFA TCU. D 10/30/2011 Bp Charles Franklin Brookhart Jr. m 4/13/1995 Camolyn Thayer Leach c 2.

LEACH, Fredric Francis (Alb) 585 4th Ave, Troy NY 12182 **Died 6/27/2016** B Salamanca NY 1939 s Francis & Elsie. BA Alfred U 1962; STB Ya Berk 1967; MDiv Yale DS 1974. D 6/17/1967 P 3/1/1968 Bp Lauriston L Scaife. m 7/20/1963 Diane Handy c 2. Vic S Lk's Ch Mechanicville NY 2003-2016; Pres - Bd Dir Epis Ch Hm Troy NY 2002-2003; Pres - Bd Dir Epis Ch Hm Troy NY 1993-1997; Asst Chapl Ny St Assembly 1991-2003; Bd Dir Epis Ch Hm Troy NY 1990-2003; R Trin Ch Lansingburgh Troy NY 1990-2003; S Lawr Epis Mnstry Waddington NY 1985-1990; R Trin Ch Gouverneur NY 1985-1990; R St Andr Epis & H Cross Luth Ch La Junta CO 1979-1985; Rep Of Nciw Dio Wstrn New York Tonawanda NY 1972-1979, Sprtl Life Com 1970-1979; Dir Of Activities S Bonventure Sum Yth Prog 1972-1976; R Gr Ch Randolph NY 1971-1979; Exec Secy Ch Mssn Help 1969-1971; Cur S Mk's Ch Orchard Pk NY 1967-1971; Dioc Coun Dio Albany Greenwich NY 1996-2002. Auth, "The Epis mag".

LEACH, JoAnn Zwart (Ore) 8400 Paseo Vista Dr, Las Vegas NV 89128 **Gr In The Desert Epis Ch Las Vegas NV 2016-** B Redlands CA 1950 d Floyd & Ann. BA Westmont Coll 1972; MA U CA 1974; MDiv CDSP 1985. D 6/11/1985 Bp Robert Hume Cochrane P 1/18/1986 Bp Otis Charles. m 1/14/1984 Shannon Paul Leach. Assoc R Chr Ch Par Lake Oswego OR 2000-2013; Chapl Epis Ch at Pr Princeton NJ 1997-1999; Chap of the Epiph Salt Lake City UT 1990-1999; Chaplain Dio Utah Salt Lake City UT 1990-1997; Cn Cathd Ch Of S Mk Salt Lake City UT 1988-1989; Chapl S Mk's Chap Salt Lake City UT 1985-1988; Chapl Rowland Hall/S Mk's Sch Salt Lake City UT 1985-1987. CDSP Bd Mem 2002-2008; ESMHE Strng Com 1992-1995; Pres Of ESMHE 1998-2000; Recovery Cmsn 2000.

LEACH, John Philip (WTenn) 1380 Wolf River Blvd, Collierville TN 38017 **R Ch of the H Apos Collierville TN 2008-; Pres - Stndg Com Dio W Tennessee Memphis 2012-, Dep - The GC 2009-, Dep - The GC 2009-, St. Columba Bd Dir 2008-, Stndg Com 2008-, Bp's Coun Mem 2005-2008** B Helena AR 1969 s Philip & Patricia. BBA Millsaps Coll 1991; MDiv VTS 2004. D 6/26/2004 P 1/8/2005 Bp Don Edward Johnson. m 7/10/2017 Sarah T Leach c 2. R Ch Of The Annunc Cordova TN 2004-2008.

LEACH, Marilyn May (Minn) **P S Jas Ch Marshall MN 2005-** B Norwich CT 1941 d Earl & Jean. BA U of Hawaii 1963; MA U of Missouri 1964. D 6/12/2005 Bp Daniel Lee Swenson P 12/11/2005 Bp James Louis Jelinek. c 2.

LEACH, Shannon Paul (Nev) 8400 Paseo Vista Dr, Las Vegas NV 89128 **Chr Ch Par Lake Oswego OR 2013-, R 1999-2012; P Gr In The Desert Epis Ch Las Vegas NV 2012-; Stndg Cmsn Dio Oregon Portland OR 2006-** B Denver CO 1956 s Doyce & Carolyn. BS Westminster Coll 1979; MDiv CDSP 1985. D 12/22/1984 P 1/18/1986 Bp Otis Charles. m 1/14/1984 JoAnn Zwart c 2. Dio Oregon OR 2000-2005; Assoc Trin Ch Princeton NJ 1997-1999; Dep GC Dio Utah Salt Lake City UT 1991-1997, COM 1993-1997, Stndg Com 1986-1992; R S Jas Epis Ch Midvale UT 1987-1997; Rowland Hall/S Mk's Sch Salt Lake City UT 1985-1987; Chapl S Marg's Chap Salt Lake City UT 1985-1987; Yth Min All Souls Par In Berkeley Berkeley CA 1984-1985.

LEACOCK, Rob (Ark) 8605 Verona Trl, Austin TX 78749 **Epis Collgt Sch Little Rock AR 2016-** B Gainesville FL 1979 s Robert & Rebecca. AB Davidson Coll 2001; MDiv Yale DS 2005. D 6/24/2006 P 2/3/2007 Bp James Monte Stanton. m 8/14/2004 Stefanie West Leacock c 3. Upper Sch Chapl S Andrews Epis Sch Austin TX 2010-2016; Assoc S Mich And All Ang Ch Dallas TX 2006-2010.

LEAHY, John Joseph (CFla) 1007B Kings Way, New Bern NC 28562 B Worcester MA 1948 s John & Anne. BS Assumption Coll; MDiv GTS 1998. D 6/20/1998 P 6/12/1999 Bp Gordon Scruton. m 4/19/1969 June Leahy c 2. Pstr S Mary

Of The Ang Epis Ch Orlando FL 2006-2010; Pstr S Paul's Epis Ch Gardner MA 2000-2006; Cur/PIC S Mich's-On-The-Heights Worcester MA 1998-2000.

LEAMAN, Kris (Ia) 120 1st St Ne, Mason City IA 50401 **Ch Of The Sav Clermont IA 2016-; Supply Cler St. Paul's Luth Ch Mason City Iowa 50401 2015-** B Mason City, Iowa 1955 d Roman & Kathleen. Working on Angl Stds Bexley-Seabury; Working on Angl Stds CDSP; BA Buena Vista U 1994; TEEM Cert Wartburg TS 2016. D 2/15/2015 P 8/16/2015 Bp Alan Scarfe. m 10/11/1975 Jay Michael Leaman c 2. Hosp Chapl Mercy Hosp No Iowa Mason City Iowa 50401 2015.

LEANILLO OSB, Ricardo Ivan (SwFla) 5033 9th St, Zephyrhills FL 33542 **D Gr Ch Tampa FL 2013-; D S Eliz's Epis Ch Zephyrhills FL 2013-, D 2003-2004** B Sacramento CA 1947 s Ricardo & Ethel. AA Pasco-Hernando Cmnty Coll 1975; BA U of So Florida 1977; Cert S Leo U 1984. D 1/18/2003 Bp John Bailey Lipscomb. m 8/10/1996 Kimberly Ann Anderson c 5. D Serv Philippine Indep Ch Tampa FL 2004-2005. Oblate Ord of S Ben 2005.

LEANNAH, Scott Robert (Mil) 3734 S. 86th St., Milwaukee WI 53228 **Vic S Mary's Epis Ch Summit WI 2003-** B Escondide CA 1966 s Robert & Susan. BA Marq 1988; MDiv S Fran Sem 1993. Rec 11/23/2003 Bp Steven Andrew Miller. m 7/29/2006 Virginia R Kuemmel c 1. Exec Coun Dio Milwaukee Milwaukee WI 2009-2012, Dep, GC 2009-, Pres, Stndg Com 2008-2010, Secy, Stndg Com 2005-2007, Camp Webb Sprtl Dir 2004-.

LEARY, Charles Randolph (SO) 133 Croskey Boulevard, Medway OH 45341 **Ret 2000-** B Mingo WV 1930 s William & Mary. BA Davis & Elkins Coll 1953; MDiv Tem 1957; PDS 1958. D 11/22/1958 P 5/23/1959 Bp William P Roberts. m 12/27/1950 Juanita M Leary c 4. Supply Cler S Andr's Ch Dayton OH 1995-2000; S Jas Ch Piqua OH 1985-2000; S Mk's Ch Sidney OH 1985-2000; Supply P S Paul's Epis Ch Greenville OH 1985-2000; S Chris's Ch Fairborn OH 1961-1985; Cur S Paul's Epis Ch Dayton OH 1959-1961. Auth, "Leary Fam Genealogy," *Jn Leary Sr Revolutionary War Veteran*, Off Depot, Fairborn, OH, 2013; Auth, *Mssn Readiness*, CCS, 1990; Auth, *18 Sermons*. Rotary Club 1962-2005. Best Sermon Awd - Seven Worlds Corp 1990.

LEARY, Kevin David (Ct) 15 Rimmon Rd, Woodbridge CT 06525 **D S Jas Apos 1988-** B New Haven CT 1944 s David & Cecilia. S Thos Sem Bloomfield CT; U of New Haven. D 12/3/1988 Bp Arthur Edward Walmsley. m 1/27/1968 Carolyn Leary c 4. NAAD.

LEAS, Bercry Eleanor (Mich) 7051 Wakan Ln., Corryton TN 37721 **D S Hilary's Ch Ft Myers FL 2008-; Emergency Response Chapl Dio E Tennessee Knoxville TN 2009-** B Philadelphia PA 1945 d Edgar & Mary. BA Estrn Michigan U 1967; MA Estrn Michigan U 1971; Ds Whitaker TS 1990. D 6/23/1990 Bp R aymond Stewart Wood Jr. m 5/19/2006 Douglas Naas. S Lk's Ch Knoxville TN 2008; D S Jn's Ch Royal Oak MI 1990-2001. DOK 2008; NAAD; OSL.

LEATHERMAN, Daniel Lee (Haw) 7 Pursuit, Aliso Viejo CA 92656 **Chapl S Alb's Chap Honolulu HI 2005-; Chapl S Mary And All Ang' Sch Aliso Viejo CA 2002-; Chapl California Air NG - March AFB 1999-** B Honolulu HI 1970 s David & Karen. BA U of Hawaii 1993; MDiv Epis TS of the SW 1996. D 6/25/1996 Bp George Nelson Hunt III P 1/6/1997 Bp Robert Manning Moody. m 11/17/1996 Charmaine Mee Yin Leatherman. S Mary And All Ang Sch Aliso Viejo CA 2002-2005; Assoc The Epis Ch Of S Andr Encinitas CA 2001-2005; S Marg Of Scotland Par San Juan Capo CA 1999-2002; Asst Chapl S Marg Of Scotland Sch San Juan CA 1999-2001; Chapl Oklahoma Air NG 1998-1999; Asst S Jn's Epis Ch Tulsa OK 1996-1999. Epis Armdf Chapl Assn.

LEAVITT, Christie Plehn (Nev) 1739 Carita Ave, Henderson NV 89014 **P S Matt's Ch Las Vegas NV 1986-** B Omaha NE 1949 d Robert & Rose. BA U of Nevada at Las Vegas 1973; MA U of Nevada at Las Vegas 1979. D 4/6/1986 Bp Robert Reed Shahan P 11/23/1986 Bp Stewart Clark Zabriskie. m 5/12/1973 Robert Merrill Leavitt.

LE BARRON, Bruce Erie (WK) 3218 White Tail Way, Salina KS 67401 **Cn Pstr Chr Cathd Salina KS 1995-; Ret 1992-** B Jamestown NY 1930 s Erie & Coralyn. BA SUNY 1951; MDiv Ya Berk 1955. D 5/29/1955 P 11/30/1955 Bp Frederick Lehrle Barry. c 3. R All SS Ch Nevada MO 1986-1992; Asst & Org/Chrmstr S Lk's Par Kalamazoo MI 1980-1986; Asst & Org/Chrmstr S Jn The Evang Ch Elkhart IN 1976-1980; R Chr Ch Bethany CT 1969-1976; R Trin Ch Lakeville CT 1964-1969; R S Barn Ch Burlington NJ 1962-1964; Chr Ch Magnolia NJ 1959-1962; Vic Ch Of S Jn-In-The-Wilderness Gibbsboro NJ 1959-1962; P-in-c S Barbara Tahawus NY 1957-1958; P-in-c S Chris No Creek 1957-1958; Cur All SS Ch New York NY 1955-1957; P-in-C S Tim Moreau NY 1955-1957. CBS; GAS; Mem of the SocMary; Oblate of (Benedictine) Blue Cloud Abbey; Oblate of S Gilbert of Sempringham, Engl Ord of Cister; Soc of S Marg.

LEBENS ENGLUND, Paul (Minn) 7315 N Wall St, Spokane WA 99208 **Dn Cathd Ch Of S Mk Minneapolis MN 2014-** B Yakima WA 1974 s James & Judith. BA Evergreen St Coll 1997; MDiv CDSP 2004. D 6/12/2004 P 1/8/2005 Bp James E Waggoner Jr. m 7/24/1999 Erica Lebens Englund c 2. P-in-c S Dav's Ch Spokane WA 2013-2014; Cn to the Ordnry Dio Spokane Spokane WA 2013, Cn for Congrl Dvlpmt 2007-2013, COM 2004-2007, Dep to GC

2004-; re-start Vic W Cntrl Epis Mssn Spokane WA 2008-2009; P Assoc Cathd Of S Jn The Evang Spokane WA 2004-2007. paull@spokanediocese.org

LE BLANC, Fran Andre (Telles) (Md) 204 Monument Rd, Orleans MA 02653 **P-in-c 2004-** B Rio De Janeiro BR 1953 d Andre & Elvira. BA New York Inst of Tech 1977; MBA Dart 1981; MDiv GTS 1993. D 6/12/1993 Bp Richard Frank Grein P 5/1/1994 Bp Frank S Cerveny. m 5/21/2011 Francis Wandell. Chr Ch Forest Hill MD 2004-2016; P-in-c S Ptr's Ch Great Falls SC 2004; Asst The Ch Of The H Sprt Orleans MA 2003; St Gabr Of The Annunc Columbia SC 1999-2001, 1998; Dio Upper So Carolina Columbia SC 1999, Stndg Com 1998-2003; Vic S Gabr Of The Annunc Columbia SC 1998-2001; Asst R S Jn's Epis Ch Columbia SC 1996-1998; S Hilda's And S Hugh's Sch New York NY 1994-1996; Assoc All SS Ch New York NY 1994-1995; Cur S Thos Ch New York NY 1993-1994.

LEBLANC, Tracy Jean (Ore) 15416 Ne 90th St, Vancouver WA 98682 **D S Ptr And Paul Epis Ch Portland OR 2007-** B Greeley CO 1971 d John & Michelle. Cntr for Diac Mnstry; BA Willamette U 1993; MS Portland St U 1997. D 10/21/2006 Bp Johncy Itty. m 8/21/1993 James LeBlanc c 3.

LEBRIJA, Lorenzo (Los) c/o Cathedral Center of St Paul, 840 Echo Park Ave, Los Angeles CA 90026 **Dio Los Angeles Los Angeles CA 2014-, Bd Mem, Epis Fed Cmnty Credit Un 2017-, Chair, Prog Grp on Stwdshp 2017-, Bp's Liaison to the Prog Grp on Hisp Mnstrs 2016-, Bp's Liaison to the Cmsn on LGBTQ Mnstrs 2015-** B Mexico City Mexico 1972 s Juan & Cristina. BA Florida Intl U 2000; MBA Florida Intl U 2007; MDiv GTS 2014. D 6/7/2014 P 1/17/2015 Bp Joseph Jon Bruno. m 1/17/2012 Troy Edward Elder. Assn of Fund Raising Professionals 2014. llebrija@ladiocese.org

LEBROCQ JR, Eric Francis (Tex) St. John's Episcopal Church, PO Box 1477, Sealy TX 77474 **Pstr Ldr S Jn's Epis Ch Sealy TX 2012-** B Crossett AR 1940 s Eric & Anna. BS Louisiana Tech U 1963; Louisiana Tech U 1972; U of Texas 1985; Cert Iona Sch of Mnstry 2011. D 6/18/2011 Bp C Andrew Doyle P 2/1/2012 Bp Dena Arnall Harrison. m 4/28/2001 Mary Lou Roehrig LeBrocq c 2.

LEBRON, Robert Emmanuel (Mil) 409 E. Court St., Janesville WI 53545 B New York NY 1952 s Bernard & Rose. AA SUNY 1976; BSW Florida Intl U 1980; Geisinger Med Cntr 1983; MDiv Sthrn Bapt TS 1983; Trin Epis Sch for Min 2000; Police Chapl Critical Incendent Stress Mgmt 2010; Mem Intl Conf of Police Chapl 2011; Chapl Ord of St Lk 2012. D 12/10/1995 Bp Claude Charles Vache P 6/15/1996 Bp Brice Sidney Sanders. m 8/20/2005 Robyn Lebron c 2. R Trin Ch Janesville WI 2005-2014; P-in-c Trin Epis Ch Janesville WI 2005-2009; P All SS' Epis Ch Chevy Chase MD 2004-2005. Coll Chapl, Bd Cert 1986-2000; Intl Conf of Police Chapl 2011-2013; US Navy Chapl Corp 1985-2005.

LEBUS, Jesse Williams (LI) 1670 Route 25a, Cold Spring Harbor NY 11724 **Cur St Jn's Ch Cold Sprg Harbor NY 2015-** B Winchester KY 1975 s Orie & Susan. GTS; MA U of Louisville. D 6/6/2015 P 12/5/2015 Bp Lawrence C Provenzano. m 9/13/2014 Meredith Anne Brown c 1. jwlebus@stjcsh.org

LECHE III, Edward Douglas (Oly) 205 Olympic View Dr, Friday Harbor WA 98250 **Ret 1988-** B Longview WA 1926 s Edward & Muriel. BA Cbury Coll 1951; Cert GTS 1954. D 6/29/1954 P 6/29/1955 Bp Stephen F Bayne Jr. Int Emm Ch Orcas Island Eastsound WA 1995-1996; The Epis Par of St Dav Friday Harbor WA 1967-1988; Vic Gr Ch Lopez Island WA 1967-1983; Vic S Chas Angl Par Poulsbo WA 1963-1967; Vic S Paul's Epis Ch Port Gamble WA 1961-1967; Asst S Hubert Yacolt WA 1959-1961; Asst S Lk's Epis Ch Vancouver WA 1959-1961; Vic S Jn's Epis Ch So Bend WA 1957-1959; S Ptr's Ch Seaview WA 1957-1959; Cur Chr Ch Seattle WA 1955-1957; Cur S Mary's Ch Lakewood WA 1954-1955. Illustrator, "Illustrations," *Ch Facts (Dio Wstrn New York)*, 2003; Illustrator, "Illustrations,The Epis," *Profsnl Additions*, 2003; Illustrator, "Illustrations," *The GC Daily*, 2003; Illustrator, "Illustrations," *The Olympia Churhman*, 2003; Writer, Illustrator, "Illustrations," *The Pig That Loved Potatoes-A Somewhat Whimsical Hist Of The Pig War*, Edw Douglas Leche Iii, 2000; Illustrator, "Illustrations," *The Wild Wrld By Geo And Netty Macginitie*, Longhouse, 1974.

LECLAIR, Arthur Anthony (Colo) 8221 E Fremont Cir, Englewood CO 80112 **R Gd Shpd 1978-** B Charleroi PA 1931 s A E. BA U of Dayton 1956; MA Loyola U 1969. Rec 3/1/1974 as Priest Bp William Carl Frey. m 8/22/1970 Joanne Juneau c 2. Gd Shpd Epis Ch Centennial CO 1976-1995; Dio Colorado Denver CO 1975-1976; Cur Trin Ch Greeley CO 1974-1976; R RC Ch 1960-1970. Ord Of S Lk.

LECLAIR, Paul Joseph (Mich) 1434 E 13 Mile Rd, Madison Heights MI 48071 **Dn Dio Michigan Detroit MI 2011-** B Detroit, MI 1950 s Paul & Grace. Sewanee: The U So, TS; U So TS; Whitaker Inst; BA Oakland U 1972; MAT Saginaw Vlly St U 1978. D 2/13/2010 P 11/6/2010 Bp Wendell Nathaniel Gibbs Jr. m 8/26/1972 Elizabeth LeClair c 3. D S Pat's Epis Ch Madison Hts MI 2010, P 2010-. paul.leclair143@gmail.com

LECLAIRE, Patrick Harry (Nev) 620 W B St, Fallon NV 89406 **P H Trin Epis Ch Fallon NV 2000-** B Minneapolis MN 1947 s Wallace & Dorothy. AA Wstrn Nevada Coll 1990. D 12/12/1999 P 7/16/2000 Bp John Stuart Thornton. m 3/11/1968 Loraine Bailey.

LECLERC BSG, Charles Edward (NH) 1873 Dover Rd, Epsom NH 03234 **Chapl Nrsng Hm Mnstry 2010-; Chapl Mnstry to the Dying 2000-; D S Paul's Ch Concord NH 2000-, D 2000-** B Woonsocket RI 1944 s Laureni & Claire. BS Johnson & Wales U 1991. Rec 2/1/1988 as Deacon Bp George Nelson Hunt III. D-In-Res Ch Of The Epiph Providence RI 1988-1991; Serv RC Ch 1977-1988.

LECOUTEUR II, Eugene Hamilton (Va) 6000 Grove Ave, Richmond VA 23226 **S Steph's Ch Richmond VA 2015-, 2008-2014** B Fredericksburg VA 1956 s Eugene & Janet. AB The W&M 1978; MBA Cor 1992; MDiv UTS 2008. D 6/7/2014 P 12/6/2014 Bp Shannon Sherwood Johnston.

LECROY, Anne Evelyn (ETenn) 400 N Boone St, Apt As14, Johnson City TN 37604 **Died 5/5/2016** B Summit New Jersey 1927 d Arthur & Anne. BA Bryn 1947; MA Bryn 1948; PhD U Cinc 1952; Duke 1978. Trans 6/6/2001 as Deacon Bp Charles Glenn VonRosenberg. c 3. D S Tim's Epis Ch Kingsport TN 2001-2008; Secy Dio E Tennessee Knoxville TN 1976-1982; SLC Dio E Tennessee Knoxville TN 1974-1983. *Var arts Chrsnty and Lit*, 2003; *10 Hymn Texts*, Ch Hymnal Corp, 1982; Co-Ed, *Lesser Feasts and Fasts*, Ch Pension Fund, 1980; Contrib, *Bk of Common Pryr*, Ch Pension Fund, 1979. Amer ACPE 1998; Phi Kappa Phi 1968-2000; Third Ord of S Fran (professed) 1990. Wm Fowler Awd in Tchg E Tennessee St U 1992.

LEDERHOUSE, Susan (Mass) PO Box 1586, Orleans MA 02653 **R S Ptr's Ch On The Canal Buzzards Bay MA 2010-** B Richmond VA 1954 d Peter & Susan. BA Hollins U 1975; MS U IL 1976; MDiv GTS 2005. D 6/11/2005 Bp John Palmer Croneberger P 12/17/2005 Bp Carol J Gallagher. m 8/29/1987 Howard Bruce Lederhouse. Supply P Dio Massachusetts Boston MA 2009-2010; Int The Ch Of The H Sprt Orleans MA 2008-2009; R S Jas Ch Old Town ME 2007-2008; Asst S Mary's Ch Sparta NJ 2005-2006. Beta Phi Mu 1976; Phi Beta Kappa 1975.

LEDERMAN, Maureen Elizabeth (Ct) 124 Midland Dr, Meriden CT 06450 **S Jn's Ch Guilford CT 2012-; Assoc. R, Day Sch Chapl, & Chr Ed. Dir S Thos's Ch New Haven CT 2004-** B 1977 BA providence Coll 1999; mdiv Ya Berk 2002. D 6/12/2004 P 1/29/2005 Bp Andrew Donnan Smith. m 7/13/2002 William Paul Lederman.

LEDFORD, Marcia (Mich) 959 Sherman St, Ypsilanti MI 48197 B Detroit MI 1961 d Lynn & Ruth. D 6/22/2013 P 12/22/2013 Bp Wendell Nathaniel Gibbs Jr. m 6/7/2014 Linda Karen Sankovich. Dio Michigan Detroit MI 2014-2016; S Ptr's Ch Detroit MI 2013.

LEDGERWOOD, Mary Jayne (Va) 6715 Georgetown Pike, McLean VA 22101 **S Thos Ch Greenville AL 2017-** B Waynesburg PA 1958 d Edward & Betty. MDiv VTS 2001. D 6/23/2001 Bp Peter J Lee P 1/26/2002 Bp John L Rabb. m 5/28/1994 Brian Ledgerwood. Gr Ch The Plains VA 2012-2014; VTS Alexandria VA 2012; Assoc R S Jn's Epis Ch Mc Lean VA 2008-2012; R S Andr's Epis Ch Glenwood MD 2004-2008; Assoc R S Jn's Ch Ellicott City MD 2001-2004.

LEDIARD SR, Daniel E (EO) PO Box 681, Virginia City NV 89440 **R S Jn's Ch Hermiston OR 2010-** B Salt Lake City UT 1947 s Alfred & Frances. D 10/6/2006 Bp Katharine Jefferts Schori P 6/3/2007 Bp Jerry Alban Lamb. m 8/30/1969 Jo Anne Lediard c 3. P ST PAULS Epis Ch VIRGINIA CITY NEVADA 2006-2010.

LEDIARD, Jo Anne (Spok) 1609 W 10th Ave, Kennewick WA 99336 **P-in-c S Paul's Epis Mssn Kennewick WA 2011-** B Seattle WA 1947 d Richard & Barbara. Dio of Nevada; Dplma St Marks Hosp Sch of Nrsng 1969. D 8/23/1998 Bp Stewart Clark Zabriskie P 9/16/2001 Bp Katharine Jefferts Schori. m 8/30/1969 Daniel E Lediard c 3. Dio Nevada Las Vegas 2006-2009.

LEDYARD, Christopher Martin (Az) 2331 E Adams St, Tucson AZ 85719 B Los Angeles CA 1950 s Hubert & Mary. D 6/7/2014 Bp Kirk Stevan Smith. c 2.

LEDYARD, Florence Livingstone (Md) 1021 Bosley Rd, Cockeysville MD 21030 **R S Barth's Ch Baltimore MD 2002-; R Epiph 1986-** B Detroit,MI 1950 d William & Florence. BA Colorado Womens Coll 1972; MA U 1972; MDiv VTS 1978. D 6/17/1978 Bp William Jones Gordon Jr P 6/1/1979 Bp H Coleman Mcgehee Jr. m 11/4/1974 William Canfield III. S Jas Epis Ch Mt Airy MD 2000-2002; Epiph Ch Dulaney Vlly Luthvle Timon MD 1983-1996; Asst S Dav's Par Washington DC 1978-1982.

LEE III, Alfred Harrison (Dal) 534 W 10th St, Dallas TX 75208 **Died 3/5/2016** B Estelline TX 1932 s Alfred & Lillie. BA TCU 1954; MA U of Alabama 1955; S Augustines Coll Cbury Gb 1956; BD EDS 1959; S Georges Coll Jerusalem IL 1978. D 6/20/1959 Bp Charles A Mason P 12/1/1959 Bp The Bishop Of Natal. Ret 1994-2016; Dn - Dallas Dnry 1984-1985; Exec Coun 1982-1985; Epis TS Of The SW Austin TX 1980-1983, Trst 1980-1983; Trst Bp Davies Cntr 1976-1981; Dn - Dallas Dnry 1971-1974; Com 1971-1973; R Chr Epis Ch Dallas TX 1970-1994; Exec Coun 1969-1974; Dn - Nthrn Dnry 1967-1970; S Lk's Ch Denison TX 1965-1970, R 1965-1970; P-in-c Karkloof Par In So Afr 1959-1961; Asst S Paul In Durban So Afr 1959-1961. Auth, "Window On Asia". Hon Chapl S Bride 1964; Hon Cn Dio Dal.

LEE III, Arthur Randall (SwFla) 7304 Van Lake Dr, Englewood FL 34224 **Asst S Jas Epis Ch Pt Charlotte FL 2010-; Exec Bd SW Florida Cltn against Human Trafficking 2013-; Ch Disciplinary Bd Dio SW Florida Parrish FL**

2011- B Minneapolis MN 1944 s Arthur & Ethelynn. BA San Francisco St U 1966; MDiv CDSP 1969; MLitt Oxf GB 1976. D 6/28/1969 Bp Chauncie Kilmer Myers P 9/26/1971 Bp The Bishop Of Oxford. m 8/10/1974 Rosemary Lee c 1. R S Dav's Epis Ch Englewood FL 2000-2009; R Ch Of The H Sprt Sfty Harbor FL 1985-2000; R S Mk's Ch Starke FL 1982-1985; Asst S Andr's Epis Ch Tampa FL 1977-1982. Auth, "Morphological Diversity Among The Protists," *Proc. Of 4th Intl. Conf. Of Syst. & Evol. Biology*, 1991; Auth, "Bludgeon: A Blunt Instrument For The Analysis Of Contamination In Textual Traditions," *Proc. Conf. Of The Allc*, 1990; Auth, "Cler Families In Crisis," *Families In Transition*, Epis Ch Cntr, 1984.

LEE, Betsy A. (Minn) 4901 Triton Dr, Golden Valley MN 55422 B Decorah IA 1958 d David & Lorraine. BA S Olaf Coll 1980; MDiv Luth TS at Chicago 1990; Cert Estrn Mennonite U 2001. Rec 1/24/2006 as Priest Bp Alan Scarfe. m 10/8/2013 Karen Joy Evans. R S Edw The Confessor Wayzata MN 2008-2011; Int Trin Ch Muscatine IA 2006-2008; Pstr Serv parishes in Evang Luth Ch in Amer 1990-2005; Bd Mem Epis Cmnty Serv Inc Minneapolis MN 2010-2013.

LEE, Caleb J (SC) 215 Ann St, Beaufort NC 28516 **Assoc Gr Ch Cathd Charleston SC 2014-** B Chapel Hill NC 1981 s David & Barbara. BA No Carolina St Unversity 2003; MDiv VTS 2012. D 6/9/2012 Bp Clifton Daniel III. m 9/25/2004 Allen J Jordan c 3. S Paul's Ch Beaufort NC 2012-2014.

LEE, Chen-Cheng (Tai) No. 311 Sec.2, Chieding Rd, Chieding District, Kaohsiung City 85241 Taiwan **P-in-c St. Andr's Epis Mssn Kaohsiung Taiwan 2011-; P (Vic) St. Mk's Epis Ch Pintung Taiwan 2011-; Dio Taiwan Taipei 2004-** B Taiwan 1976 s Chien-Wen & Su-Chen. BA Tainan Theol Coll Taiwan 1999; MDiv Tainan Theol Coll and Sem TW 2002; Min-hua Theol Coll, Hong Kong 2008. D 6/11/2004 P 2/19/2005 Bp Jung-Hsin Lai. m 6/26/2004 Hsin-Yi Yeh c 2. P (Vic) St. Ptr's Epis Ch Chiayi Taiwan 2006-2011; Cur St. Ptr's Epis Ch Chiayi Taiwan 2004-2006; Dencon-in-Charge H Trin Epis Ch Keelung Taiwan 2004.

LEE, Christine Kim (NY) St Mary's Episcopal Church, 521 W 126th St, New York NY 10027 **All Ang' Ch New York NY 2008-** B Indianapolis IN 1972 d Sangbok & Youngja. BA Moody Bible Inst 1994; MDiv Trin Intl U 1998; ThM Trin Intl U 2000; Dplma of Angl Stds GTS 2012. D 3/3/2012 P 9/29/2012 Bp Mark Sean Sisk. m 10/12/2002 James Younghoon Lee. S Mary's Manhattanvile Epis Ch New York NY 2012.

LEE, Daniel Ki Chul (Ga) 623 Caines Rd, Hinesville GA 31313 **Died 6/30/2017** B South Korea 1951 s Eu & Nak. Chom Shin Presb Sem; Gnrl Assembly Presb Sem. D 12/7/1997 P 12/18/1998 Bp Henry Irving Louttit. c 2. Dio Georgia Savannah GA 2001-2005.

LEE, Darry Kyong Ho (Los) 5950 Imperial Hwy Apt 47, South Gate CA 90280 B 1949 s Tai & Ok. AA Los Angeles City Coll 1972; BA U CA 1973; MS San Francisco St U 1975; MDiv CDSP 1979; PhD Case Wstrn Reserve U 1992. D 6/23/1979 P 5/1/1980 Bp Robert Claflin Rusack. m 5/6/1978 Soo Keun Lee. S Jos's Par Buena Pk CA 1999-2000; Calv Ch Cleveland OH 1989-1991; Dio Newark Newark NJ 1987-1988; Serv Ch Of Korea 1983-1988; Dio Los Angeles Los Angeles CA 1982-1986; S Andr's Par Torrance CA 1979-1981; Vic S Gabr's. Auth, "Falling Egg".

LEE, David Edward (Va) 2343 Highland Ave, Charlottesville VA 22903 **Non-par 1986-** B Harrisburg PA 1940 s William & Doris. BA Trin 1962; STB EDS 1966. D 6/17/1966 Bp Joseph Thomas Heistand P 4/1/1967 Bp Clarence Rupert Haden Jr. m 11/29/1990 Elizabeth Alice Courain. Assoc S Paul's Memi Charlottesvlle VA 1981-1985; Non-par 1979-1981; R Trin Ch Belleville MI 1972-1979; Asst S Paul's Epis Ch Flint MI 1970-1972; Asst Vic Ch Of S Mart Davis CA 1966-1970.

LEE, Deborah A (NY) 50 Guion Pl Apt 5h, New Rochelle NY 10801 **Asst P Chr Ch Warwick NY 2017-; P-in-c S Paul's Ch Chester NY 2017-** B New Rochelle NY 1970 d Fredrick & Hyacinth. MA Clincl Counslg Colorado Chr U; M.Div / Cert in Sprtl Direction GTS; BA Comparative Lit / French Wms. D 3/4/2017 Bp Mary Douglas Glasspool.

LEE, Donald DeArman (WTex) Po Box 545, Bandera TX 78003 B Corpus Christi TX 1942 s William & Christine. BS Texas A&M U 1965; MDiv Epis TS of the SW 1993. D 6/29/1993 P 1/9/1994 Bp John Herbert MacNaughton. m 6/4/1966 Karen Lee c 4. Vic Ch Of The Ascen Montell TX 2000-2011; Archd Dio W Texas San Antonio TX 1999-2007; Archd S Jn's Cathd Chap San Antonio TX 1999-2007; S Chris's Ch Bandera TX 1993-1999; Vic S Bon Ch Comfort TX 1993-1995.

✠ LEE JR, The Rt Rev Edward Lewis (WMich) 123 Glenwood Rd, Merion Station PA 19066 **Ret Bp of Wstrn Michigan Dio Pennsylvania Philadelphia PA 2000-** B Philadelphia PA 1934 s Edward & Adlyn. BA Br 1956; MDiv GTS 1959. D 5/9/1959 Bp Oliver J Hart P 11/14/1959 Bp Joseph Gillespie Armstrong Con 10/7/1989 for WMich. m 6/17/1961 Kathryn F Lee c 1. Ret Bp of Wstrn Michigan Dio Wstrn Michigan Kalamazoo MI 2002, Bp of Wstrn Michigan 1989-2002; Gnrl Bd Examing Chapl HOB 1994-2006; Bp of Wstrn Michigan Dio Wstrn Michigan Portage MI 1989-2002; Coun Coll of Preachers Washington DC 1983-1989; Dio Washington Washington DC 1983-1989; Dio Washington Washington DC 1983-1986, Com of Inquiry on Nuclear Weapons 1983-1986; R S Jn's Ch Georgetown Par Washington DC 1982-1989; Dep to

GC Convoc of Amer Ch in Europe 1976-1979; Convoc of Epis Ch in Europe Paris 1974-1982; S Jas Epis Ch Firenze 50123 1973-1982; R S Jas' Ch Florence Italy 1973-1982; St Jas Ch 1973-1982; Pstr / Liturg P S Ptr's Ch Germantown Philadelphia 1971-1973; S Ptr's Ch Philadelphia PA 1971-1973; Natl Chair EPF 1970-1973; Lectr in Homil PDS Philadelphia 1966-1970; Epis Advsr Tem Philadelphia PA 1964-1973; Asst Ch Of The Annuniciation Philadelphia PA 1964-1971; Cur The Ch Of The H Trin Rittenhouse Philadelphia PA 1959-1964. Amnesty Intl , USA 1998; EPF 1967; Sthrn Pvrty Law Cntr 1988. DD The GTS 1990.

LEE, Enoch (Tai) North 1-6, Ming-Shin Street, Hualien Taiwan **D S Lk Hualien Taiwan 2000-** B Nan-Jing City CN 1947 s Ru-Shu & Su-Qin. Cheng-Chicago U Taipei Tw 1989; BA TS of Fu-Jen U Taipei Tw 1998. D 10/28/2000 Bp John Chih-Tsung Chien. m 11/20/1976 Duan-Yi Lee c 2. Dio Taiwan Taipei 2000-2002.

LEE, George (Haw) 2468 Lamaku Pl, Honolulu HI 96816 **Ret 1992-** B New Haven CT 1927 s Wah & Rose. Ya Berk; BA Ya 1950; BD Yale DS 1955. D 9/21/1957 Bp Albert Ervine Swift P 8/14/1958 Bp Robert McConnell Hatch. m 7/19/1980 Grace Lee. MacCray Cntr Epis Campus Mnstry Honolulu HI 1989-1991; Vic St Jn the Bapt Epis Ch Waianae HI 1983-1988; S Lk's Epis Ch Honolulu HI 1978-1979; The Epis Ch in Hawaii Honolulu HI 1974-1991; Assoc Sec Urban Mnstrs Exec Coun Epis Ch 1963-1968; Vic S Simon Cyrenian Springfield MA 1958-1960; Asst S Ptr's Ch Springfield MA 1957-1958.

LEE, Grace (Va) D 4/16/2016 Bp Shannon Sherwood Johnston.

LEE, Hosea Mun-Yong (Nwk) 1600 Parker Ave Apt 3-D, Fort Lee NJ 07024 **Asst Mssnr Ch Of The Gd Shpd Ft Lee NJ 1985-** B Korea 1929 s Peter & Miryum. SocMary. D 6/8/1985 P 12/1/1985 Bp John Shelby Spong. m 3/15/1953 Martha Hys-Sook Kim.

LEE, Hyacinth Evadne (NY) 50 Guion Pl, 5H, New Rochelle NY 10801 **D Trin S Paul's Epis New Rochelle NY 1992-** B JM 1941 d Ezekiel & Sylvia. RN U Hosp W Indies Kingston JM 1965; BA Marymount Manhattan Coll 1979; MS LIU 1992. D 5/30/1992 Bp Richard Frank Grein. c 1.

LEE, James Kyung-Jin (Los) Episcopal Church of the Messiah, 614 N Bush St, Santa Ana CA 92701 **Asstg P Ch Of The Mssh Santa Ana CA 2013-; Assoc Prof U CA Irvine Irvine 2009-** B Deagu, South Korea 1970 s John & Young. BA U of Pennsylvania 1992; MA U CA Los Angeles 1995; MA U CA Los Angeles 1997; PhD U CA Los Angeles 2000; MDiv Claremont TS 2012. D 6/16/2012 Bp Diane Jardine Bruce P 1/12/2013 Bp Joseph Jon Bruno. m 8/8/1998 Julie Grace Cho c 2. Assoc Prof U CA Santa Barbara Santa Barbara 2004-2009.

LEE JR, James Oliver (Dal) 1729 S Beckley Ave, Dallas TX 75224 **Vic Trin Epis Ch Dallas TX 2014-** B Lackawanna NY 1953 s Orea. USNA 1975; BA U of Kansas 1978; JD U of Kansas 1982; MA Harvard DS 2002. D 6/5/2004 P 2/5/2005 Bp James Monte Stanton. m 8/30/1980 Kelly G Lee c 2. The Par Epis Sch Dallas TX 2012-2014; S Geo's Epis Ch Dallas TX 2010-2014; Assoc R Trin Ch Lawr KS 2006; Cur S Lk's Epis Ch Dallas TX 2005-2006.

✠ LEE, The Rt Rev Jeff (Chi) 65 E Huron St, Chicago IL 60611 **Bp of Chicago Dio Chicago Chicago IL 2008-** B Sturgis MI 1957 s Larry & Bonnie. BA U MI 1979; MDiv Nash 1985. D 4/13/1985 P 11/16/1985 Bp William Cockburn Russell Sheridan Con 2/2/2008 for Chi. m 12/29/1979 Lisa Lee c 2. R S Thos Epis Ch Medina WA 2000-2008; R S Chris's Ch Milwaukee WI 1994-2000; H Fam Epis Ch Fishers IN 1992-1994; New Ch Planter Dio Indianapolis Indianapolis IN 1991-1994, 1991-1992; Cn to Ordnry Dio Nthrn Indiana So Bend IN 1987-1991; Cur S Jn The Evang Ch Elkhart IN 1985-1987. Auth, *Opening the PB*, Cowley Press, 1998. Affirming Catholicism 2001; Associated Parishes 1999; NAAD 1986. bishop@episcopalchicago.org

LEE JR, John E (NMich) Rr 1 Box 586, Newberry MI 49868 B Jackson MI 1935 s John & Leah. BS Cntrl Michigan U 1974. D 9/20/1992 Bp Thomas Kreider Ray. m 4/22/1957 Judith E Artman. D All SS Ch Newberry MI 1993-2008.

LEE, Judith M (WNY) 36 Marion Rd E # 8540, Princeton NJ 08540 **Calv Epis Ch Williamsville NY 2015-; Asst Manakin Epis Ch Midlothian VA 2005-** B Antigonish Nova Scotia 1947 BA USC. D 6/7/2003 Bp David Bruce Joslin P 1/17/2004 Bp George Edward Councell. m 7/27/1977 Dale Bruce Haidvogel c 1. S Jn's Ch Wilson NY 2007-2015; Vic S Andr's Ch Newfane Burt NY 2005-2015; Asst Chr Ch New Brunswick NJ 2003-2005. office@standrewsburt.com

LEE, Jui-Chiang (U) 163 Tung-Ming Rd., Keelung Taiwan **Dio Taiwan Taipei 2003-** B Taipei Hsien 1973 s Wen-Jen & Yu-Chiu. D. m 6/23/2001 Shih-Yung Fung c 2.

LEE, Julia Hamilton (Ala) B Hartford CT 1945 d James & Julia. AS Centenary Coll for Wmn 1966; BA Norwich U; Vermont Coll 1996. D 10/1/2011 Bp Henry Nutt Parsley Jr. c 2.

LEE, Kirk A (At) 1195 Village Run NE, Atlanta GA 30319 B 1954 BS Rockford Coll 1976; MDiv Trin, U Tor CA 1990. Trans 1/1/2001 Bp Robert Gould Tharp. S Jas Epis Ch Marietta GA 2002-2012. Off The Most Venerable Ord of the Hosp of St Jn of Jerusalem 2011.

LEE, Marc DuPlan (Kan) 4515 W Moncrieff Pl, Denver CO 80212 **Pres Affinity Fundraising Registration Denver CO 2008-** B Poughkeepsie NY 1951 s Robert & Jeanne. BA Col 1973; MDiv EDS 1979; Cfre 1998. D 6/2/1979 Bp

Paul Moore Jr P 9/29/1980 Bp Walter Decoster Dennis Jr. m 6/24/1978 Elisabeth M Lee c 2. Metropltn Luth Mnstrs Kansas City MO 1998-1999; Pres Affinity Resources Lawr KS 1997-2007; Gr Cathd Topeka KS 1993-1998; Cn Chancllr & Dir Dvlpmt Gr Cathd San Francisco CA 1986-1993; R S Mary's Ch Mohegan Lake NY 1982-1986; Asst Cathd Of St Jn The Div New York NY 1979-1982. Auth, "Raise Capital Funds Using The Internet"; Ed, "Prairie Poetry On-Line Journ". Assn Of Fundraising Professionals 1987.

LEE, Margaret Will (Chi) 3412 54th St, Moline IL 61265 B Saint Louis MO 1949 d Louis & Betty. DMin Nash; BA Monmouth Coll 1971; MDiv Nash 2009. D 11/16/1996 Bp Keith Lynn Ackerman P 10/16/2010 Bp John Clark Buchanan. m 11/3/1972 Frank William Lee c 2. P Gr Epis Ch Galesburg IL 2013-2015; All SS Epis Ch Moline IL 2010-2013; D H Trin Epis Ch Geneseo IL 2005-2008; D H Trin Geneseo IL 2005-2008; D S Mk's Epis Ch Silvis IL 2002-2005; D Chr Ch Moline IL 1996-2002. Amer Chem Soc 1967; NAAD 1998. Monmouth Coll DSA Monmouth Coll 1996.

LEE, Maurice Charles (Spr) 3231 Alton Rd, Atlanta GA 30341 B Sydney NSW AU 1935 s William & Muriel. LTh Moore Theol Coll Sydney AU 1960. Trans 2/1/1992 Bp Edward Lloyd Salmon Jr. m 11/30/1982 Janet Inez Lee. S Paul's Epis Ch Pekin IL 2002-2003; S Mich's Epis Ch O Fallon IL 1999-2001; R S Barn Ch Havana IL 1994-1999; Asst S Phil's Ch Charleston SC 1992-1994; Serv Ch of Australia 1960-1989.

LEE, Nathaniel Jung-Chul (WA) Church of the Holy Spirit, 1624 Wooded Acres Dr, Waco TX 76710 **All SS' Epis Ch Chevy Chase MD 2015-** B Reston VA 1982 s Hyeon-Kon & Gail. BA Wheaton Coll 2004; MA Wheaton Coll 2006; MDiv TESM 2009; MDiv Trin Sch for Mnstry 2009; ThM Duke 2011. D 12/12/2009 P 2/2/2011 Bp William Howard Love. Asst S Mk's Ch Austin TX 2014-2015; Cur Epis Ch Of The H Sprt Waco TX 2013-2014.

✠ LEE, The Rt Rev Peter J (Va) 511 E Rosemary St, Chapel Hill NC 27514 **Chr Ch Georgetown Washington DC 2015-; Dio No Carolina Raleigh NC 2015-, Pres, Stndg Com 1980-1984; Chair The Friends Of Cbury Cathd In The Untd States Washington DC 2003-; Trst Ya Berk New Haven CT 1998-** B Greenville MS 1938 s Erling & Marion. BA W&L 1960; Duke 1964; BD VTS 1967; VTS 1984; Sewanee: The U So, TS 1993; DLitt W&L 1999. D 6/29/1967 Bp Edward Hamilton West P 5/8/1968 Bp William Foreman Creighton Con 5/19/1984 for Va. m 8/28/1965 Kristina K Lee c 2. Bp Provsnl of E Carolina Dio E Carolina Kinston NC 2013-2014; Int Dn The Amer Cathd of the H Trin Paris 75008 2012-2013, Int Dn 2012-2013; Dn The GTS New York NY 2010-2012, Int Dn 2010-2012; Int Gr Cathd San Francisco CA 2009-2010, Int Dn 2009-2010; Bp Dio Virginia Richmond VA 1984-2009; Vstng Lectr Epis Polity Duke Ds Durham NC 1981-1984; R Chap Of The Cross Chap Hill NC 1971-1984; Asst S Jn's Ch Lafayette Sq Washington DC 1968-1970; D-In-Trng S Jn's Cathd Jacksonville FL 1967-1968; Chair, Bd Trst The CPG New York NY 2009-2012; Chair, Bd Trst VTS Alexandria VA 1993-2009; Pres, Amer Friends Dio Jerusalem 1989-1996; Chair, HOB Comm on Natl & Intl Affrs Dom And Frgn Mssy Soc- Epis Ch Cntr New York NY 1989-1992, PBFWR 1987-1993. DSA First Freedom Fndt 2012; Distinguished Alum Awd Washington&Lee Univ 2010; Doctor of Letters Washington&Lee Univ 1998; Dupont Awd 1997; DD Stuso 1993; DD VTS 1984; Phi Beta Kappa. peterlee@christchurchgeorgetown.org

LEE, Rhonda Mawhood (NC) 914 Green St, Durham NC 27701 **Cn Dio No Carolina Raleigh NC 2014-** B Montreal Quebec CA 1966 BA McGill U 1989; MA McGill U 1991; MDiv Louisville Presb TS 2005; PhD Duke 2007. D 6/4/2005 P 12/4/2005 Bp Ted Gulick Jr. m 3/18/1997 Wayne E Lee. Assoc R S Phil's Ch Durham NC 2011-2014; Vic S Jos's Ch Durham NC 2006-2010; Cler Assoc. Calv Ch Louisville KY 2005-2006. rhonda.lee@episdionc.org

LEE, Richard Stanley (SanD) 4036 Ampudia St, San Diego CA 92110 **Ch Of The Gd Samar San Diego CA 2016-** B Leicester, England 1971 s Stuart & Rosemary. B.Eng. U of Wales, Bangor 1993; Ph.D. U of Wales, Bangor 1998; Cert in Mnstry Stds Epis Dio San Diego, Sch for Mnstry 2016. D 6/11/2016 Bp Jim Mathes. m 9/13/2013 Antonio Peȳa Ruvalcaba. richardl@goodsamchurch.org

LEE, Robert Bruce (Vt) 51 Park St., Canaan VT 05903 **P S Paul's Ch Canaan VT 2000-** B Bridgeport CT 1943 s Jack & Annette. BS U of Vermont 1965; MS U of Vermont 1967. D 10/22/2000 Bp Mary Adelia Rosamond Mcleod P 8/4/2001 Bp Thomas C Ely. m 7/1/1967 Rita Bergeron Lee c 3.

LEE III, Robert Vernon (Fla) 1131 N Laura St, Jacksonville FL 32206 B El Paso TX 1951 s Robert & Cynthia. BA Van 1973; U GA 1975; MDiv Ya Berk 1988; DMin NYTS 1992. D 4/30/1988 Bp Claude Charles Vache P 5/18/1989 Bp Jeffery William Rowthorn. m 5/18/1985 Mirte De Lee. Mem U. S. Pres's Coun On Fin Literacy 2007-2011; Bd Dir Reg ChmbrCom 2006-2008; Mem Mayor's Faith-based Advsry Bd Jacksonville FL 2003-2007; Chair Super Bowl Outreach Com Jacksonville FL 2003-2005; Mem Governor's Faith-based Advsry Bd Florida 2000-2006; Bd Dir HabHum Jacksonville Florida 2000-2005; Founding Chair & CEO FreshMinistries Jacksonville Florida 1995-2011; Bd Dir Interfaith Coun Jacksonville Florida 1995-2007; Bd Dir Florida Coun of Ch 1995-2000; R Ch Of Our Sav Jacksonville FL 1989-1994; Cur S Jn's Epis Par Waterbury CT 1988-1989; Chair Asstg Bp Selection Cmsn Dio Florida

Jacksonville 2001-2002, Asstg Bp'S Cmsn Chair 1997-2001, Exec Coun 1995-2011, Chair Strategic Plnng Cmsn 1992-1995, Chair Cmsn On Environ 1991-1996, Chair Bdgt Com 1990-1992; Bd Dir S Mary's Ch Jacksonville FL 1991-1994. Bk, "Organizing Parishioners for the Protection of the Environ," NYTS, 1992. Compass Rose Soc 1997-2001; Ord of Jn's of Jerusalem 1998-2011. Annual Diversity Awd Jacksonville Bus Journ 2013; Annual Diversity Awd Jacksonville Bus Journ 2009; Eagle Awd Jacksonville Sheriff's Off 2008; Eagle Awd Jacksonville Sheriff's Off 2008; Change Maker of the Year Jacksonville Times-Un 2006; Humanitarian of the Year Rotary 1998; Crossroads Afr Riverside Ch 1961.

LEE, Sang (Dal) 2783 Valwood Pkwy, Farmers Branch TX 75234 B Korea 1965 s Se & Moon. Trans 6/27/2008 Bp James Monte Stanton. m 10/24/1992 Eun Joo Lee c 2. S Andr's Ch Dallas TX 2008-2012.

LEE, Scott Charles (Ct) 2000 Main Street, Stratford CT 06615 **Chr Ch Stratford CT 2013-** B Meridian MS 1951 s Charles & Julia. BA U So 1973; MAT Van 1980; MDiv Sewanee: The U So, TS 1992. D 6/7/1992 P 12/20/1992 Bp William Evan Sanders. R Trin Ch Wethersfield CT 2006-2013; Cn Trin Cathd Little Rock AR 2000-2006; R S Mk's Ch Antioch TN 1994-2000; Cur Trin Ch Clarksville TN 1993-1994; Dio Tennessee Nashville TN 1992-1993; Asst for Admin Chr Ch Cathd Nashville TN 1987-1989. Auth, "The Angl Vision of The New Ch's Tchg Series Bk Revs," *Sewanee Theol Revs*, The U So, 1997; Auth, "DOCC Stdt Handbook," *DOCC Stdt Handbook*, The U So, 1993; Auth, "The Gd News of Jesus Bk Revs," *Sewanee Theol Revs*, The U So, 1993; Auth, "The Pleasure of Her Text Bk Revs," *Sewanee Theol Revs*, The U So, 1992. Phyllis M. Redfield Awd InterCommunity Mntl Hlth Common Ground Prog 2013. revsclee@aol.com

LEE, Scott R (NwT) St James the Apostle Epis Ch, 1803 Highland Hollow Dr, Conroe TX 77305 **S Barn Ch Warwick RI 2017-** B Amarillo TX 1973 s Charles & Mary. BS Texas Tech U 1996; MDiv Epis TS Of The SW 2012; MDiv Epis TS of the SW 2012. D 1/14/2012 P 9/8/2012 Bp James Scott Mayer. m 8/5/1994 Jennifer A Lee c 2. Assoc S Mary's Ch Edmond OK 2015-2017; S Jas The Apos Epis Ch Conroe TX 2012.

LEE, Shiane Marlena (NY) D 5/13/2017 Bp Andrew Marion Lenow Dietsche.

LEE, Shirley Lynne (Ak) 1205 Denali Way, Fairbanks AK 99701 **P S Matt's Epis Ch Fairbanks AK 2012-** B Fairbanks AK 1959 d Russell & Helen. Cert Antioch Law Sch 1980. D 2/13/2010 Bp Rustin Ray Kimsey P 5/27/2012 Bp Mark A Lattime. m 12/15/1979 Gary D Lee c 6. Yth Coordntr/Cmncatn Dio Alaska Fairbanks AK 2010-2011.

LEE, Solomon Sang-Woo (Chi) 9227 Cameron Ln, Morton Grove IL 60053 **D One In Chr Ch Prospect Heights IL 1988-** B Kangwha KR 1929 s Andrew & Grace. Seoul Natl U Seoul Kr 1950; Cert Sch for Deacons 1987. D 12/26/1987 Bp Frank Tracy Griswold III. m 10/7/1958 Chu Nam Lee c 3. Amer Mnstry Grant 1988.

LEE, Stedwart Warren Rubinstein (VI) 261 Mount Pleasant, Frederiksted VI 00840 **S Lk's Ch St Thos VI 2014-** B Stone Castle Tabernacle 1952 s Lawrence & Anne. U of the Vrgn Islands; BA Codrington Coll 1980. Trans 9/30/2006 Bp Edward Gumbs. m 12/29/1998 Shirlene Lee-Williams c 2.

LEE, Susan Hagood (Mass) 336 Maple St, New Bedford MA 02740 **S Lk's Epis Ch Fall River MA 1988-** B Oakland CA 1949 d Richard & Jeanne. BA Br 1971; MDiv Harvard DS 1988; PhD Bos 2003. D 6/25/1988 P 3/4/1989 Bp George Nelson Hunt III. c 2. Dioc Refugee Coordntr Dio Massachusetts Boston MA 1990-1994. "'Rice Plus': Widows and Econ Survival in Rural Cambodia," Routledge, 2006; "Traffic in Wmn," *Blackwell Encyclopedia of Sociol*, Blackwell Pub, 2006; "Female Genital Mutilation," *Blackwell Encyclopedia of Sociol*, Blackwell Pub, 2006; Auth, "Witness to Chr, Witness to Pain," *Sermons Seldom Heard*, Crossroad Pub, 1991; Ed, "Liberal and Persevering: Wmn in the Epis Dio Rhode Island," *Remembering Our SS: The RI Herstory Proj*, 1986.

LEE, Tambria Elizabeth (NC) 304 E Franklin St, Chapel Hill NC 27514 **Chapl U NC Chap Hill NC 2003-; Assoc for U Mnstry Chap Of The Cross Chap Hill NC 1993-** B Athens GA 1962 d Joseph & M Frances. BA Florida St U 1985; MDiv Yale DS 1988; DMin SWTS 1993. D 6/12/1993 P 5/1/1994 Bp Albert Theodore Eastman. m 11/21/2009 David E Brown.

LEE, Terence A (LI) 19610 Woodhull Ave, Hollis NY 11423 **S Gabr's Ch Hollis NY 2010-** B Charleston SC 1974 s Cynthia. BS Coll of Charleston 1996; MDiv Nash 2005. D 6/18/2005 P 12/10/2005 Bp Edward Lloyd Salmon Jr. m 10/10/2010 Violet Lee c 2. Cn S Jn's Cathd Albuquerque NM 2008-2010; D S Paul's Ch Bennettsville SC 2005-2008.

LEE III, Thomas Carleton (LI) 3000 Galloway Ridge Apt D104, Pittsboro NC 27312 B Niagara Falls NY 1928 s Harold & Fanny. BA Leh 1948; STB GTS 1951; STM GTS 1953. D 5/26/1951 P 5/31/1952 Bp Lauriston L Scaife. m 7/17/1954 Emily Lee. R St Jn's Ch Cold Sprg Harbor NY 1963-1993; Asst Min S Steph's Ch Prt Washington NY 1960-1963; R S Phil's Ch Garrison NY 1954-1960; P-in-c S Jn's Epis Ch Ellicottville NY 1953-1954; Gr Ch Randolph NY 1951-1954; Ret; Fell and Tutor The GTS New York NY 1951-1953.

LEE, Thomas Moon (Tenn) 510 Mable Mason Cv, La Vergne TN 37086 **R H Sprt Nashville TN 2002-** B Seoul KR 1962 d Young & Myung. BA Han Young U Seoul KR 1986; BTh Calvin TS Korea 1989; MDiv Ch of God TS 1993; Cert Ang Stud Sewanee: The U So, TS 2001; DMin Regent U 2002. D 12/16/2001 P 6/23/2002 Bp Bertram Nelson Herlong. m 4/21/1990 Jung Hwa Lee c 2. H Sprt Ch Nashville TN 2008-2013, 2001-2006. "A Study of the Ch Growth Through Healing Mnstry," Regent U Virginia Bch.

LEE, Wanhong Barnabas (Md) St John's Episcopal Church, 9120 Frederick Rd, Ellicott City MD 21042 **S Jn's Ch Ellicity City MD 2012-** B Seoul Korea 1958 s Ho & Soon. Trans 2/1/2009 Bp Ted Gulick Jr. m 1/4/2017 Eunyoung Leah Lee c 4. Dio Maryland Baltimore MD 2011-2012; Assoc Chr Ch Elizabethtown KY 2009-2010.

LEE, Wen-Hui (Tai) 5F No. 7 Kee-King 2nd Road, Kee Lung City 20446 Taiwan B Chang-Hwa TW 1953 s Kun-York & Tsai-Lien. BS Natl Taiwan Ocean U 1977; MDiv Tainan Theol Coll and Sem TW 1986; Cert St Lukes Theol Educ CTR Atlanta GA 1988; So E Asia Grad Sch of Thoelogy 1993. D 8/17/1986 Bp Poi-Yeung Cheung P 6/1/1988 Bp John Chih-Tsung Chien. m 8/26/1979 Cho-Fang Lin. Dio Taiwan Taipei 1991-2001, 1986-1987, Del: GC in Philadelphia 1997, Dir: Mnstry of Liturg 1995-2001, Mem: H Ord Com 1995-2001, Mem: Stndg Com 1995-2001, Del: CCEA Full Conv In Singapore 1995, Del: EAM Conf in San Francisco 1993, Del: CCEA Yth Mnstry Conf in Malaysia 1991, Dir: Mnstry of Educ & Mssn 1990-1994; P-in-c H Trin Epis Ch In Kee-Lung TW 1990-2001; Lectr St Jn's U TW 1990-1993; P-in-c St Lk's Epis Ch In Hua-Lien TW 1989-1990; P-in-c St Mk's Epis Ch In Ping-Tung TW 1988-1989; Cur St Paul's & St Tim's Epis Ch In Kaoshiong TW 1988-1989; D-In-Trng S Lk's Epis Ch Atlanta GA 1987-1988; D-in-Taining St Lk's Theol Educ CTR Atalanta GA 1987-1988; D St Mk's Epis Ch In Ping-Tung TW 1986-1987; Cur St Paul's & St Tim's Epis Ch In Kaoshiong TW 1986-1987.

LEE III, William Forrest (Md) Po Box 2188, Mountain Lake Park MD 21550 **R Our Fr's Hse The Log Ch Oakland MD 1992-; Vic S Jn's Ch Oakland MD 1992-; S Matt's Par Oakland MD 1992-; Stndg Com Dio Maryland Baltimore MD 2002-** B Boston MA 1948 s William & Natalie. BS Ithaca Coll 1971; MDiv CDSP 1989; DMin SWTS 2004. D 6/25/1989 Bp Rustin Ray Kimsey P 7/1/1990 Bp Bob Gordon Jones. m 6/26/2002 Mary Kathleen Gibbs c 3. S Barth's Ch Cokeville WY 1989-1992; Vic S Jas Ch Kemmerer WY 1989-1992; Com Dio Wyoming Casper 1991-1992.

LEECH, John (Oly) PO Box 65807, Tucson AZ 85728 **Supply P S Paul's Ch Tombstone AZ 2017-** B.A. U CA, Santa Cruz 1979; MDiv CDSP 1984; Cert Seattle U 2009; Cert Seattle U 2009; DMin SFTS 2013. D 11/6/2004 P 8/12/2006 Bp Jerry Alban Lamb. R S Alb's Ch Edmonds WA 2007-2013; Assoc Trin Epis Cathd Sacramento CA 2005-2007; D S Patricks Ch Kenwood CA 2004-2005. john.leech@yahoo.com

LEED, Rolf (WMo) 226 N Main St, Clinton MO 64735 B Honolulu HI 1941 s Bjarne & Alice. MDiv Brigham Young U 1964; MDiv SWTS 1969; ACPE Bapt Med Cntr 1983. D 9/13/1969 Bp Francis E I Bloy P 3/14/1970 Bp Norman L Foote. c 3. S Paul's Epis Ch Clinton MO 1994-2006; Dio W Missouri Kansas City MO 1985-1988; S Andr's Ch Kansas City MO 1985; Vic Gr Epis Ch Liberty MO 1984-1986; Assoc S Andr's 1983-1984; All SS Ch Pratt KS 1980-1983; Chr Ch Kingman KS 1980-1983; Vic Gr Ch Anth KS 1980-1983; Dio Wstrn Kansas Hutchinson KS 1979-1982; R Emm Ch Kellogg ID 1976-1980; Vic S Andr's Mulian KS 1976-1980; H Trin Epis Ch Wallace ID 1975-1978; Vic S Jas Ch Mtn Hm ID 1969-1976; Vic S Jas Mccall ID 1969-1976.

LEEHAN, Jim (Ind) 7047 Vuelta Vistoso, Santa Fe NM 87507 B La Moure ND 1939 s Floyd & Florence. BA Crosier Hse of Stds 1964; STB Crosier Hse of Stds 1966; MA Case Wstrn Reserve U 1972; MSSA Case Wstrn Reserve U 1975; DMin Ohio Methodist TS 1986. Rec 1/6/1981 as Priest Bp John Harris Burt. c 3. Vic Ch Of The Gd Shpd Ft Defiance AZ 2003-2007; Vic Gd Shpd Mssn Ft Defiance AZ 2003-2007; Vic Navajoland Area Mssn Farmington NM 2003-2007; Assoc R Outreach S Paul's Epis Ch Indianapolis IN 1995-2003; Asst Fac Chr TS Indianapolis 1994-1996; Dir of Campus Mnstry U Chr Mvmt Cleveland OH 1974-1994; Campus Min RC Ch 1966-1973; Pres, Stndg Com The Epis Ch In Navajoland Coun Farmington NM 2006-2007; Cler Wellnes Com Dio Indianapolis Indianapolis IN 1996-2003, Trnr Sexual Misconduct Prevention 1994-2003. Auth, "Psychol," *Grp Treatment for adult Survivors of Abuse*, Sage, 1996; Auth, "Sprtlty," *Defiant Hope: Sprtlty for Survivors of Fam Abuse*, Westminster/ Jn Knox, 1993; Auth, "Pstr Care," *Pstr Care for Survivors of Fam Abuse*, Westminster/ Jn Knox, 1989; Auth, "Psychol," *Grown-Up Abused Chld*, Chas AThomas, 1985.

LEEMHUIS, Guy Anthony (Los) 260 N Locust St, Inglewood CA 90301 **D S Geo's Ch Riverside CA 2016-; D H Faith Par Inglewood CA 2015-** B Los Angeles CA 1968 s Melvin & Paige. BA U CA, Los Angeles 1990; JD Loyola Law Sch 1994; MDiv Claremont TS 2016. D 12/20/2014 Bp Joseph Jon Bruno. guyleemhuis@gmail.com

LEES, Everett (Okla) 2613 W Broadway St, Broken Arrow OK 74012 **Vic Chr Epis Ch Tulsa OK 2013-** B Oklahoma City OK 1976 s Donald & M Ann. DMin VTS; BBA U of Oklahoma 2000; MDiv Epis TS of the SW 2009. D 1/16/2009 P 7/24/2009 Bp Edward Joseph Konieczny. m 5/3/2003 Kristin K Lees c 3. Chr Ch Tulsa Dio Oklahoma Oklahoma City OK 2011-2012, Stndg

L

Com 2011-; Cur S Pat's Epis Ch Broken Arrow OK 2009-2011. everett@christchurchtulsa.org

LEESON, Gary William (Los) 4457 Mont Eagle Pl, Los Angeles CA 90041 B Laurium MI 1944 s Ralph & Margalene. BA Drury U 1966; BD Nash 1969. D 2/12/1969 Bp Edward Randolph Welles II P 8/1/1969 Bp Donald H V Hallock. R All SS Par Los Angeles CA 1999-2007; P Ch Of The Epiph Los Angeles CA 1986-1988; Asst Trin Epis Par Los Angeles CA 1984-1986; R S Jas Ch W Bend WI 1972-1979; P S Aidans Ch Hartford WI 1972-1973; Cur Trin Ch Janesville WI 1969-1972. Hon Cn of the Cathd Cntr The Bp of Los Angeles 2007.

LEFEBVRE, Eugene Francis (Pa) 635 Willow Valley Sq Apt H-509, Lancaster PA 17602 **Ret 1991-** B New York NY 1929 s Francis & Antoinette. BA Estrn Kentucky U 1952; BA Estrn Kentucky U 1952; MDiv Epis TS in Kentucky 1957; MA Villanova U 1971; MA Villanova U 1971; U of Durham GB 1984. D 6/14/1956 P 6/14/1957 Bp William R Moody. m 6/21/1952 Gladys Lefebvre c 3. Assoc All SS Ch San Diego CA 1995-2003; Chapl AmL 1984-1992; Chapl CAP 1982-1992; R S Tim's Ch Roxborough Philadelphia PA 1960-1991; Hd Mstr S Tim's Sch 1960-1991; Vic S Mary's Ch Williamsport PA 1959-1960; R S Jn Dayton KY 1957-1959. Auth, "Sharing," *Chrsnty Today*; Auth, "Chr Today," *Chrsnty Today*; Auth/Ed, *The Healing Message*. CCU 1961-1978; Chapl Healing Pryr Fllshp 1983-2000; ECM 1988; Ord of S Lk 1960.

LEFEVRE, Ann Raynor (Be) 1190 Bianca Dr Ne, Palm Bay FL 32905 B Portland OR 1934 d Spencer & Eleanor. AA Brevard Cmnty Coll 1969; BA U of Cntrl Florida 1971; MA Stetson U 1972; MA Moravian TS 1991. D 5/23/1991 Bp James Michael Mark Dyer. m 12/23/1979 Carl Anthony Lefevre c 4. D Ch of Our Sav Palm Bay FL 2002-2009; D S Lk's Ch Lebanon PA 1991-1995. NAAD.

LEGER, Don Curtis (WLa) 919 Anthony Ave, Opelousas LA 70570 **Asst To R Ch Of The Epiph 1998-** B Opelousas LA 1956 s Curtis & Shirley. AS LSU 1980; Bp Sch Mnstry 1997. D 6/24/1998 Bp Robert Jefferson Hargrove Jr. m 6/28/1975 Jeanette Marie Leger c 2. S Paul's Ch Abbeville LA 2010-2011; Dio Wstrn Louisiana Alexandria LA 2000-2007; S Barn Epis Ch Lafayette LA 1999-2007.

LEGGE, Don Edward (Tex) 1809 Barton Hills Dr, Austin TX 78704 B Paducah TX 1931 s Edward & Margaret. BA U of Texas 1954. D 6/19/1999 Bp Claude Edward Payne P 1/5/2000 Bp Leopoldo Jesus Alard. c 2. All SS Ch Cameron TX 1999-2007.

LEGNANI, Robert Henry (NJ) 22 Ashley Dr, Delran NJ 08075 **Chapl to Ret Cler and Spouses Dio New Jersey Trenton New Jersey 2013-** B Mount Holly NJ 1946 s Felix & Gertrude. BA Ups 1969; MDiv PDS 1974; STM GTS 1980; Cert Coll of Preachers 1991; Cler Ldrshp Inst 2000. D 4/27/1974 P 11/16/1974 Bp Albert Wiencke Van Duzer. m 12/3/1977 Susan T Legnani c 2. P-in-c S Steph's Ch Riverside NJ 2011-2013; R S Steph's Epis Ch Beverly NJ 1988-2012; Chapl Glouchester Cnty NJ Cmnty Coll 1984-1988; Pres Camden-Woodbury Cler 1983-1984; Chapl Psych Hosp Camden Cnty NJ 1980-1988; Vic H Trin Epis Ch Wenonah NJ 1978-1988; Cathdl Maj Chapt Trin Cathd Trenton NJ 1978-1981; Boys Conf Dio New Jersey Trenton NJ 1975-1982, Chapl to Ret Cler and Spouses 2013-, Cler Wellness Com 1996-1997, Dn Burlington Convoc 1992-1996, Ed Bd Nwspr 1990-2003, Chair of Cmsn of Cler Salaries 1986-1989, Cmsn of Cler Salaries 1981-1985, Boys Conf 1975-1980; Cur H Cross Epis Ch Plainfield NJ 1974-1978; Vic St Andrews Ch Plainfield NJ 1974-1978. Auth, "When is it Rt to Close a Ch?," *Living Ch*, 1994; Auth, "Ch News Column," *Beverly Bee*. HSEC 1974.

LEHMAN, Katherine Megee (Cal) 705 W Main St, Kerrville TX 78028 B Austin TX 1946 d Robert & Nancy. BA Santa Clara U 1970; MDiv CDSP 1982; DMin CDSP 1999. D 6/19/1982 P 6/1/1983 Bp William Edwin Swing. m 6/11/1966 Henry Clay Lehman c 2. R S Bede's Epis Ch Menlo Pk CA 1990-2012; Assoc R S Steph's Par Bel Tiburon CA 1984-1990; Asst R S Steph's Epis Ch Orinda CA 1982-1984. Auth, "Go and Tell the Others," *God's Friends*, St. Greg Nyssa Ch, 1992; Auth, "Arts in the Ch Model," *CDSP DMin thesis*, GTU Libr, 1990; Auth, "Sing & Dance Chld Of God," Hinshaw Mus, 1980. Associated Parishes 1984-1994. CDSP DD Berkeley 2006.

LEHMAN, Susan C (SwVa) 550 E 4th St #U, Cincinnati OH 45202 B Canton OH 1941 d Thomas & Katharyn. BA Mia 1963; MA Xavier U 1973; MA U Chi 1984. D 5/28/1977 P 11/30/1977 Bp John Mc Gill Krumm. m 5/5/1974 John Dalzell. Vic Ch of the Gd Shpd Inc Blue Grass VA 2001-2006; Vic S Andr's Ch Clifton Forg VA 1995-1999; Sweet Briar Coll Sweet Briar VA 1985-2001; H Sprt Epis Ch Cincinnati OH 1978-1982; Chr Ch - Glendale Cincinnati OH 1977-1980.

LEHMANN, Richard B (Alb) 24 Summit Ave, Latham NY 12110 **D S Andr's Ch Schenectady NY 2001-** B Jamaica NY 1954 s Richard & Ruth. BS No Cntrl Coll 1978; Gordon-Conwell TS 1981; Mercer TS 1989. D 6/9/2001 Bp Daniel William Herzog P 11/22/2008 Bp William Howard Love. m 9/18/1982 Christine Lehmann c 2. S Matt's Ch Latham NY 2010-2015; Ch Of The H Cross Troy NY 2008-2009.

LEHRER, Christian Anton (Cal) 800 Pomona St, Crockett CA 94525 **D S Mk's Par Crockett CA 2009-** B Albany NY 1963 s Vinzenz & Joan. BA The Coll of

S Rose 1986; MA Dominical U 2001; Diac Stds Sch for Deacons Berkeley CA 2007; MTS Jesuit TS 2013. D 6/6/2009 Bp Marc Handley Andrus.

LEIBHART, Linda Dianne (Roch) 9406 Chipping Dr, Richmond VA 23237 B York PA 1952 d Lamar & June. BS Millersville U 1974; MDiv VTS 1980. D 6/13/1980 Bp Dean Theodore Stevenson P 2/1/1981 Bp Charlie Fuller Mcnutt Jr. Ch of the Redeem Addison NY 2010-2014; S Mths Epis Ch Midlothian VA 1999-2000; Off Of Bsh For ArmdF New York NY 1989-2012; S Paul's Ch Troy PA 1985-1989; S Jas Ch Mansfield PA 1982-1985; Dio Cntrl Pennsylvania Harrisburg PA 1980-1984; Asst All SS Ch Hanover PA 1980-1982; Asst Epis Deaf Missions Harrisburg PA 1980-1982.

✠ LEIDEL JR OJN, The Rt Rev Edwin Max (EMich) 430 W Brentwood Ln, Milwaukee WI 53217 **Assoc Chr Ch Milwaukee WI 2015-, P Assoc 1970-1975** B Baltimore MD 1938 s Edwin & Gertrude. BS U of Wisconsin 1961; MDiv Nash 1964; DMin Sewanee: The U So, TS 1990; DD Nash 1997; DD Huron U Coll 2004; Coaching Certification Cler Ldrshp Inst 2007. D 2/22/1964 P 8/22/1964 Bp Donald H V Hallock Con 9/7/1996 for EMich. m 6/20/1964 Ira P Leidel c 2. Provsnl Bp Dio Eau Claire Eau Claire WI 2010-2012; Congrl Coach Ch of Can (Huron) London ON Can 2007-2010; Comgrgational Coach Dio Huron London Ontario 2007-2010; Epis Visitor Visitor to the Ord of Julian of Norwich 2006-2012; Bp Dio Estrn Michigan Saginaw MI 1996-2006; Corner Stone Field Rep Dio Minnesota Minneapolis MN 1994-1996; Prov VI Exec Coun 1988-1993; R S Chris's Epis Ch S Paul MN 1986-1996; Dn Chr Ch Cathd Darwin Australia 1981-1982; Dn - So Cntrl Deanry Dio Indianapolis Indianapolis IN 1977-1980; R S Tim's Ch Indianapolis IN 1975-1986; R S Steph's Ch Racine WI 1967-1970. Auth, "Awakening Grassroots Sprtlty," iUniverse, 2004; Auth, "Claiming a Distinctive Character for the Ord," Dio Minnesota, 1994; Auth, "Bp, P or D?," Dio Minesota, 1993; Auth, "Perceptions of Minstry Roles in Relatns to Three Primary Functions of Mnstry," Doctoral Disertation, 1990. Ord of Julian of Norwich 2006; Sis of S Mary 1968; The Cmnty of Aiden and Hilda 2002. DD Hur U, London, ON 2004; DD Nash Sem, Nashotah, WI 1998. ed@leidel.us

LEIDER, Jennifer (O) St. Paul's Episcopal Church, 798 S. Coy Rd., Oregon OH 43616 B Charlotte NC 1982 d Dwight & Frances. MA Case Wstrn Reserve U 2005; BA Case Wstrn Reserve Unversity 2005; MDiv EDS 2008. D 6/13/2009 P 5/8/2010 Bp Mark Hollingsworth Jr. m 9/2/2006 Stephen George Leider c 1. S Michaels In The Hills Toledo OH 2015-2016; R S Paul's Ch Oregon OH 2010-2015; Chapl Res Mercy St Vinc Med Cntr 2009-2010; Asst S Paul's Epis Ch Medina OH 2008-2009.

LEIDHEISER-STODDARD, Margaret Clare (SO) St. John's Episcopal Church, 700 High St, Worthington OH 43085 **S Jn's Ch Worthington OH 2016-** B Raleigh NC 1981 d Edward & Nancy. MDiv PSR; MA Queen's U (Can); Dplma The Bex Seabury Wstrn Sem Fed. D 6/11/2016 P 6/10/2017 Bp Thomas Edward Breidenthal. m 6/30/2007 Jonathan Paul Leidheiser-Stoddard c 1.

LEIFUR, Teresa (CGC) 1110 E Gadsden St, Pensacola FL 32501 **Supply S Anna's Ch Atmore AL 2011-** B Pensacola FL 1945 d Jesse & Artie. AA Pensacola St Coll 1978; BA U of W Florida 1988; MDiv Candler TS Emory U 1994. D 5/27/1995 P 1/27/1996 Bp Charles Farmer Duvall. m 4/12/1968 Duane Eugene Leifur c 3. Chapl W Florida Hosp 2003-2013; R S Jn's Ch Pensacola FL 2001-2005; Vic Imm Ch Bay Minette AL 1996-2001; Dio Cntrl Gulf Coast Pensacola FL 1995-1996; Cur S Monica's Pensacola FL 1995-1996. OSH (Assoc) 1982.

LEIGH, W Joseph (NJ) 238 Twilight Ave, Keansburg NJ 07734 **P-in-c S Mary's Ch Keyport NJ 2006-, 1992; Non-par 2004-** B Denver CO 1952 s Walter & Jane. BA Metropltn St Coll of Denver 1974; MDiv SWTS 1978. D 6/29/1978 Bp William Carl Frey P 2/2/1979 Bp Arthur Anton Vogel. m 12/26/1987 Barbara Redepenning. The Ch Of S Uriel The Archangel Sea Girt NJ 2000-2004, Asst P 2000-2004, Cur 1980-1982; Vic Ch Of S Clem Of Rome Belford NJ 1992-2000; Int All SS Epis Ch Lakewood NJ 1990-1991; S Jas Memi Ch Eatontown NJ 1985-1990; Gr Ch Merchantville NJ 1983-1984; S Mk's Ch Denver CO 1979-1980; Cur S Phil's Ch Joplin MO 1978-1979. wjleigh52@yahoo.com

LEIGH-KOSER, Charlene M (CPa) 6219 Lincoln Hwy, Wrightsville PA 17368 **Asst S Andr's Epis Ch York PA 2003-, Asst to R 1986-2008** B Lancaster PA 1949 d Charles & Esther. BS Millersville U 1971; MDiv EDS 1977. D 6/10/1977 Bp Dean Theodore Stevenson P 5/1/1978 Bp Roger W Blanchard. c 1. P-in-c All SS Ch Selinsgrove PA 2010-2011; St Marks Luth Ch York PA 2003-2006; S Paul's Epis Ch Harrisburg PA 2001-2002; All SS Ch Hanover PA 1986-1988; Dioc Pstr Mnstry 1984-1986; P-in-c Ch Of The Gd Shpd Webster City IA 1981-1984; Asst Chr Ch Needham Hgts MA 1978-1980; D S Ptr's Ch Beverly MA 1977-1978.

LEIGH-TAYLOR, Christine Heath (NCal) 4231 Oak Meadow Rd, Placerville CA 95667 B Los Angeles CA 1943 d Denys & Charlotte. BA U CA Los Angeles 1964; MS California Sch of Profsnl Psychol 1988; MDiv CDSP 2000. D 12/1/2001 P 6/1/2002 Bp William Edwin Swing. m 12/24/1988 David Ollier Weber c 3. R S Clem's Ch Rancho Cordova CA 2005-2014; Assoc. R For Yth Mnstry S Ambr Epis Ch Foster City CA 2002-2005; Lead Chapl; Lay Chapl Trnr Mendocino Coast Dist Hosp Ft Bragg CA 2000-2002; Yth Min S Mich And All Ang Ch Ft Bragg CA 2000-2002. Auth, "Bus Ldrshp As A Sprtl Discipline," *The Physcn Exec*, 2000; Auth, "Storytelling In Healthcare Orgnztn," *The Physcn Exec*, 2000.

LEIGHTON, Blake Eugene (NCal) St Michael and All Angels Episc. Ch., PO Box 124, Fort Bragg CA 95437 **Died 1/15/2016** B Fort Bragg CA 1945 s Granville & Marion. Chico St Coll 1966; BA Sonoma St U 1978; CDSP 1981. D 10/21/2011 P 4/13/2012 Bp Barry Leigh Beisner. Mus Dir/Org S Mich And All Ang Ch Ft Bragg CA 1996-2016.

LEIGHTON, Christopher (Ct) 33 Dora Cir, Bridgeport CT 06604 B Boston MA 1954 s Paul & Susan. BA U of Massachusetts 1976; MDiv TESM 1979. D 9/29/1979 P 3/29/1980 Bp Robert Bracewell Appleyard. m 10/13/1973 Janet Leighton c 4. R S Paul's Ch Darien CT 1998-2015; R S Jas' Epis Ch Cambridge MA 1994-1998; R S Dav's Epis Ch Peters Township PA 1985-1994; R All SS Ch Aliquippa PA 1979-1985. Auth, "Withinsight," Poets' Corner Press, 1972. Bro Of S Andrews 1983; Ch Army (Bd Trst) 1999.

LEIGHTON, Jack Lee (Tex) 135 E Circuit Dr, Beaumont TX 77706 **Ret 1999-** B Wichita KS 1934 s Walter & Vera. BA Rice U 1957; BD Epis TS of the SW 1962. D 6/20/1962 Bp John Elbridge Hines P 6/10/1963 Bp Frederick P Goddard. c 1. S Steph's Ch Beaumont TX 1999; R S Geo's Epis Ch Port Arthur TX 1993-1999; Vic Ch Of The Incarn Houston TX 1986-1993; Assoc S Chris's Ch Houston TX 1984; Asst Emm Ch Houston TX 1978-1983; 1966-1978; Asst S Mk's Ch Houston TX 1964-1966; M-in-c S Lk's El Campo TX 1962-1964.

LEIGHTON, Tim (Spr) **D S Matt's Epis Ch Bloomington IL 2017-** D 3/25/2017 Bp Daniel Hayden Martins.

LEIKER, Diana Louise (WNY) D 12/10/2016 Bp Ralph William Franklin.

LEIN, Clay A (Tex) 1102 Highland St., Houston TX 77009 **S Jn The Div Houston TX 2014-** B Inglewood CA 1961 s Larry & Erlys. Gordon-Conwell TS; SE Missouri St U; BS U of Missouri 1984; MBA Arizona St U 1990; MDiv TESM 1995; DMin Gordon-Conwell TS 2014. D 6/10/1995 Bp Robert Reed Shahan P 1/6/1996 Bp Edward Lloyd Salmon Jr. m 5/21/1983 Jill E Lein c 3. Sr Pstr S Phil's Epis Ch Frisco TX 2002-2014; Asst Chr Epis Ch Plano TX 1996-2001; No Amer Mssy Scty Charlotte NC 1996; Asst Chr the King Pawleys Island SC 1995-1996. Auth, "Ordnry Faith," Xulon Press. clein@sjd.org

LEINBACH, Jeanne A (O) 2747 Fairmount Blvd, Cleveland Heights OH 44106 **S Paul's Epis Ch Cleveland OH 2015-; COM Dio Ohio Cleveland 2016-** B Hartford CT 1960 d Russell & Jacqueline. BA Mt Holyoke Coll 1982; MBA Cor 1986; MDiv SWTS 2007. D 6/2/2007 Bp Bill Persell P 12/15/2007 Bp Victor Alfonso Scantlebury. c 2. Assoc Chr Ch Winnetka IL 2007-2015; Stndg Com Dio Chicago Chicago IL 2014-2015. jleinbach@stpauls-church.org

LEININGER, Austin L (ECR) 532 Center St, Santa Cruz CA 95060 **Calv Epis Ch Santa Cruz CA 2017-; Assoc S Paul's Epis Ch Ft Collins CO 2013-** B Eugene OR 1973 s Jack & Dorothy. BA U CA 2000; MDiv CDSP 2006; MA GTU 2007. D 6/3/2006 Bp William Edwin Swing P 12/2/2006 Bp Marc Handley Andrus. m 8/2/2003 Elizabeth J Northrop c 3. Ch Of The Epiph San Carlos CA 2009-2010; Asst Ch Of S Mart Davis CA 2006-2008. aleininger@calvarysantacruz.org

LEIP, Harry Louis (Mo) 600 N Euclid Ave, Saint Louis MO 63108 **D Trin Ch S Louis MO 2011-; COM Dio Missouri S Louis MO 2014-2018, Dss Anne Hse - Strng Com 2013-2014, Dss Anne Hse - Bd Mem 2012-2013, Diocesean Coun 2011-2013, Epis Sch for Mnstry - Bd Mem 2011-2013** B St Louis MO 1965 s Harry & Georgia. BS Missouri St U 1987. D 1/29/2011 Bp George Wayne Smith. harry@trinitycwe.org

LEISERSON, Joanna (SO) 2218 Oakland Ave, Covington KY 41014 **Calv Ch Cincinnati OH 2016-; Cn for Chr Formation Epis Soc Of Chr Ch Cincinnati OH 2005-** B Alameda CA 1949 d David & Betsy. BA U CA 1970; BA U CA 1972; MA U CA 1974; MDiv Gonzaga U 2004. D 7/10/2004 P 1/8/2005 Bp James E Waggoner Jr. c 4. The Epis Ch Of The Ascen Middletown OH 2015-2016; Int S Anne Epis Ch W Chester OH 2013-2015; Cn for Sprtl Formation and Mssn Chr Ch Cathd Cincinnati OH 2005-2014; Dir Of Educ & Cmncatn S Steph's Epis Ch Spokane WA 2005; Cathd Of S Jn The Evang Spokane WA 1995-2000. Auth, "Weaving God's Promises," *Weaving God's Promises for Chld*, Morehouse Educ Resources; Auth, "Weaving God's Promises," *Weaving God's Promises for Chld*, Morehouse Educ Resources.

LEITE, Dessordi Peres (WA) **Ch Of S Steph And The Incarn Washington DC 2016-; P-in-c S Jas Ch Oakland CA 2012-** Trans 6/14/2014 as Priest Bp Marc Handley Andrus.

LEMA, Julio M (At) 1379 Craighill Ct, Norcross GA 30093 **S Davids Ch Brunswick GA 2007-** B Columbia 1942 s Julio & Martha. RC Sem Cartagena Columbia 1961; U of Bolbariana Meddllein Columbia 1967. D 7/10/2007 P 1/10/2008 Bp J Neil Alexander. m 6/28/1964 Maria Dora Lema c 3. S Dav's Ch Roswell GA 2007-2010; Consult To Hisp Families Self Employed 2004-2007.

LEMAIRE JR, Michael E (Cal) 2220 Cedar St, Berkeley CA 94709 **P All Souls Par In Berkeley Berkeley CA 2010-** B Burlington VT 1966 s Michael & Lois. BA Ham 1988; MDiv Jesuit TS 2000; Cert Ang Stud CDSP 2010. D 6/5/2010 P 12/4/2010 Bp Marc Handley Andrus. m 11/1/2008 Joseph Anthony Delgado. On Lok Lifeways San Francisco CA 2011.

LEMAY, Anne Rae (NJ) 576 West Ave, Sewaren NJ 07077 **Hd Of Yth Serv Franklin Township Libr Somerset NJ 1997-** B Manchester NH 1953 d Emile

& Colette. Cert Kean U; BA Rutgers The St U of New Jersey 1975; MLS Rutgers The St U of New Jersey 1989. D 10/21/2000 Bp David Bruce Joslin. m 12/29/2000 Kenneth L Erb c 2. Seamens Ch Inst New York NY.

LEMBURG, David Wesley (Miss) 1350 Courthouse Rd, Gulfport MS 39507 **Asst Par Of The Medtr-Redeem Mccomb MS 2015-, 2004-2009; Chapl ArmdF Ret Hm 2010-** B Houston TX 1974 BA U of Arkansas 2001; MDiv GTS 2004. D 8/27/2004 Bp Larry Maze P 5/29/2005 Bp Duncan Montgomery Gray III. m 8/23/2003 Melanie Dickson c 2. S Geo's Epis Ch Honolulu HI 2014; S Nich Epis Ch Aiea HI 2014; Vic H Trin Ch Crystal Sprg MS 2007-2009.

LEMBURG, Melanie Dickson (Miss) 1909 15th Street, Gulfport MS 39501 **S Columb's Ch Ridgeland MS 2015-** B Jackson MS 1976 d Stephen & Debra. BA Rhodes Coll 1998; MDiv GTS 2004. D 5/6/2004 P 12/1/2004 Bp Duncan Montgomery Gray III. m 8/23/2003 David Wesley Lemburg c 2. R S Ptr's By The Sea Gulfport MS 2009-2015; R Par Of The Medtr-Redeem Mccomb MS 2004-2009.

LEMERY, Gary Conrad (RI) 45 Bay View Drive North, Jamestown RI 02835 B Woonsocket RI 1949 s Conrad & Lorraine. BS Roger Wms 1972; MDiv S Marys Sem and U 1977; DMin EDS 1992. Rec 11/1/1983 as Priest Bp George Nelson Hunt III. m 6/11/1982 Kathleen Ann Lemery. Int S Ann's-By-The-Sea Block Island RI 2012-2013; R Ch Of The Trsfg Providence RI 2000-2009; R S Jn The Div Ch Saunderstown RI 1994-2000; Ch Of The Ascen Wakefield RI 1993-1994; S Mk's Epis Ch Riverside RI 1987-1992; Vic S Thos' Alton Wood River Jct RI 1983-1987; Vic S Eliz's Ch Hope Vlly RI 1983-1986; S Jas Epis Ch At Woonsocket Woonsocket RI 1980-1981; Epis Chars Pres Dio Rhode Island Providence RI 2008-2010.

LEMLER, James (Ct) Christ Church, 254 E Putnam Ave, Greenwich CT 06830 B Mishawaka IN 1952 s Forrest & Juanita. BA DePauw U 1973; Oxf GB 1974; MDiv Nash 1976; DMin Chr TS 1981; Cert Par Dvlpmt Inst New York NY 1985. D 6/11/1976 P 12/1/1976 Bp William Cockburn Russell Sheridan. m 10/23/1976 Sharon F Lemler c 3. R Chr Ch Greenwich CT 2007-2017; DFMS Dir of Mssn TEC New York NY 2004-2008; Dir of Mssn Epis Ch Cntr New York NY 2004-2007; 20/20 T/F Of The Natl Ch 2000-2003; Dn & Pres Bexley Seabury Fed Chicago IL 1998-2004; Dn S Jn The Div Chap Evanston IL 1998-2004; Stndg Cmsn On Dom Mssn And Evang 1997-2000; Ch In Metropltn Areas Stndg Cmsn On The 1995-1998; Vstng Prof Chr TS 1982-1983; R Trin Ch Indianapolis IN 1981-1998; Provost S Richard's Sch IN 1981-1984; Chapl Depauw U Greencastle IN 1980-1981; Epis Cmnty Serv 1979-1983; Bd Epis Cmnty Serv 1979-1980; Cn Precentor Chr Ch Cathd Indianapolis IN 1977-1980; Asst To The Dn The Cathd Ch Of S Jas So Bend IN 1976-1977; Dep Gc Dio Indianapolis Indianapolis IN 1988-2000, Bd Metropltn Campus Mnstry 1981-1987, Urban Strtgy Cmsn 1977-1980. Auth, "Transforming Congregations," *Ch Pub*, 2008; Auth, "Groundwork I, II, III," *DFMS*, 2007; Auth, "Serving Those In Need," *Jossey-Bass*, 1999; Auth, "Trst Educ & The Congregregational Bd," *Trst Ldrshp Dvlpmt*, 1996; Auth, "Numerous arts, Monographs and Blue Bk Reports". Ord Of S Ben, Confrater 1980. Sagmore Of The Wabash St Of Indiana 1998.

LEMLEY, Daniel James (SwFla) 701 Orange Ave, Clearwater FL 33756 **Assoc Ch Of The Ascen Clearwater FL 2016-** B Tampa FL 1978 BA Rol 2003; MDiv VTS 2015. D 12/5/2015 P 7/1/2016 Bp Dabney Tyler Smith. m 1/12/2008 Sara Roach Sara Blackwell Roach. Yth Dir H Innoc Epis Ch Valrico FL 2010-2013. daniell@churchofascension.org

LEMLEY, Kent Christopher (At) 764 Springlake Ln NW, Atlanta GA 30318 **S Anne's Epis Ch Atlanta GA 2015-; Fac Georgia St U Atlanta GA 1997-; Epis Chars Fndt Dio Atlanta Atlanta GA 2013-, Cmsn on Higher Educ 2010-2012; Lobbyist Epis Dio Atlanta 2013-** B Ft Myers FL 1946 s Kermit & Ann. BA Furman U 1968; MBA Georgia St U 1973. D 8/6/2011 Bp J Neil Alexander. m 7/15/2000 Karen Kirkpatrick Lemley. S Paul's Epis Ch Newnan GA 2013-2014; D H Innoc Ch Atlanta GA 2011-2013.

LEMMING, Craig Peter (Minn) St John The Evangelist Episcopal Church, 60 Kent St, Saint Paul CO 55102 B Harare Zimbabwe 1982 s Vincent & Linda. BMUS New Engl Conservatory 2005; MMUS Indiana U 2008; MMUS Indiana U 2008; MDiv Untd TS 2017; MDiv Untd TS 2017. D 6/20/2015 P 6/27/2017 Bp Brian N Prior. S Jn The Evang S Paul MN 2016.

LEMON, Karen Dillenbeck (WK) 20081 Sw 20th Ave, Pratt KS 67124 **P All SS Ch Pratt KS 2001-, P 1999-; P S Mk's Ch Med Ldg KS 2001-, 1999-; Chairman, COM Dio Wstrn Kansas Hutchinson KS 2012-, Dep to GC 2011-** B New York NY 1945 d Douglas & Elizabeth. K SU 1966; BA Newman U 2006; MTS Newman U 2011; MTS Other 2011. D 6/5/1998 P 3/27/1999 Bp Vernon Edward Strickland. m 8/20/1966 John Lemon c 3. Chr Ch Kingman KS 1999-2001. vicar_karen@yahoo.com

LEMONS, Catherine L (Minn) 12621 Old Columbia Pike, Silver Spring MD 20904 **R Chr Ch Austin MN 2011-** B Raymondville TX 1947 d Sam & Evelyn. BS Texas A&M U Kingsville 1969; MDiv VTS 2010. D 7/23/2009 Bp James Louis Jelinek P 7/29/2010 Bp Brian N Prior. m 12/29/1974 Richard M Lemons c 3. Trin Ch Anoka MN 2010-2011.

LENNON, Evelyn Cromartie (Minn) 65a Lovell Rd, Fryeburg ME 04037 B Cordova AK 1952 d George & Beatrice. BA U of Texas 1976; MA Untd

Sem 1992; MS Augsburg Coll 1994. D 10/14/1995 Bp Sanford Zangwill Kaye Hampton. c 1.

LENNOX, Daniel Duncan (Nwk) 707 Washington St, Hoboken NJ 07030 **S Lk's Par Darien CT 2015-** B St Catharines Ontario 1980 s Robert & Barbara. BA McGill U 2003; MDiv Ya Berk 2006; STM Bos 2007. D 6/14/2008 Bp Andrew Donnan Smith P 12/14/2008 Bp Peter J Lee. m 8/25/2007 Abigail Lennox c 2. R All SS Epis Par Hoboken NJ 2013-2015; S Matt's Ch Bedford NY 2009-2013; Chr Ch Alexandria VA 2008-2009. dlennox@allsaintshoboken.com

LENNSTROM, Brian Lee D 7/6/2017 Bp Gregory Harold Rickel.

LENOIR, Robert Scott (Miss) 2005 Lauban Ln, Gautier MS 39553 **Asstg P S Jn's Epis Ch Ocean Sprg MS 2012-; Co-Coordntr of Disaster Relief Team Dio Mississippi Jackson MS 2011-, Coordntr of Cmncatn 2008-** B McComb MS 1954 s James & Elizabeth. BA Millsaps Coll 1977; MDiv Sewanee: The U So, TS 1988. D 5/25/1988 P 12/25/1988 Bp Duncan Montgomery Gray Jr. m 2/9/1978 Harriett Lenoir c 1. P Assoc The Chap Of The Cross Madison MS 2010-2011; S Mary's Ch Lexington MS 2006-2008; Vic S Pierre's Epis Ch Gautier MS 2001-2005; S Jas Ch Greenville MS 1995-2000, R 1995-2000, Cur 1988-1990; R S Steph's Epis Ch Indianola MS 1990-1995; P-in-c Ch Of The Redeem Greenville MS 1988-1990. Cmnty of St. Jos 2010.

LENT, Morris J (SC) 1855 Houghton Dr, Charleston SC 29412 **Ret 2001-** B Boonville MO 1941 s Morris & Luella. BS USMA 1964; JD U of Virginia 1970; MDiv Sewanee: The U So, TS 1978. D 6/17/1978 Bp Hunley Agee Elebash P 2/24/1979 Bp Gray Temple. m 9/2/1967 Harriett Lent c 1. Int All SS Ch Hilton Hd Island SC 2001-2003; Chapl Porter-Gaud Sch Charleston SC 1987-2001; R S Jas Ch Charleston SC 1980-1987; Asst S Mich's Epis Ch Charleston SC 1978-1980. Auth, "A Bk, A Rabbit, & Mouth Full Of Fruit," Journ Of Theol.

LENTEN, John William (NMich) 11 Longyear Dr, Negaunee MI 49866 **S Jn's Ch Negaunee MI 2007-; VP Range Bank 2001-** B Islepeming MI 1960 s Wilfred & Marian. BS Nthrn Michigan U 1982. D 9/13/2006 P 4/22/2007 Bp James Arthur Kelsey. c 3.

LENTZ, Benjamin Lee (Be) 9758 N. Rome Rd., Athens PA 18810 **Long Term Supply Gr Ch Waverly NY 2011-; Trin Ch Athens PA 2011-** B Paterson NJ 1950 s Lee & Ruth. BA Bloomfield Coll 1973; MDiv EDS 1976. D 6/5/1976 Bp George E Rath P 12/11/1976 Bp John Shelby Spong. m 8/25/1973 Andrea Lentz c 1. Cluster P Emm Ch Elmira NY 2007-2011; R Ch Of The Redeem Sayre PA 1991-2007; R S Ptr's Ch Dartmouth MA 1980-1991; Chr Ch Pompton Lake NJ 1980; Old No Chr Ch Boston MA 1980; Vic S Gabr's Ch Oak Ridge NJ 1977-1980; St Josephs Ch Newark NJ 1977.

LENTZ JR, Julian Carr (ECR) 1001 Sleepy Hollow Ln, Plainfield NJ 07060 B Maryville TN 1951 s Julian & Mary Nell. BA Maryville Coll 1973; MDiv VTS 1977. D 6/22/1977 Bp William Evan Sanders P 4/2/1978 Bp William F Gates Jr. m 6/21/2010 Julianne Nagel c 4. Palmer Trin Sch Palmetto Bay FL 2005-2014; All SS' Epis Day Sch Carmel CA 1998-2000; S Andr's Ch Saratoga CA 1989-1998; Chapl Bp's Sch San Jose CA 1983-1989; The Bp's Sch La Jolla CA 1983-1989; Cn S Andr's Cathd Jackson MS 1980-1983; R S Paul's Ch Memphis TN 1978-1980; S Paul's Epis Ch Chattanooga TN 1977-1978.

LENZO, Alex (RG) 1525 33rd Cir SE, Rio Rancho NM 87124 **S Fran Ch Rio Rancho NM 2015-** B Austin TX 1986 s Gary & Gay. BA and Theol Stds Wheaton Coll 2009; MDiv PrTS 2012. D 6/14/2014 P 6/12/2015 Bp Michael Vono. m 5/26/2012 Rebecca Lynn Winship Lenzo. S Tim's Ch Roxborough Philadelphia PA 2014-2015; St Jas Sch Philadelphia PA 2014-2015. contributer, "For day twenty," Thoughts for Young Servnt, Dio Pennsylvania, 2013. lenzoalexander@gmail.com

LEO, Agnes Patricia (Haw) 665 Paopua Loop, Kailua HI 96734 B UK 1940 D 11/19/1995 Bp George Nelson Hunt III. D S Andr's Cathd Honolulu HI 2010-2012; D Ch Of The Epiph Honolulu HI 2001-2008; D Emm Epis Ch Kailua HI 1995-2000. Ord Of S Lk.

LEO, Denise Florence (Pa) 400 S Jackson St, Media PA 19063 **D Ch Of S Jn The Evang Essington PA 1997-** B Drexel Hill PA 1957 d Ralph & Florence. MA Cleveland St U 1980; Cert Pennsylvania Diac Sch 1994; MEd Widener U 1995. D 9/24/1994 Bp Allen Lyman Bartlett Jr. m 6/4/1988 Stephen Nicholas Leo c 1. Dir Chld'S Rel Educ Trin.

LEO, Jason Elliman (SO) 3780 Clifton Ave, Cincinnati OH 45220 **Cn Dio Sthrn Ohio Cincinnati OH 2016-, 1994-2015; R Calv Ch Cincinnati OH 2000-** B 1966 s James. BA Buc; MDiv GTS; MDiv GTS. D 6/24/1992 Bp John Herbert MacNaughton P 1/6/1993 Bp Earl Nicholas Mc Arthur Jr. m 8/25/1990 Jeanne E Folts c 1. Trin Epis Ch London OH 1998-2000; S Geo Ch San Antonio TX 1992-1994; Dir Yth Mnstrs Dio Sthrn Ohio.

LEO, John (Be) 295 Brown St, Wilkes Barre PA 18702 **Assoc R H Cross Epis Ch Wilkes Barre PA 2001-; Supply P Dio Bethlehem Bethlehem PA 1997-** B Winooski VT 1921 s Abraham & Zaraef. BA U of Vermont 1950; BTh Bex Sem 1953; MA California St Polytechnic U 1965; U of Birmingham Birmingham GB 1970; U of Edinburgh GB 1973; Cantess Cbury GB 1980. D 6/11/1953 Bp Vedder Van Dyck P 12/16/1953 Bp William Crittenden. Pstr S Andr's Ch Nanticoke PA 2008-2014; Supply P S Ptr's By-The-Sea Epis Ch Morro Bay CA 1990-1992; P-in-c S Ben's Par Los Osos CA 1986-1987; Supply P Dio El

Camino Real Salinas CA 1983-1997; Int S Paul's Ch Cambria CA 1977-1979; Int S Barn Ch Arroyo Grande CA 1969-1970, DeptCe 1965-1968; Tchr of Engl CA Men's Colony (Prison) San Luis Obispo CA 1965-1982; Dio California San Francisco CA 1965-1970; Chapl AF 1961-1964; Vic Chap Of The Gd Shpd Hawk Run PA 1953-1961.

LEON, Luis (WA) 1525 H St NW, Washington DC 20005 **R S Jn's Ch Lafayette Sq Washington DC 1994-** B Guantanamo CU 1949 s Luis & Concepcion. BA U So 1971; MDiv VTS 1977. D 6/22/1977 Bp William Hopkins Folwell P 6/17/1978 Bp Thomas Augustus Fraser Jr. m 6/27/1981 Lucille Leon c 2. Adj Fac Bexley Seabury Fed Chicago IL 1993-2002; R Trin Par Wilmington DE 1988-1994; R S Paul's Epis Ch Paterson NJ 1982-1988; Dir, Refugee Prog Dio Maryland Baltimore MD 1980-1982; Asst S Ptr's Epis Ch Charlotte NC 1977-1980. DD U So 1999.

LEON, Sadoni (Hai) c/o Diocese of Haiti, Boite Postale 1309, Port au Prince Haiti Haiti **Dio Haiti Port-au-Prince HT 2008-** B 1976 s Marc & Rose. D 1/25/2006 P 2/18/2007 Bp Jean Zache Duracin. m 12/21/2010 Daphnide Jean Philippe.

LEONARD, Henry Alan (USC) 254 Crooked Tree Dr, Inman SC 29349 **R S Marg's Epis Ch Boiling Spgs SC 2005-** B Pittsburgh PA 1964 s Henry & Eva. BA Ripon Coll Ripon WI 1986; MEd Nthrn Illinois U 1993; MDiv CDSP 1996. D 6/15/1996 Bp Frank Tracy Griswold III P 12/15/1996 Bp Charles I Jones III. m 6/5/1993 Brenda Heidhoff Leonard c 1. Chapl Off Of Bsh For ArmdF New York NY 1999-2005; Asst Ch Of The H Sprt Missoula MT 1996-1998. St Chapl of the Year VFW 2010.

LEONARD, Jaime (Va) D 6/10/2017 Bp Shannon Sherwood Johnston.

LEONARD, Sean T (Mass) Saint Dunstans Episcopal Church, 18 Springdale Ave, Dover MA 02030 **S Dunstans Epis Ch Dover MA 2016-** B Attleboro MA 1973 s Thomas & Kathie. BS Bridgewater Coll 1995; MDiv VTS 2006. D 6/3/2006 Bp Michael Whittington Creighton P 1/11/2007 Bp Nathan Dwight Baxter. m 8/7/1999 Chrishelle A Leonard c 2. R S Mk's Ch Orchard Pk NY 2008-2016; Asst The Epis Ch Of S Jn The Bapt York PA 2006-2008; Asst to the R The Epis Ch of St. Jn the Bapt York PA 2006-2008; Spprt Spec Living Word Acad Leola PA 2002-2003. revsean@saintdunstansma.org

LEONARD, Thomas Edgar (Az) 11 Avineda de la Herran, Tubac AZ 85646 **Ret Asso Cler St. Phil's in the Hills Tucson 2004-** B Walla Walla WA 1936 s Edgar & Marie. U of Oregon 1956; BA U of Arizona 1959; MDiv CDSP 1962. D 6/9/1962 Bp Arthur Kinsolving P 12/1/1962 Bp John Joseph Meakin Harte. m 12/18/1975 Ines M Leonard c 5. R S Chris's Ch Sun City AZ 1995-2000; Chair Dio.Substance Abuse Com 1982-1995; R S Barth's Epis Ch Livermore CA 1982-1995; R Trin Ch Canton MA 1978-1982; R Chr The King Ch Tucson AZ 1974-1977, Vic 1966-1973; Chair Dio Lay Readers Dio of Arizona 1969-1972; Vic S Geo's Epis Ch Holbrook AZ 1962-1964. Auth, "Dioc Plcy On Alcosm"; Auth, "In Memoriam; Rebecca".

LEONARD-PASLEY, Tricia (Ct) 680 Racebrook Rd, Orange CT 06477 **S Andr's Ch Milford CT 2014-** B Bronx NY 1965 d David & Marguerite. BA Boston Coll 1987; MTS Weston Jesuit TS 1994; MAR Yale DS 2013. D 6/8/2013 P 1/18/2014 Bp Ian Theodore Douglas. m 5/18/1991 Kevin R Leonard-Pasley c 5.

LEONCZYK JR, Kenneth George (Dal) 425 D St SE Apt 304, Washington DC 20003 B Marlton NJ 1977 s Kenneth & Kathleen. BA U So Sewanee 2000; Cert Ang Stud Ya Berk 2002; MA Yale DS 2002; JD Yale Law Sch 2009. D 1/31/2004 P 8/14/2004 Bp James Monte Stanton. m 5/30/2009 Ashley Ridgway Leonczyk. Evang-in-Res Chr the King Ch 2011-2012; Asstg P Chr Ch Greenwich CT 2009-2010; Int P (similar to Int R) S Jas Epis Ch New Orleans LA 2006-2007; SMU Chapl Dio Dallas Dallas TX 2005-2006; Cn Pstr S Matt's Cathd Dallas TX 2005; P-in-c The Epis Ch of the Intsn Carrollton TX 2005; Dioc Cur H Trin Epis Ch Garland TX 2004-2005; P Dio Connecticut Meriden CT 2008-2012. Auth, "Var Legal arts," Covington & Burling LLP, Covington & Burling LLP, 2011; Auth, "RLUIPA & Eminent Domain ...," Texas Revs of Law & Politics, U of Texas- Austin, 2009; Auth, "Lenten Reflections ...," Gathered Around the Throne, St. Matt's Cathd (Dallas, TX), 2004. Cn of the Cathd St. Matt's Cathd (Dallas,TX) 2005; Cn of the Cathd Epis Ch of Sudan (Kadugli Nuba Mts. Dio) 2004.

LEONETTI, Stephen James (NCal) PO Box 6194, Vacaville CA 95696 B Glendale CA 1946 s Robert & Margaret. BA U CA 1968; MA Claremont Coll 1974; MDiv GTS 1978. D 6/20/1981 P 1/11/1982 Bp Robert Claflin Rusack. m 11/29/1974 Judith Leonetti. Dio No Carolina Raleigh NC 1997-2000; Dio Nthrn California Sacramento CA 1997-2000; R Epiph Epis Ch Vacaville CA 1995-2011; Dio Oregon Portland OR 1992-1995, 1988-1990, Chair, Evang Cmsn 1993-1995, Chair, COM 1985-1990; S Jas' Epis Ch Coquille OR 1992-1995; R Gr Epis Ch Medford MA 1990-1992; Ch Of The Resurr Eugene OR 1984-1988; Dio Los Angeles Los Angeles CA 1981-1984; Mssnr for Congrl Dvlpmt Dio Los Angeles Los Angeles CA 1981-1984.

LEON-LOZANO, Cristobal (EcuC) Casilla 13-05-179, Manta Ecuador **Litoral Dio Ecuador Guayaquil 1997-** B Guayaquil EC 1961 s Pedro & Teodocia Finlandia. BA Antonio Ruiz Flores 1995; Sete 4 Years 1997. D 7/14/1996 P 3/22/1998 Bp Terencio Alfredo Morante-Espana. m 2/25/1983 Ita Ofelia Chila c 3.

LEOPOLD, Bobby (ETenn) 1616 Read Ave, Chattanooga TN 37408 **Southside Abbey Chattanooga TN 2016-; ECF Inc New York NY 2011-** B Charleston SC 1979 s Robert & Sophie. BA U of Tennessee 2004; BA U of Tennessee 2005; MDiv VTS 2008. D 5/31/2008 P 1/10/2009 Bp Charles Glenn VonRosenberg. m 6/4/2005 Lisa Woodard Leopold. Mssnr, Southside Abbey Dio E Tennessee Knoxville TN 2012-2015; Assoc R S Paul's Epis Ch Chattanooga TN 2011-2012, Asst R 2008-2012. rkleopold@gmail.com

LEPLEY, Rebecca Ruth Baird (EMich) 539 N William St, Marine City MI 48039 **S Paul's Epis Ch Harsens Island MI 2012-** B Monongahela PA 1945 d Clinton & June. Whitaker TS; BS Indiana U of Pennsylvania 1967; ThM St Johns Prov Sem Plymouth MI 1985. D 1/18/1984 Bp William Jones Gordon Jr P 6/1/1985 Bp H Coleman Mcgehee Jr. m 6/17/1967 Robert Lepley c 3. S Mk's Epis Ch Marine City MI 1988-2009; Int Gr Ch Mt Clemens MI 1987-1988; Archd Dio Michigan Detroit MI 1986-1992; Asst R S Chris-S Paul Epis Ch Detroit MI 1985-1987; Asst S Mk's Ch Detroit MI 1984-1985.

LEROUX, Donald Francis (ND) 319 S 5th St, Grand Forks ND 58201 B Salem MA 1952 s Robert & Frances. AS Cmnty Coll of the AF 1992. D 6/30/2007 Bp Michael Smith. m 11/23/1974 Mary Leroux c 4.

LEROUX JR, Grant Meade (Ga) 5 Mooregate Square, Atlanta GA 30327 B Flushing NY 1941 s Grant & Louisa. BA U So 1968; MDiv TESM 1980. D 6/14/1980 P 12/13/1980 Bp Robert Bracewell Appleyard. m 6/22/1968 Claire Leroux. Int Ch Of The Redeem Greensboro GA 2009-2010; Int All SS Ch Warner Robins GA 2006-2007; Int S Steph's Ch Milledgeville GA 2004-2005; Int The Epis Ch Of The Nativ Dothan AL 2003-2004; R Ch Of The H Nativ St Simons Is GA 1987-2003; Asst Trin Cathd Little Rock AR 1983-1987; R Ch Of The Epiph Avalon PA 1980-1983.

LE ROY, Melinda Louise Perkins (WNC) 4 Flycatcher Way Unit 302, Arden NC 28704 B Albany NY 1944 d James & Anna. BA Col 1969; MA Col 1970; Cert Portland St U 1987. D 1/10/1991 Bp Robert Louis Ladehoff. m 3/17/1990 Joseph Patrick Dominic LeRoy. Cnvnr Dioc Cmsn to End Racism Oregon 2005-2012; D S Paul's Par Oregon City OR 2001-2006; D All SS Ch Portland OR 1991-2001.

LERUD, **Nathanael D** (Ore) Trinity Episcopal Cathedral, 147 NW 19th Ave, Portland OR 97209 **Cn For Sprtl Formation Trin Epis Cathd Portland OR 2009-; COM Dio Oregon Portland OR 2012-** B Portland OR 1982 s David & Claudia. BA Whitman Coll 2004; MDiv GTS 2007. D 6/9/2007 Bp James E Waggoner Jr P 12/29/2007 Bp Richard Lester Shimpfky. m 4/4/2013 James Joiner. Cur Chr Ch Ridgewood NJ 2007-2009; Trst Listening Hearts Mnstrs 2012-2017. Contrib, "Sundays and Seasons," *Sunday and Seasons: Preaching,* Augsburg Fortress, 2015; Contrib, "Sundays and Seasons," *Sundays and Seasons 2015,* Augsburg Fortress, 2015; Contrib, "Sundays and Seasons," *Sundays and Seasons 2014,* Augsburg Fortress, 2014. nathan@trinity-episcopal.org

LESCH, Robert Andrew (Minn) 828 5th St Ne, Minneapolis MN 55413 **P-in-c Gr In Royalton 1983-** B 1924 s Arthur & Ruth. BFA U MN 1956. P 6/1/1960 Bp Hamilton Hyde Kellogg. m 10/22/1976 Pam Lesch c 3. P-in-c Ch Of Our Sav Little Falls MN 1983-1994; Serv S Thos Ch Minneapolis MN 1967-1982; M-in-c All SS Epis Indn Mssn Minneapolis MN 1959-1967.

LESESNE JR, Gray (Ind) 1100 W 42nd Street, Suite 235, Indianapolis IN 46208 **Ch Planter and Vic Dio Indianapolis Indianapolis IN 2015-, Bp Search Com 2015-** B West Columbia SC 1975 s William & Ellen. BA Presb Coll 1997; MDiv VTS 2001; DMin VTS 2013. D 6/15/2001 P 4/17/2002 Bp Dorsey Henderson. m 7/1/2017 Ethan Bradley. Cn Chr Ch Cathd Indianapolis IN 2008-2015; R All SS' Epis Ch Glen Rock NJ 2003-2008; Asst R S Barth's Ch No Augusta SC 2001-2003; Mem, Joint Stndg Com on Plnng and Arrangements Dom And Frgn Mssy Soc- Epis Ch Cntr New York NY 2009-2015; Mem, Dioc Coun Dio Newark Newark NJ 2005-2008. Auth, "Narratives and newcomers : an exploration for lay leaders," *Doctoral dissertation,* VTS, 2013; Co-Auth, "Send us out : a Curric for Soc Mssn," *Indep study Pub,* VTS, 2001. gray@goodsamaritanbrownsburg.org

LESEURE, Laurence James (NY) 530 E 234th St Apt 1F, Bronx NY 10470 B Peoria IL 1946 s Kenneth & Anna. BA Wabash Coll 1968; MDiv Yale DS 1971; MA Ya 1972; MPhil Ya 1975. D 6/12/1971 P 12/18/1971 Bp Joseph Warren Hutchens. S Steph's Epis Ch Woodlaw Bronx NY 2004-2010; Dio New York New York NY 2000-2004; Ch Of The Trsfg New York NY 1999-2000, Asst 1976-1979; S Jn's Ch Centralia IL 1997-1998; Vic S Thos Ch Salem IL 1997-1998; Non-par 1984-1997; Vic Chr Tashua CT 1982-1984; Asst Trin Par New York NY 1979-1983; Asst Chr Ch New Haven CT 1971-1976.

LESH, Ryan Edwin (NY) 7423 S Broadway, Red Hook NY 12571 **Vic Chr Ch Red Hook NY 2006-** B Greeley CO 1959 s Edwin & Billie. BS Van 1982; MD U Roch 1986; MDiv CDSP 2006. D 3/19/2005 P 9/23/2006 Bp Mark Sean Sisk.

LESIEUR, Betsy Ann (RI) 200 Heroux Blvd # 2001, Cumberland RI 02864 B Pawtucket RI 1945 d Irving & Elsie. Rhode Island Sch for Deacons. D 7/13/1985 Bp George Nelson Hunt III. c 1. D S Paul's Ch Pawtucket RI 2002-2013; S Geo And San Jorge Cntrl Falls RI 2000-2002; D Chr Ch In Lonsdale Lincoln RI 1999-2000, Asst 1985-1998; Dio Rhode Island Providence RI 1998, 1990-1997; Cathd Of S Jn Providence RI 1992-2000; Res Serving Coordntr Blackstone Falls Cntrl Falls RI 1990-1996.

LESLIE, **Joanne** (Los) 1351 Grant St, Santa Monica CA 90405 **Bp Search Com Dio Los Angeles Los Angeles CA 2015-, COM 2011-2015, Archd 2011-** B Ottawa Ontario Canada 1944 d John & Patricia. BA Reed Coll 1966; ScD JHU 1983; Cert Theol Stud CDSP 2001. D 6/8/2002 Bp Chester Lovelle Talton. m 12/22/2013 Walter Johnson c 3. D and Cn Pstr St Johns Pro-Cathd Los Angeles CA 2008-2011, Archd 2008-; Par D H Faith Par Inglewood CA 2002-2007. "Wmn, Wk, and Chld Welf in the Third Wrld," Westview Press, 1989; "Food Plcy:Integrating Supply, Distribution, and Consumption," The JHU Press, 1987. jleslie@ladiocese.org

LESLIE, Jo Marie (Md) D 6/10/2017 Bp Chilton Richardson Knudsen.

LESLIE III, **Richard B** (ECR) 520 Lobos Ave, Pacific Grove CA 93950 **COM Dio El Camino Real 2013-** B San Jose CA 1948 s Richard & Dorothea. BA Santa Clara U 1970; MDiv CDSP 1977. D 6/25/1977 Bp Chauncie Kilmer Myers P 5/27/1978 Bp William Foreman Creighton. m 5/29/1971 Kathleen Lynn Leslie c 5. Stndg Com Dio El Camino Real 2007-2012; Bp Search Com Mem Dio El Camino Real 2006-2007; Bd Mem Epis Hm Fndt Lafayette CA 2002-2008; Dioc Coun Mem Dio El Camino Real 2001-2003; R Ch of S Mary's by the Sea Pacific Grove CA 2000-2015; Field Educ Supvsr CDSP Berkeley CA 1983-2000; R S Jas Ch Fremont CA 1981-2000; Chapl (Maj) US-AR San Francisco CA 1978-1990; Assoc R S Mk's Epis Ch Santa Clara CA 1978-1981; Cur S Fran' Epis Ch San Francisco CA 1977-1978; Chapl San Francisco Gnrl Hosp San Francisco CA 1977-1978; Pres of Stndg Com Dio El Camino Real Salinas CA 2011-2012, 1984-2011, 1982-1983; Pres of Stndg Com Dio California San Francisco CA 1999-2000, Stndg Com 1996-2000. Ralph B Atkinson Awd Monterey Cnty Chapt of the ACLU 2009.

LESSMANN, **Mary Therese** (Dal) 8011 Douglas Avenue, Dallas TX 75225 **S Mich And All Ang Ch Dallas TX 2016-** B Corpus Christi TX 1964 d Donald & Corinne. BBA Texas A&M U 1986; MDiv SMU Perkins 2009. D 6/6/2009 Bp James Monte Stanton P 2/26/2010 Bp Paul Emil Lambert. m 4/16/1988 William Russell Lessmann c 2. Vic Ch Of The Gd Samar Dallas TX 2013-2015; Assoc R St Andrews Ch McKinney TX 2009-2013; Intern Ch Of The Annunc Lewisville TX 2008-2009; Dir of Educational Prog Ch Of The Incarn Dallas TX 2005-2008; COM Dio Dallas Dallas TX 1997-2003. mlessmann@saintmichael.org

LESTER, Elmore William (LI) 1440 Tanglewood Pkwy, Fort Myers FL 33919 **Ret 1993-** B Saint Clair MI 1932 s Elmore & Doris. BA U of Arizona 1955; MDiv Epis TS of the SW 1960. D 9/29/1959 Bp Richard Stanley Merrill Emrich P 12/1/1960 Bp James Pernette DeWolfe. H Cross Trussville AL 1992-1993; R All SS Ch Brooklyn NY 1965-1993; Vic S Dav's Epis Ch Cambria Heights NY 1963-1965; Chapl (Captain) US-A 1961-1963; Vic S Andrews-By-The-Lake Epis Ch Harrisville MI 1959-1960. Auth, "Mr. Drum Major," *Bk,* Hal Leonard Mus, 1957. Kappa Kappa Psi 1954. Mahatma Gandhi Peace Prize Awd Com 2007; Hon Cn Cathd Of S Cyp 1980; Dioc Serv cross Dio Kumasi 1979; Bronz Star US Army 1963.

LE SUEUR, Susan Dianne Lassey (NH) 18 Gaita Dr, Derry NH 03038 B El Centro CA 1949 d Russell & Elvira. BA California St U 1986; ETSBH 1988; MA Creighton U 1992; Andover Newton TS 1994; MDiv Sewanee: The U So, TS 1996. D 6/24/1996 Bp James Edward Krotz P 12/21/1996 Bp Harold Anthony Hopkins Jr. c 2. R Ch Of The Trsfg Derry NH 2002-2011; R S Anne's Ch Calais ME 1996-2002.

LESWING, **James Bartholomew** (Chi) 1125 Franklin St, Downers Grove IL 60515 B Philadelphia PA 1948 s Herbert & Gladys. BA Dickinson Coll 1970; MDiv Yale DS 1973. D 6/9/1973 P 12/15/1973 Bp Leland Stark. m 8/1/2012 William Perry Crosbie c 2. R S Andr's Ch Downers Grove IL 1988-2014; R S Ptr's Epis Ch Monroe CT 1979-1988; Cn Cathd Ch Of S Paul Burlington VT 1975-1979; Asst S Paul's Epis Ch Chatham NJ 1973-1975; Dio Chicago Chicago IL 1988-2003.

LETHIN, Judith Lynn Wegman (Ak) 3509 Wentworth St, Anchorage AK 99508 **D S Mary's Ch Anchorage AK 2000-** B Boise ID 1944 d William & Rosalind. EFM Sewanee: The U So, TS; BA Albany Law Sch 1986; MA Albany Law Sch 1992; MDiv Vancouver TS CA 2003. D 2/1/2000 P 2/1/2004 Bp Mark Lawrence Macdonald. m 10/20/1963 Kris Walter Lethin c 4.

LETHIN, Kris Walter (Ak) 175 Main St, Seldovia AK 99663 **D S Geo In The Arctic Kotzebue AK 2000-** B Glendale CA 1940 s Clarke & Marjorie. BBA U of Alaska 1962; EFM Sewanee: The U So, TS 1995. D 2/1/2000 Bp Mark Lawrence Macdonald. m 10/20/1963 Judith Lynn Wegman Lethin c 4. D/Vol Pilot Wings Of The Sprt - Aviation Mnstry - Alaska 1986-2005.

LEVENSALER, Kurt H (NCal) St Timothy's Church, 1550 Diablo Rd, Danville CA 94526 B Visalia CA 1973 BA Biola U 1996; DAS Ya Berk 2004; MDiv Yale DS 2004. D 6/20/2004 Bp Jerry Alban Lamb P 1/10/2005 Bp Peter J Lee. m 7/30/2006 Leighanne Levensaler c 2. Assoc S Tim's Ch Danville CA 2011-2013; Dir of Outreach Mnstrs Trin Epis Cathd Portland OR 2006-2009; Assoc Imm Ch-On-The-Hill Alexandria VA 2006; Cler Res/Lilly Fell Chr Ch Alexandria VA 2004-2006. Wm Palmer Ladd Prize Ya Berk 2003.

LEVENSON JR, Russell J (Tex) St Martin's Episcopal Church, 717 Sage Rd, Houston TX 77056 **R S Mart's Epis Ch Houston TX 2007-** B Birmingham AL 1962 s Russell & Lynne. DMin Beeson DS; BA Birmingham-Sthrn Coll

L

1984; MDiv VTS 1992; DMin Beeson DS 1997. D 6/13/1992 P 1/6/1993 Bp Robert Oran Miller. m 1/6/1993 Laura N Levenson c 3. Stndg Com Dio The Cntrl Gulf Coast 2005-2007; R Chr Epis Ch Pensacola FL 2002-2007; Exec Com Dio Wstrn Louisiana 1998-2001; R Ch Of The Ascen Lafayette LA 1997-2002; Assoc S Lk's Epis Ch Birmingham AL 1993-1997; Asst Chapl Sewanee U So TS Sewanee TN 1992-1993. Auth, "Provoking Thoughts," St. Mart's Ch, 2010; Auth, "Preparing Room," St. Mart's Ch, 2010; Auth, "Var arts," *Angl Dig*; Auth, "Var arts," *Chistianity Today*; Auth, "Var arts," *Decision mag*; Auth, "Var arts," *Epis Life*; Auth, "Var arts," *Sewanee Theol Revs*; Auth, "Var arts," *LivCh*; Auth, "Var Article," *Virginia Sem Journ*. Comm Partnr Fllshp Founding Bd Advisors 2009; Sigma Alpha Epsilon Fraternity 1980. Distinquished Alum of the Year Beeson DS 2011; Pres Stdt's Serv Awd Birmingham-Sthrn Coll 1984.

LEVESCONTE, Suzanne Joy Kreider (SO) Trinity Episcopal Church, 115 N 6th St, Hamilton OH 45011 **R Trin Ch Hamilton OH 2015-, P-in-c 2013-2015; ECSF (Epis Cmnty Serv Fndt, Bd Pres Dio Sthrn Ohio Cincinnati OH 2016-, ECSF (Epis Cmnty Serv Fndt), Bd Mem 2015-2016, Faith-in-Life Grants Com, Mem 2013-2015** B Ephrata PA 1955 d Jacob & Anna. BS Mia 1986; MDiv Earlham Sch of Rel 2009; MDiv Earlham Sch of Rel 2009; STM GTS 2011; Dip Ang Stud GTS 2011. D 6/29/2011 P 6/9/2012 Bp Thomas Edward Breidenthal. c 2. Cur S Pat's Epis Ch Dublin OH 2011-2013; Founding/Supporting Mem RENEW (Renew the No End from Within) Hamiliton Ohio 2013-2016. CT, Glendale, OH - Assoc 2014.

LEVINE, Paul H (ECR) 720 S 3rd St Apt 5, San Jose CA 95112 B Monmouth IL 1946 s Hervert & Pearl. BA U Denv 1968; MDiv Nash 1971. D 12/27/1970 Bp Edwin B Thayer P 7/1/1971 Bp William Hampton Brady. S Mk's Epis Ch Santa Clara CA 1992-1995; R S Fran' Epis Ch Turlock CA 1976-1989; Assoc S Paul's Epis Ch Visalia CA 1974-1976; Asst To Dn St Paul's Epis Cathd Fond Du Lac WI 1971-1974.

LEVY, Sandra Maria (Va) 9107 Donora Dr, Richmond VA 23229 **Theol-in-Res S Jn's Ch Richmond VA 2004-** B Louisville KY 1943 d James & Thelma. BA Indiana U 1970; PhD Indiana U 1974; MDiv VTS 1994. D 6/25/1994 P 1/7/1995 Bp Alden Moinet Hathaway. m 12/18/2010 Paul Achtemeier c 2. R S Mk's Ch Richmond VA 1997-2004; Assoc R E Lee Memi Ch (Epis) Lexington VA 1994-1997. Auth, "The Flourishing Life," Cascade Books, 2012; Auth, "Imagination and the Journey of Faith," Wm. B. Eerdmans Pub Co, 2008; Auth, "Suffering and Post-Mod Consciousness," *ATR*, 1998; Auth, "Coleridges Rime of the Ancient Mariner: Theodicy in a New Key," *ATR*, 1996; Auth, "Behavior and Cancer," Jossey-Bass, 1985. AAR 2007; APA 1975; Soc for Biblic Lit 2003; SCNC 1998-2000.

LEVY, William Turner (NY) 22121 Lanark St, Canoga Park CA 91304 **Provost Viewpoint Sch Calabasas CA 1979-; Non-par 1961-** B Far Rockaway NY 1922 s Jacob & Florence. BA CUNY 1942; MA Col 1947; PhD Col 1953. D 6/8/1952 P 6/1/1953 Bp Horace W B Donegan. Cur All Ang' Ch New York NY 1952-1960. Auth, "Wm Barnes: The Man & The Poems"; Auth, "The Chairman"; Auth, "Affectionately," *Ts Eliot*.

LEWALLEN, Jerrilee Parker (Ala) 174 Carpenter Cir, Sewanee TN 37375 B Fayetteville GA 1944 d George & Clyde. BA U of Texas 1966; JD Indiana U 1977; MDiv Sewanee: The U So, TS 1998; DMin Sewanee: The U So, TS 2009. D 5/13/1998 Bp Henry Nutt Parsley Jr P 12/1/1998 Bp Robert Oran Miller. m 2/24/1979 Thomas L Lewallen. Otey Memi Par Ch Sewanee TN 2006-2008; S Columba-In-The-Cove Owens X Rds AL 2004-2006; D-in-c/ R S Tim's Epis Ch Athens AL 1998-2004; COM Dio Alabama Birmingham 2001-2011. Auth, "Making Your Way to the Pulpit: Hethcock's Homil Goes to the Par," Wipf and Stock, 2011.

LEWALLEN, Theresa Cammarano (Va) St Albans Episcopal Church, 6800 Columbia Pike, Annandale VA 22003 B New York NY 1954 d Frank & Margaret. MA Trin Washington U; BA Randolph-Macon Coll 1976. D 4/16/2016 Bp Shannon Sherwood Johnston. c 1.

LEWELLEN, Donald S (Chi) 523 W Glen Ave, Peoria IL 61614 B Olney IL 1934 s Stephen & Bernadine. BS Estrn Illinois U 1956; MS Estrn Illinois U 1962; PhD Clayton U 1981. D 11/1/1986 Bp Donald James Parsons. m 12/27/1970 Janet Kay Lewellen c 3. D St Paul's Epis Ch Peoria IL 1999-2007, D 1987-1998; Dio Quincy Peoria IL 1995-1999; Archd S Jas Epis Ch Lewistown IL 1995-1999; D S Fran Epis Ch Chillicothe IL 1994-1995.

LEWELLIS, Bill (Be) 3235 Clear Stream Dr, Whitehall PA 18052 **Bp's Rep on Bd Dir Epis Hse Allentown 1988-** B Girardville PA 1937 s William & Mary. BA S Chas Borromeo Sem 1960; Lic Sacr Theol Gregorian U 1964. Rec 11/1/1999 as Priest Bp Paul Victor Marshall. m 5/23/1981 Monica R Lewellis c 3. P-in-c Gr Epis Ch Allentown PA 2001; Cmncatn Min/Ed Dio Bethlehem Bethlehem PA 1986-2010, Cn Theol 1998-, Cmncatn Min/Ed 1986-2010; Cmncatn Dir/Vocation Dir RC Ch 1963-1981; Bp's Rep on Bd Dir Kirby Epis Hse 2007-2012; Bp's Rep on Bd Dir Epis Hse Allentown PA 1988-2015. Co-Auth, "Your Faith You Life: An Invitation to the Epis Ch," Morehouse, 2009; Auth, "Some 170 Columns," *Var Daily Newspapers*, Var Daily Newspapers. ECom 1988. Cn Theol Dio Bethlehem, ECUSA 1998; Dom Prelate/Monsignor Dio Allentown, RC Ch 1977; Chapl To His Holiness/Monsignor Dio Allentown, RC Ch 1971.

LEWIS III, Adam (Del) 115 E 90th St Apt 5C, New York NY 10128 **1994-** B Marianna FL 1937 s Adam & Lois. BA Florida St U 1960; STB Ya Berk 1966; BFA Ya 1972; MFA Ya 1973; DD Ya 1986; Ya 1986. D 6/11/1966 P 3/18/1967 Bp Walter H Gray. m 10/21/2011 Thomas K Chu c 1. R Chr Ch Christiana Hundred Wilmington DE 1983-1995; R Trin By The Cove Naples FL 1980-1983; R S Paul's Ch Fairfield CT 1973-1980; Vic Zion Epis Ch N Branford CT 1968-1970; Asst Min S Lk's Par Darien CT 1966-1968. Auth, "Billy Baldwin: The Great Amer Decorator," Rizzoli, 2010; Auth, "The Great Lady Decorators: The Wmn Who Defined Interior Design 1870-1955," Rizzoli, 2010; Auth, "Albert Hadley: The Story of Amer's Preeminent Interior Designer," Rizzoli, 2005; Auth, "Van Day Truex: The Man Who Defined Twentieth Century Taste and Style," Viking, 2001.

LEWIS III, Albert Davidson (ETenn) 340 Chamberlain Cove Rd, Kingston TN 37763 **Dioc Cmsn 1976-; Departments of Mssn & Coll Wk 1969-** B Alexandria LA 1938 s Albert & Louise. BA Tul 1960; MDiv Sewanee: The U So, TS 1963. D 6/24/1963 Bp Girault M Jones P 5/1/1964 Bp Iveson Batchelor Noland. m 11/13/1959 Jan H Lewis c 4. Vic Gr Point Cap and Retreat Cntr 2001-2007; R Ch Of The Resurr Loudon TN 1991-2001; Asst R Ch Of The Gd Shpd Lookout Mtn TN 1986-1991; Vic Ch Of The Ascen Hattiesburg MS 1977-1986; Chapl U of Sthrn Mississippi 1977-1986; Chapl Mississippi St U in Starkville 1974-1977; Chair - Dept of Camps 1972-1976; Chair of the Dept of Coll Wk 1970-1974; Vic Ch Of The Resurr Starkville MS 1969-1971; R S Paul's Newport AR 1966-1969; Cur Gr Memi Hammond LA 1963-1966; Chapl SE Louisiana Coll 1963-1966. ESMHE.

LEWIS, Alice LaReign (EMich) 437n County Road 441, Manistique MI 49854 B Corunna MI 1936 d Ole & Florence. D 9/15/1998 P 5/30/1999 Bp Thomas Kreider Ray. m 12/3/1955 Richard J Lewis c 4. P-in-c Chr Epis Ch Owosso MI 2014.

LEWIS, Allen Lee (SD) 4705 S Wildwood Cir, Sioux Falls SD 57105 B Charlotte NC 1941 s Harry & Jane. BA Augustana Coll 1980; MDiv Sewanee: The U So, TS 1983. D 6/29/1983 P 2/23/1984 Bp Conrad H Gesner. m 1/28/1963 Brenda Lewis c 4. P-in-c Ch Of S Mary And Our Blessed Redeem Flandreau SD 1988-2006; S Thos Epis Ch Sturgis SD 1988-1989; Dio So Dakota Pierre SD 1987-1995, Cn to the Ordnry 1987-1988; Bd Pres S Mary Epis Ch Springfield SD 1986-1988; P-in-c Yankton Mssn 1986-1987; Chr Epis Ch Yankton SD 1983-1987. Ord of S Lk.

LEWIS, Barbara (Tex) 1401 Calumet St. unit 312, Houston TX 77004 B New York NY 1947 d Ralph & Thelma. BA Mt Holyoke Coll 1968; MS Col 1975; MDiv GTS 1998. D 10/24/1993 P 5/29/1999 Bp Franklin Delton Turner. c 1. R St Andrews Epis Ch Houston TX 2005-2013; Int Gr Epis Ch Alvin TX 2004-2005; Assoc R S Thos The Apos Epis Ch Houston TX 2000-2004; Assoc R Lord Of The St Epis Mssn Ch Houston TX 1998-2000; D S Andr's Ch Yardley PA 1993-1998.

LEWIS, Barbara Ann (Nev) 1511 Cardinal Peak Ln Unit 101, Las Vegas NV 89144 **D Gr In The Desert Epis Ch Las Vegas NV 1997-** B Chicago IL 1930 d Reginald & Lillian. Chicago Teachers Coll 1951; Roosevelt U 1952. D 6/22/1997 Bp Stewart Clark Zabriskie. c 2. Dioc Secy Epis Dio Nevada Las Vegas NV 2001-2010; Mem, Sr Coun Dio Nevada Las Vegas 2011. UBE 2000-2009.

LEWIS, Barbara J (Pa) 19115 Avalon Way, Lawrenceville NJ 08648 **P-in-c Of Our Sav Secaucus NJ 2011-** B Abington PA 1943 d William & Elizabeth. BA Gwyneed Mercy Coll Gwyneed Vlly PA 1991; MDiv EDS 1995. D 6/10/1995 P 6/1/1996 Bp Allen Lyman Bartlett Jr. c 4. R S Jas Ch Greenridge Aston PA 1997-2010; Assoc S Mary's Ch Sparta NJ 1995-1997. Assoc OHC 1975.

LEWIS, Betsey Converse (Ct) 43 Flying Point Rd, Branford CT 06405 **Died 1/18/2017** B New Haven CT 1923 d Thornton & Margaret. BA Smith 1945; MA U of Delaware 1969. D 12/7/1991 Bp Arthur Edward Walmsley. m 12/4/1948 Kendall Lewis c 3. D S Lk's Epis Ch New Haven CT 1991-2017. Auth, "A Guide For Developing A Hospice Orientation Prog". NAAD. Coffin-Forsberg Fellowowship (Ds) Ya.

LEWIS, Catherine Blanc (Roch) 7086 Salmon Creek Rd, Williamson NY 14589 B New York NY 1939 d William & Particia. BA Bryn 1961; MDiv Bex Sem 1984. D 6/8/1985 P 6/1/1986 Bp William George Burrill. m 9/5/1964 Richard B Lewis. Int Ch Of The Ascen Rochester NY 2000, Asst to R 1985-1991, Pstr Asst 1983-1985; Chr Ch Pittsford Pittsford NY 1992-1998; Asst to R S Lk's Ch Fairport NY 1991-1992.

LEWIS, Charles Robert (Alb) 3711 Glen Oaks Manor Dr, Sarasota FL 34232 **Ret 1998-** B Independence MO 1936 s Robert & Emabel. BS U CO 1958; MDiv Nash 1965. D 3/20/1965 P 9/1/1965 Bp Donald H V Hallock. R Ch Epis Hudson NY 1973-1997; Asst Treas Dio W Missouri Kansas City MO 1970-1973; Gr And H Trin Cathd Kansas City MO 1970-1973; Vic Trin Epis Ch Marshall MO 1967-1970; Cur Trin Ch Janesville WI 1965-1967. Delta Upsilon; Delta Sigma Phi.

LEWIS, Cynthia Jean (RG) D 6/25/1985 P 5/22/1986 Bp Richard Mitchell Trelease Jr.

LEWIS, Earl James (Del) 1313 Lee St E Apt 112, Charleston WV 25301 B Baltimore MD 1935 s Earl & Sara. BA W&L 1958; BD VTS 1964. D 6/22/1964 P 5/1/1965 Bp Harry Lee Doll. c 4. Mssnr Dio Delaware Wilmington 1995-2001; Dio No Carolina Raleigh NC 1987-1994; Vic Ch Of The Incarn Pittsfield Twp Ann Arbor MI 1985; R S Andr's Ch Ann Arbor MI 1982-1984; R S Jn's Epis Ch Charleston WV 1974-1982; Dn Estrn Convoc 1971-1974; R Trin Epis Ch Martinsburg WV 1968-1974; Cur S Anne's Par Annapolis MD 1964-1968. Auth, *Strike Terror No More (1 Chapt)*, Chalice Press, 2002; Auth, *The Gulf War: Ch & Peacemaking*, No Carolina Coun of Ch, 1997; Auth, *W Virginia Pilgrim*, Seabury Press, 1976. DD VTS 2000.

LEWIS, Ernest Loran (NCal) 640 Hawthorne Ln, Davis CA 95616 **Assoc Ch Of S Mart Davis CA 2011-** B Fresno CA 1935 s Harold & Esther. AB Fresno St U 1958; MD Washington U 1963; Cert Epis Sch for Deacons 2002; Cert CDSP 2013. D 9/8/2002 Bp Jerry Alban Lamb P 10/1/2011 Bp Barry Leigh Beisner. m 11/23/1964 Mary Ann Lewis c 4.

LEWIS JR, Giles Floyd (Tex) 786 Glendalyn Ave, Spartanburg SC 29302 B Orlando FL 1927 s Giles & Florence. BS Clemson U 1949; MDiv Sewanee: The U So, TS 1957. D 7/17/1957 P 3/25/1958 Bp Clarence Alfred Cole. c 4. H Cross Trussville AL 2000-2003; Mssy Ch of the Adv Spartanburg SC 1994-1998; Assoc S Jn The Div Houston TX 1972-1990; R S Barth's Ch Nashville TN 1967-1972; Assoc Chr Ch Cathd Lexington KY 1964-1967; Assoc Chr Ch Greenville SC 1963-1964; All SS Epis Ch Clinton SC 1957-1960; Min in charge Ch Of The Epiph Laurens SC 1957-1960.

LEWIS, Harold Thomas (Pgh) 315 Shady Ave, Pittsburgh PA 15206 **Adj Prof Pittsburgh TS 1997-; ECF Inc New York NY 1980-** B Brooklyn NY 1947 s Frank & Muriel. BA McGill U 1967; MDiv Ya Berk 1971; U of Cambridge 1973; Dplma St Georges Coll Jerusalem 1990; Ya Berk 1991; PhD U of Birmingham Birmingham Gb 1994. D 6/12/1971 Bp Jonathan Goodhue Sherman P 12/21/1971 Bp William Carl Frey. m 2/7/1970 Claudette Nathalie Lewis c 1. Vstng Lectr Coll of the Trsfg Grahamstown So Afr 2004; Chair, Advsry Coun, Angl Observer to UN Archbp of Cbury 1997-2013; R Calv Ch Pittsburgh PA 1996-2013; Int S Mk's Ch Brooklyn NY 1995-1996; Prof Geo Mercer TS Garden City NY 1994-1996; Tutor The GTS New York NY 1985-1986; Stff Off Blk Mnstrs Epis Ch Cntr New York NY 1983-1994; Vstng Professoor Angican Sem Dio Bukavu Zaire 1980; R S Monica's Epis Ch Washington DC 1978-1982; Comissary To Bp Of Bukavu Zaire Bukavu Zaire 1976-1984; R Dio Washington Washington DC 1973-1978; Asst S Mary The Less Cambridge Engl 1972-1973; Iglesia Epis Espiritu Santo Tela 1971-1972; P-in-c Iglesia Epis Santisima Trinidad La Ceiba At 1971-1972; Bd Trst SWTS 2000-2006; SCWM Dio Pittsburgh Pittsburgh PA 1998-1999, Gnrl Bec 1996-2000; V-Chair Bd Trsts Ya Berk New Haven CT 1986-1991. Auth, "A Ch for the Future So Afr as Crucible for Anglicanism in a New Century," Ch Pub Inc, 2007; Auth, "Chr Soc Witness," Cowley Press, 2001; Auth, "Elijah'S Mantle: Pilgrimage," *Politics And Proclamation*, Ch Pub Inc, 2001; Auth, "Yet w A Steady Beat: The Afr Amer Struggle For Recognitionn In The Epis Ch," Trin Press, 1996; Ed/Compsr, "Lift Every Voice & Sing Ii: An Afr-Amer Hymnal," Ch Hymnal Corp, 1993; Auth, "In Season," *Out Of Season: A Collection Of Sermons*, Dfms, 1992; Auth, "arts & Revs". Advsry Coun, Ang Observer to UN 1998-2012; Bd, Hist Soc of Epis Ch 2004-2011; ECF Fellows Forum 2000-2009; UBE 1968. STM hon GTS 2013; HOD HOD Medal 2012; Dn's Cross for Servnt Ldrshp VTS 2009; Doctor of Cn Law Seabury-Wstrn Theol Sem 2001; DD Berk 1991; Hon Cn Dio Bukavu (Congo) 1980.

LEWIS JR, Howarth Lister (SeFla) 1110 Sand Drift Way, West Palm Beach FL 33411 **Cn for Deacons Dio SE Florida Miami 2004-, 1992-; D-in-c S Geo's Epis Ch & Cmnty Cntr Riviera B 2001-; D H Trin Epis Ch W Palm Bch FL 1992-** B New York NY 1934 s Howarth & Edith. BA U of Florida 1957. D 3/23/1992 Bp Calvin Onderdonk Schofield Jr. m 6/8/1957 Dianna Jean Lewis c 3. D-in-c S Geo's Epis Ch Riviera Bch FL 2001-2008; D S Patricks Ch W Palm Bch FL 1998-2001. NAAD. Coll of Fellows Amer Inst Archits 2001; H Smith Awd Amer Inst Archits; Anth Pullara Awd Florida Assn Amer Inst Archits. hlewis@lewis-architecture.com

LEWIS JR, Irwin Morgan (SVa) 4449 N Witchduck Rd, Virginia Beach VA 23455 **R Chr and S Lk's Epis Ch Norfolk VA 2010-, Assoc 1991-1998, Asst 1980-1983** B Bronxville NY 1952 s Irwin & Dorothy. BA W&M 1974; MEd W&M 1975; MDiv VTS 1980. D 5/31/1980 P 3/1/1981 Bp Claude Charles Vache. m 8/12/1989 Catherine Lewis c 1. Cn to the Ordnry Dio Sthrn Virginia Newport News VA 2003-2010, Chair - Spir Cmsn 1983-1986; R Old Donation Ch Virginia Bch VA 1998-2003; R S Mk's Ch Hampton VA 1983-1991; Cur The Epis Ch Of The Adv Norfolk VA 1980. Auth, "Confirmed To Serve". Soc Of S Jn The Evang.

LEWIS, Jason (Ky) 204 Monroe Ave, Belton MO 64012 **Cn Dio Kentucky Louisville KY 2013-; Vic St Mary Magd Epis Kansas City MO 2007-** B Walkins Glen NY 1978 s William & Donna. MDiv Nazarene TS 2004; CAS Geo Herbert Inst For Pstr Stds 2006. D 6/2/2007 P 12/1/2007 Bp Barry Howe. m 12/19/1998 Amy Lynn Lewis c 3. St Mary Magd Epis Ch Loch Lloyd MO 2007-2013.

LEWIS, Jeffrey Clement (RI) St George's School, PO Box 1910, Newport RI 02840 B Galveston TX 1965 s John & Polly. BA U of Texas 1989; MDiv Bangor TS 2004. D 11/1/2004 P 6/10/2006 Bp Chilton Richardson Knudsen. m 5/22/1993 Susan Boyd Geehr-Lewis c 3. S Giles Ch Jefferson ME 2006-2008; On-call Chapl Penobscot Bay Med Cntr Rockport Maine 2005-2009; Assoc Cler The Epis Ch Of S Jn Bapt Thomaston ME 2005-2006; Cler Intern S Mk's Ch Waterville ME 2004-2005. revcapjclewis@gmail.com

LEWIS, John (WTex) St. Benedict's Workshop, 315 E Pecan St, San Antonio TX 78205 **St Ben's Workshop San Antonio TX 2013-; Co-Dir The Work-Shop San Antonio Texas 2005-; Dir of Formational Outreach Epis TS Of The SW Austin TX 2016-; Dn, Exam Chapl; Mssnr for Chr Formation Dio W Texas San Antonio TX 2013-** B Beaumont TX 1952 s Z & Edith. BA Houston Bapt U 1974; Juris Doctor U of Houston 1977; MDiv VTS 1997; D.Phil. Oxf GB 2004. D 6/19/1997 P 11/15/2001 Bp James Edward Folts. m 10/22/1988 Patricia Bridwell. S Mk's Epis Ch San Antonio TX 2001-2012; P-t Fac Mem, Dept of Rel Trin U San Antonio Texas 2003-2013. Jn G. Lewis, "Looking for Life: The Role of Theo-Ethical Reasoning in Paul's Rel," *Journ for the Study of the NT Supplement Series*, Continuum/T&T Clark, 2005. Angl Assn of Biblic Scholars 2005; SBL 2002; Sprtl Dir' Intl 2005. john.lewis@ssw.edu

LEWIS, John Walter (Me) 33 Knowlton St, Camden ME 04843 B Gainesville TX 1937 s Elbert & Jennie. Rice U - Rel Stds; MD U of Texas Med Branch 1967; JD Yale Law Sch 1982. D 6/18/2005 Bp Chilton Richardson Knudsen. m 2/10/1995 Roberta Laemmle Lewis c 4.

LEWIS, Karen Cichowski (Mich) 218 W Ottawa St, Lansing MI 48933 **P-in-c S Paul's Epis Ch Lansing MI 2013-** B Madison WI 1956 d William & Mary. BA Cntrl Michigan U 1978; MDiv SWTS 1995. D 6/8/1996 P 5/31/1997 Bp R aymond Stewart Wood Jr. c 3. Int Trin Ch Geneva NY 2010-2013; Cn Dio Cntrl New York Liverpool NY 2006-2010; Cn To The Ordnry Dio Estrn Oregon Cove OR 2002-2006; Asst To Bp For Chr Formation Dio Michigan Detroit MI 2000-2002; Asst R S Jn's Ch Plymouth MI 1998-2000; All SS Epis Ch Pontiac MI 1996-1998.

LEWIS, Kate (Los) 265 W Sidlee St, Thousand Oaks CA 91360 **Chapl St. Jn's Reg Med Cntr 2011-** B Lodi CA 1958 BA Loyola Marymount U 1980; BA Loyola Marymount U 1980; MDiv CDSP 2002. D 6/2/2002 P 1/11/2003 Bp Joseph Jon Bruno. m 7/9/2008 Patricia Dee Hendrickson c 1. Vic Emm Epis Ch Kailua HI 2008-2011; Assoc St Cross Epis Ch Hermosa Bch CA 2003-2008; Chapl Res UCLA Med Cntr Los Angeles CA 2002-2003. Assn of Profsnl Chapl 2013.

LEWIS, Katherine Twyford (Minn) 13000 St. Davids Rd, Minnetonka MN 55305 **St Dav's Epis Ch Minnetonka MN 2009-** B Alexandria VA 1964 d Earl & Judith. BA Denison U 1986; MDiv VTS 1996. D 6/29/1996 Bp Herbert Thompson Jr P 2/15/1997 Bp Kenneth Lester Price. c 2. Cn Cathd Ch Of S Mk Minneapolis MN 1998-2002; P E Cntrl Ohio Area Mnstry Bridgeport OH 1997-1998; Trin Ch Bellaire OH 1997-1998. klewis@stdavidsparish.org

LEWIS, Kenneth Rutherford (Ala) 708 Fairfax Dr, Fairfield AL 35064 **Black Belt Comm. Dio Alabama 2005-; Dep Sheriff Jefferson Cnty Sheriff's Off Birmingham AL 1994-** B Sheffield AL 1946 s William & Eloise. BA Miles Coll 1976. D 10/30/2004 Bp Henry Nutt Parsley Jr. m 9/29/1985 Peggy Ann Lewis c 4. Bailiff St Of Alabama Birmingham AL 1993-1994; Asst. Dir. Of Security Birmingham Race Course Birmingham AL 1992-1993; Sergeant Birmingham Police Dept. Birmingham AL 1972-1992.

LEWIS, Kenrick Ewart (Mass) 309 New York Ave, Jersey City NJ 07307 B Belize HN 1931 s Roland & Florrie. BS U of The W Indies 1956; DIT S Ptr Theol Coll 1959; BD EDS 1969; STM Andover Newton TS 1970; STM Bos 1986. D 5/1/1959 P 6/1/1960 Bp The Bishop of Jamaica. c 3. Trin Ch Bellaire OH 1998-2001; Trin Ch Montclair NJ 1998-2001; Dio New York New York NY 1988-2003; Dir Of Pstr Care S Lk/Roosevelt Hosp Cntr 1988-2003; S Lk's-Roosevelt Hosp Cntr New York NY 1988-2003; S Jn's S Jas Epis Ch Boston MA 1985-1988. UBE, Massachusetts Cleric Assn.

LEWIS, Laurie Ann (Kan) 3705 Edgemont St, Wichita KS 67208 **Gr Epis Ch Winfield KS 2013-; Trin Ch Arkansas City KS 2013-; Chapl Epis Campus Mnstry Wichita KS 2010-; Elected Mem of Disciplinary Bd Dio Kansas Topeka KS 2012-, Mem of Campus Mnstry Coun (Form known as Higher Educ Com) 2009-** B Denver CO 1974 d Jewel & LaVerna. BBA Wichita St U 1998; MDiv VTS 2008. D 6/7/2008 P 12/6/2008 Bp Dean E Wolfe. m 8/19/2000 Thomas Ray Lewis c 2. P S Stephens Epis Churchrch Wichita KS 2009-2013; Cur Trin Epis Ch El Dorado KS 2008-2009. gracewinfiledks@gmail.com

LEWIS, Lawrence Bernard (WMo) 415 Market Street, Osceola MO 64776 **Ret 1997-** B Osceola MO 1932 s Bernard & Myrtle. BA U of Missouri 1954; MA U of Missouri 1955; U of Paris FR 1961; MDiv Bex Sem 1973. D 6/9/1973 Bp George Leslie Cadigan P 12/19/1973 Bp Arthur Anton Vogel. m 6/20/1964 Ruth Gilman c 3. Dn Nrthrn Deanry Dio W Missouri Kansas City MO 1996-1997, Eccl Crt 1991-1995, Centennial Com 1990, Prov VII CE Cmsn 1989-1990, Dioc Coun 1989, Sprtl Dir Happ 1987-1988, Chair DeptCE & Yth 1986; Vic S Paul's Ch Maryville MO 1992-1997; S Oswald In The Field Skidmore MO 1985-1997; P-in-c S Paul's Epis Ch Clinton MO 1980-1985; Chapl,

507

half time U of Missouri Med Cntr Columbia MO 1977-1979; Chapl, half time Mid-MO Mntl Hlth Cntr Columbia MO 1976-1979; R Chr Ch Epis Boonville MO 1973-1979. Auth, "Osceola: A Town on the Border," 2016.

LEWIS JR, Lloyd Alexander (LI) 5501 Seminary Rd Apt 812, Falls Church VA 22041 **Hon Asst S Paul's Par Washington DC 2000-; Mem GBEC 2009-** B Washington DC 1947 s Lloyd & Alice. AB Trin Hartford CT 1969; MDiv VTS 1972; MA Ya 1975; MPhil Ya 1981; PhD Ya 1985. D 5/27/1972 Bp Robert Bruce Hall P 12/2/1972 Bp Richard Beamon Martin. Mem Gnrl Bd Examing Chapl 2009-2015; Prof VTS Alexandria VA 2000-2012, Assoc Prof of NT 1985-1991, 1982-1991, Asst Prof of New Testamentew Testament 1978-1981; Mem Gnrl Bd Examing Chapl 2000-2006; Adj Biblic Lang The GTS New York NY 1995-2000; Hon Asst Par Of S Jas Of Jerusalem By The Sea Long Bch NY 1993-2000; Dn Dio Long Island Garden City NY 1991-2000; Dn and Dep for Educ Geo Mercer TS Garden City NY 1991-2000; Honary Asst S Geo's Ch Washington DC 1978-1991; Hon Asst S Monica's Ch Hartford CT 1974-1978; Cur S Geo's Ch Brooklyn NY 1972-1974; Bd Dir St. Steph's And St. Agnes Sch Alexandria VA 2009-2012; Mem GBEC 2000-2006; Mem Coll of Bishops Strng Com 1997-2001. Auth, "Colossians, Philemon," *True to Our Native Land*, Fortress, 2007; Auth, "The Philemon-Paul-Onesimus Triangle," *Stony the Road We Trod*, Fortress, 1991. SBL 1976. DD VTS 1992; Cn Theol Dio Long Isand 1991.

LEWIS, Mabel Burke (NY) 40 Barton St, Newburgh NY 12550 B Orange NJ 1940 d Charles & Mabel. BA Wheaton Coll at Norton 1962; MDiv UTS 1982. D 12/15/1982 Bp Paul Moore Jr P 1/6/1985 Bp Walter Decoster Dennis Jr. Dio New York New York NY 2003-2009, 1985-1993; S Anne's Ch Washingtonville NY 2003-2009; S Thos Epis Ch New Windsor NY 2003-2009; S Ptr's Epis Ch Peekskill NY 2002, Outreach Chapl And Cur 2000-2002; S Peters Ch Peekskill NY 2000-2002; R Ch Of The Ascen Greenpoint Brooklyn NY 1995-2000; Consult S Aug's Ch New York NY 1993-1995; S Martha's Ch Bronx NY 1991-1993; Assoc S Mary's Manhattanville Epis Ch New York NY 1984-1986.

LEWIS, Mark (Nwk) PO Box 93, Rensselaerville NY 12147 B Howell County MO 1960 s Gary & Willie Mae. BA U So 1982; U of Virginia 1985; MDiv VTS 1990. D 6/2/1990 Bp Peter J Lee P 1/19/1991 Bp Robert Poland Atkinson. m 8/3/2011 K Dennis Winslow. Vic Ch Of Our Sav Secaucus NJ 1994-2010; Asst Chr Ch Ridgewood NJ 1991-1994; Cur S Steph's Epis Ch Culpeper VA 1990-1991; Trst Chr Hosp; Adj Prof Jersey City S Coll. Auth, *Var Literary & Hist Periodicals*.

LEWIS, Matthew W (Tenn) 900 Broadway, Nashville TN 37203 **Chr Ch Cathd Nashville TN 2016-** B Oak Harbor Washington 1984 s Charles & Jere. BA U of W Georgia 2007; MDiv Duke DS 2011. D 5/25/2013 Bp Mike Milliken P 11/25/2013 Bp Scott Anson Benhase. Yth Dir The Ch Of The Gd Shpd Augusta GA 2013-2016.

LEWIS, Maurine Ann (Mil) 1717 Carl St, Fort Worth TX 76103 **Ret 2008-** B Kansas City MO 1942 d Richard & Helen. BA U of No Texas 1976; MA U of No Texas 1981; MDiv CDSP 1990. D 6/27/1992 P 1/31/1993 Bp Richard Lester Shimpfky. c 3. R S Dunst's Ch Madison WI 1997-2008; Assoc Gr Cathd Topeka KS 1994-1997; Cur S Phil The Apos Scotts Vlly CA 1992-1994; S Lk's Ch Los Gatos CA 1992-1993; Stndg Com Dio Milwaukee Milwaukee WI 2000-2008; COM Dio Kansas Topeka KS 1994-1997.

LEWIS III, Philip Gregory (Oly) B Philadelphia PA 1932 D 6/25/2005 Bp Vincent Waydell Warner. m 9/1/1978 Laura Elizabeth Lewis.

LEWIS, Philip M (Spr) 420 N. Plum St., Havana IN 62644 **R S Barn Havana IL 2005-** B Ypsilanti MI 1955 s Curtis & Thelma. BA Hartwick Coll 1978; MDiv Cranmer Theol Hse 2001. D 11/1/2001 P 5/1/2002 Bp Daniel William Herzog. m 6/30/1979 Alison G Lewis c 4. S Barn Ch Havana IL 2004-2010; R S Jn's Epis Ch Mt Vernon IN 2003-2004; S Ptr's Ch Albany NY 2001-2002.

LEWIS, Richard H (CNY) none, none NY 13442 **Ret 2001-** B Riverside NJ 1936 s Charles & Elizabeth. BA Wilmington Coll 1958; MA U MI 1960; BD VTS 1963; MS Rutgers The St U of New Jersey 1971. D 6/29/1963 Bp Richard Stanley Merrill Emrich P 1/6/1964 Bp Robert Lionne DeWitt. m 6/4/1962 Sarah V Lewis c 2. Headwaters Epis Mssn Boonville NY 1993-2001; S Mk's Ch Port Leyden NY 1993-2001; S Paul's Ch Constableville NY 1993-2001; R Trin Ch Boonville NY 1993-2001; R The Epis Ch Of The Cross Ticonderoga NY 1984-1993; Trin Ch Whitehall NY 1984-1993; Vic S Barn Epis Ch Monmouth Jct NJ 1981-1984; Vic S Barn Ch Kutztown PA 1980-1981; R No Par Epis Ch St. Clair PA 1975-1980; P-in-c S Jn The Evang Ch New Brunswick NJ 1970-1975; Asst Cathd Ch Of S Paul Detroit MI 1966-1969; P-in-c St Thos Ch Detroit MI 1964-1966, D 1963.

LEWIS, Richard Irvin (Spr) D 5/31/2016 P 12/8/2016 Bp Daniel Hayden Martins.

LEWIS, Robert Michael (Neb) 11251 SW Highway 484, Dunnellon FL 34432 **R S Steph's Ch Grand Island NE 2013-** B Saint Petersburg FL 1977 s Billy & Doreen. AA St Petersburg Coll 1997; BA U of So Florida 2004; MDiv Nash 2007. D 6/2/2007 Bp John Wadsworth Howe P 1/6/2008 Bp Peter Hess Beckwith. m 7/7/2001 Ellen K Lewis c 1. Ch Of The Adv Dunnellon FL 2009-2013; Vic All SS Ch Morton IL 2007-2009. CBS 2004; GAS 2004; SocMary 2004.

LEWIS, Sarah Elizabeth (Md) 576 Johnsville Rd, Eldersburg MD 21784 **VP for Mssn Epis Mnstrs To The Aging Eldersburg MD 2010-, VP for Mssn 2010-; Fairhaven Sykesville MD 1991-** B Tallahassee FL 1955 d Benjamin & Elizabeth. AA S Marys Coll 1975; BA U of Virginia 1978; MDiv SWTS 1988. D 6/12/1988 P 12/17/1988 Bp Frank S Cerveny. Int H Trin Epis Ch Essex MD 1990-1991; Int S Mths' Epis Ch Baltimore MD 1989.

LEWIS, Sarah V (CNY) PO Box 4353, Rome NY 13442 **Supply P S Anne's Ch Lowell MA 2017-; Long Term Supply P S Dav's Barneveld NY 2010-** B Grayling MI 1940 d Sylvester & Eunice. U MI 1960; AS Med Coll of Virginia 1962; BA Wayne 1968; MA Bex Sem 2000. D 12/6/2003 P 8/7/2004 Bp Gladstone Bailey Adams III. m 6/4/1962 Richard H Lewis c 2. P Assoc Gr Epis Ch Utica NY 2009-2010; Int Chapl Luth Care Mnstrs Clinton NY 2006; Utica-Rome Dist Chapl Dio Cntrl New York Liverpool NY 2004-2010, COM's Ord for Mnstry Team Mem 2007-2010, Safe Ch Trnr 2004-2008; Pstr Assoc All SS Ch Utica NY 2004-2008; Asst Chapl Luth Care Mnstrs Clinton NY 2004-2006. Soc of S Marg 2003.

LEWIS, Sharon Lynn Gottfried (SwFla) 3773 Wilkinson Rd, Sarasota FL 34233 B Trenton NJ 1943 d Joseph & Anne. BEd Trenton St Coll 1965; MS Nova SE U 1984; MDiv Sewanee: The U So, TS 1993. D 6/26/1993 P 1/8/1994 Bp Rogers Sanders Harris. Ch Of The H Sprt Osprey FL 1995-2009; S Wlfd's Epis Ch Sarasota FL 1993-1994. Dok Curs.

LEWIS, Stephen Charles (Okla) B 1943 D 6/19/2004 Bp Robert Manning Moody. m 6/25/1988 Nancy Lewis.

LEWIS, Theodore Longstreet (WA) 20235 Laurel Hill Way, Germantown MD 20874 **Theol-in-Res All SS' Epis Ch Chevy Chase MD 2005-; Commissary for Amer Angl Ch of Congo 2001-** B Hempstead NY 1926 s Edward & Margaret. BA Hav 1949; MIA Harv 1951; MDiv VTS 1964. D 6/27/1964 Bp Paul Moore Jr P 1/25/1965 Bp William Foreman Creighton. c 2. Dio Washington Washington DC 1973-2004, Supply P 1973-2001; Serv Congreg in Viet Nam Zaire Korea Laos Var countries 1965-1973; Cur S Columba's Ch Washington DC 1964-1965. "Vietnam and the Sxlty Issue in the Ch," *Washington Dio Nwspr*, 1999; "Pilgrimage to Boga [Congo]," *Virginia Sem Journ*, 1997; Auth, "To Restore the Ch: Radical Redemp Hist to Now," *(Bk)*, self, 1996; "Cranmer's Journey," *Virginia Sem Journ*, 1990.

LEWIS JR, Theodore Radford (SC) 106 Line St, Charleston SC 29403 B Galveston TX 1946 s Theodore & Carrie. BA U of Houston 1970; MDiv Epis TS of the SW 1982. D 6/22/1982 Bp Maurice Manuel Benitez P 2/2/1983 Bp Gordon Taliaferro Charlton. m 11/29/1968 Martha D Lewis c 2. R Calv Ch Charleston SC 1992-2013; R S Lk The Evang Houston TX 1983-1991; Chapl TX Sthrn U-Houston 1983-1991; Assoc S Jas Epis Ch Houston TX 1982-1983; Stndg Com So Carolina Charleston SC 1997-2000, Rel Div Mayors Coun on Homelessness/Homeless 1994-1996; Chair Prov VII Mssn Proj Area Dio Texas Houston TX 1990-1991. OHC 1982. Outstanding Cmnty Serv Chas. Chapt Negro Wmn 2006; Plaque for Cmnty Serv Delta Sigma Theta Sorority 1999; Omega Psi Phi Man of the Year Mu Alpha Chapt 1999; Plaque for Serv as Police Chap Coastal Police Chapl 1996; Assault on Illiteracy Prog Awd Houston Illiteracy Assoc. 1990; Omega Psi Phi Man of the Year Nu Phi Chapt 1990.

LEWIS, Thom (SVa) 2702 W Market St, Greensboro NC 27403 B High Point NC 1946 s William & Maude. MDiv Savonarola TS Scranton. Rec 4/19/2001 Bp David Conner Bane Jr. P-in-c S Chris's Epis Ch Hobbs NM 2009-2012; Int R Gr Ch Carlsbad NM 2008-2009; Calv Ch Bath Par Mc Kenney VA 2003-2008; Asst Ch Of The Epiph Danville VA 2001-2003.

LEWIS, Timothy J (LI) Po Box 264, Wainscott NY 11975 **R S Ann's Epis Ch Bridgehampton NY 2001-** B Carmarthen Wales 1956 s Elvet & Jean. BA U of Wales 1977; BTh Salisbury & Wells Theol Coll Sem GB 1986. Trans 7/24/2001 Bp Orris George Walker Jr. m 1/12/1994 Sandra Lewis c 1. rector@optonline.net

LEWIS, Walter England (Nwk) 60 Dryden Rd, Montclair NJ 07043 **Pstr Assoc/Asstg P St. Jas Epis Ch Montclair NJ 2006-** B Radford VA 1938 s James & Elizabeth. BA U of Virginia 1961; MDiv VTS 1964; DMin Drew U 1983. D 6/27/1964 Bp William Foreman Creighton P 1/9/1965 Bp Paul Moore Jr. c 3. Int S Clem's Ch Hawthorne NJ 2002-2003; P-in-c S Paul's Ch N Arlington NJ 1999-2001; Int Ch Of The Trsfg No Bergen NJ 1988-1990; 1985-1999; Dir Restoration Mnstrs Dio Newark Newark NJ 1985-1999; Assoc S Ptr's Ch Essex Fells NJ 1980-1985; R Chr Epis Ch E Orange NJ 1977-1980; Assoc S Jas Ch Montclair NJ 1972-1977; R St Georges Ch Leonardtown MD 1965-1972. "No Room in the Inn," *The Voice (Dioc Nwsltr)*, Dio Newark, 2004; Auth, "Exam Time," *Acts 29 (mag)*, ERM, 1987; Auth, "Help One Another Make Him Known - Equipping the Laity to Share the Gd News," *Drew U D. Min. Thesis*, U Microfilms Internaitonal, 1983.

LEWIS, William Benjamin (WA) 14110 Royal Forest Ln, Silver Spring MD 20904 B Freetown NE SL 1942 s William & Gladys. BA How 1969; MA How 1972; PhD How 1981; MDiv How 1991. D 6/15/1991 P 5/1/1992 Bp Ronald Hayward Haines. m 11/29/1969 Tabitha Abiola Lewis c 4. Vic S Phil The Evang Washington DC 1996-2014; S Paul's Rock Creek Washington DC 1991-1996.

LEWIS, William George (CFla) 442 Sanderling Dr, Indialantic FL 32903 **Ret 1995-** B Aliquippa PA 1929 s Albert & Ada. MEd U Pgh 1954; MDiv PDS 1958. D 6/7/1958 Bp William S Thomas P 12/21/1958 Bp Austin Pardue. m 9/29/1990 Beverly K Lewis c 3. H Trin Epis Ch Melbourne FL 1980-1994, R 1980-1994; Archd Dio Pittsburgh Pittsburgh PA 1972-1980; R Chr Epis Ch No Hills Pittsburgh PA 1964-1972; S Geo's Ch Waynesburg PA 1958-1964.

LEWIS-HEADDEN, Margaret (Oly) P.O. Box 1997, 1036 Golf Course Rd., Friday Harbor WA 98250 **D The Epis Par of St Dav Friday Harbor WA 2009-** B Riverside CA 1941 d Frank & Margaret. CDSP; Fuller TS; TS-Honolulu; U of Idaho; U of Washington; VTS; BS U MN 1965. D 11/11/1983 Bp Edmond Lee Browning. m 8/21/2008 William Perry Headden. Emm Epis Ch Mercer Island WA 2002-2003; Ch Of The Resurr Bellevue WA 2000-2002; S Andr's Ch Seattle WA 1990-1998; D Asst To R S Andr's 1988-2000; D Chr Ch Seattle WA 1985-1988; D Par of St Clem Honolulu HI 1983-1985.

LEWIS-THEERMAN, Kristina D (NY) 91 Church St, Seymour CT 02630 **S Lk's Ch Katonah NY 2015-** B Wadesboro NC 1952 d Joseph & Pauline. BS Coll of Charleston 1987; MS U of Florida 1991; PhD U of Florida 1994; MDiv GTS 2005. D 6/4/2005 P 1/7/2006 Bp Thomas C Ely. m 6/20/2015 Paul Theerman c 4. R Trin Ch Seymour CT 2009-2015; Asst S Mary's Epis Ch Barnstable MA 2005-2009.

LEY, James Lawrence (Pa) 101 Lydia Ln, West Chester PA 19382 B Philadelphia PA 1945 D 6/21/2003 Bp Charles Ellsworth Bennison Jr. m 7/1/1989 Frances Ley c 2. Ch Of The Redeem Springfield PA 2003-2004.

LEYS, Donovan I (LI) 20931 111 Avenue, Queens Village NY 11429 **P and R S Steph's Epis Ch Jamaica NY 2006-** B JM 1961 s Seymour & Margaret. Untd Theol Coll of the W Indies Kingston JM 1985; BA U of The W Indies 1985. Trans 5/29/1995 Bp Orris George Walker Jr. m 7/8/2005 Sandra E Legall-Leys c 1. R The Ch Of The Epiph And S Simon Brooklyn NY 1995-2006; Assoc P S Aug's Epis Ch Brooklyn NY 1992-1994; D / P Serv Angl Ch of Jamaica W Indies Jamaica 1985-1987.

L'HOMME, Robert Arthur (Chi) 8501 Timber Ln, Lafayette IN 47905 **Sunday Assoc St Johns Epis Ch Lafayette IN 2005-** B Worcester MA 1941 s Arthur & Georgina. BA Assumption Coll 1963; MA Assumption Coll 1964; MDiv Nash 1969. D 6/23/1969 Bp Gerald Francis Burrill P 12/20/1969 Bp James Winchester Montgomery. m 4/15/1989 Carol A L'Homme. Dn St Paul's Epis Ch Peoria IL 1991-2004; Chapl Shapiro Dvlpmt Cntr 1982-1991; R S Paul's Ch Kankakee IL 1972-1991. Auth, "Weekly Rel Column," *The Indianapolis News*, 1965. OHC. Casper News Awd.

L'HOMMEDIEU, J Gary (CFla) 1433 Fairview St, Orlando FL 32804 B Rockville Centre NY 1951 s Ronald & Audrey. MA U of Cntrl Florida; BA Tufts U 1973; MDiv EDS 1979. D 6/2/1979 P 12/1/1979 Bp Paul Moore Jr. m 8/26/1978 Judith S M Myers c 4. Cn Cathd Ch Of S Lk Orlando FL 2002-2015; Int Ch Of The Redemp Southampton PA 2001-2002; Dio Pennsylvania Philadelphia PA 1997; R Ch of the Atone Morton PA 1984-1997; The Ch Of The Atone Morton PA 1984-1997; R Ch Of The Redeem Rensselaer NY 1981-1984; Asst S Mary's Epis Ch Manchester CT 1979-1981. jgarylh@aol.com

LIAO KING-LING, Samuel (Tai) 1-105-7 Hangchow South Road, Taipei Taiwan **P-in-c S Mk In Ping-Tung 1981-** B 1947 s George & Wen-Farn. Fong-Chia U Commerce 1971; MDiv Tainan Theol Coll and Sem TW 1981. D 9/21/1980 P 7/1/1981 Bp Poi-Yeung Cheung. m 3/27/1976 Chin-Fang Su c 1. Dio Taiwan Taipei 1981-2008; Cur S Jn's Cathd Taipei Taiwan 1980-1981.

LIBBEY, Elizabeth Weaver (USC) 1140 Fork Creek Rd, Saluda NC 28773 B Richmond VA 1947 d Robert & Vera. BS Winthrop U 1968; MA U of So Carolina 1974; MDiv VTS 1984. D 6/9/1984 P 5/1/1985 Bp William Arthur Beckham. m 6/18/1984 Robert Edward Libbey c 1. BEC 1990-1992; S Fran of Assisi Chapin SC 1986-1999; S Alb's Ch Lexington SC 1984-1986.

LIBBEY, Robert Edward (USC) 16 Salisbury Drive #7410, Asheville NC 28803 B Boston MA 1939 s Robert & Thelma. BA U So 1961; MDiv Sewanee: The U So, TS 1969. D 6/26/1969 P 1/24/1970 Bp Gray Temple. m 6/18/1984 Elizabeth Weaver Libbey c 3. Int Ch Of The H Cross Tryon NC 2001-2002; Int S Mk's Ch Gastonia NC 2000-2001; Dn Cntrl Deanry Dio Upper So Carolina Columbia SC 1992-1994; Ecum Off 1979-1991; R Epis Ch Of S Simon And S Jude Irmo SC 1979-1999; R Chr Epis Ch Lancaster SC 1973-1979; Asst Par Ch of St. Helena Beaufort SC 1971-1973; D-in-c St Anne's Epis Ch Conway SC 1969-1971; Trin Ch Myrtle Bch SC 1969-1971.

LIBBY, Glenn Maurice (Los) 835 W 34th Street 203, Los Angeles CA 90089 **P-in-c S Phil's Par Los Angeles CA 2010-, P 2008-2009, Assoc 2001-2002; Dioc Coun Dio Los Angeles Los Angeles CA 1999-; Bd Trst CDSP Berkeley CA 2011-** B Waterville ME 1953 s Willis & Norma. BA U of Maine 1974; MA USC 1977; MBA San Diego St U 1987; MDiv Ya Berk 1995; PhD USC 2001. D 6/3/1995 Bp Jack Marston Mckelvey P 1/4/1996 Bp John Shelby Spong. Asstg St. Jn's Par 2004-2007; St Johns Pro-Cathd Los Angeles CA 2001-2003; Chapl The Cbury USC Fndt Inc Los Angeles CA 1996-2015. Ahmanson Fllshp USC 2000; LAS Fllshp USC 1999; Hooker Fllshp And Muehl Prize For Preaching Yale DS 1995; Phi Beta Kappa 1974; Phi Kappa Phi 1973.

LIBBY, Richardson Armstrong (Ct) 235 King George Street, Annapolis MD 21401 **Assoc S Anne's Par Annapolis MD 1999-; Ret 1997-; Chapl Cathd of St Ptr & St Paul Washington DC 2008-** B Norwalk CT 1932 s Richardson & Josephine. BA Trin Hartford CT 1954; STB GTS 1960. D 6/18/1960 Bp Angus Dun P 12/21/1960 Bp Oliver L Loring. m 6/3/1961 Kathryn B Blunck c 2. Imterim St Andr the Fisherman Mayo MD 2004-2005; R Trin Ch Branford CT 1988-1997; R Gr Ch Newington CT 1971-1988; R S Jn's Epis Ch Niantic CT 1963-1965; Cur Gr Epis Ch Bath ME 1960-1963; Chair, Cmncatn Com Dio Connecticut Meriden CT 1976-1981. AFP 1978; Soc of King Chas, Mtyr 1987.

LIBBY, Robert Meredith Gabler (SeFla) 200 Ocean Lane Dr Apt 408, Key Biscayne FL 33149 **Ret 1998-** B Flushing NY 1930 s Francis & Ethel. BA Emory U 1952; MDiv Sewanee: The U So, TS 1958; STM Sewanee: The U So, TS 1972. D 6/19/1958 P 1/2/1959 Bp Randolph R Claiborne. m 5/23/1975 Katherine Libby. R S Chris's By-The-Sea Epis Ch Key Biscayne FL 1990-1998; Gd Samar Epis Ch Orange Pk FL 1981-1990; Dep Gc Dio Florida Jacksonville 1978-1990; S Andr's Ch Jacksonville FL 1977-1978; S Marg's-Hibernia Epis Ch Fleming Island FL 1977-1978; Chapl Dir Of Dvlpmt Epis HS Jacksonville FL 1971-1977; Jacksonville Epis HS Jacksonville FL 1971-1977; Exec Secy Of The Radio/Tv Dept ECEC 1967-1971; R S Cathr's Ch Jacksonville FL 1960-1967; Cn S Paul's Epis Ch Atlanta GA 1958-1960. Auth, "Coming To Faith," Iuniverse, 2001; Auth, "Gr Happens," 1994; Auth, "The Forgiveness Bk," 1992. frboblibby@aol.com

LIBERATORE, James Vincent (Tex) 2535 Broadway St, Pearland TX 77581 **R S Andr's Epis Ch Pearland TX 1995-** B Philadelphia PA 1950 s Eugene & Florence. BS Stevens Inst of Tech 1972; MDiv Epis TS of the SW 1985. D 6/14/1985 Bp William Carl Frey P 1/1/1986 Bp Maurice Manuel Benitez. m 6/13/1970 Christine Liberatore c 2. Stff Chapl S Lk's Epis Hosp Houston TX 1994-1995; R Trin Epis Ch Baytown TX 1987-1994; Asst to R S Dunst's Epis Ch Houston TX 1985-1987. Alb Inst, Bread for Wrld, Associated Parishes; Exec Bd; Habitat.

LICARI, Luigi (Cal) 904-9 Deer Park Crescent, Toronto ON M4V 2C4 Canada **D St. Ptr & Paul Old Cath Par Amsterdam 2005-** B Ilion NY 1949 s Bennie & H Ruth. St Bernards Sem Rochester NY; BA S Jn Fisher Coll 1971; BA Sch for Deacons 1995. D 12/7/1996 Bp William Edwin Swing. m 11/11/2005 Maxie Masanori Sakamakie. D S Jn's Ch New York NY 2002-2005; D S Cyp's Ch San Francisco CA 2000-2002; D S Aid's Ch San Francisco CA 1996-2000. NAAD 1995; Oasis/CA 1995.

LIDDLE, Vincent T (Pa) 1226 Cedar Rd, Ambler PA 19002 **P Assoc St Matthews Epis Ch Maple Glen PA 2009-** B Clarks Summit PA 1933 s Harry & Marie. BA Mary Immac Sem 1957; PhD Inst of Philosophers U in Louvain BE 1966. Rec 6/20/1981 as Priest Bp Lyman Cunningham Ogilby. m 7/31/1970 Rosemary I Liddle c 1. Assoc P St. Steph's ProCathedral Wilkes Barre PA 2007-2009; Int Vic Resurr Epis Ch Naples FL 2003-2005, Assoc 1998-2002; P Assoc S Matt's Ch Maple Glen PA 1998; R Ch Of The Mssh Lower Gwynedd PA 1981-1998. Auth, "The Personalism of Maurice Nedoncelle," *Philos Stds*, 1966.

LIDDY, Jeffery T (Pa) 922 Main Street, Ste. 406, Lynchburg VA 24504 **Adj Instrc. Virginia Epis Sch 2011-** B Fairfield IA 1952 s Robert & Dorothy. BA U of Iowa 1977; MDiv SWTS 1982; Cert S Georges Coll Jerusalem IL 1997; Cert Coll of Preachers 1999; Cert Sarum Coll Salisbury Gb 2002. D 6/25/1982 P 6/18/1983 Bp Walter Cameron Righter. c 2. Chapl Westminster-Cbury Of Lynchburg Lynchburg VA 2010-2012; Fdng Bd Mem Samar Food Bank 2006-2011; Pennypack Dnry Dio Pennsylvania Philadelphia PA 2005-2009; Mem, Dioc Coun Dio Pennsylvania 2005-2008; R All SS Ch Philadelphia PA 2004-2009; R S Jn's Epis Ch Naperville IL 1994-2004; R S Jn's Ch Wichita KS 1987-1993; Asst Ch Of The Ascen Clearwater FL 1985-1987; Vic Ch Of The Epiph Centerville IA 1982-1985; Dioc Coun Dio Kansas Topeka KS 1990-1993. Alb Inst 1988-2004; AAPC 1987-2011; Bro Of S Andr 1994-2004; Ord Of S Lk 1987-1993. Seabury-Wstrn Prize Seabury-Wstrn Sem 1982.

LIEB, James Marcus (ECR) PO Box 293, Ben Lomond CA 95005 B Los Angeles CA 1946 s Philip & Bernice. Bachelors U CA, Santa Cruz 1974; BA Epis Sch for Deacons 1985. BA Other 1985. D 12/3/1988 Bp William Edwin Swing. m 10/2/1971 Catherine Lieb c 3. D Calv Epis Ch Santa Cruz CA 2002-2004; D S Jas Ch Fremont CA 1988-2002.

LIEBENOW, Robert Ervin (Chi) 8 Laurel Place Dr, Asheville NC 28803 **Ret 1989-** B Chicago IL 1925 s Emil & Myrtle. BA Carroll Coll 1946; MDiv Nash 1949. D 6/16/1949 P 12/1/1949 Bp Wallace E Conkling. c 2. R Trin Epis Ch Wheaton IL 1968-1989; P-in-c S Ambr Epis Ch Ft Lauderdale FL 1956-1959; Asst All SS Prot Epis Ch Ft Lauderdale FL 1954-1956; Cur Gr And S Ptr's Ch Baltimore MD 1950-1954; P-in-c S Andr Ch Grayslake IL 1949-1950.

LIEBER, William Louis (SanD) 8975 Lawrence Welk Dr Spc 77, Escondido CA 92026 **Vol Assoc Gr Epis Ch Of The Vlly Mssn San Marcos CA 2008-, Vol Assoc 2000-2006; Res Dio San Diego Bp Mathes 2006-; Ret 1999-** B Detroit MI 1936 s John & Lucia. U of Detroit Mercy 1957; Nthrn St U Aberdeen SD 1959; Michigan TS 1970; SWTS 1971. D 6/29/1970 Bp Richard Stanley Merrill Emrich P 1/1/1971 Bp Archie H Crowley. m 2/9/1957 Joy A Lieber c 5. Int Gr Epis Ch Of The Vlly Mssn San Marcos CA 2006-2008; P in charge S Chris-S

Paul Epis Ch Detroit MI 1977-1999; Dn of the Down River Convoc Dio Michigan Detroit MI 1974-1976, 1970-1976; Vic S Jn Temperance MI 1970-1977; St Johns Ch Temperance MI 1970-1977.

LIEBERT-HALL, Linda Ann (CFla) Shepherd of the Hills, 2540 W Norvell Bryant Hwy, Lecanto FL 34461 **D Shpd Of The Hills Epis Ch Lecanto FL 2008-** B Tulsa 1959 d Robert & DeLoris. BS Washington U; JD S Louis U 1985. D 6/22/2007 Bp Michael Smith. m 5/9/1987 Michael Gregory Hall.

LIEBLER, John Stephen Baxter (CFla) 2254 6th Avenue SE, Vero Beach FL 32962 B Coral Gables FL 1954 s John & Mary. BA U of Notre Dame 1976; MA U of Notre Dame 1977; MDiv Sewanee: The U So, TS 1981. D 5/31/1981 P 12/1/1981 Bp Calvin Onderdonk Schofield Jr. m 1/8/1983 M Cynthia Schnell c 2. R S Andr's Epis Ch Ft Pierce FL 2002-2016; R S Ptr The Fisherman Epis Ch New Smyrna FL 1992-2002, Vic 1987-1991; Chapl Epis Campus Mnstry At Ucf Orlando FL 1985-1987; Chapl Dio Cntrl Florida Orlando FL 1985; Cur The Epis Ch Of The Gd Shpd Tequesta FL 1981-1984.

LIEF, Richard C (SanD) 3212 Eichenlaub St, San Diego CA 92117 B Providence RI 1940 s Richard & Jane. BA U of Redlands 1962; MDiv VTS 1965; DMin Claremont TS 1979. D 9/26/1965 P 5/21/1966 Bp John Brooke Mosley. m 6/23/1962 Carolyn A Lief c 2. Cn for Performing/Visual Arts Cathd Ch Of S Paul San Diego CA 1997-2001; Int Ch Of The Gd Shpd Bonita CA 1997-1998; Int S Jn's Ch Fallbrook CA 1996; Pstr Assoc S Barth's Epis Ch Poway CA 1994-1997; The Epis Ch Of S Andr Encinitas CA 1994-1995; Hosp Chapl S Jas By The Sea La Jolla CA 1991-1998; Chapl Epis Cmnty Serv Natl City CA 1990-1994; Int Dn Trin Cathd San Jose CA 1987-2003; Vic and R S Dav's Epis Ch San Diego CA 1970-1990; Asst S Fran' Par Palos Verdes Estates CA 1967-1970; Asst Imm Ch Highlands Wilmington DE 1965-1967; COM Dio San Diego San Diego CA 1986-1995, Bd Dir Dioc Corp 1986-1989, Dep of GC 1985-1991, Soc Concerns 1982-1985, Stndg Com 1981-1985, Chair Fin Com 1980-1981. Auth, *The Role of the Sprtl Dir in the Curs Mvmt*, 1979. Dir Acad for Sacr Dramatic Arts San Diego CA 1990-1994. Hon Cn St. Paul's Cathd, San Diego, CA 2015; Int Dn Emer Trin Cathd, San Jose, CA 2011.

LIEM, Jennifer E (NCal) PO Box 855, Tahoe City CA 96145 B 1974 d Charles & Clare. BA Ft Lewis Coll 1999; MDiv SWTS 2005. D 6/10/2006 P 12/9/2006 Bp Robert John O'Neill. Asst Gr Mssn Ch Tallahassee FL 2016, Assoc 2016-; Vic Noel Porter C&C Tahoe City CA 2009-2016; Vic S Nich Mssn Tahoe City CA 2009-2016; Assoc R S Lk's Ch Denver CO 2007-2009; Cur S Steph's Ch Longmont CO 2006-2007.

LIERLE, Deane Kae (Okla) 5037 E Via Montoya Dr, Phoenix AZ 85054 B Quincy IL 1932 s Alva & Susie. BA Culver-Stockton Coll 1954; MDiv Lexington TS 1957; DMin Phillips U 1980; Cert CDSP 1988. D 1/2/1988 Bp William Jackson Cox P 6/4/1988 Bp Gerald Nicholas Mcallister. m 12/2/1989 Margaret Lawrence Lierle c 2. Asst All SS Ch Phoenix AZ 2000-2006; Int All SS Ch Phoenix AZ 1998-2000; R S Lk's Epis Ch Ada OK 1992-1994; Trin Ch Tulsa OK 1988-1992.

LIESKE, Mark Stephen (Los) 3833 Artadi Dr, Spanish Springs NV 89436 **Pstr & CFO Living Stones Ch Reno NV 2011-** B Santa Monica CA 1953 Post Grad Dplma Wstrn Sem; BA Pepperdine U 1978; MDiv CDSP 1981; MBA Golden Gate U 2002. D 6/20/1981 P 1/10/1982 Bp Robert Claflin Rusack. m 11/11/1989 San San Tin c 2. Vic S Clare Of Assisi Rancho Cucamonga CA 1988-1989; R S Geo's Par La Can CA 1987-1988; Assoc R All SS Par Beverly Hills CA 1983-1987; Asst R & Sch Chapl S Jas Par Los Angeles CA 1981-1983.

LIETZ, Dennis Eugene (Chi) 935 Knollwood Rd, Deerfield IL 60015 **D S Greg's Epis Ch Deerfield IL 1996-** B Hendricks MN 1934 s Albert & Della. BS So Dakota St U 1956; MS So Dakota St U 1958. D 2/3/1996 Bp Frank Tracy Griswold III. m 9/22/1959 Helen Lietz c 5.

LIEW, Richard (NY) 168 Long Hill Road, Oakland NJ 07436 **Dir of CPE S Jos's Epis Chap Far Rockaway NY 1994-** B Ipoh Perak MY 1940 s Liew & Hilda. BTh Trin TS Sg 1964; STM Drew U 1971; STM Drew U 1971; Cert Blanton-Peale Grad Inst 1973; PhD Mellon U 1973; Cert NYU Med Sch 1980; Cert NYU Med Sch 1980; DMin NYTS 2000. D 2/18/1978 Bp Harold Louis Wright P 10/1/1978 Bp Paul Moore Jr. m 2/14/2014 Sow Chin Wong c 1. Dir Clincal Pstr Educ In Epis Hlth Serv 1994-2009; Epis Hlth Serv Far Rockaway NY 1994-2009; Dir Of Pstr Care & Educ NY Hosp At Cornell Med Cntr 1990-1994; Dir Of Pstr Care Dept Untd Hosp Med Cntr 1987-1990; Epis Mssn Soc New York NY 1978-1984; Chapl Epis Mssn Soc 1974-1984; Stff Counslr Long Island Coun Of Ch 1974-1976; Pstr Methodist Ch 1962-1974. Co-Ed, "Pstr Care Of The Mentally Disabled: Advancing The Care Of The Whole Person," Haworth Press, Inc, 1994. Approved Fell, The Intl Coun of Sex Educ & Parenthood of the Amer U 1981; Assn for Grp Psych 1980; Bd Cert Chapl, Assn of Profsnl Chapl 1977; Clincal Mem, Amer Assn for Mar And Fam Ther 1979; CPE Supvsr, ACPE 1981; Diplomate, AAPC 1979; Diplomate, Coll of Pstr Supervision & Psych 1993. Distinguished Serv Coll of Pstr Supervision & Psych 2010; The Rev. Dr. Jacob W. Diller Awd for Excellence & Distinguished Serv in Pstr Care Epis Hlth Serv, Dio Long Island 2010; Outstanding Achievement Epis Heath Serv, Dio Long Island 2006; Intl Clincl Pstr Eductor ACPE

2001; Distinguished Vol Mayor & Coun, Borough of Franklin Lakes, New Jersey 1996.

LIGGETT JR, James Edgar (NwT) 3518 Hyde Park Ave, Midland TX 79707 **Mem GC JSC on Prog Bdgt and Fin 2012-; Ret Ret 2012-** B El Dorado KS 1949 s James & Cordelia. BA U of Houston 1971; MDiv EDS 1977. D 6/18/1977 P 12/20/1977 Bp Gerald Nicholas Mcallister. c 1. R S Nich' Epis Ch Midland TX 2007-2012; R The Epis Ch Of S Mary The Vrgn Big Sprg TX 1994-2007; R S Thos Ch Garden City KS 1989-1994; R Gr Epis Ch Winfield KS 1980-1989; Vic S Jude's Ch Wellington KS 1980-1989; Cur Gr Ch Muskogee OK 1977-1980; Chair, Conv Deputation Dio NW Texas Lubbock TX 2012, Chair of the GC Deputation 2009-2015, Vice-Chair, Bp Search Com 2007-2008, Mem and Pres (2006) , Stndg Com 2004-2006, Dep to GC 2003-2015, GC Dep 2003-2012, Dioc Webmaster 2003-2010, Chair, COM 1998-2008, Dir, D Formation Prog 1996-, Mem, COM 1996-, Dn, Permian Basin Dnry 1995-2002; Rdr, Gnrl Ord Examinations Dio Kansas Topeka KS 1989-1995; Mem, Coun for the Dvlpmt of Mnstry Prov VI 1984-1989.

✠ LIGHT, The Rt Rev A(rthur) Heath (SwVa) 2524 Wycliffe Ave Sw, Roanoke VA 24014 **Ret Bp of SwVa Dio SW Virginia Roanoke VA 1996-, Bp 1979-1996** B Lynchburg VA 1929 s Alexander & Mary. BA Hampden-Sydney Coll 1951; MDiv VTS 1954. D 6/11/1954 P 6/24/1955 Bp George P Gunn Con 6/2/1979 for SwVa. m 6/12/1953 Sarah Ann Light c 4. Joint SCWM 1991-1994; Pres Prov III 1982-1993; R Chr and S Lk's Epis Ch Norfolk VA 1967-1979; R S Mary's Ch Kinston NC 1964-1967; R Chr Ch Eliz City NC 1958-1964; Chr Ch Boydton VA 1954-1958; R S Jas Ch Boydton VA 1954-1958; S Jn's Epis Ch Chase City VA 1954-1958; S Tim's Epis Ch Clarksville VA 1954-1958; VP Kyosato Educ Experiment Proj (KEEP) Japan. Auth, "God, the Gift, the Giver," Epis Ch Cntr. DD Hampden-Sydney Coll 1987; DD St Paul's Coll 1979; DD VTS 1979.

LIGHTCAP, Torey Lynn (Kan) 835 SW Polk St, Topeka KS 66612 **Dio Kansas Topeka KS 2015-** B Weatherford OK 1972 s Leland & Lura. BA Oklahoma Bapt U 1994; MS Oklahoma St U 1996; MDiv Epis TS of the SW 2004. D 6/12/2004 Bp Robert John O'Neill P 1/8/2005 Bp Rayford Baines High Jr. m 1/9/1993 Jacqueline Whitney c 2. Dio Iowa Des Moines IA 2014-2015; R S Thos' Epis Ch Sioux City IA 2009-2015; P-in-c S Barn Ch Glenwood Spgs CO 2006-2009; Assoc S Jas The Apos Epis Ch Conroe TX 2004-2006. Coll of Pstr Leaders 2006; Gathering of Leaders 2010; Omicron Delta Kappa 1994. Polly Bond Awards for Writing ECom 2007; Polly Bond Awd for Web Design ECom 2004. tlightcap@episcopal-ks.org

LIGHTSEY, Pamela Sue Willis (Ga) 2700 Pebblewood Dr, Valdosta GA 31602 **D S Paul's Ch Macon GA 2013-** B Jacksonville FL 1950 d Douglas & Doris. BA Valdosta St U 1972. D 5/28/1989 Bp Harry Woolston Shipps. m 4/8/1977 Johnny Carroll Lightsey c 2.

LIGHTSEY, Richard Brian (NI) 602 W Superior St, Kokomo IN 46901 **R S Andr Epis Ch Kokomo IN 2000-** B Bakersfield CA 1959 s Otis & Rita. AA Bakersfield Cmnty Coll 1980; BS California St U 1982; MDiv Amer Bapt Sem of the W 1989. D 6/8/1996 P 12/18/1996 Bp David Mercer Schofield. m 9/16/1989 Deanne Lightsey c 3. All SS Ch Bakersfield CA 1996-2000.

LIGON, Michael Moran (EC) 517 Brandywine Cir, Greenville NC 27858 B Clarksburg WV 1949 s James & Mary. BS U NC 1972. D 9/22/1988 Bp Brice Sidney Sanders. m 5/8/1971 Lynda Kay Ligon c 2. D S Tim's Ch Wilson NC 1997-2000, D 1993-1996; D Dio E Carolina Kinston NC 1988-1993.

LIKOWSKI, James Boyd (Ore) 2818 Lilac St, Longview WA 98632 **Ret 1990-** B Laguna Beach CA 1925 s James & Martha. BA U CA 1949; BD CDSP 1963. D 6/24/1963 P 2/10/1964 Bp James Walmsley Frederic Carman. Asst Chapl Legacy Gd Samar Hosp Portland OR 1983-1990; R S Aid's Epis Ch Portland OR 1970-1982; Sr Assoc S Paul's Epis Ch Salem OR 1967-1970; Ch Of The Gd Shpd Prospect OR 1965-1967; Vic S Mart's Ch Shady Cove OR 1965-1967; Cur S Geo's Epis Ch Roseburg OR 1963-1964.

LIKWARTZ, Judy Saima (Ore) Po Box 51447, Casper WY 82605 **S Steph's Ch Casper WY 2005-** B Pocatello ID 1941 d Donald & Saima. BS U of Wyoming 1994; BSW U of Wyoming 1995. D 2/5/2000 Bp Bruce Caldwell. m 5/30/2004 Don J Likwartz c 2. D Ch Of S Andr's In The Pines Pinedale WY 2000-2004. NAAD 2000.

LILE JR, James Elbert (WMo) **R All SS Ch Nevada MO 2017-** D 11/4/2016 P 5/18/2017 Bp Martin Scott Field.

LILES, Allison Sandlin (Ala) 6615 Saddleback Ct, Crozet VA 22932 **Int Exec Dir EPF Ithaca NY 2012-** B Decatur AL 1980 d Steven & Carol. BA Birmingham-Sthrn Coll 2002; MDiv VTS 2006. D 5/25/2006 Bp Marc Handley Andrus P 12/20/2006 Bp Henry Nutt Parsley Jr. m 5/27/2006 Eric James Liles c 2. Ch of Our Sav Charlottesvlle VA 2015-2016; Assoc St Thos Epis Ch Huntsville AL 2010-2012; Asst H Trin Epis Ch Auburn AL 2007-2010; Chapl S Pat's Epis Day Sch Washington DC 2006-2007.

LILES, Eric James (Va) Saint Paul's Church, PO Box 37, Ivy VA 22945 B Bakersfield CA 1978 s Jimmy & Dolly. BA Texas A&M U 1999; MDiv VTS 2007; DMin TS 2015; DMin Sewanee: The U So, TS 2015. D 5/17/2007 Bp Neff Powell P 12/11/2007 Bp Henry Nutt Parsley Jr. m 5/27/2006 Allison Sandlin c 2. R S Paul's Ch Charlottesville VA 2012-2017; Assoc S Jn's Ch Decatur AL

2010-2012; R S Steph's Epis Ch Smiths Sta AL 2007-2010; Yth Dir S Matt's Ch Austin TX 2000-2004; Yth Dir All SS Epis Ch Stafford TX 2000. Epis Ntwk for Econ Justice 2007-2010.

LILES, Linda Kathleen (NY) 120 W 69th St, New York NY 10023 **R Chr And S Steph's Ch New York NY 1998-** B Beebe AR 1950 d Doyle & Naomi. BFA Kansas City Art Inst 1975; MDiv Ya Berk 1988; STM Ya Berk 1990. D 6/11/1988 P 3/18/1989 Bp Herbert Alcorn Donovan Jr. m 11/15/2014 Susan Delong Ball. Assoc Trin Epis Ch Southport CT 1994-1998; S Ptr's Epis Ch Cheshire CT 1991-1994, Assoc 1991-1994, Assoc 1988-1990; Int Zion Epis Ch N Branford CT 1990-1991. Menil Schlr Yale 1989.

LILLARD SR, Eddie Lee (NJ) 1819 Columbus Ave, Neptune NJ 07753 **D S Thos Epis Ch Red Bank NJ 2004-; D S Aug's Epis Ch Asbury Pk NJ 2000-** B Middleton OH 1932 s Joseph & Joyce. D 10/21/2000 Bp David Bruce Joslin. m 6/14/1953 Adaline Jordan.

LILLEY, Lin S (RG) St. Alban's Episcopal Church, 1810 Elm St, El Paso TX 79930 **S Alb's Ch El Paso TX 2017-; Int P-in-c S Thos Of Cbury Epis Ch Albuquerque NM 2013-, 2010-2011** B Lampasas County TX 1948 d Virgil & Mary. BA Tarleton St U 1970; MA W Texas St U 1971; PhD U of Iowa 1992; Dplma in Chr Mnstry TESM 2010. D 9/18/2010 Bp William Carl Frey P 10/8/2011 Bp Michael Vono. Int S Mk's Epis Ch Durango CO 2015-2016. linslilley@gmail.com

✠ LILLIBRIDGE, The Rt Rev Gary Richard (WTex) PO Box 6885, San Antonio TX 78209 B San Antonio TX 1956 s Richard & Carol. BS Texas St U San Marcos 1978; MDiv VTS 1982. D 6/23/1982 Bp Stanley Fillmore Hauser P 1/5/1983 Bp Scott Field Bailey Con 2/21/2004 for WTex. m 10/12/1985 Catherine Lillibridge c 3. Bp of W Texas Dio W Texas San Antonio TX 2004-2017, Archd 1995-2004; R S Dav's Epis Ch San Antonio TX 1998-2003; R Ch Of The Adv Brownsville TX 1992-1995; R S Jas Epis Ch Del Rio TX 1988-1992; Partnr In Mnstry Estrn Convoc Kenedy TX 1988; S Tim's Ch Cotulla TX 1986; Asst Ch Of The Gd Shpd Corpus Christi TX 1982-1984. Distinguished Alum Texas St U 2010; DD Sewanee 2006; DD VTS 2004. gary.lillibridge@dwtx.org

LILLICRAPP, Arthur Reginald (NCal) 9401 Century Oaks Ln, Elk Grove CA 95758 **Pstr/Chapl Wilmer Eye Inst Of JHU Hosp Baltimore MD 1984-** B Rockville Center NY 1947 s Arthur & Irene. Cert Addictions Counslr; Lic Int Mnstry Prog; BA Laf 1969; MDiv GTS 1974; MS Loyola U 1986; Cert GTS 1998. D 6/8/1974 Bp Paul Moore Jr P 12/1/1974 Bp Harold Louis Wright. Gr Epis Ch Wheatland CA 2012-2013; Ch Of S Mart Davis CA 2009-2014; Mgr Sprtl Care Kaisor Permanente Med Cntr Sacramento CA 2007-2017; Assoc Trin Epis Cathd Sacramento CA 2007-2011; S Paul's Epis Ch Oroville CA 2005-2007; Dir. Pstr Care Shasta Reg Med Cntr Redding CA 2000-2007; S Jas Epis Ch Mt Airy MD 1999-2000; Ch Of The H Cross Cumberland MD 1997-1999; Int S Mk's Ch Highland MD 1996-1997; Dir Of Pstr Care Howard Cnty Gnrl Hosp Columbia MD 1986-1996; R S Jn's Ch Mt Washington Baltimore MD 1979-1985; Trin Ch Towson MD 1976-1979; Asst Chr And S Steph's Ch New York NY 1974-1976. AAPC, Coll Of Chaplai 1986-1996; Assn of Profsnl Chapl 2000; Bd Cert Chapl, CPSP 2010; Int Mnstry Ntwk, Licienced Int Pstr 1997. Employee of the Year Kaiser Med Sacramento CA 2016; Employee of the Year Shasta Reg Med Cntr, Redding CA 2004; Who'S Who Rel 1977. moralle@comcast.net

LILLIE, Paul Andrew (Haw) 3311 Campbell Avenue, Honolulu HI 96815 **R S Mk's Ch Honolulu HI 2009-** B St Louis MO 1975 s James & Nadine. BMus Millikin U 1997; ThM Trin Luth Sem 2000; MDiv Bex Sem 2004. D 6/4/2004 P 2/5/2005 Bp Michael Garrison. m 12/15/2008 Jayson John O'Donnell. Cn S Paul's Cathd Buffalo NY 2006-2008; Appointed Mssy / Jerusalem ECUSA/ Mssn Personl New York NY 2005-2006; P Exec Coun Appointees New York NY 2005-2006; YA Serv Corps / Jerusalem ECUSA/Mssn Personl New York NY 2004-2005; D Ecusa / Mssn Personl New York NY 2004. paul.lillie@ stmarkshonolulu.org

LILLIS, Rosemary (Roch) 1222 Sunset Ave, Asbury Park NJ 07712 B Mineola NY 1950 d Ernest & Angela. BS Molloy Coll 1972; ACPE 1989; MDiv UTS 1994; MS Col 1996; Int Crit Incid Stress Mgmt Fndt 2000. D 6/4/1994 Bp John Shelby Spong P 12/17/1994 Bp Jack Marston Mckelvey. c 2. Trin Ch Asbury Pk NJ 2011-2012; S Geo's Ch Hilton NY 2009-2011; S Mk's And S Jn's Epis Ch Rochester NY 2008; S Lk's Ch Brockport NY 2007-2008; S Andr's Ch Harrington Pk NJ 2005-2007; S Mths' Epis Ch Baltimore MD 2003-2004; Prog Coordntr Organ donation and Crisis Chapl Johns Hopkins Hosp Baltimore MD 2001-2003; Int The Ch Of The H Apos Halethorpe MD 2000-2001; Chapl Providence Hosp Holyoke MA 1998-1999; Chapl Wmn & Chld's Hosp Charleston WV 1996-1998; Soc Wk Intern Newark Beth Israel Med Cntr NJ 1995-1996; P-in-c Ch Of The Gd Shpd Ringwood NJ 1994-1996; Soc Wk Intern Hackensack Med Cntr NJ 1994-1995; Dir of Pstr Care Momentum Proj for HIV/AIDS NYC 1990-1991.

LILLPOPP, Donald R (Ct) 7314 Aloe Dr, Spring Hill FL 34607 **Ret 1998-** B Greenfield MA 1933 s Robert & Catherine. BA U of Massachusetts 1956; STB Ya Berk 1959. D 6/13/1959 Bp William A Lawrence P 12/19/1959 Bp Robert McConnell Hatch. m 1/6/1960 Joanne Lillpopp c 3. Int R S Eliz's Epis Ch Zephyrhills FL 2003-2004, 1992-2002; Assoc S Andr's Epis Ch Sprg Hill FL

1999-2005, 1996-1998; R Chr Epis Ch Norwich CT 1980-1998; R Chr Ch Roxbury CT 1973-1980; 1970-1973; Asst Trin Ch On The Green New Haven CT 1968-1970; R S Paul's Ch Windsor VT 1966-1968; Trin Ch Claremont NH 1966-1968; R S Ann's Ch Burlington VT 1964-1966; S Matt's Ch Enosburg Fls VT 1964-1966; Cur Imm Ch Bellows Falls VT 1961-1964; S Mary's Epis Ch Thorndike MA 1959-1960; Asst S Ptr's Ch Springfield MA 1959-1960; Ex-Coun Dio Connecticut Meriden CT 1982-1986.

LILLVIS, David Matthew (Mich) 4708 State Park Hwy, Interlochen MI 49643 B Ashtabula OH 1948 s Matias & Irene. BA Wayne 1970; MDiv EDS 1973; Dplma Henry Ford Hosp Sch of Nrsng 1983. D 6/30/1973 Bp H Coleman Mcgehee Jr P 4/6/1974 Bp Albert A Chambers. m 9/19/1970 Meredith Hunt c 2. R under Contract Trin Ch Three Rivers MI 2006-2013; P in Res S Ptr's Ch Detroit MI 1992-2005; Int S Lk's Ch Utica MI 1991; Int S Phil And S Steph Epis Ch Detroit MI 1989-1991; Int Trin Ch Detroit MI 1989; R S Eliz's Ch Redford Chart Township MI 1976-1981; Cur Ch Of S Jn The Evang Hingham MA 1973-1976.

LILLY, Elizabeth (WNC) 2953 Ninth Tee Dr, Newton NC 28658 **Bd Dir Valle Crucis Conf Cntr Valle Crucis NC 2010-** B Wilson NC 1956 d James & Barbara. BA Meredith Coll 1978; MDiv Andover Newton TS 1985. D 5/29/2004 Bp Bob Johnson P 1/22/2005 Bp Porter Taylor. m 7/9/1993 Henry Thomas Lilly c 1. P Mssnr Epis Ch Of S Ptr's By The Lake Denver NC 2012-2014, Assoc 2004-2007; R Ch Of The Epiph Newton NC 2007-2011; Assoc Pstr Trin Reformed Untd Ch of Chr 1991-1993; Assoc Pstr Amherst Congrl Ch Untd Ch of Chr 1989-1991; Stff Chapl High Point Reg Hosp 1987-1989; Pstr Pleasant Ridge Untd Ch of Chr 1985-1989; Lifelong Chr Formation Com Dio Wstrn No Carolina Asheville NC 2005-2011.

LILLY, Elizabeth Louise (SO) 152 W Weisheimer Rd, Columbus OH 43214 **Iconographer 1996-** B Chicago IL 1933 d Robert & Mary. Mstr Iconographers; BA OH SU 1955; MAR Trin Luth Sem 1978; MDiv Trin Luth Sem 1979; DMin Untd TS Dayton OH 1987. D 6/28/1976 Bp John Mc Gill Krumm P 9/23/1984 Bp William Grant Black. c 2. Trin Ch Columbus OH 2002, Asst 1976-1980; Dir - Dioc Resource Cntr Dio Sthrn Ohio Cincinnati OH 1996-2002; S Ptr's Epis Ch Delaware OH 1995-1996; Assoc S Jn's Ch Worthington OH 1994-1998, Assoc 1988-1993; Vic S Paul's Epis Ch Logan OH 1991-1993; Assoc S Jas Ch Painesville OH 1985-1987; P-in-c & Exec Dir S Jn's Hm For Girls Painesville OH 1985-1987; St Johns Hm Cleveland OH 1985-1987; R Gd Shpd Norwood OH 1983-1985; Vic S Dav Vandalia OH 1982-1983; Asst Chr Epis Ch Dayton OH 1980-1982; Sprtl Dir Curs and Kairos 1973-1987. Auth, "Speak To Me," *Wmn Uncommon Prayers*, Morehouse Pub, 2000; Auth, "Icons,By Cmsn," 1996; Auth, "It Is Finished: A Faithful Par Closes Itself," ,*Dissertation*, UTS Dayton, OH, 1979; Auth, "God'S Sign Lang; The Faith of the Ch in Symbols," Self-Pub, 1978. Oblate: SHN 1970.

LIM, You-Leng Leroy (Los) 12172 9th St, Garden Grove CA 92840 B SG 1964 s Chin-Hoe & Yun-Nee. UTS; BA Pr 1990; MDiv Harvard DS 1995; MBA Harv 2001. D 5/20/1995 Bp Barbara Clementine Harris P 1/13/1996 Bp Frederick Houk Borsch. Asst S Mary Mariposa CA 1996-1998; S Mary's Epis Ch Los Angeles CA 1996-1998; Chapl U CA At Irvine 1996-1998. Auth, "Boundary Wars"; Auth, "Our Families Our Values".

LIMA, Roy Allen (Fla) 259 Duncan Dr, Crawfordville FL 32327 **D H Comf Epis Ch Tallahassee FL 2017-** B Jacksonville FL 1951 s Pasquale & Reitha. The Angl Inst Live Oak FL; BS U of Florida 1978. D 5/27/2007 Bp Samuel Johnson Howard. m 6/30/1979 Diane Lima c 2. D Ch Of The Adv Tallahassee FL 2010-2017; D Mssnr S Teresa Of Avila Crawfordville FL 2008-2010.

LIMATO, Richard Paul (NY) 225 W 99th St, New York NY 10025 B Mt Vernon NY 1951 s Gennaro & Constance. BA Ford 1973; MS Iona Coll 1978; EdD Ford 1998. D 5/13/2017 Bp Andrew Marion Lenow Dietsche. c 1.

LIMATU, Hector Roberto (Los) 42900 Chapantongo, Hidalgo Mexico **Imm Mssn El Monte CA 2012-; Vic Var Congregations In Hidalgo 1992-** B Guatemala City GT 1960 s Roberto & Amparo. TS of Guatemala Gt 1985; S Andrews TS MX 1992. D 10/31/1992 P 5/1/1993 Bp Sergio Carranza-Gomez. m 11/12/1994 Emilia Limatu-Pinto c 4. Ch Of Our Sav Par San Gabr CA 2012-2015; Dio Mex Mex City MOR 1992-2006. padrelimatu@hotmail.com

LIMBACH, Mary Evelyn (Eau) 2034 Upper Ridge Road, Port Washington WI 53074 B Evergreen Park IL 1954 d Casper & Mary. S Fran Sch of Nrsng Peoria IL 1975; Cert So Dakota St U 1985; BD S Josephs Coll Windham ME 1990; MDiv Sewanee: The U So, TS 1993. D 5/1/1993 Bp Roger John White P 11/1/1993 Bp John Clark Buchanan. c 2. R All SS Ch Nevada MO 1993-1999.

LIMBURG, Megan (Va) St Christopher's School, 711 Saint Christophers Rd, Richmond VA 23226 **S Mary's Whitechapel Epis Lancaster VA 2017-** B Charlottesville VA 1962 d Samuel & Mary. BA U of Virginia 1984; MEd U of Virginia 1989; MA UTS 1995; DMin Bapt TS of Richmond 2006. D 6/9/2012 P 12/15/2012 Bp Shannon Sherwood Johnston. m 7/20/1996 Timothy Cornelius Limburg. Gr Ch Kilmarnock VA 2014-2017; S Chris's Sch Richmond VA 2012-2014.

LIMEHOUSE III, Frank F (Ala) 3538 Lenox Rd, Birmingham AL 35213 B Orangeburg SC 1943 s Frank & Jean. BA Wofford Coll 1966; MDiv VTS 1989. D 6/29/1989 Bp Christopher FitzSimons Allison P 6/1/1990 Bp Edward Lloyd

L

Salmon Jr. m 8/5/1973 Jane M Limehouse c 2. Dn The Cathd Ch Of The Adv Birmingham AL 2005-2014; R Par Ch of St. Helena Beaufort SC 1995-2005; R S Barth's Epis Ch Hartsville SC 1991-1994; Asst R S Jas Ch Charleston SC 1989-1991.

LIMO, John Edward (Los) 15757 Saint Timothy Rd, Apple Valley CA 92307 **S Tim's Epis Ch Apple Vlly CA 2016-** B Kissi Kenya 1962 s Julius & Idalia. Dplma in Theol Great Lakes U of Kisumu 1993; MDiv Intl TS 2009. Trans 6/16/2015 as Priest Bp Joseph Jon Bruno. m 12/2/1992 Violet Atieno Violet Atieno Odhiambo c 2. office@sttimshd.org

LIMOZAINE, Bruce John (Ark) 30 Gettysburg N, Cabot AR 72023 **D/P S Steph's Epis Ch Jacksonville AR 2001-** B Washington DC 1942 s Jean & Hanora. BA Coll of Emporia 1971; MS U of Wisconsin 1975; U Denv 1979. D 4/28/2001 P 12/9/2006 Bp Larry Maze. m 8/4/1996 Shaun Lenee Limozaine c 3. Athena'S hon Soc Coll Of Emporia 1971.

LIMPERT JR, Robert Hicks (Alb) 731 Old Piseco Road, Piseco NY 12139 B Saranac Lake NY 1945 s Robert & Harriet. BA Hobart and Wm Smith Colleges 1967; STB GTS 1970. D 6/13/1970 Bp Allen Webster Brown P 12/19/1970 Bp Charles Bowen Persell Jr. P-in-c Adirondack Mssn Pottersville NY 1991-2013, 1970-1988; Cn Chancllr Cathd Of All SS Albany NY 1988-1991. Cn Cathd of All SS, Albany, NY 2002.

LIMPITLAW, John Donald (Ct) 140 Whidah Way, Wellfleet MA 02667 **Guardian ad Litem Collier Cnty Crt Naples FL 2007-; Patient Vol Avow Hospice of Naples FL 2004-** B New York NY 1935 s Robert & Olga. BA Trin Hartford CT 1956; MAR Ya Berk 1992. D 6/13/1992 P 12/23/1992 Bp Arthur Edward Walmsley. m 5/21/1960 Susan Elizabeth Limpitlaw c 3. Assoc Trin Epis Ch Southport CT 1997-1999; Vic Chr Ch Easton CT 1992-1997; VP Macmillan Inc New York NY 1977-1989; VP Warnaco Inc Bridgeport CT 1969-1977; Dir S Mk's Day Care Cntr Operation Hope. Integrity 2006-2010. Who's Who in Amer.

LIN, Justin Chun-Min (Tai) 3/F, 262 Chung-Hsiao I Road, Hsin Hsing Dis, Kaohsiung 800 Taiwan **Dio Taiwan Taipei 1999-** B 1969 s Fu-Chun & Chun. S Jn & S Mary Inst of Tech; BS Fu-Jen Cath U 1997. D 3/27/1999 P 1/8/2000 Bp John Chih-Tsung Chien. m 2/28/2000 Fen-Ju Hsieh c 2. D S Paul's.

LIN, Lily Li-Feng (Tai) 23 Wu-Chuan West Road Sec. 1, Taichung TAIWAN Taiwan **St Jas Epis Ch Taichung W Dist 2006-; Dio Taiwan Taipei 2005-** B Taipei 1975 s Zong-Ren & Zhao. RSB Caulty of Theologe; BA Fu-Jen Cath U. D 6/11/2005 P 7/22/2006 Bp Jung-Hsin Lai. m 10/9/2004 Yu-Ta Lin c 2.

LIN, Samuel Ying-Chiu (Tai) #280 Fuhsing S Rd, Sec 2, C/O Diocese Of Taiwan, Taipei Taiwan **Vic Adv 1985-** B 1954 s Chhing-Chhuan & Chen-Chu. BA Natl Cheng-Kung U Tw 1977; MDiv Tainan Theol Coll and Sem TW 1983; MPhil U Coll Dublin 1990. D 7/10/1983 P 7/1/1984 Bp Poi-Yeung Cheung. m 2/19/1980 Jane C C Lee c 2. Dio Taiwan Taipei 1983-2014; P-in-c S Mich's Hostel Tainan Taiwan 1983-1985; Cur S Paul's Ch Kaohsiung Taiwan 1983-1985. "Meditation Of Gospel Lesson (Chinese)," Taiwan Epis Ch, 1997.

LIN, Shu-Hwa (Tai) 1 F #29 Alley 6, Lane 168 Chung-her Rd, Keelung Taiwan 20347 Taiwan **D St Steph's Ch - Keelung Taiwan 2009-** B Taiwan 1948 d Yun-Peng & Yeh-Chu. MDiv Chinese Evang Sem; BA Fung-Chia U. D 11/21/2009 Bp Jung-Hsin Lai. c 2. Dio Taiwan Taipei 2009-2015.

LINARES-RIVERA, Ivette (PR) **Dio Puerto Rico Trujillo Alto PR 2004-, 2001-2003** B 1973 d Noel & Luz. MDiv S Ptr and S Paul Epis Sem PR 2002. D 10/13/2002 P 10/5/2003 Bp David Andres Alvarez-Velazquez. m 4/19/2008 Francisco Javier Cáceres-Santiago c 1.

LINBOOM, Bradley A. (Chi) **Ch Of The H Nativ Clarendon Hls IL 2016-** B Sterling, IL 1978 s Roger & Carol. Bachelor of Mus Ashland U 2001; Mstr of Mus The U of Akron 2003; Mstr of Div VTS 2016. D 12/19/2015 P 6/21/2016 Bp Jeff Lee. m 8/6/2005 Christina L Godefrin.

LINCOLN, Matthew R (WNY) Trinity Church, 371 Delaware Ave, Buffalo NY 14202 **Trin Epis Ch Buffalo NY 2015-** B Saint Louis MO 1958 s Charles & Claire. U Chi; BA Earlham Coll 1984; MDiv GTS 1991. D 10/16/1991 P 4/26/1992 Bp Ronald Hayward Haines. m 9/26/1987 Catherine E Carr c 2. R S Jn's Ch No Haven CT 1998-2015; Cur S Chris's Ch Chatham MA 1995-1998; Cur S Fran Ch Potomac MD 1991-1995; Dn, New Haven Dnry Dio Connecticut Meriden CT 2000-2006; Chair, Evang Com Dio Massachusetts Boston MA 1996-1998; Cmsn Liturg & Mus Dio Washington Washington DC 1993-1995. mlincoln@trinitybuffalo.org

LINCOLN, Richard Kent (Los) 15114 Archwood St, Van Nuys CA 91405 B Lubbock TX 1945 s Eldon & Helen. BA U Denv 1967; MDiv GTS 1976; MA Natl U 1982. D 6/12/1976 P 12/1/1976 Bp Paul Moore Jr. m 3/28/1970 Catherine Lincoln. Asst S Simon's Par San Fernando CA 1994-1995; Directing Chapl Gd Samar Hosp Los Angeles CA 1990-1994; Gd Samar Hosp Los Angeles CA 1990; Non-par 1988-1990; P S Mich and All Ang Epis Ch Studio City CA 1984-1988; Assoc S Mart-In-The-Fields Par Winnetka CA 1983-1984; Assoc S Mk's Par Altadena CA 1983; Chapl The Bp's Sch La Jolla CA 1981-1982; Chapl Bp Sch La Jolla CA 1980-1983; Assoc Chr Ch Coronado CA 1980-1981; Assoc St. Barth Ch New York NY 1977-1978; Non-par 1976-1978; Assoc S Clem's Ch New York NY 1975-1976.

LINCOLN, Thomas Clarke (Nwk) 1156 Carolina Cir Sw, Vero Beach FL 32962 B Mount Vernon NY 1934 s Alan & Elizabeth. BA Wms 1956; MDiv VTS 1966. D 6/11/1966 P 12/14/1966 Bp Leland Stark. m 6/15/1957 Renee Marie Lincoln. S Thos Ch Lyndhurst NJ 1998-1999, Int 1998-1999, Int 1992-1994; Trin Epis Ch of Bergen Cnty Allendale NJ 1995, 1989; Int S Jn's Epis Ch Montclair NJ 1991; Int S Ptr's Ch Mtn Lks NJ 1990-1991; Vic The Ch Of The Sav Denville NJ 1967-1968.

LIND, Douglass Theodore (Ct) 17080 Harbour Point Dr Apt 1017, Fort Myers FL 33908 **P Assoc Calv Ch Stonington CT 2009-** B St Paul MN 1939 s Olaf & Jennie. AB Harv 1961; MDiv UTS 1964; PhD SE U 1974; DMin GTF So Bend IN 1989; ThD GTF So Bend IN 2007. D 6/10/2006 Bp Andrew Donnan Smith P 2/10/2007 Bp James Elliot Curry. m 7/31/1965 Penelope Lind. P Assoc Ch Of S Mich And All Ang Sanibel FL 2009-2011; supply P S Mary's Epis Ch Manchester CT 2007-2012; Cur S Jas Ch New London CT 2006-2007; Par Assoc First Presb Ch Stamford Ct. 1999-2004; Pstr to pastors Presb of New York New York City 1995-1999; Partnr Sigma Grp LLC. 1983-2011; Pres TriSource Grp Inc. 1983-1992; Advsry Dir Ayers Whitmore & Co 1976-1983; Assoc Pstr Wilton Presb Ch Wilton Ct. 1973-1995; Ther & Bd chair Hudson River Counslg Serv Rye New York 1973-1983; Mgmt Consult Reed & DiSalvo Assoc New York City 1973-1976; Sr Min No Av Presb Ch New Rochelle N.Y. 1967-1973.

LIND, Tracey (O) 80 E. 252nd St., Euclid OH 44132 B Columbus OH 1954 d Stanley & Winne. BA U of Toledo 1977; MA U Cinc 1979; MDiv UTS 1987. D 6/13/1987 Bp Paul Moore Jr P 12/10/1987 Bp John Shelby Spong. m 8/12/2010 Emily B Ingalls. Dn Trin Cathd Cleveland OH 2000-2017; R S Paul's Epis Ch Paterson NJ 1989-2000; Assoc Chr Ch Ridgewood NJ 1987-1989. "Interrupted By God: Glimpses from the Edge," Pilgrim Press, 2004. Dio Newark Cantenbury Schlrshp Dio Newark 1994; Maxwell Fellowowship Uts 1987.

LINDAHL, Rosa Vera (Ala) **Ch Of The Ascen Montgomery AL 2015-; Consult ECF Inc New York NY 2014-; P Mssnr S Ambr Epis Ch Ft Lauderdale FL 2010-; Bd Mem Cahawba MHA 2015-** B Cali Colombia 1959 d Gunnar & Ann. BA Loyola U 1983; MDiv Sewanee: The U So, TS 1987. D 7/16/2005 P 5/12/2006 Bp Leo Frade. m 7/9/1988 Sherod Earl Mallow c 1. S Paul's Epis Ch Lowndesboro AL 2015; P Mssnr All SS Prot Epis Ch Ft Lauderdale FL 2005-2014. Auth, "Out of Many, One," *ECF Vital Practices*, ECF, 2011. Transformational Mnstrs Fell ECF 2010.

LINDBERG, Robert Morris (CPa) 16 Winch Hill Rd, Swanzey NH 03446 **Pstr Adv Luth Ch 2010-** B Waukegan IL 1950 s Ernest & Signe. BA Sthrn Illinois U 1975; MS Sthrn Illinois U 1976; Chr Sem/Seminex 1977; MDiv Bex Sem 1986. D 8/6/1986 Bp Richard Mitchell Trelease Jr P 2/7/1987 Bp Harold Barrett Robinson. m 11/14/1987 Maryann L Lindberg c 2. R Chr Ch Berwick PA 2004-2009; R Chr Epis Ch Warren OH 1994-2004; R S Mths Ch Hamilton NJ 1989-1994; Cn S Paul's Cathd Buffalo NY 1986-1989. Distinguished Grad Awd Lake Cnty Coll 1986.

LINDELL, John Allen (Mont) 6629 Merryport Ln, Naples FL 34104 **Co-Chair Recovery Mnstrs Com Dio SW Florida Parrish FL 2006-** B Chicago IL 1943 s Julian & Irvina. BA Parsons Coll 1964; MDiv Epis TS in Kentucky 1984; DMin GTF 1988. D 12/15/1985 P 6/15/1986 Bp Don Adger Wimberly. m 5/23/1992 A A Lindell. Dvlpmt Dir Sunrise Cmnty 2004-2007; Substance Abuse Counslr Psychotherapeutic Serv Inc. Naples 2000-2004; R S Fran Epis Ch Great Falls MT 1997-1999; S Paul's Ch Ft Benton MT 1997-1999; S Matt's Hse Naples FL 1993-1996; Assoc S Paul's Ch Naples FL 1987-1993; Vic S Tim's Barnes Mtn Irvine KY 1985-1987. Auth, "Sinned Againstness," *Fellows Yearbook of GTF*, 1989. Life Tenured Fell Grad Theolgical Fndt 1989.

LINDELL, Thomas Jay (Az) 4460 N Camino Del Rey, Tucson AZ 85718 **D S Phil's In The Hills Tucson AZ 2000-** B Red Wing MN 1941 s Carl & Florence. BS Gustavus Adolphus Coll 1963; Ph.D. U of Iowa 1968; none U CA San Francisco 1969; none U of Washington 1969; none Westcott Hse Cambridge UK 1997; none Wycliffe Hall Oxford UK 1999; none Wycliffe Hall Oxford UK 2000; none Wycliffe Hall Oxford, UK 2001. D 10/14/2000 Bp Robert Reed Shahan. m 2/25/2000 Marilyn Jean Anderson c 2. Mem, Com on Sci, Tech, and Faith Exec Coun ECUSA 2004-2009; D's Coun Dio Arizona Phoenix AZ 2006-2015, COM 2002-2010. Soc of Ord Scientists 2003.

LINDEMAN, Eileen Cornish (RI) 830 Mohican Way, Redwood City CA 94062 **Vic S Ann's-By-The-Sea Block Island RI 2013-** B Grand Island NE 1954 d Arthur & Dena. BS U of Nebraska 1976; MA Creighton U 1994. D 5/28/1995 P 2/11/1996 Bp James Edward Krotz. m 4/2/1976 Mitchell James Lindeman c 3. Dio Rhode Island Providence RI 2013-2014; Int R S Bede's Epis Ch Menlo Pk CA 2012-2013; Epis Cmnty Serv Natl City CA 2001-2002, 1996-1998; The Bp's Sch La Jolla CA 1999-2000; Chr Ch Coronado CA 1997-2006; Asst S Mk's On The Campus Lincoln NE 1995-1996; Chapl S Monica Lincoln NE 1994-1996. Cath Fllshp Of Epis Ch.

LINDEMAN, Matthew James (Ct) PO Box 400, Southport CT 06890 B New Haven CT 1982 s Mitchell & Eileen. MDiv Ya Berk; BA Earlham Coll 2005; MDiv Yale DS 2012. D 6/6/2015 Bp Gayle Harris P 12/19/2015 Bp Laura Ahrens. m 7/8/2005 Anna G Einstein c 1. Yth Dir Trin Epis Ch Southport CT 2013-2017.

LINDEMAN, Mitchell James (Cal) 139 Ocean Avenue, Cranston RI 02905 B Tacoma WA 1956 s William & Marilyn. BA U of Nebraska 1980; MDiv Ya Berk 1983. D 6/15/1983 P 12/16/1983 Bp James Daniel Warner. m 4/2/1976 Eileen Cornish c 3. R Chr Ch Portola Vlly CA 2006-2014; R Chr Ch Coronado CA 1996-2006; R S Matt's Ch Lincoln NE 1990-1996; R S Thos' Epis Ch Falls City NE 1985-1990; Asst All SS Epis Ch Omaha NE 1983-1985. Cath Fllshp Epis Ch 1987. Fund Schlr Fund for Theol Educ 1981.

LINDENBERG, Juliana T (NC) 231 N Church St, Rocky Mount NC 27804 B Orlando, FL 1970 d Jimmie & Vicki. BA The Coll of Wooster 1997; MDiv Candler TS Emory U 2001. D 6/26/2010 Bp Don Edward Johnson. m 6/16/2000 David Lindenberg c 2. Vic S Mk's Epis Ch Roxboro NC 2015-2016; Asst Ch Of The Gd Shpd Rocky Mt NC 2011-2013; St Geo's Indep Sch Collierville TN 2010-2011.

LINDER, Callie Maebelle (Mich) 2034 S 69th East Pl, Tulsa OK 74112 D 1987- B Elgin TX 1923 d Oscar & Clara. PhD Indiana U 1970; Sewanee: The U So, TS 1986. D 6/27/1987 Bp H Coleman Mcgehee Jr.

LINDER, Mark Allen (Ky) 2500 Crossings Blvd # 518, Bowling Green KY 42104 B Little Rock AR 1945 s Bernard & Ellen. BS U of Arkansas 1970; MDiv VTS 1973. D 6/25/1973 Bp Christoph Keller Jr P 4/16/1974 Bp Reginald Heber Gooden. m 12/28/1968 Patricia G Linder c 3. Transition Off Dio Kentucky Louisville KY 2007-2013, Dep GC 2000-2007, Pres Stndg Com 1996-1999; R Chr Epis Ch Bowling Green KY 1994-2007; R Trin Ch Pine Bluff AR 1985-1994; Chapl NG 1977-1994; R S Paul's Epis Ch Batesville AR 1977-1985; Assoc Chr Ch Overland Pk KS 1975-1977; P-in-c S Aug's Ch Ft Smith AR 1974-1975; S Jn's Epis Ch Ft Smith AR 1973-1975; Stndg Com Dio Arkansas Little Rock AR 1986-1989, Exec Coun 1982-1985, CE Cmsn 1973-1981.

LINDER, Philip Conrad (Lex) 25 Otranto Lane, Columbia SC 29209 S Jn's Ch Versailles KY 2011- B Flushing NY 1960 s Conrad & Leona. BS Villanova U 1982; MDiv GTS 1985; DMin Columbia TS 1993; BA The GTF 2006. D 5/20/1985 Bp Robert Campbell Witcher Sr P 12/21/1985 Bp Henry Boyd Hucles III. m 8/14/1982 Ellen N Linder c 3. Dn Trin Cathd Columbia SC 1999-2011; R H Trin Par Decatur GA 1990-1999; S Mart In The Fields Ch Atlanta GA 1987-1990; Asst Gr Epis Ch Massapequa NY 1985-1987. "A P's Journ of Hope - God and 9/11," IUniverse, Inc.; Auth, "H Trust," LivCh; Auth, "The Run Within," LivCh. Soc of S Jn the Evang 1998-2006.

LINDH-PAYNE, Kristofer Hans (Md) 2216 Pot Spring Rd., Timonium MD 21093 Assoc R Epiph Ch Dulaney Vlly Luthvle Timon MD 2009- B Baltimore MD 1977 s Hans & Patricia. BA S Marys Coll of Maryland 1999; MA Loyola Coll Baltimore MD 2003; MDiv SWTS 2009. D 6/13/2009 Bp John L Rabb. m 8/28/2004 Heather Lindh-Payne.

LINDLEY, James B (Ore) 97955 Hallway Rd, PO Box 3190, Harbor OR 97415 Vic S Tim's Ch Brookings OR 2008- B Crescent City CA 1967 s Jim & Kathrine. BS Willamette U 1989; Dio Oregon Cntr for the Diac 2006; VTS 2007. D 9/5/2007 Bp Johncy Itty P 6/14/2008 Bp Robert Louis Ladehoff. m 8/13/1988 Paige Lindley c 2.

LINDLEY, Susan Shea (Okla) 1202 W Elder Ave, Duncan OK 73533 B San Mateo CA 1943 d John & Mary. BSFS Geo 1965; JD U of Texas 1970; MDiv Phillips TS 2007. D 6/23/2007 Bp Robert Manning Moody P 1/19/2008 Bp Edward Joseph Konieczny. m 4/24/1971 George W Lindley c 1. S Lk's Ch Chickasha OK 2013; Vic Dio Oklahoma Oklahoma City OK 2008-2012.

LINDQUIST, Mary Dail (Vt) 16 Bradley Ave, Brattleboro VT 05301 R S Mich's Epis Ch Brattleboro VT 2011-; Vic The Epis Ch On W Kauai 2004- B Batavia NY 1968 d Ray & Phyllis. BA Br 1991; MDiv PrTS 1995; STM GTS 2000. Trans 2/11/2004 Bp Wayne Wright. m 7/23/2000 Kurt Brian Johnson. Vic Epis Ch On W Kaua'i Eleele HI 2004-2011; Assoc R S Dav's Epis Ch Wilmington DE 2000-2003; Dir of Chr Formation Trin Ch Princeton NJ 1997-1999.

LINDSAY JR, Spencer Hedden (La) 273 Monarch Dr Apt L-26, Houma LA 70364 B Houma,LA 1948 s Spencer & Doris. BA Centenary Coll of Louisiana 1970; MDiv SWTS 1973. D 6/25/1973 P 4/1/1974 Bp Iveson Batchelor Noland. m 6/11/2014 Earl Clifford Woodard. P-in-c H Apos New Orleans LA 1978-1982; Chr Of The H Apos New Orleans LA 1977-1982; Vic S Mary's Ch Chalmette LA 1976-2003; Cur S Lk's Ch Baton Rouge LA 1973-1976. Integrity.

LINDSEY, Barrett Kelland (Oly) 2511 E 40th Ave, Spokane WA 99223 Died 3/23/2017 B Oklahoma City OK 1941 s Lucien & Dolores. BA U of Oklahoma 1963; STB U Tor 1966. D 6/17/1966 Bp Chilton R Powell P 1/1/1967 Bp Frederick Warren Putnam. m 6/14/1998 Barbara Jean Lindsey. Ret 1998-2017; Int S Steph's Epis Ch Spokane WA 1997-1998; Int S Paul's Epis Ch Mt Vernon WA 1995-1997; Dio Olympia Seattle 1994; Chr Ch Seattle WA 1980-1994; Assoc R Chr Ch Par Lake Oswego OR 1977-1980; Cn Pstr S Andr's Cathd Honolulu HI 1973-1977; Assoc R S Jn's Ch Oklahoma City OK 1970-1973; Vic S Lk The Beloved Physcn Idabel OK 1969-1970; Vic S Mk's Ch Hugo OK 1967-1970; Cur S Paul's Ch Altus OK 1966-1967.

LINDSEY, Kenneth Lewis (Me) 649 W River Rd, Augusta ME 04330 Ret 1988- B Barre MA 1924 s Lewis & Mattie. NEU 1945; LTh Epis TS in Kentucky 1963; U of Kentucky 1964; Coll of Preachers 1976. D 6/22/1963 Bp Robert McConnell Hatch P 12/21/1963 Bp Oliver L Loring. m 7/6/1991 Christine Ann Davis c 1. Asst S Barn Ch Berlin NH 1991-1998; Dio Maine Portland ME 1987-1988, Dioc Coun 1972-1986, Cler Compstn Rev Com 1971, Chairman Cltn for Missions 1982-1987; Vic S Lk's Ch Farmington ME 1982-1987; P-in-c Chr Epis Ch Eastport ME 1975-1982; R S Anne's Ch Calais ME 1967-1982; R S Lk Woodland ME 1967-1982; St Lukes Ch Woodland ME 1967-1982; Vic All SS Macwahoc ME 1963-1967; S Hugh Ch Lincoln ME 1963-1967; S Thos Ch Winn ME 1963-1967. AmL 1945; Veteran's of Frgn War (VFW) 1988. Liberation Appreciation Dplma from Normandy Republique of Francaise 2001; Hon Cn St. Lk's Cathd Portland 1986; Purple Heart US ARMY 1945; Bronze Star US ARMY 1945. chrisken91@gmail.com

LINDSEY, Richard Carroll (SC) 3001 Meeting St, Hilton Head Island SC 29926 R All SS Ch Hilton Hd Island SC 2003-; Bd Mem Dominican Dvlpmt Grp 1999-; COM So Carolina Charleston SC 2013-, Stndg Com 2013- B Baltimore MD 1949 s Erle & June. BS Towson St U 1972; MDiv EDS 1976. D 5/30/1976 P 1/1/1977 Bp David Keller Leighton Sr. m 5/25/1974 Jane Lindsey c 2. Chapl S Paul Sch Clearwater FL 1992-2003; R S Alfred's Epis Ch Palm Harbor FL 1990-2003; R Nativ Epis Ch Bloomfield Township MI 1985-1990; R Chr Ch W River MD 1980-1985; Asst S Jn's Ch Reisterstown MD 1976-1980.

LINDSLEY, James Elliott (NY) Maplegarth, Box 881, Millbrook NY 12545 B Morristown NJ 1930 s James & Alice. BA Bard Coll 1952; STM GTS 1955; GTS 2006. D 6/11/1955 P 12/17/1955 Bp Benjamin M Washburn. m 11/19/1960 Barbara N Lindsley. Vic Ch Of S Nich On The Hudson New Hamburg NY 2003-2007; S Paul's And Trin Par Tivoli NY 1977-1992; Hstgr Dio New York New York NY 1970-1992; P-in-c Chr Ch Harrison NJ 1967-1969; R Chr Ch Corning NY 1966-1967; R S Steph's Ch Millburn NJ 1957-1966; Asst S Jas Ch Montclair NJ 1955-1957; Hstgr Dio Newark Newark NJ 1963-1966. "First Winter," Trst of the Morristown Green; Auth, "S Ptr'S Ch Of Morristown"; Auth, "S Jas' Ch Of New York City"; Auth, "Certainly Splendid Hse"; Auth, "Ch Club Of New York"; Auth, "This Planted Vine". Washington Assn Of New Jersey 1960.

LINDSTROM JR, Donald Fredrick (CGC) 269 Rainbow Falls Road, Franklin NC 28734 B Atlanta GA 1943 s Donald & Susie. ABJ U GA 1966; MDiv VTS 1969; JD Woodrow Wilson Coll of Law 1977; U of W Florida 1983. D 6/28/1969 Bp Randolph R Claiborne P 3/6/1970 Bp Milton Legrand Wood. m 12/30/1983 Marcia Pace c 1. Chapl Greenville Alabama Police and Fraternal Ord of Police 1997-2010; R S Thos Ch Greenville AL 1997-2009; Chapl Butler Cnty Alabama Sheriff 1997-2005; Chapl Meridian Police Lauderdale Cnty Sheriff FOP 1991-1997; R The Epis Ch Of The Medtr Meridian MS 1991-1997; Vic H Sprt Epis Ch Gulf Shores AL 1988-1991; Asst Chr Epis Ch Pensacola FL 1981-1982; R All SS Ch Pawleys Island SC 1978-1981; Chapl Chapl Atlanta Police Dept Atlanta 1975-1978; Asst S Mart In The Fields Ch Atlanta GA 1975-1978; Vic Gd Shpd Epis Ch Austell GA 1971-1975; Police Off/Detective Sergeant Atlanta (Ga) Police Dept 1970-1975; Chapl Appleton Ch Hm for Girls Macon Georgia 1969-1971; Cur Chr Ch Macon GA 1969-1971; Ecum Off Dio Cntrl Gulf Coast Pensacola FL 1997-2010, Ecum Off 1989-1997; Ecum Off Dio Mississippi Jackson MS 1991-1996. producer/writer, "The Autumn Years," Radio-TV Div, ECUSA, 1968; producer/writer, "Cry for Help," Radio-TV Divison, ECUSA, 1968. Amer Assn for Mar and Fam Ther: Clincl 1985-2010; Bd for Chld Advocacy Cntr 1988-1991; Chambellan Prov/Bailli Chaine des Rotisseurs 1993-2000; Intl Conf of Police Chapl,Mstr Chapl 1991; NW Florida Chapt, Natl Kidney Fndt (Pres) 1987-1990; OHC (Assoc) 1971; Rotary Intl 1978. Outstanding Citizen of the Year Greenville Alabama Jaycees 2005; Ldrshp Atlanta Ldrshp Atlanta 1974; Superior Awd for Gnrl News Associated Press Broadcasters 1963; Superior Awd for News Specials Associated Press Broadcasters 1963. frfredl@icloud.com

LINDSTROM, Justin Alan (Okla) Saint Paul's Cathedral, 127 NW 7th St, Oklahoma City OK 73102 Dn S Paul's Cathd Oklahoma City OK 2012- B Escondido CA 1972 s Joel & Jeanne. BA Texas Luth U 1994; MDiv Epis TS of the SW 1999. D 8/28/1999 Bp Claude Edward Payne P 8/29/2000 Bp Leopoldo Jesus Alard. m 6/22/1996 Susan A Lindstrom c 2. S Aid's Ch Cypress TX 2002-2012; The Great Cmsn Fndt Houston TX 2002-2005; Asst S Mart's Epis Ch Houston TX 1999-2002. deanlindstrom@stpaulsokc.org

LINDSTROM, Marjorie Dawson (Nwk) 91 Francisco Ave, Rutherford NJ 07070 Assoc Gr Ch Newark NJ 2007-; Assoc P Gr Ch Newark NJ 2006-; Seamens Ch Inst New York NY 2005- B Hackensack NJ 1951 d George & Roberta. BA Ohio Wesl 1973; MA NYU 1977; MDiv GTS 2005. D 6/12/2005 Bp John Palmer Croneberger P 1/21/2006 Bp Carol J Gallagher. m 7/20/1974 Michael A Lindstrom c 2. Calv Ch Bayonne NJ 2013.

LINDWRIGHT, Philippa Elin (Ore) 3600 SW 117th Ave Apt 149, Beaverton OR 97005 S Barth's Ch Beaverton OR 2012- B Palo Alto CA 1987 d Thomas & Jennifer. BA Earlham Coll 2008; MDiv EDS 2012. D 6/30/2011 P 6/28/2012 Bp Brian N Prior. pippa@stbartsbeaverton.org

LINEBAUGH, Jonathan Andrew (CFla) 5910 NE 22nd Ter, Fort Lauderdale FL 33308 B Fairfax VA 1982 s Craig & Susan. BS Mssh Coll 2005; MDiv TESM

513

2008. D 6/7/2008 Bp Robert William Duncan P 7/8/2015 Bp Gregory Orrin Brewer. m 6/6/2004 Megan Linebaugh c 1.

LING, James K (Tai) 4149 N Kenmore Ave # 28, Chicago IL 60613 B Chen Kang CN 1924 s Wann & Liao. Li Phone Arts Coll Cn 1948; BTh Allnce Sem Hk 1957; Tainan Theol Coll and Sem TW 1965; MTh Heav People Sem 1975. D 8/24/1965 P 2/1/1966 Bp James Chang L Wong. m 1/1/1962 Ruth Ru Te Ling c 3. Dio Mauritius Phoenix 1974-1978; Pres Chinese Mssn Mauritius 1972-1980; Vic H Trin Keelung Taiwan 1966-1971; Dio Taiwan Taipei 1965-1977. Auth, "Traveler In The Globe," 2003; Auth, "The Way To Be Happy," 1982.

LING, Steven (Ct) Trinity Episcopal Church, 345 Main St, Portland CT 06480 **Trin Ch Seymour CT 2016-** B Lansing MI 1951 s Clarence & Dorothy. BA Albion Coll 1973; MA MI SU 1978; MDiv Ya Berk 2007. D 3/25/2007 Bp Paul Victor Marshall P 11/10/2007 Bp James Elliot Curry. m 11/2/1985 Thea Katherine Ling c 2. P Asst Ch Of The H Trin Middletown CT 2008-2013; P-in-c Trin Ch Portland CT 2007-2016.

LINGLE, Mark Duane (Ct) 503 Old Long Ridge Rd, Stamford CT 06903 **S Fran Ch Stamford CT 2015-, P-in-c 2013-** B Park Rapids MN 1966 s Emmett & Shirley. BA Concordia Coll 1988; MDiv Luther Sem 1992. Rec 10/1/2013 as Priest Bp Ian Theodore Douglas. m 12/30/1994 Marnie Beth Sadlowsky.

LINK, Michael Roger (Nev) 11844 Orense Dr, Las Vegas NV 89138 **Treas Natl Ntwk Of Epis Cler Assn Lynnwood WA 2009-** B Davenport IA 1941 s Floyd & Elizabeth. BA U of Iowa 1962; MDiv SWTS 1965. D 6/24/1965 P 1/1/1966 Bp Gordon V Smith. m 9/1/1962 Linda M Nyenhuis c 2. P-t Int P All SS Epis Ch Las Vegas NV 2016-2017, Asstg P 2001-2016; P-t Int P S Mart's In The Desert Pahrump NV 2016-2017; Transitions Off Dio Nevada Las Vegas 2004-2011; R S Phil's Epis Ch Rochester MI 1980-2001; Cn for Educ. and Prog. Dvlpmt St Paul's Epis Ch Peoria IL 1973-1979; R S Lk's Ch Ft Madison IA 1968-1973; Vic S Paul Epis Ch Creston IA 1965-1968; Trin Ch Winterset IA 1965-1968. AGO 1960; Angl Associations of Musicians 1981.

LINLEY, Eliza (ECR) 210 Lake Court, Aptos CA 95003 **Calv Epis Ch Santa Cruz CA 2016-; Asstg P Epis Ch of St Jn the Bapt Aptos Aptos CA 2000-** B Sacramento CA 1952 d James & Margaret. BA Smith 1974; MA U CA 1978; MDiv CDSP 1990. D 12/7/1990 P 12/8/1991 Bp William Edwin Swing. m 1/7/1989 David William Richardson. Vstng Chapl CDSP Berkeley CA 1997-1999, chair, Bd Trst 2007-2013, Trst 2001-2013; Asstg P S Phil The Apos Scotts Vlly CA 1996-2000; Int S Jn's Epis Ch Oakland 1995-1996; S Alb's Ch Albany CA 1993-1995; S Anselm's Epis Ch Lafayette CA 1992; Yth Min All Souls Par In Berkeley Berkeley CA 1991-1992; Trst ECBF No Chesterfield VA 1993-2002. Epis Ch in the Visual Arts 2002.

LINN, David Neill (Cal) Po Box 212, Moraga CA 94556 **Died 6/12/2017** B San Jose CA 1939 s Ronald & Mildred. BA California St U 1967; MDiv CDSP 1969. D 6/28/1969 P 10/1/1970 Bp Chauncie Kilmer Myers. Supply P Dio California San Francisco CA 1972-1973; Assoc Chapl Herrick Hosp Berkeley CA 1969-1972. Ord Of S Lk 2000.

LINNENBERG, Daniel M (Roch) 267 Brooklawn Dr, Rochester NY 14618 **Asst Prof U Roch 2008-** B Humboldt TN 1953 s John & Mary. BA Bowling Green St U 1976; MAEd Wstrn Kentucky U 1983; MDiv Nash 1987; EdD U Roch 2008. D 11/11/1987 P 5/29/1988 Bp David Reed. m 8/22/1975 Virginia Mary Skinner-Linnenberg. R Ch Of The Ascen Rochester NY 2000-2009; Int S Mk's And S Jn's Epis Ch Rochester NY 1999-2000; P-in-c Ch Of The Nativ Boyne City MI 1994-1998; Asst S Paul's Ch Maumee OH 1988-1992; Cur Trin Epis Ch Owensboro KY 1987-1988. dlinnenberg@warner.rochester.edu

LINSCOTT, John Burton (NC) 830 Durham Rd, Wake Forest NC 27587 **D S Johns Epis Ch Wake Forest NC 2008-** B Kona HI 1946 s Burton & Genie. Diac Stds Duke 2007. D 6/14/2008 Bp Michael B Curry. m 12/11/1995 Susan E Linscott c 3.

LINSCOTT, Stephanie (Tex) 3838 N Braeswood Blvd, Apt 257, Houston TX 77025 B Baytown TX 1960 d Stephen & Judy. BA U of Houston 1989; MDiv Epis TS of the SW 1996. D 12/3/1997 P 10/18/2002 Bp Claude Edward Payne. S Lk's Epis Hosp Houston TX 1998-1999; Trin Ch Houston TX 1997-1999; Trin Ch Galveston TX 1997-1998.

LINTON, Adam Stuart (Mass) 204 Monument Rd, Orleans MA 02653 **R The Ch Of The H Sprt Orleans MA 2009-** B San Rafael CA 1954 s Stuart & Patricia. AA Coll of Marin 1975; DIT S Tikhon Orth TS So Canaan PA 1980; MDiv Gordon-Conwell TS 1990. Rec 10/17/1997 as Priest Bp Frank Tracy Griswold III. m 7/17/1977 Lori A Linton c 5. Dep, GC Dio Utah 2006-2009; Liturg & Mus Com Chair Dio Utah 2005-2009; Dio Utah 2003-2006; R Ch Of The Gd Shpd Ogden UT 2000-2009; R S Lk's Ch Dixon IL 1997-2000; Serv Orth Ch in Amer 1980-1996. Cler Ldrshp Proj Class XIII.

LINVILLE, Harriet Burton (ECR) 10372 S W Windwood Way, Portland OR 97225 **P Trin Epis Cathd Portland OR 2015-** B Mount Clemens MI 1943 d Fitz & Margery. AB U MI 1965; BA U MI 1965; AM U MI 1968; MA U MI 1968; Cert Ang Stud CDSP 1981. D 10/20/1982 P 11/1/1983 Bp Rustin Ray Kimsey. c 2. R S Ptr's By-The-Sea Epis Ch Morro Bay CA 1996-2011; Int Ch Of Our Sav Pasco WA 1993-1995; Int Ch Of The H Sprt Missoula MT 1993; supply P Dioc of Spokane 1992-1993; Curs Dio Estrn Oregon Cove OR

1987-1992, Stndg Com, Dioc Coun 1986-1994, Dioc Ecum Off 1984-1996, Dep GC 1979-1991; R S Jn's Ch Hermiston OR 1986-1992; Par Asst The Par Of S Mk The Evang Hood River OR 1986, Par Asst 1982-1986; Dep GC Dio El Camino Real Salinas CA 2007-2010, Dioc Ecum Off 1997-2008, Stndg Com 1997-2007; Exec Bd EDEO Ft Myers FL 1987-2005. Auth, "In Chr There Is No E Or W," *Epis*, 1988.

LINZEL, Claire Benedict (SwFla) 411 Nottinghill Gale St. #805, #1207, Arlington TX 76014 **Ret 2008-** B Akron OH 1930 d Clarence & Rhoda. BA Drew U 1951; MS Indiana U 1967; MDiv CDSP 2003. D 6/24/1995 Bp Telesforo A Isaac. m 6/29/1957 August Edward Linzel c 4. S Andr's Ch Grand Prairie TX 2006-2007; D S Alb's Epis Ch Arlington TX 2004-2006; D All Souls Par In Berkeley Berkeley CA 2001-2003; D Ch Of The H Sprt Sfty Harbor FL 1996-2000; D Ch Of The Redeem Sarasota FL 1995-1996. Soc of S Fran, Third Ord, Life Professed 1962.

LIOTTA BSG, Thomas Mark (NY) 629 County Route 12, New Hampton NY 10958 **Dir of Mus S Jas' Ch Goshen NY 2000-** B Troy NY 1942 s Sylvester & Mary. DC Teachers Coll Washington DC. D 5/14/2005 Bp Mark Sean Sisk. m 6/21/2010 James Mahoney.

LIPP, Beth Ann (ND) P.O. Box 1241, Bismarck ND 58502 B New Ulm MN 1958 d George & Janet. AA Bismarck St Coll 1978; BS U of Mary 1998. D 6/8/2007 Bp Michael Smith. m 8/12/1978 Dennis Lipp c 3.

LIPPART, Thomas Edward (NMich) 5207 Eleuthra Circle, Vero Beach FL 32967 B Upper Darby PA 1937 s John & Mary. BS Michigan Tech U 1959; BD Nash 1965; Cert VTS 1989. D 6/12/1965 Bp Robert Lionne DeWitt P 12/11/1965 Bp Albert Ervine Swift. m 6/21/1964 Ira P Leidel c 2. Ret Dio Nthrn Michigan Marquette MI 1997-2011, Mssnr SoCntrl Reg 1990-1997, Chapl to Ret Cler + spouses 2003-2011, Mssnr SoCntrl Reg 1990-2003, Dioc Coun 1978-1997, Dioc Coun 1978-1989, Stnd Com 1974-1977, Cmncatns, chairman 1971-1985, Nomntns Com Bp 1971-1981, Cmncatns, chairman 1971-1973; So Cntrl Reg Manistique MI 1992-1997; S Steph's Ch Escanaba MI 1971-1991; Vic S Jn's Ch Iron River MI 1967-1971; Vic S Mk's Ch Crystal Falls MI 1967-1971; Asst Ch Of S Asaph Bala Cynwyd PA 1965-1967, Asst 1965-1967. "Beryllides - A Discussion," *Journ of Metals*, AIMME, 1962.

LIPPE, Amanda J (ETenn) PO Box 29, Norris TN 37828 **S Fran' Ch Norris TN 2017-** B Barbados 1976 d Christopher & Wendy. BS Florida Atlantic U 1999; MS Florida Atlantic U 2001; MDiv Sewanee: The U So, TS 2008. D 2/26/2012 P 5/10/2013 Bp Leo Frade. m 2/16/2008 Jason E Lippe. S Thos Epis Par Miami FL 2013-2017. priest-in-charge@stfrancisnorris.org

LIPPITT, Dudley Hand (Ga) 1704 11th Ave, Albany GA 31707 **D S Paul's Ch Albany GA 1989-** B Pelham GA 1930 d C W & Mary. Georgia St U 1989. D 5/14/1989 Bp Harry Woolston Shipps. m 8/20/1954 Samuel Brown Lippitt c 4.

LIPSCOMB III, C(Harles) Lloyd (SwVa) 501 V E S Rd Apt B513, Lynchburg VA 24503 **Ret 1998-** B Buffalo NY 1936 s Charles & Mary. BA U Roch 1958; MDiv Harvard DS 1961; VTS 1962. D 6/16/1963 P 6/21/1964 Bp William Henry Marmion. m 8/22/1964 Elizabeth Johnston Lipscomb c 3. R S Barn Ch Lynchburg VA 1971-1998; Trin Epis Ch Lynchburg VA 1971-1998; S Paul's Ch Saltville VA 1967-1971; Vic S Thos' Epis Ch Abingdon VA 1967-1971; Asst S Paul's Epis Ch Winston Salem NC 1964-1967; Asst Emm Epis Ch Staunton VA 1963-1964. R Emer S Barn and Trin Ch 2001.

LIPSCOMB III, John W (CFla) 317 S Mary St, Eustis FL 32726 B Vero Beach FL 1966 s John & Karyl Ann. Ashbury TS; BA Johnson U 2002; MDiv Nash 2011. D 6/11/2011 Bp Hugo Luis Pina-Lopez P 12/11/2011 Bp John Wadsworth Howe. m 7/18/1987 Karen Lipscomb c 3. S Thos Epis Ch Eustis FL 2011-2017.

LIPSCOMB, Randall Steve (Kan) 3324 NW Bent Tree Ln, Topeka KS 66618 **Dn Gr Cathd Topeka KS 2001-** B Cartersville GA 1951 s Harry & Sara. AS Georgia St U 1981; BS Kennesaw St U 1987; MDiv Sewanee: The U So, TS 1991. D 6/8/1991 P 1/1/1992 Bp Frank Kellogg Allan. m 7/22/1976 Robyn Denise Lipscomb c 1. R Ch of the Resurr Sautee Nacoochee GA 1995-2001; Assoc Gr-Calv Epis Ch Clarkesville GA 1993-1995; Vic S Mary Magd Ch Columbus GA 1991-1993. Auth, "Proper Prefaces and Offertory Sentences for Years A, B, C," Ch Pub Grp, 2009; Auth, "Adv Sermons," *Sewanee Theol Revs*, The STUSo, 1998.

LIPSEY, Howard Martin (Chi) 62 Malden Ave, La Grange IL 60525 B Oak Park IL 1934 s Albert & Margaret. BA U MI 1956; STB Ya Berk 1966. D 6/11/1966 Bp James Winchester Montgomery P 12/16/1966 Bp Gerald Francis Burrill. m 12/16/1961 Glenda Karen Lipsey c 2. Vic Gr Ch Pontiac IL 1969-1970; Cur S Greg's Epis Ch Deerfield IL 1967-1969.

LIRIANO MARTINEZ, Jorge Antonely (NJ) 3050 River Rd, Camden NJ 08105 B Gaspar Hernandez DR 1958 s Josto & Bienvenida. D 5/9/2015 Bp William H Stokes. m 11/24/1990 Luz Liriano.

LIRO, Judith Reagan (Tex) 4301 N I H 35, Austin TX 78722 B San Antonio TX 1942 d Edgar & Byrne. BA Colorado Coll 1964; MDiv Epis TS of the SW 1984. D 11/27/1984 Bp Maurice Manuel Benitez P 6/1/1985 Bp Gordon Taliaferro Charlton. m 6/4/1964 Joseph J Liro c 2. Associaterector S Geo's Ch Austin TX 1984-2013.

LISBY, Gregory C (WMass) All Saints Episcopal Church, 10 Irving Street, Worcester MA 01609 **R All SS Ch Worcester MA 2015-** B Indianapolis IN 1979 s Ricky & Karen. BSW Indiana U 2002; MSW Indiana U 2003; MDiv GTS 2006. D 6/24/2006 P 1/22/2007 Bp Cate Waynick. m 6/6/2014 Timothy H Burger c 2. R Chr Ch Ridgewood NJ 2010-2015; R Ch Of The Ascen Cranston RI 2008-2010; Assoc S Mart's Ch Providence RI 2006-2008. greg@allsaintsw.org

LITMAN, Eric Robert (Mass) 1991 Massachusetts Ave, Cambridge MA 02140 **S Jas' Epis Ch Cambridge MA 2015-** B Nashua NH 1978 s Robert & Barbara. BS Norwich U 2000; MDiv Gordon-Conwell TS 2009; Angl Stds Cert The EDS 2014; Angl Stds Cert The EDS 2014. D 6/6/2015 P 1/9/2016 Bp Gayle Harris. m 6/29/2002 Emily Robbins Litman c 2.

LITSEY, Kim Jeanne (Ct) 915 Main St, South Glastonbury CT 06073 B Corona CA 1956 d Theodore & Mary. BA U CA, Fullerton 1980; MFA U CA, Irvine 1982; MDiv Yale Div Schhol, Ya 2009; MDiv Yale Div Schhol, Ya 2009; MDiv Yale DS 2009; MDiv Yale DS, Ya 2009. D 10/5/2014 Bp Laura Ahrens P 12/20/2016 Bp Ian Theodore Douglas. S Lk's Ch So Glastonbury CT 2015-2016.

✠ **LITTLE II, The Rt Rev Edward Stuart** (NI) 52231 Brendon Hills Dr, Granger IN 46530 B New York NY 1947 s Stuart & Bessie. BA USC 1968; MDiv SWTS 1971; DD SWTS 2000. D 6/19/1971 Bp Gerald Francis Burrill P 12/18/1971 Bp James Winchester Montgomery Con 3/18/2000 for NI. m 3/22/1968 Sylvia Gardner c 2. Bp of NI Dio Nthrn Indiana So Bend IN 2000-2016; BEC Dio San Joaquin 1992-2000; R All SS Ch Bakersfield CA 1986-2000; Chapl CA St U Long Bch CA 1976-1979; R S Jos's Par Buena Pk CA 1975-1986; Asst S Mich's Mssn Anaheim CA 1973-1975; Cur S Matt's Ch Evanston IL 1971-1973; Chair Dioc Vision/Structure Com Epis Dio San Joaquin Modesto CA 1994-1997, Stndg Cmsn Evang 1989-1993. Auth, "Bk," *Joy in Disguise: Meeting Jesus in the Dark Times*, Morehouse, 2009; Auth, "Bk," *Ears to Hear: Recognizing and Responding to God's Call*, Morehouse, 2003; Auth, "arts," *Journey Through Word*; Auth, "arts," *Living Ch*. Phi Beta Kappa 1967. DD SWTS 2000.

LITTLE, Geoffery Alan (Ct) 358 Lenox Street, New Haven CT 06513 B Springfield MA 1960 s Derek & Dawn. BA Bow 1982; MDiv TESM 1992; ThM Fuller TS 2004. D 6/13/1992 Bp Arthur Edward Walmsley P 3/1/1993 Bp Jeffery William Rowthorn. m 7/20/2002 Blanca Saborit c 2. Ch Mssn Soc Usa Inc New Haven CT 1998-2000; P-in-c S Jas' Ch New Haven CT 1994-2010; Prog Off Ovrs Ministers Study Cntr New Haven CT 1992-1998; Ovrs Mnstrs Study Ctr New Haven CT 1992-1998; Asst R S Jn's Ch New Haven CT 1992-1994; SAMS Ambridge PA 1988-1992; Recruitment Off SAMS Ambridge PA 1988-1992; Mssy SAMS Arequipa Peru 1985-1988. Auth, "Discerning Your Mssy Call."

LITTLE, Harry Robert (CNY) 22366 County Route 42, Carthage NY 13619 **Ret 1990-** B Brooklyn NY 1927 s Harry & Arabella. Long Island Dioc TS 1962. D 4/28/1962 P 12/21/1962 Bp James Pernette DeWolfe. c 4. R Gr Ch Carthage NY 1980-1990; Gr Ch Copenhagen NY 1980-1989; Cur Trin Ch Northport NY 1969-1980; P-in-c S Michaels & All Ang 1963-1969; P-in-c S Mk's Epis Ch Medford NY 1962-1969; Chapl Pilgrim St - Edgewood St Hosps Brentwood NY 1962-1963. New York St Assn Of Fire Chapl.

LITTLE, Tracie L (EMich) 543 Michigan Ave, Marysville MI 48040 **R S Jude's Epis Ch Fenton MI 2016-** B Bistroff Moselle France 1962 d Wayman & Patricia. BA U of Wstrn Ontario CA 1984; MDiv Hur CA 2004. Trans 11/15/2004 as Deacon Bp Edwin Max Leidel Jr. m 10/5/2013 David Little c 2. Dio Estrn Michigan Saginaw MI 2010-2015; Asst Gr Epis Ch Port Huron MI 2006-2008; Gr Epis Ch Port Huron MI 2006; R All SS Epis Ch Marysville MI 2004-2016; Stdt Placement Serv Angl Ch of Can 2003-2004.

LITTLEFIELD, Jeff (Ore) 11265 SW Cabot St, Beaverton OR 97005 **R S Barth's Ch Beaverton OR 2011-; Dn,Sunset Convoc Dio Oregon Portland OR 2013-** B Salt Lake City UT 1966 s Diane. BA Willamette U 1988; Seattle U TS and Mnstry 2001; MDiv CDSP 2004. D 6/26/2004 Bp Vincent Waydell Warner P 12/4/2004 Bp William Edwin Swing. Assoc R Epis Par Of S Jn The Bapt Portland OR 2004-2007; Assoc R S Steph's Epis Ch Orinda CA 2004-2007. frjefflittlefield@gmail.com

LITTLEJOHN, Lucrecia M (Tex) 6307 Hickory Holw, Windcrest TX 78239 **Ret Texas 2012-** B Panama PA 1950 d Jose & Ana. Cert Colegio Felix Olivares PA 1969; BA U of Texas 1994; MDiv Sewanee: The U So, TS 1997. D 6/24/1997 Bp Robert Boyd Hibbs P 2/1/1998 Bp James Edward Folts. m 7/31/1973 Ian P Littlejohn. Cn Pstr Chr Ch Cathd Houston TX 2002-2012; Santa Fe Epis Mssn San Antonio TX 1997-2002.

LITTLEJOHN, Norman Richard (Alb) B Massena NY 1949 BS Clarkson U 1972; Cert St Lawr Lewis BOCES 1988; Cert Dn Sch Trin Ch Postdam Ny 3yrs Ord 2003. D 6/28/2003 Bp Daniel William Herzog. m 5/10/1986 Catherine Jane LaFouce c 2.

LITTLEPAGE, Dorothella Michel (Mass) 74 S Common St, Lynn MA 01902 **P-in-c Dio Massachusetts Boston MA 2015-, 2014** B Huntsville AL 1984 d Willie & Harriett. BS Spelman Coll 2006; MDiv VTS 2011. D 12/18/2010 P 6/26/2011 Bp J Neil Alexander. S Steph's Memi Ch Lynn MA 2011-2013. rev. dmlittlepage@gmail.com

LITTLETON, William Harvey (Ga) PO Box 20633, Saint Simons Island GA 31522 B Macon GA 1928 s George & Virginia. BA Emory U 1948; BD Candler TS Emory U 1951; PhD U of Edinburgh Edinburgh Gb 1956; STM Sewanee: The U So, TS 1960. D 6/12/1960 P 12/1/1960 Bp Randolph R Claiborne. m 6/22/1951 Patricia Hammond c 3. Int S Patricks Ch Albany GA 1992-1993; Res Int P Chr Ch Epis Savannah GA 1990-1992; R S Andr's Epis Ch Douglas GA 1981-1990; The Great Cmsn Fndt Houston TX 1977-1978; S Paul's Ch Waco TX 1976-1981; Cn Pstr Chr Ch Cathd Houston TX 1973-1976; R S Mk's Ch Beaumont TX 1966-1968; Dn of Convoc H Trin Par Decatur GA 1963-1966; Exec Bd S Steph's Ch Milledgeville GA 1961-1963; Asst S Lk's Epis Ch Atlanta GA 1960-1961; Asst To Chapl Sewanee U So TS Sewanee TN 1959-1960; Serv Methodist Ch 1950-1957; Liturg Cmsn Dio Texas Houston TX 1977-1980, BEC 1974-1980, Mem of The Bd 1974-1977; Dio Georgia Savannah GA 1963-1968; Dio Atlanta Atlanta GA 1961-1966. Auth, "Gd Morning Forever," 1966.

LITTMAN, Val J (Eur) Altos Del Maria,, 314 Toscana II, Sora Panama B Lockport NY 1948 s Walter & Rose. MDiv S Jn Vianney Sem 1973; MS Loyola U 1981. Rec 10/1/1980 Bp James Winchester Montgomery. m 12/2/1978 Linda Korolewski. Coun of Advice, Elected 2009 Convoc of Epis Ch Europe 2009-2011; Vic, Gr Ch Herault Convoc of Epis Ch in Europe Paris 2009-2011; Mssn Cong Dvelopment Convoc of Epis Ch Europe 2003-2011; VP, Dir Fam Assistance Prog Nthrn Trust Corp Chicago Illinois 1991-2001; H Trin Ch Skokie IL 1990-1991; Int S Alb's Ch Chicago IL 1988-1989; Employee Assistance Prog account Mgr, Arthur Andersen Parkside Med Serv Chicago Illinois 1986-1988; limited Priv Pract Psych and Consult Priv Pract Chicago Illinois 1981-2001; Dio Chicago Chicago IL 1981-1986; Asst Cathd Of S Jas Chicago IL 1980-1991. Auth, "A Bright Sun & Long Shadows," *Memoire / Bk*, Trafford Pub, 2007. Employee Assistance Professionals Assn 1980-2002; NASW 1980-2002.

LITTRELL, James H (Pa) 339 Dover Rd, South Newfane VT 05351 B Lexington VA 1943 s Ira & Mary. BA Davidson Coll 1965; PDS 1970. D 6/6/1970 P 5/1/1971 Bp Robert Lionne DeWitt. m 10/12/1979 Lm Skypala c 1. R S Mary's Ch Hamilton Vill Philadelphia PA 1997-2012; H Apos And Medtr Philadelphia PA 1996, 1980-1991; Ch of the H Comm Philadelphia PA 1982-1992; Non-par 1979-1982; Chapl Hob Geneva NY 1977-1979; Hobart And Wm Smith Colleges Geneva NY 1977-1978; Trin Epis Ch Buffalo NY 1973-1977; Voyage Hse 1970-1973; DCE Ch Of S Mart-In-The-Fields Philadelphia PA 1968-1972; Chapl Chld's Hosp Philadelphia PA 1967-1968. Int Mnstry Ntwk. Citizenship Awd Natl Coun Of Christians & Jews 1995.

LITWINSKI, Anthony (Eur) Mauritiusplatz 1, Wiesbaden MI D65183 Germany B Highland Park MI 1947 s Harry & Dorothy. BA Sacr Heart Sem 1969; STB Pontifical Gregorian U Rome IT 1972; STL Pontifical Gregorian U Rome It 1976; Westphalian Wilhelm Universty 1980; MBA City U of Seattle 1988. Rec 6/2/2001 as Priest Bp William Edwin Swing. m 4/19/1986 Jana Lee Johnsen. R Ch of S Aug of Cbury 65189 Wiesbaden 2010-2014; R S Jas Epis Ch Kamuela HI 2003-2010; Cn Bursar Gr Cathd San Francisco CA 2001-2002; Sem Stff Presb Tch 1989-1995; P RC Ch 1973-1980; Planned Giving Cmsn The Epis Ch in Hawaii Honolulu HI 2008-2010, Asst Treas 2005-2008, Dioc Coun 2003-2008; Fin Com Dio California San Francisco CA 1996-2002.

LITZENBERGER, Caroline Jae (Ore) 1605 NE Clackamas St Apt 300C, Portland OR 97232 **Mem Dio Of Oregon COM For Baptismal Mnstry 2004-** B Tacoma WA 1942 BS U of Washington 1964; MA Portland St U 1989; PhD U of Cambridge 1993; Cert Theol Stud CDSP 2003. D 5/10/2003 Bp Robert Louis Ladehoff P 1/3/2004 Bp Johncy Itty. c 1. Int Chr Ch Par Lake Oswego OR 2013-2014; S Matt's Epis Ch Portland OR 2011-2013; Dio Oregon Portland OR 2010, 2006-2009; S Anne's Epis Ch Washougal WA 2010; Asst Epis Par Of S Jn The Bapt Portland OR 2003-2004; S Mich And All Ang Ch Portland OR 2003-2004. "Communal Ritual Concealed Belief: Layers Of Response To The Regulation Of Ritual In Reformation Engl," Camb Press, 2004; "Defining The Ch Of Engl: Rel Change In The 1570s," Schlr Press, 1998; "Loc Responses To Rel Changes: Evidence From Gloucestershire Wills," 16th Century Journ Pub, 1998; "The Engl Reformation And The Laity," Camb Press, 1997.

LITZENBURG JR, Thomas Vernon (SwVa) 316 Jefferson St, Lexington VA 24450 B Baltimore MD 1933 s Thomas & Charlotte. BA W&L 1957; BD Yale DS 1961; MA Pr 1963; PhD Pr 1965. P 5/1/1963 Bp William Henry Marmion. m 8/21/1976 Jayne S Litzenburg c 3. Chapl Bryn & Hav PA 1959-1960; Hon Asst Trin Ch Swarthmore PA 1962-1964. Auth, "Intellctl Honesty & Rel Commitment".

LIU, Ting-Hua (Tai) I-105-7 Hang Chou South Road, Silo Taiwan **Serv Ch In Tawiwan 1967-** B 1939 s Pu-Ching & Kuei. MDiv Tainan Theol Coll and Sem TW; BD Tainan Theol Coll and Sem TW 1966. D 5/21/1967 P 11/30/1967 Bp James Chang L Wong. m 1/16/1967 Su-Tsu Liu. Vic S Mich's 1985-1987; Vic Gr Taipei Taiwan 1974-1985; P-in-c S Ptr & Kou Bei Mssn 1968-1974; Dio Taiwan Taipei 1967-2004; P-in-c S Ptr's Chiayi Taiwan 1967-1973. Auth, "Angl Chant In Chinese".

L

LIVELY, James W (SwVa) 11610 Chantilly Ct, Clermont FL 34711 **R S Paul's Epis Ch Salem VA 2012-** B Indianapolis IN 1962 s Daniel & Elizabeth. BA U of Cntrl Florida 1997; MDiv Sewanee: The U So, TS 2002. D 6/8/2002 P 12/7/2002 Bp John Wadsworth Howe. m 11/16/1996 Tracy B Lively c 2. R S Mths Epis Ch Clermont FL 2006-2011; Chr Ch Grosse Pointe Grosse Pointe Farms MI 2003-2006; Asst S Jas Epis Ch Ormond Bch FL 2002-2003.

LIVELY, Paula Kay (WMo) 601 E Benton St, Monett MO 65708 **Dio W Missouri Kansas City MO 2014-** B Oklahoma City OK 1948 d Paul & Dortha. Cert Geo Herbert Inst 2013. D 5/3/2014 P 11/7/2014 Bp Martin Scott Field. m 12/16/1977 Roswell Michael Lively.

LIVERMORE, Charles Whittier (ETenn) 7604 Windwood Dr, Powell TN 37849 B Rochester MN 1949 s George & Nancy. BA Westminster Coll 1971; MDiv VTS 1978. D 7/2/1978 Bp William Evan Sanders P 5/12/1979 Bp William F Gates Jr. m 6/17/1978 Diane Smith c 1. Trin Epis Ch Gatlinburg TN 1999-2014; Non-par Detoxification Rehab. Inst Knoxville TN 1989-1999; Ch Of The Gd Shpd Knoxville TN 1983-1987; P-in-c S Mary Magd Ch Fayetteville TN 1979-1985; Dio Tennessee Nashville TN 1979-1983; D St Jas Epis Ch at Knoxville Knoxville TN 1978-1979.

LIVERPOOL, Herman Oswald (Fla) 3405 Nw 48th Ave, # JJ413, Lauderdale Lakes FL 33319 **Died 3/17/2017** B GY 1925 s Joseph & Hilda. Codrington Coll; BA U of The W Indies 1977; MTh Ibis 1985. Trans 11/1/1983. m 6/1/1953 Lucielle Liverpool c 3. Ret 1995-2017; P-in-c S Cyp's St Aug FL 1983-1995; Dio Florida Jacksonville 1983-1992; R S Aug & S Mary E Coast Demeara 1980-1983; P-in-c H Redeem Georgetown 1977-1980. "Play," *Ruth and Naomi*, 2008; Auth, "Play," *The Prodigal Son*, 2007; Auth, *A Second Collection of Poems*, 2000; Auth, "The Days Last Ride," *Melodies of the Soul by the Natl Libr of Poetry*, 1998; Auth, "An Immigrants Dilemma," *Passages of Light by the Natl Libr of Poetry*, 1997; Auth, *Collection of Poems*. Bro of S Andrews 2000; Fndr of Friends of S Cyp; Intl Soc of Poets 2000; Vicars Landing -A Ret Cmnty 1988-1991. Hon DD IBIS 1986.

LIVINGSTON, Bill (Miss) 37 Sheffield Place, Brevard NC 28712 **Dio Wstrn No Carolina Asheville NC 2015-, Mem of Pstr Response Team 2012, Mem of Pstr Response Team 2011-; Fac Mem CREDO Memphis TN 2012-; Fac Mem Cntr for Mnstry Jackson MS 2010-; Consult Wm V. Livingston 1977-; Consult/Sprtl Dir Wm V. Livingston Brevard NC 1977-; Fac Mem Credo Inst Inc. Memphis TN 2011-; Epis Relief & Dvlpmt Journey Partnr Mem Ecusa / Mssn Personl New York NY 2010-** B Vicksburg MS 1951 s Edward & Marjorie. BA Mississippi St U 1973; MEd Delta St U 1975; MDiv Epis TS of the SW 1999. D 3/13/1999 Bp C Wallis Ohl P 10/2/1999 Bp Alfred Marble Jr. m 8/26/1977 Diane Howard Livingston c 3. P-in-c S Phil's Ch Brevard NC 2013-2015; Cn Dio Mississippi Jackson MS 2009-2011, Mem of Exec Com 2003-2009, Chair of Stndg Com 2008-2009, Mem of Stndg Com 2006-2008, Vice-Pres of Exec Com 2005-2006, All S's Sch Trst 2000-2011; Int S Alb's Ch Hickory NC 2009-2011; R Ch Of The Resurr Starkville MS 2002-2006; R Chr Epis Ch Vicksburg MS 1999-2002; Mem of Alum Strng Com Epis TS Of The SW Austin TX 2004-2009. Co-Auth, "Case Stds in Disaster Mnstrs," *Disaster Mnstry Handbook*, Inter Varsity Press, 2015; Co-Auth, "Study of a Rel Denomination's Response to Hurricane Katrina," *Natural Hazard Revs*, 2015; Auth, "When Disaster Strikes," *Vstry Papers*, 2013; co-Auth, "Attendee Help Seeking Behavior after Hurricane Katrina in Mississippi and Louisiana," *Intl Journ of Emergency Mntl Hlth*, 2011; Auth, "From Honeymoon to Disillusionment to Reconstruction: Recognizing Healthy and Unhealthy Coping Mechanisms," *Disaster Sprtl Care: Practical Cler Responses to Cmnty, Reg and Natl Tragedy*, SkyLight Paths, 2008. Paul Harris Fell Paul Harris Fell 1992; DSA Natl Coun of Cmnty Mntl Hlth Centers 1989; Pike Cnty Boss of the Year Bus and Profsnl Wmn 1987.

LIVINGSTON, Diane Howard (WNC) 37 Sheffield Place, Brevard NC 28712 **D S Ptr's By The Sea Gulfport MS 2007-** B Vicksburg MS 1949 d Ernest & Joy. BA SMU 1972; MA Mississippi Coll 1977. D 1/4/2003 Bp Alfred Marble Jr. m 8/26/1977 Bill Livingston c 3. D Ch Of The H Fam Mills River NC 2012-2013; D S Alb's Ch Hickory NC 2010-2011, D 2010-2011; Chapl Coast Epis Schools Inc Long Bch MS 2008-2011; Chapl Coast Epis Sch Pass Chr MS 2008-2009; D Chr Ch Bay S Louis MS 2006-2007; D Chr Ch Bay St. Louis MS 2006-2007; Chapl/Case Mgr Luth-Epis Serv Mnstry Jackson MS 2005-2008; D Ch Of The Resurr Starkville MS 2004-2006, D 2003-2006; The Epis Ch Of The Gd Shpd Columbus MS 2003-2004. Pike Cnty Citizen of the Year Enterprise Journ 1987.

LIVINGSTON, James John (Los) 31641 La Novia Ave, San Juan Capistrano CA 92675 **Chapl S Marg Of Scotland Par San Juan Capo CA 2011-; S Marg's Epis Sch San Juan Capo CA 2011-** B Montgomery AL 1976 s Lee & Martha. BA U of Florida 1998; MS Florida Coll of Integrated Med 2005; MDiv VTS 2011. D 6/4/2011 Bp John Bryson Chane P 1/7/2012 Bp Diane Jardine Bruce. m 12/26/2006 Joanne Mariel McCall c 2.

LIVINGSTON, James Leo (NMich) 3135 County Road 456, Skandia MI 49885 B 1940 D 12/17/2000 P 7/1/2001 Bp James Arthur Kelsey. m 6/21/1986 Gwendolyn Kay Hetler.

LIVINGSTON, Philip Irving Conant (SJ) 17 Linda Vista Dr, Monterey CA 93940 **Died 7/5/2017** B San Jose CA 1931 s Frank & Jessie. BA Ripon Coll

Ripon WI 1954; MDiv Nash 1957. D 1/29/1957 P 8/17/1957 Bp William Hampton Brady. m 9/2/1973 Kateri Picou Livingston c 1. Ret 1993-2017; Non-par 1973-1993; Vic Ch Of S Mary Of The Snows Eagle River WI 1970-1972; Vic Ch Of The H Apos Oneida WI 1967-1969; Cn To Bp Dio Fond du Lac Appleton WI 1960-1972; R S Bon Plymouth WI 1958-1960; S Paul's Ch Plymouth WI 1958-1960; Cur S Andr's Ch Baltimore MD 1957-1958. Auth, "Brethren In Unity," Par Press, Fond Du Lac, Wi, 1963.

LIZ LOPEZ, Ramon A (PR) PO Box 6814, Elizabeth NJ 07202 **Dio Puerto Rico Trujillo Alto PR 2009-, 1997-2004** B Tambori Domincan Republic 1954 s Juan & Gregoria. CAS San Pedro Y San Pablo Sem Trujillo Allo Puerto Rico; MDiv Word Educ Serv PR. m 12/4/1993 Jacqueline Liz c 2. Vic Gr Epis Ch Eliz NJ 2004-2009.

LJUNGGREN, M Lorraine (NC) 5400 Crestview Rd, Raleigh NC 27609 **Trst, Epis Dio No Carolina Dio No Carolina Raleigh NC 2016-, Invstmt Com 2013-2016, Pres, Stndg Com 2011-2013** B Columbia SC 1949 d Robert & Margaret. AA Palm Bch Cmnty Coll 1969; BA Florida St U 1971; MDiv Sewanee: The U So, TS 1991. D 5/25/1991 Bp Calvin Onderdonk Schofield Jr P 1/4/1992 Bp Bob Johnson. m 5/2/1992 James Melnyk. R S Mk's Epis Ch Raleigh NC 1999-2016; R S Jn's Epis Ch Marion NC 1992-1999; Chapl Kanuga Confererences Inc Hendersonvlle NC 1991. Interfaith Allnce for Justice 1995; New Hope Road Allnce, Inc 2014-2016. Woods Ldrshp Awd U So 1989.

LJUNGGREN, Timothy Merle (Mont) 62 Greenway Dr, Goshen IN 46526 **P-in-c Ch Of The Incarn Great Falls MT 2004-** B Tucson AZ 1957 s Philip & Cecelia. BA SUNY 1991; MDiv Bex Sem 1994. D 6/3/1994 P 4/24/1995 Bp Andrew Fairfield. m 5/9/2014 Linda M Ljunggren c 4. S Jn Of The Cross Bristol IN 1997-2004; Trin Ch Milwaukee WI 1994-1997. rector.incarnation@gmail.com

LLERENA FIALLOS, Angel Polivio (EcuC) Apartado 89, Guaranda, Provincia De Bolivar Ecuador **Vic Iglesia Epis Del Ecuador Quito 1990-** B Godranda EC 1967 s Manuel & Isabel. Coll; Sem 3 Yrs. D 5/1/1990 Bp Adrian Delio Caceres-Villavicencio. m 3/12/1981 Maritza Esthela Martinez Dovilar.

LLOYD II, Arthur Selden (Mil) 1104 Mound St Apt A, Madison WI 53715 **Died 8/4/2015** B Osaka JP 1927 s James & Louisa. BA U of Virginia 1950; BD VTS 1956; STM Yale DS 1968; MS U of Wisconsin 1974. D 6/1/1956 Bp Frederick D Goodwin P 12/19/1956 Bp Henry W Hobson. m 9/24/1960 Susan Ellsworth Scherr c 2. Ret 1992-2015; 1978-1991; Com MHE Dio Milwaukee Milwaukee WI 1968-1977, Prov Vic 1968-1976, 1988-1993; S Fran Hse U Epis Ctr Madison WI 1968-1977; St Fran Hse Madison WI 1968-1977, Chapl 1968-1977; Brazil Comp Dioc Com Dio Indianapolis Indianapolis IN 1961-1967, Dept Coll Wk 1961-1964; Asst The Ch of the Redeem Cincinnati OH 1956-1961. Auth, "Freire," *Conscientization & Adult Educ*. Epis Ntwk for Econ Justice 1996; EUC 1980. Phi Beta Kappa.

LLOYD, Bonnie Jean (Tenn) 1420 Wilson Pike, Brentwood TN 37027 **D Ch Of The Gd Shpd Fitchburg MA 2014-** B Oak Park IL 1945 d George & Marion. Dio TN D Sch Sewanee: The U So, TS; BSEdu Nthrn Illinois U 1968; MBA U of Indianapolis 1987. D 1/25/2014 Bp John Bauerschmidt. c 2.

LLOYD, Dennis Calvin (Pa) 811 Dover Rd, Wynnewood PA 19096 B Everett WA 1954 s Calvin & Barbara. BA U of Washington 1977; MDiv Nash 1980. D 8/6/1981 P 6/22/1982 Bp Robert Hume Cochrane. m 6/17/1995 Pamela Satterfield c 3. R Ch Of The H Apos Wynnewood PA 2008-2016; P-in-c Ch Of The H Trin Nashville TN 1991-2008; 1988-1991; Asst S Simon's On The Sound Ft Walton Bch FL 1983-1988; Cur S Andrews Epis Ch Port Angeles WA 1981-1983.

LLOYD, Elizabeth Anne (Chi) 322 Farragut St, Park Forest IL 60466 **D Ch Of The H Fam Pk Forest IL 2002-** B Duluth MN 1937 d Bruce & Margaret. BA U MN 1959. D 2/2/2002 Bp Bill Persell. m 2/23/1963 George Stephen Lloyd c 2. AED (Assn for Epis Deacons) 2001.

LLOYD, Emily A (NY) 487 Hudson St, New York NY 10014 **P The Ch Of S Lk In The Fields New York NY 2014-** B Las Vegas NV 1985 d William & Edith. BA U NC 2008; MDiv Ya Berk 2012. D 9/15/2012 Bp Laura Ahrens P 4/6/2013 Bp James Elliot Curry. m 10/13/2012 Stephen James Lloyd c 1. Calv Ch Stonington CT 2012-2014. elloyd@stlukeinthefields.org

LLOYD, James Edward (NJ) Apdo Postal 803, La Cristsina 50-5, Ajijic CHI-APAS 45920 Mexico B Portland OR 1939 s Cleo & Dorothy. BS Portland St U 1963; BD Nash 1966. D 6/22/1966 Bp James Walmsley Frederic Carman P 12/1/1966 Bp Hal Raymond Gross. m 6/14/2010 Robin Edgar Lawrason. Timber Creek Epis Area Mnstry Gloucester City NJ 1997; Pres Of The Nj Epis Cler Assn 1994-1996; S Lk's Ch Westville NJ 1994-1996; Cmsn On Human Sxlty 1992-1997; Chair - Dioc Aids Taskforce 1986-1994; Liturg Cmsn 1984-1997; Dioc Bicentennial Cmsn 1982-1985; S Barn Ch Burlington NJ 1980-1994; Chair - Ctte Elctns In Pa 1978-1980; Cmsn On Cler Salaries & Pensions 1978-1980; Chair - Cath Fllshp 1978-1979; Secy Of The Dnry 1977-1980; Assoc Ch Of S Lk And Epiph Philadelphia PA 1977-1980; Pres Of The CCU 1977-1978; Dioc Conv Com 1975-1980; Secy Of The CCU 1975-1977; Cur S Clements Ch Philadelphia PA 1974-1977; Ch Of The Epiph Lake Oswego OR 1973-1974; Liturg Cmsn Dio Oregon Portland OR 1973, Dioc Coun 1972-1973, Chair On The Dioc Ecum Com 1971-1973; Asst The Epis Ch Of The Gd

Samar Corvallis OR 1972-1973; Yth Cmsn & Dept Of CE 1968-1971; S Chris's Ch Port Orford OR 1966-1971; Vic S Jn-By-The-Sea Epis Ch Bandon OR 1966-1971; Liturg Cmsn Dio Pennsylvania Philadelphia PA 1984. Chapl Fndr & Patriots Of Amer; CBS, GAS, Epis Actor'S Gld, Chapl Mltry Ord Crusades. Human Awd 1979.

LLOYD, John Janney (NY) 115 Iroquois Rd, Yonkers NY 10710 **Ret 1992-** B Wakayama JP 1920 s James & Louisa. BA U of Virginia 1941; MDiv VTS 1947; MA Harv 1954. D 2/1/1947 Bp Henry St George Tucker P 8/9/1947 Bp Frederick D Goodwin. m 12/19/1953 Elisabeth Lloyd c 5. Vic S Jos's Ch Bronx NY 1998-2000; Int All SS Epis Ch Vlly Cottage NY 1995-1997; P-in-c Metropltn Japanese Mnstry 1994-1997; Int S Jas' Ch No Salem NY 1992-1994; Mssnr Metropltn Japanese Mnstry 1986-1992; S Andr's Epis Ch Hartsdale NY 1986-1991; R Calv Ch Tamaqua PA 1983-1986; R S Jas' Ch Drifton PA 1983-1986; No Lackawanna Vlly Par Olyphant PA 1980-1983; Assoc All SS Ch Worcester MA 1973-1980; R S Andr's Ch Belmont MA 1968-1973; Mssy Dio Kyoto Japan 1947-1968; R S Mary Kyoto Japan 1947-1949.

LLOYD, Kevin Michael (RI) 67 Mount Hope Ave, Jamestown RI 02835 **R S Matt's Par Of Jamestown Jamestown RI 2006-; Mem of Stndg Com Dio Rhode Island Providence RI 2013-, Mem of Cmsn on Congrl Dvlpmt 2010-2012, Secy of Conv 2007-** B Urbana IL 1971 s Harry & Susan. BA Wake Forest U 1993; MDiv VTS 2001. D 6/4/2001 P 11/24/2002 Bp Bob Johnson. m 1/7/2000 Julia A Lloyd c 2. Asst R Ch Of The Ascen Hickory NC 2002-2006; Resrch Asst to Archbp of Cbury Lambeth Palace London Untd Kingdom 2001-2002. The Harris Awd VTS 2001; cl Wake Forest U 1993.

LLOYD, Lucia Kendall (Va) PO Box 158, Tappahannock VA 22560 **R S Steph's Ch Heathsville VA 2008-** B Philadelphia PA 1968 d Wallace & Susan. BA Davidson Coll 1990; MA Yale DS 1994; MA Mid 1995; MDiv VTS 2005. D 6/18/2005 P 12/19/2005 Bp Peter J Lee. m 6/29/1996 Marshall Lloyd c 2. S Thos' Ch Richmond VA 2005-2008; Stndg Com Dio Virginia Richmond VA 2012-2015, GC 1st Alt Dep 2012, Bp Nomin Com 2011-2012, Bp Transition Com 2006-2007.

LLOYD, Mally (Mass) 4 Berkeley Street, Cambridge MA 02138 **Ch Of S Jn The Evang Duxbury MA 2017-; RNL Assoc Plymouth MA 2016-** B Bryn Mawr PA 1953 d Joseph & Margaret. Wheaton Coll 1972; BA Br 1975; Andover Newton TS 1989; MDiv EDS 1996. D 6/5/1996 Bp M(Arvil) Thomas Shaw P 2/8/1997 Bp Arthur Edward Walmsley. m 1/1/2011 Katherine H Ragsdale c 3. Dio Massachusetts Boston MA 2008-2016; Chr Ch Par Plymouth MA 2002-2008; Int Chr Ch Needham Hgts MA 2001, Assoc 1996-2000. EWC 1995; Massachusetts Cler Assn 1996; Philips Brooks Club 2000; Recently Ord Cler, Co-Cnvnr 1998-2009. mallloyd2@aol.com

LLOYD, Robert Baldwin (SwVa) 3204 Mathews Ln., Blacksburg VA 24060 **Ret 1991-** B Nojiri Japan 1926 s James & Louisa. BA U of Virginia 1951; BD VTS 1954; Epis TS in Kentucky 1982; VTS 1983. D 6/4/1954 P 6/1/1955 Bp Robert Fisher Gibson Jr. c 3. S Paul's Mssn Amherst VA 1990-2007; Bd Dir EUC 1983-1988; Com 1980-1983; Natl Cmsn For Soc & Spec Mnstry 1978-1980; Exec Dir Of Apso 1969-1991; EAM Kingsport TN 1969-1991; Chapl VPI Dept Of Coll 1958-1969; Emm Chap Blacksburg VA 1954-1997; M-in-c Ch of the Incarn Mineral VA 1954-1958; Exec Bd Dio SW Virginia Roanoke VA 1990-1992, Exec Bd 1984-1989. Auth, "Poems, Var"; Auth, "Coun Sthrn Moutains In Transition"; Auth, "The Need For Phase-Out Of Strip Mining"; Auth, "Quarterly"; Auth, "Art 1"; Auth, "Plumblines"; Auth, "Admidst Devstatn & Desprtn Appalachians Celebrate Lifes Wholeness"; Auth, "Tn Churchman"; Auth, "Redemp Denied: An Appalachian Rdr"; Auth, "Remembrance"; Auth, "The Return"; Auth, "What Is A Mo?"; Auth, "Alas," *Oh Desecrated Mountains*.

LLOYD III, Samuel Thames (Mass) 206 Clarendon St, Boston MA 02116 **P-in-c Trin Ch Epis Boston MA 2011-, R 1993-2005** B Brookhaven MS 1950 s Samuel & Marie. BA U of Mississippi 1971; MA Geo 1975; PhD U of Virginia 1981; MDiv VTS 1981. D 6/24/1981 P 4/16/1982 Bp Duncan Montgomery Gray Jr. m 7/3/1976 Marguerite M Lloyd c 2. Dn Cathd of St Ptr & St Paul Washington DC 2005-2011; R Ch Of S Paul And The Redeem Chicago IL 1984-1988; S Paul's Memi Charlottesvlle VA 1983-1984; Asst Prof U of Virginia 1981-1984. Auth, *"Gd News for Castaways: Thoughts of a U Chapl,"EvangES Nwsltr*, 1992; Auth, *Var Revs,Journ of Rel, Virginia Sem Journ, Sewanee Theol Revs*. Ord of S Jn 2008. DD VTS 2003; DD U So 1996. slloyd@trinitychurchboston.org

LLOYD, Sharon Lee (Vt) 386South St, Middlebury VT 05753 **Non-par 1993-** B Cincinnati OH 1946 d Dale & Adelaide. MDiv GTS; BA U of Maryland 1970; VTS 1974. D 2/10/1979 P 11/1/1979 Bp Morgan Porteus. m 7/25/1986 Arthur Grindon c 1. Vic S Paul's Epis Ch Wells VT 1991-1993; Asst S Steph's Ch Middlebury VT 1987-1990; Assoc Chr And S Steph's Ch New York NY 1984-1987; Co-R S Andr's Epis Ch Lincoln Pk NJ 1981-1982; S Jn's Ch Stamford CT 1979-1981; Fell The GTS New York NY 1982-1986. Auth, "Var arts".

LLUMIGUANO AREVALO, Nancy (EcuC) Sarmiento, Quito Ecuador **Iglesia Epis Del Ecuador Quito 2012-, 2006-2009; Vicaria Iglesia Epis Del Eduador Catedral El Senor 2006-** B Guarando Bolivar 1977 d Jose & Maria. m 12/25/2004 Mauro Armijos c 1.

LO, Kwan (Los) 133 E Graves Ave, Monterey Park CA 91755 B Hong Kong 1954 s Cheung & Yuk. BD Chung Chi Coll 1984; MBA Sterling U 1991; LLB Lon GB 1999. Trans 12/5/2007 Bp Joseph Jon Bruno. m 8/30/1982 Mei Chung Lau c 2. R S Gabr's Par Monterey Pk CA 2007-2015.

LOBBAN, Andy (Cal) Grace Cathedral, 1100 California St, San Francisco CA 94108 **S Barth's Epis Ch Livermore CA 2016-** B Palo Alto CA 1975 s Peter & Nina. SB MIT 1997; MA U CA 1999; MDiv Epis TS of the SW 2011. D 6/29/2011 Bp David Mitchell Reed. m 6/12/1999 Olga Lobban c 2. Gr Cathd San Francisco CA 2012-2016; Gd Samar Cmnty Serv Dio W Texas San Antonio TX 2011-2012. rector@saintbartslivermore.com

LOBDELL, Gary Thomas (Oly) 2610 E Section St Unit 92, Mount Vernon WA 98274 B Spokane WA 1953 s Harry & Dolores. BS WA SU 1975; MS WA SU 1978; MA Seattle U 1993; MDiv CDSP 2004. D 6/26/2004 Bp Vincent Waydell Warner P 1/8/2005 Bp Charles Franklin Brookhart Jr. m 7/12/1975 Carrie Lobdell c 2. Assoc P S Aid's Epis Ch Stanwood WA 2007-2010; R Ch Of The H Fam Mills River NC 2005-2007; Asst Ch Of The H Sprt Missoula MT 2004-2005.

LOBS, Donna Burkard (CFla) 128 Legacy Dr, Advance NC 27006 **Ret 2002-** B Abingdon PA 1942 d Frank & Lillian. BS E Stroudsburg U 1964. D 12/26/1987 Bp Frank Tracy Griswold III. m 3/21/1964 George Richard Lobs c 4. D Trin Ch Vero Bch FL 2008-2010; D Cathd Ch Of S Lk Orlando FL 1994-2002; D S Mk's Ch Geneva IL 1987-1993. Mourners Path Facility 1999; NAAD 1989; Ord of S Lk 1994; Steph Mnstry 1998.

LOBS III, George Richard (CFla) 128 Legacy Dr, Advance NC 27006 B Philadelphia PA 1942 s George & Marjorie. BS E Stroudsburg U; MDiv PDS; MDiv PDS; DMin Trin-Deerfield; DMin Trin-Deerfield. D 5/25/1968 P 4/20/1969 Bp Frederick Warnecke. m 3/21/1964 Donna Burkard Lobs. P in Charge Trin Ch Vero Bch FL 2008-2012; Dn Cathd Ch Of S Lk Orlando FL 1993-2006; R S Mk's Ch Geneva IL 1979-1993; R S Steph's Epis Ch Mckeesport PA 1973-1979. Auth, "arts".

LOCH, C Louanne (Fla) Holy Trinity Episcopal Church, 100 NE 1st St, Gainesville FL 32601 **R S Paul's By-The-Sea Epis Ch Jaxville Bch FL 2016-; Bd Mem and Pres CEEP Austin TX 2009-** B Charleston SC 1962 d Louis & Frances. BS Mississippi Coll 1983; Mississippi Coll 1991; MDiv VTS 1995; U of Phoenix 2003; Cert U of Notre Dame 2006. D 6/17/1995 Bp Alfred Marble Jr P 2/1/1996 Bp Robert Wilkes Ihloff. m 11/21/1998 Walter Eric Loch. BEC Dio Florida Jacksonville 2010-2013, Fin Com 2013-, Chair, Conv Nomin Com 2010, Exec Com 2009-2010; R H Trin Epis Ch Gainesville FL 2007-2016; R S Jn's Epis Ch Fayetteville NC 2003-2007; S Mths' Epis Ch Baltimore MD 1999-2003; Chapl Garrison Forest Girls Sch 1998-1999; Com on Evang Dio Maryland Baltimore MD 1997-2003, Cmsn on Const and Cn 1996-2000, Bp Com on Chr/Jewish Relatns 1995-1997, Bp Com on Chr/Jewish Relatns 1995-1997; Asst S Thos' Ch Garrison Forest Owings Mills MD 1995-1999; Curs Dio Mississippi Jackson MS 1990, Curs 1990. Curs 1990; Soc S Aid and Hilda 1995.

LOCH, Jerry Lynn (Chi) 446 Somonauk St, Sycamore IL 60178 **D S Ptr 1989-** B Bloomington IL 1945 s Harold & Florence. Eureka Coll 1965; Truman St U 1966; S Lk Hosp Sch Nrsng 1968; S Jn Hosp Sch Anesthesiology 1970; BS Chicago St U 1974; BA Chicago St U 1981; MS Columbia Pacific U 1983; Cert Shalem Inst Washington DC 1984; PhD Emory U 1986; Chicago Deacons Sch 1989. D 12/2/1989 Bp Frank Tracy Griswold III. m 9/18/1977 Kay Lynn Loch c 3.

LOCHER, Elizabeth A (Va) Msalato Theological College, PO Box 264, Dodoma Tanzania Tanzania B Chicago IL 1986 d John & Debra. BA The W&M 2008; MDiv VTS 2012. D 6/2/2012 Bp Ted Gulick Jr P 12/14/2013 Bp Shannon Sherwood Johnston. m 8/21/2010 Benjamin James Locher c 1. Gr Epis Ch Alexandria VA 2013-2016; Exec Coun Appointees New York NY 2012-2013; Dom And Frgn Mssy Soc- Epis Ch Cntr New York NY 2012.

LOCHNER, Charles Nugent (NJ) 2106 5th Ave, Spring Lake NJ 07762 B Utica NY 1944 s Walter & Kathryn. BA La Salette Sem Ipswitch MA 1967; STB CUA 1970; STB Other 1970; MA CUA 1971; MRE S Thos U Houston TX 1973; MS Iona CollegeNew RocelleNY 1985. Rec 5/17/1997 Bp John Shelby Spong. m 6/7/1980 Jeanie M Lochner c 5. R S Ptr's Ch Spotswood NJ 2001-2008; Int Gr Ch Van Vorst Jersey City NJ 2000-2001; Int Ch Of The Atone Tenafly NJ 1997-2000; Co-Fndr/Counslr Hearts and Crafts Counslg Ramsey NJ 1990-2000. Compsr, "Winter In My Life," JC Enterprises, 1986; Compsr, "Just One Man," JC Enterprises, 1986; Contributer, "Being Human in the Face of Death," IBS Press.

LOCK, John Mason (NJ) Trinity Episcopal Church, 65 W Front St, Red Bank NJ 07701 **P-in-c Trin Epis Ch Red Bank NJ 2013-** B Alburquerque NM 1982 s William & Judith. BA U of Delaware 2003; MDiv TESM 2008. D 6/7/2008 Bp William Carl Frey P 5/9/2009 Bp Edward Joseph Konieczny. m 6/10/2006 Bonnie J Lock c 4. Cur All Souls Epis Ch Oklahoma City OK 2008-2013.

LOCKE, Carol Ann (Los) 61 Painter St Apt 1, Pasadena CA 91103 B Buffalo NY 1947 d William & Catherine. BS SUNY 1968; MA Luth TS 1970. D 1/18/2003 Bp John Bailey Lipscomb. c 3. D All SS Par Los Angeles CA 2006-2008; Dir Of Yth Mnstrs S Hilary's Ch Ft Myers FL 2003-2004.

517

LOCKE, Kathleen Newell (Nwk) 15 Norwood Ave, Summit NJ 07901 **P/Chapl VNA Hospice Morristown NJ 2005-; P/Chapl Morristown Meml Hosp Morristown NJ 1999-; P/Chapl Overlook Hosp Summit NJ 1994-** B Raleigh NC 1937 d William & Nell. AB Duke 1959; MDiv Drew U 1995. D 11/1/2003 P 5/15/2004 Bp John Palmer Croneberger. c 2. Chapl St Clare's Hosp Denville/Dover NJ 1997-1999. Assn of Epis Healthcare Chapl 1999.

LOCKE, Ralph Donald (CNY) 11 Orange St, Marcellus NY 13108 **Vic Gr Ch Willowdale Geneva NY 2001-, D 1992-2000** B Geneva NY 1931 s Dayton & Mary. BA SUNY 1987; MDiv Bex Sem 1992. D 6/13/1992 P 1/2/1993 Bp William George Burrill. m 2/19/1955 Nancy Arlene Wright. Vic S Jn's Ch Marcellus NY 1993-2001. Grand Chap New York Masonic Lodge 1994.

LOCKE, William Russell (RI) 63 Pidge Avenue, Pawtucket RI 02860 **Trin Ch N Scituate RI 2016-; S Andr's By The Sea Little Compton RI 2015-** B Erie PA 1953 s Clarence & Joan. U IL 1973; BA U of Massachusetts 1981; MDiv EDS 1986. D 12/27/1993 P 7/9/1994 Bp George Nelson Hunt III. m 8/23/1980 Ethel R Locke c 2. S Ptr's By The Sea Narragansett RI 2014-2015; S Mart's Ch Providence RI 2013-2014; R S Paul's Ch Pawtucket RI 2002-2013; R Ch Of The Gd Shpd Pawtucket RI 1994-2002; Chair, Hisp Mnstry Com Dio Rhode Island Providence RI 2015, Dioc Coun 2010-2015, GC Dep 2006-2015, Stndg Com 2006-2010, GC Dep 2004-2013. Soc Of Cath Priests 2009; Soc of S Marg 1977.

LOCKETT, Donna A (CGC) 102 Shadow Ln, Troy AL 36079 B Brookville PA 1941 D 7/26/2003 P 6/26/2004 Bp Philip Menzie Duncan II. c 2. Ch Of The Epiph Enterprise AL 2008-2011; S Jas Ch Eufaula AL 2004-2005; S Mk's Epis Ch Troy AL 2003.

LOCKETT, Harold J (At) B Houston TX 1954 s Richard & Doris. M.Div C.H. Mason TS; BBA U of Texas @ El Paso, Texas 1981; Dplma in Angl Stds Prog VTS 1984; DMin CH Mason TS 2002. D 4/30/2005 P 11/6/2005 Bp J Neil Alexander. m 12/21/1985 Carol P Marsh-Lockett c 2. Assoc S Paul's Epis Ch Atlanta GA 2013-2014; Cur 2005-2006; Chapl Dio Atlanta Atlanta GA 2006-2013; P-in-c S Tim's Epis Ch Decatur GA 2006-2013; R S Tim's Decatur GA 2006-2010; Chapl/ Dir Absalom Jones Cntr & Chap Atlanta GA 2005-2010. ALPHA PHI ALPHA FRATERNITY, INC 1986.

LOCKETT, Tina Lynn (Pgh) 809 Maplewood Ave, Ambridge PA 15003 **Dn of Stdt and Dir of Admssns TESM Ambridge PA 2005-** B Atlanta GA 1966 d Thomas & Donna. BS Troy U 1988; MEd Troy U 1990; MDiv TESM 2001. D 12/8/2001 P 6/22/2002 Bp Robert William Duncan. TESM Ambridge PA 2005-2009, 2005-2009; Ch Of The Ascen Pittsburgh PA 2002-2005, Asst R 2001-2005.

LOCKHART SR, Ronald Wayne (Pa) PO Box 1330, Malvern PA 19355 **S Mary's Epis Ch Stone Harbor NJ 2000-; 1970-** B Van Buren AR 1931 s William & Reba. BS U of Tulsa 1956; MDiv Crozer TS 1962; U of Pennsylvania 1964; EDS 1966. D 6/11/1966 Bp Robert Lionne DeWitt P 10/1/1966 Bp Albert Ervine Swift. m 7/12/1969 Sandra S Slevin c 1. Chr Ch Media PA 1997-1998; R Ch Of The Redeem Springfield PA 1968-1970; Cur S Paul's Ch Philadelphia PA 1966-1968; Serv Bapt Ch 1961-1965.

LOCKLEY, Linda Sue (SwFla) 6006 Braden Run, Bradenton FL 34202 B New Castle PA 1955 d Robert & Joanne. BA Eckerd Coll; AA Manatee Cmnty Coll. D 6/20/1993 Bp Rogers Sanders Harris. m 4/5/1975 Wayne Stanley Buckner c 3.

LOCKWOOD II, Frank Robert (Alb) 14 Spencer Blvd, Coxsackie NY 12051 B Cornwall NY 1968 s Frank & Susan Anne. AA Herkimer Cnty Cmnty Coll 1991. D 5/10/2008 P 4/1/2012 Bp William Howard Love. m 9/6/1997 Joanne Charlene Lockwood c 2.

LOCKWOOD, Marcia Miller (ECR) PO Box 345, Carmel Valley CA 93924 **Godly Play Trnr Dio El Camino Real Monterey CA 2011-; Assoc P S Dunst's Epis Ch Carmel CA 2008-** B Kalamazoo MI. 1936 d Rudel & Elizabeth. BS NWU 1958; MDiv CDSP 1983. D 12/27/1987 P 6/29/1988 Bp Donald Purple Hart. m 6/21/1958 George S Lockwood c 4. COM Dio El Camino Real Monterey CA 2002-2008; Alum Counsel CDSP Berkeley CA 1997-2001; Assoc Ch of S Mary's by the Sea Pacific Grove CA 1992-2008; Cn S Andr's Cathd Honolulu HI 1988-1991; Founding Pres Hospice of Kona 1985-1987.

LODDER, Herbert Kingsley (Md) 130 W Seminary Ave, Lutherville MD 21093 **Exec Dir Pstr Counselling Serv of Maryland 2010-** B Syracuse NY 1933 s Clifford & Eleanor. BA Duke 1955; MDiv VTS 1958; MA GW 1967; MPA U of Baltimore 1980; MS Loyola Coll 1986. D 6/16/1958 Bp Malcolm E Peabody P 11/21/1959 Bp Walter M Higley. m 2/2/1980 Frances Lodder c 5. Chapl Johns Hopkins Bayview Med Cntr 2004-2009; Assoc R Ch Of The H Comf Luthvle Timon MD 1994-2000; Vic Ch Of The Resurr Baltimore MD 1982-1992; Exec Dir JHU Sch of Med Resrch Unit 1980-2004; Var Epis Ch -substitution 1980-1982; Exec Dir Mantra Drug Counselling Cntr 1975-1980; Assoc R S Jn's Ch Ellicott City MD 1973-1974; Asst to the R S Andr's Epis Ch Arlington VA 1962-1972; Mssy S Andr's Ch Evans Mills NY 1958-1962. ESCRU 1968-1972. Outstanding Serv Awd MD Drug Abuse Admin 1984.

LODER, Debra Jayne (Az) D 6/10/2017 Bp Kirk Stevan Smith.

LODWICK, James Nicholas (NY) 925 W Washington St, South Bend IN 46601 B Cincinnati OH 1938 s Edward & Virginia. BA Ya 1960; BD EDS 1963; MA U of Notre Dame 1994. D 6/9/1968 Bp Roger W Blanchard P 12/13/1968 Bp Russell T Rauscher. Hisp Mssnr Dio Nthrn Indiana So Bend IN 2003; Int S Jas' Epis Ch Goshen IN 1999-2000; Int S Alb's Epis Ch Ft Wayne IN 1998; Vstng Lectr GTS 1997; Vstng Lectr Yale-Berk New Haven CT 1997; Assoc S Mich And All Ang Ch So Bend IN 1991-1997; Assoc S Jas Ch New York NY 1984-1991; The Ch of S Matt And S Tim New York NY 1979-1984; R The Ch of S Edw The Mtyr New York NY 1976-1979, Cur 1969-1972; Dio New York New York NY 1968-1977. CBS 1972; Soc of Cath Priests 2011.

LOEFFLER, George C (Be) 46 Wessnersville Rd, Kempton PA 19529 **Died 10/28/2016** B Orange NJ 1931 s George & Ethel. BA Leh 1953. D 11/18/1967 Bp Leland Stark. m 11/23/2016 Barbara Knaebel Bowen c 2. Chapl to the Ordnry Dio Bethlehem Bethlehem PA 1966-2016.

LOESCHER, Candyce Jean (Ky) St. Mark's Episcopal Church, 2822 Frankfort Ave, Louisville KY 40206 **S Mk's Epis Ch Louisville KY 2016-; VP, Trst & Coun Dio Kentucky Louisville KY 2013-, Pres of Stndg Com 2010-2012, Dn Four Rivers Dnry 2009-2014, Trst & Coun 2008-2009, Co Chair, Mssn Funding 2008-** B St Louis MO 1949 d Gene & Dorothy. BFA Memphis Coll of Art 1979; MDiv VTS 2007. D 12/21/2006 Bp J Neil Alexander P 9/29/2007 Bp Ted Gulick Jr. m 9/5/1987 Warren S Loescher. R S Mary's Ch Madisonville KY 2007-2016.

LOEWE, Richard (Los) 1907 W West Wind, Santa Ana CA 92704 **Ret 1987-** B Chicago IL 1913 s Sidney & Olga. ETSBH; JD Loyola U; NWU. D 9/12/1970 Bp Francis E I Bloy P 3/1/1971 Bp Victor Manuel Rivera. m 8/2/1947 Jane Wilson. Non-par 1974-1987; Assoc S Steph's Par Whittier CA 1970-1974.

LOFGREN, Claire (NY) St. Joseph of Arimathea, 2172 Saw Mill River Road, White Plains NY 10607 **P-in-c The Ch Of S Jos Of Arimathea White Plains NY 2013-, Int 2008-2009** B Oakland CA 1954 d Edward & Lenore. BA U CA 1976; Tchr Cert Mills Coll 1985; MDiv CDSP 1989; CTh U of Durham GB 1989; STM Sewanee: The U So, TS 1995. Trans 1/8/1993 Bp Bertram Nelson Herlong. Dio New York New York NY 2010-2013; S Paul's Ch Sprg Vlly NY 2010-2013; Assoc S Jn's Ch Cornwall NY 2004-2008; Assoc EDS Cambridge MA 1999-2003; Soc Of St Marg Duxbury MA 1998-2003; AssociateRector Jn's Epis Ch Charleston WV 1995-1998; Assoc Otey Memi Par Ch Sewanee TN 1994-1995; Serv Ch of Engl 1990-1993. Auth, "Sprtl Formation For Priesthood," *Sewanee Theol Revs,* U So, 1996. Convenor, SOSc No Amer Chapters 1998-2007; Epis Ch Ntwk on Sci Tech and Faith 1993; Soc of Ord Scientists (SOSc) 1991; Sprtl Dir Intl 1994-2006. revclofgren@yahoo.com

LOFMAN, Donald Stig (NY) 12 Depot St, Middletown NY 10940 **Assoc Gr 1990-** B Alexandria VA 1944 D 4/14/1973 Bp James Winchester Montgomery. c 1. D Ch Of The Resurr Hopewell Jct NY 2001-2003.

LOGAN, Christie Larson (Oly) 720 E Road Of Tralee, Shelton WA 98584 **S Hugh Of Lincoln Allyn WA 2003-** B Philadelphia PA 1942 D 11/30/2002 P 6/10/2003 Bp Sanford Zangwill Kaye Hampton. c 3.

LOGAN, Jeffery Allen (FtW) Psc 817 Box 43, Fpo AE 09622 **Off Of Bsh For ArmdF New York NY 2000-** B Fort Riley KS 1956 s Robert & Jeanne. BA DePauw U 1978; MDiv Epis TS of the SW 1983. D 8/14/1983 P 6/24/1984 Bp Archibald Donald Davies. m 9/4/1993 Anne Elizabeth Logan. R S Paul's Epis Ch Gainesville TX 1996-2000; R S Lk's Ch Mineral Wells TX 1989-1994; Vic Our Lady Of The Lake Clifton TX 1986-1989; Dio Ft Worth Ft Worth TX 1985-1989; R S Mk's Ch Bridgeport CT 1985-1986; Cur S Tim's Ch Ft Worth TX 1983-1985. CCU; ESA; Mltry Chapl Assn; SSC. Who'S Who In Rel 1987.

LOGAN JR, John Alexander (Tex) 2808 Sunset Blvd, Houston TX 77005 B La Grange TX 1928 s John & Juanita. BA U of Texas 1948; JD U of Texas 1950; MDiv VTS 1953; MA U of Virginia 1979. D 7/2/1953 P 7/1/1954 Bp John Elbridge Hines. Cn Emer Chr Ch Cathd Houston TX 2000, 1982-1996; Cn to Ordnry Dio Texas Houston TX 1996-2000, Ret-Cn Emer 2000-, Stndg Com 1994-1997, Secy 1986-; The Great Cmsn Fndt Houston TX 1996-1997; Chapl S Lk Hosp 1980-1982; S Lk's Epis Hosp Houston TX 1980-1981; S Jas' Epis Ch La Grange TX 1980; Asst The Ch of the Gd Shpd Austin TX 1965-1977, Asst 1953-1955; P-in-C S Tim Waco TX 1955-1965. Auth, "Dowered w Gifts," 1989.

LOGAN, Linda Marie (CNY) 405 N Madison Ave, Pierre SD 57501 **Trin Ch Boonville NY 2009-** B Honolulu HI 1951 d John & Norma. BA Idaho St U 1972; MA Van 1974; MDiv CDSP 1997. D 1/12/1997 P 7/12/1997 Bp John Stuart Thornton. Headwaters Epis Mssn Boonville NY 2003-2009; Cntrl Dn Dio So Dakota Pierre SD 2000-2003, Dioc Yth Coun 1998-2000; Assoc R Trin Epis Ch Pierre SD 1997-2003; Dio E Tennessee Knoxville TN 1986-1990. Ed, "The E Tennessee Epis," Associated Ch Press, 1990. Epis Cmnctr; Pierre/Ft Pierre Min. Rel Jrnlst Of The Year Tennessee Assn Of Ch 1990; Honorable Mention For Great Excellence The E Tennessee Epis Associated Ch Press 1990; Polly Bond Awd ECom 1987.

LOGAN, Michael Dennis (Alb) St Mark's Church, P.O. Box 331, Malone NY 12953 **Died 7/24/2016** B Ogdensburg NY 1955 s Earl & Marjorie. AAS Suny Canton 1985. D 6/11/2005 Bp Daniel William Herzog. m 8/31/2016 Paula Logan c 3. S Mk's Ch Malone NY 2008-2013.

LOGAN, William Stevenson (Mich) 1514 Chateaufort Pl, Detroit MI 48207 B Detroit MI 1920 s William & Evelyn. BS U of Pennsylvania 1941; MA Chrysler

Inst of Engr Detroit MI 1943; BD EDS 1951; MA U MI 1980. D 6/30/1951 Bp Richard Stanley Merrill Emrich P 12/30/1951 Bp Russell S Hubbard. m 12/1/1951 Mary Adelaide Logan c 1. Actg Dn Cathd Ch Of S Paul Detroit MI 1993-1995, Exec VP Cathd Fndt 1985-1992; CODE Strng Com Dio Michigan Detroit MI 1980-1983, Archd 1973-1985, Pres MI Cmsn UMHE 1970-2002, VP Michigan Coun Chairman 1969-1972, Exec Dir Dept Prog 1963-1973, Chair Dept CSR 1960-1968; R S Mart Ch Detroit MI 1952-1963; Asst Chr Ch Detroit MI 1951-1952. CODE. Hon Cn S Paul Cathd 1968.

LOGAN JR, Willis (Va) 100 W Jefferson St, Charlottesville VA 22902 **S Mk's Ch Fincastle VA 2017-** B Roanoke VA 1978 s George & Helen. BA Mid 2001; MSL Geo 2008; MDiv Duke Div 2014; MDiv Duke DS 2014. D 6/7/2014 Bp Shannon Sherwood Johnston. m 6/12/2004 Ashley F Logan c 3. Chr Epis Ch Charlottesvlle VA 2014-2016.

LOGAN, Yvonne Luree (NY) 1185 Park Ave Apt 12j, New York NY 10128 B Los Angeles CA 1960 d Samuel & Mary. BA U CA Los Angeles 1983; MS London Sch of Econ London Engl 1991; MDiv UTS 2004. D 3/11/2006 P 9/23/2006 Bp Mark Sean Sisk. m 9/30/1994 Martin Luree Sankey c 2.

LOGSDON, Tami Davis (NwT) 4207 Emil Ave, Amarillo TX 79106 B Amarillo TX 1957 d Max & Sandra. Amarillo Coll; TCU; W Texas A&M U. D 10/29/1999 Bp C Wallis Ohl. D S Andr's Ch Amarillo TX 1999-2000.

LOGUE, Frank (Ga) 111 Clinton Ct, Saint Marys GA 31558 **Cn Dio Georgia Savannah GA 2010-, 2000-2007** B Montgomery AL 1963 s Thomas & Judy. BA Georgia Sthrn U 1984; MDiv VTS 2000. D 2/5/2000 P 8/26/2000 Bp Henry Irving Louttit. m 9/7/1985 Victoria S Logue c 1. King Of Peace Kingsland GA 2008-2010. flogue@gaepiscopal.org

LOGUE, Mary Ann Willson (Ct) 173 Livingston St, New Haven CT 06511 **Ret 1994-** B Clinton MA 1927 d Edward & Ruth. BA Smith 1948; MDiv Ya Berk 1985. D 6/13/1987 Bp Arthur Edward Walmsley P 3/18/1988 Bp Clarence Nicholas Coleridge. m 6/10/1950 Frank Logue. Assoc Chr Ch New Haven CT 1998-2002; Assoc P Ch of the H Sprt W Haven CT 1996-1998; Assoc S Jn's Epis Par Waterbury CT 1990-1994; Asst Chr Ch Stratford CT 1987-1990. Ord Of S Helena 1995.

LOHMANN, John J (Mich) 296 Ackerson Lake Dr., Jackson MI 49201 **P S Andr's Epis Ch Livonia MI 2009-** B Detroit MI 1933 s Peter & Elisabeth. BA U So 1959; MDiv Sewanee: The U So, TS 1962; MBA Ohio U 1982. D 6/29/1962 Bp Hamilton Hyde Kellogg P 1/1/1963 Bp William R Moody. c 3. Int S Andr's Epis Ch Valparaiso IN 2007-2008; Yoked Par S Jn's Ch Clinton MI 2004-2007; R S Ptr's Ch Tecumseh MI 1998-2005; R Sprt of Gr Luth Epis Ch W Bloomfield MI 1969-1976; Ch Of Our Sav Gallatin TN 1964-1968; Yoked Par S Jos Of Arimathaea Ch Hendersonvlle TN 1964-1968; Cur Chr Ch Cathd Lexington KY 1962-1964. Amer Soc for Quality 1976-1996; Mensa. Assoc Alum Nash 2010; Cert Relibility Engr ASQC 1982; Cert Quality Engr ASQC 1979; Acad of Par Cler Founding Pres 1969; Phi Beta Kappa; Who's Who In Sci & Engr.

LOHSE, Dana May (Wyo) Po Box 291, Kaycee WY 82639 B Buffalo WY 1930 d Daniel & Eva. BA U of Wyoming 1971. D 7/11/1997 Bp William Harvey Wolfrum P 6/1/1998 Bp Bruce Caldwell. m 11/24/1952 Glen Raymond Lohse.

LOKEN, Gail Mitchell (Ak) 5101 Omalley Rd, Anchorage AK 99507 **Chr Ch Anchorage AK 2012-** B Santa Monica CA 1954 d Malcolm & Joan. BS U of Puget Sound 1976; Tchr Cert U of Washington 1979; MDiv Vancouver TS 2014. D 10/22/2011 P 6/1/2013 Bp Mark A Lattime. m 5/30/1977 Alan K Loken c 2. S Ptr's Ch Seward AK 2014-2016.

LOKEY, Michael Paul (Eas) 29618 Polks Rd, Princess Anne MD 21853 **S Paul's Marion Sta Princess Anne MD 2005-** B Yakima WA 1946 D 9/15/2001 Bp Martin Gough Townsend P 10/2/2002 Bp Charles Lindsay Longest. m 6/22/1973 Viola Mae Wagner c 3. mplokey@gmail.com

LOLCAMA, Thirza A (Oly) 10630 Gravelly Lake Dr SW, Lakewood WA 98499 B Yakima WA 1941 d Edward & Helen. D 10/17/2009 Bp Gregory Harold Rickel. m 12/18/1960 Robert C Lolcama c 2. D S Mary's Ch Lakewood WA 2012-2013.

LOLK, Otto Lothar Manfred (Pa) 3135 Clark Ave, Trevose PA 19053 B Bremen Germany 1936 s Otto & Elsie. BA Montclair St U 1969; MDiv GTS 1973; PhD Iona Coll 1979; MA Blanton-Peale Grad Inst 1985. D 6/9/1973 Bp Leland Stark P 12/16/1973 Bp George E Rath. c 3. Pres Rhawnhurst Min 1991-2008; All SS Ch Rhawnhurst Philadelphia PA 1985-2008; R S Ptr's Epis Ch Livingston NJ 1981-1985; R Ch Of S Mary The Vrgn Ridgefield Pk NJ 1975-1981; Asst R S Paul's Epis Ch Paterson NJ 1973-1975. Ord Of S Jn The Bapt - Menham, NJ 1970.

LOMAS, Bruce Alan (Mass) 3 Gould St, Melrose MA 02176 **R Trin Par Melrose MA 2001-** B Providence RI 1952 s Herbert & Dorothy. BA Rhode Island Coll 1989; MDiv VTS 1992. D 6/20/1992 Bp George Nelson Hunt III P 1/1/1993 Bp Edward Lewis Lee Jr. m 6/2/1973 Jane Lomas c 2. S Barn Ch Wilmington DE 1998-2001; R S Mich's Aubrn ME 1995-1998; The Par of S Mich's Auburn ME 1995-1998; Gr Ch Grand Rapids MI 1992-1995; Asst To R Grand Rapids MI 1992-1995.

LOMBARDO, Janet Marie Vogt (NH) 67 Ridge Rd, Concord NH 03301 **Trin Ch Claremont NH 2015-** B Park Ridge NJ 1959 d Victor & Marie. VTS; BA Rutgers The St U of New Jersey 1981; MEd Rutgers The St U of New Jersey 1983; MDiv EDS 1997. D 2/15/1998 P 12/1/1998 Bp Douglas Edwin Theuner. m 8/6/1983 Mark Anthony Lombardo c 2. S Paul's Ch Lancaster NH 2013-2015; S Barn Ch Berlin NH 2013; Ch Of S Jn The Evang Dunbarton NH 2011; S Andr's Ch New London NH 2008-2011; Cur Trin Epis Ch Tilton NH 1998-2005.

LONDON OHC, Daniel Deforest (Los) 2451 Ridge Rd, Berkeley CA 94709 **Chr Ch Sausalito CA 2015-; Epis Sch For Deacons Berkeley CA 2013-** B Stanford CA 1983 s Robert & Janet. Cert of Angl Stds CDSP; Bachelor of Arts Westmont Coll; MA Fuller TS 2008; PhD Grad Theol Un 2016. D 6/8/2013 Bp Joseph Jon Bruno P 1/11/2014 Bp Mary Douglas Glasspool. m 5/20/2016 Ashley London Bacchi. CDSP Berkeley CA 2013-2014; Ch Of Our Sav Par San Gabr CA 2007-2009. Auth, "Judging God: Lrng from the Jewish Tradition of Protest Against God," *Journ of Comparative Theol*, 2016; Auth, ""Pray Interly": Julian of Norwich's Sprtlty of Pryr," *Compass: A Revs of Topical Theol*, 2015; Auth, "Bk Revs," *ATR*, 2013. AAR 2010; Coll Theol Soc 2010; Colloquium on Violence and Rel 2012; Sigma Tau Delta Engl hon Soc 2005; Soc for the Study of Chr Sprtlty 2010. Raymund Schwager Best Paper Awd Colloquium on Violence and Rel 2013; Most Outstanding Rel Stds Stdt Awd Westmont Coll 2005. vicar.redeemer@gmail.com

LONDON, Gary Loo (Los) 122 S California Ave, Monrovia CA 91016 **Asst S Thos The Apos Hollywood Los Angeles CA 2013-** B Burley ID 1940 s Loo & Maycelle. MDiv SWTS 1991. D 6/15/1991 P 1/1/1992 Bp Frederick Houk Borsch. R S Lk's Epis Ch Monrovia CA 1995-2011; Trin Par Fillmore CA 1993-1995; S Bede's Epis Ch Los Angeles CA 1991-1992.

LONE, Jose Francisco (Hond) **Dio Honduras San Pedro Sula 2006-; Iglesia Epis Hondurena San Pedro Sula 2006-** B Copan Honduras 1973 s Francisco & Amelia. ThD Programa Diocesano Educ Teologica 2003. D 10/28/2005 Bp Lloyd Emmanuel Allen. m 8/9/2002 Cori Vanessa Vanessa Sanchez Irias c 2.

LONERGAN, Kathleen Guthrie (Mass) 119 Washington Street, c/o St James Episcopal Church, Groveland MA 01834 **S Jas Ch Groveland Groveland MA 2014-** B New York NY 1979 d Michael & Roxana. BA Tufts U 2001; MDiv Harvard DS 2005; Dip Ang Stud GTS 2008. D 6/6/2009 Bp M(Arvil) Thomas Shaw. m 10/6/2012 Christopher M Kowaleski c 1. Asst R Par Of Chr Ch Andover MA 2011-2014; Non-stipendiary Assoc Trin Par of Newton Cntr Newton Cntr MA 2010-2011; Dir of Yth Mnstrs Dio Massachusetts Boston MA 2009-2011, Disciplinary Com Mem 2010-, Conv Strng Com 2009-. sjcgclergy@gmail.com

LONERGAN, Robert Thomas (Ore) 601 Taylor St, Myrtle Creek OR 97457 **Vic Ch Of The Ascen Riddle OR 1992-** B Aberdeen WA 1935 s Robert & Angeline. Oregon Sch of Rel; BA Linfield Coll 1963; MA Linfield Coll 1972; U So 1992. D 1/27/1984 Bp Matthew Paul Bigliardi P 8/25/1992 Bp Robert Louis Ladehoff. m 9/23/1961 Loris C Townsend c 1. Ch Of The H Sprt Sutherlin OR 1992-2011.

LONERGAN, Wallace Gunn (Ida) 812 E Linden St, Caldwell ID 83605 **Assoc S Dav's Epis Ch Caldwell ID 1997-; Assoc Dio Idaho Boise ID 1997-** B Potlatch ID 1928 s Willis & Lois. AA Lower Columbia Coll 1948; BA The Coll of Idaho 1950; MBA U Chi 1955; PhD U Chi 1960. D 2/23/1997 P 11/30/1997 Bp John Stuart Thornton. m 2/17/2007 Joan Penoyer. Auth, "Mnstry & Higher Educ," *Advance*; Auth, "Ldrshp Trng & Its Role in Ch," *Ch Educ Finding*. Vstng Schlr Intl Angl Exch Prog Rikkyo U.

LONERGAN JR, Willis Gerald (Oly) 6114 E Evergreen Blvd, Vancouver WA 98661 **Assoc S Lk's Epis Ch Vancouver WA 1998-, 1972-1998, Asst 1951-1971; Ret 1989-** B Nampa ID 1924 s Willis & Lois. BA U of Washington 1949; Cert CDSP 1951; MA U of Detroit Mercy 1975. D 6/29/1951 P 11/1/1952 Bp Stephen F Bayne Jr. m 6/26/1948 Geraldine Evelyn Lonergan. All SS Epis Ch Pontiac MI 1983-1989; Exec Asst to Bp Dio Michigan Detroit MI 1974-1985, ExCoun 1973-1984, Secy Dioc Conv 1973-1984, Assoc Dir Dept Prog 1966-1973; Chair DeptCE S Steph's Epis Ch Spokane WA 1961-1964; Epis Ch Of The Redeem Republic WA 1956-1961; Vic S Jn's Epis Ch Colville WA 1956-1961; Vic S Matthews Auburn WA 1954-1956; Vic S Anne Camas WA 1951-1954; Dio Spokane Spokane WA 1961-1964. Assn of Rel and Applied Behavioral Sci; CODE.

LONG, Amy Laurel (WK) B Silver Spring, MD 1982 Bachelor of Arts Hanover Coll 2005; Mstr of Div PrTS 2008. D 12/12/2015 P 12/10/2016 Bp Mike Milliken. m 12/28/2013 Brandon Long.

LONG, Benjamin Isaac (Tex) 1941 Webberville Rd, Austin TX 78721 B Rockford IL 1977 s Michael & Cheri. MDiv Epis TS Of The SW 2012; MDiv Epis TS of the SW 2012. Trans 2/4/2010 as Priest Bp C Andrew Doyle. m 1/1/2005 Amy E Wright. S Jas Ch Austin TX 2011-2012.

LONG, Beth (At) 165 Meredith Ridge Rd, Athens GA 30605 B Nicosia CY 1952 d Melvin & L Jeanne. BA U Tor 1974; MA U of St Michaels Coll 1980; U So 1989; VTS 1990. D 6/15/1991 P 1/11/1992 Bp Ronald Hayward Haines. c 3. R S Greg The Great Athens GA 2006-2016; R Trin Ch Lakeville CT 1999-2006; Vic S Jn's Ch Ashfield MA 1992-1999; Chapl Phila Presb Hosp 4 Chapls 1991-1992; Dre S Dunst's Epis Ch Beth MD 1991-1992. Human Relatns Cmsn Ashfield Ma.

LONG, Betty Ann (WMass) 2 Viking Ln, Sandwich MA 02563 B Vintondale PA 1946 d Albert & Sue. BS Rhode Island Coll 1969; MDiv EDS 1985. D 6/1/1985 P 6/14/1986 Bp John Bowen Coburn. c 2. P-in charge Trin Epis Ch Shrewsbury MA 2007-2012; Int R S Cyp's Epis Ch Hampton VA 2005-2007; Assoc R Ch Of The Epiph Norfolk VA 2005; Int R S Steph's Ch Newport News VA 2002-2005; Assoc R S Jn's Ch Hampton VA 2001-2002; Assoc R Hickory Neck Ch Toano VA 1998-1999; Vic S Simon's-By-The-Sea Virginia Bch VA 1994-1995; Assoc R S Mart's Epis Ch Williamsburg VA 1990-1994; Asst R The Ch Of The Gd Shpd Acton MA 1985-1989. Int Mnstry Int Mnstry Ntwk 2002.

LONG, Cynthia A (NCal) 7041 Verdure Way, Elk Grove CA 95758 **S Matt's Epis Ch Sacramento CA 2014-, D 2008-2013, D 2007-; D S Mich's Epis Ch Carmichael CA 2014-; Dir Coleman Hlth Outreach at St Matt's CRC 2008-** B Vallejo CA 1954 d William & Patricia. RN S Lk Sch of Nrsng 1979; BD H Name U 2002; BA Sch for Deacons 2007. D 6/9/2007 Bp Barry Leigh Beisner. m 7/1/1979 Mark Long c 2.

LONG, Eric (SwVa) PO Box 257, Roanoke VA 24002 **S Jn's Ch Roanoke VA 2014-** B Milton FL 1971 s John & Edna. BA U of Memphis 1993; MDiv Nazarene TS 1996; CAS Sewanee: The U So, TS 1999. D 6/26/1999 P 1/15/2000 Bp Barry Howe. m 12/25/1993 Shelley R Henderson-Long c 2. R S Chris's Ch Pensacola FL 2007-2014; Founding P St Mary Magd Epis Ch Loch Lloyd MO 2006-2007; Assoc S Anne's Ch Lees Summit MO 1999-2001. elong@stjohnsroanoke.org

LONG, Gail (SVa) 2441 Tuxedo Pl, Albany GA 31707 B Fort Benning GA 1944 d Jay & Elizabeth. BS U CO 1968; MS California St U 1981; MDiv TESM 2000. D 9/23/2000 P 5/22/2001 Bp Dorsey Henderson. c 1. R S Geo's Epis Ch Newport News VA 2005-2010; Coordntr - Cbury Way Dio Upper So Carolina Columbia SC 2004-2005; Int R Gr Epis Ch Anderson SC 2002-2004; Asst To The R S Chris's Ch Spartanburg SC 2000-2002. Auth, "Personal Sprtlty And BCP," *Crosswalk*, Dio Upper So Carolina, 1999. Cbury Way 2000; Christians For Biblic Equality 1998.

LONG II, John Michael (Neb) 1615 Brent Blvd, Lincoln NE 68506 **D Ch Of The H Trin Lincoln NE 2004-** B Lincoln NE 1961 s John & Marilyn. U of Nebraska 1994. D 8/1/2004 Bp Joe Goodwin Burnett. m 4/25/1998 Mary Lu Long c 2.

LONG OSB, Lewis Harvey (Az) 28 W Pasadena Ave, Phoenix AZ 85013 **Died 3/2/2017** B Denver MO 1931 s Lewis & Lavina. BA U of Missouri 1951; STB GTS 1957. D 6/21/1957 P 12/21/1957 Bp Edward Clark Turner. Assoc R All SS Ch Phoenix AZ 1995-2000; S Mary's Epis Ch Phoenix AZ 1959-1993; R S Jn's Ch Abilene KS 1957-1959. Ord of S Ben.

LONG, Robert Carl (WMo) 4301 Madison Ave Apt 218, Kansas City MO 64111 B Chicago IL 1927 s Carl & D Irene. BA U of Kansas 1949; MD U of Kansas 1953. D 12/20/1986 Bp John Forsythe Ashby. m 9/2/1950 Ellen O Long c 4.

LONG, Shirley Dube (WNC) Po Box 72, Deep Gap NC 28618 **D Par Of The H Comm Glendale Sprg NC 1999-** B Miami FL 1944 d Raymond & Margaret. BS Florida St U 1966; MA Appalachian St U 1969. D 12/18/1999 Bp Bob Johnson. m 4/8/1980 Donald Finley Long.

LONG, Thomas Mcmillen (Colo) 4155 E Jewell Ave Ste 1117, Denver CO 80222 B Denver CO 1949 s Lawrence & Elizabeth. BA U Denv 1972; MDiv VTS 1975. D 1/5/1975 P 9/1/1975 Bp William Carl Frey. c 1. Assoc The Ch Of The Ascen Denver CO 2002-2011; Assoc S Tim's Epis Ch Littleton CO 1995-2001; Non-par 1989-1995; Assoc Chr Epis Ch Denver CO 1984-1988; R S Barth's Ch Estes Pk CO 1978-1984; Cur Ch Of The Ascen Pueblo CO 1975-1978. AAPC.

LONGACRE, Seth T (Cal) 4171 Parkside Pl, Carlsbad CA 92008 **Mem Dio California Dept. Of Wrld Missions 2005-** B Tarrytown NY 1962 s Jay & Ada. BA U Chi 1983; MBA Golden Gate U 1990; MLa Naropa U 1999; BA Sch for Deacons 2004; DMin U of Creation Sprtlty Oakland CA 2006. D 12/4/2004 Bp William Edwin Swing. D St. Bede's Epis Ch 2004-2006.

LONGBOTTOM, Rob (CFla) 3891 Cedar Hammock Trl, Saint Cloud FL 34772 **The Ch Of S Lk And S Ptr S Cloud FL 2013-** B Techachapi CA 1974 s David & Kendal. BA U CA 1997; MDiv TESM 2002. D 2/16/2002 P 9/21/2002 Bp David Mercer Schofield. m 4/2/2005 Amee M Longbottom c 3. R S Jn's Ch Ogdensburg NY 2005-2013; Asst S Paul's Epis Ch Visalia CA 2002-2005; CPE Intern Chld's Hosp Los Angeles 2001; GC Alt Dio Albany Greenwich NY 2009; Dioc Coun Epis Dio Albany 2008-2011. Pi Sigma Alpha 1997.

LONGE, Neal Patrick (Alb) 58 Reber St, Colonie NY 12205 **Chapl Fraternal Ord of Police Albany NY 2017-; Chapl Amsterdam Fire Dept Amsterdam NY 2014-; Chapl Montgomery Cnty Emergency Mgmt Fonda NY 2012-; R S Ann's Ch Amsterdam NY 2012-; Chr the King Cntr Bd Mem Dio Albany Greenwich NY 2016-, Dn - Wstrn Mohawk Dnry 2013-2016** B Albany NY 1979 s Patrick & Sherry. BMus SUNY Coll at Potsdam 2001; AAS Fulton-Montgomery Cmnty Coll 2006; MA S Marys Sem & U Baltimore 2006; Dip Ang Stud TESM 2010. D 5/30/2009 P 6/30/2010 Bp William Howard Love. m 11/27/2004 Lisa M Verville c 2. Cur S Mich's Albany NY 2010-2011; D Intern Chr Ch Schenectady NY 2009-2010.

✠ LONGEST, The Rt Rev Charles Lindsay (Md) 7200 3rd Ave., C-035, Sykesville MD 21784 B Catonsville MD 1933 s George & Mamie. BA U of Maryland

1956; MDiv Ya Berk 1959; DD Ya Berk 1989. D 6/26/1959 Bp Noble C Powell P 4/5/1960 Bp Harry Lee Doll Con 10/14/1989 for Md. m 6/9/1956 Barbara H Longest c 2. Asstg Bp Dio Easton Easton MD 2001-2003; Bp Suffr of Md Dio Maryland Baltimore MD 1989-1997, Ret Bp Suffr of Md 1998-, Chair Dioc Com Mssn 1972-1983; R Ch Of The H Cross Cumberland MD 1973-1989; Vic Epis Ch Of Chr The King Baltimore MD 1963-1973; Asst S Barth's Ch Baltimore MD 1960-1973; Asst H Trin Epis Ch Essex MD 1959-1960. ASSP 1962; OHC 1962. DD Berk 1989.

LONGHI, Anthony Peter (Chi) 1850 Landre Ct, Burlington WI 53105 B New Rochelle NY 1947 s Peter & Concetta. BA Concordia Coll 1980; MDiv TESM 1985. D 1/26/1985 P 7/27/1985 Bp Alden Moinet Hathaway. m 5/7/2011 Julie P Babenko-Longhi c 1. S Jn's Epis Ch Mt Prospect IL 2002-2003; R S Paul's Ch Mchenry IL 1993-2002; P-in-c Ch of SS Thos and Lk Patton PA 1985-1993; Chapl Ebersburg Cntr Ebersburg PA 1985-1993; S Thos Ch Nthrn Cambria PA 1985-1993. Auth, *The Cord.*

LONGHITANO, Maria Vittoria (Eur) via Benevenuto Cellini 24, Corsico MI 20094 Italy B Enna Italy 1974 d Antonio & Graziella. MD Fac of Philosphy 2001. Rec 10/17/2013 as Priest Bp Pierre W Whalon. m 4/7/2007 Andrea Lanza.

LONGO, John Alphonsus (Haw) 9901 N Oracle Rd, Apt 8103, Tuscon AZ 97062 **Died 2/1/2016** B Brooklyn NY 1936 s John & Margaret. BA USC 1980; S Jn Coll GB 1981; MDiv TESM 1983. D 12/9/1986 Bp Robert Hume Cochrane P 10/1/1987 Bp Robert Louis Ladehoff. m 5/8/1993 Barbara Dailey c 2. S Mary's Epis Ch Honolulu HI 1995-1999; Dio Oregon Portland OR 1991-1995; S Jn's Epis Ch Toledo OR 1989-1991; S Lk's Ch Grants Pass OR 1988-1989; D-In-Trng Ch Of The Trsfg Darrington WA 1986-1987.

LONGSTAFF, Thomas Richmond Willis (Me) 39 Pleasant St, Waterville ME 04901 **Rep Hse of Representatives St of Maine 2010-** B Nashua NH 1935 s William & Evelene. MDiv Bangor TS 1964; BA U of Maine 1964; PhD Col 1973; Hebr Un Coll Jerusalem 1974; MA Colby Coll 1984. D 3/3/1974 P 7/1/1974 Bp Frederick Barton Wolf. m 8/17/1969 Cynthia Curtis c 5. Per-Diem Stff Chapl Maine Gnrl Med Cntr Waterville ME 2003-2011; Chapl Waterville Fire Dept Waterville ME 1991-1993; Serv Chr Ch 1967-1968; Serv Methodist Ch 1960-1965; Non-par. Co-Auth, "Excavations at Sepphoris," *Sepphoris*, Brill, 2006; Auth, "A Synopsis Of Mk (Cd)," Trin Press Intl , 2002; Auth, "One Gospel From Two; Mk'S Use Of Matt And Lk," Trin Press Intl , 2002; Auth, "What Are Those Wmn Doing At The Tomb Of Jesus?," *A Feminist Comp To Matt*, Sheffield Acad Press, 2001; Auth, "Palynology And Cultural Process," *Archeol In The Galilee*, Scholars Press, 1997; Auth, "Computer Rcrdng, Analysis, And Interp," *The Oxford Encyclopedia Of Archeol In The Near E*, 1997; Auth, "Abba, God, H Sprt, Most High, Image Of God, +More," *Harper'S Bible Dictionary*, 1996; Auth, "Synoptic Abstract: Vol. Xv Of The Computer Bible," Biblic Resrch Assoc, 1978; Auth, "Evidence Of Conflation In Mk?," Scholars Press, 1977. Amer Schools Of Oriental Resrch 1978-2008; Cath Biblic Assn Of Amer 1965-2008; Israel Exploration Soc 1978-2008; SBL 1965-2008; Studiorum Novi Testamentum Societas 1975-2008. Fell Woodrow Wilson Fndt 1964.

LONGSTRETH, William Morris (Pa) 1146 Handview Circle, Pottstown PA 19464 **Non-par 1969-** B Philadelphia PA 1933 s William & Laura. BA Hav 1959; STM PDS 1963; MA Villanova U 1970. D 6/8/1963 P 12/1/1963 Bp Joseph Gillespie Armstrong. m 6/25/1960 Barbara Caroline Heylmun. Int Chr Ch Bridgeport PA 1970-1978; DCE S Mary's Epis Ch Ardmore PA 1966-1969; Cur S Lk And S Simon Cyrene Rochester NY 1963-1966. Auth, "De-Liberation". jevans@stpetersplace.org

LONSWAY, Rose Anne (O) St Peter's Episcopal Church, 45 W Winter St, Delaware OH 43015 **Gr Epis Ch Willoughby OH 2015-** B Painesville OH 1948 d Edward & Gladys. BSN Avila U 1981; MA Webster U 1984; MDiv Bex 2013; MDiv Bex Sem 2013. D 6/29/2013 P 6/14/2014 Bp Thomas Edward Breidenthal. c 2. S Ptr's Epis Ch Delaware OH 2013-2015.

LONTO, Michael J (WNY) 99 Wildwood Av, Salamanca NY 14779 **Vic S Jn's Epis Ch Ellicottville NY 2009-; Chapl City of Salamanca Fire Dept 2008-; R S Mary's Ch Salamanca NY 2007-** B New York NY 1956 s Francis & Elizabeth. BS S Johns U 1978; MDiv TESM 2006. D 7/29/2006 Bp Robert William Duncan P 3/18/2007 Bp David Mercer Schofield. m 7/26/1986 Christine Lonto c 4. S Mary Epis Ch Red Bank Templeton PA 2006-2007; S Mich's Wayne Township Wayne Township PA 2006-2007; S Paul's Epis Ch Kittanning PA 2006-2007; Moral Ldrshp Off CAP 2003-2009; Prog/Analyst Cnty Of Kern 1991-2002.

LOOMIS, Julia Dorsey Reed (SVa) 416 Court St, Portsmouth VA 23704 B Portsmouth VA 1945 d Robert & Anna. BA Randolph-Macon Wmn's Coll 1967; Fulbright Georg August U Goettingen Germany 1968; MA Br 1970; MDiv Ya Berk 1992. D 6/7/1992 P 1/5/1993 Bp Frank Harris Vest Jr. m 6/14/1969 David E Loomis c 3. Assoc S Andr's Ch Norfolk VA 2005-2007; Int Ch Of The Gd Shpd Norfolk VA 2002-2004; Assoc S Thos Epis Ch Chesapeake VA 2000-2002; Int Bruton Par Williamsburg VA 1996-1999; D Emm Ch Virginia Bch VA 1992-1996. Auth, "Wisdom Calls at the Threshold," *Faith at Wk*, 2006; Auth, "Who is Chr for Us Today," *Reflections*, Yale DS, 1992. EPF

2000. Julia A. Archibold High Schlrshp Prize Berkeley/Yale DS 1992; Downes Prize for Publ Reading of Scripture Berkeley/Yale DS 1992; Phi Beta Kappa Randolph-Macon Wmn's Coll 1967.

LOOP, Dick (Ore) 36489 Florence Ct., Astoria OR 97103 **Ret Dio Oregon Portland OR 2012-, Mem of Bd Trst 2007-2012** B Okmulgee OK 1945 s Alfred & Ruth. U of Washington 1967; BS San Jose St U 1969; MS U CA 1971; MDiv Epis TS of the SW 1998. D 6/25/1995 P 12/16/1995 Bp John Stuart Thornton. m 8/3/2001 Marilyn L Loop c 2. Gr Epis Ch Astoria OR 2006-2012, R 2002-2005; Vic Mtn Rivers Epis Cmnty Idaho Falls ID 1995-2002; S Mk's Epis Ch Idaho Falls ID 1995-2002; S Paul's Ch Blackfoot ID 1995-2002.

LOOR CEDENO, Mariana De Jesus (EcuL) 22 Ava & 3er Callejon P, Bahia De Caraquez Ecuador **Litoral Dio Ecuador Guayaquil 2004-** B 1956 d Vicente & Jacinta. DIT Litoral Sem Guayaquil Ec. D 3/22/1998 P 7/14/2002 Bp Terencio Alfredo Morante-Espana. m 10/12/1996 Narciso Cevallos c 4. Vic Cristo Rey Catedral Guayaquil Ecuador 2002-2004.

LOPER, Jerald Dale (Minn) 1524 Country Club Rd, Albert Lea MN 56007 B Albert Lea MN 1931 s Dale & Hattie. D 12/14/1981 Bp Robert Marshall Anderson. m 7/27/1963 Elizabeth Plummer c 2. Calv Ch Waseca MN 1982-1983; Asst Chr Ch Albert Lea MN 1981-2013; Chapl In Nrsng Hm; Dioc Diac Trng Prog.

LOPEZ, Abel E (Los) 2396 Mohawk St Unit 7, Pasadena CA 91107 **Ch Of The Mssh Santa Ana CA 2013-** B CUBA 1969 s Reinaldo & Adis. Set Matanzas Cu; MDiv Epis TS of the SW 2000. D 6/11/2005 P 1/14/2006 Bp Joseph Jon Bruno. m 4/22/2006 May Ling Lopez c 3. Sr Assoc All SS Ch Pasadena CA 2005-2013. rector@messiah-santaana.org

LOPEZ, Antonio (Nev) 832 N Eastern Ave, Las Vegas NV 89101 **S Lk's Epis Ch Las Vegas NV 2013-** B Oxnard CA 1948 s Antonio & Maria. MDiv St Jn's Sem 1982. Rec 10/20/2012 as Priest Bp Dan Thomas Edwards. m 7/3/2013 Lorenzo Gabaldon.

LOPEZ, Bienvenido Taveras (DR) Iglesia Episcopal Divina Providencia, Calle Marcos Del Rosario #39 Republica Dominicana Dominican Republic **Dio The Dominican Republic (Iglesia Epis Dominicana) Gazcue Santo Domingo 2008-** B Republica Dominicana 1967 s Ramon & Leonida. Lic Centro de Estudios Teologicos; Lic Dominicana O & M 2004. D 2/4/2007 P 2/10/2008 Bp Julio Cesar Holguin-Khoury. m 11/25/2001 Benigna Arias c 2.

LOPEZ JR, Eddie (Ct) 35 S Franklin St, Wilkes Barre PA 18701 **Dio Connecticut Meriden CT 2013-; P Iglesia Betania Norwalk CT 2012-, Missional P 2012-; Dir of Sprtl Care & Pstr Educ Greenwich Hosp Greenwich CT 2009-** B New York 1960 s Eddie & Juanita. BS Nyack Coll 1983; Cert Luth Med Cntr 1987; MDiv NYTS 1989; STM UTS 1992; Cert No Gnrl Hosp 2007. D 6/24/2011 Bp Paul Victor Marshall P 1/5/2012 Bp John Palmer Croneberger. m 9/29/2007 Rosanna Rosado c 4. Asst S Steph's Epis Ch Wilkes Barre PA 2011-2013, Asst P 2012; Sr Organizer New York Lawyers for the Publ Interest NYC 2007-2009; Adj Prof NYTS NYC 2007-2008; Adj Prof Cuny Jn Jay Coll ofCriminal Justice NYC 2006-2007; Dvlpmt Dir Gr Ch Cmnty Cntr White Plains NY 2006-2007; Stff Chapl Harlem Med Cntr NYC 2006-2007; Cmpgn Dir CUNY Labor Murphy Instiitute NYC 2005-2006; Prog Dir Gnrl Bd Global Mnstrs NYC 2000-2004; Exec Dir Natl Coun of Ch NYC 1996-2000; Adj Prof NYTS NYC 1995-1998; Adj Prof Mercy Coll Dobbs Ferry NY 1992-1995; Pstr La Resurreccion Meth Ch Bronx NY 1988-2005; Stff Chapl New York City Dept of Corrections NYC 1984-1990.

LOPEZ, Mary Alice (SwFla) 504 Columbia Dr, Tampa FL 33606 B Tampa FL 1951 BA Salem Coll Winston-Salem NC. D 6/14/2003 Bp John Bailey Lipscomb. m 7/11/1974 Victor Manuel Lopez c 3.

LOPEZ, Oscar Obdulio (Hond) 12 Calle, 10-11 Avenue Bo Cabanas, San Pedro Honduras **Vic Iglesia Epis San Andres San Pedro Sula 1989-; Iglesia Epis San Lucas San Pedro Sula 1989-** B San Pedro Sula Cortes HN 1951 s Maria. D 1/6/1989 P 1/25/1995 Bp Leo Frade. m 5/11/1990 Marta Isabel Oseguera c 1. Dio Honduras San Pedro Sula 1989-2016.

LOPEZ, Pedro Nel (Tex) Saint Peter's Church, 705 Williams St, Pasadena TX 77506 **S Ptr's Ch Pasadena TX 2011-** B Colombia 1968 s Pedro & Lucrecia. Bachelors Universidad San Buenaventura Bogota CO 1991; MDiv. M.A. Cath Theol Un 1997; MDiv. M.A. Other 1997. Rec 11/22/2003 as Priest Bp Victor Alfonso Scantlebury. m 8/31/2002 Estella Herrera c 2. Ch Of The Redeem Elgin IL 2006-2011; S Mich's Ch Barrington IL 2004-2006; Santa Teresa de Avila Chicago IL 2004.

LOPEZ JR, Ramiro Eduardo (WTex) 1247 Vista Del Juez, San Antonio TX 78216 **R S Geo Ch San Antonio TX 2004-** B Corpus Christi TX 1964 s Ramiro & Juanita. Del Mar Coll 1985; BA Texas St U San Marcos 1988; MDiv Sewanee: The U So, TS 1995. D 6/29/1995 Bp James Edward Folts P 1/25/1996 Bp Robert Boyd Hibbs. m 5/25/1991 Kendra M Lopez c 2. Ch Planter Dio W Texas San Antonio TX 2003-2004; Vic St Ptr & St Paul Ch Mssn TX 2002-2003; Asst R S Jn's Ch McAllen TX 1998-2002; Asst R S Alb's Ch Harlingen TX 1995-1998.

LOPEZ, Sarah (Ia) D 1/28/2012 Bp Alan Scarfe.

LOPEZ, Sunny (Chi) 3115 W Jerome St, Chicago IL 60645 **Assoc Gr Ch Chicago IL 2008-; Bethany Methodist Corp Chicago IL 2000-; Corp Dir Of Mssn**

And Sprtl Care Bethany Hm And Methodist Hosp Chicago IL 1992-; Dir Of Pstr Care The Methodist Hm Chicago IL 1988-** B Ottawa IL 1949 d Harry & Laverne. BA Mundelein Coll 1982; MDiv Garrett-Evang TS 1987; DMin Chicago TS 1997. D 12/7/1991 Bp Frank Tracy Griswold III. m 9/30/1978 Frank Lopez c 2. D Cathd Of S Jas Chicago IL 1994-2006. Apc (Assn Of Profsnl Chapl) 1999; EPF 1991; For (Fllshp Of Recon) 1999; No Amer Assn Of The Diac 1991; The Natl Assn Of Female Executives 2000. S Steph's Awd For Peace And Justice Mnstry No Amer Assn Of The Diac 2001.

LOPEZ, Uriel (Tex) 40 Center St, Elgin IL 60120 **Vic The Great Cmsn Fndt Houston TX 2015-** B Paez, Colombia 1971 s Pedro & Lucrecia. MDiv Cath Theol Un 1999; MA Cath Theol Un 2000. Rec 8/31/2011 as Priest Bp Jeff Lee. m 3/1/2011 Maria L Mateus Cuesta c 2. R Ch Of The Redeem Elgin IL 2011-2015. urloc51@gmail.com

LOPEZ-CHAVERRA, Hector (SwFla) Episc Ch St. Francis, P.O. Box 9332, Tampa FL 33674 B Aguagas Colombia 1937 s Antonio & Ines. Bachelor & Sem Stds; BA Sem Chr P 1971. D 6/30/1973 P 8/4/1974 Bp Adrian Delio Caceres-Villavicencio. m 5/19/1974 Olga S Lopez c 2. Vic S Fran Ch Tampa FL 2002-2013; Serv Ch in Colombia 1988-1993; Iglesia Epis Del Ecuador Quito 1984-1987; Iglesia Epis En Colombia Bogota 1977-1993; Serv Ch in Ecuador 1973-1987.

LOPEZ ZAMUDIO, Rocio Patricia (Okla) PO Box 10722, Midwest City OK 73140 B Mexico 1972 d Raymundo & Maria. IONA 2017. D 6/30/2017 Bp Edward Joseph Konieczny. m 1/24/1996 Jorge Alberto Dela Rosa Munoz c 2.

LOPOSER, Ellen Fogg (Spok) St Andrew's Episcopal Church, 2404 N Howard St, Spokane WA 99205 B Tacoma WA 1946 d Charles & Alice. BS/BA WA SU 1968; MA Arizona St U 1977. D 6/27/2010 Bp James E Waggoner Jr. m 8/18/1990 Bernard Andre Loposer c 2.

LOR, Cher John (Minn) Holy Apostles Episcopal Church, 2200 Minnehaha Ave E, Saint Paul MN 55119 B Laos 1960 s Yong & Zoua. D 6/20/2015 P 6/21/2016 Bp Brian N Prior. c 3.

LORA, Juan B (Ct) 16 Paul St, Danbury CT 06810 **Hisp Mssnr 1983-** B 1925 s Jose & Mercedes. Santo Tomas De Aquino Sem 1950. Rec 12/1/1979 as Priest Bp Paul Moore Jr. Trin Par Norwalk CT 1989-1992; Vic Iglesia Betania Norwalk CT 1987-1993; Dio Connecticut Meriden CT 1981-1988; Holyrood Ch New York NY 1981; Serv RC Ch.

LORD, James Raymond (Ky) 3001 Myrshine Dr, Pensacola FL 32506 **Chr Epis Ch Pensacola FL 2012-; Ret 1997-** B Dublin GA 1934 s James & Susie. BA Presb Coll 1956; BD PrTS 1961; ThM Duke 1964; PhD Duke 1968. D 12/26/1972 P 4/29/1973 Bp Hanford Langdon King Jr. Adj Prof of Theol Brescia U Owensboro KY 2000-2003; R Trin Epis Ch Owensboro KY 1991-1997; R S Lk's Ch Louisville KY 1986-1991; R Gr Ch Hopkinsville KY 1978-1986; Vic S Mart's-In-The-Fields Mayfield KY 1975-1978; S Ptr's of the Lakes Gilbertsville KY 1974-1978; Assoc. Prof. of Hmnts Coll of Idaho Caldwell ID 1973-1974; Asst. Prof. of Philos & Rel Coll of Idaho Caldwell ID 1969-1973; Instr of Rel Duke Durham NC 1964-1969; GC Dep Dio Kentucky Louisville KY 1994-1997, Stndg Com 1992-1994, Dep GC 1988-1991, Stndg Com 1988-1990, Trst and Coun 1987-1994, Stndg Com 1982-1984, Trst and Coun 1977-1980. Auth, "Bk Revs," *Newman Stds Journ*, 2006; Transltr, "Jesus (by Hans Conzelmann)," Fortress Press, 1973. Cath Biblic Assn 1972.

LORD, Mary George (NwPa) 2425 Glendale Ave, Erie PA 16510 **D S Ptr's Ch Tulsa OK 2007-** B Erie PA 1948 d Ralph & Marie. Gannon U 1966. D 6/24/2006 Bp Robert Manning Moody. m 5/30/1987 Charles David Lord c 3.

LORD, Philip Warren (WNY) 5013 Van Buren Rd, Dunkirk NY 14048 **Chapl 108th Scottish Highlander hon Squadron (U.S. AF) 2012-** B Philadelphia PA 1940 s John & Edna. BA Hobart and Wm Smith Colleges 1963; MDiv GTS 1966; CLU The Amer Coll Bryn Mawr PA 1987; Cert The Amer Coll Bryn Mawr PA 1988. D 6/11/1966 Bp Leland Stark P 12/7/1966 Bp John Henry Esquirol. m 10/8/1966 Susan Lord c 1. S Paul's Epis Ch Angola NY 2001-2010; S Alb's Ch Silver Creek NY 1997-2000, 1994-1996; R Ch Of S Jn The Bapt Dunkirk NY 1973-1982; Asst Gr Ch Lockport NY 1971-1973; Cur S Steph's Ch Providence RI 1968-1970; Cur S Jn's Ch Stamford CT 1966-1968. EPF 2011; Ord of S Ben - S Greg's Abbey, Three Rivers, 1959; Sis of the H Nativ - P Assoc 1969.

LORD, Richard (Va) 543 Beulah Road Northeast, Vienna VA 22180 **Int Assoc R S Paul's Ch Charlottesville VA 2017-** B Washington DC 1953 s David & Julie. BA CUA 1976; MDiv VTS 1981; STM Ya Berk 1992. D 6/20/1981 P 12/20/1981 Bp John Thomas Walker. m 11/26/1976 Deborah Ann Greene c 3. R Ch Of The H Comf Vienna VA 1994-2016; R Chr And Epiph Ch E Haven CT 1989-1994; R S Mart's Epis Ch Monroeville PA 1984-1989; Ch Of The Apos Fairfax VA 1981-1984. Compass Rose Soc 2001. Hon Cn Schlr Chr Ch 1992. rlord1@gmail.com

LORD, Robert Charles (CFla) 1312 Bridgeport Drive, Winter Park FL 32789 **All SS Ch Of Winter Pk Winter Pk FL 2006-; R All SS Episcoapl Ch Winter Pk FL 2006-** B Washington DC 1953 s David & Julie. BA Florida Atlantic U 1977; MDiv Nash 1980; DMin Fuller TS 2002. D 6/22/1980 P 1/26/1981 Bp Calvin Onderdonk Schofield Jr. m 6/14/1975 Nancy Lord c 2. Dep GC Dio Kansas Topeka KS 2000-2006, 2000-2003; R S Mich And All Ang Ch Mssn

KS 1996-2006; R Trin Ch Greeley CO 1988-1996; R S Mich's Ch Colonial Heights VA 1984-1988; Assoc Ch Of The Apos Fairfax VA 1982-1983; Assoc S Dav's Epis Ch Lakeland FL 1981-1982; Asst S Mk The Evang Ft Lauderdale FL 1980-1981; Dep GC Dio Colorado Denver CO 1994-2000. OHC.

LORD-WILKINSON, Randall A (WA) Church of the Ascension, 205 S Summit Ave, Gaithersburg MD 20877 **Ch Of The Ascen Gaithersburg MD 2007**- B Charleston WV 1955 s Paul & Eunice. BA W Virginia U 1978; MDiv Harvard DS 1982. D 5/28/1983 Bp John Bowen Coburn P 5/19/1984 Bp Roger W Blanchard. m 1/1/1994 Cynthia L Lord-Wilkinson c 2. R S Paul's Epis Ch Bremerton WA 1995-2007; R S Ptr's Ch Salem MA 1985-1995; S Andr's Ch Framingham MA 1983-1985; COM Dio Olympia Seattle 1999-2007, Cmsn on Liturg and Mus 1998-1999.

LORENSON, Ruth Lorraine (LI) 9 Warton Pl, Garden City NY 11530 **Non-par 1975**- B Brooklyn NY 1937 d David & Lenora. RN Med Cntr Jersey City NJ 1957; BS Coll of New Jersey 1958; Mercer Cnty Cmnty Coll 1976. Trans 6/13/1990. m 6/21/1958 Leslie Lorenson. Soc Of S Fran.

LORENZ, Constance (LI) 49 Hudson Watch Dr, Ossining NY 10562 **Mssnr S Paul's Ch Great Neck NY 2010**- B Brooklyn NY 1949 Cert Mercer TS 1997. D 6/28/1997 Bp Orris George Walker Jr. m 10/9/1971 Leslie Lorenz c 2. All SS Ch Great Neck NY 2015; Dio Long Island Garden City NY 2010-2014; D Cathd Of The Incarn Garden City NY 2007-2010; D Ch Of S Alb The Mtyr S Albans NY 2001-2005; D Gr Ch Jamaica NY 2000-2001; D Zion Ch Douglaston NY 1997-2000.

LORENZE, James Dennis (Eau) 2304 Country Club Ln, Eau Claire WI 54701 **D Chr Ch Cathd Eau Claire WI 1998**- B Freeport IL 1942 s Leo & Clara. Coll Med Tech. D 4/18/1998 Bp William Charles Wantland. m 4/9/1983 Debra Helen Lorenze c 2.

LORENZETTI, Dominick J (SJ) **S Paul's Epis Ch Modesto CA 2015**- Rec 12/20/2014 as Priest Bp David C Rice.

LORING III, Richard Tuttle (Mass) 114 Badger Ter, Bedford MA 01730 **Bridge P St. Andr's Epis Ch Hanover MA 2017-; Ret Dio Massachusetts Boston MA 1995**- B Boston MA 1929 s Richard & Helen. BA Harv 1951; STB GTS 1957; ThD GTS 1968. D 6/22/1957 Bp Anson Phelps Stokes Jr P 1/25/1958 Bp Oliver L Loring. Sabbatical Coverage S Jn's Ch Newtonville MA 2016; Bridge P Trin Epis Ch Wrentham MA 2014-2015; Transitional P All SS Epis Ch of the No Shore Inc Danvers MA 2013-2014; Int S Mk's Ch Westford MA 2008-2011; Int S Paul's Ch Millis MA 2007-2008; Int Calv Epis Ch Danvers MA 2006-2007; Int Ch Of The H Nativ S Weymouth MA 2004-2006; Int S Jn's Ch Charlestown (Boston) Charlestown MA 2003-2004; Int Gr Ch Norwood MA 2001-2003; Int Gr Epis Ch Medford MA 2001; Int Asst Chr Ch Needham Hgts MA 2000-2001; Int Emm Ch Braintree MA 1999-2000; Int Asst Ch Of S Jn The Evang Hingham MA 1998-1999; Int Asst S Andr's Ch Framingham MA 1998-1999; Int Gr Ch Newton MA 1998; Long-Term Supply P S Mich's Epis Ch Holliston MA 1996-1998; Long-Term Supply P Ch Of The Ascen Fall River MA 1995-1996; Dio Massachusetts Boston MA 1994-2004, 1982-, 1982-, 1972-1975, Assessment Revs Com 1994-2004; Exec Secy GBEC 1983-1990; Supplement Accounts Boston MA 1976-1977; Stndg Com Dio Massachusetts Boston MA 1975-1984; Ecum Coun Chelsea MA 1975-1982; Com on Examinations for Ord Dio Massachusetts Boston MA 1971-1975; R S Lk's/San Lucas Epis Ch Chelsea MA 1968-1995; Chapl, Elmira Reformatory Dio Cntrl New York Liverpool NY 1966-1967; Asst Gr Epis Ch Elmira NY 1963-1968; Sum Chapl St Mary's Hosp Bayside NY 1962; Sum Asst Ch Of The Trsfg New York NY 1960; Asst St Pauls Chap New York NY 1960; Asst S Jn's Of Lattingtown Locust Vlly NY 1959-1963; Fell and Tutor The GTS New York NY 1959-1963; Cur The Par Of All SS Ashmont-Dorches Boston MA 1957-1959. Auth, "S Lk's Epis Ch in Chelsea Massachusetts 150 Years 1841-1991," privately printed - Chelsea, MA, 1991. Cler Club of Boston 1969-1990; Libr and Archv Bd 1982; Marg. Coffin PB Soc, Boston 1982; Parsons Club Cambridge 1969-2010. Nash Fllshp Dio MA 1977.

LORING, William Delano (Ct) 15 Pleasant Drive, Danbury CT 06811 **Assoc S Paul's Ch Brookfield CT 2004-; Exec Com (Ed, 2016-17) Angl Soc 1970**- B Saint Petersburg FL 1937 s Henry & Lydia. BA JHU 1965; Drew U 1965; MDiv PDS 1965; GTS 1969; MS Wstrn Connecticut St U 1987. D 12/18/1965 P 6/18/1966 Bp Alfred L Banyard. m 7/15/2004 Diane Marie Amison- Loring c 2. Assoc Ch Of The Epiph Southbury CT 2002-2004; P-in-c Chr Ch Waterbury CT 1999-2001; Int Chr Ch Trumbull CT 1999; Int Imm S Jas Par Derby CT 1998-1999; P-in-c Chr Ch Patterson NY 1990-1997; P-in-c S Lk's Epis Ch New Haven CT 1982-1983; Vic S Jn's Ch Sandy Hook CT 1972-1982; P-in-c S Jas Ch Callicoon NY 1971-1972; Consult SLC Epis Ch 1970-1976; Chapl S Mary Sch Peekskill NY 1969-1971; Asst (Non-stipendiary) S Jos's Ch Queens Vlg NY 1968-1969; Vic S Andr The Apos Highland Highlands NJ 1965-1967; Exec Coun Dio Connecticut Meriden CT 2008-2016, Exec Coun 2000-2001, Fin Com 1988-2008, Exec Coun 1983-1986, Liturg Cmsn, Sec. 1976-1988, Evang Com 1976-1981, Fin Com 1974-1983, A R C w/ Dio Bridgeport (RC) 1974-1980. "Boone Porter: An Appreciation," *The Angl*, 1999; "What's Wrong w the New Confessions," *Living Ch*, 1971; Auth, "The Beatific Vision of Thos

Aquinas," *ATR*, 1969. Angl Soc 1962; CCU 1972; Ord of S Ben, S Greg Abbey, Confrator 1970.

LOSCH, Richard Rorex (Ala) Po Box 1560, Livingston AL 35470 **S Alb's Ch Gainesville AL 1994**- B Boston MA 1933 s Paul & Helen. BA Ya 1956; MDiv Ya Berk 1959; MEd No Carolina St U 1989. D 6/11/1959 Bp Walter H Gray P 3/15/1960 Bp John Henry Esquirol. S Paul's Ch Greensboro AL 2005-2008; P-in-c S Jas' Ch Livingston AL 1994-2003; Asst S Tim's Ch Raleigh NC 1986-1989; Non-par 1983-1989; Asst S Mich's Ch Marblehead MA 1970-1986; Asst. Headmaster The Tower Sch Marblehead MA 1969-1981; Chapl Watkinson Sch Hartford CT 1966-1969; Yth Dir Dio Connecticut Meriden CT 1964-1966; R S Jn's Ch Sandy Hook CT 1961-1966; Cur Trin Ch Torrington CT 1959-1961. Auth, "All the People in the Bible," Eerdmans, 2008; Auth, "The Uttermost Part of the Earth," Eerdmans, 2005; Auth, "The Many Faces of Faith," Eerdmans, 2001. LitD (Hon.) U of W Alabama 2009; Kappa Mu Epsilon (Mathematics) U of W Alabama 1998; Phi Kappa Phi No Carolina St U 1989.

LOUA, Cece Alfred-S (Mich) 1021 Norwich Drive, Troy MI 48084 **S Matt's And S Jos's Detroit MI 2013-; Chapl Res Wm Beaumont Hosp Royal Oak MI 2013-; P Assoc for Pstr Care Dio Michigan Detroit MI 2007**- B Republic of Guinea 1962 s Kpeliwolo & Mami. BA Pontifical Gregorian U 1991; BA Universite Jesuite de Paris Paris FR 1998; MTh Universite Jesuite De Paris Paris FR 2000; MA Wayne 2005. Rec 7/6/2006 Bp Wendell Nathaniel Gibbs Jr. m 8/30/2014 Therese Haba c 1. Nativ Epis Ch Bloomfield Township MI 2012; All SS Ch Detroit MI 2010-2012; Asst Cathd Ch Of S Paul Detroit MI 2006-2010. casloua@gmail.com

LOUD JR, Johnson D (Minn) 740 Shane Park Cir Apt 2, Prescott WI 54021 **Vic Ch Of The Mssh Prairie Island 1998**- B Red Lake MN 1942 s Johnson & Clemence. BS S Cloud St U 1965; MDiv CDSP 1997. D 6/27/1987 Bp Edmond Lee Browning P 5/1/1988 Bp Robert Marshall Anderson. c 2. Ch Of The Mssh Prairie Island Welch MN 1997-2014; Int S Antipas Ch Redby MN 1997-1998; Int S Jn's Missions Redby MN 1997-1998.

LOUDEN, Molly O'Neill (Ct) 37 Gin Still Ln, West Hartford CT 06107 **S Jas's Ch W Hartford CT 2004**- B Toledo OH 1943 d Richard & Vera. AA U of Florida 1962; BS Florida Sthrn Coll 1967; MDiv Ya Berk 1983; DMin GTF 2003. D 9/16/1984 Bp Arthur Edward Walmsley P 4/27/1985 Bp Clarence Nicholas Coleridge. m 8/11/1962 Bruce Louden c 3. Cur S Andr's Ch Meriden CT 1984-1988; Par Intern S Mk's Ch New Britain CT 1983-1984.

LOUDENSLAGER, Samuel Charles (Ark) 20000 Hwy 300-Spur, Bigelow AR 72016 B Ardmore OK 1955 s Charles & Dorothy. BA U of Memphis 1980; MS New Mex St U 1983. D 11/23/2002 Bp Larry Maze. m 2/12/1983 Teresa Loudenslager. Eccelesiastical Crt, Mem Dio Arkansas Little Rock AR 2004-2007, Dioc Jubilee Off 2002-2006, Div of Stwdshp, Mem 1998-2000. NAAD 2001.

LOUGHRAN JR, Eugene James (SwFla) 633 Coquina Court, Fort Myers FL 33908 B Salem NJ 1940 s Eugene & Grace. BA Hobart and Wm Smith Colleges 1962; MDiv PDS 1965. D 5/1/1965 P 11/6/1965 Bp Alfred L Banyard. m 8/25/1963 Elizabeth Loughran. R S Jn The Div Epis Ch Sun City Cntr FL 1983-1999; R S Paul's Ch Mt Vernon OH 1974-1983; R S Barn Ch Brackenridge PA 1969-1974; R S Paul's Ch Monongahela PA 1967-1969; Cur Calv Epis Ch Flemington NJ 1965-1967.

LOUGHREN, James Patrick (Dal) 4879 Lake Shore Dr, Bolton Landing NY 12814 **S Lk's Epis Ch Dallas TX 2015-; Dn Dio Albany Greenwich NY 2005**- B Potsdam NY 1955 BA St Lawr 1981; Wadhams Hall Sem 1987; MDiv S Johns Sem Boston 1991; MA S Johns Sem Boston 1991. Rec 4/16/2003 as Priest Bp Daniel William Herzog. c 1. Vic Gr Ch Hoolehua HI 2013-2015; R Ch Of S Sacrement Bolton Landing NY 2004-2013.

LOUIS, Richard Mortimer (Nwk) 2395 Quill Ct, Mahwah NJ 07430 **R Emer St. Jn's Memi Ch Ramsey NJ 2000**- B Brooklyn NY 1933 s Mortimer & Olga. BA Colg 1955; MDiv EDS 1959. D 6/11/1959 P 12/19/1959 Bp Horace W B Donegan. m 11/5/1966 M Kristan B Louis c 2. Assoc Chr Ch Ridgewood NJ 2002; R S Jn's Memi Ch Ramsey NJ 1978-2000; R S Mk's Ch Teaneck NJ 1971-1978; Cur Chr Ch Hackensack NJ 1970-1971; Sr Chapl E Midtown Prot Chapl NYC NY 1965-1970; Chapl S Lukes Hosp NYC 1961-1965; Cur Ch of the Epiph NYC NY 1959-1961; Mem Stndg Commitee Dioces of Newark NJ. Cbury Schlr Dio Newark 1988.

LOUIS DEAN SKIPPER, James Louis Dean (Ala) 1426 Gilmer Ave, Montgomery AL 36104 **P-in-c St. Paul's Epis Ch Carlowville AL 2006-; Chapl Montgomery Epis Campus Mnstry Montgomery AL 2004**- B Dothan AL 1950 s Louie & Geraldine. BA U of Alabama 1973; MA Hollins U 1974; MFA U of Iowa 1976; MDiv Epis TS of the SW 1998. D 5/26/1998 Bp Henry Nutt Parsley Jr P 12/2/1998 Bp Robert Oran Miller. m 6/1/2001 Susan Williams c 2. So Talladega Cnty Epis Mnstry Sylacauga AL 2011-2015; St. Matt's Epis Ch Madison AL 2010-2011; S Paul's (Carlowville) Carlowville AL 2006-2010; Dio Alabama Birmingham 2004-2010; Assoc Steph's Epis Ch Birmingham AL 2000-2004; Int Ch of the Epiph Guntersville AL 1999-2000; Ch Of The Epiph Guntersville AL 1998-2000; Asst R Ch of the Epiph Guntersville AL 1998-1999. "The Wk Ethic of the Common Fly," Settlement Hse Press, 2007;

"The Fourth Watch of the Night," Swan Scythe Press, 2001; Auth, "Deaths That Travel w the Weather," Orchesis Press, 1992; Auth, "Sm Song of the New Moon," Bellwether Press, 1977. fatherskipper@gmail.com

LOUISE SSM, Sister Catherine (Mass) 17 Louisburg Sq, Boston MA 02108 B New York NY 1916 d Edward & Kate. Brearly Sch; BA Bryn 1938; MA Col 1941. D 11/1/1978 Bp Morris Fairchild Arnold P 12/1/1979 Bp John Bowen Coburn. Sis Soc Of S Marg.

LOUTREL, William Frederic (Ct) 1090 Ridge Rd, Hamden CT 06517 **Vol Asst. P S Thos's Ch New Haven CT 2000-** B Newton MA 1951 s Louis & Dora. BS RPI 1973; MDiv GTS 1978. D 6/10/1978 P 3/17/1979 Bp Morgan Porteus. m 1/19/2006 Thomas Michael Fynan. R S Jn's Ch E Hartford CT 1984-1989; Chr Ch Cathd Indianapolis IN 1980-1984; Cn Dio Indianapolis Indianapolis IN 1980-1984; Cur S Mich's Ch Naugatuck CT 1978-1980.

✠ LOUTTIT, The Rt Rev Henry Irving (Ga) 611 E Bay St, Savannah GA 31401 B West Palm Beach FL 1938 s Henry & Amy. BA U So 1960; BD VTS 1963. D 6/11/1963 Bp Henry I Louttit P 4/25/1964 Bp Albert R Stuart Con 1/21/1995 for Ga. m 6/14/1962 Jayne Louttit c 1. Bp Of Georgia Dio Georgia Savannah GA 1995-2010; R Chr Ch Valdosta GA 1967-1994; D-In-C Trin Ch Statesboro GA 1963-1964; Mem NCCC 1996-2000; SCCM Dom And Frgn Mssy Soc- Epis Ch Cntr New York NY 1988-1997; Trst VTS Alexandria VA 1984-1989. ADLMC; RWF; S Alb & S Sergius. DD STUSo 1996; DD VTS 1993; Phi Beta Kappa.

LOVE, Leon Lewis (CNY) 5 Gail Dr, Waverly NY 14892 B Elmira NY 1938 s Clarence & Cecilia. BS Mansfield U of Pennsylvania 1969; MDiv Bex Sem 1972. D 5/27/1972 P 3/17/1973 Bp Dean Theodore Stevenson. m 8/27/1984 Ann Mair Love c 2. Chr Ch Wellsburg NY 1998-2003; Emm Ch Elmira NY 1998-2003; Vic Gr Ch Waverly NY 1998-2003; S Jn's Epis Ch Elmira NY 1998-2003; Chemung Vlly Cluster Elmira NY 1996-2003; Non-par 1991-1998; R S Jn's Ch Wilson NY 1989-1991; St Mk Epis Ch No Tonawanda NY 1987-1989; Non-par 1981-1986; Chr Enrichment Cntr Flint MI 1978-1981; R Chr Flint MI 1978-1981; R S Matt's Epis Ch Sunbury PA 1977-1978; S Mary's Ch Williamsport PA 1972-1977.

✠ LOVE, The Rt Rev William Howard (Alb) PO Box 211, Lake Luzerne NY 12846 **Bp of Albany Dio Albany Greenwich NY 2006-** B Dallas TX 1957 s James & Frances. BA Texas St U San Marcos 1980; MS SUNY 1988; MDiv Nash 1991. D 6/22/1991 P 3/1/1992 Bp David Standish Ball Con 9/16/2006 for Alb. m 10/22/1983 Karen Elizabeth Love. R S Mary's Ch Lake Luzerne NY 1992-2006; Dn's Vic Cathd Of All SS Albany NY 1991-1992. bishoplove@albanydiocese.org

LOVEKIN, Arthur Adams (RG) 10501 Lagrima De Oro Rd NE, Apt 4208, Albuquerque NM 87111 **Cn Emer S Jn's Cathd Albuquerque NM 2004-, Clincl Psychol 1976-1986; Ret 1992-** B Boston,MA 1928 s Osgood & Marion. BA Stan 1951; BD CDSP 1954; STM Sewanee: The U So, TS 1962; PhD Fuller TS 1975. D 6/12/1954 P 12/19/1954 Bp Arthur Kinsolving. m 6/18/1977 Ann Lewis Lovekin c 8. Fndr Vic Ch Of The H Cross Edgewood NM 1995-1998; Asst Chapl Gd Samar Hosp Los Angeles CA 1987-1992; Fndr; Exec Dir Samar Counslg Cntr Albuquerque NM 1987-1992; Asst S Paul's Pomona Pomona CA 1973-1974; Fndr Vic S Jn's Mssn La Verne CA 1962-1969; Assoc S Lk's Epis Ch Monrovia CA 1960-1962; Fndr Vic S Dav's Epis Page AZ 1959-1960; Vic St Johns Epis-Luth Ch Williams AZ 1956-1960; Supt and Chapl Julia C. Emery Sch for Girls Liberia 1955-1956; Asst Gr St Pauls Epis Ch Tucson AZ 1954-1955. Co-Auth, "Glossolalia: Behavioral Sci Perspective on Spkng in Tongues," Oxf Press, 1985. AAPC 1978-2003; Amer Bd Profsnl Psychol 1986-2003; APA 1973-2003; APA, Div 36: The Psycholog 1980-2003; Commision of Mnstry 1978-1985; Cmsn of Mnstry 1991-1997. Diplomate AAPC 1990; Diplomate Amer Bd Profsnl Psychol 1986.

LOVELACE, David (CPa) 140 N Beaver St, York PA 17401 **Dep to GC Dio Cntrl Pennsylvania Harrisburg PA 2000-** B Richmond VA 1948 s Ray & Charlotte. AA Ferrum Coll 1968; BA Emory and Henry Coll 1970; MDiv VTS 1976; MST Columbia TS 1990. D 5/22/1976 Bp John Alfred Baden P 3/19/1977 Bp Hunley Agee Elebash. m 7/8/1989 Elaine Alvina Lovelace c 3. Com Coordntr, Natl Ch Prov III 2005-2011; R The Epis Ch Of S Jn The Bapt York PA 1996-2017; R S Paul's Epis Ch Newnan GA 1982-1996; Asst Ch Of The Gd Shpd Rocky Mt NC 1979-1982; S Jas Epis Ch Belhaven NC 1976-1979; Stndg Com Pres Dio Atlanta Atlanta GA 1995-1996. Auth, "Min to the Poor," *Congressional Record.*

LOVELADY, Eldwin M (Oly) 3700 14th Ave SE, Unit 3, Olympia WA 98501 **S Ben Epis Ch Lacey WA 2016-; Assoc P S Mary's Ch Lakewood WA 2011-; Chapl to Ret Cler / Spouses Dio Olympia Seattle 2013-, Caring for All Creation Cmsn 2012-** B Morrilton AR 1945 s Earnest & Louise. AAS US-AF 1986; BS Pk U 1989; MDiv Sewanee: The U So, TS 1993. D 5/29/1993 Bp Frank Jeffrey Terry P 12/4/1993 Bp David Charles Bowman. m 8/1/1974 Deborah Lovelady c 4. Cong Dvlpmt Consult St. Jn's Sudanese Mssn Tukwila WA 2011-2013; Sunday supply and Pstr Care St. Lk's Epis Ch Elma WA 2011-2013; Int R S Lk's Epis Ch Vancouver WA 2010-2011; R All SS Epis Ch Las Vegas NV 2004-2009; R S Ptr's Ch Westfield NY 1998-2004; Cur S Lk's Epis Ch Jamestown NY 1993-1998; Multicultural Mnstry Off Dio Neva-

da Las Vegas 2008-2009; Liturg Cmsn Dio Wstrn New York Tonawanda NY 1993-1998. Cmnty of S Mary 1992.

LOVELESS, Phillip Lyman (SanD) Episcopal Community Center, 2083 Sunset Cliffs Blvd, San Diego CA 92107 B San Diego CA 1938 s Carl & Margaret. D 2/14/2015 Bp Jim Mathes. m 11/3/1971 Georgina Loveless. ploveless@edsd.org

LOVETT, G David (ETenn) 7900 High Heath, Knoxville TN 37919 **Asst S Steph's Epis Ch Oak Ridge TN 2011-; Pstr Counslr First Bapt Ch Knoxville 2008-; Pstr Counslr Pstr Counslg for Growth 2001-** B Knox County TN 1948 s Raymond & Mildred. BS U of Tennessee 1970; MDiv SE Bapt TS 1980; DMin Garrett-Evang TS 1996. D 5/29/2010 P 5/28/2011 Bp Charles Glenn VonRosenberg. m 2/8/1991 Anne E Elkins c 2. Transitional D Ch Of The Gd Shpd Knoxville TN 2010-2011. associaterector@ststephensor.org

LOVING, John Harnish (NwT) 8009 Ladera Verde, Austin TX 78739 B Richmond VA 1938 s Harnish & Elizabeth. Cbury Coll; BA U Rich 1961; MDiv GTS 1967; S Georges Coll Jerusalem IL 1985. D 6/22/1967 P 5/23/1968 Bp George P Gunn. m 6/24/1967 Nancy W Loving c 2. Asst The Ch of the Gd Shpd Austin TX 2008-2009; P-t Asst Ch of the Gd Shpd Austin TX 2007-2009; Int and Supply Wk Dio Texas Austin TX 2004-2007; Alum/ae Bd GTS 1998-2004; Chair, COM Dio NW Texas 1995-1998; BEC Epis Ch 1994-2006; GC Del Dio NW Texas 1994-2000; Bd Trst Sem of the SW Austin 1993-1996; R Emm Epis Ch San Angelo TX 1990-2003; R Gr Epis Ch Ponca City OK 1983-1990; R Johns Memi Epis Ch Farmville VA 1969-1983; Cur Ch Of The Ascen Norfolk VA 1967-1969; Stndg Com Dio NW Texas Lubbock TX 1999-2000, Long-R Plnng & Structure 1994-1998; Trst Epis TS Of The SW Austin TX 1993-1996. Auth, "Adv IV: The Visitation," *LivCh,* 1997. jloving3@austin.rr.com

LOW, James Robert (Ct) 60 Shadagee Rd Unit 22, Saco ME 04072 B Beverly MA 1939 s James & Nettie. BA Harv 1960; MA Wesl 1966; BD EDS 1969. D 6/21/1969 Bp Anson Phelps Stokes Jr P 5/6/1970 Bp John Melville Burgess. m 3/18/1972 Linda C Low c 3. S Matt's Epis Ch Lisbon Falls ME 2005-2007; Calv Ch Suffield CT 1998-2004; Mssnr Gr Ch Broad Brook CT 1998-2004; H Trin Epis Ch Enfield CT 1998-2004; No Cntrl Reg Mnstry Enfield CT 1998-2004; S Andr's Epis Ch Enfield CT 1998-2004; R Epiph Par Walpole MA 1987-1998; Assoc R S Barn Ch Falmouth MA 1972-1987; Asst R All SS Ch Chelmsford MA 1969-1972; COM Dio Massachusetts Boston MA 1990-1998, Falmouth Coun on Aging 1983-1989, 1978-1982, Dioc Coun 1977. Rev Jim Low Day Town of Falmouth 1987.

LOW, Melvin Leslie (Ia) 1310 Sierra Dr NE Apt 14, Cedar Rapids IA 52402 B Everett MA 1938 s Melvin & Jean. BA Gordon Coll 1972; MDiv Nash 1975; U of Notre Dame 1979. D 4/22/1975 Bp Charles Thomas Gaskell P 11/15/1975 Bp Alexander D Stewart. Vic Trin Ch Emmetsburg IA 1997-2007; Ch Of S Thos Algona IA 1997-2006; 1987-1996; R Gr Ch Cedar Rapids IA 1983-1986; R S Mk's Ch Waupaca WI 1978-1983; R S Paul's Ch Windsor VT 1976-1978; Dio Wstrn Massachusetts Springfield 1975-1976; Asst Trin Epis Ch Ware MA 1975-1976. Soc of S Jn the Evang.

LOW, Raymond Albert (Mass) 5 Buttonwood Rd, Marshfield MA 02050 **Ret 2003-; R Emer S Lk's Epis Ch Scituate MA 2003-, R 1963-2002** B Melbourne VIC AU 1931 s Roy & Mavis. LTh Ridley Coll Melbourne AU 1957; BA Estrn Nazarene Coll 1972; MEd Boston St Coll 1982; MA Estrn Nazarene Coll 1987. Trans 6/1/1963 as Priest Bp Anson Phelps Stokes Jr. m 11/7/1959 Joan Elizabeth Low c 3. S Jn's Epis Ch Saugus MA 2000-2002; Dn Dio Massachusetts Boston MA 1999-2002; Cur S Paul's Ch Brockton MA 1961-1963; Serv Ch in Australia 1958-1961. Search for Justice and Equality in Palestine/Israel - Pres 1992-2002. Scituate Citizen of the Year Awd ChmbrCom 1993.

LOW, Salin Miller (Ct) 12 Meadowview Ct, Canton CT 06019 **Donations & Bequests, Bd Mem Dio CT Meriden CT 2015-; Dioc Fin Cmte Dio CT Meriden CT 1997-** B Norman OK 1949 d Edward & Julia. W&M 1969; BBA U of Oklahoma 1971; MBA U of Tulsa 1984; MDiv VTS 1990. D 6/23/1990 Bp Robert Manning Moody P 5/3/1991 Bp Allen Lyman Bartlett Jr. Bp & Dioc. Exec Cmte Dio CT Hartford CT 2006-2011; Planned Giv Cmte Dio Connecticut Meriden CT 1996-2003; BEC Dio CT Hartford CT 1996-2001; R S Jn's Ch Pine Meadow CT 1993-2014; Stwdshp Cmte Dio Pennsylvania Philadelphia PA 1992-1993; Asst Chr Ch Philadelphia Philadelphia PA 1990-1993.

LOW, William Harrison (Ct) 12 Meadowview Ct, Canton CT 06019 **Died 9/19/2016** B Hyannis MA 1928 s Alfred & Lillian. Oxford Sch of Bus Admin Cambridge MA 1949; Ya Berk 1965; STM Yale DS 1974. D 6/12/1965 Bp Charles Francis Hall P 12/1/1965 Bp Donald J Campbell. m 1/19/1997 Salin Miller Low c 2. Assoc S Paul's Epis Ch Bantam CT 2000-2007; P-t Chapl S Mich's Chap So Kent CT 1996-2016; Ret 1993-2016; R S Alb's Ch Simsbury CT 1978-1993; Dept Mssns Dio Connecticut Meriden CT 1967-1978; ExCoun 1980-1993; All SS Chap Hartford CT 1966-1978; Vic All SS Mssn Hartford CT 1966-1978; All SS' Epis Ch E Hartford CT 1966-1978; S Mk's Ch Ashland NH 1965-1966; P-in-c Trin Ch Meredith NH 1965-1966.

LOWE, Dianne Louise (Spok) St James Episcopal Church, 1410 NE Stadium Way, Pullman WA 99163 **Chapl Pullman Reg Hosp 2012-; D S Jas Pullman WA 2012-** B Detroit MI 1949 d Wayne & Josephine. PhD Pacific Wstrn U

1988. D 10/21/2012 Bp James E Waggoner Jr. c 1. Assn of Epis Deacons 2012; Assn of Profsnl Chapl 2013.

LOWE, Edward Charles (Ga) PO Box 168, Saint Marys GA 31558 **S Matt's Epis Ch Flat Rock MI 2005-** B Aurora IL 1951 s Clifford & Helen. Moody Bible Inst 1973; MA Moody Bible Inst 1996; DMin TESM 2006. D 6/2/2007 P 12/15/2007 Bp John Wadsworth Howe. m 4/20/1974 Catherine Grace Lowe c 3. Chr Ch S Marys GA 2009-2012; Asst S Barn Ch Deland FL 2007-2009; S Ptr's Epis Ch Lake Mary FL 2005-2007.

LOWE JR, Eugene Yerby (NY) 624 Colfax St, Evanston IL 60201 **Assoc Provost NWU 1995-** B Staten Island NY 1949 s Eugene & Miriam. BA Pr 1971; MDiv UTS 1978; MA UTS 1982; PhD UTS 1987. D 6/3/1978 P 12/1/1978 Bp Paul Moore Jr. m 11/4/1989 Jane Pataky Henderson. Asst Calv and St Geo New York NY 1978-1983; Asst H Comm In New York City 1978-1983.

LOWE, Harold Chapin (Dal) 2212 Saint Andrews, McKinney TX 75070 **Sacramentalist H Fam 1984-** B Wichita KS 1950 s Harold & Eris. BD U of Kansas 1973; MA Pepperdine U 1980. D 11/27/1983 P 6/1/1984 Bp Leonardo Romero-Rivera. m 5/3/1974 Norma Camargo c 2. Cn To Ordnry Dio No Mex 1984-1986. Auth, "Journ Of Indstrl Engr". NAAD. Ralph Jas Awd 1984; Fulbright Schlr 1973.

LOWE JR, J Fletcher (Del) 1600 Westbrook Ave Apt G-27, Richmond VA 23227 B Greenville SC 1932 s John & Marie. BA W&L 1954; MDiv GTS 1959. D 6/20/1959 P 7/16/1960 Bp Clarence Alfred Cole. m 6/27/1959 Mary Frances Adamson c 3. Vacation Supply The Amer Cathd of the H Trin Paris 75008 2001; Int R Emm Epis Ch Geneva 1201 2000; Exec Dir Virginia Interfaith Cntr for Publ Plcy Richmond VA 1997-2004; P-in-c S Paul's Within the Walls Rome 1997; Int Ch of the Ascen Munich 1996-1997; Int S Jn's Ch Richmond VA 1995-1996; Int S Jas Epis Ch Firenze 50123 1994; Chapl, Tchr, Coach The Epis Acad Newtown Sq PA 1993-1994; Bd Mem PBFWR New York NY 1988-1992; R Imm Ch Highlands Wilmington DE 1985-1993; Bd Mem, Chair Natl Hunger Com New York NY 1974-1982; R Ch Of The H Comf Richmond VA 1970-1985; Exec Dir - Dept of CSR Dio Virginia Richmond VA 1967-1970, Cmsn on Lay Mnstry, Dio Virginia 1995-2002, Stndg Committe, Pres, Dio Virginia 1983-1985, Stndg Com 1981-1985, Stndg Com, Dio Virginia 1981-1985, Human Needs Com, Dio Virginia 1981-1984, Exec Bd, Dio Virginia 1978-1980, Exec Com, Dio Virginia 1973-1980, Liturg Cmsn, Dio Virginia 1967-1976; Vic S Barn Ch Lynchburg VA 1963-1967; Vic Ch Of The Ascen Seneca SC 1959-1963; Bd Mem Voicesd for Virginia's Chld 2007-2016; Bd Mem Hsng Opportunities Made Equal (Hm) Richmond VA 2004-2015; Comp Dio Cmsn (Dio Pretoria, SA) Dio Delaware Wilmington 1987-1990, Dioc Coun 1987-1990, Dioc T/F on Cler/Lay Profsnl Compstn 1987-1990; Mem, Chair Richmond Mnstrl Assn 1967-1982; Chr Soc Relatns Com, Chair Dio SW Virginia Roanoke VA 1965-1967, Liturg Cmsn 1965-1967, Virginia Coun of Ch, Exec Com 1965-1967, Exec Com 1964-1967; Mem, Chair Lynchburg Mnstrl Assn 1963-1967. Co-Ed, "Radical Sending: Go to Love and Serve," *Radical Sending: Go to Love and Serve*, Ch Pub/Morehouse, 2016; Auth, "Baptism:the Event and the Adventure," *Baptism: The Event and the Adventure*, LeaderResources, 2006; Auth, "Wrshp and the Mnstry of the Baptized," *As We Gather to Pray*, Epis Ch Cntr, 1996; Co-Ed, "Mnstry in Daily Life: A Guide to Living the Baptismal Cov," *Mnstry in Daily Life: A Guide to Living the Baptismal Cov*, The Epis Ch Cntr, 1996; Auth, "Misc. Soc justice, Liturg & Baptismal Mnstry arts in Natl, Dioc, Loc and Ecum Pub"; Auth, "Selected Sermons , 1978-90," *Selected Sermons*, The Epis Ch Cntr. Cntr for Baptismal Living, Bd Mem 1998-2006; Episcopalians on Baptismal Mssn 2006. Soc Justice Maker VA Interfaith Cntr for Publ Plcy 2012; R Emer Ch of the H Comf, Richmond, VA 2009; Distinquished Alum Awd GTS 2007; Commendation Virginia St Senate and Hse of Delegates 2004; Commonwealth Awd, Interfaith advocacy and Relatns Coun for Amer's First Freedom 2003; Hon Cn S Ptr's Cathd, Dio Bukedi, Uganda 1982; Virginia Citizenship Awd Anti-Defamation League, Virginia Chapt 1976; All-Amer (lacrosse) Washington & Lee U 1954; ODK - Ldrshp Soc Washington & Lee U 1954. jflowe@aol.com

LOWE, John Leon (Ind) 200 Glennes Ln Apt 205, Dunedin FL 34698 B Indianapolis IN 1928 s Russel & Ethel. BA Pasadena Coll 1954; BD Butler U 1957; MA Butler U 1969. D 6/30/1957 P 1/4/1958 Bp John P Craine. m 2/5/1950 Patricia Lowe c 3. Assoc Ch Of The Ascen Clearwater FL 1998-2007; Vic S Johns Ch Indianapolis IN 1959-1965; Chapl (part time) Wmn Prison 1959-1964; Vic S Mich's Ch Noblesville IN 1957-1959. Intl Soc of Theta Phi 1957; Pres Indiana Acad of Rel 1976.

LOWE, Lori Marleen (Chi) 5116 W Malibu Ct, McHenry IL 60050 **P-in-c S Paul's Ch Mchenry IL 2012-** B Atlanta GA 1947 d Billy & Marion. U of W Georgia 1966; BA Georgia St U 1969; MDiv Candler TS Emory U 1983. D 6/7/1986 P 12/21/1988 Bp Charles Judson Child Jr. m 1/8/2000 William Pearman Mclemore c 3. Transitional R S Aug's Epis Ch Wilmette IL 2011-2012; Int S Marg's Ch Annapolis MD 2009-2010; R S Mk's Epis Ch Lagrange GA 1995-2009; Int S Thos Epis Ch Columbus GA 1994-1995; S Bede's Ch Atlanta GA 1991-1994; Chr Ch Norcross GA 1987-1991; Asst S Barth's Epis Ch Atlanta GA 1986-1987; Dir, Discerning Young Vocations Experience (DYVE) Dio

Atlanta Atlanta GA 1999-2009. Auth, "Wmn Of The Word". Cmnty Of S Mary. Omicron Delta Kappa Ldrshp Soc.

LOWE, Robert Steven (Chi) 2009 Regency Ct, Geneva IL 60134 **D S Mk's Ch Geneva IL 2005-** B Joplin MO 1947 s Billy & Ardeth. BD U of Arkansas 1970; MS Arizona St U 1971. D 2/5/2005 Bp Bill Persell. m 7/18/1969 Lela Lowe c 2.

LOWE JR, Thomas (RG) Episcopal Church of St. John, P.O. Box 449, Alamogordo NM 88310 **R S Jn's Epis Ch Alamogordo NM 2011-** B San Angelo TX 1948 s James & Martha. BA U of No Texas 1971; DDS U of Texas 1975; MPH U MN 1980; DBCS TESM 2006. D 10/21/2006 P 5/6/2007 Bp Jeffrey Neil Steenson. c 2. Captain (0-6) USPHS 1976-1996; Pres Otero Hunger Cltn 2012-2013; COM Dio The Rio Grande Albuquerque 2010-2011, Mem, Stndg Com 2008-2011, Chair, Bp Search Com 2008-2010, Pres, Stndg Com 2005-2006, Stndg Com Pres 2005-2006, Stndg Com Mem 2002-2006, Mem, Stndg Com 2002-2005, Dioc Coun Mem 1999-2002, Mem, Dioc Coun 1998-2002; Bd Dir Lincoln Cnty Humane Soc New Mex 2006-2008; Pres Eagle Creek Conservation Assn New Mex 2005-2007; Bd Mem Wells Fargo Bank New Mex 1999-2002; VP Ballet New Mex 1997-2000; Clnc Operating Com Whitman Walker Clnc Washington DC 1992-1996; Bd Dir Epis Caring Response to AIDS Washington DC 1991-1995; Bd Dir Washington Free Clnc Washington DC 1991-1995. co-Auth, "Prevalence of latex-specific IgE antibodies in Hosp Personl," *Annal of Allergy, Asthma, and Immunology*, Amer Coll of AAI, 1996; co-Auth, "Use of Tamoxifen and HRT in Wmn at High Risk for Breast Cancer," *Journ of the Natl Cancer Inst*, Natl Cancer Inst, 1996; Auth, "Human Tissue Regulation," *FDA Med Bulletin*, Food and Drug Admin, 1994; Auth, "Tattoos," *FDA Med Bulletin*, Food and Drug Admin, 1994; Auth, "Pedicle Screws," *FDA Med Bulletin*, Food and Drug Admin, 1994; co-Auth, "Condom Use for Prevention of Sexual Transmission of HIV Infection," *Journ of the AMA*, AMA, 1993; co-Auth, "Recommendation for Prevention of HIV and Hepatistis Infection in Hosp Personl," *Morbidity and Mortality Weekly Report*, Centers for Disease Control, 1987; co-Auth, "Condoms for Prevention of HIV," *Morbidity and Motality Weekly Report*, Centers for Disease Control, 1987; co-Auth, "The US Surgeon Generals Statement on AIDS and Condoms," *Surgeon Generals Statement*, Off of the US Surgeon Gnrl, 1987; co-Auth, "Infection Risks from Transplanted Corneas," *Morbidity and Mortality Weekly Report*, Centers for Disease Control, 1986; co-Auth, "Acanthamoeba Keratitis in Contact Lens Users," *Morbidity and Mortality Weekly Report*, Centers for Disease Control, 1986; Auth, "Regulating Sperm Banks," *Regulatory Affrs Focus*, Regulatory Affrs Profsnl Soc, 1966. Soc for the Sci Study of Sex 1993; Soc of Ord Scientists 2008. Fell Amer Coll of Epidemiologists 2007; Mntl Hlth Hall of Fame Reg Spprt Ntwk, Clark Cnty, WA 2007; Fell Amer Coll of Dentists 1992; Exemplary Serv Medal US Surgeon Gnrl 1992.

LOWE, Walter James (At) 1647 N Rock Springs Rd NE, Atlanta GA 30324 **Prof Of Theol Candler TS At Emory U 1971-** B Madison WI 1940 s James & Lois. BA DePauw U 1962; BTh U of Louvain 1963; BD Yale DS 1967; PhD Ya 1972. D 6/24/1967 Bp John P Craine. m 6/30/1979 Barbara DeConcini. Auth, "Mystery & The Unconscious: A Study In The Thought Of Paul Ricoent"; Auth, "Evil & The Unconscious"; Auth, "Theol & Difference: The Wound Of Reason". Conf Angl Theol.

LOWERY, Donald Andrew (NC) 210 S Chestnut St, Henderson NC 27536 **R The Ch Of The H Innoc Henderson NC 2005-** B Burlington VT 1956 s Andrew & Carolyn. BA Lee U 1979; MA Loyola Coll 1984; MDiv VTS 1987. D 6/20/1987 Bp Albert Theodore Eastman P 4/23/1988 Bp William Gillette Weinhauer. R Ch Of The Gd Shpd York SC 1991-2005; Asst S Mk's Ch Gastonia NC 1987-1991; Ch Silver Com for the Consecration of Samuel Rodman Dio No Carolina Raleigh NC 2017, Historic Properties Cmsn 2017-, St. Jas Kittrell Historic Ch Com 2017-, E Reg P Search Com 2009-2010, Old St. Jn's Com 2005-; Sprtl Dir For Happ Dio Upper So Carolina Columbia SC 2002-2005, Sprtl Dir For Curs 2001, Cmsn On Racism 1997-2000, Com St Of Ch 1994-1996, VP Cathd Coll Bd 1992-1993. Soc Of King Chas The Mtyr 2007. Henry Richardson Awd York Place, The Epis Chld'S Hm 2004.

LOWERY, Hermon Lee (Ga) 2705 Michael Rd, Albany GA 31721 **S Paul's Ch Albany GA 2013-** B Repton AL 1955 s Bill & Frances. MDiv Sewanee: The U So, TS 1990. D 6/2/1990 P 4/27/1991 Bp Charles Farmer Duvall. m 11/23/2009 Linda D Lowery c 2. Ch of the H Sprt Alabaster AL 2002-2013; Vic Ch Of The Resurr Centerville UT 1995-2002; Dio Utah Salt Lake City UT 1995-2002; S Paul's Ch Mobile AL 1990-1995; Dio Cntrl Gulf Coast Pensacola FL 1990. hleelowery@gmail.com

LOWNEY, James Edward (Ind) 2651 California St, Columbus IN 47201 B Spokane WA 1947 s James & Elizabeth. BA U of Portland 1970. D 10/22/2011 Bp Cate Waynick. c 1.

LOWREY, Edward Sager (NwPa) Box 54, 107 Harvey Road, Foxburg PA 16036 **Vic Memi Ch Of Our Fr 1988-** B Warren PA 1938 s Edward & Emma. BA U of Wstrn Ontario CA 1960; LTh Huron Angl Sem London On CA 1962; MTh Pittsburgh TS 1975. D 6/29/1962 Bp William Crittenden P 12/21/1963 Bp Winfred Hamlin Ziegler. m 9/14/1963 Melanie Lowrey. Ch Of Our Fr Foxburg PA 1989-2001, Vic 1962-1964; Non-par 1983-1987; R Trin Ch St Clair Shrs

MI 1980-1982; P S Aid's Ch Michigan Ctr MI 1979-1980; Dn Sw Convoc Dio Michigan Detroit MI 1977-1979; Chapl Mi St Prison 1976-1980; S Paul's Epis Ch Jackson MI 1976-1979; R S Matt's Epis Ch Homestead PA 1972-1975; R Trin Epis Ch Beaver PA 1966-1972; Cur S Jn's Ch Bangor ME 1964-1966; Bec Dio NW Pennsylvania Erie PA 1991-1993.

LOWREY III, Pierce Lang (At) 3830 Randall Farm Rd, Atlanta GA 30339 **Dio Atlanta Atlanta GA 2014-, 2006-2009; Epis Ch Cntr New York NY 2013-; Vic St Ben's Epis Ch 2006-; Vic St Ben's Epis Ch 2005-; Bd Mem Prot Hour/Day One Atlanta GA 2004-** B Austin TX 1953 s Pierce & Rosemari. MDiv Candler TS Emory U; Georgia Inst of Tech; BA Georgia St U. D 9/29/2004 Bp J Neil Alexander P 4/3/2005 Bp Frank Kellogg Allan. m 11/12/1988 Julie Marie Lowrey c 4. S Anne's Epis Ch Atlanta GA 2013-2014, 2005-2006; The GTS New York NY 2010-2013; St Ben's Epis Ch Smyrna GA 2010.

LOWRY, David B (LI) Po Box 51777, New Orleans LA 70151 **Geo Mercer TS Garden City NY 2010-** B Boston MA 1946 s David & Helen. BA Ham 1968; MDiv GTS 1975; PhD Indiana U 1988. D 1/15/1972 Bp Joseph Warren Hutchens P 7/1/1972 Bp Charles Alfred Voegeli. m 8/29/1970 Mary Lowry c 1. Dir Desmond Tutu Cntr The GTS New York NY 2010-2012, 2009-2010; R Chr Ch Manhasset NY 2004-2013, Asst 1974-1976, 1972-1975; Dn Chr Ch Cathd New Orleans LA 1986-1990; Assoc Prof Of Biblic Stds Mercer TS 1981-1986; Cn-In-Res Cathd Of The Incarn Garden City NY 1980-1986; R Ch Of The Nativ Indianapolis IN 1978-1980; Actg Chapl Holderness Sch Plymouth NH 1972-1974; VP Trst of the Estate belonging to the Dio Long Island Dio Long Island Garden City NY 2007-2010.

LOWRY, Robert Lynn (Tex) Trinity in the Woodland Texas, 3901 S Panther Creek Dr, The Woodlands TX 77381 B Kansas City MO 1936 s Earl & Francis. Texas A & M U; Iona Sch for Mnstry 2012. D 6/16/2012 Bp C Andrew Doyle. m 9/23/1954 Louise Wricht Lowry.

LOWRY III, William M (Ark) PO Box 224, Tunica MS 38676 **S Theo's Epis Ch Bella Vista AR 2016-; Ch Of The Epiph Tunica MS 2013-** B Clarksdale MS 1974 s William & Margaret. BS Mississippi Coll 2001; MDiv Sewanee: The U So, TS 2013; MDiv The TS at The U So 2013. D 9/14/2013 P 4/12/2014 Bp Duncan Montgomery Gray III. m 9/17/2005 Ivee Ayn Lowry c 2. The Chap Of The Cross Madison MS 2007-2010. wilmlow3@gmail.com

LOW-SKINNER, Debbie (Cal) 137 Redding Rd Apt C, Campbell CA 95008 **P-in-c Chr Epis Ch Sei Ko Kai San Francisco CA 2015-; Co-Chair Asian Cmsn of Dio Calif 2017-; VP, Engl Japanese Amer Rel Fed 2017-** B San Francisco CA 1952 d Donald & Ida. BS U of San Francisco 1974; MS Santa Clara U 1991; MDiv CDSP 1997; Cert Int Mnstry Prog 2002. D 6/21/1997 P 12/27/1997 Bp Richard Lester Shimpfky. Pstr Assoc S Andr's Ch Saratoga CA 2012-2014; Int R S Barth's Epis Ch Livermore CA 2010-2012; P in Res Epis Ch Of S Mk The Evang Bellmore NY 2009-2010; Int Gr Epis Ch Massapequa NY 2009; R Chr Ch Garden City NY 2003-2010; P in Charge S Mart's Epis Ch New Bedford MA 2000-2003; Cur All SS Ch Carmel CA 1998-2000; Assoc Vic Ch Of The H Sprt Campbell CA 1997-1998; Nomin Com Mem Dio California San Francisco CA 2011-2012; Epis Asiamerican Mnstry Cmsn Secty Dio Long Island Garden City NY 2009-2010, Co-Chair Bp Coadj Search Commitee 2008-2009, Dioc Coun Mem 2003-2008; Pres Garden City Cler Fllshp Garden City NY 2006-2010; Cathd Chapt Clerk Cathd Of The Incarn Garden City NY 2005-2010; Alum Coun Mem CDSP Berkeley CA 2005-2008; Dioc Coun Mem Dio Massachusetts Boston MA 2001-2003; Dioc Coun Mem Dio El Camino Real Salinas CA 1999-2000. EWC 1997-2014; Int Mnstry Ntwk 2002; OSL the Physcn 1999-2014; OHC 1997; Soc of Wmn Engr 1979-2003. revdeb95008@gmail.com

LOY, Reed J (NH) 885 Shore Rd, Cape Elizabeth ME 04107 **S Andr's Epis Ch Contoocook NH 2017-** B Exeter NH 1986 s James & Sarah Jane. BA U of New Hampshire 2008; MDiv CDSP 2015. D 6/6/2015 P 1/17/2016 Bp A Robert Hirschfeld. m 8/18/2012 Linden P Rayton c 1. S Alb's Ch Cape Eliz ME 2015-2017.

LOYA, Craig William (Neb) 113 N 18th St, Omaha NE 68102 **Dn Trin Cathd Omaha NE 2013-** B North Platte NE 1977 s Ernesto & JaNelle. BA Hastings Coll 1999; Dip Ang Stud Ya Berk 2002; MDiv Ya Berk 2002. D 10/11/2002 P 5/3/2003 Bp Creighton Leland Robertson. m 8/14/2004 Melissa Loya c 2. Cn to the Ordnry Dio Kansas Topeka KS 2011-2013, Cn to the Ordnry 2009-2013, Campus Mssnr 2007-2013; P-in-c Ch Of The Gd Shpd Fairhaven MA 2006-2007; S Mart's Epis Ch New Bedford MA 2006-2007; Int Asst R Gr Ch New Bedford MA 2004-2005; Vic Rosebud Epis Mssn Mssn SD 2002-2004. cloya@trinityepiscopal.org

LOYD, Janet Ellen (Oly) 56738 Sturgeon Rd, Darrington WA 98241 **P-in-c Ch Of The Trsfg Darrington WA 2012-** B Pasadena CA 1957 d Everil & Vesta. MA Claremont Grad U; BA Pomona Coll 1979. D 2/15/2011 P 6/20/2012 Bp Gregory Harold Rickel.

LOYD, Michael Corman (Kan) D 6/17/2017 Bp George Wayne Smith.

LOYOLA, Leo (Haw) Diocese o f Hawaii, 229 Queen Emma Sq, Honolulu HI 96813 **P-in-c S Jn's By The Sea Kaneohe HI 2013-** B Cavite City Philippines 1970 s Julio & Wilhelmina. BA U of Hawaii 1993; MDiv VTS 2012. D 5/27/2012 P 12/16/2012 Bp Robert Leroy Fitzpatrick. m 9/1/2007 Melody Eve Loy-

ola. Calv Epis Ch Kaneohe HI 2015-2017; Calv Epis Ch Preschool And Day Care Cntr Kaneohe HI 2015; The Epis Ch in Hawaii Honolulu HI 2012-2014.

LOZAMA, Abiade (Hai) **Dio Haiti Port-au-Prince HT 2009-** B Mirebalais Haiti 1979 s Michael & Solange. BTh Seminaire de Theologie EEH 2007; MA VTS 2011. D 11/1/2009 P 6/29/2010 Bp Jean Zache Duracin. m 2/13/2012 Djempscie A Lozama.

LOZANO, Kathleen Barbara (Los) St Matthias Episcopal Church, 7056 Washington Ave, Whittier CA 90602 B Boston MA 1938 d Clinton & Verna. BA California St U - Long Bch 2000; MA California St U, Fullerton 2001; D Claremont U 2012. D 2/7/2012 Bp Joseph Jon Bruno. c 3.

LUAL, Anderia Arok (Az) Diocese of Arizona, 114 W Roosevelt St, Phoenix AZ 85003 **Vic St Paul the Apos Sudanese Mssn Phoenix AZ 2015-** B 1956 s Lual & Deng. MTS Iliff TS 2006. Trans 9/4/2008 Bp Kirk Stevan Smith. Vic Dio Arizona Phoenix AZ 2008-2015; P Dio Colorado Denver CO 2002-2007.

LUBELFELD, Nicholas Paul Needham (Va) 4460 Edan Mae Ct, Annandale VA 22003 **Instr Whitaker TS 1982-** B Detroit MI 1950 s Prof & Joan. BA U MI 1972; Dip Theol Stud U of Durham Engl 1976; MDiv VTS 1978. D 6/17/1978 Bp William Jones Gordon Jr P 6/3/1979 Bp H Coleman Mcgehee Jr. m 5/22/1978 Elizabeth Lubelfeld c 2. Pstr Assoc Ch Of Our Redeem Aldie VA 2007-2009; Assoc The Falls Ch Epis Falls Ch VA 1994-2007; R Trin Ch Arlington VA 1986-1993; Serv Chr Conciliation Serving Cntrl MI 1983-1986; S Paul's Epis Ch Lansing MI 1978-1986. Auth, "I can't get the update to Wk".

LUCAS, Albert (HB) 4440 Meadow Creek Cir, Sarasota FL 34233 **Died 11/4/2016** B Philadelphia PA 1924 s Albert & Frances. PDS 1951. D 6/2/1951 Bp William P Remington P 12/1/1951 Bp Lane W Barton. m 5/19/1979 Patricia Ann Lucas. St Fran Hosp Hartford CT 1975-1977; Chapl-In-Trng Hartford Hosp CT 1973-1975; R S Alb's Simbury CT 1967-1973; Pres Joint Vstry Cov Par MD 1966-1967; R S Alb's Williamsort MD 1966-1967; R S Anne's Epis Ch Smithsburg MD 1966-1967; R S Jn's Par Hagerstown MD 1962-1967; R Trin Ch Bend OR 1959-1962; R S Steph's Epis Ch Orinda CA 1955-1959; R S Andr's Epis Ch Prineville OR 1951-1955. Cert Chapl Coll Of Chapl (Amer Prot Hosp Assn). 1st Citizens Awd Jr ChmbrCom 1953.

LUCAS, Alison C (ECR) 19315 Vineyard Ln, Saratoga CA 95070 **Ldr Centering Pryr 2012-; Chapl Ord of S Lk 2012-** B Wilmington DE 1925 d Allan & Edith. AA Centenary Coll 1946; BS U of Pennsylvania 1948; MS U of Hartford 1979; MA S Mary Coll Moraga CA 1980; BA Sch for Deacons 1991. D 12/2/1991 Bp Richard Lester Shimpfky. c 3. Sch Chapl / Rel Tchr S Andr's Sch Saratoga CA 1996-2009; D S Phil's Ch San Jose CA 1992-2012; Acad Dn S Andr's Sch Saratoga CA 1979-1990; Trnr New Engl Trng Inst 1965-1978; Rel Educ Consult Dio Maryland Baltimore MD 1964-1969. Auth, "Fam Life & Sex Educ," *Curric*, Simsbury, Conn., Publ Schools, 1968. Ord of S Lk 1990. Distinguished Alum Awd Centenary Coll 2002.

LUCAS, Jason Bryan (Minn) St. Edward Episcopal Church, 865 Ferndale Rd. N, Wayzata MN 55391 **R S Edw The Confessor Wayzata MN 2015-, 2014-2015** B Kearny AZ 1979 s James & Yolanda. BA U of Phoenix 2010; MDiv CDSP 2013; MDiv CDSP 2013. D 6/28/2012 P 6/27/2013 Bp Brian N Prior. m 7/18/2012 Matthew Johnson. Asst Gr Ch New Bedford MA 2013-2014. Intl Angl Liturg Consult 2014; Societas Liturgica 2014. frjason@stedwards-mn.org

LUCAS, Jeremy P (Ore) 1060 Chandler Rd, Lake Oswego OR 97034 **Chr Ch Par Lake Oswego OR 2014-** B Birmingham AL 1971 BA U of Alabama; MDiv GTS 2004. D 6/5/2004 P 12/2/2004 Bp Henry Nutt Parsley Jr. m 6/10/2015 Siobhan Passmore c 1. Ch Of The H Sprt Episco Battle Ground WA 2011-2014; Exec Coun Appointees New York NY 2008-2011; D-in-c S Tim's Epis Ch Athens AL 2004-2008. rector@ccparish.org

LUCAS, Kimberly Danielle (WA) 1830 Connecticut Ave NW, Washington DC 20009 **R S Marg's Ch Washington DC 2012-** B Fayetteville NC 1970 d D D & Marian. BS Wake Forest U 1992; MDiv UTS 1995. D 6/29/1996 Bp Robert Carroll Johnson Jr P 4/19/1997 Bp Ronald Hayward Haines. m 11/19/2009 Mark D Retherford c 4. S Ambroses Ch Raleigh NC 2005-2011; Chr Epis Ch No Hills Pittsburgh PA 1999-2001; Asst S Lk's Ch Trin Par Beth MD 1996-1999. klucas@stmargaretsdc.org

LUCAS, Mary Louise (Mass) 136 Bay Street #501, Hamilton L8P 3H8 Canada B Toronto ON CA 1948 d Harry & Mary. BA York U 1970; MDiv Harvard DS 1975. Trans 6/1/1987 Bp David Elliot Johnson. R S Jn's Ch Winthrop MA 1987-1990; Asst Ch Of S Jn The Evang Boston MA 1982-1985; Serv Ch Of Can 1975-1981.

LUCAS, Paul Nahoa (Haw) 47-074 Lihikai Dr, Kaneohe HI 96744 **S Jn's By The Sea Kaneohe HI 2016-** B Palo Alto CA 1959 s George & Ruth. BA U of Hawaii - Manoa 1982; JD Santa Clara Sch of Law 1987. D 10/23/2015 P 8/27/2016 Bp Robert Leroy Fitzpatrick. m 5/26/1984 Kathleen Kawehi Neumann c 3.

LUCAS, Rigal (Hai) Box 1309, Port-Au-Prince Haiti **Dio Haiti Port-au-Prince HT 1992-** B Maissade HT 1961 s Odver & Aneclea. Cert Sem of Theol Montrouis 1992. D 12/1/1992 Bp Luc Anatole Jacques Garnier P 9/21/1993 Bp Jean Zache Duracin. m 12/28/1995 Sherline Desarmes Lucas c 2.

LUCAS, T Stewart (Md) Church of the Nativity, 419 Cedarcroft Rd, Baltimore MD 21212 **P-in-c The Ch Of The Nativ Cedarcroft Baltimore MD 2014-, P-in-c 2013-2014** B Macon GA 1976 s David & Mary. BS U GA 1998; MDiv VTS 2001. D 6/9/2001 Bp Robert Gould Tharp P 1/5/2002 Bp John L Rabb. m 1/1/2013 Douglas Albert Campbell. Assoc R S Marg's Ch Annapolis MD 2007-2013; Assoc R Memi Ch Baltimore MD 2001-2007. stewart@ nativitycomforter.org

LUCAS, Wanda Beth (Ga) 524 Suncrest Blvd, Savannah GA 31410 B Guthrie OK 1938 d Carl & Opal. BS Oklahoma St U 1960; CPE 1996. D 12/12/1995 Bp Henry Irving Louttit. m 12/21/1958 Michael Arthur Lucas c 5. D S Fran Of The Islands Epis Ch Savannah GA 1995-2013; Chapl Memi Med Cntr Savannah GA 1995-1996. ACPE.

LUCENT, Robert Brian (SanD) 629 Judson St, Escondido CA 92027 **Trin Ch Escondido CA 1995-** B Paterson NJ 1927 s Santos & Margaret. BA Hobart and Wm Smith Colleges 1948; BD SWTS 1952. D 6/29/1951 Bp William Blair Roberts P 2/5/1952 Bp Conrad H Gesner. m 1/10/1952 Moina MacPherson Lucent c 2. Ch Of The H Fam Fresno CA 1976-1992; Epis Dio San Joaquin Modesto CA 1976-1982; All SS Epis Ch Omaha NE 1965-1972; Vic S Paul's Epis Ch Grinnell IA 1965-1972; Vic St. Fran Ch Sioux City NE 1965-1972; Chapl USNR 1965-1969; Chapl USNR Active Duty 1962-1965; P-in-c Dio Louisiana New Orleans LA 1957-1958; Dio So Dakota Pierre SD 1952-1956; S Matt's Epis Ch Rapid City SD 1952-1956; P-in-c Cheyenne River Indn Mssn Cheyenne Agcy SD 1952-1955; Asst Rosebud Epis Mssn Mssn SD 1951-1952.

LUCEY, David (Va) 399 Hope St., Bristol RI 02809 **S Fran Epis Ch Great Falls VA 2015-** B Nansemond County VA 1957 s Dennis & Grace. BA Hampden-Sydney Coll 1979; MBA Wake Forest U 1981; MDiv GTS 1999. D 2/6/1999 P 9/11/1999 Bp Richard Frank Grein. m 4/25/1987 Katherine H Harmer c 5. R S Mich's Ch Bristol RI 2009-2015; Assoc R The Ch Of The H Sprt Lake Forest IL 2005-2009; The Par Of S Mary And S Jude NE Harbor ME 2002-2005; Asst Min S Matt's Ch Bedford NY 1999-2002. Omicron Delta Epsilon 1979; Phi Aplha theta 1979; Soc of the Pilgrims 2002.

LUCHS, Lewis Richard (Chi) 6417 81st St, Cabin John MD 20818 **Non-par 1966-** B Portsmouth OH 1935 s Fred & Evelyn. BA Beloit Coll 1957; MD SWTS 1961. D 6/24/1961 Bp Charles L Street P 12/1/1961 Bp Gerald Francis Burrill. m 7/13/1963 Susan Jean Robertson. P-in-c S Andr In Zomba Nyasaland 1964-1966; Vic S Andr In Zomba Nyasaland 1963-1964; Cur Emm Epis Ch Rockford IL 1961-1963.

LUCK, Diana Nelson (Dal) 6912 Merrilee Ln, Dallas TX 75214 **Asst S Matt's Cathd Dallas TX 1996-** B Holland MI 1939 d Lewis & Lola. Lic Angl TS 1995; U of Texas in Arlington 1996. D 6/29/1996 Bp James Monte Stanton. m 5/30/1987 George Edmund Luck c 3. Dio Dallas Dallas TX 2001-2004, Mem, COM 2000-2011, Archd 2000-2010.

LUCK JR, George Edmund (Dal) 6912 Merrilee Ln, Dallas TX 75214 **Ret 1999-; Inst. Old Test & Sprtlty Angl TS Dallas TX 1972-** B Houston TX 1933 s George & Allene. Daniel Baker Coll 1953; BA U of No Texas 1955; MDiv PDS 1958; Nash 1967. D 6/18/1958 P 12/20/1958 Bp John Joseph Meakin Harte. m 5/30/1987 Diana Nelson Luck c 3. Int Dn S Matt's Cathd Dallas TX 2001-2002, Cn 1999-2000; Pres Stndg Com Dio Dallas Dallas TX 1994-1995, COM 1990-1996, Stndg Com 1992-1995, ExCoun 1974-1991; R H Trin Ch Rockwall TX 1987-1999; R S Chris's Ch And Sch Ft Worth TX 1978-1987; Assoc S Jn's Epis Ch Dallas TX 1969-1978; R S Wm Laud Epis Ch Pittsburg TX 1967-1969; Chapl S Anselm Cbury Hse Arlington TX 1962-1967; Vic H Trin Forney TX 1960-1962; Ch Of Our Merc Sav Kaufman TX 1958-1962; P-in-c S Thos Ch Ennis TX 1958-1959. OHC 1952.

LUCK, G Thomas (CNY) 310 Montgomery St., Syracuse NY 13202 **Cn Theol Dio Cntrl New York 2007-; Co-Fndr, Mem of the Bd Cathd Sq Dvlpmt Corp Syracuse NY 2010-; Co-Fndr Cathd Sq Nbrhd Assn 2010-; Bd Mem Samar Cntr Syracuse NY 2004-** B Philadelphia PA 1955 s George & Jane. Cntrl Coll London 1977; BA Austin Coll 1978; MDiv Nash 1981; Cler Ldrshp Proj Class IX 2001; ALM Harv 2008; Maxwell Sch Syr 2009; Kellogg Sch NWU 2012; DMin CDSP 2014; DMin CDSP 2014; DMin CDSP 2014. D 6/20/1981 P 5/31/1982 Bp Archibald Donald Davies. m 6/20/2015 Jane Brostrom Lewis c 4. Dioc Bd Dio Cntrl New York 2009-2013; Dn St Paul's Syracuse Syracuse NY 2004-2014; Dep-GC Dio Cntrl New York 2004-2013; Stndg Com Dio Cntrl New York 2004-2008; Fin Com Dio Cntrl New York 2004; R Epis Ch Of S Mary The Vrgn Falmouth ME 1991-2004; R The Ch Of The Redeem Rochester NH 1986-1991; Cur S Jn's Ch Portsmouth NH 1983-1986; Cur Ch Of The Epiph Richardson TX 1981-1983. Auth, "Var arts," *The Post-Standard/syracuse.com*, Syracuse Media Grp; Auth, "Var arts," *The Post-Standard/syracuse.com*, Syracuse Media Grp. EPF; Epis Publ Plcy Ntwk; Episcopalians for Global Recon; Fllshp of St. Jn, The SSJE 1995. Ch of the Cathd Ondo Dio Ch of Nigeria Angl 1997; The Crucis Cross Camp Crucis, Granbury, TX 1973.

LUCKENBACH, David Andrew (Tex) 1709 S College Ave, Tyler TX 75701 **R Chr Epis Ch Tyler TX 2009-** B Limestone ME 1968 s Carl & Carolyn. BA Texas A&M U 1991; MDiv Sewanee: The U So, TS 1998. D 6/24/1998 Bp Robert Boyd Hibbs P 2/5/1999 Bp James Edward Folts. m 5/5/1999 Silvia Luckenbach c 3. S Mk's On The Mesa Epis Ch Albuquerque NM 2002-2009;

S Lk's Epis Ch San Antonio TX 2000-2002; Ch Of The Adv Brownsville TX 1998-2000. dluckenbach@christchurchtyler.org

LUCKETT JR, David Stafford (Miss) 4241 Otterlake Cove, Niceville FL 32578 B Alexandria LA 1933 s David & Anna. BS LSU 1958; MDiv Bex Sem 1962; MEd Mississippi Coll 1985. D 6/16/1962 P 12/22/1962 Bp John P Craine. m 6/15/1958 Janice C Luckett c 3. Assoc S Andr's By The Sea Epis Ch Destin FL 2011, Int 2009; Int S Andr's Cathd Jackson MS 2005-2007; Int Trin Ch Apalachicola FL 2004-2005; Int Ch Of The Epiph Crestview FL 2000-2004; R & Headmaster All SS' Epis Sch Vicksburg MS 1984-1999; R S Paul's Epis Ch Meridian MS 1974-1984; Vic S Tim's Ch Indianapolis IN 1971-1972; Cur S Lk's Ch Baton Rouge LA 1969-1971; R S Jas Ch New Castle IN 1965-1969; Vic S Jn's Ch Washington IN 1962-1965; Chapl for 27 yrs (Col) US-Army (Ret).

LUCKEY, Marion Isabelle Aiken (NMich) 1531 Vardon Rd, Munising MI 49862 **P S Jn's Ch Munising MI 1991-** B Newark NJ 1940 d Raymond & Margaret. MI SU; Wstrn Michigan U; BA Cntr Coll 1962; MA Nthrn Michigan U 1967. D 6/3/1990 P 1/6/1991 Bp Thomas Kreider Ray. m 8/1/1964 Thomas Hannan Luckey.

LUCKEY III, Thomas Hannan (NMich) E9430 E. Munising Ave. #2, Munising MI 49862 B Louisville KY 1939 s Thomas & Justine. BS Manchester Coll 1961; MA Nthrn Michigan U 1967; Cert Cntrl Michigan U 1970. D 9/8/1996 Bp Thomas Kreider Ray. m 8/1/1964 Marion Isabelle Aiken Luckey c 2. D S Jn's Ch Munising MI 1996-2007, D 1996-.

LUCKRITZ, Denzil John (Chi) 558 Kingsway Dr, Aurora IL 60506 **Trin Epis Ch Aurora IL 2015-** B Clinton IA 1954 s John & Lila. BA U of Nthrn Colorado 1976; MDiv SWTS 1989. D 6/8/1989 Bp William Carl Frey P 12/16/1989 Bp Frank Tracy Griswold III. m 8/6/1977 Lisa A Speer c 2. R S Ptr's Ch Osterville MA 2010-2015; R S Jn The Evang Lockport IL 1990-2010; Asst R The Epis Ch Of S Jas The Less Northfield IL 1989-1990; Dir of Oprtns Bexley Seabury Fed Chicago IL 1988-1991.

LUDBROOK, Helen Christine (Mo) 1422 Lawnwood Dr, Des Peres MO 63131 B Brisbane Queensland AU 1942 d Arthur & Marjorie. Eden TS; U of So Australia Au 1964; MDiv Sewanee: The U So, TS 1984. D 6/15/1984 P 3/25/1985 Bp William Augustus Jones Jr. m 1/17/1964 Philip A Ludbrook c 3. Assoc R S Mart's Ch Ellisville MO 1991-2007, Asst 1987-1990; Asst S Tim's Epis Ch S Louis MO 1984-1987.

LUECKENHOFF, James Joseph (WLa) 1518 Griffith St, Lake Charles LA 70601 B Jefferson City MO 1939 s Arthur & Eleanor. BA CUA 1970. Rec 9/1/1999 as Priest Bp Robert Jefferson Hargrove Jr. m 10/2/1987 Linda Lueckenhoff. Trin Epis Ch Deridder LA 2006-2011; Epis Ch Of The Gd Shpd Lake Chas LA 2002-2011, Asst 1990-.

LUECKERT, Diana Rowe (NCal) 4800 Olive Oak Way, Carmichael CA 95608 **Asst S Fran Epis Ch Fair Oaks CA 2000-** B Oakland CA 1933 d Ralph & Mary. AA Coll of Marin 1969; BD California St U 1976; Cert Olympia TS 1987. D 12/3/1991 P 6/1/1992 Bp Vincent Waydell Warner. m 8/3/1976 Drury Waller Wood. P-in-c S Paul's Epis Ch Sacramento CA 2002-2005; P S Christophers Epis Ch Westport WA 1992-2000.

LUEDDE, Christopher S (Roch) 31 Kitty Hawk Dr, Pittsford NY 14534 B Saint Louis MO 1951 s Fullerton & Jeanne. BA U of Kansas 1973; MDiv Pittsburgh TS 1976. D 8/19/1976 Bp Robert Bracewell Appleyard P 3/12/1977 Bp Lloyd Edward Gressle. m 1/6/1973 Susan K Luedde c 2. R S Thos Epis Ch Rochester NY 1996-2009; R S Paul's Ch Maumee OH 1987-1996; Int Trin Ch Toledo OH 1985-1987; Vic S Mk's Epis Ch Bridgeport MI 1978-1985; Asst Trin Epis Ch Carbondale PA 1976-1978. Oxford Roundtable affiliate of Oxf, Eng. 2008; Oxford Roundtable affiliate of Oxf, Eng. 2007; Who'S Who In Rel 92-93; El Shaddai Biblic Stds Lld; Jas H Brooks Bible Prize Westminster Coll.

LUETHE, Robin Lewis (Oly) 789 Highway 603, Chehalir WA 98532 B Bremerton WA 1940 s Alfred & Olivia. BA Whitman Coll 1962; MDiv GTS 1965. D 6/29/1965 P 3/30/1966 Bp Ivol I Curtis. m 12/27/1968 Lois Mae Luethe c 3. S Anne's Epis Ch Washougal WA 1991-1998; R Epiph (now St Tim) Chehalis WA 1972-1990; S Tim's Epis Ch Chehalis WA 1972-1989; Chapl US-NR 1969-1972; Cur S Lk's Epis Ch Vancouver WA 1965-1969. Auth, "arts," *Living Ch.*

LUFKIN, Alison C (Colo) PO Box 1305, Leadville CO 80461 **S Geo Epis Mssn Leadville CO 2004-** B Elmhust IL 1963 BA Wheaton Coll. D 7/19/2003 P 9/20/2005 Bp William Jerry Winterrowd. m 9/7/1985 George S Lufkin c 2. Dio Colorado Denver CO 2014-2017.

LUFKIN, George S (Colo) PO Box 243, Leadville CO 80461 B Tucson AZ 1963 s George & Carolyn. BA Wheaton Coll 1985; MBA Pace U 1989; Colgate-Rochester Div 1990. D 1/16/2005 Bp Robert John O'Neill P 7/20/2005 Bp William Jerry Winterrowd. m 9/7/1985 Alison C Connor c 2. Dio Colorado Denver CO 2014-2017.

LUGER, Virginia M (ND) 821 N 4th St Apt 3, Bismarck ND 58501 **D S Lk's Ch Ft Yates ND 1996-** B Milwaukee WI 1928 d Ezra & Lauretta. Cert Jamestown Coll 1949; AA Stndg Rock Cmnty Coll 1976; BS U of Mary 1989. D 11/22/1996 Bp Andrew Fairfield. m 5/22/1948 Ferdinand Luger c 4. Auth, "No Dakota Veterans Cemetery: A Haven Of Peace," *No Dakota Rea/Rtc.* Tribune Goodwill Awd The Bismarck Tribune 2003; Nominee, Golden Rule Awd J.C. Penney 2000.

LUGO, Beverley Lee (Ida) 411 10th Ave S, Nampa ID 83651 B Fairbanks AK 1968 d Floyd & Gloria. BA NW Nazarene U 1991; MS U of Phoenix 2009. D 3/19/2017 Bp Brian James Thom. m 4/23/2010 Ruben Lugo c 1.

LUHRING, Peggy Williams (SVa) 4449 N Witchduck Rd, Virginia Beach VA 23455 B Memphis TN 1948 d Henry & Mildred. BS U GA 1971; MA Bowie St Coll 1981; MSW Norfolk St U 1988. D 6/14/2008 Bp John Clark Buchanan. m 10/29/2011 Henry Garrett Luhring. D Old Donation Ch Virginia Bch VA 2012-2016; D All SS' Epis Ch Virginia Bch VA 2008-2012.

LUI, David Suikwei (Cal) 1011 Harrison St # 202, Oakland CA 94607 B China 1944 CDSP. D 6/7/2003 P 12/6/2003 Bp William Edwin Swing. m 12/9/1967 Selina Lui c 2. R Ch Of The Incarn San Francisco CA 2003-2016.

LUJAN, Mary Royes (EO) Po Box 25, Hood River OR 97031 B Summerville OR 1968 d George & Valerie. BS Estrn Oregon U 1996; MDiv VTS 2001. D 6/5/2001 P 6/5/2002 Bp William O Gregg. m 10/20/2007 Ken Michael Lujan. Diocesean Coun Mem Dio Estrn Oregon 2004-2007; R The Par Of S Mk The Evang Hood River OR 2003-2008; Palmer Memi Ch Houston TX 2001-2002.

LUKANICH, Emily A (Colo) Christ Episcopal Church, PO Box 1000, Vail CO 81658 **Epis Ch Of The Trsfg Vail CO 2016-** B Camp Lejeune NC 1977 d Jonathan & Janet. BA U IL 1999; MDiv VTS 2014. D 5/24/2014 P 11/22/2014 Bp Mark Bourlakas. m 11/22/2008 Christopher J Lukanich c 2. Cur Chr Ch Blacksburg VA 2014-2016. emily@episcopalvail.com

LUKAS, Arlene (WNC) 416 N Haywood St, Waynesville NC 28786 B Chicago IL 1949 d Lawrence & Gertrude. MA Roosevelt U 1981; MDiv Starr King Sch for the Mnstry 1993; DAS VTS 2001. D 6/23/2001 Bp Michael B Curry P 3/16/2002 Bp Bob Johnson. Gr Ch In The Mountains Waynesville NC 2008-2015; S Aug's Epis Ch Wilmette IL 2004-2008; T To R S Phil's Ch Brevard NC 2001-2004. mountainpriest1847@gmail.com

LUKAS, Randolph Edgar (Alb) PO Box 827, New Lebanon NY 12125 **D Ch Of Our Sav New Lebanon NY 2010-** B Queens NY 1957 s Edgar & Gloria. BA CUNY Queens Coll 1986. D 6/5/2010 Bp William Howard Love. m 10/11/1987 Carol Anne Lukas c 2.

LUKENS JR, Alexander M (Colo) 536 Seneca Cir, Walsenburg CO 81089 B Helena MT 1938 s Alexander & Julia. U of Heidelberg 1959; BA German Ya 1960; BD CDSP 1964; Dine Coll Shiprock NM 2006. D 6/11/1964 Bp Joseph Summerville Minnis P 3/12/1965 Bp Charles Francis Hall. Assoc Dir Pstr Care and Educ Presb/St. Lk's Med Cntr Denver CO 1976-1989; Chapl-in-Res Presb Med Cntr 1973-1975; Chapl Intern Presb/ St. Lk's Med Cntr Denver CO 1973-1975; Asst S Barn Epis Ch Denver CO 1970-1973; Chapl St Dept of Corrections Huntsville TX 1969-1970; 1965-1967; Asst San Juan Mssn Farmington NM 1965-1967; Asst Gr Ch Manchester NH 1964-1965. "Thoughts on the Sacr and the Demonic," *Navajo Stds Conf*, 2009. ACPE 1973.

LUKENS, Ann Pierson (Oly) 2015 Killarney Way, Bellevue WA 98004 **Chair, Bd Dir Dio Olympia Seattle 2010-, Bd Dir 2008-, Coun 1996-2000, D 1993-1996** B Harrisonburg VA 1946 d Earl & Mary. BA Br 1971; MDiv Seattle U 1993; DMin Columbia TS 2007. D 11/12/1993 P 7/9/1994 Bp Vincent Waydell Warner. m 7/8/1967 Terence P Lukens c 3. R S Mich And All Ang Ch Issaquah WA 2000-2013; S Thos Epis Ch Medina WA 1994-2000.

LUKENS, Matthew M (Haw) 183 Alala Rd, Kailua HI 96734 **Assoc Emm Epis Ch Kailua HI 2015-** B Birmingham AL 1986 s Matthew & Vicki. BA Unversity of Virginia 2009; MDiv Ya Berk 2013. D 6/8/2013 Bp Shannon Sherwood Johnston. Cur Par of St Clem Honolulu HI 2013-2014.

LULEY, William Tracy (Mo) 1101 Sulphur Spring Rd, Manchester MO 63021 B Lynwood CA 1953 s Charles & Adelaide. BBA Wstrn Michigan U 1977; MDiv Nash 1983. D 5/13/1983 Bp William Cockburn Russell Sheridan P 11/25/1983 Bp Charles Bennison Sr. m 5/22/1982 Mary Luley c 3. R S Lk's Epis Ch Manchester MO 1996-2014; Vic Ch Of The Ascen Epis Springfield MO 1992-1996; R Trin Epis Par Waterloo IA 1988-1992; R S Andr's Ch Big Rapids MI 1985-1988; Cur Emm Ch Petoskey MI 1983-1985.

LULLO, Milania (WNY) 200 Cazenovia St, Buffalo NY 14210 B Buffalo NY 1955 d Chester & Mary. EFM 2009. D 12/26/2009 Bp Michael Garrison. c 2.

LUMBARD, Carolyn Mary Dunsmore (Roch) 326 Frederick Douglas St, Rochester NY 14608 B Durham NC 1945 d Arthur & Doris. Duke 1965; BA Ups 1969; MDiv VTS 1990. D 6/2/1990 P 12/1/1990 Bp John Shelby Spong. m 6/25/1988 Thomas Lumbard c 2. Dio Rochester Henrietta 2000-2007; S Alb's Ch Oakland NJ 1997-2000; Vic Chr Ch Belleville NJ 1992-1997; Assoc S Paul's Epis Ch Morris Plains NJ 1990-1992.

LUMLEY, Dale Allen (WK) 906 W Wheat Ave, Ulysses KS 67880 **Vic Ch Of The Epiph Concordia KS 2007-** B New York NY 1947 s Thomas & Julia. BA GW 1983; MDiv VTS 1990. Trans 12/1/1994 Bp Orris George Walker Jr. m 1/12/1985 Miriam Lumley. S Jn's Ch Ulysses KS 2010-2012; Dio Wstrn Kansas Hutchinson KS 2007-2010; H Trin Epis Ch Madera CA 1998-2005; All SS Ch Brooklyn NY 1994-1997; Serv Ch Of Can 1991-1994. frdalelumley@hotmail.com

LUNA JR, Eulalio Gallardo (WTex) 234 W Mariposa Dr, San Antonio TX 78212 **Ret 2002-** B San Antonio TX 1942 s Eva. BA Trin U San Antonio 1965;

MDiv Epis TS of the SW 1977. D 6/20/1977 P 1/29/1978 Bp Scott Field Bailey. m 6/7/1968 Mary Grace Luna c 3. R All SS Epis Ch San Benito TX 1987-2002, R 1978-1987; R Chr Ch Epis Laredo TX 1982-1987; Texas Mltry Inst San Antonio TX 1977-1978; Chapl Tx Mltry Inst San Antonio 1977-1978. Intl Ord Of S Lk The Physcn 1984.

LUNA, Julie Ann (Minn) D 6/27/2017 Bp Brian N Prior.

LUND, Joseph Walter (WA) 70381 Placerville Rd, Rancho Mirage CA 92270 **Asstg Cler S Marg's Epis Ch Palm Desert CA 2006-** B Minot ND 1946 s John & Marie. BS U of Akron 1968; JD Geo 1973; MDiv VTS 1991; DMin SWTS 1998. D 6/15/1991 Bp Ronald Hayward Haines P 12/20/1991 Bp James Winchester Montgomery. m 12/10/2011 James P Kelley. R S Dav's Par Washington DC 1996-2003; Assoc Chr Ch Par Kensington MD 1991-1996. SKCM 1990. Mem of the Bd Epis Comm. Serv 2007; Co-Chair Epis Peace Cmsn 1998.

LUND, Judith Ann (Ark) 8280 Spanker Ridge Dr, Bentonville AR 72712 **Chapl Cir of Life Hospice Springfield AR 2007-; St. Thos Epis Ch Springfield AR 2006-; Chapl St. Mary's Hosp Rogers AR 2004-** B Minneapolis MN 1940 d Elmer & Anna. MA Luther TS 1998; Cert Theol Stud Epis TS of the SW 2004. D 12/4/2004 P 6/11/2005 Bp Larry Maze. m 4/22/1961 William V Lund c 2.

LUND, Virginia U Sapienza (Mil) 1101 Greenough Dr W, Apt. E-6, Missoula MT 59802 B Detroit MI 1938 d Paul & Giovanina. Whitaker TS 1984; MA EDS 1985. D 12/21/1985 P 12/5/1987 Bp H Coleman Mcgehee Jr. c 2. Chapl St Fran Hse Madison WI 1991-2003, Asst Chapl 1988-1990; Cur S Gabr's Epis Ch Eastpointe MI 1987-1988; The Whitaker Inst of Theol Detroit MI 1986-1988; Instr Whitaker TS Detroit MI 1986-1987. Auth, "Revolutionary Forgiveness: Feminists Reflections on Nicaragua," 1986. EWC 1990.

LUNDAK, Joel D (Neb) 1702 1st Ave, Nebraska City NE 68410 **Died 10/9/2016** B Fort Lewis WA 1941 s Edward & Mary. BA U of Nebraska 1963; STB GTS 1966; MA U of Nebraska 1981; PhD U of Nebraska 1988. D 6/9/1966 P 12/1/1966 Bp Russell T Rauscher. m 6/19/2004 Helen Lundak c 4. Chapl St Mary's Ch Nebraska City NE 1998-2016, 1998-1999; Prof Of Psych Peru St Coll 1989-2016; Ch Of The H Trin New York NY 1982-1998; S Andr's Ch Seward NE 1982-1998, P-in-c 1978-1998; H Trin Ch York NE 1982-1995; Chapl Nebraska Dept Of Corrections 1981-1985; R S Johns Ch Albion NE 1971-1974; Vic Incarn In Papillon NE 1969-1971; Gr Epis Ch Huron SD 1967-1969, R 1967-1969; S Andr's Ch Omaha NE 1966-1967, Cur 1966-1967. Auth, "A Wellness Approach To Rehab In A Maximum Security Prison"; Auth, "Wellness Perspectives". Best Correctional Practices Awd 1998.

LUNDBERG III, Nelson John (Alb) 36 Plaza Avenue, Governor's Sq, Rensselaer NY 12144 **Died 12/1/2016** B Albany NY 1941 s Nelson & Geraldine. STB GTS; BA Marist Coll. D 6/3/1967 Bp Allen Webster Brown P 12/2/1967 Bp Charles Bowen Persell Jr. H Name Boyntonville Hoosick Falls NY 1992-2005; P-in-c Chr's Ch Duanesburg NY 1977-1979; P-in-c S Bon Ch Guilderland NY 1970-1979; Cur Chr Ch Epis Hudson NY 1968-1970; Cur S Paul's Ch Troy NY 1967-1968.

LUNDBERG, Richard Evard (Chi) 811 E Central Rd Apt 239, Arlington Heights IL 60005 **Died 11/12/2016** B Mishawaka IN 1925 s Gustave & Blanche. BA Yankton Coll 1949; STB GTS 1959. D 5/26/1951 P 12/8/1951 Bp Wallace E Conkling. c 4. Ret 1990-2016; R S Simons Ch Arlington Hts IL 1975-1990; R S Paul's Par Riverside IL 1968-1975; Dn Denver Deanry Dio Colorado Denver CO 1965-1968, 1960-1966, Chair Div Yth 1958-1966, Coll Wk Div DeptCE 1958-1964; Chapl Fed Correctional Inst 1959-1968; R St Georges Englewood CO 1957-1968; Vic S Tim's Epis Ch Rangely CO 1956-1957; S Eliz's Ch Whiterocks UT 1954-1957; P-in-c Ch Of The H Sprt Randlett UT 1953-1954; S Paul's Epis Ch Vernal UT 1953-1954; Vic S Paul's Ch Dekalb IL 1951-1953; Stndg Com Dio Chicago Chicago IL 1974-1990, Pres Epis Cooprtv 1969-1973. Sprtl Dir, Grad Sums GTS 1987.

LUNDELIUS, Carolyn S (WA) 5801 Nicholson Lane Apt 1923, Rockville MD 20852 **Ret Dio Washington 2003-** B Bryan TX 1931 d William & Heulette. AA Stephens Coll 1950; BS TCU 1983; Lic Angl TS 1984; U So 1995. D 11/24/1984 Bp Archibald Donald Davies P 11/20/1991 Bp Ronald Hayward Haines. c 2. P-in-c Gr Epis Ch Silver Sprg MD 2004-2005; R S Mary Magd Ch Silver Sprg MD 1999-2002, Assoc 1993-1996; P-in-c S Andr's Epis Ch Coll Pk MD 1997-1999; P-in-c Gd Shpd Epis Ch Silver Sprg MD 1996-1997; Asst Gr Ch Washington DC 1990-1993; Sch Chapl The Epis Ch Of The Trsfg Dallas TX 1987-1990; Assoc Chr The King Epis Ch Ft Worth TX 1985-1986. The OSL 2001.

LUNDEN, Michael Carl (NY) 118 S Church St, Goshen NY 10924 **R S Jas' Ch Goshen NY 2000-** B Tampa FL 1962 s Jean. BS SUNY at Buffalo 1985; Cert S Hyacinth Coll & Sem Granby MA 1990; MDiv GTS 1997. D 6/14/1997 P 12/13/1997 Bp Richard Frank Grein. m 9/24/2011 Sharon R Hedgepeth c 2. P-in-c Ch Of The Ascen And H Trin W Pk NY 1997-2000; Dio New York New York NY 1997-2000.

LUNDGREN, Linda Lou (Minn) 8 3rd St, Proctor MN 55810 B Teaneck NJ 1954 d Harold & Violet. D 11/21/1993 P 6/18/1994 Bp Sanford Zangwill Kaye Hampton. m 7/14/1973 Robert Lundgren. R Chr Ch.

LUNDGREN, Richard John (Chi) 13129 Lake Mary Dr., Plainfield IL 60585 **Assoc R S Edw The Mtyr and Chr Epis Ch Joliet IL 2007-; Assoc St. Edw**

And Chr 2007- B Chicago 1964 s Norman & Carol. BA Villanova U 1987; MDiv Cath Theol Un 1994; Cert Ang Stud SWTS 2007; Cert Ang Stud SWTS 2007. Rec 6/7/2007 Bp Victor Alfonso Scantlebury. m 10/11/2013 Robert Francis Davis. rlundgren@secec.net

LUNDIN, George Edward (Miss) 705 Southern Ave, Hattiesburg MS 39401 B Chicago IL 1942 s George & Evelyn. BA Ohio Wesl 1964; PhD U Pgh 1973; MDiv Sewanee: The U So, TS 1982. D 6/20/1982 Bp H Coleman Mcgehee Jr P 5/1/1983 Bp James Barrow Brown. m 5/7/2015 Judith Koock Lundin c 2. Chap Of The Cross Rolling Fork MS 2008-2011; S Paul's Ch Woodville MS 2001-2008; Vic S Eliz's Mssn Collins MS 1987-2001; S Lk's Ch New Orleans LA 1984-1987; Trin Ch New Orleans LA 1982-1984. Auth, "Ms Philological Assn"; Auth, "Contemporary Rel Ideas". Ford Fllshp; Woodrow Wilson Fell.

LUNDQUIST, Robert O (WNC) 419 Turnpike Rd, Mills River NC 28759 Chapl Dio Wstrn No Carolina Asheville NC 2013-; R Ch Of The H Fam Mills River NC 2009- B Washington DC 1956 s Donald & Patricia. BA W&M 1978; MDiv SWTS 1985. D 6/28/1985 P 5/11/1986 Bp William Evan Sanders. m 12/31/1983 Pamela Mumby c 1. P-in-c S Paul's Epis Ch Ft Collins CO 2005-2008; R St Gabr the Archangel Epis Ch Englewood CO 1998-2004; Evang Off Dio Sthrn Virginia Newport News VA 1995-1998; Vic & R Gd Samar Epis Ch Virginia Bch VA 1989-1998; Asst Trin Ch Manassas VA 1986-1989; D Ch Of The Gd Shpd Lookout Mtn TN 1985-1986. rector@ourholyfamily.org

LUNNUM, Lindsay (LI) Zion Episcopal Church, 243-01 Northern Blvd, Douglaston NY 11363 R Zion Ch Douglaston NY 2013- B Bellevue WA 1977 d Ronald & Linda. BA Seattle Pacific U 1999; MDiv Ya Berk 2008. D 3/15/2008 P 9/20/2008 Bp Mark Sean Sisk. m 11/24/2009 James A Mcgeveran c 2. S Barn Ch Irvington NY 2010-2013; Asst S Mart's Ch Providence RI 2008-2010.

LUNTSFORD, Sharon Lorene (ND) Po Box 18, Alexander ND 58831 Coorinator of Peer Bridge No Dakota Wstrn Sunrise ND 2002-; Dio Idaho ID 1994- B Watford City ND 1940 d Leonard & Selma. Minot St U 1958; Jamestown Coll 1959. D 1/29/1994 Bp John Stuart Thornton P 12/18/2009 Bp Michael Smith. m 3/13/1976 Robert Charles Luntsford c 1. Pres. of Silver Creek Cmnty Serv Inc. Dio Idaho Boise ID 1994-2000.

LUONI, Richard B (CFla) 2499 N Westmoreland Dr, Orlando FL 32804 R S Mich's Ch Orlando FL 2015- B Parkelsburg WV 1963 s Billy & Naomi. BS Concord U 1988; MDiv SFTS 2005. D 12/3/2005 P 6/3/2006 Bp William Edwin Swing. m 8/29/2009 Cynthia K Luoni. R S Geo's Epis Ch Summerville SC 2008-2015; Dio California San Francisco CA 2006.

LUPFER JR, William B (NY) 120 Broadway Fl 38, New York NY 10271 Trin Par New York NY 2014-; S Jn The Evang Ch Portland OR 2000- B Berwyn IL 1961 s William & Virginia. U of Lancaster Lancaster Gb 1982; BA U CO 1983; MDiv Ya Berk 1987; DMin SWTS 2003. D 6/12/1993 P 5/14/1994 Bp Albert Theodore Eastman. m 8/4/1990 Kimiko K Lupfer c 2. Trin Epis Cathd Portland OR 2003-2014; R S Jn's Ch Plymouth MI 1997-2003; Assoc Ch Of The H Comf Kenilworth IL 1993-1997. Psychol Stds And Cler Consult Prog 1999. Lilian Claus Schlr Yale Berkeley 1985. wlupfer@trinitywallstreet.org

LUPTON JR, James Harold (Ark) 241 Riverview St., Belhaven NC 27810 P-in-c S Geo Epis Ch Engelhard NC 1997- B Washington NC 1931 s James & Grace. BA Duke 1954; MA U of Pennsylvania 1960; MDiv Epis TS of the SW 1985. D 1/18/1986 Bp Stanley Fillmore Hauser P 7/1/1986 Bp Scott Field Bailey. c 3. Chair, Ecum Cmsn Dio E Carolina Kinston NC 1999-2003; S Alb's Ch Stuttgart AR 1989-1997; Vic S Ptr Tollville AR 1989-1997; St Ptr's Epis Ch Devalls Bluff AR 1989-1997; R Gr Ch Weslaco TX 1988-1989; S Peters Epis Sch Kerrville TX 1986-1988; S Ptr's Epis Ch Kerrville TX 1986-1988; Secy Arkansas Interfaith Conf.

LUSIGNAN, Louise Jennet (WA) 10450 Lottsford Road, Mitchellville MD 20721 Ret Washington DC 2013- B Berkeley CA 1943 d Francis & Louise. B.A. Pomona Coll; MAT Antioch U New Engl 1967; MLS U of Wstrn Ontario CA 1971; MDiv VTS 1988. D 6/11/1988 Bp John Thomas Walker P 1/5/1989 Bp Ronald Hayward Haines. m 8/10/1974 Michael Reeves Lusignan. Assoc R for Pstr Mnstrs S Jn's Epis Ch Mc Lean VA 2000-2013; S Columba's Ch Washington DC 1988-2000.

LUSK JR, Karl (Ky) 236 Ridgeview Dr, New Haven KY 40051 Chapl Nelson Cnty Chapl' Response Team 2011-; R Ch Of The Ascen Bardstown KY 2009-; Chapl Coordntr Flaget Memi Hosp Bardstown KY 2009-; Chair, Dioc Bdgt Com Dio Kentucky Louisville KY 2013-, Trst and Coun 2012-, Trst and Coun 2010-2011, Co-chair, Dioc Bdgt Com 2010-, Chair, Dept. for Mssn and Evang 2009-, Dioc Disaster Coordntr 2008-, Dioc Disaster Coordntr 2007- B Lexington KY 1945 s Karl & Ruby. BS Iowa St U 1967; AT Sthrn Illinois U 1968; MA Louisville Presb TS 2007. D 4/14/2007 P 10/27/2007 Bp Ted Gulick Jr. m 2/20/1982 Anne T Lusk c 2. Vic S Thos Ch Campbellsvlle KY 2007-2009.

LUTAS, Donald Mckenzie (Mich) 6114 28th St, Detroit MI 48210 R S Cyp's Epis Ch Detroit MI 1991- B Saint Thomas Jamaica WI 1955 s Walter & Nettie. Untd Theol Coll of the W Indies Kingston JA 1978; BA U of The W Indies 1978; STM GTS 1984; MLS U of Detroit Mercy 1995; DMin GTF 2002. Trans 7/1/1987 Bp Claude Charles Vache. m 10/15/2007 Belinda Delan-

co Whitney c 1. Vic S Jas Epis Ch Portsmouth VA 1986-1991; Serv Ch in Jamaica 1979-1986.

LUTES, Kathleen Monson (Mil) 2224 Cedar Dr, Rapid City SD 57702 P-in-c Trin Ch Janesville WI 2015- B Minneapolis MN 1957 d Juel & Patricia. BS U MN 1979; MA S Cathr U 1986; MDiv Epis TS of the SW 2002. D 6/15/2002 P 4/23/2003 Bp James Louis Jelinek. m 11/24/1984 Richard K Lutes c 2. R S Andr's Epis Ch Rapid City SD 2004-2015; D S Jn's Ch Of Hassan Rogers MN 2003; S Mart's By The Lake Epis Minnetonka Bch MN 2002-2003; Asst to the R/Chr Educaiton St. Lk's Epis Ch Minneapolis MN 1992-1999. kathymonsonlutes@gmail.com

LUTHER, Carol Luther (Cal) St Paul's Episcopal School, 46 Montecito Ave., Oakland CA 94610 Vic Dio California San Francisco CA 2015-; S Paul's Day Sch Of Oakland Oakland CA 2007-, 1999-2004; Chapl St. Paul's Epis Sch Oakland CA 2007- B Berkeley CA 1950 d John & Mary. BA Scripps Coll 1972; MDiv CDSP 1997. D 6/5/1999 P 11/20/1999 Bp William Edwin Swing. m 11/25/1973 Jay W Luther c 1. P-in-c S Aid's Mssn Bolinas CA 2014-2015; S Paul's Ch Oakland CA 2014-2015, Assoc & Sch Chapl 1999-2004; Vol Ch Of The Nativ San Rafael CA 2011; Vic Ch Of The Redeem San Rafael CA 2004-2007. cluther@well.com

LUTHRINGER, George Francis (Los) 4876 Via Cupertino, Camarillo CA 93012 Died 11/13/2015 B Springfield IL 1934 s Marshall & Martha. BS MIT 1957; MS MIT 1957; BD CDSP 1966. D 6/25/1966 P 12/31/1966 Bp Roger W Blanchard. m 10/2/1982 Beatrice Ann A Pentecost. Asstg P S Columba's Par Camarillo CA 2004-2015; S Fran Of Assisi Epis Ch Simi Vlly CA 1992-1995; 1969-1992; R Resurr Cincinnati OH 1966-1969. Auth, "Considering Abortion? Clarifying What You Believe," Educational Series No. 9, Rel Cltn for Abortion Rts, 1992; Auth, "The Ethics of Ordnry Time," Nutrition in Clincl Pract, Amer Soc for Parenteral and Enteral Nutrition, 1991. Rep to Dioc Coun 2001-2006.

LUTTER, Linda F (Chi) 5725 Stearns School Rd, Gurnee IL 60031 B San Diego CA 1949 d Frederick & Emma. Assoc Coll of Lake Cnty 2001. D 12/20/2014 Bp Jeff Lee. m 10/4/1975 Glenn Henry Lutter c 2.

LUTTRELL, John Sidney (LI) 295 Old Kings Hwy, Downingtown PA 19335 B Norman OK 1943 s John & Josephine. BA Ya 1965; STB GTS 1968; PhD Hebr Un Coll 1977. D 5/28/1968 P 12/18/1968 Bp Chilton R Powell. m 6/1/1968 Rosemary M Perkins c 2. Dn Dio Long Island Garden City NY 2000, Chairman, COM 1996-2002; R S Lk's Ch Sea Cliff NY 1987-2008; P-in-c Chr Memi Epis Ch El Reno OK 1986-1987; Dio Oklahoma Oklahoma City OK 1986-1987; Headmaster S Jn's Ch Oklahoma City OK 1982-1985; Chapl Casady Sch Oklahoma City OK 1980-1982; Fac Cincinnati Cnty Day Sch 1978-1979; Cur S Lk's Ch Tulsa OK 1968-1969. SBL 1968-1982. The Fndr's Medallion Hebr Un Coll 2008; Henry Knox Sherrill Fllshp Ya 1965. jsid43@verizon.net

LUTZ, Alison W (NY) National Route 3, Cange Haiti Haiti S Aug's Chap Nashville TN 2015- B Redbank NJ 1976 d John & Tracy. BA Emory U 1999; MDiv Candler TS Emory U 2004; MDiv Candler TS@Emory 2004; Angl Stds Berk @ Yale 2012. D 3/3/2012 P 9/29/2012 Bp Mark Sean Sisk. Chr Ch Of The Ascen Paradise Vlly AZ 2013-2014; Sr Advsr Partnr In Hlth 2008-2013. Article, "Econ Inequality as God's Law?: Considering the Nature of Econ Life," ATR, 2013.

LUTZ, Randall Robert (RG) 2365 Brother Abdon Way, Santa Fe NM 87505 R S Bede's Epis Ch Santa Fe NM 2006- B Danville PA 1958 s Robert & Margaret. TESM; BA Bloomsburg U of Pennsylvania 1980; Cert The Sch for Mnstry 2007. D 10/21/2006 Bp Jeffrey Neil Steenson P 11/10/2007 Bp William Carl Frey.

LUTZ, Richard Herbert (LI) Cashelmara 40, 23200 Lake Road, Bay Village OH 44140 Ret 1998- B New York NY 1937 s Stephen & Amelia. BA,cl Adel 1958; STB GTS 1961. D 4/8/1961 P 10/28/1961 Bp James Pernette DeWolfe. R S Geo's Ch Hempstead NY 1987-1997; R S Matt's Ch Woodhaven NY 1965-1986, Cur 1961-1963; Cur & Headmaster All SS Ch San Diego CA 1963-1965; Stndg Com, 1980-1988 Dio Long Island Garden City NY 1980-1988, Dep, Prov II Syn, 1978 1978, Dep to GC, 1976, 1979 1976-1979, Ch Charity Fndt Bd, 1973-1982 1973-1982, Fam Consult Serv Bd, 1972-98, Pres, 1982-88 1972-1998, Liturg Cmsn, 1970-1981 1970-1981, COM, 1967 - 1978 1967-1978. Mem of GAS; P Assoc Our Lade of Walsingham; SocMary 2012; SSC.

LUTZ, Ruth Jeanne (RG) 1330 Renoir Ct., Las Cruces NM 88007 Dn, SW Dnry Dio The Rio Grande Albuquerque 2012- B Indianapolis IN 1947 d Robert & Ruth. BA U of Texas 1970; MA New Mex St U 1972; DMin Austin Presb TS 2008. D 2/29/1988 P 9/21/1988 Bp William Davidson. m 12/27/1969 William Lutz c 2. S Chris's Epis Ch El Paso TX 2012-2015; Luth-Epis Coordntng Com Evang Luth Ch in Amer 2008-2011; Pstr Peace Luth Ch Las Cruces NM 2003-2011; Int Pstr S Jn's Cathd Albuquerque NM 2003; Assoc R S Andr's Epis Ch Las Cruces NM 1997-2003; Asstg Cler 1991-1997; Chapl New Hope Hospice 1996-1997; Chapl Mesilla Vlly Hospice 1991-1995; Asstg Cler S Mary's Epis Ch Albuquerque NM 1989-1991. Auth, "Benediction," LivCh, 1996; Auth, "All Sung Out, Except Grandma," LivCh, 1993. DOK 1972; Intl Ord of S Lk the Physcn 2001; Soc of St. Ben 2003. Wmn of Faith City of Las Cruces / CareSource Cmnty Mnstrs, Inc. 2003.

LUTZ, William Charles (CNY) 82 Scott Ave, Elmira NY 14905 B Plainfield NJ 1952 s Charles & Marjorie. BA Heidelberg U 1974; MDiv GTS 1978; DMin Bangor TS 1997. D 6/3/1978 P 12/2/1978 Bp Albert Wiencke Van Duzer. m 6/17/1978 Heather Anne Conelley c 3. R Trin Ch Elmira NY 1999-2016; Stndg Com Dio New Hampshire Concord NH 1995-1999, Stwdshp Com 1992-1994, Chair Cler Dvlpmt Com 1993-1995, Evang Com 1988-1992, Yth Com 1987; R Ch Of Our Sav Milford NH 1987-1999; Dio Wstrn Massachusetts Springfield 1984-1987; Vic S Chris's Ch Fairview Chicopee MA 1984-1987; Chapl Belmont Chap at S Mk's Sch Southborough MA 1982-1984; St. Mk's Sch of Southborough Inc. Southborough MA 1982-1984; S Andr's Ch Turners Fall MA 1979-1982; Asst S Jas' Ch Greenfield MA 1979-1982; Asst Gr Ch Merchantville NJ 1978-1979. OHC 1975.

LWEBUGA-MUKASA, Katherine N (WNY) 168 Schimwood Ct, Getzville NY 14068 D S Phil's Ch Buffalo NY 1989- B Northampton MA 1947 d Thomas & Marion. BA Smith 1969; MA San Diego St U 1974; MS Sthrn Connecticut St U 1979. D 12/2/1989 Bp Arthur Edward Walmsley. m 5/29/1970 Jamson S Lwebuga-Mukasa.

LYCETT, Horace Abbott (Colo) 1223 Center St, Goodland KS 67735 B Baltimore MA 1933 s Isaac & Caroline. BA Colorado St U 1956; MDiv Nash 1963. D 6/29/1959 P 2/2/1960 Bp Joseph Summerville Minnis. c 3. P-in-c S Paul's Epis Ch Goodland KS 2004-2011; Dio Colorado Denver CO 1999-2002; R All SS Epis Ch Denver CO 1971-1999; Vic S Paul's Epis Ch Ft Collins CO 1964-1968; S Mk's Ch Craig CO 1959-1964; Vic S Paul's Epis Ch Steamboat Sprngs CO 1959-1964. Auth, "Var arts," LivCh, 1979. EUC 2000; Sis Of Charity 1950.

LYGA, Robert Michael (Minn) N36457 State Road 93/121, Independence WI 54747 Supply P S Barn Ch Clear Lake WI 2000-; S Phil's Ch Turtle Lake WI 2000- B Independence WI 1938 s Marcel & Helen. BS U of Wisconsin 1961; MD Nash 1968. D 6/24/1968 P 4/14/1969 Bp Hamilton Hyde Kellogg. R H Trin Intl Falls MN 1992-2000; Vic S Ptr's Ch Warroad MN 1992-2000; R S Matt's Epis Ch Minneapolis MN 1969-1992; Cur St. Aid New Brighton MN 1969-1974.

LYLE, Jerry (Tex) St. Joseph's Episcopal Church, PO Box 797, Salado TX 76571 B Austin TX 1950 s John & Iota. Austin Cmnty Coll; U of Texas Austin; Austin Cmnty Coll 1973; U of Texas Austin 1976; Iona Sch of Mnstry 2008; Iona Sch of Mnstry 2008. D 2/10/2008 Bp Don Adger Wimberly. m 3/20/1971 Pat Lee Levensailor c 2. jlyle25468@gmail.com

LYLE, Patsy Rushworth (La) 19344 Links Ct, Baton Rouge LA 70810 Nrsng Hm Mnstry Baton Rouge Dnry 1981- B Baton Rouge LA 1934 d Locksley & Nell. BS LSU 1956. D 12/19/1986 Bp Charles Edward Jenkins III. m 9/8/1956 John Donald Clyde c 2. Sprtl Dir Epis Ch Of The H Sprt In Baton Rouge Baton Rouge LA 1994-2005; Chair Dio Louisiana New Orleans LA 1988-2005; Dnry Cmsn On Aging 1987-1993; D S Marg's Epis Ch Baton Rouge LA 1986-1994. NAAD 1979; Sprtl Dir Intl 1994.

LYLE, Randall Robert (Ia) 2350 Glass Rd NE, Cedar Rapids IA 52402 Asst Chr Ch Cedar Rapids IA 2010-; Assoc Prof Non-par S Mary U 1993- B Scottsbluff NE 1952 s Robert & JoDeen. BA Loretto Heights Coll 1977; MDiv SWTS 1982; PhD Iowa St U 1992. D 6/2/1982 Bp William Harvey Wolfrum P 12/29/1982 Bp Walter Cameron Righter. m 6/4/1977 Karla Lyle c 4. St Fran Epis Ch San Antonio TX 2001-2003; R Gr Ch Boone IA 1989-1993; Ch Of The Gd Shpd Webster City IA 1989-1992; Exec Coun Appointees New York NY 1984-1989; Vic Los Colos Sierras de Cordoba Argentina 1984-1989; Cur S Andr's Ch Des Moines IA 1982-1984. "Neurofeedback Treatment of Type 1 Diabetes: Perceptions of Quality of Life and Stabilization of Insulin Treatment.," Journ of Neurotherapy, Haworth, 2006; "Client Experiance of Gender in Therapeutic Re;ationships: An Interpretive Ethnography.," Fam Process, Blackwell, 2001; "QUalitative Resrch in Fam Ther.," Journ of Mar and Fam Ther, AAMFT, 2001; "Life Cycle Dvlpmt: Divorce and the Hisp Fam," Fam Ther w Hispanics, Allyn & Bacon, 2000; "The Narrative Ethics and the Ethics of Narrative: The Implications of Ricoeur's Narrative Model for Fam Ther," The Journ of Systemic Therapies, 2000. rlyle@mtmercy.edu

LYLE, William Edward (SO) 1547 Stratford Dr, Kent OH 44240 Int Supply Chr Epis Ch Kent OH 2000- B Mount Hope WV 1926 s Ernest & Margie. BA Kent St U 1950; MA U MI 1952; BD Bex Sem 1961. D 6/29/1961 Bp Archie H Crowley P 12/1/1961 Bp Richard Stanley Merrill Emrich. m 5/6/2009 Phyllis Lyle c 4. Int S Paul's Epis Ch Logan OH 1988-1989; Int Ch Of The Epiph Nelsonville OH 1985-1991; Non-par 1984-1987; R S Paul's Epis Ch Of E Cleveland OH 1982-1984; Non-par 1981-1982; R Gr Ch Ravenna OH 1976-1981; Non-par 1968-1969; Assoc S Mart's Ch Chagrin Fall OH 1967-1968; Non-par 1966-1967; Asst Min All SS Epis Ch Pontiac MI 1961-1963; P-in-c S Paul In Ohio.

LYMAN, Janyce Rebecca (Cal) 115 Sheridan Way, Woodside CA 94062 B Marshall MI 1954 d Howard & Janyce. BA Wstrn Michigan U 1976; MA CUA 1979; PhD Oxf GB 1983. D 6/5/1993 P 6/1/1994 Bp William Edwin Swing. m 7/27/1985 Andrew Bridges c 2. Samuel Garret Prof of Ch Hist CDSP Berkeley CA 1994-2005. "Natural Resources: Tradition without Orthodoxy," ATR, 2002;

"Early Chr Traditions," Cowley Pub, 1999; Auth, "Christology and Cosmology," Oxf Press, 1993.

LYNCH JR, Bobby (WNC) Po Box 561, Rutherfordton NC 28139 D S Gabr's Ch Rutherdforton NC 1980- B Rutherfordton NC 1940 s Thurman & Lillie. D 5/29/1975 Bp William Gillette Weinhauer. m 3/9/1963 Helen Edgerton c 3.

LYNCH, Daniel Luke (WVa) 123 Hidden Valley Ests, Scott Depot WV 25560 B Mullens WV 1930 s Daniel & Ruth. BA U of Virginia 1957; MDiv VTS 1991. D 6/11/1991 P 6/1/1992 Bp John Henry Smith. m 10/10/1983 Pamela Susan Kelsey. Vic S Jas Ch Charleston WV 1991-2002.

LYNCH, David (WMo) 16808 S State Route D, Belton MO 64012 R Ch Of The Resurr Blue Sprg MO 2016- B Flint MI 1954 s William & Olive. BA Adrian Coll 1976; MDiv VTS 2012. D 6/2/2012 P 1/5/2013 Bp Dean E Wolfe. m 12/30/1977 Deborah A Lynch c 1. St Mary Magd Epis Ch Loch Lloyd MO 2014-2015; Int Trin Ch Atchison KS 2014; S Jas Ch Wichita KS 2012-2014.

LYNCH, Gwynn (SanD) 13319 Fallen Leaf Rd, Poway CA 92064 Gr Epis Ch Of The Vlly Mssn San Marcos CA 2017- B St. Louis MO 1961 d David & Judith. MDiv Claremont TS; BS California St U 1983. D 6/11/2005 P 12/11/2005 Bp Jim Mathes. m 5/4/1985 Frank Peter Freund c 3. Vic S Mary's In The Vlly Ch Ramona CA 2010-2016; Dioc Coun Mem Dio San Diego San Diego CA 2007-2010, Safeguarding God's People Trnr 2006-, Safeguarding God's People Trng Coordntr 2006-; All Souls' Epis Ch San Diego CA 2005-2010.

LYNCH, John J (RI) 4109 Big Bethel Rd, Tabb VA 23693 Dio Rhode Island Providence RI 2016-; Chapl, Prov III DOK Woodstock GA 2015-, Chapl, Dio Sthrn Virginia 2012-2015 B Mt. Airy NC 1982 s Larry & Celeste. Trin TS; BA Wake Forest U 2002; Dip Theol Stud Universidad Catolica De Honduras HN 2003; MA Trin TS 2009; Ph.D. Trin TS 2014. D 10/28/2005 P 1/6/2008 Bp Lloyd Emmanuel Allen. m 11/14/2003 Cecilia Lynch c 1. R Chr The King Epis Ch Yorktown VA 2010-2016; Substitute Chapl The Cbury Sch Greensboro NC 2009-2010; Cn for Liturg Dio Honduras 2008-2009; Dio Honduras San Pedro Sula 2006-2009; Prof (NT, Gk, Anglicanism) Programa Diocesano de Educacion Teologica San Pedro Sula Ho 2006-2009; D and Mssnr Iglesia Epis de la Epifania Villanueva 2006-2007; Iglesia Epis Hondurena San Pedro Sula 2005-2009; Catedral Epis El Buen Pstr San Pedro Sula 2005-2006; Chapl/ Tchr Escuela Epis El Buen Pstr 2002-2009. Auth, "The Logos as Reason, Word, and Love in the Theol of Jos Ratzinger," CreateSpace/Kindle Digital Pub, 2014; Ed, "Our Daily Prayers: Devotions Drawn from the Historic Bk of Common Pryr and Other Traditional Angl Sources," CreateSpace/Kindle Digital Pub, 2012; Auth, "The Creeds: A Study for Individuals and Groups," CreateSpace/ Kindle Digital Pub, 2011; Transltr, "Orden para la celebración de la Santa Comunión del Libro de Oración Común de la Iglesia de Inglaterra (1662)," CreateSpace/ Kindle Digital Pub, 2009; Ed and Contrib, "Comments on Certain Passages of The Thirty-Nine arts," CreateSpace/ Kindle Digital Pub, 2009; Ed and Contrib, "Natl Apostasy and the Case of Cath Subscription Considered w an Essay on the Life of the Reverend Jn Keble," CreateSpace/ Kindle Digital Pub, 2009; Auth, "Los Santos en el cuerpo de la Iglesia," Forw Mvmt, 2008; Auth, "Devoción Mariana en la Iglesia," Forw Mvmt, 2008; Contrib, "Educación cristiana o formación catequética," IX Prov of the Epis Ch, 2007. Priests Assoc of the H Hse of Our Lady of Walsingham 2010. ctkrector@aol.com

LYNCH, Pamela S (EMich) 525 Weiss Rd, Gaylord MI 49735 P S Andr's Epis Ch Gaylord MI 2012-, P 2012- B Detroit MI 1956 d Frank & Viola. BSN Wayne 1977; MSN Wayne 1987. D 4/21/2012 P 10/20/2012 Bp Steven Todd Ousley.

LYNCH, Suzanne Mchugh Stryker (WMo) 1342 S Ventura Ave, Springfield MO 65804 Stff Chapl Cmnty Hospices of Amer Springfield MO 2006-; D S Jas' Ch Springfield MO 1994- B Omaha NE 1949 d Hird & Suzanne. AAS Monticello Jr Coll 1969. D 1/25/1994 Bp John Clark Buchanan. m 6/27/1970 James P Lynch c 2. S Jn's Ch Springfield MO 1995-2006. dcn-h0n@sbcglobal.net

LYNCH, William David (NC) 8849 Ray Rd, Raleigh NC 27613 B Asheville NC 1941 s William & Nona. BM Ob 1962; MM Eastman Sch of Mus of the U Roch 1964; DMA Eastman Sch of Mus of the U Roch 1969. D 2/18/2012 Bp Michael B Curry. m 1/14/1967 Marilyn S Lynch c 2.

LYNN, Connor Kay (Los) 1902 Park Ave Apt 316, Los Angeles CA 90026 B Taft CA 1931 s Bedford & Winnie. BA Stan 1952; BD CDSP 1956; CDSP 1973. D 6/17/1956 Bp Sumner Walters P 12/22/1956 Bp Robert E Campbell. St Mary in Palms Los Angeles CA 1990-2003; Mssy CPWA 1985-1989; Exec Coun Appointees New York NY 1985-1989; R Epis Ch Of S Anne Stockton CA 1983-1985. Ord of S Ben Cam. - Oblate 1998; OHC 1963.

LYNN, Jacqueline Goler (Chi) ElderCARE Waukegan IL 2015- B Atlanta GA 1948 d Benjamin & Martha. BA U of Wisconsin 1971; U IL 1983. D 2/2/2002 Bp Bill Persell. c 2. Cathd Of S Jas Chicago IL 2009-2015. jlynneldercare@sbcglobal.net

LYON, Don (CFla) 1628 Bent Oaks Blvd, DeLand FL 32724 P-in-c S Jas Epis Ch Ormond Bch FL 2013- B Newport RI 1947 s Walter & Ruth. BS U of Massachusetts 1971; MA U of Iowa 1972; MDiv Bex Sem 1980. D 6/7/1980 Bp Morris Fairchild Arnold P 5/23/1981 Bp Robert Shaw Kerr. m 9/9/1967 Karen

L Lyon c 2. P-in-c Epis Ch Of The H Sprt Apopka FL 2011-2013; R S Barn Ch Deland FL 1995-2011; R S Steph's Epis Ch Wilkes Barre PA 1988-1995; R S Mk's Ch Newark NY 1984-1988; Vic Calv Ch Underhill VT 1980-1984. Ord of S Ben 1995; Ord of S Lk 1996. donlyon16@gmail.com

LYON IV, James Fraser (USC) 1512 Blanding St, Columbia SC 29201 **R Ch Of The Gd Shpd Columbia SC 1991-** B Cheraw SC 1956 s James & Marcine. BA Winthrop U 1978; MA Winthrop U 1980; MDiv SWTS 1983; EdD U of So Carolina 2003. D 6/11/1983 P 5/12/1984 Bp William Arthur Beckham. m 6/14/1980 Sallie L Lyon c 2. R Ch Of The Gd Shpd York SC 1986-1991; Asst S Martins-In-The-Field Columbia SC 1983-1986. Angl Euch League 1992; Soc-Mary 1992. Phi Alpha Theta.

LYON, Lauren (Ia) Trinity Church, 320 E College St, Iowa City IA 52240 **Trin Ch Iowa City IA 2014-** B Des Moines IA 1954 d Ivan & Marilyn. BA U CA 1986; MDiv Ya Berk 1994. D 6/4/1994 P 12/3/1994 Bp John Clark Buchanan. m 8/15/1993 Nelson McGee. Dir of Cmncatn Dio W Missouri Kansas City MO 2013-2014; S Mary's Epis Ch Kansas City MO 2005-2014; S Fran Acad Inc. Salina KS 2004-2005; Assoc S Matt's Ch Kansas City MO 2000-2001; S Andr's Ch Kansas City MO 1999-2000; S Ptr's Ch Harrisonville MO 1997-1999; Gr Ch Carthage MO 1995-1996; D Gr And H Trin Cathd Kansas City MO 1994. trinityic@trinityic.org

LYON, Susan Loy (Ark) 1000 N Mississippi St, Little Rock AR 72207 B St Louis MO 1951 d Richard & Dorothy. BA The Colorado Coll 1973; DDS U of Texas, Dental Branch 1977. D 8/8/2015 Bp Larry Benfield. m 6/20/1976 Thomas F Hudson c 3.

LYONS JR, James Hershel (Nev) All Saint's Episcopal Church, 4201 W Washington Ave, Las Vegas NV 89107 **P-in-c S Chris's Epis Ch Boulder City NV 2010-** B Ft Sill Lawton OK 1964 s James & Naomi. Rec 12/9/2007 Bp Jerry Alban Lamb.

LYONS, Leroy A (NJ) 1208 Prospect Ave, Plainfield NJ 07060 B 1938 s Wilfred & Louisa. Rutgers The St U of New Jersey; GOE Codrington Coll 1964; LTh Hur CA 1969; STB GTS 1970; STM GTS 1971. Trans 2/24/1971 Bp Alfred L Banyard. m 8/26/1990 Michelle Graham-Lyons c 2. R S Mk's Ch Plainfield NJ 1971-2010; Serv Ch Of Trinidad 1963-1967.

LYONS, Lorraine M (Alb) 1154 Hedgewood Ln, Niskayuna NY 12309 B Baltimore MD 1957 d Roger & Joanna. BS U of Delaware 1979; MDiv S Bernards TS and Mnstry 2000. D 6/11/2000 P 12/16/2000 Bp Daniel William Herzog. c 2. S Mk's Ch Hoosick Falls NY 2007-2013; Assoc R S Steph's Ch Schenectady NY 2000-2003.

LYONS, Patricia M (WA) **Chr Ch Capitol Hill Washington DC 2016-; St. Steph's And St. Agnes Sch Alexandria VA 2005-** B Bronxville, NY 1973 d Lorna. BA Harvard Coll 1995; Mstr of Div Harvard DS 1998; Doctor of Mnstry VTS 2008. D 11/21/2015 P 6/11/2016 Bp Mariann Edgar Budde. m 3/18/2013 Elisabeth Margaret Kimball. Auth, "The Soul of Adolescence," *The Soul of Adolescence*, Ch Pub, 2008.

LYTHGOE, Amy Underhill (Colo) **D 2016-; S Jn's Epis Ch Boulder CO 2016-; Middle Sch Chapl St Elizabeths Sch Denver CO 2015-** B Lansing MI 1966 B.A. W&M. D 6/18/2016 P 6/10/2017 Bp Robert John O'Neill. c 3. Contract Chapl St Anth Hosp Lakewood CO 2015-2016; Yth Min S Ambr Epis Ch Boulder CO 2013-2016. alythgoe@sesden.org

LYTLE, Ashley Alexandra Gabriella (At) 515 E Ponce De Leon Ave, Decatur GA 30030 **St Ben's Epis Ch Smyrna GA 2017-; Other Lay Position The Epis Ch Of S Ptr And S Paul Marietta GA 2009-** B Oakland CA 1987 d Guy & Maria. BA The TS at The U So 2009; BA The U So 2009; BA The U So 2009; MDiv Candler TS 2015. D 12/20/2014 P 6/20/2015 Bp Robert Christopher Wright. The Ch of the Common Ground Atlanta GA 2016; H Trin Par Decatur GA 2015-2016.

LYTLE, Ronald (Wyo) 1222 Rosewood Ln, Powell WY 82435 **Ret 2007-** B Donnelly ID 1935 s Donald & Evelyn. BS U of Wyoming 1961. D 3/2/1988 P 9/14/1988 Bp Charles I Jones III. m 6/12/1960 Kathryn M Lytle c 4. S Jn's Ch Powell WY 2002-2007; Mnstry Dvlp - Reg 1 Dio Wyoming Casper 1999-2007, Ret Cler Chapl 2011-; S Andr's Ch Basin WY 1999-2007; S Andr's Ch Meeteetse WY 1999-2007; R Gr Ch Rice Lake WI 1991-1999; Asst S Lk's Ch Billings MT 1988-1991.

M

MAAS, Benjamin Wells (Va) 1374 S Brook St, Louisville KY 40208 **S Jas' Epis Ch Warrenton VA 2013-** B Williamsburg VA 1974 BA U of Virginia 1997; MDiv VTS 2003. D 5/17/2003 P 12/6/2003 Bp Ted Gulick Jr. m 6/1/2002 Anna Hope Maas c 2. S Andr's Ch Louisville KY 2004-2013; S Jas Ch Pewee Vlly KY 2003-2004.

MAAS, Jan Alfred (NY) 2121 Jamieson Ave Unit 1909, Alexandria VA 22314 B Syracuse NY 1940 s Alfred & Catherine. BMus U of Wisconsin 1963; MDiv GTS 1973; MLS SUNY 1994. D 6/9/1973 P 12/9/1973 Bp Horace W B Donegan. c 1. R Ch Of The Ascen And H Trin W Pk NY 1984-1993; Ed - Epis New

Yorker Dio New York New York NY 1976-1984, Dioc Coun 1986-1989; P-in-c Ch Of The Incarn New York New York NY 1974-1975, Asst 1973-1974. Assoc: CHS 1985.

MABERRY, Lois Rayner (WLa) D 1/30/2016 Bp Jacob W Owensby.

MACARTHUR III, Robert Stuart (Mo) 334 Maple Ridge Road, Center Sandwich NH 03227 **Non-par 1969-** B Detroit MI 1942 s Robert & Elizabeth. BA Dart 1964; STB Ya Berk 1967. D 6/10/1967 Bp Leland Stark P 1/6/1968 Bp Charles Francis Hall. m 6/11/1966 Marguerite Ann MacArthur. Cur S Thos Ch Hanover NH 1967-1969. Auth, "Glory Hallelu".

MACATEE, Louise Mae (Los) Church of the Epiphany, 5450 Churchwood Dr, Oak Park CA 91377 B Burbank CA 1946 d Russell & Maxine. D 6/4/2016 P 1/14/2017 Bp Joseph Jon Bruno. c 1.

MACAULEY JR, Robert Conover (Vt) 175 Hills Point Road, Charlotte VT 05445 B New York NY 1966 s Robert & Alma. BA Wheaton Coll 1988; MS Oxf GB 1989; MDiv Ya Berk 1993; STM Ya Berk 1994; MD Ya 1995. D 6/10/1995 Bp Clarence Nicholas Coleridge P 9/29/1996 Bp Robert Wilkes Ihloff. m 1/1/2001 Pamela Burton-Macauley. P-in-c S Paul's Epis Ch On The Green Vergennes VT 2002-2006; Asst P Ch Of The H Apos New York NY 2000-2001; Asst P Par of St Paul's Ch Norwalk Norwalk CT 1998-1999; Asst P Memi Ch Baltimore MD 1995-1998.

MACBETH, Andy (WTenn) 1640 Harbert Ave, Memphis TN 38104 **Int Epis Ch Of S Jn The Bapt Breckenridge CO 2015-; P-in-c Ch Of The H Cross W Memphis AR 2013-; Bd Trst VTS Alexandria VA 2001-, Bd Trst 1998-2012** B Chester PA 1949 s Andrew & Lois. BA Randolph-Macon Coll 1971; MDiv EDS 1975; DMin VTS 2000. D 6/11/1975 P 1/6/1976 Bp Emerson Paul Haynes. m 6/7/1969 Sybil Jane Prouse c 2. Int Chr Ch Grosse Pointe Grosse Pointe Farms MI 2010-2012; R Calv Ch Memphis TN 2004-2011; R Estrn Shore Chap Virginia Bch VA 1988-2004; R S Jas Ch Painesville OH 1981-1988; Assoc Chr Ch Shaker Heights OH 1978-1981; Asst Trin By The Cove Naples FL 1975-1978; Stndg Com 2008-2011; Stndg Committtee Dio W Tennessee Memphis 2008-2010; Chair COM Dio Sthrn Virginia Newport News VA 2003-2004, Stndg Com 1999-2002, Stndg Com 1998-2000, Chair Evang Cmsn 1994-1998, Chair CE Dept 1994-1996, Chair DeptCE 1992-1993; Chair Stwdshp Cmsn Dio Ohio Cleveland 1986-1988, Stwdshp Cmsn 1986-1988, Chair, Par Educ Div 1984-1986, Plnng Cmsn 1982-1985. Auth, "Praying in Black and White: A Hands-on Pract for Men," *Bk*, Paraclete, 2011; Auth, "Dearly Beloved: Navigating Your Ch Wedding," *Bk*, Seabury, 2007; Auth, "Envisioning Your Life in the Third Age," *doctoral thesis*, 2000.

MACCOLL, Craig (Colo) 5876 E Kettle Pl, Centennial CO 80112 **R Gd Shpd Epis Ch Centennial CO 2005-** B Pasadena CA 1952 s Eugene & Leeanne. BA U Chi 1974; MA U Chi 1976; Cert Oxf GB 1980; MDiv Nash 1981. D 6/22/1981 P 12/21/1981 Bp James Winchester Montgomery. m 2/2/1985 Ann Burmond Hiestand c 2. Int S Fran Of Assisi Epis Wilsonville OR 2004-2011, 1988-1997; Dio Oregon Portland OR 2003-2005, Dn, Sunset Convoc 1990-1995; Exec Dir Vision Action Ntwk in Washington Cnty Beaverton OR 2002-2003; R Ch Of Recon San Antonio TX 1997-2001; Dir of Pstr Serv Wm Temple Hse Portland OR 1985-1989; Vic S Gabr Ch Portland OR 1985-1987; Cur S Mich's Ch Barrington IL 1981-1983; Tchr St. Paul's Sch Concord NH 1977-1978. AAPC 1990-2008.

MACCOLLAM, Joel Allan (Alb) 240 Belflora Way, Oceanside CA 92057 **Died 5/5/2017** B Albany NY 1946 s Allan & Jacqueline. BA Ham 1968; Col 1969; MDiv GTS 1972. D 6/3/1972 P 12/15/1972 Bp Allen Webster Brown. m 5/3/1975 Jann Marie MacCollam c 2. 1979-2017; Assoc S Mk's Par Glendale CA 1978-1979; R S Steph's Ch Schuylerville NY 1974-1978; LocTen S Jas Ch Oneonta NY 1973-1974; Cur S Jn's Epis Ch Troy NY 1972-1973; Evang Cmsn Dio Los Angeles Los Angeles CA 1978-1979. Auth, *Carnival of Souls*, Seabury, 1980; Auth, *The Way Doctrine*, Intervarsity, 1980; Auth, *The Weekend That Never Ends*, Seabury, 1979. Hon LLD California Grad TS 1987.

MACCONNELL, James Stuart (Wyo) 403 15th St #1, Dallas Center IA 50063 B Kingston NY 1930 s Eugene & Alice. DC Natl Coll of Chiropractic Lombard IL 1958; MDiv SWTS 1973. D 5/12/1973 Bp Quintin Ebenezer Primo Jr P 12/8/1973 Bp James Winchester Montgomery. m 6/21/1959 Carolyn June Mac-Connell c 3. Ch Of The Resurr W Chicago IL 1994-1995; P S Clare's Epis Ch Pleasanton CA 1990-1994; Assoc S Jos's Ch Lakewood CO 1988-1989; R Ch Of S Thos Rawlins WY 1986-1987; Int P Dio Milwaukee Milwaukee WI 1984-1986, 1981-1982; Assoc S Mich's Epis Ch Racine WI 1982-1983; Chapl S Lk's Epis Hosp 1981-1982; Vic S Laurence Epis Ch Effingham IL 1975-1980; Cur S Matt's Ch Evanston IL 1973-1974. Auth, *Living Ch*; Auth, *Mar & Fam Counslg*. EME, Natl Presenting Cler Couple 1978-1988; Seabury Fell Mnstry 1979.

MACDONALD, Daniel (Mass) 147 Concord Rd, Lincoln MA 01773 **Transitional D All SS' Epis Ch S Burlington VT 2010-** B Boston MA 1981 s Bradley & Barbara. BA Carleton Coll 2004; MDiv Ya Berk 2008. D 6/5/2010 Bp Gayle Harris P 1/8/2011 Bp M(Arvil) Thomas Shaw. m 5/31/2008 Laura Sponseller c 3. S Anne's In The Fields Epis Ch Lincoln MA 2012-2017.

MACDONALD, David Roberts (LI) 253 Glen Ave, Sea Cliff NY 11579 **R S Lk's Ch Sea Cliff NY 2011-; Cmdr Ord of S Jn 2001-** B Ancon Canal

Zone Panama 1954 s Malcolm & Francis. BA California St Polytechnic U 1976; Nash 1985; MDiv SWTS 1987; MA U of Wales 2004; PhD GTF 2007. D 8/22/1987 P 4/8/1988 Bp Reginald Heber Gooden. m 10/3/1999 Betty W MacDonald c 3. Chapl Washington Natl Cathd Washington DC 2005-2011; R Chr Ch Durham Par Nanjemoy MD 2004-2011; R S Lk's Ch Denison TX 2002-2003; R S Paul's Epis Angl Ch Frederiksted St Croix VI 1999-2001; Asst R S Paul's Epis Ch Shreveport LA 1997-1999; Cathd Stff Cathd Of S Jn The Evang Spokane WA 1996-1997; Trst, Dioc Invstmt Trust Epis Dio San Joaquin Modesto CA 1994-1996, Co-Chair, Evang & Renwl Cmsn 1990-1993; S Mart Of Tours Epis Ch Fresno CA 1994-1996; Epis Chapl Fresno St U Fresno CA 1992-1993; Chr Ch Lemoore CA 1991, 1988-1990; Active Duty Army Off Of Bsh For ArmdF New York NY 1990-1991; Cur S Geo's Epis Ch Laguna Hills CA 1987-1988; Chapl Cathd of St. Ptr & St. Paul Washington DC US 2006-2011; Bd Dir Collington Ret Cmnty Dio Washington Washington DC 2006-2010. Auth, "Padre - E.C. Crosse & The Devonshire Epitaph," Cloverdale Books, 2007; Auth, "The Transit of the Angl Mind to the Maryland Colony," Cloverdale Books, 2007; Auth, "Theol and Certainty," *LivCh (Feb. 6)*, LivCh Fndt, 2005. C.St.J. The Ord of S Jn 2013; Fell Angus Dunn Fndt 2004.

MACDONALD, Gilbert John (EMich) 331 West Mill Street, Oscoda MI 48750 B Halifax NS CA 1928 s Fredwick & Mary. BA U of Kings Coll Halifax NS CA 1949; BBA Ns Bus Coll CA 1951; BD The Coll of Emm and S Chad CA 1954. m 6/17/1954 Rosemarie Kathleen MacDonald c 4. Hope - S Jn's Epis Ch Oscoda MI 1985-1992, 1968-1976; Vic All SS Houghton Lake MI 1966-1968; Vic S Mk Tracy MN 1964-1966; R S Jas Ch Marshall MN 1964-1966; Chapl U Minnesota 1964-1966; All SS Epis Indn Mssn Minneapolis MN 1960-1964; Co-R Chr Epis Ch Grand Rapids MN 1960-1964; Serv Ch Of Can 1954-1960.

MACDONALD, Heyward Hunter (Md) 2551 Summit Ridge Trail, Charlottesville VA 22911 **none Ret Charlottesville VA 2003-** B Richmond VA 1940 s Donald & Anne. BS U of Virginia 1964; MBA U NC 1965; MDiv VTS 1973; DMin VTS 1990. D 5/26/1973 P 5/18/1974 Bp Robert Bruce Hall. m 8/22/1970 Sandra Marie Macdonald c 2. R S Jas Ch Monkton MD 1981-2003; R Westover Epis Ch Chas City VA 1975-1981; Cur Chr Epis Ch Luray VA 1973-1975. Auth, "Everything Changed: The VietNam War and Amer Culture," *http://www.amazon.com/dp/B00UICGHMA*, Amazon - Kindle, 2015; Auth, "Stwdshp Theol and Pract: A Process For Leaders of Congregations," *http://www.lulu.com/content/455137*, Lulu Web Pub, 2006; Auth, "Pearl of Great Price, Oral Hist of a Fam during WWII," *http://www.lulu.com/content/467721*, Lulu Web Pub, 2006; Auth, "Calling of Vstry As Servnt of the People of God," *Forw Mvmt*, Forw Mvmt, 2001; Auth, "Return to VietNam," *https://sites.google.com/site/vietnamreturn/*, self Pub, 2001; Auth, "Theol and Mar: A Theol Primer for Cler and Others Who Seek a Deeper Meaning for Mar," *VTS Doctoral Dissertation*, unpub, 1990. Bishops' Awd for Ord Mnstry Bp of Maryland 2003.

MACDONALD, Jean A (Vt) 7 N College St, Montpelier VT 05602 B Malden MA 1952 d Roderick & Virginia. BS U of New Hampshire 1974; MA EDS 1994. D 12/12/1997 P 6/26/1998 Bp Mary Adelia Rosamond Mcleod. m 2/12/2011 Meg Alison Powden c 2. R S Andr's Epis Ch St Johnsbury VT 2008-2016, Asst 1997-2000; Chr Ch Island Pond VT 2003-2007. jeanmac829@gmail.com

MACDONALD, Linda Jean (Mich) 1780 Nemoke Trl, Haslett MI 48840 **Archd Dio Michigan Detroit MI 2005-** B Grand Rapids MI 1942 d Lee & Margaret. BS Wstrn Michigan U 1964; MA MI SU 1970; Whitaker TS 1994. D 6/11/1994 Bp R aymond Stewart Wood Jr. Archd Diosese of MI 2004-2012; D Asst S Kath's Ch Williamston MI 1995-2004.

✠ MACDONALD, The Rt Rev Mark Lawrence (Ak) 2228 Penrose Ln., Fairbanks AK 99709 **Natl Indigenous Bp Angl Ch of Can 2007-** B Duluth MN 1954 s Adrian & Sue. BA Scholastica Toronto Toronto On CA 1975; MDiv U Tor CA 1978. D 2/1/1979 P 8/1/1979 Bp Robert Marshall Anderson Con 9/13/1997 for Ak. m 11/11/1989 Virginia Mac Donald c 3. Bp Of Alaska Dio Alaska Fairbanks AK 1997-2007; Dio Minnesota Minneapolis MN 1993-1997; S Antipas Ch Redby MN 1993-1997; Vic S Jn-In-The-Wilderness Red Lake MN 1993-1997; Vic Ch Of The Gd Shpd Ft Defiance AZ 1989-1993; Reg Vic Navajoland Area Mssn Farmington NM 1989-1993; R S Steph's Epis Par Portland OR 1984-1989; S Jn's Epis Ch Mauston WI 1981-1984; Vic S Mary's Epis Ch Tomah WI 1981-1984; The Par of St Paul's Epis Ch Duluth MN 1979-1981; Res Chapl S Lk's Hosp Duluth MN 1978-1980. Associated Parishes; ACPE; Tertiary Of The Soc Of S Fran.

MACDONALD, Susan Savage (Va) 1527 Senseny Rd, Winchester VA 22602 **S Paul's On-The-Hill Winchester VA 2014-** B Ithaca NY 1953 d John & Victoria. BMus Virginia Commonwealth U/Sch of the Arts 1979; MA GW 1982; JD Penn St-Dickinson Sch of Law 1997; M.Div. Luth TS at Gettysburg 2011. D 12/15/2007 P 6/14/2008 Bp William Michie Klusmeyer. m 2/21/1992 Randolph R Macdonald c 1. P-in-c Gr Epis Ch Kearneysville WV 2010-2013; Assoc Trin Ch Shepherdstown WV 2007-2013.

MACDONALD, Terrence Cameron (O) 207 Weed St, New Canaan CT 06840 **Serv S Chris 1978-** B 1938 s Cameron & Helen. U MI 1960; BA U of Toledo 1961; BD Bex Sem 1964. D 6/13/1964 P 3/1/1965 Bp Nelson Marigold

Burroughs. m 8/10/1968 Jean MacDonald. Asst S Matt's Ch Bedford NY 1970-1977; Non-par 1967-1970; Cur S Paul's Ch Akron OH 1964-1967.

MACDONALD, Walter Young (Mich) 2796 Page Ave, Ann Arbor MI 48104 B Boston MA 1941 s Herman & Marion. BA Davidson Coll 1964; MDiv EDS 1969; MS U MI 1971; Cntr For Humanistic Stds 1981. D 6/10/1969 Bp Robert Bruce Hall P 5/1/1970 Bp Archie H Crowley. m 8/14/1965 Louisa MacDonald. Non-par 1969-1971.

MACDONELL, Alexander Harrison (Nwk) 216 Heath Vlg, Hackettstown NJ 07840 **Ret 1994-** B Savannah GA 1927 s Alexander & Kathryn. BA Col 1950; MDiv VTS 1968. D 5/25/1968 Bp William S Thomas P 12/21/1968 Bp Robert Bracewell Appleyard. m 8/19/1950 Clare Mac Donell c 4. Chapl for Ret Cler Dio Newark Newark NJ 1996-1998; R and Dir, Joint Mnstry All SS Ch Bergenfield NJ 1992-1993; R S Lk's Epis Ch Haworth NJ 1980-1993; R S Steph's Epis Ch Pittsburgh PA 1971-1980; R Chr Ch Brownsville PA 1969-1971. Cbury Schlrshp Dio Newark 1985.

MACDOUGALL, Matthew Bradstock (NwPa) 343 E Main St, Youngsville PA 16371 B Lancaster PA 1981 s Malcolm & Linda. LTh VTS 2009. D 6/13/2009 Bp Nathan Dwight Baxter P 2/20/2010 Bp Sean Walter Rowe. P-in-c S Fran Of Assisi Epis Ch Youngsville PA 2009-2013.

MACDOWELL, Barry Scott (Ind) 138 S 18th St, Richmond IN 47374 B Lansing MI 1945 s George & Ortha. BA MI SU 1969; MA U MI 1969. D 6/24/1993 Bp Edward Witker Jones. m 5/6/1969 Carolyn Kay MacDowell c 3.

MACDUFFIE OSB, Bruce Lincoln (CNY) 836 5th Ave. West, Dickinson ND 58601 **P The Ch Of The Epiph Sherburne NY 2010-, Vic 2001-2010, R 1994-2000** B Newburyport MA 1936 s William & Bertha. BA Blackburn Coll 1959; MEd Bos 1969; MDiv SWTS 1984; DMin SWTS 1998. D 5/8/1985 P 11/30/1985 Bp Harold Anthony Hopkins Jr. m 6/10/1975 Gloria Lee MacDuffie c 4. Assoc adj. Prof Dickinson St U Dickinson ND 2005-2011; S Jn's Epis Ch Dickinson ND 2005-2011; R S Paul's Ch Oxford NY 2002-2005, R 1994-1999; Dio Cntrl New York Liverpool NY 1999-2004, Prncpl, New Cler Acad 1996-2003; R S Thos Ch Hamilton NY 1999-2002; Calv Epis Ch Mc Donough NY 1997-1999; Emm Ch Norwich NY 1994-1999; R S Jas' Epis Ch Dalhart TX 1991-1994; Dio Minnesota Minneapolis MN 1988-1991; Supvsng P Leech Lake Indn Reserv 1988-1991; Rgnl Vic Dio No Dakota Fargo ND 1985-1988. "Comparing Study Bibles," *Dio No Dakota web site*, Dio No Dakota, 2006. Associated Parishes 1982-2002; St. Greg's Abbey 1982. blmacduffie@frontier.com

MACEK, Kathryn Ellen (EO) PO Box 1001, La Grande OR 97850 **R S Ptr's Ch La Grande OR 2012-, Int 2011** B Adams MA 1946 d Robert & Jacqueline. BMus Mt St Marys Coll 1968; MDiv CDSP 2010. D 4/30/2011 P 10/16/2011 Bp Bavi Edna Rivera. m 9/5/1981 Thorman F Hulse c 2. Dioc Coun Dio Estrn Oregon Cove OR 2013-2016. stpeterslagrande@gmail.com

MAC EWEN, Suzanne Marie (Wyo) Po Box 137, Evanston WY 82931 **D S Paul's Epis Ch Evanston WY 2011-** B Chicago IL 1941 d Francis & Agnes. Andover Newton TS; Missouri Wstrn St U. D 8/14/2003 Bp Bruce Caldwell.

MACFARLANE, Robert John (Chi) 3724 Farr Ave, Fairfax VA 22030 **Ret 1998-** B Sioux City IA 1931 s Robert & Esther. BS Iowa St U 1954; MA U of Iowa 1958; STB GTS 1968. D 6/22/1968 P 12/19/1968 Bp Gordon V Smith. m 6/25/1971 Maria Byrd Keith c 1. Chapl Wstrn Prov Cmnty S Mary 1982-1986; R S Barn' Epis Ch Glen Ellyn IL 1979-1998; Asst Trin Cathd Davenport IA 1974-1978; P-in-c All SS Epis Ch Storm Lake IA 1968-1974; P-in-c S Steph's Epis Ch 1968-1974. EPF 1991.

MACFIE JR, Tom (Tenn) 117 Carruthers Rd, Sewanee TN 37375 **Chapl Sewanee U So TS Sewanee TN 2006-; U Chapl and Dn U So Sewanee TN 2006-** B Greenville SC 1958 s Thomas & Ellen. BA U So 1980; MDiv Sewanee: The U So, TS 1989. D 5/19/1989 P 12/16/1989 Bp William Gillette Weinhauer. m 3/21/1987 Pamela Macfie c 1. R Otey Memi Par Ch Sewanee TN 1997-2006; R S Barn Ch Tullahoma TN 1989-1997. Auth, "Seeking a Deeper Knowledge of God: Centering Pryr and the Life of a Par," *Sprtlty, Contemplation and Transformation*, Lantern Books, 2008; Auth, "Looking For the Enchanted Place," *Sewanee Theol Revs*, 1998. Dn of All SS' Chap U So 2009; Participant, Natl Cler Renwl Prog 2003.

MACGILL, Martha Nell (Md) **Emm Ch Cumberland MD 2014-** B Alexandria VA 1958 d Winfield & Anna. BA Davidson Coll 1980; JD U of Virginia 1984; LLM NYU 1986; MDiv VTS 1995. D 6/3/1995 P 1/1/1996 Bp Peter J Lee. m 6/13/1981 Richard B Kelleher c 2. Memi Ch Baltimore MD 2000-2014; S Steph's Ch Richmond VA 1996-1997. administrator@emmanuelparishofmd.org

MACGILL III, William D (WVa) 5909 cedar landing rd, Wilmington NC 28409 B Newport News VA 1944 s William & Eloise. BA Hampden-Sydney Coll 1967. D 6/14/1997 P 6/13/1998 Bp John Henry Smith. m 4/4/1982 Sybil Owen Macgill. P St. Mary's Epis Ch Burgaw No carolina 2008-2010; R Chap on the Mt 2002-2006; Vic S Jn's Ch Marlinton WV 2000-2006; P S Thos Epis Ch Wht Sphr Spgs WV 1998-2001; Ch Of The Incarn Ronceverte WV 1998-2000.

MACGOWAN JR, Kenneth Arbuthnot (Colo) 3440 S Jefferson St Apt 1136, Falls Church VA 22041 **Ret 1996-** B Quincy FL 1924 s Kenneth & Mary. BS U So 1947; MA Mex City Coll Mex City Mx 1948; JD Harv 1951; MDiv VTS 1984. D 6/23/1984 Bp Peter J Lee P 5/22/1985 Bp David Henry Lewis Jr. c 4.

Cn Mssnr Dio Colorado Denver CO 1994-1996; Non-par 1990-1994; Vic & R Trin Ch Manassas VA 1986-1990; Int S Paul's Ch Haymarket VA 1985-1986; Asst Vic All SS Epis Ch Woodbridge VA 1984-1985; COLM Dio Virginia Richmond VA 1988-1990. Auth, "arts, Wrshp, The Word," & The Wrld; Auth, "arts," Acts 29. Aac; ERM. Phi Beta Kappa; Phi Beta Kappa.

MACGREGOR, Laird Stanley (WK) 322 S Ash St, Mcpherson KS 67460 **Dio Wstrn Kansas Hutchinson KS 2006-; Vic S Anne's Ch Mcpherson KS 2006-** B Medicine Lodge KS 1966 s John & Barbara. BS U of Kansas 1988; MDiv Sewanee: The U So, TS 2006. D 5/9/2006 P 11/25/2006 Bp James Marshall Adams Jr.

MACIAS PEREZ, Franklin Oswaldo (EcuL) CALLE AMARILIS FUENTES N, 603 Y CALLE D, GUAYAQUIL 09-01-5250 Ecuador **Litoral Dio Ecuador Guayaquil 2015-** B Quevedo Los Rios 1965 s Carlos & Teresa. D 10/11/2014 Bp Terencio Alfredo Morante-Espana. m 2/12/2009 Aida Pastora Loor c 4.

MACINNIS, Elyn G (NY) 64 Memorial Rd, Providence RI 02906 B New York NY 1951 d Richard & Betty. BA Kirkland Coll 1973; MDiv Harvard DS 1977. D 2/14/1993 Bp Kuang-Hsun Ting P 8/1/1993 Bp William George Burrill. m 12/30/1974 Peter P Macinnis c 2. Min Trin Cong Shanghai China 2008-2017; Min Cong of the Gd Shpd Beijing China 1995-2004; Exec Coun Appointees New York NY 1994-2010; Min S Paul's Intl Cong 1989-1995; Serv Untd Ch Of Chr 1977-1993. Auth, "Character Reflections," 2011; Auth, "Powers Principalities & People," Methodist Bd GLOBAL Mnstrs, 1979. The Rabbi Mart Katzenstein Awd Harv DS 2004.

MACINTIRE, Morgan Montelepre (La) 2050 Bert Kouns, Shreveport LA 71118 **Chr Ch Covington LA 2015-; R S Jas Epis Ch Shreveport LA 2012-, P-in-c 2011-2015, 2010-2011** B Shreveport LA 1982 d John & Elizabeth. BA Rhodes Coll 2004; MDiv VTS 2008. D 6/7/2008 Bp D Avid Bruce Macpherson P 8/8/2009 Bp David Colin Jones. m 6/4/2005 Angus Alan MacIntire c 1. Chapl Dio Wstrn Louisiana Alexandria LA 2011-2014; Asst Trin Ch Manassas VA 2008-2010; Secy of Cmncatn S Mk's Cathd Shreveport LA 2004-2006.

MACINTOSH, Neil Keith (Kan) Charismead, 11A Browns Road, The Oaks, NSW 2570 Australia B Newtown VIC AU 1935 s Alexander & Evelyn. ThL Moore Theol Coll Sydney 1961; BD Lon GB 1963; THS Australia Coll of Theol 1967; AA Libr Assoc of Australia 1976; MA Macquarie U 1977. Trans 4/1/1989 as Priest Bp Gerald Nicholas Mcallister. m 8/14/1965 Denise Ve Macintosh c 3. Serv Angl Ch of Australia Sydney Australia 2003-2007; Serv Ch of the Prov of the W Indies 1997-2003; Angl Dio the Bahamas and the Turks and Caicos Islands Nassau 1997-2000; St. Monica's Angl Ch 1997-2000; R S Paul's Epis Ch Coffeyville KS 1989-1997; Serv Angl Ch of Australia Sydney Australia 1961-1982. Auth, "Richard Johnson," Blackwell Dict. of Evang Biography, Blackwell, 1995; Auth, "Mary Johnson," Australian Dict. of Evang Biography, Evang Hist Assoc., 1994; Auth, "Richard Johnson," Australian Dict. of Evang Biography, Evang Hist Assoc., 1994; Auth, "Richard Johnson, Chapl to the Colony of New So Wales," Libr of Australian Hist, 1978.

MACK, Alan E (Oly) **Died 10/9/2016** B 1940 s Earl & Marion. AB Harv 1962; MDiv Ya Berk 1967. D 8/10/1967 Bp Ivol I Curtis P 2/10/1968 Bp Donald H V Hallock. c 4. Dio Olympia Seattle 2008-2010; P-in-c St Ptr's Epis Par Seattle WA 2005-2007; S Mk's Cathd Seattle WA 2004; All SS Epis Ch Seattle WA 1973-1979; St. Tim's and St. Greg's S Jn's Ch Kirkland WA 1969-1973; Cur Chr Ch Milwaukee WI 1967-1969. Ed, "Icons: The Fascination and the Reality," Riverside Bk Co, Inc., 1995; Ed, "St. Spiridon's Cathd: A Century in Seattley of," St. Spiridon Cathd Press, 1995.

MACK, Arthur Robert (Mich) 13 Dover Ln., Hendersonville NC 28739 B Watertown NY 1942 s Arthur & Sarah. BS USMA 1964; MDiv GTS 1971. D 5/5/1971 Bp Clarence Edward Hobgood P 2/27/1972 Bp Chilton R Powell. m 2/12/1983 Susan G Mack c 4. R S Jn's Ch Westland MI 1998-2008; R Trin Ch Lancaster NY 1989-1997; R The Ch Of The Epiph Sherburne NY 1981-1989; S Ptr's Epis Ch Cazenovia NY 1980; St Paul's Syracuse Syracuse NY 1980, Cur 1971-1973; Trin Ch Lowville NY 1980, Int R 1979-1980; Off Of Bsh For ArmdF New York NY 1973-1979. Ord of S Lk 1974; OHC 1970.

MACK, Ross Julian (NI) Po Box 462, Valparaiso IN 46384 **1984-** B Lansing MI 1949 s Walter & June. BA Hope Coll 1971; MDiv Nash 1974; BSME Valparaiso U 1986. D 4/19/1974 P 11/2/1974 Bp Charles Thomas Gaskell. m 7/31/1971 Patricia M Mack c 1. R S Andr's Epis Ch Valparaiso IN 1977-1984; Asst Trin Ch Milwaukee WI 1974-1976.

MACKAY III, Donald (Oly) 9727 NE Juanita Dr, Unit #311, Kirkland WA 98034 B Billings MT 1940 s Donald & Virginia. BA Trin Hartford CT 1962; MDiv VTS 1965. D 6/24/1965 P 12/28/1965 Bp Chandler W Sterling. m 7/11/1964 Rosemary MacKay c 5. R S Jn's Ch Kirkland WA 1990-2005; R S Lk's Ch Billings MT 1967-1990; Vic Whitefish Mssn Field Columbia Falls MT 1965-1967. Auth, "Chr's Own Forever," Self Pub - St. Jn'S Ch, 2002. Chapl Ord Of S Lk 1989-1994.

MACKE, Beth (Ind) 4713 Housebridge Rd, Corydon KY 42406 **R S Steph's Epis Ch New Harmony IN 2017-, P-in-c 2014-2016** B St Louis MO 1964 d James & Barbara. BS Sprg Hill Coll 1985; PhD Emory U 1993; MDiv Sewanee: The U So, TS 2001. D 6/9/2001 Bp Robert Gould Tharp P 12/22/2001 Bp J Neil Alexander. m 5/11/2011 Mark D Sellars c 1. Adj Instr Sociol Ken-

tucky Wesleyan Coll 2014-2017; Adj Instr Henderson Cmnty Coll Henderson KY 2010-2014; Vic Dio Indianapolis Indianapolis IN 2010-2013; R S Paul's Ch Henderson KY 2007-2010; R S Mary's Epis Ch Middlesboro KY 2003-2007; Sr Asst to the R S Dav's Ch Roswell GA 2002-2003; Cur S Geo's Epis Ch Griffin GA 2001-2002. Amer Sociol Assn 2000.

MACKENDRICK, Gary Winfred (Ore) 3014 Main Street, Forest Grove OR 97116 B Dublin TX 1945 s Elby & Daphnae. CEU U of Oregon; BA W Texas A&M U 1967; MDiv Iliff TS 1971; MCPC Gonzaga U 1977; MA Gonzaga U 1977. D 10/16/1977 P 2/19/1978 Bp John Raymond Wyatt. m 10/1/1999 Janet Elaine MacKendrick c 3. Vic / Int S Andr's Ch Portland OR 1984-1985; Ch Of The Epiph Lake Oswego OR 1983-1985; Pstr Counslr Epis Par Of S Jn The Bapt Portland OR 1983-1985; Gr Epis Ch Astoria OR 1979-1983; S Steph's Epis Ch Spokane WA 1978-1979. Auth, Etchings; Auth, Jewish & Hellenistic Background Churchr Ch; Auth, The Sons of S Mich. Coll of Chapl. The Mich Lambert, Ph.D., Awd for Clincl Excellence 2003.

MACKENZIE JR, Albert Harold (SO) 37 Abbey Ln, Washington NC 27889 **Ret 1992-** B Gallipolis OH 1928 s Albert & Martha. BFA Ohio U 1959; MDiv VTS 1962. D 6/17/1962 Bp Roger W Blanchard P 1/5/1963 Bp Samuel B Chilton. m 8/5/1951 Dorothy Mackenzie. Supply P Emm Ch Farmville NC 2008-2013; S Jn's / S Mk's Grifton NC 2003-2008; P-in-c Zion Epis Ch Washington NC 1998-2002; Supply P S Jas Epis Ch Belhaven NC 1995-1998; Chapl Gallipolis Vol Fire Dept 1984-1992; Gr Ch Pomeroy OH 1977-1978; R S Ptr's Ch Gallipolis OH 1964-1992; Asst Gr Epis Ch Alexandria VA 1962-1964. Rotarian of the Year 1995; Outstanding Serv Awd BB/S 1988; Fireman of the Year 1988.

MACKENZIE, A(Lexander) James (NCal) 3988 NW Walnut Ct., Corvallis OR 97330 B Anchorage AK 1946 s William & Margaret. BA U of Montana 1969; Olympia TS 1982; MDiv Nash 1992. D 6/24/1988 Bp Robert Hume Cochrane P 1/18/1992 Bp Rustin Ray Kimsey. c 3. R Chr Ch Eureka CA 2002-2005; Pres Stndg Com Ch Of The Redeem Pendleton OR 1992-2002; Asst St Philips Epis Ch Waukesha WI 1989-1991; Asst S Andr's Epis Ch Tacoma WA 1988-1989; Dio Estrn Oregon Cove OR 1992-1998. Ka Papa (Ha Cmnty Of Ch); NAAD; RWF. tartan18@gmail.com

MACKENZIE, John Anderson Ross (WNY) 11819 Eastkent Sq, Richmond VA 23238 B Edinburgh Scotland GB 1927 s Donald & Edith. MA U of Edinburgh GB 1949; BD U of Edinburgh Edinburgh GB 1952; PhD U of Edinburgh GB 1962; Lic Lund U 1964. D P 9/19/1998 Bp David Charles Bowman. m 7/14/1951 Flora Margaret MacKenzie c 3. Assoc S Lk's Epis Ch Jamestown NY 2000-2006; Int S Paul's Epis Ch Mayville NY 1998-1999. Doctor of Humane Letters Shenandoah U, Winchester VA 1997.

MACKENZIE, Jonathan (NH) 52 Brick Kiln Rd, Chelmsford MA 01824 **Asst S Anne's Ch No Billerica MA 2012-** B Ticonderoga NY 1938 s Harry & Kate. BA Un Coll Schenectady NY 1960; MDiv GTS 1967. D 6/3/1967 P 12/21/1967 Bp Allen Webster Brown. m 6/3/2000 Carol MacKenzie c 4. Sacramentalist S Mk's Ch Westford MA 2011-2012; Asst All SS Ch W Newbury MA 2007-2010; S Jn's Epis Ch Lowell MA 2005-2007; R S Jas Epis Ch Laconia NH 1994-2004; S Lk's Ch Mechanicville NY 1988-1994, R 1982-1988; Trin Epis Ch Mechanicville NY 1988-1991; Trin Ch Boonville NY 1987-1988; Chr Ch Coxsackie NY 1982-1988; S Lk's Ch Catskill NY 1982-1987; R S Lk's Epis Ch Smethport PA 1978-1982; Vic Ch Of The Gd Samar Mckeesport PA 1976-1978; S Jn's Epis Ch Troy NY 1975-1976; Chapl S Agnes Sch Loudonville NY 1974-1975; R Chr Ch Walton NY 1970-1974; Cur Chr Ch Cooperstown NY 1967-1970.

MACKENZIE, Katharine Helen (Los) 948 W Sierra Nevada Way, Orange CA 92865 **Asst Ch Of The Mssh Santa Ana CA 2000-** B Los Angeles CA 1957 d John & Elizabeth. BA California St U 1979; JD Loyola U 1982; MDiv ETSBH 1997. D 6/14/1997 Bp Chester Lovelle Talton P 1/1/1998 Bp Frederick Houk Borsch. m 6/4/1977 Robert Stanley MacKenzie. S Aug By-The-Sea Par Santa Monica CA 1997-2000.

MACKENZIE, Lester V (Los) 428 Park Ave, Laguna Beach CA 92651 **Corp of the Dio - Dir Dio Los Angeles Los Angeles CA 2015-, GC Cler Dep 2011-, Exam Chapl 2010-, 2008-** B South Africa 1974 s Ernest & Charmaine. LTh VTS 2007. D 6/9/2007 P 1/12/2008 Bp Joseph Jon Bruno. m 7/25/2004 Angela M MacKenzie c 2. Assoc for Emerging Mnstrs The Par Of S Matt Pacific Plsds CA 2009-2016; Cur St Johns Pro-Cathd Los Angeles CA 2007-2009. lmackenzie@stmaryslb.org

MACKENZIE, Mary Catherine (Oly) 16060 Ne 28th St, Bellevue WA 98008 **S Jn's Epis Ch Snohomish WA 2016-** B Seattle WA 1957 d William & Nancy. BSE U of Washington 1979; MSE U of Washington 1985; MDiv SWTS 2005. D 6/25/2005 P 1/14/2006 Bp Vincent Waydell Warner. m 4/28/1979 Wesley S Ono c 2. S Lk's Ch Tacoma WA 2015; Newcomer Mnstry Coordntr Ch Tacoma WA 2013-2014; YA Mssnr Chr Ch Seattle WA 2009-2012; Cur Trin Epis Ch Everett WA 2006-2007; Cur Emm Epis Ch Mercer Island WA 2005-2006. Cler Assn of the Dio Olympia 2005.

MACKENZIE, Vanessa Mildred (Los) 1739 Buckingham Rd, Los Angeles CA 90019 **R Epis Ch Of The Adv Los Angeles CA 2000-** B Johannesburg ZA 1959 Trans 12/1/2000 Bp Chester Lovelle Talton.

MACKENZIE, Vincent Victor (Cal) 110 Bella Vista Ave, Belvedere CA 94920 **Died 8/3/2016** B Peoria IL 1929 s Victor & Alma. BS Bradley U 1953; JD U IL 1954; S Georges Coll Jerusalem IL 1991; BA Sch for Deacons 1992. D 12/4/1993 Bp William Edwin Swing P. m 9/15/1956 Carolyn Elaine MacKenzie c 3. Dioc Hunger Cmsn 1988-2016. Bread For The Wrld.

MACKEY, George Rudolph (Los) 801 Haslam Dr, Santa Maria CA 93454 **Ret 1999-** B Casper WY 1929 s George & Esther. BS U of Nebraska 1958; MDiv CDSP 1966. D 6/13/1966 P 12/19/1966 Bp James W Hunter. m 12/18/1977 Judith P Mackey. R S Ptr's Par Santa Maria CA 1985-1999; S Jas' Epis Ch Coquille OR 1981-1985; S Mk's Ch Myrtle Point OR 1981-1985; Vic S Paul's Epis Mssn Powers OR 1981-1985; P S Paul's Epis Ch Salem OR 1977-1981; Ch Of The H Comm Rock Sprg WY 1969-1977; Vic All Souls Edgerton WY 1966-1969; Vic Chr Epis Ch Glenrock WY 1966-1969.

MACKEY, Guy (RG) 312 N. Orchard Ave., Farmington NM 87401 **St Johns Epis Ch Farmington NM 2009-** B Suffern NY 1972 s Jeffrey & M(artha). BS Chadwick U 1993; MDiv Cranmer Theol Hse 1998. D 9/15/1999 P 3/18/2000 Bp Robert Jefferson Hargrove Jr. m 12/20/1997 Cheryl L Mackey c 2. Chr Memi Ch Mansfield LA 2001-2009; Cur Gr Epis Ch Monroe LA 1999-2001.

MACKEY, Jeffrey A (Fla) 500 Grove Street, Melrose FL 32666 B Kingston NY 1952 s Allen & Vivian. STD Laud Hall TS; BSc Nyack Coll 1974; MDiv Macon Bapt TS 1978; DMin GTF 1990; Cert GTS 1993; ThD Evangel Chr U 2011; PhD Trin TS 2011. D 2/22/1993 P 9/14/1993 Bp David Bruce Joslin. m 12/18/1971 M(artha) LaVanne Webster c 3. R Trin Epis Ch Melrose FL 2008-2011; R S Mk's Ch Orchard Pk NY 2007-2008; Acad Dn TESM Ambridge PA 2005-2007; Dio New York New York NY 2003-2004; Int S Greg's Epis Ch Woodstock NY 2003-2004; R S Jn's Epis Ch Kingston NY 2002-2003; Ass't VP & Dn Nyack Coll Nyack NY 2000-2005; Ass't VP/Dn of Coll of Arts and Sciences Nyack Coll [Ext of Mnstry] Nyack NY 1999-2005; R Epis Ch Of S Mk The Evang Bellmore NY 1997-1999; Vic Leonidas Polk Memi Epis Mssn Leesville LA 1996-1997; Vic Polk Memi Ch Leesville LA 1996-1997; R Trin Epis Ch Deridder LA 1996-1997; Vic Gr Epis Ch Waterville NY 1994-1996; Assoc R Gr Epis Ch Utica NY 1993-1996, Vic 1991-1992; Assoc Gr Ch Utica NY 1991-1996; Serv Chr & Mssy Allnce Ch 1971-1991; Sr Pstr Mnstry in Chr & Mssy Allnce 1971-1991; Chair, BEC Dio Florida 2008-2013. Auth, "But I Repeat Myself," The Wilson Press, 2011; Auth, "Chr's Centripetal Cross -2nd ed," The Wilson Press, 2011; Auth, "The Four Fold Gospel," The Wilson Press, 2010; Auth, "Take Your Chants," GROVEPUBLISHING, 2010; Auth, "A Hidden Surprise," iUniverse, 2008; Auth, "Hidden Mirth: The Gr Behind the Goodness," Pleasant Word, 2005; Auth, "And Jesus Everything: Conversations w A.B. Simpson," Blackfriar Books, 2000; Auth, "Prophet of Justice, Prophet of Life," Ch Pub, Inc., 1996; Auth, "Where Love & People Are," Wyndham Hall Press, 1990; Auth, "A Wrshp Manifesto," Brentwood Chr Press, 1989; Auth, "Chr's Centripetal Cross," Brentwood Chr Press, 1989; Auth, "Indicatives & Imperatives," Brentwood Chr Press, 1987. Angl Ord of Preachers [Dominicans] - Fndr/Mem 1999; SBL 2001. DD GTF 2005; D.Litt. Evang Coll & Sem 2004; D.H.L. S Paul TS 2001; S.L.D. Ridgedale TS 1975.

MACKEY, Judith P (Los) 801 Haslam Dr, Santa Maria CA 93454 **Dio Los Angeles Los Angeles CA 1999-** B Wilkinsburg PA 1942 d Charles & Lois. U Pac 1963; BA Chapman U 1991; Chapman U 1994. D 2/21/1986 Bp Robert Louis Ladehoff. m 12/18/1977 George Rudolph Mackey c 1. D S Ptr's Par Santa Maria CA 1986-1999. CHS; Integrity; NAAD.

MACKEY, Peter David (Mich) 614 Company St, Adrian MI 49221 B Pottsville PA 1940 s Sheldon & Marie. BA Ursinus Coll 1962; BD Lancaster TS 1965. D 6/24/1974 P 10/25/1974 Bp Dean Theodore Stevenson. c 1. R Chr Ch Adrian MI 1998-2002; S Jn's Epis Ch Bowling Green OH 1993-1996; R S Andr's Epis Ch York PA 1985-1993; R S Jas Bedford PA 1974-1985; Serv Untd Ch Of Chr 1965-1974.

MACKILLOP, Alan Bruce (SanD) 73 Windward Ln, Manchester NH 03104 B Cambridge MA 1936 s Kenneth & Mildred. BA Willamette U 1958; MDiv GTS 1970. D 4/8/1961 P 10/28/1961 Bp James Pernette DeWolfe. m 6/9/1958 Erica Dorothy MacKillop c 2. Pstr Asst, p/t Gr Epis Ch Concord NH 2014-2015; P-in-c S Andr's Ch Ayer MA 2005-2009; S Jn's Epis Ch Saugus MA 2003-2005; Int S Andr's Epis Ch Ayer MA 2001-2002; S Andr's Ch La Mesa CA 1979-1998; Ch Of The H Comm Mahopac NY 1976-1979; Cur Ch Of The Resurr New York NY 1967-1971; R Gr Epis Ch Port Jervis NY 1964-1967; Cur S Jn's Ch New York NY 1961-1964; Envirn Just Cmsn Phil Brooks Clb Dio Massachusetts; Ecum Cmsn Evang Cmsn Dio New York; Dio Coun Envirn Just Dio San Diego. Cltn for the Abolition of the Death Penalty, NH 2010; Cmnty of S Mary 1977; Mart Luther King Jr. Cltn, NH 2010; NAACP 1961; OHC 1962; Our Lady of Walsingham 1991; Soc of Cath Priests 2014. Cmnty Serv NAACP 2014.

MACKIN, Mary Ruetten (SwVa) St John's Episcopal Church, PO Box 257, Roanoke VA 24002 B Chippewa Falls WI 1946 d Hubert & Doris. BA Bethel Coll 1968; MA Ohio U 1977; MDiv VTS 2012. D 5/21/2012 P 12/11/2012 Bp Neff Powell. m 12/14/1985 Cooper Richerson Mackin.

MACKINTOSH, Leigh (NY) St Michael's Church, 225 W 99th St, New York NY 10025 **S Mich's Ch New York NY 2015-** B South Boston VA 1984 d Douglas & Jennifer. BA Lynchburg Coll 2007; MDiv Ya Berk 2013. D 3/1/2014 Bp Mark Bourlakas P 10/4/2014 Bp Allen Shin. The Ch of S Ign of Antioch New York NY 2014-2015; The Ch of S Matt And S Tim New York NY 2014-2015.

MACKNIGHT, Jeff (WA) 5450 Massachusetts Ave, Bethesda MD 20816 **R S Dunst's Epis Ch Beth MD 1999-** B Saint Louis MO 1959 s Frank & Barbara. BS Nebraska Wesl 1981; MDiv VTS 1984. D 6/15/1984 P 12/1/1984 Bp James Daniel Warner. m 10/10/1987 Leslie H MacKnight c 2. R S Phil's Epis Ch Laurel MD 1993-1999; R S Greg's Epis Ch Parsippany NJ 1988-1993; Asst Ch Of The Atone Tenafly NJ 1986-1988; Cur S Matt's Ch Lincoln NE 1984-1986. Ed, "Leaven," *Journ of NNECA*, NNECA, 1998. Lilly Endwmt Pstr Renwl Grant Lilly Endwmt 2006. rector@stdunstansbethesda.org

MACKOV, Elwyn Joseph (WVa) 118 Five Point Ave, Martinsburg WV 25404 **S Phil's Ch Chas Town WV 2008-** B Brooklyn NY 1940 s Joseph & Emma. MDiv GTS; BA Moravian TS 1965; STB GTS 1968. D 6/15/1968 P 12/21/1968 Bp Jonathan Goodhue Sherman. m 6/24/1995 Janette S Mackov. Emm Ch Keyser WV 1999-2006; H Trin Ch Logan WV 1997-2000; S Pauls Epis Ch Williamson WV 1997-2000; Mssnr Sthrn Appalachian Cluster 1997-2000; Sthrn Appalachian Cluster Williamson WV 1996-1999; Nelson Cluster Of Epis Ch Rippon WV 1995-1996; R All Souls Memi Epis Ch Washington DC 1974-1988; R Emm Epis Ch Great River NY 1970-1974; Cur All SS Ch Bayside NY 1968-1970.

MACLEAN, Peter Duncan (LI) P.O. Box 848, Colchester VT 05446 **Ret 1993-** B New York NY 1930 s Charles & Grace. BA Trin Hartford CT 1952; MDiv GTS 1955. D 4/16/1955 P 11/5/1955 Bp James Pernette DeWolfe. m 10/3/1970 Margaret Ellen Maclean. R S Lk's Ch Alburg VT 2002-2004; Int Chr Ch Sag Harbor NY 1994-1996; S Mary's Epis Ch Shltr Island NY 1976-1993; Dio Long Island Garden City NY 1976-1977; Ch Of The Mssh Mayodan NC 1974-1977; Asst Trin Ch Northport NY 1973-1974; R S Jas Epis Ch S Jas NY 1967-1970; Chapl USN 1964-1967; R S Ann's Ch Sayville NY 1960-1964; R Trin Epis Ch Lewiston ME 1957-1960; Min in charge Ch Of The Ascen Greenpoint Brooklyn NY 1955-1957.

MACLEOD, Jay (NH) Episcopal Church Of St Andrew, PO Box 294, New London NH 03257 **S Andr's Ch New London NH 2013-** B Stoughton MA 1961 s John & Nancy. AB Harvard Coll 1984; MA Oxf 1987; MDiv Lincoln Theol Coll 1993. Trans 10/11/2013 as Priest Bp A Robert Hirschfeld. m 10/29/1988 Sally Marie Asher c 3. jay@standrewsnl.org

MACLEOD III, Norman (Vt) 2 Church St, Woodstock VT 05091 B Southington CT 1947 s Norman & Helen. BA Clark U 1970; MA Adel 1981; MDiv Ya Berk 1989. D 7/1/1989 P 2/4/1990 Bp George Nelson Hunt III. m 9/18/1982 Elizabeth C Stevens c 3. R S Jas Ch Woodstock VT 2011-2017; Int S Jn's Epis Par Waterbury CT 2010-2011; Int Par Of S Jas Ch Keene NH 2008-2010; R Chr Ch Guilford CT 1997-2008; Vic S Aug's Ch Kingston RI 1991-1997; Epis Chapl U Of Rhode Island 1991-1997; Assoc Gr Ch In Providence Providence RI 1989-1991.

MACLIN, Charles Waite (Me) Po Box 1259, Portland ME 04104 **Non-par 1979-** B Winston-Salem NC 1934 s Henry & Lucy. BA Guilford Coll 1956; MDiv VTS 1959; Fllshp 1970. D 6/21/1959 P 12/13/1959 Bp Richard Henry Baker. c 2. Dn Reg Dio Virginia Richmond VA 1976-1978; R Chr Epis Ch Winchester VA 1974-1978; Dept Chr Trng Dio Maryland Baltimore MD 1968-1974, Chair Yth Com & Mem Deptce 1968-1971, Excoun 1971-1973; Assoc R The Ch Of The Redeem Baltimore MD 1967-1974; R S Jos's Ch Durham NC 1962-1966; S Paul's Epis Ch Cary NC 1959-1962; Min In Charge Trin Ch Fuquay Varina NC 1959-1962. Me Pstr Counselors Assn.

MACMILLAN, Cameron P (CFla) **Ch Of The Gd Shpd Maitland FL 2016-** B 1984 s Patrick & Cindy. B.A. U MI 2013; Masters Nash 2016. D 1/16/2016 P 7/17/2016 Bp Gregory Orrin Brewer. m 8/29/2010 Hannah Rose Fralick c 1.

MACNABB, Anne St Clair Coghill (Md) 20370 Marguritte Sq, Sterling VA 20165 **Trin Ch Waterloo Elkridge MD 2015-** B Fairfax VA 1970 BA Mary Baldwin Coll 1992; MDiv VTS 2004. D 6/26/2004 P 1/10/2005 Bp Peter J Lee. c 1. Asst R S Matt's Epis Ch Sterling VA 2008-2015; S Dunst's Ch Mc Lean VA 2007-2008; S Thos Epis Ch Mclean VA 2004-2007. info@trinityelkridge.org

MACNALLY, Janet Lee (Minn) **D S Chris's Epis Ch S Paul MN 2007-; Speech/ Theatre Coach St. Marg's Highschool 2000-** B St Paul MN 1950 BS U MN Duluth 1972. D 6/28/2007 Bp James Louis Jelinek. m 9/8/1973 William MacNally c 2.

✠ **MACNAUGHTON, The Rt Rev John Herbert** (WTex) 230 W Sunset Rd Apt 1113, San Antonio TX 78209 B Duluth MN 1929 s Herbert & Jennie. BA U MN 1951; MDiv Bex Sem 1954; D.D. Sewanee: The U So, TS 1985; D.D Bex Sem 2003. D 6/20/1954 P 2/28/1955 Bp Stephen E Keeler Con 2/6/1986 for WTex. m 6/25/1954 Shirley Ross c 5. Bp of W Texas Dio W Texas San Antonio TX 1986-1995; R Chr Epis Ch San Antonio TX 1975-1986; R S Steph The Mtyr Ch Minneapolis MN 1972-1975; R Trin Ch Excelsior MN 1967-1972; Dn The Epis Cathd Of Our Merc Sav Faribault MN 1958-1968; R H Trin Intl Falls MN 1954-1958; Vic S Ptr's Ch Warroad MN 1954-1958. Auth, *More Blessed to Give*, CPG, 1983; Auth, *Stwdshp Myths & Methods*, Seabury Press, 1975. Apos in Stwdshp The Epis Ntwk in Stwdshp 2006.

M

MACNEICE, Alan Donor (Haw) 29Eo Street 178, Commond Choy Chom, Phnom Penh Cambodia B Drogheda County Louth IE 1934 s Herbert & Evelyn. Trin Dublin IE; U Coll Dublin. Trans 12/27/1983 Bp John Shelby Spong. St Thos Ch Hanalei HI 1999-2006; Stndg Com The Epis Ch in Hawaii Honolulu HI 1999-2003, Cmncatns Chair 1995-1999, Dioc Coun 1994-1998, Dep Gc 1997-2003, Co Chair Bp Search Com 1995-1996; R Chr Memi Ch Kilauea HI 1993-2006; Int S Steph's Ch Millburn NJ 1991-1992; Int Chr Ch Glen Ridge NJ 1990-1991; Asstg S Bern's Ch Bernardsville NJ 1987-1989; S Alb's Ch Oakland NJ 1984-1986; S Barth's Epis Ch Ho Ho Kus NJ 1983-1984; Supply P Dio Newark Newark NJ 1981-1983; Serv Ch Of Nthrn Ireland Jamaica & Engl 1964-1981. Auth, "The Forgotten Country," *Garden Island*, 2002; Auth, "P Visits Cambodia," 2000; Auth, "Bp Spong In Hawai'i," *The Voice*, 1987; Auth, "An Int P Speaks," *The Voice*, 1986.

MACORT, John Gilbert (Ct) 5227 Rancho Ave, Sarasota FL 34234 **Ret 1998**- B Philadelphia PA 1937 s John & Louise. BA Hav 1960; MDiv EDS 1963; MA La Salle U 1971. D 6/8/1963 P 12/14/1963 Bp Joseph Gillespie Armstrong. m 5/1/1965 Sally-Jean Macort c 3. R S Andr's Ch Madison CT 1982-1998; Wooster Sch Danbury CT 1980-1982; Assoc The Epis Ch Of Beth-By-The-Sea Palm Bch FL 1973-1980; Assoc Trin Epis Ch Ambler PA 1969-1973; Assoc S Thos' Ch Whitemarsh Ft Washington PA 1963-1968. Auth, "A Seeker's Theol, (Chrsnty Reinterpreted as Mysticism)," *A Seeker's Theol, (Chrsnty Reinterpreted as Mysticism)*, 2017; Auth, "The Curse of a Questioning Mind," *The Curse of a Questioning Mind (Jas Gibson Harkins)*, Create Space/ Amazon, 2012; Auth, "A Reasonable Cov," *A Reasonable Cov*, Audubon Press, 1995; Auth, "An Outline of Ceremonies for the Euch Liturg-co Auth w Jn A. Schultz," *An Outline of Ceremonies for the Euch Liturg-co Auth w Jn A. Schultz*, Trin Press, 1972.

MACPHAIL, Alexander Douglas (SwVa) 1101 Franklin Rd SW, Roanoke VA 24016 **R Chr Epis Ch Roanoke VA 2015**- B Harrisonburg VA 1974 s Ralph & Alice. BA Bridgewater Coll 1997; MDiv VTS 2002. D 6/15/2002 P 12/16/2002 Bp Peter J Lee. m 5/24/2003 Karin L Chambers c 2. R Emm Ch Woodstock VA 2008-2015; R S Andr's Ch Mt Jackson VA 2008-2015; Chr Epis Ch Gordonsville VA 2004-2007; Cur Aquia Ch Stafford VA 2002-2004. CSB 2008; SocMary 2008. amacphail@christroanoke.org

MACPHAIL, Karin L (Va) 335 Eagle Street, Woodstock VA 22664 B Poughkeepsie NY 1972 d Charles & Susan. BA U of Texas 1994; MDiv VTS 2004. D 6/26/2004 P 1/18/2005 Bp Peter J Lee. m 5/24/2003 Alexander Douglas MacPhail c 2. P-in-c Cunningham Chap Par Millwood VA 2010-2015; Assoc R & Chapl S Paul's Memi Charlottesvlle VA 2004-2005.

✠ **MACPHERSON, The Rt Rev D Avid Bruce** (WLa) 3108 Garden Hill Cir, Edmond OK 73034 **Supplemental Epis Oversight Chr Ch St. Jn's Par Accokeek 2017-; Asstg Bp All Souls' OKC Dio Oklahoma 2013-; DEPO Bp St. Paul's Darien CT Dio Connecticut 2012-; Mem Sewanee U So Bd Trst 1999**- B Winnipeg Manitoba Canada 1940 s Kenneth & Rose. Cypress Coll Cypress CA 1974; DIT ETSBH 1978; Claremont TS 1979. D 2/17/1980 P 9/20/1980 Bp Robert Claflin Rusack Con 10/9/1999 for Dal. m 7/25/1958 Susan D Hegele c 2. Bp of Wstrn Louisiana Dio Wstrn Louisiana Alexandria LA 2002-2012; Bp Suffr Dio Dallas Dallas TX 1999-2002, Cn to the Ordnry 1993-1999; Mem ETSS Austin Bd Trst 1993-2007; Cn to the Ordnry Dio Los Angeles Los Angeles CA 1988-1993; Vic S Jn's Mssn La Verne CA 1981-1988; Pres Prov VII Fairfax VA 2005-2009, VP 2002-2005; PBp's Coun of Advice Dom And Frgn Mssy Soc- Epis Ch Cntr New York NY 2002-2009; Prov Chapl DOK-Prov VII 2000-2006; Bd H Trin Epis Sch Heath UT 1995-2002; Bd Mem Epis TS Of The SW Austin TX 1993-2007; Bd Trst Angl TS Dallas TX 1993-2002; VP Cathd Gardens Corp Dallas TX 1993-2002; Bd GDCC/CCM Dallas TX 1993-1998; Bd InterRel Cncl of Sthrn California 1991-1993; Pres Sthrn California Ecum Coun 1991-1993; Bd Trst ETSC 1990-1993; VP Sthrn California Ecum Coun 1989-1991; Bd PVCC Claremont CA 1987-1989. BroSA 1967. DD Nash, Nashotah 2009; DD U So, Sewanee 2003; Polly Bond Awd ECom 1996; Hon Cn Cathd Cntr of S Paul Cong of S Athan 1993.

MACQUEEN, Karen B (Los) 23730 Gold Nugget Ave, Diamond Bar CA 91765 B Welland Ontario Canada 1945 D 12/13/2003 P 6/12/2004 Bp Joseph Jon Bruno. Assoc R S Paul's Pomona Pomona CA 2004-2012.

MACSWAIN, Robert Carroll (EC) University Of The South School Of Theology, 335 Tennessee Ave., Sewanee TN 37383 **Assoc Prof of Theol Sewanee U So TS Sewanee TN 2015-, Instr of Theol and Chr Ethics 2009-2015** B Hampton VA 1969 s Travis & Joyce. BA Liberty U 1992; MDiv PrTS 1995; ThM U of Edinburgh 1996; Dip VTS 2000; PhD U of St Andrews 2010. D 6/30/2001 Bp The Archbishop Of Canterbury P 2/2/2002 Bp Clifton Daniel III. Ramsey Fell and Chapl S Chad's Coll U of Durham Durham 2005-2008; Sum Int P S Paul's Ch Beaufort NC 2004; Asst to the R S Mary's Ch Kinston NC 2001-2004; Resrch Asst to the Archbp of Cbury Lambeth Palace London UK 2000-2001. Co-Ed, "Div Generosity and Human Creativity: Theol Through Symbol, Painting and Archit (essays by Dav Brown)," Routledge, 2017; Co-Ed, "God in a Single Vision: Integrating Philos and Theol (essays by Dav Brown)," Routledge, 2016; Ed, "Scripture, Metaphysics, and Poetry: Austin Farrer's The Glass of Vision w Critical Commentary," Ashgate, 2013; Auth, "Solved by Sac-

rifice: Austin Farrer, Fideism, and the Evidence of Faith," Peeters, 2013; Co-Ed, "Theol, Aesthetics, and Culture: Responses to the Wk of Dav Brown (co-edited w Taylor Worley)," Oxf Press, 2012; Co-Ed, "The Cambridge Comp to C. S. Lewis (co-edited w Mich Ward)," Camb Press, 2010; Co-Ed, "The Truth-Seeking Heart: Austin Farrer and His Writings (co-edited w Ann Loades)," Cbury Press, 2006; Co-Ed, "Grammar and Gr: Reformulations of Aquinas and Wittgenstein (co-edited w Jeffrey Stout)," SCM Press, 2004.

MACVEAN-BROWN, Shannon L (Ind) 8850 Woodward Ave, Detroit MI 48202 **Cn Chr Ch Cathd Indianapolis IN 2014**- B Detroit MI 1967 d Paul & Jacqueline. BFA Kendall Coll of Art And Design 1989; MDiv SWTS 2005. D 12/18/2004 P 7/2/2005 Bp Wendell Nathaniel Gibbs Jr. m 10/24/1992 Phillip H Macvean c 1. R S Matt's And S Jos's Detroit MI 2006-2013, 2005; Cur Ch Of The Resurr Ecorse MI 2005-2006. shannonm@cccindy.org

MACWHINNIE II, Anthony Eugene (CGC) 7810 Navarre Pkwy, Navarre FL 32566 **S Monica's Cantonment FL 2014**- B Pensacola FL 1969 s Anthony & Susan. BS U of W Florida 1993; MDiv Epis TS of the SW 2008. D 6/7/2008 P 5/2/2009 Bp Philip Menzie Duncan II. m 10/13/2012 Elizabeth Anagnostis MacWhinnie c 1. R St Aug of Cbury Navarre FL 2010-2014; P-in-c S Thos By The Sea Panama City Bch FL 2008-2010.

MADDEN, John Erwin (LI) PO Box 398, Laurel NY 11948 **Supply P S Cuth's Epis Ch Selden NY 2003-; Ret 1998**- B New York NY 1937 s James & Lilly. BA CUNY 1959; MDiv Nash 1962; GTS 1963; S Vladimirs Orth TS 1966. D 4/28/1962 P 12/1/1962 Bp James Pernette DeWolfe. m 6/28/1992 Gail R Madden. Dio Long Island Garden City NY 1983-1984; Ch Of S Jn The Bapt Ctr Moriches NY 1980-1997; R S Thos Of Cbury Ch Smithtown NY 1970-1980; R Chr Ch Cobble Hill Brooklyn NY 1967-1970; R Epiph Ozone Pk NY 1964-1967; P-in-c S Gabr's Ch Brooklyn NY 1962-1964; S Lydia's Epis Ch Brooklyn NY 1962-1964.

MADDISON, Benjamin B (NJ) **H Trin Epis Ch Wenonah NJ 2017**- B Philadelphia PA 1987 s Alvin & Jacqueline. BA Rutgers U 2009; MDiv VTS 2015. D 11/1/2014 P 6/13/2015 Bp William H Stokes. m 6/17/2011 Ashley D Hutchinson. S Alb's Epis Ch Waco TX 2015-2017. rector@holytrinitywenonah.org

MADDON, Ernest Clinton (Okla) 1411 the Lakes Ct, Keller TX 76248 **Ret S Phil's Epis Ch Ardmore OK 2009**- B Okmulgee OK 1947 s Norman & Dorothy. BA Cntrl St U 1972; MDiv Epis TS of the SW 1994. D 6/25/1994 P 12/17/1994 Bp Robert Manning Moody. m 12/21/1968 Paula J Maddon c 2. R St Phil's Epis Ch Ardmore OK 1996-2009, Int 1995-1996, Cur 1994-1995; Int S Phil's Epis Ch Ardmore OK 1995-1996.

MADDOX III, William Edward (NC) 5718 Catskill Court, Durham NC 27713 **Non-par 1987**- B Bryn Mawr PA 1944 s William & Dorothy. BA U of Maryland 1967; PDS 1970; Tem 1972. D 6/6/1970 P 12/1/1970 Bp Robert Lionne DeWitt. m 1/15/1977 Cleopatra Maddox c 1. Chapl S Aug's Coll Raleigh NC 2008-2010; R S Tit Epis Ch Durham NC 2002-2008; R S Phil's Epis Ch Jacksonville FL 2000-2001; Chapl Off Of Bsh For ArmdF New York NY 1980-1999; Chapl US-A 1980-1986; R S Marg's Ch Dayton OH 1976-1979; P-in-c S Mary's Epis Ch Philadelphia PA 1974-1976; P-in-c S Mary Epis Ch Chester PA 1970-1972. Metropltn Untd Ch Dayton; UBE.

MADDUX, Carole Frauman (At) 9695 Hillside Dr, Roswell GA 30076 **D The Ch Of Our Sav Atlanta GA 2008**- B Waycross GA 1959 d Walter & Sally. BIS Georgia St U 1991; MS Merc 1994. D 8/6/2006 Bp J Neil Alexander. m 12/31/1988 Delane Paul Maddux c 2. D St. Aid's Epis Ch Alpharetta GA 2006-2007. "A D's Word and Voice are as Important as Her Example," *Pathways*, Dio Atlanta, 2006. DOK 1999-2006; NAAD 2006.

MADDUX, Donald Jess (Oly) 706 West Birch Street, Shelton WA 98584 B Longview WA 1938 s Delbert & Daisy. BS OR SU 1960; MDiv GTS 1964. D 6/29/1964 Bp William F Lewis P 6/5/1965 Bp Ivol I Curtis. m 12/30/1968 Carolyn L Maddux c 1. P in Charge S Jn's Epis Ch Olympia WA 2008-2009, Hisp Mnstry 2003-2015; Int S Paul's Epis Ch Bremerton WA 2007-2008; Int S Barn Epis Ch Bainbridge Island WA 2006-2007; Assoc for Hisp Mnstry S Jn's Ch Olympia WA 2004-2015; Dio Rep Hisp Mnstry Ntwk Prov VIII Dio Olympia Seattle 1997-2002, 1990-1992; R S Germains Epis Ch Hoodsport WA 1976-1992; S Hugh Of Lincoln Allyn WA 1975-1977; S Nich Ch Tahuya WA 1975-1977; R The Ch Of S Dav Of Wales Shelton WA 1970-2002; Serv Ch of Engl 1966-1968; Ret 1964-2002; Cur Ch Of The Ascen Seattle WA 1964-1966. Auth, "arts," *Angl Dig*; Auth, "arts," *Crossroads*; Auth, "arts," *Living Ch*. Intl Pres for RWF 1990-1995.

MADDY, Marta Tuff (Minn) **S Andr's By The Lake Duluth MN 2015-; Total Mnstry Mentor St. Mary's Epis Ch Ely Minnesota 2011**- B Minneapolis MN 1955 BA Carleton Coll 1977; MDiv GTS 2005. D 6/15/2005 P 12/15/2005 Bp James Louis Jelinek. m 8/16/1980 Michael Merle Maddy c 3. S Andr's Ch Cloquet MN 2013-2014; Trin Epis Ch Hermantown MN 2013; P-in-c S Jn's Ch Eveleth MN 2007-2015; P-in-c S Jas Epis Ch Hibbing MN 2006-2013; Asst The Par of St Paul's Epis Ch Duluth MN 2005-2006.

MADER, Carol Ann (Mich) 6092 Beechwood Drive, Haslett MI 48840 **P-in-c S Jas' Epis Ch Dexter MI 2010-; R S Aug of Cbury Mason MI 1993**- B Detroit MI 1957 d Ivan & Doris. BA Albion Coll 1979; MA Butler U 1982; MDiv Chr TS 1986; CAS SWTS 1987. D 6/24/1987 P 2/1/1988 Bp Edward Witker Jones.

c 2. P-in-c S Aug Of Cbury Mason MI 2001-2008; Int S Matt's Ch Indianapolis IN 1997-2000; Vic All SS Ch Seymour IN 1990-1994; Asst R S Paul's Epis Ch Indianapolis IN 1987-1990. Phi Beta Kappa 1979.

MADISON, David (FtW) 1420 4th Ave Ste 29, Canyon TX 79015 **Admin SW Assn of Epis Schools Canyon TX 2015-; Dir of Rel Stds All SS' Epis Sch Ft Worth TX 2007-** B Baton Rouge LA 1974 s Edwin. D.Min. VTS; BA Austin Coll 1996; JD Baylor U 1999; MDiv Nash 2004. D 3/13/2004 P 9/14/2004 Bp Jack Leo Iker. All SS' Epis Sch Of Ft Worth Ft Worth TX 2007-2015; Cur All SS' Epis Ch Ft Worth TX 2004-2007. CBS 2001; SocMary 2001. dmadison@swaes.org

MADISSON LOPEZ, Vaike Marika (Hond) Km. 119 Crr al Norte, Jugo de Cane, Siguatepeque 21105 Honduras **Iglesia Epis Hondurena San Pedro Sula 2006-; Chapl El Buen Pstr Epis Sch San Pedro Sula Honduras 2005-; D San Patricio Epis Ch El Progreso. Honduras 2005-** B Puerto Cortes Honduras 1959 d Arnold & Maria. Diocesano Educ Programa Teologica 2007. D 10/28/2005 P 11/23/2007 Bp Lloyd Emmanuel Allen. m 4/28/1979 Hildebrando Molina c 4. Dio Honduras San Pedro Sula 2006-2016, Rgstr 2003-.

MADRID, Hector Orlando (Hond) Apartado Postal 30, Siguatepeque, Comayagua Honduras **Iglesia Epis S Juan Apostol Siguatepeque 1992-; Iglesia Epis San Bartolome Apostol Siguatepeque Co 1992-; Iglesia Epis San Matias Apostol Siguatepeque 1992-; Iglesia Epis Santiago Apostol Siguatepeque Co 1992-; Mision Epis Siguatepeque 1992-; Mision Epis Siguatepeque 1992-; Vic Proteccion Santa Lucia Concepcion del Norte Sa 1992-; Dio Honduras San Pedro Sula 1989-** B Concepcion Norte HN 1958 s Napoleon & Juliana. D 1/6/1989 P 3/1/1995 Bp Leo Frade. m 3/14/1980 Reina Isabel Lopez.

MADSEN, David Lloyd (SanD) Saint Alban's Episcopal Church, 490 Farragut Cir, El Cajon CA 92020 **R S Alb's Epis Ch El Cajon CA 2013-; Bd Dir Epis Refugee Ntwk of San Diego 2014-; Area Mssnr Epis Dio San Diego 2013-; CEO The Welcome Ch of El Cajon 2013-** B La Junta CO 1951 s Robert & Betty. BS Cornerstone U 2002; MSM Cornerstone U 2004; MDiv GTS 2008; DMin NYTS 2012. D 6/9/2008 P 12/21/2008 Bp Robert R Gepert. m 8/28/1973 Naomi M Madsen c 2. P in Charge Ch Of S Jn The Evang Essington PA 2009-2013; Fire Dept Chapl Tinicum Township Fire Dept Tinicum Township 2009-2013; P Welcome Ch Cler Team 2009-2013; Prog Manger Ecclesia Mnstrs of New York New York 2008-2009; Res Chapl VA Hosp of NY NY 2008-2009; Sum Prog Mgr Ch Of The H Apos New York NY 2008.

MADSON, Peter G (CFla) 509 Derby Dr, Altamonte Springs FL 32714 **Non-par 1993-** B Lexington KY 1937 s George & Jane. BA Oglethorpe U 1959; STB GTS 1962. D 7/3/1962 Bp Henry I Louttit P 1/1/1963 Bp James Loughlin Duncan. c 2. SAMS Ambridge PA 1987-2015; Epis Ch Of The Resurr Longwood FL 1987-1993; Cur Chr Ch Longwood FL 1980-1985; Non-par 1973-1980; Vic S Fran Of Assisi Ch Bushnell FL 1972-1973; Asst Gr Epis Ch Of Ocala Ocala FL 1968-1969; Vic S Marg's Ch Inverness FL 1967-1968; Vic Ch Of The H Cross Valle Crucis NC 1966-1967; S Mary Of The Hills Epis Par Blowing Rock NC 1966-1967; Vic S Mary Beaver Creek NC 1966-1967; Cur S Andr's Epis Ch Tampa FL 1964-1966; Vic S Jas Epis Ch Pt Charlotte FL 1963-1964; Vic S Nath No Port Charlotte FL 1963-1964; Cur S Mk's Epis Ch Venice FL 1962-1963.

MAESEN, William August (Chi) Po Box 4380, Chicago IL 60680 **Trnr St. Leonards IL 2005-; Consult Catheral Shltr Chicago IL 2004-; Ret 1999-** B Albertson NY 1939 s August & Wilhelmina. BA Oklahoma City U 1961; LLB LaSalle Ext U 1965; MA Indiana St U 1968; PhD U IL 1979; MI SU 1981; SWTS 1985; BA Sthrn California U for Profsnl Stds 2004. D 12/2/1989 Bp Frank Tracy Griswold III. m 11/21/1989 Carolee Maesen c 3. Chapl Joliet Area Cmnty Hospice 1999-2006; Mem Bd Cathdl Cathd Shltr Chicago IL 1998-2003; Chapl VITAS Hospice IL 1994-1999; D Chr Ch Joliet IL 1989-1992; Dir of Residential Care Cathd Shltr Chicago IL 1980-1983; Chapl Serv USAF Reserves 1962-1968; Bp Coun Dio Wstrn Michigan Kalamazoo MI 1979-1981. Auth, "Fraud in Mntl Hlth Pract," *Admin & Plcy in Mntl Hlth*, 1991. DSA St of Illinois 2001; "Who's Who in Rel".

MAFLA SILVA, Daniel Antonio (Colom) Carrera 6 No 49-85, Piso 2, Bogota Colombia B Cali Valle Colombia 1979 s Guillermo & Amelia. Dip Seminario Teologia Bautista; Universidad Bautista. D 2/20/2010 Bp Francisco Jose Duque-Gomez. m 7/29/2000 Luz Erika Varela Cardona c 1.

MAGALA, Joy (Los) 8341 De Soto Ave, Canoga Park CA 91304 **St Marks Epis Ch Van Nuys CA 2005-** B Mulago Uganda 1953 d Ignatius & Ekiria. Trans 5/26/2005. m 1/22/1983 Samuel E Magala c 5.

MAGDALENE, Deborah (NY) 12 Saterlee Pl, Wappingers Falls NY 12590 **Zion Epis Ch Wappingers Falls NY 2012-** B Los Angeles CA 1952 d James & Nancy. BA Humboldt St U 1989; MA Humboldt St U 1991; MDiv GTS 2009. D 2/7/2009 P 9/5/2009 Bp Henry Irving Louttit. S Alb's Epis Ch Augusta GA 2009-2012; Ldrshp Coun Mem and Sis for Vocations The Ord of St Helena 2001-2010.

MAGEE, Frederick Hugh (Spok) 17 North Street, ST. ANDREWS - KY16 9PW Great Britain (UK) B London UK 1933 s John & Faith. BA Ya 1956; Westcott Hse Cambridge 1959. D 12/20/1959 P 12/18/1960 Bp William Derrick Lindsay

Greer. m 10/14/1989 Yvonne Houston Magee c 3. Serv Scottish Epis Ch Untd Kingdom 2006-2009; Cmncatn Off Dio Spokane Spokane WA 2003-2005; Cmncatn Off Dio Spokane Spokane WA 2001-2002; Reg Mssnr Lower Yarima Villa Reg Mnstry Prosser WA 1999-2002; RurD Wenatcher Dnry Weantcher WA 1996-2003; Vic S Jas Epis Ch Cashmere WA 1991-2003; Vol P Trin Ch San Francisco CA 1987-1991; Serv Scottish Epis Ch Untd Kingdom 1973-1987; P-in-c S Jn's Epis Ch Donora PA 1963-1964; P-in-c Trin Epis Ch Monessen PA 1963-1964; Serv Ch of Engl Untd Kingdom 1959-1962. Auth, "How do we Know the Course is from Jesus?," *Miracle Worker*, UK Miracle Ntwk, 2011; Auth, "An Upgrader's Guide," CreateSpace, 2010; Auth, "Is 'A Course in Miracles' Chr?," *Miracle Worker*, UK Miracle Ntwk, 2007; Auth, "Let's Not Wrshp Jesus," *Miracle Worker*, UK Miracle Ntwk, 2006; Auth, "Terrorism," *Miracles Monthly*, Cmnty Miracles Cntr, 2005; Auth, "Heaven," *Insight*, Insight Fndt for ACIM, 1998; Auth, "A Personal Testimony," *Miracles Monthly*, Cmnty Miracles Cntr, 1998; Auth, "Which Jesus?," *Insight*, Insight Fndt for ACIM, 1997; Auth, "Salvation," *Insight*, Insight Fndt for ACIM, 1996; Auth, "Atone Without Sacrifice," *Insight*, Insight Fndt for ACIM, 1994; Auth, "Giving Christmas New Meaning," *Insight*, Insight Fndt for ACIM, 1993; Auth, "Jesus and the Euch," *C.M.C. Nwsltr*, California Miracles Cntr, 1990. Hon Cn Cathd Ch of St. Paul, Dundee 2008.

MAGERS, James Hugh (WTex) 4934 Lakeway Dr, Brownsville TX 78520 **Ret 1997-** B Abilene TX 1940 s Hugh & Hazel. BA Texas A&M U 1963; BD VTS 1968. D 5/18/1968 Bp Samuel B Chilton P 12/18/1968 Bp George Henry Quarterman. m 6/1/1963 Joan Magers c 2. S Dav's Epis Ch San Antonio TX 2004; Ch Of The Adv Brownsville TX 2002-2003; S Lk's Epis Ch San Antonio TX 2001-2002; St Andr Epis Ch Ft Worth TX 2000-2001; Int R 1997-2000; Dir Stwdshp Epis Ch Cntr New York NY 1993-1996; Dept Of Missions Dallas TX 1986-1992; Non-par 1985-1996; Cn To Ordnry Dio W Texas San Antonio TX 1982-1985; R Ch Of The Redeem Eagle Pass TX 1977-1982; S Jn's Epis Ch Odessa TX 1975-1977; Chr Memi Epis Ch El Reno OK 1971-1974; Locten Chr Boise City OK 1969-1975; Vic S Jas' Epis Ch Dalhart TX 1969-1975; S Paul's Epis Ch Dumas TX 1969-1975; Cur Gr Ch Vernon TX 1968-1969; S Lk's Epis Ch Childress TX 1968-1969; Trin Ch Quanah TX 1968-1969. Auth, "Mssn Statements"; Auth, "Action Plans"; Auth, "Par Narrative". Epis Ntwk For Stwdshp; EvangES.

MAGGIANO, Grey (Md) Memorial Episcopal Church, 1407 Bolton St, Baltimore MD 21217 **Memi Ch Baltimore MD 2016-** B Phoenix AZ 1981 s Ronald & Laurie. BA Wms 2003; MPP Geo 2006; MDiv VTS 2013. D 6/8/2013 Bp Shannon Sherwood Johnston P 12/21/2013 Bp Leo Frade. m 4/14/2007 Monica Castillo Maggiano c 2. D Trin Cathd Miami FL 2013-2016. gmaggiano@memorialepiscopal.org

MAGIE, William Walter (Ia) 301 S 2nd St, Polk City IA 50226 B Albia IA 1947 s Wilfred & Kathryn. AA Centerville Cmnty Coll 1969; BA Acadia U 1972; EFM 1993. D 3/17/1993 Bp Chris Christopher Epting. m 2/26/1966 Francis Jane Magie c 2.

MAGILL, Elizabeth Anne (Tex) 301 E 8th St, Austin TX 78701 **P Dio Texas Houston TX 2014-** B Washington DC 1984 d John & Susan. BA W&M 2006; MDiv Ya Berk 2009. D 6/6/2009 Bp Peter J Lee P 12/6/2009 Bp Shannon Sherwood Johnston. Assoc S Dav's Ch Austin TX 2009-2011; Intern Epis Ch At Yale 2008-2009.

MAGILL, Peter George (CFla) 8310 Crosswicks Dr, Orlando FL 32819 **R H Fam Ch Orlando FL 1997-** B Montreal QC CA 1949 s Donald & Dorothea. BTh McGill U 1973; MDiv Hur CA 1975. Trans 11/1/1982 Bp Frank S Cerveny. m 1/13/1973 Jane M Magill c 3. R S Steph's Ch Norfolk VA 1989-1997; R S Lk's Epis Ch Jackson TN 1986-1989; Assoc - Rel Eductr San Jose Epis Ch Jacksonville FL 1982-1986; Serv Ch of Can 1975-1982. H Cross 1973.

MAGLIULA OHC, Robert James (NY) Holy Cross Monastery, PO Box 99, West Park NY 12493 **Superior OHC 2017-** B Brooklyn NY 1949 s Amadio & Lucy. BA CUNY 1972; MPS Pratt Inst 1976; ATR AATA 1977; MDiv UTS 1982; Cert Benedictine Formator's Prog (Rome) 2011. D 6/5/1982 P 1/9/1983 Bp Paul Moore Jr. Dir of Formation OHC 2013-2017; Prncpl H Cross Sch (So Afr) 2010-2013; Dir H Cross Schlrshp Fund (So Afr) 2007-2013; H Cross Monstry W Pk NY 2006-2013; R The Epis Ch Of Chr The King Stone Ridge NY 1989-2006; Chapl Epis Mssn Soc New York NY 1983-1989; Sr Chapl Goldwater Memi Hosp New York City NY 1983-1989; Chapl S Lk-Roosevelt Hosp Cntr NYC 1982-1983; Assoc S Mary's Manhattanville Epis Ch New York NY 1982-1983.

✠ **MAGNESS, The Rt Rev James Beattie** (SVa) Diocese of Southern Virginia, 11827 Canon Blvd Ste 101, Newport News VA 23606 **Bp Asstg Dio Sthrn Virginia Newport News. VA 2017-** B Saint Petersburg FL 1946 s Jack & Rose. BS Wstrn Carolina U 1974; MDiv Epis TS of the SW 1977; Dplma CPE 1981; DMin Yale DS 1999. D 6/25/1977 P 5/20/1978 Bp William Gillette Weinhauer Con 6/19/2010 for Armed Forces and Federal Ministires. m 6/27/1970 Carolyn Ann Magness c 2. Bp Suffr for the ArmdF and Fed Mnstrs Epis Ch Cntr New York NY 2010-2017; Cn for Mssn Dio Sthrn Virginia Newport News VA 2009-2010; Int R Galilee Epis Ch Virginia Bch VA 2007-2009; Pres Virtual Life Solutions LLC Columbia 2005-2007; Cn to the Ordnry Dio Kentucky

Louisville KY 2004-2007; Navy Chapl Off Of Bsh For ArmdF New York NY 1980-2003; DCE and Yth Ch Of S Jn In The Wilderness Flat Rock NC 1977-1980; S Paul's Ch Edneyville NC 1977-1980. Auth, "Forms & Rituals Of Pstr Care," *The Navy Chapl.* ACPE 1980; St. Greg's Abbey 1990. bishopassist@diosova.org

MAGNUS, Elsie Linda (ND) PO Box 704, Walhalla ND 58282 **D S Ptr's Ch Walhalla ND 2007-** B Langdon ND 1948 d Merle & Mary. BS U of No Dakota 1968; BS U of No Dakota 1968. D 6/30/2007 Bp Michael Smith. m 6/17/1967 Bruce Magnus c 3.

MAGNUS, Robert Frederick (Be) 105 Baird Rd, Mars Hill NC 28754 **Adj Cleric Epis Ch Of The H Sprt Mars Hill NC 1997-** B Orange NJ 1934 s Robert & Cora. BA Pr 1955; STM NYTS 1981. D 4/19/1969 P 10/1/1969 Bp Alfred L Banyard. c 4. R All SS Epis Ch Lehighton PA 1989-1996; S Jn's Epis Ch Palmerton PA 1989-1996; R Trin Ch Athens PA 1986-1989; Int Chr Ch New Brunswick NJ 1986; R Gd Shpd Amanzimtoti Republic of So Afr 1983-1985; Asst S Paul Durban Republic of So Afr 1981-1982; R The Epis Ch Of The H Comm Fair Haven NJ 1973-1981; Cur S Lk's Ch Gladstone NJ 1969-1972.

MAGNUSON, George Peter (Colo) 2015 Glenarm Pl, Denver CO 80205 B Chicago IL 1934 s Raymond & Astrid. AA No Pk Coll 1954; BA U MN 1956; BD No Pk TS Chicago IL 1960; MA McCormick TS 1966; DMin McCormick TS 1973. D 6/9/2007 P 12/8/2007 Bp Robert John O'Neill. m 5/31/1998 Carrie Doehring c 5.

MAGNUSON, Paulette Williams (Tex) D 6/21/2014 P 1/13/2015 Bp Dena Arnall Harrison.

MAGOON, George Arthur (NC) 5299 S Ventura Way, Centennial CO 80015 **Ret 1993-** B Littleton NH 1924 s John & Ina. BA Dart 1949; MEd Springfield Coll 1950; Ya Berk 1957. D 6/10/1957 P 12/21/1957 Bp Charles Francis Hall. m 12/30/1949 Joanne M Magoon c 6. H Trin Ch Raleigh NC 1984-1989; S Jn's Ch Henderson NC 1984-1989; P-in-c H Trin Townsvillle NC 1983-1993; S Jas Epis Ch Hendersonvlle NC 1983-1993; S Mths Ch Louisburg NC 1977-1985; P-in-c S Jas Kittrell NC 1974-1993; S Jas Ch Henderson NC 1974-1989; S Paul's Ch Louisburg NC 1974-1982; Priest-in-Charge St. Mths Ch Louisburg NC 1974-1982; Dio No Carolina Raleigh NC 1974-1976; Lower Sch Hd St. Cathr's Sch Richmond VA 1970-1974; Asst/Headmaster Trin Epis Sch Galveston TX 1968-1970; Asst St Paul's Syracuse Syracuse NY 1965-1968; P-in-c Ivie Memi Ch of the Mssh Bethlehem Bethlehem NH 1961-1965; Chapl & Tchr St. Mary's-in-the-Mountains Littleton NH 1961-1965; Ch Of The Epiph Lisbon Lisbon NH 1957-1961; Asst S Lk's Ch Woodsville NH 1957-1961.

MAGUIRE III, Bernard Leonard (Pa) 224 Flourtown Rd, Plymouth Meeting PA 19462 B Wilmington DE 1945 s Bernard & Elizabeth. BA Trin 1967; MDiv EDS 1972. D 6/3/1972 Bp William Henry Mead P 6/1/1973 Bp Frederick Hesley Belden. Washington Memi Chap Vlly Forge PA 2002-2004; R Calv Ch Conshohocken PA 1978-2002; H Apos And Medtr Philadelphia PA 1976-1978; Vic Memi Chap Of The H Comm Philadelphia PA 1976-1978; Cur Trsfg Edgewood RI 1974-1976; Ch Of The Trsfg Providence RI 1972-1976.

MAHAFFEY, Glenn G (CNY) 201 S Wilbur Ave, Sayre PA 18840 B Birmingham AL 1956 s Joseph & Joyous. BA Wstrn St U 1978; MDiv SWTS 1985. D 6/14/1985 Bp William Carl Frey P 12/14/1985 Bp William Harvey Wolfrum. m 4/23/2000 Naomi Miner-Mahaffey c 3. Ch Of The Redeem Sayre PA 2012-2015; R S Ptr's Ch Rockland ME 2008-2012; R Emm Ch Norwich NY 2000-2008; R Ch of Our Sav No Platte NE 1989-1997; Asst R Ch Of The Ascen Pueblo CO 1987-1989; Vic Epis Ch Of S Jn The Bapt Granby CO 1985-1987; Trin Ch Kremmling CO 1985-1987.

MAHAFFY II, Richard James (WMass) D 5/28/2016 P 1/21/2017 Bp Doug Fisher.

MAHAN, Charles Earl (Kan) 444 Brightfield Trl, Manchester MO 63021 **S Lk's Epis Ch Manchester MO 2017-** B Tomball TX 1966 s Charles & Jo. BA Concordia U 1989; MDiv Luth Sem Prog in the SW 1993. Rec 2/13/2006 as Priest Bp Gary Richard Lillibridge. m 6/13/1993 Shannon A Mahan c 2. R S Jn's Ch Wichita KS 2011-2017; R S Matt's Ch Edinburg TX 2006-2011; Pstr Serv Evang Luth Ch in Amer 1993-2006. Bp Elliott Soc 2007. fatherearl@stlukesec.org

MAHER JR, John (Va) 14331 Forest Row Trl, Midlothian VA 23112 **Vic S Fran Epis Ch 2013-; Ch Planter Dio Arizona Peoria AZ 2006-; Vic Prince of Peace Epis Ch 2005-** B Philadephia PA 1952 s John & Barbara. BA Kutztown U 1974; MDiv GTS 1979; DMin Fuller TS 1992. D 6/16/1979 P 5/28/1980 Bp Lyman Cunningham Ogilby. m 2/14/1975 Carol D Madden c 2. Vic Dio Arizona Phoenix AZ 2005-2012; R S Mary 's Ch Elverson PA 1981-2005; S Mk's Ch Philadelphia PA 1979-1981; Cur S Mk's Ch Philadelphia PA 1979-1981.

MAHER, Joseph Anthony (CFla) 5997 Heron Pond Dr, Port Orange FL 32128 **Ret 1998-** B Philadelphia PA 1929 s Patrick & Margaret. BA Villanova U 1952; MA CUA 1956; PhD NYU 1971. Rec 4/1/1981 as Priest Bp William Hopkins Folwell. m 7/1/1978 Catherine M Maher. S Mary's Epis Ch Daytona Bch FL 2003-2013; R Ch Of The H Chld Ormond Bch FL 1983-1997; Gr Epis Ch Of Ocala Ocala FL 1981-1983; COM Dio Cntrl Florida Orlando FL 1996-1998.

Auth, "Stations of the Cross for the Elderly," Liquori Pub, 1978. Alb Inst; ES-MA.

MAHON, Laurence Franklin (EO) 8501 Ne Wilson Creek Rd, Ashwood OR 97711 **D S Mk's Epis and Gd Shpd Luth Madras OR 2002-** B Walla Walla WA 1931 s Kenneth & Doris. Portland St U. D 5/1/2002 Bp William O Gregg. m 7/2/1950 Patricia Marie Mahon c 2.

MAHONEY, James Michael (Ida) 1912 Delmar St, Boise ID 83713 **Supply S Steph's Boise ID 1968-** B Salmon ID 1936 s James & Marian. Idaho St U 1958; Boise St U 1970. D 12/13/1968 P 12/21/1969 Bp Norman L Foote. m 6/4/1957 Jennie Ross Mahoney c 2.

MAHOOD, Sharon M (Ia) 3705 Washington Ave, Des Moines IA 50310 B Springfield MO 1945 d George & Janet. BA U of Kansas 1967; MA U MN 1969; PhD U of Kansas 1971; MDiv GTS 1989. D 6/4/1989 Bp Lyman Cunningham Ogilby P 1/1/1990 Bp Chris Christopher Epting. R S Andr's Ch Des Moines IA 2004-2011; Cn Admin Dio Iowa Des Moines IA 2001-2003; R S Anne's Epis Ch S Paul MN 1998-1999; R S Ptr's Ch Bettendorf IA 1991-1998; P-in-c The Cathd Ch Of S Paul Des Moines IA 1989-1991.

MAHURIN, Shanda M (SwFla) 1021 Greenturf Rd., Spring Hill FL 34608 B Jersey City NJ 1950 d Joseph & Victoria. BA Goucher Coll 1972; MDiv PrTS 1976. D 8/6/1985 P 4/6/1986 Bp William Grant Black. m 10/19/1997 Randal Mahurin c 3. R S Andr's Epis Ch Sprg Hill FL 2005-2012; Int R S Mk's Ch Marco Island FL 2004-2005; Chapl Hospice of Cntrl Virginia Richmond VA 1997-1998; Int R S Ptr's Par Ch New Kent VA 1997-1998; Chapl Westminster-Cbury Ret Cmnty 1996-1997; Assoc R S Paul's Ch Richmond VA 1987-1996; Asst R S Andr's Ch Dayton OH 1985-1987. Auth, "Counselors in Perplexity; Comp in Joy," *Counselors in Perplexity; Comp in Joy,* self-Pub, 1986. Phi Beta Kappa 1972. Wailes Prize in NT Stds Princeton TS 1975.

MAIER, Andrea R (Oly) 10841 Whipple Street, No. 105, North Hollywood OR 91602 **St Fran Epis Mssn Outreach Cntr San Bernardino CA 2015-; Cler Assist in Cong S Mk's Par Glendale CA 2011-** B 1955 d Raymond & Miriam. BA U of Washington 1984; BA U of Washington 1984; BA U of Washington 1984; MDiv GTS 1996. D 6/8/1996 P 1/18/1997 Bp Frederick Houk Borsch. Epis Communities & Serv Pasadena CA 2012-2013; S Andr's Epis Ch Ojai CA 2007-2010; Dio Olympia Seattle 2005; R S Lk's Epis Ch Vancouver WA 2002-2004; Assoc R St. Barth Ch New York NY 1998-2001; Asst to R Ch Of Our Sav Silver Sprg MD 1996-1998; Dio Los Angeles Los Angeles CA 1988-1993.

MAIER, Beth Ann (Vt) 1924 Blake St A, Berkeley CA 94704 B Oak Ridge TN 1949 d Robert & Evelyn. BA Swarthmore Coll 1970; MD Case Wstrn Reserve Sch of Med 1975. D 1/6/2009 Bp Thomas C Ely. m 5/31/1975 Robert Finucane c 3.

MAIL, Mary J(ean) (Mil) 509 East University, Bloomington IN 47401 B Buffalo NY 1952 d John & Mary. BA IL Wesl 1974; MDiv CDSP 1981; MA Indiana U 1982. D 6/24/1981 P 3/17/1982 Bp Edward Witker Jones. R S Mk's Ch Beaver Dam WI 1999-2015; Assoc Trin Epis Ch Bloomington IN 1993-1995; Asst 1981-1984; Int S Paul's Epis Ch Greenville OH 1987-1988; Cn To The Ordnry Dio Indianapolis Indianapolis IN 1984-1987; DRE S Mk's Par Berkeley CA 1979-1981.

MAILS, Ryan F (NC) D 6/17/2017 Bp Anne Hodges-Copple.

MAINWARING, Monica Burns (SanD) 1114 9th St, Coronado CA 92118 B Glendale CA 1978 d Robert & Rita. B.A U CA at Davis 2000; MDiv Harvard DS 2006; B.A U CA at Davis 2006; B.A U CA at Davis 2006. D 5/30/2015 P 12/19/2015 Bp Jim Mathes. m 9/24/2005 Simon J Mainwaring c 3. Chr Ch Coronado CA 2015-2017; Ch Of The Gd Samar San Diego CA 2015.

MAINWARING, Simon J (SanD) Christchurch School, 49 Seahorse Ln, Christchurch VA 23031 B Manchester, UK 1974 s Rodney & Myfanwy. BA Oxf GB 1996; BA Westcott Hse Cambridge 2002; MA Oxf GB 2003; CTh Westcott Hse Cambridge 2003; ThM Harv 2004; MA Westcott Hse Cambridge 2006. Trans 7/23/2007 Bp Marc Handley Andrus. m 9/24/2005 Monica Burns c 3. S Andr's By The Sea Epis Par San Diego CA 2010-2017; Christchurch Sch Christchurch VA 2007-2010.

MAIOCCO III, Joseph F (SwFla) 500 Park Shore Dr, Naples FL 34103 **R S Jn's Ch Naples FL 2008-** B Beaufort SC 1958 s Joseph & Barbara. BSW W Virginia U 1980; MDiv TESM 1984. D 6/2/1984 P 12/1/1984 Bp Alden Moinet Hathaway. m 9/20/1980 Janet Beth Maiocco. Adv Epis Ch Westlake OH 1999-2008; S Barn Ch Bay Vill OH 1991-1993; Off Of Bsh For ArmdF New York NY 1987-1991; Dio Pittsburgh Pittsburgh PA 1984-1987.

MAITREJEAN, J Patrick (Cal) 1549 Circulo Jacona, Rio Rico AZ 85648 B Nogales,AZ 1941 s John & Viola. BA U of Arizona 1964; STM ETSC 1969; Grad Theol Un 1981. D 6/10/1969 P 6/4/1970 Bp David Reed. Vic Chr The Lord Epis Ch Pinole CA 1981-2005; Archd Of Colombia 1976-1979; Pstr Un Ch Bogota Colombia 1976-1977; Pstr Un Ch Bogota Colombia 1973-1974; R S Alb's Bogota Colombia 1972-1979; Iglesia Epis En Colombia Bogota 1969-1981; Asst S Geo Medellin Colombia 1969-1972.

MAJKRZAK, Albert Walter (Chi) 1222 Carpenter Street, Madison WI 53704 **H Cross Epis Ch Wisconsin Dells WI 2016-** B East Orange NJ 1944 s Joseph & Sophie. MDiv Epis TS in Kentucky 1979; BS SUNY 1979. D 5/13/1979 Bp

Addison Hosea P 12/16/1979 Bp Victor Manuel Rivera. m 10/22/1966 Karen V Majkrzak c 3. R Chr Ch Waukegan IL 1997-2005; R Chr Ch Ansonia CT 1988-1997; Evang Off Dio Milwaukee Milwaukee WI 1986-1988; R S Mk's Ch S Milwaukee WI 1981-1988; Ch Of The Resurr Clovis Clovis CA 1980-1981; S Lk Selma CA 1979-1981. holycrosswd@frontier.com

MAJOR, John Charles (Be) 220 Montgomery Ave, West Pittston PA 18643 **R Trin Epis Ch Pittston PA 2001-; Dioc Coun Dio Bethlehem Bethlehem PA 2010-** B Williamsport PA 1960 s Joseph & Mary. BA Mansfield U of Pennsylvania 1982; U of Scranton 1983; MDiv Chr the King Sem 1987. Rec 12/18/1999 as Priest Bp Paul Victor Marshall. m 7/27/1996 Sandra Valli Major. P-in-c The Epis Ch Of S Clem And S Ptr Wilkes Barre PA 2012-2016; R Prince Of Peace Epis Ch Dallas PA 2009-2012; Int S Jas-S Geo Epis Ch Jermyn PA 2000-2001; Asst Pstr RC Ch Scranton PA 1987-1996.

MAJOR, Joseph Kenneth (SeFla) 1835 Nw 54th St, Miami FL 33142 B Miami FL 1936 s Joseph & Alice. BA S Aug 1959; DIT Mercer TS 1968. D 6/29/1968 Bp Richard Beamon Martin P 1/25/1969 Bp James Loughlin Duncan. c 1. Dio SE Florida Miami 1980-1983; Cmsn Black Mnstrs 1977-1980; Ch Of The Incarn Miami FL 1969-2008, Assoc 1968-1969; Trst Trin Cathd Miami FL 1980-1983. Auth, "Gensis Of A Par"; Auth, "What Can Be Salvaged ?".

MAJOR, Philip S (CNY) St Paul's Syracuse, 310 Montgomery St Ste 1, Syracuse NY 13202 **St Paul's Syracuse Syracuse NY 2016-** B Summit NJ 1961 s Russell & Flora. BA Ob 1984; BMed Oberlin Conservatory 1984; MDiv Bos TS 2010. D 7/22/2010 P 1/25/2011 Bp Vicky Gene Robinson. m 5/2/1987 Nancy A Bronder c 2. R S Mk's Epis Ch Casper WY 2011-2015; Assoc for Multi-Generational Mnstrs S Mk's Epis Ch Burlington MA 2010-2011; S Andr's Ch New London NH 2002-2009. revmajors@stpaulsyr.org

MAKES GOOD, Daniel Harry (SD) Po Box 28, Wanblee SD 57577 **Died 4/30/2016** B Allen SD 1937 s Antione & Olive. D 6/29/1975 Bp Walter H Jones P 4/26/1980 Bp Harold Anthony Hopkins Jr. m 10/4/1960 Mercy Broken Makes Good. Dio No Dakota Fargo ND 1982-1985; D Pine Ridge Mssn 1975-2016.

MAKINS, Claire T (NwT) **Cur Ch of the Heav Rest Abilene Abilene TX 2017-** D 12/3/2016 P 6/3/2017 Bp James Scott Mayer.

MAKOWSKI, Chester Joseph (Tex) 1410 Jack Johnson Blvd., Galveston TX 77550 **Vic S Aug's Epis Ch Galveston TX 2008-; Chairman of the Bd The Wm Temple Fndt Galveston TX 2010-** B El Paso TX 1963 s Chester & Wanda. BA U of St Thos 1984; JD U of Houston 1991; Cert Iona Sch for Mnstry 2009. D 6/20/2009 P 1/21/2010 Bp C Andrew Doyle. m 6/28/2003 Mary Wolter c 2.

MALANUK, Patricia Craig (USC) 6045 Lakeshore Dr, Columbia SC 29206 **Cn Pstr Trin Cathd Columbia SC 2012-, Cn for Mssn and Outreach 2012-, 1996-2000** B Columbia SC 1947 d Charles & Juanita. BA U of So Carolina 1969; Luth Theol Sthrn Sem 1992; MDiv Sewanee: The U So, TS 1995. D 6/10/1995 P 5/14/1996 Bp Dorsey Henderson. m 6/18/2005 Robert Malanuk c 3. Int S Steph's Epis Ch Ridgeway SC 2002-2003; D S Jn's Epis Ch Columbia SC 1995-1996. Trst U So 1996.

MALARKEY, Shawn O (Pgh) 33 Alice St, Pittsburgh PA 15205 **Trin Cathd Pittsburgh PA 2017-; Ch Of The Nativ Pittsburgh PA 2015-** B Butler PA 1974 s Thomas & Lesley. BS The Penn 1996; BA Duquesne U 1998; MA S Vinc Sem 2001; MDiv S Vinc Sem 2002. Rec 6/16/2015 as Priest Bp Dorsey McConnell. m 10/14/2006 Jolean M Gioia c 2. Other Lay Position Dio Pittsburgh Pittsburgh PA 2008.

MALAVE TORRES, Hector (PR) B 1940 m 10/27/1963 Luz M Ramos Velez. Dio Puerto Rico Trujillo Alto PR 2004-2012, 1991-2003.

MALCOLM, Frieda (Eas) 1006 Beaglin Park Dr Apt 201, Salisbury MD 21804 **R S Alb's Epis Ch Salisbury MD 2001-; Dep, GC Dio Easton Easton MD 2017-, Mem, Dioc Coun 2016-, Alt Dep, GC 2015-2017, Co-Chair, Nom Com for Bp XI 2015-2016, Mem, COM 2011-2017, Dn, Sthrn Convoc 2008-, Mem, Stndg Com 2006-2009, Dep, GC 2005-2015, Personl and Compstn Com 2003-2014, 2003-2009, Mem, COM 2003-2006, Vice-Pres, Dioc Coun 2003-2005** B Miami FL 1954 d John & Janet. DMin VTS; ABS Smith 1975; MS SUNY-Albany 1979; MDiv Sewanee: The U So, TS 1987. D 6/21/1987 Bp James Barrow Brown P 6/15/1988 Bp George Phelps Mellick Belshaw. c 1. Asst Trin Ch Towson MD 1995-2001; Int Trin Ch Moundsville WV 1994-1995; Exec Dir Highland Educational Proj Dio W Virginia Charleston WV 1991-1993; Gr Ch Welch WV 1990-1993; S Lk's Epis Ch Welch WV 1990-1993; The Sthrn Cluster Northfork WV 1990-1993; Int Chr Ch Middletown NJ 1990; Chapl Trenton Area Campus Mnstry Trenton NJ 1988-1989; Asst S Matt's Ch Pennington NJ 1987-1990. DuBose Awd for Serv U So 2005. pastormalc@comcast.net

MALCOLM, Karen Gottwald (Alb) D 5/30/2015 Bp William Howard Love.

MALCOLM, Kenneth A (Colo) 910 E 3rd Ave, Durango CO 81301 **Cn Dio Colorado Denver CO 2015-** B Ft Smith AK 1963 s Douglas & Jo-Sue. BA Austin Coll 1986; MA Texas Tech U Lubbock TX 1991; MDiv Epis TS of the SW 2007. D 6/16/2007 Bp Peter J Lee P 12/21/2007 Bp Dena Arnall Harrison. m 6/13/1999 Elizabeth P Pfautz c 2. S Mk's Epis Ch Durango CO 2012-2014; Faith Relatns Dir Comfort the Chld Intl Austin Texas 2010-2004; Assoc R S Dav's Ch Austin TX 2008-2011, 2007; Asstg Fac Epis TS Of The SW Austin

TX 2008; Prog Dir Dio Virginia Richmond VA 2000-2004. "Death's Reflection of Life: Italian Hagiographical Representations of Death in the 11th, 12th, and 13th Centuries," Texas Tech U Press, 1991; "Death and Soc: the 11th and 12th Centuries," *26th Intl Congr of Medieval Stds*, Kalamazoo, 1990. ken@episcopalcolorado.org

MALCOLM, Patricia Ann (Del) PO Box 1374, Dover DE 19903 **D Chr Ch Dover DE 2009-** B Yonkers NY 1951 d William & Addie. BA Delaware St U 1998. D 12/5/2009 Bp Wayne Wright. m 6/30/1973 Walter R Malcolm c 3.

MALDONADO-MERCADO, Roberto (Ore) 2700 W Powell Blvd Apt 3144, Gresham OR 97030 **Dio Oregon Portland OR 2013-; H Cross Epis Ch Boring OR 2013-** B Manati PR 1959 s Roberto & Sara. BA U of Puerto Rico 1982; Seminario Evangelico de Puerto Rico PR 1984; MDiv Estrn Bapt TS 1987; CAS Epis TS of the SW 1988. D 10/29/1988 Bp Franklin Delton Turner P 11/4/1989 Bp Allen Lyman Bartlett Jr. m 4/10/2017 Leticia Ramirez-Figueroa c 1. R S Simon's Par San Fernando CA 2000-2013; Vic Los Tres Santos Reyes Baltimore MD 1996-1999; S Andr's Epis Ch Ft Pierce FL 1994-1996; Dio Pennsylvania Philadelphia PA 1988-1991.

MALE JR, Henry Alfred (Be) 80 Kal Shore Rd, Norway ME 04268 B Atlantic City NJ 1930 s Henry & Adelaide. BA Hobart and Wm Smith Colleges 1952; LTh GTS 1955; Coll of Preachers 1970; DMin Wartburg TS 1982. D 4/30/1955 P 11/5/1955 Bp Alfred L Banyard. c 3. Serv as Pstr ELCA Cong 2006-2007; P-in-c S Barn Ch Rumford ME 1994-2006; R Ch Of The Epiph Glenburn Clarks Summit PA 1967-1993; Civilian Chapl. Ft. Monmouth Eatontown NJ 1956-1967; R S Mary's Ch Keyport NJ 1956-1967; Vic Our Sav Cheesequake NJ 1956-1962. Auth, "Conversion to Ecum," *Ecumical Trends*, 1993. No Amer Acad of Ecuminists 1985-1986. Hon Cn Nativ Cathd, Bethlehem 1985.

MALERI, Karen D (Me) 112 Randolph Avenue, Milton MA 02186 **Dir Of Pstr Care Dept Havenwood Heritage Heights 2004-** B Guantanamo Bay Cuba 1953 d Robert & Mitzi. MDiv EDS 2001. D 11/6/2004 P 5/14/2005 Bp Chilton Richardson Knudsen. c 2. S Mich's Ch Milton MA 2010-2013; Havenwood-Heritage Heights Concord NH 2004-2008.

MALIA, Linda Merle (WNY) 209 Columbus Ave, Buffalo NY 14220 **Assoc S Simon's Ch Buffalo NY 2003-** B St. Catherine's Ontario CA 1952 d Ronald & Isabella. ThD U Tor; BA SUNY 1994; MA Colgate Rochester Crozer DS 1998; MA CRDS 1998. D 6/22/2002 P 11/15/2003 Bp Michael Garrison. m 8/8/1981 William Malia. S Jude's Ch Buffalo NY 2008-2010. revpeaches@yahoo.com

MALIA, Phyllis Terri (CFla) D 9/27/2014 Bp Gregory Orrin Brewer.

MALIAMAN, Irene Egmalis (Haw) ECIM, 911 N Marine Corps Dr, Tamuning GU 96913 Guam **Dio Micronesia Tumon Bay GU 2009-; Arch-D The Epis Ch of S Jn the Div Tamuning GU 2009-** B Philippines 1963 d Valentin & Catherine. ThB S Andrews TS 1987; MDiv S Andrews TS 2002. Trans 5/1/2011 Bp Robert Leroy Fitzpatrick. m 6/8/1991 Alfred Maliaman c 1. P St Pauls Epis Ch Saipan MP 2006-2009; Dio Nthrn Luzon Tabuk 1992-1993; Dio Cntrl Philippines Queson City 1988-1990.

MALIN, Katherine Murphy (Mass) 147 Concord Rd, Lincoln MA 01773 **S Anne's In The Fields Epis Ch Lincoln MA 2009-** B Greenwich CT 1964 d Randall & Lucinda. BA Ya 1987; MDiv GTS 2006. D 3/11/2006 P 9/23/2006 Bp Mark Sean Sisk. m 5/4/1996 Bruce E Smith c 3. Cur Chr Ch Bronxville NY 2006-2009.

MALIONEK, Judith Webb (Alb) D 10/30/2016 Bp William Howard Love.

MALIONEK, Thomas V (Alb) St Paul Church, Po Box 637, Kinderhook NY 12106 **S Paul's Ch Kinderhook NY 2015-; Assoc R All SS' Epis Ch Chevy Chase MD 2010-** B Newburyport MA 1954 s Vincent & Stasia. BA U of Virginia 1976; MA U of Virginia 1978; MA Nash 2009. D 12/12/2009 P 12/18/2010 Bp William Howard Love. m 2/8/1986 Judith Webb Judith Gail Webb c 2.

MALLARY JR, Raymond DeWitt (NY) 80 Lyme Rd #161, Hanover NH 03755 **Ret 1991-** B Springfield MA 1926 s Raymond & Gertrude. BA Dart 1948; STB GTS 1951. D 6/10/1951 P 12/9/1951 Bp Horace W B Donegan. c 3. R All SS Ch New York NY 1960-1991; Assoc DCE for Coll Wk Dio New York NY 1957-1960; Vic Trin Ch Fishkill NY 1953-1956; Asst Cathd Ch Of S Paul Burlington VT 1951-1952. DD AIC (not Epis affiliated) 1973; Phi Beta Kappa Dart 1948.

MALLETT, Juli (Oly) 114 20th Ave SE, Olympia WA 98501 **Cur S Jn's Epis Ch Olympia WA 2017-** B Washington Pennsylvania 1985 d Carolyn. MDiv EDS 2015. D 12/17/2016 P 6/20/2017 Bp Gregory Harold Rickel. m 1/27/2014 Lee C Zeman. Assoc S Mary's Ch Lakewood WA 2016-2017; Intern S Tim's Epis Ch Chehalis WA 2015.

MALLETTE STEPHENS, Hershey Mallette (NC) D 2/20/2016 Bp Anne Hodges-Copple P 7/16/2016 Bp Andrew Marion Lenow Dietsche.

MALLIN, Caroll Sue Driftmeyer (SeFla) 1150 Stanford Dr, Coral Gables FL 33146 **Asst S Lk 1981-** B Indianapolis IN 1933 d Edgar & Helen. MS Barry U; BA Florida Intl U. D 12/15/1981 Bp Calvin Onderdonk Schofield Jr. c 2. Cmncatn Coordntr Epis Ch Miami FL 1974-1981.

MALLON, Beth Kohlmeyer (Ore) PO Box 445, Wilsonville OR 97070 **Archd Dio Oregon Portland OR 2011-; D S Fran Of Assisi Epis Wilsonville OR 2007-** B Oakland CA 1959 d Leland & Mary. BA Oregon Coll of Educ 1982;

MBA U of Nebraska 1989; BA Sch for Deacons 2004; BA The Epis Sch for Deacons 2004. D 9/11/2004 Bp Jerry Alban Lamb. m 7/19/1980 Kevin Frederick Mallon c 2. D Gr Epis Ch Fairfield CA 2004-2007. bethm@diocese-oregon.org

MALLONEE, Anne Floyd (NY) 19 E 34th St, New York NY 10016 **Hon Cler S Thos Ch New York NY 2016-; Chf Eccl Off The CPG New York NY 2014-; Hon Cn Cathd Ch Of S Mk Minneapolis MN 2002-, Actg Dn 2000-2002, Sub-Dn 1999-2000, Cn Pstr 1997-1999** B Wichita KS 1958 d Robert & Barbara. BA U of Kansas 1979; MDiv Ya Berk 1986. D 6/7/1986 Bp Paul Moore Jr P 1/10/1987 Bp Richard Frank Grein. m 4/6/2002 Anthony C Furnivall. Vic Trin Par New York NY 2004-2014; Int Chr Ch Cathd Hartford CT 2002-2004; Assoc Chr Ch Overland Pk KS 1990-1996; Chapl Cbury At Kansas U Lawr KS 1986-1991; Dio Kansas Topeka KS 1986-1991; Dn's Search Com Ya Berk New Haven CT 2013-2014, Trst 2005-2013; Trst The Allnce for Downtown New York 2008-2014. Hon Cn Cathd Ch of St. Mk, Minneapolis 2002. amallonee@cpg.org

✠ MALLORY, The Rt Rev Charles Shannon (ECR) 74988 Tahoe Cir, Indian Wells CA 92210 **Ret Bp of El Camino Real Dio El Camino Real Salinas CA 1990-, Dioc Bp 1980-1990** B Dallas TX 1936 s William & Hazelle. BA U CA 1958; MDiv GTS 1961; STD GTS 1970; MA Rhodes U Grahamstown ZA 1971. Trans 1/15/1979. m 1/26/2010 Martha Burton Mallory c 5. Asst Bp Dio Oklahoma Oklahoma City OK 2000-2004, 1999, 1992-1994; Pstr Assoc S Jas By The Sea La Jolla CA 1999-2001; Sr Dir / Intl Wrld Neighbors OK City OK 1990-1992; Asst Bp of LI Dio Long Island Garden City NY 1979-1980; Bp Dio Botswana New York NY 1973-1979; Dir Mssns Ovamboland Namibia 1963-1969; Mssy to Afr ECUSA 1961-1972.

MALLORY, Richard Deaver (Az) 455 Hope St Apt 3-D, Stamford CT 06906 **Gr St Pauls Epis Ch Tucson AZ 2016-** B Anniston AL 1943 s James & Lena. BA Wake Forest U 1965; BD UTS 1971; Cert Blanton-Peale Grad Inst 1974; DMin Andover Newton TS 1978; Cert Inst of Core Energetics New York NY 2001. D 6/5/1971 Bp Horace W B Donegan P 12/18/1976 Bp Paul Moore Jr. c 1. Epis Par Of S Mich And All Ang Tucson AZ 2015; Assoc All SS Of The Desert Epis Ch Sun City AZ 2013-2015; S Thos Of The Vlly Epis Clarkdale AZ 2010-2013; Epis Ch of Chr the Healer Stamford CT 2005-2006; Int Trin Epis Ch Southport CT 2004-2005; Int S Barn Epis Ch Greenwich CT 2002-2003; Int Gr Epis Ch Norwalk CT 1999-2000; Int All Ang' Ch New York NY 1979-1980.

MALLORY, Steven Michael (Okla) 1808 Cedar Ln, Ponca City OK 74604 **D Gr Epis Ch Ponca City OK 1996-** B Ponca City OK 1952 s Ira & Bette. AA No Oklahoma Coll Tonkawa OK 1972; BA Oklahoma St U 1980; MS Oklahoma St U 1982. D 6/22/1996 Bp Robert Manning Moody. m 6/13/1987 Vicki Lynn DeShazer. Chr Motorcycle Assn; Lic Profsnl Counslr; Police Chapl; Vietnam Veterans Of Amer; Ymca.

MALLOW, Sherod Earl (SeFla) 2131 Sw 23rd Ave, Fort Lauderdale FL 33312 B Selma AL 1945 s Edwin & Juanita. BS Troy U 1972; MDiv Sewanee: The U So, TS 1986; DMin SWTS 1999. D 11/19/1986 Bp Furman Charles Stough P 5/1/1987 Bp Robert Oran Miller. m 7/9/1988 Rosa Vera Lindahl c 1. R All SS Prot Epis Ch Ft Lauderdale FL 1999-2014, Assoc 1997-1998; R S Elis's Epis Ch Memphis TN 1991-1996; S Barn' Epis Ch Hartselle AL 1989-1991; Mssnr Dio Alabama Birmingham 1989-1990; R H Cross-St Chris's Huntsville AL 1987-1988; Mssnr Trin Epis Ch Florence AL 1986-1987.

MALLOY, Nancy (Colo) Saint Laurence's Episcopal Mission, 26812 Barkley Rd, Conifer CO 80433 **S Laurence's Epis Mssn Conifer CO 2014-** B Chicago IL 1947 s Erwin & Hattie. BA Wstrn Illinois U 1988; MDiv SWTS 1992. D 6/10/2000 P 1/6/2001 Bp William Jerry Winterrowd. c 1. R Ch Of The H Comm Lake Geneva WI 2008-2013; Emm Epis Ch Athens GA 2007-2008; P Par Ch Of S Chas The Mtyr Ft Morgan CO 2001-2007; S Aid's Epis Ch Boulder CO 2001; Calv Ch Rochester MN 1998-2000.

MALLOY, Patrick L (NY) The General Theological Seminary, 440 W 21st St., New York NY 18102 **Cathd Of St Jn The Div New York NY 2016-; Prof The GTS New York NY 2014-, Prof 2009-2014** B Cumberland MD 1956 s Leo & Joella. BA La Salle U 1978; MA Tem 1980; MA U of Notre Dame 1985; PhD U of Notre Dame 1991. Rec 6/29/2001 as Deacon Bp Paul Victor Marshall. S Jn's Cathd Denver CO 2015-2016; P Ch of S Jn on the Mtn Bernardsville NJ 2013-2015; R Gr Epis Ch Allentown PA 2002-2011; COM Dio Bethlehem Bethlehem PA 2003-2009. Auth, "Revs of H Conversation Sprtlty for Worhsip," *Spiritus*, 2011; Auth, "Gr in the City: Urban Mnstry in the New Normal," *ATR*, 2010; Auth, "Rick Warren Meets Greg Dix: The Liturg Mvmt Comes Knocking at the Megachurch Door," *ATR*, 2010; Auth, "Celebrating the Euch," Ch Pub, 2007; Auth, "Unexpected Clues in a Seventeenth-Century Angl Recension of a RC Devotional Bk," *Bodleian Libr Record*, 2007; Auth, "The Re-Emergence of Popular Rel Among Non-Hisp Catholics in the Untd States," *Wrshp*, 1989. Cn Liturg Dio Bethlehem 2011; Chf Precentor The GTS 2004. pmalloy@stjohndivine.org

MALM, Robert Hiller (Va) 3601 Russell Rd, Alexandria VA 22305 **R Gr Epis Ch Alexandria VA 1989-** B New Bedford MA 1951 s Robert & Nancy. BA U NC 1974; MDiv Ya Berk 1977. D 6/18/1977 P 6/17/1978 Bp Thomas Augustus Fraser Jr. m 6/5/1982 Leslie E Malm c 4. R Chr Ch Portsmouth NH

1983-1989; Asst The Ch Of The Adv Boston MA 1980-1983; Blue Ridge Sch Dyke VA 1979-1980; S Mary's Epis Ch High Point NC 1979, 1977-1979, Asst 1977-1979. Soc Of S Jn The Evang - Assoc.

MALONE, Bonnie (Oly) 24219 Witte Rd SE, Maple Valley WA 98038 **S Geo Epis Ch Maple Vlly WA 2010-** B Stanford CA 1973 BS Creighton U. D 6/6/2003 P 12/6/2003 Bp Barry Howe. m 9/2/1995 Carl O Malone c 2. Assoc R Calv Ch Memphis TN 2004-2009; Dio W Missouri Kansas City MO 2004.

MALONE JR, Elmer Taylor (NC) 308 Wilcox St., Warrenton NC 27589 **R Trin Ch Scotland Neck NC 2011-** B WilsonNC 1943 s Elmer & Mildred. BS Campbell U 1967; MA U NC 1975; No Carolina Diac Prog 1991; Other 1998; So Carolina Read for H Ord 1998. D 6/1/1991 Bp Robert Whitridge Estill P 6/13/1998 Bp Edward Lloyd Salmon Jr. c 2. Supply P S Jn's Ch Henderson NC 2006-2009; Vic Chap Of The Gd Shpd Ridgeway NC 2004; Asst S Tim's Ch Raleigh NC 2004; P-in-c St Jas Epis Ch Kittrell NC 2000-2011; P-in-c S Jn's Ch Battleboro NC 2000-2001; D Chap Of The Cross Chap Hill NC 1991-1995; Pub & Records Dio No Carolina Raleigh NC 1990-2003, Chair, Historic Properties Cmsn 2005-2016, Secy, Historic Properties Cmsn 1997-2004, Alt Dep to GC 1997-1999, Hstgr 1996-2006, Del, N. C. Coun of Ch 1996-2002, Ecum Relatns Cmsn 1995-2002, Secy of the Dio 1992-2003, Dioc Coun Dept. of Records & Hist 1992-1996, Cmncatn Cmsn 1991-2003; Lectr NC Cntrl U Durham NC 1977-1984. Auth, "The Epis Ch in No Carolina During the War Between the States," Literary Lantern Press, 2013; Auth, "Competing Claims of Authority Roil So Carolina," *Epis Journ*, Epis Journ, 2013; Auth, "Remembering Malcolm Fowler," *No Carolina Folklore Journ*, N. C. Folklore Soc, 2012; Auth, "Prevaricating w all the Masters of Antiquity," *No Carolina Folklore Journ*, N. C. Folklore Soc, 2009; Auth, "Mssy Dist of Asheville," *Encyclopedia of No Carolina*, UNC Press, Chap Hill, 2006; Auth, "Edwin Wiley Fuller," *Sthrn Writers: A New Biographical Dictionary*, Lousiana St U Press, 2006; Auth, "Malone's New Hist Map of Georgia," Literary Lantern Press, 2005; Auth, "Malone's New Literary Map of Georgia," Literary Lantern Press, 2002; Auth, "Malone's New Literary Map of Florida," Literary Lantern Press, 2001; Auth, "Come Hell or High Water: Determined Couple in N. C. Marry During Flood," *LivCh*, Living Ch Fndt, 1999; Auth, "Malone's New Literary Map of NC," Literary Lantern Press, 1990; Auth, "The View from Wrightsville Bch," Literary Lantern Press, 1988; Auth, "The Rev. Edm Noah Joyner," *Dictionary of N. C. Biography, Vol. 3*, UNC Press, Chap Hill, 1988; Auth, "Sonnet for an Unknown Clergyman," *Engl & Roanoke: A Collection of Poems, 1584-1987*, NC Div Cultural Resources, 1988; Co-Auth, "Literary NC: A Hist Survey," NC Div Cultural Resources, 1986; Auth, "U NC in Edwin W. Fuller's 1873 Novel Sea-Gift," *No Carolina Hist Revs*, NC Div Cultural Resources, 1976; Auth, "The Tapestry Maker," Jn F. Blair, 1972; Auth, "The Cleared Place of Tara," Pope Printing, Dunn, N. C., 1970; Illustrator, "Hist of the Caduceus Motif," *Journ of the AMA*, AMA, 1967. ECom 1993-2003. Vstng Sci Inst for Mathematics in the Geosciences, Nat. Cntr for Atmos. Resrch 2013; Collaboration in Mathematics and Geosciences Natl Sci Fndt 2007; Weather and Climate Impacts Assessment Natl Cntr for Atmospheric Resrch 2006; Awd of Excellence--Feature Writing ECom 2004; Awd of Excellence--Humor, written ECom 2000; Awd of Excellence--Editorials ECom 1997; Awd of Excellence--News Writing ECom 1997; Who's Who in Cmnty Serv Who's Who 1997; Cratis Williams Prize NC Folklore Soc 1979; Smithwick Awd NC Soc of Cnty and Loc Historians 1977.

MALONE, Michael James (Dal) 430 Greenwood Drive, Petersburg VA 23805 **R Farnham Ch Richmond VA 2001-** B Hamburg NY 1955 s Frank & Irene. U of Virginia 1975; LTh Nash 1993. D 5/18/1993 Bp Edward Harding MacBurney P 4/25/1994 Bp James Winchester Montgomery. S Jn's Ch Warsaw VA 2001-2014; Com Mus & Liturg Dio Dallas Dallas TX 2000-2001, ExCoun 1999-2001, Wstrn Convoc Chair 1999-2001, Com Addiction & Recovery 1998-2001; R S Mk's Ch Irving TX 1997-2001; Chapl Petersburg Fire Dept 1995-1997; P-in-c S Jn's Ch Petersburg VA 1994-1997; P-in-res Emm Ch At Brook Hill Richmond VA 1993-1997; Comm on Alco and Drugs Dio Sthrn Virginia Newport News VA 1996-1997; Com Sm Ch 1996-1997; Comm on Addiction and Recovery Dio Virginia Richmond VA. The Soc of King Chas the Mtyr 2005.

MALONE, Tim (WA) 2609 N Glebe Rd, Arlington VA 22207 B Washington DC 1960 s David & Anita. BA DeSales U 1983; MA GW 1996; MDiv VTS 2009. D 6/13/2009 P 1/16/2010 Bp John Bryson Chane. m 6/28/1992 Leslie Malone c 1. Asst to the R S Mary's Epis Ch Arlington VA 2009-2017.

MALONE, Trawin E (Tex) 4115 Paint Rock Dr., Austin TX 78731 **R Chr Epis Ch Cedar Pk TX 2014-; Dioc Wellness T/F Dio Texas Houston TX 2016-** B Fayetteville AR 1951 s Theodore & Frances. BGS U of Texas at Dallas 1980; MDiv Epis TS of the SW 1983; MEd U of No Texas 1992; DMin SWTS 2004. D 6/11/1983 Bp Robert Elwin Terwilliger P 6/5/1984 Bp Donis Dean Patterson. m 8/26/1995 Melissa R Malone. Cn for Reg Mnstry Dio No Carolina Raleigh NC 2008-2014; R Ch Of The Atone Sandy Sprg GA 2002-2008; Eccl Crt S Mart's Epis Ch Metairie LA 1999-2002, Chr Formation 1993-1998; Chapl S Mart's Epis Sch Metairie LA 1993-1999; R Ch Of The Gd Shpd Terrell TX 1991-1993; Asst The Epis Ch Of The Trsfg Dallas TX 1985-1991; Cur S

Jas Ch Dallas TX 1983-1985; Congrl Dvlpmt Cmsn Dio Atlanta Atlanta GA 2005-2008; Dio Louisiana New Orleans LA 1999-2002; Yth Cmsn Dio Dallas Dallas TX 1984-1987.

MALONEY, Linda M (Vt) Po Box 294, Enosburg Falls VT 05450 **Dioc Ecum Off Dio Vermont Burlington VT 2013-** B Houston TX 1939 d David & Alta. BA S Louis U 1963; PhD S Louis U 1968; MA U of So Carolina 1981; MA S Louis U 1983; ThD U of Tuebingen DE 1990; DAS GTS 2001. D 10/15/2002 P 4/23/2003 Bp James Louis Jelinek. c 3. Int Calv Ch Underhill VT 2009-2011; P-in-partnership S Matt's Ch Enosburg Fls VT 2005-2009. Auth, "The Captain from Connecticut," U.S. Naval Inst, 2013; Co-Auth, "Proclamation Easter," Fortress Press, 2003; Auth, "All That God Had Done w Them," Ptr Lang, 1995; Auth, "The Captain from Connecticut," NEU Press, 1984.

MALONEY, Raymond Burgess (NCal) 517 White Birch Ln, Windsor CA 95492 **Died 2/17/2016** B Southbridge MA 1935 s Philip & Helena. MDiv S Johns Sem 1963; MA Assumption Coll 1976; CAGS Rhode Island Coll 1987. Rec 6/1/1992 as Priest Bp George Nelson Hunt III. Asst St Pauls Epis Ch Hillsdale CA 2012-2016; Ch Of The Gd Shpd Cloverdale CA 2002-2008; Chr Epis Ch Windsor CA 1999-2000; 1995-2016; Vic S Thos Alton RI 1994-1995; Asst S Geo And San Jorge Cntrl Falls RI 1992-1994; Serv RC Ch 1963-1981. Ord of S Lk.

MALONEY, Sean Patrick Henry (WTex) 622 Airline Rd, Corpus Christi TX 78412 **R S Barth's Ch Corpus Christi TX 2008-** B Gary IN 1974 s James & Darlene. MDiv Sewanee: The U So, TS 2008. D 12/15/2007 P 6/25/2008 Bp Edward Stuart Little II. m 6/20/1998 Jessica Maloney c 2.

MALOTTKE, William Neill (Spr) 553 Thunderbird Trl, Carol Stream IL 60188 **Died 9/16/2015** B Oak Park IL 1934 s Clarence & Charlotte. BA Illinois Coll 1955; MA Ya 1956; BD SWTS 1959. D 6/11/1959 P 6/24/1960 Bp Charles A Clough. m 4/23/1960 Carla Cave c 2. Hon Cn The Cathd Ch Of S Paul Springfield IL 2013-2015; R Emer Trin Ch 1996-2015; V-Chair - SCSC 1992-1994; SCSC 1988-1994; Dn - NW Dnry 1988-1992; Mem Structure Commision 1985-1991; Dir: Div of Admin and Fin Dio Springfield Springfield IL 1985-1989, Stndg Com 1982-1989, Dir: Div of Mssn and Wrshp 1981-1985, Stndg Com 1976-1984; SCSM 1985-1988; Mem Commision on Ch Mus 1981-1985; Dep GC 1979-1991; EvConf Sch Ch Mus 1977-1982; Alt Dep GC 1976-2015; R Trin Ch Jacksonville IL 1970-1996; Chapl EvConf Sch Ch Mus 1967-1978; R S Jn's Epis Ch Charlotte MI 1965-1970; Cn Precentor Cathd Of S Jas Chicago IL 1962-1965; Vic S Jas Epis Ch Dahlgren IL 1959-1962; Trin Ch Mt Vernon IL 1959-1962; Vic Trin Ch Mt. Vernon IL 1959-1962. Auth, *(Compsr) An Ord for Compline*, 1976. R Emer Trin Ch 1996; LHD Illinois Coll 1979; Phi Beta Kappa 1955.

MALSEED, Caroline Frey (Ak) 4032 Deborah Dr., Juneau AK 99801 **S Brendan's Epis Ch Juneau AK 2011-, 2004** B Auburn NY 1950 d James & Elizabeth. BA Hiram Coll 1972; MA Cor 1977; MDiv Bex Sem 1980. D 2/1/1981 P 5/8/1982 Bp Robert Rae Spears Jr. P-in-c S Ptr's Ch Washington NJ 1992-1998; Dio Pennsylvania Philadelphia PA 1992-1993; Asst R Calv Epis Ch Summit NJ 1989-1991; R Chr Ch Bethel VT 1985-1986; Asst R S Eliz's Ch Ridgewood NJ 1983-1984; Pstr'S Asst S Mk's And S Jn's Epis Ch Rochester NY 1982-1983; Ch Of The Gd Shpd Webster NY 1980-1981.

MALTBIE, Colin Snow (Minn) 1000 Shumway Ave, Faribault MN 55021 **Shattuck-S Mary's Sch Faribault MN 2015-** B Bloomington IN 1979 s Daniel & Karen. BA San Francisco St U 2001; MA U of St Thos 2005; MDiv VTS 2011. D 7/29/2010 P 6/30/2011 Bp Brian N Prior. m 7/13/2002 Aurora M Kubach c 2. R S Ptr's Epis Ch Kasson MN 2012-2015; S Lk's Epis Ch Rochester MN 2011-2012. colin.maltbie@s-sm.org

MANASEK, Robert Wesley (Neb) St Francis Episcopal Church, PO Box 1201, Scottsbluff NE 69361 **Asstg P S Fran Epis Ch Scottsbluff NE 2009-, P 2009-** B Omaha NE 1949 s Joseph & Laura. BA U of Nebraska at Omaha 1971; MA U of Nebraska at Omaha 1975. D 4/18/2006 P 5/12/2007 Bp Joe Goodwin Burnett. m 12/29/1972 Barbara J Manasek c 2.

MANASTERSKI, Myron Julian (CFla) 2901 Sw 91st St # 2907, Ocala FL 34476 B Sewickley PA 1956 s Chester & Olga. BA Washington and Jefferson U 1978; MEd Duquesne U 1981; MDiv TESM 1986; AA Inst of Pstr Stds Chicago 1991; MS U Pgh 1994. D 6/7/1986 Bp Alden Moinet Hathaway P 7/22/1987 Bp Clarence Cullam Pope Jr. m 8/23/1986 Marianne Manasterski. Gr Epis Ch Of Ocala Ocala FL 2003-2006; S Alb's Epis Ch Murrysville PA 1999-2002; S Jn's Epis Ch Memphis TN 1995-1999; Non-par 1992-1995; Int Trin Epis Ch Beaver PA 1991-1992; Non-par 1989-1991; Cur Dio Ft Worth Ft Worth TX 1986-1989; St Andr Epis Ch Ft Worth TX 1986-1989.

MANCHESTER, Sean (RI) 19 Trinity Pkwy, Providence RI 02908 **St Fran Epis Ch Coventry RI 2011-; Chapl Dio Rhode Island Providence RI 2000-; Non-par 1993-** B Los Angeles CA 1954 s Arthur & Marlene. EDS; BA Providence Coll 1978; MDiv Andover Newton TS 1984; MSW Smith 1994. D 7/13/1985 P 4/19/1986 Bp George Nelson Hunt III. m 6/7/1991 Michelle Manchester. S Aug's Ch Kingston RI 1998-1999; Assoc For Campus Mnstry U Of New Mex & S Thos Of Cbury 1988-1992; S Thos Of Cbury Epis Ch Albuquerque NM 1988-1991; Chapl Rhode Island Coll 1987-1988; Cur S Mich's Ch Bristol RI 1985-1987.

MANCIL, Eric Nathan (Ala) **St. Cathr's Epis Ch Chelsea AL 2017-; Dio Cntrl Gulf Coast Pensacola FL 2013-** D 11/22/2014 P 6/12/2015 Bp Philip Menzie Duncan II.

MANDELL, Cuthbert Heneage (Eas) 2010 Schooner Dr, Stafford VA 22554 B Lake Charles LA 1948 s Cuthbert & Ernestine. BA LSU 1970; JD LSU 1973; MDiv VTS 1994. D 6/11/1994 Bp James Barrow Brown P 6/1/1995 Bp John Henry Smith. m 12/21/1974 Rebecca Mandell c 3. R Aquia Ch Stafford VA 2001-2011; R Ch Of The Gd Shpd Wareham MA 1997-2001; St Stephens Romney WV 1995-1997; Vic Emm Ch Moorefield WV 1994-1997; S Steph's Ch Romney WV 1994.

MANDERBACH, Aaron (Ct) 1207 Meadow Rdg, Redding CT 06896 **Vic S Faith Ch Havertown PA 2045-2047; Vic Trin Ch Boothwyn PA 2040-2045; Ret 1980-** B Philadelphia PA 1912 s Edward & Freida. BA Tem 1934; BD Ya Berk 1937; Ya 1974. D 5/24/1937 P 12/15/1937 Bp Francis M Taitt. m 6/29/1968 Judith M Manderbach c 4. Int Trin Ch Lakeville CT 1995-1996, Int 1985-1994; Int S Andr's Ch Kent CT 1992-1993; Int Chr Ch Canaan CT 1983-1984; Int Chr Ch Sharon CT 1982-1983; R S Steph's Ch Ridgefield CT 1950-1980, R 1947-1950. Grad Soc Of Berk 1937.

MANDEVILLE, Kathleen C (NY) Po Box 450, Tivoli NY 12583 **Chapl Bard Coll NY 1996-** B Amarillo TX 1954 d Howard & Georgia. BA Bard Coll 1976; MDiv EDS 1983. D 6/4/1983 P 4/1/1984 Bp Paul Moore Jr. R S Clem's Ch New York NY 1992-1993, Vic 1986-1991, Cur 1983-1984.

MANDRELL, H Dean (Ak) B Lyons KS 1937 s Morgan & Ruth. BA SW Coll Winfield KS 1963. D 12/7/1975 Bp Matthew Paul Bigliardi P 2/10/2002 Bp Mark Lawrence Macdonald. m 5/27/1960 Carol Mandrell. S Barth's Ch Palmer AK 2001-2011.

MANGELS III, John (NCal) 6725 Hillglen Way, Fair Oaks CA 95628 **P-in-c S Jn's Epis Ch Marysville CA 2015-** B Livermore CA 1952 s John & Jeanne. BA U CA 1975; MDiv CDSP 1979. D 4/7/1983 P 1/1/1984 Bp John Lester Thompson III. m 7/26/1980 Anne Mangels. S Andr's In The Highlands Mssn Antelope CA 2007-2008; R S Geo's Ch Carmichael CA 1994-2012; P-in-c S Mich Ch Alturas CA 1993-1994; Vic Gd Shpd Epis Ch Susanville CA 1987-1994; Vic S Andr's Ch Meeteetse WY 1984-1987.

MANGUM, Frank Burnett (Tex) 14041 Horseshoe Cir, Woodway TX 76712 **Ret Epis Ch 1996-** B Natchez MS 1932 s Frank & Billie. BA Millsaps Coll 1954; MDiv Sewanee: The U So, TS 1957; STM Sewanee: The U So, TS 1965; Chr Ch Coll GB 1978; Coll of Preachers 1981; U of Durham GB 1991. D 7/3/1957 P 3/17/1958 Bp Robert Raymond Brown. Epis Fndt of Texas Dio Texas 1995-1998; R Chr Ch Nacogdoches TX 1993-1996; Bd Trst U So 1993-1995; Secy, Bp Quin Fndt Dio Texas 1985-1990; R S Paul's Ch Houston TX 1983-1993; Chapl S Lk Hosp Houston TX 1979-1983; S Lk's Epis Hosp Houston TX 1979-1983; Chair, Dept of CE Dio Texas 1974-1975; Secy, Exec Bd Dio Texas 1974-1975; Exec Bd Dio Texas 1973-1975; Bd Trst U So 1972-1980; R Ch Of The H Comf Angleton TX 1969-1979; R S Andr's Ch Rogers AR 1968-1969; Texas Epis Sch Assn 1966-1968; Bd Trst U So 1966-1968; Assoc R S Paul's Ch Waco TX 1961-1968; R S Lk's Epis Ch N Little Rock AR 1960-1961, Vic 1957-1960. DuBose Awd STUSo 2005.

MANIACI, Maria Kathleen (NMich) 824 Dakota Ave, PO Box 411, Gladstone MI 49837 **D Trin Ch Gladstone MI 1997-** B Elkhart IN 1946 d George & Louella. D 6/1/1997 Bp Thomas Kreider Ray. c 3. NAAD 1999.

MANION, James Edward (Del) 20 Olive Ave, Rehoboth Beach DE 19971 B Masury OH 1937 s Joseph & Rose. BA Huntington Coll 1963; MA U of Kentucky 1964; MDiv Epis TS in Kentucky 1969. D 5/24/1969 P 11/1/1969 Bp William R Moody. m 8/25/1962 Betty J Manion. All SS and St Georges Ch Rehoboth Bch DE 1981-1999; R Trin Ch Uppr Marlboro MD 1976-1980; Assoc Emm Par Epis Ch Sthrn Pines NC 1974-1976; Chapl De St Police 1971-1974; R S Phil's Ch Laurel DE 1970-1974; Asst Ch Of The Gd Shpd Lexington KY 1969-1970.

MANIYATT, John Kuriakose (Md) 4 E University Pkwy, Baltimore MD 21218 B Arakuzha India 1959 s John & Leelamma. BSc Nirmala Coll; MDiv Jnana Deepa Vidyapeeth 1989; MDiv Jnana Deepa Vidyapeeth 1989; MS Loyola U 2006. Rec 12/8/2013 as Priest Bp Eugene Taylor Sutton. m 4/30/2007 Chin-Mei Maniyatt.

MANLEY JR, Derrill Byrne (NwT) 1615 S Carpenter Ln, Cottonwood AZ 86326 B Phoenix,AR 1951 s Derrill & Inez. California Wstrn U 1970; BA U of Arizona 1973; MDiv EDS 1977; PhD Texas Tech U 1986. D 6/18/1977 Bp Joseph Thomas Heistand P 10/1/1978 Bp Willis Ryan Henton. m 8/11/1973 Cynthia A Manley c 3. S Thos Of The Vlly Epis Clarkdale AZ 1997-2004; S Matt's Ch Austin TX 1986-1988; Non-par 1983-1987; R Ch Of The H Trin Midland TX 1978-1982; Chapl Austin St Hosp 1977-1978.

MANLEY, Wendy T (Cal) 1090 Brookfield Rd., Berlin VT 05602 B Summit NJ 1939 d John & Norma. U of Connecticut; BA Madonna U 1990; MDiv Ya Berk 1993. D 6/19/1993 Bp R aymond Stewart Wood Jr P 3/1/1994 Bp Gethin Benwil Hughes. m 6/18/1960 Robert G Manley c 2. Supply P Dio Indianapolis Indianapolis IN 2002-2003; S Jn's Epis Ch Oakland CA 1998-2000; Ch Of The Gd Shpd Cloverdale CA 1996; Pstr'S Asst Ch Of The Gd Samar San Diego CA 1993-1994.

MANN, Alice B (Mass) 51 Leroy Ave, Haverhill MA 01835 **Sr Consultant Alb Inst Bethseda MD 1995-** B Philadelphia PA 1949 d Edward & Mary. BA U of Pennsylvania 1970; MDiv PDS 1974; MA Temple Gb 1995. D 6/15/1974 P 1/1/1977 Bp Lyman Cunningham Ogilby. m 7/11/2009 Thomas Grannemann. The Alb Inst Beth MD 1995-2010; Non-par 1993-1995; Int Trin Ch Asbury Pk NJ 1991-1993; S Andr's Ch Trenton NJ 1988-1991; Vic S Mich's Ch Trenton NJ 1988-1991; Vic S Jn The Evang Yalesville CT 1981-1988; Vic S Gabr's Epis Ch Philadelphia PA 1980-1981; Assoc Ch Of Our Sav Jenkintown PA 1974-1979; Ch Of S Asaph Bala Cynwyd PA 1974-1979. Auth, "Raising The Roof," The Alb Inst, 2002; Auth, "Can Our Live?," The Alb Inst, 2001; Auth, "The In-Between Ch," The Alb Inst, 2000; Auth, "Cler Ldrshp In Sm Cmntys," Ascen Press, 1985; Auth, "Incorporation Of New Members In Epis Ch," Ascen Press, 1983.

MANN, Carl Douglas (Ia) 19372 140th St, Danville IA 52623 **P-in-c Chr Epis Ch Burlington IA 2016-** B Cedar Rapids IA 1957 s Thomas & Helen. BA Luther Coll 1980; MDiv Nash 2006. D 12/3/2005 P 6/10/2006 Bp Alan Scarfe. m 11/27/1982 Jane Roberts c 2. R S Alb's Ch Sprt Lake IA 2006-2016. revrhino@christchurchonline.com

MANN, Charles Henry (SwFla) 5900 N Lockwood Ridge Road, Sarasota FL 34243 **R Ch of the Nativ Sarasota FL 2004-** B Winter Haven FL 1954 s Earl & Frances. BA U of So Florida 1977; MDiv TESM 1998. D 6/6/1998 Bp John Wadsworth Howe P 12/6/1998 Bp John Bailey Lipscomb. m 12/17/1977 Debra J Mann c 4. Assoc R S Jn's Ch Naples FL 1998-2004. mannch@aol.com

MANN, Frederick Earl (SwFla) 7835 Moonstone Dr, Sarasota FL 34233 **P-in-c S Bede's Ch St. Petersburg FL 2014-; Ret 2011-** B Lakeland FL 1950 s Earl & Frances. AA Polk Jr Coll Winter Haven FL 1970; BA U of Florida 1972; MDiv Nash 1978. D 6/29/1978 Bp William Hopkins Folwell P 12/29/1978 Bp Arthur Anton Vogel. m 10/10/1981 Denise Mann c 2. R S Andr's Ch Kansas City MO 2004-2011; The Cathd Ch Of S Jas So Bend IN 1993-2003; R H Cross Epis Ch Sanford FL 1986-1992; R S Mths Epis Ch Clermont FL 1982-1986; Asst Emm Ch Orlando FL 1980-1982; Assoc Chr Epis Ch Springfield MO 1978-1980; Congrl Dvlpmt Cmsn Dio W Missouri Kansas City MO 2008-2011, Congrl Dvlpmt Cmsn 2005-2011; Bd Mem Kansas City Cmnty Kitchen 2005-2011; Stndg Com Dio Nthrn Indiana So Bend IN 1999-2003, Dn 1993-1999; Stndg Com Dio Cntrl Florida Orlando FL 1989-1992, Dioc Bd 1986-1988, Dioc Bd 1986-1988, Dn Inst Chr Stds 1983-1985. Auth, "Bible Rdr Fllshp Series: 1, 2," *1,2,3 Jn and Jude*, BRF, 1985. Alum Assn of Nash - Wrdn 1998-2004; Ord of S Lk - Chapl 1987; OHC 1975; SHN 1977-2011.

MANN III, Harold Vance (WNC) 15 Creekside View Dr, Asheville NC 28804 B Miami FL 1941 s Harold & Ella. BA Randolph-Macon Coll 1964; MDiv Sewanee: The U So, TS 1977. D 6/5/1977 Bp William Henry Marmion P 5/4/1978 Bp James Barrow Brown. m 7/4/2007 Margaret Mann c 2. R S Thos Epis Ch Burnsville NC 2008-2011; Int Trin Epis Ch Watertown NY 2005-2006; Int S Jn's Epis Ch Midland MI 2004-2005; Dn Dio Sthrn Virginia Newport News VA 2000-2004; R S Paul's Epis Ch Suffolk VA 1993-2004; Dn Reg I Dio Virginia Richmond VA 1988-1992; R S Steph's Epis Ch Culpeper VA 1984-1993; R S Anne's Par Scottsville VA 1980-1984; Asst S Mk's Cathd Shreveport LA 1978-1980; Cur S Augustines Ch Metairie LA 1977-1978.

MANN, Henry Rezin (SanD) 7981 Hemingway Ave, San Diego CA 92120 **Asst S Dunst's Epis Ch San Diego CA 2003-, Asst to R 1987-2002** B Jacksonville FL 1932 s Walter & Ruth. BA San Diego St U 1958; JD U of San Diego 1967; DIT ETSBH 1987; MA Claremont TS 1988. D 6/13/1987 P 12/19/1987 Bp Charles Brinkley Morton. m 7/17/1954 Shirley B Mann c 3. Cn Dio San Diego San Diego CA 1998-1999, Asst to Bp 1993-1997; Asst to Bp Dio San Diego 1992-1995; Vic S Columba's Epis Ch Santee CA 1989-1995.

MANN, Louise (Mass) 8399 Breeding Rd, Edmonton KY 42129 B Philadelphia PA 1941 d Edward & Mary. BS Chestnut Hill Coll 1963; MEd Tem 1968; MA Chr TS 1974; MDiv EDS 1984. D 6/24/1984 Bp Edward Witker Jones P 10/18/1985 Bp John Bowen Coburn. c 3. The Ch Of The H Name Swampscott MA 1996-2004; Assoc R Chr Ch Exeter NH 1989-1996; Asst R S Andr's Ch New London NH 1986-1989. Auth, "Listening for the Sacr in the Faith Cmnty," Dio Massachusetts, 1994. No Amer Mnstrl Fell 1984.

MANN, Lucretia Winslow (ECR) 5271 Scotts Valley Dr, Scotts Valley CA 95066 B Lowell MA 1952 BA Wellesley Coll 1974; MS U of Florida 1990; PhD U of Florida 1993; MDiv EDS 2013. D 10/26/2013 P 10/11/2014 Bp Mary Gray-Reeves. c 3.

MANN, Mary Anne (Ct) 36 Convent Drive 1a31, Bethesda MD 20892 **Non-par 1988-** B Trenton NJ 1944 d Edward & Mary. BS Philadelphia Coll of Art 1972; MA Goddard Coll 1983; MDiv GTS 1984; PhD NEU 1998. D 6/16/1984 Bp Lyman Cunningham Ogilby P 5/1/1985 Bp William Bradford Hastings. Vic S Jn's Ch Guilford CT 1984-1988; Consult/Instr Dio Pennsylvania Philadelphia PA 1976-1980. Auth, "Conformed To Chr," *Structures & Standards In Par Dvlpmt*.

MANNEN, Daniel Joseph (CFla) 414 Pine St, Titusville FL 32796 B Frankfort KY 1947 s Daniel & Julie. BA St Bern Coll; DMN St Mary's U; MA.TN Washington Theol Un. Rec 12/12/2015 as Priest Bp Gregory Orrin Brewer. m 11/26/1982 Elizabeth Ann Schmitz.

MANNING, Gary Briton (Mil) 1717 Church St., Wauwatosa WI 53213 **R Trin Ch Milwaukee WI 2004-** B Jacksonville FL 1959 BA Lee U. D 6/9/2002 Bp Stephen Hays Jecko P 12/14/2002 Bp Carol J Gallagher. m 2/27/1988 Tabitha Leah Manning c 1. Assoc Chr and S Lk's Epis Ch Norfolk VA 2002-2004.

MANNING, Gene Bentley (Tenn) 900 Broadway, Nashville TN 37203 B Chattanooga TN 1955 d James & Ethel. BS U of Tennessee 1977; MEd Van 1991; MDiv Sewanee: The U So, TS 2001; DMin SWTS 2010; DMin SWTS 2010. D 6/23/2001 P 4/21/2002 Bp Bertram Nelson Herlong. m 4/14/1978 James P Manning c 3. Sub Dn Chr Ch Cathd Nashville TN 2008-2017; Assoc R S Geo's Ch Nashville TN 2002-2007; Dio Tennessee Nashville TN 2001-2002; S Phil's Ch Nashville TN 2001.

MANNING, Jeanette Belle (SO) 164 Community Dr, Dayton OH 45404 **S Marg's Ch Dayton OH 2004-** B Aberdeen SD 1943 D 6/12/2004 Bp Kenneth Lester Price. m 6/12/1971 Lawrence Ray Manning c 4. Mem of Cler Wellness Committe Dio Sthrn Ohio Cincinnati OH 2004-2006.

MANNING, Jean Louise (NMich) 1344 M-64, Ontonagon MI 49953 B Ontonagon MI 1957 d William & Ellen. D 4/1/1990 P 10/7/2000 Bp Thomas Kreider Ray. m 8/16/1975 Charles Manning. Assoc Ch Of The Ascen Ontonagon MI 1990-2008.

MANNING, Ronald Francis (CFla) 70 Town Ct Apt 307, Palm Coast FL 32164 **Epis Ch of the Blessed Redeem 2004-; Ret R Ch of the Blessed Redeem Palm Bay FL 2003-** B Hayes Clarendon JM 1933 s Solomon & Muriel. Jamaica Sch of Agriculture 1954; Inst for Chr Stuides 1983. D 9/21/1983 Bp William Hopkins Folwell P 9/30/1990 Bp John Wadsworth Howe. m 8/17/1955 Leila Joyce Monica Manning c 4. Assoc S Thos Flagler Cnty Palm Coast FL 2000-2003; R S Tim's Epis Ch Daytona Bch FL 1990-1999; D Cathd Ch Of S Lk Orlando FL 1983-1990.

MANNING, Shannon R (La) 5335 Suffolk Dr, Jackson MS 39211 **Cn Dio Louisiana New Orleans LA 2013-** B Jackson MS 1974 d William & Yvonne. BA Millsaps Coll 1997; MDiv GTS 2001. D 6/16/2001 Bp Alfred Marble Jr P 12/16/2001 Bp Duncan Montgomery Gray Jr. m 7/29/2000 Richard J Manning c 2. Assoc R S Jas Ch Jackson MS 2007-2013, 2005; Chapl S Andr's Epis Sch Jackson MS 2005-2007; S Andr's Epis Sch Ridgeland MS 2005-2007; Dio Mississippi Jackson MS 2002-2005; S Mary's Ch Lexington MS 2002-2005; Cur S Jn's Epis Ch Ocean Sprg MS 2001-2002. smanning@edola.org

MANNING, Slaven L (USC) PO BOX 220, Prosperity SC 29127 **S Fran of Assisi Chapin SC 2015-; Int Assoc R S Steph's Epis Ch Hurst TX 2008-** B Shreveport LA 1959 s Earl & Kathryn. Cert Tarrant Cnty Cmnty Coll; BA U of No Texas 1982; MDiv Nash 1985. D 12/21/1985 P 4/21/1987 Bp Donis Dean Patterson. m 2/11/1996 Linda G Manning. S Alb's Ch Davenport IA 1990-1994; Ch Of The Gd Shpd Dallas TX 1987-1990; S Lk's Ch Denison TX 1985-1986. fr.manning@gmail.com

MANNING, William Bentley (Ala) **Asst S Mary's-On-The-Highlands Epis Ch Birmingham AL 2014-** D 6/11/2014 P 12/10/2014 Bp John Mckee Sloan Sr.

MANNING-LEW, Sharon Janine (NY) 522 Washington St, Peekskill NY 10566 **Assoc S Aug's Epis Ch Croton Hdsn NY 2013-** B New York NY 1952 d Clarence & Gloria. BS Nyack Coll 2003; MDiv GTS 2007. D 3/10/2007 P 9/29/2012 Bp Mark Sean Sisk. m 11/24/1988 Shang Lew c 1. Customer Serv Mgr The Artina Grp 1984-2013.

MANNISTO, Virginia L (NMich) N4354 Black Creek Rd, Chatham MI 49816 B 1950 d Robert & Letitia. Cntrl Michigan U 1969; Nthrn Michigan U 2002. D 6/3/1990 P 1/1/1991 Bp Thomas Kreider Ray. m 3/4/2006 Charles H Mannisto c 2. Dio Nthrn Michigan Marquette MI 2005-2007, D 1990-1991; S Jn's Ch Munising MI 1991-2008, R 1991-.

MANNSCHRECK, Mary Lou Cowherd (SwVa) St Luke's Episcopal Church, 801 S Osage Ave, Bartlesville OK 74003 B Wetumka OK 1943 d Leonard & Christine. BS Oklahoma St U 1965; MEd Contral St U Edmond OK 1978; MDiv Epis TS of the SW 2007. D 6/23/2007 Bp Robert Manning Moody P 12/8/2007 Bp Edward Joseph Konieczny. c 1. Chr Ch Bluefield WV 2012-2013; S Paul's Ch Saltville VA 2010-2011; Cur S Lk's Epis Ch Bartlesville OK 2007-2009; Admin Tech St Of Oklahoma 2001-2004.

MANOLA, John Edwin (NJ) B 1917

MANOOGIAN, Phyllis (Cal) 2300 Bancroft Way, Berkeley CA 94704 B Washington DC 1949 d Charles & Anna. BA Epis Sch for Deacons; BA U of Wisconsin 1972; BA Epis Sch for Deacons 2012; BA Epis Sch for Deans 2012. D 6/14/2014 Bp Marc Handley Andrus.

MANSELLA, Thomas G (Va) 3705 S George Mason Dr, Apt 2105-S, Falls Church VA 22041 B Buenos Aires AR 1944 s Adolfo & Petrona. Dio Paraguay Asunción Py; Instituto Biblico Buenos Aires AR 1970; Dio Argentina Buenos Aires AR 1971. Trans 3/1/1989 Bp Peter J Lee. m 12/2/1972 Elizabeth Mansella c 3. Archd Dio Argentina 2011-2012; R, St Jn's Cathd Dio Argentina 2009-2011; Translation Serv Coordntr Epis Ch Cntr New York NY 2005-2009; S Mich's Epis Ch Arlington VA 1997-2004; Vic Iglesia Epis San Marcos Alexandria VA 1994-1997; Vic La Iglesia De Cristo Rey Arlington VA 1989-1999; Mssnr Dio Virginia Richmond VA 1987-1989; Serv Dio Argentina 1981-1987; Serv Dio Paraguay 1971-1981. Auth, "Security and Sfty Issues for

540

the 21st Century Off," *The ATA Chronicle*, Amer Translators Assn, 2003; Auth, "Anglicanism And Ecum," *Panama*, 1986.

MANSFIELD, Charles Kirk (Vt) 157 Parker Hill Rd, Bellows Falls VT 05101 **D Imm Ch Bellows Falls VT 2003-** B Norwalk CT 1924 s Charles & Ethel. Norwalk Cmnty Coll Norwalk CT. D 6/7/2003 Bp Thomas C Ely. m 11/14/1953 Gloria Carol Mansfield c 4.

MANSFIELD, Gregory James Edward (SeFla) St. Bernard de Clairvaux Episcopal Church, 16711 West Dixie Highway, North Miami Beach FL 33160 **R S Bern De Clairvaux N Miami Bch FL 2010-** B Martinsville IN 1957 s Jerry & Marcia. BA Huntington Coll 1980; EdM Harv 1986; DMin GTF 1990. D 6/24/1986 P 3/1/1987 Bp Edward Witker Jones. Asst The Ch Of The Guardian Ang Lake Worth FL 2007-2010; Chapl St. Mary's Hosp W Palm Bch FL 2006-2010; R S Andr's Ch Kansas City MO 1996-2000; Cn To Ordnry Dio W Missouri Kansas City MO 1993-1995; Assoc R S Paul's Ch Kansas City MO 1988-1993; Cur Gr Ch Muncie IN 1986-1988. Co-Auth, "Let's Go: Greece," St. Mart's Press; Co-Auth, "Let's Go: Italy," St. Mart's Press. Soc of Cath Priests 2010.

MANSFIELD, Mary Robb (Vt) 32 Wood Rd, North Middlesex VT 05682 **Died 3/21/2016** B Brattleboro VT 1940 d Hermon & Bertha. BA U of Vermont 1977; MS Syr 1983; MDiv Colgate Rochester Crozer DS 1994; MDiv CRDS 1994. D 7/16/1994 P 6/5/1995 Bp David Bruce Joslin. m 6/24/1962 Richard Henry Mansfield c 3. Ret 2008-2016; R S Jn's In The Mountains Stowe VT 1999-2008; Chemung Vlly Cluster Elmira NY 1996-1997; S Jn's Epis Ch Elmira NY 1995-1997; Cur S Paul's Ch Owego NY 1994-1996; Investigative comm. to consider Dioc-wide fund raiser Dio Vermont 2011-2012; Mem of same-sex Mar Com Dio Vermont 2006-2007.

MANSFIELD, Meribah Ann (SO) 2282 Fernleaf Lane, Columbus OH 43235 **S Alb's Epis Ch Of Bexley Columbus OH 2012-; D S Jn's Ch Columbus OH 2012-** B Bronxville NY 1949 d George & Ann. BA Witt 1971; MLS Wstrn Michigan U 1972; Sch for Diac Formation, Dio Sthrn Ohio 2012. D 6/2/2012 Bp Thomas Edward Breidenthal. m 11/27/1987 Donald Bruce Mansfield c 2.

MANSFIELD JR, Richard Huntington (Ct) 41 Gatewood, Avon CT 06001 **Ret 2002-; Dn Chr Ch Cathd Hartford CT 1991-, Cn 1982-1991** B Mount Vernon NY 1937 s Richard & Marjory. BA Rol 1960; STM Ya Berk 1963. D 12/27/1965 Bp Horace W B Donegan P 6/10/1966 Bp Charles Francis Boynton. m 6/4/1960 Sharon B Kelley c 4. Dn Bex Sem Columbus OH 1977-1982; R H Trin Epis Ch Oxford OH 1970-1977; Cur S Matt's Ch Bedford NY 1966-1970; Fac S Andr's Sch Boca Raton FL 1963-1966; Stndg Com Dio Connecticut Meriden CT 1997-2001, Exec Coun 1986-1996, COM 1983-. Auth, "Holding Cbury Accountable," *Wit*, 1987; Auth, "Footwashing," *Epis*, 1986; Auth, "Sem Educ," *Living Ch*, 1982; Auth, "Wmn as Agents of God," *Wit*, 1982. SIM 2002. DD Ya 1979.

MANSFIELD, Victor Claibourne (WNC) PO Box 531, Skyland NC 28776 B Raleigh NC 1955 s Raymond & Jessie. BA Methodist U 1977; MDiv VTS 1982. D 6/7/1982 Bp Hunley Agee Elebash P 6/18/1983 Bp Robert Whitridge Estill. c 2. R Calv Epis Ch Fletcher NC 2000-2015; R S Thos' Epis Ch Abingdon VA 1989-2000; Asst H Trin Epis Ch Greensboro NC 1986-1989; Asst S Ptr's Epis Ch Charlotte NC 1982-1986.

MANSIR, Kerry Rhoads (Me) **CE Dir S Barth's Epis Ch Yarmouth ME 2013-** D 6/17/2017 Bp Stephen Taylor Lane.

MANSON, Anne Leslie Yount (Va) The Prestwould, 612 West Franklin St. #12C, Richmond VA 23220 B Richmond VA 1944 d Robert & Eva. AB W&M 1967; MDiv UTS Richmond 1985; MDiv UTS in Va. 1985; Cert VTS 1986. D 6/11/1986 P 3/30/1987 Bp Peter J Lee. c 1. R Cunningham Chap Par Millwood VA 2006-2010; Vic Ch of the Incarn Mineral VA 1998-2006; R Ch Of The Creator Mechanicsvlle VA 1988-1997; Int Gr Epis Ch Goochland VA 1988; D S Mary's Epis Ch Richmond VA 1986-1987; Exec Bd Dio Virginia Richmond VA 1996-1998, Cmsn for So Afr Partnership 1995-1996, Pres 1990-1995, Pres 1989, Stndg Jury 1987-1996, Com on Fam Life, Human Sxlty, and Abortion 1987-1992; Homil, appointed Sectn Ldr UTS in Va. 1992; Pres, Richmond Cler 1990-1991. Contrib, "A Costly Love," *Epis Ch website*, Epis Ch, 2001; Contrib, "A Costly Love," *Epis Ch website, Sermons that Wk*, Epis Ch, 2001; Contrib, "In Memory of St. Fran," *The Angl Dig*, Unknown, 2000. Kappa Delta Pi At Wm & Mary 1966. Walter D Moore Fllshp For Grad Stds UTS in Va. 1985; W T Thompson Schlr UTS in Va. 1983.

MANSON, Malcolm (Cal) 35 Keyes Avenue, San Francisco CA 94129 **Assiant (Non-stip) Gr Cathd San Francisco CA 2001-** B Melton Mowbray UK 1938 s James & Williamina. BA Oxf GB 1961; MA Oxf GB 1964. D 6/25/1977 Bp Chauncie Kilmer Myers P 6/27/1978 Bp William Foreman Creighton. m 4/11/1982 Snowden J Manson. The Epis Ch Of S Mary The Vrgn San Francisco CA 2000-2002; Sch Hd Gr Cathd San Francisco CA 1990-1999; Cn Epis Par Of S Jn The Bapt Portland OR 1986-1990; Assoc St Johns Epis Ch Ross CA 1977-1982.

MANTILLA-BENITEZ, Haydee (EcuC) Avenue Libertad Parada 8, Esmeralda Ecuador B Guayaquil EC 1948 d Luis & Teresa. Sem 1989. D 12/18/1988 P 5/1/1990 Bp Adrian Delio Caceres-Villavicencio. Iglesia Epis Del Ecuador Quito 1993-2010.

MANUEL, Anandsekar Joseph (LI) 3907 61st St, Woodside NY 11377 **S Paul's Ch Woodside NY 2002-** B Vellore India 1953 Trans 12/11/2002 Bp Orris George Walker Jr. m 10/11/1982 Agnes Shanthakumari Manuel c 1.

MANZANARES, Zoila Manzanares-Rodriguez (Ind) 6613 El Paso Dr, Indianapolis IN 46214 B El Salvador CA 1960 d Roberto & Bertha. Inst of Tech Centro Americano Engr 1984; MDiv Epis TS of the SW 1994. D 6/24/1995 Bp Oliver Bailey Garver Jr P 1/1/1996 Bp Frederick Houk Borsch. m 11/6/2009 Robin L Cole. Cn Chr Ch Cathd Indianapolis IN 2007-2017; Trin Epis Par Los Angeles CA 2003-2005; Pueblo Nuevo Epis Ch Los Angeles CA 2001-2003; H Faith Par Inglewood CA 1995-1998.

MANZO, Peter Thomas (NJ) 69 Penn Rd, Voorhees NJ 08043 B Bayonne NJ 1947 s Valentine & Rita. AB Geo 1968; MBA Col 1972; JD Cor 1972; Cert Ang Stud GTS 1999. Rec 11/18/1998 as Deacon Bp Joe Doss. m 3/25/1989 Joan U Manzo c 3. R S Barth's Ch Cherry Hill NJ 2002-2016; Cur S Lk's Ch Gladstone NJ 1999-2002; D Gr Epis Ch Plainfield NJ 1998-1999; D St. Pat RC Ch Chatham NJ 1982-1988. Auth, "Will we see our pets in the Resurr?," *LivCh -- online*, 2012; Auth, "Why we're Getting Thrown Out," *LivCh*, 2005.

MAPPLEBECKPALMER, Richard Warwick (Cal) 472 Dale Rd, Martinez CA 94553 B 1932 s Richard & Frances. BA Corpus Christi Coll Cambridge 1956; Ripon Coll Cuddesdon 1958; MA Corpus Christi Coll Cambridge GB 1960. Rec 6/1/1988 as Priest Bp William Edwin Swing. m 4/29/1973 Lindzi Mapplebeckpalmer. Gr Inst For Rel Lrng Berkeley CA 1994-2004; R S Clements 1988-1989; S Clem's Ch Berkeley CA 1988-1989; Par P Ch Of Engl 1958-1988.

MARANVILLE, Irvin Walter (Vt) 6809 23rd Ave W, Bradenton FL 34209 **Ret 1995-** B Wallingford VT 1928 s Stephen & Madeline. AS Champlain Coll 1972. D 10/19/1986 Bp Robert Shaw Kerr. m 9/5/1951 Joyce Margaret Maranville c 3.

MARANVILLE, Joyce Margaret (Vt) 6809 23rd Ave W, Bradenton FL 34209 **Ret 1995-** B London UK 1931 d Arthur & Rosamond. Pryor Bus Acad. D 10/19/1986 Bp Robert Shaw Kerr. m 9/5/1951 Irvin Walter Maranville c 4.

✠ MARBLE JR, The Rt Rev Alfred (NC) 301 N Elm St Ste 308C, Greensboro NC 27401 **Died 3/29/2017** B Oneonta NY 1936 s Alfred & Charlotte. BA U of Mississippi 1958; U of Edinburgh GB 1965; BD Sewanee: The U So, TS 1967. D 6/22/1967 P 5/1/1968 Bp John Maury Allin Con 6/15/1991 for Miss. m 1/5/1974 Helen Nadine Harper c 2. Ret Bp Of Mississippi Dio Mississippi Jackson MS 2003-2017, Bp Of Miss 1993-2003, 1991-2003, Bp Coadj 1991-1993; Stff Asst To Bp Dio E Carolina Kinston NC 1984-1991, 1983-1991; The Epis Ch Of The Medtr Meridian MS 1978-1983; S Ptr's Ch Oxford MS 1972-1978; Ch Of The Nativ Water Vlly MS 1971-1978; Chapl U MS 1971-1974; Vic H Cross Epis Ch Olive Branch MS 1969-1971; S Timothys Epis Ch Southaven MS 1969-1971; Cur S Jas Ch Jackson MS 1967-1969.

MARCANTONIO, John (Nwk) 39 Johnson Rd, West Orange NJ 07052 B Elizabeth NJ 1951 s Henry & Carmela. MA Pontifical Coll Josephinum 1983; MS Ford 1989; Dip Ang Stud GTS 2010. Rec 11/13/2010 as Priest Bp Mark M Beckwith. m 1/3/2008 Kimberly Gunning-Marcantonio c 1.

MARCETTI, Alvin Julian (RI) 81 Warren Ave, East Providence RI 02914 B Modesto CA 1941 s William & Evelyn. BA San Jose St U 1966; MA Santa Clara U 1976. Trans 5/14/2015 as Priest Bp W Nicholas Knisely Jr. m 12/11/2013 Mark R Sutherland.

MARCH, Bette Ann (Wyo) 34 Thomas The Apostle Rd, Cody WY 82414 B Bozeman MT 1940 d Clifford & Jessie. California St U; AD Ln Cmnty Coll 1978; BD S Josephs Coll No Windham ME 1982. D 10/16/2004 Bp Bruce Caldwell. m 3/1/1994 Everett Alan March c 2. Occupational Hlth Nurse Us W Denver CO 1981-2000.

MARCH, Joan Amanda (Mass) **Emm Ch Boston MA 2015-** D 6/3/2017 Bp Gayle Harris.

MARCHAND, R Richard (NY) 1 Kingsley Ave, Staten Island NY 10314 B Seattle WA 1959 s Frederick & Patricia. BA Whitman Coll 1982; MDiv GTS 2008; Cert Academia de Espanol Guatemala 2009. D 1/26/2008 P 8/6/2008 Bp Bavi Edna Rivera. R Ch Of The Ascen Staten Island NY 2010-2016; Assoc The Ch of S Matt And S Tim New York NY 2008-2010; D The Ch Of S Lk In The Fields New York NY 2008. Soc of Cath Priests 2009-2010.

MARCHL III, William Henry (NC) 719 S 1st St, Smithfield NC 27577 B Pittsburgh PA 1964 s William & Mary. BA Ken 1986; MDiv Ya Berk 1992. D 1/3/1993 P 7/8/1993 Bp Alden Moinet Hathaway. m 8/3/1991 Laura L Marchl c 1. R S Paul's Epis Ch Smithfield NC 2003-2006; P Cur S Steph's Ch Durham NC 1998-2002; Trin Ch Coshocton OH 1995-1998; The Ch Of The Adv Jeannette PA 1993-1995; Calv Ch Pittsburgh PA 1993-1994; P S Barth's Ch Scottdale PA 1993-1994. Auth, "arts," *Living Ch*. SocMary. Jn Crowe Ransom Poetry Prize; Phi Beta Kappa.

MARCIALES ARENAS, Alberto Camilo (Colom) Carrera 6 No 49-85, Piso 2, Bogota Colombia B Cucuta Norte de Santander Colombia 1942 s Luis & Isabel. BA Colegio La Salle 1962; Lic Universidad de Pamplona 1993; Universidad de Pamplona 1999. D 12/13/2008 P 3/22/2009 Bp Francisco Jose Duque-Gomez. m 8/13/1966 Marleny Blanca Leal de Marciales c 4.

MARCOUX, Stephen Kent (WA) St George's Parish, 160 U St NW, Washington DC 20001 **P-in-c S Geo's Ch Washington DC 2013-** B Lafayette LA 1961 s Harvey & Mary. BS U of New Orleans 1986; CAS Ya Berk 1997; MDiv Yale DS 1997; MBA Yale Sch of Mgmt 1997. D 5/30/1998 Bp Charles Edward Jenkins III P 10/7/1999 Bp Ronald Hayward Haines. m 5/14/2000 Ellen Burke Kennedy c 2. Asst R Gr Epis Ch Silver Sprg MD 2008-2010; P Ch Of S Steph And The Incarn Washington DC 1998-2003. kmarcoux@stgeorgesdc.org

MARCURE, Johanna (CNY) 209 E Main St, Waterville NY 13480 **Gr Epis Ch Syracuse NY 2012-** B Ft Jackson SC 1962 d Richard & Anne. BA U of Mass-achusetts 1994; MDiv Andover Newton TS 2009. D 3/21/2009 P 3/13/2010 Bp Gordon Scruton. c 3. Gr Epis Ch Waterville NY 2010-2012. jmarcure@aol.com

MARCUSSEN, Bjorn Birkholm (SanD) 731 G St C3, Chula Vista CA 91910 B Copenhagen DK 1942 s Tage & Hildeborg. MA Copenhagen Sem Copenhagen Dk 1972; MS Royal Danish Grad Sch of Educ Copenhagen Dk 1974. Rec 2/1/2000 as Priest Bp Gethin Benwil Hughes. Cler-in- Charge of Hisp Mnstry Cathd Ch Of S Paul San Diego CA 2012-2014; R S Phil The Apos Epis Ch Lemon Grove CA 2001-2011; Dio San Diego San Diego CA 2001-2005; Vic S Eliz's Epis Ch San Diego CA 2000-2001.

MAREE, Donna L (Pa) 2112 Delancey St, Philadelphia PA 19103 **R Trin Memi Ch Philadelphia PA 2011-; R Chr Epis Ch Warren OH 2006-** B Pittsfield MA 1955 d Ruth. BS Smith 1997; MDiv EDS 2000. D 10/26/2002 P 6/21/2003 Bp Herbert Thompson Jr. m 5/14/2006 Charles E Carr c 3. R Chr Epis Ch Warren OH 2006-2011; Asst. for New Members Trin Epis Ch Buffalo NY 2003-2006; Indn Hill Ch Cincinnati OH 2002-2003. secretary@christchurchwarren.org

MAREK, Joseph J (Tenn) 204-A Courthouse Dr., Salmon ID 83467 **Vic Ch Of The Redeem Salmon ID 2009-** B Milwaukee WI 1936 s Joseph & Sophia. St Bonaventure Minor Sem 1954; BA Wisconsin Inst 1960; LLB La Salle Ext U Sch of Law 1966. D 2/14/2004 P 9/12/2004 Bp Bertram Nelson Herlong. m 10/26/1957 Penny Marek c 2. R S Matt's Epis Ch Mcminnville TN 2006-2008; Vic S Andr's Epis Ch New Johnsonville TN 2004-2006.

MARGERUM, Michael C (Nev) 11205 Carlsbad Rd, Reno NV 89506 B Seattle WA 1948 s Richard & Barbara. BS OR SU 1971; BS Golden Gate U 1973. D 12/7/1985 Bp William Benjamin Spofford. m 10/11/1975 Donna Painter. Hospice.

MARGRAVE, Thomas Edmund Clare (NY) 29 William St, Cortland NY 13045 **Cmdr Chapt 406 Mltry Ord of the Purple Heart 2014-; Par P S Ptr's Ch Bainbridge NY 2014-; Chapl City of Cortland NY Vol Fire Dept 2011-; Vol Responder Disaster Serv Amer Red Cross 2011-; Supply Off/Reg Dir New York St Assn of Fire Chapl 2011-; Reg Disaster Sprtl Care Advsr Wstrn and Cntrl New York Reg of the Amer Red Cros 2017-; Cortland Cnty Cmnty Vol Ldr Cntrl New York Chapt of the Amer Red Cross 2015-** B Washington DC 1945 s Oliver & Lella. BS USMA 1968; MA Syr 1973; DAS Ya Berk 1993; MDiv Yale DS 1993. D 8/21/1993 P 9/14/1994 Bp David Bruce Joslin. m 5/25/1975 Marianne Krieger c 3. Post Cmdr Tioughnioga VFW Post 2354 Cortland NY USA 2015-2017; Chapl Town of Cornwall NY PBA 2009-2011; Mem, Chapl Com New York St Assn of Fire Chiefs 2008-2011; Mem and Chair Cornwall Cares About Yth 2005-2011; Disaster Chapl Disaster Chapl Serv of New York 2004-2011; Chapl Highland Engine Co #1 Cornwall NY 2004-2011; R S Jn's Ch Cornwall NY 2004-2011; Bd Mem Cortland Cnty Coun of Ch 2000-2004; Bd Mem Cortland Loaves and Fishes 2000-2004; Chapl City of Cortland NY Vol Fire Dept 1999-2004; Bd Mem Cortland Cnty Coun of Ch 1999-2004; Bd Mem and Co-Pres Cortland Cnty Mntl Hlth Cmnty Needs Bd 1999-2004; R Gr Epis Ch Cortland NY 1999-2004, R Emer 2013-; Com Mem Untd Way of Chenango Cnty 1998-2011; Cluster Team Vic Emm Ch Norwich NY 1993-1999; Bd Mem Chenango Cnty HeadStart 1993-1995; Mem, Prog Com, Mid-Hudson Reg Dio New York New York NY 2005-2011, Mem, Bd and Com for Campus Mnstry 2004-2011, Mem, Exec Com, Mid-Hudson Reg 2004-2007; Mem, Bd for the Fndt of the Dio Dio Cntrl New York Liverpool NY 2003-2004, Mem, Campus Mnstry Com 2001-2004, Chair, Justice, Peace and Integrity of Creation Com 1999-2004, Curs Sec Lead Sprtl Advsr 1994-2001. Alb Inst 1993; Associated Parishes 1993-2005; Soc of Cath Priests, NA 2008. Disaster Preparedness and Response Serv Vol Awd Cortland Cnty Chapt of the Amer Red Cross 2013; Disaster Preparedness and Response Serv Vol Awd Cortland Cnty Chapt of the Amer Red Cross 2012; Rotarian of the Year Rotary Club of New Windsor Cornwall, NY 2011.

MARICONDA, Thomas Nicholas (Ct) 36 Main St, Newtown CT 06470 B 1952 s Salvatore & Mary Rose. BA Estrn Connecticut St U 1976. D 9/10/2011 Bp Laura Ahrens. m 11/18/2008 Walter M Dembowski.

MARIN, Carlos Heli (CFla) 438 Magpie Ct, Kissimmee FL 34759 **P H Faith Ch Saline MI 2006-; S Chris's Ch Orlando FL 2006-** B Calarca-Q-Colombia 1952 s Hernando & Belarmina. U Quindio Armenia-Colombia 1977; BA Dio Armenia Armenia-Colombia 1980; MDiv Asbury TS 2011. Rec 5/28/2005 Bp John Wadsworth Howe. m 10/18/1974 Esperanza Baquero c 3.

MARINCO, Judith Ann (Mich) 1434 E 13 Mile Rd, Madison Heights MI 48071 **D S Pat's Epis Ch Madison Hts MI 2010-** B Flint MI 1950 d Frank & Doris. AA Ferris St U 1972. D 11/6/2010 Bp Wendell Nathaniel Gibbs Jr. m 8/15/1970 Vincent Michael Marinco c 2.

MARINCO, Vincent Michael (Mich) 1434 E 13 Mile Rd, Madison Heights MI 48071 **Reverend D S Pat's Epis Ch Madison Hts MI 2010-** B Detroit MI 1948 s Vincent & Betty Jane. BS Ferris St U 1972. D 2/13/2010 P 11/6/2010 Bp Wendell Nathaniel Gibbs Jr. m 8/15/1970 Judith Ann Marinco c 2.

MARINO, Matthew A (Az) 114 W Roosevelt Street, Phoenix AZ 85003 **S Jn The Div Houston TX 2015-** B Phoeniz AZ 1964 s Marty & Dorothy. Fuller TS; BA Grand Canyon U 1987; MEd Arizona St U 2005; Cert in Urban Stds Fuller TS 2007; MDiv Phoenix Sem 2015. D 7/17/2011 Bp Kirk Stevan Smith. m 2/18/1989 Kari Marino c 2. Neely Grant Bd Dio Arizona Phoenix AZ 2011-2015, Cn for Yth/YA 2010-2014; P St Judes Epis Ch Phoenix AZ 2008-2015; Yth Off Prov VIII San Diego CA 2013-2015.

MARIS, Margo Elaine (Ore) 13201 Se Blackberry Cir, Portland OR 97236 **Non-par 1994-** B Portland OR 1942 d Earl & Clarice. BA Willamette U 1964; MA GW 1967; L&C 1967; MDiv CDSP 1978; Portland St U 1978. D 1/22/1978 Bp David Ritchie Thornberry P 1/1/1979 Bp Bob Gordon Jones. c 1. Dio Minnesota Minneapolis MN 1999-2003, Cn To Ordnry 1987-1994, 1981-1994; Int All SS Ch Portland OR 1995-1996; S Andr's Epis Ch Minneapolis MN 1985-1987; Int S Chris's Epis Ch S Paul MN 1985-1987; R H Trin Epis Ch Elk River MN 1980-1984; Chapl U Of Wyoming 1978-1980; Asst S Matt's Epis Cathd Laramie WY 1978-1979; Yth Alternatives 1970-1971; Dn Of Wmn Coll 1965-1968; Co-Chair On The Sexual Exploitation Com. Contrib, "Breach Of Trust:"; Auth, "Sexual Exploitation By Hlth Care Professionals & Cler 94"; Auth, "Healing The Wounds Of The Ch"; Auth, "Victim/Survivor".

MARKEVITCH, Diane Mary (Mil) 17 Dumont Cir, Madison WI 53711 B Green Bay WI 1947 d Joseph & Marquarite. BBA U of Wisconsin 1984; MDiv SWTS 1999; Cert Sprtl Direction 2006. D 4/24/1999 P 10/24/1999 Bp Roger John White. m 7/3/1971 Ronald G Markevitch c 1. R Trin Epis Ch Platteville WI 2006-2012; R H Cross Epis Ch Wisconsin Dells WI 1999-2006; Cur S Dun-st's Ch Madison WI 1999-2001.

MARKHAM, Eva Melba Roberts (Ky) 1604 Whippoorwill Rd., Louisville KY 40213 **D Resurr Ch Louisville KY 1997-** B Madisonville KY 1951 d Samuel & Mayme. BA U of Louisville 1969; MS U of Evansville 1980; EdD U of Louisville 2000. D 4/29/1989 Bp David Reed. m 6/1/1974 Kenneth Markham c 2. D Ch Of The Adv Louisville KY 2010-2011. ermark01@louisville.edu

MARKHAM, Ian (Va) 3737 Seminary Rd, Alexandria VA 22304 **Dn & Pres VTS Alexandria VA 2007-** B Crediton Devon UK 1962 s Stephen & Beryl. BD Lon GB 1985; MLitt U of Cambridge 1989; PhD U of Exeter 1995. D 6/9/2007 Bp Andrew Donnan Smith P 12/11/2007 Bp Peter J Lee. m 7/4/1987 Lesley P Markham c 1. Dn & Prof Hartford Sem 2001-2007. Auth, "Liturg Life Principles," Ch Pub, 2009; Ed, "A Wrld Rel Rdr - Third Ed," Wiley-Blackwell, 2009; Auth, "Understanding Chr Doctrine," Wiley-Blackwell, 2008; Auth, "Do Morals Matter," Wiley-Blackwell, 2007. Fell of King's Coll, London King's Coll, London U 2013; Hon DD VTS 2013.

MARKIE, Patrick Gregory (Minn) 770 Parkview Ave, Saint Paul MN 55117 B Saint Paul MN 1947 s Cecil & Florence. D 6/29/2006 Bp James Louis Jelinek. m 2/14/1975 Roxanna Markie c 1.

MARKLE, Ann (ETenn) 1076 Sparta Hwy, Crossville TN 38572 **Pensions Com Dio E Tennessee Knoxville TN 2008-** B Terre Haute IN 1952 d Richard & Mary. BS Indiana St U 1976; MS Indiana St U 1979; MS SUNY 1989; MDiv Ya Berk 1999; Cert Haden Inst 2007. D 6/26/1999 P 1/8/2000 Bp Michael Garrison. R S Raphael's Epis Ch Crossville TN 2002-2014; Asst Calv Epis Ch Williamsville NY 1999-2002. Auth, "Bldg a Labyrinth," *E Tennessee Epis*, 2009; Auth, "When Recon Is Impossible," *Bulletin of the Worker Sis/Brothers of the H Sprt*, 2004. Gvrng Bd (Interfaith) Ntwk Of Rel Communities 1999-2001. E Williams Muehl Prize In Preaching Berkley DS 1999.

MARKS, Chas (WMo) 2732 Benton Blvd, Kansas City MO 64128 **S Aug's Ch Kansas City MO 2017-; S Fran Cmnty Serv Inc. Salina KS 2017-; Sr Advsr for Cmnty & Ch Relatns The S Fran Fndt 2017-** B Newton KS 1972 s Larry & Judith. BA Wichita St U 1995; MA St Meinrad TS 1997; Cert in Priesthood Stds Bp Kemper Sch of Mnstry 2011. D 11/7/2014 P 5/16/2015 Bp Martin Scott Field. m 9/10/2008 Barry Nipp. S Mary's Epis Ch Kansas City MO 2015-2016. chas.marks@st-francis.org

MARKS, Patrica (Ga) 814 W Alden Ave, Valdosta GA 31602 B New York City 1943 d LeRoy & Mary. BA Douglass Coll 1965; PhD MI SU 1970. D 11/22/2003 Bp Henry Irving Louttit. m 11/30/1968 Dennis Marks. D Chr Ch Valdosta GA 2003-2004. "The 'Arry Ballads," McFarland Pub Co., 2006; "Sarah Bernhardt's First Amer Tour," McFarland Pub Co., 2003; "Bicycles, Bangs, and Bloomers: The New Wmn in the Popular Press," U Press of Kentucky, 1990; "The Smiling Muse: Victoriana in the Comic Press," Associated U Press-es, 1985; "Amer Literary and Drama Revs," G.K. Hall, 1984. No Amer Assoc. for the Diac 2003.

MARKS, Sharla J (FtW) 2431 St Gregory St, Arlington TX 76013 **UTA Campus Mnstry S Alb's Epis Ch Arlington TX 2011-, D 2009-** B Oklahoma City OK 1946 d Eugene & Virginia. BS Texas Womans U 1968; MUP Texas A&M U

1977; Lic Angl TS 2002. D 1/6/2001 Bp Jack Leo Iker. m 7/27/1967 Constant Roberts Marks c 2.

MARKS SR, William Parker (USC) 51 Otterside Ct, Middlebury VT 05753 B Tarboro NC 1930 s William & Margaret. BS E Carolina U 1955; MDiv VTS 1960. D 6/18/1960 Bp Richard Henry Baker P 12/20/1960 Bp Thomas Augustus Fraser Jr. m 9/23/2010 Deborah Gist Marks c 2. R S Mich's Epis Ch Easley SC 1991-2002; 1974-1991; All SS' Epis Ch Concord NC 1962-1974; P-in-c S Andrews Ch Durham NC 1960-1962. Auth, "The Golden Doorstop," Meadowbrook Pub, 1977.

MARLER, Malcolm Lewis (Ala) B Selma AL 1955 s Albert & Martha. BA Clemson U 1977; MDiv Sthrn Bapt TS 1980; DMin Sthrn Bapt TS 1988. D 5/21/2013 Bp Santosh K Marray P 1/15/2015 Bp John Mckee Sloan Sr. m 7/4/2004 Mary Bea Krohn.

MARLIN, John Henry (Okla) 1818 Coventry Lane, Oklahoma City OK 73120 **Vic Emer Casady Sch Oklahoma City OK 2008-, 1993-2008** B Muskogee OK 1939 s John & W Augusta. BA Oklahoma City U 1961; MDiv VTS 1966; MA GW 1967; MEd Marymount U 1987. D 6/25/1966 P 5/1/1967 Bp William Foreman Creighton. All Souls Epis Ch Oklahoma City OK 1993-2008; S Edw Chap Oklahoma City OK 1988-2001; R Meade Memi Epis Ch Alexandria VA 1972-1977; Chapl St Steph Sch Alexandria VA 1969-1988; Asst Min The Ch Of The Epiph Washington DC 1966-1969. Vic Emer Casady Sch 2008.

MARMON, Mark Mccarter (Tex) 10416 Highway 6, Hitchcock TX 77563 **Vic All SS Epis Ch Hitchcock TX 2013-** B San Antonio TX 1956 s Harvey & Jo. BS Texas Tech U 1980; MDiv Iona Sch for Mnstry 2013. D 6/15/2013 P 12/21/2013 Bp C Andrew Doyle. m 11/20/1999 Shelley B Marmon. markmarmon@gmail.com

MARONDE, James A (Los) **S Lk's Mssn Fontana CA 2011-; Dir St Lukes Outreach Cntr 2011-** B 1949 MDiv GTS 1978; PhD Wm Lyon U 1987. D 6/17/1978 P 1/20/1979 Bp Robert Claflin Rusack. m 7/18/2003 Denise Peters c 5. P-in-c S Nich Par Encino CA 2005-2010; S Steph's Epis Ch Valencia CA 2003-2004; R S Mart-In-The-Fields Par Winnetka CA 1985-1995; Assoc S Alb's Epis Ch Los Angeles CA 1978-1985. jamesmaronde@gmail.com

MARONEY III, Gordon Earle (Ark) PO Box 202, Smackover AR 71762 B 1948 s Gordon & Myrtle. BS Sthrn Arkansas U 1972; MEd Sthrn Arkansas U 1979. D 12/3/2004 P 7/15/2005 Bp Larry Maze. Tchr Camden Fairview HS Camden AR 1978-2012.

MARQUAND, Betty Harlina (Colo) 1521 Windsor Way Unit 8, Racine WI 53406 **Ret 1998-; D S Lk's Ch 1991-; Chapl S Lk's Hosp 1991-** B Oak Creek CO 1926 d Isaac & Flora. AA Colorado Womens Coll 1944; BA U CO 1946; MDiv Nash 1985. D 1/22/1985 Bp William Carl Frey. c 2. D All SS Ch Tybee Island GA 1988-1989; D S Matt's Ch Kenosha WI 1985-1987.

MARQUES, Barbara (Va) 7411 Moss Side Ave, Richmond VA 23227 **R S Jn's Ch W Point VA 2014-** B Chicago IL 1949 d Bernard & Elizabeth. MDiv Sewanee: The U So, TS 2007. D 6/16/2007 P 12/18/2007 Bp Peter J Lee. c 2. Chr Ch Glen Allen VA 2011-2014; Dio Virginia Richmond VA 2010-2011; Ptr Paul Dvlpmt Cntr Of The Epis Ch Richmond VA 2007-2012; S Ptr's Epis Ch Richmond VA 2007-2010; Probation Supvsr Henrico Jvnl Crt Dept Of Jvnl Justice 1998-2007.

MARQUESS, Judith Ann (Vt) 212 Woodhaven Dr # 5d, White River Junction VT 05001 **D S Paul's Epis Ch White Riv Jct VT 2002-** B Rockville Center NY 1937 d Douglas & Grace. BA CUNY 1958. D 9/21/2002 Bp David Bruce Joslin. c 2.

MARQUEZ, Juan I (DR) Calle Santiago 114, Gazcue, Santo Domingo Dominican Republic **Dio The Dominican Republic (Iglesia Epis Dominicana) Gazcue Santo Domingo 2009-, 1977-1981; Vic Gnrl Epis Ch In Dominican Republic 2009-** B San Pedro de Macoris Dom Republic 1947 s Rafael & Ana. BA Inst Advncd Stds DO 1971; MDiv ETSC 1976. D 5/1/1977 P 6/4/1978 Bp Telesforo A Isaac. m 6/15/2011 Carmen Luisa De Jesus Guaba c 3. Intl Partnership Off Epis Ch Cntr New York NY 2001-2008; Chr Epis Ch Ballston Spa NY 1994; S Jn's Ch Cohoes NY 1993; S Mary's Ch Lake Luzerne NY 1991-1992; Chapl NY St Dept of Correctional Serv 1989-2001; Cmnty Chapl NY St Dept of Correctional Serv 1987-1989; Dio New York New York NY 1986-1988; Mision San Juan Bautista Bronx NY 1986-1988; Vic San Juan Bautista New York NY 1986-1988; Vic Hisp Ministers Rochester NY 1982-1986; Dio Rochester Henrietta 1982-1985; Assoc Holyrood Ch New York NY 1981-1982; Vic S Gabr Macoris Dominican Republic 1977-1981.

MARQUIS JR, James F (ETenn) 2017 Kirby Rd, Memphis TN 38119 **Ret 1998-; Dep (Pheonix) GC- Epis Ch Cntr New York NY 1990-, Alt Dep (Detroit) 1968-1990** B New York NY 1930 s James & Thelma. Coll of Preachers Washington DC; BA Tusculum Coll 1951; MDiv Sewanee: The U So, TS 1972. D 6/25/1972 Bp William Evan Sanders P 7/21/1972 Bp John Vander Horst. m 2/23/1952 Emma Shipley c 3. Supply P S Matt's Ch Dayton TN 2004-2010; Chapl Dio E Tennessee Knoxville TN 1994-1995; R S Mart Of Tours Epis Ch Chattanooga TN 1984-1997; S Paul's Epis Ch Murfreesboro TN 1975-1984; Vic S Andr's Epis Ch New Johnsonville TN 1972-1975; Judge Eccl Trail Crt 1992-1997; Bp and Coun Dio E Tennessee 1990-1996; Chapl Middle Tenesse

St U 1975-1984. Who'S Who In Rel 1975; Outstanding Young Men Of Amer 1965.

MARR JR OSB, Andrew (Chi) 56500 Abbey Rd, Three Rivers MI 49093 **Abbot S Greg's Abbey Three Rivers MI 1972-; St Greg's Abbey Three Rivers MI 1972-** B Detroit MI 1947 s Robert & Dorothy. BA Kalamazoo Coll 1969; Untd TS of the Twin Cities 1970; MDiv Nash 1972. D 5/24/1988 P 11/29/1988 Bp Frank Tracy Griswold III. Auth, "The Forest of Windwllynn," St. Greg's Abbey Press, 2014; Auth, "From Beyond to Here: Merendael's Gift and Other Stories," iUniverse, 2012; Auth, "Creatures We Dream of Knowing: Stories of Our Life Together," iUniverse, 2011; Auth, "Tools for Peace," iUniverse, 2007; Auth, "b in the Darkest Time of Year," iUniverse, 2004.

MARR, Jon Aidan (RG) 906-B Old Las Vegas Hwy, Santa Fe NM 87505 **Ret 1994-** B Denver CO 1933 s John & Helen. BA U CO 1956; BD Nash 1959; Urban Trng Cntr 1968; Coll of Preachers 1972. D 6/29/1959 P 2/2/1960 Bp Joseph Summerville Minnis. R & Abbot S Andr's Ch Denver CO 1969-1984; Vic S Barth's Ch Estes Pk CO 1959-1968. "Men Athirst For God," Familian/OHF, 1984. OHF.

MARRAN, Pauline Matte (NY) 80 Lyme Rd Apt 219, Hanover NH 03755 **Died 11/23/2016** B Detroit MI 1923 d Joseph & Beulah. Cert Detroit Commercial Coll Detroit MI 1943; Cert Fndt for Admin Reearch 1962; EFM Sewanee: The U So, TS 1994. D 5/30/1992 Bp Richard Frank Grein. m 9/13/1981 Robert John Marran. Epis Hosp Chapl Bd Mem Dartmouth Hitchcock Med Ctr Lebanon NH 2000-2011; D S Thos Ch Hanover NH 2000-2007; D Ch Of The Gd Shpd Granite Spgs NY 1992-2000. Assn for Epis Deacons 1992.

✠ MARRAY, The Rt Rev Dr Santosh K (Ala) The Diocese of Easton, 314 North St, Easton MD 21601 **Bp Dio Easton Easton MD 2016-; Mem Stndg Cmsn on Cmncatn and Tech 2013-; Mem, Stndg Cmsn on Cmncatn & Info Tech Dom And Frgn Mssy Soc- Epis Ch Cntr New York NY 2013-** B Corentyne, Guyana 1957 s Gurdat & Chanderwati. Dplma Codrington Coll 1981; BA U of the W Indies, Barbados 1981; DMin Bex Sem 2002; LLM U of Wales, Cardiff, UK 2006; Mstr of Law U of Wales, Cardiff, Wales, UK 2006; STM GTS 2009. Trans 9/10/2003 Bp Stephen Hays Jecko. m 9/10/1977 Nalini V Marray c 2. Asst Bp of Alabama Dio Alabama Birmingham 2012-2016; Asst Bp of E Carolina Dio E Carolina Kinston NC 2009-2012; Bp Dio Seychelles Indn Ocean 2005-2008; R S Phil's Epis Ch Jacksonville FL 2003-2005; Mem Archbp of Cbury Pstr Visitors 2009-2012; Mem Angl Comm Cov Design Grp 2006-2009. Auth, "Chr Outreach and Advocacy in Sm Congregations," *Crosscurrent Article*, Dio E Carolina, 2010; Auth, "Chr Outreach and Advocacy in Sm Cong," *Crosscurrent Article*, Dio E Carolina, 2010; Auth, "Sprtlty of the Par P Based on Acts 2:37-47," *Dissertation for STM Sprtlty*, GTS, 2009; Auth, "Sprtlty of the Par P," *Dissertation: STM Chr Sprtlty*, GTS, NY, 2009; Auth, "Sprtlty in Cn Law," *Dissertation for LLM Cn Law*, U of Wales, UK, 2006; Auth, "Sprtlty in Angl Cn Law," *Dissertation: LLM Cn Law*, U of Wales, Cardiff, UK, 2006; Auth, "Lay Trng & Sprtl Formation for Ldrshp and Mnstry," *Dissertation: DMin*, CRDS/Bex, 2002. DD Bex Sem 2008; Thos Philips Memi - excellence in Liturg Ya Berk 2001. bishop@dioceseofeaston.org

MARRERO CAMACHO, Luis Fernando (PR) B 1923 D 10/26/1986 P 12/20/1987 Bp Telesforo A Isaac. m 7/17/1962 Marian Bocanegra.

MARRONE, Michael J (Mass) 410 Washington St, Duxbury MA 02332 B New York NY 1943 s Dominick & Catherine. BA Pace U; MDiv EDS 1974. D 6/8/1974 Bp Paul Moore Jr P 5/1/1975 Bp Frederick Barton Wolf. m 8/1/1970 Catherine Ann Marrone. R Ch Of S Jn The Evang Duxbury MA 1987-2005; Renwl & Evang Com Dio Massachusetts Boston MA 1987-1988; Chair - Ctte Admission Of Parishes & Missions 1985-1986, Liturg Cmsn 1984-1987; R S Mk's Ch Westford MA 1977-1987; Chr Ch Gardiner ME 1974-1977.

MARSDEN, Richard Conlon (SwFla) 222 S Palm Ave, Sarasota FL 34236 B Bridgeport CT 1952 s Richard & Eileen. BA Norwich U 1974; MRE Gordon-Conwell TS 1986; MDiv TESM 1990. D 9/7/1990 Bp Rogers Sanders Harris P 4/24/1991 Bp Edward Harding MacBurney. m 12/27/1975 Gail E Marsden. Asst Ch Of The Redeem Sarasota FL 1996-2006, Assoc R 1996-; Asst Chr Ch Bradenton FL 1990-1996.

MARSH, Abigail (Colo) 6931 E Girard Ave, Denver CO 80224 B Denver CO 1947 d Mordecai & Helene. AA Monticello Coll Godfrey IL 1967; BA U Denv 1969; Cert Colorado D Sch Denver CO 2001. D 11/10/2001 Bp William Jerry Winterrowd. D S Thos Epis Ch Denver CO 2002-2013.

MARSH, Caryl Ann (U) 829 E 400 S Apt 110, Salt Lake City UT 84102 **Bd First VPres Girl Scouts of Utah 2004-** B Bromley Kent UK 1938 d Godfrey & Irene. Inst of Bankers London 1958; BA San Jose St U 1974; MDiv CDSP 1977. D 6/25/1977 Bp Chauncie Kilmer Myers P 6/25/1978 Bp John Raymond Wyatt. R S Paul's Ch Salt Lake City UT 1989-2004; Dir Of Chr Growth & Dvlpmt Dio Spokane Spokane WA 1985-1989, Prov YA Prog Co-ordntr 1984-1989, HDep St of the Ch Cmttee 1985-1991, Dep, Gen Conv 1982-1989; Vic S Paul's Ch Cheney WA 1980-1985; S Tim Med Lake WA 1980-1985; P-in-c All SS Ch Richland WA 1979-1980, Assoc 1977-1980; Pres. Stndg Com Dio Utah Salt Lake City UT 2002-2004, HDep Nom Cmttee Pres Bp 1994-1997, Dep, Gen Conv 1991-1997, Pres. HDep Coun of Advice

1991-1997; Bd Trst CDSP Berkeley CA 2000-2013; Bd Legal Aid Soc 1992-1998; Bd Untd Way 1991-1997.

MARSH IV, Charles Wallace (At) St. James' Episc Church, 161 Church St. N.E., Marietta GA 30060 **Cathd Of S Phil Atlanta GA 2011-** B Nashville TN 1978 s Charles & Jean. BA U So 2001; MDiv Ya Berk 2007. D 2/3/2007 P 8/11/2007 Bp Henry Irving Louttit. m 5/29/2010 Margaret Ann Marsh. S Jas Epis Ch Marietta GA 2009-2011; Assoc R S Paul's Ch Albany GA 2007-2009; Lay Chapl U So 2001-2004.

MARSH, Elizabeth (Mass) 368 Kings Hwy W, 358 Farwood Rd, Haddonfield NJ 08033 B New York NY 1948 d James & Elizabeth. BA U of New Hampshire 1973; MDiv Andover Newton TS 1981. D 6/29/1981 P 10/23/1982 Bp Frederick Barton Wolf. m 11/24/1979 Michael Joseph Feicht. Vic S Dav's Epis Ch Halifax MA 1984-1990; Int S Paul's Epis Ch Hopkinton MA 1983-1984.

MARSH, Gayle Mardene (Minn) 1644 Cohansey St, Saint Paul MN 55117 **P-in-c All SS Ch Northfield MN 2006-** B Grove City PA 1957 d Dean & Margaret. ADN New Mex St U 1977; BSN New Mex St U 1985; MDiv Fuller TS 1988; CAS VTS 1989; Cert Christos Cntr for Sprtl Direction 2004. D 8/2/1989 P 8/22/1990 Bp Terence Kelshaw. m 4/23/2012 Robyn Schmidt. Ch Of The H Cross Dundas MN 2008-2009; Dio Minnesota Minneapolis MN 2007-2010, 1998; Sr Assoc S Chris's Epis Ch S Paul MN 1998-2006; P-in-c Shpd Of The Prairie Eden Prairie MN 1993-1998; R H Trin Epis Ch Elk River MN 1991-1993; S Brendan's Ch El Paso TX 1989-1991.

MARSH, Karl Edwin (Neb) 1873 S Cherry Blossom Ln, Suttons Bay MI 49682 **Lic Profsnl Counslr St of Michigan 2000-; Ret 1998-** B Battle Creek MI 1934 s William & Mildred. BA U MI 1956; MDiv SWTS 1959; MA Ball St U 1974. D 6/20/1959 Bp Benjamin M Washburn P 12/23/1959 Bp Francis W Lickfield. m 1/17/1959 Barbara L Marsh. S Mk's Epis Pro-Cathd Hastings NE 1976-1998; Assoc Psychol Hastings Reg Cntr Hastings NE 1975-1998; R S Jas Ch Piqua OH 1967-1974; Vic S Steph's Epis Ch Hobart IN 1964-1967; Vic S Mich's Ch Noblesville IN 1961-1964; Cur Gr Ch Grand Rapids MI 1959-1961. Auth, *Instructed Euch*, Little Farms Pub, 1974; Auth, *Our Whole Being*, Little Farms Pub, 1974. Natl Certied Counslr Natl Bd Cert Counselors; Cert Clincl Mntl Hlth Counslr Natl Bd Cert Counselors.

MARSH, Keith A (Pa) Church of the Messiah, PO Box 127, Gwynedd PA 19436 **R Ch Of The Mssh Lower Gwynedd PA 2005-** B Camp Atterbury IN 1952 s Charles & Renee. BS Indiana U 1974; MDiv VTS 1991. D 6/22/1991 P 3/21/1992 Bp George Nelson Hunt III. m 10/9/1982 Deborah A Marsh c 3. Dn Chr Ch Cathd Louisville KY 1996-2005; S Matt's Epis Ch Louisville KY 1991-1996.

MARSH, Mike (WTex) 343 N. Getty, Uvalde TX 78801 **R S Phil's Ch Uvalde TX 2005-; Discernment Com, Mem Dio W Texas San Antonio TX 2008-, Exam Chapl, Mem 2006-** B Killeen TX 1960 s Byron & Janice. BS U of Texas at El Paso 1982; JD Texas Tech U 1985; MDiv Sewanee: The U So, TS 2003; DMin Pittsburgh TS 2012. D 6/12/2003 Bp Robert Boyd Hibbs P 1/6/2004 Bp James Edward Folts. m 9/1/1995 Cynthia Ann Beaver c 2. Adj Fac Epis TS Of The SW Austin TX 2014, 2013; Asst R S Ptr's Epis Ch Kerrville TX 2003-2005. marshmk@stphilipsuvalde.org

MARSH JR, Robert Francis (Fla) 2462 C H Arnold Rd, Saint Augustine FL 32092 B Jacksonville FL 1945 s Robert & Thelma. BBA Georgia St U 1976; MDiv Sewanee: The U So, TS 1982. D 6/13/1982 P 12/18/1982 Bp Frank S Cerveny. m 7/25/1968 Diane Marsh c 3. P-in-c S Mk's Ch Palatka FL 2014-2002, 2014-, R 1992-2002; P-in-c Ch Of The Recon S Aug FL 2006-2007; Chapl Jacksonville Epis HS Jacksonville FL 2002-2011; Reg Cn Dio Florida - River Reg 1997-2002; R Dio Flordia - St Jn's River Cluster Mnstry 1995-2000; P-iu-Charge St Marys Epis Ch Palatka FL 1992-2002; S Cathr's Ch Jacksonville FL 1991-1992; Int S Jn's Cathd Jacksonville FL 1991; Dio Florida Jacksonville 1989-1990, River Reg Cn 1997-2002; R S Jas Epis Ch Perry FL 1986-1989; Asst S Ptr's Ch Jacksonville FL 1984-1986; Asst H Comf Epis Ch Tallahassee FL 1982-1984. Ed, "Rel Fiction," *Jeshua*, 1989. GC Cler 4 Dio Florida 2006; Pres Stndg Com 2004; GC Cler 3 Dio Florida 2003; GC Cler 4 Dio Florida 2000; Pres Conlee Hse Batterd Wmn Shltr Bd 1999; Chair Div Of Yth Mnstrs 1990; Chair Substance Abuse Com 1982.

MARSHALL, Carol Phillips (USC) Christ Episcopal Church, PO Box 488, Lancaster SC 29721 **Ch Of The Ascen Seneca SC 2009-** B Orangeburg SC 1950 d Ernest & Carolyn. Erskine Coll; BA U of So Carolina 1972; MDiv Sewanee: The U So, TS 1999. D 6/12/1999 P 10/4/2006 Bp Dorsey Henderson. m 6/2/2007 Donald Bruce Marshall c 2. Chr Epis Ch Lancaster SC 2006-2009; D St Alb's Epis Ch 2003-2006.

MARSHALL, David Allen (Oly) P.O. Box 33029, Seattle WA 98133 **S Dunst-The Highlands Shoreline WA 2009-; R S Dunst's Ch w the Henry Memi Chap Seattle WA 2009-** B San Francisco CA 1961 BS California St U 1985; MA VTS 2003. D 6/28/2003 P 1/17/2004 Bp Vincent Waydell Warner. m 6/18/1983 Alice Joan Marshall c 3. Gd Samar Epis Ch Sammamish WA 2006-2008; Asst S Steph's Epis Ch Seattle WA 2003-2006.

MARSHALL, David J (SanD) Grace Episcopal Church, 1020 Rose Ranch Road, San Marcos CA 92069 **S Jn's Epis Ch Chula Vista CA 2012-** B Tacoma WA 1969 s John & Nancy. BA S Martins U 1991; MDiv CDSP 2007. D 6/9/2007 P

6/7/2008 Bp James E Waggoner Jr. m 5/21/1995 Christina R Marshall c 4. R Gr Epis Ch Of The Vlly Mssn San Marcos CA 2008-2012; Cur S Lk's Ch Coeur D Alene ID 2007-2008.

MARSHALL III, Elliott Wallace (Chi) 710 Crab Tree Lane, Bartlett IL 60103 B Salisbury MD 1943 s Elliott & Winifred. BA Randolph-Macon Coll 1965; MDiv Epis TS in Kentucky 1971; Sewanee: The U So, TS 1977; Cantess Cbury GB 1978; Coll of Preachers 1985; S Georges Coll Jerusalem IL 1992. D 5/29/1971 P 12/19/1971 Bp Addison Hosea. m 10/8/2011 Pu Nam c 3. R Ch Of The Incarn Bloomingdale IL 1997-2003; R Trin Ch Elkton MD 1990-1995; R S Fran Ch Denham Spgs LA 1982-1989; Chr Epis Ch Eastville VA 1977-1982; R Emm Ch Cape Chas VA 1977-1982; Hungars Par Machipongo VA 1977-1982; R Chr Epis Ch Buena Vista VA 1975-1977; Asst R Chr Epis Ch Charlottesvlle VA 1972-1974; Vic Adv Ch Cynthiana KY 1971-1972; Dioc Coun of Easton Dio Easton Easton MD 1993-1996; Chair of Liturg Cmsn Dio Louisiana New Orleans LA 1984-1988, Dn, Baton Rouge Dnry 1983-1989; Dn, Estrn Shore Convoc Dio Sthrn Virginia Newport News VA 1977-1982.

MARSHALL III, Howard R (NJ) 6313 Wyndam Rd, Pennsauken NJ 08109 **Died 6/13/2017** B Camden NJ 1948 s Howard & Jeanette. BA Glassboro St U 1981; MDiv Nash 1984. D 6/2/1984 Bp George Phelps Mellick Belshaw P 12/1/1984 Bp Vincent King Pettit. m 2/22/1969 Christina R Green. Non-par 1987-2017; Trin Ch Moorestown NJ 1984-1985.

MARSHALL, John Anthony (WNY) 7145 Fieldcrest Dr, Lockport NY 14094 **P-in-c S Mich And All Ang Buffalo NY 2009-; Dn Niagara Dnry Dio Wstrn New York NY 2005-; Chair, Hlth Care Mnstrs Dio Wstrn New York Tonawanda NY 2004-** B Buffalo NY 1953 s Clyde & Jean. BA Wadhams Hall Sem Coll 1976; MDiv Chr the King Sem 1980. Rec 6/1/1997 as Priest Bp Paul Victor Marshall. m 6/25/1994 Mary Rita Marshall c 4. R Chr Ch Lockport NY 1999-2009; R The Epis Ch Of S Clem And S Ptr Wilkes Barre PA 1997-1999. ACPE 1993-1999; Coll of Chapl 1993-1999; Natl Coll of Cath Chapl 1990-1993.

MARSHALL, John Harris (NwT) **D The Epis Ch Of S Mary The Vrgn Big Sprg TX 2002-** B 1946 D 10/27/2002 Bp C Wallis Ohl.

MARSHALL, Lewis Edwin (NY) 176 Dean St, Brooklyn NY 11217 **All SS Ch Staten Island NY 2009-** B Nashville AR 1957 s Emmett & Nina. BA S Jos Sem Coll 1979; MDiv GTS 1992. D 6/13/1992 Bp James Barrow Brown P 12/1/1992 Bp Orris George Walker Jr. m 6/5/2008 Alan William Balicki. S Ann And The H Trin Brooklyn NY 1993-1995; Asst S Ann & H Trin 1992-1995.

MARSHALL, McAlister Crutchfield (Va) 2316 E Grace St # 8011, Richmond VA 23223 B Cleveland OH 1929 s McAlister & Isabel. BA U of Virginia 1954; BD Bex Sem 1957; STM Sewanee: The U So, TS 1971; DMin Van 1979. D 6/10/1957 Bp Frederick D Goodwin P 5/31/1958 Bp Robert Fisher Gibson Jr. m 11/26/1951 Doris Marshall c 2. P-in-c S Asaph's Par Ch Bowling Green VA 1992-2001; Assoc Emm Ch At Brook Hill Richmond VA 1991-2002, 1979; S Jn's Ch Richmond VA 1986-1990; Imm Ch Mechanicsvlle VA 1984-1985; Dn Dio Virginia Richmond VA 1978-1979, Chair 1972-1977; Chf Chapl Prince Wm Hosp Manassas VA 1969-1979; R Trin Ch Manassas VA 1967-1978; R Ch Of S Jas The Less Ashland VA 1960-1967; All SS Ch Richmond VA 1957-1960; Ch Of The H Comf Richmond VA 1957-1960. Auth, "Hymns," *Hymn Soc of Amer*.

✠ MARSHALL, The Rt Rev Paul Victor (Be) 2234 Overlook Ln, Fogelsville PA 18051 B New York NY 1947 s Victor & Frances. BA Concordia Coll 1969; MDiv Concordia Sem S Louis 1973; ThD GTS 1982; DCnL Epis Sem Lexington 1999. D 2/4/1978 P 6/10/1978 Bp William Hampton Brady Con 6/29/1996 for Be. m 5/31/1969 Diana S Hilty c 2. Bp Of Bethlehem Dio Bethlehem Bethlehem PA 1996-2013; Ch Of S Jas The Apos New Haven CT 1991-1993; Assoc Prof Ya Berk New Haven CT 1989-1996; Prof Liturg & Homil Mercer TS Garden City NY 1986-1988; Trst Epis Fndt For Educ 1984-1988; Assoc Prof Liturg & Homil Mercer TS Garden City NY 1984-1986; R Chr Ch Babylon NY 1982-1989; Asst Trin LI City NY 1979-1982; Chapl US-Army 1972-1980; Serv Luth Ch 1972-1977; Cmsn On Life & Human Hlth Dio Long Island Garden City NY 1986-1988. Auth, "Messages in the Mall," CPG; Auth, "One, Cath and Apostolic," CPG; Auth, "Same-Sex Blessisng: Stories & Rltes," CPG; Auth, "The Bp is Coming," CPG; Auth, "Angl Liturg In Amer," CPG; Auth, "The Voice Of A Stranger," CPG; Auth, "Preaching For The Ch Today," CPG. Amer Psychoanalytic Assn 2007; No Amer Acad Of Liturg 1982; Societas Liturgica 1979. Jn D. Verdery Awd NAES 2004; DD GTS 1996.

MARSHALL, Richard G (Ala) 6944 Cypress Spring Ct, Saint Augustine FL 32086 **Ret 1991-** B Detroit MI 1928 s Richard & Hazel. BS Lawr Tech U 1961; MDiv Epis TS of the SW 1981. D 6/12/1981 P 12/15/1981 Bp Furman Charles Stough. m 8/1/2009 Gloria Elaine Johnson c 5. Int S Steph's Epis Ch Huntsville AL 1998-1999; P-in-c H Cross-St Chris's Huntsville AL 1994-1998; R S Andr's Epis Ch Sylacauga AL 1981-1990. Auth, "My Journey w Jesus and Jo," *My Journey w Jesus and Jo and Poems by Jo*, Brushpanther Press/lulu.com, 2008; Auth, "Pryr: The Begining Of The Journey," *The Cross*, BroSA, 1981.

MARSHALL, Robert (RI) 191 County Rd, Barrington RI 02806 **R S Jn's Ch Barrington RI 2010-** B Wilson, NC 1969 s Thomas & Elizabeth. BS Barton

544

Coll 1992; MDiv VTS 2006. D 6/3/2006 P 12/9/2006 Bp Michael B Curry. m 11/5/2012 Tatiana M Marshall c 1. Asst S Jn's Ch Lynchburg VA 2006-2010.

MARSHALL JR, William Shattuck (Be) 12 Holiday Ct, Kingston PA 18704 **Asst S Steph's Epis Ch Wilkes Barre PA 2010-; R The Epis Ch of S Clem and S Ptr Wilkes 2004-** B New York NY 1942 s William & Marjorie. BS SUNY 1965; MEd U Pgh 1968; MS Adams St Coll 1987; Cert Mercer TS 1989. D 6/17/1989 Bp Orris George Walker Jr P 6/24/2000 Bp Paul Victor Marshall. m 5/5/1968 Madelinediv Barbara Pascarella c 2. The Epis Ch Of S Clem And S Ptr Wilkes Barre PA 2002-2010; Chair Dioc Recovery Cmsn Dio Bethlehem Bethlehem PA 2000-2006, 2000-2002, Asst 1999-2000, Ds Advsry Com 1991-1995, COM 1989-1995; Vic S Nichol Womeldorf PA 2000-2002; S Jn's Epis Ch Palmerton PA 1999-2000; Pres NECAD 1995-1998; D Chr Oyster Bay NY 1993-1998; D Epis Ch of Gr and Resurr E Elmhurst NY 1991-1993; Ch Of Chr The King E Meadow NY 1989-1991; Chair Bps Com Dio Long Island Garden City NY 1985-1998. Auth, *Recovery is More than Words*, 1993; "Mir: The Magic of Medjugorje," *The Deakones*, 1990. NASW 1981; NAAD 1989-2000; Recovery Mnstrs of the Epis Ch 1983.

MARSTON, Robert Dandridge (SVa) 128 Prince St Unit 47, Tappahannock VA 22560 B Washington DC 1952 s Robert & Ann. BA U of Virginia 1975; MDiv VTS 1979; DMin Sewanee: The U So, TS 1988. D 6/23/1979 Bp Robert Bruce Hall P 5/1/1980 Bp David Henry Lewis Jr. m 8/19/1978 Maria B Marston c 2. R S Andr's Epis Ch Newport News VA 1993-2014; Pres Orange Cnty Mnstrl Assn VA 1988-1989; VTS Alexandria VA 1986-1987; R S Thos Epis Ch Orange VA 1985-1993; P-in-c 1984-1985; EFM Mentor 1983-1985; S Fran Ch Greensboro NC 1982-1985; Bd Chapl Serv Ch Of Va VA 1981-1982; Pres Culpeper Mnstrl Assn VA 1981-1982; Secy Of Reg I In Va 1980-1982; Asst Little Fork Epis Ch Rixeyville VA 1979-1982; Asst S Steph's Epis Ch Culpeper VA 1979-1982; Supvsr Of Field Wk Dio Virginia Richmond VA 1986-1989, Mssnr 1980-1985. Auth, "Experiencing The Presence Of God During Times Of Need: A Case Study". Bro Of S Andr OHC. Outstanding Young Men Amer 1986; Who'S Who Young Amer 90.

MARTA, Dale Charles (Mo) 112 N Ray Ave, Maryville MO 64468 B Rochester PA 1956 s Thomas & Martha. BA Penn 1978; MDiv VTS 1982. D 6/5/1982 Bp Albert Wiencke Van Duzer P 6/1/1983 Bp Charles Farmer Duvall. m 8/23/1980 Janet Kay Marta c 3. Off Of Bsh For ArmdF New York NY 1995-1999; R S Mart's By The Lake Epis Minnetonka Bch MN 1990-1995; R Ch Of The Gd Shpd Pitman NJ 1987-1990; Trin By The Cove Naples FL 1983-1987; Chr Epis Ch Pensacola FL 1982-1983.

MARTENS, Ann F (Va) 3050 N Military Rd, Arlington VA 22207 B Roanoke VA 1953 BA U Rich; MA Webster U; MDiv VTS 2005. D 6/18/2005 Bp Peter J Lee P 12/21/2005 Bp David Colin Jones. Asst R S Ptr's Epis Ch Arlington VA 2006-2016; Asst Trin Ch Arlington VA 2005-2006.

MARTIN, Alexander David (SO) St Timothy's Episcopal Church, 8101 Beechmont Ave, Cincinnati OH 45255 **Assoc S Tim's Epis Ch Cincinnati OH 2013-** B Ashtabula OH 1986 s Gerald & Cheryl. BA The OH SU 2009; MDiv GTS 2013. D 6/29/2013 P 6/14/2014 Bp Thomas Edward Breidenthal. m 12/7/2011 Robert J Hoon. alexm@sainttimothys.com

MARTIN, Alison Jane (WNY) PO Box 234, Youngstown NY 14174 B Buffalo NY 1953 d John & Helen. Dplma Buffalo Gnrl Hosp Sch of Nrsng 1980; BS SUNY 1991; MDiv Bex Sem 1994. D 6/11/1994 P 12/17/1994 Bp David Charles Bowman. c 1. S Paul's Epis Ch Lewiston NY 2015-2016; St Johns Epis Youngstown NY 2014-2017; P-in-c S Pat's Ch Buffalo NY 2011-2014; Vic S Aid's Ch Alden NY 2009-2010; Chapl Hospice Buffalo 2004-2014; R Trin Ch Lancaster NY 1999-2003; Dio Wstrn New York Tonawanda NY 1995-1998; R S Jn's Ch Wilson NY 1994-1999.

MARTIN, Andrea Brooke (WA) 163 Oak Street, Hillsdale MI 49242 **H Faith Ch Saline MI 2017-; Asst R Chr & H Trin Ch Westport CT 2004-** B Kincheloe AFB MI 1975 d Randall & Cassandra. BA U of Notre Dame 1998; MDiv Ya Berk 2002. D 6/7/2003 P 6/5/2004 Bp M(Arvil) Thomas Shaw. m 1/8/2005 Christopher Scott Martin c 1. Assoc R S Pat's Ch Washington DC 2008-2013; Chr And H Trin Ch Westport CT 2004-2007; Chr Ch Alexandria VA 2003-2004; Cler Res Chr Ch Alexandria VA 2002-2004. andreamartin975@gmail.com

MARTIN, Barbara Jane (SwFla) 230 Dent Dr, Naples FL 34112 **Died 1/1/2017** B Mount Vernon NY 1926 d George & Bessie. D 6/13/1998 Bp John Bailey Lipscomb. c 5. Seas.D Angl Ch of St. Jas Port-Au-Port Can 2005-2017; D Ch of the Epiph 2004-2005; D Resurr Epis Ch Naples FL 1999-2017; Chapl Naples Cmnty Hosp 1998-2002; D S Paul's Ch Naples FL 1998-1999.

MARTIN, Chad Travis (Tex) 4900 Jackwood St, Houston TX 77096 **S Mart's Epis Ch Houston TX 2013-** B Springfield MO 1976 s Howard & Carolyn. BMus U of Mary Hardin-Baylor 1999; MM SW Missouri St 2001; MDiv VTS 2009. D 6/20/2009 Bp C Andrew Doyle P 1/8/2010 Bp Rayford Baines High Jr. m 6/2/2007 Cinnamon Martin c 1. Dir of Fam Mnstrs S Thos Ch Houston TX 2009-2013.

MARTIN, Charles Percy (Pgh) 220 Columbia St, Johnstown PA 15905 **Ret 1996-** B Detroit MI 1930 s Percy & Mildred. BA U Pgh 1952; BD Bex Sem 1955. D 6/25/1955 Bp William S Thomas P 12/17/1955 Bp Austin Pardue. R S Mk's Ch Johnstown PA 1978-1995; R All SS Epis Ch Verona PA 1962-1978; R Emm Ch Pittsburgh PA 1961-1962; Secy Of Conv Dio Pittsburgh Pittsburgh PA 1960-1995.

MARTIN, Christopher (Cal) 1123 Court St, San Rafael CA 94901 **R S Paul's Epis Ch San Rafael CA 2004-** B Wilmington DE 1968 s Peter & Victoria. BA Ya 1990; MDiv Ya Berk 1996. D 6/22/1996 Bp Vincent Waydell Warner P 2/1/1997 Bp Andrew Donnan Smith. m 11/9/2009 Chloe A D Martin c 2. Assoc R All SS Par Beverly Hills CA 1999-2004; Asst Chr Ch Cathd Hartford CT 1997-1999. Auth, "The Restoration Proj," Forw Mvmt, 2013; *Gathering the NeXt Generation*, Morehouse, 2000. Soc of S Jn the Evang 1995.

MARTIN, Christopher S (Fla) PO Box 330500, Atlantic Beach FL 32233 **P Assoc All SS Epis Ch Jacksonville FL 2015-, Int Asst 2013, P-in-c 2013** B Decatur IL 1942 s Percy & Barbara. BA Concordia Sr Coll 1964; MDiv Concordia TS 1968; MA Webster U 1970. D 6/10/1984 P 1/6/1985 Bp Frank S Cerveny. m 1/18/1992 Sandra L Langston c 2. Dio Florida Jacksonville 1985-1991, Dep - 2009 GC 2008-2011; R S Mary's Epis Ch Green Cv Spg FL 1984-2007.

MARTIN, Clyde Albert (SO) 1600 N Breiel Blvd, Middletown OH 45042 B Painesville OH 1933 s Walter & Lydia. OH SU; Diac Sch Dio Sthrn Ohio 1994. D 11/11/1994 Bp Herbert Thompson Jr. m 6/14/1955 Mary Carolyn Martin c 2. D The Epis Ch Of The Ascen Middletown OH 1994-2007.

MARTIN, Derrick Antonio (SeFla) 17 Fernhill Ave, Buffalo NY 14215 **Dn - Schuylkill Dnry 1992-** B 1944 s Solomon & Madlyn. Untd Theol Coll of The W Indies Kingston Jm 1971; Lic U of The W Indies 1971; BA U of The W Indies 1975; STM GTS 1980; DMin Estrn Bapt TS 1996. D 6/1/1971 P 7/1/1972 Bp The Bishop Of Jamaica. m 2/14/2009 Jean Alexander-Martin c 2. S Kevin's Epis Ch Opa Locka FL 2003-2005; St. Monica's Angl Ch 2002-2003; Angl Dio the Bahamas and the Turks and Caicos Islands Nassau 2001; S Phil's Ch Buffalo NY 1998-2000; R Calv St Aug Epis Ch Philadelphia PA 1986-1998; Serv Ch Of Bahamas 1982-1986; Serv Ch Of Jamaica 1971-1982. Bro Of S Andr.

MARTIN, Donald Graham (WK) 1715 W 5th St, Colby KS 67701 **P-in-c S Paul's Epis Ch Goodland KS 2011-, D 1986-2011; P-in-c S Fran Epis Ch Russell Sprg KS 1995-; S Lk's Epis Ch Scott City KS 1995-; Vic Ascen-On-The-Prairie Epis Ch Colby KS 1991-** B Saint Louis MO 1946 s William & Winifred. BA Trin 1968; Chicago TS 1973. D 12/19/1986 P 7/22/1992 Bp John Forsythe Ashby. m 4/6/1991 Evelyn Irene Martin c 4. Coun Mem Dio Wstrn Kansas Hutchinson KS 2010-2015, Dioc Coun 2010-, Cmsn on the Mnstry 2009-2011, Stndg Com 2002-2009, Dioc Coun 1996-2001; Bd Mem Heartland Rural Counslg Serv Colby KS 2001-2015. Phi Beta Kappa 1968.

MARTIN JR, Ed (NJ) 1281 Venezia Ave, Vineland NJ 08361 B Wilmington DE 1942 s Edward & Margaret. BA Widener U 1964; MDiv VTS 1971; MA Webster U 1977; DMin VTS 1987. D 6/10/1971 P 1/15/1972 Bp William Henry Mead. m 5/29/1965 Christianna R Martin c 3. Chapl: Morgue Amer Red Cross Wrld Trade Cntr & St. Paul's Chap 2001-2002; Search Consult Dio New Jersey 1996-2011; R S Andr's Epis Ch Bridgeton NJ 1994-2003; Chapl FDU-Rutherford Campus 1982-1994; R Gr Epis Ch Rutherford NJ 1982-1994; R S Barth's Epis Ch Ho Ho Kus NJ 1977-1982; Chapl Off Of Bsh For ArmdF New York NY 1975-1977; Chapl (Capt) U.S. Army Ft Leonard Wood MO 1975-1977; Dio Delaware Wilmington 1971-1975; Pres,De Epis Cler Assn S Jn The Bapt Epis Ch Milton DE 1971-1975. Contrib, "Sprtl Healing," *Psychol Today*, 1989; Auth, "Trng Laity In Visitation w The Aging," *DMin Dissertation*, VTS, 1987. Letter of Appreciation Bp: Dio New Jersey 2003; Certificates of Spec Congressional Recognition Congr of the Untd States 2003; Letters of Appreciation Congr of the Untd States: Hse of Representatives 2003; Letter of Appreciation Gvnr: St of New Jersey 2003; Cert of Appreciation Gvnr: St of New York 2003; Letters of Apprerciation Off of the Mayor: City of New York 2003; Cert of Appreciation Par of Trin Ch, New York City 2003; Letter of Appreciation The White Hse, Washington, D.C. 2003; Letters of Appreciation Untd States Senate 2003; Remington Cup VTS 1971.

MARTIN, George H (Minn) 12305 Chinchilla Ct W, Rosemount MN 55068 **Presenter/Consult Start-Up Start-Over 1987-** B Toledo OH 1942 s John & Gretchen. BA Hobart and Wm Smith Colleges 1964; BD Bex Sem 1967; DMin VTS 1990. D 6/17/1967 Bp Nelson Marigold Burroughs P 2/1/1968 Bp John Harris Burt. m 3/28/1964 Caroline J Martin c 4. Int S Marg's Epis Ch Palm Desert CA 2009-2010; Int S Barth's Epis Ch Poway CA 2005-2006; Int Chr Ch Red Wing MN 2004-2005; Int Chr Ch Par La Crosse WI 2002; Int S Mk's Barrington IL 2000-2007; Int S Andr's Epis Ch Amarillo TX 2000-2001; Cong. Stds Prog Adj Fac Seabury Wstrn Sem 1994-2003; Vic SS Martha And Mary Epis Ch S Paul MN 1987-2000; R S Lk's Ch Minneapolis MN 1975-1986; Cur All SS Epis Ch Omaha NE 1972-1975; Asst Ch Of The H Trin Lincoln NE 1969-1972; Cur S Jn's Epis Ch Cuyahoga Fls OH 1967-1969; Chair Bex Sem Columbus OH 1990-1994, Bd Trst 1986-1989. Auth, "Door-To-Door Ministy," Ch Ad Proj, 2002; Auth, "Rt Start: Birthing New Congregations In The New Millenium," Ch Ad Proj, 2000; Auth, "Advert Loc Ch: Handbook For Prom," Ch Ad Proj, 1999; Auth, "From Disciple To Apos," Ch Ad Proj, 1996. Intl Assn Police Chapl 1996.

MARTIN JR, George Oliver (WK) B Buffalo NY 1933 s George & Helen. D 6/4/1988 Bp John Forsythe Ashby. m 7/26/1991 karen Kline Martin c 5.

MARTIN, Gregory Alexander (Cal) 162 Hickory St, San Francisco CA 94102 **Chapl Vol Stanford Hosp and Clinics Palo Alto CA 2012-; D Ch Of The Adv Of Chr The King San Francisco CA 2009-** B Vancouver Canada 1946 s Hubert & Catherina. BA York U 1976; MDiv Other 1980; MDiv Other 1980; MDiv Trin, Toronto, Can 1980. Trans 12/28/2011 as Deacon Bp Marc Handley Andrus.

MARTIN, Hallock (SeFla) 5042 El Claro N, West Palm Beach FL 33415 B Charleston SC 1950 s Franklin & Margaret. Cntr Coll 1971; BS U of Tennessee 1976; MDiv Sewanee: The U So, TS 1988. D 6/11/1988 P 3/18/1989 Bp Harry Woolston Shipps. m 6/9/1974 Lydia Martin c 3. R H Sprt Epis Ch W Palm Bch FL 1993-2016; Vic S Lk's Epis Hawkinsville GA 1989-1993; Trin Ch Cochran GA 1988-1993.

MARTIN, Irene Elizabeth (Oly) PO Box 83, Skamokawa WA 98647 **P S Jas Epis Ch Cathlamet WA 1992-** B Southsea UK 1946 d Harold & Evelyn. BA York U 1969; U Tor 1970; MLS U of British Columbia Vancouver BC CA 1975. D 1/25/1992 P 8/14/1992 Bp Vincent Waydell Warner. m 4/25/1973 Kent Martin. Auth, "Bch Heaven," *Hist of Wahkiakum Cnty*, WA SU Press, 1997; Auth, *Legacy & Testament: The Story of the Columbia River Gillnetters*, WA SU Press, 1994. RWF. Govenor Heritage Awd Washington Gvnr 2000; Jas Castles Awd Cntr for Columbia River Hist 1998. imartin@iinet.com

MARTIN, James Mitchell (WVa) 177 Edison Dr, Huntington WV 25705 **Asst S Jn 1971-** B Huntington WV 1928 s Adam & Vera. BS Georgia Inst of Tech 1951. D 6/11/1971 P 2/1/1972 Bp Wilburn Camrock Campbell. m 9/13/1971 Dorothy Jane Fuller.

MARTIN JR, John Charles (Md) 610 Brookfield Ave, Cumberland MD 21502 B Cumberland MD 1950 s John & Dorothy. BS U of Maryland 1972. D 6/6/2009 Bp John L Rabb. m 11/20/1987 Donna Jean Martin c 2.

MARTIN, John Gayle (Pa) 8114 Heacock Ln, Wyncote PA 19095 **Ret 1998-** B Bessemer AL 1941 s John & Marjorie. BA Birmingham-Sthrn Coll 1962; MDiv Sewanee: The U So, TS 1967; Cert Pstr Trng Inst Philadelphia PA 1993. D 6/10/1967 P 5/4/1968 Bp George Mosley Murray. m 6/23/1967 Robin Pierce Martin. Int R Memi Ch Of The H Nativ Jenkintown PA 2004-2006; Int Ch Of The Redeem Springfield PA 2003-2004; Int S Jn's Ch Bala Cynwyd PA 2001-2003; Int H Innoc S Paul's Ch Philadelphia PA 1999-2001; R Chr Ch And S Mich's Philadelphia PA 1982-1998; R S Alb's Ch Hoover AL 1975-1982; R Ch Of The Epiph Guntersville AL 1971-1975; Asst S Jas Par Wilmington NC 1969-1971; Vic S Mary's Epis Ch Andalusia AL 1967-1969; S Thos Ch Greenville AL 1967-1969. AAPC.

MARTIN, Kathleen A (NY) 900 W End Ave, New York NY 10025 B Saint Petersburg FL 1949 d Edward & Sheila. D 6/14/1997 P 12/1/1997 Bp Richard Frank Grein.

MARTIN, Kenneth Earl (Fla) 125 Holly View, Holly Lake Ranch TX 75765 **P S Lk's Epis Ch Lindale TX 2012-; P St Marys Epis Ch Palatka FL 2008-** B Dalhart TX 1948 s Wayland & Earlene. Seward Jr Coll 1970; BBA W Texas A&M U 1972; MDiv Epis TS of the SW 1978. D 6/10/1978 P 6/9/1979 Bp Willis Ryan Henton. m 6/7/1969 Vicki Jean Martin c 4. R S Paul's Fed Point E Palatka FL 2003-2006; Asstg P S Lk's Epis Ch N Little Rock AR 1999-2002; Chapl S Fran Hse 1994-1998; S Steph's Epis Ch Jacksonville AR 1993-1999; Chair - Dept Christn Ed Dio Arkansas Little Rock AR 1993-1994, Chair - Stew Cmsn 1994-1996, Dir Of The Handicap Camp 1993, Dn Of The NE Convoc 1990-1992, 1989; R Ch Of The Gd Shpd Forrest City AR 1987-1993; S Andr's Paradis Luling LA 1986-1987; Vic S Tim's Ch La Place LA 1984-1987; Dept Of Missions Dallas TX 1984; Vic S Philips Epis Ch Sulphur Spgs TX 1982-1983; Cur S Dav's Ch Garland TX 1981-1982; S Lk's Epis Ch Levelland TX 1981; Dio NW Texas Lubbock TX 1978-1981, Secy 1982-1983; Vic The Epis Ch Of The Gd Shpd Brownfield TX 1978-1981.

MARTIN, Kevin E (Dal) 202 Kickapoo Creek Ln, Georgetown TX 78633 **Cong Dev Off Dio Oklahoma Oklahoma City OK 2012-** B Cleveland OH 1946 s Glenn & Clarissa. DD Nashotah Sem; BA U of No Texas 1968; MDiv Ya Berk 1971; Advncd CPE 1978. D 6/17/1971 P 12/19/1971 Bp Theodore H McCrea. m 6/13/1964 Sharon D Smith c 2. Dn S Matt's Cathd Dallas TX 2005-2012; Cn for Cong Dev Dio Cntrl Florida Orlando FL 2004-2008; Dir Vital Ch Mnstrs Plano TX 2003-2007; Chr Epis Ch Plano TX 2003-2005; Assoc Vital Ch Mnstry Plano TX 2003-2005; Cn for Cong Dev Dio Texas Houston TX 1998-2002; The Great Cmsn Fndt Houston TX 1993-1997; Dir Ldrshp Trng ERM Evergreen CO 1990-1994; Acts 29 Mnstrs Thomasville GA 1990-1993; R S Lk's Epis Ch Seattle WA 1984-1990; R S Matt's Epis Ch Westerville OH 1979-1984; Chapl Beth Hosp Cincinnati OH 1978-1979; R Emm Epis Ch Stamford CT 1973-1977; Cur S Matt's Epis Ch Wilton CT 1971-1973. Auth, "5 Keys for Ch Leaders," *Bk*, Ch Pub, 2007; Auth, "The Myth of the 200 Barrier," *Bk*, Abingdon, 2005; Auth, "Stwdshp and Giving," TENS, 2003; Contrib, "2020," *2020 Report*, The Epis Ch, 2002; Contributing Auth, "Chr Ch, Denver," *Inner City Parishes*, Abingdon, 1992; Auth, "Mssn and Evang," *New Wineskins for Global Mssn*, ECMS, 1992; Auth, "Preaching to the Bereaved," *Coll of Preachers Nwsltr*, Coll of Preachers, 1985; Contributing Auth, "Authentic Preaching," *Coll of Preachers Nwsltr*, Coll of Preachers, 1984. 2020 Taskforce 2000-2003;

ERM 1985-1993; Ldrshp Ntwk Ed Bd 1993-1999. DD Nashotah Sem 2015. deankevinmartin@gmail.com

MARTIN, Lydia Adriana Peter (Md) 10800 Greenpoint Rd, Lavale MD 21502 **Stff Chapl Naad Cumberland MD 2005-** B Kortgene The Netherlands 1941 BS U of No Dakota 1964; BA Frostburg St U 1976; MS Frostburg St U 1983; Cert Sthrn California Sensory Integration Tests 1983. D 6/2/2007 Bp John L Rabb. m 1/24/1964 James Oscar Martin c 2. Occupational Ther Aota Cumberland MD 1976-2001.

MARTIN, Lyle Fay (Neb) 906 Main St, Gregory SD 57533 **Died 6/16/2017** B Erwin SD 1926 s Joseph & Hannah. D 11/18/1988 P 10/20/1990 Bp Craig Barry Anderson. m 6/25/2007 Moyra L Mason c 3. P Trin Epis Ch Winner SD 1993-1996; P Chr Ch Sidney NE 1990-2001; D S Jas Epis Ch Belle Fourche SD 1988-1990. Homeless Awd Min Assoc 1997.

MARTIN, Mary J (NY) 900 W End Ave Apt 10-C, New York NY 10025 B Saint Petersburg FL 1949 d Edward & Sheila. BA Hollins U; MDiv UTS; MDiv UTS; MA UTS; PhD UTS. D 6/1/1996 P 12/7/1996 Bp Richard Frank Grein. Asst Par Of Trin Ch.

MARTIN, Mary Nadine (Az) 7750 E Oakwood Cir, Tucson AZ 85750 **D Ch Of S Matt Tucson AZ 2013-** B Atlanta GA 1939 d Robert & Florine. BA Georgia St U 1978. D 10/14/2006 Bp Kirk Stevan Smith. m 7/26/1987 William Jeffrey Martin c 2. Sci Writer/ Ed Centers For Disease Control And Prevention 1967-1998.

MARTIN, Nancee (Oly) 10560 Fort George Road, Fort George Island FL 32226 **Adj Prof Florida St Coll at Jacksonville 2011-; Stndg Com Dio Florida Jacksonville 2010-, BEC 2009-, Campus Mnstry Coop, Chairperson 2008-2010, Global Recon Cmsn (MDGs), Chairperson 2007-2010; Bd Trst Sewanee U So TS Sewanee TN 2006-** B Jacksonville FL 1952 d Walter & Pansy. BA U of Florida 1974; MA U of No Florida 1976; MDiv Sewanee: The U So, TS 2000; DMin Sewanee: The U So, TS 2008. D 6/10/2000 P 1/13/2001 Bp William Jerry Winterrowd. c 4. Cn S Mk's Cathd Seattle WA 2014-2017; R S Geo Epis Ch Jacksonville FL 2010-2014; P-in-c S Mich's Ch Gainesville FL 2009-2010; Chapl Ch Of The Incarn Gainesville FL 2007-2010; Assoc S Jn's Epis Ch Boulder CO 2002-2007; Cur S Andr's Ch Denver CO 2000-2002. Bk reviewer, "Sprtl Dir's Intl ," *Presence mag*, SDI, 2009; Contrib, "Lifting Wmn Voices: Prayers to Change the Wrld," *Bk*, Morehouse, 2009; Contrib, "Wmn at the Well," *Bk*, Judson Press, 2003. Amer Soc For Psychoprophal In Obst 1982-1987; Natl Cert Counselors 1996. Griffin Schlr Stuso 2000; Preaching in Excellence Prog Washington D.C. 1999.

MARTIN, Nancy D (WVa) 222 5th Ave, Hinton WV 25951 B Lansing MI 1949 d Edward & Lavon. MI SU 1970. D 12/3/2011 Bp William Michie Klusmeyer. m 9/4/1976 Darrell L Martin c 2.

MARTIN, Paul Dexter (WLa) 275 Southfield Road, Shreveport LA 71105 **Asst R S Paul's Epis Ch Shreveport LA 1997-; Commsion on Mnstry Dio Wstrn Louisiana Alexandria LA 2010-, Trst, U So 2006-, Co-chair, Evang Cmsn 2000-, Dioc Sprtl Dir, Curs 1998-** B Cincinnati OH 1950 s Francis & Mary. BA Wabash Coll 1972; MDiv Sewanee: The U So, TS 1975. D 6/14/1975 Bp John P Craine P 6/27/1976 Bp John McKie. m 11/25/1978 Christine Anne Martin c 3. Ch Of The Incarn Alexandria LA 1995-1997; R S Jn's Epis Ch Minden LA 1990-1994; Asst R S Jn's Epis Ch Charlotte NC 1980-1989; Serv Ch of Engl 1975-1980; Trst, U So Dio No Carolina Raleigh NC 1996-1999, Dioc Yth Cmsn 1991-1999.

MARTIN, Rene Elizabeth (Md) Buckingham's Choice, 3200 Baker Cir, Adamstown MD 21710 **Buckingham's Choice Adamstown MD 2015-** B Cherokee IA 1960 d Teddy & Wilma. BSN U of Iowa 1982; MA U of Iowa 1993; PhD U of Iowa 1996; Post-Doctoral Fell U of Iowa 1998; MDiv GTS 2012. D 12/17/2011 P 6/17/2012 Bp Alan Scarfe. m 5/6/1994 Jerry Marvin Suls c 1. S Paul's Epis Par Pt Of Rocks MD 2014-2015. renny.martin@integrace.org

MARTIN, Rex L (Wyo) PO Box 64, Hartville WY 82215 **Vol Ch Of Our Sav Hartville WY 2006-** B 1956 s Sherman & Daylene. EFM The U So TS 2005. D 7/22/2006 P 1/6/2007 Bp Bruce Caldwell. m 6/26/1982 Rhonda Martin c 2.

MARTIN JR, Robert James (SwFla) 9727 Bay Colony Dr, Riverview FL 33578 B Philadelphia PA 1936 s Robert & Anna. BS VMI 1960; MDiv UTS Richmond 1965; ThM PrTS 1976; DMin Sewanee: The U So, TS 1993. D 11/1/1994 Bp Rogers Sanders Harris P 5/24/1995 Bp Telesforo A Isaac. m 6/23/1963 Betsy Priscilla Payne. Asst to R S Ptr's Ch Plant City FL 2005-2008, Int 2002-2003; Int Gr Ch Tampa FL 2004-2005; Int S Mary's Ch Dade City FL 2003-2004; R All Ang By The Sea Longboat Key FL 2000-2004; Asst to R St Johns Epis Ch Tampa FL 1995-2000.

MARTIN, Robin Pierce (Pa) 8114 Heacock Ln, Wyncote PA 19095 B Mobile AL 1947 d Arvin & Barbara. BA U of Alabama 1978; MDiv Luth TS 1984. D 6/28/1984 Bp Furman Charles Stough P 4/25/1985 Bp Lyman Cunningham Ogilby. m 6/23/1967 John Gayle Martin c 2. R Ch Of The Adv Hatboro PA 1987-2013; S Mary's Epis Ch Ardmore PA 1984-1987.

MARTIN, Terry L (NJ) 220 Fairview Ave, Hammonton NJ 08037 **R S Steph's Ch Waretown NJ 2010-** B San Luis Obispo CA 1954 s Gladwyn & Anna. AA U of Wisconsin 1984; BS U of Wisconsin 1987; MDiv Nash 1990. D 12/30/1989 P 7/25/1990 Bp William Louis Stevens. m 6/21/2003 Cheryl A Calletta c

1. Epis Ch Cntr New York NY 2008-2009; Vic Ch Of The H Sprt Tuckerton NJ 2005-2008; Ch Of S Mary's By The Sea Pt Pleas Bch NJ 2003-2005; S Chris's Ch Spartanburg SC 2001-2002; S Jas Ch Paso Robles CA 1993-2000; Asst To Dn St Paul's Epis Cathd Fond Du Lac WI 1990-1993.

MARTIN, William Henderson (RG) PO Box 640161, El Paso TX 79904 **Ret 1988-; Chapl S Lk Hosp NYC - St Hosp Mentally Ill Philadelphia PA 1967-** B Sonora TX 1924 s John & Willie. BA McMurry U 1949; BA U of No Texas 1954; MA U of No Texas 1955; MDiv GTS 1965. D 5/7/1965 P 11/13/1965 Bp C J Kinsolving III. m 12/21/1946 Joan Herndon Martin. St Pauls Ch 1983; R Chr the King El Paso TX 1969-1982; H Sprt Epis Ch El Paso TX 1969-1982; Asst Cathd Of St Jn The Div New York NY 1967-1969; Vic S Mary's Ch Lovington NM 1965-1967. Auth, *The Organ Concerti of GF Handel*, 1955. OGS 1965.

MARTIN OSB, William Jeffrey (Az) 7750 E Oakwood Cir, Tucson AZ 85750 B Washington DC 1932 s William & Cora. BA U of Nebraska 1957; MS U of Utah 1963; PhD U of Utah 1965. D 10/14/2006 Bp Kirk Stevan Smith. m 7/26/1987 Mary Nadine Martin c 2. D Ch Of S Matt Tucson AZ 2009-2014. NEAC 1993-1995.

MARTIN, William L (Be) 5114 Hilltop Cir, East Stroudsburg PA 18301 **R S Brigid's Ch Nazareth PA 2011-** B South Kingstown RI 1948 s Frederick & Emma. BA U of Rhode Island 1970; MDiv Ya Berk 1973. D 6/16/1973 P 12/21/1973 Bp Frederick Hesley Belden. m 8/6/1977 Gloria Hull. R S Steph's Ch Westborough MA 2002-2010; R S Steph's Epis Ch Clifton Hgts PA 1995-2002; R S Lk's Ch Hope NJ 1990-1995; R Cunningham Chap Par Millwood VA 1986-1989; R All SS Ch Chelmsford MA 1982-1986; R S Paul's Ch Windsor VT 1979-1982; Vic Trin Milton VT 1976-1979; Asst S Paul's Ch Plainfield CT 1975-1976; Cur S Thos Ch Greenville RI 1973-1975; Dioc Coun Dio Bethlehem 2015.

MARTIN, William Thomas (At) 3207 Pristine View, Williamsburg VA 23188 B Hannibal MO 1942 s Junius & Dorothy. BA Culver-Stockton Coll 1966; MDiv Andover Newton TS 1970. D 12/27/1969 Bp George Leslie Cadigan P 7/15/1970 Bp Leland Stark. m 8/24/1968 Virginia G Martin c 2. Int S Clare's Epis Ch Blairsville GA 2000-2009; R Ch Of The Ascen Cartersville GA 1994-2007; Dn Montgomery Dnry 1984-1988; R All Hallows Ch Wyncote PA 1980-1994; Asst Ch Of The Redeem Bryn Mawr PA 1975-1980; Jvnl Off Pemiscot Cnty MO 1972-1975; Vic S Lk and S Jn's Caruthersvlle MO 1972-1975; Cur S Thos Ch Dover NH 1970-1972. Assoc of H Cross Monstry 1973; Ecum Oblate Mt Sav Monstry 1983.

MARTIN, William V (Okla) PO Box 1153, Pryor OK 74362 B Tulsa OK 1944 s William & Lottie. BA Pr 1966; MBA SMU 1972; MDiv SWTS 1996. D 6/15/1996 P 12/1/1996 Bp Larry Maze. m 6/25/1966 Carole W Martin c 2. Vic St Mart of Tours Epis Ch Pryor OK 2013-2016; Dio Oklahoma Oklahoma City OK 2009-2012; Dio Colorado Denver CO 2006-2009; All SS' Epis Sch Vicksburg MS 2000-2006; S Marg's Epis Ch Little Rock AR 1998-2000; Trin Cathd Little Rock AR 1996-1998.

MARTINDALE, James Lawrence (NMich) 14 Stonegate Hts, Marquette MI 49855 **Presb St. Jn's Epis Ch 2007-; S Jn's Ch Negaunee MI 2006-** B Green Bay WI 1937 s James & Mary. BS Nthrn Michigan U 1967. D 9/13/2006 P 4/22/2007 Bp James Arthur Kelsey. m 11/30/1963 Kathleen D Martindale c 3.

MARTINDALE, Kyle Thomas (Neb) 9302 Blondo St, Omaha NE 68134 **Assoc All SS Epis Ch Omaha NE 2016-** B Germany 1987 s Richard & Jenny. Bachelor of Arts Hastings Coll 2009; M.Div. VTS 2016. D 4/15/2016 P 10/29/2016 Bp Scott Scott Barker. m 5/24/2016 Patricia Lauren D Zu Iga. kmartindale@allsaintsomaha.org

MARTINDALE, Richard James (Ky) 5 S Green St, Henderson KY 42420 **S Paul's Ch Henderson KY 2012-** B South Bend IN 1957 s Donald & Shirley. U of Nebraska; BA JHU 1979; MDiv VTS 1995. D 6/3/1995 P 12/1/1995 Bp Brice Sidney Sanders. m 10/22/1983 Jenny L Martindale c 2. R Trin Epis Ch Columbus GA 2005-2012; Vic S Jn's Mssn Harvard NE 1998-2005; Dn S Mk's Epis Pro-Cathd Hastings NE 1998-2005; Cur S Jn's Ch Decatur AL 1995-1998.

MARTINER, John William (Del) 65 Continental Dr, Harwich MA 02645 **Adj Cler S Chris's Ch Chatham MA 2010-** B New Haven CT 1940 s John & Genevieve. BS Cntrl Connecticut St U 1962; MDiv Ya Berk 1965; DMin Hartford Sem 1986. D 6/1/1965 Bp Walter H Gray P 4/1/1966 Bp John Henry Esquirol. m 6/19/1965 Elizabeth B Martiner c 2. Adj Cler S Monica's Epis Ch Naples FL 2009-2013; Assoc S Mary's Epis Ch Bonita Sprg FL 2009; Transition Consult Dio Delaware Wilmington 2002-2006, Bp Search Com 1998-2001, 1000-1997; Trst Ya Berk New Haven CT 1997-2003; R Chr Ch Christiana Hundred Wilmington DE 1995-2006; Chair - Com 1988-1992; S Thos Epis Ch Rochester NY 1983-1995; Sub-Dn - Bridgeport Dnry 1978-1980; Chapl Police Dept Trumbull CT 1974-1983; R Gr Epis Ch Trumbull CT 1973-1983; R Emm Epis Ch Cumberland RI 1968-1972; Cur S Paul's Ch Wallingford CT 1965-1968; AFP; Exec Coun Dio Connecticut Meriden CT 1978-1980; Exec Coun Dio Rhode Island Providence RI 1971-1974. Auth, "The Chr Funeral," 1991; Auth, "Ltrgy-A Vehicle For Soc Mnstry," 1986. Fvc. Kappa Delta Pi 1961.

MARTINEZ, Gregorio Bernardo (NwT) 907 Adams Ave, Odessa TX 79761 **Vic Iglesia Epis de Santa Maria Midland TX 2001-** B Carazo Carazo NI 1946 s Simeon & Enriqueta. Loyola U 1970; Universidad Nacional De Nicara Managua Ni 1973; Cert Theol Stud Epis TS of the SW 1994. D 10/30/1994 P 5/20/1995 Bp Sam Byron Hulsey. m 9/6/1969 Lylliam Urbina Martinez c 2. Vic San Miguel Arcangel Odessa TX 1999; P Dio NW Texas Lubbock TX 1995-2012, Hisp Mnstry 1994-; Hisp Mnstry S Jn's Epis Ch Odessa TX 1994-1995. syndicatemage@yahoo.com

MARTINEZ, Jose (Ct) 155 Wyllys St, Hartford CT 06106 **Vic Dio New York New York NY 2013-** B Guatemala 1961 s Cupertina. BS Carlos Martinez Duran Coll 1988; MDiv GTS 2006; BS SUNY 2006. D 6/9/2007 P 12/15/2007 Bp Andrew Donnan Smith. m 1/30/2008 Herminia Martinez c 3. Ch of our Sav Plainville CT 2012-2013; Ch Of The Gd Shpd Hartford CT 2007-2013, 1996-2007; Dio Oregon Portland OR 1996-2001; Prog & Bdgt Com Dio Connecticut Meriden CT 2011-2013. APLM (Assoc Parishes for Liturg & Mnstry 2007. curajlm@gmail.com

MARTINEZ, Kim Renee (RG) Po Box 1434, Santa Cruz NM 87567 B Denver CO 1953 The Sch For Mnstry; BA San Francisco St U 1980; MA U of New Mex 1984. D 6/21/2003 P 10/2/2004 Bp Terence Kelshaw. m 5/31/1996 Joseph A Martinez.

MARTINEZ, Lucy Anne Roberts (At) 539 Wagner Way Ne, Kennesaw GA 30144 B Knoxville TN 1941 d John & Juanita. King Coll 1962; Indiana St U 1983; Chicago Deacons Sch 1991. D 12/7/1991 Bp Frank Tracy Griswold III. m 7/22/1961 Inocencio Martinez c 3. S Clem's Epis Ch Canton GA 1997-2004; D S Mary Epis Ch Crystal Lake IL 1991-1995. EFM Mentor 1985-1990; NAAD; SHN 1977.

MARTINEZ, Mario Ancizar (NY) 802 Broadway, New York NY 10003 B Montenegro Quindio CO 1940 s Rafael & Teresa. Intl Assn of Counselors & Therapists Ngh; NGH Natl Gld of Hypnotists; EPH Institutio Filosoficoco 1962; BTh Pontificio ateneo Salesiano 1969; MEd Universidad Mariana 1972. Rec 12/1/1987 as Priest Bp Robert Campbell Witcher Sr. m 3/8/1975 Blanca Bastidas c 3. S Ptr's Ch Port Chester NY 2002-2006, P Assoc 2002-; Mssnr Mision San Pablo New York NY 1998-2005; S Andr's Ch Beacon NY 1998-2000; Mssnr La Iglesia Del Buen Pstr Newburgh NY 1997-2000; Dio New York New York NY 1996-1997; Hisp Mssnr Chr Ch Poughkeepsie NY 1994-2000; Asst The Ch of S Matt And S Tim New York NY 1989-1996, 1988-1996; Serv RC Ch 1969-1974. "Many arts," *Nwspr Impacto*, 2001.

MARTINEZ AMENGUAL, Margarita (Hond) **Dio Honduras San Pedro Sula 2006-** B Puerto Cortes 1948 d Arnaldo & Juana. Programa Dioc De Ed Teol; Universidad Pedagogica. D 10/28/2005 Bp Lloyd Emmanuel Allen. c 2.

MARTINEZ AMENGUAL, Roberto Aaron (Hond) **Dio Honduras San Pedro Sula 2006-; Iglesia Epis San Pablo Apostol San Pedro Sula 2006-** B Puerto Cortes, Cortes 1954 s Arnaldo & Juana. D 10/29/2005 Bp Lloyd Emmanuel Allen. m 2/11/1984 Bienvenida Rodriguez c 3.

MARTINEZ-JANTZ, Jeanie (Va) 5821 Bush Hill Dr, Alexandria VA 22310 **Int Olivet Epis Ch Alexandria VA 2013-** B Shawnee OK 1956 d Gene & Frances. BA No Carolina St U 1983; MDiv VTS 2007. D 4/29/2007 P 1/5/2008 Bp Leo Frade. m 3/1/1986 Carlos Felipe Martinez c 2. Asst R S Andr's Ch Burke VA 2009-2013. SBL 2005.

MARTINEZ-MORALES, Roberto (Los) 1011 S Verdugo Rd, Glendale CA 91205 **Vic Iglesia Epis De La Magdalena Mssn Glendale CA 2006-** B Mexico Distrito Federal 1971 s Roberto & Maria. Cetis 1998; BD Seminario de San Andres 2000. D 12/17/1999 P 7/1/2000 Bp Sergio Carranza-Gomez. m 12/27/1996 Yanci Guerrero-Yanez c 2. R Dio Mex 2001-2006; Vic Dio Mex Hidalgo 2000-2001; Dio Mex Mex City MOR 1999-2006.

MARTINEZ RAPALO, Arturo (Hond) IMS SAP Dept 215. PO BOX 523900, Miami FL 33152 Honduras B 1953 s Ramon & Serapia. D 3/11/2007 Bp Lloyd Emmanuel Allen. m 3/11/1977 Miranda Trinidad Azucena Fernandez c 5.

MARTINEZ-RAPALO, Ramon (Hond) B 1947 m 4/5/1998 Miriam Suyapa-Ochoa c 3. Dio Honduras San Pedro Sula 1998-2011.

MARTINEZ TOLEDO, Eduardo (PR) **Dio Puerto Rico Trujillo Alto PR 2005-** B 1953 s Juan & Rosa. Bachillerato Seminario para Sacredote. Rec 4/27/2002 as Priest Bp Bernardo Merino-Botero. m 8/15/1992 Claudia Esperanza Cardenas c 2. Iglesia Epis En Colombia Bogota 2002-2005.

MARTINEZ TORO, Jorge De Jesus (Colom) Carrera 80 #53a-78, Medellin, Antioquia Colombia B 1955 s Jorge & Lucia. BA Sem S Jose 1969; BA Inst S Carlos 1971. P 1/1/1996 Bp Bernardo Merino-Botero. m 11/27/1999 Esmeralda Cardona. Iglesia Epis En Colombia Bogota 1995-2016.

MARTIN FUMERO, Emilio Samuel (DR) **Clerico Dio Of The Republic Santo Domingo DO 2011-; Clérigo Dio Of The Republic Santo Domingo DO 2011-; Dio The Dominican Republic (Iglesia Epis Dominicana) Gazcue Santo Domingo 2011-** B Cuba 1951 s Juan & Ana. Trans 8/1/2011 Bp Julio Cesar Holguin-Khoury. m 12/12/2005 Maria Gonzalez Paso c 3. Sacerdote Diocesis de Cuba Cardenas Matanzas Cuba 1990-2011.

MARTINHAUK, Jeff (SanD) 2728 6th Ave, San Diego CA 92103 **Assoc Cathd Ch Of S Paul San Diego CA 2016-** B Bethesda MD 1970 s Donald & Judy. BBA SMU 1992; MDiv Epis TS of the SW 2009. D 3/12/2011 P 1/7/2012 Bp

Diane Jardine Bruce. c 2. S Tim's Epis Ch Apple Vlly CA 2013-2016; Chapl Seton Healthcare Fam 2010-2012; Chapl Res Seton Healthcare Fam 2009-2010. Integrity USA 2006. martinhaukj@stpaulcathedral.org

MARTINICHIO, John Robert (CNY) 89 Fairview Ave, Binghamton NY 13904 **R S Paul's Ch Endicott NY 2012-, P-in-c 2011-2012; Vice-Chair Dioc Bd Dio Cntrl New York Liverpool NY 2010-, Chair, COM 2009-2012, Dn of Binghamton Dist 2007-2012, Co-Chair Pstr Response Team 2005-2011, Safe Ch Trnr 2004-** B Binghamton NY 1958 s John & Joanne. AA SUNY 1979; BA Wadhams Hall Sem Coll 1981; MDiv Chr the King Sem 1985; AAS Simmons Sch of Mortuary Sci 1993. Rec 10/19/2002 as Priest Bp Gladstone Bailey Adams III. m 9/4/1993 Barbara A Martinichio c 2. P in Charge St. Paul's Epis Ch Endicott NY 2011; R Chr Ch Binghamton NY 2002-2011; Coordntr Safe Ch Prog. johnrobert58@stny.rr.com

MARTINO, Rose Marie (LI) 612 Forest Ave, Massapequa NY 11758 B New York NY 1941 d Frederick & Marie. BS SUNY 1994; Mercer TS 1998. D 6/10/1998 Bp Orris George Walker Jr. c 3. S Gabr's Ch Brooklyn NY 2012-2013; The Ch Of The Ascen Rockville Ct NY 2008-2012; D Cathd Of The Incarn Garden City NY 2000-2008; Asst Chr Ch Oyster Bay NY 1998-2000; Teach Lem 1 And 2 Mercer TS Garden City NY. Auth, "D In The Stock Mrkt Wrld," *Wmn Uncommon Prayers*, Morehouse Pub, 2000; Auth, "The Space Between (Poem)," *Natl Libr Of Poetry*, 1994. NAAD 1994.

MARTIN-RHODES, Lilla Rebecca (LI) 27002 Arrowbrook Way, Wesley Chapel FL 33544 B JM 1939 d Rudolphus & Rosetta. BA CUNY 1978; MA CUNY 1978; Mercer TS 1994. D 6/15/1994 Bp Orris George Walker Jr. m 9/28/1985 Eugene Rhodes c 3.

✠ **MARTINS, The Rt Rev Daniel Hayden** (Spr) 821 S 2nd St, Springfield IL 62704 **Bp of Springfield Dio Springfield IL 2011-; Chair of Dir Nash Nashotah WI 2012-; Bd Mem LivCh Fndt 2012-** B Rio de Janeiro BR 1951 s Elson & Ollie. BA Westmont Coll 1973; MA U Arizona 1975; MDiv Nash 1989. D 6/18/1989 Bp Robert Louis Ladehoff P 12/20/1989 Bp James Barrow Brown Con 3/19/2011 for Spr. m 8/27/1972 Brenda Fay Ormsbee c 3. R S Anne's Epis Ch Warsaw IN 2007-2011; Adj Prof San Joaquin Sch for Mnstry Fresno CA 2003-2007; R S Jn's Epis Ch Stockton CA 1994-2007; Vic S Marg's Epis Ch Baton Rouge LA 1991-1994; Cur S Lk's Ch Baton Rouge LA 1989-1991; Exam Chapl Dio Nthrn Indiana So Bend IN 2008-2011; RurD Epis Dio San Joaquin Modesto CA 2000-2007, Exam Chapl 1999-2007, Secy of Conv 1994-1998. Comm Partnr Bishops 2011. DD Nash 2011. bishop@episcopalspringfield.org

MARTZ, Jeannie (Los) 3107 Pepperwood Ct, Fullerton CA 92835 **R Trin Epis Ch Orange CA 2007-** B Evanston IL 1950 d John & Valerie. BA McGill U 1972; MDiv Ya Berk 1990. D 6/9/1990 P 3/16/1991 Bp James Russell Moodey. c 2. Dio SE Florida Miami 2007; Assoc R S Mk's Ch Palm Bch Garden FL 1995-2007; Assoc R S Mart's Ch Chagrin Fall OH 1990-1995.

MARTZ, Stephen Bryant (Chi) 947 Oxford Rd, Glen Ellyn IL 60137 **Pres C.G. Jung Inst of Chicago 2015-; Jungian analyst & Sprtl Dir Priv Pract 1987-** B Washington DC 1951 s Buford & Naomi. BA U of Maryland 1976; MDiv Cath Theol U 1988; DMin Chicago TS 1995; Dplma CG Jung Inst 2007. D 6/18/1994 P 12/17/1994 Bp Frank Tracy Griswold III. m 6/17/1989 Carla Amato-Martz c 2. R Ch Of Our Sav Elmhurst IL 2011-2014; Co-Dir,Clincl Trng Prog C.G. Jung Inst of Chicago 2010-2012; Vic S Nich w the H Innoc Ch Elk Grove Vlg IL 1995-2011; S Hilary's Ch Prospect Hts IL 1995. "Remembering Fr. Paul Murray," *The Washington Blade*, 2009; "In Your Dreams," *Luth Wmn Today*, 2008. Serv to Ch Cmnty Assn of Chicago Priests 1986.

MARX, Jeffery Wayne (WTenn) 484 Riding Brook Way, Collierville TN 38017 **R S Andr's Epis Ch Collierville TN 2001-** B Chicago IL 1956 s Francis & Barbara. BA S Meinrad Coll 1977; MA Cath U of Louvain 1983; MA Cath U of Louvain 1984; MS U of Tennessee 1993. Rec 3/1/1999 Bp James Malone Coleman. m 7/9/1993 Ann D Dooley c 3. Cn S Mary's Cathd Memphis TN 1999-2001. Auth, "Fundamentalism, A Cath Response," *Verbum*, 1983. Rotary 2001. PTA Lifetime Achievement Shelby Cnty Sch System 2011; Serv To Yth Natl Conf Of Christians & Jews 1990.

MASADA, Jennifer Ann (Ia) 912 20th Ave, Coralville IA 52241 **P New Song Epis Ch Coralville IA 2010-** B Kimball NE 1965 d Teruo & Rita. BMus U of Nebraska Omaha 1988; PhD U of Iowa 1993. D 7/26/2009 P 1/31/2010 Bp Alan Scarfe. m 4/23/1994 Kirk Corey c 2.

MASILLEM, Benedict Baguyos (Ak) 6510 E 10th Ave Apt B, Anchorage AK 99504 B San Fernando La Union PH 1970 s Jacinto & Lorenza. BTh S Andrews TS Manila PH 1992; MDiv S Andrews TS Manila PH 2010; MA S Andrews TS Manila PH 2010. Trans 9/20/1999 Bp Mark Lawrence Macdonald. Supply/Part Time P S Christophers Ch Anchorage AK 2008-2013, 2001-2002; Filipino Mnstry Mssnr Dio Alaska Fairbanks AK 2001-2004; Pstr-In-Serv Thanksgiving Mssn 1992-1994.

MASON, Alan Newell (Ct) 211 Senexet Rd, Woodstock CT 06281 B Pawtucket RI 1938 s Lyman & Rubina. BS U of Rhode Island 1960; MDiv Ya Berk 1963; MPA U Cinc 1970. D 6/22/1963 P 5/1/1964 Bp John S Higgins. m 1/29/2000 Susan M Mason c 2. S Phil's Epis Ch Putnam CT 1991-2004; Non-par

1969-1991; Dir Ch Hse 1964-1968; Inner City Mssy Cathd Of S Jn Providence RI 1963-1968.

MASON, Alice Joan Magnuson (WNC) 106 Lanterns Wick Trl, Sylva NC 28779 **Died 12/22/2016** B Grand Rapids MI 1934 d Albert & Edna. U So; Wayne; AA Grand Rapids Cmnty Coll 1954. D 4/13/1985 Bp William Gillette Weinhauer. c 4. D S Dav's Ch Cullowhee NC 1993-2016; D S Cyp's Ch Franklin NC 1985-1991.

MASON, Brooks Kevin (SanD) Cathedral Church of Saint Paul, 2728 6th Ave, San Diego CA 92103 B Charleston WV 1954 s Brooks & Garnet. CEU online CDSP/CALL; BA W Virginia U 1979; Cert of Study Bloy Hse, ETSC 2012. D 4/7/2013 Bp Jim Mathes. Cathd Ch Of S Paul San Diego CA 2013, D 2013-, 2005-2013. masonb@stpaulcathedral.org

MASON, Bruce (Ct) PO Box 443, Litchfield CT 06759 B Brockton MA 1936 s Harry & Mildred. BS Springfield Coll 1958; MSW U of Connecticut 1969; Cert Sthrn Connecticut St U 1981. D 12/1/1990 Bp Arthur Edward Walmsley. m 2/5/1966 Sandra Burrows Mason c 3. Dir, Spec Serv Naugatuck CT Sch Dist 1999-2001; D Trin Ch Torrington CT 1995-2008; D S Mich's Ch Litchfield CT 1990-1995; Asst Dir Naugatuck CT Sch Dist 1988-1999; Soc Worker Naugatuck CT Sch Dist 1970-1988.

MASON, Bruce Edmund (Alb) PO Box 211, Lake Luzerne NY 12846 B Evanston IL 1971 s David & Margaret. BA Ham 1993; MA GW Washington DC 1997; BTh Wycliffe Hall Oxford GB 2007. D 6/9/2007 P 12/22/2007 Bp William Howard Love. m 12/23/1995 Shay Mason c 2. R S Mary's Ch Lake Luzerne NY 2007-2011; Cmncatn Dir Amer Angl Coun 2000-2004; Asst Truro Epis Ch Fairfax VA 1997-2000.

MASON JR, Charles Thurston (Ind) 224 N Alden Rd, Muncie IN 47304 B Springfield OH 1939 s Charles & Josephine. BA Ob 1962; STB PDS 1966. D 6/11/1966 Bp Robert Lionne DeWitt P 2/4/1967 Bp George Alfred Taylor. m 6/6/1970 Charlotte Lynne Mason c 2. R Gr Ch Muncie IN 1984-2002; R S Paul's Ch Lock Haven PA 1976-1984; S Alb's Epis Ch Salisbury MD 1970-1976.

MASON, Christopher P (SwVa) 128 Laurel Mountain Estates Drive, Todd NC 28684 B Savannah GA 1949 s Cecil & Lorraine. BA U So 1971; MDiv Sewanee: The U So, TS 1974; MA E Carolina U 1992; EdD California Coast U 2006. D 6/7/1974 Bp George Paul Reeves P 1/1/1975 Bp Robert Claflin Rusack. m 4/27/1994 Jeannette C Cawl c 3. S Lk's Epis Ch Mechanicsburg PA 2014-2015; R Chr Epis Ch Marion VA 2008-2011; Prncpl Oak Hill Acad Mouth of Wilson VA 2005-2009; Vic St Patricks Ch Pooler GA 2002-2005; Upper Sch Hd St. Andr's by the Marsh Sch 2001-2005; Chapl Blue Ridge Sch St. Geo VA 1992-2001; R S Steph's Ch Goldsboro NC 1986-1992; Assoc S Jas Par Wilmington NC 1982-1986; Chapl Chr Sch Arden NC 1977-1982; Vic S Phil's Ch Hinesville Hinesville GA 1975-1977; Cur All SS-By-The-Sea Par Santa Barbara CA 1974-1975. "Crossing Into Manhood: A Men's Stds Curric," Cambria Press: Youngstown, NY, 2007.

MASON, David Raymond (O) 2277 N Saint James Pkwy, Cleveland Heights OH 44106 B Hagerstown MD 1936 s Edwin & Camilla. BA W Virginia U 1959; STB GTS 1962; MA U Chi 1969; PhD U Chi 1973. D 6/13/1962 P 12/19/1962 Bp Wilburn Camrock Campbell. m 6/29/1963 Margaret Mason. Assoc S Paul's Epis Ch Cleveland OH 1978-2008; Assoc Prof Of Rel Stds JCU Cleveland OH 1977-1982; Asst Prof Of Rel Stds JCU Cleveland OH 1972-1977; Fell Epis Ch Fndtn 1970-1971; Vic All SS Ch Charleston WV 1962-1966. Auth, "A Christology Of Universal Redemptive Love," *Dialog*, 2002; Auth, "Time & Providence," 1982; Auth, "Can God Be Both Perfect & Free?," *Rel Stds*, 1982; Auth, "Can We Speculate On How God Acts ,," *Journ Of Rel*, 1977. AAR 1971; Metaphysical Soc Of Amer 1977; Soc For The Study Of Process Philosophies 1972. Grail Fac Fell JCU 1979.

MASON, Eric (Oly) Church of the Redeemer, 6211 NE 182nd St, Kenmore WA 98028 B Denver CO 1966 s Patrick & Christine. BA Valparaiso U 1990; MDiv Ya Berk 1999; MACP Seattle TS and Psychol 2011. D 10/18/2012 P 6/13/2013 Bp Gregory Harold Rickel. Gr Ch Bainbridge Island WA 2013-2016.

MASON, Jack Malleroyal (Eas) 114 S Harrison St, Easton MD 21601 B Wilmington NC 1943 s Jack & Lilly. BS E Carolina U 1965; MEd Towson U 1972. D 5/2/2004 P 10/8/2011 Bp Bud Shand. m 8/7/1965 Frances G H Mason c 2. Pupil Serv Anne Arundel Cnty Schools Annapolis MD 1968-2002.

MASON, Joan M (NJ) 417 Washington St, Toms River NJ 08753 **R Chr Ch Toms River Toms River NJ 2003-** B Lakewood NJ 1953 d Vincent & Virginia. BA Rutgers The St U of New Jersey 1975; EFM Sewanee: The U So, TS 1995; MDiv GTS 1998. D 6/6/1998 Bp David Standish Ball P 12/12/1998 Bp Vincent King Pettit. m 4/28/2012 Jeffrey Howard Mason c 2. Assoc R S Ptr's Ch Medford NJ 1998-2003; Deploy Off Dio Albany Greenwich NY 1991-1995, GC Dep 1994 & 1994-1997; Supvsr Shell Oil Co Houston Texas 1976-1983; GC Alt Dep 2003 Dio New Jersey Trenton NJ 2003. Cnvnt St. Jn Bapt--Assoc 2008; DOK 2011; Ord of S Lk 2002.

MASON, Joel Clark (NY) 39 Morton Pl, Chappaqua NY 10514 **Core Fac: Wrshp, Sprtlty, & Preaching Drew U 2005-** B Chattanooga TN 1955 s Joel & Sarah. Iliff TS 1978; MDiv Duke DS 1981; Sewanee: The U So, TS 1984; DMin Drew U 2005; Mstr of Arts Other 2012; Mstr of Arts Sacr Heart U 2012. D 7/1/1984 Bp William F Gates Jr P 3/3/1985 Bp William Evan Sanders. m

5/14/1981 Mary Jo Mason c 1. R Ch Of S Mary The Vrgn Chappaqua NY 1996-2014; R Chr Epis Ch Oil City PA 1990-1996; S Mk's Ch Dalton GA 1987-1990; Dio E Tennessee Knoxville TN 1985-1987; P-in-c S Thos Ch Elizabethton TN 1985-1987; S Jn's Epis Cathd Knoxville TN 1984-1985. Auth, "Virtual Sprtl Formation: A Journey Without Steps," VDM Verlag, 2008. Gold Medal Acad Excellence Sacr Heart U 2012; Democracy In Action Rec League of Wmn Voters of Metro Columbus 2010; Graduation w dist Drew U 2005; Paul Harris Fell Rotary 2001.

MASON, John Skain (HB) Rr 2 Box 542b, Inwood WV 25428 **Non-par 1989-** B Springfield OH 1936 s Charles & Josephine. BA DePauw U 1958; STB PDS 1963. D 6/8/1963 Bp Joseph Gillespie Armstrong P 5/1/1964 Bp John Brooke Mosley. m 7/4/1989 Sharon Mason c 3. S Andr The Fisherman Epis Mayo MD 1988-1989; Ch Of The Gd Shpd Greer SC 1987-1988; Chr Ch Alexandria VA 1986-1987, 1976-1977; S Patricks Ch Falls Ch VA 1985; Int Mnstry 1984-1989; Ecum Mnstry w Methodist Ch 1978-1984; S Ptr's Epis Ch Arlington VA 1978; Vic S Matt's Epis Ch Sterling VA 1974-1976; Non-par 1968-1974; R S Paul Piney MD 1966-1968; S Paul's Epis Ch Piney Waldorf MD 1966-1968; Assoc R S Alb's Epis Ch Mc Cook NE 1965-1966; Cur Calv Epis Ch Hillcrest Wilmington DE 1963-1965.

MASON, Judith Ann (Chi) 5445 N Sheridan Rd Apt 2404, Chicago IL 60640 **Died 11/13/2015** B Auburn NY 1949 d Edward & Evelyn. BA DePaul U 1999. D 2/2/2003 Bp Bill Persell.

MASON, Keith Wentworth (WMass) 130 Highland Ave, Leominster MA 01453 **Died 9/17/2015** B Tangier NS Canada 1927 s James & Myrtle. LTh U of Kings Coll Halifax CA 1951; VTS 1980. Trans 9/1/1966 Bp Robert McConnell Hatch. m 5/1/1953 Maureen Drope c 5. Ret 1994-2015; R S Mk's Ch Leominster MA 1966-1994; Dio Wstrn Massachusetts Springfield 1966-1993, Ecum Off 1980-1986; LocTen S Andr's Ch Longmeadow MA 1965-1966; Captain, Militia Padre/Chapl Royal Can Army 1953-1969; Serv Angl Ch of Can 1951-1965. "Search for Tomorrow," Axiom Press, 2009.

MASON, Lawrence Walker (SVa) 2355 Brookwood Rd, Richmond VA 23235 **Ret 1998-** B Ashland VA 1933 s Albert & Blanche. BA U Rich 1957; VTS 1960. D 6/28/1960 P 6/25/1961 Bp Frederick D Goodwin. Manakin Epis Ch Midlothian VA 1967-1998; R S Lk's Ch Powhatan VA 1967-1998; Chapl S Paul Coll Hong Kong 1965-1967; R Our Sav Sandston VA 1964-1965; R Cople Par Hague VA 1960-1964.

MASON, Lisa P (WTex) 1300 Wiltshire Ave, San Antonio TX 78209 **Asst R S Dav's Epis Ch San Antonio TX 2009-** B Corpus Christi TX 1964 d John & Eloise. BA SMU 1984; MDiv Epis TS of the SW 2009. D 5/27/2009 Bp Gary Richard Lillibridge P 12/3/2009 Bp David Mitchell Reed. m 12/21/1984 Kirk B Mason c 2.

MASON, Marilyn Joyce Smith (Los) PO Box 743, Bristol RI 02809 B Bristol RI 1935 d Lowell & Mary. BEd Rhode Island Coll 1956; MA CDSP 1958; MA U of Nevada at Las Vegas 1972. D 6/8/1996 P 1/1/1997 Bp Chester Lovelle Talton. c 2. S Ptr's Par Rialto CA 2005-2007; S Lk's Mssn Fontana CA 2001-2007; S Clare Of Assisi Rancho Cucamonga CA 1998-2000.

MASON, Philip Caldwell (Colo) 280 Peregrine Dr, San Marcos TX 78666 B Fort Worth TX 1940 s Sidney & Katherine. MDiv Epis TS of the SW 1996. D 6/7/1997 P 12/1/1997 Bp William Jerry Winterrowd. m 9/22/1989 Susan Mason c 3. S Laurence's Epis Mssn Conifer CO 2003-2009; R S Matt's Parker CO 1999-2003, Cur 1997-1998.

MASON OJN, Samuel Alison (NC) 2181 Jameson Ave Unit 1207, Alexandria VA 22314 B Mobile AL 1944 s Philip & Emma. BA U So 1966; MDiv VTS 1973; DMin Drew U 1999. D 6/6/1973 P 12/1/1973 Bp Furman Charles Stough. Int R Trin Epis Ch 2016-2017; Assoc for Pstr Care S Paul's Epis Ch Alexandria VA 2009-2015; Int Ch Of The Ascen Montgomery AL 2005-2006; COM Dio No Carolina Raleigh NC 1991-1994; R S Steph's Ch Durham NC 1990-2003; R S Jn's Epis Ch Mobile AL 1983-1990; R S Mths Epis Ch Tuscaloosa AL 1977-1983; R S Lk's Ch Scottsboro AL 1973-1977. Oblate of Ord of Julian of Norwich 2005.

MASON, Victoria Anne (Tex) 6500 Halsey Court, Austin TX 78739 **D S Jn's Epis Ch Austin TX 2015-; T/F Mem Discernment Process T/F Dio Texas Austin 2014-; Chair Com for the Diac Dio Texas 2008-** B Seattle WA 1948 d Gerald & Barbara. BA U of Texas 1970; MS Universtiy of Wisconsin Stout Menomonie 1974; Cert Iona Sch for Mnstry, Dio Texas 2007. D 2/9/2007 Bp Don Adger Wimberly. m 2/14/1976 Roy D Larsen c 3. D Iglesia San Francisco de Asis Austin TX 2012-2013, D 2010-2012; D El Buen Samaritano Epis Mssn Austin TX 2009-2010; D S Dav's Ch Austin TX 2007-2009; Mem Iona Initiative T/F 2010-2012; Fac Iona Sch for Mnstry 2009-2012. NAAD 2005. deaconvic@austinstjohns.org

MASQUELETTE, Eizabeth Daggett (Tex) 2204 Welch St, Houston TX 77019 B Austin TX 1927 d David & Elizabeth. Hollins U 1945; BA U of Texas 1948; MTS St. Mary's RC Sem Houston, TX 1976; MTS St. Mary's RC Sem, Houston, TX 1976; MTS U of St Thos, Houston, TX 1976; MDiv Epis TS of the SW 1978; BA U of Texas 2048. D 12/5/1978 P 6/8/1979 Bp James Milton Richardson. m 3/17/1948 Philip Abbott Masquelette c 4. Cler Asst St Fran Episcpal Ch Houston TX 1999-2011; Assoc S Fran Ch Houston TX 1996-1998;

Chr The King Ch Houston TX 1982-1996; The Great Cmsn Fndt Houston TX 1982-1996; Asst Ch Of The Epiph Houston TX 1978-1981. Auth, "Adv Recollections," Speedy, 2000; Auth, "Adventures of BoffinBear: A Chld's Story for Adults," Speedy, 1999; Auth, "Back to the Beginning," *Wmn Journ*, Brigid's Place, 1999. Ord of S Helena.

MASSENBURG, Barbara Jean (Ak) 7962 N Tongass Hwy, Ketchikan AK 99901 **Asst P S Jn's Ch Ketchikan AK 2005-, Vic 2002-2004, D 2000-2005** B Akron OH 1936 d Verne & Olive. BA Hiram Coll 1958; Wstrn Reserve U 1959. D 10/15/2000 Bp Frederick Warren Putnam P 11/30/2005 Bp Mark Lawrence Macdonald. c 1.

MASSENBURG, Raymond Douglas (WA) 1514 15th St NW, Washington DC 20005 **S Lk's Ch Washington DC 2011-** B Chicago, IL 1967 s Willie & Sheila. MBA Pur 1992; PhD U IL 2006; MDiv SWTS 2010. D 6/5/2010 P 12/19/2010 Bp Jeff Lee. m 7/3/2002 Yvonne Massenburg c 2. Asst R Ch Of S Paul And The Redeem Chicago IL 2010-2011.

MASSEY, Hoyt B (SwFla) Po Box 2161, Franklin NC 28744 **Ret 1990-; Chair - Stndg Liturg Cmsn 1975-** B Saint Petersberg FL 1927 s Hoyt & Mary. BS Florida St U 1952; LTh Sewanee: The U So, TS 1965. D 6/24/1965 P 12/1/1965 Bp Henry I Louttit. c 3. Int S Paul's Chap Magnolia Sprgs AL 1995-2000; Int S Agnes Epis Ch Franklin NC 1993-1994; Int S Jn Sylvia NC 1991-1993; Int S Jas Florence Italy 1990-1991; Dio SW Florida Parrish FL 1979-1990; P-in-c All Ang By The Sea Longboat Key FL 1979-1980; Dn of the Tampa Dnry 1977-1978; Pres - Stndg Cmsn 1977-1978; Stndg Cmsn 1974-1978; R St Johns Epis Ch Tampa FL 1968-1978; Vic S Chris's Ch Orlando FL 1967-1968; Cur S Mich's Ch Orlando FL 1965-1967.

MASSEY, Nigel John (NY) 111 E 60th St Penthouse, New York NY 10022 **R French Ch Of S Esprit New York NY 1994-** B 1960 s John & Margaret. BA U of Birmingham Gb 1981; MA Oxf GB 1987; Cert Theol Stud Oxf GB 1987; Dip Selly Oak Coll Birmingham Gb 1990. Trans 5/14/1996 Bp Walter Decoster Dennis Jr. m 6/24/2012 John Blair Wyker. Serv Ch Of Engl 1987-1996. Hugenot Soc Of Amer 1994; S Georges Soc 1996.

MASSIE IV, Robert Kinloch (Mass) 140 Sycamore St, Somerville MA 02145 **P S Jas' Epis Ch Cambridge MA 1998-** B New York NY 1956 s Robert & Suzanne. BA Pr 1978; MDiv Ya Berk 1982; DBA Harv 1989. D 6/2/1982 P 4/20/1983 Bp Paul Moore Jr. m 11/20/1982 Anne E Tate c 1. P-in-c Chr Ch Somerville MA 1986-1988; P-in-c Chr Ch Cambridge Cambridge MA 1985-1988; Asst & Chapl Gr Epis Ch New York NY 1982-1984. Auth, "A Song in the Night," *A Memoir of Resilience*, Doubleday, 2012; Auth, "Loosing Bonds: US & So Afr In Apartheid Years," Doubleday, 1998; Auth, "From Prophets To Profits," *Manhattan Inc*, 1985; Co-Ed, "The Big Bus Rdr," Pilgrim Press, 1980; Auth, "Setting Their Lives In Motion," *Ny Times Sunday mag*, 1979; Auth, "The Constant Shadow". Joan Bavaria Awd Ceres 2009; Damyanova Awd Tufts U 2008; Sr Fulbright Awd Untd States Govt 1993; Henry Luve Ethics Fllshp Harv 1987.

MASTER II, George (Pa) 6838 Woodland Avenue, Philadelphia PA 19142 **Police Chapl Philadelphia Police Dept 2009-; Int Vic S Dismas Epis Mssn At Graterford Philadelphia PA 2009-, Asst Vic 1995-2009, Int Vic 1994-1995, Int Vic 2009-; Pstr S Jas Ch of Kingsessing Philadelphia PA 2009-; Dioc Coun Mem Dio Pennsylvania Philadelphia PA 2010-** B Lake Placid NY 1947 s Henry & Florence. Colorado Sch of Mines 1966; BS U of Massachusetts 1977; MDiv Ya Berk 1987. D 10/24/1987 Bp Walter Decoster Dennis Jr P 4/23/1988 Bp Vincent King Pettit. m 10/15/2011 Doris Master. Pstr S Aug's Philadelphia PA 2003-2009, Pstr 2000-2009; Int S Paul's Ch Chester PA 1998-2000; P-in-c S Mart's Epis Ch Upper Chichester PA 1995-1998; Int Vic S Mary's Epis Ch Philadelphia PA 1994-1995; S Mk's Ch Honey Brook PA 1994; Asst Min The Epis Ch Of The Adv Kennet Sq PA 1991-1994; Cur S Mary's Ch Haddon Heights NJ 1987-1991.

MASTERMAN, Brenda Patricia (RG) 119 N Golfview Road, Box 9, Lake Worth FL 33460 **D S Andr's Ch Lake Worth FL 2001-** B Huntington WV 1946 BA Palm Bch Atlantic U 2004. D 9/1/2001 Bp Leo Frade. c 2.

MASTERMAN, Frederick James (SeFla) 15170 N Rugged Lark Dr, Tucson AZ 85739 B Niagara Falls NY 1937 s Frederick & Marion. BA SUNY 1959; STB GTS 1963. D 6/15/1963 P 5/23/1964 Bp Lauriston L Scaife. m 12/23/2004 Becky Ann Masterman c 2. Int Chr The King Ch Tucson AZ 2011-2013; Assoc S Greg's Ch Boca Raton FL 2001-2004; Cn Dio SE Florida Miami 1988-2001; R Ch Of The Ascen Miami FL 1978-1988; R S Steph's Ch Niagara Falls NY 1971-1975; Vic S Andr's Ch Newfane Burt NY 1967-1971; S Jn's Ch Wilson NY 1967-1971; Cur S Mths Epis Ch E Aurora NY 1963-1966. Auth, "arts," *Ch Hist mag*.

MASTERMAN, Patricia Dinan (NwT) 2700 W 16th Ave Apt 272, Amarillo TX 79102 **Died 12/15/2016** B Amarillo TX 1927 d Wilfrid & Frances. BA Colorado Coll 1949. D 10/25/1985 Bp Sam Byron Hulsey. c 2. Ret 1999-2016; Archd S Andr's Epis Ch Amarillo TX 1993-1999; Stff All SS' Epis Ch Ft Worth TX 1988-1993; Ed Dio NW Texas Lubbock TX 1972-1988.

MASTERS, Ralph Leeper (Tex) 459 Medina Dr, Highland Village TX 75077 **Asst Ch Of The Annunc Lewisville TX 2003-** B Saint Joseph MO 1929 s Ralph & Juanita. BS U of Texas 1955; STM Epis TS of the SW 1958. D 6/1/

1958 Bp James Parker Clements P 6/1/1959 Bp John Elbridge Hines. P-in-c S Mart's Epis Ch Copperas Cove TX 1992-2001; R S Mary's Epis Ch Inc Lampasas TX 1988-1992; R S Mich And All Ang Lake Chas LA 1966-1987; Chapl Mcneese St Coll LA 1966-1978; R S Phil Houston TX 1961-1966; Vic Chr Ch Matagorda TX 1958-1961; S Jn's Epis Ch Palacios TX 1958-1961.

MASTERSON, Liz Rust (Del) 1 Southerly Ct., Apt. 606, Towson MD 21286 **P Assoc Trin Ch Towson MD 2015-** B Milford DE 1946 d Manford & Virginia. BA Randolph Coll 1968; MA NWU 1970; MA U of Delaware 1983; MDiv GTS 2006. D 6/8/2006 P 12/12/2006 Bp Wayne Wright. c 2. S Thos's Par Newark DE 2015; Gd Shpd Epis Ch Wilmington DE 2009-2010; R S Nich' Epis Ch Newark DE 2006-2015. Assoc - Epis Carmel of St. Teresa 2008; Assoc - OSH 1984.

MATARAZZO, Laura Rice (Nwk) 10 Doe Hollow Lane, Belvidere NJ 07823 B Cleveland OH 1951 d Norman & Betty. BA U So 1973; MDiv Drew U 2001. D 4/13/2002 Bp John Palmer Croneberger P 10/19/2002 Bp Rufus T Brome. m 6/1/1973 Robert Joseph Matarazzo c 4. S Lk's Ch Hope NJ 2011-2014; S Mary's Ch Belvidere NJ 2011-2014; Calv Epis Ch Summit NJ 2002-2008.

MATHAUER, Margaret Ann (Vt) 7 Holy Cross Rd, Colchester VT 05446 **D All SS' Epis Ch S Burlington VT 1991-** B Cincinnati OH 1943 d Paul & Otillia. BS Bowling Green St U 1965; MEd Bowling Green St U 1967; Cert U of Vermont 1973; MEd Trin 1979. D 7/30/1991 Bp Daniel Lee Swenson. c 4.

MATHENY, Clint Michael (CFla) 130 N Magnolia Ave, Orlando FL 32801 **Cathd Ch Of S Lk Orlando FL 2015-** B Memphis TN 1950 s Clint & Hermina. D 12/9/2006 Bp John Wadsworth Howe. m 5/26/1984 Linda Matheny c 1. servantleader@me.com

MATHER, Nicholas S (Spok) **Cur Cathd Of S Jn The Evang Spokane WA 2015-** B Moses Lake WA 1987 s Jay & Susan. BA Gonzaga U 2008; MDiv VTS 2015. D 10/19/2014 P 6/6/2015 Bp James E Waggoner Jr. m 7/26/2014 Krista M Mather. nmather@stjohns-cathedral.org

MATHER-HEMPLER, Portia (ECR) 950 - 30th Street, Port Townsend WA 98368 B Port Townsend WA 1949 d Howard & Portia. Ripon Coll Cuddesdon, Oxford, UK; BA U of Oregon 1972; MDiv CDSP 1984; DASD SFTS 2008. D 6/29/1984 Bp David Rea Cochran P 6/7/1985 Bp Charles Shannon Mallory. m 10/6/1990 James Paul Hempler. supply P Trin Cathd San Jose CA 2015; Co-Dir Contemplative Cntr of Silicon Vlly Saratoga CA 2011-2014; Supply P S Fran Epis Ch San Jose CA 2011; Sprtl Dir & founding Dir of Cntr Contemplative Cntr of Silicon Vlly Saratoga CA 2010-2015; Supply P Epis Ch in Almaden San Jose CA 2009; Assoc R S Andr's Ch Saratoga CA 1991-2006; Assoc R S Jn's Epis Ch Olympia WA 1987-1990; Assoc All SS Epis Ch Palo Alto CA 1984-1987; Mem, Stwdshp Cmsn Dio El Camino Real Salinas CA 2005-2010; Mem, CE Cmsn Dio Olympia Seattle 1987-1990. Auth, "How to Call People to Tchg Mnstry of the Ch," *AWARE*, The Epis Ch, 1979. NNECA 1988-1990; Sprtl Dir Intl 1998.

MATHES, Hester Shipp (WTenn) 4645 Walnut Grove Rd, Memphis TN 38117 **Ch Of The H Comm Memphis TN 2014-** B Memphis TN 1974 d Charles & Cornelia. BA W&M 1996; MDiv VTS 2014. D 6/28/2014 P 1/3/2015 Bp Don Edward Johnson. m 10/3/1998 Andrew Alexander Mathes c 2. Calv Ch Memphis TN 1997-2000.

✠ MATHES, The Rt Rev Jim (SanD) 2083 Sunset Cliffs Blvd, San Diego CA 92107 **VTS Alexandria VA 2017-** B Dallas TX 1959 s George & Kathleen. BA U So 1982; MDiv VTS 1991. D 6/22/1991 Bp William Evan Sanders P 3/22/1992 Bp Philip Alan Smith Con 3/5/2005 for SanD. m 8/15/1981 Teresa S Mathes c 2. Bp of San Diego Dio San Diego San Diego CA 2005-2017; Cn to the Ordnry Dio Chicago Chicago IL 2001-2005; R The Epis Ch Of S Jas The Less Northfield IL 1994-2001; Asst Min All SS' Epis Ch Belmont MA 1991-1994; Prot Chapl Mclean Hosp Belmont MA 1991-1994. Phi Beta Kappa 1981. bishopmathes@edsd.org

MATHESON, M Jennings Jennings (Ct) 74 South St # 809, Litchfield CT 06759 B Greensboro NC 1950 d Kenneth & Frances. BA Sweet Briar Coll 1972; MDiv GTS 1983. D 3/22/1984 Bp Walter Decoster Dennis Jr P 12/1/1984 Bp Paul Moore Jr. m 6/24/1989 Robert Clements c 1. S Paul's Epis Ch Shelton CT 2012-2014; R S Mich's Ch Litchfield CT 1997-2012; R S Wstrn Massachusetts Springfield 1990-1997; Dn, So Berkshire Dnry; Gr Ch Great Barrington MA 1990-1997; Trin Epis Ch Southport CT 1984-1989; Hosp Chapl Ch Of The Incarn New York NY 1983-1984; ; Liturg and Mus Cmsn; Dn, Wickfield Dnry Dio Connecticut Meriden CT.

MATHEUS, Rob (SO) 6300 Kinver Edge Way, Columbus OH 43213 **Assoc St. Alb's Epis Ch Bexley OH 2004-** B Pueblo CO 1953 s Robert & Charlotte. BA Coe Coll 1975; MDiv SWTS 1979. D 6/23/1979 P 1/19/1980 Bp Walter Cameron Righter. m 6/14/2003 Donna George. S Alb's Epis Ch Of Bexley Columbus OH 2004-2010; Vic Ch Of The Gd Samar Amelia OH 2001-2004; Adv Ch Cynthiana KY 2000-2001; S Raphael's Ch Lexington KY 1987-2000; R S Paul's Epis Ch Greenville OH 1981-1987; Cur S Andr's Ch Des Moines IA 1979-1981.

MATHEW, Cherian (ND) B Kerala India 1941 s Cherian & Anna. D 11/17/1990 P 6/21/1991 Bp Andrew Fairfield. m 6/15/1965 Blanche Marie Mathew c 2.

MATHEWS, Keith Elizabeth (SO) 662 N 600 E, Firth ID 83236 B Charleston WV 1948 d Robert & Elizabeth. BA W Virginia U 1970; Bex Sem 1972; MDiv CDSP 1974; VTS 1992; Sabbatical Dio Chr Ch NZ 1997. D 10/4/1975 Bp Wilburn Camrock Campbell P 1/5/1977 Bp Robert Poland Atkinson. m 6/15/1974 James Patrick Roeder. R S Mary's Epis Ch Hillsboro OH 1999-2004; R S Mk's Ch Lake City MN 1998-1999; Founding R S Jn's-of-the-Mesa Parachute CO 1994-1998; R S Jn's Epis Ch New Castle CO 1992-1998; R S Barn Ch Glenwood Spgs CO 1992-1997; R Trin Ch Scotland Neck NC 1988-1992; R S Thos' Epis Ch Syracuse NY 1983-1988; Int Dio Cntrl New York Liverpool NY 1981-1983; Trin Epis Ch Watertown NY 1981-1982; S Ann's Ch N Martinsvlle WV 1977-1981; D S Matt's Ch Charleston WV 1975-1976. OHC 1970; SMOTJ 1998. Rossiter Fllshp Bex 1988; Rossiter Fllshp Bex 1985; Phi Beta Kappa W Virginia U 1970.

MATHEWS, Koshy (Pa) 103 Potters Pond Dr, Phoenixville PA 19460 **R S Ptr's Ch Phoenixville PA 2006-** B Tiruvalla Kerala India 1948 s P C & Annamma. BS U of Kerala Kottayam IN 1970; MDiv PrTS 1977; MEd Harv 1981; DMin EDS 2000. D 6/2/2001 Bp Barbara Clementine Harris P 6/8/2002 Bp M(Arvil) Thomas Shaw. m 5/28/1977 Susan Koshy c 2. Int R The Par Of S Chrys's Quincy MA 2005; Int R Epiph Par Walpole MA 2004-2005; Assoc R Chr Ch Needham Hgts MA 2001-2004; Chr Epis Ch Sheffield MA 2001-2004; Dioc Intern S Ptr's Ch Weston MA 2000-2001. saintpetersphoenix@gmail.com

MATHEWS, Miriam Atwell (Md) 3433 Manor Ln, Ellicott City MD 21042 **D S Jn's Ch Ellicott City MD 2002-** B Howard County MD 1943 d Richard & Ethel. Cert Maryland Bankers Sch 1979; Rutgers The St U of New Jersey 1987; EFM Sewanee: The U So, TS 1996. D 6/14/1997 Bp Charles Lindsay Longest.

MATHEWS, Ranjit (Mass) 7 Pond St, Randolph MA 02368 **S Jas Ch New London CT 2017-** B Brighton MA 1979 s Koshy & Susan. BA GW 2001; MDiv UTS 2005; MDiv UTS 2005. D 6/3/2006 Bp M(Arvil) Thomas Shaw P 1/6/2007 Bp Gayle Harris. m 8/12/2006 Johanna J Kuruvilla c 1. Epis Ch Cntr New York NY 2013-2017, 2010-2011; Assoc The Par Ch Of S Lk Long Bch CA 2011-2013; Exec Coun Appointees New York NY 2011; Asst S Mich's Ch Milton MA 2006-2009; Internet Consult/Asst Human Dvlpmt And Capability Assn 2005-2006.

MATHEWS JR, Thomas Etienne (Nwk) 5 Surrey Ln, Madison NJ 07940 **R S Lk's Ch Phillipsburg NJ 2007-** B Newark NJ 1974 BS Trenton St Coll; MDiv EDS 2003. D 6/7/2003 P 12/6/2003 Bp John Palmer Croneberger. m 9/12/1998 Tanya Mathews c 2. Cur Gr Ch Madison NJ 2003-2007.

MATHEWS, Weston (SwVa) 6000 Grove Ave, Richmond VA 23226 **Gr Ch The Plains VA 2017-; S Steph's Ch Richmond VA 2014-** B Winchester VA 1980 s William & Susan. BA W&M 2004; MA W&M 2005; MDiv VTS 2014. D 5/24/2014 Bp Mark Bourlakas P 12/6/2014 Bp Shannon Sherwood Johnston. m 6/23/2007 Hannah M Mathews.

MATHEWSON, Colin J (SanD) St Paul's Episcopal Cathedral, 2728 6th Ave, San Diego CA 92103 **S Lk's Ch San Diego CA 2017-** B San Diego CA 1980 s Peter & Penny. BA Stan 2002; MDiv Sewanee: The U So, TS 2013; MDiv The TS at The U So 2013. D 4/20/2013 P 10/19/2013 Bp Jim Mathes. m 7/21/2006 Laurel Stewart c 2. Dio San Diego San Diego CA 2016; Cathd Ch Of S Paul San Diego CA 2013-2016.

MATHEWSON, Kathryn Carroll (ETenn) 412 silverberry, Pittsboro NC 27312 B Buffalo NY 1944 d Kenneth & Jean. BA Sweet Briar Coll 1966; MDiv Aquinas Inst of Theol 1996; CATS SWTS 1997; DMin Aquinas Inst of Theol 2011; DMin Other 2011; DMin Other 2011. D 7/29/1996 P 7/29/1997 Bp Peter Hess Beckwith. m 10/12/1968 David Mathewson c 2. Assoc R S Tim's Ch Signal Mtn TN 2003-2011; Asst R Epis Ch Of The Redeem Greenville SC 1998-2003; P-in-c S Thos Epis Ch Glen Carbon IL 1997-1998.

MATHEWSON, Laurel (SanD) St Paul's Cathedral, 2728 6th Ave, San Diego CA 92103 **S Lk's Ch San Diego CA 2017-** B LaGrande OR 1983 d Reed & Elizabeth. BA Stan 2005; MDiv Sewanee: The U So, TS 2013; MDiv The TS at The U So 2013. D 4/20/2013 P 10/19/2013 Bp Jim Mathes. m 7/21/2006 Colin J Mathewson c 2. Dio San Diego San Diego CA 2016; Cathd Ch Of S Paul San Diego CA 2013-2016. The Freeman Prize for Acad Merit The U So: TS 2011. mathewsonl@stpaulcathedral.com

MATHIAS, Barbara Helen (Minn) 110 S Oak St, Lake City MN 55041 B Wabasha MN 1953 d Richard & Elizabeth. D 6/20/2015 P 6/21/2016 Bp Brian N Prior. m 5/12/1973 Peter Michael Mathias c 3.

MATHIESON, James West (SVa) 183 Grove Park Cir, Danville VA 24541 B Winthrop MA 1938 s David & Ruth. BA Lynchburg Coll 1960; MDiv Sewanee: The U So, TS 1966. D 6/24/1966 Bp George P Gunn P 6/9/1967 Bp David Shepherd Rose. m 8/1/1959 Joan Mathieson c 3. S Paul's Epis Ch Suffolk VA 2006-2007; R Ch Of The Epiph Danville VA 1993-2004; R S Andr's Ch Rocky Mt NC 1975-1993; R Emm Epis Ch Chatham VA 1969-1975; Asst R S Mich's Ch Richmond VA 1966-1969.

MATHIS, Judy (CFla) 86 Dianne Dr., Ormond Beach FL 32176 **D St. Jas Epis Ch Ormond Bch FL 2003-** B Cincinnati OH 1941 BA U of Miami 1963; MS Syr 1981. D 12/13/2003 Bp John Wadsworth Howe. m 4/16/1964 Horace Mathis c 2. S Jas Epis Ch Ormond Bch FL 2007-2013.

MATHIS, Thelma Monique (At) 306 Peyton Rd SW, Atlanta GA 30311 **Assoc S Ptr's Ch Rome GA 2013-** B Fort Monmouth NJ 1965 d Gordon & Rosalyn. BA Emory U 1987; MSW U GA 1992; MDiv Sewanee: The U So, TS 2008. D 12/21/2007 P 8/9/2008 Bp J Neil Alexander. m 5/2/2009 Vincent L Mathis c 1. Sewanee U So TS Sewanee TN 2011-2013; Assoc R S Paul's Epis Ch Atlanta GA 2008-2011.

MATHISON, Mary Alice (CGC) 28788 N Main St, Daphne AL 36526 **S Paul's Epis Ch Daphne AL 2014-** B Fort Walton Beach FL 1984 d Robert & Virginia. BA Sewanee: The U So, TS 2007; BA The TS at The U So 2007; MDiv VTS 2014. D 12/14/2013 P 8/2/2014 Bp Philip Menzie Duncan II.

MATIJASIC, Ernie (SwFla) 401 W Shoreline Dr #253, Sandusky OH 44870 B Pittsburgh PA 1952 s Ernest & Mary. SWTS; BA Penn 1973; MDiv VTS 1978. D 6/3/1978 Bp Robert Bracewell Appleyard P 12/31/1978 Bp William Henry Marmion. c 3. R Gr Epis Ch Sandusky OH 1989-2009; R Trin Epis Ch So Boston VA 1984-1989; P-in-c S Marg's Epis Ch Waxhaw NC 1983-1984; Asst Ch Of The H Comf Charlotte NC 1981-1984; Asst S Paul's Epis Ch Lynchburg VA 1978-1981. Rotary 1990.

MATIS, Glenn Marshall (Pa) 45 Latham Ct, Doylestown PA 18901 **Org Fam of God Luth Ch Buckingham PA 2011-; Chapl Bucks Cnty Correctional Facility 2008-** B Bryn Mawr PA 1947 s Arthur & C. BME Shenandoah U 1969; MA Glassboro St U 1974; MDiv EDS 1976; MS Marywood U 1981; Providence Sch of Div 2010; D.D. Providence Sch of Div 2010. D 6/12/1976 P 5/21/1977 Bp Lyman Cunningham Ogilby. m 8/16/1975 Patricia Ann Coates. Pres Stndg Com Dio Pennsylvania 2007-2010; R Ch Of The Resurr Philadelphia PA 1989-2006; Ch Of The H Nativ Wrightstown PA 1980-1989; Dio Pennsylvania Philadelphia PA 1978-1979, Intake Off 2011; Ch Of The Redeem Springfield PA 1976-1978. Glenn M. Matis, "Cler in Difficult Calls," *Leaven*, 2014; Auth, "The Impact of Dual-Career Marriages on the Priesthood & Ch," *Leaven*, 1990. gmatis@verizon.net.

MATISSE, Jacqueline Edith (SO) 232 E Main St, Lebanon OH 45036 **R S Pat's Epis Ch Lebanon OH 1991-** B New Orleans LA 1948 d Albert & Nancy. BA Albion Coll 1970; MA St Johns Prov Sem Plymouth MI 1984; MDiv VTS 1988. D 6/25/1988 Bp Henry Irving Mayson P 1/14/1989 Bp H Coleman Mcgehee Jr. Dir Camping Progs Dio Sthrn Ohio Cincinnati OH 1991-1994; Chr Ch - Glendale Cincinnati OH 1988-1991; Assoc Chr Ch Glendale OH 1988-1991.

MATLACK, David Russell (NY) Po Box 703, Southwest Harbor ME 04679 **Ret 1982-** B Philadelphia PA 1922 s David & Elizabeth. MDiv EDS 1949; MBA CUNY 1975; SB Harv 2044. D 6/23/1949 Bp Oliver J Hart P 1/1/1950 Bp Joseph Gillespie Armstrong. m 7/22/1950 Margery A Matlack c 3. Non-par 1968-1982; R S Barn Ch Irvington NY 1964-1968; R S Mich's Epis Ch Arlington VA 1956-1964; R S Mk's Epis Ch Penn Yan NY 1950-1956. Auth, "Cost Effectivness Of Spinal Cord Injury Cntr Treatment," Natl Paraplegia Fndt, 1974.

MATLAK, David John (Mil) 1101 Forest Ave, Richmond VA 23229 **Other Lay Position S Matt's Ch Richmond VA 2013-** B Salt Lake City UT 1977 s Michael & Rosemarie. BS Wheaton Coll 2000; MDiv Nash 2013. D 6/13/2015 P 1/20/2016 Bp Steven Andrew Miller. m 8/12/2000 Caroline A Smith c 4.

MATNEY, Rex H (Kan) The Church of the Covenant, PO Box 366, Junction City KS 66441 **D Intrnshp Ch Of The Cov Jct City KS 2012-; D Intrnshp S Paul's Epis Ch Clay Cntr KS 2012-** B Amarillo TX 1943 s Rex & Frances. BGS Chaminade U of Honolulu; Grad Stds K SU; Kansas Sch for Mnstry 2012. D 6/2/2012 Bp Dean E Wolfe. m 11/20/1990 Jolana Montgomery-Matney c 1.

MATOTT, Michele Louise (RI) 80 Fisher Road Unit 90, Cumberland RI 02864 **Ch Of The Trsfg Providence RI 2014-; S Mary's Ch E Providence RI 2013-; Admin McAuley Vill 2010-** B Albany NY 1958 d Ellsworth & Jean. BS Muskingum Coll 1980; MDiv UTS 1986; DMin SWTS 2008. D 11/22/1992 P 9/1/1993 Bp George Nelson Hunt III. m 1/6/2006 Marguerite Mclaughlin c 4. Chr Epis Ch Norwich CT 2011, Int 2011; S Alb's Ch Danielson CT 2008-2010; S Thos Ch Greenville RI 1996-2008, 1995-1996; Chapl S Eliz's Hm 1993-1996; S Eliz's Hm Providence RI 1993-1996; Chapl S Mary's Hm for Chld 1993-1994; DCE Gr Ch In Providence Providence RI 1992-1995.

MATSON, David John (Me) 26 Heron Lane, Harpswell ME 04079 **R S Matt's Epis Ch Hallowell ME 2011-; Adj Fac Bangor TS 2006-; Dio Maine Portland ME 1998-** B Worcester MA 1961 s Arthur & Nancy. BA Bates Coll 1983; MDiv EDS 1998; MDiv VTS 1998. D 8/15/1998 Bp Chilton Richardson Knudsen P 6/5/1999 Bp Gordon Scruton. m 9/19/2009 Jessica Gorton c 2. Vic S Barn Ch Augusta Augusta ME 2009-2016; P St Mths Epis Ch Brunswick ME 2008-2009; R S Nich Epis Ch Scarborough ME 2004-2008; Int S Ptr's Epis Ch Londonderry NH 2002-2004; Int Ch Of The Gd Shpd Rangeley ME 2001-2002; Dio Wstrn Massachusetts Springfield 1998-2001; Asst S Steph's Ch Westborough MA 1998-2001.

MATTER, Janice Louise (Me) 5 Boynton Ln, Billerica MA 01821 B Altoona PA 1941 D 4/26/2003 Bp Chilton Richardson Knudsen. c 3. D Ascen Memi Ch Ipswich MA 2003-2007.

MATTERS, Rick (ECR) 181 S Corinth Ave, Lodi CA 95242 B Spokane WA 1950 s Clyde & Anna. BA Whitworth U 1973; MDiv GTS 1984; STM GTS 1991. D 6/11/1985 Bp Robert Hume Cochrane P 6/1/1986 Bp William Gillette

Weinhauer. m 5/20/1972 Andrea K Matters c 3. R All SS Ch Carmel CA 2007-2015; R S Jn The Bapt Lodi CA 1993-2007; Assoc R Trin Epis Ch Everett WA 1987-1993; Asst Trin Epis Ch Asheville NC 1985-1987.

MATTHEW, John Clifford (Ida) 5301 E Warm Springs Ave E102, Boise ID 83716 **Non-par 1994-** B Anderson IN 1927 s Mark & Mary. BA Hanover Coll 1951; MDiv Louisville Presb TS 1954; MEd The Coll of Idaho 1991. D 11/20/1994 P 5/28/1995 Bp John Stuart Thornton. m 1/20/1991 Judy Aileen Mckay. Vic Emm Ch Hailey ID 1994-1996; Exec Presb Presbyteries of Boise Kendall Estrn Oregon 1973-1989; Reg/Natl Stff Presb Bd Natl Missions 1960-1973; Pstr Presb Ch 1955-1960; Mem The Coll of Idaho Bd Trst 1980-1992. DD The Coll of Idaho 1977.

MATTHEWS, Alan Montague Basil (SJ) PO Box 76, Vallecito CA 95251 **Died 12/3/2015** B London UK 1937 s Hanibal & Winifred. BA Hon Theol Exeter U UK 1986; Dio Oxford Oxf 2002. Trans 2/19/2009 Bp Jerry Alban Lamb. m 4/22/2006 Cheryl Parker. Vic S Clare of Assisi Epis Ch Avery CA 2011-2015; S Mk's Epis Ch Tracy CA 2010-2012; P-in-c Epis Dio San Joaquin Modesto CA 2009-2015.

MATTHEWS JR, Allen Russel (WTex) Po Box 348, Luling TX 78648 **Ret 2000-** B Stephenville TX 1935 s Allen & Lelia. SW U Georgetown TX 1956; BA U of Houston 1959; MDiv Epis TS of the SW 1977. D 6/21/1977 P 1/15/1978 Bp Scott Field Bailey. m 5/23/1956 Jane Rogers Matthews c 3. R Trin Ch Victoria TX 1988-2000; Dio W Texas San Antonio TX 1981-1988, Trst of the Ch Corp 1980-1981, Mem, Exec Bd 1996-1998, Mem, Stndg Com 1992-1995; S Marg's Epis Ch San Antonio TX 1979-1984; S Fran By The Lake Canyon Lake TX 1979-1981; M-in-c H Trin Carrizo Sprg TX 1977-1979.

MATTHEWS, Anne (Miss) P. O. Box 804, Brookhaven MS 39602 **R Ch Of The Redeem Brookhaven MS 2010-; Co-Ldr Lincoln Cnty Mssn Mississippi 2015-** B 1951 d Jamie & Mary. BA SW U 1973; MA U of Texas 1975; MS U of Texas 1991; Cert Mnstry Acad Iona Sch 2005. D 6/24/2006 Bp Don Adger Wimberly P 2/17/2007 Bp Claude Edward Payne. m 1/24/1987 Randolph Raynolds. Vic S Thos' Epis Ch Rockdale TX 2005-2010.

MATTHEWS, Bonnie Anne (Ct) Trinity Episc Church, 120 Sigourney St, Hartford CT 06105 B Derby CT 1955 d William & Vivienne. D 9/15/2012 Bp Laura Ahrens. c 1.

MATTHEWS, Daniel Paul (NY) 1047 Amsterdam Ave, New York NY 10025 **Co-Chair Dvlpmt Cathd of St Jn Div New York NY 2004-** B Chicago,IL 1933 s Robert & Martha. BA Rol 1955; BD CDSP 1959; Coll of Preachers 1972. D 6/29/1959 Bp John Vander Horst P 2/1/1960 Bp Theodore N Barth. m 10/4/1960 Diane Kendrick Vigeant Matthews c 3. R Trin Par New York NY 1987-2004; R S Lk's Epis Ch Atlanta GA 1980-1987; R S Jn's Epis Cathd Knoxville TN 1972-1980; R S Dav's Epis Ch Nashville TN 1965-1972; Asst Ch Of The H Comm Memphis TN 1961-1965; Min in charge Ch Of The H Comf Monteagle TN 1959-1961; Min in charge St Jas Epis Ch Sewanee TN 1959-1961. OBE Ord of the British Empire/British Embassy, Washington D.C. 2006; DD U So TS/ Sewanee, TN 1992; DD GTS/ New York, NY 1987; LHD Rol/ Winter Pk, FL 1986; DD CDSP/ Berkeley, CA 1984.

MATTHEWS JR, Daniel Paul (At) 435 Peachtree St, Atlanta GA 30308 **R S Lk's Epis Ch Atlanta GA 2003-** B Memphis TN 1961 s Daniel & Diane. BS U So 1984; MDiv VTS 1989. D 6/18/1989 P 5/20/1990 Bp William Evan Sanders. m 8/15/1987 Sarah Barnes Matthews c 2. R S Paul's Epis Ch Kingsport TN 1996-2003; Assoc S Mk's Epis Ch Jacksonville FL 1993-1996; Assoc S Paul's Epis Ch Chattanooga TN 1989-1992.

MATTHEWS, Donald William (CNY) 375 W Clinton St, Elmira NY 14901 B Pittsburgh PA 1960 s Donald & Marilyn. BS Ashland U 1983; MDiv Bex Sem 1991. D 6/15/1991 P 1/1/1992 Bp James Russell Moodey. m 7/2/1983 Margaret R Matthews c 2. Dio Cntrl New York Liverpool NY 2005; R Gr Epis Ch Elmira NY 1997-2017; Cluster P/Vic Chr Epis Ch Geneva OH 1991-1997; The Cluster Of Ch In NE OH Ashtabula OH 1991-1997; Trin Jefferson OH 1991-1997. Associated Parishes; Assn Ord Oblates Of Sacr Heart Of Jesus; OHC.

✠ MATTHEWS, The Rt Rev Frank Clayton (Va) PO Box 12686, New Bern NC 28561 **Mng Dir Coll for Bishops 2008-; Bp Off of Pstr Dvlpmt Ecusa / Mssn Personl New York NY 1998-** B Raleigh NC 1947 s Walter & Ellinore. BA Hampden-Sydney Coll 1970; MDiv VTS 1973. D 6/23/1973 Bp Thomas Augustus Fraser Jr P 4/3/1974 Bp Bennett Jones Sims Con 9/11/1993 for Va. m 6/7/1969 Martha H Matthews c 1. Epis Ch Cntr New York NY 1998-2017; Bp Suffr Dio Virginia Richmond VA 1993-1998, Cn 1987-1998; R Emm Ch At Brook Hill Richmond VA 1980-1987; Asst Chr Ch New Bern NC 1976-1979; H Innoc Ch Atlanta GA 1973-1976. Auth, "Formulat," *Formulations & Discussions*. DD VTS 1993; Ldrshp Atlanta Awd 1975.

MATTHEWS III, James Houston (WNC) 2232 Water Oak Ln, Gastonia NC 28056 B Gastonia NC 1947 s James & Annabelle. BA Belmont Abbey Coll 1974; MDiv GTS 1977. D 6/25/1977 Bp William Gillette Weinhauer P 5/2/1978 Bp James Barrow Brown. m 5/29/1972 Sharon Matthews c 3. R All SS' Epis Ch Gastonia NC 1991-2005; R All SS Ch Cayce SC 1986-1991; R Ch Of The Epiph Opelousas LA 1980-1986; Cur Ch Of The Ascen Lafayette LA 1977-1980; Stndg Comm. Pres Dio Wstrn No Carolina Asheville NC 2001-2005.

M

MATTHEWS, Joyce (Mich) 37906 Glengrove Dr, Farmington Hills MI 48331 **Assoc Chr Ch Cranbrook Bloomfield Hills MI 2005-** B Detroit MI 1947 d Gunzie & Gertrude. BS U MI 1974; MS U MI 1976; MDiv SWTS 2005. D 12/18/2004 P 7/2/2005 Bp Wendell Nathaniel Gibbs Jr. m 7/28/1973 Lauriant Matthews c 2. Respiratory Clincl Spec Trin Healthcare Farmington Hills MI 1994-1999.

MATTHEWS, Kevin (NC) 625 Candlewood Drive, Greensboro NC 27403 **Chapl Dio No Carolina Raleigh NC 2006-; Chapl S Mary's Hse Epis/Angl Campus Greensboro NC 2006-** B Baltimore MD 1956 s Robert & LaMoyne. BA U of Maryland Baltimore Cnty 1978; MDiv VTS 1984; ABD Duke 2004. D 5/9/1984 Bp Albert Theodore Eastman P 3/3/1985 Bp David Keller Leighton Sr. Int St Elizabeths Epis Ch Apex NC 2005-2006; Int Chap Of Chr The King Charlotte NC 1996; Assoc S Tit Epis Ch Durham NC 1993-2000; Int S Mich And All Ang Hyattsville MD 1992; Vic S Phil The Evang Washington DC 1988-1991; Asst to Bp of Maryland Dio Maryland Baltimore MD 1987-1988, 1984-1987; P-in-c Cathd Of The Incarn Baltimore MD 1987, Asst to Dn 1985-1987; Asst S Phil's Ch Annapolis MD 1984-1985.

MATTHEWS, Mary Theresa (RI) Woodson Dr 2721, 2721 Woodson Dr, Mckinney TX 75070 **P-in-c S Wm Laud Epis Ch Pittsburg TX 2009-** B Scranton PA 1952 d Thomas & Mary. BTh U of Scranton 1994; MDiv Ya Berk 1999. D 4/17/1999 P 10/23/1999 Bp Paul Victor Marshall. c 2. S Ann's-By-The-Sea Block Island RI 2005-2006; S Mk's Epis Ch Moscow PA 1999-2002.

MATTHEWS, Patricia Gail (Ark) D 3/19/2016 P 10/1/2016 Bp Larry Benfield.

MATTHEWS, Richard L (Minn) 8895 Bradford Pl, Eden Prairie MN 55347 B Rochester NH 1946 s Elton & Virginia. BS U of Massachusetts 1970; MS U of Pennsylvania 1980; MBA Indiana U 1989. D 5/16/1986 P 12/16/1986 Bp William Cockburn Russell Sheridan. m 8/23/1969 Jacqueline A Matthews c 2. Chapl - Sr Care Ctr H Trin Epis Ch Elk River MN 2006-2008; R Trin Ch Anoka MN 2004-2013; Chair - Dioc Coun Dio Minnesota 1994-1995; R S Paul's Ch Minneapolis MN 1993-2004; Asst R S Lk's Ch Baton Rouge LA 1991-1993; R H Fam Ch Angola IN 1987-1991; Assoc Trin Ch Ft Wayne IN 1986-1987.

MATTHEWS, William Thompson (CFla) **S Edw's Sch Vero Bch FL 2015-** D 5/24/2014 P 1/13/2015 Bp Gregory Orrin Brewer.

MATTIA, Joan Plubell (Va) 1 Egyetem Ter, Debrecen 4032 Hungary **Vstng Prof U of Debrecen 2012-** B Clearfield PA 1953 d Earl & Irene. BA Geo Mason U 1985; MDiv VTS 1988; PhD U of Birmingham Birmingham GB 2007. D 6/18/1988 P 3/15/1989 Bp Peter J Lee. m 1/21/1978 Louis Joseph Mattia c 1. Adj Fac Geo Mason U Fairfax VA 2008-2012; Adj Fac VTS Alexandria VA 2008-2012; The Leads Fndt Herndon VA 2008-2009; S Peters-In-The-Woods Epis Ch Fairfax Sta VA 2007; Exec Coun Appointees New York NY 1999-2002; Mssy Serv Angl Ch of Tanzania 1999-2002; Co-R S Mich's Ch Gainesville FL 1991-1999; S Marg's Ch Woodbridge VA 1991; Assoc Trin Ch Arlington VA 1989-1990; Asst S Jas' Epis Ch Leesburg VA 1988-1989. PhD dissertation, "Walking the Rift: Idealism and Imperialism in E Afr, 1890-1911," *PhD dissertation*, U of Birmingham, 2007.

MATTIA JR, Louis Joseph (Va) 622 Worchester St, Herndon VA 20170 **Bus Dvlpmt Consult Fed Engr Vienna VA 2008-** B Washington DC 1952 s Louis & Irene. BS Pur 1974; MDiv VTS 1988; Cert GW 2007. D 6/18/1988 P 3/15/1989 Bp Peter J Lee. m 1/21/1978 Joan Plubell Mattia. Chr Epis Ch Lucketts Leesburg VA 2011-2012, 2011-2012, 2010-2011; Ch Of The Gd Shpd Bluemont VA 2011; Assoc R Ch Of The H Comf Vienna VA 2003-2008; Mssy Mawapwa Tanzania Dfms 1999-2003; Exec Coun Appointees New York NY 1999-2002; Co-R S Mich's Ch Gainesville FL 1991-1999; S Marg's Ch Woodbridge VA 1989-1991; Asst S Jas' Epis Ch Leesburg VA 1988-1989. "Conversation w Sanji," *Publish Amer*, 2005.

MATTILA, Daniel E (Ct) 104 Walnut Tree Hill Rd, Sandy Hook CT 06482 **Asst S Mk's Ch Bridgewater CT 2014-; Psych, Priv Pract Cognitive Ther Inst of Westport 2005-; Psych Cognitive Ther of Westport CT 2003-; Psych Cognitive Ther of New York 1997-; Psych Cognitive Ther Cntr of New York 1996-** B Santa Clara CA 1968 s William & Gloria. BA Hamline U 1991; Dip Ang Stud Ya Berk 1994; MDiv Yale DS 1994; MSW U of Connecticut 1997. D 9/29/1994 P 3/31/1995 Bp James Louis Jelinek. P-in-c S Jn's Ch Sandy Hook CT 2001-2006; Assoc S Jas Epis Ch Danbury CT 1999-2001; P-in-c Calv St Geo's Epis Ch Bridgeport CT 1997-1999; Asst S Jn's Ch Bridgeport CT 1994-1996. Auth, "Chapt: Schema Focused Ther For Depression," *Comparative Treatments For Depression*, Springer, 2002. Who'S Who In Amer 2003; Founding Fell Acad Of Cognitive Ther 2000; Phi Beta Kappa 1991.

MATTLIN, Margaret Baker (Minn) 2085 Buford Ave, Saint Paul MN 55108 **D Ch Of The H Apos 2005-** B Saint Paul MN 1945 d Harold & Mary. BA Hamline U 1967; MLS Hamline U 1988. D 8/14/1996 Bp Sanford Zangwill Kaye Hampton. D Ch Of The Ascen Stillwater MN 1997-1999.

MATTSON, Jennifer Elizabeth (CPa) 241 Sherman Ave Apt 3, New Haven CT 06511 **S Thos Ch Lancaster PA 2017-** B Washington DC 1979 d Peter & Vicki. BS Shippensburg U 2001; MDiv Ya Berk 2005. D 6/11/2005 P 10/4/2006 Bp Michael Whittington Creighton. m 12/17/2005 Craig Fenn c 4. Archd S Jn's Epis Ch Lancaster PA 2006-2015.

MATTSON, Sherry (Ind) 11974 State Highway M26, Eagle Harbor MI 49950 B Detroit MI 1949 d Raymond & Ella. BA Simmons Coll 1971; MDiv Epis TS of the SW 1979; Cert Haden Inst 2009. D 6/16/1979 P 5/31/1980 Bp H Coleman Mcgehee Jr. m 9/6/1993 Richard Thorp Draper c 2. campus Min Dio Indianapolis Indianapolis IN 2004-2005, Dep to GC 2003-2006; P-in-c All SS Ch Seymour IN 2000-2003, P 1997-2000; Int S Dav's Ch Beanblossom Beanblossom IN 2000; Chapl Dio Sthrn Virginia Newport News VA 1988-1998; Jackson Field Hm Jarratt VA 1988-1998; R S Dav's Ch Cullowhee NC 1981-1988; Chapl Oakland U Columbus MI 1979-1981; S Steph's Ch Troy MI 1979-1980. Mayor'S Cmsn On Human Relatns Madison In 1999-2003.

MATYLEWICZ, Stephen Jerome (Be) 116 Riverview Ln, Jermyn PA 18433 B Scranton PA 1934 s Stephen & Genevieve. Dioc Prog. D 6/2/1977 P 10/28/1978 Bp Lloyd Edward Gressle. m 1/18/1968 Maureen Wayman. Chr Ch Forest City PA 1993-2004; R Trin Epis Ch Carbondale PA 1993-2004; Asst Ch Of The Epiph Glenburn Clarks Summit PA 1985-1994; Asst No Lackawanna Vlly Mnstry 1977-1983.

MAUAI, Brandon Lee (ND) 500 S Main Ave, Sioux Falls SD 57104 B Fort Yates ND 1984 s Benedict & Karen. D 6/9/2007 Bp Michael Smith. m 11/17/2007 Angela Goodhouse-Mauai c 4. Yth Dir Dio So Dakota Pierre SD 2011-2013.

MAUGHAN III, Matthew Webster (O) 1226 Waverly Rd, Sandusky OH 44870 **Stff Chapl and Dir of Stff Dvlpmt Stein Hospice Serv Inc. Sandusky 2006-** B Richmond VA 1946 s Matthew & Myra. U of Virginia 1967; Jas Madison U 1968; BS Virginia Commonwealth U 1973; MEd Virginia Commonwealth U 1975; MDiv GTS 1986. D 6/7/1986 P 5/28/1987 Bp Claude Charles Vache. m 3/19/1967 Joy C Maughan c 2. Int Pstr S Paul's Epis Ch Put In Bay OH 2008-2010; Stein Hospice Serv Inc Sandusky OH 2006-2011; Assoc R Gr Epis Ch Sandusky OH 2002-2006; R S Jn's Ch Suffolk VA 1988-2002; Glebe Ch Suffolk VA 1988-1998; Asst to the R Emm Epis Ch Hampton VA 1986-1988.

MAULDEN, Kristina Ann (Okla) 501 S Cincinnati Ave, Tulsa OK 74103 **Assoc R Trin Ch Tulsa OK 2007-; Fresh Start Fac Dio Oklahoma Oklahoma City OK 2010-, COM 2009-, Reg Dn 2008-2012** B Mount Clemens MI 1967 d Zachariah & Sharon. BS U MI 1989; U of Texas 1992; MDiv TESM 1995. Trans 9/2/2003 Bp John Wadsworth Howe. m 11/29/1996 Anthony Wayne Maulden c 2. Vic H Fam Epis Ch Fishers IN 2003-2006; Asst Epis Ch Of The Resurr Longwood FL 1999-2003.

MAUMUS, Priscilla Guderian (La) Episcopal Diocese of Louisiana, 1623 Seventh St., New Orleans LA 70115 B New Orleans LA 1947 d Emmett & Gwendolyn. BA Newcomb Coll 1969; MA Tul 1981. D 12/1/2007 Bp Charles Edward Jenkins III. m 1/20/1973 Craig Maumus c 1. Archd Dio Louisiana New Orleans LA 2010-2016; D Chr Ch Cathd New Orleans LA 2010-2015; D S Mart's Epis Ch Metairie LA 2008-2010; Chapl Lambeth Hse 2006-2013. Assn of Epis Deacons 2006.

MAUNEY, James Patrick (RI) P.O Box 1236, Sagamore Beach MA 02562 B ParisTN 1942 s James & Eleanor. BA Duke 1965; MDiv EDS 1972. D 6/17/1972 P 12/17/1972 Bp Frederick Hesley Belden. m 3/19/1966 Mardi J Mauney c 1. Dir of Angl & Global Relatns Epis Ch Cntr New York NY 1991-2005, Dep - Angl Relatns 1989-1991, Coordntr of Ovrs Mnstrs 1982-1987; Serv Ch in Brazil 1977-1982; Exec Coun Appointees New York NY 1977-1982; Asst S Mart's Ch Providence RI 1975-1977; Cur S Paul's Ch N Kingstown RI 1972-1975. DD EDS 2005; Hon Cn Dio DR 1993.

MAURAIS, Robert Irwin (CFla) 175 Groveland Rd, Mount Dora FL 32757 **R Emer St. Edw the Confessor Mt Dora FL 2009-** B Davenport IA 1931 s Robert & Plooma. BS NWU 1955; MDiv SWTS 1958. D 6/14/1958 Bp Charles L Street P 12/20/1958 Bp Gerald Francis Burrill. m 6/20/1953 Lois N Maurais c 4. Int P-in-c S Edw The Confessor Mt Dora FL 2008-2009, R 1979-1996; S Matt the Apos Epis Ch Miami FL 1981-1996; Asst Ch Of The Redeem Sarasota FL 1972-1978; Chapl S Petersburg Jr Coll 1971-1972; Headmaster Cbury Sch of Florida St. Petersburg FL 1968-1971; Asst S Thos' Epis Ch St Petersburg FL 1968-1971; Cn Eductr Cathd Ch Of S Lk Orlando FL 1967-1968; Headmaster The Cathd Sch Orlando FL 1967-1968; LocTen S Aug's Epis Ch St Petersburg FL 1965-1966; Asst. Headmaster Berkeley Preparatory Sch Tampa FL 1961-1967; Asst St Johns Epis Ch Tampa FL 1961-1965; Cur S Andr's Epis Ch Tampa FL 1960-1961; Cur Trin Epis Ch Wheaton IL 1958-1959; Stndg Com, Pres Dio Cntrl Florida Orlando FL 1993-1996, Stndg Com 1984-1992, Curs Cmsn 1983-1985, Dn, Ocala/Leesburg Dnry 1980-1984, Asst.Ecum Off 1979-1981; Chair Com Ecum Rel Dio SW Florida Parrish FL 1973-1979, Chair Com Schs 1969-1972.

MAURER, David Stuart (Los) 909 Maplewood Ave, Ambridge PA 15003 **Died 1/5/2016** B Los Angeles CA 1951 s Arthur & Betty. BS California St U 1974; Cert Childrens Hosp Sch of Physical Ther 1980; MDiv TESM 2007. D 6/9/2007 P 1/12/2008 Bp Joseph Jon Bruno. m 6/5/1976 Karen Maurer c 2. Co-Vic S Clare Of Assisi Rancho Cucamonga CA 2011, Co-Vic 2008-2016; Physical Ther Orthapaedic & Sports Physical Ther 2000-2004.

MAURER, Karen (Los) 777 N. Acacia Ave., Rialto CA 92376 **S Wilfrid Of York Epis Ch Huntington Bch CA 2014-; Full Time S Clare Of Assisi Rancho Cucamonga CA 2011-** B Downey CA 1954 d John & Patricia. BA USC

1976; MDiv TESM 2007. D 6/9/2007 P 1/12/2008 Bp Joseph Jon Bruno. c 2. Sprtl Dir Curs 2008-2011; Full Time S Ptr's Par Rialto CA 2007-2014.

MAURER, Sally Beth (NJ) St Johns Episcopal Church, 76 Market St, Salem NJ 08079 B Camden NJ 1955 d Robert & Jane. BS U of Delaware 1998; MS Rutgers 2001. D 5/5/2012 Bp George Edward Councell. m 6/11/2010 Oscar L Maurer c 3. stjohnssalemnj@comcast.net

MAURY, James Ludlow (Ga) PO Box 61297, Savannah GA 31420 B St Louis MO 1944 s Ludlow & Louise. MSW U of Alabama 1973; PhD CUA 1982; MDiv Ya Berk 2014. D 5/31/2014 P 1/24/2015 Bp Scott Anson Benhase. m 10/7/2008 Daniel Edward Snyder.

MAXFIELD, Christian D (Mil) 519 S Michigan St, Prairie Du Chien WI 53821 **S Jn's Ch Naples FL 2015-** B Illinois 1979 s Donald & Kathryn. MDiv Nash 2007. D 6/30/2007 P 1/5/2008 Bp Keith Lynn Ackerman. m 9/16/2003 Kate L Maxfield. R H Trin Epis Ch Prairie Du Chien WI 2010-2015; Yth, YA and Fam Mnstry St Paul's Epis Ch Peoria IL 2007-2010.

MAXSON, John Hollis (Haw) 447 Kawaihae St, Honolulu HI 96825 **Ret 1990-** B Oceanside CA 1929 s Elmer & Lulu. BA U of Hawaii 1958; BD CDSP 1961. D 6/4/1961 Bp George Richard Millard P 12/16/1961 Bp Harry Sherbourne Kennedy. m 5/2/1953 Ethel Moosun Maxson c 3. Ch Of The H Nativ Honolulu HI 1983-1989; Asst S Chris's Ch Kailua HI 1964-1969; Vic H Innoc' Epis Ch Lahaina HI 1961-1964.

MAXWELL, Anne M (La) 259 W Hickory St, Ponchatoula LA 70454 **Assoc Chr Ch Covington LA 2009-** B Spartenburg SC 1965 d George. D 6/7/2003 P 1/11/2004 Bp J Neil Alexander. m 5/20/2003 William Ryan Hussey c 1. P-in-c All SS Epis Ch Ponchatoula LA 2009; H Trin Par Decatur GA 2004-2007; S Dunst's Epis Ch Atlanta GA 2003-2004.

MAXWELL, Barbara Jean (O) 120 Charles Ct, Elyria OH 44035 **Chapl S Jos's Epis Chap Far Rockaway NY 2000-** B Newport VT 1944 d Roger & Marietta. BS Cleveland St U 1984; MA JCU 1994; BA Cleveland St U 2003. D 11/13/2004 Bp Mark Hollingsworth Jr. c 2.

MAXWELL, Elizabeth Gail (NY) 225 W. 99th St., New York NY 10025 **P Ch Of The Ascen New York NY 2015-** B Madison WI 1956 d Robert & Margaret. BA Duke 1977; MDiv PrTS 1982. D 6/11/1983 P 12/16/1983 Bp John Shelby Spong. c 1. Int S Mich's Ch New York NY 2011-2014, Int R 2011-; Assoc R/Prog Dir Ch Of The H Apos New York NY 1989-2011; R S Matt's Ch Paramus NJ 1983-1989. info@ascensionnyc.org

MAXWELL JR, George (At) 2744 Peachtree Road NW, Atlanta GA 30305 **Vic Cathd Of S Phil Atlanta GA 2005-** B Columbia SC 1956 s George & Virginia. BA U NC 1979; JD Duke 1982; MDiv Candler TS Emory U 2004. D 2/26/2005 P 8/20/2005 Bp J Neil Alexander. m 6/15/1999 Sally R Weaver c 3. Int Dir Emmaus Hse Atlanta GA 2004. SW Georgia 40 under 40 The Albany Herald 2012; Mart Luther King Jr Intl Bd Preachers Morehouse Coll 2011.

MAXWELL, George Motier (Ga) 115 E Gordon St, Savannah GA 31401 **Died 8/28/2016** B Augusta GA 1930 s Grover & Corrie. VTS; BS VMI 1951; MDiv VTS 1961. D 6/26/1961 P 6/26/1962 Bp Clarence Alfred Cole. m 7/9/1954 Virginia Maxwell c 3. Ret 1991-2016; Sprtl Dir Dio Georgia Savannah GA 1991-2001; R Chr Ch Epis Savannah GA 1973-1990; R Ch Of The H Comf Sumter SC 1967-1973; Asst Ch Of The Redeem Sarasota FL 1966-1968; R S Chris's Ch Spartanburg SC 1961-1966. DD VTS 1989.

MAXWELL, James (Mich) 281 W Drayton St, Ferndale MI 48220 B Yonkers NY 1939 s Frank & Mary. BA Col 1960; MDiv VTS 1964. D 6/6/1964 P 12/19/1964 Bp Horace W B Donegan. m 8/28/1965 Martha Eloise Maxwell c 3. Total Mnstry Mssnr S Marg's Ch Hazel Pk MI 1996-2004; Mssnr Dio Michigan Detroit MI 1996-2000, Asst Deploy Off 1994-2000, Chair, Urban Affrs 1982-1993, Stndg Com, Pres 2001-2002, GC Dep. 1996-2002; R S Lk's Ch Ferndale MI 1979-2004; R Ch Of The Gd Shpd And S Jn Milford PA 1973-1979; R Ch Of S Jn The Evang Philadelphia PA 1967-1973; Cur Trin Ch Covington KY 1964-1967. Epis Peace Fllshp (EPF) 1968; EvangES (EES) 1965; Fran Scott Key Soc of VA Sem 2009; Soc for Increase of Mnstry (SIM) 1965. Investor Partnr McGehee Interfaith Trust Fund 2009; Fndr/Long-time Bd Mem-So Oakland Shltr (SOS) 2008; DD Ursinus Coll 2008; Human Serv Profsnl Cmnty Serv of Oakland 1989.

MAXWELL, Kevin Burns (Cal) 2 Meadow Park Circle, Belmont CA 94002 **Prof of Philosphy and Rel Notre Dame de Namur U Belmont CA 1986-** B Yakima WA 1941 s J Alex & Mary. BA Gonzaga U 1964; MA Gonzaga U 1966; DIT Kachebere Sem 1971; STM Jesuit TS 1973; MA Rice U 1978; PhD Rice U 1983. Rec 12/1/1990 as Priest Bp William Edwin Swing. m 7/16/1988 Josephine L Murphy. Schlr-in-res Trsfg Epis Ch San Mateo CA 1990-2002; Serv RC Ch 1971-1986. "Oral Dynamics of Bagobo Culture," *Tambara Journ*, Ateneo de Davao U, 1986; "Bemba Myth and Ritual: The Impact of Literacy on an Oral Culture," *Amer U Stds*, Ptr Lang, 1983.

MAXWELL, Max (Ct) Grace Episcopal Church, 4 Madison Ave, Madison CT 06443 **Gr Ch Madison NJ 2016-** B Midland MI 1954 s Martin & Mary. BA Stan 1977; MDiv UTS 1994; STM GTS 1998. D 2/6/1999 P 9/11/1999 Bp Richard Frank Grein. m 7/19/2009 Paul Kline. Int S Tim's Ch Fairfield CT 2015-2016; R Gr Epis Ch Hartford CT 2004-2014; Asst Min Ch Of The Incarn New York NY 2000-2004; Novc H Cross Monstry W Pk NY 1998-2000; Bd

Mem Parkville Cmnty Assn Hartford CT 2012-2015; Stndg Com Dio Connecticut Meriden CT 2011-2016, Millennium Dvlpmt Goals Com 2006-2014, Bp and Exec Coun 2006-2011, Cont Educ Com 2005-2014; Bd Mem Hartford Gay and Lesbian Hlth Collective Hartford CT 2008-2012. gracemadisoninterim@gmail.com

MAXWELL, Sally Dawn (Minn) St David's Episcopal Church, 304 E 7th St, Austin TX 78701 **S Jas Epis Ch Hibbing MN 2013-** B Duluth MN 1953 d Clinton & Lillian. BS Coll of St Scholastica 1978; MA Coll of St Scholastica 1990; Dip Ang Stud Epis TS of the SW 2008; MDiv Untd TS of the Twin Cities 2008. D 7/26/2007 P 7/8/2008 Bp James Louis Jelinek. m 12/1/1985 Dean Gies c 3. The Par of St Paul's Epis Ch Duluth MN 2010-2013; S Andr's By The Lake Duluth MN 2010.

MAXWELL, William F. (U) 515 Van Buren St, Port Townsend WA 98368 **Assoc Gr Ch Bainbridge Island WA 1993-, Vic 1992-1993; Ret 1990-; Nonstip Asst S Paul's Epis Ch Port Townsend WA 1990-** B Philadelphia PA 1925 s William & Bessie. SWTS 1949; Coll of Preachers 1958; Coll of Preachers 1958; BA cl SMU 2046; MDiv cl SWTS 2047. D 3/25/1947 Bp Harry Tunis Moore P 9/21/1949 Bp Charles A Mason. m 7/2/1977 Sue Barnhardt Maxwell c 3. Int St. Jas Epis Salt Lake City UT 1998; Dn Cathd Ch Of S Mk Salt Lake City UT 1978-1990; R S Jn's Epis Ch Tulsa OK 1972-1978; Dn Cathd Of S Jas Chicago IL 1964-1972; R S Jas Ch Bozeman MT 1961-1964; R S Chris's Epis Ch Oak Pk IL 1954-1961; Chapl NWU Evanston IL 1950-1954; Vic S Lk's Epis Ch Stephenville TX 1949-1950; D-in-c S Matt's Ch Comanche TX 1947-1948. Auth, "Poetry," *Still Paying Attention*, 2014; Auth, "Poetry," *Paying Attention*, 2012; Co-Auth, "Manual," *Sxlty: A Div Gift*; Auth, "Use Guide," *The Bible for Today's Ch*. Trng & Consulting Serv - Dio Olympia 1990-2008. Dn Emer St. Mk's Cathd, Salt Lake City 1990; DD Seabury-Wstrn 1968.

MAY, Amanda Rutherford (Cal) 613 Parkhaven Ct, Pleasant Hill CA 94523 **S Mich And All Ang Concord CA 2017-; Vic S Jn's Epis Ch Clayton CA 2013-** B San Diego CA 1950 d George & Anna Gwyn. BA Stan 1971; MS Lon/London Sch of Econ 1973; Bethel Sem W 1991; MDiv CDSP 1993. D 6/5/1993 P 12/21/1993 Bp Gethin Benwil Hughes. c 2. H Sprt Ch Dio California San Francisco CA 2013-2016; Int R S Ptr's Epis Ch Redwood City CA 2012-2013; Int R Chr Ch Sausalito CA 2010-2012; Exec Dir The Cntr for Today's Pilgrim San Diego CA 2007-2010; Cler/ Cler Alt GC San Diego CA 2000-2009; Exec Dir/CEO Epis Cmnty Serv Natl City CA 1994-2006; Asst The Epis Ch Of S Andr Encinitas CA 1994. Auth, "A Table in the Wilderness," *Preaching as Prophetic Calling: Sermons That Wk XII*, Morehouse Pub, 2004; Auth, "The End Times," *Preaching Through the Year of Mk: Sermons That Wk VIII*, Morehouse Pub, 1999. amandamay438@gmail.com

MAY, Charles Scott (At) 3750 Peachtree Rd NE Apt 811, Atlanta GA 30319 **Cler Assoc All SS Epis Ch Atlanta GA 2001-; Ret 1996-** B Little Rock AR 1931 s Guy & Louise. BA W&L 1953; BD Sewanee: The U So, TS 1957. D 6/29/1957 P 3/17/1958 Bp Robert Raymond Brown. R S Jas Epis Ch Marietta GA 1973-1996; Assoc Trin Cathd Columbia SC 1972-1973, Asst 1966-1971; Chapl Ma Gnrl Hosp Boston MA 1971-1972; R S Paul's Newport AR 1958-1966; Cur Chr Epis Ch Little Rock AR 1957-1958; Pres Kennestone Hosp Chapl' Assoc. 1977-1978; Mem of Bd Trst Cobb Cmnty Symphony 1975-1978; Mem at Lg Cobb Cnty Symposia 1975-1976; Mem of Advsry Com Cobb Cnty Georgia Travelers Aid 1974-1976; Mem Kennestone Hosp Chapl' Assoc. 1973-1980; Dn of Marietta Convoc Dio Atlanta Atlanta GA 1973-1974; Bd Dir Mid Carolina Coun on Alcosm 1973-1974; VP Columbia Ministers' Assn 1970-1971; Mem of Bp and Coun Dio Upper So Carolina Columbia SC 1969-1971; Mem at Lg Richland Co. Chapt Amer Red Cross 1966-1970; Chairman Dept of CE Dio Arkansas Little Rock AR 1964-1965, Dep to GC St. Louis, Missouri 1964, Mem of Exec Coun Dio Arkansas 1963-1965, Del to Syn of Seventh Provionce, Albuquerque, N.M. 1963, Dir of Sr High Camp 1962-1965, Mem of Bd Trst All SS Epis Sch, Vicksburg, Mississippi 1962-1964, Del to Syn of Seventh Prov, Austin, Texas 1960, Yth Advsr 1959-1964.

MAY, David Hickman (Va) 93 Eubank Dr, Kilmarnock VA 22482 **R Gr Ch Kilmarnock VA 2006-** B Tacoma WA 1959 s Boyd & Patricia. BA U of Tennessee 1981; MFA Virginia Commonwealth U 1987; MDiv Sewanee: The U So, TS 1993. D 6/12/1993 P 12/1/1993 Bp Peter J Lee. m 2/4/1989 Emily S May c 2. R S Andr's Ch Richmond VA 1996-2006; Asst Ch Of Our Sav Charlottesvlle VA 1993-1996. grace.rector1@verizon.net

MAY JR, Frederick Barnett (NJ) 916 Lagoon Ln., Mantoloking NJ 08738 B New York NY 1948 D 10/21/2000 Bp David Bruce Joslin. m 11/9/1991 Kathleen Dunn c 1.

MAY JR, James B (Fla) 16178 Williams Pl, King George VA 22485 **Chr Ch Monticello FL 2013-** B Orlando FL 1954 s James & Janice. BS Florida St U 1976; MA Jacksonville U 1981; MDiv SWTS 1991. D 2/27/1993 P 8/1/1993 Bp Bob Gordon Jones. m 8/9/1980 Katherine A May c 1. S Paul's Owens King Geo VA 2004-2013; S Ptr's Epis Ch Sheridan WY 1998-1999, Yth Min 1991-1993; R S Jas' Ch Indn Hd MD 1997-2004; Vic S Barth's Ch Cokeville WY 1993-1997; Vic S Jas Ch Kemmerer WY 1993-1997.

MAY IV, Lynde Eliot (Mil) 982 Hunters Trl, Sun Prairie WI 53590 **Asstg P Cathd Ch Of S Ptr St. Petersburg FL 2007-, Int 1998-2006; Ret 1996-** B

Bridgeport CT 1933 s Lynde & Florence. BS Ya 1955; MDiv Ya Berk 1958; MEd Rhode Island Coll 1970. D 6/7/1958 P 3/7/1959 Bp John S Higgins. m 1/31/1959 Diane A May c 3. Asst P S Jn The Div Epis Ch Sun City Cntr FL 2000-2001; Int S Eliz's Epis Ch Zephyrhills FL 1996-1998; Int S Mary's Par Tampa FL 1994-1996; R S Lk's Ch Madison WI 1983-1994; Ch Of S Jn Chrys Delafield WI 1978-1983; S Jn's Mltry Acad Delafield WI 1978-1981; U Sch Milwaukee Milwaukee WI 1976-1978; Chapl S Andr Sch Barrington RI 1965-1976; S Andrews Sch Barrington RI 1965-1976; R S Mk's Ch Warren RI 1960-1965; Cur Chr Ch Westerly RI 1958-1960.

MAY, Maureen May (Neb) The Oaks, 2015 County Road R, Fremont NE 68025 **D S Jas' Epis Ch Fremont NE 2013-** B Nottingham GB 1939 d Clifford & Irene. CPE; EFM Sewanee: The U So, TS 1992. D 10/30/1993 Bp James Edward Krotz. m 1/24/1960 Ronald May c 1. Vol Chapl Clarkson Hosp Omaha NE 1996-1997.

MAY, Philip Walter (WTex) 700 S Upper Broadway St, Corpus Christi TX 78401 **Ch Of The Gd Shpd Corpus Christi TX 2010-** B Ontario Canada 1957 s Sidney & Elaine. BA U of Wstrn Ontario CA 1980; MA U of Wstrn Ontario CA 1982; MDiv Trin 1989; MDiv Trin 1989. Trans 10/27/2010 Bp Gary Richard Lillibridge. m 12/30/2012 Alice J Stewart c 2.

MAY, Richard Ernest (Va) Po Box 155, Campton NH 03223 B Evanston IL 1946 s Ernest & Gladys. BS U of Delaware 1969; MDiv VTS 1979; MA Norwich U 1989. D 5/24/1979 Bp William Hawley Clark P 6/1/1980 Bp Philip Alan Smith. m 12/28/1968 Barbara Anne May c 2. S Ptr's Epis Ch Bridgton ME 1996-1998; H Trin Epis Ch Swanton VT 1993-1994; Chair - Dept Rel Woodberry Forest Sch Woodberry Forest VA 1989-1993; U Chapl Norwich U Northfield VT 1987-1989; Prot Chapl Norwich U Northfield VT 1983-1987; R S Mary's Epis Par Northfield VT 1983-1987; Bruton Par Williamsburg VA 1982-1983; Dio Sthrn Virginia Newport News Va 1982-1983; Chapl Wm & Mary Williamsburg VA 1982-1983; Asst Ch Of The Gd Shpd Nashua NH 1979-1982; Chapl Daniel Webster Coll Nashua NH 1979-1982.

MAY, Richard Leslie (SVa) 349 Archers Mead, Williamsburg VA 23185 **Ret 1997-** B Omaha NE 1934 s Edgar & Mary. BA U of Nebraska 1956; JD Creighton U 1962; MDiv Bex Sem 1967; DMin NYTS 1982; STM GTS 1986. D 6/24/1967 P 12/21/1967 Bp Russell T Rauscher. c 2. R Bruton Par Williamsburg VA 1987-1996; Trin Educ Fund New York NY 1978-1987; Exec Asst Trin Par New York NY 1977-1979; R Ch Of The Epiph Jacksonville FL 1969-1977; P S Jn's Ch Valentine NE 1967-1969; S Jn's Epis Ch Cody NE 1967-1969.

MAY, Thomas Richard (NJ) 65 W Front St, Red Bank NJ 07701 B Camden NJ 1947 s Clayton & Olga. BA Shelton Coll 1970; MDiv Reformed Epis Sem 1973. D 6/1/2010 P 12/3/2010 Bp George Edward Councell. m 5/23/1970 Mary Grace May c 1.

MAYBERRY, Richard (Ct) 16 Southport Woods Drive, Southport CT 06890 **Asst S Matt's Epis Ch Wilton CT 2010-; Ret 2008-** B Delano CA 1945 s Theodore & Elsie. BS U of Oregon 1967; MDiv GTS 1971. D 6/20/1971 P 1/6/1972 Bp Charles Alfred Voegeli. R S Fran Ch Stamford CT 1978-2007; Asst S Mk's Ch Mt Kisco NY 1971-1978. illustrator, *P's Handbook*, Morehouse-Barlow, 1983; illustrator, *A Manual for Acolytes*, Morehouse-Barlow, 1981. Assn of Angl Mus. R Emer St Fran Ch, Stamford CT 2007.

MAYBIN, Maxine Roberta (Colo) 915 Yuma St Apt 124, Colorado Springs CO 80909 **D S Raphael Epis Ch Colorado Sprg CO 1992-** B Boston MA 1923 d Mack & Eva. BS DePaul U 1979; Bishops Inst for Diac Formation 1992. D 10/24/1992 Bp William Jerry Winterrowd. c 4. Chapl Memi Hosp AIDS Cltn CO Sprgs CO. Auth, "Significance of Slow Ventricular Tachycardi and Slow Ventricular Couplets during Ambulatory ECG Monitoring," *Amer Journ of Cardiology*, 1979. Chi Eta Phi, Iota Eta Chapt - Colorado Sprg, CO 1991; Ord of the DOK 1989; Sigma Theta Tau, Inc. - Natl hon Soc of Nrsng - Gam 1980.

MAYCOCK, Roma Walker (Va) 5210 Patriots Colony Dr, Williamsburg VA 23188 B Des Moines IA 1936 d Howard & Ardus. BS Iowa St U 1958; MDiv VTS 1983. D 6/11/1983 Bp Robert Bruce Hall P 5/12/1984 Bp David Henry Lewis Jr. m 6/21/1958 Paul Dean Maycock c 5. R S Steph's Ch Catlett VA 1985-2005; Gr Ch Casanova VA 1985-1990; Asst S Aid's Ch Alexandria VA 1983-1985.

MAYEN, John Mabior (SD) 1415 S Bahnson Ave, Sioux Falls SD 57105 B South Sudan 1981 D 11/6/2005 Bp Creighton Leland Robertson. c 4.

MAYER, Annette Cleary (FtW) **D Associated Parishes Inc. Ft Worth TX 2015-; Hospice Chapl Universal Hlth Serv 2007-** B Niagara Falls, NY 1952 MDiv Brite DS 2015. D 10/22/2015 Bp James Scott Mayer. m 2/19/1977 Donald Ferdinand Mayer.

MAYER, Charles David (NY) B Oceanside NY 1955 s Charles & Mary. BA Ob 1977; MDiv Harvard DS 1982; Cert Blanton-Peale Grad Inst 1992; Cert Blanton-Peale Grad Inst 1992; Cert Blanton-Peale Grad Inst 1994; Psy.D. GTF 2008. D 6/1/1996 P 12/7/1996 Bp Richard Frank Grein. m 1/25/1986 Claudia Powell Mayer. Assoc Ch Of The Incarn New York NY 1996-1998; Serv Meth Ch 1982-1993. Contrib, "One-Parent," *One-Chld Families*, Amer Inst For Resrch, 1980. Amer Assn Pstr Coun; Assn Clin Mem Amer Grp Psychther Assn; Assn Mem Amer Assn Of Mar & Fam Ther.

✠ MAYER, The Rt Rev James Scott (NwT) 1802 Broadway, Lubbock TX 79401 **Bp of NW Texas Chap of the Trsfg Lubbock TX 2009-; Bp of NW Texas Dio NW Texas Lubbock TX 2009-** B Dallas TX 1955 s James & Mary. BBA Texas Tech U 1977; MDiv Epis TS of the SW 1992. D 6/20/1992 Bp Donis Dean Patterson P 3/25/1993 Bp James Monte Stanton Con 3/21/2009 for NwT. m 2/4/1978 Katherine K Mayer c 2. R Ch of the Heav Rest Abilene Abilene TX 1994-2009; Asst S Jas Epis Ch Texarkana TX 1992-1994. D.D. U So 2011; D.D. Sem of the SW 2010. bishopmayer@nwtdiocese.org

MAYER, Linda Margaret (Spok) PO Box 1226, Chelan WA 98816 **Cmnty P S Andr's Ch Chelan WA 2010-** B 1943 D 6/13/2009 P 6/5/2010 Bp James E Waggoner Jr. m 6/15/1974 Rudolph Mayer c 3.

MAYER JR, Nicholas Max (WTex) Po Box 1265, Castroville TX 78009 **H Trin Carrizo Sprg TX 2005-** B Little Rock AR 1933 s Nicholas & Omie. US-NA 1957; BA U of Arkansas 1960; BD VTS 1967. D 6/14/1967 P 4/4/1968 Bp George Henry Quarterman. c 2. R S Phil's Ch Uvalde TX 1971-1994; Ch Of The Ascen Montell TX 1971-1991; P-in-c S Mk's Epis Ch Coleman TX 1968-1970; Cur Ch of the Heav Rest Abilene Abilene TX 1967-1971.

MAYER, Peter Woodrich (Md) 1601 Pleasant Plains Rd, Annapolis MD 21409 **R S Marg's Ch Annapolis MD 2010-** B Keene NH 1969 s Douglas & Susan. BA Providence Coll 1992; MDiv VTS 2001. D 6/9/2001 Bp Daniel William Herzog P 1/19/2002 Bp Albert Theodore Eastman. m 7/9/2005 Allison H Mayer c 2. R Emm Epis Ch Cumberland RI 2005-2010; Asst S Jn's Ch Lafayette Sq Washington DC 2001-2005; Cmsn on Cong Dvlpmt Dio Rhode Island Providence RI 2008-2010.

MAYER, Robert James (ECR) 20920 Mcclellan Rd, Cupertino CA 95014 **Died 12/27/2016** B Lynn MA 1932 s Max & Joanne. MIT 1950; Harv 1952; BA Brandeis U 1957; CDSP 1969. D 4/5/1966 P 7/26/1971 Bp George Richard Millard. m 4/12/1958 Joanna Conway Mayer c 4. Volntr Chapl Santa Clara Vlly Med Cntr 1991-2016; H Fam Epis Ch San Jose CA 1989; Assoc S Lawr Campbell CA 1966-1973; Chair Dept Mssns Dio El Camino Real Salinas CA 1985-1986, Chair Dept Mssns 1981-1984.

MAYER, Sandra Crow (CGC) 5158 Border Dr N, Mobile AL 36608 B 1941 U of So Alabama; U So. D 7/21/2000 P 2/4/2001 Bp Charles Farmer Duvall. R S Jn's Ch Monroeville AL 2009-2012; Trin Epsicopal Ch Atmore AL 2001-2008; The Ch Of The Redeem Mobile AL 2000-2001; Wilmer Hall Mobile AL 1991-2000.

MAYERS, Tom (Mich) 3837 W. 7 Mile Rd., Detroit MI 48221 B GY 1955 s Charles & Caroline. CTh Centro de Estudios Teologicos 1984; MEd Cambridge Coll 1993; DMin EDS 1998. Trans 8/2/1995 Bp Don Edward Johnson. m 12/27/1984 Altagracia P Mayers c 3. All SS Ch Detroit MI 2008-2010; S Mk's Ch Dorchester MA 1995-2007; Asst P S Mk's Ch Brooklyn NY 1990-1991; Asst P S Simeon's Ch Bronx NY 1989-1990; Asst P S Ann's Ch Of Morrisania Bronx NY 1988-1989; P-In-C Espiritu Santo Brooklyn NY 1987-1991; Asst P Ch Of S Thos Brooklyn NY 1987-1988.

MAYES, Amy Kathryn (Wyo) 519 E Park Ave, Riverton WY 82501 B Powell WY 1950 d Jewell & Roberta. D 8/23/2013 P 4/26/2014 Bp John Smylie. c 3.

MAYFIELD, Donna Jeanne (O) 515 N Chillicothe Rd, Aurora OH 44202 **Hospice Chapl Vstng Nurses Assoc Cleveland OH 2006-** B Houston TX 1948 d Donald & Doris. TCU; BD S Edwards U Austin TX 1985; MDiv Epis TS of the SW 1986. D 6/24/1986 Bp Maurice Manuel Benitez P 5/1/1987 Bp Gordon Taliaferro Charlton. c 3. S Phil's Epis Ch Akron OH 2010-2013; S Paul's Epis Ch Cleveland OH 2004; R S Jn's Epis Ch Cuyahoga Fls OH 1999-2004; S Mart's Ch Chagrin Fall OH 1996-1999; All SS Epis Sch Lubbock TX 1994-1996; Chapl All SS Epis Sch Lubbock TX 1994-1996; S Chris's Epis Ch Austin TX 1992-1993; Assoc Dir Pstr Educ & Fam Counslg Cntr Austin TX 1989-1993; Asst S Dav's Ch Austin TX 1986-1988; Assoc Counslr Pstr Educ & Fam Counslg Cntr Austin TX 1984-1989. Auth, "Old Liberty and the Cross," *LivCh*, 2003; Auth, "Just Call Me Donna," *LivCh*, 1987; Auth, "New Frontiers' Wmn In The Ord Mnstry Ap Bulletin," 1986; Auth, "Open".

MAYFIELD JR, Ellis (ETenn) 1449 Stagecoach Rd, Sewanee TN 37375 B Fort Meade MD 1952 s Ellis & Susan. BS U So 1973; MDiv SWTS 1979. D 8/6/1979 Bp Richard Mitchell Trelease Jr P 5/16/1980 Bp William Evan Sanders. c 4. Athletic Dir S Andr's Chap S Andrews TN 1997-1999; Chapl S Andr's-Sewanee Sch Sewanee TN 1995-2013; R Ch Of The Gd Samar Knoxville TN 1979-1995.

MAYHALL, Monna S (Tenn) 1509 Jaybee Ct, Franklin TN 37064 **Assoc S Paul's Ch Franklin TN 2005-** B Alabama 1963 D 10/1/2005 Bp Stephen Hays Jecko P 4/15/2007 Bp James Monte Stanton. m 4/9/1988 Douglas Jackson Mayhall c 1. monna@stpaulsfranklin.com

MAYHEW, Nancy (EMich) D 6/17/2017 Bp Steven Todd Ousley.

MAYHOOD, Gary William (LI) 509 W Plane St, Hackettstown NJ 07840 B New York NY 1947 s Alexander & Evelyn. BA Pacific Luth U 1969. D 12/21/1974 P 6/28/1975 Bp Jonathan Goodhue Sherman. Clerk Dio Long Island Garden City NY 1975-1976; Cur S Marg's Fresh Meadow NY 1974-1975.

MAYNARD, Beth H (Spr) 702 W Green St, Champaign IL 61820 **R Emm Memi Epis Ch Champaign IL 2014-** B Nashville TN 1962 d Robert & Jane. BA Amh 1984; MDiv Bos TS 1993; Cert SWTS 1994. D 6/4/1994 Bp David Elliot Johnson P 6/10/1995 Bp John Henry Smith. m 4/19/1986 Mark C Dirksen. S

Jn's Ch Beverly MA 2013; P Ch Of The Redeem Chestnut Hill MA 2011-2012; Fndr/Chapl Mill St Hse Cmnty Beverly MA 2005-2012; R Ch Of The Gd Shpd Fairhaven MA 2000-2004, P-in-c 1997-2000; Chapl U of Mass Dartmouth MA 2000-2002; Asst R S Gabr's Epis Ch Marion MA 1997-2000; Epis Chapl Marshall U Huntington WV 1994-1997; Asst Trin Ch Huntington WV 1994-1997. Ed, "Get Up Off Your Knees: Preaching the U2 Catalog," Cowley, 2003; Auth, "How to Evangelize a GenXer (NOT)," Forw Mvmt, 2001; Contrib, "The Bread of Life," Morehouse Pub, 2000; Auth, "Meditations for Lay Eucharistic Ministers," Morehouse Pub, 1999. Phi Beta Kappa 1984. bmaynard@gmail.com

MAYNARD, Dennis Roy (SanD) 49 Via Del Rossi, Rancho Mirage CA 92270 B Arkansas City KS 1945 s Hue & Roxie. AA Arkansas City Cmnty Coll 1964; AA Cowley Coll 1964; BA Westmar Coll 1966; MDiv SWTS 1969; DMin SWTS 2001. D 6/21/1969 P 12/1/1969 Bp Chilton R Powell. m 8/13/1983 Nancy Major c 4. R S Jas By The Sea La Jolla CA 1997-2003; Vice R S Mart's Epis Ch Houston TX 1995-1997; R Chr Ch Greenville SC 1980-1995; R Ch Of The Epiph Richardson TX 1972-1980; Vic/R St. Mk's Dallas Texas (Became Ch of the Epiph) 1971-1972; Cur Gr Ch Muskogee OK 1969-1970; Vic S Philips Muskogee OK (Merged w Gr Ch) 1969-1970. Auth, "Even Jesus Needed Money," *Even Jesus Needed Money*, Dionysus Pub, 2017; Auth, "The Messy Magnolia," *The Magnolia Series Bk Nine*, Dionysus Pub, 2017; Auth, "The Magnolia At Christmas," *The Magnolia Series Bk Eight*, Dionysus Pub, 2014; Auth, "Healing For Pastors and People After A Sheep Attack," *Healing For Pastors & People After A Sheep Attack*, Dionysus Pub, 2013; Auth, "Preventing A Sheep Attack," *Preventing A Sheep Attack*, Dionysus Pub, 2013; Auth, "The Changing Magnolia," *The Magnolia Series Bk Seven*, Dionysus Pub, 2011; Auth, "When Sheep Attack," *When Sheep Attack*, Dionysus Pub, 2011; Auth, "The Magnolia At Sunrise," *The Magnolia Series Bk Six*, Dionysus Pub, 2010; Auth, "The Sweet Smell of Magnolia," *The Magnolia Series Bk Five*, Dionysus Pub, 2009; Auth, "The Pink Magnolia," *The Magnolia Series Bk Four*, Dionysus Pub, 2008; Auth, "Pruning The Magnolia," *The Magnolia Series Bk Three*, Dionysus Pub, 2007; Auth, "When The Magnolia Blooms," *The Magnolia Series Bk Two*, Dionysus Pub, 2006; Auth, "Behind The Magnolia Tree," *The Magnolia Series Bk One*, Dionysus Pub, 2005; Auth, "Forgive & Get Your Life Back," *Forgive & Get Your Life Back*, Dionysus Pub, 2003; Auth, "Forgiven, Healed & Restored," *Forgiven, Healed & Restored*, Dionysus Pub, 1997; Auth, "The Money Bk," *The Money Bk*, Dionysis Pub, 1997; Auth, "Those Episkopols," *Those Episkopols*, Dionysus Pub, 1997; Frequent Contrib, "Angl Dig," *Angl Dig*. Who's Who Among Outstanding Americans U. S. Registry 1995; Oxford's Who's Who Oxford 1993.

MAYNARD, Jane F (Oly) 6732 N Parkside Ln, Tacoma WA 98407 B Southbridge MA 1954 d Paul & Rita. BA U of Pennsylvania 1975; MA U IL 1979; MDiv CDSP 1992; MA Claremont TS 1998; PhD Claremont TS 2001. D 1/12/1992 P 7/26/1992 Bp John Stuart Thornton. m 12/29/2001 James C Treyens c 3. R Chr Ch Tacoma WA 2010-2014; P-in-c S Thos Epis Ch Medina WA 2008-2009; P-in-c Epiph Par of Seattle Seattle WA 2007-2008; P-in-c Gd Samar Epis Ch Sammamish WA 2004-2006; Dn, DSOMAT Dio Olympia Seattle 2004, Stndg Com 2012-, Stwdshp and Planned Giving Cmsn 2007-2014, Bd Mem, Dioc Sch of Mnstry and Theol 2004-2010; Ass Pfr PastoralTheology &Dir of Field Ed. CDSP Berkeley CA 2001-2003, Dir of Field Educ 1995-2000; Asstg P All SS' Ch San Francisco CA 1998-2001; Asstg P S Mk's Epis Ch Upland CA 1995; Admssn & Pstrl Counslr Claremont TS CA 1993-1994; Assoc Chapl S Alphonsus Rgnl Med Cntr Boise ID 1992-1993. Co-Ed, "Pstr Bearings: Lived Rel and Pstr Theol," Lexington Books, 2010; Auth, "Transfiguring Loss: Julian of Norwich as a Guide for Survivors of Traumatic Grief," The Pilgrim Press, 2006; Auth, "Reflection," *New Westminster Dictionary of Chr Sprtlty*, Westminster Jn Knox, 2005; Auth, "Purgatory:Place or Process? Wmn Views on Purgatory in 14-15th Century Britain," *Stds in Sprtlty*, 2002; Auth, "Finding Rel and Sprtl Meaning in AIDS Related Multiple Loss: The Contributions of Showings to a Constructive Theol," *Wmn Chr Mystics Speak to Our Times*, Sheed & Ward, 2001. scl U of Pennsylvania 1975; Phi Beta Kappa U of Pennsylvania 1975. jmaynardm@gmail.com

MAYNARD, Joan Pearson (SO) 2661 Haverford Rd, Columbus OH 43220 B Austin TX 1940 d Forest & Jennie. BA Baylor U 1962; BSW Wright St U 1981; MS U of Dayton 1984; MA Luth TS 1992. D 1/23/1993 Bp Herbert Thompson Jr. m 1/6/1962 Robert Howell Maynard c 1. Chapl OH SU Med Cntr.

MAYO, H(Arold) Jonathan (Be) 3900 Mechancsville Rd, Whitehall PA 18052 **S Steph's Ch Whitehall PA 2014-; R S Geo's Epis Ch Hellertown PA 2010-** B Carbondale PA 1953 s Arthur & Harriet. BA Wilkes Coll 1975; MDiv S Vladimirs Orth TS 1980. Rec 3/14/2004 Bp Keith Whitmore. m 5/20/2013 Hazel Pamela Mayo c 2. P-in-c Ch Of S Thos And S Jn New Richmond WI 2004-2010.

MAYOM, Abraham Mabior (SD) **P-in-c Dio So Dakota Pierre SD 2014-** B Sudan 1977 s Dhuka & Achiek. D 11/6/2005 P 5/7/2006 Bp Creighton Leland Robertson. c 1.

MAYOR, Mike (Oly) 10630 Gravelly Lake Dr SW, Lakewood WA 98499 **Consult, Stwdshp Dvlpmt Dio Utah Salt Lake City UT 2008-, Alt, GC 2007-2013, Mem, Dioc Fin Com 2005-, Chair, Dioc Evang Com 2004-2007,** **Mem, Dioc Coun 2004-2007, Sum Camp Chapl, Camp Tuttle 2004-, Chair, Mssn Resource Team 2003-2008, Consult, Congrl Dvlpmt 2003-, Exam Chapl 2003-** B Lexington Park MD 1966 s Robert & Kathleen. BA San Diego St U 1995; MDiv SWTS 1996; Cert SWTS 2006. D 6/8/1996 P 12/21/1996 Bp Gethin Benwil Hughes. m 8/3/2005 Liana Lee Mayor c 1. S Mary's Ch Lakewood WA 2014-2016; R All SS Ch Salt Lake City UT 2002-2014; GOE Rdr BEC 2001-2010; R S Steph's Ch Severn Par Crownsville MD 1998-2002; Nave Chapl Cathd of St Ptr & St Paul Washington DC 1997-1999; Asst R S Thos Epis Ch Towson MD 1996-1998; Consult, Congrl Dvlpmt Dio Maryland Baltimore MD 2000-2003, Sum Camp Chapl, Bp Claggett Cntr 2000-2002, Chair, Dioc Conv Plnng Com 2000-2001, Co-Chair, Plnng Com for Natl YA Conf 1999-2001, Chair, Dioc Evang Com 1998-2002, Chair, Evang Com 1997-2000. Auth, "Liberal or Conservative: Labels Miss the Whole Picture," *Salt Lake Tribune*, Nwspr Agcy Corp, 2008; Auth, "Angl Power - It's About Power Not Sex," *Salt Lake Tribune*, Nwspr Agcy Corp, 2007; Contrib, "Responding w Integrity to an Unjust War," *The Dioc Dialogue*, Epis Dio Utah, 2002. Polly Bond Awd of Merit ECom 2004; Mahlon Norris Gilbert Awd SWTS 1996.

MAYORGA-GONZALEZ, Mary (Ct) 3 Oakwood Ave., Lawrence MA 01841 B 1939 d Anasis & Clementina. U of Costa Rica Cr 1978; MA Epis TS of the SW 1986; MDiv EDS 1989. D 5/30/1992 P 1/23/1993 Bp David Elliot Johnson. m 4/2/1978 Armando Gonzalez. Grtr Hartford Reg Mnstry E Hartford CT 2001-2004; St Jas Epis Ch Hartford CT 2001-2004; P in Charge Bethany Epis Ch Norwalk CT 2000-2001; Dio Massachusetts Boston MA 1994-2000; Hisp Congregations P S Lk's/San Lucas Epis Ch Chelsea MA 1992-2007; Cltn For Hisp Mnstrs Pepperell MA 1992-1994.

MAYPOLE, Sara (Va) 6988 Woodchuck Hill Rd, Fayetteville NY 13066 B Topeka KS 1941 d John & Bertha. BFA U of Kansas 1963; MDiv EDS 1979; DMin Fuller TS 1996. D 6/2/1979 Bp Paul Moore Jr P 4/13/1980 Bp Horace W B Donegan. m 5/3/2003 Thomas A Maypole. Int S Barth's Ch Estes Pk CO 2008-2009; Adj Prof of Pstr Theol VTS Alexandria VA 1996-2001; R S Marg's Ch Woodbridge VA 1991-2003; Evang and Renwl Cmsn Dio Connecticut Meriden CT 1989-1990, Advsry Bd 1988-1991; R S Ptr's Ch So Windsor CT 1985-1991; Assoc Chr Ch Christiana Hundred Wilmington DE 1983-1985; S Paul's Epis Ch Pittsburgh PA 1979-1983. Auth, *Overcoming Resistance to Renwl*; Auth, *Who Will Cast the 1st Stone.*

MAYRER, Jane Goodhue (Md) 2010 Sulgrave Ave, Baltimore MD 21209 **Cathd Of The Incarn Baltimore MD 2001-** B Pueblo CO 1947 BA Stamford U 1969; JD U of Alabama 1976. D 6/2/2001 Bp Robert Wilkes Ihloff. m 1/6/1996 Andrew Mayrer c 1.

MAYS, Foster (Kan) Epiphany Episcopal Church, P.O. Box 367, Sedan KS 67361 **R Ch Of The Epiph Sedan KS 2013-; Dn, SE Convoc Dio Kansas Topeka KS 2016-, Pres, Coun of Trst 2016-** B Greenwood SC 1959 s Marshall & Jane. BS U of So Carolina 1981; MBA GW 1991; MDiv Sewanee: The U So, TS 2013. D 12/21/2012 P 6/30/2013 Bp Paul Victor Marshall. m 11/16/1991 Linda L Leinbach c 2. epiphanysedan@gmail.com

MAYS-STOCK, Barbara L (RI) 50 Charles St, Cranston RI 02920 B Newport RI 1954 d Judson & Anna. Andover Newton TS; BA Providence Coll 1977; Rhode Island Sch for Deacons 1994. D 3/20/1994 Bp George Nelson Hunt III. m 3/4/1978 Roger William Stock c 1. D Cathd Of S Jn Providence RI 2006-2011, D 1994-1999; Co-Chair COM Dio Rhode Island 2006-2009; Mem Dioc Coun Dio Rhode Island 2005-2006; Secy Secy to Conv Dio Rhode Island 2004-2008; D Ch Of The Ascen Cranston RI 2000-2008; Chair Dioc AIDS T/F 1992-2002; Chair RI St Coun ofChurches Interfaith Hiv/Aids Taskforce 1992-2000; COM Dio Rhode Island Providence RI 2006-2009.

✠ MAZE, The Rt Rev Larry (Ark) 102 Midland St, Little Rock AR 72205 **Ret Bp of Arkansas Dio Arkansas Little Rock AR 2006-, 1994-2006, Bp of Ark 1993-2006** B Havre MT 1943 s Archie & Goldie. BS No Montana Coll 1968; MS Montana St U 1969; MDiv Epis TS of the SW 1972. D 6/25/1972 P 1/17/1973 Bp Jackson Earle Gilliam Con 6/11/1994 for Ark. m 4/12/2017 George James Abbott-Maze c 4. Ch Of The Nativ Greenwood MS 1988-1994; R All SS Ch Jackson MS 1981-1988; S Jas Epis Ch Port Gibson MS 1977-1981; Chapl S Andr Sch Jackson MS 1974-1978; S Andr's Epis Sch Ridgeland MS 1974-1978; Asst Ch Of The H Sprt Missoula MT 1972-1974. DD TS U So 1995; DD Epis TS of the SW 1994. lemaze@sbcglobal.net

MAZGAJ, Marian Stanislaus (WVa) PO Box 206, Valley Grove WV 26060 **Died 4/7/2016** B Gaj PL 1923 s Joseph & Josephine. MA U of Cracow PL 1951; STD U of Cracow PL 1954; JCL CUA 1958; JCD CUA 1970; MA Duquesne U 1972. Rec 10/1/1981 as Priest Bp Robert Poland Atkinson. m 6/27/1972 Mildred J Ankrom c 2. Asst S Matt's Ch Wheeling WV 1997-2013; Chapl CAP Clarksburg WV 1988-2016; R S Paul's Ch Weston WV 1986-1995; R S Steph's Epis Ch Steubenville OH 1983-1986; Vic S Mich's Ch Kingwood WV 1982-1983; Asst Trin Ch Morgantown WV 1981-1983; Serv RC Ch 1952-1972. Auth, *Vstng Hm in Poland After 33 Years & Wrld War II True Stories*, McClain, 1993; Auth, *Communist Govt of Poland as Affecting Rts of the Ch from 1944-1960*, CUA, 1970; Auth, "Numerous arts," *Herald Star*, 1961; Auth, "Numerous arts," *Charleston Gazette*; Auth, "Numerous arts," *Other Pub*; Auth, "Numerous arts," *The Franciscan Monthly*; Auth, "Numerous arts," *The Intel-*

M

ligencer; Auth, "Numerous arts," *The Steubenville Register*; Auth, "Numerous arts," *Wheeling News Register*.

MAZINGO, Stephen L (Fla) Saint Peter's Church, 801 Atlantic Ave, Fernandina Beach FL 32034 **P S Ptr's Ch Fernandina Bch FL 2013-; Dom And Frgn Mssy Soc- Epis Ch Cntr New York NY 2008-** B Jacksonville NC 1981 s Larry & Carol. BA Appalachian St U 2004; MDiv VTS 2007. D 6/9/2007 P 12/8/2007 Bp Clifton Daniel III. m 1/21/2012 Abigail Lee Mazingo c 1. S Jas Par Wilmington NC 2008-2013; Exec Coun Appointees New York NY 2007-2008. smazingo@stpetersparish.org

MAZUJIAN, Harry (NJ) 44 Broad St, Flemington NJ 08822 B East Orange NJ 1953 s Irvand & Valerie. BA Drew U 1975; MDiv GTS 1988. D 6/6/1988 Bp Robert Campbell Witcher Sr P 12/10/1988 Bp Orris George Walker Jr. m 8/4/1979 Ruth Mazujian c 3. R Calv Epis Ch Flemington NJ 1998-2017; R St Jn the Bapt Epis Ch Linden NJ 1992-1998; Vic S Mk's Ch Hammonton NJ 1990-1992; Asst S Mary Anne's Epis Ch No E MD 1988-1990. Ord Of H Cross.

MAZZA, Joseph (Colo) 1737 Mayview Rd, Jacksonville FL 32210 B Long Island NY 1940 s Thomas & Frances. D 6/13/2009 Bp Thomas Edward Breidenthal. m 12/31/1993 Carol A Mazza c 2.

MAZZA, Joseph Edward (FdL) 4569 Glidden Dr, Sturgeon Bay WI 54235 **Ret 1992-** B Naperville IL 1929 s Joseph & Ethel. VTS; BA Ripon Coll Ripon WI 1951; MDiv SWTS 1954. D 6/19/1954 P 12/20/1954 Bp Gerald Francis Burrill. m 9/7/1957 Susan Mazza c 5. Vic S Lk's Epis Ch Sis Bay WI 1999-2004; Int Chr the King/H Nativ (Sturgeon Bay) Sturgeon Bay WI 1995-1996; Dn Evanston Deanry Dio Chicago Chicago IL 1991-1992; R S Aug's Epis Ch Wilmette IL 1971-1992; R S Paul's Epis Ch Beloit WI 1962-1971; Cn Cathd Of S Jas Chicago IL 1956-1961; Vic The Annunc Of Our Lady Gurnee IL 1954-1956. Conf of St. Greg's Abbey 1952; Fllshp of St. Jn (SSJE) 1993.

MAZZACANO, Leslie G (NJ) 379 Huntington Drive, Delran NJ 08075 **D Trin Ch Moorestown NJ 2007-; Non-par 2001-** B Philadelphia PA 1952 d Robert & Mary. AA Pierce Jr Coll 1971. D 10/31/1998 Bp Joe Doss. m 10/6/1979 John K Mazzacano. D Gr Ch Pemberton NJ 1998-2001.

MAZZARELLA, Virginia Teresa (Roch) 327 Mendon Center Rd, Pittsford NY 14534 **St Paul's Luth Ch Dansville NY 2012-; Pstr Zion Luth Ch 2012-** B Jackson Hgts NY 1958 d Anthony & Justine. BA Dickinson Coll 1979; MEd Duquesne U 1983; MDiv Pittsburgh TS 1990. D 6/2/1990 P 12/13/1990 Bp Alden Moinet Hathaway. m 7/23/1999 Charles A Ennis c 6. Joint Pastorate S Mths Epis Ch Rochester NY 2008-2009; S Jn's Ch Canandaigua NY 2006-2008, 2002; Gr Ch Lyons NY 2005-2006; S Mk's Ch Newark NY 2003-2004; Int S Lk's Ch Branchport NY 2002-2003; S Geo's Ch Hilton NY 2001-2002; R Gr Ch Scottsville NY 1999-2000; R S Andr's Epis Ch Caledonia NY 1999-2000; S Thos Epis Ch Rochester NY 1995-1998; Asst P S Mich's Ch Geneseo NY 1994-1996; Vic Trin Ch Freeport PA 1992-1993; Vic Ch Of The H Innoc Leechburg PA 1991-1993. Larry G Nagel Memi Prize In Pstr Care Pittsburgh TS; Sylvester S Marvin Fellowowship Pittsburgh TS; Thos Jamison Schlrshp Pittsburgh TS.

MCADAMS, James Lee (Ala) 3775 Crosshaven Dr, Birmingham AL 35223 **Gr Ch Cullman AL 2015-** B Birmingham AL 1971 s Stanley & Helen. BBA Faulkner U 2004; MDiv Sewanee: The U So, TS 2008. D 5/24/2008 Bp John Mckee Sloan Sr P 12/16/2008 Bp Henry Nutt Parsley Jr. m 7/27/1991 Kimberly Carter c 3. Asst R S Steph's Epis Ch Birmingham AL 2008-2015.

MCADAMS, Kathy (Mass) PO Box 51003, Boston MA 02205 **S Jn's Ch Sharon MA 2017-; Vision Team Ldr - Dom Pvrty Working Grp Dom And Frgn Mssy Soc- Epis Ch Cntr New York NY 2008-** B Washington DC 1965 d Merton & Bette. AA Arapahoe Cmnty Coll 1985; BA Metropltn St Coll of Denver 1987; MDiv CDSP 2000. D 12/2/2000 P 6/2/2001 Bp William Edwin Swing. m 12/15/2006 Ellen Mary M Grund. S Mk's Epis Ch Burlington MA 2015; Civic Engagement & Stabilization Prog Working Groups Massachusetts & Boston Reg Ntwk Cmpgn to end homeless 2009-2010; Exec Dir Ecclesia Mnstrs Boston MA 2006-2013; Advsry Bd / Cmnty Relatns Com Urban Mnstry of Palo Alto 2002-2004; Asst/Actg R All SS Epis Ch Palo Alto CA 2001-2005; Int Dir - Homeless Mnstry Old Presb Ch - San Francisco 2000-2001; D / Eucharistic Min - Rite I S Lk's Ch San Francisco CA 2000-2001; Co-Ldr of Christmas Retreat for People w AIDS San Damiano Friary - Danville CA 2000; Chapl Alta Bates Med Cntr - Berkeley CA 1999; Tchg Asst - Pstr Care CDSP Berkeley CA 1999, Alum Coun 2009-; Asst to the Pres - Oasis/California (LGBT Mnstry) Dio California San Francisco CA 1998-2001; Sem S Tim's Ch Danville CA 1998-2000; St Yth Proj Coordntr w Larkin St Yth Cntr All SS' Ch San Francisco CA 1997; Assoc Dir Ecum Hse - San Francisco St U - SF CA 1993-1994.

MCAFEE JR, Ernest (Dal) 1106 Richland Oaks Drive, Richardson TX 75081 **Epis Ch Of The Ascen Dallas TX 2013-** B Memphis TN 1938 s Ernest & Ila. BA Van 1960; MBA Pepperdine U 1980; MDiv Epis TS of the SW 1985; DMin Drew U 1992. D 6/19/1985 Bp Scott Field Bailey P 12/19/1985 Bp Stanley Fillmore Hauser. m 6/4/1960 Diana D McAfee. Int Chr Epis Ch Dallas TX 2010-2013; Pstr Asst Epsicopal Ch Of The Ascen 2005-2010; R S Barn Ch Garland TX 1998-2005; S Richard's Of Round Rock Round Rock TX 1997-1998; S Lk's Epis Ch Salado TX 1990-1997; D Trin-By-The-Sea Port

Aransas TX 1985-1990. Auth, "Generations," Forw Mvmt Press, 1997. ernest.mcafee@ascensiondallas.org

MCALEER, Ruth Bresnahan (Kan) 8700 Metcalf Ave Apt 102, Shawnee Mission KS 66212 **Died 8/19/2015** B Newburyport MA 1931 d Thom & Catharine. Brigham Hosp Sch of Nrsng Boston MA 1954; BA Barat Coll 1976; MA Webster U 1978; SWTS 1991; CPE St Lukes Med Cntr Milwaukee Wisconsin 1992. D 6/20/1992 P 12/19/1992 Bp Frank Tracy Griswold III. c 3. S Mich And All Ang Ch Mssn KS 2004-2008; Reserve Chapl S Lk's Med Cntr Kansas City MO 2002-2006; Chr Ch Overland Pk KS 2001-2003; Ethics Com S Lk's Hlth Care Systems Overland Pk KS 1999-2015; Epis/ELCA Coordntng Team Dioceses of Kansas and W Missouri 1999-2005; Eccles. Crt Dio Kansas Topeka KS 1998-2005, Dn 1998-2003, Dn NE Convoc 1998-2003, Chapl to Ret Cler and Spouses 2004-2015; R Gr Epis Ch Ottawa KS 1996-1999; Asst S Steph's Ch Troy MI 1994-1995; Asst Trin Ch Highland Pk IL 1992-1993; Res Chapl S Lk's Med Cntr Milwaukee WI 1991-1992. "Daily Meditations," *Forw day by Day*, Forw Day By Day, 2004. Coll Chapl 1993-1997; Soc of S Jn the Evang 1993.

MCALHANY, Julie Ann (Me) St John's Episcopal Church, 234 French St, Bangor ME 04401 B Newberry SC 1954 d William & Margaret. BA Furman U 1976; MA U of Maine 1988; MS Maine Maritime Acad 2008. D 6/25/2011 Bp Stephen Taylor Lane. m 10/20/2010 Lorraine Estella Schinck c 2.

MCALLEN, Robert (WTex) 1112 S Westgate Dr, Weslaco TX 78596 **Vic Epiph Epis Ch Raymondville TX 2003-** B Brownsville TX 1934 s Argyle & Margaret. BS Rice U 1956; Studied under Cn 9 Prog 2005. D 8/30/2006 P 3/25/2007 Bp Gary Richard Lillibridge. m 12/29/1959 Margaret McAllen c 3. Bro S Andr.

MCALLISTER, Loring William (Minn) B Winnemucca Nevada 1937 s Glendon & Isabel. BA GW 1960; MA U of Kansas 1966; PhD U of Kansas 1968. m 4/29/1967 Lucy Jean McAllister. D S Mary's Basswood Grove Hastings MN 1982-2001; D S Lk's Epis Ch Hastings MN 1975-1982.

MCALPINE, James Paul (Mass) 2 Victoria Ct Apt 208, York ME 03909 **Ret 1994-** B Torrington CT 1931 s John & Julia. BA Trin 1953; BD EDS 1956; MA New Sch U 1973. D 12/22/1956 Bp Archie H Crowley P 10/1/1957 Bp Walter H Gray. c 4. R Gr Ch Newton MA 1984-1994; Ch of theTransfiguration Bretton Woods NH 1983-1984; R Chr Ch No Conway NH 1975-1984; Natl Higher Educ Mnstrs 1969-1975; Ecum Min Oakland U 1963-1966; R St Mich & Gr Ch Rumford RI 1959-1963; P-in-c All SS Ch Ivoryton CT 1957-1959. laker150@comcast.net

MCALPINE, Thomas Hale (FdL) PO Box 46017, Madison WI 53744 **Chapl S Mary's Chap Wautoma WI 2007-** B Stockton CA 1950 s Arthur & Joy. BA U CA 1971; MA Fuller TS 1976; PhD Yale DS 1984. D 5/22/2004 Bp Sergio Carranza-Gomez P 11/27/2004 Bp Joseph Jon Bruno. m 12/30/1978 Elvice S McAlpine c 1. R S Ptr's Ch (S Mary's Chap) Ripon WI 2007-2015; R S Jas Ch Manitowoc WI 2006-2007; Dio Los Angeles Los Angeles CA 2004-2006; Assoc S Jn's Par Sn Bernrdno CA 2004-2006. "Facing The Powers," Wipf & Stock, 2002; "By Word Wk & Wonder," Wipf & Stock, 2002; "Sleep Div And Human In The OT," Sheffield Acad Press, 1986.

✠ MC ARTHUR JR, The Rt Rev Earl Nicholas (WTex) Po Box 734, Wimberley TX 78676 **Died 7/17/2016** B Houston TX 1925 s Earl & Nanabelle. BA Rice U 1948; MDiv VTS 1963; VTS 1988; Sewanee: The U So, TS 1990. D 7/10/1963 Bp Everett H Jones P 1/18/1964 Bp Richard Earl Dicus Con 1/6/1988 for WTex. c 4. Bp Dio W Texas San Antonio TX 1988-1993, Curs Sprtl Dir 1986-2016, Curs Sprtl Dir 1980-1982; Liaison Natl Curs Com & Hob 1988-1992; R S Steph's Epis Ch Wimberley TX 1981-1987; R All SS Epis Ch Corpus Christi TX 1967-1981; Assoc H Sprt Epis Ch Houston TX 1965-1967; R Ch Of The Annunc Luling TX 1963-1965.

MCAULAY, Roderick Neil (NCal) 7803 Stefenoni Ct, Sebastopol CA 95472 **Lectr Lectr in Cn Law CDSP 2010-** B Sacramento CA 1944 s John & Edith. BA Occ 1966; JD Stan Sch of Law 1969; MDiv CDSP 1999. D 6/26/1999 Bp Vincent Waydell Warner P 1/5/2000 Bp Richard Lester Shimpfky. m 7/25/1970 Mary McAulay c 1. Supply P The Ch of the Incarn Santa Rosa California 2014-2015; Disciplinary Bd The Epis Dio Nthrn California Sacramento CA 2010-2011; Presiding Judge, Eccl Crt 2009, COM, Mem and chairman 2002-2013, Chairman, Dioc COM 2010-2013; R S Steph's Epis Ch Sebastopol CA 2001-2010; Assoc All SS Epis Ch Palo Alto CA 1999-2001.

MCBAY, Susannah E (Tex) 717 Sage Rd, Houston TX 77056 **S Mart's Epis Ch Houston TX 2014-** B England 1985 d Barry & Margaret. Profsnl Cert in Educ Leeds U 2009; Post Grad Dplma St Jn's Coll 2013; MA Oxf 2014; MA Oxf 2014; Post-Grad Dplma St Jn's Theol Coll, Nottingham 2014. Trans 10/31/2014 Bp C Andrew Doyle. m 6/1/2013 Stephen Claude Mcbay. Auth, "God's Voice - Calling," *Awesome Voices*, Gilead Pub, 2013. smcbay@stmartinsepiscopal.org

MCBEATH, Susan Audrey (Ind) 13088 Tarkington Commons, Carmel IN 46033 **D S Chris's Epis Ch Carmel IN 1995-** B Madison WI 1939 d Ivor & Lida. BS U of Wisconsin 1961; MS U of Wisconsin 1962; MA Chr TS 1987. D 6/23/1995 Bp Edward Witker Jones. c 1. NAAD.

MCBRIDE, Bill (WLa) 9105 Colonial Gdns, Shreveport LA 71106 **Dn TS Dio Wstrn Louisiana Shreveport 2005-** B Meridian MS 1950 s William & Diana.

M

BA Rhodes Coll 1972; MA NW St U 1979; PhD Van 1989; Angl TS 2005. D 6/4/2005 P 5/17/2006 Bp D Avid Bruce Macpherson. m 8/6/1978 Cheryl Wisenbaker McBride c 1. R S Mths Epis Ch Shreveport LA 2007-2015; Cur S Tim's Ch Alexandria LA 2005-2007; Tchr Louisiana Sch For Math Sci And Arts Natchitches LA 1983-2007; Mem, Cmsn on Yth and YA Mnstry Dio Wstrn Louisiana Alexandria LA 2008-2011. SBL 1996.

MCBRIDE, David Patrick (Tex) 12572 Foster Rd, Los Alamitos CA 90720 **Died 6/20/2017** B Shreveport LA 1927 s Jackson & Mary. BA U of Texas 1947; MDiv VTS 1950; MA SUNY 1971. D 7/10/1950 P 3/24/1951 Bp Clinton Simon Quin. m 3/31/1974 Nancy Jeanette McBride c 3. Ret 1988-2017; Chapl VA Hosp Long Bch CA 1974-1988; ArmdF and Fed Ministires New York NY 1968-1987; Chapl VA Hosp Northport NY 1968-1974; Chapl (LCDR) USNR Active Duty Var 1955-1968; R H Trin Epis Ch Dickinson TX 1954-1955, Min in charge 1951-1953; Min In Charge S Mich's Ch La Marque TX 1950-1951. (affiliation: Bp of ArmdF; Six Mltry hon US Navy; Assorted Veterans Affrs (VA) hospitals.

MCBRIDE, Ronald Winton (Cal) 34043 Calle Mora, Cathedral City CA 92234 **Assoc S Ptr's Epis Ch San Francisco CA 1999-; Ret 1990-** B Ashland OH 1925 s Charles & Blanche. BA Wheaton Coll 1949; The Biblic Sem New York NY 1952; STB Ya Berk 1954. D 12/23/1954 Bp Horace W B Donegan P 6/24/1955 Bp Charles Francis Boynton. c 5. Assoc S Paul In The Desert Palm Sprg CA 2001-2005; Chapl Dio California San Francisco CA 1996-1998, Admin 1989-1995; Engl Chapl Gd Shpd Taipei Taiwan 1986-1988; Chapl S Lk Hosp San Francisco CA 1970-1986; S Lukes Hosp San Francisco CA 1970-1986; Vstng Instr CDSP Berkeley CA 1970-1983; Vstng Instr PDS 1964-1970; Instnl Chapl Epis Cmnty Servs Philadelphia PA 1963-1970; Vic Ch Of The Trsfg Towaco NJ 1961-1963; R S Paul's And Resurr Ch Wood Ridge NJ 1957-1961; Asst Min Calv and St Geo New York NY 1954-1957. Auth, "Cottage To Cathd: A Narrative Of The Tawain Epis Ch," Richard T Corsce.

MCBRYDE, Greer (CFla) 1155 C.R. 753 South, Webster FL 33597 **Chapl Hlth Cntrl Pk Winter Garden FL 2005-** B Greenville SC 1945 d Walter & Margaret. AA Valencia Cmnty Coll 1981; Inst for Chr Stds Florida 1996; MDiv Asbury TS 2004. D 11/23/1996 P 1/15/2005 Bp John Wadsworth Howe. m 8/21/1963 Clyde McBryde c 2. Assoc R Ch Of The Mssh Winter Garden FL 2005-2011; D All SS Ch Of Winter Pk Winter Pk FL 2002-2004; EFM Mentor U So TN 1997-2001; D Emm Ch Orlando FL 1996-2001. Auth, "Through The Vlly of the Shadow of Death," *Through the Vlly of the Shadow of Death*, self-Pub, 2010. Ord of S Lk 1997. Outstanding Serv Awd Mart Luther King, Jr. Commemoration Soc, Inc. 2009; Intern. Soc. of Theta Phi Asbury TS-Fla 2004.

MCCABE, Chad P (WMass) **Dio Wstrn Massachusetts Springfield 2016-** D 1/5/2014 Bp Edward Lloyd Salmon Jr P 9/14/2014 Bp Daniel William Herzog.

MCCABE III, Charles Peyton (WMich) 325 West Center, Hastings MI 49058 B Charleston WV 1953 s Charles & Lois. BA Marshall U; MDiv VTS 1987. D 9/20/1987 Bp William Franklin Carr P 5/1/1988 Bp Robert Poland Atkinson. m 12/29/1973 Frankie McCabe c 1. Chair - Estrn Dnry Dio Wstrn Michigan Kalamazoo MI 1993-2002, 1992-2007; R Emm Ch Hastings MI 1990-2007; Assoc R The Memi Ch Of The Gd Shpd Parkersburg WV 1987-1989.

MCCABE, Paul Charles (At) 1785 Benningfield Dr Sw, Marietta GA 30064 **Ch Of The Annunc Marietta GA 2009-** B Atlanta GA 1969 s Patrick & Vera. BS Georgia St U 1993; MDiv Sewanee: The U So, TS 2007. D 12/21/2006 P 6/30/2007 Bp J Neil Alexander. m 1/20/2006 Adrian W McCabe c 1. Cur S Edw's Epis Ch Lawrenceville GA 2007-2009.

MCCAFFREY, Susan Maureen (CFla) 4110 S Ridgewood Ave, Port Orange FL 32127 **D Gr Epis Ch Inc Port Orange FL 2011-** B Philadelphia PA 1944 d Amerigo & Helen. LGPN Estrn Voc Tech Sch; Montgomery Cnty Cmnty Coll 1988; Diac Stds Inst of Chr Stds 2011. D 12/11/2010 Bp John Wadsworth Howe. m 5/19/2001 William McCaffrey c 2.

MCCAIN, Michael T. (Ark) B Little Rock, Arkansas 1989 B.S.B.A. U of Arkansas, Walton Coll of Bus 2011. D 3/19/2016 P 10/1/2016 Bp Larry Benfield. mccaimt0@sewanee.edu

MCCALEB, Douglas William (SeFla) 464 NE 16th Street, Miami FL 33132 **Dn Trin Cathd Miami FL 2006-** B Burbank CA 1949 s Sidney & Rose. BA U CA 1971; MDiv GTS 1987. D 6/13/1987 P 4/24/1988 Bp Peter J Lee. R Chr Epis Ch Winchester VA 1995-2005; Asst S Jn's Ch Lafayette Sq Washington DC 1993-1994; S Jn's Epis Ch Mc Lean VA 1987-1992. Auth, "Va Epis (1990-1992)". dean@trinitymiami.org

MCCALL, Chad (Tex) **S Dav's Ch Austin TX 2015-** B Chicago IL 1971 s Charles & Jacqueline. BA Davidson Coll 1993; MBA Georgia Inst of Tech 1995; MDiv Duke DS 2005. D 6/18/2011 P 2/5/2012 Bp C Andrew Doyle. m 7/24/1999 Rhone R McCall c 2. S Ptr's Ch Weston MA 2010-2015. chad.m@stdave.org

MCCALL JR, Jack Keith William (Me) 300 Page St, San Francisco CA 94102 **Non-par 1992-** B Rochester IN 1948 s Jack & Mildred. BA U of Maine 1970; MDiv GTS 1976. D 3/25/1975 P 1/31/1976 Bp Frederick Barton Wolf. Gr Cathd San Francisco CA 1990-1991; Asst Chr Ch Portola Vlly CA 1988-1989; Int S Ann's Epis Ch Windham Windham ME 1985-1986; Deploy Off Dio Maine Portland ME 1983-1985, 1983-1984, Asst To Bp Of Me 1979-1983,

1979-1982; S Giles Ch Jefferson ME 1976-1978; Asst Cathd Ch Of S Lk Portland ME 1975-1976.

MCCALL, Ramelle Lorenzo (Md) 730 Bestgate Rd, Annapolis MD 21401 **Ch Of The H Trin Baltimore MD 2017-** B Baltimore MD 1981 s Leroy & Benita. BS Stevenson U 2003; MDiv Wake Forest U 2006; Cert Ang Stud VTS 2011. D 6/4/2011 P 12/10/2011 Bp Eugene Taylor Sutton. S Mich And All Ang Ch Baltimore MD 2012-2017; D S Phil's Ch Annapolis MD 2011-2012. smaa_md@verizon.net

MCCALL, Richard David (LI) 5117 N Chatham Dr, Bloomington IN 47404 B Baltimore MD 1947 s Henry & Olivia. BA McDaniel Coll 1968; MA Indiana U 1972; MDiv Nash 1979; PhD CDSP 1998. D 5/31/1979 P 1/26/1980 Bp Edward Witker Jones. m 7/10/1999 Terry A Meacham c 1. Provost S Jn's Chap Cambridge MA 2005-2010; Int Par Of The Mssh Auburndale MA 2004-2005; Prof EDS Cambridge MA 1999-2010; Dn CDSP Berkeley CA 1998-1999, Lectr 1994-1997; Int All Souls Par In Berkeley Berkeley CA 1996-1997; R S Paul's Ch Glen Cove NY 1986-1994; Chapl S Mary Garden City NY 1982-1984; Cn Cathd Of The Incarn Garden City NY 1981-1986; Asst R S Steph's Ch Terre Haute IN 1979-1981; Chapl GBEC 2003-2010. Auth, "Angl Wrshp in No Amer," *Encyclopedia of Rel in Amer*, CQ Press, 2010; Auth, "Do This: Liturg as Performance," Univ. of Notre Dame Press, 2007; Auth, "Imagining the Other: Aesthetic Thology," *Rel and the Arts*, 2006; Auth, "Drama and Wrshp," *New Dictionary of Liturg and Wrshp*, 2003; Auth, "The Shape of the Eucharistic Pryr," *Wrshp*, 2000; Auth, "In My Beginning is My End: The Future Shape of Liturg," *ATR*, 1999; Auth, "Performing Drama. Liturg, and Being-as-Event," *Doxology*, 1998; Auth, "Enacting Presidency, Diaconia, and Ch," *Open*, 1997; Auth, "Theopoetics: The Acts of God in the Act of Liturg," *Wrshp*, 1997; Auth, "Anamnesis or Mimesis," *Ecclesia Orans*, 1996. IALC 2003; No Amer Acad of Liturg 1997; Societas Liturgica 2002. Fell ECF 1996.

MCCALL, Terry A (Mass) 5117 N Chatham Dr, Bloomington IN 47404 B South Bend IN 1950 d Justin & Mary. BS U of Maryland 1971; MS Indiana U 1976; MDiv SWTS 1984; PhD OH SU 1995. D 6/25/1984 Bp Edward Witker Jones P 12/29/1984 Bp William Grant Black. m 7/10/1999 Richard David Mccall c 1. Int R S Paul's Ch Brookline MA 2008-2009; S Jas' Epis Ch Cambridge MA 2007-2008; S Andr's Ch Framingham MA 2005-2007; Trin Ch Concord MA 2001-2003; The Ch Of Our Redeem Lexington MA 2000-2005; Int Dio Massachusetts Boston MA 2000-2003; R Epis Ch Of S Ptr And S Mary Denver CO 1997-1999; Assoc P Epis Ch Of The Ascen Dallas TX 1995-1996; 1992-1995; Epis Mnstry To The Oh St U Columbus OH 1990-1992; Epis Chapl S Steph's Epis Ch And U Columbus OH 1990-1992; P-in-c S Paul's Ch Columbus OH 1989-1990; Assoc S Mk's Epis Ch Columbus OH 1986-1989; R Our Sav Ch Mechanicsburg OH 1984-1986.

MCCALLISTER, Katlin E (Az) 3738 N Old Sabino Canyon Rd, Tucson AZ 85750 B New Brunswick NJ 1987 d Thomas & Robin. BS U of Arizona 2011; MDiv VTS 2014. D 10/22/2013 Bp George Edward Councell P 5/24/2014 Bp William H Stokes. Asst S Alb's Epis Ch Tucson AZ 2014-2016.

MCCALLUM, Bruce Allan (FdL) PO Box 561, Waupaca WI 54981 **D S Mk's Ch Waupaca WI 2011-** B Chicago IL 1942 s Robert & Fernella. U IL; Amer Coll 1967. D 5/7/2011 Bp Russell Edward Jacobus. m 12/28/1963 Karen McCallum c 3.

MCCANDLESS, Clelie Fleming (Miss) 8245 Getwell Rd, Southaven MS 38672 **S Mk's Ch Gulfport MS 2016-** B New Orleans LA 1955 d Fenvrick & Clyde. MDiv Sewanee: The U So, TS 2011. D 6/4/2011 P 1/21/2012 Bp Duncan Montgomery Gray III. m 10/10/1980 William Howard McCandless c 3. S Timothys Epis Ch Southaven MS 2011-2016.

MCCANDLESS, Richard Lawrence (O) 1106 Bell Ridge Rd., Akron OH 44303 B Savannah GA 1946 s Edward & Sara. BS mcl MI SU 1966; MS MI SU 1967; MDiv VTS 1970; DMin Lancaster TS 1984. D 6/20/1970 P 5/19/1971 Bp Philip Alan Smith. m 9/10/1966 Patricia McCandless c 3. R S Paul's Ch Akron OH 1992-2006; Dn & R Cathd Ch Of S Steph Harrisburg PA 1985-1992, Pres, St. Steph's Epis Sch 1985-1992; GC Alt Dep S Jn's Epis Ch Sharon PA 1979-1985; R of Par Par Mssn Rising Sun MD 1977-1979; Dio Easton Easton MD 1976-1979, Cmsn on Minsitry chair 1978-1980, Stndg Cmsn Secy 1978-1980, CE Cmsn chair 1977-1980, BACAM chair 1975-1980; R S Mk's Epis Ch Perryville MD 1974-1979; Assoc R All SS Ch Richmond VA 1972-1974; Cur (multi-charge Par w St. Jas Leesburg VA) Our Sav Oatlands VA 1970-1972; Cur S Jas' Epis Ch Leesburg VA 1970-1972; Ethics Com Akron Chld's Hosp Akron OH 1999-2013; Dioc Coun Dio Ohio Cleveland 1994-1996, Ecum chair 1993-1998, COM 1992-2006, BACAM chair 1992-2005; Bd Dir Victim Assistance Prog Akron OH 1993-2013; COM Plnng co-chair Prov III Baltimore MD 1986-1988, Prov COMs Strng Com 1982-1985; BACAM chair Dio Cntrl Pennsylvania Harrisburg PA 1985-1992, Cmsn on Minsitry chair 1985-1992, Pres of St. Steph's Epis Sch 1985-1992; Dioc Coun Dio NW Pennsylvania Erie PA 1984-1986, BACAM chair 1981-1986, COM chair 1981-1986, Chair of BACAM, Chair of COM 1979-1985; Bd Dir, co-Fndr Shenango Vlly Foodbank Sharon PA 1983-1985; Cncl examination Rdr Board of Exam Chapl 1983-1984; Bd Dir Buhl Chld's Hm Mercer PA 1982-1985; Bd Dir, co-Fndr Hospice of the Shenango Vlly Sharon PA 1982-1984; VP, co-Fn-

M

dr Shenango Vlly Foodbank 1982-1984; Plnng Com Great Lakes Ch Ldrshp Sch 1979-1982; Bd Dir Epis Hm for Ladies Richmond VA 1973-1976; BA-CAM Exam Dio Virginia Richmond VA 1972-1975. Co-Auth, "Only Love Can Make It Easy," *Bk*, Twenty Third Pub, 1988; Auth, "More than 30 arts and Revs," *Journ, mag, websites*, 1996-present. Bioethics Ntwk of Ohio 2005; Bluecoats of Summit Cnty OH 1995; Reality Ther Assn 1990-1998; Rel Educ Assn 1972-1992; Natl Sci Fndt Grad Fllshp MI SU 1966; Tau Beta Pi (Engr hon Soc) MI SU 1966; BS mcl in 3 years MI SU 1966.

MCCANDLESS, Richard William (Kan) 3028 Washington Ave, Parsons KS 67357 B Mitchell SD 1932 s Richard & Mildred. BA U of No Dakota 1954; STB EDS 1962. D 6/16/1962 Bp George Leslie Cadigan P 12/21/1962 Bp Gordon V Smith. m 4/25/1985 Jean McCandless. H Trin. Reg Mnstry Parsons KS 1994-2001; Vic Calv Ch Yates Cntr KS 1993-2003; Vic Gr Ch Chanute KS 1993-2003; Vic S Tim's Ch Iola KS 1993-2003; Dn Dio Kansas Topeka KS 1984-2003; R S Jn's Parsons KS 1984-2003; S Jn's Ch Parsons KS 1983-1994; R Trin Epis Ch El Dorado KS 1971-1983; Cn Gr Cathd Topeka KS 1967-1971; Vic St Andr's Ch Clear Lake IA 1962-1967.

MCCANN, Christopher Richard (O) 16267 Oakhill Rd, Cleveland Heights OH 44112 **P-in-c S Lk's Epis Ch Chardon OH 2006-** B Windsor Nova Scotia 1963 s R & Beverley. BA U of Kings Coll Halifax NS CA; MDiv Atlantic TS 1998. Trans 6/5/2006 as Priest Bp Mark Hollingsworth Jr. R Angl Ch of Can 1998-2006.

MCCANN, John Harrison (WMo) 1492 Hemlock Ct, Liberty MO 64068 **Assoc Gr Epis Ch Liberty MO 2012-** B Fort Sam Houston TX 1945 s Willis & Catherine. BA U of Kansas 1967; MDiv VTS 1971. D 6/11/1971 Bp Edward Randolph Welles II P 12/17/1971 Bp Arthur Anton Vogel. m 3/5/1993 Susan Griffen. Chair, COM Dio W Missouri Kansas City MO 1992-2012, Archd 1991-2012, Cn 1985-1991, 1972-1973, Fin Com 1991-2012; Dn Metropltn Dnry MO 1982-1984; Assoc S Paul's Ch Kansas City MO 1973-1985; Cur Chr Epis Ch Springfield MO 1971-1973. johnpcd@gmail.com

MCCANN, Michael Louis (HB) **Non-par 1978-** B Bay City MI 1943 s Wilfred & Geraldine. BS Cntrl Michigan U 1966; Epis TS in Kentucky 1972. D 6/1/1972 Bp Addison Hosea P 12/1/1972 Bp Archibald Donald Davies. m 8/3/1974 Rita R Podoski. S Lk's Epis Ch Milwaukee WI 1973-1974; S Jn's Ch Ft Worth TX 1972-1973.

MCCANN, Michael Wayne (At) 975 Longstreet Cir, Gainesville GA 30501 **P Assoc Gr Epis Ch Gainesville GA 2006-, 1980-1987** B Kansas City MO 1947 s Wayne & Elinor. BA Hav 1968; MTS Harvard DS 1971. D 6/26/1971 P 4/1/1972 Bp John Melville Burgess. m 7/17/1987 Candace Lighton c 2. Asst Gr Gainesville GA 1980-1986; R Trin Ch Hampton NH 1974-1980; Cur S Chrys's Wollaston MA 1971-1974; The Par Of S Chrys's Quincy MA 1971-1974.

MCCANN, Robert Emmett (Cal) 4023 Canyon Rd, Lafayette CA 94549 B Chicago IL 1931 s Peter & Mary. BA Glennon Coll St Louis MO 1953; MDiv Kenrickglennon Sem 1957; MEd Washington U 1966. Rec 10/1/1976 as Priest Bp Chauncie Kilmer Myers. m 12/15/1967 Sylvia McCann c 2. S Matt's Epis Ch San Mateo CA 2005-2007; Serv Angl Ch of Can 2003-2007; Ch Of Our Sav Mill Vlly CA 2002-2007; Int S Giles Ch Moraga CA 1999-2000; Nonpar 1996-1998; Int S Clem's Ch Berkeley CA 1995-1996; Dir Planned Giving Dio California San Francisco CA 1991-1997; S Jn's Epis Ch Oakland CA 1976-1991; Serv RC Ch 1957-1966. Auth, "Congrl Guide To Planned Giving," 1997. Allin Fllshp Ecum Institue; Procter Fellowowship "Anglicanism, Globalism And Ecum" EDS.

MCCANN, Sandra Briggs (At) B Washington PA 1944 d David & Harriett. BS Maryville Coll 1966; MD Tem Sch of Med 1970; MDiv VTS 2003. D 10/17/2004 P 7/3/2005 Bp J Neil Alexander. m 4/15/1972 Martin McCann c 2. Exec Coun Appointees New York NY 2004-2016. Hon doctorate VTS 2015; Cn Dio Cntrl Tanganyika 2012. mccanns@mindspring.com

MCCANN, Susan Griffen (WMo) 1492 Hemlock Ct, Liberty MO 64068 B New York NY 1943 d Richard & Sara. BA Mt Holyoke Coll 1964; MS U of Kansas 1986; MDiv Epis TS of the SW 1996. D 6/8/1996 P 12/14/1996 Bp John Clark Buchanan. m 3/5/1993 John Harrison McCann. R Gr Epis Ch Liberty MO 1996-2015. AAMFT; ACSW; LMCSW; NASW.

MCCARD, John (At) 3110 Ashford Dunwoody Rd Ne, Atlanta GA 30319 **R St Jas Ch Richmond VA 2017-; R S Mart In The Fields Ch Atlanta GA 2004-; R St. Mart in the Fields Ch Atlanta GA 2004-** B Tampa FL 1965 s Ray & Rosalyn. BA Ob 1988; MDiv GTS 1992; STM Nash 2003; DMin VTS 2007. D 7/25/1992 P 6/6/1993 Bp Herbert Thompson Jr. m 6/15/1991 Cynthia K McCard c 3. R S Mk's Ch Marco Island FL 1998-2004; S Mk's Epis Ch San Antonio TX 1997-1998; Asst R S Paul's Epis Ch Dayton OH 1992-1996. jmccard@doers.org

MCCARLEY, Melanie (Mass) Zion Church, 221 E. Washington St., Charles Town WV 25414 **S Paul's Ch Dedham MA 2016-; COM Dio W Virginia Charleston WV 2011-, Comp Dio Com 2011-, Dn of Estrn Dnry 2004-, Dioc Coun 2004-; Prov III VP Prov III Baltimore MD 2009-** B Falls Church VA 1966 d Terry & Rita. Ya Berk; BA MWC 1988; MDiv VTS 1991. D 6/13/1992 Bp Robert Poland Atkinson P 8/28/1993 Bp Edward Witker Jones. m 11/9/1991 Philip Earl McCarley. R Zion Epis Ch Chas Town WV 2001-2016; Emm

Ch Rapidan VA 1998-2001; Vic S Steph's Elwood IN 1994-1997; Assoc H Fam 1992-1994; H Fam Epis Ch Fishers IN 1992-1994. mmccarley@stpauls-dedham.org

MCCARROLL SSG, Connie Jo (SO) 4381 S.Rangeline Rd., West Milton OH 45383 **D S Andr's Ch Dayton OH 2014-** B Dayton OH 1946 d Lawrence & Thelma. BS Wright St U 1968; MS Wright St U 1970; DO MI SU 1976; DSO Sch for the Diac 1995. D 10/28/1995 Bp Herbert Thompson Jr. D S Paul's Epis Ch Greenville OH 2012-2014; D Ch Of The Gd Shpd Athens OH 2009-2011; D S Geo's Epis Ch Dayton OH 1995-2010. Vol of Year Ohio Osteopathic Assn 2011; Hall of hon Milto-Un Schools Milton -Un Schools W Milton Ohio 2009; Living Water Awd Kettering Med Cntr/ Adventist Hosp Systems 2004.

MCCARROLL, Sandra Kim (Nev) 1806 Hilton Head Dr, Boulder City NV 89005 **R S Chris's Epis Ch Boulder City NV 2005-** B American Falls 1937 d Max. BA U Chi 1961; MA Un Coll Schenectady NY 1968. D 4/10/2005 P 10/15/2005 Bp Katharine Jefferts Schori. m 9/12/1959 Bruce McCarroll c 1. P S Chris's Epis Ch Boulder City NV 2005-2010.

MCCARRON, Charles F (LI) 11 Violet Ave, Mineola NY 11501 **P-in-c S Mary's Epis Ch Shltr Island NY 2015-; Fam Consult Serv Dio Long Island 2005-; Memberdiocesan COM Dio Long Island 2004-** B The Bronx NY 1955 BA Ford 1978; MDiv Maryknoll TS 1985; MA St Bonaventure U 1989; JD CUNY 1991; DAS GTS 2001. Rec 6/3/2002 Bp Orris George Walker Jr. Dio Long Island Garden City NY 2010-2011, Cn 2005-; Epis Cmnty Serv Long Island 1927 Bay Shore NY 2007-2014; P-in-c Ch Of The Resurr Kew Gardens NY 2003-2007. "Anth Of Padua," Franciscan Inst Pub, 1994; "Lawr Of Brindisi," Franciscan Inst Pub, 1989; "Franciscan Spirituals And Capuchin Reform," Franciscan Inst Pub, 1987. chairlief@aol.com

MCCART, Thomas K (Roch) 1793 Dunaway Ct, Indianapolis IN 46228 **Died 5/27/2017** B Oklahoma City OK 1948 s Virgil & Dorethea. BA SW Oklahoma St U 1971; MA U of New Mex 1974; MDiv CDSP 1978; Oxf GB 1981; MA Van 1993; PhD Van 1994. D 9/15/1978 P 5/24/1979 Bp Richard Mitchell Trelease Jr. Assoc R S Paul's Ch Rochester NY 2002-2011; Int Par of St Clem Honolulu HI 2000-2001; R S Mk's Epis Ch Upland CA 1996-2000; Cn Precentor Chr Ch Cathd Indianapolis IN 1990-1996; Dio Tennessee Nashville TN 1989; Chr Ch Cathd Nashville TN 1987-1988; Chapl TCU Ft Worth TX 1981-1986; Cur Trin Epis Ch Ft Worth TX 1981-1985. Auth, "Matter & Manner of Praise," Scarecrow Press, 1998. AAM 1975; Assn of Dioc Liturg & Mus Comm 1979-2000. Fllshp ECF 1988. tkmccart@gmail.com

MCCARTHY, Bartlett Anderson (Dal) 7335 Inwood Rd, Dallas TX 75209 **Non-par 1988-** B Refusio TX 1943 s Richard & Jane. BD U MN 1966; MDiv GTS 1970. D 6/29/1970 Bp Hamilton Hyde Kellogg P 6/10/1971 Bp The Bishop Of Tokyo. m 10/3/1987 Kalita Beck. S Mich And All Ang Ch Dallas TX 1984-1987; Breck Sch Minneapolis MN 1980-1983; Chapl Brech Sch Minneapolis MN 1979-1983; Assoc S Mart's By The Lake Epis Minnetonka Bch MN 1976-1979; Asst Chapl U Epis Cntr 1974-1976; R S Ptr's Ch Cass Lake MN 1971-1974; Asst S Alb Tokyo Japan 1970-1971; Asst Ch Of The H Trin New York NY 1968-1970.

MCCARTHY, Bill (Ore) 5060 SW Philomath Blvd, PMB 165, Corvallis OR 97333 **Ret 2006-** B Tacoma WA 1941 s Denward & Florence. BS OR SU 1966; U Cinc 1970; MDiv Nash 1975. D 6/14/1975 Bp Quintin Ebenezer Primo Jr P 12/13/1975 Bp James Winchester Montgomery. m 4/22/1962 Bernice McCarthy c 2. Vice Chair of Bd Samar Hlth Serv Corvallis OR 1989-2006; R The Epis Ch Of The Gd Samar Corvallis OR 1989-2006; Share/Food Waukegan IL 1985-1989; R Chr Ch Waukegan IL 1981-1989; Curs Off/Sprtl Dir Dio Chicago Chicago IL 1977-1985; Vic One In Chr Ch Prospect Heights IL 1977-1981; Cur S Mich's Ch Barrington IL 1975-1977; Stndg Com Dio Oregon Portland OR 1993-1997. Assn For Psychol Type. Who'S Who In Healthcare Marquis 2002; Who'S Who In Rel Marquis.

MCCARTHY, Ian (Fla) St. Mary's Episcopal Church, 623 SE Ocean Blvd, Stuart FL 34994 **Asst St Fran in the Field Ponte Vedra FL 2016-** B Tallahassee FL 1977 s Samuel & Patrina. BS U of Florida 2001; MDiv TESM 2007. Trans 5/11/2012 as Priest Bp William Howard Love. m 10/30/2010 Nicole Atkinson Mccarthy c 3. S Mary's Ch Stuart FL 2014-2015; Asst Galilee Epis Ch Virginia Bch VA 2012-2014, Yth Dir 2001-2012.

MCCARTHY, Jean Elizabeth Rinner (Ia) 2906 39th St, Des Moines IA 50310 B Mount Pleasant IA 1943 d Donald & Vaughn. BA U of Iowa 1965; MA S Johns U 1988; MDiv SWTS 2000. D 5/27/2000 P 2/24/2001 Bp Chris Christopher Epting. m 8/29/1964 Michael Lynn McCarthy c 2. R S Mk's Epis Ch Des Moines IA 2001-2015; D The Cathd Ch Of S Paul Des Moines IA 2000-2001; Dir Of Chr Formation 1996-1999.

MCCARTHY, Martin Franklin (NC) 4205 Quail Hunt Lane, Charlotte NC 28226 B Washington DC 1952 s Maurice & Barbara. BA Emory and Henry Coll 1974; MDiv VTS 1978. D 6/3/1978 P 6/4/1979 Bp John Alfred Baden. m 5/9/1981 Cindy L McCarthy c 2. Kanuga Conf Cntr 2001-2006; Fndng Bd Trst Trin Epis Sch So Charlotte NC 1999-2004; R S Jn's Epis Ch Charlotte NC 1995-2008; Dn Dio Virginia Richmond VA 1988-1991; Pres Virginia Epis Cler Assn 1988-1989; R Epiph Epis Ch Richmond VA 1982-1995; Asst S Dunst's Ch Mc Lean VA 1978-1982.

MCCARTHY, Melissa (Los) 6860 Poppyview Dr, Oak Park CA 91377 **Vic Ch Of The Epiph Oak Pk CA 2009-, P-in-c 2008-2009, Assoc 2006-; Dio Los Angeles Los Angeles CA 2011-** B Bakersfield CA 1972 d Michael & Linda. BA U CA 1998; MDiv CDSP 2005; MDiv CDSP 2005. D 6/11/2005 Bp Chester Lovelle Talton P 1/14/2006 Bp Joseph Jon Bruno. Ballet Instr Self-Employed 1992-2003.

MCCARTHY, Nancy Horton (SeFla) 24 Highbridge Xing, Apt 1002, Asheville NC 28803 **Adj P All Soul's Cathd Asheville NC 2013-; Adj The Cathd Of All Souls Asheville NC 2013-** B Newark NJ 1934 d Leonard & Gladys. BA Ob 1956; MDiv VTS 1988. D 10/4/1982 P 11/30/1988 Bp Calvin Onderdonk Schofield Jr. c 1. Assoc S Greg's Ch Boca Raton FL 2009-2013, Assoc 1988-1999; P Assoc St. Greg's Epis Ch Boca Raton FL 2009-2013; P-in-c S Mary's Epis Ch Of Deerfield Deerfield Bch FL 1999-2009; Asst S Jn's Ch Hollywood FL 1982-1985. Ord of Julian of Norwich 1984. Phi Beta Kappa Ob 1956.

MCCARTHY JR, Stephen Joseph (Mass) 2017 6th Ave N, Birmingham AL 35203 B Boston MA 1987 s Stephen & Phoebe. AB Vassar Colleg 2010; AB Vassar Colleg 2010; AB Vas 2010; AB Vas 2010; MDiv Ya Berk 2014. D 6/6/2015 Bp Gayle Harris P 12/12/2015 Bp Santosh K Marray. Cur The Cathd Ch Of The Adv Birmingham AL 2015-2016.

MCCARTY, Marjorie McDonall (EC) 100 E Sherwood Dr, Havelock NC 28532 B New York NY 1939 d Bertrand & Mildred. BA La Roche Coll 1979; MDiv Pittsburgh TS 1982. D 6/5/1982 P 12/1/1982 Bp Robert Bracewell Appleyard. c 4. R S Chris's Ch Havelock NC 1996-2008; P-in-res Ware Epis Ch Gloucester VA 1988-1996; Dioc Pstr Care Dept 1982-1988; Dio Pittsburgh Pittsburgh PA 1982-1988.

MCCARTY, Mary Sharon (WA) 1831 Parkers Creek Road, Port Republic MD 20676 **R S Mary's Aquasco Aquasco MD 1997-** B Three Rivers MI 1951 d John & Virginia. BS U CA 1979; MDiv CDSP 1987. D 6/13/1987 Bp Charles Brinkley Morton P 12/1/1988 Bp John Thomas Walker. m 6/23/1984 Jeffrey Samuel Buyer. Int Chr Ch Durham Par Nanjemoy MD 2012-2017; Int Chr Ch W River MD 2010-2011; Int Ch Of Middleham Lusby MD 2007-2008; R S Paul's Par Prince Geo's Cnty Brandywine MD 1997-2006; Chapl Queen Anne Sch Upper Marlboro MD 1995-1997; Queen Anne Sch Uppr Marlboro MD 1995-1997; Asst R S Paul's Epis Ch Piney Waldorf MD 1988-1995.

MCCARTY, Patricia (WTenn) 1720 Peabody Ave., Memphis TN 38104 **S Lk's Epis Ch Jackson TN 2015-** B Memphis TN 1958 d Thomas & Billie. BA U of Tennessee 1980; JD Cecil C Humphrey Sch of Law 1983; MDiv Epis TS of the SW 2009. D 6/7/2009 P 1/16/2010 Bp Don Edward Johnson. Cur Gr - S Lk's Ch Memphis TN 2009-2015.

MCCARTY, Steven Lynn (Md) Saint Andrew's Episcopal Church, 22 Cumberland St, PO Box 189, Clear Spring MD 21722 **Vic S Andr's Ch Clear Sprg MD 2011-** B Hagerstown MD 1959 s Roger & Marlene. AA Hagerstown Cmnty Coll 1980; BS Frostburg St U 1990; Cert Sewanee: The U So, TS 2006; MA Nash 2011. D 6/10/2006 Bp Robert Wilkes Ihloff P 6/12/2011 Bp Eugene Taylor Sutton. m 11/8/1981 Melanie McCarty c 2. BroSA 2000; Soc of Cath Priests 2011; SocMary 2012; The CBS 2008.

MCCARTY, Willis Barnum Coker (Fla) 5303 Ortega Blvd Apt 208, Jacksonville FL 32210 B Jacksonville FL 1930 s Harvey & Nellie. BA Ccollege of Arts and Sci U So 1954; MDiv Sewanee: The U So, TS 1956; DD Sewanee: The U So, TS 1993. D 6/20/1956 P 4/15/1957 Bp Edward Hamilton West. m 8/6/1956 Betty Ann McCarty c 3. Int S Jn's Cathd Jacksonville FL 1999-2000; Int S Ptr's Ch Fernandina Bch FL 1996-1997; Int S Thos' Epis Ch St Petersburg FL 1995-1996; R S Mk's Epis Ch Jacksonville FL 1971-1995; R S Andr's Epis Ch Panama City FL 1962-1971; Dir of Yth Flo Florida Jacksonville 1959-1962; Chapl (COL) Florida NG 1957-1987; R Trin Ch Apalachicola FL 1956-1959.

MCCASLIN, H Kenneth (Pa) 694 Kennedy Ln, Wayne PA 19087 **D S Dav's Ch Wayne PA 2017-** B Augusta ME 1955 s Henry & Jacqueline. BS U of Phoenix 2004; MAR Luth TS 2013. D 6/14/2008 Bp Edward Lewis Lee Jr. m 6/26/1982 Cheryl Rene McCaslin. Vlly Forge Dnry D Mssnr Calv Ch Conshohocken PA 2014-2016; D Chr Epis Ch Pottstown PA 2010-2013. Hlth Level Seven Fell Hlth Level Seven, Intl 2010. revhkenm@gmail.com

MCCASLIN, Robert Allan (WNC) 5198 NC Highway 194 S, Banner Elk NC 28604 **R Ch Of The H Cross Valle Crucis NC 2012-; Dn - Mtn Dnry Dio Wstrn No Carolina Asheville NC 2015-** B Deerfield IL 1954 s William & Nora. Cert Soc for HR Managment 2001; CPE U of Arkansas Med Cntr 2007; Off of Congrl Dvlpmt The Epis Ch 2008; MDiv Sewanee: The U So, TS 2009. D 3/21/2009 Bp Larry Maze P 9/27/2009 Bp Larry Benfield. m 11/26/2005 Patricia Pan Adams-Mccaslin c 2. R Ch Of The H Cross W Memphis AR 2010-2012, D in Charge 2009-2010. Soc for HR Mgmt 1986-2006. CE Prize for Creativity & Excellence in Biblic Stds TS, Sewanee, TN 2009; Shettle Prize for Excellence in Liturg Reading TS, Sewanee, TN 2009.

MCCAUGHAN, Patricia Susanne (Los) 1554 N. Shelley Avenue, Upland CA 91786 **R and Headmaster S Geo's Epis Ch Laguna Hills CA 2015-, Assoc P 2010-2015, Assoc R 2007-2008; Epis Ch Cntr New York NY 2006-; Prov VII, VIII Correspondent Epis News Serv Los Angeles CA 2005-; Correspondent Epis News Serv New York NY 2004-; Cmncatn Profsnl Dio Los Angeles Los Angeles CA 1999-** B Detroit MI 1953 d Donald & Madge. BA Wayne 1975; MS Col 1983; MDiv GTS 1997. D 6/21/1997 P 5/31/1998 Bp Raymond Stewart Wood Jr. m 5/30/1998 Keith Akio Yamamoto. St Fran Epis Mssn Outreach Cntr San Bernardino CA 2011-2015; Asst R S Mary's Par Laguna Bch CA 2002-2007; P-in-c S Fran Of Assisi Par Sn Bernrdno CA 1999-2002; D-in-c S Martha's Ch Detroit MI 1997-2006; D-in-c Cathd Ch Of S Paul Detroit MI 1997-1999; Dio Michigan Detroit MI 1997-1998. pmccaughan@ladiocese.org

MCCAULEY, Claud Ward (SwVa) 612 W Franklin St, Richmond VA 23220 **Died 12/28/2015** B Roanoke VA 1928 s John & Elizabeth. BA Hampden-Sydney Coll 1952; MDiv VTS 1955. D 6/3/1955 Bp Frederick D Goodwin P 6/23/1962 Bp Robert Fisher Gibson Jr. m 9/9/1962 Jane Gaunt c 2. Vic Gr Ch Bremo Bluff VA 2001-2007; Dn Augusta Convoc VA 1998-2000; Dioc Exec Bd Dio SW Virginia Roanoke VA 1996-1999, Chair-Stwdshp Com 1999-2000, Exec Bd 1973-1995, Pres (1971)-Stndg Com 1969-1972; Vic S Lk's Ch Hot Sprg VA 1995; Dn New River Convoc VT 1994-1995; R Gr Ch Radford VA 1993-1995; All SS Ch Richmond VA 1977-1993; Del GC Minneapolis-St. Paul MN 1976-2015; Delgate Gnrl Convetion Houston TX 1970-2015; Chapl Vpi Blacksburg VA 1970-1975; R Chr Ch Blacksburg VA 1964-1976; R Epis Ch Of Our Sav Midlothian VA 1956-1963. Ord Of S Lk 1978.

MCCAULEY, Margaret Hudley (Los) 4215 W 61st St, Los Angeles CA 90043 **D St Johns Pro-Cathd Los Angeles CA 2012-; D H Nativ Par Los Angeles CA 2007-** B Chicago IL 1943 d General & Cynthia. BA California St U Los Angeles 1965; MA California St U 1979; Cert Theol Stud ETSBH 2006. D 12/2/2006 Bp Joseph Jon Bruno. m 7/3/1965 Ronald Lee McCauley c 2. Admin Los Angeles Unified Sch Dist 1971-2005. DOK 2006.

MCCAULEY, Shana (Ore) 1550 Diablo Rd, Danville CA 94526 **P-in-c S Edw's Ch Silverton OR 2009-** B San Antonio, TX 1978 d David & Myong. BA U of Washington 2000; MDiv SWTS 2006. D 6/24/2006 Bp Vincent Waydell Warner P 12/2/2006 Bp Marc Handley Andrus. m 12/1/2009 Ryan S McCauley c 1. Assoc S Tim's Ch Danville CA 2006-2008.

MCCAULLEY, Barbara Marie (Ia) 620 Briarstone Dr Apt 28, Mason City IA 50401 **VP, Mssn and Ethics Mercy Med Cntr Mason City IA 2008-** B Mason City IA 1952 d Dale & Edna. BA U of Iowa 1975; MDiv U of Dubuque 1980. D 10/16/2002 Bp George Elden Packard P 5/24/2003 Bp Alan Scarfe. c 1. Gr Epis Ch Chas City IA 2010-2013; Stff Chapl, Int Dir Mercy Med Cntr Mason City IA 1989-2008.

MCCAUSLAND, John Lesher (NH) 457 Reservoir Dr, Weare NH 03281 **Assoc S Andr's Epis Ch Contoocook NH 2013-** B Chicago IL 1939 s John & Clara. BA Harv 1961; LLB Harvard Law Sch 1964; MDiv Nash 1983. D 6/11/1983 Bp Quintin Ebenezer Primo Jr P 12/17/1983 Bp James Winchester Montgomery. m 6/15/1965 Anne Darrow McCausland c 2. Vic H Cross Epis Ch Weare NH 1997-2004; R S Matt's Ch Evanston IL 1992-1997; R S Chas Ch St. Chas IL 1985-1992; Cur S Mich's Ch Barrington IL 1983-1984. Chapl SCHC 1998-2002; EPF 1998; Fllshp of St. Jn 1984.

MCCAW, Mary Ann (Oly) 6 Lincoln Rd, Wellesley MA 02481 B New York NY 1948 d Frank & Agatha. BA Bard Coll 1971; MDiv EDS 1974; CTh Seattle U Inst For Ecum Stds 1994. D 7/9/1994 P 1/16/1995 Bp Vincent Waydell Warner. m 2/1/1976 Robert McCaw. Sr Asst Dir Harborview Med Cntr Seattle WA 1988-1992. ACPE.

MCCLAIN, Daniel W (Md) 4 E University Pkwy, Baltimore MD 21218 **S Dav's Ch Baltimore MD 2017-** B Las Vegas NV 1977 s George & Sheryl. MA Trin Evang DS 2003; MPhil CUA 2012; PhD CUA 2017. D 1/15/2017 Bp Chilton Richardson Knudsen. m 7/14/2001 Katherine E Glahn c 4.

MCCLAIN, Marion Roy Sam (FtW) 3650 Chicora Ct Apt 330, Fort Worth TX 76116 B Paris TX 1938 s Roy & Elizabeth. BS Texas A&M U at Commerce 1960; MS Texas A&M U at Commerce 1963; MTh SWTS 1979; DMin Austin Presb 1984. D 6/24/1977 P 12/1/1977 Bp Robert Elwin Terwilliger. m 8/20/1960 Anndrea McClain c 1. R S Lk's Epis Ch Stephenville TX 1978-2009; Cur The Epis Ch Of The H Nativ Plano TX 1977-1978.

MCCLAIN, Mikel (Ore) 7875 SW Alden St, Portland OR 97223 **Asst S Barth's Ch Beaverton OR 2012-** B Houston TX 1948 s Glen & Edna. BA U of Houston 1974; MDiv Epis TS of the SW 1977. D 9/23/1977 P 5/1/1978 Bp Richard Mitchell Trelease Jr. m 1/14/2006 Marilyn Mills Walkey c 3. S Barn Ch Bonanza OR 2003-2004; R S Paul's Ch Klamath Fall OR 2003-2004; R Gd Shpd Of The Hills Cave Creek AZ 1988-2003; R Ch Of The Epiph Houston TX 1986-1988; R Ch Of The Resurr Austin TX 1983-1986; Stwdshp & Evang Departments Dio Texas Houston TX 1978-1988; Assoc R Trin Epis Ch Baytown TX 1978-1983; Assoc R All SS Epis Ch El Paso TX 1977-1978. Ord Of S Lk.

MCCLAIN, Rebecca Lee (Oly) Saint Paul's Cathedral, 2728 6th Ave, San Diego CA 92103 B Lakeland FL 1947 d Fred & Mildred. Baylor U; BA Trin U San Antonio 1969; MA Epis TS of the SW 1977; MDiv Epis TS of the SW 1985. D 8/29/1985 Bp Anselmo Carral-Solar P 4/1/1986 Bp Gordon Taliaferro Charlton. c 3. Int Dn Cathd Ch Of S Paul San Diego CA 2013-2014; Cn Mssnr S Mk's Cathd Seattle WA 2008-2012; Godly Play Fndt Seattle WA 2007-2009; Exec Dir Godly Play Fndt Ch Of Our Sav Par San Gabr CA 2007-2008; Exec Dir CDO Epis Ch Cntr New York NY 2005-2007; Exec Dir CDO Epis Ch Cntr

M

New York NY 2005-2007; Dn Trin Cathd Phoenix AZ 1995-2005; Dio Arizona Phoenix AZ 1991-2005, Cn to the Ordnry 1989-1991; Natl Stwdshp Consult 1990-1994; Hosp Chapl S Lk's Epis Hosp Houston TX 1987-1988; CE Ch Of The Epiph Houston TX 1986-1987; Chr Formation and Liturg Ch Of The Resurr Austin TX 1985-1986. Auth, *Mssn Statements*. Wmn of Year YWCA 1994.

MCCLAIN, William Allen (NCal) 6825 Sterchi Ln, Montague CA 96064 B Colorado Springs CO 1927 s Raymond & Belle. BA DePauw U 1951; MDiv CD-SP 1966. D 6/19/1966 Bp James Albert Pike P 1/21/1967 Bp Chauncie Kilmer Myers. m 11/10/1951 Sally McClain. P S Barn Ch Mt Shasta CA 1990-1997; 1970-1989; Cur Chr Ch Portola Vlly CA 1966-1970.

MCCLASKEY, Steven Lloyd 2020 21st St, Rock Island IL 61201 B Los Angeles CA 1942 s Charles & Jeanne. BA San Diego St U 1968; MDiv Nash 1973. D 9/15/1973 Bp Robert Claflin Rusack P 3/1/1974 Bp Richard S Watson. m 11/16/2002 April J McClaskey c 2. Trin Epis Ch Rock Island IL 2002-2007, R 2002-; R All SS Ch San Diego CA 1985-2002, Assoc R 1983-1985, 1973-2002; Vic The Ch Of Chr The King Alpine CA 1974-1983; Chapl San Diego St U 1973-1976. SSC.

MCCLEERY III, Bill (SO) 7265 Edgewood Ln, Athens OH 45701 B Lancaster OH 1945 s William & Esther. BA OH SU 1967; MDiv PrTS 1970; Cert Ang Stud Bex Sem 2007. D 2/2/2008 Bp Kenneth Lester Price P 12/5/2008 Bp Thomas Edward Breidenthal. m 3/2/2011 Anna Linea Warmke. Vic Ch Of The Epiph Nelsonville OH 2008-2015; Vic S Paul's Epis Ch Logan OH 2008-2015.

MCCLELLAN, Robert Farrell (NMich) Po Box 841, Saint Helena CA 94574 **1965-** B Chicago IL 1934 s Robert & Katherine. BA MI SU 1956; BD CDSP 1959; PhD MI SU 1964. D 6/28/1959 Bp Richard Stanley Merrill Emrich P 7/1/1961 Bp Archie H Crowley. m 6/23/1956 Sara F McClellan c 4. S Paul's Ch Marquette MI 1964-1965; Vic S Annes Ch Dewitt MI 1962-1964; Vic S Geo's Ch Cordova AK 1959-1960. Auth, "The Heathen Chinese," OH SU, 1966; Auth, "Amer Image of China," MI SU, 1964.

MCCLELLAN, Thomas Lee (Pa) Po Box 642, Lafayette Hill PA 19444 **P-in-c Calv Ch Conshohocken PA 2015-** B Wilmington DE 1942 s William & Mary. BA Muhlenberg Coll 1965; MDiv EDS 1970; U of Cambridge 1974; S Georges Coll Jerusalem IL 1976. D 6/6/1970 P 3/6/1971 Bp Robert Lionne DeWitt. Bd Mem Widows' Corp 2000-2010; Dn Wissahickon Dnry 1987-1993; Bps Res Interfaith Wit for Peace 1984-1989; R S Mary's At The Cathd Philadelphia PA 1977-2014; Asst Chapl of Sacr Stds Dept S Andrews Sch Of Delaware Inc Middletown DE 1976-1977; Assoc S Dav's Ch Wayne PA 1974-1976; Pstr Asst The Epis Ch Of The Adv Kennet Sq PA 1970-1972. *arts*, 2003. Bp White Par Libr Assn 2004; Bp White PB Soc 2001.

MCCLELLAND, Carol Jean (EO) 12019 SE 15th St, Vancouver WA 98683 **D S Mk's Epis and Gd Shpd Luth Madras OR 1998-** B Portland OR 1937 d Sherman & Lilly. U of Washington; BS OR SU 1959; MEd Portland St U 1982. D 10/11/1998 Bp Rustin Ray Kimsey. m 9/13/1958 Douglas McClelland. Steph Mnstry.

MCCLENAGHAN, Malcolm Eugene (NCal) 2020 Brady Ln, Roseville CA 95747 **Ret 1991-** B Lancaster OH 1923 s Donald & Frances. BA No Cntrl Coll 1945; MDiv Evang TS 1947. D 12/6/1950 Bp Nelson Marigold Burroughs P 6/12/1951 Bp Beverley D Tucker. m 6/5/1949 Elaine H McClenaghan c 1. Int S Mary's Elk Grove CA 1994-1996; Int Ascen Epis Ch Vallejo CA 1992-1993; Archd The Epis Dio Nthrn California Sacramento CA 1984-1990; R S Matt's Ch Kenosha WI 1972-1984; R S Paul's Epis Ch Modesto CA 1965-1972; Dn Trin Epis Cathd Sacramento CA 1959-1965; R S Jas Ch Of Sault S Marie Sault Sainte Marie MI 1957-1959; Cn Gr And H Trin Cathd Kansas City MO 1955-1957; R S Paul's Ch Toledo OH 1950-1954; Serv Evang Untd Bretheran Ch 1947-1950. Appreciation Citation Natl Conferenced Of Christians & Jews 1983.

MCCLOGHRIE, K(athleen) Lesley (NY) 4259 Forest Hills Dr, Fortuna CA 95540 **Assoc P S Fran Ch Fortuna CA 2013-** B Gateshead County Durham UK 1947 d Raymond & Margaret. BA U of Manchester 1969; MDiv CDSP 1999. D 11/20/1999 P 6/3/2000 Bp William Edwin Swing. m 7/24/1969 Keith Mccloghrie c 3. Vic Ch Of The H Trin Pawling NY 2003-2012; Dio New York New York NY 2003-2012; Assoc R Gr Ch Middletown NY 2000-2003; Chld's Mnstrs Coordntr S Bede's Epis Ch Menlo Pk CA 1999-2000. klmccloghrie@ gmail.com

MCCLOSKEY JR, Robert Johnson (SeFla) Po Box 1691, West Jefferson NC 28694 B York PA 1942 s Robert & Janet. BA Stetson U 1963; STB GTS 1967. D 6/24/1967 Bp Anson Phelps Stokes Jr P 6/1/1968 Bp Frederic Cunningham Lawrence. m 6/15/1968 Kathleen Anne Fran McCloskey c 3. Assoc S Mary Of The Hills Epis Par Blowing Rock NC 2008-2009, R 1976-1982; Assoc S Paul's Ch Wilkesboro NC 2008-2009; Assoc Ch Of The Incarn Miami FL 2002-2006; Stff Off Lambeth Conference 1998 1998; Serv Ch in Engl 1990-2005; R S Steph's Ch Coconut Grove Miami FL 1989-1999; R S Ptr's by-the-Sea Epis Ch Bay Shore NY 1982-1989; R S Mk's Ch Westford MA 1972-1976; R S Jas Epis Ch Teele Sq Somerville MA 1969-1972; Epis Chapl Tufts in Medford MA 1969-1972; Cur Gr Epis Ch Medford MA 1967-1969; S Jn's Cathd Jacksonville FL 1959-1962; CPE Bd Cntrl Islip St Hosp NY; Lectr Coll of Preachers; Fac Mississippi & Sewanee Ch Mus Conferences; Chair-Ecum Cmsn Dio

SE Florida Miami 1993-1999, Chair - Dioc Liturg & Mus Ctte 1990-1993; Chair-Dioc.Liturg Com Dio Long Island Garden City NY 1983-1987; Chair-Dioc.Liturg & Mus Ctte Dio Wstrn No Carolina Asheville NC 1976-1981; Chair-Dioc.Liturg & Mus Ctte Dio Massachusetts Boston MA 1969-1975. Auth, *Brit Composing for ICET Texts.* ADLMC, Associat 1968-2000; Cmnty Chr Serv Agcy Natl Conf Christia 1989-1993; EDEO 1974-1996; Epis Soc for Cultural Racial Unity [ESCRU] 1963-1972; Epis Soc to MHE [ESMHE] 1970-1972; Grtr Miami Rel Leaders 1989-2000; HOPE Inc 1989-1991; No Carolina ARC Cmsn 1976-1982; No Carolina Bapt Epis Dialogue 1976-1981.

MCCLOUD, Christine Lorraine (Nwk) 816 Prospect St, Union NJ 07083 **Turning Point Cmnty Svcs 2000-** B Newark NJ 1961 d Stanley & Inez. D 6/3/2006 Bp John Palmer Croneberger. c 2.

MCCLOUD, Linda (Lex) 4057 Mooncoin Way Apt 7102, Lexington KY 40515 B Topmost KY 1946 d Everett & Bonnie. BBA Belmont U 1985; MDiv Sewanee: The U So, TS 2005. D 2/5/2005 P 8/5/2005 Bp Henry Irving Louttit. P-in-c Ch Of The H Trin Georgetown KY 2015-2016; Int S Lk's Ch Billings MT 2015; Vic Dio Montana Helena MT 2008-2015, Dep to GC 2012, Pres of Stndg Com 2011-2013, Dioc Coun Mem 2008-2010; Vic Dio Georgia Waverly GA 2007-2008; Vic Dio Georgia Moultrie GA 2005-2007; Dioc Coun Mem Dio Georgia Savannah GA 2005-2007.

MCCLOUGH, Jeffrey David (Chi) 3801 Central Ave, Western Springs IL 60558 **Pstr Counslr Counslg Ministers Inc 1986-** B Chicago IL 1941 s William & Myrtice. BA Ripon Coll Ripon WI 1963; MDiv SWTS 1966; MA SWTS 1969. D 6/11/1966 Bp James Winchester Montgomery P 12/17/1966 Bp Gerald Francis Burrill. m 6/29/1985 Caroline McClough c 2. Counslg Mnstrs Glenview IL 1988-1997; Dio Chicago Chicago IL 1986-1987, Com 1977-1980; Pstr Counslr S Dav's Ch Glenview IL 1981-1986; Pstr Counslr Gr Ch Chicago IL 1969-1980; Assoc Trin Ch Chicago IL 1968-1969; Cur Cathd Of S Jas Chicago IL 1966-1968.

MCCLOY, Randolph McKellar (WTenn) 42 S Goodlett St, Memphis TN 38117 B Memphis TN 1936 s Elise. MD U of Tennessee Med Sch 1961; MS U MN 1966; MA Memphis TS 2010. D 11/21/2009 Bp Don Edward Johnson. m 1/1/1979 Linda Kay McCloy c 3.

MCCLURE, Robert Coke (Neb) Saint Matthew's Church, 312 W 16th St, Alliance NE 69301 **Calv Ch Hyannis NE 2013-; R S Matt's Ch Allnce NE 2013-** B Berkeley CA 1954 s Frank & Augusta. BA Dart 1976; Mstr of Div PrTS 1980; Cert of Angl Stds CDSP 2010. D 2/11/2010 P 8/12/2010 Bp Brian James Thom. m 9/16/2005 Tamara K McClure c 5. Chr Epis Ch Harlan KY 2010-2013; P-in-c Dio Lexington Lexington 2010-2013; S Mk's Ch Hazard KY 2010-2012; Pstr First Presb Ch Pocatello Idaho 1986-1993. Auth, "Lessons for Revolutionaries," *Viewpoint*, PTS, 1977. Who's Who in the W Who's Who 1990; Friar Club Alum Awd PrTS 1980. rectorstm@gmail.com

MCCLURE JR, William James (EMich) 232 North 'E' Street, Cheboygan MI 49721 **R Trin Epis Ch Alpena MI 2015-** B Clare MI 1959 s William & Shirley. BS Cntrl Michigan U 1982; MDiv VTS 2001. D 7/22/2001 P 7/23/2002 Bp Edwin Max Leidel Jr. m 6/10/2006 Deborah D McClure c 1. S Andr's Epis Ch Gaylord MI 2011-2012; R S Jas' Epis Ch Cheboygan MI 2001-2015.

MCCOART JR, Charles Carroll (Va) Emmanuel Episcopal Church, 1608 Russell Rd, Alexandria VA 22301 **Emm Epis Ch Alexandria VA 2013-** B Washington DC 1960 s Charles & Barbara. Angl Stds at the Dio Virginia; MDiv Mt St Mary's Sem 1990; MDiv Mt St Mary's Sem 1990. Rec 2/9/2013 as Priest Bp Shannon Sherwood Johnston. ccmccjr@gmail.com

MCCOID, Dean Bailey (ECR) 25 Oakmore Dr, San Jose CA 95127 **Died 6/14/2016** B Vallejo CA 1925 s Chester & Virginia. BA Dickinson Coll 1950. D 1/30/1965 Bp George Richard Millard. m 6/27/1953 Carolyn Anne Watts c 3. Ret 1999-2016; Dio El Camino Real Salinas CA 1982-1999; Trin Cathd San Jose CA 1982-1999; Asst S Phil's Ch San Jose CA 1965-1982.

MCCOLL, Scott Joseph (Eur) B San Diego California 1951 s Winston & Virginia. BA St. Fran Sem, San Diego 1976; STB / MA The Amer Coll of Leuven 1980. Rec 4/27/2016 as Priest Bp Pierre W Whalon. m 7/25/2014 Jeremy M Law.

MCCOMAS, Scot A (FtW) 223 S Pearson Ln, Keller TX 76248 **R S Mart In The Fields Ch Keller TX 2015-** B Dallas TX 1966 s Frederic & Mary. BA SMU 1991; MDiv Harvard DS 1999; STM GTS 2003. D 1/10/2004 Bp Leo Frade P 8/27/2004 Bp Michael B Curry. S Lk's Epis Ch Dallas TX 2014-2015; H Trin Ch Rockwall TX 2013-2014; Upper Sch Chapl The Par Epis Sch Dallas TX 2012-2015; Cur Gr Ch Madison NJ 2010-2011; Asst S Ptr's Epis Ch Charlotte NC 2004-2009; Chapl Palmer Trin Sch Miami FL 1999-2002.

MCCOMBS, Lauren (Cal) 1040 Border Rd, Los Altos CA 94024 B San Jose CA 1955 d Robert & Sallie. BA U CA Santa Barbara 1977; BA Sch for Deacons 2011. D 12/3/2011 Bp Marc Handley Andrus. c 2. Chr Epis Ch Los Altos CA 2012-2014.

MCCONCHIE, Leann Patricia (WNY) 119 Royal Pkwy E, Williamsville NY 14221 **D S Paul's Epis Ch Harris Hill Buffalo NY 2014-; D The Epis Ch Of The Gd Shpd Buffalo NY 2007-** B Detroit MI 1955 BS U of Detroit Mercy 1978. D 5/6/2004 Bp Michael Garrison. m 10/17/1981 William Edward McConchie c 1. Cn S Paul's Cathd Buffalo NY 2004-2007.

MCCONE, Susan Jonal (Ct) 80 Green Hill Rd, Washington CT 06793 **R S Jn's Ch Washington CT 2012-, R 2010-; Bp's Dioc Exec Coun Dio CT 2011-** B Minneapolis MN 1949 d John & Alyce. BA Smith 1971; JD Col 1974; MDiv Yale DS 1998; Cert Ang Stud Ya Berk 1999. D 6/8/2002 P 1/11/2003 Bp Andrew Donnan Smith. m 10/24/1982 Robert Paul Wessely. P-in-c Chr Ch Par Epis Watertown CT 2008-2009; Dir of Dvlpmt Epis Ch Cntr New York NY 2007-2011; Dio Connecticut Meriden CT 2005-2006; Dio New York New York NY 2005-2006; P-in-c S Jn's Epis Ch Bristol CT 2005-2006; Chr Ch Poughkeepsie NY 2003-2005; Chapl Vas Poughkeepsie NY 2003-2005; Cur Chr Ch New Haven CT 2002-2003. Auth, "Holiness of Beauty," *AAM Journ*, 2002. Affirming Angl Catholicism Exec Bd 1999-2009; Andr Inst of Angl Sprtlty and Mus, Co-Dir 2011; Assoc, CHS, New York 2000; Bd Dir, Amer Friends of Angl Cntr in Rome 2005-2008.

MCCONKEY, David Benton (Alb) 6 Albion Place, Northampton NN1 1UD Great Britain (UK) **Serving Ch of Engl Untd Kingdom 2003-; Serv Ch of Engl Untd Kingdom 2003-** B Salina KS 1953 s Howard & Grace. BA Kansas Wesl 1975; MMus Ya 1977; MDiv Ya Berk 1979; PhD GTF 2008. D 10/28/1983 P 7/1/1984 Bp John Forsythe Ashby. R S Eliz of Hungary Zimbabwe 1994-2003; Lectr Bp Gaul Theol Coll Zimbabwe 1994-2002; Vstng Adj Instr Nash Nashotah WI 1994; Cn Capitular Cathd Of All SS Albany NY 1988-1993; R Ch Of The H Cross Warrensburg NY 1986-1994; Cur & Org-Chm S Lk's Ch Louisville KY 1984-1986; D Chr Cathd Salina KS 1983-1984; Trst Dio Albany Greenwich NY 1989-1993. AGO, Hymn Soc Amer, Epis Sy; SSC 1987. Evelyn Light Fell Soc for the Maintenance of the Faith 2006.

✠ MCCONNELL, The Rt Rev Dorsey (Pgh) Episcopal Diocese of Pittsburgh, 4099 William Penn Hwy, Suite 502, Monroeville PA 15146 **Bp of Pittsburgh Dio Pittsburgh Pittsburgh PA 2012-** B Omaha NE 1953 s John & Sally. BA Ya 1975; MDiv GTS 1983. D 6/4/1983 P 12/4/1983 Bp Paul Moore Jr Con 10/20/2012 for Pgh. m 6/8/1980 Elizabeth Jane McConnell c 1. R Ch Of The Redeem Chestnut Hill MA 2004-2012; R S Alb's Ch Edmonds WA 1995-2004; R The Ch Of The Epiph New York NY 1989-1995; Chapl Epis Ch At Yale New Haven CT 1985-1989; Cur S Thos Ch New York NY 1983-1985; Chapl S Geo Assn IBEW Loc #3 New York NY 1981-1995. Auth, "Apos of Joy," Blue Moon Press, New Haven, 1989. Fulbright Schlr 1975. dmcconnell@episcopalpgh.org

MCCONNELL JR, James Bert (CFla) 2916 Palm Dr, Punta Gorda FL 33950 **Vic S Ann's Epis Ch Wauchula FL 2006-** B New Orleans LA 1942 s James & Joyce. Loyola U; BS S Mary Dominican 1977; MDiv Sewanee: The U So, TS 1986. D 6/14/1986 P 12/20/1986 Bp Willis Ryan Henton. m 9/4/1965 Carolyn McConnell c 2. R H Trin Epis Ch Gillette WY 2004-2006; S Barn' Epis Ch Hartselle AL 2002-2004; Ch Of The Resurr Rainbow City AL 2000-2001; R The Epis Ch Of The Redeem Avon Pk FL 1996-2000; R All SS Epis Ch Deltona FL 1993-1995; R S Paul's Ch Woodville MS 1990-1993; Assoc Trin Ch Natchez MS 1988-1990; Vic S Andr's Ch Lake Chas LA 1987-1988; Cur S Thos' Ch Monroe LA 1986-1987.

MCCONNELL, Theodore A (Alb) 106 East Farm Woods Ln, Fort Ann NY 12827 **Ret Ret 1994-** B Burlington IA 1938 s John & Helen. Cert Epis TS of the SW; BA Gri 1960; STB Yale DS 1963; STM Yale DS 1968; MS Concordia Coll 2000; MA Concordia Coll 2004; PhD Concordia Coll 2005. D 6/26/1965 Bp John Melville Burgess P 4/17/1966 Bp Robert Fisher Gibson Jr. P-in-c S Tim Glens Falls NY 1988-1994; P-in-c S Tim's Ch Moreau NY 1987-1994; R Ch Of The H Cross Warrensburg NY 1983-1984; Ed Dir M-B Co Dio Massachusetts Boston MA 1980-1984; Fortress Press Philadelphia PA 1977-1980; Ed Seabury Press- Epis Ch Cntr New York NY 1976-1977; Ed Pilgrim Press Philadelphia PA 1969-1975; Asst Min Chr Ch Cambridge Cambridge MA 1966-1968; Cur S Ptr's Epis Ch Arlington VA 1965-1966. Auth, "Success and the Cler," Inkwater, 2015; Auth, "The Great Fleeceman and Other Stories," Inkwater, 2011; Auth, "Finding a Pstr," Harper, 1986; Auth, "Ch on the Wrong Road," Regnery Gateway, 1986; Auth, "The Shattered Self," Pilgrim Press, 1971.

MCCONNELL, Theodore Howard (Va) 7319 Habeas Ct., Mechanicsville VA 23111 **P-in-c S Paul's Epis Ch Millers Tavern VA 2017-** B Pontiac MI 1947 s Howard & Althea. BA Alma Coll 1970; MA Cntrl Michigan U 1974; MDiv VTS 1985. D 1/24/1981 Bp William Jones Gordon Jr P 7/27/1985 Bp Emerson Paul Haynes. m 8/16/1969 Anita M McConnell c 3. Int Ware Epis Ch Gloucester VA 2012-2014; Int Kingston Par Epis Ch Mathews VA 2011-2012; Int Calv Ch Tarboro NC 2010-2011; Int S Lk's Ch Tarboro NC 2010-2011; R S Paul's Epis Ch Wilmington NC 2007-2010; Dn St Paul's Epis Cathd Fond Du Lac WI 2003-2007; R Chr Epis Ch Gordonsville VA 1997-2003; R S Mart's Epis Ch Richmond VA 1990-1997; Asst Ch Of The Redeem Sarasota FL 1985-1990; Asst S Jn's Epis Ch Alma MI 1981-1982.

MCCONNEY, J Anne (Neb) 413 S 78th St Apt 8, Omaha NE 68114 B Omaha NE 1932 d Lawrence & Fern. Cottey Coll 1951; BA U of Nebraska 1954; MA U of Nebraska 1978; MDiv Ya Berk 1984. Trans 4/1/1992 Bp James Edward Krotz. Dir/ Ed Of Pub All SS Epis Ch Omaha NE 2002-2010; Dio The Rio Grande Albuquerque 1995-1996, Ed 1994-1996; H Trin Epis Ch - Mssn Raton NM 1994-1995; Vic Trin Memi Epis Ch Crete NE 1993-2001; Dio Nebraska Omaha NE 1992-2000, Ed 1991-1993; Vic St Aug of Cbury Epis Ch Elkhorn NE 1992-1993; St Augustines Of Cbury Epis Mssn Elkhorn NE 1992-1993; Serv Ch Of Can 1986-1991. Auth, "Pilgrim Songs," *Episcpal Life*, 2000; Auth, "Our December Hearts," Morehouse, 1999; Auth, "Lesser Observances," *Epis Life*, 1994. ECom 1994. Multiple Polly Bond Awards ECom 1994.

MCCOOK, Carla Benae (SwFla) 1929 Par Pl, Sarasota FL 34240 **S Marg Of Scotland Epis Ch Sarasota FL 2016-** B Saint Petersburg FL 1973 d Charles & Shelia. BA Flagler Coll 1995; MDiv VTS 2004. D 5/22/2004 Bp John Wadsworth Howe P 11/30/2004 Bp Neff Powell. m 4/23/1994 Shane P McCook c 3. Bp's Asst for Chr Formation Dio Milwaukee Milwaukee WI 2011-2016; Pres Stndg Com of the Dio Milwaukee 2009-2011; Secy Stndg Com of the Dio Milwaukee 2007-2009; R S Thos Of Cbury Ch Greendale WI 2006-2011; Second VP Epis Conf of the Deaf 2005-2008; Asst R S Paul's Epis Ch Salem VA 2004-2006. Auth, "Living the Adventure: A Living Compass Sum Camp Curric," *Living the Adventure: A Living Compass Sum Camp Curric*, Living Compass, 2014. stmargaretrector@gmail.com

MCCORMICK, Brendan (Ct) 5 Sea Ln, Old Saybrook CT 06475 **Vic All SS Ch Ivoryton CT 2008-** B Chicago IL 1943 s William & Irene. Lic Sacr Theol S Anselmo 1971; MA Providence Coll 1978. Rec 10/1/1983 as Priest Bp Arthur Edward Walmsley. m 6/11/1977 Rosemary McDermott-McCormick c 1. S Paul's Ch Wallingford CT 1988-2007; Asst R S Mk's Ch New Britain CT 1983-1988; Tchr Cbury Sch New Milford CT 1978-1983; Tchr Marmion Acad Aurora IL 1971-1976.

MCCORMICK, Matthew W (SC) Messiah Episcopal Church, 1631 Ford Pkwy, Saint Paul MN 55116 **Mssh Epis Ch S Paul MN 2016-; P Ch Of The H Cross Sullivans Island SC 2008-** B Hickory NC 1978 s John & Lynn. MTh Luther Sem; BA Coll of Charleston 2001; MDiv TESM 2007. D 12/1/2007 Bp Edward Lloyd Salmon Jr P 6/1/2008 Bp Mark Joseph Lawrence. m 9/18/2004 Lisa Christian McCormick c 1. Assoc S Phil's Ch Charleston SC 2008-2013. m. mccormick@messiahepiscopal.org

MCCORMICK, Phyllis Ann (SwFla) 2850 Countrybrook Dr Apt 13, Apt. 13, Palm Harbor FL 34684 **D S Chris's Ch Tampa FL 1998-** B Brooklyn NY 1938 d Frank & Teresa. BA Marymount Manhattan Coll 1960; JD New York Law Sch 1982. D 6/13/1998 Bp John Bailey Lipscomb. D H Trin Epis Ch In Countryside Clearwater FL 1999-2005.

MCCORMICK, Reid T (CFla) 210 Church St, Greenville AL 36037 **S Andr's Epis Ch Ft Pierce FL 2017-** B Jacksonville FL 1957 s John & Jean. BS Auburn U 1979; MDiv Sewanee: The U So, TS 1997. D 6/8/1997 Bp Stephen Hays Jecko P 12/13/1997 Bp Bob Johnson. m 1/23/1982 Jacqueline J McCormick c 2. R S Thos Ch Greenville AL 2011-2017; Assoc S Mich's Ch Orlando FL 2003-2011; R Emm Ch Orlando FL 2000-2002; Assoc All SS Ch Of Winter Pk Winter Pk FL 1998-1999; Asst Ch Of The Ascen Hickory NC 1997-1998.

MCCORMICK, Thomas Ray (Del) PO Box 1478, Bethany Beach DE 19930 B Lewistown, PA 1938 s Ray & Margaret. MA Shippensburg St Coll; AB Lenoir Rhyne Coll 1960. D 12/5/2009 Bp Wayne Wright. m 8/4/1956 Susanne R McCormick c 3.

MCCOWN, William R (Ala) 3816 Cromwell Dr, Birmingham AL 35243 **R S Paul's Ch Franklin TN 2017-; Ch Of The Nativ Epis Huntsville AL 2013-** B Hunstville, AL 1962 s James & Jeanne. D 6/1/2004 P 12/2/2004 Bp Henry Nutt Parsley Jr. m 9/25/1993 Laura R McCown c 2. The CPG New York NY 2009-2012; S Mary's-On-The-Highlands Epis Ch Birmingham AL 2004-2009. rusty@stpaulsfranklin.com

MCCOY OHC, Adam Dunbar (NY) Mount Calvary Monastery, 505 E Los Olivos St, Santa Barbara CA 93105 **Prior Mt Calv Monstry Santa Barbara CA 2014-** B Chicago IL 1946 s Duncan & Morna. BA MI SU 1969; MA Cor 1972; PhD Cor 1973; MDiv CDSP 1979. D 5/31/1979 P 12/29/1979 Bp Wesley Frensdorff. Bursar OHC W Pk NY 2008-2013; Novc Mstr OHC W Pk NY 2008-2010; Adj Prof GTS New York NY 2003-2008; Bd Trst Hse of the Redeem New York NY 2002-2015; R The Ch of S Edw The Mtyr New York NY 2001-2008; Dn, Dnry 9 Dio Los Angeles Los Angeles CA 1998-2001, Comm. on Mnstry 1996-1997; Chapl Anaheim CA Police Dept Anaheim CA 1996-2001; R S Mich's Mssn Anaheim CA 1992-2001; Novc Mstr OHC Santa Barbara CA 1984-1990; Prior Mt Calv Retreat Hse Santa Barbara CA 1981-1990; Hisp Cmsn Dio New York New York NY 2005-2008. Auth, "H Cross: A Century of Angl Monasticism," Morehouse-Barlow, 1987. OHC 1973. Phi Beta Kappa MI SU 1969. adamdmccoy@gmail.com

MCCOY, David Ormsby (SO) 24 Old Coach Road, Athens OH 45701 B Portsmouth OH 1938 s Walter & Thelma. AB Ken 1960; STB GTS 1964. D 6/13/1964 P 12/19/1964 Bp Roger W Blanchard. m 4/30/2011 Christine B Knisely c 2. Retirees and Spouses/Partnr and Surviving Spouses Dio Sthrn Ohio Cincinnati OH 2009-2013, Dn Angl Acad 1994-1998; Assoc S Andr's Ch Pickerington OH 1998-2011; Legis Rep Ohio Coun Of Ch Columbus OH 1989-1994; Int Ch Of S Edw Columbus OH 1988; R S Steph's Epis Ch And U Columbus OH 1978-1989, R 1978-1987, Assoc 1973-1978, Assoc 1973-1978, Asst 1964-1967; Stff Natl Hmnts Series 1971-1973; R Chr Ch Xenia OH 1967-1971. Democracy In Action Rec League of Wmn Voters of Metro Columbus 2010.

MCCOY, Elaine K (O) 3785 W 33rd St, Cleveland OH 44109 B Newark NJ 1945 d Francis & Sarah. BA Leh 1981; PhD U of Adelaide Au 1987; MDiv EDS 2005. D 6/14/2005 P 1/12/2006 Bp Mark Hollingsworth Jr. m 8/20/2008 Patricia Lida Hanen c 4. Ch Of The Ascen Lakewood OH 2012-2013; Gr Epis Ch Sandusky OH 2009-2010; S Andr's Epis Ch Elyria OH 2007-2009; Epis W Side Shared Mnstry Cleveland OH 2006.

MCCOY, Frances Jean (SwVa) 1001 Virginia Ave NW, Norton VA 24273 **Dn Of The Abingdon Convoc 1992-** B Connellsville PA 1943 d Francis & Barbara. BA Antioch Coll 1966; MA Marshall U 1968; MDiv VTS 1985. D 6/5/1985 Bp Robert Poland Atkinson P 12/1/1985 Bp William Franklin Carr. All SS Epis Ch Norton VA 1990-2008; S Mk's Ch S Paul VA 1990-2008; Coordntr Of Prog & Educ Dio W Virginia Charleston WV 1987-1990; Emm Ch Moorefield WV 1985-1987. Auth, "Lets Begin Here". EvangES.

MCCOY, Robert Martin (Md) 521 Sixth St., Annapolis MD 21403 **Chapl Ginger Cove - Cont care Ret Cmnty 2008-** B Washington DC 1942 s David & Elizabeth. D 6/2/2007 Bp John L Rabb. m 4/8/1988 Jean K Kay c 4. D S Mart's-In-The-Field Day Sch Severna Pk MD 2011-2012; S Jas' Par Lothian MD 2007-2011; D S Mk's Chap Deale Deale MD 2007-2011.

MCCOY, William Keith (NJ) 14 Second Street, Edison NJ 08837 **D S Jn's Ch Somerville NJ 2001-** B Cambridge MA 1954 s William & Irene. AB Harv 1976; MLS Drexel U 1978. D 4/13/1985 Bp George Phelps Mellick Belshaw. Instr Dioc Sch for Deacons 2008-2014; D Gr Epis Ch Plainfield NJ 1987-2000; D Chr Ch New Brunswick NJ 1985-1987; All SS Ch Highland Pk NJ 1985-1986; Archd Dio New Jersey Trenton NJ 2005-2014, Chair Com On Diac 1994-2002. Columnist, "Welcome to the Dio St. Ives," *Diakoneo*, Assoc. of Epis Deacons, 2005. Fund for the Diac 2001. S Steph's Awd NAAD 1999.

MCCRACKEN-BENNETT, Richard J (SO) 9019 Johnstown Alexandria Rd, Johnstown OH 43031 B Bucyrus OH 1949 s Richard & Patricia. BA U of Findlay 1971; MDiv S Meinrad TS 1976; DMin SWTS 2002. Rec 12/21/1989 as Priest Bp William Grant Black. m 11/1/1980 Nancy McCracken c 2. All SS Epis Ch New Albany OH 2000-2014; Nthrn Miami Vlly Cluster Urbana OH 1997; Vic Ch Of The H Trin Epis Bellefontaine OH 1994-1997; Vic Ch Of The Epiph Urbana OH 1992-1997; Vic Our Sav Ch Mechanicsburg OH 1990-1996.

MCCRAY-GOLDSMITH, Julia (Ore) 147 NW 19th Ave, Portland OR 97209 **Trin Epis Cathd Portland OR 2016-** B Los Angeles CA 1961 d Richard & Sandra. MA Creighton U 2011; MDiv CDSP 2014; MDiv CDSP 2014. D 12/7/2013 P 6/14/2014 Bp Marc Handley Andrus. m 5/31/1987 John T McCray-Goldsmith c 2. CE Dir Dio California San Francisco CA 2016, 2003-2013. juliam@diocal.org

MCCREARY, Ernest Cannon (USC) 8530 Geer Hwy, Cleveland SC 29635 **Ret 1989-** B Cynthiana KY 1926 s Ernest & Marie. BA U So 1950; MDiv VTS 1953. D 6/28/1953 Bp John J Gravatt P 5/10/1954 Bp Clarence Alfred Cole. c 4. Vic S Andr's Epis Ch Greenville SC 1984-1988; Asst Chr Ch Greenville SC 1971-1984; Cur S Steph's Epis Ch Ridgeway SC 1969-1971; Chapl Dio Upper So Carolina Columbia SC 1963-1978; Vic S Lk's Ch Newberry SC 1957-1961; Vic Trin Ch Abbeville SC 1953-1957.

MCCREATH, Amy Ebeling (Mass) 23 Gilbert St, Waltham MA 02453 **Ch Of The Gd Shpd Watertown MA 2010-** B Kettering OH 1965 d Harry & Martha. BA Pr 1987; MA U of Wisconsin 1991; MDiv SWTS 1998. D 4/23/1998 P 12/18/1998 Bp Roger John White. m 3/20/1993 Brian K McCreath c 2. EDS Cambridge MA 2015-2017; Dio Massachusetts Boston MA 2001-2010, Chapl to MIT 2001-; S Chris's Ch Milwaukee WI 1998-2001. Coun of APLM 2000.

MCCRICKARD, Bonnie Mixon (Ala) Church of the Nativity, 208 Eustis Ave SE, Huntsville AL 35801 **Ch Of The Nativ Epis Huntsville AL 2014-** B Huntsville AL 1972 d William & Linda. BA Trin U 1994; MA Washington U 1996; MSW Washington U 1996; BA Belmont U 2009; BA Belmont U 2009; MDiv Sewanee: The U So, TS 2014; MDiv The TS at The U So 2014. D 6/7/2014 P 12/13/2014 Bp John Bauerschmidt. m 2/26/2000 Matthew Price McCrickard. bmccrickard@nativity-hsv.org

MCCRUM, Lewis Lamb (NJ) 415 Washington St, Toms River NJ 08753 **D Chr Ch Toms River Toms River NJ 1990-** B Newark NJ 1942 s William & Virginia. BA Pratt Inst 1965. D 6/9/1990 Bp George Phelps Mellick Belshaw. m 6/26/1965 Mary Jane McCrum c 2.

MCCUE, Allan Homer (Mass) 12 Regwill Ave, Wenham MA 01984 **Ret 1996-** B Topeka KS 1931 s Howard & Blanche. BA Antioch Coll 1953; BD EDS 1956. D 6/24/1956 Bp Edward Clark Turner P 12/26/1956 Bp Henry W Hobson. m 9/22/1956 Cynthia B Mccue c 3. Int S Chris's Ch Chatham MA 2002-2003; Int Chr Ch S Hamilton MA 1994-1997; Int S Mary's Epis Ch Rockport MA 1992-1994; S Ptr's Ch Beverly MA 1966-1992; Vic H Sprt Epis Ch Cincinnati OH 1958-1965; Asst Gr Ch Cincinnati OH 1956-1958. Cmsn Wider Mssn Dio Massachussetts 1992-2005; Jubilee Fund Dio Massachussetts 2000-2008; Mass. Schlrshp Africans Studying in Amer Co-Chair 2001-2011; Rep to Global Epis Mssn 1998-1999.

MCCUE, Michael Edlow (WMass) 123 Eileen Dr, Rochester NY 14616 **Chapl California Dept. of Corrections & Rehab Susanville 2005-** B Oakland CA 1949 s Patrick & Virginia. BA San Jose St U 1973; MDiv CDSP 1980. D 11/8/1980 Bp Charles Shannon Mallory P 1/10/1982 Bp John Raymond Wyatt.

m 9/17/1977 Maureen Anne Walsh c 2. P-in-c H Sprt Mssn Lake Almanor CA 2012-2013, 2010-2011; P-in-c Gd Shpd Epis Ch Susanville CA 2011-2014; Chapl High Desert St Prison Susanville CA 2005-2013; Int S Mich's Ch Lansdowne PA 2001-2002; R S Jn's Epis Ch Honeoye Falls NY 1996-2000; Zion Ch Avon NY 1996-2000; Chapl California Dept. of Corrections & Rehab Vacaville C 1985-1996; Chapl California St Prison- Solano Vacaville CA 1985-1996; Chapl Santa Clara Cnty Jail San Jose CA 1982-1985; Chapl Santa Clara Cnty Jail San Jose CA 1982-1985; Cur S Barn Ch Arroyo Grande CA 1980-1981. Amer Correctional Chapl Assn 1982; EPF 1971; HSEC 1980.

MCCULLOCH, Kent Thomas (Oly) 10630 Gravelly Lake Dr Sw, Lakewood WA 98499 **Chair - Nomin Com 1981-; BEC 1980-; Bd Trst 1980-** B Portland OR 1946 s John & Elizabeth. BA California St U 1970; MDiv CDSP 1976. D 7/25/1976 Bp Hal Raymond Gross P 8/1/1977 Bp Matthew Paul Bigliardi. c 2. R S Mary's Ch Lakewood WA 1985-2007; Exam Chapl 1981-1984; S Andr's Ch Portland OR 1980-1984; S Barth's Ch Beaverton OR 1979-1980; Chr Ch Par Lake Oswego OR 1976-1979; Dioc Coun Dio Olympia Seattle 1993-1996, Curs 1986-1992. Auth, "Living Ch".

MCCULLOUGH, Brian Duncan (SanD) 332 N Massachusetts St, Winfield KS 67156 B Wichita KS 1945 s Fredrick & Jacquelyn. BA U of Missouri 1968; MDiv GTS 1971; MA Kean U 1985. D 6/12/1971 P 11/26/1971 Bp George Leslie Cadigan. m 7/30/1986 Kimberlin A Fowler c 4. Non-Stipend Gr Ch Winfield KS 1995-2007; Vic All SS Epis Ch Brawley CA 1991-1992; Gr Ch Middletown NY 1990-1991; Gr Epis Ch Winfield KS 1978-1980; Ch Of The Redeem Houston TX 1976-1978; Trin Par New York NY 1972-1976. Psi Chi hon Soc 1982. Psi Chi Natl Psychol Hon Soc 1982.

MCCULLOUGH, Mary (Pa) 708 S. Bethlehem Pike, Ambler PA 19002 **Assoc R Trin Epis Ch Ambler PA 2008-** B Abington PA 1953 d Walter & Margaret. Luth TS; MS Neumann Coll 2003; MDiv GTS 2008. D 6/14/2008 P 1/10/2009 Bp Edward Lewis Lee Jr. m 4/3/1976 David McCullough c 2. Ch Sch Coordntr All Hallows Ch Wyncote PA 2000-2005.

MCCUNE, Henry Ralph (Dal) 11560 Drummond Dr, Dallas TX 75228 **Ret 2001-** B Birmingham AL 1939 s John & Caroline. BA Baylor U 1960; MDiv SW Bapt TS 1965. D 8/26/1979 P 8/1/1980 Bp Archibald Donald Davies. m 8/5/1973 Janice Jeffrey c 2. R H Trin Epis Ch Garland TX 1981-2001; Chapl S Matt's Cathd Dallas TX 1980-1981; Dio Dallas Dallas TX 1979-1980; The Epis Ch Of The Resurr Dallas TX 1979.

MCCURDY III, Alexander (Pa) 613 Maplewood Avenue, Wayne PA 19087 **Assoc S Dav's Ch Wayne PA 2008-; Adj Assoc St. Dav's Ch Wayne PA 2006-** B Philadelphia PA 1939 s Alexander & Flora. BA Wesl 1961; BD EDS 1964; MA Wayne 1973; CG Jung Inst 1977; PhD Un Inst & U Cincinnati OH 1986. D 6/11/1964 Bp Walter H Gray P 3/1/1965 Bp John Henry Esquirol. m 11/16/1991 Patricia Tyson McCurdy c 2. H Apos And Medtr Philadelphia PA 1979-1980; 1971-2006; Asst Chapl Epis Acad Philadelphia PA 1965-1969; Asst S Paul's Ch Philadelphia PA 1965-1969; Cur Trin Epis Ch Southport CT 1964-1965. Auth, "Establishing & Maintaining the Analytical Structure," *Jungian Analysis*, Open Crt Press, 1982. amccurdy@stdavidschurch.org

MCCURRY MILLIKEN, Cathleen Ann (Mil) 1734 Fairhaven Dr., Cedarburg WI 53012 **Par D S Jas Ch W Bend WI 2009-** B Richland WA 1963 d John & Anna Mary. AB Duke 1985; AM Duke 1989. D 6/2/2007 Bp Steven Andrew Miller. m 6/20/1987 Charles Kenneth Milliken c 2.

MCCURTAIN, Glad (SwFla) 261 1st Ave SW, Largo FL 33770 **S Anne Of Gr Epis Ch Seminole FL 2016-; Mem, Fin Com Dio SW Florida Parrish FL 2009-, Mem, Dioc Coun 2006-, Sprtl Dir., Curs Sec 2004-2008** B Pensacola FL 1947 d Grover & Fauntleroy. BA U of W Florida 1969; MDiv SWTS 2003. D 6/24/1995 Bp Telesforo A Isaac P 6/14/2003 Bp John Bailey Lipscomb. m 9/7/1968 James Hume Mccurtain c 4. S Jn's Epis Ch Clearwater FL 2003-2014; JPIC Off Cathd Ch Of S Ptr St. Petersburg FL 1998-2000; D H Trin Epis Ch In Countryside Clearwater FL 1995-1998.

MCCUSKER III, Thomas Bernard (Va) Orchid Garden Homes, 229/103 Thepprasit Road. Moo 12, Chonburi 20260 Thailand **Int Dir Of Chapl Goodwin Hse Ret Cmnty 2005-; Sabbatical P Ch Of The Resurr 2004-** B Boston MA 1946 s Thomas & Harriett. MA Duquesne U; BA Ashland U 1969; MDiv VTS 1978. D 6/3/1978 Bp Robert Bracewell Appleyard P 4/1/1979 Bp Charles Francis Hall. Goodwin Hse Incorporated Alexandria VA 2005-2007; Ch Of The Resurr Alexandria VA 2004; Int S Lk's Ch Alexandria VA 2001-2003; Int S Barn Ch Annandale VA 2000-2001; Int S Paul's Epis Ch Alexandria VA 1998-1999; Ch Of The Gd Shpd Burke VA 1979-1997.

MCDADE, Shelley D (LI) 12 W 11th St, New York NY 10011 **P-in-c S Jn's Ch Brooklyn NY 2015-** B Wilmington DE 1961 d William & Lucille. BA Ashland U 1983; MDiv GTS 2010. D 3/13/2010 P 9/25/2010 Bp Mark Sean Sisk. Assoc R Ch Of The Ascen New York NY 2010-2014. mtrshelley@ascensionnyc.org

MCDANIEL, Eleanor Becker (SwVa) **Dio SW Virginia Roanoke VA 2016-; Cur Trin Ch Staunton VA 2016-** B 1977 d David. M.Div. Sewanee: The U So, TS; B.A. U of Virginia; M.Ed. Van. D 5/14/2016 P 12/10/2016 Bp Mark Bourlakas. c 2.

MCDANIEL, Elna Irene (Eau) 408 W Nott St, Tomah WI 54660 **S Jn's Epis Ch Mauston WI 2003-; D S Mary's Epis Ch Tomah WI 2002-** B 1943 D 11/23/2002 Bp Keith Whitmore. m 9/9/1960 Kenneth Richard McDaniel c 5.

MCDANIEL, Judith Maxwell (Oly) 3971 Point White Dr NE, Bainbridge Island WA 98110 B Oklahoma City OK 1940 d Don & Martha. BA U of Texas 1961; U of Washington 1971; MDiv GTS 1985; PhD U of Washington 1994. D 6/12/1978 P 6/30/1984 Bp Robert Hume Cochrane. m 6/7/1961 Jackson L McDaniel c 2. Adj Prof of Homil Seattle U Seattle Washington 2013; Prof Homil VTS Alexandria VA 1990-2011; R S Jn's Epis Ch Gig Harbor WA 1987-1990; Assoc R S Jn's Epis Ch Olympia WA 1985-1986; Assoc S Mk's Cathd Seattle WA 1979-1983; D S Barn Epis Ch Bainbridge Island WA 1978-1979; Cathd Chapt Dio Olympia Seattle 1987-1990, Bd & Fac, TS 1986-1990, Mem, COM 1985-1990, Treas, Cler Assn 1982-1983, Mem, COM 1979-1983. Auth, "Homiletical Perspective: Matt 8:18-22; Matt 8:23-27; Matt 8:28-9:1," *Feasting on the Gospels*, Westminster Jn Knox Press, 2013; Auth, "Gr in Motion: the Intersection of Wmn Ord and VTS," RiverPlace Cmncatn, 2011; Auth, "The Preaching Cong, a Mirror of the Gospel," *Staying One, Remaining Open*, Morehouse Pub, 2010; Auth, "Homiletical Perspective: Day of Pentecost, Trin Sunday, Proper 3, Year B," *Feasting on the Word*, Westminster Jn Knox Press, 2009; Auth, "The Interpreter of Dreams: Preaching to Effect Change," Hervormde Teologiese Stds 62(4), 2006; Auth, "A Change of Character," *Sermons from Preaching Excellence Prog, Vol. XV*, Bk Masters, Inc., 2006; Auth, "Redescribing Reality as Scriptural Sabbath," *Preaching as Prophetic Calling: Sermons that Wk XII*, Morehouse Pub, 2004; Auth, "Remember," Virginia Sem Journ, 2003; Auth, "The Place of the Bible in the Virginia Sem Curric: Homil," *Tchg the Bibile in the New Millennium*, ATR, 2002; Ed, "Preaching Gr in the Human Condition," 2001; Auth, "A Votive For The Preaching Of The Gospel," *Sermons That Wk X*, Morehouse Pub, 2001; Auth, "He Came To Proclaim A Message," *Preaching Mk: The Recovery Of A Narrative Voice*, Chalice Press, 1999; Auth, "The Prchr As Theol And Tchr," *Preaching Through The Year Of Mk: Sermons That Wk Viii*, Morehouse Pub, 1999; Auth, "Rhetoric Reconsidered: Preaching As Persuasion," Sewanee Theol Revs, 1998; Auth, "Let Every Heart Prepare Him Room," *The Living Pulpit*, 1997; Auth, "Disciples And Discipline," *Virginia Sem Journ*, 1996; Auth, "What You See Is What You Get," *Sermons That Wk V*, FMP, 1995. Acad Of Homil 1990; CHS; Societas Homiletica 1993. Howard Chandler Robbins Prof Of Homil VTS 2002; Treas Societas Homiletica 1999; Pres Societas Homiletica 1997; Exec Bd Societas Homiletica 1995; Chair COM/Dio Olympia 1987.

MC DARBY, Mark Daniel (Alb) 8 Summit St, Philmont NY 12565 **D S Mk's Epis Ch Philmont NY 2006-** B Hudson NY 1960 s Raymond & Esther. D 6/10/2006 Bp Daniel William Herzog. m 8/11/2006 Catherine Marie Mc Darby c 2.

MCDERMOT, Joanna (NwPa) 19556 E Cole Rd, Meadville PA 16335 B Athens GA 1936 d John & Mary. Duquesne U; Franciscan U of Steubenville; BS Linc 1957. D 1/23/1999 Bp Robert Deane Rowley Jr. m 12/27/1961 Richard Frederick McDermot. D Chr Ch.

MCDERMOTT, James Patrick (LI) 1709 Rue Saint Patrick Apt 504, Montreal QC H3K 3G9 Canada **Int Currently Serving Angl Ch Of Can 2005-** B New York NY 1948 s Roland & Mary. BA SUNY 1970; MS SUNY 1983; Cert Mercer TS 1989. P 6/1/1990 Bp Orris George Walker Jr. m 3/22/1969 Veronica DeSantis. P Asst S Anselm's Ch Shoreham NY 1990-2004; Asst Ch of S Jude Wantagh NY 1989-1990.

MCDERMOTT, Jane Leslie (O) 2918 Kirkhaven Dr, Youngstown OH 44511 **Extended Supply S Aug's Epis Ch Youngstown OH 2008-** B Buffalo NY 1946 d Raymond & Ida. Case Wstrn Reserve U 1967; BA U of Akron 1970; MDiv SWTS 1978. D 6/24/1978 P 2/24/1979 Bp John Harris Burt. R S Andr Ch Canfield OH 1991-2001, Int 1989-1991; Int S Steph's Ch E Liverpool OH 1988-1989; R Trin Ch New Phila OH 1983-1988; St. Jn's Hm/ girls Dio Ohio Cleveland 1982; Int S Tim's Ch Macedonia OH 1979-1982; Chapl Univ Hosp 1979-1982; Asst Ch Of The Trsfg Cleveland OH 1978-1979; Asst Emm Epis - Cleveland Ohio 1978-1979. Auth, "Var arts".

MCDERMOTT, John Roy (Md) 4493 Barberry Ct, Concord CA 94521 **Asstg P S Jn's Epis Ch Clayton CA 2011-** B Pueblo CO 1937 s Roy & Beatrice. AB cl Harv 1959; BA Harv 1959; MDiv CDSP 1962; STM UTS 1965. D 6/24/1962 Bp James Albert Pike P 6/8/1963 Bp George Richard Millard. m 5/27/1961 Laurel Lee McDermott c 4. Asstg P Memi Ch Baltimore MD 1976-2005; Asst Broadmoor Cmnty Ch Colorado Sprg CO 1965-1966; Asstg P All SS Ch Baldwin NY 1964-1965; Cur S Fran Epis Ch San Jose CA 1962-1964.

MCDERMOTT, Matthew (Cal) 580 Colorado Ave, Palo Alto CA 94306 **R S Mk's Epis Ch Palo Alto CA 1995-** B Lorain OH 1957 s William & Dorothea. AA Lorain Cnty Cmnty Coll 1977; BA San Francisco St U 1982; MDiv CDSP 1987. D 6/6/1987 P 6/4/1988 Bp William Edwin Swing. m 11/5/1983 LeeAnne McDermott c 3. Asst to R Trin Par Menlo Pk CA 1989-1995; Asst to R S Steph's Epis Ch Orinda CA 1987-1989.

MCDERMOTT, Nelda Grace (Ark) 1204 Hunter St, Conway AR 72032 **D S Ptr's Ch Conway AR 2001-** B Blue Springs MS 1937 d Wilburn & Grace. MS Blue Mtn Coll 1961; MS U of Cntrl Arkansas 1984; D Formation Prog 2001. D 11/3/2001 Bp Larry Maze. m 6/4/1961 Cecil Wade McDermott.

MCDONALD, Catherine Jane Walter (Minn) 9671 Clark Cir, Eden Prairie MN 55347 **Chapl Hastings Veterans Hm MN 2003-** B Conde SD 1938 d Barton & Eunice. BS Nthrn St U Aberdeen SD 1962; MDiv Untd TS of the Twin Cities 1977. D 4/24/1977 P 4/1/1978 Bp Philip Frederick McNairy. m 12/27/1961 John McDonald c 2. Dio Minnesota Minneapolis MN 1990-2012; Chapl MN Wmn Correctional Facility MN 1989-2003; Chapl Fergus Falls Reg Treatment Cntr MN 1980-1989; 1977-1982.

MCDONALD, Dawn (CFla) 1457 Barn Owl Loop, Sanford FL 32773 **Vic The Ch Of The H Presence Deland FL 2012-** B Canada 1958 d John & Reba. British Columbia Inst of Tech BC Can 1989; BTh The Coll of Emm and S Chad CA 1995; DMin GTF 2009; MDiv The Coll of Emm and S Chad CA 2009. Trans 3/31/2010 Bp John Wadsworth Howe. m 4/24/1998 Neville Joseph Crichlow. Int/P in Charge St. Mary Magd Ft Nelson B.C. Can 2008-2009; Dioc rep for Dio Yukon AFP 2006-2007; Exec Com Mem Dio Yukon 2005-2007; R St. Mary Magd Ft Nelson B.C. Can 2005-2007; R H Cross Vancouver B.C. Can 1998-2005; Dioc Cmncatn Com Dio New Westminster 1998-2002; Lay Evang H Cross Vancouver B.C. Can 1997-1998; Coordntr Tentmaker Intl for Chr Kobe Japan 1991-1992. dpreacherdawn@cfl.rr.com

MCDONALD, Durstan R (Tex) 811 E 46th St, Austin TX 78751 B New York NY 1937 s Douglas & Carolyn. BA Trin Hartford CT 1958; STB PDS 1963; PhD U of Pennsylvania 1968; Hobart and Wm Smith Colleges 1979; DHL Epis TS of the SW 2004. D 6/9/1963 P 12/13/1963 Bp Joseph Gillespie Armstrong. m 6/14/1958 Ruth J McDonald c 5. Int Dn The Amer Cathd of the H Trin Paris 75008 2003; Epis TS Of The SW Austin TX 1984-2002; Dn Chr Chap Austin TX 1983-2002; Trin Educ Fund New York NY 1978-1983; Dir Trin Inst Nyc 1977-1983; Trin Par New York NY 1977-1983; Hobart And Wm Smith Colleges Geneva NY 1967-1977; Chapl Hob Geneva NY 1967-1977; Asst Trin Oxford PA 1963-1965. Auth, "W N Pittenger: A Bibliography"; Auth, "Macrina: Fourth Cappadocian?"; Ed, "The Myth," *Truth Of God Incarnate*. Hon Doctor of Humane Letters ETSS 2004; Hon DD Hob 1979.

MCDONALD, James D (Ark) 511 Coley Dr, Mountain Home AR 72653 **S Paul's Epis Ch Batesville AR 2017-** B Pocahontas AR 1958 s Charles & Lois. BA U of Arkansas 1980; MS U of Arkansas 1998; MDiv Sewanee: The U So, TS 2009. D 3/21/2009 Bp Larry Maze P 9/23/2009 Bp Larry Benfield. m 12/27/1978 Catherine L McDonald c 3. S Andr's Ch Mtn Hm AR 2009-2017; Chair, Bd Trst Camp Mitchell Epis Ch Morrilton AR 2006-2008.

MCDONALD, James Ross (Alb) 1937 The Plz, Schenectady NY 12309 **R S Steph's Ch Schenectady NY 1989-; Stndg Com Dio Albany Greenwich NY 1996-** B El Paso TX 1955 s William & Julie. BA Ken 1977; MS U Chi 1983; MDiv McCormick TS 1985; DMin PrTS 1996. D 6/15/1985 Bp James Russell Moodey P 4/4/1986 Bp Donald Maynard Hultstrand. m 2/20/2011 Lisa McDonald c 2. Vic S Lk's Ch Springfield IL 1988-1989; S Jn's Epis Ch Decatur IL 1985-1989. Auth, "Understanding How Ch Members Reflect Theol On Daily Life Experiences," 1997.

MCDONALD, James Roy (NY) PO Box 161897, Austin TX 78716 **1970-** B Brownwood TX 1942 s Jimmy & Helen. BA TCU 1965; STB Ya Berk 1968; MA Col 1973; PhD NYU 1980. D 6/1/1968 Bp Charles A Mason P 2/1/1969 Bp William Elwood Sterling. m 6/5/1999 Mary Guerrero. Pstr Counslr S Ann And The H Trin Brooklyn NY 1976-1979; Instr The GTS New York NY 1971-1975; Asst Calv and St Geo New York NY 1968-1969. "Enterprise Risk Mgmt and Improved Shareholder Value," *Perspectives in Bus*, St. Edw's U, 2006; "Decision Point: Mng Career Change in a Changing Wrld," CareerLynz Intl , 1994.

MCDONALD, James Wallace (SJ) 627 Goshen Ave, Clovis CA 93611 **Non-par 1975-** B Myrtle Bch SC 1943 s James & Edna. BA California St U 1965; MDiv SWTS 1968; MS California St U 1977; MPA California St U 1989. D 6/29/1968 P 1/25/1969 Bp Clarence Rupert Haden Jr. m 2/2/1974 Cheryl Susanne Spurgeon. Chapl California St U Fresno 1973-1974; Assoc R S Columba Ch Fresno CA 1972-1974; Vic S Barth Burney CA 1969-1972; Vic S Mich's Ch Anderson CA 1969-1972; St Bartholomews Ch Burney CA 1969-1972; Cur Ch Of The Incarn Santa Rosa CA 1968; The Epis Dio Nthrn California Sacramento CA 1968. Who'S Who In Rel; Who'S Who In The Wrld; Phi Kappa Phi.

MCDONALD, Janet Strain (Va) Po Box 233, Free Union VA 22940 **Serving Mssn Dio Haiti Port-au-Prince HT 2007-, Serving Mssn 2007-** B Birmingham AL 1957 d John & Juanelle. BA Emory U 1980; MA U of Virginia 1987; MDiv Sewanee: The U So, TS 1998; DMin Other 2010; DMin Other 2010; DMin Wesley TS, Washington, D.C. 2010. D 6/19/1999 Bp Peter J Lee P 5/23/2000 Bp David Colin Jones. m 8/16/1980 Jay Adams McDonald c 2. Mssnr Blue Ridge Mssn Team Dio Virginia VA 2004-2007; Dio Virginia Richmond VA 2001-2007; S Geo's Ch Stanley VA 2001; Intern Cur St Jas Epis Ch Sewanee TN 1999-2000. "Art and Sprt," *Designing and Tchg a Sem course in Theol on the Arts*, Arts: The Arts in Rel on Theol Stds, 2002; Auth, "Albemarle Country, Virginia Furniture 1750-1850," *mag Antiques*, 1998; Auth, "Alabama Quilts," 1980.

M

MCDONALD, Karen Loretta (WMich) 89513 Shorelane Dr, Lawton MI 49065 B Buchanan MI 1939 RN Bronson Sch of Nrsng. D 4/4/2001 Bp Edward Lewis Lee Jr. m 6/25/1960 James McDonald c 3.

MCDONALD, Lauren (SVa) Spiritworks Foundation, 5800 Mooretown Rd, Williamsburg VA 23188 **Bruton Par Williamsburg VA 2016-; Directory of Cmnty Programming SpiritWorks Fndt 2012-** B East Point GA 1969 d Edwin & Page. BA U So 1991; MDiv SWTS 2008. D 2/1/2008 Bp John Clark Buchanan P 8/23/2008 Bp O'Kelley Whitaker. Campus Chapl S Steph's Ch Newport News VA 2012-2016; Assoc R Hickory Neck Ch Toano VA 2008-2011.

MCDONALD, Marc Edwin (Kan) 828 Commercial St, Emporia KS 66801 **S Andr's Epis Ch Emporia KS 2017-** B Cincinnati OH 1971 s Blake & Anne. BA Mid Amer Nazarene U 1992; MDiv Phillips TS 2001. D 6/6/2015 P 12/13/2015 Bp Kirk Stevan Smith. m 5/1/1993 Linda Marie McDonald c 1. Vic St Johns Epis-Luth Ch Williams AZ 2015-2017, Other Lay Position 2014-2015. pastormem@gmail.com

MCDONALD, Mark William (CGC) Church Of The Advent, 12099 County Road 99, Lillian AL 36549 **Ch Of The Adv Lillian AL 2014-** B Monroe LA 1966 s William & Shirley. BBA U of Louisiana 1990; MBA U of So Alabama 1992; MDiv Sewanee: The U So, TS 2000. D 6/3/2000 P 2/17/2001 Bp Charles Farmer Duvall. m 6/4/1994 Joni Angelea McDonald c 4. P-in-c Imm Ch Bay Minette AL 2011-2014; P in Charge Trin Epsicopal Ch Atmore AL 2011-2014; S Paul's Epis Ch Daphne AL 2009-2010; R The Epis Ch Of The Epiph New Iberia LA 2002-2009; Cur S Lk's Epis Ch Mobile AL 2000-2001. mark@adventlillian.org

MCDONALD III, Norval Harrison (Md) 309 Royal Oak Dr, Bel Air MD 21015 **Dir, Sprtl Care Upper Chesapeake Hlth Bel Air MD 2004-** B Baltimore MD 1957 s Norval & Bettie. BA Loyola Coll 1979; MDiv Ya Berk 1982; MDiv VTS 1985. D 9/13/1984 P 5/1/1985 Bp David Keller Leighton Sr. m 8/18/1979 Janice Lynn McDonald. Oncology Chapl Johns Hopkins Hosp Baltimore MD 2001-2004; Int Ch Of The Redemp Baltimore MD 2000-2002; Stff Chapl Hospice Of Baltimore Towson MD 2000-2001; Stff Chapl Mercy Med Cntr Baltimore MD 2000; Dir, Pstr Care Ch Hm & Hosp Baltimore MD 1993-2000; Deer Creek Par Darlington MD 1986-1993; R Gr Memi Ch Darlington MD 1986-1993; Cur Emm Ch Bel Air MD 1984-1986. Assn Of Profsnl Chapl 1999.

MCDONALD, Vickie Lynn (SwFla) D 12/3/2016 Bp Dabney Tyler Smith.

MCDONALD, William Kenneth (Mich) 421 East Ellen Street, Fenton MI 48430 B Sedgwick CO 1941 s Beaty & Irene. BA U of Iowa 1963; MDiv Drew U 1967; U of Edinburgh GB 1967. D 1/9/1970 Bp Richard Stanley Merrill Emrich P 5/27/1970 Bp Archie H Crowley. c 2. P-in-c Ch Of The Resurr Clarkston MI 1997-2003; P-in-c S Paul's Epis Ch Corunna MI 1986-1991; S Kath's Ch Williamston MI 1985-1986; S Mich's Epis Ch Lansing MI 1984-1985; S Jude's Epis Ch Fenton MI 1977-1978; P-in-c St. Bede's Epis Ch Linden MI 1975-1976; Asst Chr Epis Ch Flint MI 1969-1972; Pstr Halsey Meth Ch Grand Blanc MI 1967-1969.

MCDONNELL, Brian K (Md) 8 Loveton Farms Ct, Sparks MD 21152 **Construction Superintendant Erachem Baltimore MD 1990-** B Trenton NJ 1953 s William & Edith. BS Sprg Garden Coll 1975; EFM Sewanee: The U So, TS 2004. D 6/5/2004 Bp Robert Wilkes Ihloff. c 1. Sexton S Thos' Ch Garrison Forest Owings Mills MD 2008-2015.

MCDONNELL, George Anne (ECR) PO Box 3811, Lacey WA 98509 **S Mk's Epis Ch Santa Clara CA 2016-; Vic S Ben Mssn Lacey WA 2005-** B Point Pleasant NJ 1969 d Gordon & Joyce. BA Coll of S Eliz 1991; MDiv SWTS 2002. D 5/18/2002 Bp Roger John White P 1/25/2003 Bp Vincent Waydell Warner. m 2/20/2013 Elizabeth A McDonnell c 2. Vic S Ben Epis Ch Lacey WA 2005-2016; Assoc for Yth and YA S Thos Epis Ch Medina WA 2002-2005. "I Remember A Different Story," *The Olympian*, The Olympian Nwspr, Olympia WA, 2007; "The Devil Is In The Details," *The Olympian*, The Olympian Nwspr, Olympia WA, 2007.

MCDONNELL III, Richard P (Ga) 3 Wexford on the Green, Hilton Head Island SC 29928 B New York NY 1945 s Edward & Josephine. BA Belknap Coll 1971; BS SUNY 1974; MA LIU 1976; MDiv UTS 1977; PhD NYU 1979; ML-ITS S Marks TS So Un KY 1983; DMin Grad Theol Fund 1992; DMin Grad Theol Fund 1992. Trans 5/1/1984 Bp George Paul Reeves. m 8/7/1972 Maureen Christine McDonnell c 5. S Fran Of The Islands Epis Ch Savannah GA 2006-2009; Assoc Redeem Hilton Hd SC 1992-2002; Chapl Whiskey Rd Fox Hounds & Aiken Hounds 1986-1992; Vic The Epis Ch Of The Annunc Vidalia GA 1984-1986; Serv Ch Of Can 1979-1982. Auth, "The Dr. Peeples Files"; Auth, "Cranmer On Euch," *The Angl*; Auth, "The Momophysite Position In Christological Controversies," *The Angl*. Amer Hist Soc; Angl Soc; Bible And Common PB Soc Of The Epis Soc; Ch Hist Soc; Hilton Hd Island Hist Soc, VP 1997; Skcm. Cn Theol Anglica Bp of the So W 1991; Hon Cn S Andrews Cathd 1990.

MCDOUGALL, Robert Franklin (Mich) 641 Michigan Avenue, Apt 304, Frankfort MI 49635 **Died 11/16/2015** B Ypsilanti MI 1929 s Arthur & Beulah. BA Estrn Michigan U 1951; MDiv Ya Berk 1956; Ldrshp Acad for New Directions 1975. D 6/23/1956 P 12/23/1956 Bp Dudley B McNeil. m 6/21/1953 Dorothy

M McDougall c 2. S Christophers Ch Northport MI 1993-2001; Ret 1990-2015; Epiiscopal Chapl Jackson Prisions 1979-1992; Epis Chapl Sthrn MI Prison 1979-1992; R S Paul's Epis Ch Jackson MI 1978-1989; Dir of Cmncatn No Dio Michigan Detroit MI 1976-1978, Bd Dir for the MI Coun of Ch 1974-1977, Nthrn Convoc 1974-1976, Exec Coun 1986-1990, Exec Coun 1986-1990, Dn of the SW Convoc 1981-1985, Alt Dep GC 1979-1982, Alt Dep GC 1979-1980, Pres of the Stndg Com 1977-1978, Pres of the Stndg Com 1977-1978, Pres of the Bd Dioc Paper 1976-1982, Pres of the Bd Dioc Paper 1976, Stndg Com 1974-1978, Stndg Com 1974-1975, Dn McCoskry Convoc 1971-1973; Vic S Eliz Higgins Lake MI 1974-1978; S Eliz's Epis Ch Roscommon MI 1974-1978; Team Mnstry Grp Ldr Nthrn I-75 Resorts Corridor Northport MI 1974-1977; R S Alb's Highland Pk MI 1969-1974; Trst Assn Dio Wstrn Michigan Kalamazoo MI 1966-1969, Chair on the Dept of CE 1965; Epis Chapl Albion Coll MI 1961-1969; R S Jas' Epis Ch Of Albion Albion MI 1961-1969; Trst of the Stdt Fndt U MI 1961-1969; Founding Chapl Starr Commonwealth for Boys Albion MI 1961-1963; Vic S Mk's Epis Ch Paw Paw MI 1957-1960; Cur S Paul's Ch Muskegon MI 1956-1957; Epis Chapl Jackson Prisions 1979-1992.

MCDOUGLE, Jane (Cal) 537 Chenery Street, San Francisco CA 94131 **Ch Of The H Innoc San Francisco CA 2013-** B Exeter England 1957 d James & Jean. BEd Homerton Coll Cambridge Gb 1979; DMA Stan 1989; MDiv CDSP 2005. D 6/4/2005 P 12/3/2005 Bp William Edwin Swing. m 7/29/2013 Paul Bendix c 1. S Bede's Epis Ch Menlo Pk CA 2005-2013. jmcdougle44@gmail.com

MCDOWELL, Artie Samuel (RG) Po Box 5505, Clovis NM 88102 **Died 5/24/2017** B Montgomery AL 1929 s Artie & Metta. Dio The Rio Grande Instrn; BBA U of Memphis 1951; MEd Estrn New Mex U 1977. D 1/26/1983 Bp Richard Mitchell Trelease Jr P 9/5/1990 Bp Terence Kelshaw. m 7/30/1966 Susan A McDowell c 2.

MCDOWELL, Glenda Irene (WNC) Cathedral of All Souls, 9 Swan St, Asheville NC 28803 B Morganton NC 1950 d Wilford & Willie. AA Blanton's Jr Coll 1983. D 1/21/2012 Bp Porter Taylor. c 2.

MCDOWELL, Harold Clayton (LI) 27 Private Rd, Medford NY 11763 **Ret 1994-** B Brooklyn NY 1927 s Harold & Gudrun. BA Adams St Coll; CTh Mercer TS. D 9/27/1969 P 5/16/1970 Bp Jonathan Goodhue Sherman. m 12/7/1947 Kathryn L McDowell. Int Chr Ch Bellport NY 1993-1994; Mssn Dio Long Island Garden City NY 1978-1979, Stwdshp 1975-1977; S Pat's Ch Deer Pk NY 1970-1992; Asst S Cuth's Epis Ch Selden NY 1969-1970; Asst S Mich & All Ang Gordon Heights NY 1969-1970.

MCDOWELL, James Lynn (SwFla) 2808 Valley Park Dr., Little Rock AR 72212 **Ret 2004-** B Tullahoma TN 1942 s Carl & Mary. BA Van 1964; MDiv Sewanee: The U So, TS 1978. D 6/24/1978 Bp William Evan Sanders P 5/6/1979 Bp William F Gates Jr. c 1. Stwdshp Chair Dio SW Florida Parrish FL 1998-2000; R S Alb's Epis Ch St Petersburg FL 1994-2004; Cn to the Ordnry Dio Arkansas Little Rock AR 1987-1994, Chair Dept Stwdshp 1985-1986; R Gr Ch Pine Bluff AR 1982-1986; R The Epis Ch Of The Mssh Pulaski TN 1979-1982; D S Geo's Ch Germantown TN 1978-1979. CODE 1987-1994; FD Maurice Soc 1983-1990.

MCDOWELL JR, John Sidebotham (CPa) 125 Beverly Rd, Ashland VA 23005 **R Ch Of The Trsfg Blue Ridge Summit PA 2010-; R Calv Chap Beartown Blue Ridge Summit PA 2009-** B Wellesboro PA 1942 s John & Josephine. AA Hershey Jr Coll Hershey PA 1962; BA Dickinson Coll 1964; MDiv VTS 1971. D 6/11/1971 Bp Dean Theodore Stevenson P 6/24/1972 Bp Thomas Augustus Fraser Jr. m 5/16/1970 Harriet R McDowell c 3. Int All SS' Epis Ch Hershey PA 2007-2008; R Ch Of S Jas The Less Ashland VA 1996-2005; Pres And Bd Mem CODE 1990-1994; Chair - Dept Of Missions Dio Cntrl Pennsylvania Harrisburg PA 1982-1995, Cn 1980-1995, Chair - Sch of Chr Stds 1982-1995, GC Dep 1982-1995; R The Memi Ch Of The Prince Of Peace Gettysburg PA 1973-1982; Cur Emm Par Epis Ch Sthrn Pines NC 1971-1973.

MCDOWELL, Joseph Lee (CFla) 116 Jamaica Dr, Cocoa Beach FL 32931 **Links Of Hope Rockledge FL 2002-** B Washington DC 1939 s Ridgely & Marguerite. BA U of Virginia 1961; MDiv Gordon-Conwell TS 1970; EDS 1971. D 6/26/1971 P 2/1/1972 Bp William Foreman Creighton. m 9/10/1965 Helen C McDowell c 5. Int R Gloria Dei Epis Ch Cocoa FL 2004-2005, Assoc 1996-2001; Dn Of The Keys Dnry In SE Florida 1992-1994; R S Jas The Fisherman Islamorada FL 1990-1994; Bd Trst Epis Wrld Mssn 1983-1990; R S Paul's Ch Winona MN 1980-1990; R All SS Ch Oakley Av MD 1971-1980; Exec Bd Dio SE Florida Miami 1991-1994.

MCDOWELL, Maria Gwen (Ore) D 6/10/2017 Bp Michael Hanley.

MCDOWELL, Mia Chelynn Drummond (USC) PO Box 726, Spartanburg SC 29304 **S Matt's Epis Ch Spartanburg SC 2015-** B Greenville SC 1969 d Johnny & Linda. Cert Greenville Tech Coll 1994; BA Anderson U 2002; MDiv The TS at The U So 2015. D 6/6/2015 P 1/14/2016 Bp William Andrew Waldo.

MCDOWELL, Todd S (Mo) Grace Episcopal Church, 514 E Argonne Dr, Kirkwood MO 63122 **R Gr Ch S Louis MO 2009-** B Evansville IN 1962 s Jerry & Sonja. BBA Fontbonne U; MDiv SWTS 2000. D 6/11/2000 Bp Peter Hess Beckwith P 12/16/2000 Bp John Bailey Lipscomb. m 8/27/1994 Sabine S McDowell c 2. S Ptr's Epis Ch S Louis MO 2008-2009; The Angl/Epis Ch Of Chr The King Frankfurt am Main 60323 2007-2008; Cn Vic The Amer Cathd of the H Trin Paris 75008 2005-2007; Assoc R Trin By The Cove Naples FL 2000-2005; Dioc Coun Dio Missouri S Louis MO 2010-2014, chair - DHP Com 2010-2013; Coun of Advice Convoc of Epis Ch in Europe Paris 2005-2008; chair - Cler Compstn Com Dio SW Florida Parrish FL 2003-2005, Dioc Coun 2001-2005. todd.mcdowell@gracekirkwood.org

MCDOWELL-FLEMING, David Howard (CGC) 3560 Briar Cliff Dr, Pensacola FL 32505 B Melbourne VIC AU 1944 s Arthur & Margaret. DIT Melbourne Coll of Div 1972; MDiv Duke DS 1976; CAS GTS 1987; PhD Logos Grad Sch 2004. D 7/22/1987 P 5/1/1988 Bp Charles Farmer Duvall. m 12/23/1975 Martha A McDowell-Fleming c 2. R S Monica's Cantonment FL 1991-2007; Int S Jn's Epis Ch Mobile AL 1990-1991; Cur All SS Epis Ch Mobile AL 1987-1990; Methodist Chapl Duke Hosp Durham NC 1972-1973. "The Deconstruction Of A Dio," Logos, 2004.

MCDUFFIE, John Stouffer (WA) 5320 Westpath Way, Bethesda MD 20816 **R Chr Ch Prince Geo's Par Rockville MD 1998-** B Morrison IL 1950 s James & Mary. S Johns Coll 1970; BA Bos 1972; MSW U NC 1974; MDiv VTS 1987. D 6/6/1987 Bp Claude Charles Vache P 4/16/1988 Bp James Russell Moodey. m 6/8/1996 Mary Stuart Addis c 3. R S Dunst's Epis Ch Beth MD 1989-1998; Cur S Paul's Ch Akron OH 1987-1989. Auth, "What The Thunder Said," *Rel & Intellectual Life*, 1998.

MCELRATH, James Devoe (WNC) 22 Edgewater Ln, Canton NC 28716 B 1935 s Wiley & Ruth. BS Wstrn Carolina U 1956; MA U NC 1959. D 12/9/1995 Bp Bob Johnson. m 8/4/1956 Nancy Evans McElrath c 2. Cler Coordntr Hospice Of Haywood Cnty NC. Franciscan Assn.

MCELROY, Catherine DeLellis (NY) 191 Larch Ave, Teaneck NJ 07666 B Wilmington DE 1935 d Vincent & Josephine. BA U of Delaware 1960; S Cecilia Conservatory 1963; MDiv UTS 1985. D 6/3/1978 Bp Paul Moore Jr P 1/1/1979 Bp Richard Beamon Martin. Pstr Asst Ch Of The Intsn New York NY 1975-1979.

MCELROY, Gary Austin (O) 8437 Eaton Dr, Chagrin Falls OH 44023 **Ret 2005-** B Denver CO 1937 s Louis & Victoria. BS Col 1961; MDiv GTS 1964; STM Ya Berk 1969; Cert Ya 1970; Oxf GB, Mansfield Coll 1973; MSW U IL 1976. D 4/4/1964 P 10/1/1964 Bp Walter C Klein. m 5/30/1964 Elizabeth M McElroy c 3. P-in-c S Clements Epis Ch Greenville PA 2009-2010; P-in-c Ch Of The Epiph Strongsville OH 1997; Dir of All SS Counslg Cntr All SS Ch Cleveland OH 1986-1995; S Mk's Ch Cleveland OH 1985-1986; Dir AAA Chr Counselors 1983-2006; Dir of Counslg Cntr Chr Ch Shaker Heights OH 1982-1983; Vice-Pres - Bd - Pstr Counslg Cntr 1978-1982; Pres - Nrsng Hm Mnstry 1978-1981; Pstr Counslr Mntl Hlth Serv In Springfield 1976-1982; Chapl Clark Cnty Coun Of Ch 1976-1980; Chapl Chap Of S Jn The Div Champaign IL 1970-1975; Dir Of The ECF U IL 1970-1975; R S Andr's Ch Northford CT 1969-1970; Cur DCE Gr Ch White Plains NY 1967-1969; Chapl New York Cornell Hosp 1967-1969; P-in-c H Sprt Hamden CT 1966-1967; Asst S Jn's Ch New Haven CT 1966-1967; Cur S Jn The Evang Ch Elkhart IN 1964-1966; Cmsn on Soc Serv Dio Ohio Cleveland 1973-1975, Dept of CE 1971-1973. Auth, "Jas De Koven & The Wi Election Of 1874". ESMHE, AAPC, EPF. Fell AAPC 1978.

MCELROY, Jamie (Miss) 3921 Oakridge Dr, Jackson MS 39216 **R S Jas Ch Jackson MS 2013-; Coun of Deacons Dio SW Florida Parrish FL 2011-** B Washington DC 1973 s James & Sally. BA Ya 1995; MDiv CDSP 2008. D 12/5/2009 P 6/5/2010 Bp Marc Handley Andrus. m 7/27/1996 Peyton Craig McElroy c 2. Cn for Evang & Outreach Cathd Ch Of S Ptr St. Petersburg FL 2010-2013; S Bede's Epis Ch Menlo Pk CA 2009-2010; Dir of Serv Lrng Trin Sch Menlo Pk CA 2009-2010; Prog Dir Los Ayudantes Tutoring & Mentoring Redwood City CA 2008-2010.

MCELWAIN, David Marc (Wyo) 3594 Stampede Ranch, Cheyenne WY 82007 **Chapl VetA Hosp Cheyenne Wyoming 2013-; P S Mk's Ch Cheyenne WY 2011-** B Newcastle PA 1955 s Harry & Viola. BS Arizona St U 1977; MDiv Cntrl Bapt TS 1986; Cert CDSP 2008. D 6/9/2007 P 2/9/2008 Bp Clifton Daniel III. m 6/1/1985 Linda Pauline McElwain c 7. Chapl Us Navy 1990-2010; Serv Amer Bapt Ch 1985-1989. david.mcelwain2@va.gov

MCEWEN, Michael Thomas (Okla) 514 Big Rock Rd, PO Box 338, Medicine Park OK 73557 **Chapl (Lt Col, Ret) St. Barbara's Epis Cong Ft. Sill OK 2010-; LADC Lic Counslr (Priv Pract) Lawton OK 2008-** B Vienna Austria 1948 s Carl & Lois. BS U of Cntrl Oklahoma 1975; MA U of Oklahoma 1976; BA Oklahoma City U 1981; MDiv VTS 1988; DMin Phillips TS 1999. D 5/7/1988 P 11/9/1988 Bp Brice Sidney Sanders. m 11/22/1968 Vycke McEwen c 2. Assoc S Andr's Epis Ch Lawton OK 2008-2010; Prov Coordntr Prov of the SW (Prov VII) 2008-2009; Chapl (Lt Col) US Army Ft Carson CO 2003-2008; P-in-c S Dav's Ch Oklahoma City OK 2001-2005; Assoc S Mary's Ch Edmond OK 1999; S Mk's Epis Ch Weatherford OK 1997-1999; St Greg's U Shawnee OK 1995-1999; P-in-c S Tim's Epis Ch Pauls Vlly OK 1995-1997; P-in-c S Ptr's Ch Coalgate OK 1992-1995; R Emm Epis Ch Shawnee OK 1989-1992; Asst R S Jn's Epis Ch Fayetteville NC 1988-1989. Auth, "Combat Stress: What Congregations nedd to Know," *www.tec-Chapl.org/CombatStressPPT_3-1.htm*, The Epis Ch, 2008; Auth, "Wmn in the Bible," *www.episcopalchurch.org/41685_81935_ENG_HTM.htm*, The Epis Ch, 2007; Auth, "Seven Pearls of

Sprtlty," FMP, 2002; Auth, "God, Creation, Freedom, and Evil," *Living Ch*, 2001; Auth, "101 Favorite Bible Stories," FMP, 2000. Amer Benedictine Acad 1989; Oblate Ord of S Ben 1989. The DSM Bp Suggragan for Fed Chaplaincies, The Epis Ch 2008.

MCFADDEN, Cheryl Culley (EC) D 6/3/2017 Bp Robert Stuart Skirving.

MCFARLAND, Earl Everett (RG) 8960 Stetson Pl, Las Cruces NM 88011 B Omaha NE 1934 s Earl & Isabelle. BA California St U 1960; MA California St U 1965; TESM 2001. D 7/28/2001 Bp Terence Kelshaw. m 5/28/1970 Joy Elizabeth McFarland c 4. D S Andr's Epis Ch Las Cruces NM 2001-2003.

MCFARLANE, Robert Bruce (Mass) 21 Euclid Ave, Lynn MA 01904 B Lynn MA 1934 s John & Matilda. BA Tufts U 1955; MDiv Ya Berk 1958; MEd Tufts U 1968. D 6/21/1958 Bp Frederic Cunningham Lawrence P 1/4/1959 Bp Henry Knox Sherrill. m 8/18/1985 Susan Eileen McFarlane c 4. 1970-1966; Asst S Mk's Ch Southborough MA 1966-1970; R Ch Of The H Trin Marlborough MA 1960-1966; Asst The Cathd Ch Of S Paul Boston MA 1958-1960.

MCGARRY, Susan Ellen (Vt) Saint Stephen's Church, 3 Main St, Middlebury VT 05753 **R S Steph's Ch Middlebury VT 2012-** B New Haven CT 1953 d John & Jean. BA Ob 1974; MDiv EDS 1978; PhD U MI 2009. D 6/24/1978 P 3/1/1979 Bp John Harris Burt. c 2. R S Aid's Ch Ann Arbor MI 1990-2012; Epis Stdt Fndt Ann Arbor MI 1989-1990; Asst Chapl Epis Stdt Fndt U MI At Ann Arbor 1989-1990; Chapl Ob OH 1985-1988; S Andr's Ch Ann Arbor MI 1978-1984.

MCGARRY-LAWRENCE, Marla Terese (Ore) 2136 NE Cesar E Chavez Blvd., Portland OR 97212 B Merced CA 1952 d Russell & Doris. Cert Cntr for Diac Mnstry 1994; BA Marylhurst U 1998. D 9/29/1994 Bp Robert Louis Ladehoff. m 9/18/1971 Gary L Lawrence c 2. D S Ptr And Paul Epis Ch Portland OR 2015-2017; S Matt's Epis Ch Portland OR 2010-2013; S Mich And All Ang Ch Portland OR 2002-2010, 2000-2002, D 1994-2002.

MCGARVEY, Philip Peter (Md) 3671 Lily St, Oakland CA 94619 **Non-par 1974-** B Philadelphia PA 1944 s John & Betty. BA Dickinson Coll 1966; STB Ya Berk 1969. D 6/23/1969 Bp Harry Lee Doll P 12/1/1969 Bp John Henry Esquirol. c 1. Asst Min S Lk's Epis Ch New Haven CT 1969-1970.

MCGAVERN III, Cecil George (Tex) 15015 Memorial Dr, Houston TX 77079 **Ch Of The Gd Shpd Tomball TX 2014-** B Lompoc CA 1970 s Cecil & Edith. BS U of So Florida 1992; MDiv Epis TS Of The SW 2013; MDiv Epis TS of the SW 2013. D 6/15/2013 Bp C Andrew Doyle. m 3/6/1993 Melissa Lynn McGavern c 4. Emm Ch Houston TX 2013-2014. george@emmanuel-houston.org

MCGAVRAN, Frederick Jaeger (SO) 3528 Traskwood Cir, Cincinnati OH 45208 **Chapl Epis Ret Serv Cincinnati OH 2010-** B Columbus, OH 1943 s James & Marion. BA Ken 1965; JD Harvard Law Sch 1972; Sch for Diac Mnstry 2010. D 6/12/2010 Bp Thomas Edward Breidenthal. m 1/5/1980 Elizabeth McGavran c 2. Trst The Epis Cmnty Serv Fndt 2011-2013. Auth, "The Butterfly Collector," *The Butterfly Collector*, Black Lawr Press, 2009. The Literary Club of Cincinnati 1996.

MCGEE JR, Hubert (Ind) 1609 Rivershore Rd, Elizabeth City NC 27909 **P-in-c St Lukes Epis Ch Currituck NC 2004-** B Fort Lauderdale FL 1928 s Hubert & Jean. U NC; AA San Mateo Jr Coll 1950; BS E Carolina U 1956. D 6/24/1987 P 3/5/1988 Bp Edward Witker Jones. m 7/1/1950 Beverly Clark c 3. P-in-c S Mary's Ch Gatesville NC 2002-2004; P-in-c Chr Ch Eliz City NC 1998-2001; Vic S Lk's Epis Ch Cannelton IN 1988-1998.

MCGEE, Kyle Marland (Ct) 11133 Town Walk Dr, Hamden CT 06518 **P-in-c St. Mk's Epis Ch Bridgeport CT 2006-** B Columbus OH 1942 s Lawrence & Dorothy. BA DePauw U 1963; MDiv Yale DS 1967. D 6/17/1967 P 12/17/1967 Bp Roger W Blanchard. c 2. P-in-c S Jn The Evang Yalesville CT 2000-2005; Int S Ptr's Epis Ch Oxford CT 1997-2000; Int S Mk's Ch Bridgeport CT 1993-1994; R S Paul And S Jas New Haven CT 1987-1991; Urban Mssn Off Dio Connecticut Meriden CT 1981-1987; Prot Chapl Geo Washington DC 1972-1981; Asst Min Ch Of S Steph And The Incarn Washington DC 1969-1972; Asst Min and Campus Min Chr Epis Ch Dayton OH 1967-1969.

MC GEE, Vern Wesley (Spok) 1000 E. Craig Ave, Ellensburg WA 98926 **Died 9/23/2015** B Spokane WA 1939 s George & Lela. MA U of Washington 1968; PhD U of Texas 1986; MDiv GTS 2008. D 6/7/2008 P 12/13/2008 Bp James E Waggoner Jr. R Gr Ch Ellensburg WA 2009-2015.

MCGEE, William Earl (ETenn) 3404-A Taft Hwy, Signal Mountain TN 37377 B Knoxville TN 1948 s George & Elinor. BS U of Tennessee 1970; MA U of Tennessee 1976; EdD U of Tennessee 1982. D 6/16/2001 Bp Charles Glenn VonRosenberg. m 6/16/1973 Roslyn Vanstone.

MCGEE-STREET, Eleanor Lee (Ct) 35 Killdeer Rd, Hamden CT 06517 B Baltimore MD 1943 d John & Eleanor. MS CUA; BA U of Maryland; MA Ya. D 10/27/1974 Bp William Foreman Creighton P 9/7/1975 Bp George West Barrett. m 7/30/2000 Claude Parke Street. S Lk's Ch Westcliffe CO 2001-2002; Prof Ya Berk New Haven CT 1987-1997; R S Paul And S Jas New Haven CT 1987-1991; Clncl Soc Wkr Epis Soc Serv Dio Connecticut Meriden CT 1982-1987; Priv Pract - Psych 1981-2000; Assoc Chapl Trin 1981-1985; Dio Washington Washington DC 1974-1981; Chapl Amer U Washington DC 1971-1981. Auth, "Wrestling w The Patriarchs; Retrieving Wmn Voices In Preaching," Abingdon Press, 1996; Auth, "Wmn & Preaching Mnstry," *Yale DS*

565

M

Journ, 1983; Auth, "The Rite To Be Female/Male". Wmn Of The Year Awd Amer U.

MCGEHEE, Andrew Austin (At) 1790 Lavista Rd NE, Atlanta GA 30329 B Atlanta GA 1984 s William & Andrea. BA The U of Mississippi 2006; MDiv The GTS 2015. D 12/20/2014 P 6/20/2015 Bp Robert Christopher Wright. m 8/19/2012 Tiffany Lynn McGehee c 1. S Barth's Epis Ch Atlanta GA 2015-2017.

MCGEHEE, J Pittman (Tex) 1307 Westover Rd, Austin TX 78703 **Dir Broadacre Cntr Houston TX 1991-** B Fort Smith AR 1943 s Jarrett & Mary. BS Oklahoma St U 1966; MDiv VTS 1969; CG Jung Inst 1996. D 6/21/1969 Bp Chilton R Powell P 12/29/1969 Bp Robert Rae Spears Jr. m 8/29/1964 Bobby L McGehee c 2. Dn Chr Ch Cathd Houston TX 1980-1991; R Chr Epis Ch Tyler TX 1978-1980; Assoc S Fran In The Fields Harrods Creek KY 1973-1978; Assoc S Paul's Ch Kansas City MO 1969-1973; Dep, GC Dio Texas Houston TX 1985-1988, Pres, Mnstrl Allnce 1980-; Chair, Dept of CE Dio Kentucky Louisville KY 1976-1978. Auth, "Growing Down," Ink Brush Press, 2013; Auth, "The Paradox of Love," Bright Sky Press, 2011; Auth, "Raising Lazarus," Amazon, 2009; Auth, "Words Made Flesh," Amazon, 2008; Auth, "The Invisible Ch," Praeger, 2008; Auth, "Herbie," 1970. DD Epis TS of the SW 1988.

MCGEHEE, Lionel Eby (NY) 225 W 99th St, New York NY 10025 B Delhi LA 1964 s Thomas & Lynda. BA NE Louisiana U 1988; MDiv SWTS 1993. D 6/12/1993 Bp Robert Jefferson Hargrove Jr P 5/1/1994 Bp Roger W Blanchard. Asst R S Mich's Ch New York NY 1997-2000; Asst Par Of Chr Ch Andover MA 1993-1997; Counslr All SS Vicksburg MS 1988-1990.

MCGEHEE, Stephen (USC) The Episcopal Church Of The Advent, 141 Advent St, Spartanburg SC 29302 **S Steph's Ch Richmond VA 2017-; Mem, COM Dio Upper So Carolina Columbia SC 2015-; Chairman of Kanuga Endwmt Bd Kanuga Confererences Inc Hendersonvlle NC 2015-** B Richmond VA 1955 s Carden & Caroline. Dplma St. Chris's (Epis) Sch 1974; BA W&L 1979; Cert of Banking Stonier Grad Sch of Banking 1985; Cert in Banking Stonier Grad Sch of Banking 1985; Cert U So-EFM Prog 1997; MDiv VTS 2012; MDiv VTS 2012. D 12/17/2011 Bp J Neil Alexander P 10/27/2012 Bp Robert Christopher Wright. m 6/16/1979 Ruth Antell McGehee c 3. Assoc R for Pstr Care Ch Of The Adv Spartanburg SC 2012-2017; Sr Wrdn All SS Epis Ch Atlanta GA 2005-2006; Mem, Bd Dir Cov Cmnty Inc Atlanta GA 1994-1997. Phi Kappa Sigma Fraternity 1974-1979. Phi Beta Kappa Washington and Lee Univefrsity 1979; mcl W&L 1979. smcgehee@churchofadvent.org

MCGILL, James Calvin (Tex) 6339 E Mystic Mdw, Houston TX 77021 **Pstr Spanish Lang Cong Chr Ch Cathd 2008-; Cn Chr Ch Cathd Houston TX 2005-; Bd Gvnr IHS Hosp Houston Houston TX 1995-; Dioc Hisp Cmsn Dio Texas Houston TX 1991-, Dioc Liturg Cmsn 1996-1999** B Dallas TX 1950 s Charlie & Virgina. BS USMA 1973; MDiv Sewanee: The U So, TS 1991. D 6/29/1991 Bp Terence Kelshaw P 12/4/1992 Bp William Elwood Sterling. m 7/21/1973 Elizabeth Rose Fleming c 2. Cn Mssnr Chr Ch Cathd Houston TX 2005-2015; Dn E Harris Convoc Houston TX 1998-2002; R S Paul's Ch Houston TX 1994-2004; Assoc R S Ptr's Ch Pasadena TX 1991-1994. iakwbos01@gmail.com

MCGILL JR, William James (CPa) Po Box 682, Cornwall PA 17016 B Saint Louis MO 1936 s William & Ethel. PhD Harv; MA Harv; BA Trin Hartford CT. D 4/28/1973 P 6/1/1974 Bp Robert Bracewell Appleyard. m 6/18/1960 Ellen Buck. P-in-c S Jas Ch Lancaster PA 1994-2010; Int S Andr's Epis Ch York PA 1993-1994; Non-par 1990-1993; Int S Thos Ch Lancaster PA 1989-1990; Int S Paul's Ch Manheim PA 1988-1989; Non-par 1987-1988; Non-par 1986-1988; Non-par 1984-1986; Non-par 1983-1988; Prof W&J Washington PA 1980-1984; P-in-c S Geo's Ch Waynesburg PA 1975-1983; Assoc Prof Hist W&J Washington PA 1972-1980; Dn W&J Washington PA 1972-1975; Non-par Alma Coll Alma MI 1962-1972; Non-par Wstrn Md Coll Westminster MD 1960-1962. Auth, "Geo Herbert," *R.S. Thos And The Argument w God*, 2003; Auth, "arts," *Rock Sprg Chronicles*, Fithian, 1999; Auth, "Maria Theresa," 1972; Ed, "Spitball".

MCGIMPSEY, Ralph Gregory (Mich) 8207 Nice Way, Sarasota FL 34238 **P in Res S Bon Ch Sarasota FL 2000-** B Cleveland OH 1937 s John & Muriel. BA Mia 1959; MDiv Bex Sem 1964. D 6/13/1964 P 12/18/1964 Bp Nelson Marigold Burroughs. c 2. Cn Provost Cathd Ch Of S Paul Detroit MI 1989-1999; R St. Dav's Epis Ch Garden City MI 1973-1989; R S Paul's Epis Ch Brighton MI 1967-1973; Asst Min S Jn's Epis Ch Saginaw MI 1964-1967; Cathd Chapt Dio Michigan Detroit MI 1985-1999.

MCGINLEY, Charles Richard (Md) 18024 Sand Wedge Dr, Hagerstown MD 21740 **R S Mk's Ch Lappans Boonsboro MD 1988-, 1973-1987** B Hagerstown MD 1926 s Edward & Frances. AA Hagerstown Jr Coll 1948; BS Bos 1949; MDiv VTS 1957. D 6/7/1957 Bp Frederick D Goodwin P 5/25/1958 Bp Robert Fisher Gibson Jr. m 8/24/1950 Katherine Lorraine McGinley c 3. R S Paul's Ch Sharpsburg MD 1973-1980; R S Matt's Epis Ch Newton KS 1968-1973; Assoc Gd Samar Epis Ch San Jose CA 1965-1968; R Emm Ch Virginia Bch VA 1959-1965; Assoc S Steph's Ch Richmond VA 1957-1959.

MCGINN, John Edward (Mass) 29 Oak Ridge Rd, East Sandwich MA 02537 **Bridge P St. Steph's Epis Ch Cohasset MA 2017-** B Hartford CT 1947 s John & Josephine. BA U of Connecticut 1969; MDiv EDS 1980. D 6/14/1980 P 12/

1/1980 Bp Morgan Porteus. m 11/15/1969 Marion G McGinn c 2. R S Jn's Ch Sandwich MA 1995-2013; R S Paul's Ch Southington CT 1982-1995; Asst Chr Chr Ch Westerly RI 1980-1982.

MCGINNIS, Richard H(arry) (Fla) 1312 Wisconsin St., Apt. 137, Hudson WI 54016 **Ret 1994-** B Philadelphia PA 1929 s Robert & Frances. BA Seattle Pacific U 1951; GTS 1954. D 6/29/1954 P 6/29/1955 Bp Stephen F Bayne Jr. c 3. S Andr's Ch Darien GA 1988-1994; Assoc S Dav's Ch Jacksonville FL 1984-1994; R Trin Epis Ch Watertown SD 1978-1984; R Trin Epis Ch Winner SD 1967-1978; Vic Chr Ch Anvik AK 1961-1967; Cur Trin Par Seattle WA 1957-1961; Vic Ch Of The Redeem Kenmore WA 1954-1957; Asst Ne Lake Mssn Kirkland WA 1954-1955. Auth, "Mar Mnstry," *Mar Mnstry Trng Outline*, Self, 1993; Auth, "Mar Mnstry," *Mar Mnistry Pstr's Manual*, Self, 1992. AAC 1999; Curs 1971; Forw In Faith N. A. 1997; Kairos 1990; Mar Savers 1996; Ord Of S Lk 1986. Lifetime Achievmnt Mar Savers 2001.

MCGINTY, John P (LI) 33 Jefferson Street, Garden City NY 11530 **R S Anselm's Ch Shoreham NY 2016-; Dn Gd Shpd Epis Chap Garden City NY 2012-** B Salem MA 1957 s John & Mary. AB St Jn Sem Coll 1979; STD No Amer Coll 1990; STD Pontifical Gregorian U 1990. Rec 11/19/2011 Bp Lawrence C Provenzano. Dn Geo Mercer TS Garden City NY 2012-2016; Gr Ch Brooklyn NY 2012; Dio Long Island Garden City NY 2011-2012. jmcginty@stanselmsofshoreham.org

MCGINTY, William Joseph (Be) 110 Ave M., Matamoras PA 18336 B Derry City IE 1948 s John & Margaret. BD Lon GB 1979; MA Lon GB 1983; MA Inst of Rel Educ Yonkers NY 1997; DMin Drew U 2008. Rec 9/29/2001 as Priest Bp Paul Victor Marshall. m 11/29/1997 Maryann McGinty c 1. R Ch Of The Gd Shpd And S Jn Milford PA 2003-2012; S Jas-S Geo Epis Ch Jermyn PA 2002-2003.

MCGIRR, Joyce Bearden (Nwk) B Paterson NJ 1942 d Leonard & Gwendolyn. BA Montclair St 1966; MA Montclair St 1985; Cert GTS 2010; Cert The GTS 2010; MDiv GTS 2014; MDiv The GTS 2014. D 6/14/2014 P 1/10/2015 Bp Mark M Beckwith. m 12/15/1979 John Timothy McGirr c 1.

MCGLANNAN, Dorian (Mich) 6217 137th Pl SW, Edmonds WA 98026 B Baltimore MD 1952 d Francis & Joan. Bos 1971; BA S Olaf Coll 1975; S Marys Sem 1982; MDiv GTS 1984. D 11/18/1985 P 11/1/1986 Bp Albert Theodore Eastman. m 8/25/1990 Joseph A Cospito c 3. R S Jn's Ch Plymouth MI 2005-2013; R Ch Of The Gd Shpd Fed Way WA 1997-2005; Natl Excoun Epf Epis Ch Cntr New York NY 1990-1992; Assoc R Epiph Par of Seattle Seattle WA 1989-1997; Int S Paul's Epis Ch Prnc Frederck MD 1988-1989; Asst Ch Of The Mssh Baltimore MD 1985-1988.

MCGLASHON JR, Hugh (CFla) PO Box 3303, Haines City FL 33845 **Ret 1998-** B Rochester NY 1932 s Hugh & Rosalind. BS U of So Dakota 1961; MDiv PDS 1973; ThM NBTS 1986. D 4/26/1975 P 11/1/1975 Bp Albert Wiencke Van Duzer. m 3/27/1954 Lois McGlashon c 3. Int S Mk's Epis Ch Haines City FL 2009-2010, R 1991-2009; Chapl Chap Of S Mary & S Martha Bp Gray Inn Davenport FL 2000-2006; Dn of the SW Dnry Dnry Haines City FL 1995-1999; Chapl BGI Davenport FL 1990-1993; Dn of the Keys Dnry Keys Dnry Key W FL 1988-1990; R S Paul's Ch Key W FL 1988-1990; Int All SS Ch Bay Hd NJ 1987-1988; R Ch Of The H Sprt Lebanon NJ 1980-1987; R Chr Ch Palmyra NJ 1976-1980; Cur S Andr's Ch Mt Holly NJ 1975-1976; Liaison of Yth Wk and Inter-Dioc Relation Dio Haiti Port-au-Prince HT 1968-1987.

MCGOVERN, Gerald Hugh (HB) 2600 Lake Michigan Dr Nw, Grand Rapids MI 49504 B Granite City IL 1933 s Hugh & Wilma. BS Sthrn Illinois U 1955; BS SWTS 1958. D 6/24/1958 P 6/11/1959 Bp Charles A Clough. m 9/5/1953 Betty Lou McGovern c 3. Vic S Jn's Ch Centralia IL 2002; Vic S Anne's Epis Ch Warsaw IN 1963-1967; S S Thos Ch Salem IL 1958-1962.

MCGOWAN, Carole Jean (RG) 425 University Blvd NE, Albuquerque NM 87106 **Exam Chapl Dio The Rio Grande Albuquerque 2009-; Bd Mem New Mex Conf of Ch Albuquerque NM 2006-** B Buffalo NY 1946 d William & Lou. BA Vas 1968; MA Ya 1972; MDiv Nash 1979. D 6/14/1980 Bp Morgan Porteus P 3/25/1981 Bp Arthur Edward Walmsley. R S Thos Of Cbury Epis Ch Albuquerque NM 1990-2013; P-in-c S Ptr's Epis Ch Bloomfield NY 1989-1990; Int R S Mk's Ch Newark NY 1988-1989; Int Assoc S Thos Epis Ch Rochester NY 1987; Dir Epis Ch Rela Crds/Bex/Crozer Bex Sem Columbus OH 1984-1990; Asst The Ch of the Redeem Cincinnati OH 1980-1984; Asst to the Bishops Dio Connecticut Meriden CT 1980; SCSD, Chair Epis Ch Cntr New York NY 1994-1997, SCSD, Co-Chair 1991-1993. Polly Bond Awd ECom 1997.

MCGOWAN, Diane Darby (Minn) 5029 2nd Ave S, Minneapolis MN 55419 **D St Geo's Epis Ch Minneapolis MN 2013-; D S Thos Ch Minneapolis MN 2003-** B Rhinebeck NY 1948 d Robert & Elizabeth. U Denv 1968; EFM U of So 1989; MBA U of St Thos 1991. D 5/18/2003 Bp James Louis Jelinek. m 9/12/1991 Mitchell Bruce Pearlstein c 4. D S Phil's Ch S Paul MN 2003-2013.

MCGOWAN, Sandra Maria (Alb) D 5/30/2015 Bp William Howard Love.

MCGOWEN, Willetta Hulett (Ga) 900 Gloucester St, Brunswick GA 31520 B Brunswick GA 1951 d William & Margaret. D 6/15/2009 Bp Henry Irving Louttit. m 10/6/1984 Mitchell McGowen c 3.

MCGRADY, Jacqueline Ann (Mass) PO Box 2847, Nantucket MA 02584 B Falmouth MA 1964 d John & Patricia. BA Amh 1987; MDiv Harvard DS 1990; GTS 1991. D 5/30/1992 P 5/29/1993 Bp David Elliot Johnson. m 12/10/1994 Peter Swenson c 2. R S Mk's Epis Ch Burlington MA 1999-2005; Asst Ch Of The Gd Shpd Nashua NH 1993-1999; Asst S Phil's Ch Garrison NY 1992-1993.

MCGRANE, Kevin John (Mo) 3664 Arsenal St, Saint Louis MO 63116 B St Louis MO 1950 s Harold & Margaret. BA U of Missouri 1978; Grad Cert Fin Educ Inst 1984; ESM Dplma Epis Sch for Mnstry 2013. D 11/21/2014 Bp George Wayne Smith. m 7/23/1973 Mary Catherine McGrane c 3.

MCGRATH, Victoria (Nwk) 113 Center Ave, Chatham NJ 07928 **R All SS Ch Millington NJ 2002-; Chapl RSCM Kings Coll Course PA 1998-** B New York NY 1956 d Abbot & Barbara. BA Wells Coll 1978; MA Col 1987; MDiv Drew U 1994. D 6/4/1994 Bp Jack Marston Mckelvey P 12/4/1994 Bp John Shelby Spong. m 8/23/1980 John Byram McGrath c 2. Alum/i Exec Bd Secy Drew TS Madison NJ 2004-2009; Int All SS' Epis Ch Glen Rock NJ 1999-2002; Bd Mem Overlook Hosp Cpaliancy Bd Summit NJ 1995-1999; Asst R Chr Ch Short Hills NJ 1994-1999; Dioc Bdgt and Fin Com Dio Newark Newark NJ 2009-2011, Vice-Pres, Dioc Coun; Cnvnr, Strng Com; Co-Chair, Equipping Action Team 2008-2011, Cler Peer Coach 2008-2010, COM Formation Liason for Previously Ord 2005-2010, Co-Chair, Bp's Search/Nomin Com 2005-2007, Co-Chair, Bp Search/Nomin Com 2005-2006, Formation Advsr for Previously Ord Cler 2005-, St. Mart's Hse Fund Bd - Pres, Vice-Pres 2002-, COM, Screening Co-Chair; Educ Chair 1996-2004, Yth Mnstrs Bd 1996-2003, Min for Recently Ord Cler Grp 1995-2005, Recently Ord Cler Mentor 1995-1998, Dioc Nomin Com 1994-1995. Cmnty of S Mary - Assoc 1976-2005; Cmnty of St. Jn Bapt - Assoc 2005.

MCGRAW, Jean (SC) 1878 Oleander Ct, Charleston SC 29414 **P-in-c 2013-** B Charleston SC 1946 d Charles & Delilah. BS Coll of Charleston 1967; MDiv Epis TS of the SW 2010. D 6/5/2011 Bp Stacy F Sauls P 12/21/2011 Bp Chilton Richardson Knudsen. m 4/30/1967 Stanley Earle McGraw c 3. Epis TS Of The SW Austin TX 2014-2016, 2014, 2013, 2013, Stdt Bd Rep 2010-2011; P-in-c St Fran Epis Ch Charleston SC 2013-2017; St Andr's Mssn Charleston SC 2012, Dir of Chr Ed 2005-2007; D Calv Epis Ch Ashland KY 2011-2013.

MCGRAW, Stanley Earle (At) 1878 Oleander Ct., Charleston SC 29414 **P-in-c S Jas Epis Ch Prestonsburg KY 2010-** B Spartanburg SC 1942 s Ray & Willie. BA Wofford Coll 1964; MDiv VTS 1969. D 6/23/1969 P 1/1/1970 Bp Gray Temple. m 4/30/1967 Jean Mcgraw c 3. P-in-c S Mk's Epis Ch Charleston SC 2013-2015; Int S Fran Par Temple TX 2007-2010; Asst St Andr's Mssn Charleston SC 2004-2007; P-in-c Chr Epis Ch Sparta NC 1999-2003; Dio Atlanta Atlanta GA 1997-1999, Dir of Spec Mnstrs 1981-1992, Dn of Convoc 1979-1981, Instnl Chapl 1979-1981, Hon Cn 1979-, Chapl to DOK 1977-, Chairperson of Evang Com 1973-1986, Dn of Convoc 1973-; R S Jn's Epis Ch Atlanta GA 1995-1997; Vic Ch Of The H Comf Atlanta GA 1993-1995; Assoc R Emmaus Hse Epis Ch Atlanta GA 1980-1983; R Ch Of The Epiph Atlanta GA 1971-1979; Asst R Par Ch of St. Helena Beaufort SC 1969-1971. Mntl Hlth Wk Awd Fulton Cnty 1993; Mntl Hlth Wk Commendation 93 Dekalb Cnty.

MCGRAW, Tara L (SwFla) **R S Paul's Ch Naples FL 2009-, P-in-c 2007-2009, Assoc 2005-2016; Const & Cn Com Dio SW Florida Parrish FL 2005-** B Coral Gables FL 1957 BBA U of Miami 1977; JD U of Miami 1981; MDiv VTS 2005. D 6/18/2005 P 12/21/2005 Bp John Bailey Lipscomb. m 4/29/2000 John Patrick McGraw. Vic Resurr Epis Ch Naples FL 2005-2007. frtara@saintpaulsnaples.org

MCGREEVY, Molly Paine (Ct) 503 Old Long Ridge Rd, Stamford CT 06903 **Died 11/1/2015** B New York NY 1936 d Hugh & Helen. BA Vas 1958; MDiv GTS 1986. D 6/10/1989 Bp Paul Moore Jr P 12/1/1989 Bp Walter Decoster Dennis Jr. m 5/21/1976 Earl Warren Hindman c 3. Assoc S Fran Ch Stamford CT 1996-2003; Tutor The GTS New York NY 1989-1996; The Ch Of S Lk In The Fields New York NY 1989-1995.

MCGREGOR, Patricia Cox (SeFla) PO Box 399, Ambridge PA 15003 **SAMS Ambridge PA 2008-** B Denver CO 1959 d Gerry & Audrey. DMin Gordon-Conwell TS; BS Ursinus Coll 1981; MAR Trin Evang DS 1990. Trans 8/1/2008 Bp Leo Frade. m 7/27/1985 Todd A McGregor c 2. Global Teams Forest City NC 1988-2003.

MCGUGAN, Terry (Colo) 2950 S University Blvd, Denver CO 80210 **R Chr Epis Ch Denver CO 2013-** B Boston MA 1964 s Arthur & Janet. AA Emory U 1984; BA Emory U 1986; MDiv GTS 1992. D 5/28/1992 P 12/1/1992 Bp Harry Woolston Shipps. m 5/15/2010 JoEllen M McGugan c 2. R S Mich's Epis Ch Racine WI 1995-2012; Assoc S Mart In The Fields Ch Atlanta GA 1993-1995; Vic S Fran Ch Camilla GA 1992-1993; Vic The Epis Ch Of S Jn And S Mk Albany GA 1992-1993.

MCGUINNESS, David (NC) 4330 Pin Oak Dr, Durham NC 27707 B Dublin IE 1943 s Ignatius & Sarah. MDiv S Kierans Coll Kilkenny IE 1973. Trans 9/7/2002 Bp Michael B Curry. R S Steph's Epis Ch Erwin NC 2003-2015. michael.curry@episdionc.org

MCGUIRE, Malcolm (Pa) 1300 Lombard St Apt 711, Philadelphia PA 19147 B Plattsburg NY 1935 s Ritchie & Lillian. BA New York Sch of Mus 1964; MDiv PDS 1970; STM PDS 1973; EdD Tem 1984; MEd Tem 1991. D 6/6/1970 P 12/19/1970 Bp Horace W B Donegan. P-in-c Ch Of The Crucif Philadelphia PA 2002-2004, P-in-c 1975-1979; R S Alb's Ch Roxborough Philadelphia PA 1989-1994; Dio Pennsylvania Philadelphia PA 1988-2000; Non-par 1980-1986; Asst S Mk's Ch Philadelphia PA 1971-1974; Cur Ch Of S Lk And Epiph Philadelphia PA 1970-1971. Ed, "Coll Tem 84". Alumnini Serv Awd Tem 1984.

MCGUIRE, Mark Alan (WMo) 908 SW Hackney Ct, Lees Summit MO 64081 **R S Paul's Epis Ch Lees Summit MO 2002-; chair, Cler Compstn Com Dio W Missouri Kansas City MO 2013-, Mem COM 2003-2009** B Warrensburg MO 1951 s Harry & Beverly. BS U of Cntrl Missouri 1974; MDiv Sewanee: The U So, TS 2002. D 6/8/2002 P 12/7/2002 Bp Barry Howe. m 9/1/1984 Donna Jean McGuire.

MCGURK, Brian (Mass) 625 Main St, Chatham MA 02633 **R S Chris's Ch Chatham MA 2003-** B Waterbury CT 1956 s Francis & Shirley. PhD Sthrn California U of Hlth Sciences 1982; BA Trin 1990; MDiv Ya Berk 1992. D 6/13/1992 Bp Arthur Edward Walmsley P 12/20/1992 Bp Clarence Nicholas Coleridge. m 10/3/2015 Diana Lynn Galazzo c 3. R S Ptr's Par Ch New Kent VA 1998-2003; Asst R S Mary's Epis Ch Richmond VA 1994-1998; Cur S Matt's Epis Ch Wilton CT 1992-1993; S Mk New Canaan CT 1990-1992.

MCHALE, Stephen (Cal) 1700 Santa Clara Ave, Alameda CA 94501 **Chr Ch Alameda CA 2013-** B Rome Italy 1973 s John & Laurie. BA Whitman Coll 1996; MDiv CDSP 2008. D 6/28/2008 Bp Bavi Edna Rivera. m 7/24/2004 Holly C Larsen c 2. Ch Of The Resurr Pleasant Hil CA 2008-2013. stephen@christchurchalameda.org

MCHALE O'CONNOR, Mary Colleen (WNY) 1 East Main Street, Le Roy NY 14482 **R S Mk's Epis Ch Le Roy NY 2005-** B Binghamton NY 1957 d Edward & Nancy. BA Mid 1979; MDiv EDS 1988. D 4/6/2002 P 10/6/2002 Bp Roger John White. m 8/17/1985 Christopher Duane O'Connor c 5. P-in-c S Paul's Ch Watertown WI 2002-2005.

MCHENRY, Richard Earl (FtW) 1010 Willowcreek Rd, Cleburne TX 76033 B Tucson AZ 1932 s Alfred & Mary. BA Missouri Vlly Coll 1954; MDiv Mc-Cormick TS 1959. D 5/20/1967 Bp Robert Rae Spears Jr P 10/9/1967 Bp Edward Randolph Welles II. R Ch Of The H Comf Cleburne TX 1991-2004; Cmnty Ministers Dio Ft Worth TX 1989-1993, Nomin Com For Bp Coadj 1992-1994, Exec Coun 1989-1991; All SS' Epis Ch Ft Worth TX 1984-1991; Dn Of The Sthrn Dnry 1978-1979; R Gr Ch Carthage MO 1976-1983, Asst 1967-1975; Serv Presb Ch; Liturg Cmsn Dio W Missouri Kansas City MO 1969-2004. CCU, NOEL, Fllshp S Alb & S Sergius, Epis Syn Amer, SSC. R Emer.

MCHUGH III, John Michael (NJ) 324 Rio Grande Blvd Nw, Albuquerque NM 87104 **Imm 1992-** B Trenton NJ 1948 s John & Dorothy. BA Glassboro St U 1969; MDiv EDS 1975. D 4/26/1975 Bp Albert Wiencke Van Duzer P 1/1/1976 Bp Morris Fairchild Arnold. Non-par 1989-1991; Stff S Mk's On The Mesa Epis Ch Albuquerque NM 1981-1988, Asst 1977-1980; Chapl S Jos's Hosp Albuquerque NM 1977-1981; Fac Instr Of Pstr Stds Loyola U Chicago IL 1976-1982; Intrnshp S Jn Arlington MS 1975-1976.

MCILHINEY, David B (NH) 701 E High St Apt 211, Charlottesville VA 22902 **Chapl Blue Ridge Sch Dyke VA 2010-** B Gainesville FL 1942 s William & Zelda. BA Harv 1964; BD UTS 1968; PhD Pr 1977. D 6/8/1968 P 12/21/1968 Bp Horace W B Donegan. Chapl S Paul's Memi Charlottesvlle VA 2004-2009; R Trin Ch Claremont NH 1986-2001; Chapl Phil Exeter Aca Exeter NH 1977-1986; Chapl S Thos Ch Hanover NH 1973-1977. Auth, "A Gentleman in Every Slum," Pickwick, 1988.

MCILMOYL, William Joseph (NCal) 1314 Spring St, Saint Helena CA 94574 B Troy NY 1949 s Sherman & Charlotte. BA Hobart and Wm Smith Colleges 1972; MDiv SWTS 1988. D 6/22/1988 P 12/21/1988 Bp William Hopkins Folwell. m 6/8/1985 Sandra Swetnam c 2. R Gr Ch S Helena CA 1993-2016; Asst S Jas Epis Ch Ormond Bch FL 1988-1993. frmac@grace-episcopal.org

MCILROY, Ellen Lafleur (Cal) 5555 Montgomery Dr Apt 59, Santa Rosa CA 95409 **Died 7/27/2016** B Tokyo JP 1931 d James & Gwynneth. BA Bryn 1952; PhD Syr 1963; Grad Theol Un 1976. D 6/24/1972 P 1/16/1977 Bp Chauncie Kilmer Myers. Ret 1987-2016; Assoc Ch Of The Epiph San Carlos CA 1985-1987; Chair, Com on the Ord of Wmn S Jas Ch Oakland CA 1974-1976; S Aid's Ch San Francisco CA 1972-1974; Com on Sxlty Dio California San Francisco CA 1972-1976.

MCILVAIN, Jean Christine (Pgh) 5622 Alan St, Aliquippa PA 15001 **D Chr Epis Ch No Hills Pittsburgh PA 2003-** B Beaver Falls PA 1946 d Robert & Vivian. BS Clarion U of Pennsylvania 1968. D 12/5/1998 Bp Robert William Duncan. D Prince Of Peace Epis Ch Aliquippa PA 1998-2003.

MCILVEEN, Richard William (Me) 26 Concord St, Portland ME 04103 **Non-par 1981-** B 1947 s William. BA Penn 1969; MDiv GTS 1973. D 5/27/1973 Bp William Crittenden P 1/1/1974 Bp James Stuart Wetmore. m 12/31/1975 Anna Maria McIlveen. Chapl Reg Memi Hosp Brunswick ME 1979-1981; Vic S Barth's Epis Ch Yarmouth ME 1979-1981; Int S Ann's Epis Ch Windham Windham ME 1976-1977; S Jn's Ch Presque Isle ME 1976; Vic For S Ann'S Ch For The Deaf Dio New York New York NY 1974-1975.

MCINDOO, Lisa S (WTenn) Diocese Of West Tennessee, 692 Poplar Ave, Memphis TN 38105 **Dio W Tennessee Memphis 2016-** B 1966 d Richard & Virginia. Mstr of Div Sewanee: The U So, TS 2016. D 6/4/2016 P 12/11/2016 Bp Don Edward Johnson. m 1/17/2002 William Hudson Mcindoo c 1.

MCINERNEY, Joseph Lee (Cal) 1421 Oxford St, Berkeley CA 94709 B San Jose CA 1944 s Joseph & Norma. Stan; U of Leeds Gb; U of Pennsylvania. D 1/12/1970 P 1/13/1971 Bp George Richard Millard. P-in-c Chr Ch Creswell NC 1974-1975; S Andr's Ch Columbia NC 1974-1975; S Geo Epis Ch Engelhard NC 1974-1975.

MCINNIS, Victor Erwin (Miss) Po Box 63, Lexington MS 39095 **Off Of Bsh For ArmdF New York NY 1997-** B Centerville MS 1957 s Clifton & Francis. BS U of Sthrn Mississippi 1987; MDiv Sewanee: The U So, TS 1991. D 6/3/1991 Bp Duncan Montgomery Gray Jr P 8/1/1992 Bp Alfred Marble Jr. D Gr Ch Carrollton MS 1991-1997; D S Mary's Ch Lexington MS 1991-1994.

MCINTIRE, Rhonda (RG) 17 Camino Redondo, Placitas NM 87043 **R San Gabr the Archangel Epis Ch Corrales NM 2012-, 2009-2010** B Pampa TX 1950 d James & Glorine. BA Valparaiso U 1972; MDiv Epis TS of the SW 1996. D 6/22/1996 Bp Claude Edward Payne P 6/4/1997 Bp Terence Kelshaw. m 6/10/1978 Timothy R McIntire c 1. R S Andr's By The Sea Epis Par San Diego CA 2004-2008; Vic S Jn's Epis Ch Chula Vista CA 2003-2004; Cn S Jn's Cathd Albuquerque NM 1996-2002. rhonda.mcintire@q.com

MCINTOSH, David Kevin (Ct) 1 North Main Street, PO Box 309, Kent CT 06757 **Chair, COM Epis Ch in Connecticut 2014-; P Assoc S Andr's Ch Kent CT 2012-; Physcn- Med/Peds Wstrn Connecticut Med Grp 2011-; Med Stff New Milford Hosp 2000-; COM Dio Connecticut Meriden CT 2011-** B Miami, FL 1964 s Donald & Patricia. BS Duke 1986; MD U of Miami 1991; MDiv GTS 2010. D 6/12/2010 Bp Ian Theodore Douglas P 1/22/2011 Bp James Elliot Curry. m 12/19/2005 Charles Daniel Barr. Assoc. Prof. of Med Univ. of Vermont Sch of Med 2011; Asstg P Trin Ch Torrington CT 2010-2012. Connecticut Epis Cler Assn 2010; Soc of Cath Priests 2009.

MCINTOSH, Eric (Pgh) St James Episcopal Church, 11524 Frankstown Rd, Pittsburgh PA 15235 **S Jas Epis Ch Pittsburgh PA 2013-** B Pittsburgh PA 1966 s Fred & Henrietta. MDiv Pittsburgh TS; Carnegie Mellon U 1984; BS U Pgh 2008. D 6/15/2013 P 1/11/2014 Bp Dorsey McConnell. m 7/13/1991 Monique McIntosh c 3.

MCINTOSH, Justin M (Va) 4332 Leeds Manor Road, Markham VA 22643 **R Epis Ch Of Leeds Par Markham VA 2011-; Com on Priesthood Dio Virginia Richmond VA 2011-, Young P Initiative 2009-** B Alexandria VA 1983 s Dennis & Susan. Bachelor of Arts W&M 2005; Dplma of Angl Stds Ya Berk 2009; Mstr of Div Yale DS 2009. D 11/14/2009 Bp Shannon Sherwood Johnston P 5/15/2010 Bp David Colin Jones. m 6/28/2008 Elena T Mcintosh c 3. Assoc S Thos Epis Ch Mclean VA 2009-2011. Cn of the Dio Long Island The Cathd of Garden City 2011. jmac53083@gmail.com

MCINTOSH, Kendra Lea (Nwk) 26 W 84th St, New York NY 10024 B Shawnee Mission KS 1964 D 6/14/2003 P 1/28/2004 Bp James E Waggoner Jr. S Thos Ch Lyndhurst NJ 2007-2010; S Jas Ch New York NY 2003-2005.

MCINTOSH, Mark Allen (Chi) 65 E Huron St, Chicago IL 60611 B Evanston IL 1960 s Gilbert & Katherine. BA Ya 1982; BA Oxf GB 1985; MDiv GTS 1986. D 6/14/1986 Bp James Winchester Montgomery P 12/1/1986 Bp Frank Tracy Griswold III. m 8/10/1985 Elizabeth Anne McIntosh. Cathd Of S Jas Chicago IL 1986-1989; Sem Asst S Thos In New York City 1985-1986; Sem Asst S Mary Magd Oxford Engl 1983-1985.

MCINTOSH, Randy Eugene (WK) 138 S 8th St, Salina KS 67401 **S Jn's Mltry Sch Salina KS 2013-; Vic Epis Ch Of The Incarn Salina KS 2008-** B Salina KS 1953 s Wendell & Lillian. D 9/1/2007 P 2/14/2009 Bp James Marshall Adams Jr. Chr Cathd Salina KS 2007-2008; Sexton 1998-2004; Dio Wstrn Kansas Hutchinson KS 2006-2007.

MCINTOSH, Wayne S (SD) Trinity Episcopal Church, 500 14th Ave NW, Watertown SD 57201 B Winnipeg Manitoba 1961 s George & Henrietta. BA U of Manitoba 1987; BTh McGill U Quebec 1991; MDiv Montreal TS CA 1991. Trans 2/1/2008 Bp Creighton Leland Robertson. m 9/18/1982 Lorraine G McIntosh c 4. R Trin Epis Ch Watertown SD 2008.

MCINTYRE, Calvin Carney (NY) 4401 Matilda Ave, Bronx NY 10470 **R Ch Of The Gd Shpd Wakefield Bronx NY 2000-, Vic 1998-2016** B Saint Ann Jamaica 1951 s Herbert & Mary. Cert Ch Teachers Coll Jamaica WI 1973; Dplma Untd Theol Coll of the W Indies Kingston JM 1980; LTh Trin 1987; Dplma Blanton Peale Grad of Hlth & Rel NY 1992; BA Coll of New Rochelle 1992; MDiv Trin 2000. Trans 3/5/1992 as Deacon Bp Orris George Walker Jr. m 9/19/1981 Camille D Mcintyre. Asst S Paul's Ch-In-The-Vill Brooklyn NY 1997-1998; Asst Ch Of SS Steph And Mart Brooklyn NY 1995; P-in-c Ch Of The Redeem Brooklyn NY 1993-1994; Asst Ch Of S Thos Brooklyn NY 1990-1993; Serv Ch of W Indies 1980-1982. St. Geo's Soc of New York 2009.

MCINTYRE III, Charles Ernest (NwT) 2429 Santa Cruz Ln, Odessa TX 79763 **Died 8/31/2016** B Sparrows Pt MD 1924 s Charles & Grace. BA Loyola U 1950; MDiv Sewanee: The U So, TS 1975. D 11/25/1956 Bp C J Kinsolving III P 6/11/1975 Bp Willis Ryan Henton. m 8/12/1944 Margaret E McIntyre. Int Team R S Mk's Epis Ch Pecos TX 1994-2016; Ret 1993-2016; Assoc S Jn's

Epis Ch Odessa TX 1981-1992; Trin Epis Ch Marble Falls TX 1979-1981; R S Paul Burnet Cnty TX 1978-1981; Dio NW Texas Lubbock TX 1975-1979, Com Mssn 1975-1978, Chair Mssn Cmsn 1986-1988; Gr Ch Vernon TX 1975-1979; Trin Ch Quanah TX 1975-1979; Asst S Alb's Ch El Paso TX 1956-1964. Bd PACT.

MCINTYRE, Gregory Edward (NC) 258 W Franklin Blvd, Gastonia NC 28052 **P S Alb's Ch Davidson NC 2013-** B Athens GA 1975 s Gregory & Margaret. BS Unversity of Georgia 2001; MDiv GTS 2011; MDiv The GTS 2011. D 12/18/2010 P 9/17/2011 Bp Porter Taylor. m 10/22/2000 Kathleen E McEvoy c 2. Assoc S Mk's Ch Gastonia NC 2011-2013; S Jas Ch Black Mtn NC 2004-2010.

MCINTYRE, John George (Md) 326 Pintail Dr, Havre De Grace MD 21078 B Baltimore MD 1939 s Charles & Grace. BS Loyola U 1961; BD Bex Sem 1964. D 9/19/1964 P 6/22/1965 Bp Harry Lee Doll. m 8/26/1972 Linda G McIntyre. R H Trin Ch Churchville MD 1997-2004; R S Mary's Epis Ch Pocomoke City MD 1990-1997; R S Jn's Epis Ch Bellefonte PA 1986-1990; Dio Wstrn Massachusetts Springfield 1983-1986; R Trin Epis Ch Shrewsbury MA 1983-1986; R S Andr's Ch Manchester NH 1978-1983; Chr Ch Chaptico MD 1974-1977; R Ch Of The Guardian Ang Baltimore MD 1972-1974; P Chr Ch Worton MD 1968-1971; R S Jn Betterton MD 1968-1971; S Steph's Ch Earleville MD 1968-1971; Vic S Paul Perry Hall MD 1966-1968; R S Geo Manchester MD 1965-1966; Cur Ch Of The Ascen Westminster MD 1964-1966.

MCINTYRE, Moni (Pgh) 4601 5th Ave #825, Pittsburgh PA 15213 **R Ch Of The H Cross Pittsburgh PA 2005-, D 2002-2016, P-in-c 2002-2005, Asst 2000-2002; Asst Prof Duquesne U 1990-** B Detroit MI 1948 d Angus & Cathryn. BA U of Detroit Mercy 1970; MA Estrn Michigan U 1972; MA U of Windsor 1979; MDiv SS Cyril and Methodius Sem 1983; PhD U of St Michaels Coll 1990. D 6/10/2000 P 12/16/2000 Bp Robert William Duncan. Auth, "The Black Ch and Whiteness: Looking for Jesus in Strange Places," *Christology and Whiteness: What Would Jesus Do?*, Routledge, 2012; Co-Ed, "Light Burdens Heavy Blessings," Franciscan, 2000; Co-Ed, "Readings in Ecology & Feminist Theol," Sheed & Ward, 1995; Auth, "On Choosing the Gd in the Face of Genocide," *Genocide Forum*, 1995; Auth, "Sin, Evil and Death in the New Age," *The Way*, 1993; Auth, "Soc Ethics and the Return to Cosmology," Ptr Lang, 1992; Auth, "Chr Soc Ethics and Hlth Care," *The Way*, 1992; Auth, "The Image of God in Rel Autobiography," *Grail*, 1991. AAR 1989; Soc of Chr Ethics 1989. Highly Effectve Eductr Awd DCPublic Schools 2012; Racial Justice Awd YWCA 2012.

MCJILTON, Sheila N (WA) St Philip's Church, 522 Main St, Laurel MD 20707 **R S Phil's Epis Ch Laurel MD 2007-** B Kingsport TN 1953 d Tolbert & Anne. Mars Hill Coll; BA Salisbury U 1976; MDiv VTS 1999. D 5/23/1999 P 12/11/1999 Bp Martin Gough Townsend. m 12/31/2014 Patricia Hendrickson c 1. Int R S Dav's Epis Ch Wilmington DE 2006-2007; P-in-c S Paul's Ch Centreville MD 2003-2006; VTS Alexandria VA 2001; Asst R Chr Ch Par Kent Island Stevensville MD 1999-2003. Auth, "Reflection on Genesis 22:1-14 (poem)," *VTS Journ*, 1998; Auth, "Ash Wednesday," *ATR Sprg 2000 Vol82 No2*; Auth, "Who Sleep on H Stones," *ATR Winter 2000 Volume 82 No 1*; Auth, "Leave-taking," *VTS Journ August 2000*. Exec Com on Status of Wmn.

MCKAIG, Byron James (Los) Mount Mesa, Box 1572, Lake Isabella CA 93240 **Died 6/23/2016** B Los Angeles CA 1935 s James & Elvira. BA U CA 1957; BD CDSP 1966. D 9/9/1967 P 3/1/1968 Bp Francis E I Bloy. m 6/30/1984 Gladys Dean McKaig c 3. Asst S Lk's Ch Bakersfield CA 1990-1997; Asst S Ptr's Epis Ch Kernville CA 1984-1989; Asst Incarn 1974-1981; Assoc R S Marg's Epis Ch So Gate CA 1972-1974; P-in-c S Anne Lynwood CA 1971-1972; Assoc R S Paul's Pomona Pomona CA 1968-1971; Asst Imm Mssn El Monte CA 1967-1968.

MCKAY, Judy Aileen (Ida) 6251 S Paperbirch Ave, Boise ID 83716 **Ret 1996-** B Oakland CA 1941 d Stanley & Jean. BA U CA 1963; MDiv SFTS 1977. D 11/20/1994 P 5/25/1995 Bp John Stuart Thornton. m 1/20/1991 John Clifford Matthew. Vic Emm Ch Hailey ID 1995-1996; Assoc Exec Syn of the Pacific P.C.(U.S.A.) 1987-1992; Pstr EvergreenPresbyterian Ch 1983-1987; Asst Pstr Calv Presb Ch San Francisco CA 1981-1983; Asst Pstr First Presb Ch Pocatello ID 1980; Dir Camp Sawtooth Ketchum ID 1979-1980; Pstr Cmnty Presb Rigby iD 1977-1978; Serv Presb Ch 1972-1992. Co-Auth, "CE in the Sm Ch," Judson Press, 1988. Assoc. of Presb Ch Educators 1977.

MCKAY, Paige Higley (NwT) 1101 Slide Rd, Lubbock TX 79416 B Amarillo TX 1967 d Thomas & Brenda. BA Texas Tech U 1989; Dioc D Formation 2012. D 12/1/2012 Bp James Scott Mayer. m 9/5/1992 Michael Edward McKay c 2.

MCKAY IV, Robert (NwPa) 1267 Treasure Lk, Du Bois PA 15801 B Cincinnati OH 1942 s Robert & Dorothy. BA Hobart and Wm Smith Colleges 1964; MDiv PDS 1967. D 4/22/1967 P 10/28/1967 Bp Alfred L Banyard. c 2. R Ch Of Our Sav Dubois PA 2001-2009; Chr Epis Ch E Tawas MI 1995-2001; R Hope - S Jn's Epis Ch Oscoda MI 1995-2001; Lakeshore Epis Area Parishes Oscoda MI 1995-2001; R S Andrews-By-The-Lake Epis Ch Harrisville MI 1995-2001; Trin Epis Ch Chambersburg PA 1983-1993; R Chr Ch Bordentown NJ 1974-1983; R S Mk Pleasantville NJ 1969-1974; Asst Min S Lk's Epis Ch Metuchen NJ 1967-1969.

MCKAY, William Martin (RG) **D S Paul's Peace Ch Las Vegas NM 2006-** B Hartford CT 1935 s Kenneth & Evelyn. Basic Chr Stds TESM 2006. D 10/21/2006 Bp Jeffrey Neil Steenson. m 9/18/1978 Elizabeth McKay c 5.

MCKEAN, Deborah Adams (Me) PO Box 137, Cushing ME 04563 **D S Ambr Par Claremont CA 2013-** B Memphis TN 1939 d Thomas & Marie. BA Mt Holyoke Coll 1960; MLS U of Rhode Island 1972. D 6/23/2007 Bp Chilton Richardson Knudsen. m 7/1/1961 Philip McKean c 2. D The Epis Ch Of S Jn Bapt Thomaston ME 2006-2011.

MCKEE, Christianne Louise (Spok) 1909 W. Clearview Dr., Ellensburg WA 98926 **S Mich's Epis Ch Yakima WA 2015-** B Fort Worth TX 1953 d Marvin & Christianne. BA U of Dallas 1976; MDiv Nash 1987. D 6/13/1987 P 6/12/1988 Bp Donis Dean Patterson. m 10/26/2013 Cindy Marie Bruns c 1. Dir H Ground Cntr for Sprtlty 2012-2014; Supply P Ch of the Resurr Roslyn WA 2011-2012; P H Trin Epis Ch Sunnyside WA 2010-2011; Assoc The Epis Ch Of S Thos The Apos Dallas TX 1997-2009; P-in-c St. Steph's Epis Ch Sanger TX 1996-1997; Int S Barn Epis Ch Denton TX 1994-1995, Int 1994-1995, Cur 1987-1989; Vic All SS Ch 1991-1994; Asst Epis Ch Of The Ascen Dallas TX 1989-1991; Campus Min U of No Texas Texas Wmn's U 1987-1989; Chair, Wrshp Com for Dioc Conv Dio Spokane Spokane WA 2011; Dioc Cmsn on HIV/AIDS Dio Dallas Dallas TX 1994-1995, Com for the Consecration of a Bp 1993. EWC 1989; Integrity 1990. christianne.mckee@yahoo.com

MCKEE II, Daniel Deupree (Ark) 500 Hazelton Dr., Madison MS 39110 **Died 1/4/2017** B Vicksburg MS 1945 s William & Helen. BA Millsaps Coll 1967; ETS, Edinburgh, Scotland 1970; MDiv Sewanee: The U So, TS 1971; DMin Sewanee: The U So, TS 1991. D 6/20/1971 P 5/27/1972 Bp John Maury Allin. m 2/24/1973 Diane McKee c 2. Subdean Trin Cathd Little Rock AR 2004-2010; Int S Steph's Epis Ch Huntsville AL 2003-2004; Int Ch Of The Nativ Epis Huntsville AL 2002-2003; Cn Dio Arkansas Little Rock AR 1995-2002, Stndg Com 2006-2009, ExCoun 1983-1993; R S Paul's Newport AR 1982-1995; S Matt's Epis Ch Kosciusko MS 1978-1979; Vic Imm Winona MS 1977-1982; Vic S Mary's Ch Lexington MS 1977-1982; Vic S Chris's Ch Jackson MS 1974-1977; Vic All SS Ch Inverness MS 1971-1974; S Thos Ch Belzoni MS 1971-1974. Auth, *Laborers in the Vineyard.*

MCKEE, Elizabeth Shepherd (NC) 408 Woodlawn Ave, Greensboro NC 27401 **D Dio No Carolina Raleigh NC 1993-** B Luebo ZR 1953 d Charles & Anne. BA Florida St U 1974; MS U NC 1977; D Formation Prog 1993. D 6/6/1993 Bp Robert Whitridge Estill. m 1/15/1994 Raymond Joseph Huger.

MCKEE, Helen Louise (SVa) 405 Avondale Dr., Danville VA 24541 **P-in-c Trin Ch Gretna VA 2011-; Dir of Pstr Care / Chapl Danville Reg Med Cntr Danville VA 2008-** B San Francisco 1936 d August & Alpha. BS U CA Los Angeles 1960; MDiv VTS 2006. D 6/24/2006 Bp Vincent Waydell Warner P 2/18/2007 Bp Bavi Edna Rivera. c 4. Asst Chr Epis Ch Danville VA 2008-2013; Int S Steph's Epis Ch Longview WA 2007; Ch Of The Epiph Danville VA 2006-2008; Asst R St. Paul on the Hill Winchester VA 2006-2007; Pohick Epis Ch Lorton VA 2004-2006. DOK 1998.

MCKEE, Lewis Kavanaugh (WTenn) 57 Wychewood Dr, Memphis TN 38117 **Asst Cler Calv Ch Memphis TN 2002-; Non-par 1988-** B Memphis TN 1921 s William & Marion. S 5/4/1980 Bp William F Gates Jr P 5/1/1981 Bp William Evan Sanders. m 8/6/1943 Heloise M McKee. Asst R S Jn's Epis Ch Memphis TN 1986-1988; D Ch Of The H Comm Memphis TN 1980-1986.

MCKEE, Martha Marcella (NJ) 11 Exeter Ct, East Windsor NJ 08520 **Vic Ch Of The H Sprt Tuckerton NJ 2009-; Chapl The Evergreen (CCRC) Moorestown NJ 2003-** B Houston TX 1953 d Robert & Clara. BS U of Texas 1973; MPA U of Missouri-Kansas City 1978; MDiv GTS 2003. D 6/7/2003 Bp David Bruce Joslin P 12/13/2003 Bp George Edward Councell. m 6/22/1985 James Lee Olander. Evergreens Chap Moorestown NJ 2003-2009; The Evergreens Moorestown NJ 2003-2009.

MCKEE, Michael Dale (Los) 815 Emerald Bay, Laguna Beach CA 92651 B 1946 D 12/1/1972 P 4/1/1973 Bp Robert Claflin Rusack. m 8/25/1967 Cynthia McKee c 2. Asst Dir Cntr For Hlth Serv Sch Med At U Of.

MCKEE, Stephen Lee (Okla) 501 S Cincinnati Ave, Tulsa OK 74103 **R Trin Ch Tulsa OK 2001-** B Mount Vernon IL 1950 s Charles & Mary. BS Van 1973; BTh Chichester Theol Coll 1981. D 5/8/1982 P 2/19/1983 Bp George Paul Reeves. m 10/2/1982 Lindsey L McKee c 1. R Ch Of The H Comm S Louis MO 1994-2001; R St Ptr & All SS Epis Ch Kansas City MO 1990-1994; Chapl Assoc S Paul's Ch Kansas City MO 1986-1990; Cur S Paul's Ch Albany GA 1982-1985; D in Trng S Paul's Ch Augusta GA 1982. Outstanding Serv Awd Mart Luther King, Jr. Commemoration Soc, Inc. 2009.

MCKEE, Susan Rose (CGC) PO Box 29, Bon Secour AL 36511 **S Paul's Chap Magnolia Sprgs AL 2011-; D S Ptr's Epis Ch Bon Secour AL 2011-; Dio Cntrl Gulf Coast Pensacola FL 2011-** B Waterbury CT 1954 d John & Helen. AS U of Bridgeport 1974. D 2/10/2011 Bp Philip Menzie Duncan II. c 3. The Epis Cmnty 2011.

MCKEE, Todd Anderson (Vt) 105 Hickory Rdg, White River Junction VT 05001 **D S Barn Ch Norwich VT 2013-** B Hagerstown MD 1969 s George & Nancy. BA Mssh Coll 1990; MDiv PrTS 1993; Cert EDS 1996. D 12/16/

2012 P 10/4/2013 Bp Thomas C Ely. Geth Ch Proctorsville VT 2013-2016. gethsemanechurchvt@gmail.com

MCKEEVER, Anne Dryden (NCal) 2620 Capitol Ave., Sacramento CA 95816 B Klamath Falls OR 1952 d Harold & June. AB U CA 1974; MDiv CDSP 2009. D 6/13/2009 P 12/12/2009 Bp Barry Leigh Beisner. m 6/12/1976 Casey McKeever c 2. P Trin Epis Cathd Sacramento CA 2010-2014.

✠ MCKELVEY, The Rt Rev Jack Marston (Roch) 8 Grove St, Rochester NY 14605 **Trst Colgate Rochester Crozer DS 2010-; Trst Colgate Rochester Crozer DS 1999-** B Wilmington DE 1941 s George & Dorothy. BA U of Delaware 1963; MDiv VTS 1966; VTS 1992. D 9/17/1966 Bp John Brooke Mosley P 5/13/1967 Bp Richard Henry Baker Con 4/20/1991 for Nwk. m 8/29/1964 Linda B Mc Kelvey c 4. PBp's Coun of Advice, Pres of Prov HOB 2000-2006; Pres of Prov Prov II 2000-2006; Bp of Rochester Dio Rochester Henrietta 1999-2008; Bd Mem Epis Sr Life Com 1999-2008; Trst Hobart & Wm Smith 1999-2008; Com on Pstrl Dvlpmt HOB 1993-2011; Bp Suffr of Newark Dio Newark Newark NJ 1991-1999; R S Paul's Ch Englewood NJ 1979-1991; Vic H Trin (Old Swedes) Wilmington DE 1970-1979; Vic Trin Par Wilmington DE 1970-1979; Par & Dioc Consult 1968-1988; Vic S Jn the Bapt Milton DE 1966-1970; Int S Martin's Com HOB. Auth, "Cir Dancing w God - A Tool for Congrl Dvlpmt," 2007; Auth, "Old Swedes Ch-A Photographic Tour," 1974; Auth, "Adult Educ Curric on Teachable Moments"; Auth/Ed, "Inter-Met: Bold Experiment in Theol Educ," Alb Inst. Sigma Phi Epsilon Citation Sigma Phi Epsilon Fraternity 2010; DD VirginiaTheological Semmary 1992.

MCKENNA, Cynthia Ann (Okla) P.O. Box 187, Boerne TX 78006 **Ther Counslg Boerne TX 2005-** B Roswell NM 1961 d Boyd & Erminia. U of New Mex 1982; BS Texas Tech U 1986; MEd Texas Tech U 1989; MDiv Epis TS of the SW 1996; MA S Marys U 2003. D 8/26/1996 Bp Sam Byron Hulsey P 3/2/1997 Bp Robert Manning Moody. m 10/14/2014 Melanie Fain. Ther Alamo Rape Crisis Cntr San Antonio TX 2003-2006; Chapl All SS Chap Tulsa OK 1998-2002; Holland Hall Sch Tulsa OK 1998-2002; Assoc S Dunst's Ch Tulsa OK 1996-1998.

MCKENNA, Keith (NY) 429 Lakeshore Drive, Putnam Valley NY 10579 B Poughkeepsie NY 1934 s Jefferson & Rae. BA Pace U 1956; MS Pace U 1983; Marymount Manhattan Coll 1997; NYTS 1999. D 5/15/1999 Bp Richard Frank Grein. m 9/18/1959 Ann Therese McKenna c 2. D S Aug's Epis Ch Croton Hdsn NY 2007-2013; D S Ptr's Epis Ch Peekskill NY 2002-2007; D All SS Ch Harrison NY 2000-2001; D S Mary's Ch Mohegan Lake NY 1999-2000. Amer Fed of Teachers 1967.

MCKENNEY, Mary Lou R (ECR) **Strategic Plnng Com Dio El Camino Real Monterey CA 2012-; Fin Com Dio El Camino Real Salinas CA 2002-** B 1949 MDiv Vancouver TS CA 1999. Trans 12/1/2002 Bp Richard Lester Shimpfky. m 10/26/1986 John A McKenney. R All SS Epis Ch Watsonville CA 2002-2010; Vic St. Mary's Epis Ch- Tegucigalpa Honduras 2000-2001; D St. Helen's Angl Ch- Vancouver B.C. Can 1998-1999.

MCKENNEY, Walter (Ct) 38 Clover Dr, West Hartford CT 06110 B Albany GA 1934 s Elijah & Jennie. Cert Hartford Sem 1982; Capital Cmnty Coll 1996. D 10/23/1999 Bp Clarence Nicholas Coleridge. m 5/12/1962 Ida Anita Turner. NAAD.

MCKENZIE, Bryan Keith (FtW) 2117 Ruea St, Grand Prairie TX 75050 **Vic S Jos 1987-** B Gastonia NC 1957 s Thomas & Francis. BA Baylor U 1981; MDiv SWTS 1986. D 7/12/1986 P 8/1/1987 Bp Clarence Cullam Pope Jr. Dio Ft Worth Ft Worth TX 1986-1990. Soc H Trin.

MCKENZIE, Jennifer Gaines (Va) Christ Church, 118 N Washington St, Alexandria VA 22314 B Escambia County FL 1963 d Robert & Doris. BA Auburn U 1988; Cert Bloy Hse 1993; MDiv VTS 2004. D 6/26/2004 Bp Peter J Lee P 1/6/2005 Bp Charles Lovett Keyser. m 3/26/1988 Kenneth Alan McKenzie c 3. Vic The Ch Of The Epiph Oak Hill VA 2013; Vic Dio Virginia Richmond VA 2012; Ch Of The Gd Shpd Burke VA 2010-2011; Assoc R Chr Ch Alexandria VA 2007-2009; Asst R S Dav's Par Washington DC 2004-2007. "Benedictine Sprtlty In The Par," *Congregations*, Alb Inst, 2004.

MCKENZIE JR, William Bruce (Ore) 1873 Sw High St, Portland OR 97201 **Ret 1999-** B Bellingham WA 1931 s William & Mary. BA Seattle Pacific U 1957; BA S Edwards Coll Seattle WA 1959; MDiv S Thos Sem Seattle 1963; MA U of San Francisco 1973; PhD Stan 1979. Rec 8/1/1973 as Priest Bp James Walmsley Frederic Carman. m 8/10/1969 Darlene A McKenzie c 3. S Barth's Ch Beaverton OR 1982-1998; Vic Ch Of The Resurr Eugene OR 1978-1982; Dio Oregon Portland OR 1976-1979; Asst Trin Epis Cathd Portland OR 1973-1976; Serv RC Ch 1963-1973.

MCKENZIE-HAYWARD, Renee (Pa) 34 East Hodges Ave, Philadelphia PA 19121 **Dio Pennsylvania Philadelphia PA 2011-; Vic to the Advoc and Chapl to Temple Univ. Geo W So Ch of Advoc Philadelphia PA 2011-** B Chester PA 1955 d Grover & Sara. BS U of Pennsylvania 1976; MDiv Estrn Bapt TS 1992; MA Tem 1995; DAS GTS 2001; PhD Tem 2005. D 6/2/2001 P 12/8/2001 Bp David Bruce Joslin. m 3/16/1985 Isaac Hayward c 2. R Calv St Aug Epis Ch Philadelphia PA 2003-2011; Assoc Gr Ch In Haddonfield Haddonfield NJ 2001-2003. Auth, "Being the Advoc," *Angl and Epis Hist Journ,*

2015; "A Womanist Soc Ontology," Dissertation Tem, 2005; "A Womanist Experience Of God". revrenee@churchoftheadvocate.org

MCKEON, Julia McKay (Cal) 1590 Cabrillo Hwy S, Half Moon Bay CA 94019 B 1952 d Neil & Olive. BA NWU 1974; MM NWU 1976; MDiv CDSP 2015; MDiv CDSP 2015. D 6/13/2015 Bp Marc Handley Andrus P 12/5/2015 Bp Chester Lovelle Talton. m 6/5/1982 John J McKeon c 2.

MCKEON JR, Richard R (NY) Church of the Messiah, PO Box 248, Rhinebeck NY 12572 **R Ch Of The Mssh Rhinebeck NY 2010-** B Bronxville NY 1955 s Richard & Shirley. BA Mid 1977; Coll of the Resurr 1984; STM Ya Berk 1985. D 6/8/1985 P 12/14/1985 Bp Horace W B Donegan. Dio New York New York NY 1996-2010; Zion Ch Dobbs Ferry NY 1988-2010; Chapl Andrus Chld's Hm 1987-2010; Cur S Jn's Ch Getty Sq Yonkers NY 1985-1988. SocOLW.

MCKIM, Laurie J. (WTex) Church of the Advent, 104 W Elizabeth St, Brownsville TX 78520 **Asst R Ch Of The Adv Brownsville TX 2012-** B Independence MO 1956 d Kim & Barbara. BS U of Missouri 1993; MDiv Epis TS of the SW 2012; MDiv Sem of the SW 2012. D 7/24/2004 Bp Barry Howe P 6/2/2012 Bp Martin Scott Field. c 3. D S Matt's Ch Kansas City MO 2004-2009. rector@adventbrownsville.org

MCKINLEY, Ellen Bacon (Ct) 47 Valley Rd # B1, Cos Cob CT 06807 **Ret 1998-** B Milwaukee WI 1929 d Edward & Lorraine. BA Bryn 1951; MDiv Ya Berk 1976; STM GTS 1979; PhD UTS 1988. D 12/18/1980 P 7/9/1981 Bp Arthur Edward Walmsley. Cathd Chapt All SS Ch Princeton NJ 1992-1997; Int Trin Ch Princeton NJ 1990-1991; Trst Donations & Bequests Dio Connecticut Meriden CT 1988-1991, Com Mar & Human Sxlty 1988-1990, Epis Elctn Com 1986-1987; Asst S Sav's Epis Ch Old Greenwich CT 1982-1990; Cur S Paul's Ch Riverside CT 1981; Dio New Jersey Trenton NJ 1992-1996. EWC.

MCKINLEY, Mele Senitila Tuineau (Ore) 1817 E Alsea Hwy, Waldport OR 97394 B Fonoifua TO 1956 d Viliami & Lesioli. Oregon Cntr for the Diac 1993. D 12/18/1993 Bp Robert Louis Ladehoff. m 6/2/1978 David Leroy McKinley c 2. Auth, "Leipua Of Love".

MCKINNEY, Barbara Jean (Ia) 1435 Park Ave, Des Moines IA 50315 **Died 7/10/2016** B Des Moines IA 1935 d Fred & Emily. BS S Fran Coll Loretto PA; Cert Sprtl Direction; U of Iowa; RN Iowa Luth Hosp Sch Nrsng 1957; Cert Hlth Mnstry 1986; CPE Iowa Luth Hosp Sch Nrsng 1986. D 12/5/1993 Bp Chris Christopher Epting P 11/20/2010 Bp Alan Scarfe. m 8/20/1960 John F McKinney c 4. P The Cathd Ch Of S Paul Des Moines IA 2010-2016, D 1997-2010; D S Lk's Ch Des Moines IA 1993-1996; Min Of Hlth & Par Nurse S Jn Luth 1986-2011; Bd Iowa Interfaith Aids Ntwk 2016. Ord Of S Lk.

MCKINNEY, Catherine R (Va) Varina Episcopal Church, 2385 Mill Rd, Henrico VA 23231 **Varina Epis Ch Henrico VA 2013-** B Memphis TN 1954 d Max & Barbara. BS U of Tennessee 1984; MDiv VTS 2001. D 3/23/2003 P 10/26/2003 Bp Edwin Max Leidel Jr. m 3/21/1976 William Daniel McKinney. Imm Ch Mechanicsvlle VA 2013; Emm Epis Ch Hampton VA 2011-2013; S Barn Epis Ch No Chesterfield VA 2009-2011; S Andr's Ch Norfolk VA 2007-2009; All SS Ch So Hill VA 2006-2007; Geth Ch Proctorsville VT 2005; D All SS Epis Ch Marysville MI 2003-2004; S Andr's Epis Ch Algonac MI 2003-2004.

MCKINNEY, Chantal Bianca (NC) 242 Flintshire Rd., Winston-Salem NC 27104 **Chr Beloved Cmnty Winston Salem NC 2016-** B High Point NC 1977 d Robert & Evelyn. BS Appalachian St U 1998; MDiv VTS 2002; DMin Chicago TS 2009. D 6/22/2002 Bp Michael B Curry P 4/26/2003 Bp James Gary Gloster. m 9/24/2005 Bryson J McKinney c 2. Assoc Dio No Carolina Raleigh NC 2015-2016, Dn of Winston-Salem Convoc 2009-2012; Ch Of The Ascen At Fork Advance NC 2014-2016; Assoc R S Paul's Epis Ch Winston Salem NC 2008-2013; Asst R S Mary's Epis Ch High Point NC 2004-2008; Assoc R S Fran Ch Greensboro NC 2002-2004. chantalbmckinney@gmail.com

MCKINNEY, Douglas Walton (Los) 401 S Detroit St Apt 311, Los Angeles CA 90036 B Portland OR 1948 s John & Doris. CDSP; BA L&C 1970; MDiv SFTS 1973; California Inst of Integral Stds 1989. D 3/2/1981 P 5/21/1982 Bp William Edwin Swing. Int S Jos's Par Buena Pk CA 2008; Ch Of The Ascen Tujunga CA 2006-2007, Int 2003-2004; Int All SS Epis Ch Oxnard CA 2005-2006; S Fran Mssn Norwalk CA 2000-2002; The Epis Ch Of S Jn The Evang San Francisco CA 1991-1993; Int S Cyp's Ch San Francisco CA 1986-1988; S Paul's Epis Ch Walnut Creek CA 1982-1986; Ch Of The Gd Samar San Francisco CA 1981-1982; Cur/D Iglesia Epis Del Buen Samaritano San Francisco CA 1981-1982; Sprtl Dir S Jas Epis Ch San Francisco CA 1989-1999. California Ass'N Of Mar And Fam Therapists 1999; Camaldolese Benedictine Ord 1995.

MCKINNON, Michael John (Mass) 9 Svenson Ave, Worcester MA 01607 B New Haven CT 1968 s James & Ernestine. BA Cntrl Connecticut St U 1991; MDiv Ya Berk 1994; Nash 1997. Trans 10/1/1998 Bp Keith Lynn Ackerman. c 1. Ch Of The H Trin Marlborough MA 2004-2007; S Andr's Ch Peoria IL 1998-2004; Serv Ch Of Can 1995-1998.

MCKINNON, Stanley A (Ark) PO Box 767, Siloam Springs AR 72761 **R Gr Ch Siloam Sprg AR 2008-** B Carrollton MO 1959 s Ronald & Geraldine. BA Texas Tech U 1983; MDiv Asbury TS 1987; STM Ya 1989; STM Ya 1989. D 12/3/2006 Bp Larry Maze P 6/9/2007 Bp Larry Benfield. m 5/15/1983 Laurie B McKinnon c 2. Chaplian Jn Br 1999-2008.

MCKNIGHT, James F (Cal) 801 S Plymouth Ct Unit 817, Chicago IL 60605 **Asstg P Gr Ch Chicago IL 2011-** B Chicago IL 1941 s James & Vivian. BS DePaul U 1964; MDiv CDSP 1999. D 6/5/1999 P 11/20/1999 Bp William Edwin Swing. c 2. Assoc R Chr Epis Ch Los Altos CA 2000-2010; D S Jas Epis Ch San Francisco CA 1999.

MCKNIGHT, Leta Jeannette Zimmer (Vt) 75 South, Box 434, Lyndonville VT 05851 B Utica NY 1930 d Homer & Genieve. Bangor TS. D 6/9/1981 P 2/1/1982 Bp Robert Shaw Kerr. m 9/3/1950 Alfred Forest McKnight. S Ptr's Mssn Lyndonville VT 1985-1995; Caledonia Mnstrl Assn; Lyndon Area Ecum Coun.

MCKONE-SWEET, Mark C. (SanD) 16275 Pomerado Rd, Poway CA 92064 **R S Barth's Epis Ch Poway CA 2014-; Tchr, Chrsnty 101 The Epiph Sch Dorchester MA 2012-; BOD, At-Lg The Prot Chapl Newton-Wellesley Hosp 2012-** B Cambridge MA 1969 s Frank & Elizabeth. BA Wheaton Coll at Norton 1992; MBA NEU Boston MA 2002; MDiv EDS 2007. D 6/2/2007 P 1/12/2008 Bp M(Arvil) Thomas Shaw. m 6/7/2003 Kathleen E Mckone c 2. R S Dunstans Epis Ch Dover MA 2009-2014; Asst R S Paul's Ch Natick MA 2007-2009; Yth Min Par Of S Paul Newton Highlands MA 1997-1999; Dir Of Sales Equal Exch Inc W Bridgewater MA 1992-2004; Cler Assn BOD Co-Pres Dio Massachusetts Boston MA 2010-2012, Stndg Com 2010-, BOD, Mass Epis Cler Assocation 2008-, Cler Assn BOD, At-Lg 2008-. revmark@stbartschurch.org

MCLACHLAN, Devin Shepard (Mass) 38 Beaufort Place, Thompsons Lane, Cambridge CB5 8AG Great Britain (UK) **Fndr Plan Bede Chicago IL 2014-** B Chicago IL 1973 s Donald & Mary. BA Harv 1996; MDiv EDS 2002. D 6/12/2004 Bp M(Arvil) Thomas Shaw P 1/8/2005 Bp Gayle Harris. m 6/10/2006 Iza Riana Hussain. Int Chapl Brent Hse (U Of Chicago) Chicago IL 2014, P Assoc 2011-2014; R Par Of The Mssh Auburndale MA 2007-2011, 2005-2007; S Mk's Cathd Seattle WA 2004; Trst (Secy) EDS Cambridge MA 2007-2014. revmcdev@gmail.com

MCLAIN III, Paul King (WTenn) 102 N 2nd St, Memphis TN 38103 **Calv Ch Memphis TN 2015-** B Jackson MS 1960 s Paul & Marilyn. Bachelor of Bus Admin U of Mississippi 1982; Mstr of Arts in Liberal Arts S Johns Coll Santa Fe NM 2004; Dplma in Angl Stds Ya Berk 2007; Mstr of Div Yale DS 2007. D 6/7/2008 P 12/6/2008 Bp Dean E Wolfe. m 11/9/2002 Ruth L McLain. Sub-Dn and Cn Trin Cathd Little Rock AR 2010-2015, Cn and Assoc P 2010-2012; D Trin Ch Lawr KS 2009-2010, Cur 2008-2010, Transitional D 2008; Chapl Res Wesley Med Cntr Wichita KS 2007-2008; Mem, Com on Resolutns Dio Arkansas Little Rock AR 2015, Chair, Com on Elctns 2013, Mem, Bd Trst 2011-; Mem, COM Dio Kansas Topeka KS 2009-2010. Ya Berk Grad Soc 2007; Soc of Cath Priests of the Epis Ch and the Angl Ch of Can 2011-2012. St. Geo's Coll Awd Ya Berk 2007. pmclain@trinitylittlerock.org

MCLAREN, Beth A (WMich) 230 North Kalamazoo Mall, #402, Kalamazoo MI 49007 B Coatesville PA 1956 d Samuel & Doris. BA Taylor U 1978; MDiv Ya Berk 1983; Epiph Certification Prog 2006. D 6/9/1984 P 2/2/1985 Bp Arthur Edward Walmsley. m 5/20/1978 James Thomas McLaren c 3. S Lk's Par Kalamazoo MI 2007-2010, 2005; S Thos Epis Ch Battle Creek MI 2003; Asst R S Andr's Ch Meriden CT 1991-1995; Int Sr Mssnr Grtr Hartford Reg Mnstry E Hartford CT 1991; R St Jas Epis Ch Hartford CT 1986-1990; Cur S Mk's Ch Mystic CT 1984-1986.

MCLAREN, Christopher Todd (RG) 6730 Green Valley Place NW, Los Ranchos NM 87107 **R S Mk's On The Mesa Epis Ch Albuquerque NM 2011-** B Lynwood CA 1967 s Bruce & Jean. BS Willamette U 1989; MDiv Epis TS of the SW 2000. D 6/10/2000 Bp Robert Louis Ladehoff P 1/26/2001 Bp Charles Edward Jenkins III. m 12/31/1993 Maren McLaren c 3. Assoc R S Mich And All Ang Ch Albuquerque NM 2006-2011; Asst. for Yth Mnstry Dio Louisiana New Orleans LA 2003-2005; R S Geo's Epis Ch New Orleans LA 2000-2006, Assoc R 2000-2004.

MCLAUGHLIN, Debra Kay (SeFla) 1704 Buchanan St, Hollywood FL 33020 B Norman OK 1950 d Otto & Ida. BA U of Texas 1969; Diac Track Dioc Sch of Chr Stds 2009. D 5/31/2014 Bp Leo Frade. c 2. Jas L Duncan Conf Cntr Delray Bch FL 2008-2011.

MCLAUGHLIN, Eleanor L (NH) 38 Nekal Ln, Randolph NH 03593 **Del WCC Meeting on Ord of Wmn 1978-** B Boston MA 1935 d Sidney & Virginia. BA Wellesley Coll 1957; MA Rad 1958; PhD Harv 1968. D 2/2/1980 P 5/8/1971 Bp John Bowen Coburn. m 1/2/2010 Elizabeth Hess c 2. R S Barn Ch Berlin NH 2006-2007; Vic Chr Ch So Barre MA 1996-2001; Dio Wstrn Massachusetts Springfield 1995-2001; Int S Paul's Epis Ch Stockbridge MA 1995-1996; Adj Prof Of Wmn Stds Westfield St Coll 1994-2000; S Ptr's Ch Springfield MA 1994-1995; Gr Ch Amherst MA 1991-1994; Dn of Coll Chap Mt Holyoke So Hadley MA 1989-1991; Int S Paul's Ch Dedham MA 1987-1988, Asst 1986-1987; Asst S Ptr's Epis Ch Cambridge MA 1985-1986; Asst Ch Of S Jn The Evang Boston MA 1981-1983, 1980-1982; Mem Dio The Rio Grande Albuquerque 1979-1989; Mem , Faith & Ord Natl Coun of Ch 1976-1980; Assoc Prof Of Ch Hist Andover Newton TS 1975-1989; Chair, Taskforce Wmn & Rel Natl Orgnztn for Wmn 1973-1974; Assitant Prof Of Hist Wellesley Coll 1964-1974; Chair, Cmsn on Wmn & Mnstry Dio Massachusetts Boston MA 1974-1980. Auth, "Feminist Christologies: Re-Dressing the Tradition," *Recon-*

structing the Chr Symbol, ed. M. Stevens, Paulist Press, 1993; Auth, "Priestly Sprtlty," *ATR:66,1984*, Ascen Press, 1984; Auth, "Anglo-Catholicism And The Wmn Mvmt," *Essays Cath & Radical, eds. Leech,Williams*, London, 1984; Auth, "Wmn Of Sprt"; Auth, "Nashotah Revs"; Auth, "Chr My Mo: Feminine Naming & Metaphor In Medieveal Sprirituality"; Auth, "Priestly Spririotuality". Allnce For Theol Ethics & Ritual (Water) 1985-1993; Boston Ministers Club 1983-1989; Cath Fllshp Of Epis Ch 1982-1990; Cntr For Progressive Chrsnty 2000-2002; The Soc of Cath Priests 2010. Resrch Awd Cmsn On Lay Mnstry, Epis Ch 1975; Kent Fell Soc For Rel In Higher Educ 1958; Phi Beta Kappa Wellesley Coll 1956.

MCLAUGHLIN, John Norris (Mass) 406 Paradise Rd Apt 1b, Swampscott MA 01907 **Ret 1988-** B Bridgewater MA 1924 s Everett & Ellen. BS NEU 1945; BD EDS 1949. D 6/8/1949 P 12/10/1949 Bp Norman B Nash. m 10/1/1949 Louise Phyllis Ray c 3. Vic The Ch Of S Mary Of The Harbor Provincetown MA 1979-1987; R S Paul's Ch Newburyport MA 1970-1978; R S Ptr's Ch Dartmouth MA 1963-1970, P 1959-1962; R Calv Ch Suffield CT 1955-1959; R Trin Epis Ch Weymouth MA 1950-1955; Min In Charge S Jn's Epis Ch Franklin MA 1949-1950. Selected Who's Who Among Students in Amer Universities & Colleges 2045.

MCLAUGHLIN, Marlys Jean (Az) 10926 W Topaz Dr, Sun City AZ 85351 B Anoka MN 1928 d Calvin & Georgena. U So; EFM 1994. D 2/8/1997 Bp Robert Reed Shahan. m 8/15/1946 Jack Dwane. D S Chris's Ch Sun City AZ 1997-2009.

MCLEAN JR, James Rayford (Ark) PO Box 524, Leland MI 49654 B Natchitoches LA 1941 s James & Evelyn. BS Sthrn Arkansas U 1963; Theol Coll Gb 1967; BD Sewanee: The U So, TS 1968; DMin Sewanee: The U So, TS 2008. D 6/18/1968 P 12/1/1968 Bp Robert Raymond Brown. m 5/4/1999 Ellen M McLean c 2. S Paul's Epis Ch Batesville AR 1990-1998; Cn Mssnr Dio Arkansas Little Rock AR 1985-1990, 1972-1976, Com 1947-1974; S Ptr's Ch Conway AR 1985-1990; H Trin Epis Ch Hot Sprg AR 1983-2006; R S Lk's Ch Hot Sprg AR 1976-1985; Asst Chr Epis Ch Charlottesvlle VA 1971-1972; Vic S Andr's Ch Mtn Hm AR 1968-1971.

MCLEAN, Jean Medding (Mont) **S Andr's Ch Basin WY 2004-** B Greensboro NC 1945 D 3/7/2004 Bp Vernon Edward Strickland P 9/14/2004 Bp Bruce Caldwell. m 7/12/1977 Paul Dickens Mclean c 2.

MCLEAN, Katherine Sharp (La) **Trin Ch New Orleans LA 2015-** B New Orleans LA 1958 d Wiley & Maude. BA Tulane 1980; MBA U of Texas at Austin 1985; MDiv Ya Berk 2013. D 4/13/2013 P 1/4/2014 Bp Morris King Thompson Jr. m 11/24/2007 William Speight McLean. Cur S Mich & S Geo S Louis MO 2013-2015.

MCLEAN, Richard (WTex) 3821 Sandia Dr, Plano TX 75023 B Woolsey GA 1935 s Oliver & Ella. BA Merc 1958; MDiv Sthrn Bapt TS 1964; MA Rice U 1986; CTh Epis TS of the SW 1989. D 6/23/1989 Bp Earl Nicholas Mc Arthur Jr P 1/1/1990 Bp John Herbert MacNaughton. m 6/8/1956 Gayle Laverne McLean. S Eliz's Epis Ch Buda TX 1994-1996; The Ch Of The H Sprt Dripping Spgs TX 1994-1996; Vic S Mich's Epis Ch San Antonio TX 1989-1993; Dio W Texas San Antonio TX 1989; Serv Sthrn Bapt Ch 1962-1987.

MCLEAVEY, Lauren (Mass) St Anne's Episcopal Church, PO Box 134, North Billerica MA 01862 **S Anne's Ch No Billerica MA 2016-** B Denvers MA 1980 d James & Linda. BA Syr 2002; MDiv GTS 2013. D 6/1/2013 P 12/7/2013 Bp Lawrence C Provenzano. m 9/7/2013 Frank A Warren. Emm Epis Ch Great River NY 2013-2016; P-in-c S Mk's Ch Islip NY 2013-2016. rector@stannes-billerica.org

MCLELLAN, Brenda Jean (Mont) 350 Janet St Apt 2b Apt 2b, Helena MT 59601 B New Haven CT 1943 d Richard & Edith. BA Carroll Coll 1981; MDiv The Coll of Emm and S Chad CA 1990. D 8/5/1989 P 6/3/1990 Bp Charles I Jones III. c 5. Dioc Coun Dio Montana Helena MT 1996-2008, 1993-1995, COM 1994-2007; S Jn's Ch/Elkhorn Cluster Townsend MT 1990-2010; Chapl Hospice 1990-1997; P-in-c Ch Of The Nativ/Elkhorn Cluster Helena MT 1990-1993. Rugg Prize For Cmnty Relatns 1990; 8th Metropltn of Rupertsland Prize for Liturg Coll of Emm & S Chad 1989; Outstanding Sr Schlr Carroll Coll 1981.

MCLEMORE, Ann Rossington (Miss) 3921 Oakridge Dr, Jackson MS 39216 **S Jas Ch Jackson MS 2014-; Serving Stndg Com 2011-; Serving COM 2009-; Serving Latino Mnstry Com 2009-; Chapl Pinellas Pk Fire Dept 2009-** B St Louis MO 1952 d Donald & Mary. BA Trin U San Antonio 1974; Lic The Angl TS 2000. Trans 1/20/2004 as Priest Bp John Bailey Lipscomb. R S Giles Ch Pinellas Pk FL 2009-2013; Serv Congrl Dvlpmt Com 2008-2012; Dn Dnry Ft Myers FL 2005-2009; Serv Stndg Com 2005-2008; Vic S Jn's Epis Ch St Jas City FL 2004-2009; Serv Angl Ch of Mex 1999-2003; Stndg Com Mem Dio SW Florida Parrish FL 2005-2008. Person of the Year Ft. Myers FL News-Express Nwspr 2005. amclemore@stjjax.org

MCLEMORE, William Pearman (Chi) 5116 W Malibu Ct, McHenry IL 60050 **S Paul's Ch Mchenry IL 2013-; Ret 2001-** B West Point NY 1937 s Ephraim & Edith. BA Florida St U 1962; M.Div. VTS 1965. D 6/22/1965 P 4/1/1966 Bp Edward Hamilton West. m 1/8/2000 Lori Marleen Lowe c 3. R S Steph's Epis Ch Smiths Sta AL 1990-2000; R Dio Alabama Birmingham 1990-1992,

Pres of the Stndg Com 1987, Chair Dept of Par Dvlpmt 1978-1982, Chair Dept of Par Dvlpmt 1978-1982, Pres 1978-1982; R H Trin Epis Ch Auburn AL 1974-1986; R S Paul's Epis Ch Jesup GA 1969-1973; Assoc Chr Epis Ch Pensacola FL 1968-1969; Vic Chr Ch Cedar Key FL 1965-1968; Archv and Hstgr Dio Atlanta Atlanta GA 2002-2009. Auth, "A Gift of Laughter," *Tribute to Rainbow Vill, Atlanta, GA*, The Brack Grp, Tucker, GA, 2007; Auth, "The Ch Year in Cartoons," St Steph's, Phenix City, AL, 1989; Auth, "Cartoons by Bill McLemore," H Trin, Auburn, AL, 1984; Auth, "An Introdcution to NT Gk," The Auth, 1977. RWF 1966-1986. Best Original Cartoon Natl Nwspr Assn 1971. wmclemore37@gmail.com

MCLEOD, Harrison Marvin (USC) Christ Church, 10 N Church St, Greenville SC 29601 **R Chr Ch Greenville SC 2008-** B 1960 s Henry & Mary. BS U of Alabama 1983; MDiv Epis TS of the SW 1993. D 6/5/1993 P 12/11/1993 Bp Robert Oran Miller. m 8/5/1989 Jennifer B McLeod c 2. R Chr Epis Ch Tyler TX 2002-2008; R Gd Shpd Decatur AL 1997-2002; Asst All SS Epis Ch Birmingham AL 1993-1997.

MCLEOD III, Henry Marvin (Vt) 301 Georgetown Cir, Charleston WV 25314 **Ret 2000-** B Mobile AL 1937 s Henry & Margaret. BA U of Alabama 1959; JD Cumberland Sch of Law 1966; MDiv Sewanee: The U So, TS 1979. D 5/20/1979 P 12/17/1979 Bp Furman Charles Stough. m 11/25/1970 Mary Adelia Rosamond c 5. R S Jas Epis Ch Essex Jct VT 1994-2000; Co-R S Jn's Epis Ch Charleston WV 1983-1993; Co-R S Tim's Epis Ch Athens AL 1979-1983. Juris Doctor, mcl Cumberland Sch of Law 1966. hmmcleod@suddenlink.net

MCLEOD, James Wallace (ECR) 34400A Mission Blvd Apt 1109, Union City CA 94587 **Ret 1996-** B San Francisco CA 1934 s John & Ivy. BA San Francisco St U 1957; MDiv CDSP 1960; DMin VTS 1977; Fell Coll of Preachers 1983; Fell S Georges Coll Jerusalem IL 1983. D 6/26/1960 P 5/27/1961 Bp James Albert Pike. m 6/25/1960 Frankie McLeod c 4. Int S Fran Epis Ch San Jose CA 1999-2000; R All SS Epis Ch Palo Alto CA 1996-2010, R 1970-1993; Cn to Ordnry Dio El Camino Real Salinas CA 1993-1996, 1980-1992; CDSP Berkeley CA 1989-1992; Vic S Tim's Ch Danville CA 1967-1970; Assoc Trin Par Menlo Pk CA 1966-1967, 1960-1963; Vic S Clem's Ch Rancho Cordova CA 1963-1966. Auth, *A P Looks at the Diac*, 1983.

✠ MCLEOD, The Rt Rev Mary Adelia Rosamond (Vt) 301 Georgetown Cir, Charleston WV 25314 B Birmingham AL 1938 d Edward & Mary. LTh Sewanee: The U So, TS 1980. D 6/11/1980 P 12/1/1980 Bp Furman Charles Stough Con 11/1/1993 for Vt. m 11/25/1970 Henry Marvin Mcleod c 5. Ret Bp of Vermont Dio Vermont Burlington VT 2001-2005, Bp of Vermont 1993-2000; Secy HOB 1998-2001; Pstr Dvlpmt 1994-2001; Natl Cn Com GC 1988-1994; Archd So Reg Dio W Virginia Charleston WV 1988-1991; R S Jn's Epis Ch Charleston WV 1983-1993; R S Tim's Epis Ch Athens AL 1980-1983. Contrib, "A Voice Of Our Own," 1996. DD U of Charleston 1996; DD EDS 1994; LHD Smith 1994.

MCLEOD, Robert Boutell (CFla) 6661 N Placita Alta Reposa, Tucson AZ 85750 B Oxnard,CA 1954 s John & Suzette. BA Pitzer Coll 1976; MA NWU 1978; MDiv VTS 1986. D 6/11/1986 Bp Peter J Lee P 5/3/1987 Bp Christopher FitzSimons Allison. m 12/23/1980 Nancy S McLeod c 5. R Chr The King Epis Ch Orlando FL 1996-2001; Asst S Alb's Epis Ch Wickenburg AZ 1993-1996; R Par Ch Of S Chas The Mtyr Ft Morgan CO 1989-1992; Chr the King Pawleys Island SC 1987-1988; D S Mart's Ch Doswell VA 1986-1987; The Fork Ch Doswell VA 1986-1987. Auth, "Everything You Know is Wrong: The Case for a New Reformation," Fenestra Books, 2005.

MCLEOD, Sandra Kirby (CGC) St Agath's Church, 150 Circle Dr, DeFuniak Springs FL 32435 **S Agatha's Epis Ch Defuniak Spgs FL 2012-** B Decatur AL 1947 d Grady & Mildred. BA Calhoun Coll Athens Coll 1974; MS Florence U 1976; PhD U of Alabama 1981; MDiv GTS 2012; MDiv The GTS 2012. D 12/21/2011 P 6/23/2012 Bp Philip Menzie Duncan II. m 9/19/1980 Thomas Alex McLeod c 3. sandrakm47@aol.com

MCLEOD, Timothy Reeves (NC) PO Box 1336, Burlington NC 27216 **Ch Of The H Comf Burlington NC 2015-** B Richmond VA 1986 s Robert & Nancy. BA Indiana U 2010; MDiv Duke DS 2015. D 2/20/2016 Bp Anne Hodges-Copple P 9/10/2016 Bp Peter J Lee. m 8/21/2009 Caitlin Montgomery Mcleod.

MCLEON IV, Richard (WTex) PO Box 698, Henderson TX 75653 **Asstg P S Jn's Epis Ch Carthage TX 2013-; Supply P Dio W Texas San Antonio TX 2012-, Mssnr, Estrn Convoc Partnr in Mnstry 2009-2012** B Dallas TX 1962 s Richard & Sandra. BS Texas A&M U 1985; MBA Sul Ross St U 1998; Cert Iona Sch for Mnstry 2010. D 6/2/2010 Bp David Mitchell Reed P 12/12/2010 Bp Gary Richard Lillibridge. m 12/10/1988 Patricia H McLeon c 2. Mssnr Partnr In Mnstry Estrn Convoc Kenedy TX 2010-2012. Bp Elliot Soc 2013. richard@rcelectric.org

✠ MCLOUGHLIN, The Rt Rev Jose Antonio (WNC) 924 N Robinson Ave, Oklahoma City OK 73102 **Bp Dio Wstrn No Carolina Asheville NC 2016-** B San Juan PUERTO RICO 1969 s William & Caridad. BA U of Cntrl Florida 1993; MDiv VTS 2005. D 6/18/2005 P 12/18/2005 Bp Peter J Lee Con 10/1/2016 for WNC. m 6/26/1993 Laurel L Mcloughlin c 2. Cn to the Ordnry Dio Oklahoma Oklahoma City OK 2008-2016; Assoc R/Sch Chapl S Steph's Ch Coconut

M

Grove Miami FL 2006-2008; Asst R Chr Epis Ch Winchester VA 2005-2006. bishopjose@diocesewnc.org

MCLUEN, Roy Emery (CGC) 25450 144th Place SE, Kent WA 98042 B Oakland CA 1945 s Ramon & Mildred. BS Iowa St U 1968; MA U of Iowa 1971; DMA U of Iowa 1973; MDiv Sewanee: The U So, TS 1988. D 5/1/1990 P 2/1/1991 Bp Chris Christopher Epting. m 5/18/1968 Kathy Lyn Mcluen c 3. R S Andr's Epis Ch Panama City FL 2002-2010; R S Anselm Epis Ch Lehigh Acres FL 1997-2002; Vic S Mk's Ch Maquoketa IA 1991-1997; D S Tim's Epis Ch W Des Moines IA 1990-1991. Auth, "Var Mus arts". Ord Of S Lk.

MCMAHAN, Larry Wayne (CGC) 3902 E Jamie Ln, Bloomington IN 47401 B Lafayette IN 1947 s Donald & Violet. BA DePauw U 1969; MDiv Yale DS 1972; CPE Emory U 1990. D 7/1/1972 Bp John P Craine P 1/25/1973 Bp William Hopkins Folwell. Int S Jn's Ch Monroeville AL 2007-2008; S Mich's Ch Ozark AL 2006; Int S Simon's On The Sound Ft Walton Bch FL 2003-2004; R S Lk's Ch Marianna FL 2002-2003; Dio Cntrl Gulf Coast Pensacola FL 1994-2004, Cmsn On Sprtl Growth 1994-2000; R S Matt's Ch Mobile AL 1993-2001; Assoc R S Mich And All Ang Ch Stone Mtn GA 1984-1988; Chapl S Richard's Epis Sch IN 1979-1980; R S Mk's Ch Plainfield IN 1978-1983; P-in-c S Mary's Epis Ch Martinsville IN 1978-1982; Non-par 1976-1978; P-in-c Gr Epis Ch Menominee MI 1975-1976; Chapl S Edw's Prep Sch Vero Bch FL 1973-1975; Cur Trin Ch Vero Bch FL 1972-1975; Cmsn On Evang & Renwl Dio Indianapolis Indianapolis IN 1979-1984; Cmsn On Yth Dio Cntrl Florida Orlando FL 1973-1975. "Lyrics to Choir Anthem," *O Epiph Star*, St. Jas Mus Pub., 2003; "Severla Poems in Anthology," *Carry Onward*, self-Pub, 1998.

MCMANIS, Dennis Ray (SwFla) 12606 Rockrose Glen, Lakewood Ranch FL 34202 B Salina KS 1949 s Ray & Erma. D 1/18/2002 Bp John Bailey Lipscomb. m 7/3/1969 Linda E McManis c 2. Archd Dio SW Florida Parrish FL 2008-2016, Archd 2004-2005; Dir Off of Disaster Response Dio Louisiana New Orleans LA 2006-2017; D Calv Ch Indn Rk Bc FL 2002-2005. dmcmanis@episcopalswfl.org

MCMANUS, Bridget (CNY) 531 Cumberland Ave, Syracuse NY 13210 S Jas Ch Pulaski NY 2005- B Syracuse NY 1971 D 12/18/2002 Bp Victor Alfonso Scantlebury P 6/28/2003 Bp Bill Persell. m 8/22/1998 William Hunt c 2. Gr Epis Ch Syracuse NY 2012-2013; All SS Epis Ch Chicago IL 2000-2003. sallyheiligman@cs.com

MCMANUS, Mary Christie (Cal) 215 10th Ave, San Francisco CA 94118 B Saint Louis MO 1948 d Donnell & Patricia. BA U CA 1970; BEd Cntrl Washington U 1976; MBA Estrn Washington U 1985; BA Sch for Deacons 1995. D 12/7/1996 Bp William Edwin Swing. S Jn's Epis Ch Clayton CA 2007-2012; D S Jas Epis Ch San Francisco CA 1996-2000.

MCMANUS, Michael J (Colo) P. O. Box 33022, Palm Beach Gardens FL 33420 Ch Of The Trsfg Evergreen CO 2014- B West Palm Beach FL 1954 s John & Virginia. BA S Vinc De Paul Sem 1977; MDiv S Vinc De Paul Sem 1981; Dip Ang Stud VTS 2009. Rec 12/20/2008 as Deacon Bp Leo Frade. m 7/28/1984 Cathleen W McManus c 2. S Mk's Ch Palm Bch Garden FL 2011-2014; P-in-c S Geo's Epis Ch Riviera Bch FL 2009-2014.

MCMICHAEL JR, Ralph Nelson (Spr) 1210 Locust St, Saint Louis MO 63103 P-in-c S Andr's Epis Ch Edwardsville IL 2014-, Int 2013-2014; Instr S Mary the Vrgn Ch Nashotah WI 1988- B Frankfurt DE 1956 s Ralph & Marinell. CUA; BA Los Angeles Trade Tech Coll 1978; MDiv Nash 1981. D 6/13/1981 P 6/5/1982 Bp Willis Ryan Henton. m 8/2/1986 Susan Jan McMichael c 3. S Andr's Ch Carbondale IL 2013; Int S Mich's Epis Ch O Fallon IL 2011-2012; Cn Dio Missouri S Louis MO 2005-2010; S Mich & S Geo S Louis MO 2001-2005; Nash Nashotah WI 1988-2001; Cur S Mk's Ch Arlington TX 1987-1988; Stff S Tim's Ch Ft Worth TX 1985-1987; Non-par 1982-1985; Ch Of The Ascen Lafayette LA 1981-1982; Dio Wstrn Louisiana Alexandria LA 1981-1982. Auth, "ATR". Naal.

MCMILLAN, Bruce Dodson (Miss) Po Box 596, Holly Springs MS 38635 P Assoc S Ptr's Ch Oxford MS 2010-; Dn of Nthrn Convoc Dio MS 2008-; R Chr Ch Holly Sprg MS 1995-; Mem of the Stndg Com Dio Mississippi Jackson MS 2012-, Dn - Nthrn Convoc 2008-, 1998-2007, Stndg Com, Exec Com, Fin Com 1995- B Jackson MS 1954 s William & Kathleen. BA U So 1976; MDiv Epis TS of the SW 1988. D 6/4/1988 P 5/20/1989 Bp Alex Dockery Dickson. Vic Calv Ch Michigan City MS 1997-2000; Assoc R Ch Of The H Comm Memphis TN 1992-1995; Sewanee U So TS Sewanee TN 1990-1996; Gr Epis Ch Paris TN 1988-1992, D-In-Trng 1988-1989; Cur Dio W Tennessee Memphis 1988, Fin Coun, Exec Com 1994-1995. CBS 1987.

MCMILLAN, John Nixon (Alb) 4531 Ethel St, Okemos MI 48864 S Paul's Epis Ch Albany NY 2009- B Sault Ste. Marie Ontario Canada 1948 s Hugh & Mary. BA Wilfrid Laurier U 1985; MA U of Iowa 1991; PhD U of Iowa 1997; MDiv Yale DS 2004. D 12/20/2003 P 6/26/2004 Bp Wendell Nathaniel Gibbs Jr. m 6/19/1976 Barbara A McMillan. Trin Epis Ch Grand Ledge MI 2008-2009; Gr Ch Grand Rapids MI 2006-2007; All SS Epis Ch Pontiac MI 2004-2006; All SS Ch E Lansing MI 1994-2002.

MCMILLEN II, Chuck (WTenn) St James Episcopal Church, PO Box 838, Union City TN 38281 S Jas Epis Ch Un City TN 2013-; Ch Hm Bd Dio W Tennessee Memphis 2013-, Cler Dep to 78th GC 2013-, Bp & Counsel 2012-

B Oakland CA 1961 s Michael & Eleanor. BA Memphis St U 1994; MDiv VTS 2012. D 6/2/2012 P 12/8/2012 Bp Don Edward Johnson. m 9/25/1994 Jeanne Gillia Myrick c 1.

MCMILLIN, Andrea McMillin (NCal) 1600 Knox Ave, Bellingham WA 98225 Cn The Epis Dio Nthrn California Sacramento CA 2014- B Little Rock AR 1966 d At & D Stoddard. BA Hendrix Coll 1989; MDiv Ya Berk 1994. D 11/16/1996 P 5/24/1997 Bp Larry Maze. m 6/12/1994 John Scott Stockburger c 2. Chr Epis Ch Blaine WA 2009-2014; Dio Olympia Seattle 2008-2012; Asst St. Paul's Epis Ch 2004-2005; S Thos Ch Springdale AR 1998-1999; Trin Cathd Little Rock AR 1996-1998.

MCMULLEN, Andrew L (Haw) Saint Matthias Episcopal Church, 18320 Furrow Rd, Monument CO 80132 St Michaels & All Ang Ch 2016- B Kansas City MO 1964 s Larry & Marilyn. BA U CO 1986; JD U of Missouri 1990; MDiv Epis TS of the SW 2006. D 6/3/2006 Bp Barry Howe P 12/21/2006 Bp William Jones Skilton. m 10/12/2012 Renate M Mcmullen c 8. S Mths Epis Ch Monument CO 2013-2016; S Ptr's Ch Honolulu HI 2011-2012; Dio Colorado Denver CO 2010-2011; R Ch Of The Ascen Pueblo CO 2009-2011; Assoc R Trin By The Cove Naples FL 2006-2009.

MCMURREN, Jay Junior (Ore) 578 23rd St Ne, Salem OR 97301 Ret 1998- B Portland OR 1928 s Jess & Eva. BBA U of Oregon 1952; BD VTS 1968. D 6/26/1968 P 1/6/1969 Bp James Walmsley Frederic Carman. m 9/22/1984 Margaret H McMurren c 2. Assoc S Paul's Epis Ch Salem OR 1993-1997; Stwdshp Cmsn Dio Oregon Portland OR 1980-1989, Stndg Com 1982-1985; R Gr Memi Portland OR 1973-1993; Chapl U Or-Eugene 1970-1973; Vic S Matt's Epis Ch Eugene OR 1968-1973.

MCMURREN, Margaret H (Ore) 1525 Glen Creek Rd Nw, Salem OR 97304 Vic The Epis Ch Of The Prince of Peace Salem OR 1993- B Portland OR 1947 d William & Jean. BA Geo Mason U 1974; CDSP 1978. D 12/29/1992 P 6/29/1993 Bp Robert Louis Ladehoff. m 9/22/1984 Jay Junior McMurren c 3.

MCMURTRY, Herbert Charles (Ak) 1915 Lindsay Loop, Mount Vernon WA 98274 Ret 1994- B Guysborough NS CA 1931 s Percy & Mary. BA Un Coll Barbourville KY 1954; MDiv CDSP 1957; MA Reed Coll 1971; DMin Jesuit TS 1982. D 6/24/1957 Bp Stephen F Bayne Jr P 6/24/1958 Bp Frank A Rhea. m 8/23/1998 Nichola C McMurtry c 2. R The Ch Of The H Trin Juneau AK 1992-1994; S Jas The Fisherman Kodiak AK 1986-1992; Exec Coun Appointees New York NY 1986-1987, 1984-1986; S Mary's Ch Anchorage AK 1985-1994; P-in-c The Epis Ch of S Jn the Div Tamuning GU 1983-1986; Dio Micronesia Tumon Bay GU 1983; R S Jn The Evang Ch Portland OR 1978-1983; P-in-c H Cross Epis Ch Boring OR 1976-1978; Asst Chr Ch Par Lake Oswego OR 1972-1976; Asst All SS Ch Portland OR 1968-1972; 1966-1968; Asst Emm Epis Ch Mercer Island WA 1964-1966; Ch Of The Resurr Bellevue WA 1960-1964; Vic S Marg's Epis Ch Bellevue WA 1960-1964; Vic Ch Of The H Sprt Vashon WA 1957-1960; S Lk's Ch Tacoma WA 1957-1960.

MCNAB, Charles Bruce (Colo) 2 Park Plaza Rd, Bozeman MT 59715 B Texarkana AR 1945 s Charles & Audrey. BA Austin Coll 1967; MA (ABD) Pr 1969; MDiv GTS 1972. D 4/10/1972 Bp Theodore H McCrea P 11/11/1972 Bp Stephen F Bayne Jr. m 6/14/1992 Joan T Tempel c 4. R Chr Epis Ch Aspen CO 2004-2011; R S Jn's Epis Ch Midland MI 1997-2003; R Chr Epis Ch Denver CO 1985-1994; R S Andr's Epis Ch Panama City FL 1977-1985; Cur S Paul's Epis Ch Lakewood CO 1974-1977; Hon. Cur H Trin Ch Winchmore Hill London 1973-1974; P Assoc All SS Ch Princeton NJ 1972-1973; Asst in Instrn Pr Princeton NJ 1972-1973; Vic Chr Ch. Bangkok Thailand 1995-1997. Auth, "Believing is Seeing: a Guide for Responding to Jn's Gospel," *Believing is Seeing: a Guide for Responding to Jn's Gospel*, Wipf & Stock, 2016; Auth, "Finding the Way: Restarting Your Journey w Jesus," *Finding the Way: Restarting Your Journey w Jesus*, Wipf & Stock, 2013; Auth, "Let Your Light Shine," *Let Your Light Shine*, Xlibris, 2010; Auth, "Obligations of the Ch in Engl Soc: Mltry Arrays of the Cler, 1369-1418," *Ord and Innovation in the Middle Ages*, Pr Press, 1976; Co-Ed, "Ord and Innovation in the Middle Ages," *Ord and Innovation in the Middle Ages*, Pr Press, 1976. Fell ECF 1973; Fell Woodrow Wilson Natl Fllshp Fndt 1967.

MCNAB, Joan T (Colo) 536 W North St, Aspen CO 81611 B Lincoln NE 1935 d William & Ruth. BA OH SU 1957; MDiv Iliff TS 1991. D 12/15/1991 Bp William Harvey Wolfrum. m 6/14/1992 Charles Bruce McNab c 3. Chr Epis Ch Aspen CO 2004-2013; D S Jn's Epis Ch Midland MI 1997-2000; D Serv Chr Ch Bangkok Thailand 1995-1997; Pstr Care Assoc Chr Epis Ch Denver CO 1991-1994. NAAD.

MCNABB, Christopher W (NJ) The GTS New York NY 2016- D 5/19/2017 Bp William H Stokes.

MCNAIR, David Miller (WNC) The Episcopal Church of the Holy Spirit, PO Box 956, Mars Hill NC 28754 R Epis Ch Of The H Sprt Mars Hill NC 2010- B Portsmouth VA 1965 s Donald & Joyce. BA Wake Forest U 1988; MDiv Sthrn Bapt TS 1993; Cert Ang Stud Sewanee: The U So, TS 2008; Cert Ang Stud U So TS 2008. D 6/8/2008 P 12/14/2008 Bp Porter Taylor. m 10/5/1996 Cynthia Lynn Michie c 2. S Jas Ch Black Mtn NC 2008-2010, 1996-2008; Dio Wstrn No Carolina Asheville NC 1996-2007.

MCNAIR, Kent Stevens (NCal) 2200 Country Club Dr., Cameron Park CA 95682 B Los Angeles CA 1949 s Edward & Ann. BA Tem 1979; MDiv Reformed Epis Sem 1980; ThM PrTS 1981; DMin Fuller TS 1996. D 9/29/1981 Bp Edward McNair P 4/19/1982 Bp John Lester Thompson III. c 2. R Faith Epis Ch Carmeron Pk CA 1992-2012; Archd The Epis Dio Nthrn California Sacramento CA 1987-1992; Cn Trin Epis Cathd Sacramento CA 1984-1987, Cur 1981-1984.

MCNAIRY, Philip Edward (Minn) 2287 Bevans Cir, Red Wing MN 55066 B Cincinnati OH 1937 s Philip & Cary. BS Trin Hartford CT 1960; MDiv VTS 1970. D 6/29/1970 Bp Hamilton Hyde Kellogg P 2/14/1971 Bp Philip Frederick McNairy. m 12/14/1976 Mary L McNairy c 3. R Chr Ch Red Wing MN 1995-2003; Dio Olympia Seattle 1990-1993, Stndg Com 1991-1993; R S Steph's Epis Ch Longview WA 1988-1993; R Gr Epis Ch Sandusky OH 1984-1988; R Trin Ch Allnce OH 1979-1984; R Ch Of The Gd Shpd Athens OH 1973-1978; Asst S Matt's Ch Bedford NY 1970-1973; Dioc Coun Dio Minnesota Minneapolis MN 1997-2003; Dioc Coun Dio Ohio Cleveland 1982-1988. Paul Harris Fell Rotary Club 2002.

MCNALLY, Jennifer Steckel (Minn) 2035 Charlton Rd, Sunfish Lake MN 55118 **S Anne's Epis Ch S Paul MN 2016-** B Milwaukee WI 1970 d William & Gail. BA U of Wisconsin 1992; JD Willamette U 1996; MDiv Untd TS 2006. D 6/20/2015 P 6/21/2016 Bp Brian N Prior. m 8/2/1997 William Branden McNally c 3.

MCNAMARA, Beth Cooper (Md) 8015 Rider Ave, Towson MD 21204 **Stff Assoc Epis Socail Ministers 1986-** B Washington DC 1949 d Wesley & Helen. BA Ohio Wesl 1971; MLa JHU 1974; MDiv VTS 1986. D 6/7/1986 P 4/1/1987 Bp Albert Theodore Eastman. m 6/10/1970 David King McNamara c 1. S Paul's Epis Par Pt Of Rocks MD 1990-1993; Asst Ch Of The Resurr Baltimore MD 1987-1990; Dioc Refugee Coordntr 1986-1988; Asst S Jas' Epis Ch Parkton MD 1986-1987.

MCNAMARA, Joseph Francis (CPa) Po Box 474, Mansfield PA 16933 **Asst Nthrn Tier Cluster Par In Mansfield 1985-** B Baltimore MD 1946 s Frank & Mary. BA Kings Coll Wilkes-Barre PA 1973; MA Maywood Coll 1975; PhD Un Grad Sch 1979; MDiv VTS 1984. D 6/8/1984 P 5/1/1985 Bp Charlie Fuller Mcnutt Jr. m 4/1/1978 Ann McNamara c 1. Visitin P S Jn's Ch Westfield PA 2001; S Andr's Ch Tioga PA 1991-2011; S Jas Ch Mansfield PA 1985-1990. Amer Acadamy Of Forensic Examiners 1997; Amer Bd Psychol Specialties, Diplomate 1997; APA 1980; Pennsylvania Psychol Assn 2001. Distinguished Tchg Awd (Tchr Of The Year) Pa Coll Of Tech At Penn St 1991.

MCNAMARA, Kim (Oly) PO Box 156, Allyn WA 98524 B New Rochelle NY 1954 d James & Lynne. MA Antioch U - Seattle 1995; PhD Antioch U 2008. D 4/10/2015 P 10/13/2015 Bp Gregory Harold Rickel. m 7/20/1974 John F McNamara c 2.

MCNAMARA, Patrick (NH) Holy Trinity, 768 Main St, Greenport NY 11944 **Ch Of The H Trin Greenport NY 2013-** B Clinton MA 1947 s Joseph & Josephine. BA La Salette Missionaries 1976; MDiv Washington Theol Un 1979. Rec 7/9/2013 Bp A Robert Hirschfeld. P-in-c Ch Of The Redeem Mattituck NY 2014-2015, 2013-2014.

MCNAUGHTON, Bonnie Eleanor (Los) 2571 Via Campesina Unit G, Palos Verdes Estates CA 90274 **D Chr Ch Par Redondo Bch CA 2012-** B Minneapolis MN 1942 d Thomas & Gardys. Cert Dio No Dakota Diac Trng Prog 2007; Cert Other 2007. D 6/22/2007 Bp Michael Smith. c 2. D S Thos Ch Ft Totten ND 2007-2012.

MCNAUGHTON, Margaret (WA) 720 Upland Pl, Alexandria VA 22314 B Detroit MI d J & C. Colorado St U 1974; BS MI SU 1976; MDiv VTS 1982; Andover Newton TS 1986; DMin Wesley TS 1999. D 6/20/1982 Bp H Coleman Mcgehee Jr P 6/10/1983 Bp Morgan Porteus. Assoc Dn For Cmnty Life, Ethnic Mnstrs and Admssns VTS Alexandria VA 1995-2009; Assoc R S Alb's Par Washington DC 1986-1995; Assoc R S Mk's Ch Foxborough MA 1982-1985. Auth, "A View From The Other Side: Life In Cmnty For Spouses Of Seminarians," *DMin Thesis*. Alb Inst Resrch Fell.

MCNAUL, Robert Guthrie (Nev) 1909 Camino Mirada, North Las Vegas NV 89031 **Chairman Epis Recovery Mnstrs Las Vegas NV 2010-; Ret 1991-; Ret 1991-** B Denver CO 1942 s James & Sara. BA U Denv 1965; MDiv CDSP 1968; Moore Theol Coll Sydney Australia 1971; Seattle U 1982. D 7/25/1968 Bp Joseph Summerville Minnis P 2/1/1969 Bp Edwin B Thayer. m 12/28/2002 Nancy McNaul c 1. S Phil Amarillo TX 1988-1991; Vic S Phil Amarillo TX 1988-1991; Int All SS Ch Tacoma WA 1986-1988; Asst Emm Epis Ch Mercer Island WA 1984-1985; Asst S Eliz's Ch Seattle WA 1983-1984; Asst S Jn's Ch Kirkland WA 1982-1983; Int S Paul's Epis Ch Mt Vernon WA 1981-1982; R Ch Of Our Sav Pasco WA 1972-1980; Serv Ch of Australia 1970-1972; Cur Epiph Epis Ch Denver CO 1968-1970.

MCNEELEY, David Fielden (Hai) 566 Standish Rd, Teaneck NJ 07666 **Hon Asstg Cler S Thos Ch New York NY 2001-; P Dio Haiti Port-au-Prince HT 1987-, Numerous Com positions 1982-1996** B Knoxville TN 1950 BA U So 1972; MPHTM Tul 1978; MD Tul 1978; Cert GTS 1987; S Pauls Sem Haiti 1987. D 6/12/1988 P 12/14/1988 Bp Luc Anatole Jacques Garnier. m 12/13/1985 Marise Bayard c 3. Mssy Exec Coun Appointees New York NY 1999-2004; Mssy Med Mssy PCUSA/ECUSA 1982-1996. Auth, "numerous,"

Over 70 Pub in Profsnl Journ. Numerous Profsnl Med societies; Soc of S Marg 1974. DD (Hon) U So TS 1996; Outstanding Alum Tulane Sch of Publ Hlth & Tropical Med 1986.

MCNEELY, Virginia Diane (NCal) Trinity Cathedral, 2620 Capitol Ave, Sacramento CA 95816 **D All SS Memi Sacramento CA 2013-** B Melrose Park IL 1944 d John & Anne. BA Stan 1966; MS California St U E Bay 1972; BTS Sch for Deacons - Berkeley 2012. D 6/9/2012 Bp Barry Leigh Beisner. c 2.

MCNEER, Charles Conrad (SwVa) 490 Court St Apt 6, Abingdon VA 24210 **Pres Standard Bannner Coal Corp 1992-** B Huntington WV 1934 s Henry & Ruth. BA Duke 1956; MDiv VTS 1963; Menninger Clnc 1973; MS U of Kansas 1990. D 6/23/1963 P 5/2/1964 Bp William Henry Marmion. Dir. & Soc Worker Counslg & Consult Serv 1973-2000; Ch Of St Thos Holton KS 1973-1977; Dio Kansas Topeka KS 1973-1977; S Phil's Epis Ch Topeka KS 1973-1977; P-in-c S Thos Holton Topeka KS 1972-2000; Dir Gdnc & Cnslng Sullins Coll Bristol VA 1968-1971; Vic S Mk's Ch S Paul VA 1966-1968; P-in-c S Steph Nora VA 1966-1968; Chapl Abingdon Convoc Colls Bristol VA 1963-1966. NASW 1990.

MCNELLIS, Kathleene Kernan (RG) 6200 Coors NW, Albuquerque NM 87120 B Camden NJ 1944 d William & Caroline. Ball St U 1964; BA U of Texas 1968; Oxf GB 1998. D 8/24/1986 Bp Richard Mitchell Trelease Jr P 5/23/2000 Bp Terence Kelshaw. c 2. Cn Dio The Rio Grande Albuquerque 2011-2014; Vic S Fran On The Hill El Paso TX 2009-2011; P-in-c All SS Epis Ch El Paso TX 2008-2010; S Chris's Epis Ch El Paso TX 2007-2011, D 1988-1991; Vic S Brendan's Ch El Paso TX 2002-2007; P-in-c St Lk's Epis Ch Anth NM 2000-2001; Chapl Pro Cathd Epis Ch Of S Clem El Paso TX 1991-2000.

MCNIEL, Donna (SJ) 4401 4th St N Apt 242, Arlington VA 22203 B Belen NM 1971 BA Austin Coll 1994; MDiv Louisville Presb TS 1999; Cert Ang Stud Sewanee: The U So, TS 2002; Cert Ang Stud Sewanee: The U So, TS 2002; DMin EDS 2008; DMin EDS 2008. D 6/7/2003 P 12/6/2003 Bp Barry Howe. Exec Dir New Mex Conf of Ch Albuquerque NM 2011-2016; U Multifaith Chapl U Pac Stockton CA 2007-2011; Assoc S Thos's Par Newark DE 2004-2007; Vic S Jn's Ch Neosho MO 2004; Chapl Dio W Missouri Kansas City MO 2001-2002.

MCNISH, Jill L (Pa) 199 W Baltimore Ave, Clifton Heights PA 19018 B Kearny NJ 1952 d Howard & Margaret. BA U of Virginia 1973; JD Rutgers The St U of New Jersey 1976; MDiv UTS 1997; PhD UTS 2002. D 5/31/1997 Bp Jack Marston Mckelvey P 12/11/1997 Bp John Shelby Spong. m 10/11/2014 Clare Yellin c 2. R S Steph's Epis Ch Clifton Hgts PA 2011-2015; Int S Steph's Ch Waretown NJ 2009-2010; P-in-c Trin Epis Old Swedes Ch Swedesboro NJ 2007-2008; Int S Mary's Ch Sparta NJ 2004; Int S Greg's Epis Ch Parsippany NJ 2002-2003; Int Gr Ch Un City NJ 2001-2002; S Mk's Ch W Orange NJ 1999-2000; Ch Of The H Trin W Orange NJ 1998; S Lk's Epis Ch Montclair NJ 1997-1998. Auth, "Getting Real About God, Sin, Suffering and Evil," U Press of Amer, 2011; Contrib, "Encyclopedia of Psychol and Rel," Springer, 2011; Auth, Haworth Press, 2004; Auth, "Uses of Theories of Depth psychologyin Ord Mnstry and the Instnl Ch," *Journ of Pstr Care and Counslg*, 2002; Auth, "The Passionate Aggression in Creation and the Human Psyche," *Koinonia Fall*, 2000; Auth, "Viewing the Veil: The Sprtlty of Depression, Voice, September," *p8*, 1999; Auth, "Pstr Care Implications," *Lectionary Homil*. AAR; SBL, Psychol and the Bible Steeri. Hudnut Awd for Preaching UN Sem 1997; ECom Awd.

MCNULTY, Lynne Herrick (Roch) 28 Gillette St, Rochester NY 14619 **D S Steph's Ch Rochester NY 1986-** B Buffalo NY 1948 d Roy & Yvonne. BA Keuka Coll 1970; MA St Bernards Sem Rochester NY 1987. D 6/28/1986 Bp William George Burrill. m 3/11/1972 Brian Joseph McNulty c 2.

✠ MCNUTT JR, The Rt Rev Charlie Fuller (CPa) 5225 Wilson Ln Apt 2137, Mechanicsburg PA 17055 **Ret Bp of Cntrl Pennsylvania Dio Cntrl Pennsylvania Harrisburg PA 1996-, Co-Chair, PA Conf. of Inter-Ch. Coop. 1986-1995, Bp of Cntrl Pennsylvania 1982-1995, Bp Coadj 1980-1985** B Charleston WV 1931 s Charlie & Mary. BA W&L 1953; MDiv VTS 1956; MS Florida St U 1970. D 6/11/1956 P 12/19/1956 Bp Wilburn Camrock Campbell Con 11/8/1980 for CPa. m 3/3/1962 Alice Turnbull McNutt c 3. Chf Operating Off Epis Ch Cntr New York NY 1995-1997; Pres Pennsylvania Coun of Ch 1989-1995; ExCoun ECUSA 1988-1994; Pres APSO 1985-1987; Dio W Virginia 1977-1980; Dio W Virginia 1975-1979; R Trin Epis Ch Martinsburg WV 1974-1980; Dep Gnrl Convetion 1973-1979; Cn, Archd Dio Florida Jacksonville 1972-1974, Dir Consult Plnng 1970-1974, Consult Plnng 1968-1971; R S Lk's Epis Ch Jacksonville FL 1962-1968; Asst S Jn's Epis Ch Tallahassee FL 1960-1962; Chr Memi Ch Williamstown WV 1956-1960; Trin Ch Parkersburg WV 1956-1960; Mem, Bd Trst VTS Alexandria VA 1976-1980. Auth, "Is PPBS Feasible in Epis Dio?," *Thesis for MS Degree in Urban and Reg Plnng,* Florida St U, 1970. Phi Beta Kappa 1953. Doctor of Divnity Lebanon Vlly Coll of Pennsylvania 1996; Doctor of Dvinity VTS 1981.

MCNUTT, Robin Lee (Neb) 3020 Belvedere Blvd, Omaha NE 68111 B Omaha NE 1951 d Robert & Gloria. D 8/15/2004 Bp Joe Goodwin Burnett. c 2.

MCPARTLIN, Julie (Alb) Harbour Island Club #203, 5101 Highway A1a, Vero Beach FL 32963 B New York NY 1948 d Robert & Hester. BA Connecticut Coll 1969; MDiv GTS 1996. D 5/25/1996 P 11/30/1996 Bp David Standish

Ball. m 6/28/1969 Kenneth J McPartlin c 2. P-in-c S Jas' Epis Ch Lake Geo NY 1998-2014, R 1996-1997. revjuls@aol.com

MCPEAK, Helen C (Oly) 415 S 18th St, Mount Vernon WA 98274 **S Paul's Epis Ch Mt Vernon WA 2016-; Assoc Epis Ch of the Epiph 2005-** B Oakland CA 1965 d Ross & Dorothy. BS U CA 1988; MDiv CDSP 1997. D 5/30/1997 P 12/13/1997 Bp Jerry Alban Lamb. m 8/10/1991 Robert A Mcpeak c 2. Komo Kulshan Cluster Mt Vernon WA 2013-2015; Epis Ch of the Epiph Las Vegas NV 2005-2012; Trin Ch Sonoma CA 2002-2004; The Epis Dio Nthrn California Sacramento CA 2002-2003; Asst R S Patricks Ch Kenwood CA 1997-2000.

MCPHAIL, Donald Stewart (SC) 22 Saint Augustine Dr., Charleston SC 29407 B Montreal QC CA 1933 s Melville & Gladys. BA Concordia U 1959; Cr Mirfield Yorks Gb 1961; MDiv GTS 1962. D 4/28/1962 P 12/21/1962 Bp James Pernette DeWolfe. m 4/26/1969 Randall R Mcphail c 3. Exam Chapl Gr Ch Cathd Charleston SC 1992-2005; Assoc S Lk's Epis Ch Hilton Hd Island SC 1991; Dn S Jn's Cathd Denver CO 1981-1991; S Ptr's by-the-Sea Epis Ch Bay Shore NY 1963-1981; Cur The Ch Of The Ascen Rockville Ct NY 1963; So Carolina Charleston SC 1992-2005; Stndg Com Dio Colorado Denver CO 1986-2005. EvangES.

MCPHEE, Gizelle Valencia (SeFla) PO Box 12943, Miami FL 33101 B Miami FL 1959 d George & Gloria. BA Fisk U 1980; MS Tennessee St U 1987. D 5/30/2015 Bp Leo Frade.

MCPHERSON, Clair W (NY) 1234 Midland Ave #5E, Bronxville NY 10708 **Assoc Prof of Ascetical Theol The GTS New York NY 2011-; Prof Fordham Coll Lincoln Cntr 2007-** B (unknown) 1949 s Walter & Bonnie. PhD Washington U 1979; MDiv GTS 1982. D 6/19/1982 Bp Quintin Ebenezer Primo Jr P 12/12/1982 Bp James Winchester Montgomery. m 4/10/1971 Connie McPherson c 3. Ch Of The Trsfg New York NY 2012-2017, Assoc P 2006-2011; Adj Prof NYU 2006-2011; R Trin S Paul's Epis New Rochelle NY 1989-2005; Adj Prof Bexley Seabury Fed Chicago IL 1985-1989; R S Lk's Ch Dixon IL 1984-1989; Asst Cathd Of S Jas Chicago IL 1982-1984. Auth, "Gr at this Time," *Gr at this Time*, Morehouse Pub, 1999; Auth, "Keeping Silence," *Sprtlty & Hist of Anglo-Saxon Engl*, 1998; Auth, "Understanding Faith," *Understanding Faith*, Morehouse Pub, 1997; Auth, "The Sea A Desert," *Amer Benedictine Revs*, 1985. Conf Angl Theol 1985; Medieval Acad Amer 1985; Soc for the Study of Chr Sprtlty 2011.

MCPHERSON, Phebe Lewald (Md) 214 Wardour Dr, Annapolis MD 21401 **Epiph Epis Ch Odenton MD 1988-** B Richmond VA 1950 d James & Ella. BA Goucher Coll 1972; MDiv SWTS 1975; DMin VTS 2006. D 2/13/1977 P 12/3/1977 Bp David Keller Leighton Sr. m 6/21/1997 William Bruce McPherson c 1. Comission on Ch in Sm Communities Epis Ch Cntr New York NY 1988-1994; Dio Maryland Baltimore MD 1987-1988, Dep Gc 1982-1994, 1979, Stndg Com 1997-; Memi Ch Baltimore MD 1979-1987; Assoc S Barth's Ch Baltimore MD 1977-1979. Bp'S Awd Dio Maryland 2006.

MCPHERSON, Thomas Dale (SwFla) 6 Post Pointe Cir, Valdosta GA 31602 B Marshall MI 1941 s Allen & Marion. BS MI SU 1964; MA Cntrl Michigan U 1974. D 5/25/1994 Bp Harry Woolston Shipps. m 6/20/1964 Carolyn McPherson c 2. D Chr Ch S Marys GA 1996-2008.

MCPHERSON, William Bruce (Md) 214 Wardour Drive, Annapolis MD 21401 **1992-** B Cleveland OH 1940 s William & Margaret. BA Trin 1962; MBA Loyola U 1973; MDiv GTS 1991. D 3/10/1992 P 1/1/1993 Bp Albert Theodore Eastman. m 6/21/1997 Phebe Lewald c 3. S Jn's Ch Georgetown Par Washington DC 2011-2012; Gr Epis Ch Silver Sprg MD 2009-2011; Int R S Andr's Epis Ch Coll Pk MD 2008-2009; Int H Trin Epis Ch Bowie MD 2006-2008; Int St. Jn's Epis Ch Ellicott City MD 2005-2006; S Jn's Ch Ellicott City MD 2004-2006; Int Precentor Washington Natl Cathd Washington DC 2004-2005; Cathd of St Ptr & St Paul Washington DC 2004; Int S Steph's Ch Severn Par Crownsville MD 2002-2003; S Ptr's Epis Ch Arlington VA 2001-2002; Ch Of The Gd Shpd Towson MD 1999-2001; All SS Epis Par Sunderland MD 1998-1999.

MCQUADE, **Lynne** (NY) 900 Palmer Rd Apt 7-L, Bronxville NY 10708 B Yonkers NY 1941 d Alan & Margaret. RN S Lukes Hosp Sch of Nrsng 1962; BA Marymount Manhattan Coll 1973; MPH Col Sch of Publ Hlth 1974; MDiv GTS 1982. D 6/5/1982 Bp Paul Moore Jr P 4/10/1983 Bp William Evan Sanders. m 5/11/1991 Joseph T McQuade. Supply S Mk's Epis Ch Yonkers NY 2008-2010; S Jn's Ch So Salem NY 2008; Assoc Par of Chr the Redeem Pelham NY 1997-1999; Assoc S Barth's Ch In The Highland White Plains NY 1995-1997; Assoc S Andr's Epis Ch Hartsdale NY 1991-1995; Cur Chr Ch Bronxville NY 1986-1990; Assoc S Paul's Ch Franklin TN 1983-1986; Chapl S Barn Nrsng Hm Chattanooga TN 1982-1983. Assn Bro of S Greg - Assoc 1996; Cmnty of S Mary - Assoc 1987. Sigma Theta Tau Natl Nrsng hon Soc 1977. revldm@optonline.net

MCQUEEN, **Dale** (Oly) 3230 Chanute Dr., Lake Havasu city AZ 86406 B Seattle WA 1945 s Avery & Dorothy. BS City U of Seattle 1996; MDiv SWTS 1999. D 6/26/1999 Bp Sanford Zangwill Kaye Hampton P 1/8/2000 Bp Bruce Caldwell. m 10/19/1985 Carol Joyce McQueen. R S Andr's Epis Ch Aberdeen WA 2002-2013; R All SS Epis Ch Torrington WY 1999-2002.

MCQUEEN, **Henry P** (WA) St John's Church, 3427 Olney Laytonsville Rd, Olney MD 20832 **S Jn's Ch Olney MD 2016-** B Lancaster PA 1959 s James & Mildred. BBA Stetson U 1982; MBA Drexel U 1984; MDiv VTS 2012. D 4/22/2012 Bp Nathan Dwight Baxter P 12/15/2012 Bp Herman Hollerith IV. m 12/17/1987 Diane H Hertz c 1. Assoc Hickory Neck Ch Toano VA 2012-2016. rector@stjec.org

MCQUEEN II, James Douglas (SanD) All Saints Church, 625 Pennsylvania Ave, San Diego CA 92103 **All SS Ch San Diego CA 2012-** B Peoria IL 1983 s James & Norma. BS Eureka Coll 2006; MDiv Nash 2008. D 12/8/2007 P 6/14/2008 Bp Keith Lynn Ackerman. m 6/3/2010 Sarah L McQueen c 1. R All SS Chap Elkhart Lake WI 2011-2012; Cur Gr Epis Ch Sheboygan WI 2008-2012. jdmcqueenii@gmail.com

MCQUEEN, **Paul** (CFla) 1332 Bramley Ln, Deland FL 32720 B Oakland IL 1945 s Hubert & Glenna. BS Florida St U 1968; MDiv Nash 1981. D 6/21/1981 P 1/17/1982 Bp William Hopkins Folwell. c 3. R Epis Ch Of The Resurr Longwood FL 2009-2017, 2007-2009, 2004-2005; Exec Dir Cbury Retreat And Conf Cntr Oviedo FL 1990-2009; R Gloria Dei Epis Ch Cocoa FL 1982-1990; Asst Trin Ch Vero Bch FL 1981-1982. Episcopl Campus & Conf Centers, Inc. 1990; IACCA 1991.

MCQUERY, **Andrew Michael** (Ore) D 6/10/2017 Bp Michael Hanley.

MCQUIN, Randall Lee (Kan) 3141 Fairview Park Dr Ste 250, Falls Church VA 22042 **Non-par 1988-** B Medicine Lodge KS 1951 s Robert & Beverly. BA U of Kansas 1973; JD U of Kansas 1976; MDiv Yale DS 1979. D 6/16/1979 Bp Edward Clark Turner P 12/1/1979 Bp William Davidson. R S Paul's Ch Manhattan KS 1984-1987; S Lk's Epis Ch Scott City KS 1979-1984.

MCQUITTY, Elizabeth Grace (Los) **St Johns Pro-Cathd Los Angeles CA 2016-** D 6/3/2017 Bp Diane Jardine Bruce.

MCRAE, Marcia O (EC) 511 E Broughton St, Bainbridge GA 39817 **S Fran Ch Goldsboro NC 2016-; P-in-c S Jn's Epis Ch Bainbridge GA 2013-** B San Antonio TX 1948 BA Valdosta St Coll 1970; Sewanee: The U So, TS 2011. D 8/20/2010 P 4/16/2011 Bp Scott Anson Benhase. m 12/19/1970 John Henry McRae c 1. Cur S Thos Epis Ch Thomasville GA 2011-2012.

MCREE, Timothy Patrick (WNC) 274 Sunset Hts, Canton NC 28716 **Cathechumenate Commitee 1996-; Prison Mnstry 1996-; R S Andr's Epis Ch Canton NC 1995-** B Hickory NC 1955 s George & Barbara. AA Caldwell Cmnty Coll and Tech Inst 1977; BS Appalachian St U 1980; MDiv Sewanee: The U So, TS 1992. D 6/6/1992 P 1/1/1993 Bp Don Edward Johnson. m 8/14/1976 Beverly Adams c 2. 1994-1998; Gr Ch Asheville NC 1992-1995; Asst R Gr Ch Asheville NC 1992-1995.

MCSPADDEN, Christine (Cal) **Bd Dir Forw Mvmt of the Epis Ch Cincinnati OH 2008-** B Charlottesville VA 1964 d Frederick & Constance. BA U of Virginia 1986; MDiv Ya Berk 1995. D 6/8/1996 Bp Clarence Nicholas Coleridge P 12/7/1996 Bp Richard Frank Grein. m 8/19/1989 David Ford McSpadden. Trin Epis Ch Santa Barbara CA 2016-2017; Ch Of The Incarn San Francisco CA 2016; Assoc: P Vic St. Paul's Cathd 2014-2015; Assoc The Epis Ch Of S Mary The Vrgn San Francisco CA 2013-2014; Cn for Cathd LIfe Gr Cathd San Francisco CA 2010-2012; P-in-c S Lk's Ch San Francisco CA 2004-2008; Assoc St. Barth Ch New York NY 1996-1999. Contrib, "Soul Proclamations: Singing the Magnificat w Mary," Forw Mvmt, 2015; Contrib, "A Journey w Lk," *50 Day Bible Challenge*, Forw Mvmt, 2015; Contrib, "October daily meditations," *Forw Day by Day*, Forw Mvmt, 2015; Contrib, "Preaching Scripture Faithfully," *Chr Reflections*, Inst for Faith and Lrng, 2014; Auth, "Resurr Living," Forw Mvmt, 2013; Auth, "Observing Lent," Forw Mvmt, 2013; Contrib, "The Art Of Reading Scripture Preaching Scripture Faithfully In A Post-Christiandom Ch," Pub By Eerdmans, 2003. Preaching Excellence Awd Coll of Preachers 1994.

MCSWAIN, **William D** (SC) 7313 Highway 162, Hollywood SC 29449 B Lakeland FL 1946 s William & Carolyn. BA U NC; DMin UTS 1976. D 10/4/1986 Bp William Arthur Beckham P 2/14/1987 Bp Rogers Sanders Harris. m 6/2/1984 Janet M McDuffee c 1. P-in-c Chr Ch Denmark SC 2008-2012; R S Geo's Epis Ch Schenectady NY 1999-2007; S Anna's Ch New Orleans LA 1995-1999; R Intsn Epis Ch Stevens Point WI 1991-1995; Vic Ch Of The Cross Columbia SC 1988-1990; Ch Of The Gd Shpd Columbia SC 1987-1988; D S Martins-In-The-Field Columbia SC 1986-1987. ACPE.

MCTERNAN, Vaughan Durkee (Colo) 2609 Rigel Drive, Colorado Springs CO 80906 B Denver CO 1950 BA Trin 1973; MDiv Ya Berk 1978; MDiv Ya Berk 1978; MDiv Yale DS 1978; PhD Denver U And Iliff TS 1998. D 7/17/2004 P 1/25/2005 Bp Steven Andrew Miller. m 3/26/1977 Kevin J McTernan c 2. Ch Of Our Sav Colorado Sprg CO 2013-2014; Assoc Ch Of The Ascen Pueblo CO 2010-2013; Vstng Asst Prof Colorado Coll 2007-2009; P-in-c S Dav Of The Hills Epis Ch Woodland Pk CO 2006-2010; Vstng Asst Prof Beloit Coll 2001-2005; Vstng Asst Prof Lycoming Coll 1998-2000; Instr Colorado Coll 1992-1997.

MCVEY, Arthur William (Kan) 9218 Cherokee Pl, Leawood KS 66206 **P-in-c S Matt's Ch Kansas City MO 2013-, 2010-2013** B Hamilton ON CA 1942 s James & Margaret. BD S Augustines Scarboro Ontario CA; MA Wilfrid Laurier U. Trans 2/13/1979 Bp Edward Clark Turner. m 4/5/1975 Linda G McVey c 3.

R Calv Epis Ch Sedalia MO 2003-2010. *Value Proposition Marketing*, Woods and Waters, 2000. frbill.stmatt@sbcglobal.net

MCVEY, Brian (Tenn) 4403 High Ct, Davenport IA 52804 **P Ch Of The Adv Nashville TN 2015-; Account Exec Sam Co Fin Serv 2001-** B Charleston, WV 1967 s George & Janis. St Anne/Wycliffe Hall; BA Hampden-Sydney Coll 1990; U of Dallas Inst of Phil Stds 1992; MDiv TESM 2006; MDiv TESM 2006. D 12/17/2005 P 7/1/2006 Bp Alan Scarfe. m 8/11/1991 Karen E Phillips c 7. S Alb's Ch Davenport IA 2006-2014; S Steph's Ch E Liverpool OH 2005-2006.

MCWHORTER, Betty (NY) 1304 NW Meadows Drive, McMinnville OR 97128 B Tampa FL 1949 d Ernest & Elizabeth. BS Auburn U 1970; Candler TS Emory U 1984; MDiv U of St Thos 1987. D 6/6/1987 P 5/16/1988 Bp Charles Judson Child Jr. m 11/27/1970 James B McWhorter c 3. R S Mary's-In-Tuxedo Tuxedo Pk NY 2007-2015; Com On Soc Responsibility In Investments GC 2000-2007; Epis Cler Assn Dio Washington Washington DC 1998-2007, Epis Caring Response To Aids 1997-2000, Stwdshp Cmsn 1996-1998; R S Pat's Ch Washington DC 1995-2007; Int S Peters-In-The-Woods Epis Ch Fairfax Sta VA 1995; Int S Jn's Epis Ch Mc Lean VA 1993-1995; Dioc Rep Prov Vii Ce Cmsn Dio Texas Houston TX 1990-1993; S Fran Ch Houston TX 1987-1993. SCHC - Chapl 1996-1999. bettysmcwhorter@gmail.com

MCWHORTER, Shirley R (Mich) St Thomas Episcopal Church, 2441 Nichols Drive, Trenton MI 48183 **Vic S Thos Ch Trenton MI 2007-** B Middlesex UK 1949 d Dennis & Christina. AA Brevard Cmnty Coll 1993; BA U of Cntrl Florida 1995; MDiv Sewanee: The U So, TS 1999. D 6/19/1999 Bp John Wadsworth Howe P 12/18/1999 Bp Clifton Daniel III. m 9/20/1969 Gary L McWhorter c 4. Dio Sthrn Ohio Cincinnati OH 2006-2007; Asst S Cyp of Carthage Columbus OH 2006-2007; Vic S Nich Of Myra Epis Ch Hilliard OH 2002-2006; Dir, Par Fam Mnstrs, Assoc R S Ptr's Epis Ch Washington NC 1999-2000. Ord of S Lk; Phi Kappa Phi. revshirleymcw@yahoo.com

MCWHORTER, Stephen Dexter (Va) 570 Lovely Ln, Sylacauga AL 35151 **Instr in Ethics UAB Med Sch 2017-** B Charleston WV 1941 s Joseph & Joan. BA W Virginia U 1963; MDiv EDS 1967. D 6/12/1967 P 12/20/1967 Bp Wilburn Camrock Campbell. Int S Jn's Epis Ch Southampton NY 2014-2016; Int Chr Ch Frederica St Simons Is GA 2010-2013; Int S Thos Epis Ch Birmingham AL 2007-2008; Int Epis Ch Of The Ascen Birmingham AL 2006; R S Dav's Ch Ashburn VA 1992-2005; Hd of Cler Trng Dio Virginia Richmond VA 1990-1992; Robert Shuller Mnstrs Orange CA 1987-1988; R S Paul's Epis Ch Walnut Creek CA 1978-1987; Chapl S Edm's Acad 1970-1977; R The Ch Of The Redeem Pittsburgh PA 1970-1977; Chapl, Marshall U, Asst Trin Ch Dio W Virginia Charleston WV 1967-1970; Chapl Marshall U Huntington WV 1967-1970.

MEACHAM, Carlyle Haynes (Vt) Po Box 115, Washburn IL 61570 **Ret 1991-** B Dickinson Center NY 1926 s Leon & Hazel. BA Atlantic Un Coll 1949; STB Harvard DS 1953; STM Harvard DS 1954; Cert SWTS 1965. D 5/29/1965 P 11/20/1965 Bp Albert A Chambers. m 1/3/1981 Donna S O'Dell c 2. R S Mart's Epis Ch Fairlee VT 1988-1991; S Paul's Epis Ch Pekin IL 1984; Int Trin Ch Lincoln IL 1981-1982; All SS Ch Morton IL 1979; Vic S Anne Ch Ann IL 1965-1966; Serv Unitarian Ch 1954-1964.

MEACHEN, Jerome Webster (Ct) 20 W Canal St Apt 423, Winooski VT 05404 B Oklahoma City OK 1930 s Jerome & Mildred. BA Ob 1951; MS UTS 1953. D 12/6/1967 Bp William Loftin Hargrave. m 6/25/1952 Marielouise Emery Meachen c 5. S Jn's Ch Stamford CT 1990-1998; Asst S Paul's Ch Darien CT 1986-1990; Pstr's Asst S Paul's Ch Riverside CT 1983-1986; Pstr's Asst Chr Ch Epis Savannah GA 1974-1983; Pstr's Asst Ch Of The Redeem Sarasota FL 1966-1974; Ret. Auth, *The Hymnal 1982*. AAM.

MEAD, Alan Champ (CPa) 3159 Silver Sands Circle #103, Virginia Beach VA 23451 **Ch Of H Apos Virginia Bch VA 2016-; Cmncatn Min Int Mnstry Ntwk Baltimore MD 2015-; Ch Of The Ascen Norfolk VA 2014-** B Utica NY 1945 s Warren & Evelyn. BA Utica Coll 1975; MDiv EDS 1979. D 6/9/1979 Bp John Bowen Coburn P 1/30/1980 Bp Harold Barrett Robinson. m 8/17/1968 Patricia A Mead c 2. Int S Paul's Epis Ch Dayton OH 2011-2012; Int S Paul's Epis Ch Indianapolis IN 2009-2011; Int S Jn's Ch Richmond VA 2008-2009; Int S Paul's Memi Charlottesvlle VA 2006-2008; Int Ch Of The Epiph Glenburn Clarks Summit PA 2005-2006; Int Chr Ch Reading PA 2004; COM Dio Cntrl Pennsylvania Harrisburg PA 1998-2004; Eccl Trial Crt Dio Cntrl Pennsylvania Harrisburg PA 1998-2003; Convenor - Convoc Dio Cntrl Pennsylvania Harrisburg PA 1998-2001; R Chr Ch Berwick PA 1995-2004; R Emm Ch W Roxbury MA 1989-1995; Co-Vic Ch Of The H Nativ Seekonk MA 1987-1989; R S Mk's Epis Ch Riverside RI 1983-1987; R S Andr's Ch New Berlin NY 1981-1983; S Matt's Ch So New Berlin NY 1981-1983; Cur S Lk's Epis Ch Jamestown NY 1979-1981; Pres Natl Ntwk Of Epis Cler Assn Lynnwood WA 2003-2007.

MEAD, Andrew Craig (NY) 321 Wandsworth Street, Narragansett RI 02882 B Rochester NY 1946 s Gaylord & Margery. BA DePauw U 1968; BD Yale DS 1971; MLitt Oxf GB 1974. D 6/11/1971 Bp John P Craine P 12/18/1971 Bp Joseph Warren Hutchens. m 1/1/1972 Nancy Anne Hoxsie c 2. R S Thos Ch New York NY 1996-2014; R The Ch Of The Adv Boston MA 1985-1996; R The Ch Of The Gd Shpd Rosemont PA 1978-1985; Cur The Par Of All

SS Ashmont-Dorches Boston MA 1975-1978; Cur S Jn The Evang Yalesville CT 1973-1975; S Paul's Ch Wallingford CT 1973-1975; Serv Ch of Engl 1971-1973. R Emer St. Thos Ch Fifth Av 2014; DD Nash 2002; Off of the British Empire Queen Eliz II 2002. amead@saintthomaschurch.org

MEAD, Carol Lynn (Miss) 105 Montgomery Hl, Starkville MS 39759 **S Ptr's By The Lake Brandon MS 2013-** B Harvey IL 1955 d George & Lorraine. BA Mississippi U for Wmn 1977; MDiv Ya Berk 2009. D 5/30/2009 Bp Joe Goodwin Burnett P 12/2/2009 Bp Duncan Montgomery Gray III. Chapl/Cur Ch Of The Resurr Starkville MS 2009-2013. thenewmead@yahoo.com

MEAD, Loren Benjamin (WA) 3440 S Jefferson St Apt 1478, Falls Church VA 22041 **Assoc S Alb's Par Washington DC 1994-** B Florence SC 1930 s Walter & Dorothy. MA U of So Carolina 1951; BA U So 1951; MDiv VTS 1955. D 6/20/1955 P 6/21/1956 Bp Thomas N Carruthers. c 4. Fndng Pres Alb Inst Inc. Herndon 1974-1994; The Alb Inst Beth MD 1974-1992; Dir Proj Test Pattern (The PB's Advsry Comm. on Evang.) Was 1969-1974; R Ch Of The H Fam Chap Hill NC 1957-1969; R Trin Epis Ch Pinopolis SC 1955-1957. Co-Auth (w Billie Alb), "Creating the Future Together," Alb Inst, 2008; Auth, "A Change of Pastors," Alb Inst, 2005; Auth, "Fin Meltdown in the Mainline?," Alb Inst, 1998; Auth, "Five Challenges for the Future Ch," Alb Inst, 1996; Auth, "Transforming the Cong for the Future," Alb Inst, 1993; Auth, "The Once & Future Ch," Alb Inst, 1991; Auth, "New Hope for Congregations," Seabury Press, 1972; Auth, "The Whole Truth"; Auth, "More Than Numbers"; Auth, "Critical Moment". Acad Par Cler 1970; Int Pstr Ntwk 1975. The Bp's Awd Bp of Dio Washington 2005; Henry Knox Sherrill Awd ECF 1999; DD Ya Berk 1987; DD VTS 1985; DD U So 1984.

MEAD, Matthew Hoxsie (NY) 1415 Pelhamdale Avenue, Pelham NY 10803 **Par of Chr the Redeem Pelham NY 2015-; Chair of Bdgt Com Dio New York New York NY 2013-, Dn of the Sawmill Cler 2012-2015, Bdgt Com 2012-, Com To Elect A Bp 2010-2011, COM 2009-, Ecum Cmsn: Epis & Meth Dialogue 2009-, Hisp Grants Com 2008-2010, Dioc Coun 2007-2013, Congrl Spprt Plan Com 2007-** B Boston MA 1976 s Andrew & Nancy. BA U Chi 1998; M. Div Ya Berk 2004. D 3/13/2004 P 9/18/2004 Bp Mark Sean Sisk. m 6/5/2004 Nicole D Mead c 2. R Ch Of The Gd Shpd Granite Spgs NY 2009-2015; Cur for Liturg & Educ Ch Of S Mary The Vrgn New York NY 2004-2009. matthew@christchurchpelham.org

MEADE, Elizabeth G (Chi) 406 Peck Rd, Geneva IL 60134 **D S Chas Ch St. Chas IL 2004-** B Quicy MA 1952 Skidmore Coll. D 2/2/2002 Bp Bill Persell P 6/14/2014 Bp Chris Christopher Epting. m 5/16/1981 Gary Lawrence Meade c 2. Ch Of The H Nativ Clarendon Hls IL 2015. rectorchn@sbcglobal.net

MEADE, Gary J (WTenn) St. Mary's Episcopal Church, 108 N. King Ave., Dyersburg TN 38024 **R S Mary's Epis Ch Dyersburg TN 2007-** B Albuquerque NM 1961 s Thomas & Caroline. BA Rice U 1983; JD U of New Mex 1995; MDiv TESM 2001. D 7/28/2001 P 2/23/2002 Bp Terence Kelshaw. c 2. Int R S Mary's Epis Ch Albuquerque NM 2007; Asst to the Dn S Jn's Cathd Albuquerque NM 2001-2006. gmeade@stmarysdyersburg.org

MEADERS JR, Calvin Judson (Miss) 200 E Academy St., Canton MS 39046 **R Chap Of The Cross 1989-** B Newton MS 1947 s Calvin & Minnie. AA Clarke Memi 1967; BA Mississippi Coll 1969; MDiv New Orleans Bapt TS 1980; MEd Mississippi St U 1983; Cert Sewanee: The U So, TS 1989. D 5/26/1989 P 12/1/1989 Bp Duncan Montgomery Gray Jr. m 12/18/1979 Nancy Dixon Meaders c 2. R Gr Epis Ch Canton MS 1995-2012; Chap Of The Cross Rolling Fork MS 1989-1995; Serv Sthrn Bapt Ch 1982-1985.

MEADERS III, Calvin Judson (Miss) 305 S Commerce St, Natchez MS 39120 **S Phil's Ch Jackson MS 2016-** B Meridian MS 1983 s Calvin & Nancy. BA U of Mississippi 2007; BA U of Mississippi 2007; MDiv Epis TS Of The SW 2013; MDiv Epis TS of the SW 2013. D 6/1/2013 P 1/12/2014 Bp Duncan Montgomery Gray III. m 5/23/2009 Rebecca Horton Meaders c 3. Trin Epis Day Sch Natchez MS 2013-2016.

MEADOWCROFT, Jeffrey Whittaker (USC) D 6/22/1967 Bp Gray Temple P 7/1/1968 Bp Archie H Crowley.

MEADOWS JR, Richard (WA) Grace Episcopal Church, 1607 Grace Church Rd, Silver Spring MD 20910 **Gr Epis Ch Silver Sprg MD 2016-** B Buffalo NY 1957 s Richard & Mary. MDiv Virginia Un U 2005; MDiv Virginia Un U 2005; Cert Ang Stud VTS 2010. D 6/18/2011 Bp Herman Hollerith IV P 12/31/2011 Bp Dorsey Henderson. m 12/24/1998 Linda Mose Meadows c 4. R S Lk's Epis Ch New Haven CT 2013-2016; The Epis Ch Of S Jn The Bapt Orlando FL 2011-2013.

MEAIRS, Babs Marie (SanD) 11650 Calle Paracho, San Diego CA 92128 B Palo Alto CA 1950 d Laddin & Beverlee. BA U CA Davis 1972; MDiv CDSP 1979; MA TCU 1988. D 10/14/1979 Bp Archibald Donald Davies P 12/1/1993 Bp William Edwin Swing. m 2/26/1994 Edward Leonard Busch. Field Coordntr Off of the Bp Suffr for Chaplaincies New York NY 2007-2010; Epis Ch Cntr New York NY 2007-2009; Chapl Veterans Affrs Med Cntr San Diego CA 2001-2007; Chapl VetA Med Cntr Dallas TX 1996-2001; Chapl Off Of Bsh For ArmdF New York NY 1994-2007; Asst S Chris's Ch And Sch Ft Worth TX 1990-1991; Chapl All SS Epis Sch Ft Worth TX 1984-1989; Chapl All SS' Epis Ch Ft Worth TX 1984-1989; Asst Trin Epis Ch Ft Worth TX 1979-1983.

M

MEANS, Carl T (Wyo) 300 Mt. Arter Loop, Lander WY 82520 **Shoshone Epis Mssn Ft Washakie WY 1999-** B Hetzel WV 1937 s Obie & Mary. D 6/30/1990 P 1/18/1991 Bp Terence Kelshaw. m 9/26/2007 Linda R Wilson c 4. Reg Mssnr Dio Wyoming Casper 1999-2008; Non-par Dio The Rio Grande Albuquerque 1990-1999, 1990.

MEANS, Jackie (Ind) 834 Mount Dora Ln, Indianapolis IN 46229 B PeoriaIL 1936 d Theodore & Minnette. Chr TS. D 4/6/1974 Bp John P Craine P 1/1/1977 Bp Donald James Davis. m 3/31/2001 William D Lyons. Asst S Matt's Ch Indianapolis IN 2013-2016; Vic S Geo Epis Ch W Terre Haute IN 2002-2004; Dir of Prison Mnstrs Epis Ch Cntr New York NY 1998-2006; R S Mk's Ch Plainfield IN 1991-1998, R 1986-1990; Dio Indianapolis Indianapolis IN 1977-1990. Auth, "Wrld Bk Encyclopedia". ACPE, Acca, In Chapl Assn, Ord Of Ascen 1988. Who'S Who Of Wmn In Rel 1977.

MEARS JR, Preston Kennard (NH) 15101 Candy Hill Rd, Upper Marlboro MD 20772 **1974-** B East Orange NJ 1940 s Preston & Marion. BA Hav 1962; BD EDS 1966; MPA NEU 1985. D 6/11/1966 P 12/18/1966 Bp Leland Stark. m 1/12/1963 Laurie Mears c 3. Assoc S Jas Epis Ch Bowie MD 2006-2008; R Ch Of The Trsfg Derry NH 1970-1974; Cur S Ptr's Ch Morristown NJ 1966-1970.

MEASE, Carole Ann (CPa) 359 Schoolhouse Rd, Middletown PA 17057 **Crna Penn St Hershey Med Cntr Hershey PA 2001-** B Lebanon PA 1948 d William & Dorothy. BA Lebanon Vlly Coll 1971; AA Harrisburg Area Cmnty Coll 1981; Cert Harrisburg Hosp Sch of Nurse Anesthesia 1986. D 6/6/2000 Bp Michael Whittington Creighton.

MEAUX, Amy Dafler (Lex) 320 W Main St, Danville KY 40422 **Trin Epis Ch Danville KY 2011-** B Beaufort SC 1974 d Richard & Christy. BA NW St U 1997; MDiv Epis TS of the SW 2002. D 12/28/2001 P 7/10/2002 Bp Charles Edward Jenkins III. m 7/24/1999 Jared Morgan Meaux c 2. S Mich And All Ang Ch Dallas TX 2004-2011; Asst R Trin Ch New Orleans LA 2002-2004.

MEBANE JR, Willie Henry (WNY) 128 Pearl St, Buffalo NY 14202 **P S Paul's Cathd Buffalo NY 2014-** B Durham NC 1952 s Willie & Carrie Elizabeth. BA U NC 1975; MDiv Ya Berk 2006. D 6/13/2009 P 1/16/2010 Bp Andrew Donnan Smith. m 12/25/1973 Ilona Mebane c 2. Cur Trin Cathd Cleveland OH 2009-2014.

MECK III, Daniel Stoddart (Md) 5620 Greenspring Avenue, Baltimore MD 21209 **July Vic S Mart's In The Field Sum Chap Biddeford Pool ME 2007-; Chapl S Paul's Sch Brooklandville MD 2007-** B Harve de Grace MD 1964 s Daniel & Patsie. BS U of Maryland 1986; MDiv VTS 2000. D 6/10/2000 Bp John L Rabb P 12/9/2000 Bp Robert Wilkes Ihloff. m 9/8/1990 Kelly J Meck c 3. Assoc S Dav's Ch Baltimore MD 2000-2007.

MECK, Nancy E (SVa) 13530 Heathbrook Rd, Midlothian VA 23112 **Johns Memi Epis Ch Farmville VA 2014-** B Fairmont WV 1954 d William & Helen. AB Mary Baldwin Colleg 1977; MS W Virginia U 1980; PhD W Virginia U 1985; MDiv Epis TS of the SW 2000. D 6/3/2000 Bp Barry Howe P 2/6/2001 Bp Peter J Lee. m 12/23/2005 Michael Mccarthy. Assoc R Ch Of The Redeem Midlothian VA 2007-2014; Assoc R S Steph's Ch Richmond VA 2000-2005. nancyemeck@aol.com

MECKLING, Judith B (Pa) 730 S Highland Ave, Merion Station PA 19066 **Ch Of S Jude And The Nativ Lafayette Hill PA 2015-; Vic All Souls Ch For The Deaf Philadelphia PA 2007-** B Philadelphia PA 1952 d Gustav & Jane. BA Estrn U 1974; MS Cor 1979; MDiv GTS 1985. D 6/8/1985 Bp O'Kelley Whitaker P 3/17/1986 Bp Robert Louis Ladehoff. Dio Pennsylvania Philadelphia PA 2007-2014; Chapl Norristown St Hosp Norristown PA 2005-2006; P-in-c Hse Of Pryr Philadelphia PA 2003-2004; Hospice Chapl Abington Memi Hosp 2002-2007; Chapl Germantown Hm Philadelphia PA 2000-2002; Assoc S Gabr's Epis Ch Philadelphia PA 1998-2000; Chapl Legacy Gd Samar Hosp Portland OR 1990-1996; Non-par Co-Fndr and Dir Sophia Cntr Lake Oswego 1988-1992; Asst Chr Ch Par Lake Oswego OR 1985-1988. Assn Of Profsnl Chapl; Cler Fam Ntwk; Sprtl Dir Intl .

MEDELA, Jean Milor (Hai) c/o Diocese of Haiti, Boite Postale 1309, Port au Prince Haiti Haiti **Dio Haiti Port-au-Prince HT 2008-** B 1978 s Jean & Ulysse. D 1/25/2006 P 2/18/2007 Bp Jean Zache Duracin. m 6/19/2008 Mona J P Medela c 2.

MEDINA, Ernesto R (Neb) 16611 Castelar St, Omaha NE 68130 **R S Martha's Epis Ch Papillion NE 2009-** B San Diego CA 1960 s Ernest & Maria. BA U CA San Diego 1984; MDiv CDSP 1988. D 6/4/1988 P 12/10/1988 Bp Charles Brinkley Morton. m 4/24/1992 Susan J Powers c 2. Dn for Urban Mssn Trin Cathd Omaha NE 2007-2009; Provost Cathd Cntr Of S Paul Cong Los Angeles CA 2000-2007; Mssnr for CE Dio Los Angeles Los Angeles CA 1995-2007; Int S Edm's Par San Marino CA 1994-1995; Asst To R S Mk's Epis Ch Upland CA 1990-1994; Cur/Assoicate Trin Ch Escondido CA 1988-1990. Co-Ed, "Awake My Soul," Epis Ch Cntr, 2000. Pres ADLMC 1997.

MEDINA, Felix R (PR) Po Box 2156, Bridgeport CT 06608 B 1937 s Ramon & Filomena. Harvard DS; MDiv Epis Sem Puerto Rico 1963. D 6/22/1963 P 12/21/1963 Bp Albert Ervine Swift. m 10/12/1963 Victoria M Cruz c 4. S Lk's/S Paul's Ch Bridgeport CT 1993-2002; The Ch of S Matt And S Tim New York NY 1987-1988; Serv Puerto Rico.

MEDINA MEJIA, Jorge Reynaldo (Hond) **Iglesia Epis Hondurena San Pedro Sula 2006-** B Tegucigalpa F.M. 1960 s Emilio & Eercilia. DIT Programa Diocesano Educacion Teologica 2002. D 10/28/2005 Bp Lloyd Emmanuel Allen. m 5/16/1981 Iris Esther Esther Avila Medina c 4. Dio Honduras San Pedro Sula 2006-2011.

MEDLEY, James W (SVa) 808 Gates Ave Apt B5, Norfolk VA 23517 **Ch Of The Gd Shpd Norfolk VA 2014-** B Richmond VA 1963 s Wayland & Jo Anne. BA Virginia Commonwealth U 2002; MDiv Epis TS of the SW 2008. D 2/1/2008 P 8/1/2008 Bp John Clark Buchanan. m 5/20/2017 Janelle L Mason c 2. Assoc Estrn Shore Chap Virginia Bch VA 2010-2014; R All SS Ch So Hill VA 2008-2010. james.medley@goodshepherdnorfolk.org

MEECH, Michelle (NY) 4800 Woodward Ave, Detroit MI 48201 **S Jn's Epis Ch Kingston NY 2016-** B Youngstown, OH 1968 d David & Judith. BA Indiana U of Pennsylvania 2010. D 4/13/2010 P 10/14/2010 Bp Bavi Edna Rivera. Mnstry Dvlp Dio Michigan Detroit MI 2012-2016; Dir, Cont Educ CDSP Berkeley CA 2010-2012; Asst S Alb's Ch Albany CA 2010-2012.

MEEKS, Edward Gettys (USC) 405 S. Chapel Street, Baltimore MD 21231 B Atlanta GA 1952 s William & Carrie. BA U of So Carolina 1974; DIT Coll of the Resurr 1978. D 8/23/1978 P 7/11/1979 Bp George Moyer Alexander. m 5/30/2012 John Greeley Earls. P Assoc Ch Of The Gd Shpd York SC 2003-2005; P-in-c Ch Of The Nativ Un SC 2002-2005; P-in-c S Ptr's Ch Great Falls SC 1999-2002; R S Mary's Ch Asheville NC 1983-1998; R Chr/St Paul's Epis Par Hollywood SC 1979-1983; Epis Ch on Edisto Edisto Island SC 1979-1983; Asst Ch Of The Gd Shpd Columbia SC 1978-1979. Phi Beta Kappa Alpha Chapt, U of So Carolina 1974. egmeeks@aol.com

MEENGS, John Richard (WMich) 622 Lawndale Ct, Holland MI 49423 B Chicago IL 1938 s John & Ada. AA Worsham Coll 1960; Cert Sewanee: The U So, TS 2001. D 6/15/2002 Bp Edward Lewis Lee Jr. m 8/11/1984 Rose Marie Meengs c 1. D All SS Ch Saugatuck MI 2002-2013. BroSA 1998; Fllshp of St. Jn 1998.

MEGEATH, Sally Holme (Colo) 343 Canyon St, Lander WY 82520 **D S Thos Epis Ch Denver CO 2013-** B Denver CO 1943 d James & Mary. Metropltn St Coll of Denver 1990. D 5/7/2005 Bp Bruce Caldwell. m 4/23/1988 Joe D Megeath c 3.

MEGGINSON JR, Marshall Elliot (HB) 5689 Utrecht Rd, Baltimore MD 21206 **Vic S Barn 1969-** B New York NY 1933 s Marshall & Mildred. BA U of Maryland 1958; BD Epis TS of the SW 1963. D 6/17/1963 Bp Frederick P Goddard P 5/1/1964 Bp John Elbridge Hines. m 2/14/2005 Else Boswell. Cur Chr Ch Winnetka IL 1966-1969; Vic All SS Bridge City TX 1963-1966.

MEGINNISS, David Hamilton (Ala) 801 Pin Brook Lane, Tuscaloosa AL 35406 **R Chr Ch Tuscaloosa AL 2005-** B Dothan Al 1954 s Benjamin & Annette. MA U of Alabama 1977; JD U of Alabama 1980; MDiv Sewanee: The U So, TS 2001. D 5/31/2001 Bp Henry Nutt Parsley Jr P 12/4/2001 Bp Onell Asiselo Soto. m 11/24/2009 Barbara O Meginniss c 1. R Trin Ch Wetumpka AL 2001-2005.

MEHEUX, Sybil Adlyn (CFla) 543 Corporation St, Holly Hill FL 32117 B Westmoreland Jama CA 1933 d Linford & Iva. Bethlehem Tchr Trng Coll Associations 1954; BA U of The W Indies 1974; MEd CUNY 1984. D 6/6/1998 Bp John Wadsworth Howe. m 6/16/1962 Montrose Augustus Meheux. D Gr Epis Ch Inc Port Orange FL 1998-2000.

MEIER, Kermit Irwin (Ore) 1209 Fleet Landing Blvd, Atlantic Beach FL 32233 **Asst Chr 1986-** B Brainerd MN 1918 s Fred & Helen. Muskegon Jr Coll Muskegon MI 1938; BA Albion Coll 1940; STB Bex Sem 1943. D 6/22/1971 P 1/1/1973 Bp James Walmsley Frederic Carman. m 8/12/1944 Marian Elizabeth Liddell. Non-par 1977-1985; Serv Methodist Ch 1943-1967; Chapl USN 1943-1965.

MEISS, Marion (Be) 46 S. Laurel St., Hazleton PA 18201 B Hazelton PA 1943 d Joseph & Rose. D 9/29/2007 Bp Paul Victor Marshall. m 6/13/1964 Albert George Meiss c 2.

MEISTER, Deborah Anne (WA) 3001 Wisconsin Ave. NW, Washington DC 20016 **R S Alb's Par Washington DC 2011-, R 2011-** B New York NY 1968 d Robert & Margaret. BA Harv 1990; PhD U CA 1999; MDiv Ya Berk 2002. D 6/23/2002 Bp Joseph Jon Bruno P 12/14/2002 Bp Marc Handley Andrus. R Chr Ch New Brunswick NJ 2006-2011; Assoc R S Lk's Epis Ch Birmingham AL 2002-2006.

MEISTER, Stephen George (Roch) 400 S Main St, Newark NY 14513 B Lansing MI 1946 s Orley & Freda. BS Rochester Inst of Tech 1996. D 3/29/2008 Bp Jack Marston Mckelvey. m 11/22/1968 Jo Ann Meister c 3.

MEISTER BOOK, Nancy D (Az) B Lincoln NE 1942 d Ralph & Martha. D 1/23/2010 Bp Kirk Stevan Smith. m 5/1/2010 James B Book c 3.

MEJIA, Jairo (ECR) 12149 Saddle Road, Carmel Valley CA 93924 **Ret 1994-** B Aguadas Caldas CO 1922 s Jesus & Margarita. Seminario Conciliar de Medellin 1944; Lic Universidad & Javeriana 1945; Lic Collegio Pio Latino Americano 1946; MA Santa Clara U 1976. Rec 9/1/1985 as Deacon Bp Charles Shannon Mallory. m 9/2/1970 Geraldine Rose Mejia c 1. Vic St Paul's/San Pablo Epis Ch Salinas CA 1988-1994; Asst Hisp Mssn Salinas & Monterey CA 1983-1988; sev Positions RC Ch Medellin Colombia 1945-1970. Auth, *Paso a Paso con la*

Biblia, Ed CLIE, Barcelona, Spain, 1994; Auth, *Curso de Liturgia*, Edit Bedout,, Medellin, Colombia, 1962; Auth, *Tratado de la Divina Gracia*, Edit. Bedout, Medellin, Colombia, 1960.

MEJIA, Jose Arnaldo (Hond) Calle Principal, La Estrada HN Honduras B Ajuterique Comavagua 1950 s Gregoria. BA Instituto Immaculado 1970; Seminario Nuestra Senora Sumapa 1974; Seminario Teologicia Salazar 1976; Universidad Ibamisionera 1985. Rec 9/20/2003 Bp Lloyd Emmanuel Allen. c 2. Dio Honduras San Pedro Sula 2005-2015.

MEJIA, Nelson Yovany (Hond) Roatan Islas De La Bahia, Apartado 193, Roatan, Coxen Hole Honduras **Dio Honduras San Pedro Sula 2006-; Iglesia Epis Hondurena San Pedro Sula 2006-** B Siguatepeque Comyagua 1972 s Miguel & Leila. DIT Programa Diocesano De Educaccion 2003; DIT Universidad Biblica Latinoamericana 2005. D 10/29/2005 Bp Lloyd Emmanuel Allen. m 1/19/2002 Kara Ann Thompson De Mejia c 2.

MEJIA ESPINOSA, Jose Vicente (EcuC) Avenue La Castellana 40-06, Zona 8, Guatemala City 01008 Guatemala **Asst To Dn S Jas Cathd In Guatemala 1987-** B Fredonia Ant CO 1932 s Vincente & Bernice. BA Sem Conciliar De Medellin 1955; BTh Sem Conciliar De Medellin 1959. Rec 1/1/1988 as Priest Bp Armando Roman Guerra Soria. m 1/7/1980 Maria Teresa Catalina Louys De Mejia. Iglesia Epis Del Ecuador Quito 1996-2001; Dio Guatemala New York NY 1987-1996. Auth, "Tugurianos Y Oligarquias 70 Las Siete Palabras".

MELBERGER, MaryJo (Pa) 734 Twining Way, Collegeville PA 19426 **P Assoc Ch Of The Mssh Lower Gwynedd PA 2010-** B Philadelphia PA 1943 d Joseph & Marion. BS Elizabethtown Coll 1965; DAS GTS 1991; MDiv Luth TS 1992. D 6/13/1992 P 5/22/1993 Bp Allen Lyman Bartlett Jr. m 12/26/1964 Kenneth E Melberger c 3. Epis Chapl Chautauqua Inst Chautauqua NY 2012; Int R Ch Of The H Apos Wynnewood PA 2006-2008; Assoc R S Thos' Ch Whitemarsh Ft Washington PA 2003-2006; Lower Sch Chapl The Epis Acad Newtown Sq PA 2001-2003; R S Jn's Ch Bala Cynwyd PA 1999-2001; Asst Ch Of The H Comm Memphis TN 1995-1999; Conf Coordntr Cler Ldrshp Proj Cordova TN 1994-1995; Asst The Ch Of The H Trin Rittenhouse Philadelphia PA 1992-1994; Bd Mem Samar Counselling Cntr Philadelphia PA 2010-2015; COM Dio W Tennessee Memphis 1997-1999; Bd Mem Samar Counselling Cntr Memphis TN 1996-1999; Cmsn on Human Sxlty Dio Pennsylvania Philadelphia PA 1992-1993. Alb Inst 1995-2015; OHC 1991; The SCHC 2015.

MELCHER, John Robert (Mich) 2441 Nichols St, Trenton MI 48183 B Minneapolis MN 1950 s Robert & Lorraine. BA S Louis U 1973; MA S Louis U 1975; MDiv U Tor CA 1981; GTS 1990. Trans 5/1/1990 Bp Robert Marshall Anderson. m 2/15/1986 Elizabeth Ann McNamara c 1. R S Thos Ch Trenton MI 1998-2006; R S Paul's Epis Ch Mayville NY 1993-1998; Assoc R All SS' Epis Ch Chevy Chase MD 1990-1993; DCE & Dvlpmnt S Mart's By The Lake Epis Minnetonka Bch MN 1987-1989; Chapl S Jos's Hosp S Paul MN 1984-1985; Pstr Rosebud Sioux Reserv S Fran Mssn SD 1982-1983. Auth, "Testimony Usa Senate: Hlth Care Crisis On Rosebud Reserv". Soc Jof Esus.

MELCHIONNA, Elizabeth Marie Marie (NC) 104 Nuttal Pl, Chapel Hill NC 27514 **Chap Of The Cross Chap Hill NC 2016-** B Roanoke VA 1980 d Olin & Elizabeth. BA Davidson Coll 2002; Dplma Ya Berk 2006; MDiv Yale DS 2006; Cert Yale Inst of Sacr Mus 2006; Cert Estrn Mennonite U 2013. D 6/4/2006 P 8/23/2007 Bp Neff Powell. m 12/10/2011 William Sandidge Roberts c 2. Cn S Jn's Cathd Denver CO 2013-2016; Epis Campus Min Davidson Coll 2009-2013; Assoc R S Alb's Ch Davidson NC 2009-2013; Asst R S Mary's Epis Ch Arlington VA 2007-2009; Fell Inst. for the Study of Rel Culture and Peace Thailand 2006-2007; Instr of Theol and Liturg McGilvary Coll of Div Chiang Mai Thailand 2006-2007; Disciplinary Bd Dio Colorado Denver CO 2015-2016; Cathd Ridge Bd 2014-2016; Galilee Cmsn Dio No Carolina Raleigh NC 2012-2013, COM for the Priesthood 2011-2013, Israel Palestine T/F 2011-2013, Com on Accessibility 2010-2013, Com on MHE 2009-2013. Monthly Meditation, "April 2017," *Forw Day by Day*, Forw Mvmt, 2017; Bk Revs, "The Ch and Conflict Resolution in So Afr and Rwanda; The Sacrifice of Afr: A Political Theol for Afr," *Angl and Epis Hist*, 2013. Fllshp of S Jn (SSJE) 2007. rector@thechapelofthecross.org

MELENDEZ, Michael Paul (Mass) 138 Tremont St, Boston MA 02111 B Wichita Falls TX 1952 s Carlos & Alice. MSW Bos 1983; PhD Case Wstrn Reserve U 2007. D 6/5/2010 Bp Gayle Harris.

MELIN, Marilyn Joyce (Chi) 206 South Maple Street, Libertyville IL 60048 B Chicago IL 1944 d Marshall & Marion. BA Mundelein Coll 1978; MDiv SWTS 1985. D 2/10/1985 Bp James Winchester Montgomery P 9/1/1985 Bp Frank Tracy Griswold III. c 2. S Mary Epis Ch Crystal Lake IL 2008-2009; S Leonards Oratory Chicago IL 1987-1990; S Aug's Epis Ch Wilmette IL 1985-1988; S Lawr Epis Ch Libertyville IL 1985.

MELIS, Alberto Manuel (Tex) 305 N 30th St, Waco TX 76710 B Havana Cuba 1949 s Rafael & Olga. BA Florida Atlantic U 1981; MS Florida Intl U 1999; Dplma Theol Iona Sch for Mnstry 2015. D 6/20/2015 Bp C Andrew Doyle. m 9/22/1972 Carol Irving c 2.

MELLISH, Roy Whyle (La) PO Box 1825, Morgan City LA 70381 **Ret 2009-** B Santiago Chile 1941 s John & Violet. Cert ETSC 1971; S Georges Coll Jerusalem IL 1998; Oxf GB 2003; Durham Ecum Conf 2005. D 8/7/1971 P 2/12/1972 Bp Reginald Heber Gooden. c 1. R Trin Epis Ch Morgan City LA 1993-2008; R S Steph's Ch Innis LA 1990-1993; Ch Of The Epiph Houston TX 1989-1990; The Great Cmsn Fndt Houston TX 1987-1990; P-in-c Iglesia el Buen San Pedro Sula Honduras 1984-1987; Exec Coun Appointees New York NY 1976-1987; P-in-c Iglesia Santa Margarita Honduras 1976-1984; St Georges Ch 1972-1976; Dio Panama 1971-1976; Serv Epis Ch of Panama 1971-1976. Tertiary of the Soc of S Fran 1979.

MELLO, Iris Elaine (RI) 88 Albert Ave, Cranston RI 02905 **D S Mary's Ch Warwick RI 2007-** B East Providence RI 1939 d William & Edith. BS Roger Wms 1990; MS U of Rhode Island 1993. D 7/13/1985 Bp George Nelson Hunt III. m 10/12/1957 Charles Edward Mello c 4.

MELLO, Jeffrey William (Mass) 130 Aspinwall Ave, Brookline MA 02446 **Adjct Fac EDS Cambridge MA 2010-; R S Paul's Ch Brookline MA 2009-** B Warwick RI 1968 s Charles & Iris. BA Rhode Island Coll 1991; MSW Simmons Coll Boston MA 2000; MDiv EDS 2007. D 6/2/2007 P 1/12/2008 Bp M(Arvil) Thomas Shaw. m 12/12/2004 Paul Daigneault c 1. Assoc R Chr Ch Cambridge Cambridge MA 2007-2009; Mem, Epis Transition Com Dio Massachusetts Boston MA 2013-2014, Lectr, Diac Trng Prog 2013-, Dn, Chas River Dnry 2011-, Trnr, Cler Safe Ch Refresher 2008-. EPF 2007. jmello@stpaulsbrookline.org

MELLO, Mary Ann (RI) B Cincinnati OH 1964 d John & Susan. D 6/15/2013 Bp W Nicholas Knisely Jr. c 1.

MELLO-MAKI, Christine Helene (NMich) 470 North Us 141, Crystal Falls MI 49920 **D S Mk's Ch Crystal Falls MI 1997-** B Royal Oak MI 1938 d Manuel & Eleanor. ADB Suomi Coll 1958; ADN Jc Mott Jr Coll 1979; BD Lake Superior St U 1986. D 6/22/1997 Bp Thomas Kreider Ray. m 9/5/1959 Warren William Maki.

MELLON, Robert E (Pa) 10551 Machrihanish Cir, San Antonio FL 33576 **Ret 2006-** B Philadelphia PA 1941 s Joseph & Elizabeth. Dioc COLM; Cert Pennsylvania Diac Sch 1996. D 9/26/1996 Bp Franklin Delton Turner. m 9/5/1999 Gail V Mellon. The Ch Of The Trin Coatesville PA 2003-2006; S Jas' Epis Ch Downingtown PA 1999-2003; D S Mary's Philadelphia PA 1997-1999; S Jas Ch Collegeville PA 1996-2006.

MELLOTT, Emily Alice (NJ) 207 W Main St, Moorestown NJ 08057 **Trin Ch Moorestown NJ 2016-** B Chicago IL 1973 AB Bryn 1995; MDiv CDSP 2005. D 6/18/2005 Bp Bill Persell P 1/21/2006 Bp Victor Alfonso Scantlebury. R Calv Ch Lombard IL 2008-2016; Asst to the R S Ptr's Epis Ch S Louis MO 2005-2008. trinity@trinitymoorestown.org

MELNYK, James (NC) 5400 Crestview Rd, Raleigh NC 27609 **P-in-c S Paul's Epis Ch Smithfield NC 2010-; COM Dio No Carolina Raleigh NC 2004-** B Mount Vernon NY 1955 s Walter & Rita. BA U of So Carolina 1977; MDiv Sewanee: The U So, TS 1989. D 6/10/1989 P 5/19/1990 Bp William Arthur Beckham. m 5/2/1992 M Lorraine Ljunggren c 1. Ch Of The H Fam Chap Hill NC 2009-2010; Dio Pennsylvania Philadelphia PA 2005; Asst & Co-Pstr S Mk's Epis Ch Raleigh NC 2000-2009; Int S Lk's Epis Ch Durham NC 1999-2000; P-in-c The Cathd Of All Souls Asheville NC 1997-1998, P-in-c 1997-1998, 1991-1999, Assoc 1991-1997, Assoc 1991-1997; P-in-c S Andr's Epis Ch Greenville SC 1990-1991; Chr Ch Greenville SC 1989-1991. Interfaith Allnce for Justice 1995-1998.

MELTON, Betty Anne (Miss) **D S Paul's Epis Ch Meridian MS 2016-; Com on Mnstry w LGBT Persons Dio Mississippi Jackson MS 2010-** B Pascagoula, MS 1945 d Thomas & Annie. Assoc of Sci Mississippi Gulf Coast Cmnty Coillege 1965; Bachelor of Sci U of Sthrn Mississippi 1967; Mstr of Educ Mississippi St U 1975; A.C. Marble Sch for Theol Formation 2016. D 6/4/2016 Bp Brian Seage.

MELTON, Brent (Va) 210 Ellington St, Fayetteville NC 28305 **R All SS Ch Richmond VA 2013-** B Wilmington NC 1975 s Norman & Margarete. BS Coll of Charleston 1999; MDiv Sewanee: The U So, TS 2005. D 6/25/2005 P 4/8/2006 Bp Clifton Daniel III. m 5/21/2005 Kathryn U Melton c 2. R Chr Ch Eliz City NC 2007-2013; Asst Min S Jn's Epis Ch Fayetteville NC 2005-2007; Tchr New Hanover Cnty Sch Wilmington NC 2001-2002; Tchr Charlottesville City Schools Charlottesville VA 1999-2001. bmelton@allsaintsrichmond.org

MELTON, Heather L (LI) 288 Harrison Ave, Harrison NY 10528 **Epis Ch Cntr New York NY 2013-** B Washington Court House OH 1978 d Thomas & Julie. BS Kent St U 2001; MDiv CDSP 2008; MA Grad Theol Un 2009. D 5/31/2008 P 1/10/2009 Bp Robert John O'Neill. m 1/30/2010 Jk Melton c 2. Dom And Frgn Mssy Soc- Epis Ch Cntr New York NY 2013; R Chr Ch Garden City NY 2011-2013; Cur S Ambr Epis Ch Boulder CO 2008-2011; Dir of Yth & YA Mnstrs S Jn's Epis Ch Boulder CO 2000-2005. hmelton@episcopalchurch.org

MELTON, Jk (Colo) Fordham University, Department of Theology, 441 E Fordham Rd, Bronx NY 10458 **All SS Ch Harrison NY 2016-; Doctoral Candidate Ford 2013-2018** B Murray UT 1979 s James & Kay. BA U CO 2002; MDiv GTS 2013; Ph.D. Ford 2018; Ph.D. Other 2018. D 1/26/2013 Bp Robert John O'Neill P 7/27/2013 Bp Lawrence C Provenzano. m 1/30/2010 Heather L Payton. S Lk's Ch Somers NY 2015-2016; P-in-c Chr Epis Ch Lynbrook NY 2013-2014. meltonjk@gmail.com

MELTON, Jonathan Randall (Mil) 1360 Regent St # 157, Madison WI 53715 **Chapl S Fran Hse U Epis Ctr Madison WI 2012-; St Fran Hse Madison WI 2012-** B Austin TX 1980 s M(Ark) & Karen. Indiana U at So Bend IN 2001; BA Wheaton Coll 2003; MDiv Duke DS 2007. D 12/21/2006 P 9/18/2007 Bp Edward Stuart Little II. m 12/31/2005 Rebekah L Melton c 2. R S Chris's By The Sea Portland TX 2009-2012; Asst To The R S Helena's Epis Ch Boerne TX 2007-2009.

MELTON, M(Ark) Randall (WTex) 721 St. Louis Street, P.O. Box 139, Gonzales TX 78629 **R S Jas' Epis Ch Kemp TX 2017-; R Epis Ch Of The Mssh Gonzales TX 2008-; Curs Sec Dio W Texas San Antonio TX 2014-, Liturg and Mus Com 2012-, Dn NW Convoc 2010-2012, Cont Educ Com 2010-, New Cler Mentor 2009-2011, BEC 2009-** B Dallas TX 1953 s Jack & Anna. BS E Texas St U 1976; MDiv Epis TS of the SW 1983. D 6/11/1983 Bp Robert Elwin Terwilliger P 5/9/1984 Bp Donis Dean Patterson. m 1/5/1978 Karen L Melton c 3. R S Mich And All Ang Ch So Bend IN 1999-2008; Bp's Mssnr for Mssn and Prog Dio Dallas Dallas TX 1996-1999, COM 1994-1997; Vic All SS Ch 1994-1995; Asst P and Sch Chapl S Jn's Epis Ch Dallas TX 1988-1994; R S Mths' Epis Ch Athens TX 1986-1988; Asst P Epis Ch Of The Redeem Irving TX 1984-1986; D Chr Epis Ch Dallas TX 1983-1984; Vice-Pres Gonzales Mnstrl Allnce 2012-2013.

MEMBA, Joseluis (NJ) PO Box 502, Red Bank NJ 07701 **S Thos Epis Ch Red Bank NJ 2016-** B Equatorial Guinea 1971 s Jeronimo & Maria. Urbaniana U 2001; MTh Urbaniana U 2001; Mstr Cn Law Pontifical Lateran U 2003; MA The Pontifical Lateran Universit 2003; Mstr Cn Law The Pontifical Lateran Universit 2003; Doctor Cn Law Pontifical Lateran U 2004; PhD The Pontifical Lateran Universit 2004; Doctor Cn Law The Pontifical Lateran Universit 2004. Rec 5/30/2015 as Priest Bp Leo Frade. m 8/17/2008 Rosalinda Memba. S Ambr Epis Ch Ft Lauderdale FL 2015. stthomasredbank@yahoo.com

MENAUL, Marjorie Ann (CPa) 6288 Peach Tree Rd, Columbus OH 43213 B Columbus OH 1947 d Robert & Marilyn. BA U MI 1969; MA U CA 1971; MA U Chi 1986; MDiv Nash 1989. D 6/17/1989 Bp Frank Tracy Griswold III P 1/6/1990 Bp R aymond Stewart Wood Jr. R S Paul's Ch Bloomsburg PA 1995-2012; Asst S Andr's Ch Ann Arbor MI 1989-1995; Stndg Com Mem Dio Cntrl Pennsylvania Harrisburg PA 2005-2008, Pres, Stndg Com 2003-2004, Dep, GC 2003-, Stndg Com Mem 2001-2003, Alt Dep, GC 2000-. "Ascen of the Lord," *The Abingdon Wmn Preaching Annual*, Abingdon, 2002; "I Samuel 1 & 2," *Interp*, UTS, 2001. Epis Cler Assn of Cntrl PA 1998; EWC 1995. Cn St, Steph's Cathd, Harrisburg 2008.

MENDENHALL, Elborn E (Kan) 2477 SW Brookhaven Ln, Topeka KS 66614 **Ret 1990-** B Garden City KS 1928 s Lester & Bessie. BS K SU 1951; MS Harv 1953; STB GTS 1959; K SU 1974. D 4/25/1959 P 2/12/1960 Bp Arnold M Lewis. m 7/20/1972 Burney Bailey c 3. 1988-1990; Calv Ch Yates Cntr KS 1987-1988; Int S Tim's Ch Iola KS 1987-1988; Vic S Mk's Ch Blue Rapids KS 1983-1986, Vic 1970-1982; Vic S Lk's Ch Wamego KS 1972-1976; H Innoc' Epis Ch Como MS 1966-1970; H Cross Epis Ch Olive Branch MS 1966-1967; Vic S Timothys Epis Ch Southaven MS 1966-1967; R H Trin Ch Cincinnati OH 1961-1965; Cur Gr Epis Ch Utica NY 1959-1961. CT 1963; Ord S Ben 1959; Ord of S Lk 1983.

MENDEZ, Noe (Dal) The Holy Nativity Episcopal Church, 2200 18th St, Plano TX 75074 **Iglesia de la Santa Natividad Plano TX 2016-** B Oaxaca Mexico 1962 s Felipe & Fidelfa. Escuela Normal de Maestros Mesico 1982; MDiv Instituto Teologico San Mateo Dallas 2006. D 11/10/2007 Bp James Monte Stanton P 6/3/2009 Bp Paul Emil Lambert. m 1/27/1984 Maria Luisa Mendez c 4. P The Epis Ch Of The H Nativ Plano TX 2010-2016.

MENDEZ, Richard (U) RR2 Box 64, Pocatello ID 83202 B Pocatello ID 1948 s Magdaleno & Alvina. Idaho St U 1972; AAS Haskell Indiana Jr Coll 1974; Cert SWTS 1989. D 3/30/1990 P 11/30/1990 Bp Bob Gordon Jones. m 4/8/1975 Josephine Ann Mendez c 3. Dio Utah Salt Lake City UT 1995-2011; Dio Wyoming Casper 1992-1994; Vic Our Fr's Hse Lander WY 1991-1995; Rgnl Min Mtn And Desert Indn Missions (Id Wy Ut Nv Mt) 1990-1995; Shoshone Epis Mssn Ft Washakie WY 1990-1991.

MENDEZ, Troy Douglas (Az) Trinity Cathedral, 100 W Roosevelt St, Phoenix AZ 85003 **Trin Cathd Phoenix AZ 2014-** B Houston TX 1972 s Roy & Sandra. BBA U of Notre Dame 1994; MDiv VTS 2009. D 6/6/2009 P 1/9/2010 Bp Sergio Carranza-Gomez. Assoc R S Marg's Epis Ch Palm Desert CA 2011-2013; Cur Ch Of Our Sav Par San Gabr CA 2009-2011. troy@trinitycathedral.com

MENDEZ COLON, Ana Rosa (PR) Urb. Venus Gardens Calle Peliux 1770, San Juan PR 00926 **Dio Puerto Rico Trujillo Alto PR 2007-** B Puerto Rico 1954 d Enrique & Dolores. D 5/1/2005 P 8/27/2006 Bp David Andres Alvarez-Velazquez. m 10/18/1985 Sixto Rodriguez Rios c 3.

MENDOZA, Christine Love (Tex) 3201 Windsor Rd, Austin TX 78703 **Cur The Ch of the Gd Shpd Austin TX 2013-** B San Antonio TX 1970 d Gary & Frances. BA U NC 1992; MDiv Epis TS Of The SW 2013; MDiv Epis TS of the SW 2013. D 6/15/2013 Bp C Andrew Doyle P 1/18/2014 Bp Dena Arnall Harrison. m 6/13/1999 Jonathan Mao Mendoza c 1.

MENDOZA, Loretta J (Mil) 2708 Red Fawn Ct, Racine WI 53406 **Bd Cert Stff Chapl Wheaton Franciscan Healthcare All SS Racine WI 2011-** B Edinburg TX 1952 d Benito & Irene. Cert Milwaukee Area Tech Coll 1982; Cert St Fran Sem Milwaukee WI 1992; MDiv SWTS 2002. D 4/6/2002 Bp Roger John White P 3/25/2003 Bp Chilton Richardson Knudsen. m 5/22/1971 Gilbert Mendoza c 1. All SS Med Cntr Racine WI 2003-2008; Asst S Jas Epis Ch Milwaukee WI 2003. loretta.mendoza@ascension.org

MENDOZA CEDENO, Eduardo (EcuL) **P Iglesia Epis Del Ecuador Quito 1996-** B Porto Viejo-Manabi 1957 s Victor & Rosa. D 2/2/1986 Bp Adrian Delio Caceres-Villavicencio P 6/7/1992 Bp Martiniano Garcia-Montiel. c 3. Litoral Dio Ecuador Guayaquil 1991-1993.

MENDOZA MARMOLEJOS, Milquella Rosanna (DR) **Dio The Dominican Republic (Iglesia Epis Dominicana) Gazcue Santo Domingo 2007-** B 1969 D 2/12/2006 Bp Julio Cesar Holguin-Khoury. c 2.

MENDOZA PEREZ, Julio Cesar (Ve) Iglesia Episcopal de Venezuela, Centro Diocesano Av. Caroní No. 100, Colinas de Bello Monte Caracas 1042-A Venezuela **Dio Venezuela Caracas 2014-** B 1956 s Jose & Romelia. Divina Pastora Y Santa Rosa de Lima; Licenciaso Divina Pastora Y Santa Rosa de Lima; Licenciaso en Iilosofia y Teologia Divina Pastora Y Santa Rosa de Lima; Universidad Cntrl de Venezuela 1997; Licenciado en Educacion U of Cntrl de Venezuela 1997; UCLA 2011; Lic in Educ UCLA 2011; Magister Scientiarum ed Historia UCLA 2011; Lic in Educ U of Cntrl de Venezuela 2199. Rec 10/19/2013 as Priest Bp Orlando Jesus Guerrero. m 8/25/1990 Josefina Dominguez de Mendoza c 3.

MENDOZA QUIROZ, Hugo Eligio (EcuL) Calle #19, #208, Calderon Ecuador B Calderon Ecuador 1942 D 3/22/1998 P 4/13/2008 Bp Terencio Alfredo Morante-Espana. m 11/19/1976 Ramona Edita Parraga Cobena c 5. Litoral Dio Ecuador Guayaquil 2006-2014.

MENEELEY, Beverly Ann (Be) B West Oakdale PA 1943 d James & Elizabeth. Luzerne Cnty Cmnty Coll; Bp's Sch 2012. D 3/2/2014 Bp Sean Walter Rowe. m 6/30/1962 Ronald Dale Meneeley c 3.

MENELAS, Frederic (Hai) **Dio Haiti Port-au-Prince HT 2009-** B Gros Morne Haiti 1971 s Esdras & Macola. BTh Seminaire de Theologie 2007; MA VTS 2011. D 11/1/2009 P 6/29/2010 Bp Jean Zache Duracin. m 6/7/2011 Wislande Lubin Menelas c 1.

MENGER, James Andrew (Ga) 3521 Nassau Dr, Augusta GA 30909 **P-in-c S Mary's Ch Augusta GA 2002-; Asst R The Ch Of The Gd Shpd Augusta GA 2001-** B Augusta GA 1950 s Earl & Betty. Sewanee: The U So, TS; MA Clemson U 1975; MEd U of So Carolina 1983; Cert Camb 1988; DMin GTF 1989. D 2/3/2001 P 8/23/2001 Bp Henry Irving Louttit. m 2/6/1982 Glenda Menger. Serv Sthrn Bapt Ch 1976-1997. Amer Acad Of Bereavement 2000. Fell GTF 1989.

MENJIVAR, Natividad (Okla) St Mark's Episcopal Church, 6744 S Kings Hwy, Alexandria VA 22306 **Dio Oklahoma Oklahoma City OK 2014-; Vic Santa Maria Virgen Epis Oklahoma City OK 2014-** B Honduras 1967 s Vicente & Maria. BA Nuestra Senora de Suyapa; Lic Nuestra Senora de Suyapa; Angl Stds (1yr) VTS. Rec 9/29/2012 as Priest Bp Shannon Sherwood Johnston. m 6/25/2005 Ana A Menjivar c 2. S Mk's Ch Alexandria VA 2012-2014; S Marg's Ch Woodbridge VA 2012-2013. anagv77@yahoo.com

MENJIVAR, Nicholas (NC) Po Box 218, Durham NC 27702 B SV 1942 s Francisco & Maria. BA S Jos Sem 1969; MA S Jos Sem 1973. Rec 4/14/1996 Bp Frederick Houk Borsch. m 8/11/1994 Maria Gladys Menjivar c 2. Iglesia El Buen Pstr Durham NC 2000-2007; Vic Hisp Mssn S Phil's Ch Durham NC 1998-2000; Dio No Carolina Raleigh NC 1998-1999; Dio Los Angeles Los Angeles CA 1997-1998; All SS Epis Ch Oxnard CA 1996-1997.

MENNELL, John A (Nwk) 75 S Fullerton Ave, Montclair NJ 07042 **R S Lk's Epis Ch Montclair NJ 2006-** B Santa Monica CA 1965 s Robert & Antoinette. BA U of Notre Dame 1987; MDiv GTS 2005. D 5/14/2005 P 11/26/2005 Bp Herbert Thompson Jr. m 5/2/2008 Sonia E Waters c 3. Assoc P S Mich's Ch New York NY 2005-2006.

MENSAH, Albert Wellington (Chi) B 1934 D 1/20/1963 Bp Gerald Francis Burrill. m 6/11/1964 Catherine A Mensah.

MENZI, Donald Wilder (Mich) 5 E 10th St, New York NY 10003 **Non-par 1967-** B Ypsilanti MI 1937 s Leonard & Margaret. BD Bex Sem 1936; BA Ob 1960; CUNY 1969; PhD NYU 1978. D 6/29/1963 Bp Richard Stanley Merrill Emrich P 2/1/1964 Bp Roger W Blanchard. m 11/28/1958 Judy Barich c 3. P-in-c S Andr's Addyston OH 1966-1967; Asst Min Calv Ch Cincinnati OH 1963-1966. Hud Fell Cuny-Hunter; Levi A Olin Fell Hebr Un Coll.

MERCADO GALARZA, Wilfredo (PR) B Yuaco PR 1944 s Alejandro & Ramonita. Estudios Generales. D 2/8/1998 P 7/5/2003 Bp David Andres Alvarez-Velazquez. m 3/5/1979 Eva Vazquez. Sacerdote Dio Puerto Rico Trujillo Alto PR 2004-2011, Sacerdote 2003.

MERCER JR, Charles Spencer (Md) The Episcopal Church Of St Mary The Virgin, 3121 Walbrook Ave, Baltimore MD 21216 **R Ch Of S Mary The Vrgn Baltimore MD 2012-; Chapl DOK Dio Maryland Baltimore MD 2011-** B Baltimore MD 1952 s Charles & Anna. Assoc of Arts Cmnty Coll of Baltimore 1979; St. Marys 1987. Rec 5/25/2006 as Deacon Bp Robert Wilkes Ihloff. m 3/

11/2005 Karen Mercer. Asst S Barth's Ch Baltimore MD 2011-2012; Chapl Gd Samar Hosp 2005. stmarysw@verizon.net

MERCER, Emmanuel A (Pa) Saint Paul's Church, 22 E Chestnut Hill Ave, Philadelphia PA 19118 **S Paul's Ch Philadelphia PA 2011-** B Sekondi Ghana 1971 s James & Georgina. LTh St Nich TS 1998; MDiv Candler TS Emory U 2004; STM Yale DS 2005; MA VTS 2009. Trans 4/18/2006 Bp Dorsey Henderson. m 6/14/2003 Monique D Glivens c 3. Cn For Yth Mnstry Trin Cathd Columbia SC 2005-2009; All SS Epis Ch Atlanta GA 2001-2004; Asst St. Ptr's Angl Ch Tarkwa 1998-2000. atomercer11@gmail.com

MERCER JR, Roy Calvin (CFla) 4932 Willowbrook Cir, Winter Haven FL 33884 **Non-par 1968-** B Wyandotte MI 1934 s Roy & Ruth. BA Ob 1956; BD VTS 1962; MEd U of Florida 1971; PhD U of Florida 1975. D 6/9/1962 P 12/1/1962 Bp Nelson Marigold Burroughs. m 12/2/1983 Wilma Marie Mercer c 2. Assoc Chapl Ch Of The Incarn Gainesville FL 1964-1968; Assoc Chr Ch Lima OH 1962-1964. Phi Delta Kappa; Phi Kappa Phi; Kappa Delta Pi.

MERCER, Thomas Robert (NY) Po Box A, Granite Springs NY 10527 B Liverpool UK 1941 s Joseph & Georgina. BA Oxf GB 1963; MA Oxf GB 1966; U of Leeds Gb 1967. Trans 1/1/1982. S Paul's Ch- Morrisania Bronx NY 2003-2006; R Ch Of The Gd Shpd Granite Spgs NY 1996-2003; R S Jas Epis Ch Fordham Bronx NY 1991-1995; Vic All SS Epis Ch Skowhegan ME 1987-1991; Asst The Ch Of The Atone Morton PA 1986-1987; Dio Liberia Monrovia 1971-1982; Vic S Teresa Voinjama Liberia 1968-1986.

MERCER LADD, Morgan (LI) D 1/14/2017 Bp Lawrence C Provenzano.

MERCHANT, John Edward (At) 474 Sunset Dr., Asheville NC 28804 B Harrisonburg VA 1946 s John & Nellie. BA U So 1968; MDiv VTS 1973. D 6/7/1973 P 2/25/1974 Bp Wilburn Camrock Campbell. c 2. S Geo's Epis Sch Milner GA 2000-2003; Headmaster St Geo's Sch Griffin GA 2000-2003; Chapl H Innoc Sch Atlanta GA 1998-2000; H Innoc' Epis Sch Atlanta GA 1998-2000; Gr-S Lk's Epis Sch Memphis TN 1991-1998; Headmaster Gr-St Lk's Sch Memphis TN 1991-1998; Chapl S Jas Sch S Jas MD 1985-1991; St Jas Sch Hagerstown MD 1985-1991; S Mk's Epis Sch Ft Lauderd FL 1982-1985; Dn, Actg Headmaster S Mk's Sch Ft Lauderdale FL 1982-1985; Chapl Jacksonville Epis HS 1978-1982; Jacksonville Epis HS Jacksonville FL 1978-1982; Vic S Andr's in the Vill Ch Barboursville WV 1975-1978; Asst S Matt's Ch Wheeling WV 1973-1975. Gvrng Bd NAES 1985-1991. Ruth Jenkins Awd for Exemplary Serv Nat. Assoc. of Epis Schools 2000.

MERCHANT SSAP, Patricia (At) 120 Warren St NE, Atlanta GA 30317 **Int P-in-c S Alb's Ch Monroe GA 2017-** B Monterey CA 1947 d Charles & Aileen. BS Jas Madison U 1969; MDiv VTS 1974. D 5/24/1974 Bp John Alfred Baden P 1/2/1977 Bp Robert Bruce Hall. m 10/10/1987 Louis Squyres. Int S Thos Epis Ch Columbus GA 2013-2014; The Ch Of Ascen And H Trin Cincinnati OH 2007-2009; R Indn Hill Ch Cincinnati OH 2000-2008; Int Chr Ch Cathd S Louis MO 1998-2000; Dio Atlanta Atlanta GA 1998; The Epis Ch Of The Nativ Fayetteville GA 1991-1998; S Lk's Epis Ch Atlanta GA 1985-1990; Emm Ch Virginia Bch VA 1982; Non-par Non-par 1981-1984; Asst S Paul's Ch Richmond VA 1977-1980; Asst Imm Ch-On-The-Hill Alexandria VA 1974-1977.

MERCHANT II, Wilmot T (SC) 801 11th Avenue North, North Myrtle Beach SC 29582 **R S Steph's Epis Ch N Myrtle Bch SC 2002-, Asst 2000-2001** B Gbarnga Bong County LR 1961 s Wilmot & Martha. BA Cuttington U 1986; Cert S Georges Coll Jerusalem IL 1987; MDiv EDS 1992; ThM Weston Jesuit TS 1993; DMin Drew U 2000. Trans 4/20/2000 Bp Edward W Neufville II. m 12/23/1989 Eugenia C Merchant c 2. P-in-c Trin Ch Of Morrisania Bronx NY 1996-1999; Assoc S Paul's Epis Ch Paterson NJ 1993-1995; Asst S Barth's Epis Ch Cambridge MA 1991-1992; Serv Ch Of W Afr 1986-1989.

MERCURE, Joan Carol (Minn) 4557 Colfax Ave S, Minneapolis MN 55419 B Farmington MN 1955 d Fred & Mary. BA Augsburg Coll 1988; MDiv Untd TS 2013. D 1/24/2013 P 6/27/2013 Bp Brian N Prior. c 1.

MEREDITH, Carol Ann (Colo) 316 Oakland St, Aurora CO 80010 **n/a n/a 2000-** B Manchester UK 1948 Kedron Pk Teachers Coll 1968; BS Friends U 1991; MA Friends U 1994; MDiv SWTS 2004. D 2/13/1992 Bp William Edward Smalley P 1/17/2004 Bp Dean E Wolfe. m 2/6/1970 Howard W Meredith c 2. R S Steph's Epis Ch Aurora CO 2009-2016; Int S Andr's Ch Denver CO 2007-2009; Assoc Gd Shpd Epis Ch Wichita KS 2005-2007; P-in-c S Jn's Ch Wichita KS 2004-2005; Chapl Wesley Med Cntr 1986-2001; Spec Ed Tchr Kansas 1970-1978.

MERFY, Florence Martha (Nev) 1515 Shasta Dr Apt 1510, Davis CA 95616 **Ret 1997-** B Union OR 1922 d Victor & Florence. BA Reed Coll 1943; MEd U of Nevada at Las Vegas 1978. D 11/1/1987 Bp Stewart Clark Zabriskie. c 3. D All SS Epis Ch Las Vegas NV 1987-1997. SHN.

✠ MERINO-BOTERO, the Rt Rev Bernardo (Colom) Calle 97 - No 16-51, Apt 303 Edificio Royal Plaza, Bogota Colombia B Venecia Antioquia CO 1930 s Cristobal & Sofia. Mss Sem Colom. Rec 11/15/1971 as Priest Bp Reginald Heber Gooden Con 6/29/1979 for Colom. m 4/1/1971 Josefina Merino-Botero. Ret Bp of Colombia Iglesia Epis En Colombia Bogota 2002, 1979-2001, Chair on the Stndg Com 1975-1978; Bp of Colombia Dio Colombia 1979-2002; Archd of Colombia Dio Colombia 1975-1979; Serv Angl Ch of Cntrl Amer 1971-1975. Auth, *Biography of Bp Builes*; Auth, *El Mensajero*. Javerianos.

MEROLA SR, Carl Robert (CFla) 705 Victory Lane, Hendersonville NC 28739 **S Matt's Epis Ch Sterling VA 2001-** B Wilkinsburg PA 1935 s Domenic & Lucy. BSME Carnegie Mellon U 1960; MBA U Pgh 1968; EFM Sewanee: The U So, TS 1983. D 3/16/1984 Bp William Hopkins Folwell. m 4/13/1957 Jeanne Lynn Merola c 5. Ch Of The H Fam Mills River NC 2002-2006; Asst Epis Ch of the New Cov Winter Sprg FL 1984-1999.

MEROLA JR, Carl Robert (Va) 402 Valencia Cir, Oviedo FL 32765 **R S Matt's Epis Ch Sterling VA 2001-** B Pittsburgh PA 1958 s Carl & Jean. BA Kings Coll 1980; MDiv Trin Evang DS 1985. D 5/14/1986 P 12/1/1986 Bp William Hopkins Folwell. m 6/14/1986 Linda Ann Merola. S Jas Epis Ch Ormond Bch FL 1996-2001; S Eliz's Epis Ch Sebastian FL 1988-1994; Cur S Andr's Epis Ch Ft Pierce FL 1986-1988; Com.

MERONEY, Anne Elrod (At) 4919-B Rivoli Dr, Macon GA 31210 B Henderson NC 1943 d Joseph & Florence. BA Georgia St U 1974; JD Woodrow Wilson Coll of Law 1977; MDiv Candler TS Emory U 2002. D 6/8/2002 P 1/5/2003 Bp J Neil Alexander. c 2. All Ang Epis Ch Eatonton GA 2013-2015; Chr Ch Macon GA 2004-2005; Asst R S Anne's Epis Ch Atlanta GA 2002-2004.

MERRELL, Robin Nicholas (Cal) 3886 Balcom Rd, San Jose CA 95148 B Spokane WA 1937 s Merton & Carmen. BA U of Idaho 1959; BD CDSP 1964; MA Santa Clara U 1986. D 6/20/1964 P 12/19/1964 Bp John Joseph Meakin Harte. m 11/26/2013 Randolf James Rice c 1. Asstg Mision Nuestra Sra De Guadalupe San Jose CA 1998-2000; S Phil's Ch San Jose CA 1988-1998; Non-par 1982-1987; Indn Epis Mnstry San Francisco CA 1976-1981; Dio California San Francisco CA 1973-1976; R S Mk's Ch King City CA 1969-1973; S Dav's Epis Page AZ 1964-1966; Vic St Johns Epis-Luth Ch Williams AZ 1964-1966. Auth, "Hometowns"; Auth, "A Mem Of The Fam".

MERRICK, Barbara Robinson (Ky) 8110 Saint Andrews Church Rd, Louisville KY 40258 B Madisonville KY 1951 d RW & Mary Frederica. BA Wstrn Kentucky U 1974; MA U of Louisville 1988. D 6/24/2014 Bp Terry Allen White. c 2.

MERRILL, George Richard (Md) 9046 Quail Run Rd, Saint Michaels MD 21663 **Non-par 1976-; Dir Baltimore Pstr Counslg Serv 1973-** B Staten Island NY 1934 s Elliott & Irma. BA Hobart and Wm Smith Colleges 1956; STB Ya Berk 1960; Amer Fndt of Rel & Psych 1965. D 6/11/1960 P 12/1/1960 Bp Horace W B Donegan. m 12/10/1983 Josephine Merrill c 2. Asst Ch Of The Resurr Baltimore MD 1974-1976; Asst S Steph's Epis Ch Bloomfield CT 1966-1973; Chapl Blue Hills Hosp Hartford CT 1965-1973; Assoc All Ang' Ch New York NY 1962-1965; Cur St Johns Ch W Hartford CT 1960-1962. Auth, "Anxiety: Friend Or Foe". AAPC; ACPE.

MERRILL, Richard Hull (ECR) 1755 W Ridgeview Circle, Palm Springs CA 92264 **Died 6/8/2017** B Seattle WA 1929 s Elmer & Inez. BA U CA 1951; JD U CA 1956; MDiv VTS 1971. D 6/26/1971 Bp Chauncie Kilmer Myers P 12/20/1971 Bp George Richard Millard. c 4. Asstg S Paul In The Desert Palm Sprg CA 2010-2013; Ret 1994-2017; Vic S Paul's Ch Cambria CA 1990-1994; Assoc Epis Ch in Almaden San Jose CA 1987-1988; Dio El Camino Real Salinas CA 1987; Vic S Lk's Ch Hollister CA 1981-1986; Assoc S Geo's Ch Salinas CA 1979-1981; R S Ptr's Epis Ch Red Bluff CA 1972-1978; Cur S Paul's Ch Oakland CA 1971-1972.

MERRILL JR, Robert Clifford (Tex) 1321 Upland Dr #5192, Houston TX 77043 B Brooklyn NY 1958 s Robert & Phyllis. BS U of Virginia 1980; PhD U of Notre Dame 1983; N/A Iona Sch of Mnstry (Dio TX) 2008. D 6/28/2008 Bp Don Adger Wimberly P 1/24/2009 Bp Rayford Baines High Jr. m 11/26/1983 Carmen Sepulveda c 1. R S Barth's Ch Hempstead TX 2006-2014.

MERRILL, Russell Walter (EMich) 262 Raleigh Pl, Lennon MI 48449 **D S Paul's Epis Ch Corunna MI 1984-** B Owosso MI 1944 s Russell & Margaret. Cert Whitaker TS. D 6/25/1983 Bp William Jones Gordon Jr P 12/21/2003 Bp Edwin Max Leidel Jr. m 1/20/1968 Jennifer Lynn Alexander. stpauls48817@yahoo.com

MERRIMAN, Michael Walter (Minn) 2012 Stain Glass Dr, Plano TX 75075 **Asst The Epis Ch Of The Trsfg Dallas TX 2004-** B Austin TX 1939 s Walter & Jane. BA U of Texas 1963; STB GTS 1966. D 6/15/1966 Bp Charles A Mason P 12/1/1966 Bp William Paul Barnds. m 1/21/1967 Charlotte A Merriman. Wrdn S Mk's Coll 1997-2004; Prncpl St. Mk's Coll, Townsville Australia, Dio N. Queensland St Marks Coll Townsville Queensland 1997-2004; P-in-c Geth Ch Minneapolis MN 1994-1997; SLC 1988-1994; Vstng Lectr CDSP Berkeley CA 1984-1987; Precentor and Vice Dn Gr Cathd San Francisco CA 1982-1992; Instr Angl Theol Sem 1981-1982; R Gd Shpd Granbury TX 1979-1982; R Camp Crucis Granbury TX 1978-1979; Int Dio Dallas Dallas TX 1976-1978, Chair Of The Yth Div 1969-1974; R S Andr's Ch Grand Prairie TX 1976; R S Barn Ch Garland TX 1967-1974; Chapl Midwestern U Wichita Falls TX 1966-1967; Chair Of The Liturg Cmsn Dio California San Francisco CA 1983-1989. Auth, "The Rite Light," *The Rite Stuff*, Ch Pub, 2008; Auth, "The Baptismal Mystery & The Catechumenate," Ch Pub, 1989; Auth, "Our Living Wrshp," Ch Pub. Associated Parishes 1976. mmerriman@transfiguration.net

MERRIN, Susie (Colo) **R S Andr's Ch Manitou Sprg CO 2014-** D 8/18/1990 Bp Charles I Jones III P 10/15/2005 Bp Charles Franklin Brookhart Jr.

M

MERRITT, Claudia W (Va) 3401 Hawthorne Avenue, Richmond VA 23222 **Assoc S Steph's Ch Richmond VA 2008-, 2005** B Los Angeles CA 1947 d Harold & Miriam. BA Carnegie Mellon U 1970; MBA Van 1972; MDiv PrTS 1976. D 8/20/1977 Bp Henry Irving Mayson P 4/8/1978 Bp H Coleman Mcgehee Jr. m 11/2/2002 Craig Merritt c 4. Ch Of S Jas The Less Ashland VA 2014-2016; CE Dir S Paul's Ch Richmond VA 2012-2014; Int St. Paul's Epis Ch Millers Tavern VA 2006-2008; S Paul's Epis Ch Millers Tavern VA 2006-2007; S Andr's Ch Richmond VA 2006; Assoc R (Int) S Steph's Ch Richmond VA 2005-2006; Int S Ptr's Port Royal Port Royal VA 2003-2005; Int S Jn's Ch W Point VA 2002-2003; Ch Of The H Comf Richmond VA 1996-2001; S Lk's Epis Ch Durham NC 1993-1995; S Thos Epis Ch Reidsville NC 1992-1993; Int S Jn's Ch Bala Cynwyd PA 1989-1990; Asst Ch Of S Mart-In-The-Fields Philadelphia PA 1987-1989; Chr Ch And S Mich's Philadelphia PA 1986-1987; Stwdshp Off Dio Pennsylvania Philadelphia PA 1982-1987; Asst S Thos' Ch Whitemarsh Ft Washington PA 1980-1981; H Faith Ch Saline MI 1977-1979; Vic H Faith Ch Saline MI 1977-1979. merrittclaudia@gmail.com

MERRITT, Frederick Deen (Neb) B Chadron NE 1934 s Ferdinand & Elvina. D 5/7/1988 Bp James Daniel Warner. m 3/18/1962 Barbara Lundeen.

MERRITT, Robert E (CFla) 864 Summerfield Dr, Lakeland FL 33803 B Saint Petersburg FL 1940 s Edward & Mae. BS Florida St U 1965; MDiv Sewanee: The U So, TS 1975. D 6/17/1975 P 2/1/1976 Bp William Hopkins Folwell. m 12/27/2008 Barbara G Merrit c 3. All SS Epis Ch Lakeland FL 1997; Asst S Steph's Ch Lakeland FL 1984-1990; S Lk The Evang Ch Mulberry FL 1980; Asst R S Dav's Epis Ch Lakeland FL 1975-1980. remerritt@tampabay.rr.com

MERROW, Andrew T P (Va) 2609 North Glebe Road, Arlington VA 22207 **VTS Alexandria VA 1988-; R S Mary's Epis Ch Arlington VA 1985-** B Alexandria VA 1954 s Edward & Helen. BA U of Vermont 1976; MDiv VTS 1981. D 6/7/1981 Bp Robert Bruce Hall P 3/12/1982 Bp David Henry Lewis Jr. m 9/27/2008 Cameron Merrow c 2. VTS Alexandria VA 2012, 2011, 2011, 2006, 2004, 2003, 2002, 1999, 1998, 1994, 1993, 1990-1992; Assoc R Chr Ch Alexandria VA 1981-1985. Cn St. Mathrews Cathd 2006.

MERTZ, Annie Pierpoint (Cal) St. Paul's Episcopal School, 116 Montecito Ave, Oakland CA 94610 **S Paul's Day Sch Of Oakland Oakland CA 2015-; Assoc S Paul's Nrsry And Day Sch Alexandria VA 2014-** B Berkeley CA 1985 d Claude & Susan. BS U CA 2007; MDiv VTS 2014. D 6/14/2014 P 12/6/2014 Bp Marc Handley Andrus. m 8/16/2014 Andrew Mackay Mertz c 1. P S Paul's Epis Ch Alexandria VA 2014-2015. amertz@spes.org

MERTZ, Mary Ann (Pa) 116 Lancaster Pike, Oxford PA 19363 **R S Christophers Epis Ch Oxford PA 2011-; Mem of Hisp Mnstry T/F Dio Pennsylvania Philadelphia PA 2012-, Mem of Liturg Cmsn 2012-** B Louisville KY 1951 d Thomas & Martha. BA Bellarmine U 1972; MTS S Meinrad TS 1994; DMin Louisville Presb TS 2006; Dip Ang Stud GTS 2009. D 6/19/2009 P 12/21/2009 Bp Ted Gulick Jr. m 11/21/1975 Kenneth Louis Mertz c 1. The Epis Acad Newtown Sq PA 2009-2011. Doctorate, "Clothe as Chr: The P within the Body of the Faihtful," Louisville Presb Sem, 2006. Ntwk of Biblic Storytellers, Intl 2011. Doctorate w dist Louisville Presb Sem 2006.

MERZ, John (LI) 129 Kent Street, Brooklyn NY 11222 **P-in-c Ch Of The Ascen Greenpoint Brooklyn NY 2010-; Chapl NYU New York NY 2005-; S Matt's Ch Pennington NJ 2005-** B Brooklyn NY 1965 s Joseph & Mary. BA CUNY 1994; MDiv Yale DS 2004. D 3/13/2004 P 9/18/2004 Bp Mark Sean Sisk. m 8/10/2010 Tara Anderson c 2. P-in-c Dio Long Island Garden City NY 2010-2016; Dio New York New York NY 2005-2010.

MESA, Prospero Eugenio (La) 3104 Verna St, Metairie LA 70003 **Died 2/17/2017** B Havana CU 1928 s Prospero & Ana. BS U of Havana Cu 1947; MA U of Havana Cu 1954; STB UTS Mantanzas CU 1964; EdD U of Havana Cu 1965. Trans 12/1/1981. m 4/23/1966 Raquel C Mesa c 3. Ret 1992-2017; Dio Louisiana New Orleans LA 1989, 1982-1986; Assoc S Jn's Ch Kenner LA 1987-1992; Upper Sch Chapl S Mart's Epis Sch 1987-1992; S Mart's Epis Sch Metairie LA 1987-1992; Ch Of The H Sprt New Orleans LA 1986-1987; Gr Ch New Orleans LA 1984-1985; Exec Coun Appointees New York NY 1964-1981; Serv Ch of Cuba 1964-1980.

MESENBRING, David Gary (Oly) 1245 10th Ave E, Seattle WA 98102 B Des Moines IA 1951 s Victor & June. BA Kalamazoo Coll 1973; MA U Chi 1975. Rec 7/24/2011 as Priest Bp Gregory Harold Rickel. m 6/1/1991 Maria Jesus Jimenez-Mesenbring c 2. Sr Assoc S Mk's Cathd Seattle WA 2011-2012; Exec Dir Seafarers' Hse Ft Lauderdale FL 1991-2006.

MESERVEY, Norman Rix (WNC) 84 Church St, Franklin NC 28734 B Elmira NY 1937 s Norman & Lydia. BA Syr 1960; MA Syr 1963; MDiv EDS 1977. D 6/19/1977 Bp Frederic Cunningham Lawrence P 1/15/1978 Bp Roger W Blanchard. m 4/22/1995 Lorie Meservey. R S Agnes Epis Ch Franklin NC 1994-2002; P-in-c Ch Of The Redeem Bensalem PA 1990-1994; Non-par 1988-1990; Asst Trin Ch Oxford Philadelphia PA 1986; R S Alb's Ch Philadelphia PA 1983-1985; S Alb's Ch Roxborough Philadelphia PA 1983-1985; R All SS Par Whitman MA 1978-1983; Asst The Cathd Ch Of S Paul Boston MA 1977-1978. Auth, "Be Not Afraid"; Auth, "Setting Rite Ii"; Auth, "Benedic," *Anima Mea.*

MESLER JR, Raymond Clyde (NY) 7470 W Glenbrook Rd Apt 313, Milwaukee WI 53223 **Ret 1990-** B Bolivar NY 1927 s Raymond & Marion. BMus U of No Texas 1949; MDiv UTS 1984; STM UTS 1985. D 1/27/1985 Bp Albert Wiencke Van Duzer P 2/19/1986 Bp Otis Charles. c 3. S Paul's Ch Milwaukee WI 2002-2005; Asst P St Mths Epis Ch Waukesha WI 1997-1999; P S Simon's Ch Staten Island NY 1986-1990; Asst to R Chr And S Steph's Ch New York NY 1985-1986.

MESLEY, Gordon Warwick (WMo) 2021 S Hummel Dr, Independence MO 64055 **Min of the Chap S Lk's Hosp 2007-** B Kansas City MO 1929 s George & Blanche. Graceland Coll Lamoni IA 1948; BA U of Nthrn Iowa 1952. D 2/13/1999 Bp Barry Howe. m 8/26/1995 Evelyn Ruth Allen. Chapl S Lk's Hosp 2006.

MESSENGER, Ray Stillson (CNY) 3877 Milton Ave Apt 235, Camillus NY 13031 B Auburn NY 1937 s Robert & Katherine. BS Worcester Polytechnic Inst 1962; MBA U Roch 1970; Bex Sem 1988. D 6/22/1988 P 1/21/1989 Bp William George Burrill. m 9/27/1961 Susan R Rogers c 4. Pres Fndt for Epis Ch at Cor Ithaca 1994-1997; R S Jas' Ch Clinton NY 1991-2001; Asst S Jas Ch Skaneateles NY 1988-1991; V-Chair Dioc Bd Dio Cntrl New York Liverpool NY 1993-1995. Pi Tau Sigma Hon Mechanical Engr Fraternity 1962.

MESSENGER, William Glen (Mass) 84 Lexington St, Belmont MA 02478 **Exec Ed Theol of Wk Proj 2009-; Exec Ed Theol of Wk Proj Inc. Boston 2006-** B Fairborn OH 1960 s William & Gwendolyn. BS Case Wstrn Reserve U 1982; MBA Harv 1988; MDiv Bos TS 1997; DMin Gordon-Conwell TS 2007. D 6/6/1998 P 5/29/1999 Bp M(Arvil) Thomas Shaw. m 9/14/1991 Kimberly Mae Messenger c 2. Ch Planter Dio Massachusetts Boston MA 2004-2008; Bus Ldr-shp & Sprtlty Ntwk S Tim's Epis Ch Mtn View CA 2002-2006; Dir, Mockler Cntr Gordon-Conwell TS 1999-2008; Dir and Adj Prof Mockler Ctr For Faith & Ethics In The Workplace 1999-2008; Asst R All SS' Epis Ch Belmont MA 1998-2001. Ed, "Theol of Wk Bible Commentary," Hendrickson Pub, 2014.

MESSENGER-HARRIS, Beverly Ann (CNY) 124 W Hamilton Ave, Sherrill NY 13461 B Buffalo NY 1947 d James & Eleanor. BA Hobart and Wm Smith Colleges 1972; MDiv Bex Sem 1975. D 6/16/1975 P 1/1/1977 Bp Ned Cole. m 5/21/1976 James Harris. 1991-1993; Vic Oneida Area Epis Consortium 1988-1991; Oneida Area Epis Consortium Oneida NY 1987-1991; St Andrews Epis Ch Rome NY 1986-1987; Int Chr Ch Manlius NY 1985-1986; R Geth Ch Sherrill NY 1984-1991, R 1977-1981; S Geo's Ch Utica NY 1984-1985; Asst Gr Epis Ch Utica NY 1982-1984; In-charge Zion Ch Rome NY 1975-1977.

MESSER, Charles Wilson (Pa) PO Box 452, Glen Riddle PA 19037 **P H Apos And Medtr Philadelphia PA 2014-** B Lake Wales Fl 1971 s David & Gale. AA Polk Cmnty Coll 1993; BA Trevecca Nazarene U 1997; MDiv Nazarene TS 2001; CAS Sewanee: The U So, TS 2002. D 6/7/2003 P 12/6/2003 Bp Barry Howe. m 11/21/2011 Diane M Messer c 3. R Resurr Epis Ch Rockdale Aston PA 2009-2014; Assoc The Ch Of The Redeem Baltimore MD 2005-2009; Asst St Mary Magd Epis Ch Loch Lloyd MO 2003-2004; Asst Cler S Mary Magd Epis Ch Kansas City MO 2002-2005.

MESSER, Julia Weatherly (SVa) 5181 Princess Anne Rd, Virginia Beach VA 23462 **Estrn Shore Chap Virginia Bch VA 2015-** B Columbia SC 1983 d Jakob & Betsy. BA Mary Baldwin Coll 2006; MDiv VTS 2010. D 6/12/2010 P 12/18/2010 Bp Herman Hollerith IV. P Emm Ch Virginia Bch VA 2010-2015.

MESSER, Kenneth Blaine (Ia) D 12/12/2015 P 2/26/2017 Bp Alan Scarfe.

MESSERSMITH, Daphne S (CPa) PO Box 125, Cornwall PA 17016 B York PA 1950 d William & Josephine. BA Washington U 1972; Cert Ang Stud GTS 1994. D 6/12/1981 Bp Dean Theodore Stevenson P 6/18/1994 Bp Charlie Fuller Mcnutt Jr. m 12/27/2003 Merton E Messersmith c 3. Int R Trin Epis Ch Buffalo NY 2013-2014; R Ch of the Nativ-St Steph Newport PA 2005-2013; Cn Pstr Cathd Ch Of S Steph Harrisburg PA 2001-2005; R Calv Chap Beartown Blue Ridge Summit PA 1997-2001; R Ch Of The Trsfg Blue Ridge Summit PA 1997-2001; Int S Lk's Ch Lebanon PA 1996-1997; The Epis Acad Newtown Sq PA 1994-1996, 1991-1993; Asst Chapl Epis Acad Merion PA 1991-1996; D Asst S Jn's Epis Ch Lancaster PA 1990-1991; Asst Chapl Epis Acad Merion PA 1983-1986; D S Andr's Epis Ch York PA 1981-1983. daphne@pa.net

MESSERSMITH, Merton E (CPa) 909 Alison Ave, Mechanicsburg PA 17055 B Harrisburg PA 1947 s Herbert & Lois. BA Hobart and Wm Smith Colleges 1969; MDiv PDS 1972. D 5/27/1972 P 4/1/1973 Bp Dean Theodore Stevenson. m 12/27/2003 Daphne S Killhour c 2. R S Lk's Epis Ch Mechanicsburg PA 1998-2008; Chapl Dio Cntrl Pennsylvania Harrisburg PA 1984-1998; Dio Pennsylvania Philadelphia PA 1984-1998; R S Paul's Ch Newport KY 1980-1984; S Paul's Ch Louisville KY 1980-1983; Ch Of The Trsfg Blue Ridge Summit PA 1976-1980.

MESSICK, Joshua E (Eas) PO Box 3400, Meridian MS 39303 **S Mary's Epis Ch Pocomoke City MD 2016-; The Epis Ch Of The Medtr Meridian MS 2014-** B Easton MD 1989 s Scott & Tina. BA Salisbury U 2011; MDiv VTS 2014. D 6/7/2014 Bp Bud Shand P 1/24/2015 Bp Brian Seage. m 7/19/2014 Jordan M Messick.

MESSIER, Daniel Joseph (Az) 600 S La Canada Dr, Green Valley AZ 85614 **R Epis Ch Of S Fran-In-The-Vlly Green Vlly AZ 2011-** B Claremont NH 1953 s Victor & Gilberte. BA S Mich's Coll 1975; MA CUA 1978. Rec 2/6/

1994 as Priest Bp Edward Lloyd Salmon Jr. m 11/24/2006 Phyllis J Messier c 3. R S Mk's Epis Ch Charleston SC 2002-2011; P-in-c St. Mk's Epis Ch Charleston SC 2001-2002; R S Thos Epis Ch N Charleston SC 1996-2001; Asst R Gr Ch Cathd Charleston SC 1994-1996; Assoc Pstr RC Ch 1980-1986. dan@stfrancisgvaz.org

MESSINA JR, Michael Frank (CFla) 94 Pecan Run, Ocala FL 34472 B Duluth MN 1943 s Michael & Ann. AA Duluth Area Vocational 1970; Cert Prchr Lewis Sch of Mnstry 1984. D 8/5/1987 P 8/24/1988 Bp Richard Mitchell Trelease Jr. m 11/21/1973 Sandra Kay Flyckt c 4. R S Pat's Ch Ocala FL 1996-2015; Asstg P S Anne's Ch Crystal River FL 1993-1996, 1992; Vic Ch Of The Adv Dunnellon FL 1990-1992; S Marg's Ch Inverness FL 1989-1990; D Jordana De Fe Rgnl Mnstry Dio The Rio Grande Albuquerque 1987-1989. Chapl For Ord Of S Lk.

MESTETH, Rhoda Yvonne (SD) Po Box 9, Pine Ridge SD 57770 B Pine Ridge SD 1938 d Peter & Sophie. MS Black Hill St U. D 6/16/2002 P 10/28/2004 Bp Creighton Leland Robertson.

MESTRE JR, José Wilfredo (Ct) 2340 North Ave Apt. 7D, Bridgeport CT 06614 **D S Jn's Ch Bridgeport CT 2013-; Chaplin St. Vinc's Med Cntr Bridgeport CT 2005-** B Manati PR 1951 s Jose & Delia. NW Chr Coll Eugene OR 1972; Inter Amer U of Puerto Rico 1978; Fairfield U 1993; Auburn TS 1997; GTS 2006. D 12/9/2000 Bp Andrew Donnan Smith. D Calv St Geo's Epis Ch Bridgeport CT 2007-2010; S Lk's/S Paul's Ch Bridgeport CT 2003-2007; D Calv Epis Ch Bridgeport CT 2000-2002. Auth, "Poesia (Poems)," *TERTULIA*, Ediciones del Chorro, 1990; Auth, "Una Poeta Sacerdotal," *TERTULIA*, Ediciones del Chorro, 1988; Auth, "Mujer de Vanguardia: Elena Vigo," *TERTULIA*, Ediciones del Chorro, 1987.

METCALF, Michael Patrick (Dal) 3205 Landershire Ln, Plano TX 75023 **Healing Proj 1998-; Com On Mnstry To Persons w Hiv/Aids 1995-; Instr Of Systematic Theol 1993-** B Tulsa OK 1950 s Frederick & Thelma. BA U of Dallas 1973; MDiv Nash 1982; MA Amberton U 1998. D 6/26/1982 Bp Archibald Donald Davies P 4/1/1983 Bp Robert Elwin Terwilliger. c 1. Epis Search Com 1991-1992; R Ch Of The Epiph Richardson TX 1990-2002; 1989-1992; 1987-1989; S Jn's Epis Ch Corsicana TX 1986-1990; Dn Of The Estrn Dnry 1985-1986; R S Dunst's Ch Mineola TX 1984-1986; Cur The Epis Ch Of The H Nativ Plano TX 1982-1984; Chair On The Dioc Cmsn Of Healing Ministers. Associated Parishes; Assn Sprtl Ethical Rel Values Counslg; NNECA, Dallas Epis Cleric Assn.

METCALFE, Steven Todd (WNY) 20 Milton St, Williamsville NY 14221 **R S Jas' Ch Batavia NY 2010-** B Dayton OH 1950 s Watson & Janet. BA U Cinc 1979; MDiv EDS 1983. D 6/11/1983 P 1/6/1984 Bp William Grant Black. c 1. R Calv Epis Ch Williamsville NY 1993-2010; R The Epis Ch Of The Gd Shpd Buffalo NY 1987-1993; Asst. R Chr Ch - Glendale Cincinnati OH 1983-1987; Chr Ch Cathd Cincinnati OH 1983-1987. stmcfe.64@gmail.com

METELLUS, Donald (Hai) B 1981 s Exavier & Odette. Lic Seminaire de Theologie 2011. D 7/29/2012 P 3/13/2014 Bp Jean Zache Duracin. Dio Haiti Port-au-Prince HT 2012-2015.

METHENY JR, Lloyd Erwin (NCal) 11070 Hirschfeld Way #66, Rancho Cordova CA 95670 **Ret 1989-** B Kimball NE 1927 s Lloyd & Eva. BA U of Nebraska 1950; BTh PDS 1954. D 4/22/1954 P 12/21/1954 Bp Howard R Brinker. Vic S Clem's Ch Rancho Cordova CA 1980-1989; LocTen S Tim's Ch Gering NE 1961-1962; P-in-c Ch Of The Gd Shpd Bridgeport NE 1955-1959; R Ch Of The H Apos Mitchell NE 1954-1980; BEC Dio Nebraska Omaha NE 1963-1972. Omicron Delta Kappa; Theta Chi.

METHVEN, Susanne (Okla) PO Box 1783, Salina KS 67402 **S Fran Cmnty Serv Inc. Salina KS 2016-** B Halton England 1957 d Alexander & Ingeborg Andrea. BA Hollins U 1978; MBA Harv 1980; MS U of Nevada at Las Vegas 2003; MDiv Epis TS of the SW 2007; Cert Sojourn Insitute 2011. D 10/6/2006 Bp Katharine Jefferts Schori P 7/21/2007 Bp Robert Manning Moody. Assoc R S Jn's Epis Ch Tulsa OK 2007-2016. Auth, *If only I had known: avoiding common mistakes in couple Ther*, WWNorton, 2005. sbmethven@hotmail.com

METHVIN, Thomas G (Dal) 3966 McKinney Ave, Dallas TX 75204 **R S Phil's Epis Ch Frisco TX 2015-** B Starkville MS 1965 BA Louisiana Coll 1987; MDiv New Orleans Bapt TS 2003. Trans 11/17/2008 Bp James Monte Stanton. m 9/3/1994 Steffanie Methvin c 2. R Ch Of The Incarn Dallas TX 2008-2015; Min Of Discipleship Chr Epis Ch Plano TX 2004-2006. greg@stphilipsfrisco.org

METIVIER, Catherine A (Okla) B Tulsa OK 1954 BS U of Texas 1978; DDS U of Texas 1985; MDiv VTS 2005. D 6/25/2005 P 12/21/2005 Bp Robert Manning Moody. c 2. Vic Dio Oklahoma Oklahoma City OK 2005-2009.

METOYER, Eric (Cal) Episcopal Diocese Of California, 1055 Taylor St, San Francisco CA 94108 **Assoc for Congrl Mnstry Dio California San Francisco CA 2012-; Assoc S Cyp's Ch San Francisco CA 2012-, D 2011-2012** B Jersey City NJ 1960 s Victor & Marie. BA Wms 1988; MDiv CDSP 2011. D 12/3/2011 P 6/2/2012 Bp Marc Handley Andrus. m 8/3/1991 Jessica Noel Morin c 1. ericm@diocal.org

METTLER, Garrett M (Los) 8 Sunnyside Ave., Pleasantville NY 10570 **Trin Ch Fishkill NY 2015-** B Goleta CA 1975 BS California St Polytechnic U 1997; MDiv VTS 2002. D 6/22/2002 Bp Richard Lester Shimpfky P 1/11/2003 Bp Joseph Jon Bruno. m 1/10/1998 Rebecca Lynn Mettler c 1. Wooster Sch Danbury CT 2012-2015; Int S Jn's Ch Pleasantville NY 2011-2012; R S Tim's Epis Ch Apple Vlly CA 2005-2011; S Geo's Acad Laguna Hills CA 2002-2004; Assoc S Geo's Epis Ch Laguna Hills CA 2002-2004.

METZ, susanne (ETenn) 335 Tennessee Ave, Sewanee TN 37383 **R St. Jn the Bapt Battle Creek TN 2007-; Fac TS Sewanee TN 2003-** B Philadelphia PA 1950 d Albert & Elizabeth. BA Immaculata U 1972; MA W Chester U of Pennsylvania 1982; BA Immaculata U 1983; MDiv Sewanee: The U So, TS 1996; DMin Sewanee: The U So, TS 2003. D 12/7/1996 P 6/28/1997 Bp Robert Gould Tharp. Sewanee U So TS Sewanee TN 2001-2011; Cntr For Mnstry In Sm Ch Memphis TN 1998-2001; Assoc St. Jn the Bapt Battle Creek TN 1996-2007; S Jn The Bapt Battle Creek TN 1996-1998. "You Will Lead Me by the Rt Road," *Sewanee Theol Revs*, TS, Sewanee, 2005; Ed, *Tuesday Morning: Mnstry and Liturg Preaching Journ*, TS, Sewanee.

METZGER, Carl (Pa) 100 E Lehigh Ave, Philadelphia PA 19125 B Lavelle PA 1939 s Othneil & Dorothy. BA U Pgh 1961; MA Villanova U 1984. D 6/11/1983 P 12/1/1986 Bp Lyman Cunningham Ogilby. c 1. S Alb's Ch Roxborough Philadelphia PA 1995-2005; Epis Hosp Philadelphia PA 1987-2000; Vic S Lk's Ch Philadelphia PA 1986-1987; The Ch Of The H Trin Rittenhouse Philadelphia PA 1983-1987. emmanuelchurch@cavtel.net

METZGER, Curtis (NH) PO Box 1541, Concord NH 03302 **All SS Epis Ch Littleton NH 2016-** B 1957 s J Hayes & Katherine. BA U of New Hampshire 1983; MDiv U Tor CA 1986. Trans 1/17/2007 Bp Vicky Gene Robinson. m 12/17/2016 Douglas Hartford. P-in-c S Steph's Ch Pittsfield MA 2007-2014; R S Steph's Ch Pittsfield NH 2006-2016.

METZGER, Jim (Mo) 3402 Sawgrass Ln, Cincinnati OH 45209 **Ret 1997-** B Cincinnati OH 1934 s Ralph & Katharine. BA Ohio Wesl 1956; MA VTS 1963; Coll of Preachers 1971; UCincinnati Dept of Psych Fam Ther Inst 1983; Lic Marr& Fam Ther 2005. D 6/15/1963 P 12/1/1963 Bp Roger W Blanchard. m 8/26/1961 Hope H Metzger c 3. R S Ptr's Epis Ch S Louis MO 1989-1997; R Indn Hill Ch Cincinnati OH 1973-1989; R Ch Of The Incarn Penfield NY 1966-1973; Asst Ch Of S Edw Columbus OH 1963-1965. Outstanding Cmnty Rep. Cease Fire, Cincinnati, ohio 2006; City of Cincinnati, Comm. Problem Oriented Policing Cincinnati and Comm. Prob. Oriented Policing CPOP 2005; Dn Emer St. Mich's Cathd - Boise, ID 1988; ,Fell Coll of Preachers 1971.

METZLER, Carolyn Walburn (Me) 1611 Sunset Gardens Rd SW, Albuquerque NM 87105 **P-in-c Big Bend Epis Mssn Alpine TX 2013-; Mem, Com On Baptismal Mnstry Dio Maine 2005-; Vic St Thos 2004-** B Chicago IL 1955 BA Hope Coll. D 6/14/2003 P 3/13/2004 Bp Chilton Richardson Knudsen. m 6/2/1984 Eric Metzler c 2. Dio Maine Portland ME 2004-2009; S Thos Ch Winn ME 2004-2009. Honorable Mention Polly Bond Awd For Cmncatn 2003. cwmetzler@gmail.com

METZLER, Martie (Mo) 5305 Kenrick View Drive, Saint Louis MO 63119 **Emm Epis Ch S Louis MO 2013-** B Monroe LA 1950 d George & Eleanor. MDiv Bex Sem 1984. D 6/23/1984 P 5/31/1985 Bp O'Kelley Whitaker. m 7/16/1977 Paul Arthur Metzler c 2. P-in-c Ch Of The H Innoc W Orange NJ 2010-2013; Assoc R of Pstr Care and Mew Mem Incorporati S Jas Ch New York NY 2005-2010; Dir of Pstr Care Interreligious Coun of Cntrl NY Syracuse NY 2003-2005; Cn St Paul's Syracuse Syracuse NY 1991-2003; Syracuse Area Interreligious Coun Syracuse NY 1988-1991; Chapl Crouse Irving Memi Hosp 1987-1992; Assoc R Gr Ch Baldwinsville NY 1985-1987; Int S Andr Delta NY 1984-1985; Int S Mk's Ch Clark Mills NY 1984-1985; Paris Cluster Chadwicks NY 1984. m.metzler.chi@gmail.com

METZLER, Paul Arthur (CNY) 5305 Kenrick View Dr, Saint Louis MO 63119 **Assoc Ch Of The Trsfg New York NY 2007-; Dir, Cmnty & Prog Serv VNSNY Hospice Care Manhattan NY 2005-** B Brooklyn NY 1944 s Arthur & Edna. AA Concordia Jr Coll 1964; BA Concordia Sr Coll 1966; MDiv Concordia TS 1970; STM Concordia TS 1971; DMin Concordia TS 1992; Dio Angl Stds 1995. D 6/17/1995 P 5/16/1996 Bp David Bruce Joslin. m 7/16/1977 Martie Sallwasser c 2. Assoc Ch Of The H Innoc W Orange NJ 2010-2013; Cathd Precentor St Paul's Syracuse Syracuse NY 1994-1999; Serv Var positions ELCA Syracuse NY 1971-1994. AAPC; Assn for Death Educ & Counslg; Assn for Epis Heathcare Chapl 1996; Clincl Mem AAMFT; Coun of Hospice Professionals. paul.metzler2010@gmail.com

MEUSCHKE, Marty O (Ga) 145 River Ridge Loop, Hortense GA 31543 B Washington DC 1945 s Jack & Verda. D 4/24/2007 Bp Henry Irving Louttit. m 5/13/1973 Paula Meuschke c 2.

MEYER, Alan King (Az) 5909 SW Karla Ct, Portland OR 97239 **Non-par 1989-; Arizona Chapl Assn 1984-** B San Francisco CA 1952 s Donald & Eleanor. BA U of Arizona 1979; U of Arizona 1979; MDiv CDSP 1983. D 6/11/1983 P 11/1/1984 Bp Joseph Thomas Heistand. m 12/29/1977 Ann Meyer. S Jn's Epis Ch Bisbee AZ 1985-1988; S Paul's Ch Tombstone AZ 1985-1988; Bisbee Mnstrl Assn 1984-1988; Vic S Lk's Willcox AZ 1984-1985; Assoc R S Paul's Epis Ch Salem OR 1983-1984; . ACPE. Phi Alpha Theta 1972; Www Vigil Ord Of Teh Arrow 1972; Alpha Phi Omega B.S.A. 1970.

M

MEYER, Erika K (NY) 240 E. 31st St., New York NY 10016 **Ch Of The Gd Sh-pd New York NY 2009-** B New York NY 1963 d John & Kathleen. BA U MI 1988; MDiv CDSP 1994. D 6/18/1994 P 2/1/1995 Bp R aymond Stewart Wood Jr. c 2. S Barn Of The Vlly Cortez CO 2002-2009; Int Gr Ch Waterford NY 2000-2001; Dio Utah Salt Lake City UT 1996-1998; Int Chapl Rowland Hall S Mk's Sch 1996-1997; Assoc Thumb Epis Area Mnstry Dio Estrn Michigan Saginaw MI 1994-1995; Thumb Epis Area Mnstry Deford MI 1994-1995.

MEYER, John Anthony (LI) 423 Falcon Ridge Drive, Sheridan WY 82801 **Int S Ptr's Epis Ch Sheridan WY 2010-, Asst 2003-2010** B Brooklyn NY 1939 s John & Mildred. Mercer TS 1978. D 6/23/1979 P 12/22/1980 Bp Robert Campbell Witcher Sr. m 8/26/1962 Deanne Meyer c 4. Int S Lk's Epis Ch Buffalo WY 2002-2003; R S Marg's Ch Plainview NY 1982-2002; Cur H Trin Epis Ch Vlly Stream NY 1979-1982. jdmeyer423@charter.net

MEYER, John Paul (Mich) 1353 Labrosse St, Detroit MI 48226 B Minneapolis MN 1935 s Ernest & Ellen. BA U MN 1957; BD UTS 1960; non-degree GTS 1964; unfinished PhD Sthrn Illinois U 1972. D 11/9/1960 P 5/1/1961 Bp Horace W B Donegan. m 6/25/1960 Kathleen B Meyer c 4. S Ptr's Ch Detroit MI 1981-2002; Ch Of The Mssh Detroit MI 1978-1979; R S Anne's In The Field Madison OH 1972-1977; R Trin Jefferson OH 1972-1977; Vic S Anne Anna IL 1971-1972; Chapl Sthrn Illinois U - Carbondale 1967-1972; Asst S Paul's and Trin Chap Alton IL 1964-1967; Asst All SS Ch Brooklyn NY 1962-1964; Cur S Ptr's Epis Ch Lakewood OH 1960-1962.

MEYER, Mark David (Colo) 1365 Fairview Ave, Canon City CO 81212 **R Chr Ch Cn City CO 1998-** B Elmhurst IL 1954 s Morgan & Carol. BA Colorado Coll 1976; MDiv·Epis TS of the SW 1979. D 11/30/1979 P 5/30/1980 Bp William Carl Frey. R S Mary's Epis Ch Blair NE 1992-1998; R S Mk's Epis Ch Plainview TX 1983-1992; Cur S Jos's Ch Lakewood CO 1980-1983; Cur Epiph Epis Ch Denver CO 1979-1980. markdmeyer@q.com

MEYER, Nancy Ruth (Chi) St Peter's Episcopal Church, 621 W Belmont Ave, Chicago IL 60657 **D S Ptr's Epis Ch Chicago IL 2008-; Bd Mem The Ch Hm Chicago IL 2007-** B Elmhurst IL 1946 d Walter & Ruth. BSN U of Washington 1970; MSN Wayne 1979; Dplma Sewanee: The U So, TS 1989; Dplma U So TS 1989; Dioc Sch for D Formation & Trng Chicago IL 2007. D 1/19/2008 Bp Victor Alfonso Scantlebury.

MEYER, Robert (FdL) PO Box 184, Tremont IL 61568 **Ret 1995-** B Toledo OH 1935 s Walter & Vera. BA Ob 1957; PhD Duke 1961; STB GTS 1971. D 4/16/1971 P 10/15/1971 Bp Francis W Lickfield. m 2/3/1962 Robin Witwer c 2. Cn St Paul's Epis Ch Peoria IL 2001-2012; Vic Ch Of The H Nativ Jacksonport Sturgeon Bay WI 1989-1995; Dio Fond du Lac Appleton WI 1989-1995, Liturg Cmsn 1984-1985; Vic S Mk's Ch Waupaca WI 1984-1989; St Olaf's Epis Ch Amherst WI 1984-1989; Chr Ch Lexington MO 1981-1984; Vic Dio W Missouri Kansas City MO 1981-1984, Sprtl Dir Curs 1982-1984; Chapl Lewistown Fire Dept Lewistown IL 1977-1981; Dio Quincy Peoria IL 1973-1981; S Jas Epis Ch Lewistown IL 1973-1981; S Ptr's Ch Canton IL 1971-1974. Cn Honoris Causis Cathd Ch of S Paul (Dio Quincy)/Peoria 2001; Bp's Awd of Ord S Paul Dio Quincy 1978; Phi Beta Kappa Duke 1961; Sigma Xi Duke 1960; Phi Lambda Upsilon Duke 1959.

MEYER, Wendel William (Mass) 347 Emerald Bay Cir Unit S7, Naples FL 34110 B Evanston IL 1949 s Wendel & Marion. BA U So 1971; MDiv GTS 1978; STM GTS 1980; PhD U of Cambridge 1986. D 6/18/1978 Bp William Evan Sanders P 5/27/1979 Bp Robert Bracewell Appleyard. m 1/1/1995 Ann Wevling c 2. Actg Pusey Min The Memi Ch at Harv Cambridge MA 2010-2012; R S Jn's Ch Beverly MA 1999-2009; Assoc Min The Memi Ch at Harv Cambridge MA 1997-1999; R S Ptr's Ch Philadelphia PA 1989-1997; Cn S Paul's Cathd Buffalo NY 1986-1989; 1982-1986; Cur Chr Ch New Haven CT 1979-1982. Auth, *Var arts.*

MEYERS, David Craig (WMich) Church Of The Holy Spirit, 1200 Post Dr NE, Belmont MI 49306 **S Ptr's By-The-Lake Ch Montague MI 2015-; Vic Ch of the H Sprt Belmont MI 2008-** B Muskegon MI 1953 s Eugene & Arlene. BA MI SU 1976; MA MI SU 1977; MA U of Detroit Mercy 1979; EdD Wstrn Michigan U 2001. D 5/3/1986 Bp Howard Samuel Meeks P 1/22/2011 Bp Robert R Gepert. m 10/7/1978 Merry Kim Meyers c 2. D S Jn the Apos Epis Ch Ionia MI 2008-2009; D S Paul's Ch Greenville MI 1986-2008.

MEYERS, Frederick W (Rick) (Colo) 420 Cantril St, Castle Rock CO 80104 B Sturgis MI 1946 s Ralph & Coral. BA MI SU 1970; MA MI SU 1970; MDiv Iliff TS 1978; STM Nash 1980; DMin GTF 1991. D 6/29/1979 P 5/28/1980 Bp William Carl Frey. m 12/23/1966 Rita K Meyers c 2. R Chr's Epis Ch Castle Rock CO 1991-2015; Asst S Barn Epis Ch Denver CO 1990-1991; Asst S Thos Epis Ch Denver CO 1988-1989; Vic S Matt's Parker CO 1980-1988; Asst Chapl Ch Of S Jn Chrys Delafield WI 1979-1980; Exec Coun Dio Colorado Denver CO 1992-1996, EDEO 1984-1991.

MEYERS, Michael William (Az) 300 N Constitution Dr, Tucson AZ 85748 B 1943 D 10/5/2002 Bp Robert Reed Shahan. m 9/27/1966 Patricia Meyers c 2.

MEYERS, Ruth (Cal) Church Divinity School Of The Pacific, 2451 Ridge Rd, Berkeley CA 94709 **P All Souls Par In Berkeley Berkeley CA 2010-; Hodges-Haynes Prof of Liturg CDSP Berkeley CA 2009-** B Passaic NJ 1957 d Richard & Dorothy. Cardinal Stritch U; BS Syr 1977; MDiv SWTS

1985; MA U of Notre Dame 1989; PhD U of Notre Dame 1992. D 6/5/1985 Bp Otis Charles P 4/13/1986 Bp William Gillette Weinhauer. m 6/10/1989 Daniel L Britton c 1. GC Dep Dio Chicago Chicago IL 2006-2009; Adj Fac Bexley Seabury Fed Chicago IL 1995-2009; Sum Sch Fac U Of Notre Dame 1994-1998; Int Trin Epis Ch Marshall MI 1993; Rep Of Prov V Syn Dio Wstrn Michigan Kalamazoo MI 1992-1995, 1992-1994, Dioc Liturg 1991-1998, Pstr Care Com 1991-1995, Consulting Team 1990-1991; Int S Paul's Epis Ch St Jos MI 1987-1988; Asst R Ch Of The Ascen Hickory NC 1985-1986. Auth, "Steph, D and Mtyr; Nativ of Jn the Bapt; Thos, Apos; Mary Magd, Apos; Barth, Apost," *New Proclamation Commentary on Feasts, H Days, and Other Celebrations,* Fortress, 2007; Auth, "Fresh Thoughts on Cnfrmtn." *ATR,* 2006; Auth, "Rites of Initiation," *The Oxford Guide to BCP Worldwide,* Oxf Press, 2006; Auth, "The Promise and Perils of Liturg Change," *ATR,* 2004; Auth, "Baptism 4: Angl; Baptismal Vows, Renwl of; Ord of Wmn," *New Westminster Dictionary of Liturg and Wrshp,* Westminster Jn Knox, 2002; Auth, "Journeys of Faith," *The Conviction of Things Not Seen,* Brazos Press, 2002; Ed and Contrib, "Gleanings: Essays on Expansive Lang w Prayers for Var Occasions," Ch Pub, 2001; Auth, "The Gift of Authority: New Steps in Angl/RC Relatns," *Ecum Trends,* 2001; Auth, "By Water and the H Sprt: Baptism and Cnfrmtn in Anglicanism," *Engaging the Sprt,* Ch Pub, 2001; Auth, "Cont the Reformation," Ch Pub, 1997; Ed, "A PB for the 21st Century," Ch Hymnal, 1996; Ed and Contrib, "Chld at the Table," Ch Hymnal, 1995; Ed, "Baptism and Mnstry," Ch Hymnal, 1994; Ed and Contrib, "How Shall We Pray?," Ch Hymnal, 1994. Associated Parishes Coun 1996.

MEYERS, Timothy Mark (NC) **S Jas Par Wilmington NC 2016-** D 6/11/2016 P 12/17/2016 Bp Anne Hodges-Copple.

MEZACAPA, Nicklas A (Minn) 111 3rd Ave SW, Rochester MN 55902 B Cleveland OH 1949 s Anthony & Helen. BA Heidelberg U 1971; MDiv Bex Sem 1981. D 6/27/1981 Bp John Harris Burt P 1/3/1982 Bp Charles Bennison Sr. m 7/25/1970 Edna Suzanne Tremayne c 2. R Calv Ch Rochester MN 1986-2016; R S Johns Ch Cedar Rapids IA 1984-1986; Asst S Lk's Par Kalamazoo MI 1981-1984. Auth, *A10 Spprt Grp;* Auth, *Angl Dig;* Auth, *Living Ch.*

MICHAEL, Mark A (WA) 10033 River Rd, Potomac MD 20854 **S Fran Ch Potomac MD 2016-** B Hagerstown MD 1978 s Dennis & Jo. BA Duke 2000; BTh Oxf GB 2003. D 4/8/2006 Bp John L Rabb P 10/14/2006 Bp Robert Wilkes Ihloff. m 7/2/2005 Allison Zbicz c 2. S Tim's Ch Herndon VA 2015-2016; R Chr's Ch Cooperstown NY 2009-2015; R S Paul's Ch Sharpsburg MD 2007-2009; Asst Chapl St Jas Sch Hagerstown MD 2006-2009. CBS 2003; SocMary 2003. mmichael@stfrancispotomac.org

MICHAELS, Glen Francis (Alb) Po Box 2123, Plattsburgh NY 12901 **P Assoc, Vol Trin Ch Plattsburgh NY 2004-; Asst Atty Gnrl St of New York 2000-** B Chicago IL 1955 s Russell & Elaine. U Chi 1974; BA CUA 1978; JD Ya 1982; MDiv CDSP 1992. D 12/5/1992 P 12/1/1993 Bp William Edwin Swing. c 3. R S Jn's Ch Essex NY 1996-2000; Ch Of The Gd Shpd Houlton ME 1994-1996; R Open Heart Healing Cmnty Piedmont CA 1993-1994; D S Paul's Ch Oakland CA 1993.

MICHAELS, Laurie Jane (Chi) 647 Dundee Ave, Barrington IL 60010 **D S Mich's Ch Barrington IL 2010-** B Detroit MI 1953 d Waldo & Margaret. BS Geo 1974; AD St Marys Coll 1979; AD St Marys Coll 1981; Natl U Grad Sch Nurse Prog 1996; Dio Chicago Deacons Sch 2009. D 2/6/2010 Bp Jeff Lee. m 8/17/1974 Gregory H Michaels c 2. Bp Anderson Hse Chicago IL 2010-2015.

MICHAELSON, Peter Ruhl (RI) 2 Gaspee Point Dr, Warwick RI 02888 **Vic S Mary's Ch E Providence RI 2012-; Ret Warwick RI 2006-; Hon. Chapl The Mssn to Seafarers Narragansett Bay 2006-** B Milwaukee WI 1942 s Stanley & Elizabeth. Defense Languate Inst 1962; BA U of Utah 1967; BD EDS 1970; DMin SWTS 1998. D 6/24/1970 Bp Richard S Watson P 3/1/1971 Bp Lyman Cunningham Ogilby. m 9/3/1965 Wanda Michaelson c 2. Dvlpmt Off Rhode Island St Coun of Ch 2011-2013; S Jn The Div Ch Saunderstown RI 2010-2012; Int R S Mk's Ch Warwick RI 2008-2009; S Ann's-By-The-Sea Block Island RI 2006-2007; Asst S Barn Ch Warwick RI 2002-2009; Exec Secy Serv No Amer Maritime Mnstry Assn. 2001-2005; Ecum Off Dio Rhode Island Providence RI 1995-2000; Ch of the Epiph Rumford RI 1993-2000; St Mich & Gr Ch Rumford RI 1993-2000; Stff to Bp of Idaho Dio Idaho Boise ID 1992-1993, Ecum Off 1986-1991, Prog Dir of Yth Camps 1985, Dioc Coun 1983-1984, Prog Dir of Yth Camps 1979-1982, Chair on Prog Dept 1983-1986, Chair on Evang & Renwl 1979-1984; Vic Ch Of H Nativ Meridian ID 1978-1992; Sprtl Dir Curs Dioceses of Mass. Idaho and RI 1976-1993; Assoc S Andr's Ch Framingham MA 1970-1978. Auth, "Settling the Homeless," *Living Ch;* Auth, "Conflict in the Ch," *Living Ch.* Cler Assn. of RI - Epis 2006; EPF 1968; No Amer Maritime Mnstry Assn. 2001; OSL 1976; The Mssn to Seafarers 2001; Urban Caucus 1976-1995.

MICHAUD, Bruce Alan (EMich) 2090 Wyndham Ln, Alpena MI 49707 B Alpena MI 1947 s Gene & Betty. BA MI SU 1969; MDiv VTS 1972. D 6/26/1972 Bp Richard Stanley Merrill Emrich P 9/20/1973 Bp H Coleman Mcgehee Jr. m 10/11/2002 Margaret L Michaud c 2. R Trin Epis Ch Alpena MI 2002-2014; R S Paul's Ch Louisville KY 1985-2002; R S Albans Epis Ch Bay City MI 1981-1985; R S Andr's Epis Ch Algonac MI 1974-1981; Asst Gr Epis

M

Ch Port Huron MI 1972-1974; Stndg Com Pres Dio Estrn Michigan Saginaw MI 2013-2014. Gospel & Our Culture Ntwk 1990.

MICHAUD, David Norman (Eas) St Peter's Church, 115 Saint Peters St, Salisbury MD 21801 **GC Off Consult Epis Ch Cntr New York NY 2014-, 2012; P-in-c S Ptr's Ch Salisbury MD 2013-** B Lynn MA 1963 s Norman & Patricia. ABS U CA 1985; MDiv GTS 2007. D 6/2/2007 P 12/21/2007 Bp Bud Shand. m 6/13/1987 Kelli Lankford Michaud c 2. R S Andr's Epis Ch Princess Anne MD 2007-2013; Dep GC Dio Easton Easton MD 2014-2016, Co Chair, Dioc Discernment Com 2014-2015, Mem, Disciplinary Bd 2011-2016, First Alt Dep GC 2011-2014, Chair, Dioc Grants Com 2010-2015, VP, Dioc Coun 2009-2013, Mem, Nomin Com 2007-2013; Chair Grtr Princess Anne Mnstrl Assn 2009-2013; Database Mgr GC Sec: 2006-2012 2006-2012. Auth, "A Hist of the Dio Easton: How the First Parishes, Geography and Urbanization Shaped the Dio," *Same as Title (Sr hon Thesis)*, GTS & digitally: Dio Easton, 2007.

MICHAUD, Eleanor Jean (Eau) B Chicago IL 1939 D 2/19/2005 P 8/20/2005 Bp Keith Whitmore. m 11/14/1970 Ronald Jaksch Michaud c 2.

MICHAUD, Jean Fruitho (Hai) c/o Diocese of Haiti, Boite Postale 1309, Port au Prince Haiti Haiti **Dio Haiti Port-au-Prince HT 2008-** B 1976 s Michaud. D 1/25/2006 P 2/18/2007 Bp Jean Zache Duracin. m 10/13/2011 Kercia Eugene Michaud.

✠ **MICHEL, The Rt Rev Rodney Rae** (LI) 600 E Cathedral Rd Apt G304, Philadelphia PA 19128 **Ret Bp Suffr of Long Island Dio Long Island Garden City NY 2007-, Suffr Bp of Long Island 1997-2007; Asstg Bp Dioocese of Pennsylvania 2007-** B Petersburg NE 1943 s Marion & Phyllis. Nebraska Wesl 1963; BS U of Nebraska 1965; BD SWTS 1970. D 6/21/1970 P 12/1/1970 Bp Russell T Rauscher Con 4/12/1997 for LI. Dio Pennsylvania Philadelphia PA 2009-2011; R, Chair, Stndg Com S Ptr's by-the-Sea Epis Ch Bay Shore NY 1991-1997; Cn Pstr Cathd Of The Incarn Garden City NY 1987-1991; R S Paul's Epis Ch Grand Forks ND 1982-1987; Chair, COM Dio Nebraska Omaha NE 1979-1981, Mem, COM, Stndg Com 1972-1979; R S Fran Epis Ch Scottsbluff NE 1972-1982; S Mk's Ch Gordon NE 1970-1972; Vic S Mary's Ch: Holly Rushville NE 1970-1972. Epis Visitor: Bro of S Greg 1997; Ord of S Lk 1975; SHN 1995; SocMary 1970. DD SWTS. cnb41137@yahoo.com

MICHELFELDER, Susan Rebecca (SO) 30 W Woodruff Ave, Columbus OH 43210 **R S Steph's Epis Ch And U Columbus OH 2016-** B Toledo OH 1951 d George & Dorothy. BA Capital U 1980; MA Luth TS at Chicago 1987; MDiv CDSP 1999. D 6/19/1999 Bp Kenneth Lester Price P 3/25/2000 Bp Clarence Wallace Hayes. Gr Ch The Plains VA 2014-2016; S Mart's Epis Ch Charlotte NC 2013-2014; Int Chr Ch Middletown NJ 2010-2013; P-in-c Trin Epis Ch Everett WA 2009-2010; P-in-c Epiph Par of Seattle Seattle WA 2008-2009; Int S Ptr's Epis Ch Delaware OH 2005-2007; R S Ptr's Ch Gallipolis OH 2001-2005; R Chr Ch By-The-Sea Colon Panama 2000-2001; Mssy Dio Panama 1999-2001; R Dio Panama 1999-2001; D Chr Ch By-The-Sea Colon Panama 1999-2000; D Dio Sthrn Ohio Cincinnati OH 1999. Associated Parishes. rebecca_michelfelder@icloud.com

MICHELL, Neal O (Dal) 5100 Ross Ave, Dallas TX 75206 **Dn S Matt's Cathd Dallas TX 2013-** B Dallas TX 1953 s James & Jimmie. BA U of Texas 1976; JD U of Houston 1979; MDiv Sewanee: The U So, TS 1986; DMin Fuller TS 2003. D 6/13/1986 Bp Stanley Fillmore Hauser P 12/13/1986 Bp John Herbert MacNaughton. m 8/5/1978 Varita Michell c 4. Cn to the Ordnry Dio Dallas Dallas TX 2008-2012, Cn for Strategic Dvlpmt 2001-2007; Int R S Lk's Epis Ch Dallas TX 2007-2008; R S Jn's Ch New Braunfels TX 1998-2001; Ch Of The Redeem Germantown TN 1992-1998; R S Tim's Ch Indianapolis IN 1992-1998; R S Barn Epis Ch Fredricksburg TX 1988-1991; Vic H Trin Carrizo Sprg TX 1986-1988; P-in-c S Tim's Ch Cotulla TX 1986-1988. Auth, "Beyond Bus as Usual: Vstry Ldrshp Dvlpmt, Second Ed," Ch Pub, 2016; Auth, "How to Hit the Ground Running: A Quick Start Guide to Congregations w New Ldrshp," Ch Pub, 2005. Who's Who Among Executives SE Executives Ass'n 1997; Dwight Gk Medal U So, Sch of Theol 1986.

MICHELS, Sandie B (Ind) 5910 Black Oak Lane, Ft. Worth TX 76114 **P-in-c S Elis Ch Ft Worth TX 2012-; Ret 2009-** B San Bernardino CA 1945 d Raymond & Donna. BA CUNY 1969; MDiv GTS 1975; STM GTS 2011. D 6/26/1975 Bp Archibald Donald Davies P 4/25/1977 Bp Richard Mitchell Trelease Jr. Asst S Jn's Ch New York NY 2009-2011; S Fran In The Fields Zionsville IN 1986-2009; Assoc S Mart's Ch Ellisville MO 1979-1986; Dio The Rio Grande Albuquerque 1978-1979; S Clem's Epis Par Sch El Paso TX 1975-1978.

MICHIE, Michael Williams (Dal) 8701 Tiercels Dr, Mckinney TX 75070 **St Andrews Ch McKinney TX 2008-** B Mineral Wells TX 1968 s Joe & Juliana. BA U of Texas 1990; MPA Texas St U San Marcos 1992; MA Oral Roberts U 1993; Cert Theol Stud Epis TS of the SW 1998. D 11/1/1999 P 11/2/2000 Bp Claude Edward Payne. m 8/10/1991 Laurie L Michie c 3. Dio Dallas Dallas TX 2004-2007, Pres, Stndg Com 2011-2012, Dep, GC 2010-, Stndg Com 2009-2012, Del, Prov Syn 2008-2009, Exec Coun 2006-2009; Chr The King Ch Houston TX 2003; The Great Cmsn Fndt Houston TX 2002-2004; S Barn Ch Austin TX 2000-2002; Asst R S Richard's Of Round Rock Round Rock TX 1999-2000. Auth, "Communities of Transformation," *Vstry Paper*, ECF, 2013; Auth, "Daily Off Daily," Online Daily Off Serv, 2011.

MICHNO, Dennis Glen (Eau) 34615 County Highway J, Bayfield WI 54814 **P in charge Chr Ch Bayfield WI 1996-** B Chicago IL 1947 s Thaddeus & Jeanne. BS S Johns U Collegeville 1969; Juilliard Sch 1971; MDiv GTS 1977; STM GTS 1983. D 5/19/1977 P 11/19/1977 Bp Harold Louis Wright. R Trin Epis Ch Stoughton MA 1991-1995; Asst The Ch Of The H Sprt Orleans MA 1988-1991; Asst S Dav's Epis Ch S Yarmouth MA 1987-1988; Cathd Of St Jn The Div New York NY 1984-1987; Cur All SS Ch New York NY 1977-1984; Dir of Mus All SS Ch New York NY 1971-1984. Auth, *A P's Handbook*, 1983; Auth, *A Manual for Acolytes*, 1981. Assn of Angl Mus; CHS. Bp's Cross Paul Moore, New York 1981.

MICKELSON, Margaret Belle (Ak) PO Box 849, Cordova AK 99574 **S Geo's Ch Cordova AK 2009-** B Lima OH 1947 d George & Mary Jane. BA Mia 1970; MS U MI 1972; MDiv CDSP 2007. D 12/4/2006 P 6/12/2007 Bp Mark Lawrence Macdonald. c 1.

MIDDLETON, Mark Leslie (Chi) 509 Hessel Blvd, Champaign IL 61820 **Supply P Gr Ch Pontiac IL 2013-; Asst To R S Matt 1980-** B Champaign IL 1949 s Glenn & Lois. MS Baden-Powell U; BA NWU 1972; MDiv SWTS 1976; MBA U Chi 1981. D 5/8/1976 Bp Quintin Ebenezer Primo Jr P 11/1/1976 Bp James Winchester Montgomery. m 4/29/1995 Paula Massey c 2. Supply P Ch Of The Gd Shpd Momence IL 2008-2013; Supply P 2007-2013; Dir of Fin HabHum Champaign Chapt 2006-2008; HabHum for Champaign Cty 2006-2007; Vic S Alb's Ch Chicago IL 2001-2004; Vic St Cyprians Ch Chicago IL 1999-2001; Cler team Mnstry S Mk's Ch Evanston IL 1998-1999; Indstrl Chapl Illinois Municipal Ret Fund 1993-2004; Indstrl Chapl Standard Oil Co of Indiana-AMOCO 1988-1992; Indstrl Chapl Luth Gnrl Hlth Care System (Advoc HCS) 1984-1988; Cler team Mnstry S Matt's Ch Evanston IL 1980-1992; Indstrl Chapl Standard Oil Co of Indiana-AMOCO 1980-1984; Ch Of The H Apos Wauconda IL 1978-1980; The Ch Of S Jn The Evang Flossmoor IL 1976-1978. Auth, "Mortuary Sci and the Quest for the Moral High Ground in Jude 9.," *Bibliography*, Word Press, 2014. Natl Assn For The Self- Supporting Active Mnstry. Wood Badge BSA 2002; Anderson Schlr 1975; H B Whipple Schlr 76; Kramer Prize Theol 75 SWTS.

MIDDLETON III, Richard Temple (Miss) 944 Royal Oak Dr, Jackson MS 39209 B Jackson MS 1942 s Richard & Johnie. BS Linc 1963; MEd Linc 1965; EdD U of Sthrn Mississippi 1972; Fell Sewanee: The U So, TS 1993. D 7/3/1993 Bp Duncan Montgomery Gray Jr P 2/27/1994 Bp Alfred Marble Jr. m 8/10/1968 Brenda Marie Middleton c 2. R S Mk's Ch Jackson MS 2003-2014; Vic S Mary's Ch Vicksburg MS 1993-2003. Auth, "Afr Americans & Dry Bones," *The Boule Journ*, 2008; Auth, "Stop The Foolishness, Hit The Books," *Close Up mag*, 1999; Auth, "Remember These Things," *The Boule Journ*, Sigma Pi Phi Fraternity, 1998; Auth, "A Recent Miss. Crt Decision Affects Educ & Wmn Rts," *Negro Educational Revs*, 1979. Exec Coun Epis Ch 1988.

MIDDLETON, Tracie Gail (FtW) PO Box 24761, Fort Worth TX 76124 **D Trin Epis Ch Ft Worth TX 2016-; Dio Ft Worth Ft Worth TX 2014-** B Dallas TX 1976 d Russell & Virginia. BA Austin Coll 1998; Iona Sch for Mnstry Dio Texas 2009; MA Lamar U 2011. D 2/22/2009 Bp Don Adger Wimberly. D S Steph's Epis Ch Hurst TX 2011-2016; D S Jn's Epis Ch Silsbee TX 2009-2011; Chapl Vidor Firefighters' Assn Vidor TX 2007-2011; Port Chapl Pt. Arthur Intl Seafarers' Cntr Pt. Arthur TX 2005-2009. Assn for Epis Deacons 2014. tracie.middleton@edfw.org

MIDENCE VALDES, Jose Francisco (Hond) Comercio, Tela Honduras **Dio Honduras San Pedro Sula 1989-; Vic H Sprt 1989-** B Tegucigalpa DC HN 1965 s Alfonso & Alba. Santa Maria Sem 1989. D 1/6/1989 Bp Leo Frade. m 2/6/2004 Veronica Pereira-Lara c 5.

MIDWOOD JR, John Earle (Pa) 300 North Lawrence, Philadelphia PA 19106 B Trenton NJ 1946 s John & Isabel. BS Tem 1971; MDiv EDS 1974; DMin SWTS 2000. D 6/15/1974 P 1/31/1975 Bp Lyman Cunningham Ogilby. m 9/12/1969 Faith A Bustard c 1. Epis Cmnty Serv Philadelphia PA 2000-2013; Archd Dio Pennsylvania Philadelphia PA 1989-2000; Ch Of S Jn The Evang Philadelphia PA 1984-1989; Asst Chr Ch Philadelphia Philadelphia PA 1978-1984; The Epis Acad Newtown Sq PA 1974-1978.

MIDYETTE III, Charles Thomas (EC) 122 Queen St, Beaufort NC 28516 B 1940 s Charles & Margaret. BA U So 1963; MDiv VTS 1966; LLD S Pauls Coll Lawrenceville 1987; DD VTS 2003. D 6/29/1966 P 1/6/1967 Bp Thomas H Wright. m 11/23/1979 Margaret Midyette c 1. R S Paul's Epis Ch Greenville NC 1994-2004; R S Phil's Ch Durham NC 1978-1994; R S Paul's Ch Beaufort NC 1971-1978; R S Paul's Epis Ch Clinton NC 1968-1971; Asst S Steph's Ch Goldsboro NC 1966-1968. Auth, "Sermons From S Phil'S: Selections 1912-1994," 2001; Auth, "Hunger Notes"; Auth, "Jub".

MIDZALKOWSKI, Sarah Frances (Mich) 765 Grove Street, East Lansing MI 48823 **Cbury MI SU E Lansing MI 2007-** B Gainesville Florida 1970 d Joseph & Sally. BA U of Florida 1992; MDiv VTS 2004. D 3/13/2004 P 9/18/2004 Bp Mark Sean Sisk. Trin Ch Fredericksbrg VA 2004-2007.

MIEDKE, Warren Giles (Tex) 13131 Fry Rd, Cypress TX 77433 **D S Aid's Ch Cypress TX 2011-** B Algona IA 1938 s Ralph & Mary. Iona Sch 2011. D 6/18/2011 Bp C Andrew Doyle. m 6/25/1960 Marilyn J Miedke c 2.

M

583

MIESCHER III, Walter Henry (Kan) 2630 N Ridgewood Ct, Wichita KS 67220 **D S Barth's Ch Wichita KS 1999-** B Portland OR 1945 s Walter & Francis. BS Nthrn Arizona U 1976; EFM Sewanee: The U So, TS 1989; Kansas Sch of Mnstry 1999. D 10/6/1999 Bp William Edward Smalley. m 7/21/1990 Cheryl Lee Gunter c 2. NAAD.

MIHALYI, David (CNY) 472 Washington St, Geneva NY 14456 B Lowville NY 1950 s Charles & Helen. BS SUNY 1972; MDiv Colgate Rochester Crozer DS 1977; MDiv CRDS 1977. D 9/17/1977 P 6/17/1979 Bp Ned Cole. m 12/7/2001 Mary Lee Mihalyi. Dio Cntrl New York Liverpool NY 1989-1991; Vic Gr Ch Willowdale Geneva NY 1982-1985; R S Paul's Ch Waterloo NY 1981-2012; Assoc All SS Angl Ch Rochester NY 1979-1980.

MIKAYA, Henry C (WMich) Box 1315, Gabrone Botswana B Kasunqu MW 1940 s Henock & Doris. Cert S Cyp Theol Coll 1970; S Johns Sem 1971; Cert Coll Ascen 1975; MBA Mecy Coll 1983; MDiv Drew U 1992; MA Trin 1994. Trans 9/1/1990 Bp John Shelby Spong. m 11/26/1966 Mary Veronica Kalonga. Exec Coun Appointees New York NY 1999-2002; H Trin Epis Ch Wyoming MI 1996-1999; R Epis Ch Of SS Jn Paul And S Clem Mt Vernon NY 1992-1996; Chr Epis Ch E Orange NJ 1990-1991; Serv Ch Of Malawi 1971-1979. Newark Cler Assn.

MIKEL, Joseph F (Oly) 15945 Cascade Ln Se, Monroe WA 98272 **The Ch Of S Dav Of Wales Shelton WA 2016-** B Spokane WA 1948 s Wallace & Janet. Grays Harbor Cc 1968; Seattle Cmnty Coll 1968; BA U of Washington 1971; MDiv GTS 1974. D 7/15/1974 P 7/26/1975 Bp Ivol I Curtis. m 10/5/1969 Peggy Martha Mikel. Ch Of The Ascen Seattle WA 1983; S Paul's Ch Walla Walla WA 1977-1979; Com 1975-1977; S Steph's Epis Ch Longview WA 1974-1977. Soc Of S Jn The Evang.

MILAM, David Ross (Mass) 108 Lakeside Ave, Lakeville MA 02347 **R Ch Of Our Sav Middleboro MA 2004-** B El Paso TX 1960 s Earl & Brenda. BS U of Maine 1988; MDiv Sewanee: The U So, TS 2001. D 6/9/2001 Bp Robert Jefferson Hargrove Jr P 2/17/2002 Bp Gerry Wolf. m 8/13/1983 Ruth L Milam c 3. Cur Trin Ch Newport RI 2001-2004.

MILAM, Thomas Richerson (SwVa) 715 Forest Hills Dr, Wilmington NC 28403 B Winchester VA 1965 s John & Louise. BA W Virginia U 1988; MDiv Va Berk 1993; MD U of Virginia 1998. D 6/12/1993 P 12/15/1993 Bp Peter J Lee. m 6/17/1995 Noelle Valley Milam c 4. S Jas Par Wilmington NC 2010, 2008-2009, Asst 2002; S Paul's Memi Charlottesvlle VA 1995-1998, 1993-1994; Chr Epis Ch Charlottesvlle VA 1994.

MILAN JR, Jesse (Kan) 7103 Waverly Ave, Kansas City KS 66109 B Depue OK 1928 s Clarence & Willie. BS U of Kansas 1953; MS U of Kansas 1954; EdS Emporia St U 1969; Baker U 2000. D 6/3/2006 Bp Dean E Wolfe. m 6/13/1954 Alversa Brewster c 4. Asst Prof of Educ Baker U Boldwin KS 1969-2002. Dr of Educ Baker U 2001.

MILANO, Mary Lucille (Chi) 8765 W Higgins Rd, Chicago IL 60631 **S Alb's Ch Chicago IL 2004-; Dir For Hunger Educ Evang Luth Ch In Amer - Churchwide Off 2002-** B Chicago IL 1952 d Daniel & Catharine. BA Mundelein Coll 1973; MDiv McCormick TS 1977; JD Nthrn Illinois U 1978; DMin GTF 1994; U of Leicester 2002. D 6/11/2000 Bp Peter Hess Beckwith P 7/30/2002 Bp Victor Alfonso Scantlebury. c 1. Asst Cathd Of S Jas Chicago IL 2002-2003; Evang Luth Ch in Amer Chicago IL 2001-2003; Asstg D S Andr's Ch Paris IL 2000-2001. Auth, "Hunger No More - Intl ," Bread For The Wrld Inst, 2003; Auth, "Peace Is In Our Hands: Bldg A Vocabulary Of Peace Through Th," *Law Related Educ*, Illinois St Bar Assn, 2002; Auth, "The Forcible Transfer Of Palestinians To Gaza," *The Globe*, Illinois St Bar Assn, 2002; Auth, "A Primer On Impeachment," Illinois St Bar Assn, 1998; Auth, "Ethical Issues And The Internet," Illinois St Bar Assn, 1998; Auth, "Practicing Law Across St Boundaries," *The Globe*, Illinois St Bar Assn, 1998; Auth, "Mortgage Foreclosure," *Basic Real Estate Pract*, Iicle, 1988. ABA 1978; Assn For Practical And Profsnl Ethics 1993; Coll Theol Soc 1991; Illinois St Bar Assn 1978; Intl Bar Assn 1995; Italian Amer Political Cltn Of Illinois 1999; Justinian Soc Of Lawyers 1978; Ord Of The Easter Star - Grand Chapt Of Illinois 1977. Judith Shanahan Memi Ldrshp And Serv Awd S Mary Of The Woods Coll 2001; DSA For Career Achievement And Publ Serv Nthrn Illinois U Coll Of Law Alum Assn 1998; DSA Illinois St Bar Assn 1990; Ldrshp Awd GSA, Chicago Dist Coun 1988; Mem And Vice Chair City Of Chicago Bd Ethics 1987; Anna L And Jas Nelson Raymond Fell NWU Coll Of Law 1977; Fell Soc For Values In Higher Educ 1975; Fell Danforth Fndt 1973.

MILES, Frank William (Colo) 1175 Vine St Apt 207, Denver CO 80206 **Ret 1996-** B Springfield OH 1936 s William & Barbara. BS USMA 1958; MDiv Nash 1968; Marq 1971; NW St U 1972; EdD U Denv 1980; PrTS 1982. D 7/25/1968 Bp Joseph Summerville Minnis P 1/25/1969 Bp Edwin B Thayer. m 6/17/1984 Kathryn Miles c 1. Asst S Barn Epis Ch Denver CO 1996-1998; Non-par 1987-1990; R Intsn Epis Ch Denver CO 1982-1987; Vic S Mart In The Fields Aurora CO 1978-1982; Asst Chr Epis Ch Denver CO 1975-1978; Instr At The Acad Ft Polk LA 1974-1975; Hosp Chapl 1973-1974; Chapl Ft Polk LA 1971-1975; Chapl S Jn's Mltry Acad Delafield WI 1970-1971; Vic S Paul's Epis Ch Steamboat Sprngs CO 1969-1970; Vic S Mk's Ch Craig CO 1968-1970; S Jas' Epis Ch Meeker CO 1968-1969. Auth, "Stages Human

Dvlpmt". Mltry Chapl, Assn Assn Of Chr Therapists. Air Medal W/Oak Leaf Cluster; Meritorious Serv Medal,; Bronze Star,.

MILES, Glenworth Dalmane (LI) 2714 Lurting Ave, Bronx NY 10469 **R S Geo's Ch Brooklyn NY 2002-** B Manchester JM 1960 s Arthur & Sylvia. AA Queensborough Cmnty Coll 1983; BA CUNY 1988; MDiv GTS 1991; DMin Drew U 2001. D 6/8/1991 P 12/14/1991 Bp Richard Frank Grein. Dio New York New York NY 1996-2001; P-in-c S Martha's Ch Bronx NY 1995-2001; Vic Gr Ch (W Farms) Bronx NY 1992-1995; D S Lk's Epis Ch Bronx NY 1991-1992; Chapl Lady of Mercy Med Cntr 1989-1990. OHC 1979; The BroSA 2004. Balm in Gilead HIV/AIDS Awd The Balm in Gilead 2006; Cmnty Serv Awd Lion's Club of New York 2005; Medal for exceptional Pstr care to the people of God The Soc of St Jn the Evang and Theol, Dio 2000.

MILES, James B (HB) **Min Reston Epis Cong 1976-** B Holden MA 1937 s James & Mary. BA Dart 1959; MA Rhode Island Coll 1967. D 5/22/1976 Bp John Alfred Baden P 6/11/1977 Bp Robert Bruce Hall. m 12/23/1961 Joan Earlene Miles c 2. S Anne's Epis Ch Reston VA 1976-1980.

MILES JR, John Pickett (SVa) 268 Mill Stream Way, Williamsburg VA 23185 **Ret 2004-** B Rochester NY 1942 s John & Alice. BA U NC 1966; MDiv VTS 1969. D 6/24/1969 P 6/1/1970 Bp Thomas Augustus Fraser Jr. m 6/12/1965 Helen K Miles c 2. R S Mart's Epis Ch Williamsburg VA 1975-2004; Asst H Trin Par Epis Clemson SC 1971-1975; Asst Calv Ch Tarboro NC 1969-1971.

MILES, Kristin K (Ct) 661 Old Post Rd, Fairfield CT 06824 **Trin Par New York NY 2014-** B Washington DC 1972 d Allan & Linda. BA Wellesley Coll 1994; MDiv Harvard DS 2000. D 6/11/2011 P 12/17/2011 Bp Laura Ahrens. m 7/17/1999 Chris Miles c 3. S Paul's Ch Fairfield CT 2011-2012.

MILES, Richard Alan Knox (NC) 634 Parkway Blvd, Reidsville NC 27320 **R S Thos Epis Ch Reidsville NC 2011-; Dn of Greensboro Convoc Dio No Carolina Raleigh NC 2012-** B Sanger CA 1950 s William & Mabel. BA Fresno Pacific U 1972; MDiv PrTS 1977; DMin SFTS 1997; Angl Stds ETSBH 2005. D 4/23/2005 Bp Sergio Carranza-Gomez P 1/14/2006 Bp Frank Tracy Griswold III. m 7/3/1976 Daun Miles c 2. P-in-c S Thos Of Cbury Par Long Bch CA 2010; D S Fran' Par Palos Verdes Estates CA 2005; Dir of Mus Bert Lynn Middle Sch Torrance CA 1998-2006; Sr Pstr Presb Ch 1977-1997; Supply P Dio Los Angeles Los Angeles CA 2006-2011. Soc of Cath Priests 2011; The Ord of St. Lazarus 1990. Sr Chapl The Ord of St. Lazarus 2014. rector@stthomasreidsville.org

MILES, Thomas Dee (Kan) 1308 Overlook Dr, Manhattan KS 66503 **Coun of Trst Dio Kansas Topeka KS 2011-** B Omaha NE 1947 s Richard & Ruth. BA U of Nebraska at Kearney 1970; MDiv Sewanee: The U So, TS 1976. D 6/28/1976 P 12/1/1976 Bp William Davidson. m 6/1/1968 Susan J Miles c 1. R S Paul's Ch Manhattan KS 2002-2012; P-in-c S Tim's Ch Gering NE 1994-2002; R Ch Of The H Apos Mitchell NE 1992-2002; Assoc All SS Epis Ch Omaha NE 1990-1992; S Eliz's Ch Holdrege NE 1978-1988; S Aug's Ch Meade KS 1977-1978; P-in-c S Tim's Epis Ch Hugoton KS 1977-1978; Dio Wstrn Kansas Hutchinson KS 1976.

MILFORD, Sara M (Ark) 228 Spring St, Hot Springs AR 71901 **All SS Ch Bentonville AR 2017-; S Lk's Ch Hot Sprg AR 2015-** B Rogers AR 1977 d Kenny & Pamela. BA Hendrix Coll 2001; MDiv The TS 2015; MDiv The TS at The U So 2015. D 3/17/2015 P 9/14/2015 Bp Larry Benfield. m 6/13/1998 Casey Trenton Milford c 4.

MILHAN, Pamela Hope Arnold (SwFla) D 6/13/2015 Bp Dabney Tyler Smith.

MILHOAN, Charles Everett (Az) 4102 W Union Hills Dr, Glendale AZ 85308 **D S Jn The Bapt Epis Ch Glendale AZ 2009-; Chairperson PC4Free Computer Mnstry 2003-; Instr - D Formation Acad Dio Arizona Phoenix AZ 2017-, Spec Liturg Coordntr 2016-, D Coun Mem 2015-, Sprtl Dir - Arizona Curs Sec 2015-; Asst Dn Camp 60's More or Less 2009-** B Amarillo TX 1950 s George & Ruth. Ord D Formation Acad - Dio Arizona. D 1/24/2009 Bp Kirk Stevan Smith. m 7/30/1977 Stacy Brown c 2. Vol DuetAZ 2010-2012.

MILHOLEN, Linda Scott (WMo) PO Box 109, Houston MO 65483 **P Ch Of The Trsfg Mtn Grove MO 2014-, D 2010-2015** B Hot Springs AR 1946 d Cleberne & Opal. BS Georgia Inst of Tech 1970; MD Emory U 1974; Cert Bp Kemper Sch for Mnstry 2014. D 7/6/1996 Bp Don Adger Wimberly P 4/26/2014 Bp Martin Scott Field. m 6/4/1964 Garland Milholen. D S Alb's Ch In The Ozarks Ch Bolivar MO 2002-2009; D Epis Ch of Our Sav Richmond KY 1996-2001.

MILHOLLAND, Nancy Elizabeth (Mass) 58 Stanford Heights Ave, San Francisco CA 94127 B New York NY 1959 d Harry & Helen. BA Dart 1983; MDiv SWTS 1992. D 5/30/1992 Bp David Elliot Johnson P 2/27/1993 Bp R aymond Stewart Wood Jr. Gr Ch Millbrook NY 1995-1996; Assoc S Jn's Epis Ch Saginaw MI 1992-1995. Auth, "The First 9 Weeks," *Brooklyn Bridge*, 1999.

MILHON-MARTIN, Jana (Los) 569 Carleton Pl, Claremont CA 91711 **Other Lay Position S Jn's Mssn La Verne CA 2010-** B Pomona, CA 1966 d James & Dorothy. BA Azusa Pacific U 1989; M.Div Claremont TS 2016. D 6/4/2016 P 1/14/2017 Bp Joseph Jon Bruno. m 5/23/1998 Victor Lee Martin c 3. jana_mimartin@hotmail.com

MILIAN, Mario Emilio (SeFla) 5690 N Kendall Dr, Coral Gables FL 33156 **Chapl U.S. AF Reserve Command 2013-; R S Thos Epis Par Miami FL**

2011-, Assoc R 2008-2011 B CU 1976 s Mario & Annie. BIS Arizona St U 2005; MDiv CDSP 2009. D 7/15/2000 Bp Leo Frade P 2/10/2001 Bp Robert Reed Shahan. m 7/11/1996 Julie Anne Alvelo Espinosa c 2. R All SS Epis Ch Oxnard CA 2006-2008; Assoc R S Matt's Ch Chandler AZ 2000-2006. mmilian@stepsmia.org

MILIEN, Marivel (SeFla) 6744 N Miami Ave, Miami FL 33150 **Iglesia Epis Santisima Trinidad Miami FL 2014-; D St Paul et Les Martyrs D'Haiti Miami FL 2007-** B Dominican Republic 1966 d Juan & Paula. D 10/28/2007 Bp Leo Frade P 11/9/2013 Bp Julio Cesar Holguin-Khoury. m 12/22/1991 Smith Baptiste Smith Milien c 3.

MILIEN, Smith Baptiste Smith (SeFla) 6744 North Miami Ave, Miami FL 33150 **P St Paul et Les Martyrs D'Haiti Miami FL 2008-; Vic S Jos/S Thos Boca Chica Dominican Republic 1986-** B Gressier Port-au-Prince HT 1959 s Ecclesiaste & Zulema. BA Centro de Estudios Teologicos 1986. D 10/26/1986 P 12/20/1987 Bp Telesforo A Isaac. m 12/22/1991 Marivel Milien c 3. Iglesia Epis Santisima Trinidad Miami FL 2013-2014; R Episcopan Bakery Barahona DR 2006-2007; Vic Iglesia Epis San Tito Jimani DR 2004-2007; Tchr Centro De Estu Dios Teologicos Santo Domingo DR 2003-2007; Recetor Jesus Peregrino Chld's Shltr Barahona DR 2003-2007; Archd So Reg Dio DR 2003-2007; Vic Iglesia Epis San Jorge Azua DR 2000-2003; Vic Iglesia Epis La Resurreccion Consuelo DR 1991-1994; R San Gabr Elem Sch Consuelo DR 1991-1994; Dio The Dominican Republic (Iglesia Epis Dominicana) Gazcue Santo Domingo 1986-2007; Vic Iglesia Epis San Gabr.

MILKOVICH, Edward Frank (Los) 28211 Pacific Coast Hwy, Malibu CA 90265 B Raton New Mexico 1954 s Edward & Angelina. AA Coll of the Canyons 1974; BA California St U 1976; MDiv CDSP 2017. D 6/3/2017 Bp Diane Jardine Bruce. m 6/4/2011 Lorraine Senna c 3.

MILLAR, Chuck (Mich) 14818 Oakes Rd, Perry MI 48872 **Ret 1992-** B Lansing MI 1933 s Charles & Pamelia. BA Albion Coll 1955; BD Yale DS 1958; MA MI SU 1975. D 6/28/1958 P 7/18/1959 Bp Richard Stanley Merrill Emrich. m 6/18/1955 Susan Millar c 4. Non-par 1972-1992; Ecumical Assoc Lansing MI 1967-1972; R Trin Epis Ch Flushing MI 1960-1966; Vic S Geo Epis Ch Centerline MI 1958-1960.

MILLAR, John Dunne (Az) 7245 E Manzanita Dr, Scottsdale AZ 85258 B Detroit MI 1940 s James & America. BS Geo Mason U 1974; MBA Loyola U 1978; MDiv VTS 1985. D 6/22/1985 P 4/1/1986 Bp Peter J Lee. c 1. Dio Arizona Phoenix AZ 2006; S Aug's Epis Ch Tempe AZ 2002-2006; Trin Epis Ch El Dorado KS 1999-2002; Non-par 1995-1998; Ch Of S Phil And S Jas Denver CO 1992-1995; R Chr Epis Ch Ballston Spa NY 1988-1992; Cur The Ch Of The Mssh Glens Falls NY 1987-1988; Asst Chr Epis Ch Winchester VA 1985-1987.

⚓ MILLARD, The Rt Rev George Richard (Cal) 501 Portola Rd # 8107, Portola Valley CA 94028 B Dunsmuir CA 1914 s George & Constance. CDSP; STM PSR; MA Santa Clara U; BA U CA 1935; BD EDS 1938. D 7/6/1938 Bp Archie Noel Porter P 6/14/1939 Bp Henry Knox Sherrill Con 2/2/1960 for Cal. Convoc of Epis Ch in Europe Paris 1980-2001; Chr Epis Ch Los Altos CA 1980-2000; Asstg Bp of California Dio California San Francisco CA 1980-2000, Bp 1960-1976; Exec Coun Appointees New York NY 1978-1980; Epis Ch Cntr New York NY 1977-1978; R Chr Ch Alameda CA 1951-1960; R S Jas Epis Ch Danbury CT 1941-1951; Cur S Jn's Epis Par Waterbury CT 1939-1941; Cur S Jas Ch New York NY 1938-1939; Trst The CPG New York NY 1969-1979.

MILLARD, Michael Wayne (WLa) 405 Washington Ave, Mansfield LA 71052 B Little Rock AR 1968 s Irvin & Sherrill. BA U of Dallas 1990; MDiv Nash 2008. D 6/7/2008 P 3/7/2009 Bp D Avid Bruce Macpherson. m 4/23/1994 Samantha D Millard c 3. R Chr Memi Ch Mansfield LA 2010-2017; Cur S Mk's Cathd Shreveport LA 2008-2010.

MILLER, Alan Clayborne (Fla) 1637 Nw 19th Cir, Gainesville FL 32605 B Birmingham AL 1949 s Albert & Eleanor. BA Emory U 1971; MA U of Florida 1981; PhD U of Florida 1984; MDiv Sewanee: The U So, TS 1992. D 6/20/1992 P 12/20/1992 Bp John Wadsworth Howe. m 10/23/1976 Shelia Flemming Miller c 2. Serv S Fran Of Assisi Epis Ch Lake Placid FL 1992-1998. Auth, "A Handbook For Wilderness Counslr"; Auth, "Gender Constancy In Pre-Sch Chld". APA.

MILLER, Alden Scott (Oly) 211 Calle del Verano, Palm Desert CA 92260 **Asstg Cler St. Marg of Scotland Palm Desert CA 2005-** B Los Angeles CA 1945 s Alden & Agnes. BA USC 1966; ETSBH 1985; MA Claremont TS 1986; MA Claremont TS 1986. D 6/22/1986 Bp Robert Claflin Rusack P 1/24/1987 Bp Oliver Bailey Garver Jr. m 4/1/2000 Lorraine Ann Miller c 1. S Lk's Epis Ch Vancouver WA 2000-2002; S Andr's Ch Seattle WA 1997; S Steph's Epis Ch Seattle WA 1989-1997; Asst R All SS Par Beverly Hills CA 1986-1989.

MILLER, Alfred Franklin (EO) 665 E Gladys Ave, Hermiston OR 97838 B Portland OR 1959 s Charles & Doreen. BS OR SU 1983; MDiv Ya Berk 1990. D 6/30/1990 Bp Rustin Ray Kimsey P 1/1/1991 Bp David Charles Bowman. m 8/21/1982 Michelle Leslie Miller c 2. S Lk's Epis Ch Vancouver WA 2000-2001; S Jn's Ch Hermiston OR 1999-2000; Dio Estrn Oregon Cove OR 1993-1998; Cur S Lk's Epis Ch Jamestown NY 1990-1993.

MILLER, Ann C (Ct) 99 Timberwood Rd, West Hartford CT 06117 B Saint LouisMO 1947 d William & Ann. BA Smith 1969; MDiv VTS 1989. D 6/10/

1989 P 12/10/1989 Bp Arthur Edward Walmsley. m 11/9/1996 Barry William Miller. S Ann's Epis Ch Old Lyme CT 2009-2010; St Johns Ch W Hartford CT 2008-2009, Int Asst 2008-2009, Int 1999-2000; Int Trin Epis Ch Williamsport PA 2007-2008; Int Emm Ch Covington VA 2006-2007; Int Calv Epis Ch Santa Cruz CA 2005-2006; Dio El Camino Real Salinas CA 2005; Int Epis Ch Cntr New York NY 2004-2005; Int Cathd Of The Incarn Garden City NY 2003; Dio Wstrn Massachusetts Springfield 2002-2003; Int Trin Par Lenox MA 2002-2003; Int S Jas Ch New London CT 2000-2001; Deploy Off Dio Connecticut Meriden CT 1995-1999; S Jas's Ch W Hartford CT 1993-2001; Chapl Trin Chap Hartford CT 1991-1995; Ya Berk New Haven CT 1989-1991; Epis Ch At Yale New Haven CT 1989-1991; Asst Chapl Epis Ch at Ya New Haven CT 1989-1991. Auth of one Chapt, "Renewing Denominational Linkages," *Temporary Shepherds*, Alb Inst, 1998. Soc for the Increase of Mnstry Exec Com 1993-2003.

MILLER, Anthony Glenn (Los) 350 S Madison Ave Apt 207, Pasadena CA 91101 B Los Angeles CA 1959 s Isaac & Lillian. BA USC 1984; MDiv GTS 1988; STM Yale DS 1995; STM Ya 1995; STM Ya 1995; EdM Harv 1996. D 6/25/1988 P 1/21/1989 Bp Frederick Houk Borsch. P S Barn' Par Pasadena CA 2002-2011; P S Aug And S Mart Ch Boston MA 1999-2001; Assoc S Ptr's Epis Ch Cambridge MA 1995-1998; Dio Long Island Garden City NY 1988-1992. agm@post.harvard.edu

MILLER, Arthur Burton (ECR) 2050 California St Apt 20, Mountain View CA 94040 B Des Moines IA 1922 s Howard & Amy. BA Whitworth U 1949; BEd Whitworth U 1950; MA U of Oregon 1962; PhD U of Oregon 1964. D 12/14/1988 P 6/1/1989 Bp Charles Shannon Mallory. m 9/11/1942 Lucy Minerva Smith. D Trin Cathd San Jose CA 1988-2001.

MILLER, Barbara Ruth (ECR) 5318 Palma Ave, Atascadero CA 93422 **S Jas Ch Paso Robles CA 2015-** B Princeton NJ 1953 d Thomas & Mary. BA California Polytechnic St U 2011; MDiv CDSP 2014; MDiv CDSP 2014. D 2/15/2014 P 8/15/2014 Bp Mary Gray-Reeves. c 3. S Steph's Epis Ch Sn Luis Obispo CA 2000-2003. BRMILLER8620@SBCGLOBAL.NET

MILLER, Barry William (Ct) 99 Timberwood Rd, West Hartford CT 06117 B Monessen PA 1939 s Charles & Olga. BS Penn 1961; MDiv GTS 1966. D 6/14/1966 Bp Ned Cole P 6/13/1967 Bp Walter M Higley. m 11/9/1996 Ann C Miller c 2. Int R.E. Lee Memi Lexington VA 2006-2007; Int R R E Lee Memi Ch (Epis) Lexington VA 2006; Int Vic S Phil The Apos Scotts Vlly CA 2004-2006; Int St. Phil the Apos Scotts Vlly CA 2004-2006; Int R Trin Ch Fishkill NY 2003-2004; Int Chapl Seabury Ret Cmnty Bloomfield CT 2001-2003; Vic S Steph's Epis Ch Bloomfield CT 1998-2003; P-in-c Chr Ch Waterbury CT 1997-1998; Int Chr Ch Avon CT 1997; Assoc S Jas Epis Ch Danbury CT 1995-1997; Assoc S Steph's Ch Ridgefield CT 1994-1995; Int S Andr's Ch New Haven CT 1993; Int All SS Epis Ch Meriden CT 1992-1993; Int S Andr's Ch Meriden CT 1990-1991; Int Pstr and P Assoc Var Parishes 1968-1998; Assoc Trin Epis Ch Cranford NJ 1968-1973; Cur Gr Ch Jamaica NY 1968; Cur Zion Ch Rome NY 1966-1967. Contrib, "Being an Afterpastor," *Transitional Mnstry*, Ch Pub, 2009. NNECA 2003-2012. revsmiller@gmail.com

MILLER, Charlene Ida (Tex) 14300 66th St N Lot 900, Clearwater FL 33764 B Phillipsburg NJ 1955 d Charles & Marie. BS Trenton St Coll 1977; MDiv Moravian TS 1983; MEd Kutztown U 1996. D 5/6/1984 P 4/28/1985 Bp James Michael Mark Dyer. m 5/7/1983 John Martin Miller c 3. Hd of Sch Trin Sch of Texas Longview TX 2004-2010; Dn of Students All SS Ch Phoenix AZ 2001-2004; Dn Stdts All SS Sch Vicksburg MS 1996-2004; Dn of Students All SS' Epis Sch Vicksburg MS 1996-2001; R S Barn Ch Kutztown PA 1989-1996; Int S Jas-S Geo Epis Ch Jermyn PA 1988-1989; R S Mk's Epis Ch Moscow PA 1985-1988; Int Chapl Easton Hosp Easton PA 1984-1985; D Trin Ch Easton PA 1984-1985.

MILLER, Charles Bernard (SVa) 302 Brittania Dr., Williamsburg VA 23185 **Died 4/8/2017** B Winston Salem NC 1947 LLB No Carolina Cntrl U. D 6/15/2002 P 1/28/2003 Bp David Conner Bane Jr. m 6/5/2002 Barbara Pitts. Int S Barn' Ch Greensboro NC 2005-2006.

MILLER, Christopher H (Va) 1000 Saint Stephens Rd, Alexandria VA 22304 **Imm Ch Mechanicsvlle VA 2017-; St. Steph's And St. Agnes Sch Alexandria VA 2015-** B Boston MA 1987 s Edward & Virginia. AB Harvard Coll 2010; MDiv VTS 2015. D 6/6/2015 Bp Shannon Sherwood Johnston P 12/12/2015 Bp Susan Goff. m 6/27/2015 Sarah HT Taylor c 1.

MILLER, Christopher James-Alan (At) 3098 Saint Annes Ln Nw, Atlanta GA 30327 **S Anne's Epis Ch Atlanta GA 2016-** B York PA 1987 s Terry & Lisa. BA Coastal Carolina U 2012; MDiv Candler TS 2016. D 12/19/2015 P 6/25/2016 Bp Robert Christopher Wright. cmiller@saintannes.com

MILLER, Clark Stewart (NI) 319 7th St, Logansport IN 46947 **S Eliz's Epis Ch Culver IN 2013-; D Trin Epis Ch Logansport IN 2010-** B Logansport IN 1955 s Theodore & Eunice. BS Indiana St U 1978; MS Indiana St U 1983. D 12/20/2009 P 7/9/2010 Bp Edward Stuart Little II. m 6/2/1984 Debra Miller c 4.

MILLER, David Dallas (Dal) 1700 N Westmoreland Rd, Desoto TX 75115 B Salisbury MD 1978 s Paul & Joanne. BAS Dallas Bapt U 2004; MDiv

SMU Perkins 2010. D 6/26/2010 Bp Paul Emil Lambert. m 8/29/2009 Keeley Chorn c 2. S Matt's Cathd Dallas TX 2013-2017; Cbury Epis Sch Desoto TX 2011-2012; D S Anne's Epis Ch Desoto TX 2010-2012, Cur 2010-. dmiller@episcopalcathedral.org

MILLER, David Walton (Los) 1037 16th St Apt 1, Santa Monica CA 90403 B San Bernardino CA 1950 s Donald & Patricia. BA U CA Santa Barbara 1973; MDiv VTS 1977. D 6/25/1977 Bp Chauncie Kilmer Myers P 6/25/1978 Bp William Foreman Creighton. m 8/4/1979 Sarah Rodgers c 3. R The Par Of S Matt Pacific Plsds CA 1993-2008; R Ch Of The Epiph San Carlos CA 1983-1993; Assoc R S Jas Par Los Angeles CA 1979-1983; Gr Cathd San Francisco CA 1977-1979. Honoray Cn of the Cathd Cntr of St. Paul Dio Los Angeles 2006.

MILLER, Donald Stewart (Cal) 45602 State Highway 14, Stevenson WA 98648 **Lectr Clark Coll Vancouver WA 2003-; Ret 1998-** B Seattle WA 1932 s Atwill & Helen. BA Whitman Coll 1954; MDiv GTS 1957; DMin Claremont TS 1985. D 9/28/1957 Bp Stephen F Bayne Jr P 6/1/1958 Bp Frank A Rhea. m 12/29/1962 Judith Ann Miller c 2. R S Matt's Epis Ch San Mateo CA 1986-1997; R Ch Of Our Sav Par San Gabr CA 1975-1985; R Trin Epis Ch Everett WA 1970-1975; R S Andr's Epis Ch Aberdeen WA 1964-1970; Vic Ch Of The H Sprt Vashon WA 1960-1964; Cur Ch Of The Ascen Seattle WA 1957-1960; Dioc Coun Dio California San Francisco CA 1984-1987; Excoun Dio Olympia Seattle 1974-1977, Excoun 1967-1973. Auth, "Pehlivan: Turkish Sport, Islamic Sprt," *Intl Revs*, 1998; Auth, "Reformation Of The Liturg Year," Claremont, 1986; Auth, "A Pilgrim'S Progress"; Auth, "arts," *Angl Dig*; Auth, "arts," *Pulpit Dig*.

MILLER, Duane Alexander (WTex) D 6/29/2017 Bp David Mitchell Reed.

MILLER JR, Edward Oehler (Va) 6715 Georgetown Pike, Mclean VA 22101 **R S Jn's Epis Ch Mc Lean VA 1996-; Chair of Trst Ch Schools Dio Virginia Richmond VA 2014-, Trst 2013-** B New York NY 1948 s Edward & Ann. BA Harv 1970; MDiv EDS 1973. D 6/10/1973 Bp John Harris Burt P 2/24/1974 Bp The Bishop Of Quebec. m 10/28/1978 Virginia H W Miller c 2. R All SS' Epis Ch Belmont MA 1984-1996; Asst Min Trin Ch Epis Boston MA 1976-1984; P-in-c Quebec Labrador Fndt Inc Ipswich MA 1975-1976; P-in-c Serv Angl Ch of Can 1975-1976; Chapl The Choate Sch Wallingford CT 1974-1975; Chapl Choate Rosemary Hall Sch Wallingford CT 1973-1975; Calv and Geo New York NY 1973; Stndg Com Pres Dio Virginia Richmond VA 2011-2012, Stndg Com 2009-2012; Bd Gvnr Chair Christchurch Sch Christchurch VA 2009-2014, Bd Gvnr 2004-2014; Stndg Com Vice-Pres Dio Massachusetts Boston MA 2004-2005, Co-Chair, Nomin Com for a Bp Coadj 1993-1994, Stndg Comittee 1992-1995, Stndg Com 1992-1995, Chair COM 1986-1990; Com on Corp Responsibility Exec Coun Appointees New York NY 2003-2009. emiller@stjohnsmclean.org

MILLER JR, Edwin Lee (Okla) 3300 N Vermont Ave, Oklahoma City OK 73112 **Ret Asst Santa Maria Virgen Oklahoma City OK 2004-** B Houstonia MO 1937 s Edwin & Frances. BA U of Texas 1965; MDiv Epis TS of the SW 1968; MA U of Oklahoma 1993. D 7/3/1968 Bp Frederick P Goddard P 5/1/1969 Bp James Milton Richardson. m 2/16/1990 Rita A Crockett. Int S Dav's Ch Oklahoma City OK 2000-2002; Asst S Mary's Ch Edmond OK 1988-2002; Int Trin Ch Guthrie OK 1985; Int Epis Ch Of The Resurr Oklahoma City OK 1984-1985; Int S Tim Paul's Vlly OK 1983-1984; Int Var Congreg 1982-1986; Int S Matt's Ch Enid OK 1982-1983; Fac Ecum Inst Chicago IL 1974-1981; R S Alb's Ch Houston TX 1969-1974; Asst S Mart's Epis Ch Houston TX 1968-1969. Auth, "Attachment Failure and Trauma," *Psychosynthesis and Healing Trauma*, Assoc for Advancement of Psychosynthesis, 2011; Auth, "Psychosynthesis and a Chr Sprtl Philos," *Psychosynthesis and Sprtlty*, Assoc for Advancement of Psychosynthesis, 2008.

MILLER, Elizabeth (Me) 286 Lincoln St, South Portland ME 04106 B Doylestown PA 1944 d William & Mary. BA U of Sthrn Maine 1972; MDiv Bangor TS 2002. D 6/1/2002 P 12/8/2002 Bp Chilton Richardson Knudsen. m 11/22/1961 Robert Thomas Miller. Chr Ch Norway ME 2012-2014; S Mk's Ch Augusta ME 2004-2011; S Matt's Epis Ch Hallowell ME 2004-2005; Cur Epis Ch Of S Mary The Vrgn Falmouth ME 2002-2004.

MILLER, Elizabeth M (Be) 44 E Market St, Bethlehem PA 18018 **Trin Ch Bethlehem PA 2003-** B St. Louis MO 1954 d Alexander & Sara. Sewanee: The U So, TS. D 5/31/2003 Bp Paul Victor Marshall. m 5/26/1990 Terry Lee Miller. liz@trinitybeth.org

MILLER, Eric Lee (SO) 321 Worthington Ave., Cincinnati OH 45215 **Chapl Wyoming Fire Dept. Wyoming OH 2012-; R The Ch Of Ascen And H Trin Cincinnati OH 2010-** B Parkersburg WV 1977 s Mark & Margaret. BA W Virginia U 2000; MDiv VTS 2003. D 9/19/2002 P 6/7/2003 Bp William Michie Klusmeyer. m 5/11/2002 Rosemary R Miller c 2. R S Steph's Epis Ch Beckley WV 2005-2010, GC Dep 2009; Cur S Jn's Ch Huntington WV 2003-2005.

MILLER JR, Ernest Charles (NY) 611 Broadway Rm 520, New York NY 10012 B Norwalk CT 1956 s Ernest & Edith. BA Franklin & Marshall Coll 1978; MA U MI 1979; MDiv Nash 1982; PhD Oxf GB 1990. D 6/26/1982 Bp Archibald Donald Davies P 5/1/1983 Bp Robert Elwin Terwilliger. m 7/25/1987 Judith F Miller c 1. R Ch Of The Trsfg New York NY 2000-2005; S Paul's Ch Water-

town WI 1997-2000; S Anskar's Epis Ch Hartland WI 1997; Prof S Mary the Vrgn Ch Nashotah WI 1996-2000; S Simon The Fisherman Epis Ch Port Washington WI 1996; Nash Nashotah WI 1995-2000; Serv Ch In Engl 1984-1996; Cur S Andr's Ch Dallas TX 1982-1984. Auth, "Toward A Fuller Vision: Orthodoxy & The Angl Experience"; Auth, "Praying The Euch". Sub Chapl The Most Vunerable Ord Of The Hospitals Of St Jn Of Judea 2000.

MILLER, Fred (CPa) 547 Brighton Place, Mechanicsburg PA 17055 **Pres Transitional Mnstrs of the Epis Ch 2011-** B Wilmington DE 1950 s John & Emma. BA Glassboro St U 1972; PDS 1974; MDiv EDS 1975; Cert SWTS 2001. D 4/26/1975 P 10/25/1975 Bp Albert Wiencke Van Duzer. m 5/19/1973 Kristine Lynn Miller c 3. Int Chr Epis Ch Williamsport PA 2014-2015; Assoc R S Andr's Ch St Coll PA 2013-2014; P-in-c S Lk's Epis Ch Altoona PA 2011-2013; Int S Jas Ch Wichita KS 2010-2011; Int Chr Ch Somers Point NJ 2008-2010; R All SS' Epis Ch Hershey PA 1989-2008; P-in-c Sum Chap S Jn's Ch Avalon NJ 1984-1987; R Gr Ch Pemberton NJ 1981-1989; Vic Trin Epis Old Swedes Ch Swedesboro NJ 1977-1981; Cur S Paul's Epis Ch Westfield NJ 1975-1977; Alt Dep GC 2006-2009; Chair - Bp Search Com Dio Cntrl Pennsylvania Harrisburg PA 2005-2006, Pres - Stndg Com 2004-2005, Cler Convoc Convenor 1998-2007, COM 1991-1997, Chair - Liturg and Mus Cmsn 1991-1996, Dioc Coun 1990-1996; Dep Prov II Syn Dio New Jersey Trenton NJ 1982-1989. Epis Cler Assn 1987-2017; Int Mnstrs of the Epis Ch 2008-2015. Cn of Cathd Bp 2014. fmiller10251975@gmail.com

MILLER, Frederic (LI) 41 Reid Ave., Port Washington NY 11050 **S Geo's Ch Hempstead NY 2017-** B Glen Ridge NJ 1951 s Paul & Susan. BA Pr 1973; MPhil Oxf 1976; MDiv GTS 2013. D 6/1/2013 P 12/7/2013 Bp Lawrence C Provenzano. m 5/15/1982 Katherine C Hill c 1. S Marg's Ch Plainview NY 2016; Int St Jn's Ch Cold Sprg Harbor NY 2015-2016; Cur Chr Ch Oyster Bay NY 2013-2015; P-in-c S Bede's Epis Ch Syosset NY 2013-2014; Chair, Com to Nominate a Bp Coadj Dio Long Island Garden City NY 2008-2009; Wrdn (except 2005-7) S Steph's Ch Prt Washington NY 1999-2011. Geo Cabot Ward Prize for Best Reading of the Bible and the Serv of the Ch The GTS 2013; Bp of Newark Preaching Prize The GTS 2013.

MILLER, Isaac J (Pa) 18th & Diamond, Philadelphia PA 19121 **P Calv St Aug Epis Ch Philadelphia PA 2011-** B Raleigh NC 1943 s Houser & Ida. BA Morehouse Coll 1964; MDiv EDS 1968. D 9/13/1975 Bp Joseph Warren Hutchens P 5/1/1976 Bp Morgan Porteus. m 7/11/1970 Rose S Miller c 1. Dio Pennsylvania Philadelphia PA 1991-2009; R Geo W So Ch of Advoc Philadelphia PA 1989-1990; Assoc The Afr Epis Ch Of S Thos Philadelphia PA 1986-1989; R S Tim's Decatur GA 1982-1985; R Cbury Cmnty Atlanta GA 1978-1982; Dio Atlanta Atlanta GA 1978-1982; Asst R S Paul And S Jas New Haven CT 1975-1978.

MILLER, James Barrett (NCal) 550 Seagaze Dr Apt 19, Oceanside CA 92054 **Ret H Trin Nevada City CA 1989-** B San Bernardino CA 1949 s Donald & Patricia. BA U CA Santa Barbara 1971; MDiv VTS 1974; PhD Fuller TS 1982. D 6/10/1974 Bp Robert Poland Atkinson P 5/24/1975 Bp Wilburn Camrock Campbell. c 3. Bk Revs Ed HSEC Appleton WI 1982-2008; R H Trin Ch Nevada City CA 1980-1989; Asst S Jn's Epis Ch Charleston WV 1975-1977; Chapl to Marshall U Trin Ch Huntington WV 1974-1975; Vice Chair, Comission on Mnstry The Epis Dio Nthrn California Sacramento CA 1981-1987; Alum/ae Exec Commitee VTS Alexandria VA 1981-1984. Auth, "The First Bk of Homilies and the Doctrine of H Scripture," *Angl and Epis Hist*, 1997; Auth, "The Struggle of Memory Against Forgetting," *Hist mag PECUSA*, 1984; Auth, "Scripture in the Engl Reformation 1526-1553," U Microfilms Intl , 1982; Auth, "The Theol of Wm Sparrow," *Hist mag PECUSA*, 1977.

MILLER, James Lower (NY) 126 Goldens Bridge Rd, Katonah NY 10536 **Non-par 1968-** B Concordia KS 1927 s Charles & Ruth. BA U of Maryland 1956; BD EDS 1959; STM Andover Newton TS 1969. D 6/20/1959 P 12/19/1959 Bp Angus Dun. m 5/14/1960 Marcia Nan Allen c 1. P-in-c Chr And S Steph's Ch New York NY 1965-1968; Asst S Aug's Ch New York NY 1961-1963; Asst S Paul And S Jas New Haven CT 1960-1961; Asst All Souls Memi Epis Ch Washington DC 1959-1960.

MILLER, Janice Mary Howard (NI) 2117 E Jefferson Blvd, South Bend IN 46617 **D The Cathd Ch Of S Jas So Bend IN 1998-; D S Mich 1994-** B Honeoye Falls NY 1939 d Raymond & Nina. Gordon Coll; U Roch; BA No Pk U 1963; MS NWU 1964; Dio Cntrl Florida Inst Chr Stds 1990. D 12/14/1991 Bp John Wadsworth Howe. m 7/10/1975 Richard Roy Miller c 3. D H Cross Epis Ch Sanford FL 1991-1993. Intl Osl-Physcn.

MILLER, Jean Louise (EC) 9191 Daly Rd., Cincinnati OH 45231 **D S Jas The Fisherman Epis Ch Shallotte NC 2010-** B Hershey PA 1950 d John & Bertha. AA Tem 1970. D 6/14/2008 Bp Thomas Edward Breidenthal. m 1/20/1973 Gary Lee Miller c 2.

MILLER, Jerry Lee (WMo) 4258 E Whitehall Dr, Springfield MO 65809 **P-in-c Trin Epis Ch Lebanon MO 2012-** B Columbus IN 1945 s Arnold & Marjorie. BA Indiana U 1972; MDiv Nash 1975. Trans 2/5/2004 Bp Mark Sean Sisk. m 11/27/1996 Elizabeth Elaine Miller. R S Jn's Ch Springfield MO 2003-2012; R Zion Epis Ch Wappingers Falls NY 1998-2003; All SS Epis Ch Farmington MO 1988-1997; Vic S Pauls Epis Ch Ironton MO 1988-1997;

Asst S Andr's Ch Stillwater OK 1986-1988; R All SS' Epis Ch Duncan OK 1981-1985; P-in-c Ch Of S Jn The Bapt Elkhart IL 1978-1981; Trin Ch Lincoln IL 1978-1981; Cur S Mich And All Ang Ch Mssn KS 1975-1978. trinityepiscopalmo@gmail.com

MILLER, Jo Anne (Ore) P.O. Box 413, Bandon OR 97411 **Vic S Jn-By-The-Sea Epis Ch Bandon OR 2007-** B Medford OR 1949 d Cyrus & Frances. BS Sthrn Oregon U 1971; MDiv CDSP 2005. D 10/8/2005 P 6/28/2006 Bp Johncy Itty. m 5/29/1969 Teddy Charles Miller c 2. Dio Oregon Portland OR 2008-2009.

MILLER, Joel (ECR) 160 Robideaux Rd, Aptos CA 95003 B Glendale CA 1948 s Steven & Patricia. BS California St Polytechnic U 1970; MDiv Fuller TS 1975; TESOL Wm Carey U 1985. D 6/13/1998 P 1/16/1999 Bp David Mercer Schofield. m 4/2/1983 Maria Christina Miller c 4. Emm Epis Ch Geneva 1201 2016-2017; R Calv Epis Ch Santa Cruz CA 2006-2016; R S Fran' Epis Ch Turlock CA 2000-2006; Asst to R S Paul's Epis Ch Modesto CA 1998-2000. "Riding the Fence Lines," BWD Pub, 2003.

MILLER, Joe Ted (Okla) 2732 Walnut Rd, Norman OK 73072 B Ponca City OK 1941 s Ted & Mary. MA CUA 1964; STM GTS 1973; DMin McCormick TS 1980. Rec 7/1/1973 as Priest Bp James Stuart Wetmore. m 5/28/1973 Estelle Karl Miller c 4. S Jn's Ch Norman OK 1981-2003; R S Elis's Epis Ch Memphis TN 1974-1981; Asst S Jn's Ch Larchmont NY 1973-1974.

MILLER, John Edward (Alb) PO Box 12, Ancram NY 12502 **Vic Calv Epis Ch Cairo NY 1998-; P-in-c Gloria Dei Epis Ch Palenville NY 1998-** B Batavia NY 1948 s Frank & Phyllis. BA SUNY 1970; MDiv PDS 1974. D 12/22/1973 Bp Allen Webster Brown P 9/14/1974 Bp Wilbur Emory Hogg Jr. m 12/30/1972 Kathie F Fleming c 1. P-in-c S Mk's Epis Ch Philmont NY 1986-1997; R S Lk's Ch Willmar MN 1982-1984; R S Jn's Ch Moorhead MN 1980-1982; Vic Ch Of The Nativ Star Lake NY 1974-1978.

MILLER, John Edward (Va) 4209 Monument Ave, Richmond VA 23230 B Richmond VA 1948 s John & Marion. BA W&L 1970; MDiv UTS Richmond 1974; ThM UTS Richmond 1977; PhD UTS Richmond 1982. D 12/12/1981 P 6/25/1982 Bp Robert Bruce Hall. m 11/17/2012 Deborah B Miller c 1. R S Mary's Epis Ch Richmond VA 1982-2015. Auth, *Ch Renwl Groups*, Virginia Epis; Auth, *EFM Curric Year 4*, The U So; Auth, *The Relevance of Process Theol*, Virginia Epis.

MILLER, John Leonard (NY) 23 Cedar Ln, Princeton NJ 08540 B Philadelphia PA 1928 s Harry & Dora. STB Harvard DS; STM Harvard DS; ThD Harvard DS; Harv; DIT U of St Andrews; MA Ya. D 6/15/1974 P 12/1/1974 Bp Jonathan Goodhue Sherman. m 9/27/2016 Ronald M Monteverde. Asst Prof Of Rel Connecticut Coll; Asst S Mich.

MILLER JR, John Meredith (Vt) 34 County Route 59, Buskirk NY 12028 B Pensacola FL 1943 s John & Jane. BA Duke 1965; MDiv GTS 1968; (Spec Stdt) VTS 1979; MSS Bryn 1984. D 6/29/1968 Bp William Foreman Creighton P 1/4/1969 Bp Jonathan Goodhue Sherman. m 10/5/1968 Adele Maslen c 3. P-in-Partnership S Mk's-S Lk's Epis Mssn Fair Haven VT 2013-2016; Vic Gr Ch Broad Brook CT 2008-2012; R Chr Ch Roxbury CT 2001-2008; R S Mk's Ch Westford MA 1996-2001; Int S Thos' Ch Whitemarsh Ft Washington PA 1994-1996; Int S Anne's Ch Abington PA 1992-1994; Int Chr Epis Ch Villanova PA 1991-1992; Int Ch Of The H Nativ Wrightstown PA 1989-1991; Vic Chr Ch Bridgeport PA 1986-1989; S Ptr's Ch Glenside PA 1984-1986, 1982-1984; Int S. Ptr's Epis Ch Glenside PA 1982-1984; Rep The GTS New York NY 1977-1982; R Ch Of The H Comf Vienna VA 1976-1982; Vic S Jas Ch Brookhaven NY 1972-1975; Cur, Assoc Ch Of The Trsfg Freeport NY 1968-1972; Bd Dir Fair Haven Concerned Fair Haven VT 2014-2016; Com 1-D on the Vocational Diac Dio Connecticut Meriden CT 2010-2012, Transition Com for the Election of a Dioc Bp 2009-2011, Liturg Instr, Vocational Diac Trng Prog 2007-2011; Coun on Aging, Chair 03-07 Town of Roxbury Roxbury CT 2002-2008; Dio Massachusetts Area Cnvnr, Natl Trnr BeFriender Mnstry St. Paul MN 1998-2001; Com on Human Sxlty and the Ch, Adult Curric Dvlp Dio Pennsylvania Philadelphia PA 1991-1992; Bd Managers, Yth Detention Cntr, Chair 86 Cnty of Montgomery Norristown PA 1984-1986; Natl Epis Curs Com Natl Epis Curs Off Aldie VA 1980-1982; Coordntr of CE Sum Conf Dio Virginia Richmond VA 1980-1981, Com on Resolutns 1979-1980, Com on Study of Div of the Dio 1978-1980, Com on Ch Status, chair '78 1977-1978; Liturg Cmsn Dio Long Island Garden City NY 1974-1975; Radio Mnstry, Prog Dir Long Island Coun of Ch Garden City NY 1971.

MILLER, John Preston (Me) 223 Lakes At Litchfield Dr, Pawleys Island SC 29585 **Died 12/24/2016** B Cambridge MA 1933 s John & Marguerite. BA U of Massachusetts 1954; STM EDS 1957. D 6/1/1957 P 12/1/1957 Bp William A Lawrence. c 4. P-in-c S Andr's Ch Winthrop ME 1996-1998; Int Chr And Epiph Ch E Haven CT 1995; Int Ch of the H Sprt W Haven CT 1994-1995; Chair - Com On Vocational Diac 1982-1988; Com 1982-1988; Treas Prov 1 1982-1985; R Ch Of The H Trin Middletown CT 1981-1995; Chair On Bd S Lk's Hm Outreach Mnstry 1981-1993; Prov I Middletown CT 1980-1982; Exec Secy Of Prov I Prov 1 1979-1982; Chair On VIM Dio Maine 1978-1981; Vstng Lectr Bangor TS 1976-1977; R S Jn's Ch Bangor ME 1967-1981; R H Trin Epis Ch Southbridge MA 1959-1967; Asst S Paul's Ch Holyoke MA 1957-1959;

Exec Bd Alum Assn EDS Cambridge MA 1980-1983; Stndg Com Dio Maine Portland ME 1970-1977. Auth, "Selected Sermons". Angl Soc.

MILLER, John Sloan (La) 12679 N Highmeadow Ct, Baton Rouge LA 70816 **S Steph's Ch Innis LA 2016-** B Lake Charles LA 1963 s Joseph & Mary. BS McNeese St U 1987; MDiv Sewanee: The U So, TS 2004. D 6/5/2004 P 4/2/2005 Bp D Avid Bruce Macpherson. m 9/19/1987 Celene Cassa Miller c 3. P-in-c S Fran Ch Denham Spgs LA 2014-2015; Assoc R/Asst Hd of Sch S Jas Epis Ch Baton Rouge LA 2006-2014; Cur St Jas Epis Ch and Sch Alexandria LA 2004-2006.

MILLER, Joseph Potter (Los) B 1924 D 9/12/1970 Bp Francis E I Bloy P 3/27/1971 Bp Victor Manuel Rivera. m 9/19/1953 Doris Chott.

MILLER, Judith Joelynn Walker (Oly) PO Box 1782, Westport WA 98595 B Shelton WA 1952 d Edward & Gertrude. RN NYU 1993; BD S Martins Coll Lacey WA 2000; MS Gonzaga U 2004. D 11/19/1997 Bp Sanford Zangwill Kaye Hampton. m 6/26/1971 Ronald James Walker c 1. D S Christophers Epis Ch Westport WA 1997-2013.

MILLER JR, Kenneth Charles (Mil) 3906 W Mequon Rd, Mequon WI 53092 **R S Bon Ch Thiensville WI 2010-** B Bristol TN 1973 s Kenneth & Betty. BA King Coll 1995; MDiv VTS 2005. D 6/18/2005 Bp Charles Glenn VonRosenberg P 1/21/2006 Bp Dean E Wolfe. m 12/15/1995 Tania Marie Miller c 3. R S Paul's Epis Ch Smithfield NC 2007-2010; asst. R S Jas Ch Wichita KS 2005-2007.

MILLER, Kurt David (Ga) 3665 Bermuda Cir, Augusta GA 30909 **Vic Ch Of The Atone Hephzibah GA 2010-, Vic 1998-2007; Adj Prof Georgia Mltry Coll Martinez GA 1995-** B Newark NJ 1938 s Kenneth & Florence. AAS New York Inst of Tech 1973; BT New York Inst of Tech 1978; MS Bos 1981; MDiv Erskine TS 1996; DMin Erskine TS 2001. D 3/12/1986 Bp Harry Woolston Shipps P 6/1/1997 Bp Henry Irving Louttit. c 1. Respite P S Aug Of Cbury Ch Augusta GA 1997-1998; D S Alb's Epis Ch Augusta GA 1986-1994. Auth, "Disseration," *Bldg the Body of Chr Through the Love of God in a Sm Grp Fllshp*, Erskine TS, 2001.

MILLER, Laura Jean (Alb) 41 Gardiner Pl, Walton NY 13856 B Fairbanks AK 1954 d Robert & Beverly. D 5/10/2008 Bp William Howard Love. m 3/25/1984 Lawrence Miller c 1.

MILLER, Laurence Henry (Be) 31 Tecumseh Pass, Millsboro DE 19966 B Minneapolis MN 1936 s Henry & Josephine. BA Wesl 1958; MA Indiana U 1959; BD VTS 1962. D 9/15/1962 P 6/1/1963 Bp John Brooke Mosley. R S Ptr's Epis Ch Hazleton PA 1997-2001; Reg Mssnr S Phil's Ch Quantico MD 1995-1997; W Wicomico Cnty Cluster Quantico MD 1995-1997; Gr Epiph Ch Philadelphia PA 1986-1995; R Ch Of The Epiph Philadelphia PA 1986-1991; S Dav's Ch Salem NH 1970-1986; Asst Ch Of The Gd Shpd Nashua NH 1965-1970; Dio Delaware Wilmington 1962-1965; S Jn The Bapt Epis Ch Milton DE 1962-1965.

MILLER, Leewin Glen (SwFla) 4279 70th St Cir E, Palmetto FL 34221 **Asst S Jn The Div Epis Ch Sun City Cntr FL 2012-** B Detroit MI 1940 s Leslie & Agnes. BS U of No Alabama 1966; MDiv Epis TS in Kentucky 1980. D 5/11/1980 P 6/1/1981 Bp Addison Hosea. m 9/1/1962 Yoniece Miller c 2. R S Mary's Epis Ch Palmetto FL 1996-2009; R Ch Of S Edw Columbus OH 1989-1995; R Gr Ch Pomeroy OH 1983-1989; Vic S Jn's Ch Corbin KY 1980-1983; Pstr Winchester Presb Winchester KY 1976-1980; Evang/Renwl Cmsn Dio Sthrn Ohio Cincinnati OH 1985-1989, Com Profsnl Dev 1984. Narrator, "Natl PSA Proj for Epis Ch"; Auth, "40 Days!"; Auth, "Inside The Husk"; Auth, "Awesome Power Of Habit"; Auth, "Awareness, the Missing Ingredient"; Auth, "There Is More Than Just One Way To Say I Love You"; Host; Auth and Presenter, "Publ in the Loc Ch," *Natl PSA Proj for the Epis Ch*.

MILLER JR, Louis (USC) 129 Heathwood Rd, Union SC 29379 B Portsmouth VA 1940 s Louis & Mary. BA U of So Carolina 1970; MDiv Sewanee: The U So, TS 2005. D 5/28/2005 Bp Porter Taylor P 12/9/2005 Bp Henry Irving Louttit. m 12/27/1974 Mary A Griffin c 3. Calv Ch Pauline SC 2012-2016; Vic Ch Of The Nativ Un SC 2012-2016; Mssn Chapl Dodge St Prison Chester Ga 2006-2012; R Chr Epis Ch Dublin GA 2005-2012; Dn of the Piedmont Convoc Dio Upper So Carolina Columbia SC 2012-2014; Chairma, Transition Com Dio Georgia Savannah GA 2008-2010, Dn Cntrl Convoc 2007-2012. Ord of S Vinc Acolytes 1979.

MILLER, Marion R (Tenn) Po Box 1903, Monterey CA 93942 **The CPG New York NY 2013-; S Andr's Ch Marianna AR 2012-, 2006-2009** B Denver CO 1953 d Bruce & Barbara. BA NE Illinois U 1975; MDiv SWTS 1984. D 6/24/1984 P 3/1/1985 Bp Joseph Thomas Heistand. c 1. Explorefaithorg Memphis TN 2003-2010; Credo Inst Inc. Memphis TN 2002-2005; Calv Ch Memphis TN 2002-2004; Dio El Camino Real Salinas CA 2000-2001, 1997-1999; Dio Idaho Boise ID 1988-1997, Dir Of The Diac Formation 1988-1990; Ch Of The H Sprt Bullhead City AZ 1986-1988; Rural Dir Of Bp'S Sch Mnstry Dio Arizona Phoenix AZ 1986-1988; Vic H Cross Dolan Sprg AZ 1985-1988; Vic Trin Epis Ch Kingman AZ 1985-1988; Epis Chapl Nthrn Arizona U At Flagstaff 1985-1986; Assoc R Ch Of The Epiph Flagstaff AZ 1985; S Jn The Bapt Epis Ch Glendale AZ 1984-1985. Oblate Ascen Priority Ord Of S Ben.

MILLER, Mark Joseph (Oly) 913 2nd St, Snohomish WA 98290 B Minneapolis MN 1951 s Robert & Betty. BA Pacific Luth U 1975; MDiv Nash 1979;

St Petersburg Theol Acad RU 1993. D 7/21/1979 P 7/8/1980 Bp Robert Hume Cochrane. m 4/16/1994 Julie D Wilkenson c 1. R S Jn's Epis Ch Snohomish WA 1997-2016; R S Ptr's Ch Huntington WV 1996-1997; P-in-c Ch Of The H Apos Bellevue WA 1994-1995; Assoc S Paul's Ch Seattle WA 1987-1993; Vic S Jos And S Jn Ch Lakewood WA 1981-1987; Chapl Annie Wright Sch Tacoma WA 1981-1983; Asst S Andrews Epis Ch Port Angeles WA 1979-1981; Dioc Coun Dio Olympia Seattle 2014-2017, Ecum Off 1989-1993. Angl Soc 1997; Seattle - St. Petersburg Sis Ch Prog 1988.

MILLER, Monroe Richard (NI) 17716 Downing Dr, Lowell IN 46356 B Portland OR 1945 s Monroe & Alismarie. BS Ferris St U 1969. D 1/4/1989 Bp Francis Campbell Gray P 4/28/2002 Bp Edward Stuart Little II. c 2. P-in-c Chr The King Epis Ch Huntington IN 2005-2014; Asstg P S Andr's Epis Ch Valparaiso IN 2002-2004, D 1989-2002; Supply S Andr's By The Lake Epis Ch Michigan City IN 2002-2003. NAAD 1989-2003.

MILLER, Nancy Fay (RI) 82 Rockmeadow Rd, Westwood MA 02090 B Boston MA 1938 d Ralph & Vera. Wheelock Coll 1958; BA Simmons Coll 1988; Rhode Island Sch for Deacons 1995. D 6/24/1995 Bp J Clark Grew II. m 2/22/1958 Richard Watson Miller c 4. Dn Ch Of The Gd Shpd Pawtucket RI 1999-2000; Exec Dir Dio Rhode Island Providence RI 1996-2000, 1995-; COM S Mart's Ch Providence RI 1995-1999. Friends Of The Fllshp; NAAD; SCHC.

MILLER, pastor (Be) 2227 NW 79th Ave, Doral FL 33122 **Ch Of The Gd Shpd Hartford CT 2013-** B Opalika AL 1978 d John & Sue. AA Edison Cmnty Coll Ft Myers FL 2001; BFA Florida Atlantic U 2003; MDiv EDS 2008. D 6/16/2007 P 4/19/2008 Bp Leo Frade. Exec Coun Appointees New York NY 2008-2009.

MILLER, Patricia L (WMo) 1840 Hickory Station Cir, Snellville GA 30078 B Atlanta, GA 1950 d Harold & Sarah. RN Georgia Bapt Hosp Sch of Nrsng Atlanta GA 1971; BSN Med Coll of Georgia 1978; MSN Med Coll of Georgia 1979; MDiv Epis TS of the SW 1996; DMin St Pauls TS Kansas City MO 2005. D 6/7/1997 P 12/7/1997 Bp William Jerry Winterrowd. Int S Aid's Epis Ch Milton GA 2016-2017; Vic S Mich's Epis Ch Independence MO 2015-2016, Vic 1999-2015; Pres-elect & Pres Natl Epis Curs 2009-2011; Assoc S Ambr Epis Ch Boulder CO 1997-1999; Chapl S Dav's Hosp Austin TX 1994-1996. motherpat@staidans.org

MILLER, Patrick Jameson (Tex) 3514 Corondo Ct., Houston TX 77005 **R S Mk's Ch Houston TX 2008-; Dep, GC Dio Texas Houston TX 2011-, Dn, E Harris Convoc 2009-, Bp Transition Com 2008-2010, Secy, Stndg Com 2006-2009, Trst, Camp Allen 2006-; Trst Epis TS Of The SW Austin TX 2006-** B Gulfport MI 1966 s Felix & Nan. BA Austin Coll 1990; MDiv Epis TS of the SW 2000. D 6/17/2000 Bp Claude Edward Payne P 6/27/2001 Bp Don Adger Wimberly. m 11/20/1999 Allison Standish Miller c 2. S Mk's Epis Sch Houston TX 2008-2014; Cn for Chr Formation Chr Ch Cathd Houston TX 2003-2008; Asst R S Richard's Of Round Rock Round Rock TX 2000-2003. Auth, "Spoken: A Collection of Sermons," MTpages, 2010; Auth, "Empty: A Pilgrim's Memoir," MTpages, 2009. Texas Lyceum 2005-2011.

MILLER, Paula (Mich) 1325 Champaign Rd, Lincoln Park MI 48146 **S Mich And All Ang Epis Ch Lincoln Pk MI 2013-** B Pittsburgh PA 1946 d Jack & Mary. BS Wheeling Jesuit U 1968; PhD U of Virginia 1972; MDiv Ecum TS 2011. D 6/22/2013 P 12/22/2013 Bp Wendell Nathaniel Gibbs Jr. m 5/29/1971 Stephen Joseph Miller c 4. stmichaelslp@gmail.com

MILLER, R Cameron (Roch) 164 Washington St, Geneva NY 14456 **P-in-Partnership Trin Ch Geneva NY 2016-** B Muncie IN 1953 s Robert & Virginia. BA Skidmore Coll 1976; MDiv EDS 1980; Coll of Preachers 1989. D 6/24/1980 P 3/21/1981 Bp Edward Witker Jones. m 6/12/1982 Kathryn W Miller c 4. P-in-Partnership S Mk's Epis Ch Newport VT 2013-2016; Adj, Rel Stds Canisius Coll Buffalo NY US 2008-2013; R Trin Epis Ch Buffalo NY 1999-2013; R S Steph's Epis Ch And U Columbus OH 1989-1999; R S Matt's Ch Indianapolis IN 1982-1989; Asst St Johns Epis Ch Lafayette IN 1980-1982. Poet, "Listening to Dark Ang," *Poetry Quarterly*, Prolific Press, 2016; Auth, "Mo Teresa's God," *The Poet's Quest for God (autumn release)*, Eyewear Press, 2016; Auth, "The Steam Room Diaries," Tumbleweed Books, CA, 2015; Poet, "My Fr Died Last Night, Wind on Snow," *Inwood Indiana*, Prolific Press, 2015; Poet, "Eleven Below in Vermont, Alone Again at the Wok 'N Roll," *Waiting Series and Where I Live Series*, Silver Birch Press, 2015; Auth, "The Next Voice You Hear," Trin Ch Press, 2012. Hon Doctorate Jesus the Liberator Sem 2008.

MILLER, Richard (Pa) 1521 Ashby Rd, Paoli PA 19301 **Ret 1999-** B Philadelphia PA 1941 s Charles & Mary. BA Witt 1963; MDiv PDS 1966; STM GTS 1968; SFTS 1976. D 6/11/1966 Bp Robert Lionne DeWitt P 12/21/1966 Bp Jonathan Goodhue Sherman. m 8/21/1965 Linda Webber Miller c 3. Pa Dioc Coun Dio Pennsylvania Philadelphia PA 1981-1984; S Fran-In-The-Fields Malvern PA 1979-1999; Assoc All SS' Epis Ch Chevy Chase MD 1970-1979; Asst Hdmstr Par Sch Gr Epis Ch Massapequa NY 1968-1970; Cur Adv Ch Of The Adv Westbury NY 1966-1968.

MILLER, Richard Sevier (Ida) 1312 Wisconsin St Apt 232, Hudson WI 54016 **Died 10/4/2015** B Milwaukee WI 1927 s George & Inez. BA Carroll Coll 1950; GTS 1953; Cert No Dakota St U 1972. D 5/17/1953 P 11/30/1953 Bp William

Jones Gordon Jr. c 6. Asst P S Phil's Boise ID 1994-2008; Ret 1992-2015; Ret 1992-2015; Int S Lk's Epis Ch Idaho Falls ID 1990-1992; All SS Epis Ch Omaha NE 1986-1987; Vic S Paul's Indn Mssn Sioux City IA 1981-1986; Dio So Dakota Pierre SD 1974-1981; Geth Epis Ch Sisseton SD 1972-1981; S Jas Epis Ch Waubay SD 1971-1981; S Lk's Sta Veblen SD 1971-1981; P-in-c S Mary's Epis Ch Peever SD 1971-1981; Vic Trin Ch Wahpeton ND 1969-1971; Vic Chr Ch Chamberlain SD 1961-1969; R Trin Ch Baraboo WI 1956-1961; Min in charge S Jn's Ch Allakaket AK 1953-1956. Auth, "Power of the Higher One in AA's 12 Steps," 1987.

MILLER, Robert Mcgregor (Pa) 2039 Serendipity Way, Schwenksville PA 19473 B Honolulu HI 1948 s Frank & Margaret. BS USMA 1972; MS USAF Inst of Tech Wright-Pater 1980; MDiv VTS 1995. D 6/10/1995 P 12/16/1995 Bp Frank Harris Vest Jr. m 6/10/1972 Linda Sue Boyd c 2. S Jn's Ch Norristown PA 2012; P-in-c Trin Ch Gulph Mills Kng Of Prussia PA 2008-2011; Int S Alb's Ch Roxborough Philadelphia PA 2006-2008; Int S Ptr's Ch Phoenixville PA 2003-2006; R Ch Of The Mssh Lower Gwynedd PA 1999-2003; R The Epis Ch Of The Adv Norfolk VA 1995-1999.

MILLER, Robert William (Minn) 11030 Batello Dr, Venice FL 34292 B San Francisco CA 1942 s Gerald & Betty. U MN; U CA 1964; BA San Francisco St U 1967; MDiv Nash 1971; U of St. Thos 1991; U MN 1993. D 6/27/1970 P 2/28/1971 Bp Chauncie Kilmer Myers. m 8/18/1975 Margaret Anne Ehlen. Assoc The Epis Ch Of The Gd Shpd Venice FL 2008-2015; P-in-c Trin Ch Litchfield MN 2002-2004; Hisp Mssnr Chr Ch Albert Lea MN 1999-2000; Instr/Tech Deaf Blind Serv of MN Minneapolis MN 1997-2008; Dio Minnesota Minneapolis MN 1997-1998; P-in-c La Mision El Santo Nino Jesus S Paul MN 1997-1998; P-in-c S Matt's Epis Ch Minneapolis MN 1993-1997; R S Jas On The Pkwy Minneapolis MN 1990-1993; Epis Par of Ames Ames IA 1988-1990; Dir El Porvenir Agricultural Sch Choluteca Honduras 1986-1988; Dir St.Mary's Tech Inst Tegucigalpa Honduras 1984-1988; Serv Ch in Honduras 1980-1989; Exec Coun Appointees New York NY 1979-1988; Chapl La Casa de Maria Retreat Santa Barbara CA 1976-1979; Asst S Paul's Ch Oakland CA 1974-1976; P-in-c S Dorothy's Rest Camp Meeker CA 1970-1973; AIDS T/F Dio Iowa Des Moines IA 1989-1990; Dioc Ecum Off Dio Honduras San Pedro Sula 1975-1987. Auth, w Eyes Wide Open, LN Press, 1998; Auth, Hm is Where the Heart Wants to Be, LN Press, 1993; Auth, A Time of Hope, Morehouse, 1979; Auth, A Gift of Time, Morehouse, 1977; Auth, Chld's Liturgies, Paulist Press, 1976. CT 1971; Immac Heart Cmnty 1975.

MILLER, Roger Edward (CFla) 11620 Claymont Circle, Windermere FL 34786 B Albany NY 1936 s Edward & Arlie. BS Worcester Polytechnic Inst 1959; MS Florida Inst of Tech 1969; MDiv SWTS 1976. D 6/29/1976 P 1/13/1977 Bp William Hopkins Folwell. m 12/8/1962 Rita E Miller c 3. R S Geo Epis Ch The Villages FL 1998-2006; R Chr Ch Longwood FL 1985-1998; R S Marg's Ch Inverness FL 1978-1985; Cur Trin Ch Vero Bch FL 1976-1978; Stndg Com Dio Cntrl Florida Orlando FL 1991-1994, Curs Cmsn 1986-1990, Evang Cmsn 1983-1985, Dioc Bd 1980-1982, Hondurasg Cmsn 1978-1979.

MILLER, Ronald Homer (Md) 830 W 40th St. Apt 860, Baltimore MD 21211 B Butler PA 1936 s Walter & Marion. BA Ya 1960; STB GTS 1964; STM GTS 1968; PhD Ford 1972. D 6/19/1964 Bp George F Gunn P 5/1/1965 Bp David Shepherd Rose. m 5/20/1961 Mary Hotchkiss Miller c 1. Int Ch Of S Mary The Vrgn Baltimore MD 2010-2012; Int Ch Of The Adv Baltimore MD 2000-2003; Asst S Jas' Epis Ch Baltimore MD 1999-2000, Assoc R 1991-1997; Coordnt AP Baltimore MD 1998-2002; Assoc for Ord Mnstry Dio Maryland Baltimore MD 1990-1994, Liturg Cmsn 1972-1977, BEC 1975-1977; Assoc R S Barth's Ch Baltimore MD 1989-1990, Assoc 1974-1977; Dio Pittsburgh Pittsburgh PA 1987, Dioc Coun & Vice Pres 1978-1982, BOEC 1977-1986; Bd, Dn, & Fac Fac Trng Prog for Mnstry Pittsburgh PA 1978-1984; R S Alb's Epis Ch Murrysville PA 1977-1986; Asst Trin Par New York NY 1971-1972; Asst Zion Epis Ch Wappingers Falls NY 1967-1968; Cur S Jn' Ch Washington DC 1965-1967; Cur Ch Of The Epiph Danville VA 1964-1965. Auth, "An Instructed Euch," OPEN, 1978; Auth, "A Study Guide for the H Euch PBCP," Morehouse Pub, 1977; Auth, "Liturg Materials in the Acts of Jn," Studia Patristica XIII, 1971. ADLMC 1973-1989; Ord of S Helena 1978; RACA 1986; Societas Liturgica 1972-2004.

MILLER, Sarah HT (Tex) 5286 Santa Maria Dr, Mechanicsville VA 23116 B Houston TX 1986 d Walker & Susan. BA Rice U 2008; MDiv VTS 2015. D 6/20/2015 Bp C Andrew Doyle P 1/9/2016 Bp Mariann Edgar Budde. m 6/27/2015 Christopher H Miller c 1. S Jn's Ch Lafayette Sq Washington DC 2015-2017; Other Lay Position H Sprt Epis Ch Houston TX 2009-2012.

MILLER, Sarah Leanne (Neb) PO Box 2421, Fremont NE 68026 **Cur Dio Nebraska Omaha NE 2015-** B Huntsville AL 1988 d Roger & Cynthia. BA U So 2010; MDiv Sewanee: The U So, TS 2015. D 7/11/2015 Bp Santosh K Marray.

MILLER, Stephen Arthur (WNC) 290 Hillside Oaks Dr, Jefferson NC 28640 B Saline MI 1947 s Harold & Delores. BA MI SU 1969; MDiv Sewanee: The U So, TS 1982. D 6/7/1982 Bp Hunley Agee Elebash P 12/18/1982 Bp William Evan Sanders. m 12/28/1968 Susan Miller c 1. R Par Of The H Comm Glendale Sprg NC 1999-2013; Int S Barn Ch Dillon SC 1996-1998; Int The Ch Of The Cross Bluffton SC 1996; Int S Thos Ch Savannah GA 1995; Int

S Mk's Epis Ch Charleston SC 1993-1994; Bd Dir Bp Gasden Ret Cmnty 1988-1993; R S Jude's Epis Ch Walterboro SC 1984-1993; Atone Ch Walterboro SC 1984-1988; Cur S Mary's Ch Kinston NC 1982-1984; Trst Sewanee U So TS Sewanee TN 1983-1984.

⌖ **MILLER, The Rt Rev Steven Andrew** (Mil) 804 E Juneau Ave, Milwaukee WI 53202 **Bp of Milwaukee Dio Milwaukee Milwaukee WI 2003-** B Detroit MI 1957 s Ben & Doris. BA MI SU 1979; MDiv GTS 1984; DD GTS 2004; GTS 2004. D 6/30/1984 Bp Henry Irving Mayson P 12/30/1984 Bp H Coleman Mcgehee Jr Con 10/18/2003 for Mil. m 2/4/1989 Cynthia Celeste Miller. VTS Alexandria VA 2002; Dn Reg XV Dio Virginia Richmond VA 1999-2003, Ecum Cmsn 1994-1998, Pres of the Stndg Com 2002-2003; R S Alb's Epis Ch Annandale VA 1996-2003; R Chr Epis Ch Gordonsville VA 1990-1996; Instr Cntrl Methodist Coll 1988-1990; Vic Chr Ch Epis Boonville MO 1986-1990; Dio W Missouri Kansas City MO 1986-1990; S Mary's Ch Fayette MO 1986-1990; Cur Chr Epis Ch S Jos MO 1984-1986. CdI Trainers 2001-2011. Bp's Shield Dio W Missouri 1988. bishop11@diomil.org

MILLER, Susan Heilmann (ECR) 25020 Pine Hills Dr, Carmel CA 93923 **Coun Mem Dio El Camino Real 2005-; Vic, St. Mths' Epis Ch Dio El Camino Real 2003-** B Yuba City CA 1945 d Paul & Helen. BA Stan 1966; MS Col 1969; MA Stan 1973; PhD Stan 1976; MDiv CDSP 2003. D 6/28/2003 P 1/10/2004 Bp Richard Lester Shimpfky. m 6/24/1967 Allen C Miller. Chapl Jn XXIII AIDS Mnstry Salinas CA 2003-2008; S Mths Ch Seaside CA 2003-2008; Chair, Dio Peace & Justice Commisssion Dio El Camino Real 2006. Preaching & Theol subscription to Interp for excelle CDSP 2003; Preaching Excellence ECF 2003.

MILLER, Thomas Paul (NY) 165 Christopher St Apt 5W, New York NY 10014 **Cn for Liturg and Arts Cathd Ch of S Jn the Div New York NY 2003-** B West Reading PA 1949 s Joseph & Shirley. BA U Pgh 1971; MDiv UTS 1989; STM GTS 1998. D 6/9/1990 P 12/15/1990 Bp Richard Frank Grein. Cathd Of St Jn The Div New York NY 2003-2013; Dio New York New York NY 1996-2003; S Greg's Epis Ch Woodstock NY 1994-1995; S Mich's Ch New York NY 1990-1994. CHS, Assoc of 1991; SSJE, Fllshp of 2002.

MILLER, Todd (Mass) 12 Ridge Ave., Newton MA 02459 **R Trin Par of Newton Cntr Newton Cntr MA 2006-; R Trin Par of Newton Cntr Newton Cntr MA 2006-** B Racine WI 1969 s David & Marilyn. BA S Olaf Coll 1991; MDiv VTS 2004. D 6/19/2004 P 1/22/2005 Bp Joseph Jon Bruno. m 11/26/1999 Ashley Paige Miller c 2. Par Of Chr Ch Andover MA 2004-2006; S Paul's Epis Ch Ventura CA 1999-2002.

MILLER, Victoria C (Ct) 350 Sound Beach Ave, Old Greenwich CT 06870 B Philadelphia PA 1953 d Sidney & Jean. BA Smith 1975; MBA Harv 1979; MDiv GTS 1990; ThD GTS 1998. D 6/9/1990 P 12/15/1990 Bp Richard Frank Grein. R S Sav's Epis Ch Old Greenwich CT 2002-2017; Asst to R S Steph's Ch Ridgefield CT 1998-2002; Dir The CPG New York NY 1994-1998; Assoc P Chr And S Steph's Ch New York NY 1990-1998. Auth, "The Lambeth arts: Doctrinal Dvlpmt And Conflict In The Sixteenth Century Engl," *Latimer Hse Stds*, Latimer Hse, 1994; Auth, "Wm Wake And The Reunion Of Christians," *Angl & Epis Hist*, 1993; Auth, "Ecclesiology, Scripture, & Tradition In The Dublin Agreed Statement," *Harvard Theol Revs*, 1993.

MILLER, William B (La) PO Box 1745, Lihue HI 96766 **R Chr Ch Covington LA 2015-** B 1959 BS Abilene Chr U 1981; MDiv McCormick TS 1986; CITS Epis TS of the SW 1991. D 10/2/1989 Bp Maurice Manuel Benitez P 4/3/1990 Bp Anselmo Carral-Solar. R S Mich And All Ang Ch Lihue HI 2006-2015; R Trin Ch Houston TX 1999-2006; S Jas Ch Austin TX 1991-1998; The Great Cmsn Fndt Houston TX 1991-1998; S Jn The Div Houston TX 1989-1991, 1986-1989. Auth, *The Gospel According to Sam*, Seabury Books, 2005.

MILLER, William Charles (Pgh) 18297 W 155th Ter, Olathe KS 66062 **Prncpl WCM Consulting specializing in Theol Educ 2013-** B Minneapolis MN 1947 s Robert & Cleithra. AB Indiana Wesl 1968; MLS Kent St U 1974; PhD Kent St U 1983; MARS Cntrl Bapt TS 1988; MBA Mid Amer Nazarene U 1997; STM Nash 2001. D 12/7/2006 P 6/30/2007 Bp Keith Lynn Ackerman. m 7/25/1969 Brenda Miller c 2. Ch Of The Nativ Pittsburgh PA 2012-2013, Asstg P 2007-2012, 2006-2012; Dir, Accreditation Assn of Theol Schools in the US and Can 2011-2013. Ch of Engl Record Soc 2002; Forw in Faith NA 2007; The CBS 2004. wcm.consulting@outlook.com

MILLER, William Robert (CPa) 182 Dew Drop Rd Apt G, York PA 17402 **Engl Prof York Coll York PA 1989-** B Anniston AL 1959 s William & Joyce. BA Eckerd Coll 1982; MA Hollins U 1983; PhD SUNY 1989. D 6/11/2005 Bp Michael Whittington Creighton. c 1.

MILLER, William T (Fla) 25928 Kilreigh Dr, Farmington Hills MI 48336 **Piedmont Ch Madison VA 2014-; Int Pstr Bethlehem Luth Ch 2011-** B Jacksonville FL 1978 BA U So 2001; MDiv VTS 2005; STM Luth TS at Gettysburg 2012; STM Luth TS at Gettysburg 2012. D 6/5/2005 P 12/11/2005 Bp Samuel Johnson Howard. m 1/14/2006 Lauren Edith Miller. Assoc Chr Ch Cranbrook Bloomfield Hills MI 2005-2009. millersoak@hotmail.com

MILLER IV, Woodford Decatur (CFla) 2508 Creekside Dr., Fort Piece FL 34981 **Camp Wingmann Avon Pk FL 2014-** B 1969 s Woodford & Josephine. AA Polk Cmnty Coll 1994; BA U of So Florida 1995; MDiv TESM 2007. D 6/2/

2007 P 12/9/2007 Bp John Wadsworth Howe. m 3/20/1993 Sindy Renee Miller c 2. S Paul's Epis Ch New Smyrna Bch FL 2010-2014; Asst R/Acad Chapl S Andr's Epis Ch Ft Pierce FL 2007-2010.

MILLER-MUTIA, Sylvia J (RG) 425 University Blvd NE, Albuquerque NM 87106 **S Thos Of Cbury Epis Ch Albuquerque NM 2015-** B Fort Collins CO 1976 d Mark & Anne. BFA U of Utah 1997; MA PSR 2002; Cert Ang Stud CDSP 2009; CTS CDSP 2010. D 6/5/2010 P 12/4/2010 Bp Marc Handley Andrus. m 1/5/2002 Donnel Miller-Mutia c 3. Yth and Fam Min S Greg Of Nyssa Ch San Francisco CA 2010-2015; S Steph's Par Bel Tiburon CA 2003-2010.

MILLETTE, Carol Leslie (RI) 19 Midway Dr, Warwick RI 02886 **D S Ptr-S Andr 1985-** B Pawtucket RI 1942 d Harold & Gertrude. Rhode Island Sch For Deacons. D 4/5/1986 Bp George Nelson Hunt III. D S Lk's Ch Pawtucket RI 2011; Dioc Advoc For Chld And Fam.

MILLICAN JR, Ford Jefferson (La) 3919 Morris Pl, Jefferson LA 70121 **P S Mart's Epis Ch Metairie LA 2006-; S Mart's Epis Sch Metairie LA 2005-** B Baton Rouge LA 1967 s Ford & Jacquelyn. BA LSU 1990; MDiv Epis TS of the SW 1999. D 2/28/1999 P 9/7/1999 Bp Charles Edward Jenkins III. m 8/7/1993 Lisa Gayle Millican c 2. Dio Louisiana New Orleans LA 1999-2005; Chapl Ch Of The H Sprt New Orleans LA 1999.

MILLIEN, Jean-Elie (Hai) Ecole Le Bon Samaritan, 26 Rue Jonathas, Carrefour 06134 Haiti B Gressier Port-au-Prince HT 1934 s Joseph & Dormela. MDiv ETSC 1964; MDiv ETSC 1964; Licence Eld 1968; Eld 1968. D 5/14/1964 Bp Charles Alfred Voegeli P 12/1/1964 Bp James Loughlin Duncan. c 5. P-in-c Dio Haiti Port-au-Prince HT 1996-1998, 1964-1987; Vic S Jn's Ch Stamford CT 1992-1996; Vic-In-Charge Ascen Ch New Haven CT 1991-1992; P Assoc Dio Connecticut Meriden CT 1991-1992; Asst S Andr's Epis Ch Miami FL 1989-1991; P-in-c S Matt's Grande Riviere Haiti 1983-1988; P-in-c SS Innocence Port De Paix Haiti 1977-1983; Vic S Marcos Rio Haina Dominican Republic 1972-1974; P-in-c Redemp In Gonaives 1969-1972; P-in-c S Sav Cayes Haiti 1966-1969; Vic S Sav Cayes Haiti 1965-1966; Vic Epiph In Port-Au-Prince Port-Au-Prince Haiti 1964-1965; Dir Of Pension S Pierre In Port-Au-Prince Port-Au-Prince Haiti 1964-1965.

MILLIEN, Wilner (PR) B 1934 s Estinor & Lauramise. MDiv Seminario Epis del Caribe 1963; MBA Wrld U 1984. D 6/22/1963 Bp Albert Ervine Swift P 12/22/1963 Bp Charles Alfred Voegeli. m 6/30/1964 Raymonde Delienn c 3. Dio Puerto Rico Trujillo Alto PR 2004-2006; 1987-2003, 1963-1970.

MILLIGAN, Donald Arthur (Mass) 222 Bowdoin St, Winthrop MA 02152 B Charleston SC 1943 s Walter & Ruth. BA Hobart and Wm Smith Colleges 1970; MDiv GTS 1973. D 6/9/1973 P 12/15/1973 Bp John Melville Burgess. m 2/9/1985 Kathleen Milligan c 3. R S Jn's Ch Winthrop MA 1991-2008; R St Jn the Bapt Epis Ch Linden NJ 1984-1991; S Barn-In-The-Dunes Gary IN 1978-1983; R S Jn's Ch Sharon MA 1974-1978; Cur Gr Epis Ch Lawr MA 1973-1974. OHC, Ord Of S Anne.

MILLIGAN, Kathleen Sue (Ia) 3714 Pennsylvania Ave Apt. I-86, Dubuque IA 52002 **Chr Ch Cedar Rapids IA 2016-** B Des Moines IA 1949 d James & Lura. BA Morningside Coll 1971; MDiv Garrett-Evang TS 1981. D 4/18/1986 P 11/1/1986 Bp Walter Cameron Righter. R S Jn's Epis Ch Dubuque IA 2006-2016; Pres- Stndg Com Dio Iowa Des Moines IA 2001-2002; R S Alb's Ch Davenport IA 1996-2006; Vic Trin Ch Emmetsburg IA 1987-1996; Ch Of S Thos Algona IA 1986-1996; Int S Andr Clear Lake IA 1986-1987. Ed, "Iowa Epis," 1988. sjed@mwci.net

MILLIGAN, Michael (U) 28 Ridgeview Drive, Bountiful UT 84010 **Ret P Cathd Ch Of S Mk Salt Lake City UT 2008-** B Atlanta GA 1942 s Horace & Louise. Oxford Coll of Emory U 1962; BA U of W Georgia 1967; MDiv Sewanee: The U So, TS 1970; Georgia St Univ 1980. D 6/27/1970 Bp Randolph R Claiborne P 3/6/1971 Bp Milton Legrand Wood. m 11/6/1982 Katherine Clark January c 3. R Ch Of The Resurr Centerville UT 2004-2007; P-in-c S Paul's Peace Ch Las Vegas NM 1998-2000; Vic Epis Ch Of The H Fam Santa Fe NM 1996-2004; Int S Bede's Epis Ch Santa Fe NM 1993-1995; Int The Epis Ch Of S Ptr And S Paul Marietta GA 1992-1993; P-in-c Gr-Calv Epis Ch Clarkesville GA 1991-1992; Fam Ther Atlanta Inst for Fam Stds 1989-1990; R S Julian's Epis Ch Douglasville GA 1985-1989; Chapl Coordntr Of Pstr Care All SS Epis Ch Atlanta GA 1981-1984; Grad Stdt Georgia St U 1976-1981; Chair Long-R Plnng T/F Dio Atlanta Atlanta GA 1973-1976; S Cathr's Epis Ch Marietta GA 1973-1976; R S Paul's Ch Macon GA 1970-1973. Ed, "Ed," *S Lk's Journ of Theol*, TS, Univ of So, 1970; Assoc. Ed, "Assoc. Ed," *S Lk Journ Theol*, TS, Univ of So, 1969. Woods Ldrshp Awd TS, Univ of So 1968.

MILLIKEN, Jean Louise (Va) 3732 N Oakland St, Arlington VA 22207 **Nonpar Pstr Counslg Ntwk Arlington VA 1986-** B Pittsburgh PA 1943 d Clyde & Lois. BA Westminster Coll 1965; MDiv Candler TS Emory U 1978; DMin Wesley TS 1992. D 6/10/1978 Bp Charles Judson Child Jr P 12/6/1980 Bp Bennett Jones Sims. m 11/6/1965 William Milliken c 2. Assoc Chr Ch Alexandria VA 2006-2009; Pstr Assoc Cathd of St Ptr & St Paul Washington DC 2002-2006; Int S Ptr's Epis Ch Arlington VA 2001-2002; S Andr's Epis Ch Arlington VA 1987-1988; Ch Of The Resurr Alexandria VA 1984-1985; Chapl S Lk's Epis Ch Atlanta GA 1980-1983; D S Tim's Decatur GA 1979-1980; Dio

Atlanta Atlanta GA 1978-1979. Auth, "Faith At Wk mag," 1992; Auth, "Power And Mnstry". Advncd Clinician Imago Relation Ther; AAPC.

✠ **MILLIKEN, The Rt Rev Mike** (WK) 1 N. Main Sreet - Suite 418, Hutchinson KS 67501 **Bp of Wstrn Kansas Dio Wstrn Kansas Hutchinson KS 2011-; Bp Asstg Dio Kansas Topeka KS 2017-** B Lexington KY 1947 s Jack & Ruby. BA U of Kentucky 1970; MDiv Epis TS in Kentucky 1973; MA Xavier U 1992. D 5/26/1973 P 11/30/1973 Bp Addison Hosea Con 2/19/2011 for WK. m 8/2/1969 Kathleen Smith c 1. Instr in Biblic Lit Hutchinson Cmnty Coll Hutchinson KS 2006-2010; R Gr Epis Ch Hutchinson KS 1998-2014; Lectr in Theol Xavier U Cincinnati OH 1992-1993; R Gr Epis Ch Florence KY 1977-1998; Vic S Matthews Ch Lexington KY 1973-1977. Soc of S Marg. bishopmilliken@gmail.com

MILLIKIN, Gregory Loyd (Los) 228 S Pitt St, Alexandria VA 22314 **S Paul's Epis Ch Alexandria VA 2015-** B Henrico City VA 1979 s William & Virginia. BA U NC 2001; MDiv VTS 2015. D 6/6/2015 Bp Diane Jardine Bruce P 1/16/2016 Bp Joseph Jon Bruno. m 11/14/2014 Andrew Brooks Rutledge.

MILLNER JR, Bollin Madison (Va) 8 N Laurel St, Richmond VA 23220 **R Gr & H Trin Epis Ch Richmond VA 2003-** B Richmond VA 1954 s Bollin & Shirley. BA U Rich 1976; MA VTS 1979; Duke 1983. D 4/15/1984 P 4/21/1985 Bp Robert Whitridge Estill. m 7/24/1976 Katherine A Kelly c 2. Ch Of The Gd Shpd Rocky Mt NC 1992-2003; R Imm Ch King and Queen Courthouse VA 1986-1992; S Jn's Ch W Point VA 1986-1992; S Steph's Ch Durham NC 1984-1986; Stndg Com Dio Virginia Richmond VA 2000-2003, New Congrl Dvlpmt 1998-1999, Asst Deploy Off 1989-1997. Phi Beta Kappa.

MILLOTT, Diane Lynn (SwFla) 4510 Pilgrim Mill Road, Cumming GA 30041 B Muskegon MI 1945 d Frances & Alice. BBA U of No Florida 1976; MA U of So Florida 1994. D 6/18/2005 Bp John Bailey Lipscomb. m 10/23/1988 Robert Thomas Millott c 2. D S Hilary's Ch Ft Myers FL 2010-2011; D S Jn's Epis Ch St Jas City FL 2006-2010; Acquisition Libr Ret Lee Cnty Libr System 1989-2011.

MILLOTT, Donna Evans (SwFla) 1236 Santa Barbara Blvd, Cape Coral FL 33991 B Cleveland OH 1947 d Lester & Frances. Kent St U. D 6/29/1991 Bp Rogers Sanders Harris. c 4. D S Hilary's Ch Ft Myers FL 1991-2011.

MILLOTT, Robert Thomas (SwFla) 4510 Pilgrim Mill Road, Cumming GA 30041 **D S Columba Epis Ch Suwanee GA 2012-** B Cleveland OH 1944 s Wilbur & Helen. BS U of So Florida. D 6/14/2003 Bp John Bailey Lipscomb. m 10/23/1988 Diane Lynn Millott. D S Lk's Ch Ft Myers FL 2005-2011; D Lamb Of God Epis Ch Ft Myers FL 2003-2005.

MILLS, Alice Marie (USC) St Mary's Episcopal Church, 170 Saint Andrews Rd, Columbia SC 29210 **Asst for Mem Care S Mary's Ch Columbia SC 2013-; COM Dio Upper So Carolina Columbia SC 2014-** B Asheville NC 1958 d Robert & Mildred Anne. BS No Carolina St U 1980; MDiv Sewanee: The U So, TS 2010. D 5/23/2010 Bp Porter Taylor P 11/30/2010 Bp Barry Leigh Beisner. m 7/2/2016 John Christopher Mills c 2. Asst S Mary's Epis Ch Napa CA 2010-2012. stmarysoffice@att.net

MILLS JR, Arthur Donald (SO) 2696 Cedarbrook Way, Beavercreek OH 45431 B Ft Chaffee AR 1958 s Arthur & Dorothy. BS W Virginia Wesleyan Coll 1979; MS AF Inst of Tech 1983. D 6/14/2008 Bp Thomas Edward Breidenthal. c 1. D S Andr's Ch Dayton OH 2008-2011.

MILLS, Byron Keith (Az) 596 W. Ord Mountain Rd, Globe AZ 85501 **R S Jn The Bapt Globe AZ 2002-, D 2001-** B Globe AZ 1952 s Von & Elwanda. BA U of Phoenix 1988. D 10/27/2001 P 11/9/2002 Bp Robert Reed Shahan. m 9/29/1972 Rayla Alene Beason c 4. Chapl Arizona Dept of Corrections 2001-2005.

MILLS, Carol Ann (Tex) 205 Hillcrest Dr, Alvin TX 77511 **D Gr Epis Ch Alvin TX 2009-** B Chicago IL 1944 d Donald & Annie. U MI; BS Estrn Michigan U 1967; MLS Texas Womans U 1973; BA California Sch for Deacons 1984. D 6/8/1985 Bp William Edwin Swing. m 4/17/1971 Joseph Milton Mills c 1. D S Paul's Ch Houston TX 1997-2009; Asst S Chris 1990-1996; D Chr Epis Ch Plano TX 1985-1988.

MILLS, Christen H (Mass) **Epiph Par Walpole MA 2016-** D 6/7/2014 Bp M(Arvil) Thomas Shaw P 1/10/2015 Bp Alan Gates.

MILLS, David Knight (SO) 172 Clark Point Rd # 696, Southwest Harbor ME 04679 **1972-** B Evanston IL 1930 s Ellsworth & Mary. BA Wms 1952; MDiv VTS 1957. D 6/8/1957 Bp William A Lawrence P 12/1/1957 Bp Richard Stanley Merrill Emrich. m 6/16/1956 Audrey Mills c 2. Bd New Creation Healing Cntr Plaistow NH 2000-2006; Bd Inst of Chr Renwl Plaistow NH 1997-2006; Newsong Mnstry SW Harbor 1975-1976; R Ch Of Our Sav Cincinnati OH 1960-1972; Cur All SS Epis Ch Pontiac MI 1957-1960. Auth, *The Sea Around Us ME Coast Guide*.

MILLS III, Edward James (ETenn) 2104 Lamont St, Kingsport TN 37664 B Charleston WV 1954 s Edward & Betty. BA W Virginia Wesleyan Coll 1977; MDiv VTS 1980. D 6/15/1980 P 6/1/1981 Bp Robert Poland Atkinson. m 8/21/1976 Karen Lee Mills. R S Paul's Epis Ch Kingsport TN 2005-2014, 1994-1996; Asst Ch Of The Gd Samar Knoxville TN 2001-2004; S Thos' Epis Ch Abingdon VA 2000-2001; All SS' Epis Ch Morristown TN 1999-2000; Emm Epis Ch Bristol VA 1998-1999; S Thos Epis Ch Knoxville TN 1997-1998; S Jn's Epis Ch Johnson City TN 1996-1997; S Andr's in the Vill

Ch Barboursville WV 1985-1994; Vic S Mk's Epis Ch Berkeley Spg WV 1982-1984; Asst S Mk's Epis Ch St Albans WV 1981-1982; D Chr Ch Clarksburg WV 1980-1981. "An Unexpectal Yet Brdden Journey," Intergrity Monograph.

MILLS, Eric Christopher (FdL) 347 Libal St, De Pere WI 54115 **R S Anne's Epis Ch De Pere WI 2010-** B Milwaukee WI 1960 s Gerald & Elayne. BA U of Texas 1989; MDiv Nash 1998. D 6/27/1998 P 1/22/1999 Bp Jack Leo Iker. m 10/11/1985 Susan G Moore c 3. Assoc R Chr Ch Bradenton FL 2007-2010; Chapl Off Of Bsh For ArmdF New York NY 2001-2007; Asst S Vinc's Cathd Bedford TX 1998-2001.

MILLS, Fred Thomas (Ky) 685 West Dr, Madisonville KY 42431 **D Dio Kentucky Louisville KY 1987-** B Salisbury NC 1927 s Fred & Hazzie. BS Bowling Green Coll of Commerce 1949. D 6/14/1987 Bp David Reed. m 8/31/1950 Barbara Ann Mills c 4. NAAD.

MILLS III, Joseph Edmund (LI) 1118 9th St Apt 9, Santa Monica CA 90403 **Non-par 1968-** B Brooklyn NY 1941 s Joseph & Dorothy. BA Hobart and Wm Smith Colleges 1963; STB GTS 1966. D 6/16/1966 Bp Jonathan Goodhue Sherman P 12/1/1966 Bp Robert Claflin Rusack. Cur S Aug By-The-Sea Par Santa Monica CA 1966-1968.

MILLS JR, Joseph Milton (Tex) 205 Hillcrest Dr, Alvin TX 77511 **D Gr Epis Ch Alvin TX 2009-** B Dallas TX 1945 s Joseph & Odessa. BS U of Texas 1967; MS LSU 1970; PhD The Australian Natl U 1977; BA California Sch for Deacons 1984. D 6/8/1985 Bp William Edwin Swing. m 4/17/1971 Carol Ann Mills c 3. D S Paul's Ch Houston TX 1997-2009; D S Chris's Ch League City TX 1990-1997; D Chr Epis Ch Plano TX 1985-1990.

MILLS, Joy Anna Marie (Pa) 2103 Quail Ridge Dr, Paoli PA 19301 B Darby PA 1942 d Arthur & Margaret. Vas 1962; BA Br 1964; MDiv EDS 1986; Fell AAPC 1988; MA in Pstr Mnstry Boston Coll 1988. D 6/13/1987 Bp David Elliot Johnson P 4/16/1988 Bp Allen Lyman Bartlett Jr. m 11/6/2004 Arthur C Benedict c 3. non-stipendiary P S Ptr's Germantown PA 1994-1997; Asst Chapl Epis Ch At Pr NJ 1991-1994; Pstr Assoc S Dav's Ch Wayne PA 1990-1992; Ch Of S Asaph Bala Cynwyd PA 1987-1990; Ch Of Our Sav Jenkintown PA 1987-1989. Auth, "My Living into His Dying," *Journeys: Essays from the Heart of Pstr Counslg*, Amer Assn of Pstr Counslg, 2008; Auth, "Living into Dying," *Journ of Pstr Care and Counslg*, Journ of Pstr Care Pub, Inc., 2003; co-Auth, "God's Sweet Surprises: Ang, Mentors, Friends May Fllshp Serv," *CWU*, CWU, 1999; Auth, "Lighting, Troubling, Raising, and Widening: Re-Imagining Revival/Decade Impressions," *Journ of Wmn Ministires*, Episcopal Ch Pub Co., 1998; Auth, "Fourth Wrld Conf on Wmn," *Equal wRites*, RC Wmn Ord Conf, 1996; Auth, "Biblic Stories of Wmn: Death Dealing or Life Giving?," *The Renfrew Perspective*, The Renfrew Fndt, 1996. AAPC 1992; Wmn of Faith 1990-1995. joymills9@gmail.com

MILLS III, Ladson Frazier (SC) 3114 Mayfair Ln, Johns Island SC 29455 B Rock Hill SC 1951 s Ladson & Doris. BA Cit 1973; MDiv Sewanee: The U So, TS 1980; DMin GTF 1999. D 6/14/1980 P 12/1/1980 Bp Gray Temple. c 2. R Chr Ch Frederica St Simons Is GA 2006-2011; Ch Of The Ascen Knoxville TN 1997-2006; Pres Of The Stndg Com 1993-1994; R Trin Ch Myrtle Bch SC 1991-1997; Chair Of The Dept Spec Ministers 1986-1988; So Carolina Charleston SC 1984; Ch Of Our Sav Johns Island SC 1981-1991; S Jn's Epis Par Johns Island SC 1980; Trst Sewanee U So TS Sewanee TN 1984-1988. Auth, "It'S Christmas".

MILLS, Michael S (Dal) 11122 Midway Rd, Dallas TX 75229 B Demopolis AL 1968 s Robert & Carol. BS U of Montevallo 1989; MA U of Montevallo 1991; MDiv Nash 1995; JD U of Alabama Sch of Law 2009. D 9/14/1995 P 3/1/1996 Bp Keith Lynn Ackerman. m 11/28/1987 Susan Lee c 2. P-in-c Ch Of The Gd Shpd Dallas TX 2013, R 2013-; Supply Dio Dallas 2012-2013; Supply P Dio Dallas Dallas TX 2011-2013; Dn S Matt's Cathd Dallas TX 2002-2005; Ch Of The Incarn Dallas TX 2000-2002, Cur for CE 2000-2002, Cur for Yth, Singles, & Young Marrieds 1995-1998; P-in-c H Trin Par Pelton UK 1998-2000.

MILLS, Nancy Thompson (Ga) PO Box 3136, Thomasville GA 31799 **Vic Ch Of The Gd Shpd Thomasville GA 2007-; Stndg Com Dio Georgia Savannah GA 2010-, Dioc Counsel 2005-2007** B Philadelphia PA 1944 d Frederic & Mary Ruth. Sewanee: The U So, TS 2004. D 6/10/2003 P 12/20/2003 Bp Henry Irving Louttit. m 11/15/1980 Luther Rice Mills. P Mssnr S Anne's Ch Tifton GA 2004-2007; Chapl Hospice of SW Georgia 2001-2004.

MILLS, Stephen (ECR) 713 Helen Drive, Hollister CA 95023 B South Weymouth MA 1946 s William & Marjorie. BA Claremont Men's Coll 1970; JD U Pac McGeorge Sch of Law 1976; MDiv CDSP 1984. D 6/10/1984 P 12/21/1984 Bp John Lester Thompson III. m 6/16/1990 Eleanor Wakefield-Mills c 6. Adj Fac San Jose St U 2014; Int S Ptr's By-The-Sea Epis Ch Morro Bay CA 2012-2013; Chapl St. Brutus's Secure Cntr for Incurably Criminal Boys 2010-2015; R Epis Ch in Almaden San Jose CA 2002-2009; Vic H Fam Epis Ch Rohnert Pk CA 1984-2002; Presiding Judge, Eccl Crt Dio El Camino Real Salinas CA 2008-2009, Bp Search Com 2007; Dioc Coun The Epis Dio Nthrn California Sacramento CA 1986-1987. Co-Auth, "Revs of Current Legis," *Pacific Law Journ*, McGeorge Sch of Law, 1974.

M

MILLS, Susan (SO) 526 McLaughlin St, Richmond CA 94805 B Hazard KY 1939 d James & Mildred. BA Indiana U 1961; MA Indiana U 1966; MDiv GTS 1976. D 6/12/1976 Bp Paul Moore Jr P 3/5/1977 Bp James Stuart Wetmore. R S Andr's Ch Dayton OH 2000-2006; R S Paul's Jeffersonvlle IN 1989-2000; Liturg Off Dio Delaware Wilmington 1984-1989, 1983-1989; Hosp Chapl S Jn's Ch New York NY 1983-1989, Asst 1976-1982; S Steph's Ch Harrington DE 1983-1989; S Marg's Ch Bronx NY 1982-1983; Tchr S Lk Sch In New York City 1976-1979; Liturg & Mus Cmsn Dio Indianapolis Indianapolis IN 1989-2000. Ord Of S Helena.

MILLS, Wallace Wilson (Ida) B Camden SC 1944 s Wilson & Barbara. AB Harvard Coll 1967; JD U of So Carolina Sch of Law 1973; MDiv EDS 2015. D 7/23/2014 P 5/14/2015 Bp Brian James Thom. m 2/8/1969 Elizabeth Wilson Mills c 3. wmills@mindspring.com

MILLSAP, William Richard (Nev) PO Box 2246, Reno NV 89505 **Assoc R Trin Epis Ch Reno NV 2010-** B Oakland CA 1957 s Russel & Carolyn. BA U of Nevada at Reno 1980; MA U of Nevada at Reno 1983; CDSP & Dioc Trng 2006. D 1/31/2006 P 7/31/2006 Bp Katharine Jefferts Schori. c 2.

MILLS-CURRAN, Lori (Mass) 7 Kimball Rd, Westborough MA 01581 **D Dio Massachusetts Boston MA 2016-; Secy, Stndg Cmsn on Ecum & Interfaith Re The Epis Ch New York NE 2006-; Mem, Stndg Cmsn on Ecum & Interfaith Relat The Epis Ch New York NY 2003-** B Inglewood CA 1956 d Charles & Ruth. BA U CA 1978; JD U CA 1982; MDiv Weston Jesuit TS 2001. D 8/24/1988 Bp William Davidson. m 8/27/1977 William C Mills-Curran c 3. D S Andr's Ch Framingham MA 2007-2016; D S Paul's Ch Natick MA 2001-2006; D S Paul's Ch N Kingstown RI 1990-1998; D S Matt Albuquerque NM 1988-1989; Yth Mnstry Coordntr Dio Rhode Island Providence RI 1992-1994. DOK; Natl Gld: Catchesis of the Gd Shpd. Phi Beta Kappa.

MILLS-POWELL, Mark Oliver Mclay (Eur) The Dower House Cottage Upton Grey, Basingstoke, Hampshire R6251RY Great Britain (UK) **R Trin 1988-** B 1955 s Neil & Rosamond. BA U of Durham Gb 1978; MDiv VTS 1982. Trans 10/1/1988 Bp John Thomas Walker. m 8/21/1981 Dana Sedgwick Mills c 2. Old Fields Chap Hughesville MD 1988-1994; Trin Epis Par Hughesville MD 1988-1994; Serv Ch Of Engl 1983-1986. Auth, "Praying In The Shadow Of The Bomb". Soc Of S Fran.

MILNER JR, Raymond Joseph (SanD) 200 E 22nd St Apt 32, Roswell NM 88201 B Williston ND 1930 No Dakota U Grand Forks ND 1952. D 1/9/2007 Bp Jeffrey Neil Steenson. m 8/2/1954 Mary Martha Milner c 2.

MILTENBERGER, Gordon (Dal) 10 Oak Village Rd, Greenville TX 75402 **Ret Ret 1990-** B Saint Louis MO 1928 s George & Dorothy. BA Harv 1950; STB Ya Berk 1953; STM Ya Berk 1958. D 6/20/1953 P 12/21/1953 Bp Charles A Mason. m 2/23/1957 Dolores Shepherd c 2. Resurr Gr Epis Ch Dallas TX 2002; R All SS Epis Ch Dallas TX 1973-1990; R Ch Of The H Comf Cleburne TX 1967-1973; Chapl TCU Ft Worth TX 1960-1967; Vic S Mary the Vrgn Wichita Falls TX 1958-1960; P-in-c S Paul's Ch Westbrook CT 1956-1958; Vic S Lk's Epis Ch Stephenville TX 1954-1956; Cur S Matt's Cathd Dallas TX 1953-1954.

MINARIK JR, Harry J (ETenn) 69 Hickory Trail, Norris TN 37828 **R S Fran' Ch Norris TN 2009-, P-in-c 2007-, D 2006-2016** B Atlanta GA 1949 s Harry & Jaqueline. BA E Tennessee St U 2003; MDiv Sewanee: The U So, TS 2006; MDiv Sewanee: The U So, TS 2006; MDiv Sewanee: The U So, TS 2006. D 5/27/2006 P 1/6/2007 Bp Charles Glenn VonRosenberg. m 5/20/1994 Sonya Minarik c 3. Dept. Supvsr U.S. Fence 2003.

MINDRUM, Alice Anderson (Ct) 60 Range Rd, Southport CT 06890 B Aurora IL 1949 d Gene & Marjorie. BA U of Iowa 1972; MA Ya Berk 1994. D 6/8/2002 P 12/14/2002 Bp Andrew Donnan Smith. m 8/22/1970 Thomas L Mindrum c 3. S Tim's Ch Fairfield CT 2013-2015; P-in-c Calv St Geo's Epis Ch Bridgeport CT 2009-2011; S Paul's Ch Fairfield CT 2007-2009, 2006, 2006, 2004-2005; Chr Ch Bethany CT 2006-2009; Chr Ch Ansonia CT 2006; Gr Epis Ch Norwalk CT 2006, 2002-2004.

MINEAU, Charles Douglas (NMich) B Gladstone MI 1949 s Clifford. D 6/11/2014 P 12/14/2014 Bp Rayford J Ray. m 5/19/2007 Helen Mineau.

MINER, Bob (Ct) 15 Morningside Ter, Wallingford CT 06492 **Ret 2000-** B Westerly RI 1939 s John & Lila. BA Leh 1961; STB Ya Berk 1964; Cert Trin Dublin IE 1989. D 6/20/1964 P 3/27/1965 Bp John S Higgins. m 8/22/1964 Gladys T Miner c 2. Int S Jn's Epis Par Waterbury CT 2011-2012; Int S Ann's Epis Ch Old Lyme CT 2010-2011; Int Trin Ch Branford CT 2009-2010; Int S Paul's Ch Wallingford CT 2007-2009; Vic All SS Ch Ivoryton CT 2006-2007; Int S Ptr's Epis Ch Bennington VT 2003-2005; Int Trin Chap Hartford CT 2003; Assoc Grtr Hartford Reg Mnstry E Hartford CT 2002-2003; Bd Mem Epis Soc Serv 1987-1989; R S Sav's Epis Ch Old Greenwich CT 1974-2000; Dn Lower Naugatuck 1973-1974; R Imm Ch Ansonia CT 1971-1974; R Imm S Jas Par Derby CT 1966-1974; Asst Chr Ch In Lonsdale Lincoln RI 1964-1966. EDEO (Pres: 1998-2002) 1980-2006; EPGM (Treas 2003- Cnvnr 2007-2008) 2002-2011. Hugh White Awd ENEJ 2010; Cn Chr Ch Cathd, Hartford 1998.

MINER, Darren R (Cal) 1750 29th Ave, San Francisco CA 94122 **P-in-c Ch Of The Incarn San Francisco CA 2016-, Assoc 2011-2016, Assoc 2010-2011, D 2010** B Salinas, CA 1959 s Ronald & Wilma. BA U CA 1980; CPhil U CA

1983; MDiv CDSP 2006; MA Grad Theol Un 2006. D 6/5/2010 P 12/4/2010 Bp Marc Handley Andrus. m 7/28/2008 Mathew Kochumalayil Chacko. Co-Chair, Dnry Coordntng Com Dio California San Francisco CA 2014-2015, Pres, San Francisco Dnry 2013-2015, VP, San Francisco Dnry 2012-2013, Mem, Dioc Com on Nomin 2011-2015. Angl Assn of Biblic Scholars 2007; AP 2010; Integrity USA 1992; Soc of Cath Priests 2010. Trabert-Graebner Gk Scriptural Schlr's Awd CDSP 2005. comebefed@aol.com

MINER, David R. (Fla) 3212 Wind Lake Ln, Tallahassee FL 32312 **Voltuneer Chapl Prison Chapl Florida 2010-** B Denver, CO 1946 s George & F. Bachelors of Sci Excelsior Coll 1984; Masters of Sci Florida St U 1989. D 11/7/2015 P 7/13/2016 Bp Samuel Johnson Howard. c 1.

MINER II, James Stevens (SO) 276 North Ardmore Road, Columbus OH 43209 **Ret 1998-** B Columbus OH 1942 s Ralph & Phyllis. BA Ya 1964; BD Epis TS of the SW 1967. D 6/17/1967 P 12/16/1967 Bp Nelson Marigold Burroughs. m 6/5/1965 Elizabeth Wilbur Miner c 2. Assoc S Alb's Epis Ch Of Bexley Columbus OH 1999-2002; Int S Lk's Ch Granville OH 1997-1998; Int S Paul's Epis Ch Dayton OH 1996-1997; R Trin Ch Columbus OH 1986-1996; Exec Asst to Bp Dio Ohio Cleveland 1980-1986; R S Paul's Epis Ch Medina OH 1975-1980; Assoc S Jn's Ch Youngstown OH 1969-1975; Cur Gr Epis Ch Sandusky OH 1967-1969.

MINER-PEARSON, Anne Arlene (Minn) 15601 Island Road, Burnsville MN 55306 B Kansas City MO 1941 d Paul & Dorothy. Untd TS of the Twin Cities; BS U of Kansas 1963; MDiv SWTS 1983; DMin SWTS 1995. D 6/29/1983 P 1/18/1984 Bp Robert Marshall Anderson. m 5/22/1983 Daniel Pearson. Ch Of The Nativ Burnsville MN 2004-2007; Dio Minnesota Minneapolis MN 1998-2003; R All Souls' Epis Ch San Diego CA 1996-1998; R S Anne S Paul MN 1986-1996; S Anne's Epis Ch S Paul MN 1986-1996; Int S Mary's Ch S Paul MN 1984-1986; Asst S Clem's Ch S Paul MN 1983-1984. Auth, "Sermon," *Abingdon Wmn Preaching Annual Year A*, Abingdon Press; Auth, *Essays & Interviews on Wmn Sprtlty*; Auth, *Mar & Sprtlty: Revisiting the Mar Cov*; Auth, "Sacr Strands," *Sermons by Minnsota Wmn*; Auth, *The Spiral Path*.

MINERVA SR, Royal Edward (Fla) B New York NY 1930 s Dominic & Emma. Dio Florida Sch of Mnstry; BA Jones Coll Jacksonville FL 1979. D 12/8/2002 Bp Samuel Johnson Howard. m 6/20/1952 Mildred Minerva c 1.

MINGLEDORFF, Paschal Schirm (Ga) 9541 Whitfield Ave, Savannah GA 31406 **Respite P S Ptr's Epis Ch Savannah GA 2001-** B Savannah GA 1935 d William & Doris. S Marys Jr Coll Raleigh NC 1953; U GA 1954; Armstrong Atlantic St U 1978; Cert Sewanee: The U So, TS 1992; Sewanee: The U So, TS 2000. D 4/18/1995 P 12/18/1999 Bp Henry Irving Louttit. m 7/11/1960 Frederick William Mingledorff c 3. Int S Eliz of Hungary Richmond Hill GA 2000-2001; D S Fran Of The Islands Epis Ch Savannah GA 1998-1999; D S Thos Ch Savannah GA 1995-1998.

MINICH, Henry Nichols Faulconer (SeFla) 250 Pantops Mountain Rd Apt 5406, Charlottesville VA 22911 **Chapl Emer Dio SE Florida Miami 1994-, Chapl 1990-1994, Dn 1983-1994** B West Chester PA 1931 s Ralph & Margaret. BA U of Virginia 1953; MDiv VTS 1958; STM Sewanee: The U So, TS 1968; JD U of Miami 1976. D 5/10/1958 Bp Oliver J Hart P 11/15/1958 Bp Angus Dun. m 8/30/1975 Helen De Russy Minich c 3. Int S Anne's Par Scottsville VA 2004-2005; Assoc 1998-2003; Chr Epis Ch Charlottesvlle VA 1999-2000; Int Trin Epis Ch Charlottesvlle VA 1995-1996; Chapl Chap of the Venerable Bede Coral Gables FL 1970-1994; Chapl U Miami 1964-1994; Vic H Sacr Hollywood FL 1961-1964. *Var arts in Bioethics*, 2003. CBS 1996; GAS 1996; Oblate Ord of S Ben. VP's Awd for Serv U of Miami 1994; Hon Cn Trin Cathd 1991; Who's Who in Rel 1974.

MINIFIE, Charles Jackson (NY) 23 Sherman Dr, Hilton Head Island SC 29928 **Assoc Gr Ch Cathd Charleston SC 2011-** B Providence RI 1941 s Benjamin & Frances. BA Trin Hartford 1963; MDiv EDS 1966. D 6/4/1966 P 12/17/1966 Bp Horace W B Donegan. m 5/30/2009 Justina Lasley c 4. R Chr Ch Bronxville NY 1995-2003; Int Calv Epis Ch Summit NJ 1993-1994; Int S Lk's Par Darien CT 1992-1993; Pres Coll Prchrs WDC Washington DC 1983-1992; Pres of Coll of Preachers Cathd of St Ptr & St Paul Washington DC 1983-1991; Dir Capital Giving, Asst. Chapl Mt Holyoke Coll So Hadley MA 1981-1983; VP Hartford Sem Fndt CT 1979-1980; VP The Hartford Sem Fndt Hartford CT 1979-1980; R Trin Ch Newport RI 1973-1978; Assoc Trin Epis Cathd Portland OR 1969-1973; Asst S Thos Ch New York NY 1966-1969. Auth, "Wm Reed Huntington & Ch Unity," *Hist mag*, 1966. Ord of S Jn 1989.

MINIFIE, Thomas Richardson (Oly) 1311 Bonneville Ave Apt C, Snohomish WA 98290 B Corpus Christi TX 1944 s Benjamin & Frances. BA Mt Un Coll 1967; MDiv PDS 1971. D 6/5/1971 P 12/18/1971 Bp Horace W B Donegan. m 1/23/1976 Jennifer Reed. S Phil Ch Marysville WA 1997-2004; Asst S Jn's Ch Kirkland WA 1994-1997; R S Paul's Ch Malden MA 1991-1994; Assoc R S Lk's Epis Ch Seattle WA 1985-1991; R S Lk's Ch Marietta OH 1980-1985; Assoc S Paul's Ch Dedham MA 1974-1980; Chapl Boston St Hosp Boston MA 1973-1976; Cur So Berkshire Dnry Stockbridge MA 1971-1973.

MINNICH-LOCKEY, Laura Karen (Va) 79 Laurel St, Harrisonburg VA 22801 **S Steph And The Gd Shpd Elkton Elkton VA 2016-; P Dio Virginia Richmond VA 2001-; Mssnr Jas Madison Epis Cmnty Harrison VA 2001-** B

Stuttgart Germany 1962 d Lawrence & Jeanne. BS Texas St U San Marcos 1984; MEd Texas St U San Marcos 1988; BS VTS 1993. D 6/6/1993 Bp Earl Nicholas Mc Arthur Jr P 12/6/1993 Bp Steven Charleston. m 6/6/1992 Russell Garrett Lockey c 3. S Fran Of Assisi Ch Philadelphia MS 1997-2001; Vic S Fran of Assisi Ch Philadelphia MS 1996-2001; Asst The Epis Ch Of The Medtr Meridian MS 1996-1997; Int The Ch Of The H Trin Juneau AK 1994-1995. Auth, "Context Effect & Its Effect on Memory," ERIC.

MINNICK, Margaret (Ct) 381 Main St Box 187, Middletown CT 06457 B Weymouth MA 1950 d Wallace & Elizabeth. BA U of Massachusetts 1973; MDiv Bex Sem 1978. D 3/19/1982 P 11/1/1982 Bp Lloyd Edward Gressle. m 6/16/1979 David W Minnick. Ch Of The H Trin Middletown CT 1995-2014; S Mk's Ch New Canaan CT 1985-1995; Asst S Fran Ch Greensboro NC 1983-1985; S Lk's Ch Lebanon PA 1982-1983; Lebanon Cnty Chr Ministers 1979-1982.

MINNIS, Joseph Abell (FdL) PO Box 486, Boulder Junction WI 54512 **Died 5/10/2017** B Joliet IL 1935 s Joseph & Mary Katherine. U CO 1959; Nash 1962. D 6/18/1962 P 12/21/1962 Bp Joseph Summerville Minnis. m 9/1/1957 Sue A Minnis c 4. Ret 1999-2017; Int S Anne's Epis Ch De Pere WI 1997-1999; S Jn's Ch Shawano WI 1991-1997; S Jn's Epis Ch New London WI 1991-1997; Dio Fond du Lac Appleton WI 1991-1995; Emm Ch Rushford MN 1989-1991; Vic Ch Of S Jn Chrys Golden CO 1964-1965; Vic Ch Of The H Comf Broomfield CO 1962-1967; Trst Dio Colorado Denver CO 1969-1972. Auth, "A Fam's Journey to Christmas".

MINNIX, George Myers (NI) 2008 Raintree Dr Apt 4, Elkhart IN 46514 **Died 7/29/2016** B Elkhart IN 1939 s Lloyd & Marietta. BA W&M 1961; MDiv Nash 1964. D 1/25/1964 P 7/25/1964 Bp Walter C Klein. S Chris's Ch Crown Point IN 1996-2001; Chapl Emer Howe Mltry Sch Howe IN 1986-2016; S Mk's Par Howe IN 1974-1986; Chapl Howe Mltry Sch Howe IN 1969-1986; Howe Mltry Sch Howe IN 1969-1986; Vic H Fam Ch Angola IN 1964-1969; Vic S Chas The Mtyr Butler IN 1964-1966.

MINOR, Albert Neely (ETenn) 7006 Brickton Way, Knoxville TN 37919 **Chapl to Ret Dio. of E Tennessee 2012-; Assoc St. Jas Par Knoxville TN 2000-** B Jennings LA 1930 s Stephen & Alberta. BA U So 1952; GTS 1955; STB GTS 1967; MS U of Tennessee 1979. D 6/20/1955 Bp George Mosley Murray P 12/18/1955 Bp Randolph R Claiborne. m 7/29/1955 Carroll Minor c 4. Assoc St Jas Epis Ch at Knoxville Knoxville TN 2006-2010; Coordntr of Chaplaincies to Ret Cler and Surviving Prov IV 1999-2007; Int S Andr's Ch Harriman TN 1997-1998; Int Ch Of The Gd Samar Knoxville TN 1995-1996; Int S Fran' Ch Norris TN 1994-1995; Mem Advsry Grp for Mnstrs in Higher Educ 1990-1993; Coordntr Prov. IV Coordnr - Mnstrs in Higher Educ 1990-1993; Mem Coun for Human Needs (of the GC) 1984-1987; Vic & Chapl St. Mich and All Ang - Tyson Hse Stdt Fdn. Knoxvi 1979-1994; Bd Appalachian People's Serv Orgnztn 1973-2012; Mem Advsry Grp for Mnstrs in Higher Educ 1968-1971; Chapl S Mich And All Ang Knoxville TN 1964-1994; Chapl Tyson Hse Stdt Fndt Knoxville TN 1964-1994; Epis Chapl Univ. of Tennessee - Tyson Hse Stdt Fdn. Knoxville TN 1964-1994; Vic St. Alb's Ch Montezuma Ga./ 1956-1958; Vic & R S Andr's Epis Ch Ft Vlly GA 1955-1958; Vic All SS Episcopal Ch Warner Robbins Ga 1955-1957; Chapl to Ret Cler and Surviving Spouses Dio E Tennessee Knoxville TN 1999-2007, Chair Dioc Ecum Cmsn 1984-1986. Auth, "A Tie w The Little People," *Living Ch*; Auth, "Moving Toward Cath Unity," *Plumbline*. EDEO; ESMHE. Al Minor Day City of Knoxville 1994.

MINOR, Cheryl Vasil (Mass) 65 Common Street, Belmont MA 02478 **Co-R All SS' Epis Ch Belmont MA 1997-; Dir Godly Play Resources Kansas 2012-; Godly Play Trnr, Editior Godly Play Fndt Colorado 2001-** B Concord MA 1963 d Thomas & Nancy. BA Bos 1985; MDiv VTS 1991; Ph.D. Northcentral U 2013. D 6/1/1991 P 2/15/1992 Bp David Elliot Johnson. m 6/28/1986 Paul Lawrence Minor c 2. Assoc Gr Epis Ch New York NY 1993-1997; Chapl/Tchr S Barn Elem Sch Philadelphia PA 1991-1993; D S Lk's Ch Philadelphia PA 1991-1992.

MINOR, Paul Lawrence (Mass) 65 Common St., Belmont MA 02478 **Co-R All SS' Epis Ch Belmont MA 2008-, 1997-2006; Chapl Colonel Army NG 1996-; Chapl Army NG 1996-; Bp's Coun of Advice Off Of Bsh For ArmdF New York NY 2015-; Advsry Coun Veterans Affrs Boston 2013-** B Baltimore MD 1962 s Fred & Elizabeth. BA Bos 1985; MDiv VTS 1991; MA Northcentral U 2011; Ph.D. Newburgh Sem 2013. D 6/1/1991 P 2/15/1992 Bp David Elliot Johnson. m 6/28/1986 Cheryl Vasil c 2. Assoc Gr Epis Ch New York NY 1993-1997; Cur S Lk's Ch Philadelphia PA 1991-1993. paul.l.minor2.mil@mail.mil

MINSHEW, James Keener (SeFla) Po Box 1596, Port Salerno FL 34992 B Hartford AL 1942 s Monroe & Eunice. BS Florida St U 1965; MDiv Sewanee: The U So, TS 1983. D 6/16/1983 P 12/21/1983 Bp Calvin Onderdonk Schofield Jr. m 6/28/2003 Janice P Minshew c 4. R S Lk's Epis Ch Stuart FL 1985-2008; Cur S Andr's Epis Ch Miami FL 1983-1985. Epis Recovery Mnstrs 1983; RACA 1992.

MINSHEW, Nancy Elizabeth (CFla) 3735 Us Highway 17 92 N, Davenport FL 33837 **D Asst Chap Of S Mary & S Martha Bp Gray Inn Davenport FL 2002-; D S Mk's Epis Ch Haines City FL 1999-** B Baltimore MD 1952 d Steven & Laura. D 1/16/1999 Bp John Wadsworth Howe. m 8/26/1993 Ronald Eugene Minshew.

MINTER, Larry Clifton (Ky) 5409 Hickory Hill Rd, 5409 Hickory Hill Rd, Louisville KY 40214 **S Paul's Epis Ch Evansville IN 2015-** B Hugo OK 1954 s Clifton & Kathleen. BA Oklahoma Bapt U 1976; SW Bapt TS 1979; MDiv Sthrn Bapt TS 1981; Cert SWTS 1988; Louisville Presb TS 2005; Cler Ldrshp Inst 2008; Kentuckiana Pstr Counselling Consortium 2008. D 5/31/1988 P 4/4/1989 Bp David Reed. m 9/1/1980 Jane B Minter c 1. Chr Ch Epis Hudson OH 2013-2015; Int S Tim's Epis Ch Perrysburg OH 2013; Int St Johns Epis Ch Lafayette IN 2011-2013; Int Ch Of The Ascen Frankfort KY 2008-2011; R S Ptr's Epis Ch Louisville KY 2004-2008; Int The Epis Ch Of The Mssh Pulaski TN 2003-2004; R S Columba-In-The-Cove Owens X Rds AL 1999-2003; R St. Columba Huntsville AL 1999-2003; Vic All SS Ch Un WV 1996-1999; R S Jas' Epis Ch Lewisburg WV 1991-1999; Cur S Lk's Ch Louisville KY 1988-1991. AAPC 2006. larrycminter@gmail.com

MINTER, Michael William (FdL) 314 Bellevue Rd, Highland NY 12528 **1976-** B Louisville KY 1946 s Sheriden & Ruby. BA NWU 1968; MDiv Nash 1973; MA U of Wisconsin 1976; PhD Ford 1981; PhD Hofstra U 1985. D 5/31/1973 P 12/21/1973 Bp Charles Gresham Marmion. Asst Ch Of The H Apos Oneida WI 1975-1976; Dio Fond du Lac Appleton WI 1974-1976; Vic S Jn's Ch Shawano WI 1974-1975; S Jn's Epis Ch New London WI 1974-1975; Dio Kentucky Louisville KY 1973.

MINTER, Russell Deane (Tex) 364 Beckett Point Rd, Port Townsend WA 98368 B Santa Monica CA 1926 s Bruce & Norah. BA U CA 1949; MA U CA 1951; MA U CA 1952; MDiv CDSP 1963. D 9/5/1963 P 3/6/1964 Bp Francis E I Bloy. m 11/11/2000 Elizabeth Arnel Minter c 2. R Chr Ch Eagle Lake TX 1989-1998; Chapl St. Lk's Epis Hosp Houston TX 1983-1989; Cullen Memi Chap Houston TX 1979-1983; Chapl Ben Taub Genral Hosp Houston TX 1974-1978; Vic S Steph Newhall Saugus CA 1966-1973; Cur S Aug By-The-Sea Par Santa Monica CA 1963-1966.

MINTON, Anne Mansfield (Mass) 35 Riverwalk Way Unit 303, Lowell MA 01854 B Rochester NY 1941 d Leo & Helen. BA Coll of New Rochelle 1962; MA CUA 1968; PhD NYU 1979; MA Andover Newton TS 1995. D 6/24/1993 P 1/7/1994 Bp Douglas Edwin Theuner. m 6/20/2004 Janice M Luti. Int Emm Ch Braintree MA 2004-2005; Int Emm Epis Ch Braintree MA 2004-2005; S Matt And The Redeem Epis Ch Boston MA 2003; R Chr Ch Somerville MA 1996-2000; Int Gr Epis Ch Concord NH 1994-1995; All SS Epis Ch Attleboro MA 1993-1994; Asst All SS Attleboro NH 1993-1994.

MINTURN, Benjamin Bradshaw (WA) 122 Ewarts Pond Rd, Hendersonville NC 28739 **Diplomate Coll of Pstr Supervision and Psych 1992-; Ret Hendersonville NC 1990-; Clincl Mem The Amer Assn for Mar and Fam Ther 1980-; Clincl Mem The AAMFC 1973-** B Chicago IL 1929 s Benjamin & Jeanette. BA Trin 1951; BD VTS 1954; MDiv VTS 1965. D 6/4/1954 Bp Robert Fisher Gibson Jr P 11/1/1954 Bp Goodrich R Fenner. m 4/3/1976 Lynda B Minturn c 3. Dir/Pres Mar and Fam Inst Washington DC 1970-1990; The Chesapeake Fndt Washington DC 1969-1971; R Ch Of The Ascen Silver Sprg MD 1957-1964; Chapl/Intern of CPE St Hosp Topeka KS 1956-1957; Vic S Mart-In-The-Fields Edwardsville KS 1954-1956.

MINTURN, Sterling Majors (NY) 5555 N Sheridan Rd Apt 607, Chicago IL 60640 **Assoc Epis Ch Of The Atone Chicago IL 2005-** B Slidell LA 1933 s Sterling & Maree. BS NW St U 1956; MDiv GTS 1962. D 6/27/1962 Bp Iveson Batchelor Noland P 5/4/1963 Bp Girault M Jones. Assoc S Geo's Epis Ch Maplewood NJ 2003-2004; Assoc P All SS Ch Orange NJ 1992-2002; Assoc P S Jn's Ch New York NY 1969-1992; Chapl New York Fed Detention Hse New York NY 1968-1975; Cur Trin Par New York NY 1964-1968; Asst Min S Clem's Ch New York NY 1962-1963.

MINTZ, Elsa H (Pa) 3716 Abercrombie Court, Mount Pleasant SC 29466 B Baltimore MD 1956 d Robert & Joan. AB Ken 1978; MDiv EDS 1982; MS Loyola U 1993. D 10/12/1982 Bp David Keller Leighton Sr P 9/14/1983 Bp Charlie Fuller Mcnutt Jr. c 1. R S Andr's Epis Ch Glenmoore PA 1995-2015; Asst Cathd Of The Incarn Baltimore MD 1992-1993; Assoc S Jn's Ch Roanoke VA 1986-1991; Cn Cathd Ch Of S Steph Harrisburg PA 1982-1986.

MINX, Patricia Ann (Kan) 105 S Indian Wells Dr, Olathe KS 66061 B La Crosse WI 1946 d William & Helen. BA Avila Coll 1978; MA Loyola U 1988. D 9/27/2003 Bp William Edward Smalley. m 9/2/1995 Francis B Minx. D S Lk's Epis Ch.

MIONSKE, Wayne Allan Robert (FdL) 4537 N 92nd St # U202, Wauwatosa WI 53225 **Ret 1998-** B Chicago IL 1937 s Carl & Viola. MDiv Luth TS at Chicago 1963; MEd U of Wisconsin 1969; Cert Nash 1982. D 4/2/1982 P 8/6/1982 Bp Charles Thomas Gaskell. Supply P S Nich Epis Ch Racine WI 2000-2006; H Trin Epis Ch Waupun WI 1985-1998; Ed FDL Clarion 1985-1995; Dio Fond du Lac Appleton WI 1985-1991; S Andr's Ch Kenosha WI 1982-1985; Dio Milwaukee Milwaukee WI 1982; Serv Luth Ch 1963-1979. Assoc, Ord of Julian of Norwich 2006.

MIRATE, Galen Alderman (Ga) 3338 Plantation Dr, Valdosta GA 31605 **S Patricks Ch Albany GA 2016-; Supply P Dio Georgia Savannah GA 2013-** B Charleston SC 1955 d Hugh & Annabel. Sewanee: The U So, TS; BS Emory

U 1977; JD U GA 1981. D 2/4/2006 P 8/7/2006 Bp Henry Irving Louttit. m 7/11/1992 Donald Mirate c 1. P Ch Of The Gd Shpd Thomasville GA 2013; Asst R Ch Of Chr The King Valdosta GA 2012-2013; Vic S Marg Of Scotland Epis Ch Moultrie GA 2007-2011; Assoc P Chr the King Epis Ch Valdosta GA 2006-2007.

MIRON, Jane Elizabeth (CPa) **Archd Dio Cntrl Pennsylvania Harrisburg PA 2014-** B Lancaster PA 1949 d Earl & Anna. BS Millersville U 1971. D 2/12/2005 Bp Michael Whittington Creighton. m 9/8/1973 David Miron c 2.

MISKELLEY, Audrey (Cal) **S Paul's Epis Ch Walnut Creek CA 2016-** B Independence MO 1959 BA Columbus St U 1989; MA U of Tennessee 1991; MDiv VTS 2005. D 6/18/2005 Bp Charles Glenn VonRosenberg P 1/19/2006 Bp Stacy F Sauls. m 10/24/1993 Charles Miskelley c 3. S Aid's Ch San Francisco CA 2015-2016; Int S Tim's Ch Danville CA 2015; Assoc S Steph's Epis Ch Orinda CA 2013-2014; Cn Evang Chr Ch Cathd Lexington KY 2005-2011. miskelley1@gmail.com

MISNER, Mary Jane Brain (Mil) N1639 Six Corners Rd, Walworth WI 53184 B Waukeegan IL 1936 d Theodore & Mildred. RN S Lk Hosp Sch Nrsng 1957; U of Wisconsin 1976; Nash 1989. D 10/21/1989 Bp Roger John White. m 10/5/1957 Daniel Wayne Misner c 4. D & Dir'S Asst S Jn In The Wilderness Elkhorn WI 2001-2002; D & Dir'S Asst S Lk's Ch Whitewater WI 1992-2001; Asst Ch Of The H Comm Lake Geneva WI 1989-1992. Cmnty Of S Mary; Ord Of S Lk.

MISSNER, Heath McDonell (Chi) 470 Maple St, Winnetka IL 60093 B New York NY 1944 d Alexander & Patricia. BA Wellesley Coll 1966; MA NWU 1967. D 2/6/2010 Bp Jeff Lee. c 4.

MITCHEL III, Glen Henry (Hank) (Los) 1072 Casitas Pass Road #317, Carpinteria CA 93014 B Los Angeles CA 1951 s Glen & Cynthia. BA U Pac 1973; MDiv CDSP 1977. D 6/15/1991 P 1/11/1992 Bp Frederick Houk Borsch. m 10/5/1991 Maricela Mitchel c 1. Assoc Trin Epis Ch Santa Barbara CA 2009; Vic Ch Of The Epiph Oak Pk CA 1994-2008; Asst S Mart-In-The-Fields Par Winnetka CA 1991-1994; Chapl S Mart's Sch CA 1991-1994.

MITCHELL, Barbara Louise (Alb) **S Jas' Epis Ch Lake Geo NY 2017-** D 6/3/2017 Bp William Howard Love.

MITCHELL JR, Charles Albert (Los) 111 S 6th St, Burbank CA 91501 B Tacoma WA 1944 s Charles & Florence. BA U of Puget Sound 1966; STB ATC 1969. D 12/19/1969 P 12/21/1970 Bp Jackson Earle Gilliam. m 5/10/1969 Seiko Bernice Shikaze. R S Jude's Epis Par Burbank CA 1997-2016; Ch Of The Gd Shpd Reedley CA 1994-1997; S Jas Epis Cathd Fresno CA 1989-1994; Ch Of The Ascen Forsyth MT 1974-1989; Emm Ch Miles City MT 1974-1989; H Trin Epis Ch Troy MT 1969-1974; S Lk's Ch Libby MT 1969-1974; S Mich And All Ang Eureka MT 1969-1974. revcamitchell@aol.com

MITCHELL, Dawn-Victoria (Mo) 3206 Pleasant St, Hannibal MO 63401 **R Trin Ch Hannibal MO 2010-** B Melrose MA 1972 d Richard & Linda. BS W Virginia Wesleyan Coll 1994; MDiv S Paul TS 1998; CAS SWTS 2000. D 6/3/2000 P 12/5/2000 Bp Barry Howe. Pstr Serv Meth Ch ME 2008-2010; Emm Epis Ch Wakefield MA 2006-2007; Assoc R Calv Ch Columbia MO 2000-2006. ESMHE 2001-2004.

MITCHELL III, James Franklin (WTex) 1164 Vista Bonita, New Braunfels TX 78130 **Died 10/6/2015** B Breckenridge TX 1932 s Harvey & Mary. BS U of Houston 1955; MDiv Epis TS of the SW 1973; DMin Drew U 1993. D 6/20/1973 Bp Scott Field Bailey P 6/18/1974 Bp James Milton Richardson. m 5/4/1957 Mary M von der Goltz. Ret 1998-2015; R St Fran Epis Ch San Antonio TX 1982-1997; Prov Vii Rgnl Coordntr Evang Dio W Texas San Antonio TX 1980-1998; Assoc S Mk's Ch Beaumont TX 1976-1982; All SS Ch Cameron TX 1973-1976; S Thos' Epis Ch Rockdale TX 1973-1976; The Great Cmsn Fndt Houston TX 1973-1976; Bd Trsts Epis TS Of The SW Austin TX 1993-1997.

MITCHELL, Joe T (NC) 505 Mountain Rd, Asheboro NC 27205 **The Epis Ch Of Gd Shpd Asheboro NC 2015-** B Bristol VA 1984 s Preston & Susan. BA Cntr Coll 2006; MDiv GTS 2012. D 8/18/2012 Bp Neff Powell. Chr Ch Cathd Lexington KY 2012-2015; S Thad Epis Ch Aiken SC 2007-2009. jtmitchell5@gmail.com

MITCHELL, John Patrick (NJ) PO Box 261, Cape May NJ 08204 **R Ch Of The Adv Cape May NJ 2008-; Dn of Atlantic Convoc Dio New Jersey Trenton NJ 2012-, Stndg Com on Const and Cn, Chair 2010-** B Muncie IN 1945 s Omer & Euva. BA Ya 1967; JD Indiana U 1970; MPhil Drew U 2001; CAS GTS 2002; PhD Drew U 2007. D 5/31/2003 Bp John Palmer Croneberger P 12/13/2003 Bp Rufus T Brome. m 8/17/1968 Dorothy T Mitchell c 3. Int Gr Epis Ch Westwood NJ 2005-2008; Trst Turrell Fund 2003-2008; Assoc Ch Of The Mssh Chester NJ 2003-2005; Stndg Cmsn on Const and Cn Dio Newark Newark NJ 2005-2008.

MITCHELL, John Stephen (Vt) 372 Canterbury Rd, Manchester Center VT 05255 **R Zion Ch Manchestr Ctr VT 1995-** B Wellesley MA 1948 s Charles & Eltress. BA Berkshire Chr Coll 1982; MDiv Ya Berk 1985. D 8/24/1985 Bp Alexander D Stewart P 6/14/1986 Bp Andrew Frederick Wissemann. m 6/7/2009 Jane L Uva c 4. S Lk's Ch Farmington ME 1988-1995; Asst S Jn's Ch Naples FL 1987-1988; Par Of S Jas Ch Keene NH 1985-1987.

MITCHELL, Judith N (RI) 24 Hart St, Providence RI 02906 B Providence RI 1942 d Raymond & Mary. BA Rhode Island Coll 1966; MA Br 1967; PhD U of Connecticut 1981. D 6/26/1993 P 12/1/1993 Bp George Nelson Hunt III. m 2/10/1965 Raymond E Mitchell c 3. S Jn The Div Ch Saunderstown RI 2012-2014; R SS Matt and Mk Barrington RI 2002-2012; Cur S Alb.

MITCHELL, Karin Rasmussen (NJ) 125 Orchard Ave, Hightstown NJ 08520 **R S Dav's Ch Cranbury NJ 2005-** B Teaneck NJ 1955 d Carl & Mabel. BA Rutgers The St U of New Jersey 1977; MS Rutgers The St U of New Jersey 1985; MDiv PrTS 2001; Cert GTS 2002. D 6/22/2002 P 12/21/2002 Bp David Bruce Joslin. m 10/20/1979 David Frank Mitchell c 3. Vic S Fran Ch Dunellen NJ 2003-2005; Assoc The Ch Of The H Innoc Bch Haven NJ 2002-2003. Womens Epis Caucus 1992.

MITCHELL, Katherine N (EC) 515 Pamlico River Dr, Washington NC 27889 **Chapl Brigham and Wmn Hosp Boston MA 1995-** B Washington NC 1945 d John & Katherine. MA Emml 1995; DMin Andover Newton TS 2003. D 6/5/2004 Bp M(Arvil) Thomas Shaw. m 6/22/1974 Albert Phillips Mitchell c 3. D Trin Ch Randolph MA 2011-2017; D Ch of the Gd Shpd 2004-2007. AAPC 1995-2010; AEHC 1996; Assn of Profsnl Chapl 2001. Dennis Thompson Schlrshp 2008; Partnr in Excellence 2008; Dennis Thompson Schlrshp Brigham and Wmn Hosp 2004; Partnr's In Excellence Brigham and Wmn Hosp 2002.

MITCHELL, Lisa Sauber (NJ) 380 Sycamore Ave, Shrewsbury NJ 07702 **R Chr Ch Epis Shrewsbury NJ 1997-** B Bartlesville OK 1957 d Charles & Josella. BS Oklahoma St U 1979; MA Fuller TS 1987; STM Nash 1988. D 9/16/1989 Bp Oliver Bailey Garver Jr P 3/24/1990 Bp Frederick Houk Borsch. c 2. R S Jn's Epis Ch Vinita OK 1991-1997; Assoc R S Jos's Par Buena Pk CA 1989-1990; DCE S Paul's Ch Milwaukee WI 1988; Stndg Com Dio New Jersey Trenton NJ 2005-2010, EFM Dioc Coordntr 2002-, Dioc Coun 2000-2003, Comp Dio Com 1999-2011, Liturg and Mus Cmsn 1997-1999; Dioc Coun Dio Oklahoma Oklahoma City OK 1995. "Sermons That Wk". christchurchshrewsbury@verizon.net

MITCHELL, Marilyn Dean (NC) 90 Worcester Rd Unit 12, Washington Depot CT 06794 **D La Iglesia de la Sagrada Familia Newton Grove NC 2010-** B McPherson KS 1937 d Albert & Adeline. BA U of Connecticut 1974; MLS Emporia St U 1983; MDiv Yale DS 1994. D 9/17/2005 Bp Andrew Donnan Smith. c 3. D S Jn's Ch New Milford CT 2005-2009; S Jn's Epis Par Waterbury CT 2005; Adm. Assist First Congrl Ch Washington CT 2000-2010. Soc of S Jn Evang 1992. Robert Watson Schlr Yale DS 1992.

MITCHELL, Pat Rhonda (NY) 732 Scarsdale Rd, Tuckahoe NY 10707 **Cn for Chr Formation Dio New York New York NY 2005-** B Bronx NY 1949 d Lewis & Muriel. BA Mt Holyoke Coll 1970; MS Col 1974; MPhil Col 1977; MDiv Ya Berk 2002. D 3/16/2002 P 9/21/2002 Bp Mark Sean Sisk. c 1. Assoc R St. Barth Ch New York NY 2002-2005. Berk Grad Soc Coun 2006-2015.

MITCHELL, Preston Wade (SwVa) B Munich Germany 1952 s Joe & Marjorie. MA E Tennessee St; BA Cit. D 2/22/2013 Bp Neff Powell. m 12/20/2009 Patty Baumgartner c 2.

MITCHELL JR, Richard Cope (Colo) 3107 Nevermind Ln, Colorado Springs CO 80917 B Chickasha OK 1951 s Richard & Sara. BA Wheaton Coll 1975; Cert Wesley TS 1979; MDiv Gordon-Conwell TS 1980; CAS Nash 1985; Nash 2000. D 6/15/1985 P 5/3/1986 Bp Gerald Nicholas Mcallister. m 3/8/1981 Suzan Mitchell c 4. S Andr's Ch Cripple Creek CO 2015-2017; All SS Epis Ch Torrington WY 2013-2014; Epis Ch Of S Jn The Bapt Granby CO 2012-2013; Spec Mobilization Spprt Plan Washington DC 2004-2011; Pension Fund Mltry New York NY 2003-2004; S Fran Epis Ch Scottsbluff NE 2003-2004, 2002-2003; P-in-c S Paul's Ch Watertown WI 2000-2002; S Aidans Ch Hartford WI 2000; Gr Epis Ch Cortland NY 1996-2000; R S Anne's Ch Millington TN 1992-1996; S Tim's Epis Ch Rangely CO 1992, Vic 1987-1989; Dio Colorado Denver CO 1990-1992, Stndg Com 1988-1992; R S Jas' Epis Ch Meeker CO 1989-1991; Cur Epis Ch Of The Resurr Oklahoma City OK 1985-1987. copemitchell@msn.com

MITCHELL, R(Obert) James (Kan) Via Roma, Wichita KS 67230 **Asst St. Steph's Wichita KS 2005-** B Grand Rapids MI 1930 s Waldemar & Margaret. BA MI SU 1952; MTh Bex Sem 1963. D 6/11/1963 Bp Charles Ellsworth Bennison Jr P 12/1/1963 Bp Charles Bennison Sr. m 8/24/1990 Judith Thompson Mitchell c 6. Asst S Stephens Epis Churchrch Wichita KS 2006-2009; P-in-c S Alb's Epis Ch Wichita KS 2002-2005; P Mssnr S Jas Ch Wichita KS 1997-2002; 1970-1997; Asst Min S Paul's Ch Rochester NY 1966-1969; Vic S Dav's Ch Lansing MI 1963-1966.

MITCHELL, Sadie S (Pa) 600 E Cathedral Rd, Apt H320, Philadelphia PA 19128 B Philadelphia PA 1922 d Joseph & Lucinda. BS Tem 1942; MS U of Pennsylvania 1968; EdD Nova SE U 1978; MDiv Philadelphia Luth TS 1984; MDiv Philadelphia Luth TS 1990. D 6/20/1987 Bp Lyman Cunningham Ogilby P 5/31/1988 Bp Allen Lyman Bartlett Jr. m 1/1/1976 Charles Mitchell c 3. Assoc The Afr Epis Ch Of S Thos Philadelphia PA 1990-2012; Asst P S Mk's Ch Philadelphia PA 1988-1990; Asst. P St. Jn's Epis Ch Narberth PA 1988-1989; Chapl Com Dio Pennsylvania Philadelphia PA 1987-1999, Chair Stwdshp Cmsn 1969-1971; Asst. P St. Lk's Epis Ch Philadelphia PA 1987-1988. Philadel-

M

phia Theol Inst 1981-2006; SBL 1982-1990; UBE 1969. Hon Bd Mem Epis Cmnty Serv 1990.

MITCHELL, Thomas James (WNY) 7145 Fieldcrest Drive, Lockport NY 14094 **P-in-c Chr Ch Lockport NY 2012-; Cler Rep. to Dioc Coun Dio Wstrn New York Tonawanda NY 2013-, Cler Rep. to Dioc Coun 2009-2013** B Buffalo NY 1947 s Thomas & Marion. Cath U; BA S Jn Vianney Sem 1969; MA S Jn Vianney Sem 1974; AA Trocaire Coll 1989. D 6/2/2009 P 12/12/2009 Bp Michael Garrison. m 8/9/2012 Thomas Ralabate c 1.

MITCHELL, Tim (Ky) 901 Baxter Ave, Louisville KY 40204 **Mem, Bd Trst The CPG New York NY 2009-; R Ch Of The Adv Louisville KY 2008-; Mem of Bd Dio California San Francisco CA 2006-, Invstmt Com Mem 2005-** B Louisville KY 1959 s Joseph & Mary. BA U of Notre Dame 1981; U of Salamanca 1982; MS Geo 1984; MDiv U of S Mary of the Lake Mundelein Sem 1992; DMin PSR 2005. Rec 6/1/2002 as Priest Bp William Edwin Swing. Trin Ch San Francisco CA 2006-2007; Ch Of The H Innoc San Francisco CA 2004-2005; S Paul's Ch Oakland CA 2003-2004; Reg Dir and Invstmt Advsr Chr Bros Invstmt Serv San Francisco CA 1995-2007; Assoc Pstr (and D) H Name Cathd Par Chicago IL 1992-1995. "The Ovrs List," *Bk, co-Auth*, Augsburg Pub Hse, 1985. Phi Beta Kappa Phi Beta Kappa Arts and Sciences hon Socity 1981.

MITCHELL, Winifred L (Colo) 3821 Elk Ln, Pueblo CO 81005 B Denver CO 1947 d Arthur & Dorothy. BA U CO 1970; MA U CO 1975; PhD U CO 1986; MDiv Epis TS of the SW 2007. D 6/14/2007 P 12/20/2007 Bp James Louis Jelinek. m 5/25/1974 Paul F Brown c 2. Ch Of S Ptr The Apos Pueblo CO 2011-2014; H Trin Epis Ch Luverne MN 2009-2011; P-in-c S Mart's Epis Ch Fairmont MN 2007-2011; Prof Of Anthropology Minnesota St U 1982-2004; Exam Chapl Dio Minnesota Minneapolis MN 2009-2011, COM 2008-2011. Anthropologist, "The Aymara," *The Encyclopedia of Men and Wmn*, Human Relatns Area Files Press, 2004; Anthropologist, "Wmn Age Hierarchies and the Prestige of Suffering," *Wmn among Wmn*, U IL Press, 1998; Anthropologist, "Pragmatic Literacy and Empowerment," *Anthropology and Educ Quarterly 25:3*, Amer Anthropological Assn, 1994; Anthropologist, "Lighting Sickness," *Natural Hist 102 (11)*, Amer Museum of Natural Hist, 1993. Amer Anthropological Assn 1979-2004. Jonathan M. Daniels Fllshp EDS and Daniels Fndt 2006; Fulbright Schlrshp Fulbright Cmsn 1983; Inter-Amer Fndt Fllshp Inter-Amer Fndt 1983.

MITCHENER, Gary Asher (O) 13800 Shaker Blvd Apt 206, Cleveland OH 44120 B Saint Louis MO 1939 s Paul & Elaine. BA Pacific U 1960; BD EDS 1966; MTh Harvard DS 1986. D 6/25/1966 P 1/8/1967 Bp George Leslie Cadigan. m 10/10/1987 Judith C Claghorn c 2. Int S Alb Epis Ch Cleveland OH 2007-2009; Int Chr Epis Ch Kent OH 2003-2006; Int Ch Of The Epiph Euclid OH 2000-2002; Cn Pstr Trin Cathd Cleveland OH 1992-2000; R Ch Of The Gd Shpd Fitchburg MA 1986-1992; R Dio Wstrn Massachusetts Springfield 1986-1992; Chapl Dartmouth U Hanover NH 1977-1985; Assoc R S Thos Ch Hanover NH 1977-1985; Vic S Lk's Ch Woodsville NH 1971-1974; Cur Calv Ch Columbia MO 1966-1969. Natl Sci Fndt Grad Fllshp 1970.

MITCHICAN, Jonathan A (Pa) 1000 Burmont RD, Drexel Hill PA 19026 **R The Ch Of The H Comf Drexel Hill PA 2008-** B 1980 MDiv Ya Berk 2006. D 6/3/2006 P 12/16/2006 Bp Bud Shand. m 5/21/2005 Gina S Mitchican c 2. Assoc R S Ptr's Ch Salisbury MD 2006-2008.

MITHEN III, Thomas Scott (Ga) 516 E Broughton St, Bainbridge GA 39817 B Greenville AL 1954 s Thomas & Isabel. BS Troy U 1977. D 10/21/2009 Bp Henry Irving Louttit. m 8/13/1977 Naomi Mithen c 2.

MITMAN, John Louis (Ct) 31 Steep Hollow Ln, West Hartford CT 06107 **Assoc Gr Epis Ch Hartford CT 2013-; Exec Dir/Dvlpmt Soc for Increase of Mnstry W Hartford CT 2001-; All SS Conf Cntr Bd 1992-** B Washington DC 1940 s Louis & Dorcas. BA Randolph-Macon Coll 1962; STB Ya Berk 1965. D 6/12/1965 Bp Charles Francis Hall P 12/11/1965 Bp Harvey D Butterfield. m 6/9/1962 Ruth Mitman c 2. Assoc Chr Ch Cathd Hartford CT 2002-2013; Soc For The Increase Of Mnstry W Hartford CT 2001-2010; R S Jas's Ch W Hartford CT 1990-2001; R The Cathd Ch Of S Paul Des Moines IA 1985-1990; Chapl & Lectr Benedictine Experience Cbury Cathd 1982-1986; Cbury Cathd Trust of Amer 1981-1987; Cbury MI SU E Lansing MI 1974-1985; Dir of Interns & Fellows Dart Hanover NH 1971-1974; Precentor S Jn's Cathd in Hong Kong 1970-1971; Vic ProTem S Mich's Lancing 1969-1970; Chapl St. Jn's Cathd Hong Kong 1969-1970; Cur S Thos Ch Hanover NH 1965-1972; Chair on Trsfg Lodge Convoc; Dioc Com Dio Michigan Detroit MI 1984-2001, Pres, Stndg Com 1982-1983, Stndg Com 1979-1981. Auth, "Premarital Counslg: A Practical Manual for Cler & Lay Counselors," Seabury Press, 1981.

MIX, Lucas John (Az) Lucas Mix, 26 Oxford St, Cambridge MA 02138 **Resrch Assoc Harv 2013-** B Seattle WA 1975 s William & Susan. BA U of Washington 1997; PhD Harv 2004; MDiv CDSP 2007. D 6/30/2007 Bp Bavi Edna Rivera P 1/6/2008 Bp Gregory Harold Rickel. Chapl Dio Arizona Phoenix AZ 2009-2013; Chapl Epis Campus Mnstry U of Arizona Tucson 2009-2013; Supply P Dio Olympia Seattle 2008-2009; Cur Ch of the Apos Seattle WA

2007-2008. "Life in Space: Astrobiology for Everyone," Harv Press, 2009. Soc of Ord Scientists 2010.

MIZIRL, Sandra M (Tex) 3015 Fleeton Rd, Reedville VA 22539 **S Mary's Fleeton Reedville VA 2014-; Coll Mssnr Texas A&M Coll Sta TX 1999-; Coll Coordntr Prov VII Fairfax VA 2009-** B Oklahoma City OK 1947 d George & Mary. BA U of Oklahoma 1979; MDiv Sewanee: The U So, TS 1998. D 6/20/1998 Bp Claude Edward Payne P 6/21/1999 Bp Leopoldo Jesus Alard. m 5/22/1970 Larry Alan Mizirl c 1. Dio Texas Houston TX 2013-2014, Dn-Cntrl Convoc 2006-2008, co-Fac transitional deacons 2002-2008, Div of Liturg-Chair 2002-2007, Div of Wrshp-Chair 2002-2007, Div of Coll Mnstry-Chair 1999-2013; The Great Cmsn Fndt Houston TX 1999-2013; Trin Epis Ch The Woodlands TX 1998-1999; Vstng Com Sewanee U So TS Sewanee TN 2004-2010. Auth, "Coll Pilgrimage," *The Diolog*, Dio Texas, 2011; Auth, "Angl Sprtlty," *Texas Epis*, Dio Texas, 2008; Auth, "Front-Line Of Life," *From The Mtn*, U So, 2000. Griffin Fllshp U So 1998; Woods Ldrshp Awd U So 1995.

MKHIZE, Danana Elliot (La) 1222 N Dorgenois St, New Orleans LA 70119 B 1938 s Difile & Annie. AFTS Fed TS 1968; BA U of So Afr Pretoria ZA 1968; DIT U of Birmingham Gb 1973; DMin Claremont TS 1983. Trans 7/29/1985 Bp Robert Claflin Rusack. m 1/1/1968 Ruth Buyisiwe Mkhize. R S Lk's Ch New Orleans LA 1996-1999; R S Mart's Epis Ch Compton CA 1989-1996, Vic 1985-1988, P-in-c 1982-1984; Serv Angl Ch Of So Afr 1967-1979.

MOBERLY, Paul Benjamin (Vt) D 1/7/2017 Bp Thomas C Ely.

MOBLEY, James E (SO) 955 Matthews Dr, Cincinnati OH 45215 **D S Simon Of Cyrene Epis Ch Cincinnati OH 2012-** B Chattanooga TN 1930 s John & Janie. Morristown N&I Coll; Mt St Marys Sem 1978. D 1/26/1975 Bp John Mc Gill Krumm. m 12/25/1954 Sharon Faye Walton c 2. Chapl Of Pstr Mnstry S Lk's In Lincoln Heights. Grtr Cincinnati Chapl.

MOCKRIDGE III, Oscar Alling (Nwk) 358 Stiles Ct, West Orange NJ 07052 **Died 4/24/2017** B Newark NJ 1937 s Oscar & Georgie. BA Pr 1959; MDiv ETS Cambridge MA 1965; MDiv ETSBH 1965; MDiv ETSBH 1965; MPA NYU 1975. D 6/12/1965 Bp Leland Stark P 12/18/1965 Bp George E Rath. m 9/7/1963 Anne Mockridge c 2. S Lk's Epis Ch Montclair NJ 2011-2015; Pstr Assoc Gr Ch Madison NJ 2000-2004; Ther Cntr for Mntl Hlth NYC New York 1993-2000; Admin. Coordntr Cmnty Mntl Hlth Cntr Paterson NJ 1974-1978; 1973-2000; Coordntng Consult Dio Newark Newark NJ 1972-1974; R The Ch Of The Annunc Oradell NJ 1970-1972; R Trin Ch Irvington NJ 1967-1970; Cur S Ptr's Ch Mtn Lks NJ 1965-1967.

MOCZYDLOWSKI, Ann Louise Hare (WA) 10120 Brock Dr, Silver Spring MD 20903 B Reading PA 1953 d Clyde & Rose. D 6/9/2000 Bp Michael Whittington Creighton P 2/25/2001 Bp Jane Hart Holmes Dixon. m 6/8/1985 William Wesley Moczydlowski c 2. R S Mary Magd Ch Silver Sprg MD 2010-2015; Ch Of Our Sav Silver Sprg MD 2005; Asst Gr Epis Ch Silver Sprg MD 2000-2004.

MODESITT, Lori Jane (Wyo) 1357 Loomis St, Wheatland WY 82201 **Mnstry Dvlp Dio Wyoming Casper 2012-, Mnstry Dvlp 2011; P All SS Ch Wheatland WY 2002-** B Rock Island IL 1954 d Francis & Lola. D 2/7/2002 P 9/21/2002 Bp Bruce Caldwell. m 7/19/1980 Walter Lee Modesitt.

MOEHL, Thomas Joseph (Ore) 12360 Summit Loop SE, Turner OR 97392 **Vic Ch Of Chr The King On The Santiam Stayton OR 2001-** B Klamath Falls OR 1949 s Richard & Martha. BS L&C 1971; MBA OR SU 1981. D 6/16/2001 P 12/21/2001 Bp Robert Louis Ladehoff. m 3/20/1971 Linda Kindred c 3.

MOELLER, Linda Lee Breitung (NJ) 13 Blossom Dr, Ewing NJ 08638 **R Sts Steph and Barn Epis Ch Florence NJ 2015-, Vic 2006-2015; Dir Sch for Deacons Dio New Jersey Trenton NJ 2002-, Chair, Bp's Advsry Com on Liturg 2000-2009** B Port Jefferson NY 1950 d York & Liria. STM The GTS; BA Barry U 1991; MDiv GTS 1995. D 6/4/1988 P 6/24/1994 Bp Calvin Onderdonk Schofield Jr. m 12/31/1987 Harold Carl Moeller. Int Chapl S Mich's/Rutgers U New Brunswick NJ 2003-2004; Asst to the R S Lk's Epis Ch Metuchen NJ 1999-2003; Assoc P Trin Par New York NY 1995-1999; Assoc P Ch Of The Heav Rest New York NY 1994-1995; D/Asst Chr And S Steph's Ch New York NY 1993-1994; D/Asst S Mary Magd Epis Ch Pompano Bch FL 1988-1992. Auth, *Baptism: Inclusion or Exclusion*; Auth, *Cnfrmtn: Sacramental Rite or Rite of Discipline and Politics*; Auth, *Investiture of PBp: New Way to Gather.* Assn of Angl Mus 2000; No Amer Acad of Liturg; Societas Liturgica.

MOERMOND, Curtis Roghair (Ia) B O'Brien County IA 1941 AA S Pauls Coll Concordia MO 1963; BS Concordia Teachers Coll Seward NE 1965; BD Concordia TS 1969; MDiv Concordia TS 1973; DMin Concordia TS 1988. D 12/18/2004 P 6/25/2005 Bp Alan Scarfe. c 4. Gr Ch Cedar Rapids IA 2009-2013; Int S Thos' Epis Ch Sioux City IA 2005-2008. curt@crgraceepiscopal.org

MOFFAT JR, Alexander Douglas (FtW) B 1933 D 6/10/1958 P 12/13/1958 Bp Richard S Watson.

MOHN, Michael Collver (Va) 1527 Senseny Rd, Winchester VA 22602 B Detroit MI 1938 s Frederick & Inez. BA Stetson U 1961; MDiv VTS 1970; S Georges Coll Jerusalem IL 1981; S Georges Coll Jerusalem 1993. D 6/6/1970 P 1/1/1971 Bp Robert Lionne DeWitt. m 5/24/1969 Janice Lynn Mohn c 1. R Meade Memi Par White Post VA 2005-2007; Emm Epis Ch Delaplane Delaplane VA 1999-2003; S Jas' Epis Ch Leesburg VA 1998-1999, Int 1984-1985; H Land Com Dio Virginia Richmond VA 1988-1996, Yth Com 1985-1994;

594

Chapl Com Winchester Memi Hosp 1987-1992; S Pauls On The Hill Epis Ch Ossining NY 1984-2003; S Paul's On-The-Hill Winchester VA 1984-1998; Ch Of The Ascen Hickory NC 1982-1984; Vic S Paul's Epis Ch Morganton NC 1978-1982; Vic St Mary's and St Steph's Epis Ch Morganton NC 1978-1982; Natl Ch Committees On Yth 1974-1978; Assoc R S Bon Ch Sarasota FL 1974-1978; Vic S Mart's Epis Ch Williamsburg VA 1972-1974; Asst Chr Ch Philadelphia Philadelphia PA 1970-1972; Chapl Magee Memi Hosp Philadelphia PA 1970-1972. Comt, Evang Educ Sch; Ord of the Sis of the Resurection 1978. info@goodshepherdbluemont.com

MOHRINGER, Johannes Red Cloud (Ind) The Four Winds 2880w 250n, Lebanon IN 46052 **Died 2/15/2017** B Haarlem NL 1926 s William & Thona. BA Millikin U 1957; BD Chr TS 1960. D 1/9/1960 P 7/1/1960 Bp John P Craine. m 5/18/1955 Johanna A Mohringer. Ret 1992-2017; Non-par 1975-2017; S Thos Ch Franklin IN 1974-1975; Worker P-in-c S Steph's Elwood IN 1967-1973; Cn Theol S Paul's Cathd Oklahoma City OK 1966-1971, Asst To Dn 1962-1965; Cur S Jn's Epis Ch Tulsa OK 1965-1966; Vic S Ptr's Ch Lebanon IN 1960-1962. Amer Indn Med Soc; Ny Acad Of Sciences.

MOISE, Burnet (SeFla) Trans 5/8/2000 as Priest Bp Calvin Onderdonk Schofield Jr.

MOISE, Joe (LI) 1227 Pacific St, Brooklyn NY 11216 B 1939 s Montesquieu & Leraisse. Coll of S Pierre HT 1963; ETSC 1968. D 12/2/1967 P 6/1/1968 Bp Charles Alfred Voegeli. Dio Long Island Garden City NY 1985-1989; S Barth's Ch Brooklyn NY 1984-2005; Asst & In-Charge Haitian Mnstry S Bartholemew 1984-1989; Vic S Paul The Apos In Dominican Republic 1979-1983; Headmaster Colegio E'Pis Jesus Nazareno Dominican Republic 1978-1983; Vic H Cross Mssn In Dominican Republic 1978-1983; Dio The Dominican Republic (Iglesia Epis Dominicana) Gazcue Santo Domingo 1976-1983; Vic Cathd Ch of All SS St Thos VI 1975-1976; Dio Vrgn Islands Charlotte Amalie St Thom VI 1975-1976; P-in-c Missions Gros-Morne & Gonaives In Haiti 1971-1975; P-in-c Missions Cayes Area Haiti 1969-1971; Mssy In Carolina 1967-1968.

MOJALLALI, Darius (Alb) 13 High St, Delhi NY 13753 **S Jn's Ch Delhi NY 2011-; R S Ptr's Ch Stamford NY 2011-** B Boston MA 1952 s Rahim & Roselle. BA Connecticut Coll 1975; MDiv PrTS 1981; Cert Ang Stud GTS 1982. D 6/18/1983 P 12/21/1983 Bp Wilbur Emory Hogg Jr. m 9/3/1999 Stephanie Leis c 3. P-in-c S Dav's Ch Feeding Hills MA 2008-2011; R S Steph's Ch Delmar NY 1988-2008; S Paul's Ch Salem NY 1983-1988; R S Paul's Epis Ch Greenwich NY 1983-1988. dmojo26@me.com

MOLE, James Frederick (Pa) 10 E 3rd St, Waynesboro PA 17268 **Died 2/4/2016** B Princeton WV 1924 s Frederick & Edith. BS Concord U 1950; MDiv PDS 1961; Cert U of Pennsylvania 1965; MEd Tem 1973. D 5/13/1961 P 11/18/1961 Bp Oliver J Hart. c 2. P Assoc S Mary's Epis Ch Waynesboro PA 1999-2014; Dn Fairmount Deanry Dio Pennsylvania Philadelphia PA 1972-1980; Vic S Nathanael Philadelphia PA 1961-1989; S Nathanaels Ch Philadelphia PA 1961-1989. Cerrtificate of Appreciation for Devoted Serv Archdiocesan Sr Citizens Coun 1987.

MOLEGODA, Niranjani S (Ct) 232 Durham Rd, Madison CT 06443 **S Andr's Ch Madison CT 2016-; R Gr Ch Jefferson City MO 2007-** B Colombo LK 1958 d William & Seelawathi. BA Agnes Scott Coll 1981; MS U of Colombo Lk 1984; MDiv Ya Berk 1993. D 9/8/1996 P 5/17/1997 Bp M(Arvil) Thomas Shaw. Int S Jas' Epis Ch Cambridge MA 2006-2007; P-in-c The Ch Of S Mary Of The Harbor Provincetown MA 2003-2006; Assoc R Chr Ch Cambridge Cambridge MA 1999-2003; S Anne's In The Fields Epis Ch Lincoln MA 1999; Soc Of St Marg Duxbury MA 1998.

MOLINA-MOORE, Amanda E (WA) PO Box 3510, Wilmington DE 19807 **S Columba's Ch Washington DC 2016-; Cur Chr Ch Christiana Hundred Wilmington DE 2015-** B New York NY 1984 d Oscar & Lydia. BA Rutgers U 2006; MDiv PrTS 2013; Dplma in Angl Stds VTS 2015. D 6/13/2015 P 1/16/2016 Bp Clifton Daniel III. m 8/17/2013 John H Molina-Moore. amolinamoore@christchurchde.org

MOLINE, Mark Edwin (Az) 2000 Shepherds Lane, Prescott AZ 86301 B Lawrence KS 1945 s Harold & Dollie. BS Amer U 1976; MDiv Candler TS Emory U 1998. D 6/26/1999 Bp Richard Lester Shimpfky P 2/5/2000 Bp Frank Kellogg Allan. m 7/8/1966 Judith Ann Moline c 2. R S Lk's Ch Prescott AZ 2007-2013; Vic Dio Atlanta Atlanta GA 2003-2006; R Gd Shpd Epis Ch Austell GA 2001-2003; Assoc S Teresa Acworth GA 1999-2000.

MOLITORS, Elizabeth Anne (Chi) 393 N Main St, Glen Ellyn IL 60137 **R The Annunc Of Our Lady Gurnee IL 2013-** B Toledo OH 1962 d Thomas & Lois Ruth. BA Mia 1983; MBA DePaul U 1998; MDiv SWTS 2009. D 6/6/2009 P 12/5/2009 Bp Jeff Lee. c 1. Assoc R S Mk's Epis Ch Glen Ellyn IL 2009-2013.

MOLLARD, Elizabeth McCarter (CPa) 235 N Spruce St, Elizabethtown PA 17022 B Providence RI 1941 d Edward & Cynthia. BA U of New Hampshire 1962; MA U of Missouri 1981; MDiv VTS 2002. D 6/8/2002 P 1/4/2003 Bp Michael Whittington Creighton. m 12/7/1963 Francois R Mollard c 3. R S Lk's Epis Ch Mt Joy PA 2002-2008.

MOLLER, Nels D (Ida) 902 E Lakeview Ln, Spokane WA 99208 **Par Mem/Asstg P St. Dav's Epis Chrurch Spokane WA 2006-; S Jas Ch Burley ID 2001-; Trin Memi Epis Ch Rupert ID 1994-** B Rupert ID 1936 s Nels & De-

loris. BS U of Idaho 1960; Cert U CA 1972; EFM Sewanee: The U So, TS 1992. D 1/29/1994 P 8/7/1994 Bp John Stuart Thornton. m 3/23/1985 Patricia Mai Burns c 4. St Matthews Epis Ch Rupert ID 1994-2006.

MOLLISON, Carol Suzanne (Okla) 721 N Thomas St, Altus OK 73521 **D S Paul's Ch Altus OK 2004-** B Oklahoma City OK 1943 d Malcom & Dorothy Jo. BA U of Oklahoma 1965; MAPA U of Oklahoma 1967; MA U of Oklahoma 1967; JD U of Oklahoma 1974. D 6/19/2004 Bp Robert Manning Moody P 2/7/2015 Bp Edward Joseph Konieczny.

MOLNAR, Annette June (RG) St Elizabeth's Episcopal Church, 1 Morse Rd, Sudbury MA 01776 B Hamilton Ontario Canada 1932 d Luke & Hazel. Prchr Lewis Sch of Mnstry. D 11/7/1984 Bp Richard Mitchell Trelease Jr. c 3. D S Bede's Epis Ch Santa Fe NM 1984-2005.

MOLONY, Roberta Diane (Chi) 2009 Boehme St, Lockport IL 60441 **Chapl DOK 2008-; D S Jn The Evang Lockport IL 2001-** B Chicago IL 1941 d Fred & Violet. D 2/3/2001 Bp Bill Persell. m 10/30/1993 William J Molony c 4.

MOMBERG, Thomas A (WTenn) 3235 Overland Place, Memphis TN 38111 B Cincinnati OH 1949 s Robert & Elizabeth. BA Br 1971; MDiv GTS 1986. D 6/14/1986 P 12/13/1986 Bp Frank Tracy Griswold III. m 11/13/2004 Eyleen Hamner Farmer c 2. Int S Matt's Epis Ch Louisville KY 2013-2014; R All SS Ch Frederick MD 2008-2013; Assoc R Ch Of The H Comm Memphis TN 2002-2008; Chapl Res Methodist Healthcare Memphis TN 2001-2002; P-in-c S Thos Ch Somerville TN 2001-2002; Chapl Bp Spencer Place Inc Kansas City MO 2000-2001, Chapl 2000-2001; R Trin Ch Lawr KS 1995-2000; R S Mk's Ch Erie PA 1990-1995; Assoc R S Paul's Epis Ch Pittsburgh PA 1988-1990; Cur Gr Ch Oak Pk IL 1986-1988. Cler Ldrshp Proj 1996.

MONAHAN, Anne (WA) 404 S Lee St, Alexandria VA 22314 **Pstr Asst S Paul's Epis Ch Alexandria VA 2006-** B Schenectady NY 1938 d Armand & Magdalene. BS Syr 1959; MDiv VTS 1982. D 6/9/1982 P 5/27/1983 Bp David Henry Lewis Jr. m 9/9/1961 William J Monahan c 3. Actg Field Educ Dir VTS 2001-2006; Dio Delaware Wilmington 2000-2004; Int S Aid's Ch Alexandria VA 1997-1999; Int S Mk's Ch Alexandria VA 1996-1997; Int S Alb's Epis Ch Annandale VA 1993-1996; Int The Ch Of The Redeem Beth MD 1992-1993; Int All SS Ch Alexandria VA 1991-1992; Int S Mary Magd Ch Silver Sprg MD 1989-1991; Int S Mary's Chap Ridge Ridge MD 1987-1989; Int Asst R S Fran Ch Potomac MD 1986-1987; Assoc S Dav's Par Washington DC 1983-1986; Cur The Ch of S Clem Alexandria VA 1982-1983; Stndg Com Dio Washington Washington DC 1990-1992, Dep, GC 1988-1991. EPF 1982-1992; Fllshp of S Jn 1999-2015; Int Ntwk 1986-1994.

MONASTIERE, Sally Melczer (Los) 1335 North Hills Drive, Upland CA 91784 **Asst S Mk's Epis Ch Upland CA 2011-** B Phoenix AZ 1946 BA Scripps Coll 1967; MA Claremont Grad U 1970; MDiv CDSP 2001. D 10/12/2002 P 5/3/2003 Bp Joseph Jon Bruno. Epis Communities & Serv Pasadena CA 2005-2011; Asst Trin Epis Ch Orange CA 2003-2005.

MONCRIEFF, Stephanie Christan Patterson (Tex) 3401 Bellaire Dr S, Fort Worth TX 76109 B Houston TX 1987 d Randall & Linda. B.S U of Houston 2009; BS U of Houston 2009; MDiv Brite DS 2016. D 6/25/2016 Bp C Andrew Doyle. m 6/26/2010 Jeremy Scott Moncrieff.

MONETTE, Ruth Alta (Los) 104-5990 E Blvd, Vancouver BC V6M3V4 Canada B Des Plaines IL 1977 d William & Elizabeth. BA Hobart and Wm Smith Colleges 1999; MDiv EDS 2004. D 6/11/2005 Bp Chester Lovelle Talton P 1/14/2006 Bp Joseph Jon Bruno. Serv Angl Ch of Can 2007-2008; Cbury Westwood Fndt Los Angeles CA 2005-2006; H Faith Par Inglewood CA 2005-2006; Chapl Cbury Westwood Fndt 2004-2006.

MONGE-MANCIA, Israel (Hond) **Dio Honduras San Pedro Sula 1998-** B 1969 m 8/6/2004 Sandra Estela Mejia-Avila c 3.

MONGE-SANTIAGO, Juan (NJ) 213 Madison Ave, Lakewood NJ 08701 **P-in-c All SS Epis Ch Lakewood NJ 2015-** B Fajardo Puerto Rico 1963 s Juan & Binicia. BBA Universidad Interamericana 2000; MBA Universidad Interamericana 2002; MDiv Other 2006; MDiv Other 2006; MDiv Seminario San Pedro Y San Pablo 2006. D 8/27/2006 P 2/11/2007 Bp David Andres Alvarez-Velazquez. c 2. Cn of Stwdshp Dio Puerto Rico Trujillo Alto PR 2006-2015, D 2005-2006, Secy of Stndg Com 2013; Vic Mision El Buen Pstr Fajardo PR 2006-2015; Supvsr Of Mfg Eaton 2004-2005; Purchasing Mgr Corning 1990-2003. padrejuan@optimum.net

MONICA, Ted (Fla) 6661 Man O War Trail, Tallahassee FL 32309 **Chair of Liturg Com Dio Florida Jacksonville 2011-, Dioc Coun 2009-, Dioc Ecum Com 2009-, Reg Cn 2009-** B Watertown NY 1959 s Oliver & Rosemarie. BA Wadhams Hall Sem Coll 1982; MDiv Chr the King Sem 1986. Rec 4/8/1998 as Priest Bp Daniel William Herzog. c 2. R H Comf Epis Ch Tallahassee FL 2009-2015; R S Jn's Ch Johnstown NY 2002-2009; R Ch Of The Gd Shpd Elizabethtwn NY 1998-2002; Reg Dn Dio Albany Greenwich NY 2006-2009; Reg Dn 2005-2009, Conv Plnng Com 2003-2009, Conv Plnng Com 2000-2009, Liturg Com 1999-2009, Instr, D Trng Sch 1999-2003. Compsr, "Hymn: We Are The Body of Chr," 2002.

MONICA, Teri A (Alb) Trinity Episc Church, 18 Trinity Pl, Plattsburgh NY 12901 **Trin Ch Plattsburgh NY 2016-** B Plattsburgh NY 1958 d Walter & Carol. BA SUNY 1985; MA SUNY 2001; MA S Bernards TS and Mnstry Albany

2007. D 6/9/2007 P 12/8/2007 Bp William Howard Love. c 2. Asst H Comf Epis Ch Tallahassee FL 2011-2016; S Jn's Epis Ch Tallahassee FL 2011-2013; Ch Of The Ascen Carrabelle FL 2009-2011; S Teresa Of Avila Crawfordville FL 2009-2010; Asst S Jn's Ch Johnstown NY 2007-2009.

MONK, Edward R (Dal) Saint John's Church (Episcopal), 101 N. 14th Street, Corsicana TX 75110 **R S Jn's Epis Ch Corsicana TX 2003-** B Dallas TX 1972 s J D & Betty. BA Baylor U 1995; MDiv Nash 1999. D 11/29/1998 P 5/29/1999 Bp Keith Lynn Ackerman. m 7/1/1995 Virginia N Newberry c 3. Yth Off Dio Quincy Peoria IL 2000-2003, VP, Dioc Coun 2001-2003, Fin Com Chairman 1999-2003, Liturgies Instr for Dioc Mnstry 1999-2003; Cn St Paul's Epis Ch Peoria IL 1999-2003; D Trin Ch Milwaukee WI 1998; Bd Pres Corsicana ISD Corsicana TX 2015-2017. Co-Auth, "So You're Called to be a Bp," Dovetracts, Inc, 2006. CCU 1999; CBS 1995; GAS 2005; Soc of King Chas the Mtyr 2007; SSC 1999. Distinguished Akumni Nash 2016; Hon Dioc Cn Dio Quincy 2003. frmonk@stjohnscorsicana.com

MONNAT, Thomas Leonard (Pa) 213 Earlington Road, Havertown PA 19083 B Syracuse NY 1948 s Leonard & Florence. BA Villanova U 1970; MDiv GTS 1978. D 6/14/1978 P 10/1/1979 Bp Lyman Cunningham Ogilby. m 6/21/1997 Nancy Monnat c 3. P in charge The Ch Of The Atone Morton PA 1998-2007; Asst/Int R All SS Ch Wynnewood PA 1995-1998; R Geth Ch Minneapolis MN 1983-1994; S Steph The Mtyr Ch Minneapolis MN 1979-1982; Chapl-in-Res Abbot NW Hosp in Minneapolis 1978-1979; Asst S Nich Minneapolis MN 1978-1979.

MONNOT, Elizabeth Lockwood (NCal) 1225 41st Avenue, Sacramento CA 95922 **Co-R All SS Memi Sacramento CA 2006-; COM The Epis Dio Nthrn California Sacramento CA 2015-** B Waterbury CT 1967 d Robert & Isabel. BA Ob 1989; ALM Harv 1997; MDiv CDSP 2002. D 6/22/2002 P 1/25/2003 Bp Richard Lester Shimpfky. m 9/28/2002 Michael John Monnot c 3. Asst R Gr Ch S Helena CA 2002-2005. revbmonnot@allsaintssacramento.org

MONNOT, Michael John (NCal) 1225 41st Ave, Sacramento CA 95822 **Co-R All SS Memi Sacramento CA 2006-; Mem, Bd Trst The Epis Dio Nthrn California Sacramento CA 2014-, Campus Mnstry Cmsn, Chair 2009-** B Burlingane CA 1961 s John & Constance. BA U CA 1985; MDiv CDSP 2002. D 12/4/2004 P 6/4/2005 Bp William Edwin Swing. m 9/28/2002 Elizabeth Lockwood Hawley c 1. Asst S Patricks Ch Kenwood CA 2005-2006. revmonnot@allsaintssacramento.org

MONREAL, Anthony A (SJ) 9323 South Westlawn, Fresno CA 93706 B Dos Palos CA 1959 s Anthony & Guillermina. BA S Jn Sem Coll Camarillo CA 1983; MDiv Pontifical Coll Josephinum 1988; MS Natl U 1993; EdD GTF 2005. Rec 6/1/1994 as Priest Bp David Mercer Schofield. m 6/20/1992 Linda Carey. P S Jas Epis Cathd Fresno CA 1994-1999; D Our Lady of Guadalupe Fresno CA 1993-1994; Serv RC Ch 1988-1991.

MONROE, George Wesley (Chi) 2866 Vacherie Ln, Dallas TX 75227 **Ret 2002-** B Texarkana TX 1940 s John & Bernadine. BA Baylor U 1962; MDiv Nash 1968. D 6/26/1968 Bp Charles A Mason P 12/28/1968 Bp William Paul Barnds. Assoc To Exec Dir Bp Anderson Hse Chicago IL 1993-2002; Exec Dir Dio Chicago Chicago IL 1984-1993; Epis Chars And Cmnty Serv (Eccs) Chicago IL 1984-1993; R Chr Ch Portsmouth NH 1976-1981; Vic S Barn' Epis Ch Glen Ellyn IL 1973-1976; Asst Ch Of The Ascen Chicago IL 1971-1973; Cur S Lk's Ch Evanston IL 1969-1971; Cur S Jn's Ch Ft Worth TX 1968-1969. Novel, "A Perfect Gift," Lulu Press, 2010.

MONROE, Sarah Beth (Oly) PO Box 1248, Westport WA 98595 **Chapl on the Harbor Westport WA 2014-; D S Andr's Epis Ch Aberdeen WA 2013-** B Los Gatos CA 1983 d Randall & Gina. BA Evergreen St Coll 2010; MDiv EDS 2013. D 10/18/2012 P 4/23/2014 Bp Gregory Harold Rickel.

MONROE, Virginia Hill (Ala) 430 Newman Ave. Se, Huntsville AL 35801 **Assoc S Steph's Epis Ch Birmingham AL 1997-** B Gadsden AL 1943 d James & Lee. Cerification SURSUM CORDA, Dio So Carolina; RN U of Alabama 1964; MDiv Sewanee: The U So, TS 1994; DMin Sewanee: The U So, TS 2005. D 5/21/1994 P 12/3/1994 Bp Robert Oran Miller. c 1. R Ch Of The Gd Shpd Cashiers NC 2002-2015; Assoc Chr Ch Greenville SC 1999-2002; Assoc Ch Of The Nativ Epis Huntsville AL 1994-1996; Chair, Stndg Com Dio Wstrn No Carolina Asheville NC 2013, Stndg Com 2010-2013, Chair, COM 2006-2008, COM 2003-2008, Mem, Search Com for 5th Bp of WNC 2003-2004.

MONROE LOES, Brenda Frances (At) 304 E 6th St, West Point GA 31833 B Chicago Heights IL 1962 d Martin & Carol. BS Pur 1984; MDiv Epis TS of the SW 1998. D 11/23/1998 Bp Herbert Alcorn Donovan Jr P 1/15/2000 Bp Ronald Hayward Haines. m 2/26/2011 Joseph H Loes. P-in-c S Jn's W Point GA 2010-2015; R S Jas Epis Ch Clayton GA 2001-2005; Asst R S Jn's Ch Olney MD 1999-2000.

MONSON, Scott B (Minn) 1015 Sibley Memorial Hwy Apt 303, Saint Paul MN 55118 **Chem Hlth Spec Ramsey Cnty Proj Remand St. Paul MN 2017-; Tchg Fac U MN Minneapolis MN 2013-; P-in-c S Mary's Basswood Grove Hastings MN 2012-** B St Peter MN 1956 s Carl & Bernice. BA Gustavus Adolphus Coll 1986; MA Minnesota St U Mankato 1989; MDiv SWTS 2001; Grad Cert U MN 2012. D 10/15/2002 P 4/23/2003 Bp James Louis Jelinek. Prog Dir 3Rs NuWay Counslg Cntr Minneapolis MN 2015-2016; Dir of Clincl Serv

Transitions Recovery Prog St. Paul MN 2012-2015; Assoc S Paul's On-The-Hill Epis Ch Minneapolis MN 2010-2012; Addiction Counslr Univ. of MN Med Cntr-Fairview Minneapolis MN 2010-2012; R Chr Ch Austin MN 2003-2009. Amer Counslg Assn 2012; Assn of Sprtlty, Ethics, and Rel Values in Counslg 2013. Seabury-Wstrn Serv Awd SWTS 2001. stmaryschurch@gmx.com

MONSOUR, John Vincent (SwFla) 2114 W Destiny Point Cir, St George UT 84790 B Pawtucket RI 1947 s George & Eleanor. CG Jung Inst; Washington Sch of Psych; BA Providence Coll 1969; MA Washington Theol Un 1974; DMin Andover Newton TS 1977. Rec 10/4/1995 as Priest Bp Rogers Sanders Harris. Dir of Mnstry Dvlpmt Dio SW Flordia Sarasota FL 2004-2009; Dio SW Florida Parrish FL 2004-2008; Assoc All SS Ch Tarpon Spgs FL 2000-2004; Int St Cathr of Alexandria Epis Ch Temple Terrace FL 1998-1999; Samar Counslg Cntr Tampa FL 1996-2009; Assoc S Mk's Epis Ch Of Tampa Tampa FL 1994-1996. Fell, Amer Assoc. Pstr Counselors (AAPC) 1998. Cmnty Serv Awd The Red Cross 2005.

MONTAGNO, Karen (Mass) 536 Main St # 2, Medford MA 02155 **Dir Congrl Resources and Trng Dio Massachusetts Boston MA 2010-; Colleague Bethany Hse of Pryr Arlington MA 2008-** B Portsmouth VA 1955 d George & Willie. BSW OH SU 1977; MA OH SU 1979; MDiv VTS 1995. D 6/24/1995 P 5/4/1996 Bp Herbert Thompson Jr. c 3. Int S Cyp's Ch Boston MA 2010-2011; Chr Ch Cambridge Cambridge MA 2001-2010, 1999; Dn of Students & Cmnty Life EDS Cambridge MA 1996-2009; Asst Dio Sthrn Ohio Cincinnati OH 1995-1996; Cur S Matt's Epis Ch Westerville OH 1995-1996. Auth, *Called by Jesus*; Auth, *Epis Curric for Yth*, Morehouse Pub; Auth, *Peace and Justice*; Auth, *Sprtlty*. Soc of S Jn the Evang 1994; UBE, Massachusetts Chapt, Chapl 2000. ,Polly Bond Awd ECom 2004.

MONTAGUE, Cynthia Russell (ECR) 17574 Winding Creek Rd, Salinas CA 93908 **Epis Ch Of The Gd Shpd Salinas CA 2003-; Jail Chapl Dio El Camino Real Salinas CA 2002-; Chapl Monterey Cnty Jail Salinas CA 2002-** B Washington DC 1953 d Homer & Lillian. BA Brandeis U 1975; MDiv Andover Newton TS 1986. D 5/4/2002 Bp Richard Lester Shimpfky. m 9/24/2008 Marilyn Jeanne Westerkamp c 2. D Assoc Trin Ch Gonzales CA 2002; CPE Chapl Emma Pendleton Bradley Hosp Providence RI 1986-1987; Sem Ch of St. Aug & St. Mart Boston MA 1985-1986; CPE Chapl Boston City Hosp Boston MA 1985. Integrity USA 1977. Jonathan Edwards Soc Andover Newton TS 1986.

MONTALTO, Alfred Patrick (NY) 841 4th Ave, North, Apt 65, St. Petersburg FL 33701 **Ret 2001-** B Poughkeepsie NY 1943 s Alfred & Helen. MA Marist Coll 1966; BA Marist Coll 1966; MDiv Ya Berk 1969; STM Ya Berk 1977. D 6/7/1969 P 12/20/1969 Bp Horace W B Donegan. The Ch Of S Steph Staten Island NY 2000-2001; Dio New York New York NY 1998-2000; S Barth's Ch In The Highland White Plains NY 1997-1998; Ch Of The Gd Shpd Wakefield Bronx NY 1986-1997; P-in-c S Andr's Ch Bronx NY 1985-1986; All SS Ch Harrison NY 1971-1976. NYPD Citizen of the Year; "Who's Who in Rel".

MONTANARI, Albert Ubaldo (WNY) 135 Old Lyme Dr Apt 4, Williamsville NY 14221 **Ret 1990-** B Rochester NY 1926 s Joseph & Anna. BS Buffalo St Coll 1958; MDiv Pittsburgh TS 1965. D 6/3/1978 Bp Harold Barrett Robinson P 10/1/1978 Bp Philip Frederick McNairy. m 4/28/1947 Mary Montanari c 1. Asst H Apos Epis Ch Tonawanda NY 1990-1996, Cur 1978-1981; R S Pat's Ch Buffalo NY 1986-1989, Vic 1981-1985; Serv Presb Ch 1965-1978.

MONTELLA, Christopher (Los) **D S Mart-In-The-Fields Par Winnetka CA 2016-** B Bayshore NY 1971 s Anthony & Jean. Mstr of Div EDS 2015. D 6/4/2016 P 1/14/2017 Bp Joseph Jon Bruno.

MONTES, Alejandro Sixto (Tex) 10426 Towne Oak Ln, Sugar Land TX 77478 **Vic San Mateo Epis Ch Bellaire TX 1993-** B Lima PE 1944 s Miguel & Teresa. Cert Cntrl Amer TS GT 1978; Lic Cntrl Amer TS GT 2000. D 6/24/1989 Bp Maurice Manuel Benitez P 2/5/1990 Bp Anselmo Carral-Solar. m 8/5/1967 Laura Montes c 3. The Great Cmsn Fndt Houston TX 1993-2008; Iglesia San Mateo Houston TX 1989-2016.

MONTES, Alex G (Tex) 11608 Glen Knoll Dr, Manor TX 78653 **Vic St Mary Magd Epis Ch Manor TX 2008-; Vic The Great Cmsn Fndt Houston TX 2008-** B 1967 s Alejandro & Laura. MDiv VTS 2005. D 6/11/2005 P 12/13/2005 Bp Don Adger Wimberly. m 7/20/2005 Hong Duc T Montes c 3. S Paul's Ch Waco TX 2005-2008; Ch Of The Redeem Houston TX 1994-1998.

MONTES, Eli (Kan) St Francis Community Services, 4155 E Harry St, Wichita KS 67218 **S Jn's Ch Wichita KS 2016-; S Fran Cmnty Serv Inc. Salina KS 2013-; Latino/Multicultural Mssnr Dio Nebraska Lexington NE 2006-** B El Paso TX 1960 d Gregorio & Evangelina. U of Texas 1982; U of New Mex 1983; AAS El Paso Cmnty Coll El Paso TX 1987; BS U of Phoenix 1997; MDiv Sewanee: The U So, TS 2002. D 7/27/2002 Bp Terence Kelshaw P 7/26/2003 Bp Don Adger Wimberly. m 6/4/1988 Joel A Montes c 4. Trin Ch Victoria TX 2011-2013; S Christophers Ch Cozad NE 2010-2011; Dio Nebraska Omaha NE 2007-2010; On Track Mnstry Lexington NE 2006; Asst R S Steph's Ch Beaumont 2004-2005; S Steph's Ch Beaumont TX 2004-2005; P-in-c S Geo's Epis Ch Port Arthur TX 2003-2004; The Great Cmsn Fndt Houston TX 2002-2004; Hisp Mssnr St. Matt's Beaumont TX 2002-2003. DOK 2005.

MONTGOMERY, **Brandt Leonard** (WLa) Episcopal Church of the Ascension, 1030 Johnston Street, Lafayette LA 70501 **Chapl Ascen Day Sch Lafayette LA 2014-; Dismantling Racism Cmsn Chairman Dio Wstrn Louisiana Alexandria LA 2017-, Disciplinary Bd Mem 2016-2017, Yth & YA Cmsn Mem 2015-2016; Interfaith Subcommittee Mem The Lambda Chi Alpha Fraternity Carmel Indiana 2017-; Jr Bd Dir of the Natl Alum Assn Mem U of Montevallo Montevallo Alabama 2015-** B Talladega AL 1985 s John & Dudley. BA The U of Montevallo 2007; MDiv GTS 2012. D 5/27/2012 P 12/2/2012 Bp John Mckee Sloan Sr. Ch Of The Ascen Lafayette LA 2014; Cur Cbury Chap and Coll Cntr Tuscaloosa AL 2012-2014; BEC Mem Dio Alabama Birmingham 2013-2014, Cmsn on Sprtlty Mem 2013-2014, Dioc Coun Mem 2013-2014, Dept of Mnstry for Higher Educ Mem 2012-2014. Auth, "Gr in Creation: Preaching Gr in Genesis 1-3," *The Living Pulpit*, The Living Pulpit, Inc., 2016; Auth, "Gospel Hosp--From Jesus to Us, From Us to Others," *The Living Pulpit*, The Living Pulpit, Inc., 2012. Ord of Omega 2007; Phi Alpha Theta Natl Hist hon Soc 2004; The HSEC 2017. Paul Harris Fell Rotary Intl Fndt 2013; Geo Cabot Ward Prize The GTS 2012; Alum of the Year Lambda Chi Alpha Sigma-Epsilon Chapt 2008. bmontgomery@aesgators.org

MONTGOMERY, **Bruce** (NJ) 1310 Tullo Rd, Martinsville NJ 08836 **R S Mart's Ch Bridgewater NJ 1982-** B Toledo OH 1950 s Charles & Mona. BA Albion Coll 1972; PrTS 1975; MDiv GTS 1977. D 6/11/1977 Bp Jonathan Goodhue Sherman P 5/30/1978 Bp Robert Campbell Witcher Sr. m 12/18/1976 Lani Lynn Montgomery c 3. Asst S Anne's Ch Abington PA 1977-1982.

MONTGOMERY, **Catharine Whittaker** (SwVa) 2231 Timberlake Dr, Lynchburg VA 24502 B Durham NC 1944 d William & Catherine. BA Randolph-Macon Coll 1994; Cert VTS 1998. D 5/22/1999 P 1/22/2000 Bp Neff Powell. m 3/16/1963 John Robert Montgomery c 2. P-in-c Gr Memi Ch Lynchburg VA 2006-2016; Assoc S Paul's Epis Ch Lynchburg VA 1999-2006; Educational Consortium Dio SW Virginia Roanoke VA 1999. Omicron Delta Kappa 1993; Psi Chi 1993. Phi Beta Kappa Randolph-Macon Wmn'S Coll 1994.

MONTGOMERY, **Ellen Maddigan** (WNY) 41 Saint Georges Sq, Buffalo NY 14222 B Buffalo NY 1929 d Arthur & Lillian. GTS; BA SUNY 1981; MDiv U Tor CA 1985. D 6/22/1985 P 4/1/1986 Bp Harold Barrett Robinson. m 3/31/1951 H Ernest Montgomery c 3. Pstr Care Trin Epis Ch Buffalo 1997-1999; Int Ascen Epis Ch 1995-1997; Dir of Pstr Care Hospice Buffalo NY 1991-1995; Dio Wstrn New York Tonawanda NY 1991-1992; Mssn Counslr Trin Epis Ch Buffalo NY 1989-1999; Asst S Mk's Ch Orchard Pk NY 1985-1986. Capture a Heart Awd Homespace, Inc. 2004; Vision Awd Canaan Hse 2003.

MONTGOMERY, **Ian** (FdL) 26 Gaskill Rd, Chester VT 05143 **Mssy P SAMS 2009-** B London UK 1944 s Hector & Anne. LLB U of St Andrews 1966; FCA Inst For Chart Accountants 1969; CTh Oxf GB 1975; DMin Sewanee: The U So, TS 2002. Trans 8/1/1979 as Priest Bp Alexander D Stewart. m 10/9/1976 Polly Montgomery c 2. S Lk's Ch Cambridge NY 2014-2016; S Dav's Ch Austin TX 2014-2015; R S Thos Ch Menasha WI 1997-2009; R S Barth's Ch Nashville TN 1992-1997; R S Phil's Ch New Orleans LA 1983-1992; Dio Wstrn Massachusetts Springfield 1978-1983; Serv Ch Of Engl 1975-1978.

MONTGOMERY, **Ian Bruce** (ECR) 19 Montrose Ave, Bryn Mawr PA 19010 **The Ch Of The Gd Shpd Rosemont PA 2015-; Pres Via Media Grp 2012-; Chapl Holland Lodge 8 NYC NY 1998-** B Bremerhaven Germany 1966 s Richard & Diana. U of S Andrews 1988; BA U Pgh 1991; MDiv GTS 1998. D 6/13/1998 Bp Robert Gould Tharp P 12/19/1998 Bp George Phelps Mellick Belshaw. m 3/31/2005 Lydia J Montgomery c 2. Epis Prog Dir Thrivent Fin for Lutherans 2010-2012; Exec Dir & Chapl Mnstry to Manhattan New York NY 2009-2010; R All SS Epis Ch Palo Alto CA 2005-2008; Asst Ch of S Mary the Vrgn New York NY 2004-2005; Trin Epis Ch Red Bank NJ 2002-2004; Cn Pstr The Amer Cathd of the H Trin Paris 75008 2000-2001; Secy/Treas Dio New Jersey Trenton NJ 1998-2000; Cur S Geo's-By-The-River Rumson NJ 1998-2000. Fllshp of S Jn (SSJE) 2005. montgomery.goodshepherd@gmail.com

✠ MONTGOMERY, **The Rt Rev James Winchester** (Chi) 5555 N Sheridan Rd Apt 809, Chicago IL 60640 B Chicago IL 1921 s James & Evelyn. BA NWU 1943; STB GTS 1949; STD GTS 1963; Nash 1963; SWTS 1969; LLD Shimer Coll 1969; LHD Iowa Wesleyan Coll 1974. D 6/18/1949 P 12/17/1949 Bp Wallace E Conkling Con 9/29/1962 for Chi. JCCMA 1976-1980; Ret Bp of Chicago Dio Chicago Chicago IL 1970-1987, SCL 1970-1976, Bp Coadj of Chicago 1965-1971, Bp Suffr of Chicago 1962-1965, Ret Bp of Chicago 1960-1987, Ret Bp of Chicago 1959-1987, Ret Bp of Chicago 1954-1987, Stndg Com 1960-1962, Cathd Chapt 1959-1962, ExCoun, Dn So Deanry 1954-1962; Serv Bexley Seabury Fed Chicago IL 1985-1988; Serv Nash Nashotah WI 1962-1988; R The Ch Of S Jn The Evang Flossmoor IL 1951-1962; Cur S Lk's Ch Evanston IL 1949-1951; Trst The CPG New York NY 1975-1988; Trst The GTS New York NY 1964-1982, Trst 1961-1963. Phi Beta Kappa 1943.

MONTGOMERY, **Jennifer Born** (Va) 4000 Lorcom Ln, Arlington VA 22207 **Trin Ch Newtown CT 2017-** B Atlanta GA 1954 d Robert & Ethel. BA Shorter Coll 1988; MDiv VTS 1998. D 6/13/1998 P 4/20/1999 Bp Peter J Lee. m 2/10/2001 Joseph E Glaze c 3. R S Andr's Epis Ch Arlington VA 2009-2017; R S Jas' Ch Clinton NY 2002-2009; Asstg Vic Chr Ch Glen Allen VA 1998-2002.

MONTGOMERY, **John Alford** (Lex) B Mount Holly NJ 1936 D 6/1/1974 Bp Addison Hosea. m 7/14/1962 Carol Tabler c 4.

MONTGOMERY, **John Fletcher** (USC) 2827 Wheat St, Columbia SC 29205 **R S Jn's Epis Ch Columbia SC 1999-** B 1964 BA Furman U; MDiv VTS; MDiv VTS. D 6/18/1994 P 1/7/1995 Bp John Wadsworth Howe. m 6/11/1988 Sarah Michaels Montgomery. All SS Epis Ch Deltona FL 1996-1999; Ch Of The Redeem Bryn Mawr PA 1994-1996; Trin Ch Vero Bch FL 1989-1991.

MONTGOMERY, **Lee Allen** (U) 70 N 200 W, Cedar City UT 84720 **P Dio Utah Salt Lake City UT 2015-** B Lone Grove OK 1950 s Lee & Carmen. MEd E Cntrl OSU 1975; PhD U of No Texas 1981. D 6/14/2008 P 2/12/2009 Bp Carolyn Tanner Irish. m 10/7/1978 Alison Kim McLeod c 2. S Jude's Ch Cedar City UT 2014; Sprt of the Desert Ivins UT 2008-2014.

MONTGOMERY, **Tyler Lindell** (SVa) PO Box 3520, Williamsburg VA 23187 **Chapl Bruton Par Williamsburg VA 2015-** B Providence RI 1987 s Archibald & Phyllis. BA U of Pennsylvania 2009; MDiv Berkeley Epis Sem 2015. D 6/6/2015 P 12/16/2015 Bp Herman Hollerith IV. m 6/24/2017 Mary C Montgomery. tmontgomery@brutonparish.org

MONTIEL, **Robert Michael** (WTenn) 103 S Poplar St, Paris TN 38242 B Gadsden AL 1951 s Gonzalo & Voncile. BS Georgia Inst of Tech 1973; JD U of Alabama 1976; MDiv Sewanee: The U So, TS 1991. D 6/1/1991 P 1/1/1992 Bp Charles Farmer Duvall. m 6/28/2013 Antoinette Montiel c 3. R Gr Epis Ch Paris TN 2000-2006; R Chr The King Epis Ch Normal IL 1994-2000; Trin Epsicopal Ch Atmore AL 1991-1994; D-In-Trng S Anna's Ch Atmore AL 1991-1992. Tertiary Of The Soc Of S Fran.

MONTILEAUX, **Charles Thomas** (SD) Po Box 246, Kyle SD 57752 B Porcupine SD 1960 s Francis & Barbara. Rio Salado Cmnty Coll; BA U of Dubuque 1983; MA U of Dubuque 1985; MDiv U of Dubuque 1987. D 6/22/1986 P 6/1/1987 Bp Craig Barry Anderson. m 7/14/1979 Cheryl Alverine c 2. Dio So Dakota Pierre SD 1987-1989; On Sabbatical.

MONTJOY IV, **Gid** (Md) 609 Collins Creek Dr., Murrells Inlet SC 29576 B Paris TX 1944 s William & Alice. BBA U of Mississippi 1966; Cert Mississippi Coll 1970; MDiv TESM 1983; DMin Sewanee: The U So, TS 1989. D 6/23/1984 P 1/18/1985 Bp Duncan Montgomery Gray Jr. m 5/17/2002 Cynthia Montjoy c 3. Discernment Coordntr Epis Dio Maryland 2011-2013; Assoc S Anne's Par Annapolis MD 1995-2010; R H Trin Epis Ch Auburn AL 1987-1995; Vic S Mk's Ch Raymond MS 1985-1987; Vic Ch Of The Creator Clinton MS 1984-1987; Eccl Crt Dio Maryland Baltimore MD 2005-2008, 1999-2004. Auth, "Chr in the Wrld," *CE in the Dio Alabama*, Dio Alabama, 1993; Auth, "Starting a New Cong in the Epis Ch," *Starting a New Cong in the Epis Ch*, D. Minn Proj, 1989; Auth, "What One needs to Know About Conservatorship and Guardianships in Chancery Crt," *What One Needs to Know About the Crt System in Mississippi*, Mississippi Bar Assn, 1978.

MONTOOTH, **Cynthia Hooton** (SwFla) 15 Knob Hill Circle, Decatur GA 30030 **D Assoc St. Hilary's Epis Ch 2004-** B Hollister CA 1942 d Wade & Alice. BA The Curtis Inst of Mus 1961; Lic Sch for Diac Formation Ellenton FL 2004. D 6/12/2004 Bp John Bailey Lipscomb. m 1/18/1974 Gene Montooth c 4. D Assoc S Hilary's Ch Ft Myers FL 2004-2008.

MONTOYA CARPIO, **S Leonardo** (EcuC) Apartado #17-01-3108, Quito Ecuador **Archd Of Cuenca 1989-; R Epis Ch In Ecuador 1983-; Dir Of Missions Universitaria Quito Ecuador 1981-** B Loja EC 1949 s Filoteo & Maria. Salamanca U 1978; Lic Cntrl U 1985; Cuenca U 1988. D 2/7/1982 P 3/1/1983 Bp Adrian Delio Caceres-Villavicencio. m 8/1/1987 Clara Ordonez. Iglesia Epis Del Ecuador Quito 2005-2009, 1982-2003. Auth, "Pensamiento Latinoamericano Xaverian U, La Legitima Defensa De La Persona," *Doctoral Thesis*, 1988. Apd.

MONTROSE, **Richard Sterling** (LI) 712 Franklin St, Westbury NY 11590 **D'S Asst Jamaica NY 1997-; Retured Westbury. NY 2010-** B Orange NJ 1927 s Levi & Marie. BS LIU 1958; Cert Mercer TS 1995. D 10/18/1997 Bp Rodney Rae Michel. m 1/22/1956 Florence Hilda Brown.

MONZON-MOLINA, **Eduardo** (Hond) Apartado 2598, San Pedro Honduras **Assoc Par Of San Jose 1986-** B Guatemala City GT 1943 s Francisco & Estela. San Carlos U Gt 1966; EDS 1968; MDiv ETSC 1969. D 5/31/1969 P 12/1/1969 Bp William Carl Frey. m 5/2/1970 Hilda Perez De Monzon c 2. Cn Catedral Epis El Buen Pstr San Pedro Sula 2000-2007; SAMS Ambridge PA 1989-2007; Chair - Cmsn On Stwdshp 1986-1987; Coord - Dioc Ldrshp Dev - Costa Rica 1984-1987; Sec - Com 1975-1979; Pres- Com On Ecum 1975-1978; Cn-In-Charge S Jas Cathd In Guatamala 1974-1979; Exam Chapl 1971-1979; Pres - Const & Cn 1971-1978; Dioc Power Of Atty 1971-1972; Dio Guatemala New York NY 1969-1980. Auth, "Crisis Confrontation," *Crisis Preparedness*. SAMS 1987-2008. Vstg Fell Austin Sem 1979.

MOODY, **John Wallace** (NY) 42 W 9th St Apt 18, New York NY 10011 **Profsnl Artist and art Consult 1992-; Ret 1991-** B Glenside PA 1926 s Harold & Lulu. BA Un Coll Schenectady NY 1950; MDiv EDS 1953; MA NYU 1969. D 6/6/1953 P 12/20/1953 Bp Henry W Hobson. Assoc Pstr Mnstrs Trin Par New York NY 1988-1991; Interfaith Dept if Pstr Care The Vill Nrsng Hm New York NY 1987-1988; Dir Pstr Care Vill Nrsng Hm NYC 1987-1988; Int S Jn's Ch New York NY 1987; Int S Jn In-The-Wilderness Copake Falls

NY 1986-1987; Dir of Prog Dvlpmt Manhattan Plaza Assoc New York NY 1983-1987; Dir Prog Dvlpmt Manhattan Plaza NYC 1983-1986; R S Pauls On The Hill Epis Ch Ossining NY 1976-1983; Dir Cntr Forum Ch Of S Paul The Apos Baltimore MD 1974-1976; Assoc Dir Lower Manhattan Culture Coun & Downtown Mnstry Coordntr 1974-1975; Cmnty and Cultural Affrs 1969-1974; Vic 1954, R 1964 Ch Of S Edw Columbus OH 1954-1968; Cur S Alb's Epis Ch Of Bexley Columbus OH 1953-1954; Bp and Chapt Dio Sthrn Ohio Cincinnati OH 1966-1967, Exam Chapl 1962-1967. Artist, "Variety of Gallery Exhibitions," *1992-to present*, 2013; Auth, "Mnstry to the Aging," *Alb Inst*, 1982; Auth, "Liturg and the Arts," *Cath Wrld*, 1962; Auth, "Recent Article in a Climate of Change," *Chr Century*, 1960. Epis Ch and the Visual Arts 2002. Prog Awd to Trin Ch Arts & Bus Coun of NYC 1973.

✠ MOODY, The Rt Rev Robert Manning (Okla) 4001 Oxford Way, Norman OK 73072 **Ret Bp of Oklahoma Dio Oklahoma Oklahoma City OK 2007-, Trst 1988-2007** B Baltimore MD 1939 s Irving & Ann. BA Rice U 1962; U of Texas 1963; MDiv VTS 1966; S Georges Coll Jerusalem IL 1981. D 6/21/1966 P 5/29/1967 Bp James Milton Richardson Con 2/6/1988 for Okla. m 4/19/1968 Beryl Lance Moody c 4. HOB, GC ECUSA New York NY 1988-2006; R Gr Epis Ch Alexandria VA 1975-1987; R S Jas Ch Riverton WY 1970-1975; Asst S Jn The Div Houston TX 1968-1970; P-in-c S Mths Ch Waco TX 1967-1968; Chapl Baylor U Waco TX 1966-1968; Vic S Jas Ch McGregor TX 1966-1968; Epis TS Of The SW Austin TX 1988-1992; Trst VTS Alexandria VA 1982-1987. EvangES 1975-1987. Distinguished Alum St. Jn's Sch, Houston, Texas 2010; Distinguished Alumus Rice U 2005; DD VTS 1988.

MOON, Abigail White (Fla) 211 N Monroe St, Tallahassee FL 32301 **Chr Formation and Mssn S Jn's Epis Ch Tallahassee FL 2011-** B Columbus GA 1975 d Lawrence & Signe. BA U of So 1997; MDiv Sewanee: The U So, TS 2011. D 2/11/2011 Bp Scott Anson Benhase P 9/6/2011 Bp Samuel Johnson Howard. m 8/4/2007 Robert Allen Moon. Yth Dir The Ch Of The Gd Shpd Augusta GA 2005-2008.

MOON, Anthony Bernard (Okla) 2401 N. Westminster Road, Arcadia OK 73007 **Congrl Consult S Aug Of Cbury Oklahoma City OK 2012-; Dio Oklahoma Oklahoma City OK 2012-, Mem, Comission on Mnstry 2009-** B Blackwell OK 1952 s Sylvester & Mary. BA Cntrl St U 1975; MEd Cntrl St U 1979; PhD U of Oklahoma 1995; Dioc D Formation Prog 1997. D 6/21/1997 Bp Robert Manning Moody. m 4/5/1985 Marian Jean Moon c 3. D S Mary's Ch Edmond OK 1997-2012. "Coming to Terms w Being Lost," *Sermons That Wk (Series)*, Morehouse Pub, 2004.

MOON, Catherine Joy (Cal) The Curate's House, 7 Walton Village, Liverpool AL L4 6TJ Great Britain (UK) **Serving Angl Ch in the U.K. 2004-** B London UK 1948 d George & Eileen. Royal Acad of Mus London GB 1972; BA Sch for Deacons 1984; Cert GTS 1985. D 6/9/1984 P 6/8/1985 Bp William Edwin Swing. CSF Mnstry Prov 1987-1994.

MOON JR, Don Pardee (Chi) 438 N Sheridan Rd # A500, Waukegan IL 60085 B Manila PH 1936 s Don & Sibyl. BS Cor 1957; MS NYU 1958; BD Nash 1965. D 6/12/1965 Bp James Winchester Montgomery P 12/1/1965 Bp Gerald Francis Burrill. m 1/18/1985 Joanne M Armstrong. P-in-c Ch Of The H Apos Wauconda IL 2005-2007; Shimer Coll Waukegan IL 1995-2003, 1967-1977; Chr Ch Waukegan IL 1992-2003; Pres Shimer Coll Waukegan IL 1978-2004; Dn & Bus Mgr Shimer Coll Waukegan IL 1971-1978; Instr & Pstr Counslr Shimer Coll Waukegan IL 1967-1971; R The Ch Of S Anne Morrison IL 1965-1969.

MOON, James Fred (WMo) 43 Old Mill Ln, South Greenfield MO 65752 B Springfield MO 1933 s William & Gladys. BA Drury U 1955; MDiv SWTS 1958. D 5/31/1958 P 12/18/1958 Bp Edward Randolph Welles II. m 5/12/1979 Cheryl C Calvin c 5. P in Charge St. Stephens Epis Ch Monett MO 2010-2012; P-in-c S Thos a'Becket Epis Ch Cassville MO 2003-2010; Trin Epis Ch Lebanon MO 2001-2003; S Steph's Ch Monett MO 1992-1996; Dio W Missouri Kansas City MO 1964-1994; Chapl U MO-KS City 1964-1980; Chapl Cntrl MO St Coll-Warrensburg 1962-1963; R Chr Ch Warrensburg MO 1958-1963. ESMHE 1988. Bp's Shield 1997; Bp's Shield 1969.

MOON, Mary Louise (Oly) 927 S Sheridan Ave, Tacoma WA 98405 **D S Columba's Ch 2004-; D S Catherines Ch Enumclaw WA 2002-** B Town of Broom NY 1935 d Mahlon & Catherine. BS Cor 1956. D 6/29/2002 Bp Vincent Waydell Warner.

MOON, Richard Warren (Neb) Po Box 1012, West Plains MO 65775 B Richmond Hgts MO 1954 s William & Virginia. BA Colorado Coll 1976; MA U Chi 1977; JD U CO 1980; MDiv Nash 1991. D 6/11/1991 P 12/1/1991 Bp John Clark Buchanan. m 6/2/1979 Connie F Moon c 2. Chr Ch Epis Beatrice NE 2006-2010; Eccl Crt Dio W Missouri Kansas City MO 1994-1995, Stndg Com 1995; R All SS Ch W Plains MO 1993-2006; Assoc To R Gr Ch Carthage MO 1991-1993.

MOON, Robert Michael (Los) 1294 Westlyn Pl, Pasadena CA 91104 B Santa Monica CA 1962 BA NWU 1984; JD SW U Sch of Law Los Angeles CA 1988; MDiv GTS 2003. D 6/14/2003 P 1/24/2004 Bp Joseph Jon Bruno. S Richard's Epis Ch Skyforest CA 2005-2008; The Ch Of The Ascen Sierra Madre CA 2003-2005.

MOONEY, Michelle Puzin (Mil) 2633 N Hackett Ave Apt A, Milwaukee WI 53211 **D S Mk's Ch Milwaukee WI 2001-** B Wichita Falls TX 1942 d Lucien & Andre. BS U of Texas 1964; MS U of Wisconsin 1980. D 4/21/2001 Bp Roger John White. m 12/7/1991 Richard F Mooney c 3. The Gathering: Ecum Healing Mnstry 1988-2001.

MOONEY, Noreen O'Connor (LI) 1 Berard Blvd, Oakdale NY 11769 B Bronx NY 1940 d Hugh & Elizabeth. BA Col 1968; MDiv GTS 1983. D 12/10/1983 Bp Robert Campbell Witcher Sr P 2/18/1989 Bp Orris George Walker Jr. S Paul's Ch Oxford NY 2001; Chenango Cluster Norwich NY 2000; S Jas Ch Brookhaven NY 1991-1995; Dio Long Island Garden City NY 1987-1991; St Jas Ch Sag Harbor NY 1986-1987; S Johns Epis Hosp Far Rockaway NY 1985-1986; Asst All SS Ch Great Neck NY 1983-1985.

MOORE, Albert Lee (NC) 8705 Gleneagles Dr, Raleigh NC 27613 B Philadelphia PA 1937 s Albert & Harriet. MDiv Shaw DS 1994. D 12/20/1997 Bp Robert Carroll Johnson Jr. m 6/17/1972 Ernstein Saint Claire Moore c 4. D Chr Epis Ch Raleigh NC 1998-2010.

MOORE, Allison (Nwk) 11 N Broadway, Irvington NY 10533 **S Barn Ch Irvington NY 2017-** B Pasadena CA 1957 d James & Lois. BA Simmons Coll 1978; MS Ya 1980; MA Harvard DS 1984; PhD Bos 1989. D 6/8/1991 P 12/14/1991 Bp Richard Frank Grein. c 2. S Mk's Ch In The Bowery New York NY 2015-2017; R Ch Of The Gd Shpd Ft Lee NJ 1996-2015; Exec Dir Gd Shpd Cmnty Serv Inc. 1996-2011; Int H Cross Epis Ch Plainfield NJ 1995-1996; Cur Gr Ch White Plains NY 1991-1994. Allison M. Moore, "Cler Moms: Survival GUide to balancing Fam and Cong," Seabury, 2008. Families of Cler Untd in Spprt 2004; Soc for Values in Higher Educ 1981. allisonm@stbarnabas.org

MOORE, Andrew Y (WTenn) 254 E Putnam Ave, Greenwich CT 06830 **S Mary's Epis Ch Richmond VA 2017-** B Elkhurt IN 1981 s Charles & Susan. BA Indiana U 2012; MDiv Yale DS 2015. D 5/30/2015 Bp Don Edward Johnson P 12/19/2015 Bp Ian Theodore Douglas. Chr Ch Greenwich CT 2015-2017; Other Lay Position Calv Ch Memphis TN 2010-2012. amoore@christchurchgreenwich.org

MOORE, Andy J (NJ) 229 Goldsmith Ave, Newark NJ 07112 **S Eliz's Ch Eliz NJ 2008-, R 2008-; Cathd Chapt Trin Cathd Trenton NJ 2010-** B Trinidad & Tobago 1963 BA Codrington Coll 1993. Trans 11/3/2003 Bp George Edward Councell. m 8/5/1995 Natalie Roberts c 3. Dir Seamens Ch Inst New York NY 2003-2008; Dir The Seamen's Inst of New York & New Jersey New York NY 2003-2008; Chapl S Jos's Par Day Sch Queens Vill NY 2001-2003; Serv Angl Ch Dio Trinidad and Tobago 1989-2001. fatherandymoore@gmail.com

MOORE, Anne Elizabeth Olive (Ore) 630 B St, Silverton OR 97381 **The Epis Ch Of The Prince Of Peace Salem OR 2005-; COM Dio Oregon Portland OR 2011-** B Indianapolis IN 1950 d George & Sally. BA Pur 1972; MS Portland St U 1996; MDiv CDSP 2005. D 10/8/2005 P 4/28/2006 Bp Johncy Itty. m 9/2/1980 James R Moore c 3. S Hilda's Ch Monmouth OR 2008-2014.

MOORE JR, Charles Nottingham (SVa) 12800 Nightingale Drive, Chester VA 23836 **P-in-c Merchants Hope Epis Ch Prince Geo No Prince Geo VA 2010-** B Hopewell VA 1944 s Charles & Edwina. BS W&M 1966; MEd W&M 1969; MDiv Gordon-Conwell TS 1973; DMin Andover Newton TS 1974. D 6/9/1976 P 6/1/1985 Bp John Bowen Coburn. m 5/25/2002 Deborah Jean Moore c 2. Int S Jn's Epis Ch Saugus MA 2009; Adjust Prof of Applied Ethics Salem St U 2005-2009; R S Lk's Epis Ch Malden MA 2000-2009; Supply P MA 1996-2000; Int S Jn's Epis Ch Gloucester MA 1994-1996, Dir--Chr Ch Counslg Cntr 1975-1993; Supply P 1986-1994; Forensic Psychol Dept of Mntl Hlth 1980-2010; Dir--Chr Ch Counslg Cntr Chr Ch S Hamilton MA 1975-1983; Pstr Psych Cape Ann Mntl Hlth Cenger 1974-1980. APA.

MOORE, Charles Owen (Pa) 4631 Ossabaw Way, Naples FL 34119 **Ret 1995-** B Hamilton OH 1932 s Buford & Gladys. BA Ob 1954; MDiv GTS 1958. D 6/11/1958 P 12/22/1958 Bp Horace W B Donegan. c 3. R S Mk's Ch Philadelphia PA 1981-1995; Chair Dio Chicago Chicago IL 1968-1981, Stndg Com 1976-1979; R S Giles' Ch Northbrook IL 1966-1981; Asst Ch Of The Resurr New York NY 1963-1966, Cur 1959-1962; Cur S Jas Ch New York NY 1958-1959; COM Dio Pennsylvania Philadelphia PA 1987-1992. Phi Beta Kappa.

MOORE, Charlotte Elizabeth (Eas) D 6/8/2001 P 1/23/2003 Bp Michael Whittington Creighton.

MOORE, Cheryl P (U) 2378 East 1700 South Street, Salt Lake City UT 84108 **Int Chapl U Of Utah Salt Lake City UT 2002-** B Cambridge MA 1946 d Jesse & Mary. BA San Francisco St U 1974; MDiv EDS 1983. D 5/10/1986 Bp Otis Charles P 2/2/1987 Bp George Edmonds Bates. m 6/10/1989 Daniel Lee Andrus c 1. S Jas Epis Ch Midvale UT 2005; Dio Utah Salt Lake City UT 2002-2005, 1989-1998; Cathd Ch Of S Mk Salt Lake City UT 2001, 1990-1991; All SS Ch Salt Lake City UT 1988-1989; Chapl Westminster Coll Salt Lake City UT 1986-1998.

MOORE, Christopher Chamberlin (Pa) 51 Springhouse Ln, Media PA 19063 **Mem Brandywine Collaborative Mnstry 2016-; Credo Inst Inc. Memphis TN 2008-** B Summit NJ 1943 s John & Johanna. BA Muhlenberg Coll 1965; MA Drew U 1968; MDiv Andover Newton TS 1975. D 4/27/1974 P 12/21/1974 Bp Albert Wiencke Van Duzer. m 10/14/1978 Janice K Moore c 2. Instr Credo Inst Memphis TN 2008-2016; Deploy Dio Delaware Wilmington 2007-2008;

Assoc All SS and St Georges Ch Rehoboth Bch DE 2006-2013; R The Ch Of The H Comf Drexel Hill PA 1994-2006; Cmncatn, Deploy, Asst to the Bp Dio New Jersey Trenton NJ 1990-1994; R S Andr's Ch New Bedford MA 1984-1990; Dio San Diego San Diego CA 1981; Asst S Lk's Ch San Diego CA 1980-1984; S Alb's Epis Ch El Cajon CA 1979-1981; Asst Gr Ch Merchantville NJ 1974-1977. Auth, "Solitude: A Neglected Path to God," Cowley Press, 2001; Auth, "Opening the Cler Parachute," Abingdon Press, 1995; Auth, "What I Really Want To Do," CBP (Chalice), 1989; Auth, "Rel Column, 2002-2006," *The Pennsylvania Epis.* Soc of the Cincinnati 1994. Emmy Awd for Rel Broadcasting Natl Assn of Television Arts and Sciences, San Diego 1981. ccmsoulman@aol.com

MOORE, Clifford Allan (Wyo) P.O. Box 1086, #3 Valley Dr., Sundance WY 82729 B Concord CA 1936 s Walter & Edna. BA Chapman U 1958; MDiv SWTS 1997. D 6/11/1997 Bp Jerry Alban Lamb P 12/11/1997 Bp Bruce Caldwell. m 4/14/1957 Katherine JoAnne Moore c 4. Int S Lk's Epis Ch Buffalo WY 2010-2011; Dioc Coun Mem Dio Wyoming Casper 2004-2008, Mnstry Dvlp - SE Wy 2000-2003; All SS Ch Wheatland WY 1997-1999; Ch Of Our Sav Hartville WY 1997-1999. Knights hon Soc 1958.

MOORE III, Clint (Chi) 750 Pearson Street Apt 902, Des Plaines IL 60016 **Chapl Rainbow Hospice Pk Ridge IL 1994-** B Corpus Christi TX 1950 s Clint & Elinor. BA U So 1972; MDiv SWTS 1992; MA Loyola U Chicago 2001; PhD Loyola U Chicago 2008. D 6/13/1992 Bp James Barrow Brown P 12/19/1992 Bp Frank Tracy Griswold III. m 4/3/1988 Jane Peters Moore c 2. Clincl Ethics Fell Luth Gnrl Hosp Pk Ridge IL 1996-1998; Asst Trin Ch Highland Pk IL 1993-1995; Advoc Hlth Care Oak Brook IL 1993-1994; Pstr Fell Luth Gnrl Hosp Trauma Serv Pk Ridge IL 1993-1994. Assn for Death Educ and Counslg 2001; Bd Cert Chapl Assn Profsnl Chapl 1992. Fell in Thanatology Assn for Death Educ and Counslg 2005.

MOORE, Courtland Manning (FtW) 2341 Monticello Cir, Plano TX 75075 B Tulsa OK 1929 s Courtland & Mary. BA U of Oklahoma 1950; MDiv CDSP 1953; DMin SWTS 2000. D 6/21/1953 P 12/21/1953 Bp Chilton R Powell. m 10/10/1959 Barbara Williams c 3. P-in-c Ch Of The Annunc Lewisville TX 2011-2013; Ret P Asst Ch of the Annunc Lewisville TX 2001-2010; Ret/Int Mnstrs Dio Dallas Dallas TX 1994-2001; R S Alb's Epis Ch Arlington TX 1983-1994; Reg Refugee/Migration Field PBFWR New York NY 1980-1983; Chair - Prov VII Refugee Com Prov VII 1978-1983; Cn Dio Dallas Dallas TX 1971-1983, Dioc Transition Min 1974-1983; R S Mk's Ch Irving TX 1965-1971; R All SS Epis Ch Weatherford TX 1962-1965; R S Dav's Ch Oklahoma City OK 1955-1962; Vic S Mk's Ch Seminole OK 1953-1955; Dioc Transition Min Dio Ft Worth Ft Worth TX 2010-2013, Cn 2009. Hon Cn Dio Dallas 2002.

MOORE, Daniel T (Va) 553 Galleon Dr, Naples FL 34102 **Trin By The Cove Naples FL 2015-; COM, Presb Mem, 2016-present Dio SW Florida Parrish FL 2016-** B Falls Church VA 1982 s William & Sylvie. BA Jas Madison U 2005; MA U of Virginia 2009; MDiv Duke DS 2015. D 6/6/2015 Bp Shannon Sherwood Johnston P 12/6/2015 Bp Dabney Tyler Smith. m 12/30/2006 Kristin M Sandberg c 4. dmoore@trinitybythecove.com

MOORE, David (Oly) 116 Rossel Lane, PO Box 702, Eastsound WA 98245 B Denver CO 1947 s Glenn & Margaret. BA New Coll of Florida 1970; U of Edinburgh GB 1972; MDiv Sewanee: The U So, TS 1975; DMin U So & Van 1987. D 6/11/1975 P 12/27/1975 Bp Emerson Paul Haynes. m 7/31/1976 Sarah Tippett Moore c 4. Int R S Jn's Epis Ch Kula HI 2010-2012; P-in-c S Marg's Epis Ch Bellevue WA 2005-2007; Chapl Iolani Sch Honolulu HI 2002-2005; Chapl S Alb's Chap Honolulu HI 2002-2005; Assoc Dn Sewanee U So TS Sewanee TN 1996-2002; R S Jn's Ch Royal Oak MI 1992-1996; Bp's Cn for Educ & Prog Dio Utah Salt Lake City UT 1988-1992; R S Ptr's Ch La Grande OR 1981-1988; Assoc R S Bon Ch Sarasota FL 1975-1981.

MOORE, Delrece Lorraine (Colo) 3665 Overton St, Colorado Springs CO 80910 B 1945 D 11/13/2004 Bp Robert John O'Neill. m 9/30/1979 Luther Moore.

MOORE, Denise Maureen (Alb) D 5/30/2015 Bp William Howard Love.

MOORE, Diane Marquart (WLa) 211 Celeste Dr, New Iberia LA 70560 B Franklinton LA 1935 d Harold & Dorothy. LSU 1954; U of SW Louisiana 1990; Bishops Sch of Mnstry, Dio Wstrn Louisiana LA 2000. D 11/30/1999 Bp Robert Jefferson Hargrove Jr. c 2. Dir Inst Of Dracons 2004-2005; Mem Mem Sprtlty Cmsn 2002-2005; The Epis Ch Of The Epiph New Iberia LA 2001-2005; Dio Wstrn Louisiana Alexandria LA 2001-2004, COM 1998-2005, Long-R Plnng 1998-1999; Dir Solomon Hse 1998-2005; Trst Epis TS Of The SW Austin TX 1997-2005. Auth, "Everything Is Blue," Border Press, 2012; Auth, "Chant of Death," Pinyon Pub, 2010; Auth, "Avery Island," Acadian Hse, 2001; Auth, "Mart'S Quest," Blue Heron Publ, 1995; Auth, "Live Oak Gardens," Acadian Hse, 1993; Auth, "Their Adventurous Will: Profiles Of Memorable Louisiana Wmn," USL Acadiana Press, 1984; Auth, "Iran: In A Persian Mrkt," Type Co., 1980; Auth, "33 other books to date". Assoc., St. Mary's Cnvnt, Sewanee 2007; Healthy Kids Advsry Bd 1999-2005; Lifetime Mem Of Lafayette Publ Libr 2000; Lifetime Mem Of The GSA 2000; No Amer Soc Of Deacons 2000. St.Geo Epis Awd Natl Epis Ch 2007; Dist Gvnr Rotary Dist 5930 2004; Emmett Broussard Awd For Outreach Mnstrl Allnce Of Iberia Par 2002; Inspirational Poetry: Deep So Writer'S Conf 1967.

MOORE, Dominic C (Az) 533 E Main St, Lexington KY 40508 **S Matt's Ch Chandler AZ 2014-** B Woodruff SC 1983 s Lewis & Rosemary. BA Hobart and Wm Smith Colleges 2005; MDiv CDSP 2011. D 6/18/2011 Bp Prince Grenville Singh P 12/21/2011 Bp Chilton Richardson Knudsen. m 7/13/2004 Jesse W Moore. Cur Ch Of The Gd Shpd Lexington KY 2011-2014. dominiccmoore@gmail.com

MOORE, Donald Ernest (Eas) 3946 Rock Branch Rd, North Garden VA 22959 B 1947 D 6/15/1988 P 11/20/1988 Bp Daniel Lee Swenson. m 8/29/1970 Margaret Moore. Gr Ch Red Hill Va No Garden VA 1994-1998; Mcilhany Par Charlottesville VA 1994-1998; S Paul's Berlin MD 1989-1992.

MOORE III, Edward Fitzroy (Tex) 13515 King Cir, Cypress TX 77429 B Saint Louis MO 1927 s Edward & Helen. BA Drake U 1951; MDiv Drake U 1963; MEd U of Missouri 1967; Cert U of Missouri 1968. D 5/5/1990 P 12/15/1990 Bp William Augustus Jones Jr. m 6/6/1952 Patricia Ann Moore c 3. P-in-c S Alb's Epis Ch Fulton MO 1994-1999; Asst P Calv Ch Columbia MO 1991-1994.

MOORE, Frederick Ashbrook (NCal) 1675 Chester Ave, Arcata CA 95521 B New Haven CT 1950 s Frederick & Sally. D 5/27/2005 Bp Jerry Alban Lamb.

MOORE, Helen N (Ct) 24 Goodwin Circle, Hartford CT 06105 B Chattanooga TN 1942 d Frank & Jane. PhD Bos; BSW Regis 1982; MEd Harv 1984; MDiv Harvard DS 1987. D 5/30/1992 Bp David Elliot Johnson P 2/21/1993 Bp John Mc Gill Krumm. m 11/3/1973 Thomas Moore c 4. R S Paul's Ch Richmond VA 2006-2007; R Trin Epis Ch Southport CT 2003-2004; R S Lk's Par Darien CT 2002-2003; Dn Cathd Of S Jas Chicago IL 1999-2001; R S Hubert's Epis Ch Mentor OH 1997-1999; Assoc R Trin Ch Epis Boston MA 1992-1997.

MOORE, James Raymond (Haw) 911 N Marine Corps Dr, Tamuning GU 96913 Guam B St Paul MN 1942 s Samuel & Florence. BA Augsburg Coll 1966; MA U of Guam 1970. D 1/15/2009 Bp George Elden Packard. c 3.

MOORE, James Wesley (WMo) 18151 Dearborn St, Stilwell KS 66085 B Osawatomie KS 1939 s Wesley & Calista. Bethany Coll; DDS U of Missouri 1964; Cert Med Residency 1966. D 2/3/1996 Bp John Clark Buchanan. m 7/23/1960 Patricia Elaine Moore c 3. D The Epis Ch of S Jn the Div Tamuning GU 2009-2013; D S Andr's Ch Kansas City MO 1995-2014. Chapl Intl Ord of S Lk Physcn.

MOORE, Joseph I (NJ) 1 Water St, Pennsville NJ 08070 **Died 7/14/2016** B Philadelphia PA 1942 s Clarence & Anna. BA Ken 1964; MBA U of Pennsylvania 1966; MDiv SWTS 1975. D 6/14/1975 Bp Quintin Ebenezer Primo Jr P 12/13/1975 Bp James Winchester Montgomery. m 2/5/1966 Sharon P Moore. Ret 2005-2016; R S Geo's Ch Pennsville NJ 2001-2005; Int S Thos' Epis Ch Glassboro NJ 1999-2001; Int S Jn The Evang Ch Lansdowne PA 1997-1999; R Trin Epis Ch Ambler PA 1993-1996; R Incarn H Sacr Epis Ch Drexel Hill PA 1977-1993; Cur Chr Ch Waukegan IL 1975-1977.

MOORE, Judith (O) 7125 North Hills Blvd NE, Albuquerque NM 87109 B East Cleveland OH 1944 d Herbert & Alzada. BA Muskingum Coll 1966; MA Kent St U 1974; MDiv Colgate Rochester Crozer DS 1984; MDiv CRDS 1984. D 6/30/1984 P 2/1/1986 Bp James Russell Moodey. Lead Pstr Epis Shared Mnstry NW OH 1993-1997; Epis Shared Mnstry Of NW Ohio Sherwood OH 1988-1997; Vic Trin Ch Bryan OH 1988-1993; Int S Tim's Ch Macedonia OH 1987-1988; Gr Epis Ch Willoughby OH 1985-1987.

MOORE, Julia Gibert (Miss) 208 S Leflore Ave, Cleveland MS 38732 **Calv Epis Ch Cleveland MS 2006-** B Cleveland MS 1938 BA U of Mississippi 1958; MEd Delta St U 1982; EdD Delta St U 1984. D 4/29/2000 Bp Alfred Marble Jr P 12/21/2000 Bp Duncan Montgomery Gray III. m 4/19/1958 Dana Moore c 1. All SS Ch Inverness MS 2005-2007; Int Chap of the Cross Rolling Fork MS 2001-2002.

MOORE, Katherine JoAnne (Wyo) PO Box 246, Sundance WY 82729 **P Ch Of The Gd Shpd Sundance WY 2009-** B Yreka CA 1938 d Arnold & Muriel May. D 8/7/2008 P 2/14/2009 Bp Bruce Caldwell. m 4/14/1957 Clifford Allan Moore c 4. Assoc - CHS 2001; DOK 1990.

MOORE, Kathleen Mary (SwFla) **D Dio SW Florida Parrish FL 2016-** D 12/3/2016 Bp Dabney Tyler Smith.

MOORE, Linda Turman (NCal) 155-A Derek Dr, Susanville CA 96130 B Ross CA 1941 d Hobart & Frances. BA Ob 1963; MA Amer U 1973; MS U of Maryland 1991; MDiv VTS 1993. D 6/12/1993 Bp Ronald Hayward Haines P 3/1/1994 Bp Edward Cole Chalfant. c 2. The Epis Dio Nthrn California Sacramento CA 1997-2009; Gd Shpd Epis Ch Susanville CA 1996-2009; Asst Trin Epis Ch Lewiston ME 1993-1995.

MOORE, Lynda Foster (WNC) 138 Murdock Ave, Asheville NC 28801 **Ret 2003-** B Spartanburg SC 1939 d Hugh & Edith. BA MWC 1961; MA Appalachian St U 1971; Shalem Inst for Sprtl Formation 1987; MDiv VTS 1992. D 6/6/1992 P 12/12/1992 Bp Frank Kellogg Allan. m 7/9/2009 Dianna Gardner Hays c 1. R Ch Of The Mssh Murphy NC 2001-2003; Assoc Ch Of The H Cross Tryon NC 1995-2001; Int Epis Ch Of The H Sprt Cumming GA 1994, Asst 1992-1993.

599

M

MOORE, Margaret Jo (NCal) 516 Clayton Ave, El Cerrito CA 94530 **Assoc Ch Of The Incarn Santa Rosa CA 1996-; R H Wisdom Cmnty 1995-** B Santa Monica CA 1945 d Russell & Dorothy. RN S Lukes Sch of Nrsng 1966; BA California Sch for Deacons 1989; MDiv CDSP 1994. D 7/13/1994 P 1/19/1995 Bp Jerry Alban Lamb. m 6/27/1993 Ed Kahn c 2. S Patricks Ch Kenwood CA 1994-1995.

MOORE, Mark Ross (Ct) 85 Viscount Dr Unit 12c, Milford CT 06460 **Atty Legal Aid Mnstry Bridgeport CT 2007-** B New Haven CT 1949 s Luther & Marjorie. Alleg; BA Sthrn Connecticut St U 1973; MEd Bos 1977; MDiv EDS 1985; CSD Cntr for Rel Dvlpmt Cambridge MA 1986; JD Quinnipiac U 2004. D 6/4/1986 Bp John Bowen Coburn P 5/16/1987 Bp Douglas Edwin Theuner. c 1. P-in-c S Jn's Ch Sandy Hook CT 2008-2010; R Gr Epis Ch Trumbull CT 1999-2007; Int S Ptr's Epis Ch Milford CT 1998-1999; Int S Fran Ch Holden MA 1997-1998; Int Gr Ch N Attleboro MA 1996-1997; Chapl Mntl Hlth Mnstry Belmont MA 1994-1996; R Chr Ch In Lonsdale Lincoln RI 1992-1995; R S Jn The Evang Mansfield MA 1988-1992; R S Jn the Evang Mansfield MA 1988-1992; Cur S Jn's Ch Portsmouth NH 1986-1988. ACPE 1986; Soc of S Jn the Evang 1984. Outstanding Ldrshp Awd MA Assoc. for Retarded Citizens 1991.

MOORE, Mark T (Mil) ST PAUL'S EPISCOPAL CHURCH, 413 S 2ND ST, WATERTOWN WI 53094 **S Thos Of Cbury Ch Greendale WI 2012-** B 1952 s Thomas & Joyce. BS Cardinal Stritch U 1990; MDiv SWTS 2005; MTS SWTS 2007. D 6/3/2006 P 12/9/2006 Bp Bill Persell. m 9/17/2016 Sandra Elizabeth Moore c 2. R S Paul's Ch Watertown WI 2006-2012.

MOORE, Mary Diane (Oly) 7796 S Harrison Cir, Centennial CO 80122 B Saint Joseph MO 1942 d Charles & Thelma. BA U of Kansas 1964; Cert NW Missouri St U Maryville MO 1965; Bp Inst Diac Formation 1992; MA Regis U 1992; CSD S Thos Sem 1993. D 10/24/1992 Bp William Jerry Winterrowd. m 6/4/1966 Arthur Howard Moore c 3. Asst S Matt's Parker CO 2000-2001; Coordntr Of Vol - Gc Dio Colorado Denver CO 1998-2000, 1996-2000, Adm Liaison Com 1994-1998, D 2002-; D Metro So Dnry 1993-1998; Gd Shpd Epis Ch Centennial CO 1993. Auth, "Journey Into The Cross," *Mary'S Hope*, 2002; Auth, "Healing For Wounded Souls," *Mary'S Hope*, 2002; Auth, "Lament And Transitions," *Wmn Uncommon Prayers*, Morehouse Pub, 2000; Auth, "Easter-ing And Sprt Stroke," *Wmn Uncommon Prayers*, Morehouse Pub, 2000; Auth, "Pistachio Chld," *Wmn Uncommon Prayers*, Morehouse Pub, 2000; Auth, "Col-lect The Silence," *Prisms Of The Soul*, Morehouse, 1996. NAAD 1992; Sprtl Directory Intl 1996.

MOORE, Mary Navarre (ETenn) 715 E Brow Rd, Lookout Mountain TN 37350 B Chattanooga TN 1949 d Carl & Laura. BA Emory U 1971; CPA St of Tennessee 1981; MDiv Candler TS Emory U 2000. D 1/23/1999 Bp Robert Gould Tharp P 2/3/2001 Bp Charles Glenn VonRosenberg. m 9/30/1995 Walter Moore c 1. Asst Ch Of The Gd Shpd Lookout Mtn TN 2001-2007.

MOORE, Matthew Edward (LI) 139 Saint Johns Pl, Brooklyn NY 11217 B Pasadena CA 1958 s Richard & Mabel. AB U CA 1981; MA San Francisco St Unviersity 1985; MA U Chi 1990; PhD U IL at Chicago 2000. D 1/14/2017 Bp Lawrence C Provenzano. m 7/13/2013 Thomas Christopher Muller.

MOORE, Melvin Leon (Va) 219 Cornwallis Ave, Locust Grove VA 22508 **Chapl/ EMT Lake of The Woods Vol. Rescue Squad 2007-** B Oklahoma City OK 1938 s Ovie & Lucille. BS U of Oklahoma 1962; MEA GW 1969; MDiv VTS 1995. D 11/27/1995 Bp Frank Clayton Matthews P 6/13/1996 Bp Peter J Lee. m 9/4/1981 Nancy G Moore c 4. Vic Emm Ch Rapidan VA 2002; Asst R S Matt's Ch Richmond VA 1995-2002.

MOORE, Michael D (Fla) **Chapl Cmnty Hospice NE Florida 2011-** D 6/12/2005 P 2/26/2006 Bp J Neil Alexander.

MOORE, Michael Osborn (NH) 7321 Brad St, Falls Church VA 22042 **P Assoc S Lk's Ch Alexandria VA 2008-, Int 1986-1987** B Detroit MI 1935 s Edward & Mary. BA Colg 1958; MDiv VTS 1965. D 6/12/1965 Bp Beverley D Tucker P 2/24/1966 Bp Nelson Marigold Burroughs. m 6/20/1959 Patricia Hill Moore. Assoc S Lk's Epis Ch Alexandria VA 2003-2008; Int Assoc R S Lk's Epis Ch Alexandria VA 2001-2003; Int Ch of Our Redeem Aldie VA 2000-2001; P-in-c S Dunst's Epis Ch Beth MD 1998-1999; S Steph's Epis Ch Espanola NM 1997-2001, 1991-1996, 1985-1990; S Jn's Ch Chevy Chase MD 1997-1998; P-in-c S Jn's Norwood Par Chevy Chase MD 1997-1998; Int Assoc R Ch Of The Gd Shpd Burke VA 1995-1997; S Bede's Epis Ch Santa Fe NM 1995-1997; Int S Chris's Ch Springfield VA 1992-1994; Int All Hallows Par So River Edgewater MD 1991-1992; P-in-c S Geo's Ch Washington DC 1990-1991; S Paul's Peace Ch Las Vegas NM 1989-1991, 1976-1988; Int Trin Ch Manassas VA 1988-1990; S Paul's Rock Creek Washington DC 1987-1988; P-in-c S Paul's Rock Creek Par DC 1987-1988; R S Andr's Epis Ch Contoocook NH 1985-1986; Trin On The Hill Epis Ch Los Alamos NM 1983-1984; S Patricks Ch Falls Ch VA 1970-1985; R S Pat's Epis Ch Falls Ch VA 1970-1984; Chapl Randoph-Macon Womens' Coll Lynchburg VA 1968-1970; S Jn's Ch Lynchburg VA 1968-1970; Asst R Ch of Our Sav Akron OH 1965-1968.

MOORE, Muriel Elizabeth (WNC) 355 Red Oak Trl, Boone NC 28607 **Died 1/2/2016** B Montreal QC CA 1934 d Robert & Edna. Appalachian St U; BA Sir Geo Wms Montreal CA 1953. D 12/18/1999 Bp Bob Johnson. m 7/31/1981 James Grant Moore c 3. Ch Of The H Cross Valle Crucis NC 1993-2016. DOK; Ord of S Lk; OHC.

MOORE, Nancy Lee (Me) 403 Harrison Rd, Norway ME 04268 **Chr Ch Norway ME 2014-** B Brunswick ME 1967 d George & Ada. BA Mid 1989; MDiv Bos TS 2000. D 6/23/2001 P 1/19/2002 Bp Chilton Richardson Knudsen. Dpr Excellence Coordntr Dio Maine Portland ME 2003-2007; Vic Ch Of The Mssh Dexter ME 2002-2005; S Aug's Epis Ch Dovr Foxcroft ME 2001-2014; Vic S Johns Epis Ch Brownville ME 2001-2014; Exec Dir Trin Epis Ch Lewiston ME 2001-2003.

MOORE, Orral Margarite (Neb) 714 N 129th Plz, Omaha NE 68154 B Newark NJ 1933 d Nicholas & Orral. D 5/31/1996 Bp James Edward Krotz. m 4/23/1955 Frank Martin Murphy. D All SS Epis Ch Omaha NE 1996-2010.

MOORE, Pamela Andrea (NCal) Po Box 4791, Santa Rosa CA 95402 **D Ch Of The Incarn Santa Rosa CA 2001-; S Andr's In The Redwoods Monte Rio CA 2001-** B San Diego CA 1951 d Charles & Camilla. BA Sch for Deacons; MA CUNY 1990. D 9/16/2001 Bp Jerry Alban Lamb.

MOORE, Patricia Elaine (NCal) 342 Wilson St, Petaluma CA 94952 **The Bp's Ranch Healdsburg CA 2009-, Chapl 2009-** B New Orleans LA 1941 d Daniel & Helen. BA Mid 1963; MS NWU 1964; MA Claremont TS 1981; PhD U of New Mex 2000. D 11/19/1982 P 6/28/1986 Bp Charles Brinkley Morton. c 2. S Andr's In The Redwoods Monte Rio CA 2002; Ch Of The Incarn Santa Rosa CA 2000-2007; Asstg P S Bede's Epis Ch Santa Fe NM 1996-1999; All Souls' Epis Ch San Diego CA 1989-1993; Epis Cmnty Serv Natl City CA 1989-1990; Chapl Epis Cmnty Serv San Diego CA 1986-1990; Dio San Diego San Diego CA 1985-1988; D S Dav's Epis Ch San Diego CA 1982-1985. patmasrev@gmail.com

MOORE, Paul R (RG) Church Of The Good Shepherd, PO Box 2795, Silver City NM 88062 **R Ch Of The Gd Shpd Silver City NM 2012-** B Quito EC 1957 Taylor U; MIA Intl Sch for Intl Trng 1985; Seminario Ecuatoriano de Teologia Epis EC 1991; MSF Sem of the SW 2012. D 5/19/1990 Bp Adrian Delio Caceres-Villavicencio P 11/16/1991 Bp Jose Neptali Larrea-Moreno. m 6/3/1978 Karisse Ann Cone c 3. R S Chris's Ch Killeen TX 2000-2012, Dioc Curs Sec Sprtl Advsr 2009-2011; R Gr Ch Weslaco TX 1992-2000; P-in-c Adv-S Nich Ch Quito 1991-1992; P-in-c Ch Of Our Sav Dallas TX 1983-1991; Cross Cultural Trnr and Cmnty Dvlpmt Spec Wycliffe Bible Translators 1983-1991; Multicultural Mnstry Com Dio W Texas 1996-1999; Stwdshp of Creation Dio W Texas 1995-1998. Auth, "Fruits of the Sprt in Practical Life/Frutos del Espíritu en la Vida Práctica," *Fruits of the Sprt in Practical Life/Frutos del Espíritu en la Vida Práctica*, Stillpoint by the Sea, San Antonio, TX, 2008. Soc for Intercultural Educ, Trng and Resrch 1986-1990. padrequiteno@gmail.com

MOORE JR, Ralph M (Me) 191 West Meadow Rd., Rockland ME 04841 **Trst, Fac The Watershed Sch Camden Maine 2003-; Founding Trst, Tchr The Watershed Sch Rockland Maine 2001-** B Los Angeles CA 1936 s Ralph & Frankie. BA Stan 1957; MDiv UTS 1961; DMin EDS 1995. D 12/21/1972 P 5/9/1973 Bp Robert Lionne DeWitt. m 11/30/1985 Bridget Gallagher Buck c 3. R S Ptr's Ch Rockland ME 1996-2007; Actg Dn of Students and Cmnty Life EDS Cambridge MA 1995-1996; P-in-c All SS Ch Stoneham MA 1992-1995; Mssy Exec Coun Appointees New York NY 1987-1991; El Buen Pstr, San Jose Dio Costa Rica San Jose 1987-1990; Vic, St. Mk's, Bluefields Dio Nicaragua New York NY 1986-1987; Asst Ch Of S Mart-In-The-Fields Philadelphia PA 1984-1986; P-in-c S Mary's Ch Hamilton Vill Philadelphia PA 1976, Assoc 1973-1983; Stff and Exec Dir The Chr Assn at the U of Pennsylvania 1973-1985; Dir of Film Prog Walnut St Theatre Philadelphia PA 1971-1973; Secy for Yth Prog UCC Bd for Homeland Mnstrs Philadelphia PA 1965-1970; Pstr Highland Untd Ch of Chr Portland Oregon 1961-1965; Pstr Knight Cmnty (UCC) Ch Grand View Idsho 1959-1960. Auth, "The Jesus Deck," US Game Systems, 1973; Auth, "In Celebration," *Untd Ch Resources*, Untd Ch Press, 1970; Auth, "Breakout," *Yth Mnstry Resources*, Friendship Press, 1968.

MOORE, Richard Wayne (La) 4500 Lake Borgne Ave, Metairie LA 70006 B Washington DC 1947 s Harry & Lois. AA Florida Jr Coll 1973; BA U of No Florida 1974; MDiv VTS 1977; MS Valdosta St U 1984. D 6/12/1977 P 12/1/1977 Bp Frank S Cerveny. m 6/29/1996 Karen Moore c 3. R S Phil's Ch New Orleans LA 1997-2003; Trin Epis Ch Baton Rouge LA 1993-1997; Chapl S Mart's Epis Sch Metairie LA 1990-1995; S Mart's Epis Sch Metairie LA 1990-1993; R Trin Ch Statesboro GA 1988-1990; Dioc Coordntr Of Higher Educ In Ga 1986-1988; Dio Georgia Savannah GA 1986-1988; Asst R Chr Ch Valdosta GA 1984-1986; Chapl Valdosta St Coll 1984-1986; Asst R Frederick Par Winchester VA 1979-1984; Vic S Paul's On-The-Hill Winchester VA 1979-1984; Chr Epis Ch Winchester VA 1979-1980; Asst R H Comf Epis Ch Tallahassee FL 1977-1979.

MOORE, Robert (Cal) 4230 Langland St, Cincinnati OH 45223 B Cleveland OH 1937 s Robert & Margaret. AA El Camino Coll 1964; BS California St U Long Bch 1967; California St U Hayward CA 1969; MDiv CDSP 1977. D 11/25/1978 P 11/3/1979 Bp Chauncie Kilmer Myers. m 2/16/1979 Bavi Edna Rivera c 3. Ch Of The H Trin Richmond CA 2003-2004; R S Anselm's Epis Ch Lafayette CA 1992-1997; Dio El Camino Real Salinas CA 1986-1992; S Geo's Ch Sali-

M

nas CA 1984-1987; St Johns Epis Ch Ross CA 1979-2003; Pstr Epis Dio San Joaquin Modesto CA 2008. rbyronmoore@gmail.com

MOORE, Robert Allen (Minn) 19 Lea Road, Whittle-le-Woods, Chorley, Lancs PR6-7PF Great Britain (UK) **Ret 1997-** B San Jose CA 1932 s Byron & Rosamond. BA U Pac 1954; Lon GB 1955; STB Bos 1958; STM Bos 1959. D 2/10/1963 Bp Hamilton Hyde Kellogg P 6/1/1963 Bp Philip Frederick McNairy. m 3/17/2006 Roger Stubbings c 1. Serv Ch of Engl 1978-1997; Chapl Anoka Cnty Police 1975-1980; R Trin Ch Anoka MN 1971-1980; Chapl (Lieutenant Cmdr) US Navy 1968-1971; Chapl US Naval Reserve 1967-1988; P-in-c Emm Ch Adams NY 1964-1968; Zion Ch Pierrepont Manor NY 1964-1968; Cur S Jn In The Wilderness S Paul MN 1963-1964, 1957-1962; Vic S Tim's Forest Lake MN 1963-1964; Serv Methodist Ch 1957-1962; Stwdshp Consult Dio Minnesota Minneapolis MN 1979-1980, Reg Dn 1977-1978.

MOORE, Robert Joseph (Tex) 3285 Park Falls Ct., League City TX 77573 **S Mich's Ch La Marque TX 2014-; Ret 2005-; still Ret but also Asst Gd Shpd Epis Ch 1207 Winding Way Friendswood 2005-** B Galveston,TX 1950 s Darwin & Jane. BA U So 1972; MDiv Epis TS of the SW 1975; DMin Sewanee: The U So, TS 1993. D 6/17/1975 Bp Scott Field Bailey P 6/17/1976 Bp James Milton Richardson. m 6/18/1983 Nancy Elizabeth Moore c 2. Assoc Ch Of The Gd Shpd Friendswood TX 2005-2014; R S Barth's Ch Hempstead TX 1996-2005, Int R 1995; Chapl The U of Houston Houston TX 1987-1995; Vic Ch Of The Resurr Houston TX 1984-1995; Assoc S Chris's Ch Houston TX 1979-1984; The Great Cmsn Fndt Houston TX 1975-1996; Chapl Prairie View A&M U Prairie View TX 1975-1979; S Fran Of Assisi Epis Prairie View TX 1975-1979; S Paul's Ch Katy TX 1975-1977. Auth, *Narrative Hist of the Black Epis Ch in the Dio Texas*, 1993.

MOORE JR, Robert Raymond (SwVa) 110 Clinton Avenue, Big Stone Gap VA 24219 **Vic Chr Epis Ch Big Stone Gap VA 1993-** B Toronto ON CA 1948 s Robert & Ellenor. Rhodes Coll; BS U of Tennessee 1970; MS U of Memphis 1974. D 10/20/1993 P 6/1/1994 Bp A(rthur) Heath Light. m 12/16/1972 Harriet Ingram.

MOORE, Robin Adair (Oly) Po Box 584, Grapeview WA 98546 B Bend OR 1938 d Charles & Frances. Willamette U; BA U of Washington 1962; MA Portland St U 1972; MDiv EDS 1985; ThM Weston Jesuit TS 1985. D 6/15/1985 P 5/24/1986 Bp Herbert Alcorn Donovan Jr. m 4/12/1969 Richard R Moore c 2. Dio Olympia Seattle 1994-2002; S Hugh Of Lincoln Allyn WA 1988-1999; Vic S Nich Ch Tahuya WA 1988-1993; S Mk's Epis Ch Jonesboro AR 1986-1988; Dio Arkansas Little Rock AR 1985-1986. Cath Fllshp; Living Stones; RWF.

MOORE, Rodney Allen (Colo) 221 S Salem Ct, Aurora CO 80012 B Stromsburg NE 1942 s Kenneth & Pauline. BS U of Nebraska 1963; MEd U of Nebraska 1970; MDiv Nash 1975; DMin SWTS 2003. D 5/30/1975 Bp Robert Patrick Varley P 12/1/1975 Bp George T Masuda. m 8/19/1967 Mary Helen Bucknell c 2. Int Chr Epis Ch Denver CO 2012-2013; Vic Ch Of The H Comf Broomfield CO 2007-2010; P-in-c S Steph's Epis Ch Aurora CO 2006-2007, R 1986-2006; Dio Colorado Denver CO 1998-2006, Chair Yth Cmsn 1989-1997, Com on Par Redevelopment 2005-2013, Dn of the Metro E Dnry 1993-1996; EFM Mentor 1982-2000; R S Alb's Epis Ch Mc Cook NE 1979-1986; R S Barn Ch Omaha NE 1978-1979; Vic S Eliz's Ch Holdrege NE 1975-1978; Bd Dir Living the Gd News 1992-1993; Bd the Trin Ranch Dio Nebraska Omaha NE 1987-1994, Pres of the Stndg Com 1986, Stndg Com 1985-1987, Pres of the Holdredge Mnstrl Assn 1985-1986, Dept of Mssn 1983-1985, Dept of Mssn 1983-1984, Alt Dep GC 1982-1985, Eccl Crt 1982-1984, Pres of the Holdredge Mnstrl Assn 1982-1983, Plnng Strtgy Cmsn 1981-1983, Vice-Chair on the Exec Coun 1981-1983, Chair Yth Cmsn 1980-1986, Chair Yth Cmsn 1980-1982, Cmsn on Ch Growth 1978-1979, Liturg Cmsn 1978-1979, Exec Coun 1977.

MOORE, Stephen Edward (Oly) 350 sunset ave n, Edmonds WA 98020 **Vic All SS Ch Bellevue WA 1997-** B Tacoma WA 1946 d Edward & Jean. BA WA SU 1973; MA WA SU 1974; JD U of Washington 1977; Dplma Dioc TS Olympia 1979; Dioc TS Olympia 1979; U So 1996. D 6/27/1992 P 6/12/1993 Bp Vincent Waydell Warner. m 2/14/1970 Deanna Leslie Dunn c 2. Chapl GBEC 2003-2015; Cler Dep GC 2000-2012; Int S Jn The Bapt Epis Ch Seattle WA 1995-1996; Assoc Trin Par Seattle WA 1993-1995. Auth, "Ch Words: Origin & Meaning," Forw Mvmt Press, 1996. Angl Soc 1992; Cler Assn Of The Dio Olympia 1992.

MOORE, Steven Paul (CNY) St Mary's Episcopal Church, 1917 3rd St, Napa CA 94559 B Glens Falls NY 1976 s Paul & Joanne. Cert of Angl Stds CDSP 2012. Rec 10/30/2012 as Priest Bp Barry Leigh Beisner. m 7/2/2011 Erin Rose Moore. Asst S Mary's Epis Ch Napa CA 2012-2014.

MOORE, Theodore Edward (NJ) 17 Cray Ter., Fanwood NJ 07023 **S Eliz's Ch Eliz NJ 2011-; Gr Epis Ch Plainfield NJ 2005-** B Florence SC 1936 s Theodore & Catherine. BS Morehouse Coll 1957; MBA Ford 1972. D 6/11/2005 Bp George Edward Councell. m 6/2/2007 Karen Frances Moore c 3.

MOORE JR, Tillman Marion (Ak) 2316 Via Carrillo, Palos Verdes Estates CA 90274 **Ret 1993-** B Amarillo TX 1927 s Tillman & Velma. BS Iowa St U 1949; MD Washington U 1953. D 6/21/1967 P 8/1/1968 Bp William Jones Gordon Jr. m 12/22/1950 Shirley Louise Moore. Asst S Fran' Par Palos Verdes Estates CA 1970-1988; Asst S Thos' Mssn Hacienda Hgts CA 1967-1970. Auth, "Ak

Churchmen". Natl Assn For The Self- Supporting Active Mnstry, Fllshp S Jas Of Jerusalem, Fllshp S Alb & S Sergius.

MOORE, Trenton Scott (Wyo) **Assoc Ch Of Our Sav Jacksonville FL 2016-; S Jn's Epis Ch Jackson WY 2014-** D 10/2/2014 P 7/11/2015 Bp John Smylie.

MOORE, Vassilia Shelton (SwFla) 16500 Gulf Blvd Apt 755, North Redington Beach FL 33708 B New York NY 1941 d Wilson & Vassilia. BS Col 1966; MDiv Sewanee: The U So, TS 1991. D 6/13/1992 Bp Rogers Sanders Harris P 1/1/1993 Bp David Reed. Asst Chr Epis Ch Bowling Green KY 1992-1993. S Mary Cnvnt.

MOORE JR, William Henry (Spr) 141 Candlewood Dr, Wallace NC 28466 B Natchez MS 1926 s William & Hazel. Epis Dio Sthrn Ohio 1990; Methodist TS 1990. D 11/19/1990 P Herbert Thompson Jr P 6/29/2002 Bp Peter Hess Beckwith. m 6/29/1981 Jacque O Moore. Archd Dio Springfield Springfield IL 1992-2003; D-In-C S Jn's Ch Columbus OH 1990-1992. Auth, "Mystagouge"; Auth, "Links-Stwdshp"; Auth, "Linked To The Body Of Chr". Hon Cn Cathd Ch of St. Paul 2004; S Steph Awd Naad 2000; One O'clock Awd No Texas U 1978; Outstanding Cadet Awd Gulf Coast Mltry Acad 1942.

MOORE JR, W Taylor (Miss) 22002 Halliburton Cv, Oxford MS 38655 B Bluefield WV 1949 s Walter & Betty. Phillips Exeter Acad 1967; BA Duke 1971; MDiv UTS 1974; DMin SWTS 2000. D 10/23/1977 P 5/7/1978 Bp David Keller Leighton Sr. m 7/22/1978 Nancy C Deane c 2. R S Ptr's Ch Oxford MS 2001-2015; R S Chris's By-The River Gates Mills OH 1990-2001; R Chr Epis Ch Spotsylvania VA 1983-1990; Epis Chapl Goucher Coll Towson St U Baltimore MD 1979-1982; Asst R Trin Ch Towson MD 1979-1982; Gr Ch Elkridge MD 1978-1979.

MOOREHEAD, Constance Fay Peek (Oly) 3030 S Findlay St, Seattle WA 98108 **Died 6/9/2017** B Des Moines IA 1926 d Charles & Ethel. Drake U; Seattle U 1957; Dio Olympia Dioc TS 1997. D 6/28/1997 Bp Vincent Waydell Warner. c 2. D S Clem's Epis Ch Seattle WA 1997-2013. Anti-racism Com Chair 2003; Dep 2006; EUC Bd Mem 2003.

MOOREHEAD, Kate Bingham (Fla) 240 N Belmont St, Wichita KS 67208 **Dn S Jn's Cathd Jacksonville FL 2009-** B New Haven CT 1970 d Timothy & Susan. D 6/14/1997 P 2/1/1998 Bp Clarence Nicholas Coleridge. m 8/13/1994 James D Moorehead c 3. R S Jas Ch Wichita KS 2003-2009; R S Marg's Epis Ch Boiling Spgs SC 1999-2003; St Johns Ch W Hartford CT 1997-1999.

MOORE-LEVESQUE, Christa Marie (Roch) 2000 Highland Ave, Rochester NY 14618 **Cur S Thos Epis Ch Rochester NY 2015-** B Framingham MA 1988 d Wayne & Melanie. M.Div Duke DS; BA Wm Smith 2011; MA Hobart and Wm Smith Colleges 2012. D 5/13/2015 P 11/21/2015 Bp Prince Grenville Singh. m 4/16/2016 John Moore. christa@stthomasrochester.org

MOORER, Dawson Delayne (O) 281 E 244th St Apt D5, Euclid OH 44123 B Tulsa OK 1954 s Darwin & Margaret. Baylor U 1973; BA NWU 1976; MS U of Texas 1980; MDiv SWTS 1989. D 6/17/1989 P 12/1/1989 Bp Frank Tracy Griswold III. m 6/21/1980 Sheila Elizabeth McGinn c 2. Calv Ch Sandusky OH 2002-2004; P-in-c No Cntrl Epis Shared Mnstry Port Clinton OH 2002-2004; S Thos' Epis Ch Port Clinton OH 2002-2004; P-in-c Zion Ch Monroeville OH 2002-2004; Mssn In Charge S Paul Epis Ch Norwalk OH 2001-2004; Int R S Andr's Ch Cleveland OH 2001-2002; R Ch Of The Epiph Euclid OH 1998-2000; Int R S Jas Epis Ch Wooster OH 1996-1997; Int R Chr Ch Oberlin OH 1995-1996; S Mk's Ch Cleveland OH 1993-1994; Assoc; Int R The Epis Ch Of S Jas The Less Northfield IL 1991-1992; Asst To Dn Cathd Of S Jas Chicago IL 1989-1991. SBL.

MOORHEAD, Bill (Ia) 107 Washington Park Rd, Iowa City IA 52245 **P Assoc Trin Ch Iowa City IA 1989-** B Fort Wayne IN 1942 s Donald & Ruth. AB Harv 1963; MDiv Nash 1966; MA U of Iowa 1999. D 3/5/1966 P 9/10/1966 Bp Donald H V Hallock. m 5/9/1971 Wendy N Nurnberg c 2. Int Chapl, Univ of Iowa Dio Iowa Des Moines IA 1990-1992; R S Jas Epis Ch Oskaloosa IA 1980-1989; R Chr Ch Cntrl City NE 1977-1980; P-in-c S Christophers Ch Cozad NE 1976-1977; Vic S Pauls Epis Ch Arapahoe NE 1973-1977; Cur S Jas Ch Wichita KS 1971-1973; Cur Chr Ch Par La Crosse WI 1971; Novc OHC W Pk NY 1968-1971; Vic S Barth's Ch Pewaukee WI 1966-1968.

MOOTE, Kimberly Ann (NMich) E9494 Maple St, Munising MI 49862 **D S Jn's Ch Munising MI 1996-** B Kremling CO 1957 d Edward & Janelle. D 3/6/1996 Bp Thomas Kreider Ray. m 7/15/1978 Gordon Moote c 3.

MOQUETE, Clemencia Rafaela (NY) 821 Central Trinity Avenue, Bronx NY 10456 B DO 1952 d Rafael & Gladys. D 6/8/1991 P 12/1/1991 Bp Richard Frank Grein. Mid Hudson Catskill Rural and Migrant Min Poughkeepsie NY 1998; Dio New York New York NY 1996-1998; Hisp Mnstry New York NY 1992-1995.

MORALES, Carlton Owen (NC) Po Box 21011, Greensboro NC 27420 **Stff Chapl Moses Cone Hosp Greensboro NC 1985-** B JM 1928 s Henry & Zerita. BA Guilford Coll; S Peters Theol Coll JM 1958; S Georges Coll Jerusalem IL 1978; Duke 1982; VTS 1988. D 6/1/1957 P 6/14/1958 Bp The Bishop Of Jamaica. m 12/1/1948 Louise Lamb c 3. Ch Of The Redeem Greensboro NC 1966-1999; Dio No Carolina Raleigh NC 1966-1976. Soc Of S Jn The Evang.

M

MORALES, Evelyn Ruth (NC) 2009 Hickswood Rd, High Point NC 27265 B San Diego CA 1942 d Raoul & Belia. BA U CA 1969; MEd U NC 1973. D 6/3/2006 Bp Michael B Curry. c 3.

MORALES JR, Frank R (NY) 3115 S High St, Arlington VA 22202 **All Souls Ch New York NY 2015-; Assoc Cmnty Of Mnstry Of Chr Bronx NY 1976-** B New York NY 1949 s Frank & Betty. D 9/5/1976 Bp Paul Moore Jr P 3/1/1977 Bp Harold Louis Wright. m 6/14/1971 Leslie Ruth Morales. S Barn Ch Ardsley NY 2012; Trin Ch Of Morrisania Bronx NY 1993; S Ann's Ch Of Morrisania Bronx NY 1980-1982; Chr Ch Poughkeepsie NY 1976-1979.

MORALES, Loyda E (NY) 347 Chiquita Court, Kissimmee FL 34758 **Dio New York New York NY 2005-, COM 2009-2013, Congrl Spprt Plan 2007-2013, Epis Chars 2006-2008** B San Juan PUERTO RICO 1960 d Roberto & Irma. BA U of Puerto Rico 1984; MA U of Puerto Rico 1992; MDiv GTS 2005. D 3/19/2005 P 9/17/2005 Bp Mark Sean Sisk. Vic The Ch Of S Steph Staten Island NY 2005-2013; Bishops Vic The Ch of St Steph Staten Island NY 2005-2013; Supvsr, Methods And Procedures Banco Popular Of No Amer New York NY 2001-2004.

MORALES, Roberto (Va) B 1933 m 1/3/1958 Irma Rodriguez c 4. San Jose Ch Arlington VA 1991-2000; La Iglesia De Cristo Rey Arlington VA 1991-1994; S Ann's Ch Of Morrisania Bronx NY 1986-1990; Dio Puerto Rico Trujillo Alto PR 1977-1979.

MORALES COLON, Francisco Javier (PR) **Dio Puerto Rico Trujillo Alto PR 2010-** B Arroyo PR 1977 s Francisco & Carmen. D 11/22/2009 P 8/15/2010 Bp David Andres Alvarez-Velazquez.

MORALES GAVIRIA, Jose Ricardo (Colom) Barrio Las Delicias, El Bagne, Antioquia Colombia **Vic Annunc 1987-** B Libano Talima CO 1942 s Jose & Soledad. D 2/11/1986 P 1/1/1987 Bp Bernardo Merino-Botero. Iglesia Epis En Colombia Bogota 1987-2007.

✠ **MORALES MALDONADO, The Rt Rev Rafael L** (PR) Iglesia Episcopal Puetorriquene, PO Box 902, Saint Just PR 00978 Puerto Rico **Dioc Bp Dio Puerto Rico Trujillo Alto PR 2017-, 2012-2017** B Toa Alta PR 1963 s Ramon & Carmen. MEd Universidad de Puerto Rico 1989; Cert. in Angl Stds San Pedro y San Pablo Sem Trujillo Allo Puerto Rico 2010. Rec 10/27/2010 as Deacon Bp David Andres Alvarez-Velazquez Con 7/22/2017 for PR. m 6/9/2007 Vanessa Marrero. obisporafael@episcopalpr.org

MORALES-VEGA, Emilia (PR) D10 Calle Pomarrosa, Guaynabo PR 00969 **Cn Catedral San Juan Bautista Santurce PR 1995-** B 1946 d Fernando & Josefina. Maestria Seminario Divinidad Evangelico de Puerto Rico; Maestria Seminario Other; MA U of Puerto Rico. c 3. Dio Puerto Rico Trujillo Alto PR 2004-2013, P 1993-2003; Vic Mision San Esteban Guaynabo PR 1993-2011; Directora Directora Centro Pre-Escolar La Encarnacion 1992-1995; D Parroquia La Encarnacion Hato Rey PR 1990-1991; Tchr Dept of Educ in PR 1968-1992. Founders Awd Integrity Maine 2013; Bd Mem of the Year Preble St 2013; Maestria en Divinidad mcl Seminario Evangelico de Puerto Rico 1997; Bachillerato mcl Universidad de Puerto Rico 1968.

MORAN, John Jay (Mont) 2415 Hauser Blvd, Helena MT 59601 **D S Ptr's Cathd Helena MT 1999-** B Fort Meade SD 1939 D 10/23/1999 Bp Charles I Jones III. m 3/24/1961 Sharron Kay O'Neill c 2.

✠ **MORANTE-ESPANA, The Rt Rev Terencio Alfredo** (EcuL) Ulloa 213 Y Carrion, Box 17-0-353-A, Quito Ecuador **Bp Of Ecuador Litoral Dio Ecuador Guayaquil 1994-, Bp of Ecuador Litoral 1986-** B Vinces Los Rios EC 1946 s Vicente & Dolores. Seminario Alianza Guayaquil 1971; Seminario Alianza Guayaquil 1971. D 5/18/1975 P 4/14/1976 Bp Adrian Delio Caceres-Villavicencio Con 10/12/1994 for EcuC. m 8/15/1977 Olga De Jesus Arevalo Morante c 1. Bp Iglesia Cristo Rey Guayaquil Gu 1994-2000; Vic Iglesia Santiago Apostolo Enrique Drouet Peninsula 1988-1994; Vic Iglesia Sagrada Familia Cuenca 1975-1988; Iglesia Epis Del Ecuador Quito 1975-1985.

MORA VILLEGA, Carlos Donato (EcuL) Amarilis Fuentes 603 Calle D Ave Trujillo, Guayaquil Ecuador **Litoral Dio Ecuador Guayaquil 2015-** B 1958 Centro Teologico San Patricio; Centro Teologico San Patricio; cio. D 10/11/2014 Bp Terencio Alfredo Morante-Espana. m 8/14/1981 Amelia Cruz Barzola Lozano c 2.

MORCK, Christopher Robert (Mass) Grace Episcopal Church, 133 School St, New Bedford MA 02740 **R Gr Ch New Bedford MA 2015-, P-in-c 2012-2015** B Huntingdon PA 1975 s Robert & Patricia. BA Wheaton Coll 1997; MA Boston Coll 2006. D 5/30/2009 Bp Wilfrido Ramos-Orench P 10/2/2010 Bp Luis Fernando Ruiz Restrepo. m 6/1/1997 Patricia Jean Ohnsorg Morck c 2. Dom And Frgn Mssy Soc- Epis Ch Cntr New York NY 2009-2012; Exec Coun Appointees New York NY 2009-2012.

MORE, James Edward (Ida) 645 Liberty Ln, Emmett ID 83617 **Died 9/17/2016** B Denver CO 1924 s James & Helen. BA U of Wyoming 1965; BD VTS 1968. D 6/19/1968 P 12/1/1968 Bp James W Hunter. m 9/6/1947 Harriet Loine Lowe c 1. R S Mary's Ch Emmett ID 1981-1986; Assoc S Jas Ch Payette ID 1975-1981; S Andr's Epis Ch Sedona AZ 1972-1975; Assoc Vic S Dav's Epis Page AZ 1972-1975; Vic Chr Ch - Epis Newcastle WY 1970-1972; Vic S Jn The Bapt Ch Glendo WY 1969-1970; R All SS Ch Wheatland WY 1968-1970.

MOREAU, Joseph Raoul (LI) 15524 90th Ave, Jamaica NY 11432 B Gorman Commune HT 1922 s Dorcius & Marie. ETSBH 1948; Epis TS 1948. D 7/1/1948 P 7/1/1949 Bp Charles Alfred Voegeli. m 7/4/1950 Marie Therese Simone Moreau. Asst Cathd S Trin Port-Au-Prince Haiti 1969-1973; P-in-c Redemp Gonaives Haiti 1966-1969; P-in-c S Simeon Croix-Des-Bouquets Haiti 1958-1966; P-in-c S Esprit Cape Haitian Haiti 1956-1958; P-in-c S Ptr Mireballs Haiti 1955-1956; Vic S Mk's Leborgne Haiti 1948-1949.

MOREAU, Walter Jerome (NJ) 211 Willow Valley Sq # D-319, Lancaster PA 17602 **Ret 1989-** B Indiana PA 1926 s Walter & Ruth. BA Hobart and Wm Smith Colleges 1947; STB GTS 1950. D 4/15/1950 P 10/14/1950 Bp Austin Pardue. c 1. R S Mary's Ch Haddon Heights NJ 1975-1988; Dn Nthrn Convoc Dio New Jersey Trenton NJ 1974-1975, Pres Nthrn Cler 1966-1973, 1963-1965, Dept Mus 1960-1962; R S Lk the Evang Roselle NJ 1959-1975; Stff Cathd Ch Of S Mk Minneapolis MN 1956-1959; R The Ch Of The Adv Jeannette PA 1951-1956; P-in-c S Barn Ch Brackenridge PA 1950-1951.

MOREHEAD, Carol (WTex) St Mark's Episcopal Church, 315 E Pecan St, San Antonio TX 78205 **P S Mk's Epis Ch San Antonio TX 2013-** B Kansas City MO 1962 d William & Betty. BA Abilene Chr U 1985; Grad Stds in Rel Pepperdine U 1987; MDiv Epis TS Of The SW 2013; MDiv Epis TS of the SW 2013. D 1/9/2013 Bp David Mitchell Reed P 7/13/2013 Bp Gary Richard Lillibridge. m 5/1/1986 Daniel Blake Morehead c 3. cmorehead@stmarks-sa.org

MOREHOUS, Amy Hodges (ETenn) 800 S. Northshore Dr., Knoxville TN 37919 B Knoxville TN 1972 d Nancy. BA U of Tennessee 1994. D 12/9/2006 Bp Charles Glenn VonRosenberg. m 3/11/1997 David Morehous c 1. D Ch Of The Ascen Knoxville TN 2010-2016, CE Dir 2010-; Dio E Tennessee Knoxville TN 2001-2004.

MOREHOUSE JR, Merritt Dutton (FdL) 1920 Green Tree Road, Washington Island WI 54246 B Evanston IL 1936 s Merritt & Louise. BA Ya 1959; Cert Whitaker TS 1994. D 6/11/1994 Bp R aymond Stewart Wood Jr. m 7/23/1973 Joyce Louise Clasen Morehouse. D S Lk's Epis Ch Sis Bay WI 2000-2011; Archd Dio Michigan Detroit MI 1998-2000; D Chr Ch Cranbrook Bloomfield Hills MI 1996-2000. Ed/Writer, "Diakoneo (Journ)," *Diakoneo*, Assn for Epis Deacons.

MOREHOUSE, Rebecca (Cal) 21 Sonora Way, Corte Madera CA 94925 **Vol Of The Nativ San Rafael CA 2005-; Par D Epsicopal Ch of the Nativ San Rafael CA 2004-; Attitudinal Healing Grp Fac San Quentin St Prison San Quentin CA 2002-** B Laconia NH 1945 d Stephen & Frances. BA Smith 1967; BA Sch for Deacons 2004. D 12/4/2004 Bp William Edwin Swing. c 2. Epis Sch For Deacons Berkeley CA 2005-2016.

MOREHOUSE, Timothy Lawrence (NY) 200 Riverside Dr Apt 7B, New York NY 10025 **Chapl Trin Sch New York NY 2004-** B Ames IA 1963 s Lawrence & Georgia. BA Harv 1985; MDiv PrTS 1991; MA Harv 1995; STM GTS 2001. D 6/22/2002 P 5/31/2003 Bp Charles Ellsworth Bennison Jr. timothy. morehouse@trinityschoolnyc.org

MORELL, Ellen Jones (Ky) 8110 Saint Andrews Church Rd, Louisville KY 40258 **Bd Dir Waycross Epis C&C 2005-** B Indianapolis IN 1942 BS Indiana U 1964; MDiv Chr TS 2002. D 6/28/2003 P 2/8/2004 Bp Cate Waynick. Chr Ch Elizabethtown KY 2012-2014; S Ptr's Epis Ch Louisville KY 2009-2012; Dio Indianapolis Indianapolis IN 2008-2009; Ch Of The Nativ Indianapolis IN 2003-2008.

MORELLI, John (NY) 210 E 181 St Apt 1A, Bronx NY 10457 **D Cathd Ch of St. Jn the Div New York NY 2004-** B New York NY 1935 s John & Carmen. Hisp Pstr Inst. D 5/10/1987 Bp Paul Moore Jr. m 4/27/1963 Amelia Rodriquez. San Andres Ch Yonkers NY 1996-2002, D 1996-2002; Ch Of The H Trin New York NY 1995-1996, D 1995-, 1987-1994, D 1987-1992; S Ptr's Ch Port Chester NY 1994-1996, D 1994-; Dio New York New York NY 1993-1994; S Ann's Ch Of Morrisania Bronx NY 1993-1994, D 1993-1994.

MORELLI, Thomas Carlo Anthony (SanD) 1114 9th St, Coronado CA 92118 **D Dio San Diego San Diego CA 2016-** B Audubon NJ 1947 s Carlo & Mary. BS Rider U 1974; EXMBA Stan 1989. D 2/14/2015 Bp Jim Mathes. m 11/17/2007 Polly H Priscilla Howe c 5.

MORESCHI, Alexander Thomas (Ga) D 5/31/2014 Bp Scott Anson Benhase.

MORETZ, Matthew John (NY) 325 Park Ave, New York NY 10022 **Assoc St. Barth Ch New York NY 2012-, D 2006; Mem of Bdgt Com Dio New York New York NY 2016-** B Augusta GA 1979 s John & Susan. BA Davidson Coll 2001; MDiv GTS 2006. D 2/4/2006 P 8/9/2006 Bp Henry Irving Louttit. m 8/6/2016 Megan Irene Brandt-Meyer. Cur Chr's Ch Rye NY 2007-2012; Asstg Cler Hisp Epis Cntr San Andres Ch Yonkers NY 2006-2007; Cur S Paul's Ch Yonkers NY 2006-2007; Dir of Chr Formation Chr Ch Frederica St Simons Is GA 2001-2003; Mem of the Bd Trst The GTS 2013-2016. Producer, "Fr Matt Presents," *Fr Matt Presents*, YouTube, 2006. Soc of Cath Priests 2016. moretz@stbarts.org

MOREY, Gordon Howell (Mil) N4111 Pine St, Brodhead WI 53520 **Ret 1994-** B Providence RI 1942 s Earl & Florence. BS Florida St U 1965; MDiv Sewanee: The U So, TS 1969. D 3/8/1970 P 6/27/1971 Bp James Loughlin Duncan. m 6/6/1964 Carol Morey. Asst S Lk's Epis Ch Milwaukee WI 1981-1988; Gr Ch

Madison WI 1978-1980; R S Mary Magd Epis Ch Pompano Bch FL 1974-1978; Asst All SS Prot Epis Ch Ft Lauderdale FL 1970-1974.

MORFORD, Norman L (Ind) PO Box 55085, Indianapolis IN 46205 B Fort Wayne IN 1934 s Elbert & Harriet. BA DePauw U 1956; BD SMU 1960. D 10/14/1973 P 5/1/1974 Bp John P Craine. m 12/19/1958 Pamela P Morford c 3. R S Tim's Ch Indianapolis IN 2001-2008, Int 1992-2000; Int Trin Ch Anderson IN 1998-2000; Int S Ptr's Ch Lebanon IN 1994-1995; Int S Matt's Ch Indianapolis IN 1987-1991; Int S Fran In The Fields Zionsville IN 1986-1987; Int Gr Ch Muncie IN 1983-1984; P-in-c Trin Ch Connersville IN 1977-1978; Assoc S Phil's Ch Indianapolis IN 1973-1975; Serv Methodist Ch CA & IN 1960-1973.

MORFORD, Samuel Allen (Neb) 9302 Blondo St, Omaha NE 68134 B Chanute KS 1939 s Darrell & Lillian. BA Kansas U 1964. D 5/24/1990 Bp James Edward Krotz. m 6/8/1963 Edna Cruz Morford c 2.

MORGAN, Barbara Jean (Alb) 24 Silver St Apt G8, Great Barrington MA 01230 B Newark,NJ 1938 d Harry & Myra. U of Delaware 1958; BS Lesley U 1978; MEd NEU 1981; MDiv EDS 1988. D 2/16/1991 P 10/1/1992 Bp R aymond Stewart Wood Jr. S Jn In-The-Wilderness Copake Falls NY 1998-2007; Cred Com Chair Dio Estrn Michigan Saginaw MI 1994-1997; Exec Dir Shltr Inc 1992-1998; Trin Epis Ch Alpena MI 1992-1998; D S Andr's Ch Ann Arbor MI 1991-1992; Assoc R Dio Michigan Detroit MI 1992-1993. Soc of S Jn the Evang 1978.

MORGAN, Daniel (Ct) 489 Mansfield Ave, Darien CT 06820 B Royal Oak MI 1965 s Frank & Mildred. BA Gordon Coll 1987; MDiv TESM 1993. D 6/12/ 1993 Bp Arthur Edward Walmsley P 1/1/1994 Bp Harry Woolston Shipps. m 1/30/2008 Kristin Morgan c 3. S Paul's Ch Darien CT 1999-2010; Chr Ch Epis Savannah GA 1993-1999; Fllshp Of Christians In Us & Schools 1987-1990; Reg Dir Of Yth Mnstry.

MORGAN, David Forbes (Colo) 740 Clarkson St, Denver CO 80218 **Gr Epis Ch Georgetown CO 1999-; Dir Contemplative Outreach for Pryr Fllshp Denver CO 1983-; Prior Ord of Chr Centered Ministers Denver CO 1973-** B Toronto ON CA 1930 s Forbes & Ruth. MDiv Rocky Mtn Coll; MDiv Rocky Mtn Coll; DLitt Tem; DC U of the Natural Healing Arts 1954; ThB Rocky Mtn Coll 1958; MDiv Coll of the Rockies 1968. D 1/6/1982 Bp William Carl Frey P 11/22/1982 Bp William Harvey Wolfrum. m 9/7/1956 Delores M Morgan. Cn S Jn's Cathd Denver CO 1982-1995. Auth, *Chr Centered Mnstrs; A Response to God's Call*; Auth, *Songs w A Message*. Contemplation Outreach LTD Intl ; OGS; Ord of Chr Centered Ministers; Ord of S Lk. Who's Who in Hlth; Alpha; Who's Who in the Wrld; Who's Who in Rel.

MORGAN, Dennis Lee (Eas) 6242 Oxbridge Dr, Salisbury MD 21801 **P-in-c S Mary's Epis Ch Tyaskin MD 2014-; P-in-c S Paul's Ch Vienna MD 2013-; Chapl Peninsula Reg Med Cntr 2009-** B Crisfield MD 1955 s Marvin & Helen. BA Salisbury U 1976; MTS VTS 2013. D 11/10/2007 P 5/3/2014 Bp Bud Shand. m 8/15/1987 Esther Jane Rockwell. mortsdeli@aol.com

MORGAN, Diane Elizabeth (Mich) 25710 Beech Ct, Redford MI 48239 **Chapl to Ret Cler & Families Dio Michigan Detroit MI 2015-, Chapl 2008-2015** B Detroit MI 1940 d Anthony & Dorothy. BS Wayne 1973; MDiv Bex Sem 1990. D 6/23/1990 P 6/15/1991 Bp R aymond Stewart Wood Jr. m 8/30/2011 Karen White c 4. Vic Nativ Epis Ch Bloomfield Township MI 2009-2011; Long term supply P Gr Epis Ch Southgate MI 2004-2006; Gr Epis Ch Southgate MI 2004-2005; Dir of Sprtl Care Beaumont Hosp Royal Oak MI 1997-2006; Chapl Beaumont Hosp Royal Oak MI 1992-1997; R S Mart Ch Detroit MI 1991-1997; CPE Res Chld's Hosp of Detroit Detroit MI 1990-1991. Auth, "Reiki and Hosp Chapl," *Reiki Intl* , Reiki Intl , 2001. Assembly of Epis Hlth Care Chapl 1996; Bd Cert - Assn of Profsnl Chapl 1995; Cert Thanatologist- ADEC 2006.

MORGAN, Dwight Dexter (SeFla) 2201 S.W. 25th Street, Coconut Grove FL 33133 B Corn Island NI 1954 s Winston & Justina. BA Instituto Nacional 1974; Casa San Miguel 1978; Dioc TS 1999. D 5/14/1978 Bp George Edward Haynsworth P 6/1/1999 Bp Calvin Onderdonk Schofield Jr. c 1. Ch Of The H Comf Miami FL 2002-2009; S Bern De Clairvaux N Miami Bch FL 2001.

MORGAN, Ed (Colo) 5952 E Irish Pl, Centennial CO 80112 **Asst S Mich And All Ang' Ch Denver CO 2012-; Pool Chapl The Denver Hospice 2007-** B Indianapolis IN 1944 s James & Mary. BA Pur 1966; MDiv Nash 1983. D 6/ 4/1983 Bp William Carl Frey P 12/14/1983 Bp William Harvey Wolfrum. m 12/30/1967 Sara K Morgan c 2. Cn Dio Colorado Denver CO 2001-2004; S Steph's Epis Ch Aurora CO 2000-2005; R S Mk's Epis Ch Little Rock AR 1996-2001; R S Barth's Ch Estes Pk CO 1985-1996; Cur S Jos's Ch Lakewood CO 1983-1985.

MORGAN, E F Michael (Pa) 33 Baltusrol Way, Springfield NJ 07081 **P-in-c Gr Epis Ch Hulmeville PA 2010-; Appointed P Zion Epis Ch Chas Town WV 2017-** B Shreveport LA 1943 s Elmer & Alice. BA U of Pennsylvania 1964; MA Ob 1966; STB PDS 1970; PhD Ohio U 1990; MEd Ohio U 1996. D 6/6/1970 P 5/1/1971 Bp Robert Lionne DeWitt. m 1/6/2015 Rosa V Morgan c 2. Exec Dir Epis Preaching Fndt Springfield New Jersey 2009-2010; R S Jn's Ch Bala Cynwyd PA 2003-2007; R Ch Of The Gd Shpd Athens OH 1979-2002; Asst Ch Of The Redeem Chestnut Hill MA 1972-1979; Asst Rgstr Harvard DS Cambridge MA 1971-1972. Auth/Ed, "Preaching Jesus - 2010," Epis Preaching

Fndt, 2010; Auth, "Faithful Living: Faithful Dying," Morehouse, 2000; Auth/ Ed, "Preaching Jesus," Epis Preaching Fndt. EvangES 1998. Legis Congressional Fell Brookings Inst-US Hse Rep. 2013; Hlth Level Seven Fell Hlth Level Seven, Intl 2010; Res Fell U So, Sewanee 2007; Cmnty Serv Awd Chld's Rts Coun 2006; Merrill Fllshp Harvard DS 2001; Fellowowship Coll of Preachers 1990. efmorgan1@gmail.com

MORGAN, Elaine Ludlum (Nev) 402 W Robinson St, Carson City NV 89703 B Los Angeles CA 1929 d William & Helen. TS Dio Olympia; Claremont Coll 1949; BA Pomona Coll 1949; MA USC 1953. D 6/30/1984 Bp Robert Hume Cochrane. m 4/8/1949 Robert Norman Morgan c 2. Ch Of Coventry Cross Minden NV 1999-2009; D Dio Nevada Las Vegas 1996-2011; D S Ptr's Epis Ch Carson City NV 1990-1995; D All SS' Epis Ch Vancouver WA 1984-1990. Auth, "Coventry Cross Cuisine," Morris Pub, 1998; Auth, "Rel arts," Nevada Appeal Nwspr,Carson City, 1996; Auth, "In The Kitchen w Wmn Of St. Mk'S," *Coventry Crossings (1997-2000)*, Ptr Geddes Press, 1962; Auth, "Pipes Of Pan," Pasadena Cmnty Coll Press, 1947. Carson City Mnstrl Assn; NAAD; Vlly Chr Fllshp (Gardnerville). Phi Beta Kappa Pomona Coll 1949; Pi Lambda Theta Pomona C Ollege Chapt 1948.

MORGAN III, Harold Edgar (USC) 204 Derby Ln, Clinton SC 29325 **R All SS Epis Ch Clinton SC 2006-** B Wilmington DE 1948 s Harold & Martha. BA Cit 1970; MDiv Sewanee: The U So, TS 1977. D 6/11/1977 P 3/5/1978 Bp George Moyer Alexander. m 4/28/1973 Mamie Elizabeth Morgan. R Ch Of The Gd Shpd Galax VA 2000-2006; Int Ch Of The Resurr Greenwood SC 1998-2000; CE Asst Chr Ch Greenville SC 1996-1998, Chapl 1984-1995; S Barth's Ch Cokeville WY 1979-1984; Vic S Jas Ch Kemmerer WY 1979-1984; Asst S Chris's Ch Spartanburg SC 1977-1979.

MORGAN, Heather M (Mo) 1400 Forum Boulevard, Suite 38, Columbia MO 65203 **Coordntr of Coll Age and Cmnty Mnstry Missouri Meth Ch 2011-** B LaGrange IL 1964 d William & Susan. BA Duke 1986; MDiv SWTS 1994. D 6/18/1994 Bp Robert Jefferson Hargrove Jr P 12/17/1994 Bp Frank Tracy Griswold III. m 8/1/2009 Rex A Morgan. New Horizons Meth Ch Columbia MO 2012-2017; Ch Planter/Pstr Dio Missouri S Louis MO 2007-2011; Mssy Vic Ch Of The H Sprt Greensboro NC 2002-2007; Chapl Cbury Sch Greensboro NC 1999-2001; Asst R Chr Epis Ch Springfield MO 1996-1999; Asst to the R S Greg's Epis Ch Deerfield IL 1994-1996.

MORGAN, James Charles (Tex) 235 Royal Oaks St, Huntsville TX 77320 B Massillon OH 1943 s James & Grace. BA Steph F Austin St U 1965; MDiv VTS 1969. D 7/1/1969 P 5/1/1970 Bp James Milton Richardson. St Ptr The Fisherman Trin TX 1999-2002; S Steph's Ch Huntsville TX 1994-2015; The Great Cmsn Fndt Houston TX 1972-1975, 1969-1971; S Mary's Ch W Columbia TX 1971-1993; R S Mk's Epis Ch Richmond TX 1971-1974; S Mk's Ch Houston TX 1971; M-in-c S Lk's Rusk TX 1969-1971; St Lukes Ch Rusk TX 1969-1971; M-in-c Trin Ch Jacksonville TX 1969-1971.

MORGAN JR, James Hanly (WVa) 520 11th Ave., Huntington WV 25701 **D Trin Ch Huntington WV 2005-** B Huntington WV 1937 s James & MaryAnn. BS W Virginia U 1959. D 9/29/2008 Bp William Michie Klusmeyer. m 3/25/ 1961 Elizabeth Morgan c 4.

MORGAN, J. Gregory (NY) St. Simon the Cyrenian Church, 135 Remington Place, New Rochelle NY 10801 **All SS Epis Par Hoboken NJ 2015-; D Ch Of S Simon The Cyrenian New Rochelle NY 2015-** B Camden NJ 1943 s Max & Betty. BA U of Washington 1965; Certificats Université d'Aix-Marseille 1966; Certificats Université d'Aix-Marseille 1966; MA U MI 1967; MA Penn St 1995; MDiv GTS 2012; MDiv The GTS 2012. D 6/2/2012 P 12/1/2012 Bp Martin Scott Field. m 11/29/2013 Thomas Merrick Reefer c 1. Asst to the R Chr Chr And S Steph's Ch New York NY 2012-2014; Dir of Dvlpmt Friendship Hse/Cathr's Place KC MO 2007-2009; Fam Counslr Serv Corp Intl KC MO 2004-2007; Adj Instr Metropltn Cmnty Coll KC MO 2003-2009; Marketing Assoc Bp Spencer Place KC MO 2002; Headmaster The Harrisburg Acad PA 1989-2000; Headmaster Prot Epis Cathd Fndt Washington DC 1980-1989; Pres W Shore Libr Assn (PA) 1998-2000; Secy Harper W. Spong Schlrshp Fndt 1993-2000; Pres Assn of Indep Schools of Grtr DC 1988-1989. Writer, "My Favorite Prof," *Columns mag*, U of Washington, 1999; Auth, "The Hbg. Acad Early Years," *U Archive*, Penn St Harrisburg, 1995; Writer, "Measures for Tough Times," *Indep Sch mag*, Natl Assn of Indep Schools, 1994; Writer, "Indep. Schools Remarkably Effective," *Nwspr op-ed*, Harrisburg Patriot-News, 1993. Sem Rep Epis Preaching Fndt Seminar 2011; Sum Res Ripon Coll, Cuddesdon, UK 2011; Winner Winifred H. Clark Prize, Gnrl Sem 2011; Schlrshp Rec Soc for the Increase of the Mnstry 2010; Mentor EFM, Sewanee, TN 2006.

MORGAN, Keely (Minn) 60 Kent St, Saint Paul MN 55102 **Epis Hm St Paul MN 2013-** B Fort Smith AR 1981 d William & Mary. BA Hamline U 2006; MDiv Luther TS 2010. D 7/23/2009 Bp James Louis Jelinek P 7/29/2010 Bp Brian N Prior. Asst R S Jn The Evang S Paul MN 2010-2012.

MORGAN, Kimberly Ann (Nev) 305 N Minnesota St, Carson City NV 89703 **Assoc S Ptr's Epis Ch Carson City NV 2010-** B Washington DC 1956 d Richard & Barbara. BA U of Nevada at Reno 1977; JD U of Oklahoma 1980; CTS CDSP 2008. D 7/25/2009 P 2/13/2010 Bp Dan Thomas Edwards. m 12/ 28/1985 John Slider.

MORGAN, Mamie Elizabeth (USC) 204 Derby Lane, Clinton SC 29325 **R S Lk's Ch Newberry SC 2007-** B Greenville SC 1953 d Paul & Alma. BA U of So Carolina 1974; MDiv Sewanee: The U So, TS 1979. D 11/1/1980 P 11/1/1981 Bp Bob Gordon Jones. m 4/28/1973 Harold Edgar Morgan. Int Chr Ch Blacksburg VA 2005-2007; R Chr Ch Bluefield WV 2000-2005; Int S Thad Epis Ch Aiken SC 1999-2000; Epis Ch Of The Redeem Greenville SC 1998; S Jn's Ch Winnsboro SC 1995-1997; Clincl Chapl Sc Dept Of Mntl Hlth 1989-1994; Clincl Pstr-In-Res Spartanburg Reg Med Cntr SC 1988-1989; Epiph Ch Spartanburg SC 1987-1989; S Barth's Ch Cokeville WY 1980-1984; Asst S Jas Ch Kemmerer WY 1980-1984. Int Ministers Ntwk 1997; Prof Trng In Int Mnstry. Woods Ldrshp Awd U So 1976.

MORGAN, Marilyn Kay (Ark) 1475 Stone Crest Dr, Conway AR 72034 B Conway AR 1947 d Friedman & Mary Aline. BSE U of Cntrl Arkansas 1970; MSE U of Cntrl Arkansas 1976. D 5/5/2007 Bp Larry Benfield. D S Ptr's Ch Conway AR 2007-2008.

MORGAN, Michael T (Mont) West 3817 Fort Wright Drive 1-204, Spokane WA 99204 B San Francisco CA 1949 s Alfred & Hazel. BA Uscd 1971; MDiv EDS 1975. D 8/2/1975 P 9/1/1976 Bp Wesley Frensdorff. Dio Montana Helena MT 1993-1995, Bd Trst 1980-1981, Secy Pk Cnty Ministers Assn 1981-1982; Bd Dir Jr Citizens Camp Montana Coun Of Ch 1980-1988; S Andr's Ch Livingston MT 1979-1992; S Jn's Ch Emigrant MT 1979-1992; Advsr Of The Yth Cmsn Dio Nevada Las Vegas 1975-1979; Cur S Steph's Epis Ch Reno NV 1975-1979.

MORGAN, Michele H. (WA) 301 A St NE, Washington DC 20002 **S Mk's Ch Washington DC 2015-** B Calgary 1963 d John & Beatrice. BA S Cathr U 1986; MDiv GTS 2004. D 6/10/2004 P 12/16/2004 Bp James Louis Jelinek. m 8/18/2013 MIchelle V Dibblee. Breck Sch Minneapolis MN 2014-2015; S Jn The Bapt Epis Ch Minneapolis MN 2011-2012, Transitional R 2011-2012, Int Chld/Yth 2008; Int P S Jas On The Pkwy Minneapolis MN 2009-2011; Int P S Jn's Ch S Cloud MN 2009; Assoc Ch Of The Ascen Stillwater MN 2004-2007.

MORGAN, Pamela S (Ark) 1410 E Walnut St., Rogers AR 72756 **R S Thos Ch Springdale AR 2009-** B Little Rock AR 1955 d Calvin & Sibyl. BA St Mary-Of-The-Woods Coll 1999; MDiv Sewanee: The U So, TS 2001. D 2/22/2001 P 9/15/2001 Bp Larry Maze. m 9/24/1973 Kevin Ryan Morgan c 3. S Andr's Ch Mtn Hm AR 2003-2008; S Mk's Epis Ch Little Rock AR 2001-2003.

MORGAN, Philip (Va) 17476 Hawthorne Ave, Culpeper VA 22701 **R Emm Ch Rapidan VA 2015-, Vic 2015-, Vic 2006-2015** B Swansea Wales 1951 s Haydn & Edith. BS Lon GB 1975; BD U of Wales GB 1978; MBA Columbia Sthrn U 2009. Trans 9/18/1985 Bp William Cockburn Russell Sheridan. m 9/14/1974 Carol L Morgan c 3. Chapl Blue Ridge Sch Dyke VA 2004-2010; Chapl Blue Ridge Sch St. Geo VA 2004-2010; R Little Fork Epis Ch Rixeyville VA 2000-2003; Chapl All SS Chap Howe IN 1986-2000; Chapl Howe Mltry Sch Howe IN 1986-2000; R S Mk's Par Howe IN 1986-2000; Howe Mltry Sch Howe IN 1985-2000, Bd Trst Mem 2011-; Vic H Fam Ch Angola IN 1985-1986; Gdnc Dir Howe Mltry Epis Sch Howe IN 1985-1986; Cur S Jn The Evang Ch Elkhart IN 1984-1985; Cur S Mary in Swansea w H Trin & S Jas 1983-1984; Cur Morriston 1981-1983; Chapl Morriston Hosp 1981-1983; Serv Ch in Wales 1978-1984; Cur S Nich in Swansea 1978-1981; Chapl W Glamorgan Inst of Higher Educ 1978-1981. Auth, "Gospel Talks," CelticPress, 2013; Auth, "Walk Once More w Me," CelticPress, 2011; Auth, CelticPress, 2010; Auth, CelticPress, 2009; Auth, CelticPress, 2008; Auth, "The First b," *LivCh*, The Ch-in-Wales; Auth, "What is Pryr," *The Welsh Churchman*, The Ch-in-Wales; Auth, "Chr Initiation," *The Welsh Churchman*, The Ch-in-Wales. Lifetime Assoc St. Mary's Ch, Swansea, Wales St. Mary's, Swansea, Wales 1984.

MORGAN, Ralph Baier (Tex) **S Cyp's Ch Lufkin TX 2015-** B Houston TX 1958 s Ralph & DeAlva. BA Houston Bapt U 1983; MDiv Epis TS of the SW 2006. D 6/24/2006 Bp Don Adger Wimberly P 1/11/2007 Bp Dena Arnall Harrison. m 5/12/2001 Terri S Morgan c 3. R Chr Ch Eagle Lake TX 2009-2015; S Lk's Epis Hosp Houston TX 2009; Asst S Dunst's Epis Ch Houston TX 2006-2009; Dn Chr Ch Nacogdoches TX 1996-1997; Yth Dir Ch Of The H Apos Katy TX 1992-2003; Dn Adv Epis Sch Stafford TX 1991-1996; Yth Dir All SS Epis Ch Stafford TX 1989-1991; Yth Dir Ch Of The H Sprt 1985-1989; Yth Dir S Jn The Div Houston TX 1984-1986. rector@stcyprianschurch.org

MORGAN, Randall Carl (SC) St Jude's Episcopal Church, 907 Wichman St, Walterboro SC 29488 B Parkersburg WV 1948 s Douglas & Ruth. BA Glenville St Coll 1979; MDiv VTS 1985. D 6/5/1985 Bp Robert Poland Atkinson P 12/1/1985 Bp William Franklin Carr. R S Jude's Epis Ch Walterboro SC 2005-2011; P S Paul's Ch Athens TN 2001-2005; Vic Ch Of The Gd Shpd Greer SC 1988-2001; S Fran Ch Potomac MD 1987-1988; Olde S Jn's Ch Colliers WV 1985-1986.

MORGAN V, Richard (RI) 19 Castle Way, Westerly RI 02891 **Assoc Chr Ch Westerly RI 1985-** B Hartford CT 1941 s Richard & Avice. BA Dart 1963; MDiv EDS 1970. D 12/21/1972 Bp Morgan Porteus P 6/29/1973 Bp Matthew George Henry. m 2/15/1974 Betty Morgan c 2. P-in-c S Eliz's Ch Hope Vlly RI 2008-2012; Vic S Mths Ch Coventry RI 1993-2007; Res Chaplin - Yawgoog Scout Reserv BSA and Camp Ho Rhoda Isle St Coun of Ch 1992-2017; R Beckford Par Shenandoah Cnty VA 1983-1985; R Emm Ch Woodstock VA 1983-1985; R S Andr's Ch Mt Jackson VA 1983-1985; Vic

Sum Chap 1973-1983; Vic Trin & Resurr Little Switzerland Shenandoah Cnty NC 1973-1983; Vic Trin Ch Spruce Pine NC 1973-1983. Bro Way Cross 1975. The Ord Of S Geo Rhode Island St Coun of Ch/ Providence, RI 2000.

MORGAN, Richard Thomas (Pa) Church of the Good Samaritan, 212 W Lancaster Ave, Paoli PA 19301 **Dn Ch Of The Gd Samar Paoli PA 2012-** B United Kingdom 1970 BA U of Cambridge - Peterhouse 1991; MA U of Cambridge - Peterhouse 1995; Cert for Theol graduates U of Oxford - Wycliffe Hall 1996. Trans 1/26/2012 Bp Charles Ellsworth Bennison Jr. m 2/20/1999 Margaret Ruth Morgan c 5.

MORGAN, Ruth Margaret (RG) 8017 Krim Dr. NE, Albuquerque NM 87109 **Asst to the R Hope in the Desert Eps Ch 2011-** B Racine WI 1954 d John & Iola. BA Coll of Santa Fe 2000; MA Webster U 2003; TESM 2009. D 9/19/2009 P 9/25/2010 Bp William Carl Frey. m 9/13/1997 Felix Morgan c 4. P-in-c S Fran Ch Rio Rancho NM 2010-2011, D 2009-2010, Admin Asst to the R 2006-2009.

MORGAN, Walter (ETenn) 3475 Edgewood Cir Nw, Cleveland TN 37312 B Monroe LA 1936 s Gordon & Mary. BS Tul 1959; MDiv Nash 1979; Cert Mid Atlantic Assn 1982. D 5/10/1979 P 11/14/1979 Bp James Barrow Brown. m 6/25/1960 Janet Mahaffey c 2. Int Ch Of The Adv Louisville KY 2002; B&C Dio E Tennessee Knoxville TN 1991-1993, COM Chair 1995-1999, COM 1993-1994, Design Team Plnng & Structure 1991-1992; R S Lk's Ch Cleveland TN 1989-2002; Design Team Par Act Consult Trng Dio Wstrn Louisiana Alexandria LA 1986-1987, Dispatch Bus 1984-1988, Par Growth Consult 1984-1988, Chair Camp Hardtner Cmsn 1983-1988, Cdo 1982-1988, Cn Ordnry 1981-1988, Dep GC 1985-1988. craigmorgan1@verizon.net

MORGAN-HIGGINS, Stanley Ethelbert (Nwk) 3828 Leprechaun Ct, Decatur GA 30034 B Panama PA 1938 s Clifford & Edna. BA RP U Panama; MD ETSC 1975. D 10/31/1976 P 8/26/1979 Bp Lemuel Barnett Shirley. m 5/27/1989 Cecily A Morgan c 2. R Ch Of The H Comm Paterson NJ 1991-2002; P-in-c S Agnes And S Paul's Ch E Orange NJ 1990-1991; S Cyp's Epis Ch Hackensack NJ 1990-1991; St Agnes Ch E Orange NJ 1990-1991; St Marys & St Margarets Ch 1982-1988; St Stephens Mssn 1982-1988; Chr Ch By The Sea 1979-1981; Serv Ch in Panama 1976-1990; Dio Panama 1976-1989.

MORICAL, Robin E (CFla) 1631 Ford Pkwy, Saint Paul MN 55116 **All SS Epis Ch Deltona FL 2014-** B Riverside CA 1964 d Layton & Naomi. BA MN 1992; MDiv Nash 2008. D 5/31/2008 P 5/30/2009 Bp John Wadsworth Howe. m 6/24/1989 James H Morical c 3. Assoc Ch of the Incarn Oviedo FL 2010-2014; D Assoc Mssh Epis Ch S Paul MN 2009-2010. rmorical@gmail.com

MORIN, Geoffrey S (Pa) 841 Shenton Road, West Chester PA 19380 B Methuen MA 1965 s Rudolph & Elizabeth. BA Duke 1987; MDiv Ya Berk 1994. D 6/11/1994 Bp Clarence Nicholas Coleridge P 4/1/1995 Bp R aymond Stewart Wood Jr. c 1. Assoc Ch Of The Gd Samar Paoli PA 1997-2006; Chr Ch Grosse Pointe Grosse Pointe Farms MI 1994-1997.

MORISSEAU, Robert Edward Lee (NY) 502 Forest Gln, Pompton Plains NJ 07444 **Asstg Cler Cathd of S Jn the Div New York NY 2002-** B Saint Louis MO 1932 s Clarence & Corinne. BA Missouri Vlly Coll 1954; MDiv EDS 1957. D 6/15/1957 P 12/21/1957 Bp Arthur C Lichtenberger. m 6/25/1960 Caroline B Morisseau c 3. Cathd Of St Jn The Div New York NY 1995-1998; R S Jn's Ch New City NY 1969-1994; R S Jn's Epis Ch Oneida NY 1962-1969; Asst S Ptr's Epis Ch S Louis MO 1957-1962; Chapl to Ret Cler and spouses Dio New York New York NY 1996-2007.

MORITZ III, Bernard Eugene (SwVa) 4022 Fauquier Ave, Richmond VA 23227 B Natchez MS 1941 s Joseph & Jane. BA Mississippi St U 1963; MDiv Nash 1973; STM Sewanee: The U So, TS 1983. D 6/11/1973 P 5/19/1974 Bp John Maury Allin. m 3/14/1964 Jeanelle Lowe Moritz c 2. R Ascen Epis Ch Amherst VA 1999-2006; R S Mk's Ch Amherst VA 1999-2005; Supply P Dio Alabama Birmingham 1988-1999; Vic Our Sav Birmingham AL 1986-1988; Vic Our Sav Madison AL 1985-1988; Assoc R Ch Of The Nativ Epis Huntsville AL 1984-1986; Asst R S Paul's Ch Fayetteville AR 1981-1984; Vic Ch Of The Redeem Brookhaven MS 1977-1981; Vic All SS Ch Inverness MS 1974-1977; S Thos Ch Belzoni MS 1974-1977; Cur S Paul's Ch Columbus MS 1973-1974. Cmnty of S Mary, P Assoc 1979.

MORIYAMA, Jerome Tomokazu (WA) Rossbrin Cove, Schull, Co. Cork Ireland **Non-par 1978-** B Tokyo 1943 s Tomokiyo & Yoshie. BA Keio U Tokyo 1968; MA Keio U Tokyo 1970; MDiv EDS 1975; MA Lon SOAS 1979; PhD Lon SOAS 1984. D 6/7/1975 P 5/20/1976 Bp William Foreman Creighton. m 12/1/1973 Ann Mary Gamwell c 2. Exec Coun Appointees New York NY 1975-1985; Mssy S Mk's Theol Coll In Dar-Es-Salaam Tanzania 1975-1978. Daniel O'Connor and others, "Part 2: Perspectives 8. Bldg a Hm-grown Ch Jerome T Moriyama," *Three Centuries of Mssn -The Untd Siciety for the Propogation of the Gospel 1701-2000*, USPG and Continuum Intl Pub Grp, 2000.

MORLAN, Lynette K (SJ) 2803 Stratford Dr, San Ramon CA 94583 **R Epis Ch Of S Anne Stockton CA 2009-, P-in-c 2008-** B Sacramento CA 1951 BS California St U. D 6/5/2004 P 12/4/2004 Bp William Edwin Swing. m 8/28/1971 David L Morlan c 2. Yth Min S Barth's Epis Ch Livermore CA 2004-2008.

M

MORLEY, Anthony J (Minn) 825 Summit Ave #806, Minneapolis MN 55403 B Switzerland 1930 s Felix & Isabel. BA Hav 1951; U of Vienna 1952; MDiv EDS 1955. D 6/18/1955 Bp Angus Dun P 12/8/1955 Bp Horace W B Donegan. m 3/11/1978 Ruth Olson c 4. Pilot Dio Coordntr Exec Coun New York NY 1968-1970; Dir of Resrch Dio Missouri S Louis MO 1965-1968; R Trin Ch S Louis MO 1958-1965; Fell and Tutor The GTS New York NY 1955-1958. 1978; Auth, "A Legis Guide to Sch Fin," *Civil Rts Dig*, 1972.

MORLEY, Richard Matthew (NJ) 140 S Finley Ave, Basking Ridge NJ 07920 **R S Mk's Ch Basking Ridge NJ 2009-** B Wilmington DE 1974 s Richard & Sarah. BA S Josephs U Philadelphia PA 1996; MDiv Candler TS Emory U 2002. D 6/8/2002 Bp John L Rabb P 12/15/2002 Bp Robert Wilkes Ihloff. m 6/24/2000 Karen Renee Morley c 2. Vic S Ptr's Ch Lonaconing MD 2002-2010; Dio Maryland Baltimore MD 2002-2009.

MORLEY, William Harris (NC) 3454 Rugby Rd, Durham NC 27707 **P Assoc Chap Of The Cross Chap Hill NC 2002-; Non-par 1991-** B Columbus OH 1951 s Buel & Dorothy. TCU 1970; BA U of Kansas 1973; MDiv Nash 1978; DMin GTF 1991; MBA GTF 1991. D 6/17/1978 Bp Quintin Ebenezer Primo Jr P 12/16/1978 Bp James Winchester Montgomery. m 5/24/2003 Arlene J Diosegy c 2. R S Tim's Epis Ch W Des Moines IA 1983-1991; Vic S Paul's Ch Mchenry IL 1979-1983; Cur S Jn's Epis Ch Naperville IL 1978-1979. Auth, "Exec Coaching:An Annotated Bibliography," Cntr For Creative Ldrshp, 2000. OHC 1979.

MORNARD, Jean Elisabeth (SD) 1400 21st St SW Lot 110, 208, Huron SD 57350 **R Gr Epis Ch Huron SD 2012-** B Duluth MN 1955 d John & Jo. Dplma CIDEF U Catholique de lOuest 1976; BA U MN 1983; MDiv (cl) GTS 2012. D 6/30/2011 P 6/28/2012 Bp Brian N Prior. m 6/27/1987 Michael F Mornard.

MORONEY, Kevin John (Pa) 440 W 21st St, New York NY 10011 **The GTS New York NY 2016-** B Summit NJ 1961 s Robert & Joyce. BS Vlly Forge Chr Coll 1986; MDiv GTS 1992; MLS Rutgers The St U of New Jersey 2000; PhD Milltown Inst of Theol and Philos 2008. D 6/13/1992 P 2/1/1993 Bp George Phelps Mellick Belshaw. m 8/24/2006 Rosemary Elizabeth Curran c 2. S Chris's Ch Gladwyne PA 2015-2016; R Chr Epis Ch Villanova PA 2009-2015; Assoc R S Dav's Ch Wayne PA 2005-2009; P-in-c St. Jn's Sandymount 2001-2004; Chapl and Lectr in Liturg Ch of Ireland Theol Coll 2000-2005; Chapl S Jas Sch MD 1998-2000; St Jas Sch Hagerstown MD 1998-2000; All SS Epis Ch Lakewood NJ 1994-1998; R All SS NJ 1994-1998; Asst Pstr S Lk's Epis Ch Metuchen NJ 1992-1994. Auth, "Imperfect, w Peace," *LivCh*, 2009; Auth, "Some Results of a Survey of the BCP 2004," *Ch of Ireland Gazette*, 2005; Auth, "Rebirth, Renwl, Revs," *Search*, 2004; Auth, "Angl Catholicism in the Dio Dublin," *Search*, 2002. moroney@gts.edu

MORONTA, Buddelov (Va) **Gr Ch White Plains NY 2017-** B New York 1970 s Adolfo & Octavia. BA UNIBE 1993; BA PUCMM 1998; BA CET 2008; MA VTS 2012. D 2/14/2010 P 2/20/2011 Bp Julio Cesar Holguin-Khoury. Vic S Mk's Ch Alexandria VA 2015-2017; S Tim's Ch Herndon VA 2015-2016; Dio The Dominican Republic (Iglesia Epis Dominicana) Gazcue Santo Domingo 2010-2015.

MORPETH, Robert Park (Ala) 521 20th St N, Birmingham AL 35203 **Dio Alabama Birmingham 1997-, Dep for Fin & Admin 1997-** B Columbus GA 1951 s James & Julia. BS Columbus U 1974; MDiv Sewanee: The U So, TS 1978. D 6/10/1978 Bp Charles Judson Child Jr P 5/1/1979 Bp Bennett Jones Sims. m 1/29/1994 Susan Jones. Epis Black Belt Mnstry Greensboro AL 1990-1997; Assoc S Thos Epis Ch Columbus GA 1988-1990; Int S Mary Magd Ch Columbus GA 1986-1988; Chapl US-AR 1985-1994; Chapl Georgia NG 1984-1985; Chapl Florida NG 1981-1984; Asst S Mk's Epis Ch Jacksonville FL 1981-1983; Asst Chr Ch Macon GA 1979-1981; Dio Atlanta Atlanta GA 1978-1979. rmorpeth@dioala.org

MORRIGAN, Cedar Abrielynne (Minn) 309 13th St Sw, Little Falls MN 56345 B 1957 AA Anoka-Ramsey Cmnty Coll 1977; BS S Cloud St U 1981. D 4/1/2002 Bp Frederick Warren Putnam P 10/6/2002 Bp Daniel Lee Swenson. m 9/30/1984 Johanna V(Irginia) S(Tella) Morrigan c 1.

MORRILL, Bonnie G (Dal) 5314 Somerset Dr., Rowlett TX 75089 **D H Trin Rockwall TX 2007-; S Matt's Cathd Dallas TX 2005-; D H Trin Rockwall 2003-** B Greeley CO 1946 d John & Laura. BA Sch for Deacons 1999. D 5/22/1999 Bp Richard Lester Shimpfky. m 6/10/1966 Charles Clifford Morrill c 3. H Trin Ch Rockwall TX 2003-2004; D Epis Ch Of The Gd Shpd Salinas CA 1999-2003. Epis Conf of the Deaf of the Epis Ch in the 1985; Ord of S Lk 1999.

MORRIS, Alfred E (Pa) 505 E Catherine St, Chambersburg PA 17201 **Died 12/6/2016** B Philadelphia PA 1934 s Alfred & Viola. BS Tem 1957; BS CRDS 1961. Trans 1/22/1991 Bp Allen Lyman Bartlett Jr. m 8/2/1958 Barbara Ruth Ludlam c 4. Ret 1999-2016; Non-par 1993-1999; R Ch Of S Jn The Evang Essington PA 1991-1993; Serv Ch Of Can 1985-1990.

MORRIS, Alfred John (Ct) 9201 Sw 192nd Court Rd, Dunnellon FL 34432 **Died 1/20/2016** B Pawtucket RI 1925 s Charles & Charlotte. BA Barrington Coll 1959; Gordon-Conwell TS 1961; California Bapt U 1963; CDSP 1966. D 9/10/1966 P 3/11/1967 Bp Francis E I Bloy. m 12/22/1956 Dorothy Krautter c 3. Ret 1988-2016; R Ch Of The Gd Shpd Shelton CT 1970-1988; Assoc S Paul's Ch Pawtucket RI 1968-1970; Assoc S Paul's Pomona Pomona CA 1966-1968; Serv Bapt Ch 1958-1964.

MORRIS, Anthony Grant (Alb) 163 N Pole Rd, Melrose NY 12121 **Died 11/7/2016** B Mansfield Notts UK 1924 s Arthur & Alison. BA Harv 1949; BD Harvard DS 1959. D 5/1/1959 Bp Frederic Cunningham Lawrence P 11/1/1959 Bp Conrad H Gesner. S Paul's Ch Troy NY 1982; Non-par 1978-2016; S Ptr's Ch Albany NY 1975-1977; R Ch Of The H Cross Troy NY 1960-1972; Vic W Area Cheyenne River Indn Mssn Dupree SD 1959-1960.

MORRIS, Bonnie (WNY) 20 Milton Street, Williamsville NY 14221 **S Jas' Ch Batavia NY 2015-** B Oklahoma City OK 1961 d William & Mary. Bex Sem; BA S Marys Coll of Maryland 1983; MBA SUNY at Buffalo 2001; MDiv Chr the King Sem 2011. D 12/20/2008 Bp Michael Garrison P 7/21/2011 Bp Ralph William Franklin. m 5/27/1989 Timothy Patrick Morris c 2. Asst R Calv Epis Ch Williamsville NY 2011-2015.

MORRIS, Charles Hamilton (Mo) 2140 Farnsworth Dr, O Fallon MO 63368 **Died 12/26/2016** B Kerrville TX 1932 s Otho & Ethel. AA Schreiner U 1952; BA U of Texas 1954; MDiv VTS 1957; DMin VTS 1980. D 7/15/1957 Bp Everett H Jones P 2/28/1958 Bp Richard Earl Dicus. m 8/10/1957 Janet Eleanor Morris c 3. Asstg P Ch Of The Gd Shpd S Louis MO 1997-1999; Asstg P Ch Of The Trsfg Lake S Louis MO 1994-2016; S Hilary's Ch Prospect Hts IL 1994-1996; R S Andr's Ch S Louis MO 1980-1996; Vic St Fran Ch S Louis MO 1966-1979; Asst S Mich & S Geo S Louis MO 1965-1966; Chapl Washington U St. Louis MO 1965-1966; Asst S Mart's Epis Ch Houston TX 1962-1965; P-in-c Calv Ch Menard TX 1959-1962; S Jas Epis Ch Ft McKavett TX 1959-1962; M-in-c S Jas Ch Hallettsville TX 1957-1959; Trin Epis Ch Edna TX 1957-1959; Comp Dio Com Dio Missouri S Louis MO 1996-2002, Stndg Com (Pres., '95) 1992-1995, Dioc Coun 1989-1991. Faith Aloud 2000.

MORRIS, Charles Henry (Be) 24 Forsythia Dr, Harwich MA 02645 B West Chester PA 1941 s Charles & Miriam. BS W Chester U of Pennsylvania 1963; MDiv PDS 1969. D 6/7/1969 Bp Chandler W Sterling P 12/13/1969 Bp Robert Lionne DeWitt. m 8/24/1963 Wilma J Morris c 2. Int Asst Ch of the H Sprt 2010-2012; Int Asst Ch of the H Sprt 2009-2011; P-in-c St. Jn's Palmerton PA 2006-2007; R Trin Epis Ch Pottsville PA 1995-2005; Assoc S Mary's Epis Ch Barnstable MA 1989-1995; R S Paul's Ch Coll Point NY 1978-1989; Epis Ch Of S Mk The Evang Bellmore NY 1975-1978; Headmaster The Adv Sch Westbury NY 1971-1978; Cur Ch Of The Adv Westbury NY 1969-1975. NAES 1980-1984. Cn Pstr Dio Bethlehem 1999.

MORRIS, Clayton L (Cal) 30 Devoe St Apt 2B, Brooklyn NY 11211 B EugeneOR 1946 s Joseph & Betty. BA Willamette U 1968; MDiv CDSP 1971; MA Grad Theol Un 1971; PhD Grad Theol Un 1986. D 6/22/1971 Bp James Walmsley Frederic Carman P 1/2/1972 Bp Chauncie Kilmer Myers. c 2. Ltrgics Off Epis Ch Cntr New York NY 1991-2010; Assoc P/Min S Mk's Epis Ch Palo Alto CA 1986-1991; Ch Of The H Trin Richmond CA 1986; All Souls Par In Berkeley Berkeley CA 1982-1985; Lectr in Mus CDSP Berkeley CA 1982-1984; Org/Chrmstr S Paul's Ch Oakland CA 1979-1980; R S Mk's Ch King City CA 1974-1979; Assoc Min S Andr's Ch Saratoga CA 1971-1974. Auth, "The PB in Cyberspace," *Oxford Guide to BCP*, Oxf Press, 2006; Auth, "H Hosp," *H Hosp: Wrshp and the Baptismal Cov*, Ch Pub Inc, 2005; Auth, "The Future of Liturg Text," *A PB for the 21st Century*, Ch Pub Inc, 1996; Ed, "As we gather to pray," *As We Gather to Pray: An Epis Guide to Wrshp*, Ch Pub Inc, 1996; Auth, "Incarn into Culture," *The Chant of Life*, Ch Pub Inc. Associated Parishes Coun 1991; Assn Angl Musicians 1980; ADLMC 1978-2002; Consult on Common Texts 1991-2009; Intrenational Angl Liturg Consultaion 1992-2009; NAAL 1997.

MORRIS, Danielle DuBois (CFla) 444 Covey Cv, Winter Park FL 32789 **D All SS Ch Of Winter Pk Winter Pk FL 2000-** B 1947 AA Andr Jr Coll 1968; BA Rol 1972; Cert U of Cntrl Florida 1999. D 12/11/1999 P 5/19/2007 Bp John Wadsworth Howe. m 1/6/1977 Charles Anthony Morris. S Mich's Ch Orlando FL 2007-2013; Ex. Dir, Cler Position Walking The Mourner's Path Winter Pk FL 1996-2005. Auth, "Adventures Unlimited," *Walking The Mourner'S Path Workbook*. Amer Acad Of Bereavement.

MORRIS, David John (Pa) 449 Newgate Ct Apt B2, Andalusia PA 19020 **S Lk's Ch Philadelphia PA 2013-** B Plainfield NJ 1958 s Raymond & Helen. BA Tem 1990; MDiv GTS 1994. D 11/12/1994 P 12/2/1995 Bp Allen Lyman Bartlett Jr. m 11/26/2008 Douglas S Cline. Chapl/Dir of Pstr Care Temple U Hosp--Epis Div Philadelphia PA 2000-2005; Tem Hosp Philadelphia PA 2000-2005; All SS Ch Rhawnhurst Philadelphia PA 1999-2006; R All SS Crescentville Philadelphia PA 1999-2006; Vic Ch Of The Gd Shpd Ringwood NJ 1997-1999; Dio Newark Newark NJ 1997-1999; Assoc S Andr's In The Field Ch Philadelphia PA 1994-1997. Episc. Cmnty Serv--Chapl Adv Comm. Phil PA 2001-2005; NEHM 2005.

MORRIS, David Wayne (NY) 15 Pine St, Lake Peekskill NY 10537 **D Ch Of The H Comm Mahopac NY 2007-** B Ossining NY 1951 s Edward & Ruth. BA Franklin Pierce Coll 1975; AA Franklin Pierce Coll 1982; MS Pace U 1988. D 6/4/1994 Bp Richard Frank Grein. m 11/27/1976 Charlotte Patricia Morris c 1. D S Ptr's Epis Ch Peekskill NY 1994-2007.

MORRIS, Donald Richard (Vt) 280 Round Rd, Bristol VT 05443 **P S Steph's Ch Middlebury VT 2009-** B Schenectady NY 1930 s Ernest & Carmen. BA Harv 1951; MA Harv 1957. D 6/24/1978 P 3/1/1979 Bp John Thomas Walker. m 6/2/1984 May Foster Bowers Morris c 2. Cn Pstr Ch of Our Sav Killington VT 1995; R S Paul's Epis Ch On The Green Vergennes VT 1991-1995; St Pauls Ch Bristol VT 1991-1995; R Chr-S Paul Hollywood SC 1984-1991; Chr/ St Paul's Epis Par Hollywood SC 1984-1991; Epis Ch on Edisto Edisto Island SC 1984-1990; R Ch Of The H Comm Washington DC 1979-1984.

MORRIS, Gregg A (Chi) 1125 Franklin St, Downers Grove IL 60515 **R S Andr's Ch Downers Grove IL 2015-** B Peoria IL 1963 s Jack & Gladys. BA Taylor U 1986; MA Azusa Pacific U 1994; MDiv VTS 2011. D 6/4/2011 Bp Eugene Taylor Sutton P 12/10/2011 Bp Joe Goodwin Burnett. m 12/30/1995 Laura O Laura Diane Olsen c 2. S Jn's Ch Ellicott City MD 2011-2015; Ch Of Our Sav Par San Gabr CA 1994-1997. gmorris@saintandrewschurch.net

MORRIS, Janie Kirt (Tex) 439 NW 44th Street, Oklahoma City OK 73118 **Chair Wrld Mssn Bd 2013-** B Oklahoma City OK 1945 d Glenn & Lila. BA U of Oklahoma 1967; MDiv Epis TS of the SW 1990. D 6/23/1990 P 2/1/1991 Bp Robert Manning Moody. c 2. Dn W Harris Cler 2007-2009; Exam Chapl Com for the Diac 2006-2009; Quin Fndt Trst Dio Texas 2004-2009; R Emm Ch Houston TX 2003-2014; R Emm Epis Ch Shawnee OK 1992-2003; Asst R S Mary's Ch Edmond OK 1991-1992; Yth Min/Sch Chapl All SS Epis Ch Austin TX 1990-1991.

MORRIS, Jim (Pa) 203 Devon Dr, Exton PA 19341 **Int All SS Ch Rhawnhurst Philadelphia PA 2011-** B Bryn Mawr PA 1933 s Edgar & Helen. BA Ursinus Coll 1956; MDiv Epis TS of the SW 1963; AA Amer Fndt of Rel & Psych 1967; VTS 1996; Cert Oxf GB 1998; Cert Oxf GB 1998; DMin VTS 2000. D 6/8/1963 P 12/1/1963 Bp Joseph Gillespie Armstrong. m 9/10/1966 Shirley Joan Clark c 2. Int Ch Of Our Sav Jenkintown PA 2006-2010; Int The Ch Of The Ascen Claymont DE 2004-2005; S Martha's Epis Ch Bethany Bch DE 2002-2003; P-in-c S Mart's Epis Ch Fairlee VT 2002-2003; S Paul Ch Exton PA 1982-2003; Actg R Ch Of The Redemp Southampton PA 1981-1982; Hospice Com Dio Pennsylvania Philadelphia PA 1980-1983; Assoc Chr Ch Ithan PA 1979-1981; Chr Epis Ch Villanova PA 1979-1981; Chapl Ch Farm Sch Paoli PA 1971-1979; Asst Min S Mary's Epis Ch Ardmore PA 1967-1969; Stff Dept Mssns Dio New York New York NY 1966-1967; Vic S Mary Annunc Philadelphia PA 1963-1966. Auth, "Hlth & Med In The Angl Tradition," *Journ Of Chr Healing*, 1984; Auth, "Bridging Renwl: A Cmnty Bldg Process That Celebrates Diversity In Unity".

MORRIS, John (Vt) 37 Thompson Rd, East Corinth VT 05040 B Lincoln NE 1943 s Robert & Margaret. BA Midland U 1965; Bos 1967; STB GTS 1968. D 6/14/1968 P 12/13/1968 Bp Russell T Rauscher. m 5/28/1966 Susan M Morris c 3. R S Mart's Epis Ch Fairlee VT 2002-2013; Int R S Lk's Ch Chester VT 2000-2002; St Mary's in The Mountains Epis Wilmington VT 1985-2000, R 1972-1979; 1973-1999; Dio New York New York NY 1968-1971; Cur The Ch of S Edw The Mtyr New York NY 1968-1971. Auth, "First Comes Love: the ever-changing face of Mar," *First Comes Love?*, Pilgrim Press, 2007; Auth, "Living by the Word," *Chr Century*, Chr Century, 2002; Auth, "essays," *Educational Ldrshp*, Educational Ldrshp, 1992; Auth, "essays," *Teachers' Journ*, Teachers' Journ, 1992.

MORRIS III, John Glen (Va) 1021 Aquia Dr, Stafford VA 22554 **Asst R Aquia Ch Stafford VA 2004-** B Burlington NC 1970 BA Wake Forest U. D 6/26/2004 P 1/10/2005 Bp Peter J Lee. morris@aquiachurch.com

MORRIS, John Karl (NCal) 3663 Solano Ave Apt 204, Napa CA 94558 **Assoc S Mary's Epis Ch Napa CA 2011-, D 1994-2006, Assoc 2011-** B Denver CO 1939 s Bryce & Grace. U CO; BS USNA 1961; MS MIT 1973; OE MIT 1973; BA California Sch for Deacons 1988; CAS CDSP 2011. D 2/19/1992 Bp Jerry Alban Lamb P 9/8/2011 Bp Barry Leigh Beisner. c 4. D H Sprt Epis Ch Houston TX 1993-1994; D S Mary's Epis Ch Napa CA 1992-1993. "Regulatory Consideration in the Design of Teusion Leg Platforms," SPE Journ Soc of Petroleum Egineer, 1988; "Measurement of Low-Wavenumber Components of Turbulout Boundary Layer Wall Pressure Fluctuations," ASA Journ Acoustic Soc of Amer, 1973. jkmorris1961@gmail.com

MORRIS, John William (CPa) St. John's Episcopal Church, 321 W. Chestnut St., Lancaster PA 17603 **Archd S Jn's Epis Ch Lancaster PA 2005-** B York PA 1952 s Elmer & Nancy. BA Susquahanna U 1974; MDiv EDS 1979. D 6/15/1979 P 2/10/1980 Bp Dean Theodore Stevenson. m 8/24/1974 Cynthia Kay Cromis c 2. R S Thos Epis Ch Mclean VA 1988-2005; R S Marg's Epis Ch Parkville MD 1983-1988; Asst St Martins-In-The-Field Ch Severna Pk MD 1979-1983.

MORRIS, Jonathan Edward (USC) 717 Dupre Dr, Spartanburg SC 29307 **R Ch Of The Adv Spartanburg SC 2009-; Dn - Piedmont Convoc Dio Upper So Carolina Columbia SC 2011-, Eccl Disciplinary Bd 2011-** B Williamsburg VA 1966 s Harry & Lillian. BA Roa 1988; MSW Virginia Commonwealth U 1993; MDiv GTS 2001. D 2/23/2001 P 9/14/2001 Bp Neff Powell. m 5/15/1993 Ellen Elizabeth Morris c 4. R Calv Ch Louisville KY 2004-2009; Assoc R Trin Ch Staunton VA 2001-2004. nmorris@churchofadvent.org

MORRIS, Julie H. (Los) P.O. Box 2305, Camarillo CA 93011 B Fullerton CA 1970 d John & Gerlinde. BA Loyola Marymount U 1992; MA Boston Coll 1994; MDiv Claremont TS 2001. D 6/16/2001 Bp Robert Marshall Anderson P 1/12/2002 Bp Frederick Houk Borsch. m 9/21/1996 Paul DeBusschere c 3. P The Abundant Table S Paula CA 2010-2012; R Trin Ch Fillmore CA 2007-2010; R Trin Par Fillmore CA 2006-2010; S Columba's Par Camarillo CA 2005-2007, 2001-2005; Chapl California St U Channel Islands CA 2004-2008.

MORRIS, Kevin L (LI) 176 Palisade Ave, Jersey City NJ 07306 **P The Ch Of The Ascen Rockville Ct NY 2012-** B Melbourne FL 1979 s Larry & Sandra. BA U of Miami 2000; MDiv Yale DS 2004. D 4/17/2004 P 11/30/2004 Bp Leo Frade. m 5/21/2016 Keith A Voets. Chr Hosp Jersey City NJ 2008-2012; Ch Of The Resurr New York NY 2004-2005.

MORRIS, Richard Melvin (O) 55 Countryside Dr, Cumberland RI 02864 B North Attleboro MA 1923 s George & Etta. BA Br 1947; BD EDS 1950. D 5/31/1950 P 12/1/1950 Bp Norman B Nash. m 12/29/1951 Marjorie Morris c 6. R S Ptr's Epis Ch Lakewood OH 1965-1985; R S Thos' Epis Ch Syracuse NY 1952-1965; Asst All SS' Epis Ch Belmont MA 1950-1952; Chair of The Stndg Com Dio Ohio Cleveland 1988-1989, Chairman of the Dept of CE 1985-1988, Chair of the Dept Chr Soc Relatns 1971-1985, Chair of the Dept of Chr Soc Relatns 1967-1970, Exec Coun 1967-1968; Exec Coun Dio Cntrl New York Liverpool NY 1962-1965.

MORRIS, Roberta Louise (Los) 1733 N New Hampshire Ave, Los Angeles CA 90027 B Winsor Ontario 1953 d Robert & Mary. MA,PhD York U; BA U Tor 1973; MDiv St Mich's Coll 1979. Trans 5/12/2015 as Priest Bp Joseph Jon Bruno. c 2.

MORRIS, Robert Corin Veal (Nwk) 422 Clark, South Orange NJ 07079 **Interweave Summit NJ 2001-** B Detroit MI 1941 s John & Lorene. BA Ya 1963; STB GTS 1966. D 6/29/1966 Bp Chauncie Kilmer Myers P 1/26/1967 Bp Richard Stanley Merrill Emrich. m 7/26/1969 Suzanne Bate Morris. Chr Ed. Asst. The Ch Of The Sav Denville NJ 1985-1988; Asstg P S Bern's Ch Bernardsville NJ 1983-1985; Calv Epis Ch Summit NJ 1968-1997; Asstg P S Ptr's Ch Essex Fells NJ 1967-1968; Assoc R St. Jas Epis Ch Detroit MI 1966-1967; Fac, Epis Coll Stdt Gatherings Epis Ch Cntr New York NY 1985-1994. Contrib, "Provocative Gr:," Upper Room Books, 2006; Auth, "Suffering and the Courage of God," Paraclete, 2005; Auth, "Prayers to Green the Earth," Interweave, 2004; Auth, "Wrestling w Gr: A Sprtlty for the Rough Edges," Upper Room Books, 2003; Auth, "Sprtl Formation Bible: Sprtl Exercises for Isaiah," Zondervan/Upper Room, 1999. DD The GTS 2009; Cert of Merit Epis Dio Newark 1993; Phi Beta Kappa Key Phi Beta Kappa 1963.

MORRIS III, Robert Lee (Va) B Raleigh NC 1958 s Robert & Jacqueline. BA Bridgewater Coll 1980; MDiv Bethany TS 1985; Angl Stds VTS 2011. D 6/9/2012 P 12/15/2012 Bp Shannon Sherwood Johnston. m 5/31/1980 Deborah Crouse Morris c 2.

MORRIS, Robert Lee (Fla) 601 Alhambra Ln N, Ponte Vedra Beach FL 32082 B South Charleston WV 1947 s Lewis & Thursta. BA W Virginia U 1969; MDiv GTS 1973. D 6/7/1973 P 2/24/1974 Bp Wilburn Camrock Campbell. m 8/26/1973 Cathleen Linda Gillis c 2. Assoc Pstr Care Chr Epis Ch Ponte Vedra FL 2004-2014; Assoc S Dunst's Epis Ch Houston TX 1999-2004; Vic All SS Epis Ch Brighton Heights Brighton Heights PA 1994-1999; Asst Chr Epis Ch No Hills Pittsburgh PA 1992-1994; Asst All SS Ch Aliquippa PA 1985-1990; P-in-c Cathd of the Isles Millport Scotland 1974-1985; D S Pauls Epis Ch Williamson WV 1973-1974; Dio W Virginia Charleston WV 1973.

MORRIS, Sarah (SwVa) 1962 Tyler Rd, Christiansburg VA 24073 **Chr Ch Pearisburg VA 2012-; Dir of Cbury Stdt Mnstrs Gr Ch Radford VA 2011-** B 1959 d Warren & Jane. BA Berea Coll 1981; MDiv U of New Mex 1982; MDiv Sewanee: The U So, TS 1996; MDiv The TS at The U So 1996. D 3/26/2012 P 10/6/2012 Bp Neff Powell. m 5/7/2005 Robert Earl Morris. S Steph's Ch Richmond VA 2004-2008; The Ch Of The Gd Shpd Augusta GA 1996-2004.

MORRIS, Stephen B (SwFla) 140 4th St N, St Petersburg FL 33701 **Cathd Ch Of S Ptr St. Petersburg FL 2008-; Chapl The Epis Sch Of Dallas Dallas TX 1993-** B Alexandria LA 1965 s James & Dorothy. BBA Loyola U 1988; MDiv Epis TS of the SW 1994. D 10/30/1993 P Robert Jefferson Hargrove Jr P 5/1/1994 Bp James Monte Stanton. m 6/29/2013 Christina B Morris c 6. S Jas Epis Ch Ormond Bch FL 2004-2008; S Lk's Ch Salisbury NC 2000-2003; Upper Yellowstone Epis Ch Livingston MT 1999-2000; The Epis Ch Of The Gd Shpd Vidalia LA 1996; Epis Sch Of Dallas Dallas TX 1993-1995.

MORRIS, Thomas Rand (Tex) PO Box 173, Sewanee TN 37375 **All SS Epis Sch Tyler TX 2013-** B Lake Charles LA 1962 s Walter & Bonnie. BA LSU 1986; MDiv PrTS 1990. D 6/7/1999 Bp Robert Jefferson Hargrove Jr P 2/5/2000 Bp Frank Kellogg Allan. m 4/11/1999 Hadley Simmonds Morris c 1. S Mary's Sewanee Sewanee TN 2009-2013; R S Paul's Ch Wilkesboro NC 2004-2009; R Trin Ch Spruce Pine NC 2001-2004; Assoc R All SS Epis Ch Atlanta GA 1999-2001.

MORRIS-KLIMENT, Nicholas M (Mass) 44 Seminole Rd, Acton MA 01720 **Chr Ch Needham Hgts MA 2014-** B Philadelphia PA 1963 s Robert & Janet. BA Ya 1985; MA Br 1988; Br 1990; MDiv Ya Berk 2001. D 6/15/2002 P 5/31/2003 Bp M(Arvil) Thomas Shaw. m 12/20/1997 Jameson Lynn Morris-Kliment c 2. P-in-c S Paul's Ch Lynnfield MA 2012-2014; Asst Trin Ch Concord MA 2004-2012; Asst S Ptr's Ch Weston MA 2002-2004. nick@ccneedham.org

MORRISON, Enid Ann (Ind) 8320 E. 10th St., Indianapolis IN 46219 B London England 1937 d Frederick & Enid. AGS Indiana U-Pur-Indianapolis 1985; BGS Indiana U-Pur 1987; MTS Chr TS 1997. D 10/26/2008 Bp Cate Waynick. c 2. D S Matt's Ch Indianapolis IN 2008-2013. Amer Epis Diac 2006.

MORRISON, Glenn David (Mich) 171 W Pike St, Pontiac MI 48341 B Pontiac MI 1960 s Merritt & Eleanor. D 6/14/2014 Bp Wendell Nathaniel Gibbs Jr. m 4/30/2011 Pamela Morrison c 3.

MORRISON JR, Henry T Nick (Az) Po Box 610, Ketchum ID 83340 B Mount Pleasant NY 1939 s Henry & Mary. BA U MN 1963; PEDI Imede Lausanne Ch 1971; MA Yale DS 1980. D 6/24/1982 Bp Robert Marshall Anderson P 3/1/1983 Bp David Bell Birney IV. m 3/10/1979 Karen Anne Morrison c 6. Asstg Chr Ch Of The Ascen Paradise Vlly AZ 1993-1998; Non-par 1991-1993; Asst Ch Of The Epiph Epis Minneapolis MN 1986-1991; Non-par 1984-1986; Emm Ch Hailey ID 1983-1984; R S Thos Epis Ch Sun Vlly ID 1983-1984. Auth, "Intercept". Knights Of Malta (Ord S Jn Jerusalem).

MORRISON, James R (La) 1329 Jackson Ave, New Orleans LA 70130 **S Andr's Epis Ch New Orleans LA 2014-** B Houma LA 1961 s Chester & Joanne. BA St Meinrad Coll 1983; MDiv St Mary of the Lake 1987; MDiv St Mary of the Lake 1987; Angl Stds Sewanee: The U So, TS 2013; Angl Stds The TS at The U So 2013. Rec 5/22/2013 as Priest Bp Morris King Thompson Jr. Trin Ch New Orleans LA 2013-2014. jmorrison@standrewsnola.com

MORRISON, John Ainslie (SO) Calvary Episcopal Church, 3766 Clifton Ave, Cincinnati OH 45220 **Emer Prof of Pediatrics Cinti Chld's Hosp (Cardiology) 2009-** B Cincinnati OH 1939 s Marion & Mary. BA U Cinc 1962; BD EDS 1965; MA U Cinc 1971; PhD U Cinc 1977. D 9/25/1965 P 3/27/1966 Bp Roger W Blanchard. m 8/17/1963 Patricia Wright. Vol Asst Calv Ch Cincinnati OH 1998-2013; Resrch Prof and Emer Prof of Pediatrics Chld's Hosp Med Cntr Div of Cardiology 1988-2013; P-in-c S Steph's Epis Ch Cincinnati OH 1987-1991; H Sprt Epis Ch Cincinnati OH 1975-1976; Asst Min Chr Ch - Glendale Cincinnati OH 1965-1968. Auth, "200 arts & Chapters On Med & Epidemiology". Felllow, Amer Coll of epidemiology 1979-2009.

MORRISON III, John E (LI) 510 Manatuck Blvd, Brightwaters NY 11718 **Int S Jn's Ch Huntington NY 2007-** B New York NY 1941 s John & Constance. BA Dart 1963; MEd Hofstra U 1968; MLS SUNY 1973; CTh Mercer TS 1980. D 6/7/1980 Bp Robert Campbell Witcher Sr P 5/15/1982 Bp Henry Boyd Hucles III. m 6/5/1965 M Susan Morrison. Asst S Ptr's by-the-Sea Epis Ch Bay Shore NY 1999-2011; Geo Mercer TS Garden City NY 1994-2000; Instr Theol Mercer 1982-1996; Asst Gr Epis Ch Massapequa NY 1980-1999. Auth, "Idea Of Cov In Narnia"; Auth, "God Means What He Says: Cs Lewis On Forgiveness"; Auth, "Bulletin Of Ny Cs Lewis Soc"; Auth, "A Pleasure Is Full Growth Only When It'S Remembered".

MORRISON, Karl Frederick (NJ) 75 Linwood Circle, Princeton NJ 08540 **Assoc All SS Ch Princeton NJ 2004-** B Birmingham AL 1936 s Karl & Margaret. BA U of Mississippi 1956; MA Cor 1957; PhD Cor 1961. D 5/9/1998 P 4/10/1999 Bp Joe Doss. m 8/29/1964 Anne Caroline Morrison c 2. P-in-c The Epis Campus Mnstry at Rutgers New Brunswick NJ 2003; D Chr Ch New Brunswick NJ 1998-2003. Co-Ed, "Stds in Medieval Empathies," Brepols, 2013; Co-Ed, "Seeing the Invisible," Brepols, 2005; Auth, "Understanding Conversion," U of Virginia Press, 1992; Auth, "Conversion and Text," U of Virginia Press, 1992; Auth, "Hist as a Visual Art," Pr Press, 1990; Auth, "I am You," Pr Press, 1988; Auth, "The Mimetic Tradition of Reform," Pr Press, 1982; Auth, "Europe's Middle Ages," Scott, Foresman, 1970; Auth, "Tradition and Authority," Pr Press, 1969; Auth, "Carolingian Coinage," Amer Numismatic Soc, 1967; Auth, "The Two Kingdoms," Pr Press, 1964; Auth, "Rome and the City of God," Amer Philos Soc, 1964; Co-Transltr, "Imperial Lives and Letters," Col Press, 1962. Amer Cath Hist Soc 1970; Amer Hist Assn 1965; Amer Soc of Ch Hist 1970; Medieval Acad of Amer 1960; Soc of Biblic Theologians 1999. Vstng Mem Inst for Advncd Study 2004; Carey Sr Fac Fell U of Notre Dame 2001; Haskins Medal Medieval Acad of Amer 1994; Fell Medieval Acad of Amer 1986.

MORRISON, Larry Clair (NJ) PO Box 100, Front Royal VA 22630 B West Buffalo Township PA 1940 s Robert & Helen. BA Pr 1970; MDiv Westminster TS 1975. D 6/5/1982 P 10/1/1982 Bp Albert Wiencke Van Duzer. m 12/22/1972 Priscilla Jane Morrison c 1. P-in-c S Jn The Evang Ch Blackwood NJ 1997-1999; Supply P S Jn's Epis Ch Maple Shade NJ 1996-1997; Non-par 1992-1996; Vic Ch Of S Jn-In-The-Wilderness Gibbsboro NJ 1984-1992; Cur Trin Cathd Trenton NJ 1982-1984; Serv Presb Ch 1975-1981.

MORRISON, Leroy Oran (NwT) 6535 Amber Dr, Odessa TX 79762 B Sharon PA 1953 s Oran & Ruth. AA Penn 1992. D 5/24/1998 Bp Robert Deane Rowley Jr. m 4/25/1975 Kathy Sue DeHoff c 2.

MORRISON, Mary K (ECR) 443 Alberto Way Unit B221, Los Gatos CA 95032 B Sacramento CA 1946 d Robert & Janet. BA U CA 1969; Cert U CA 1970; BTS Sch for Deacons 1985; MDiv CDSP 2000. D 6/24/2000 P 4/26/2001 Bp Richard Lester Shimpfky. m 7/15/2008 Claudia Jo Weber c 2. GC Dep Dio El Camino Real 2010-2013; R S Jas Ch Paso Robles CA 2008-2013; Stndg Com

Dio El Camino Real 2006-2009; Chair, Transition Com Dio El Camino Real 2005-2007; Dioc Coun Dio El Camino Real 2003-2006; Pstr Assoc S Lk's Ch Los Gatos CA 2002-2008, Asstg Cler 2000-2002; Prog Dir CDSP Berkeley CA 2000-2002.

MORRISON, Mikel Anne (Oly) 760 Kristen Ct, Santa Barbara CA 93111 **D S Andr's Epis Ch Ojai CA 2000-** B Cleveland OH 1941 d Stephen & Ethel. BA Coll of Wooster 1962; MS U IL 1964; Oxf GB 1989; MA Fuller TS 1990. D 6/27/1992 Bp Chester Lovelle Talton. m 6/10/1964 Rollin John Morrison c 2. D S Mich's U Mssn Isla Vista CA 1992-2004. NAAD.

MORRISON, Paul Charles (NC) 77 W Coolidge St #227, Phoenix AZ 85013 **1988-** B Conneaut OH 1933 s Paul & Mary. BA Case Wstrn Reserve U 1955; MDiv Bex Sem 1964; ThM Duke 1971. D 6/13/1964 Bp Nelson Marigold Burroughs P 1/1/1965 Bp Robert Lionne DeWitt. c 4. Chapl Jn Umstead Hosp Butner PA 1975-1980; R S Jos's Ch Durham NC 1968-1975; R Chr Ch Albemarle NC 1966-1968; Cur S Mk's Ch Philadelphia PA 1964-1966.

MORRISON, Pauline (Ore) St John's Episcopal Church, 110 NE Alder St, Toledo OR 97391 **Facility Chapl Pinnacle Healthcare 2008-; Chapl Pinnacle Healthcare Inc 2008-; Bd Mem St. Anselm of Cbury Campus Mnstrs Corvallis 2008-; S Jn's Epis Ch Toledo OR 2007-; Law Enforcement Chapl, Vol Lincoln City Police Dept & Lincoln Cnty Sheriff's Of 2004-; Fire Chapl, Vol No Lincoln Fire & Rescue Dist #1 OR 2004-** B Santa Ana CA 1950 d Paul & Anita. AS Judson Bapt Coll Portland OR 1971; Portland St U 1976; Oregon Cntr for the Diac 2004. D 9/18/2004 Bp Johncy Itty. c 2. Int Chapl Samaritan Pacific Communities Hosp/Hospice OR 2005-2006; COM Dio Oregon Portland OR 2005-2010, Peace & Justice Cmsn 2004-2007. 2016 Chf's Awd No Lincoln Fire & Rescue Dist #1 2017; 2015 Sheriff's Awd Lincoln Cnty Sheriff's Off 2016; 2015 Spprt Person of the Year No Lincoln Fire & Rescue Dist #1 2016. monnshadowducky@yahoo.com

MORRISON, Richard (Az) 720 West Elliot Road, Gilbert AZ 85233 **Vice-Chncllr Dio Arizona Phoenix AZ 2014-, Chncllr 1992-2011, Chair of Cn Com 1992-, Prlmntrn 1992-** B Mesa AZ 1947 s Eunice. BS Nthrn Arizona U 1970; JD U of Houston 1977; MA SFTS 1991. D 2/8/1997 P 6/28/2003 Bp Robert Reed Shahan. m 12/8/1973 Elaine Morrison c 2. Int S Matt's Ch Chandler AZ 2012-2014, Vstng P 2011; D 2000-2003; P Ch Of The Epiph Tempe AZ 2005-2012, D 1997-2005; R Ch Of The Epiph Flagstaff AZ 2003-2005; Chair of COM Dio Arizona 2008-2010; Chair of Cn Com Dio Arizona 1993-2013. Blue Key 1968-1970; Ord of the Barons 1976; Phi Eta Sigma 1966; Phi Kappa Phi 1969. Doctor of Humane Letters Nthrn Arizona U 2015; Centennial Hist Awd in Rel Town of Gilbert, Arizona 2011; Doctor of Humane Letters U of Arizona 2011; Distinguished Achievement Arizona St U 1989.

MORRISON JR, Robert Dabney (EC) 119 Briarwood St., Lynchburg VA 24503 **Ret 2007-** B Lynchburg VA 1941 s Robert & Margaret. BS Davidson Coll 1963; MDiv VTS 1971. D 6/4/1971 P 12/9/1971 Bp William Henry Marmion. m 8/9/1969 Julia R Morrison c 2. R S Jn's Epis Ch Wilmington NC 2000-2007; R S Mths Epis Ch Midlothian VA 1979-2000; R S Jas Ch Roanoke VA 1974-1979; Assoc S Dav's Ch Wayne PA 1971-1973.

MORRISON, Robert Paterson (Ore) Po Box 789, Lincoln City OR 97367 B Kilmaurs Scotland GB 1944 s Robert & Edith. Duquesne U; BD U of Edinburgh Edinburgh Gb 1969; STM Drew U 1970; BA Portland St U 1976. D 6/28/1983 P 6/1/1984 Bp Matthew Paul Bigliardi. c 3. S Jas Ch Lincoln City OR 2000-2010, 1987-2000, Vic 1987-1991; Asst Trin Epis Cathd Portland OR 1984-1987; Chapl Gd Samar Hosp & Med Cntr Portland OR 1983-1984; Legacy Gd Samar Hosp Portland OR 1983-1984; Serv Presb Ch 1970-1976. Fllshp S Alb & S Sergius.

MORRISON, Samuel Warfield (FdL) 101 S Wythe St, Pentwater MI 49449 **R S Jas' Epis Ch Of Pentwater Pentwater MI 2007-** B Iowa City IA 1951 s William & Elizabeth. BS Wstrn Michigan U 1972; MA SWTS 1975. D 6/2/1975 P 6/2/1976 Bp Charles Bennison Sr. m 7/8/1972 Jane M Gustafson c 3. Vic S Paul's Ch Plymouth WI 1996-2007; St Bon Ch Hilbert WI 1996-2004; R S Aid's Ch Michigan Ctr MI 1986-1996; Vic S Paul's Ch Greenville MI 1978-1986; Cur S Lk's Par Kalamazoo MI 1978; R S Ptr's By-The-Lake Ch Montague MI 1976-1977; D Dio Wstrn Michigan Kalamazoo MI 1975-1976; S Dav's Ch Lansing MI 1975-1976. Cler Assn; Curs; Ord of S Lk.

MORRISON-CLEARY, Douglas Vaughn (Minn) B Newcastle Australia 1965 s James & Lurline. D 6/8/2006 P 12/21/2006 Bp James Louis Jelinek. m 10/5/1991 Jennifer Morrison-Cleary c 2. Cong of the Gd Shpd Keewatin MN 2007-2009; S Paul's Ch Virginia MN 2007-2008; Assoc In Mnstry/LP Cong Of The Gd Shpd 2005-2006.

MORRIS-RADER, Patricia (Ore) 8045 Sw 56th Ave, Portland OR 97219 **Gr Epis Ch Astoria OR 2007-** B Brementon WA 1939 d George & Liela. BA Linfield Coll 1963; MS OR SU 1978. D 9/29/2001 Bp Robert Louis Ladehoff. m 6/8/2002 Donald D Rader c 2. D S Jn The Evang Ch Portland OR 2007-2012; D Epis Par Of S Jn The Bapt Portland OR 2001-2006.

MORRISS, Jerry Davis (Dal) 132 Baywood Blvd, Mabank TX 75156 B Matador TX 1941 s Malcolm & Eunice. Baylor U 1961; U of No Texas 1967; BA Sch for Deacons 1991. D 12/7/1991 Bp William Edwin Swing P 2/15/2003 Bp James Monte Stanton. m 12/29/1961 Carroll Reeves Morriss. R S Jas' Epis Ch Kemp

M

TX 2003-2016, D 1994-2002; Dio Dallas Dallas TX 2001-2002, Cmsn on Rural Ch Mnstry 2006-; D S Clem's Ch Berkeley CA 2001-2002, 1991-2000; D H Cross Epis Ch Castro Vlly CA 1992-1994. Amer Assn Chr Counslrs.

MORRISSETTE, Paul E (WMass) 14 Enaya Circle, Worcester MA 01606 B Berlin NH 1930 s Henry & Lumina. BA S Marys Sem & U Baltimore 1952; StMarys Sem Baltimore MD 1957; MEd Rivier Coll 1970; MS Univ of NH 1973; DMin Boston Univ 1976; DMin Boston Univ 1976. Rec 12/16/1987 as Priest Bp Andrew Frederick Wissemann. m 11/20/1983 Judith A Morrissette. Supply Chr Ch So Barre MA 2005-2007; P-in-c Chr Memi Ch No Brookfield MA 1996-2000; Int S Matt's Ch Worcester MA 1991-1993; Int H Trin Epis Ch Southbridge MA 1989-1990; Clinician/Dir Worcester Pstr Counslg Cntr 1982-1989; Serv Dio Manchester, NH RC Ch 1957-1982. Auth, "Rollo May and Sartre: Their Relatedness and their Contributions to Counslg," *AMHC Forum*, The Assn of Mntl Hlth Chapl, 1975; Auth, "The Role Functions of Chapl At New Hampshire Hosp," *AMHC Forum*, The Assn of Mntl Hlth Cler, Inc., 1975; Auth, "Taking a Second Look at Psych Treatment: Ther Is Not Enough," *Hosp and Cmnty Psychiaty*, 1975; Auth, "A study of Rel Values: Psych Patients Are Compared To Non- Patietnts," *AMHC Forum*, The Assn pf Mntl Hlth Chapl, 1974; Auth, "CPE For Sis," *The Camillian*, NACC, XII, 1974; Auth, "Three Chapl Models," *AMHC News Letters*, 1973. AAPC; Massachusets Lic Clincl Psychol; Massachusetts Psychol Assn 1995.

MORROW, Andrea (Mich) 2803 1st St, Wyandotte MI 48192 **S Steph's Ch Wyandotte MI 2015-** B Tecumseh MI 1967 d Robert & Judith. BA U MI 1988; MA U MI 1989; MDiv Ecum TS 2014. D 6/13/2015 P 12/12/2015 Bp Wendell Nathaniel Gibbs Jr. m 8/3/2003 John Timothy Morrow c 2.

MORROW, Daniel R (CPa) 101 Pine St, Harrisburg PA 17101 **Dio Cntrl Pennsylvania Harrisburg PA 2016-** B Henryetta OK 1977 s David & Deborah. BA Oklahoma Bapt U 2001; MDiv Claremont TS 2006. D 6/9/2007 P 1/12/2008 Bp Joseph Jon Bruno. m 8/28/2012 Teresa S Morris. S Paul's Par Oregon City OR 2011-2016; S Clem's-By-The-Sea Par San Clemente CA 2007-2008; Yth Dir S Jn's Mssn La Verne CA 2005-2007.

MORROW, Gabriel Charles Daniel (Mont) PO Box 41, Burnt Hills NY 12027 B Santa Barbara CA 1974 s Richard & Nancy. BS Le Tourneau U 1996; MDiv Nash 2014. D 5/31/2014 Bp William Howard Love P 12/14/2014 Bp Charles Franklin Brookhart Jr. m 8/17/1996 Angela Franzen c 2. Cur S Ptr's Cathd Helena MT 2014-2017. rector@calvarybh.org

MORROW JR, Harold Frederick (CPa) 2453 Harrisburg Pike, Lancaster PA 17601 **D S Edw's Epis Ch Lancaster PA 2010-; Disaster Response Cmsn Dio Cntrl Pennsylvania Harrisburg PA 2010-** B Columbia PA 1952 s Harold & Lillian. Sch of Chr Stds 2010. D 10/31/2010 Bp Nathan Dwight Baxter. m 9/23/1972 Deborah J Morrow c 3. Assn for Epis Deacons 2010.

MORROW, Jerry Dean (Mass) 89 Msgr Patrick J Lydon Way, Dorchester MA 02124 B Macomb IL 1944 s Harold & Vera. BA MacMurray Coll 1966; SMM UTS 1968; MDiv UTS 1971; Bos 1976. D 6/5/1971 P 12/18/1971 Bp Horace W B Donegan. c 3. T/F on Catechumate Dio Massachusetts Boston MA 1993-1997, Chair, Mus Cmsn 1985-1992, Liturg Cmsn 1982-1984; R S Jn's Ch Sharon MA 1983-2016; Coordntr YA Netwk S Matt And The Redeem Epis Ch Boston MA 1980-1982; Mssnr All SS Par Brookline MA 1979-1981; P-in-c S Lk's And S Marg's Ch Allston MA 1977-1979; Asst Zion Ch Douglaston NY 1971-1972. Associated Parishes 1984; ADLMC 1984-2002; Soc of Cath Priests 2009.

MORROW, John Thomas (NJ) Po Box 424, Pine Beach NJ 08741 **Ret 1996-** B Philadelphia PA 1934 s Lester & Lillie. BA U So 1957; STB PDS 1960. D 4/30/1960 P 11/1/1960 Bp Alfred L Banyard. m 6/21/1958 Marilyn Morrow c 3. Mem Trial Crt Dioc. Of NJ 2003-2006; Chair Of The Bd Managers S Mart's Retreat Hse Gladstone NJ 1970-1979; R S Lk's Ch Gladstone NJ 1965-1996; Min S Bern's Sch Gladstone NJ 1965-1970; R S Geo's Epis Ch Helmetta NJ 1962-1965; Cur Gr Ch Merchantville NJ 1960-1962; Dn Of The Watchung Convoc. Cmnty Of S Jn The Bapt. Hon Cn Trin Cathd.

MORROW, Mildred K (WNC) 9 Swan St, Asheville NC 28803 **The Cathd Of All Souls Asheville NC 2013-, Cn 2012-2013** B Kingsport TN 1973 d Robert & Sarah. BSW U of Tennessee 2001; MSW U of Tennessee 2007; MDiv EDS 2010; MDiv EDS 2010. D 11/9/2013 P 5/10/2014 Bp Porter Taylor. m 8/10/2007 Jules N Smith c 1.

MORROW, Penelope (Eas) St Paul's by-the-Sea Episcopal Church, PO Box 1207, Ocean City MD 21843 B San Luis Obispo CA 1943 d Lynn & Jean. BA Salisbury U; AA Wor-Wic Cmnty Coll. D 10/4/2008 Bp Bud Shand. m 12/26/1992 Douglas Ralph Hastings c 2.

MORROW, Quintin Gregory (FtW) 917 Lamar St, Fort Worth TX 76102 B Yuma AZ 1963 s Richard & Billie. BA Chr Heritage Coll 1991; MDiv TESM 1994. D 6/11/1994 P 2/24/1995 Bp Gethin Benwil Hughes. m 1/12/1991 Kathryn Morrow c 2. St Andr Epis Ch Ft Worth TX 2001-2005; R S Anne's Epis Ch Oceanside CA 1995-2001; Cur S Barth's Epis Ch Poway CA 1994-1995.

MORSCH, Joel James (SwFla) 1903 - 85th Court NW, Bradenton FL 34209 **Chr Ch Bradenton FL 2006-; Bd Mem Fndt for Hisp and Latino Mnstry Inc. 2013-; Chairman, Dioc Fin Com Dio SW Florida Parrish FL 2011-,**

Dioc Endwmt Bd 2011-, Dioc Fin Com 2010-, Dioc Coun 2007-, Dioc Coun 2006-; Bd Mem S Steph's Epis Sch Bradenton FL 2006- B Aurora IL 1950 s Byron & Betty. BA U of Wisconsin 1972; MDiv Nash 1998. D 12/8/1997 P 7/5/1998 Bp Keith Lynn Ackerman. m 1/11/1992 Barbara Bell Morsch c 3. R The Epis Ch Of The Resurr Franklin TN 2002-2006; Assoc R S Jn's Epis Ch Naperville IL 1998-2002; Stndg Com Dio Tennessee Nashville TN 2005-2006. joelmorsch@gmail.com

MORSE, Alice Janette (Mich) 3899 Ryan's Ridge, Monroe MI 48161 B Howell MI 1947 d Walter & Ellamae. BA Estrn Michigan U 1971; MDiv Nash 1986. D 6/30/1987 Bp Henry Irving Mayson P 8/1/1993 Bp Roger John White. c 3. R Trin Epis Ch Monroe MI 2003-2015; S Paul's Ch Milwaukee WI 1999-2003; P-in-c S Andr's Ch Kenosha WI 1994-1997; Non-par 1987-1994.

MORSE, Davidson Rogan (FtW) 2916 Caprock Ct, Grapevine TX 76051 B Macon GA 1970 BA Mississippi St U. D 3/22/2003 P 9/30/2003 Bp Jack Leo Iker. m 7/30/1994 Amy Carolyn Morse c 4. Assoc R St Andr Epis Ch Ft Worth TX 2006-2009; Cur S Laurence Epis Ch Southlake TX 2003-2006.

MORSE, Elizabeth Bovelle (Ore) 661 NW Kersey Dr, Dallas OR 97338 B Portland OR 1954 d William & Jean. Montana St U 1973; BS OR SU 1976; MDiv CDSP 1988. D 6/24/1988 Bp Charles Shannon Mallory P 1/11/1989 Bp Donald Purple Hart. c 1. Vic S Thos Epis Ch Dallas OR 2012-2014; R S Mich The Archangel Par El Segundo CA 2004-2011; Seamens Ch Inst Of Los Angeles San Pedro CA 2003-2004, 1999-2000; S Thos Of Cbury Par Long Bch CA 2000-2002; St Cross Epis Ch Hermosa Bch CA 1997-1999; S Fran' Par Palos Verdes Estates CA 1992-1994; S Ptr's Par San Pedro CA 1991; Vic Epis Ch On W Kaua'i Eleele HI 1989-1991; S Jn's Ch Eleele HI 1989-1991; Vic S Paul's Kekaha W Kauai HI 1989-1991; Asst Ch Of Our Sav Mill Vlly CA 1988-1989.

MORT, Kevin Duane (SwFla) D 12/8/2012 Bp Dabney Tyler Smith.

MORTON, James Parks (NY) 285 Riverside Dr Apt 13-B, New York NY 10025 **Pres Interfaith Cntr New York NY 1997-** B Houston TX 1930 s Vance & Virginia. BA Harv 1951; BA U of Cambridge 1953; STB GTS 1954; MA U of Cambridge 1959; The New Sem 1985; Pratt Inst 1992; GTS 1996. D 6/12/1954 P 12/18/1954 Bp Horace W B Donegan. m 12/30/1954 Pamela Morton c 4. Dn Cathd Of St Jn The Div New York NY 1972-1997; Dir Urban Trng Cntr for Chr Mssn Chicago IL 1964-1972; Secy for Urban Wk ECEC New York NY 1962-1964; Assoc P in charge Gr Ch Van Vorst Jersey City NJ 1954-1962. Auth, "Lightworks: Explorations in Art," *Culture & Creativity*; Auth, "Intro," *Emergence: Rebirth of Sacr*; Auth, "Haut Liex: An Appreciation of Rene Dubus," *Orion*. Lindisfarne Assn; Ord of S Jn-Jerusalem. Distinguished Medal Barnard Coll 1987; Jn Phillips Awd Phillips-Exeter Acad 1985.

MORTON, John Andrew (WNC) Po Box 185, Flat Rock NC 28731 **R Ch Of S Jn In The Wilderness Flat Rock NC 1999-** B Lancaster SC 1947 s Turner & Mary. BA Wofford Coll 1969; JD U of So Carolina 1974; LLM GW 1985; MDiv VTS 1994. D 6/5/1994 P 12/14/1994 Bp Bob Johnson. m 5/24/1992 Paula Morton c 2. Assoc S Jn's Epis Ch Chula Vista CA 1997-1999; S Phil's Ch Brevard NC 1994-1997.

MORTON SR, Kell (Pa) 316 High St, Pottstown PA 19464 B Toledo OH 1947 s Raymond & Betty. BS U of Toledo 1972; MDiv Nash 1978. D 6/24/1978 P 12/1/1978 Bp William Hampton Brady. m 6/16/1972 Constance C Morton c 4. P-in-c S Jn's Ch Norristown PA 2006-2011; R Chr Epis Ch Pottstown PA 1991-2005; R Gr Ch Riverhead NY 1984-1991; Supt S Dav Epis Sch 1984-1991; Dioc Dir Liturg Com Dio Fond du Lac Appleton WI 1982-1984, 1980-1984; St Ambr Epis Ch Antigo WI 1980-1984; S Barn Epis Ch Tomahawk WI 1980-1981; Cur Trin Epis Ch Oshkosh WI 1978-1980. CBS; Soc-Mary; SocOLW; Soc Of The H Nativ.

MORTON, Paula (WNC) 901 Big Raven Ln, Saluda NC 28773 B Burlington NC 1960 d Robert & Elois. BA Wstrn Carolina U 1986; MDiv VTS 1994. D 6/5/1994 P 12/7/1994 Bp Bob Johnson. m 5/24/1992 John Andrew Morton. R Ch Of The Trsfg Saluda NC 2011-2013, 2002-2010; Spec Mobilization Spprt Plan Washington DC 2010-2011; Pension Fund Mltry New York NY 2005-2006; Gr Ch Morganton NC 2000-2001; Off Of Bsh For ArmdF New York NY 1996-1999; Cur Calv Epis Ch Fletcher NC 1994-1996.

MORTON, Ronald Dean (ETenn) 5401 Tiffany Ln, Knoxville TN 37912 B San Jose CA 1952 s Harold & Melva. BA Natl U 1983; MA Alliant U 1986. D 3/12/2012 Bp George Young III. m 3/27/1987 Cynthia A Mobley c 2.

MORTON, William Paul (EO) 1025 NE Paula Dr, Bend OR 97701 **Non-par 1971-** B Philadelphia PA 1945 s William & Dorothy. BA Dickinson Coll 1967; MDiv Ya Berk 1970; STM Ya Berk 1971. D 6/16/1970 P 4/1/1971 Bp Robert Lionne DeWitt. m 8/9/1969 Katharine Dresch Langham. Missional P Epis Ch Of The Trsfg Sis OR 2011; Missional P Dio Estrn Oregon Cove OR 2010-2011, Stndg Com & Dioc Coun 2009-2012. Rotary 1998. wpm1025@bandbroadband.com

MORTON III, Woolridge Brown (Va) 212 Wirt St NW, Leesburg VA 20176 B Charlottesville VA 1938 s Woolridge & Louisa. BA U of Virginia 1961; Ministere Des Affaires Culturelles Paris Fr 1966. D 6/2/1974 Bp Edmond Lee Browning P 12/1/1974 Bp Albert Ervine Swift. m 6/26/1965 Margaret Anita Templeton. P Assoc Gr Ch The Plains VA 1996-2007; Asst R Trin Ch Fredericksbrg VA 1977-1991; Assoc R S Ptr's Epis Ch Purcellville VA 1976-1986; Cur S

Paul's Within The Walls Rome 1974-1975. Auth, "A Call For Bold Ldrshp," *Seaching For Sacr Space*, Ch Pub Co., 2002. Honary Mem Amer Inst Of Architects 1993; Fell Us/Icoms 1990.

MOSCOSO, Servio Rhadames (NJ) 38 W End Pl, Elizabeth NJ 07202 **Vic Gr Epis Ch Eliz NJ 1996-, 1985** B San Pedro Macoris DO 1950 s Servio & Julia. BD U of Santo Domingo Santo Domingo Do 1974; MDiv S Andrews TS MX 1979. D 10/7/1979 P 12/14/1980 Bp Telesforo A Isaac. m 8/31/1975 Angela Moscoso c 3. The Great Cmsn Fndt Houston TX 2009-2011; San Jose Epis Ch Eliz NJ 1986-2009; Vic Iglesia Epis Cristo el Rey Puerto Plata 1981-1985; Vic Dio The Dominican Republic (Iglesia Epis Dominicana) Gazcue Santo Domingo 1979-1985; Iglesia Epis San Marcos Haitiana Ft Lauderdale FL 1979-1981. Auth, "Religiosidad Paopular Dominicana," 1979. OHC 1977.

MOSELEY, Christine Carr (Vt) PO Box 125, Newport VT 05855 B Boston MA 1948 d Theodore & Phyllis. RN Chld's Hosp Sch of Nrsng 1969. D 12/18/2016 P 6/16/2017 Bp Thomas C Ely. m 6/24/1978 Thomas A E Moseley c 3.

MOSER, Albert E (Alb) 133 Saratoga Rd Apt. 109-8, Glenville NY 12302 **D Chr Epis Ch Ballston Spa NY 1998-** B Reading PA 1928 s Paul & Helen. BS Lebanon Vlly Coll 1953; MS SUNY 1959. D 10/16/1965 Bp Allen Webster Brown. m 11/23/1950 Mary Jane Moser c 3. S Andr's Ch Schenectady NY 1965-1998. Scotia-Glenville Lions Serv Club 1954. Melvin Jones Fell Lions Intl 1985.

MOSER, Frederick Perkins (Vt) 5167 Shelburne Rd, Shelburne VT 05482 **Ecum/Interreligious Off Dio Vermont Burlington VT 2016-, Natl Workshop on Chr Unity Rep 2017-; Trin Ch Shelburne VT 2015-; Exec Com Moderator Vermont Ecum Coun 2017-** B Middletown CT 1953 s Theodore & Beatrice. BA Connecticut Coll 1975; MDiv Yale DS 1979; DMin EDS 2004. D 6/13/1981 Bp Arthur Edward Walmsley P 2/13/1982 Bp William Bradford Hastings. m 5/28/1988 Kim Hardy c 2. Bd Mem Wayland Hsng Partnership 2013-2015; Field Educ Supvsr Harvard Divintiy Sch Cambridge MA 2007-2015; Ecum/Interreligious Off Dio Massachusetts Boston MA 2006-2015, Admin of Cler Cont Educ Fund 2006-2015, Dioc Coun Mem 2006-2015, Dir, Bd Dir, Massachusetts Coun of Ch 2006-2015, Natl Workshop on Chr Unity, Rep 2006-2015, COM 1995-1997; Cnvnr Wayland Interfaith Cler Assn Wayland MA 2000-2015; R Ch Of The H Sprt Wayland MA 1994-2015; GOE Rdr GBEC 1994-2001; Chapl Hobart And Wm Smith Colleges Geneva NY 1984-1994; Assoc S Mary's Epis Ch Manchester CT 1981-1984; Yth Dir St Peters Epis Ch Morristown NJ 1979-1981; Tchr Trin Sch New York NY 1979-1981; Asst Chapl Carleton Coll Northfield MN 1977-1978; Coordntr of Dioc Ecum and Interreligious Off Epis Prov Of New Engl Portland ME 2009-2013; Moderator Massachusetts Cmsn on Chr Unity 2009-2011; COM Dio Rochester Henrietta 1987-1994. revfredmoser@gmail.com

MOSER, Gerard Stoughton (Eur) 15 Hoopoe Ave., Camps Bay, Cape Town 8005 South Africa B Knoxville TN 1938 s Arthur & Sara. BA U So 1960; MDiv GTS 1964. D 6/30/1964 Bp William Evan Sanders P 5/1/1965 Bp John Vander Horst. m 7/10/1992 Carole Hambleton-Moser c 2. R Emm Epis Ch Geneva 1201 1976-2000; 1973-1976; Asst Min S Paul's Ch Rochester NY 1968-1973; Vic S Mary Magd Ch Fayetteville TN 1966-1967; Cur Gr - S Lk's Ch Memphis TN 1964-1966.

MOSER, Patricia Mariann (Chi) 621 W Belmont Ave, Chicago IL 60657 B Chicago IL 1950 d George & Marian. BA Webster Coll 1971; MFA Carnegie-Mellow U 1974; JD De Paul U 1980. D 6/28/2014 Bp John Clark Buchanan.

MOSER, Paul Henry (Md) 15 Brooks Rd, Bel Air MD 21014 B Ossining NY 1938 s Henry & Mary. BD Ken; BA W Virginia Wesleyan Coll 1960; BD Bex Sem 1963; Ldrshp Acad for New Directions 1975. D 6/5/1963 P 12/1/1963 Bp William Camrock Campbell. m 5/1/1965 Christine W Moser c 4. GC Dep Dio Maryland Baltimore MD 1979-1984, Co-Chair Of The VIM 1978-2009; R Emm Ch Bel Air MD 1977-2008; Stndg Com Dio W Virginia Charleston WV 1973-1982, Dn 1972-1976, Exec Coun 1970-1972; Chapl Shpd Coll 1969-1977; Vic Trin Ch Shepherdstown WV 1969-1977; R Chr Memi Ch Williamstown WV 1965-1969; Vic Gr Ch St Marys WV 1965-1969; Asst S Matt's Ch Wheeling WV 1963-1965.

MOSES, Donald Harwood (Kan) 2201 Sw 30th St, Topeka KS 66611 B Fort Wayne IN 1933 s Horace & Harriet. MDIV Nash; Nash; BS K SU 1956; MDIV Nash 1968; Stwdshp-MIL/WMO/OK EpCh- Stwdshp Trng 1974; U of Wisconsin 1974; Inerim Mnstry Int Mnstry Trng 1996. D 3/8/1968 Bp Edward Randolph Welles II P 9/28/1968 Bp Robert Rae Spears Jr. m 9/9/1956 Shirley R Moses c 3. Int St. Andrews Epis Ch Emperia KS 2003-2005; Int S Paul's Ch Manhattan KS 2001-2002; Int S Lk's Ch Wamego KS 1998-2000; Int S Ptr's Ch Pittsburg KS 1996-1997; Brewster Place (The Congrl Hm) Topeka KS 1992-1993; Chapl Brewster Pl Ret Cmnty 1989-1996; Shawnee Coun Advocacy Coun on Aging 1989-1994; S Dav's Epis Ch Topeka KS 1989; 1986-1988; Coun on Mssns Dio Oklahoma Oklahoma City OK 1982-1986; Vic S Paul's Ch Claremore OK 1982-1986; Yth Div Educ conf Dio W Missouri Kansas City MO 1979-1981; R S Ptr's Ch Harrisonville MO 1978-1982; R S Fran Ch Menomonee Falls WI 1971-1978; Coll Wk Chair Dio Milwaukee Milwaukee WI 1971-1975; Vic Trin Epis Ch Mineral Point WI 1969-1971; Trin Epis Ch

Platteville WI 1969-1971; Chapl UWI -Platteville 1969-1971; Cur Ch Of The Gd Shpd Kansas City MO 1968-1969. RWF 1968; Soc of S Jn the Evang 1966.

MOSES, George David (WVa) 20 Alexander Drive, Morgantown WV 26508 B Charleston WV 1947 s Richard & Lorise. BS W Virginia U 1970; MDiv GTS 1973; MA W Virginia U 1983; EdD W Virginia U 1990. D 6/7/1973 P 2/1/1974 Bp Wilburn Camrock Campbell. m 2/9/1975 Holly Christine Carnahan c 2. Clincl Asst. Prof Dept. Behavioral Med WV U Morgantown 1989-1995; Exec Dir/Pstr Counslr Morgantown Pstr Counslg Cntr Inc Morgantown WV 1988-2012; W Virginia U Dio W Virginia Charleston WV 1984-1988, Comission on Mnstry 1980-1987, Dioc Coun 1980-1982; Grad Stdt WV U Morgantown WV 1982-1990; Vic S Barn Bridgeport WV 1978-1982; Int Gr Ch Ravenswood WV 1977-1978; Asst Ch Of The Redeem Houston TX 1974-1977. Auth, "Doctoral Dissertation," *Dyadic Adjustment: Its Impact on Ther Burnout,* 1990. Amer Assn Pstr Counslg Assn - Fell 1999; Amer Counslg Assn - Profsnl 1983.

MOSES, Michael David (Minn) 11078 Nichols Spring Dr, Chatfield MN 55923 B Mankato MN 1951 s Charles & Edna. BS Minnesota St U Mankato 1985; MBA Minnesota St U Mankato 1986. D 7/29/2006 Bp Daniel Lee Swenson P 3/25/2007 Bp James Louis Jelinek. m 8/9/1975 Susan Moses c 3. Mem, Total Mnstry Team St Matt's Epis Ch.

MOSES, Robert Emilio (CFla) 145 E Edgewood Dr, Lakeland FL 33803 **R S Dav's Epis Ch Lakeland FL 2013-, Asst to the R, DRE 2008-** B Lakewood OH 1971 s Robert & Mary Ann. BS Florida St U 1992; STB Other 1998; STB Pontifical Gregorian U, Rome, Italy 1998; STL Other 2000; STL Pontifical Gregorian U, Rome, Italy 2000. Rec 5/31/2008 Bp John Wadsworth Howe. m 9/27/2003 Nancy Brink Moses c 2. rmoses@stdavidslakeland.com

MOSES, Sarah Marie (Miss) B Jackson TN 1974 d John & Marie. BA Furman U 1996; MDiv Harvard DS 2002; PhD Boston Coll 2011. D 6/14/2014 Bp Duncan Montgomery Gray III P 5/2/2015 Bp Brian Seage. m 9/7/2002 William Schenck c 2. Cur Chr Ch Holly Sprg MS 2013-2016. Auth, "Ethics and the Elderly," Orbis Books, 2016.

MOSHER, David Rike (SwFla) 6764 122nd St, Seminole FL 33772 **Ret 1990-** B Los Angeles CA 1924 s Ezra & Norine. BA U Denv 1949; MDiv Ya Berk 1952. D 3/25/1952 Bp Walter H Gray P 10/12/1952 Bp Harold L Bowen. m 11/26/2000 Maureen Sommerville Anderson. Sum Asst H Trin Spruce Pine NC 1990-1996; Sum Asst S Lk's Epis Ch Asheville NC 1989-1990; Int Ch Of The H Sprt Osprey FL 1987-1988; Cathd Ch Of S Ptr St. Petersburg FL 1980-1989; Longterm CARE Admin Dio SW Florida 1959-1990; Dio Colorado Denver CO 1959-1984; R Calv Ch Golden CO 1952-1959. Fell Amer Coll of Healthcare Admin 1985; Hon Past Pres Amer Hlth Care Assn 1985; Phi Beta Kappa U Denv 1949.

MOSHER, Steve (ETenn) 314 W. Broadway Ave, Maryville TN 38801 **R S Andr's Ch Maryville TN 2009-** B Atlanta GA 1962 s David & Cynthia. BBA U GA 1985; MDiv Sewanee: The U So, TS 2004. D 6/5/2004 P 12/2/2004 Bp J Neil Alexander. m 11/29/1986 Kirsten K Mosher c 2. Assoc R Ch Of The Nativ Epis Huntsville AL 2004-2009.

MOSIER, James David (EO) 1237 Sw 12th St, Ontario OR 97914 **R S Matt's Epis Ch Ontario OR 2010-, D 1985-2010** B The Dalles OR 1946 s Ernest & Eleanor. BA U of Portland 1968. D 9/21/1985 Bp Rustin Ray Kimsey P 5/22/2010 Bp Bavi Edna Rivera. m 7/12/1969 Vicki Sue Dehaven c 2. Ecumenist of the Year Ecum Mnstrs of Oregon 2006; Kappa Delta Pi hon Soc 1966.

MOSIER, William (Ore) 39361 Mozart Ter Unit 101, Fremont CA 94538 **D S Hilda's Ch Monmouth OR 1994-** B The Dalles OR 1946 s Ernest & Elenor. BS Wstrn Oregon U 1984; MS Wstrn Oregon U 1986; Oregon Cntr for the Diac 1994. D 10/29/1994 Bp Robert Louis Ladehoff. m 8/13/2011 Beverly Mosier. The Epis Conf of the Deaf 1985. Elected Pres Epis Conf of the Deaf 2004; Meritorius Serv Awd Epis Conf of the Deaf 1999; Elected Bd Mem Epis Conf of the Deaf 1997.

MOSKAL, Jason Edward (LI) 3350 82nd St, Jackson Heights NY 11372 **D S Mk's Ch Jackson Heights NY 2013-** B Brooklyn NY 1977 s Edward & Christina. BBA Tem 1999. D 6/7/2014 Bp Lawrence C Provenzano. deaconmoskal@gmail.com

MOSLEY, Carl Ernest (Eas) 111 76th St Unit 205, Ocean City MD 21842 **Hosp Chapl Atlantic Gnrl Hosp Berlin MD 2007-** B Washington DC 1942 s Carl & Helen. ABA Benjamin Franklin U 1968; BS Benjamin Franklin U 1972; Dip Theol Stud VTS 2007; MMin Nash 2011. D 11/13/2007 P 4/21/2012 Bp Bud Shand. m 10/23/1987 Virginia Mosley. carlmosleyccsc@msn.com

MOSQUEA, Jose Luis (DR) **Dio The Dominican Republic (Iglesia Epis Dominicana) Gazcue Santo Domingo 2007-** B Rio San Juan 1971 D 2/12/2006 Bp Julio Cesar Holguin-Khoury.

MOSS JR, Alfred Alfonso (Chi) 1500 N Lancaster St, Arlington VA 22205 **S Andr's Epis Ch Arlington VA 1993-; 1975-** B Chicago IL 1943 s Alfred & Ruth. BA Lake Forest Coll 1965; STB EDS 1968; MA U Chi 1972; PhD U Chi 1977. D 6/15/1968 Bp James Winchester Montgomery P 12/21/1968 Bp Gerald Francis Burrill. c 1. Assoc Chapl U Chi 1970-1975; Cur The Ch Of The H Sprt Lake Forest IL 1968-1970. Auth, *Dangerous Donations: Nthrn Philantrophy and Sthrn Black Educ 1902-1930,* Col of Missouri Press, 1999; Auth,

609

M

"Alexander Crummell," *Black Leaders of the 19th Century*; Auth, *From Slavery To Freedom: A Hist of Afr Americans*; Auth, *The Amer Negro Acad*. HSEC 1994; UBE. DD Virginia Theoligal Sem 2006.

MOSS III, David M (At) 3880 N Stratford Rd Ne, Atlanta GA 30342 B Saint Louis MO 1943 s Harry & Helen. BA Washington U 1966; MDiv SWTS 1969; STM SWTS 1970; PhD NWU 1974; ThD Somerset U Gb 1990. D 6/22/1969 Bp James Loughlin Duncan P 4/13/1970 Bp James Winchester Montgomery. m 5/5/1984 Denise S Moss. Chapl Lenbrook Sq In Atlanta GA 1989-1993; Asst All SS Epis Ch Atlanta GA 1979-2004; Seabury Inst For Pstr Psych 1979-1985; Tchng Stff Cntr For Rel & Psych In Chicago IL 1975-1980; Chapl NWU In Evanston IL 1975-1979; Advoc Hlth Care Oak Brook IL 1973-1975; Chapl Luth Gnrl Hosp In Pk Ridge IL 1972-1975; Asst R S Chrys's Ch Chicago IL 1969-1974; Chair Dio Chicago Chicago IL 1972-1979. Ed, "Orgnztn & Admin Pstr Counslg Centers," Abingdon, 1981; Ed, "Journ Of Pstr Care"; Ed, "Alcoholic'S 12 Steps Into Life," Forw Mvmt; Ed, "Pstr Psychol"; Ed, "Amer Journ Of Pstr Counslg"; Ed, "Dialogues In Depth Psychol & Rel"; Ed, "Journ Rel & Hlth". Aamft; AAPC; Amer Coll Forensic Examiners; APA; ACPE; CDSP. DD SWTS 1997; Vstng Schlr Freud Museum 1991.

MOSS, Denise S (At) B Saint Louis MO 1942 d John & Claire. BA Merc 1981; MDiv Merc 2000; DMin SWTS 2005. D 2/21/2004 P 1/16/2007 Bp J Neil Alexander. m 5/5/1984 David M Moss c 2. R Ch Of The Medtr Washington GA 2007-2012; R S Alb's Ch Elberton GA 2007-2012; Asst S Tim's Epis Ch Calhoun GA 2000-2002; Clincl Chapl Cov Cmnty Inc. 1997-2000. Auth, "Feed Your Wk: Dispelling dangerous myth in a dangerouls Wrld," Libr of Congr, 2005.

MOSS III, Frank Hazlett (WMass) 17910 NW Chestnut Lane, Portland OR 97231 B Fredericksburg VA 1945 s Frank & Nancy. BA Pr 1967; MDiv EDS 1970; MBA U of New Haven 1988. D 6/20/1970 Bp Philip Alan Smith P 5/15/1971 Bp Robert Bruce Hall. m 12/28/1968 Elizabeth Moss c 2. Int Ch Of The Redeem Pendleton OR 2006-2010; Dio Wstrn Massachusetts Springfield 1999-2006; S Jas' Ch Greenfield MA 1999-2006; R Trin Ch Ft Wayne IN 1990-1999; S Andr's Ch Meriden CT 1979-1990; Geth Ch Proctorsville VT 1974-1979; P-in-c S Lk's Ch Chester VT 1974-1979; Cur Gr Epis Ch Utica NY 1972-1974; Chapl S Anne Sch Charlottesville VA 1971-1972; Cur S Paul's Memi Charlottesvlle VA 1970-1972.

MOSS, J Eliot Blakeslee (WMass) 7 Kestrel Ln, Amherst MA 01002 **Vic S Jn's Ch Ashfield MA 2008-; GC Alt Dep Dio Wstrn Massachusetts Springfield 2010-, Dioc Coun 2008-; Cathd Chapt Chr Ch Cathd Springfield MA 2007-** B Staunton VA 1954 s William & Mary. BS MIT 1975; MS MIT 1978; PhD MIT 1981. D 6/19/2004 P 4/23/2005 Bp Gordon Scruton. m 5/29/1976 Hannah Allen Abbott c 2. Asst Ch Of The Atone Westfield MA 2005-2008, D 2004-2005. Fllshp S Jn; Fllshp of the Way of the Cross 2004.

MOSS SR, Ledly Ogden (SeFla) 4020 Nw 187th St, Carol City FL 33055 **D Epis Ch Of The H Fam Miami FL 1992-** B 1931 s Wellington & Melwese. D 4/4/1992 Bp Calvin Onderdonk Schofield Jr. m 10/24/1962 Muriel Martha Moss c 4.

MOSS, Susan Maetzold (Minn) 175 Woodlawn Ave, Saint Paul MN 55105 **Vice Chair ECMN Cir of the Beloved-Epis Serv Corps 2016-** B Red Wing MN 1950 d James & Elizabeth. BA Bowling Green St U 1972; MA Luther TS 1976; MDiv Untd TS of the Twin Cities 1984; GTS 1985; Seminario De San Andres 2001. D 6/11/1984 P 10/23/1985 Bp Robert Marshall Anderson. m 8/24/1974 Thomas Verne Moss c 3. Int Asst R S Jn The Evang S Paul MN 2012-2013; Vic La Mision El Santo Nino Jesus S Paul MN 2008-2011; Upper Sch Rel Breck Sch Minneapolis MN 2000-2008; Cn Dio Minnesota Minneapolis MN 1999-2008, Treas; Vice Chair ECMN Cuba Cmsn 2013-, Instr, Assessments: ECMN Sch for Formation 2011-, VP; Pres: Stndg Com-elected 2010-2015, Reg Dn: E Metro Area 2008-2012, Stff Liason Mssn Strtgy Ntwk 2005-2007, Vice Chair, Co Chair COM 1996-2000, Exam Chapl 1996-, Chair Wellness Com 1988-1990; R S Jas On The Pkwy Minneapolis MN 1993-1998; Int R S Lk's Ch Minneapolis MN 1992-1993; Assoc S Jn The Bapt Epis Ch Minneapolis MN 1989-1990; Assoc Ch Of The Epiph Epis Minneapolis MN 1984-1987; Dir of YA Mnstry S Steph The Mtyr Ch Minneapolis MN 1982-1984; Vstng Fell Epis TS Of The SW Austin TX 2008.

MOSSBARGER, David Jefferson (NwT) 1402 Wilshire Dr, Odessa TX 79761 **R S Barn' Epis Ch Of Odessa Odessa TX 2003-** B La Jolla CA 1958 s John & Jane. BA SMU 1980; MDiv Epis TS of the SW 1985. D 6/15/1985 P 12/21/1985 Bp Donis Dean Patterson. m 12/27/1986 Deborah L Snyder c 3. Gr Ch Llano TX 1997-2002; Prov VII CE Com 1996-1999; Chr Asst Mnstry Pres 1996-1997; Kerrville Mnstrl Allnce Pres 1994-1995; S Peters Epis Sch Kerrville TX 1991-1997; Asst R S Ptr's Epis Ch Kerrville TX 1991-1997; S Geo's Epis Ch Dallas TX 1990-1991; Dept Of Missions Dallas TX 1987-1990; Cur S Lk's Epis Ch Dallas TX 1985-1986; Dept Of CE Dio W Texas San Antonio TX 1993-1997.

MOSSO, Karen Ann (Ind) 721 Roma Ave., Jeffersonville IN 47130 **Ret 2007-** B Saint Paul MN 1945 d Earl & Carla. BS U MN 1967; MA Minnesota St U Mankato 1975; MDiv Bex Sem 1978. D 6/24/1978 P 7/13/1980 Bp Robert Marshall Anderson. R S Paul's Jeffersonvlle IN 2002-2007; Int S Mk's Epis

Ch Huntersville NC 2001-2002; Int All SS Epis Ch Charlotte NC 1999-2001; St Louis Urban Partnership S Louis MO 1996-1998; Dio Missouri S Louis MO 1995-1996; Int Trin Ch Litchfield MN 1993-1994; S Matt's Epis Ch Minneapolis MN 1992-1993; Supply Dio Minnesota Minneapolis MN 1989-1993; Asst S Edw's Ch Duluth MN 1988-1989; The Par of St Paul's Epis Ch Duluth MN 1988-1989; R S Lk's Epis Ch Hastings MN 1983-1988; Epis Cmnty Serv Inc Minneapolis MN 1978-1983; Chapl Gilfillan Cntr Bemidji MN 1978-1983. Oblate, Our Lady of Gr, Beech Grove, IN 2011; Wmn Touched by Gr, Our Lady of Gr Monstry 2003; Wmn Touched by Gr, Our Lady of Gr Monstry, Beech Grove,IN 2003.

MOTE, Donna Susan (At) 1296 Fork Creek Trl, Decatur GA 30033 **Chapl Dio Atlanta Atlanta GA 2013-, Cnvnr, Mnstry Innovations T/F 2014-; Sewanee U So TS Sewanee TN 2013-; Vice Chair, Bd Dir The Sabbath Hse Bryson City NC 1999-** B Atlanta GA 1964 d Bernard & Marcella. BA Shorter Coll 1986; MDiv Sthrn Bapt TS 1990; PhD Emory U 2012. D 5/22/2013 P 12/21/2013 Bp Robert Christopher Wright. m 6/25/2016 Mary R England. Co-Auth, "The Go Guide: 10 Steps for Innovations in Mnstry from Lk 10," H Innoc' Press, 2016; Auth, "Twin Legacies," *In the Shade of the Sycamore Tree: Ministers Reflect on the Subject of Wealth*, The Intermundia Press, 2015. AAR 1989. innovate@episcopalatlanta.org

MOTE, Doris Ellen (Ind) 2018 Locust St, New Albany IN 47150 B Anderson IN 1938 d Henry & Louise. BA Ball St U 1960; MDiv Untd TS Dayton OH 1973. D 6/22/1974 P 1/29/1977 Bp John Mc Gill Krumm. c 3. R S Paul's Epis Ch New Albany IN 1992-2004; Int Ch Of The Trsfg Braddock Heights MD 1990-1991; Chr Ch Forest Hill MD 1989-1990; H Cross Ch St MD 1989-1990; Int H Cross MD 1989-1990; Ch Of The H Evangelists Baltimore MD 1988-1989; Vic H Evang Baltimore MD 1987-1989; Dio Maryland Baltimore MD 1986-1991; Assoc R S Barth's Ch Baltimore MD 1980-1986; Chr Epis Ch Dayton OH 1975-1979; Dio Sthrn Ohio Cincinnati OH 1975-1979.

MOTE, Larry H. (RG) 1016 E 1st St, Portales NM 88130 **Vic Trin Ch Portales NM 2006-** B Claude TX 1943 s Paul & Mildred. BBA Estrn New Mex U 1978; Basic Chr Stds Trin/ Rio Grande Sch For Mnstry 2006. D 5/20/2006 P 11/30/2006 Bp Jeffrey Neil Steenson. m 2/14/1987 Nancy Mote c 7. BroSA 2007-2011; The Intl Ord of St Lk the Physcn 2008.

MOTES, Brantley Eugene (Ala) Po Box 5556, Decatur AL 35601 B Sylacauga AL 1936 s Dewitt & Dorma. BA Athens St U 1960; MDiv Van 1964; DMin Van 1976. D 6/4/1993 Bp Furman Charles Stough P 12/1/1993 Bp Robert Oran Miller. m 5/21/1983 Glenda Carol Sanders. Gd Shpd Decatur AL 1995-1997; Dio Alabama Birmingham 1993-1995; H Cross-St Chris's Huntsville AL 1993-1994; Serv Meth Ch 1962-1998. Phi Tau Chi.

MOTHERSELL, Lawrence Lavere (Roch) Po Box 1, Geneseo NY 14454 **Profsnl Campus Ministers Div 1981-** B Potter NY 1939 s Sheldon & Kathleen. Colgate Rochester Crozer DS; CRDS; BS SUNY 1961; MA SUNY 1967. D 9/20/1981 P 3/1/1983 Bp Robert Rae Spears Jr. m 6/20/1959 Patricia Ann Gage. Sci Cmsn On Sprtl Care. Auth, "Mainstreaming". Ch Mssn Deaf People, Wrld Congr Jewish Deaf.

MOTIS, John Ray (CFla) Church of the Good Shepherd, 221 S 4th St, Lake Wales FL 33853 **D The Epis Ch Of The Gd Shpd Lake Wales FL 2012-** B Friend NE 1957 s Edmund & Ruth. D 12/8/2012 Bp Gregory Orrin Brewer. m 6/22/1995 Laura Smith Motis c 2.

MOTT, Pam (WMass) 148 Dorwin Dr, West Springfield MA 01089 **Dio Wstrn Massachusetts Springfield 2013-** B White Plains NY 1957 d Willard & Charlotte. CAS Ya Berk; BA SUNY 1978; MDiv Yale DS 1985. D 6/8/1991 P 12/15/1991 Bp Richard Frank Grein. R S Mary's Ch Portsmouth RI 2004-2013; Cn Trin Epis Cathd Portland OR 1998-2004; R S Eustace Ch Lake Placid NY 1994-1998; Cur Gr Ch Millbrook NY 1991-1994. pmott@diocesewma.org

MOTTL, Christine Elizabeth (Pa) 27074 St. Peter's Church Rd., Crisfield MD 21817 **Bd Mem HabHum 2009-; Dir of Stds Providence TS 2007-** B New York NY 1951 d Alfred & Ann. Colgate Rochester Crozer DS; CRDS; BA SUNY 1972; MA SUNY 1975; MDiv Trin TS Newburgh IN 1999. D 5/5/2000 P 11/5/2000 Bp James Edward Krotz. m 7/8/1978 Paul Edward Mottl c 2. R S Paul's Ch Doylestown PA 2009-2015; Chapl Dio Nebraska Omaha NE 2004-2009; Chapl The Nebraska Med Cntr 2004-2009; Int Ch Of The H Apos Mitchell NE 2003-2004; Chapl All SS Med Cntr Racine WI 2003; Coordntr of Epis Serv S Lk's Hosp Racine WI 2002-2003; R Calv Ch Hyannis NE 2000-2002; Chapl Hospice 1999-2003; Bd Mem Box Butte Gnrl Hosp Allnce NE 1998-2002. Co-Auth, "Through the Eye of a Needle," Morris Pub, 2012. Assoc of Profsnl Chapl 2004. DD, D.D. Prov. Theo. Sch. 2007; Bd Cert Chapl, BCC Assoc of Profsnl Chapl 2004.

MOTTL, Paul Edward (Neb) 27074 St. Peters Church Road, Crisfield MD 21817 **Dn / Pres Providence TS 2005-; Eccumenical Cn of the Coll of Cn Natl Old Cath Cathd of Chr 2015-** B Bay Shore NY 1944 s Edward & Claire. BA Adel 1965; MRE Methodist TS in Ohio 1970; MDiv Colgate Rochester Crozer DS 1993; PhD Sheffield Univ 2003. D 4/24/1993 Bp Orris George Walker Jr P 11/1/1993 Bp George Clinton Harris. m 7/8/1978 Christine Elizabeth Hinek c 2. Rdr Epis Ch BEC 2006-2011; Ehtics Bd Fremont Med Cntr 2005-2009; R S Jas' Epis Ch Fremont NE 2005-2009; Reg Yth Coordntr Dio

Nebraska Omaha NE 2005-2008, Bp & Trst 2007-2009, Exec Cmsn 1998-2007; Calv Ch Hyannis NE 2003; Chapl Allnce Fire Dept 1998-2005; R S Matt's Ch Allnce NE 1997-2005; Asst S Ptr's by-the-Sea Epis Ch Bay Shore NY 1994-1997; Chapl Suffolk Cnty Coun BSA 1994-1997; Cn to the Ordnry Dio Pennsylvania Philadelphia PA 1993-2009, Chair, BEC 2009-; P-in-c S Ptr's Epis Ch Williston ND 1993-1994; COM Dio No Dakota Fargo ND 1993-1994. Co-Auth, "Through the Eye of a Needle," Morris Pub, 2012; Auth, "Heartland Hope," Morris Pub, 2000. FA 1992-1996; Naval Inst 1979; USCG Aux 2016. dean@providencetheo.org

MOUA, Bao (Minn) Holy Apostles Episcopal Church, 2200 Minnehaha Ave E, Saint Paul MN 55119 B Thailand 1980 d Chong & Chao. D 6/20/2015 P 6/21/2016 Bp Brian N Prior. m 12/21/2002 Tza Thao.

MOUER, Patty (WNC) 500 Christ School Road, Asheville NC 28704 **R S Lk's Epis Ch Asheville NC 2004-** B Richmond VA 1963 d James & Dorothy. BA Br 1986; MS U of Tennessee 1993; MDiv Van 1994. D 6/10/2000 P 12/9/2000 Bp Bob Johnson. m 5/26/1990 Joseph R Mouer c 2. Asst to the R Gr Ch Asheville NC 2000-2004.

MOUGHTY, Kelly Patricia (Me) 115 E Fairfax Street, Falls Church VA 22046 **The Falls Ch Epis Falls Ch VA 2015-** B Stamford CT 1983 d Brian & Donna. BA GW 2005; MDiv Ya Berk 2012. D 6/9/2012 Bp James Elliot Curry P 12/14/2012 Bp Stephen Taylor Lane. m 7/17/2015 Alexander Alden Peterson. S Alb's Ch Cape Eliz ME 2012-2015. kmoughty@thefallschurch.org

MOUILLE, David Ronald (Kan) 4786 Black Swan Dr, Shawnee KS 66216 B Church Pt LA 1942 s Joseph & Enola. BA Notre Dame Sem Grad TS 1964; STB CUA 1968; STM GTS 1972; MEd U of Kansas 1982; PhD KANSAS U 1990. Rec 5/1/1971 as Priest Bp Iveson Batchelor Noland. m 7/2/1995 Amy Mouille. S Mart-In-The-Fields Edwardsville KS 1981-1990; R Gr Epis Ch Ottawa KS 1976-1980; Asst S Mich And All Ang Ch Dallas TX 1973-1976; Asst Par of Chr the Redeem Pelham NY 1971-1973; Asst Trin S Paul's Epis New Rochelle NY 1970-1971; Serv RC Ch 1968-1970. AAPC.

MOULDEN, Michael Mackreth (NC) 401 Plainfield Road, Greenborough NC 27455 **R St. Frances Epis Ch Greensboro NC 2007-** B Washington DC 1951 s William & Mary. BA Guilford Coll 1974; MDiv Sewanee: The U So, TS 1979. Trans 10/8/2003 Bp Stephen Hays Jecko. m 5/15/2015 Laura Shuster Moulden c 2. R S Fran Ch Greensboro NC 2007-2015; Chapl St. Vinc Hosp Jacksonville FL 2006-2007; Ch Of Our Sav Jacksonville FL 2006; S Jn's Cathd Jacksonville FL 2006; Chr Epis Ch Cleveland NC 2004-2005; Trin Epis Sch Charlotte NC 2003-2005; Chapl Trin Epis Sch Charlotte NC 2003-2005; R All SS Epis Ch Jacksonville FL 1998-2003; R S Eliz's Epis Ch Knoxville TN 1992-1998; R Epis Ch of the Gd Shpd Charleston SC 1988-1992; R S Ann's Ch Nashville TN 1983-1988; Dio Tennessee Nashville TN 1980-1983; Vic S Jas Cumberland Furnace TN 1980-1983; D-in-Trng S Steph's Epis Ch Oak Ridge TN 1979-1980; ; Chair - Yth Dept; COLM Dep to Gen Conv; EFM Mentor Dioc Coun.

MOULINIER, Deirdre Ward (Az) D 6/7/2014 Bp Kirk Stevan Smith.

MOULTON, Elizabeth Jean (Be) 109 Cruser St, Montrose PA 18801 B Louisville KY 1941 d Newton & Elizabeth. BS U IL 1963; MS Nthrn Illinois U 1972; MDiv Luth TS at Gettysburg 1987. D 6/12/1987 P 5/10/1988 Bp Charlie Fuller Mcnutt Jr. m 5/20/1962 John R Moulton c 2. Chr Ch Susquehanna PA 2006-2010; Supply S Mk's New Milford PA 2006-2010; R S Paul's Ch Montrose PA 1999-2005; Supply Prince Of Peace Epis Ch Dallas PA 1998; R Chr Ch Stroudsburg PA 1992-1998; Vic S Alb's Ch Littleton NC 1992; Gr Ch Weldon NC 1988-1992; R S Anna's Ch Littleton NC 1988-1992; Vic All SS Ch Roanoke Rapids NC 1988-1991; Asst Mt Calv Camp Hill PA 1987-1988.

MOULTON, Eric Morgan (EC) 1219 Forest Hills Dr, Wilmington NC 28403 **S Jn's Epis Ch Wilmington NC 2014-** B Atlanta GA 1972 s John & Linda. BA U GA 1994; MATS Reformed TS 2009; STM Sewanee: The U So, TS 2015; STM The TS at The U So 2015. D 1/19/2014 P 7/23/2014 Bp Gregory Orrin Brewer. m 3/5/1994 Serinda M Moulton c 7. Yth Dir Dio Cntrl Florida Orlando FL 2003-2013.

MOULTON II, John Adkins (Fla) 1631 Blue Heron Ln, Jacksonville Beach FL 32250 **Cler Fund Raiser Food For The Poor Coconut Creek FL 1999-** B Richmond VA 1944 s John & Martha. BA U NC 1967; MDiv UTS 1970; Ripon Coll Cuddesdon 1971; DMin VTS 1986; S Georges Coll Jerusalem IL 1989. D 6/24/1970 P 10/17/1971 Bp William Moultrie Moore Jr. m 1/28/1967 Harriet Moulton c 2. Assoc S Geo Epis Ch Jacksonville FL 2001-2008; R S Paul's By-The-Sea Epis Ch Jaxville Bch FL 1993-2000; R Ch Of The Redeem Midlothian VA 1979-1993; R S Paul's Epis Ch Wilmington NC 1975-1979; Assoc H Trin Epis Ch Fayetteville NC 1973-1975; Cur Bruton Par Williamsburg VA 1971-1973; Fundraiser Food for the Poor Inc. Coconut Creek 2000-2014; Exec Bd Dio Sthrn Virginia Newport News VA 1987-1993, Commisssion on Mnstry 1981-1993, Liturg Cmsn 1981-1987; Exec Bd Dio E Carolina Kinston NC 1977-1979. OHC 1973.

MOULTON, Roger Conant (Mass) 291 Washington St, Arlington MA 02474 **Ret 1993-** B Boston MA 1929 s Stanley & Lina. BS Babson Coll 1950; MDiv EDS 1960. D 6/18/1960 Bp Anson Phelps Stokes Jr P 1/8/1961 Bp Dudley S Stark. m 7/11/1953 Barbara Holden Moulton c 3. P-in-c S Mk's Epis Ch Burlington

MA 2005-2006; Asstg P Par Of The Epiph Winchester MA 2004-2008; Asstg P All SS Ch Chelmsford MA 2001-2003; Asst The Ch Of Our Redeem Lexington MA 1997-1999; Seamens Ch Inst Newport RI 1993; Co-Cnvnr Watertown Mnstry Assn 1980-1982; R Ch Of The Gd Shpd Watertown MA 1979-1993; Int Ch Of Our Sav Arlington MA 1979; Ecum All SS Epis Ch Portsmouth OH 1977-1978; R S Jn's Ch Huntington WV 1972-1975; Assoc S Mk's Epis Ch Columbus OH 1968-1972; R Trin Ch Newark OH 1964-1968; Cur S Paul's Ch Rochester NY 1960-1964. Auth, "E-Mail From Amer," *Sherborne Scene-Devon, U.K.*, Ecum Monthly, 2001. Phillips Brooks Club, Boston 1980-1992. Honoree of the Year Nature Conservancy, Boston 1996.

MOUNCEY, Perry Kathleen (CNY) 127 Brookview Ln, Liverpool NY 13088 **Reverend S Matt's Ch Moravia NY 2007-** B Toronto Canada 1948 d Theodore & Susan. RN St Josephs Sch of Nrsng 1970; Loc Dioc Formation Prog 2006. D 10/7/2006 P 6/9/2007 Bp Gladstone Bailey Adams III. m 9/16/1972 Douglas W Mouncey c 2. Gr Ch Mex NY 2009.

MOUNTFORD, Helen Harvene (Los) 1566 Edison St, Santa Ynez CA 93460 B Dallas TX 1942 d Roger & Harvene. BS U of Iowa 1964; JD U of Kansas 1969. D 11/1/1985 Bp Richard Frank Grein. c 2. D Ch Of The Incarn San Francisco CA 1999-2000; D S Marg's Ch Lawr KS 1997-1999; Archd Dio Kansas Topeka KS 1994-1999; D S Mich And All Ang Ch Mssn KS 1985-1997. NAAD.

MOUNTFORD SR, Robert Tatton (CFla) 160 Heron Bay Cir, Lake Mary FL 32746 **Ret 1999-** B 1933 m 2/12/1952 Mildred Mountford. Assoc R S Ptr's Epis Ch Lake Mary FL 1999; Trin Ch Saco ME 1988-1999.

MOURADIAN, Victoria Kirk (Los) 1411 Dalmatia Dr., San Pedro CA 90732 **All SS-By-The-Sea Par Santa Barbara CA 2013-; Kensington Epis Hm Alhambra CA 2008-; Chapl The Epis Hm 2008-** B Chicago IL 1950 d Kenneth & Helen. Cert Ang Stud ETS at Claremont; BA USC 1973; MA Fuller TS 2007. D 6/7/2008 P 1/10/2009 Bp Joseph Jon Bruno. c 3. Epis Communities & Serv Pasadena CA 2008-2013; Cur S Bede's Epis Ch Los Angeles CA 2008-2013.

MOUSIN, Thomas Nordboe (Mass) 29 Lakeview Rd, Winchester MA 01890 **R S Jn's Ch Charlestown (Boston) Charlestown MA 2011-, R 2011-; Mem, Dioc Coun Dio Massachusetts Boston MA 2012-** B Hackensack NJ 1956 s Carl & Dorothy. BA Dart 1978; MDiv UTS 1983; Cert Theol Stud EDS 2011. D 12/14/2010 P 6/25/2011 Bp Thomas C Ely. m 5/1/2011 Thomas James Brown. D Ch Of The Gd Shpd Reading MA 2011.

MOWERS, Culver Lunn (CNY) Po Box 130, Brooktondale NY 14817 B Syracuse NY 1942 s Jack & Erma. BA Syr 1964; MDiv EDS 1968. D 6/14/1968 Bp Walter M Higley P 5/28/1969 Bp Ned Cole. m 10/24/2003 Pauline Mowers. R S Thos Epis Ch Slaterville Sprg NY 1972-2012; R S Mk's Ch Candor NY 1972-1979; P-in-c St Johns Epis Ch Berkshire NY 1972-1975; P-in-c All SS Ch 1968-1972; P-in-c S Paul's Ch Brownville NY 1968-1972; P-in-c S Paul's Ch Watertown NY 1968-1971. culliem@earthlink.net

MOWERS, David M (Mil) 1631 Ford Pkwy, Saint Paul MN 55116 **R Trin Ch Baraboo WI 2017-** B Kirkland IL 1985 s Ted & Peggy. BA No Cntrl U 2007; MA Bethel Sem 2012. D 6/26/2014 P 6/20/2015 Bp Brian N Prior. m 10/12/2013 Elizabeth A Mowers c 2. S Mart's By The Lake Epis Minnetonka Bch MN 2015-2017.

MOWERY, Donald (WTenn) 231 Baronne Pl, Memphis TN 38117 **Ret 1995-; Consult Urban Chld Inst 1995-; Consult Urban Chld Inst 1995-** B Chattanooga TN 1931 s Clarence & Myrtle. BS U of Tennessee 1953; MDiv Ya Berk 1956. D 7/1/1956 Bp Theodore N Barth P 1/18/1957 Bp John Vander Horst. m 4/10/1983 Julie B Mowery. Asstg S Jn's Epis Ch Memphis TN 1995; Dio W Tennessee Memphis 1968-1995; Bridges Inc Memphis TN 1963-1995; Stff S Mary's Cathd Memphis TN 1963-1995; R S Andr's Ch Nashville TN 1956-1963. Bp's Mnstry Awd Dio W Tennessee 1985.

MOYER, Dale Luther (SeFla) 4851a Nursery Rd, Dover PA 17315 B New Ringgold PA 1937 s Irvin & Catherine. BA Albright Coll 1959; BD Evang TS 1962; STM Nash 1970. D 6/14/1964 Bp James Winchester Montgomery P 12/19/1964 Bp Gerald Francis Burrill. m 7/2/1966 Donna S Moyer. P-in-c S Paul's Ch Columbia PA 1998-2003; S Jn's Epis Ch Midland MI 1996-1997; R S Mart's Epis Ch Pompano Bch FL 1987-1996; R S Paul's Ch Wallingford CT 1978-1987; R Par Of Chr The King Willingboro NJ 1970-1978; Dce S Jas Epis Ch Danbury CT 1969-1970; Vic H Cross Kansas City 1968-1969; R S Mart-In-The-Fields Edwardsville KS 1966-1968; Cur S Dav's Ch Glenview IL 1964-1966. CHS.

MOYER, J Douglas (Be) 205 North Seventh Street, Stroudsburg PA 18360 **R Chr Ch Stroudsburg PA 2011-; Dio Bethlehem Bethlehem PA 2009-, Pres of Stndg Com 2016-, Secy of Conv 2016-** B Chester PA 1949 s James & Charlotte. BA Penn 1971; BS Widener U 1981; MDiv Nash 2009. D 2/2/2009 Bp John Palmer Croneberger P 9/29/2009 Bp Paul Victor Marshall. m 12/19/1983 Michelle M Merlo c 3. Asst Chr Ch Reading PA 2011, 2009-2011.

MOYER, Laureen H (Cal) 412 Centre Ct, Alameda CA 94502 **Assoc Chr Ch Alameda CA 2012-, Assoc 2008-2012** B Albany NY 1946 d John & Beatrice. BA U of Tennessee 1968; MA Washington Theol Un 2001; VTS 2002; MFA CA Inst of Integral Stds 2015. D 9/19/2002 P 6/7/2003 Bp William Michie Klusmeyer. c 2. Int S Andr's Epis Ch San Bruno CA 2010-2011; P-in-c Gr Epis Ch Kearneysville WV 2006-2007; Assoc Nelson Cluster Of Epis Ch Rippon WV 2004-2005; S Phil's Ch Chas Town WV 2002-2005; Assoc St Johns Epis

Ch Harpers Ferry WV 2002. "Which is Better: Grid Listing or Grp Question Design for Data Collection in Establishment Surveys?," *Resrch Report Series*, U.S. Census Bureau, 1999; "Problem w Determining and Listing Grp. Qtrs. in Prep. for Enumeration," *Proceedings of the Survey Methods Sectn*, Amer Statistical Assn, 1998; "How Do People Answer Income Questions?," *Publ Opinion Quarterly*, AAPOR, 1998. Soc of Cath Priests (SCP) 2013.

MOYER, Michael David (Eas) 1 Church St, Berlin MD 21811 **R S Paul's Berlin MD 1999-** B Pottstown PA 1967 s David & Linda. AGS Montgomery Cnty Cmnty Coll 1987; MDiv Bangor TS 1992; BA U of Maine 1992; STM Nash 1996. D 6/21/1997 Bp Allen Lyman Bartlett Jr P 12/22/1997 Bp Jack Leo Iker. c 1. Cathd Ch Of The Nativ Bethlehem PA 2015-2016; Assoc All SS' Epis Ch Ft Worth TX 1997-1999. CBS; GAS; OGS 2012; P Assoc -- All SS Sis of the Poor; SocMary.

MOYER, Michelle M (Be) 321 Wyandotte St, Bethlehem PA 18015 **Cathd Ch Of The Nativ Bethlehem PA 2015-** B Easton PA 1956 d Carmen & Antoinette. BA W Chester U 1978; MDiv Moravian Thelogical Sem 2013. D 3/2/2014 P 1/24/2015 Bp Sean Walter Rowe. m 12/19/1983 J Douglas Moyer c 2. canonmichelle@nativitycathedral.org

MOYERS, William Riley (SwFla) 2008 Isla De Palma Cir, Naples FL 34119 **Chaplian Avow Hospice Naples FL 2010-; Bp Gray Fndt Dio SW Florida Parrish FL 2011-** B Peoria IL 1944 s Arthur & Lenor. Illinois St U; Illinois Cntrl Coll 1974. D 11/2/2003 Bp Keith Lynn Ackerman. m 1/25/1969 Cheri Lynne Moyers c 1. D S Monica's Epis Ch Naples FL 2009-2013, Cler Ldr of Steph Mnstry 2011-; St Paul's Epis Ch Peoria IL 2003-2007.

MOYLE, Sandra K (Fla) Holy Cross Faith Memorial Episcopal Church, 88 Baskervill Dr, Pawleys Island SC 29585 **Asst H Cross Faith Memi Epis Ch Pawleys Island SC 2013-** B Huntingdon PA 1949 d Ralph & Mary. BA Virginia Wstrn Cmnty Coll 1969; BA Old Dominion U 1972; MDiv VTS 1997. D 6/14/1997 Bp Rogers Sanders Harris P 1/15/1998 Bp John Bailey Lipscomb. Dio Florida Jacksonville 2007-2008, Chair, Liturg and Wrshp Cmsn 2005-2008; Assoc R S Mk's Epis Ch Jacksonville FL 2003-2013; Asstg R St Johns Epis Ch Tampa FL 1997-2002; Anchor-Reporter GC Epis News Serv New York NY 2003; Stndg Com Dio SW Florida Parrish FL 2001-2003.

MOYSER, George H (SC) 58 Raven Glass Ln, Bluffton SC 29909 **Emer Prof U of Vermont Burlington Vermont 2011-; Mem Epis Forum of So Carolina 2013-** B York UK 1945 s Herbert & Violet. BA U of Manchester UK 1966; MA U of Essex UK 1968; MA U MI 1972; PhD U MI 1976; Montreal TS CA 1994. D 5/31/1994 P 12/18/1994 Bp Mary Adelia Rosamond Mcleod. m 7/26/1969 Stella Mary Moyser c 1. Emer Prof/ Instr U of Vermont Burlington Vermont 2010-2011; Int/Supply S Matt's Ch Enosburg Fls VT 2010; Int/Supply S Lk's Ch S Albans VT 2009-2010; Deptl Chair U of Vermont Burlington Vermont 1996-2010; R Calv Ch Underhill VT 1994-2006; Prof U of Vermont Burlington Vermont 1987-2010; Asst/Assoc Prof U of Manchester Engl 1972-1987; New Parishes Com So Carolina Charleston SC 2014; Eccl Crt Dio Vermont Burlington VT 2009-2012, Eccl Crt 2008-2011. Auth, "Rel and Politics," *The Roubledge Compinion to the Study of Rel*, Routledge, 2009; Auth, "The WCC," *Encyclopedia of Politics and Rel*, CQ Press, 2007; Auth, "European Rel in Comparison Perspective," *Political Theol*, 2005; Ed, "Politics & Rel In The Mod Wrld," Routledge, 1991; Co-Auth, "Ch & Politics In A Secular Age," Clarendon Press, 1988; Ed, "Ch & Politics Today," T & T Clarke, 1985. Amer Political Sci Assn 1970-2010; Fllshp Of Soc Of S Jn The Evang 1993; Friends Of York Min 1995; The Angl Soc 1997. The Robert V. Daniels Awd for Outstanding Contributions to Intl Educ U of Vermont 2010; Emer Prof U of Vermont 2010.

MOZELIAK JR, Leon Clement (CNY) St. Paul's Church and All Saints Church, 204 Genesee Street and 153 South First Street, Chittenango NY 13037 **Par P All SS' Epis Ch Fulton NY 13069 2017-; Par P St. Paul's Epis Ch Chittenango NY 13037 2017-; R Gr Epis Ch Utica NY 2011-** B Carbondale PA 1951 s Leon & Mary. BA S Marys Sem & U Baltimore 1977; Exec MBA U of New Haven 1989; MDiv GTS 1996; DMin SWTS 2010. D 6/14/1997 P 12/20/1997 Bp Clarence Nicholas Coleridge. m 11/25/1978 Lynn Ellen Terragna c 2. Int Trin Epis Ch Hamburg NY 2009-2011; Int S Paul's Epis Ch Harris Hill Buffalo NY 2007-2009; R S Thad Epis Ch Aiken SC 2000-2007; Pres Mead Hall Epis Day Sch Aiken SC 2000-2006; R Trin Epis Ch Collinsville CT 1998-2000; Cur S Ptr's Epis Ch Cheshire CT 1997-1998, Pstr Assoc 1996-1997; COM Dio Wstrn New York Tonawanda NY 2009-2011, COM 2008-2011, Dioc Ins Cmsn 2008-2011, Cler Compstn Com 2007-2011, Dioc Ins Com 2007-2011; Bp's Dep for Mssn Congregations Dio Upper So Carolina Columbia SC 2006-2007, Exam Chapl 2004-2007, Exam Chapl 2003-2006, Pres of the Exec Coun 2003-2005, Pres of the Stndg Com 2003-2005, Dioc Ins Com 2002-2007, Dioc Ins Com 2001-2005, Dn of the Gravatt Convoc 2000-2003. frleonm@yahoo.com

MOZINGO, Brandon Thomas (Pgh) **Trin Cathd Pittsburgh PA 2016-** D 6/3/2017 Bp Dorsey McConnell.

MRAZ, Barbara E (Minn) 4201 Sheridan Ave S, Minneapolis MN 55410 B 1944 d Harry & Agnes. BS U MN 1966; MA U MN 1970. D 1/25/1982 Bp Robert Marshall Anderson. m 8/2/1969 Richard Mraz c 2. D S Jn The Evang S Paul

MN 2002-2013; Dn St Dav's Epis Ch Minnetonka MN 1988-2013; Dn S Jn The Bapt Epis Ch Minneapolis MN 1988-2000. Auth, "Sacr Strands".

MROCZKA, Mary Ann (Roch) 77 Plum Drive Apt F, Dansville NY 14437 **Fac Assoc for Mnstry Ldrshp Bethel Sem San Diego San Diego CA 2009-; GOE Rdr Gnrl Ord Exams 2002-; Int /Supply P 1990-; Stndg Com Dio Rochester Henrietta 2013-** B Washington DC 1949 d Joseph & Virginia. BS U of Dayton 1973; MRE SW Bapt TS 1977; MDiv Bex Sem 1979; BA Marist Coll 1993; MS No Carolina St U 2000; Duke DS 2005; PhD No Carolina St U 2005; Cert U of San Diego 2008; San Diego City Coll 2010. D 9/22/1984 Bp Robert Rae Spears Jr P 11/30/1985 Bp William George Burrill. R St Peters Memi Ch Dansville NY 2012-2015; Assoc St. Steph's Cathd San Deigo CA 2006-2008; Assoc - diversity Fac Cntr for Tchg & Lrng NCSU Raleigh 2002-2005; Int S Barth's Ch Pittsboro NC 2001; Assoc Ch Of The H Trin Pawling NY 1989-1990; Assoc Estrn Dutchess Min Coun Pawling NY 1986-1990; Chapl Goldwater Hosp New York NY 1985-1986; D Tri-Cnty Epis Area Mnstry Monticello NY 1985; Ldr of Missions OSH NY 1981-1985; Safe Ch Curric Com Dio San Diego San Diego CA 2006-2008; Bd Mem SE Counslg & Consulting Cntr 2006; Bd Mem, NCSU Campus Mnstry Dio No Carolina Raleigh NC 2003-2004, Anti-Racism Com 2002-2005. OHC 1985. Alum Schlrshp Psychol Dept, NCSU 2004; Hon Soc Psi Chi 1993; Hon Soc Alpha Chi 1992; Rossiter Schlr Bex 1984.

MUDD, Gwynneth Jones (SVa) 797 Casual Ct, Virginia Beach VA 23454 **R S Steph's Ch Norfolk VA 2009-** B CA 1937 d Edmund & Eileen. U of Maryland 1957; BS U of Virginia 1972; MS Geo Mason U 1980; Geo Mason U 1981; VPI 1981; MDiv VTS 1992. D 6/13/1992 Bp Robert Poland Atkinson P 12/1/1992 Bp Peter J Lee. c 4. Vic Ch Of S Edw Columbus OH 2005; S Paul's Ch Columbus OH 2002-2004; R S Lk's Ch Granville OH 1998-2002; Cn Pstr Chr Ch Cathd Lexington KY 1997-1998, P-in-c 1996-1997, Cn Pstr 1995-1996; Asst R S Ptr's Epis Ch Washington NC 1993-1995; Asst R S Aid's Ch Alexandria VA 1992-1993; Chapl, Cler Spouses Dio Sthrn Ohio Cincinnati OH 2002-2005, Dioc Curs, Sprtl Dir 1999-2004; Chair, Comission on Mnstry Dio E Carolina Kinston NC 1994-1995, Yth Cmsn 1994-1995, COM 1993-1995, Exec Coun 1993-1995. Ord Of S Lk 1995-1998; Sigma Alpha Iota 1956; Steph Mnstry 1995. Phi Delta Kappa Virginia Tech 1984; Fell ECF ECF 1968.

MUDGE, Barbara Duffield Covington (Ore) 88427 Trout Pond Ln, Bandon OR 97411 **Died 5/24/2016** B Laguna Bch CA 1930 d Luther & Harriet. BA Occ 1952; MA ETSBH 1981; Cert CDSP 1982. D 11/4/1982 Bp Robert Claflin Rusack P 5/8/1983 Bp George West Barrett. c 3. Pres Pres Bandon Mnstrl Assn 2005-2007; VP Everyone at the Table inc. 2004-2016; Mem Comp Dio Com 2004-2006; Ecum Coordntr Prov 8 2002-2004; S Paul Epis Ch Norwalk OH 1999-2016; S Jn-By-The-Sea Epis Ch Bandon OR 1999-2006; Chapl CPC 1997-2003; Pres Sthrn CA Ecum Coun 1994-1995; Vic S Fran Of Assisi Epis Ch Simi Vlly CA 1986-1995; S Mary's Par Laguna Bch CA 1984-1986; Chapl So Coast Med Cntr 1982-1986; Simi Vlly Interfaith Cltn for Hmless/Needy 2016; Ecum Off Dio Oregon Portland OR 2002-2006, Judge of Eccl Trial Crt 2002-2006. OHC 1992. Wmn of Achievement Bus & Profsnl Wmn Club 1980; Cn 93 Cathd Cntr; 85 in Rel YWCA.

MUDGE, Hannah (Alb) Oaks of Righteousness Episcopal Ministry, 2331 15th St, Troy NY 12180 B Greenwich CT 1984 d Shaw & Julia. AAS SUNY Delhi 2001; BM Wheaton Coll 2006; MDiv TESM 2010; MDiv Trin Sch for Mnstry 2010. D 6/5/2010 P 12/18/2010 Bp William Howard Love. Dio Albany Greenwich NY 2012-2016.

MUDGE OHC, Hiram Thomas (Kan) PO Box 99, West Park NY 12493 **Monk OHC W Pk NY 2011-** B Cincinnati OH 1938 s Hiram & Virginia. BA Cor 1960; MDiv Nash 1964. D 2/22/1964 P 8/22/1964 Bp Donald H V Hallock. Prior OHC W Pk NY 2006-2011; Dir of Guesthouse Mnstrs OHC W Pk NY 2002-2006; Novc Mstr OHC W Pk NY 1998-2002; Asst Superior OHC W Pk NY 1990-1998; Prior H Sav Priory Pineville SC 1983-1990; Novc Mstr OHC W Pk NY 1973-1982; Prior Whitby Monstry Grapevine TX 1971-1973; OHC W Pk NY 1967-1973; R S Lk's Ch Whitewater WI 1965-1967. Auth, *Tracts & arts on the Pryr Life*. Phi Kappa Phi; Phi Beta Kappa.

MUDGE, Julia Hamilton (Alb) 204 Worthington Ter, Wynantskill NY 12198 **Mem, Liturg & Ch Mus Com Dio Albany Greenwich NY 1998-** B Houston TX 1956 d Bill & Blanche. BA Ob 1979; MA S Bernards TS and Mnstry 2004. D 6/12/2004 Bp Daniel William Herzog P 1/1/2005 Bp David John Bena. m 6/13/1981 Shaw Mudge c 3. SAMS Ambridge PA 2009-2014; Asst Chr's Ch Duanesburg NY 2004-2009. "Welcome Song (Mus composition)".

MUDGE, Melanie A (NC) 2820 Rue Sans Famille, Raleigh NC 27607 B Raleigh NC 1945 d Harley & Althea. BS Virginia Commonwealth U 1967; MDiv Sewanee: The U So, 1999. D 5/26/1999 Bp Robert Carroll Johnson Jr P 2/12/2000 Bp James Gary Gloster. S Thos Epis Ch Sanford NC 2015-2016; S Lk's Ch Salisbury NC 2013-2014; R Emm Epis Ch Winchester KY 2006-2013; R Epis Ch Of The H Sprt Cumming GA 2002-2006; Asst R All SS Ch Roanoke Rapids NC 1999-2002. Preaching Excellence Awd 1999.

MUDGE JR, Shaw (Alb) 25 Rushforde Dr, Manchester CT 06040 **S Ptr's Ch So Windsor CT 2016-** B Greenwich Connecticut 1953 s Shaw & Patricia. BA Dickinson Coll 1976; MDiv TESM 1988; DMin TESM 2004. D 6/14/1997 Bp

Clarence Nicholas Coleridge P 8/29/1998 Bp Daniel William Herzog. m 6/13/1981 Julia Hamilton Mudge c 3. Hon Assoc Trin Ch Tariffville CT 2014-2016; Exam Chapl Angl Dio Belize Cntrl Amer 2013-2016; Dir, Angl Theol Inst Angl Dio Belize Cntrl Amer 2012-2016; Fndr, Fac Mem Global Online Angl Theol Coll Prog 2012-2016; SAMS Ambridge PA 2009-2016; Mem, HOD St of the Ch Com ECUSA GC 2003-2009; Evang Com ECUSA GC 2003-2006; R Chr's Ch Duanesburg NY 2002-2009; Secy of the Dio Dio Albany Greenwich NY 2000-2009, GC Dep (Deputation Chair 2006) 2003-2006, GC, Joint Evang Com Mem (HOD Secy 2006) 2003-2006, GC, St of the Ch Com Mem 2003-2006, Salary and Benefits Com Mem/Chair 1999-2010, Chf Archit, D Formation Prog Curric 1999-2004; R Chr Ch Walton NY 1998-2002; P-in-c S Paul's Ch Bloomville NY 1998-2002. PB Coordntr, "(Spanish Ed)," *Bk of Common Pryr*, The Ch in the Providence of the W Indies, 2016; Auth, "D Formation Prog Curric in the Dio Albany," *Doctoral Thesis*, Trin Sch for Mnstry, 2004; Ed, "Journ of Dioc Conv," *Conv Journ 2000-2008*, Dio Albany; Ed, "Web site of the Dio Belize," *Offcl Web site of the Dio Belize, 2014 to 2016*, Angl Dio Belize. voyag7747@gmail.com

MUELLER, Denise Ray (SO) 412 Sycamore St., Cincinnati OH 45202 **D S Jn's Ch Worthington OH 2010-, Legis Liaison 2009-2010; Cnvnr, Soc Justice & Publ Plcy Dio Southerm Ohio Cincinnati OH 2009-** B Lincoln IL 1951 d Forrest & Chiquita. OH SU 1972; Angl Acad 2008. D 6/14/2008 Bp Thomas Edward Breidenthal. m 5/28/1999 Karen Roberta Peeler. Assn of Epis Deacons 2008.

MUELLER, Heather (Haw) PO Box 628, Kapa'au HI 96755 **P-in-c S Andr's Ch Taft CA 2013-; P-in-c Kohala Epis Mssn Kapaau HI 2012-** B Radford VA 1942 d Robert & Esther. BS MI SU 1966; MDiv CDSP 1978. D 6/21/1979 P 4/22/1981 Bp Edmond Lee Browning. c 2. Min of Hosp St. Geo's Coll Jerusalem 2011-2012; R S Jn's Epis Ch Kula HI 1981-2010; H Innoc' Epis Ch Lahaina HI 1980-1981; Seabury Hall Makawao HI 1979-1981; Chapl/Tchr Seabury Hall Makawao HI 1978-1981. Auth, "Hist Of S Jn'S," *Kula*, 2000. EWC 1982-1988; NNECA 1991.

MUELLER, Mary Margaret (WTex) 1045 Shook Ave Apt 105, San Antonio TX 78212 B San Antonio TX 1944 d James & Margaret. BA Trin 1967; MDiv Sewanee: The U So, TS 1982. D 6/24/1982 Bp Stanley Fillmore Hauser P 1/6/1983 Bp Scott Field Bailey. Int Gr Ch Llano TX 2003-2010; Asst S Mk's Epis Ch San Antonio TX 1993-2001; Dir Of Pstr Care San Antonio Hospice TX 1990-1991; Asst Chr Epis Ch San Antonio TX 1982-1990.

MUELLER, Susan Richards (Mil) 7018 Colony Dr, Madison WI 53717 B Evanston IL 1946 d Stanleigh & Olive. Loyola U 1967; BS U of Wisconsin 1968; MA U of Wisconsin 1970; Nash 1983. D 4/7/1984 Bp Charles Thomas Gaskell. m 6/22/1968 William Mueller c 2. Archd Dio Milwaukee Milwaukee WI 2006-2013, Dir -Deacons' Formation Prog 2001-2005, Commision on Mnstry 1991-2000; D S Andr's Ch Madison WI 2003-2010; D Gr Ch Madison WI 1996-2000; D S Dunst's Ch Madison WI 1987-1996; D St Fran Hse Madison WI 1984-1987. NAAD 1984; NAAD 1984.

MUES, Steven Wayne (Kan) 144 Lake Mountain Dr, Boulder City NV 89005 B Arapahoe NE 1948 s Wayne & Dorothy. BA U of Nebraska 1970; MDiv PDS 1973; DMin Untd TS of the Twin Cities 1994. Trans 11/3/2003 Bp James Louis Jelinek. m 9/2/1969 Marilyn K Mues. R S Stephens Epis Churchrch Wichita KS 2005-2013; S Judes Ranch Boulder City NV 2003-2005; R S Lk's Epis Ch Rochester MN 1989-2003; R Ch Of The H Trin Lincoln NE 1984-1989, Cur 1974-1983; P-in-c S Pauls Epis Ch Arapahoe NE 1978-1984. Auth, "A Thinking Person'S Ch," *LivCh*, 2000; Auth, "Hist Theol Characteristics Making Evang Difficult," *ATR*, 1995; Auth, "Time," *Sermons That Wk*, Forw Mvmt Press, 1994. Louisville Inst Grant Rec 2000.

MUGAN JR, Robert Charles (WNC) 894 Indian Hill Rd, Hendersonville NC 28791 B Sioux City IA 1940 s Robert & Hazel. Marq 1964; BA S Louis U 1966; MA S Louis U 1969; MA S Louis U 1973; MA S Louis U 1973. Rec 4/16/1994 as Priest Bp Alfred Marble Jr. m 6/27/1981 Susan H Mugan c 1. Int Ch Of The H Cross Tryon NC 2013-2016; R Ch Of The Trsfg Bat Cave NC 1997-2012; Chap Of The Cross Chap Hill NC 1996-1997; Asst Pstr Chap of the Cross Madison MS 1996-1997; Asst R S Ptr's By The Lake Brandon MS 1994-1996; Serv RC Ch 1972-1977.

MUHLHEIM, Nancy Colleen Collins (Ore) 98 Fairway Loop, Eugene OR 97401 **D S Mary's Epis Ch Eugene OR 2001-** B Portland OR 1944 d Francis & Isis. BA U of Oregon 1965; Dio Oregon Cntr for the Diac 2001; Dio Oregon Cntr for the Diac 2001. D 9/29/2001 Bp Robert Louis Ladehoff. m 9/11/1965 Wilson Caughey Muhlheim c 2. CHS 1998.

MUINDE, Sandra Laverne (FdL) 311 Division St, Oshkosh WI 54901 **D Trin Epis Ch Oshkosh WI 2011-** B Milwaukee WI 1950 d Alfonso & Shirley. D 5/7/2011 Bp Russell Edward Jacobus. m 6/21/1969 Samuel Muinde c 3.

MUIR, George Daniels (Ga) St. Paul's Church, 605 Reynolds St., Augusta GA 30901 **Int R S Paul's Ch Augusta GA 2013-** B Goldsboro NC 1954 s J & Martha. BA U NC 1976; MDiv VTS 1982. D 6/7/1982 Bp Brice Sidney Sanders P 1/21/1983 Bp Hunley Agee Elebash. m 8/20/1977 Susan Byers Muir c 3. Int R All SS Ch Richmond VA 2012-2013; Int R Trin Epis Ch Asheville NC 2010-2012; R Gr Epis Ch Hinsdale IL 2001-2010; Assoc Gr & H Trin Epis Ch

Richmond VA 1989-2000; R S Paul's Ch Beaufort NC 1984-1989; Asst S Jn's Epis Ch Fayetteville NC 1982-1984. Bd, Ymca 1989-2000; COM 1994-1997; Dir Middle Atlantic Paridh Trng Prog 1989-2000; Goe Rdr 1987-1994; Stndg Com 1986-1989.

MUIR, Richard Dale (Chi) 181 Wildwood Rd, Lake Forest IL 60045 **Ret 1996-** B Cincinnati OH 1932 s Virgil & Virginia. BS Mia 1954; MDiv Bex Sem 1967; DMin Hartford Sem 1981. D 6/17/1967 Bp Nelson Marigold Burroughs P 2/6/1968 Bp John Harris Burt. m 8/8/1959 Ruth A Muir c 3. Assoc The Ch Of The H Sprt Lake Forest IL 1992-1996; R S Mk's Barrington IL 1986-1991; Int Gr Ch Vineyard Haven MA 1985-1986; R S Steph's Ch Cohasset MA 1970-1984; Pres Bex Alum Bex Sem Columbus OH 1969-1976; Cur S Paul's Ch Akron OH 1967-1970.

MUKHWANA-NAFUMA, Joel Eric (NY) B Uganda 1941 s Daniel & Susana. CTh Bp Tucker Theol Coll Mukono Ug 1969; LTh VTS 1975; BA U of Charleston 1981; MA Marshall St U 1983; MDiv VTS 1983. Trans 12/3/2004 Bp Mark Sean Sisk. m 10/30/1970 Juliana Auma Nafuma c 3. P-in-c Trin Ch Mt Vernon NY 2004-2013; Dio New York New York NY 2003-2012. Auth, "Imbalu, Gisu Initiation Rite," UMI Dissertation Serv, 1991; Auth, "The Faith of Magd," 1980. Naming of Joel Nafuma Refugee Cntr Epis Ch, Rome 1985.

MULAC, Pam (Los) 7585 N Park Crest Ln, Prescott Valley AZ 86314 **Vic S Alb's Epis Ch Wickenburg AZ 2009-** B Salem OH 1944 d Elmer & Dorothy. Bryn 1964; BA U Chi 1966; MDiv SWTS 1974; PhD NWU 1988. D 9/21/1974 Bp James Winchester Montgomery P 12/13/1978 Bp Charles Bennison Sr. m 8/8/1987 George R Larsen. Dio Los Angeles Los Angeles CA 2001-2005; R S Steph's Par Whittier CA 1998-2005; Int S Mich's Epis Ch Riverside CA 1996-1998; Int S Tim's Epis Ch Apple Vlly CA 1995-1996; Bloy Hse Claremont CA 1994-1998; Chapl Foothill Presb Hosp Glendora CA 1994-1995; Foothill Presb Hosp Glendora CA 1994-1995; Asst S Geo's Par La Can CA 1994-1995; Asst All SS Ch Pasadena CA 1992-1993; Asst S Ambr Par Claremont CA 1988-1991; Asst S Mk's Epis Ch Upland CA 1984-1987; Adj Instr Bexley Seabury Fed Chicago IL 1979-1981. AAPC 1973; ACPE 2000; OHC 1973. Resrch Awd Aapc Pacific Reg 1989.

MULDER, Timothy John (Nwk) 2 Hunt Lane, Gladstone NJ 07934 **R Chr Ch Short Hills NJ 2010-; Epis Preaching Fndt Springfield NJ 2005-; Assoc Prof of Homil & Liturg New Brunswick TS New Brunswick NJ 2005-** B Englwood NJ 1954 s Edwin & Luella. BA Hope Coll 1976; MDiv PrTS 1982; DMin Drew U 1991. D 2/11/1998 P 8/1/1998 Bp Joe Doss. m 9/29/2007 Linda Walker c 2. Prof New Brunswick TS New Brunswick NJ 2008-2010; The Epis Preaching Fndt 2006-2008; R S Lk's Ch Gladstone NJ 1998-2006; Asst 1998; S Bern's Ch Bernardsville NJ 1998, Assoc 1996-1998; Assoc 1996-1998; Pstr RCA Bedminster & Wayne NJ 1982-1996. Auth, "Adv/Christmas Year C 2009-12010," *New Proclamation*, Fortress Press, 2009; "My, How You've Changed," *Sermons and Comments*, Epis Preaching Fndt, 2006; Auth, "Never the Point of the Story," *Preaching through the Year of Lk*, Morehouse Pub, 2000; Auth, *Liturg & Life*, Reformed Ch Press, 1996; Ed, *Sprtl Discipline of Tithing*, Reformed Ch Press, 1993. Cmnty of St. Jn Bapt 2006.

MULDOON, Maggie R (Minn) 18350 67 Avenue, Cloverdale BC V3S 1E5 Canada B Minneapolis MN 1939 d Cosmas & Mary. BA U of St Thos 1980; MDiv U Tor CA 1990. Trans 11/5/2002 Bp James Louis Jelinek. c 5. Int S Lk's Epis Ch Rochester MN 2003-2004; P-in-c S Paul's Ch Winona MN 2002-2003.

MULFORD, Marie Lynne (WVa) 2585 State Route 7 N, Gallipolis OH 45631 **P River Bend Cluster Pt Pleasant WV 2013-, 2003-2008; P Gr Ch Ravenswood WV 2005-; R St. Jn's Epis Ch Ripley WV 2005-; R River Bend Epis Mnstrs Pt. PLeasant WV 2003-** B Chicago IL 1948 d Willard & Shirley. BA OH SU 1971; MA OH SU 1978; MDiv Bex Sem 2012. D 9/19/2002 P 6/7/2003 Bp William Michie Klusmeyer. m 8/21/1983 James Mulford. P S Jn's Ripley WV 2002. Ldrshp Awd Bex Sem 2012; DD SWTS 2012.

MULKIN, Suzanne Devine (CFla) 875 Brock Rd, Bartow FL 33830 **Vol Chapl Lake Wales Med Cntr Lake Wales FL 2012-; D The Epis Ch Of The Gd Shpd Lake Wales FL 2008-** B Queens NY 1948 d Raymond & Marion. Reformed TS; AA Vernon Crt Jr Coll 1968; BA Barrington Coll 1971; Cert Natl Inst For Lay Trng New York NY 1978; Cert Inst for Chr Stds Florida 1998. D 12/11/1999 Bp John Wadsworth Howe. m 6/19/1976 Michael Mulkin. D All SS Epis Ch Lakeland FL 2004-2006; D S Steph's Ch Lakeland FL 2002-2003; D H Trin Epis Ch Bartow FL 1999-2002. DOK 2016; NAAD 1999; OSL 2005.

MULL, Judson Gary (At) 499 Trabert Ave Nw, Atlanta GA 30309 **Cler Assoc All SS Epis Ch Atlanta GA 1994-** B Chattanooga TN 1946 s Julian & Grace. BA U GA 1972; MDiv Sewanee: The U So, TS 1977. D 6/11/1977 Bp Bennett Jones Sims P 3/4/1978 Bp Charles Judson Child Jr. Cler Assoc Cathd Of S Phil Atlanta GA 1984-1993; Asst R S Anne's Epis Ch Atlanta GA 1978-1984; D/P Emm Epis Ch Athens GA 1977-1978.

MULLALY JR, Charles Francis (Va) 888 Summit View Ln, Charlottesville VA 22903 B Washington DC 1942 s Charles & Virginia. BA E Carolina U 1967; MS Sthrn Illinois U 1979; MA Baylor U 1981; MDiv VTS 1994. D 6/11/1994 P 12/1/1994 Bp Peter J Lee. m 6/18/1966 Leith Mullaly c 3. Emm Epis Ch Greenwood VA 1997-2012; Asst S Ptr's Epis Ch Arlington VA 1994-1997.

MULLARKEY, Meghan Kathleen (Oly) **Emm Epis Ch Mercer Island WA 2015-** B Arlington VA 1983 d Daniel & Barbara. BA Elon U 2006; MDiv The Seattle TS and Psychol 2012; Angl Stds Cert CDSP 2016. D 12/17/2016 P 6/20/2017 Bp Gregory Harold Rickel. m 6/8/2013 Lucas David Abernathy c 1. Yth Dir S Marg's Epis Ch Bellevue WA 2013-2015.

MULLEN, Melanie B (WA) St Paul's Episcopal Church, 815 E Grace St, Richmond VA 23219 **Dom And Frgn Mssy Soc- Epis Ch Cntr New York NY 2017-; Epis Ch Cntr New York NY 2017-** B Johnson City NY 1974 d Ronald & Martha. BA U NC 1996; MDiv VTS 2012. D 6/2/2012 P 1/26/2013 Bp Mariann Edgar Budde. Assoc S Paul's Ch Richmond VA 2012-2017; Dio Washington Washington DC 2012. mmullen@stpauls-episcopal.org

MULLEN, Sean E (Pa) St Mark's Church, 1625 Locust St, Philadelphia PA 19103 **R St Mk's Ch Philadelphia PA 2006-; S Mk's Ch Philadelphia PA 2002-** B Jersey City NJ 1967 s Richard & Anne. BA W&M 1989; MDiv GTS 1996. D 6/1/1996 P 12/1/1996 Bp Richard Frank Grein. Assoc St Mk's Ch Philadelphia PA 2002-2006; Chapl to Archbp of Perth 1998-2002; Asst R All SS Ch Richmond VA 1996-1998.

MULLER, Denise Holly (Az) D 6/10/2017 Bp Kirk Stevan Smith.

MULLER, Donald Joseph (NJ) 4 Christopher Mill Rd, Medford NJ 08055 **R S Ptr's Ch Medford NJ 2004-** B New York NY 1953 s Edward & Edith. BA Manhattan Coll 1975; MDiv Nash 1980; DMin GTF 1997. D 6/7/1980 P 12/1/1980 Bp Paul Moore Jr. m 9/5/1982 Margaret Lynn Muller c 2. Dn-Burlington Convoc Dio New Jersey Trenton NJ 2004-2007, Dioc Coun 1990-1994, Chair - Evang Comm 1988-1995, Evang Cmsn 1987-1995, Dept Of Cmncatn 1986-; R S Steph's Epis Ch Wilkes Barre PA 1996-2004; Bd Trst Sthrn Ocean Cnty Hosp 1993-1996; R The Ch Of The H Innoc Bch Haven NJ 1986-1996; R Ch Of The Div Love Montrose NY 1982-1986; Cur Par of Chr the Redeem Pelham NY 1980-1982; Dir Sum Yth Conf Dio New York New York NY 1981-1985. Cmnty of S Mary - P Assoc 2012. Cn Dio Bethlehem 1999.

MULLER JR, John (Colo) 513 E 19th St, Delta CO 81416 **Ret 2008-** B Philadelphia PA 1942 s John & Elizabeth. BA U of Pennsylvania 1964; MDiv VTS 1969. D 6/7/1969 Bp Chandler W Sterling P 12/7/1969 Bp David Ritchie Thornberry. m 10/14/1967 Linda Muller c 2. Bd Dir Cmnty Care Hospice 1980-1984; S Lk's Epis Ch Delta CO 1977-2008; Stff Ch Of The Redeem Houston TX 1976-1977; Vic S Barn Of The Vlly Cortez CO 1971-1975; S Paul's Ch Mancos CO 1971-1975; Asst S Mk's Epis Ch Casper WY 1969-1971; Exec Coun Dio Colorado Denver CO 1979-1985, Dioc Coun 1972-1978.

MULLER, Michael Anthony (Nwk) St Peter's Episc Church, 215 Boulevard, Mountain Lakes NJ 07046 B Toowoomba Australia 1970 s Noel & Carol. Rec 10/15/2016 as Priest Bp Mark M Beckwith. m 4/6/1999 Aida Elizabeth Sosa c 2.

MULLER, Thomas G (Eur) Via Bernardo Rucellai, 9, Florence Italy B Frankfurt DE 1956 s Horst & Marta. BA Ya 1979; Alanus U 1985; MDiv EDS 2001. D 11/17/2002 P 6/20/2003 Bp Pierre W Whalon. S Jas Epis Ch Firenze 50123 2002-2004, Stdt Min 2002-; St Jas Ch 2002-2004.

MULLER JR, William C (Vt) 522 W 4th Ave, Mitchell SD 57301 **Trin Ch Rutland VT 2014-** B Poughkeepsie NY 1961 s William & Katherine. BA Marist Coll 1988; MDiv CDSP 2006. D 3/11/2006 Bp Mark Sean Sisk P 9/16/2006 Bp Creighton Leland Robertson. m 9/5/2013 Cynthia K Muller c 4. R S Mary's Epis Ch Mitchell SD 2006-2014.

MULLIGAN IV, Edward B (At) Holy Innocents' Episc Ch, 805 Mount Vernon Hwy NW, Atlanta GA 30327 B Kingston PA 1952 s Edward & Ellen. BA Amh 1975; JD S Louis U Law Sch S Louis MO 1981; MDiv Ya Berk 2006. D 6/3/2006 Bp Vicky Gene Robinson. m 8/29/1992 Pamela L Mulligan c 3. Hd Chapl H Innoc' Epis Sch Atlanta GA 2012-2015; P-in-c S Columba's Chap Middletown RI 2011-2012; P Emm Chap Manchester MA 2009-2011; Hd Chapl S Geo's Sch Middletown RI 2008-2012; Hd Chapl Salisbury Sch Salisbury CT 2006-2008.

MULLIN, Mark Hill (Okla) 2091 Brownstone Ln, Charlottesville VA 22901 B Chicago IL 1940 s Francis & Alma. BA Harv 1962; BA Oxf GB 1964; MDiv GTS 1968; MA Oxf GB 1968. D 6/15/1968 P 3/1/1969 Bp James Winchester Montgomery. m 7/23/1964 Martha Jane Mullin c 3. Hdmstr Casady Sch Ok City OK 1998-2002; Casady Sch Oklahoma City OK 1998-2002; Cathd of St Ptr & St Paul Washington DC 1978-1999; Hdmstr S Albans Sch Washington DC 1977-1997; Blue Ridge Sch Dyke VA 1976-1977; Asst Hdmstr Blue Ridge Sch S Georges VA 1976-1977; Dn Choate Sch Wallingford CT 1973-1976; The Choate Sch Wallingford CT 1968-1976; Chapl Choate Sch Wallingford CT 1968-1973. Auth, "The Headmaster's Run," Rowman and Littlefield Educ, 2008; Auth, "Educ for the 21st Century," Madison Books, 1991; Auth, "Wstrn Europe 84," Stryke-Post, 1984; Auth, "Should Buffalo Bob Come to Chap?," *NAIS Journ*, 1975.

MULLINS, Andrew Jackson W (NY) 230 E 50th St Apt 4C, New York NY 10022 **P-t Assoc P All SS Ch New York NY 2012-; R Emer The Ch of the Epiph 2011-; Trst U of Charleston 2011-** B Charleston WV 1939 s Andrew & Sallye. BA Bethany Coll 1962; STM GTS 1967; Col 1978; Cert Inst For Not-For-Profit Mgmt 1978. D 6/12/1967 P 12/16/1967 Bp Wilburn Camrock Campbell. m 6/15/1996 Cathy West c 4. R Emer The Ch Of The Epiph New York NY 1998-2011; V-Dn S Mk's Cathd Seattle WA 1990-1998; The Assoc R St. Barth Ch New York NY 1968-1990; Dir S Bartholomews Cmnty Club 1968-1980; Vic Gr Ch Ravenswood WV 1967-1968; S Jn's Ripley WV 1967-1968; Chair of Assessment Bd. Dio New York New York NY 2006-2011. Auth, "A Hist Of Missions In The Dio W Virginia". Hon Cn Dio Olympia 1998; Who'S Who In Rel. amullins@stbarts.org

MULLINS, Edward L (Mich) 730 E Knot Ct, Corolla NC 27927 **Int Chr Ch Eliz City NC 2013-** B Wheeling WV 1944 s Ezekiel & Mayme. BBA Marshall U 1966; MDiv VTS 1971; Cert of Stds PrTS 1982; PrTS 1982; Cert of Stds Harv 1987; Harv 1987. D 6/11/1971 P 2/26/1972 Bp Wilburn Camrock Campbell. m 6/30/1973 Diana M Mullins c 2. Freelance Photographer Photographer 2003-2011; Int R Epis Ch Of S Fran-In-The-Vlly Green Vlly AZ 2000-2011; R Chr Ch Cranbrook Bloomfield Hills MI 1996-2009; R S Barth's Epis Ch Poway CA 1985-1996; R Emm Ch Cumberland MD 1978-1984; Assoc Gr Epis Ch Silver Sprg MD 1974-1978; Vic S Mk's Epis Ch Berkeley Spg WV 1971-1974. Auth, "Guidelines For Congrl Growth," *Dio San Diego*, Dioc, 1989; Auth, "Outline Notes on The NT," *Self Pub*, S Barth's, 1988; Auth, "Outline Notes On The OT," *Self Pub*, S Bartholomews, 1988; Auth, "Article on Ch Growth," *Alive Now*, Grp, 1973. Epis Ch Visual Arts 2007. Wrld Sabbath Peace Awd Outstanding Wk bewteen Rel 2009; ECVA's Pub Rel Arts 2007; Herald Awd Best Ecum Event TV 2004; Herald Awd Best Rel Prog TV 2003; Hometown Awd Best Rel TV Interview Show 2002. emullins.photos@gmail.com

MULLINS, Judith Pierpont (Oly) 80 E Roanoke St Apt 16, Seattle WA 98102 B Waterbury CT 1938 d Elvin & Bernice. AS Dn Coll 1958; Lic U of Tennessee 1966. D 6/22/1996 Bp Vincent Waydell Warner. m 6/25/1960 Donald Hugh Mullins.

MULLINS, Perry Emerson (Dal) **S Ptr's Ch Mc Kinney TX 2017-** D 6/14/2014 P 4/25/2015 Bp Paul Emil Lambert.

MULLINS, Walter Earl (Md) 6922 Hollenberry Rd, Sykesville MD 21784 B Nash County NC 1945 s Walter & Nancy. BA E Carolina U 1967; MDiv SE Bapt TS 1972; Inst Pstr Psychol 1975; Advncd CPE 1978. D 6/12/1982 P 4/1/1983 Bp John Thomas Walker. c 4. All SS Ch Frederick MD 2013-2016; R S Barn Epis Ch Sykesville MD 2000-2013; R S Paul's Ch Dedham MA 1988-1992; Assoc S Jn Georgetown MD 1983-1985; S Jn's Ch Georgetown Par Washington DC 1983-1985; VTS Alexandria VA 1983-1984; Dir For The Dept Of Pstr Care Colombia Hosp In Washington D.C. 1978-1983; Assoc Manassas Ch VA 1972-1976.

MULLIS, Robert Bradley (NC) 405 Baymount Dr., Statesville NC 28625 **R Trin Epis Ch Statesville NC 2003-** B Winston-Salem NC 1961 s Starret & Pauline. BA Davidson Coll 1983; MA U NC 1991; MDiv Duke DS 1996; Cert Ang Stud VTS 1996. D 6/29/1996 P 6/21/1997 Bp Robert Carroll Johnson Jr. m 8/13/1994 Ellyn Bain Mullis c 2. Dioc Coun Mem Dio No Carolina Raleigh NC 2006-2008; Asst Ch Of The Nativ Raleigh NC 1996-2003.

MULVEY, Dorian L (Az) 8951 E. Sutton Drive, Scottsdale AZ 85260 **R S Anth On The Desert Scottsdale AZ 2008-** B New York NY 1954 d Harold & Dorothy. BA CUNY 1975; MBA NYU 1981; MDiv SWTS 1998. D 6/20/1998 Bp Chilton Richardson Knudsen P 12/21/1998 Bp Herbert Alcorn Donovan Jr. m 5/30/1976 George M Mulvey c 2. R Ch Of The Ascen Seattle WA 2003-2008; The Epis Ch Of S Jas The Less Northfield IL 1998-2003. Bd Dir, Olympia 2005-2008; Bdgt Com, Chicago 2001-2003; Chr Formation Comission, Chicago 2000-2003.

MULVEY JR, Thomas Patrick (Mass) **Emm Ch Braintree MA 2009-** B Boston MA 1955 BS Stonehill Coll 1977; JD Suffolk U 1985; MDiv EDS 2001. Trans 9/6/2005 Bp M(Arvil) Thomas Shaw. m 12/11/1982 Elizabeth Mulvey c 2. Asst Ch Of S Jn The Evang Hingham MA 2004-2007.

MUMFORD, Nigel William David (SVa) B England 1954 s Michael. D 6/11/2005 P 12/17/2005 Bp Daniel William Herzog. m 9/15/2001 Lynn French Mumford c 2. The Rev. Dio Albany Greenwich NY 2005-2013. PTSD healing, "After The Trauma, The Battle Begins," *After the Trauma the Battle Begins. Post Trauma Healing*, Oratory Press, 2011; Healing, "The Forgotten Touch," *The Forgotten Touchm More Stories of Healing*, Seabury Press, 2007; Healing, "Hand to Hand from Combat to Healing," *Hand to Hand from Combat to Healing*, Ch Pub, 2002. Kennedy Lifetime Achievement Awd Grove City Coll 2011; Paul Harris Fell Rotary 1999; Preaching Excellence Prog Yale DS 1999; Wittnauer Humanitarian Awd New York Wittnauer 1998.

MUMITA, Joseph Thairu (Mass) Grace Episcopal Church, 67 Norwood St, Everett MA 02149 B Kajiado Kenya 1973 s Robert & Gladys. Trans 9/28/2016 as Priest Bp Alan Gates. m 6/12/1999 Grace Ruguru Thairu c 3.

MUMMA-WAKABAYASHI, Diane Carole (Spr) D 6/22/2017 Bp Daniel Hayden Martins.

MUN SSP, Paul Shinkyu (Tenn) Church Of The Holy Spirit, 5325 Nolensville Pike, Nashville TN 37211 **R H Sprt Ch Nashville TN 2013-** B Tokyo, Japan 1944 s Yongoh & Yangja. MDiv Sthrn Bapt TS 1989; PhD Other 1995; PhD Sthrn Bapt TS 1995; Dip Ang Stud Other 2004; Dip Ang Stud SungKongHoe Angl U Korea 2004. D 9/28/2007 P 3/31/2008 Bp John Clark Buchanan. m 10/24/1973 Grace Mun c 2. Pres The Assn of Korean Epis Ch 2009; Vic Gr Epis

Ch Virginia Bch VA 2008-2012; Prof Regent U Virginia Bch VA 1998-2011; Pres Assn of Korean Epis Ch 2009.

MUNCIE, Margaret Ann (NY) 1 Chipping Court, Greenville SC 29607 **Exec Dir Cbury Counslg Cntr Greenville SC 2011-** B New York NY 1948 d James & Doris. BA Hood Coll 1970; MDiv GTS 1974; Bd Cert Chapl 1984; Cert U MI 1984; Cert U of So Caroline 2012. D 6/15/1974 P 4/25/1977 Bp Jonathan Goodhue Sherman. m 7/27/1974 Stephen M Bolle c 2. Chapl The Healthcare Chapl Inc New York NY 2002-2009; Fac Dio Sthrn Ohio Cincinnati OH 1994-2000; VP The GTS New York NY 1992-1993, Seminar Moderator 1978-1991; Chapl St Lukes Cntr Cincinnati OH 1990-2000; Chapl The Deupree Ret Com 1990-2000; Chapl Greenwich Chapl Serv Greenwich CT 1982-1990; Chapl Greenwich Chapl Serv Inc Greenwich CT 1982-1990; Non-par Supply Cler 1980-1982; Asst S Matt's Ch Bedford NY 1978-1980; Chapl Area Colls Poughkeepsie NY 1974-1977; Bishops Advsry Com New York NY 1974-1976; Field Educ Supvsr Ya Berk New Haven CT 1984-1990; Cmsn On Aging Dio New York New York NY 1983-1989. Contrib, "arts of Chapl," *Plainviews*, The HealthCare Chapl, 2013; Auth, "Sensory Stimulated Wrshp," 2003; Ed, "Aging Nwsltr," 1994; Co-Auth, "Dvlpmt Of Sprtl Awareness Prog In Ltc Settings," 1993. ACPE; Assn Prof Chapl; ESMA; Forsa.

MUNCIE, Steve D. (LI) 65 Joralemon Street, Brooklyn NY 11201 **P-in-c Chr Ch Gardiner ME 2016-** B Fort Knox KY 1955 s Russell & Wilma. BA Mia 1976; MDiv Van 1979. D 6/29/1982 P 1/18/1983 Bp William Grant Black. m 12/28/2013 Peter Conrad Bals c 2. R Gr Ch Brooklyn NY 2004-2016; Cn Dio Sthrn Ohio Cincinnati OH 2000-2004; R S Fran Epis Ch Springboro OH 1982-2000. CT, Assoc 2000.

MUNDIA, Wilberforce Omusala (NC) 204 W Salisbury St, Pittsboro NC 27312 **S Barth's Ch Pittsboro NC 2011-** B Kima Kenya 1955 s James & Fanice. BA Oak Hill Coll 1981; MTS Trin Luth Sem 1984; ThD Bos 1995. Trans 1/3/2012 as Priest Bp Michael B Curry. m 4/10/1982 Alice D Mundia c 3. mundialism@gmail.com

MUNDY, Robert Lowry (RG) **Chapl The Great SW Dist of Civitan Intl 2010-; Vic S Matt's Mssn Los Lunas NM 2006-** B Las Cruces NM 1963 BS New Mex St U 1988; Basic Chr Stds TESM 2005. D 7/30/2005 P 8/19/2006 Bp Jeffrey Neil Steenson. m 7/17/1999 Karen Lee Mundy. COM Dio The Rio Grande Albuquerque 2009-2011, Cathd Chapt 2008-2009. Valencia Civitan Club 2008; Valencia Cnty Jvnl Justice Bd 2011; Valencia Cnty Resiliency Corp. 2011. Paul Harris Fell Chama Rotary Club 2006.

MUNGOMA, Stephen Masette (Los) 1401 W 123rd St, Los Angeles CA 90047 B Mbale UG 1949 s Nicholas & Kezia. BA Makerere U 1972; MA Makerere U 1977; MA Fuller TS 1987; PhD Fuller TS 2003. Trans 6/1/2000 Bp Frederick Houk Borsch. m 1/6/1973 Rachel Masete Kakai c 4. S Patricks Ch And Day Sch Thousand Oaks CA 2005-2006; P-in-c S Tim's Par Compton CA 2000-2006; Serv Ch In Uganda 1991-1994.

MUNOZ, Antonio (Dal) 5100 Ross Ave, Dallas TX 75206 **S Barn Ch Garland TX 2017-** B Mexicali Baja Mexico 1963 s Manuel & Maria. MA Universidad Autonoma de Baja CA 1985; Cert S Andrews TS Guadalajara MX 1990; Seminario San Andres 1990. D 11/30/1990 P 10/27/1991 Bp Samuel Espinoza-Venegas. c 4. Cn For Hisp Mnstry S Matt's Cathd Dallas TX 2003-2016; La Iglesia De San Pablo Seaside CA 1994-2003; Vic Mssn San Pablo Monterey CA 1994-2002; Vic Iglesia San Mateo Yeatesville NC 1993-1994; Dio E Carolina Kinston NC 1993; Dio Wstrn Mex Zapopan Jalisco 1990-1993; Vic Santa Maria Vrgn Hermosillo 1990-1993.

MUNOZ, Frank Peter (SanD) Navy Region Southwest, San Diego CA 92136 **S Ptr's Epis Ch Del Mar CA 2014-; Adj Prof Cntrl Texas Coll 2007-; Chapl Off Of Bsh For ArmdF New York NY 2004-; Chapl USN San Diego CA 2004-** B CUBA 1958 s Victoria. DMin (in process) Fuller TS; BA Loyola Marymount U 1983; Jesuit TS 1984; MA Mt St Marys Coll Los Angeles CA 1989; CTh ETSBH 1996; MA Natl U 2006; Naval War Coll 2008. D 6/1/1996 P 1/18/1997 Bp Frederick Houk Borsch. m 7/3/1982 Estella Munoz c 2. S Michaels By-The-Sea Ch Carlsbad CA 2013; Chapl & Dir of Rel Stds S Anne's Sch 2003; Sr. Assoc for Chr Ed. S Geo's Epis Ch Laguna Hills CA 2002-2003; R All Ang Ch Miami FL 1999-2002; Asst to the Dn Trin Cathd Miami FL 1997-1998; D S Barn' Epis Ch Los Angeles CA 1996-1997. semperfipadre@yahoo.com

MUNOZ, Maria E (Los) Nuestra Senora de Las Americas, 2610 N. Francisco, Chicago IL 60647 B Los Angeles CA 1957 d Fernando & Maria. BA Pr 1980; California St Los Angeles 1990; MDiv Epis TS of the SW 2005. D 6/11/2005 Bp Chester Lovelle Talton. La Iglesia De Nuestra Senora De Las Americas Chicago IL 2014-2017; Cathd Of S Jas Chicago IL 2012-2015; P-in-c Trin Epis Par Los Angeles CA 2006-2012; Spec Educ Tchr Los Angeles Unified Sch Dist 1985-2002.

MUNOZ-LABRA, Manuel J (PR) B Cienfuegos Cuba 1929 s Victor & Josefa. BTh Seminario Evangelico De Matanza 1958; PhD Universidad De Oriente Cu 1963. D 4/13/1958 P 2/24/1959 Bp Alexander Blankingship. m 6/5/1961 Oneida F Munoz c 2. Dio Puerto Rico Trujillo Alto PR 1980-2000, 1972-1979. "Lit," Juan De Valdes:His Living & Writings, 1958. Ymca Of The Usa, E Field Cluster Awd 1992; Bp Medal Bp Reus Awd 1978.

MUNOZ PENA, P. Munoz (PR) Paseo De La Reina 2703, Ponce PR 00716 Puerto Rico **Dio Puerto Rico Trujillo Alto PR 2006-** B Santo Domingo DR 1960 s Juan & Yolanda. Rec 6/17/1990 Bp David Andres Alvarez-Velazquez. m 8/15/2004 Marion Gelpi Longoria.

MUNOZ QUINTANA, Dimas D (PR) Po Box 8106, Humacao PR 00792 **Dio Puerto Rico Trujillo Alto PR 2005-** B Chicago IL 1954 s Dimas & Carmen. D 10/13/2002 P 10/3/2004 Bp David Andres Alvarez-Velazquez. m 7/10/1981 Vilma Rios Mercado c 4.

MUNRO BSG, Edward Henry (Md) 12310 Firtree Ln, Bowie MD 20715 **D St. Phil's Annapolis 2013-** B New York NY 1943 s Edward & Cecilia. Dio Maryland D Trng Prog; Nthrn Virginia Cmnty Coll 1972; U of Maryland 1977; Cert Sewanee: The U So, TS 1985. D 6/15/1991 Bp Albert Theodore Eastman. m 12/8/1962 Barbara Gail Munro c 4. D St. Chris's Linthicum MD 2006-2013; D S Phil's Ch 2004-2006; Dir Baltimore Intl Seafarer's Cntr Baltimore MD 1993-2004; D Chap of the Redemp Locust Point Baltimore 1992-1996; D The Ch of the H Apos 1991-1992. No Amer Maritime Mnstry Assn. Hon Chapl Missions to Seamen.

MUNRO, Joann Reynolds (Ct) 27 Chateau Margaux, Bloomfield CT 06002 **Died 5/8/2016** B Walla Walla WA 1934 d Harry & Sarah. BS U of Idaho 1956; MA NYU 1975; MDiv Ya Berk 1985. D 6/13/1987 P 2/1/1988 Bp Arthur Edward Walmsley. m 6/22/1996 David L Simpson c 2. Cn for Transitional Mnstry Dio Connecticut Meriden CT 1999-2006; R S Mich's Ch Naugatuck CT 1993-1999; S Paul's Ch Fairfield CT 1987-1993. "It's a Journey: Calling a P to Your Par," The Epis Dio Connecticut. Cn Chr Ch Cathd 2005; Cn Chr Ch Cathd 2000; Cler Ldrshp Proj, Class IX Trin Ch, Wall St, NYC.

MUNRO, Michael (Kan) 804 Cottonwood Dr, Lansing KS 66043 **R S Paul's Ch Leavenworth KS 2000-** B San Mateo CA 1952 s Francis & Theresa. AA Coll of San Mateo 1972; BA WA SU 1974; MDiv CDSP 1983; Cert Cler Ldrshp Proj - Class XXI 2008. D 6/25/1983 P 6/9/1984 Bp William Edwin Swing. m 8/20/1983 Machrina Loris Blasdell c 2. Vic S Mths Epis Ch San Ramon CA 1995-2000; St Johns Epis Ch Ross CA 1992-1995; Int S Anselm's Epis Ch Lafayette CA 1991-1992; P-in-c Emm Epis Ch Delaplane Delaplane VA 1987; Asst Min Ch Of The Gd Shpd Burke VA 1985-1987; Asst Min Chr Epis Ch Los Altos CA 1983-1985; Dn, NE Convoc Dio Kansas Topeka KS 2004-2015, Bp Search Com 2003-2004. Third Ord, Soc of S Fran 1982.

MUNROE, Jim (WMass) 235 State St Apt 413, Springfield MA 01103 B Boston MA 1946 s William & Jeannette. BA Wms 1972; MDiv VTS 1975. D 6/15/1975 P 1/6/1976 Bp Alexander D Stewart. Dn Chr Ch Cathd Springfield MA 1998-2015, 1982-1983; S Jn's Ch Northampton MA 1983-1998; Stff Off Dio Wstrn Massachusetts Springfield 1982-1983; Int S Thos Epis Ch Auburn MA 1982; Asst Gr Epis Ch New York NY 1977-1981; S Andr's Ch Turners Fall MA 1975-1977; S Jas' Ch Greenfield MA 1975-1977.

MUNROE, Sally G (Colo) 1127 Westmoreland Rd, Colorado Springs CO 80907 B Charleston WV 1942 BS SMU. D 6/8/2002 P 12/14/2002 Bp William Jerry Winterrowd. S Andr's Ch Manitou Sprg CO 2010-2013; Ch Of S Mich The Archangel Colorado Spg CO 2002-2009.

MUNSELL, Richard Francis (Colo) B Sheridan WY 1952 s Douglas & Elizabeth. MDiv St Jn's U 1979; MAT Grad Theol Un 1995; Mstr of Strategic Stds w dist Air U/Air War Coll 2006. Rec 1/26/2013 as Priest Bp Robert John O'Neill. m 12/23/2009 Debra Lynn Munsell.

MUNSON, Peter A (Colo) 9972 W 86th Ave, Arvada CO 80005 **R S Ambr Epis Ch Boulder CO 2001-** B London UK 1957 s Holger & Coranelle. BA U CO 1979; JD U CO 1982; MDiv VTS 1991. D 6/15/1991 P 12/1/1991 Bp William Jerry Winterrowd. m 8/1/1987 Julia S Smith c 2. Vic S Martha's Epis Ch Westminster CO 1992-2001; Cur Ch Of S Jn Chrys Golden CO 1991-1992.

MUNZ, Catherine A (WMass) 5 Willow Circle, Easthampton MA 01027 **R S Jn's Ch Northampton MA 2008-** B Detroit MI 1953 d Charles & Jo Ann. Schoolcraft Cmnty Coll; ABS Nthrn Michigan U 1976; MDiv GTS 1993. D 6/19/1993 P 7/2/1994 Bp R aymond Stewart Wood Jr. m 5/26/1978 William D Phelps c 2. R S Brendan's Epis Ch Franklin Pk PA 1998-2008; S Jn's Ch Royal Oak MI 1993-1997; Com on the Status of Wmn Exec Coun Appointees New York NY 2004-2009. Contrib, "Wmn Uncommon Prayers," Morehouse Pub, 2000.

MURANGI, Samuel Bacwa (Pa) 8201 Frankford Ave, Philadelphia PA 19136 **Emm Ch Philadelphia PA 2015-** B Fort-Portal 1966 s Samuel & Mary. Theol Bp Tucker Coll; MSS Bryan Mawr Coll; MDiv Luth Theologial Sem; Theol Bp Tucker Coll 1993; MSS Bryan Mawr Coll 2000. Trans 12/7/2015 Bp Clifton Daniel III. m 12/31/2011 Yvonne Kasiimo Murangi c 2.

MURASAKI-WEKALL, Ellen S (Los) 330 East Cordova St Unit 366, Pasadena CA 91101 **Consult Pasadena CA 1990-; Sprtl Dir Pasadena CA 1990-** B Cologne DE 1930 d Ludwig & Lucy. BS NYU 1956; MS USC 1961; PhD Colorado Chr U 1973; ETSBH 1986. D 11/9/1996 Bp Chester Lovelle Talton P 1/22/2005 Bp Joseph Jon Bruno. m 10/13/1984 Gene Wekall. P for Engl-Spkng Cong Cathd Cntr Of S Paul Cong Los Angeles CA 2010-2012; Assoc Ch Of The Ascen Tujunga CA 2008-2010; Int S Steph's Luth Ch Granada Hills CA 2006-2007; Assoc R S Geo's Par La Can CA 2005-2006, D 1996-2005. "Grp Wk w Adolescents," Journ of Psychol, 1963.

MURAY, Leslie Anthony (Mich) 241 Douglas Ave, Lansing MI 48906 B Budapest HU 1948 s Remus & Marianna. BA Whittier Coll 1971; BA Claremont TS 1973. P 10/1/1975 Bp John Joseph Meakin Harte. All SS Ch Brooklyn MI 1999-2001, 1997-1998; P S Jn's Epis Ch S Johns MI 1990-1996; Non-par 1988-1990; Cbury MI SU E Lansing MI 1986-1989; R S Jn The Bapt Globe AZ 1986-1988; S Geo's Epis Ch Holbrook AZ 1984-1985; S Paul's Epis Ch Winslow AZ 1984-1985; Non-par 1982-1984; R Epiph On The Desert Gila Bend AZ 1980-1981; Epis Cmnty Serv Phoenix AZ 1978-1979; S Lk's At The Mtn Phoenix AZ 1976-1978; Dio Arizona Phoenix AZ 1975-1976.

MURBARGER, Jason Andrew (CFla) Trinity Episcopal Church, 2365 Pine Ave, Vero Beach FL 32960 **S Mary's Epis Ch Daytona Bch FL 2016-; Trin Ch Vero Bch FL 2013-** B Lansing MI 1969 s John & Judy. BSBA Cit 1992; MBA S Mart's U 1997; MDiv Nash 2013. D 5/14/2013 P 12/9/2013 Bp Daniel Hayden Martins. m 7/24/1992 Sharon Marie Murbarger c 2.

MURCHIE, Alan Cameron (Ct) 78 Green Hill Rd, Washington CT 06793 **Calv Ch Stonington CT 2015-** B Torrington CT 1963 s George & Carol. BA Ya 1985; MDiv Ya Berk 2007. D 6/11/2011 Bp Laura Ahrens P 1/14/2015 Bp Ian Theodore Douglas. S Jn's Ch Washington CT 2011-2013; Chr's Ch Rye NY 2000-2002.

MURCHISON, Joel Williams (EC) 259 W 19th St, Chattanooga TN 37408 **Non-par 1973-** B Wilmington NC 1924 s David & May. BS U NC 1948; MDiv VTS 1952. D 6/23/1952 Bp Thomas H Wright P 6/18/1953 Bp Richard Stanley Merrill Emrich. Chapl Epis Mssn Soc 1963-1973; Mssnr Cntrl Amer 1962-1963; R S Columba Ch Detroit MI 1957-1962, Asst 1953-1957; Cur Chr Ch Cranbrook Bloomfield Hills MI 1952-1953. Integrity-E.T. 2001.

MURDOCH, Judith Carolyn (Fla) 4227 Columbia Rd, Martinez GA 30907 B Plainfield NJ 1943 d John & Eleanor. BS Monmouth U 1975; MS Nova SE U 2000. D 1/29/2011 Bp Scott Anson Benhase. m 7/25/1981 Francis J Murdoch c 3.

MURDOCH, Julie B (WVa) 75 Old Cheat Rd., Morgantown WV 26508 B Bethesda MD 1958 BBA W&M 1980; JD W&M 1983; MDiv VTS 2004. D 7/26/2003 P 6/13/2004 Bp John Bryson Chane. m 9/6/1986 Scott Orlo Murdoch c 3. R S Thos a Becket Epis Ch Morgantown WV 2008-2016; Asst to R S Barn' Ch Leeland Uppr Marlboro MD 2004-2008; D H Trin Epis Ch Bowie MD 2003-2004.

MURDOCH, Richard Dorsey (SVa) 214 Archers Mead, Williamsburg VA 23185 **Ret VA 2000-** B Frederick MD 1939 s Richard & Martha. BA U of Maryland 1961; MDiv VTS 1970; MBA Syr 1989; DMin Asbury TS 1991. D 6/27/1970 P 2/1/1971 Bp William Foreman Creighton. m 2/1/1964 Jane Lynn Murdoch c 2. VA 1995-2000; Chapl (LTC) US-A Ft Riley KS 1994-1995; Chapl (LTC) US-A Baumholder and Hanau Germany 1992-1994; Chapl (MAJ) US-A Ft Monmouth NJ 1989-1992; Chapl (MAJ) US-A Ft Campbell KY 1984-1988; Chapl (CPT) US-A Bamberg Germany 1981-1983; Off Of Bsh For ArmdF New York NY 1978-1995; Chapl (CPT) US-A Ft Polk LA 1978-1980; WV 1976-1978; S Jn Wheeling WV 1976-1977; R Gr Ch Elkridge MD 1973-1976; Assoc R S Phil's Epis Ch Laurel MD 1970-1973.

MURDOCH JR, William Henry (Me) Po Box 639, Damariscotta ME 04543 **Ret 1995-** B Philadelphia PA 1931 s William & Hannah. Penn 1956; BA Villanova U 1968; MDiv EDS 1971. D 6/19/1971 P 2/1/1972 Bp Robert Lionne DeWitt. m 9/12/1953 Jane Murdoch c 2. Estrn Upper Peninsula Epis Convoc Moran MI 1999-2001; R S Giles Ch Jefferson ME 1993-1994, Vic/R 1979-1986; Archd Dio Iowa Des Moines IA 1989-1993; Vic Ch Of The Epiph Centerville IA 1986-1989; Gr Ch Albia IA 1986-1989; Vic S Andr's Ch Chariton IA 1986-1988; R S Fran-In-The-Fields Malvern PA 1973-1978; Cur Trin Memi Ch Binghamton NY 1971-1973.

MURDOCK, Audrey Jean (Ct) 831 Stafford Ave, Bristol CT 06010 B Burnley Lancashire UK 1938 d Dennis & Evelyn. BA Southport Coll Southport GB 1952; GTS 2000. D 6/15/2000 P 10/19/2000 Bp Mary Adelia Rosamond Mcleod. c 2. Int P St Marks/St Lukes Castleton Fair Haven 2010-2012; Vic S Jn's Epis Ch Bristol CT 2006-2009; Rectr Trin Ch Jersey Shore PA 2002-2005; Assoc R Trin Ch Rutland VT 2000-2001. Auth, "Hist of Trin Epis Ch," *Rutland VT 1794-1994*, 1994. SSJE 1994.

MURDOCK, Brian J(oseph) P(Aul) (Mass) 38 Highland Park Ave, Roxbury MA 02119 **Died 10/16/2016** B Peabody MA 1954 s Urban & Helen. Gordon-Conwell TS; UTS; BA Boston Coll 1977; MDiv GTS 1985. D 6/4/1986 Bp John Bowen Coburn P 4/1/1987 Bp David Elliot Johnson. Gr Ch Vineyard Haven MA 2014-2016; P In Res Emm Ch W Roxbury MA 2004-2011; Int S Paul's Epis Ch Hopkinton MA 2002-2004; Fndr & Exec Dir Malcolm-Garrison-King Cmnty Hse Roxbury MA 1999-2016; Assoc S Mary's Epis Ch Boston MA 1997-2004; Chapl & Dir Of Recovery Suffolk Cnty Sheriff's Dept 1990-2002; R Ch Of S Jn The Evang Boston MA 1986-1990; S Jn's Ch Charlestown (Boston) Charlestown MA 1986-1990; Vstng Chapl Bunker Hill Cmnty Coll 2016; Charlestown Ecum Coun 2016. Soc Of S Jn The Evang - Assoc.

MURDOCK, Thomas Lee (Cal) 14821 N E Eugene St, Portland OR 97230 **Died 5/17/2017** B San Mateo CA 1934 s James & Lillian. BA Willamette U 1957; NWU 1958; MDiv CDSP 1962; VTS 1982. D 6/11/1962 P 12/1/1962 Bp James Walmsley Frederic Carman. c 4. Asst Gr St Pauls Epis Ch Tucson AZ 1995-2007; Assoc Iglesia Epis Del Buen Samaritano San Francisco CA 1992-2017; Ret 1988-2017; Consult Gd Samar Cntr San Francisco CA 1988-2017; S Jn-By-The-Sea Epis Ch Bandon OR 1988-2017; Assoc S Mk's Par Berkeley CA 1988-2017; Pres Of The Epis Chars 1988-1989; Pres Of The San Mateo Epis Cler 1985-2017; R Trsfg Epis Ch San Mateo CA 1984-1987; 1973-1976; R Emm Ch Coos Bay OR 1970-1984; R S Aid's Epis Ch Portland OR 1966-1970; Stndg Com Dio Oregon Portland OR 1977-1980, Stndg Com 1969-1976; Bd Trst CDSP Berkeley CA 1975-1990. U Fell NWU; Legislativee Res Untd States Senate 85th Congr.

MURGUIA, James Raphael (WTex) 6904 West Ave, San Antonio TX 78213 B San Antonio TX 1968 s Clemente & Priscilla. U So 1988; BA Texas A&M U 1992; MDiv Epis TS of the SW 1998. D 6/3/1998 P 2/5/1999 Bp James Edward Folts. m 6/20/1998 Elisabeth B Murguia c 2. S Geo Ch San Antonio TX 2012-2014; S Dav's Epis Ch San Antonio TX 2004-2011; R S Phil's Ch Uvalde TX 2000-2004; Cur Ch Of The Gd Shpd Corpus Christi TX 1998-2000.

MURIUKI, James (Spr) 493 S Jackson St, Montgomery AL 36104 **Vic Ch Of The Redeem Cairo IL 2014-** B Nyeri Kenya 1962 s Gerald & Eva. Dplma Asumbi Teachers' Trng Coll, Kenya 1982; Dplma of Theol St. Paul's Untd Theol Coll, Kenya 1991; B.Th Birmingham Easonian B. bible Coll 1999; M.Div Beeson DS, Samford U 2002. Trans 10/3/2012 as Priest Bp John Mckee Sloan Sr. m 9/5/1992 Jane W Kamau c 2. Gd Shpd Ch Montgomery AL 2012-2014.

MURPH, Jeffrey David (Pgh) 530 10th St, Oakmont PA 15139 **Chapl UPMC St. Marg Hosp 2005-; R S Thos Memi Epis Ch Oakmont PA 1994-** B Concord NC 1959 s Charles & Doris. BA U NC 1980; MDiv VTS 1986. D 12/14/1986 Bp Robert Whitridge Estill P 12/1/1987 Bp Frank Harris Vest Jr. m 10/11/1986 Meloni J Murph c 3. Assoc S Paul's Epis Ch Winston Salem NC 1986-1994; Stndg Com Dio Pittsburgh Pittsburgh PA 2008-2012, Stndg Com 1997-2008.

MURPHEY, William Frederick (CPa) 2306 Edgewood Rd, Harrisburg PA 17104 **R Bangor Ch Of Churchtown Narvon PA 2008-; Ret 1998-; Co-chair Planned Giving Comm Dio Cntrl Pennsylvania Harrisburg PA 2006-, Chapl to Be Retire Cler & Spouses 2004-** B Scranton PA 1932 s Howard & Frances. BA Leh 1954; STB Ya Berk 1957. D 6/15/1957 P 12/21/1957 Bp Frederick Warnecke. m 5/24/1958 Marian Lois Murphey c 2. Int S Jn's Ch Marietta PA 2000-2002; S Andr's Epis Ch Shippensburg PA 1984-1998; The Epis Hm for the Aged Shippensburg PA 1984-1998; Cn Pstr Cathd Ch Of S Steph Harrisburg PA 1979-1984; R S Paul's Ch Wellsboro PA 1974-1979; R All SS Ch Hanover PA 1965-1974; R S Steph's Ch Whitehall PA 1960-1965; Cur Trin Ch Bethlehem PA 1957-1960. Hon Cn S Steph's Cathd/Harrisburg PA 1991.

MURPHREE, James Willis (Dal) 5426 Meadowcreek Dr Apt 2037, Dallas TX 75248 B Fort Worth TX 1934 s J W & C D. BA Ya 1957; MDiv UTS 1970; Cert PDS 1971. D 2/26/1972 P 12/1/1972 Bp William Henry Mead. S Lk's Epis Ch Dallas TX 1996-2003; Asst Ch Of The Epiph Richardson TX 1984-1989; Asst All SS Epis Ch Dallas TX 1982-1984; P-in-c Ch Of The Epiph Dallas TX 1979-1982; Asst Chr Epis Ch Dallas TX 1977-1979; Chapl Parkland Hosp & Terrell St Hosp 1975-1977; Pres Inst Of Rel And Hlth 1973-1975; Cur S Alb's Ch Wilmington DE 1972-1973. AEHC.

MURPHY, Diane Gensheimer (Va) 9374 Mount Vernon Cir, Alexandria VA 22309 **Assoc Chr Ch Alexandria VA 2006-, P Assoc 2006-; Real Estate Advsr Dayspring 2012-; Trst Virginia Dioc Hm 2011-** B Erie PA 1948 d Herbert & Jeanne. BA Gannon U 1970; MA U of Maryland 1971; PhD U of Maryland 1978; MDiv VTS 2003. D 6/14/2003 P 12/20/2003 Bp Peter J Lee. m 6/6/1980 James Jerome Murphy c 1. S Paul's Epis Ch Alexandria VA 2005, Asst 2003-2005; Chapl Washington Hosp Cntr 2002; Dioc Hm Bd Trst Dio Virginia Richmond VA 2011-2012; Goodwin Hse Pstr Advsry Com 2010-2012.

MURPHY, Edward John (NJ) 10 Rupells Rd, Clinton NJ 08809 **S Ptr's Ch Washington NJ 2012-** B Brooklyn NY 1946 s Edward & Helen. BA CUNY; Drew U; MA FD; EID Rutgers The St U of New Jersey. D 5/22/1999 Bp Joe Doss P 1/15/2000 Bp Herbert Alcorn Donovan Jr. m 8/26/1972 Marguerite Murphy. Pstr Assoc S Mart's Ch Bridgewater NJ 2008-2011; R S Paul's Epis Ch Bound Brook NJ 2002-2008; Calv Epis Ch Flemington NJ 2000-2001; Ch Of The H Sprt Lebanon NJ 1999-2002. APA.

MURPHY JR, Edward John (CNY) 7639 Reed Ter, Lowville NY 13367 **Shared Epis Mnstry E Lowville NY 2006-; Tchr Asst/Tchr Carthage Cntrl Sch 1998-** B Brooklyn NY 1952 s Edward & Marie. Bex Sem; BS Tennessee Tech U 1979; MS SUNY 1988. D 10/7/2006 P 6/16/2007 Bp Gladstone Bailey Adams III. m 7/20/1996 Susan Everard. emurphy1952@gmail.com

MURPHY, Genevieve Margaret (Va) 501 Simmons Gap Road, Box 172, Earlysville VA 22936 **Died 4/21/2016** B York Yorkshire UK 1934 d Louis & Elsie. BA Mary Baldwin Coll 1982; MEd U of Virginia 1985; EdD U of Virginia 1990; MA VTS 1998. D 12/10/1998 P 6/10/1999 Bp Peter J Lee. c 2. R Buck Mtn Epis Ch Earlysville VA 1998-2006. office@mcilhany.org

MURPHY, Gwyneth MacKenzie (NY) St Mary the Virgin Episcopal Church, 191 South Greeley Ave, Chappaqua NY 10514 **S Jn's Ch New York NY 2016-; Sprtl Dir Dioceses of Utah Caifornia New York 1995-; Retreat Ldr Dioceses of Utah California New York 1995-; Sacr Dance Tchr, Choreographer, Performer Dioceses of Utah California New York 1993-** B Mount Vernon NY 1955 d Frank & Bronwen. BA Barnard Coll of Col 1976; JD Ford

1981; MDiv Harvard DS 1991; Cert Sursum Corda Sprtl Dir Trng 2006. D 12/18/1994 P 6/1/1995 Bp George Edmonds Bates. Ch Of The Gd Shpd Granite Spgs NY 2015-2016; P Ch Of S Mary The Vrgn Chappaqua NY 2014-2015; Int S Greg's Epis Ch Woodstock NY 2013-2014; S Andr's Epis Ch New Paltz NY 2011-2012, Vic 2008-; Muslim-Chr Relatns Com Dio New York New York NY 2007-2012, SUNY New Paltz Chapl 2007-2012, Epis Muslim Relatns Com 2013-, Prog Plnng Com 2007-; Chapl CNS Hospice Salt Lake City UT 2004-2006; Retreat Ldr, Int Dio Utah Salt Lake City UT 2004, Stndg Com 1996-1998, COM 2003-2006; Assoc Pstr Cathd Ch Of S Mk Salt Lake City UT 2002-2003; Assoc R S Jn's Epis Ch Oakland CA 2000-2001; Pstr Assoc Gr Cathd San Francisco CA 1998-2000; R S Mich's Ch Brigham City UT 1996-1998; Hosp Chapl Epis Cmnty Serv Inc Salt Lake City UT 1995-1996, 1995; Adj Fac, Theol Westminster Coll and Weber St U Utah 1994-1998; Inerim Assoc Zion Luth Ch Salt Lake City 1994-1995; Strng Com Utah Conf On Wmn In Rel 1993-1997; Assoc All SS Ch Salt Lake City UT 1993-1996. Auth, "Var," *GraceCom Website*, Gr Cathd, San Francisco; Auth, "Var," *Utah Dioc Dialogue*, Dio Utah. Sacr Dance Gld 1995; Utah Pstr Care Assoc 1994-1998. Wmn of the Year YWCA Salt Lake City 2003.

MURPHY JR, Hartshorn (Los) 1630 Greenfield Ave. Apt 105, Los Angeles, Los Angeles CA 90025 B Baltimore MD 1948 s Hartshorn & Mildred. BA U of Maryland 1970; MDiv VTS 1973. D 5/24/1973 P 2/1/1974 Bp David Keller Leighton Sr. m 5/27/1973 Marla C Murphy c 1. R S Aug By-The-Sea Par Santa Monica CA 1997-2009; Archd For Congrl Dvlpmt Dio Los Angeles Los Angeles CA 1988-1997; R S Phil's Par Los Angeles CA 1980-1988; R S Geo Milwaukee WI 1975-1980; St Georges Ch Milwaukee WI 1975-1980; Cur Ch Of The H Nativ Baltimore MD 1973-1975.

MURPHY, James T (SwFla) 1605 Banchory Cir, Walhalla SC 29691 **R Chr Angl Cashiers NC 2009-** B Cleveland OH 1952 s James & Pauline. Cert OH SU 1973; BS U of So Florida 1989; MDiv Sewanee: The U So, TS 1993. D 6/26/1993 P 1/6/1994 Bp Rogers Sanders Harris. m 8/20/1988 Sharon L Murphy c 1. R Emm Angl New Bern NC 2005-2009; Mssy P The Angl Ch of Rwanda Kigali Rwanda 2004-2012; R Chr Angl Manasota FL 2004-2005; R Ch of the Nativ Sarasota FL 1995-2004; Asst R S Dav's Epis Ch Englewood FL 1993-1995; Yth Dir Ch Of The H Sprt Osprey FL 1986-1990. AFP 1990; Bro Of S Andr 1993; ERM 1987; Fllshp Wit 1992-1997; Intl Ord Of S Lk 1988.

MURPHY, Jo-Ann Rapp (Va) 3605 S Douglas Rd, Miami FL 33133 **Asst S Steph's Ch Coconut Grove Miami FL 2009-** B Queens NY 1941 d John & Hulda. BA Mar 1963; Cert 1985; MDiv VTS 1987; Cert Shalem Inst 1993; DMin Drew U 1998. D 6/13/1987 Bp Peter J Lee P 5/14/1988 Bp David Henry Lewis Jr. c 2. Chapl Hospice of Virginia Richmond VA 2006-2009; Dir. Chr. Formation Ware Epis Ch Gloucester VA 2005-2008; Ch Of The H Comf Richmond VA 2002-2006; Ch Of The Gd Shpd Burke VA 1998-2002; R S Paul's Epis Ch Morris Plains NJ 1997-1998; Ch Of The Trsfg Towaco NJ 1989-1997; Asst to R Ch Of The Resurr Alexandria VA 1987-1989. Writer, "Conv Daily," 1979; Writer/Ed, "Voice Dio Newark"; Ed, "Rauch". Ord of S Helena 1989.

MURPHY, Linda Estelle (Va) 15 Hamilton St, Colonial Beach VA 22443 **D S Ptr's Ch Oak Grove Oak Grove VA 2013-** B Woburn MA 1947 d Howard & Martha. Dip Theol Stud VTS 2005. D 2/5/2011 Bp Shannon Sherwood Johnston. m 6/14/1997 Cyrus Murphy c 6. Pstr Assoc Imm Ch-On-The-Hill Alexandria VA 2010-2012. lem1624@aol.com

MURPHY, Michael John (Tenn) 219 Jennings Cir, Tullahoma TN 37388 **R S Barn Ch Tullahoma TN 2007-** B Waukesha WI 1975 s William & Dorothy. BA MI SU 1999; MDiv Nash 2002. D 12/6/2001 P 9/1/2002 Bp Keith Lynn Ackerman. m 8/2/1997 Erica E Murphy c 1. Asst S Ptr's Ch Columbia TN 2002-2007.

MURPHY, Michael Robert (SVa) 2315 Mary Goodwyn Rd., Powhatan VA 23139 **Emm Epis Ch Powhatan VA 2005-** B Portsmouth OH 1944 s Robert & Margaret. OH SU 1964; MDiv Epis TS in Kentucky 1978; BS U of Kentucky 1978. D 5/14/1978 P 12/1/1978 Bp Addison Hosea. m 11/28/1964 Sally Murphy. Police Off Chr Ch Amelia Ct Hs VA 1996-2004; S Matt's Epis Ch Chesterfield VA 1996-1997; Archd Dio Sthrn Virginia Newport News VA 1990-1996; R S Dav's Epis Ch No Chesterfield VA 1980-1989; R S Paul's Ch Newport KY 1978-1980; Dio Lexington Lexington 1976-1980.

MURPHY, Patricia Ann (Kan) 7515 W 102nd St, Overland Park KS 66212 B Tampa FL 1943 d Morris & Virginia. AA Richland Coll; Kansas Sch of Mnstry 2002; Other 2002. D 3/1/2003 Bp William Edward Smalley. c 2. Chair HELP 317 Kansas City KS 2004-2011; D S Paul's Ch Kansas City KS 2003-2010.

MURPHY JR, P L (Dal) **Int S Chris's Ch Dallas TX 2007-** D 6/15/1978 P 12/18/1978 Bp Scott Field Bailey.

MURPHY, Richard William (RG) 4717 Sundial Way, Santa Fe NM 87507 **Chapl St Senate New Mex 2013-** B New Haven CT 1945 s Richard & Margaret. AA GTS 1968; BA S Johns Sem 1970; MDiv GTS 1988; DMin GTF 2003. D 6/3/1989 P 6/23/1990 Bp David Elliot Johnson. m 4/6/1974 Carol Fransen c 1. Bd Dir Pstr Counslg Cntr Santa Fe NM 2010-2014; R S Bede's Epis Ch Santa Fe NM 1997-2011; Field Educ Supvsr EDS Cambridge MA 1993-1997; R The Par Of S Chrys's Quincy MA 1991-1997; Cur S Ptr's Ch Osterville MA 1989-1991. Fllshp of SSJE 1985; SBL 1988. The Sultan and the S

Peace Awd Unity Productions Fndt 2017; Ruby Awd Mt Vernon Soroptimists 2013; Living the Dream Awd Theater Residency Proj 2003.

MURPHY, Robert A (WMo) 4225 Sw Clipper Ln, Lees Summit MO 64082 B Kansas City MO 1937 s Al & Dorothy. BA Cntrl Methodist U 1960. D 3/27/1993 Bp John Clark Buchanan. m 8/11/1962 B Kathleen Murphy c 3. D St Ptr & All SS Epis Ch Kansas City MO 1993-2006.

MURPHY JR, Russell Edward (Wyo) 11506 Wornall Rd, Kansas City MO 64114 **Vol Chapl St Lk's Hosp So Overland Pk KS 2013-** B Saint Louis MO 1945 s Russell & Marion. BA Washington U 1967; MA U of Missouri 1972; MDiv S Paul TS 1980; Nash 1982. D 8/6/1982 P 2/9/1983 Bp Arthur Anton Vogel. c 1. R S Lk's Epis Ch Buffalo WY 2007-2010; Mssnr S Steph's Epis Ch De Tour Vill MI 2002; R / Mssnr S Jas Ch Of Sault S Marie Sault Sainte Marie MI 2001-2007; Vic Dio Utah Salt Lake City UT 1999-2001; Vic S Mich's Ch Brigham City UT 1998-2000; Calv Epis Ch Osceola AR 1998-1999; Vic Dio Arkansas Little Rock AR 1998-1999; S Steph's Ch Blytheville AR 1998-1999; R S Paul's Ch Fayetteville AR 1993-1997; R S Jn's Epis Ch Mankato MN 1984-1993; Cur Chr Epis Ch S Jos MO 1982-1984; Chapl-Ni-Res S Lk's Hosp Kansas City MO 1980-1981; Chapl Intern Trininty Luth Hosp Kansas City MO 1979-1980. Mn Coun Ch, Alb Inst 1986-1993; WY Cltn of Chruches 2007.

MURPHY, Susan Marie (Me) 37 Chancery Lane, Sanford ME 04073 **R S Geo's Epis Ch Sanford ME 2008-** B Pittsfield MA 1946 d Francis & Sophie. BA Elms Coll 1971; Westfield St Coll 1976; Westfield St Coll 1981; MDiv EDS 1999. D 5/22/1999 P 12/4/1999 Bp Chilton Richardson Knudsen. m 8/29/2015 Teresa Louise Marriott. Chapl Maine Correctional Cntr Windham ME 2006-2008; D Aroostook Epis Cluster Caribou ME 2001-2006, P 1999-2006.

MURPHY, T Abigail (LI) 15 Stewart Ave, Stewart Manor NY 11530 **P-in-c S Elis's Epis Ch Floral Pk NY 2000-; S Thos' Epis Ch Floral Pk NY 2000-** B Indianapolis IN 1959 d Leroy & Ruth. Taylor U 1979; MA Bos 1981; MDiv SWTS 1995. D 6/23/1995 P 3/25/1996 Bp Orris George Walker Jr. m 6/3/1995 Roy Murphy. Cur Cathd Of The Incarn Garden City NY 1995-1999. Associated Parishes 1995-1998; EWC 1995.

MURPHY, Terri Marie (WA) 15575 Germantown Rd, Germantown MD 20874 **Ch Of The Ascen Silver Sprg MD 2012-; Indstrl Revs Bd Shady Grove Adventist Hosp Rockville MD 2010-** B Winthrop MA 1951 d Lawrence & Edna. AA Northshore Cmnty Coll 1971; BA U of Massachusetts 1974; MEd Suffolk U 1975; Cert Shaelm Inst for Sprtl Formation 2007; Cert Shalem Inst for Sprtl Formation 2007; MTS Wesley TS 2012. D 9/22/2012 Bp Mariann Edgar Budde. c 3. DRE S Nich Epis Ch Germantown MD 2012-2014; Profsnl Advsry Grp Shady Grove Adventist Hosp Rockville MD 2009-2011; Chapl Vol Montgomery Cnty Correctional Facility 2005-2008. Assn of Epis Deacons 2012.

MURPHY, Thomas Christopher (WA) 3700 Massachusetts Avenue, NW, Apartment 531, Washington DC 20016 B Stamford CT 1948 s Thomas & Patricia. BA Sacr Heart U 1972; MTS VTS 2007. D 6/9/2007 P 1/19/2008 Bp John Bryson Chane. m 12/10/1977 Mary Jane Rieser c 1. Assitant To The R Chr Ch Georgetown Washington DC 2007-2014; Dir Of Ch Relatns Bread For The Wrld 1997-2005.

MURPHY, Thomas Edward (Spok) 215 Tolman Creek Rd Unit 34, Ashland OR 97520 **Supply P Dio Oregon Portland OR 2005-; Ret Ret 2001-** B Natick MA 1935 s Edward & Gladys. BA U of Redlands 1957; MDiv Berkeley Bapt DS 1961; CAS EDS 1966. D 6/29/1966 P 2/24/1967 Bp Ivol I Curtis. m 11/24/1979 Huberta Imilda Murphy c 3. P-in-c S Mk's Ch Yreka CA 2009-2010; Asst S Mk's Epis Par Medford OR 2006-2009; P-in-c S Paul's Mssn Cres City CA 2006-2007; Int S Dav's Ch Spokane WA 2003-2004; P-in-c S Jn's Epis Ch Colville WA 2001-2003; Vic S Paul's Ch Cheney WA 1994-2001; R S Andr's Ch Spokane WA 1989-2001; R S Lk's Ch Ft Madison IA 1986-1988; Dio Olympia Seattle 1986; Dioc Stwdshp Com Dio Olympia 1980-1990; R H Trin Ch Seattle WA 1979-1986; Vic S Christophers Epis Ch Westport WA 1979-1983; Assoc S Eliz's Ch Seattle WA 1973-1978; Vic S Marg Seattle WA 1973-1978; Chapl Chas Wright Acad Tacoma WA 1973-1974; Vic S Dav Emm Epis Ch Shoreline WA 1967-1973; Assoc Min Epiph Par of Seattle Seattle WA 1966-1967. CHS 1992.

MURPHY, Thomas Lynch (WNC) 9 Swan St, Asheville NC 28803 **P The Cathd Of All Souls Asheville NC 2010-** B Oklahoma City OK 1977 s Thomas & Nancy. BA U NC 2000; MTS Harvard DS 2005; Cert Ang Stud VTS 2008. D 5/23/2010 P 12/11/2010 Bp Porter Taylor. m 5/29/2004 Amanda Murphy c 2.

MURPHY, Thomas M (Nwk) 38 Duncan Avenue, Jersey City NJ 07304 **R S Paul's Ch In Bergen Jersey City NJ 2013-** B Jersey City NJ 1967 s Thomas & Catherine. BA New Jersey City U 1989; MA St Peters Coll Jersey City NJ 1991; MDiv GTS 2007. D 6/2/2007 P 12/22/2007 Bp Mark M Beckwith. m 7/12/1997 Susan R Suarez. Assoc Gr Ch Madison NJ 2011-2013, 2007-2010, Cur 2007-2010; Chapl Ch Of The Incarn Gainesville FL 2010-2011; R S Mich's Ch Gainesville FL 2010-2011; Cathd Chapt Trin And S Phil's Cathd Newark NJ 2009-2010.

MURPHY, Timothy Hunter (Ala) 801 The Trce W, Jasper AL 35504 B Decatur AL 1949 s Charles & Anne. BS U of Alabama 1972; MDiv VTS 1978. D 6/14/1978 P 12/15/1978 Bp Furman Charles Stough. m 12/20/2009 Kate Dolye Davis Murphy c 4. R S Mary's Epis Ch Jasper AL 2008-2017; Vic Ch Of The

H Nativ St Simons Is GA 2006-2008; R Trin Epis Ch Florence AL 1995-2006; R Trin Epis Ch The Woodlands TX 1993-1995; R S Lk's Ch Scottsboro AL 1984-1993; R Ch Of The H Comf Sumter SC 1983-1984; R S Ptr's Epis Ch Talladega AL 1980-1983; R Trin Epis Ch Alpine AL 1980-1983; Cur S Jn's Ch Decatur AL 1978-1980.

MURPHY, Warren Charles (Wyo) 50 Diamond View Rd, Cody WY 82414 **Prog Dir Thos the Apos Retreat Cntr 2010-; Environ Projects Dir Wyoming Assn of Ch 2010-** B Philadelphia PA 1944 s Warren & Frances. BA Bridgewater Coll 1967; MDiv EDS 1972. D 6/24/1972 P 1/15/1973 Bp Harold Barrett Robinson. m 6/25/1977 Katharine Linde c 2. Dir Wyoming Assn of Ch 2004-2009; R Chr Ch Cody WY 1989-2004; Vstng P Shoshone Epis Mssn Ft Washakie WY 1986-1989; S Andr's Mssn Atlantic City WY 1982-1989; P in Charge Trin Ch Lander WY 1982-1989; R S Paul's Epis Ch Dixon WY 1977-1982; Asst Trin Trin Epis Ch Buffalo NY 1973-1977; Chair , COM Dio Wyoming Casper 2003-2010, Stndg Com 1992-2003, Dioc Coun 1989-1992, GC Dep 1988-2011, Chair Ch Cltn 1984-1992. Auth, "On Sacr Ground: A Rel and Sprtl Hist of Wyoming," *Bk*, Wordsworth Pub, 2011.

MURPHY, William McKee (WMich) N 2794 Summerville Park Road, Lodi WI 53555 B Champaign IL 1946 s William & Eunice. BA U of Wisconsin 1969; MDiv Nash 1973. D 4/28/1973 Bp Donald H V Hallock P 10/27/1973 Bp Charles Thomas Gaskell. m 8/26/1989 Mary Elizabeth Neall c 3. Mayor City of Sturgis Sturgis MI 2000-2002; R St Jn's Epis Ch of Sturgis Sturgis MI 1989-2003; R Geth Epis Ch Marion IN 1976-1989; P-in-c S Alb's Ch Sussex WI 1974-1976; P-in-c S Barth's Ch Pewaukee WI 1973-1976; Caseworker Vocational Rehab Counslr Madison WI 1969-1970.

MURRAY, Austin B (Haw) 2853 Panepoo St, Kihei HI 96753 B Monaghan IE 1950 s Eamonn & Rose. U Coll Dublin 1973; ThM S Patricks Coll/Sem 1974; GTS 1989; MTh New Brunswick TS 1995. Rec 9/12/1987 as Priest Bp Vincent King Pettit. c 5. P-in-c Trin Ch By The Sea Kihei HI 2008-2016; R S Steph's Ch Waretown NJ 1989-2008; Ch Sch Dir S Jas Ch Long Branch NJ 1987-1988; Asst St. Jas Long Branch NJ 1984-1988; Asst St Barn RC Bayville NJ 1976-1980; Ed/Dir 'The Monitor' Dioc Nwspr Trenton NJ 1976-1980; Asst Immac Concep RC Somerville NJ 1974-1976.

MURRAY IV, Bill S (WTenn) 8011 Douglas Avenue, Dallas TX 75225 **S Mich And All Ang Ch Dallas TX 2014-** B Memphis TN 1973 s William & Lela. BA U of Memphis 1997; MDiv VTS 2006. D 6/10/2006 P 2/15/2007 Bp Don Edward Johnson. m 3/1/2003 Jessica M Murray c 2. R S Elis's Epis Ch Memphis TN 2007-2014; Cur S Geo's Ch Germantown TN 2006-2007; Yth Dir Gr - S Lk's Ch Memphis TN 1998-2003; Stndg Com, Pres Dio W Tennessee Memphis 2010-2012, St. Columba Bd, Chair 2009-2013, Ch Hm Bd, Chair 2006-2009, Happ Strng Com, Chair 1999-2003. bmurray@saintmichael.org

MURRAY, Cicely Anne (Pa) 600 E Cathedral Rd Apt D104, Philadelphia PA 19128 B Harpenden Herts UK 1927 d Percy & Constance. MS Middlesex Hosp London GB 1949; Pennsylvania Diac Sch 1996. D 11/2/1996 Bp Allen Lyman Bartlett Jr. D S Mary's Ch Wayne PA 1998-2005; D S Matt's Ch Maple Glen PA 1996-1998. NAAD 1995; Soc of Comp of H Cross 1982.

MURRAY, Diane Marie (FdL) W5766 Winooski Rd, Plymouth WI 53073 **R S Jas Ch Manitowoc WI 2009-; Dir, Sum Camp Dio Fond du Lac Appleton WI 2006-** B Pocatello ID 1957 d Leo & Betty. U of Wisconsin 1982; Milwaukee Area Tech Coll 1996; BA Marian Coll of Fond Du Lac 2001; Lakeland Coll 2002. D 8/23/1998 P 5/23/2009 Bp Russell Edward Jacobus. c 3. Yth Mnstry Coordntr Dio Fond du Lac Appleton WI 2006-2012, Coordntr, Yth Mnstry 2006-; D S Paul's Ch Plymouth WI 2000-2007; D S Ptr's Epis Ch Sheboygan Falls WI 1998-2000. Bp's Cross Dio Fond du Lac 2003.

MURRAY, Elizabeth Ann (CFla) 144 Sea Park Blvd, Satellite Beach FL 32937 B East Chicago IN 1951 d John & Shirley. U of Wisconsin 1972; BA U of Nthrn Colorado 1974. D 12/8/2001 Bp John Wadsworth Howe. m 6/21/1980 Douglas Alan Ludwig. Yth Dir S Jn's Ch Melbourne FL 2008-2015.

MURRAY JR, George Ralph (Eas) 4453 Eastwicke Dr, Salisbury MD 21804 **Asstg D S Ptr's Ch Salisbury MD 2015-; Chapl Deers Hd Hosp Cntr 2003-; Character Dvlpmt Instr CAP 2002-** B Washington DC 1936 s George & Dorothy. Dio Easton Sch for Total Mnstry; Other; AA Montgomery Coll 1959; BS Amer U 1963; MA Geo 1981. D 4/6/2002 Bp Charles Lindsay Longest. m 8/19/1955 Mary Barbara Murray c 2. Pstr Assoc All Hallow's Ch Snow Hill MD 2009-2013; D Pstr S Mary's Epis Ch Tyaskin MD 2006-2009, Asstg D 2002-2006; Supply Dio Easton Easton MD 2005-2006; D Pstr S Paul's Epis Ch Hebron MD 2004-2005.

MURRAY III, John William (CGC) 1326 Live Oak Ln, Jacksonville FL 32207 B Charleston SC 1940 s John & Mary. BS Emory U 1961; BS Coll of Charleston 1964; MDiv VTS 1967. D 6/22/1967 P 6/1/1968 Bp Gray Temple. m 8/27/1966 Sara Ann Lofton Murray c 2. R H Trin Epis Ch Pensacola FL 1983-2002; Assoc S Barth's Epis Ch Atlanta GA 1975-1983; Cur S Jn's Atlanta GA 1971-1975; R Chr Ch Denmark SC 1967-1971; Vic S Alb's Ch Blackville SC 1967-1971. OHC.

MURRAY, Kat (Okla) 1255 Canterbury Blvd, Altus OK 73521 B Huntington WV 1963 d Hershell & Imogene. BA Marshall U 1985; MDiv VTS 1991; MBA U of Phoenix 2000; DO OSU-COM 2008; SW OK Fam Med Residency 2011.

D 6/11/1991 P 6/13/1992 Bp John Henry Smith. P-in-c S Paul's Ch Altus OK 2009-2014; Fam Med Res SW Oklahoma Fam Med Residency Lawton OK 2008-2011; S Basil's Epis Ch Tahlequah OK 2004-2006, R 2000-2003; Asst Trin Ch Tulsa OK 1998-2000; Int Cathd Of S Lk And S Paul Charleston SC 1997-1998; Int S Jn's Epis Par Johns Island SC 1996-1997; Chapl Off Of Bsh For ArmdF New York NY 1994-1996; Chapl USN 1994-1996; Vic Nelson Cluster Of Epis Ch Rippon WV 1991-1994.

MURRAY, Kathleen (NJ) **P-in-c S Mk's Epis Ch Keansburg NJ 2013-** B Phillipsburg NJ 1960 d Joseph & Joann. BS Rosemont Coll 1983; MPA Col 2004; MDiv GTS 2013; MDiv The GTS 2013. D 11/2/2012 P 10/3/2013 Bp George Edward Councell. m 5/30/2013 Martha Mae Dooley. kmurray@gts.edu

MURRAY, Laura Jane (Oly) 7701 Skansie Ave, Gig Harbor WA 98335 **S Jn's Epis Ch Gig Harbor WA 2014-** B Bethel AK 1962 d J Lloyd & Geneva. AA Rogers St Coll 1988; BA U of Washington 2010; MDiv Epis TS Of The SW 2014; MDiv Epis TS of the SW 2014. D 12/21/2013 P 7/22/2014 Bp Gregory Harold Rickel. m 4/3/2001 Michael C Murray.

MURRAY, Lewellyn St Elmo (LI) 590 Flatbush Ave Apt 9M, Apt. 9-M, Brooklyn NY 11225 B Colon PA 1926 s F Robert & Ida. Merc TS. D 6/17/1978 P 1/1/1981 Bp Robert Campbell Witcher Sr. m 11/24/1955 Dorothy Hinds. P-in-c S Lydia's Epis Ch Brooklyn NY 1981-2013; Non-par 1978-1981. E Bklyn Ch, OHC. Bd Cert Chapl Assn of Profsnl Chapl 2011; Cn of the Dio Long Island The Cathd of Garden City 2011. lydiaans@verizon.net

MURRAY, Lois Thompson (SeFla) 1521 Alton Rd # 219, Miami Beach FL 33139 B PA 1942 d Jack & Lois. MDiv PrTS; BA Swarthmore Coll 1965. D 7/23/2004 Bp Leo Frade P 2/18/2005 Bp James Hamilton Ottley. c 2.

MURRAY, Mac (WMass) 23 Dana Park, Hopedale MA 01747 **R Trin Epis Ch Milford MA 2006-** B Buffalo NY 1952 s Gerard & Eleanor. BS New Mex St U 1976; PMD Harv 1986; MDiv VTS 2002. D 6/15/2002 P 12/18/2002 Bp Peter J Lee. m 6/12/1976 Merline Roush c 2. Asst R Gr Ch The Plains VA 2002-2006. fr.mac@trinitychurchmilford.org

MURRAY, Michael Hunt (Va) 700 Port St Apt 226, Easton MD 21601 **Ret 1988-** B Cambridge UK 1922 s Cecil & Veronica. BA Harv 1948; MA JHU 1950; BTh ETSBH 1965; CAS W&M 1982. D 6/24/1965 P 12/1/1965 Bp Robert McConnell Hatch. m 11/16/1955 Eliane C Cadilhac c 1. Dir Quest Cntr for Personal & Sprtl Growth 1983-1988; R Ware Epis Ch Gloucester VA 1975-1983; R S Mich & All Ang Cuernavaca Mex 1969-1975; Cmncatn Off of the Dept of Prom ECEC 1966-1969; Cur All SS Ch Worcester MA 1965-1966. Auth, "Chance or Providence," Easterly Press, MD, 2001; Auth, "The Thought of Teilhard de Chardin," Seabury Press, NY, 1966; Auth, "In Sight of Eden," Jonathan Cape, London, 1961. Amer Assn Counslg & Devolpment, VA Mntl Hlth 1979; Amer Teilhard de Chardin Assoc. 1964.

MURRAY, Milton Hood (Fla) 3750 Peachtree Rd NE # 422, Atlanta GA 30319 **Ret 1991-** B Athens GA 1929 s William & Tulley. BS U GA 1950; Cert CPE 1956; MDiv VTS 1958. D 6/21/1958 Bp Robert E Gribbin P 12/22/1958 Bp Randolph R Claiborne. c 1. Assoc Chr Epis Ch Ponte Vedra FL 1999-2004, Assoc R 1984-1991; Stndg Com Dio Atlanta Atlanta GA 1976-1979, Chair Dept Par Serv 1971-1975, Dep GC 1970, Chair Bd Gvnrs 1964-1969; R S Bede's Ch Atlanta GA 1970-1984; Chair Camp Mikell Bd. of Govs. Atlanta GA 1964-1970; R S Steph's Ch Milledgeville GA 1964-1970; Vic Gr-Calv Epis Ch Clarkesville GA 1958-1964.

MURRAY, Noland Patrick (Ark) 14300 Chenal Pkwy Apt 1316, Little Rock AR 72211 B Springfield MO 1934 s Woody & Clara. BA Baylor U 1955; BD Sthrn Bapt TS 1958; PhD Duke 1963. D 5/7/1977 P 3/15/1978 Bp Christoph Keller Jr. c 3. S Mk's Epis Ch Jonesboro AR 1983-1999; R All SS Epis Ch Russellville AR 1978-1982; Cur S Paul's Ch Fayetteville AR 1976-1978; Dep, GC Dio Arkansas Little Rock AR 1976-1982. Auth, "Living Beyond Your Losses," Morehouse Pub, 1997; Auth, "Creationism and Evolution: The Real Issues," 1981.

MURRAY, Robert Scott (SJ) 1104 Kitanosho-Cho, Ohmihachiman, Shiga 523-0806 Japan B Visalia CA 1957 s Robert & Norma. Nash; S Jn Coll Sante Fe NM; BS California St U 1980; MDiv CDSP 1986. D 7/25/1987 P 5/1/1988 Bp Victor Manuel Rivera. m 7/10/1988 Hiroko Murray. St Stephans Ch Kyoto 1993-1994; S Thos Of Cbury Mammoth Lakes CA 1990-1992; Asst P Ch Of The H Fam Chap Hill NC 1988-1989; Mssnr-In-Charge Ch Of The Epiph Corcoran CA 1987-1988.

MURRAY, Robin George Ellis (SwFla) 27439 Edenfield Dr, Wesley Chapel FL 33543 **Assoc S Mary's Ch Dade City FL 2013-** B Glenelg AU 1935 s George & Lillian. BA MI SU 1959; MBA MI SU 1963; MDiv VTS 1968; Amer Inst of Fam Relatns 1975; Bethel Bible Inst Madison WI 1976; DMin Andover Newton TS 1982. D 6/29/1968 Bp Archie H Crowley P 1/11/1969 Bp Richard Stanley Merrill Emrich. m 9/8/1962 Dorothy R Murray. Assoc S Mary's Par Tampa FL 2008-2011; Sr Chapl Hernando Cnty Sheriff's Dept 1996-2004; Ret S Andr's Epis Ch Sprg Hill FL. 1986-2004; R S Andr's Epis Ch Sprg Hill FL 1986-2004; R S Paul's Ch Lynnfield MA 1978-1986; Off Of Bsh For ArmdF New York NY 1973-1978; Assoc The Falls Ch Epis Falls Ch VA 1970-1972; Asst Chr Ch Dearborn MI 1968-1969; Dn of Hernando/Pasco Dio SW Florida Parrish FL 2000-2002, Dn of Clearwater 1996-2000; Sr Chapl Hernando Cnty

Sheriff's Dept 1996-2004; Trst HCA Oak Hill Hosp 1996-2002. Auth, "Symptomatology & Mgmt Of Acute Grief As Experienced By Death & Dying," *Doctoral Thesis*, 1982. Acad Of Par Cler; ACPE. Schlrshp Rec Soc for the Increase of the Mnstry 2010; Colonel, U S Army Chapl Dept of Defense 1995; Outstanding Young Men Of Amer 1971.

MURRAY III, Roderic Lafayette (Ala) 634 Timber Ln, Nashville TN 37215 **Consult/Instr St.Thos/Nashville CPE Partnership 2010-; Adj Prof Belmont U Sch of Rel Nashville TN 2004-; Ch Pension Fund Benefici 2002-** B Beattyville KY 1940 s Roderic & Mattie. U of Kentucky 1960; BA Wstrn Kentucky U 1962; MDiv Van 1969; Sewanee: The U So, TS 1971; Van 1971; DDiv Van 1972. D 5/24/1969 Bp William R Moody P 11/30/1969 Bp John Vander Horst. m 6/4/1966 Jennie B Murray c 2. Assoc Chr Ch Cathd Nashville TN 2007-2012, Cur 1999-2006; Chapl Untd States Dept of Veteran Affrs Nashville TN 2001-2003; R Ch Of The Nativ Epis Huntsville AL 1988-2001; Dn S Andr's Cathd Jackson MS 1980-1988; Chapl S Andr Sch Jackson MS 1980-1985; R S Paul's Ch Augusta GA 1975-1980; R S Andr's Ch Maryville TN 1971-1975. Auth, "arts Var mag". Fllshp Un Theiologal Sem 1986; Fllshp Emory 1984; S.T.D. (Doctor of Sacr Theol) Epis TS 1983; Fllshp VTS 1983; Outstanding Citizen Awd Human Relatns Cmsn 1980.

MURRAY III, Thomas Holt (WTex) 1120 Lake Dr, Kerrville TX 78028 **S Peters Epis Sch Kerrville TX 2005-; Assoc S Ptr's Epis Ch Kerrville TX 2005-** B Oklahoma OK 1965 s Thomas & Julia. BS Texas A&M U 1987; MA U of Mary Hardin-Baylor 1989; MA VTS 1996. D 12/5/1998 Bp Leopoldo Jesus Alard P 12/13/1999 Bp Claude Edward Payne. m 7/6/2004 Julie Ann Murray c 1. Dio Texas Houston TX 2005; R S Mich And All Ang' Epis Ch Longview TX 2004-2005; Asst Trin Ch Marshall TX 2003-2004; All SS Epis Sch Tyler TX 2000-2002; Chapl All SS Epis Sch Tyler TX 2000-2002; Assoc P Chr Epis Ch Tyler TX 2000-2002; P S Cuth's Epis Ch Houston TX 1998-2000.

MURRAY, Thomas P (Fla) 4129 Oxford Ave, Jacksonville FL 32210 **R S Mk's Epis Ch Jacksonville FL 2015-** B Madison WI 1968 s Richard & Martha. BA No Carolina St U 1992; MDiv Sewanee: The U So, TS 1999. D 5/29/1999 P 12/4/1999 Bp Edward Lloyd Salmon Jr. m 11/12/2009 Perrin Steele c 4. Assoc R S Paul's Epis Ch Winston Salem NC 2006-2015; R S Dav's Ch Cheraw SC 2003-2006; Assoc For Fam Mnstry Par Ch of St. Helena Beaufort SC 1999-2003. tmurray@stmarksjacksonville.org

MURRAY, Trilby Ometa (Chi) 3801 S Wabash Ave, Chicago IL 60653 B Barbados West Indies 1948 d Milton & Beryl. D 6/28/2014 Bp John Clark Buchanan.

MURRAY, Vincent Devitt (Oly) 306 Lopez Ave, Port Angeles WA 98362 **Ret 2000-** B Jersey City NJ 1935 s William & Jeannette. BA Loyola U 1959; PHL Loyola U 1960; MA Ford 1961; STB Wood 1967; MA GW 1972. Rec 11/12/1993 as Priest Bp Vincent Waydell Warner. m 10/5/1974 Anne Carlyle Hastings c 1. Faith Ch Kingston WA 1995-2000; Serv RC Ch 1966-1973.

MURRAY-SMITH, Jihan Brittany (Chi) **S Chrys's Ch Chicago IL 2017-** D 12/19/2015 Bp Jeff Lee.

MURRELL, William Lewis (NY) 2400 Johnson Ave Apt 10c, Bronx NY 10463 **Int P All Souls Ch New York NY 1998-; Asst Intsn New York City 1996-; Hon Asst Ch Of The Intsn New York NY 1982-** B BB 1922 s Arthur & Inez. BA SUNY 1978; SUNY 1981; NYTS 1983; GTS 1986; MEd U of No Texas 1994. D 6/6/1983 Bp Paul Moore Jr P 9/1/1989 Bp James Stuart Wetmore. m 12/29/1971 Luisa Pommou. P-in-c Ch Of The Ascen Mt Vernon NY 1992-1996; Int Trin Ch Of Morrisania Bronx NY 1991-1992; Pstr Assoc Intsn New York City 1989-1991; D Intsn New York City 1983-1989.

MURSULI, Modesto E (SeFla) 399A Himrod St, Brooklyn NY 11237 **S Thos Epis Par Miami FL 2014-; P St Margarets and San Francisco de Asis Epis Ch Hialeah FL 2013-; Vic Iglesia de la Santa Cruz (LI) 2008-** B Camaguey CU 1952 s Orlando & Maria. TS of Havana Havana CU 1980; CIAM Rome IT 1989; Angl Educ Havana CU 1993. Trans 4/20/1999 as Priest Bp Robert Reed Shahan. m 4/26/1990 Annie Gomez Montalvan c 1. Dio Long Island Garden City NY 2008-2012; Vic Dio Arizona Phoenix AZ 1999-2008; Iglesia Epis De San Pablo Phoenix AZ 1999-2008; Vic Iglesia de San Pablo (AZ) 1999-2008; Mssnr Epis Ch of Honduras 1997-1998; R Epis Ch of Cuba 1992-1997; R RC Ch 1980-1990.

MUSGRAVE, David Charles (Chi) 11112 Bayberry Hills Dr, Raleigh NC 27617 B New York NY 1948 s Howard & Dorothy. BA Hobart and Wm Smith Colleges 1970; MDiv GTS 1973; DMin Eden TS 1978. D 6/16/1973 Bp Jonathan Goodhue Sherman P 12/15/1973 Bp George Leslie Cadigan. m 8/22/1970 Donna B Musgrave c 1. R S Aug's Epis Ch Wilmette IL 1993-2010; R S Alb's Ch Indianapolis IN 1984-1993; R S Mk's Ch S Louis MO 1978-1984; Asst Ch Of The H Comm S Louis MO 1973-1978.

MUSHORN, Richard C (LI) 2206 Cloverleaf Cir SE, Cleveland TN 37311 B Kew Gardens NY 1946 s Harold & Frances. BA Cathd Coll of the Immac Concep 1966; MDiv Our Lady of Ang Sem Niagara U 1971. Rec 12/1/1987 as Priest Bp Robert Campbell Witcher Sr. R Epis Ch Of S Mk The Evang Bellmore NY 1990-1994; Dio Long Island Garden City NY 1989-1990; Vic Chr Ch Brentwood NY 1988; Cur All SS Epis Sunnyside NY 1987-1989; Cur All SS' Epis Ch Long Island City NY 1987-1988; Asst St Jane Frances DeChantal Easton PA

1978-1979; Asst Cathd of St Catharine Allentown PA 1975-1978; Asst St Pat RC Ch Pottsville PA 1971-1975; Asst St Lawr the Mtyr Catasauqua PA 1971.

MUSOKE-LUBEGA, Benjamin Kiwomutemero (NY) 27 Compton Dr, East Windsor NJ 08520 **P & Dir of Faith in Action Trin Par New York NY 2005-, 1989-1990** B MengoUG 1956 s Benjamin & Theorphilis. BA Shimer Coll 1975; BD Bp Tucker Theol Coll Mukono Ug 1980; MA McCormick TS 1985; STM Nash 1987. Trans 9/25/1990 Bp William Grant Black. m 7/16/1994 Edith L Musoke-Lubega c 2. Epis Ch Cntr New York NY 2002-2005; R S Matt's And S Jos's Detroit MI 1997-2002; H Sprt Epis Ch Cincinnati OH 1991-1997; Vic H Sprt Detroit MI 1988-1997; Serv Ch Of Uganda 1980-1984; Chair - Cmnty Educ & Fund Raising Natl Coun Of Ch Of Chr In The USA. Cmnty Of Trsfg.

MUSSATTI, David James (Nev) Po Box 5572, Incline Village NV 89450 **Assoc S Pat's Ch Incline Vlg NV 1982-** B Los Angeles CA 1934 s James & Louise. BA San Jose St U 1957; MA U of Nevada at Reno 1968; EdD U Pac 1981. D 3/17/1982 P 11/1/1982 Bp Wesley Frensdorff. m 7/25/1981 Stephanie Irene Finlay c 4. Bro of S Andr 1958; Ord of S Lk 1999. Phi Delta Kappa 1968; Phi Beta Kappa 1957; Phi Kappa Phi 1957.

MUSSELMAN JR, William Stanley (Pa) 93 Willow Way, Lansdale PA 19446 **Died 12/29/2016** B Norristown PA 1929 s William & Kathryn. BA Ge 1951; BD PDS 1954. D 6/5/1954 Bp Joseph Gillespie Armstrong P 12/11/1954 Bp Oliver J Hart. c 3. Ch Of The H Sprt Harleysville PA 1995-2000; Asst S Jn's Epis Ch Carlisle PA 1990-1993; Ret 1989-2016; R Chr Ch Epis Ridley Pk PA 1956-1989; Cur Ch Of Our Sav Jenkintown PA 1954-1956.

MUSSER, Lisa (WTenn) 8011 Douglas Avenue, Dallas TX 75225 **Assoc for Pstr Care S Mich And All Ang Ch Dallas TX 2012-** B New Orleans LA 1974 d Barbara. BA Sprg Hill Coll 1996; MDiv GTS 2005. D 6/4/2005 Bp Mark Hollingsworth Jr P 12/11/2005 Bp Samuel Johnson Howard. m 6/20/2015 David N Musser c 1. Assoc R for Formation and Servnt Mnstrs Ch Of The H Comm Memphis TN 2011-2012; Pres Natl Assoc for Epis CE Dir 2011-2012; Assoc R for Formation Chr Ch Grosse Pointe Grosse Pointe Farms MI 2007-2011; Asst R S Ptr's Ch Fernandina Bch FL 2005-2007; Yth Min S Paul's Ch Akron OH 2000-2002; Pres Nat Assoc for Episc CE Dir (Forma) 2011-2012. Gathering of Leaders 2011; Natl Assn for Epis CE Dir (NAECED) 2008-2012. lflores@saintmichael.org

MUSTARD, George Thomas (SwVa) 6437 Monarch Ct, Hoschton GA 30548 **Asst S Mary And S Martha Ch Buford GA 2012-** B Tazewell VA 1944 s George & Lina. BA Berea Coll 1974; MDiv VTS 1977; VTS 1984. D 6/12/1977 P 12/18/1977 Bp William Henry Marmion. m 11/27/1965 Shirley Snider Mustard c 2. Asst S Jn's Ch Roanoke VA 2009-2011; R S Jn's Ch Bedford VA 1999-2008; Chr Ch Pocahontas VA 1991-1999; R S Mary's Ch Bluefield VA 1991-1999; Trin Ch Richlands VA 1991-1999; R The Tazewell Cnty Cluster Of Epis Parishes Tazewell VA 1991-1998; R S Geo's Epis Ch Griffin GA 1986-1991; R S Jas Ch Roanoke VA 1980-1986; Asst Chr Epis Ch Roanoke VA 1977-1979. "Preaching as Prophetic Calling," *Harvest Evang*, Morehouse Pub. Alling and Schlafer, Editors. Phi Kappa Phi.

MUSTERMAN, Amanda Ellen (Lex) PO Box 633, Somerset KY 42502 **S Pat Ch Somerset KY 2015-** B Somerset KY 1978 d John & Gerry. BA TCU 2000; MDiv Candler TS @Emory 2004; Cert in Yth and Theol PrTS 2012; MDiv Candler TS @Emory 2014; MDiv Candler TS @Emory 2014. D 3/7/2015 P 9/19/2015 Bp Doug Hahn. Other Lay Position Chr Ch Cathd Lexington KY 2008-2013. rev@stpatsomerset.org

MUTCHLER, Marlene Kay-Scholten (Ore) 147 Nw 19th Ave, Portland OR 97209 **Dio Oregon Portland OR 2016-; Trin Epis Cathd Portland OR 2016-** B Ludington MI 1967 d Dale & Mary. BA MI SU 1989. D 2/6/2016 P 9/6/2016 Bp Michael Hanley. m 6/23/1990 Wade Norman Mutchler c 2.

MUTH, David Philip (NCal) 1429 Spring Valley Dr, Roseville CA 95661 **Nonpar 1987-** B New Orleans LA 1933 s Philip & Dorothy. BS Tul 1955; MDiv Sewanee: The U So, TS 1967; JD U NC 1985. D 6/29/1967 P 1/1/1968 Bp William G Wright. m 6/4/1960 Deborah Jean Muth. Vic S Andr-Highlands No Highland CA 1973-1987; S Andr's In The Highlands Mssn Antelope CA 1973-1986; Cur Gr Ch New Orleans LA 1969-1973; LocTen S Paul's Epis Ch Wilmington NC 1967-1968.

MUTH, Donald Charles (La) 4920 Cleveland Pl, Metairie LA 70003 **Serv Ch of Engl 2003-; Int R S Lk's Ch New Orleans LA 2000-; Ret 1998-** B New Orleans LA 1933 s Philip & Dorothy. BA Tul 1955; SWTS 1958. D 6/18/1958 Bp Girault M Jones P 5/23/1959 Bp Iveson Batchelor Noland. m 5/24/1958 Nancy E Muth c 4. Int S Paul's Ch New Orleans LA 2002-2003, Int 1998-2001; Asst S Mart's Epis Ch Metairie LA 1985-1997; Chair Dio Chicago Chicago IL 1972-1976, Advsry Liturg Cmsn 1968-1976; Ch Of The H Nativ Clarendon Hls IL 1966-1985; Cur Gr Ch New Orleans LA 1961-1966; Cur S Paul's Ch Abbeville LA 1958-1961; Ch Of The Ascen Lafayette LA 1958-1960; Chapl U SoWstrn Lafayette LA 1958-1960.

MUTOLO, Frances (Colo) 85 Long Bow Cir, Monument CO 80132 **D S Andr's Ch Manitou Sprg CO 2009-** B McKeesport PA 1953 d Frank & Angela. RN Mercy Hosp Sch of Nrsng 1973. D 11/11/2000 Bp William Jerry Winterrowd.

M

m 4/20/1977 Michael M Malivuk c 2. D Ch of the Gd Shpd Colorado Spg CO 2003-2008; D Chr's Epis Ch Castle Rock CO 2000-2003.

MUTZELBURG, Michael Kenneth (Mich) 110 W South Holly Rd, Fenton MI 48430 **Died 1/1/2017** B Detroit MI 1940 s Herman & Ruth. BA Wayne 1967; MDiv Ya Berk 1970; MS U MI 1985. D 6/29/1970 Bp Archie H Crowley P 3/12/1971 Bp Richard Stanley Merrill Emrich. m 1/28/2017 Linda Lou Mutzelburg c 1. R S Pat's Epis Ch Madison Hts MI 1992-1995; S Andr's Epis Ch Flint MI 1989-1992; P-in-c S Paul's Epis Ch Corunna MI 1982-1987; Trin Epis Ch Flushing MI 1974-1977; Asst Min S Andr's Ch Ann Arbor MI 1970-1974. Acad of Cert Soc Workers; NASW.

MYCOFF JR, Walter Joseph (SO) 892 W Webster Rd, Summersville WV 26651 B Pittsburgh PA 1942 s Walter & Marguerite. BA Ohio U 1964; MDiv VTS 1971. D 6/11/1971 P 2/1/1972 Bp Wilburn Camrock Campbell. m 6/19/1965 Martha H Mycoff c 3. P-in-c St.Matthews Westerville Ohio 2007-2008; Cn Dio Sthrn Ohio Cincinnati OH 2005-2008; R The Epis Ch Of The Ascen Middletown OH 1997-2005; Vic All Souls Epis Ch No Ft Myers FL 1990-1997; R Trin Ch Morgantown WV 1983-1990; Chapl W Virginia AF NG 1979-1994; R S Andr's Ch Oak Hill WV 1972-1983; Vic Ascen Chinton WV 1971-1972; R Ch Of The Incarn Ronceverte WV 1971-1972; P-in-c S Matt's Epis Ch Westerville OH 2007-2008. Personalities Of The So Awd.

MYERS, Amy Slaughter (Md) Epiphany Episcopal Church, 2216 Pot Spring Rd, Timonium MD 21093 **Epiph Ch Dulaney Vlly Luthvle Timon MD 2016-** B Richmond VA 1970 d James & Azma. BA U NC at Chap Hill 1991; MA U of Pennsylvania 1992; PHD JHU 2000; Cert Loyola U Maryland 2016. D 1/16/2016 Bp Chilton Richardson Knudsen P 9/3/2016 Bp Eugene Taylor Sutton. m 8/17/1996 Paul David Myers c 3. Other Lay Position Cathd Of The Incarn Baltimore MD 2010-2014.

MYERS, Annwn (Miss) 335 Tennessee Avenue, Sewanee TN 37383 **Assoc U Chapl All SS' Chap U So Sewanee TN 1989-; Sewanee U So TS Sewanee TN 1989-** B Aurora IL 1953 d Paul & Beatrice. BA Millsaps Coll 1981; MDiv VTS 1984. D 6/23/1984 P 5/24/1985 Bp Duncan Montgomery Gray Jr. m 1/23/1988 Samuel Dixon Myers c 2. S Andr's Cathd Jackson MS 1989; The Chap Of The Cross Madison MS 1989, Int R 1988-1989; Chapl S Andr's Epis Day Sch Jackson MS 1988-1989; Asst R S Jn's Epis Ch Pascagoula MS 1987-1988, Cur 1984-1986.

MYERS, Bethany Leigh (Colo) 800 N Saint Asaph St # 202, Alexandria VA 22314 B Sterling CO 1983 d Robert & Linda. BA Willamette U 2005; MSW U of Connecticut 2009; MDiv Ya Berk 2010. D 11/20/2010 Bp Robert John O'Neill. m 6/12/2010 Nicholas A Myers. Ch Of Our Sav Colorado Sprg CO 2014-2015.

MYERS, Brooke (Mo) 4141 Flora Pl, Saint Louis MO 63110 **R Ch of the H Comm 2002-** B Charleston SC 1951 s deRosset & Barbara. BA Coll of Charleston 1974; MDiv CDSP 1979. D 6/7/1980 P 12/22/1980 Bp John Lester Thompson III. m 9/30/1995 Anne Hunter Kelsey c 2. R Ch Of The H Comm S Louis MO 2002-2013; R H Cross Epis Ch Castro Vlly CA 1989-2001; Asst All Souls Par In Berkeley Berkeley CA 1986-1989; Vic S Tim's Ch Gridley CA 1980-1986; Co-Pstr Chr The King Quincy CA 1979-1980.

MYERS III, Bruns M (Miss) 107 Sundown Rd, Madison MS 39110 **Asst S Phil's Ch Jackson MS 2003-, Asst 2003-, P 2003-, Cur 2002** B Jackson MS 1950 s Bruns & Evelyn. BA Belhaven Coll 1986; MDiv Reformed TS 1988. D 6/21/2001 Bp Duncan Montgomery Gray III P 1/24/2002 Bp Alfred Marble Jr. Chapl / Ethicist MS Methodist Rehab Cntr Jackson MS 1990-2006. Kappa Alpha Ord, Alpha Upsilon Chapt 1972. Gd Will Cmnty Serv Awd Gd Will Industries Of Mississippi 2000; Golden Deeds Awd Exch Club Of No Jackson 1996; ABS Awd In Biblic Stds Belhaven Coll 1986; Mich Landon Grad Schlrshp Awd Mississippi Dept Of Rehab Serv 1986.

MYERS, David John (WMo) 12599 Timberline Dr, Garfield AR 72732 **D St. Thos a Beckett Cassville MO 2006-** B Pueblo CO 1940 s Lawrence & Dorothy. Cntrl Bapt TS; U of Kansas. D 2/1/2003 Bp Barry Howe. m 12/30/1989 Susan Ann Myers c 2. D St. Paul's Lee's Summit MO 2003-2006; Chapl Northcare Hospice Inc. No Kansas City KS 2003-2005.

MYERS, Elizabeth Williams (Be) 798 Willow Grove St # 3a, Hackettstown NJ 07840 **S Ptr's Ch Mt Arlington NJ 2010-** B New York NY 1935 d Darwood & Elizabeth. BA Smith 1957; MDiv EDS 1962. D 5/24/1974 Bp John Alfred Baden P 1/14/1977 Bp Dean Theodore Stevenson. Int S Lk's Ch Hope NJ 2008-2010; Int Panther Vlly Ecum Ch Hackettstwn NJ 2007-2008; Int Trin Carbondale PA & Chr 2005-2007; Assoc Chr Ch Newton NJ 2002-2004; P Epis Ch in Navajoland 2000-2002; R Ch Of The Gd Shpd And S Jn Milford PA 1980-2000; Assoc Chr Ch Cranbrook Bloomfield Hills MI 1978-1980; Int S Jas Ch Lancaster PA 1974-1978; Asst to R Emm Ch Middleburg VA 1973-1974. ewmyers904@gmail.com

MYERS, Fredrick Eugene (SanD) 1111 E Ramon Rd Unit 80, Palm Springs CA 92264 **Ret 2000-** B Elyria OH 1935 s Ford & Alberta. AA Lorain Cnty Cmnty Coll 1975; BA Ob 1977; MDiv SWTS 1980. D 6/28/1980 Bp John Harris Burt P 1/1/1981 Bp Charles Bennison Sr. m 11/7/1954 Janet Yvonne Myers. Dn Of The Traverse Dnry Dio Wstrn Michigan Kalamazoo MI 1989-1993, Exec Coun 1987-1993, Stndg Com 1995-1997, Stndg Com 1985-1994; R S Paul's Epis

Ch Elk Rapids MI 1982-2000; Asst Gr Epis Ch Traverse City MI 1980-1982; Grand Traverse City Area Mssn Traverse City MI 1980-1982.

MYERS, Jeannette (NCal) 38 Payran Street, Petaluma CA 94952 B Petaluma CA 1950 d William & Irene. BA Sonoma St U 1975; MDiv CDSP 1979; CTS Jesuit TS 1987. D 11/1/1979 P 10/23/1983 Bp John Lester Thompson III. c 2. Ch Of The H Apos Hilo HI 2001-2004; S Jude's Hawaiian Ocean View Ocean View HI 1999-2001; R Ch Of S Jn The Evang Boston MA 1996-1999; Dio California San Francisco CA 1991-1996; Prchr Food For The Poor Mssn Outreach Florida 1991-1996; Asst Chr Ch Alameda CA 1988-1991; DCE S Clem's Ch Berkeley CA 1987-1988; Vic S Clare Assisi Challenge Forbestown CA 1983-1986; Nonpar 1981-1982; Co-Pstr Chr The King Quincy CA 1979-1980.

MYERS, John Geenwood (WLa) 833 Clarence St, Lake Charles LA 70601 **R Ch of the Gd Shepard Lake Chas LA 2004-; R Epis Ch Of The Gd Shpd Lake Chas LA 2004-** B Ridgway PA 1956 s Paul & Mabel. BA Alleg 1979; MDiv SWTS 1990. D 6/2/1990 Bp Donald James Davis P 4/20/1991 Bp Robert Deane Rowley Jr. m 6/9/1990 Joan Myers c 2. R Emm Ch Petoskey MI 1995-2004; Asst R S Andr's Ch Downers Grove IL 1992-1995; P in charge Gr Ch Lake City PA 1990-1992.

MYERS, Jonathan (WNC) St Stephen Episcopal Church, 4805 NE 45th St, Seattle WA 98105 **Yth Dir Emm Epis Ch Mercer Island WA 2010-** B Greenville OH 1979 s Galen & Sondra. BA Indiana Wesl 2002; MDiv The Seattle TS and Psychol 2009. D 10/18/2012 P 6/13/2013 Bp Gregory Harold Rickel. Dio Wstrn No Carolina Asheville NC 2015-2017; S Andr's Ch Seattle WA 2013-2015.

MYERS, Max Arthur (Ct) 247 New Milford Tpke, Marble Dale CT 06777 B Coffeyville KS 1943 s Arthur & Gwendolyn. BA Cornell Coll 1965; BD Harvard DS 1968; PhD Harv 1976. D 12/13/1999 P 6/18/2000 Bp Michael Garrison. m 7/14/1984 Maureen Elizabeth Myers c 3. S Andr's Epis Ch Marble Dale CT 2007-2015; S Mary's Epis Ch Gowanda NY 2002-2007; P-in-c S Mary's Ch Salamanca NY 2001-2002; S Steph's Ch Olean NY 2000-2002; Cn Theol S Paul's Cathd Buffalo NY 2000. Auth, "Christmas On Celluloid," *Christmas Unwrapped*, Trin Press Intern, 2001; Auth, "Stds In The Theol Ethics Of Ernest Troeltsch," Edwin Mellen Press, 1991; Auth, "The Contemporary Crisis Of Marxism And Our Responsibility," *Thought: A Revs Of Culture And Ideas*, 1987; Auth, "Toward What Is Rel Thinking Underway," *De-Construction And Theol*, Crossroads, 1982; Auth, "Ideology And Legitimation As Necessary Concepts For Chr Ethics," *Journ Of The AAR*, 1981; Auth, "Santa Claus As An Icon Of Gr," *Ibid*. AAR; Conf Of Angl & Luth Theol; Soc Of Chr Ethics.

MYERS, Nicholas A (Colo) 6050 N Meridian St, Indianapolis IN 46208 **S Tim's Epis Ch Littleton CO 2016-** B South Bend IN 1983 s James & Trudy. BA Wabash Coll 2005; MDiv Yale DS 2009. D 5/31/2009 Bp Edward Stuart Little II P 12/7/2009 Bp Shannon Sherwood Johnston. m 6/12/2010 Bethany Leigh Davidson c 1. Vic S Paul's Epis Ch Indianapolis IN 2015-2016; Assoc P Gr And S Steph's Epis Ch Colorado Sprg CO 2011-2015; Cler Res Chr Ch Alexandria VA 2009-2011.

MYERS, Rebecca (CPa) St John's Church, 701 Engineer St, Corbin KY 40701 **R Ch of the Nativ-St Steph Newport PA 2015-; Admin S Agnes Hse Lexington KY 2013-; P-in-c S Jn's Ch Corbin KY 2013-** B Ft Smith AR 1956 d Robert & Mary. BASW Shippensburg U of PA 1984; MSW U of Kansas 1996; MDiv GTS 2013; MDiv The GTS 2013. D 1/26/2013 P 7/27/2013 Bp Mariann Edgar Budde. c 2. Dio Lexington Lexington 2013-2015; Mem, So Afr Partnership Com Dio Washington Washington DC 2007-2010; Mem, Mssn and Outreach Com Cathd of St Ptr & St Paul Washington DC 2006-2009. Auth, "Healing the Disaster of Slavery: The Maafa Suite at St. Paul's Bapt Ch Brooklyn NY," *Angl and Epis Hist*, The HSEC, 2014. rev.myers2013@gmail.com

MYERS JR, Robert Keith (Chi) 7050 N Oakley Ave, Chicago IL 60645 **Co-Dir of Mssn Misericordia Heart of Mercy Cntr 2011-** B Clinton IA 1945 s Robert & Corine. BA Illinois Coll 1968; MDiv SWTS 1975; PhD NWU 1984. D 6/14/1975 P 12/13/1975 Bp James Winchester Montgomery. c 2. Co-Dir of Mssn Misericordia Heart of Mercy Cntr; Chicago IL 60660 2011-2017; R Ch Of The H Comf Kenilworth IL 1986-2011, Assoc R 1979-1985, Cur 1975-1978. Auth, "The Relatns Between Dreams & Dreamers In Mod Psychol Lit," *Doctoral Dissertation*, NWU, 1984. Friend; Soc Of S Jn The Evang 1988. Bp Whipple Schlr SWTS 1975.

MYERS II, Robert Ware (Ind) 8014 River Bay Drive West, Indianapolis IN 46240 **Chapl to the Ret Cler & Surviving Spouses Dio Indianapolis Indianapolis IN 2011-** B Gainesville FL 1944 s Robert & Alice. BA Jacksonville U 1967; MDiv Sewanee: The U So, TS 1973. D 6/13/1973 P 5/7/1974 Bp Edward Hamilton West. m 6/23/1979 Evelyn Wiley Myers c 1. Assoc S Paul's Epis Ch Indianapolis IN 2008-2010, 2000-2006; Sacramentalist S Tim's Ch Indianapolis IN 2006-2008; S Chris's Epis Ch Carmel IN 1991-2000; Chr Ch Cathd Indianapolis IN 1984-1991; Assoc S Chris's Ch Pensacola FL 1979-1984; H Innoc Ch Atlanta GA 1978-1979; Vic Ch Of The Epiph Jacksonville FL 1975-1977; S Mary's Ch Jacksonville FL 1975-1977; S Fran Of Assisi Epis Ch Tallahassee FL 1974-1976; Dio Florida Jacksonville 1973-1978. Auth, "Play," *The White Horse*, 1992; Auth, "Play," *What's Best For Billy?*, 1992; Auth, "Play," *Airwaves*, 1991.

MYERS, Roy Clarence (WLa) 1906 Evangeline Dr, Bastrop LA 71220 B Glenshaw PA 1949 s Julius & Viola. BA Geneva Coll 1971; MDiv Epis TS in Kentucky 1977; DMin Covington TS 1986. D 6/26/1977 P 12/11/1977 Bp Robert Bracewell Appleyard. m 8/28/1971 Benetta L Myers c 1. R Chr Ch Bastrop LA 2004-2007; R H Trin Epis Ch Wyoming MI 2000-2004; R S Jas Ch Manitowoc WI 1998-2000; R S Tim's Ch Bp CA 1992-1998; P-in-c Gr Ch Pomeroy OH 1990-1992; Vic Gr Ch Ravenswood WV 1986-1992; S Andr's Epis Ch Rose City MI 1981-1986; Vic Trin Epis Ch W Branch MI 1981-1986; R Chr Ch Brownsville PA 1977-1981; Serv Presb Ch 1975-1977. EFAC.

MYERS, Thomas (NJ) 2502 Central Ave, North Wildwood NJ 08260 B Plainfield NJ 1942 s Richard & Jane. B.A. U NC 1965; niveau maitrise IPFE de la Sorbonne 1966; DEUG Institut Prot Theologie 1999; BTh Cambridge Theol Fed GB 2004; Cert Ang Stds Nash 2007. D 5/31/2007 P 12/21/2007 Bp George Edward Councell. c 3. P-in-c S Simeon's By The Sea Wildwood NJ 2008-2014; Assoc The Ch Of S Uriel The Archangel Sea Girt NJ 2007-2008; Pstr Asst Amer Cathd in Paris 2003-2004; Pstr Asst to French Mssn Convoc of Epis Ch in Europe Paris 2002-2004.

MYERS, William Francis (Va) 11142 Beaver Trail Ct, Reston VA 20191 **Ret 1993**- B Washington DC 1933 s Raymond & Matilda. BA U of Maryland 1955; MDiv VTS 1960; MA Colg 1970; DMin Wesley TS 1979. D 6/18/1960 P 12/1/1960 Bp Angus Dun. S Jn's Epis Ch Mc Lean VA 1972-1993; R S Thos Ch Hamilton NY 1967-1970; R Trin Ch S Chas MO 1963-1967; S Geo's Ch Glenn Dale MD 1960-1963; Vic S Jas Epis Ch Bowie MD 1960-1963. Auth, "Brightness Of His Presence".

MYHR, Laura Parmer (WNC) 100 Summit Street, Marion NC 28752 B Nashville TN 1946 d Henry & Mitylene. E Tennessee St U 1967; BS U of Tennessee 1974; MDiv Van 1990; Sewanee: The U So, TS 1992. D 6/14/1992 P 2/21/1993 Bp William Evan Sanders. m 7/6/2008 Harold Henline c 3. R S Jn's Epis Ch Marion NC 2000-2008; Cn Pstr S Jn's Epis Cathd Knoxville TN 1995-2000; Asst S Phil's Ch Nashville TN 1992-1995; Chapl S Thos Hosp Nashville 1992-1995.

MYNATT, Belva Charlene (WMo) 3523 S Kings Hwy, Independence MO 64055 B Independence MO 1942 d Charles & Belva. BA U of Missouri 1964; MS U of Cntrl Missouri 1972; Pk U 1987; Rockhurst U 1988; S Paul TS Kansas City MO 1988. D 1/18/1989 Bp Arthur Anton Vogel. m 8/1/1964 Kenneth Edward Mynatt c 2. Epis Soc Serv Dio W Missouri Kansas City MO 1996-1998, Co-Dn WMO Sch for Mnstry 2000-2010, Strng Com Parenting Life Skills 1996-1999, Chair Hisp Mnstry 1987-1995; D S Anne's Ch Lees Summit MO 1991-2008; D Trin Ch Independence MO 1989-1991. Auth, "First Article, Scrub Oaks and Pines," *LivCh*, 1990; Auth, *Seventh Grade Spanish Curric*, 1965. NAAD 1989. Bp's Shield Dio W Missouri 2008; Loc org Mortar Bd UMKC 1964; Torch and Scroll, Loc Phi Beta Kappa UMKC 1964.

MYRICK, Harry Eugene (RG) 708 E Lockhart Ave, Alpine TX 79830 **Ret 1992**- B Gallup NM 1927 s John & Mary. BA U of New Mex 1957; MDiv CDSP 1960. D 6/10/1960 P 4/11/1961 Bp C J Kinsolving III. Providence Memi Hosp El Paso TX 1984-1992; Chapl Providence Memi Hosp El Paso TX 1984-1992; R S Fran On The Hill El Paso TX 1976-1984; Assoc Pro Cathd Epis Ch Of S Clem El Paso TX 1960-1976.

MYRICK, William Harris (Mil) 503 E Walworth Ave P.O. Box 528, Delavan WI 53115 B Sault Saint Marie MI 1946 s William & Betty. BS Nthrn Michigan U 1981; MDiv Nash 1984. D 2/23/1984 P 9/22/1984 Bp Thomas Kreider Ray. Chr Epis Ch Of Delavan Delavan WI 1998-2012; Chr Ch Epis Madison WI 1992-1998; inter R Chr Ch Epis Madison 1990-1991; R Gr Ch Madison WI 1987-1992; Epis Ch-Wstrn Reg Crystal Falls MI 1987; R Chr Ch Calumet MI 1984-1987; Dio Nthrn Michigan Marquette MI 1984-1986. Auth, "Index Guide," *BCP*.

MYSEN, Andrea Leigh (Chi) 411 Laurel Ave, Highland Park IL 60035 **Dio Chicago Chicago IL 2014**- B Pensacola FL 1964 BBA TCU 1986; MA Denver Sem 1995; MDiv SWTS 2004. D 3/30/2004 P 9/30/2004 Bp Victor Alfonso Scantlebury. m 1/9/2004 Rene Mysen c 2. R Trin Ch Highland Pk IL 2005-2014; Cur All SS Epis Ch Chicago IL 2004-2005.

N

NABE, Clyde Milton (Mo) 4742 Burlington Ave N, Saint Petersburg FL 33713 **Non-par 1965**- B Saint Louis MO 1940 s Loretta. BS Pur 1962; MA U of Missouri 1965; MA Pur 1972; PhD Pur 1975. D 12/22/1979 P 11/30/1980 Bp Albert William Hillestad. m 8/25/1962 Jo Ann Reisner c 4. Affiliated Cler Cathd Ch Of S Ptr St. Petersburg FL 2005-2006; Affiliated Cler S Bede's Ch St. Petersburg FL 2001-2005; P S Thos Epis Ch Glen Carbon IL 1985-1990; Asst Min S Paul's and Trin Chap Alton IL 1982-1983; R S Gabr Wood River IL 1981-1985; Asst Min S Andr's Epis Ch Edwardsville IL 1979-1981; Affiliated Cler Trin Ch S Louis MO 1990-2001. Auth, "Death & Dying/ Life & Living," *6th Ed.*, Wadsworth, 2009; Auth, "Mystery & Rel: Newman'S Epistemology Of Rel," 1988; Auth, "Morality Of Rel Beliefs," *Rel Stds*, 1986; Auth, "Confessionalism & Philos Of Rel," *Amer Journ Theol & Philos*, 1983.

NACHTRIEB, John David (Chi) 131 N Brainard Ave, La Grange IL 60525 **D Ch Of The Trsfg Palos Pk IL 1998**- B Chicago IL 1948 s Robert & Elizabeth. BA DePauw U 1970; Cert Chicago D Sch Chicago IL 1997. D 2/7/1998 Bp Herbert Alcorn Donovan Jr. m 1/23/1971 Beverly Lynn Nachtrieb c 2.

NAECKEL, Lynn Miles (Minn) Po Box 43, Ranier MN 56668 **H Trin Intl Falls MN 2006-, Lay Prchr 1995-2005** B Kansas City MO 1938 d Arno & Mildred. BA NWU 1960; MA NWU 1970; PhD NWU 1972. D 10/23/2005 Bp Daniel Lee Swenson P 7/8/2006 Bp James Louis Jelinek. c 1.

NAEF, Linda (Miss) 655 Eagle Ave, Jackson MS 39206 **Chapl S Andr's Sch 1993**- B Philadelphia PA 1953 d Richard & Jane. BS U of Sthrn Mississippi 1974; MS U of Sthrn Mississippi 1976; MS U of Sthrn Mississippi 1978; MDiv EDS 1986; ThD Harv 1995. D 5/31/1986 Bp Duncan Montgomery Gray Jr P 5/1/1987 Bp Otis Charles. m 11/24/1982 Richard Lewis Hudson. S Andr's Epis Sch Ridgeland MS 1994-1996; Asst R S Mich's Ch Milton MA 1991-1992; S Paul's Ch Brookline MA 1989-1990, 1987.

NAEGELE III, John Aloysius (CPa) 982 Spa Rd. Apt. 201, Annapolis MD 21403 **Assoc S Phil's Ch Annapolis MD 2007**- B Philadelphia PA 1933 s John & Natalie. BA W Liberty St Coll 1955; LTh Epis TS in Kentucky 1963; MDiv Epis TS in Kentucky 1986. D 12/1/1963 P 7/1/1964 Bp William R Moody. m 8/21/1988 Ellen W Naegele c 3. Int S Lk's Epis Ch Mechanicsburg PA 2002-2004; Int Hope Epis Ch Manheim PA 2001-2002, R 1992-2001; Non-par CEO - Sarah Todd Hm- Cont Care Cmnty 1985-1992; R Trin And S Phil's Epis Ch Lansford PA 1977-1984; Non-par USA - Off of Econ Opportuniy 1966-1974; P-in-c S Mk's Ch Hazard KY 1962-1966.

NAGATA, Ada (Los) Church of Our Saviour, 535 West Roses Road, San Gabriel CA 91775 **Epis Ch Of Our Sav New York NY 2016**- B Hongkong China 1953 d Nam & Lin-Chan. BSN California St U 1999; BSN California St U, Dominguez Hills 1999; MDiv ETSBH 2007; DMin EDS 2015. D 6/9/2007 P 1/12/2008 Bp Joseph Jon Bruno. m 9/21/1985 Ronnie Nagata c 1. Ch Of Our Sav Par San Gabr CA 2009-2016. awongnagata@churchofoursaviour.org

NAGEL, Virginia Otis Wight (CNY) 100 Wilson Pl, Syracuse NY 13214 **Dep Genral Conv CNY NY 2003-; P-in-c Henry Winter Syle Mnstry w The Deaf Dio Albany 1991-** B Schenectady NY 1939 d Otis & Marjorie Marie. BA Gallaudet U 1959; MDiv Estrn Bapt TS 1988. D 11/22/1986 Bp Lyman Cunningham Ogilby P 6/1/1988 Bp Allen Lyman Bartlett Jr. m 10/3/1959 Robert V Nagel c 3. Mssnr Ephphatha Mssn For The Deaf Gates NY 1998; Pres Epis Conf Of The Deaf 1996-2002; First Vice-Pres Epis Conf Of The Dear 1994-1996; Ephphatha Epis Par Of The Deaf Syracuse NY 1988-2009; Dio Cntrl New York Liverpool NY 1988-2008; Dio Pennsylvania Philadelphia PA 1987-1988; Jubilee Intern All Souls Ch For The Deaf Philadelphia PA 1986-1988. Auth, "Sunday Sermons For Everyday People," *Year A*, Privately Printed, 2002; Auth, "Bcp Lections Translated Into Amer Sign Lang," *Year B*, Privately Printed, 2002; Auth, "BCP Lections Translated Into Amer Sign Lang," *Years A, B & C*, Privately Printed, 2002; Auth, "Sunday Sermons For Everyday People," *Years B & C*, Privately Printed, 2002; Auth, "Jubilee Journ," 1988; Auth, "To Remember Means To Live," *Bapt Ldr*, 1988. ECom 1989-1996; Epis Conf Of The Deaf 1961; Ord Of S Lk 1977; OHC, Assoc 1970. Thos Gallaudet Awd Epis Conf Of The Deaf 2004.

NAGLE, George Overholser (CNY) 65 Glenwood Dr, Saranac Lake NY 12983 B West Reading PA 1936 s Warren & Elizabeth. BA Cor 1957; STB Ya Berk 1960; STM Sewanee: The U So, TS 1972. D 6/18/1960 P 6/29/1961 Bp Walter M Higley. m 6/13/1959 Margaret B Nagle c 3. Efm Mentor 1989-2000; Sr Chapl Adirondack Correctional Facility 1985-1999; Sr Chaplian Clinton Correctional Facility 1983-1985; Sr Chapl Dry Hill Correctional Facility 1982-1983; P-in-c S Jn In The Wilderness (Sum Chap) Paul Smiths NY 1977-1996; P-in-c S Mk's Ch Malone NY 1976-1977; Plcy Analyst Adirondack Pk Agcy 1974-1981; Chapl Hse Gd Shpd Utica NY 1967-1974; R S Steph's Ch New Hartford NY 1967-1974; R Chr Epis Ch Jordan NY 1961-1996, D 1960-1961. Auth, "Rel Attitudes And Symbols In The Writing Of Jn Updike".

NAGLEY, Stephanie Jane (WA) 6030 Grosvenor Lane, Bethesda MD 20814 **R S Lk's Ch Trin Par Beth MD 2003**- B Colfax WA 1953 d Harold & Violet. BSN Estrn Washington U 1975; MSN U of Texas 1977; PhD Case Wstrn Reserve U 1984; MDiv VTS 1993. D 6/5/1993 Bp James Russell Moodey P 2/1/1994 Bp Gethin Benwil Hughes. m 8/22/2008 Joann Marie Halle. Assoc R S Mk's Ch Washington DC 1999-2003; CPG Credo Proj The CPG New York NY 1997-1999; Assoc R S Jas By The Sea La Jolla CA 1993-1999; Bd Trst VTS Alexandria VA 1992-2003. Harris Awd VTS 1993.

NAGY, Robert A (NJ) 33396 Alagon Street, Temecula CA 92592 **All SS Ch Bay Hd NJ 2015**- B Bridgeport CT 1952 s Frank & Joan. BS Arizona St U 1981; MBA Arizona St U 1984; MDiv Sewanee: The U So, TS 1994. D 6/11/1994 P 12/17/1994 Bp Robert Reed Shahan. m 8/10/1974 Beatrice J Dobi c 2. Vic S Thos Epis Ch Temecula CA 2006-2015; R Trin Ch Portsmouth VA 2002-2006; R Prince Of Peace Epis Ch Dallas PA 1998-2002; S Mary's Epis Ch Phoenix AZ 1995-1998; Dio Arizona Phoenix AZ 1994-1995; Cur Trin Cathd 1994-1995. admin@allsaintsbayhead.org

N

NAIRN, Frederick William (Minn) 5895 Stoneybrook Dr, Minnetonka MN 55345 B IE 1943 s Frederick & Maureen. GOE Trin Dublin IE 1967; Luther TS 1987; DMin 1988. Trans 8/5/1987 Bp Robert Marshall Anderson. m 8/10/2002 Mary Jo Montenegro c 1. S Anne's Epis Ch De Pere WI 1999-2000; S Paul's Ch Brainerd MN 1998; R Ch Of The Epiph Epis Minneapolis MN 1987-1996; Int St Geo's Epis Ch Minneapolis MN 1986-1987; Exch R St Dav's Epis Ch Minnetonka MN 1985-1986; Serv Ch of Engl 1970-1984; Raf Chapl 1970-1974; Serv Ch of Ireland 1967-1970.

NAKAMURA RENGERS, Katherine Toshiko (Ala) 521 20th St N, Birmingham AL 35203 **Dio Alabama Birmingham 2011-** B Birmingham AL 1985 BMus NWU 2007; MDiv VTS 2011. D 5/20/2011 Bp John Mckee Sloan Sr P 12/13/2011 Bp Henry Nutt Parsley Jr. m 5/22/2010 Josiah Daniel Rengers. S Lk's Epis Ch Birmingham AL 2012-2016.

NAKATSUJI, Dorothy Masako Kamigaki (Haw) 1725 Fern St, Honolulu HI 96826 **Ret 1996-** B Peru WY 1932 d Nobuo & Ida. MS U of Utah 1962; Dio Trng Prog HI 1983. D 11/11/1983 Bp Edmond Lee Browning. m 6/23/1962 Ronald M Nakatsuji c 1. D Par of St Clem Honolulu HI 2002-2007, 1990-1991. Naeyc; NAAD; Third Ord At Soc Of S Fran.

NAKAYAMA, Timothy Makoto (Oly) 700 6th Ave S Apt 321, Seattle WA 98104 **Ret 1992-** B Vancouver BC CA 1931 s Gordon & Lois. BA U of British Columbia Vancouver BC CA 1953; ATC 1956; LTh ATC 1964. Trans 3/28/1966 as Priest Bp Ivol I Curtis. m 9/18/1961 Lois Keiko Nakayama c 4. Serv Ch in Japan 1991-2000; P in Charge All Soul's Epis Ch Chatan Okinawa 1991-1992; R Dio Olympia Seattle 1977-1991; R St Ptr's Epis Par Seattle WA 1977-1991, Par P, Appointed Natl Convenor, Epis Asiamerica Mnstry, Japanese Convoc 1973-1991; Serv Ch in USA 1966-1991; Serv Ch in Can 1956-1966. Auth, "Wrld War II internment as a Japanese-Can Chld," *Too Young To Fight*, Stoddard, 1999; Auth, "Hist of Angl Japanese Missions in Can," *Can Ch Hist Journ*, 1967. Cmnty of Nazareth 1993. Epis Asiamerica Mnstry Cross Natl EAM 1985; Bp's Cross Bp Curtis of Olympia 1972.

NAKO, James Walter (Chi) 9300 S Pleasant Ave, Chicago IL 60643 B Chicago IL 1937 s Walter & Eleanora. MA U Chi 1953; MDiv scl SWTS 1962. D 6/23/1962 Bp Charles L Street P 12/1/1962 Bp Gerald Francis Burrill. R Emer Ch of the H Nativ Chicago IL 2010-2012; R Ch Of The H Nativ Chicago IL 1992-2010; Min of Pstr Care Chr Ch River Forest IL 1981-1991; R Gr Ch Chicago IL 1966-1972; Asst to Dn Cathd Of S Jas Chicago IL 1962-1965.

NALVEN, Claudia (Chi) 327 S 4th St, Geneva IL 60134 **Asst. R S Mk's Ch Geneva IL 2007-** B Mt Kisco, NY 1958 d Joseph & Josephine. BS Nyack Coll 1999; MDiv TESM 2006. D 3/30/2007 P 10/12/2007 Bp Henry W Scriven. c 2.

NANCARROW, Arthur Paul (Mich) 148 W Eagle Lake Dr, Maple Grove MN 55369 **Ret 1993-** B Houghton MI 1930 s Arthur & Elsie. BA Ripon Coll Ripon WI 1952; MDiv SWTS 1955; MA U of Detroit Mercy 1973. D 6/15/1955 P 12/18/1955 Bp Herman R Page. m 10/12/1955 Deborah A Nancarrow c 3. Archd Dio Michigan Detroit MI 1986-1992, Asst to Bp for Faith & Wrshp 1973-1978, Assoc Dir Whitaker TS 1964-1978, Assoc Dir Whitaker TS 1964-1978, Stndg Comm 1982-1985; R S Jude's Epis Ch Fenton MI 1978-1992; The Whitaker Inst of Theol Detroit MI 1964-1978; Dn Gr Epis Ch Menominee MI 1958-1964; Vic Ch Of The Ascen Ontonagon MI 1956-1958; S Marks Ch Ewen MI 1956-1958; Asst S Jas Ch Of Sault S Marie Sault Sainte Marie MI 1955-1956; Stndg Comm Dio Nthrn Michigan Marquette MI 1959-1964. Hon Cn S Paul's Cathd 1993; Phi Beta Kappa Ripon Coll 1983.

NANCARROW, Paul Steven (SwVa) 25 Church St, Staunton VA 24401 **R Trin Ch Staunton VA 2008-** B Ontonagon MI 1956 s Arthur & Deborah. BA Ripon Coll Ripon WI 1978; MA U MN 1984; MDiv SWTS 1986; PhD Van 2000. D 6/28/1986 P 2/24/1987 Bp Henry Irving Mayson. m 4/29/2006 Lee Morris c 2. R St Geo's Epis Ch Minneapolis MN 1999-2008; Int S Barth's Ch Nashville TN 1997-1999; Int Otey Memi Par Ch Sewanee TN 1996-1997; P-in-c The Epis Ch Of The Resurr Franklin TN 1995-1996; P Ch Of Our Sav Gallatin TN 1993-1995; Assoc Chr Ch Dearborn MI 1988-1993; Asst Gr Epis Ch Port Huron MI 1986-1988. "The Call of the Sprt: Process Sprtlty in a Relational Wrld," P&F Press, 2005; Auth, "Wisdom's Info," *Zygon: Journ Rel & Sci*, 1997; Auth, "Realism and Anti-Realism," *Process Stds*, 1995. rector@trinitystaunton.org

NANCEKIVELL, Diane (NJ) 1008 Hemenway Rd, Bridport VT 05734 **Assoc Cathd Ch Of S Paul Burlington VT 2011-** B Montreal QC CA 1946 d Arthur & Beatrice. BEd U of Alberta Edmonton AB CA 1976; MEd S Michaels Coll Vermont 1984; MDiv Bangor TS 1992. D 11/7/1998 P 5/1/1999 Bp Joe Doss. m 5/21/1994 Thomas Roland Baskett c 1. Dn Trin Cathd Trenton NJ 2000-2006; S Paul's Epis Ch Westfield NJ 1998-2000.

NANNY, Susan Kathryn (Mo) 2831 Eads Ave, Saint Louis MO 63104 B Tulsa OK 1955 d Joe & Patricia. BS U of Texas 1977; MDiv SWTS 1989. D 6/17/1989 Bp Robert Manning Moody P 1/1/1990 Bp Bob Gordon Jones. Cn Chr Ch Cathd S Louis MO 2000-2008; Int S Fran Epis Ch Eureka MO 1997-2000; Trin Ch S Louis MO 1989-1994; Epis City Mssn St Louis MO 1989-1990.

NANTHICATTU, Jacob Philip (NY) 182 Ridge Rd, Valley Cottage NY 10989 **S Paul's And Resurr Ch Wood Ridge NJ 2015-** B Kottayam India 1963 s Chacko & Aleyamma. BA Un Biblic Sem 1990; MA Untd Theol Coll 1998;

Doctor of Theol T.M.A Inst of Counslg 2008. Trans 9/27/2014 Bp Andrew Marion Lenow Dietsche. m 1/3/1994 Mariam Jacob c 2. All SS Epis Ch Vlly Cottage NY 2014-2015; Dir/Rel Counslr All SS Ch 2009-2014.

NANTON-MARIE, Allan Anselm (Fla) PO Box 1-5442, Fort Lauderdale FL 33318 B Port of Spain Saint George TT s Anselm & Ira. Dip Jamaica Bible Coll; BA SUNY Empire St Coll 1975; UTS 1975; MDiv Yale DS 1978; Cert NYU 1986. D 12/8/1996 P 6/15/1997 Bp Stephen Hays Jecko. Int Vic S Kevin's Epis Ch Opa Locka FL 2002-2004; LocTen S Agnes Ch Miami FL 2000-2002; LocTen Dio SE Florida Miami 2000; Asst to the R Dio Florida Jacksonville 1996-1999; S Paul's By-The-Sea Epis Ch Jaxville Bch FL 1996-1998, Par Mssnr 1995-1996; Bd Mem Caribbean Med Relief Assn Los Angeles CA 1987-1991; Advsry Bd Mem New York St Div of Human Rts New York New York 1983-1992; Conciliator New York St Div of Human Rts New York New York 1983-1992; Exec Bd Caribbean-Amer Congr Brooklyn New York 1981-1986; Chairman Sr Citizens Serv of Morrisania Bronx New York 1979-1981; M-in-c New York Conf of the Meth Ch; NY 1974-1981; Evang W Indies Mssn Port of Spain Trinidad & Tobago 1972-1974. Auth, "Caribbean Roots People: The Struggle for Amerindian Survival in the Caribbean," (In press) Cedar Press, Barbados, W.I.; Auth, "Mandate for Caribbean Rituals in Rel Drama," (In press)Jnl of Intl Theol Cntr Atlanta GA. Phi Alpha Delta Law Fraternity, Intl 1987.

NAPOLIELLO, Susan Foster (NCal) 2412 Foothill Blvd No. 31, Calistoga CA 94515 **D S Lk's Mssn Calistoga CA 2015-** B San Francisco CA 1948 d Ben & Margaret. BA U CA - Santa Barbara 1982; BA U CA - Santa Barbara 1982; MA U CA - Santa Barbara 1986; MA U CA - Santa Barbara 1986; MA San Francisco St U 1992; MA San Francisco St U 1992; BA Sch for Deacons 2012; BA Sch for Deacons 2012. D 12/7/2013 Bp Marc Handley Andrus. m 11/12/1999 Edward Russell Napoliello. Fac The Epis Sch for Deacons 2013-2017.

NARAIN, Errol Lloyd (Chi) 125 E 26th St, Chicago IL 60616 B Durban ZA 1949 s Haricharan & Mona. LSED Springfield Durban ZA 1971; Assoc Fed TS AFTS 1980; Assoc Fed TS Other 1980; BA U of Natal 1981; MA U Chi 1985. Trans 4/1/1988 Bp Albert Theodore Eastman. m 12/29/1973 Louisa S Narain c 3. R Trin Ch Chicago IL 1989-2015; Int S Marg's Epis Ch Parkville MD 1988-1989; Chapl S Paul Sch Baltimore MD 1987-1988; Angl Ch of Sthrn Afr 1980-1987. Auth, *Word & Witness*. So Afr Sci and Rel Forum 2012. Fulbright Schlr Fulbright 1984.

NARVAEZ, Alfonso Anthony (WTex) PO Box 8004, Reston VA 20195 B New York NY 1930 s Alfonso & Isabel. BA CUNY 1962; MS Col 1964; MPS NYTS 1984; Dplma Inst Pstr Hisp 1985. D 6/8/1985 P 6/1/1986 Bp John Shelby Spong. m 4/18/1971 Dabney Narvaez c 4. Supply Cler Chr Ch Creswell NC 2006-2010; Asst S Paul's Epis Ch Edenton NC 2000-2003; P-in-c Chr Ch Epis Laredo TX 1993-1998; Vic Trin Ch Paterson NJ 1986-1993; Reporter The New York Times 1969-1993.

NARVAEZ ADORNO, Jose A. (PR) **Asst Vic Iglesia Epis Puertorriquena Arecibo PR 2014-; Vic Iglesia Epis Puertorriquena Utuado PR 2009-** B Corozal, PR 1944 s Sebastian & Juana. BA Seminario San Vicente De Paul 1968; MD Seminario San Vicente De Paul 1972; MD Seminario San Vicente De Paul 1972. Rec 6/1/1988 as Priest Bp Francisco Reus-Froylan. m 6/13/2003 Rebecca Caridad Lopez Ortiz c 3. Vic Dio Puerto Rico Trujillo Alto PR 2009-2014, Vicario 2004-2005, 2002-2003, 1989-1991, Vicario 1982-1987; Vic Iglesia Epis Puertorriquena Arecibo PR 2003-2009; Archd Iglesia Epis Puertorriquena Lares PR 2000-2003; Asst Vic Iglesia Epis Puertorriquena Arecibo PR 1990-2000; Vic Iglesia Epis Puertorriquena Lares PR 1983-1990; Vic Iglesia Epis Puertorriquena Arecibo PR 1980-1983; P Iglesia Catolica Romana Arecibo PR 1968-1975; Dir Hospice Care/Arecibo PR 2002-2013; Gerente Med Care/Arecibo PR 1984-2002; Dir San Lucas Hm Care Ponce PR 1979-1980; Profesor Universidad Interamericana Arecibo PR 1975-1979; Profesor Departamento de Educacion Corozal PR 1975-1977.

NASH, Cynthia Gordon (WNC) 15 Hemlock Ave, Spruce Pine NC 28777 B Winston-Salem NC 1958 d Clyde & Margaret. BS No Carolina St U 1980. D 1/9/2016 Bp Porter Taylor. m 7/12/1980 Charles Fredrick Nash c 1.

NASH, Penny Annette (Va) 6000 Grove Ave, Richmond VA 23226 **S Steph's Ch Richmond VA 2014-** B Louisburg NC 1955 d Willis & Catherine. BA Florida St U 1978; MDiv Candler TS Emory U 2008. D 12/21/2007 Bp J Neil Alexander P 8/9/2008 Bp Keith Whitmore. m 6/16/1989 Thomas A Cox c 2. Assoc R for Yth, Chld & Families Bruton Par Williamsburg VA 2011-2014; S Simon's Epis Ch Conyers GA 2010; Assoc R S Pat's Epis Ch Atlanta GA 2008-2010.

NATERS-GAMARRA, Floyd J (Los) 620 S Gramercy Pl Apt 421, Los Angeles CA 90005 **Died 5/15/2016** B Colon Colon PA 1941 s Septimo & Policarpa. MDiv ETSC 1966; U of Panama Panama City PA 1967. D 6/11/1966 P 12/17/1966 Bp Reginald Heber Gooden. c 2. Asst S Mary's Epis Ch Los Angeles CA 2007-2016; S Phil's Par Los Angeles CA 2003-2006; Dio Los Angeles Los Angeles CA 2000-2003, Mssnr Multicultrl Mnstries & Congreg Dvlpmnt 1999-2003; Dio Massachusetts Boston MA 1995-1999; Cnvr Ethnic Cler 1995-1999; Chapl Ube Mass 1993-1999; Dioc Hisp Com 1990-1999; S Steph's Epis Ch Boston MA 1989-1994; Dio Pennsylvania Philadelphia PA 1988-1989;

S Barn Kensington Philadelphia PA 1983-1988; S Mary's Manhattanville Epis Ch New York NY 1982-1983; Hisp Epis Cntr San Andres Ch Yonkers NY 1979-1982; Chr Ch By The Sea 1976-1979; Dio Panama 1974-1979.

NATHANIEL, Mary (Ak) PO Box 56, Chalkyitsik AK 99788 **Dio Alaska Fairbanks AK 2014-** B Fort Yukon AK 1946 d Fred & Sophie. Cook Coll & TS Tempe AZ. D 6/30/1990 Bp George Clinton Harris P 12/26/2003 Bp Mark Lawrence Macdonald. m 3/26/1983 David Nathaniel c 4.

NATIONS, Christopher Cameron (CFla) 338 E Lyman Ave, Winter Park FL 32789 **Asst All SS Ch Of Winter Pk Winter Pk FL 2015-** B Jackson MS 1989 s James & Janet. BA The U IL 2012; MDiv The TS at The U So 2015. D 1/2/2015 Bp Daniel Hayden Martins P 7/8/2015 Bp Gregory Orrin Brewer. m 7/21/2012 Carly Alane Newton. frcameronn@allsaintswp.com

NATOLI, Anne Marie (EC) 305 Myrtle St, Ashland VA 23005 **Ecclesiashcal Crt Dio E Carolina Kinston NC 2004-** B Watertown NY 1950 d Anthony & Ethel. DMin Austin Presb Sem; BS Russell Sage Coll 1972; MS Med Coll of Virginia 1979; MDiv VTS 1998. D 5/26/1998 P 12/8/1998 Bp Henry Irving Louttit. c 1. R Gr Ch Whiteville NC 2003-2015; S Paul's Ch Albany GA 1999-2003; Dio Georgia Savannah GA 1998. Oblate, Ord of Julian of Norwich 2006; Ord of S Lk.

NATTERMANN, Margaret Ann (WMich) 06685 M-66n, Charlevoix Estates Lot 124, Charlevoix MI 49720 B Philadelphia PA 1948 d Elmer & Edith. BS Alma Coll 1970; MDiv SWTS 1991. D 7/6/1991 P 6/26/1993 Bp Edward Lewis Lee Jr. Ch Of The Nativ Boyne City MI 2006-2014; Int Chr Epis Ch Charlevoix MI 1998-1999; Emm Ch Petoskey MI 1994-1995, 1992-1993.

NATZKE, Vicki (FdL) 7221 Country Village Dr, Wisconsin Rapids WI 54494 **P Ch of St Jn the Evang Wisconsin Rapids WI 2004-** B Wis Rapids WI 1955 d Charles & Joan. BS U of Wisconsin 1978; MEd U of Wisconsin 1983; MDiv Nash 2002. D 12/8/2001 P 6/8/2002 Bp Russell Edward Jacobus. m 8/7/1981 David Ken Natzke c 2. Assoc S Thos Ch Menasha WI 2002-2004.

NAUGHTON, Ezra A (VI) 398 N St Sw, Washington DC 20024 B 1926 s James & Mary. BS Dist of Columbia Teachers Coll 1962; MA How 1965; PhD CUA 1973; MA Washington Theol Consortium 1993. D 12/7/1993 Bp Egbert Don Taylor P 3/1/1995 Bp James Winchester Montgomery. m 5/8/1989 LaVerne Glasgow. Dio Washington Washington DC 1993-1998; Ret. Cath Fllshp Of Epis Ch; Cath Fllshp Of Epis Ch; Washington Dc Cleric Assn; Washington Dc Cleric Assn.

NAUGHTON, Mary Anne (SeFla) 3300A S Seacrest Blvd, Boynton Beach FL 33435 B Brooklyn NY 1943 d John & Nora. BS Ford 1966; MA Ford 1970; MA Ford 1985; Angl Dplma Bexley - Seabury 2015. D 5/30/2015 Bp Leo Frade. m 10/30/1972 William Joseph Naughton c 2.

NAUGHTON, Sharon Yvonne (EMich) St Paul's Episcopal Church, 711 S Saginaw St, Flint MI 48502 B Grand Rapids MI 1937 d Anthony & Isla. BA U of Detroit Mercy 1959. D 10/11/2003 Bp Edwin Max Leidel Jr. Dio Estrn Michigan Saginaw MI 2008-2009.

NAUGLE, Gretchen Rohn (Neb) l535 North 69th Stret, Lincoln NE 68505 B Allentown PA 1943 d Benjamin & Elizabeth. BA Pur 1964; MA U of Iowa 1980; MDiv Luth TS 1994. Rec 9/3/2009 as Priest Bp Joe Goodwin Burnett. m 6/2/1963 Ronald C Naugle c 1. Assoc S Lk's Ch Wymore NE 2010-2015; P Chr Ch Epis Beatrice NE 2010-2013; S Chas The Mtyr Fairbury NE 2010-2011; Int Gr Ch Par -Epis Columbus NE 2009-2010.

NAUMANN, John Frederick (Mont) 1241 Crawford Dr., Billings MT 59102 B Toowoomba Queensland AU 1940 s John & Elsie. Lic S Fran Sem 1966. Trans 3/21/1989 as Priest Bp Charles I Jones III. R S Steph's Ch Billings MT 1989-2005; Serv Ch of Australia 1966-1989.

NAUMANN, Richard Donald (Wyo) 1251 Inca Dr, Laramie WY 82072 **D S Matt's Epis Cathd Laramie WY 2005-; Archd Dio Wyoming Casper 2011-** B Columbia MO 1946 s Hugh & Geraldine. BA U of Missouri 1971; MEd U of Missouri 1972; EdS U of Wyoming 1998. D 2/17/2005 Bp Bruce Caldwell. m 11/16/1968 Mary Barninger Naumann c 2. Chapl Hospice of Laramie Laramie WY 2001-2014. AED 2005.

NAUSKA, Gayle Lynn Carey (Ak) 1703 Richardson Dr, Anchorage AK 99504 **owner - LPC Nauska Counslg Anchorage AK 2010-; P S Mary's Ch Anchorage AK 2007-** B Normal IL 1955 d Omer & Carol. AAS U of Alaska 1988; BA Alaska Pacific U 1990; MS U of LaVerne 1993; MDiv Vancouver TS CA 2009; Cert U of Alaska Anchorage 2010. D 5/11/1997 Bp Albert Theodore Eastman P 3/25/2004 Bp Mark Lawrence Macdonald. m 12/6/1980 Norman Nauska. S Christophers Ch Anchorage AK 2014-2016; Chr Ch Anchorage AK 2003-2007; D All SS' Epis Ch Anchorage AK 1997-2001. AAPC 1994; Amer Counslg Assn 2010.

NAWROCKI, Cynthia Lynn (WMich) 3006 Bird Ave Ne, Grand Rapids MI 49525 **Chapl Bronson Hosp 2003-** B Lansing MI 1947 d Ivan & Marian. D 9/20/2003 Bp Robert R Gepert. m 12/29/1984 Frederick Edwin Nawrocki c 3. D S Mk's Ch Grand Rapids MI 2006-2010; D S Andr's Ch Grand Rapids MI 2003-2008.

NAYLOR, Susan B (Mo) 2905 Wingate Ct, Saint Louis MO 63119 B Ypsilanti MI 1957 d Warren & Ramona. Dplma Barnes Hosp Sch of Nrsng 1991; Dplma The Epis Sch for Mnstry 2002. D 6/3/2004 Bp George Wayne Smith. m 8/

17/1996 Earl Carleton Naylor. D S Mart's Ch Ellisville MO 2010-2012; D / Pstr Assoc Emm Epis Ch S Louis MO 2004-2010; Par Nurse, RN Dss Par Nurse Mnstrs St. Louis MO 1998-2010. "Mnstry Of Hlth And Wholeness: A Par Nrsng Prog," Circut Rider mag /, 2001.

NAZRO JR, A(Rthur) Phillips (Tex) 1201 Castle Hill St Apt 302, Austin TX 78703 **Died 7/10/2016** B New York NY 1937 s Arthur & Frances. BA Rice U 1958; BS Rice U 1959; BD Epis TS of the SW 1966. D 6/8/1966 Bp James Milton Richardson P 5/29/1967 Bp Frederick P Goddard. m 5/29/1964 Lucy Nazro c 4. All SS Epis Ch Austin TX 2001-2009; S Steph's Epis Sch Austin TX 1983-1994; Asst Chapl S Steph Sch 1981-1994; Assoc Trin Ch Galveston TX 1978-1980; R S Paul's Epis Ch Orange TX 1975-1978; Asst R Ch Of The Ascen Clearwater FL 1970-1975; S Jn's Epis Ch Sealy TX 1968-1970; R S Mary's Ch Bellville TX 1968-1970; S Mk's Ch Gladewater TX 1966-1967; Min in charge S Mich And All Ang' Epis Ch Longview TX 1966-1967. Texas Coun for the Hmnts 1997-2002.

NDAI, Domenic M (Pa) 801 Macdade Blvd, Collingdale PA 19023 B 1947 s Ndai & Beth. Kamwenja Coll 1968; BD S Paul Untd TS 1985; STM GTS 1989; MA Evang TS 1996. Trans 2/1/1998 Bp Allen Lyman Bartlett Jr. m 8/10/1974 Anne Wairimu Muthoga c 6. Trin Ch Boothwyn PA 1997-2013.

NDISHABANDI, William K (NJ) 147 Daniel Lake Blvd, Jackson MS 39212 **S Aug's Epis Ch Asbury Pk NJ 2016-** B Kilembe Uganda 1959 BA Haggai Inst for Ldrshp; BA Afr Bible Coll 1995; MA Reformed TS 1999; DCE Carolina U of Theol 2002. Trans 11/1/2002 as Priest Bp Duncan Montgomery Gray III. m 5/24/1986 Naomi M Ndishabandi c 5. Int All SS Ch Jackson MS 2008-2009, R 2006-; Dio Mississippi Jackson MS 2004-2016; Vic S Jn's Ch Leland MS 2001-2006; Vic Ch Of The Redeem Greenville MS 1999-2006. staugustineap@gmail.com

NDUNGU, Samuel Kirabi (Pa) 6361 Lancaster Ave, Philadelphia PA 19151 **The Afr Epis Ch Of S Thos Philadelphia PA 2017-** B Kiambu 1979 s Joseph & Annah. BDiv St Paul's TS 2011; MA Andersonville TS 2012. Trans 10/25/2016 as Priest Bp Daniel Gutierrez. m 5/2/2008 Sylvia Wambui Kirabi c 1.

NEAD III, Prescott Eckerman (USC) 714 Michaels Creek, Evans GA 30809 B Albany,NY 1947 s Prescott & Clara. BA Alfred U 1972; MDiv Sewanee: The U So, TS 1975. D 5/31/1975 P 12/20/1975 Bp Wilbur Emory Hogg Jr. m 6/9/2001 Susan Porterfield c 3. Vic S Aug Of Cbury Aiken SC 1990-2005; R All SS Epis Ch Clinton SC 1984-1990; Coordntr Dio Upper So Carolina Columbia SC 1981-1990; Asst R Ch Of Our Sav Rock Hill SC 1980-1984; R S Andr's Epis Ch Douglas GA 1979-1980; R S Paul's Ch Albany GA 1976-1979; R Chr's Ch Duanesburg NY 1975-1976.

NEAKOK, Willard Payne (Ak) **Dio Alaska Fairbanks AK 2014-** D 8/25/2005 P 2/12/2006 Bp Mark Lawrence Macdonald.

NEAL, Deonna Denice (WA) eSchool of Graduate PME, 600 Chennault Cir, Maxwell Afb AL 36112 B Glendale CA 1972 d William & Jodelle. BS The US-AF Acad 1994; MDiv GTS 2002; MPhil Oxf GB 2005; PhD Other 2010; PhD The U of Notre Dame 2010. D 6/15/2002 P 5/5/2004 Bp John Bryson Chane. Promising Schlr Awd ECF 2003.

NEAL, James Frederick (Oly) 1831 E South Island Dr, Shelton WA 98584 **P S Hugh Of Lincoln Allyn WA 2003-** B Hailey ID 1941 s Harry & Maxine. BS Idaho St U 1963. D 11/30/2002 Bp Sanford Zangwill Kaye Hampton P 6/23/2003 Bp Vincent Waydell Warner. m 6/1/1962 Wilma Larae Bingham.

NEAL, Kristi Hasskamp (WNC) 100 Spring Ln, Black Mountain NC 28711 **Archd Dio Wstrn No Carolina Asheville NC 2011-, Archd 2011-** B Marion NC 1947 d Harry & Patricia. BA Duke 1969; MEd Wstrn Carolina U 1979. D 1/28/2006 Bp Porter Taylor. m 11/28/1998 John Culbreth c 2.

NEAL, Linda (ECR) 41-884 Laumilo St, Waimanalo HI 96795 B Dayton KY 1949 d Lloyd & Mary. D 12/18/1985 Bp Edmond Lee Browning.

NEAL JR, Millard Fillmore (SwFla) 14820 Rue De Bayonne, Clearwater FL 33762 **Asstg P Cathd Ch of S Ptr S Petersburg Fl 2009-; Cn/Pstr Cathd Ch of S Ptr S Petersburg FL 2007-** B Clearwater FL 1929 s Millard & Nettie. BS Bethune-Cookman Coll 1950; S Mary U 1971; MDiv Iliff TS 1973. D 6/11/1988 Bp Gerald Francis Burrill P 2/1/1989 Bp James Winchester Montgomery. c 3. Vic Cathd Ch of S Ptr S Petersburg Fl 2008; Asstg P Cathd Ch of S Ptr S Petersburg Florida 2007-2008; P-in-c Cathd Ch of S Ptr S Petersburg FL 2004-2005; Cn Dio SW Florida Parrish FL 2002-2004; Asstg P Cathd Chuirch of S Ptr S Petersburg 1999-2005; P-in-c All S's Cathd St. Thos VI 1999; Cn Cathd Ch Of S Ptr St. Petersburg FL 1998-2008; Int S Jn's Epis Ch Clearwater FL 1996-1997; Assoc Pstr S Mk's Epis Ch Of Tampa Tampa FL 1990-1995; Assoc R S Giles Ch Pinellas Pk FL 1989-1990.

NEAL, Scott (Vt) PO Box 410, Arlington VT 05250 **R S Paul's Epis Ch White Riv Jct VT 2015-** B Lincoln NE 1957 s William & Maxine. BS U of Maine 1979; MDiv GTS 2007. D 11/29/2006 P 12/1/2007 Bp Thomas C Ely. m 2/16/1980 Elizabeth Neal c 2. R S Jas Epis Ch Arlington VT 2007-2015.

NEAL, William Everett (FdL) B Santa Rosa CA 1940 D 1/10/1965 P 8/9/1965 Bp William Hampton Brady.

NEALE, Alan James Robert (Pa) 316 S 16th St, Philadelphia PA 19102 **R The Ch Of The H Trin Rittenhouse Philadelphia PA 2004-** B London UK 1952 s James & Lilian. BS Lon GB 1973; BA Oxf GB 1976; CTh Oxf GB 1977; MA

Oxf GB 1979. Trans 12/2/1988 Bp Craig Barry Anderson. m 3/9/1987 Wendy E Neale c 4. R S Columba's Chap Middletown RI 1991-2004; Assoc Trin Ch Newport RI 1991; R S Paul's Ch Brookings SD 1988-1990. ajrn316@gmail.com

NEARY, Marlyn Mason (NH) 1935 Us Route 3, Colebrook NH 03576 **Vic S Steph's Epis Mssn Colebrook NH 1998-** B Barton VT 1946 d Percy & Eva. D 3/14/1998 P 9/20/1998 Bp Douglas Edwin Theuner. m 2/25/1967 William Neary.

NEAT, William Jessee (Lex) 311 Washington St, Frankfort KY 40601 **R Ch Of The Ascen Frankfort KY 2011-** B Glasgow KY 1953 s James & June. BS Estrn Kentucky U 1975; MA Wichita St U 1981; MDiv GTS 1999. D 6/11/1999 P 5/13/2000 Bp Michael Whittington Creighton. m 12/16/1973 Virginia S Neat c 1. R Chr Ch Chaptico MD 2003-2011; Assoc R S Jas Ch Lancaster PA 1999-2003. OHC - Assoc (AHC) 1991; Soc of Cath Priests (SCP) 2013. rector@ascensionfrankfort.org

NEBEL, Sue (Chi) 2023 Lake Ave, Wilmette IL 60091 **D S Aug's Epis Ch Wilmette IL 2015-** B Grand Rapids MI 1940 d Edson & Elisabeth. BA Albion Coll 1961; MA U CO 1963; PhD NWU 1969; MDiv SWTS 2007. D 2/7/1998 Bp Herbert Alcorn Donovan Jr. m 7/13/1967 Henry Martin Nebel c 2. D Gr Ch Chicago IL 2011-2014; D S Simons Ch Arlington Hts IL 2008-2011; D The Annunc Of Our Lady Gurnee IL 2004-2008; D Gr Ch Oak Pk IL 2001-2005; D Ch Of The H Fam Lake Villa IL 1999-2000; D S Matt's Ch Evanston IL 1998-1999. Assn for Epis Deacons 1998. Recognition Of Diac Mnstry In The Traditional Of St. Step N Amer Assn For The Dracuete 2005.

NECKERMANN, Ernest Charles (Los) 1107 Foothills Dr, Newberg OR 97132 B Oak Park IL 1937 s Edwin & Martha. BA Elmhurst Coll 1962; STB PDS 1965; MA Untd States Intl U 1977. D 6/24/1965 P 1/2/1966 Bp Chandler W Sterling. m 12/6/1995 Barbara A Sager c 1. St Columbas Epis Ch Big Bear City CA 2000-2003; P-in-c S Paul's Mssn Barstow CA 1995-2000; 1990-1991; Asst R The Epis Ch Of S Andr Encinitas CA 1988-1990; 1981-1987; S Ptr's Epis Ch Del Mar CA 1977-1981; All SS Epis Ch Columbia Falls MT 1968-1976; Vic S Matt's Ch Columbia Fls MT 1968-1976; Vic Chr Ch Sheridan MT 1965-1967; S Paul's Ch Virginia City MT 1965-1967; Trin Ch Ennis MT 1965-1967; Dioc Yth Dir Dio Montana Helena MT 1966-1976.

NEDELKA, Jerome Joseph (LI) PO Box 2016, Miller Place NY 11764 **Bp's Chapl to Ret Cler Dio Long Island Garden City NY 2009-, Archdnry of Suffolk 1998-2009, Great So Bay Dnry 1979-1998, Bp's Chapl to Ret Cler 2005-2009; Ret Dio Long Island Garden City NY 2000-; Chapl NY St Assn of Fire Chapl 1979-** B Flushing NY 1938 s Frank & Marie. Cert Germaine Sch of Photography 1954; BA Wag 1959; MDiv PDS 1965. D 6/19/1965 P 12/21/1965 Bp Jonathan Goodhue Sherman. m 10/9/1960 Ruth A Nedelka c 2. Presiding Judge Eccl Crt Dio Long Island 2006-2009; Instr Eucharistic Ministers Course Dio Long Island Garden City NY 1980-1999; Chapl Islip Fire Dept 1979-2000; R S Mk's Ch Islip NY 1978-2000; Vic Ch Of Chr The King E Meadow NY 1968-1978; Cur All SS Ch Bayside NY 1965-1967; Trst Epis Hlth Serv Far Rockaway NY 1980-2014; Assoc Chapl Hse of Representatives D.C 1973; Assoc Chapl New York St Senate 1968-1974. Chair, Dio.Com. on Environ, "We're Drowning in Our Own Garbage," *Tidings*, Dio Long Island, 1970. New York St Assn of Fire Chapl 1979; Ord of S Lk 1980-2000; P Assoc, OHC 1965. Lifetime Achievement Awd Dio Long Island Camp DeeWolfe 2017; Cn of the Cathd of the Incarn Dio Long Island 2002; Bp's Cross for Distinguished Dioc Serv Dio Long Island 2000; R Emer S Mk's Ch,Islip,NY 2000; Distinguished Trst Untd Hosp Fund/Epis Hlth Serv 2000; Paul Harris Fell Rotary Intl 1995.

NEDS, Walter Eugene (SeFla) 2674 Winkler Ave Apt 411, Fort Myers FL 33901 **Died 12/22/2015** B Lima OH 1926 s John & Florence. Creighton U 1945; LTh VTS 1962; LTh VTS 1976. D 6/9/1962 Bp Nelson Marigold Burroughs P 12/22/1962 Bp William Foreman Creighton. c 3. Ret 1991-2015; Asst to Bp for Mnstry Dio SE Florida Miami 1979-1990; LocTen H Sprt Epis Ch W Palm Bch FL 1977-1979; Asst St Margarets and San Francisco de Asis Epis Ch Hialeah FL 1975-1977; Asst Ch Of The Ascen Miami FL 1974-1975; Vic S Jas The Fisherman Islamorada FL 1972-1974; Assoc Chr Ch Cranbrook Bloomfield Hills MI 1965-1972; Asst S Thos' Par Washington DC 1962-1965. Auth, *The Orgnztn Bridge*, Self-Pub, 1974.

NEED, Merrie Anne Dunham (Colo) 7726 S Trenton Ct, Englewood CO 80112 **S Anne's Epis Sch Denver CO 2005-; Chapl St. Anne's Epis Sch Denver CO 2005-** B Denver CO 1947 d Herbert & June. U of Puget Sound 1966; BA U CO 1969; MEd U of Delaware 1976; U of Sthrn Mississippi 1979; MDiv Bex Sem 1991. D 6/13/1992 P 11/16/1993 Bp William George Burrill. m 7/20/1974 Harry Need c 1. Gd Shpd Epis Ch Centennial CO 2004-2005; Chapl Denver Wmn Correctional Facility Denver CO 2002-2003; The Ch Of The Ascen Denver CO 2002; Peace in Chr Ch Eliz CO 2000-2002; Asst Chr's Epis Ch Castle Rock CO 1999-2000; Non-par Dio Colorado Denver CO 1998-1999; Zion Ch Avon NY 1995; Calv/St Andr's Par Rochester NY 1993-1994.

NEEL, Doug (Colo) 225 S Pagosa Blvd, Pagosa Springs CO 81147 **Dio Colorado Denver CO 2012-; Reg Mssnr Dio Colorado 2011-; R S Pat's Epis Ch Pagosa Sprg CO 2008-** B Fort Benning GA 1954 s Earl & Alice. BD U of

Arkansas 1976; MDiv Nash 1983. D 6/11/1983 Bp Robert Elwin Terwilliger P 5/5/1984 Bp Donis Dean Patterson. m 6/25/1989 Sarah Neel c 3. Stndg Com Dio Colorado 2010-2011; Instr, Sacr Theol Angl TS Dallas TX 2003-2004; R H Trin Ch Rockwall TX 2000-2004; Assoc The Epis Ch Of The Trsfg Dallas TX 1999-2000; Adj P Trsfg Dallas TX 1997-1998; Instr, Sacr Theol Angl Sch of Theol ogy Dallas TX 1985-1987; Rep, BEM Taskforce Grtr Dallas Coun of Ch Dallas TX 1985-1987; Cur S Lk's Epis Ch Dallas TX 1983-1986; Cmsn of Liturg Dio Dallas Dallas TX 1986-1987, Cmsn of Evang 1984-1987.

NEELEY II, Harry Edwin (Mont) 100 W Glendale St #8, Dillon MT 59725 **Ret 1994-; Dir Tri Cnty Tri Par Wood Bank Mnstry 1994-** B Sioux Falls SD 1934 s Thomas & Alice. Ldrshp Acad for New Directions; BS Augustana Coll 1957; BD Epis TS of the SW 1964. D 5/30/1964 P 12/1/1964 Bp James W Hunter. m 8/22/1954 Valrae Neeley c 3. S Andr's Ch Philipsburg MT 1992-1994; S Marks Pintler Cluster Anaconda MT 1987-1994; S Mich Ch Alturas CA 1984-1986, Vic 1982-1984, Vic 1971-1981; Calv Epis Ch Red Lodge MT 1981-1984; Our Sav Epis Joliet MT 1981-1984; Vic S Jude Mssn Field Red Lodge MT 1981-1984; S Paul's of the Stillwater Ch Absarokee MT 1981-1984; R St Jas Epis Ch Dillon MT 1977-1981; Vic S Lk's Ch Lakeview OR 1976-1977; Dn The Epis Dio Nthrn California Sacramento CA 1974-1976; R S Lk's Epis Ch Monrovia CA 1970-1971; Dir S Jude Chld Ranch Boulder City WY 1969-1970; R H Trin Epis Ch Thermopolis WY 1965-1969; Chair C&C Dio Wyoming Casper 1965-1967, Exec Coun 1965-1967; Stndg Com Dio Montana Helena MT 1980-1983.

NEEL-RICHARD, Joanne Louise (Ct) 39 Mckinley Ave, New Haven CT 06515 B San Francisco CA 1945 d Harry & Phyllis. BS U Pgh 1966; MDiv Ya Berk 1988; MS Col 1993. D 6/12/1988 Bp Frank S Cerveny P 1/28/1989 Bp Clarence Nicholas Coleridge. m 12/31/2008 Mary Anne Osborn c 3. Chr Ch New Haven CT 2008-2009; Int Pstr Ch of the H Sprt W Haven CT 2008-2009; P-in-c Trin Ch Wethersfield CT 2001-2006; Dio Connecticut Meriden CT 1999-2007, Stndg Com 1999-2004, Stndg Com Pres 2003-2004; Grtr Waterbury Mnstry Waterbury CT 1998-2001; All SS Ch Wolcott CT 1997-2001; P-in-c S Geo's Ch Middlebury CT 1997-2001; Trin Ch Litchfield CT 1997-2001; Int Old S Andr's Ch Bloomfield CT 1996-1997; Chr Ch Stratford CT 1990-1996; Asst Trin Ch Torrington CT 1988-1990; Int Ch of the H Sprt W Haven CT. Connecticut Soc Clincl Soc Workers Ethics Chair 1996-2000.

NEELY, Christopher Fones (SO) 3580 Shaw Ave 409, Cincinnati OH 45208 B Cincinnati OH 1927 s Uberto & Barbara. BS MIT 1948; MS U of Tulsa 1949; MDiv CDSP 1961; Shalem Inst for Sprtl Gdnc Washington DC 1987. D 6/25/1961 Bp James Albert Pike P 1/19/1962 Bp Roger W Blanchard. c 3. Vic S Phil's Ch Cincinnati OH 1995-2001; Chapl Sprtl Care Serv Hosp Cincinnati OH 1982-1984; R S Jas Westwood 1968-1989; R S Jas Epis Ch Cincinnati OH 1967-1988; R The Epis Ch Of The Ascen Middletown OH 1961-1967. *October*, October Fwd Day by Day, 1991.

NEFF, Shanna (WTex) St Pauls Episcopal Church, PO Box 1148, San Antonio TX 78294 **S Paul's Ch Brady TX 2014-** B Cleveland TX 1963 d Louis & Barbara. BA U of St Thos 1985; MDiv VTS 1991. D 6/22/1991 Bp Maurice Manuel Benitez P 3/26/1992 Bp William Elwood Sterling. m 6/29/1991 Stephen Suarez c 2. Trin Ch Longview TX 2009-2012; Dio Oklahoma Oklahoma City OK 2002-2008; S Aug Of Cbury Oklahoma City OK 2001-2002; H Sprt Epis Ch Houston TX 2000-2001; R S Jn's Epis Ch Silsbee TX 1995-2000; All SS Epis Ch Hitchcock TX 1993-1995; S Fran Epis Day Sch Houston TX 1993; S Mk's Epis Sch Houston TX 1993; S Cyp's Ch Lufkin TX 1991-1992.

NEFSTEAD, Eric (Cal) 275 Burnett Ave Apt 8, San Francisco CA 94131 **Instr Episcolar Sch For Deacons 2005-; Exec Dir, Sojourn Chapl San Francisco Gnrl Hosp 2004-; Sojourn Chapl At San Francisco Generial Hosp 2004-** B Staples MN 1966 s Melvin & Sonja. BA S Olaf Coll 1988; MDiv UTS 1995; CAS CDSP 2005. D 6/1/2002 P 6/7/2003 Bp William Edwin Swing. Sojourn Multifaith Chapl San Francisco CA 2010-2011, 2004-2006.

NEGLIA, Dwight (Nwk) 116 Oakmont Dr, Mays Landing NJ 08330 B Long Island NY 1943 s Louis & Gladys. BA LIU CW Post 1966; MDiv PDS 1969. D 6/14/1969 P 12/1/1969 Bp Jonathan Goodhue Sherman. m 1/22/1966 Nancy E Neglia c 2. R S Agnes The Little Falls NJ 1997-2006; R S Jn's Ch Dover NJ 1981-1997; R Trin Epis Ch Beaver PA 1972-1981; Cur S Geo's Ch Hempstead NY 1969-1972. Ord of S Lk.

NEIDLINGER, Theodore (NI) 125 S Mccann St, Kokomo IN 46901 **Assoc Chr The King Epis Ch Huntington IN 2014-, 2013-2014** B Peoria IL 1950 s Paul & Mildred. BS Indiana St U 1972; MHA Indiana U 1976. D 10/9/1991 Bp Francis Campbell Gray P 2/8/2002 Bp Edward Stuart Little II. m 12/17/1971 Dianne Neidlinger c 2. Asstg P S Andr Epis Ch Kokomo IN 2010-2014, Asstg P 2002-2004, P 1991-2002; P-in-c Trin Epis Ch Logansport IN 2005-2010; Cn for Diac Dio Nthrn Indiana So Bend IN 2000-2002.

NEIGHBORS, Dolores (Chi) 5555 S Everett Ave Apt C-4, Chicago IL 60637 **Hon Cn Cathd Of S Jas Chicago IL 2003-, Hon Cn 2003-, Asstg Cler 2001-2002, Cn Pstr 1997-2000** B Chicago IL 1929 d Roscoe & Ruth. Cert Kennedy-King Coll 1948; Chicago St U 1973; MDiv SWTS 1988. D 6/18/1988 P 12/1/1988 Bp Frank Tracy Griswold III. c 3. Ch Of S Paul And The Redeem Chicago IL 2003-2006; S Chrys's Ch Chicago IL 2000-2001; Dio Chicago Chicago IL 1997-2000; S Edm's Epis Ch Chicago IL 1990-1997; Assoc Ch Of The Epiph Chicago IL 1988-1990. Ntwk of Biblic Story Tellers 1990-2000; UBE 1980-2011.

NEIL, Earl Albert (WA) 4545 Connecticut Ave Nw Apt 929, Washington DC 20008 B Saint Paul MN 1935 s Earl & Katherine. BA Carleton Coll 1957; BD SWTS 1960; MS U CA 1973. D 6/18/1960 Bp Hamilton Hyde Kellogg P 12/17/1960 Bp Edward Clark Turner. m 4/2/1992 Angela Kazzie-Neil c 1. Int Calv Ch Washington DC 1997-2000; Cn Cathd of St Ptr & St Paul Washington DC 1994-1997; Chapl Prov So Afr 1990-1993; Exec Natl Mssn In Ch & Soc Ecec 1986-1994; Stff Off Cltn For Human Needs 1977-1986; Epis Ch Cntr New York NY 1974-1994; R S Aug's Ch Oakland CA 1967-1974; Co-Vic Chr Chicago 1964-1967. Hon DD SWTS 1989; Carl Alum Awd Carleton Coll 1971; Outstanding Young Man In Amer 1970.

NEIL, Judy Kay (Ala) Grace Episcopal Church, 5712 1st Ave N, Birmingham AL 35212 B Paducah KY 1952 d William & Rose. D 10/1/2016 Bp John Mckee Sloan Sr. c 2. jivey1@bellsouth.net

NEILSEN, Eloise (RI) 20 Exeter Blvd, Narragansett RI 02882 B Pawtucket RI 1930 d Harold & Matilda. RN Newton-Wellesley Hosp Sch of Nrsng Lower Falls MA 1951; Sch for Deacons 1988. D 2/4/1989 Bp George Nelson Hunt III. m 8/22/1953 Erling Hugh Neilsen c 4. Chapl Washington Cnty Hospice Narragansett RI 1989-1994. NAAD; Ord of Julian of Norwich 1987. S S Steph's Awd for Diac Mnstry NAAD 1997.

NEILSON, Albert Pancoast (Del) 10 Chickadee Dr, Topsham ME 04086 **Ret 2002-** B Philadelphia PA 1930 s Harry & Alberta. BA Ya 1952; STB GTS 1957; STM NYTS 1972. D 6/1/1957 Bp Charles Francis Hall P 12/12/1957 Bp Richard Stanley Merrill Emrich. c 3. Non-par 1991-2002; Assoc Trin Par Wilmington DE 1964-1990; Vic S Clare Of Assisi Epis Ch Ann Arbor MI 1957-1963. AAPC, Fell 1976.

NEILSON, John Robert (NJ) 39 Yarmouth Ct, Scotch Plains NJ 07076 **Ret 1997-; Ret 1997-** B New York NY 1932 s John & Elizabeth. BA Lycoming Coll 1958; MDiv PDS 1961. D 4/21/1961 P 10/28/1961 Bp Alfred L Banyard. m 5/11/1963 Sandra Neilson. R All SS' Epis Ch Scotch Plains NJ 1969-1997; Vic S Barth's Ch Cherry Hill NJ 1963-1969; Cur Gr Ch Merchantville NJ 1961-1962. Chapl Ord of the Noble Comp of the Swan 1992; Oblate - OSB, Portsmouth Abbey, RI. Phi Alpha Theta.

NEILSON, Kurt Brian (Ore) 2736 SE 63rd Ave, Portland OR 97206 **Legacy Gd Samar Hosp Portland OR 2014-; Adj Fac/pilgrimage Ldr Franciscan Sprtl Cntr 2011-** B Huntington NY 1958 s Henry & Margaret. S Fidelis Coll 1978; BA SUNY 1980; MTS Cath Theol Un 1988; MDiv SWTS 1991. D 6/15/1991 Bp Frank Tracy Griswold III P 1/1/1992 Bp Hays H. Rockwell. m 9/27/1986 Diane Urbano-Neilson c 3. Chapl PRN Serenity Hospice 2013-2014; Sprtl Care intern Legacy Gd Samar Hosp 2012-2013; Co-Dir Acad for Formation and Mssn 2010-2014; S Ptr And Paul Epis Ch Portland OR 2000-2014, R 1995-2000; Cur Emm Epis Ch S Louis MO 1991-1995; Chapl Advncd S Fran Hosp of Evanston 1990-1991; Chapl Res U Chi Hospitals 1988-1989. "Urban Iona," Morehouse 2007. Assn for Clincl-Pstr Educ 1989; Coll of Pstr Supervision and Psych 2014. kbneilson@lhs.org

NEILSON, Lisa Rene (FtW) 902 George Bush Dr, College Station TX 77840 **Dio Texas Houston TX 2016-** B Denver CO 1962 d Russell & Frances. B.A. Syr 1985; M.Div. VTS 2016. D 1/15/2016 Bp James Scott Mayer P 9/22/2016 Bp Rayford Baines High Jr. m 7/9/1988 Robert Dane Neilson c 2. lisa@episcoags.org

NEILY, Robert Edward (Mich) 704 15th St Apt 360, Durham NC 27705 **Hon Cn Cathd Ch of S Paul Detroit MI 2006-** B Swampscott MA 1938 s Fred & Gertrude. BA San Jose St U 1959; MDiv CDSP 1962; MA San Jose St U 1970. D 6/24/1962 Bp James Albert Pike P 6/18/1963 Bp George Richard Millard. m 4/13/1996 Martie W Wernz c 2. R S Mich's Ch Grosse Pointe MI 1980-2006; R S Jn's Par Sn Bernrdno CA 1971-1980; Assoc R Ch Of Our Sav Par San Gabr CA 1969-1971; Asst S Clem's Ch Berkeley CA 1966-1969; Vic S Jn The Div Epis Ch Morgan Hill CA 1964-1966; Ch Of S Jos Milpitas CA 1964-1965; Asst S Mk's Epis Ch Santa Clara CA 1962-1964.

NEIMAN, Judi Ann (WMich) 34462 1st St, Paw Paw MI 49079 B Flint MI 1938 d Francis & Geraldine. AA Aquinas Coll 1958; RN Mercy Cntrl Nrsng Sch 1961; Dplma Div Word Intl Cntr 1971; Dioc study Prog 1987; Cert CPE 1990. D 10/13/1990 Bp Edward Lewis Lee Jr. Chapl Bronson-Lakeview Cmnty Hosp 1991-2006; D Coordntr Dio Wstrn Michigan Kalamazoo MI 1991-2002; D S Mk's Epis Ch Paw Paw MI 1990-2006; Chapl Hospice of SW Michigan 1990-2003. NAAD 1992-2006. Diac Awd Naad 2000.

NEITZEL, Anna C (Dal) 6525 Inwood Road, Dallas TX 75209 B Dallas TX 1946 d Howard & Mary. BS U of Texas 1992; MTS SMU Perkins 2004. D 6/4/2005 Bp James Monte Stanton. m 12/27/1967 James Neitzel c 2. D The Epis Ch Of S Thos The Apos Dallas TX 2009-2013; Dir. Missions Trips & Pilgrimages S Mich And All Ang Ch Dallas TX 2005-2007.

NELSON, Ann Jean (Colo) 2002 Warwick Ln, Colorado Springs CO 80909 **Ret 1996-** B Providence RI 1935 d Edgar & Zabelle. BA Br 1956; MA Br 1959; Cert Epis TS of the SW 1984. D 12/27/1984 Bp William Carl Frey P 6/27/1985 Bp William Harvey Wolfrum. R S Andr's Ch Cripple Creek CO 1991-1996; Asst S Fran Of Assisi Colorado Spg CO 1986-1990; Com Diac Dio Colorado Denver CO 1995-2002, COM 1987-1994. Auth, "A P Looks at D Formation," *DiaKoneo*, 1999. NAAD 1995.

NELSON III, Benjamin Howard (WTex) 3039 Ranch Rd 12, San Marcos TX 78666 **S Mk's Ch San Marcos TX 2012-** B Sewanee TN 1974 s Benjamin & Cammie. BA Millsaps Coll 1996; MDiv Sewanee: The U So, TS 2002. D 6/24/2002 Bp Robert Boyd Hibbs P 2/28/2003 Bp James Edward Folts. m 12/14/2002 Linda Latchford Nelson c 1. P All SS Ch Kapaa HI 2008-2012; Asst to the R S Paul's Epis Ch Chattanooga TN 2004-2008; Cur Ch Of The Gd Shpd Corpus Christi TX 2002-2004.

NELSON SR, Bob (SanD) 330 11th St, Del Mar CA 92014 **D Dio San Diego San Diego CA 2016-, Camp Stevens Bd Mem 2011-2014, Dioc Coun 2004-2007, Com on Ord Mnstry 2003-2006, Property Com Mem 1998-2010; Archd Epis Dio San Diego 2016-** B Saint Louis MO 1939 s Arthur & Lillian. AA El Camino Coll 1960; BS U CA, Los Angeles 1962; ETSBH 1998; ETSBH 2000. D 6/9/2001 Bp Gethin Benwil Hughes. c 4. Cler in Charge S Anne's Epis Ch Oceanside CA 2010-2012; D/Par Admin St. Ptr's Epis Ch Del Mar CA 2007-2009; D S Ptr's Epis Ch Del Mar CA 2005-2009; D Ch Of The Gd Samar San Diego CA 2001-2003. Rotary Grp Study Fell Rotary Intl Fndt 1974. rnelson@edsd.org

NELSON, Charles Herbert (LI) 194-51 Murdock Ave, Saint Albans NY 11412 **D Assist (Prison Mnstry w the Bro of S Andrews) S Gabr's Ch Hollis NY 2017-; Vol Interfaith Hosp 2012-; S Steph's Epis Ch Jamaica NY 2011-; D S Paul's And Resurr Ch Wood Ridge NJ 2004-; Assoc Clincl Chaplin The Coll of Pstr Supervision and Psycholtherapy 2013-; Assoc Pstr Counslr The Coll of Pstr Supervision and Psych 2013-** B Newark NJ 1938 s Thomas & Mabel. Mercer TS; Mercer TS Garden City N.Y.; Newark TS Newark N.J.; Other; St Jn Hosp Far Rockaway N.Y. D 6/5/2004 Bp John Palmer Croneberger. m 4/1/2000 Veronica Nelson c 1. D Asst Dio Long Island Garden City NY 2011-2016; D S Phil's Ch Brooklyn NY 2010; D S Dav's Epis Ch Cambria Heights NY 2008-2011; D S Jos's Ch Queens Vlg NY 2006-2008; S Agnes And S Paul's Ch E Orange NJ 2006-2007; Mnstry Soc Justice Mnstry Newark 1996-1999; Prison Mnstry Yth Hse of Newark 1996-1999. Brookfeild Lion's Club 2015; Bro of St Andr 1996; Queen's Fed of Cler 2014; UBE 1996. Cert of Recognition Trin Cathd 1990.

NELSON, Charles Nickolaus (Minn) Rt 2 Box 283, Park Rapids MN 56470 B Minneapolis MN 1930 s Oscar & Anna. D 5/30/1986 Bp Harold Anthony Hopkins Jr. m 5/30/1955 Adele Elizabeth Nelson c 3. D Geth Cathd Fargo ND 1986-1995. NAAD, ABS.

NELSON, David Scott (Tex) 19330 Pinehurst Trail Dr, Humble TX 77346 **R Chr The King Epis Ch Humble TX 2011-** B Houston TX 1979 s Steven & Susan. BBA S Marys U San Antonio TX 2002; MDiv VTS 2005. D 6/13/2009 Bp Mark Hollingsworth Jr P 1/30/2010 Bp David Charles Bowman. m 7/25/2009 Beth Anne Nelson c 1. Campus Mssnr/D in Charge S Jn's Epis Ch Bowling Green OH 2009-2011.

NELSON, Elizabeth Anne (Ida) B Fort Worth TX 1955 d Michael & Percy. BA U of No Texas 1976. D 5/1/2011 P 11/6/2011 Bp Brian James Thom. m 4/16/1987 Andrew Otis Nelson c 2. Assoc P S Antony Of Egypt Silverdale WA 2013.

NELSON, Elizabeth Lane (CFla) 705 Jefferson Ave, Lehigh Acres FL 33936 **R S Fran Of Assisi Epis Ch Lake Placid FL 1999-, R 1998-** B Fall River MA 1948 d Everett & Lottie. BD U of Rhode Island 1991; MDiv VTS 1996. D 12/1/1998 P 6/13/1999 Bp John Wadsworth Howe. m 5/14/2011 Joel D Nelson c 5. BStA Chapl 1996; DOK Dioc Chapl 2006; Cert of S Lk 1994.

NELSON, Genevieve Elizabeth (SVa) 7400 Hampton Blvd, Norfolk VA 23505 B Fort Ord CA 1988 d Carl & Jillian. BA U CO 2016. D 4/16/2016 Bp Herman Hollerith IV. m 5/14/2007 Wayne Chancey Nelson.

NELSON, Geri Lee (Ga) 129 Viewcrest Dr, Hendersonville NC 28739 B Pikeville KY 1948 d Frelin & Edith. D 12/18/1999 Bp Robert Carroll Johnson Jr. m 6/9/1990 Richard A Nelson. S Thos Ch Savannah GA 2005-2012; D Ch Of The H Fam Mills River NC 1999-2001.

NELSON, James Craig (WTex) 2500 N 10th St, McAllen TX 78501 **R S Jn's Ch McAllen TX 2011-** B Woodward OK 1949 s Gene & Eula. SW Oklahoma St U 1969; BS Oklahoma St U 1971; MDiv VTS 1989. D 6/17/1989 P 1/1/1990 Bp Robert Manning Moody. m 9/7/1968 Linda R Nelson c 1. R Ch Of The Gd Shpd Friendswood TX 2000-2011; R Epis Ch Of The Resurr Oklahoma City OK 1989-2000.

NELSON, James Lowell (Mass) 1218 Heatherwood, Yarmouth Port MA 02675 **Died 11/28/2016** B Owatonna MN 1926 s Robert & Carol. BS U of Arizona 1950; MDiv Bex Sem 1964. D 6/1/1964 Bp Anson Phelps Stokes Jr P 5/30/1965 Bp Frederic Cunningham Lawrence. m 3/28/1976 Anne V R Nelson. Ret 1990-2016; R Ch Of The H Nativ S Weymouth MA 1972-1989; Founding S Dav's Epis Ch S Yarmouth MA 1966-1973; Cur S Andr's Ch Framingham MA 1964-1965. Boston Cleric Club 1964-1990.

NELSON, J Douglas (SD) 21 rue du Sourdonnet, Les Mathes SD 17570 France **Pasteur Eglise Reformee De Vincennes 1993-** B Whitefish MT 1952 s Thurlow & Joann. BA MI SU 1974; MDiv Colgate Rochester Crozer DS 1978;

N

MDiv CRDS 1978. D 11/10/1978 Bp George T Masuda P 7/1/1979 Bp Walter H Jones. m 7/11/1981 Christel Thobois. Pasteur Eglise Reformee De S Quentin France 1985-1993; Non-par 1983-1985; Chapl S Ptr Angl Chantilly France 1982-1983; Chr Epis Ch Milbank SD 1978-1981; Dio So Dakota Pierre SD 1978-1981; M-in-c S Mary Webster SD 1978-1981; M-in-c S Mary's Epis Ch Webster SD 1978-1981.

NELSON, Jeffrey Scott (Neb) 1714 Short Street, North Platte NE 69101 **R Ch of Our Sav No Platte NE 2010-; Bp and Trst Com Dio Nebraska Omaha NE 2012-** B Milwaukee WI 1959 s Kenneth & Sharon. BA Valparaiso U 1982; MDiv Luth TS at Chicago 1986; ThD Luther TS 1997. Rec 1/7/2010 Bp James Louis Jelinek. c 3. S Fran Of Assisi Epis Ch Lake Placid FL 2013. Auth, "Chr Has No Body Now But Yours: Sermons for Lent and Easter," Parson's Porch, 2015; Auth, "Lg Grp Wrshp Resource," *2016 Luth Outdoor Mnstry Curric*, Evang Luth Ch in Amer, 2015. rector.cosnp@gmail.com

NELSON, Joseph Reed Peter (NJ) 715 Magie Ave, Elizabeth NJ 07208 **Nhcac Hlth Cntr 1994-; Non-par 1993-** B Tuscaloosa AL 1941 s Hugh & Sarah. BA U NC 1964; BD EDS 1967; MS Col 1971; PhD NYU 1976. D 12/18/1970 P 6/1/1971 Bp Horace W B Donegan. m 3/16/1968 Lynne Nelson c 1. Int St Jn the Bapt Epis Ch Linden NJ 1991-1992; Vice-Pres Of External Affrs Interfaith Med Cntr Brooklyn NY 1985-1991; Non-par 1983-1991; Dio Connecticut Meriden CT 1979-1981; Vic Ascen Ch New Haven CT 1971-1983; Serv All Ang' Ch New York NY 1970-1971. Karatana 1971. Morehead Schlr U Nc 1959; Spec Citation For Serv 83 Mayor; Ml King Awd 82 New Haven Publ Schs.

NELSON, Joshua D (NI) B Portsmouth OH 1987 s Eli & Charla. D 12/23/2016 P 6/24/2017 Bp Doug Sparks.

NELSON, Julie (ECR) 532 Tyrella Ave Apt 30, Mountain View CA 94043 B Fort Rucker AL 1969 d James & Judy. BS California St U Fresno 1993; MDiv GTS 2008. D 6/21/2008 Bp Mary Gray-Reeves P 1/24/2009 Bp Eugene Taylor Sutton. c 2. P Assoc for Evang Gd Samar Epis Ch San Jose CA 2011-2013; Assoc R St Martins-In-The-Field Ch Severna Pk MD 2008-2010.

NELSON, Julie F (NwPa) 140 Oyster Pond Rd, Falmouth MA 02540 **Died 7/29/2016** B Philadelphia PA 1931 d William & Isabel. BA Col 1972; CTh EDS 1992; MDiv VTS 1994. D 7/8/1995 P 1/13/1996 Bp Robert Deane Rowley Jr. Ch of the Ascen Munich 2001-2002; COM Dio NW Pennsylvania Erie PA 1996-2002; Vic Ch Of The H Cross No E PA 1995-2002; Chapl Brevillier Vill Erie PA 1995-1996.

NELSON, Leilani Lucas (Cal) 3973 17th St, San Francisco CA 94114 B Honolulu HI 1948 d Joseph & Lois. L&C; U of Hawaii; BTh California Sch for Deacons 1988. D 12/2/1989 Bp William Edwin Swing. m 12/27/1973 Lowell Thomas Nelson c 2. S Andr's Epis Ch San Bruno CA 2002-2010; D Fam Assoc S Paul's Epis Ch Burlingame CA 1999-2002; Yth Min S Matt's Epis Ch San Mateo CA 1990-1999; Ch Adminstrator S Fran' Epis Ch San Francisco CA 1988-1990.

NELSON JR, Levine S (Pa) Po Box 1105, Norristown PA 19404 B Buffalo NY 1945 s Levine & Marian. BA Hobart and Wm Smith Colleges 1967; MDiv PDS 1970. D 6/29/1970 Bp Harold Barrett Robinson P 4/27/1973 Bp Robert Lionne DeWitt. m 7/3/1967 Holly Munn. Asst All SS Ch Norristown PA 1986-2008; Non-par 1977-1985; Asst S Christophers Epis Ch Oxford PA 1972-1976; Asst H Sacr Highland Pk PA 1970-1972.

NELSON, Raymond A (SVa) 3850 Pittaway Dr, Richmond VA 23235 **Headmaster Trin Epis Sch 1986-** B Brooklyn NY 1932 s Raymond & Georgena. Wms 1954; Harv 1957; EDS 1960. D 10/9/1966 Bp George E Rath P 12/1/1967 Bp Leland Stark. m 8/13/1955 Rosemary Davenport King. Asst The Epis Ch Of The Adv Kennet Sq PA 2009-2013; Cur S Lk's Ch Gladstone NJ 1966-1967; Serv Fed Of Ch.

NELSON, Richard A (Ga) 7607 Lynes Ct, Savannah GA 31406 B Cadillac MI 1953 s Leonard & Ruth. BA Cntrl Michigan U 1976; MDiv SWTS 1983. D 3/25/1983 Bp Quintin Ebenezer Primo Jr P 9/29/1983 Bp James Winchester Montgomery. m 6/9/1990 Geri Lee Nelson c 2. R S Thos Ch Savannah GA 2004-2017; R Ch Of The H Fam Mills River NC 1997-2004; Assoc S Jas Epis Ch Hendersonvlle NC 1993-1997; Asstg S Wlfd's Epis Ch Sarasota FL 1989-1992; S Bon Ch Sarasota FL 1988-1989; R S Alb's Ch Chicago IL 1985-1987; Cur Ch Of The Ascen Chicago IL 1983-1985. Assoc, CT 1994.

NELSON JR, Richard L (NwT) Po Box 82, Burton TX 77835 **Salem Evang Luth Ch Brenham TX 2016-; Pstr (R) Greenvine Emm Luth Ch Burton TX 2007-** B Sedalia MO 1976 s Carol. BA U of Missouri 1998; MDiv Epis TS of the SW 2004. D 6/5/2004 P 12/11/2004 Bp C Wallis Ohl. m 8/22/1997 Karen Rochelle Nelson c 2. Pstr Emm Luth Ch of Greenvine Burton TX 2007-2014; Chapl All SS Epis Sch Lubbock TX 2004-2007; Assoc R S Steph's Ch Lubbock TX 2004-2007. revrichnelson@gmail.com

NELSON, Rita Beauchamp (Del) 30895 Crepe Myrtle Dr Unit 66, Millsboro DE 19966 **Gvnr Appointed Bd Mem/Treas Chld Placement Revs Bd 2014-; Secy/Treas/Cmncatn Integrity Delaware 2011-** B Detroit MI 1939 d Edgar & Antoinette. BS Sacr Heart U, Fairfield, CT 1975; MBA U of Connecticut, Storrs, CT 1981; MDiv VTS 1999; Cert in Spriitual Direction Franciscan U, Steubenville, Ohio 2000; Cert in Spriitual Direction Franciscan U, Steubenville, Ohio 2003. D 6/12/1999 P 12/12/1999 Bp John Bailey Lipscomb. m 3/21/1980

Ralph William Peters c 2. Diac Formation Dir Dioc Coun Inc Wilmington DE 2005-2012; R S Phil's Ch Laurel DE 2005-2009; R The Ch Of The Ascen Claymont DE 2001-2005; Cur S Jn's Epis Ch Clearwater FL 1999-2000; Bd Mem/Treas Integrity Delaware Chapt 2011-2014; Bd Mem/Treas Primeros Pasa Early Lrng Centere 2007; Bd Mem Laurel Boys & Girls Club 2005-2008; Mem Dio. of DE COM 2003-2013; COM Dio Delaware Wilmington 2003-2013, Personl Com 2002-2005; Bd Mem Claymont Cmnty Cntr 2002-2005; Mem Dio. of DE Personl & Plcy Com 2001-2003. Auth, "Always Kristen," *Bk*, Create Space, 2017; Auth, "It's 'T' Time," *LivCh*, LivCh, 2003; Auth, "Jesus Wept," *AM-BO*, VTS, 1998; Auth, "Quiet Day," *Catalog*, VTS, 1997. Integrity 2009-2012. revrita23@gmail.com

NELSON JR, Robert Mitchell (Nev) 3609 Casa Grande Ave, Las Vegas NV 89102 **Ret 1995-** B Evanston IL 1941 s Robert & Ruth. BS U of New Mex 1966. D 5/19/1987 P 11/1/1987 Bp Stewart Clark Zabriskie. m 8/15/1964 Kathy Amanda Atchison. Cn To The Ordnry Dio Nevada Las Vegas 2002-2014.

NELSON, Robert William (Ak) 93 Laukahi St, Kihei HI 96753 B Torrance CA 1939 s Lee & Marie. AA El Camino Coll 1958; BA U CA 1961; Rel.D TS at Claremont 1965; Grad Cert U of Geneva/WCC 1971. D 1/7/1979 P 12/1/1979 Bp David Rea Cochran. c 2. Chapl Maui Memi Med Cntr 2011-2017; Vol Coordntr Hale Kau Kau 2001-2017; Pstr Counslg Consult & Supvsr Samar Centers (Anchorage Fairbanks Honolulu) 1983-2006; Assoc R S Mary's Ch Anchorage AK 1979-2001; Dir Untd Campus Mnstry Fairbanks AK 1969-1974; Serv Methodist Ch 1965-1979. AAPC, AAMFT 1965-2001; Mar Fam Ther 1976-2001. bobnorma@me.com

NELSON, Roger (Mass) 557 Salem St, Malden MA 02148 **Assoc Par Of The Epiph Winchester MA 2003-** B Weymouth MA 1940 s Carl & Marjorie. BA Trin Hartford CT 1962; MDiv EDS 1966. D 6/25/1966 P 6/3/1967 Bp Anson Phelps Stokes Jr. c 1. R S Jn's Epis Ch Saugus MA 1973-2003; Cur Epis Ch Of S Thos Taunton MA 1966-1973. Bd Ch & Hm Soc 1973; Marg Coffin PB Soc 1998. Phi Beta Kappa Trin, Hartford, CT 1961; Pi Gamma MU Trin, Hartford, CT 1961.

NELSON, Sarah Lee (Del) Saint James Episcopal Church, 2 S Augustine St, Newport DE 19804 **S Jas Epis Ch Newport Newport DE 2002-; St Jas the Great Epis Ch Newport Bch CA 2002-; Non-par 1993-** B Washington DC 1957 d Thomas & Margaret. BA Duke 1979; MS CUA 1982; MDiv Duke DS 1986. D 6/13/1987 Bp Edward Lewis Lee Jr P 6/17/1989 Bp John Shelby Spong. c 5. The Epis Ch Of The Adv Kennet Sq PA 1995-1997; Vic S Gabr's Ch Oak Ridge NJ 1990-1993; Asst to R S Ptr's Ch Mtn Lks NJ 1988-1990; Asst Chapl S Agnes Sch Alexandria VA 1987-1988; D S Ptr's Epis Ch Arlington VA 1987-1988.

NELSON-AMAKER, Melana (WA) 8001 Annapolis Rd, New Carrollton MD 20784 **S Chris's Ch New Carrollton MD 2014-** B Pittsburgh PA 1955 d Frank & Alberta. BA Carnegie Mellon U 1981; MDiv Pittsburgh TS 1988. D 6/4/1988 P 5/20/1989 Bp Alden Moinet Hathaway. m 9/26/1981 Derek Leon Amaker. S Phil's Ch Annapolis MD 2010-2011; Trin Ch Washington DC 2009-2010; VTS Alexandria VA 2008-2012; Trin Epis Ch Charlottesvlle VA 1996-2007; Sacramentalist All SS Ch Aliquippa PA 1993-1994; Int Ch Of The Epiph Avalon PA 1990-1992; Cur Emm Ch Pittsburgh PA 1989-1990; Int Ecum Cmnty Of Recon Pittsburgh PA 1987-1988.

NELSON-LOW, Jane (Spok) 719 W. Montgomery Ave, Spokane WA 99205 B San Jose CA 1943 d Clifton & Margaret. Arizona St U 1961; BA Linfield Coll 1970; MDiv CDSP 1991. D 6/18/1991 Bp Robert Louis Ladehoff P 2/27/1992 Bp William Benjamin Spofford. c 3. H Trin Epis Ch Wallace ID 2004-2010; Vic Emm Ch Kellogg ID 2004-2007; Assoc Cathd Of S Jn The Evang Spokane WA 2000-2004; Sr Assoc S Barn On The Desert Scottsdale AZ 1998-2000; Asst Chr Ch Par Lake Oswego OR 1991-1998.

NEMBHARD, Ralston Bruce (CFla) 8413 Clematis Ln, Orlando FL 32819 B Manchester Jama CA 1955 s David & Iris. BA U of The W Indies 1981; STM Ya Berk 1988. Trans 1/19/1998 Bp John Wadsworth Howe. m 9/4/1982 Heather Yvonne Nembhard c 2. R The Epis Ch Of S Jn The Bapt Orlando FL 1997-2009; Serv Ch Prov W Indies 1981-1997. Auth, "Prayers From The Cross," 1983; Auth, "You & Your Neighbour In A Broken Wrld," 1982. BSA; Steadfast Ministers.

NEMES, John Dale (Oly) 16920 Se 40th Pl, Bellevue WA 98008 **Asst S Marg 1986-; D S Lk's Epis Ch Elma WA 1981-** B Glenwood MN 1944 s John & Beth. BS U MN 1969; LLD Wm Mitchell Coll 1974. D 12/14/1981 Bp Robert Marshall Anderson. m 8/20/1966 Mary Elizabeth Brooks c 2. Asst S Paul's Ch Winona MN 1982-1986.

NERN JR, William B (Cal) B Wheeling WA 1940 s William & Ruth. BA Bethany Coll 1962; MDiv CDSP 1971. D 6/26/1971 Bp George Richard Millard P 1/2/1972 Bp Chauncie Kilmer Myers. c 2. Epis Cmnty Serv San Francisco CA 1987-1994; Epis Sanctuary San Francisco CA 1986-1993; Ch Of The Redeem San Rafael CA 1974-1986; Asst S Andr's Ch Saratoga CA 1971-1974.

NERUD, Barbara Jeanne (Neb) B Norrill NE 1931 d Glen & Ethel. D 9/6/2005 Bp Joe Goodwin Burnett. m 8/27/1950 Jack Nerud c 4. D Dio Nebraska Omaha NE 2005-2011.

NESBIT, Pamela (Pa) 16 Belmont Sq, Doylestown PA 18901 **Archd Cathd Ch of Our Sav Philadelphia PA 2016-; Dio Pennsylvania Philadelphia PA 2013-** B Montebello CA 1947 d Bud & Silva. BA U CA 1968; MA Tem 1970; PhD Tem 1976; Pennsylvania Diac Sch 1996. D 9/22/1996 Bp Franklin Delton Turner. m 11/26/1988 C Clifton Nesbit c 1. D S Paul's Ch Doylestown PA 2012-2015; D Ch Of The H Nativ Wrightstown PA 2009-2011; D S Andr's Ch Yardley PA 1999-2008; D Gd Shpd Ch Hilltown PA 1996-1998. Assn for Epis Deacons 1993; Diakonia of the Americas and Caribbean 2007.

NESBIT JR, William (Chi) 917 Wildwood Ct, St. Charles IL 60174 **Gr Ch Jefferson City MO 2017-** B Chicago Heights IL 1958 s William & Nancy. AS Valparaiso U 1979; BS U IL 1982; MDiv SWTS 1996. D 6/15/1996 P 12/1/1996 Bp Frank Tracy Griswold III. m 9/22/1984 Beverly Kaye Nesbit c 2. Gr Epis Ch New Lenox IL 2016-2017; S Chris's Epis Ch Oak Pk IL 2015-2016; R S Chas Ch St. Chas IL 2000-2015; Asst R S Andr's Ch Downers Grove IL 1996-2000; Stndg Com Dio Chicago Chicago IL 2005-2010, Dioc Coun 1998-2004, Yth Coun 1996-2004. billnesbit@att.net

NESBITT, John Russell (EO) 3846 NE Glisan St, Portland OR 97232 **R S Dav's Epis Ch Portland OR 1990-** B Poughkeepsie NY 1936 s Garven & Mary. BS SUNY 1958; MS WA SU 1980; SWTS 1998. D 12/16/1973 Bp James Walmsley Frederic Carman P 1/2/1987 Bp Rustin Ray Kimsey. m 8/20/1960 Ellen Ascherfeld Nesbitt c 2. Vic S Lk's Ch Lakeview OR 1986-1990; S Andr's Epis Ch Florence OR 1974-1979. NNECA 1988; ORCA 1988.

NESBITT, Margot Lord (Okla) 1703 N Hudson Ave, Oklahoma City OK 73103 B Tonbrigde Kent UK 1927 d Douglas & Octave. BA U of Oklahoma 1950; BFA U of Oklahoma 1971; MA U of Oklahoma 1975; Cert Oklahoma Diac Trng Sch 1988; PhD U of Oklahoma 1988; Epis TS of the SW 1994. D 6/26/1988 Bp Gerald Nicholas Mcallister P 6/18/1994 Bp Robert Manning Moody. m 6/6/1948 Charles Rudolph Nesbitt c 3. P S Paul's Cathd Oklahoma City OK 1994-2012. Benedictine Oblate 1995. Hon Cn Dio Oklahoma 1997.

NESBITT, Paula Diane (Cal) 577 Forest St., Oakland CA 94618 **The Epis Ch Of S Mary The Vrgn San Francisco CA 2017-; Vstng Schlr Grad Theol Un Berkeley CA 2011-; non-stipendiary P Assoc All Souls Par In Berkeley Berkeley CA 2002-; GBEC, Mem GC- Epis Ch Cntr New York NY 2012-2018; Com on the Status of Wmn, Chair Exec Coun Appointees New York NY 2012-, Com on the Status of Wmn, Mem 2009-2012; Cont Indaba Evaltn Team Angl Comm Off London 2009-** B Seattle WA 1948 d John & Ellen. BS U of Oregon; MDiv Harvard DS 1987; MA Harv 1987; PhD Harv 1990. D 7/5/1991 Bp Robert Louis Ladehoff P 2/26/1992 Bp William Jerry Winterrowd. m 3/26/2000 L Kirk Kirk Miller. Vstng Assoc Prof U CA Berkeley CA 2001-2011; Actg Dir C.M. Williams Inst for Ethics and Values U. of Denver 1999-2001; Vstng Assoc Prof U Denv Denver CO 1998-1999; Asst S Barn Epis Ch Denver CO 1991-2001; Asst/Assoc Prof Iliff TS Denver CO 1990-1998; Bd Mem Rel Resrch Assn 2007-2011; Grad Fllshp Selection Com ECF Inc New York NY 1995-2000; BEC, Mem Dio Colorado Denver CO 1992-1996. Adaptor/Ed, "Living Recon," Forw Mvmt, 2014; Auth, "Mnstry in Occupational Transformation," *A Point of Balance: The Weight and Measure of Anglicanism*, Morehouse, 2012; Auth, "Keepers of the Tradition: Rel Professionals and their Careers," *Handbook of the Sociol of Rel*, Sage, 2007; Ed, "Rel and Soc Plcy," AltaMira, 2001; Auth, "Epis Ch and Bk of Common Pryr," *Contemporary Amer Rel*, Macmillan Libr Reference, 2000; Co-Auth, "Wmn Status in the Ch," *Gender Mosaics*, Roxbury Press, 2000; Auth, "Feminization of the Cler in Amer," Oxf Press, 1997; Auth, "Sexual Orientation as a Justice Issue Dilemmas of Postmodern Soc Philos and Rel for Civil Rts," *Soc Justice Resrch*, 1997; Auth, "First and Second Career Cler," *Journ for the Sci Study of Rel*, 1995; Auth, "Mar, Parenthood and the Mnstry," *Sociol of Rel*, 1995. SSA 2005. Distinguished Article Awd Amer Sociol Assn, Sociol of Rel Sectn 1997.

NESHEIM, Donald Oakley (Minn) 10785 Valley View Rd #114, Eden Prairie MN 55344 **Ret 2003-; Dio Minnesota 2003-** B Dupree SD 1937 s Melvin & Marjorie. BD U of Nebraska 1971; GW 1973; MDiv Sewanee: The U So, TS 1984. D 6/17/1984 Bp Walter H Jones P 12/21/1984 Bp Craig Barry Anderson. c 3. Long Term Supply Epiph Epis Ch S Paul MN 2007-2008; P-in-c S Matt's Epis Ch Minneapolis MN 1997-1999; Cn Adminstrator Dio Minnesota Minneapolis MN 1992-2002; R S Andr's Epis Ch Minneapolis MN 1992-2002; P-in-res S Chris's Epis Ch S Paul MN 1991-1992; Dn of the Pine Ridge Dnry Dio So Dakota Pierre SD 1987-1991, Adminstrator of the Pine Ridge Dnry 1985-1986; R S Katharine's Ch Mart SD 1984-1991. Ord of S Lk 1981. Legion of Merit US-A 1977.

NESIN, Leslie Frances (Me) Po Box 358, Howland ME 04448 **Transitional D S Mart's Epis Ch Palmyra ME 2003-** B Dayton OH 1944 RN JHU. D 4/26/2003 P 11/9/2003 Bp Chilton Richardson Knudsen. Ch Of The Gd Shpd Houlton ME 2004-2011; Dio Maine Portland ME 2003-2004.

NESMITH, Elizabeth Clare (LI) 305 Carlls Path, Deer Park NY 11729 **P-in-c Chr Ch Babylon NY 2011-** B Marietta GA 1953 BS Wstrn Carolina U 1976; MA U IL 1981; MDiv GTS 2005. D 6/11/2005 P 2/11/2006 Bp John Palmer Croneberger. S Bon Epis Ch Lindenhurst NY 2014-2017; S Ptr's by-the-Sea Epis Ch Bay Shore NY 2011-2014; Exec Dir, Epis Chars Dio Long Island

Garden City NY 2007-2011; Epis Chars of Long Island Inc. Garden City NY 2007-2011; S Jn's Of Lattingtown Locust Vlly NY 2005-2007.

NESS, Jerry (Neb) 803 Avenue E Pl, Kearney NE 68847 B Chicago IL 1952 BA Wabash Coll 1976; MA Loyola U 1996; MDiv SWTS 1999. D 6/19/1999 Bp Bill Persell P 12/17/1999 Bp James Louis Jelinek. R S Lk's Ch Kearney NE 2007-2017; Asstg P Cathd Of S Jas Chicago IL 2002-2007; R Ch Of The Medtr Chicago IL 2002-2007; R S Mart's Epis Ch Fairmont MN 1999-2002.

NESS, Louisett Marie (Chi) 466 W Jackson St, Woodstock IL 60098 **D Ch Of The Incarn Bloomingdale IL 2008-** B 1948 D 2/5/2005 Bp Bill Persell. c 4.

NESS, Zanne Bartlett (ND) 1971 Mesquite Loop, Bismarck ND 58503 **Cn Dio No Dakota Fargo ND 2011-, Cn Mssnr 2011-; Asstg P St. Geo's Epis Ch 2011-** B Canadian TX 1941 d William & Fermanetta. BS W Texas A&M U 1987; MA W Texas A&M U 1990; PhD U of So Dakota 1994. D 6/8/2007 P 2/12/2011 Bp Michael Smith. m 7/19/2003 Terrance Ness c 3. zannec@bis.midco.net

NESTA, Paul A (NI) **S Paul's Epis Ch Laporte IN 2015-** Trans 9/9/2014 as Deacon Bp Paul Emil Lambert.

NESTLEHUTT, Abigail Crozier (Pa) Po Box 517, Saint Michaels MD 21663 **S Ptr's Ch In The Great Vlly Malvern PA 2016-** B Boston MA 1969 d William & Prudence. BA Ya 1991; MDiv Harvard DS 1995; STM GTS 1998. D 12/19/1998 P 12/4/1999 Bp M(Arvil) Thomas Shaw. m 1/13/2001 Mark S Nestlehutt c 2. Dio Easton Easton MD 2015; P-in-c All Faith Chap Miles River Par Easton MD 2012-2015; Assoc R Chr Ch St Michaels Par S Mich MD 2003-2010; Assoc R S Chrys's Ch Chicago IL 2001-2003; Asst to R S Barn Ch Falmouth MA 1999-2001. abigail@dioceseofeaston.org

NESTLEHUTT, Mark S (Eas) 115 West Chestnut, PO Box 517, Saint Michaels MD 21663 B Atlanta GA 1962 s Milton & Betty. AB U GA 1984; BA Georgia St U 1985; MA Georgia St U 1986; MDiv EDS 1997. D 6/5/1999 P 6/3/2000 Bp M(Arvil) Thomas Shaw. m 1/13/2001 Abigail Crozier c 2. S Mary's At The Cathd Philadelphia PA 2017; R Chr Ch St Michaels Par S Mich MD 2003-2016; Assoc R S Chrys's Ch Chicago IL 2001-2003; Bp's Stff Dio Massachusetts Boston MA 2000-2001, Pstr Response Team 1998-2000, Assessement Revs Com 1996-2000; Cur Ch Of S Jn The Evang Hingham MA 1999-2000; Rel Tchr Epiph Sch Dorchester MA 1998-2000; Rel Tchr The Epiph Sch 1998-2000; Stndg Com Dio Easton Easton MD 2015-2006, Fin Com 2014-2008, Personl & Compstn Com 2014-, Chair, Comp Dio Relatns 2007-2014. Auth, *Sprtlty for You*, Forw Mvmt Press, 1999; Auth, "Chalcedonian Christology," *Journ of Ecum Stds*, Temple Press, 1998; Auth, "Anglicans in Greece," *Angl and Epis Hist*, 1996. mark@christstmichaels.org

NESTLER, Mary June (U) 8700 S. Kings Hill Dr, Cottonwood Heights UT 84121 **Exec Off Dio Utah Salt Lake City UT 2007-, Cn for Mnstry Formation 2006-2010** B Colorado Springs CO 1951 d Karl & Margaret. BMus The Curtis Inst of Mus 1975; MDiv GTS 1979; MA S Mary Sem Baltimore MD 1985; CPhil U CA 1992. D 6/12/1979 Bp David Keller Leighton Sr P 12/16/1979 Bp Robert Bruce Hall. c 2. The Epis Ch In Utah Salt Lake City UT 2006; Schlr In Res S Jas Par Los Angeles CA 1998-2006; Asst All SS Ch Pasadena CA 1993-1997; Dn and Pres Bloy Hse Claremont CA 1992-2006, 1989-1990, 1982-1986; P-in-c Epis Ch Of S Andr And S Chas Granada Hills CA 1991-1992; P-in-c S Geo's Mssn Hawthorne CA 1989-1991; Asst to R St Gregorys Epis Ch Long Bch CA 1983-1986; Instr Ch Hist Epis Theol Sch Claremont 1981-1990; P-in-c S Jn's And H Chld Wilmington CA 1981; Chapl Pilgrim Sch 1980-1984; Asst All SS Par Beverly Hills CA 1980-1981; Chapl S Marg's Sch Tappahannock VA 1979-1980. Cn Of Cathd Cntr Of S Paul Bp Borsch Of Dio Los Angeles 2001; Fell The ECF 1985. mjnestler@episcopal-ut.org

NESTOR, Elizabeth M (RI) 57 South Rd, Wakefield RI 02879 **Clincl Prof of Emergency Med Br Med Sch 2011-; Attending Physcn Rhode Island Hosp 1994-; Vice Chair of Fac Dvlpmt Dept of EM Brown Med Sch 2014-; Clincl Prof of Emergency Med Brown Med Sch 2011-; Attending Physcn Rhode Island Hosp 1994-** B Wakefield RI 1952 d Thomas & Mary. BA U of Rhode Island 1973; MDiv Yale DS 1979; MD NWU 1991. D 6/29/1979 Bp Frederick Hesley Belden P 12/23/1980 Bp George Nelson Hunt III. Attending Physcn Miriam Hosp 1994-2008; Asst S Aug's Ch Kingston RI 1994-2000, Asst Vic 1983-1987, Asst Vic 1983-1987; Asst Gr Ch Chicago IL 1987-1991; Epis Chapl U Of Rhode Island In Kingston 1983-1987; Asst Ch Of The Redeem Bryn Mawr PA 1982; Dio Connecticut Meriden CT 1980-1981; Int S Andr's Ch New Haven CT 1979-1982. Auth, "The Only Law I've Got," *Acad Emergency Med*, AEM, 2012; Auth, "I speak Doctor," *Acad Emergency Med*, AEM, 2012; Auth, "The Challenges of Treating Pain in the Emergency Dept," *Med and Hlth Rhode Island*, Med Soc of RI, 2011; Auth, "The Intimate Sci," *Acad Emergency Med*, AEM, 2009; Auth, "The Obligation of Narrative," *Canadien Journ of Emergency Med*, CJEM, 2006. Fell Of The Amer Coll Of Emergency Physicians 1996; Soc for Acad Emergency Med 2006. Milton Hamolsky Outstanding Physcn of the Year RI Hosp Med Stff Assn 2013; Jacek Franaszek Fac Tchg Awd Brown Emergency Med Residency 2012; Jacek Franaszek Fac Tchg Awd Brown Emergency Med Residency 2010; Excellence in Tchg Awd Brown Med Sch 2008; Wmn Physcn of the Year RIMWA 2008; Outstanding Physcn UEMF

2008; Tchg Recognition Awd Brown Med Sch 2006; Fllshp and Resrch Grant Smithkline Beecham 1988.

NETTLETON, Edwin Bewick (Colo) Po Box 22, Lake City CO 81235 **R Pilgrims Rest Ministers 1991-** B Oakmont PA 1940 s Lewis & Marion. BS Texas Tech U 1962; BD Epis TS of the SW 1966; DD Epis TS of the SW 1989; Epis TS of the SW 1989. D 6/3/1966 P 12/1/1966 Bp George Henry Quarterman. m 9/3/1960 Mary F Nettleton. S Jas Ch Lake City CO 2005-2010; 1988-1991; R S Jas Epis Ch Taos NM 1976-1991; S Vincents Hse Galveston TX 1969-1976; R S Vinc's Hse Galveston TX 1969-1976; Chr Ch San Aug TX 1967-1969; S Jn's Epis Ch Carthage TX 1967-1969; Vic S Jn's Epis Ch Cntr TX 1967-1969; Cur S Chris's Epis Ch Lubbock TX 1966-1967; The Epis Ch Of The Gd Shpd Brownfield TX 1966-1967. Auth, "Why Were You Searching for Me," *Bk*, Peak Pub, 2006.

NETTLETON, Jerome Paul (Eas) 525 E 6th St, Cookeville TN 38501 **D St. Mich's Ch and U Cntr Cookeville TN 2001-** B Omaha NE 1937 s Paul & Beryl. BS U of Maryland. D 9/15/2001 Bp Martin Gough Townsend. m 11/27/1958 Myrna Sue Nettleton.

NETZLER, Sherryl Kaye (Nev) 1631 Esmeralda Pl, Minden NV 89423 B New Zealand 1948 d Trevor & Lola. D 10/6/2006 Bp Katharine Jefferts Schori P 9/14/2008 Bp Dan Thomas Edwards. m 8/2/1974 Serwind Netzler c 2.

NEUBAUER, Nicholas Lawrence (Nev) **Transitional D Gr In The Desert Epis Ch Las Vegas NV 2016-** B Las Vegas, Nevada 1979 s Lawrence & Christina. Bachelor of Arts U of Nevada, Las Vegas 2004; Mstr of Soc Wk U of Nevada, Las Vegas 2007. D 4/14/2016 P 2/27/2017 Bp Dan Thomas Edwards. m 10/12/2008 Brooke B Boemio c 3. NASW 2004. Bd Certification ACS 2009; Clincl Mem ATSA 2009.

NEUBAUER, Zachary David (CFla) B Alliance OH 1985 s David & Penny. Pstr Stds Moody Bible Inst 2007; MDiv TESM 2017. D 1/30/2017 Bp Gregory Orrin Brewer. m 12/29/2007 Erica Simone Gardner c 3.

NEUBERGER, Jeffrey Lynn (Spok) 9106 N Bradbury St, Spokane WA 99208 B Sioux Falls SD 1949 s Harold & Mavis. BS So Dakota St U 1977; MDiv SE Bapt TS 1981. D 9/8/2004 P 5/7/2005 Bp Daniel William Herzog. m 6/11/1981 Kathryn Arthur c 3. Ch Of The Resurr Veradale WA 2011-2012; Conv Coordntr Dio Spokane Spokane WA 2011, Cn for Admin 2009-2010; Wing Chapl, Fairchild AFB USAF Spokane WA 2004-2008.

NEUBURGER, James Edward (USC) 301 W Liberty St, Winnsboro SC 29180 B St Louis MO 1947 s Maurice & Elizabeth. BA U of Notre Dame 1969; Cert Ang Stud Sewanee: The U So, TS 2006. D 6/24/2006 P 6/25/2008 Bp Dorsey Henderson. m 5/29/1969 Carol Neuburger c 3. R S Jn's Ch Winnsboro SC 2008-2015.

NEUFELD, Ellen Christine (Alb) 6349 Milgen Rd Apt 12, Columbus GA 31907 B Jamaica NY 1950 d William & Catherine. BS SUNY 1974; MS SUNY 1979; MA Ford 1982; Cert Ang Stud GTS 1993. D 1/6/1994 Bp John Shelby Spong P 7/1/1994 Bp Jack Marston Mckelvey. m 1/11/1986 Michael John Neufeld. Trin Ch Rensselaerville Rensselaerville NY 2013-2015; S Lk's Ch Chatham NY 2007-2011; Trin Ch Gloversville NY 2004-2005; Ch Of The Ascen Troy NY 2001-2004; S Thos Of Cbury Thomaston GA 1998-1999; Trin Epis Ch Columbus GA 1998; Ch Of The Gd Shpd Sumter SC 1996-1997; S Aug's Epis Ch Pinewood SC 1996-1997; S Dav's Ch Cheraw SC 1996; Asst to R S Lk's Epis Ch Montclair NJ 1994-1995; D / Asst To R S Mk's Ch Teaneck NJ 1994.

NEUFELD, Michael John (Alb) 52 Sacandaga Rd, Scotia NY 12302 **R S Andr's Ch Schenectady NY 2000-; Off Of Bsh For ArmdF New York NY 1997-** B Jamaica NY 1953 s Michael & Ethel. BA Seton Hall U 1974; MA Ford 1983; Cert Ang Stud GTS 1993. D 1/6/1994 Bp John Shelby Spong P 7/10/1994 Bp Jack Marston Mckelvey. m 1/11/1986 Ellen Christine Neufeld. Chapl Us A Ft Benning GA 1997-2000; Asst Gr Epis Ch Camden SC 1995-1997; Asst S Lk's Epis Ch Montclair NJ 1994-1995; S Mk's Ch Teaneck NJ 1994.

NEUHARDT, Kerry Coford (Az) 975 E Warner Rd, Tempe AZ 85284 **Ch Of Our Sav Lakeside AZ 2014-; Chapl Nthrn Arizona U In Flagstaff 1991-; Prov Viii Yth Coun 1985-** B Butte MT 1954 s Roy & Shirley. BA Carroll Coll 1978; MDiv Epis TS of the SW 1981. D 9/21/1982 Bp Leigh Allen Wallace Jr P 3/1/1983 Bp Jackson Earle Gilliam. m 10/19/1984 Diana Lynn Fields c 2. Navajoland Area Mssn Farmington NM 2012-2014; S Jn's Ch Christiansted St Croix VI 2011-2012; P-in-c S Jas The Apos Epis Ch Tempe AZ 2002-2011; Pstr Asst S Barn On The Desert Scottsdale AZ 1998-2002; S Steph's Ch Phoenix AZ 1998-1999; Serv Ch In Australia 1997-1998; R S Andr's Epis Ch Sedona AZ 1990-1997; All SS Ch Phoenix AZ 1985-1990; Fam & Yth Coordntr All SS' Epis Dayschool Phoenix AZ 1985-1990; Assoc R Trin Epis Ch Everett WA 1983-1985; Epis Campus Chapl Montana St U At Bozeman 1982-1983; Asst S Jas Ch Bozeman MT 1982-1983. Ord Of S Lk.

NEUHAUS, Beverly Ruth (NY) 277 Garrison Ave, Staten Island NY 10314 **Died 12/11/2015** B Staten Island NY 1944 d Edward & Ruth. BA S Johns U 1987. D 6/4/1994 Bp Richard Frank Grein. m 10/3/1964 Robert Neuhaus c 2. D S Jn's Ch Staten Island NY 2010-2015; D S Simon's Ch Staten Island NY 1998-2005; D Chr Ch New Brighton Staten Island NY 1994-1997.

NEUHAUS, Theodore James (Minn) 290 Dayton Ave Apt 1w, Saint Paul MN 55102 B Milwaukee WI 1940 s Lawrence & Marjorie. BS U of Wisconsin-Mil-

waukee 1963; Coll of the Resurr 1966; DA Ashworth U 2005; D.Arts Ashworth U 2005. D 8/15/1975 Bp Philip Frederick McNairy P 11/23/1982 Bp Robert Marshall Anderson. Int S Paul's Ch Minneapolis MN 2004-2006, 1999-2004; S Paul's On-The-Hill Epis Ch Minneapolis MN 1999-2004; Int Ch Of The Epiph Epis Minneapolis MN 1997-1998; Int Gr Ch Amherst MA 1995-1996; Int S Jn's Ch Massena NY 1993-1995; Int S Jn The Bapt Epis Ch Minneapolis MN 1992-1993; Int S Jas On The Pkwy Minneapolis MN 1987-1990; Int H Trin Epis Ch Elk River MN 1985-1986; P-in-C S Mathais Mssn St. Paul Pk MN 1983-1984; Int S Clem's Ch S Paul MN 1981-1983; Asst The Angl/Epis Ch Of Chr The King Frankfurt am Main 60323 1978-1981; D S Chris's Epis Ch S Paul MN 1975-1978. CBS 1962; Friends of St Geo and Descendants of the Knights of the Garter 1982; GAS 1962; Sovereign Mltry Ord of the Temple of Jerusalem 2001.

NEVELS JR, Harry V (O) 2532 Potomac Hunt Ln Apt 1B, Richmond VA 23233 **Chapl St. Paul's Coll Lawrenceville VA 2006-** B Savannah GA 1938 s Harry & Mary. Coll of Preachers; Savannah St Coll 1958; GW 1959; VTS 1962; U GA 1964; Case Wstrn Reserve U 1990. D 6/16/1962 P 5/1/1963 Bp Albert R Stuart. m 12/29/1962 Susie Nevels c 1. Ch Of The Trsfg Cleveland OH 1982-1998; R Emm Cleveland OH 1982-1992; S Aug's Ch New York NY 1976-1982, Vic 1974-1976; Trin Par New York NY 1974-1976; R S Matt's Ch Savannah GA 1968-1974; Vic The Epis Ch Of S Jn And S Mk Albany GA 1962-1968.

NEVILLE, Barry Paige (Eas) St Paul's Episcopal Church, PO Box 429, Berlin MD 21811 B Salisbury MD 1958 s William & Ruth. BA Salisbury St Coll 1982; MA Salisbury St U 1985. D 5/4/2013 Bp Bud Shand. m 3/23/1985 Karen Callahan Neville.

NEVILLE, Robert E (Ct) 5170 Madison Ave, Trumbull CT 06611 **Gr Epis Ch Trumbull CT 2015-; Chr Ch Trumbull CT 2014-** B St Louis MO 1953 s John & Laura. BA Lindenwood Coll 1977; MDiv CDSP 2012; MDiv CDSP 2012. D 1/26/2013 P 8/3/2013 Bp Mary Gray-Reeves. m 10/10/2009 Margaret Davidson c 2. Epis Ch of St Jn the Bapt Aptos Aptos CA 2013. rector@christchurchtashua.com

NEVILLE, Robyn M (Va) 1299 Quaker Hill Dr, Alexandria VA 22314 B Wilmington NC 1976 BA W&M. D 6/14/2003 P 12/20/2003 Bp Peter J Lee. m 11/23/2002 Robert Samian Reeder. The GTS New York NY 2012-2013; Asst H Trin Par Decatur GA 2010-2012; Chr Ch Cambridge Cambridge MA 2006; Asst S Andr's Ch Burke VA 2003-2005.

NEVIN-FIELD, Claire Margaret (Pa) 816 Derby Dr, West Chester PA 19380 **Asst S Ptr's Ch Philadelphia PA 2006-; Asst R St. Ptr's Ch Philadelphia PA 2006-** B Cannock England 1963 d Ronald & Sadie. BSN U of Delaware 1984; MS U of Pennsylvania 1994; MDiv GTS 2006. D 6/10/2006 P 12/16/2006 Bp Charles Ellsworth Bennison Jr. m 4/5/1980 Robert Andrew Field c 2. nevinfield@stpetersphila.org

NEVINS, Nancy Ruth (WMo) 416 SE Grand, Lee's Summit MO 64063 **PRN Chapl S Lk's Hosp So Overland Pk Kansas 2011-; D S Paul's Epis Ch Lees Summit MO 2011-** B Kansas City MO 1945 d Percy & Mary. Lamar U 1981; LSU 1982. D 6/5/2010 Bp Barry Howe. m 12/28/1991 Stanley Nevins c 5.

NEW, Robert Henry (SVa) 2804 Cove Ridge Road, Midlothian VA 23112 **Died 11/20/2016** B Rochester MN 1927 s Gordon & Ethel. MDiv Bex Sem; BA U MN 1961; Bex Sem 1964; Cert Gestalt Inst 1978. D 6/13/1964 P 2/2/1965 Bp Nelson Marigold Burroughs. m 7/7/1951 Marian New. LocTen S Dav's Epis Ch No Chesterfield VA 2003-2004; Asst R S Mich's Ch Richmond VA 1998-2000, Int 1988-1989; Int Emm Ch Virginia Bch VA 1996-1997; Ret 1995-2016; Int S Steph's Ch Newport News VA 1995-1996; Int Trin Ch Portsmouth VA 1993-1994; Int Chr Epis Ch Raleigh NC 1992-1993; Vic Trin Epis Ch Highland Sprg VA 1990-1992; Int Estrn Shore Chap Virginia Bch VA 1986-1988; Int S Tim's Epis Ch S Louis MO 1985-1986; Int S Andr's Ch Ann Arbor MI 1984-1985, Int R 1983-1984; Gr Epis Ch Sandusky OH 1983-1984; Assoc Chapl Riverside Hosp 1982-1984; Int Ch Of The Epiph Euclid OH 1982-1983; R S Tim's Epis Ch Perrysburg OH 1977-1982; Assoc S Paul's Ch Akron OH 1973-1977; R S Paul's Ch Mt Vernon OH 1973-1974; Asst S Paul Epis Ch Norwalk OH 1964-1967. Acad Of Par Cler 1971-1995; Acad Of Par Cler Bd 1986-1988; Acad Of Par Cler Bd 1982-1984.

NEWAGO, Michael Jeffrey (Eau) PO Box 816, Bayfield WI 54814 **Dio Springfield Springfield IL 2017-; S Andr's Ch Ashland WI 2017-** B Ashland WI 1972 s Leonard & Susan. BA Quincy U 1996; MA Nash 2017. D 10/29/2016 Bp William Jay Lambert III. m 10/25/2003 Karen Goodlet c 1.

NEWBERRY, Hancella Warren (SO) 840 Middlebury Dr N, Worthington OH 43085 **CPE Prog Mgr Ohio St Univ Med Cntr 2010-** B Fort Sill OK 1957 d Hancel & Annabelle. BA W&M 1978; MDiv Harvard DS 1981. D 6/7/1982 Bp David Henry Lewis Jr P 1/31/1983 Bp William Grant Black. m 4/4/1987 Mervin Orin Newberry c 3. Dir of Chapl Serv and Clincl Pstr Educat Mt Carmel W Hosp Columbus OH 2002-2010; CPE Supvsr and Prog Mgr Mt Carmel W Hosp Columbus OH 1991-2002; CPE Supervisory Res Mt Carmel Med Cntr Columbus OH 1989-1991; Int Ch Of S Edw Columbus OH 1988-1989; Int S Jas Epis Ch Columbus OH 1987-1988; Stff Chapl Mt Carmel E Hosp Columbus OH 1987; Stff Chapl Chr Hosp Cincinnati OH 1985-1986; Res Chapl Beth

Hosp Cincinnati OH 1984-1985; Chapl Chap of the H Chld at Chld's Hosp Cincinnati OH 1982-1984; Stff Chapl Chld's Hosp Med Cntr Cincinnati OH 1982-1984.

NEWBERRY III, Jay Lamar (Mass) 205 Oxbow Rd, Wayland MA 01778 **Non-par 1969-** B Detroit MI 1936 s Jay & Anna. BA U MI 1958; BD EDS 1966. D 6/25/1966 P 5/1/1967 Bp Anson Phelps Stokes Jr. m 3/14/1964 Jane Wendell Newberry. Gr Ch Norwood MA 2000-2001; S Ptr's Ch Osterville MA 1999-2000; S Ptr's Ch Beverly MA 1998-1999; S Anne's Ch Lowell MA 1996; S Eliz's Ch Sudbury MA 1990; Gr Ch Newton MA 1983-1984; S Paul's Ch Peabody MA 1983; S Paul's Ch In Nantucket Nantucket MA 1982; R S Jn's Ch Frostburg MD 1968-1969; Cur The Ch Of Our Redeem Lexington MA 1966-1967.

NEWBERT, Russell Anderson (WNY) 185 Norwood Ave, Buffalo NY 14222 B Gardiner ME 1937 s Russell & Gwendolyn. BS U of Maine 1959; STB GTS 1964; MA U of Notre Dame 1989. D 6/13/1964 Bp Oliver L Loring P 12/12/1964 Bp Roger W Blanchard. R S Simon's Ch Buffalo NY 1975-1998; R S Paul's Ch Martins Ferry OH 1972-1975; Cur Ch Of S Mich And All Ang Cincinnati OH 1964-1972.

NEWBERY, Charles Gomph (LI) 1322 Shattuck Ave., #306, Berkeley CA 94709 **Ret 1994-** B Chicago IL 1928 s Alfred & Helen. BA Ya 1951; STB GTS 1954. D 6/12/1954 P 12/18/1954 Bp Benjamin M Washburn. m 6/23/1954 Jane Newbery c 5. R S Jn's Of Lattingtown Locust Vlly NY 1974-1994; R S Jn's Ch Roanoke VA 1969-1974; R Chr Ch New Brunswick NJ 1966-1969; Vic All SS Ch Princeton NJ 1960-1966; Asst Trin Ch Princeton NJ 1956-1960; Cur Chr Ch Poughkeepsie NY 1954-1956. DD GTS 1986.

NEWBOLD SR, Simeon Eugene (Va) PO Box 540668, Opa Locka FL 33054 **P-in-c S Kevin's Epis Ch Opa Locka FL 2012-** B Miami FL 1954 s David & Catherine. BSW Tuskegee U 1977; MEd Tuskegee U 1979; MDiv SWTS 1989; DMin Samuel Dewitt Proctor TS 2005. D 12/23/1989 P 1/1/1992 Bp Calvin Onderdonk Schofield Jr. m 8/21/1982 Audrea Newbold c 2. Dio SE Florida Miami 2008-2012; Assoc Ch Of The Incarn Atlanta GA 2008-2010; Dio Virginia Richmond VA 2006-2008; Chapl/Vic S Paul's Coll Lawranceville VA 2005-2006; Vic S Paul's Coll Lawranceville VA 2005-2006; Cler Rep to Syn/Dio Virginia Prov III 2002-2005; R S Ptr's Epis Ch Richmond VA 2000-2005; Dio Cntrl Florida Orlando FL 1994-2000; Comm on Mnstry Mem Dio Cntrl Florida Orlando FL 1993-1996; R Ch Of S Simon The Cyrenian Ft Pierce FL 1992-1994; Asst Mssh-S Barth Epis Ch Chicago IL 1989-1991; Convenor Black Epis Seminarians 1988-1989; Epis Cmsn of Black Mnstry Epis Ch Cntr New York NY 1988-1989. Reseacher/Writer, "Choosing Life Over Death: The Dvlpmt of a Strategic Growth Plan for S Ptr's Epis Ch," Samuel DeWitt Proctor TS, 2005. simeonnewbold@yahoo.com

NEWBY, Robert LaVelle (Colo) 18 Folsom Pl, Durango CO 81301 B Topeka KS 1934 s Robert & Loretta. BS Sterling Coll 1962; BD Denver Sem 1967. D 6/10/1995 P 1/27/1996 Bp William Jerry Winterrowd. m 8/4/1957 Shirley Newby c 4. St. Fran of Assisi Mssn So Fork CO 2006-2007; S Pat's Epis Ch Pagosa Sprg CO 2004-2005; Ch Of The Gd Samar Gunnison CO 1999-2002; Asst S Mk's Epis Ch Durango CO 1998-1999, D 1995; Supply St Johns Epis Ch Farmington NM 1997-1998; S Geo Epis Mssn Leadville CO 1996-1998.

NEWBY, William Russell Michael (WLa) 705 N. Moffet Ave, Joplin MO 64801 **Died 10/18/2016** B Moberly MO 1950 s William & Janice. BA Cntrl Methodist U 1972; MEd U of Missouri 1975; MDiv Nash 1983. D 6/29/1981 P 7/1/1983 Bp Charles Thomas Gaskell. m 8/9/1975 Deborah Newby. R S Jas Epis Ch Shreveport LA 2003-2005; S Jn's Ch Neosho MO 1993-2003; Vic S Nich Ch Noel MO 1993-1995; Assoc S Phil's Ch Joplin MO 1988-1993; Int Trin Ch Michigan City IN 1988; R S Mich And All Ang Ch So Bend IN 1986-1988; Cn Mssnr To The Deaf Dio Ft Worth Ft Worth TX 1983-1986; Assoc R S Steph's Epis Ch Hurst TX 1983-1986; Dio Milwaukee Milwaukee WI 1981-1983; P-n-c, All Souls deaf Cong S Jas Epis Ch Milwaukee WI 1981-1983; Secy-Gnrl Ord Of St Vinc Little Neck NY 1981-1996. Ed, "The Angl Way"; Auth, "Osv Tracts". Assn Chr Therapists; Ord Of S Ben, Cbsaint, Som, Epis Conf Of The Deaf Of The Epis Ch In The USA, SSC, Secy Gnrl Ord S Vincents. Counslr Of The Year Natl Counslr Assn 1981.

NEWCOMB, Blair Deborah (Md) PO Box 301, Center Sandwich NH 03227 **Non-par 1989-** B Ithaca NY 1947 d Edward & Carol. BA Mt Holyoke Coll 1969; MEd Duke 1972; MDiv Ya Berk 1980; PhD U MI 1999. D 6/14/1980 P 2/15/1981 Bp Alexander D Stewart. m 1/11/2011 Paul J Henle. Assoc The Ch Of The Redeem Baltimore MD 1986-1989; Chapl Presb Hosp Oklahoma City OK 1983-1984; Asst Trin Ch On The Green New Haven CT 1981-1983; S Steph's Ch Westborough MA 1981. Amer Soc For Legal Hist; Amer Soc Of Ch Hist; Medieval Acad. Vstng Fellowow Univ Of Richmond 1999; Inst For The Hmnts Fellowowship U MI 1995; Lurcy Fllshp 1993.

NEWCOMB, Deborah Johnson (Va) 25260 County Route 54, Dexter NY 13634 B Watertown NY 1949 d John & Catherine. BA Dickinson Coll 1972; MDiv Sewanee: The U So, TS 1987; DMin Sewanee: The U So, TS 1995. D 6/27/1987 P 1/16/1988 Bp George Lazenby Reynolds Jr. m 5/26/2001 Robert Newcomb c 3. R Emm Ch King Geo VA 2000-2004; R Hanover w Brunswick Par - S Jn King Geo VA 2000-2004; Int Trin Ch Uppr Marlboro MD 1999-2000; Assoc

The Ch Of The Redeem Baltimore MD 1996-1999; Assoc Chr Ch Alexandria VA 1988-1995; P-in-c S Barn Ch Tullahoma TN 1988, D 1987-1988.

NEWCOMB, Thomason League (NY) 35 Parkview Ave 4L, Bronxville NY 10708 - **Ret 2015-** B New York NY 1947 s Wyllys & Frances. BA Baldwin-Wallace Coll 1969; MDiv GTS 1975. D 6/21/1975 Bp John Harris Burt P 2/14/1976 Bp Gray Temple. m 6/29/1974 Lee Ann S Stutzman c 3. Assessment Comm Dio NY Epis Chars 2003-2009; R Ch Of S Jas The Less Scarsdale NY 2000-2015; Dn, Bridgeport Dnry Dio Connecticut Meriden CT 1996-1998; R S Tim's Ch Fairfield CT 1983-2000; Happ Dir Dio Georgia Savannah GA 1980-1983; Asst Chr Ch Epis Savannah GA 1978-1983; Asst S Mich's Epis Ch Charleston SC 1975-1978.

NEWCOMBE, David Gordon (NY) 113 Gilbert Road, Cambridge CB4 3NZ Great Britain (UK) B Bronxville NY 1952 s Gordon & Virginia. BA U of Vermont 1975; MDiv GTS 1978; STM GTS 1982; PhD U of Cambridge 1990. D 5/18/1978 Bp Harold Louis Wright P 11/1/1979 Bp Harvey D Butterfield. m 6/26/1976 Barbara Lynn Johnson c 4. Chapl St Jn's Coll Sch Cambridge UK 1985-1987; Ch Of S Jas The Less Scarsdale NY 1979-1985. Auth, "Jn Hooper," Davenant Press, 2009; Auth, "Jn Hooper," *Cambridge Dictionary of Chrsnty*, Camb Press, 2009; Auth, "Nich Hawkins," *New Oxford Dictionary of Natl Biography*, Oxf Press, 2004; Auth, "Jn Hooper," *New Oxford Dictionary of Natl Biography*, Oxf Press, 2004; Auth, "Jn Ponet," *New Oxford Dictionary of Natl Biography*, Oxf Press, 2004; Auth, "Wm Rokeby," *New Oxford Dictionary of Natl Biography*, Oxf Press, 2004; Auth, "Jas Stanley," *New Oxford Dictionary of Natl Biography*, Oxf Press, 2004; Auth, "Richard Mayew," *New Oxford Dictionary of Natl Biography*, Oxf Press, 2004; Auth, "Geoffrey Blythe," *New Oxford Dictionary of Natl Biography*, Oxf Press, 2004; Auth, "Henry Man," *New Oxford Dictionary of Natl Biography*, Oxf Press, 2004; Auth, "Hugh Inge," *New Oxford Dictionary of Natl Biography*, Oxf Press, 2004; Auth, "Jn Kite," *New Oxford Dictionary of Natl Biography*, Oxf Press, 2004; Auth, "Jn Skip," *New Oxford Dictionary of Natl Biography*, Oxf Press, 2004; Auth, "Chas Booth," *New Oxford Dictionary of Natl Biography*, Oxf Press, 2004; Auth, "Jn Howden," *New Oxford Dictionary of Natl Biography*, Oxf Press, 2004; Auth, "Cuth Tunstall," *New Oxford Dictionary of Natl Biography*, Oxf Press, 2004; Ed, "Facsimilie of Foxe's Bk of Martyrs, 1583...on CD-ROM," Oxf Press, 2001; Auth, "Electric Foxe, A Digital Case Hist.," *Jn Foxe: An Hist Perspective*, Ashgate Press, 1999; Auth, "A Finding List of editions of Jn Foxe's Acts and Monuments.," *Jn Foxe and the Engl Reformation*, Scolar Press, 1997; Auth, "The Visitation of the Dio Gloucester and the St of the Cler, 1551.," *Transactions of the Bristol and Gloucestershire Archeol Soc*, 1996; Auth, "Henry VIII and the Engl Reformation," Routledge, 1995; Auth, "Jn Hooper's visitation and examination of the Cler in the Dio Gloucester, 1551," *Reformations Old and New: essays on the socio Econ impact of Rel change, c. 1470 - 1630.*, Scolar Press, 1995.

NEWELL, John E (SVa) 501 Old Town Dr, Colonial Heights VA 23834 B Cleveland OH 1951 s John & Mildred. BA U Denv 1974; MDiv Nash 1989. D 6/12/1989 Bp John Wadsworth Howe P 12/13/1989 Bp William Hopkins Folwell. m 3/15/1975 Courtney Hawley c 3. Ch Of The Redeem Midlothian VA 2015-2016; S Mich's Ch Colonial Heights VA 1993-2013; Gr Epis Ch Inc Port Orange FL 1989-1993.

NEWHART, David George (CFla) 120 Larchmont Ter, Sebastian FL 32958 **R S Eliz's Epis Ch Sebastian FL 2007-; Stndg Com Dio Cntrl Florida Orlando FL 2017-, Dioc Bd 2011-2016, Congrl Dvlpmt 2011-2013, Chair Inst of Chr Stds 2010-, COM 2010-, Sprtl Dir Curs Cmsn 2008-2011, Cler Events Cmsn 2008-2009** B Scranton PA 1955 s William & Barbara. BS Arizona St U 1982; MDiv TESM 2005. D 5/28/2005 Bp John Wadsworth Howe P 12/11/2005 Bp Gary Richard Lillibridge. m 7/22/1998 Matilda M Pirlo c 2. Cur S Helena's Epis Ch Boerne TX 2005-2007. stelizabethsepis@bellsouth.net

NEWLAND, Benjamin John (Colo) Saint John's Episcopal Church, 1419 Pine St, Boulder CO 80302 **Assoc S Jn's Epis Ch Boulder CO 2014-; Chapl US Army Reserve 2011-** B Richland WA 1975 s Dennis & Judy. BA Gonzaga U 1997; MDiv CDSP 2000. D 6/24/2000 Bp John Stuart Thornton P 1/7/2001 Bp Barry Howe. m 6/12/2004 Jieun Kim Newland. R Chr Epis Ch Puyallup WA 2007-2014; Assoc S Andr's Ch Madison CT 2006-2007; Asst Gr And H Trin Cathd Kansas City MO 2000-2005. bnewland@stjohnsboulder.org

NEWLAND, William Trent (Va) 43506 Shalimar Pointe Ter, Leesburg VA 20176 **Died 3/30/2016** B Roanoke VA 1934 s William & Josephine. BS VMI 1958; MDiv VTS 1966. D 9/17/1966 Bp John Brooke Mosley P 5/1/1967 Bp William Foreman Creighton. m 6/12/1958 Ann Crawford Newland c 3. S Thos Epis Ch Mclean VA 2003-2016; S Jas' Epis Ch Leesburg VA 1993-2006; Pstr Counslr Ch Of The H Comf Vienna VA 1986-2003; Pstr Counslr Pstr Counslg Centers of Grtr Washington Washington 1971-1986; P-in-c S Jn's Epis Ch Arlington VA 1967-1971; Cur S Jn's Epis/Angl Ch Mt Rainier MD 1966-1967. Amer Assn of Mar and Fam Therapists 1975; AAPC 1973.

NEWLIN, Melissa Dollie (ECR) 1965 Luzern St, Seaside CA 93955 B Fort Knox KY 1946 d Charles & Mary. BA San Francisco St U 1972; MDiv CDSP 1973. D 6/23/1973 Bp Chauncie Kilmer Myers. m 10/5/1985 Jeff Lucas. Santa Lucia

Chap Big Sur Carmel CA 1991-2007; D All SS Ch Carmel CA 1991-2004; Natl Coun Of Ch New York NY 1978-1979; S Andr's Ch Hanover MA 1976-1977.

NEWLUN, Connor J (Va) Aquia Episcopal Church, PO Box 275, Stafford VA 22555 **S Paul's Ch Hanover VA 2015-** B Winchester VA 1984 s Thomas & Karen. AA Nthrn Virginia Cmnty Coll 2006; BA U of Virginia 2009; MDiv VTS 2013. D 6/8/2013 P 12/14/2013 Bp Shannon Sherwood Johnston. m 9/3/2005 Sarah L Newlun c 2. Asst Aquia Ch Stafford VA 2013-2015. newlun@aquiachurch.com

NEWMAN, Georgia Ann (At) D 5/17/2008 Bp J Neil Alexander.

NEWMAN JR, Harry George (Spr) 5 Hackberry Ln, Springfield IL 62704 **Died 8/30/2015** B Hammond IN 1928 s Harry & Dorothy. BA; MA. m 9/20/1952 Elizabeth Johnson. Asst Chr Ch Springfield IL 1986-2015.

NEWMAN II, James Arthur (Los) 1445 Westerly Ter, Los Angeles CA 90026 **R S Bede's Epis Ch Los Angeles CA 1990-** B Long Beach CA 1949 s James & Lillian. BS U MN 1973; MDiv VTS 1978. D 6/24/1978 P 2/2/1979 Bp Robert Marshall Anderson. m 2/16/2014 Michael Mullins. Int Chapl Cbury Irvine Fndt Irvine CA 1990; Int Chr Ch Par Redondo Bch CA 1988-1990; R and Chapl All SS Ch Northfield MN 1980-1988; Ch Of The H Cross Dundas MN 1980-1988; Asst S Chris's Epis Ch S Paul MN 1978-1980; Reg Dn Dio Los Angeles Los Angeles CA 2001-2016. AAM 2009-2017; Assn of Dioc Liturg & Mus Commissions 1982-2002; EPF 1978; ESMHE 1980-1992; Integrity 1976; OHC 1974. rector@stbedesla.org

NEWMAN, Michael Werth (Pa) 1806 Half Mile Post South, Garnet Valley PA 19060 B Boston MA 1944 s Byron & Mary. MDiv S Marys Sem and U 1974; MEd U of Maine 1980; STM GTS 1984. Rec 10/25/1983 as Deacon Bp Frederick Barton Wolf. m 1/18/1982 Melda Mary Newman. Supply S Mart's Epis Ch Upper Chichester PA 2000-2004; Supply Dio Pennsylvania Philadelphia PA 1999; Cler Deploy Com 1995-1999; R Chr Ch Epis Ridley Pk PA 1991-1999; R Chr Ch Stroudsburg PA 1986-1991; Bd Exam Chapl 1986-1987; Exec Bd 1986-1987; Liturg Cmsn 1985-1987; R Trin Ch Buchanan VA 1984-1986; Serv/Pstr RC Ch 1974-1981. AAPC 1978. Citizen Year Botetourt Cnty 1986.

NEWMAN JR, Murray Lee (Va) 10450 Lottsford Rd Apt 1206, Mitchellville MD 20721 **Ret 1996-** B Checotah OK 1924 s Murray & Sally. BA Phillips U 1945; MA Phillips U 1947; BA Other 1951; BA U of Basel, Switzerland 1952; ThD UTS 1960; S Georges Coll Jerusalem 1984; Ecumenical Inst Jerusalem 1986; Institut Catholique De Paris 1992. D 1/29/1956 P 9/26/1956 Bp William A Lawrence. m 6/6/1946 Janice Hood Newman c 4. Prof VTS Alexandria VA 1956-1996. Auth, "Erodus," *Forw Mvmt*, 2000; Auth, "The Old Convenantand The New," *Sead*, 2000; Auth, "Genesis," *Forw Mvmt*, 1999; Auth, "Interp Of Scripture," *The Afr Amer Jubilee*, 1999; Auth, "People Of The Cov," 1962; Auth, "Israels Prophetic Heritage"; Auth, "Stds In Deuteronomy"; Auth, "Idb Supplement"; Auth, "Rahab & Conquest"; Auth, "The Cont Quest For The Hist Cov". Cath Of Biblic Assn; SBL.

NEWMAN, Richard Barend (Pa) 14 Princess Ln, Newtown PA 18940 **Ret 2001-** B Trenton NJ 1936 s John & Jennie. Moody Bible Inst 1957; BA Westmont Coll 1960; MA Tem 1971. D 11/2/1991 Bp Franklin Delton Turner. m 6/19/1965 Dorothy Jean Newman c 2. Trin Ch Buckingham PA 1999-2000; Dio Pennsylvania Philadelphia PA 1995-1997; Cur S Lk's Ch In The Cnty Of Buck Newtown PA 1994-1995; Asst Washington Memi Chap Vlly Forge PA 1992-1994. Auth, "A Photographic View Of Bucks Cnty, Pa," *Bucks Cnty Town And Country Living*, 1999; Auth, "Farms & Barns Of Bucks Cnty".

NEWMAN, Ryan Douglas (Haw) PO Box 429, Kapaa HI 96746 **All SS Ch Kapaa HI 2013-; Chapl Campbell Hall Sch N Hollywood CA 2002-; Bd Mem Hillsides Pasadena CA 2011-** B Tarzana CA 1976 s Stephen & Charlotte. BA USC 1998; MDiv VTS 2002. D 6/29/2002 P 1/11/2003 Bp Joseph Jon Bruno. Campbell Hall Vlly Vlg CA 2002-2013.

NEWMAN, Thomas Frank (SD) 10 Red Oak Rd, Shawnee OK 74804 B Waukesha WI 1945 s Howard & Gertrude. BA U of Texas 1974; MDiv Sewanee: The U So, TS 1977. D 6/26/1977 P 6/16/1978 Bp Walter H Jones. m 2/5/1966 Shirlene Newman c 2. Dio So Dakota Pierre SD 2004-2006, 1977-1980; Mssnr Mini Sosa Cluster Chamberlain SD 2004-2006; Chr Epis Ch Forrest City AR 2004; Ch Of The Gd Shpd Forrest City AR 2004, 1996-2000; Mssnr Delta Cluster Mnstry AR 2000-2004; Delta Epis Cluster Mnstry Forrest City AR 2000-2003; R S Andr's Ch Marianna AR 1995-2000; P Ch Of The Epiph Dallas TX 1986-1995; P Dio Oklahoma Oklahoma City OK 1983-1985; S Mk's Ch Seminole OK 1983-1985; R S Thos Epis Ch Sturgis SD 1980-1982; P Trin Epis Ch Mssn SD 1977-1980.

NEWNAM, Elizabeth (Cal) 555 4th St Unit 530, San Francisco CA 94107 B Galveston TX 1943 d Frank & Martha. BA Randolph-Macon Coll 1965; MA Eastman Sch of Mus 1967; Florida St U 1972; MDiv CDSP 1989. D 5/31/1989 P 12/1/1989 Bp Sam Byron Hulsey. Assoc Trin Ch San Francisco CA 1999-2005; P-in-c S Barn Ch San Francisco CA 1996-2005; Epis Ch Of S Geo Canyon TX 1989-1995; ; Dn Of The Panhandle Dnry.

NEWSOM, James Cook (WTenn) St George's Independent School, 3749 Kimball Ave, Memphis TN 38111 B Memphis TN 1954 s William & Sarah. Cert Theol Stud U So Sewanee TN; BA U of Memphis 1977; MDiv Memphis TS 2007. D 1/19/2008 P 8/9/2008 Bp Don Edward Johnson. m 4/27/1997 Patti Newsom c 6. St Geo's Indep Sch Collierville TN 2009-2015; Bishops Vic S Matt's Ch Covington TN 2007-2009.

NEWTON, Alissabeth Anne (Oly) Diocese Of Olympia, 1551 10th Ave E, Seattle WA 98102 **S Columba's Epis Ch Kent WA 2014-** B Roseville CA 1978 d Clark & Yvonne. BA Seattle U 2000; MDiv Seattle U 2014; MDiv Seattle U 2014. D 12/21/2013 P 7/22/2014 Bp Gregory Harold Rickel. m 4/2/2005 Andrew Alan Moore c 2. Dio Olympia Seattle 2014-2015; S Paul's Ch Seattle WA 2014, Chld's Formation Dir 2009-2011.

NEWTON, John David (Minn) 1631 Ford Pkwy, Saint Paul MN 55116 B Halifax Nova Scotia 1948 s John & Flora. MA McGill U 1973; Dip Min Stud Montreal Dioc Theol Coll 1974. Trans 11/1/2004 Bp James Louis Jelinek. m 9/7/1973 Karen A Newton c 3. R Mssh Epis Ch S Paul MN 2004-2015; P Angl Ch of Can 1974-2004. jdnewtonii@gmail.com

NEWTON IV, John Wharton (Tex) 209 W 27th St, Austin TX 78705 **Cn Dio Texas Houston TX 2011-, Campus Mssnr 2008-** B Beaumont TX 1981 s John & Martha. BBA U of Texas 2004; MDiv VTS 2008. D 6/28/2008 Bp Don Adger Wimberly P 1/31/2009 Bp Dena Arnall Harrison. m 10/27/2012 Emily Hunt Newton c 2. Epis TS Of The SW Austin TX 2013; The Great Cmsn Fndt Houston TX 2008-2011. jnewton@epicenter.org

NEYLAND, Thomas Allen (Colo) PO Box 228, Hygiene CO 80533 B Beaumont TX 1936 s Allen & Winnie. BA U of Texas 1959; MDiv SWTS 1963; Ldrshp Acad for New Directions 1989; Grad Int Mnstry Ntwk 1996. D 6/15/1963 Bp James Winchester Montgomery P 3/21/1964 Bp Theodore H McCrea. m 4/23/1972 Charlotte A Neyland c 4. Supply H Cross Epis Mssn Sterling CO 2010-2011; Int The Ch Of Chr The King (Epis) Arvada CO 2006-2007; Int S Mk's Ch Cheyenne WY 2004-2005; Int S Andr's Ch Omaha NE 2002-2003; Int Trin Ch Ennis MT 2001-2002; Int S Jas Epis Ch Wheat Ridge CO 2000-2001; Int S Jos's Ch Lakewood CO 1999-2000; Int S Alb's Epis Ch Mc Cook NE 1998-1999; Int Ch of Our Sav No Platte NE 1997-1998; R Par Ch Of S Chas The Mtyr Ft Morgan CO 1992-1996; R - Reg Coordntr S Mk's Epis Ch Pecos TX 1990-1991; Dio WK SE Rgnl Coordntr Dio Wstrn Kansas Hutchinson KS 1988-1990; R S Jn's Ch Great Bend KS 1985-1990; R S Paul's Epis Ch Coffeyville KS 1981-1985; R S Thos Ch Ennis TX 1977-1980; Int Ch Of The H Apos Ft Worth TX 1976-1977; Dio Arizona Phoenix AZ 1971-1972, 1968-1970; Chapl S Aid's Epis Ch Boulder CO 1967-1968; Cur All SS' Epis Ch Ft Worth TX 1965-1967; Vic S Mart's Ch Lancaster TX 1963-1964; Sabbatical supply S Matt's Epis Cathd Laramie WY 2009. Phi Mu Alpha 1957-1960.

NEYLON, Jean Carla (Md) B 1936

NG, Joshua (Los) 15930 Annellen St, Hacienda Heights CA 91745 **S Thos' Mssn Hacienda Hgts CA 2005-** B Kota Kinabalu Sabah 1963 s Huat-Lang & Jingguni. Trans 8/30/2005 as Priest Bp Joseph Jon Bruno. m 11/23/1991 Pit-Lin Chin c 4.

NGUYEN, Duc Xuan (Los) 9097 Crocus Ave, Fountain Valley CA 92708 B 1941 s Ba & Lai. BA U Saigon Vn 1965; MDiv Golden Gate Bapt TS 1971; MLS CUNY 1975; PhD Drew U 1978. D 2/27/1984 P 7/7/1984 Bp Robert Claflin Rusack. m 5/29/1977 Thuan Nguyen c 1. Ch Of Redeem Mssn Garden Grove CA 1985-1992; Dir Indochinese Ministers Of Wrld Vision.

NGUYEN, Hong Xuan (Los) 10795 Garza Ave, Anaheim CA 92804 B Caobang VN 1936 s Ba & Lai. Claremont TS; BA Saigon U 1967; MS Natl Inst Admsntr 1974; MDiv CDSP 1990. D 6/16/1990 P 1/1/1991 Bp Frederick Houk Borsch. m 11/18/1962 Baoan Thi Le c 4. Prof Un U CA 2006-2010; Vic Ch Of Redeem Mssn Garden Grove CA 1991-2005. Auth, "The Story of Sadhu Sundar Singh, A Life Fully Dedicated to God's Kingdom (Vietnamese)," Self, 2010; Transltr, "The Pract of the Presence of God (Vietnamese)," Self, 2008; Auth, "A Moment Of Meditation (Vietnamese)," Allnce Bk Stores, 1970. Vietnamese Interfaith Coun of USA 2017; Vietnamese Mnstrl Fllshp of Sthrn California 1991.

NI, Huiliang (Los) St Edmunds Episcopal Church, 1175 S San Gabriel Blvd, San Marino CA 91108 **Ch Of Our Sav Par San Gabr CA 2014-** B Shanghai China 1962 s Ni & Cha. BA E China Normal U 1984; BA Oak Hill Theol Coll GB 1994; MA E China Normal U Shanghai China 1997. D 6/9/2007 P 1/12/2008 Bp Joseph Jon Bruno. m 2/14/1989 Yuanzhi Wu c 1. Kairos Cmncatn Serv Intl Alhambra CA 2011-2013; Assoc, PhD S Edm's Par San Marino CA 2007-2012; Stdt Claremont Grad U 1997-2007.

NICHOLS, Alice S (Ky) 216 E 6th St, Hopkinsville KY 42240 **R Gr Ch Hopkinsville KY 2011-; Chairperson Aaron McNeil Hse Hopkinsville KY 2017-; Dn Four Rivers Dnry of the Dio Kentucky 2016-** B Wadesboro NC 1947 d Vernon & Margaret. BA Meredith Coll 1969; MSW U of Tennessee Sch of Soc Wk 1972; MDiv Van 2004. D 4/14/2007 P 10/27/2007 Bp Ted Gulick Jr. c 1. R Chr Ch Elizabethtown KY 2007-2011; Chairperson Human Relatns Cmsn Hopkinsville KY 2015-2016; Pres, Stndg Com Dio Kentucky Louisville KY 2014-2015.

NICHOLS, Catherine Palmer (Vt) PO Box 554, East Middlebury VT 05740 B North Conway NH 1944 d Fessenden & Ethel. MDiv Epis Divinitiy Sch; AB Harv 1966; MM U MI 1970; MM U MI 1971; MDiv EDS 1983. D 5/28/1983 Bp John Bowen Coburn P 3/14/1984 Bp Maurice Manuel Benitez. m 12/17/2012 Robert Bruce Borden c 2. P Jerusalem Gathering E Middlebury VT 2013-2016; Cn Pstr Trin Epis Cathd Portland OR 2005-2012; Int S Jn's Ch

Portsmouth NH 2004-2005; R S Steph's Ch Middlebury VT 1991-2003; Cn Pstr Chr Ch Cathd Houston TX 1985-1991; Asst to R H Sprt Epis Ch Houston TX 1983-1985; Mus & Liturg Cmsn, Chair Dio Vermont Burlington VT 1993-2003, Dioc Coun 1991-1997; Cler Pstr Care Com Dio Texas Houston TX 1987-1991, COM 1984-1985, Exam Chapl 1983-1986; Mus Cmsn Dio Massachusetts Boston MA 1980-1983. EWC 1998; Middlebury Area Cler 1991-2004; St. Jn's Soc, EDS 1991-2004. Preaching Prize EDS 1983; Avon Schlr Suffern HS 1962. revcpn@gmail.com

NICHOLS, Kevin Donnelly (NH) 21 Hampshire Hills Dr, Bow NH 03304 **Chair, Bp Search Com Dio New Hampshire Concord NH 2011-** B Inglewood CA 1962 s Thomas & Virginia. BA S Bonaventure U 1984; MDiv S Marys Sem and U 1992. Rec 12/1/1999 as Priest Bp Douglas Edwin Theuner. m 4/20/1996 Patti O Nichols c 3. R S Andr's Epis Ch Contoocook NH 2006-2014; R S Steph's Ch Pittsfield NH 2000-2006; Asst Chr Ch Exeter NH 2000.

NICHOLS, Liane Christoffersen (Ia) 2013 Minnetonka Dr, Cedar Falls IA 50613 **D S Lk's Epis Ch Cedar Falls IA 1992-** B Dubuque IA 1934 d Iver & Veronica. BA U of Nthrn Iowa 1956; MA St Coll of Iowa 1966. D 10/18/1992 Bp Chris Christopher Epting. c 3. NAAD 1993.

NICHOLS III, Robert George (Tex) 15 Hannon Ave, Mobile AL 36604 **S Ptr's Ch Chattanooga TN 2014-** B Jackson MS 1955 s Robert & Mary. BA Millsaps Coll 1977; MDiv VTS 1988; DMin Sewanee: The U So, TS 1995; Basic Int Mnstry Ntwk 2005. D 5/26/1988 P 10/26/1989 Bp Duncan Montgomery Gray Jr. m 5/29/1993 Diana K Nichols c 2. Emm Memi Epis Ch Champaign IL 2013-2014; Chap Of S Jn The Div Champaign IL 2011-2012; S Ptr's Ch Jackson AL 2008-2011, 2005-2007; R S Chris's Ch Houston TX 2007-2008; S Jn's Ch Monroeville AL 2003-2006; S Lk's Epis Ch Mobile AL 2000-2003; Asst R S Mk's Epis Ch Little Rock AR 1997-2000; Chr Epis Ch Little Rock AR 1997; Ch Of The Ascen Hattiesburg MS 1996-1997; All SS Epis Ch Mobile AL 1990-1996; Chapl Wilmer Hall Chld's Hm AL 1990-1993; Cur S Jn's Epis Ch Pascagoula MS 1988-1990.

NICHOLS, Sarah Winn (Los) 837 S Orange Grove Blvd, Pasadena CA 91105 B Madison WI 1965 d Stephen & Mary. BS Van 1986; MDiv Fuller TS 2004; Cert CDSP 2005. D 6/11/2005 Bp Joseph Jon Bruno P 1/14/2006 Bp Frank Tracy Griswold III. Dir of Pstr Care Epis Communities & Serv Pasadena CA 2008-2016; Dio Los Angeles Los Angeles CA 2007, Dioc Stwdshp Prog Grp 2006-; Assoc R S Mich and All Ang Epis Ch Studio City CA 2005-2007. Contributing Auth, "Caring for Protestants: Asking the Rt Questions," *Living w Grief: Sprtlty and End-of-Life Care*, Hospice Fndt of Amer, 2011; Auth, "Exam the Impact of Sprtl Care in Long Term Care," *Omega: The Journ of Death and Dying*, Baywood Pub Co., Inc., 2011. sarahwnichols@icloud.com

NICHOLSON, Aleathia Dolores (Tenn) 3729 Creekland Ct, Nashville TN 37218 **D Chr Ch Cathd Nashville TN 2007-** B Salisbury NC 1937 d John & Leathia. BS Hampton U 1959; MA U of Connecticut 1965; EdS Geo Peabody Coll of Van 1969; Lic Epis TS in Kentucky 1989. D 10/28/1989 Bp George Lazenby Reynolds Jr. D S Anselm's Epis Ch Nashville TN 2002-2007; D/Asst S Mths Ch Nashville TN 1989-2000. Contributing Auth, *Encyclopedia of Afr-Amer Culture and Hist, Supplement*, Macmillan Reference USA/Gale Grp Imprint, 2001; Contributing Auth, *Notable Black Amer Men*, Gale Resrch, 1998; Contributing Auth, *Notable Black Amer Wmn-Volume Two*, Gale Resrch, 1996; Contributing Auth, *Notable Black Amer Wmn-Volume One*, Gale Resrch, 1992. Intl Ord Of S Lk Physcn 2001-2002; NAAD 2001. Fell Tennessee Collaborative Ldrshp Acad 1996; Experienced Tchr Fllshp in the Hmnts Peabody Coll 1968.

NICHOLSON, Anne L (Md) 1830 Connecticut Ave NW, Washington DC 20009 **S Jas' Par Lothian MD 2016-** B Baltimore MD 1987 d Matthew & Nancy. BA Lake Forest Coll 2009; MDiv GTS 2014; MDiv The GTS 2014. D 1/11/2014 Bp Robert Wilkes Ihloff P 10/11/2014 Bp Eugene Taylor Sutton. m 5/30/2015 Leonardd Scott Lipscomb c 1. Asst S Marg's Ch Washington DC 2014-2016. anicholson@stmargaretsdc.org

NICHOLSON, Donald Robert (HB) 104 42nd St. NW, Bradenton FL 34209 **Died 8/10/2015** B Hartford CT 1935 s Robert & Mary. BA GW 1960; STB Ya Berk 1964; DMin Acad of Chinese Healing Arts Sarasota FL 1999. D 6/22/1964 P 6/3/1965 Bp Harry Lee Doll. m 11/27/2004 Beverly Hunt c 2. P-in-c S Raphael's Ch Ft Myers Bch FL 2013-2015; Int Gd Samar Epis Ch Clearwater FL 2008-2009; Chapl Cmnty Coll Of Manatee 2003-2015; Asst Chr Ch Bradenton FL 1997-2006; 1970-2015; Dio Wstrn Massachusetts Springfield 1968-1970; Asst S Ptr's Ch Springfield MA 1968-1970; Ch Of The H Sprt 1966-1968; Vic H Sprt Aberdeen MD 1964-1968; Dio Maryland Baltimore MD 1964-1966.

NICHOLSON, Kedron (Fla) 245 Kingsley Ave, Orange Park FL 32073 **R Gr Epis Ch Orange Pk FL 2014-; S Patricks Ch Albany GA 2013-** B Columbus GA 1977 d Michael & Eleanor Drake. BA U GA 1998; MDiv VTS 2002. Trans 9/29/2003 Bp J Neil Alexander. m 3/5/2011 James C Nicholson c 2. Calv Ch Americus GA 2012-2013; Assoc R S Jn's Ch Montgomery AL 2008-2011; Gr Ch The Plains VA 2006-2008; Epis Ch Cntr New York NY 2005-2006; S Tim's Ch Herndon VA 2003-2005; Asst H Innoc Ch Atlanta GA 2002-2003. VTS Alum Exec Coun 2008-2010.

NICHOLSON, Wayne Philip (WMich) 405 E High St, Mount Pleasant MI 48858 **R S Jn's Ch Mt Pleasant MI 2006-** B Los Angeles CA 1948 s Eugene & Shirley. BA U of Washington 1971; MDiv GTS 2002. D 6/1/2002 Bp William Edwin Swing P 12/7/2002 Bp Catherine Scimeca Roskam. m 6/26/2014 William Dension Kelley. P-in-c Dio New York New York NY 2002-2006; S Paul's Ch Chester NY 2002-2006.

NICKEL, Rebecca (Ind) St. Timothy's Episcopal Church 2601 E. Thompson Road, Indianapolis IN 46227 **P-in-c S Tim's Ch Indianapolis IN 2011-** B McPherson KS 1957 d John. AA Cntrl Coll 1978; BA Azusa Pacific U 1980; MDiv Fuller TS 1986; Iliff TS 1997. D 6/6/1998 P 12/16/1998 Bp William Jerry Winterrowd. m 7/24/1981 David B Nickel c 2. Waycross Epis C&C Morgantown IN 2011, 2010; S Paul's Epis Ch Gas City IN 2010-2012; P-in-c Dio Indianapolis Indianapolis IN 2008-2015; S Steph's Elwood IN 2008-2011; P-in-c H Fam Ch Angola IN 2007; Dio Nthrn Indiana So Bend IN 2004-2006; R Trin Ch Ft Wayne IN 2001-2004; Assoc S Jn's Epis Ch Boulder CO 1999-2000; Cur S Andr's Ch Denver CO 1998-1999.

NICKELSON, Marian L (Ak) 1133 Walnut Ave, Kenai AK 99611 **D S Fran By The Sea Ch Kenai AK 1997-; D S Fran by the Sea Kenai AK 1997-; Chairman Dio Alaska Prison Mnstry T/F 2010-** B Livingston MT 1937 d H Lawrence & Ruby. Montana St U 1957; Montana St U 1957; BS Montana St U 1960; BS Montana St U 1960; MS Montana St U 1969; MS Montana St U 1969. D 5/15/1997 Bp Albert Theodore Eastman. m 11/25/1960 Ray Clifford Nickelson. No Amer Assn of Deaconate. dmpbdk@gmail.com

NICKERSON, Audra M (WMich) 141 Broad St N, Battle Creek MI 49017 **D Dio Wstrn Michigan Kalamazoo MI 1986-** B Marshall MI 1926 d Blaine & Mabel. BA MI SU 1948. D 5/3/1986 Bp Howard Samuel Meeks. m 1/6/1951 Ralph Dale Nickerson c 1. Ord Of S Ben.

NICKERSON, Bruce Edward (Mass) 77 South Rd, Bedford MA 01730 B Boston MA 1938 s Bernard & Edith. AS Tufts U 1960; BA Tufts U 1965; MA NEU 1967; PhD Indiana U 1976. D 6/23/1990 Bp George Nelson Hunt III. m 9/1/1973 Joanna Gay Nickerson. D S Ptr's Epis Ch Cambridge MA 2012-2015; D S Eliz's Ch Wilmington MA 2009-2012; D S Barth's Epis Ch Cambridge MA 2000-2009; D Chr Ch Somerville MA 1991-2002; D S Jas Epis Ch At Woonsocket Woonsocket RI 1990-1991. NAAD.

NICKERSON JR, Donald Albert (Me) Po Box 855, Intervale NH 03845 B Boston MA 1939 s Donald & Mildred. BS Springfield Coll 1961; STB Ya Berk 1964. D 6/20/1964 Bp Anson Phelps Stokes Jr P 6/4/1965 Bp John Melville Burgess. m 8/25/1962 Susan M Nickerson c 3. Epis Ch Cntr New York NY 1989-1998, Liaison To Trien Com Wrld Mssn Com 1982-1985; Exec & Secy Off New York NY 1986-1988; R S Paul's Ch Brunswick ME 1974-1986; R Chr Ch No Conway NH 1966-1974; Cur Trin Par of Newton Cntr Newton Cntr MA 1964-1966; Dio Maine Portland ME 1982-1986; Stndg Com Dio New Hampshire Concord NH 1973-1974.

NICKLES, Amanda L (Fla) PO Box 10472, Tallahassee FL 32302 **Vic Gr Mssn Ch Tallahassee FL 2010-** B Columbia SC 1956 d Robert & Carole. MDiv TESM 2003. Trans 3/13/2004 Bp Robert William Duncan. c 2. R The Ch Of The Gd Shpd Canajoharie NY 2004-2009.

NICKLES, Brenda Joyce (Alb) 12 Woodbridge Ave., Chatham NY 12037 B Catskill NY 1953 d Herbert & Helen. D 5/10/2008 P 3/29/2015 Bp William Howard Love. c 3.

NICKLES, Megan Woods (Wyo) 349 N Douglas St, Powell WY 82435 **S Jn's Ch Powell WY 2005-** B Powell WY 1964 d William & Dolores. BA U of Wyoming 1986. D 6/30/2005 P 2/10/2006 Bp Bruce Caldwell. m 8/19/1989 Lloyd Steven Nickles c 3. Dio Wyoming Casper 2012-2016. mnickles@bresnan.net

NICOLL, Tom (NY) 16 Claret Dr, Greenville SC 29609 B Greenville SC 1953 s Ernest & Mary. BA Davidson Coll 1975; MA U of Virginia 1981; MDiv GTS 1982. D 6/12/1982 P 5/21/1983 Bp William Arthur Beckham. m 8/7/1982 Mary F Nicoll c 2. R S Jn's Ch Larchmont NY 1993-2013; Assoc Chr Ch Charlotte NC 1990-1993; Vic H Trin Epis Ch Essex MD 1984-1989; Asst Chr Epis Ch Charlottesvlle VA 1982-1984. Omicrom Delta Kappa; Phi Beta Kappa.

NICOLOSI, Gary (Nwk) St. James Westminster Church, 115 Askin Street, London ON N6C 1E7 Canada **R St. Jas Westminster Ch London ON 2010-; Chair, Post Ord Trng Prog Dio Huron London Ontario 2012-** B Brooklyn NY 1950 s Joseph & Carol. BA Ford 1972; MA Geo 1973; JD Tem 1976; MDiv U Tor CA 1983; DMin Pittsburgh TS 1997. Trans 4/16/1985 Bp William George Burrill. m 4/30/1983 Heather Bruce Nicolosi c 1. Congrl Dvlpmt Off Dio British Columbia Victoria 2007-2010; R S Ptr's Ch Morristown NJ 2005-2007; R S Barth's Epis Ch Poway CA 1997-2005; R S Thos Ch Lancaster PA 1990-1997; Cn For Mnrtrs Cathd Ch Of The Nativ Bethlehem PA 1987-1990; Gr Ch Scottsville NY 1985-1987; R S Andr's Epis Ch Caledonia NY 1985-1987; Incumbent Ch Of Can 1983-1985; Chair, Strategic Plnng Implementation Team Dio British Columbia Victoria BC 2008-2010. Auth, "The Why Question," *The Angl Journ*, 2013; Auth, "Believing in a Wrld Like This," *The Angl Journ*, 2013; Auth, "Called to Mssn," *The Angl Journ*, 2013; Auth, "Come Hm Again," *The Angl Journ*, 2011; Auth, "The Sprtl Compass of the Ch," *The Angl Journ*, 2011; Auth, "One Chr's Perspective on Norway," *The*

Angl Journ, 2011; Auth, "The Case For Open Comm," *The Angl Journ*, 2011; Auth, "What Steve Jobs Can Teach the Ch," *The Angl Journ / ENS*, 2011; Auth, "Anxious Times Demand a Courageous Response," *Networking*, 2009. Awd of Merit The Can Ch Press 2012; Awd of Merit The Associated Ch Press 2011; DD U So 2001; DD EDS 1998. gary.nicolosi@gmail.com

NIEHAUS, Thomas Kenneth (WNC) 12503 N Woodberry Dr, Mequon WI 53092 **P Assoc S Bon Ch Thiensville WI 2012-** B Cincinnati OH 1939 s Sylvester & Lucille. BA Xavier U 1963; MA U Cinc 1964; PhD U of Texas 1976; MLS U of Texas 1976; MDiv Sewanee: The U So, TS 1993. D 7/10/1993 Bp James Barrow Brown P 1/1/1994 Bp Bob Johnson. m 6/13/1964 Julia Niehaus c 2. R Emer S Thos Epis Ch Burnsville NC 2004, R 1997-2003; S Jn's Ch Sylva NC 1993-1997; Dioc Ecum Off Dio Wstrn No Carolina Asheville NC 1998-2004; Asst Prof of Hist Tul New Orleans LA 1988-1990; Dir, Latin Amer Libr Tul New Orleans LA 1977-1990. Auth, "Liberation Theol," *Encyclopedia of Latin Amer Hist*, Chas Scribner's Sons, 1993; "Cath Rt in Contemp. Brazil," *Rel in Latin Amer. Life & Liter.*, Baylor U Press, 1980; "Lorenzo Hervas y Panduro, S.J.," *Archivum historicum Societatis Iesu*, Rome: Jesuit Hist Soc, 1975. Fulbright Prof Cntrl U of Venezuela 1983; Fulbright Schlr (grad Stdt) U of Madrid, Spain 1967.

NIELSEN III, Peter W (O) 5811 Vrooman Rd, Painesville OH 44077 **P-in-c S Ptr's Epis Ch Ashtabula OH 2015-; Cedar Hills C&C Painesville OH 2004-; Ord D, Exec Dir Cedar Hills Camp & Conf Cntr Painesville OH 1993-** B Darby PA 1955 s Peter & Lois. Shpd U 1989. D 11/13/2004 P 11/7/2014 Bp Mark Hollingsworth Jr. m 6/28/1975 Laura J Nielsen c 4. Dio Ohio Cleveland 2004-2014. ECCC, Inc. 1987.

NIEMAN, John S (Me) PO Box 234, Newcastle ME 04553 **S Andr's Ch Newcastle ME 2016-** B Passaic NJ 1959 s Thomas & Audrey. BA Drew U 1984; MDiv Harvard DS 1987. D 5/30/1987 P 12/12/1987 Bp John Shelby Spong. m 7/28/1984 Margaret S Snider c 1. R H Trin Par Epis Clemson SC 2006-2016; R S Andr's Ch Ann Arbor MI 1997-2006; R S Mary's Ch Sparta NJ 1993-1997; R S Dunst's Ch Ellsworth ME 1990-1993; Cur S Eliz's Ch Ridgewood NJ 1987-1989. Auth, *Epis Life*. Phi Beta Kappa 1983.

NIEMEYER, David (Va) 501 W Nine Mile Rd, Highland Springs VA 23075 **S Mk's Ch Richmond VA 2012-** B Hattiesburg MS 1953 s Carl & Betty Sue. BS U of Sthrn Mississippi 1977; MDiv S Meinrad TS 1982; MA U of Notre Dame 1986; MS U of St Thos 1994. Rec 6/7/2008 Bp Peter J Lee. m 5/20/1989 Arielle F Niemeyer c 2. Vic Dio Virginia Richmond VA 2009-2012, Co-Chair, Com on Race Relatns 2009-; Vic Trin Epis Ch Highland Sprg VA 2008-2012. Amer Assn of Mar and Fam Ther 1993; Virginia Assn of Mar and Fam Ther 2002.

NIESE JR, Alfred Moring (NJ) 6 Apple Tree Dr, Brunswick ME 04011 **Ret 1998-** B New York NY 1937 s Alfred & Anne. BA Rutgers The St U of New Jersey 1959; STB GTS 1963; STM NYTS 1971. D 6/8/1963 P 12/21/1963 Bp Leland Stark. m 2/5/1966 Bronda M Niese c 2. S Aug's Epis Ch Dovr Foxcroft ME 1999-2001; Int S Paul's Ch Brunswick ME 1999-2000; R Ch of S Jn on the Mtn Bernardsville NJ 1980-1997; Chr Ch Short Hills NJ 1976-1980; Ch Of The Atone Fair Lawn NJ 1967-1976; Asst Trin And S Phil's Cathd Newark NJ 1963-1967; Pres Stndg Com Dio New Jersey Trenton NJ 1996-1997, Chair Dioc Com for Unified Bdgt 1991-1995, Chair Dio Bdgt Com 1989-1990, Dioc Fndt 1985-1988, Chair D Polity Com 1984. AAPC 1975-1985. R Emer Ch of St. Jn on the Mtn 2002.

NIETERT, Jack Frederick (SC) 2830 W Royal Oaks Dr, Beaufort SC 29902 **P St Marks Chap Port Royal SC 2009-; Trst Dio SC 2013-** B New York NY 1941 s Rudolph & Elsa. BA Hobart and Wm Smith Colleges 1963; MDiv GTS 1966. D 6/16/1966 P 12/21/1966 Bp Jonathan Goodhue Sherman. m 6/23/1990 Christina N Nelson c 2. team Mnstry St Mk's Epis Ch Port Royal SC 2009-2014; Int All SS Ch Tybee Island GA 2008-2009; S Jn's Epis Ch Halifax VA 2007-2008; Int Trin Epis Ch So Boston VA 2007-2008; Vic All SS Epis Ch Hampton SC 1999-2007; Int S Jas Ch Charleston SC 1998; R Ch Of The Gd Shpd Kansas City MO 1989-1998; Assoc S Andr's Ch Mt Pleasant SC 1975-1989; R Gr Ch Hastings Hds NY 1974-1975; R Zion Ch Dobbs Ferry NY 1969-1975; Asst S Jas Ch Hyde Pk NY 1966-1969. Hon Cn, Gr and H Trin Cathd 1997.

NIPPS, Leslie (Cal) 592 Jean St #202, Oakland CA 94610 **Pstr Counslr Leslie Nipps Counslg Oakland CA 2009-; Vol Mgr Meals On Wheels of San Francisco San Francisco CA 2008-** B Mount Kisco NY 1963 d John & Helen. BA Cor 1987; MDiv GTS 1994. D 6/4/1995 P 12/16/1995 Bp Joe Doss. Tchr W Cnty Detention Facility Richmond CA 2007-2008; S Mich And All Ang Concord CA 2003-2006; Dir Of Fam And Chld'S Mnstrs S Greg Of Nyssa Ch San Francisco CA 2001-2003; Asst S Mk's Epis Ch Toledo OH 1998-2001; Vic Ch Of The H Sprt Tuckerton NJ 1995-1998. Auth, "Practical Postmodernism For Parishes," 'Open'. AP, 2001. Coun Mem AP (Aplm) 2001.

NISBETT, Joshua Mastine (LI) 11738 Cross Island Pkwy, Cambria Heights NY 11411 **R S Dav's Epis Ch Cambria Heights NY 1985-; Chapl S Jos's Par Day Sch Queens Vill NY 1985-** B Nevis West Indies 1946 s Clarence & Alice. BA Untd TS 1975. D 6/29/1974 P 7/1/1975 Bp The Bishop Of Antigua. m 12/4/1976 Enid Fay Nisbett c 3.

NISSEN, Peter Boy (WK) 312 S Kansas Ave, Norton KS 67654 **Chapl Nortain Vlly Hope Treatment Cntr 1996-** B Seattle WA 1946 s Boy & Roma. BA U

of British Columbia 1969; MDiv Vancouver TS CA 1973. P 5/1/1975 Bp Furman Charles Stough. S Andr's Ch Hays Hays KS 1999-2011; 1997-1998; Serv Ch Of The Epiph Concordia KS 1996-1998; Kansas Army NG Chapl USANG 1994-2001; Vic Trin Epis Ch Norton KS 1993-1996; Off Of Bsh For ArmdF New York NY 1980-1993; Assoc S Mk's Epis Ch Casper WY 1979-1980; Serv Angl Ch of Can 1973-1979.

NITZ, Theodore Allen (Spok) 2300 NW Ridgeline Drive, Pullman WA 99163 **Archd S Jas Pullman WA 1991-; Archd Dio Spokane Spokane WA 2003-** B Oakland CA 1946 s Jack & Beverly. BA U of Washington 1968; MA WA SU 1975; PhD WA SU 1999. D 9/26/1982 Bp Harold Anthony Hopkins Jr. m 8/16/1970 Sharon Ann Nitz c 2. D/Asst Dio No Dakota Fargo ND 1988-1991; S Geo's Epis Ch Summerville SC 1988-1991; D/Asst Zion Ch Rome NY 1984-1988; R Bp's Acad for Mnstry Dvlpmt Fargo ND 1982-1984; Asst Geth Cathd Fargo ND 1982-1984. "Messengers, Agents, and Attendants: Deacons in the Body of Chr," *Diakoneo*, 2006; "Commentary on New D Cn w Ormonde Plater," *Diakoneo*, 2003. HSEC 1994; NAAD 1982.

NIX JR, William Dale (NwT) 11355 Nix Ranch Road, Canadian TX 79014 B Amarillo TX 1941 s William & Mary. CDSP 1963; BA Texas A&M U 1963; MDiv Epis TS of the SW 1975. D 6/7/1975 P 6/18/1976 Bp Willis Ryan Henton. m 8/3/1963 Nelwyn H Nix c 3. Panhandle Reg Mssnr Dio NW Texas Lubbock TX 2000-2003, Cn to the Ordnry 1981-1986, 1978-1981; Pres Stndg Com Dio of NW Texas 1993-1996; R S Andr's Epis Ch Amarillo TX 1992-2000; Gvrng Bd NAES New York NY 1987-1994; Pres Stndg Com Dio of Ft Worth 1987-1990; Dn All SS' Epis Ch Ft Worth TX 1986-1992; GC Dep 1982-2003; Del Prov 7 Syn 1978-2002; R Steph's Ch Lubbock TX 1977-1981; Cur S Jn's Epis Ch Odessa TX 1975-1977; Joint Stndg Cmsn on Prog Bdgt & Fin Epis Ch Cntr New York NY 1994-2003. Chapl Ord of St. Jn of Jerusalem 1987; Oblate OSB 1993. Hon Cn Dio NW Texas 1986; Who's Who in Rel 1985.

NIXON, Barbara Elizabeth (Ct) 399 Windward Way, Sacramento CA 95831 **Vic S Lk's Ch Galt CA 2006-** B Detroit MI 1954 d Glenn & Irma. BA Kirkland Ham 1976; MA Col 1981; Chr Stds Dplma Regent Coll Vancouver CA 1983; Dip Ang Stud Ya Berk 1987; MDiv Yale DS 1987. D 6/13/1987 Bp Arthur Edward Walmsley P 6/17/1989 Bp William Bradford Hastings. m 1/10/1998 James R Wirrell. Assoc P All SS Memi Sacramento CA 2003-2005; Int R Varina Epis Ch Henrico VA 2000-2001; Chapl S Chris's Sch Richmond VA 1998-2000; Assoc P and Supply Serv Angl Ch of Can / British Columbia 1994-1998; Assoc R S Paul's Ch Fairfield CT 1994; P-in-c Angl Ch of Ireland Limerick and Cnty Clare 1993-1994; P in Charge and Supply P Serv Angl Ch of Can / Ottawa 1992-1993; P-in-c Dio Ottawa Ottawa ON 1992; Asst R S Jn's Epis Ch Vernon Rock Vernon Rockville CT 1990-1992; Asst R All SS Epis Ch of the No Shore Inc Danvers MA 1989; Chapl S Paul's Sch Concord NH 1987-1988. Curs 1989. Who's Who In Amer Wmn.

NIXON, James Thomas (At) 2700 Bennington Dr Ne, Marietta GA 30062 B Kingston PA 1948 s James & Constance. Lic Penn 1968; BD U Cinc 1980; MDiv Sewanee: The U So, TS 1990. D 5/26/1990 Bp John Maury Allin P 3/16/1991 Bp Alex Dockery Dickson. m 5/22/1971 Joan Anita Lange c 2. R S Cathr's Epis Ch Marietta GA 1998-2015; Vic Gr Epis Ch New Lenox IL 1992-1998; S Thos The Apos Humboldt TN 1990-1992. Woods Ldrshp Awd U So 1988.

NIXON, Thomas E (CGC) 1580Deese Road, Ozark AL 36360 B Batavia NY 1948 s Donald & Janet. BA SUNY 1973; MEd Bos 1976; MDiv EDS 1976; DMin Sewanee: The U So, TS 1996. D 9/25/1982 P 8/1/1983 Bp Charles Farmer Duvall. c 2. S Mich's Ch Ozark AL 2007-2010, Vic 2007-, 1982-1991; Ch Of The Epiph Enterprise AL 2004-2007, 1992-1995; P-in-c Ch of the Epiph Enterprise AL 2004-2007.

NNAJI, Udochukwu Benjamin (NY) 1905 Morris Ave, Bronx NY 10453 **S Edm's Ch Bronx NY 2016-** B Agbaza 1975 s Humphrey & Esther. Theol Dplma St Paul's U Coll 2001; BA U of Nigeria 2001; MSC U of Lugano 2007; Theol Dplma St Paul's U Coll 2011; BA U of Nigeria 2011; MSEd Lehman Coll 2016. Trans 7/21/2016 as Priest Bp Andrew Marion Lenow Dietsche. m 11/20/2010 Juliana Chioma Nnaji c 4. frudoben@yahoo.com

NOALL, Nancy J(O) (WA) 312 Hillmoor Dr, Silver Spring MD 20901 B Clarksburg WV 1936 d Joseph & Mabel. Kent St U 1957; LTh VTS 1981. D 6/20/1981 Bp John Thomas Walker P 1/6/1982 Bp William Benjamin Spofford. m 7/20/1957 William F Noall c 3. R S Paul's Epis Ch Piney Waldorf MD 2000-2006; P-in-c S Mk's Ch Fairland Silver Sprg MD 1998-2000; Int S Jn's Epis Ch Zion Par Beltsville MD 1995-1997; Int S Tim's Ch Herndon VA 1990-1994; Int S Mk's Ch Alexandria VA 1987-1989; Asst S Paul's Epis Ch Alexandria VA 1981-1987.

NOBLE, Anthony Norman (SanD) 625 Pennsylvania Ave, San Diego CA 92103 **R Emer All SS Ch San Diego CA 2011-, R 2003-2011; Locum duty C of E Dio in Europe 2011-** B Australia 1947 s Norman & Alice. BTh S Barn Coll AU 1978. Serv Angl Ch of Australia 1979-2003. Ord of St Corentin 1995; SSC 1980; SSM 1998; Shrine of Our Lady of Walsingham 1980. rector@allsaintschurch.org

NOBLE, Mitzi McAlexander (WA) 508 Tranquility Rd., Moneta VA 24121 **Dvlpmt Off Epis Conf of the Deaf 2002-; Ret 2001-** B Kingsport TN 1941 d

632

Buren & Ruby. RBA Shpd U 1985; How 1988; Wesley TS 1988; MDiv GTS 1990. D 6/15/1991 Bp Ronald Hayward Haines P 12/21/1991 Bp Orris George Walker Jr. m 6/29/1957 Paul Benjamin Noble c 2. Int Ch Of The Atone Washington DC 2004-2005; P-in-c S Barn' Epis Ch of The Deaf Chevy Chase MD 2000-2001; Stwdshp and Planned Giving Dio Washington 1998-2001; P-in-c H Sprt Epis Ch Germantown MD 1998-1999; R Trin Ch Lakeville CT 1993-1998; Asst S Jn's Of Lattingtown Locust Vlly NY 1991-1993; Pstr in Charge Dio Jamaica W Indies Vaughnsfield Ch 1985-1986; Liturg Advsr, Chap of the H Sprt Dio Washington Washington DC 1998-1999; Ecum Comm. Dio Connecticut Meriden CT 1993-1998. Auth, *Planned Giving Bklet*. Angl-Luth Soc; The Angl Soc.

NOBLE, William Conner (NJ) 1941 Wayside Rd, Tinton Falls NJ 07724 **P-in-c S Jas Ch Long Branch NJ 2015-** B Vidalia GA 1940 s Bennett & Lucy. BA U So 1962; MDiv GTS 1969; MS USC 1980; DMin GTF 1995; Cert Postgraduate Cntr For Mntl Hlth New York NY 2002; Cert Blanton-Peale Grad Inst 2006; Cert Blanton-Peale Grad Inst 2006; PsyD GTF 2010. D 6/14/1969 P 3/8/1970 Bp Albert R Stuart. m 6/19/1976 Liliane G Noble c 4. P-in-c S Jas Memi Ch Eatontown NJ 1997-2002; Exec Asst To Bp Armdf Epis Ch Cntr New York NY 1995-2002; Off Of Bsh For ArmdF New York NY 1975-1995; Chapl US-Army 1975-1995; Chapl S Barn' Ch Leeland Uppr Marlboro MD 1972-1975; Vic Trin Ch Statesboro GA 1970-1972; Cur S Paul's Ch Albany GA 1969-1970. Auth, "'Reflections On A Vision," *Journ Of Rel And Hlth*, Blanton-Peale Inst, 2003; Auth, "In The Shadow Of Death," *A New Conversation*, Ch Publilshing Co, 2001; Auth, "arts And Bk Revs," *LivCh*, LivCh, 1985; Auth, "A Theol Of Mnstry," *Mltry Chapl Revs*, 1982. Amer Assn Of Mar And Fam Therapists 2002; AAPC 2002; Natl Assn for the Advancement of Psychoanalysis 2006. wcnoble@aol.com

NOBOA VITERI, Eugenio Terencio (EcuC) Casilla 0901-5250, Guayaquil Ecuador **Vic Iglesia San Marcus 24ava y la O Guayas 1984-; Iglesia San Pedro Guayaquil 1984-; Iglesia Todos los Santos 25ava y la S Guayaquil Gu 1984-** B Parroquia Simon Bolivar EC 1955 s Terencio & Ninfa. D 12/16/1984 Bp Adrian Delio Caceres-Villavicencio P 6/1/1992 Bp Martiniano Garcia-Montiel. Litoral Dio Ecuador Guayaquil 1991-2008.

NOCHER, Janet Gregoire (FtW) 4408 Foxfire Way, Fort Worth TX 76133 **Older Adult Mnstrs Co-Chair Prov VII Fairfax VA 2014-; Chapl Baylor Inst for Rehab 2012-; Chapl Baylor Hlth Care System 2007-; Dioc Chair Epis Relief and Dvlpmt New York NY 2008-** B Miami FL 1940 d Louis & Sarah. U of Florida 1960; Angl TS 1995. D 6/5/1996 Bp Jack Leo Iker. c 2. COM Dio Ft Worth Ft Worth TX 2008-2012; COM for the Diac 1996-2008; D Trin Epis Ch Ft Worth TX 2000-2013; D S Chris's Ch And Sch Ft Worth TX 1996-2000.

NOE, William Stanton (Va) Po Box 2078, Ashland VA 23005 **1984-** B Greenville NC 1929 s Alexander & Sarah. U Vienna 1953; BA U So 1954; U Heidelberg DE 1955; MDiv Sewanee: The U So, TS 1961; PhD U of Virginia 1973. D 6/21/1961 P 3/1/1962 Bp Thomas H Wright. P-in-c Ch Of Our Sav Montpelier VA 1964-1984; P-in-c Ch of the Incarn Mineral VA 1963-1964; P-in-c Trin Louisa VA 1963-1964; Vic S Ptr's By-The-Sea Swansboro NC 1961-1963.

NOEL, Virginia Lee (Mo) 15826 Clayton Rd Apt 131, Ellisville MO 63011 **Ret 1998-** B Little Rock AR 1934 d William & Mabel. BS U of Wisconsin 1957; MDiv Nash 1977; S Louis U 1989. D 4/16/1977 Bp Charles Thomas Gaskell P 2/16/1980 Bp Robert Marshall Anderson. c 4. Cn Chr Ch Cathd S Louis MO 1984-1986; Screening Com Dio Minnesota Minneapolis MN 1980-1984, Epis Cmnty Serv, Bd Mem 1980-1984; Assoc S Geo S Louis Pk MN 1980-1984; St Geo's Epis Ch Minneapolis MN 1980-1984; Chapl H Trin/U Epis Cntr Minneapolis MN 1979-1980; Cntrl City Ch Coordntr Dio Milwaukee Milwaukee WI 1977-1979; S Andr's Ch Milwaukee WI 1977-1979; Asst S Geo Milwaukee WI 1977-1979; EFM, mentor Dio Missouri S Louis MO 1984-1993; Chr Soc Action Com Dio Milwaukee Milwaukee WI 1977-1979. Auth, "Darkness," *Plumbline*, 1977; Auth, "Mysticism: Its Relatns to Other Spiritualities," *Nashotah Revs*, 1976. Ord of S Helena, Assoc 1984.

NOETZEL, Joan Lois (SeFla) 7300 W Lake Dr, West Palm Beach FL 33406 B Rye NY 1932 d Cornelius & Joan. BA Palm Bch Atlantic U; AA Lasell Coll 1952. D 11/27/1987 Bp Calvin Onderdonk Schofield Jr. m 10/1/1955 Everett Llewellyn Noetzel. D H Trin Epis Ch W Palm Bch FL 1987-2002.

NOISY HAWK SR, Lyle Maynard (SD) 1702 E Highway 44 Lot 171, Rapid City SD 57703 B Fort Yates ND 1942 s Edward & Nancy. Cert Theol Stud Nash 1973; BA So Dakota St U 2000; MS So Dakota St U 2004. D 6/15/1973 P 12/21/1974 Bp Walter H Jones. m 1/1/1966 Mary Emily Noisy Hawk c 4. Geth Epis Ch Sisseton SD 1995-2000; Vic Bp Whipple Mssn Morton MN 1990-1995; Vic Living Waters Ch Denver CO 1989-1990; Geth Epis Ch Wanblee SD 1988-1989; Chapl/Consult Dept. of Vet. Affrs Ft. Meade SD 1976-1989; Vic S Matt's Epis Ch Rapid City SD 1976-1989; Dio So Dakota Pierre SD 1973-1999; Pine Ridge Mssn Pine Ridge SD 1973-1976. Fam of the Year SDSU/Alumini 2001.

NOLAN, Richard Thomas (Ct) 451 Heritage Drive, Apt 1014, Pompano Beach FL 33060 B Waltham MA 1937 s Thomas & Elizabeth. BA Trin Hartford CT 1959; MDiv Hartford Sem 1963; MA Ya 1967; PhD NYU 1973; Harv 1991. D 6/29/1963 Bp John Melville Burgess P 6/1/1965 Bp Frederic Cunningham Lawrence. m 6/4/2009 Robert Charles Pingpank. Ret P-in-res S Andr's Ch Lake Worth FL 2002-2004; Ret Hon Life Cn Chr Ch Cathd Hartford CT 1994-2004; P-t S Paul's Epis Ch Bantam CT 1974-1988; & Math Tchr in Cathd Choir Sch Cathd Of St Jn The Div New York NY 1963-1964; . Ed, "Soul Mates: More Than Partnr," *online Ed*, www.nolan-pingpank.com, 2004; "The Diac Now," *online Ed*, Corpus/Wrld, 2002; Auth, "Living Issues In Ethics," *online Ed*, iUniverse, 2002; Ed, "Living Issues in Ethics," *revised Ed*, iUniverse, 2000; Ed, "www.Philos-Rel.org," *www.Philos-Rel.org*, online educational website, 2000; Ed, "Living Issues In Philos," *9th Ed*, Oxford, 1995; Auth, "Living Issues in Ethics," *Chinese Ed*, Huaxia, 1988; Ed, "Living Issues In Philos," *8th Ed*, Wadsworth, 1986; Ed, "Living Issues In Philos," *Indonesian Ed*, PT Bulan Bintang, 1984; Ed, "Living Issues in Ethics," *1st Ed*, Wadsworth, 1982; Auth, "Living Issues In Philos," *7th Ed*, Wadsworth, 1979; "The Diac Now," *1st Ed*, Corpus/Wrld, 1968. AAR 1965; Amer Philos Assn 1965; Angl Assn of Biblic Scholars 1998; Hemlock Soc of Florida 1994; Integrity, Inc 1980; Interfaith Allnce 2000; Lambda Legal 2001. Soc of Rgnts Cathd of S Jn the Div 2004.

NOLAND, Elisabeth Hooper (RG) 2 Pino Pl, Santa Fe NM 87508 **D Epis Ch Of The H Fam Santa Fe NM 2004-** B Waltham MA 1939 d Richard & Katharine. Goucher Coll; BA Trin TS Albuquerque. D 7/28/2001 Bp Terence Kelshaw. m 6/27/1987 Charles Donald Noland c 1.

NOLTA, Hugh Gregg (NCal) 556 E Sycamore St, Willows CA 95988 **Died 3/17/2016** B Willows CA 1942 s Dale & Gretchen. D 10/30/2010 P 7/9/2011 Bp Barry Leigh Beisner. m 6/28/1971 Vicki Ann Nolta c 3.

NOON, Anna Catherine Christian (Md) 5203 Falls Road Ter Apt 1, Baltimore MD 21210 **S Jn's Ch Ellicott City MD 2015-** B Springfield TN 1970 d Dennis & Carol. BA U So 1992; MDiv GTS 2010. D 6/12/2010 P 12/18/2010 Bp Herman Hollerith IV. Asst S Dav's Ch Baltimore MD 2013-2015; Assisant R S Jn's Ch Hampton VA 2010-2013. anoon@stjohnsec.org

NOONAN, Deborah Anne (Az) 2331 E. Adams St., Tucson AZ 85719 B Panorama City CA 1979 d John & Catherine. BA U of Virginia 2001; MDiv Ya Berk 2010. D 6/6/2009 P 7/10/2010 Bp Kirk Stevan Smith. m 5/26/2012 Jesse Zink. Asst Dio Arizona Phoenix AZ 2010-2012; Cn Trin Cathd Phoenix AZ 2010-2012.

NORBY, Laura L (Mil) 508 Rupert Rd, Waunakee WI 53597 B Kankakee IL 1949 d Lloyd & Jeanine. BA Wartburg Coll 1971; MA Peabody Coll 1972; EdS Peabody Coll 1973; ADN Maysville Cmnty and Tech Coll 1978. D 6/5/1993 Bp Roger John White. m 11/1/1983 Terry Norby. D Dio Milwaukee Milwaukee WI 1993-2003.

NORCROSS, Steve (Ore) 8949 SW Fairview Pl, Portland OR 97223 **Dir Wm Temple Hse Portland OR 1999-** B Charleston WV 1941 s Robert & Helen. BA W Virginia U 1963; MDiv SMU Perkins 1966; Cert CDSP 1968; Sewanee: The U So, TS 1975; VTS 1998. D 8/5/1968 P 5/15/1969 Bp Ivol I Curtis. m 10/19/1985 Sandra Norcross c 2. P-in-c Ascen Par Portland OR 2004-2011; Int S Jn's Epis Ch Olympia WA 2002-2003, 1968-1970, Cur 1968-1970; Chapl Wm Temple Hse Portland OR 2002; Int All SS Ch Hillsboro OR 1999-2002; R S Mart's Ch Lebanon OR 1991-1999; Int Epis Par Of S Mich And All Ang Tucson AZ 1987-1988; R S Mk's Ch Havre MT 1983-1987; R Meade Memi Epis Ch Alexandria VA 1980-1983; Chapl Supvsr Sibley Memi Hosp WDC 1978-1980; Chapl Intern S Eliz Hosp WDC 1976-1977; Int S Jas Epis Ch Westernport MD 1975-1976; R Ch Of The Gd Shpd Charleston WV 1972-1974; Assoc Chr Ch Tacoma WA 1970-1972. Auth, *The Bivocational Option*, The Sm Ch / Alb Institue, 2000; Auth, *Var arts Hymnody & Ch Mus*. ADLMC; CBS 1975; EPF 1968; Integrity 1980; OHC 1972.

NORDQUIST, Conrad (Los) 4063 Ruis Ct, Jurupa Valley CA 92509 **Asst All SS Epis Ch Riverside CA 2001-** B Minneapolis MN 1933 s Conrad & Lucy-Lee. BS U MN 1955; LTh SWTS 1959; MA USC 1977. D 6/20/1959 P 12/21/1959 Bp Philip Frederick McNairy. c 3. R S Jn The Div Epis Ch Costa Mesa CA 1977-2000; Prof Bloy Hse Claremont CA 1974-1984; Assoc S Nich Par Encino CA 1965-1978; Asst Chr Ch Las Vegas NV 1963-1964; Cur Ch Of The Mssh Santa Ana CA 1960-1963; Vic S Ptr's Ch Warroad MN 1959-1960.

NORDSTROM JR, Eugene Alexander (HB) **Non-par 1969-** B Portland OR 1939 s Eugene & Kathleen. BA Whitman Coll 1962; STB ATC 1965; MS U of Washington 1967; DSW USC 1973. D 12/21/1965 Bp Ivol I Curtis. Stff S Lk's Epis Ch Vancouver WA 1967-1969. Auth, "A Study Of Love In Parent-Chld Relationships"; Auth, "Experiment In Upgrading The Nonprofessional Worker".

NORDWICK, Brian P (ECR) 670 Clearview Dr, Hollister CA 95023 **Cn for Admin & Fin Dio El Camino Real Salinas CA 2004-** B Medford OR 1953 s Harry & Jeanette. BS California Luth U 1976; BA California Sch for Deacons 1993. D 5/28/1994 Bp Richard Lester Shimpfky. m 3/20/1982 Sheila Marie Nordwick c 1. D S Steph-In-The-Field. brian@edecr.org

NORGARD, David Lee (Los) PO Box 691458, West Hollywood CA 90069 **Prncpl OD180 Consulting LLC W Hollywood CA 2005-; P Assoc All SS Par Beverly Hills CA 2012-; Chair AULA Alum Assn Los Angeles CA 2011-** B Hibbing MN 1958 s Theodore & Gladys. BA Augsburg Coll 1980; MDiv Ya Berk 1983; MAOM Antioch U 2008. D 6/11/1984 P 12/20/1984 Bp

Robert Marshall Anderson. m 10/11/2011 Joseph Edward Oppold. Assoc for Congrl Dvlpmt Cathd Ch Of S Paul San Diego CA 2004-2005; VP for Prog Epis Cmnty Serv Natl City CA 2003-2004; Exec Dir Epis Cmnty Serv Inc Minneapolis MN 2000-2003; R The Epis Ch Of S Jn The Evang San Francisco CA 1994-2000; Exec Dir & Mssnr The Oasis Newark NJ 1990-1994; Assoc All SS Epis Par Hoboken NJ 1990-1992; Asst R Ch Of The H Apos New York NY 1985-1990. Awd Of dist Among Recent Graduates Yale DS 1995; Dn'S Citation For Cmnty Serv Berk 1983. david@od180consulting.com

NORGREN, William Andrew (NY) 120 East 79th Street Apt. 2D, New York NY 10075 **Ret Ret 1995-; Hon Asst S Thos Ch New York NY 1995-** B Frostburg MD 1927 s William & Martha. BA W&M 1948; STM GTS 1953; BLitt Oxf GB 1959. D 5/31/1953 P 12/20/1953 Bp Horace W B Donegan. Theol Consult Epis Ch Cntr New York NY 1995, Ecum Off 1980-1994, Asst Ecum Off 1979, Asst Ecum Off 1975-1978; Gvrng Bd NCCC 1979-1995; Hon Assoc Trin Par New York NY 1975-2015, Pstr Asst 1972-1974; Pstr Asst Ch Of The Ascen New York NY 1972; Observer 2nd Vatican Coun 1963-1965; Advsr WCC Assembly 1961-1991; Exec Dir Cmsn on Faith & Ord NCCC New York NY 1959-1971; Chapl Ch of Engl Chr Ch Catheral Oxford 1955-1958; Asst Ch Of The Resurr Kew Gardens NY 1953-1955; Fell/Tutor The GTS New York NY 1953-1955. Auth, "Faith and Ord in the USA," Wm B. Eerdmers Pub Co, 2011; Ed, "Ecum of the Possible," Forw Mvmt Press, 1994; Ed, "Toward Full Commitment & Concordat of Agreement," Forw Mvmt Press, Augsburg, 1991; Ed, "Implications of the Gospel," Forw Mvmt Press, Augsburg, 1988; Ed, "Living Room Dialogues," Paulist Press, Friendship Press, 1965. DD Ya Berk, New Haven, CT 1995; DD GTS, New York 1984.

NORMAN, Curt (EMich) St. John's Episcopal Church, 123 N Michigan Ave, Saginaw MI 48602 **S Jn's Epis Ch Saginaw MI 2016-** B Norfolk VA 1969 s Worth & Patricia. BA U of No Texas 1996; MDiv Sewanee: The U So, TS 2001. D 6/9/2001 Bp D Avid Bruce Macpherson P 5/18/2002 Bp James Monte Stanton. m 1/11/2003 Margaret I Norman c 2. R S Lk's Epis Ch Stephenville TX 2011-2016; Assoc Ch of the H Faith Santa Fe NM 2009-2011; R S Lk's Ch Denison TX 2004-2009; Assoc S Ptr's Epis Ch Del Mar CA 2003-2004; Cur Chr Epis Ch Plano TX 2001-2003. curt@stjohns-saginaw.org

NORMAN, Harold Gene (Dal) 406 Dula Cir., Duncanville TX 75116 B Waco TX 1927 s Ulma & Lena. BA U of Texas 1950; MDiv Bex Sem 1954. D 7/2/1954 P 7/1/1955 Bp Clinton Simon Quin. m 2/16/1974 Patsy Vinson c 1. R S Gabr's Duncanville TX 1985-1986; Dept Of Missions Dallas TX 1984-1985; St Gabriels Ch Desoto TX 1975-1986; Vic S Gabr's Duncanville TX 1975-1985; R S Geo's Epis Ch Dallas TX 1970-1975; Vic Santiago Apos In Guatamala City 1965-1970; Vic All SS Managua Nicaragua 1961-1965; R S Barth's Ch Hempstead TX 1956-1960; Cur St Andrews Epis Ch Houston TX 1954-1956. Auth, "Manual Para Lectores Laicos," 1963.

NORMAN, Joseph Gary (Alb) PO Box 800, Morris NY 13808 **D Zion Ch Morris NY 2006-** B Richmond VA 1959 s Joseph & Nancy. BA U of Virginia 1981; MA W&M 1987. D 6/10/2006 Bp Daniel William Herzog. m 8/15/1987 Stacia Gregory c 2.

NORMAN, Lynn (CGC) Trinity Episcopal Church, 1900 Dauphin St, Mobile AL 36606 **Trin Epis Ch Mobile AL 2012-** B Chattanooga TN 1979 s Lynn & Suzanne. BA U So 2001; MDiv VTS 2006; MDiv VTS 2006. D 5/27/2006 P 1/21/2007 Bp Charles Glenn VonRosenberg. m 7/18/2012 Sara N Norman c 1. Calv Epis Ch Cleveland MS 2009-2012; Asst S Steph's Epis Ch Oak Ridge TN 2006-2009; Asst-Cntrl Files Cbl And Assoc 2002-2003. rector@trinitychurchmobile.org

NORMAN JR, Richard Hudson (WLa) 405 Glenmar Ave, Monroe LA 71201 **Gr Epis Ch Monroe LA 2013-** B Alexandria LA 1958 s Richard & Frances. Wake Forest U 1977; NW St U Natchitoches 1980; BS LSU 1984; MA LSU 1988; STM GTS 1993; MDiv GTS 1993. D 6/6/1992 P 5/15/1993 Bp Robert Jefferson Hargrove Jr. m 5/29/1993 Adrienne Judith Mckee c 2. Cn Liturg Cathd Ch Of S Mk Minneapolis MN 2005-2013; R Epis Ch Of The Redeem Greenville SC 2002-2005; Serv Ch In Engl 1997-2002; Assoc R All SS' Epis Ch Chevy Chase MD 1995-1997; R S Paul's Ch Abbeville LA 1993-1995; D The Ch of S Matt And S Tim New York NY 1992-1993; Pstr Asst The Amer Cathd of the H Trin Paris 75008 1991-1992; Joint Fin Com (Coun and Trst) Dio Minnesota Minneapolis MN 2012, Mgmt Com (Coun) 2012, 2011 Dioc Conv Liturg Com 2011, Dioc Liturg Com for the Consecration of a New Bp 2010, Dn of Reg 8 2009-2011, Cmsn on Liturg 2005-2010; 2004 Dioc Conv Liturg Plnng Com Dio Upper So Carolina Columbia SC 2004; Bp's Advsry Coun on Aspirants for Mnstry 2002-2005; Plannning Com for the Edmonton Epis Area Trien Cler Conf for 2001 Ch Of Engl London 2000-2002, Stndg Com (Fin), W Barnet Dnry 1999-2002, Gvnr, St. Andr's C of E Primary Sch, Southgate 1997-1998, Stndg Advsry Coun on Rel Educ in the Borough of Enfield 1997-1998; Gvnr, St Mary's C of E HS, Hendon Dio London Dn'S Crt LONDON 2000-2002, Gvnr, St. Jn's C of E Primary Sch, Hendon 1999-2002; Elected Rep Hse of Cler London Dioc Syn 2000-2002; Com Mem W Barnet Sch Capitation Fees Working Party UK 1999-2000; Exec Com Mill Hill Ch LEP Mill Hill London 1998-2002; Chairman Soc Responsibility Com Mill Hill LEP London 1998-2002; Com Mem Addison Av Working Grp Enfield Dnry 1997-1998;

Chapl Chapl to the Metroplltn Police Southgate London 1997-1998; Dioc Ins Com Dio Washington Washington DC 1996-1997, Dioc Personl Committe 1996-1997; Dioc Sch for Mnstry (Tchg Fell) Dio Wstrn Louisiana Alexandria LA 1994-1995, Chapl Bd, U of SW Louisiana 1994, Cmsn on Liturg 1993-1995, Bd Dir, The Well (Ch Army), Lafayette, LA 1993-1994. rector@gracechurchmonroe.org

NORMAN, Tex (CFla) B Austin TX 1950 s Richard & Jo Ann. BA Oklahoma Chr Coll 1972; BA E Cntrl U 1976; Inst of Chr Stds 1996. D 3/23/1996 Bp John Wadsworth Howe. m 8/4/1972 Kathie E Ervenson-Norman c 1.

NORMAND, Ann Dennison (Tex) 1225 Texas Ave., Houston TX 77002 B Beaumont TX 1942 d George & Elouise. BS Texas Tech U 1964; Baylor U 1984; MDiv Austin Presb TS 1995; Cert VTS 1995; DMin Austin Presb TS 2001. D 6/17/1995 Bp Claude Edward Payne P 2/18/1996 Bp Leopoldo Jesus Alard. c 4. Cn to the Ordnry Dio Texas Houston TX 2008-2014; R Trin Epis Ch Marble Falls TX 1998-2008; Asst to the R S Paul's Ch Waco TX 1995-1998. Auth, "The Vow of Stability: Rooting the Contemporary Epis Par in Benedictine Sprtlty," Austin Presb TS, 2001. Cler Renwl Grant Lilly Endwmt, Inc. 2005; WP Newell Memi Fllshp Austin Presb TS 1995. denny08@me.com

NORMANN, Margaret Ella Monroe (Ct) 888 B Heritage Vlg, Southbury CT 06488 B Providence RI 1931 d Parker & Margaret. BA Vas 1952; MA NYU 1966; MS Sthrn Connecticut St U 1978. D 6/15/1993 Bp Walter Decoster Dennis Jr. m 7/17/1953 Conrad Neil Normann c 4. D S Paul's Ch Woodbury CT 2002-2005; D Ch Of The H Comm Mahopac NY 1996-2002; Chapl Four Winds Psych Cntr Katonah NY 1993-1999. Auth, "Stand Up & Be Counted," 1990; Auth, "In My Hm Town," 1989; Auth, "There Goes The Nbrhd," Nys Dept Of Mntl Hlth; Auth, "Swear To Uphold". Spec Citation Westchester Cnty Bd Legislators 1994; Cert Of Nerit For Wk w Homeless Gvnr Cuomo 1991; Mickey Loland 2nd Annual Hope For The Homeless Awd St Of Ny 1991; DSA Lincoln Sch 1988.

NORRIS, David (Ct) 5 Briar Brae Rd, Stamford CT 06903 B 1935 BA Harv; MS Iona Coll; MDiv UTS; MDiv UTS; MA UTS; PhD UTS. D 10/20/1982 P 11/1/1983 Bp William Bradford Hastings. m 6/11/1958 Gunilla Dryselius. Serv Presb Ch.

NORRIS JR, Edwin Arter (Chi) 2866 Vacherie Ln, Dallas TX 75227 **Ret 1994-; Nash Nashotah WI 1990-, 1978-1989** B Akron OH 1929 s Edwin & Elizabeth. BA U Denv 1955; Nash 1956; Nash 1986. D 6/15/1962 P 10/28/1963 Bp James Reginald Mallett. Dio Chicago Chicago IL 1982-1985; Dio Chicago Chicago IL 1977-1980; R Ch Of The Ascen Chicago IL 1971-1993; Cur S Paul Hammond IN 1964-1965; Mem S Greg's Abbey Three Rivers MI 1956-1970; Dep GC Dio Chicago Chicago IL 1988-1991, Dep GC 1982-1985, Dep GC 1976-1982. CCU, ECM, ESA.

NORRIS, John Roy (Okla) 6310 E 111th Place, Tulsa OK 74137 **Died 1/7/2017** B Oklahoma City OK 1940 s John & Eleanor. Cntrl St Coll Chadron NE 1960; BS Oklahoma City U 1964; MDiv Epis TS in Kentucky 1977; DMin Phillips Grad Sem 1988. D 6/18/1977 Bp Gerald Nicholas Mcallister P 12/18/1977 Bp Frederick Warren Putnam. m 11/21/1962 Linda C Norris c 2. Chapl S Simeon's Epis Hm 1986-2006; Chapl S Simeons Epis Hm Tulsa OK 1986-2005; R S Ptr's Ch Tulsa OK 1982-1986; S Jn's Ch Oklahoma City OK 1977-1982; Cur Dio Oklahoma Oklahoma City OK 1977-1980.

NORRIS, Mark Joseph Patrick (Neb) 155 Strozier Rd # B, West Monroe LA 71291 B Omaha NE 1961 s Richard & Roberta. BA Creighton U 1990; MTh S Johns U 1995; CTh Epis TS of the SW 1999; CPE Nebraska Med Cntr 2003. Rec 1/17/1999 as Priest Bp Robert Jefferson Hargrove Jr. Ch Of The Trsfg Evergreen CO 2010-2013; S Mary's Epis Ch Blair NE 2006-2009; H Fam Epis Ch Omaha NE 2003-2005; R S Pat's Epis Ch W Monroe LA 1999-2002.

NORRIS, M Brent (WNC) 337 Charlotte St, Asheville NC 28801 **R S Mary's Ch Asheville NC 2005-** B Easley SC 1962 s Robert & Margie. BA Furman U 1984; MDiv Sewanee: The U So, TS 1996; DMin Columbia TS, Decatur, GA 2013; DMin Other 2013. D 5/31/1996 P 12/7/1996 Bp Henry Irving Louttit. m 2/24/1989 Cynthia B Baker c 1. Preist in Charge Iglesia Nuestro Salvador Asheville NC 2007-2009; R Gr Ch Cullman AL 1999-2005; Cur Chr Ch Frederica St Simons Is GA 1996-1999. CSM Assoc 1996. rector@stmarysasheville.org

NORRIS III, Paul Haile (At) 951 Williams St, Madison GA 30650 **R S Columba Epis Ch Suwanee GA 2004-** B Atlanta GA 1965 s Paul & Carolyn. BA Davidson Coll 1987; MDiv GTS 1994. D 6/4/1994 P 12/10/1994 Bp Frank Kellogg Allan. m 7/27/1991 Theresa B Norris c 2. Dio Atlanta Atlanta GA 2002-2003; The Epis Ch Of The Adv Madison GA 1996-2002; S Mk's Ch Dalton GA 1994-1996.

NORRIS, Rollin Bradford (Mich) 1626 Strathcona Dr, Detroit MI 48203 **Ret 1994-; Ret 1994-** B Nevilly FR 1934 s Whitton & Carolyn. BA Harv 1956; BD EDS 1959. D 6/20/1959 Bp Hamilton Hyde Kellogg P 12/20/1959 Bp Philip Frederick McNairy. m 7/18/1959 Margo Norris c 1. Int Chr Ch Dearborn MI 1993; Int S Jn's Ch Royal Oak MI 1991-1992; Int Dio Michigan Detroit MI 1990-1994; Int S Lk's Ch Utica MI 1990-1991; R All SS Ch Detroit MI 1985-1990; R S Paul's Epis Ch Port Huron MI 1971-1985; Assoc Chr Ch Cran-

N

brook Bloomfield Hills MI 1968-1971; Vic Ch Of The Resurr Minneapolis MN 1962-1968; Cur S Lk's Ch Minneapolis MN 1959-1962.

NORRIS, Stephen Allen (Ga) 2493 Chandler Dr, Valdosta GA 31602 **S Barn Epis Ch Valdosta GA 2016**- B Valdosta GA 1975 s Kenneth & Terrie. BA SE U 1997; MDiv VTS 2003; MS Valdosta St U 2015. D 2/8/2003 P 8/20/2003 Bp Henry Irving Louttit. m 8/9/1997 Stephany A Norris c 2. St Jas Ch Valdosta GA 2016; S Andr's Epis Ch Douglas GA 2013-2015; S Fran Of The Islands Epis Ch Savannah GA 2012-2013; Dir of Pstr Care So Georgia Med Cntr Valdosta GA 2004-2012; yes S Jn's Ch Moultrie GA 2003-2004. Assn of Profsnl Chapl 2007. norris.stephen9@gmail.com

NORRIS, Susy (NJ) 6355 Pine Dr., Chincoteague VA 23336 B Jefferson City MO 1943 d Harold & Alice. BD DePauw U 1965; SMM UTS 1968; MDiv Drew U 1981; none GTS 1986. D 6/14/1986 P 1/10/1987 Bp George Phelps Mellick Belshaw. m 8/20/1966 Kenneth Scott Norris c 2. P Assoc Gr Ch Newark NJ 2008-2009; P Gr St Pauls Ch Trenton NJ 2000-2008; Dir D Formtn Dio New Jersey Trenton NJ 1997-2002; R H Trin Ch So River NJ 1993-1994; Field Spvsr The GTS New York NY 1991-1994; Assoc Gr Epis Ch Plainfield NJ 1991-1993; Asst Min S Jn's Ch Eliz NJ 1986-1987; Chapl Overlook Hosp Summit New Jersey 1980-1983. Claiming the Blessing 2006-2009; Cmnty Of S Jn The Bapt 1984; EWC 1976-1982; Integrity 1982; Interfaith Hosp Ntwk 1994-2006; NAAD 1992; Oasis New Jersey 2004-2009.

NORRO, Hugo Pablo (Los) 4200 Summers Ln Unit 15, Klamath Falls OR 97603 B Buenos Aires Argentina 1942 s Hector & Giovanna. BA California St U 1973; BS California St U Los Angeles 1975; MDiv CDSP 1985; PsyD USC 2001. D 6/15/1985 P 12/21/1985 Bp Oliver Bailey Garver Jr. m 8/19/2006 Bernice Norro c 3. R S Jos's Par Buena Pk CA 2001-2008; Int S Jas' Par So Pasadena CA 2000-2001; R S Mary's Epis Ch Mitchell SD 1988-2000; Asst S Wilfrid Of York Epis Ch Huntington Bch CA 1985-1988.

NORTH, Bob (Chi) 7 Huron Trce, Galena IL 61036 **R Gr Epis Ch Galena IL 2001-; PT SUNDAY'S S Paul's Ch Savanna IL 2001**- B Rochester MN 1942 s Clarence & Phyllis. BA Macalester Coll 1964; BD Bex Sem 1967; DMin Luther TS 1982. D 7/25/1967 P 4/6/1968 Bp Hamilton Hyde Kellogg. m 5/27/1967 Karen North c 4. R Gr Epis Ch Galena IL 2001-2011; R Gr Epis Ch Freeport IL 1995-2001; Mssy S Lk's Ch Pk City UT 1993-1995; Dio Utah Salt Lake City UT 1992-1995; Calv Cathd Sioux Falls SD 1990-1992; R Gr Ch Holland MI 1983-1989; R Chr Epis Ch Grand Rapids MN 1976-1982; Asst S Mary's Ch S Paul MN 1974-1976; Assoc St Dav's Epis Ch Minnetonka MN 1970-1973; R Epiph Epis Ch S Paul MN 1967-1970. Galena Cultural Arts Allnce Pres 2006; Habitat of Jo Daviess Cnty Founding Pres 2005; YMCA Founders 1980; Bush Ldrshp Fellowowship 1973. robertdavidnorth@gmail.com

NORTH, Joseph James (Alb) 144 Prospect Ave, Gloversville NY 12078 **Trin Ch Gloversville NY 2002**- B Binghamton NY 1946 D 9/8/2002 Bp David John Bena P 3/7/2009 Bp William Howard Love. m 6/13/1970 Monica Young.

NORTH JR, William Miller (Tex) 570 Marietta Ave, Swarthmore PA 19081 B Buffalo NY 1942 s William & Carolyn. BA Coll of Wooster 1964; Col 1967; MDiv UTS 1967; Cert Blanton-Peale Grad Inst 1971. D 8/1/1995 P 3/5/1996 Bp Hays H. Rockwell. m 6/26/1965 Mary D North c 2. S Lk's Epis Hosp Houston TX 2005-2007; Dir of Chapl Serv St. Lk's Epis Hlth System Houston TX 2005-2007; Chapl to the Cler Dio Arizona Phoenix AZ 2005; Int Assoc Dn Trin Cathd Phoenix AZ 2005; Assoc Chr Ch Of The Ascen Paradise Vlly AZ 1999-2004; Assoc S Mich & S Geo S Louis MO 1993-1999; Exec Dir Care and Counslg Inc and TheEpiscopal City Mssn S 1975-1993; Mem of Bd Dir Chester Eastside Inc Chester 2014-2017. Amer Assn of Mar and Fam Therapists; AAPC; Soc of S Jn the Evang.

NORTHCRAFT, Linda Louise (Mich) 19120 Eldridge Ct, Southfield MI 48076 B Cumberland MD 1945 d Howard & Sidna. BS Frostburg St U 1967; MA Wstrn Maryland Coll 1973; MDiv Ya Berk 1987. D 6/20/1987 P 5/19/1988 Bp Albert Theodore Eastman. m 6/22/2011 Ellen Cora Ehrlich. R S Jn's Ch Royal Oak MI 1997-2012; S Mths' Epis Ch Baltimore MD 1990-1997; Int S Mary Anne's Epis Ch No E MD 1989; Ch Of The H Comf Luthvle Timon MD 1987-1989; COM Dio Michigan Detroit MI 1999-2003; Com of the Episcopate Dio Maryland Baltimore MD 1994-1997, COM 1990-1996, Liturg Com 1990-1994, COM 1990-1993, Peace & Justice Cmsn 1987-1989. Chas E Mersick Prize for Preaching Yale DS 1987.

NORTHUP, Frederick Bowen (At) 1118 Chicory Lane, Asheville NC 28803 **Fndr and Pres Athletes for a Better Wrld Atlanta GA 1998**- B Asheville,NC 1945 s Isaac & Josephine. Institut des Etudes Politiques 1966; BA U So 1968; MDiv GTS 1973. D 6/16/1973 Bp Robert E Gribbin P 6/23/1974 Bp William F Gates Jr. m 6/29/1968 Jule S Northup c 2. Assoc S Geo's Epis Ch Griffin GA 2002-2003; Fndr/Pres Athletes For A Better Wrld Atlanta GA 1998-2002; Dn S Mk's Cathd Seattle WA 1988-1998; R Epis Ch Of The Gd Shpd Lake Chas LA 1982-1988; Asst St. Barth Ch New York NY 1978-1982; Cn Convoc of Epis Ch in Europe Paris 1975-1978; Cn The Amer Cathd of the H Trin Paris 75008 1975-1978; Asst S Jn's Epis Ch Memphis TN 1973-1975. Auth, "Winning More Than The Game," Amazon, 2012; Auth, 1985; Auth, 1980. Huguenot Soc 1968.

NORTHUP, Lesley Armstrong (NY) 1298 NE 95th St, Miami FL 33138 **Dn, The hon Coll Florida Intl Univ 2004-; Assoc Profof Rel Stds, hon Coll Dn Florida Intl U 2003-; Cn Theol Dio Bethlehem Bethlehem PA 1996**- B Bronx NY 1947 d Edmund & Ruth. BA U of Wisconsin 1970; MDiv EDS 1980; MA CUA 1983; PhD CUA 1991. D 6/7/1980 P 1/19/1981 Bp Paul Moore Jr. c 1. Instr U of Maryland 1988-1993; Instr of Liturg VTS Alexandria VA 1987; Exec Secy Natl Epis. Cltn on Alco and Drugs 1985-1986; Instr in Liturg Howard Univ Sch of Div 1984; Educ Coordntr S Aug's Epis Ch Washington DC 1983-1985; Chapl USNR 1977-1999. Ed, "Years 1999-2004," *Rel Documents, No Amer Annual*, Amer Intl Press, 2004; Co-Ed, "Leaps & Boundaries: Lit Rev in the 21st Cent," Continuum/Morehouse, 1997; Auth, "Ritualizing Wmn," Pilgrim Press, 1997; Auth, "The 1892 Revs of BCP," Edwin Mellen Press, 1993; Ed, "Wmn and Rel Ritual," Pstr Press, 1993. Florida Hmnts Coun 2001-2007; HSEC 2005; Nat Coun of hon Colleges 2004; No Amer Acad of Liturg 1997; Societas Liturgica 1997. Cn Theol Dio Bethlehem 1996.

NORTHWAY, Daniel Page (Kan) 3531 SW Ashworth Ct, Topeka KS 66614 B Oneida NY 1942 s David & Virginia. Topeka Inst for Psychoanalysis; Ya 1965; BA U of Miami 1970; MD U of Miami 1974; EFM TS 1978; EFM Sewanee: The U So, TS 1978; Menninger Clnc 1979. D 9/29/1988 Bp Richard Frank Grein P 8/1/1989 Bp John Forsythe Ashby. m 3/6/1970 Kathryn Ann Sweeney c 2. Assoc Trin Ch Lawr KS 2008-2010; 1991-2000; Vic S Mk's Ch Blue Rapids KS 1988-2008; S Paul's Ch Marysville KS 1988-2008; Mem COM 1990-1998. OHC, RWF, Associated P.

NORTON, Ann Elizabeth (EMich) PO Box 217, Otter Lake MI 48464 B Detroit MI 1946 d David & Doris. BA Cntrl Michigan U 1968. D 9/23/2008 P 3/21/2009 Bp Steven Todd Ousley. m 8/15/1970 Joseph Norton c 2.

NORTON JR, James Frederick (Ia) 1621 E River Ter, Minneapolis MN 55414 **Non-par 1987**- B Cleveland OH 1946 s James & Barbara. BA Baldwin-Wallace Coll 1969; MDiv Bex Sem 1981. D 9/24/1981 Bp Harold Anthony Hopkins Jr P 3/1/1982 Bp William Grant Black. m 12/27/1970 Susan Lee Croy. R S Jn's Ch Mason City IA 1984-1986; Asst R Chr Epis Ch Of Springfield Springfield OH 1981-1984; Amer Mnstry Fllshp 1977-1980. Ord Of S Lk.

NORTON, Jerry R (Ak) **Epiph Ch Kivalina AK 1974**- B Kivalina AK 1942 s Daniel & Betty. D 7/28/1974 Bp William Jones Gordon Jr. m 1/15/1967 Rebecca Swan c 1.

NORTON, Marlee R (Va) 2416 N Florida St, Arlington VA 22207 **Gr Epis Ch Hulmeville PA 2014-; P-in-c S Jas Epis Ch Bristol PA 2014-, 2009-2012** B Chicago 1955 d Donald & Jane. BA U of Iowa 1977; BA U of Iowa 1977; MDiv VTS 2006. D 6/16/2007 Bp Peter J Lee P 12/17/2007 Bp David Colin Jones. Dio Pennsylvania Philadelphia PA 2012-2013; VP of Intl Prog Natl Telecommunications 1986-2003. marleenorton@gmail.com

NORTON, Mary (NwPa) 218 Center St, Ridgway PA 15853 **P-in-c Emm Ch Corry PA 2014-; Dnry Dn Dio NW Pennsylvania Erie PA 2009-, Dioc Hlth Team 2008-2010, Prov 3 Syn Rep 2007-, Stndg Com 2007**- B Pittsburgh PA 1957 d Thomas & Mary. BA Alleg 1979; MBA Duquesne U 1988; MDiv VTS 2006. D 10/29/2005 P 6/10/2006 Bp Robert Deane Rowley Jr. P-in-c Gr Epis Ch Ridgway PA 2009-2014; P-in-c S Agnes' Epis Ch S Marys PA 2009-2014; Ch Of Our Sav Dubois PA 2009. The Ford Chair VTS 2006.

NORTON, Mary Julyan (Ak) St Georges In the Arctic Church, Po Box 269, Kotzebue AK 99752 B Castro Valley CA 1955 d James & Margaret. Tchg Cred California St U - E Bay; coursework CDSP; BA Lewis & Clark Coll; coursework U of Alaska. D 8/2/2015 P 2/18/2017 Bp Mark A Lattime. m 9/30/1989 Ernest Norton c 5.

NORVELL, John David (Okla) 530 Northcrest Dr, Ada OK 74820 B 1952 s James & Billie. BS Oklahoma St U 1976; MDiv Epis TS of the SW 1988. D 6/18/1988 Bp Gerald Nicholas Mcallister P 3/17/1989 Bp Robert Manning Moody. m 7/17/2003 Susan Norvell c 1. R S Lk's Epis Ch Ada OK 1995-2017; Ch Of The Redeem Okmulgee OK 1990-1995; S Paul's Cathd Oklahoma City OK 1988-1990.

NOVAK, Barbara Ellen Hosea (Spok) 1107 E 41st Ave, Spokane WA 99203 B Spokane WA 1949 d Noel & Margaret. BA WA SU 1972; MA Sthrn Illinois U 1974. D 11/19/1978 Bp John Raymond Wyatt. m 8/29/1981 Terry Novak.

NOVAK, Margaret Anne (Oly) 15502 30th Ave Ne, Shoreline WA 98155 B Bellingham WA 1940 d John & Margaret. BS WA SU 1962; MA Seattle U 1991. D 6/24/2000 Bp Sanford Zangwill Kaye Hampton. m 8/11/1962 Stuart Raymond Novak c 3. S Andr's Ch Seattle WA 2002-2005.

NOVAK, Nick (Tex) 5215 Honey Creek, Baytown TX 77523 B San Antonio TX 1950 s Donald & Oleta. AA San Jacinto Coll 1975; BBA U of Houston Clear Lake 1984; MDiv TESM 1991. D 6/23/1991 P 2/17/1992 Bp Maurice Manuel Benitez. m 5/9/1971 Pamela Gay Novak c 2. R Trin Epis Ch Baytown TX 2001-2016; S Mk's Ch Bay City TX 1994-2001; Vic S Paul's Epis Ch Woodville TX 1991-1994; The Great Cmsn Fndt Houston TX 1991-1994.

NOVAK-SCOFIELD, Eleanor Patricia (SwVa) 124 E Main St, Abingdon VA 24210 B New Haven CT 1946 d Joseph & Helen. BA Sacr Heart U 1972; MS Virginia Commonwealth U 2011. D 12/3/1988 Bp Arthur Edward Walmsley.

NOVES, W David Peter (WNY) 840 Bataan Ave, Dunkirk NY 14048 **P-in-c S Mary's Epis Ch Gowanda NY 2008**- B Buffalo NY 1943 s William &

635

N

Doris. BA SUNY 1966; STB Ya Berk 1969; DMin GTF 1991. D 6/21/1969 Bp Lauriston L Scaife P 12/9/1976 Bp John Harris Burt. m 6/22/1968 Diane R Noves c 4. R Gr Ch Randolph NY 1997-2007; P-in-c Chr Ch Punxsutawney PA 1987-1997; Chaplian Dubois Reg Med Cntr 1987-1997; R Emm Ch Corry PA 1978-1987; Assoc Ch Of Our Sav Akron OH 1975-1978; Cur S Paul's Ch Akron OH 1969-1971.

NOWLIN, Ben Gary (Mo) 61 Dames Ct, Ferguson MO 63135 B Fort Smith AR 1953 s Ben & Reba. BA U of Cntrl Arkansas 1975; PhD U of Oklahoma 1981; MDiv Epis TS of the SW 1984. D 6/16/1984 Bp William Jackson Cox P 5/1/1985 Bp Herbert Alcorn Donovan Jr. m 12/20/1975 Susan Nowlin c 1. S Steph's Ch S Louis MO 1993-2001; S Jas Ch Magnolia AR 1992-1993; S Mary's Epis Ch El Dorado AR 1990-1991; Dio Arkansas Little Rock AR 1989-1990; R S Mk's Ch Crossett AR 1987-1989; Asst R S Paul's Ch Fayetteville AR 1984-1987.

NOYES, Daphne B (Mass) Church of the Advent, 30 Brimmer St, Boston MA 02108 **D The Ch Of The Adv Boston MA 2008-; Chapl Massachusetts Gnrl Hosp Boston MA 1994-** B Boston MA 1947 d Thomas & Tenney. St Vladimir's Sem 1994; MA EDS 1995; Partnr Healthcare System CPE Cntr 1996; HealthCare Dimensions 1999; Amer Red Cross 2001; Dioc D Prog 2001; Beth Israel Dss Med Cntr 2008; Col Med Cntr 2009; GW 2010; Harvard Med Sch 2012. D 10/6/2001 Bp M(Arvil) Thomas Shaw. c 2. D Ch Of S Jn The Evang Boston MA 2001-2007; Emm Ch Boston MA 2001-2007; The Cathd Ch Of S Paul Boston MA 2001-2007; Pt. Care Svcs. Interdisciplinary Advsry C'tee Massachusetts Gnrl Hosp 2012-2013; Ethics in Clincl Pract Com Massachusetts Gnrl Hosp 2011-2013; Dom Violence Working Grp Massachusetts Gnrl Hosp 2008-2011. Contrib, "Deacons and Their Stories," *Many Servnt: An Intro to Deacons,* Cowley, 2004; Contrib, "Forgiveness," *The H Intimacy of Strangers,* Jossey-Bass, 2002. Assembly of Epis Healthcare Chapl 1996-2006; Assn of Epis Deacons (life Mem) 2011; Assn of Profsnl Chapl 1996-2006; NAAD 2001-2005. Chr Ldrshp Awd Chr Cmnty Cmsn 2013; Partnr in Excellence Massachusetts Gnrl Hosp 2009; Polly Bond Awd ECom 2004; Fell AAPC 1998.

NSENGIYUMVA, Samuel (Md) 1223 Huron Trail, Sheboygan Falls WI 53085 **Ch Of The Ascen Westminster MD 2014-** B Cyeru Rwanda 1961 s Petero & Agnesta. BA SeminaryDaystar U Nairobi Kenya 1996; MA Associated Mennonite Biblic Sem 1999. Trans 8/11/2004 as Priest Bp Russell Edward Jacobus. m 12/26/1987 Marie Rose Nirere c 4. R S Ptr's Epis Ch Sheboygan Falls WI 2003-2014; H Fam Ch Angola IN 1999-2003; Asst Riruta Par Nairobi Kenya 1996-1998; D Riruta Par Nairobi Kenya 1993-1996; Exec Coun Dio Fond du Lac Appleton WI 2005-2011, Stndg Com 2004-2008. nsengasa@yahoo.com

NSUBUGA, Thomas (WLa) 538 Main St, Grambling LA 71245 **S Mk's Cathd Shreveport LA 2015-; VP , Campus Mnstry Bd Grambling St U Grambling Louisiana 2010-** B Uganda 1969 s Lameka & Agiri-Norah. BA Makerere U 1992; BD Bp Tucker Theol Coll 1995; MDiv Cranmer Theol Hse 2001. Trans 12/23/2008 Bp D Avid Bruce Macpherson. m 1/4/1997 Erinah E Nsubuga c 2. S Lk's Chap Grambling LA 2008-2015.

NTAGENGWA, Jean Baptiste (Mass) 138 Tremont St, Boston MA 02111 **Dir of Transition Mnstry Dio Massachusetts Boston MA 2012-** B Rwanda 1966 s Francois & Marisiyana. BD St Pauls U Limuru-Kenya 1998; MTS Harvard DS 2001; ThD Bos TS 2008. Trans 5/29/2008 Bp M(Arvil) Thomas Shaw. m 8/21/1993 Christine Ntagengwa c 3. Dir of Clients Serv Refugee Immigration Mnstry Malden MA 2011-2012; P-in-c S Jn's S Jas Epis Ch Boston MA 2011-2012; Asst P Ch Of The H Sprt Mattapan MA 2009-2011. Auth, "Bk," *Overcoming Cycles of Violence in Rwanda: Ethical Ldrshp and Ethnic Justice,* Edwin MellenPress, 2010.

NUAMAH, Father Reggie (LI) 3607 Glenwood Rd, Brooklyn NY 11210 B 1948 Trans 5/13/2002 Bp Orris George Walker Jr. m 8/7/1979 Rebecca Nuamah c 1. Int S Paul's Epis Ch Bound Brook NJ 2011-2017, 2008-2010; S Mary's Ch Brooklyn NY 2001-2008. stpaulsbbnj@verizon.net

NULL, John A (WK) 636 East Iron, Salina KS 67401 **Cn Theol Dio Wstrn Kansas Hutchinson KS 2005-** B Birmingham AL 1960 s William & Peggy. BA SMU 1982; MDiv Yale DS 1985; STM Yale DS 1989; PhD U of Cambridge 1995. D 8/31/1985 Bp John Forsythe Ashby P 6/8/1986 Bp Christopher FitzSimons Allison. Caritas Fndt Of Wstrn Kansas Salinas KS 2003-2016; Chapl Goodenough Coll London UK 1996-1999; Chapl Fettes Coll Edinburgh Scotland 1994-1995; R S Andr's Epis Ch Liberal KS 1988-1990; Ch Of S Jn By The Sea W Haven W Haven CT 1987-1988; S Jas' Ch New Haven CT 1987-1988; Asst & Chapl Gr Epis Ch New Haven NY 1985-1987. "Thos Cranmers Theol of the Heart," *Trin Journ for Theol and Mnstry,* 2007; "The Marian Exiles in Switzerland," *Jahrbuch für Europäische Geschichte,* 2006; "Real Joy: Freedom to be Your Best," Hännsler, 2004; "Jn Redman, the Gentle Ambler," *Westminster Abbey Reformed, ed. Knighton and Mortimer,* Ashgate, 2003; "Thos Cranmer's Doctrine of Repentance: Renewing the Power to Love," Oxford, 2000. Fell Royal Hist Soc 2008; Spec Discretionary Grant Rec ECF 2006; Guggenheim Fell Jn Simon Guggenheim Memi Fndt 2006; NEH Fell Natl Endwmt for the Hmnts 2005; Grant Rec HSEC 2002; Fulbright Schlr Fulbright Fndt 1990.

NUNEZ, Carlos E (Ore) 3052 Se 158th Ave, Portland OR 97236 B Santiago CL 1936 s Carlos & Marina. BTh UTS Buenos Aires AR 1961; MDiv UTS Buenos Aires AR 1964; DMin SFTS 2000. D 6/22/2002 Bp Robert Louis Ladehoff. c 2. H Cross Epis Ch Boring OR 2002.

NUNEZ, Timothy Charles (CFla) 10481 Se 68th Ct, Belleview FL 34420 **Cn Dio Cntrl Florida Orlando FL 2014-** B Bartow FL 1961 BA U of Florida. D 5/24/2003 P 12/7/2003 Bp John Wadsworth Howe. m 10/21/1988 Mary N Nunez c 4. R Epis Ch Of S Mary Belleview FL 2003-2014. tnunez@cfdiocese.org

NUNLEY, Janet W (NY) 137 N Division St, Peekskill NY 10566 **P-in-c S Ptr's Epis Ch Peekskill NY 2013-, Assoc P 2001-2013** B Gulfport MS 1954 d Lolan & Sibyl. BA Trin U San Antonio 1975; MDiv EDS 1992. D 12/10/1994 Bp George Nelson Hunt III P 7/15/1995 Bp Barbara Clementine Harris. m 12/7/2016 Susan T Erdey. Int Dir of Cmncatn & Marketing EDS Cambridge MA 2011-2012, 2010; Dio New York New York NY 2010-2013; P S Thos Epis Ch New Windsor NY 2010-2012; P St Fran of Assisi Montgomery NY 2009-2013; Dep for Cmncatn Epis Ch Cntr New York NY 2005-2009, Dep Dir, Epis News Serv 2000-2004; Bd Mem ECom 1998-2001; Cmncatn Dir Dio Rhode Island Providence RI 1997-2000; R S Ptr's And S Andr's Epis Providence RI 1996-2000; Assoc P Ch Of The H Trin Tiverton RI 1995-1996, D 1994-1995. Co-Auth, "Many Parts One Body: How the Epis Ch Works," Ch Pub, 2009; Auth, "How Many Lightbulbs Does It Take To Change A Chr?," Ch Pub, 2008; Auth, "Understanding the Windsor Report," Ch Pub, 2005; Auth, "Var arts," *Epis News Serv,* 2000. ECom 1990-2009. jnunley@stpeterspeekskill.org

NUNN, Frances Louise (Va) Po Box 206, Monterey VA 24465 **Cur S Geo 1978-** B Washington DC 1925 d Ira & Esther. BA Vas 1948; JD GW 1952. D 10/14/1978 Bp Robert Bruce Hall P 11/1/1982 Bp David Henry Lewis Jr. Epis Ch Cntr New York NY 1989.

NURDING, Brian Frank (Haw) 1144 Kumukumu St. Apt. E, Honolulu HI 96825 **Ret 1998-** B Tacoma WA 1935 s Frank & Jessie. BA Stan 1957; MDiv CDSP 1960. D 6/24/1960 P 3/13/1961 Bp William F Lewis. m 6/2/1990 Joe Ellen Nurding c 2. Int Waikiki Chap Honolulu HI 2000-2001; Int Gd Samar Epis Ch Honolulu HI 1997; Int S Ptr's Ch Honolulu HI 1995-1997; R Par of St Clem Honolulu HI 1979-1990; R S Jn The Bapt Epis Ch Seattle WA 1970-1979; R Gr Ch Ellensburg WA 1964-1970; Asst Trin Epis Ch Everett WA 1960-1964. Alum Preaching Prize CDSP 1960.

NUSSER-TELFER, Hiltrude Maria (O) 9868 Ford Rd, Perrysburg OH 43551 **Stff Chapl ProMedica Flower Hosp Sylvania OH 1997-** B 1937 d Karl & Margareta. Bus Sch Industries and Handels Kammer 1956; BA Cath U Louvain 1992; MA Katholike Universitaet 1994; Dplma GTS 2002; DMin GTF 2010. D 6/8/2002 Bp Arthur Williams Jr P 12/18/2002 Bp J Clark Grew II. D Epis Shared Mnstry Of NW Ohio Sherwood OH 2002. Auth, "Pstr Care," *Outcomes of Faith During Hospitalization A Case Study Method,* Auth Hse, 2010. Assn of Profsnl Chapl 2004; Epis Hlth Care Chapl Assn 2002; Flower Hosp Aux 1999; Flower Hosp Gld 1999; Ohio Chapl Orgnztn 2008.

NUTTER, James Wallace (Tex) 6221 Main St, Houston TX 77030 B Minden LA 1956 s James & Alice Anne. BA Bates Coll 1979; MDiv Nash 1983. D 5/28/1983 P 12/11/1983 Bp Frederick Barton Wolf. m 6/30/2007 Lucy Nutter c 2. R Palmer Memi Ch Houston TX 1994-2013; R S Ptr's Ch Rockland ME 1987-1994; Cur Cathd Ch Of S Lk Portland ME 1983-1987. Soc Of S Jn The Evang.

NWACHUKU, Chukwuemeka Polycarp (Chi) St Andrew's - Pentecost Evanston, 1928 Darrow Ave, Evanston IL 60201 **Vic St. Andrews Pentecost Epis Ch Evanston IL 2007-, 2001-** B Owerri Nigeria 1968 s Emmanuel & Cicelia. BEd Alyan Ikoku (Nsukka); MTS Seabury-Wstrn; Dplma Th Trin UTS; Dplma Rel Trin UTS. Trans 12/19/2013 as Priest Bp Jeff Lee. m 5/22/2004 Doreen O Nwachuku c 2.

NYATSAMBO, Tobias Dzawanda (NH) PO Box 737, Ashland NH 03217 **R S Jas Epis Ch Laconia NH 2011-** B Kadoma Zimbabwe 1947 s Masiwa & Norah. DRS All Nations Chr Coll UK 1980; MRE Gordon-Conwell TS 1991. Trans 9/11/2008 Bp Vicky Gene Robinson. m 12/23/1973 Rozina Nyatsambo c 3. P-in-c S Mk's Ch Ashland NH 2007-2009.

NYBACK, Rachel (Los) 1818 Monterey Blvd, Hermosa Beach CA 90254 **R St Cross Epis Ch Hermosa Bch CA 2004-** B California 1970 d Warren & Gretchen. BA Smith 1992; MA Claremont Grad U 1995; MDiv VTS 2004. D 6/19/2004 P 1/22/2005 Bp Joseph Jon Bruno. Fam Assoc St Cross by the Sea Epis Ch 2004-2009.

NYBACK, Warren (Los) 242 E Alvarado St, Pomona CA 91767 **Died 5/6/2017** B Los Angeles CA 1939 s Martin & Beula. BA USC 1961; BD CDSP 1964. D 9/10/1964 P 3/1/1965 Bp Francis E I Bloy. m 8/23/2004 Michael Witmer c 1. 1995-2017; Com - Gay/Lesbian Cmnty 1995-2017; 1993-1995; 1985-1990; Alt Dep Gc 1985-1988; Prog Of CE & Trng 1980-1981; Rep Of Bd Hillsides Epis Ch Hm For Chld 1980-1981; 1973-1978; S Paul's Pomona Pomona CA 1972-2001; Rep Of The Bd Hillsides Epis Ch Hm For Chld 1970-1975; Pres Par Manor Compton CA 1967-1972; Headmaster Par Sch Compton CA 1967-1972; R S Tim's Par Compton CA 1967-1972; Cur The Par Ch Of S Lk Long Bch CA 1964-1967.

NYBERG, Kristina Yvette (Los) 700 S. Myrtle Avenue, Apt 514, Monrovia CA 91016 **Grp Chapl (USAF) Los Angeles AFB 2015-** B New York NY 1962 d Eino & Amelia. BS USAF Acad 1986; MDiv TESM 1994. D 6/5/1994 P 12/12/1994 Bp Edward Lloyd Salmon Jr. c 3. Stff Chapl (USAF) AF Chapl Corps Coll Ft Jackson SC 2012-2015; Prot Chapl (USAF) RAF Mildenhall U.K. 2009-2012; CPE Res USAF Lackland AFB San Antonio TX 2008-2009; Prot Chapl (USAF) USAF Sheppard AFB TX 2004-2008; Prot Chapl (USAFR) USAF Reserves Whiteman AFB MO 1998-2004; Vic Trin Epis Ch Lebanon MO 1997-2001; Asst R S Mich's Epis Ch Charleston SC 1995-1997; Asst R S Paul's Epis Ch Lees Summit MO 1994-1995.

NYE, Linda Wade (NC) Grace Memorial Episcopal Church, 871 Merrimon Ave, Asheville NC 28804 **Ch Of The Epiph Eden NC 2010-** B Concord NC 1959 d Jack & Doris. BA Wstrn Carolina U 1981; MDiv Sewanee: The U So, TS 2007. D 6/9/2007 P 12/15/2007 Bp Porter Taylor. m 3/3/1984 Steven Nye. Assoc Gr Ch Asheville NC 2007-2009.

NYE, Max Ormsbee (Nev) 150 Cortona Way Apt 331, Brentwood CA 94513 **P S Alb's Epis Ch Brentwood CA 2010-; Ret 1988-; Dn Shasta Dnry 1979-** B Oakland CA 1928 s Berthold & Virginia. U CA 1953; VTS 1971. D 6/26/1971 P 12/1/1971 Bp Chauncie Kilmer Myers. m 6/30/1951 Nadeane Berry c 4. Assoc S Thos Epis Ch Temecula CA 2003-2010; Int R S Fran Ch Pauma Vlly CA 2002; Founding Chapl Mendocino Coast Dist Hosp 1998-2001; Assoc S Mich And All Ang Ch Ft Bragg CA 1997-2001; Assoc Epis Ch Of S Fran-In-The-Vl-ly Green Vlly AZ 1995-1997; Int Chr Memi Ch Kilauea HI 1992; Assoc R Trin Epis Ch Reno NV 1990-1995; P Gr Ch Martinez CA 1987-1988; R All SS Epis Ch Redding CA 1982-1986; Vic Gd Shpd Epis Ch Susanville CA 1978-1982; R St Johns Epis Ch Ross CA 1973-1977; R Trin Oakland CA 1971-1973.

NYEIN, Zachary Charles (ETenn) 20 Belvoir Ave, Chattanooga TN 37411 **Gr Ch Chattanooga TN 2016-** B Knoxville TN 1989 s Tun & Cathy. B.M. The U of Tennessee 2011; MDiv 2016; MDiv Ya Berk 2016; MDiv Ya Berk 2016. D 2/6/2016 P 9/21/2016 Bp George Young III. znyein@saygrace.net

NYGAARD, Richard Lowell (NwPa) B 1940 s Leo & Amanda. bachelor of Sci USC 1969; bachelor of Sci USC 1969; bachelor of Sci USC 1969; juris doctor U MI 1971; juris doctor U MI 1971; juris doctor U MI 1971; doctor of laws Edinboro U of Pennsylvania 1993; doctor of laws Edinboro U of pennsylvania 1993; doctor of laws edinboro U of pennsylvania 1993. D 6/11/2016 Bp Sean Walter Rowe. m 4/10/1965 Martha Jean Marks.

NYGAARD, Steven Bickham (NMich) 6144 Westridge 21.25 Dr, Gladstone MI 49837 B Evanston IL 1948 s Dorrance & Margaret. D 5/4/2002 Bp James Arthur Kelsey. m 4/18/1987 Pamela Martin-Nygaard c 1.

NYRE-THOMAS, Beryl Jean (Los) 1117 Bennett Ave, Long Beach CA 90804 **Asst The Par Ch Of S Lk Long Bch CA 2005-, 2000-2004** B London UK 1936 d Maurice & Evelyn. BA Gld Hall Sch Mus 1956; BA California St U 1975; MA California St U 1978; MA ETSBH 1986. D 6/22/1986 Bp Robert Claflin Rusack P 1/10/1987 Bp Oliver Bailey Garver Jr. m 1/4/2005 Gordon Thomas c 1. Ch Of The H Comm Gardena CA 2001-2004; Assoc St Gregorys Epis Ch Long Bch CA 1989-2000; Asst S Anselm Of Cbury Par Garden Grove CA 1986-1989; Refugee Coordntr Dio Los Angeles Los Angeles CA 1982-1985.

NYSTROM, Brian Eric (Wyo) PO Box 1690, Jackson WY 83001 **S Jn's Epis Ch Jackson WY 2017-** B Chicago IL 1954 s Bertil & Betty. D 6/6/2015 P 12/9/2015 Bp John Smylie. c 2.

O

OAK, Carol Pinkham (Md) St. John's Episcopal Church, 9120 Frederick Road, Ellicott City MD 21042 B Jamaica NY 1954 d Gilbert & Doris. BA U CO 1976; MDiv Ya Berk 1985; DMin SWTS 2003. D 8/24/1985 Bp Andrew Frederick Wissemann P 4/27/1986 Bp Robert Rae Spears Jr. m 10/11/1986 Jeffrey C Oak c 2. R S Jn's Ch Ellicott City MD 2006-2016; Assoc Chr Ch Alexandria VA 2000-2006; Consult Dio Washington Washington DC 1999-2001; R S Jas' Ch Goshen NY 1990-1999; Asst All SS Ch Staten Island NY 1988-1990; Cur S Jas Ch New York NY 1985-1987; Assoc Fac Coll of Preachers Washington DC 2002-2007; Com to Elect a Bp Dio New York New York NY 1997-1998, Pres of the Stndg Com 1997-1998. Auth, "Creating the Conditions for New Pastors' Success," *Congregations*, The Alb Inst, 2006; Auth, "Help, The R Is Pregnant," *Alb Inst*, The Alb Inst, 1994.

OAKES, Leonard (Cal) 777 Southgate Ave, Daly City CA 94015 **Vic H Chld At S Mart Epis Ch Daly City CA 2009-** B Philippines 1971 s Benedicto & Teresa. Trans 6/6/2009 Bp Marc Handley Andrus. m 4/27/1993 Haidee Oakes c 3.

OAKES, Louise K (NC) 201 N Walbridge Ave Apt 335, Madison WI 53714 B Watertown WI 1936 d Raymond & Cora. AA U of Wisconsin 1957; ACS Herzing Inst Madison WI 1973; Cert Nash 1984; Cert SWTS 1992. P 1/1/1994 Bp Roger John White. c 4. Vic Ch Of The H Sprt Greensboro NC 1997-2001; Vic S Helena's Ch Burr Ridge IL 1994-1996; D S Matt's Ch Evanston IL 1991-1994; D Gr Ch Madison WI 1987-1991.

OAKES OJN, Sara Elizabeth Herr (Cal) 622 Terra California Dr Apt 7, Walnut Creek CA 94595 B New York NY 1933 d Edwin & Aline. BA U of Detroit Mercy 1981; Michigan TS 1982. D 6/22/1983 Bp H Coleman Mcgehee Jr P 8/17/1994 Bp Jerry Alban Lamb. m 1/1/1975 Robert C Oakes. Asst S Giles Ch Moraga CA 1997-1999; D S Anselm's Epis Ch Lafayette CA 1988-1994; Pstr Assoc S Paul's Epis Ch Walnut Creek CA 1987-1988; Non-par 1985-1986; D All SS Epis Ch Pontiac MI 1983-1984. OHC 1977; Wrdn Of Oblates For Ord Of Julian Of Norwich 1985.

OAKLAND, Mary Jane (Ia) 1612 Truman Dr, Ames IA 50010 B Madison SD 1944 d Charles & Lilah. BS So Dakota St U 1967; MS Iowa St U 1970; PhD Iowa St U 1985. D 6/7/1995 Bp Chris Christopher Epting P 6/18/2005 Bp Alan Scarfe. m 8/13/1966 David Oliver Oakland c 3. S Paul's Ch Marshalltown IA 2006-2015, R 2006-2015; D Epis Par of Ames Ames IA 1995-2001; Chair of COM Dio Iowa Des Moines IA 2009-2015. The Ord of Julian of Norwich-Oblate 1984.

OASIN, Elizabeth Jayne (NJ) 344 B Delancey Pl, Mount Laurel NJ 08054 **P-in-c Ch Of The Atone Laurel Sprg NJ 2012-** B PhiladelphiaPA 1944 d J Arthur & Marion. BA How 1968; MA Tem 1970; MDiv EDS 2000. D 5/20/2000 Bp David Bruce Joslin P 4/28/2001 Bp Herbert Alcorn Donovan Jr. c 2. Assoc Trin Cathd Trenton NJ 08618 2004-2007; Assoc S Ptr's Ch Medford NJ 2001-2010; Stff Off for Anti-Racism and Gender Equality Epis Ch Cntr New York NY 2000-2010. "Kaleidscopic God," *Race and Power*, Morehouse, 2003; "Pryr to a Sheltering God," *Wmn Uncommon Prayers*, Morehouse, 2000. scl How 1968.

OATS, Louis (NC) 1325 Hickory Lane, Dandridge TN 37725 **Hdmstr Trin Epis Sch Charlotte NC 1999-** B Nashville TN 1951 s Paul & Bettye. BA U So 1973; MDiv SWTS 1980; DMin Columbia TS 1998. D 6/29/1980 P 5/1/1981 Bp William Evan Sanders. m 4/10/1976 Sharon E Oats c 2. Chr Epis Ch Cleveland NC 2012; S Steph's Ch Durham NC 2012; Hd of Sch S Jas Epis Sch Of Corpus Christi Inc. Crp Christi TX 2011-2012; Hd of Sch Trin Epis Sch Charlotte NC 2000-2011; R All SS' Epis Ch Morristown TN 1987-1999; Asst to R Ch Of The Ascen Knoxville TN 1984-1987; Dio Tennessee Nashville TN 1981-1984; Vic S Thos Ch Elizabethton TN 1981-1984; D-in-trng Ch Of The H Comm Memphis TN 1980-1981. Auth, *Preparing for Priesting: A Trng Prog*, CTS Press, 1998. Untd Way Vol Awd 1989.

OBARSKI, Sandra Ruth (Minn) 1111 Lowell Cir, Apple Valley MN 55124 **Part TIme Geth Ch Minneapolis MN 2006-** B Milwaukee WI 1938 d Arnold & Ruth. RN Milwaukee Cnty Gnrl Hosp Sch of Nrsng 1959; AS Inver Hills Cmnty Coll 2004; Diac Stds D Formation Prog 2006. D 6/29/2006 Bp James Louis Jelinek. m 9/17/1960 Marvin Obarski c 2. Ch Of The Nativ Burnsville MN 1993-1995. Assn for Epis Deacons 2007.

OBENCHAIN, John Colin (Pa) 98 Ayers Dr, Rising Sun MD 21911 **P-in-c S Jn's Ch Gap PA 2007-** B Chester PA 1943 s Colin & Lillian. BA Heidelberg U 1966; MDiv PDS 1969. D 8/29/1969 P 2/1/1970 Bp Chandler W Sterling. m 4/5/2005 Beverly A Obenchain c 2. The Epis Ch Of The Adv Kennet Sq PA 2000-2001; R S Christophers Epis Ch Oxford PA 1972-1999; R Incarn H Sacr Epis Ch Drexel Hill PA 1970-1972; Asst S Paul's Ch Philadelphia PA 1969-1970.

OBERHEIDE, Richard Dean (Ala) 155 N Twining St, Montgomery AL 36112 B Kansas City MO 1949 s Harold & Virginia. BA Winona St U 1975; MDiv SWTS 1978. D 6/24/1978 Bp Robert Marshall Anderson P 1/6/1979 Bp Charles Bennison Sr. m 9/18/1971 Nancy Oberheide c 2. Gr Ch Sheffield AL 2004-2014; Off Of Bsh For ArmdF New York NY 1984-2004; Vic S Jn's Ch Fremont MI 1978-1984. Auth, "Easter In The Er," *Sermons That Wk*, Random Hse, 1996; Auth, "Best AF Sermons 1985."

OBIER, Cynthia Andrews (La) 4255 Hyacinth Ave, Baton Rouge LA 70808 **Archit St Fire Marshal Baton Rouge LA 1996-** B Opelika AL 1957 d Newton & Ann. BA LSU 1980. D 9/13/2003 Bp Charles Edward Jenkins III. m 12/18/1982 Robert Row Obier. D Trin Epis Ch Baton Rouge LA 2003-2014.

OBREGON, Ernesto M (Ala) 5424 Wisteria Trce, Trussville AL 35173 **Serv Patriarchate of Antioch Damscus Syria 2006-** B Havana CU 1951 s Patricio & Gloria. Ken; TESM; AA Dekalb Cmnty Coll Clarkston GA 1973; MA Ashland TS 1975; MA Other 1975; BS Kent St U 1977; MA Cleveland St U 1981; MS Florida Inst of Tech 2013. D 11/1/1990 P 4/1/1991 Bp The Bishop Of Peru and Bolivia. m 7/8/1978 Denise Ruth Lockney c 3. Hisp Mssnr Dio Alabama Birmingham 2000-2004; R Christo Redentor Areguipa Peru Prov of Sthrn Cone 1993-2000; Archd Reg III Dioceses Of Peru & Bolivia Prov of Sthrn C 1990-2000; Mssy SAMS Ambridge PA 1989-1993; Serv Allnce Of Renwl Ch 1981-1989. Bro Of S Andr 1990-2000.

O'BRIEN, Charles Harold (WMass) 738 Simonds Rd, Williamstown MA 01267 **Asst S Jn's Ch Williamstown MA 1989-** B Oshkosh WI 1927 s Erwin & Margaret. BA U of Notre Dame 1951; MA U of Notre Dame 1952; STB Gregorian U 1957; STL Gregorian U 1959; PhD Col 1967. Rec 10/9/1979 as Priest Bp Donald James Parsons. m 12/21/1964 Elvy Setterqvist. Vic S Paul's Ch Warsaw IL 1984-1989; Assoc S Geo's Ch Macomb IL 1979-1984; Prof Wstrn Illinois U at Macomb 1972-1994; Serv RC Ch 1958-1964. Auth, "Death of a Robber Baron," Kensington Books, 2013; Auth, "Assassins' Rage," Severn Hse, 2008; Auth, "Cruel Choices," Severn Hse, 2007; Auth, "Black Gold," Poisoned Pen

O

Press, 2002; Auth, "Mute Witness," Poisoned Pen Press, 2001; Auth, "Ideas of Rel Toleration in Austria," Amer Philos Assn, 1969; Auth, "Jansenist Cmpgn for Toleration of Protestants," *Journ of Hist of Ideas*.

O'BRIEN, Craig Edward (Ga) 201 E 49th St, Savannah GA 31405 **P Assoc S Jn's Ch Savannah GA 2007-** B Halifax Nova Scotia Canada 1972 s Daniel & Valerie. BA U of Kings Coll Halifax NS CA 1995; MDiv Wycliffe Hall Oxford GB 1997. Trans 10/22/2004 Bp Leo Frade. The Ch Of The Guardian Ang Lake Worth FL 2005-2007; Par P The Ch Of The Guardian Ang Lantana FL 2003-2007.

O'BRIEN, Donald Richard (SwFla) **D Redeem 1980-** B Opelika AL 1952 AA Manatee Cmnty Coll 1972. D 6/11/1980 Bp Emerson Paul Haynes. m 8/4/1972 Deborah O'Brien.

O'BRIEN, Eileen Elizabeth (Tex) **Cur Dio Texas Houston TX 2016-** D 6/21/2014 Bp Dena Arnall Harrison P 1/14/2015 Bp C Andrew Doyle.

O'BRIEN, Julie Lynn (Az) 1735 S College Ave, Tempe AZ 85281 **R S Steph's Ch Phoenix AZ 2012-** B Bloomington IN 1956 MDiv Epis TS of the SW 2009. D 6/7/2008 P 6/13/2009 Bp Kirk Stevan Smith. c 1. Vic Epis Ch of the H Sprt Phoenix AZ 2009-2012; D S Aug's Epis Ch Tempe AZ 2008.

O' BRIEN, Richard L (Nev) Christ Church, 200 S Maryland Pkwy, Las Vegas NV 89101 **Epis Ch of the Epiph Las Vegas NV 2016-; Assoc Chr Ch Las Vegas NV 2013-** B Somerville MA 1965 s Lawrence & Patricia. BA U of Massachusetts 1987; BA U of Massachusetts 1987; MS Bos 2005; MS Bos 2005. D 4/6/2013 P 10/26/2013 Bp Dan Thomas Edwards. m 5/25/2017 Jennifer L O'Brien c 3. Mnstry Dvlpmt Cmsn Dio Nevada Las Vegas 2013-2014.

O'BROCHTA, Joseph William (Lex) **D Trin Ch Covington KY 2016-** D 1/9/2016 Bp Doug Hahn.

O'CALLAGHAN, Beth (WA) 15575 Germantown Rd, Germantown MD 20874 **S Nich Epis Ch Germantown MD 2017-; P-in-c S Fran Of Assisi Cherokee NC 2014-** B Pittsburgh PA 1958 d Horace & Prudence. BS U of Maryland 1980; MHS JHU 1987; MDiv VTS 2009. D 6/13/2009 P 1/16/2010 Bp John Bryson Chane. m 10/15/2010 Marla Aizenshtat. R S Mary's Ch Ronkonkoma NY 2012-2017; Asst R Ch Of The Ascen Gaithersburg MD 2009-2012. rector@saintnicks.com

O'CARROLL, Bryan (SwFla) 912 63rd Ave W, Bradenton FL 34207 **S Geo's Epis Ch Bradenton FL 2011-** B Michigan 1967 s Kevin & A Lorraine. BA Eckerd Coll 2008; MDiv Nash 2011. D 2/27/2011 P 8/28/2011 Bp Dabney Tyler Smith. m 8/31/1991 Susan Leslie O'Carroll c 3.

OCCHIUTO, Joseph John (LI) Rec 12/5/2015 Bp Lawrence C Provenzano.

O'CONNELL, Kelly Ann (Los) St Stephen's Church, 24901 Orchard Village Rd, Santa Clarita CA 91355 **S Steph's Epis Ch Valencia CA 2012-** B Euclid OH 1967 d Jerome & Bernadette. BA Ken 1989; MDiv EDS 1995. D 6/5/1999 P 6/4/2000 Bp M(Arvil) Thomas Shaw. m 5/18/2014 Christina Laberge. R S Mk's Epis Ch Toledo OH 2005-2012; Int S Lk's Epis Ch Scituate MA 2004-2005; Asst to R S Anne's In The Fields Epis Ch Lincoln MA 2000-2004; Bp's Aide Dio Massachusetts Boston MA 1999-2000. revkelly@st-stephens.org

O'CONNELL, Patricia Marie (WMass) D 6/10/2017 Bp Doug Fisher.

O'CONNOR, Andrew T (Kan) 9605 W Greenspoint St, Wichita KS 67205 **R Gd Shpd Epis Ch Wichita KS 2009-; Mem, Coun of Trst Dio Kansas Topeka KS 2016-, Pres, SW Convoc 2012-2013, COM 2010-; Instr The Bp Kemper Sch for Mnstry Topeka KS 2010-** B Glendale CA 1978 s Lawrence & Mary. AB Boston Coll 2000; MDiv VTS 2005. D 6/11/2005 Bp Chester Lovelle Talton P 1/14/2006 Bp Frank Tracy Griswold III. m 8/10/2002 Heather S Killpatrick-O'Connor c 5. P-in-c S Mk's Par Altadena CA 2007-2009; Assoc R All SS-By-The-Sea Par Santa Barbara CA 2005-2007; Asst Chapl/Lay Min Cbury USC Los Angeles CA 2001-2002; Urban Intern Epis Urban Intern Prog Inglewood CA 2000-2001; Bd Dir The Cbury USC Fndt Inc Los Angeles CA 2008-2009. gsrector@sbcglobal.net

O'CONNOR, Christopher Duane (WNY) 30 Favor St, Attica NY 14011 B Fort Wayne IN 1958 s Bartholomew & Martha. AB Assumption Coll Worcester MA 1980; MTS Weston TS 1985; MDiv Cath Theol Un 1999. D 7/20/2013 P 5/3/2014 Bp Ralph William Franklin. m 8/17/1985 Mary Colleen McHale O'Connor c 5. St Mk Epis Ch No Tonawanda NY 2016-2017; S Lk's Epis Ch Attica NY 2014-2016; Chr Ch Albion NY 2014-2015. chrisoconnor@rochester.rr.com

O'CONNOR, Maureen Nicole (Chi) **Calv Ch Lombard IL 2017-** D 5/31/2016 P 12/17/2016 Bp Jeff Lee.

O'CONNOR JR, Terrence (NJ) 2998 Bay Ave, Ocean City NJ 08226 **Ch Of S Mk And All SS Absecon Absecon NJ 2016-** B Philadelphia PA 1970 s Terrence & Joanne. BS The Penn 1993; MA Rowan U 2003; MDiv The Luth TS at Philadelphia 2015. D 11/1/2014 P 6/8/2015 Bp William H Stokes. H Trin Epis Ch Wenonah NJ 2015. smasoffice@aol.com

ODA-BURNS, John MacDonald (Cal) 611 La Mesa Dr, Portola Valley CA 94028 **Asst S Bede's Epis Ch Menlo Pk CA 2011-; Ret 1996-; Ret 1996-** B Exeter UK 1931 s Hector & Marjorie. AKCL Lon Kings Coll 1956; S Bon Coll Warminster GB 1957. Trans 4/1/1967 Bp Chauncie Kilmer Myers. m 5/18/1985 Marjorie Oda-Burns c 3. Assoc P Chr Ch Portola Vlly CA 2002-2009, R 1971-1996; Assoc Trsfg Epis Ch San Mateo CA 1999-2002; Pstr Trin Par

Menlo Pk CA 1967-1971; Serv Ch of Bahamas 1964-1967; Serv Ch of So Afr 1959-1964; Serv Ch of Engl 1957-1959.

ODDERSTOL, Sarah Dodds (WA) St. Mary's Episcopal Church, 306 S Prospect Avenue, Park Ridge IL 60068 **Chapl Pk Ridge Police Dept Pk Ridge Illinois 2010-** B Philadelphia PA 1964 BS The Amer U; MDiv VTS 2003. D 6/14/2003 P 2/21/2004 Bp Carol J Gallagher. m 12/29/1990 Eric Odderstol c 2. The Ch Of The H Sprt Lake Forest IL 2013-2015; R S Mary's Ch Pk Ridge IL 2008-2012; Int R S Cyp's Epis Ch Hampton VA 2007-2008; Assoc R S Ptr's By The Sea Gulfport MS 2005-2007; Cur All Souls' Epis Ch San Diego CA 2004-2005; Asstg P Chr Ch Coronado CA 2004.

ODEKIRK, Dennis Russell (Los) 830 Columbine Ct, San Luis Obispo CA 93401 **Ret Ret 2001-** B Mauston WI 1938 s Charles & Evelyn. BA Lawr 1959; U of Brussels Brussels BE 1960; BD SWTS 1963; MA U of Notre Dame 1977; PhD U CA 1990; PhD U CA, San Diego 1990. D 6/3/1963 Bp William Hampton Brady P 12/21/1963 Bp Charles Bennison Sr. m 6/20/1959 Charlene Elizabeth Odekirk c 4. R All SS-By-The-Sea Par Santa Barbara CA 1993-2001; R S Mich's Epis Ch Carmichael CA 1986-1993; Sr Asst S Jas By The Sea La Jolla CA 1981-1986; Prov 5 Coordntr A-RC T/F 1979-1983; EDEO Coordntr Prov V 1979-1981; DepGC A-RC T/F 1973-1979; R S Jn's Epis Ch of Sturgis Sturgis MI 1968-1981; Asst S Thos Epis Ch Battle Creek MI 1966-1968; Vic S Fran Ch Orangeville Shelbyville MI 1963-1966; Ecum Off Dio Wstrn Michigan Kalamazoo MI 1977-1981. Auth, *Bk Revs*.

O'DELL, Thomas Peyton (WMich) 123 W Washington St, Lexington VA 24450 B Hodgenville KY 1950 s John & Helen. BS Murray St U 1973; JD W&L 1976; MDiv GTS 1987. D 7/22/1987 P 3/6/1988 Bp David Reed. m 5/25/2014 Linda O'Dell c 3. R All SS Epis Ch Omaha NE 2006-2014; P-in-c R E Lee Memi Ch (Epis) Lexington VA 2000-2005; R S Jn's Ch Roanoke VA 1992-2000; Asst R S Fran In The Fields Harrods Creek KY 1987-1992.

ODGERS, Marie Christine Hanson (Neb) 8800 Holdrege St, Lincoln NE 68505 B Fremont NE 1932 d Willard & Mathilda. BA Nebraska Wesl 1955; AS Nebraska Wesl 1993. D 4/29/2010 Bp Joe Goodwin Burnett. m 5/31/1955 Richard Varney Odgers c 2.

ODIERNA, Robert William (NH) Po Box 412, Nashua NH 03061 B New York NY 1949 s Frank & Carolyn. BA Hobart and Wm Smith Colleges 1971; MDiv GTS 1975; Cert Blanton-Peale Grad Inst 1981; DMin Andover Newton TS 1996. D 6/7/1975 Bp Jonathan Goodhue Sherman P 12/1/1975 Bp George E Rath. m 12/22/2011 Heidi Odierna c 3. R Ch Of The Gd Shpd Nashua NH 1986-2017; Dir The Waterbury Pstr Counslg Cntr 1983-1986; R All SS Epis Ch Oakville CT 1977-1986; P-in-c Chr Ch Ridgewood NJ 1975-1977. AAPC. info@cgsnashua.org

ODOM, Robert Martial (Dal) 5923 Royal Ln, Dallas TX 75230 **The Par Epis Sch Dallas TX 2014-** B Baton Rouge LA 1968 s Harold & Bonnie. BA LSU 1990; MDiv Nash 2001. D 12/27/2000 P 9/8/2001 Bp Charles Edward Jenkins III. m 6/17/1995 Mary Inez Odom c 2. P S Jn's Epis Ch Dallas TX 2014-2015; R S Lk's Epis Ch Dallas TX 2008-2014; Assoc S Jas Epis Ch Baton Rouge LA 2004-2008; Cur Chr Ch Covington LA 2001-2004.

O'DONNELL, Elizabeth Gibbs (Me) 16726 Lauder Ln, Dallas TX 75248 B Jamestown NY 1942 d Stanton & Grace. BS Cor 1964; MA U Denv 1966. D 6/19/2004 Bp Chilton Richardson Knudsen. c 2. D The Epis Ch Of The Trsfg Dallas TX 2009-2017; D S Jn's Ch Bangor ME 2005; Par Admin St. Jn's Epis Ch Bangor ME 1983-1993.

O'DONNELL, John J (NH) 315 Mason Rd, Milford NH 03055 **Non-par (NH Lic. Pstr Psych) 1980-** B Holyoke MA 1932 s John & Evelyn. BS U of Massachusetts 1954; Sem of Niagara Niagara NY 1960; DMin Andover Newton TS 1975. Rec 11/1/1974 as Priest Bp Robert Shaw Kerr. m 10/13/1973 Mary Wynne. Chapl NH Hosp 1975-1980; Serv RC Ch 1957-1973. Amer Assn for Mar & Fam Ther; AAPC; ACPE; NHAPP.

O'DONNELL, Michael Alan (Alb) 4940 Shirley Pl, Colorado Springs CO 80920 **R S Jn's Ch Ogdensburg NY 2013-** B Bryn Mawr PA 1956 s William & Valia. BS Manhattan Coll 1979; MA Palmer TS 1981; PrTS 1982; MA Cincinnati Chr Sem 1983; PhD K SU 1986. Trans 6/24/2004 as Priest Bp Keith Lynn Ackerman. m 6/9/1987 Rachel O'Donnell c 3. VP & CDO Cath Chars of Colorado Sprg Colorado CO 2009-2013; P-in-c Gr And S Steph's Epis Ch Colorado Sprg CO 2007-2009, P-in-c 2007, 1. Clncl Pstr Counslr & Asstg P 2. Assoc R 2004-2006; P L'Eglise Epis au Rwanda 2001-2004. Auth, "What a Son Needs from His Dad," *Bk*, Baker Books, 2011; Auth, "The Oz Syndrome," *Bk*, ACU Press, 2001; Auth, "How A Man Prepares His Sons for Life," *Bk*, Bethany Hse, 1996; co-Auth, "Question of hon," *Bk*, Harper Collins/Zondervan, 1996; co-Auth, "Gd Kids," *Bk*, Doubleday, 1996; Auth, "Hm from Oz," *Bk*, Word Pub, 1994; co-Auth, "Heart of the Warrior (for fathers)," *Bk*, ACU Press, 1993. Franciscan Ord of Div Compassion (Oblate) 2001. Cath Press Awd for Best Fam Life Column Cath Press Awd 2012; Outstanding New Tchr of the Year Cmnty Hse Middle Sch 2009.

OECHSEL JR, Russell Harold (Tex) 15811 Mesa Gardens Dr, Houston TX 77095 **D S Mary's Epis Ch Cypress TX 2007-** B Oak Park, IL 1948 s Russell & Rita. BS Nthrn Illinois U 1974; The Iona Sch for Mnstry 2007. D 2/9/2007 Bp Don Adger Wimberly. m 11/21/1998 Linda Sue Oechsel c 3.

OESTERLIN, Peter William (RG) 3232 Renaissance Dr SE, Rio Rancho NM 87124 B Milwaukee WI 1933 s Ernst & Gertrude. BA U of Vermont 1959; STB GTS 1962. D 6/6/1962 P 12/15/1962 Bp Harvey D Butterfield. m 8/26/2010 Kathy Ellen Oesterlin c 2. R S Matt's Epis Ch Newton KS 2002-2004; Int Trin Ch Lawr KS 2000-2002; Int Gr Epis Ch Winfield KS 1999-2000; Int Trin Ch Arkansas City KS 1999-2000; Trin Epis Ch El Dorado KS 1998-1999; Int Gd Shpd Epis Ch Wichita KS 1996-1998; S Jn's Ch Wichita KS 1994-1998; Int Gr Epis Ch Ottawa KS 1993-1994; Chf of Chapl Serv Veteran's Admin Med Cntr Topeka KS 1985-1993; Chf of Chapl Serv Veteran's Admin Med Cntr Dayton OH 1980-1985; P-in-c S Andr's Epis Ch Mccall ID 1977-1979; Chapl Veteran's Admin Med Cntr Bosie ID 1975-1980; ArmdF and Fed Ministires New York NY 1969-1993; Chapl Veteran's Admin Med Cntr Washington DC 1969-1975; Vic Atone Brooklyn NY 1967-1969; Chapl Veteran's Admin Med Cntr White River Jct 1963-1967; S Paul's Epis Ch White Riv Jct VT 1962-1968; Cur S Paul's Epis Ch White River Jct VT 1962-1968; Cur S Jas Ch Woodstock VT 1962-1963; BEC Dio Vermont Burlington VT 1963-1967. Coll of Chapl 1967.

OETJEN, Sandra Lee (Nev) 4613 Steeplechase Ave, North Las Vegas NV 89031 **Chairperson, Cmsn on Ord and Licensing Dio Nevada Las Vegas 2010-** B Reno NV 1948 d William & Adelma. CDSP; Sewanee: The U So, TS; UNR. D 10/14/2006 Bp Katharine Jefferts Schori. m 3/13/1993 Jack Oetjen c 1. NAAD (No Amer Assoc. for the Diac) 2006.

O'FLINN, Nancy C (Ala) **S Martins-In-The-Pines Ret Comm Birmingham AL 2016-** D 11/3/2012 Bp John Mckee Sloan Sr.

O'FLYNN, Donnel (Mont) Christ Church, 215 3rd Ave E, Kalispell MT 59901 **R S Thos Ch Hamilton NY 2004-** B Helena MT 1952 s John & Dorothy. BA St Johns Coll Annapolis MD 1974; MDiv VTS 1985. D 6/8/1985 P 1/4/1986 Bp John Thomas Walker. m 6/28/1985 Janet c Christhilf c 2. R Gr Ch Vineyard Haven MA 1998-2004; Vic S Jn The Evang Yalesville CT 1989-1998; Cur Chr Ch New Haven CT 1985-1989.

OFOEGBU, Daniel Okwuchukwu (Dal) Church Of The Ascension, 8787 Greenville Ave., Dallas TX 75243 **Vic Dio Dallas Dallas TX 2013-** B Nkpologwu, Nigeria 1957 s Chikezie & Agnes. BA Tougaloo Coll 1987; LM Angl TS 2005; MTS Nash 2011. D 8/19/2006 Bp James Monte Stanton P 9/6/2008 Bp Paul Emil Lambert. m 8/27/1992 Roseline Ofoegbu c 5. Asst Epis Ch Of The Ascen Dallas TX 2011-2012. emmanuelanglicanc@yahoo.com

OGBURN JR, John Nelson (NC) 330 W Presnell St Apt 44, Asheboro NC 27203 B Greensboro NC 1932 s John & Jean. BS U NC 1955; JD U NC 1957. D 5/31/1992 Bp Robert Whitridge Estill. m 2/18/1961 Edith Ogburn. D S Andr's Ch Haw River NC 1993-1999; D The Epis Ch Of Gd Shpd Asheboro NC 1992-1999.

OGBURN, William L (Pgh) 55 Main St, North Kingstown RI 02852 **The Ch Of S Lk In The Fields New York NY 2016-** B Atlanta GA 1982 s James & Lisa Ann. BA Presb Coll 2005; MDiv GTS 2014; MDiv The GTS 2014. D 5/15/2013 P 6/21/2014 Bp Dorsey McConnell. m 7/12/2016 Jonathan Philip Vantassel. Asst S Paul's Ch N Kingstown RI 2014-2016.

OGDEN, Virginia Louise (Alb) 51 Brockley Dr, Delmar NY 12054 **The Ch Of The Gd Shpd Canajoharie NY 2012-** B New York City 1949 d Julius & Mildred. MA St Bernards TS And Mnstry Rochester NY 2006. D 6/10/2006 Bp Daniel William Herzog P 1/6/2007 Bp William Howard Love. m 5/24/1980 Kenneth Ogden c 2. Int S Steph's Ch Delmar NY 2008-2010.

OGEA, Herman Joseph (WLa) 110 W 13th St, PO Box 912, Jennings LA 70546 **P Trin Ch Crowley LA 2009-** B Lake Charles LA 1947 s Jasper & Gladys. MDiv Notre Dame Sem Grad TS; CAS Sewanee: The U So, TS. Rec 6/23/2000 as Priest Bp Robert Jefferson Hargrove Jr. m 4/2/1994 Kathleen Lambert Doherty-Ogea. S Barn Epis Ch Lafayette LA 2004-2005; R Chr Ch Bastrop LA 2004-2004.

OGIER JR, Dwight (At) 125 Betty Street, Clarkesville GA 30523 **Int S Jn's Ch Christiansted St Croix VI 2012-; Chapl Clarkesville Fire Dept 2011-; Chapl to Ret Cler Dio Atlanta Atlanta GA 2004-** B Fort Benning GA 1942 s Dwight & Constance. BA U So 1964; MDiv Ya Berk 1971; VTS 1977; DMin Pittsburgh TS 1989. D 6/20/1971 Bp James Loughlin Duncan P 4/29/1972 Bp Albert Ervine Swift. m 7/20/1962 Barbara Watts Ogier c 2. Int St Peters Epis Ch St Croix VI 2009-2010; Serv Luth Ch Cumming GA 2008-2009; Int Ch of the Nativ Fayettville GA 2005-2006; Asst S Dav's Ch Roswell GA 2001-2002; Assoc H Trin Par Decatur GA 1999-2001; Chapl Forsyth Cnty Sheriff Off 1997-2002; Chapl Forsyth Cnty Fire Dept 1995-2011; R Epis Ch Of The H Sprt Cumming GA 1994-1999; S Aug Coll Bd Assn 1992-1994; Dio No Carolina Raleigh NC 1991-1992; Assoc R S Mich's Ch Raleigh NC 1987-1994; Chapl S Lk's Day Sch Mobile AL 1984-1988; Assoc S Lk's Epis Ch Mobile AL 1984-1987; Vic H Fam Ch Orlando FL 1981-1984; R H Trin Epis Ch Bartow FL 1977-1981; Asst S Mk's Epis Ch Jacksonville FL 1972-1977; Cur H Trin Epis Ch W Palm Bch FL 1971-1972; Trst Sewanee U So TS Sewanee TN 1990-1994, Trst 1984-1989. Auth, *Forsyth Cnty News*. OHC 1978.

OGLE, Albert Joy (NY) 3634 Seventh Ave Unit 6B, San Diego CA 92103 **Vic S Ptr's Ch Millbrook NY 2014-** B Belfast IE 1954 s Albert & Thelma. BD U of Wales 1975; Trin-Dublin IRE 1976; PGCE Lon GB 1977; MA Trin-Dublin

IRE 2007. Trans 2/1/1982 as Priest Bp Robert Claflin Rusack. m 2/13/2016 Mile Petrov. P Res Cathd Ch Of S Paul San Diego CA 2007-2015; Dio Los Angeles Los Angeles CA 2007, Cn for Intl Recon 2006-2008; R S Geo's Epis Ch Laguna Hills CA 1999-2006, Int Pstr 1997-1998; Assoc Trin Hollywood CA 1991-1995; Assoc All SS Ch Pasadena CA 1987-1991; Serv Ch of Ireland 1977-1982. Chapt, "Returning to Places of Wounded Memory," *The Sprt of Place*, U of Laval, 2010; Chapt, "Pstr Handbook for HIV," *The Gospel Imperative in the Midst of AIDS*, 1989; Auth, "Cnfrmtn Prog," *Stand Out in a Crowd*, 1978. Cn Dio Los Angeles 2003; Epis Relief and Deveopment Off Dio Los Angeles 2003. aogle@cox.net

OGLE SR, Louis Knox (La) 43 Hyacinth Dr, Covington LA 70433 **Stff Chapl St. Tammany Par Hosp Covington LA 1999-** B Galveston TX 1942 BA SE Louisiana U 1985. D 2/23/2002 Bp Charles Edward Jenkins III. m 2/3/1962 Margaret Berger Ogle c 3. D S Mich's Epis Ch Mandeville LA 2006-2011; Chapl New Orleans Police Dept. New Orleans LA 1998-1999.

OGLESBY, Charles Lucky (NC) 325 Glen Echo Ln Apt J, Cary NC 27518 **D Dio No Carolina Raleigh NC 1997-, D 1987-1996** B Breckenridge TX 1935 s Thomas & Ava. BA U of Texas 1957; MA U of Kentucky 1971; EdD No Carolina St U 1979. D 10/4/1987 Bp Robert Whitridge Estill. m 7/11/1992 Hilda Phillips c 2. D St Elizabeths Epis Ch Apex NC 2000-2002; D Dio Wstrn No Carolina Asheville NC 1993-1997. NAAD.

OGLESBY, Keith W (At) **Epis Ch Of The H Sprt Cumming GA 2009-** B Atlanta GA 1958 s Joseph & Margaret. BA Georgia St U 1980; MDiv Candler TS Emory U 2007. D 12/21/2006 P 6/27/2007 Bp J Neil Alexander. m 9/1/1979 Lynn Oglesby c 3. Asst S Aid's Epis Ch Milton GA 2007-2009.

OGLESBY, Patricia A (Pa) 1734 Huntington Tpke, Trumbull CT 06611 **Dir Of The Dept Pstr Care Amer Oncologic Hosp 1980-** B Washington DC 1950 d Nicholas & Alma. BA Connecticut Coll 1971; MDiv Yale DS 1976. D 6/18/1977 P 5/13/1978 Bp William Hawley Clark. P-in-c S Faith Ch Havertown PA 2003-2015, 1996-1997; Trin Epis Ch Trumbull CT 1997-2002; Nevil Memi Ch Of S Geo Ardmore PA 1994-1996; S Paul's Ch Elkins Pk PA 1993-1994; Epis Cmnty Serv Philadelphia PA 1987-1993; Trin Ch Swarthmore PA 1985-1986; P-in-c S Aidans Ch Cheltenham PA 1981-1982; Serv Ch of St Andrews & St Matthews Wilmington DE 1979-1980; Dio Delaware Wilmington 1979-1980.

OGUIKE, Martin U (NJ) 17 Woodbridge Ave, Sewaren NJ 07077 **R Raritan Bay Epis Team Mnstry Sewaren NJ 2003-** B NG 1956 s Harold & Cordelia. DIT Trin Umuahia Ng 1983; MPhil U of Birmingham Gb 1988; PhD U of Port-Harcourt Ng 2005. Trans 1/1/2003 Bp David Bruce Joslin. m 11/17/1990 Ngozi Martin-Oguike c 4. Vic S Cyp's Epis Ch Hackensack NJ 1999-2002. moguike@aol.com

OGUS, Mary Hutchison (EC) 175 9th Ave, New York NY 10011 **S Paul's Ch Beaufort NC 2016-** B Lake Charles LA 1954 BA U Denv. D 6/14/2003 P 6/26/2004 Bp Clifton Daniel III. m 12/2/1989 Richard Ogus. Trin Epis Ch Chocowinity NC 2016; R S Paul's Epis Ch Clinton NC 2004-2010; D The Ch Of The Epiph New York NY 2003-2004.

OGWAL-ABWANG, Benoni Y (NY) 135 Remington Pl, New Rochelle NY 10801 B Adilang UG 1942 s Yovani & Gladys. Cert Theol Stud Buwalasi Theol Coll 1962; DIT Bp Tucker Theol Coll Mukono Ug 1968; BD Hur CA 1974. Trans 6/1/1990 Bp Edmond Lee Browning. m 9/25/1971 Alice N Okoth-Ogwal c 1. Ch Of S Simon The Cyrenian New Rochelle NY 2001-2009; S Paul's Epis Ch Harrisburg PA 1989-2001; Bp Of Nthrn Uganda Nthrn Uganda 1974-1989. Hononary DD Hur U, London, Ontarion 1975.

OH, David Yongsam (Nwk) 1224 McClaren Drive, Carmichael CA 95608 **S Peters Ch Bogota NJ 1990-** B Sinchun Korea 1933 s Chang & Sun. BD Presb Theol Coll 1960; BA Sung Jeon U 1962; BD S Michaels TS 1967; VTS 1978; MDiv SFTS 1996. Trans 2/21/1990 as Priest Bp John Shelby Spong. m 8/15/1972 Anna Oh. S Mich's Epis Ch Carmichael CA 1991-2013; R Angl Ch of Korea 1967-1990.

OH, KyungJa (SO) Bexley Seabury Seminary Federation, 1407 E 60th St, Chicago IL 60637 **P Bex Sem Columbus OH 2014-** B Chicago IL 1951 d Fred & Esther. BA IL Wesl 1973; MDiv SWTS 2000. D 6/15/2002 P 12/21/2002 Bp Bill Persell. m 1/3/2012 Melissa McNeill c 2. Ch Of The Adv Cincinnati OH 2011-2014; Vic S Chad Epis Ch Loves Pk IL 2003-2011; Asst The Annunc Of Our Lady Gurnee IL 2002. kjoh@bexleyseabury.edu

O'HAGIN, Zarina Eileen Suarez (Vt) 215 Corner Rd, Hardwick VT 05843 B Ruislip UK 1954 d Harry & Czarina. BA U Chi 1976; JD U Chi 1984. D 2/7/1998 Bp Herbert Alcorn Donovan Jr. c 1. D S Jn The Bapt Epis Hardwick VT 2000-2015; D Ch Of S Paul And The Redeem Chicago IL 1998-2000.

O'HARA, Christina Swenson (SD) 2707 W 33rd St, Sioux Falls SD 57105 **R Ch Of The Gd Shpd Sioux Falls SD 2017-** B Toronto Canada 1968 d John & Catherine. BA Mid 1991; MDiv Sioux Falls Sem 2010. D 4/30/2011 P 12/10/2011 Bp John Tarrant. m 6/8/1991 David O'Hara c 3. Cn Calv Cathd Sioux Falls SD 2012-2016.

O'HARA, Ellen (NY) 141 Fulton Ave Apt 609, Poughkeepsie NY 12603 **Mem Cler Critical Concerns Dio New York New York NY 2007-** B New York NY 1942 d Thomas & Rebecca. BA CUNY 1964; MA Ford 1969; MDiv GTS 1997.

D 6/14/1997 P 12/13/1997 Bp Richard Frank Grein. R S Paul's Ch Pleasant Vlly NY 1997-2012. Soc Of S Jn The Evang.

O'HARA-TUMILTY, Anne (Los) 26029 Laguna Court, Valencia CA 91355 **Bd Mem Epis Hm Cmnty 2006-; R S Jas' Par So Pasadena CA 2002-** B Utica NY 1950 d James & Mary. BA California St U 1988; ETSBH 1991; MDiv Claremont TS 1993. D 6/13/1993 Bp Chester Lovelle Talton P 1/1/1994 Bp Frederick Houk Borsch. m 8/29/1981 David Tumilty c 2. Assoc All SS Par Beverly Hills CA 1993-2002; Dio Los Angeles Los Angeles CA 1988-1990; AIDS Cmsn Dio Los Angeles Los Angeles CA. amtoht@aol.com

O'HEARNE, John Joseph (WMo) 4550 Warwick Blvd Apt 1212, Kansas City MO 64111 B Memphis TN 1922 s John & Norma. Hendrix Coll 1940; BS Rhodes Coll 1944; MD U of Tennessee 1945; MS U CO 1951. D 5/30/1992 P 12/1/1992 Bp John Clark Buchanan. m 12/30/1982 Barbara V O'Hearne c 4. Auth, "Nonverbal Behavior In Groups &"; Auth, "Comprhensive Grp Psychol".

✠ **OHL, The Rt Rev C Wallis** (NwT) 3205 Skye Ridge Dr, Norman OK 73069 B Bay City TX 1943 s Charles & Marguerite. BA U So 1965; MDiv Nash 1974; DD Nash 1998; DD Sewanee: The U So, TS 1998. D 12/20/1973 P 6/20/1974 Bp Chilton R Powell Con 6/28/1997 for NwT. m 9/4/1964 Sheila K Ohl c 3. Provsnl Bp of Ft Worth Dio Ft Worth Ft Worth TX 2009-2012; Bp of NW Texas Dio NW Texas Lubbock TX 1997-2008; R Ch Of S Mich The Archangel Colorado Spg CO 1991-1997; Dep GC 1982-1991; R S Mich's Epis Ch Norman OK 1977-1991; Dn Bp's TS TS 1976-1978; Prof Hist Bp's TS TS 1975-1978; Assoc S Paul's Cathd Oklahoma City OK 1974-1977; Eccl Crt Dio Colorado Denver CO 1992-1995; Stndg Com Dio Oklahoma Oklahoma City OK 1987-1990, Chair COM 1985-1991, Chair - BEC 1983-1991; Trst Nash Nashotah WI 1977-1981. Auth, "Into the Household of God," *Into the Household of God*, 1989. Hon Doctorate Bokchita Bible Coll and Truck Stop 2006; Hon DD Nash 1998; Hon DD STUSo 1998. cwo1021@aol.com

OHLEMEIER, Mark William (Kan) **Cur Chr Epis Ch Springfield MO 2017-** D 6/17/2017 Bp George Wayne Smith.

OHLIDAL, Susan Marie (Vt) D 5/15/2014 P 1/17/2015 Bp Thomas C Ely.

OHLSON, Elizabeth Anderson (NJ) 5752 West Ave, Ocean City NJ 08226 **D H Trin Epis Ch Ocean City NJ 2003-** B Winchester MA 1939 d Elmer & Mary. Pennsylvania Johnson Cnty Cmnty Coll; Penn 1959; Penna Acad of the Fine Arts 1962; BFA U of Kansas 1980. D 2/3/1996 Bp Frank Tracy Griswold III. m 7/29/1961 Richard Frank Ohlson. D Ch Of The H Nativ Clarendon Hls IL 1996-2001. SCHC 1990.

OHLSTEIN, Allen Michael (Kan) 310 W 17th St, Leavenworth KS 66048 **Dir, Anti-Hunger Ntwk Epis Cmnty Serv Kansas City MO 2005-** B Paterson NJ 1949 s Herbert & Anna. BA Seton Hall U 1971; MPA Jacksonville St U 1978. D 6/11/2005 Bp Dean E Wolfe. m 10/14/2000 Kimberly S McMillan c 4. Trin Cathd Little Rock AR 2010-2011; Epis Cmnty Serv Kansas City MO 2005-2009. NAAD 2004.

OHMER, John (Va) The Falls Church Episcopal, 115 E Fairfax St, Falls Church VA 22046 **R The Falls Ch Epis Falls Ch VA 2012-** B Grand Rapids MI 1961 s Donald & Sofka. BA Wabash Coll 1984; Van 1985; MDiv VTS 1994. D 6/24/1994 Bp Edward Witker Jones P 1/22/1995 Bp Peter J Lee. m 12/17/1988 Mary Elizabeth Ohmer c 2. The Falls Ch Epis Day Sch Falls Ch VA 2012-2013; R S Jas' Epis Ch Leesburg VA 1999-2012; Assoc R S Mary's Epis Ch Arlington VA 1994-1999.

O'KEEFE, Lloyd Frost (O) 970 Cottage Gate Dr, Kent OH 44240 **Ret 2002-** B Columbus OH 1939 s Thomas & Agnes. BA Heidelberg U 1962; BD VTS 1967. D 6/17/1967 P 12/16/1967 Bp Nelson Marigold Burroughs. m 12/27/1966 Roberta B O'Keefe. Epis Cmnty Serv Fndt Cleveland OH 1991-1998; Akron Area Assn Of Ch 1989-1991; Dio Ohio Cleveland 1988-2002, Asst To Bp Peace/Justice 1988-2001; Gr Ch Ravenna OH 1987-1988; Hunger Action Enabler Eastminster Presb Youngstown OH 1983-1989; R Chr Epis Ch Kent OH 1971-1980; Assoc Chr Epis Ch Warren OH 1969-1971; Cur Trin Ch Toledo OH 1967-1969. EPF 1988.

OKEREKE, Ndukaku Shadrack (Dal) 9624 Valley Mills Ln, Dallas TX 75227 B Nigeria 1950 s Isaiah & Phube. BS Bp Coll 1995; MDiv TESM 2005. Trans 8/15/2003 Bp James Monte Stanton. m 6/2/1984 Christiana Okereke c 4. St Peters Angl Ch Dallas TX 2006-2010.

OKKERSE, Kenneth Howland (FdL) 4078 Valley View Trl, Sturgeon Bay WI 54235 **Died 1/29/2017** B Rye NY 1928 s Bertram & Jennie. BA U of Virginia 1951; GTS 1955. D 6/11/1955 Bp Benjamin M Washburn P 12/21/1955 Bp Henry Hean Daniels. c 3. Int Chr Ch Green Bay WI 2000-2017; S Paul's Epis Ch Suamico WI 2000-2001; Int S Jas Ch Manitowoc WI 1997-1998; Asst R S Anne's Epis Ch De Pere WI 1994-1997; R Intsn Epis Ch Stevens Point WI 1990-1991; R S Andr's Ch Millinocket ME 1985-1990; Chr the King/H Nativ (Sturgeon Bay) Sturgeon Bay WI 1981-1985; Vic Ch Of The H Nativ Jacksonport Sturgeon Bay WI 1981-1985; Vic H Nativ Jacksonport WI 1981-1985; Yth Camps Dio Fond du Lac Appleton WI 1980-1982; Asst R S Thos Ch Menasha WI 1978-1981; Ch Of The Epiph Norfolk VA 1973-1978; Dio Coun Dio Maine Portland ME 1985-1990. Sis Of H Nativ.

OKRASINSKI, Ronald Stanley (Va) Po Box 420, Colonial Beach VA 22443 **Liturg Cmsn 1978-** B Irvington NJ 1941 s Stanley & Helen. GTF; BA Seton Hall U 1963; MDiv Immac Concep Sem 1968; VTS 1979; DMin U of Notre Dame 1986. Rec 6/1/1980 as Priest Bp Robert Bruce Hall. m 5/27/1972 Claudette J Okrasinski c 2. Chapl Cathd of St Ptr & St Paul Washington DC 1996; Dn of Reg I in Virginia 1984-1989; 1981-1986; Plnng Com 1981-1983; R S Mary's Ch Colonial Bch VA 1980-2013; S Geo's Ch Fredericksburg VA 1980, Asst 1978-1980; Serv RC Ch 1968-1977; Cmncatn Com. Auth, *Liturg*.

OKTOLLIK, Carrie Ann (Ak) PO Box 446, Point Hope AK 99766 **Dio Alaska Fairbanks AK 2017-** B Kotzebue AK 1952 d Howard & Emily. D 2/13/2010 Bp Mark Lawrence Macdonald P 2/18/2017 Bp Mark A Lattime. m 8/31/1973 Martin Oktollik c 3. S Thos Ch Point Hope AK 2010-2016.

OKUNSANYA, Adegboyega Gordon (At) 711 Saint Saginaw Street, Flint MI 48502 B Igbara-Oke ON NG 1942 s Isaac & Julie. Ripon Coll Cuddesdon Oxford Gb 1966; Westminster Coll 1969; Emml 1981; PrTS 1981; MDiv Van 1985; DMin Van 1988. Trans 2/17/1992 Bp R aymond Stewart Wood Jr. m 12/11/1965 Jean Okunsanya. R Ch Of The Incarn Atlanta GA 2005-2011; Dio Atlanta Atlanta GA 2003-2004; S Paul's Epis Ch Flint MI 2000-2003; S Jn The Div Epis Ch Burlington WI 2000; Dio Milwaukee Milwaukee WI 1998-2000, Dep Cong Dvlpmt 1992-1998; Cathd Ch Of S Paul Detroit MI 1991-1998; Int Sewanee U So TS Sewanee TN 1988-1989; Assoc S Ann's Ch Nashville TN 1987-1988. Auth, "Issues Of Death Comparative Analysis On Jewish, Wstrn," *Afr Funeral Rites*; Auth, "Wstrn," *Afr Funeral Rites*. Iha; Ord For SS Of S Mary.

OKUSI, George Otiende (Los) 312 S Oleander Ave, Compton CA 90220 **S Thos Of Cbury Par Long Bch CA 2015-; Emergency On Call Chapl UCLA Santa Monica Hosp - Santa Monica 2012-; Counslr St. Tim's Tower and Manor for Seniors 2009-; Emergency On Call Chapl UCLA Ronald Reagan Hosp - Westwood 2009-; Chapl St. Tim's Epis Day Sch - Compton California 2007-; Bd Mem Ecum Interfaith Mnstry of Los Angeles 2012-; Bd Mem Interfaith Minstry in the Dio 2011-** B Kisumu 1964 s Petro & Lona. Dip Theol Stud St Johns Sch of Mssn 1990; MDiv Intl TS 2004; DMin Intl TS 2006. Trans 4/29/2010 Bp Joseph Jon Bruno. m 12/11/1993 Christine A Otiende. R S Tim's Par Compton CA 2009-2014; Dioc Chapl Girl's Friendly Soc in the Dio 2012-2015; Bd Members Prog Grp on HIV/AIDS 2011-2014; Bd Mem Prog of Black Mnstry 2010-2013. calleb48@yahoo.com

OLANDESE, Jan Susan (Nev) 2830 Phoenix St, Las Vegas NV 89121 **Online Fac/Sprtlty & Fiction The Oates Inst 2005-** B Seattle WA 1948 d Jerry & Freda. BA California St U 1970; MA U of Nevada at Las Vegas 1972; MDiv Oxf GB 2000; MDiv CDSP 2001; CPE U of Iowa 2002. D 5/29/2001 Bp Katharine Jefferts Schori P 12/1/2001 Bp William Edwin Swing. m 2/26/2010 Carlo Olandese. Chapl and Bereavement Coordntr Affnity Hospice of Life Las Vegas NV 2009-2010; Chapl S Rose Dominican Hospitals Henderson NV 2003-2009; Chapl Res U of Iowa Hospitals Iowa City IA 2001-2004; Assoc R S Fran' Epis Ch San Francisco CA 2001-2002. Preface Auth, "Indra's Jewels (Bk)," *Indra's Jewels*, Smallworks Press, 2014; Co-Auth, "Sex and Satanism in Susan Howatch's The High Flyer and The Heartbreaker," *Sprtl Identities: Lit and the Post Secular Imagination*, Ptr Lang Intl Acad Pub, 2010; Co-Auth, "Scandalous Risks: Sex, Scandal and Sprtlty in the Sixties," *Scandalous Truths: Essays by and about Susan Howatch*, Susquehanna U Press, 2005; Co-Auth, "Revs of The Novel, Sprtlty and Mod Culture," *The Angl Cath*, 2003; Co-Auth, "Psychic Sprtlty and Theol Romance in Susan Howatch's," *Chrsnty and Lit*, 2001. Assn of Profsnl Chapl 2003; Clark Cnty Mnstrl Assn 2003. Who's Who in Amer Marquis Who's Who 2015; Who's Who in Amer Marquis Who's Who 2014; Who's Who in Amer Marquis Who's Who 2013; Who's Who in Amer Marquis Who's Who 2012; Gold Medal Acad Excellence Sacr Heart U 2012; Who's Who in Amer Marquis Who's Who 2011; Sprt Awd Sojourn Chapl at SFGH 2011; Who's Who in Amer Marquis Who's Who 2010.

OLBRYCH, Jennie Clarkson (SC) 26 Saint Augustine Dr, Charleston SC 29407 **Vic S Jas Santee Ch Mc Clellanville SC 2006-** B Columbia SC 1950 d Andrew & Sarah. S Marys Jr Coll Raleigh NC 1969; BA U of So Carolina 1977; MDiv VTS 1988; DMin PrTS 2012. D 6/23/1988 P 5/13/1989 Bp Christopher FitzSimons Allison. m 6/2/1979 John A Olbrych c 5. Assoc Chapl Lower Sch Porter-Gaud Sch Charleston SC 2008-2016; R Epis Ch of the Gd Shpd Charleston SC 1998-2005; Cn for Int Mnstry S Steph's Epis Ch Charleston SC 1996-1997; Cn for Int Mnstry Epis Ch of the Gd Shpd Summerville SC 1995, Asst to R 1989-1993; Cn For Int Mnstry S Mich's Epis Ch Charleston SC 1994; Cn for Int Mnstry So Carolina Charleston SC 1993-1998, COM 2012-2013, Dep to GC 2003 2002-2003, Dn of Charleston Convoc 1999-2012, Dn of W Charleston Convoc 1999-2002, Cong Dvlpmnt Com 1996-2006; Cn for Int Mnstry S Jude's Epis Ch Walterboro SC 1993-1994; Asst to Dn Cathd Of S Lk And S Paul Charleston SC 1988. Auth, "The Bonds of Affection: Assessing Cler Ldrshp Effectiveness Using Adult Attachment Theory," *UMI*, ProQuest LLC, 2012. stjamesec@tds.net

OLDFATHER, Susan Kay (Kan) PO Box 187, Kingsville MD 21087 **S Mary's Epis Ch Woodlawn Gwynn Oak MD 2015-** B Bloomington IN 1947 d Frank & Mary Ellen. Dip Ang Stud Sewanee: The U So, TS; MLS U of Maryland Coll Pk 1994; MDiv Jesuit TS 2003. D 6/6/2009 P 6/5/2010 Bp Dean E Wolfe. c 2. Int R S Jn's Ch Kingsville MD 2010-2013.

OLDHAM ROBINETT, Lynn Margaret (Cal) 211 Forbes Ave, San Rafael CA 94901 **P Ch Of The H Innoc Corte Madera CA 2006-** B Oakland CA 1966 d Donald & Susan. BA U CA 1988; MDiv CDSP 1998. D 12/5/1998 P 6/5/1999 Bp William Edwin Swing. m 8/31/1997 Ryan Robinett c 3. S Paul's Epis Ch San Rafael CA 1999-2005, Asst R 1998-1999.

OLDS, Kevin (Ct) 4670 Congress St, Fairfield CT 06824 **S Tim's Ch Fairfield CT 2017-** B Oswego NY 1975 s Don & Sherry. BA Un Coll 1997; MDiv Drew U 2008; STM GTS 2010. D 11/14/2009 P 6/19/2010 Bp George Edward Councell. m 7/4/2009 Jill Olds c 2. R S Jn's Epis Ch Saugus MA 2010-2017.

OLDSTONE-MOORE, Jennifer (SO) St Anne Episcopal Church, 6461 Tylersville Rd, West Chester OH 45069 **S Andr's Epis Ch Wshngtn Ct Hs OH 2015-** B Baltimore MD 1961 d Michael & Elizabeth. Bexley-Seabury; BA Swarthmore Coll 1983; MA U Chi 1987; PhD U Chi 2000; Angl Cert GTS 2015. D 6/6/2015 P 7/4/2016 Bp Thomas Edward Breidenthal. m 9/19/1987 Christopher Raymond Oldstone-Moore c 3. Auth, "Scientism and Mod Confucianism," *The Sage Returns: Confuican Revival in Contemporary China*, SUNY, 2015; Auth, "Chinese Rel Traditions," *Understanding the Rel of the Wrld*, Wiley-Blackwell, 2015; Auth, "Sustained Experiential Lrng: Modified Monasticism and Pilgrimage," *Tchg Theol and Rel*, Wabash, 2009; Auth, "Confucianism, Daoism," *Estrn Rel*, Duncan Baird, 2005; Auth, "Taoism," Oxf Press, 2003; Auth, "Confuciansm," Oxf Press, 2002; Auth, "Confucianism, Daoism, Buddhism," *China: Empire and Civilization*, Oxf Press, 2000; Auth, "Chinese Rel Traditions," *Wrld Rel: The Illustrated Guide*, Oxf Press, 1999; Auth, "Alchemy and the Journey to the W," *Journ of Chinese Rel*, Indiana, 1998. rev.jennifer@saintanne-wc.org

O'LEARY, Jane (Md) 6011 Chesworth Rd., Baltimore MD 21228 **D Ch Of The Guardian Ang Baltimore MD 2003-** B Rochester NY 1949 d John & Joyce. BA GW 1971; MS Sthrn Connecticut St U 1976; MSW U of Maryland 2004. D 12/2/1989 Bp Arthur Edward Walmsley. m 11/20/2005 William Thomas Mundy c 3. Eccl Crt Dio Maryland Baltimore MD 2008-2011; D Chr Epis Ch Norwich CT 2000-2002; Asst Archd Dio Connecticut Meriden CT 1997-2002, Eccl Crt 1995-2002, Ecclesiatical Crt 1995-2002; Chr Epis Ch Middle Haddam CT 1997-1998; D S Jas Ch Preston CT 1990-1996; D S Paul's Epis Ch Willimantic CT 1990-1991. NAAD 1989.

OLIVER, Eugene Emery (O) 250 East Alameda St #418, Santa Fe NM 87501 **Died 11/26/2015** B Independence, KS 1926 s Leonard & Juanita. BA OH SU 1959; MDiv Bex Sem 1962. D 6/9/1962 P 12/15/1962 Bp Nelson Marigold Burroughs. m 4/19/1947 Blanche Marie Conaway c 2. R Emer St Paul's Steubenville Ohio 1987-2015; Ret 1986-2015; Fin Dept Dio Ohio Cleveland OH 1976-1979; R S Paul's Ch Steubenville OH 1965-1986; Cur S Paul's Ch Akron OH 1962-1965; Dept Cler & Lay Mnstrs Dio Ohio Cleveland 1968-1972, ExCoun 1968-1971, DeptMssn 1967-1971, Dept Prom 1965-1968.

OLIVER, Kyle M (NY) St. Michael's Church, 225 W 99th St, New York NY 10025 **S Mich's Ch New York NY 2016-** B Port Huron MI 1984 s Christopher & Joanne. BS U of Wisconsin-Madison 2006; MS U of Wisconsin-Madison 2009; MDiv VTS 2012. D 4/21/2012 P 11/29/2012 Bp Steven Andrew Miller. m 5/26/2012 Kristin Lee Saylor. Digital Mssnr & Instr VTS Alexandria VA 2015-2016, Digital Mssnr & Lrng Lab Coordntr 2012-2015; Asst P S Paul's Par Washington DC 2012-2015. Lifetime Distinguished Serv Dio Cntrl PA 2013; LECUSA/ECL Cert of Appreciation Liberian Epis Communities in USA 2013; Yoder Prize for Essay on Love VTS 2012; Harris Awd for Acad Excellence & Ldrshp VTS 2012; Second Place, Stdt Essay Competition LivCh 2011. koliver@saintmichaelschurch.org

OLIVER, Nancy Diesel (CFla) 2951 Mulberry Dr, Titusville FL 32780 **Full time Chapl Brevard Cnty Jail 2017-; D Cathd Ch Of S Lk Orlando FL 2015-** B St Louis MO 1954 d Elmer & Carroll. BSW U of Cntrl Florida 2010. D 9/12/2015 Bp Gregory Orrin Brewer. m 12/28/1974 Robert L Oliver c 11. noliver@stlukescathedral.org

OLIVERO, Cesar Olivero (SwFla) 17241 Edgewater Dr, Port Charlotte FL 33948 **M-in-c S Jas Epis Ch Pt Charlotte FL 2003-** B Elmhurst NY 1959 Lic VTS. D 6/14/2003 P 12/19/2003 Bp John Bailey Lipscomb. m 12/27/2014 Pamela Kay Olivero c 5. Dio SW Florida Parrish FL 2003.

OLIVO, David A (WA) 1525 H St NW, Washington DC 20005 **Asst S Jn's Ch Lafayette Sq Washington DC 2014-; Chattanooga Epis Campus Mnstry Bd Chair Dio E Tennessee Knoxville TN 2013-, Bp and Coun Mem 2012-; Conf Com Mem CEEP 2012-** B Portsmouth VA 1986 s David & Maxine. BA Milligan Coll 2008; MDiv Sewanee: The U So, TS 2011. D 6/4/2011 Bp Charles Glenn VonRosenberg P 12/12/2011 Bp George Young III. m 7/6/2013 Catherine R Outten Olivo c 2. Cur S Paul's Epis Ch Chattanooga TN 2011-2014.

OLLER, Janet Petrey (Ind) St John's Episcopal Church, PO Box 445, Crawfordsville IN 47933 **P-in-c S Jn's Epis Ch Crawfordsvlle IN 2012-** B Washington DC 1952 d Harry & Genevieve. BA U CO 1973; JD U of Houston 1983; MDiv SWTS 2009. D 6/20/2009 Bp Cate Waynick P 1/24/2010 Bp Duncan Montgomery Gray III. m 6/12/1999 Jeffery S Oller. Int S Andr's Epis Ch Greencastle IN 2011-2012; Asst R and Chapl S Ptr's Ch Oxford MS 2009-2011; Anti-Racism Com Dio Indianapolis Indianapolis IN 2012-2014, Const and Cn Com 2012-, Anti-Racism Com 2011-2014, Stndg Com 2011-2014, Safe-

guarding God's People Trnr 2011-; Judicial Crt Dio Mississippi Jackson MS 2010-2011.

OLMEDO-JAQUENOD, Nina (Cal) 1321 Webster St, Alameda CA 94501 B Rosario Santa Fe AR 1928 d Carlos & Irma. MA U of Bueno Aires AR 1942; MRE New Orleans Bapt TS 1957; MDiv CDSP 1980; MA California St U 1981. D 6/24/1978 Bp William Foreman Creighton P 6/1/1980 Bp John Raymond Wyatt. Mssn Outreach Speaker Food For The Poor Inc. Provices V &Vi 1992-1993; Chapl S Agustine Coll Chicago IL 1991-1992; Non-par 1986-1990; P-in-c S Mths Epis Ch San Ramon CA 1984-1985; Vic S Fran Assisi Brentwood CA 1983-1985; Fndr And Dir Centro Consejero Christos Brentwood CA 1980-1985; Centro Hispano (Siruiendo El Delta) Walnut Creek CA 1979-1985; Vic S Alb's Epis Ch Brentwood CA 1978-1980; Dio California San Francisco CA 1978-1979. Auth, "Var arts," *Journ Of Wmn Ministers*; Auth, "Chld'S Stories & Poetry," *Versos Para Ninos*; Auth, "Var arts," *Wit*.

OLMSTED, Nancy Kay Young (RI) Po Box 245, Lincoln RI 02865 B Duluth MN 1947 d Telford & Evelyn. BA Gri 1969; JD U Chi 1972; MDiv EDS 1990. D 8/4/1990 P 2/23/1991 Bp Douglas Edwin Theuner. m 8/23/1969 David Olmsted. Chr Ch In Lonsdale Lincoln RI 1994-2005; S Paul's Ch Pawtucket RI 1990-1993. Phi Beta Kappa; Phi Beta Kappa.

OLOIMOOJA, Edith Ipiso (Los) 3303 W Vernon Ave, Los Angeles CA 90008 **Chr The Gd Shpd Par Los Angeles CA 2016-** B Kenya 1985 BA Bible Coll of E Afr. D 2/5/2012 P 1/12/2013 Bp Joseph Jon Bruno. m 12/10/2007 Joseph Mtende Oloimooja c 6.

OLOIMOOJA, Joseph Mtende (Los) 1501 N Palos Vevoler Dr. #128, Harbor City CA 90710 B Kenya 1972 s Kanchori & Lente. Bible Coll of E Afr Kenya 1994; MDiv Intl TS 2003. Trans 11/1/2005 as Priest Bp Joseph Jon Bruno. m 12/10/2007 Edith Ipiso c 6. Chr The Gd Shpd Par Los Angeles CA 2010-2016; Epis Ch Of The Adv Los Angeles CA 2007-2010; Asstg P St Mary in Palms Los Angeles CA 2006-2007.

OLSEN, Christie (WNC) 1812 Lower Ridgewood Blvd., Hendersonville NC 28791 **Admin S Jas Epis Ch Hendersonvlle NC 2015-; Cn for Cmnty Life Washington Natl Cathd Washington DC 2007-** B New York NY 1964 d James & Judith. BA Sweet Briar Coll 1986; Cert Ang Stud Ya Berk 2002; MDiv Yale DS 2002. D 6/15/2002 Bp M(Arvil) Thomas Shaw P 6/27/2003 Bp James Monte Stanton. R S Fran Of Assisi Gulf Breeze FL 2010-2015; S Mich And All Ang Ch Dallas TX 2008-2010, 2002-2007, Assoc for Pstr Care 2002-2007; Cathd of St Ptr & St Paul Washington DC 2007-2008; S Peters-In-The-Woods Epis Ch Fairfax Sta VA 2007. Daugthers of the King 2005. christie@stjamesepiscopal.com

OLSEN, Daniel Kevin (Pa) Box 681, Oaks PA 19456 **R St Pauls Epis Ch Oaks PA 1995-** B Indianapolis IN 1954 s Bernhard & Elizabeth. Ball St U 1973; BA Taylor U 1976; MA No Pk TS 1978; MDiv TESM 1992. D 6/3/1992 Bp Edward Harding MacBurney P 12/1/1992 Bp Alexander D Stewart. m 4/25/1981 Katharine Ellen Olsen c 3. Cur All SS Ch Wynnewood PA 1992-1995. Amer Angl Coun; Angl Comm Ntwk.

OLSEN, David Logie (Ore) 10445 Sw Greenleaf Ter, Tigard OR 97224 **Ret 1999-** B Portland OR 1936 s Oscar & Melva. L&C 1954; BA U Denv 1959; MDiv Nash 1972. D 8/10/1972 P 2/15/1973 Bp James Walmsley Frederic Carman. m 9/7/2014 Peter Andrew Carney. Chr Ch S Helens OR 1990-1999; Treas Cler Assn Dio Oregon Portland OR 1986-1998, Bd of Trst 1979-1987, Liturg Cmsn 1974-2000, Treas Cler Assn 1972-1973; R S Dav's Epis Ch Portland OR 1980-1990; S Jn's Epis Ch Toledo OR 1973-1980; S Lk's Ch Waldport OR 1973-1980; Vic S Steph's Ch Newport OR 1973-1980; Asst All SS Ch Portland OR 1972-1973.

OLSEN, Donna Jeanne Hoover (Ind) 2601 East Thompson Road, Indianapolis IN 46227 B Chicago IL 1943 d Donald & Cosette. BA U of Indianapolis 1974; MA Chr TS 1993; U of Iowa 1999; Ivy Tech St Coll 2010. D 6/23/1995 Bp Edward Witker Jones. m 6/7/1963 Harold Nelvin Olsen c 3. Int Chapl S Richard's Sch Indianapolis IN 2001-2005; Chapl Trin Ch Indianapolis IN 2001-2003; D S Tim's Ch Indianapolis IN 1995-2001; DRE S Paul's Epis Ch Indianapolis IN 1995, DRE 1989-1995; DRE Chr Ch Cathd Indianapolis IN 1982-1989. Auth, "Journey to Easter," *Journey to Easter*; Auth, "Ldr Resources," *Ldr Resources*; Auth, "Ldr Resources," *Ldr Resources*; Auth, "Words of Truth," *Words of Truth*.

OLSEN, Jean Barry (RI) 35-C W Castle Way, Charlestown RI 02813 B Providence RI 1943 d Bernard & Florence. D 7/13/1985 Bp George Nelson Hunt III. Chapl Kent Cnty Meml Hosp 1987-1990.

OLSEN JR, Lloyd Lein (CFla) 992-B E Michigan St, Orlando FL 32806 **Adj Prof of Theol and Philos Barry U Miami FL 2006-** B Richmond VA 1951 s Lloyd & Martha. BGS U MI 1984; MDiv VTS 1984; DMin Reformed TS 2004; PhD GTF Oxf Prog 2011. D 10/11/1984 Bp H Coleman Mcgehee Jr P 9/30/1985 Bp William Hopkins Folwell. m 2/21/1982 Ginette E Olsen c 2. S Geo Epis Ch The Villages FL 2013-2015; The Ch Of S Lk And S Ptr S Cloud FL 2012; Assoc Cathd Ch Of S Lk Orlando FL 2011-2012, Assoc 2002-2007; R Epis Ch Of The H Sprt Apopka FL 2007-2011; S Mary Of The Ang Epis Ch Orlando FL 2006; P-in-c S Chris's Ch Orlando FL 2002-2005; R S Paul's Epis Ch Jackson MI 1991-1998; Doctoral Stdt Post-Grad Stds 1989-2002; R S Ptr's Ch

O

Fernandina Bch FL 1989-1991; Assoc R S Mich's Ch Orlando FL 1987-1989; Asst R Trin Ch Vero Bch FL 1985-1987. Auth, "Summa Creatio: A Theodicy of Successive Creation," 2011; Auth, "Theodicy And Chr Mnstry: The Practical Theol Of Suffering," 2004. GTF, Active Fell 2011; Soc of Chr Philosophers 2012.

OLSEN, L Michael (RG) St James Episcopal Church, 208 Camino de Santiago, Taos NM 87571 **Chapl - Taos Squadron CAP New Mex Wing 2014-; P-in-c S Jas Epis Ch Taos NM 2013-** B Denver CO 1948 s Lawrence & Lela. Dplma US Army War Coll; BA Pk U 1976; MA Webster U 1980; ETSBH 2007; MDiv CDSP 2008. D 6/7/2008 P 1/10/2009 Bp Joseph Jon Bruno. m 5/21/1966 Cassandra A Potter c 2. D St Cross Epis Ch Hermosa Bch CA 2008-2013; COM Dio Los Angeles Los Angeles CA 2009-2013. frmike@stjamestaos.org

OLSEN, Meredith DK (Md) 4127 Chadds Crossing, Marietta GA 30062 **S Barn Epis Ch Sykesville MD 2016-** B Drexel Hill PA 1975 d Joseph & Jayne. BA Birmingham-Sthrn Coll 1998; MDiv Candler TS Emory U 2002; STM GTS 2005. D 6/12/2005 P 7/26/2006 Bp J Neil Alexander. m 8/21/1999 Derek A Olsen c 2. All Hallows Par So River Edgewater MD 2011-2013; S Mk's Ch Highland MD 2010-2011; S Jn's Ch Reisterstown MD 2008-2009; S Marg's Ch Carrollton GA 2007-2008; The Epis Ch Of S Ptr And S Paul Marietta GA 2006.

OLSEN, Robert M (NCal) 8070 Glen Creek Way, Citrus Heights CA 95610 **D S Geo's Ch Carmichael CA 2011-** B Maderra CA 1947 s Hans & Ida. BA California St U 1969; MS USC 1988; BA Sch for Deacons 2001. D 7/28/2001 Bp Jerry Alban Lamb. m 9/14/1968 Sandra J Olsen c 2. Epis Cmnty Serv The Epis Dio Nthrn California Sacramento CA 2001-2014, COLM 1995-2014.

OLSON, Alice Ingrid (Minn) 7218 Hill Rd, Two Harbors MN 55616 B Duluth MN 1947 d Walter & Ina. D 6/17/2001 Bp James Louis Jelinek. m 7/2/1966 Quentin William Olson. D S Andr's By The Lake Duluth MN 2002-2013.

OLSON, Anna Burns (Los) 4274 Melrose Ave, Los Angeles CA 90029 **S Mary's Epis Ch Los Angeles CA 2011-** B Hanover NH 1971 BA Stan 1993; MDiv UTS 1998. D 6/24/2000 Bp Joseph Jon Bruno P 1/6/2001 Bp Frederick Houk Borsch. c 2. The Par Ch Of S Lk Long Bch CA 2008-2011; Cler & Laity Untd for Econ Justice 2006-2008; P-in-c Trin Epis Par Los Angeles CA 2002-2006; H Faith Par Inglewood CA 2000-2002, Assoc R 1998-2000. ao90004@gmail.com

OLSON, Britt Elaine (Oly) 262 Swenson Ct., Auburn CA 95603 **P-in-c S Lk's Epis Ch Seattle WA 2015-** B Fairbanks AK 1959 d Charles & Zoe. BA U of Oregon 1981; MDiv CDSP 1996. D 6/15/1996 P 12/13/1996 Bp Robert Louis Ladehoff. m 8/11/2007 Bryon H Hansen. Cn to the Ordnry The Epis Dio Nthrn California Sacramento CA 2006-2014; Cn for Evang & Cong. Dev. Dio El Camino Real Salinas CA 2005-2006; R S Paul's Epis Ch Sparks NV 1998-2005; Asst to the R Chr Ch Par Lake Oswego OR 1996-1998; Prog Assoc S Mich And All Ang Ch Portland OR 1992-1993; Prog Dir Ecum Mnstry of OR Emergency Food Portland 1991-1993. britt@stlukesseattle.org

OLSON, Corinna (SeFla) 8888 SW 131st Ct Apt 205, Miami FL 33186 **P-in-c S Lk The Physcn Miami FL 2006-** B Baton Rouge LA 1958 d John & Karen. BA Florida Atlantic U 1982; MDiv GTS 2004. D 4/17/2004 P 12/10/2004 Bp Leo Frade.

OLSON, Ellen Elizabeth (Neb) 609 Avenue C, Plattsmouth NE 68048 B Sioux City IA 1946 D 1/6/2003 Bp James Edward Krotz. m 4/24/1965 Merlin Leroy Olson.

OLSON, John Seth (Ala) 202 Gordon Dr SE, Decatur AL 35601 **S Jn's Ch Decatur AL 2013-** B Birmingham AL 1984 s Eric & Barbara. B.A. Sewanee: The U So; MDiv Epis TS of the SW 2013. D 5/29/2013 Bp John Mckee Sloan Sr P 12/11/2013 Bp Santosh K Marray. m 1/4/2017 Kimberly Meuth. seth@stjohnsdecatur.org

OLSON, Thomas Mack (NCal) 300 West St, Vacaville CA 95688 **R Epiph Epis Ch Vacaville CA 2012-** B Sanger CA 1967 s Thomas & Donna. BA U CO 1993; MDiv Iliff TS 2006. D 9/10/2011 P 3/24/2012 Bp Barry Leigh Beisner. m 5/17/2014 Jeremiah David Karagan. fathermack.epiphany@gmail.com

OLSSON, Paul V (Nwk) 32 Hillview Ave, Morris Plains NJ 07950 **Trst Hse of the Gd Shpd Hackettstown NJ 2011-; Co-Chair Morris Cnty (NJ) Long-Term Recovery Com 2011-; Chapl Morris Plains Fire Dept 2006-; R S Paul's Epis Ch Morris Plains NJ 2003-; Bd Trst Hse Of The Gd Shpd Hackettstown NJ 2011-** B Woodbury NJ 1963 s Victor & Virginia. BA JHU 1985; MIA Col 1987; MDiv GTS 1999. D 2/6/1999 P 9/11/1999 Bp Richard Frank Grein. Asst Chr And S Steph's Ch New York NY 1999-2003; Cathd Chapt Dio Newark Newark NJ 2013-2016, Bp's Advsry Com on HR 2010-, Com on Constitutions and Cn 2009-2013, COM, Diac Ord Com 2004-2012, Dist Rep. to Dioc Coun 2004-2008.

OLULORO, Emmanuel Bola (Az) 848 E Dobbins Rd, Phoenix AZ 85042 B Nigeria 1949 s Gabriel & Yeye. BS Norfolk St U 1983; MBA/MS Marylhurst U 1992. D 6/6/2015 Bp Kirk Stevan Smith. m 1/29/2001 Stella O Oloye c 2.

OLVER, Matthew S C (Dal) 6431 Vista Ave, Wauwatosa WI 53213 **Asst Prof of Liturg and Pstr Theol Nash Nashotah WI 2014-; BEC Dio Dallas Dallas TX 2017-, BEC 2012-2013, Exec Coun, Dio Dallas 2008-2011, Ecum Off 2005-2010, Epis Rep, Ecum Young Cler Conf Plnng Team, Baltimore, MD 2005-2007; elected Mem No Amer Acad of Liturg (NAAL) 2016-; Bd Mem**

LivCh Fndt Milwaukee WI 2016-; Mem Intl Angl Liturg Consult (IALC) 2015-; elected Mem Societas Liturgica 2015-; Writer Cov Weblog (LivCh Fndt) Milwaukee W 2008- B Waynesboro PA 1980 Phd Marq; BA Wheaton Coll 2001; MDiv Duke DS 2005. D 11/1/2005 P 5/27/2006 Bp James Monte Stanton. m 7/27/2001 Kristen Casey c 2. Asst R Ch Of The Incarn Dallas TX 2008-2013, Cur for Yth and Young Families 2006-2008; Cur and Sch Chapl S Jn's Epis Ch Dallas TX 2005-2006; Chapl Chld's Med Cntr Dallas TX 2005; Angl-RC Theol Consult in the USA (ARC-USA) Epis Ch Cntr New York NY 2008-2014; Cnvnr Disaster Preparedness Plan for the City of Dallas 2008; Off-Dio Dallas EDEO Ft Myers FL 2005-2010. Auth, "¿The Bavarian¿s Surprise: Ratzinger¿s Sprt of the Liturg as the Sprt of the Coun¿," *Nova et Vetera*, 2017; Auth, "¿The Eucharistic Materials in Enriching our Wrshp 1: A Consideration of its Trinitarian Theol¿," *ATR*, 2016; Auth, "¿A Note on the Silent Cn in the Missal of Paul VI and Cardinal Ratzinger¿," *Antiphon*, 2016; Auth, "¿Contraception¿s Authority: An Angl¿s Liturg and Synodical Thought Experiment...," *Journ of Ecum Stds*, Journ of Ecum Stds, 2015; Auth, "¿Documented Ecum: Why the Angl Cov is the Hope for Anglicanism and its Ecum Calling," *Pro Communione: Theol Essays on the Angl Cov*, Pickwick Pub/Wipf and Stock, 2012; Auth, "Impassioned Unity: The Sprtl Grammar of Cbury's Visit to Rome," *Esprit*, Jan/Feb, 2007; co-Auth, "True Ecum," *LivCh*, 1921-01-01, 2007; Auth, "A New Annunc," *Esprit*, April, 2006; Auth, "Re-Reception: A Fundamental Tool for Chr Unity," *LivCh*, 1915-01-01, 2006. No Amer Acad of Liturg 2016; No Amer Patristic Soc 2007; Societas Liturgica 2015; The AAR (AAR) 2005; The No Amer Acad of Ecumenists (NAE) 2005. Hoyt Hickman Awd for Outstanding Liturg Schlrshp Duke DS 2005; mcl, Mstr of Div Duke DS 2005. molver@nashotah.edu

O'MALLEY, Donald Richard (WNC) 101 Piney Rd, Hayesville NC 28904 B Camden NJ 1952 D 6/7/1997 P 12/21/1997 Bp Bob Johnson. m 6/8/1974 Deborah O'Mallley. Ch Of The Gd Shpd Hayesville NC 1997-2003.

OMERNICK, Marilyn (Los) 1418 Montecito Dr, Los Angeles CA 90031 B Stevens Point WI 1955 BS Viterbo U 1977; MA MI SU 1980; MS MI SU 1983; MDiv ETSBH 1999. D 6/26/1999 P 1/8/2000 Bp Frederick Houk Borsch. m 6/17/2008 Carol A Grosvenor. Chr Ch Par Redondo Bch CA 2015-2016; S Paul's Pomona Pomona CA 2015; S Mich The Archangel Par El Segundo CA 2011-2014; P-in-c S Mary's Epis Ch Los Angeles CA 2008-2011; S Mich and All Ang Epis Ch Studio City CA 2007, P-in-c 2007, Int 2003-2004; P-in-c S Jn's Mssn La Verne CA 2006-2007; Int St Johns Pro-Cathd Los Angeles CA 2004-2005; Int S Alb's Epis Ch Los Angeles CA 2004; Sr Assoc St Cross Epis Ch Hermosa Bch CA 1999-2003. laomernick@yahoo.com

ONATE-ALVARADO, Gonzalo Antonio (EcuC) Apartado Postal #5250, Guayaquil Ecuador **Natl Dir Soc Improvement Epis In Ecuador 1986-** B Celica Loja EC 1957 s Gerardo & Ana. U Cuenca 1981; MA U Havana 1983; Cert Cntr Theol Stds 1985. D 2/2/1986 Bp Adrian Delio Caceres-Villavicencio. m 8/31/1981 Deyce Aquilar-Ordonez. Litoral Dio Ecuador Guayaquil 1987-1991; Iglesia Epis Del Ecuador Quito 1986. Auth, "Var Lectures On Publ Hlth U Of Cuenca".

O'NEIL, Janet Anne (Mo) 808 N Mason Rd, Saint Louis MO 63141 B St Paul MN 1944 d Percy & Jeanne. BA Lawr 1966; MEd U of Missouri 1989. D 5/17/2007 Bp George Wayne Smith. m 8/20/1966 Michael O'Neil c 2. D S Tim's Epis Ch S Louis MO 2007-2015.

O'NEILL, Bruce Douglas (Cal) 2833 Claremont Blvd, Berkeley CA 94705 **R S Clem's Ch Berkeley CA 1997-** B Walnut Creek CA 1966 s Robert & Inge. BA U CA 1988; MDiv VTS 1994. D 6/4/1994 P 6/3/1995 Bp William Edwin Swing. m 7/2/1994 Michele Elizabeth O'Neill c 1. Asst R S Bede's Epis Ch Menlo Pk CA 1994-1997.

O'NEILL, Joanne Carbone (Nwk) 97 Highwood Ave., Tenafly NJ 07670 B Bronx NY 1948 d Rocco & Rita. BA Rutgers The St U of New Jersey 1983; MS Ford 1993. D 12/9/2006 Bp Carol J Gallagher. m 4/16/1983 James O'Neill. S Barn Epis Ch Williston FL 2007-2008; D Ch Of The Atone Tenafly NJ 2006-2010.

✠ O'NEILL, The Rt Rev Robert John (Colo) 7937 E 24th Ave, Denver CO 80238 **Bp of Colorado Dio Colorado Denver CO 2003-** B Pasadena CA 1955 s Richard & Joanne. BA TCU 1977; MDiv Yale DS 1981. D 6/28/1981 Bp William Grant Black P 1/1/1982 Bp William Carl Frey Con 10/4/2003 for Colo. m 8/6/1977 Virginia L O'Neill c 3. R Par Of The Epiph Winchester MA 1991-2003; Cn S Jn's Cathd Denver CO 1981-1991. Auth, "Exploring The Liturg," S Jn'S Cathd, 1991; Auth, "Focus On Lk," *Living The Gd News*, 1991. bishoponeill@coloradodiocese.org

O'NEILL, Vincent DePaul (Haw) 98-939 Moanalua Rd, Aiea HI 96701 **Ret Nevada 2008-** B Hartford CT 1938 s John & Gertrude. BA S Columbans Sem 1961; MDiv S Columbans Sem 1965; MEd NEU 1970; MA Cntrl Michigan U 1974; DMin SFTS 1980. Rec 11/1/1975 as Priest Bp Edwin Lani Hanchett. m 3/10/1969 Maria C O'Neill. R S Tim's Ch Aiea HI 1984-2007; Chapl Police Chapl 1977-2008; Cn Pstr S Andr's Cathd Honolulu HI 1977-1984; The Epis Ch in Hawaii Honolulu HI 1977-1978, Ecum Off 1988-2008. Auth, "Toward A Theol Of AA".

O

O'NEILL, William Haylett (Chi) 4899 Montrose Blvd. Apt. 703, Houston TX 77006 **Died 1/16/2017** B Houston TX 1939 s Haylett & Kate. BA U of No Texas 1967; MDiv SWTS 1970; MSW Loyola U 1980. D 6/18/1970 Bp Theodore H McCrea P 5/4/1971 Bp James Winchester Montgomery. Asstg P Palmer Memi Ch Houston TX 1999-2017; Adj Prof Field Educ Bexley Seabury Fed Chicago IL 1984-1991; R S Jn's Epis Ch Chicago IL 1982-1993; Soc Worker Cath Chars Holbrook Cntr for Counslg 1980-1993; Non-par Grad Sch 1978-1982; P-in-c Gr Ch Chicago IL 1972-1978; Asst Chr Ch Winnetka IL 1970-1972.

ONG, Dian Marie (Ia) 803 W Tyler Ave, Fairfield IA 52556 **D S Mich's Ch Mt Pleasant IA 1997-** B Anamosa IA 1940 d Arthur & Helen. BA Parsons Coll 1962. D 9/17/1997 Bp Chris Christopher Epting. m 7/27/1996 John Nathan Ong c 2. DOK 1996; Sis of S Helena 1996.

ONG, Merry Chan (Cal) 1011 Harrison St, Oakland CA 94607 **Exec Coun Dio California 2012-; Int Chr Epis Ch Sei Ko Kai San Francisco CA 2010-; After Sch Prog. Dir, Ch Admin True Sunshine Par San Francisco CA 2002-, Ch Admin, Prog. Dir 2002-2006** B Philippines 1957 d Manuel & Leticia. BBA U of Santo Tomas 1980; MEd Notre Dame Coll 1997; MDiv Biblic Sem of the Philippinese 2000; MDiv Biblic Sem of the Philippinese 2000; Cert Ang Stud Ch of the DS in Pacific 2007. D 6/13/2008 P 6/6/2009 Bp Marc Handley Andrus. c 1. Area Mssnr Dio California San Francisco CA 2009-2010; R Epis Ch Of Our Sav Oakland CA 2009-2010, R 2010-; D S Jas Epis Ch San Francisco CA 2008-2009, D 2008-2009.

ONKKA, Marcia Rauls (Minn) 1200 Autumn Dr Apt 211, Faribault MN 55021 **Ret 1994-** B Paynesville MN 1926 d J H & Hazel. U MN 1946. D 2/14/1990 Bp Sanford Zangwill Kaye Hampton. m 5/25/1946 Paul William Onkka. D All SS Ch Northfield MN 1992-1994; Ch Of The H Cross Dundas MN 1992-1994; D The Epis Cathd Of Our Merc Sav Faribault MN 1990-1992. NAAD.

ONKKA SR, Paul William (Minn) 1200 Autumn Dr Apt 211, Faribault MN 55021 **Ret 1993-** B Virginia MN 1919 s Elno & Inga. BS U MN 1943. D 2/14/1990 Bp Sanford Zangwill Kaye Hampton. m 5/25/1946 Marcia Rauls Onkka. D S Paul's Ch Yuma AZ 2001-2007; D The Epis Cathd Of Our Merc Sav Faribault MN 1990-1993. NAAD.

ONYENDI, Matthias E (Tex) B MBA Nigeria 1968 s Godwin & Catherine. Dip Theol Stud Imm Coll 1993; MA U of Ibadan 1997; Dip Virginia Theol Sem 2001. Trans 10/31/2006 Bp Don Adger Wimberly. m 2/13/1999 Goodness Onyendi c 3. S Fran Of Assisi Epis Prairie View TX 2006-2007; Vic St Marg's Epis Ch 2004-2006; R St Mary Epis Ch 2004-2006.

OPARE-ADDO, Frederick Akwetey (LI) 13304 109th Ave, South Ozone Park NY 11420 **P S Jn's Ch So Ozone Pk NY 2014-** B Accra Ghana 1956 s Robert & Josephine. LTh St. Nich Theol Coll 1986; DPS U of Birmingham 2000; BCPC/BCCC Epis Hlth Serv 2003. Trans 9/16/2014 Bp Lawrence C Provenzano. c 2.

OPAT, Kris (Pgh) 1066 Washington Rd, Pittsburgh PA 15228 **P-in-c S Dav's Epis Ch Peters Township PA 2012-** B Pittsburgh PA 1980 s Robert & Lou Ann. BSME Grove City Coll 2002; MDiv TESM 2008. D 6/7/2008 Bp Robert William Duncan P 12/13/2008 Bp David Colin Jones. m 9/24/2011 Shauna Mcinnes. Assoc R S Paul's Epis Ch Pittsburgh PA 2008-2013; D in Charge Three Nails Mssy Fllshp Pittsburgh PA 2008-2009.

OPEL, William A (NH) 395 Locust Road, Eastham MA 02642 **Ret 1988-** B Kansas City MO 1926 s Frederick & Bertha. BA Harv 1949; BD EDS 1952; MA UTS 1954; EdD UTS 1960; AB Harv 2049. D 6/14/1952 Bp Goodrich R Fenner P 12/13/1952 Bp Granville G Bennett. m 6/9/1951 Nina Ule Opel c 3. Int Faith Epis Ch Merrimack NH 1984-1987; Int S Barn Ch Berlin NH 1984; Int Ch Of The Gd Shpd Reading MA 1982-1983; R S Dunstans Epis Ch Dover MA 1980-1982; R St Johns Broad Creek Ft Washington MD 1971-1980; Assoc Dir Peace Corps Ghana & Botswana 1967-1971; Exch P St. Mich & All Ang Lower Sydenham SE London 1966-1967; Tchr/Chapl St. Agnes Sch Alexandria VA 1963-1979; R S Thos Epis Ch Mclean VA 1961-1967; Assoc R All SS' Epis Ch Chevy Chase MD 1959-1961; Field Educ Dir/Instr Philadelphia Div Sem Philadelphia PA 1957-1959; Chapl/Tchr St. Geo's Sch Newport RI 1955-1957; Chapl/Tchr Trin-Pawling Sch Pawling NY 1954-1955; Asst Gr Ch Jamaica NY 1952-1954; Exch P St. Mich's Lower Sydenham London 1966-1967; Instr, Dir. Field Educ Philadelphia Div Sem Philadelphia PA 1957-1959; Chapl/Tchr St. Geo's Sch Newport RI 1955-1957; Chapl/Tchr Trin-Pawling Sch Pawling NY 1954-1955. Auth, "The Jackdaw and the Peacock: Biblic Mistranslations and Chr Traditions," St. Johann Press, 2014.

O'PRAY, Denis Michael (Minn) 2412 Seabury Ave, Minneapolis MN 55406 B Buffalo NY 1941 s George & Elsie. BA Hobart and Wm Smith Colleges 1963; MA U MN 1970. D 6/11/1975 P 3/25/1976 Bp Philip Frederick McNairy. m 8/30/1964 Lynette C O'Pray c 3. Vic Ch Of The Nativ Burnsville MN 2008-2015; R Ch Of Our Sav Par San Gabr CA 1990-2007; Assoc R All SS Ch Pasadena CA 1983-1990; R S Jas On The Pkwy Minneapolis MN 1976-1983; Dio Minnesota Minneapolis MN 1976; Cur S Lk's Epis Ch Jamestown NY 1975-1976.

OPRENDEK, Matt (LI) 33 Jefferson ave, Garden City NY 11530 **Dio New York New York NY 2016-** B Elk Grove Village IL 1967 s Frederic & Jayne. BA Baylor U 1989; Bachelor in Mus Baylor U 1989; JD U of Texas Sch of Law

1996; JD U of Texas Sch of Law 1996; MDiv GTS 2012; MDiv The GTS 2012. D 5/26/2012 P 12/1/2012 Bp Vicky Gene Robinson. m 10/12/2012 Eric Allen Doescher. P-in-c Chr Ch Garden City NY 2013-2016; Dio Long Island Garden City NY 2013-2014; Chr Ch Exeter NH 2012-2013. rector@christchurchgc.org

ORBAUGH, Phyllis Rae (RG) 6626 Shpaati Ln, Cochiti Lake NM 87083 B Clay City IL 1938 d Raymond & Viola. Cert Oklahoma City SW Oklahoma City OK; U of Tulsa; Cbs TESM 2001. D 7/28/2001 Bp Terence Kelshaw. c 3. Ch of the H Faith Santa Fe NM 2001-2004; S Mths Epis Ch Shreveport LA 1980-1992. Albuquerque Hospice Soc 2006; Mem of Hon Literary Soc 2005.

ORCHARD, Carolyn Gertrude (NMich) 311 S 4th St, Crystal Falls MI 49920 **P S Mk's Ch Crystal Falls MI 1991-** B Stambaugh MI 1936 d Frank & Gertrude. BSN U MI 1959. D 5/20/1990 P 1/27/1991 Bp Thomas Kreider Ray. m 6/16/1956 David George Orchard c 3. D Dio Nthrn Michigan Marquette MI 1990-1991.

O'REAR, Lisa (O) **S Andr Epis Ch Mentor OH 2017-** B Bedford IN 1959 d Daniel & Mildred. BA DePauw U 1982; JD Washington U 1985; MDiv Bex 2012; MDiv Bex Sem 2012. D 6/9/2012 Bp Mark Hollingsworth Jr P 6/23/2013 Bp Arthur Williams Jr. m 10/24/1992 Kermit Luther Lassen c 1. S Paul's Ch Fremont OH 2016-2017; S Mk's Epis Ch Wadsworth OH 2015; Dio Ohio Cleveland 2013; S Pat's Ch Brunswick OH 2012-2015; S Barn Ch Bay Vill OH 2012-2013.

O'REILLY, Eileen (SO) 6873 Fieldstone Pl, Mason OH 45040 **Cmsn on Congrl Life Dio Sthrn Ohio Cincinnati OH 2011-, 2010, 2001-2003; R All SS Ch Cincinnati OH 2009-, R 2009-** B San Francisco CA 1947 d Austin & Sarah. BA San Francisco St U 1970; JD Natl U 1975; USC 1986; MDiv Trin Dublin IE 1995; MDiv Trin Dublin IE 1995; MDiv Trin Dublin IE 1995. Trans 11/1/2001 as Priest Bp Kenneth Lester Price. m 9/17/2008 Dana Speer. The Epis Ch Of The Ascen Middletown OH 2008-2009; S Andr's Epis Ch Wshngtn Ct Hs OH 2007-2008; Int H Trin Epis Ch Oxford OH 2005-2006; Int S Jas Ch Piqua OH 2001; R Dio Kilmore Cootehill Par Grp Cavan 1996-2000.

O'REILLY, John Thomas Jack (SwFla) 5321 Laurelwood Pl, Sarasota FL 34232 B Hartford CT 1937 s Myles & Violet. D 6/13/1998 Bp John Bailey Lipscomb. m 1/17/1959 Ina Marie Johnson.

O'REILLY, Patricia (Los) 402 S. Oakland Ave Apt 6, Pasadena CA 91101 **Dir Friends In Deed 2006-** B Boston MA 1950 d Patrick & Sara. BA Boston Coll 1971; MA Boston Coll 1972; MDiv EDS 1982. D 6/5/1982 Bp John Bowen Coburn P 1/22/1983 Bp Robert Claflin Rusack. c 4. Ecum Coun Pasadena Area Ch Pasadena CA 2006-2013; Mssh Luth Ch Pasadena CA 2005-2006; S Fran Mssn Norwalk CA 2002-2004; Chapl The Par Of S Matt Pacific Plsds CA 1995-2002; Asst S Aid's Epis Ch Malibu CA 1992-1994; Cathd Cong Los Angeles CA 1987-1995; Dir Epis Chaplncy La Cnty Facilities Dio Los Angeles Los Angeles CA 1987-1995; Epis Chapl USC Med Cntr LA 1987-1992; S Phil's Par Los Angeles CA 1987-1989; Co-R Ch Of The Epiph Los Angeles CA 1982-1987.

OREM, Becky Jane Tilton (NwT) St Paul's on-the-Plains Episcopal Church, 1510 Avenue X, Lubbock TX 79401 B Lubbock TX 1953 d William & Polly. BS Texas Tech U 1975; MS Texas Tech U & Hlth Sciences Cntr 1985; D Formation Prog in Dio NWTX 2011. D 12/3/2011 Bp James Scott Mayer. m 11/14/1998 John Marshall Orem c 2.

ORENS, Elizabeth Mills Pickering (Md) St James Church, 19200 York Rd, Parkton MD 21120 **Hon Asst All Souls Memi Epis Ch Washington DC 2013-** B Washington DC 1939 d George & Charlotte. Dplma Juilliard Sch 1961; BA Amer U 1963; MRE UTS 1967; MA Col 1969; ABD Drew U 1976; MDiv EDS 1978. D 10/19/1978 Bp John Shelby Spong P 10/14/1979 Bp George E Rath. m 6/6/1971 John R Orens c 1. R S Jas' Epis Ch Parkton MD 2007-2011; Chapl Cathd of St Ptr & St Paul Washington DC 1987-2007; Chapl Natl Cathd Sch Washington DC 1987-2007; Assoc Dio Wstrn Massachusetts Springfield 1982-1987; Assoc R Gr Ch Amherst MA 1982-1987; S Andr's Ch Belmont MA 1979-1980, 1978-1979; Rel Tchr Dwight Sch For Girls Englewood New Jersey 1971-1973; Pres/Chairman of the Bd Interfaith Conf of Metropltn Washington 1998-2002; Ecum Cmsn Dio Washington Washington DC 1991-2007. Auth, "Bk Revs," *Julia Gatta's The Nearness of God*, The Sewanee Revs, 2010; Auth, "Article," *The Heir of Redclyffe*, Fllshp Papers, 1990. SSJE 1987.

ORESKOVICH JR, Steve John (Mont) 1405 Sunflower Dr, Missoula MT 59802 B Butte MT 1945 s Steve & Zorka. BA Carroll Coll 1973; MTh Aquinas Inst of Theol 1975; VTS 1981. D 8/16/1981 P 3/1/1982 Bp Jackson Earle Gilliam. m 6/22/1973 Brenda Oreskovich. Directing D Formation 1989-1991; Ch Of The H Sprt Missoula MT 1981-2010; Chair Of Rel Stds Loyola HS 1978-1980; DRE H Trin 1977-1978.

ORIHUELA, Roberto Opolinar (Va) 7000 Arlington Blvd, Falls Church VA 22042 **La Iglesia de Santa Maria Falls Ch VA 2012-** B Bolivia 1959 s Aida. BTh Cath U of Bolivia 1990; BPh Cath U of Bolivia 1990; VTS 2011. Rec 11/20/2011 as Priest Bp David Colin Jones. m 5/6/2002 Helkha Peredo-Pinto. roberto.orihuela@yahoo.com

O'RILEY, Lori Cameron (At) **Assoc S Pat's Epis Ch Dublin OH 2016-** B Ft Stewart GA 1976 d Patrick & Anne. BS Shorter U 2000; MEd U of W GA 2006;

O

MDiv The U So TS 2016. D 12/19/2015 P 6/25/2016 Bp Robert Christopher Wright.

ORLANDO, Helen Marie (NJ) 10 Iris Ct, Marlton NJ 08053 **Mem, Dioc Global Goals T/F Dio New Jersey Trenton NJ 2011-, Mem, Bd Missions 2008-2010, Mem, Comp Dio Com 2007-2011** B Toledo OH 1951 d George & Corrine. Burlington Cnty Med Reserve Corps; Rutgers The St U of New Jersey; U MN 1972; Courses towards BA (Smith) U MN 1972; BA Smith 1973; Completed EFM 1997; Graduated D Formation Prog, Dio NJ 2000; Cert EfM Mentor Sewanee: The U So, TS 2003; Cert Disaster Chapl, NDIN Disaster Chapl Trng 2011. D 10/21/2000 Bp David Bruce Joslin. m 6/23/1973 Michael Thomas Orlando c 2. Chapl Burlington Cnty Med Reserve Corps New Jersey 2013-2015; Admin Asst S Ptr's Ch Medford NJ 2006-2007, Par Admin 2003-2006, D 2000-; Mentor EFM 2003-2009. Assn of Epis Deacons (AED) 1997. dcnhelen@stpetersmedford.org

ORME-ROGERS, Charles Arthur (Mil) 7634 Mid Town Rd - #212, Madison WI 53719 **CPE Supvsr Meriter Hlth Serv and Hosp Inc. 2010-; Asst St. Paul's Episcoal Ch Carondelet MO 2006-** B Robinson Illinois 1949 s Roy & Ardis. BA Wabash Coll 1973; MA U of Notre Dame 1979; MDiv Eden TS 2006; Cert Epis Sch for Mnstry 2008; ACPE Res and Supervisory Stdt St Lukes Epis/ Presb Hosp 2008; Supvsr ACPE 2013; Supvsr Other 2013. D 5/31/2006 P 1/6/ 2007 Bp George Wayne Smith. m 12/11/1976 Catherine Marie Orme c 2. CPE Res St. Lk's Hosp 2005-2010; S Matt's Epis Ch Warson Woods Kirkwood MO 2004-2005. "A field dependency explanation of age differences in the persuasibility of irrelevant stimuli," *Intl Journ of Aging and Human Dvlpmt*, 1979; "Examination of stimulus persistence as the basis for superior visual identification performance among adults," *Journ of Gerontology*, 1978. ACPE 2008. Divinitatis Doctor Edinburg TS 2012; cl Wabash Coll 1973.

ORMOS, C Patrick (WTex) 12933 Latchwood Ln, Austin TX 78753 B Paris FR 1951 s Paul & Jacqueline. BA Indiana U 1975; MA Chicago TS 1977; Dip Min Stud Montreal TS CA 1978; STM McGill U 1990; DMin SWTS 1997. Trans 1/1/1992 Bp Francis Campbell Gray. c 1. R St Fran Epis Ch San Antonio TX 2007-2011; R S Andr's Epis Ch Valparaiso IN 1991-2007; Int Gr Epis Ch Freeport IL 1990-1991; Serv Angl Ch of Can 1978-1990. Auth, "The Place of Self-Revelation in Preaching," *Pract of Mnstry in Can*.

ORNDORFF, Vivian (Tex) 3901 S Panther Creek Dr, The Woodlands TX 77381 **Trin Epis Ch The Woodlands TX 2014-** B Cincinnati OH 1964 d Donald & Carol. BFA U Cinc 1989; BFA U Cinc 1989; MDiv Epis TS Of The SW 2014; MDiv Epis TS of the SW 2014. D 6/7/2014 Bp Dean E Wolfe. m 9/18/1993 Patrick Andrew Orndorff c 2. vorndorff@trinitywoodlands.org

O'ROURKE, Brian (Los) 1325 Monterey Road, South Pasadena CA 91030 B Wiesbaden Germany 1976 s Kelly & Cynthia. BS Menlo Coll 1998; BS Menlo Coll 1998; MDiv VTS 2011. D 6/11/2011 Bp Diane Jardine Bruce P 1/14/2012 Bp Jim Mathes. m 9/28/2002 Jennifer O'Rourke c 1. S Jas' Par So Pasadena CA 2014-2017; Ch Of The Epiph Oak Pk CA 2012-2014; P Assoc S Marg's Epis Ch Palm Desert CA 2011-2012.

O'ROURKE, David Carter (Colo) 2425 Colorado Ave, Boulder CO 80302 **Assoc Chapl Colorado Dept of Corrections 2016-; D S Aid's Epis Ch Boulder CO 2015-** B Queens NY 1964 s Daniel & Anne. BA SUNY Plattsburgh 1989. D 6/13/2015 Bp Robert John O'Neill. m 7/29/2000 Rebecca O'Rourke c 2.

OROZCO, Benjamin Manuel (SanD) 3568 Elmwood Ct, Riverside CA 92506 **All SS Epis Ch Riverside CA 2004-** B Glendale AZ 1933 s Antonio & Esther. BA U CA 1959; BD CDSP 1962; U of Texas 1971. D 6/28/1962 Bp Everett H Jones P 1/4/1963 Bp Richard Earl Dicus. m 6/25/1967 Irene Emma Orozco c 2. Vic S Andr's By The Lake Lake Elsinore CA 1995-1998, P 1977-1978; Vic S Gabr's Ch Duncanville TX 1966-1970; Cur S Paul's Epis Ch San Antonio TX 1964-1966; P Santa Fe Epis Mssn San Antonio TX 1963-1964. SSC.

ORPEN JR, J Robert (Chi) 5550 S Shore Dr Apt 512, Chicago IL 60637 **Ret 1986-** B Providence RI 1921 s John & Mary. BA Br 1942; STB GTS 1948; STM Nash 1949. D 3/31/1948 P 4/23/1949 Bp Granville G Bennett. m 5/30/ 1957 Lavinia Orpen c 3. Asst S Mich's Ch Barrington IL 1990-2009; Assitant P Cathd Of S Jas Chicago IL 1985-2012; Dn Chicago W Dnry 1974-1986; R S Steph Chicago IL 1969-1989; P-in-c St Stephens Ch Chicago IL 1969-1985; R Ch Of The Adv Chicago IL 1958-1986; R S Geo Bronx NY 1954-1958; Vic S Geo Bronx NY 1953-1954; Vic H Trin Epis Ch Fallon NV 1949-1953; Assoc Mssn Fallon Nv 1949-1953; Asst S Matt's Ch Kenosha WI 1948-1949; Dio Coun Dio Chicago Chicago IL 1974-1986, Spanish Supply P 1970-1973, Dio Coun 1961-1969; Chair Dept & Prom Dio Nevada Las Vegas 1950-1951.

ORR, Daniel Longsworth (O) 433 E Maple St, Bryan OH 43506 **Gr Epis Ch Mansfield OH 2015-; Asst D Epis Shared Mnstry Of NW Ohio 2004-** B Decatur GA 1971 BA Ob. D 1/30/2004 Bp J Clark Grew II P 10/6/2004 Bp Mark Hollingsworth Jr. m 5/31/1997 Ann Longsworth Orr c 2. S Paul's Ch Fremont OH 2006-2014; Dio Ohio Cleveland 2004-2006; Epis Shared Mnstry Of NW Ohio Sherwood OH 2004.

ORR, Kristin Elizabeth (Chi) P. O. Box 25, Flossmoor IL 60422 **Dn, Joliet Dnry Dio Chicago Chicago IL 2012-, Dioc Coun Mem 2005-** B Berkeley CA 1958 d Charles & Carol. BS Ya 1980; MS U of Washington 1982; PhD U of Washington 1985; MDiv VTS 1991. Trans 3/11/2004 Bp Chilton Richardson Knud-

sen. R The Ch Of S Jn The Evang Flossmoor IL 2004-2017; R S Pat's Ch Brewer ME 1999-2003; S Mk's Ch Houston TX 1991-1999; Dioc Liturg Cmsn Dio Texas Houston TX 1995-1999.

ORRALA MONCADA, Francisco (EcuL) **Litoral Dio Ecuador Guayaquil 2015-** B Guayaquil Ecuador 1947 D 10/11/2014 Bp Terencio Alfredo Morante-Espana. m 1/21/1985 Claudina Pacheco De Orrala c 4.

ORRIN, Dyana Vail (Ak) 1501 N Adams St, Fredericksburg TX 78624 B Glendale CA 1937 d Ande & Lillian. AA Anchorage Cmnty Coll 1983; BA Alaska Pacific U 1988; MDiv CDSP 1991; DMin Vancouver TS CA 2004; DMin Vancouver TS CA 2004. D 12/19/1987 Bp George Clinton Harris P 9/1/1991 Bp Steven Charleston. c 1. Asst P St. Barn Epis Ch Fredericksburg Texas 2007-2012; R S Jas The Fisherman Kodiak AK 2005-2006; R S Dav's Epis Ch Wasilla AK 1992-2005; Asst Dio Alaska Fairbanks AK 1991-1992; Chapl U of Alaska Anchorage Alaska 1991. DOK 2008; OHC 1989.

ORSBURN, Kenneth Ray (Okla) B Holdenville OK 1984 s Kenneth & Patsi. BA E Cntrl U 2006; MDiv Wycliffe Coll 2013; MDiv Wycliffe Coll Toronto CA 2013. D 12/22/2012 P 7/6/2013 Bp Edward Joseph Konieczny. m 4/12/2015 Soha Orsburn. Cur S Jn's Epis Ch Tulsa OK 2013-2015. korsburn@sjtulsa.org

ORSO, Thomas Ray (NY) 100 DeHaven Drive #405, Yonkers NY 10703 **Gr Ch White Plains NY 2016-** B Williamsport PA 1947 s Max & June. BFA Witt 1969; MDiv EDS 1977; MS Wstrn Connecticut St U 1991. D 6/18/1977 P 9/9/1978 Bp William Hawley Clark. S Jn's Of Lattingtown Locust Vlly NY 2014-2015; Int S Mk's Ch Westhampton Bch NY 2013-2014; Cn For Deploy Dio New York New York NY 2001-2012; P-in-c S Andr's Epis Ch Staten Island NY 2000-2001; P-in-c S Mk's Epis Ch Yonkers NY 1997-2000; R Ch Of The Ascen And H Trin W Pk NY 1981-1983; Chapl Trin Pawling Sch Pawling NY 1977-1991; Trin-Pawling Sch Pawling NY 1977-1981.

ORT, Larry Victor (SD) St. Paul's Episcopal Church, 726 6th St, Brookings SD 57006 **S Paul's Ch Brookings SD 2014-** B Wauseon OH 1947 s Victor & Edna. BA Sprg Arbor U 1969; MA MI SU 1976; PhD MI SU 1997. D 10/6/2012 P 6/24/2013 Bp John Tarrant. m 10/14/1995 Judith Ann Burger c 2.

ORTEGA, Guido Andres (EcuC) Avenue Amazonas 4430 Y Villalengua, Casilla 17116 Ecuador **Iglesia Epis Del Ecuador Quito 2012-, 1999-2010** B Bolivar Carchi EC 1965 s Maria. U Cath Ecu 5 Yrs. m 4/21/1995 Jenny J P Quiroz. Vic Iglesia Nueva Jerusalem Pelileo Tu 1999-2010.

ORTEZ, Jose Leonel (SeFla) **Santa Cruz-Resurr Epis Ch Biscayne Pk FL 2003-** B 1965 s Enrique & Eva. MA Honduras 1990; BA Honduras 1994. Rec 4/15/1998 Bp Calvin Onderdonk Schofield Jr. m 4/1/2016 Diocelina Montanez Fuerte c 3. Pstr - Sch Prncpl Iglesia Epis Epifania - Escuela Villanueva Hoduras 2001-2002; Dio Honduras San Pedro Sula 1998-2002; Mssy Diocesis of Honduras San Pedro Sula 1998-2001; Assistance Pstr Cristo Redentor Tegucigalpa 1997-1998.

ORTIZ, Michelle Alisa (At) 1015 Old Roswell Rd, Roswell GA 30076 **S Dav's Ch Roswell GA 2015-** B Pensacola FL 1977 d Charles & Patricia. BA U of Cntrl Florida 1998; MDiv Sewanee: The U So, TS 2012; MDiv The TS at The U So 2012. D 12/10/2011 Bp Dabney Tyler Smith. m 1/2/1999 Edgardo Ortiz c 3. P H Innoc Epis Ch Valrico FL 2012-2015; Yth Dir Dio SW Florida Parrish FL 2012-2014.

ORTT, William Jeffrey (Eas) 111 S Harrison St, Easton MD 21601 **R Chr Ch S Ptr's Par Easton MD 1999-** B Niagara Falls NY 1958 s John & Molly. na Niagara U 1978; BA SUNY at Buffalo 1980; BA SUNY at Buffalo 1980; MDiv GTS 1986; DMin Drew U 1993. D 5/31/1986 P 5/29/1987 Bp Harold Barrett Robinson. m 5/19/1990 Susan Elizabeth Ortt. R S Steph's Ch Newton IA 1990-1999; Asst S Fran Ch Greensboro NC 1986-1990. OHC 1985. fatherbill@christchurcheaston.org

ORTUNG, Thomas Edward (Oly) 105 State St, Kirkland WA 98033 B Poughkeepsie NY 1962 s Edward & Teresa. BA SUNY at Albany 1999; MDiv Nash 2007. D 6/9/2007 Bp William Howard Love P 1/25/2009 Bp Gregory Harold Rickel. m 7/1/1989 Jami L Ortung c 3. Dio Olympia Seattle 2011-2012; S Lk's Ch Cambridge NY 2007-2008.

ORVILLE, Lynn D (RI) PO Box 491, Little Compton RI 02837 **S Andr's By The Sea Little Compton RI 2017-; Dio Maine Portland ME 2016-; Dio Virginia Richmond VA 2012-** B Jackson MI 1958 d James & Eloise. BS Bellevue U 1991; MDiv VTS 1998. D 4/21/1998 P 10/23/1998 Bp James Edward Krotz. m 9/30/1978 Douglas Duvall Orville c 1. P-in-c S Clem's Epis Ch Greenville PA 2009-2010; Vic S Barth's Epis Ch Bemidji MN 2005-2007; Chapl Epis Cmnty Serv Bemidji MN 2004-2005; R Gr Epis Ch Chadron NE 2000-2004; Cn Pstr Cathd Of S Paul Erie PA 1998-1999; Dioc Coun Exec Com Dio Minnesota Minneapolis MN 2007-2008, Dioc Coun 2005-2008; Stndg Com Dio Nebraska Omaha NE 2001-2004. rector@standrewlc.org

ORWIG, Dana Lynn Maynard (Okla) 2710 Nw 17th St, Oklahoma City OK 73107 **DCE S Jn's Ch Oklahoma City OK 2005-, DCE 1992-2004; Asst Chapl S Jn's Epis Sch Inc. Oklahoma City OK 1992-** B Julesburg CO 1954 d Judson & Gladys. Texas Tech U 1974; BA U of Texas 1978. D 6/27/1992 Bp Robert Manning Moody. m 9/21/1974 Steven Rhea Orwig c 2. NAAD.

OSBERGER, Charles Edward (Eas) 14084 Old Wye Mills Rd, Wye Mills MD 21679 **R Old Wye Ch Wye Mills MD 1986-** B Houston TX 1954 s Charles

& Margeurite. BA USC 1976; MA Fuller TS 1978; MDiv TESM 1980. D 6/5/ 1982 P 12/1/1982 Bp Robert Bracewell Appleyard. c 2. R S Lk's Chap Queenstown MD 1986; Assoc S Mart's Ch Chagrin Fall OH 1982-1985. Bd India Mssn; Bro Of S Andr; Ecmc Casa; Theol Stdt Fllshp.

OSBORN, Mary Anne (Ct) 560 Lake Dr., Guilford CT 06437 **R Chr Epis Ch Middle Haddam CT 2012-** B Mobile AL 1951 d Prime & Grace. BA Florida St U 1974; MA U of No Florida 1976; MDiv EDS 1986. D 6/8/1986 P 12/14/1986 Bp Frank S Cerveny. m 12/31/2008 Joanne Louise Neel. Int Zion Epis Ch N Branford CT 2009-2011; Assoc S Paul's Ch Fairfield CT 1999-2007; Assoc Trin Ch Torrington CT 1999; Middlesex Area Cluster Mnstry Higganum CT 1998-1999; S Paul And S Jas New Haven CT 1996-1998; Dir of the Cntr for Sprtlty & Aging S Paul & S Jas 1995-1998; Asst Dir Interfaith Vol Caregivers 1990-1994; Dir of Pstr Serv Tandet Cntr for Cont Care Stamford CT 1988-1990; Chapl Hartford Hosp Hartford CT 1986-1988.

OSBORN, Sherrell E (Vt) 1142 Prindle Rd Apt B, Charlotte VT 05445 **Bp Booth Conf Cntr Burlington VT 2015-, 2014-2015** B Springfield MA 1961 d Jonathan & Sue. BS Green Mtn Coll 1983; MEd Bos 1987; Dip Ang Stud Ya Berk 2002; MDiv Yale DS 2002. D 6/21/2003 P 12/20/2003 Bp Andrew Donnan Smith. Camp Prog Coordntr Camp Agape Vermont 2009-2012; R S Mk's Ch Springfield VT 2006-2012; Assoc R S Mich's Ch Milton MA 2003-2006. Seminarians Interacting Yale DS 2001; Jess H. and Hugo A. Norenbuerg Preaching Prize Yale DS 2000; Pres's Publ Serv Fllshp Ya 2000. sosborn@dioceseofvermont.org

OSBORN DE ANAYA, Chan (NAM) 1115 Main St, Vicksburg MS 39183 **Cn St Michaels Epis Ch Upper Fruitland NM 2015-; Cn The Epis Ch In Navajoland Coun Farmington NM 2015-; Navajoland Area Mssn Farmington NM 2011-** B Florence AL 1951 RN Coll of Santa Fe. D 6/21/2003 Bp Terence Kelshaw P 1/3/2004 Bp Duncan Montgomery Gray III. m 11/30/1996 Vernon L Anaya c 2. R Chr Epis Ch Vicksburg MS 2003-2010. ecncanaya@gmail.com

OSBORNE, Charles Edward (ETenn) 1540 Belmeade Dr, Kingsport TN 37664 B Mount Croghan SC 1929 s Edward & Emeline. BS U NC 1951; MS U of Maine 1953; PhD NWU 1956. D 6/21/1981 Bp William Evan Sanders. m 8/6/1955 Columbine Vera Amici c 2. S Columba's Epis Ch Bristol TN 2002-2007; D S Chris's Ch Kingsport TN 1997-2002; D S Paul's Epis Ch Kingsport TN 1981-1996.

OSBORNE, Jamie (Ala) D 5/13/2017 Bp John Mckee Sloan Sr.

OSBORNE, Janne Alr (Tex) PO Box 150535, Austin TX 78715 B Skalskor DK 1952 d Merritt & Inga. Austin Coll 1973; BD U of Texas 1989; MDiv VTS 1994. D 7/6/1994 Bp John Herbert MacNaughton P 1/18/1995 Bp James Edward Folts. c 2. Assoc S Mich's Ch Austin TX 2005-2015; R S Alb's Epis Ch Waco TX 2002-2005; Assoc R S Dav's Ch Austin TX 1997-2002; Ch Of Our Sav Aransas Pass TX 1994-1997; Vic Trin-By-The-Sea Port Aransas TX 1994-1997; Secy S Mich's Epis Ch San Antonio TX 1989-2004; CE Coordntr S Alb's Epis Ch Arlington TX 1984-1989. Sis of the H Sprt 2006.

OSBORNE, Ralph Everett (FdL) 2420 Marathon Ave, Neenah WI 54956 **R S Thos Ch Menasha WI 2010-** B Chicago IL 1956 s Ralph & Martha. DePaul U 1974; BA Olivet Nazarene U 1978; MA U of Missouri Kansas City 1983; MDiv Nazarene TS 1985. D 6/17/1995 P 1/6/1996 Bp David Bruce Joslin. m 8/12/1978 Cindy Jo Osborne c 4. Dio Cntrl New York Liverpool NY 2005; R Zion Epis Ch Greene NY 1996-2010; S Dav's Ch Fayetteville NY 1995-1996.

OSBORNE, Richard L (RG) 102 Southfork Cir, Pottsboro TX 75076 **Ret 2008-** B Syracuse NY 1942 s Leo & Dorothy. Le Moyne Coll 1963; BA St Bernards Sem Rochester NY 1964; MDiv S Bernards TS and Mnstry 1968. Rec 6/26/1995 Bp William Edward Smalley. m 5/30/1992 Constance Osborne c 1. S Chris's Epis Ch Wichita KS 2007-2008; S Chris's Epis Ch Hobbs NM 2005-2007; Vic St Chris's 2005-2007; S Mary's Ch Lovington NM 2002-2007.

OSBORNE, Ronald Douglas (Ia) 2325 E Highview Dr., Des Moines IA 50320 B Kearney NE 1940 s Rolland & Esther. BA Westmar Coll 1962; BD SWTS 1965; U of Iowa 1989; Creighton U 1993; Cert St Jos Cntr 1995; DMin SWTS 2005. D 6/24/1965 P 1/1/1966 Bp Gordon V Smith. m 4/6/1991 Sara Jane Hauff c 2. R All S's Epis Ch Indianola IA 2010-2016; Assoc S Andr's Ch Des Moines IA 2007-2014; R Trin Epis Par Waterloo IA 1998-2006; Vic S Mart's Ch Perry IA 1990-1998; Coll Field Des Moines IA 1972-1990; Chapl Epis Chapl at U Of Iowa Iowa City IA 1965-1990. Auth, "Mar Of Christians And Jews," Plumbline, 1984; Auth, "Rendering Resrch From Caesar," Plumbline, 1982. Affirming Angl Catholicism 1966. Chapl Sons Of Knutt--Lake Wobegon 1998.

OSBORNE, William Paul (Spok) 5720 S Perry St, Spokane WA 99223 **S Steph's Epis Ch Spokane WA 2011-** B Tacoma WA 1955 s Robert & Evelyn. BA Gri 1977; MS Humboldt St U 1991; MDiv CDSP 2001. D 1/14/2001 Bp Mark Lawrence Macdonald P 8/5/2001 Bp Jerry Alban Lamb. m 1/7/1995 Margaret Ann Drumm c 5. S Mich And All Ang Ch Ft Bragg CA 2009-2011, 2006-2009; Asst P S Mary's Epis Ch Napa CA 2001-2006.

OSBORNE-MOTT, Susan Elizabeth (NJ) 503 Asbury Ave, Asbury Park NJ 07712 B Minneapolis MN 1950 d Lawrence & Mary. BA U MN 1974; MDiv SWTS 2007. D 6/2/2007 Bp Bill Persell P 12/15/2007 Bp Victor Alfonso Scant-

lebury. m 8/24/1985 Bradley A Mott c 2. S Mary's Epis Ch Stone Harbor NJ 2012-2014; Asst R Trin Ch Asbury Pk NJ 2008-2012.

OSGOOD, John A (NY) 201 Old Mountain Rd N, Nyack NY 10960 B New Berlin NY 1948 BA Un Coll Schenectady NY 1970; Dip U of Birmingham GB 1972; MDiv GTS 1973; STM GTS 1975. D 6/9/1973 Bp Paul Moore Jr P 12/20/1973 Bp Horace W B Donegan. m 6/20/1985 Maribeth B Goewey c 2. Cn Ordnry Dio New York New York NY 1996-2014, Stndg Com 1988-1992, Chair Angl-Roman Cath Com 1976-1983; R Gr Ch Middletown NY 1979-1996; Tutor The GTS New York NY 1977-1983; R The Epis Ch Of Chr The King Stone Ridge NY 1975-1979; Cur Chr Ch Of Ramapo Suffern NY 1973-1975; Chapl Rockland Cmnty Coll Suffern NY 1973-1975. Auth, *Angl-RC Consult Inter-Par Dialogue*; Auth, *Ecum Study Guide on Authority*; Auth, *Ecum Study Guide on Mnstry & Ord*.

OSGOOD, Thomas Marston (Cal) 6471 Coopers Hawk Rd, Klamath Falls OR 97601 **Asst S Paul's Ch Klamath Fall OR 2006-; Ret 2001-** B Pittsburgh PA 1932 s Thomas & Dorothy. BA Ya 1954; BD CDSP 1957. D 6/23/1957 Bp Russell S Hubbard P 3/1/1958 Bp William Jones Gordon Jr. c 3. Chapl Epis Hm Fndt In Lafayette 1978-2001; Epis Sr Communities Lafayette CA 1978-2001; Non-par 1977-1978; Chapl Doctors Hosp 1975-1977; Assoc Epiph Par of Seattle Seattle WA 1969-1975; Vic S Lk's Ch Sequim WA 1964-1969; Cur S Steph's Epis Ch Longview WA 1962-1964; Vic S Geo In The Arctic Kotzebue AK 1957-1962.

O'SHEA, Nancy Corinne Tucker (WTenn) 6294 Venus Ave, Bartlett TN 38134 **D All SS Epis Ch Memphis TN 2016-; COM Dio W Tennessee Memphis 2016-, Stndg Com 2010-2014, Disciplinary Bd 2010-** B Kansas City MO 1942 d Dean & Martha. BS U of Missouri 1964. D 10/28/1985 Bp Arthur Anton Vogel. m 8/10/1985 Donald Patrick O'Shea. D Imm Ch Ripley TN 2009-2015; Chapl S Fran Hosp Memphis TN 2000-2009; D S Mary's Cathd Memphis TN 1986-1999. DOK 1987; Oblates of St. Ben 1980.

O'SHEA, Susan J (Oly) 234 Wood Ave SW #410, Bainbridge Island WA 98110 B San Diego CA 1944 d Fredrick & Madeline. BS U of Kansas 1979; MDiv Epis TS of the SW 1988. D 6/19/1988 Bp Richard Frank Grein P 9/1/1991 Bp Vincent Waydell Warner. m 5/10/1980 Jerry N O'Shea c 1. Chapl/Dir Chap of S Martha and S Mary of Bethany Seattle WA 1991-2008, Chapl/Dir 1991-2011; Port Chapl Mssn to Seafarers Seattle WA 1990-1991; Urban Chapl S Mk's Cathd Seattle WA 1989-1991.

OSHRY, Michael A (Spok) 5225 S Cree Dr, Spokane WA 99206 **Ret Ret 2017-** B Crawfordsville IN 1955 s Harold & Barbara. Ball St U; MDiv Chr TS; BS Indiana Wesl; CAS SWTS. D 6/18/2005 P 5/28/2006 Bp Cate Waynick. c 1. Cardiology Stff Chapl Sacr Heart Med Cntr Spokane WA 2012-2017; Guest Celebrant S Mary's Epis Ch Martinsville IN 2009-2012; Guest Celebrant S Geo Epis Ch W Terre Haute IN 2006-2012; Assoc P S Chris's Epis Ch Carmel IN 2005-2009; ER/Trauma Stff Chapl S Vinc's Hosp Indianapolis IN 2002-2012. Assn of Profsnl Chapl 2008.

OSMUN, Andrew (Ct) 41 Park Circle, Milford CT 06460 **Chr And Epiph Ch E Haven CT 2016-; Missional P Chr and The Epiph Ch 2014-** B Wilmington DE 1948 s William & Priscilla. BA Wms 1971; Cert Theol Stud Oxf GB 1975. D 10/5/1975 P 4/4/1976 Bp Robert Bracewell Appleyard. m 8/31/1974 Terry O Osmun c 2. R S Ptr's Epis Ch Milford CT 1999-2012; S Lk's Ch Chester VT 1980-1999; Vic Geth Ch Proctorsville VT 1980-1985; Vic Ch Of The Trsfg Clairton PA 1975-1980; Cur S Steph's Epis Ch Mckeesport PA 1975-1980. Soc of Angl Missionaries and Senders 1976.

OSNAYA-JIMENEZ, Uriel (Tex) 9600 Huntington Place Dr, Houston TX 77099 **Vic The Great Cmsn Fndt Houston TX 2014-; Vic Iglesia Epis Santa Maria Virgen Houston TX 2008-, 1990-1997** B Mexico City MX 1956 s Aaron & Evangelina. BA Jose Vasconcelos 1976; Cert S Andrews TS Ph 1979; Cert Epis TS of the SW 1980. D 12/1/1979 Bp Donald James Davis P 1/23/1982 Bp Robert Elwin Terwilliger. m 9/28/2012 Maria Florencia Itzep c 2. S Matt's Cathd Dallas TX 1982-1990; Dio Dallas Dallas TX 1981, Asst Hisp Mnstry 1980-1982. CHS.

OSORIO-CAMACHO, Nabor (Ve) **Dio Venezuela Caracas 2004-** B 1952 D 12/19/1992 P 6/29/1993 Bp Onell Asiselo Soto. c 1.

OST, Gary (Cal) 499 Ellsworth St Apt A, San Francisco CA 94110 **Asstg P S Aid's Ch San Francisco CA 2012-** B Renton WA 1947 s Wilbert & Irene. BA U of Washington 1969; MDiv CDSP 1972. D 8/26/1972 P 12/1/1973 Bp Ivol I Curtis. m 3/5/2014 Michael A Embry c 2. Dio California San Francisco CA 2000-2007; ECharF 1986-1992; R S Lk's Ch Walnut Creek CA 1982-2007; R S Eliz Seattle WA 1977-1979; S Eliz's Ch Seattle WA 1977-1979; Vic S Lk's Ch Sequim WA 1974-1977; Cur S Lk's Ch Tacoma WA 1972-1974. Integrity; Tertiary Of The Soc Of S Fran.

O'STEEN, Joe Arnold (LI) 1665 Waterford Dr, Lewisville TX 75077 B Hope AR 1935 s Alpha & Ola. BA Henderson St U 1957; MDiv UTS 1960; GTS 1961; Blanton-Peale Grad Inst 1971; New York Cntr for Psychodrama Trng Brooklyn NY 1978. D 6/10/1961 P 12/16/1961 Bp Horace W B Donegan. Assoc S Andr's Epis Ch Pearland TX 1999-2014; Assoc Ch Of The Redeem Brooklyn NY 1980-1993; Counsellor for PhD,s Col (NY Ny) 1973-1992; Counslr, Off of Admin. Col 1972-1992; Asst S Ann And The H Trin Brooklyn NY 1971-1976;

645

Hse Parent Jewish Chld Care Assoc. of New York 1971-1973; Counslr Jewish Chld Care Assn of New York 1970-1972; Org/Cantor St. Thos Albanian Orth Ch Bridgeport CT 1970; Vic S Anselm's Ch Shoreham NY 1967-1971; Asst Ch Of S Jas The Less Scarsdale NY 1964-1966; Asst Chr Ch Greenwich CT 1961-1964. Amer Soc for Grp Psych & Psychodrama 1973-1990. MCL Henderson St U 1957.

OSTENSO MOORE, Anna Victoria (Minn) 519 Oak Grove St, Minneapolis MN 55403 **Cathd Ch Of S Mk Minneapolis MN 2015-** B Minneapolis MN 1980 d Brian & Jane. BA Mid 2003; MA King's Coll 2006; MA King's Coll 2006; MA King's Coll, Unversity of London 2006. D 6/20/2015 P 6/21/2016 Bp Brian N Prior. m 10/18/2014 David Ostenso Moore. Yth Dir Ch Of The Nativ Burnsville MN 2007-2015. annaom@ourcathedral.og

OSTENSON, Roy Oliver (SwFla) 4009 Wonderland Hill Ave, Boulder CO 80304 **Died 4/13/2017** B Hallock MN 1921 s Edwin & Lillian. BA Montana St U 1948; BD EDS 1951; Coll of Preachers 1963; MA Wstrn Michigan U 1982. D 8/6/1951 P 2/6/1952 Bp Henry Hean Daniels. m 1/19/1945 Sondra Ostenson. Ret 1989-2017; Dir Dio SW Florida-Ch Counslg Cntr Naples 1985-1989; Ther Dio SW Florida-Ch Counslg Cntr Naples 1983-1985; Dio SW Florida Parrish FL 1982-1989; Gr Ch Grand Rapids MI 1968-1983; R S Matt Warson Woods MO 1960-1968; Chapl U Roch Dio Rochester Henrietta 1954-1960; Vic Chr Poplar MT 1951-1954; Vic S Matt's Ch Glasgow MT 1951-1954.

OSTERTAG, Edward Frederick (Oly) 11650 26th Ave SW, Burien WA 98146 **Died 5/11/2017** B Albuquerque NM 1925 s Carl & Kathryn. BA U So 1950; MDiv GTS 1952; Colorado St U 1966. D 6/22/1952 Bp James M Stoney P 3/27/1953 Bp C J Kinsolving III. c 4. P-in-c Chr Ch Hillsboro NM 1991-2001; St Pauls Epis Ch Truth Consq NM 1991-1998; R S Barn Epis Ch Denver CO 1984-1990; 1981-1984; R S Lk's Epis Ch Ft Collins CO 1960-1981; Vic S Matt Alburquerque NM 1956-1960; Dn Albuquerque Convoc 1955-1959; Stndg Com Dio Colorado Denver CO 1965-1967, Dn 1962-1964, Trst 1961. Human Relatns Awd 1982.

OSTLUND, Holly Lisa (SeFla) 15730 88th Pl N, Loxahatchee FL 33470 B Miami FL 1954 d Grant & Mary. BS U of Tennessee 1976; MA Barry U Miami 2002; Cert Epis TS of the SW 2002. D 2/8/2003 P 9/6/2003 Bp Leo Frade. c 2. S Mk's Ch Palm Bch Garden FL 2009-2013; Trin Ch Towson MD 2009; Dio SE Florida Miami 2007-2009; P-in-c The Ch in the Grove Loxahatchee FL 2006-2009; Asst R S Mary's Epis Ch Stuart FL 2003-2006.

OSTRANDER, Paul Copeland (Okla) 2321 Northwest 48th Street, Oklahoma City OK 73112 **S Alb's Ch Cushing OK 2003-** B Ponca City OK 1926 s Quintus & Martha. BA U of Oklahoma 1950; SWTS 1964; Epis TS in Kentucky 1966; Cert Presb Hosp Oklahoma City OK 1982. D 6/17/1966 P 10/17/1968 Bp Chilton R Powell. c 4. Trin Ch Guthrie OK 2006-2007, 2005-2006; Chapl Hospice of Oklahoma Cnty Inc Oklahoma City 1991-1999; Vic Nativ Yukon OK 1986-1989; Vic S Raphael Yukon OK 1982-1986; Vic Chr Memi Epis Ch El Reno OK 1977-1986; Dio Oklahoma Oklahoma City OK 1976-1989; S Mich And All Ang Ch Lindsay OK 1974-1977; P S Tim's Epis Ch Pauls Vlly OK 1974-1977; Vic S Paul's Epis Ch Holdenville OK 1972-1974; Cur S Jn's Ch Norman OK 1971-1972; S Jas Epis Ch Oklahoma City OK 1970-1971; S Marg's Ch Lawton OK 1970-1971; Asst S Paul's Cathd Oklahoma City OK 1967-1969; Cur All SS Epis Ch Miami OK 1966-1967.

OSTUNI, Elizabeth Ellen (Nwk) 10 Hampton Downes, Newton NJ 07860 **D S Mary's Ch Sparta NJ 2013-; Archd Ch Of The Gd Shpd Sussex NJ 2009-** B Parsons KS 1937 d Walter & Ferne. BA U of Kansas 1959; MA U of Kansas 1972; Cert GTS 2001. D 6/5/2004 Bp John Palmer Croneberger. m 9/9/1984 Lawrence Ostuni c 3. D S Jn's Ch Dover NJ 2004-2008. "Successful Cmncatn w Alzheimer's Disease Patients," *Elsivir*; "Getting Through: When someone you care for has Alzheimer's Disease," *Speech Bin.*

O'SULLIVAN, Ann Kathlyn (Me) D 6/13/2015 Bp Stephen Taylor Lane.

OSWALD, Todd D (USC) 2200 Wilson Rd, Newberry SC 29108 B 1964 D 7/1/2006 P 1/20/2007 Bp Edward Lloyd Salmon Jr. Trin Ch Abbeville SC 2015-2017.

OTA, David Yasuhide (Cal) 900 Edgewater Blvd, Foster City CA 94404 **R S Ambr Epis Ch Foster City CA 1997-** B San Francisco CA 1954 s Ichiro & Mary. BS U CA 1976; MDiv CDSP 1983. D 6/25/1983 Bp William Edwin Swing P 6/10/1984 Bp Edmond Lee Browning. m 2/4/1984 Karen Swanson c 1. Vic/R Gd Samar Epis Ch Honolulu HI 1983-1997; Campus Min U HI The Epis Ch in Hawaii Honolulu HI 1983-1988, GC Dep 1987-1996; Pres, Stndg Com Dio California San Francisco CA 2010-2011, Mem, Stndg Com 2009-2013, GC Dep 2005-2013. dyota@mindspring.com

OTIS, Violetta Lansdale (Me) 17 Foreside Rd, Falmouth ME 04105 B Evanston IL 1947 d James & Violetta. AA Bradford Jr Coll 1967; BA U of Wisconsin 1969; MDiv EDS 1998. D 7/2/1998 P 1/30/1999 Bp Chilton Richardson Knudsen. c 2. P-in-c Trin Epis Ch Lewiston ME 1999-2006.

OTT, Janet Sanderson (Miss) 1200 Meadowbrook Rd Apt 44, Jackson MS 39206 **S Mk's Ch Raymond MS 2011-** B Laurel MS 1951 d Joe & Ann. BS Mississippi Coll 1989; MDiv EDS 1996. D 6/22/1996 P 3/1/1997 Bp Alfred Marble Jr. m 3/31/1970 Luther Smith Ott c 2. Assoc Ch Of The Creator Clinton MS 2003-2007; S Columb's Ch Ridgeland MS 1996-2003.

OTT, Luther Smith (Miss) 1200 Meadowbrook Road, #44, Jackson MS 39206 B Oxford MS 1949 s Thomas & Lorraine. BA Millsaps Coll 1971; JD U of Mississippi 1973; MA EDS 1996. D 4/15/1998 P 10/28/1998 Bp Alfred Marble Jr. m 3/31/1970 Janet Sanderson Ott c 2. The Chap Of The Cross Madison MS 2012-2014; Ch of the H Trin Vicksburg MS 2011-2012; S Paul's Epis Ch Meridian MS 2010-2011; Ch Of The Creator Clinton MS 2002-2006; Cur S Phil's Ch Jackson MS 1998-2000.

OTT, Paula Lee (Lex) 2410 Lexington Rd, Winchester KY 40391 B Cincinnati OH 1951 d Eli & Arvilla. BSEd U Cinc 1973; MEd U of Kentucky 1979. D 6/5/2011 Bp Stacy F Sauls. m 6/18/1978 John Stephen Ott c 1.

OTT, Robert Michael (ECR) 1490 Mark Thomas Dr., Monterey CA 93940 **S Jn's Chap Monterey CA 2009-** B Seoul Korea 1947 D 5/30/2004 Bp Samuel Johnson Howard P 12/5/2004 Bp Edward Lloyd Salmon Jr. m 12/14/1974 Bonnie Ellen Ott c 2. Ch Of The H Cross Sullivans Island SC 2004-2009. bobstjohnschapel@redshift.com

OTTAWAY, Richard Napoleon (NJ) 16 Bell Ter, Bernardsville NJ 07924 B Ypsilanti MI 1931 s Henry & Ruth. BA Ecu 1954; MDiv VTS 1957; PhD U of Manchester 1979. D 6/27/1957 P 5/1/1958 Bp Thomas H Wright. m 6/28/1981 Elaine Ottaway c 2. Part Time Epis Ch Of S Thos Taunton MA 2008-2009; Ch of S Jn on the Mtn Bernardsville NJ 1992-1995; Non-par 1974-1992; The Ch & Industry Inst Winston Salem NC 1969-1972; Wake Forest U Ch & Indstrl Inst 1966-1970; Chapl Winston-Salem Area NC 1964-1966; Chapl E Carolina Univeristy Greenville NC 1959-1964; Cur S Paul's Epis Ch Greenville NC 1959-1964; D S Paul's Ch Vanceboro NC 1957-1958; Trin Epis Ch Chocowinity NC 1957-1958; Dioc Coun Dio No Carolina Raleigh NC 1970-1973; Chair Of The Pitt Cnty Inter-Racial Com Dio E Carolina Kinston NC 1962-1964. Auth, "Humanising The Workplace"; Auth, "Intro-Ing Orgnztns Behavior".

OTTERBURN, Margaret K (Nwk) 50 Route 24, Chester NJ 07930 **R Ch Of The Mssh Chester NJ 2007-** B Stoke-on-Trent GB 1946 d Benjamin & Winifred. BS Lon GB 1968; MA Belfast U Belfast 1975; MDiv Drew U 1999. D 6/1/2002 P 12/7/2002 Bp John Palmer Croneberger. m 7/26/1969 Michael S Otterburn c 3. Cathd Ch Of S Mk Minneapolis MN 2004-2007; Cur Gr Ch Newark NJ 2003-2004.

OTTERY JR, Willis Dee (NH) 83 Irving Dr, Weare NH 03281 **Died 10/2/2015** B Fond du Lac WI 1927 s Willis & Irene. BS U of Wisconsin 1950. D 11/1/1997 Bp Douglas Edwin Theuner. m 3/26/1994 Linda Messenger Ottery c 4. D S Paul's Ch Concord NH 2007-2015; S Andr's Epis Ch Contoocook NH 2000-2007; D Ch Of S Jn The Evang Dunbarton NH 1997-2000. Auth, *A Man Called Sampson*, Penobscot, 1989. NAAD 1995. Recognition of Diac Mnstry in the Tradition of S Step Natl Amer Assn for the Diac 2001.

✠ **OTTLEY, The Rt Rev James Hamilton** (LI) 3 E Fairway Ct, Bay Shore NY 11706 B Colon PA 1936 s Lipton & Mirell. STB ETSC 1964; MS ETSC 1973; Epis TS of the SW 1980; VTS 1982; Epis TS of the SW 1986; Sewanee: The U So, TS 1986; Ya Berk 1991. Trans 4/30/2000 Bp Orris George Walker Jr Con 1/21/1984 for RP. m 1/15/1965 Lillian Ottley c 4. Asst Bp Dio SE Florida Miami 2001-2004; Dio Honduras San Pedro Sula 2000-2001; Ch Of The Mssh Cntrl Islip NY 1999-2001; Asst Bp Dio Long Island Garden City NY 1999-2000; Angl Observer Untd Nations 1995-1999; Epis Ch Cntr New York NY 1994-1999; Bp Of Panama Angl Ch In Cntrl Amer 1984-1995; Mntl Hlth Prog 1978-1994; Dio The Dominican Republic (Iglesia Epis Dominicana) Gazcue Santo Domingo 1978-1984; St Pauls Ch 1977-1984; Exec Secy Prov IX 1976-1984; Dio Panama 1964-1994; Serv Angl Ch In Cntrl Amer (Panama) 1964-1984. Auth, "Making Sense Of Things"; Auth, "We Are Angls"; Auth, "The Challenge Of The Past," *The Challenge Of The Future.*

OTTO, Ronald Lee (EMich) St Andrews Church, PO Box 52, Harrisville MI 48740 B Toledo OH 1941 s Arthur & Grace. Mutual Mnstry Spprt Team. D 10/23/2011 P 4/28/2012 Bp Steven Todd Ousley. m 8/25/1985 Susan Wanty Otto.

OTTO, Susan Wanty (EMich) St Andrews Church, PO Box 52, Harrisville MI 48740 B Ann Arbor MI 1955 d John & Joan. Cert Alpena Cmnty Coll; BS MI SU; Mutual Mnstry Spprt Team. D 10/23/2011 P 4/28/2012 Bp Steven Todd Ousley. m 8/25/1985 Ronald Lee Otto.

OTTSEN, David (Tex) 3007 Live Oak Dr., Brenham TX 77833 B Charles City IA 1952 s George & Katherine. BA Coe Coll 1974; MDiv Epis TS of the SW 1982. D 4/2/1982 Bp Charles Thomas Gaskell P 3/1/1983 Bp William Jackson Cox. m 5/25/1974 Deborah Ottsen c 1. R S Ptr's Epis Ch Brenham TX 2008-2017; S Paul's Ch Mishawaka IN 1997-2008; Mssnr Dio Nthrn Indiana So Bend IN 1994-1996; R S Andr Broken Arrow OK 1988-1994; St Andrews Ch Broken Arrow OK 1988-1994; Cn S Paul's Cathd Oklahoma City OK 1985-1988; Cur S Andr's Ch Stillwater OK 1982-1985; Stndg Com Dio Oklahoma Oklahoma City OK 1992-1994. Drum Major Awd Mayors' Off, Mishawaka and So Bend, IN 2003; Drum Major Awd Mayors' Off, Mishawaka and So Bend, IN 2001.

OU, Chun Shih (Tai) 200 Chu Chang 1st Road, Kaohsiung Taiwan **Bd Tainan Theol Coll 1969-; Exam Chapl 1967-; Vic S Paul 1967-** B Kao Sung TW 1934 s Ching & Hsi. BTh Tainan Theol Coll and Sem TW 1962; Tokyo Cntrl TS 1967. D 4/25/1965 P 2/1/1966 Bp James Chang L Wong. m 2/24/1959

Tong-Yin Ou c 4. Dio Taiwan Taipei 1967-1999; Mssy Hsiackang Hsiang Taiwan 1965-1967.

OUGHTON, Marjorie Knapp (Pa) Church St Paul's, 301 E 9th St, Chester PA 19013 **Chapl H Redeem Hlth System 2014-** B Philadelphia PA 1944 d Joseph & Ruth. BS Wag 1965; MBA Marymount U Arlington VA 1987; Cert Theol Stud NW Hse of Theol Stds 2008; Cert Theol Stud NW Hse of Theol Stds 2008. D 2/28/2009 Bp Sanford Zangwill Kaye Hampton. c 2.

OUSLEY CSF, David Kenneth (Alb) Saint Eustace Episcopal Church, 2450 Main St, Lake Placid NY 12946 **D Vic S Jas Ch Au Sable Forks NY 2005-; Vic St. Jas 2004-; D Assoc, Vol Trin Ch Plattsburgh NY 2001-; Stndg Com Dio Albany Greenwich NY 2009-** B Bellingham WA 1943 Wstrn Washington U; MA Nash 2008. D 6/29/2002 Bp Daniel William Herzog P 2/27/2008 Bp William Howard Love. m 6/5/1965 Cheryl Beatrice Ousley c 3.

OUSLEY, John Douglas (NY) 209 Madison Ave, New York NY 10016 **Incarn Cntr 1986-; R Ch Of The Incarn New York NY 1985-** B Kansas City MO 1947 s Jack & Nancy. BA Ya 1969; MRE NYTS 1971; MTh Lon GB 1972; MA New Sch U 1975. D 11/12/1972 P 9/30/1973 Bp Horace W B Donegan. m 9/28/2013 Dana Lynne Ousley c 2. Pres Incarn Cntr 1986-1998; S Paul's Within the Walls Rome 1981-1985; The Amer Cathd of the H Trin Paris 75008 1978-1981; Lectr Inst of Theol Cath of St Jn Dv 1973-1978; Asst S Thos Ch New York NY 1973-1978. Auth, "arts," *ATR*; Auth, "arts," *Rel Stds*; Auth, "arts," *Wall St Journ*. Cler Liaison - NYPD 2004; Cmnty of S Mary; Soc of Chr Philosophers; Sons of the Amer Revolution. Phi Beta Kappa. ousleyjd@churchoftheincarnation.org

OUSLEY, Patrick Lance (Oly) 1551 10th Ave E, Seattle WA 98102 **S Jn's Ch Kirkland WA 2015-** B Dallas TX 1964 s John & Faye. BBA Baylor U 1987; MDiv Sewanee: The U So, TS 2001. D 6/16/2001 Bp Claude Edward Payne P 6/19/2002 Bp Don Adger Wimberly. m 4/13/1991 Jenness Bundy c 2. Cn Dio Olympia Seattle 2011-2015; R S Thos Ch Wharton TX 2004-2011; Int Dioc Yth Mnstry Coordntr Dio Texas Houston TX 2003; Asst R S Dunst's Epis Ch Houston TX 2001-2004.

✠ OUSLEY, The Rt Rev Steven Todd (EMich) 1821 Avalon Ave, Saginaw MI 48638 B Palestine TX 1961 s John & Faye. BA Baylor U 1983; MS Texas A&M U 1984; MDiv Epis TS of the SW 1991; DMin SWTS 2004. D 6/22/1991 P 2/1/1992 Bp Maurice Manuel Benitez Con 9/9/2006 for EMich. m 10/27/1984 Ann M Schumann-Ousley c 3. Bp of Estrn Michigan Dio Estrn Michigan Saginaw MI 2006-2017, Mssnr for Congrl Dvlpmt 2001-2006; R S Fran Par Temple TX 1997-2001; R Ch Of The H Comf Angleton TX 1993-1997; Cur The Ch of the Gd Shpd Austin TX 1991-1993. DD Seabury-Wstrn 2008; DD Sem of the SW 2007. tousley@eastmich.org

OUTMAN-CONANT, Robert Earl (Mass) 482 Beech St, Rockland MA 02370 **Ret Dio Mass 2011-** B Middlebury VT 1947 s Robert & Dorothy. Mntl Hlth Cert Commonwealth of Massachusettes; BA W Maryland Coll 1969; MDiv VTS 1973; DMin Andover Newton TS 1981. D 6/7/1973 P 3/13/1974 Bp David Keller Leighton Sr. m 10/3/1981 Judith Outman-Conant c 2. R S Jn's Epis Ch Holbrook MA 1995-2011; Sprtl Advsr Cusillo Renwl Mvmt 1994-2011; Mentor EFM 1994-2010; Assoc R Ch Of The H Nativ S Weymouth MA 1992-1995, P Assoc 1987-1992; Pstr Counslr Souter Counceling Cntr 1982-1996; R Trin Epis Ch Rockland MA 1977-1986; Assoc R S Mk's Ch Brooklyn NY 1976-1977; Cur Par Of Chr Ch Andover MA 1973-1975. AAPC 1981; Amer Assn of Pstr Counselors - Fell 1996.

OUTWIN, Edson Maxwell (WNY) 316 Park Ave, Medina NY 14103 B New York NY 1943 s Edson & Mary. ABS Washington U 1965; MDiv GTS 1969. D 6/14/1969 Bp Leland Stark P 5/26/1973 Bp George E Rath. m 6/8/1968 Kay Outwin c 2. Dn Genesee Reg Dnry 2007-2009; Vic S Jn's Ch Medina NY 2002-2009; S Mich's Epis Ch Oakfield NY 2002-2009; Vic S Mary's Epis Ch Gowanda NY 1997-2002; Dio Rochester Henrietta 1989-1990; Vic Allegany Cnty Epis Mnstry Belfast NY 1985-1989; P-in-c Gr Ch N Attleboro MA 1985; P-in-c S Ptr's Ch On The Canal Buzzards Bay MA 1982-1984; Asst Gr Ch Middletown NY 1978-1979; Asst All Ang' Ch New York NY 1973-1977; Cur Chr Ch Hackensack NJ 1969-1970. LAND 1966; Phi Delta Theta 1962.

OVENSTONE, Jennifer (SanD) 810 Mockingbird Ln Apt 301, Towson MD 21286 **Assoc R S Jn's Ch Ellicott City MD 2008-** B Dundee Scotland 1978 BA Azusa Pacific U 2000; MDiv VTS 2003. D 6/7/2003 Bp Gethin Benwil Hughes P 1/17/2005 Bp Desmond Mpilo Tutu. m 2/12/2013 Sidney Smith. Cler Res S Geo's Epis Ch Griffin GA 2005-2008; S Paul's Par Baltimore MD 2005-2008; Cler Res Chr Ch Alexandria VA 2003-2005.

OVERALL, Martha Rollins (NY) 345 E 86th St Apt 16-D, New York NY 10028 **S Ann's Ch Of Morrisania Bronx NY 1996-, Vic 1993, Asst 1991-1992** B New York NY 1947 d John & Vera. BA Rad 1969; JD NYU 1976; MDiv UTS 1991; Ursinus Coll 2000. D 6/8/1991 P 12/14/1991 Bp Richard Frank Grein. c 1. Pres - Stndg Com Dio New York New York NY 2001-2002, Stndg Com 1998-2001, 1996-2001, Dio Coun 1995-2002, 1993-, Ecum Cmsn 1991-1999. Auth, *Var arts*. Trin Transformational Fllshp Trin Ch Wall St 2006; DD Ya Berk 2001.

OVERFIELD, Brenda (SVa) 2817 Mohawk Drive, North Chesterfield VA 23235 **S Mths Epis Ch Midlothian VA 2014-** B 1959 d Rolland & Katherine. BA U

of Missouri 1981; MDiv GTS 1993. D 4/24/1993 P 11/7/1993 Bp Orris George Walker Jr. Archd Dio Long Island Garden City NY 2011-2014; R H Trin Epis Ch Vlly Stream NY 1998-2014; All SS Ch Great Neck NY 1998; Int All SS' Epis Ch Great Neck NY 1997-1998; Asst S Thos Of Cbury Ch Smithtown NY 1995-1998; Epis Hlth Serv Far Rockaway NY 1993-1998; Dir of Pstr Care S Jn's Epis Hosp Smithtown NY 1993-1997; Asst Ch of S Jude Wantagh NY 1993-1995. Chair, COM 1998-2001; Chair, Dept of Mssn 2006-2011; Congrl Dvlpmt, Prov II 2006-2011; Dioc Coun 2006-2011; Trst of the Estate, Dioc. of LI 2006-2010. Bd Cert Chapl Assn of Profsnl Chapl 1995. bsoverfield@stmatmidlo.com

OVERGAARD, Emily Lodine (Minn) D 6/26/2014 Bp Brian N Prior.

OVERTON, Donald Ernest (EC) 4106 Dove Park Blvd, Louisville KY 40299 **Ret Supply P 2000-; Supply P S Lk's Epis Ch Cannelton IN 2013-; Supply P Peace Epis Ch Rockport IN 2005-** B Alliance NE 1936 s Kenneth & Dorothy. BS U of Nebraska 1957; MDiv SWTS 1960; MA U of New Mex 1970. D 6/15/1960 P 12/21/1960 Bp Howard R Brinker. m 6/4/1957 Idona A Overton c 2. R Chr Epis Ch Hope Mills NC 1995-2000; R Ch Of The H Sprt Bellevue NE 1988-1993; Fac US-A Ft Monmouth NJ 1982-1984; Chapl Off Of Bsh For ArmdF New York NY 1967-1988; Chapl US-A 1967-1988; Vic Epis Ch Of The Incarn Salina KS 1964-1967; Chapl S Jn Mltry Sch Salina KS 1964-1967; Vic S Chas The Mtyr Fairbury KS 1964-1967. Chapl H Redeem 1960-1964.

OWEN, Charles Bryan (La) St Luke's Episcopal Church, 8833 Goodwood Blvd, Baton Rouge LA 70806 **R S Lk's Ch Baton Rouge LA 2015-, 2013-2015** B Memphis TN 1969 s Sterling & Ruby. BA Ken 1991; MA Van 1994; PhD Van 2000; Cert Ang Stud Sewanee: The U So, TS 2001. D 9/18/2001 Bp Alfred Marble Jr P 3/20/2002 Bp Duncan Montgomery Gray III. m 5/31/1997 Julie Ann Nolte c 2. P S Andr's Cathd Jackson MS 2006-2012; R Epis Ch Of The Incarn W Point MS 2001-2006. frbryanowen@stlukesbr.org

OWEN, David Allen (Ct) 92 E Hill Rd, Canton CT 06019 B Toledo OH 1936 s Allen & Marion. BA W&L 1958; STM EDS 1962. D 6/9/1962 P 12/1/1962 Bp Nelson Marigold Burroughs. m 11/27/1986 Anne B Batterson c 2. Trin Epis Ch Collinsville CT 1997-1998; Int Dio Connecticut Meriden CT 1996-1998; Adj Fac U Of Hartford In Connecticut 1991-1992; R Old S Andr's Ch Bloomfield CT 1983-1996; Kent Sch Kent CT 1977-1983; Chapl Kent Sch Kent CT 1977-1983; Assoc The Ch Of The H Sprt Lake Forest IL 1970-1976; Stff Gr Ch Chicago IL 1966-1970; Chapl U IL In Chicago 1966-1970; Cur S Chrys's Ch Chicago IL 1962-1966.

OWEN, Donald Edward (Ala) 1921 Chandaway Ct, Pelham AL 35124 **D (nonstipendiary) The Epis Ch Of S Fran Of Assisi Pelham AL 2004-** B Florence AL 1949 s Wallace & Mittie. BA U of Alabama 1974; MA U of Alabama 1977; BS U of Alabama 1989; MBA Samford U 1999. D 10/30/2004 Bp Henry Nutt Parsley Jr. m 7/7/1972 Teresa Owen c 1.

OWEN II, G Keith (O) 18001 Detroit Ave, Lakewood OH 44107 **R S Ptr's Epis Ch Lakewood OH 2004-; Vstng P Trsfg Sum Chap Whitefield NH 1994-** B Petersburg VA 1959 s Gordon & Mable. Non Degree Cleveland St U; BA U of Virginia 1982; MDiv GTS 1988; PrTS 2005. D 6/9/1988 P 3/16/1989 Bp Claude Charles Vache. m 9/4/1994 Monica Miller c 3. Exec Secy No Amer Com St. Georges Coll Jerusalem 2005-2014; R S Paul's Epis Ch Albany NY 1994-2004; Assoc R S Steph's Ch Newport News VA 1988-1994. Study Grants For Leaders Louisville Inst 2000. keithowen@stpeterslakewood.org

OWEN, Harrison Hollingsworth (WA) **Pres H.H.Owen and Co. 1978-** B Evanston IL 1935 s Raymond & Mary. BA Wms 1957; BD VTS 1960; MA Van 1965. D 5/14/1960 Bp Oliver J Hart P 7/1/1961 Bp Chilton R Powell. m 8/12/1967 Ethelyn Abbott Owen c 5. Dir VA Scholars Prog VetA 1977-1978; Dir Off of Educ, Prevention and COntrol Natl Institutes of Hlth (NHLBI) 1974-1976; Dir Reg Med Prog 1970-1974; Assoc Dir Of The Peace Corps In Liberia US Peace Corps 1967-1969; Assoc Team Mnstry S Marg's Ch Washington DC 1965-1967; Coll Chapl Cathd Of The Incarn Baltimore MD 1960-1962. Auth, "Wave Rider: Ldrshp for High Performance in a Self Organizing Wrld," Berrett-Koehler, 2008; Auth, "Open Space Tech: A User's Guide (3rd Ed)," Berrett- Koehler, 2008; Auth, "The Pract of Peace," Human Systems Dynamics Inst., 2004; Auth, "The Power of Sprt," Berrett-Koehler, 2003; Auth, "The Sprt of Ldrshp," Berrett-Koehler, 2000; Auth, "Expanding our Now," Berrett Koehler, 1997; Auth, "The Millennium Organiztion," Abbott Pub, 1993; Auth, "Riding the Tiger," Abbott Pub, 1992; Auth, "Sprt: Transformation and Dvlpmt in Orgnztn," Abbott Pub, 1987. Share the Wealth Awd Orgnztn Dvlpmt Ntwk 2007.

OWEN, Jennifer Marie (NY) **Cur Chr Ch Greenwich CT 2012-** B La Mirada CA 1977 d Christopher & Carol. BA NYU 1998; MA NYU 2003; MDiv Ya Berk 2012. D 3/3/2012 P 9/29/2012 Bp Mark Sean Sisk. m 6/30/2012 Sam Owen. jowen@christchurchgreenwich.org

OWEN, Ron (Fla) 1100 Stockton Street, Jacksonville FL 32204 **P-in-c Ch Of The Gd Shpd Jacksonville FL 2017-** B Sikeston MO 1949 s Bryan & Jean. BA U of Kentucky 1971; JD U of Florida Coll of Law 1973; MDiv VTS 2008. D 6/1/2008 P 12/7/2008 Bp Samuel Johnson Howard. m 6/5/1993 Janet Davis Owen c 2. P-in-c S Paul's Epis Ch Quincy FL 2015; Assoc R H Trin Epis Ch Gainesville FL 2011-2014; Asst R S Ptr's Ch Fernandina Bch FL 2010-2011;

O

Chf of Stff for Dom Prog FreshMinistries Inc Jacksonville FL 2008-2009; P Assoc S Eliz's Epis Ch Jacksonville FL 2008-2009. rowen@gsjax.church

OWEN, Sam (NY) 661 E 219th St, Bronx NY 10467 **Dio New York New York NY 2012-; Haitian Cong of the Gd Samar Bronx NY 2012-** B Winston-Salem NC 1960 s Louis & Nancy. BA Tul 1982; MBA U of Miami 1992; MDiv Ya Berk 2012. D 6/16/2012 Bp John O'Neill P 12/19/2012 Bp Andrew Marion Lenow Dietsche. m 6/30/2012 Jennifer Marie Owen c 2.

OWEN, Shelby Ochs (SwVa) 222 Fayette St, Staunton VA 24401 **R Emm Ch Staunton VA 2013-** B Chattanooga TN 1958 d Martin & Celia. BA W&M 1980; MDiv VTS 2005. D 6/4/2005 P 12/15/2005 Bp David Conner Bane Jr. m 8/15/1981 Stephen Owen c 3. Assoc Trin Ch Staunton VA 2009-2012; Assoc S Paul's Ch Charlottesville VA 2007-2009; Asst R for Yth and Fam Mnstrs S Anne's Epis Ch Reston VA 2005-2007. priest-emmanuelstaunton@verizon.net

OWENS IV, Bernard J (NC) 4407 Westbourne Rd, Greensboro NC 27410 **R S Andr's Ch Greensboro NC 2010-** B Charlotte NC 1975 s Bernard & Janet. BA U NC 1997; DAS Ya Berk 2004; MDiv Yale DS 2004. D 12/17/2005 P 6/25/2006 Bp Michael B Curry. m 10/4/2010 Johanna Owens c 1. Assoc R S Paul's Epis Ch Cary NC 2006-2010; Chapl Res - Pediatricds UNC Hospitals Chap Hill NC 2005-2006; Dioc Intern Gr Epis Mssn Clayton NC 2004-2005; Trin Epis Ch Southport CT 2002-2003.

OWENS, Brent (Lex) Christ Church Cathedral, 166 Market St, Lexington KY 40507 **D Chr Ch Cathd Lexington KY 2012-** B Phildelphia PA 1962 BS Indiana U 1984; JD Stetson U 1987; MDiv Epis TS of the SW 2005. D 4/17/2005 Bp Leo Frade P 10/29/2005 Bp Kirk Stevan Smith. m 7/20/1985 Malinda S Owens c 3. R S Alb's Ch Monroe GA 2008-2012; Cur S Barn On The Desert Scottsdale AZ 2005-2008. bowens@ccclex.org

OWENS JR, Donald P (La) 712 Saddleridge Drive, Wimberley TX 78676 **Emer Prof Tul Sch of Med 2015-; LMFT Louisiana 2002-; Chapl/ Prof Epis Mnstry To Med Educ New Orleans LA 2000-; Lic Profsnl Counslr Louisiana 2000-; LMFT Oklahoma 1991-; Lic Profsnl Counslr Oklahoma 1986-** B Fort Worth TX 1942 s Donald & Marguerite. Arlington St Arlington TX 1962; BA Trin U San Antonio 1966; MDiv Pittsburgh TS 1969; PhD U of Oklahoma 1986. D 6/11/1975 P 10/17/1975 Bp Chilton R Powell. m 4/9/1966 Barbara John c 4. Chapl and Prof of Med and Psych Tul Sch Of Med 2000-2015; Dio Louisiana New Orleans LA 2000-2012; P-in-c S Tim's Ch La Place LA 2000-2012; Int S Dav's Ch Oklahoma City OK 1999-2000, Int 1995-1997; Int S Jas Epis Ch Oklahoma City OK 1997-1998; Int Epis Ch Of The Nativ Yukon OK 1995-1997; Int S Fran Ch Edmond OK 1989-1990; Int Emm Epis Ch Shawnee OK 1987-1989; Dio Oklahoma Oklahoma City OK 1982-2000; Chapl S Anselm Cbury Norman OK 1975-2000; Cur S Jn's Ch Norman OK 1975-1981; Serv Untd Presb Ch 1969-1975; Chair Knight Chair of Hmnts and Med Ethics Emer Tul Sch of Med 2007-2015. Auth, "Healing and Hope in the midst of Devastation: Reflections on Katrina in the light of 9/11," *Journ of Rel and Hlth*, Journ of Rel and Hlth, Volume 50, Issue 1, 2011; Auth, "The Med Sch Cur: An Examination of Stdt Need," *Journ of Rel and Hlth*, Journ of Rel and Hlth Volume 50, Issue 3, 2011; Auth, "Organ Donation by a Prisoner: Legal and Ethical Considerations," *Journ Louisiana St Med Soc*, Journ Louisiana St Med Soc, Vol. 162, 2010; Auth, "Hist of the Epis Mnstry to Med Educ," *Churchwork*, Epis Dio Louisiana, 2008; Auth, "Psych Issues and Answers Following Hurricane Katrina," *Acad Psych*, Acad Psych, 31:200-204, 2007; Auth, "Beyond Sprtlty: The role of Med Sch Chapl," *Healing Mnstry*, Healing Mnstry, Volume 14, Number 4, Fall, 2007; Auth, "Perspectives on the Cancer Death of a Med Stdt," *Amer Journ of Hospice and Palliative Care*, Journ of Hospice and Palliative Care, Vol 22, No 5, 2005; Auth, "Allowing Patients To Die: Practical Ethical And Rel Concerns," *Journ of Clincl Oncology*, Journ Of Clincl Oncology Vol 21 No 15, 2003. Amer Assn for Mar and Fam Ther 2003; Amer Counslg Assn 2001; Amer Psych Assn 1998; Amer Soc for Bioethics and Hmnts 2000; Arnold P. Gold Humanism in Med hon Soc 2006; ESMHE 1985-2003; Louisiana Counslg Assn 2000. Distinguished Alum Awd Pittsburgh TS 2002.

OWENS, Gene Waller (At) 3260 Indian Valley Trl, Atlanta GA 30341 B Atlanta GA 1933 d Hugh & Lauree. BA Merc 1983; Cert EFM 1995. D 10/28/1995 Bp Frank Kellogg Allan. m 7/26/1980 J Robert Owens c 3. D Ch Of The H Comf Atlanta GA 1999-2003; D S Bede's Ch Atlanta GA 1995-1998. NAAD 1994.

OWENS, John Alfred (Fla) 4180 Julington Creek Rd, Jacksonville FL 32223 B Annapolis MD 1947 s William & Audry. Angl Inst of Theol 2007. D 6/1/2008 P 12/7/2008 Bp Samuel Johnson Howard. m 10/19/1968 Ellen B Owens c 2. Asst Ch Of Our Sav Jacksonville FL 2013.

OWENS, Jonathan Michael (Cal) 777 Southgate Ave, Daly City CA 94015 B Tulsa OK 1980 s Harry & Cathryn. BA Epis Sch for Deacons; AA NE Oklahoma A&M Coll 2001; BA SW Oklahoma St U 2003. D 6/2/2012 Bp Marc Handley Andrus. H Chld At S Mart Epis Ch Daly City CA 2012-2013.

OWENS, Miriam Elizabeth (Roch) 515 Oakridge Dr, Rochester NY 14617 **P-in-c Ch Of The Incarn Penfield NY 2008-** B Amityville NY 1937 d Joseph & Edith. BA Queens Coll 1959; MDiv Bex Sem 1980. D 10/18/1980 P 10/17/1981 Bp Robert Rae Spears Jr. m 7/12/1960 Raymond L Owens c 3. R S Jn's Epis Ch Honeoye Falls NY 1983-1988, Int R 1981-1983; Ch Of The Ascen Rochester NY 1982-1999.

OWENS, Robert Michael (At) P.O. Box 86, 637 University Ave, Sewanee TN 37375 **Founding Dir The Forgiveness Clnc 2013-; Assoc Cmnty of S Mary the Vrgn (CSM) 1982-; Cn (Hon) Angl Cathd St. Geo Cape Town 1991-** B Birmingham AL 1947 s Robert & Edythe. BS U of Alabama 1969; MS U of Alabama 1970; MS U GA 1973; MDiv Sewanee: The U So, TS 1983. D 6/11/1983 P 4/1/1984 Bp Charles Judson Child Jr. m 10/13/2006 Jeannine Clements c 4. R Ch Of The Trsfg Rome GA 2002-2011; R Trin Epis Ch Asheville NC 1994-2000; Appointed Mssy Exec Coun Appointees New York NY 1994; Vstng Cn Cathd of S Geo Cape Town 1992-1994; Archbp Tutu Dio Atlanta Atlanta GA 1991-1994, Archbp Tutu 1987-1994, Comp Mssnr in Educ 1985-1987, Chair, Comp Dio Com 1983-1985; Chapl to Archbp Tutu Dio Capetown 1990-1991; Dir of Trng for Ministers Dio Kimberley-Kuruman 1987-1989; Assoc R The Epis Ch Of S Ptr And S Paul Marietta GA 1985-1990; Assoc R S Paul's Ch Macon GA 1983-1985; Founding Dir, Dioc Alcosm Recovery Team (DART) Angl Dio Cape Town CPSA 1990-1994; Chapl to the Archbp (Tutu) Angl Ch of the Prov of So Afr (CPSA) 1990-1991; Consult to the Bp for Cler Care Angl Dio Kimberly & Kuruman CPSA 1985-1987. Cmnty of S Mary 1983; Tertiary Ord S Mary the Vrgn 1983; Tertiary Ord of the Precious Blood of Jesus 1987. Cn Angl Dio Capetown, Ch. of the Prov. of Sthrn Afri 1991.

OWENS, U'Neice Yvette (Ga) 4033 Foxborough Blvd, Valdosta GA 31602 **Admin Secy 23rd Med Grp 1990-** B Austin TX 1963 d Pauris & Laura. Pk U. D 6/28/2006 Bp Henry Irving Louttit. m 8/19/1990 Augustine Owens c 4.

✠ **OWENSBY, The Rt Rev Jacob W** (WLa) 335 Main St, Pineville LA 71360 **Bp of Wstrn Louisiana Dio Wstrn Louisiana Alexandria LA 2012-; Bp Mt Olivet Chap Pineville LA 2012-** B Spartanburg SC 1957 s James & Trudy. BA Emory U 1980; MA Emory U 1983; PhD Emory U 1985; MDiv Sewanee: The U So, TS 1997; DD TS 2013; DD Sewanee: The U So, TS 2013. D 6/8/1997 P 12/7/1997 Bp Stephen Hays Jecko Con 7/21/2012 for WLa. m 4/30/1983 Joy B Bruce c 3. Dn S Mk's Cathd Shreveport LA 2009-2012; R Emm Epis Ch S Louis MO 2003-2008; R S Steph's Epis Ch Huntsville AL 1999-2003; Asst S Mk's Epis Ch Jacksonville FL 1997-1999. Auth, "Gospel Memories," Morehouse, 2016; Auth, "Connecting the Dots," WestBow Press, 2012; Auth, "Dilthey and the Narrative of Hist," Cor Press, 1994; Auth, "Your Untold Story," Ch Pub. bishopjake@diocesewla.org

OWREN, David (NCal) 99 Pampas Ln, Fortuna CA 95540 B Schenectady NY 1947 s Harvey & Doris. BA San Jose St U 1969; MDiv Pacific Luth TS 1974; ThM Pacific Luth TS 1977. Rec 12/30/2005 Bp Jerry Alban Lamb. m 7/25/1992 Carol Arnold Owren c 2. Vic S Fran Ch Fortuna CA 2006-2010.

OWSLEY, Rebecca D (EMich) Christ Episcopal Church, 202 W Westover St, East Tawas MI 48730 B Bloomington IN 1942 d Charles & Janice. BA Mia 1979; Coppage Gordon Sch for Mnstry (Dioc) 2012. D 4/21/2012 P 10/20/2012 Bp Steven Todd Ousley. c 5. P-in-c Chr Epis Ch E Tawas MI 2013-2016.

OWUSU-AFRIYIE, Kwabena (Pa) 811 Longacre Blvd, Yeadon PA 19050 **P-in-c H Cross Epis Ch Plainfield NJ 2013-; R St Mich's Epis Ch Yeadon PA 2004-** B Kumasi Ghana 1954 s Sampson & Adwoa. Teachers Coll Ghana 1971; BTh Trin Ghana 1979; MTS VTS 1988; Geo Mason U 1990. Trans 1/1/2005 Bp Charles Ellsworth Bennison Jr. m 9/8/2011 Mabel Owusu-Afriyie c 7. S Mich's Ch Lansdowne PA 2004-2013; Asst S Paul's Ch Bailey's Crossroads Falls Ch VA 1990-1993; Int Asst S Andr's Epis Ch Arlington VA 1987-1988.

OXFORD, Scott Alexander (WNC) 520 New Haw Creek Rd, Asheville NC 28805 B Morganton NC 1957 s John & Nancy. BS Appalachian St U 1980; MDiv Sewanee: The U So, TS 1987; DMin Drew U 1994. D 5/15/1987 P 11/22/1987 Bp William Gillette Weinhauer. c 2. R S Jas Ch Black Mtn NC 2003-2016; Cn To Bp Dio Wstrn No Carolina Asheville NC 2000-2003, Stndd Com 1988-1994, Stndg Com 2005-, Chair Stwdshp Cmsn 1990-1997; R Ch Of The H Cross Valle Crucis NC 1993-1999; Chapl Hospice 1988-1993; R S Paul Lake Jas NC 1988-1993; R St Mary's and St Steph's Epis Ch Morganton NC 1988-1993; Assoc R Ch Of The Ascen Hickory NC 1987-1988. Auth, "St"; Auth, "Re-Memberance At Christmas". OHC 1998. scottox28@gmail.com

P

PACE, Bradley Warren (Ind) St Johns Episcopal Church, 600 Ferry St, Lafayette IN 47901 **R St Johns Epis Ch Lafayette IN 2013-; Adj Prof Youngstown St U Youngstown OH 2011-** B Louisville KY 1975 s Robert & Teressa. BA Berea Coll 1997; MA U of Arkansas 1999; PhD U IL at Urbana-Champaign 2006; MDiv SWTS 2008. D 6/7/2008 P 12/6/2008 Bp Jeff Lee. m 1/6/1998 Mary K Elder c 3. R S Jn's Ch Youngstown OH 2010-2013; Assoc Trin Epis Ch Wheaton IL 2008-2010. Auth, "Publ Reason and Publ Theol," ATR, 2009.

PACE, David Frederick (ECR) 514 Central Ave, Menlo Park CA 94025 B Haverhill MA 1940 s Frederick & Dorothy. STM Jesuit TS; BS Menlo Coll; STB U of San Francisco. D 3/4/1977 Bp Chaunie Kilmer Myers P 4/1/1978 Bp Wesley Frensdorff. Ch Of S Jos Milpitas CA 2002-2005; R S Jas' Ch Monterey CA 1998-2000; S Ptr's Ch Honolulu HI 1997-1998; Dir Of Pstr Care S Rose Hosp In Hayward 1986-1997; Chr Ch Alameda CA 1981-1985; Trin Par Menlo Pk CA 1980-1981.

PACE, David Taylor (Ore) 1729 Northeast Tillamook St, Portland OR 97212 B Honolulu HI 1941 s John & Kathryn. BS OR SU 1965; Oregon Hlth Sci U Dental Sch 1968; MDiv CDSP 1972. D 8/10/1972 P 6/1/1973 Bp James Walmsley Frederic Carman. m 1/22/1966 Jeanne Frances Pace c 1. Oregon Epis Sch Portland OR 2001-2002; Chapl, Tchr, Coach Oregon Epsicopal Sch Portland OR 1980-2002; Ch Of The Trsfg Brightwood OR 1978-1980; 1977-1980; S Mich And All Ang Ch Portland OR 1975-1979; Asst S Barn Par Portland OR 1972-1974.

PACE, James Conlin (NY) 145 W 46th St Apt 5, New York NY 10036 **Asst Ch Of S Mary The Vrgn New York NY 2011-** B Bradenton FL 1954 s Jack & Jayne. BA U So 1976; BSN Florida St U 1978; MSN Van 1981; PhD U of Alabama 1986; DSN U of Alabama 1986; PhD U of Alabama Birmingham 1986; MDiv Van 1988. D 6/25/1988 P 4/22/1989 Bp George Lazenby Reynolds Jr. Supply P Dio TN 2007-2011; Evening Chapl Van Med Cntr 2006-2008; S Anselm's Epis Ch Nashville TN 2006-2007; S Clem's Epis Ch Canton GA 1996-2002; S Jn's Epis Ch Mt Juliet TN 1995; Asstg P S Mk's Nashville TN 1989-1992; Chapl Alive Hospice 1988-1994; D'S Asst S Mk's Nashville TN 1988-1989. jcp12@nyu.edu

PACE, Joseph Leslie (Ct) 1 Gold St, Apt 16E, Hartford CT 06103 **S Lk's Ch So Glastonbury CT 2017-; Int S Mk's Ch New Britain CT 2015-** B Knoxville TN 1951 s Norman & Doris. BA U So 1973; MDiv GTS 1979; MA Hartford Sem 2000. D 6/17/1979 Bp William F Gates Jr P 6/1/1980 Bp William Evan Sanders. R St Johns Ch W Hartford CT 1991-2013; Asst S Geo's Ch Nashville TN 1984-1991; Dio Tennessee Nashville TN 1980-1984; Vic S Raphael's Epis Ch Crossville TN 1980-1984; D S Lk's Epis Ch Jackson TN 1979-1980; Stndg Com Dio Connecticut Meriden CT 2011-2014, Com 1992-1998, Rdr Goe 1984-1991. Auth, "Var Bk Revs". Muslim-Chr Relatns, Hartford Sem: Advsry Committ 1999; Soc For Increase Of Mnstry: Exec Com 1995; Soc Of S Marg: Assoc; SCHC: Chapl. Ord of Hosp of St. Jn Jerusalem 2006.

PACE, Robert F (NwT) 6200 Adirondack Trl, Amarillo TX 79106 **R S Andr's Epis Ch Amarillo TX 2016-, Assoc 2012-2016** B Freeport TX 1966 s Harvey & Joyce. MA TCU; BA Austin Coll 1988; PhD TCU 1992; MDiv Epis TS of the SW 2012. D 12/10/2011 P 6/18/2012 Bp James Scott Mayer. m 6/4/1988 Jill A Walters c 1. Pres of the Stndg Com, 2015-2016 Dio NW Texas Lubbock TX 2015-2016. Ed, "Buffalo Days: Stories from J. Wright Mooar," St Hse Press, 2005; Auth, "Halls of hon: Coll Men in the Old So," LSU Press, 2004; Co-Auth, "Frontier Texas: Hist of a Borderland to 1880," St Hse Press, 2004; Co-Ed, "Fear God and Walk Humbly: The Agricultural Journ of Jas Mallory, 1843-1877," U of Alabama Press, 1997. rpace@standrewsamarillo.org

PACE, Stephanie Anne Heflin (O) 3677 Hughstowne Dr, Akron OH 44333 **R S Matt's Epis Ch Brecksville OH 2010-** B 1956 d Martin & Sydney. Trans 7/26/2001 Bp J Clark Grew II. m 4/15/1978 Hugh D Pace c 3. P-in-c S Barn Ch Trion GA 2008-2010; R New Life Epis Ch Uniontown OH 2001-2007.

PACHECO, Jose (SanD) 209 Clay St, Weed CA 96094 B 1941 s Jose & Adelina. Immac Concep Sem 1967. Rec 8/1/1994 as Priest Bp Jerry Alban Lamb. m 7/15/1972 Linda Alvarado c 4. S Andr's By The Lake Lake Elsinore CA 2006-2009; Dio San Diego San Diego CA 1998-2005; S Barn Ch Mt Shasta CA 1994-1998.

✠ PACKARD, The Rt Rev George Elden (NY) 26 Oakwood Ave, Rye NY 10580 B New Rochelle NY 1944 s George & Catherine. BA Hobart and Wm Smith Colleges 1966; US-A Chapl Sch 1973; MDiv VTS 1974; US-A Advncd Course Command and Gnrl Stff 1987; DD VTS 2000; VTS 2000. D 6/5/1974 P 12/15/1974 Bp William Henry Marmion Con 2/12/2000 for Armed Forces and Federal Ministires. m 6/18/1999 Brook Hedick Packard c 3. Bp Suffr for Armed Serv & Fed Mnstrs Epis Ch Cntr New York NY 1999-2010; P-in-c Chr's Ch Rye NY 1997-1999; P-in-c The Ch Of The Epiph New York NY 1995-1997; Supply P S Jn's Ch New Rochelle NY 1992-1993; Cn to the Ordnry Dio New York New York NY 1989-1995, Chair, Dioc Bdgt Com 2000-2002; Chapl US-A Reserves 1981-1997; R Gr Ch Hastings Hds NY 1980-1989; R Chr Ch Martinsville VA 1976-1980; Asst S Paul's Epis Ch Lynchburg VA 1974-1976; Chapl EPF Ithaca NY 2013-2015. Co Auth, "Pstr Tchg," *Pstr Tchg on Just War*, HOB, 2003. First Infantry Div 1995; The Druid Soc 1965. September 11th 2001.

PACKARD, Jeffrey Alan (Va) 220 Morgan Ln, Spotsylvania VA 22551 **R Chr Epis Ch Spotsylvania VA 2000-** B Bellefonte PA 1966 s Richard & Janet. BA Penn 1989; MDiv VTS 1995; Sewanee: The U So, TS 1999. D 6/9/1995 Bp Charlie Fuller Mcnutt Jr P 2/10/1996 Bp Michael Whittington Creighton. m 7/1/1989 Sian A Packard c 3. All SS Ch Brookland PA 1996-2000; Vic Chr Ch Coudersport PA 1996-2000; Cur S Andr's Ch St Coll PA 1995-1996. Auth, "Experiencing H Week," LivCh, 2008; Auth, "The Scam Artist," LivCh, 2002; Auth, "Faith Like a River," Preaching Through the Year of Lk: Sermons that Wk IX, Morehouse Pub, 2000; Auth, "Ang in the Flames," LivCh, 2000.

PACKARD, Laurence Kent (Va) 9350 Braddock Rd, Burke VA 22015 B Rockville Centre NY 1952 s Henry & Jane. DMin PrTS; BA Wake Forest U 1975; U of Tennessee 1976; MDiv VTS 1979. D 6/28/1979 Bp William F Gates Jr P 5/3/1980 Bp William Evan Sanders. m 11/1/1980 Melissa Armour. Ch Of The Gd Shpd Burke VA 1997-2015; S Cathr's Epis Ch Marietta GA 1989-1996; Dept Of Chr Nurture Dio Wstrn Louisiana Alexandria LA 1985-1989, Dept Of CE 1984-1989; Asst to R S Mk's Cathd Shreveport LA 1983-1989; Dio W Tennessee Memphis 1983; Vic S Jn's Ch Mart TN 1980-1983; Dio Tennessee Nashville TN 1980-1982, Yth Advsr 1979-1983; D-In-Trng S Elis's Epis Ch Memphis TN 1979-1980; Bd Dir S Columba's Epis Ch Bristol TN 1981-1983. Auth, "Being There: A New Vision Of Yth Mnstry"; Auth, "Celebrating Yth Mnstry". Ord Of S Mary.

PACKARD, Linda Axelson (Chi) 2 Currant Ct, Galena IL 61036 B Chicago IL 1942 d William & Elin. BA Lawr 1964; MDiv McCormick TS 1989; Cert SWTS 1989; Cert Int Mnstry Prog 1992. D 12/2/1989 P 7/2/1990 Bp Frank Tracy Griswold III. m 10/18/1980 C Anthony Packard c 3. Int Gr Epis Ch Galena IL 2010-2011; R Ch Of Our Sav Chicago IL 1997-2008; Int Gr Ch Oak Pk IL 1994-1997; Pres, Stndg Commitee Dio Chicago Chicago IL 1993-1996; Asst S Greg's Epis Ch Deerfield IL 1993-1994; Int St. Andrews Pentecost Epis Ch Evanston IL 1992; Stff Chapl Evanston Hosp Evanston IL 1990-1994; Admssns Coordntr Bexley Seabury Fed Chicago IL 1990-1992; Chapl U Chi Hospitals Chicago IL 1989-1990. Coll Chapl.

PACKARD, Nancy Meader (Be) 359 Whitehall Rd, Hooksett NH 03106 **Assoc S Alb's Epis Ch Reading PA 2013-** B Waterville ME 1946 d Harold & Arlene. MEd Notre Dame Coll 1983; Cert EDS 1997; MA Notre Dame Coll 1997. D 6/17/2001 P 12/22/2001 Bp Douglas Edwin Theuner. c 2. R S Mary's Epis Ch Reading PA 2004-2012; Gr Ch Manchester NH 2001-2004.

PACKARD, William L (Va) D 6/10/2017 Bp Shannon Sherwood Johnston.

PACKER CSJB, Barbara J (Nwk) Po Box 240, Mendham NJ 07945 **Dvlpmt Off S Jn Bapt Cnvnt Mendham NJ 2010-** B Abington PA 1942 d Walter & Margaret. BS Millersville U 1963; MDiv Drew U 1989. D 6/10/1989 P 2/19/1994 Bp George Phelps Mellick Belshaw. Superior S Jn the Bapt Cnvnt Mendham NJ 1997-2010; S Jn's Ch Eliz NJ 1989-1995; Asst Superior S Jn Bapt Cnvt Mendham NJ 1988-1997; Asst to Hdmstr S Jn Bapt Sch Mendham NJ 1976-1983. Auth, "The Calling of S Pat," *Living Ch*, 1997; Auth, "S Teresa & The Priority of Pryr," *Living Ch*, 1996; Auth, "Catherineof Siena," *Living Ch*, 1996; Auth, "In A Quiet Time & Place," *Living Ch*, 1992. Cmnty of St. Jn Bapt 1964.

PADASDAO, Imelda Sumaoang (Haw) 1326 Konia St, Honolulu HI 96817 **Assoc S Eliz's Ch Honolulu HI 2008-** B Masikil Bangui Ilocos PH 1953 d Florentino & Iluminada. Cannons Coll of Commerce 1973; Hawaii Sch of Bus 1976; Dio Hawaii Diac Trng Prog HI 1986. D 12/14/1986 P 10/7/1990 Bp Donald Purple Hart. Dioc Coun S Pauls Ch Honolulu HI 1990-1999; Treas The Epis Ch in Hawaii Honolulu HI 1977-1990, 1990-.

PADDOCK, Andrea Lee (Los) 31551 Catalina St,, Laguna Beach CA 92651 **Sprtl Care Vol Mssn Hosp Laguna Bch Ca 2010-; Dio Los Angeles Los Angeles CA 2007-** B Oakland CA 1944 d Dexter & Dorothy. BA U CA 1966; California St U 1969; ETSBH 2006. D 12/2/2006 Bp Chester Lovelle Talton. c 3. Sr Adult Mnstry S Marg Of Scotland Par San Juan Capo CA 2006-2009; Int Chapl The Covington: An Epis Hm Cmnty Aliso Viejo Ca 2006. Assn for Epis Deacons 2007.

PADDOCK, John Sheldon (SO) 1837 Ruskin Rd, Dayton OH 45406 **R Chr Epis Ch Dayton OH 1999-** B Rochester NY 1946 s William & Jane. BA U Roch 1968; MDiv VTS 1972; DMin Untd TS 2004. D 6/15/1972 P 12/24/1972 Bp John Mc Gill Krumm. m 1/19/1974 Ann V Paddock c 8. R Gr Epis Ch Bath ME 1988-1999; R Gr Ch Great Barrington MA 1980-1988; R S Paul's Epis Ch Greenville OH 1974-1980; Asst Ch Of S Edw Columbus OH 1972-1974. johnpaddock@daytonchristepiscopal.com

PADGETT, John Elliott (WTex) 12431 Modena Bay, San Antonio TX 78253 B McKenzie TN 1943 s John & Martha. BS USNA 1965; MS Untd States Naval Postgraduate Sch 1972; MDiv Epis TS of the SW 1988. D 5/23/1988 Bp Earl Nicholas Mc Arthur Jr P 12/1/1988 Bp John Herbert MacNaughton. m 6/17/2006 Leslie Watson Zapata Padgett c 2. Cn Mssnr Partnr In Mnstry Estrn Convoc Kenedy TX 2005-2011; R S Andr's Epis Ch San Antonio TX 1995-2005; Vic/R S Chris's By The Sea Portland TX 1990-1995; Asst/Int R S Thos Epis Ch And Sch San Antonio TX 1988-1990. Ord Of S Lk - Chapl 1992.

PADGETT, Judy Malinda Pitts (At) 980 W Mill Bnd Nw, Kennesaw GA 30152 B Knoxville TN 1945 d John & Nan. D 10/18/1998 Bp Onell Asiselo Soto. m 10/19/1963 Robert Micheal Padgett. D S Cathr's Epis Ch Marietta GA 1998-2003.

PADILLA, Manuel Jack (NMich) 711 Michigan Ave, Crystal Falls MI 49920 **Reg Cleric For The Wstrn Reg Dio Nthrn Michigan Marquette MI 1988-; Epis Ch-Wstrn Reg Crystal Falls MI 1988-** B Paterson NJ 1955 s Diego & Laurinda. BA U of Maryland 1982; MDiv SWTS 1988; DMin SWTS 2004. D 12/22/1987 P 6/1/1988 Bp Thomas Kreider Ray. m 6/22/1974 Margaret E Padilla c 2. Mssnr/P S Mk's Ch Crystal Falls MI 1988-2013. mpadilla@up.net

PADILLA, Margaret E (NMich) 711 Michigan Ave, Crystal Falls MI 49920 **P S Mk's Ch Crystal Falls MI 1997-** B Crystal Falls MI 1953 d Norbert & Mary.

D 12/4/1996 P 6/22/1997 Bp Thomas Kreider Ray. m 6/22/1974 Manuel Jack Padilla c 2.

PADILLA-MORALES, Luis (PR) **Dio Puerto Rico Trujillo Alto PR 2004-, 1999-2003; R Dio Puerto Rico (S Andr's Par) 2000-** B 1965 BA Other 1989; BA Sem. Regina Cleri (RCC) 1989; Cert. Estudios Anglicano Other 1999; Cert. Estudios Anglicano Sem. Epis San Pedro Y San Pablo 1999; MA Pontificia Universidad Católica de Puerto Rico 2006; MA Pontificia Universidad Católica de Puerto Rico 2006. m 10/18/1997 Melva Irizarry Clavell. R RC Ch- San Antonio Abad Par 1994-1995; R RC Ch- Our Lady of Miracle Par 1992-1994; Vic Dio Puerto Rico S Just PR US 1989-1992; Asst (P) RC Ch- S Jos's Par 1989-1992.

PADRON, Pilar Felicia (WNY) D 6/3/2017 Bp Sean Walter Rowe.

PADZIESKI, Virginia Sue (Minn) 7 Terrace Point, P. O. Box 788, Grand Marais MN 55604 B Independence KS 1952 d Douglass & Doris. U of Oklahoma 1970; Simpson Coll 1971; Winchester Art Coll 1985. D 10/17/1992 Bp Sanford Zangwill Kaye Hampton. m 10/8/1983 Robert Joseph Padzieski. Stndg Com Dio Minnesota Minneapolis MN 1996-1998, Dioc Coun 1994-1996; D Calv Ch Rochester MN 1992-2013.

PAE, Joseph S (LI) 191 Kensington Rd, Garden City NY 11530 **S Paul's Ch Great Neck NY 2010-** B Chunan South Korea 1971 BA U of Pennsylvania 1994; MDiv Ya Berk 2001. D 6/24/2003 P 1/17/2004 Bp Orris George Walker Jr. m 5/12/2007 Ju Young Lee-Pae c 2. P-in-c All SS Ch Great Neck NY 2015, R 2015-; Dio Long Island Garden City NY 2010-2014; Cn Cathd Of The Incarn Garden City NY 2004-2010; P Chr Ch Alexandria VA 2003-2004.

PAE, Keun-Joo (Nwk) 76 E Main St, Newark OH 43055 B Gang-nung ROK 1974 d Joo-Seon & Myung-Sook. BEd Seoul Natl U of Educ 1997; MDiv Ya Berk 2003; PhD UTS 2009. D 6/2/2012 P 12/15/2012 Bp Mark M Beckwith.

PAGANO, Joseph Samuel (Md) **S Anne's Par Annapolis MD 2010-** B Fontana CA 1964 s Stephen & Mary. BA U of Pennsylvania 1987; MDiv PrTS 1993; PhD Marq 2001. D 6/5/2004 P 12/8/2004 Bp Steven Andrew Miller. m 8/26/1990 Amy Elizabeth Richter. R Emm Ch Baltimore MD 2006-2010; Asst S Paul's Ch Milwaukee WI 2005-2006; S Jas Epis Ch Milwaukee WI 2001-2002.

PAGE, Donald Richard (Ct) 11 Nassau Rd., Somers Point NJ 08244 **Ret 2008-** B Audubon NJ 1943 s Victor & Allene. AA Pierce Jr Coll 1965; BA Trenton St Coll 1968; MDiv PDS 1971. D 4/24/1971 P 10/23/1971 Bp Alfred L Banyard. m 6/13/1970 Elizabeth R Page c 2. Sunday Celebrant No Cntrl Reg Mnstry Enfield CT 1996-2008; Sprtl Care Dir Evergreen Hlth Care Cntr 1993-2008; Calv Ch Suffield CT 1993-2007; Gr Ch Broad Brook CT 1993-2007; H Trin Epis Ch Enfield CT 1993-2007; Sunday Celebrant S Andr's Epis Ch Enfield CT 1993-2007; Chapl Johnson Memi CT 1992-2008; R Gr Ch Stafford Sprg CT 1979-1992; Rep AFP Dio New Jersey Trenton NJ 1978-1979; R S Mk's Ch Hammonton NJ 1973-1979; R S Mich's Ch Trenton NJ 1971-1973; Aids T/F Dio Connecticut Meriden CT 1987-1990. Assn Of Epis Chapl 1992-2008; Coll Of Chapl 1992-2008. Citation For Cleric Activities Kessler Hosp 1979.

PAGE, Herman (Kan) Po Box 5167, Topeka KS 66605 **Died 9/17/2015** B Boston MA 1927 s Herman & Lois. BA Harv 1950; MDiv EDS 1952. D 6/1/1952 P 12/13/1952 Bp Herman R Page. m 6/6/1952 Mary Waldo c 3. Asst 1990-2015; Assoc S Dav's Epis Ch Topeka KS 1990; Int Dio Kansas Topeka KS 1987-1990; Vic S Phil's Epis Ch Topeka KS 1980-1987; R S Andr's Epis Ch Liberal KS 1967-1980; Assoc Secy ECEC Hm Dept Roanridge MO 1963-1967; R Trin Epis Ch Houghton MI 1957-1963; Vic S Jn's Ch Iron River MI 1952-1957; S Mk's Ch Crystal Falls MI 1952-1957.

PAGE JR, Hugh Rowland (NI) 1526 Cedar Springs Ct, Mishawaka IN 46545 **Non-par 1984-; GBEC GC- Epis Ch Cntr New York NY 2015-; Hon Cn The Cathd Ch Of S Jas So Bend IN 2015-; BEC Dio Nthrn Indiana So Bend IN 2013-** B Baltimore MD 1956 s Hugh & Elaine. BA Hampton U 1977; Pittsburgh TS 1978; MDiv GTS 1980; STM GTS 1983; MA Harv 1988; PhD Harv 1990; DMin GTF 2006. D 6/28/1980 P 12/30/1980 Bp David Keller Leighton Sr. m 8/7/2004 Jacquetta E Page. Supply P Trin Ch Michigan City IN 2011-2013; Int Vic Alexander Crummell Cntr Highland Pk MI 1984; Tutor The GTS New York NY 1982-1983; R S Jos's Epis Ch Fayetteville NC 1981-1982; Asst to the R S Jas' Epis Ch Baltimore MD 1980-1981. Hon Cn Cathd of St. Jas, So Bend, IN 2015.

PAGE, Marilyle Sweet (Roch) 6 Cadence Ct, Penfield NY 14526 B Saint Louis MO 1942 d Martin & Vera. BS Ohio U 1964; MDiv Bex Sem 1975; DMin Bex Sem 1986. D 6/7/1975 Bp John Mc Gill Krumm P 1/4/1977 Bp Robert Rae Spears Jr. P-in-c Ephphatha Mssn for the Deaf Rochester NY 2001-2008; R S Mk's And S Jn's Epis Ch Rochester NY 2001-2008, 2001; P-in-c Chr Ch Rochester NY 2000; Int The Ch Of The Epiph Gates NY 1999; Ext of Mnstry Counslg & Consult Serv Rochester NY 1997-2008; Int S Thos Epis Ch Rochester NY 1995-1996; R Ch Of The Atone Westfield MA 1989-1995; R S Ptr's Epis Ch Henrietta NY 1985-1989; Assoc S Steph's Ch Rochester NY 1977-1979; Dio Rochester Henrietta 1975-1984. Auth, "The Ch & The Alco Addicted Fam: A Co-Dependent Perspective," *D. Min. Thesis*, 1986. AAMFT 1990-2010; AAPC 1995-2008; MFT Lic 1993. Outstanding Serv Awd as Pres Genesee Vlly Chapt - NY Assn for MFT 2000.

PAGE, Michelle Rene (EC) 18115 State Road 23 Ste 112, South Bend IN 46637 **Non-par 1982-** B San Antonio TX 1954 d Orah & Barbara. Ya; BA Gri 1977; MDiv GTS 1980. D 11/22/1980 Bp James Winchester Montgomery P 12/1/1981 Bp Hunley Agee Elebash. Vic S Andr's Ch Goldsboro NC 1981-1982; Vic S Aug's Epis Ch Kinston NC 1981-1982.

PAGE, Rufus Lee (NCal) 2525 11th Ave, Sacramento CA 95818 **Non-par 1992-** B Ionia MI 1934 s Rufus & Mary. BA Shimer Coll 1955; STB PDS 1958. D 4/26/1958 P 11/1/1958 Bp Alfred L Banyard. m 10/17/1982 Gayle Page c 3. Assoc All SS Memi Sacramento CA 1990-1992; Non-par 1970-1990; Assoc S Matt's Epis Ch Sacramento CA 1969-1970; R S Paul's Epis Ch Sacramento CA 1966-1968; Cur S Steph's Par Whittier CA 1962-1966; Cur S Jas Par Los Angeles CA 1960-1962; In-Charge S Barn By The Bay Villas NJ 1958-1960. Auth, "Funk & Wagnalls New Encyclopedia"; Auth, "Students Needs As A Clergyman Sees Them Ca Educ Agcy 73". Annual Awd For Outstanding Soc Wk For A Non-Profsnl Natl Assn Soc Wkrs 1968.

PAGE JR, William Russell (Mass) 217 Holland St Pt 2A, Somerville MA 02144 B Evanston IL 1949 s William & Ann. BA Trin 1971; MDiv GTS 1975. D 6/14/1975 Bp Quintin Ebenezer Primo Jr P 12/1/1975 Bp James Winchester Montgomery. P Bro Soc Of S Jn The Evang 1984-2005; P S Jn's Chap Cambridge MA 1979-2014; Soc-St Jn The Evang Cambridge MA 1979-2005; Novc Soc Of S Jn The Evang 1979-1981; Asst Ascen Memi Ch Ipswich MA 1975-1978.

PAGLIARO, Lois Anne (NY) 18818 89th Ave, Hollis NY 11423 B New York NY 1948 d Salvatore & Muriel. BA CUNY 1977; MDiv EDS 1980. D 6/7/1980 Bp Paul Moore Jr. The Ch Of S Lk In The Fields New York NY 1986-2003.

PAGLINAUAN, Cristina (Md) 5603 N Charles St, Baltimore MD 21210 **Assoc R The Ch Of The Redeem Baltimore MD 2010-** B Newark NJ 1970 d Teodulo & Wilhelmina. AB Harv 1992; MDiv GTS 2010. D 6/19/2010 Bp John L Rabb P 1/6/2011 Bp Eugene Taylor Sutton. m 11/24/2007 David Lloyd Warner c 2.

PAGUIO, Ruth Alegre (ECR) 212 Swain Way, Palo Alto CA 94304 B Philippines 1969 d Wilfrido & Leonor. MDiv CDSP; BA Harris Memi Coll; MEd Tariac St U Tariac Philippines. D 12/21/2005 P 8/24/2006 Bp Sylvestre Donato Romero. m 6/5/2004 Adorlito Paguio. P S Jn's Epis Ch Stockton CA 2015; Lay H Fam Epis Ch San Jose CA 2005, Vic 2005-; Dss Meth Ch 1990-2001.

PAHL JR, James Larkin (NC) 302 College St, Oxrford NC 27565 **R S Steph's Ch Oxford NC 2008-** B Winston Salem NC 1971 s James & Alice. BA No Carolina St U 1995; MDiv VTS 2005. D 6/26/2005 P 1/6/2006 Bp Michael B Curry. m 3/2/1996 Susan Norris Pahl c 4. Asst S Jas Par Wilmington NC 2005-2008.

PAIN, Mary Reed (Mil) 10400 W Dean Rd Apt 102, Milwaukee WI 53224 **D S Simon The Fisherman Epis Ch Port Washington WI 2005-; Chapl Waukesha Memi Hosp Waukesha WI 2005-** B Cambria WI 1938 d James & Ethel. BA U of Wisconsin 1960; MA SWTS 1962. D 12/7/2002 Bp Roger John White. m 11/17/1967 Jack Pain c 2. EFM Mentor Dio Milwaukee Milwaukee WI 2002-2006; D S Fran Ch Menomonee Falls WI 2002-2005.

PAINE, Michael Jackson (WVa) 13 Byron St, Boston MA 02108 **Non-par 1968-** B Boston MA 1940 s Francis & Frances. BA Pr 1962; BD UTS 1965. D 6/9/1965 P 12/15/1965 Bp Wilburn Camrock Campbell. m 8/22/1964 Victoria Landel Moore. R Trin Ch Morgantown WV 1966-1968; Chapl W Virginia U 1966-1968; Cur S Matt's Ch Charleston WV 1965-1966.

PAINTER JR, Borden Winslow (Ct) 110 Ledgewood Rd, West Hartford CT 06107 B Brooklyn NY 1937 s Borden & Gladys. BA Trin Hartford CT 1958; MA Ya 1959; STB GTS 1963; PhD Ya 1965. D 6/11/1963 P 12/21/1963 Bp Horace W B Donegan. m 8/29/1959 Ann Deborah Dunning. Dio Connecticut Meriden CT 1974-1987; 1967-1979; Asst S Jn's New Haven CT 1963-1966. "Mussolini's Rome," Palgrave-Macmillan, 2005; Auth, "Renzo DeFelice and Historiography of Italian Fascism," *Amer Hist Revs*; Auth, "Angl Terminology in Recent Tudor and Stuart Historiography," *Angl and Epis Hist*; Auth, "The Vstry in Colonial New Engl," *Hist mag of the Prot Epis Ch*; Auth, "The Vstry in the Middle Colonies," *Hist mag of the Prot Epis Ch*; Auth, "Bp Walter H Gray & the Angl Cong of 1954," *Hist mag of the Prot Epis Ch*. DD GTS 2005.

PAINTER, R Scott (Tex) **S Steph's Epis Ch Houston TX 2016-** D 6/25/2016 Bp C Andrew Doyle.

PALACIN, Manuel Enrique (PR) B 1935 Dio Puerto Rico Trujillo Alto PR 2004-2007, 1980-2003, 1964-1979.

PALACIO BEDOYA, Luis Hernan (Colom) Carrera 6 No 49-85, Piso 2, Bogota Colombia B Yarumal Antioguia 1959 s Javier & Matha. D 10/18/2008 Bp Francisco Jose Duque-Gomez.

PALAGYI, Addyse Lane (Ore) 3697 Croisan Creek Rd S, Salem OR 97302 **Mssy to Ukraine Dio Oregon Portland OR 2008-, Mssy to China 2006-, Mssy to Hungary 2005-, Mssy to China 2006-; Mssy To China Dio Oregon 2004-; D S Thos Epis Ch Dallas OR 2000-** B Salem OR 1927 d Addison & Gladys. BA Willamette U 1949; MA Stan 1952; PhD SUNY 1975; Cntr for the Diac 2000. D 9/30/2000 Bp Robert Louis Ladehoff. c 4. "Families: The Artistic Chld," *Fam Focus mag*, 1997; "Tapestries," The E River Anthology Addison Pacific, 1992; "Behavior Modification Through Theatre," Parker, 1980;

"The Assembly Prog," Parker, 1975; "The Writer's Corner (monthly column 1992--1998)," *Mid-Vlly Arts mag.*

PALARINE, John R (Fla) 12236 Mandarin Rd, Jacksonville FL 32223 **Yth Dir Dio SW Florida Parrish FL 2015**- B Saint Paul MN 1948 s Fiori & Lorayne. BA S Thos 1970; MDiv SWTS 1973. D 6/29/1973 P 3/22/1974 Bp Philip Frederick McNairy. m 10/26/1991 Joanne E Palarine c 2. VTS Alexandria VA 2003, 2002, 2001, 1999; Att Dep Dio Florida Jacksonville 2000-2003, Stndg Com 2007-2009, 2000-2006, Dioc Coun 1997-1999; R Ch Of Our Sav Jacksonville FL 1996-2013; Pstr Response Team Ch Of The Ascen Clearwater FL 1992-1996; Cn For Yth & Educ Dio Cntrl Florida Orlando FL 1981-1991; Dio Minnesota Minneapolis MN 1979-1981, Natl Ch Yth Coordntr 1978-1981, Yth Coordntr 1973-1974; Asst S Jn The Evang S Paul MN 1976-1978; Cur S Ptr's Epis Ch Chicago IL 1974-1976.

PALASI, Dario G (LI) 13424 96th St, Ozone Park NY 11417 **P-in-c St Jn's Epis Ch Flushing NY 2004-, P-in-c 2002-2003** B Ca-ew, Bulalacao, Mankayan, Philippines 1960 s Menio & Besina. AA U of Asia 1981; MDiv S Andrews TS 1985; MDiv S Andrews TS 1985. Trans 3/5/2003 Bp Orris George Walker Jr. m 12/28/1989 Catherine Palasi c 3. Dio No Cntrl Philippines Baguio City 1990-1993; Dio Cntrl Philippines Queson City 1986-1989.

PALLARD SR, John J (CFla) PO Box 142, Peckham Lane RR#2, Coventry RI 03/01/2816 B Scramton PA 1945 s John & Mary Ann. BA Oblate Coll 1969; MRE Fairfield U 1975; MA Oblate Coll 1975; EdD Boston Coll 1982; MEd Niagara U Niagara Falls NY 1982. Rec 10/9/2008 as Priest Bp John Wadsworth Howe. m 4/3/2002 Erin Pallard c 1. Epis Ch Of The H Sprt Apopka FL 2013-2017; R S Barn Ch Warwick RI 2009-2013; Dio Rhode Island Providence RI 2009; P-in-c St Fran Epis Ch Coventry RI 2008-2013. P-Tchr, "The Ch's Soc Mssn," Cntr for Lrng, 1979.

PALLARES ARELLANO, Jorge Enrique (Los) 10154 Mountair Ave, Tujunga CA 91042 **Int S Simon's Par San Fernando CA 2014-; S Lk's Of The Mountains La Crescenta CA 2012-** B Puebla Mexico 1957 s Enrique & Lidia. BA Universidad Autonoma de Puebla 1980; Dip Comunidad Teologica de Mex 2005; BA Seminario de San Andres MX 2005. Trans 11/5/2008 Bp Joseph Jon Bruno. m 8/1/1987 Rosa Patricia Pezzat de Pallares c 2. Vic Ch Of The Ascen Tujunga CA 2008-2012; Vol P Iglesia Anglicana De Mex 2006-2008. jorgepallaresa2007@hotmail.com

PALMA, Jose (WMo) 420 West 14th St, Kansas City MO 64105 **P-in-c Dio W Missouri Kansas City MO 2009-; Assoc Gr Ch Carthage MO 2009-** B SV 1963 s Jose & Maria. BA Santiago De Maria Usulutan SV 1993. Rec 8/25/2001 as Priest Bp Claude Edward Payne. m 11/18/1994 Mercedes Palma c 4. The Great Cmsn Fndt Houston TX 2004-2008; Pstr Iglesia San Francisco de Asis Austin TX 2001-2008.

PALMER, Alison (WA) 70 Lookout Rd, Wellfleet MA 02667 B Medford MA 1931 d Charles & Lois. BA Br 1953; MA Bos 1970; Dio Washington Spec Preparatory Prog 1974. D 6/9/1974 Bp William Foreman Creighton P 9/7/1975 Bp George West Barrett. 1999-2003; Assoc The Ch Of The H Sprt Orleans MA 1995-1998; Assoc Min Chap Of S Jas The Fisherman Wellfleet MA 1982-1983; 1976-1981; Assoc Min S Columba's Ch Washington DC 1974-1975. Wm Scarlett Awd Epis Ch Pub Soc 1994.

PALMER JR, Archie (Nwk) 459 Passaic Ave Apt 315, West Caldwell NJ 07006 **Int Min The Ch Of The Annunc Oradell NJ 2011-, Int Min 2005-2011** B Chattanooga TN 1939 s Archie & Elizabeth. BA Wms 1962; MDiv PDS 1969. D 6/14/1969 P 12/17/1969 Bp Leland Stark. m 6/24/1967 Lynne Palmer c 1. Int Min Chr Ch Hackensack NJ 2011; Int Min Chr Ch Pompton Lake NJ 2007-2010; Int Min S Andr And H Comm Ch So Orange NJ 2004-2005; Int Min Trin Ch Cliffside Pk NJ 2004-2005; Int Min S Lk's Epis Ch Haworth NJ 2002-2003; Int Min S Andr's Epis Ch Lincoln Pk NJ 2001; Non-par 1984-2001; R Trin Epis Ch Cranford NJ 1982-1984; Chapl New Jersey Army NG 1979-1982; R Trin Epis Ch Kearny NJ 1971-1982; Asst to R S Jas Ch Montclair NJ 1969-1971. Trst For Bloomfield Coll 2000.

PALMER, Beth (Miss) 1415 Baum St, Vicksburg MS 39180 **R Ch of the H Trin Vicksburg MS 2012-** B Danville PA 1953 d Samuel & Ethel. BS Bloomsburg U of Pennsylvania 1975; MBA Penn 1981; MDiv VTS 2003. D 6/14/2003 P 12/20/2003 Bp Peter J Lee. m 11/27/1981 David Ralph Rorick c 1. R S Jn's Ch W Point VA 2003-2012. revbeth@holytrinityvicksburg.org

PALMER, Brian G (ECR) 2700 Eton Rd, Cambria CA 93428 **S Paul's Ch Cambria CA 2015-** B 1949 s Charles & Jean. MDiv VTS 2009. D 1/24/2009 Bp Chester Lovelle Talton P 8/10/2014 Bp Joseph Jon Bruno. The Par Of S Matt Pacific Plsds CA 2009-2015.

PALMER, Earle Jason (Ak) Po Box 1002, Ward Cove AK 99928 **Died 2/12/2016** B Elma WA 1930 s Ben & Ina. D 10/9/1972 P 4/1/1973 Bp William Jones Gordon Jr. m 5/24/1963 Lana Jaquith. Asst P S Jn's Ch Ketchikan AK 1978-2016.

PALMER, John Avery (ECR) 981 South Clover Ave, San Jose CA 95128 **Chapl/ Pstr Care S Fran Epis Ch San Jose CA 2013-; CACert. Dis. Shltr Func. Ass. Ser. Team Santa Clara Soc Serv Agcy; Santa Clara Co. CA 2011-; Pres Cypress Sr Cntr Advsry Coun; San Jose CA 2010-; Asst Chapl H Sprt Mssn Lake Almanor CA 2010-; Asst Instr SeniorNet Comput. Class.(Willows/Cypress Cntrs); SJ CA 2010-; D/H Sprt Mssn; Lake Al-**

manor, CA The Epis Dio Nthrn California Sacramento CA 2009-; **Med Vol. for Disaster Relief Santa Clara Co. Publ He./Emergency Med. Serv; CA 2008-; Police Chapl Santa Clara Police Dept; Santa Clara CA 1995-; Ord's Chapl Sov. Ord St. Jn of Jer. Knights Hospitaller; SJ 1989-; Chapl Coordntr SC Cnty AIDS Interfaith Resources; Campbell CA 1986-; Chapl / Dir Necessities & More Inc.; Campbell CA 1985-; Chap.; Dis/Hlth Serv. Amer Red Cross(Silicon Vlly Chapt.); San Jose CA 1976-; Pres, Advsry Cmsn for Persons w Disabil Santa Clara Cnty Bd Supervisors; SCCo. CA 1976-; Lead, Dio's Disaster/Emergency Preparedness Com Dio El Camino Real Salinas CA 2011-, Presiding Judge, Eccl Trial Crt 2010-2011; Dio's Liaison, Natl Epis Hlth Mnstrs S Paul's Epis Ch Indianapolis IN 2009-; Pres.: Adv. Cmsn/Persons w Diasabilities Santa Clara Cnty Bd Supervisors 1976-** B Cooperstown, New York 1944 s Kenneth & Helen. BS OH SU 1969; MA U CA/Berkeley Sch of Publ Hlth 1971; BS CDSP 1988; PhD Canbourne U 2005. D 9/20/1991 Bp Richard Lester Shimpfky. m 9/2/1989 Sherrill Carlton Martinez c 2. Chapl/Pstr Care Ch Of The H Sprt Campbell CA 2000-2002; Chapl / Pstr Care S Mk's Epis Ch Santa Clara CA 1991-1999; Jail Chapl Santa Clara Cnty Correctional Institions; San Jose CA 1989-2000; AIDS Chapl SF Gnrl Hosp; San Fransisco CA 1988-2000; Hosp Chapl Santa Clara Cnty Vlly Med Cntr; San Jose CA 1987-1997; Liaison, Dio El Camino Real Natl Epis Hlth Mnstrs. Auth, "Hlth Instrn in California's Publ Schools," *Hlth Framework in California*, CA St Dept of Ed., 1977; Auth, "Childrens' Mntl Hlth," *NMHA*, NMHA, 1972. (Am Red Cross) Vol. Org. Active in Disasters (VOAD) 1976; Amer Publ Hlth Assn 1971; Intl Conf of Police Chapl 1996; No Amer Assn Diac 1988. Hall Of Fame Mt. Markham HS 2007; Knight of Gr Ord of S Jn of Jerusalem, Knights Hospitallier 2003; Employee of the Year Santa Clara Cnty Hlth & Hosp System 1998; Knight of hon Ord of S Jn of Jerusalem, Knights Hospitallier 1989; Employee of the Year Santa Clara Cnty Publ Hlth Dept 1982; Pres'sScholarship Awd The OH SU 1968; Natl hon Soc W Winfield Cntrl Sch 1960.

PALMER, John M (NY) 33 E 10th St Apt 2-G, New York NY 10003 B Kansas City MO 1945 s Milo & Carrie. BA Wm Jewell Coll 1967; STB GTS 1970. D 6/20/1970 Bp Robert Rae Spears Jr P 1/1/1971 Bp Edward Randolph Welles II. Assoc S Jn's Ch New York NY 1998-2000; Dir Of Spec Par Ministers Trin Par New York NY 1984-1988; Trin Educ Fund New York NY 1979-1986; R Ch Of The Trsfg Bat Cave NC 1977-1979; Asst To Bp Of SE Florida Dio SE Florida Miami 1975-1977, 1974-1977, Yth Coordntr 1973-1975; Asst S Steph's Ch Coconut Grove Miami FL 1970-1973. Auth, "Unicorn". Comt.

PALMER, Richard Rainer (Colo) 400 Summit Blvd Unity 1503, Broomfield CO 80021 **Ret 1992-; Ret 1992-** B Bogota CO 1928 s Thomas & Marguerite. BS U Denv 1954; MDiv Nash 1959. D 6/29/1959 P 2/1/1960 Bp Joseph Summerville Minnis. R S Lk's Ch Denver CO 1983-1992; R Ch Of S Mich The Archangel Colorado Spg CO 1967-1983; R Chr The King Epis Ch Ft Worth TX 1963-1967; Vic Chr Epis Ch Aspen CO 1959-1963; Chair - COM Dio Colorado Denver CO 1971. Auth, "7 Ways God Helps You," 1969.

PALMER, Richard William (Wyo) 4753 Estero Blvd Apt 1601, Fort Myers Beach FL 33931 **Ret 1996-** B Cleveland OH 1923 s Leon & Myrtle. BA Pr 1944. D 6/30/1984 P 3/1/1985 Bp John Harris Burt. m 11/27/1969 E Allyene Chrisman. P Lamb Of God Epis Ch Ft Myers FL 2000-2002; S Raphael's Ch Ft Myers Bch FL 1998-2003; Dio Wyoming Casper 1992-1994, Archd 1985-1991; D S Lk Bath WY 1984-1985; Pres Equipment Co Dio Colorado Denver CO 1975-1994.

PALMER, Sara Elizabeth (NC) 108 W Farriss Ave, High Point NC 27262 **R H Trin Epis Ch Oxford OH 2016-** B Redhill, Surrey England 1957 d David & Elizabeth. BA Bristol U 1979; Tchr Cert King Alfreds Teachers Trng Coll 1980; MDiv VTS 2010. D 6/19/2010 P 1/15/2011 Bp Michael B Curry. m 2/22/1986 David J Palmer c 1. Asst to the R S Mary's Epis Ch High Point NC 2010-2016. holytrector@gmail.com

PALMGREN, Charles Leroy (At) 4482 Hunters Ter, Stone Mountain GA 30083 B Peoria IL 1933 s Elmer & Iantha. BA Drake U 1955; MA U Chi 1963; PhD Un Grad Sch 1972. D 10/2/1985 Bp William Carl Frey P 10/1/1986 Bp Peter J Lee. m 8/17/1957 Marian Robertson. Asst S Ptr's Epis Ch Arlington VA 1985-1988. Soc Of S Fran.

PALUMBO, Candace Ann (Alb) D 6/3/2017 Bp William Howard Love.

PANASEVICH, Eleanor Jones (Mass) 104 Oak St, Weston MA 02493 B New York NY 1941 d Albert & Eleanor. BA Smith 1963; MDiv EDS 1995. D 6/6/1998 Bp Barbara Clementine Harris P 5/29/1999 Bp M(Arvil) Thomas Shaw. m 4/22/1978 Leo Panasevich c 1. S Mich's Ch Milton MA 2001-2003; Asst R S Ptr's Epis Ch Cambridge MA 1999-2001, D 1998-1999.

PANG, Lisa A (Haw) 911 N Marine Corps Dr, Tamuning GU 96913 Guam B Seattle WA 1956 d Glen & Dolores. BA WA SU 1979. D 1/15/2009 Bp George Elden Packard. m 7/21/1979 Patrick Pang c 4.

PANG, Pui-Kong Thomas (Mass) 138 Tremont St, Boston MA 02111 **Exec Dir Epis Boston Chinese Serv 2005-; Exec Dir Grtr Boston Chinese Cmnty Serv Inc 2000-** B Hong Kong,HK 1954 s Chun & Gick. BA Chinese U HK 1982; MEd Boston Coll 1988; DMin Bos 1996. Trans 11/25/1998 as Priest Bp M(Arvil) Thomas Shaw. m 1/1/1983 Wendy Pik-Chay Luk c 2. Asiamerica

Mnstry The Cathd Ch Of S Paul Boston MA 2000-2013; Mssnr, Chinese Mnstrs Dio Massachusetts Boston MA 1996-2013.

PANKEY, Steven J (CGC) 1780 Abbey Loop, Foley AL 36535 **Chr Epis Ch Bowling Green KY 2017-** B Harvey IL 1980 s John & Patricia. BS Millersville U 2002; MDiv VTS 2007. D 6/9/2007 P 1/24/2008 Bp Nathan Dwight Baxter. m 3/1/2003 Catherine R Pankey c 2. Assoc R S Paul's Ch Foley AL 2007-2016.

PANNELL, Terry (Mass) 519 Commercial St, Provincetown MA 02657 **R The Ch Of S Mary Of The Harbor Provincetown MA 2006-** B Ripley MS 1956 s Clayton & Dollie. BS U of No Alabama 1985; MTS Van 2001; MDiv Sewanee: The U So, TS 2003. D 6/7/2003 P 3/6/2004 Bp D Avid Bruce Macpherson. S Clem's Ch New York NY 2006; Asst Dio Wstrn Louisiana Alexandria LA 2003-2006; Asst Ch of the H Cross Shreveport LA; P-in-c St Clem's Epis Ch New York City NY; R St. Mary of the Harbor Provincetown MA. Writer, "Rite of Passage," *The Spire*, Van Off of Cmncatn & Pub, 2004. ptownvicar50@gmail.com

PANTLE, Thomas Alvin (Dal) 617 Star St # 81, Bonham TX 75418 B Portland OR 1939 s Alvin & Marian. BS Portland St U 1963; LTh SWTS 1966. D 6/22/1966 Bp James Walmsley Frederic Carman P 1/1/1967 Bp William Evan Sanders. S Dunst's Ch Mineola TX 2002-2011; Vic All SS Ch Atlanta TX 1998-2002; Vic S Mart Epis Ch New Boston TX 1998-2002; Ch Of The H Trin Bonham TX 1995-1997; The Epis Ch Of The H Nativ Plano TX 1993-1994, 1969-1974, R 1969-1974; P-in-c S Edw's Ch Silverton OR 1989-1998; Dio Oregon Portland OR 1988-1991; S Mary's Ch Woodburn OR 1984-1988; Int Ch Of The Resurr Eugene OR 1982-1983; The Epis Ch Of The Gd Samar Corvallis OR 1981-1982; Int S Mary's Epis Ch Eugene OR 1980-1981; Non-par 1978-1980; R Ch Of The H Cross Paris TX 1974-1978; Vic Resurr Lenoir City TN 1966-1969; The Epis Ch Of The Resurr Franklin TN 1966-1969.

PANTON, Rosalyn Way (Ga) 2200 Birnam Pl, Augusta GA 30904 **D S Alb's Epis Ch Augusta GA 1994-** B Augusta GA 1942 d Raymond & Mary. BA Fisk U 1964. D 10/28/1994 Bp Henry Irving Louttit. c 2. Ord Of S Helena.

PAOLOZZI, Joann Lee (Oly) 211 Summit Ave E Apt 212, Seattle WA 98102 B Pendleton OR 1941 d Don & Alma. BEd Estrn Oregon U 1963; Cert Westcott Hse Cambridge 1987; MDiv CDSP 1989. D 6/27/1989 P 5/1/1990 Bp Robert Louis Ladehoff. c 1. Dio Olympia Seattle 2002-2003; S Matt Ch Tacoma WA 2001-2002; R S Tim's Epis Ch Chehalis WA 1992-2001; Asst S Mich And All Ang Ch Portland OR 1989-1991. Dok.

PAPANEK, Nicolette (Kan) 545 Greenup St #3, Covington KY 41011 **P-in-c S Alb's Epis Ch Of Bexley Columbus OH 2017-** B San Francisco CA 1951 d Victor & Winifred. BA Webster U 1985; MDiv SWTS 2002. D 4/6/2002 P 10/12/2002 Bp William Edward Smalley. Int Epis Ch Of The Resurr Oklahoma City OK 2015-2017; Int St Aug of Cbury Epis Ch Elkhorn NE 2014-2015; Int St Augustines Of Cbury Epis Mssn Elkhorn NE 2014; S Bede's Epis Ch Santa Fe NM 2012-2014; Int R Trin Ch Covington KY 2010-2012; Int Trin Ch Russellville KY 2009-2010; Int Chr Epis Ch Bowling Green KY 2007-2008; Int S Jn's Ch Wichita KS 2006-2007; Int S Thos The Apos Ch Overland Pk KS 2004-2006; Cur/Assoc R Gd Shpd Epis Ch Wichita KS 2002-2004.

PAPAZOGLAKIS, Elizabeth Brumfield (Alb) 912A Route 146, Clifton Park NY 12065 **Assoc R S Geo's Ch Clifton Pk NY 2017-; Asst S Mk's Ch Malone NY 2013-** B 1950 d John & JoAnn. BS LSU 1977; MA Nicholls St U 1990; MA Sacr Heart TS Hales Corners 2009. D 6/6/2009 P 5/1/2010 Bp Steven Andrew Miller. m 9/17/1977 Thomas W Pakis c 3. R S Jn's Ch Massena NY 2013-2015; Asst to the R Trin Ch Milwaukee WI 2010-2013; Consult Chapl ProHealthCare 2009-2013; D Dio Milwaukee Milwaukee WI 2009-2010; Mus Dir S Barth's Ch Pewaukee WI 2009; Zion Epis Ch Oconomowoc WI 2002-2007.

PAPAZOGLAKIS, Thomas W (Alb) 912a Route 146, Clifton Park NY 12065 **R S Geo's Ch Clifton Pk NY 2017-** B Brooklyn NY 1955 s James & Janis. BA LSU 1978; MBA Tul 1989; MDiv Nash 2002. D 12/27/2001 Bp Charles Edward Jenkins III P 6/30/2002 Bp Roger John White. m 9/17/1977 Elizabeth Brumfield c 3. Asst S Jn's Ch Massena NY 2013-2015; R S Mk's Ch Malone NY 2013-2015; P-in-c/Vic S Barth's Ch Pewaukee WI 2002-2012. Helen S. Appelberg Vision in Ldrshp Awd Cmnty of Hope Intl 2009. fr.tomp@gmail.com

PAPE, Cynthia Dale (Mass) 1 Linden St, Quincy MA 02170 B Flemington NJ 1956 d Richard & Beverly. NEU; AA Roger Willliams Coll. D 6/6/2009 Bp M(Arvil) Thomas Shaw. m 8/13/2004 Anne Campbell Moore.

PAPILE, Jim (Va) 3241 Brush Dr, Falls Church VA 22042 **Trnr/Mentor Educ for Ministrty 1996-** B Chelsea MA 1951 s James & Phyllis. U of New Hampshire 1971; BS Geo Mason U 1989; MDiv VTS 1992. D 6/13/1992 Bp Robert Poland Atkinson P 12/1/1992 Bp Peter J Lee. m 10/7/1978 Barbara Kay Evans c 5. Dioc Com of the Priesthood Dio Virginia 2000-2017; R S Anne's Epis Ch Reston VA 1999-2016; Epis EvangES Arlington VA 1998-1999; S Patricks Ch Falls Ch VA 1994-1999; Dioc Com On Educ Dio Virginia 1992-1995; Asst to R Imm Ch-On-The-Hill Alexandria VA 1992-1994. Treas EES 1997-2016.

PAPINI, Heber Mauricio (Okla) 9100 E 21st St, Tulsa OK 74129 B Cumari Goias BR 1950 s Uberdon & Maria. BA Fach Brazil Br 1981; MDiv Epis TS of the SW 1993. D 10/28/1995 Bp Leopoldo Jesus Alard P 5/1/1996 Bp Claude

Edward Payne. c 4. R S Ptr's Ch Tulsa OK 2013-2016; Dio Oklahoma Oklahoma City OK 2012; Nuestra Senora De Guadalupe Waukegan IL 2010-2011; Trin Ch Houston TX 2004; R S Ptr's Ch Pasadena TX 2000-2009; Vic S Alb's Ch Houston TX 1995-2000; The Great Cmsn Fndt Houston TX 1995-2000.

PAPPAS, Christopher A (RI) 211 Galland Close NW, Edmonton AB T5T 6P6 Canada B Plainfield NJ 1962 BS Trin Hartford CT 1980; PhD U of Connecticut 1992; MDiv Ya Berk 2004; DAS Ya Berk 2004. D 12/13/2003 Bp Keith Whitmore. m 5/16/1970 Elisabeth J Thompson c 4. R Chr Ch Westerly RI 2008-2010; Serv Angl Ch of Can 2004-2008. rector@holytrinity.ab.ca

PAPPAS III, Jim (At) 735 University Ave, Sewanee TN 37383 **St. Matt's Epis Ch Madison AL 2016-; Asstg P Sis of St Mary Sewanee TN 2011-** B Belleville IL 1973 s James & Rose. Quincy U; Althoff Cath HS 1991; BA McKendree U 1997; MDiv Sewanee: The U So, TS 2005. D 12/20/2008 P 2/10/2010 Bp J Neil Alexander. m 5/25/2008 Jennifer Davis Michael c 1. Int S Mary Magd Ch Fayetteville TN 2014-2016; P-in-c Trin Ch Winchester TN 2010.

PARACHINI, David Charles (Ct) 42 Blue Jay Dr, Northford CT 06472 B Philadelphia PA 1942 s Harold & Ruth. BA U of Pennsylvania 1965; BTh Hur CA 1968; STM Andover Newton TS 1969. Trans 12/1/1970 Bp John Melville Burgess. m 5/24/1965 Mary Parachini c 1. Int S Steph's Ch E Haddam CT 2011-2012; R Gr Epis Ch Windsor CT 2001-2011; Int S Andr's Ch Madison CT 1998-2001; Dio Connecticut Meriden CT 1997-2005; Int Imm S Jas Par Derby CT 1997-1998; Int Chr Ch Guilford CT 1995-1997; Litchfield Hills Reg Mnstry Bridgewater CT 1991-1995; Area Mssnr Litchfield Hills Reg Mnstry Bridgewater CT 1991-1995; Int St Johns Ch W Hartford CT 1990-1991; Ya Berk New Haven CT 1986-1990; Asst Dn Ya Berk New Haven CT 1986-1990; St Geo's Epis Ch Minneapolis MN 1986; Int S Jas On The Pkwy Minneapolis MN 1984-1985; Minnesota Epis Fndt Inc Minneapolis MN 1981-1986; Int S Clem's Ch S Paul MN 1981-1983; Int S Matt's Ch S Paul MN 1979-1980; Gr Ch Newton MA 1970-1972. Auth, "Prog In a Cnty Jail"; Auth, "A Guide to Human Serv for Sch Managers". Fllshp Natl Educ Plcy 1976.

PARADINE, Philip James (Va) 118 Monte Vista Ave., Charlottesville VA 22903 B London UK 1946 s Albert. BS Lon GB 1967; MA U of Ottawa 1976; MDiv VTS 1997; DMin SWTS 2003. Trans 4/4/1998 Bp Peter J Lee. m 2/5/1994 Carter Kimsey c 4. P-in-c S Paul's Epis Ch Port Townsend WA 2005-2006; Vic S Lk's Simeon Charlottesville VA 2003-2012; Int Trin Epis Ch Martinsburg WV 2003-2005; R S Thos Epis Christiansbrg VA 1999-2003; Asst R Emm Epis Ch Alexandria VA 1997-1999.

PARADISE, Gene Hooper (Ga) 10 Iron Bound Pl NW, Atlanta GA 30318 **Ret Georgia 2012-** B Nashville TN 1936 s Ira & Lois. BA Van 1958; MDiv Epis TS in Kentucky 1983. D 1/22/1983 P 10/28/1983 Bp George Paul Reeves. Assoc for Sr. Pstr Care S Lk's Epis Ch Atlanta GA 2002-2011; Cur The Ch Of Our Sav Atlanta GA 2000-2001; Dio Georgia Savannah GA 1987-1995; R S Mich's Ch Waynesboro GA 1984-1999; Asst R S Thos Ch Savannah GA 1983-1984.

PARADISE, Scott Ilsley (Mass) 305 Badger Terrace, Bedford MA 01730 **Died 9/13/2015** B Winchester MA 1929 s Scott & Alma. BA Ya 1950; BD EDS 1953. D 6/6/1953 Bp Norman B Nash P 6/13/1954 Bp The Bishop Of Sheffield. m 12/20/1958 Jeanne McKay c 2. Ret 1994-2015; Dio Massachusetts Boston MA 1978-1994; Chapl MIT Cambridge MA 1978-1994; Boston Indstrl Mssn Cambridge MA 1965-1978; Founding Dir Boston Indstrl Mssn Cambridge MA 1965-1978; Assoc Dir Indstrl Mssn Detroit MI 1957-1965; Sheffield Indstrl Mssn Sheffield Engl 1953-1957. Auth, "Unequal Battle," *MA Audubon*, 1969; Auth, "Vandal Ideology," *The Nation*, 1969; Auth, "Detroit Indstrl Mssn: A Personal Narrative," Harper & Row, 1968. EPF; ESMHE 1978-1994.

PARAISON, Edwin Mardochee (DR) Calle Tony Mota Ricart #16, Box 132, Barahona Dominican Republic B Cap Haitien HT 1962 s Jean & Yolande. D 10/26/1986 P 12/1/1987 Bp Telesforo A Isaac. m 8/26/1990 Angie Dinorah Polanco Monegro. Dio The Dominican Republic (Iglesia Epis Dominicana) Gazcue Santo Domingo 1986-1994; Mssy. Anti-Slavery Awd 1994; Haitian Consul In Dominican Republic.

PARAISON, Maud (Hai) PO Box 5826, Fort Lauderdale FL 33310 B 1945 d Enoch & Madeleine. Dioc Sch for Mnstry; BA Florida Intl U; AA Miami-Dade Cmnty Coll; So Florida Theol Cntr for Theol Stds. D 5/26/1994 P 12/19/1998 Bp Calvin Onderdonk Schofield Jr. c 4. Ch Of The Intsn Ft Lauderdale FL 2000-2008; H Sacr Hollywood FL 1999-2000; St Paul et Les Martyrs D'Haiti Miami FL 1994-1998.

PARAN, William John (Mich) 435 S Gulfstream Ave Unit 1005, Sarasota FL 34236 **Ret 1994-** B Springfield MA 1928 s John & Marion. BS U of Detroit Mercy 1952; MDiv Bex Sem 1968. D 6/29/1968 P 12/30/1968 Bp Archie H Crowley. m 7/26/2003 Patricia Ann Paran. Int S Thos Epis Ch Battle Creek MI 1994; S Andr's Ch Grand Rapids MI 1991-1992; Int S Paul's Epis Ch Port Huron MI 1990-1991; S Paul's Epis Ch Lansing MI 1985-1991; R S Jas Ch Piqua OH 1974-1985; Assoc R S Jn's Epis Ch Midland MI 1968-1974. Life Mem MI Assn CPA's.

PARDINGTON III, George Palmer (Ore) 3033 Ne 32nd Ave, Portland OR 97212 **Assoc St.Steph's Ch 2004-; Ret 1997-** B Mobile AL 1939 s George & Mary. BA W&L 1961; MDiv GTS 1966; PhD Grad Theol Un 1972; STM GTS 1988. D 6/29/1966 Bp Iveson Batchelor Noland P 5/11/1967 Bp Girault M Jones. m

6/7/1965 Anne S Pardington c 2. S Marg's Epis Ch Marylhurst OR 2001-2003; Chapl Assoc S Steph's Epis Par Portland OR 1995-1997; Portland Metro Epis Campus Mnstry Portland OR 1992-1997; Epis Par Of S Jn The Bapt Portland OR 1985-1991; Chapl and Dir Portland Metro Epis Campus Mnstry Portland OR 1993-1997; Dio Oregon Portland OR 1978-1984; Vic Chr Epis Ch Danville VA 1974-1978; Ch Of The Epiph Danville VA 1974-1978; Chapl/ Rel Tchr Chatham Hall Sch Chatham VA 1972-1974; 1968-1972; Cur and Chapl Gr Memi Hammond LA 1966-1968. Auth, *Rel Experience and Process Theol*, Paulist, 1976; Auth, "Transcendance & Models of God," *ATR*; Auth, "H Ghost is Dead, H Sprt Lives," *ATR*; Auth, "Theol & Sprtl Renwl," *ATR*. ARIL 1985-1998; ESMHE 1978-1998; SVHE 1995-1998; Soc of S Jn the Evang 1985. Fllshp ECF 1968; Phi Beta Kappa 1960.

PARDO ARCINIEGAS, Angel Maria (Colom) c/o Diocese of Colombia, Cra 6 No. 49-85 Piso 2, Bogota, BDC Colombia **Iglesia Epis En Colombia Bogota 2016-** B Colombia 1961 s Efren & Rosario. Lic Filosofia y Teologia Universidad Mariana 1987; Teologo Los Sagrados Corazones 1989. Rec 8/27/1989 as Priest Bp Francisco Jose Duque-Gomez. m 5/5/2011 Liliana R Caipe c 4.

PARDOE III, Edward Devon (Ct) St Barnabas Episcopal Church, 954 Lake Ave, Greenwich CT 06831 **R S Barn Epis Ch Greenwich CT 2012-** B Abington PA 1956 s Edward & Edith. BS Trin 1978; MDiv UTS 2005; STM GTS 2010. D 3/7/2009 P 9/12/2009 Bp Mark Sean Sisk. m 4/26/1986 Helen Mahoney Pardoe c 4. Asst Gr Epis Ch New York NY 2010-2012. rectorstb@optonline.net

PARHAM, Alfred Philip (RG) 6148 Los Robles Dr, El Paso TX 79912 **Ret 1996-** B Fort Benning GA 1930 s Alfred & Elisa. BA Ya 1952; MDiv Epis TS of the SW 1963; Coll of Preachers 1972; DMin SFTS 1983. D 6/30/1963 Bp Richard Earl Dicus P 1/8/1964 Bp Everett H Jones. m 3/7/1953 Ruth A Parham c 3. R S Alb's Ch El Paso TX 2007-2011; Int H Sprt Epis Ch El Paso TX 2005-2006; Int S Jn's Epis Ch Alamogordo NM 2004-2005; Vic S Brendan's Ch El Paso TX 1997-2000; Asst S Fran On The Hill El Paso TX 1991-1994; Chapl Pstr Counslg Serv Of El Paso El Paso TX 1990-1995; R S Steph's Epis Ch Wimberley TX 1988-1989; Int Ch Of The Resurr Windcrest TX 1987-1988; Chapl S Mary Hall San Antonio TX 1983-1988; Asst S Paul's Epis Ch San Antonio TX 1982-1988; R S Thos Epis Ch And Sch San Antonio TX 1966-1981; P-in-c S Tim's Ch Cotulla TX 1965-1966; P-in-c All SS Epis Ch Pleasanton TX 1963-1966; Chapl to the Ret Dio The Rio Grande Albuquerque 2009-2011; Pres, Epicopal Recovery Mnstrs Dio W Texas 1984-1986; Del to Texas Conferences of Ch Dio W Texas 1968-1981. Auth, "Feeling Free," Xlulon, 2008; Auth, "Feeling Free," *Emotional Recovery*, Xulon, 2008; Auth, "Letting God," *Meditations in Recovery*, Harper'S, 1987. Yale Club Pres San Antonio Tx 1975.

PARINI, Barbara Dennison Biggs (Mass) 2957 Barbara St., Ashland OR 97520 B Brooklyn NY 1931 d Thomas & Florence. AA Centenary Coll 1951; BA S Thos Aquinas Grand Rapids MI 1984; MDiv VTS 1988. D 6/11/1988 P 2/26/1989 Bp Lyman Cunningham Ogilby. m 1/24/1953 Joseph Anthony Parini c 3. Assoc S Mary's Epis Ch Bonita Sprg FL 2002-2004, Asst 2000-2001; Vic Chr Ch Sag Harbor NY 1996-1999; Vic S Dav's Epis Mssn Pepperell MA 1993-1994; All SS Ch Chelmsford MA 1991-1992; Cur S Andr's Ch Grand Rapids MI 1988-1991. Oblate Ord Julian of Norwich 1988-2006.

PARISH, Nurya Love (WMich) 1025 3 Mile Rd NE, Grand Rapids MI 49505 **Ch of the H Sprt Belmont MI 2016-; Mem, Dioc Coun Dio Wstrn Michigan Kalamazoo MI 2013-, Mem, Bp Search Team 2012-2013** B Las Vegas NV 1971 d John & Sherrill. BA U of Redlands 1992; MDiv Harvard DS 1996; Cert SWTS 2011. D 5/23/2011 P 12/3/2011 Bp Robert R Gepert. m 3/4/2000 David Parish c 2. Assoc S Andr's Ch Grand Rapids MI 2011-2016, Sem 2010-2011, Chld's Mnstry Dir. 2009-2010; Assoc Min Fountain St Ch Grand Rapids Michigan 2002-2006; New Cong Min Epiph Cmnty Ch Fenton Michigan 1997-2001; Chapl Wake Forest Food Faith & Rel Ldrshp Intensive 2015.

PARK, Ciritta Boyer (WA) 6201 Dunrobbin Dr, Bethesda MD 20816 **The Ch Of The Redeem Beth MD 2015-** B South Bend IN 1959 d Byron & Betty. BA Pur 1980; D Formation Prog 1989; EFM 1990; MDiv Bex Sem 2006. D 11/9/1990 Bp William Grant Black P 6/24/2006 Bp Kenneth Lester Price. m 8/16/1980 Stephen William Park c 1. Assoc R S Pat's Epis Ch Dublin OH 2006-2015, D 2003-2006; Pres C. B. Pk & Assoc LLC 1995-2006; D S Paul's Ch Columbus OH 1992-2003; D S Steph's Epis Ch And U Columbus OH 1990-1992; Dep Dir Assn. on Higher Educ and Disabil 1988-1995; Conv Mgr NEAC Washington DC 1995-2000. Auth, "Easter Vigil Sermon," *Sermons that Wk: Prophetic Preaching*, Epis Preaching Fndt, 2004; co-Auth, "Accessible Meetings & Conventions," *same*, Assn. on Higher Educ. & Disabil, 2002. Amer Soc of Assn Executives 1988-2003; Integrity/Intl 1991; NEAC 1991-2000; NAAD 1989-2005. Auth of the Year Profsnl Conv Mgmt Assn. 1998; Best Educ Pub Amer Soc of Assn. Executives 1992; Best FIrst Auction Publ Broadcasting Serv 1984.

PARK, Cynthia B (At) 13560 Cogburn Road, Milton GA 30004 **Asst Gr Epis Ch Gainesville GA 2014-; The Ch of S Clem Alexandria VA 2008-; D H Comf Epis Ch 2006-; D Gr Epis Ch Mt. Meigs AL 2004-** B Dallas TX 1952 d Forest & Richard. BA S Leo U Norfolk VA 1989; PhD Cath U 2000; MS Troy U 2000; MTS VTS 2008. D 10/30/2004 Bp Henry Nutt Parsley Jr P 6/11/2012 Bp Ted Gulick Jr. m 4/21/2001 John J Park c 4. S Aid's Epis Ch Milton GA 2012-2014; Gr Epis Ch Pike Road AL 2004-2006. cynthia@gracechurchgainesville.org

PARK III, Howard Franklin (Mo) 14133 Baywood Village Dr, Chesterfield MO 63017 **Asstg Cler Ch Of The Trsfg Lake S Louis MO 2002-; Ret 1998-** B Philadelphia PA 1933 s Howard & Mary. BA Ya 1955; MDiv VTS 1962. D 6/16/1962 P 1/23/1963 Bp George Leslie Cadigan. m 3/31/1975 Helen Park c 3. S Mart's Ch Ellisville MO 1965-1998; Cur Chr Ch Cathd S Louis MO 1962-1965; Stndg Com Dio Missouri S Louis MO 1977-1988.

PARK, John Hayes (Hond) 520 Park Rd, Ambridge PA 15003 B New Brighton PA 1945 s Robert & Jennie. TESM; BA Geneva Coll 1967; AM Duke 1970; MDiv Epis TS of the SW 1984. D 6/2/1984 Bp Alden Moinet Hathaway P 7/2/1985 Bp Sam Byron Hulsey. m 5/29/1976 Susan Delgado-Park c 2. Dn Angl Cathd of the Gd Shpd Lima Peru 2004-2013; SAMS Ambridge PA 1995-2010; Vic Trinidad Trinidad Honduras 1991-2003; Vic Visitación BVM Concepción del Norte Honduras 1991-2001; Vic H Sprt Tela Honduras 1991-1999; Vic San Lucas Delicias Del Norte & Cristo Rey Exitos De Anch 1991-1996; Archd Dio Honduras San Pedro Sula 1990-2003, Dn of Omoa and Puerto Cortés 1987-1990, Archd 1991-2003; Exec Coun Appointees New York NY 1985-1994; Vic San Marcos San Marcos & 7 other Ch in Omoa Honduras 1985-1991; Int Ch of the Heav Rest Abilene Abilene TX 1985. Cn Buen Pstr Cathd, San Pedro Sula 2000.

PARK, Patricia (NCal) D 8/13/2016 Bp Barry Leigh Beisner.

PARK, Stephen Radcliffe (NH) 4060 Barrows Point Rd, Nisswa MN 56468 B Washington DC 1947 s Edward & Betty. BS Shimer Coll; MDiv VTS 1980. D 10/21/1973 P 11/1/1974 Bp John Alfred Baden. m 2/29/1992 Denise Zapffe Park c 1. Kairos Sprtl Dir 1991-1994; Prison Mnstry 1991-1994; Ch Fund Raising 1989-1994; Non-par 1984-1994; Ch Computer Consult 1984-1989; Curs Secy 1981-1984; Vic Faith Epis Ch Merrimack NH 1981-1984; Cur Ch Of The H Comf Vienna VA 1974-1976; Cur Chr Ch Alexandria VA 1973-1974; Alco & Drug Abuse Com; Coordntr Of The Merrimack Interfaith Coun; Dn Of The Sthrn Convoc.

PARK, Theodore A(llen) (Minn) 19 S 1st St Apt B2208, Minneapolis MN 55401 **Int S Anne's Epis Ch S Paul MN 1996-** B Saint Louis MO 1951 s Alvin & Jean. BA U MN 1975; MA S Cathr U 1991; DAS GTS 1993; DMin Untd TS 2010. D 6/24/1993 Bp Robert Marshall Anderson P 2/21/1994 Bp Sanford Zangwill Kaye Hampton. m 8/14/2015 Dennis Vernon Christian. R Chr Ch Red Wing MN 2015, 2010-2011; Geth Ch Minneapolis MN 2013-2015; S Andr's By The Lake Duluth MN 2012-2013; S Jas On The Pkwy Minneapolis MN 2004-2009, R 2002-2003, P 2000-2001; Int S Alb's Epis Ch Edina MN 1998-2000; Chair, Liturg Com Dio Minnesota Minneapolis MN 1996-2002; Assoc St Dav's Epis Ch Minnetonka MN 1995-1996. Cntr for Progressive Chrsnty. Phi Beta Kappa 1975.

PARKE, John Holbrook (WMass) 213 Reeds Landing, Springfield MA 01109 **Died 3/15/2017** B Amherst MA 1916 s Hervey & Ethel. BA Pr 1938; MDiv GTS 1942. D 6/7/1942 P 2/3/1943 Bp William A Lawrence. m 7/10/1982 Eleanor Parke c 4. Asst S Dav's Ch Feeding Hills MA 1989-2001; Int All SS Ch So Hadley MA 1986-1987; Ret 1982-2017; Asst The Falls Ch Epis Falls Ch VA 1980-1982; R S Steph's Ch Heathsville VA 1978-1980; Vic Chr Ch Rochdale MA 1971-1978; R S Barn On The Desert Scottsdale AZ 1965-1970; R St Jas the Great Epis Ch Newport Bch CA 1955-1965; R Gr Ch Norwood MA 1952-1955; R S Jn's Ch Worcester MA 1946-1952; Chapl US-Army 1944-1946; S Andr's Ch Turners Fall MA 1942-1944; Asst S Jas' Ch Greenfield MA 1942-1944. Auth, "Manual of Chr Healing"; Auth, "Cler Manual for Chr Healing". Natl Wrdn, Ord of S Lk 1971-1978; Ord of S Lk 1952.

PARKER, Andrew David (Tex) 11838 Riverview Dr, Houston TX 77077 **Emm Ch Houston TX 2016-** B Bartlesville OK 1957 s Harry & Phyllis. Bachelor's Texas Tech U 1978; Mstr's Texas A&M U 1984; MDiv Ya Berk 1989. D 6/9/1989 P 12/11/1989 Bp Sam Byron Hulsey. m 10/17/1987 Elizabeth Parker c 3. R S Tim's Epis Ch Lake Jackson TX 2001-2016; Assoc S Andr's Epis Ch Amarillo TX 1993-2001; Asst Ch of the Heav Rest Abilene Abilene TX 1989-1993. Auth, "Keeping The Promise," Morehouse, 1994. Bd No Amer Assn For The Catechumenate 1996-2006.

PARKER, Betsee (Va) 110 W Franklin St, Richmond VA 23220 B Minneapolis MN 1951 d Owen & Betsy. BA Wellesley Coll 1982; MDiv Harvard DS 1985. D 6/11/1988 Bp David Elliot Johnson P 4/1/1993 Bp Barbara Clementine Harris. m 3/17/1984 Michael Rod Zalutsky c 2. S Jas' Epis Ch Leesburg VA 1994-1998; Emm Ch Middleburg VA 1994; Trin Ch Fuquay Varina NC 1988-1996.

PARKER, Carol Ann (EO) 9333 Nw Winters Ln, Prineville OR 97754 **Non-par 1992-** B Glascow MT 1944 d Lowell & Dorothy. Cntrl Oregon Cmnty Coll Bend OR. D 3/15/1992 P 9/5/1992 Bp Rustin Ray Kimsey. m 8/12/1961 Jerold Corwin Parker.

PARKER, David Clinton (Ind) 224 Davis Ave, Elkins WV 26241 B Springfield MA 1949 s Ward & Helen. BA Wilmington Coll 1980; MDiv GTS 1983. D 6/4/1983 P 12/14/1983 Bp William Grant Black. m 6/29/2001 Connie S Townsend c 3. R S Matt's Ch Indianapolis IN 1991-1997; S Barn Bridgeport WV 1990-1991; R Ch Of The Heav Rest Princeton WV 1985-1990; Asst S Mk's Epis Ch Columbus OH 1983-1985.

PARKER, Dennis J (Ore) 4320 SW Corbett Ave, Unit # 317, Portland OR 97239 **Campus Chapl Portland St U Portland OR 2009-** B Morristown NJ 1952 s Thomas & Loretta. BFA Emerson Coll 1982; MDiv CDSP 2003. D 6/22/2002 P 1/11/2003 Bp Robert Louis Ladehoff. m 1/17/2014 Michael S Sagun. R S Steph's Epis Par Portland OR 2008-2016, 2004-2008; Ch Of The Resurr Eugene OR 2004-2008; Supply Chapl Providence Hlth Systems Portland OR 2003-2006; Cur Chr Ch Par Lake Oswego OR 2002-2004; Assoc Legacy Gd Samar Hosp Portland OR 2001-2004; GC Del Dio Oregon Portland OR 2010-2012, COM Chair 2010-. revdennisj@comcast.net

PARKER, Donald Harry (Mass) 28 Cambridge Cir., Smithfield RI 02917 **Assoc S Thos Ch Greenville RI 2015-; Chapl, R.I. OSL 2014-** B Bridgeport CT 1943 s Albert & Mildred. BA Cntrl Connecticut St U 1965; MDiv Ya Berk 1968; MS Sthrn Connecticut St U 1978. D 6/11/1968 Bp Walter H Gray P 3/1/1969 Bp John Henry Esquirol. m 8/21/1965 Carol A Parker c 2. Int Emm Epis Ch Cumberland RI 2010-2013; Int S Jn's Ch Ashton RI 2009-2010; Int S Mary's Ch Warwick RI 2006-2008; Int S Ptr's Ch Dartmouth MA 2004-2006; Int S Jas Epis Ch At Woonsocket Woonsocket RI 2001-2004; Int S Paul's Ch Brockton MA 1999-2001; R Ch Of The H Nativ Seekonk MA 1986-1998; S Lk's Epis Ch E Greenwich RI 1981-1985; Assoc S Lk's Warwick RI 1981-1985; S Jn's Ch Sodus NY 1979-1981; Chapl U Of Bridgeport CT 1976-1978; Chr Ch Trumbull CT 1974-1979; R Chr Tashua CT 1974-1978; Vic Chr Harwinton CT 1970-1974; S Ptr's Ch Plymouth CT 1970-1974; Cur Trin Ch Wethersfield CT 1968-1970.

PARKER, Elizabeth (Tex) 200 Oyster Creek Dr, Lake Jackson TX 77566 **Palmer Memi Ch Houston TX 2016-** B Bellefonte PA 1954 d William & Betty. BA Penn 1976; MDiv Ya Berk 1988. D 6/11/1988 Bp Paul Moore Jr P 2/18/1989 Bp William Bradford Hastings. m 10/17/1987 Andrew David Parker c 3. Assoc R S Tim's Epis Ch Lake Jackson TX 2001-2016; S Andr's Epis Ch Amarillo TX 1993-2001; Chapl St. Andr's Epis Sch Amarillo TX 1993-2000; Dn Dio NW Texas Lubbock TX 1990-1991; Ch of the Heav Rest Abilene Abilene TX 1989-1993; D Chr Ch Greenwich CT 1988-1989. Catechesis of the Gd Shpd 1993.

PARKER, Gary Joseph (LI) 9 Barrow St. #3B, New York NY 10014 **P-in-c S Steph's Ch Prt Washington NY 2015-; Int S Paul's Epis Ch Glen Cover WY 2006-** B Potsdam NY 1948 s Joseph & Florence. BA SUNY 1971; MDiv GTS 1975. D 6/15/1974 P 12/16/1974 Bp Wilbur Emory Hogg Jr. c 1. Int Gr Ch Morganton NC 2013-2015; Ch Of S Mich The Archangel Colorado Spg CO 2012-2013; S Ann's Ch Sayville NY 2009-2011; Int S Paul's Ch Glen Cove NY 2006-2009; Epis Ch Cntr New York NY 2004-2006; Dir of VA, Healthcare, Prison & Maritime Chaplaincies The Epis Ch Cntr 2004-2006; Chapl Off Of Bsh For ArmdF New York NY 1983-2004; R Trin Ch Whitehall NY 1982-1983; Chapl USN 1980-2005; The Epis Ch Of The Cross Ticonderoga NY 1977-1982; Cur S Andr And H Comm Ch So Orange NJ 1974-1977. Third Ord Franciscan Soc 1995.

PARKER, James Frank (HB) 2409 Cheshire Woods Rd, Toledo OH 43617 B Omaha NE 1946 s Frank & Viola. BS U of Nebraska 1983; MDiv Sewanee: The U So, TS 1987. D 8/24/1987 Bp James Daniel Warner P 5/1/1988 Bp Arthur Williams Jr. m 6/10/1967 Wanda Marie Eddy. All SS Epis Ch Toledo OH 1991; All SS Ch Mcalester OK 1990-1991; Asst S Andr's Epis Ch Toledo OH 1987-1989.

PARKER JR, James N (Ga) 402 E 46th St, Savannah GA 31405 **R S Geo's Epis Ch Savannah GA 2004-, D 1997-1998** B Camp Kilmer NJ 1948 s James & Inez. Sewanee: The U So, TS; BA Augusta St U 1970; MS Bos 1975. D 8/24/1982 Bp George Paul Reeves P 11/16/1998 Bp Henry Irving Louttit. m 10/23/1999 Leslie D Parker c 3. Vic St Patricks Ch Pooler GA 1998-2000; D in Charge S Eliz's Epis Ch Richmond Hill GA 1994-1997; D The Collgt Ch of St Paul the Apos Savannah GA 1992-1994, D 1982-1991; D S Ptr's Epis Ch Savannah GA 1990-1992; D S Thos Ch Savannah GA 1986-1989. CBS 1982.

PARKER, Jesse Leon Anthony (Md) 105 W 6th St, New Castle DE 19720 **Hon Vic S Paul's Par Baltimore MD 1991-, Cur 1981-1991** B Saint Augustine FL 1951 s Jesse & Verna. BA S Mary TS & U 1974; MDiv GTS 1981. D 10/17/1981 P 6/28/1982 Bp David Keller Leighton Sr. m Gene Sartori c 1. Mem Dioc Coun 2013-2015; Mem Dioc Liturg Com 2011-2015; Mem Dioc COM 2010-2014; Chapl Maryland Defence Force 2009-2016; Steer Comm Rel Cltn For Civil Mar Equality Equality Maryland 2005-2013; R S Jn's Ch Huntingdon Baltimore MD 1991-2016; Bd Mem Prisoner's Aid Assn of Maryland 1983-1991; Secy OGS 1981-1991; Asst Chapl Ch Hm & Hosp Baltimore MD 1981-1984; Dioc Coun Dio Maryland Baltimore MD 2013-2015, Mem, Com on Liturg and Mus 2010-2015, Dioc COM 2010-2014, Dioc Ecum Off 2010-2014, Mem, Com on Aging 1991-1994. GAS 1979; OGS 1981-1992; Ord of S Ben (Confrater) 1986; SocMary 1989; SocOLW 2009.

PARKER, Mark (NCal) D 8/27/2016 P 4/8/2017 Bp Barry Leigh Beisner.

PARKER, Matthew Ross (Dal) **S Jos's Par Buena Pk CA 2005-** B Plano TX 1979 MDiv Nash 2005. D 6/4/2005 Bp James Monte Stanton. Ch Of The Gd Shpd Dallas TX 2013-2014; Cur Ch Of The Annunc Lewisville TX 2005-2006.

PARKER, Robert Coleman (Tex) 832 W Jones St, Livingston TX 77351 B Philadelphia PA 1936 s William & Mary. Epis TS of the SW. D 6/12/1972 Bp Richard Earl Dicus P 12/1/1972 Bp Harold Cornelius Gosnell. R S Paul's Epis Ch Orange TX 1998-2003; S Lk's Ch Livingston TX 1993-1998; The Great Cmsn Fndt Houston TX 1993-1997; Non-par 1984-1993; Asst All SS Epis Ch Austin TX 1977-1984; Asst S Barth's Ch Corpus Christi TX 1974-1977; Vic Ch Of Our Sav Aransas Pass TX 1972-1974.

PARKER, Ronald Mark (FtW) 200 N Bailey Ave, Fort Worth TX 76107 B Kansas City MO 1952 s Robert & Mary. D 10/22/1999 Bp Roger John White. m 10/24/1987 Denise Dawn Rodenhause. All SS' Epis Sch Of Ft Worth Ft Worth TX 2000-2004; All SS' Epis Ch Ft Worth TX 2000.

PARKER, Ronald Wilmar (Pa) 254 Williams Rd, Bryn Mawr PA 19010 B Philadelphia PA 1938 s Charles & Nydia. BA Combs Mus 1962; BMusEd Combs Mus 1975; MA GTS 1978; MPS NYTS 1980; DMin GTF 1986; DMin U of Notre Dame 1986; Cert Oxf GB 2002. D 6/2/1979 P 12/1/1979 Bp Albert Wiencke Van Duzer. m 4/20/1963 Josephine Parker c 1. Exec Comm Merion Dnry Ardmore PA 2000-2003; Emer Chr Epis Ch Villanova PA 1992-2009; Adj Prof Pstr care St. Sophia Orth Sem 1985-1989; R S Paul's Epis Ch Bound Brook NJ 1980-1992; Dn Nthrn Convoc Watchung NJ 1980-1983; Cur S Lk's Epis Ch Metuchen NJ 1979-1980; Dioc Nomin Com Dio Pennsylvania Philadelphia PA 1998. Auth, "GTF Yearbook," *(sermons)*, GTF, 1986; Auth, "Living Ch," *(Var mag arts)*, 1986; Auth, "St. Jn's Mass," *S Jn's Mass*, 1976. CBS; Ord of S Lk 1979; Ord of S Lk - Chapl. Outstanding Life Achievement in Mus & Mnstry Abraham Lincoln HS 2005.

PARKER JR OHC, Roy Earl (Mass) Holy Cross Monastery, West Park NY 12493 B Los Angeles CA 1933 s Roy & Amy. BS MIT 1955; MDiv EDS 1964; STM Jesuit TS 1981. D 6/20/1964 P 1/25/1967 Bp Anson Phelps Stokes Jr. Chapl Manhattan Plaza AIDS Proj NYC 1989-1992; Serv Ch in Jamaica 1971-1972; Stff Dio Massachusetts Boston MA 1970-1971; Liturg Com Dio New York New York NY 1985-1992. OHC 1972; Soc of S Jn the Evang 1958-1970.

PARKER, Stephanie Eve (Oly) 4805 NE 45th St, Seattle WA 98105 **Chr Epis Ch Sparta NC 2016-; R S Steph's Epis Ch Seattle WA 2010-** B Anchorage AK 1962 d Paul & Cora. MDiv VTS 2003. D 2/8/2003 P 8/14/2003 Bp Henry Irving Louttit. Assoc S Paul In The Desert Palm Sprg CA 2005-2009; Vic Ch Of The Gd Shpd Swainsboro GA 2003-2005.

PARKER JR, Stephen Dwight (Ct) 4607 Chandlers Forde, Sarasota FL 34235 B New York NY 1940 s Stephen & Elizabeth. BA W&M 1964; MDiv Ya Berk 1967. D 6/14/1967 P 2/5/1968 Bp Albert Ervine Swift. m 8/2/1985 Barbara F Parker c 2. S Jn's Epis Ch Fishers Island NY 1997-2008; Chapl Salisbury Sch 1994-2005; Asst R S Jas The Fisherman Islamorada FL 1993-1994; R S Matt's Epis Ch Wilton CT 1978-1993; R Trin Epis Ch Collinsville CT 1969-1978; Cur S Lk's Par Darien CT 1967-1969; Exec Coun Dio Connecticut Meriden CT 1988-1990, COM 1982-1987. Auth, "Bridges, Reconnecting Sci and Faith," Tate Pub, 2012. Endowed Chapl Chair Salisbury Sch class of 59 2004; Sr Class Awd Salisbury Sch 1995; Epis Evang Fndt Sermon Prchng Prize 1992.

PARKER, Susan Dozier (Az) D 6/10/2017 Bp Kirk Stevan Smith.

PARKER, William Curtis (NJ) 200 Armitage Court, Lincoln University PA 19352 **R S Andr's Ch Louisville KY 2013-; Bd Mem Int Mnstry in the Epis Ch 2012-; Mem Int Mnstry Ntwk (IMN) 2010-; COM Dio Kentucky Louisville KY 2014-** B Seaford DE 1958 s Joseph & Pearl. U of Delaware 1978; City Coll of San Francisco 1982; BA U of San Francisco 1984; MDiv GTS 1996. D 6/22/1996 Bp Vincent Waydell Warner P 12/7/1996 Bp Richard Frank Grein. m 6/17/2016 Robert Stephen Monitto. Int R Ch Of The Ascen Parkesburg PA 2011-2013; R Epis Ch Of The Epiph Ventnor City NJ 2007-2010; R S Bede's Epis Ch Syosset NY 1999-2007; Cur/Int Vic Ch Of S Mary The Vrgn New York NY 1996-1999; Cnvnr: Bp's Advsry Coun on Same-Gender Blessing Rite Dio Pennsylvania Philadelphia PA 2012-2013; Com on the Diac Dio New Jersey Trenton NJ 2008-2010, Atlantic City Mssn Bd 2007-2010; Commision on Mnstry Dio Long Island Garden City NY 2000-2007, Dioc Bdgt Com 2000-2007. Affirming Angl Catholicism 1996. bparker@mysaintandrews.org

PARKIN, Jason Lloyd (Chi) 222 Kenilworth Ave, Kenilworth IL 60043 **R Ch Of The H Comf Kenilworth IL 2011-, Assoc 1987-1991** B Chicago IL 1958 s Joseph & Louise. BMus Chicago Coll of Performing Arts Chicago IL 1979; MMus NWU 1980; MDiv Nash 1985; DMin SWTS 1998. D 6/15/1985 Bp Frank Tracy Griswold III P 12/21/1985 Bp James Winchester Montgomery. m 6/16/1984 Janice Dymitro c 3. R The Epis Ch Of S Mary The Vrgn San Francisco CA 2000-2011; R Trin Ch Iowa City IA 1991-2000; Asst Gr Epis Ch Hinsdale IL 1985-1987; Assessment Revs Com Dio California San Francisco CA 2010-2011, Dioc Assessment Revs Com 2010-2011, Bd, Ohlhoff Recovery Prog 2007-2011, Bd, Cathd Sch for Boys 2003-2008, Mus and Liturg Cmsn 2002-2009, Cmsn on Mus and Liturg 2001-2004; Bd Mem Ohlhoff Recovery Prog 2007-2011; Bd Mem Cathd Sch for Boys 2002-2007; Cler Wellness Cmsn Dio Iowa Des Moines IA 1996-2000, Ways and Means Com 1996-2000, Ways and Means Com 1995-2000, Const & Cn Com 1994-2000, New Ch Starts Cmsn 1994-1998, Cler Wellness Cmsn 1993-1996, New Ch Starts Com 1993-1996. Phi Beta Kappa 1979. jlparkin@holycomforter.org

PARKINSON, Caroline (Va) 4614 Riverside Drive, Richmond VA 23225 B Washington DC 1943 d Sydney & Elizabeth. BA U of Virginia 1965; Amer U 1969; MDiv VTS 1984. D 6/14/1986 P 1/11/1987 Bp John Thomas Walker. m 10/10/1998 James T Parkinson c 2. P Assoc St Jas Ch Richmond VA 2012-2017; R Gr Ch The Plains VA 1997-2010; Assoc R S Alb's Par Washington DC 1986-1997. Auth, "From Ashes To Fire," *Trin News Occasional Paper*, 1994.

PARKS, James Joseph (Fla) B Jacksonville FL 1936 D 12/8/2002 Bp Samuel Johnson Howard. m 9/6/1958 Barbara Parks. D (Vol) S Alb's Epis Ch Chiefland FL 2007-2008.

PARKS, Kenneth Thomas (Ark) 1001 Kingsland Rd, Bella Vista AR 72714 B Atlanta GA 1945 s Roy & Lillian. BA Henderson St U 1970; MA U of Arkansas 1971; PhD U of Mississippi 1979; MDiv Sewanee: The U So, TS 1987. D 3/6/1988 P 9/9/1988 Bp Herbert Alcorn Donovan Jr. m 7/7/1968 Brenda Kay Parks c 1. R S Theo's Epis Ch Bella Vista AR 2005-2015; R S Barth's Ch Corpus Christi TX 1997-2005; R S Barth's Epis Ch Ft Smith AR 1989-1997; Cur S Lk's Ch Hot Sprg AR 1988-1989; Dio Arkansas Little Rock AR 1988. Auth, "The Way of the Cradle"; Auth, "Adv Meditations". Oblate, Ord of Julian of Norwich 1985. DuBose Awd for Serv The TS U So 2011.

PARKS, Larry Joseph (EMich) St John the Baptist, PO Box 217, Otter Lake MI 48464 B Flint MI 1945 s Kenneth & Betty. BA Oakland U 1972. D 3/21/2009 Bp Steven Todd Ousley. m 6/18/1965 Sarah J Arnold c 3.

PARKS, Sarah J (EMich) St John the Baptist, PO Box 217, Otter Lake MI 48464 **P-in-c Gr Epis Ch Lapeer MI 2016-** B Lapeer MI 1944 d Cyrene & Marion. D 9/23/2008 P 3/21/2009 Bp Steven Todd Ousley. m 6/18/1965 Larry Joseph Parks c 3.

PARKS, Theodore Edward Michael (Mil) PO Box 590, Milwaukee WI 53201 **Asst S Ptr's Ch Milwaukee WI 2011-, D 2007, D 2003; Asst All SS' Cathd Milwaukee WI 2009-** B Chathan NY 1944 s Elba & Caroline. BS SUNY 1967; MDiv Nash 1971; BBA U of Wisconsin 1984. D 1/25/2003 Bp Roger John White P 7/26/2003 Bp Keith Whitmore. P-in-c Epis Ch Of The Resurr Mukwonago WI 2003-2006; Mem of Exec Coun Dio Milwaukee Milwaukee WI 2006-2010.

PARLIER, Susan Taylor (USC) 1238 Evergreen Ave, West Columbia SC 29169 **Lexington Interfaith Cmnty Serv 1990-** B Wilmington DE 1952 d Dixon & Louise. BA Col 1973; MS Virginia Commonwealth U 1975; MA Luth Theol Sthrn Sem 2003. D 12/14/2002 Bp Dorsey Henderson. m 4/12/1980 John Russell Metz c 1.

PARMAN IV, Fritz Quinn (ETenn) St. Paul's Episcopal Church, 305 W 7th St, Chattanooga TN 37402 B Jacksonville FL 1983 s Fritz & Vicki. BA U of No Florida 2007; MDiv Sewanee: The U So, TS 2013; MDiv The TS at The U So 2013. D 12/9/2012 P 5/26/2013 Bp Samuel Johnson Howard. m 4/2/2005 Rachelle J Parman c 2. S Paul's Epis Ch Chattanooga TN 2014-2017; Asst S Paul's By-The-Sea Epis Ch Jaxville Bch FL 2013-2014; S Jn's Cathd Jacksonville FL 2007-2010.

PARMETER JR, George (SD) Po Box 1361, Huron SD 57350 **Chapl Fndr & Mem Huron Reg Med Cntr 1995-** B Deer River MN 1946 s George & Margeret. BA Bemidji St U 1969; SWTS 1972; Johnston Inst 1973; Ldrshp Acad for New Directions 1976; Alte 86 88 1988; SWTS 1997; Knights Templars H Land Pilgrimage 1998. D 6/28/1973 P 4/1/1974 Bp Philip Frederick McNairy. m 10/26/1974 Gayle Harriet Parmeter c 3. R Gr Epis Ch Huron SD 1993-2010; R Ch Of The H Comm Lake Geneva WI 1989-1993; Chair Of The So Big Horn Basin Chapl Bd 1987-1989; Yth Ministers Coordntr Dio Wyoming Casper 1985-1988, Stndg Com 1980-1983, Del Of Prov Vi Syn 1986-1987, Fin Com 1985, EYC Cler Advsr 1982-1984, EYC Cler Advsr 1979-1981; So Big Horn Basin Chapl Bd 1983-1989; Chf Chapl Hot Sprg Cnty Law Enforcement Chapl Prog 1983-1989; R H Trin Epis Ch Thermopolis WY 1979-1989; Dioc Coun Dio Minnesota Minneapolis MN 1975-1979, Stff Dir 1974-1986, Bd Cass Lake Epis Camp 1974-1979, Com Of Indn Wk 1974-1979, 1973-1979; Breck Memi Mssn Ponsford MN 1974-1979; P-in-c S Columba White Earth MN 1974-1979; Trin Epis Ch Pk Rapids MN 1974-1979. Auth, "Dioc Yth Mnstrs Structure Plan".

PARMLEY, Ingram Cannon (WNC) 924 Plantation Dr, Lenoir NC 28645 **Died 6/22/2016** B Sewanee TN 1938 s Ingram & Rebecca. BA Scarritt Coll 1961; MA Scarritt Coll 1962; MDiv Duke DS 1964; MA Peabody Coll 1965; PhD No Carolina St U 1973. D 4/20/1974 P 12/14/1974 Bp Gray Temple. m 5/24/1959 Jane D Parmley c 3. S Jas Epis Ch Lenoir NC 1994-2004; Dir Convenant Cntr 1986-1994; Vic Chr Florence SC 1979-1984; Asst Prof Fran Marion Coll 1972-1986. Auth, "Mntl Hlth Tech".

PARNELL, Scott Daniel (WTex) D 6/4/2017 Bp Gary Richard Lillibridge.

PARNELL, William Clay (Mass) 138 Tremont St, Boston MA 02111 **Cn Dio Massachusetts Boston MA 2016-** B Atlanta GA 1956 s James & Salena. BA U GA 1977; MA U GA 1979; MDiv VTS 1989. D 6/12/1989 Bp Calvin Onderdonk Schofield Jr P 2/2/1990 Bp James Winchester Montgomery. m 11/10/2012 Thomas B Arndt. Archd for Mssn Dio New York New York NY 2010-2016; Trst Chr Hosp / Cbury Hlth Serv Jersey City NJ 1999-2010; Pres Chr Ch Commu Dvlmpt Corp Hackensack NJ 1997-2010; R Chr Ch Hackensack NJ

1994-2010; Asst to the R S Mary's Epis Ch Arlington VA 1989-1994; Alum Assn Exec Com VTS Alexandria VA 2009-2013. Phi Kappa Phi U GA 1977. bparnell@diomass.org

PARODI, Louis M (NJ) Po Box 192682, San Juan PR 00919 **Died 8/9/2016** B Genoa 1926 s James & Madeline. BA Lyceum Savona 1948; MTh Gregorian U 1954; PhD Gregorian U 1957; MEd U of Puerto Rico 1970; MEd Kean U 1981. Rec 3/1/1971 as Priest Bp Francisco Reus-Froylan. m 4/2/1971 Ludovica M Parodi. Ret 2003-2016; Asst La Encarnacion Par 1986-2003; Prof Of Hmnts Educ & Ethics Inter-Amer U 1984-2003; San Jose Epis Ch Eliz NJ 1977-1984; P Mssy & Prof RC Ch 1951-1970. Auth, "Educacion Espspecial Y Sus Servicios, Spec Educ," *2nd Ed*, 2002; Auth, "Ecumenismo: Confluencia De Valores," *Ecum Theol Textbook*, 1997; Auth, "La Sexualidad Humana," *Sex Educ*, 1993; Auth, "La Cathechesi," *Educ Of Catechumens*, 1957. Lmp Fndt For Spec Educ 1997. Acad Recognition Inter Amer U Of Puerto Rico 2000.

PARR, Heather Katheryn (Ore) 835 E 43rd Ave, Eugene OR 97405 B Portland OR 1948 d Gregory & Vera. U of Oregon; BA Dalhousie U 1984. D 10/18/1997 Bp Robert Louis Ladehoff P 6/12/2004 Bp Johncy Itty. c 2. Exec Coun Appointees New York NY 2004-2005; Dio Oregon Portland OR 2001; S Mary's Epis Ch Eugene OR 1997-2000. Ord Of S Lk.

PARRIS, Cheryl A E (Ga) 1401 Martin Luther King Jr Blvd, Savannah GA 31415 **S Paul's Ch Sprg Vlly NY 2015-** B Bronx NY 1968 d Kenneth & Cynthia. BS Iona Coll 1988; MA NYU 1991; MA Bex Sem 2000; MDiv Bex Sem 2002. D 12/21/2002 P 9/13/2003 Bp Michael Garrison. R S Matt's Ch Savannah GA 2007-2013; S Jas' Ch Batavia NY 2006; St Bonaventure U St Bonaventure NY 2002-2007; D S Steph's Ch Olean NY 2002-2006. "Words From The Hill: Black Stdt Caucus 1997-2000," Colgate Rochester DS, 2000; "Bp. Geo Barrett'S Role In The Fight-Kodak Conflict: An Examination Of Epis Authority And Soc Justice," Colgate Rochester DS, 2000.

PARRIS, Kenneth W (Cal) **D Gr Cathd San Francisco CA 2017-; Sr Police Chapl Bay Area Rapid Transit Police Dept Oakland CA 2014-; Deptl Chapl Alameda Cnty Sheriff's Off 2013-; Character Dvlpmt Instr, CAP Chapl Corps CAP U.S. AF Aux 2002-; Police Chapl Oakland Police Dept Oakland CA 1995-; Asst to the CAP Vice Cmdr (Colonel) CAP US AF Aux 2016-** D 12/2/1995 Bp William Edwin Swing.

PARRISH, David LeRoy (Neb) 647 Sussex Dr, Janesville WI 53546 **Ret 1993-** B Marshfield WI 1937 s Clarence & Georgia. BA U MN 1960; MDiv SWTS 1963. D 6/29/1963 P 5/19/1964 Bp Hamilton Hyde Kellogg. m 9/2/1961 Karen Lorraine Parrish c 3. Chapl (Lt. Col.) Wing Chapl-WI CAP NE/WI 1990-2005; Dio Nebraska Omaha NE 1990-1993; R Ch Of The H Trin Lincoln NE 1989-1993; Int S Andr's Ch Kansas City MO 1985-1986; Assoc Chapl S Lk Hosp Kansas City MO 1982-1989; St Lk's So Chap Overland Pk KS 1982-1989; St Ptr & All SS Epis Ch Kansas City MO 1982-1983; Other Lay Position Dio Minnesota Minneapolis MN 1978-1980, Dioc Coun 1968-1977; R Trin Ch Litchfield MN 1977-1982; S Mk's Ch Erie PA 1975-1977; Chf Chapl Hamot Med Cntr Erie PA 1974-1977; S Mths Ch St Paul Pk MN 1971-1974; P-in-c S Mths St. Paul Pk MN 1971-1974; Chapl S Mary's Hosp Minneapolis MN 1970-1974; Chapl Res Fairview Hosp Minneapolis MN 1969-1970; Asst S Paul's Ch Minneapolis MN 1969-1970; S Helen's Ch Wadena MN 1968-1969; Ch Of Our Sav Little Falls MN 1965-1969; P-in-c Gr Ch S Steph MN 1965-1969; Cur S Jn's Epis Ch Mankato MN 1963-1965. Coll of Chapl; Assembly of Epis Hospitals and Chapl 1970. Who's Who Rel 1975.

PARRISH JR, Joe (NJ) 300 E 56th St Apt 2B, New York NY 10022 **Assoc Pstr Ch of Engl (i-Ch.org) Dio Oxford Engl 2004-** B Knoxville TN 1941 s Joseph & Virginia. BS U of Tennessee 1963; PhD Harv 1969; MBA Harv 1974; GTS 1986; MDiv UTS 1986. D 6/7/1986 P 12/11/1986 Bp Paul Moore Jr. m 6/7/1975 Janice Z Parrish. Unified Bdgt Com Dio New Jersey Trenton NJ 1991-1993, Alt to GC 2012, Dioc Coun 2010-2013, Exec Com - Hisp Cmsn 2001-, Chair, Environ Cmsn 1998-; R S Jn's Ch Eliz NJ 1989-2013; Asst S Jn's Ch New York NY 1989-2000; Assoc R Trin Epis Ch Southport CT 1988-1989; St. Barth Ch New York NY 1986-1993; Asst R All Ang' Ch New York NY 1986-1988; Cur-So Bronx Ch Dio New York New York NY 1986-1988; Asst S Jas Ch New York NY 1986-1987; Asst S Simeon's Ch Bronx NY 1986-1987; Rapporteur - Indaba D Lambeth Conf - Kent Engl 2008; Sec Lambeth Conf - Kent Engl 1998. Auth, "Water, Environ and Sprtlty," *Epis Life*, Epis Ch, 1992. ACPE 1985; Cmnty of S Jn the Bapt 1989; NNECA 1989. Distinguished Trst Awd Untd Hosp Fund of NY 2013; Cmnty Bd 6, Co-Chair, Publ Sfty, Environ, Transportation Com Manhattan Borough Pres 2012; D.D. VTS 2010; Hon Doctorate Jesus the Liberator Sem 2008; Cmnty Bd 6 Manhattan Borough Pres 2008; Bd Dir Trin Epis Acad 2004; Chas T. Weber Awd Natl Kidney Fndt Profsnl Stff Assn 2003; Cert of Appreciation for Ground Zero Chapl Red Cross and The Epis Ch 2001; Environ Achievement New Jersey Environ Fed 2000; Creativity Awd Harvard Bus Sch 1974.

PARRISH, Judy Kay (SwVa) 989 Pigeon Hill Rd, Roseland VA 22967 B Norfolk VA 1945 d Bernard & Eva. BS Oklahoma St U 1972; MA W&M 1998; MDiv Sewanee: The U So, TS 2001. D 6/9/2001 Bp David Conner Bane Jr P 12/21/2001 Bp John Lewis Said. Gr Epis Ch Massies Mill VA 2011-2012; Nelson Par

Cluster Lovingston VA 2002-2011; P-in-c Trin Ch Arrington VA 2002-2011; Cur S Paul's Ch Delray Bch FL 2001-2002.

PARRISH, Larry A (Neb) PO Box 117, Falls City NE 68355 **R S Thos' Epis Ch Falls City NE 2010-** B Richmond Heights MO 1946 s Dale & Margaret. AB Butler Cnty Cmnty Coll 1966; BA SW Coll Winfield KS 1968; MDiv S Paul TS 1973. D 10/28/2009 P 5/4/2010 Bp Joe Goodwin Burnett. m 9/22/1984 Mary Parrish c 3.

PARRISH, William Potter (SwVa) 3708 Manton Dr, Lynchburg VA 24503 **Ret 1992-** B Carrolltown PA 1925 s Harry & Ruth. BS S Fran Coll Loretto PA 1949; MS Geo 1952; PhD Geo 1955; Cert VTS 1959. D 6/12/1959 Bp Frederick D Goodwin P 7/1/1960 Bp Robert Fisher Gibson Jr. Asst S Jn's Ch Lynchburg VA 1992; R Emm Epis Ch Chatham VA 1988-1992; Vic Trin Ch Gretna VA 1988-1992; Non-par 1983-1987; Vic S Ptr's Ch Altavista VA 1973-1982; Asst S Paul's Epis Ch Lynchburg VA 1966-1971; Non-par 1962-1965; Asst Truro Epis Ch Fairfax VA 1960-1961; D Trin Epis Ch Washington VA 1959-1960. Auth, "Var arts," *Living Ch.*

PARROTT, Sally F (USC) 100 Deerfield Dr, Greer SC 29650 B Albany GA 1951 d William & Sally. BA Van 1976; MDiv Sewanee: The U So, TS 1993. D 6/12/1993 P 5/1/1994 Bp William Arthur Beckham. m 6/16/1973 John Flick Parrott c 2. Chr Ch Greenville SC 2007-2009, 1993-1996; S Jas Epis Ch Greenville SC 2001-2004.

PARRY, James William (ETenn) 2740 Joneva Rd, Knoxville TN 37932 **D S Eliz's Ch 1986-** B Knoxville TN 1928 s Lawrence & Gladys. BD U of Tennessee 1954. D 1/26/1986 Bp William Evan Sanders. m 9/13/1948 Georgia Ruth Parry c 3.

PARRY-MOORE, Joyce Marie (Oly) St James Episcopal Church, 24447 94th Ave S, Kent WA 98030 **S Jas Epis Ch Kent WA 2015-** B Seattle WA 1961 d Mark & Sally. BA Wstrn Washington U 1982; Cert Boston Conservatory 1986; MDiv PSR 2010; MDiv PSR 2010. D 6/4/2010 Bp Marc Handley Andrus P 3/31/2011 Bp Mark A Lattime. m 6/8/1996 Patrick Moore c 5. S Barth's Epis Ch Livermore CA 2012-2015; Seamens Ch Inst New York NY 2011.

PARSELL, Harry Irvan (SwFla) 738 Pinellas Point Dr S, St Petersburg FL 33705 **Vic S Matt's Ch St Petersburg FL 2010-** B Saint Albans NY 1953 s Harry & Erie. BA Stetson U 1975; MDiv Nash 1980. D 6/22/1980 Bp William Hopkins Folwell P 1/21/1981 Bp Emerson Paul Haynes. R Ch Of The Annunc Holmes Bch FL 2003-2010; R S Barth's Ch St Petersburg FL 1989-2003; Asst Gd Samar Epis Ch Clearwater FL 1983-1989; Asst S Thos' Epis Ch St Petersburg FL 1980-1983; Cncl Dn Dio SW Florida Parrish FL 2008-2010, 2000-2007, COM 1999-2001, COM 1998-2001, Comp Dioc Com 1998-1999, Congrl Dvlpmt Comm 1997-2000, Dioc Coun 1997, Ch Ext Com 1993-1996, Com Cont Educ For Cler 1986-1992, Yth Cmsn 1984-1988, Ecum Cmsn 1981-1985. stmatthewsbythebay@gmail.com

✠ **PARSLEY JR, The Rt Rev Henry Nutt** (Ala) Episcopal Diocese of Easton, 314 North St, Easton MD 21601 **Serv Angl Comm 2008-; Bd Colleges and Universities of the Angl Comm 2007-** B Memphis TN 1948 s Henry & Barbara. BA U So 1970; MDiv GTS 1973; DD GTS 1998; DD Sewanee: The U So, TS 1998. D 6/16/1973 P 4/1/1974 Bp Gray Temple Con 9/28/1996 for Ala. m 8/8/1970 Rebecca Allison Parsley c 1. Bp Dio Easton Easton MD 2014; Bd Angl Cntr In Rome 2003-2012; Chncllr U So Sewanee TN 2003-2009; Bp of Alabama Dio Alabama Birmingham 1999-2012, Coadj 1996-1998; Trst U So Sewanee TN 1996-2012; Kanuga Prog Com Dio No Carolina Raleigh NC 1987-1992, Bd, PBp's Fund 1990-1993, Dioc Coun 1990-1992, Dep, GC 1989-1995; R Chr Ch Charlotte NC 1986-1996; R Epis Ch of the Gd Shpd Summerville SC 1982-1986; Exec Coun So Carolina Charleston SC 1981-1986, BEC 1978-1986, Stndg Com, Chair 1983-1986, Exam Chapl 1978-1986, Dep, GC 1976-1986; R All SS Ch Florence SC 1977-1982; Asst S Phil's Ch Charleston SC 1975-1977; Asst Trin Ch Myrtle Bch SC 1973-1975; Bd Alabama Faith Coun 2007-2009; Bd Angl Cntr in Rome 2003-2012; Chncllr U So Sewanee TN 2003-2009; Chair Theol Com of the HOB 1999-2010; Regent U So Sewanee TN 1999-2009; Trst U So Sewanee TN 1996-2012; Bd Porter-Gaud Sch Charleston SC 1975-1980. Auth, "I Really Miss Those Vstry Meetings," *Vstry Papers*, 2013; Auth, "Conflict and Controversy: Bringing Wounds and Blessings," *Vstry Papers*, 2004. Omicron Delta Kappa 1970; Phi Beta Kappa 1970. DD GTS 1997; DD U So, Sewanee 1997. hparsley@dioceseofeaston.org

PARSLEY, Jamie A (ND) 117 20 Ave. N., Fargo ND 58102 **P-in-c S Steph's Ch Fargo ND 2008-** B Fargo ND 1969 s Albert & Joyce. MFA Vermont Coll 1999; MA Nash 2008. D 7/25/2003 Bp Andrew Fairfield P 6/11/2004 Bp Michael Smith. Exec Asst to the Bp/Asst for Cmncatn Dio No Dakota Fargo ND 2006-2012, Dep to GC 2012, Chair of COM 2010-2012, Dep to GC 2010-, COM 2007-2012, Ed, The Sheaf 2002-2012; All SS Ch Vlly City ND 2006-2008; P Geth Cathd Fargo ND 2004-2008; Rep, Epis News Serv Advsry Commitee Prov VI 2010. Auth, "Bk," *That Word*, No Star, 2014; Auth, "Bk," *The Downstairs Tenant and Other Stories*, The Inst for Reg Stds, 2014; Auth, "Bk," *Crow*, Enso, 2012; Auth, "Bk," *Fargo, 1957; an elegy*, The Insitute for Reg Stds, NDSU, 2010; Auth, "Bk," *This Grass: poems*, Enso, 2009; Contrib, "prayers," *Evang Luth Wrshp Pstr Care*, Augsburg, 2008; Auth, "Bk," *Just Once: poems*, Loonfeather, 2007; Auth, "Bk," *Ikon: poems*, Enso, 2005; Auth,

"Bk," *no stars, no moon: new and selected haiku*, Mellen, 2004; Contrib, "A Pryr on the Feast Day of Jonathan Myrick Daniels," *Race and Pryr: Collected Voices Many Dreams*, Morehouse, 2003; Contrib, "Jesus in Showbiz," *Up Off Your Knees: Preaching the U2 Songbook*, Cowley, 2003; Auth, "Bk," *earth into earth: poems*, Enso, 2000; Auth, "Bk," *The Wounded Table.: prose poems*, Pudding Hse, 1999; Auth, "Bk," *Cloud: a poem in 2 acts*, Mellen, 1997; Auth, "Bk," *The Loneliness of Blizzards: poems*, Mellen, 1995; Auth, "Bk," *Paper Doves, Falling and other poems*, Sunstone, 1992. Fllshp of SSJE 2002; Oblate of St. Ben 1992; Soc of Cath Priests 2009. Assoc Poet Laureate of No Dakota 2004; Assoc Poet Laureate of No Dakota 2004. apium@aol.com

PARSONS, Ann Roberts (Ak) Po Box 1445, Sitka AK 99835 B Evanston IL 1925 d Keith & Helen. Chicago Art Inst Chicago IL. D 5/1/1984 Bp George Clinton Harris. m 6/21/1947 Francis John Parsons. Dn - SE Dnry (Juneau 1981-1984; Sec - Com Dio Alaska Fairbanks AK 1977-1985.

PARSONS, Berry Ed (LI) 20 Apache Ln, Sedona AZ 86351 B Brownsville TX 1946 s Givon & Nida. BA U Cinc 1969; MDiv GTS 1975. D 6/7/1975 Bp William Foreman Creighton P 6/7/1976 Bp Robert Bruce Hall. P-in-c S Jn's Epis Ch Ft Hamilton Brooklyn NY 2004-2008; Vic Ch Of S Fran Of Assisi Levittown NY 1994-2004; Vic Epis Ch of The Resurr Williston Pk NY 1994-2004; Vic S Phil And S Jas Ch New Hyde Pk NY 1992-1994; The Ch of S Ign of Antioch New York NY 1988-1990; P-in-c Ch Of The Ascen And S Agnes Washington DC 1985; S Andr's Epis Ch Arlington VA 1983-1984; Vic H Cross Mclean VA 1979-1983; Cur S Dunst's Ch Mc Lean VA 1975-1983.

✠ **PARSONS, The Rt Rev Donald James** (Spr) 6901 N Galena Rd Apt 111, Peoria IL 61614 **Died 1/4/2016** B Philadelphia PA 1922 s Earl & Helen. DCL Nash; BA Tem 1943; ThB PDS 1946; MTh PDS 1948; ThD PDS 1952; PDS 1974. D 2/1/1946 Bp William P Remington P 10/6/1946 Bp Arthur R Mc Kinstry Con 9/8/1973 for Q. c 3. Ramsey Prof of Ascetical Theol Nash Nashotah WI 2001-2016, Dn & Pres 1963-2000, Prof 1956-1962, Instr NT 1950-1955; Bp Dio Quincy Peoria IL 1973-1987, Ret Bp of Quincy 1988-2016; R S Ptr's Ch Smyrna DE 1949-1950; Instr NT Philadelphi DS 1948-1950; Imm Ch Highlands Wilmington DE 1946-1949; Asst The Ch Of The H Trin Rittenhouse Philadelphia PA 1946-1947. Auth, *Euch: Rite 2*, Seabury Press; Auth, *In Time w Jesus*, Par Press; Auth, *Lifetime Road to God*, Par Press. Epis Visitor, All SS Sis of Poor 2005; Epis Visitor, S Greg Abbey 1996-2000.

PARSONS, Susan Diane (Cal) **P-in-c S Ptr's Epis Ch Redwood City CA 2013-** B Beaumont TX 1952 d John & Grova. BA Sonoma St U 1994; MA CDSP 1997; MA CDSP 1997. D 6/5/2004 P 12/4/2004 Bp William Edwin Swing. c 2. Assoc The Epis Ch Of S Mary The Vrgn San Francisco CA 2011-2012; Assoc S Fran Of Assisi Ch Novato CA 2004-2011. susan@stpetersrwc.org

PARSONS, Timothy Hamilton (CNY) 12 Oak Ave, Norway ME 04268 **P S Barn Ch Rumford ME 2006-; Grants Revs Com Dio Maine Portland ME 2007-** B Boston MA 1941 s Kenneth & June. BA Ge 1964; MDiv VTS 1968; DMin Drew U 1977. D 6/8/1968 Bp Leland Stark P 6/4/1969 Bp Paul Moore Jr. m 12/23/1983 Susan S Parsons c 3. R S Matt's Epis Ch Liverpool NY 1993-2006; Emm Ch Adams NY 1990-1993; R Zion Ch Pierrepont Manor NY 1990-1993; S Ptr's Ch Rochelle Pk NJ 1989-1990; R S Andr's Ch Harrington Pk NJ 1986-1989; Ch Of The H Comm Norwood NJ 1986-1987; R S Jn's Ch Clinton IA 1981-1986; Ce Com Dio Sthrn Ohio Cincinnati OH 1978-1981; Gr Ch Hastings Hds NY 1972-1978; Assoc Zion Ch Dobbs Ferry NY 1972-1975; Asst P In Charge S Pat's Ch Washington DC 1970-1972; Asst S Phil The Evang Washington DC 1968-1970.

PARSONS-CANCELLIERE, Rebecca Anne (Be) Episcopal Parish Of Saint Mark And, 21 Race St, Jim Thorpe PA 18229 **Chapl Care Alternatives Hospice 2009-; D Epis Par Of S Mk And S Jn Jim Thorpe PA 2009-** B Kingston PA 1961 d Winfield & Jeanne Carol. BS Millersville U 1983; MDiv Moravian TS 1997. D 2/2/2009 Bp John Palmer Croneberger P 9/24/2016 Bp Sean Walter Rowe. m 9/18/1999 Thomas Cancelliere c 2.

PARTANEN, Robert Carl (Cal) 62 Valais Ct, Fremont CA 94539 **D S Anne's Ch Fremont CA 2006-; Proj Mgr ATT San Ramon CA 1991-** B Syracuse NY 1947 s John & Alice. BS San Jose St U 1972; BA Sch for Deacons 2003. D 6/3/2006 Bp William Edwin Swing. m 3/31/2000 Diana Lynn Miller c 1. No Amer Assoc. of Deacons 2001.

PARTEE CARLSEN, Mariclair Elizabeth (Pa) Saint Mary's Church Hamilton Village, 3916 Locust Walk, Philadelphia PA 19104 **S Mary's Ch Hamilton Vill Philadelphia PA 2013-** B Atlanta GA 1977 d Norman & Amanda. BA U GA 1999; JD U GA 2002; MDiv GTS 2007. D 12/21/2006 P 7/8/2007 Bp J Neil Alexander. m 5/5/2013 Mitchell David Partee Carlsen c 1. Cn Cathd Ch Of The Nativ Bethlehem PA 2009-2013; Assoc R Trin Ch Solebury PA 2007-2009.

PARTENHEIMER, Gary Hoffman (Pa) East Hall - Northfield Mt Hermon, Northfield MA 01360 **Rel Stds Dept Northfield Mt Hermon Sch 1977-** B Philadelphia PA 1949 s Raymond & Ella. BA Dart 1971; MDiv EDS 1977. D 6/11/1977 Bp Lyman Cunningham Ogilby P 6/1/1978 Bp John Brooke Mosley. m 6/23/1979 Sarah Hoffman. cl Soc; Phi Beta Kappa.

PARTHUM III, Charles Frederick (Mass) 1415 N Victoria Cir, Elm Grove WI 53122 **Ret Ret Elm Grove WI 2008-** B Kansas City MO 1947 s Charles & Mary. BS U of Wisconsin 1969; JD U of Wisconsin 1975; MDiv VTS 1987.

P

D 6/13/1987 Bp Ronald Hayward Haines P 6/19/1988 Bp Robert Whitridge Estill. c 2. Dn Calv Cathd Sioux Falls SD 2006-2008; Int S Steph's Epis Ch Wilkes Barre PA 2004-2006; Int S Jn's Ch Cornwall NY 2002-2004; Int S Steph's Ch Westborough MA 2001-2002; Int S Paul's Epis Ch Willimantic CT 1999-2001; Int Emm Epis Ch Wakefield MA 1997-1999; R S Ptr's Ch Weston MA 1992-1997; Chairman ReEntry Raleigh NC 1989-1992; Asst to R Chr Epis Ch Raleigh NC 1987-1992; Bd Dir Diamond City Partnership Dio Bethlehem Bethlehem PA 2005-2006, Bd Dir Reach Mnstry 2004-2006; Bd Dir Isaiah 58 Mnstrs Dio Connecticut Meriden CT 1999-2001; Chairman Isaiah 58 Mnstrs Willimantic CT 1999-2001; Bd Cbury Sch Wakefield MA 1997-1999; Bd Dir Cbury Sch Dio Massachusetts Boston MA 1997-1999, Mssn Plcy & Plnng Cmte 1994-1996, Const & Cns Cmte 1993-1998, Cler Conf Plnng/Revs 1993-1994; Ch Bd Dir ReEntry Dio No Carolina Raleigh NC 1991-1992, COM 1990-1992; Chairman ReEntry Prog Raleigh NC 1989-1992; Bd Urban Mnstry Cntr Raleigh NC 1988-1992. Connecticut Int Mnstry Assn 1999-2001; Exec Bd, Wis Law Rev 1974-1975; Int Mnstry Ntwk 1999; Natl Assn of Epis Int Mnstry Specialists 2000-2006; Transition Mnstry Ntwk 2007. AG hon US Dept Justice 1983; Ord Coif Univ Wisconsin 1975.

PARTINGTON, Richard Ogden (Pa) 4116 Twin Silo Dr, Blue Bell PA 19422 **Ret 1985-** B Philadelphia PA 1922 s Harold & Ida. BS Tem 1944; STB Tem 1947; STM Tem 1949. D 12/28/1951 Bp Oliver J Hart P 6/1/1952 Bp William P Roberts. c 2. Vic Ch Of S Jude And The Nativ Lafayette Hill PA 1952-1985; Asst Chr Ch And S Mich's Philadelphia PA 1951-1952; Serv Methodist Ch 1942-1951.

PARTLOW, John Michael Owen (WVa) 809 Chestnut Ct, Winnetka IL 60093 B Parkersburg WV 1951 s Walter & Mary. BA W Virginia U 1974; MDiv VTS 1988. D 6/1/1988 Bp Robert Poland Atkinson P 6/1/1989 Bp William Franklin Carr. m 10/9/1976 Gloria Sheerin. Chr Ch Winnetka IL 1990; D-In-Trng Trin Epis Ch Martinsburg WV 1988-1990.

PARTLOW SSG, Ruth Goodrich (SVa) 3409 W Point Ct, North Chesterfield VA 23235 B Hannibal MO 1940 d Howard & Ruth. BA Duke 1962; MA Regent U 1983; MDiv SWTS 1989. D 6/24/1989 Bp Claude Charles Vache P 3/4/1990 Bp Bob Johnson. m 6/23/1962 Robert Greider Partlow c 2. Int Co-R S Matt's Epis Ch Chesterfield VA 2010; Int Co-R Johns Memi Epis Ch Farmville VA 2007-2008; Co-R S Lk's Ch Powhatan VA 1999-2006; Co-R Chr Epis Ch Of Springfield Springfield OH 1992-1999; Int S Cyp's Ch Franklin NC 1992; R S Jn's Epis Ch Franklin NC 1990-1992; Non-par 1989.

PARTRIDGE, Cameron Elliot (Cal) 34 Hatch Rd, Medford MA 02155 **S Aid's Ch San Francisco CA 2016-; Adj EDS Cambridge MA 2014-; Lectr Harvard DS Cambridge MA 2011-; Counslr to Epis/Angl Students Harvard DS Cambridge MA 2010-; A050 T/F on the Study of Mar Dom And Frgn Mssy Soc- Epis Ch Cntr New York NY 2013-, Campus Mnstry Prov Coordntr, Prov 1 2012-** B Berkeley CA 1973 s David & Rebecca. BA Bryn 1995; MDiv Harvard DS 1998; STM Ya Berk 2001; ThD Harvard DS 2008. D 6/12/2004 Bp M(Arvil) Thomas Shaw P 1/8/2005 Bp Gayle Harris. m 10/25/2005 Kateri Paul c 2. Epis Chapl at Bos Dio Massachusetts Boston MA 2011-2016; Int Epis Chapl at Harv Epis Chapl At Harvard & Radcliffe Cambridge MA 2010-2011; Lectr on Stds of Wmn, Gender and Sxlty Harv Cambridge MA 2009-2012; Vic S Lk's And S Marg's Ch Allston MA 2006-2010; D Chr Ch Somerville MA 2004-2005. Auth & Co-Ed, "Preaching on the Hinges of the H: Toward a Homil Theol of the Chr Liturg Year," *Preaching and the Theol Imagination*, Ptr Lang, 2015; Auth, "Toward an 'Irregular' Embrace: The Philadelphia Ordinations and Transforming Ideas of the Human," *Looking Forw, Looking Backward: Forty Years of Wmn Ord*, Ch Pub, 2014; Auth, "Side Wound, Vrgn Birth, Trsfg," *Theol and Sxlty Vol. 18 No. 2*, Maney Pub, 2013; Auth, "Skandalon of Conjoinment: Angl Ecclesial Embodiment," *The Open Body: Essays in Angl Ecclesiology*, Ptr Lang, 2012. AAR 2005; No Amer Patristics Soc 2006; SBL 2007.

PARTRIDGE, Edmund Bruce (Nwk) 9849 Martingham Cir, St Michaels MD 21663 B Orange NJ 1932 s Harold & Dorothy. BA U Pgh 1959; MDiv GTS 1962; LHD London Inst GB 1972. D 6/9/1962 P 12/1/1962 Bp Leland Stark. Int S Geo's Epis Ch Newport News VA 2003-2006; Dio Newark Newark NJ 1992-1993, R Distressed Congregations 1978-1990, 1971-1975, Bp's Dep for Distressed Congregations 1978-1990; Dn Trin And S Phil's Cathd Newark NJ 1990-1992; R S Jas Ch Wichita KS 1968-1971; Excutive Coun Exec & Secy Off New York NY 1964-1968; Cur S Ptr's Ch Essex Fells NJ 1962-1964; Keynote Speaker US ArmdF European Command Epis Ch Lay Readi 1966-1967; Respresentated Div of Layman's Wk Exec Coun Wrld Coun of Ch in Amer 1965; Respresenive for ECUSA Ch of Engl Div of Laity 1964-1968; Exec Secy Adult Educ Exec Coun Appointees New York NY 1964-1968. Auth, "The New Sprtlty for Laymen," Forw Mvmt; Auth, "Anger, Rage & Resentment," St. Ive's Press; Auth, "The Guide for Lay Readers," Morehouse / Barlow; Auth, "Seabury Press," Seabury Press. GTS Alum Assn 1962; Newark Epis Cler Assn 1982; Virginia Epis Cler Assn 2002. Hon Cn Trin & S Phil's Cathd 1994; Bp's Outstanding Serv Awd 1993.

PARTRIDGE JR, Henry Roy (Me) 3 Old Colony Ln, Scarborough ME 04074 B Tuskegee AL 1947 s Henry & Olive. MS U MI 1971; MA U MI 1983; PhD U MI 1985; MDiv Harvard DS 1988. D 6/4/1988 P 12/1/1988 Bp Edward

Cole Chalfant. m 9/22/1978 Susan Elizabeth Partridge c 3. R S Ann's Epis Ch Windham Windham ME 1997-2005; Int S Dav's Epis Ch Kennebunk ME 1996-1997; Cur Cathd Ch Of S Lk Portland ME 1988-1989.

PARTRIDGE, Ivan Harold (Nwk) Po Box 235, Cotuit MA 02635 **Died 4/2/2017** B Stockport, England 1925 s Harold & Dorothy. BA Hobart and Wm Smith Colleges 1950; MDiv GTS 1953. D 6/1/1953 P 1/1/1954 Bp Benjamin M Washburn. m 6/17/1950 Jean Partridge c 4. Ret 1989-2017; Com Of Miscellaneous Resolutns 1986-1987; Natl Coun For The Dvlpmt Of Mnstry 1977-1982; 1977-1981; Sec - Nati'L Ntwk Epis Cler Assn 1970-1978; Liturg Cmsn 1970-1973; Dept Of CE 1969-1971; Chair Of The Dept 1966-1969; Plnng Com 1965-1970; Alt Dep Gc 1964-1967; Chair Of The Yth Wk Prov 2 1963-1970; 1960-1974; Chair Of The Yth Wk Div 1960-1966; Chair Of The Cmsn Of Cler Salaries 1959-1971; Dept Of CE 1958-1966; R All SS' Epis Ch Glen Rock NJ 1956-1988; Asst R S Lk's Epis Ch Montclair NJ 1953-1956; Acts/VIM Bd Dio Newark Newark NJ 1981-1985, Pres Of The Newark Cler Assn 1971-1980.

PASALO, Annalise Marie Castro (Haw) **Chapl The Epis Ch in Hawaii Honolulu HI 2016-** D 6/25/2016 P 1/14/2017 Bp Robert Leroy Fitzpatrick.

PASALO JR, Ernesto Castro (Haw) **The Epis Ch of W O'ahu Aiea HI 2016-** B Wailuku HI 1985 s Ernesto & Florencia. BS U of Hawaii 2015; MDiv VTS 2015; MDiv VTS 2015. D 6/13/2015 P 1/9/2016 Bp Robert Leroy Fitzpatrick. Ch Of The Epiph Honolulu HI 2015-2016.

PASAY, Marcella Claire (CFla) 11251 SW Highway 484, Dunnellon FL 34432 B Webster MA 1946 d Gerard & Doris. AS Quinebaug Vlly Cmnty Coll 1983. D 12/10/2011 Bp John Wadsworth Howe. m 5/23/1969 Alexander Pasay c 2.

PASCHALL JR, Fred William (NC) 4341 Bridgewood Ln, Charlotte NC 28226 B Burlington NC 1935 s Fred & Emily. BS No Carolina St U 1958; MA Sewanee: The U So, TS 1992; DMin Sewanee: The U So, TS 1996. D 6/25/1978 Bp William F Gates Jr P 6/1/1979 Bp William Evan Sanders. m 2/14/1964 Winston Paschall. Chr Ch Charlotte NC 1998-2003, Asst to R 1994-1996; Asst to R S Jn's Epis Ch Charlotte NC 1990-1994; P-in-c S Tim's Ch Signal Mtn TN 1988-1989, P-in-c 1984-1987; Int Chr Ch Epis S Pittsburg TN 1987-1988; P-in-c S Alb's Epis Ch Hixson TN 1983-1984; Assoc Ch Of The Gd Shpd Lookout Mtn TN 1982-1990; Assoc S Mart Of Tours Epis Ch Chattanooga TN 1981-1982; D S Lk's Ch Cleveland TN 1978-1979.

PASHTURRO, James Joseph (Mich) **S Jn's Ch Howell MI 2016-; S Steph's Ch Hamburg MI 2016-** B Methuen, MA 1965 s James & Louanne. Masters Bexley-Seabury; Masters U of Massachusetts Lowell 1994. D 12/12/2015 P 6/11/2016 Bp Wendell Nathaniel Gibbs Jr. m 10/1/1999 Gabriela Turro c 3.

PATIENCE, Rodger L (FdL) 130 Cherry Ct, Appleton WI 54915 **Ch Of The H Apos Oneida WI 2017-; Mentor EFM (EfM) 2011-; GC Dep (2018) Dio Fond du Lac Appleton WI 2016-, Deacons' Coun Mem 2015-2016, EFM Coordntr 2014-, COM Mem 2012-2015; Chapl, Alum Assn Kemper Hall Kenosha WI 1996-** B Winter Haven FL 1968 s Lindsay & Christine. Bexley-Seabury; Bexley-Seabury; Bexley-Seabury; Kellogg Cntr for Nonprofit Mgmt; BA Estrn Illinois U 1989; Cert Sch for Deacons - Dio Chicago 1995. D 2/3/1996 Bp Frank Tracy Griswold III P 12/17/2016 Bp Matthew A Gunter. m 5/13/1989 Katharina Elisabeth Prohaska. D S Thos Ch Menasha WI 2010-2016; D S Lk's Ch Racine WI 2007-2010; D S Lk's Ch Whitewater WI 2002-2007; Instr, Sch for Deacons Dio Milwaukee Milwaukee WI 1998-2010, D 1996-1998; D Ch Of The H Comm Lake Geneva WI 1996-2001; D S Paul's Ch Milwaukee WI 1996. Auth, "Exsultet Redux," The Angl, Angl Soc of the USA, 2013; Contrib, "An Epis Dictionary of the Ch," Ch Pub Inc, 2000. Assn for Epis Deacons (NAAD) 1993-2016; Conf, St. Greg's Abbey 1995; Fllshp of St. Jn, SSJE 1996.

PATNAUDE, Robert J (O) 7146 Hesperides Dr, Warrenton VA 20186 **Non-par 1989-** B Saratoga Sprgs NY 1949 s Robert & Elsa. Hobart and Wm Smith Colleges 1969; BS SUNY 1971; MDiv Bex Sem 1974. D 6/15/1974 Bp Wilbur Emory Hogg Jr P 12/14/1974 Bp H Coleman Mcgehee Jr. m 9/15/2012 Susan Patnaude c 2. R Chr Ch Shaker Heights OH 1987-1988; R Trin Par Menlo Pk CA 1976-1987; Asst S Jas Epis Ch Birmingham MI 1974-1976. Auth, "The Wlzard of Que," White Rhino Press, 2013; Auth, "Livonia - Lady of the Shadows," White Rhino Press, 2013; Auth, "Meditations for the Middle of the Night," White Rhino Press, 2013; Auth, "Lullababes," White Rhino Press, 2013; Auth, "Habits of Heroes," Visual Voice Tech, 2012; Auth, "Wisdom of Our Fr," White Rhino Press, 2012; Auth, "Subtraction," White Rhino Press, 2005; Auth, "Penny," White Rhino Press, 2002; Auth, "Living Simultaneously," White Rhino Press, 1999; Auth, "Leading From The Maze," Ten Speed Press, 1997. Cleric Of Year Awd Kiwanis Intl 1985.

PATRONIK JR, Joseph Andrew (SanD) PO Box 1283, Marina CA 93933 B Chicago IL 1951 s Joseph & Mary. BS OH SU 1973; MBA Santa Clara U 1980; U of Geneva Ch 1987; MDiv CDSP 1988. D 6/4/1988 P 6/3/1989 Bp William Edwin Swing. m 10/6/1990 Leslie Patronik c 4. R S Fran Ch Pauma Vlly CA 2003-2013.

PATSTON, John Ralph Ansell (NI) 502 N James St, Ludington MI 49431 **Ret 1994-** B Vancouver BC CA 1927 s Percival & Lydia. BA U So 1954; BD Nash 1957; Rutgers The St U of New Jersey 1966; STM Nash 1979. D 6/15/1957 Bp Charles L Street P 12/21/1957 Bp Gerald Francis Burrill. c 5. Int S Paul's Ch Truth Or Consequences NM 1997-1999; R S Paul's Ch Henderson

KY 1986-1994; Gr Epis Ch Of Ludington Ludington MI 1970-1986; R S Jas' Epis Ch Of Pentwater Pentwater MI 1970-1986; Vic Ch of the Medtr Harbert MI 1968-1970; Asst Dir, Cathd Shltr Cathd Of S Jas Chicago IL 1966-1968; P Chr The King Epis Ch Huntington IN 1960-1966; Cur Chr Ch Waukegan IL 1957-1960. Auth, "The Symbolism Of The Cntr & The Euch". SSC 1976.

PATTEN, Kenneth Lloyd (Hond) **Non-par 1969-** B Glace Bay NS CA 1941 s Frederick & Florence. BA Kings Coll Edmonton Ab CA 1961; STB U Tor CA 1965. Serv Ch In Honduras 1967-1969; Serv Ch Of Can 1963-1967.

PATTERSON JR, Baldo Alfred Kaleo (Haw) 229 Queen Emma Sq, Honolulu HI 96813 **The Epis Ch of W O'ahu Aiea HI 2016-** B Oahu HI 1954 s Baldo & Helen. MDiv Bangor TS 1985; DMin Chicago TS 2000. D 10/25/2013 P 9/27/2014 Bp Robert Leroy Fitzpatrick. m 7/28/1984 Nancy M Patterson c 5. Asst S Nich Epis Ch Aiea HI 2014-2015.

PATTERSON, Barbara Anne Bowling (At) 437 S Candler St, Decatur GA 30030 B Tucson AZ 1952 d Lawson & Anne. Candler TS Emory U; BA Smith 1973; MDiv Harvard DS 1977; PhD Emory U 1994. D 6/9/1984 P 5/1/1985 Bp Charles Judson Child Jr. m 7/30/1977 Joe Steadman Patterson. Dn S Jn's Atlanta GA 1984-1985; Asst Prof In The Rel Dept Emory U Atlanta GA. Auth, "Campus Calling"; Auth, "Redeemed Bodies Simone Weil: Distance & Fasting". Soc Of S Jn The Evang.

PATTERSON, Beverly A (WTex) 3701 Cimarron Blvd Apt 2604, Corpus Christi TX 78414 **Coastal Bend Partnr in Mnstry Corpus Christi TX 2016-** B Hondo TX 1958 d Otway & Geraldine. BS Amberton U 2002; MDiv Sewanee: The U So, TS 2009. D 6/20/2009 Bp James Monte Stanton P 4/2/2011 Bp Gary Richard Lillibridge. c 4. R S Andr's Ch Port Isabel TX 2011-2016; Partnr In Mnstry Estrn Convoc Kenedy TX 2010-2011; Dio W Texas San Antonio TX 2010, Nomin Com Mem 2013-2014; Sch Hlth and Curric Com Point Isabel ISD 2011-2014. mtrbev11@gmail.com

PATTERSON JR, Dennis Delamater (At) St Luke's Episc Ch, 435 Peachtree St NE, Atlanta GA 30308 **P-in-c Ch Of The H Cross Decatur GA 2017-** B Norfolk VA 1977 s Dennis & Annie. BA Norfolk St U; MDiv UTS; Cert Ang Stud VTS. D 4/19/2008 P 10/25/2008 Bp John Clark Buchanan. m 5/21/2005 Monica Edwards Patterson c 2. S Lk's Epis Ch Atlanta GA 2012-2016; R S Cyp's Epis Ch Hampton VA 2008-2012. dennis@stlukesatlanta.org

PATTERSON, Jane (WTex) Seminary of the Southwest, P.O. Box 2247, Austin TX 78768 **Asst Prof Epis TS Of The SW Austin TX 2013-, Int 2013-, Associated Fac 2010-2013, 2003-2005; Asstg Dir St Ben's Workshop San Antonio TX 2013-; Co-Dir The WorkShop 2005-; Mssnr for Adult Formation Dio W Texas San Antonio TX 2013-, Exam Chapl 2008-2013; Bd Mem Angl Assn of Biblic Scholars 2010-** B Miami FL 1954 d James & Claudia. BA Smith 1977; MTS SMU 1992; CTh Epis TS of the SW 1993; PhD SMU 2009. D 1/18/1994 P 6/15/1995 Bp John Herbert MacNaughton. m 11/22/1997 Lorenzo D Patterson c 2. Asst R S Mk's Epis Ch San Antonio TX 2005-2012; S Lk's Epis Ch San Antonio TX 2003; Assoc All SS Epis Ch Corpus Christi TX 2001-2002; Ch Of Recon San Antonio TX 1995-2000. Co-Auth, "Calling All Years Gd: Chr Vocation Throughout Life's Seasons," Eerdmans, 2017; Auth, "Keeping the Feast: Metaphors of Sacrifice in 1 Corinthians and Philippians," SBL, 2015. AAR 1993; Angl Assn Of Biblic Scholars 1996; Cltn for Mnstry in Daily Life 2005-2010; SBL 1993. Fllshp ECF 1994.

PATTERSON, John (SJ) 9 Simpson Close, Barrow on Humber, North Lincolnshire DN19 7BL Great Britain (UK) **Ret 1993-** B Croydon Surrey UK 1927 s Eric & Gladys. GOE Bishops Coll Cheshunt GB 1961; MA Regent St Polytechnic/Univ of Westminster London GB 1976; MA Regent St Polytechnic/Univ of Westminster London GB 2003. D 12/1/1961 P 12/1/1962 Bp The Bishop of Oxford. m 6/8/1949 Olive Jean Patterson c 2. Chapl (Major) CAP CA 1983-1990; Dn, Sierra Dnry Epis Dio San Joaquin Modesto CA 1979-1990, Dioc Coun 1987-1990, Dioc Coun 1979-1986; R S Mich's Epis Par Ridgecrest CA 1978-1989; Chapl (Squadron Ldr) Royal AF Great Britain (UK) 1965-1972; Serv Ch of Engl Germany & Middle E 1961-1978. Chapl of the Year NV Wing CAP 1985.

PATTERSON, John Willard (NJ) 2885 Citrus Lake Dr, Naples FL 34109 **Ret 1991-** B Hackensack NJ 1926 s John & Edna. Seton Hall U; BA U NC 1948; MDiv GTS 1951; Montclair St U 1956. D 5/26/1951 P 12/8/1951 Bp Benjamin M Washburn. m 3/31/1964 Elena Patterson c 1. S Monica's Epis Ch Naples FL 1995-2011; R Epis Ch Of The Epiph Ventnor City NJ 1984-1991; Vic S Jas Memi Ch Eatontown NJ 1976-1984; S Andr The Apos Highland Highlands NJ 1976; Vic S Paul Manalapan NJ 1973-1974; Asst S Ptr's Ch Freehold NJ 1973-1974; Non-par S Ch Of The H Comm Paterson NJ 1954-1955; Vic Ch Of S Mary The Vrgn Ridgefield Pk NJ 1951-1954.

PATTERSON, Keith F (Roch) **S Lk And S Simon Cyrene Rochester NY 2016-** B Syracuse NY 1957 s George & Eleanor. BA SUNY Coll@ Potsdam 1979; MDiv EDS 2008; MDiv EDS 2008; MDiv EDS 2008. D 5/31/2013 P 1/18/2014 Bp Thomas C Ely. P S Paul's Ch Concord NH 2014-2016; Asst S Jas Epis Ch Arlington VT 2014.

PATTERSON, Michael Steven (Nev) PO Box 1041, Fernley NV 89408 B Alameda CA 1948 s Robert & Dolores. D 7/25/2009 P 3/27/2010 Bp Dan Thomas Edwards. m 4/29/1995 Connie Patterson c 4. Dio Nevada Las Vegas 2014-2016.

PATTERSON, Peggy Pittman (Del) 10 Concord Ave, Wilmington DE 19802 **Chapl Hospice Santa Fe NM 2008-** B Macon GA 1944 d Charles & Margaret. BA Sweet Briar Coll 1967; MRE SMU 1969; MRE SMU 1969; M.Div SMU Perkins 1985; Mstr of Rel Educ SMU Perkins 1985; Cert SMU Perkins Sch Theol 1986. D 6/17/1989 P 5/26/1990 Bp Donis Dean Patterson. c 3. Assoc R Ch of the H Faith Santa Fe NM 2011-2016; Dep Gc Dio Delaware Wilmington 1997-2000, Dioc Coun 1997-2002; Dn Cathd Ch Of S Jn Wilmington DE 1995-2005; Cn Pstr S Matt's Cathd Dallas TX 1989-1995; Chair Rel Dept The Epis Sch Dallas 1978-1989; Excoun Fin Com Dio Dallas Dallas TX 1992. Auth, "Cathederals In The Twenty First Century," Wash Natl Cathederals, 2000. AAM (AAM) 1999; EWC; Integrity Inc.

PATTERSON, Robert Place (Md) 3 Cobb Ln, Topsham ME 04086 **Ret 1994-** B Taunton MA 1930 s Alvah & Alice. BA Bos 1952; MDiv Ya Berk 1955; Harvard DS 1957. D 6/25/1955 Bp Norman B Nash P 1/21/1956 Bp Anson Phelps Stokes Jr. c 4. Bd the Evang ES 1991-2005; Inst for Chr/Jewish Stds Bd 1986-1999; Co-Fndr of the Chr/Jewish Dialogue Grp Dio Maryland Baltimore MD 1982-1987, Chr Crossroads Oprtns Commitee 1988-1992, Stndg Com 1985-1987, Dep GC 1979-1984, Dioc Coun 1977-1978, Dioc Coun 1968-1976; Coll of Preachers Washington DC 1973-1978; R The Ch Of The Redeem Baltimore MD 1965-1993; Assoc Chr Ch Cranbrook Bloomfield Hills MI 1961-1965; R S Mary's Epis Ch Rockport MA 1958-1961; Assoc Ch Of The Redeem Chestnut Hill MA 1957-1958; Cur St Johns Ch W Hartford CT 1955-1956. Auth, *Reflections*, Ch of the Redeem, 1990; Auth, *Selected Sermons*. Bp's Awd for Distinguished Serv Dio Maryland 1989.

PATTERSON, Timothy J (NC) 607 N Greene St, Greensboro NC 27401 **R H Trin Epis Ch Greensboro NC 1996-, R 1996-, Asst 1989-1996** B Upper Darby PA 1952 s Robert & Helen. BA Duke 1975; MDiv Duke DS 1980; CAS GTS 1989. D 6/3/1989 P 8/15/1990 Bp Robert Whitridge Estill. m 10/30/1982 Kathleen E Forbes.

PATTERSON JR, William Brown (NC) 195 N Carolina Ave, Sewanee TN 37375 **Ret 2002-** B Charlotte NC 1930 s William & Eleanor. BA U So 1952; MA Harv 1954; BA Oxf GB 1955; MDiv EDS 1958; MA Oxf GB 1959; PhD Harv 1966; Hon. DLitt U So 2012. D 6/29/1958 Bp Edwin A Penick P 2/8/1959 Bp Richard Henry Baker. c 4. Mellon Appalachian Fell U of Virginia Charlottesville VA 1992-1993; Prof of Hist U So Sewanee TN 1991-2005; ExCom EDS Alum/ae Assn EDS Cambridge MA 1984-1987; Ed Bd S Lk's Journ of Theol 1984-1987; Dn of Coll of Arts and Sciences U So Sewanee TN 1980-1991; S Alb's Ch Davidson NC 1971-1978; Trst U So Sewanee TN 1969-1971; Fell Natl Endwmt for the Hmnts Cambridge Engl 1967-1968; Asst-Assoc-Prof of Hist Davidson Coll Davidson NC 1963-1980; Asst Chr Ch Hackensack NJ 1961-1962; Asst Gr Ch No Attleboro MA 1958-1961; The GTS New York NY 1961-1962. Contrib, "Richard Hooker and Reformed Theol," Vandenhoeck & Ruprecht, 2017; Auth, "Wm Perkins and the Making of a Prot Engl," Oxf Press, 2014; Auth, "The Liberal Arts at Sewanee: A Hist of Tchg and Lrng at the U So," U So, 2009; Auth, "King Jas VI & I & Reunion of Christendom," Cambridge U Press, 1997; Contrib, "Richard Hooker and the Construction of Chr Cmnty," Med & Ren Texts & Stds, 1997; Contrib, "This Sacr Mnstry: Angl Reflections for Jn Booty," Cowley Press, 1990; Auth, "Var arts on Hist". Amer Soc of Ch Hist 1963; Eccl Hist Soc (UK) 1967; Royal Hist Soc 2000. Distinguished Fac Awd U So 2002; Albert C. Outler Prize in Ecum Ch Hist Amer Soc of Ch Hist 1999; Rhodes Schlr Rhodes Trust 1953; Phi Beta Kappa U So 1951.

PATTERSON-URBANIAK, Penelope Ellen (CFla) 676 Nettles Ridge Rd, Banner Elk NC 28604 **Asst R Emm 1992-** B New Rochelle NY 1948 d John & Mary. BFA U GA 1970; MDiv Sewanee: The U So, TS 1992. D 6/20/1992 P 1/1/1993 Bp John Wadsworth Howe. m 7/8/1985 Ronald Lee Urbaniak. Emm Ch Orlando FL 1993-1999; S Mich's Ch Orlando FL 1992.

PATTISON, Benno David (At) 634 W Peachtree St Nw, Atlanta GA 30308 **Ch Of The Epiph Atlanta GA 2006-** B Cincinnati OH 1963 s Edward & Myrna. BA U GA 1985; MDiv GTS 1988. D 6/4/1988 P 6/1/1988 Bp Harry Woolston Shipps. m 5/8/1999 Laura Pattison c 6. S Lk's Epis Ch Atlanta GA 2001-2006; All SS Epis Ch Atlanta GA 1991-1997; Assoc R S Aug Of Cbury Ch Augusta GA 1988-1991.

PATTISON, Ruth Lindberg (At) 1501 Dinglewood Dr, Columbus GA 31906 B Pittsburgh PA 1958 d William & Lucille. BS Indiana U 1980; TESM 1984; MDiv Candler TS Emory U 1994. D 6/4/1994 P 12/1/1994 Bp Frank Kellogg Allan. m 5/29/1988 David Cummings c 4. Assoc S Anne's Epis Ch Atlanta GA 2009-2017; Chld's Chr Ed Dir S Thos Epis Ch Columbus GA 2008-2009, 1994-1997; Assoc Trin Epis Ch Columbus GA 1999-2003.

PATTON, David C (Mich) B San Diego CA 1929 BA MI SU 1951; MDiv ETS-BH 1954; MA San Francisco St U 1969. D 6/26/1954 Bp Richard Stanley Merrill Emrich P 4/9/1955 Bp Archie H Crowley. m 7/24/1982 Margaret Patton. S Mary's/Santa Maria Virgen Imperial Bch CA 1986-1991; S Fran In The Redwoods Mssn Willits CA 1983-1986; H Trin Epis Ch Ukiah CA 1978-1986. "Dynamis," St Geo Orth Cathd Wichita Ks, 1996.

PATTON, Kathleen (Oly) 1645 24th Ave, Longview WA 98632 **R S Steph's Epis Ch Longview WA 2011-, P in Charge 2010-2011, Assoc R 2000-** B Cherry Point NC 1958 d Harvey & Jane. U CA 1978; BA U CA 1980; MDiv CDSP 1990. D 6/9/1990 P 6/8/1991 Bp William Edwin Swing. m 4/6/1991 Richard Lee Green c 1. Co-R S Mk's Ch Yreka CA 1995-2000; Consult - - Chld's Mnstry Ch Of The Epiph San Carlos CA 1994-1995; Assoc R S Steph's Par Bel Tiburon CA 1990-1994; Conv Deputation Dio Olympia Seattle 2006-2009.

PATTON, Thomas Dunstan (Spr) **Chapl Logan Correctional Cntr Lincoln IL 1999-** B Springfield IL 1947 s Robert & Helen. BA U IL 1969; MDiv McCormick TS 1996; DAS VTS 1997. D 6/8/2003 P 6/29/2004 Bp Peter Hess Beckwith. c 2.

PATTON-GRAHAM, Heather Lynn (Haw) 2611 Ala Wai Blvd Apt 1206, Honolulu HI 96815 **S Alb's Chap Honolulu HI 2016-** B Dover DE 1973 d Robert & Judith. BA U of Delaware 1995; MDiv GTS 2003. D 1/18/2003 P 9/26/2003 Bp Wayne Wright. m 12/23/1995 Sandy Graham c 1. Assoc Cathd of St Ptr & St Paul Washington DC 2011-2016; S Thos' Ch Whitemarsh Ft Washington PA 2009-2011; All SS Ch Norristown PA 2006; The Epis Acad Newtown Sq PA 2005-2009; Asst R Chr Ch Christiana Hundred Wilmington DE 2003-2005.

PAUL, Jeffrey (Nev) 305 N Minnesota St, Carson City NV 89703 **Dep to GC Dio Nevada 2014-; R S Ptr's Epis Ch Carson City NV 1995-** B Cleveland OH 1954 s Donald & Florence. AA Orange Coast Coll 1975; BS California St U 1977; MDiv CDSP 1983. D 6/18/1983 Bp Albert Wiencke Van Duzer P 12/21/1983 Bp Robert Claflin Rusack. m 1/4/2014 Marietta Sophie Paul c 4. Assoc S Paul's Epis Ch Ventura CA 1990-1995; R S Andr's Par Torrance CA 1986-1989; Asst to R S Jas Par Los Angeles CA 1983-1986; S Jas' Sch Los Angeles CA 1983-1986; Dn of the NW Dist Dio Nevada Las Vegas 2008, Cmsn on Ord & Liciensing 2008-. Cmssnr's Coin Cmssnr of Prisons, St of Mississippi 2012; Paul Harris Fell Rotary Intl 2009. godguy@stpeterscarsoncity.org

PAUL, Kenneth Wayne (WLa) 720 Wilder Pl, Shreveport LA 71104 **Ret 2008-; Ret 2007-; Chair Bd H Cross Chld Placement Agcy 1984-; Chair Bd H Cross Villas hsng Elderly & Handicapped 1983-** B Alexandria LA 1935 s Newton & Mellie. BA Asbury U 1957; BD SMU 1960; DIT Oxf GB 1962; GTS 1965; Sewanee: The U So, TS 1965; MTh SMU 1972. D 6/30/1965 Bp Girault M Jones P 5/18/1966 Bp Iveson Batchelor Noland. m 9/26/1976 Virginia M Paul c 2. Pres Dio Louisiana New Orleans LA 1996-1997, P-in-res 1995-1997; R Ch Of The H Cross Shreveport LA 1968-2007; Dio Wstrn Louisiana Alexandria LA 1965-1992; S Mk's Cathd Shreveport LA 1965-1968; Serv Methodist Ch 1959-1964. Auth, "Rel & Psychol," *Louisiana Med Journ.*

PAUL, Linda Joy (Okla) 501 S Cincinnati Ave, Tulsa OK 74103 B Tulsa OK 1951 d C E Gene & Mona Lee. MEd U of Oklahoma 1972; BA Oklahoma St 1996. D 6/16/2007 Bp Robert Manning Moody. m 12/21/1986 Arthur Paul.

PAUL, Marcea Elanor (SeFla) 10600 Caribbean Blvd, Cutler Bay FL 33189 B Portland Jamaica 1954 d Vincent & Gerel. D 11/23/2013 Bp Leo Frade. c 4.

PAUL, Michael (ND) 6419 15th St S, Fargo ND 58104 **S Ptr's Epis Ch Williston ND 2015-** B Sudan 1960 s Paul & Roa. Trans 3/22/2005 Bp Robert Wilkes Ihloff. m 7/6/1985 Lona Juru Samson c 6. Dio No Dakota Fargo ND 2014-2015; S Lk's Ch San Diego CA 2006-2010; Dio Maryland Baltimore MD 2006. kijupaul@yahoo.com

PAUL, Richard (Colo) **St Matt's Epis Ch Grand Jct CO Dio Colorado Denver CO 2017-** D 6/10/2017 Bp Robert John O'Neill.

PAUL, Rocks-Anne (SwFla) 1200 4th St W, Palmetto FL 34221 B Bradenton FL 1951 d Richard & Lois. BA Sonoma St U 1995. D 6/12/2004 Bp John Bailey Lipscomb. c 3. Ch Of The H Sprt Osprey FL 2006-2012. d the King 1986.

PAUL, Wectnick (Ct) Box 1309, Port-Au-Prince Haiti B Hinche HT 1946 s Claudius & Anne. BA Lycee Dumarsais Estime 1965; BA Lycee Alexandre Petion 1966; Cert Ufcwi 1976; Ceteh 1977. D 9/18/1977 P 5/1/1978 Bp Luc Anatole Jacques Garnier. m 12/4/1980 Marie Paul c 3. Dio Connecticut Meriden CT 2005-2009; L'Eglise de L'Ephiphanie Stamford CT 1997-2009; S Jn's Ch Stamford CT 1997-2004; R Gros-Morne 1982-1994; P'S Asst S Sauveur In Cayes 1978-1982; Dio Haiti Port-au-Prince HT 1977-1995.

PAULIKAS, Steven D (LI) 286-88 7th Ave, Brooklyn NY 11215 **R All SS Ch Brooklyn NY 2013-, 2011-2013; Term Mem Coun on Frgn Relatns 2012-** B Royal Oak MI 1978 s Alfonsas & Janet. BA Ya 2001; MA Camb Cambridge Engl 2002; MDiv GTS 2008. D 6/23/2007 Bp Kenneth Lester Price P 6/28/2008 Bp Thomas Edward Breidenthal. m 10/25/2014 Jesse Lazar. Gr Ch Brooklyn NY 2008-2011; Jrnlst Freelance 2003-2005.

PAULIS, Marion Helen (SD) 201 S 4th St, Milbank SD 57252 **P-in-c Chr Epis Ch Milbank SD 2011-** B Watertown SD 1948 d Carl & Helen. FIT - NYU 1969; So Dakota St U 1970. D 4/30/2011 P 11/26/2011 Bp John Tarrant.

PAULSON, Diane Theresa (Ida) 1785 Arlington Dr, Pocatello ID 83204 **Trin Epis Ch Pocatello ID 1998-** B Chicago IL 1943 d Jacob & Theresa. BS Nthrn Illinois U 1966; MEd Indiana U 1969. D 4/25/1998 Bp John Stuart Thornton P 5/12/2001 Bp Harry Brown Bainbridge III. m 2/1/1969 Donald Leonard Paulson c 3.

PAULSON, Donald Leonard (Ida) 1785 Arlington Dr, Pocatello ID 83204 **Trin Epis Ch Pocatello ID 2998-, Asst 1998-2998** B Minneapolis MN 1944 s Donald & Eleanor. BA Hamline U 1966; MEd Indiana U 1968; PhD U of Iowa 1972. D 4/25/1998 P 10/1/1998 Bp John Stuart Thornton. m 2/1/1969 Diane Theresa Paulson.

PAULUS, Ruth B (SO) **Chapl Fairborn Fire Dept 2011-; R S Chris's Ch Fairborn OH 2005-; Cler Wellness T/F Chair Dio Sthrn Ohio Cincinnati OH 2013-** B Piqua OH 1953 d William & Ruth. Dmin SWTS; BSN Franklin U 1994; MSN Wright St U 1997; MDiv Bex Sem 2005. D 11/17/2004 P 6/25/2005 Bp Herbert Thompson Jr. m 9/18/1981 Richard J Paulus c 2.

PAVLAC, Brian Alexander (Be) 365 Rutter Ave, Kingston PA 18704 **P-in-c S Steph's Epis Ch Wilkes Barre PA 2015-, Asst 2010-2015; The Epis Ch Of S Clem And S Ptr Wilkes Barre PA 2009-** B Ohio 1956 s Charles & Elsie. BA Bowling Green St U 1978; MA Bowling Green St U 1980; MA U of Notre Dame 1982; PhD U of Notre Dame 1986. D 12/21/2009 P 6/29/2010 Bp Paul Victor Marshall. m 10/28/1981 Elizabeth Lott c 2. S Lk's Ch Scranton PA 2014. Ed and Contrib, "Game of Thrones versus Hist: Written in Blood," Wiley, 2017; Auth, "A Concise Survey of Wstrn Civilization: Supremacies and Diversities throughout Hist, Second Ed," Rowman & Littlefield, 2015; Auth, "Witch Hunts in the Wstrn Wrld: Persecution and Punishment from the Inquisition through the Salem Trials," Greenwood, 2009; Transltr, "A Warrior Bp of the 12th Century: The Deeds of Albero of Trier, by Balderich," Pontifical Inst of Medieval Stds, 2008. office@ststephenswb.org

PAXTON, Richard Edwin (Ky) 820 Broadway St, Paducah KY 42001 **D Gr Ch Paducah KY 2010-** B Paducah KY 1962 s James & Peggy. BBA Notre Dame 1984; MBA Stanford 1989; Sch of Mnstry 2009. D 5/2/2010 Bp Ted Gulick Jr. m 9/28/1985 Cheryl Paxton c 4.

PAYDEN-TRAVERS, Christine (SwVa) 1711 Link Rd, Lynchburg VA 24503 **hospice Chapl Centra Hlth Lynchburg VA 2008-** B Washington DC 1945 d Carl & Helen. BA U MI 1967; MS Col 1968; MDiv GTS 1984. D 6/11/1984 Bp Charles Bennison Sr P 5/1/1985 Bp Peter J Lee. m 9/16/1972 John Payden-Travers c 2. St Paul Evang Luth Ch 2006; R Gr Memi Ch Lynchburg VA 1997-2006; Dio SW Virginia Roanoke VA 1988-1996; R S Ptr's Epis Ch Callaway VA 1988-1996; Cur St Jas Ch Richmond VA 1984-1988.

PAYER, Donald R (Ia) 2205 Green Hills Dr, Ames IA 50014 **Fndr Matt 25 Hse-Hm for released prisoners Ames IA 2007-; Chapl Story Cnty Prison Nevada IA 1996-** B Fargo ND 1928 s Roy & Catherine. LLB U of Iowa 1954. D 12/19/1995 Bp Chris Christopher Epting. m 9/6/1952 Janet Mae Payer c 2. D Epis Par of Ames Ames IA 1995-2015.

✠ PAYNE, The Rt Rev Claude Edward (Tex) 2702 Charter House Dr, Abilene TX 79606 **Ret Bp of Texas Dio Texas Houston TX 2003-, Bp of Texas 1993-2003** B Abilene TX 1932 s Victor & Katherine. BA Rice U 1954; BS Rice U 1955; MDiv CDSP 1964. D 7/10/1964 Bp Everett H Jones P 1/14/1965 Bp Richard Earl Dicus Con 10/9/1993 for Tex. m 7/9/1955 Barbara King c 2. Chair of Strng Com Gathering of Leaders 2006-2016; Mem, Panel of Reference Angl Comm London Untd Kingdom 2005-2008; Chair of the Bd ETSSw 2001-2003; Trst Ch Pension Fund 2000-2012; Chair of the Bd St. Lk's Epis Hosp Houston TX 1995-2003; Bd Mem PBFWR 1986-1989; R S Mart's Epis Ch Houston TX 1983-1993; Asst Secy HOB 1973-1986; R S Mk's Ch Beaumont TX 1968-1983; Asst S Mk's Ch Houston TX 1966-1968; Asst Ch Of The Epiph Kingsville TX 1964-1966; Campus Mssnr TX A&I U Kingsville TX 1964-1966. Co-Auth, "Reclaiming the Great Cmsn," Jossey-Bass, 2000. Compass Rose Soc 1995. DD Sem of the SW 2013; DD GTS 2012; Distinguished Alum Rice U 1996; DD U So 1994; DD CDSP 1988.

PAYNE, Edward Thomas (SO) 8363 Cannon Knoll Ct, West Chester OH 45069 **P-in-c Gr Epis Ch Pomeroy OH 2004-; Dioc Faith & Life Com Dio Sthrn Ohio Cincinnati OH 1999-** B Cleveland OH 1948 s Brady & Betty. BA Cleveland Inst of Mus 1971; MA Cleveland Inst of Mus 1972; MDiv GTS 1996. D 5/24/1997 P 5/1/1998 Bp Herbert Thompson Jr. m 8/12/1978 Gail Annette Payne c 4. P-in-c S Fran Epis Ch Springboro OH 2010-2015; S Paul's Ch Chillicothe OH 2007-2009; Gr Ch Pomeroy OH 2006-2007; S Mary's Ch Waynesville OH 2002-2003; P-in-c St. Mary Epis Ch Waynesville OH 2001-2003; R S Simon of Cyrene Epis Ch Cincinnati OH 2000-2001; S Simon Of Cyrene Epis Ch Cincinnati OH 1997-2001; Chf Precentor GTS New York NY 1995-1996; Guest Lectr GTS New York NY 1993-1995. UBE 1997. Cert for Serv as Chf Precentor The Gnrl Sem New York 1996; The Seymour Prize for Extemporaneous Preaching The Gnrl Sem New York 1995.

PAYNE, Harold Womack (Ark) 3412 W 7th St, Little Rock AR 72205 **Ret 2003-** B Moore County NC 1941 s Augustus & Edna. BA Pfeiffer Coll Misenheimer NC 1963; BD VTS 1966. D 6/29/1966 P 6/24/1967 Bp Thomas Augustus Fraser Jr. Vic S Mk's Ch Hope AR 2002-2003; Mssnr S Jn's Ch Camden AR 2000-2003; Mssnr S Jas Ch Magnolia AR 2000-2002; Dio E Tennessee Knoxville TN 1996-1999; Vic S Thos Ch Elizabethton TN 1995-1996; Vic S Mary Magd Ch Troy NC 1992-1995; P Gr Ch Chanute KS 1988-1991; Neosho Vlly Epis Cluster Chanute KS 1988-1991; Stff Mnstry Devmt Dio Nevada Las Vegas 1979-1988; S Paul's Ch Salisbury NC 1975-1976; Novc Ch Of The Ascen And H Trin W Pk NY 1971-1975; Asst S Mart's Epis Ch Charlotte NC 1969-1971; Vic S Andr's Ch Haw River NC 1967-1969; D Chr Ch Walnut Cove NC 1966-1967; D S Phil Germanton NC 1966-1967.

PAYNE, John Douglas (FtW) 4902 George St, Wichita Falls TX 76302 **P-in-c The Epis Ch of Wichita Falls Wichita Falls TX 2008-; Ret 2006-** B Monahans TX 1937 s John & Annie. BA NWU 1959; USA Security Agcy Sch 1960; MDiv GTS 1965. D 6/22/1965 Bp Girault M Jones P 5/5/1966 Bp Iveson Batchelor Noland. m 8/14/1965 Mildred K Payne c 2. R All SS Ch Wichita Falls TX 1973-2006; Cmdr Chapl Corps USNR 1972-1997; R Ch Of The Epiph Opelousas LA 1968-1973; Cur St Jas Epis Ch and Sch Alexandria LA 1965-1968; Mem COM Dio Ft Worth Ft Worth TX 1995-2006, Pres - Stndg Commitee 1988-1989, Dn of the Nthrn Dnry 1985-1992, Chair - COM 1983-1985; Chair - Post Com (COM) Dio Dallas Dallas TX 1978-1981, COM 1976-1978, Exec Coun 1976-1978; Louisiana Ch Conf Dio Louisiana New Orleans LA 1970-1972. Columnist, "Rel Page," *Wichita Falls Times-Record News,* Scripps-Howard, 2004.

PAYNE, Nona Marie Jones (Dal) 736 Valiant Cir, Garland TX 75043 B Winthrop AR 1931 d Thomas & Pearl. Lic Sacr Theol Dio Dal Angl TS 1986; BA U of Texas 1987. D 6/20/1992 Bp Donis Dean Patterson. c 1. Asst Ch Of Our Sav Dallas TX 1997-1999; Campus Mnstry In Eastfield Coll Cmnty Of Ch Dallas TX 1995-1998; D The Epis Ch Of The Trsfg Dallas TX 1986-1997.

PAYNE, Pamela Kathryn (Ala) **S Mich's Epis Ch Fayette AL 2016-** D 5/21/2016 P 12/17/2016 Bp John Mckee Sloan Sr.

PAYNE, Richard Leeds (Mass) Po Box 289, Brewster MA 02631 **Ret 1998-** B Boston MA 1933 s William & Alice. BA Wms 1954; BD EDS 1957; MEd Boston Coll 1972. D 6/8/1957 Bp William A Lawrence P 12/16/1957 Bp Lane W Barton. m 6/6/1953 Joan W Payne c 4. Non-par 1985-1998; Vic S Steph's Ch E Haddam CT 1982-1985; Non-par 1970-1982; Asst The Ch Of S Mary Of The Harbor Provincetown MA 1969-1970; R Ch Of The Redeem Pendleton OR 1964-1969; Asst Chapl Holderness Sch Plymouth NH 1960-1964; P-in-c S Thos Ch Canyon City OR 1957-1960.

PAYNE, Susan Strauss (Ark) 1723 Center St, Little Rock AR 72206 B Malvern AR 1940 d Wilfred & Janet. BA U of Arkansas 1989; MDiv SWTS 1995. D 6/15/1995 P 12/16/1995 Bp Larry Maze. m 2/2/1991 Barry Coplin c 2. Asst to the R, Chld & Fam Mnstry Chr Epis Ch Little Rock AR 2004-2010; Vic S Mich's Epis Ch Little Rock AR 1999-2004; Dio Arkansas Little Rock AR 1998-1999, 1991-1993, Yth Coordntr 1991-1993; Mssnr S Jas Ch Magnolia AR 1998-1999; Mssnr S Jn Epis Ch 1998-1999; H Trin Epis Ch Hot Sprg AR 1997-1998; Cur S Mk's Epis Ch Little Rock AR 1995-1997.

PAYNE-CARTER, Gloria Edith Eureka (WNY) 15 Fernhill Ave, Buffalo NY 14215 B Laventille TT 1945 d Clyde & Phyllis. AAS CUNY 1969; BS CUNY 1974; MA NYU 1976; MDiv GTS 1996; Epis Hlth Serv 2001. D 4/21/1997 Bp Orris George Walker Jr P 6/5/1999 Bp Rodney Rae Michel. c 1. S Phil's Ch Buffalo NY 2005-2016; All SS Ch Bayside NY 2003-2005; Vic S Gabr's Ch Brooklyn NY 2001-2002; Epis Hlth Serv Far Rockaway NY 1998-2000; Dir Of Pstr Care Interfaith Med Cntr Brooklyn NY 1998-2000; Cur Ch Of SS Steph And Mart Brooklyn NY 1998-1999; Dio Long Island Garden City NY 1997-1998; Cur S Barn Epis Ch Brooklyn NY 1997-1998. Black Cleric Caucus Dio Li 1997-2003; CHS (Assoc) 1997-2003; ECW 1988-2003; UBE 1988-2003.

PAYNE-HARDIN, Mary Elizabeth (CGC) **S Andr's Epis Ch Panama City FL 2017-** D 12/3/2016 Bp Russell Kendrick.

PAYNE-WIENS, Reginald A (NC) 1941 Webberville Rd, Austin TX 78721 **Trin Epis Sch Charlotte NC 2015-** B Miami FL 1968 s Charles & Gladys. BA Valdosta St U 1993; MDiv VTS 1997. D 5/24/1997 P 6/6/1998 Bp Henry Irving Louttit. m 10/11/1997 Elena Wiens c 2. All SS' Epis Ch Concord NC 2013-2014; S Lk's Epis Hosp Houston TX 2013; S Jas Ch Austin TX 2010-2013; S Marg of Scotland Par San Juan Capo CA 2003-2009; Yth Min Dio SE Florida Miami 2000-2003; S Paul's Epis Ch Paterson NJ 1999-2000; S Paul's Rock Creek Washington DC 1997-1999; Asst R S Paul's Rock Creek Wdc.

PAYSON, Charles Beck (Chi) N1133 Vinne Haha Rd, Fort Atkinson WI 53538 B Portsmouth VA 1942 s Harold & Anne. AB Harv 1964; MDiv EDS 1972. D 10/3/1972 P 6/1/1973 Bp Frederick Hesley Belden. m 6/12/1964 Evelyn Payson c 3. R S Anskar's Ch Rockford IL 1993-2002; R S Peters Epis Ch Ft Atkinson WI 1977-1993; Cur Chr Ch Cooperstown NY 1973-1977; Cur Gr Epis Ch Lawr MA 1972-1973. cepayson@gmail.com

PAYSON, Deborah (Pa) 531 Maison Place, Bryn Mawr PA 19010 **Trin Ch Gulph Mills Kng Of Prussia PA 2004-** B Albany NY 1943 d George & Mary. BA W Chester U of Pennsylvania 1975; MA Luth TS 2006. D 6/18/2004 Bp Charles Ellsworth Bennison Jr. c 1.

PAYSON, Evelyn (Mil) N1133 Vinne Ha Ha Rd, Fort Atkinson WI 53538 **D S Lk's Ch Whitewater WI 2009-** B Providence RI 1943 d Herbert & Evelyn. BA Rad 1963; MLS Simmons Coll 1964. D 6/13/1992 Bp Roger John White. m 6/12/1964 Charles Beck Payson c 3. D Trin Ch Janesville WI 2004-2006, D 2004-2006; D S Anskar's Ch Rockford IL 1993-2002; S Andr's Ch Madison WI 1992-1993; D S Peters Epis Ch Ft Atkinson WI 1992-1993.

PEABODY, Morrill Woodrow (RG) Po Box 247, Lemitar NM 87823 **P Epis Ch Of The Epiph Socorro NM 2003-; Ret 2002-** B Biddeford ME 1942 s Morrill & Eleanor. BA U Pac 1965; MDiv CDSP 1969. D 9/13/1969 P 8/8/1970 Bp Victor Manuel Rivera. m 7/30/1980 Ginny Patricia Peabody c 3. Gd Samar Epis Ch Sammamish WA 2000-2002; Dio Olympia Seattle 1998-1999; Vic S Dav Emm Epis Ch Shoreline WA 1995-1998; Int S Paul's Epis Ch Bremerton WA 1994-1995; Assoc S Thos Epis Ch Medina WA 1992-1994; Asst S Marg's Epis Ch Palm Desert CA 1991-1992; Vic S Matt's Ch San Andreas CA 1989-1991; 1977-1989; S Paul In The Desert Palm Sprg CA 1976; S Ptr's Epis Ch Kernville CA 1975-1976; Yth Dir Epis Dio San Joaquin Modesto CA 1973-1974, 1972-1976; R S Phil's Ch Coalinga CA 1971-1973; Cur S Paul's Epis Ch Visalia CA 1970-1971.

PEABODY, S Walton (Pa) 234 Yahoola Shoals Dr, Dahlonega GA 30533 B Atlanta,GA 1938 s S & Louise. BA Emory U 1960; Edinburgh U 1961; MDiv Candler TS Emory U 1963; MA U Denv 1974; U of Maryland 1977; U So 1992. D 6/13/1992 P 12/12/1992 Bp William Arthur Beckham. m 3/19/1963 Jacqueline L Peabody. Chapl CFS The Sch at Ch Farm Exton 1992-2004.

PEABODY, William Nelson (Mo) 852 Water Andric Rd, Saint Johnsbury VT 05819 **Non-par 1970-** B Boston MA 1936 s Frank & Virginia. BA Cor 1959; MDiv VTS 1963; DMin Eden TS 1972. D 6/15/1963 P 12/1/1963 Bp Roger W Blanchard. m 7/2/1960 Elizabeth C Peabody c 3. Assoc Dir Educ Cntr S Louis Missouri 1968-1970; Assoc R S Paul's Ch Englewood NJ 1965-1968; Asst Ch Of The H Trin Oxford MD 1963-1965.

PEACOCK, Andrea Coffee (Ala) D 10/1/2016 Bp John Mckee Sloan Sr.

PEACOCK, Caroline (NY) St Luke In The Fields Episcopal Church, 487 Hudson St, New York NY 10014 B Hong Kong 1978 d John & Eileen. BA and BFA U MI 2000; MSW Hunter Coll 2003; MDiv GTS 2013; MDiv The GTS 2013. D 3/2/2013 P 9/7/2013 Bp Andrew Marion Lenow Dietsche. m 6/12/2010 Lauren Heather Marcewicz c 2. S Paul's Epis Ch Atlanta GA 2015-2016.

PEACOCK, George Hunt (RG) 604 Aredo De Carlos, Farmington NM 87401 **Died 7/5/2016** B Farmington NM 1940 s Wendell & Mary. Trin Sem; BA Stan 1963; MD U of New Mex 1968; MA JHU 1974. D 2/21/1998 P 3/17/1999 Bp Terence Kelshaw. m 3/11/1978 Charlotte Gibbs Carmines c 2. P-in-c S Jn's Ch Farmington NM 2007-2009; Assoc Rectort St Johns Epis Ch Farmington NM 1998-2016; Assoc Rectort Navajoland Area Mssn Farmington NM 1998-2016.

PEACOCK, Joan Louise (Va) 7515 Snowpea Ct Unit M, Alexandria VA 22306 **P Assoc Emm Epis Ch Alexandria VA 2014-; Circ&Coll Dev Asst VTS/Bp Payne Libr 2008-** B Washington DC 1955 d Bernard & Mary. BA Geo Mason U 1991; MDiv VTS 1994. D 6/11/1994 P 12/14/1994 Bp Peter J Lee. c 3. P Assoc All SS Ch Alexandria VA 2008-2013; Int Assoc S Geo's Ch Fredericksburg VA 2003-2005; R Ch Of The H Cross Dunn Loring VA 2001-2003; Assoc S Lk's Ch Alexandria VA 1994-2001; Resolutns Com Dio Virginia Richmond VA 2002-2004, Stndg Com 1997-2000, Cmsn for the Prevention of Sexual Misconduct 1995-1999, Educ Com 1994-1997. jpeacock@vts.edu

PEACOCK, Margaret Ann (NMich) Po Box 66, Saint Ignace MI 49781 **1992-** B Durham NC 1953 d William & Helen. Roa 1972; Amer Inst for Frgn Study Richmond Surrey GB 1973; BA Untd States Intl U 1975. D 9/12/1992 Bp Thomas Kreider Ray. Auth, "A Poem Called Lost," Forw Mvmt Press, 1999.

PEACOCK, Virginia A (NMich) PO Box 305, Deer Isle ME 04627 **R S Brendan's Epis Ch Deer Isle ME 2008-; Dio Maine Portland ME 1982-** B Oak Park IL 1941 d Daura & Maryella. BSEd U MI 1965; MDiv EDS 1977; MA U of St Michaels Coll Toronto 1979; PhD U of St Michaels Coll Toronto 1987. D 6/20/1982 P 11/1/1983 Bp H Coleman Mcgehee Jr. c 2. R Trin Epis Ch Houghton MI 2005-2008; S Jn's Ch Negaunee MI 1995-2005; Dio Nthrn Michigan Marquette MI 1995-2000; Gr Ch Ishpeming MI 1995-2000; Dio Michigan Detroit MI 1990-1992, 1987-1989; Epis Stdt Fndt Ann Arbor MI 1987-1995; Chapl U MI 1987-1995; Vic Ch Of The Incarn Pittsfield Twp Ann Arbor MI 1986-1987; Asst S Clem's In Toronto Ontario Can 1985-1986; Dio Toronto Toronto ON 1983-1985; Asst S Mich's & All Ang In Toronto Ontario Can 1983-1985; Asst Trin Chap In Toronto Ontario Can 1982-1983. ginnypeacock@gmail.com

PEAK, Ronald Robert (Kan) 609 Gould St, Eustis FL 32726 B Oakland CA 1944 s John & Marian. ArmdF; Ft Hays St U; San Diego City Coll; Trident Tech Coll; Dplma Epis TS of the SW 1979. D 9/25/1979 P 4/30/1980 Bp Gerald Nicholas Mcallister. c 3. R Trin Epis Ch El Dorado KS 2004-2009; R All SS Epis Ch Miami OK 2002-2004; P-in-c S Ptr's Epis Ch Key W FL 1999-2002; R Ch Of The Atone Ft Lauderdale FL 1991-1993; Port Chapl - Port Of Palm Bch Dio SE Florida Miami 1988-1991; R S Geo's Epis Ch Riviera Bch FL 1986-1991; R S Mich's Ch Hays KS 1983-1986; Assoc R S Lk's Epis Ch Bartlesville OK 1981-1983; Founding Vic Ch Of The H Cross Owasso OK 1980-1981; Cur S Lk's Ch Tulsa OK 1979-1981; M-in-c S Barn Ch Dillon SC 1978-1979.

PEALER, Judson Paul (Me) 2614 Main St, Rangeley ME 04970 B Mount Vernon OH 1950 s Arlo & Martha. BFA OH SU 1973; MDiv SWTS 1987. D 6/11/1987 P 12/11/1987 Bp Daniel Lee Swenson. m 6/19/1971 Sandra T Pealer c 3. R Ch Of The Gd Shpd Rangeley ME 2009-2015; Dio Maine Portland ME 2009-2015; P-in-c S Paul's Ch Windsor VT 2004-2009; R S Eustace Ch Lake Placid NY 1999-2004; R Emm Ch Keyser WV 1993-1999; Gr Ch Sheldon VT 1989-1993; R H Trin Epis Ch Swanton VT 1989-1993; R S Jn's Ch Highgate

Ctr VT 1989-1993; S Lk's Ch Alburg VT 1989-1993; Trin Ch Rutland VT 1987-1989.

PEARCE, Clyde Willard (Ala) 1301 Paradise Cove Ln, Wilsonville AL 35186 B Tuscaloosa AL 1940 s Rachel. D 10/30/2004 Bp Marc Handley Andrus. m 6/17/1960 Eunice Carole Pearce c 2.

PEARCE JR, Robert Charles (Kan) 1720 Westbank Way, Manhattan KS 66503 **Archd S Paul's Ch Manhattan KS 2000-; Archd Dio Kansas Topeka KS 2007-** B Denver CO 1946 s Robert & Mildred. BFA U of Alabama 1971; MA U of Alabama 1975; PhD U of Tennessee 1984. D 2/19/2000 Bp William Edward Smalley. m 12/31/1980 Demerilus Ann Pearce c 2. Chapl Mercy Hlth Cntr Manhattan KS 1998-2010.

PEARCE, Sherilyn (SO) Christ Church Cathedral, 318 E 4th St, Cincinnati OH 45202 **Cn Chr Ch Cathd Cincinnati OH 2013-** B Iowa City IA 1966 BA Baylor U 1988; MDiv Yale DS 1993. D 9/22/2012 Bp Gerry Wolf P 5/1/2013 Bp W Nicholas Knisely Jr. m 12/5/1992 Scott Alan Gunn. spearce@cccath.org

PEARCE, William Philip Daniel (ECR) 1037 Olympic Ln, Seaside CA 93955 B New Orleans LA 1926 s William & Henrietta. BA Stan 1948; Ripon Coll Cuddesdon 1957; Cert U of Leeds Gb 1964; MA U of Leeds Gb 1975. Trans 7/1/1989 Bp Charles Shannon Mallory. S Mths Ch Seaside CA 1994-1995; Dio El Camino Real Salinas CA 1990-1993; York Sch Monterey CA 1989-1992; Chapl York Sch Monterey CA 1988-1992; Serv Ch Of Engl 1960-1986; Asst S Matt's Epis Ch San Mateo CA 1957-1958. Auth, "Generation Gap," *Mambo Press*, 1983.

PEARSALL, Arlene Epp (SD) 115 N Dakota Ave Apt 117, Sioux Falls SD 57104 **Canan Pstr Calv Epis Cathd Souix Falls SD 2015-** B York NE 1943 d Jacob & Emma. BA Bethel U 1965; MA Stan 1969; PhD U IL 1991; MS U IL 1995. D 6/12/2000 Bp Creighton Leland Robertson. m 12/10/1980 Robert B Pearsall. Chapl Avera McKennan Hosp Sioux Falls SD 1999-2014. Auth, "Johnannes Pauli," *Johannes Pauli (1450-1520) on the Ch & Cler*, Edwin Mellen Press, 1994; Auth, "Johannes Pauli and the Papal Indulgences," *Reform and Counterreform: Dialectics of the Word in the Wstrn Chrsnty since Luther*, 1994; Auth, "Murders in Saxony: Dateline1500," *Clues: A Journ of Detection 14*, 1993. Assn for Epis Deacons 1999; Ch & Synagogue Libr Assn 1996-2015; Natl Ch Libr Assn 1996-2015. Assn for Epis Deacons St. Steph Awd for Servnt Ldrshp 2013.

PEARSALL, Martin A (Colo) 4939 Harvest Rd, Colorado Springs CO 80917 **Assoc Gr And S Steph's Epis Ch Colorado Sprg CO 2009-** B Norwalk CT 1946 s Raymond & Elizabeth. Epis TS of the SW; BA Alleg 1967; MA U Denv 1970. D 11/10/1983 P 5/16/1984 Bp William Harvey Wolfrum. m 6/19/1976 Mary Pearsall c 2. S Fran Of Assisi Colorado Spg CO 1986-2007; Vic H Cross Epis Mssn Sterling CO 1984-1986.

PEARSON, Albert Claybourn (Tex) 261 Fell St, San Francisco CA 94102 **Gr Epis Ch Georgetown TX 2016-; Vic Iglesia San Francisco de Asis Austin TX 2012-; P-in-c The Epis Ch Of S Jn The Evang San Francisco CA 2011-** B Lubbock TX 1978 s Anthony & Tomijann. BA New Coll 2004; MDiv CDSP 2007. D 6/13/2008 P 12/6/2008 Bp Marc Handley Andrus. m 4/8/2009 Rahel R Pearson c 1. Epis TS Of The SW Austin TX 2014-2016; Vic The Great Cmsn Fndt Houston TX 2012-2016; Ch Of The H Innoc San Francisco CA 2011-2012; Dio California San Francisco CA 2008-2010. bpearson@sfaepiscopal.org

PEARSON II, Alonzo Lawrence (FdL) 421 Lowell Pl, Neenah WI 54956 B Columbus OH 1949 s Alonzo & Barbara. BA OH SU 1973; MDiv TESM 1979. D 6/20/1981 P 5/19/1982 Bp Archibald Donald Davies. m 6/10/1972 Kathy S Pearson c 3. R S Alb's Epis Ch Marshfield WI 1997-2003; Assoc S Thos Ch Menasha WI 1988-1997; Asst Ch Of The Annunc Lewisville TX 1983-1988; Cur St Andr Epis Ch Ft Worth TX 1981-1983.

PEARSON JR, Andrew C (Ala) Cathedral Church of the Advent, 2017 Sixth Avenue North, Birmingham AL 35203 **Cn for Theol and Evang The Cathd Ch Of The Adv Birmingham AL 2015-, Cn for Theol and Evang 2011-2014; GC Dep (Alt) So Carolina Charleston SC 2012-, Dioc Coun 2008-2011** B Washington DC 1980 s Andrew & Denise. BA U of Virginia 2002; BTh Oxf GB 2007. D 4/14/2007 P 10/13/2007 Bp Edward Lloyd Salmon Jr. m 6/24/2006 Lauren S Pearson c 3. Assoc R Par Ch of St. Helena Beaufort SC 2007-2011; Dioc Coun Dio Alabama Birmingham 2013-2015. eva@cathedraladvent.com

PEARSON, Anna S (NY) 78 Main St, Hastings On Hudson NY 10706 **R Gr Ch Hastings Hds NY 2008-** B Bethesda MD 1963 d John & Hester. BA Barnard Coll of Col 1985; MDiv Ya Berk 1992; DMin Hartford Sem 2007. D 5/30/1992 P 2/15/1993 Bp David Elliot Johnson. m 5/9/1992 Charles Woods Pearson c 3. Asst St Johns Ch W Hartford CT 2000-2008; Chapl Kent Sch Kent CT 1992-2000.

PEARSON, Bryan Austin (Mass) **Assoc The Cathd Ch Of S Paul Boston MA 2017-; S Mk's Epis Ch Burlington MA 2015-** B Fort Gordon, Georgia 1980 s James & Lisa. Bachelor of Arts Armstrong St U 2005; Mstr of Div Emm Chr Sem 2009; Cert EDS 2012. Trans 1/15/2016 as Priest Bp Alan Gates.

PEARSON, Cedric Eugene (O) 14778 Dexter Falls Rd, Perrysburg OH 43551 B Fairfield AL 1945 s Junior & Flora. BA U of Virginia 1967; U MI 1968; MA Chicago TS 1973; Cert SWTS 1973; Cert Trin Sch For Mnstry 2011. D 5/12/

1973 Bp Quintin Ebenezer Primo Jr P 12/8/1973 Bp James Winchester Montgomery. m 4/22/1967 Judy Pearson c 2. P-in-c Gr Ch Defiance OH 2009-2012, R 1975-1982, R 1975-1982; Int S Andr's Epis Ch Toledo OH 2007-2009; Chapl Kingston Hlth Care Perrysburg & Sylvania OH 2005-2009; R S Tim's Epis Ch Perrysburg OH 1982-2004; Cur S Mk's Ch Evanston IL 1973-1975. Phi Beta Kappa U of Virginia Chapt of PBK 1967; Woodrow Wilson Natl Fllshp WW Natl Fllshp Fndt 1967.

PEARSON, Daniel (Minn) 1970 Nature View Lane, W. St. Paul MN 55118 B Minneapolis MN 1941 s Claude & Florence. BA U MN 1964; STB GTS 1968. D 6/24/1968 Bp Hamilton Hyde Kellogg P 3/17/1969 Bp Philip Frederick McNairy. m 5/22/1983 Anne Arlene Miner-Pearson c 2. Int S Barth's Epis Ch Poway CA 2013-2015; Int S Ptr's Epis Ch S Louis MO 2011-2012; Int S Mart's By The Lake Epis Minnetonka MN 2009-2011; Int St Dav's Epis Ch Minnetonka MN 2007-2009; Int S Steph The Mtyr Ch Minneapolis MN 2005-2007; R S Clem's Ch S Paul MN 1983-2005; R Par Of The H Trin And S Anskar Minneapolis MN 1982-1983; Chapl U Epis Cntr Minneapolis MN 1981-1983; R Trin Ch Excelsior MN 1976-1981; Cn Theol Cathd Ch Of S Mk Minneapolis MN 1972-1976; R S Paul's Epis Ch Owatonna MN 1968-1972.

PEARSON, David Ernest (NI) **S Fran Ch Chesterton IN 2015-** D 1/23/2015 P 7/23/2015 Bp Edward Stuart Little II.

PEARSON, Francis J (Be) 10 Chapel Rd, New Hope PA 18938 B Williamsport PA 1957 s William & Sarah. Geo; MDiv St Johns TS; MDiv St Johns TS; MDiv St Vinc Sem; MDiv St Vinc Sem; BS U of Scranton. Rec 7/10/2004 as Priest Bp Paul Victor Marshall. S Jas-S Geo Epis Ch Jermyn PA 2015-2016; Ch Of The Gd Shpd Scranton PA 2012-2013; P-in-c S Phil's Ch New Hope PA 2005-2012; Iconographer Self 1994-2005.

PEARSON, James Thomas (SD) Christ Episcopal Church, 513 Douglas Ave, Yankton SD 57078 **R Chr Epis Ch Yankton SD 2000-** B Sisseton SD 1954 s Julian & Charlotte. U So; BS So Dakota St U 1980; MDiv VTS 1988. D 6/28/1988 P 3/1/1989 Bp Craig Barry Anderson. m 8/25/1973 Gloria Jane Pearson c 3. Dio So Dakota Pierre SD 1988-2000; Vic H Comf Epis Ch Lower Brule SD 1988-2000; Chr Ch Chamberlain SD 1988-1989; Tutor For The Native Mnstry Prog Vancouver TS. Bro Chr Unity. christchurch@iw.net

PEARSON, Janice Von (Colo) **Our Merc Sav Epis Ch Denver CO 2006-; Our Merc Sav Mnstrs Denver CO 2006-** B 1947 D 11/13/2004 Bp Robert John O'Neill. m 8/21/1976 Alexander Pearson c 2. Ch Of S Jn Chrys Golden CO 2004-2016.

PEARSON, John Norris (Oly) 2831 Marietta St, Steilacoom WA 98388 B Everett WA 1924 s John & Margaret. BD WA SU 1949; Olympia TS 1968. D 10/5/1968 Bp Ivol I Curtis P 2/1/1979 Bp Robert Hume Cochrane. m 8/26/1949 Carol Deane Abernethy. P-in-c S Tim's In Yelm 1988-1992; Int S Jn's Ch Chehalis WA 1986-1988; Asst S Paul Dio Cyp & Gulf Ahmadi Kuwait 1980-1986; Inst Chapl Dio Olympia Seattle 1978-1980; Cur S Mary Tacoma WA 1970-1978; D H Comm Tacoma WA 1969-1970; Dioc Rep For The Dist Of Kairos. Curs; Kairos.

PEARSON, Joseph Herbert (At) 1280 Berkeley Rd, Avondale Estates GA 30002 **D H Trin Par Decatur GA 2009-** B N. Charlerol PA 1937 s Joseph & Mary. BS U of Kansas 1961. D 8/6/2006 Bp J Neil Alexander. c 2.

PEARSON, Kevin David (Oly) 16617 Marine View Dr SW, Burien WA 98166 **Chapl Chld's Hosp Seattle WA 2004-; R S Lk's Epis Ch Renton WA 2004-** B Bellingham WA 1961 s Richard & Carol. BA Seattle Pacific U 1984; MDiv GTS 1991; Cert Seattle U 2009; D.Min. (cand.) SFTS 2011; D.Min. SFTS 2015. D 6/15/1991 Bp Frank Tracy Griswold III P 2/13/1992 Bp Vincent Waydell Warner. m 2/10/2010 Thomas Kenison. R The Epis Ch Of S Jn The Evang San Francisco CA 2001-2003; Asst Cathd Of S Jas Chicago IL 2000-2001; Assoc S Lk's Ch Evanston IL 1996-1999; Int S Paul's Ch Seattle WA 1993-1994; Cur Ch Of The Ascen Seattle WA 1991-1993; Pres, Cler Assn Dio Olympia Seattle 2012-2013, Chair, Personl Cmsn 2004-2013.

PEARSON, Michael A (Pa) 2 Blount Circle, Barrington RI 02806 B Detroit MI 1950 s Archie & Mable. BA Duke 1972; MDiv PrTS 1975; GTS 1977. D 9/14/1977 P 4/7/1978 Bp William Gillette Weinhauer. m 9/13/1986 Julia M Pearson c 1. R S Mary's Ch Wayne PA 2001-2012; R S Lk's Ch Louisville KY 1992-2001; Assoc S Mk's Ch New Canaan CT 1989-1992; R Ch Of The Epiph Providence RI 1981-1989; Chapl S Mary Hm Chld No Providence RI 1978-1989; Cur S Steph's Ch Providence RI 1977-1981.

PEARSON, Patricia Waychus (Cal) 1219 Dutch Mill Drive, Danville CA 94526 **H Cross Epis Ch Castro Vlly CA 2014-, D 2014-; Com on Cn Dio California San Francisco CA 2016-, Exec Coun 2014, Gift Plnng Com Mem 2011-2012, Gift Plnng Com Mem 2011-** B Kansas City MO 1956 d Felix & Harriet. BA U of San Francisco 1978; Cert S Marys Coll 2002; BDS Epis Sch for Deacons 2010. D 6/4/2011 Bp Marc Handley Andrus. m 6/20/2008 Sharyn Leslie Mitzo. D S Lk's Ch Walnut Creek CA 2011-2014, D 2011-2014. Assn for Epis Deacons 2007.

PEARSON, William Arthur (Alb) 27 Trottingham Road, Saratoga Springs NY 12866 **D Chr Epis Ch Ballston Spa NY 2003-** B Columbus NE 1950 s William & Geraldine. D 1/11/2003 Bp Daniel William Herzog. m 5/26/1974 Elaine Lorraine Pearson c 2.

PEASE JR, Edwin C (Mass) 2 Kennedy Ln, Walpole MA 02081 B Philadelphia PA 1938 s Edwin & Rebecca. BA U of Manitoba 1963; MDiv EDS 1979; Ldrshp Acad for New Directions 1984; DMin EDS 1992. D 6/2/1979 Bp Paul Moore Jr P 2/1/1980 Bp Roger W Blanchard. m 10/6/1984 Linda J Clark. Dio Wstrn Massachusetts Springfield 1997-2004; Vic S Andr's Ch No Grafton MA 1997-2004; R Epis Ch Of S Thos Taunton MA 1996-1997; Int Chr Ch New Haven CT 1995-1996; Dep For Cong & Cler Dvlpmt Dio SW Virginia Roanoke VA 1992-1995; Dio Massachusetts Boston MA 1984-1985; R Chr Ch Medway MA 1981-1992; Cur S Anne's Ch Lowell MA 1979-1981. Acad Of Homil; Cert Int Pstr, Int Mnstry Ntwk.

PEAY, Steven Allen (Alb) 2777 Mission Rd, Nashotah WI 53058 **Assoc Prof of Ch Hist Nash Nashotah WI 2010-** B Indianapolis IN 1954 s Willard & Doris Juanita. BA Greenville Coll 1977; MA St Vinc Sem 1981; MA U Pgh 1983; MDiv S Vinc Sem 1984; PhD S Louis U 1990. Rec 8/12/2010 Bp William Howard Love. m 7/5/1996 Julie Ann Peay c 2.

PECARO, Bernard Joel (SeFla) 140 Se 28th Ave, Pompano Beach FL 33062 **R S Mart's Epis Ch Pompano Bch FL 1998-; CDR USNR Chapl Corps 1987-** B Fort Lauderdale FL 1955 s John & Josephine. BS Nova SE U 1980; MDiv Nash 1984. D 6/11/1984 P 6/11/1985 Bp Calvin Onderdonk Schofield Jr. m 9/18/1993 Sylvia Pecaro c 3. Cur S Paul's Ch Delray Bch FL 1990-1998; Cur S Mary's Epis Ch Stuart FL 1984-1990. SHN 1984. fpecaro@stmartinchurch.org

PECH, Meredith Ayer (Ore) 371 Idaho St, Ashland OR 97520 **Ldr Process Spprt Grp Linda Vista Care Cntr 2011-; Ldr Sthrn Oregon Well Spouse Spprt Grp 2007-; D Trin Epis Ch Ashland Ashland OR 1996-** B San Jose CA 1947 d Cecil & Jean. BA U CA 1969; Cert U of Oregon 1972; Cntr for the Diac Dio Oregon 1996. D 11/30/1996 Bp Robert Louis Ladehoff. m 8/20/1973 Robert Steven Pech c 3. Ashland Educ Assn 1981-2006; NEA 1972-2006; Oregon Educ Assn 1972-2006. Favorite Elem Tchr, Ashland, Oregon Sneak Preview 1996.

PECK, David W (CPa) 119 N Duke St, Lancaster PA 17602 **R S Jas Ch Lancaster PA 2008-** B Evansville IN 1966 s David & MacGregor. BA Amer U 1988; MA Camb 1994; CTM Westcott Hse Cambridge 1995. Trans 8/19/2008 Bp Nathan Dwight Baxter. m 5/30/1992 Cordelia A Moyse c 1.

PECK SR, Donald Morrow (Ore) 304 Spyglass Dr, Eugene OR 97401 B Portland OR 1936 s Edward & Hazel. U of Oregon. D 3/16/1996 Bp Robert Louis Ladehoff. m 11/23/1957 Beverly Jane Hall c 3. D S Matt's Epis Ch Eugene OR 1996-2012. NAAD.

PECK JR, Edward Jefferson (CPa) 7041 Fairway Oaks, Fayetteville PA 17222 **Ret 2004-** B Cincinnati OH 1943 s Edward & Emmadora. BA Juniata Coll 1970; MDiv PDS 1973. D 6/8/1973 P 3/25/1974 Bp Dean Theodore Stevenson. m 4/11/2010 Sandra Peck c 2. Int S Andr's Epis Ch York PA 2004-2005; Chair Untd Campus Mnstry Bd Shippensburg Univ. 1999-2015; R S Andr's Epis Ch Shippensburg PA 1999-2003; R S Paul's Epis Ch Bound Brook NJ 1994-1999; R Gr Ch Merchantville NJ 1984-1994; R S Andr's Epis Ch York PA 1978-1984; Chapl US-AR 1977-1997; R S Mary's Epis Ch Waynesboro PA 1975-1978; Cur S Jn's Epis Ch Lancaster PA 1973-1975.

PECK, Felicity Lenton Clark (ETenn) 3333 Love Cir, Nashville TN 37212 **D S Raphael's Epis Ch Crossville TN 2001-** B Falmouth UK 1942 d Edward & Bettina. Cert Croydon Tech Coll Surrey Gb. D 6/16/2001 Bp Charles Glenn VonRosenberg. m 2/21/1965 Herbert Jefferson Peck c 1. D Chr Ch - Epis Chattanooga TN 2002-2010.

PECK, Frederick (Ore) 18205 SE 42nd St, Vancouver WA 98683 B Waverly NY 1941 s Walter & Marjorie. BA Duke 1963; MDiv VTS 1966; PhD Cor 1974. D 6/25/1966 P 12/27/1966 Bp Edward Hamilton West. m 6/24/1986 Kim Huynh.

PECK, Maryjane (Mich) Christ Episcopal Church, 120 N Military St, Dearborn MI 48124 **Chr Ch Detroit MI 2016-** B Battle Creek MI 1948 d James & Frances. BA Nazareth Coll 1971; MSW Wayne 1976; MDiv Ecum Theol 2012. D 6/22/2013 P 12/22/2013 Bp Wendell Nathaniel Gibbs Jr. c 3. Chr Ch Dearborn MI 2013-2016.

PECKHAM, Ashley Hall (RI) 31 W Main Rd, Portsmouth RI 02871 B Fall River MA 1940 s Richard & Marjorie. BA Barrington Coll 1966; Merc TS 1971. D 6/27/1970 Bp John S Higgins P 10/10/1971 Bp Frederick Hesley Belden. c 2. P S Mary's Ch E Providence RI 2000-2012; New Engl Seafarers Mssn Boston MA 1998-2006; The Ch Of The H Cross Middletown RI 1993-1998; R S Barn Ch Warwick RI 1988-1991; R S Alb's Ch N Providence RI 1975-1988, R 1974-1988; Dio Rhode Island Providence RI 1975-1978; Cur Emm Ch Newport RI 1971-1974; Cur S Bon Epis Ch Lindenhurst NY 1970-1971. tcapron1970@yahoo.com

PECKHAM, Laura (Me) St Martin's Episcopal Church, 900 Main St, Palmyra ME 04965 **P-in-c S Mart's Epis Ch Palmyra ME 2013-** B Chelsea ME 1967 d Robert & Leonetta. BA U of Maine 1990; MDiv Bangor TS 2008. D 6/25/2011 P 6/23/2012 Bp Stephen Taylor Lane. m 12/5/1992 Keith A Peckham c 2. S Andr's Ch Newcastle ME 2011-2012.

PECKHAM CLARK, Margaret A (LI) 1579 Northern Boulevard, Roslyn NY 11576 **R Trin Epis Ch Roslyn NY 2003-** B Binghamton NY 1967 d Eugene & Judith. BA CUNY 1992; JD New York Law Sch 1995; MDiv GTS 2001. D 5/26/2001 Bp Andrew Fairfield P 1/26/2002 Bp Mark Sean Sisk. c 1. Asst R All Ang' Ch New York NY 2001-2003; COM Mem Dio Long Island Garden City NY 2004-2006.

PEDERSEN, John Charles (Kan) 9408 San Rafael Ave Ne, Albuquerque NM 87109 B Omaha NE 1927 s Henry & Jessie. BA U of Nebraska 1949; MDiv SWTS 1952. D 3/17/1952 P 11/3/1952 Bp Howard R Brinker. m 2/8/1954 Sharon Pedersen c 2. R Chr Ch Overland Pk KS 1982-1990; R S Matt's Epis Ch Newton KS 1978-1982; Chapl Instr Dept Rel TX Tech U Lubbock TX 1970-1978; Chapl Epis Ch Of S Geo Canyon TX 1965-1970; Chapl W TX St U Canyon TX 1965-1970; Cur S Andr's Epis Ch Amarillo TX 1962-1965; Vic Gr Ch Vernon TX 1957-1962; Trin Ch Quanah TX 1957-1962; S Mk's Ch Denver CO 1955-1957; Vic S Paul's Ch Ogallala NE 1952-1955; Vic St. Mich's Ch Imperial NE 1952-1955.

PEDRAZA ARIAS, Bladimir Ivan (Colom) Kra 17 # 76-23, Cartagena Bolivar 472 Colombia B Viracacha Boyaca Colombia 1975 s Juan & Ana. Filosofo Seminario Intermisional; Teologo Seminario Mayor Arquidiocesano; Abogado TECNAR. Rec 2/20/2016 as Priest Bp Francisco Jose Duque-Gomez. m 7/15/2015 Cintia Paola c 1.

PEDRICK, Jennifer L (RI) 1336 Pawtucket Ave, Rumford RI 02916 **Asst to R S Mary's Ch Portsmouth RI 2014-, 1998-2002; Mem of Stndg Com Dio Rhode Island Providence RI 2009-, Dep to GC 2008-, Dn, E Bay Dnry 2005-2010, Mem of COM 2003-2009** B Philadelphia PA 1966 d Daniel & Judith. BA Sweet Briar Coll 1988; MDiv Harvard DS 1998. D 6/13/1998 P 1/24/1999 Bp Gerry Wolf. m 8/20/1994 Michael John DeAngelo c 2. Ch of the Epiph Rumford RI 2002-2014; R St Mich & Gr Ch Rumford RI 2002-2014. Phi Beta Kappa Sweet Briar Coll 1988. jennifer@smcportsmouth.org

PEEK, Charles Arthur (Neb) 2010 Fifth Avenue, Kearney NE 68845 **Whitney Schlrshp Awards Com Dio Nebraska Omaha NE 2013-, Recovery Cmsn 2011-** B Greeley CO 1942 s George & Dorothy. Grad Theol Un, Berkeley; BA U of Nebraska 1964; MA U of Nebraska 1966; PhD U of Nebraska 1971. D 12/20/1970 P 6/29/1971 Bp Russell T Rauscher. m 6/19/1965 Nancy J Resler c 2. Bd Mem Mem Mssn Ntwk 2013-2014; R S Steph's Ch Grand Island NE 2008-2012, 2002-2004, Assoc 1995-2005; P-in-c Chr Ch Cntrl City NE 1989-1994; Calv Ch Hyannis NE 1987-1989; P-in-c S Jos's Ch Mullen NE 1987-1989; Reg Coordntr Dept of Evang 1982-1986; R S Lk's Ch Kearney NE 1977-1987, Reg Coordntr - Evang Prv. VIII 1983-1986; Ch Of The Epiph Flagstaff AZ 1972-1977; Vic St Johns Epis-Luth Ch Williams AZ 1972-1977. Auth, "Breezes on Their Way to Being Winds (2016 Nebraska Bk Awd winner, chosen for Talking Books)," *poetry chapbook*, Finishing Line Press, 2015; Auth, "Where We've Managed Somehow to Be," *poetry chapbook*, Wayne St Coll Press, 2014; Auth, "Critical Comp to Wm Faulkner," Greenwood, 2002; Auth, "A Wm Faulkner Encyclopedia," Greenwood, 1999. Mildred Bennett Awd Nebraska Cntr for the Bk 2011; Fulbright Sr Spec Fulbright Assn 2008; Fulbright Sr Lectr Fulbright Assn 2005; Distinguished Fac Awd Leland Holdt/Security Mutual 2005; Excellence in Tchg Awd Pratt-Heins Fndtn./U. of Nebraska 2002. cpeek.cp@gmail.com

PEEK, Guy Richardson (WNY) 6363 Transit Rd Apt 233, East Amherst NY 14051 **Died 6/13/2016** B Helena MT 1941 s Tate & Imogene. BA U of Montana 1964; MDiv Ya Berk 1967. D 6/18/1967 P 12/21/1967 Bp Chandler W Sterling. c 2. Ret 2001-2016; R S Ptr's Ch Niagara Falls NY 1992-2001; R St Johns Epis Youngstown NY 1978-1992; R Chr Ch Deposit NY 1969-1978; P-in-c Ch Of The Incarn Great Falls MT 1967-1969; Vic S Chris's Shelby MT 1967-1969; S Mk's Ch Havre MT 1967-1969; Dn, Niagara Dnry 2016.

PEEL, Margaret (Va) 543 Beulah Rd NE, Vienna VA 22180 B Nashville TN 1978 d Joe & Mary. BA Sewanee, U So 2001; MEd Belmont U 2010; MDiv VTS 2013. D 6/15/2013 P 12/18/2013 Bp John Bauerschmidt. P Ch Of The H Comf Vienna VA 2014-2017; Asst S Matt's Epis Ch Sterling VA 2013-2014.

PEEL, Richard Charles (Mont) 1726 Cannon St Apt 4, Helena MT 59601 B Harrisburg PA 1940 s Charles & Helen. BA Buc 1962; MDiv PDS 1965; MLS U of British Columbia Vancouver Bc CA 1971. D 6/26/1965 P 1/1/1966 Bp Joseph Thomas Heistand. Assoc S Ptr's Cathd Helena MT 1995-2004, Cur 1967-1994; Assoc Ch Of The Epiph Tempe AZ 1977-1995; Non-par 1970-1976; Cur The Epis Ch Of S Jn The Bapt York PA 1965-1967. Fran Jos Campbell Citation Amer Libr Assn 1994; Libr Of The Year Outreach Serv 1989; Outstanding Serv To The Blind Laura Bridgeman Awd 1975.

PEELER, Amy Lauren (Chi) 320 Franklin St, Geneva IL 60134 B Chickasaw OK 1980 d Perry & Pamela. BA Oklahoma Bapt U 2002; MDiv PrTS 2005; PhD PrTS 2011. D 9/13/2015 P 4/1/2016 Bp Edward Stuart Little II. m 12/17/1999 Lance Jonathan Peeler c 3.

PEELER, Lance Vernon (Ore) 333 NW 35th St, Corvallis OR 97330 **Gr Epis Ch Astoria OR 2013-, R 2013-; Gd Samar Med Cntr Corvallis OR 2010-** B Roseburg OR 1969 s Vernon & Patsy. BS Willamette U 1991; MDiv Epis TS of the SW 2008. D 6/25/2008 P 4/4/2009 Bp Sanford Zangwill Kaye Hampton. m 8/5/2000 Stacie Dyan-Jackson Peeler c 2. Samar Hlth Serv Corvallis OR 2010-2013; Asst The Epis Ch Of The Gd Samar Corvallis OR 2008-2015.

PEEPLES, David H (Ala) 2354 Wildwood Dr, Montgomery AL 36111 **Chapl H Cross Epis Sch Montgomery AL 2000-** B Indianapolis IN 1961 s John & Sarah. BS Trin U San Antonio 1983; MDiv Sewanee: The U So, TS 2000.

P

D 6/4/2000 P 12/12/2000 Bp Henry Nutt Parsley Jr. m 8/10/1996 Margaret F Peeples c 3. P Gr Epis Ch Pike Road AL 2005-2015; Cur S Jn's Ch Montgomery AL 2000-2005.

PEERMAN III, C(Harles) Gordon (Tenn) 4416 Harding Pl, Nashville TN 37205 **1996-** B Nashville TN 1951 s Charles & Mary. BA U of Virginia 1973; MDiv Yale DS 1976; DMin Van 1990. D 11/7/1976 P 6/1/1977 Bp Robert Bruce Hall. c 1. Assoc S Aug's Chap Nashville TN 2005-2016; Asst R for Pstr Counslg Chr Ch Cathd Nashville TN 1985-1995; 1982-1984; Asst S Steph's Ch Richmond VA 1976-1982. Auth, "Blessed Relief: What Christians Can Learn from Buddhists About Suffering," SkyLight Paths, 2008; Auth, "Anger: An Instrument of Peace," *Weavings*.

PEET, Donald Howard (Ct) PO Box 681, Sandisfield MA 01255 **Ret 1996-; Ret 1996-** B Waterbury CT 1932 s Howard & Hazel. BA U of Connecticut 1953; BD VTS 1958. D 6/11/1958 P 3/1/1959 Bp Walter H Gray. m 6/6/1953 Charlene N Peet c 3. R S Jn's Ch E Windsor CT 1979-1996; R S Andr's Ch Devon CT 1964-1979; S Andr's Ch Milford CT 1964-1979; Vic S Paul's Ch Plainfield CT 1958-1964.

PEETE, Brandon Ben (Tex) 5503 Effingham Dr, Houston TX 77035 **Asst S Steph's Epis Ch Houston TX 2013-** B Huntsville AL 1978 s Ben & Gail. BS U of Alabama 2002; MDiv Candler TS Emory U 2010. D 4/30/2011 P Keith Whitmore P 12/3/2011 Bp Rayford Baines High Jr. m 10/31/2009 Hillary S Peete c 2. All SS Epis Sch Tyler TX 2011-2013; Cur Chr Epis Ch Tyler TX 2011-2012; Yth Dir Cathd Of S Phil Atlanta GA 2005-2011; Yth Dir Ch Of The Gd Shpd Dallas TX 2002-2004.

PEETE, Nan Olive Arrington (WA) 3001 Veazey Ter Nw Apt 1208, Washington DC 20008 **Mem of the Bd The GTS New York NY 2008-** B Chicago IL 1938 d Maurice & Phoebe. BA Occ 1975; MA U of Redlands 1978; MDiv GTS 1984; SWTS 1990. D 6/16/1984 P 2/2/1985 Bp Robert Claflin Rusack. c 2. Cn For Deploy And Ord Dio Washington Washington DC 2003-2005; Cn Min Dio Sthrn Ohio Cincinnati OH 1999-2003; Assoc P Trin Par New York NY 1994-1999; Dio Atlanta Atlanta GA 1989-1994; Urban & Soc Mnstrs Cmsn Dio Indianapolis Indianapolis IN 1986-1988; R All SS Ch Indianapolis IN 1985-1988; Cur S Mk's Epis Ch Upland CA 1984-1985. Auth, "Wit"; Auth, "Shaping Our Future"; Auth, "Angl Theol Revs". Bd Dir EWC 1998-2002; UBE 1982.

PEETS, Patricia Ann Dunne (Mo) 429 Martindale Dr, Albany GA 31721 B Norman OK 1952 d Richard & Shirley. BA U of Missouri 1974. D 2/18/1996 Bp Alfred Marble Jr. m 8/25/1973 Roy Ashby Peets. D S Patricks Ch Albany GA 1996-2005.

PELKEY, Richard Elwood (Fla) 7860 SW 86th Way, Gainesville FL 32608 **R S Jos's Ch Newberry FL 2011-** B Garden Grove CA 1974 s Glenn & Christine. BMus U of Nevada Las Vegas 1996; MDiv Epis TS of the SW 2008. D 6/14/2008 Bp Barry Leigh Beisner P 12/14/2008 Bp C Andrew Doyle. m 10/23/1999 Helen K F Pelkey c 3. Assoc Trin Epis Ch Marble Falls TX 2008-2010.

PELKEY, Wayne Lloyd (Ia) 13218 State Road #17, West Plains MO 65775 B Canton NY 1946 s Lloyd & Thelma. BA U of Cntrl Missouri 1968; MDiv SWTS 1971; EMT SUNY 1973. D 6/6/1971 P 12/1/1971 Bp Allen Webster Brown. Supply P Dio Arkansas Little Rock AR 2006-2007; Supply P Dio Iowa Des Moines IA 1977-2006, Clncl Psych 1976-1983; Dio W Missouri Kansas City MO 1974-1976; S Oswald In The Field Skidmore MO 1974-1976; P S Paul's Ch Maryville MO 1974-1976; P Ch Of The Nativ Star Lake NY 1971-1974; R S Aug Hermon NY 1971-1974. Auth, "Dare We Say God"; Auth, "Curric Dvlpmt Of Sxlty Of The Mentally Retardeddare We Say God"; Auth, "Residential Needs Survey". Masters Thesis Seabury Wstrn TS 1971.

PELLA, Diane Maria (Az) Po Box 753, Hartsdale NY 10530 **Assoc S Xavier Old Greenwich CT 1996-** B New York NY 1952 d Anthony & Dora. BA NYU 1974; MBA Iona Coll 1977; MDiv Ya Berk 1989. D 10/6/1991 Bp Joseph Thomas Heistand P 4/1/1992 Bp Walter Decoster Dennis Jr. Supply P Dio Arizona Phoenix AZ 1993-1996; Assoc S Andr's Epis Ch Tucson AZ 1992-1993; Assoc S Andr's Epis Ch Hartsdale NY 1991-1992.

PELLATON, Thomas JP (NY) 2186 5th Ave Apt 7D, New York NY 10037 B New York NY 1944 s Pierre & Anne. BMus; BA Ob 1967; MFA Carnegie Mellon U 1969; MDiv Ya Berk 1991. D 6/8/1991 P 12/14/1991 Bp Richard Frank Grein. Int S Mary's Manhattanville Epis Ch New York NY 2012-2013; R The Ch Of The Ascen Rockville Ct NY 2008-2010; R Ch of the Ascen Munich 1997-2008; Assoc S Mich's Ch New York NY 1991-1997; DCOM Dio Long Island Garden City NY 2009-2011; Pres, Coun of Advice Convoc of Epis Ch in Europe Paris 2006-2008, Secy of Conv 1997-2007; Epis Chars Dio New York New York NY 1995-2007, Chair, Manhattan Cntrl IPC 1993-1996. Auth, "Dear Amer: Letters From Viet-Nam"; Auth, "Sciences Emmy For Writing Documentary Dear Amer 91". Ord of Urban Missioners 2011.

PELLEGRINI, Lucy Carr Bergen (Vt) 48 East St, Bristol VT 05443 **D S Steph's Ch Middlebury VT 2009-; Chapl Helen Porter Healthcare and Rehab Cntr 2000-; Deacons' Coun Dio Vermont Burlington VT 2009-, Deacons' Coun 2008-** B Dayton OH 1950 d Charles & Sylvia. BS Skidmore Coll 1972. D 6/5/2004 Bp Thomas C Ely. c 3. D S Paul's Epis Ch On The Green Vergennes VT 2004-2009.

PELLETIER, Ann Dietrich (RI) 57 Grandeville Ct, Apt#3323, Wakefield RI 02879 B Chicago IL 1931 d Harold & Jane. BA W&M 1954; MA Mid 1960; Rhode Island Sch For Deacons 1988. D 6/23/1990 Bp George Nelson Hunt III. D Ch Of The Ascen Cranston RI 2010-2012; D S Ptr's And S Andr's Epis Providence RI 1997-2006; D SS Matt and Mk Barrington RI 1992-1997; D S Geo And San Jorge Cntrl Falls RI 1989-1992. NAAD; Ord Of S Helena. Lind Botetort Medal Coll Of Wm & Mary 1954; Phi Beta Kappa Coll Of Wm & Mary 1953.

PELNAR, William Donald (Mil) 2544 Tilden Ave, Delavan WI 53115 **D Chr Epis Ch Of Delavan Delavan WI 2005-** B Berwyn IL 1950 D 1/13/2001 Bp Roger John White. m 5/15/1976 Michelle Ann Gifford c 3.

PEMBERTON, Barbara Louise (CFla) 668 Whispering Pines Ct, Inverness FL 34453 **Admin S Marg's Ch Inverness FL 2005-, D 2002-** B Miami FL 1952 d William & Helen. AS Hillsborough Cmnty Coll Tampa FL 1989. D 12/14/2002 Bp John Wadsworth Howe. m 6/6/1979 Kirby F Pemberton. bpemberton3@tampabay.rr.com

PENA-REGALADO JR, Jose (Hond) Col Victoria, Bloque J-3, Choloma Cortes Honduras **Dio Honduras San Pedro Sula 1995-; Iglesia Epis Santa Rosa Cisneros Villanueva Cortes 1993-; Vic Iglesia Epis de la Epifania Villanueva 1993-** B La Labor Ocotepeque HN 1957 s Ignacio & Maria. Centro U Reg Del No; Sem Mayor Nuestro Senora De Suyapa. Rec 2/1/1995 as Priest Bp Leo Frade. m 7/23/1993 Carmen Patricia Melgar Francisco-Pena c 2. Vic Iglesia Epis San Jose De La Montana San Pedro Sula 2009-2013; Serv RC Ch 1987-1993.

PENA TAVAREZ, Vicente A (DR) Iglesia Episcopal Todos Los Santos, Calle Dr. Ferry Esq Eugenio Miranda, La Romna Dominican Republic Dominican Republic **Dio The Dominican Republic (Iglesia Epis Dominicana) Gazcue Santo Domingo 2008-** B Dominican Republic 1964 s Valentin & Rosa. Lic Centro de Estudios Teologicos; Dip Ins Polotechnico JPD; BA Miami Tech Coll; Univesida UAPA. D 2/4/2007 P 2/10/2008 Bp Julio Cesar Holguin-Khoury. m 7/10/1993 Nancy Miossotte Fondeur Cabrera.

PENCE, George E (Spr) 8103 Donna Lane, Edwardsville IL 62025 B Milwaukee WI 1939 s Ivan & Virginia. BA McKendree U 1961; MA U IL 1962; No Degree SMU 1963; PhD S Louis U 1971; MTS SWTS 1979. D 6/15/1975 P 6/29/1979 Bp William Hopkins Folwell. m 12/29/1962 Ione Kolm Pence. Int R S Jn's Epis Ch Kewanee IL 2009, R 1993-2001; Int Resurr Luth Ch Godfrey IL 2005-2007; Int St. Paul's Par & Trin Chap Alton IL 2003-2005; Dioc Admin Dio Quincy Peoria IL 1996-2003; Vic Ch of the Trsfg Princeton IL 1991-1996; Chapl/Dn S Jn's Mltry Acad Delafield WI 1986-1991; Assoc R S Andr's Epis Ch Ft Pierce FL 1984-1985; Headmaster/Assoc R S Cyp's Ch Lufkin TX 1979-1984; Asst The Epis Ch Of S Jas The Less Northfield IL 1978-1979; Dn/Chapl Embry-Riddle Aeronautical U Daytona Bch FL 1972-1977; Assoc Univ Rgstr St. Louis U St. Louis Mo. 1969-1975; Dir of Admssns McKendree U Lebanon IL 1964-1969. Auth, "Bibliography of Med Ethics," *Bibliography of Med Ethics*, Self-Pub, Sem Proj, 1978. Sigma Chi 1973. Who's Who in Amer Educ Who's Who in Amer 1990; Most Prominent Eductr of Texas Texas 1983; Outstanding Young Men in Amer Who's Who in Amer 1972; Phi Delta Kappa S Louis U 1970.

PENDERGRAFT, Randall Scott (Mont) Po Box 367, Red Lodge MT 59068 **Our Sav Epis Joliet MT 2006-; Asst Vic S Alb's Epis Ch Laurel MT 2006-** B Billings MT 1949 s Lawrence & Dorothy. BS Montana St U 1972; Mnstry Formation Prog 1999. D 10/2/1999 P 4/15/2000 Bp Charles I Jones III. m 6/1/1985 Susan Blackburn. Calv Epis Ch Red Lodge MT 2017; S Paul's of the Stillwater Ch Absarokee MT 2006-2012.

PENDLETON JR SSJE, Eldride H (Mass) 21 Emery Ln, West Newbury MA 01985 **Died 8/26/2015** B McKinney TX 1940 s Eldridge & Kathryn. BA U of No Texas 1962; MA U of No Texas 1968; PhD U of Virginia 1974; MDiv Duke DS 1992. D 4/16/1993 P 11/29/1993 Bp Robert Whitridge Estill. S Jn's Chap Cambridge MA 1993-2014; Soc-St Jn The Evang Cambridge MA 1993-2005; Bro SSJE 1984-2015; Dir of Archv SSJE 2015.

PENDLETON, Mark B (NH) Christ Church, 43 Pine St, Exeter NH 03833 **R Chr Ch Exeter NH 2013-** B Cincinnati OH 1963 s Bruce & Judith. BA Florida St U 1986; MDiv GTS 1991. D 6/9/1991 Bp Frank S Cerveny P 2/1/1992 Bp John Shelby Spong. m 6/2/1990 Leslie Glover c 2. Dn Chr Ch Cathd Hartford CT 2004-2013; R Ch Of Our Sav Silver Sprg MD 1998-2004; R S Lk's Ch So Glastonbury CT 1993-1998; Asst Chr Ch Short Hills NJ 1991-1993. Cmnty Of The Cross Of Nails No Amer, Pres 2008. mpendleton@christchurchexeter.org

PENDLETON, William Beasley (NC) 1205-B Brookstown Ave. NW, Winston Salem NC 27101 **D D St. Paul's Epis Ch Winston-Salem NC 2004-; Rehab Engr NC Vocational Rehab. Serv Winston Winston-Salem NC 1987-** B Mt. Airy NC 1954 s William & Rebecca. BS No Carolina St U; No Carolina St U 1987. D 6/13/2004 Bp Michael B Curry. Proj Engr Perry Mfg Co. Mt. Airy NC 1976-1986. Bp's Com for the Diac 2007; OSL 2006; St. Frances Fllshp 2003.

PENFIELD, Joyce A. (RI) 25 Pomona Ave, Providence RI 02908 **P S Ptr's And S Andr's Epis Providence RI 2005-; Fndr & Exec. Dir. The Blessing Way Reentry & Recovery Mnstry Prov 2004-; Mem Faith Infused Recovery ef-**

forts Pawtucket RI 2012-; Dir The Blessing Way Providence RI 2004- B Urbana-Champaign IL. 1946 d John & Helen. BA Illinois St U 1968; MA Amer U 1973; PhD SUNY 1977; MA Maryknoll TS 1995; MA Other 1995; MDiv EDS 2001. D 6/2/2001 Bp David Bruce Joslin P 2/3/2002 Bp Gerry Wolf. c 3. Prison Chapl (Prot) Dio Rhode Island Providence RI 2001-2011, Mem, T/F on Same-Sex Blessings 2013, Mem, Hisp Mnstry Com 2011-, Mem Soc Concerns Com 2001-2005; Assoc Cler S Lk's Epis Ch E Greenwich RI 2001-2004. Auth Handbook, *When Cultures Meet Face to Face*, Penfield Assoc, 1997; Designer Video & Bklet, *Lang Encounters of the Best Kind*, Penfield Assoc, 1992; Auth Edited Bk, *Wmn & Lang in Transition*, St Univ. of NY Press, 1987; Pub Article, *"Proverbs as Quotes"*, U of So Afr, 1986; Auth Bk, *Communicating w Quotes: The Igbo Case*, Greenwood Press, Ct., 1983; Auth Bk, "w Jacob Ornstein-Galicia," *Chicano Engl*, Belgium Press, 1982. Outstanding Prof Rutgers U, Grad. Sch Ed. 1996; Hon Awd AARP, Rutgers U 1994.

PENICK, Fern Marjorie (Eau) 538 N 4th St, River Falls WI 54022 B Mason City IA 1942 d Donavon & Marjorie. D 7/24/1994 Bp William Charles Wantland. D Ch Of The Ascen Hayward WI 1998-2007.

PENN, John William (RG) 116 Kansas City Rd, Ruidoso NM 88345 **Ret Dio the Rio Grande Albuquerque NM 2003-; Chapl Police Chapl Lincoln Cnty NM 1990-** B Tulsa OK 1936 s John & Odessa. U of Tulsa 1955; U Denver 1956; BFA U of New Mex 1963; MDiv SWTS 1966. D 6/18/1966 Bp C J Kinsolving III P 12/21/1966 Bp George T Masuda. c 4. Cn Ltrgcs Dio The Rio Grande Albuquerque 1994-2002, Dn - SE Deanry 1993-2002, Exam Chapl - Liturg 1994-2000, Mem Dioc Coun 1993-2002, Dn SE Dnry 1990-2000, Dioc Coun 1990-2000, Chair & Vice Chair Commision on Mnstry 1980-1990, Mem/Pres. COM 1980-1990; R Epis Ch In Lincoln Cnty Ruidoso NM 1988-2003; R St Lk's Epis Ch Anth NM 1981-1988; R Ch Of The Gd Shpd Silver City NM 1978-1981; R S Matt Albuquerque NM 1972-1978; Cn Pstr Cathd Of S Jas Chicago IL 1968-1972; R S Jn's Epis Ch Dickinson ND 1966-1968; Chapl Ruidoso NM Police Dept 1993-2003; Chapl Lincoln Cnty Sheriff's Off 1992-2003; Chapl Fraternal Ord of Police Lincoln Cnty NM 1990. Auth, "arts RG Epis," *Living Ch*, 2003. Cn Liturg/ Dioc Cn Dio the Rio Grande 1994; Cn Pstr Dio Chicago 1968.

PENNEKAMP, Nancy (Cal) **Coll Instr/Fac Monitor City Coll Of San Francisco 2001-; D, Open Cathd San Francisco Night Mnstry San Francisco CA 2007-** B Oakland CA 1950 d Arthur & Eleanor. BA U CA 1972; MA Humboldt St U 1992; BTS Epis Sch for Deacons 2005; BTS Other 2005. D 12/2/2006 Bp Marc Handley Andrus. m 7/26/1987 John Cumming. Asst Chapl The Edge Chr Campus Cntr San Francisco CA 2006-2015.

PENNER, Henry Andrews (FtW) 222 S Pearson Ln, Keller TX 76248 **S Mart In The Fields Ch Keller TX 2012-** B Ft Worth TX 1946 s Theodore & Mary. BA TCU 1970; MTS Brite DS 2012. D 11/2/2012 Bp Rayford Baines High Jr. m 9/14/1996 Rhonda Penner c 1.

PENNER, Loree A (Md) 623 Monkton Rd, Monkton MD 21111 **R S Thos Epis Ch Towson MD 2011-** B Los Angeles CA 1956 d Paul & Mary. BA Bethany Coll 1982; MA California St U 1990; MDiv Sewanee: The U So, TS 2004. D 6/4/2004 Bp Jerry Alban Lamb P 12/2/2004 Bp Henry Nutt Parsley Jr. m 6/9/1984 Steven Bruce Penner c 2. Assoc R S Jas Ch Monkton MD 2005-2011; Consult All SS Chap at the Univ. of the So Sewanee TN 2004-2005; Assoc St Jas Epis Ch Sewanee TN 2004-2005. Ord of the DOK 2004.

PENNIMAN JR, Charles Frederic (Pa) 150 N 20th St Apt 500, Philadelphia PA 19103 **Died 4/22/2017** B Meridian MS 1928 s Charles & Lucile. BA Amh 1950; MDiv VTS 1957. D 6/15/1957 P 6/20/1958 Bp John Brooke Mosley. m 8/5/1960 Annette Penniman c 1. Ch Without Walls Gwynedd PA 2003-2017; Ret 1993-2017; Franklin Inst Sci Museum Philadelpia PA 1972-1993; R Trin Memi Ch Philadelphia PA 1962-1972; Vic S Mich & All Ang Endicott NY 1959-1962; Cur Gr Ch Jamaica NY 1957-1959.

PENNINGTON, Jasper Green (Mich) 204 Elm St, Ypsilanti MI 48197 B Clio MI 1939 s Walter & Hazel. BA Wstrn Michigan U 1967; MLS Wstrn Michigan U 1968; MDiv Sewanee: The U So, TS 1973; DMin GTF 1988. D 6/30/1973 Bp H Coleman Mcgehee Jr P 5/1/1974 Bp Robert Rae Spears Jr. m 10/13/1962 Carole C L Pennington c 3. R St Lk's Epis Ch Ypsilanti MI 1983-2001; Dio Maine Portland ME 1983; S Alb's Ch Cape Eliz ME 1981-1983; R S Jn's Ch Clifton Spgs NY 1978-1981; Ch Of The Ascen Rochester NY 1974-1977; Assoc Prof S Bern Sem Rochester NY 1973-1981; Ecum Off Dio Michigan Detroit MI 1986-1992. Auth, "The Penningtons & their Rel vocations through the centuries.," *As We Knew Him: reflections on M. Basil Pennington*, Paraclete Press, Brewster, Mass., 2008; Auth, "Par Hist," *Fulton J Sheen; Chronology & Bibliography*, St. Bern's Sem, Rochester NY, 1976. Dir Archbp Fulton Jn Sheen Archv 1973-1981; Exec Secy No Amer Fllshp SS Alb & Se 1989-1990.

PENNINGTON, John Joseph (Lex) 24 Thompson Ave, Ft Mitchell KY 41017 **Mem St. Paul's Food Pantry Newport Ky 2011-** B New Bedford MA 1943 s John & Sarah. BS U of Massachusetts 1965; M.P. U.S. Army 1968; MDiv VTS 1971. D 6/26/1971 P 12/29/1971 Bp John Melville Burgess. m 5/20/1973 Gail Pennington. P-in-c S Andr's Ch Ft Thos KY 2011-2012, Assoc 2011-; Bd Mem / Mem Emer Sr Serv of Nthrn Kentucky Covington KY 1996-2005; R Trin Ch Covington KY 1989-2010; R Chr Ch Par Plymouth MA 1974-1989;

Stndg Com Dio Lexington Lexington 2004-2007, Stndg Com 1996-2003, Dioc Coun 1991-1995. johnjosephpennington@yahoo.com

PENNOYER II, Robert Morgan (NY) D 3/5/2016 Bp Allen Shin P 10/15/2016 Bp Andrew Marion Lenow Dietsche.

PENNYBACKER, Kathleen Joanne (CFla) 320 S Canaday Dr, Inverness FL 34450 **Cn For Honduras Dio Cntrl Florida 2005-; D S Marg's Ch Inverness FL 1998-** B DesPlaines 1942 d John & Jennie. Texas Womans U 1963; Orange Memi Hosp Sch 1965; Inst for Chr Stds 1998. D 6/6/1998 Bp John Wadsworth Howe.

PENROD, Roger Scott (WTex) 114 S. Cypress Cir, Pharr TX 78577 **R Trin Epis Ch Pharr TX 2004-** B San Antonio TX 1953 s Roger & Texas. AA San Antonio Coll 1977; BA U of Texas 1987; MDiv Epis TS of the SW 1993; Divinitatis Doctor Other 2012. D 6/29/1993 P 1/2/1994 Bp John Herbert MacNaughton. m 11/10/1996 Alice Lee Penrod c 1. Vic S Mich's Epis Ch San Antonio TX 2003-2004; R Trin Ch San Antonio TX 1998-2003; Asst R S Thos Epis Ch And Sch San Antonio TX 1995-1998; R Trin Epis Ch Edna TX 1993-1995. Divinitatis Doctor Edinburg TS 2012; Sam Portaro Awd for creative expression in campus Mnstry Off for YA and Campus Mnstrs 2011.

PEOPLES, David Brandon (CFla) 2627 Brookside Bluff Loop, Lakeland FL 33813 **R S Steph's Ch Lakeland FL 2010-** B Orlando FL 1974 s William & Mary. BS U of Florida 1995; MDiv Sewanee: The U So, TS 2001. D 5/26/2001 Bp John Wadsworth Howe P 11/25/2001 Bp John Bailey Lipscomb. m 8/3/1996 Lourdes Maria Peoples c 5. R S Ambr Epis Ch Ft Lauderdale FL 2002-2009; Cur All SS Ch Tarpon Spgs FL 2001-2002.

PEOPLES JR, Edward Moray (Ky) 3604 Fallen Timber Dr, Louisville KY 40241 **Died 3/12/2017** B Huntington WV 1939 s Edward & Betty. BA Marshall U 1968; MDiv Sewanee: The U So, TS 1972; Louisville Presb TS 1991. D 6/19/1972 Bp David Shepherd Rose P 12/1/1972 Bp John B Bentley. Vic H Trin Ch Brandenburg KY 2011-2017; P Assoc S Matt's Epis Ch Louisville KY 2004-2009, 1993-1995; Assoc S Fran In The Fields Harrods Creek KY 1996-2003; Ch of the Gd Samar Louisville KY 1996; Stff Dio Kentucky Louisville KY 1988-1992; S Fran Sch (K-8) Goshen KY 1984-1988; Chapl S Fran Sch Goshen KY 1984-1988; Dio W Virginia Charleston WV 1979-1984; S Andr's in the Vill Ch Barboursville WV 1979-1984; R Abingdon Epis Ch White Marsh VA 1975-1979; Emm Ch Glenmore Buckingham VA 1972-1975; Emm Ch Scottsville VA 1972-1975; Vic S Anne's Ch Appomattox VA 1972-1975. mpeoples@bellsouth.net

PEPE, Carol Ann (NJ) B Brooklyn NY 1955 d Michael & Lillian. MSW/MPH Col 1984. D 5/4/2013 Bp Andrew Marion Lenow Dietsche.

PEPIN, Ken (Roch) 53 Lee Road 974, Phenix City AL 36870 **P Gr Ch Scottsville NY 2014-** B New Bedford MA 1957 s Jean & Alma. BA Worcester St Coll 1980; MDiv S Johns Sem Boston 1985; VTS 2000. Rec 6/24/2004 as Priest Bp Peter J Lee. m 4/18/1998 Mery P Pepin c 2. S Jn's Epis Ch Honeoye Falls NY 2014; S Lk's Ch Fairport NY 2013; Dio Rochester Henrietta 2012-2013; S Tim's Epis Ch Perrysburg OH 2006-2011; R S Steph's Epis Ch Smiths Sta AL 2002-2006; Vic S Jas Epis Ch Belhaven NC 2000-2002; San Mateo (S Matt's) Belhaven NC 2000-2002; Vic San Mateo Mssn Yeatesville Washington NC 2000-2002. office@saint-timothy.com

PEPPLER, Connie Jo (Ind) 4131 W Woodyard Rd, Bloomington IN 47404 **Co-Dir of D Formation Prog Epis Dio Indianapolis 2007-; D Trin Epis Ch Bloomington IN 2002-** B Anderson IN 1947 d Russell & Wanda. BA Indiana U 1970; AA Indiana Bus Coll Vincennes IN 1978; BSN Indiana U 1994; 4 year EFM 2002; 4 year Other 2002. D 6/29/2002 Bp Cate Waynick. m 3/20/1976 Michael Peppler. D S Mary's Epis Ch Martinsville IN 2002-2003.

PERALTA, Ercilia (DR) **Dio The Dominican Republic (Iglesia Epis Dominicana) Gazcue Santo Domingo 2003-** B Jarbacoa DR 1959 D 9/7/2002 Bp Julio Cesar Holguin-Khoury P 9/13/2003 Bp William Jones Skilton.

PERCIVAL, Joanna Vera (ECR) Flat 5 Waterside, Mill Lane, Uplyme, Lyme Regis, Dorset DT7 3TZ Great Britain (UK) **Trust Chapl U Hospitals Southampton 2008-** B New York NY 1952 d David & Elizabeth. O levels Guildford HS for Girls 1969; A level Guildford Polytechnic 1970; Cert Kingston Polytech 1975; BA U of San Francisco 1987; MDiv CDSP 1994; one year Dplma Swansea Metropltn U 2008; one year Dplma U of Swansea 2008. D 4/23/1994 P 11/1/1994 Bp Richard Lester Shimpfky. Vic All S's Ch Weston Green 2002-2006; Sprtlty Advsr Dio Guildford 2000-2002; Cur St Andr's Ch 1996-2000; Asst Epis Ch in Almaden San Jose CA 1994-1995. Auth, "Healing Through Gestalt Groups," *Retreats mag*, 2012; Auth, "Healing Through Gestalt Groups," *Retreats mag*, 2012; Auth, "What is Sprtl Direction?," *Retreats mag*, Retreats Assn (UK), 1997. Associated Parishes.

PERCIVAL, Jonathan Beach (NJ) 4051 Westbourne Cir, Sarasota FL 34238 B Kabul AF 1949 s LeRoy & Barbara. BA Bard Coll 1971; MDiv GTS 1975; MBA Ya 1987. D 6/14/1975 Bp Paul Moore Jr P 12/21/1975 Bp Frederick Hesley Belden. m 6/21/1986 Evaleon Hill c 1. R S Lk's Epis Ch Metuchen NJ 2000-2012; R S Andr And H Comm Ch So Orange NJ 1988-2000; R Epis Ch of Chr the Healer Stamford CT 1981-1985; R S Marg's Ch Staatsburg NY 1978-1981; Cur S Mich's Ch Bristol RI 1975-1977.

PERCIVAL, Michael John (Colo) 381 Baltusrol Dr, Aptos CA 95003 B Des Moines IA 1941 s Wright & Mary. BA Stan 1964; MA U of Wisconsin 1968; MDiv CDSP 2000. D 6/30/2000 P 1/20/2001 Bp Chris Christopher Epting. m 6/30/1991 Constance Percival. R St. Andr's Angl Ch Riberas Jalisco 2006-2010; Vic S Lk's Ch Westcliffe CO 2002-2006; Chapl St. Mk's Sch of Texas Dallas TX 2000-2002.

PERDUE, David (NwT) 1101 Slide Rd, Lubbock TX 79416 **R S Steph's Ch Lubbock TX 2010-** B Duncan OK 1949 s Jack & Georgia. BS U of Oklahoma 1972; MDiv Epis TS of the SW 2008. D 6/28/2008 P 1/3/2009 Bp Edward Joseph Konieczny. m 6/7/1968 Donna Kay Perdue c 2. Vic Ch Of The H Cross Owasso OK 2008-2010; Dio Oklahoma Oklahoma City OK 2008-2010.

PERDUE, Lane (Az) Trinity Cathdral, 100 W Roosevelt St, Phoenix AZ 85003 B New Brunswick NJ 1943 d Allen & Isabelle. Col 1965; BA Cedar Crest Coll 1983; MDiv Drew U 1990; MDiv Drew U TS 1990. D 6/22/2013 Bp Kirk Stevan Smith. c 3.

PERDUE, Thomas Hayes (EC) 3981 Fairfax Sq, Fairfax VA 22031 B Huntington WV 1969 s Thomas & Mary. BA Samford U 1993; MA Geneva Coll 1997; MDiv TESM 2002. D 11/9/2002 P 5/17/2003 Bp Robert William Duncan. m 8/12/2000 Melody Mae Perdue c 3. Assoc Ch Of The Apos Fairfax VA 2002-2005.

PEREIRA ALVAREZ, Rafael Alexis (Nev) D 12/10/2016 P 6/10/2017 Bp Dan Thomas Edwards.

PEREZ, Gregory Gerard (Nwk) 141 Broadway, Bayonne NJ 07002 **Trin Ch Bayonne NJ 2007-; R Windmill Allnce Inc. Bayonne NJ 2007-; COM Dio Newark Newark NJ 2013-, Dioc Coun 2008-2009** B Giddings TX 1960 s Butchild & Herminia. BA Coll of Santa Fe 1982; M.Div St. Meinrad TS 1986. Rec 12/15/2005 Bp John Palmer Croneberger. m 10/25/2013 Douglas Flores. P-in-c Calv Ch Bayonne NJ 2011-2012; Cur Gr Ch Van Vorst Jersey City NJ 2006-2007; CEO - AIDS Resource Cntr S Barn Ch Newark NJ 2003-2006, Exec Dir 2003-2006. Soc of Cath Priests 2009.

PEREZ, Jon Arnold (ECR) **Vic Epiph Luth & Epis Ch Marina CA 2005-** B Carmel CA 1959 Sch for Deacons 2003. D 4/16/2005 P 12/3/2005 Bp Sylvestre Donato Romero. m 10/26/2008 Robert Edward Munoz.

PEREZ JR, Juan F (Mich) B Bronx NY 1974 s Juan & Lydia. BA Manhattan Coll 1996; MSW U of Pennsylvania 1999; Epis TS Of The SW 2013; Epis TS of the SW 2013; MDiv Bex 2014; MDiv Bex Sem 2014. D 12/14/2013 P 6/14/2014 Bp Wendell Nathaniel Gibbs Jr. m 5/30/2013 Joseph H Cloutier. Dio Michigan Detroit MI 2014-2016.

PEREZ-BULLARD, Altagracia (NY) 1047 Amsterdam Ave, New York NY 10025 **Cn Dio New York New York NY 2014-** B New York NY 1961 d Ramon & Esther. BS NYU 1982; MDiv UTS 1985; STM UTS 1986. D 6/15/1991 P 5/29/1993 Bp Frank Tracy Griswold III. m 2/21/2014 Cynthia Bullard-Perez c 4. R H Faith Par Inglewood CA 2003-2014; S Phil's Par Los Angeles CA 1994-2003; Dio Chicago Chicago IL 1991-1993. Auth, "Abundant Life," *The Bk Of Wmn Sermons*, Riverhead Books, 1999; Auth, "Este Es Mi Cuerpo," *A Faith Of One'S Own Explorations By Cath Lesbians*, The Crossing Press, 1986. Who'S Who In Black Amer 2002; Econ Justice And Worker'S Rts Los Angeles Allnce For A New Econ 2002; Golden Ang Rel Advoc Awd Natl Institutes Of Mntl Hlth 2001; Outstanding Serv Awd Second Bapt Ch 2000. aperez-bullard@dioceseny.org

PEREZ MACIAS, Jesus Eduardo (Colom) Ap Aer 2704, Barranquilla, Atlantico Colombia **R S Aug 1981-** B Sta Rosa de Osos Antioquia CO 1948 s Jose & Maria. Arquidiocesano TS; Valmaria TS. Rec 3/1/1982 as Priest Bp Bernardo Merino-Botero. m 8/12/1978 Janette Cecilia Fernandez de Perez. Iglesia Epis En Colombia Bogota 1981-1998.

PEREZ MOREIRA, Hector Amado (EcuC) Cd Sauces 5 Mz 225 V2, Guayaquil Ecuador **Vic Iglesia Santiago Apostolo Enrique Drouet Peninsula 1988-; Iglesia Virgen Maria Salanguillo Santa Elena 1988-; Iglesia de la Santisima Trinidad (La Libertad) La Libertad 1988-** B Guayaquil EC 1940 s Hector & Juana. D 3/12/1988 Bp Adrian Delio Caceres-Villavicencio P 6/1/1992 Bp Martiniano Garcia-Montiel. m 1/1/2001 Eugenia Ruiz. Litoral Dio Ecuador Guayaquil 1988-2012.

PEREZ-QUINONES, Juan Pablo (PR) **Dio Puerto Rico Trujillo Alto PR 2004-, 2002-2003; R Parroquia La Encarnacion Hato Rey PR 2001-** B Puerto Rico 1958 s Juan & Dolores. MA - 1986; MA Other 1986; MA - 1993. m 12/26/1998 Alba Agosto. Asst Parroquia La Resurreccion Manati PR 2000-2001; Asst Parroquia San Pedro y San Pablo Bayamon PR 1998-2000; Asistente Iglesia La Candelaria Manati PR 1990-1996; Asistente Iglesia Santiago PR 1989-1990; Asistente Iglesia Santa Rosa Republica Dominicana 1986-1988.

PEREZ-VEGA, Rodrigo (Nwk) 214 Washington St, Hackettstown NJ 07840 B Caracas Venezuela 1967 s Nicanor & Mercedes. BS Escuela Naval de Venezuela 1990; BS Cntrl U of Venezuela 1997; MDiv GTS 2012; MDiv The GTS 2012. D 6/2/2012 P 12/15/2012 Bp Mark M Beckwith. m 10/20/2001 Michelle Perez-Vega. S Jas' Epis Ch Hackettstown NJ 2012-2013.

PERICA, Raymond William (CFla) 145 E Edgewood Dr, Lakeland FL 33803 **D S Dav's Epis Ch Lakeland FL 2015-** B Alton IL 1937 s Peter & Mary. BS St Louis Coll of Pharmacy 1959; Cert Inst for Chr Stds 2014. D 9/12/2015 Bp Gregory Orrin Brewer. m 12/28/1963 Sue Howard c 2.

PERIDANS, Dominique F (WA) 1217 Massachusetts Ave NW, Washington DC 20005 **Ch Of The Ascen And S Agnes Washington DC 2015-** B Washington DC 1963 s Jacques & Aimee. MA Ecole St Jean - France; MA Ecole St Jean - France; BS U of Steubenville 1986; MS Loyola U 2013. Rec 10/5/2013 as Priest Bp Eugene Taylor Sutton. m 6/27/2017 Edward Lawrence Newburn. S Paul's Par Washington DC 2014-2015; S Marg's Ch Annapolis MD 2013-2014; S Marg's Epis Ch Parkville MD 2013-2014. fatherdominiqueasa@gmail.com

PERINE, Everett Craig (Ct) 60 Church St, Hebron CT 06248 **Bp's and Dioc Exec Coun Dio Connecticut Meriden CT 2013-** B New York NY 1949 s Gordon & Alice. BA Mid 1971; Gordon-Conwell TS 1981; MDiv Ya Berk 1986. D 6/11/1986 P 12/21/1986 Bp Robert Shaw Kerr. c 2. R S Ptr's Epis Ch Hebron CT 2004-2017; Assoc S Barn Epis Ch Greenwich CT 2000-2004; R S Jn's Ch New Milford CT 1997-1999; R Ch Of The Gd Shpd Pitman NJ 1991-1997; Cn Res Cathd Ch Of S Paul Burlington VT 1988-1991, Cur 1986-1987. Cmnty Cross Of Nails 1981-1991.

PERKINS, Aaron C (Me) 26 Moulton Ln, York ME 03909 **Archd Dio Maine Portland ME 2014-, Archd 2014-; D S Geo's Epis Ch York ME 2008-; D St. Geo's Epis Ch York Harbor ME 2006-** B Boston MA 1968 s Richard & Cynthia. Bachelor of Archit Roger Wms 1991; BArch Roger Wms 1991. D 6/24/2006 Bp Chilton Richardson Knudsen. m 5/21/1995 Cynthia Susan Perkins c 1. Chapl Maine Correctional Cntr Windham ME 2004-2013. St. Steph Awd NAAD 2010.

PERKINS III, Albert Dashiell (Ala) 425 N Moye Dr, Montgomery AL 36109 B Chattanooga TN 1929 s Albert & Kathryn. BA U of Mississippi 1954; MDiv Sewanee: The U So, TS 1961; DMin TCU 1980. D 6/18/1961 Bp George Mosley Murray P 5/1/1962 Bp Charles C J Carpenter. m 4/6/1956 Virgie R Perkins c 3. R S Barn Epis Ch Roanoke AL 1994-1995, Vic 1961-1974; Pres Montgomery Mntsrl Un 1977-1978; S Jn's Ch Montgomery AL 1974-1995; S Jas' Epis Ch Alexander City AL 1961-1974; Secy Dio Dio Alabama Birmingham 1991-1994, Cn Revs Com 1989-1990, Evang & Renwl Dept 1979-1988, Chair Dept Mssn 1967-1978, Chair Yth Div 1965-1966. Auth, "Along The Way," *Montgomery Advert*, 1994. St Geo Medal For Scouting 1992.

PERKINS, Cecil Patrick (WMo) 1307 Holmes St, Kansas City MO 64106 B Eupora MS 1976 s Bobby & Barbara. BA Mississippi Coll 2000; MM LSU 2004; MDiv Nash 2013; MDiv Nash 2013. D 8/26/2014 P 12/16/2014 Bp Martin Scott Field. m 2/11/2017 Ezgi S Perkins. S Mary's Epis Ch Kansas City MO 2014, P 2014, P 2014-.

PERKINS, David W (Ga) None, 5157 Five Points Jewell Rd, Mitchell GA 30820 **Ch Of Our Sav Augusta GA 2016-; Advsry Grp for Ch Planting Exec Coun Appointees New York NY 2017-** B Oakdale LA 1944 s William & Ruth. STM (ABD) Sewanee: The U So, TS; BS U of Louisiana Monroe 1967; MTh New Orleans Bapt TS 1972; ThD New Orleans Bapt TS 1977; Emory U 1987; LSU 1992. D 10/25/1997 P 5/1/1998 Bp Robert Jefferson Hargrove Jr. c 2. S Andr's Epis Ch Newport News VA 2014-2016; Trin Ch Asbury Pk NJ 2012-2014; Int S Jn's Ch Versailles KY 2010-2011; Adj Prof of Gk Bapt TS Richmond VA 2009-2010; Ch planter/Vic All Souls Epis Ch Mechanicsville VA 2002-2010; Int S Marg's Ch Carrollton GA 2001-2002; Assoc S Jas Epis Ch Marietta GA 1998-2001; P-in-c S Pat's Epis Ch W Monroe LA 1998; Vic The Epis Ch Of The Gd Shpd Vidalia LA 1996-1998; Assoc Prof Theol Xavier U 1994-1995; Adj Fac, Inst of Mnstry Loyola U 1993-1998; Pstr Sthrn Bapt Cong 1989-1995; Assoc Prof NT & Gk New Orleans Bapt TS 1981-1989; Pstr Sthrn Bapt Cong 1976-1981; Chair, Com on the Diac Dio Virginia Richmond VA 2006-2009. Auth, *Var arts*. Amer Acadamy of Religioni 1995; SBL, AAR 1974. davidwperk@gmail.com

PERKINS, Ezgi S (WMo) 420 W 14th St, Kansas City MO 64105 B Izmir Turkey 1989 d Halil & Esin. BBA Drury U 2011. D 3/12/2015 P 9/14/2015 Bp Martin Scott Field. m 2/11/2017 Cecil Patrick Perkins. Asst Dio W Missouri Kansas City MO 2017, Cur 2016-2017, Cur 2015-2016.

PERKINS, Jesse S (Chi) St Michael's Episcopal Church, 647 Dundee Ave, Barrington IL 60010 **R S Mich's Ch Barrington IL 2016-; R S Mk's Epis Ch Jonesboro AR 2009-** B Hot Springs AR 1980 s Alvis & Kathy. BS U of Cntrl Arkansas 2002; MDiv SWTS 2009. D 3/21/2009 Bp Larry Maze P 9/29/2009 Bp Larry Benfield. m 6/8/2002 Kathryn A Hohrine c 1. Stndg Com Dio Arkansas Little Rock AR 2014-2016, Dn of the NE Convoc of Arkansas 2011-2014, Eccl Crt 2011-2014, First Cler Alt to GC 2012 2011-2012. jperkins@stmichaelsbarrington.org

PERKINS, Lynn Jones (RG) PO Box 4330, Gallup NM 87305 **Co-Vic Ch Of The H Sprt Gallup NM 2007-** B Atlanta GA 1947 d Oliver & Roselyn. BS U of Tennessee 1969; MS U of Tennessee 1975; MDiv TESM 2007. D 6/26/2007 Bp Jeffrey Neil Steenson P 11/10/2007 Bp William Carl Frey. m 12/27/1983 Roger S Perkins.

PERKINS, Patrick R (WMass) 679 Farmington Ave, West Hartford CT 06119 **R Dio Wstrn Massachusetts Springfield 2014-** B New Britain CT 1964 s John & Betsy. BS USNA 1987; MS RPI 1993; MDiv VTS 2009. D 6/6/2009 Bp Jeff

P

Lee P 12/19/2009 Bp James Elliot Curry. m 8/20/1988 Carol C Perkins c 2. Asst to the R St Johns Ch W Hartford CT 2009-2014. rector@stfrancisholden.org

PERKINS, Roger S (RG) 1409 Linda Drive, Gallup NM 87301 **Co-Vic Ch Of The H Sprt Gallup NM 2007-** B Louisville KY 1943 s Lloyd & Harriet. BEd Keene St Coll Keene NH 1966; MS U of Tennessee 1969; MDiv TESM 2007. D 6/27/2007 Bp Jeffrey Neil Steenson P 11/10/2007 Bp William Carl Frey. m 12/27/1983 Lynn Jones Perkins c 1. Dept. Mgr Analysas Corp 1978-1991.

PERKINSON, Edward M (O) 3 Fox Hollow, Plymouth MA 02360 B Forest Park IL 1935 s Myron & Rhoda. BA Mt Un Coll 1956; MDiv Garrett-Evang TS 1959; MA NWU 1961. D 12/21/1965 P 5/9/1966 Bp Nelson Marigold Burroughs. m 2/24/1978 Susannah Watson c 3. Asst S Paul's Ch Akron OH 2010-2012; Int Ch Of Our Sav Akron OH 2002-2003; Int Trin Ch Allnce OH 1984-1985; Assoc S Mk's Ch Canton OH 1978-1984; Vic Adv Epis Ch Westlake OH 1968-1972; Asst Chr Ch Epis Hudson OH 1965-1968. Auth, "Step Families: Another Chance," *The Script*. Amer Assn of Mar and Fam Therapists; ITAA.

PERKO, F Michael (RG) 2 Paa Ko Ct, Sandia Park NM 87047 **Cn for Cncl Affrs Dio The Rio Grande Albuquerque 2011-, Cn 2006-2011, Dioc Coun Vice-Pres/Secy 2006-2011, Mem, COM 2006-2011, Secy of Dioc Conv 2006-2011, Secy of Dioc Coun 2006-2011** B Chicago IL 1946 s Frank & Mary. AB Boston Coll 1970; AM Boston Coll 1970; MDiv Loyola U Chicago 1975; MA Stan 1976; PhD Stan 1981. Rec 9/18/2005 Bp Jeffrey Neil Steenson. m 2/5/2005 Lisa A Gruber. R S Alb's Ch El Paso TX 2011-2015, P-in-c 2011-; Dn Dioc Sch for Mnstry Albuquerque NM 2007-2012; Int Ch Of The H Cross Edgewood NM 2006-2007; Asst S Jn's Cathd Albuquerque NM 2005-2011; Serv RC Ch 1964-2004. Auth, "Cath and Amer," OSV Press, 1989; Auth, "A Time to Favor Zion," Educational Stds Press, 1988; Auth, "Enlighting the Next Generation," Garland Press, 1988; Auth, "numerous Bk Revs, Journ arts and Bk chapters". Dn Dio the Rio Grande 2007; Dioc Cn Dio the Rio Grande 2006.

PERO, David Edward (Ore) 1609 Elm St, Forest Grove OR 97116 B Abington PA 1951 s David & Henrietta. BS Estrn U 1976; BS Delaware Vlly Coll 1981. D 6/29/2013 Bp Michael Hanley. deacondepero@gmail.com

PERRA, James Francis (Md) 1401 Towson St, Baltimore MD 21230 **The Ch Of The H Apos Halethorpe MD 2015-** B Kalamazoo MI 1980 s Robert & Ann. BA MI SU 2003; MDiv Trin U Tor 2007; MDiv Trin U Tor 2007; Kellogg Cmnty Coll 2008. D 1/11/2014 P 9/9/2014 Bp Eugene Taylor Sutton. m 8/2/2008 Arianna E Apelgren Perra. Ch Of The Redemp Baltimore MD 2014-2015. office@holyapostles.ang-md.org

PERRIN, Charlie (LI) 27521 Pine Straw Rd, Leesburg FL 34748 B Brooklyn NY 1946 s Dwight & Evelyn. Adel 1965; Pratt Inst 1974; Cert Geo Mercer Memi TS 1987. D 12/15/1986 Bp Robert Campbell Witcher Sr. m 11/5/2005 Marana Perrin. Dnry D (Forest Pk) Dio Long Island Garden City NY 2014-2017, Cnvnr of Deacons 2014-2017; Cluster D S Jn's Of Lattingtown Locust Vlly NY 2011-2012; Cluster D S Lk's Ch Sea Cliff NY 2011-2012; Cluster D S Paul's Ch Glen Cove NY 2011-2012; Cluster D Trin Epis Ch Roslyn NY 2011-2012; D Gr Ch Jamaica NY 2008-2011; D S Elis's Epis Ch Floral Pk NY 2002-2008; D S Thos' Epis Ch Floral Pk NY 2002-2008; D S Mk's Ch Jackson Heights NY 2001-2002, D 1986-1990; D Ch Of S Alb The Mtyr S Albans NY 1996-2000; D All SS' Epis Ch Long Island City NY 1994-1996; D Ch Of The Redeem Astoria NY 1990-1994. Assn of Epis Deacons 1986.

PERRIN, Henry Keats (SO) 10129 Springbeauty Ln, Cincinnati OH 45231 B El Dorado AR 1945 s Howard & Vera. BA U So 1967; MDiv Sewanee: The U So, TS 1974. D 6/29/1974 P 11/1/1975 Bp Christoph Keller Jr. m 5/26/1974 Margaret Ann Perrin. S Phil's Ch Cincinnati OH 1992; Vic S Steph's Epis Ch Cincinnati OH 1991-2001; Assoc R The Ch of the Redeem Cincinnati OH 1990; Pres Of SW Ohio'S Epis Reg 1989-1990; Chair Of The Cong Dvlpmnt Com Dio Sthrn Ohio Cincinnati OH 1989-1990, 1988-1989; Int S Jas Epis Ch Cincinnati OH 1989-1990; S Jn's Ch Clinton IA 1987; Assoc R S Tim's Epis Ch Cincinnati OH 1983-1987; Vic S Andr's Ch Grove OK 1982-1983; Coun On Mssn Dio Oklahoma Oklahoma City OK 1979-1983; Vic S Jn's Epis Ch Vinita OK 1979-1983; Chair Of The Arkansas Epis Day Sch Com 1978-1979; Vic All SS Epis Ch Paragould AR 1975-1979; Chapl Arkansas St U At Jonesboro 1975-1979; Asst S Mk's Epis Ch Jonesboro AR 1975-1979; Cur S Andr's Ch Rogers AR 1974-1975. Ord Of Ascen; RACA, NECAD, Cath Fllshp Of The Epis Ch.

PERRIN, Mary Elizabeth (WMich) 2512 Highpointe Dr, Kalamazoo MI 49008 **R S Mart Of Tours Epis Ch Kalamazoo MI 2004-; Coun for Lifelong Formation, Prov V Rep Epis Ch Cntr New York NY 2011-; GC Dep Dio Wstrn Michigan Kalamazoo MI 2009-, 2001-2009** B Grand Rapids MI 1952 d Benjamin & Nettie. BA MI SU 1979; MDiv SWTS 2000. D 4/22/2001 P 10/27/2001 Bp Edward Lewis Lee Jr. m 6/15/1974 Thomas Wesley Perrin. S Andr's Ch Grand Rapids MI 2001-2004.

PERRIN, Ronald Van Orden (NY) 3409 Hollywood Ave, Austin TX 78722 **Nonpar 1965-** B Greenfield MA 1933 s Robert & Clara. BA Wesl 1955; BD UTS 1958. D 6/30/1960 P 1/1/1961 Bp Conrad H Gesner. m 6/11/1955 Janet Larson c 4. Asst Min Calv and St Geo New York NY 1963-1965; Vic Chr Epis Ch Get-

tysburg SD 1961-1963; P-in-c Sioux Indn Chap Cheyenne River Reserve SD 1961-1963.

PERRIN, Susan Elizabeth (USC) B Rockville MD 1950 d Henry & Frances. BA Jamestown Coll 1972; Cert Shalem Inst 1999; Cert Dioc Sch for Mnstry 2007. D 1/21/2006 Bp Dorsey Henderson. m 9/4/1972 Robert Anthony Perrin c 1.

PERRINO, Robert Anthony (SeFla) 1103 Duncan Cir Apt 103, Palm Beach Gardens FL 33418 B Providence RI 1933 s Anthony & Olympia. BS Providence Coll 1954. D 11/12/2003 Bp Leo Frade. m 2/7/1976 Bernice Leger c 5. S Mk's Ch Palm Bch Garden FL 2004-2010.

PERRIS, John D. (Eur) 581 Valley Rd, Upper Montclair NJ 07043 **The Angl/ Epis Ch Of Chr The King Frankfurt am Main 60323 2014-** B Oak Park IL 1960 s John & Elenor. BA Cor 1982; JD Ya 1986; MDiv GTS 1998. D 6/10/1998 P 12/10/1998 Bp Orris George Walker Jr. m 4/21/1990 Catharine D Perris c 3. R S Jas Ch Montclair NJ 2006-2014; R Chr Ch Epis Harwich Port MA 2002-2006; Assoc S Jn's Ch Roanoke VA 1998-2002; Assoc of the OHC 2003; The Angl Soc 1998. Phi Beta Kappa Cor 1981.

PERRIZO, Faith Crook (WVa) 541 Deer Ridge Ln S, Maplewood MN 55119 **Mem Mnstry Developers Collaborative 2008-** B Marietta OH 1953 d Clifford & Lillian. Cert The Wstrn Coll 1974; BA Macalester Coll 1975; MDiv SWTS 1980; Cert Academia HispanoAmericana 2012. D 6/24/1980 P 9/23/1981 Bp Robert Marshall Anderson. c 3. Int S Steph's Epis Ch And U Columbus OH 2015-2016; Cnvnr Mnstry Dvlp's Collaborative 2013-2015; Cn for Mnstry Dvlpmnt and Transitions Dio W Virginia Charleston WV 2004-2014; Plnng Grp Mem Mtn Gr: Appalachian Mnstrs Conf 2004-2014; Profsnl Dvlpmnt Com Dio Sthrn Ohio Cincinnati OH 2002-2004, Epis Ch Serv Fndt 2000-2001, COM 1997-1999, COM 1996-1999; R S Lk's Ch Marietta OH 1995-2004; Field Rep ECF New York NY 1994-1996; Asst for Mnstry/Dioc Dio Chicago Chicago IL 1990-1995, Chris Ed Dir, Gr Ch-in-the-Loop 1987-1989, 1986-1988, Search Consult 1981-1982; Vic S Fran Epis Ch Chicago IL 1984-1987; DCE & Yth S Mary's Ch Pk Ridge IL 1980-1981.

PERROTT, Ann Marie (Ct) B Beverly MA 1951 d Guy & Blanche. Gnrl Stds No Shore Cmnty Coll 1981; BS Emerson Coll 1983; MDiv EDS 2013. D 1/28/2017 Bp Laura Ahrens. m 10/2/1994 Godfrey Perrott c 1.

PERRY, Ally (WLa) 3125 Debra Ln, Westlake LA 70669 **H Trin Epis Ch Sulphur LA 2014-; Vic S Jn the Apos Pottsboro Tx 2001-** B Cincinnati OH 1949 d Edward & Queenie. BA Franconia Coll 1975; MDiv Yale DS 1978; MBA GTF 1990; St Georges Coll 1995; Hebr U of Jerusalem 1996. D 6/1/1984 P 12/21/1984 Bp Walter Cameron Righter. m 5/23/2004 Lowry Gene Perry. Int All SS Epis Ch Miami OK 2013-2014; The Rev. Ally Perry S Jn's Epis Ch Pottsboro TX 2001-2012; Vic S Anne's By The Fields Ankeny IA 1985-1997; Vic S Anne-in-the-Fields Ankeny Iowa 1985-1996; Int S Andr's Ch Des Moines IA 1984-1985; Int D/P S Andr's Clear Lake IA 1984-1985; Stndg Com Dio Dallas Dallas TX 2010-2013, COM 2004-2012, COM 2002-2012; Exec Coun Dio Iowa Des Moines IA 1990-1994, COM 1986-1990; Iowa Rel Media Serv, Bd Mem Iowa 1984-1994. Texoma Living, "article," *Sprtl, but not Rel*, 2009. Int Mnstry Ntwk 2012.

PERRY, Bonnie Anne (Chi) 4550 N Hermitage Ave # 103, Chicago IL 60640 **1996-; 1994-; Vic All SS Epis Ch Chicago IL 1992-** B San Diego CA 1962 d Raymond & Mary. SWTS; BA H Cross Coll 1984; MDiv UTS 1988; DMin 1998. D 6/2/1990 P 12/1/1990 Bp John Shelby Spong. m 12/3/2012 Martha Susan Harlow. Chair Of The Dioc Stwdshp Cmpgn 1994-1997; Dioc Cong Dvlpmnt Com 1993-1997; Int S Ptr's Ch Clifton NJ 1991-1992; Chair Of The Dioc Wmn Cmsn 1990-1992; Chr Ch Ridgewood NJ 1990-1991; Bd Inter-Rel Fllshp Of Homeless Bergen Cnty NJ 1989-1991; Mssnr Chr Ch Hackensack NJ 1988-1989. Ord Of S Helena 1998.

PERRY, Cecilia Carolyn (RI) PO Box 872, Bristol RI 02809 **Chapl Hallworth Hse Providence RI 2003-** B Bristol RI 1936 d Calbraith & Marie. BA U of Rhode Island 1970; MEd Rhode Island Coll 1977; MDiv EDS 1994. D 1/27/1996 Bp Morgan Porteus P 2/8/1997 Bp Gerry Wolf. c 3. S Mich's Ch Bristol RI 2006-2007; Supply P Ch Of The Adv Pawtucket RI 2003-2005; Int Ch Of The Mssh Providence RI 2002; R S Paul's Ch Portsmouth RI 2000-2001; Vic Calv Ch Pascoag RI 1997-2000; D S Paul's Ch N Kingstown RI 1996-1997; Yth Min/D S Paul's Epis Ch Wickford RI 1995-1997. Sis of St. Marg, Boston, MA 2003.

PERRY, David Warner (Ore) 715 Se 34th Ave, Portland OR 97214 **Assoc S Mich And All Ang Ch Portland OR 2001-** B Salem OR 1941 s Leon & Josephine. W&M 1961; BA U of Oregon 1963; STB GTS 1966; DD, hon VTS 2001; VTS 2001; DD, hon CDSP 2002; CDSP 2002. D 6/22/1966 P 12/27/1966 Bp James Walmsley Frederic Carman. m 6/19/1965 Fredrika W Perry c 2. Sprtl Life Fac L'Arche Portland Oregon 2012-2015; PB Dep for Ecum and Interfaith Relatns Epis Ch Cntr New York NY 1995-2001, Dep for Ecum and Interfaith Relatns 1994-1995, Rel Educ Coordntr 1973-1982, Bd Mem Epis Relief and Dvlpmnt 2001-2006; Assoc R All SS Ch Pasadena CA 1982-1986; Dir. CE Dio Oregon Portland OR 1971-1973; Cur Chr Ch Par Lake Oswego OR 1966-1971. Ed, "Making Sense of Things," *Making Sense of Things*, Seabury Press, 1981; Ed, "HomeGrown CE," *Homegrown CE*, Seabury Press, 1979; Ed, "AWARE

(Rel Educ Notebooks," *AWARE 10 vol.*, Epis Ch Cntr, 1974. DD VTS 2002; DD CDSP 2001; Hon Cn S Lk's Cathd, Dio Panama 1995.

PERRY, John Wallis (Vt) 431 Union St, Hudson NY 12534 B Bronx NY 1948 s John & Helen. BA Ford 1970; MDiv EDS 1999. D 6/5/1999 Bp Arthur Edward Walmsley P 12/18/1999 Bp Robert Deane Rowley Jr. m 4/22/1972 Eleanor Perry c 3. R Chr Ch Epis Hudson NY 2004-2014; R S Jas Memi Epis Ch Titusville PA 1999-2004. Cmnty Cross Nails.

PERRY, Kenneth M (Roch) PO Box 147, Geneva NY 14456 B Queens NY 1940 s Lester & Gertrude. BS SUNY 1962; MEd SUNY 1997. D 3/29/2008 Bp Jack Marston Mckelvey. m 8/25/1962 Josephine V Perry c 2.

PERRY, Margaret Rose (Az) St Francis in-the-Valley, 600 S La Canada Dr, Green Valley AZ 85614 B Jackson MI 1941 d William & Betty. AA Elgin Cnty Coll 1975; AS DuPage Glen Ellyn IL 1981. D 1/26/2008 Bp Kirk Stevan Smith. m 8/28/1959 Carl Perry c 2. D Epis Ch Of S Fran-In-The-Vlly Green Vlly AZ 2008-2014.

PERRY, Nandra Loraine (Tex) D 6/25/2016 Bp C Andrew Doyle.

PERRY, Pauline Tait (WMass) 49 Briarwood Cir, Worcester MA 01606 **Died 8/29/2016** B Springfield MA 1925 d Richard & Ethel. BA Clark U 1947; MA Assumption Coll 1975; Cert SWTS 1992. D 6/13/1992 Bp Andrew Frederick Wissemann. m 9/13/1947 Roger Newton Perry c 4. D St.Matt's Ch Worcester MA 2005-2016; D S Lk's Ch Worcester MA 1998-1999; D S Jn's Ch Worcester MA 1997-2001; D S Fran Ch Holden MA 1992-1997; D Dio Wstrn Massachusetts Springfield 2002-2016. FVC 1993; Soc of S Marg 1986-1998.

PERRY, Raymond Glenn (NMich) 251 Monongahela Rd, Crystal Falls MI 49920 **Non-par 1990-** B Crystal Falls MI 1928 s Thomas & Elsie. BD Michigan Tech U 1959. D 5/20/1990 P 12/1/1990 Bp Thomas Kreider Ray. m 1/7/1954 Helen Eckola. P (Ret) S Mk's Ch Crystal Falls MI 1990-2005.

PERRY, Robert Kendon (Ida) 411 Capitol Ave, Salmon ID 83467 **Asst Ch Of The Redeem Salmon ID 1994-** B Salmon ID 1949 s William & Aloha. D 1/29/1994 P 9/1/1994 Bp John Stuart Thornton. m 5/23/1969 Barbara Cool.

PERSCHALL JR CSF, Donald Richard (Dal) 909 W Gandy St, Denison TX 75020 **R S Lk's Ch Denison TX 2011-** B Bloomington IL 1949 s Donald & Virginia. BS U of Dubuque 1976; MDiv U of Dubuque 1978. Rec 3/1/2003 Bp Peter Hess Beckwith. m 3/25/1979 Andrea Perschall c 3. R S Mths' Epis Ch Athens TX 2006-2010; R Trin Ch Mt Vernon IL 2003-2006.

✠ PERSELL, The Rt Rev Bill (Chi) 28 Haskell Dr., Bratenahl OH 44108 **Ch Wrld Serv New York NY 2009-; Property Disputes T/F ECUSA 2005-; Bishops Working for a Just Wrld ECUSA 2002-** B Rochester NY 1943 s Charles & Emily. BA Hobart and Wm Smith Colleges 1965; MDiv EDS 1969; Intl Coll LB 1969; EDS 1981. D 6/21/1969 Bp Charles Bowen Persell Jr P 12/21/1969 Bp Robert Claflin Rusack Con 3/13/1999 for Chi. m 5/5/1973 Nancy Persell c 6. Epis Relief and Dvlpmt 2004-2010; Pres, 2001-2003 Coun of Rel Leaders Chicago IL 2001-2008; Stndg Cmsn on Ecum and Inter Faith Relatns ECUSA 2000-2006; Bp of Chicago Dio Chicago Chicago IL 1999-2008; Rush U Hosp 1999-2008; Dn Trin Cathd Cleveland OH 1991-1999; Soc Concerns & Peace Cmsn Dio Long Island Garden City NY 1983-1991, Soc Concerns & Peace Cmsn 1983-1991; Bd Pstr & Educ Servs Inc 1982-1991; R S Ann And The H Trin Brooklyn NY 1982-1991; R St Johns Pro-Cathd Los Angeles CA 1972-1982; P S Paul's Epis Ch Tustin CA 1969-1972; Trst Dio Los Angeles Los Angeles CA 1977-1981, Dept Soc Rela 1972-1976, Dept Soc Relatns 1972-1974. Phi Beta Kappa Hob 1965.

PERSON, Dorothy Jean (NMich) 208 Lane Ave, Kingsford MI 49802 B 1926 D 2/29/2004 Bp James Arthur Kelsey. m 6/7/1947 William Jay Person c 5.

PERSON, Kathryn Jeanne (NY) 1803 Glenwood Rd, Brooklyn NY 11230 **Dio New York New York NY 2014-; Sprtl Fac Credo Inst Inc. Memphis TN 2012-; Com on Status of Wmn Exec Coun Appointees New York NY 2009-** B New Orleans LA 1962 d Daniel & Sandra. BA Pr 1984; MS Col 1985; MDiv Harvard DS 1996; STM GTS 2000. D 12/19/1998 P 12/4/1999 Bp M(Arvil) Thomas Shaw. m 2/18/1996 Kamal Abdullah. S Mary's Manhattanville Epis Ch New York NY 2013-2014; Dir, Cntr for Chr Sprtlty The GTS New York NY 2009-2013; Assoc R Ch Of The H Trin New York NY 2004-2010; Assoc R Gr Ch Brooklyn NY 1999-2004. "Lifting Wmn Voices," Morehouse, 2009; "Where You Go I Shall: Gleanings From The Stories Of Biblic Widows," Cowley Pub, 2005. Fllshp of St. Jn 2002. jperson@dioceseny.org

PESSAH, Elisabeth Jayne (CFla) 1225 W Granada Blvd, Ormond Beach FL 32174 **Dio Florida Jacksonville 2016-** B Hamilton Ontario Canada 1966 d Edwin & Elizabeth. BA U of Guelph 1990; MDiv Wycliffe Coll 2011. Trans 7/8/2015 as Priest Bp Gregory Orrin Brewer. m 5/6/1995 Stephen Michael Pessah c 2.

PESSAH, Stephen Michael (CFla) 1225 W Granada Blvd, Ormond Beach FL 32174 **R Ch Of The H Chld Ormond Bch FL 2015-** B Kirkland Lake Ontario Canada 1965 s Ben & Constance. Commissioned Ch Army Trng Coll 1986; MDiv Wycliffe Coll 2005. Trans 5/27/2015 as Priest Bp Gregory Orrin Brewer. m 5/6/1995 Elisabeth Jayne Mauch c 2.

PETERMAN, Lynn C (EC) 115 John L Hurst Dr, Swansboro NC 28584 B Greenville PA 1960 d Paul & Nancy. BS U of So Carolina 1987; MS Clemson U 1991; MDiv VTS 2002. D 4/10/2002 P 10/19/2002 Bp Clifton Daniel III.

m 12/8/1993 Thomas R Peterman c 1. Assoc S Cyp's Ch New Bern NC 2006-2009; Asst S Jas Par Wilmington NC 2002-2004.

PETERS, Albert Fitz-Randolph (Del) c/o Manor House, 1001 Middleford Rd Apt 106, Seaford DE 19973 **Ret 1989-** B Washington DC 1927 s Albert & Marquerite. BA Amer U 1952; GTS 1955. D 6/18/1955 P 12/21/1955 Bp Angus Dun. Primary Pstr S Mary's Ch Bridgeville DE 2000-2005, Vic 1983-1999; Mssn Supply P Dio Delaware Wilmington 1989-2001, Sup P 1989-1997, 1983-1989; All SS Epis Ch Delmar DE 1983-1989; The Sussex Cnty Mssn Of The Epis Ch Wilmington DE 1975-1983; R S Marg's Ch Chicago IL 1962-1975; Cur Gr Ch White Plains NY 1957-1959; Cur All SS' Epis Ch Chevy Chase MD 1955-1957.

PETERS, Arthur Edward (Alb) 35 North St, Granville NY 12832 **Trin Ch Whitehall NY 2015-; D/Vic Trin Ch Granville NY 2005-** B Paterson NJ 1952 D 6/22/2003 Bp Daniel William Herzog P 3/31/2012 Bp William Howard Love. m 10/20/1979 Sue Anne Boerner. trinitygranville@gmail.com

PETERS JR, August William (WA) 1000 Hilton Ave, Catonsville MD 21228 **Ret 1997-** B Baltimore MD 1933 s August & Sarah. Cert Towson U 1953; BS U of Maryland 1957; STB Ya Berk 1961. D 7/6/1961 P 6/18/1962 Bp Noble C Powell. m 4/13/1958 Donaleen Peters c 3. Pstr Assoc S Tim's Ch Catonsville MD 2002-2013; S Paul's Par Washington DC 1985-1996; Asst to R S Paul's Rock Creek Washington DC 1985-1996; R S Lk's Par Bladensburg MD 1972-1985; Cur Chr Ch Prince Geo's Par Rockville MD 1965-1970; Vic S Alb Williamsport MD 1963-1965; Asst Emm Ch Cumberland MD 1961-1962. CAP; CBS; ESA; Foward In Faith; Soc Of All SS; Soc Of S Mary, Ward Superior.

PETERS, David W (Tex) PO Box 178, Mount Vernon IL 62864 **S Mk's Ch Austin TX 2016-** B Sellersville PA 1975 s Daniel & Diane. BA Appalachian Bible Coll 1998; MDiv Biblic TS 2002. D 11/30/2011 P 6/17/2012 Bp Daniel Hayden Martins. m 10/26/2013 Sarah Celeste Bancroft c 3. Gr Epis Ch Georgetown TX 2013-2016.

PETERS, Diana Wray (Colo) 13495 Monroe St, Thornton CO 80241 B South Joseph MO 1949 d John & Doris. S Thos Theol Sem; BS Missouri Wstrn St U 1974; MA U of Kansas 1981; MDiv CDSP 1996. D 6/8/1996 P 12/21/1996 Bp William Jerry Winterrowd. m 5/22/1981 Gary L Peters c 2. R Intsn Epis Ch Denver CO 2001-2014; All Souls Mssn Of The Deaf Denver CO 2001; S Lk's Ch Denver CO 1999-2001; Dio Colorado Denver CO 1999-2000; Cur Chr's Epis Ch Castle Rock CO 1996-1998. Celtic Cross Soc.

PETERS, Gregory William (Oly) 4424 SW 102nd Street, Seattle WA 98146 B Elkhorn WI 1961 s Joseph & Alma. BA Evergreen St Coll 1988; MDiv GTS 1995. D 6/28/1997 P 6/1/1998 Bp Vincent Waydell Warner. m 5/8/1999 Erika Diane Schreder c 2. S Jn The Bapt Epis Ch Seattle WA 2012-2013; Vic All SS Epis Ch Seattle WA 2003-2009; Int St Bede Epis Ch Port Orchard WA 2001-2003; S Mk's Cathd Seattle WA 1998-2001; S Andr's Ch Seattle WA 1997-1998.

PETERS, Helen Sarah (Ak) 1340 23rd Ave, Fairbanks AK 99701 **D S Jas' Ch 1974-** B Tanana AK 1929 d Elijah & Helen. Cert Cook Chr Trng Sch 1984. D 8/11/1974 Bp William Jones Gordon Jr. m 9/2/1956 Joseph Peters.

PETERS, John T (Minn) 14434 Fairway Dr, Eden Prairie MN 55344 **R S Alb's Epis Ch Edina MN 2000-** B Greenwich CT 1958 s John & Shirley. DPS St Johns Coll Nottingham Gb; BA U of Connecticut 1980; LTh S Johns Coll Nottingham GB 1987. Trans 10/4/1994 Bp James Louis Jelinek. R Chr Epis Ch Grand Rapids MN 1994-2000; Serv Ch Of Engl 1987-1994.

PETERS, J Patrick (CPa) 465 Zachary Dr, Manheim PA 17545 **R S Paul's Ch Columbia PA 2003-** B Trenton NJ 1946 s Martin & Edyth. BA S Mary Sem & U 1971; CUA 1974; MA JHU 1984. Rec 1/12/2002 as Priest Bp Michael Whittington Creighton. m 11/15/1980 Danielle J Peters c 4. P The Epis Ch Of S Jn The Bapt York PA 2002-2003. stpaulepchcolumbia@earthlink.net

PETERS, Peter William (Roch) 239 Yarmouth Rd, Rochester NY 14610 **Mssnr for the Vocational Discernment of all the Baptized Dio Rochester Henrietta 2013-, Vocation & Ldrshp Dvlpmt 2010-2012, Dioc Coun 1999-2010** B Tidworth UK 1939 s George & Harriet. ThL Moore Theol Coll Sydney 1962; BA U of New Engl Armidale Nsw Au 1966; MA Yale DS 1969; PhD Van 1979. Trans 6/1/1969 Bp John Vander Horst. m 5/19/2012 Sarah M Peters c 3. Int S Jn's Ch Canandaigua NY 2009-2010; P-in-c S Andr's Ch No Grafton MA 2004-2005; P-in-c S Paul's Ch Millis MA 2003-2004; R S Lk's Ch Fairport NY 1992-2003; Adj Prof Chr Ethics CRCDS 1992-1999; Chapl U Md - Coll Pk 1986-1992; Chapl Natl Cathd Sch - Wdc 1984-1986; Chapl Cranbrook Sch Kingwood TN 1982-1984; R Trin Ch Clarksville TN 1974-1982; Instr Ethics & Philos Aquinas Jr Coll Nashville TN 1970-1974; Asst S Geo's Ch Nashville TN 1970-1974; Serv Ch Of New So Wales 1963-1967. Auth, "Ch And Publ Plcy," Dio Rochester, 1999; Auth, "Some Considerations Concerning Ch & Educ For Morality"; Auth, "Evang: Angl Witness In A Pluralistic Soc"; Auth, "Ch & Publ Plcy". EPF 1987; EPF 1987; ESMHE 1986-1992; ESMHE 1986-1992; Eposcopal Urban Caucus 1987-2005; Eposcopal Urban Caucus 1987; Interfaith Allnce 1993; Interfaith Allnce 1993.

PETERS, Yejide S (NY) 1414 Greycourt Ave, Richmond VA 23227 **All SS' Epis Ch Briarcliff NY 2010-** B New York, NY 1976 d William & Jacquelyn. BA U

MI 2002; MDiv Ya Berk 2008. D 3/15/2008 Bp Mark Sean Sisk P 12/6/2008 Bp Peter J Lee. S Steph's Ch Richmond VA 2008-2010.

PETERSEN, Barbara Jean (WNC) 2047 Paint Fork Rd, Mars Hill NC 28754 **Exec Dir Cntr for Art & Sprt at St. Geo's Epis Ch 2015-** B Evanston IL 1948 d Frank & Mary. BS U of Nebraska 1970; MDiv Sewanee: The U So, TS 2000. D 5/30/2000 P 11/30/2000 Bp James Edward Krotz. m 9/4/1969 Lyle Petersen. Assoc St Georges Epis Ch Asheville NC 2010-2012, Int 2009-2010; Chapl Hospice of Madison Marshall NC 2009-2014; R Epis Ch Of The H Sprt Mars Hill NC 2002-2008; Mssnr Cluster NE 2000-2002; S Christophers Ch Cozad NE 2000-2002; S Eliz's Ch Holdrege NE 2000-2002; S Jn's Ch Broken Bow NE 2000-2002; Cur S Jn's Epis Ch Harvard NE 2000-2002; Cur S Mk's Epis Pro-Cathd Hastings NE 2000-2002; Mssnr S Pauls Epis Ch Arapahoe NE 2000-2002; S Ptr's In The Vlly Lexington NE 2000-2002. Writer/article, "Renwl of Vows," *Highland Epis*, Dio Wstrn No Carolina, 2007. Ord of S Helena, Assoc 2004-2012. CE Prize ABS 2000; Urban T Holmes III Prize U So TS 2000; Wm A Griffin Schlrshp U So TS 2000. executivedirector@centerartspirit.org

PETERSEN, Carolyn Sherman (CFla) 4708 Waterwitch Point Dr, Orlando FL 32806 **D Cathd Ch Of S Lk Orlando FL 1999-** B Cheyenne WY 1937 D 1/16/1999 Bp John Wadsworth Howe. m 8/1/1959 Leon Louis Petersen c 3.

PETERSEN, Duane Eric (WLa) 1030 Johnston Street, Lafayette LA 70501 **Assoc Ch of The Ascen Lafayette LA 2003-; Assoc R Ch Of The Ascen Lafayette LA 1998-** B Rio Hondo CA 1956 s Donald & Mavis. BS Sthrn California Coll Costa Mesa 1978; Cert Sthrn California Coll Costa Mesa 1980; MDiv TESM 1992; DMin TESM 2006. D 6/27/1992 Bp Gethin Benwil Hughes P 1/9/1993 Bp James Michael Mark Dyer. m 6/13/1981 Mirinda K Petersen c 2. Vic S Dunstans Epis Ch Modesto CA 1995-1998; Supply Cler Dio Oregon Portland OR 1994-1995; Asst R S Steph's Epis Ch Wilkes Barre PA 1992-1994.

PETERSEN, Judith (SD) 1002 2nd St, Brookings SD 57006 B Dallas TX 1935 D 4/25/2003 Bp Creighton Leland Robertson. m 10/15/1976 Daryl Dee Petersen.

PETERSEN, Scott (At) All Saints Church, 1708 Watson Blvd, Warner Robins GA 31093 **Colleague Grp Engle Preaching Fllshp- Princeton Sem 2014-; VP Ntwk of Epis Cler Associations 2014-; P-in-c All SS Ch Warner Robins GA 2013-; Bd Mem Ntwk of Epis Cler Associations 2013-** B Acton, MA 1971 s Eric & Joan. S Thos U; BA U of Massachusetts 1993; M.Div VTS 2007. D 1/6/2007 Bp Leo Frade. m 3/17/1998 Rosmira Petersen c 3. R S Paul's Ch Wilkesboro NC 2010-2013; Assoc The Epis Ch Of The Gd Shpd Tequesta FL 2007-2010.

PETERSEN, William Herbert (Roch) 49 Winding Brook Dr., Fairport NY 14450 **Epis Rep Consult of Common Texts 2011-; Adj Stndg Cmsn on Liturg & Mus 2009-; Del COCU 1978-; TEC Rep Consult on Common Texts 2011-** B Davenport IA 1941 s William & Dorothea. WCC Ecumencial Inst; BA Gri 1963; MDiv CDSP 1966; Oxf GB 1971; U CA 1971; PhD Grad Theol Un 1976; Deem Inst of Sem Mgmt 1985. D 6/24/1966 P 12/27/1966 Bp Gordon V Smith. m 7/20/1963 Priscilla E Petersen c 2. Ecum Off Dom And Frgn Mssy Soc- Epis Ch Cntr New York NY 2011; Provost Bex Sem Columbus OH 1995-2009, Dn 1983-2006; Joint Com To Elect The PBp 1994-1997; 1991-1994; Dep GC 1991-1994; GBEC 1985-1997; Alt Dep GC 1985-1988; Provost CRDS Rochester NY 1985-1987; SCER 1982-1988; Natl Luth-Epis Dialogue 1977-1991; Prof Nash Nashotah WI 1973-1983; Tchg Fell CDSP Berkeley CA 1970-1972; Fell ECF In New York City 1970-1972; Asst Trsfg Epis Ch San Mateo CA 1968-1970; P-in-c All SS Epis Ch Storm Lake IA 1966-1968; Chapl Buena Vista Coll 1966-1968; P-in-c H Comfort Cherokee IA 1966-1968; S Steph's Ch Spencer IA 1966-1968; P-in-c S Paul's Ch Rochester NY 2014; Int R Chr Ch Pittsford Pittsford NY 2012. Auth, "What Are We Waiting For? Re-Imagining Adv for Time to Come.," Ch Pub, 2017; Auth, "Ecum Ord," *Equipping the SS: Ord in Anglicanism Today*, Columba Press, 2006; Co-Auth, "Diac as Ecum Opportunity," *Hanover Report of ALIC*, ACC & Luth Wrld Fed, 1996; Co-Auth, "Implications Of The Gospel," Augsburg & Forwared Mvmt, 1988; Co-Auth, "A Hist of Mus in the Epis Ch," AAM, 1987; Auth, "On the Pattern & in the Power," *Angl Theol & Pstr Care*, Morehouse-Barlow, 1985; Auth, "Traditions Transplanted: Story Of Angl & Luth Ch In Amer," Forw Mvmt, 1981; Auth, "Clio in Ch," *Wrshp Points the Way*, Seabury, 1981. Amer Soc Ch Hist, Hist Soc Of The Episcop 1970; Angl Luth Intl Cmsn 1993-2011; Associated Parishes for Liturg & Mssn 1973; HSEC 1973; Intl Angl Liturg Conf 1995; No Amer Acad of Ecumenists 1990; No Amer Acad of Liturg 1998; Societas Liturgica 1997. Cnvnr, Adv Proj Seminar No Amer Acad of Liturg 2007; Co-Cnvnr, Angl Colloquium No Amer Acad of Liturg 2004; Pres No Amer Acad of Ecumenists 2003; DD, honoris causa CDSP 1997; Pres Coun of Epis Sem Deans 1993.

PETERSEN-SNYDER, Christine Lynn (LI) 290 Conklin St, Farmingdale NY 11735 **R S Thos Ch Farmingdale NY 2006-** B Brooklyn NY 1958 d Alfred & Marjorie. BA CUNY 2000; MDiv GTS 2004. D 5/26/2004 Bp Orris George Walker Jr P 12/18/2004 Bp Rodney Rae Michel. m 6/12/1977 Daniel Snyder c 2. Cur S Ptr's by-the-Sea Epis Ch Bay Shore NY 2004-2006. DOK 1996.

PETERS-MATHEWS, Joseph (Cal) Diocese Of California, 1055 Taylor St, San Francisco CA 94108 **Assoc Chr Ch Portola Vlly CA 2012-; Dom And Frgn Mssy Soc- Epis Ch Cntr New York NY 2011-** B Columbus GA 1986 s Bobby & Nicely. MDiv GTS 2002; MDiv The GTS 2002; BA Troy U 2009. D 12/21/2011 Bp Philip Menzie Duncan II P 12/1/2012 Bp Marc Handley Andrus. m 5/18/2013 Brandon-Richard Peters-Mathews. P Dio California San Francisco CA 2012-2016; Epis Ch Cntr New York NY 2011-2012.

PETERSON, Barbara Ann (Mass) 17 Sandy Neck Rd, East Sandwich MA 02537 B Philadelphia PA 1951 d William & Joanne. BA U of New Mex 1979; MA U of New Mex 1983; MDiv Harvard DS 1986. D 6/10/1988 P 6/17/1989 Bp Don Edward Johnson. m 7/4/1991 William Charles Wrenn c 1. R Trin Ch Marshfield MA 1999-2012; R S Matt And The Redeem Epis Ch Boston MA 1989-1999; D Chr Ch Cambridge Cambridge MA 1988-1989.

PETERSON, Bryan Anthony (Neb) 9302 Blondo St, Omaha NE 68134 B Mankato MN 1962 s Donald & Alona. D 5/22/2015 Bp Scott Scott Barker. m 6/1/1985 Tracy Nan Tracy Nan Wilson c 3.

PETERSON, Carol Elizabeth (Wyo) 1908 Central Ave, Cheyenne WY 82001 B Birkenhead England 1952 d Samuel & Irene. BS U of Wyoming 1994; MS U of Wyoming 1997. D 9/11/2008 Bp Bruce Caldwell. m 1/4/1986 Norman K Peterson c 2.

PETERSON, Diane Mildred (Ct) 5160 Madison Avenue, 4670 Congress Street, Trumbull CT 06611 B Bridgeport CT 1947 d Ralph & Phyllis. D 9/12/2009 Bp Andrew Donnan Smith. c 2. Chapl Bridgeport Hosp 2009-2010.

PETERSON JR, Frank Lon (NY) 969 Park Ave Apt 8C, New York NY 10028 **D Dio Connecticut Meriden CT 2009-; Mem - COM Dio New York New York NY 2003-** B Miami FL 1936 s Frank & Helen. Florida St U; BS NYU 1964; MA GTS 1999. D 5/18/2002 Bp Mark Sean Sisk. D S Mich's Ch New York NY 2002-2009. Auth, "The Theol and Christology of the Prologue of theGospel of Jn," GTS, 1999. Soc of S Jn The Evangeliist 1997.

PETERSON, Iris E (Be) 56 Franklin St Unit 16, Danbury CT 06810 B Chester PA 1958 d Gilbert & Charlotte. BA Cedar Crest Coll 1980; MDiv GTS 2002. D 4/6/2002 P 10/6/2002 Bp Paul Victor Marshall. Assoc R S Jas Epis Ch Danbury CT 2002-2013.

PETERSON JR, John Henry (FdL) 129 5th St, Neenah WI 54956 **Fam Ther Samar Counslg Cntr - Menasha WI 2000-** B Providence RI 1941 s John & Connie. BA U of Rhode Island 1963; MDiv Ya Berk 1966; MS U of Rhode Island 1987. D 6/18/1966 P 3/18/1967 Bp John S Higgins. m 12/30/1967 Kathleen Peterson c 3. Sr. Counslr Fam Counslg Serv - Long Island 1994-2000; S Mk's Ch Westhampton Bch NY 1994-1997; Dio Milwaukee Milwaukee WI 1988-1993; Outpatient Dir S Barn Cntr Rogers Memi Hosp Oconomowoc WI 1988-1993; R Ch Of The H Trin Tiverton RI 1973-1988; Cur S Mich's Ch Bristol RI 1967-1973; Cur Chr Ch Hackensack NJ 1966-1967. Auth, *Healing Touch*; Auth, *Origami for Christians*.

PETERSON, John Louis (WA) 1001 Red Oak Dr, Hendersonville NC 28791 B Wadena MN 1942 s John & Edythe. BA Concordia Coll 1965; STB Harvard DS 1968; ThD Chicago Inst of Advncd Theol Chicago MA 1977; DD VTS 1992; DCL Sewanee: The U So, TS 1996; DD SWTS 1997; DD Sewanee: The U So, TS 2015. D 6/6/1976 P 6/13/1977 Bp Charles Bennison Sr. m 8/20/1966 Kirsten R Peterson c 2. Dir, Cntr for Global Justice and Recon Cathd of St Ptr & St Paul Washington DC 2005-2009; Dio Washington Washington DC 2005-2009; Secy Gnrl Angl Consultative Coun 1995-2004; Secy Gnrl, Angl Comm Off Epis Ch Cntr New York NY 1995-2004; Serv Ch In Jerusalem 1983-1994; Dn, St. Georges Coll, Jerusalem Exec Coun Appointees New York NY 1982-1994; Dio Wstrn Michigan Kalamazoo MI 1976-1982, Asst To The Bp Of Wstrn Michigan 1976-1982, Cn Theol 1976-1982; Vic S Steph's Epis Ch Plainwell MI 1976-1982; Instr Bexley Seabury Fed Chicago IL 1972-1973. Auth, "A Walk In Jerusalem," Morehouse, 1998; Auth, "36 arts," *Anchor Bible Dictionary*, 1992. Hon Cn S Steph's Cathd 2008; Hon Cn All SS' Cathd 2002; Hon Cn S Paul'S Cathd 2001; Hon Cn S Mich'S Cathd 1999; Hon Cn Cbury Cathd 1995; Hon Cn S Geo Cathd 1984; Hon Cn Chr King Cathd 1982.

PETERSON JR, John Raymond (SwFla) 5020 Bayshore Blvd Apt 301, Tampa FL 33611 B Detroit MI 1936 s John & Marjorie. BA MI SU 1959; MDiv VTS 1962. D 6/29/1962 Bp Archie H Crowley P 2/1/1963 Bp Richard Stanley Merrill Emrich. m 8/22/1959 Kay Peterson. Dio SW Florida Parrish FL 1998-2001, Common Mnstry 1998-2000, Chair Of Prog 1987-1997, In Vitro Instnl Reviwe Bd 1986-1995, Chair Of The Dnry Ext Com 1984-1986, Ext Cmsn 1987-1992; R St Johns Epis Ch Tampa FL 1979-2000; R S Mk's Barrington IL 1965-1979; Asst S Paul's Epis Ch Lansing MI 1962-1965.

PETERSON, Ralph Edward (NY) 235 Walker Sreet Apt 134, Lenox MA 01240 B Duluth MN 1932 s Harold & Verna. BA U MN 1954; AMT Harv 1955; EDS 1956; MDiv Luth TS at Chicago 1960; Cert Harv Bus Sch 1977. Rec 1/24/1989 as Priest Bp Richard Frank Grein. c 1. Int Chr Ch Oyster Bay NY 2002-2004; Int Chr Ch Warwick NY 2000-2002; Int Par of Chr the Redeem Pelham NY 2000; Int Ch Of S Jas The Less Scarsdale NY 1999-2000; Int All SS' Epis Ch Briarcliff NY 1997-1998; Intl P Ch of Sweden Dio Vaxjo 1997-1998; Int S Paul's Ch Kinderhook NY 1996-1997; Int S Mk's Ch Mt Kisco NY 1994-1996; P-in-c Hse Of The Redeem New York NY 1992-1994; Henry Sloan Coffin Chair of Bible The Masters Sch Dobbs Ferry NY 1989-1992; Dir Amer Sum Inst 1984-1994; Pres The Open Cong New York City 1984-1989; Coinsultant,

668

Hlth Mnstry Archdiocese of New York 1981-1983; Sr Pstr S Ptr's Ch Luth New York City 1966-1980; Exec Dir Natl Coun of Ch NYC Dept. of Mnstry 1962-1966; Pstr Chr Ch Hammond Indiana 1960-1962. Auth, "The Healing Ch: Hlth Care Apostolate," 1981. Ch Club 1992-1996; Fllshp of St. Alb and St. Sergius 1979; Societas Sanctae Birgittae 1982. Fell The Sophia Inst 2009; Fell Soc of Art Rel and Culture 1972; D.D. Ge 1971; Acad of Par Cler Founding Pres 1969; Phi Delta Kappa Harvard 1955.

PETERSON, Richard Trenholm (Cal) 883 Roble Dr, Sunnyvale CA 94086 **Ret 2003**- B San Francisco CA 1934 s Franklin & Etta. Trin San Antonio TX 1954; Tchr Cred San Francisco St U 1968; California Sch for Deacons 1979; BA California Sch for Deacons 1984; Cert U CA 1987. D 6/28/1980 Bp William Edwin Swing. m 6/24/1962 Marilyn Ann Peterson c 2. D Emerity S Mk's Epis Ch Palo Alto CA 2000-2003; Assoc S Lk's Ch Los Gatos CA 1984-1992; Pstr Asst S Tim's Epis Ch Mtn View CA 1980-1984. *Var Mus Pub*. OHC 1976. Letter of Commendation for Wk as Ther / Counslr Phoenix Prog, El Camino Hosp 1987; Cert of Appreciation for Years of Serv Foothill-DeAnza Cmnty Coll Distr 1985; Janacek Medal Mus/Conducting Awd 1971; Cert of Merit and Appreciation USAF Chapl Off Headqu 12th AF Germany 1956.

PETERSON, Suzanne (la) Diocese of Cape Town, PO Box 1932, Cape Town 8000 South Africa **Publ Plcy & Advocacy Off Angl Dio Cape Town Prov of Sthrn Afr 2009**- B Bradenton FL 1948 d Harry & Mildred. BA Florida St U 1970; MA VTS 1972. D 12/18/1976 P 9/25/1977 Bp Walter Cameron Righter. Trin Epis Par Waterloo IA 2013-2017; Sub Dn Cathd of St. Mich & St. Geo Grahamstown So Afri 2002-2009; Exec Coun Appointees New York NY 1999-2013; Asst S Mich & All Ang Queenstown So Afr 1998-2002; The Cathd Ch Of S Paul Des Moines IA 1996-1999, 1976-1982; Mssy to So Afr 1991-1994; HOD St of the Ch Com 1988-1991; Stndg Cmsn on Peace 1988-1991; Dep GC 1985-1988; SCER 1984-1988; Iowa Inter-Ch Agcy For Peace & Justice Des Moines IA 1983-1991. Comm Res Lord Grahamstown So Afr 1994. Proctor Fell EDS 1994; Hon Cn 98 S Paul Cath. trinityoffice@ trinityepiscopalwaterloo.org

PETERSON-WLOSINSKI, Cynthia M E (Minn) 1121 W Morgan St, Duluth MN 55811 B Saint Paul MN 1950 d Glenn & Margaret. BS San Jose St U 1974; MDiv VTS 1982. D 6/24/1982 P 12/29/1982 Bp Robert Marshall Anderson. m 12/28/1983 Stephen Stanley Wlosinski c 1. Assoc Dir McCabe Renwl Cntr Duluth MN 2013-2014; S Andr's By The Lake Duluth MN 2004-2011, 1999-2003, Vic 1994-1998; Campus Mnstry U MN at Duluth Duluth MN 1986-1987; Cur S Lk's Ch Minneapolis MN 1982-1986.

PETERSON ZUBIZARRETA, Dorenda C (SeFla) **S Jn's Sch Homestead FL 2013**- B Kansas City MO 1950 Trans 1/1/2001 Bp Leo Frade. m 1/23/2002 Pedro Zubizarreta. S Paul's Ch Hamilton MT 2012-2013; Dio W Texas San Antonio TX 2010-2011; Vic S Bon Ch Comfort TX 2008-2010; All SS Epis Ch San Benito TX 2003-2008; Exec Coun Appointees New York NY 2001-2003. doriolr@aol.com

PETIPRIN, Andrew Kirk (Tenn) 3700 Woodmont Blvd, Nashville TN 37215 **Cn Dio Tennessee Nashville TN 2017**- B Plattsburgh NY 1979 s Eric & Mary. BA U Pgh 2001; MPhil Oxf GB 2003; MDiv Ya Berk 2010. D 6/5/2010 Bp John Wadsworth Howe P 12/21/2010 Bp Kirk Stevan Smith. m 12/31/2005 Amber R Petiprin c 2. R S Mary Of The Ang Epis Ch Orlando FL 2011-2017; Asst to the R Chr Ch Of The Ascen Paradise Vlly AZ 2010-2011. apetiprin@edtn.org

PETIT, Charles David (USC) 5220 Clemson Ave, Columbia SC 29206 **Assoc S Martins-In-The-Field Columbia SC 2005**- B Huntington WV 1951 BA Marshall U. D 6/14/2003 P 5/27/2004 Bp Dorsey Henderson. m 6/7/1997 Michelle S Petit c 3. D H Cross Epis Ch Simpsonville SC 2003-2005. External Serv Awd Unoiversity Of The So TS 2003.

PETITE, Robert (Chi) 4717 S. Greenwood Ave. Unit 1, Chicago IL 60615 **Int R Ch Of Our Sav Elmhurst IL 2014**- B Belloram CA 1946 s Robert & Olive. BA U of Kings Coll Halifax NS CA 1969; BA U of Kings Coll Halifax NS CA 1969; MDiv Trin, U Tor CA 1972; MDiv U Tor CA 1972; ACPE Supvsr ACPE 1996; LMFT Assn of Mar and Fam Ther 1996; BCC Profsnl Assn of Profsnl Chapl 1996; DMin Chicago TS 1998; DMin Chicago TS 1998. Trans 7/23/1993 Bp Frank Tracy Griswold III. m 10/13/2007 Mark L Tabbut c 3. The Ch Hm At Montgomery Place Chicago IL 1993-2013; Chapl And Exec Dir S Anna's Chap Chicago IL 1993-2003; R, Chapl Par P and Campus Mnstry 1971-1989. Bd Cert Chapl Assn Prof Chapl; Clincl Mem Assn Mar & Fam Ther; Supvsr ACPE.

PETLEY, Dale Alfred (Okla) 1813 Westminster Pl, Oklahoma City OK 73120 **Assoc R All Souls Epis Ch Oklahoma City OK 1997**- B Summerside CA 1958 s Melvin & Rita. BA U of Kings Coll Halifax NS CA 1979; MDiv Atlantic TS 1982. Trans 9/1/1997 Bp Robert Manning Moody. Auth, "The H Sprt". Royal Can Legion.

PETRASH, David Lloyd (Dal) 1300 Overlook Dr, Kaufman TX 75142 **Dio Dallas Dallas TX 2016-; D St. Lk's Epis Ch Denison TX 2005**- B Waxahachie TX 1948 s John & Mary. BA U of No Texas 1969; MA U of No Texas 1971; DMA U of No Texas 1975; Angl TS 2005. D 6/5/2004 P 5/29/2008 Bp James Monte Stanton. m 1/21/1984 Laura Ford c 4. S Jas' Epis Ch Kemp TX 2017; Ch Of Our Merc Sav Kaufman TX 2009-2016; S Lk's Ch Denison TX 2008-2009,

Int Hd of Sch 2007-2008; D S Steph's Epis Ch Sherman TX 2004-2005. Oblate w the OSB 2016. dpetrash@edod.org

PETROCCIONE, Jim (Nwk) 28 Ross Rd, Stanhope NJ 07874 **R Ch Of The H Comm Norwood NJ 2008**- B Elizabeth NJ 1963 s Vincent & Alice. BA U of Memphis 1995; MDiv Memphis TS 1998. D 4/13/2002 P 10/20/2002 Bp John Palmer Croneberger. m 10/4/2014 Mark Stephen Harrison. Assoc S Mary's Ch Sparta NJ 2007-2008, Assoc 2002; All SS Ch Orange NJ 2003-2006; P-in-c All SS Epis Ch Orange NJ 2002-2006; Asst S Jn's Mem'l Ch Ramsey NJ 2002-2003.

PETROCHUK, Michael Aaron (O) St Andrew's Episcopal Church, 583 W Hopocan Ave, Barberton OH 44203 **S Andr's Ch Barberton OH 2012-; Prof & Dir Walsh U No Canton Ohio 2008**- B Akron OH 1960 s Michael & Mildred. BA U of Akron 1983; MHA Xavier U 1986; PhD Cleveland St U 1999; MDiv Bex Epis Sem 2012; MDiv Bex Sem 2012. D 6/9/2012 Bp Mark Hollingsworth Jr P 3/15/2013 Bp Arthur Williams Jr. m 9/1/1990 Sherrie Lynn Petrochuk c 1. VP Akron Gnrl Hlth System Akron Ohio 1989-2008. Auth, "Breaking Down the Dogma of Hosp: Toward a New Model," *Proceedings of the Global Bus Conf*, Innovation Inst, 2014; Auth, "A Descriptive Analysis of Nrsng Satisfaction: First-Time versus Non-First-Time," *Healthcare Marketing Quarterly*, Marketing Pub, 2012; Co-Auth, "Leading the Patient Experience," *Healthcare Exec*, Amer Coll of Healthcare Executives, 2008; Co-Auth, "Career Characteristics Among Graduates of a Midwestern MHSA Prog:," *Journ of Hlth Admin Educ*, Assn of U Prog in Hlth Admin, 1999; Co-Auth, "Reforming the Hlth Care System: Implications for Hlth Care Marketers," *Healthcare Marketing Quarterly*, Marketing Pub, 1996. ACHE of Nthrn Ohio 1990; Amer Acad of Med Administrators 1986; Amer Coll of Healthcare Executives 1984; Assn of U Prog in Hlth Admin 2010; Soc of Healthcare Strtgy & Mrkt Dvlpmt 1989. Fac Assoc Awd Amer Coll of Healthcare Executives 2010; Acad Awd Mem Beta Gamma Sigma 1997; Hon Mem Sigma Beta Delta 1996; Fell Amer Coll of Healthcare Executives 1994; Fell Amer Acad of Med Admin's 1992.

PETROTTA, Anthony Joseph (Ore) PO Box 445, Wilsonville OR 97070 **P S Fran Of Assisi Epis Wilsonville OR 2005-; Adj Assoc Prof Fuller TS Nthrn California 1994**- B San Francisco CA 1950 BA Westmont Coll 1975; MA Fuller TS 1977; MPhil U of St Andrews 1984; PhD Sheffield U Engl 1990. D 7/18/2004 P 4/24/2005 Bp Jerry Alban Lamb. m 7/10/2000 Pamela Berta-Petrotta c 2. Ch Of The Incarn Santa Rosa CA 2005; S Paul's Epis Ch Benicia CA 2004-2005. co-Auth, "Pocket Dictionary of Biblic Stds," InterVarsityPress, 2002. SBL 1980.

PETTEE, Abigail Bower (Me) 33 Chestnut St, Camden ME 04843 B New York City NY 1960 d Richard & Audrey. BA Mar 1983; MA Wheaton Coll 1985; MEd Boston Coll 1993. D 6/13/2015 Bp Stephen Taylor Lane. m 9/25/1993 William Ayer Pettee c 1.

PETTENGILL, David Eugene (Az) 1558 E Gary St, Mesa AZ 85203 **Assoc S Matt's Ch Chandler AZ 2013-, Asst 1999-2012** B Polk City IA 1932 s Claude & Anna. BA Arizona St U 1958; BA Arizona St U 1958; MDiv CDSP 1960; D.D. CDSP 2011. D 6/12/1960 P 12/11/1960 Bp Arthur Kinsolving. m 9/5/1953 Lois Pettengill c 1. Asst Chr Ch Of The Ascen Paradise Vlly AZ 2010-2012, Int 1998-2009; R S Mk's Epis Ch Mesa AZ 1978-1994; Pres Yavapai Cnty Hosp Prescott AZ 1974-1977; Tchr Yavapai Cmnty Coll 1971-1977; R S Lk's Ch Prescott AZ 1967-1978; Cur Gr St Pauls Epis Ch Tucson AZ 1964-1967; R SS Phil And Jas Morenci AZ 1960-1964. Hon DD The CDSP 2011; Hon Cn To Ordnry Dio Az 1992. dalopet@gmail.com

PETTENGILL-RASURE, Rachael Marie (Mass) 453 Adams St, Milton MA 02186 **Ch Of Our Sav Milton MA 2014**- B Lawrence MA 1981 d Forrest & Cynthia. BS Nyack Coll 2004; MDiv Allnce TS 2010; Cert EDS 2014. D 6/7/2014 Bp M(Arvil) Thomas Shaw P 1/10/2015 Bp Alan Gates. m 6/2/2012 Matthew R Rasure c 1. Chapl Gr Epis Ch Medford MA 2011-2014.

PETTERSON, Ted Ross (La) 25 Signature Dr, Brunswick ME 04011 **Ret 1998**- B Amsterdam NY 1935 s John & Mary. BA Tem 1964; MDiv PDS 1970. D 6/6/ 1970 P 12/12/1970 Bp Robert Lionne DeWitt. m 4/15/1961 Joan Petterson c 2. S Paul's Ch New Orleans LA 1985-1998; The Cathd Ch Of S Paul Des Moines IA 1984-1985; The Ch Of Our Redeem Lexington MA 1974-1984.

PETTIGREW, Thomas John (Alb) 3764 Main St, Warrensburg NY 12885 **Ch Of The H Cross Warrensburg NY 2012**- B Albany NY 1984 s Karl & Meg. BA SUNY Albany 2010; MDiv Nash 2011. D 6/4/2011 P 12/21/2011 Bp William Howard Love.

PETTITT, Robert Riley (ND) 1201 49th Avenue, Rt 6, Fargo ND 58103 B Saint Cloud MN 1923 s William & Erma. D 12/21/1985 P 10/1/1987 Bp Harold Anthony Hopkins Jr. m 7/20/1946 Elizabeth Mae Bensen.

PETTY, Carol Ross (Tex) Episcopal Diocese of Texas, PO Box 2247, Austin TX 78768 **Cn Dio Texas Houston TX 2013**- B Hamilton Ohio 1953 d Max & Priscilla. BS Texas Womans U 1974; MDiv SW Bapt TS 2001; MA SW Bapt TS 2001; CTh Epis TS of the SW 2005; DMin Austin Presb TS 2012. D 6/11/ 2005 Bp Don Adger Wimberly P 12/19/2005 Bp Rayford Baines High Jr. m 5/14/2011 George Haggas Zwicker c 2. Int Ch Of The H Comf Angleton TX 2007-2013; Assoc. R Trin Ch Longview TX 2005-2007; Sem St. Lk's on the

P

Lake Epis Ch Austin TX 2004-2005; S Steph's Ch Beaumont TX 2002-2004; Assoc Chr Cmnty Ch Beaumont TX 1997-2001. cpetty@epicenter.org

PETTY JR, Jess Joseph (O) 35 B Pond St, Marblehead MA 01945 **Ret 2001-** B Berea OH 1936 s Jess & Arline. BA Baldwin-Wallace Coll 1958; MDiv Bex Sem 1961. D 6/10/1961 P 1/24/1962 Bp Nelson Marigold Burroughs. m 8/8/1969 Gillian Wilkins c 4. Int S Mary's Epis Ch Bonita Sprg FL 2004-2005; Int Cathd Ch Of S Ptr St. Petersburg FL 2002-2003; St Johns Epis Ch Tampa FL 2001-2002; Int S Jn's Epis Ch Clearwater FL 2000; Int Ch Of The Ascen Clearwater FL 1999-2000; Int Trin By The Cove Naples FL 1998-1999; Int S Hilary's Ch Ft Myers FL 1996-1997; Int Gr And H Trin Cathd Kansas City MO 1995-1996; Int S Mart's Ch Chagrin Fall OH 1994-1995; R S Paul's Epis Ch Medina OH 1981-1994; Int S Ptr's Ch Clifton NJ 1980-1981; Dn Cathd Of St Lk Balboa 1977-1980; Vic S Lk's Epis Ch Chardon OH 1973-1977; P Iglesia Anglicana de la Reg Cntrl de Amer 274 San Salvador 1963-1972; Cur Chr Ch Shaker Heights OH 1961-1963.

PETTY JR, Tyrus Cecil (Kan) 5841 Sw 26th St, Topeka KS 66614 **Dir Of Soc Wk Stormont-Vail Reg Med Cntr 1991-; Dir Of Chapl Serv Stormont-Vail Reg Med Cntr 1976-; Non-par 1975-** B Teague TX 1944 s Tyrus & Maybelle. BA TCU 1967; MDiv SWTS 1972; MS U of Kansas 1991. D 4/10/1972 Bp William Paul Barnds P 10/1/1972 Bp Edward Clark Turner. m 7/27/1968 Marjorie D McColl. S Dav's Epis Ch Topeka KS 1976-1978; Fell In The Dept Of Rel And Psychol Menninger Fndt 1975-1976; Cn Gr Cathd Topeka KS 1972-1975. Aamft; Supvrs ACPE.

PETZAK, Rodney Ross (Nev) 1965 Golden Gate Dr, Reno NV 89511 B Manistee MI 1933 s Joseph & Elsie. AA Orange Coast Coll Costa Mesa CA 1957. D 9/6/1996 P 3/1/1997 Bp Stewart Clark Zabriskie. m 9/20/1980 Sharyn L Appolloni. P S Jn's In The Wilderness Ch Glenbrook NV 1997-2011.

PEVEHOUSE, James Melvin (Tex) 24 N Masonic St, Bellville TX 77418 **R S Mary's Ch Bellville TX 2013-** B Hayward CA 1978 s Douglas & Judy. BA California St U Long Bch 2000; ThM Dallas TS 2006; Dplma in Angl Stds Epis TS of the SW 2012. D 12/10/2011 Bp Paul Emil Lambert P 12/6/2012 Bp James Monte Stanton. m 4/14/2012 Brandy Lynn Turner Pevehouse c 4. Cur Ch Of The Gd Shpd Terrell TX 2012-2013. jamespevehouse@hotmail.com

PEVERLEY, Stephen Richard (LI) 1 Araca Ct, Babylon NY 11702 B Mineola NY 1937 s Norman & Eleanor. BA Adel 1961; MA Adel 1966; Mercer TS 1978. D 6/23/1979 P 2/1/1981 Bp Robert Campbell Witcher Sr. m 7/3/1965 Susan Peverley c 4. Supply P Chr Ch Babylon NY 2010-2011, Asst 1979-2010; St Jn's Ch Cold Sprg Harbor NY 2007; Gr Epis Ch Massapequa NY 2004-2008; Epis Ch Of S Mk The Evang Bellmore NY 2004-2006, Int 1985-1986, Int 1983-1984; Int Hd Mstr St Ptr's by the Sea/Epis Day Sch 2004-2005; Int Chr Ch Manhasset NY 2003-2004; Int Chr Ch Garden City NY 2002-2003; Ch of S Jude Wantagh NY 2001-2009, Int 1998-1999, Int 1998-1999, Int 1995-1999, 1995-1997; Int S Mk's Ch Westhampton Bch NY 2000-2001; Int S Ptr's by-the-Sea Epis Ch Bay Shore NY 1997-1998; Int Trin Epis Ch Roslyn NY 1996; Int S Bon Epis Ch Lindenhurst NY 1994-1995; Int Trin Ch Northport NY 1992-1994; Int S Ann's Epis Ch Bridgehampton NY 1991-1992; Int S Phil And S Jas Ch New Hyde Pk NY 1990-1991; Int S Jas Epis Ch S Jas NY 1989-1990; Int S Paul's Ch Patchogue NY 1986-1989; Assoc Emm Epis Ch Great River NY 1980-1983. Ord Of S Lk Chapl.

PEYTON III, Allen Taylor (Alb) 2401 Ben Hill Rd, Atlanta GA 30344 **Cn Mssnr Angl Ch of The Resurr 2010-** B Copenhagen DK 1957 s Allen & Margaret. BA U So 1980; MDiv GTS 1988. D 6/11/1988 P 6/28/1989 Bp Frank Kellogg Allan. R S Paul's Epis Ch Greenwich NY 2002-2010; R S Paul's Ch Palmyra MO 1992-1995; Vic S Jas Epis Ch Clayton GA 1989-1992; D The Epis Ch Of S Ptr And S Paul Marietta GA 1988-1989. Auth, "Pondering w The Padre," http://padreallenpsblog.blogspot.com/; Auth, "Pondering w The Padre," http://padreallenpsblog.blogspot.com/.

PEYTON IV, Francis Bradley (WA) 1919 York Road, 2nd Floor, Timonium MD 21093 B Charlottesville VA 1950 s Francis & Gertrude. Deerfield Acad Deerfield MA 1968; BA U of Virginia 1972; JD U of Virginia 1975; MDiv VTS 1984. D 5/23/1984 Bp Peter J Lee P 6/11/1985 Bp David Keller Leighton Sr. m 8/1/1987 Joan A Peyton c 3. Int Sherwood Epis Ch Cockeysville MD 2013-2014; Int S Jn's Ch Kingsville MD 2004-2005; Pstr St Philips Luth Ch Baltimore MD 2001-2004; Pstr St. Phil's Luth Ch Baltimore MD 2001-2003; Epis Cler Assn Dio Washington Washington DC 1996-1999, Eccl Trial Crt 1998-2003; R S Paul's Epis Ch Piney Waldorf MD 1992-2000; Int S Anne's Par Scottsville VA 1991-1992; Chapl Westminster Cbury Hse Richmond VA 1990-1992; R Emm Ch At Brook Hill Richmond VA 1988-1990; Cur Chr Ch St Michaels Par S Mich MD 1985-1988; Asst S Jn's Ch Reisterstown MD 1984.

PEYTON, Linda (Me) 42 Flying Point Rd, Freeport ME 04032 **Mnstry to Aged 1983-** B New York NY 1952 d Bernard & Joan. BA Sarah Lawr Coll 1976; MDiv EDS 1980. D 6/7/1980 Bp Paul Moore Jr P 12/20/1980 Bp Lyman Cunningham Ogilby. m 10/29/1983 Morris C Hancock c 2. Asst Ch Of The Redeem Bryn Mawr PA 1980-1983.

PEYTON JR, Robert Lee (At) PO Box 207, Hartwell GA 30643 B Austin TX 1950 BS Louisiana Tech U 1972; MS U of Texas 1975; PhD Colorado St U

1985; MA UTS 2004; Dip Ang Stud GTS 2008. D 12/21/2007 P 6/21/2008 Bp George Wayne Smith. R S Andr's Ch Hartwell GA 2008-2014.

PEYTON, Susan Carroll (SwVa) 300 W Frederick St, Staunton VA 24401 B Aiken SC 1957 d Jack & Janet. VA MWC 1978. D 11/11/2015 Bp Mark Bourlakas. m 5/19/1984 Harry Douglas Peyton.

PEYTON, William Parish (Va) 865 Madison Ave., New York NY 10021 B Alexandria VA 1970 s Gordon & Marjorie. BA U of Virginia 1993; MDiv GTS 2006. D 6/24/2006 P 2/3/2007 Bp Peter J Lee. m 6/19/1991 Elizabeth M Peyton c 3. Assoc R S Jas Ch New York NY 2010-2017; Asst R S Paul's Ch Charlottesville VA 2006-2010; Dir St. Geo's Camp Orkney Sprg VA 2004-2008.

PFAB, Martin William (Fla) 724 Lake Stone Cir, Ponte Vedra Beach FL 32082 B Bernard IA 1935 s Henry & Regina. BA Loras Coll 1958; MDiv Mt S Bern Sem Dubuque 1962; CTh SWTS 1987. Rec 6/7/1987 as Priest Bp Walter Cameron Righter. m 11/21/1984 Penny L Pfab. S Mary's Epis Ch Green Cv Spg FL 2007-2009; Adv Ch Farmington MN 2001-2003; S Ptr's Epis Ch Kasson MN 1997-2000; Chapl Mayo Med Cntr Rochester MN 1988-2007; Dio Minnesota Minneapolis MN 1988-1997; Int Trin Epis Par Waterloo IA 1987-1988; Chapl US Army Reserve 1971-1991; Serv RC Ch 1962-1984. Assembly of the Epis Hospitals and Chapl 1988; Coll Of Chapl 1988.

PFAB, Penny L (Fla) 724 Lake Stone Cir, Ponte Vedra Beach FL 32082 **R S Paul's By the Sea Jacksonville Bch FL 2006-** B Cedar Rapids IA 1947 d John & Mildred. BD Mt Mercy Coll 1983; CTh SWTS 1994; MDiv Untd TS of the Twin Cities 1994. D 6/29/1994 Bp James Louis Jelinek P 1/7/1995 Bp Sanford Zangwill Kaye Hampton. m 11/21/1984 Martin William Pfab c 4. R S Paul's By-The-Sea Epis Ch Jaxville Bch FL 2006-2015; R S Lk's Ch Minneapolis MN 2001-2006; R S Paul's Epis Ch Owatonna MN 1995-2001; Mayo Clnc Rochester Rochester MN 1994-1995.

PFAFF, Brad Hampton (NY) 126 W 83rd St Apt 3-P, New York NY 10024 B Carlinville IL 1948 s Harold & Frieda. BA IL Wesl 1970; MDiv GTS 1975. D 3/24/1977 P 1/25/1978 Bp Harold Louis Wright. Ch Of The H Nativ Bronx NY 1997-2013; Vic Dio New York New York NY 1997-2008, P 1981-1997; Cur The Ch of S Ign of Antioch New York NY 1978-1981; Assoc Chr Ch Bronxville NY 1977-1978. CBS.

PFAFF, David Anthony (SO) 985 Forest Ave, Glendale OH 45246 **R Chr Ch - Glendale Cincinnati OH 2016-** B Oxford England UK 1964 s Richard & Margaret. BA w hon U NC 1986; MDiv GTS 1992. D 5/28/1992 Bp Robert Whitridge Estill P 5/29/1993 Bp Huntington Williams Jr. m 8/26/1989 Emily Susan Vaill c 3. The CPG New York NY 2015-2016; Cn Dio Milwaukee Milwaukee WI 2007-2014, GC Dep 2004-2012, GC Dep 2004-2012, COM Chair 2003-2007; R S Mk's Ch Milwaukee WI 1999-2007; P-in-c Ascen Memi Ch Ipswich MA 1997-1999; Assoc Chr Epis Ch Raleigh NC 1992-1997; JSCN Dom And Frgn Mssy Soc- Epis Ch Cntr New York NY 2012. david.pfaff@ christchurchglendale.org

PFAFF, Richard William (NC) 750 Weaver Dairy Rd Apt 190, Chapel Hill NC 27514 **Died 7/10/2016** B Oklahoma City OK 1936 s Frederick & Flora. AB Harv 1957; BA Oxf GB 1959; MA Oxf GB 1963; DPhil Oxf GB 1965; Cert GTS 1966. D 6/11/1966 Bp Robert Lionne DeWitt P 12/17/1966 Bp Horace W B Donegan. m 12/27/1962 Margaret Campbell c 1. P Assoc Chap of the Cross Chap Hill NC 1967-2016; Chr Ch Of Ramapo Suffern NY 1966-1967. Auth, "The Liturg in Medieval Engl. A Hist," 2009; Auth, "Liturg Calendars, Books & SS in Medieval Engl," 1998; Co-Auth & co-Ed, "The Eadwine Psalter. Text, Image, & Monastic Culture in Twelfth-Century Cbury," 1992; Auth, "Medieval Latin Liturg: Select Bibliography," 1982; Auth, "Montague Rhodes Jas," 1980; Auth, "New Liturg Feasts In Later Medieval Engl," 1970. Assn Amer Rhodes Scholars 1959; Henry Bradshaw Soc (Hon VP) 1987; Phi Beta Kappa 1957. DD GTS 2012; Fell of Medieval Acad of Amer 2000; Man of the Year Morehouse Coll 1995; DD U of Oxford 1995; Fell of Soc of Antiquaries of London 1993; Fell of Royal Hist Soc 1983.

PFEIFFER, Dorothea Koop (WNC) 2 Sweet Gum Ct, Hilton Head SC 29928 **D Dio Wstrn No Carolina 2004-; D S Lk's Epis Ch Hilton Hd Island SC 1996-** B Omaha NE 1927 d Harvey & Gertrude. BA U of Nebraska 1948; MA U Denv 1965; Illinois St U 1982; Inst of Pstr Stds Chicago 1992. D 12/18/1993 Bp Edward Harding MacBurney. m 5/27/1977 Frederick W Pfeiffer c 2. D Dio Quincy Peoria IL 1993-1996. Auth, "The View From My Car," Vantage, 2001. Chapl/ St Lukes Chapt Of Dok 1997; Cnvnt Trsfg 1988; Mem/Chapl Dok 1997.

PFISTER, Kathleen Rock (Tex) PO Box 5176, Austin TX 78763 **Cur The Ch of the Gd Shpd Austin TX 2010-** B New Orleans LA 1969 d William & Eileen. BA Amer U 1990; MDiv Epis TS of the SW 2010. D 6/19/2010 P 1/28/2011 Bp Michael B Curry. m 8/8/1997 Phillip Julian Pfister c 2. Dio No Carolina Raleigh NC 2000-2007.

PFOTENHAUER, Leon Henry (Ia) 1613 S Nicollet St, Sioux City IA 51106 B Pierre SD 1929 s William & Frances. BS So Dakota St U 1956. D 4/25/1995 Bp Chris Christopher Epting. m 5/29/1955 Lorraine Joyce Pfotenhauer c 2. D S Paul's Indn Mssn Sioux City IA 2001-2015; D Calv Epis Ch Sioux City IA 1995-2001.

PHALEN, John Richard (Los) 5772 Garden Grove Blvd Spc 487, Westminster CA 92683 B Eden NY 1936 s James & Marguerite. BA Un Coll 1958; MDiv

Ya Berk 1962; GTS 1967; Cert U CA 1977; STD SFTS 1987. D 6/22/1962 P 3/31/1963 Bp Lauriston L Scaife. m 9/23/2000 Susan Phalen c 2. Int R St Johns Pro-Cathd Los Angeles CA 2001-2009; Int Ch Of The H Comm Gardena CA 2000-2002; Chapl USAF 1964-1967; Cur Trin Epis Ch Buffalo NY 1962-1964. Auth, "Screenplay, Petals of the Midnight Rose," 2011; Auth, "Screenplay Snow Without Name," 2009; Auth, "Pathways Through theNight," *Pathways Through the Night*, Publish Amer, 2009; Auth, "Beneath the Eyes of God, The Ord," Gateways Pub, 2004; Auth, "Plays, Wastelands, Second Sunday, Midnight Video, Choir Without Song, Orphans," *Beneath the Eyes of God*, Gateways Pub, 2001; Auth, "Poems, Diary of Fallen Warriors, Snake Eyes In The Garden, Ang City Light," *Beyond the Poetry of God*, Gateways Pub, 1995.

PHAM, J Peter (Chi) St. Paul's Episcopal Church, 2430 K St, N.W., Washington DC 20037 **Hon Asstg P S Paul's Par Washington DC 2011-** B Paris France 1970 s Joseph & Catherine. AB U Chi 1990; STB Pontifical Gregorian U 1994; STL Pontifical Gregorian U 1996; STD Pontifical Gregorian U 1999; JCL Pontifical Gregorian U 2001. Rec 5/9/2008 as Priest Bp Keith Lynn Ackerman. m 6/30/2007 Soo Chu Yee. Hon Asstg P Ch Of The Resurr New York NY 2008-2011. P Assoc of the H Hse (Walsingham) 2008; Soc of King Chas the Mtyr 2012.

PHANORD, Jean Berthold (Hai) **Dio Haiti Port-au-Prince HT 2003-** B 1966 D.

PHELAN, Shane (Nwk) 43 Massachusetts Ave., Haworth NJ 07641 **Comp of Mary the Apos W Pk NY 2015-; Sis Comp of Mary the Apos 2013-; Com on the Status of Wmn Exec Coun Appointees New York NY 2012-** B Lakewood OH 1956 d William & Dorothy. BA California St U 1980; PhD U of Massachusetts 1987; MDiv Drew U 2009. D 6/6/2009 P 12/12/2009 Bp Mark M Beckwith. Pstr Our Sav Luth Ch 2010-2012; S Lk's Epis Ch Haworth NJ 2010-2012; Sis Cmnty Of St Jn Bapt 2000-2011; GC Dep Dio Newark Newark NJ 2011-2012; Stndg Com 2011-2012, Patterns of Sprtl Pract Grp 2010-2012. Ed, "We Are Everywhere," Routledge, 2007; Ed, "Playing w Fire," Routledge, 2007; Auth, "Sexual Strangers: Gays, Lesbians, and the Dilemmas of Citizenship," Tem Press, 2000; Auth, "Getting Specific: Postmodern Lesbian Politics," U Minnesota Press, 1994; Auth, "Identity Politics: Lesbian Feminism and the Limits of Cmnty," Tem Press, 1989. Medal of hon DAR 2006; Reg Schlr Rockefeller Fndt 1990; U Fell U of Massachusetts, Amherst 1981.

PHELPS, Cecil Richard (NI) 4525 Baring Ave, Box 2293, East Chicago IN 46312 B Gary IN 1938 s Cecil & Elizabeth. BA W&M 1960; STB GTS 1963. D 4/20/1963 P 10/28/1963 Bp James Reginald Mallett. Ch Of The Gd Shpd E Chicago IN 1980-2003; P S Augustines Ch Gary IN 1975-1978; Vic H Fam Ch Angola IN 1970-1974; Assoc S Greg Abbey Three Rivers MI 1967-1970; Asst The Ch of S Matt And S Tim New York NY 1964-1967; Cur S Paul's Epis Ch Munster IN 1963-1964. SSC 1973. akuttabovetherest@yahoo.com

PHELPS, Joan (Ct) 15 Freedom Way Unit 101, Niantic CT 06367 B Farmington CT 1941 d Herbert & Marie. BS U of Connecticut 1963; MA U of Connecticut 1966; MA U of Connecticut 1966; MDiv GTS 1990. D 6/9/1990 P 4/19/1991 Bp Arthur Edward Walmsley. Assoc Trin Epis Ch Hartford CT 2006-2007; Assoc S Jas's Ch W Hartford CT 2000-2006; R S Barn And All SS Ch Springfield MA 1994-1999; Asst S Paul's Epis Ch Willimantic CT 1990-1994; Asst S Jn's Epis Ch Niantic CT 1990. Ord Of S Helena.

PHELPS, John Edward (Me) 4 Glendale Rd, Kennebunk ME 04043 B Boston MA 1937 s Houston & Barbara. BA Bos 1961; MDiv VTS 1965. D 6/1/1965 Bp John Melville Burgess P 5/1/1966 Bp Anson Phelps Stokes Jr. m 6/10/1961 Janet S Phelps c 4. Int St. Steph's the Mtyr Waterboro ME 2007-2008; Dio Maine Portland ME 2000-2002, Dioc Search Com 1997-1999; Vic/R Chr Epis Ch Eastport ME 1990-2002; R S Andr's Ch Methuen MA 1977-1989; Supplement Accounts Boston MA 1971-1976; Chapl (1st Lt) US-A Resevre 1971-1973; R St Johns Ch Taunton MA 1967-1977; Cur Ch Of The H Nativ S Weymouth MA 1965-1967. Nash Fllshp Dio Massachusetts 1986.

PHELPS JR, Kenneth Oliver (Md) PO Box 40, Sunderland MD 20689 **R All SS Epis Par Sunderland MD 2004-** B Baltimore MD 1951 s Kenneth & Anne. BA Buc 1973; MDiv Luth TS at Gettysburg 1978; U of Baltimore 1985; VTS 1997. D 11/30/1999 Bp John L Rabb P 6/2/2000 Bp Robert Wilkes Ihloff. m 2/13/1988 Dianne Lynne Phelps c 3. Assoc S Thos Epis Ch Towson MD 1999-2004; Pstr Serv Luth Ch in Amer MD 1978-1985. allsaints1692@allsaints1692.org

PHELPS, Mary M (Minn) 1415 6th Ave. South, Anoka MN 55303 **R Trin Ch Anoka MN 2014-, 2013-2014** B Minneapolis MN 1951 d Douglas & Dorothy. BA S Cathr U 1990; Cert SWTS 2004; MDiv Untd TS of the Twin Cities 2005. D 6/15/2005 P 12/15/2005 Bp James Louis Jelinek. c 2. Int P S Mary's Basswood Grove Hastings MN 2010-2012; Asstg P Ch Of The Nativ Burnsville MN 2009-2010; Asst to the R St Geo's Epis Ch Minneapolis MN 2005-2007.

PHELPS, Nicholas Barclay (Pa) 1906 Trenton Ave, Bristol PA 19007 **Asst P S Mk's Ch Philadelphia PA 1999-; Ret 1998-** B Grosse Pte MI 1933 s Charles & Constance. BA Wms 1956; MDiv EDS 1959. D 6/14/1959 Bp Oliver J Hart P 12/21/1959 Bp Robert McConnell Hatch. R S Jas Epis Ch Bristol PA 1981-1997; R Trin Ch Buckingham PA 1970-1980; Chapl UCLA 1964-1970; Asst Chapl UCLA 1962-1964; Vic S Andr's Ch No Adams MA 1961-1962; Asst S Jn's Ch Williamstown MA 1959-1962. ESMHE.

PHELPS, Sarah E (Los) 306 Bayoak Dr, Cary NC 27513 B Potsdam NY 1970 d Michael & Barbara. BA SUNY at Geneseo 1993; MDiv PSR 1998. D 6/3/2006 P 1/6/2007 Bp Joseph Jon Bruno. m 5/17/2003 Michael B Phelps c 1. Assoc S Paul's Epis Ch Cary NC 2016; R S Fran' Par Palos Verdes Estates CA 2006-2015.

PHELPS, Shannon David (SanD) Po Box 234, Del Mar CA 92014 **Assoc P S Mich Sea Cardiff CA 1996-** B Pana IL 1948 s Marion & Esther. BA Stan 1980; MA Harvard DS 1990; MDiv Ya Berk 1993. D 6/5/1993 P 3/1/1994 Bp Gethin Benwil Hughes. m 9/24/1977 Kit Claire Phelps. H Cross Epis Ch Carlsbad CA 1999-2001; S Ptr's Epis Ch Del Mar CA 1993-1997.

PHELPS, Walter E (Cal) 120 Lorraine Ct, Vacaville CA 95688 **P S Brigid's Epis Ch Rio Vista CA 2006-; Ret 1989-** B Brooklyn NY 1922 s Walter & Anna. BA CUNY 1949; MA U CA 1955; BD CDSP 1959; MS U CA 1966. D 6/21/1959 P 1/9/1960 Bp James Albert Pike. m 11/20/1996 Lucretia Ann Jevne. Int Ascen Munich Germany 1992-1993; Int S Aug-Cbury Wiesbaden Germany 1991-1992; Asst P S Aid's Mssn Bolinas CA 1987-1991; S Paul's Epis Ch San Rafael CA 1982-1983, Asst 1965-1968; St Johns Epis Ch Ross CA 1965-1968; Chapl San Jose St Coll 1961-1965; Assoc S Mk's Epis Ch Santa Clara CA 1960-1961. Auth, *An Intro to Eliots Murder in the Cathd*; Auth, *Hello Thorton!; Thoughts on The Matchmaker*.

PHENNA, Timothy Peter (Colo) 1320 Arapahoe St, Golden CO 80401 **Assoc Calv Ch Golden CO 2013-** B London UK 1969 s Peter & Barbara. BTh Ridley Hall 2001; BTh Ridley Hall, Cambridge 2001. Trans 4/25/2013 as Priest Bp Robert John O'Neill. m 7/27/1991 Alisa Ann Minick c 3. tim.phenna@calvarygolden.net

PHILIP, Kristi (Spok) 22 W 37th Ave, Spokane WA 99203 B Bremerton WA 1946 d Howard & Virginia. BA U of Washington 1967; Cert CDSP 1985; MA Gonzaga U 1989. D 2/27/1977 Bp John Raymond Wyatt P 7/13/1985 Bp Leigh Allen Wallace Jr. c 2. Dio Spokane Spokane WA 2006-2011, Cn Mnstry Dvlpmt 1997-2005, Dioc Coun 1985-1989, COM 1980-1984; Cathd Of S Jn The Evang Spokane WA 2006-2007, 1985-1997; Stndg Cmsn on Sm Congregations The Epis Ch 2003-2009; D S Paul's Epis Mssn Kennewick WA 1977-1985. Auth, "A Pryr for Transition," *Wmn Uncommon Prayers*, Morehouse, 2000; Auth, "w God as our Comp," *Congregations*, Alb Inst, 1997. DD CDSP 2004; Fell Coolidge Colloquim 1993. kristip@spokanediocese.org

PHILIPS, J Kevin (ECR) 1190 Alta Mesa Road, Monterey CA 93940 **Epis Sr Communities Lafayette CA 1991-** B Kingsville TX 1955 s Ronald & Marian. BA U So 1977; MDiv Nash 1982; MA Santa Clara U 1999. D 6/5/1982 Bp Paul Moore Jr P 12/1/1982 Bp Charles Alfred Voegeli. m 5/24/2014 James Lauderdale. Chapl Heartland Hospice 2003-2009; Chapl Hospice of the Cntrl Coast 1994-2001; Pres Jn XXIII AIDS Mnstry 1990-1994; Educ Dir Monterey Cnty AIDS Proj 1990-1993; Pres/Co-Fndr The Ossining Food Pantry 1987-1989; R Trin Epis Ch Ossining NY 1985-1989; Cur S Geo's Epis Ch Schenectady NY 1982-1985; Chair Of HIV/AIDS Taskforce Dio El Camino Real Salinas CA 1991-1996; Mem of Ecum Com Dio Albany Greenwich NY 1982-1984. Ord S Mary 1985; Sons of the Amer Revolution 2004.

PHILIPS, Ronald K (Wyo) PO Box 950, Thermopolis WY 82443 B Sacramento CA 1948 s Robert & Ruth. BA U of Wyoming 1970; BS U of Wyoming 1975; MA U of Wyoming 1976. D 8/31/2013 P 3/29/2014 Bp John Smylie. m 4/21/1981 Audrey A B Philips c 2. Dio Wyoming Casper 2016.

PHILLIPS III, Arthur William (WLa) Diocese Of Western Louisiana, PO Box 20131, Alexandria VA 22320 B KS 1953 D 6/22/2002 Bp Claude Edward Payne P 1/29/2003 Bp Don Adger Wimberly. m 4/14/1973 Lynn A Phillips c 2. Vic Dio Wstrn Louisiana Alexandria LA 2013-2016; S Paul's Epis Ch Orange TX 2005-2010; All SS Epis Ch Crockett TX 2002-2004.

PHILLIPS, Benjamin T. S. (SO) **R S Geo's Epis Ch Dayton OH 2010-** B 1977 BS U of Arizona 2000; MDiv TESM 2006. D 6/3/2006 Bp Jim Mathes P 12/6/2006 Bp Don Adger Wimberly. m 1/14/2006 Amy A Phillips c 3. Asst S Jn The Div Houston TX 2006-2010. rector@stgeorgeohio.org

PHILLIPS, Beth (Cal) 815 Portola Rd, Portola Valley CA 94028 **Chr Ch Portola Vlly CA 2015-** B Missouri 1967 d John & Paula. Bachelor of Journalism U of Missouri 1989; Juris Doctorate U of Missouri 1992; Cert of Angl Stds Ya Berk 2013; MDiv Yale DS 2013. D 1/26/2013 Bp Robert John O'Neill P 7/26/2013 Bp Andrew Marion Lenow Dietsche. Asst P Chr Ch Warwick NY 2013-2015. motherbeth@ccpvw.org

PHILLIPS, Catharine Seybold (Chi) 458 Dee Ln, Roselle IL 60172 B Minneapolis MN 1955 d William & Marjorie. BA Earlham Coll 1977; MDiv SWTS 1983. D 6/23/1983 P 5/1/1984 Bp Edward Witker Jones. m 6/24/1995 Jeffrey Stephen Hill. Ch Of S Ben Bolingbrook IL 2003-2007; P-in-c Ch Of Our Sav Elmhurst IL 2000-2002; S Chas Ch St. Chas IL 1998-2000; S Dav's Epis Ch Aurora IL 1997-1998, Int R 1995-1997; S Mk's Epis Ch Glen Ellyn IL 1997; Ch Of The Incarn Bloomingdale IL 1995-1997; R S Lk's And S Marg's Ch Allston MA 1993-1995; Int Trin Epis Ch Marshall MI 1992-1993; Assoc R All SS Ch E Lansing MI 1987-1991; Epis Coun U Chi Chicago IL 1984-1987; Chapl U Of Il In Chicago 1984-1987; D Bp Brent Hse Chicago IL 1983-1984; Res Chapl NW Memi Hosp 1983-1984. ESMHE.

PHILLIPS, Craig Arnold (Va) 4818 Old Dominion Dr, Arlington VA 22207 **R S Ptr's Epis Ch Arlington VA 2002-** B Tulsa OK 1954 s Milton & Shirley. BA Br 1976; MDiv Harvard DS 1979; PhD Duke 1993. D 11/1/1980 Bp William Jackson Cox P 5/1/1981 Bp Gerald Nicholas Mcallister. m 6/11/1977 Marguerite Eustis Spruance Pool c 2. Adj Instr VTS Alexandria VA 2010, 2004; Affiliate Asst Prof Geo 2008; Dn - Conestoga Dnry Dio Pennsylvania Philadelphia PA 1999-2002, Dn, Conestoga Dnry 1999-2002, Ecum Cmsn 1998-2002; Instr Rosemont Coll Rosemont PA 1998-2002; R Incarn H Sacr Epis Ch Drexel Hill PA 1997-2002; P in Charge S Geo S Barn Ch Philadelphia PA 1996; Asst Prof Tem 1994-1997; Instr Duke 1994; Int R S Barth's Ch Pittsboro NC 1994; Vstng Lectr U NC Chap Hill NC 1993; Int R Ch Of The Gd Shpd Raleigh NC 1992-1993; Int Vic Dio No Carolina Raleigh NC 1992-1993, Ecum Cmsn 1988-1994; Int R Ch Of The Nativ Raleigh NC 1992; Int R S Tit Epis Ch Durham NC 1990-1991; Instr Duke 1989; Supply and Int P Dio No Carolina 1984-1990; Assoc R S Ptr's Epis Ch S Louis MO 1984-1986; COM Dio Oklahoma Oklahoma City OK 1981-1984; Vic S Lawr's Epis Ch Muskogee OK 1980-1984; Vic Trin Ch Eufaula OK 1980-1984; Chapl-Intern Presb Hosp Oklahoma City OK 1979-1980; Race Relatns Com Dio Virginia Richmond VA 2007-2010, Chair, Dioc BEC 2006-, COM 2006-. Auth, "Hegel, Kierkegaard," *The Blackwell Comp to the Theologians*, Wiley Blackwell, 2009; Auth, "Postmodernism, Literary Criticism, Lang, Interp, Hermeneutics, and Fundamental Theol," *Encyclopedia of Chrsnty*, Eerdmans/ Brill, 2005; Auth, "From Aesthetics to Redemptive Politics: A Political Reading of the Theol Aesthetics of Hans Urs von Balthasar and the M," UMI, 1993. AAR, 1986; Amer Soc Of Ch Hist 1976-1990; SBL 1986.

PHILLIPS, Deborah Anne (Mass) 35 Settlers Way, Salem MA 01970 **Dnry Co-Cnvnr Dio Massachusetts Boston MA 2011-, Dioc Coun 1998-2002, Chapl Dioc Young Singers Camp 1993-2002, Liturg & Mus Cmsn 1992-1995, 2005-; R Gr Ch Salem MA 1997-** B Albany NY 1954 d William & Helen. BA Bos 1976; MDiv EDS 1990. D 6/1/1991 Bp David Elliot Johnson P 5/23/1992 Bp David Bell Birney IV. m 7/16/1983 Alan Paulsen. Vic S Eliz's Ch Wilmington MA 1995-1997; Int S Gabr's Epis Ch Marion MA 1994; Asst S Mary's Ch Newton Lower Falls MA 1991-1993. Excellence in Preaching Awd Epis Evang Fndt 1989. gcis1@verizon.net

PHILLIPS, Douglas Cecil (Ind) 40 Trapelo St, Brighton MA 02135 B Columbus IN 1947 BA Indiana U 1969; MA Indiana U 1971; MDiv Indiana U 1978. D 12/21/1974 P 8/2/1975 Bp John P Craine. m 8/30/1979 Jean Marie Stoner.

PHILLIPS, Jennifer Mary (Mass) 2903 Cabezon Blvd SE, Rio Rancho NM 87124 **S Jn's Epis Ch Westwood MA 2015-** B Dartford Kent UK 1952 d Victor & Mavis. BA Wellesley Coll 1973; MDiv Andover Newton TS 1981; DMin Andover Newton TS 1984. D 6/2/1984 Bp John Bowen Coburn P 7/21/1985 Bp Edward Randolph Welles II. R S Fran Ch Rio Rancho NM 2011-2015; Vice-Chair Stndg Cmsn on Liturg & Mus 2006-2012; R S Aug's Ch Kingston RI 2000-2011; R Trin Ch S Louis MO 1995-2000; Ch Of S Jn The Evang Boston MA 1988-1995, R 1987; Chapl Brigham & Womens Hosp Dana Farber Cancer Inst Boston MA 1983-1988; Vice Chair Stndg Cmsn on Liturg & Mus 2006-2012; Co-Chair Dio MA COM 1992-1995; Dep Dep to GC 4X MA & RI 1989-2012. Auth, *Simple Prayers for Complicated Lives*, Ch Pub, Inc., 2007; Auth, *Preaching Creation*, Cowley Pub., 2000; Auth, *Prayers for Penitents*, Ch Pub, Inc.; Auth, "Pryr of the Eucharistic Cmnty & Abuse Survivor," *Sewanee Theol Revs*. Assoc Soc of S Jn the Evang 1982; Assn of Parishes for Liturg & Mus; Assn of Theol Schools Com on Accreditation 2012; Coll of Chapl; Naitonal Assn of Campus Ministers. MA - High hon Ottawa U 2003; Severinghaus Cmnty ServiceAward Wellesley Coll 1988. revjphillips@earthlink.net

PHILLIPS, Jerry Ray (La) PO Box 199, Rosedale LA 70772 B Saint Louis MO 1941 s Edgar & Zelda. AA Florida Chr Coll Tampa 1962; BA LSU 1968; Concordia TS 1972; MA Washington U 1978; EdS LSU 1997; TESM 1999; Cert Dioc Sch for Mnstry 2002; Cert McFarland Inst 2003. D 12/21/2005 P 11/19/2006 Bp Charles Edward Jenkins III. c 3. P-in-c Ch Of The Nativ Rosedale LA 2009-2013; Chr Ch Gonzales Gonzales LA 2006-2008; Int P-in-c Chr Ch Gonzales LA 2006-2008.

PHILLIPS, John Bradford (Cal) 891 Skeel Drive, Camarillo CA 93010 B Brooklyn NY 1940 s Charles & Sara. BS USNA 1962; BD EDS 1971. D 6/26/1971 Bp George Richard Millard P 4/7/1972 Bp Chauncie Kilmer Myers. m 3/26/1967 Muriel Phillips c 3. Int All SS Epis Ch Oxnard CA 2008-2009; 1979-2008; R Ch Of The H Trin Richmond CA 1974-1979; Delta Pstr Cmnty Mnstry E Contra Cnty 1972-1974.

PHILLIPS II, John Walter (CGC) 590 Parker Dr, Pensacola FL 32504 **Asst Chr Epis Ch Pensacola FL 1998-, Asst 1976-1995, 1998-; Ret Epis Ch 1998-** B Mobile AL 1931 s Sidney & Kate. BS OH SU 1952; MDiv Epis TS of the SW 1960. D 6/26/1960 Bp George Mosley Murray P 6/17/1961 Bp Charles C J Carpenter. m 5/21/1955 Ann V Vasser c 3. P-in-c S Paul's Chap Magnolia Sprgs AL 1999-2002; Vic S Anna's Ch Atmore AL 1995-1998; R Trin Epsicopal Ch Atmore AL 1995-1998; P-in-c Gd Shpd Ch Montgomery AL 1970-1976; Asst Ch Of The Ascen Clearwater FL 1967-1969; Vic Trin Ch Wetumpka AL 1961-1967; Vic All SS Ch Montgomery AL 1960-1967.

PHILLIPS, Julia Coleman (CGC) 127 Hamilton Ave, Panama City FL 32401 **P-in-c S Pat's Epis Ch Panama City FL 2001-, P-in-c 2001-, Vic 1990-2000** B Liberty MO 1928 d Mathias & Florence. JD U of Missouri 1952; BA Wm Jewell Coll 1952; DIT ETSBH 1980. D 7/25/1989 P 2/24/1990 Bp Charles Farmer Duvall. m 7/14/1965 Richard Phillips c 1. D-in-trng H Nativ Epis Ch Panama City FL 1989-1990. CPC 2002; HSEC 1980.

PHILLIPS, Kevin Alan (Va) 2094 Grant Rd, Mountain View CA 94040 B Tampa FL 1960 s Wayne & Margaret. BA Asbury U 1983; MDiv VTS 1990. D 6/17/1990 P 1/5/1991 Bp Don Adger Wimberly. m 12/7/1987 Holly K Phillips c 2. S Dav's Ch Ashburn VA 2006-2008; S Tim's Epis Ch Mtn View CA 1993-2006, R 1993-1997; Asst Chr Ch Cathd Lexington KY 1990-1993; Pres Of Dioc Coun.

PHILLIPS, Linda (Nwk) 50 State Route 24, Chester NJ 07930 **Ch Of The Mssh Chester NJ 2010-** B New York City NY 1949 d Edward & Margaret. AS Sussex Cnty Cmnty 2006. D 12/9/2006 Bp Carol J Gallagher. c 1. Chr Ch Budd Lake NJ 2010-2012.

PHILLIPS, Marie (O) 50 Sunnycliff Dr, Euclid OH 44123 **Chapl Crossroads Hospice 2014-** B Dearborn MI 1960 d George & Dorothy. BA MI SU 1982; MA Marygrove Coll 1987; MDiv EDS 1990. D 6/21/1991 Bp Henry Irving Mayson P 11/1/1994 Bp Ronald Hayward Haines. m 8/19/2013 Kristi Ann Ballinger. Int S Andr Epis Ch Mentor OH 2014-2017; Cn for Mssn Dio Ohio Cleveland 2011-2012; R Ch Of The Epiph Euclid OH 2002-2011; Assoc Epis W Side Shared Mnstry Cleveland OH 1998-2000; Chapl Hospice of Wstrn Reserve Cleveland OH 1997-2002; Chapl Hospice of S Mary's St. Mary's MD 1995-1997; Cur All Faith Epis Ch Charlotte Hall MD 1994-1996.

PHILLIPS, Michael Albin (NY) 316 E 88th St, New York NY 10128 **Vic Trin Ch Saugerties NY 2013-** B Lexington KY 1951 s Donald & Bernice. BA U of Dallas 1973; MDiv CDSP 1978. D 10/6/1979 Bp Chauncie Kilmer Myers P 9/26/1980 Bp Robert Hume Cochrane. m 7/29/1978 Sarah Easton c 2. R Ch Of The H Trin New York NY 2005-2012; Chr Ch Poughkeepsie NY 1995-2005, R 1995-2005, Assoc For Cmnty Mnstry 1982-1986; R S Phil's Epis Palatine IL 1986-1995; Cur Trin Epis Ch Everett WA 1979-1982. trinitychurch.saugerties@gmail.com

PHILLIPS, Paul Henry 1416 S Grand Blvd Apt 3, Spokane WA 99203 **R Gibson Memi Crewe VA 1977-** B Spokane WA 1941 s Paul & Elizabeth. BA U CA 1964; MA U CA 1966; PhD U CA 1975; MDiv Sewanee: The U So, TS 1997. D 6/14/1997 Bp Frank Jeffrey Terry P 12/13/1997 Bp David Conner Bane Jr. c 3. Epis Ch Of S Paul And S Andr Kenbridge VA 1997-2008; R The Epis Cluster Of Southside Lunenburg VA 1997-2008. phpccity@verizon.net

PHILLIPS JR, Raymond Leland (USC) 701 Unity St, Fort Mill SC 29715 B Towson MD 1935 s Raymond & Minnie. BS Wofford Coll 1956; MDiv Sewanee: The U So, TS 1962; Cert Appalachian Reg Hosps Inc Ape 1972. D 11/1/1962 Bp Clarence Alfred Cole P 11/1/1963 Bp John Adams Pinckney. m 6/5/1964 Nikki Ann Phillips. S Paul's Epis Ch Ft Mill SC 1974-1996; R S Andr's Epis Ch Canton NC 1972-1974; Sr Chapl-In-Res Middlesboro Appalachian Reg Hosp 1971-1972; R S Mich's Epis Ch Easley SC 1965-1971; Asst R S Thad Epis Ch Aiken SC 1962-1965.

PHILLIPS, Richard Oliver (NY) 10 Badger St, Littleton NH 03561 **Chapl Weeks Med Cntr Lancaster NH 2004-; 1973-** B Yonkers NY 1935 s John & Louise. BA Ken 1957; STB Ya Berk 1960. D 6/11/1960 P 12/17/1960 Bp Horace W B Donegan. m 6/22/1957 Judith C Phillips c 2. R S Andr's Ch Brewster NY 1969-1973; R Par of Chr the Redeem Pelham NY 1962-1969; Cur All SS Ch Bayside NY 1960-1962.

PHILLIPS, Robert Taylor (WA) 1525 Newton St NW, Washington DC 20010 **Ch Of Our Sav Washington DC 2016-** B Memphis TN 1959 s Utillus & Elene. BA U of Notre Dame 1981; MDiv Vanderbilt DS 2003; DMin Louisville Presb 2013; DMin Louisville Presb 2013; DMin Louisville Presb TS 2013. D 6/13/2015 P 1/9/2016 Bp Mariann Edgar Budde.

PHILLIPS, Robert W (CFla) 1620 Mayflower Ct Apt A-610, Winter Park FL 32792 **Ret 1984-** B Duluth MN 1920 s Chester & Doris. BA Rol 1966; MS Rol 1971; Cert Theol Stud Oxf GB 1978. D 6/15/1975 P 2/24/1979 Bp William Hopkins Folwell. m 8/28/2007 Sallie M Phillips c 1. Asst Ch Of The Gd Shpd Maitland FL 1991-2000; R All SS Epis Ch Deltona FL 1979-1984; D Dio Cntrl Florida Orlando FL 1975-1979. SSC 1983.

PHILLIPS, Roger V (Minn) 1801 Santa Maria Pl, Orlando FL 32806 **P, Total Mnstry Ch Of The Gd Samar Sauk Cntr MN 2004-, P in Res 2015-** B Philipsburg PA 1937 s Roger & Maud. U of Florida 1959; BA U of Florida 1959; Cert Sewanee: The U So, TS 2005. D 11/11/2003 Bp James Louis Jelinek P 10/24/2004 Bp Daniel Lee Swenson. m 11/13/1970 Rosemary Phillips c 4. P,Total Mnstry S Steph's Epis Ch Paynesville MN 2004-2013; Ch Of Our Sav Little Falls MN 2004-2009; Asst P S Chris's Ch Orlando FL 2004-2005; Asst St. Chris's Epis Ch 2004-2005.

PHILLIPS, Stuart John Tristram (Tenn) 654 Long Hollow Pike, Goodlettsville TN 37072 B Montreal QC CA 1933 s Arthur & Beryl. MDiv Sewanee: The U So, TS 1987; DMin Other 2010; DMin Other 2010; DMin Sewanee: The U So, TS 2010. D 7/25/1979 Bp William Evan Sanders P 6/1/1980 Bp William F Gates Jr. m 6/3/1955 Aldona Phillips. S Jas The Less Madison TN 1993-2005;

P

Gr Epis Ch Sprg Hill TN 1987-1991; Non-par 1984-1986; Assoc Ch Of The Adv Nashville TN 1981-1984; Asst S Barth's Ch Nashville TN 1979-1981.

PHILLIPS, Susan Elizabeth (Del) 18 Olive Ave, Rehoboth Beach DE 19971 B Philadephia PA 1944 d Henry & Elizabeth. BSN U of Pennsylvania 1968; MSN U of Virginia 1975. D 12/5/2009 Bp Wayne Wright. c 2.

PHILLIPS, Thomas Larison (Spr) 1015 Frank Dr, Champaign IL 61821 B Lincoln IL 1939 s Thomas & Elizabeth. BS Illinois St U 1963; MDiv Nash 1966; MS Sthrn Illinois U 1968. D 6/11/1966 P 12/19/1966 Bp Albert A Chambers. m 8/11/1962 Patricia A Phillips c 3. S Paulinus Ch Watseka IL 1994-2001; Vic Ch Of S Chris Rantoul IL 1986-2001; Assoc R Emm Memi Epis Ch Champaign IL 1978-1986; Chapl SIU Dio Springfield Springfield IL 1973-1977; Assoc S Andr's Ch Carbondale IL 1968-1973; Vic S Annes Epis Ch Caseyville IL 1966-1968. Auth, "Outdoor Living & Lrng Complement Each Other"; Auth, "Emotionally Distrurbed Chld Try Camping". ESMHE. Outstanding Ldrshp In Cmnty Mntl Hlth Awd 1977.

PHILLIPS, Wendell Roncevalle (NC) 4211 Sharon View Rd, Charlotte NC 28226 B New Rochelle NY 1939 s Wendell & Marguerite. BA Denison U 1963; MDiv GTS 1966. D 6/4/1966 P 12/17/1966 Bp Horace W B Donegan. m 8/12/1972 Linda I Phillips c 2. P Asst S Marg's Epis Ch Waxhaw NC 2010-2012; P-in-c S Mich And All Ang Epis Ch Charlotte NC 2002-2010; S Matt Ch Salisbury NC 2000-2001; Vic S Paul's Ch Salisbury NC 1993-2001; P/Org All SS Epis Ch Charlotte NC 1990-1993; Vic All SS Epis Ch Columbia Falls MT 1985-1989; P / Org S Fran Of Assisi Epis Wilsonville OR 1983-1985; Asst All SS Ch Hillsboro OR 1976-1982; R S Andr's Ch Brewster NY 1974-1975; S Geo's Ch Astoria NY 1969-1974; Cur S Jn's Epis Ch Lancaster PA 1967-1968; Mus Cmsn Dio Long Island Garden City NY 1969-1974. AGO 1975-, Bd Shltr Inc Hillsboro OR; Bd Arc of Mecklenburg Co 2003; Mus Cmsn Dio Ore 1983-1985.

PHILLIPS-GAINES, Lynn (Miss) 105 N Montgomery St, Starkville MS 39759 D Ch Of The Resurr Starkville MS 2011- B Jacksonville FL 1956 d CE & Teresa. BA Mississippi St U 1978; MS Sthrn Illinois U 1980. D 1/15/2011 Bp Duncan Montgomery Gray III. m 4/15/2005 James Russell Gaines c 1.

PHILLIPS-MATSON, Wesley A (SJ) B Los Angeles CA 1926 s Archie & Martha. MDiv CDSP 1965. D 6/24/1968 Bp Sumner Walters P 7/11/1973 Bp CE Crowther. c 1. P S Clare of Assisi Epis Ch Avery CA 1999-2001; Assoc S Jas Epis Ch Sonora CA 1991-1998; Ch of Our Sav Campbell CA 1985-1988; S Mk's Ch King City CA 1980-1983, P 1969-1972.

PHILPUTT JR, Frederick Chapman (Dal) 5811 Penrose Ave, Dallas TX 75206 B White Plains NY 1945 s Frederick & Ragnhild. BA TCU 1971; MDiv Nash 1987. D 7/25/1987 P 1/25/1988 Bp Clarence Cullam Pope Jr. m 12/29/1973 Nancy McCoy. Ch Of The Incarn Dallas TX 1992-2010; R Calv Ch Americus GA 1989-1992; Cur All SS' Epis Ch Ft Worth TX 1987-1989.

PHINNEY, James Mark (Oly) 4246 South Discovery Road, Port Townsend WA 98368 Ret 1998- B Glasgow MT 1937 s Harold & Anna. BA WA SU 1959; MDiv CDSP 1967. D 8/10/1967 P 3/30/1968 Bp Ivol I Curtis. c 2. Assoc Gr Ch Bainbridge Island WA 1999-2008; R S Paul's Epis Ch Port Townsend WA 1990-1997; Vic Dio Oregon Portland OR 1978-1990; Vic Chr Ch S Helens OR 1978-1988; R S Paul's Epis Ch Elko NV 1970-1977; S Mary's Ch Lakewood WA 1967-1970.

PHIPPS, Joy Ogburn (Ala) 3919 Westminster Ln, Birmingham AL 35243 S Steph's Epis Ch Birmingham AL 2006- B Birmingham AL 1932 d Frank & Lottie. BA Monmouth U 1974; MS Rutgers The St U of New Jersey 1980; MDiv VTS 1988. D 6/4/1988 Bp Furman Charles Stough P 12/14/1988 Bp Robert Oran Miller. c 2. Assoc S Lk's Epis Ch Birmingham AL 1990-2001; Asst Ch Of The Nativ Epis Huntsville AL 1988-1990; Stndg Com Dio Alabama Birmingham 1994-1997, COM 1988-1993.

PHIPPS, Marion Elizabeth (Chi) 5403 W Greenbrier Dr, McHenry IL 60050 R S Hugh Of Lincoln Epis Ch Elgin IL 2010- B Oak Park IL 1958 d Paul & Marion. BA Illinois St U 1980; Cert Elgin Cmnty Coll 1992; MDiv SWTS 2009. D 6/6/2009 P 12/5/2009 Bp Jeff Lee. m 1/23/1988 Michael J Phipps c 1.

PHIPPS JR, Robert Stirling (Va) Po Box 33430, San Antonio TX 78265 Chapl S Mary Hall 1994- B Baltimore MD 1935 s Robert & Rose. BA U Rich 1957; MDiv VTS 1960. D 6/1/1960 Bp Leland Stark P 1/1/1961 Bp John Elbridge Hines. m 6/2/1956 Barbee Barbee Phipps. Headmaster Chr Ch Sch Christchurch VA 1984-1994; Assoc Headmaster S Steph's Sch Austin TX 1980-1984; Chapl/Asst Headmaster S Steph's Sch Austin TX 1971-1984; Asst Chapl S Steph's Sch Austin TX 1970-1971; S Steph's Epis Sch Austin TX 1960-1984.

PIATKO, Joann M (NwPa) 26 Chautauqua Pl, Bradford PA 16701 Vic S Jos's Ch Port Allegan PA 2010- B Buffalo NY 1955 d Thomas & Margaret. AAS Trocaire Coll 1975; BA Pk U 1981; MDiv Bex Sem 2008. D 5/9/2009 P 6/6/2010 Bp Sean Walter Rowe. c 2.

PICCARD, Kathryn Ann (Mass) 68 Baldwin St Apt 2, Charlestown MA 02129 B Buffalo NY 1949 d J A & E M. BA Simpson Coll 1971; MDiv EDS 1975; ThM Harvard DS 1990. D 6/28/1975 P 3/16/1977 Bp Walter Cameron Righter. m 10/26/1997 Mary Jo Campbell. Supply P Dio Massachusetts Boston MA 1995-1998; Ch Of S Jn The Evang Boston MA 1987-1988; S Matt And The Redeem Epis Ch Boston MA 1986-1987; Dio Iowa Des Moines IA 1980; Asst Emm Ch Boston MA 1979-1982; D's Sch For Mnstry And Formation Chicago IL 1977-1980; EDS Cambridge MA 1977. Auth, "arts On Liturg". Mass Dioc Disabil Concerns Com.

PICKARD, Joe (Nwk) 91 Ann Rustin Dr, Ormond Beach FL 32176 B Hollywood CA 1945 s Judson & Jayne. BA U of Arizona 1973; MDiv VTS 1984. D 6/20/1984 P 5/1/1985 Bp Joseph Thomas Heistand. m 12/5/2011 Louis Fifer c 3. Int S Mart's Ch Maywood NJ 2009-2012; Vic Ch Of S Jn The Div Hasbrouck Hts NJ 1996-2012; Ch of S Mary The Vrgn Ridgefield Pk NJ 1996-1999; Int S Paul's Ch Montvale NJ 1994-1996; Int S Greg's Epis Ch Parsippany NJ 1993-1994; Vic Ch Of The Mssh Chester NJ 1986-1993; Asst S Dunst's Ch Mc Lean VA 1984-1986.

PICKEN, Robert Andrew (Roch) 191 Kensington Road, Garden City NY 11530 R S Paul's Ch Rochester NY 2014- B Bethpage NY 1980 s James & Barbara. BA CUA 2002; MDiv GTS 2006. D 4/25/2006 P 10/28/2006 Bp Orris George Walker Jr. Cn Cathd Of The Incarn Garden City NY 2010-2014, Cathd Chapt 2008-; P-in-c Ch Of The Ascen Greenpoint Brooklyn NY 2006-2010; VP, Bd Managers, Camp DeWolfe Dio Long Island Garden City NY 2007-2010, Dispatch of Bus, Dioc Conv 2006-. rpicken@stpaulsec.org

PICKENS, Gregory Doran (Dal) 8011 Douglas, Dallas TX 75225 Assoc S Mich And All Ang Ch Dallas TX 2011- B Oklahoma City OK 1961 BA Univ of Texas at Austin 1986; MDiv Nash 2005. D 5/14/2005 P 4/25/2006 Bp James Monte Stanton. m 1/6/2007 Noralyn D Pickens c 1. P-in-c S Mk's Ch Irving TX 2006-2011; Cur H Trin Epis Ch Garland TX 2005-2006.

PICKERAL, Gretchen Marta Benson (Minn) 404 Trout Lake Rd, Grand Rapids MN 55744 B Minneapolis MN 1952 d David & Betty. BA S Cloud St U 1977; MDiv SWTS 1992. D 6/6/1992 Bp William Augustus Jones Jr P 4/27/1994 Bp Hays H. Rockwell. m 5/12/1973 Larry Allen Pickeral c 2. S Paul's Ch Brainerd MN 2011-2016; Total Mnstry Mentor S Barth's Epis Ch Bemidji MN 2008-2013; Dio Minnesota Minneapolis MN 2006; R Chr Epis Ch Grand Rapids MN 2001-2006; Int S Mich & S Geo S Louis MO 1999-2001; P S Tim's Epis Ch S Louis MO 1998-1999; S Barn Ch Florissant MO 1997-1998, P 1997-1998, Assoc 1993-1995; Assoc Adv Crestwood MO 1996-1997; Mnstry Coordntr Dio Missouri S Louis MO 1993-1995. Auth, "Confession Of Possession," Wmn Uncommon Pryr, 2000; Auth, "Gender-Defined Sin," Wit, 1995. Minneca 2001; Moca 1992-2001; Natl Ntwk Of Epis Cler Assns 1994.

PICKERING, LouAnn (Ore) 7610 Sw 49th Ave, Portland OR 97219 Vic S Gabr Ch Portland OR 2004- B Oskaloosa IA 1954 d Morgan & Ruth. BA Pacific U 1976. D 10/18/1996 P 5/31/1997 Bp Robert Louis Ladehoff. m 9/9/1978 James M Pickering c 2. Asst Epis Par Of S Jn The Bapt Portland OR 2001-2004; Asstg P Gr Memi Portland OR 1998-2001; Chapl Epis Sch Of Portland 1996-2000.

PICKERING, William Todd (Va) 208 N 28th St, Richmond VA 23223 P-in-res S Marg's Sch Tappahannock VA 2012-; Ret Ret Richmond VA 2005- B Pittsburgh PA 1946 s Thomas & Lucile. BA Randolph-Macon Coll 1968; MDiv GTS 1971. D 6/19/1971 P 12/1/1971 Bp Robert Bracewell Appleyard. m 9/5/1970 Lee Ann Bunnell c 3. P-in-c S Jn's Epis Ch Richmond VA 2006-2013; P-in-c St. Jn's Epis Ch Tappahannock VA 2006-2013; R S Mk's Ch New Canaan CT 1997-2005; Seldon Calv Camp 1984-1991; R S Paul's Epis Ch Pittsburgh PA 1983-1997; Dioc Yth Cmsn Dio Pittsburgh 1981-1983; Com for Diac Dio Pittsburgh 1980-1985; R Chr Ch Greensburg PA 1976-1983; Cler Conf Commitee Dio Pittsburgh 1972-1975; Vic S Alb's Epis Ch Murrysville PA 1971-1976; Exec Com of Alum The GTS New York NY 1976-1982. Dio Pgh Cleric Assn 1971-1996. Who's Who in Rel 92. wmpickering@gmail.com

PICKERRELL, Nina (Cal) 1100 California St, San Francisco CA 94108 D/Vic Bayview Mssn San Francisco CA 2004-; D Gr Cathd San Francisco CA 1999- B Oakland CA 1951 d George & Evelyn. BA Sch for Deacons 1996. D 6/1/1996 Bp William Edwin Swing. m 10/28/1973 William Gene Hendirckson c 2. ESMA.

PICKUP JR, Edmund (SVa) Po Box 146, Franklin VA 23851 B Eden NC 1952 s Edmund & Edna. BA U NC 1974; JD U NC 1976; MDiv Nash 1988. D 5/27/1988 Bp Frank Harris Vest Jr P 5/31/1989 Bp Robert Whitridge Estill. R Emm Ch Franklin VA 1991-2017; Asst S Mary's Epis Ch High Point NC 1988-1991; Mem Stndg Com Dio Sthrn Virginia Newport News VA 2011-2014, Mem Exec Bd 2008-2011. Alb Inst 1987; RSCM in Amer 1995; Soc of S Marg 1992. Assoc RSCM 2011.

PICKUP JR, Ezra Alden (Vt) 37 S Main St, Alburgh VT 05440 B Hartford CT 1935 s Ezra & Lois. BA McGill U 1957; STB Ya Berk 1960. D 4/17/1960 Bp Vedder Van Dyck P 2/18/1961 Bp Harvey D Butterfield. P-in-c S Dav's Epis Ch Castleton NY 1984-1997; Consult Ch Of The H Cross Troy NY 1983-1990; Int Trin Ch Gloversville NY 1983-1984; Serv Angl Ch of Can 1982-1984; Dir & Chapl Brookhaven Hm For Boys Chelsea VT 1966-1983, D Asst 1960; Supply Chr Ch Bethel VT 1966-1982; Chr Ch Island Pond VT 1961-1966; Vic S Ptr's Mssn Lyndonville VT 1961-1966; Cur Chr Ch Montpelier VT 1960-1961; Weekend Position S Lk's Ch S Albans VT 1960-1961. Auth, Massbook/Missel (bilingual) (together w: Ainsi que / Other Devotions / Autres devotions, Montreal, 2002; Co-Ed, Le Missel Anglo-Catholique en Français, 2000; Auth/Ed, Cath, Evang &Chrsmtc Renwl. SBL 1957-2005.

PICOT, Katherine Frances (Tex) The Harnhill Centre, Harnhill, Cirencester TX GL75PX Great Britain (UK) **The Harnhill Cntr Cirencester 2014-** B Gloucester England 1973 d Lewis & Judith. BA Oxford Brookes; BA Ridley Hall 2009. Trans 10/24/2010 as Deacon Bp C Andrew Doyle. Cur S Mart's Epis Ch Houston TX 2010-2013. katep@harnhillcentre.org.uk

PICOU, Michael David (SeFla) St Stephen's Episc Ch, 2750 McFarlane Rd, Coconut Grove FL 33133 B Houma LA 1949 s Conrad & Jeanette. BA U of Miami 1972; MDiv Florida Cntr for Theol Stds 2010; STM U of So 2013; STM U of So 2013. D 3/30/2012 P 12/2/2012 Bp Leo Frade. S Steph's Epis Day Sch Miami FL 2012-2014.

PIERCE, Charles Christian (Chi) Grace Episcopal Church, 120 E 1st St, Hinsdale IL 60521 **Gr Epis Ch Hinsdale IL 2012-** B Memphis TN 1964 s Charles & Patti-Ann. BA Estrn Nazarene Coll 1987; MDiv Andover Newton TS 1992. D 11/18/1992 P 5/20/1993 Bp Edward Harding MacBurney. m 6/27/1987 Julie Ann Pierce c 4. R S Jas' Epis Ch Warrenton VA 2007-2012; Off Of Bsh For ArmdF New York NY 1999-2007; S Matt's Ch Lincoln NE 1996-1999; St Paul's Epis Ch Peoria IL 1993-1996; Ch Of S Jn The Evang Duxbury MA 1992-1993.

PIERCE, Dorothy Kohinke (CNY) PO Box 458, Chenango Bridge NY 13745 B Cooperstown NY 1947 d Theodore & Marion. BA St U Coll 1969; MS St U Coll 1981. D 11/14/2009 Bp Gladstone Bailey Adams III. m 9/28/1991 James Pierce c 3.

PIERCE, Graham Towle (Me) 35 Pine Ledge Dr, Scarborough ME 04074 B Providence RI 1930 s Frederick & Elizabeth. BA Colby Coll 1952; BD Bex Sem 1968. D 6/25/1968 P 12/21/1968 Bp Robert McConnell Hatch. m 10/9/1976 Judith H Pierce c 4. Dio Maine Portland ME 2005-2006, Admin Asst to Bp 1969-1974; R Chr Ch Biddeford ME 1997-2002; P-in-c Ch Of The Gd Shpd So Lee MA 1995-1997; All SS Epis Ch Kansas City MO 1994-1995; Int Positions 1993-1995; R S Andr's Epis Ch St Johnsbury VT 1991-1993; S Jas Epis Ch Essex Jct VT 1990-1994; Int S Lk's Ch S Albans VT 1989-1990; R S Jas Epis Ch Arlington VT 1984-1989; Vic S Ann's Epis Ch Windham Windham ME 1970-1974; Admin Intern Dio Wstrn Massachusetts Springfield 1968-1969.

PIERCE, Jacob E (NC) **S Ptr's Epis Ch Charlotte NC 2017-** D 12/13/2014 Bp Porter Taylor P 8/22/2015 Bp Anne Hodges-Copple.

PIERCE, Jay R (Lex) 205 Cardinal Ave, Versailles KY 40383 B Rockmart GA 1935 s J W & Billie. BA Coll of Mt St Jos 1978; MDiv Epis TS in Kentucky 1982. D 5/13/1978 P 5/1/1979 Bp Addison Hosea. m 5/12/1971 Patti Agnes Pierce c 2. Stwdshp Cmsn Chair 1994-1995; Int S Phil's Ch Harrodsburg KY 1992-1995; Non-par 1987-1992; Chapl VetA Hosp Lexington KY 1982-1987; Cmnty Hospice Lexington KY 1979-1980; Epis TS Lexington KY 1979-1980; D-In-Trng Ch Of The Gd Shpd Lexington KY 1978-1980; Food For The Poor Fundraising Interdenominational.

PIERCE, Nathaniel W (Eas) 3864 Rumsey Dr, Trappe MD 21673 **Prov III Ord Rep Exec Coun Appointees New York NY 2013-; Bp's Chapl HC Dio Easton Easton MD 2012-, Chapl 1990-2011, Ecum Off 2017-; Co-Trst Edw L. Ehart Trust 2012-; Cnvnr CPSP Chapt Easton MD 2005-; Wrshp Ldr S Phil's Ch Quantico MD 2002-** B Boston MA 1942 s Alvah & Anne. BS Cor 1966; MDiv CDSP 1972; MA Grad Theol Un 1972. D 5/15/1972 P 6/3/1973 Bp Ned Cole. c 3. Bd Mem and Var Off Choptank Cmnty Hlth System Denton MD 1994-2006; R Chr Epis Ch Great Choptank Par Cambridge MD 1991-2003; Dioc Coun Dio Massachusetts Boston MA 1984-1991, Stndg Cmsn on Peace (GC) 1986-1988; R All SS Par Brookline MA 1984-1990; R Gr Epis Ch Nampa ID 1975-1984; Asst Chr Ch Portola Vlly CA 1973-1975; JCP Dio Idaho Boise ID 1980-1985. Auth, "Chiara Lubich," *LivCh*, 2011; Auth, "Proposed Angl Cov," *LivCh*, 2011; Auth, "The Arrival of Feminine Theol," *LivCh*, 1997; Co-Auth, "The Voice of Conscience," EPF, 1989; Auth, "Stained Glass Windows," *LivCh*, 1987; Auth, "selected Chapt," *Rumors of War: a Moral and Theol Perspective on the Arms Race*, Seabury Press, 1982. Assoc. Ord of S Helena 1965. Bray Tubman Awd Dio Easton 2002; Who's Who in Rel 1992.

PIERCE, Patricia Daniels (NJ) 203 Wildwood Ave, Pitman NJ 08071 **Mentor EFM EFM 2011-** B Brooklyn NY 1942 d Ralph & Bertha. AA Fashion Inst of Tech 1962; BA SUNY 1992; MDiv GTS 1995. D 6/23/1995 Bp Orris George Walker Jr P 5/7/1997 Bp Brice Sidney Sanders. m 9/7/1963 John O Pierce c 2. R Ch Of The Gd Shpd Pitman NJ 1999-2014; Assoc R S Ptr's Epis Ch Washington NC 1997-1999; Int S Phil And S Jas Ch New Hyde Pk NY 1996-1997; Asst S Andr's Astoria NY 1995-1996; Chapl Pstr Care Coordntr S Mary's Hosp for Chld 1995-1996; Chapl St Mary's Hosp Bayside NY 1995-1996. Auth, "God's Time," *Wmn Uncommon Prayers*, Morehouse Pub, 2000. Wmn of the Year in Rel and Philosphy Gloucester Cnty, NJ 2006.

PIERCE, Patrick Arthur (CPa) 306 N Main Street, Mercersburg PA 17236 B Evanston IL 1949 s Charles & Carol. BA Mia 1971; MA Roosevelt U Chicago IL 1975; MDiv GTS 1979. D 6/9/1979 Bp Quintin Ebenezer Primo Jr P 12/12/1979 Bp James Winchester Montgomery. c 3. R Trin Epis Ch Chambersburg PA 2009-2014; P-in-c Mt Zion Epis Ch Hedgesville WV 2006-2009; P-in-c S Mk's Epis Ch Berkeley Spg WV 2006-2009; St Pauls Evang Luth Ch Dillsburg PA 2005-2006; Int St. Paul's Luth Ch Dillsburg PA 2005-2006; Int S Andr's Epis Ch Shippensburg PA 2004-2005; P-in-c Ch Of The Trsfg Blue Ridge Summit PA 2002-2004; Calv Chap Beartown Blue Ridge Summit PA 2002;

Int S Jn's Par Hagerstown MD 1999-2001; Int S Jas Epis Ch Westernport MD 1997-1999; R Calv Ch Cincinnati OH 1990-1997; R Ch Of The Trsfg Braddock Heights MD 1984-1990; Asst S Lk's Epis Ch Montclair NJ 1982-1984; Assoc Chr Ch Poughkeepsie NY 1979-1982; Advsry Bd Chr Mnstry Cntr Dio Sthrn Ohio Cincinnati OH 1993-1997; Yth & YA Com Dio Maryland Baltimore MD 1985-1987.

PIERCE, Roderick John (Tex) 4435 S FARM ROAD 125, SPRINGFIELD MO 65810 B Buffalo NY 1947 s John & Lois. AA Brevard Cmnty Coll 1972; BS-HCA GW 1979; MDiv Candler TS Emory U 1987. D 1/11/1988 Bp Anselmo Carral-Solar P 12/14/1988 Bp Maurice Manuel Benitez. c 2. Asst Dir, Chapl Serv St. Lk's Epis Hlth System Houston TX 1993-2009; Assoc Trin Epis Ch Baytown TX 1993; S Lk's Epis Hosp Houston TX 1991-2009; Chapl St. Lk's Epis Hosp Houston TX 1991-1993; R S Tim's Epis Ch Houston TX 1989-1991; Cur S Chris's Ch League City TX 1988-1989. Bd Cert Chapl, APC 1993; Chair, Cmsn on Quality in Pstr Serv, APC 1998-2002; Clincl Mem, ACPE 1987; Endorsed Mem, AEHC 1992; Mem, Assn of Profsnl Chapl (APC) 1991; Pres, Assembly Of Epis Healthcare Chapl (Aehc) 1997-1999. Phi Beta Kappa Bow 1987; cl w/hon Thesis Candler TS, Emory U 1987.

PIERCE, Terry Lee (Tex) PO Box 268, Taylor TX 76574 **S Jas' Ch Taylor TX 2012-** B Coronado CA 1953 d Joe & Carol. BA U of No Texas 1974; MSF Epis TS Of The SW 2014; MSF Epis TS of the SW 2014. D 6/21/2014 P 1/10/2015 Bp Dena Arnall Harrison.

PIERSON, Anne Susan (NCal) D 8/13/2016 Bp Barry Leigh Beisner.

PIERSON, Peter (Alb) PO Box 183, 156 Josh Hall Pond Road, Grafton NY 12082 **P Cathd Of All SS Albany NY 2011-** B Milwaukee WI 1950 s Paul & Patricia. BA Wms 1973; Dip Theol Stud St Johns Coll Nottingham GB 1974; DPS St Johns Coll Nottingham GB 1975; Cert VTS 1976. D 6/13/1976 Bp Alexander D Stewart P 6/1/1977 Bp Albert Wiencke Van Duzer. m 8/26/1972 Mary D Dickerson c 2. R S Jn's Epis Ch Troy NY 2010-2011; S Andr's Ch No Adams MA 2007-2010; P-in-c S Andr's Chap Blackinton MA 2003-2010; S Mk's Epis Ch Philmont NY 2002-2003; Asst S Mk's Epis Ch Jacksonville FL 1999-2000; Chapl Jacksonville Epis HS Jacksonville FL 1994-2002; Adj Tchr Epis HS Jacksonville FL 1991-1993; Yth Mnstry All Souls Epis Ch Jacksonville FL 1987-1993; R Chr Epis Ch Sheffield MA 1982-1987; Dio Wstrn Massachusetts Springfield 1982-1987; Assoc Trin Epis Ch Portland ME 1980-1982; Asst S Lk's Ch Gladstone NJ 1976-1980. FOCUS; SHORESH; SAMS.

PIERSON, Stewart (Vt) 232 High Rock Rd, Hinesburg VT 05461 **Ret 1998-** B New York NY 1937 s Richard & Dorothy. BA Colg 1959; BD UTS 1963. D 6/1/1963 P 12/20/1963 Bp Horace W B Donegan. m 8/25/1962 Julie Burger Pierson c 2. R All SS' Epis Ch S Burlington VT 1998; R S Ptr's Epis Ch Lakewood OH 1986-1998; R S Steph's Epis Ch Wilkes Barre PA 1972-1986; Cur Calv Ch Pittsburgh PA 1963-1972. Ldrshp Journalism S Peters 1984.

PIETSCH, Louise Parsons (NY) 80 Lyme Rd Apt 347, Hanover NH 03755 B New York NY 1940 d William & Louise. Fndt for Rel and Mntl Hlth; BA Col 1963; MDiv UTS 1982; DMin Drew U 1988. D 6/5/1982 Bp Paul Moore Jr P 12/21/1982 Bp James Stuart Wetmore. c 3. P Assoc S Thos Ch Hanover NH 2003-2007; S Steph's Ch Ridgefield CT 2000-2002, Pstr Assoc 2000-2002, Pstr Assoc 1998-1999; Dio New York New York NY 1997-1998, Chair Diac Form 1991-1993; P-in-c Ch Of The H Trin Pawling NY 1996; R S Lk's Ch Katonah NY 1990-1996, P-in-c 1987-1989, Assoc 1984-1987; Mem Mnstrs Cmsn 1984-1990; Bd Mem Ethics Bd Bedford NY 1984-1988; Cur S Matt's Ch Bedford NY 1983-1984. Auth, "Wmn in Prison: A Par in Search of a Mnstry (Doctoral Paper)," Drew U, 1988. Phi Beta Kappa Col 1963.

PIETTE, Joseph Leroy (Minn) 204 8th St, Cloquet MN 55720 B Moose Lake MN 1950 s James & Mary. D 7/20/2008 Bp Daniel Lee Swenson P 2/19/2009 Bp James Louis Jelinek. m 8/3/1974 Diane Elizabeth Piette c 2.

PIFKE, Lauran Kretchmar (Cal) 3400 Stevenson Blvd. #Q37, Fremont CA 94538 B Flint MI 1953 d James & Beverley. BS U IL 1975; MDiv CDSP 2006. D 6/3/2006 Bp William Edwin Swing P 12/2/2006 Bp Marc Handley Andrus. m 12/26/2006 Frederick M Hansen c 3. R S Anne's Ch Fremont CA 2007-2015; Int Calv Epis Ch Santa Cruz CA 2006.

PIGGINS, Deborah Hanwell (NJ) B Glen Ridge NJ 1945 BA Rutgers 1976; MA Rutgers, the St U of NJ 1981; MDiv GTS 2005. D 6/11/2005 P 5/27/2006 Bp George Edward Councell. H Trin Epis Ch Wenonah NJ 2015-2016; P S Andr's Ch Mt Holly NJ 2014-2015; All SS Memi Ch Navesink NJ 2012-2014; Int S Ptr's Ch Perth Amboy NJ 2009-2011; Int Ch Of The Ascen Gloucester City NJ 2008-2009; Asst Calv Epis Ch Flemington NJ 2005-2007; Chapl S Lk's Hosp Bethlehem PA 2005-2007.

PIKE, Clifford Arthur Hunt (Pa) 105 Elm St, Lawrenceburg KY 40342 B Worcester MA 1946 s Joseph & Louise. BA Transylvania U 1968; MDiv VTS 1971. D 12/8/1971 Bp William Foreman Creighton P 6/1/1972 Bp George Paul Reeves. m 7/16/1969 Nancy G Pike c 1. R The Ch Of The H Trin W Chester PA 1999-2004; S Lk's Ch Salisbury NC 1994-1999; R S Ptr's Ch Paris KY 1977-1994; Assoc S Columba's Epis Ch Bristol TN 1974-1977; Calv Ch Memphis TN 1973-1977; Asst Dio Georgia Savannah GA 1971-1973.

PIKE, David Robert (WMich) 1519 Elmwood Rd, Lansing MI 48917 **R S Dav's Ch Lansing MI 1993-; Secy 1987-; Cathd Corp 1984-** B Port Sulpher LA 1955 s Charles & Bunny. BA Grand Vlly St U 1977; MDiv EDS 1982. D 6/5/1982 Bp Charles Ellsworth Bennison Jr P 12/1/1982 Bp Charles Bennison Sr. m 5/27/1978 Nancy L Pike c 2. Dn Of The Estrn Dnry 1987-1993; 1985-1993; Epis Chapl Albion Coll Albion MI 1984-1993; R S Jas' Epis Ch Of Albion Albion MI 1984-1993; Cur S Paul's Ch Muskegon MI 1982-1984; Co-Chair Of Dioc Realignment Dio Michigan Detroit MI 1988-1990.

PIKE, Diane M (WNY) 500 Morris Ave Ste 304, Springfield NJ 07081 **Assoc S Andr's Ch Omaha NE 2016-** B Kalamazoo MI 1955 d Robert & Loraine. BA Nazareth Coll 1977; MA Oakland U 1983; MDiv Epis TS of the SW 2011. D 7/15/2011 Bp Martin Scott Field P 1/20/2012 Bp David Bruce Joslin. The Epis Preaching Fndt 2015-2016; S Paul's Epis Ch Lewiston NY 2013-2015; S Mary's Ch Portsmouth RI 2011-2013. dmpike22@yahoo.com

PIKE, Richard S (NY) St Matthew's Episcopal Church, PO Box 293, Bedford NY 10506 **Assoc R S Matt's Ch Bedford NY 2014-** B Peterborough England 1974 s John & Felicity. MA St Andrews U 1997; MDiv GTS 2014. D 3/15/2014 P 9/27/2014 Bp Andrew Marion Lenow Dietsche. m 7/3/2010 Tracy N Pike c 3. Dio New York New York NY 2015-2017. rpike@stmatthewsbedford.org

PIKE, Stephen Phillip (Ky) RCT 1 HQ Co, UIC 40145, FPO AP 96426 **Off Of Bsh For ArmdF New York NY 1991-** B Montebello CA 1956 s Joseph & Margaret. BA Baylor U 1983; MDiv Sthrn Bapt TS 1986; VTS 1988. D 5/31/1988 P 5/1/1989 Bp David Reed. m 8/7/1982 Dawna Linette Pike. Asst S Matt's Epis Ch Louisville KY 1988-1991.

PIKE, Thomas Frederick (NY) 26 Gramercy Park S Apt 9h, New York NY 10003 **Collegial Cn Trin And S Phil's Cathd Newark NJ 2008-; Gnrl Covention Com on Human Affrs Epis Ch 1974-; Trst Cathd Of St Jn The Div New York NY 1976-** B Dobbs Ferry NY 1938 s Frederick & Elizabeth. BS SUNY 1960; MDiv Ya Berk 1968; DD Ya Berk 1977; DMin NYTS 1977. D 6/1/1963 P 12/1/1963 Bp Horace W B Donegan. m 10/10/1980 Lys McLaughlin Pike c 3. Min Fllshp Oxford And Yale Parishes 1974-1975; R Calv and St Geo New York NY 1971-2008; R Calv Epis Ch New York NY US 1971-1975; Pres Of The Stndg Com 1970-1974; Chapl Leake & Watts 1966-1970; R San Andres Ch Yonkers NY 1965-1971; Cur S Mk's Ch In The Bowery New York NY 1963-1965; Trst Ya Berk New Haven CT 1969. "Filosfia del Exito," Grijalbo, Mexica, 1991; "Is It Success? Or Is It Addiction?," Nelson Pub., 1988.

PILARSKI, Terri C (Mich) 120 N Military St, Dearborn MI 48124 **R Chr Ch Dearborn MI 2011-** B Salt Lake City UT 1957 d Paul & Shannon. M.Div SWTS 1998; MSW Loyola U 1999. D 12/28/1999 P 6/28/2000 Bp Bill Persell. m 8/17/1985 Daniel Pilarski c 2. Epis Ch Of S Fran-In-The-Vlly Green Vlly AZ 2008-2010; Dn Elgin Deann Dio Chicago Chicago IL 2003; S Hilary's Ch Prospect Hts IL 2001-2008; Ch Of The H Comf Kenilworth IL 2000-2001.

PILAT, Ann Ferres (USC) St Mary's Episcopal Church, 170 St Andrews Rd, Columbia SC 29210 B Columbia SC 1950 d George & Louise. AB U of So Carolina 1971; MAT U of So Carolina 1975; MEd U of So Carolina 1990. D 1/21/2006 Bp Dorsey Henderson. c 2.

PILCHER III, William Edward (NC) 305 Jackson Rd, Mount Airy NC 27030 B Brooklyn NY 1930 s William & Caroline. BA U So 1952; MDiv GTS 1960; Cert Command and Gnrl Stff Coll 1969. D 6/21/1960 Bp Richard Henry Baker P 12/21/1960 Bp Thomas Augustus Fraser Jr. m 10/6/1979 Carolyn Dolores Pilcher c 4. Int Vic Galloway Memi Chap Elkin NC 2003-2005, Int 1997-2002, P-in-c 1981-1996; Int S Steph's Epis Ch Winston Salem NC 2000-2002; Int S Mary's Epis Ch Shltr Island NY 1993-1995; Int S Jas Ch Oneonta NY 1992-1993; Int All SS' Epis Ch Gastonia NC 1990-1991; Int Par Of The H Comm Glendale Sprg NC 1987-1989; Int Chr Epis Ch Danville VA 1986-1987; Chapl US Army 1963-1991; R Trin Ch Mt Airy NC 1963-1981; Ch Of The Adv Enfield NC 1960-1963; S Mk Ch Roanoke Rapids NC 1960-1963; P-in-c S Mk's Ch Halifax NC 1960-1963; Ovrs Mssn Cmmte Dio No Carolina Raleigh NC 1965-1967. Mltry Off Assn of Amer 1991; NC Consultants Ntwk 2001-2004; NG Assn 1983. Legion of Merit US-A 1991.

PILLOT, Anne (O) 4292 Elmwood Rd, South Euclid OH 44121 **Cmncatn Dir Assn for Epis Deacons 2013-; D Ch Of The Gd Shpd Lyndhurst OH 2011-; D S Tim's Ch Macedonia OH 2011-** B Cleveland Heights OH 1960 d Lawrence & Jane. BFA Kent St U 1985; Dio Ohio D Formation 2011. D 6/4/2011 Bp Mark Hollingsworth Jr.

PILLSBURY, Jeannette Noyes (Ia) PO Box 4, Decorah IA 52101 B Milwaukee WI 1950 d Hugh & Virginia. BA Sweet Briar Coll 1972; MEd U of Virginia 1982; PhD U of Virginia 1991. D 6/6/2010 P 12/18/2010 Bp Alan Scarfe. pillje01@luther.edu

PILLSBURY, Samuel Hale (Los) 919 Albany St, Los Angeles CA 90015 **Law Prof Loyola Law Sch 1986-** B Princeton NJ 1954 s Samuel & Katherine. ABS Harv 1976; JD Usc Law Cntr 1983; Cert ETSBH 2006. D 12/2/2006 Bp Chester Lovelle Talton. c 1.

PILTZ, Guy H (Haw) 62-2145 Ouli St, Kamuela HI 96743 B Honolulu HI 1938 s Guy & Marguerite. AB Dart 1960; BD CDSP 1963. D 5/17/1963 P 12/1/1963 Bp Harry Sherbourne Kennedy. m 6/16/1960 Josephine Irene Piltz c 3. Chapl Hawaii Preparatory Acad Kamuela HI 1994-2003; Chapl Hawaii Preparatory Acad Kamuela HI 1978-1990; S Jas Epis Ch Kamuela HI 1976-1980; Vic Kohala Missions 1973-1974; Leeward Missions Ewa Bch HI 1970-1973; Vic Leeward Missions Honolulu HI 1969-1973; Assoc S Mary's Epis Ch Honolulu HI 1968-1969; S Matt's Epis Ch Waimanalo HI 1963-1966; Vic Emm Epis Ch Kailua HI 1963-1964; Stndg Com The Epis Ch in Hawaii Honolulu HI 1969-1971.

✠ PINA-LOPEZ, The Rt Rev Hugo Luis (CFla) 2911 S Whisperbay Ct, Oviedo FL 32765 **Asstg Bp of Cntrl Florida Dio Cntrl Florida Orlando FL 2001-, Asst Bp of Cntrl Florida 1995-2000; Ret Bp Dio Honduras 2001-** B La Gloria Camaguey CU 1938 s Humberto & Hortensia. BA La Progresiva Sch of Cuba 1960; BD UTS CU 1964. Trans 2/1/1967 Bp Agueros Romualdo Gonzalez Con 8/23/1978 for Hond. m 8/5/1965 Minerva Azucena Arias c 3. R The Epis Ch Of The Redeem Avon Pk FL 1991-1995; Hisp Mssnr Dio Oklahoma Oklahoma City OK 1987-1991; Vic Santa Maria Virgen Epis Oklahoma City OK 1987-1991; Iglesia San Mateo Houston TX 1984-1987; Assoc San Mateo Epis Ch Bellaire TX 1984-1987; Exec Coun Appointees New York NY 1982-1984; Bp Dio Honduras San Pedro Sula 1978-1983; Serv Ch in Honduras 1975-1978; R S Simons Ch Miami FL 1973-1975; Asst S Thos Miami FL 1968-1973; Serv Ch of Spain 1967-1968; Serv Ch in Cuba 1964-1967. R Emer Ch of the Redeem 1995.

PINDER, Churchill Gibson (CPa) St. Stephens Episcopal Cathedral, 221 N. Front St., Harrisburg PA 17101 B Wicomico Church VA 1953 s Joseph & Gay. BA U of Virginia 1976; MDiv VTS 1983. D 8/14/1983 P 2/16/1984 Bp Rustin Ray Kimsey. m 5/28/1988 Sally Reeves Gambill c 2. Dn Cathd Ch Of S Steph Harrisburg PA 2005-2017, Cn 1986-1990; St Jn's Ch Cold Sprg Harbor NY 1995-2005; R All SS Ch Portland OR 1990-1995; S Steph's Baker City OR 1983-1986.

PINDER, Nelson Wardell (CFla) 2632 Marquise Ct, Orlando FL 32805 **Ret 1996-** B Miami FL 1932 s George & Colleen. BA Bethune-Cookman Coll 1956; Nash 1959; Urban Trng Cntr 1965; MEd Florida A&M U 1974. D 7/5/1959 Bp Henry I Louttit P 1/9/1960 Bp William Francis Moses. m 8/15/1959 Marian G Pinder c 2. R The Epis Ch Of S Jn The Bapt Orlando FL 1977-1995, Vic 1959-1969; Chapl US Senate 1977-1995; Chapl US Hse of Representatives 1973-1977. Auth, "The Legacy," Ch Pension Fund, 2003; Auth, "The Vintage Voice," Ch Pension Fund, 2003. Alpha Phi Alpha Fraternity 1999; Kappa Delta Pi (Fraternity for Educators) 1968; Phi Beta Kappa 1968. NAACP Freedom Awd 2011; Hall of Frame for Preachers More Hse 2011; Hall of Fame for Pastors Morehouse 2011; Doctor of Human Letters Voohees Coll 2011; DD VTS 2010; DD Nash 2004; Orlando Black Human Relatns Awd Orlando Black Hall of Fame and Florida Rel Hall of Fame 2002; Orlando Black Human Relatns Awd Orlando Black Hall of Fame 1987; Orlando Black Human Relatns Awd Orlando Black Hall of Fame 1978; DD Bethune-Cookman Coll 1976; Hon Cn Cathd of S Lk 1971; Alum Awd Bethune Cookman Coll 1965.

PINEO, Linda Baker (At) 3404 Doral Ln, Woodstock GA 30189 **Ch Of The Trsfg Rome GA 2013-** B Minneapolis MN 1947 d Roger & Joan. BA Mt Holyoke Coll 1969; MA Stan 1975. D 6/24/1988 P 1/5/1989 Bp Bob Gordon Jones. m 9/11/1971 Charles C Pineo c 2. Ch Of The Gd Shpd Hayesville NC 2012-2013; Int All SS' Epis Ch Gastonia NC 2010-2012; Int Ch Of The Ascen Cartersville GA 2008-2010; S Gabr's Epis Ch Oakwood GA 2006-2007; S Jas Epis Ch Marietta GA 2004-2005; S Clem's Epis Ch Canton GA 2002-2004; Assoc R Chr Epis Ch Kennesaw GA 1998-2002, Asst Cleric 1994-1997; Serv Convoc of Epis Ch in Europe Paris 1992-1994; Gd Shpd Epis Ch Centennial CO 1990-1992; Vic S Barth's Ch Cokeville WY 1988-1989; S Jas Ch Kemmerer WY 1988-1989; Chapl Dok Bd Dio Atlanta Atlanta GA 1997-2000; Chapl Ecw Bd Dio Colorado Denver CO 1990-1992.

PINHO, Joseph T (Mass) 1 Summit Dr Apt 48, Reading MA 01867 B Waterbury CT 1947 s Jose & Ivone. Rec 5/1/1997 as Priest Bp M(Arvil) Thomas Shaw. R S Eliz's Ch Wilmington MA 1998-2013; D Ch Of S Jn The Evang Boston MA 1996-1998.

PINKERTON, Patricia Edith Long (ECR) The Vicarad, St Annes Way, St.Briavels., Gloucestershire GL15 6UE Great Britain (UK) B London UK 1938 d George & Florence. BA San Jose St U 1969; MA San Jose St U 1975; CDSP 1985. D 5/4/1981 P 12/1/1982 Bp Charles Shannon Mallory. Serv Ch of Engl 1988-1997; Santa Maria Urban Mnstry San Jose CA 1985-1987; P-in-c S Theresa San Jose CA 1984-1987; Dir Santa Maria Urban Mssn 1984-1987; S Phil's Ch San Jose CA 1984-1985; Asst S Fran Epis Ch San Jose CA 1981-1982. Mow. Phi Kappa Phi.

PINKERTON, Susan B (Ct) 400 East Westminster Road, Lake Forest IL 60045 **St Johns Ch W Hartford CT 2015-** B Ft Riley KS 1952 d Bobby & Barbara. BA U of Texas 1993; JD U of Oklahoma 1997; MDiv Ya Berk 2008. D 6/28/2008 P 1/24/2009 Bp Edward Joseph Konieczny. c 3. St Paul's Epis Ch Peoria IL 2014-2015; Assoc The Ch Of The H Sprt Lake Forest IL 2011-2014; Assoc S Mk's Ch Washington DC 2008-2011; D Trin Par New York NY 2008. sbp2115@hotmail.com

PINKSTON JR, Frederick William (NC) 7225 Saint Clair Dr, Charlotte NC 28270 B Salisbury NC 1942 s Frederick & Alice. BS No Carolina St U 1965; MDiv TESM 1981. D 1/6/1982 Bp William Gillette Weinhauer P 7/1/1982 Bp

Furman Charles Stough. m 6/1/1968 Carolyn Jeanette Plecker. Assoc S Marg's Epis Ch Waxhaw NC 1989-2000; Chap Of Hope Charlotte NC 1986-1989; P-in-c Chap Of Hope Charlotte NC 1985-1989; Chr The Redeem Ch Montgomery AL 1982-1985.

PINNER JR, Joseph (ETenn) 818 Hill St, Kingston TN 37763 B Memphis TN 1950 s Joseph & Dorothy. BA Rhodes Coll 1972; MDiv VTS 1975. D 5/24/1975 P 4/1/1976 Bp William F Gates Jr. m 1/26/1981 Sharon Pinner c 3. R S Andr's Ch Harriman TN 1999-2011; Hstgr Dio Wstrn Louisiana Alexandria LA 1992-1999, 1992, PBp's Dioc Fund Coordntr 1991-1999, Chair of the Pvrty Cmsn 1991-1995, 1991, Dept of Chr Nurture 1988-1989, Pvrty Cmsn 1987-1990, CE Com 1986-1987; Vic S Lukes Ch Jennings LA 1990-1999; R S Lk's Ch Brandon MS 1989-1990; R Ch Of The Epiph Opelousas LA 1986-1989; R S Paul's Epis Ch Picayune MS 1982-1986; Chapl CAP TN 1980-1990; Dio Tennessee Nashville TN 1976-1981; Vic S Thos The Apos Humboldt TN 1976-1981; D-in-Trng S Ptr's Ch Columbia TN 1975-1976; Evang & Renwl Cmsn Dio Mississippi Jackson MS 1983-1986.

PINNOCK, Betty Lou (Ore) 459 Herbert St, Ashland OR 97520 **D S Mk's Epis Par Medford OR 2000-** B Denver CO 1932 d William & Josephine. BA U CO 1953; MEd Sthrn Oregon U 1963. D 11/4/2000 Bp Robert Louis Ladehoff.

PINTI, Daniel John (WNY) 13021 W. Main St., Alden NY 14004 **S Paul's Epis Ch Lewiston NY 2017-; S Paul's Cathd Buffalo NY 2014-** B Warren OH 1963 s Daniel & Jean. BA Kent St U 1986; MA OH SU 1988; PhD OH SU 1992; MDiv Chr the King Sem 2011. D 11/22/2008 Bp Michael Garrison P 7/2/2011 Bp Ralph William Franklin. m 8/27/1988 Maria Pinti c 3. Vic S Aid's Ch Alden NY 2011-2014. Auth, "Tyndale's Gospel of St.Jn: Translation and the Theol of Style," *Journ of Angl Stds*, 2008; Auth, "Julian's Audacious Reticence: Perichoresis and the Showings," *ATR*, 2006.

PINTO DE ARIZA, Myriam (Colom) CRA 6 #49-85, Bogota, D.C. Colombia **Iglesia Epis En Colombia Bogota 2012-** B Bogota D.C. 1951 d Luis & Lilia. Pintora (Artes) Comfenalco; Licenciada Teologia Miami Intl Sem; Maestra Preescolar Universidad Pedagogicanal. D 6/29/2012 Bp Francisco Jose Duque-Gomez. m 12/31/1971 Oscar Armando Ariza Nino c 3.

PINZON, Samuel E(duardo) (WA) 15570 Sw 143rd Ter, Miami FL 33196 B Bogota CO 1932 s Eduardo & Ana. AA Warren Wilson Coll 1957; BA Tusculum Coll 1959; MDiv UTS CU 1962; ThM PrTS 1971; ThD Covington TS 1982. D 5/14/1964 Bp David Reed P 11/14/1965 Bp William Henry Marmion. m 5/10/1961 Rosa Maria Treto Moina c 3. R San Pedro Miami FL 1990-1999; All Souls Memi Epis Ch Washington DC 1979-1980; Chairperson-Natl Cmsn on Hisp Mnstry Epis Ch in the U.S.A. 1977-1979; Chapl Hse of Mercy Washington DC 1976-1980; Vic Epis Dio Washington DC San Juan Hisp Missio 1974-1980; Mssn San Juan Washington DC 1974-1980; Com Affrs Dio Washington Washington DC 1974-1978; Serv Ch in Colombia 1967-1974; Serv Ch in Ecuador 1964-1966. Auth, *The Epis Ch in Columbia*, 1980; Auth, "La Gran Colombia," *The Chr Challenge*, 1974; Auth, "Homilia para el Dia Ecum," *Comunidad Teologica*; Auth, "El Significado de la Navidad para el Epis Anglicano," *Temas*; Auth, "Biblia v Ecum," *Vida Espiritual*; Auth, "La Praxis de la Liberacion en Miami," *Voces Luteranas*. Assn of Ministers of Grtr Miami 1982-1996; Consejo Hispano de Ministros Evangelicos / Metro Area Washingto 1978-1980; Hsng Counslg Serv - Washington, DC 1977-1980; Wilson Cntr, Washington, DC 1975-1978. Ecum Speaker representing the Prot Ch of Colo Intl Eucharistic Congr of the RC Ch 1968.

PINZON CASTRO, Luis Alberto (Colom) Carrera 6 No 49-85, Piso 2, Bogota Colombia B Buenos Dios Colombia 1948 s Teofilo & Maria Teresa. Lic Seminario Mayor-Escuela 2000; Seminario Diocesano 2003; Facultad Estudios Teologilos 2004. D 6/16/2007 P 9/14/2008 Bp Francisco Jose Duque-Gomez. m 8/24/1969 Maria Eugenia Salcedo De Pinzon c 4.

PIOTROWSKI, Mary Triplett (Az) 2035 N Southern Hills Dr, Flagstaff AZ 86004 B Oak Hill WV 1948 d John & Katharine. MDiv Epis TS of the SW; BA Hollins U 1970; MBA Ball St U 1975; MA Nthrn Arizona U 2000; MDiv Epis TS of the SW 2003. D 5/14/2003 P 12/13/2003 Bp Robert Reed Shahan. m 1/22/1972 Ronald J Piotrowski c 3. D S Andr's Epis Ch Sedona AZ 2003-2016, R 2003-.

PIOVANE, Michael (Be) Po Box 368, Trexlertown PA 18087 B Coaldale PA 1943 s Rocco & Veronica. BA S Chas Borromeo Sem 1965; BA S Chas Borromeo Sem 1965; MDiv S Chas Borromeo Sem 1969; MDiv S Chas Borromeo Sem 1969; MDiv S Chas Borromeo Sem 1969; EdD Nova SE U 1996. Rec 10/31/1993 Bp James Michael Mark Dyer. m 11/15/1986 Rita M Valenti Piovane. R S Anne's Epis Ch Trexlertown PA 1998-2015, Asstg P 1993-1998; Int S Mich's Epis Ch Birdsboro PA 1997-1998; Pstr, Diac Dir, Dioc Rel. Ed. Dir RC Ch 1969-1986. rector@stannesepiscopal.net

PIPER, Charles Edmund (NMich) 1676 Lander Ln, Lafayette CO 80026 B Rockville Center NY 1947 s Charles & Alys. BA Trin Hartford CT 1969; MDiv GTS 1972. D 6/17/1972 Bp Jonathan Goodhue Sherman P 12/21/1972 Bp Samuel Joseph Wylie. m 8/22/1970 Linda Lee Jauck c 2. So Cntrl Reg Manistique MI 2000-2010; Mssnr Gr Epis Ch Menominee MI 1989-2009; R H Trin Ch Iron Mtn MI 1979-2009; Dep GC Dio Nthrn Michigan Marquette MI 1979-1988, 1972-1979, Pres Stndg Com 1990-1994; Vic Ch Of The Gd Shpd S

Ignace MI 1974-1979; P-in-c Kincheloe (AFB) Epis Cmnty 1974-1977; Vic S Dav Sidnaw MI 1972-1974.

PIPER, Geoffrey Tindall (Mass) 124 Front St, Marion MA 02738 **R S Gabr's Epis Ch Marion MA 2008-; COM Dio Massachusetts Boston MA 2012-** B Burlington VT 1955 s Winthrop & Emilie. BA Amh 1977; MA Regent U 1981; BA Bishops U Lennoxville CA 1988. Trans 9/1/1990 Bp Andrew Frederick Wissemann. m 12/28/1983 Leslie Thayer c 3. Asst for CE Chr Ch Detroit MI 2006-2008; Asst R Sprt of Gr Luth Epis Ch W Bloomfield MI 1998-2006; Dio Wstrn Massachusetts Springfield 1990-1998; Serv Ch Of Can 1985-1990.

PIPER, Katherine (Colo) D 6/10/2017 Bp Robert John O'Neill.

PIPER, Linda Lee (NMich) 1676 Lander Lane, Lafayette CO 80026 **Dio Nthrn Michigan Marquette MI 2005-; Pres of the Stndg Com Dio Nthrn Michigan 2006-** B Brooklyn NY 1947 d Robert & Barbara. BSN U of Vermont 1969; MPH U MI 1994. D 8/13/2003 P 2/29/2004 Bp James Arthur Kelsey. m 8/22/1970 Charles Edmund Piper c 2. 2004-2013; D H Trin Ch Iron Mtn MI 2003-2013; Pres of the Stndg Com Dio Nthrn Michigan Marquette MI 2006-2011. 219b632@gmail.com

PIPER, Mary Elizabeth Meacham (Ore) 4757 Highway 66, Ashland OR 97520 **Int S Lk's Ch Grants Pass OR 2017-; Ch Of The Epiph Cape Coral FL 2012-; S Jn's Epis Ch St Jas City FL 2012-** B Minneapolis MN 1956 d Harris & Betty. BS U MN 1979; EFM 1992; Cert Cpt 1993; ORD D Formation Prog 1994; CPE Clincl Pstr Care (CPE) Units (4) 2000; Read for Ord 2000. D 6/11/1994 P 10/7/2000 Bp Charles I Jones III. m 11/5/1989 Harry C Piper c 2. S Jn-By-The-Sea Epis Ch Bandon OR 2016; S Matt's Epis Ch Gold Bch OR 2011; Co-P in charge S Mart's Ch Shady Cove OR 2004-2011; Asstg P S Jas Ch Bozeman MT 2000-2004; Hosp Chapl Bozeman Dss Hlth Svcs Bozeman MN 1999-2004; Chapl Bozeman Dss Hosp hospice 1997-1999; D Geth Ch Manhattan MT 1994-2000; COM/Baptized Dio Oregon Portland OR 2010-2011, Transition Com Co-Chair 2008-2010, Comp Dio Com 2007-, Convoc Dn 2006-2007, Dioc Coun 2006-2007, Dioc Vision Team 2005-2006; Co-ordntr of Ret Mnstrs Dio Montana Helena MT 2001-2002, BEC 1997-2000.

PIPKIN, Michael (Minn) 1730 Clifton Pl Ste 201, Minneapolis MN 55403 **Cn Dio Minnesota Minneapolis MN 2013-** B Houston TX 1976 s Robert & Jane. BA Texas Tech U 1998; MDiv VTS 2002. D 12/15/2001 P 6/22/2002 Bp C Wallis Ohl. m 11/1/2008 Molly Pipkin. The R's Assoc (Sr Assoc) S Jn's Epis Ch Charlotte NC 2011-2013; P-in-c The Falls Ch Epis Falls Ch VA 2008-2011; U.S. Navy Chapl Off Of Bsh For ArmdF New York NY 2004-2008; Chapl USN 2004-2008; Assoc R Ch Of The Gd Shpd Burke VA 2002-2004; Cur S Dav's Ch Ashburn VA 2002, 2000-2002. Auth, "Reflections on God and 9/11," *Epis News Serv*, Epis Ch, 2011; Auth, "The Romance of War (three-part series)," *Epis Cafe*, Epis Cafe, 2010; Auth, "Repealing 'Don't Ask Don't Tell' could strengthen Rel freedom in the Mltry," *Epis Life Online*, Epis News Serv, 2010; Auth, "Top 10 iPhone Apps for Organizing a P's Life," *Epis Life Online*, Epis News Serv, 2010. S Andr's Soc 2009. michael.p@episcopalmn.org

PIPPIN, Jacqueline Lynne (SanD) **Asst Cathd Ch Of S Paul San Diego CA 2017-** D 6/11/2016 P 5/6/2017 Bp Jim Mathes.

PIPPIN, Tina (At) 25 Second Avenue, Atlanta GA 30317 **Assoc Prof Of Rel Stds Agnes Scott Coll 1989-** B Kinston NC 1956 d Leon & Jean. BA Mars Hill Coll 1977; MDiv Candler TS Emory U 1980; ThM Sthrn Bapt TS 1984; PhD Sthrn Bapt TS 1987. D 5/31/1988 Bp David Reed. m 7/28/1984 Jerry Gentry. Chapl Norton-Kosaie Hosp 1988-1989; D S Matt's Epis Ch Louisville KY 1988-1989. Auth, "Death & Desire: The Rhetoric Of Gender In The Apocalypse Of Jn"; Auth, "The Postmodern Bible".

PIRET, Michael John (LI) Christ Church, 61 E Main St, Oyster Bay NY 11771 **R Chr Ch Oyster Bay NY 2016-** B Buffalo NY 1957 s Paul & Edith. BA SUNY 1979; MA U MI 1980; MLitt U of Oxford 1989; PhD U MI 1991. Trans 3/8/2016 as Priest Bp Lawrence C Provenzano. m 9/15/2009 Sian E Piret. rector@christchurchoysterbay.org

PISANI JR, Gerard Alexander (Nwk) 8602 Forester Lane, Apex NC 27539 B Pompton Lakes NJ 1938 s Gerard & Dorothy. BS Nyack Coll 1963; GTS 1966. D 6/11/1966 Bp Leland Stark P 10/15/1966 Bp George E Rath. m 11/23/2013 Dwight August Tintle. Windmill Allnce Inc. Bayonne NJ 1999-2009; R Trin Ch Bayonne NJ 1974-2009; R Chr Ch Pompton Lake NJ 1969-1974; Vic S Gabr's Ch Oak Ridge NJ 1966-1969. "The Apparent Heresy Of Jesus," Bk - Dorrance Pub, 2002.

PITA-PARRALES, Ubaldo Abilito (EcuC) Manabi Y Tayapi, Puyo Ecuador **R Ascen Puyo 1988-** B Catarama EC 1948 s Segundo & Iberible. Sem 1989. D 3/14/1987 P 12/1/1988 Bp Adrian Delio Caceres-Villavicencio. Iglesia Epis Del Ecuador Quito 1993-2003.

PITCHER, Trenton Langland (Chi) 145 E Columbia Ave, Elmhurst IL 60126 B Marshalltown IA 1938 s Elbert & Ida. BS U of Wisconsin 1962; Tufts U 1965; MDiv SWTS 1970. D 10/17/1971 P 6/18/1972 Bp James Winchester Montgomery. Chapl Bp Anderson Hse Chicago IL 1988-2003; Cn Res Cathd Of S Jas Chicago IL 1978-1988; Dio Chicago Chicago IL 1973-1977; Asst Trin Ch Highland Pk IL 1971-1978.

PITMAN JR, Omar W (WTex) 11919 El Sendero St, San Antonio TX 78233 **Died 3/20/2017** B Big Spring TX 1933 s Omar & Daphne. BA Nm Mltry Inst

P

NM 1954; MDiv GTS 1957. D 7/7/1957 P 2/4/1958 Bp C J Kinsolving III. m 11/27/1965 Mary Pitman. Cntrl Convoc Partnership In Mssn San Antonio TX 2000-2013; S Lk's Epis Ch San Antonio TX 1993-2005; Non-par 1964-1992; S Jas-Dundaff Carbondale PA 1959-1964; Vic S Jn's Ch Ft Sumner NM 1957-1959; S Mich's Ch Tucumcari NM 1957-1959.

PITMAN, Ralph William (O) 3044 Edgehill Rd, Cleveland Heights OH 44118 **Assoc Dir Spprt To At Risk Teens Cleveland OH 2000-; Assoc Dir Yth Prog Luth Metro Mnstry Cleveland OH 1999-** B Bryn Mawr PA 1947 s Ralph & Martha. BA U of Virginia 1969; MDiv EDS 1972; Virginia Commonwealth U 1987; Cert Case Wstrn Reserve U 1998; Cert Case Wstrn Reserve U 2001. D 6/28/1972 Bp Robert Lionne DeWitt P 2/9/1973 Bp Lyman Cunningham Ogilby. m 11/30/1974 Jane Buch c 2. Gr Epis Ch Willoughby OH 2001-2007; Luth Metro Mnstry Cleveland OH 1999-2007; R S Mart's Ch Chagrin Fall OH 1995-1999; S Paul's Epis Ch Cleveland OH 1991-1995, Asst 1988-1991; S Ptr's Ch Philadelphia PA 1985-1988; Asst S Steph's Ch Richmond VA 1982-1985; Chapl VA Epis Sch Lynchburg VA 1981-1982; Virginia Epis Sch Lynchburg VA 1980-1982; R S Paul's Ch Columbia PA 1976-1980; Asst Nevil Memi Ch Of S Geo Ardmore PA 1975-1976; Cmncatn Consult Dio Pennsylvania Philadelphia PA 1972-1974; Yth Cmsn Dio Ohio Cleveland 1988-1995; Chair: Cmsn on Alco and Drugs Dio Virginia Richmond VA 1985-1988. Auth, *Chld of Alcoholics in Schools*, CRIS, 1982; Auth, *Baby Jesus Childrens Wrshp Bk*, PS Mus, Inc, 1978; Auth, *The Fast I Choose-Mus & Pryr on Wrld Hunger*, PS Mus, Inc, 1974; Auth, *Cmncatn Media & Orgnztn Values: A Study of Uses of Video Tape in a Par Ch*, Consult Search, Inc, 1972. EPF.

PITT JR, Louis Wetherbee (Mass) 59 Dartmouth Ct, Bedford MA 01730 B Newark NJ 1923 s Louis & Blanche. BA Col 1944; MDiv EDS 1947. D 1/6/1947 P 10/18/1947 Bp William A Lawrence. Assoc Dn Cathd S Mary & All SS Harare Zimbabwe 1983-1986; Exec Coun Appointees New York NY 1983-1986; Cn Pstr The Cathd Ch Of S Paul Boston MA 1980-1983; Dio Massachusetts Boston MA 1979-1986; Zambia New York NY 1972-1979; Dn H Cross Cathd Lusaka Zambia 1972-1977; R All SS Par Brookline MA 1954-1972; R S Mk's Ch Foxborough MA 1949-1954; Assoc Gr Ch Manchester NH 1947-1949.

PITT-HART, Barry Thomas (SD) 1409 S 5th Ave, Sioux Falls SD 57105 B Liverpool England UK 1935 s Eric & Ida. MD U of Liverpool 1959. D 2/2/1987 Bp Craig Barry Anderson. m 5/8/1958 Mary Pitt-Hart. D Calv Cathd Sioux Falls SD 1987-1996.

PITTMAN, Albert Calhoun (WA) 403 Russell Ave # 812, Gaithersburg MD 20877 **Ret 1992-** B Greenville MS 1930 s Albert & Mollie. BA U Rich 1951; BD Colgate Rochester Crozer DS 1954; BD CRDS 1954; Kalamazoo Coll 1974; Cert VTS 1981. D 5/31/1981 Bp Charles Bennison Sr P 11/1/1981 Bp John Thomas Walker. m 8/21/1953 Julia W Pittman c 3. R Chr Ch Port Tobacco Paris La Plata MD 1981-1991; Serv Amer Bapt Ch in OH - WI - MI 1954-1979.

PITTMAN, David West (NC) 218 Pine Cove Drive, Inman SC 29349 B Greenville SC 1948 s Wayne & Dorothy. BA VMI 1970; MDiv VTS 1973. D 6/5/1973 P 12/12/1973 Bp William Henry Marmion. m 5/17/1970 Alene Belle Wright c 2. R S Ptr's Epis Ch Charlotte NC 2001-2011; R H Trin Epis Ch Gainesville FL 1986-2001; R Trin Ch Staunton VA 1973-1986.

PITTMAN, Warren Lewis (NC) 2903 County Clare Rd, Greensboro NC 27407 B Los Angeles CA 1949 s Franklin & Helen. BA Duke 1971; MDiv VTS 1974. D 6/15/1974 P 1/4/1975 Bp Robert Claflin Rusack. m 6/1/2011 Ayliffe Blake Mumford c 2. R All SS Ch Greensboro NC 1996-2015; 1993-1996; S Anselm Of Cbury Par Garden Grove CA 1980-1993; S Mich's Mssn Anaheim CA 1976-1980; Yth Dir All SS-By-The-Sea Par Santa Barbara CA 1974-1975; Chr The King Epis Ch Santa Barbara CA 1974-1975; Yth Dir Trin Epis Ch Santa Barbara CA 1974-1975. wlpplus@aol.com

PITTS, John Robert (Tex) 3652 Chevy Chase, Houston TX 77019 **Mng Prncpl Texas Star Allnce 2010-; Sr Counsel Akin Gump Straus Hauer & Feld 1997-; Gnrl Counsel Lt. Gvnr of Texas 1995-; Partnr Vinson & Elkins 1973-** B Dallas TX 1947 s Roy & Agnes. BBA SMU 1968; MBA SMU 1969; JD SMU 1972; MDiv VTS 1987. D 6/29/1987 Bp Gordon Taliaferro Charlton P 2/1/1988 Bp Maurice Manuel Benitez. m 9/7/2002 Mary Bain c 2. S Paul's Epis Ch Pflugerville TX 1998; S Matt's Ch Austin TX 1991-1996; Cn To Ordnry For Mssn & Prog The Great Cmsn Fndt Houston TX 1990-1991; Asst to R S Jn The Div Houston TX 1987-1989.

PITTS, Kristen Tossell (WA) St Andrew's Episcopal Church, 4512 College Ave, College Park MD 20740 **S Andr's Epis Ch Coll Pk MD 2016-** B Greenwood SC 1986 d Joe & Linda. B.A. Furman U; M.Div. VTS. D 6/3/2016 Bp William Andrew Waldo P 4/2/2017 Bp Mariann Edgar Budde. m 4/29/2016 Elizabeth Ida Pitts Tossell.

PITZER, Elaine Virginia (Spok) St Stephen's Episcopal Church, 5720 S Perry St, Spokane WA 99223 **D S Steph's Epis Ch Spokane WA 2012-** B Detroit MI 1943 d John & Virginia. D 10/21/2012 Bp James E Waggoner Jr. m 9/13/1980 Thomas D Pitzer c 2.

PITZER, John M (La) **S Jas Epis Ch Baton Rouge LA 2016-** Rec 5/21/2016 as Priest Bp Morris King Thompson Jr.

PIVER, Jane Duncan (Va) 53 Ridgemont Road, Ruckersville VA 22968 **Vic Gr Ch Stanardsville VA 2007-** B Rochester NY 1950 d Edward & Frances. BSN U Roch 1972; MSN U of Pennsylvania 1980; MDiv VTS 2000. D 6/24/2000 Bp Clifton Daniel III P 2/6/2001 Bp Peter J Lee. c 2. Asst Pohick Epis Ch Lorton VA 2002-2007; Vic S Andr's Ch Burke VA 2000-2002; Trin Epis Ch Lorton VA 2000-2002.

PIXCAR-POL, Tomas (PR) PO Box 3184, Guayama PR 00785 **Vic Dio Puerto Rico Trujillo Alto PR 2009-, 2004-2005, 2000-2003; Mision La Santa Cruz Lares PR 2009-** B El Quiche GT 1963 s Manuel & Petronila. Rafael Landivar U 1987; RC Sem 1989; Panama Natl U PA 1991; Cert Theol Stud Epis TS of the SW 1993. D 9/21/1993 Bp James Hamilton Ottley P 7/15/1995 Bp Clarence Wallace Hayes. Vic Dio Guatemala New York NY 2005-2009; Vic Dio The Dominican Republic (Iglesia Epis Dominicana) Gazcue Santo Domingo 1999-2003; Vic Dio Panama 1994-1997.

PIZZONIA, Wanda (Mass) Post Road & Ring'S End Road, Darien CT 06820 B Roanoke VA 1953 d Joseph & Nellie. BD Roa 1975; MDiv Ya Berk 1998. D 6/12/1999 Bp Clarence Nicholas Coleridge P 2/1/2000 Bp Andrew Donnan Smith. m 5/24/1980 Daniel G Pizzonia c 4. Ch Of The Adv Medfield MA 2004-2008; Assoc R S Lk's Par Darien CT 1999-2003.

PIZZUTO, Vincent Anthony (Cal) 171 Forrest Ave, Fairfax CA 94930 B Jersey City NJ 1967 s Vincent & Jeanine. BA St Bonaventure U 1989; MEd Boston Coll 1995; MA Cath U of Leuven 1999; PhD Cath U of Leuven 2003. Rec 12/6/2014 as Priest Bp Marc Handley Andrus. newskellig@mac.com

PLACE, Donald Gordon (WMass) 52 County Road, Pownal VT 05261 B Worcester MA 1951 s Robert & Martha. BA Wms 1974; MDiv Yale DS 1977. D 6/15/1977 P 1/14/1978 Bp Morris Fairchild Arnold. m 7/18/1981 Catherine M Place. Dio Wstrn Massachusetts Springfield 1996-2003; All S's Ch of the Berkshires No Adams MA 1996-2002; R Emm Ch Braintree MA 1989-1995; S Asaph's Par Ch Bowling Green VA 1984-1989; St Peters Ch Fredericksbrg VA 1984-1989; Vauters Ch Loretto VA 1984-1989; R S Ptr's Port Royal Port Royal VA 1983-1989; R Vauter Ch 1983-1989; S Paul's Sch Clearwater FL 1981-1983; 1979-1981; Cur Epis Ch Of S Thos Taunton MA 1977-1979. Fllshp of the Way of the Cross 2002.

PLACE, Donald Lee Andrew (NY) 111 5th Ave Apt 1206, Pittsburgh PA 15222 **Dio York Engl 1982-; Vic S Gabr & S Nich Essex Uk 1981-** B Olean NY 1937 s Harold & Margaret. Cert Diac Sch 1974; Cert GTS 1976. D 2/23/1974 Bp Kenneth Daniel Wilson Anand P 4/1/1979 Bp James Stuart Wetmore. m 6/6/1970 Mary Jane Hastings. S Steph's Epis Ch Woodlaw Bronx NY 1987-1988; Sr Cur S Tim's Middlesbrough Engl 1979-1981; Chapl S Lk & Roosevelt Hosp In New York City 1977-1979; Cur Ch Of The H Apos New York NY 1977-1978; S Ptr's Ch Bronx NY 1977-1978. Auth, "Living Ch".

PLANK, David Bellinger (LI) 26 Hampton Towne Estates, Hampton NH 03842 **Ret 2002-** B Little Falls NY 1938 s Harold & Doris. BS U Roch 1960; MDiv PDS 1967; MEd S Lawr Canton NY 1975. D 6/3/1967 Bp Allen Webster Brown P 12/24/1967 Bp Charles Bowen Persell Jr. m 6/25/1960 Francelia R Plank c 4. P-in-c S Jas Ch Brookhaven NY 1996-2002; P-in-c S Andr's Ch Mastic Bch NY 1990-2002; Asst to R S Mk's Ch Westhampton Bch NY 1984-1990; St Stephens Ch Bucksport ME 1977-1984; Trin Ch Castine ME 1977-1984; R S Phil's Ch Norwood NY 1969-1977; R Zion Ch Colton NY 1969-1977; Cur S Steph's Ch Delmar NY 1967-1969.

PLANTZ, Christine Marie (Neb) 605 S Chestnut St, Kimball NE 69145 **R S Hildas Ch Kimball NE 2013-** B Moscow ID 1946 d John & Marian. AB Shimer Coll 1968; BS Chadron St Coll 1977; MDiv SWTS 2009. D 12/11/2009 P 6/19/2010 Bp Joe Goodwin Burnett. m 5/19/1973 Charles Plantz. P-in-c Dio Nebraska Omaha NE 2010-2012, Exec Cmsn 2011-.

PLASKE, Susan Ann (Alb) 68 S Swan St, Albany NY 12210 B Albany NY 1959 d Gordon & Eileen. AAS Maria Coll 1979. D 6/4/2011 Bp William Howard Love. m 10/3/1981 Kenneth Plaske c 5.

PLATER, Ormonde (La) 150 Broadway Apt 1112, New Orleans LA 70118 **Died 8/6/2016** B New York NY 1933 s Richard & Eleanore. BA Van 1955; MA Tul 1965; PhD Tul 1969. D 7/11/1971 Bp Iveson Batchelor Noland. m 7/19/1957 Kathleen Plater c 3. Ret LA 2013-2016; D Trin Ch New Orleans LA 2007-2012; Archd Dio Louisiana New Orleans LA 1998-2005, Archd 1997-2005; D Gr Ch New Orleans LA 1996-2006; Ed of Diakoneo NAAD 1985-1995; Pres NCD 1984-1987; D S Anna's Ch New Orleans LA 1971-1995. Auth, "Deacons in the Liturg," Ch Pub, 2009; Auth, "Passion Gospels," Ch Pub, 2007; Auth, "Many Servnt," Cowley, 2004; Auth, "Intsn," Cowley, 1995; Co-Auth, "Cajun Dancing," Pelican Pub Co, 1993. Associated Parishes 1977; NAAD 1987.

PLATSON, Julie L (Ak) PO Box 1130, Sitka AK 99835 **S Ptr's By-The-Sea Sitka AK 2015-; Hospice Chapl Nathan Adelson Hospice Pahrump NV 2003-; P S Mart's In The Desert Pahrump NV 2001-, Transitional D 2000-2001** B St Petersburg FL 1961 d Daniel & Margaret. Berklee Sch of Mus 1979. D 10/1/2000 Bp George Nelson Hunt III P 5/6/2001 Bp Katharine Jefferts Schori.

PLATT, Gretchen Mary (SwFla) 1562 Dormie Dr, Gladwin MI 48624 B Biwabik MN 1936 d Ernest & Gladys. BS Estrn Michigan U 1958; MEd Wayne 1973; MEd Saginaw Vlly St U 1988. D 10/20/2002 Bp Edwin Max Leidel Jr. m 5/11/1985 Kenneth E Platt.

PLATT, Nancy Grace Van Dyke (Me) 192 Cross Hill Rd, Augusta ME 04330 B Kane PA 1937 d William & Alice. BA Hobart and Wm Smith Colleges 1959; MTASCP Montfiore Hosp 1960; SCAC SCAC Chicago IL 1975; MDiv SWTS 1975; CPE Chicago IL 1976. D 6/16/1975 Bp Quintin Ebenezer Primo Jr P 4/30/1980 Bp Morris Fairchild Arnold. c 3. R S Matt's Epis Ch Hallowell ME 1984-2003; Asst R Chr Ch Joliet IL 1983-1984; Asst Ch Of The Epiph Chicago IL 1977-1983. co-Auth, "So You Think You Don't Know One," *Ch Pub*, 2010; "Closed Doors, Open Hearts," *Forw Mvmt*, 2008; Auth, "Healing P & Par," *Addiction*, 1996; Auth, "Pstr Care To Cancer Patients," 1977; Auth, "Alcoholic's 12 Steps Into Life," 1976. APHA. CPE Resrch Awd 1976.

PLATT, Thomas Walter (Pa) 824 S New St, West Chester PA 19382 **Ret 2002-; Dn Of Stds Cbury Ecum Sem 1995-** B Harmony PA 1933 s Ira & Frances. BA Washington and Jefferson U 1955; MA U Pgh 1960; PhD U of Pennsylvania 1966; STB PDS 1967. D 6/10/1967 P 12/30/1967 Bp Robert Lionne DeWitt. m 6/1/1957 Patricia S Platt. Assoc R Emer The Ch Of The H Trin W Chester PA 1971-2002. Auth, "The Conflict Of Sci & Rel A Confusion Re-Visited"; Auth, "Fact & Value: Reflections In Contextual Relativity"; Auth, "The Pitfall Of Postmodernism Chance & Equity"; Auth, "Sci As Human Value"; Auth, "The Concept Of Violence As Discriptive," *The Concept Of Violence As Discriptive & Polemic*. Assoc R Emer Ch Of The H Trin 2002.

PLATT, Warren Christopher (NY) 255 W 23rd St Apt 3-DE, New York NY 10011 B Far Rockaway NY 1945 s William & Ida. BA Cor 1966; BD UTS 1969; PhD Col 1982. D 6/1/1969 P 12/1/1969 Bp Horace W B Donegan. Hon Asst Ch Of The Trsfg New York NY 1972-2004; Cur All SS Ch Orange NJ 1969-1970. "Translations of BCP in the Resrch Libraries," *Biblion 1, No. 1*, 1992; Auth, "The Polish Natl Cath Ch," *Ch Hist*, 1992; Auth, "Var arts"; Auth, "The Afr Orth Ch," *Ch Hist*. HSEC; SocMary.

PLATT-HENDREN, Barbara Maria (NC) 222 Normandy Dr, Clayton NC 27527 B UK 1946 d Frederick & Marguerite. BA Elmhurst Coll 1968; MRE Andover Newton TS 1970; Cert EDS 1985. D 6/1/1985 Bp John Bowen Coburn P 5/1/1986 Bp Roger W Blanchard. m 6/26/1982 Shelby Ion Hendren c 3. Gr Epis Mssn Clayton NC 1998-2013; P-inCharge Wendell Epis Explorers Wendell NC 1998-2001; P-in-c Wendell Epis Explorers 1998-2000; Int Chapl S Mary's Epis HS 1998-1999; Asst R S Jn's Ch Beverly MA 1986-1996; Asst Min S Ptr's Ch Beverly MA 1985-1986. SCHC 2008.

PLAZAS, Carlos Alberto (Chi) 1333 W Argyle St, Chicago IL 60640 **R Ch Of S Mich And All Ang Berwyn IL 1999-** B Iza Colombia 1931 s Jose & Rosa. LTh Colombia Sa CO; PhD U Chi; PhD Xavier U Colombia 1958; PhD Loyola U 1972. Rec 8/7/1972 Bp James Winchester Montgomery. m 8/26/1972 Blanca Plazas. S Aug Coll Chicago IL 1989-2000; Vic Cristo Rey Chicago IL 1979-1984; Soc And Educational Serv Chicago IL 1978-1980; Serv Ch Of Venezuela 1958-1965. Auth, "A Proposal On Mntl Hlth Educ & Consult In The Uptown Edgewater Area"; Auth, "Parent Chld Latino Cntr"; Auth, "S Aug Bilingual Cmnty Coll"; Auth, "Relationships Between The Stable m"; Auth, "A Proposal On Mntl Hlth Educ". Amer Coll Of Forensic Examinery; APA; Illinois Psychol Assn; Illionois Alco And Other Drug Abuse Profsnl Certification Assn. El Puente Awd S Aug Coll 2000; The Humanitarian Awd For The Year Pr ChmbrCom 1985; Thos & Elinor Wright Awd; DD GTS.

PLESTED, Robert William Harvey (LI) 5402 Timber Trace St, San Antonio TX 78250 B Queens NY 1939 s Leslie & Janet. BA LIU CW Post 1966; MDiv PDS 1969; Dplma Command and Gnrl Stff Coll 1984; Dplma Air War Coll 1987; MA S Marys U San Antonio TX 1990. D 6/14/1969 P 12/20/1969 Bp Jonathan Goodhue Sherman. m 12/21/1963 Denise Elizabeth Plested. Assoc Ch Of The Resurr Windcrest TX 1996-2002; Cmssnr & Chair San Antonio Fire & Police Civil Serv Cmsn 1995-2001; Int S Fran Epis Ch Victoria TX 1994-1995; Int S Alb's Ch Harlingen TX 1994; Int & Consult Var 1990-1996; Non-par 1988-1990; Dept. U.S. AF Off Of Bsh For ArmdF New York NY 1972-1988; Chapl USAF 1972-1988; Firefighter & Chapl Rocky Point NY and Bexar Cnty TX 1971-1994; Vic S Anselm's Ch Shoreham NY 1970-1972; Cur S Jn's Ch Huntington NY 1969-1970. Auth, "arts & Study Papers On Chaplncy, Mnstry & Pstr Care Mgmt," 2003; Auth, "Var Loc And Natl Pubs," 1979. Fed Of Fire Chapl 1988; Intl Conf Of Police Chapl 1979; New York St Assn Of Fire Chapl 1971; Texas Police Assn 1997. Profsnl Mltry Homors U.S. AF 1972-88 1988.

PLIMPTON, Barbara Wilson (WNC) PO Box 968, Marion NC 28752 B Worcester MA 1941 d Chester & Stella. MA EDS; BA Emml 1963; MEd Tray St U 1969; Dip Ang Stud Sewanee: The U So, TS 2007. D 9/15/2007 P 2/15/2009 Bp Porter Taylor. m 3/23/1968 Fred Plimpton.

PLOVANICH, Ede Marie (CGC) B Hattiesburg MS 1959 BS U of Mississippi 1983; MDiv Epis TS of the SW 2003. D 6/4/2006 P 4/21/2007 Bp Philip Menzie Duncan II. m 7/31/2003 Robert Plovanich c 1. The Epis Ch Of The Nativ Dothan AL 2006-2013.

PLUCKER, Susan (NCal) 1200 Fulton Ave Apt 227, Sacramento CA 95825 B Philadelphia PA 1947 d Charles & Mary Margaret. AS Northland Pioneer Coll Winslow AZ 1980; BA U of Arizona 1988; MDiv CDSP 1991. D 6/8/1991 Bp Joseph Thomas Heistand P 12/6/1991 Bp Jerry Alban Lamb. c 2. Assoc Epis Ch Of Our Sav Placerville CA 2011-2014; R S Lk's Ch Auburn CA 2004-2010; R S Ptr's Epis Ch Red Bluff CA 1993-2004; Asst Trin Ch Folsom CA 1991-1993.

PLUMMER, Catherine B (NAM) Episcopal Church in Navajoland, PO Box 720, Farmington NM 87499 **Navajoland Area Mssn Farmington NM 2012-** B Bluff UT 1949 d Albert & Lena. Cert Cook Chr Trng Sch; ECN Stff Trng; EFM. D 6/9/2012 P 5/11/2013 Bp David Earle Bailey. c 2. San Juan Mssn Farmington NM 1996-1998.

PLUMMER, Cathlena Arnette (NAM) PO Box 720, Farmington NM 87499 **Vic All SS Farmington NM 2015-; P Navajoland Area Mssn Farmington NM 2014-** B Monticello UT 1980 d Steven & Catherine. Assoc of Sci Coll of Estrn Utah at San Juan 2004; Cert of Angl Stds CDSP 2011; Cert of Angl Stds CDSP 2011; MDiv CDSP 2014; MDiv CDSP 2014. D 6/14/2014 P 11/7/2015 Bp David Earle Bailey. ecncplummer@gmail.com

PLUMMER, Dale Wilkinson (RG) 505 N. Pennsylvania, Roswell NM 88201 **R S Andr's Ch Roswell NM 2011-** B Newton KS 1958 s John & Evelyn. BS Wichita St U 1992; MDiv Sewanee: The U So, TS 2001. D 3/17/2001 P 10/14/2001 Bp William Edward Smalley. m 11/3/1984 Sharon K Plummer c 2. P-in-c Ch Of The Cov Jct City KS 2003-2011; D S Dav's Epis Ch Topeka KS 2001-2003.

PLUMMER, Lynn Whitman (NC) 8600 Mount Holly Hntrsvlle Rd, Huntersville NC 28078 B Salisbury NC 1955 s Locke & Mildred. BA Catawba Coll 1977. D 1/28/2017 Bp Anne Hodges-Copple. m 8/19/1979 Deborah Webb Deborah Jean Webb c 2.

PLUMMER, Mark Alton (NC) Grace Episcopal Church, 419 S Main St, Lexington NC 27292 **R Gr Epis Ch Lexington NC 2015-** B N Tonowanda NY 1955 s Berton & Coletta. AAS Hudson Vlly Cmnty Coll 1977; BA S Jn Fisher Coll 1998; MDiv Methodist TS in Ohio 2002; Cert Ang Stud Bex Sem 2006. D 6/23/2007 Bp Kenneth Lester Price P 6/28/2008 Bp Thomas Edward Breidenthal. m 6/21/2003 Cathleen H Carey c 2. R Gr Epis Ch Willoughby OH 2010-2013; Asst Trin Ch Columbus OH 2008-2010; D Chr Epis Ch Of Springfield Springfield OH 2007-2008. rector@gracechurchlexington.org

PLUNKET-BREWTON, Callie Dawn (Ala) 410 N Pine St, Florence AL 35630 **Assoc Trin Epis Ch Florence AL 2013-; Chapl Dio Alabama Birmingham 2011-** B Dunedin New Zealand 1976 d Rodney & Margaret. MDiv PrTS 1996; BA Texas Tech U 1996; PhD PrTS 2009. D 6/4/2011 Bp John Mckee Sloan Sr P 12/13/2011 Bp Henry Nutt Parsley Jr. m 1/8/2005 Vincent James Brewton c 3. S Jn's Ch Decatur AL 2012-2013.

PLUNKETT, Phillip Riley (Ark) 7 Sonata Trail, Little Rock AR 72205 **Asst P S Mk's Epis Ch Little Rock AR 2003-; Ret 1994-** B Little Rock AR 1932 s Benjamin & Florence. BS U of Cntrl Arkansas 1954; MEd U of Arkansas 1966; MDiv Epis TS of the SW 1970. D 6/17/1970 Bp Robert Raymond Brown P 12/1/1970 Bp Christoph Keller Jr. m 5/6/2006 Jo Ann Gates Plunkett c 2. 1992-1994; Chr Epis Ch Forrest City AR 1985-1986; P-in-c S Lk's Brinkley AR 1981-1992; Gr Ch Wynne AR 1981-1982; 1979-1980; R S Ptr Tollville AR 1973-1978; St Ptr's Epis Ch Devalls Bluff AR 1973-1978; S Alb's Ch Stuttgart AR 1970-1976.

POBJECKY, Richard Richard (CFla) 414 Pine St, Titusville FL 32796 B 1940 Rec 1/31/1975 as Priest Bp William Hopkins Folwell. m 9/15/1973 Judith A Pobjecky c 4. S Gabriels Ch Titusville FL 1977-2009; S Andr's Epis Ch Ft Pierce FL 1975-1977.

POCALYKO, Richard Peter (Pgh) 415 Stone Mill Trl Ne, Atlanta GA 30328 B Palmerton PA 1946 s Peter & Ruth. Fuller TS; BA Leh 1968; MDiv VTS 1971; PrTS 1997. D 6/26/1971 P 2/26/1972 Bp William Foreman Creighton. m 8/16/1969 Cynthia Gail Austin. Dn Trin Cathd Pittsburgh PA 2000-2004; Cathd Of S Phil Atlanta GA 1993-2000, Assoc 1990-1993; Dept Of Stwdshp Dio Atlanta Atlanta GA 1990-1994, Com 1987-1989, Strng Com Cler Assn 1982-1986, Chair - Cmsn On Consulting 1982-1983, Chair - Dept Of Stwdshp 1978-1981, Dept Of Stwdshp 1976-1977, Chair - Cmsn On Consulting 1975, Cmsn On Consulting 1974; S Dunst's Epis Ch Atlanta GA 1980-1992; Assoc S Lk's Epis Ch Atlanta GA 1973-1980; Assoc S Andr's Epis Ch Coll Pk MD 1971-1973.

POGGEMEYER JR, Lewis Eugene (U) 2849 Polk Ave, Ogden UT 84403 **D Ch Of The Gd Shpd Ogden UT 1980-** B McKeesport PA 1946 s Lewis & Aureline. BA K SU 1971. D 9/13/1980 Bp Otis Charles. m 6/7/1969 Karen Joyce West c 3. Dioc Stndg Com 1983-1986.

POGOLOFF, Stephen Mark (NC) 218 Forestwood Dr, Durham NC 27707 B Washington DC 1949 s David & Florence. BA JHU 1971; BA Oxf GB 1978; MDiv GTS 1979; MA Oxf GB 1984; PhD Duke 1990. D 8/11/1979 Bp David Keller Leighton Sr P 3/1/1980 Bp Walter Decoster Dennis Jr. m 9/23/1973 Christina Pogoloff. P-in-c St Elizabeths Epis Ch Apex NC 1993-1999; Assoc S Jos's Ch Durham NC 1984-1993; Assoc R All Ang' Ch New York NY 1980-1984; Cur S Jn's Ch Larchmont NY 1979-1980. Auth, "Isocrates & Contemporary Hermeneutics"; Auth, "Logos & Sophia: The Rhetorical Situation Of 1 Corinthians". SBL.

POGUE, Blair Alison (Minn) 2136 Carter Avenue, Saint Paul MN 55108 **R S Matt's Ch S Paul MN 2005-** B Los Angeles CA 1964 d William & Gwen. BA Whitman Coll 1986; MDiv Yale DS 2000; D.Min. Luther Sem 2013. D 6/24/2000 P 2/6/2001 Bp Peter J Lee. m 5/27/2000 Dwight J Zscheile c 1. Assoc R Ch Of The H Comf Vienna VA 2002-2005; Asst R Trin Ch Upperville VA 2000-2002. Auth, "Ongoing Discernment: The Way of Jesus," *Vstry Pa-*

pers, ECF, 2014; Auth, "St. Matt's: Living Into God's Kingdom," *Journ of Missional Pract*, Allelon, 2013; Auth, "Three Essays on Romans 8," *Feasting on the Word: Preaching the Revised Common Lectionary*, Westminster Jn Knox Press, 2011; Auth, "Cultivating a Culture of Discernment," *Vstry Papers July/August 2010*, ECF, 2010; Auth, "Kentucky Bapt Rel Culture, 1780-1860," *Kentucky: Settling The Promised Land*, U Of Kentucky Press, 1999. R. Lansing Hicks Prize Ya Berk 2000. rector@stmatthewsmn.org

POGUE, Ronald D (Tex) 5616 Shady Hill, Arlington TX 76017 B Houston TX 1948 s Alfred & Velma. BS U of Houston 1970; MDiv Candler TS Emory U 1973; DMin Houston Grad TS 1997. D 12/3/1997 Bp Claude Edward Payne P 6/1/1998 Bp Leopoldo Jesus Alard. m 2/9/1969 Gay Elva Wunderlich c 2. S Jn's Cathd Denver CO 2016-2017; R S Jn's Epis Ch Jackson WY 2015-2016; Int Chr Ch Cranbrook Bloomfield Hills MI 2012-2014; Int Calv Epis Ch Ashland KY 2012; Int Ch Of The Gd Shpd Lexington KY 2010-2012; Int Trin Ch Lawr KS 2009-2010; R Trin Ch Galveston TX 1999-2009; Cn Chr Ch Cathd Houston TX 1997-1999. Auth, *Equipping Empowering Chr Leaders in Congregations*. Theta Phi. ron@sjcathedral.org

POIRIER, Esther (Oly) 4426 133rd Ave SE, Bellevue WA 98006 B 1948 d Frank. BA Coll of Wooster 1970; MA Natl Coll of Educ 1971; MDiv CDSP 2002. D 6/29/2002 Bp Sanford Zangwill Kaye Hampton P 1/25/2003 Bp Vincent Waydell Warner. P Ch Of The Gd Shpd Fed Way WA 2006-2016; Dio Olympia Seattle 2006; Vic Ch Of Our Sav Monroe WA 2002-2006.

POISSON OSH, Ellen Francis (USC) Convent of St. Helena, 414 Savannah Barony Drive, North Augusta SC 29841 **Epis-Muslim Relatns Com - Mem Dio New York New York NY 1999-, Epis-Muslim Relatns Com 1998-2008** B New London CT 1946 d Robert & Eleanor. BA Smith 1968; MLS Teheran U Teheran IR 1972; DLS Col 1983; DTheol. D 3/18/2000 P 9/16/2000 Bp Richard Frank Grein. P-in-c All SS Ch Beech Island SC 2011-2013; Int S Aug Of Cbury Ch Augusta GA 2008-2010; Dio New York 2004-2006; Asst The Ch Of The Epiph New York NY 2000-2001. Auth, "Citizen Diplomacy in Iran," *Natl Cath Reporter, Sept 22, 2006*, 2006. Alum/ae Prize in Eccl. Hist The GTS 2000; Wmn Hist Proj Prize The GTS 2000; H Land Travel Prize The GTS 1999; H.P. Montgomery Prize The GTS 1998.

POIST, David Hahn (Va) 341 Woodlands Rd, Charlottesville VA 22901 B Baltimore MD 1940 s Emmett & Yolanda. BA W&M 1962; MDiv Ya Berk 1965; MA JHU 1969. D 6/22/1965 P 5/19/1966 Bp Harry Lee Doll. m 6/27/1970 Elizabeth Williams Poist c 2. S Paul's Memi Charlottesvlle VA 1977-2006; Chapl U of Virginia 1977-2006; Koinonia Fndt Baltimore MD 1970-1977; DP Ecum Campus Mnstry Dio Maryland Baltimore MD 1966-1970; S Paul's Par Baltimore MD 1966-1968; Asst Ch Of The Ascen Westminster MD 1965-1966; Chapl Wstrn Maryland Coll 1965-1966; Peace Cmsn Dio Virginia Richmond VA 1986-1992.

POKORNY, Wayne Douglas (Ct) 30 Woodland St Apt 11NP, Hartford CT 06105 **Assoc Gr Epis Ch Hartford CT 2000-** B Oak Park IL 1938 s Frank & Anna. BA Beloit Coll 1960; MDiv GTS 1967; DMin GTF 1986. D 6/10/1967 Bp Robert Lionne DeWitt P 2/1/1968 Bp Ned Cole. c 3. Chf Chapl US VetA Med Cntr Tomah WI 1991-2000; Chf Chapl US VetA Med Cntr Charleston SC 1988-1991; ArmdF and Fed Ministires New York NY 1987-2000; Chapl US VetA Med Cntr W Haven CT 1980-1988; Ch Of S Jn By The Sea W Haven W Haven CT 1978-1986; Dio Connecticut Meriden CT 1978-1981, Vic 1978-1981, Exec Coun 1976-1978; Natl Chapl Gld of S Barn for Nurses New York NY 1977-1983; Vice-Chapl Gld of S Barn for Nurses 1975-1977; R Trin-S Mich's Ch Fairfield CT 1974-1978; Dn, Ithaca-Cortland Dist Dio Cntrl New York Liverpool NY 1972-1974; R Calv Ch Homer NY 1969-1974; Cur Emm Ch Norwich NY 1967-1969. Auth, "arts & Bk Revs". AASECT 1981; Societas Liturgica 1977.

POLANCO DE LA CRUZ, Leonel (Ga) B 1977 s Eulogio & Francisca. Licenciado en Teologia Centro de Estudio Teologico. D 2/15/2015 P 2/13/2016 Bp Julio Cesar Holguin-Khoury. Dio The Dominican Republic (Iglesia Epis Dominicana) Gazcue Santo Domingo 2015-2016.

POLGLASE, Kenneth Alexis (Nwk) 2796 Rudder Dr, Annapolis MD 21401 **Ret 1994-** B Brooklyn NY 1931 s Alexis & Hazel. BA Wag 1953; Cert Theol Stud GTS 1956; MA FD 1972. D 9/1/1956 P 4/27/1957 Bp James Pernette DeWolfe. m 5/3/1953 Carolyn H Polglase c 4. Non-par 1985-1994; Trin Epis Ch of Bergen Cnty Allendale NJ 1964-1984; R S Mart's Ch Maywood NJ 1960-1964; Cur Gr Epis Ch Massapequa NY 1957-1960; Cur Trin Epis Ch Roslyn NY 1956-1957.

POLING, Jason Alder (Md) **Dio Maryland Baltimore MD 2016-** B New Haven CT 1972 s Wesley & Carol Ann. MDiv Sem of the E; MA St. Mary's Sem & U; BA Wms; DMin Biblic TS 2012; STM GTS 2015. D 6/7/2015 P 12/8/2015 Bp Eugene Taylor Sutton. m 8/3/1996 Mary Ann F Fasold c 2. vicar@hildas.org

POLK, Perry Willis (NCal) Grace Episcopal Church, 1405 Kentucky St, Fairfield CA 94533 **Dep Wing Chapl CAP California Wing 2013-; Squadron Chapl CAP Squadron 22 Travis AFB 2012-** B Waco TX 1940 s Willis & Florence. BBA Baylor U 1962; MBA U of Oklahoma 1967; MA NW Nazarene U 2006; MDiv CDSP 2008. D 11/22/2008 P 6/13/2009 Bp Barry Leigh Beisner. m 4/11/1970 Sylvia Marie Polk c 3. Int Gr Epis Ch Fairfield CA 2014, Int 2014-, As-

soc 2008-2014; Cert Lay Min Trng Coordntr California-Nevada Conf UMC W Sacramento 2005-2013. revperrypolk@gmail.com

POLK, Thomas Robb (RG) 90 S Longspur Dr, The Woodlands TX 77380 **Ret Dio THE RIO GRANDE 1986-** B Memphis TN 1926 s Oscar & Mary. BGE U of Oklahoma 1946; MSGE U of Oklahoma 1948; MDiv Sewanee: The U So, TS 1973; MSGE U of Oklahoma 2048. D 6/10/1973 Bp Girault M Jones P 3/12/1976 Bp Reginald Heber Gooden. c 1. R S Mary's Ch Lovington NM 1981-1986; Dio Louisiana New Orleans LA 1978; All SS Epis Ch Ponchatoula LA 1977-1980; Ch Of The Incarn Amite LA 1977-1980; Chapl Hm 1977-1979; Epis Coll Cntr Hammond LA 1977; Cur S Paul's Ch New Orleans LA 1976-1977, Asst 1975-1976; Vic All SS Ch Wheatland WY 1973-1975; All SS Epis Ch Torrington WY 1973-1975; Ch Of Our Sav Hartville WY 1973-1975; S Geo's Ch Lusk WY 1973-1975; Asst Chr Ch Epis S Pittsburg TN 1970-1973. LKOT U OF OKLAHOMA, NORMAN 1945; RIVERTON MASONIC LOGEG #26, A.F.&A.M 1956. Tau Beta Pi U of Oklahoma, Norman 1948; Sigma Xi U of Oklahoma, Norman 1946; Sigma Tau U of Oklahoma, Normal 1945.

POLLACH, Gideon Liam (LI) 125 Court Street, 11SH, Brooklyn NY 11201 **R St Jn's Ch Cold Sprg Harbor NY 2016-** B Long Beach CA 1975 s Samuel & Mary. St Albans Sch for Boys 1992; BA Trin 1996; MDiv GTS 2006. D 6/24/2006 P 2/12/2007 Bp Peter J Lee. m 6/1/2002 Sarah Broaddens Pollach c 3. Epis HS Alexandria VA 2008-2016; Assoc St. Barth Ch New York NY 2006-2007; Dir of Yth Mnstrs S Steph's Ch Richmond VA 1998-2003; Chr Ch Alexandria VA 1998-1999; Bp's Clerk The Dio Virginia Richmond VA 1997-1998. gideon@stjcsh.org

POLLARD, Richard Allen (Pgh) 1750 Hastings Mill Rd, Pittsburgh PA 15241 **Chapl (Vol) Grane Hospice 2010-** B Ridgway PA 1946 s Ernest & Mary. TESM; BS Penn 1968; JD Duquesne U 1976. D 6/12/2004 P 12/17/2004 Bp Robert William Duncan. m 11/5/1988 Susan Hurlbut Pollard c 4. R All SS Epis Ch Pittsburgh PA 2011-2014; Asst Chr Epis Ch No Hills Pittsburgh PA 2008-2012; Chapl (Vol) Heartland Hospice 2005-2010; Asst S Paul's Epis Ch Pittsburgh PA 2005-2009; Vic Ch Of The Adv Pittsburgh PA 2004-2005.

POLLARD III, Robert (NY) 400 S Ocean Blvd PHB, Palm Beach FL 33480 **Ret - Asst. P Ch of Beth by the Sea Palm Bch Florida 2010-** B Asheville NC 1927 s Robert & Mary. MIT 1944; BA Hav 1950; MDiv VTS 1954; Coll of Preachers 1966. D 6/9/1954 P 7/23/1955 Bp Matthew George Henry. m 8/18/1985 Cornelia Pollard c 2. Asst The Epis Ch Of Beth-By-The-Sea Palm Bch FL 1992; Vic S Matt's Sum Chap Sugar Hill NH 1986-2000; Evan Com Dio New York New York NY 1978-1984, Wkr P Coordntr 1977-1984, Alt Del Dio Coun 1980-1984, Chair 1965-1979; R S Paul's Ch Yonkers NY 1978-1984; Adj Prof Cathd Of St Jn The Div New York NY 1978-1979; Vic All SS Epis Ch Vlly Cottage NY 1961-1970; Cur H Trin Epis Ch W Palm Bch FL 1958-1961; Chapl Tuller Sch Tucson AZ 1956-1957; S Fran Of Assisi Cherokee NC 1954-1956; P S Jn's Ch Sylva NC 1954-1956. Auth, "Power, Love, and Chr Discipleship," *Coll of Preachers Thesis*, Self-Pub, 2007. Soc Of Colonial Wars in the St of Florida, Chapl 1986; Soc Of The Cincinnati In The St Of Virginia, Chapl 1951.

POLLEY, Bonnie Bonnabel (Nev) 1631 Ottawa Drive, Las Vegas NV 89169 **Chapl Clark Cnty Detention Cntr Las Vegas Nevada 1983-** B Lake Charles LA 1939 d Robert & Rose. Colorado Inst of Bus; U CO; U of New Mex. D 12/9/1982 Bp Wesley Frensdorff. m 8/30/1958 David Cleland Polley c 3. NAAD 1984; Ord of S Lk 1987. Chapl of the Year Salvation Army 2004.

POLLEY, Seth (Az) 5 Gardner St, Bisbee AZ 85603 B Albuquerque NM 1962 s David & Bonnie. BA U of Nevada at Reno 1986; MDiv CDSP 1992; MA U of Nevada at Reno 1998. D 4/2/1995 P 1/27/1996 Bp Stewart Clark Zabriskie. m 2/15/1997 Lori Valerie Keyne c 1. Vic/Border Mssnr Dio Arizona Phoenix AZ 2006-2013; Int Chapl Emmaus Collgt Chap at UofA Tucson AZ 2005-2006; Asst R S Jn's Ch Roanoke VA 2002-2005; Exec Coun Appointees New York NY 2001-2002, Mssy Dio Panama 2001-2002; Dio Panama 1999-2002; P-in-c St. Lk's Cathd Dio Panama Panama City 1999-2002; San Jose St. Cantebury Dio El Camino Real Salinas CA 1998; Yth Asst Chr Epis Ch Los Altos CA 1997-1999; ELM Cmnty Ch Reno NV 1995-1997; LP/ P-in-c E.L.M. Cmnty Ch Stead NV 1992-1997. Auth, "Borders and Blessings: Reflections on Our Natl Immigration Crisis from the Arizona Desert," *ATR*, 2010.

POLLINA, Roy Glen (SwVa) 311 E Church St, Martinsville VA 24112 B Oak Park IL 1951 s Roy & Dolores. BA Nthrn Illinois U 1973; MDiv Epis TS of the SW 1985. D 6/23/1985 P 5/4/1986 Bp James Barrow Brown. m 8/18/1973 Susan Pollina c 2. R Chr Ch Martinsville VA 2011-2015; P-in-c All SS Epis Ch Ponchatoula LA 2011; R S Mich's Epis Ch Mandeville LA 1986-2010; D Trin Ch New Orleans LA 1985-1986. Auth, "To Bless A Chld," *To Bless A Chld*, Ch Pub, 2009.

POLLITT, Michael James (Chi) 1376 Telegraph Rd., West Caln MI 19320 **Chf Chapl Va Hosp Coatesville PA 2002-** B Glens Falls NY 1949 s James & Dorothy. BA Providence Coll 1975; MDiv Mt S Marys Sem 1983; MA Mt St Marys Sem 1985; Cert Wstrn Michigan U 1996; DMin Cornerstone U 2001. Rec 6/25/2001 as Priest Bp Keith Lynn Ackerman. m 8/2/1993 Patricia Pollitt. Chapl/Addiction Ther Va Hosp Detroit MI 1998-2002; Chapl NG 1993-2001; Chapl U. S. Army Arlington VA 1989-1993. Auth, "Addiction, Relapse, And

Existentialism," *Chapl Today*, Assn Of Profsnl Chapl, 2003. Assembly Of Epis Healthcare Chapl 2001-2003; Natl Assn Of Veterans Affrs Chapl 1998-2003. Best Pract In Chapl Dept Of Veterans Affrs 2001.

POLLOCK, Christina (Spok) St. John the Evangelist Cathedral, 127 E. 12th Ave., Spokane WA 99202 **Died 6/2/2016** B Spokane WA 1951 d Marvin & Alyce. BA Estrn Washington U 1973; CPE D Formation Prog 1996. D 5/16/1998 Bp Frank Jeffrey Terry. m 12/18/1974 Wayne Thomas Pollock c 2. D Emm Ch Kellogg ID 2000-2002; Dio Spokane Spokane WA 1998-2004; COM Ch Of The Resurr Veradale WA 1998-2000.

POLLOCK, Douglas Stephen (Oly) 7701 Skansie Ave, Gig Harbor WA 98335 B Chicago IL 1942 s Neil & Frances. BS U IL 1965; MDiv Epis TS of the SW 1979. D 12/9/1978 P 6/17/1979 Bp Otis Charles. m 5/27/1967 Carol Ann Pollock c 2. R S Jn's Epis Ch Gig Harbor WA 1991-2010; R S Paul's Ch Klamath Fall OR 1983-1991; Ch Of The Gd Shpd Ogden UT 1980-1983; Dio Utah Salt Lake City UT 1979-1980.

POLLOCK, Elizabeth Good (Me) Po Box 896, York Harbor ME 03911 **Ret 1994-** B Van Wert OH 1926 d Roland & Myrtle. BS NWU 1948; MA Methodist TS in Ohio 1977; MDiv Methodist TS in Ohio 1979. D 4/14/1982 Bp William Grant Black P 6/2/1984 Bp Frederick Barton Wolf. m 3/26/1949 Clark Pollock. P-in-c S Steph The Mtyr Epis Ch Waterboro Cntr ME 1989-1994; Assoc S Geo's Epis Ch York ME 1984-1989; Asst S Jn's Ch Worthington OH 1982-1984; Dce Dio Sthrn Ohio Cincinnati OH 1979-1984.

POLLOCK, John Blackwell (EC) 1912 Shepard St, Morehead City NC 28557 **R S Andr's Ch Morehead City NC 2004-** B Georgetown SC 1959 s James & Elsie. Spartanburg Methodist Coll 1980; BA U of So Carolina 1983; MEd U of So Carolina 1985; Luth Theol Sthrn Sem 1994; MDiv Sewanee: The U So, TS 1996; DMin VTS 2011. D 6/8/1996 P 5/15/1997 Bp Dorsey Henderson. m 12/6/1997 Mary Withington. R S Paul's Epis Ch Clinton NC 1999-2004; Asst Chr Ch Greenville SC 1998-1999; Chapl Chr Ch Epis Sch Greenville SC 1997-1999; D S Matt's Epis Ch Spartanburg SC 1996-1997; Dep to GC Dio E Carolina Kinston NC 2006-2013, Stndg Com 2006-2009.

POLLOCK, Margaret (Va) 21517 Laytonsville Rd, Laytonsville MD 20882 **Asst S Barth's Ch Gaithersburg MD 2001-** B Washington DC 1951 d George & Nancy. Smith 1970; BA GW 1973; MBA GW 1977; MDiv VTS 1994. D 4/14/1998 P 5/8/1999 Bp Leo Frade. Epis Ch Cntr New York NY 2000-2001; Assoc S Geo's Epis Ch Arlington VA 1998-2000. Bd, Inter Ch Med Assistance; NNECA.

POLLOCK, Ronald Neal (NJ) 154 W High St, Somerville NJ 08876 **Dio New Jersey 2004-; R S Jn's Ch Somerville NJ 1998-** B Riverside NJ 1965 s Ronald & Phaedra. BA Elon U 1987; Cert S Georges Coll Jerusalem IL 1993; MDiv GTS 1994. D 6/11/1994 P 12/17/1994 Bp George Phelps Mellick Belshaw. Cur Ch of S Jn on the Mtn Bernardsville NJ 1994-1998. CHS, Nyc 1994.

POLLOCK, Ryan E (Dal) 5100 Ross Ave, Dallas TX 75206 **Dio Dallas Dallas TX 2017-** B Austin TX 1989 s Derrich & Julee. BA Criswell Coll 2014; MDiv Nash 2017. D 6/24/2017 Bp George Robinson Sumner Jr. m 8/6/2011 Jessica Jennelle Pollock.

POLVINO, Andrea Regina (WNY) 515 Columbus Ave., Waco TX 76701 B New Brunswick NJ 1958 d Joseph & Esther. BA Hobart and Wm Smith Colleges 1980; JD SUNY at Buffalo Sch of Law 1983; MDiv Sewanee: The U So, TS 2008. D 4/29/2007 Bp Michael Garrison P 11/15/2008 Bp Dena Arnall Harrison. c 1. The Great Cmsn Fndt Houston TX 2013-2015; Dio Texas Houston TX 2011; S Mary's Ch W Columbia TX 2011; Cur S Paul's Ch Waco TX 2008-2010.

POLYARD, Karen Marie (Minn) PO Box 27, Wabasha MN 55981 B Honolulu HI 1968 d Mary. BS Winona St U 1992; MS Winona St U 2006. D 6/20/2015 P 6/21/2016 Bp Brian N Prior. c 1.

POMPA, Anthony R (Be) 19 E Cochran St, Middletown DE 19709 **Dn and R Cathd Ch Of The Nativ Bethlehem PA 2007-, 1991-1995** B Jim Thorpe PA 1965 s Robert & Rose. BS Penn 1987; MDiv Epis TS of the SW 1991. D 6/8/1991 P 2/1/1992 Bp James Michael Mark Dyer. m 10/2/1993 Felicia S Pompa c 2. St Annes Epis Ch Middletown DE 2003-2007; Dio Virginia Richmond VA 1998-2003; Imm Ch Mechanicsvlle VA 1995-1998. Mk Armin Jojorian Awd Epis TS Of The SW 1991. tpompa@nativitycathedral.com

PONADER, Martha Downs (Ind) 1337 Eagle Run Dr, Sanibel FL 33957 B Sturgis MI 1933 d Howard & Elizabeth. BA Indiana U 1955; MA Butler U 1984; Chr TS 1984. D 6/24/1988 Bp Edward Witker Jones. m 6/23/1956 Wayne Carl Ponader c 4. D Dio Indianapolis Indianapolis IN 1988-1996; Ret. NAAD.

PONCE MARTINEZ, Jacqueline (PR) 1 Calle Brandon, Ensenada PR 00647 Puerto Rico **Mision Santa Cecilia Ensenada PR 2004-** B New York NY 1955 d Anastacio & Ana. Cert Theol Stud San Pedro Y San Pablo Sem S Just Puerto Rico; Universidad Interamericana San German PR; Luth TS at Gettysburg 2000. D 6/24/2000 Bp Charles Ellsworth Bennison Jr P 8/29/2004 Bp David Andres Alvarez-Velazquez. m 10/6/2007 José A Estrada c 2. Dio Puerto Rico Trujillo Alto PR 2004-2016.

POND, Finn Richard (Spok) 7315 N Wall St, Spokane WA 99208 B Santa Monica CA 1951 s Gene & Louise. BS Biola U 1974; MS OR SU 1977; PhD OR SU 1981. D 12/21/2002 Bp James E Waggoner Jr. m 8/1/1981 Jean Pond c 2.

POND JR, Walter Edward (WNY) 171 N Maple St, Warsaw NY 14569 **Ret Warsaw NY 2006-; Dio Wstrn New York Tonawanda NY 2000-** B Jacksonville FL 1933 s Walter & Marie. BA Newberry Coll 1955; MDiv Luth TS 1958; ThM Columbia TS 1964; Cert Bex Sem 1999. D 5/30/1999 P 12/5/1999 Bp Michael Garrison. m 5/19/1956 Jane McCants Weeks c 2. Vic All SS Espiscopal Ch Amherst NY 2004-2006; Reg Mnstry Dvlp The Ch Of The H Apos - Epis Perry NY 2000-2004; D S Lk's Epis Ch Attica NY 1999-2000; Adj Instr Batavia NY 1993-1995; Serv Luth Ch 1958-1983.

PONDER, James Brian (Miss) 118 N Congress St, Jackson MS 39201 **Dio Mississippi Jackson MS 2015-, GC Dep (2018) 2017-, Secy, Annual Coun of the Dio Mississippi 2016-, Secy, Dio Mississippi 2016-, Treas, Duncan M. Gray Cntr 2016-, Treas, Trst of the Dio Mississippi 2016-, Vice-Pres, Exec Com 2015, Exec Com 2014-2015, Diac Discernment Screening Com, COM 2014-, Chair, Epis Transition Com 2013-2015, A.C. Marble Sch T/F 2012-2014, COM 2012-, Sprtl Dir, Vocare in MS 2007-2008, Coll Works Com 2004-2008** B Jackson MS 1974 s James & Mary. BA Millsaps Coll 1997; MDiv GTS 2004. D 6/18/2004 P 1/22/2005 Bp Duncan Montgomery Gray III. S Paul's Epis Ch Meridian MS 2011-2015; Assoc R Gr - S Lk's Ch Memphis TN 2008-2011; Chapl Camp Bratton-Green/Gray Cntr Canton MS 2007-2008; LocTen Ch Of The Resurr Starkville MS 2006-2007, Asst R & Chapl 2004-2008; Camp Session Dir Camp Bratton-Green/Gray Cntr Canton MS 2004-2008; Chapl Epis Cbury Fllshp at Mississippi St Uni 2004-2008; Bd Mem/Vice-Pres LOVEs Kitchen Meridian MS 2012-2015; Trst Baird Charitable Trust Meridian MS 2011-2015; Chair, Dioc Stndg Com on Liturg & Mus Dio W Tennessee Memphis 2010-2011, Co-Fac, Discerning Young Vocations Experience (DYVE) 2010-2011, Dioc Liturg Coordntr & Mstr of Cermonies 2010-2011, Barth Hse (UMemphis) Advsry Com 2009-2011; Cmnty/Non-Sci Mem MSU Instnl Revs Bd Mississippi St MS 2005-2008; Cnvnr U Common Mnstry Mississippi St MS 2005-2007. bponder@dioms.org

PONG, Tak Yue (Tai) 11 Pak Po Street, Homantin Hong Kong **Prncpl All SS Middle Sch 1985-; Asst H Trin Ch 1985-** B HK 1946 s Paul & Wei. BEd Natl Taiwan Normal U 1971; MS U of Wisconsin 1972; MDiv VTS 1978; PhD Penn 1982. D 6/24/1978 Bp John Thomas Walker P 9/1/1979 Bp James T M Pong. m 8/2/1975 Li-jiuan Yu. All SS Middle Sch 1990-2010; Vic Adv In Taipei Taiwan 1983-1985; Dio Taiwan Taipei 1982-1988; Asst Prof And Chapl 1982-1985; Gr And S Ptr's Ch Baltimore MD 1979-1980; Asst Chapl Penn 1978-1981; Cur Calv Ch Washington DC 1978; Asst To Min Chinese Cmnty Ch Washington DC 1975-1978.

PONSOLDT, Megan Hollaway (Va) Grace Episcopal Church, 301 S Main St, Kilmarnock VA 22482 **The Epis Sch of Los Angeles Los Angeles CA 2011-** B Fitchburg MA 1977 d James & Peggy. BSW Virginia Commonwealth U Richmond VA 1999; MS Virginia Commonwealth U Richmond VA 2000; MDiv Ya Berk 2007. D 6/16/2007 Bp Peter J Lee P 12/16/2007 Bp Shannon Sherwood Johnston. m 9/25/2010 James Adam Ponsoldt c 1. Gr Ch Kilmarnock VA 2007-2010.

POOL, Gayland (FtW) 1870 Ederville Rd S, Fort Worth TX 76103 **Int H Trin by the Lake 2005-** B Plainview TX 1937 s Mart & Mattie. TCU; BA Texas Tech U 1959; UTS 1960; STB GTS 1962. D 4/27/1962 P 11/30/1962 Bp George Henry Quarterman. m 11/2/1991 Colice K Sherrod. Int R S Paul's Epis Ch Dallas TX 1999, 1997-1998; Asst S Greg's Epis Ch Mansfield TX 1995-1997; Associated Parishes Inc. Ft Worth TX 1995-1996; All SS' Epis Ch Ft Worth TX 1993-1997; Tarrant Area Cmnty Ch 1990-1992; R S Lk's In The Meadow Epis Ch Ft Worth TX 1985-1990; St Mich All Ang Ch 1980-1982; Chr The King Epis Ch Ft Worth TX 1974-1996; Cur S Lk's Epis Ch Dallas TX 1963-1966; Vic S Jn's Ch Andrews TX 1962-1963; The Epis Ch Of S Mary The Vrgn Big Sprg TX 1962-1963. Coun Associated Parishes 1970-2001.

POOL, Jayne (Ala) 106 Stratford Road, Birmingham AL 35209 **P S Mk's Ch Birmingham AL 2014-, P-in-c 2013; Rel Tchr Adv Epis Day Sch Birmingham AL 2007-; Rel Tchr Adv Epis Sch Birmingham AL 2007-** B Birmingham AL 1959 d James & Katherine. MA Birmingham-Sthrn Coll 1981; Candler TS Emory U 1982; MDiv Yale DS 1984; SPGP Bowen Cntr for the Study of the Fam 2009; Bowen Fam Cntr Post-Grad Prog 2009; DMin Sewanee: The U So, TS 2011. D 5/21/1998 Bp Robert Oran Miller P 12/1/1998 Bp Henry Nutt Parsley Jr. m 5/30/1981 James Marion Pool c 1. P-in-P affiliate S Mary's-On-The-Highlands Epis Ch Birmingham AL 2009-2013, 2004-2006, 1998-2002; Montgomery Epis Campus Mnstry Dio Alabama Birmingham 2002-2004, Dioc Coun 1992-2002, T/F on the Stwdshp of Creation 2004-, Stndg Com 2002-2005, Dioc Revs Bd 2001-2003, COM 1993-1996, Cmsn on Chr Formation 1991-1994; Chapl Epis Campus Mnstrs Montgomery AL 2002-2004; DCE - all ages St. Mary's-on-the-Highlands Birmingham AL 1990-1998; Cler Meth Ch 1984-1989. writer, "A Revs of "What Are You Going To Do w Your Life?"," *Sewanee Theol Journ*, The U So, 2010. Phi Beta Kappa Birmingham Sthrn Coll 1981; ABS Awd Emory U 1981. j2kpool@me.com

POOLE, Charles Lane (NCal) 6342 Paso Dr, Redding CA 96001 **Ret 1995-; Stndg Com The Epis Dio Nthrn California Sacramento CA 1978-** B Chicago IL 1933 s Charles & Helen. BS IL Wesl 1956; MTh CDSP 1959. D 7/1/1959 Bp William F Lewis P 2/27/1960 Bp William G Wright. m 7/11/1959 Evelyn R

Poole c 2. Chapl Redding Police Dept 1997-1999; Sxlty Cmsn 1991-1992; Pres of the Dioc Corp 1987-1990; Dn of the Superior California Dnry 1978-1990; R S Mich's Ch Anderson CA 1973-1995; R S Paul's Epis Ch Oroville CA 1966-1971; Assoc Trin Epis Ch Reno NV 1965-1966; Vic Chr Ch Pioche NV 1962-1965; S Barth's Ch Ely NV 1962-1965; Yth Advsr Dio Nevada Las Vegas 1961-1966; Vic S Mths Caliente NV 1961-1965; Vic S Philips-in-the-Desert Hawthorne NV 1959-1961. Hon Cn to the Ordnry Dio Nthrn California 1984.

POOLE, John Huston (CFla) 603 Spring Island Way, Orlando FL 32828 **D S Chris's Ch Orlando FL 2002-** B Franklin NJ 1947 s Huston & Marjorie. D 2/13/1982 Bp Wilbur Emory Hogg Jr. m 11/19/1965 Denice Poole. Assoc Chr Ch Gilbertsville NY 1987-1988; Assoc S Matt's Ch Unadilla NY 1982-1987.

POOLEY, Nina Ranadive (Me) 152 Princes Point Rd, Yarmouth ME 04096 **R S Barth's Epis Ch Yarmouth ME 2007-** B Providence RI 1965 d Manmohan & Gail. BA W&M 1987; MEd U of Virginia 1991; MDiv Sewanee: The U So, TS 2004. D 12/11/2004 P 9/10/2005 Bp Charles Glenn VonRosenberg. m 8/1/1993 Kenneth Thomas Pooley c 2. Assoc Chapl S Paul's Sch Baltimore MD 2006-2007; Assoc Chapl S Paul's Sch Brooklandville MD 2006-2007; Yth Min Ch Of The Gd Shpd Lookout Mtn TN 2004-2006; Mem Mssn Priorities Study Grp Dio Maine Portland ME 2009-2011, Fin Com Mem 2007-.

POOSER, William Craig (Chi) 2423 Blue Quail, San Antonio TX 78232 B Jacksonville FL 1944 s William & Louise. BA Stetson U 1967; Massachusetts Gnrl Hosp 1969; MDiv SWTS 1973; MS Texas A&M U 1985. D 6/13/1973 P 12/15/1973 Bp William Hopkins Folwell. m 2/16/1984 Patricia Pooser c 2. Ch Of The Resurr Windcrest TX 2003-2010; Int S Andr's Epis Ch Corpus Christi TX 2002-2003, 2000-2001; Supply P (Weekends) Calv Ch Menard TX 2001-2002; Trin Ch Jct TX 2001-2002; Supply P Dio W Texas San Antonio TX 1998-2000; Chapl Osf S Anth's Med Cntr Rockford IL 1991-1997; S Jude's Epis Ch Rochelle IL 1991-1993; P-in-c S Jude Rochelle IL 1990-1993; Chapl Of The 404th Chem Brigade Untd States NG Rockford IL 1989-1997; Gr Place Campus Mnstry Dekalb IL 1989-1991; Non-par 1986-1988; Gr Ch Of W Feliciana St Francisvlle LA 1985-1986; Asst S Andr's Ch Bryan TX 1980-1983; Off Of Bsh For ArmdF New York NY 1976-1981; Vic H Faith Epis Ch Port St Lucie FL 1973-1976.

POPE, Alicia Hale (RG) Trinity on the Hill, 3900 Trinity Dr, Los Alamos NM 87544 **Asst Trin On The Hill Epis Ch Los Alamos NM 2008-** B Los Alamos NM 1973 BAAS U of No Texas 1996; MPA U of New Mex 2000; Dplma TESM 2006. D 10/21/2006 Bp Jeffrey Neil Steenson P 11/10/2007 Bp William Carl Frey. m 10/6/2001 Paul Albert Pope c 2.

POPE, Charles Maurice (Ia) 505 Edgehill Dr, Saint Albans WV 25177 B Bremen GA 1947 s Hughlan & Ruby. BA U of W Georgia 1969; MDiv Sthrn Bapt TS 1972; U So 1984. D 11/30/1993 P 5/31/1994 Bp Chris Christopher Epting. m 12/22/1970 Mary B Bhame c 3. R S Paul's Epis Ch Grinnell IA 2003-2012, Int 1997-1998; Cn The Cathd Ch Of S Paul Des Moines IA 1999-2003; P-in-c S Anne's By The Fields Ankeny IA 1998-1999; P S Andr's Ch Des Moines IA 1994-1995; Counslr Employee and Fam Resources Des Moines IA 1993-1999; Counslr Plains Area Mntl Hlth Cntr. Le Mars IA 1986-1992; Mem of Com to Selcect Candidates for Bp Dio Iowa Des Moines IA 2002, Supply P 1995-2002, COM 1994-1997. "Conscientious Patriots," Epis Life, 2005; "Journey Outward," Living Ch, 2000. Natl Bd for Cert Counselors 1993-2012.

POPE III, Daniel Stuart (Roch) 406 Canandaigua St, Palmyra NY 14522 B Natick MA 1930 s Daniel & Marguerite. BA Ya 1952; STB Ya Berk 1963. D 5/10/1989 P 11/18/1989 Bp William George Burrill. m 5/21/1966 Patricia Ann Pope c 3. R S Jn's Ch Sodus NY 1997-2002; P-in-c S Steph's Ch Wolcott NY 1989-2004, D-In-C 1989.

POPE, Kristin Stina (Cal) 934 W 14th St, Port Angeles WA 98363 B Moscow ID 1950 d Kenneth & Kathleen. Emory U; BA Pitzer Coll 1973; MDiv Untd TS of the Twin Cities 1977; MA Jn F Kennedy U 2011. D 8/6/1977 Bp Philip Frederick McNairy P 4/24/1978 Bp Robert Marshall Anderson. m 7/8/2008 Sue Thompson c 2. Vic Chr Epis Ch Sei Ko Kai San Francisco CA 2010-2015, Actg Vic 2008-2009; Int H Chld At S Mart Epis Ch Daly City CA 2007-2008; H Chld At S Mart's Daly City CA 2006-2007; S Edm's Epis Ch Pacifica CA 2005-2006; Assoc Ch Of The H Innoc San Francisco CA 2003-2005; S Mk's Par Berkeley CA 2003; Int Trin Ch San Francisco CA 2002-2003; Dir Admssns CDSP Berkeley CA 1999-2002; Int S Phil's Ch San Jose CA 1999; Int Chr Ch Alameda CA 1997-1999; Asst S Barth's Epis Ch Atlanta GA 1993-1997; 1979-1993; Asst S Lk's Ch Minneapolis MN 1978-1979. Auth, *Cler Journ*; Auth, *Open Hands*.

POPE, Nadine Karen (At) PO Box 1010, Cumming GA 30028 B Oklahoma City, OK 1955 d Eugene & Natalie. D 8/6/2011 Bp J Neil Alexander. m 8/8/1992 Rodney Lee Pope c 1.

POPE, Robert Gardner (Colo) 108 Sawmill Cir, Bayfield CO 81122 **Vic S Aug's Ch Creede CO 2009-; Ret 2008-; Ret 1989-** B Newton MA 1936 s Daniel & Marguerite. BA Mar; St Jn Vianney TS RC Denver CO; MA Ya 1961; PhD Ya 1967. D 11/6/1976 P 6/9/1977 Bp Harold Barrett Robinson. m 11/22/1986 Alice Robinson c 3. S Pat's Epis Ch Pagosa Sprg CO 2004-2008, R 2004-2008; P-in-c Trin Epis Ch Hamburg NY 1988-1989; Vic Ch Of All SS Buffalo NY 1982-1986; P-in-c S Phil's Ch Buffalo NY 1981-1982, P-in-c 1977-1978; Asst

S Jn's Gr Ch Buffalo NY 1978-1981; Cur S Pat's Ch Buffalo NY 1976-1977. Auth, "The Halfway Cov," Pr, 1969. Guggenheim Fellowowship 1976.

POPE, Steven Myron (Tex) 905 Whispering Wind, Georgetown TX 78633 **Ret 2008-** B Saint Paul MN 1941 s Myron & June. BA California St U 1965; MDiv VTS 1984; DMin SWTS 2001. D 6/22/1984 Bp Joseph Thomas Heistand P 2/14/1985 Bp Maurice Manuel Benitez. m 9/1/1962 April Pope c 2. R S Andr's Ch Breckenridge TX 2005-2008; R Trin Ch Victoria TX 2001-2005; R Calv Epis Ch Richmond TX 1990-2001; Iglesia San Mateo Houston TX 1988-1990; R San Mateo Epis Ch Bellaire TX 1988-1990; Asst R S Lk's On The Lake Epis Ch Austin TX 1984-1988; Chair Div Renwl Dio Texas Houston TX 1995-1996, Bd Dir EP Amnesty Prog 1989-1994.

POPHAM, James J (CGC) Saint David's Episcopal Church, 401 S Broadway, Englewood FL 34223 **Dio Cntrl Gulf Coast Pensacola FL 2016-** B New Orleans LA 1947 s Guy & Virginia. BS Tul 1969; JD Tul Sch of Law 1972; MDiv Epis TS Of The SW 2005; MDiv Epis TS of the SW 2005. Trans 6/27/2013 as Priest Bp Dabney Tyler Smith. m 8/22/1986 Jo P Popham c 3. S Dav's Epis Ch Englewood FL 2013-2016. jimpopham@gmail.com

POPHAM, Jo P (CGC) **S Steph's Ch Brewton AL 2016-** B Monroe LA 1947 d Albert & Jo. BS Louisiana Tech U 1985; Paralegal Cert Tul 1989; MDiv Epis TS of the SW 2005. Trans 3/10/2014 Bp Dabney Tyler Smith. m 8/22/1986 James J Popham c 2. P-in-c S Nath Ch No Port FL 2014-2016. jopopham@gmail.com

POPLE, David (Ct) 95 Greenwood Ave, 22 Golden Hill St, Bethel CT 06801 B Hollis NY 1945 s John & Virginia. BA Syr 1967; MDiv Hartford Sem 1970. D 6/12/1971 Bp Joseph Warren Hutchens P 1/15/1972 Bp Morgan Porteus. m 6/21/1969 Pauline Susan Pople. R Ch Of S Thos Bethel CT 1980-2011; All SS Ch Wolcott CT 1974-1980; Dio Connecticut Meriden CT 1974-1980; Cur S Andr's Ch Meriden CT 1971-1974.

POPPE, Bernie (Nwk) 18 De Hart Rd, Maplewood NJ 07040 **R S Geo's Epis Ch Maplewood NJ 2002-** B Newport RI 1957 s Norman & Hilda. BA H Cross Coll 1979; MDiv GTS 1984. D 6/23/1984 P 1/12/1985 Bp George Nelson Hunt III. Mem and Chair COM Dioces of Newark 2005-2013; Mem Bp Transition Team Dio Newark 2005-2007; Bd Mem Hse of the Gd Shpd Hackettstown NJ 2004-2009; Chair Turning Point Cmnty Serv Irvington NJ 2003-2011; Geo Mercer TS Garden City NY 1999-2000, 1994-1995; Dn Hellgate Dnry Dio Long Island 1994-2002; R S Mk's Ch Jackson Heights NY 1992-2002; Assoc R S Ann And The H Trin Brooklyn NY 1987-1992; Cur Gr Ch Newark NJ 1984-1987.

POPPE, Kenneth Welch (Vt) 2 Cherry St, Burlington VT 05401 B Philadelphia PA 1949 s Herman & Mary. BA Hobart and Wm Smith Colleges 1971; MDiv ETSBH 1975; Col 1978; UTS 1978. D 6/14/1975 Bp Lyman Cunningham Ogilby P 3/1/1976 Bp William Hawley Clark. m 9/12/1970 Margaret S Poppe c 1. Dn And R Cathd Ch Of S Paul Burlington VT 1998-2012; R Chr Ch Shaker Heights OH 1989-1998; R S Dav's Ch Kinnelon NJ 1983-1989; Asst S Eliz's Ch Ridgewood NJ 1981-1983; P-in-c S Andr's Epis Ch Lincoln Pk NJ 1980-1981; Serv Chr Ch Short Hills NJ 1978-1980; Asst Chr Ch Christiana Hundred Wilmington DE 1975-1978. Auth, "Liturg On The Holocaust". AAR, SBL.

POPPLEWELL, Elizabeth (Ia) 1808 Nw 121st Cir, Clive IA 50325 **R S Lk's Epis Ch Cedar Falls IA 2013-, 2010-2012** B Roswell NM 1963 d Donald & Phyllis Carol. BA Drake U 1985; MDiv SWTS 2007; MDiv SWTS 2007. D 12/16/2006 P 6/16/2007 Bp Alan Scarfe. m 10/24/1987 Dennis R Popplewell c 3. Dio Iowa Des Moines IA 2013; Asst S Tim's Epis Ch W Des Moines IA 2007-2010. edpopplewell@msn.com

POPPOFF, Robin Marie (ECR) 7269 Santa Teresa Blvd, San Jose CA 95139 **D S Steph's In-The-Field Epis Ch San Jose CA 2016-** B Palo Alto CA 1956 d Ilia & Betty. Bachelor of Sci San Jose St U 1979; Assoc of Sci Heald Coll 1999; Bachelor of Diac Stds The Sch for Deacons 2016. D 6/4/2016 Bp Mary Gray-Reeves. Assn of Epis Deacons 2011. deacon@ssitf.org

PORCHER, Philip Gendron (SC) 1494 Stratton Pl, Mount Pleasant SC 29466 **Ret 1995-** B Mount Pleasant SC 1932 s Philip & Wilhelmina. BS Clemson U 1954; MDiv VTS 1957. D 6/27/1957 P 5/19/1958 Bp Thomas N Carruthers. m 8/24/1963 Georgia A Porcher c 3. Int S Thos Epis Ch N Charleston SC 2002-2003; PT Assoc S Thos Ch Chesapeake VA 1997-1999; Asst to Bp of SC Dio Sthrn Virginia Newport News VA 1975-1995, 1967-1995; R Gr Yorktown VA 1972-1975; Vic S Thos Epis Ch Chesapeake VA 1967-1972; Assoc Ch Of The Gd Shpd Sumter SC 1965-1967; Ch Of The H Comf Sumter SC 1965-1967; Chapl U SC-Columbia SC 1960-1965; P-in-c S Matt Ft Motte SC 1957-1960; P-in-c The Ch Of The Epiph Eutawville SC 1957-1960. Auth, *Why Use Int Pstr or Int Consult*. Alb Inst 1975; CODE 1982-1995; Int Mnstry Ntwk 1980.

PORTARO JR, Sam Anthony (Chi) 1250 N Dearborn St Apt 19C, Chicago IL 60610 **Fac Credo Inst Inc. Memphis TN 2006-; Consult, COM Dio Chicago Chicago IL 2005-, Stndg Com 1993-1995, Exam Chapl/COM 1983-2005, Cmsn on Higher Educ 1982-2005** B Bethesda MD 1948 s Sam & Frances. BA U NC 1970; MDiv VTS 1973; DMin PrTS 1982. D 1/25/1975 Bp Matthew George Henry P 12/20/1975 Bp William Gillette Weinhauer. m 7/3/2011 Christopher M Dionesotes. Int Dir of Field Educ The U Chi Chicago IL

1991-1992; Coordntr Of Prov V MHE 1987-1991; Epis Chapl to The U Chi Epis Ch Coun U Chi Chicago IL 1982-2005; Assoc To The R Bruton Par Williamsburg VA 1976-1982; Dio Sthrn Virginia Newport News VA 1976-1982, Cmsn on Coll Wk 1976-1982; Vic Ch Of The Epiph Newton NC 1975-1976; Pres, Alum/ae Assn Exec Com VTS Alexandria VA 2002-2003, Alum/ae Assn Exec Com 2000-2003; Coordntr for MHE Fifth Prov of the Epis Ch Epis Ch Cntr New York NY 1987-1990; Angl/RC T/F Dio Wstrn No Carolina Asheville NC 1975-1976, Cmsn on St of the Ch 1975-1976. Auth, "Transforming Vocation," Ch Pub, 2008; Auth, "Mind the Gap: Forming a New Generation for Ldrshp in an Aging Ch," Forw Mvmt Press, 2004; Auth, "Sheer Chrsnty: Conjectures on a Catechism," Cowley Pub, 2004; Auth, "Daysprings: Meditations For The Weekdays Of Adv," *Lent And Easter*, Cowley Pub, 2000; Auth, "Crossing The Jordan: Meditations On Vocation," Cowley Pub, 1999; Auth, "Brightest & Best: A Comp To The Lessons Feasts And Fasts," Cowley Pub, 1998; Auth, "Conflict And A Chr Life," Morehouse Pub, 1996; Auth, "Inquiring & Discerning Hearts: Mnstry And Vocation w YA On Campus," Scholars Press, 1993. ESMHE 1982-2003.

PORTER, Elizabeth Streeter (Ark) 10 Thunderbird Dr, Holiday Island AR 72631 **P S Jas Ch Eureka Spgs AR 2004-** B Elkhart IN 1940 D 5/4/2002 P 11/23/2002 Bp Andrew Fairfield. m 4/18/1964 Clifford Roger Porter c 2. S Geo's Epis Ch Bismarck ND 2002-2004.

PORTER III, Fulton Louis (Chi) 2720 2nd Private Rd, Flossmoor IL 60422 **R Ch Of S Thos Chicago IL 2005-; Dn, Chicago So Dnry Dio Chicago Chicago IL 2009-** B Jackson MS 1967 s Fulton & Clara. BS Morehouse Coll 1989; MD NWU 1993; MDiv SWTS 2004. D 6/12/2004 Bp Dorsey Henderson P 4/9/2005 Bp Victor Alfonso Scantlebury. m 11/26/1994 Lisa C Porter c 2. Cur S Edm's Epis Ch Chicago IL 2004-2005. Benjamin Whipple Schlr Seabury-Wstrn 2004.

PORTER, George Vernon (Ga) 1201 Fairfield St, Cochran GA 31014 **P Trin Ch Cochran GA 2005-** B Bainbridge GA 1936 s Vernon & Alice. Gordon Mltry Barnesville GA; Merc; Middle Georgia Coll. D 2/5/2005 P 8/7/2005 Bp Henry Irving Louttit. m 3/2/1974 Mary Sue Chance Porter c 5.

PORTER, Gerry (Oly) 5555 Montgomery Dr Apt N103, Santa Rosa CA 95409 **Ret 2002-** B McCook NE 1942 s Robert & Doris. BA U Denv 1964; Harvard DS 1965; MDiv EDS 1968. D 6/22/1968 P 5/31/1969 Bp Anson Phelps Stokes Jr. m 6/23/1968 Barbara W Worrell. Assoc Gr Ch Bainbridge Island WA 2005-2015; Provost S Mk's Cathd Seattle WA 1998-2000; Provost Dio Olympia Seattle 1991-2002; Provost The Cathd Ch Of S Paul Boston MA 1989-1990; Asst Dio Massachusetts Boston MA 1978-1991, 1970-1977; P-in-c S Paul's Ch Brookline MA 1976-1977; Cur/R Gr Ch Salem MA 1968-1978.

PORTER, James Robert (Az) 2200 Lester Dr NE Apt 460, Albuquerque NM 87112 B Springfield MO 1941 s James & Margaret. BA U of Texas at Arlington 1970; MDiv CDSP 1973. D 7/11/1973 P 1/18/1974 Bp Clarence Rupert Haden Jr. m 2/17/1979 Candy Porter c 2. Int S Ptr's Ch Casa Grande AZ 2008-2011; R Ch Of Our Sav Lakeside AZ 1997-2007; S Jn's Epis Ch Colville WA 1990-1997; Vic Epis Ch Of The Redeem Republic WA 1990-1996; R Trin Ch Folsom CA 1987-1990; Int Ch Of The Incarn Santa Rosa CA 1985-1987; R S Ptr's Epis Ch Red Bluff CA 1979-1985; Cur S Barn' Epis Ch Of Odessa Odessa TX 1977-1979; Cur S Jn's Epis Ch Odessa TX 1977-1979; Vic S Fran of Assisi Hse Ch Ballinger-Winters TX 1976-1977; Vic S Mk's Epis Ch Coleman TX 1976-1977; Vic Trin Ch Albany TX 1976-1977; Vic S Tim's Ch Gridley CA 1974-1976. Barbershop Harmony Soc 2000; RACA 1984; SocMary 1997.

PORTER, Joe Thomas (WTenn) 43 Carriage Ln, Sewanee TN 37375 B Rena Lara MS 1945 s Ulysses & Shirley. BA U of Memphis 1971; MDiv Sewanee: The U So, TS 1985. D 6/11/1985 P 6/11/1986 Bp Alex Dockery Dickson. m 11/24/1967 Claudia W Porter. Cur Gr - S Lk's Ch Memphis TN 2001-2007; S Lk and S Jn's Caruthersvlle MO 1999-2003; R S Mary's Epis Ch Dyersburg TN 1989-2001; P-in-c S Thos The Apos Humboldt TN 1986-1989; D S Mary's Cathd Memphis TN 1985-1986.

PORTER, John Harvey (Cal) 551 Ivy St, San Francisco CA 94102 **Exec Dir Ord of Malta Wstrn Assn U.S.A. 2000-** B CA 1944 s Robert & Susan. Rec 12/3/2005 Bp William Edwin Swing. Assoc Ch Of The Adv Of Chr The King San Francisco CA 2006-2011. P Assoc of the H Hse, OLW 2008; Soc of Cath Priests 2009.

PORTER, John Joseph (At) 215 Abington Dr NE, Atlanta GA 30328 **Tchr H Innoc Epis Sch Atlanta GA 2009-** B Newark NJ 1939 s John & Catherine. MA CUA; MA S Bonaventure U; VTS 1970. Rec 3/21/1974 as Priest Bp Matthew George Henry. m 7/14/1973 Mary Porter c 2. P-in-c H Innoc Ch Atlanta GA 2002-2009, Asst 1978-2001; R S Bede's Ch Atlanta GA 1985-2002; Cn to Bp for Cler Dvlpmt Dio Atlanta Atlanta GA 1975-1978; Cur Chr Ch Greenwich CT 1973-1975; Dir of the Cntr for Cont Educ VTS Alexandria VA 1971-1973. Ldrshp Awd Ldrshp Atlanta 1977.

PORTER, Lloyd Brian (Tex) 1701 W TC Jester Blvd, Houston TX 77008 **Ret Dio Texas 2009-** B Houston TX 1945 s Lloyd & Margaret. BA U of Texas 1968; MDiv Epis TS of the SW 1983. D 6/8/1984 P 12/13/1984 Bp Scott Field Bailey. c 2. S Mk's Ch Houston TX 2005-2008, 1990-1992; St Andrews Epis Ch Houston TX 2004-2005; The Great Cmsn Fndt Houston TX 2003-2004; Emm Ch Houston TX 2001-2002; S Jas Epis Ch Houston TX 2000-2001; S

Ptr's Ch Pasadena TX 1999-2000; R S Paul's Epis Ch Orange TX 1995-1997; S Steph's Epis Ch Houston TX 1993-1995; S Lk's Epis Hosp Houston TX 1989-1990; Chapl S Lk's Hosp Houston TX 1989-1990; R S Jas' Epis Ch La Grange TX 1986-1989; Asst R S Jn's Ch McAllen TX 1984-1986. EFM Mentor, AFP.

PORTER, Nicholas (Ct) Trinity Church, 651 Pequot Ave, P.O. Box 400, Southport CT 06890 **St Mary's in The Mountains Epis Wilmington VT 2015-; Fndr and Organizer Jerusalem Mnstrs at Acer Farm (Mid E Peace Camp) 2011-; Chapt Mem Amer Priory of the Ord of St. Jn 1999-; Re-Fndr and Hon Trst Amer Friends of the Epis Dio Jerusalem 1998-; Trst Ya Berk New Haven CT 2008-** B New York NY 1964 s Harry & Violet. BA Ya 1986; MA Amer U in Cairo 1990; MA Kings Coll Lon 1991; MDiv Ya Berk 1994. D 6/11/1994 Bp Clarence Nicholas Coleridge P 6/11/1995 Bp Samir H Kafity. m 8/10/1991 Dorothy Porter c 3. Preaching Instr St. Nersess Armenian Orth Sem New Rochelle NY 2009-1997; R Trin Epis Ch Southport CT 2005-2013; R Emm Epis Ch Geneva 1201 2000-2005; Sub-Dn &Cn Pstr The Amer Cathd of the H Trin Paris 75008 1997-2000; Exec Coun Appointees New York NY 1995-1996; Hist Instr Armenian Orth Sem of SS. Jas Jerusalem 1994-1996; Dio Jerusalem 1994-1995; Mem of Bp's Coun of Advice Convoc of Epis Ch in Europe Paris 2001-2004. Fllshp of St Alb & St Sergius 1995; Ord S Jn of Jerusalem 1995. Knight Ord of St. Jn of Jerusalem 2008.

PORTER, Pam (WMass) Po Box 19, Heath MA 01346 **Hm Care Prog Dir Franklin Cnty Hm Care Corp 2008-** B Mount Clemens MI 1948 d John & Nelle. BA U of Detroit Mercy 1973; Wayne Elem Tchg Detroit MI 1974; MDiv EDS 1986. D 6/28/1986 Bp Henry Irving Mayson P 1/17/1988 Bp Daniel Lee Swenson. m 8/3/1974 Brian Michael DeVriese c 2. Asstg P Chr Ch Cathd Springfield MA 2016-2017; Int S Jas Epis Ch Arlington VT 2006-2007; St Mary's in The Mountains Epis Wilmington VT 2000-2001, 1987-1990, Asst Vic 1987-1990; Consulting Dir NE Fndt for Chld 1996-2007; Int Chapl Mt Holyoke Coll So Hadley MA 1995-1996; Asst Gr Ch Amherst MA 1993-1996; Dio Wstrn Massachusetts Springfield 1993-1995.

PORTER, Roger Cliff (CGC) 6500 Middleburg Ct, Mobile AL 36608 **Bd Trst S Paul Sch 1975-** B Jacksonville Bch FL 1933 s Cliff & Annie. BA Stetson U 1956; MDiv VTS 1960. D 6/22/1960 P 3/1/1961 Bp Edward Hamilton West. m 8/16/1957 June Porter c 1. All SS Epis Ch Mobile AL 2003-2004; 1976-1978; S Paul's Ch Mobile AL 1970-2001; Asst R S Jn's Epis Ch Tallahassee FL 1962-1970; Chr Ch Monticello FL 1960-1962; In-Charge S Mary's Epis Ch Madison FL 1960-1962. Auth, "Selected Sermons". rcporter33@comcast.net

PORTER, Shirley (At) B Hartford CT 1955 d Ralph & Elsie. BA WA SU; MDiv VTS 2012. D 12/17/2011 Bp J Neil Alexander P 6/22/2013 Bp Robert Christopher Wright. Dio Atlanta Atlanta GA 2013-2015; S Jas Ch Macon GA 2013-2015; VTS Alexandria VA 2013, 2012.

PORTER-ACEE III, John (EC) 107 Louis St, Greenville NC 27858 **S Tim's Epis Ch Greenville NC 2016-** B Asheville NC 1978 MDiv VTS 2005. D 6/25/2005 P 1/14/2006 Bp Clifton Daniel III. m 11/16/2009 Whitney A Porter-Acee c 2. Asst To The R Chr Ch Charlotte NC 2005-2016. aceejohn@hotmail.com

PORTEUS, Bev (Eas) 27 Woods Way, Elkton MD 21921 B Freeport NY 1947 d Arthur & Beatrice. BA Buc 1969; MDiv GTS 1988. D 6/11/1988 P 12/11/1988 Bp Paul Moore Jr. m 4/9/1988 Christopher Porteus. R Trin Ch Elkton MD 1995-2010; Vic All SS Epis Ch Delmar DE 1990-1995; Asst S Ptr's Ch Salisbury MD 1990-1995; Asst Min The Epis Ch Of The Adv Kennet Sq PA 1988-1990; Stndg Com Dio Easton Easton MD 2000-2002, COM Chair 1993-1995.

PORTEUS, Christopher (Eas) 27 Woods Way, Elkton MD 21921 B Waterbury CT 1947 s Morgan & Martha. BA Bos 1973; MDiv GTS 1982. D 5/29/1982 P 4/25/1983 Bp Robert Shaw Kerr. m 4/9/1988 Bev Porteus c 1. R S Steph's Ch Earleville MD 2005-2008, 1995-2005, Int 1989-1994; H Cross Millington Massey MD 1995-; St Clements Massey MD 1995; S Mary's Epis Ch Tyaskin MD 1990-1995; Mssnr Dioc S Paul's Ch Vienna MD 1990-1995; S Paul's Epis Ch Hebron MD 1990-1995; Mssnr Dioc S Phil's Ch Quantico MD 1990-1995; S Tim's Ch Roxborough Philadelphia PA 1988-1989; Asst S Jas Epis Ch S Jas NY 1985-1988; S Ann's Ch Burlington VT 1982-1985; R S Matt's Ch Enosburg Fls VT 1982-1985.

PORTEUS, James Michael (Az) Triskele, Rinsey, Ashton, Helston TR13 9TS Great Britain (UK) B Chester-le-Street UK 1931 s Charles & Agnes. BA Oxf GB 1955; GLE Ripon Coll Cuddesdon 1957; MA Oxf GB 1958. Trans 8/1/1986 as Priest Bp Joseph Thomas Heistand. m 7/4/1998 Kate Money c 3. Serv Scottish Epis Ch 1991-2009; Epis Campus Mnstry - U of Arizona Tucson AZ 1986-1991; Chapl, Epis Campus Mnstry U of Arizona Tucson AZ 1986-1991; Serv Ch of Engl 1969-1986; Ecum Chapl Mainline Collage Mnstrs Dio of PA 1965-1969; Assoc Epis Chapl U Chi Chicago IL 1962-1965; Serv Ch of Engl 1957-1962. Hon Cn Cathd of the Isle, Isle of Cumbrae, Scotland 2006; Hon Alum CDSP 1991.

✠ PORTEUS, The Rt Rev Morgan (Ct) PO Box 782, Wellfleet MA 02667 **Ret Bp of Connecticut Dio Connecticut Meriden CT 1981-, Bp of Ct 1977-1981, Bp Coadj of Ct 1976-1977, Bp 1971-1976** B Hartford CT 1917 s Robert & Ruth. BA Bates Coll 1941; BD EDS 1943. D 9/29/1943 P 6/1/1944 Bp Frederick G

Budlong Con 10/13/1971 for Ct. c 3. Asstg Bp of Mass Dio Massachusetts Boston MA 1986-2009, 1986-2003, Asst 1982-1985; Bishops Fund Hartford CT 1971-1981; R S Ptr's Epis Ch Cheshire CT 1944-1971; Cur Trin Ch Torrington CT 1943-1944; SLC Dom And Frgn Mssy Soc- Epis Ch Cntr New York NY 1975-1980. DD Trin, Hartford, CT 1981; DD Ya Berk 1972.

PORTILLA GOMEZ, Israel Alexander (Colom) **Iglesia Epis En Colombia Bogota 2017-** B Charta Santander 1987 s Israel & Alba. Rec 12/8/2016 Bp Francisco Jose Duque-Gomez. m 7/26/2014 Linda Vosele c 1.

POST, Suzanne Marie (SwFla) 14511 Daffodil Dr Apt 1402, Fort Myers FL 33919 **Assoc P Iona Hope Epis Ch Ft Myers FL 2015-; Chapl to Ret Cler/ Ft Myers Deanary Dio SW Florida Parrish FL 2016-, Eccl Crt 2004-2007, Bp Search Com 2004-2006, COM 2003-2007** B New York NY 1963 d John & Doris. BS Pace U 1988; MDiv Yale DS 1991. D 6/8/1991 P 12/14/1991 Bp Richard Frank Grein. Ch Of S Mich And All Ang Sanibel FL 2002-2007; R S Jas' Ch No Salem NY 1994-1997; Asst Chr Chr Ch Greenwich CT 1992-1994; Cur S Thos Ch Mamaroneck NY 1991-1992; COM Dio New York New York NY 1995-1997. Auth, "Preaching as Pstr Care".

POSTON, Ronald Glen (Az) 2174 E Loma Vista Dr, Tempe AZ 85282 B Franklin KY 1951 s William & Violetta. BS Pur 1976; MA Pur 1983; MDiv Nash 1986. D 5/16/1986 P 12/12/1986 Bp William Cockburn Russell Sheridan. m 5/16/2009 Josephine Poston c 2. R Ch Of The Epiph Tempe AZ 1994-2017; Assoc All SS Ch Phoenix AZ 1991-1994; Chapl The Bp's Sch La Jolla CA 1989-1991; The Bp's Sch La Jolla CA 1989-1991; R S Phil & S Jas Ft Wayne IN 1988-1989; Trin Ch Ft Wayne IN 1986-1989; Vic S Phil & S Jas Ft Wayne IN 1986-1988; Ecum Off Dio Arizona Phoenix AZ 1998.

POTEAT, Sally Tarler (WNC) Po Box 1291, Drexel NC 28619 B Baltimore MD 1955 d Craig & Joanne. BA Duke 1977. D 12/9/1995 Bp Bob Johnson. m 10/6/ 1979 William Larry Poteat c 2. D Gr Ch Morganton NC 1996-2008.

POTEET, David Bertrand (Tex) Po Box 6828, Katy TX 77491 **Non-par 1984-** B Tulsa OK 1942 s Albert & Muriel. BS U of Texas 1965; MDiv VTS 1969. D 7/ 1/1969 Bp Scott Field Bailey P 5/1/1970 Bp James Milton Richardson. m 5/9/ 1979 Iris Poteet. S Paul's Ch Katy TX 1978-1983; The Great Cmsn Fndt Houston TX 1978-1983; S Thos The Apos Epis Ch Houston TX 1973-1978; R S Thos Seabrook TX 1973-1978; Asst S Mart's Epis Ch Houston TX 1969-1973.

POTEET, Fred (SVa) 2508 Shepherds Ln, Virginia Beach VA 23454 **Assoc Old Donation Ch Virginia Bch VA 2014-, D 2005-2006** B Huntington WV 1948 s Henry & Hilda. BS Virginia Commonwealth U 1973; VTS 2004. D 6/4/2005 Bp David Conner Bane Jr P 5/13/2006 Bp Bob Johnson. m 6/15/1969 Mary Hill c 2. Dio Colorado Denver CO 2011-2014; Int R S Jn's Ch Portsmouth VA 2009-2010; Archd Dio Sthrn Virginia Newport News VA 2008-2009, Archd 2007-2009, Yth Dir 2002-2003; P-in-c S Steph's Ch Norfolk VA 2006-2007. fpoteet@olddonation.org

POTTER, Frances Dickinson (NH) 1010 Waltham St Apt 352, Lexington MA 02421 **Ret 1987-** B Chicago IL 1929 d Truman & Jean. BA Smith 1950; MA U CA 1961; MDiv EDS 1978. D 10/20/1979 P 5/1/1980 Bp Philip Alan Smith. m 10/16/1955 Richard B Gamble c 4. Assoc R S Paul's Ch Concord NH 1984-1987; Vic Ch Of The Mssh No Woodstock NH 1981-1987; Nthrn Grafton Shared Mnstry Lisbon NH 1981-1984; S Lk's Ch Woodsville NH 1981-1984; Asst Ch Of Our Sav Milford NH 1980-1981; Chr Ch Exeter NH 1980. Phi Beta Kappa.

POTTER, Jack C (U) 231 E 100 S, Salt Lake City UT 84111 B Union City IN 1936 s James & Mary. BA Hanover Coll 1958; MA U of Delaware 1960; MDiv Bex Sem 1965. D 6/12/1965 P 12/19/1965 Bp Robert Lionne DeWitt. m 10/2/ 1987 Patricia A Potter c 4. Cathd Ch Of S Mk Salt Lake City UT 1990-2002; Gr St Pauls Epis Ch Tucson AZ 1982-1990; St Johns Epis Ch Lafayette IN 1977-1982; Dio Indianapolis Indianapolis IN 1972-1977.

POTTER, Linda Gail (Chi) 1240 NE 64th Ln, Hillsboro OR 97124 **S Mk's Epis Par Medford OR 2015-; Int R St Mk Ch Medford Oregon 2015-; R Dio Chicago IL 2003-** B Duncan OK 1949 d Ben & Myrtle. BA Portland St U 1971; S Thos Sem 1990; MDiv CDSP 1994. D 6/15/1994 P 1/20/1995 Bp Robert Louis Ladehoff. m 5/28/1971 Thomas I Potter c 2. R Trin Epis Ch Wheaton IL 2003-2014; Cn to the Ordnry Dio Oregon Portland OR 1999-2003, Dioc Chair of the Evang Com 1991-1992; R All SS Ch Hillsboro OR 1996-1999; Asst Chr Ch Par Lake Oswego OR 1994-1996; Bp's Search Com Dio Chicago Chicago IL 2006-2008, COM 2006-.

POTTER, Lorene Heath (WNY) 537 S Park Ave, Buffalo NY 14204 B Norfolk VA 1932 d William & Lorene. BA Barnard Coll of Col 1953; MA SUNY 1976; MDiv Bex Sem 1987. D 6/13/1987 P 4/1/1988 Bp David Charles Bowman. m 6/10/1953 Milton Grosvenor Potter. S Thos Ch Buffalo NY 1989-1991; Asst St Mk Epis Ch No Tonawanda NY 1987-1988. Auth, "The Afr Collection Of The Buffalo Soc Of Natural Sciences"; Auth, "Afr Arts"; Auth, "Collections".

POTTER, Meredith (Chi) 317 Satinwood Ct S, Buffalo Grove IL 60089 **S Greg's Epis Ch Deerfield IL 2013-, Vic 2005-, Assoc 1997-2005; Exec Bd Mem Faith in Action Vol 2012-; Strng Team Mem Lake Cnty Untd (IAF Orgnztn) 2004-** B Chicago IL 1934 d Charles & Mary. Tufts U; BA San Jose St U 1955; MA Wstrn Michigan U 1967; Spec in Arts Wstrn Michigan U 1968; MDiv SWTS 1985; DMin SWTS 2000. D 3/24/1985 Bp James Winchester

Montgomery P 9/29/1985 Bp Frank Tracy Griswold III. c 4. Int Dir of D. Min. in Congrl Dvlpmt Bexley Seabury Fed Chicago IL 2007-2009, Lectr in Congrl Stds and Dir. Ext, Seabury Inst 2001-2002; Bd Mem Pstr Care Bd Lake Forest Hosp 2004-2007; Asst and Supply Int P Emm Epis Ch Rockford IL 2000-2002; VP Epis Asiamerica Mnstry Coun 1996-2005; Vic One In Chr Ch Prospect Heights IL 1995-1996, 1985-1994; Sch for Deacons Fac Dio Chicago Chicago IL 1989-1994; Sprtl Dir and Mem of Sec Chicago Epis Curs 1989-1992; Vic S Mary's Ch Pk Ridge IL 1985-1995. Auth, "Alone but Not Lonely," *Gather mag*, ELCA, 2013; Auth, "Thy Will Be Done: Discerning Pryr," *Luth Wmn Today*, ELCA, 1997; Auth, "Power of Pryr," *Luth Wmn Today*, ELCA, 1996; Auth, "This Is Not The Most Important Day Of Your Life," *Preaching As The Art Of Sacr Conversation*, Morehouse Pub, 1977. EPF; Fllshp Of S Jn The Evang 1987. DSA SWTS 1994.

POTTER, Paul Christopher (Los) 10925 Valley Home Ave, Whittier CA 90603 **S Jn Chrys Ch Rcho Sta Marg CA 2017-; S Steph's Par Whittier CA 2011-** B Fontana CA 1956 s William & Georgia. BA U of San Diego 1978; MDiv S Johns Sem 1982; MDiv S Johns Sem 1982. Rec 5/16/2011 Bp Joseph Jon Bruno. c 1. The Epis Ch Of The Blessed Sacr Placentia CA 2014-2017. rev. christopherpotter@gmail.com

POTTER, Raymond J (NCal) 2224 Gateway Oaks Dr. #355, Sacramento CA 95833 **Assoc P - Vol St Marys Ch Elk Grove Sacramento CA 2008-** B Providence RI 1950 s Raymond & Claire. BA Wadhams Hall Sem Coll 1974; MDiv S Bernards TS and Mnstry 1978; DMin SWTS 1995. Rec 6/1/1988 as Priest Bp William Augustus Jones Jr. m 11/30/1985 Roberta Potter c 2. All SS Memi Sacramento CA 2000-2005; S Dunst's Ch Tulsa OK 1995-2000; S Alb's Ch N Providence RI 1990-1995; R S Alb's Centerdale RI 1990-1995; Yth Dir Dio Missouri S Louis MO 1988-1990; Asst Trin Ch S Chas MO 1988-1990; Serv RC Ch 1978-1985; Mem of Dioc Trst Fin Bd Dio Nthrn Calfornia 2003-2005; Pres of Cler Dio Oklahoma 1996-1998; Dioc Coun Dio Rhode Island Providence RI 1991-1994. Auth, "A Fifty-Two Week Model Of Cathechesis". St Geo Awd Adult BSA Narrangansett, Rhode Island 1995.

POTTER, Roderick Kenneth (Me) 16 Alton Rd Apt 215, Augusta ME 04330 **Died 2/7/2017** B Gardiner ME 1933 s Clyde & Zilphaetta. BA Bates Coll 1960; MDiv GTS 1963. D 6/8/1963 P 12/14/1963 Bp Oliver L Loring. m 6/25/1955 Barbara Potter c 2. 1980-2017; S Lk's Ch Farmington ME 1963-1981.

POTTER, Sara (NCal) 1776 Old Arcata Road, Bayside CA 95524 **R S Alb's Ch Arcata CA 2008-; Dn of Semper Virens Dnry The Epis Dio Nthrn California Sacramento CA 2012-** B Sonora CA 1970 d Donald & Janice. BA U CA 1993; Angl Stds Ya Berk 2004; MDiv Yale DS 2004. D 7/3/2004 P 1/29/2005 Bp Jerry Alban Lamb. m 6/29/2002 Aaron M Hohl c 2. Cur/Dir of Chr Formation Calv Ch Stonington CT 2004-2008.

POTTER JR, Spencer B (SeFla) 19000 SW 89th Ave, Cutler Bay FL 33157 **R S Andr's Epis Ch Miami FL 2009-** B Berlin, Vermont 1975 s Spencer & Mary. BA Bates Coll 1997; MDiv VTS 2005. D 3/19/2005 P 9/17/2005 Bp Mark Sean Sisk. m 7/6/2005 Erin Potter c 1. Assoc S Mk's Ch Palm Bch Garden FL 2007-2009; Lilly Fell S Jas Ch New York NY 2005-2007; Yth Dir Calv and St Geo New York NY 1999-2002.

POTTER-NORMAN, Ricardo T (DR) Camila Alvarez #7 Urb. Mallen, San Pedro De Macoris Dominican Republic B San Pedro de Macoris DO 1936 s Alfred & Louise. Instituto Comercial Vazques San Pedro De Macoris 1958; STB ETSC 1964. D 5/31/1964 P 12/6/1964 Bp Paul Axtell Kellogg. m 1/8/ 1965 Mercedes Benitez Potter c 2. Hon Assoc Ch Of The Medtr Bronx NY 2000-2001; Assoc Dir Epis Ch Cntr New York NY 1994-2000; Vic All Ss La Romana Dr 1980-1986; Ret Dio The Dominican Republic (Iglesia Epis Dominicana) Gazcue Santo Domingo 1980-1986, Ret 1964-; R Iglesia Epis de Todos los Santos La Romana 1980-1986; Vic Ch Of The Intsn New York NY 1976-1980; Natl Coun Of Ch New York NY 1976-1978; Trin Par New York NY 1975-1976; Vic S Steph San Pedro De Marcoris Dr 1972-1974; Vic Iglesia Epis Cristo el Rey Puerto Plata 1966-1972; Asst S Steph San Pedro De Macoris Dr 1965-1966; Asst Iglesia Epis San Andres Santo Domingo Di 1964-1965. Hon Cn Dio Cecu (Cntrl Ecuador) 1997; Hon Cn Dio Dr 1991.

POTTERTON, Carol Thayer (SO) 5825 Woodmont Ave, Cincinnati OH 45213 B Jersey City NJ 1945 d Sanford & Susan. Duke; BA Emory U 1969; MSW OH SU 1980; MA Untd TS Dayton OH 1992. D 5/4/1991 Bp Herbert Thompson Jr. c 2. D The Ch of the Redeem Cincinnati OH 2011-2016; D All SS Ch Cincinnati OH 2011-2015; D S Mary Magd Ch Maineville OH 2006-2011; D H Trin Epis Ch Oxford OH 1998-2006; D S Barn Epis Ch Cincinnati OH 1991-1998; COM Dio Sthrn Ohio Cincinnati OH 2012-2017.

POTTS, David G (SD) 1728 Mountain View Rd, Rapid City SD 57702 B Rapid City SD 1946 s Bernard & Harriet. So Dakota Sch Mines & Tech. D 11/19/1988 Bp Craig Barry Anderson. m 12/31/1989 Cheryl L Heil c 2. D S Andr's Epis Ch Rapid City SD 1988-2000.

POTTS, Kathleen (Miss) 1421 Goodyear Blvd., Picayune MS 39466 B Vicksburg MS 1951 d Frederick & Jean. BA U of Sthrn Mississippi 1975; MDiv Sewanee: The U So, TS 2002. D 6/22/2002 Bp Alfred Marble Jr P 1/11/2003 Bp Duncan Montgomery Gray III. CLERIC S Paul's Epis Ch Picayune MS 2005-2012; Cur Chap Of The Cross Rolling Fork MS 2002-2005.

P

POTTS, Matthew L (WMich) P.O. Box 298, Falmouth MA 02541 **S Barn Ch Falmouth MA 2009-** B E Grand Rapids MI 1977 s Daniel & Miyoko. BA U of Notre Dame 1999; MDiv Harvard DS 2008. D 6/9/2008 P 12/21/2008 Bp Robert R Gepert. m 8/9/2008 Colette P Potts c 2.

POULIN, Suzanne Gordon (NH) Saint John the Baptist, 118 High St, Sanbornville NH 03872 **The Epis Ch Of S Jn The Bapt Sanbornville NH 2007-; P-in-c The Epis Ch of St. Jn the Bapt Sanbornville NH 2007-** B Portland ME 1960 d John & Grace. BS Plymouth St U 1983; MDiv Andover Newton TS 2003. D 6/14/2003 P 8/7/2005 Bp Chilton Richardson Knudsen. c 2. Asst. P S Dav's Epis Ch Kennebunk ME 2005-2007.

POULOS, George William (NC) 3308 Northampton Dr, Greensboro NC 27408 **Ret 2000-** B Rome GA 1934 s James & Farris. BS U GA 1956; MDiv Sewanee: The U So, TS 1966. D 6/25/1966 P 3/11/1967 Bp Randolph R Claiborne. m 6/7/1955 Nancy Poulos c 4. R S Andr's Ch Greensboro NC 1977-1999; Assoc S Paul's Epis Ch Winston Salem NC 1975-1977; R S Tim's Decatur GA 1969-1975; Cur S Mart In The Fields Ch Atlanta GA 1966-1969; Chr Ch Walnut Cove NC 2005; Mem, COM Dio No Carolina Raleigh NC 1996-2000, Chair Dept Coll Wk 1988-1995, Mem, Dioc Coun 1987.

POUNDERS, Marci J (Dal) St James Episcopal Church, 9845 McCree Rd, Dallas TX 75238 **Assoc Epis Ch Of The Ascen Dallas TX 2016-** B Louisville KY 1961 d Lawrence & Ann. BAS U of Louisville 1983; MDiv SMU Perkins 2005. D 1/26/2008 P 11/1/2008 Bp James Monte Stanton. m 8/10/1985 Tracy Pounders c 2. Asst. S Jas Ch Dallas TX 2008-2012. Bd Certification Assn of Profsnl Chapl 2009. marci.pounders@ascensiondallas.org

POVEY, John Michael (Mass) 3901 Glen Oaks Drive E, Sarasota FL 34232 B Bristol England UK 1944 s Henry & Evelyn. BTh S Johns Coll U of Nottingham GB 1976. Trans 12/1/1978 as Priest Bp Alexander D Stewart. R S Jas' Epis Ch Cambridge MA 2000-2006; Dio Wstrn Massachusetts Springfield 1986-2000, 1980; R S Steph's Ch Pittsfield MA 1984-1986; Vic S Chris's Ch Fairview Chicopee MA 1980-1984; R Ch Of The Gd Shpd Fitchburg MA 1978-1980.

POWELL, Anne Margrete (NCal) 20248 Chaparral Cir, Penn Valley CA 95946 **D Emm Epis Ch Grass Vlly CA 2015-, D 2004-** B DK 1943 d Erik & Agnete. BA Sch for Deacons 1999. D 11/20/1999 Bp William Edwin Swing. m 2/13/2010 Lewis Powell c 3. D S Edm's Epis Ch Pacifica CA 2001-2002.

POWELL, Anthony F (Fla) 657 SE 2nd Ave, Melrose FL 32666 **R Trin Epis Ch Melrose FL 2012-** B Valdosta GA 1954 s Frank & Ruth. BA Valdosta St U 1978; MDiv Sewanee: The U So, TS 2008. D 5/31/2008 Bp John Wadsworth Howe P 12/20/2008 Bp Henry I Louttit. m 6/17/1978 Anita Ann Powell c 2. Vic Ch Of The H Nativ St Simons Is GA 2008-2012; Vic St Richard's Of Chichester Epis Mssn Jekyll Island GA 2008-2012.

POWELL, Armistead Christian (Tex) 58 St. Andrews Dr., Jackson MS 39211 B Mobile AL 1939 s Edward & Edith. BA Trin U San Antonio 1962; BD VTS 1965. D 8/11/1965 P 7/10/1966 Bp James Milton Richardson. m 8/31/1962 Virginia Dowdell Powell c 2. S Chris's Epis Ch Austin TX 2001-2002; Calv Epis Ch Bastrop TX 2000-2001; S Paul's Epis Ch Pflugerville TX 1997; All SS Epis Ch Austin TX 1967-1994; Vic S Fran Par Temple TX 1966-1967; Vic S Lk's Epis Ch Salado TX 1965-1967; St Jas Ch 1965-1966.

POWELL, Arthur Pierce (NJ) 16 Copperfield Dr, Hamilton NJ 08610 **R H Apos Epis Ch Trenton NJ 1990-** B Camden NJ 1957 s Lawrence & M Carol. BA Rutgers The St U of New Jersey 1980; MDiv GTS 1983. D 6/4/1983 Bp George Phelps Mellick Belshaw P 12/10/1983 Bp Albert Wiencke Van Duzer. m 10/26/1985 Linda Powell c 1. R The Epis Ch Of The H Comm Fair Haven NJ 1986-1990; Cur S Andr's Ch Mt Holly NJ 1983-1986; Vic S Mart-In-The-Fields Lumberton NJ 1983-1986.

POWELL, Betty (WA) **Holistic Psych Grove Transformations Inc. 2011-; Non-par 1979-; Holistic Psych Priv Pract 1976-** B Wilmington DE 1945 d Hans & Rebecca. Mt Holyoke Coll 1965; BA U of Delaware 1967; MS U NC 1969; MDiv VTS 1972; DMin Bex Sem 1975. D 6/22/1974 Bp William Foreman Creighton P 9/7/1975 Bp George West Barrett. Chr Ch Sausalito CA 2000-2004; Holistic Psych Estrn Shore Counslg Assoc Salisbury MD 1995-2003; Asst R Gr Ch Washington DC 1977-1978; Asst R S Phil's Epis Ch Laurel MD 1977-1978; Holistic Psych The Grove 1976-2011. Wmn Ord, Now, EWC.

POWELL, Blanche Lee (Del) 304 Taylor Ave, Hurlock MD 21643 **Ret 2002-** B Cambridge MD 1940 d Adam & Lula. BS Winthrop U 1961; MDiv VTS 1975. D 5/24/1975 P 1/8/1977 Bp Robert Bruce Hall. Pstr S Steph's Ch Harrington DE 2002-2006; Primary Pstr Chr Ch Delaware City DE 1994-2001; Ch Of The Nativ New Castle DE 1994-2001; Dio Delaware Wilmington 1994-2001; S Jas Epis Ch Newport Newport DE 1994-2001; S Nich' Epis Ch Newark DE 1994-2001; R Chr Ch Pearisburg VA 1984-1994; St Davids Ch Alexandria VA 1975-1982; Vic S Dav Manassas VA 1975-1981.

POWELL, Brent Cameron (WTenn) 346 Hawthorne St, Memphis TN 38112 **Chapl St. Jude's Chld's Hosp Memphis TN 1987-** B Tupelo MS 1953 s Fred & Laura. BA Blue Mtn Coll 1984; MDiv Mid-Amer Bapt TS 1987. D 12/4/2002 Bp Don Edward Johnson. m 3/6/1993 Jo Ann Powell c 3.

POWELL, Catherine Ravenel (EC) 25 Vivian Ave, Asheville NC 28801 **Dn Dio E Carolina Kinston NC 2011-** B Fayetteville NC 1952 d Robert & Catherine. BA Hollins U 1974; Inter/Met 1977; MDiv UTS 1979; Cert Catechesis of the Gd Shpd 1994. D 6/23/1979 P 1/10/1980 Bp John Thomas Walker. m 10/15/2002 Sarah Parthum c 2. R Ch Of The Servnt Wilmington NC 2008-2015; Cathd of St Ptr & St Paul Washington DC 2001-2008, Asst 1979-1985; Chapl Natl Cathd Sch 2001-2008; Washington Epis Sch Beth MD 2001-2002; R S Ptr's Ch Salem MA 1997-2001; Assoc The Ch Of Our Redeem Lexington MA 1996-1997; Assoc S Ptr's Ch Weston MA 1993-1996; P-in-c S Andr's Ch Belmont MA 1993; Vic Trin Ch Fuquay Varina NC 1990-1992; Dio No Carolina Raleigh NC 1988-1992, COM 1990-1992; Assoc R Gr Ch Washington DC 1985-1987; Chapl Natl Cathd Sch 1979-1985; Asst S Dunst's Epis Ch Beth MD 1979-1980. Chapt Auth, "Preschool Sprtlty," *Gateways to Sprtlty*, Ptr Lang Pub, 2005; Auth, "Let The Chld Come," Living the Gd News, 1990. Phi Beta Kappa Hollins Coll 1974. revcrp@gmail.com

POWELL, Christopher Atwater (Chi) Christ Church, 470 Maple St, Winnetka IL 60093 **R Chr Ch Winnetka IL 2012-** B Louisville KY 1959 s Robert & Alice. BA Tul 1981; MDiv Nash 1985. D 12/21/1985 P 6/24/1986 Bp David Standish Ball. c 2. R S Jas Ch Jackson MS 2002-2012; R Trin Ch Rutland VT 1990-2002; R S Jn The Evang Stockport NY 1986-1990. Chapl Gnrl 3rd Ord of Cubs Fans in Canaan God 2012; Ord of St. Jn of Jerusalem Queen Eliz II 2011. christopher@christchurchwinnetka.org

POWELL, David Brickman (Ala) PO Box 467, Selma AL 36702 B Orlando FL 1952 s Bruce & Mary-Frances. BA Florida Atlantic U 1976; MDiv GTS 1982. D 5/26/1982 P 12/21/1982 Bp Calvin Onderdonk Schofield Jr. m 7/11/1987 Elizabeth Jennings c 1. R S Paul's Ch Selma AL 2010-2014; Int S Jn's Ch Pensacola FL 2009; R S Andr's By The Sea Epis Ch Destin FL 2004-2009; P-in-c Ch Of The Nativ Mineola NY 2003-2004; R The Epis Ch Of The Nativ Dothan AL 1994-2002; R S Steph's Ch Brewton AL 1990-1994; Assoc S Mk's Epis Ch Venice FL 1987-1990; Asst Ch Of The Atone Ft Lauderdale FL 1986; Cur S Mk's Ch Palm Bch Garden FL 1982-1985; Fac Dioc Sch for Deacons Dio Cntrl Gulf Coast Pensacola FL 2009, Chair Dioc Cmsn on Mus and Liturg 2008-2010, Bp's Search Com 1999-2000, Stndg Com 1997-2000, Dioc Cmsn on Fin 1996-1999; Bd Dir Beckwith C&C Fairhope AL 1991-1993. dbrickmanp@aol.com

POWELL, David Richardson (NCal) 122 Main, Cloverdale CA 95425 B Cambridge MA 1935 s Wilson & Fredrika. BA CUNY 1977; MS Amer U 1981; MDiv CDSP 1986. D 6/14/1986 P 2/1/1987 Bp John Lester Thompson III. m 1/5/1995 Margaret Powell c 2. Vic Ch Of The Gd Shpd Cloverdale CA 1998-2000; The Epis Dio Nthrn California Sacramento CA 1998-2000; Chr Ch Windsor CA 1994-1998; Vic Chr Epis Ch Windsor CA 1993-1998; S Andr's In The Highlands Mssn Antelope CA 1986-1994. Associated Parishes, EPF.

POWELL, Elizabeth Jennings (Ala) P.O. Box 467, Selma AL 36702 **P-in-c Gd Shpd Ch Montgomery AL 2014-; Dept of Chr Formation Dio Alabama Birmingham 2011-** B Atlanta GA 1949 d Henry & Elizabeth. BA Agnes Scott Coll 1971; MD Van Sch of Med 1976; MDiv GTS 2005. D 6/4/2005 P 5/27/2006 Bp Philip Menzie Duncan II. m 7/11/1987 David Brickman Powell. Assoc R S Paul's Ch Selma AL 2010-2014; R St Aug of Cbury Navarre FL 2008-2009; Assoc R S Simon's On The Sound Ft Walton Bch FL 2005-2008; COM Dio Cntrl Gulf Coast Pensacola FL 2009, Fac, Dioc Sch for Deacons 2009, Stndg Com 2008-2009, Cmsn on Personal Sprtl Growth 2007-2009, Fresh Start Fac 2007-2009, Cmsn on Wrld Mssn 2006-2009; Bd Wilmer Hall Mobile AL 2007-2009. Assoc - OSH 2007. Graduated cl The Gnrl Theological Sem 2005; Chf Precentor The GTS 2004; Montgomery Prize for Highest GPA in a Jr The GTS 2003.

POWELL, Everett (Cal) 417 44th Ave, San Francisco CA 94121 B Corpus Christi TX 1934 s Everett & Imogene. BA U of Corpus Christi 1955; MA Texas A&M U 1961; PhD U of Texas 1970; Cert Ang Stud Sch for Deacons 1999. D 12/1/2001 Bp William Edwin Swing. m 6/5/1953 Gloria Katherine Powell c 1. D Ch Of The Incarn San Francisco CA 2009-2011; D The Epis Ch Of S Mary The Vrgn San Francisco CA 2001-2009. Dn Emer, Del Mar Coll 1996; Who's Who in Amer Educ 1995; Who's Who in the SW 1995.

POWELL JR, Festus Hilliard (Ark) Po Box 21162, Hot Springs AR 71903 **Non-par 1985-** B Russellville AR 1943 s Festus & Dortha. BA Alaska Tech 1968; MDiv Sewanee: The U So, TS 1972. D 5/27/1972 P 3/1/1973 Bp Christoph Keller Jr. m 6/16/1966 Brenda Powell. Vic S Ptr's Ch Conway AR 1977-1984; S Mary's Epis Ch Monticello AR 1973-1977; P-in-c S Paul Mcgeehee AR 1973-1977; S Paul's Ch Mc Gehee AR 1973-1977; Chapl U Of Arkansas In Monticello 1973-1977; Cur S Paul's Ch Fayetteville AR 1972-1973. Auth, "Var arts & Poems".

POWELL, Greg (Eas) 29497 Hemlock Ln, Easton MD 21601 **Dn Trin Cathd Easton MD 2009-** B Daytona Bch FL 1959 s John & Diane. BA Gordon Coll 1984; MDiv U Tor CA 1993. D 6/12/1993 Bp William Jerry Winterrowd P 12/1/1993 Bp Robert Gould Tharp. c 4. R S Mary's Epis Ch Pocomoke City MD 1999-2009; Chr Epis Ch San Antonio TX 1996-1999; Ch Of The Ascen Knoxville TN 1993-1995. Auth, "God'S Chosen People Exploring The Jewish Roots In Chr Faith".

P

POWELL, John Charles (NJ) 307 Red Lion Road, Southampton NJ 08088 **P-in-c S Jn's Epis Ch Maple Shade NJ 2009-** B Los Angeles CA 1944 s Charles & Carolyn. Metropltn St Coll of Denver; U CO; U Denv 1963; GTS 1984. D 8/7/1984 Bp Richard Mitchell Trelease Jr P 5/31/1985 Bp Henry Boyd Hucles III. P-in-c S Fran Ch Dunellen NJ 2006-2008; Int Gr Epis Ch Whitestone NY 2001-2004; Int S Ptr's Ch Spotswood NJ 1999-2001; Int Ch Of S Mk And All SS Absecon Absecon NJ 1998-1999; Int H Trin Ch Collingswood NJ 1997-1998; Int Gr Ch In Haddonfield Haddonfield NJ 1996-1997; Int Gr Ch Merchantville NJ 1994-1996; Int Trin Epis Ch Cranford NJ 1993-1994; Int S Geo's Epis Ch Helmetta NJ 1992; R Par Of Chr The King Willingboro NJ 1985-1991; Cur Chr Ch Manhasset NY 1984-1985. Accredited Int Specialists 1994-2000; CBS; Int Mnstry Ntwk 1994-2000. Ch And Soc Prize GTS 1983. john.charles.powell@comcast.net

POWELL, John Lynn (Cal) 180 Westbury Cir Apt 327, Folsom CA 95630 **Ret 1988-** B Wichita KS 1923 s Roxie & Minya. BA Duke 1944; BD Yale DS 1947. D 6/18/1951 P 2/1/1952 Bp Francis E I Bloy. m 6/17/1948 Shirley A Powell c 4. Asst Trin Par Menlo Pk CA 1985-1988; R S Andr's Epis Ch San Bruno CA 1958-1985; R Ch of S Mary's by the Sea Pacific Grove CA 1953-1958; Cur S Edm's Par San Marino CA 1951-1953.

POWELL, Kenneth James (Cal) All Saints Parish, 1355 Waller St, San Francisco CA 94117 B Mt Holly NJ 1950 s Walter & June. BA San Francisco St U 1984; Diac Stds Epis Sch for Deacons Berkeley CA 2007. D 12/1/2007 Bp Marc Handley Andrus. m 9/17/2005 Karen Powell c 2.

POWELL, Lewis (NCal) 20248 Chaparral Cir, Penn Valley CA 95946 **D S Jn The Evang Ch Chico CA 2016-; Indigenous Mnstrs Mssnr The Epis Dio Nthrn California Sacramento CA 2010-, Indigenous Mnstrs Mssnr 2015-, Native Amer Mssnr 2010-2015** B Churchland VA 1942 s James & Myrtle. BS U of Maryland 1964; BA Sch for Deacons 1999. D 11/20/1999 Bp William Edwin Swing. m 2/13/2010 Anne Margrete Nielsen c 2. D Emm Epis Ch Grass Vlly CA 2010-2015; Chapl U of New Mex 2001-2006; D S Thos Of Cbury Epis Ch Albuquerque NM 2000-2010; S Anne's Ch Fremont CA 1999-2000; Exec Coun Com for Indigenous Mnstrs Exec Coun Appointees New York NY 2006-2010.

POWELL, Marilyn (SC) 577 Water Turkey Retreat, Charleston SC 29412 B Oakland CA 1924 d Niels & Azalia. U So. D 7/13/1985 Bp George Lazenby Reynolds Jr. m 9/14/1943 Joseph Harllee Powell c 3. D S Steph's Epis Ch Charleston SC 2002-2005; D Ch Of Our Sav Johns Island SC 1992-2000; Team-In-Charge Ch Of The H Comf Monteagle TN 1988-1992; D St Jas Epis Ch Sewanee TN 1985-1988; Dir Mid-Cumberland Mtn Mnstry Cntr.

POWELL, Mark M (EC) St Andew's On-The-Sound Episcopal Church, 101 Airlie Rd, Wilmington NC 28403 **Trin Epis Ch Chocowinity NC 2017-** B Washington NC 1978 s Charles & Virginia. BSN E Carolina U 2001; MDiv VTS 2007. D 6/9/2007 P 6/28/2008 Bp Clifton Daniel III. S Tim's Epis Ch Greenville NC 2015-2016; S Mk's Ch Westhampton Bch NY 2012-2013; Cur S Andr's On The Sound Ch Wilmington NC 2007-2012.

POWELL, Murray Richard (Tex) 951 Curtin St, Houston TX 77018 **Asst S Mk's Ch Houston TX 2011-** B Lookout Mountain TN 1950 s Edward & Edith. BA U of Texas 1976; MDiv VTS 1977. D 6/22/1977 Bp Roger Howard Cilley P 6/1/1978 Bp James Milton Richardson. m 4/16/1983 Sarah T Powell c 2. Vic Lord Of The Streets Ch 2005-2010; The Great Cmsn Fndt Houston TX 2005-2010, 1977-1992; Asst Trin Ch Houston TX 2005-2010; R Hope Epis Ch Houston TX 1992-2005; S Jn's Epis Ch Austin TX 1984-1992; Chr Ch Cathd Houston TX 1981-1984; Chr Epis Ch Tyler TX 1978-1981; Chapl Lamar U Beaumont TX 1977-1978; Vic S Matt Ch Beaumont TX 1977-1978; St Jas Ch Houston TX 1977-1978; St Matthews Ch Beaumont TX 1977-1978.

✠ POWELL, The Rt Rev Neff (SwVa) 295 W 22nd Ave, Eugene OR 97405 **Ret Bp of SW Virginia Dio SW Virginia Roanoke VA 2013-, Bp of SW Virginia 1996-2013; Bd Trst VTS Alexandria VA 1996-** B Salem OR 1947 s G & Gretchen. Coll of Preachers; BA Claremont McKenna Coll 1970; MDiv EDS 1973. D 7/15/1973 P 1/20/1974 Bp James Walmsley Frederic Carman Con 10/26/1996 for SwVa. m 6/13/1970 Dorothy Ruth Houck c 3. Archd Dio No Carolina Raleigh NC 1983-1991; Dio Oregon Portland OR 1975-1996; Vic S Bede's Ch Forest Grove OR 1975-1983; Asst Trin Epis Cathd Portland OR 1973-1975. DD VTS 1997. ndpowell@infionline.net

POWELL JR, Peter Ross (Ct) 6 Gorham Ave, Westport CT 06880 **Asstg P Ch Of S Mary The Vrgn New York NY 2011-; P Assoc Chr And H Trin Ch Westport CT 1991-** B Philadelphia PA 1948 s Peter & Rosalie. BS No Carolina St U 1970; S Georges Coll, Jerusalem 1974; MDiv VTS 1976; ThM PrTS 1979; Coll of Preachers 1982; DMin Sewanee: The U So, TS 1997; Kennedy Sch of Govt 2000; S Georges Coll Jerusalem IL 2000; Kennedy Sch of Govt/Harvard Bus Sch 2003; Harvard Bus Sch 2006. D 6/12/1976 P 12/18/1976 Bp John Mc Gill Krumm. m 8/12/1992 Barbara Smith c 3. Pres/CEO Interfaith Hsng Assoc. Westport CT 2000-2010; Int Gr Epis Ch Norwalk CT 1993; Int S Ptr's Epis Ch Oxford CT 1992-1993; Pres/CEO Interfaith Hsng Assn Westport CT 1988-2010; R The Par Of Emm Ch Weston CT 1985-1987; Adj Prof VTS Alexandria VA 1981-1983; R Chr Ch S Jn's Par Accokeek MD 1979-1985; Assoc All SS Ch Princeton NJ 1977-1979; Tchg

Fell PrTS Princeton NJ 1976-1979; Cur S Andr's Epis Ch New Providence NJ 1976-1977. Auth, "Homeless In The Suburbs," *Festschrift for Donald Armentrout*, Sewanee, 2000. Cath Biblic Associaton 1976-2003; SBL 1975. Danver's Fell Harvard Bus Sch 2006; Fllshp Jn F. Kennedy Sch of Govt 2003; Faces Of Achievement Westport/Weston Ymca 2001; Distinguished Cmnty Serv Awd ADL 2000; Fllshp Jn F Kennedy Sch Of Govt 2000.

POWELL, R Bingham (Ore) St Mary's Episcopal Church, 1300 Pearl St., Eugene OR 97401 **R S Mary's Epis Ch Eugene OR 2012-, P-in-c 2010-2012, Cur 2007-2010** B Hillsboro OR 1981 s Neff & Dorothy. BA Wake Forest U 2003; MDiv VTS 2007. D 6/2/2007 P 12/22/2007 Bp Neff Powell. m 1/2/2010 Christine Elizabeth Tyson Zeller-Powell c 3. bingham@saint-marys.org

POWELL, Rita Teschner (Mass) Trinity Church Episcopal, 206 Clarendon St, Boston MA 02116 **Trin Ch Epis Boston MA 2013-** B Worcester MA 1978 d Russell & Anne. BA Barnard Coll of Col 1999; MDiv Ya Berk 2005. D 6/14/2008 Bp Andrew Donnan Smith P 1/17/2009 Bp Creighton Leland Robertson. m 5/4/2008 Justin A Beebe. Coordntr for Yth Mnstry Dio So Dakota Pierre SD 2008-2013; Yth Min S Mk's Ch New Canaan CT 2005-2007.

POWELL IV, Robert Jefferson (ETenn) 1101 N Broadway St, Knoxville TN 37917 **St Jas Epis Ch at Knoxville Knoxville TN 2015-** B Richmond VA 1980 s Robert & Suzan. BA Jas Madison U 2003; MDiv Emm Chr Sem 2007; DAS Sewanee: The U So, TS 2015; DAS The TS at The U So 2015. D 2/28/2015 P 9/20/2015 Bp George Young III. m 5/15/2015 Michaelangelo Martin. Other Lay Position Dio E Tennessee Knoxville TN 2014-2016.

POWELL, Sydney Roswell (NY) 3405 Grace Ave, Bronx NY 10469 **Ret 1988-** B Alligator Pond Jama CA 1923 s Hubert & Margaret. S Peters Coll Jersey City NJ 1959; GTS 1968. Trans 3/25/1969. m 7/26/1978 Daisy Powell c 3. R S Jn Black River Jamaica W Indies 1982-1988; P-in-c S Anth In Montserrat 1980-1982; P-in-c S Thos Bluefields Jamaica 1974-1979; Asst The Ch of S Matt And S Tim New York NY 1967-1972; Serv Ch Of Jamaica 1959-1967. Ecum Chr Coun.

POWELL, William Vincent (Okla) 124 Randolph Ct, Stillwater OK 74075 **Vic S Mk's Ch Perry OK 1989-, Vic 1958-1988; Ret 1988-** B Pampa TX 1927 s Earl & Olive. Oklahoma A&M Coll 1947; Oklahoma City U 1951; Nash 1958. D 12/1/1957 P 9/27/1958 Bp Chilton R Powell. c 3. Ch Of The Ascen Pawnee OK 1988-1989; Vic S Alb's Ch Cushing OK 1988-1989; R S Andr's Ch Stillwater OK 1970-1987; Chr Cathd Salina KS 1967-1970; DCE Dio Wstrn Kansas Hutchinson KS 1967-1970; Vic S Ptr's Ch Tulsa OK 1963-1967; P-in-c Trin Ch Guthrie OK 1960-1963; Vic S Mk Blackwell OK 1958-1959. Provence VII Syn-2 Terms 1979; Chair of Educ Com Provence VII 1976; Rep to Exec Coun Provence VII 1972.

POWELL IV, Woodson Lea (NC) 560 Water Tower Road, Moncure NC 27559 **Ret 2000-** B Wadesboro NC 1935 s Woodson & Evelyn. BA U NC 1957; MDiv VTS 1960. D Bp Thomas Augustus Fraser Jr P 4/29/1961 Bp Richard Henry Baker. m 8/12/1978 Susan H Powell c 3. Vic Ch Of The Adv Enfield NC 1999-2001, 1987-1995; Ch Of The Epiph Rocky Mt NC 1999-2001; Vic S Jn's Ch Battleboro NC 1999-2001, Vic 1987-1998; S Mich's Ch Tarboro NC 1999-2001; St Marys Epis Ch Speed NC 1999-2001; S Tim's Ch Raleigh NC 1999-2000; Gr Ch Weldon NC 1995-1999; Vic S Mk's Ch Halifax NC 1992-1993; R Gr Epis Ch Lexington NC 1963-1969; P-in-c S Paul's Epis Ch Thomasville NC 1960-1963. Mayor'S Civic Awd Williston Nd 1987.

POWER, William Joseph Ambrose (Dal) 8011 Douglas Ave, Dallas TX 75225 B 1931 s William & Florence. BA U Tor 1953; MA U Tor 1954; ASOR 1955; U Tor 1959; PhD U Tor 1961. D 10/8/1972 P 4/29/1973 Bp Archibald Donald Davies. m 8/5/1966 Marjorie Lucas. Assoc S Mich And All Ang Ch Dallas TX 1974-2004. SBL. DD Epis TS 1999.

POWERS JR, Clarence (LI) 139 Saint Johns Pl, Brooklyn NY 11217 B Memphis TN 1947 s Clarence & Agnes. BA U of Memphis 1970; MDiv GTS 1976. D 6/26/1976 Bp John Vander Horst P 4/14/1977 Bp William F Gates Jr. R S Jn's Ch Brooklyn NY 1987-2013; R Ch Of SS Steph And Mart Brooklyn NY 1981-1987; Vic Calv Ch Epis 1977-1980; Dio Tennessee Nashville TN 1977-1980; D Chr Ch Cathd Nashville TN 1976-1977. Auth, "Faith, Fear, And Future," *Ecum Bulletin*, 1975.

POWERS, David Allan (CGC) 959 Charleston St, Mobile AL 36604 B Reading PA 1938 s Edward & Frances. BS So Georgia Coll 1960; MA U GA 1961; MDiv Sewanee: The U So, TS 1973; DMin Sewanee: The U So, TS 1993. D 6/28/1973 P 3/1/1974 Bp George Paul Reeves. m 5/26/1979 Celeste Powers c 3. Trin Epis Ch Mobile AL 2008; S Lk's Epis Ch Birmingham AL 2003-2004; S Simon's On The Sound Ft Walton Bch FL 2000-2010; R All SS Epis Ch Mobile AL 1995-2002; R S Matt's Epis Ch Houma LA 1986-1995; Vic/R S Marg's Epis Ch Baton Rouge LA 1978-1986; Cur Epis Ch Of The Gd Shpd Lake Chas LA 1975-1978; Cur S Aug Of Cbury Ch Augusta GA 1973-1975. Woods Ldrshp Awd U So.

POWERS, Elizabeth Ann (SD) 209 S Main S, Chamberlain SD 57325 B Minneapolis MN 1950 d John & Mercedes. BA Metropltn St U; MDiv Sewanee: The U So, TS 2004. D 6/19/2004 P 12/18/2004 Bp Michael Smith. m 9/2/1995 Samuel N Robertson c 2. P-in-c Dio So Dakota Pierre SD 2008-2013; S Steph's Ch Fargo ND 2004-2008.

POWERS, Fairbairn (Nwk) 531 Harrison Ave, Claremont CA 91711 B Detroit MI 1939 d Frank & Marian. BA Smith 1960; MBA Cntrl Michigan U 1986; MDiv EDS 1992; CAGS Andover Newton TS 2009. D 11/1/1997 P 5/14/1998 Bp Douglas Edwin Theuner. m 7/10/2004 Joanna Dewey c 3. Int Ch Of The H Innoc W Orange NJ 2006-2010; Dir of Pstr Care Chr Hosp Jersey City NJ 2004-2006; Dir of Pstr Care Chr Hosp Jersey City NJ 2004-2006; Int Ch Of The Adv Medfield MA 2003-2004; Assoc S Ptr's Ch Beverly MA 2000-2003; Sr Mssnr Cntrl Berkshire Epis Commun 1998-2000; P-in-c S Agnes Ch Little Falls NJ 1997-2006; Sr Reg Mssnr Dio Wstrn Massachusetts Springfield 1997-2000; Assoc Cntrl Berkshire Epis Commun 1997-1998.

POWERS, John Carter (Okla) 2431 Terwilleger Blvd, Tulsa OK 74114 Ret Ret 2000- B Tulsa OK 1936 s Harold & Edith. BA U of Oklahoma 1958; MDiv GTS 1962; U of Cambridge 1975. D 6/21/1962 P 12/20/1962 Bp Chilton R Powell. c 3. Supply P S Bede's Ch Westport OK 2000-2017; Gnrl Secy Coll & Universities Colleges and Universities of the Angl Comm 1995-2000; The AEC New York NY 1994-2000; Exec VP Assn Epis Coll 1993-2000; Sunday Assoc Calv and St Geo New York NY 1993-2000; Dio Oklahoma Oklahoma City OK 1992-1993; R Trin Ch Tulsa OK 1975-1991; R S Mary's Ch Edmond OK 1964-1974; H Fam Ch Langston OK 1964-1968; Vic S Lk The Beloved Physcn Idabel OK 1962-1964. Soc of S Jn the Evang. Doctor of Humane Letters, Honoris Causa Cuttington U Coll (Liberia) 2001; Jas Mills Fllshp 1974; Hon Cn Dio Oklahoma; Chapl 95 S Geo's Cociety.

POWERS, Lee (NJ) 119 St. Georges Drive, Galloway NJ 08205 B Brooklyn NY 1949 s Fredrick & Dorothy. BBA U of Pennsylvania 1973; MDiv GTS 1981. D 6/6/1981 P 12/11/1981 Bp Albert Wiencke Van Duzer. m 5/28/1988 Nancy Kleinfelder c 2. Cn to the Ordnry Dio New Jersey Trenton NJ 2004-2012; Cn to the Ordnry Dio New Jersey 2004-2012; Vic Ch Of S Mk And All SS Absecon Absecon NJ 2001-2004; R S Mary's Epis Ch Daytona Bch FL 1999-2001; R S Ptr's Ch Spotswood NJ 1988-1999; Int H Trin Ch So River NJ 1987; Int Ch Of The Gd Shpd Pitman NJ 1986; Int Ch Of Our Merc Sav Penns Grove NJ 1985; Vic Trin Epis Old Swedes Ch Swedesboro NJ 1981-1984; Conf Ldr Credo Inst Inc. Memphis TN 2008-2015, Fin Fac 2000-2008.

POWERS, Nancy Chambers (Dal) 1023 Addison Ave, Pottsboro TX 75076 Pstr S Jn's Epis Ch Pottsboro TX 2013- B Houston TX 1953 BS U of Texas 1975; MEd U of No Florida 1979; Angl TS 2005. D 5/14/2005 P 4/6/2013 Bp James Monte Stanton. m 4/29/1977 Frank Norman Powers c 1. Cn Pstr S Matt's Cathd Dallas TX 2005-2013.

POWERS, Patricia Ann (SwFla) Caixa Postal 11510, Porto Alegre 91720 Brazil B Cleveland OH 1946 d Frank & Eleanor. Colgate Rochester Crozer DS; CRDS; AA Lakeland Cmnty Coll 1977; BA Cleveland St U 1979; MTh Crozer TS 1987. Trans 12/1/1990 Bp David Charles Bowman. c 2. R S Nath Ch No Port FL 2001-2012; Exec Coun Appointees New York NY 1998-2001, 1990-1992; Global Epis Mssn Ntwk 1997-1998; S Mk's Ch Buffalo NY 1992-1996; Exec Dir Of Mssn Brazilian Epis Ch 1979-1990; Serv Epis Ch Of Brasil 1979-1990. Dok, SCHC.

POWERS, R(Oy) Stephen (SVa) 1829 Pittsburg Landing, Virginia Beach VA 23464 B Koahsiung CN 1953 s James & Vivian. BA Anaheim Chr Coll 1979; MDiv GTS 1982; Harvard DS 1996. D 6/10/1982 Bp Robert Munro Wolterstorff P 12/21/1982 Bp Charles Brinkley Morton. R S Bride's Ch Chesapeake VA 2004-2015; US Navy Chapl Off Of Bsh For ArmdF New York NY 1987-2004; Chapl US Navy Chapl 1987-2004; Cur W Cntrl Epis Mssn Spokane WA 1985-1987; Cur All SS Ch Vista CA 1982-1985. SSC 1986. 4 Navy Commendation Medals US Navy; Nato Medal US Navy; Kosovo Liberation Medal US Navy; SW Asia Medal US Navy; Kuwaiti Liberation Medal US Navy; 2 Navy Achievement Medals US Navy. frstephenp@mac.com

POWERS, Sharon Kay (Mass) 49 Puritan Rd, Buzzards Bay MA 02532 B Warebam MA 1946 d Edgar & Charlotte. D 6/4/2005 Bp M(Arvil) Thomas Shaw. m 9/24/1966 John R Powers c 2. D Ch Of S Jn The Evang Duxbury MA 2012-2017.

POWERS, Steve (FdL) 311 Division St, Oshkosh WI 54901 B Indianapolis IN 1946 s Hobert & Dorothy. BA Indiana U 1968; STB GTS 1971. D 6/11/1971 P 12/21/1971 Bp John P Craine. c 1. R Trin Epis Ch Oshkosh WI 1999-2011; R Trin Epis Ch Houghton MI 1983-1999; Dio W Missouri Kansas City MO 1976-1983; Vic S Lk's Epis Ch Excelsior Sprg MO 1976-1983; Asst S Barn Ch Irvington NY 1974-1976; Cur Geth Epis Ch Marion IN 1971-1974. OHC.

POZO, Francisco (NJ) 61 Kristopher Dr, Yardville NJ 08620 Chr Ch Trenton NJ 1995- B DO 1956 s Marcelino & Rosa. BA CUA 1982; BTh S Thos Sem 1986; ThM Cath U of Paris 1989; STM GTS 1995. Rec 6/16/1994 Bp Joe Doss. m 4/4/1991 Carmen Angelin Pozo c 3. Non-par 1994-1997; Trin Epis Ch Cranford NJ 1994-1995; Serv Ch Of The Domincan Republic 1985-1990. fpchildrenfirst1@verizon.net

POZZUTO, Keith Allen (Tex) 220 8th St., Mckeesport PA 15132 Cur Dio Texas Houston TX 2017-; All SS Epis Sch Tyler TX 2016-; Asst Chr Epis Ch Tyler TX 2013- B McKeesport PA 1978 s John & Annetta. BS Geneva Coll 2004; MDIV TESM 2008. D 6/7/2008 Bp Robert William Duncan. m 5/26/2012 Melinda H Howes. pozzuto@gmail.com

PRADAT, Paul Gillespie (Ala) 12200 Bailey Cove Rd SE, Huntsville AL 35803 St Thos Epis Ch Huntsville AL 2013- B Meridan MS 1960 s Ray. BA U of Alabama 1983; MDiv Epis TS of the SW 1989. D 5/27/1989 P 12/8/1989 Bp Robert Oran Miller. m 6/24/1998 Angie Barrier Pradat c 3. The Chap Of The Cross Madison MS 2003-2004; Ch Of The Ascen Hattiesburg MS 1997-2003; Trin Ch Yazoo City MS 1992-1997; Cur S Lk's Epis Ch Birmingham AL 1989-1992.

PRADAT, Ray William (Ala) 1747 Jack Warner Pkwy Apt 208, Tuscaloosa AL 35401 Died 1/10/2017 B Birmingham AL 1930 s Joseph & Susie. BA U of Alabama 1951; MDiv Sewanee: The U So, TS 1966. D 5/30/1966 P 5/20/1967 Bp John Maury Allin. c 4. R Chr Ch Tuscaloosa AL 1973-1997; Vic Calv Epis Ch Cleveland MS 1970-1973; Gr Ch Rosedale MS 1970-1973; All SS Ch Inverness MS 1968-1970; Vic S Thos Ch Belzoni MS 1968-1970; Cur S Geo's Epis Ch Clarksdale MS 1966-1968.

PRAKTISH, Carl Robert (Va) 2572 Lemon Rd Apt 903, Honolulu HI 96815 B Clayton MO 1932 s Carl & Clara. BS U of Wisconsin 1953; MA VTS 1971. D 4/15/1972 Bp Philip Alan Smith P 5/1/1973 Bp Robert Bruce Hall. m 9/21/1951 Betty Rhomberg. Supply P Dio Virginia Richmond VA 1986-2004; Asst Ch Of The Apos Fairfax VA 1983-1986; Pryr & Praise Tchr S Paul's Ch Bailey's Crossroads Falls Ch VA 1981-1983; Int Ch Of The H Comf Washington DC 1979-1981; S Pat's Ch Washington DC 1973-1979. Auth, "Case Hist Of Tentmakers".

PRATER, Willard Gibbs (O) 50 Green St, Thomaston ME 04861 Ret 1993-; Lic Supply P Dio Maine Portland ME 1998- B Forty Fort PA 1928 s Willard & Elizabeth. BA Wilkes Coll 1951; MDiv Bex Sem 1954. D 6/9/1954 P 12/17/1954 Bp Frederick Warnecke. c 3. Lic Supply P Dio Sthrn Ohio Cincinnati OH 1995-1997; Supply P Dio Ohio Cleveland 1993-1997; R Ch Of The H Trin Epis Bellefontaine OH 1966-1993; Vic S Geo's Epis Ch Hellertown PA 1957-1966; M-in-c Chr Ch Susquehanna PA 1954-1957; M-in-c Gr Epis Ch Great Bend PA 1954-1957; S Mk's New Milford PA 1954-1957.

PRATHER, Joel A (Mil) 503 E Walworth Ave, Delavan WI 53115 Chr Epis Ch Of Delavan Delavan WI 2014- B Elmhurst IL 1973 s Gerald & Catherine. AA Coll of Dupage 1994; BS Illinois St U 1996; MDiv Nash 2009. D 10/23/2008 P 5/16/2009 Bp Keith Lynn Ackerman. m 9/5/1998 Tammy M Prather c 1. Planter - Ch of the Sav, Allen TX Dio Dallas Dallas TX 2010-2014; Cur S Phil's Epis Ch Frisco TX 2009-2010. japrather@gmail.com

PRATHER, Lynn (Ga) 3504 Professional Cir Ste A, Martinez GA 30907 Asst The Ch Of The Gd Shpd Augusta GA 2013-; H Comf Ch Martinez GA 2010- B Augusta GA 1958 d David & Elizabeth. BS Augusta St U 1996; MDiv Sewanee: The U So, TS 2010. D 2/6/2010 P 8/21/2010 Bp Scott Anson Benhase. m 6/12/1982 Stuart H Prather c 2. pratheraugusta@aol.com

PRATI, Jason M (SO) PO Box 421, New Albany OH 43054 All SS Epis Ch New Albany OH 2014- B Wheeling WV 1976 s James & Rosanne. BA Pontifical Coll Josephinum 1998; MDiv Pontifical Coll Josephinum 2002; MDiv Pontifical Coll Josephinum 2002. Rec 4/9/2013 as Priest Bp Thomas Edward Breidenthal.

PRATOR, Lloyd (Eugene) (NY) 15620 Riverside Dr W Apt 13i, New York NY 10032 Adj Instr Liturg The GTS New York NY 2007- B Martinez CA 1944 s James & Hortense. BA Stan 1966; MDiv Other 1974; Cert GTS 1992. D 6/29/1974 P 5/24/1975 Bp Chauncie Kilmer Myers. Adj Instr Liturg The GTS New York NY 2000-2013; Liturg Cmsn 1994-1998; Lower Manhattan IPC 1993-1995; R S Jn's Ch New York NY 1988-2014; All SS' Ch San Francisco CA 1979-1988; Bp's Chapl Dio California San Francisco CA 1978-1979, Chair COM 1984-1987; Cur Trsfg Epis Ch San Mateo CA 1974-1978; Trst Cathd Of St Jn The Div New York NY 1998. Auth, "A P on the Line," From The Ashes, 2001; Auth, Selected Sermons, 1987. Associated Parishes 1977-1990; Assn of Angl Mus 1990-2000. Polly Bond Awd for Rel Writing 2002.

PRATT, Dorothy (ETenn) 5409 Jacksboro Pike, Knoxville TN 37918 Ch Of The Gd Shpd Knoxville TN 2016-; R All SS' Epis Cmnty Franklin NC 2005-; R S Cyp's Ch Franklin NC 2005- B Abington PA 1957 d Charles. MA U NC 1987; MDiv GTS 2005. D 5/28/2005 P 12/10/2005 Bp Porter Taylor. c 2. All S's Par of Agnes & Cyp Franklin NC 2016; R S Agnes Epis Ch Franklin NC 2005-2016; Exec Coun Dio Wstrn No Carolina Asheville NC 2012-2015, Dn of Wstrn Dnry 2007-2010, Congrl Dvlpmt/Vitality Com 2006-2011; Bd Mem Valle Crucis Conf Cntr 2011-2017. revdorothypratt@gmail.com

PRATT JR, Earle Wilson (LI) 3240 N Caves Valley Path, Lecanto FL 34461 Ret 2002- B New Castle PA 1941 s Earle & Mary. BA Youngstown St U 1963; MA Colg 1964; MDiv EDS 1969; PhD Untd States Intl U 1973. D 6/11/1969 P 6/1/1970 Bp Ned Cole. m 2/8/2013 Valerie H Pratt. R Trin-St Jn's Ch Hewlett NY 1974-2002; Non-par 1973-1980. Auth, "Case Stds".

PRATT, Grace Atherton (Va) 8009 Fort Hunt Rd, Alexandria VA 22308 S Lk's Ch Alexandria VA 2015- B New York NY 1987 d Scottow & Camille. B.A. The U So; Sewanee; MDiv VTS 2015. D 6/6/2015 Bp Shannon Sherwood Johnston P 12/12/2015 Bp Susan Goff. m 6/7/2014 David Alderman Pratt c 1. Other Lay Position S Lk's Par Darien CT 2010-2012. grace@saintlukeschurch.net

PRATT, Jennifer Julian (Oly) 2109 N Lafayette Ave, Bremerton WA 98312 **P - Vol S Hugh Of Lincoln Allyn WA 1997**- B San Francisco CA 1948 d Phillip & Frances. BA U CA 1966; MDiv Seattle U 1996. D 11/5/1997 Bp Vincent Waydell Warner P 6/20/1998 Bp Sanford Zangwill Kaye Hampton. m 6/13/1992 William Smith.

PRATT, Mary Florentine Corley (Vt) 865 Otter Creek Hwy, New Haven VT 05472 B Saint Johnsbury VT 1949 d William & Ruth. BS U of Vermont 1972. D 1/30/1981 Bp Robert Shaw Kerr. m 8/2/1969 John Arthur Pratt. D Trin Ch Rutland VT 1993-1997; Asst S Steph's Ch Middlebury VT 1990-1993; Asst S Paul's Epis Ch On The Green Vergennes VT 1983-1990; Asst S Lk's Epis Ch New Haven CT 1981-1983; S Mk's-S Lk's Epis Mssn Fair Haven VT 1981-1983; Cmnty D.

PRATT-HORSLEY, Mary Elizabeth (ECR) 308 Lilac Dr, Los Osos CA 93402 **Died 2/26/2017** B Kenosha WI 1946 d Ernest & Ruth. AA Un Coll Cranford NJ 1982; BA Rutgers The St U of New Jersey 1986; MA California St U 1990; MDiv CDSP 1995. D 5/16/1995 P 12/2/1995 Bp Richard Lester Shimpfky. m 7/12/1969 John Anthony Horsley c 2. R S Ben's Par Los Osos CA 2000-2006; D, Asstg P S Thos Epis Ch Sunnyvale CA 1995-2000; Santa Maria Urban Mnstry San Jose CA 1995-2000; Santa Maria Urban Mnstry San Jose CA 1995-2000. scl Rutgers U, NJ 1986; Phi Beta Kappa.

PRAY, Frederick Russell (NJ) 221 Ivy Rd, Edgewater Park NJ 08010 **D S Steph's Epis Ch Beverly NJ 2005**- B Philadelphia PA 1944 s Frederick & Marie. D 4/13/1985 Bp George Phelps Mellick Belshaw. m 9/9/1967 Roberta Louise Thompson c 2. D/Asst Par Of Chr The King Willingboro NJ 1985-1993. Keiros Prison Mnstry 1981-2008; Ord S Lk 2006.

PREAS, Barbara Jean (Nev) 10328 SUMMER RIVER AV., Las Vegas NV 89144 **D Gr In The Desert Epis Ch Las Vegas NV 1994**- B Milwaukee WI 1939 d Howard & Mildred. BS U of Wisconsin 1961. D 10/1/1994 Bp Stewart Clark Zabriskie. m 7/24/1982 Rhine F Preas c 4. Claims Person Of The Year Sthrn Nevada Claims Assn 1995.

PREBLE, Charles William (Minn) PO Box 844, Saint Joseph MN 56374 **Prior Marygate Hermitage S Jos MN 1986-; Dioc Chair Of Hunger 1983**- B Santa Ana CA 1936 s Donovan & Charlotte. BA U CA 1957; BD CDSP 1960; PSR 1962; Natl Trng Lab 1976; Guelph Inst Chr Sprtlty 1978; Creighton U 1980; Arizona St U 1981; U of Nevada 1984. D 6/14/1962 Bp Ivol I Curtis P 12/14/1962 Bp Gordon V Smith. m 7/3/1963 Jana M B Preble c 2. Dn Of Reg 3 Dio Minnesota Minneapolis MN 1988-1998, Dioc Coun 1990-1992; Ch Of Our Sav Little Falls MN 1987-1997; Int S Jn's Ch S Cloud MN 1986-1987; Pres Of The Campus Chr Assn U Of Nevada 1983-1986; Chair Of The Cmsn For Evang & Renwl 1976-1980; R Dio Nevada Las Vegas 1974-1979, Stndg Com 1979-1982, Dir Of The Discovery Proj 1974-1978; R S Steph's Epis Ch Reno NV 1973-1986; 1973-1976; Secy Of The Dioc Conv Dio Utah Salt Lake City UT 1971-1973, Secy Of The Exec Coun 1970-1973; Vic S Barn Episcopal Church Tooele UT 1967-1973; Vic S Steph's Granger UT 1967-1973; Chapl S Mk's Hosp Salt Lake City UT 1967-1969; Assoc S Mich's Ch New York NY 1965-1967; Chapl Gri IA 1962-1965; Vic S Paul's Epis Ch Grinnell IA 1962-1965; Bd Epis Hse of Pryr 1987-1992; Cler Dep GC 1976-1979. Auth, "The Ruffed Grouse," *The Ruffed Grouse*, Cup and Spiral, 2012; Auth, "H Dying," *Oblate Handbook*, Liturg Press, 2009; Auth, "St. Ben's Mnstry," *S Jn's: 150 years*, Liturg Press, 2005; Auth, "The Oblate Abbot," *The Oblate Wrld*, Liturg Press, 1997. Ord Of Agape And Reconciliation; Soc Of S Marg.

PREBLE, Joan Nelson (Me) 55 Union St # 4606, Ellsworth ME 04605 B Portland ME 1940 BS Gorham St Teachers Coll Gorham ME. D 5/3/2003 Bp Chilton Richardson Knudsen. m 8/10/1963 Ralph Allen Preble c 2.

PRECHTEL, Daniel L (Chi) 2337 Greenwich Rd, San Pablo CA 94806 **Asstg P All Souls Par In Berkeley Berkeley CA 2010-; Fndr & Sprtl Guide Lamb & Lion Sprtl Gdnc Mnstrs San Pablo CA 1994**- B Battle Creek MI 1948 s Earl & Joyce. BA Wstrn Michigan U 1972; MDiv SWTS 1984; Cert Upper Room Acad of Sprtl Formation Nashville TN 1990; DMin SWTS 2002. D 6/11/1984 Bp Charles Bennison Sr P 12/22/1984 Bp Howard Samuel Meeks. m 6/10/1989 Ruth Meyers c 2. Adj Instr CALL and Theol Field Educ CDSP Berkeley CA 2010-2013; Dir Grp Sprtl Comp Prog Inst of Sprtl Comp Oak Pk IL 2008-2009; P-in-c S Aug's Epis Ch Wilmette IL 2006, 2004; Consult S Clem's Ch Harvey IL 2001-2002; Adj Fac Bexley Seabury Fed Chicago IL 1999-2008; P-in-c S Matt's Ch Evanston IL 1997; Int Asst The Annunc Of Our Lady Gurnee IL 1996-1997; R S Jn's Epis Ch Charlotte MI 1984-1995. Auth, "Light on the Path: Guiding Symbols for Insight and Discernment," *Light on the Path: Guiding Symbols for Insight and Discernment*, Morehouse-Ch Pub, 2016; Auth, "Where Two or Three are Gathered: Sprtl Direction for Sm Groups," *Where Two or Three are Gathered: Sprtl Direction for Sm Groups*, Morehouse-Ch Pub, 2012; Auth, "To Live More Nearly as We Pray: Pryr Shaping Communities," *Liturg Journ*, The Liturg Conf, 2011; Interviewed by Laura Bruno, "If I Only Had a Brain Injury," *If I Only Had a Brain Injury*, XLibris, 2008; Auth, "From Discord To Discernment," *Open: Journ Of AP*, AP, 2001; Auth, "A Chr Reawakening To The Dream," *Dream Ntwk: A Journ Exploring Dreams & Mythology*, Dream Ntwk, 2000; Auth, "Angl Sprtl Direction By Ptr Ball (Bk Revs)," *Open: Journ Of AP*, AP, 1999; Auth, "Well Sprg," 1993; Auth, "Guidelines For

Chr Living Baptismal Preparation," 1992; Auth, "Guidelines For Chr Living: Conscious Beginnings," 1992. Soc For The Study Of Chr Sprtlty 2001; Sprtl Dir Intl 1991; St. Greg'S Abbey - Three Rivers, Mi - Oblate 2000. dprechtel@llministries.com

PREECE, Mark W (Vt) 220 E 6th Ave, Conshohocken PA 19428 **S Mart's Epis Ch Fairlee VT 2014-; R Trin Ch Gulph Mills 2003**- B Norwalk CT 1953 s Warren & Deborah. BA Dart 1975; MA EDS 1978. D 6/23/2001 P 12/23/2001 Bp Charles Ellsworth Bennison Jr. m 6/25/1995 Patricia Anne Preece c 1. S Paul's Epis Ch White Riv Jct VT 2013-2014; S Jn's Epis Ch Randolph VT 2011-2013; Int Pstr Imm Ch Bellows Falls VT 2008-2011; Trin Ch Gulph Mills Kng Of Prussia PA 2003-2008; Dio Pennsylvania Philadelphia PA 2001-2003; P-in-c S Steph's Epis Ch Norwood PA 2001-2003.

PREGNALL, William Stuart (WA) 132 Lancaster Dr #410, Irvington VA 22480 **Ret 1993**- B Charleston SC 1931 s Alexander & Marion. BA U NC 1952; MDiv VTS 1958; DMin Sewanee: The U So, TS 1977. D 6/12/1958 P 5/26/1959 Bp Thomas N Carruthers. m 12/20/1952 Gabrielle J Pregnall c 3. S Geo's Ch Fredericksburg VA 1993-2001; S Mary's Chap Ridge Ridge MD 1993-1994; St Marys Par St Marys City MD 1989-1993; Dn & Pres CDSP Berkeley CA 1981-1989; Prof VTS Alexandria VA 1973-1981; Vic/R S Aug's Epis Ch Washington DC 1970-1973; Chapl LSU Baton Rouge LA 1966-1970; R S Jn's Epis Ch Charleston WV 1962-1966, Asst 1961, In-c 1958-1960; DCE So Carolina Charleston SC 1960-1961; Epis Ch Of The H Trin Ridgeland SC 1958-1960; The Ch Of The Cross Bluffton SC 1958-1960. Auth, *Epis Sem System during the Decline of the Amer Empire*, 1988; Auth, *Laity & Liturg*, 1975; Auth, "Intro," *PB Renwl*. DD CDSP 1990; Doctor in Div VTS 1987.

PREHM, Katherine T. (Spok) 3401 W Lincoln Ave, Yakima WA 98902 B Bellingham WA 1939 d Norman & Margaret. BA Wstrn Washington U 1964; EdM Wstrn Washington U 1966; Dioc Sch of Mnstry Spokane WA 1995; EFM Sewanee: The U So, TS 1997. D 6/8/1997 Bp Frank Jeffrey Terry P 6/2/2002 Bp James E Waggoner Jr. m 11/20/1970 James Prehm c 4. P S Tim's Epis Ch Yakima WA 2002-2009, D 1997-2002.

PREHN III, Walter Lawrence (NwT) 5308 Carrington Ct, Midland TX 79707 **Headmaster Trin Sch Of Midland Inc. Midland TX 2010**- B Palo Alto CA 1957 s Walter & Rebecca. BA Texas A&M U 1979; MDiv Nash 1985; PhD U of Virginia 2005. D 6/13/1985 P 12/21/1985 Bp Donis Dean Patterson. m 4/30/1988 Cecilia Prehn c 3. S Lk's Epis Ch San Antonio TX 2005-2010; Chapl & Asst Headmaster TMI-The Epis Sch of Texas San Antonio TX 1996-2001; Texas Mltry Inst San Antonio TX 1996-2001; Instr Hist/Theol Bp's Sch for Mnstry 1993-1996; R S Marg's Epis Ch San Antonio TX 1990-1996; Epis Chapl Bryn & Hav PA 1987-1990; Cur The Ch Of The Gd Shpd Rosemont PA 1987-1990; Cur Ch Of The H Cross Dallas TX 1985-1987; Chapl S Philips Epis Sch Dallas TX 1985-1987; Chair Of Liturg And Mus Cmsn Dio W Texas San Antonio TX 1990-1993. Auth, "Epis Schools: Hist & Mssn," *Handbook of Faith-based Educ in Amer*, Clio/Praeger Acad, 2011; Auth, "Bk Revs," *LivCh mag*, TLC Fndt; Auth, "poems," *LivCh, San Antonio Express-News*. Amer Hist Assn 2003; HSEC 2005; Orgnztn of Amer Historians 2003; St. Mich's Soc for the Prom of the Ch Sch 2003. Distinguished Alum Chamberlain-Hunt Acad MS 1990; Distinguished Alum Chamberlain-Hunt Acad MS 1990; cl Nash 1985.

PRENDERGAST, James David (Los) 1325 Monterey Rd, South Pasadena CA 91030 **Atty-Gnrl Counsel First Amer Title Ins. Co. 2001**- B 1943 s Edward & Ernestine. JD UC Hasting Coll of Law 1974; MAT Fuller Sem 2010; LLM Cardiff U 2014. D 6/7/2014 P 1/17/2015 Bp Joseph Jon Bruno. c 3.

PRENTICE, David Ralph (Mass) All Saints Episcopal Church, 46 Cherry St, Danvers MA 01923 B Westbrook ME 1963 s Robert & Joy. Cert EDS 2008; MDiv EDS 2012. D 6/7/2014 Bp M(Arvil) Thomas Shaw P 7/23/2016 Bp Alan Gates. m 9/22/1990 Kim Drogan Kim Ann Drogan c 1. P Emm Epis Ch Wakefield MA 2014-2015.

PRESCOTT, Vicki (Roch) 2500 East Avenue, Apartment 5H, Rochester NY 14610 B Sterling IL 1950 d Richard & Juanita. Syr; BS U IL 1973; MDiv UTS 1980. D 6/20/1981 P 6/20/1982 Bp Ned Cole. m 9/1/1973 Paul Couch c 1. R Ch Of The Incarn Penfield NY 2001-2013; R All SS Ch Cincinnati OH 1999-2001; S Barn Epis Ch Greenwich CT 1994-1998; S Fran Ch Stamford CT 1994-1995; S Steph's Ch Ridgefield CT 1993-1994; Ch Of The Resurr Oswego NY 1992; Yth Coordntr Dio Cntrl New York Liverpool NY 1990-1992; Int Chr Epis Ch Jordan NY 1988-1989; Asst St Paul's Syracuse Syracuse NY 1981-1983.

PRESCOTT, W Clarke (Los) 8830 Mesa Oak Dr, Riverside CA 92508 **Vic S Andr's By The Lake Lake Elsinore CA 2011-; Vic St Steph's Epis Ch Menifee CA 2011-; Coordntr Liga Intl Flying Doctors of Mercy 2004-; P-in Charge All SS Par Los Angeles CA 2014**- B Atlanta GA 1943 s Ralph & Ethel. BA Manhattan Coll 1969; MDiv Bex Sem 1972; MA US Intl U San Diego CA 1987; Naval Chapl Sch 1991. D 6/3/1972 Bp Paul Moore Jr P 12/16/1972 Bp Robert Rae Spears Jr. m 3/17/2007 Jeanette Prescott c 2. Asst S Geo's Ch Riverside CA 2008-2009; R All SS Epis Ch Riverside CA 1996-2005; Chapl S Marg's Epis Sch In San Juan Capistrano 1994-1996; Chapl S Marg's Epis Sch San Juan Capo CA 1994-1996; Asst Trin Par New York NY 1992-1993; Chapl USN 1982-1993; Chapl Off Of Bsh For ArmdF New York NY 1982-1992; Assoc Par Ch of St. Helena Beaufort SC 1980-1982; R S Paul's Ch Washington

687

NC 1979-1980; R Zion Epis Ch Washington NC 1978-1980; P-in-c Buen Pstr San Jose Costa Rica 1976-1977; Dio Costa Rica San Jose 1976-1977; Asst S Paul's Ch Rochester NY 1973-1976; Asst Chr Ch Pittsford Pittsford NY 1972-1973. apadre@apadre.com

PRESLER, Henry Airheart (NC) Po Box 293, Monroe NC 28111 **Assoc S Tim's Ch Raleigh NC 2010-** B Naini Tal Uttar Pradesh IN 1940 s Henry & Marion. BA U NC 1973; MA U NC 1976; MDiv GTS 1985. D 6/2/1985 P 6/7/1986 Bp Frank Harris Vest Jr. m 10/5/1963 Judith L Presler c 4. R S Paul's Ch Monroe NC 1988-2008; Vic Chap Of The Gd Shpd Ridgeway NC 1987-1988; Vic All SS Ch Warrenton NC 1986-1988; R Emm Ch Warrenton NC 1986-1988.

PRESLER, Jane Crosby (Vt) 2534 Hill West Rd., Montgomery VT 05471 **P-in-Partnership S Matt's Ch Enosburg Fls VT 2011-** B Plymouth MA 1950 d Charles & Virginia. Bard Coll 1969; BS Bos 1972; MDiv EDS 1989. D 6/3/1989 Bp David Elliot Johnson P 6/10/1990 Bp David Bell Birney IV. m 4/6/1974 Titus Leonard Presler c 4. Int Gr Ch White Plains NY 2006-2010; S Jn's Ch Staten Island NY 2006; Epis Ch Cntr New York NY 1999-2005; P-in-c S Aug And S Mart Ch Boston MA 1996-1999; All SS Ch Stoneham MA 1995-1996; Co-R S Ptr's Epis Ch Cambridge MA 1991-1995; Assoc R S Paul's Ch Dedham MA 1989-1991; Mssy in Zimbabwe 1983-1986. "Windows on Mssn (DVD)," DFMS; "The Scripture of Their Lives," Morehouse Pub. Twenty Club. Hon Cn St. Jn's Cathd in the Dio Peshawar, Ch of Pale.

PRESLER, Titus Leonard (Vt) PO Box 501, Montgomery VT 05471 **Vic St. Matt's Epis Ch Enosburg Falls VT 2014-; Prncpl Edwardes Coll Peshawar Pakistan 2011-; GC Dep Dio Vermont 2018-; Bd Mem Global Epis Mssn Ntwk 2015-** B Mussoorie Uttar Pradesh India 1950 s Henry & Marion. Procter Fell EDS; Merrill Fell Harvard DS; MDiv GTS 1972; BA Harv 1972; ThD Bos 1995. D 6/9/1979 Bp John Bowen Coburn P 2/9/1980 Bp Morris Fairchild Arnold. m 4/6/1974 Jane Crosby Butterfield c 4. Vstng Prof of Missiology Pittsburgh TS Pittsburgh PA 2014-2015; Int R St. Simon the Cyrenian Epis Ch 2009-2011; SubDean & VP Acad Affrs & Prof of Mssn & Wrld Chrsnty The GTS New York NY 2005-2009; Dn And Pres Epis TS Of The SW Austin TX 2002-2005; Lectr on Mssn GTS 2000-2002; Lectr on Preaching Harvard DS 2000-2002; EDS Cambridge MA 1993-1997; R S Ptr's Epis Ch Cambridge MA 1991-2002; Int R The Par Of S Chrys's Quincy MA 1990-1991; Assoc All SS' Epis Ch Belmont MA 1988-1990; Chr Ch Cambridge Cambridge MA 1987-1988; Exec Coun Appointees New York NY 1983-1987, Exec Coun 2003-2007, Secy, then Chair, SCWM 1997-2003; R S Dav Mssn & Bonda Ch Distr Manicaland Zimbabwe 1983-1986; Chr Ch S Hamilton MA 1979-1983; Consult Angl Cont Indaba 2009-2011; Resrch, Global Anglicanism Proj ECF Inc New York NY 2002-2006; Jubilee 2000 T/F Dio Massachusetts Boston MA 1997-2002, Nomin Com for PBp 1997-2000, Vol for Mssn Com Co-Chair 1991-2002, GC Dep 1988-2001, Stwdshp Cmsn Chair 1987-2000; Strng Com Mem Epis Partnership for Global Mssn 1995-2008. Auth, "Witness, Advocacy & Un: Anglicanism's Contribution to Chr Presence in So Asia," *Oxford Hist of Anglicanism*, Oxford, 2017; Auth, "Terrorism & Rel: A Link We Must Acknowledge, Not Deny," *Epis News Serv*, Epis News Serv, 2016; Auth, "Educ, Rel & Risk in Peshawar: A Missional Self-Examination," *Missiology*, Missiology, 2016; Auth, "Why Has Pakistan Become So Intolderant?," *Daily Beast*, Daily Beast, 2015; Auth, "Toll on the Soul: Costs of Persecution among Pakistan's Christians," *Intl Bulletin of Mssn Resrch*, Intl Bulletin of Mssn Resrch, 2015; Auth, "Persecuted in Pakistan: A Chr Eductr Survives a Beatin," *Chr Century*, Chr Century, 2014; Auth, "Hist of Mssn in the Angl Comm," *Wiley-Blackwell Comp to Angl Comm*, Wiley-Blackwell, 2013; Auth, "Going Global w God: Reconciling Mssn in a Wrld of Difference," Morehouse, 2010; Auth, "Mssn is Mnstry in Dimension of Difference," *Intl Bulletin of Mssy Resrch*, Intl Bulletin of Mssn Resrch, 2010; Auth, "Impact of Sxlty Controversy on Mssn: Case of Epis Ch," *Intl Bulletin of Mssy Resrch*, Intl Bulletin of Mssn Resrch, 2009; Auth, "Alert for Signs: Seeing and Praying through Adv," Forw Mvmt, 2007; Auth, "Listening toward Recon: A Conversation Initiative in Today's Angl Alienations," *ATR*, ATR, 2007; Auth, "Angl Comm Crisis: Complex in Politics and Causes," *Epis New Yorker*, Epis New Yorker, 2007; Auth, "Comp: An Angl Sprtlty of Mssn," *The Angl*, The Angl, 2007; Auth, "BCP in Cntrl Afr," *Oxford Comp to BCP*, Oxford, 2006; Co-Auth, "The Vitality and Promise of Being Angl," ECF, 2005; Auth, "Ldr as Catalyst: Eleven Principles of Chr Ldrshp," *Vstry Resource Guide*, ECF, 2004; Co-Auth, "Comp in Transformation: The Epis Ch's Wrld Mssn in a New Century," Morehouse, 2003; Auth, "Horizons of Mssn," Cowley, 2001; Auth, "Old & New In Wrshp & Cmnty," *ATR*, ATR, 2000; Auth, "Transfigured Night: Mssn & Culture in Zimbabwe's Vigil Mvmt," U of So Afr Press, 1999; Auth, "Rel and Politics in Zimbabwe," *Encyclopedia of Politics and Rel*, Congressional Quarterly Press, 1998; Auth, "Mssy Anglicanism Meets Afr Traditional Rel: A Restropective on Bp. Knight-Bruce's Entry Into Zimbabwe," *Missionalia*, Missionalia, 1989. Amer Soc Of Missiology 1988; Epis Partnership for Global Mssn 1992-2011; EPF 1997; Global Epis Mssn Ntwk 2015; Intl Assn Of Mssn Stds 1985. Hon Cn Theol Dio Cntrl Pennsylvania 2008; DD SWTS 2005; DD GTS 2003; Doctoral Fllshp ECF 1988.

PRESSENTIN, Elsa Ann (EMich) 7562 Alex Ct, Freeland MI 48623 B Holland MI 1944 d Paul & Vera. AB Cntrl Michigan U 1966; BA Sch for Deacons 1984. D 6/7/1986 Bp William Edwin Swing P 5/23/1998 Bp Jerry Alban Lamb. Mnstry Develoopment and Transition Mnstry Dio Estrn Michigan Saginaw MI 2008-2012, 2005-2006; Asst S Paul's Epis Ch Bad Axe MI 2000-2009; S Jn's Epis Ch Saginaw MI 2000-2003; Exec Secy Epis Conf of the Deaf 1990-1994; Vic H Sprt Ch Of The Deaf San Lorenzo CA 1989-2000; H Sprt Mssn For The Deaf San Francisco CA 1988-2000; D-in-c H Sprt Ch of the Deaf Berkeley CA 1986-1989.

PRESSEY, Stephen Palmer (Mich) 1792 Celeste Circle, Youngstown OH 44511 **Dioc Coun Detroit MI 1980-** B Baker OR 1929 s Herbert & Alma. BA Trin 1951; BD Bex Sem 1958. D 5/30/1958 P 12/19/1958 Bp Nelson Marigold Burroughs. m 12/27/1970 Constance M Jeswald c 4. Supply St. Aug Youngstown OH 2007-2013; P-in-c St. Rocco's Youngstown OH 1995-2007; R St. Jn's Temperance MI 1994-1995; S Andr's Ch Jackson MI 1985-1994; R S Kath's Ch Williamston MI 1977-1985; Vic S Rocco's Ch Youngstown OH 1969-1977; 1966-1968; R S Mk's Epis Ch Shelby OH 1958-1965. Auth, *Habakkuk*; Auth, *Jeremiah's Confession*.

PRESSLEY JR, Dennis Charles (Alb) Po Box 206, Greenwich NY 12834 **Died 7/9/2016** B Riverside NJ 1952 s Dennis & Margaret. Cert Berean U 1973. D 5/10/1999 P 11/13/1999 Bp Daniel William Herzog. m 12/8/1973 Veronica Lynn Mackey c 3. Dio Albany Greenwich NY 2003-2014, 1997-1999; Chr Ch Pottersville NY 2000-2016; Ch Of The Gd Shpd Brant Lake NY 2000-2016; S Andr's Ch Schroon Lake NY 2000-2016; S Barbara's Ch Newcomb NY 2000-2016; S Chris's Ch No Creek NY 2000-2016; Asst S Paul's Ch Brant Lake NY 2000-2016; Barry Hse Retreat Cntr Brant Lake NY 1999-2002.

PREST JR, Alan Patrick Llewellyn (Va) 3920 Custis Rd, Richmond VA 23225 B Detroit MI 1928 s Alan & Mary. BS Leh 1951; MDiv EDS 1954. D 6/9/1954 P 3/26/1955 Bp Walter H Gray. m 6/16/1956 Joan Prest c 5. Ethics Com S Mary Hosp Richmond VA 1994-2000; Adj Prof TS Richmond VA 1960-1990; Emer Prof VA Commonwealth U Richmond VA 1958-1993; Chapl S Lk Hosp Houston TX 1956-1957; Asst S Andr's Ch Meriden CT 1954-1956; Ret VA Un Universary Richmond VA. Auth, "Uncommon Pryr," Lulu Publ., 2005; Auth, "Prayers," *Hymnal for Wrshp*, NCCC, 1982; Auth, "By What Authority," *Journ Pstr Care*, Vandenhoeck, 1976; Auth, *Care for Dying*, Jn Knox, 1975; Auth, *Psychoanalytic Contributions to Cmnty Psychol*, Chas Thos, 1971; Auth, "By What Authority," Journ Pstr Care, 1970; Auth, "Suicide," *A Psych's Friend*, Journ Pstr Care. Amer Assn for Pstr Counselors 1972; ACPE 1959; Coll of Chapl 1975. Helen Flanders Dunbar Awd Coll of Pstr 2006; DD STUSo 1977.

PRESTEGARD, Joann Maxine (Oly) 55 Irving St, Cathlamet WA 98612 **Serv S Jas Epis Ch Cathlamet WA 1999-** B Woodland WA 1938 d Walter & Inez. D 10/3/1998 Bp Vincent Waydell Warner P 5/4/1999 Bp Sanford Zangwill Kaye Hampton. m 9/16/1967 Ray Elton Prestegard.

PRESTON II, James Montgomery (Tex) 1310 Malmaison Ridge Dr, Spring TX 77379 B San Antonio TX 1936 s Allan & Jenna. BA U of Houston 1963; MDiv Sewanee: The U So, TS 1967; Cert Oll Prof Tchr 1973. D 7/13/1967 Bp Everett H Jones P 1/27/1968 Bp Richard Earl Dicus. c 1. Int P S Jas' Par So Pasadena CA 1999-2000; Int S Steph's Hollywood CA 1999-2000; S Johns Pro-Cathd Los Angeles CA 1995-1997; Non-par 1983-1995; R Gr Epis Ch Houston TX 1979-1983; CPE Chapl S Lk's Hosp Houston TX 1977-1979; Dio The Dominican Republic (Iglesia Epis Dominicana) Gazcue Santo Domingo 1974-1979; Headmaster Par Sch San Pedro De Marcoris Dominican Republic 1974-1976; P-in-c Gr In Falfurrias 1968-1971; P-in-c S Jas Epis Ch Hebronville TX 1968-1971. Auth, "Mortal," *The Atlantic Contest*, 1963.

PRESTON, Leigh C (ETenn) 305 W 7th St, Chattanooga TN 37402 **Dom And Frgn Mssy Soc- Epis Ch Cntr New York NY 2007-** B Oakland, CA 1981 d Kenneth & Nancey. AB U GA Athens GA 2003; MDiv Ya Berk 2007. D 12/21/2006 P 7/1/2007 Bp J Neil Alexander. m 7/31/2004 Andrew R Thompson c 2. S Paul's Epis Ch Chattanooga TN 2014-2017; S Steph's Ch Richmond VA 2012-2014; Dio Connecticut Meriden CT 2010-2012; Grtr Hartford Reg Mnstry E Hartford CT 2008-2009; Exec Coun Appointees New York NY 2007-2008.

PRESTON, Robert George (SeFla) 401 SW 6th Ave, Hallandale Beach FL 33009 **Ret 1991-** B Tecumseh MI 1924 s John & Margaret. BA Carroll Coll 1950; Nash 1953. Trans 8/3/1955 as Priest Bp Martin J Bram. R S Andr's Epis Ch Of Hollywood Hollywood FL 1977-1991; S Anne's Epis Ch Hallandale Bch FL 1977-1991; Asst S Benedicts Ch Ft Lauderdale FL 1974-1976; Asst San Jose Epis Ch Jacksonville FL 1969-1974; Asst St Paul's Epis Ch Peoria IL 1959-1962; Vic S Jos Chicago IL 1955-1959; Serv Ch Of Can 1952-1955; Secy Dio Quincy Peoria IL 1964-1969.

PRESTON, Shannon E (Minn) **The Ch of the Gd Shpd Austin TX 2016-** D 12/16/2014 P 6/20/2015 Bp Brian N Prior.

PRESTON, Troy Lynn (Roch) Christ Episcopal Church, 33 E 1st St, Corning NY 14830 B Wellsboro PA 1973 s Leland & Rosalie. Dplma Bexley Seabury; MDiv Colgate Rochester Crozer DS; BS Mansfield U of Pennsylvania. D 4/1/2016 P 10/2/2016 Bp Prince Grenville Singh. m 6/19/2010 Kevin W Hillman. Chr Ch Corning NY 2016, R 2016-. tpreston@stny.rr.com

PRETTI, Victoria (NJ) 893 Main St, West Newbury MA 01985 **Ch Of S Mary's By The Sea Pt Pleas Bch NJ 2016-** B Winthrop MA 1958 d Joseph & Diana. ADN No Shore Coll 1984; MDiv Weston Jesuit TS 2004; Cert Epis Div 2008. D 6/6/2009 Bp M(Arvil) Thomas Shaw. m 9/27/2007 Anthony Pretti c 1. S Mary's Epis Ch Stone Harbor NJ 2014-2016; P-in-c Ch Of Our Sav Milton MA 2011-2014; All SS Ch W Newbury MA 2009-2011. administrator@ saintmarysbythesea.org

PREVATT JR, James Thomas (NC) 5104 Ainsworth Dr, Greensboro NC 27410 **Ret 2001-** B Monticello GA 1938 s James & Vida. BA Emory U 1960; BD Duke 1963; MTh Duke 1964; GTS 1965; VTS 1981. D 6/29/1965 P 6/29/1966 Bp Thomas Augustus Fraser Jr. m 4/16/1966 Muriel E Prevatt c 2. Vic S Barn' Ch Greensboro NC 1971-2001; Cur Ch Of The Atone Tenafly NJ 1965-1967. The Fllshp of St. Jn the Evang.

PREVOST, Edward Simpson (Chi) 6 Brookshire Rd, Worcester MA 01609 **Ret . 2011-; Bd Trst The GTS New York NY 2007-, Alum Assn Pres 1988-2006** B Elizabeth NJ 1944 s Sterett & Elizabeth. BA Trin 1967; BA Trin Sch 1967; MDiv GTS 1970. D 6/10/1970 Bp John Henry Esquirol P 12/20/1970 Bp Joseph Warren Hutchens. m 6/6/1970 Beverly Prevost c 2. COM Chair Dio Chicago Chicago IL 1995-1999, Com Chair 1995-1999, COM 1993-1999; R Chr Ch Winnetka IL 1992-2011; R S Paul's Ch Fairfield CT 1981-1992; R S Paul's Ch Southington CT 1973-1981; Cur S Jn The Evang Yalesville CT 1970-1973; S Paul's Ch Wallingford CT 1970-1973; COM Dio Connecticut Meriden CT 1977-1992. Auth, "R's Sermon," *On the Sabbath After 9/11*, Brandylane, 2002. Bp of Newark Preaching Prize GTS 1970.

PRICE, Ashburn Birdsall (CFla) 1781 Pocahontas Path, Maitland FL 32751 **D'S Assoc S Richard 1980-** B New York NY 1915 s Charles & Margaret. BA NYU 1936. D 1/18/1980 Bp William Hopkins Folwell. m 4/29/1943 Dorothy Brown.

PRICE, Barbara Deane (Ak) Po Box 56419, North Pole AK 99705 **D S Mk's Ch 1996-** B Lakewood OH 1944 d Richard & Florence. BA Coll of Wooster 1966; MA U of Texas 1969; MEd Duquesne U 1984; Paths To Serv Trng AK 1996; PsyD Sthrn California U For Profsnl Stds 2002. D 12/9/1996 Bp Howard Samuel Meeks. m 6/16/1990 Murray D Price. Auth, "Meditation On Adv," *Coun Of Wmn Mnstrs Dom & Frgn Mssy Soc Pecusa*, 2000; Auth, "Meditation On Untimely Death," *Coun Of Wmn Mnstrs Dom &Frgn Mssy Soc Pecusa*, 2000. AAPC; Amer Counslg Assn 1984. Appreciation Tanana Chiefs Conf 2000.

PRICE, Barbara Jean (WNY) 77 Huntington Ave, Buffalo NY 14214 **Chapl Cmnty of Spouses of the HOB 2008-; Dir The Hope Cntr 2014-; Founding Dir Morningstar Mnstrs 2008-** B Buffalo NY 1949 d LeRoy & Doris. RN EJ Meyer Memi Hosp Nrsng Sch 1970; BS S Josephs Coll 1988; MDiv Bex Sem 1997. D 6/7/1997 P 12/20/1997 Bp David Charles Bowman. m 9/26/1992 Alfred Price c 3. Dir of the Hope Cntr S Paul's Epis Ch Lewiston NY 2015, P-in-c 2015-; Congrl Transition and Dvlpmt Dio Wstrn New York Tonawanda NY 2012-2014, Cn for Congrl Dvlpmt & Deploy 1997-2004, Consult 1989-2000, Admin 1989-1992; Vic Ephphatha Epis Ch Of The Deaf Eggertsville NY 2001-2003; R S Ptr's Epis Ch Buffalo NY 2000-2014; Sub-Dn Bex Sem Columbus OH 2004-2008; Asst S Paul's Cathd Buffalo NY 1997-1998; Int Trin Ch Lancaster NY 1988-1999. Auth, "One Living in Pvrty," *Lifting Wmn Voices*, Morehouse, 2009; Auth, "From a Wmn Who Has Lost Her Baby," *Lifting Wmn Voices*, Morehouse, 2009; Auth, "A Litany w Prayers for Wmn," *Lifting Wmn Voices*, Morehouse, 2009; Auth, "Psalm For A Widow," *Wmn Uncommon Prayers*. SCHC 1997; Sprtl Dir Intl 1995. barbaraprice@episcopalwny.org

PRICE, Basil Hayes (WK) **P-in-c S Jn's Ch Great Bend KS 2017-; Pstr Intern Chr Cathd Salina KS 2015-; Pstr Intern Epis Ch Of The Incarn Salina KS 2015-** B 1950 s Basil & Buena. BS Emporia St U 1974; MS Ft Hays St U 1985; Cert Bp Kemper Sch for Mnstry 2015. D 12/12/2015 P 11/5/2016 Bp Mike Milliken. m 8/30/1974 Jane Anne Rees. bhprice2@cox.net

PRICE, Darwin Ladavis (LI) PO Box 280, Brewster MA 02631 **Ret 2009-** B Hopewell VA 1943 s Baldy & Reathella. BA U of Hartford 1967; MDiv Harvard DS 1970; EDS 1971. D 6/10/1970 Bp John Henry Esquirol P 2/21/1971 Bp Anson Phelps Stokes Jr. m 12/23/1967 Grace Price c 4. R S Lk's Ch E Hampton NY 2007-2009; Bd Trsts Pediatric Care Hiv/Aids Dio Washington Washington DC 1992-1997, Stndg Com 1991-1997; Cathd of St Ptr & St Paul Washington DC 1991-1997; R S Mary's Epis Ch Foggy Bottom Washington DC 1990-1997; R Calv Ch Suffield CT 1981-1990; Chapl, Tchr Miss Porter's Sch Farmington CT 1978-1981; Lt. Col. USAF Ny Air NG 1975-2001; S Geo's Sch Middletown RI 1975-1978; Chapl S Mary's Ch Portsmouth RI 1973-1978; Assoc The Ch Of The H Sprt Orleans MA 1972-1975; Asst All SS Par Brookline MA 1970-1972. Auth, "Coffee Hse Mnstry and the Counter Culture," *Parnass*, 1976. EME 1976-1986.

PRICE, David Lee 15967 169th Ave Se, Monroe WA 98272 **Died 2/11/2017** B Indianapolis IN 1947 s Anthony & Mary. BA U of Alaska 1995; MDiv SWTS 1999. D 5/1/1999 Bp Mark Lawrence Macdonald P 12/6/1999 Bp Sanford Zangwill Kaye Hampton. m 10/4/2003 Donna Price c 2. Ch Of The Trsfg Darrington WA 2008-2017; Supply P S Fran Epis Ch Bothell WA 2008-2017, 1999-2006.

PRICE, David William (Tex) 302 S Hardie St, Alvin TX 77511 **S Fran Ch Houston TX 2016-** B Tucson AZ 1956 s Hermon & Margaret. BA U of Arizona 1979; MDiv Epis TS of the SW 1984. D 6/16/1984 Bp Joseph Thomas Heistand P 6/1/1985 Bp Sam Byron Hulsey. m 6/27/1981 Jennifer Price c 3. R Gr Epis Ch Alvin TX 2006-2016; R S Mk's Ch Houston TX 1994-2006; R S Phil's Epis Ch Palestine TX 1990-1994; S Paul's On The Plains Epis Ch Lubbock TX 1986-1990; Cur Ch Of The H Trin Midland TX 1984-1986. dprice@sfch.org

PRICE, George Harry (SeFla) 2300 Spanish River Rd, Boca Raton FL 33432 B Mount Holly NJ 1938 s George & Naomi. BA Hobart and Wm Smith Colleges 1961; MDiv PDS 1964; STM Sewanee: The U So, TS 1974. D 4/25/1964 P 10/31/1964 Bp Alfred L Banyard. m 6/27/1964 Barbara Price c 2. R S Greg's Ch Boca Raton FL 1981-2003; R S Lk's Ch Fairport NY 1975-1981; R St Andrews Epis Ch Rome NY 1971-1975; R Trin Epis Par Hughesville MD 1966-1969; Cur H Trin Ch Collingswood NJ 1964-1965.

PRICE, George N (Me) 290 Baxter Blvd Apt B3, Portland ME 04101 B Elgin IL 1935 s Lyle & Marian. BA NWU 1957; MDiv VTS 1960. D 6/18/1960 Bp Gerald Francis Burrill P 12/17/1960 Bp Charles L Street. m 11/3/1962 Harriet H Price c 2. Cn Mssnr Dio Maine Portland ME 1990-1992, Chair of Comp Relatns 1986-1989, Chair - Commision for Outreach & Serv 1990-1992, Chair of the Liturg Com 1990-1992; R S Andr And S Jn Epis Ch SW Hbr ME 1969-1986; Assoc S Chrys's Ch Chicago IL 1966-1969; Assoc Chr Ch Winnetka IL 1960-1962; Exec Com of the Alum Assn VTS Alexandria VA 1983-1990. Doctor in Div, Honoris Causa VTS 1991; Fell Cntr for Cont Educ, VTS 1986.

PRICE, Gloria Maccormack (EC) 130 Quail Dr, Dudley NC 28333 B Winthrop MA 1931 d John & Elsa. Dio Diac Trng; NYU; San Mateo Jr Coll. D 11/2/1988 Bp Brice Sidney Sanders. m 12/24/1950 Hillery Price c 5. D S Fran Ch Goldsboro NC 1997-2000; D S Steph's Ch Goldsboro NC 1988-1997. NAAD; Ord Of S Lk.

PRICE, Harold Thomas (Ky) 409 Wendover Ave, Louisville KY 40207 **The Reverend Ch Of Our Merc Sav Louisville KY 2005-** B Cincinnati OH 1957 s Robert & Joyce. BA U Cinc 1979; MDiv Sthrn Bapt TS 1983. D 6/4/2005 P 12/10/2005 Bp Ted Gulick Jr. m 8/6/1983 Mary Virginia Burks c 2.

PRICE, John Randolph (Md) 772 Ticonderoga Ave, Severna Park MD 21146 **S Jn's Ch Olney MD 2015-; S Jn's Epis Ch Zion Par Beltsville MD 2013-** B Coolemee NC 1947 s William & Betsy. BA Laf 1969; STM GTS 1973; Cert NY Institutes of Rel and Hlth 1973; DMin VTS 1986. D 6/9/1973 P 12/22/1973 Bp Horace W B Donegan. m 8/11/2007 Laura Lee Hall c 2. Gr Ch Elkridge MD 2012-2013; Int S Mk's Ch Highland MD 2010-2012; Int Chr Ch Christiana Hundred Wilmington DE 2006-2007; Episcopate Cmsn Dio Maryland Baltimore MD 1990-1991, Liturg Com 1998-2000, Comm on the Mnstry 1990-1997; R S Anne's Par Annapolis MD 1989-2006; Asst To Bp For Diac Dio E Carolina Kinston NC 1988-1989, Evang Consult 1988-1989, Stndg Com 1988-1989, Excoun 1986-1987, Excoun 1980-1983, Liturg Cmsn 1977-1989; S Tim's Epis Ch Greenville NC 1976-1988; Deptce S Paul's Epis Ch Greenville NC 1976-1978; Assoc Ch Of The Intsn New York NY 1973-1976; Trin Par New York NY 1973-1976.

PRICE, John W (Tex) 2312 Steel Street, Houston TX 77098 **Pstr Assoc Palmer Memi Ch Houston TX 2004-; Chapl Chapl FBI 2003-** B Corpus Christi TX 1938 s William & Evelyn. BA U of Texas 1961; MDiv VTS 1964; Pecos Monstry Sch Sprtl Dirs Pecos NM 1986. D 6/29/1964 Bp Richard Earl Dicus P 1/13/1965 Bp Everett H Jones. m 6/25/1966 Arlene Price c 3. Chapl Cullen Memi Chap Houston TX 1996-2004; Chapl S Lk's Epis Hosp Houston TX 1996-2004; Chapl St Lk's Epis Hosp Houston TX 1996-2004; Sprtl Dvlpmnt Div Dio Texas Houston TX 1995-2004, Curs Strng Com 1978-1994, Dir Sum Camping Prog 1972-1977; R H Comf Epis Ch Sprg TX 1988-1996; Pres St. Geo's Crt Sr Hsing Austin TX 1982-1988; Exch R S Mary Hanwell Par Ch London Engl 1975-1976; R S Geo's Ch Austin TX 1968-1988; St Chapl (COL) TX Mltry Forces 1965-1995; Asst R S Mk's Epis Ch San Antonio TX 1965-1968; Asst R Trin Ch San Antonio TX 1964-1965. Auth, "Revealing Heaven: the Chr Case for Near-Death Experiences," *Revealing Heaven: the Chr Case for Near-Death Experiences*, HarperCollins, 2013. Internat'l Assoc Near Death Stds 2010; Near Death Experience Resrch Fndn 2001; Sprtl Dir Internat'l 2010.

PRICE, Joyce Elizabeth (WNC) 75 Echo Lake Dr, Fairview NC 28730 **Non-par 1986-** B Asheville NC 1955 d Fred & Betty. BA Warren Wilson Coll 1977; MDiv Yale DS 1981. D 6/20/1981 P 6/1/1983 Bp William Gillette Weinhauer. m 3/3/1984 Jay Carter Paul. Pstr Counslr No Cntrl Womens Cntr Dallas TX 1983-1985; Pres Of The City Allnce For Mnstry 1982-1983; Asst Ch Of The Epiph Commerce TX 1981-1983; Asst Campus Min E Texas St U In Commerce 1981-1983. City Allnce For Mnstry. Danforth Fell 1978.

PRICE, Kathleen Vermillion (WA) 199 Rolfe Rd, Williamsburg VA 23185 **Tchr Rappahanock Cmnty Coll ILL 1994-; Dir On Beads of Pryr Washington D.C. 2011-; Retreat Ldr DOK / others 1998-** B Newport News VA 1946 d Ervin & Charlotte. BS U NC 1968; Cert U of the SouthEFM 1990; MEd W&M 1991; Cert Maryknoll Inst of Afr Stds 1994; Cert. St. Geo's Coll, Jerusalem 1994; MDiv VTS 1994; Cert Myers-Briggs Type Indicator 1997; DMin How 1998; Cert CREDO I 2003; Cert Cler Ldrshp Proj XIV 2003; Cert CREDO II 2008. D 5/28/1994 P 2/11/1995 Bp Frank Harris Vest Jr. c 3. R All SS Ch Oakley Av MD 1999-2014; Asst R S Jn's Ch Chevy Chase MD 1995-1998; Asst R Gr Ch Yorktown Yorktown VA 1994-1995; Chapl, DOK Prov III Baltimore MD 2000-2006; Chapl, DOK Dio Washington Washington DC 1997-2000. *Biblic Narrative Experienced Through Visual Arts*, 1998. DOK 1990. Grant: Cler Renwl ("Following the Footsteps of Van Gogh") Lilly Fndt 2005.

✠ **PRICE, The Rt Rev Kenneth Lester** (SO) 4754 Shire Ridge Rd. W, Hilliard OH 43026 **Mem Camp and Conf Advsry Bd 2014-; Secy of the Hse HOB 2003-; Com on Plnng and Arrangements GC 2000-; Bd Mem EAM 1996-** B Charleston WV 1943 s Kenneth & Margaret. BA W Virginia U 1965; STB GTS 1968; MA Marshall U 1974. D 6/11/1968 P 12/18/1968 Bp Wilburn Camrock Campbell Con 10/29/1994 for SO. m 6/21/1968 Mary Ann Prosser c 2. Bd Mem Bexley/Seabury Fed Sem 2013-2014; Ret Bp Suffr of Sthrn Ohio Dio Sthrn Ohio Cincinnati OH 2012, Bp Suffr 1994-2011; Chair, Com on Rules GC 2012; Provsnl Bp Dio Pittsburgh Pittsburgh PA 2010-2012; Mem, Bd Dir FMP Cincinnati OH 2006-2011; Comm. to Nominate the PBp GC 2003-2006; Vice Chair of Bd Bex Sem 1999-2013; Bd Mem Epis Ret Hm 1998-2015; Mem, Bd Trst SWTS Evanston IL 1997-2006; Archd Dio W Virginia Charleston WV 1990-1994, Dn 1981-1994; R S Matt's Ch Wheeling WV 1984-1994; R Trin Ch Parkersburg WV 1974-1984, 1968-1970; Chapl Marshall U Huntington WV 1971-1974; Vic S Andr's in the Vill Ch Barboursville WV 1970-1974. DD GTS 1995. kprice@diosohio.org

PRICE, Marston (Ct) 33 Old Field hill Rd. Unit48, Southbury CT 06488 **P-in-c Ch Of The Epiph Southbury CT 2012-; Bd Mem Gr Meadows 2012-; Bd Mem Gr Meadows Southbury CT 2012-** B Washington DC 1944 s Hickman & Margaret. BA U of Miami 1969; MA U of Washington 1975; MDiv EDS 1982; Cert Mssy Traning Prog 1987; Cert Int Mnstry Trng 2000; Cert Pstr Gestault Ther Traning 2007. D 8/3/1982 Bp Robert Hume Cochrane P 5/1/1983 Bp George Nelson Hunt III. m 8/26/2006 Pamela Price c 4. R S Mich's Ch Naugatuck CT 2001-2010; Int S Paul's Epis Ch Shelton CT 2000-2001; R The Ch Of The H Sprt Orleans MA 1994-1998; R S Jn's Ch Georgetown Par Washington DC 1990-1994; R S Jn's Ch Lafayette Sq Washington DC 1990-1994; Chair - COM Dio Brasil 1987-1990; ECUSA Mssy Dio Brasil 1987-1990; ECUSA Mssy Exec Coun Appointees New York NY 1987-1990; R Gd Samar Recife Brazil 1987-1990; Assoc R Trin Ch Newport RI 1982-1987; Mem Bishops Fund Hartford CT 2003-2011. Bro of St. Andrews 2007.

PRICE, Paul Alexander (Los) 113 Tierra Plano, Rancho Santa Margarita CA 92688 **P-in-c Trin Epis Ch Redlands CA 2013-** B Berlin DE 1962 BS Azusa Pacific U. D 6/19/2004 Bp Joseph Jon Bruno P 12/19/2004 Bp Robert Marshall Anderson. m 11/1/1985 Cheryl A Simon c 1. S Geo's Ch Riverside CA 2011-2012; S Geo's Ch Riverside CA 2006-2011; Cur S Jn Chrys Ch Rcho Sta Marg CA 2004-2006. fr.paul@mac.com

PRICE, Phyllis Anne (Mass) 12191 Clipper Dr, Lake Ridge VA 22192 B New York NY 1940 d Ralph & Beatrice. BA Randolph-Macon Coll 1962; MA U Chi 1964; MA CUA 1978; Cert Ang Stud GTS 1998. D 2/6/1999 P 9/11/1999 Bp Richard Frank Grein. Trin Chap Shirley MA 2003-2004; Asst S Jas' Epis Ch Warrenton VA 2000-2002; Ce Dir Ch Of The H Trin New York NY 1999-2000.

PRICE, Raymond Estal (Wyo) 417 S 2nd St, Lander WY 82520 **Loc P Trin Epis Ch 2005-; Trin Ch Lander WY 2004-** B Niles MI 1948 s Ivan & Dorothy. BSc MI SU 1970; MA Wstrn Michigan U 1976; MPA U of Wyoming 1992; EFM U So 1993. D 2/8/2004 P 10/31/2004 Bp Bruce Caldwell. c 2. Auth, "Fool's Gold," *Poetry*, Self, 2001. Amer Assn for the Advancement of Sci 2012. Cath Press Awd for Best Fam Life Column Cath Press Awd 2012; Grad Stdt of the Year U of Wyoming 1992. rprice@wyoming.com

PRICE JR, Richard Elwyn (WNC) 185 Macon Ave Apt A-3, Asheville NC 28804 **Ret 1992-** B Florence AL 1926 s Richard & Beulah. BA Mississippi Coll 1949; BD Sthrn Bapt TS 1952; MDiv Sthrn Bapt TS 1973. D 5/20/1988 P 10/22/1988 Bp William Gillette Weinhauer. m 2/28/1953 Ellen Gray Honts c 2. Assoc S Mary's Ch Asheville NC 1996-2001; Int S Jn's Ch Asheville NC 1989-1990; Asst Gr Ch Asheville NC 1988-1989; Serv Var Ch as Min Sthrn Bapt Conv 1949-1987. Assoc, CSM; Assoc, Fllshp of St. Jn.

PRICE, Robert Paul (Tex) 1023 Compass Cove Cir, Spring TX 77379 **Leading Pstr S Dunst's Epis Ch Houston TX 2005-** B La Jolla CA 1970 s Robert & Jean. BA Stan 1996; MA Stan 1996; MDiv Yale DS 2002; MA Ya 2002. D 11/27/2001 Bp Hays H. Rockwell P 5/2/2002 Bp George Wayne Smith. m 6/29/1996 Kate Ellen Price c 3. Ch Of The Incarn Dallas TX 2004-2005; S Mich & S Geo S Louis MO 2002-2004; First Alt Dep to GC Dio Texas Houston TX 2009. Ord of St. Jn of Jerusalem 2005.

PRICE, Stephen Marsh (NY) 133 Grove Street, Peterborough NH 03458 B Zanesville OH 1941 s James & Jane Ann. BA Muskingum Coll 1964; STB GTS 1967; STM UTS 1970; Cert Amer Fndt of Rel & Psych 1973; DMin Andover Newton TS 1974. D 6/17/1967 Bp Roger W Blanchard P 12/19/1967 Bp Joseph Warren Hutchens. m 7/14/2007 Patricia Carol Liebenson c 2. Par Of S Jas Ch Keene NH 1993-1998; St. Barth Ch New York NY 1978-1984; Counslg And Human Dvlpmt Cntr New York NY 1976-1991; Interchurch Counslg Serv New York NY 1974-1976; Counslg & Human Dvlpmt Cntr New York NY 1973-1992; Cur S Mary's Epis Ch Manchester CT 1967-1969. Auth, "No More Lonely Nights: Overcoming The Hidden Fears That Keep You From Get-

ting m," Putnam, 1987. Amer Assoc for Mar And Fam Therapists 1973; AAPC 1973. stephenprice4@gmail.com

PRICE, Stephen W (Pa) 3724 E Fisherville Rd, Downingtown PA 19335 **Died 1/24/2016** B Danbury CT 1942 s Louis & Elizabeth. BA Wesl 1965; MDiv Ya Berk 1968. D 6/20/1981 P 7/1/1981 Bp Lyman Cunningham Ogilby. m 12/8/2011 Kathleen E Price. Calv Ch Conshohocken PA 2012-2016; Int S Philips 1986-2016; Asst H Trin 1980-2016; Ucc Min 1968-1970.

PRICE, Susan Medlicott (Spok) 2029 Sheridan Pl, Richland WA 99352 **Asstg P S Mk's Ch Marco Island FL 2010-** B Evansville IN 1947 BS Indiana St U 1969; PhD U of Idaho 1977. D 4/14/1999 Bp Cabell Tennis P 10/16/1999 Bp John Stuart Thornton. m 5/24/1969 William Hugh Price. Asstg P S Jn's Epis Ch Of Kissimmee Kissimmee FL 2005-2009; P S Matt's Ch Prosser WA 1999-2004.

PRICE, Terrell Wells (Roch) 23 Main St, Geneseo NY 14454 **Bd Dir Livingston Co. Cltn of Ch 2008-; D S Mich's Ch Geneseo NY 2008-; Chapl Livingston Cnty Sheriffs Dept. Geneseo NY 1998-; Chapl Geneseo Fire Dept. Geneseo NY 1975-** B Huntington NY 1936 s John & Isobel. BS SUNY; Cert EFM Univ of the So 1980; CRDS 1986; Diac Stds Bex Sem 2007. D 3/29/2008 Bp Jack Marston Mckelvey. m 8/22/1959 Dianne Price c 2. Dioc Coun Dio Rochester Henrietta 2008-2010. NAAD 2008; Third OSF 1986; Vergers Gld of Epis Ch 2001-2007.

PRICE-HADZOR, Robert Baylor (La) **S Augustines Ch Metairie LA 2017-; Trin Epis Sch New Orleans LA 2017-** B Wilkes-Barre PA 1985 s Thomas & Debra. BA Belmont U 2007; MDiv Duke DS 2010. D 5/17/2017 Bp Morris King Thompson Jr.

PRICHARD, Albert Hughes (WVa) 75 Old Cheat Rd, Morgantown WV 26508 B Wheeling WV 1943 s Arthur & Mildred. AB Davis & Elkins Coll 1966; Pittsburgh TS 1969; BS W Virginia U 1984. D 12/17/2011 Bp William Michie Klusmeyer. m 6/25/1977 Cheryl L Prichard c 2.

PRICHARD, Robert Walton (Va) Virginia Theological Seminary, 3737 Seminary Rd., Alexandria VA 22304 **Pres HSEC 2010-; Prof of Ch Hist and Instr in Liturg VTS Alexandria VA 2000-, Assoc Prof 1989-1994, Prof Of Ch Hist 1983-, 1980; Pres HSEC 2010-** B Washington DC 1949 s Edgar & Nancy. BA Pr 1971; MDiv Yale DS 1974; PhD Emory U 1983. D 5/24/1974 P 10/1/1976 Bp John Alfred Baden. m 5/27/1973 Marcia Joyce Prichard c 2. VP HSEC 2005-2010; Mem Angl RC Dialogue USA 2001-2007; Vic Gr Ch Berryville VA 1980-1983; S Mary's Memi Berryville VA 1980-1983; Int All SS Epis Ch Woodbridge VA 1979-1980; Grad Stdt Emory U 1977-1979; Cur S Geo's Epis Ch Arlington VA 1974-1977. Auth, "Hail! H Hill!," VTS, 2012; Auth, "Cohabiting Couples & Cold Feet," Ch Pub, 2008; Auth, "A Hist Of The Epis Ch, rev. ed.," Morehouse, 1999; Ed, "A Hist Of Ch Schools In The Dio Virginia," Morehouse for Ch Schools in the Dio Virginia, 1999; Auth, "The Nature Of Salvation," U IL Press, 1997; Ed, "A Wholesome Example," Bristol Books, 1993; Auth, "The Bat And The Bp," Morehouse, 1989; Auth, "Readings From The Hist Of The Epis Ch," Morehouse-Barlow, 1986. Amer Hist Assn 2006; Amer Soc of Ch Hist 1989; Conf of Angl Ch Historians 1985; HSEC 1979. Fllshp ECF 1978.

PRICHARD, Thomas Morgan (Pgh) 809 18th St, Ambridge PA 15003 **SAMS 1987-** B Alexandria VA 1952 s Edgar & Nancy. BA Ken 1974; MDiv VTS 1978. D 6/3/1978 Bp John Alfred Baden P 3/24/1979 Bp Christoph Keller Jr. m 9/17/2006 Nancy Richey Prichard. Chr Ch Overland Pk KS 2003-2005; Pres - Com Dio Colombia 1986-1987; SAMS Ambridge PA 1983-2003; Asst Trin Cathd Little Rock AR 1978-1983; Stndg Com Iglesia Epis En Colombia Bogota 1985-1986. Amer Angl Coun.

PRICKETT, Gerald Stanley (WNC) 360 Asheville School Rd., Asheville NC 28806 **R Ch Of S Mths Asheville NC 2012-; Chapl Asheville Sch Asheville No Carolina 2003-** B Toccoa, GA 1947 AB U GA 1969; MDiv Sthrn Bapt TS 1973; MEd Van 1983. D 1/13/2008 P 8/10/2008 Bp Porter Taylor. m 6/12/2000 Patricia Prickett c 3.

PRIDEMORE JR, Charles Preston (NY) PO Box 149, Ossining NY 10562 **Dio New York New York NY 2013-, 2003-2011; Cn S Lk's Ch Eastchester NY 2012-** B Fort Worth TX 1949 s Charles & Patricia. GTS; BA U of No Texas 1971. D 6/9/1984 Bp James Stuart Wetmore P 12/4/1984 Bp Paul Moore Jr. c 1. R Trin Epis Ch Ossining NY 1993-2011; Cathd Of St Jn The Div New York NY 1984-1993. Ed, *Plnng and Control of Municipal Revenues and Expenditures*, Natl Assn of Accountants, 1984; Ed, *The Capital Expenditure Decision*, Natl Assn of Accountants, 1983. Advsry Bd Epis Chars 1993; Dio New York Prison Mnstry Ntwk 2000; Dio New York Soc Concerns Cmsn 2000; Hudson No Cler 1993; Ossining Agencies Coun 1993; Ossining Mnstrl Assn 1993.

PRIEST JR, W(Illiam) Hunt (Oly) 4400 86th Ave SE, Mercer Island WA 98040 **S Ptr's Epis Ch Savannah GA 2016-; R Emm Epis Ch Mercer Island WA 2008-** B Mount Sterling KY 1964 s William & Rebecca. BA Hanover Coll 1986; MDiv Epis TS of the SW 2005. D 12/21/2004 P 8/21/2005 Bp J Neil Alexander. m 9/17/1994 Lisa Lee Priest c 1. Assoc R S Paul's Epis Ch Newnan GA 2005-2008; S Jas Ch Austin TX 2004-2005. hpriest@stpeterssavannah.org

PRINCE, Elaine (Md) 10913 Knotty Pine Dr, Hagerstown MD 21740 B Indianapolis MD 1944 d John & Dorothy. Antioch Coll; BA Ohio Wesl 1966; MA Hrod 1979; MDiv EDS 1986. D 6/7/1986 P 3/1/1987 Bp Albert Theodore

Eastman. Epis Mnstrs To The Aging Eldersburg MD 2004-2015; S Anne's Epis Ch Smithsburg MD 2001-2004; S Andr's Ch Clear Sprg MD 2001; Dio Maryland Baltimore MD 1995-2000, Dioc Coun 1995-1998, Chair Of The CE Com 1982-1983, Dioc Coun 1980-1983, Dioc Coun 1988-1991, Chair Of Yth And YA Cmsn 1980-1982; Bp Claggett Cntr Adamstown MD 1992-1995; Assoc Chr Ch Columbia MD 1986-1992; Ch Of The Ascen Westminster MD 1980-1983; DCE Emm Ch Baltimore MD 1972-1980; DCE S Barth's Ch Baltimore MD 1970-1972.

PRINGLE, Amy Fay (Los) 5332 Mount Helena Ave, Los Angeles CA 90041 **R S Geo's Par La Can CA 2005-** B Ann Arbor MI 1962 d David & Mary. BA U of MI 1988; MDiv SWTS 1992. D 6/8/2002 Bp Robert Marshall Anderson P 1/11/2003 Bp Joseph Jon Bruno. m 11/11/2005 Bryan William Jones c 3. Asst S Wilfrid Of York Epis Ch Huntington Bch CA 2002-2005. guruamy@yahoo.com

PRINGLE, Charles Derek (SVa) 419 Elizabeth Lake Dr, Hampton VA 23669 B Clones MO IE 1946 s Joseph & Isabel. BA Trin Dublin IE 1970; MA Trin Dublin IE 1972; DMin VTS 1996. Trans 9/1/1999 Bp David Conner Bane Jr. m 6/18/1976 Pamela Pringle c 3. Chr Epis Ch Smithfield VA 2013-2015; R Emm Epis Ch Hampton VA 1999-2011; Serv Ch of Can 1973-1999; Serv Ch of Ireland 1970-1973; Chair, Recon Cmsn Dio Virginia Richmond VA 2004-2006. Ed, "New Life," *Toronto*, Angl Bk Cntr, 1989; Auth, "Pstr's Page," *Welland Tribune, Ont*, 1985. Alb Inst 1994; Coll of Preachers Participant 2000; SoVE-CA 2001. Reg Dn Dio Niagara 1995; Hon Cn Dio Niagara 1987.

PRINZ, Susan Moore (USC) 6408 Bridgewood Rd, Columbia SC 29206 **S Martins-In-The-Field Columbia SC 2014-** B Sanford FL 1958 d James & Barbara. BA U of So Carolina 1980; MEd U of So Carolina 1983; PhD U of So Carolina 1998; MDiv VTS 2010. D 6/3/2010 P 6/14/2011 Bp W illiam Andrew Waldo. m 5/16/1981 Ronald J Prinz c 1. S Mich And All Ang' Columbia SC 2010-2012.

✠ PRIOR, The Rt Rev Brian N (Minn) 1730 Clifton Place Suite 201, Minneapolis MN 55403 **Bp of Minnesota Dio Minnesota Minneapolis MN 2010-** B Prosser WA 1959 s Robert & Norma. BA Whitworth U 1984; MDiv CDSP 1987. D 6/20/1987 P 4/22/1989 Bp Leigh Allen Wallace Jr Con 2/13/2010 for Minn. m 7/25/1987 Staci H Prior c 2. VP, HOD Epis Ch 2006-2009; Exec Coun Epis Ch 2000-2006; SCMD Epis Ch 2000-2006; R Ch Of The Resurr Veradale WA 1996-2009; Coordntr of Prov VIII Yth Mnstry Prov VIII 1995-2010; Exec Dir Camp Cross 1990-1996; Dir of Educ and Dvlpmt Dio Spokane Spokane WA 1990-1996; Dir of Educ and Dvlpmt Dio Spokane Spokane WA 1990-1996; Assoc R S Steph's Epis Ch Spokane WA 1987-1990. Auth, *Epis Curric for Yth*; Auth, *Yth & YA Resource Bk*. brian.p@episcopalmn.org

PRIOR, John Gregory (RI) 7 Trillium Ln, Hilton Head Island SC 29926 B Providence RI 1944 s Gerald & Emma. BA Providence Coll 1965; MDiv Sewanee: The U So, TS 1983; DMin Sewanee: The U So, TS 2005. D 6/29/1983 P 6/24/1984 Bp Christopher FitzSimons Allison. m 11/12/1966 Anna Prior c 4. Int S Mary's Ch Portsmouth RI 2013-2014; Int S Lk's Epis Ch E Greenwich RI 2010-2012; Int Gr Ch In Providence Providence RI 2009-2010; R S Andr's By The Sea Little Compton RI 2002-2009; R All SS Ch Hilton Hd Island SC 1993-2002; R St Anne's Epis Ch Conway SC 1985-1993; Asst S Jas Ch Charleston SC 1983-1985; Chair, Prog and Bdgt Dio Rhode Island Providence RI 2006-2010; Stndg Com So Carolina Charleston SC 1994-1999, Stndg Com 1985-1989.

PRIOR, Randall Leavitt (Va) 9515 Holly Prospect Ct, Burke VA 22015 **Clinician Cntr for Pstr Counslg of Virginia 2010-** B Jacksonville FL 1945 s Lyman & Gladys. BA W&L 1967; BD VTS 1970; DMin Estrn Bapt TS 1990. D 6/24/1970 Bp Edward Hamilton West P 4/16/1971 Bp George Mosley Murray. m 12/29/1966 Clotilde V Prior c 3. Adj Fac VTS Alexandria VA 2006, 2004, 2001, 1998, 1996, 1994, 1993, 1992; R S Andr's Ch Burke VA 1974-2010; Asst S Steph's Ch Richmond VA 1971-1974; P-in-c S Matt's Chipley FL 1970-1971; S Mich's Ch Gainesville FL 1970-1971. "Faith Based Serv Prog in the Publ Sector: Illustrations from Virginia," Participatory Governance Plnng Conflict Mediation, 2004. AAPC 1983; CFLE, Natl Coun on Fam Relatns 1990. rprio45@gmail.com

PRITCHARD, David Gatlin (Ct) 16 Ashlar Vlg, Wallingford CT 06492 B Washington DC 1927 s David & Elizabeth. BA CUA 1951; GTS 1954. D 6/12/1954 Bp Angus Dun P 12/18/1954 Bp Norman B Nash. m 6/26/1954 Helen L Pritchard c 4. P Assoc St. Jn's Epis Ch Waterbury CT 2005; P-in-c Chr Ch Bethlehem CT 1997-2008; Int Calv St Geo's Epis Ch Bridgeport CT 1995-1996; R Chr Ch Waterbury CT 1983-1994; Asst S Mk's Ch New Britain CT 1982-1983; St Gabr's Ch E Berlin CT 1978-1983; Cmncatns Off Dio Connecticut Meriden CT 1978-1982, Ed of The Connecticut Churchman 1978-1983; R H Apos Savannah GA 1970-1978; R Calv Ch Americus GA 1962-1970; R Chr Ch Augusta GA 1958-1962; Vic S Mary's Epis Ch Madison FL 1956-1958; Cur S Anne's Ch Lowell MA 1954-1956; P Assoc St. Jn's Epis Ch Waterbury CT 2008; Ed of The Ch in Georgia Dio Georgia Savannah GA 1975-1978. ECom 1973-1983; Epis Curs 1976.

PRITCHER, Joan Jean (At) 1098 Saint Augustine Pl Ne, Atlanta GA 30306 **Chr Ch Cathd Louisville KY 2013-** B Atlanta,GA 1954 d Gerald & Jeannine. BA

Tift Coll 1975; MRE SW Sem 1976; PhD Emory U 1985. D 6/4/1994 P 12/10/1994 Bp Frank Kellogg Allan. Trin Cathd Omaha NE 2012-2013; Int H Trin Par Decatur GA 2010-2011; Ch S Mich The Archangel Lexington KY 2008-2010; Chr Ch Macon GA 2005-2006; S Aid's Epis Ch Milton GA 2003-2004; The Epis Ch Of The Adv Madison GA 2002-2003; Ch Of The Atone Sandy Sprg GA 1994-2002.

PRITCHETT JR, Harry Houghton (NY) 1290 Peachtree Battle Ave Nw, Atlanta GA 30327 **Sr Asst to the Dn S Phil's Cathdral Atlanta GA 2005-; Ret 2001-** B Tuscaloosa AL 1935 s Harry & Margaret. BA U of Alabama 1957; MDiv VTS 1964; Cntr Coll 1981; Sewanee: The U So, TS 2007. D 6/24/1964 P 5/16/1965 Bp George Mosley Murray. m 9/1/1956 Allison Pritchett c 3. Int S Lk's Par New York NY 2004-2005; Pstr Asst to the Dn VTS Alexandria VA 2002-2003; Dn Cathd Of St Jn The Div New York NY 1997-2001; R All SS Epis Ch Atlanta GA 1981-1997; Dio Alabama Birmingham 1975-1981; Dir Field Educ Sewanee U So TS Sewanee TN 1975-1979; St Thos Epis Ch Huntsville AL 1975-1979; Asst R S Lk's Epis Ch Birmingham AL 1964-1967. Auth, *God is a Surprise Songbook*; Auth, *Morning Run: Sabbatical Reflections on the Ch & the City*; Auth, *Patterns for Par Dvlpmt*; Auth, *Sermons That Wk*. Phi Beta Kappa.

PRITCHETT JR, James Hill (WNC) 209 Nut Hatch Loop, Arden NC 28704 **Mem, Bd for Transition Mnstry GC- Epis Ch Cntr New York NY 2013-** B Atlanta GA 1956 s James & Anne. W&L 1976; BA U GA 1978; JD U GA 1981; MDiv Sewanee: The U So, TS 1991. D 6/8/1991 P 1/25/1992 Bp Frank Kellogg Allan. m 11/17/1984 Charlotte Pritchett c 2. Cn to the Ordnry Dio Wstrn No Carolina Asheville NC 2007-2016; GC Dep 2009; R S Jn's Atlanta GA 1998-2007; Assoc R All SS Epis Ch Atlanta GA 1992-1998; Assoc R The Epis Ch Of S Ptr And S Paul Marietta GA 1991-1992; Bd Mem, Secy Transition Mnstry Conf Inc. 2009-2016; GC Dep Dio Atlanta Atlanta GA 2006, Chair, New Ch Starts Cmsn 2005-2007, Co-Chair, Cong Growth & Dev. 2002-2006. Preaching Awd U So, TS 1991; Ord of the Coif hon Soc UGA Sch of Law 1981; Golden Key hon Soc UGA Chapt 1978; Phi Kappa Phi hon Soc UGA Chapt 1978; Phi Beta Kappa U of GA Chapt 1978. jimpritchett1@mac.com

PRITTS, Clarence Edward (NJ) 7 E Maple Ave, Merchantville NJ 08109 B Baltimore MD 1946 s Clarence & Eleanor. BA Frostburg St U 1968; MLa JHU 1971; MDiv GTS 1984. D 6/16/1984 Bp Albert Theodore Eastman P 2/8/1985 Bp David Keller Leighton Sr. R Gr Ch Merchantville NJ 1995-2007; R Chr Ch W River MD 1988-1995; Cur St Johns Ch W Hartford CT 1984-1988.

PRIVETTE, William Herbert (EC) 1119 Hendricks Ave., Jacksonville NC 28540 B Salisbury NC 1949 s William & Lena. BA Duke 1972; MDiv Sewanee: The U So, TS 1975. D 6/24/1975 P 3/25/1976 Bp Hunley Agee Elebash. m 5/20/1972 Karen F Privette c 3. R S Anne's Epis Ch Jacksonville NC 2002-2006; R Chr Ch Springfield IL 1992-2002; Dio Springfield Springfield IL 1992-1995, Dioc Coun 1993-2002; Assoc R S Paul's Epis Ch Dayton OH 1985-1992; S Thos' Epis Ch Ahoskie NC 1981-1985; Chr Epis Ch Hope Mills NC 1979-1981; Dio E Carolina Kinston NC 1978; Gd Shpd Epis Ch Fayetteville NC 1978; Asst S Jn's Epis Ch Fayetteville NC 1975-1978.

PRIVITERA, Linda Fisher (Mass) 21 Marathon St, Arlington MA 02474 B Pittsburgh PA 1946 d Cecil & Jean. BS Med Coll of Virginia 1968; MDiv Ya Berk 1986. D 6/13/1987 P 1/21/1988 Bp Arthur Edward Walmsley. m 12/3/2004 Melissa A Haussman c 3. R Ch Of Our Sav Arlington MA 1997-2005; Assoc R S Mk's Ch Southborough MA 1995-1996; Cler Sexual Misconduct Taskforce Dio Wstrn Massachusetts Springfield 1993-1994, 1990-1995, Prov I Aids Taskforce 1990-1993; Assoc All SS Ch Worcester MA 1990-1994; Chapl Comp Of The H Cross 1988-1989; Asst to R All SS Epis Ch Meriden CT 1987-1990. Auth, "Reviving Ophelia - Girls Ldrshp Experience," *Journ Of Wmn Mnstrs*, 1998; Auth, "The Trees," *Angl Dig*, 1994. NCA, Alb Inst; Trst Ma Bible Soc 1990-1995. Altrusa Club Serv Awd; Wmn Awd In Ldrshp Meriden 89 Ywca.

PROBERT, Walter Leslie (Mil) 125 Cedar Ridge Dr, West Bend WI 53095 **Ret 1990-** B Milwaukee WI 1925 s Walter & Mildred. BS Marq 1950. D 11/6/1960 Bp Donald H V Hallock. m 8/20/1949 Jane Beverly Lundquist c 5. Asst S Mk's Ch Milwaukee WI 1978-1990; Asst S Jas Epis Ch Milwaukee WI 1970-1977; Asst S Mart's Ch Milwaukee WI 1968-1970; Asst Chr Ch Milwaukee WI 1965-1968; Asst Chr Milwaukee WI 1965-1968; Asst Trin Erie PA 1961-1965; Asst S Jn Ch/Mision San Juan Milwaukee WI 1960-1961.

PROBST, David Charles (At) 169 Lakeport Rd., Macon GA 31210 **P-in-c S Steph's Ch Milledgeville GA 2012-** B Columbia GA 1966 s William & Gale. BA Berry Coll 1989; MDiv Candler TS Emory U 2007. D 12/21/2006 P 9/14/2007 Bp J Neil Alexander. m 1/20/1990 Marie Patellis Probst c 2. Assoc R Chr Ch Macon GA 2007-2012. fatherdavid@windstream.net

PROCTOR, F Rederick Gregory (Miss) 5527 Ridgewood Rd, Jackson MS 39211 **R Chap Of The Cross Rolling Fork MS 2015-** B Lakeland FL 1952 s William & Ruth. BA No Carolina St U 1975; MDiv VTS 1993. D 6/19/1993 Bp Huntington Williams Jr P 6/22/1994 Bp Robert Carroll Johnson Jr. m 11/18/1972 Deborah Proctor c 2. R S Paul's Epis Ch Meridian MS 2003-2009; R All SS Epis Ch Grenada MS 1997-2003; Asst to R S Cyp's Ch Oxford NC 1993-1997; Asst to R S Steph's Ch Oxford NC 1993-1997; Vice-Pres Dioc Ex-

P

ec Com Dio Mississippi Jackson MS 2004-2005, Chair-Congrl Dvlpmt Com 1998-2006. Associated Parishes for Mssn & Liturg 1993.

PROCTOR, Judith Harris (Va) St Paul's Episcopal Church, 228 S Pitt St, Alexandria VA 22314 **Vic S Paul's Epis Ch Alexandria VA 2005-; P S Paul's Epis Ch Alexandria VA 2001-** B Baltimore MD 1944 d Charles & Janet. BA Goucher Coll 1968; MS U of Maryland 1992; MSW U of Maryland 1994; MDiv VTS 1996. D 6/23/2000 P 4/17/2002 Bp Hays H. Rockwell. m 8/2/1969 Kenneth Donald Proctor c 3. Auth, "Liturg Skirmishes in the Dio Maryland, Angl and Epis Hist v. LSVIII," *no. 4*, 1999; Auth, "Therapists and the Clincl Use of Forgiveness, The Amer Journ of Fam Ther, v.21," *number 2*, 1993.

PROCTOR, Richard Gillespie (CGC) 4129 Oxford Ave., Jacksonville FL 32210 **Chr The King Epis Ch Santa Rosa Bch FL 2015-** B Tallahassee FL 1972 s Maurice & Elizabeth. BA Florida St U 1996; MDiv Columbia TS 2009; STM GTS 2011. D 12/18/2010 P 6/26/2011 Bp J Neil Alexander. m 7/25/2010 Emily Rose Proctor c 1. Assoc S Mk's Epis Ch Jacksonville FL 2013-2015; S Jn's Ch Reisterstown MD 2011-2013.

PROFFITT, Darrel D (Tex) 1225 W Grand Pkwy S, Katy TX 77494 **R Ch Of The H Apos Katy TX 2007-** B Oklahoma City OK 1956 s Jimmy & Patsy. BS U of Kansas 1979; MDiv SWTS 1991; DMin SWTS 1999. D 6/15/1991 P 12/14/1991 Bp William Edward Smalley. m 8/6/1979 Julie M Proffitt c 3. R S Marg's Ch Lawr KS 1999-2007; R Gr Ch Sterling IL 1993-1999; Assoc Ch Of The H Comf Kenilworth IL 1991-1993; Tchr Shawnee Heights USD 450 Tecumseh KS 1979-1988; Chair Congrl Dvlpmt Dio Kansas Topeka KS 2004-2007, Stndg Com 2001-2006; COM Dio Chicago Chicago IL 1994-1996. Doctoral Stds, "Dissertation," *It is No Sm Pity When We Fail to Understand Ourselves: Seeking Excellence in Congregations*, Seabury-Wstrn, 1999. Merit Awd SWTS 2004.

PROFFITT III, John (Ark) 1608 McEntire Circle, Chatsworth GA 30705 B Waynesboro VA 1951 s John & Sybil. BS Emory U 1973; MS U of Memphis 1975; MDiv Sewanee: The U So, TS 1990. D 6/16/1990 P 12/1/1990 Bp Robert Jefferson Hargrove Jr. m 6/30/1973 Margaret Proffitt c 2. Spec Tchr Saudi Aramco Cbury Grp Ras Tanura Saudi Arabia 2008-2014; The Centeburry Grp Dhahran 2008-2014; R S Mk's Epis Ch Little Rock AR 2003-2008; S Jas Epis Ch Baton Rouge LA 2001-2003; S Paul's Ch New Orleans LA 1999-2001; R S Jas Epis Ch Shreveport LA 1992-1998; Trin Ch Tallulah LA 1990-1992.

PROUD, James (Pa) 111 W Walnut Ln, Philadelphia PA 19144 B Little Falls NY 1931 s Cecil & Elsa. BA Ob 1953; LLB Ya 1956. D 6/12/1965 P 12/18/1965 Bp Horace W B Donegan. m 9/11/1987 Kathleen G Proud. Vic S Dav's Ch Philadelphia PA 1997-2006; Assoc S Jn's Ch New York NY 1976-1988; Assoc Ch Of The H Comm Paterson NJ 1972-1976; P-in-c Gr Ch (W Farms) Bronx NY 1970-1972; S Edm's Ch Bronx NY 1967-1970; Assoc S Simeon's Ch Bronx NY 1967-1970; Asst S Ptr's Ch New York NY 1965-1967. Ed, "Jn Woolman and the Affrs of Truth: The Jrnlst's Essays, Epistles, and Ephemera," *same*, Inner Light Books, 2010; Auth, "Jn Woolman and the Affrs of Truth".

✠ PROVENZANO, The Rt Rev Lawrence C (LI) Episcopal Diocese of Long Island, 36 Cathedral Avenue, Garden City NY 11530 **Bp of Long Island Dio Long Island Garden City NY 2009-; Pres/CEO Epis Hlth Serv Far Rockaway NY 2009-** B Brooklyn NY 1955 s Larry & Marie. BS SUNY 1980; MDiv Chr the King Sem 1982. Rec 12/22/1984 as Priest Bp George Nelson Hunt III Con 9/23/2009 for LI. m 1/8/1983 Jeanne M Provenzano c 3. Chf Chapl, Fire Serv Of MA 2004-2009; R S Andr's Ch Longmeadow MA 1987-2009; R All S's Ch of the Berkshires No Adams MA 1987-1994; Asst R Chr Ch Westerly RI 1984-1987; Liturg Com Dio Rhode Island Providence RI 1984-1987. Auth, "A Model Of Priestly Mnstry - The Pachomius Proj," *Sabbatical Wk*, 1999; Auth, "Reflections On The Lituges Of H Week," *The St. Jn'S Record (Par Pub.)*, 1988. Angl Soc 1986; Massachusetts Corps Of Fire Chapl 1999. Citizen Of The Year - For Outstanding Cmnty Serv Town Of Longmeadow 2002; Recognition Awd - For Serv w The Fire Dept At "Ground Zero" Fed Emergency Managment Admin 2001. lprovenzano@dioceseli.org

PROVINE, Marion Kay (Minn) 3424 Willow Ave, White Bear Lake MN 55110 **Dir of Sprtl Life Epis Hm S Paul MN 2007-** B Tallulah LA 1949 d Henry & Dorothy. BA LSU 1972; MDiv GTS 2005; MDiv GTS 2005. D 6/8/2006 P 12/21/2006 Bp James Louis Jelinek. c 3. Epis Hm S Paul MN 2007-2013.

PRUEHER JR, Roi Francis (Az) 19303 N New Tradition Rd Apt 204, Sun City West AZ 85375 **Died 8/23/2015** B La Crosse WI 1929 s Roi & Gertrude. BS USNA 1952; MS U IL 1956; PhD U IL 1967. D 10/19/1996 Bp William Charles Wantland. m 6/21/1952 Diane Prueher c 2. D Ch Of The Adv Sun City W AZ 2008-2010, D 1996-2007; D All SS Of The Desert Epis Ch Sun City AZ 1999-2008. Eta Kappa Nu.

PRUITT, Albert Wesley (CGC) 729 Brown Pl, Decatur GA 30030 B Anderson SC 1940 s James & Jennie. BA Emory U 1961; MD Emory U 1965; MDiv GTS 2000; STM GTS 2000. D 6/3/2000 P 2/2/2001 Bp Charles Farmer Duvall. m 6/3/1961 Ellanor Hanson c 1. S Jn's Ch Pensacola FL 2010; R S Fran Of Assisi Gulf Breeze FL 2002-2009; Cur S Chris's Ch Pensacola FL 2000-2002. Alpha Omega Alpha Med Soc; Amer Acad Of Pediatrics; AMA.

PRUITT, Alonzo Clemons (Va) 6552 W Shakespeare Avenue, Apt 2W, Chicago IL 60707 B Chicago IL 1951 s Alonzo & Louise. BA Roosevelt U 1975;

MSW U IL at Chicago 1978; MDiv SWTS 1984; DMin GTF 1998. D 6/16/1984 Bp Quintin Ebenezer Primo Jr P 4/1/1985 Bp James Winchester Montgomery. c 2. Calv Ch Hanover VA 2014-2016, Vic 2011-2014; Lt. Col., Chf of Chapl Richmond Sheriffs Off Richmond VA 2006-2016; R S Phil's Ch Richmond VA 2004-2009; S Phil's Ch Brooklyn NY 1993-2004; Chapl (1st Lt) US-A 1990-1998; Adj Prof of Mnstry Bexley Seabury Fed Chicago IL 1989-1991; S Geo/S Mths Ch Chicago IL 1984-1993; Dio Chicago Chicago IL 1984; Alt Dep G C Dio Long Island Garden City NY 2003, Dn 1998-2002. Auth, "Recruitment Of Minority Cler," *Hisp Ministers Journ*, The Epis Ch, 1989. Tertiary Of The Soc Of S Fran 1982; UBE 1994. Lt. Col. Alonzo Pruitt Chap Richmond City Sheriff's Off, Richmond, VA 2016; Rosenblum Awd Virginia Commonwealth U Sch of Soc Wk 2014; Cmnty Serv Awd RC Dio Richmond, Richmond, VA 2009; Publ Serv Awd Richmond City Coun 2006; Congressional Record Tribute 108th Untd States Hse of Representatives 2003; Proclamation Borough of Brooklyn, Brooklyn, NY 2003; Proclamation New York City Coun, New York, NY 2003; Proclamation New York St Asssembly 2003; DD St Paul Coll 1996; Hon Cn St Peters Cathd 1994; Cotton Memi Awd SWTS 1984; Field Prize SWTS 1984. dracpruitt@comcast.net

PRUITT JR, George Russell (Md) 1246 Summit Ave SW, Roanoke VA 24015 **Ret 1997-** B Atlanta GA 1936 s George & Nell. Truett McConnell Jr Coll 1956; Georgia St U 1959; LTh VTS 1974. D 6/10/1974 Bp Robert Poland Atkinson P 2/22/1975 Bp Wilburn Camrock Campbell. m 9/8/1956 Peggy R Reese c 3. R Ch Of The H Cross Cumberland MD 1991-1997; Vic S Mich's Epis Ch Easley SC 1986-1991; R Chr Ch Norway ME 1982-1986; S Andr's Ch Clifton Forg VA 1978-1980; R Emm Ch Covington VA 1976-1982; Vic S Ann's Ch N Martinsvlle WV 1974-1976.

PRUITT, Mark J (O) Po Box 1910, Newport RI 02840 **R S Paul's Ch Akron OH 2007-** B Pittsburgh PA 1958 s James & Ellen. U of Cambridge; BA Wheaton Coll 1980; MA VTS 1991. D 9/29/1992 Bp Stephen Whitfield Sykes P 9/1/1993 Bp Alden Moinet Hathaway. m 6/24/1989 Rebecca Jo Pruitt. S Geo's Sch Middletown RI 1999-2007; R S Ptr's Epis Ch Butler PA 1995-1999; Asst Chapl Peterhouse Chap Cambridge Uk 1992-1995; Dir Of Yth Mnstry S Jas Ch Potomac MD 1987-1992. ECF 1992-1995.

PRUITT, R Allen (At) 301 N Greenwood St, Lagrange GA 30240 **R S Mk's Epis Ch Lagrange GA 2010-** B Rome GA 1980 s Welton & Jean. BS Shorter Coll 2002; MDiv VTS 2007. D 12/21/2006 P 7/1/2007 Bp J Neil Alexander. c 1. Asst S Fran Epis Ch Great Falls VA 2007-2010. allen@stmarkslg.org

PRUSKI, Dorota (Mil) St Andrew's Episcopal Church, 1833 Regent St, Madison WI 53726 **S Andr's Ch Madison WI 2013-** B Torun Poland 1984 d Marek & Beata. BA Marq 2006; MDiv VTS 2013. D 12/15/2012 P 6/29/2013 Bp Steven Andrew Miller. associate@standrews-madison.org

PRYNE, Carla Valentine (Oly) 1745 Ne 103rd St, Seattle WA 98125 **BEC Dio Olympia Seattle 2006-, Exec Dir - Earth Mnstry 1992-1996, Pres Stndg Com 1987-1988, Bd Dir Dioc Ts 1985-1988** B Chicago IL 1954 d Michael & Mary. BA Bow 1976; MDiv Ya Berk 1979. D 7/21/1983 P 7/24/1984 Bp Robert Hume Cochrane. m 8/13/2000 Eric B Pryne c 2. P Ch Of The H Sprt Vashon WA 2010-2016; P-in-c Ch Of The Ascen Seattle WA 2008-2010; S Alb's Ch Edmonds WA 2007; Assoc Emm Epis Ch Mercer Island WA 1994-2004; Earth Mnstry Seattle WA 1992-1995; S Steph's Epis Ch Seattle WA 1992-1994; Cn Pstr & Eductr S Mk's Cathd Seattle WA 1988-1991, D 1983-1984; Serv Untd Ch Of Chr Seattle WA 1981-1983. Auth, "2 Poems By Sappho," *Gk Attitudes*, 1976. "Renewing Hope" Awd Yale DS 2008; Conservation Awd Washington Wildlife Fed 1997; Bloedel Fell 1995; Bloedel Reserve 1995; Environ Of Year Seattle Audubon 1995.

PUCA JR, Anthony J (NJ) **Gr Epis Ch Westwood NJ 2017-** B Staten Island NY 1981 s Anthony & Bonnie. BA Tem 2008; MDiv GTS 2014; MDiv The GTS 2014. D 10/22/2013 Bp George Edward Councell P 6/10/2014 Bp William H Stokes. m 9/14/2013 Paula Susana Ricca c 1. S Ptr's Ch Essex Fells NJ 2014-2016.

PUCHALLA, Daniel Andrew (Chi) 4180 N Marine Dr Apt 410, Chicago IL 60613 **Assoc Ch Of S Paul And The Redeem Chicago IL 2012-, 2008-2011** B Downers Grove IL 1983 s Christopher & Susan. BA Stetson U 2005; MDiv U Chi DS 2009. D 11/27/2011 Bp Jeff Lee P 6/2/2012 Bp Chris Christopher Epting.

PUCKETT, David Forrest King (Tex) 12535 Perthshire Rd, Houston TX 77024 B San Angelo TX 1950 s Henry & Mary-Jack. BA Texas Wesl 1974; MDiv VTS 1977. D 6/22/1977 Bp Roger Howard Cilley P 6/22/1978 Bp James Milton Richardson. m 11/29/1997 Elizabeth Puckett c 2. R H Sprt Epis Ch Houston TX 2002-2011; Bd Trst Epis TS of the SW Austin TX 1992-2006; Dn S Jn's Cathd Albuquerque NM 1992-2001; R Ch of the Heav Rest Abilene Abilene TX 1985-1992; R S Jas' Epis Ch La Grange TX 1980-1985; Asst S Dunst's Epis Ch Houston TX 1977-1980; Stndg Com Dio The Rio Grande Albuquerque 1991-2000; Stndg Com Dio NW Texas Lubbock TX 1986-1992.

PUCKETT, Douglas Arnold (USC) 111 Aiken Rd # 323, Graniteville SC 29829 **R S Paul's Ch Graniteville SC 1991-; Dir Ord Thousandfold 1987-; Dioc Exec Coun Dio Upper So Carolina Columbia SC 2015-2018; Dn Gravatt Convoc Dio Upper SC 2015-2018** B Reidsville NC 1952 s Joel & Doris. AA

Rockingham Cmnty Coll 1973; BA Gardner-Webb U 1975; Luth Theol Sthrn Sem 1978; MDiv GTS 1979; BA Georgia Rgnts U 1995. Trans 9/1/1981 Bp William Arthur Beckham. m 6/9/1979 Linda B Bedenbaugh c 2. Vic S Geo's Ch Stanley VA 1982-1991; S Paul's Ch Shenandoah VA 1982-1991; Asst S Alb's Ch Lexington SC 1981-1982; Assoc S Jn's Epis Ch Columbia SC 1980-1981; Serv St Edm's Angl Ch of Can Quebec 1979-1980. Auth, "The Ord of the Thousandfold," Forw Mvmt Press, 1988. Alpha Chi Soc 1974. dap@gforcecable.com

PUCKLE, Donne Erving (Az) 125 E Kayetan Dr, Sierra Vista AZ 85635 B London England UK 1940 s Raymond & Elizabeth. AA Phoenix Jr Coll Phoenix AZ 1960; BA Arizona St U 1963; MDiv Bex Sem 1966; Cert Pima Cmnty Coll 1993; MC U of Phoenix 1994. D 6/22/1966 P 12/26/1966 Bp John Joseph Meakin Harte. c 2. S Steph's Ch Sierra Vista AZ 2000-2005; P-in-c S Steph's Epis Ch Douglas AZ 1996-2005; Vic S Jn's Epis Ch Bisbee AZ 1993-2002, Vic 1967-1973; R Chr Ch Chippewa Fls WI 1981-1990; S Simeon's Ch Chippewa Falls WI 1981-1990; Dio Springfield Springfield IL 1979-1981; Trin Epis Ch Mattoon IL 1979-1981; Asst Chr Ch Par La Crosse WI 1976-1978; Gr Epis Ch Lk Havasu City AZ 1976, Vic 1973-1976; S Phil's Preaching Sta Parker AZ 1973-1976; Liturg Off Dio Arizona Phoenix AZ 1967-1976; S Paul's Ch Tombstone AZ 1967-1973; Chapl Par Sch Scottsdale AZ 1966-1967; Cur S Steph's Ch 1966-1967; RurD Dio Eau Claire Eau Claire WI 1985-1990. Auth, "Article," *Arizona Ch Record*; Auth, "Prayers for Adv," *Christmas and Epiph*, Forw Mvmt Press; Auth, "Handbook," *Handbook for Altar lGuild Proposed Bk of Common Pryr*. SSC 1980.

PUGH, Charles Dean (Md) 128 S Hilltop Rd, Catonsville MD 21228 **D Trin Ch Long Green MD 1998-** B VA 1937 s Charles & Martha. Catonsville Cmnty Coll; U of Baltimore; EFM Sewanee: The U So, TS 1997. D 6/14/1997 Bp Charles Lindsay Longest. m 12/15/1958 Mary Ives Maxwell.

PUGH II, Joel Wilson (Ark) 9, The Close, Salisbury SP12E B Great Britain (UK) B Little Rock AR 1932 s Robert & Mary. BA U So 1954; BD Sewanee: The U So, TS 1957; Oxf GB 1960; Sewanee: The U So, TS 1988. D 6/29/1957 P 3/17/1958 Bp Robert Raymond Brown. m 7/15/1967 Caroline Mary Stewart Pugh c 2. Chapl Chr Memi Chap Hobe Sound FL 1995-2002; Sewanee U So TS Sewanee TN 1987-1990, Pres Alum 1975-1986; Bd Mem U So Sewanee TN 1987-1990; TESM Ambridge PA 1980-1994; SCHAH 1980-1986; Dn Trin Cathd Little Rock AR 1977-1994; R The Falls Ch Epis Falls Ch VA 1972-1977; Chapl U So 1966-1972; Asst Chapl U Coll Oxf Engl 1962-1966; D-in-c Ch Of The Gd Shpd Little Rock AR 1957-1958; Advsry Bd SAMS; Dep GC Dio Arkansas Little Rock AR 1979-1991. Fllshp of Witness.

PUGH III, Willard Jerome (HB) 1700 E 56th St Apt 3806, Chicago IL 60637 **Non-par 1977-** B Louisville KY 1945 s Willard & Jane. BA Ken 1967; MDiv EDS 1970; PhD U Chi 1990. D 6/27/1970 P 5/1/1971 Bp John Harris Burt. c 1. Assoc S Mart's Ch Chagrin Fall OH 1973-1976; Cur S Andr's Epis Ch Elyria OH 1971-1973; D-In-Trng Emm Cleveland OH 1970-1971.

PUGLIESE, Richard A (Spr) 744 Parker Road, West Glover VT 05875 **Ret 2003-** B Los Angeles CA 1943 s Dominick & Equina. BA U of Washington 1966; California St U 1967; MDiv GTS 1970. D 6/24/1970 P 1/31/1971 Bp Charles Francis Hall. m 2/10/2012 Stanley Earl Corklin c 3. 1992-2003; The Cathd Ch Of S Paul Springfield IL 1984-1991; Dep GC Dio Springfield Springfield IL 1982-1991, Secy Dio 1981-1984, COM 1980-1986, Stndg Com 1983-1987; Vic S Alb's Epis Ch Olney IL 1977-1983; Vic S Mary's Ch Robinson IL 1977-1983; R S Mary's Epis Par Northfield VT 1973-1977; Cur S Paul's Ch Concord NH 1970-1973. Auth, *Hist of S Matt's Ch*, S Matt's Ch Press, 2002.

PUGLIESE, William Joseph (Ia) 108 Eden Way Ct, Cranberry Twp PA 16066 B New Kensington PA 1942 s William & Anne. BA Pontifical Coll Josephinum 1965; BD Pontifical Coll Josephinum 1969; DMin Drew U 1980. Rec 2/1/1975 as Deacon Bp Wilburn Camrock Campbell. m 2/14/1987 Arlena Ingraham Pugliese c 5. Int S Brendan's Epis Ch Franklin Pk PA 2008-2013; R Chr Ch Cedar Rapids IA 2003-2008; R S Dav's Ch Spokane WA 1996-2003; R Trin Memi Ch Warren PA 1991-1995; R Trin Ch Parkersburg WV 1985-1991; Dioc Coun S Jn Wheeling WV 1980-1985; Vic Ch Of The Gd Shpd Follansbee WV 1975-1979; Olde S Jn's Ch Colliers WV 1975-1979; Serv RC Ch 1969-1974; P-in-c St. Paul's Kittanning PA 2014-2015; Dioc Bd Dio Iowa Des Moines IA 2004-2007; Stndg Com Dio Spokane Spokane WA 2001-2003; Stndg Com Dio W Virginia Charleston WV 1984-1987. Auth, *EDEO News*, 1991; Auth, *Epis-RC Par for WV: Proposed Model*, 1980.

PULIMOOTIL, Cherian Pilo (Va) 7124 Dijohn Court Dr, Alexandria VA 22315 B 1940 s Pilo & Annamma. BA Bridgewater Coll 1975; BA Bridgewater Coll 1975; MA Middle Tennessee St U 1978; MA Middle Tennessee St U 1978; BEd Annamalai U 1985; BEd Annamalai U 1986; DMin Sewanee: The U So, TS 1986; DMin Sewanee: The U So, TS 1986. D 6/6/2009 Bp Peter J Lee P 12/6/2009 Bp Shannon Sherwood Johnston. m 10/23/1977 Ann Pulimootil c 1. R Ch of the Gd Shpd Mc Kenney VA 2014-2015; Assoc P S Mk's Ch Alexandria VA 2009-2014, P 2009-2010. cheriapp@hotmail.com

PULLIAM, James Millard (WMo) 80 Council Trl, Warrensburg MO 64093 **Ret 1993-** B Hannibal MO 1928 s Albert & Wilma. BA U of Missouri 1954; MA U of Missouri 1955; MDiv Sewanee: The U So, TS 1970. D 5/19/1970 P 5/9/

1971 Bp John Maury Allin. m 6/19/1954 Sandra Pulliam c 5. R Chr Ch Warrensburg MO 1978-1993; Calv Epis Ch Cleveland MS 1973-1978; Vic Gr Ch Rosedale MS 1973-1978; S Bernards Ch Okolona MS 1970-1973; Cur S Jn's Ch Aberdeen MS 1970-1973.

PUMMILL, Joseph Howard (Cal) 2550 Dana St Apt 2D, Berkeley CA 94704 **Ret 1988-** B Covina CA 1926 s Joseph & Volora. AA Mt San Antonio Coll 1953; BA U CA Santa Barbara 1955; MDiv Ya Berk 1958; EDS 1970. D 6/16/1958 P 2/13/1959 Bp Donald J Campbell. m 11/14/1990 Doris Ys Pummill c 2. P Ch Of Our Sav Mill Vlly CA 2000-2001; Asst The Epis Ch Of S Mary The Vrgn San Francisco CA 1991-1998, Asst 1982-1990; Mgr The Bp's Ranch Healdsburg CA 1983-1988; Vic Epis Ch On W Kaua'i Eleele HI 1977-1979; Asst Par of St Clem Honolulu HI 1975-1977; Pstr Easter Cmnty Honolulu HI 1970-1977; R Experimental Ecum Mnstry Honolulu HI 1970-1975; R S Mk's Ch Honolulu HI 1960-1969; Cur Trin Epis Ch Santa Barbara CA 1958-1969; Chair Of The Com On Campus Mnstry The Epis Ch in Hawaii Honolulu HI 1976-1977, Chair Of The Dept Of CSR 1970-1975.

PUMPHREY, Charles Michael (Ia) Naval Medical Center, Portsmouth, 620 John Paul Jones Cir, Portsmouth VA 23701 **Off Of Bsh For ArmdF New York NY 1993-** B Baltimore MD 1956 s Charles & Dorothy. BA Randolph-Macon Coll 1978; MDiv VTS 1981. D 6/27/1981 Bp David Keller Leighton Sr P 1/1/1982 Bp Paul Moore Jr. m 8/12/1978 Donna Jean Pumphrey c 3. Curs Secy Dio Iowa Des Moines IA 1992-1993, Cmncatn Cmsn 1991-1993; Vic S Paul's Ch Durant IA 1991-1993; R S Matt's Par Oakland MD 1986-1991; P-in-c S Mary's Epis Ch Tyaskin MD 1982-1986; Cur S Ptr's Ch Salisbury MD 1981-1986. Achievement Medal Usn.

PUMPHREY, David William (O) 2385 Covington Rd, Apt 201, Akron OH 44313 **Ret 1993-** B Warren OH 1927 s Claude & Sarah. BBA U Cinc 1949; MDiv Bex Sem 1955. D 6/18/1955 Bp Nelson Marigold Burroughs P 1/15/1956 Bp Beverley D Tucker. c 3. Dio Ohio Cleveland 1995-1998, ExCoun 1989-1994, Sprtl Dir Curs 1977-1988; Int S Jn's Epis Ch Cuyahoga Fls OH 1992-1993; Bd Sumner Hm Ret Cntr Akron OH 1990-2008; Bd Victim Asst Prog 1986-1991; Pstr Assoc Akron Gnrl Med Cntr Akron OH 1985-1991; Pres Interfaith Vol Caregiver Prog 1985-1990; Bd OH Hospice Assn 1977-1979; Dir Akron Chapl Fndt Akron OH 1976-1991; Assoc S Paul's Ch Akron OH 1974-1992; Assoc Ch Of The Redeem Houston TX 1973-1974; R Ch Of S Thos Berea OH 1965-1973; R S Paul's Ch Steubenville OH 1960-1964; Cur Chr Ch Shaker Heights OH 1955-1960. Int Mnstry Ntwk.

PUMPHREY, John Blair (Del) PO Box 1374, Dover DE 19903 **Reg Dir Estrn Reg ACPE 2015-; COM Dio Delaware Wilmington 2015-, Cong Consultants 2014-, Priestly Formation Com 2011-2015** B Warren OH 1947 s James & Jean. BA Ge 1969; MDiv GTS 1972. D 6/10/1972 P 12/16/1972 Bp Leland Stark. m 5/5/2007 Margaret K Kay c 2. Int Chr Ch Dover DE 2013-2014; S Barn Ch Wilmington DE 2011-2013; Dir Sprtl Wellness S Lk's Hlth System Kansas City MO 2005-2011; St Lk's Chap Kansas City MO 2005-2011; Vic Pstr Nevil Memi Ch Of S Geo Ardmore PA 2001-2005; Mgr Chapl Serv Albert Einstein Healthcare Ntwk Philadelphia PA 2000-2005; Assoc Dir Chapl Serv Christiana Care Hlth Serv Wilmington DE 1988-2000; Ch Of The H Apos Wynnewood PA 1987; Chapl Epis Cmnty Serv Philadelphia PA 1975-1988; Dir of Pstr Care Hosp of U of Pennsylvania Philadelphia PA 1974-1988; Assistan Prot Chapl Overlook Hosp Summit NJ 1972-1973. ACPE, Inc. 1978; Assn of Profsnl Chapl, Inc. 1974.

PUMPHREY, Margaret K (Del) 146 Fairhill Dr, Wilmington DE 19808 **Ch Of The Nativ New Castle DE 2012-, P 2012-, P-in-c 2004-2007** B Richland WA 1945 d William & Margaret. BA Neumann Coll Aston PA 1997; MDiv GTS 2003; MS Neumann Coll Aston PA 2006. D 1/18/2003 P 12/4/2003 Bp Wayne Wright. m 5/5/2007 John Blair Pumphrey c 4. R S Alb's Ch Wilmington DE 2010-2011; Metro Dnry Dio W Missouri Kansas City MO 2008-2010, Dn of Metro Dnry 2009-2010; Dioc Coun Mem Dio W Missouri 2008-2010; Fin Com Mem Dio W Missouri 2008-2010; Asst S Paul's Ch Kansas City MO 2008-2010; R S Aug's Ch Kansas City MO 2007-2008; Chapl Christiana Care Hlth System Wilmington DE 2003-2006; Dio Delaware Wilmington 2003-2004, Dioc Coun Mem 2005-2007; D Imm Ch Highlands Wilmington DE 2003-2004. mkpumphrey@gmail.com

PUMPHREY, Patricia Tilton (Nev) Trinity Episcopal Church, PO Box 2246, Reno NV 89505 **D Trin Epis Ch Reno NV 2013-** B Hartford CT 1941 d Cecil & Josephine. BGS U of Nevada 2000. D 10/27/2012 Bp Dan Thomas Edwards. c 2.

PUMPHREY, Thomas Claude (At) 64 Powderhorn Dr, Phoenixville PA 19460 **The Epis Ch Of S Ptr And S Paul Marietta GA 2013-** B Berea OH 1967 s David. Cleveland St U; BS Cor 1989; MDiv VTS 2004. D 6/12/2004 Bp Mark Hollingsworth Jr P 12/18/2004 Bp Charles Ellsworth Bennison Jr. m 10/18/1997 Silke Pumphrey c 2. Assoc S Dav's Ch Wayne PA 2009-2013; R S Mk's Ch Honey Brook PA 2004-2009; Nomin Com Dio Pennsylvania Philadelphia PA 2008-2010, Stwdshp Com (and chair) 2007-2010. Auth, "Hearts and Minds," *Angl Dig*, SPEAK, 2006. tpumphrey@peterandpaul.org

PUNNETT, Ian Case (Minn) 901 Portland Ave, Saint Paul MN 55104 B Wilmette, IL 1960 s Edwin & Ann. BA U IL 1998; MDiv Columbia TS 2003. D 7/

8/2008 Bp James Louis Jelinek. m 5/30/1985 Margery Campbell Punnett c 2. D S Clem's Ch S Paul MN 2009-2013.

PUNZO, Thomas Edward (WMo) 7055 N Highland Ct, Gladstone MO 64118 B Saint Joseph MO 1943 s Ferdinand & Cecelia. BA Concep Sem Coll 1965; MDiv Concep Sem Coll/Theol 1969; No Amer Coll Rome IT 1974. Rec 9/1/1981 as Priest Bp Edward Clark Turner. m 2/1/1980 Sharon Louise Punzo c 1. R Ch Of The Gd Shpd Kansas City MO 1999-2014; Int S Alb's Epis Ch Wichita KS 1997-1999; Dio Kansas Topeka KS 1996-1997, 1994; Asstng P S Dav's Epis Ch Topeka KS 1996-1997; R Ch Of The Cov Jct City KS 1984-1996; Vic Ch of SS Jn & Geo Wakefield KS 1984-1994; Assoc S Mich And All Ang Ch Mssn KS 1982-1984; P-in-c Gr Epis Ch Ottawa KS 1981-1982; Topeka Coun of Ch Topeka KS 1972-1974; Serv RC Ch 1969-1979. Auth, "Study of Ecum," *Ecum*, Archdio of Kansas City KS, 1972.

PUOPOLO JR, Angelo (SO) 2366 Kemper Ln, 1801 Rutland Ave., Cincinnati OH 45207 B Baltimore MD 1947 s Angelo & Rose. AA Catonsville Cmnty Coll 1974; BS Towson U 1975; MDiv VTS 1979. D 6/17/1979 P 6/17/1980 Bp David Keller Leighton Sr. m 2/14/1970 Mary L Puopolo c 3. Int S Andr's Epis Ch Cincinnati OH 2011-2013; Int S Jas Epis Ch Cincinnati OH 2010-2011; R Ch Of The Adv Cincinnati OH 1987-2009; Assoc R S Thos Ch Lancaster PA 1984-1987; Asst S Tim's Ch Catonsville MD 1983-1984; Vic H Cross Ch Baltimore MD 1979-1983.

PURCELL, Christine (Los) 1031 BIENVENEDA AVENUE, 1031, Pacific Palisades CA 90272 **The Par Of S Matt Pacific Plsds CA 2016-** B Los Angeles CA 1957 BA Dart 1978; MBA U of Connecticut 1988; MDiv GTS 2004. D 6/19/2004 P 2/3/2005 Bp Michael Whittington Creighton. m 6/23/1979 Robert E Purcell c 2. Ch Of The Epiph Oak Pk CA 2015; R Chr Ch Westerly RI 2013-2014; Int S Andr's Epis Ch Shippensburg PA 2010-2011; S Lk's Epis Ch Altoona PA 2009-2010; Chr Soc Mnstry Montoursville PA 2006-2008; Cur S Andr's Epis Ch Lewisburg PA 2004-2005. cpurcell@stmatthews.com

PURCELL, Mary Frances Fleming (Lex) 835 Pinkney Dr, Lexington KY 40504 **Chapl Hospice Of The Bluegrass - Lexington KY 2001-** B Cedar Falls IA 1943 d Cecil & Georgia. BA Simpson Coll 1965; MDiv Lexington TS 1983. D 6/4/1983 Bp Addison Hosea P 5/1/1986 Bp Don Adger Wimberly. m 8/8/1965 Leon Edward Purcell. Ch Of The Gd Shpd Lexington KY 1996-2001, P'S Assoc 1996-2001, Assoc 1987-1995; Int R Ch S Mich The Archangel Lexington KY 1995-1996, D 1985-1986; S Tim's Epis Ch W Des Moines IA 1992-1995, R 1992-1995; R Ch Of The Nativ Maysville KY 1989-1992; Asst R Chr Ascen Ch Richmond VA 1983-1984; The Dept Of Missions Danville KY 1983. Auth, "Harper'S Encyclopedia Of Rel Educ". SCHC. Pstr Care Awd Lexington TS 1983.

PURCELL-CHAPMAN, Diana Barnes (Roch) Po Box 492, Wellsville NY 14895 B Brooklyn NY 1933 d Erwin & Gertrude. AA SUNY; BA S Jos Coll W Hartford CT 1980; MDiv Bex Sem 1986. D 6/26/1993 P 1/22/1994 Bp William George Burrill. m 11/24/1999 Guy Chapman. Pstr Care Coordntr Dio Rochester Henrietta 1993-1999.

PURCHAL, John Jeffrey (LI) 45 Willow St. Apt. 420, Springfield MA 01103 **P-in-c S Andr's Ch Mastic Bch NY 2014-; P-in-c St Andr Epis Ch Yaphank NY 2014-** B Auroroa NE 1963 s John & Joyce. BA U of Nebraska at Kearney 1995; MDiv GTS 2004. D 6/19/2004 P 12/17/2004 Bp Gordon Scruton. S Ann's Ch Sayville NY 2013-2014; Vic S Andr's Ch Longmeadow MA 2004-2010; S Jn's Ch Millville MA 2004-2007.

PURDOM III, Allen Bradford (O) 6809 Mayfield Rd Apt 1071, Cleveland OH 44124 **Cn Dio Ohio Cleveland 2009-** B New Haven CT 1956 s Allen & Joan. U of Akron; BA U of Cntrl Florida 1979; MDiv Sewanee: The U So, TS 1996. D 6/22/1996 P 12/14/1996 Bp J Clark Grew II. m 3/17/1979 Mary J Purdom c 3. R Ch Of The Gd Shpd Lyndhurst OH 2001-2009; R Trin Ch Allnce OH 1996-2001.

PURDUM, Ellen Echols (At) 3098 Saint Annes Ln Nw, Atlanta GA 30327 **Asstg P H Trin Par Decatur GA 2014-; Ass't Dn Stdt Life & Sprtl Formation Candler TS Atlanta Georgia 2010-** B Asheville NC 1959 BA Emory U 1981; MDiv Candler TS Emory U 2001; CAS GTS 2004. D 6/5/2004 P 12/5/2004 Bp J Neil Alexander. m 6/8/1991 David Herbert Purdum. P Assoc Ch Of The Gd Shpd Covington GA 2006-2013; Dir Mnstry Fllshp Prog Fund for Theol Educ Atlanta Georgia 2006-2010; S Anne's Epis Ch Atlanta GA 2004-2006. "Mary And Martha And The Myers-Briggs," Abingdon Press, 2005.

PURDY, James Hughes (Mo) 448 Conway Meadows Dr, Chesterfield MO 63017 B Trenton NJ 1945 s James & Eloise. BA Trin Hartford CT 1967; MDiv PDS 1970. D 4/11/1970 P 10/24/1970 Bp Alfred L Banyard. m 1/22/1972 Emma S Sarosdy c 2. Asstg P Gr Ch S Louis MO 2013-2014; R S Ptr's Epis Ch S Louis MO 1998-2011; R S Jn's Ch Beverly MA 1984-1998; R S Bern's Ch Bernardsville NJ 1973-1983; Asst S Thos' Ch Garrison Forest Owings Mills MD 1970-1973. AGO 1978; CEEP 1999; EvangES of The Epis Ch 1993; Missouri Cler Assn 1998.

PURDY, Tom Clayton (Ga) Christ Church, 6329 Frederica Rd, Saint Simons Island GA 31522 **R Chr Ch Frederica St Simons Is GA 2013-** B Newport News VA 1978 s Philip & Susan. BA Millersville U 2000; MDiv Sewanee: The U So, TS 2005. D 6/11/2005 P 2/4/2006 Bp Michael Whittington Creighton. m 8/19/

2000 Donna JM Purdy c 2. R S Ptr's Ch Poolesville MD 2008-2013; Asst To The R S Jas Ch Lancaster PA 2005-2008. tom@ccfssi.org

PURKS III, James Harris (Ga) 523a 5th Ave, Albany GA 31701 **D S Paul's Ch Albany GA 2008-** B Atlanta GA 1936 s James & Mary. BA U NC 1959; MA Stan 1963. D 12/7/1999 Bp Henry Irving Louttit. D Calv Ch Americus GA 1999-2007. Ord of S Lk.

PURNELL, Erl Gould (Ct) 46 Overlook Ter, Simsbury CT 06070 B Philadelphia PA 1946 s James & Margaret. BA U Pgh 1969; MA Goddard Coll 1989; MAR Ya Berk 1993. D 8/7/1993 Bp Arthur Edward Walmsley P 2/12/1994 Bp Clarence Nicholas Coleridge. m 7/26/2002 Joanne Kimball c 4. R Old S Andr's Ch Bloomfield CT 1997-2015; Cur S Paul's Ch Riverside CT 1993-1997; Dir Dvlpmt Ya Berk New Haven CT 1991-1992. Auth, "Mainely Sermons," *Mainely Sermons*, Featherstone Press, 2017; Auth, "Mainely Poems," *Mainely Poems*, Featherstone Press, 2014; Auth, "Through Mk's Eyes," *Through Mk's Eyes*, Abingdon Press, 2006; Auth, "A Sampler Of Poems," *A Sampler of Poems*, Featherstone Press, 1998; Auth, "A Sea Kayaker'S Trip Planner & Log Bk," *A Sea Kayaker's Trip Planner & Log Bk*, GoThereDoThat, 1996. Distinguished Naval Grad U.S. Navy 1970.

PURNELL, Susan Ann (Los) 19682 Verona Ln, Yorba Linda CA 92886 B Los Angeles CA 1943 d Joseph & Ethel. BS California St U 1980; MS California St U 1982; MDiv CDSP 1989. D 6/10/1989 P 1/1/1990 Bp Frederick Houk Borsch. m 1/20/1962 Arnold Purnell. Asst S Geo's Mssn Hawthorne CA 1994; Asst S Lk's Epis Ch Monrovia CA 1991-1993; Asst S Andr's Par Fullerton CA 1990-1991; Asst R S Geo's Epis Ch Laguna Hills CA 1989-1990.

PURRINGTON, Sandra Jean (NMich) 201 E Ridge St, Marquette MI 49855 B Rice Lake WI 1942 d Russell & Dorothy. RN St Barn Sch of Nrsng 1964. D 5/14/2013 P 12/15/2013 Bp Rayford J Ray. m 8/15/1964 Burton L Purrington c 2.

PURSER, Phil Philip (USC) 635 Timberlake Dr, Chapin SC 29036 B Fayetteville NC 1947 s John & Mary. BA Methodist U 1969; MDiv Sewanee: The U So, TS 1973. D 6/23/1973 P 4/4/1974 Bp Hunley Agee Elebash. m 12/27/1970 Kay Purser c 2. R S Fran of Assisi Chapin SC 2006-2012; Cn Dio Upper So Carolina Columbia SC 2003-2005; R All SS' Epis Ch Morristown TN 2000-2003; R Epis Ch Of The Redeem Greenville SC 1981-2000; Asst S Jn's Epis Ch Columbia SC 1975-1981; R H Trin Epis Ch Hertford NC 1973-1975.

PURSLEY, George William (SO) 332 Mount Zion Rd NW, Lancaster OH 43130 **R S Jn's Epis Ch Lancaster OH 1998-** B Muncie IN 1954 s George & Billie. BA Asbury U 1976; MDiv Asbury TS 1979; MS Ohio U 1989; DMin Sewanee: The U So, TS 1998. D 12/18/1993 P 8/1/1994 Bp Herbert Thompson Jr. m 6/10/1978 Rebecca Lynn Pursley c 2. P-in-c Ch Of The Epiph Nelsonville OH 1995-1998; Vic S Paul's Epis Ch Logan OH 1994-1998; Chapl SE Correctional Inst Lancaster OH 1992-1998; Chapl Ohio Army NG 1984-2007; Assoc Prof Circleville Bible Coll (Now Ohio Chr U) 1980-1993; Dn, NE Dnry Dio Sthrn Ohio Cincinnati OH 1998-2003.

PURVIS, Howard Byrd (SVa) 245 Dexter St E, Chesapeake VA 23324 B Williamston NC 1932 s James & Cora. Cert VTS. D 10/2/1999 P 5/30/2000 Bp David Conner Bane Jr. m 2/18/1989 Delores Banks Jordan. Asst Emm Ch Virginia Bch VA 2000-2002.

PURVIS OSB, Robert David (Ind) 31 Hampshire Ct, Noblesville IN 46062 **Int Trin Ch 2005-; Ret 2001-** B Indianapolis IN 1938 s Cecil & Dorothy. Int Mnstry Prog; Butler U 1957; U of Maryland 1961; Indiana U 1964; Ind Non-Res Sem Prog IN 1975. D 9/28/1974 P 4/12/1975 Bp John P Craine. m 10/11/1958 Donna Louetta Purvis c 4. Int H Fam Epis Ch Fishers IN 2002-2003; Int All SS Ch Indianapolis IN 2001-2002; Ch Of S Mich And All Ang Sanibel FL 1997-2000; Cmssnr City Hsng Auth 1989-1996; Waycross Long-R Plnng Com 1986-1987; Exec Com Vim 1980-1982; Bd Coleman Adoption Agcy 1978-1981; S Mich's Ch Noblesville IN 1977-1997; Bd Uec 1977-1980; S Chris's Epis Ch Carmel IN 1975-1976; Dioc Bdgt Com Dio Indianapolis Indianapolis IN 1989, Bp Advsry Coun Applicnts Mnstry 1982-1988, Com 1978-1981, Chair Dioc Personl Com 1976-1977.

PURYEAR, Jim (SwFla) 339 Meadow Beauty Ct, Venice FL 34293 **R S Mk's Epis Ch Venice FL 2001-** B South Hill VA 1947 s James & Ruby. BS Old Dominion U 1972; MDiv VTS 2001. D 6/9/2001 Bp David Conner Bane Jr P 12/16/2001 Bp John Bailey Lipscomb. m 5/19/2001 Carol Brenholtz Puryear c 1. jimpuryear@stmarksvenice.com

PURYEAR, Sarah Elizabeth (Tenn) St. George's Episcopal Church, 4715 Harding Rd, Nashville TN 32705 B Portland ME 1981 d Scott & Meredith. BA Wheaton Coll 2004; MDiv Duke DS 2008. D 6/6/2009 P 1/15/2010 Bp Dabney Tyler Smith. m 9/22/2012 Daniel Hays Puryear c 1. Assoc R S Geo's Ch Nashville TN 2010-2017; Asst S Thos' Epis Ch St Petersburg FL 2009-2010.

PUTMAN, Richard Byron (Ala) 408 Thornberry Cir, Birmingham AL 35242 B Birmingham AL 1943 s Herman & Gertrude. Post-Grad Emory U; BA U of Alabama 1966; MDiv Candler TS Emory U 1974. D 10/28/1976 P 5/26/1977 Bp Furman Charles Stough. c 3. Assoc St. Matt's Epis Ch Madison AL 2013-2014; Asstg P S Thos Epis Ch Birmingham AL 2003-2013; Chapl Birmingham Epis Campus Mnstrs Birmingham AL 1981-1983; Chapl Birmingham Sthrn Coll Birmingham AL 1981-1983; R S Jn's Ch Birmingham AL 1979-1983; R S Lk's Ch Scottsboro AL 1978-1979; Chapl U of Alabama in Birmingham Birmingham AL 1976-1979; Cn Dio Alabama Birmingham 1976-1978; Cur S Andrews's Epis Ch Birmingham AL 1976-1977. Theta Phi Intl Theol Soc 1974. Cert Fin Planner CFP Bd 1992; Var Combat Medals USAF 1969; Air Medal USAF 1969.

PUTNAM, Kevin Todd (Cal) 849 Spruance Ln, Foster City CA 94404 B Portsmouth VA 1973 s Frank & Fay. BS VPI 1995; MA VPI 2000; MDiv CDSP 2003. D 8/17/2003 Bp Otis Charles P 12/4/2004 Bp William Edwin Swing. m 5/21/2000 Nelzine Delia Putnam c 1. Dio Oregon Portland OR 2006; S Andr's Sch Saratoga CA 2004-2006; S Andr's Ch Saratoga CA 2003-2013.

PUTNAM, Sarah Thompson (SC) Po Box 888, Marion SC 29571 B Nashville TN 1940 d William & Sarah. BA U of So Carolina 1961; MS U GA 1974; MDiv VTS 1997. D 3/31/1997 P 10/4/1997 Bp Edward Lloyd Salmon Jr. m 9/2/1961 Samuel Franklin Putnam. Vic Ch Of The Adv Marion SC 1998-2006; Int St Anne's Epis Ch Conway SC 1997-1998.

PUTNAM, Thomas Clyde (Ia) 397 Huron Ave, Cambridge MA 02138 **Non-par 1981-** B Des Moines IA 1948 s Clyde & Dorothy. BA Westminster Coll 1971; MDiv EDS 1977; NCPsyA CG Jung Inst 1986; PhD Un U 1988. D 6/23/1977 P 4/27/1978 Bp Walter Cameron Righter. m 8/7/1988 Susan Lawrence. Assoc Chapl Brigham Wmns Hosp Boston MA 1977-1981; Mssnr All SS Par Brookline MA 1977-1979. Auth, "A Jungian Perspective On A Repetitive Nightmare". AAPC 1978; Amer Coll Chapl 1978; Intl Assn Of Analytical Psychol 1987; New Engl Soc Of Jungian Psychoanalysts 1990; New York Assn of Analytical Psychologists 1990.

PUTZ, Shirley Joyce Baynham (Nev) 1453 Rawhide Rd, Boulder City NV 89005 B Glasgow MT 1926 d Walter & Myrtle. RN Montana Consolidated Sch of Nrsng 1947. D 7/3/1992 Bp Stewart Clark Zabriskie. m 1/19/1946 Wayne Joseph Putz.

PYATT, Petrina Margarette (NJ) 100 East Maple Ave, Penns Grove NJ 08069 B New York NY 1949 d Samuel & Juanita. BA CUNY 1988; MDiv GTS 2003. D 6/12/2004 P 1/15/2005 Bp George Edward Councell. c 2. R Ch Of Our Merc Sav Penns Grove NJ 2005-2016; Asst S Andr's Ch Bronx NY 2004-2005; Chapl Compassionate Care Hospice 2003-2005; Chair, Nomin Commttee Dio New Jersey Trenton NJ 2007-2010, Chair, Nomin Com 2006-2009, The Visioning Com 2006-2008, Mus and Liturg Com 2006-, Liturg & Mus Com Mem 2005-2007.

PYLES, Chris (CPa) 707 Park Ave, Baltimore MD 21201 **Gr And S Ptr's Ch Baltimore MD 2017-** B Washington DC 1976 s Richard & Nancy. BA Ford 1998; MDiv GTS 2005. D 3/19/2005 P 9/17/2005 Bp Mark Sean Sisk. R S Jn's Epis Ch Bellefonte PA 2010-2017; Assoc R S Lk's Ch Philadelphia PA 2007-2010; Asst to the R Washington Memi Chap Vlly Forge PA 2005-2007; Stndg Com Dio Cntrl Pennsylvania Harrisburg PA 2016-2017, Liturg Cmsn, Chair 2015-2017, RurD 2015, COM 2014-2016, Cler Wellness Initiative, Coordntr 2013-2017, Bp Search Com 2013-2014, Cler Compstn Com 2012-2013, Congrl Dvlpmt Cmsn 2011-.

PYRON JR, Wilson Nathaniel (Mo) 1422 Shady Creek Ct, Saint Louis MO 63146 **Ret 2005-** B El Dorado AR 1943 s Wilson & Kathryn. BS U of Arkansas 1965; MDiv VTS 1973. D 6/25/1973 P 3/23/1974 Bp Christoph Keller Jr. c 2. Asst Ch Of The Adv S Louis MO 2006-2009; Assoc Emm Epis Ch S Louis MO 2005-2006; R S Matt's Epis Ch Warson Woods Kirkwood MO 1999-2005; S Lk and S Jn's Caruthersvlle MO 1998-1999; R S Paul's Epis Ch Sikeston MO 1996-1999, R 1981-1986; S Lk's Ch Hot Sprg AR 1986-1996; R S Paul's Newport AR 1976-1981; Cur & Vic S Jas Ch Magnolia AR 1973-1976; Cur & Vic S Mary's Epis Ch El Dorado AR 1973-1976.

Q

QUACKENBUSH, Margaret Haight (Alb) Rr 1 Dunbar Road, Cambridge NY 12816 **D S Paul's Epis Ch Greenwich NY 1996-** B Syracuse NY 1947 d Alfred & Ruth. Core Epis Dio Albany Albany NY; D Formation Prog 1995; EFM Sewanee: The U So, TS 1995. D 11/18/1995 Bp David Standish Ball. m 4/29/1972 Peter Quackenbush.

QUAINTON, Rodney F (Chi) 1725 Northfield Square, Northfield IL 60093 **Asstg P Chr Ch Winnetka IL 2014-** B Seattle WA 1941 s Cecil & Marjorie. BA Ya 1962; BA Ya 1962; MBA Harv 1970; MBA Harv 1970; MDiv Epis TS of the SW 1988. D 6/15/1988 Bp Gordon Taliaferro Charlton P 1/6/1989 Bp Maurice Manuel Benitez. m 6/18/1999 Nanci Priest c 3. Exec Pstr First Meth Ch Birmingham MI 1999-2015; R Ch of the Heav Rest Abilene Abilene TX 1993-1995; Assoc R All SS Prot Epis Ch Ft Lauderdale FL 1990-1993; Asst to R S Dunst's Epis Ch Houston TX 1988-1990.

QUATORZE, Jean Lenord (Hai) **Dio Haiti Port-au-Prince HT 2002-** B 1969 D. m 4/7/2005 Marie Ilomene Michaud.

QUEEN, Jeffrey Denver (Lex) 3 Chalfonte Place, Fort Thomas KY 41075 **P-in-c S Andr's Ch Ft Thos KY 2012-; Trst Bex Sem Columbus OH 2009-** B Little Rock AR 1972 s James & Beverly. BA Wilmington Coll 1994; MDiv Untd TS 2000; Cert Ang Stud Bex Sem 2002. D 5/22/2004 P 2/5/2005 Bp Herbert Thompson Jr. m 11/8/1997 Richelle T Thompson c 2. R All SS Epis Ch Portsmouth OH 2006-2011; Vic S Mary Magd Ch Maineville OH 2004-2005; Pstr Meth Ch OH 1990-2002; Trst of the Ch Fndt Dio Sthrn Ohio Cincinnati OH 2006-2011, Trst of the Ch Fndt 2006-2011, Cmsn on Congrl Life 2004-2007, Cmsn on Evang 2003-2006. GAS 2004; Soc of King Chas the Mtyr 2009; SocOLW 2006.

QUEEN, Laura Virginia (Los) Church Pension Group, 19 E 34th St, New York NY 10016 **VP for Educ and Wellness The CPG New York NY 2011-** B Tampa FL 1960 d William & Laura. BS U of W Florida 1982; MDiv GTS 2003. D 6/21/2003 P 1/24/2004 Bp Joseph Jon Bruno. m 8/8/2008 Karen K Karen Clark. R S Alb's Ch Simsbury CT 2008-2011; Asst S Aug By-The-Sea Par Santa Monica CA 2005-2008; Assoc St Cross Epis Ch Hermosa Bch CA 2003-2008; Chapl Epis Communities & Serv Pasadena CA 2003-2005; Print Off The GC 2000-2011; Mssnr for Yth Dio Los Angeles Los Angeles CA 1994-2001; Mssnr for Yth Dio Massachusetts Boston MA 1989-1993. cl The GTS 2003. lqueen@cpg.org

QUEEN JR, William L (Va) 8639 Brown Summit Rd, Richmond VA 23235 **Chr And Gr Ch Petersburg VA 2016-** B Jacksonville FL 1957 s William & JoAnn. BA Eckerd Coll 1979; MIM Amer Grad Sch of Intl Mgmt Glendal 1984; MDiv VTS 1994. D 6/12/1994 P 12/11/1994 Bp Stephen Hays Jecko. m 5/3/1986 Lynn E Queen c 3. Trin Epis Ch Washington VA 2015-2016; Assoc R All SS Ch Richmond VA 2002-2015; R S Barn Epis Ch No Chesterfield VA 1997-2002; Assoc R S Paul's By-The-Sea Epis Ch Jaxville Bch FL 1994-1997. bill.queen@richmond.edu

QUEHL-ENGEL, Catherine Mary (Ia) 103 Oak Ridge Dr Se, Mount Vernon IA 52314 **Assoc P Trin Ch Iowa City IA 2006-; Chapl of the Coll Cornell Coll 1996-** B Springfield, OH 1967 d Gary & Janeen. Doctorate of Mnstry (still in progress). Washington Theol Un; BA Cornell Coll 1989; MDiv PSR 1994; MA PSR 1994. D 9/2/2005 P 4/22/2006 Bp Alan Scarfe. m 5/28/1989 Craig Engel c 1. Bd Dir Dio Iowa Des Moines IA 2006-2013, Dir of Sum Mnstrs Retreat 2006-2009, Dioc Angl Comm/Recon T/F 2006-2008.

QUESENBERRY-NELSON, Jane E (Minn) 4903 Maple Grove Rd, Hermantown MN 55811 B Duluth MN 1952 d Richard & Mildred. D 6/26/2014 Bp Brian N Prior. m 8/8/1999 Jeff L Nelson c 2.

QUEVEDO-BOSCH, Juan A (LI) 3014 Crescent St S, Astoria NY 11102 **P-in-c Ch Of The Redeem Astoria NY 2007-, R 2000-2006** B Puerto Padre Tunas CU 1955 s Juan & Maria. MTh Seminario Evangelico de Teologia 1989; MDiv U Tor CA 1990; ThM U Tor 1991. Trans 10/9/2000 Bp Orris George Walker Jr. m 4/8/2014 Juan F Aquino - Iglesias. Assoc P S Leonard's Toronto 1997-2000; Chair of the Hisp Cmsn Dio Long Island Garden City NY 2007-2011, Alt Dep to GC 2006 2006-2009, Exam Chapl 2002-2011, Dioc Coun 2002-2003, COM 2001-2011; Exam Chapl (Gnrl Bd) Dom And Frgn Mssy Soc- Epis Ch Cntr New York NY 2006-2012. Auth, "Ancestors in the cloud of witnesses : El Dia de Muertos in the Mex migrant experience in New York City," *Studia Liturgica*, 2004, vol. 34, no1, 2004; Auth, "Compasrose Liturg Tourists?," *The Chant of Life: Inculturation and the People of the Land*, Ch Pub, 2003; Auth, "The Influence of Afr Rel in Cuban Chrsnty.," *Theol in Afr*, http://theologyinafrica.com/blog/?page_id=133, 1998; Auth, "The Liturg Species," *Revising the Euch : groundwork for t*, lcuin/GROW Liturg study,, 1994; Auth, "The Visigothic-Mozarabic Liturg : Reg expression of the integrity of the Chr initiation rite 300-1085," *Thesis*, 1991. Exec. Ctte. Intl Angl Liturg Consulation 2007-2009; SOCIETAS LITURGICA and IALC Mem 1991. Hon Cn of the Cathd of the Incarn The Epis Dio Long island 2005.

✠ QUEZADA MOTA, The Rt Rev Moises (DR) Calle Costa Rica No 21, Ens. Ozama, Santo Domingo Dominican Republic **Iglesia Epis La Encarnacion La Romana 1998-; Vic Iglesia Epis de Todos los Santos La Romana 1998-; Dio The Dominican Republic (Iglesia Epis Dominicana) Gazcue Santo Domingo 1982-** B La Romana DO 1956 s Virgilio & Mercedes. Centro de Estudios Teologicos 1982. D 8/15/1982 P 5/1/1983 Bp Telesforo A Isaac Con 2/13/2016 for DR (DomRep). m 7/31/1983 Mary Jeannette Pringle de Quezada c 2. Iglesia Epis San Andres Santo Domingo Di 1998-2007; Vic Iglesia Epis San Esteban San Pedro de Macoris 1983-1988.

QUICK, Judy Goins (Ala) 224 Bentley Cir, Shelby AL 35143 **VP Global Epis Mssn Ntwk (GEMN) 2011-; D S Andr's Ch Montevallo AL 2011-; Chair Mssn and Outreach 2009-; Coordntr Epis Relief and Dvlpmt 2008-** B Jacksonville FL 1951 d Louie & Virginia. BA U of Florida 1972; MA U of Florida 1973; MBA Georgia St U 1993; EFM U So 2006. D 10/1/2011 Bp Henry Nutt Parsley Jr. m 9/11/1976 Gene Willard Quick.

QUIGGLE, George Willard (Ala) 384 Windflower Dr, Dadeville AL 36853 B Birmingham AL 1941 s George & Mary. U So; BA Birmingham-Sthrn Coll 1964; BD Candler TS Emory U 1969. D 6/21/1986 P 12/1/1986 Bp Furman Charles Stough. m 12/16/1961 Dale C Quiggle. Dio Alabama Birmingham 1998-2003; S Mich And All Ang Millbrook AL 1998-2003; P S Lk's Epis Ch Jacksonville AL 1986-1998; Grtr Birmingham Mnstrs (Ecum Urban Mssn Agcy) 1968-1985.

QUIGLEY, James E (WA) St Alban's Church, 3001 Wisconsin Ave NW, Washington DC 20016 **P S Alb's Par Washington DC 2012-; Chapl Wstrn Ken-**

tucky U Bowling Green KY 2001- B Lombard IL 1964 s John & Frances. BFA The Art Acad of Cincinnati 1987; VTS 2001; MDiv VTS 2001. D 6/3/2001 P 2/2/2002 Bp Ted Gulick Jr. m 8/19/1989 Ellen L Quigley c 1. S Geo's Epis Ch New Orleans LA 2007-2012; Assoc Chr Epis Ch Bowling Green KY 2001-2007. Alum/Alum Exec Com, VTS 2001-2003.

QUILA GARCIA, Pedro Perfecto (EcuC) Box 235, Tena Ecuador B Los Rios 1944 s Pedro & Ignacia. D 12/16/1984 P 6/1/1985 Bp Adrian Delio Caceres-Villavicencio. Iglesia Epis Del Ecuador Quito 1985-1989.

QUILL, Margaret M (Chi) Guardian Angels of Elk River, Inc., 400 Evans Avenue, Elk River MN 55330 B Milwaukee WI 1948 d Harold & Marvel. BA U of Wisconsin 1971; MA U Hawaii-Manoa Manoa HI 1974; MDiv EDS 1987. D 6/28/1987 Bp Donald Purple Hart P 1/1/1988 Bp Andrew Frederick Wissemann. P-in-c H Trin Epis Ch Elk River MN 2010-2011; Chapl Guardian Ang of Elk River Inc 2008-2006; Chapl S Lk's Epis Hosp Houston TX 2007-2008; S Lk's Epis Hosp Houston TX 2007-2008; Emm Epis Ch Rockford IL 2004-2006; Chr Ch Medway MA 1992-2004; Chapl MIT Cambridge MA 1992-1994; Vic S Steph's Ch Pittsfield MA 1990-1992; Cur All SS Ch Worcester MA 1987-1990.

QUIN, Alison Joan (NY) 3021 State Route 213 E, Stone Ridge NY 12484 **R The Epis Ch Of Chr The King Stone Ridge NY 2007-; Assoc S Nich Darnestown MD 2005-** B Washington D.C. 1959 d Frederick & Diana. BA Swarthmore Coll 1982; JD Cor 1987; MDiv VTS 2001. D 6/9/2001 Bp Jane Hart Holmes Dixon P 12/18/2001 Bp Allen Lyman Bartlett Jr. m 5/28/1983 Timothy David Shapiro c 2. S Nich Epis Ch Germantown MD 2005-2007; P-in-c S Dav's Washington DC 2003-2005; S Dav's Par Washington DC 2002-2005; Asst R S Dav's Washington DC 2002-2003; S Geo's Ch Glenn Dale MD 2002.

QUINBY, Congreve Hamilton (Alb) 51 High Grove Ct, Burlington VT 05401 **Ret 1994-** B Rochester NY 1928 s Henry & Alice. BA Wms 1950; MDiv SWTS 1958. D 6/16/1958 P 2/18/1959 Bp Donald J Campbell. m 5/31/1958 Constance Philp c 2. Stwdshp Off Dio Albany Greenwich NY 1994-1997; Stndg Com 1987-1993; R Trin Ch Potsdam NY 1985-1993; P-in-c S Aug's Ch Kansas City MO 1982-1985; Dio W Missouri Kansas City MO 1978-1982; Dept Evang & Renwl Gr And H Trin Cathd Kansas City MO 1978-1982; Corp Dio Los Angeles Los Angeles CA 1976-1978; R Chr The Gd Shpd Par Los Angeles CA 1962-1977; Vic S Jos's Par Buena Pk CA 1958-1962.

QUINES JR, Brent B (Los) The Parish of Holy Trinity and St Benedict, 412 N Garfield Ave, Alhambra CA 91801 **R Ch Of The H Trin and S Ben Alhambra CA 2012-** B Bontoc Philippines 1967 s Brent & Florence. B.TH Other 1990; B.TH St. Andr's TS, Quezon City, Philippines 1990. Trans 12/4/2012 Bp Joseph Jon Bruno. m 5/27/1994 Jasmine Sharon Kiley Quines c 2. P Dio Nthrn Philippines 1991-1993. brentspb@yahoo.com

QUINN, Carolee Elizabeth Sproull (USC) 1402 Wenwood Ct, Greenville SC 29607 **Chapl Ret Cler 2009-** B Detroit MI 1927 d William & Carolee. U of Kansas 1947; Dio SE Florida Sch for Mnstry FL 1993. D 5/20/1993 Bp Calvin Onderdonk Schofield Jr. c 3. D Epis Ch Of The Redeem Greenville SC 2012, D 1994-2012; D S Andr's Epis Ch Greenville SC 2011-2012; D S Jas Epis Ch Greenville SC 2006-2010; D S Fran Ch Greenville SC 2004-2006; Chapl Greenville Memi Hosp 1994-1995; D S Mart's Epis Ch Pompano Bch FL 1993-1994; Chapl Sea Hospice Boca Raton FL 1993-1994. NAAD.

QUINN, Catherine Alyce Rafferty (Nwk) 66 Pomander Walk, Ridgewood NJ 07450 **Cler Assoc for Fam Mnstrs S Eliz's Ch Ridgewood NJ 2011-** B Boston MA 1974 d James & Alyce. BS U So 1996; MDiv Ya Berk 2003. D 11/22/2004 P 5/22/2005 Bp Peter J Lee. m 1/15/2005 Peter Devlin Quinn c 4. Asst R S Jn's Ch Lafayette Sq Washington DC 2005-2008; Cler Res Chr Ch Alexandria VA 2004-2005.

QUINN, Eugene Frederick (WA) 5702 Kirkside Dr, Chevy Chase MD 20815 B Oil City PA 1935 s Frederick & William. BA Alleg 1957; MA U CA 1966; MA U CA 1969; PhD U CA 1970. D 6/22/1974 Bp William Foreman Creighton P 2/22/1975 Bp John Thomas Walker. m 6/16/2001 Carolyn Tanner Irish. Chapl Cathd of St Ptr & St Paul Washington DC 1987; Chr Ch S Jn's Par Accokeek MD 1985; S Columba's Ch Washington DC 1973-1978. Auth, "The French Ovrs Empire," 2000; Auth, "You & Human Rts," 1999; Auth, "Democracy At Dawn," 1998; Auth, "To Heal The Earth," 1994; Auth, "Human Rts & The Judiciary," 1994; Auth, "The Federalist Papers Rdr," 1992; Auth, "Bk Revs Of Afr Stds & Frgn Affrs"; Auth, "The Angl Ethos In Hist".

QUINN, Michele (Colo) 3153 S Forest St, Denver CO 80222 **R S Jos's Ch Lakewood CO 2008-** B Portsmouth NH 1954 d John & Joan. S Thos Sem; BA Trin 1976; MDiv Iliff TS 1997. D 6/6/1998 P 12/1/1998 Bp William Jerry Winterrowd. m 6/23/1996 Peter D Miscall c 2. Dio Colorado Denver CO 2002-2005, 2000; R Epis Ch Of S Ptr And S Mary Denver CO 2001-2008; Asst S Steph's Epis Ch Aurora CO 1999-2000.

QUINN, Peter Darrell (Ct) 120 Ford Ln, Torrington CT 06790 **P-in-c S Jn The Evang Yalesville CT 2006-; P-in-c St. Jn the Evang Yalesville CT 2005-** B Providence RI 1941 s Ernest & Marjorie. BA Barrington Coll 1973; MA Providence Coll 1976; DMin Hartford Sem 2004. D 12/22/1973 P 6/1/1974 Bp Frederick Hesley Belden. m 9/11/1965 Janet D Quinn c 2. R St Gabr's Ch E Berlin CT 1992; R Ch of our Sav Plainville CT 1985-2004; R Calv Ch Stonington CT

1977-1985; Chr Ch Westerly RI 1974-1977; Cur St Mich & Gr Ch Rumford RI 1974-1976.

QUINN, Scott (Pgh) 537 Hamilton Rd, Pittsburgh PA 15205 **Trin Cathd Pittsburgh PA 2014-; Cn Dio Pittsburgh Pittsburgh PA 2009-; R Ch of the Nativ Crafton PA 1986-** B Pittsburgh PA 1954 s Thomas & Lucille. BA U Pgh 1977; MDiv TESM 1982. D 6/5/1982 Bp Robert Bracewell Appleyard P 2/1/1983 Bp Alden Moinet Hathaway. m 6/1/1980 Vera Lee Quinn c 3. R Ch Of The Nativ Pittsburgh PA 1983-2015; Vic Ch of the Nativ Crafton PA 1983-1986; Vic S Mk Pittsburgh PA 1982-1986. squinn@episcopalpgh.org

QUINNELL, Carolyn T (CFla) PO Box 2373, Belleview FL 34421 **Par Coordntr Epis Ch Of S Mary Belleview FL 2017-; D Dio Cntrl Florida Orlando FL 2015-** B Dublin GA 1954 d Willis & Dorothy. Liberal Stds Barry U 1991. D 9/12/2015 Bp Gregory Orrin Brewer. m 4/25/1992 Robert Douglass Quinnell c 2.

QUINNELL, Robert Douglass (CFla) PO Box 2373, Belleview FL 34421 **D Epis Ch Of S Mary Belleview FL 2015-** B Waterbury CT 1946 s Robert & Marion. BS VPI and St U 1969; MS Florida Atlantic U 1973. D 9/12/2015 Bp Gregory Orrin Brewer. m 4/25/1992 Carolyn T Jackson c 3.

QUINNEY, Sarah Howell (NCal) 2351 Pleasant Grove Blvd, Roseville CA 95747 B Jacksonville FL 1984 d James & Amelia. BA Mus Florida St U 2007; BM Florida St U 2007; MDiv CDSP 2015; MDiv CDSP 2016. D 6/28/2014 P 6/12/2015 Bp Barry Leigh Beisner. Asst St Johns Epis Ch Roseville CA 2015-2017, D 2014-2015.

QUINONEZ-MERA, Juan Carlos (EcuC) **Iglesia Epis Del Ecuador Quito 2012-, 2006-2009** B Esmeraldas 1985 s Juan & Sara. Programa De Educacion Teologia; Universidad Cntrl Del Ecuador. D 2/11/2006 Bp Orlando Jesus Guerrero P 1/6/2007 Bp Wilfrido Ramos-Orench. m 7/23/2010 Wendy Arleene Berrett Buchanan.

QUINTON, Dean Lepidio (Nev) FCI La Tuna - Religious Services Dept, 8500 Doniphan Dr House 17, Anthony TX 79821 **Off Of Bsh For ArmdF New York NY 1995-** B Daqupan City PH 1949 s Crispin & Angelita. BA Div Word Sem 1971; MA Div Word Sem 1977. Rec 4/1/1995 as Priest Bp Stewart Clark Zabriskie. m 3/18/1994 Paulyn Quinton. Chapl Bureau Prisons Anth TX.

QUIROGA, Luis Alberto (LI) 14755 Sw 154th Ct, Miami FL 33196 B Bogota CO 1919 s Luis & Julia. BA Amer Coll De Bogota Bogota CO 1939; BD PrTS 1945; MTh PrTS 1946; PhD U De Antioquia CO 1950. D 4/24/1955 P 12/1/1955 Bp Albert Ervine Swift. Exec Coun Appointees New York NY 1983-1988; Chr Ch Cobble Hill Brooklyn NY 1977-1982; Dio Long Island Garden City NY 1961-1976; Chapl U In Puerto Rico 1958-1960; Dir S Jn's Cathdral Sch Rio Piedras Puerto Rico 1957-1961; Cur S Jn's Cathdral Rio Piedras Puerto Rico 1957-1961. Auth, "Word and Sacraments," 1975.

R

RAASCH, Timothy (Minn) 408 N 7th St, Brainerd MN 56401 B Macon GA 1954 s Harold & Janice. BA U CA 1976; MDiv CDSP 1982. D 6/25/1983 P 6/1/1984 Bp William Edwin Swing. S Thos Ch Lancaster PA 2016; R Dio Utah Salt Lake City UT 2015; Chr Ch Par Kensington MD 2013-2015; S Steph's Ch Grand Island NE 2012-2013; S Ptr's Epis Ch Charlotte NC 2011-2012; P-in-c S Paul's Ch Brainerd MN 2008-2011; Ch Of The Adv Louisville KY 2004-2006; S Barn Ch Norwich VT 2003-2004; Chr Ch St Michaels Par S Mich MD 2002-2003; Chair Of The Resolutns Com 1995-1996; S Fran Epis Ch San Jose CA 1994-1999; Int S Mary's Ch Portsmouth RI 1993-1994; Int Calv Ch Stonington CT 1992-1993; Int S Steph's Epis Ch Bloomfield CT 1990-1991; Chapl Hartford Hosp Hartford CT 1989-1991; R Ch Of The Nativ San Rafael CA 1986-1989; Dept Of Yth Min 1984-1985; Int Chapl Stan CA 1984-1985; Cur S Bede's Epis Ch Menlo Pk CA 1983-1986; Com Dio California San Francisco CA 1984-1989. OHC.

RABAGO-NUNEZ, Luis Antonio (U) 1211 N Redwood Rd Apt 165, Salt Lake City UT 84116 **Dio Mex Mex City MOR 2004-** B Mexico City Mexico 1973 LTh Seminario de San Andres MX. Trans 5/21/2003 Bp Carolyn Tanner Irish. m 5/1/2004 Elisa Nayeli Medina Fuentes c 2. Dio Utah Salt Lake City UT 2004; D S Steph's Ch W Vlly City UT 2003.

✠ RABB, The Rt Rev John L (Md) 4 E University Pkwy, Baltimore MD 21218 **Bd EUC 2006-** B Des Moines IA 1944 s Carleton & JoAnn. BA DePauw U 1966; MA U of Iowa 1969; MDiv EDS 1976; Cert Franciscan Intl Study Cntr Cbury GB 2004. D 6/26/1976 P 1/8/1977 Bp William Foreman Creighton Con 10/10/1998 for MD. m 4/17/1976 Sharon Rabb c 2. Pres Ecum Leaders Grp of Maryland 2005-2007; Bp Suffr of Maryland Dio Maryland Baltimore MD 1998-2010; COM Dio Atlanta Atlanta GA 1989-1998, Pres, Cler Orgnztn 1989-1993; R S Anne's Epis Ch Atlanta GA 1988-1998; Chapl U of Maryland 1980-1988; R The Ch Of The H Apos Halethorpe MD 1979-1988; Cur Ch Of The Ascen Gaithersburg MD 1976-1979. ACPE; EUC 2005. Bryce Shoemaker for Chr Unity Cntrl Maryland Ecum Coun 2005; Outstanding Alum - Profsnl Wk DePauw U 2005; Atlanta Mayor's Awd for Serv City of Atlanta 1993.

RABONE, Christian Robert (NwT) **Cur Emm Epis Ch San Angelo TX 2016-** B 1960 s Howard & Sondra. Bachelor of Arts in Mus Ed. U of Arkansas 1983; Mstr of Ed. in Admin U of No Texas 1989; Supt Degree Texas Tech U 2006; Mstr of Div Epis TS of the SW 2016. D 6/4/2016 P 1/14/2017 Bp James Scott Mayer. m 4/20/1996 Tiffany Lea Selover c 2. Lions Club 1997-2013. Accommodation Awd Crandall and Kaufman Police 1995; Hon Band Fraternity Kappa Kappa Psi 1979; Hon Mus Franternity Phi Mu Alpha Sinfonia 1979. curate@emmanuel-sa.org

RABY, Edith Gilliam (CFla) 111 S Church St, Smithfield VA 23430 B Newport News VA 1945 d Quincy & Elva. A.S. Tidewater Cmnty Coll 1972; B.A. Old Dominion U 1974; 4-year Diac Trng Institue for Chr Stds 2000. D 12/9/2000 Bp John Wadsworth Howe. c 2.

RACHAL, Paula C (NC) 2803 Watauga Dr, Greensboro NC 27408 **Chapl, Asst. Dir The Servnt Cntr Inc. Greensboro NC 2003-; Asst All SS Ch Greensboro NC 2000-** B Madison IN 1957 d Henry & Martha. BS MI SU 1980; MDiv SWTS 2000. D 6/10/2000 Bp Claude Charles Vache P 5/26/2001 Bp James Gary Gloster. m 9/15/1990 Robert T Rachal c 1. Coord. of Rel Life Stephens Coll Columbia MO 1993-1996; Lay Asst Gd Shpd Lake Chas LA 1992.

RACHAL, Robert T (NC) 2803 Watauga Dr, Greensboro NC 27408 **Supply Ch Of The Mssh Mayodan NC 2003-** B New Iberia LA 1962 s Richard & Margaret. BS LSU 1985; MDiv SWTS 1991; CSD Haden Inst 2004. D 6/8/1991 P 12/22/1991 Bp Robert Jefferson Hargrove Jr. m 9/15/1990 Paula C Rachal c 1. Campus Mnstr Trin Ch Huntington WV 1997-1999; Cbury Fllshp Huntington WV 1997-1998; Campus Mnstr Calv Ch Columbia MO 1993-1997; Asst Epis Ch Of The Gd Shpd Lake Chas LA 1992-1993; Epis Sch Of Acadiana Inc. Cade LA 1991; Asst S Barn Epis Ch Lafayette LA 1991. Auth, "Voices of Life & Hope in Cntrl Amer," *Plumbline*, 1997.

RACINE, Jean-Joel (Hai) Box 1309, Port-Au-Prince Haiti **P-in-c Leogane Mssn 1986-** B Bon Repos HT 1950 s Joseph & Marie. BA Normal Sch U Ht 1976. D 8/4/1985 P 6/1/1986 Bp Luc Anatole Jacques Garnier. m 12/16/1976 Marie Monique Senat Racine. Dio Haiti Port-au-Prince HT 2006-2012, 1985-2003. Auth, "Cours De Mathematiques 6 & 5".

RACIOPPI, Gerard Andrew (Nwk) 73 S Fullerton Ave, Montclair NJ 07042 **Ch Of The H Sprt Verona NJ 2015-** B 1970 s Salvatore & Linda. BA Iona Coll 1992; MSEd Ford Lincoln Cntr 1994; MDiv Drew TS 2015; MDiv Drew U 2015. D 12/6/2014 P 6/6/2015 Bp Mark M Beckwith. m 10/21/2013 Randall E Johnson. racioppi@holyspiritverona.org

RACKLEY, M Kathryn (O) 1730 Wright Ave, Rocky River OH 44116 **Dir Adult Formation Trin Cathd Cleveland OH 2013-** B Jacksonville FL 1962 d Otis & Betty. BA Lee U 1984; BA Stetson U 1986; MDiv Sewanee: The U So, TS 1999; MA Wisdom U 2011. D 5/29/1999 Bp Henry Irving Louttit P 11/28/1999 Bp Bob Johnson. Assoc R Chr Ch Epis Hudson OH 2006-2011; Vic R Ch Of The Ascen At Fork Advance NC 2001-2006; Asst R S Paul's Ch Wilkesboro NC 1999-2001. krackley@trinitycleveland.org

RACUSIN, Michele (SJ) 5267 San Jacinto Ave, Clovis CA 93619 **The CPG New York NY 2017-; R Ch Of The H Fam Fresno CA 2009-** B Honolulu HI 1958 d Bill & Barbara. BA U CA Los Angeles 1981; MBA Pepperdine U 1984; MDiv Mennonite Brethren Biblic Sem 2003. D 6/12/2004 Bp David Mercer Schofield P 6/4/2005 Bp William Edwin Swing. m 11/10/1984 Samuel R Racusin c 4. Assoc Gr Cathd San Francisco CA 2005-2009; D S Mary's Epis Ch Fresno CA 2004-2005; Stndg Com Epis Dio San Joaquin Modesto CA 2012-2015, Title IV Intake Off 2011-2017, Dep to GC 2009-2016, Dioc Coun 2008-2012, Bd Mem ECCO 2008-, EfM Coordntr 2008-, Sustainability Com 2008-. Amer Assn of Cert Publ Accountants 1987; California Soc of Cert Publ Accountants 1987.

RADANT, William Fred (Mil) PO Box 442, Manitowish Waters WI 54545 **P-in-c Our Sav's Phillips WI 1999-; S Marg's Epis Ch Pk Falls WI 1996-; Ret 1995-** B Oklahoma City OK 1930 s Milo & Estella. BA Oklahoma City U 1952; MA U MI 1954; MDiv Nash 1980. D 5/24/1980 P 11/29/1980 Bp Walter Cameron Righter. c 3. R S Mk's Ch Beaver Dam WI 1982-1995; P-in-c Ch Of The Epiph Centerville IA 1980-1982; P-in-c Gr Ch Albia IA 1980-1982. AFP; RWF; SHN.

RADCLIFF III, Cecil Darrell (CFla) 3010 Big Sky Blvd, Kissimmee FL 34744 **R S Jn's Epis Ch Of Kissimme Kissimmee FL 2001-** B Morgantown WV 1948 s Cecil & Betty. BA U of Cntrl Florida 1979; MDiv Sewanee: The U So, TS 1982. D 6/16/1982 P 3/1/1983 Bp William Hopkins Folwell. m 8/24/1968 Rhoda Werner Radcliff c 4. R H Trin Epis Ch Bartow FL 1995-2001; The Ch Of The H Presence Deland FL 1994-1995; R H Presence Epis Ch Deland FL 1993-1995; All SS Epis Ch Deltona FL 1985-1993; Chapl (Major) Servrd Army NG 1984-2007; Cur S Mk's Ch Cocoa FL 1982-1985. Chapl Ord of S Lk 1982.

RADCLIFF, Irene Evelyn (SO) B Charleston WV 1935 d John & Mary. BS W Virginia St U 1956; BSW OH SU 1980; MSW OH SU 1982. D 5/13/2006 Bp Kenneth Lester Price.

RADCLIFFE, Ernest Stanley (Oly) 3732 Colonial Ln Se, Port Orchard WA 98366 **Ret 1988-** B Calgary AB CA 1926 s Joseph & Claire. ATC 1952. Trans 6/1/1967. c 2. Int S Catherines Ch Enumclaw WA 1989-1992; P-in-c St Bede Epis Ch Port Orchard WA 1974-1988; Vic H Comm Tacoma WA 1969-1974; S Lk's Epis Ch Elma WA 1966-1969; Vic S Mk's Epis Ch Montesano WA 1966-1969; Asst S Paul's Ch Seattle WA 1963-1966; Serv Ch Of Can 1952-1963.

RADCLIFFE JR, William Eugene (Md) 2846 Angus Circle, Molino FL 32577 B Mount Airy NC 1944 s William & Mary. BS New Mex St U 1973; MS OH SU 1981. D 6/10/1995 Bp Charles Lindsay Longest. m 1/7/1966 Patricia Ann Radcliffe c 4. D Chr Ch Port Republic MD 1998-2007; D S Andr The Fisherman Epis Ch Edgewater MD 1997-1998; D Middleham & S Ptr's Par Lusby MD 1995-1996; Serv S Andr The Fisherman Epis Mayo MD 1983-1995.

RADKE, Pamela Kay (Nev) St Matthew's Episcopal Church, 4709 S Nellis Blvd, Las Vegas NV 89121 B San Diego CA 1947 d William & Cleo. BS U of Nevada Las Vegas 1975; MS Nova SE U 1982. D 1/21/2012 Bp Dan Thomas Edwards. c 4.

RADLEY, Charles Perrin (Me) 3701 R St NW, Washington DC 20007 **Fac Credo Inst 2002-; S Paul's K St Washington DC 2002-; Nave Chapl Cathd of St. Ptr and St. Paul Washington DC 1999-** B Washington DC 1942 s H Monroe & Ellen. BA Ken 1963; Queens TS GB 1967; Cert ETSBH 1968; MA U of Cambridge 1969; MA U of Birmingham GB 1974. D 6/29/1968 Bp William Foreman Creighton P 3/1/1969 Bp Alfred L Banyard. m 10/7/1989 Laurel Cargill Radley c 2. R S Mk's Ch Waterville ME 1989-1999; R S Paul's Ch Pawtucket RI 1984-1989; EDS Cambridge MA 1983-1984; Min Vienna Cmnty Ch Vienna Austria 1978-1983; R S Andr's Epis Ch Contoocook NH 1970-1978; Cur S Andr's Murray Hill NJ 1968-1970.

RADNER, Ephraim Louis (Colo) 410 W 18th St, Pueblo CO 81003 B New Haven CT 1956 s Roy & Virginia. BA Dart 1978; MDiv Ya Berk 1981; PhD Yale DS 1994. D 6/27/1981 P 6/1/1982 Bp William Edwin Swing. m 1/24/1987 Annette Geoffrian Brownlee c 2. Wycliffe Coll Toronto ON 2007-2014; Cn Dio Colorado Denver CO 1998; R Ch Of The Ascen Pueblo CO 1997-2007; S Jn's Ch Stamford CT 1996-1997; Emm Epis Ch Stamford CT 1994-1997; Chr Ch Shaker Heights OH 1988-1989; Calv Ch Cleveland OH 1987-1989; Gr Ch Brooklyn NY 1985-1987; Dir Ecole Theol De Matana Burundi Afr 1984-1985; Exec Coun Appointees New York NY 1981-1985; Tchr Epis Ch Burundi Bujumburg Afr 1981-1984. Auth, "The End Of The Ch," Eerdmans, 1999; Auth, "Cn And Creed," Morehouse Pub, 1998; Auth, "Inhabiting Unity," Eerdmans, 1997; Auth, "Reclaiming Faith," Eerdmans, 1993. Scholarly Engagement w Angl Doctrine 1997.

RADTKE, Warren Robert (Mass) 111 Perkins St Apt 125, Jamaica Plain MA 02130 **1980-; Sr Alum CAREER Advsr HARVARD Bus Sch 2005-** B Chicago IL 1935 s Lawrence & Meta. BS NWU 1957; M Div EDS 1964. D 6/1/1964 Bp Archie H Crowley P 2/10/1965 Bp Chauncie Kilmer Myers. m 5/14/1960 Judith Ann Lockhart c 3. Assoc R Trin Ch Epis Boston MA 2011-2012; Int HR Dir. Dio Massachusetts MA 2007; Int Exec Dir Epis City Mnstry MA 2006; Int Off Dio Massachusetts MA 2005-2006; The Credo Proj CPG 1995-2001; Acad Par Clerics 1976-1980; R Trin Par Melrose MA 1965-1981; Marguis Fell Chr Ch Cranbrook Bloomfield Hills MI 1964-1965. Auth, *Kellogg Lectures EDS 92*. Mass. Cler Assn; Phillips Brooks Club. Kellog Lecturers EDS 1992. radtkew@aol.com

RADZIK, David Robert (O) **Ch Of S Thos Berea OH 2017-** D 5/30/2015 P 2/18/2016 Bp William Howard Love.

RAEHN, J Sid (CFla) 106 Jim Dedmon Rd, Dyer TN 38330 B Orlando FL 1944 s Henry & Martha. BS Florida St U 1969; PhD Columbia St U 1995; DMin Oxf GB 2005; St Stephens Hse 2005. Trans 2/10/2006 Bp John Wadsworth Howe. m 7/9/1988 Deborah Happy Raehn c 2. Int S Phil Ch Memphis TN 2007; Pstr Care S Mich's Ch Orlando FL 2005-2006. "The 1st Blessing," *The Innkeeper*, My Story Pub, 2001. OSL 2005.

RAFFALOVICH, Francis Dawson (Dal) 306 Cobalt Cv, Georgetown TX 78633 **Ret 1988-** B Florence IT 1922 s George & Dorothy. BS U of Oklahoma 1950; Angl TS 1978. D 6/24/1977 P 7/1/1978 Bp Robert Elwin Terwilliger. m 1/6/2006 Georgia Dawson Strickland c 3. Pstr Assoc Gr Epis Ch Georgetown TX 2005-2010; R S Lk's Ch Denison TX 1983-1988; Cur And Assoc Chr Epis Ch Dallas TX 1977-1981. Auth, "Use Of Seismic Stratigraphy For Minnelusia Exploration Ne Wy"; Auth, "Geophysics".

RAFFERTY, Joseph Patrick (Be) 220 Montgomery Ave, West Pittston PA 18643 **R Prince Of Peace Epis Ch Dallas PA 2015-, 2013-2015** B Scranton PA 1956 s Joseph & Dolores. BS U of Scranton 1979; MDiv S Johns Sem 1983. Rec 12/7/2010 as Priest Bp Paul Victor Marshall. m 6/14/2005 Deborah Rafferty. S Jas-S Geo Epis Ch Jermyn PA 2012-2013.

RAFFERTY, Robert Douglas (NMich) 421 Cherry St, Iron River MI 49935 B L'Anse MI 1954 s Robert & Joan. BS MI SU 1978. D 8/4/2005 P 3/12/2006 Bp James Arthur Kelsey. m 12/20/1997 Elke Rafferty.

RAFTER, John Wesley (Me) PO Box 527, Camden ME 04843 **On-Call Chapl Pen-Bay Hosp Rockport ME 2008-; Dist Dn Dio Cntrl New York Liverpool NY 2007-, Eccl Crt 2005-2007, Conv Agenda and Arrangement Com 2005-2006** B Manchester NH 1946 s J Wesley & Ernagene. BA Estrn U 1968; MDiv Sewanee: The U So, TS 1984. D 6/9/1984 Bp William Grant Black P 12/18/1984 Bp Furman Charles Stough. m 11/29/1969 Michele Rafter c 2. R Ch Of S Thos Camden ME 2007-2015; R Dio Maine Portland ME 2007-2015,

Bishopswood Bd Dir 2013-, Bp and Coun 2011-, Chair, Dio Resolutns Com 2010-, Conflict Medtr 2009-; Dio Cntrl New York Syracuse NY 2005-2007; R S Matt's Epis Ch Horseheads NY 2003-2007; R Ch Of The Gd Samar Knoxville TN 1996-2003; Evang Resource Team Dio E Tennessee Knoxville TN 1993-2003, Profsnl Conduct Reponse Team 2000-2003, Episcopate Com 1997-1998, Stndg Com 1994-2003, 1993; S Tim's Epis Ch Kingsport TN 1992-1996; Assoc S Geo's Ch Germantown TN 1987-1992; Int S Mary's Epis Ch Jasper AL 1986-1987; R S Mich's Epis Ch Fayette AL 1984-1987; Stndg Com Dio W Tennessee Memphis 1988-1992; COM Dio Alabama Birmingham 1985-1987. Mem of Year Fayette-Lamar ARC Bd 1985.

RAGAN, Raggs (Ore) 640 Southshore Blvd., Lake Oswego OR 97034 B Lake Forest IL 1945 d Randall & Nathalie. BA Stan 1967; MA Stan 1971; MDiv CDSP 1979. D 6/24/1979 Bp Chauncie Kilmer Myers P 6/1/1980 Bp William Edwin Swing. c 2. Cn Pstr Trin Epis Cathd Portland OR 2012-2017; R S Jas Epis Ch Portland OR 2006-2012; Int R S Paul's Ch Salt Lake City UT 2004-2006, Asstg P 1990-2004; Chapl Rowland Hall/S Mk's Sch Salt Lake City UT 1994-2004; S Steph's In-The-Field Epis Ch San Jose CA 1987; CE Min S Mk's Epis Ch Palo Alto CA 1986-1988, 1985-1987, Asst R 1980-1983; Asst Dn Memi Ch Stanford CA 1985-1986; CE Min Trsfg Epis Ch San Mateo CA 1983-1984; Adj Min Memi Ch Stanford CA 1979-1980; Tchg Asst Dn Chap Stanford CA 1974-1976.

RAGLAND, Rebecca B (Mo) 1210 Locust St, Saint Louis MO 63103 **Dio Missouri S Louis MO 2015-, Chf Ecum Off 2010-, Dioc Yth Coordntr 2007-2009** B SierraLeone 1968 d Larry & Deanne. BA Asbury U 1990; MA U of Wisconsin 1994; MDiv Eden TS 2008. D 12/21/2007 P 6/21/2008 Bp George Wayne Smith. m 8/3/1991 Clyde Ragland c 2. Ch Of The H Comm S Louis MO 2009-2014. Auth, "Prayers of the People," *ATR*, Winter Vol 87 No 1, 2005. NAACP 2007; Phi Kappa Phi Acad hon Soc 1995. Grauer Awd for Excellence in Preaching and Ch Ldrshp Eden TS 2008.

RAGSDALE, Eliza Robinson (SeFla) 1750 E Oakland Park Blvd, Fort Lauderdale FL 33334 **S Mk The Evang Ft Lauderdale FL 2013-** B Florence SC 1961 d James & Carolyn. AS St Mary's Epis Sch 1979; BA Mary Baldwin Coll 1983; MSW Virginia Commonwealth U 1985; D Degree SE Florida Diac Sch 2013. D 5/31/2013 Bp Leo Frade. m 4/4/2002 Robert G Trache. motherliza@saintmarks.com

RAGSDALE, James Lewis (Colo) 3143 S Nucla St, Aurora CO 80013 B Fort Smith AR 1939 s Elmer & Fannie. AA Trinidad Jr Coll TT 1959; BA U of Nthrn Colorado 1962; MDiv Nash 1964. D 6/11/1964 P 12/1/1964 Bp Joseph Summerville Minnis. m 5/22/1965 Shirley W Ragsdale. S Eliz's Epis Ch Brighton CO 1999-2012; Vic St. Eliz Brighton CO 1999-2012; S Pat's Epis Ch Pagosa Sprg CO 1997-1998; Supply/Int P Dio Colorado Denver CO 1993-2008; R Gr Epis Ch Chadron NE 1989-1992; S Paul's Epis Ch Lamar CO 1978-1987; Asst Chr Epis Ch Denver CO 1976-1978; R S Mk's Epis Ch Durango CO 1969-1976; Vic Mssn Clear Creek CO 1964-1969.

RAGSDALE, Katherine H (Nwk) 99 Brattle St, Cambridge MA 02138 **RNL Assoc Plymouth MA 2016-** B Richmond VA 1958 d Ambler & Ann. BA W&M 1980; MDiv VTS 1987; DMin EDS 1997. D 6/3/1993 Bp John Shelby Spong P 4/9/1994 Bp Jack Marston Mckelvey. m 1/1/2011 Mally Ewing. Pres and Dn EDS Cambridge MA 2009-2016; Pres and CEO Political Resrch Assoc 2004-2009; Vic S Dav's Epis Mssn Pepperell MA 1996-2009; Advocacy Co-ordntr Epis Ch Cntr New York NY 1990-1993. Auth, "Boundary Wars: Intimacy & Distance In Healing Relationships," 1996; Auth, "Rel Issues In Dom Violence," *Albany Law Revs*, 1994. EWC; Integrity.

RAGSDALE III, Lee Morris (ETenn) **D Ch Of The Resurr Loudon TN 2016-; D Dio E Tennessee Knoxville TN 2016-** B Knoxville, TN 1951 s Lee & Ann. BA U of Tennessee at Knoxville 1976; MSW U NC at Chap Hill 1988. D 2/6/2016 Bp George Young III. m 3/30/1974 Catherine Parry.

RAHHAL, Michele Duff (Okla) 721 Franklin Dr, Ardmore OK 73401 **Chapl Oak Hall Epis Sch Ardmore OK 2000-** B Saint Louis MO 1946 d Robert & Jacquelin. BS U of New Mex 1968. D 6/24/2000 Bp Robert Manning Moody. m 7/5/1969 William Rahhal c 3. Dio Oklahoma Oklahoma City OK 2002-2008; Oak Hall Epis Sch Ardmore OK 2000-2001.

RAHM, Kent David (Va) 6604 Willow Pond Dr, Fredericksburg VA 22407 **R Trin Ch Fredericksbrg VA 1997-** B Riverhead NY 1956 s David & Laura. BA Pr 1978; MDiv GTS 1983. D 6/7/1982 Bp Robert Campbell Witcher Sr P 5/28/1983 Bp Morgan Porteus. m 10/15/1988 Joanne T Rahm c 2. Dn Dio Virginia Richmond VA 2006-2010; Dn Dio Long Island Garden City NY 1993-1997, 1986-1988; R H Trin Epis Ch Vlly Stream NY 1990-1997; Vic Epis Ch Of S Mk The Evang Bellmore NY 1989-1990; Cur Epis Ch Of S Thos Taunton MA 1982-1986; Cmsn for the Prevention of Sexual Misconduct Dio Virginia Richmond VA 1999-2010.

RAHN, Gaynell M (Va) 905 Princess Anne St, Fredericksburg VA 22401 **Assoc R S Geo's Ch Fredericksburg VA 2006-** B Savannah GA 1946 d Lawrence & Myrtis. Dio Georgia Diac Trng GA; RN Graduatey Nrsng Sch; EFM Sewanee: The U So, TS. D 9/30/1989 Bp Harry Woolston Shipps P 2/5/2000 Bp Frank Kellogg Allan. m 10/9/1965 Thomas K Rahn c 3. S Steph's Ch Pittsfield MA 2002-2005; S Mk's Ch Dalton GA 1998-2002; Ch Of The Gd Shpd Jacksonville

FL 1996-1998; D Calv Ch Memphis TN 1991-1996; D S Thos Ch Savannah GA 1989-1991. ben.hicks@stgeorgesepiscopal.net

RAICHE, Brian Michael (Mass) 26 White St, Haverhill MA 01830 **P-in-c Ch Of The Gd Shpd Reading MA 2016-** B Manchester NH 1966 s Ernest & Pauline. BS RPI 1988; MA Cath U 1995; MDiv St Aug's Sem 1995. Rec 6/6/2015 as Priest Bp Gayle Harris. m 10/12/2013 Loren Christopher Lee. Trin Epis Ch Haverhill MA 2015-2016.

RAIH, Donald Roger (WVa) 250 N Marsham St, Romney WV 26757 **Died 12/2/2016** B Freeport IL 1940 s Frederick & Ellen. BA S Meinrad Coll 1963; MRE Loyola U 1973; Nash 1982. Rec 6/1/1982 as Deacon Bp William Cockburn Russell Sheridan. m 9/1/1978 Patricia J Raih c 2. Ret 2001-2016; Vic Hampshire-Hardy Yoke Romney WV 1997-2001; St Stephens Romney WV 1997-2000; Epis Shared Mnstry Of NW Ohio Sherwood OH 1993-1997; Gr Ch Defiance OH 1993-1997; S Jn The Evang Ch Napoleon OH 1993-1997; Co-Pstr Trin Ch Bryan OH 1993-1997; Vic S Steph's Elwood IN 1986-1993; R S Paul's Epis Ch Gas City IN 1983-1993; Serv RC Ch 1967-1978; COM Dio Nthrn Indiana So Bend IN 1984-1987. Auth, *Handbook for Indiana Luth-Epis Dialogue*, Pathways/Self, 1988.

RAILEY, Robert Macfarlane (NMich) 3029 N Lakeshore Blvd, Marquette MI 49855 **mutual Mnstry P St. Paul's Epis Marquette MI 2007-** B Berkeley CA 1940 s Isham & Marie Louise. BS Stan 1962; PhD Stan 1976. D 5/9/2006 P 5/27/2007 Bp James Arthur Kelsey. m 12/29/2002 Nancy M Railey c 6.

RAINING, Hillary (Pa) 226 Righters Mill Rd, Gladwyne PA 19035 **S Chris's Ch Gladwyne PA 2014-** B Tunkhannock PA 1982 BA Moravian Coll 2005; MDiv Ya Berk 2008; DMin Drew U 2014. D 2/2/2008 P 8/15/2008 Bp Paul Victor Marshall. m 7/9/2005 Kenneth A Reinholz c 1. Assoc S Dav's Ch Wayne PA 2011-2014; Cur Trin Ch Bethlehem PA 2008-2011.

RAINS JR, Harry James (WNC) 8 Nicole Lane, Weaverville NC 28787 **St. Paul's-Lake Jas, Morganton, NC S Paul's Epis Ch Morganton NC 2009-** B Larned KS 1940 s Harry & Dorothy. BA Murray St U 1965; MDiv PDS 1968. D 4/20/1968 P 10/28/1968 Bp Alfred L Banyard. m 6/21/1980 Sharon Hawkins Rains c 3. St. Jn's Epis Ch Wytheville, VA S Jn's Epis Ch Wytheville VA 2007; R S Andr's Ch La Mesa CA 1999-2005; R Ch Of S Mich The Archangel Colorado Spg CO 1998-1999; R S Jas Ch Potomac MD 1994-1998; S Jn's Chap Manchestr Ctr VT 1986-1994; Zion Ch Manchestr Ctr VT 1986-1994; S Jn's In The Mountains Stowe VT 1981-1986; R Trin Epis Ch Lewiston ME 1978-1981; Chapl Sugarloaf Ski Area 1973-1978; R Ch Of The Gd Shpd Rangeley ME 1971-1978; Vic Chr Ch Magnolia NJ 1969-1971; Cur Gr Ch In Haddonfield Haddonfield NJ 1968-1969; Chair Resolutns Com Dio Vermont Burlington VT 1987-1991, Co-Chair Stwdshp & Evang Cmsn 1983-1986.

RAISH, John Woodham (WLa) 211 Linden St, Shreveport LA 71104 B Denver CO 1945 s Donald & Elizabeth. BA SW U Georgetown TX 1967; MDiv Nash 1980. D 6/28/1980 P 1/1/1981 Bp William Carl Frey. m 5/27/1972 Margaret H Raish c 2. R S Mths Epis Ch Shreveport LA 1997-2006; R H Trin Epis Ch Sulphur LA 1985-1997; S Andr's Epis Ch Ft Lupton CO 1981-1985; Vic S Eliz's Epis Ch Brighton CO 1981-1985; Dio Colorado Denver CO 1980; Exec Com Dio Wstrn Louisiana Alexandria LA 1998-2000.

RAJ, Vincent (ECR) P.O. Box 551, Carmel Valley CA 93950 **Fndr Cmnty of Interfaith Colleagues (CIC) 2013-** B Madras, India 1945 s Anthony & Monica. Baccalaureate Other 1965; Baccalaureate Pont. Urbaniana U, Rome 1965; Ph.L. Other 1967; Ph.L. Pont. Urbaniana U, Rome 1967; Baccalaureate Other 1969; Baccalaureate Pont. Urbaniana U, Rome 1969; STL Pont. Urbaniana U, Rome 1971. Rec 1/25/2002 as Priest Bp Richard Lester Shimpfky. m 3/27/1993 Carol B Raj c 4. Ch of S Mary's by the Sea Pacific Grove CA 2016-2017; Dio El Camino Real Salinas CA 2015; Int R All SS Epis Ch Watsonville CA 2011-2012; Dep/QC Dio El Camino Real 2008-2009; First Alt/Gen. Conv Dio El Camino Real 2005-2006; Bd Trst Dio El Camino Real 2004-2008; R S Geo's Ch Salinas CA 2002-2010. Cmnty of Interfaith Colleagues 2013; Untd Nations Assn 2009; Untd Rel Initiative 2010; Wrld Affrs Coun 2012. vincentraj.ca@gmail.com

RAJAGOPAL, Doris Elizabeth (Pa) 763 Valley Forge Rd, Wayne PA 19087 **Vic Dio Pennsylvania Philadelphia PA 2015-** B Philadelphia PA 1961 d Henry & Doris. BA Tem 1983; PhD CUNY 2000; MDiv Luth TS 2009. D 6/14/2008 P 1/10/2009 Bp Edward Lewis Lee Jr. m 6/30/1989 Subrahmanyam Rajagopal c 2. All SS Ch Collingdale PA 2010-2013; Asst S Dav's Ch Wayne PA 2008-2009.

RALPH, Michael Jay (LI) 28 Highland Rd, Glen Cove NY 11542 **S Mk's Ch Westhampton Bch NY 2014-** B Saratoga NY 1969 D 6/19/2004 P 4/11/2005 Bp Stacy F Sauls. m 7/1/2000 Aimee L Ralph c 2. S Paul's Ch Glen Cove NY 2009-2014; Ch Of The Ascen Mt Sterling KY 2006-2009; Trin Ch Covington KY 2004-2006.

RALPH, Samuel Lester (Mass) 88 King St, Reading MA 01867 B Lynn MA 1931 s Albert & Grace. BA Bos 1954; BD VTS 1958; MA Bos 1959; LLB Bos 1963; VTS 1973. D 6/21/1958 Bp Frederic Cunningham Lawrence P 12/1/1958 Bp Anson Phelps Stokes Jr. m 6/29/1964 Joyce P Ralph c 3. R Chr Ch Somerville MA 1964-1981; Asst Old No Chr Ch Boston MA 1964-1965; Asst Gr Epis Ch Medford MA 1960-1963; Cur Chr Ch Waltham MA 1958-1960. Auth, "Methods Of Law Pract In Ma," W Pub, 1965.

RALSTON, Betty Marie (Colo) Po Box 773627, Steamboat Springs CO 80477 B Greeley CO 1938 d Paul & Sybil. Dio Colorado Diac Trng Prog CO; S Lk Sch Nrsng. D 11/2/1996 Bp William Jerry Winterrowd. m 3/17/1967 Robert Sanford Ralston. D S Paul's Epis Ch Steamboat Sprngs CO 1999-2009.

RALSTON, D Darwin (O) 711 College Ave, Lima OH 45805 B Bellefontaine OH 1945 s Delva & Ethyl. BA OH SU 1972; MDiv GTS 1975. D 5/31/1975 P 12/1/1975 Bp John Mc Gill Krumm. m 6/20/1970 Andrea Ralston c 2. Dn Of Wstrn Dnry 1991-1993; R Chr Ch Lima OH 1989-2005; Ch Of St Mich And All Ang Indianapolis IN 1986-1989; Vic S Mich's & All Ang Evansville IN 1986-1989; Mssn & Strtgy Com Dio Indianapolis Indianapolis IN 1980-1989, Stndg Com 1987-1989, Wrshp Cmsn 1978-1986; Bi Par Mnstry Addyston OH 1978-1986; R Tri-Par Mnstrs Cincinnati OH 1978-1984; LocTen S Jn's Ch Worthington OH 1977-1978, Assoc R 1975-1976.

RAMAN, Neil K (LI) **Calv Ch Memphis TN 2016-** B 1987 s Kalyan & Martha. M.Div Sewanee: The U So, TS; BA The U Chi 2010. D 1/30/2016 P 9/10/2016 Bp Lawrence C Provenzano. m 1/14/2017 Elizabeth K Gassler.

RAMBO JR, Charles B (CFla) Po Box 46, Rutherfordton NC 28139 **Chr The King Epis Ch Orlando FL 2010-** B Mongomery AL 1960 s Charles & Dorothy. BA Stetson U 1991; MDiv Sewanee: The U So, TS 1997. D 6/28/1997 P 12/1/1997 Bp John Wadsworth Howe. m 8/15/1987 Carol J Rambo. S Paul's Epis Ch New Smyrna Bch FL 2006-2008; S Fran' Epis Ch Rutherfordton NC 1999-2002; D Shpd Of The Hills Epis Ch Lecanto FL 1997-1999. Ord S Lk The Physcn.

RAMBO, Thomas (SwVa) 323 Catherine St, Walla Walla WA 99362 **S Jn's Epis Ch Wytheville VA 2016-** B Addis Ababa Ethiopia 1970 s Thomas & Elinor. BA New Coll of Florida 1992; U of Kentucky 1998; MDiv Sewanee: The U So, TS 2001. D 6/9/2001 P 4/11/2002 Bp Stacy F Sauls. m 8/5/2016 Sharon Louise Rambo c 4. R S Paul's Ch Walla Walla WA 2008-2015; P-in-c Epis Ch of Our Sav Richmond KY 2004-2008; Asst To The R Ch Of The Gd Shpd Lexington KY 2001-2004.

RAMERMAN, Diane Gruner (Oly) 1216 7th St, Anacortes WA 98221 B Elmhurst IL 1942 d George & Virginia. D 8/5/2012 Bp Sanford Zangwill Kaye Hampton P 4/11/2013 Bp Gregory Harold Rickel. m 7/2/1981 Dale Byron Ramerman c 3.

RAMEY, Bernard (Va) St Alban's Episcopal Church, 6800 Columbia Pike, Annandale VA 22003 **All SS Ch Alexandria VA 2014-** B Kanagawa-Ken Japan 1976 s Donn & Sylvia. BS MIT 1998; MDiv VTS 2012. D 6/2/2012 Bp Ted Gulick Jr P 12/15/2012 Bp Shannon Sherwood Johnston. m 7/17/1999 Elinor Carson Ramey c 2. Cur S Alb's Epis Ch Annandale VA 2012-2014. fightingfriar@gmail.com

RAMEY, Lloyd Francis (Ore) 1444 Liberty St Se, Salem OR 97302 B Ironton OH 1923 s John & Myrtle. BS USC 1950. D 3/31/1965 Bp James Walmsley Frederic Carman. m 1/31/1953 Suzanne Huggins c 3. D /Asst S Paul's Epis Ch Salem OR 1965-2000.

RAMIREZ, Lucia (PR) B 1947 Dio Puerto Rico Trujillo Alto PR 2004-2009, 2000-2003.

RAMIREZ, Mark Lloyd (Chi) St Barnabas Episc Church, 22W415 Butterfield Rd, Glen Ellyn IL 60137 B San Pablo CA 1960 s Lloyd & Joyce. BS Grand Canyon U 1986; MA Wheaton Coll 1988. D 1/19/2008 Bp Victor Alfonso Scantlebury. m 8/3/1996 Anne K Ramirez c 2.

RAMIREZ-MILLER, Gerardo Carlos (NY) 351 W 24th St Apt 6-C, New York NY 10011 B New York NY 1945 s Leon & Belen. BA CUNY 1967; MDiv UTS 1986. D 1/12/1987 Bp Paul Moore Jr P 5/2/1988 Bp Jose Antonio Ramos. Supply P S Mary's Ch Carle Place NY 2001-2005; S Andr's So Fallsburg So Fallsburg NY 2000-2001; Supply P S Jas Ch Callicoon NY 2000-2001; Dio New York New York NY 2000; Sheltering Arms Chld and Fam Serv Inc New York NY 1989-2001; Epis Mssn Soc New York NY 1989-1990; Prot Chapl Coler Memi Hosp 1986-2000. Epis Actors' Gld - Life Mem 2000; OHC 1985.

RAMIREZ-NIEVES, Aida Iris (VI) PO Box 1796, Kingshill 00851 Virgin Islands (U.S.) B Bayamon PR 1954 d Victor & Brunilda. Instituto Biblico Hispano 2002. D 4/6/2013 Bp Edward Gumbs. m 8/14/1994 Antonio Torres Nieves.

RAMIREZ-SEGARRA, Cesar E (PR) PO Box 1967, Yauco PR 00698 Puerto Rico **Dio Puerto Rico Trujillo Alto PR 2008-** B Puerto Rico 1968 s Cesar & Ana. Rec 7/6/2008 Bp David Andres Alvarez-Velazquez. m 3/7/2009 Reinabelle Rosado-Gonzalez.

RAMNARAINE, Barbara Allen (Minn) St. Luke's Episcopal Church, 4557 Colfax Ave. 5, Minneapolis MN 55403 B Minneapolis MN 1934 d Rudolf & Ladene. BA Macalester Coll 1955; Dio Minnosota D Trng MN 1984. D 1/25/1984 Bp Robert Marshall Anderson. m 3/15/1955 Cecil Ramnaraine c 3. D S Paul's Ch Minneapolis MN 1989-2010; Coordntr, Epis Disabil Ntwk Dio Minnesota Minneapolis MN 1985-2011. "Assessibility Guidelines for Epis Ch"; Auth, "AccessAbility: A Manual for Ch". Oblate Ord Of S Ben.

RAMOS, Leon (PR) B 1936 s Victor & Paula. m 11/13/1981 Carmen Santos Rivera. Dio Puerto Rico Trujillo Alto PR 2004-2006, 1983-2003.

RAMOS, Mary Serena (Minn) 700 S 2nd Street, Unit 41, Minneapolis MN 55401 **Chapl U MN Masonic Chld's Hosp 2010-** B Duluth MN 1963 d Kenneth &

Jackie. BS U MN 1985; BS U MN 1985; MS U MN 1989; MS U MN 1989; MDiv CDSP 2006. D 6/8/2006 P 12/21/2006 Bp James Louis Jelinek. m 9/12/1987 Dean Arthur Ramos c 3. P S Steph The Mtyr Ch Minneapolis MN 2006-2009.

RAMOS, Pablo (U) 1904 Dale Ridge Ave, Salt Lake City UT 84116 **P Dio Utah Salt Lake City UT 2005-** B Guadalajara MX 1967 s Pablo & Elizama. MDiv S Andrews TS MX 1996. D 5/26/1996 P 12/1/1996 Bp Sergio Carranza-Gomez. m 5/19/1989 Beatriz Rodriguez c 3. Cathd Ch Of S Mk Salt Lake City UT 1998-2005; Dio Mex Mex City MOR 1996-1998; Asst R S Paul In Guanajuato. Auth, "Prot Theol 1900-60". Cmnty Of Hope S Lk Hosp Houston Tx. sanesteban1@aol.com

RAMOS, Waldemar F (PR) 560 Calle Napoles Apt 2c, San Juan PR 00924 B 1938 m 12/30/1965 Blanca J Tirado c 2. Dio Puerto Rico Trujillo Alto PR 1980-2000, 1965-1979.

RAMOS-GARCIA, Ramon (PR) B 1949 s Ramón & Lydia. Iglesia Epis PR; Enfermeria Graduado Escuela de Enfermeria Universidad de Puerto Rico 1991. c 4. Dio Puerto Rico Trujillo Alto PR 2004-2011, 1992-2003, P 1991; Enfermero Graduado Servicio Salud Hogar San Lucas IEP Ponce PR 1975-2009; Enfermero Graduado Hosp Municipal San Juan PR 1971-1975.

✠ RAMOS-ORENCH, The Rt Rev Wilfrido (PR) 77 Linnmoore St, Hartford CT 06114 **Provsnl Bp of Puerto Rico Dio Puerto Rico Trujillo Alto PR 2014-, Dir Estudio, Asst To The Bp Of Puerto Rico 1977-1979; Ret Bp Suffr of Connecticut Dio Connecticut Meriden CT 2006-, Bp Suffr of Connecticut 2000-2006, 1993-1995** B 1940 s Francisco & Maria. Caribbean Cntr for Advncd Stds; BA Pontifical Cath U of Puerto Rico 1962; MDiv ETSC 1966; GTS 1974; DMin Estrn Bapt TS 1992. D 5/29/1966 P 12/3/1966 Bp Francisco Reus-Froylan Con 1/1/2000 for Ct. m 8/17/1984 Marling Ramos-Orench. Global Partnerships Off for Prov IX Dom And Frgn Mssy Soc- Epis Ch Cntr New York NY 2009-2014; Provsnl Bp Iglesia Epis Del Ecuador Quito 2006-2009; Cntrl Epis Dnry New Britain CT 1998-2000; Assoc Mssnr Grtr Hartford Reg Mnstry E Hartford CT 1995-2000; S Lk's/S Paul's Ch Bridgeport CT 1984-1993; Vic Recon Ponce Puerto Rico 1980-1984; Cetym C A 1975-1977; Epis Sem Of The Caribbean Carolina PR 1968-1975; Asst Prof Of Pstr Theol ETSC PR 1968-1975. Auth, "Our Hist Cross Roads: Towards A New Orientation In Mssn"; Auth, "Out Of The Depths"; Auth, "Una Vision Del Ministerio Hispano En La Diocesis Epis De Ct". Aamft; Natl Hisp Cltn, The Consult, Urban Caucus. obisporamos@episcopalpr.org

RAMSAY, Frederick Jeffress (Md) 20637 N 56th Ave., Glendale AZ 85308 **Ret 2000-** B Baltimore MD 1936 s Alfred & Mette. BS W&L 1958; MS U IL 1960; PhD U IL 1962; MEd U IL 1969. D 3/12/1970 Bp Harry Lee Doll P 2/28/1971 Bp David Keller Leighton Sr. m 12/17/1982 Susan Joanne Ramsay c 6. R S Andr's Ch Pasadena MD 1991-2000; Vic S Andr's Epis Ch Glenwood MD 1987-1991; Assoc S Jn's Ch Reisterstown MD 1983-1987; Non-par 1978-1982; Assoc The Ch Of The Nativ Cedarcroft Baltimore MD 1972-1977; D-In-Trng Trin Ch Towson MD 1970-1971. Auth, "BUFFALO Mtn," do, 2007; Auth, "JUDAS, The gospel of betrayal," Perfect Niche Press, 2007; Auth, "IMPULSE," do, 2006; Auth, "SECRETS," do, 2005; Auth, "ARTSCAPE," Poisoned Pen Press, 2004; Auth, "Med & Rel"; Auth, "Effects Of Adjuvant & Antiserum On Tumor Growth"; Auth, "Investigation Of Virus-Like Material Assocd w C3 H/F9 Leukemia"; Auth, "The Baltimore Declaration"; Auth, "ten other novels," *All from poisoned Pen Press*; Auth, "ten other novels," *All from poisoned Pen Press*. Curs. Bp'S Awd For Outstanding Ord Mnstry Dio Maryland 2000.

RAMSDEN, Charles Leslie (Cal) D 6/22/1974 Bp George Leslie Cadigan P 12/28/1974 Bp Hanford Langdon King Jr.

RAMSEY, Henry Elrod (WMass) 57 Loomis Dr Apt A1, West Hartford CT 06107 **Non-par 1969-** B Atlanta GA 1938 s William & Farrar. BA U GA 1960; STB Ya Berk 1966. D 6/1/1966 Bp Randolph R Claiborne P 12/1/1966 Bp Robert McConnell Hatch. m 12/29/1960 Madge Mcleod Bowen. Asst To R S Jn's Ch Northampton MA 1967-1969; Cur S Paul's Ch Holyoke MA 1966-1967.

RAMSEY, Ronald E (SVa) 8 Meacham Rd, Cambridge MA 02140 **R S Cyp's Epis Ch Hampton VA 2014-** B Lake Wales FL 1954 s Joe & Viola. MDiv Morehouse Sch of Rel 1980; DMin Trin Luth Sem 1984; CAS EDS 1992; MPA Harv 1993. D 6/4/1994 Bp David Elliot Johnson P 12/4/1994 Bp M(Arvil) Thomas Shaw. m 11/26/1999 Jean Ramsey c 1. S Jn's Ch Arlington MA 1998-2014; Trin Ch Epis Boston MA 1994-1996; Serv Bapt Ch 1980-1990.

RAMSEY, Walter Albert (Cal) 162 Hickory St, San Francisco CA 94102 B Texas City TX 1944 BFA U of San Francisco 1977; BA Epis Sch for D 2014. D 6/13/2015 Bp Marc Handley Andrus. c 2.

RAMSEY-MUSOLF, Michael Jeffrey (Los) Department Of Physics, U. Mass Amherst, 710 N Pleasant St 416, Amherst MA 01003 **Asstg P All SS Par Los Angeles CA 2013-, Asstg P 2001-2007** B Portland OR 1961 s Lyndon & Barbara. BA Pomona Coll 1984; MA Pr 1986; PhD Pr 1989; MDiv EDS 1993. D 6/12/1993 Bp George Phelps Mellick Belshaw P 1/29/1994 Bp Frank Harris Vest Jr. m 10/1/1996 Darrel Ramsey-Musolf. Asstg P S Dunst's Ch Madison WI 2012-2013; Asstg P S Ptr's And S Andr's Epis Providence RI 1999-2000;

Asstg P S Paul's Ch Seattle WA 1996-1998; Cur Chr and S Lk's Epis Ch Norfolk VA 1993-1995. Tertiary Of The Soc Of S Fran. Young Investigator Natl Sci Fndt 1993.

RAMSHAW, Lance Arthur (Del) 106 Alden Rd, Concord MA 01742 **Non-par 1985-** B Meriden CT 1953 s Walter & Ruth. BA Ob 1974; MDiv EDS 1977; MS U of Delaware 1983; PhD U of Delaware 1989. D 6/25/1977 Bp John Harris Burt P 2/25/1978 Bp William Hawley Clark. m 9/9/1989 Abigail G Wine. Par Of The Mssh Auburndale MA 2000; Int S Barn Ch Wilmington DE 1983-1985; Int Trin Ch Elkton MD 1982-1983; Dio Delaware Wilmington 1981-1985, 1980-1981; Int S Thos's Par Newark DE 1981-1982; Int All SS and St Georges Ch Rehoboth Bch DE 1980-1981; Co-R S Paul's Ch Camden Wyoming DE 1977-1980.

RAMSHAW, Lynn Cecelia Homeyer (Chi) 12 Jolynn Drive, Ormond Beach FL 32174 B Orange NJ 1937 d Arthur & Cecelia. BA Ohio Wesl 1959; MSW Barry U 1991; MA GTS 1997. D 5/8/1980 P 6/29/1996 Bp Calvin Onderdonk Schofield Jr. c 3. Assoc The Ch Of S Jn The Evang Flossmoor IL 1999-2002; Cn Trin Cathd Cleveland OH 1997-1999; Asst S Ptr's Ch New York NY 1995-1997; St Laurence Chap Pompano Bch FL 1991-1994; Exec Dir Jubilee Mnstry St. Laurence Chap Pompano Bch FL 1991-1994; Asst S Benedicts Ch Ft Lauderdale FL 1990; COM Dio SE Florida Miami 1980-1986. Auth, "sev arts," *Luth Wmn Today aka Gather*, Fortress Press, 2010. H Wisdom Monstry 2005; OHC 1985-2004.

RAMSTAD, Philip Robert (Minn) 901 Como Boulevard East, #304, Osceda WI 54020 B Saint Paul MN 1944 s Robert & Marjorie. Pur; BA S Thos Coll Miami FL 1968; MDiv SWTS 1977. D 6/25/1977 P 2/1/1978 Bp Philip Frederick McNairy. Reserve P S Jn The Evang S Paul MN 2005-2007; Supply Dio Minnesota Minneapolis MN 2004-2007; Res P Cnvnt Of S Jn The Bapt Mendham NJ 1993-1997; R Ch Of The H Cross Dundas MN 1990-1993; All SS Ch Northfield MN 1990-1992; Non-par 1988-1989; Cur All SS Ch New York NY 1985-1986; R Chr And S Steph's Ch New York NY 1980-1985; Chr Ch Totowa NJ 1980-1985; Vic Ch Of Our Sav Little Falls MN 1977-1980; Vic Ch Of The Gd Samar Sauk Cntr MN 1977-1980; Vic Gr Royalton MN 1977-1980.

RANDALL, Anne Elizabeth (Dal) 421 Custer Rd, Richardson TX 75080 **Assoc Ch Of The Epiph Richardson TX 2009-** B Ft Worth 1967 d Edwin & Barbara. BA U of Texas 1990; MDiv SMU Perkins 2009. D 6/20/2009 P 2/2/2010 Bp James Monte Stanton. m 4/6/1991 Gardner Randall c 2.

RANDALL, Catharine Louise (Ct) 91 Minortown Rd, Woodbury CT 06798 **Prof Of French Ford 1993-** B Lafayette IN 1957 d Edward & Sally. MA Boston Coll 1981; PhD U Pgh 1986; MA Yale DS 2008. D 6/27/2007 Bp Jeffrey Neil Steenson P 11/10/2007 Bp William Carl Frey. m 1/23/1998 Randall Balmer c 3. Assoc S Jn's Ch Washington CT 2008-2009; S Paul's Ch Woodbury CT 2008.

RANDALL II, Chandler Corydon (SanD) PO Box 15605, Fort Wayne IN 46885 **Ret Dio San Diego 2000-; R Emer Trin Epis Ch Ft Wayne IN 2014-** B Ann Arbor MI 1935 s Frederick & Leta. AB U MI 1957; STB Ya Berk 1960; PhD Hebr Un Coll-Jewish Inst of Rel 1969. D 6/29/1960 Bp Archie H Crowley P 6/27/1961 Bp Roger W Blanchard. m 7/2/1960 Marian Montgomery Randall c 3. R Emer Trin Ch Ft Wayne IN 2013-1988, 2013-, R 1971-1988; Theolin-Res Chr Ch Cranbrook Bloomfield Hills MI 2000-2013; R S Ptr's Epis Ch Del Mar CA 1988-2000; Asst Prof Of The OT Earlham Coll Richmond IN 1969-1970; R S Paul's Ch Richmond IN 1967-1971; P-in-c S Andr's Addyston OH 1964-1966; Cur Gr Ch Cincinnati OH 1960-1964. Auth, "An Approach To Biblic Satire," Forw Pub, 1990; Auth, "Satire In Bible," U Microfilus, 1969; Auth, "Shaharith and Matins," *Variant*, Hebr Un Coll, 1963. Who's Who in Amer The Marquis Who's Who Pub Bd 1997; DD Ya Berk/New Haven, CT 1985.

RANDALL, Elizabeth Penney (Colo) 735 S Vine St, Denver CO 80209 **R S Andr's Ch Denver CO 2009-** B Buffalo NY 1957 d Harry & Marian. BA Smith 1979; MDiv Ya Berk 1988. D 6/11/1994 P 12/1/1994 Bp William Jerry Winterrowd. m 6/8/1985 Alan Gottlieb c 1. Cn S Jn's Cathd Denver CO 1994-2009.

RANDALL, Jeanne Rice (Ala) D 10/1/2016 Bp John Mckee Sloan Sr.

RANDALL, Richard Alan (CPa) 222 N 6th St, Chambersburg PA 17201 **Hosp Chapl Waynesboro Hosp Waynesboro PA 2002-** B Detroit MI 1944 s Robert & Barbara. BA Wayne 1967; MDiv SWTS 1970. D 6/29/1970 Bp Archie H Crowley P 1/23/1971 Bp Richard Stanley Merrill Emrich. m 7/10/1976 Martha Jean Randall c 2. Int St. Paul Evang Ch Fayetteville Pa. 2009-2010; Int St. Paul Evang Luth Ch OrrstownPA 2005-2008; R Trin Epis Ch Chambersburg PA 1987-2000; Dio Cntrl Pennsylvania Harrisburg PA 1985-2002; R H Trin Epis Ch Shamokin PA 1978-1987; Vic Gd Shpd Ch Clarion PA 1974-1977; Vic Chr Ch Punxsutawney PA 1972-1978; Vic Ch Of The H Trin Brookville PA 1972-1978; Cur All SS Ch E Lansing MI 1970-1972. ASSP 1973.

RANDALL JR, Robert James (SVa) 716 Abbey Dr, Virginia Beach VA 23455 **R Old Donation Ch Virginia Bch VA 2004-; R Old Donation Epis Ch 2004-** B Chandler AZ 1952 s Robert & Anna. BS RPI 1974; ME RPI 1975; MDiv VTS 1997. D 5/31/1997 P 2/1/1998 Bp Charles Farmer Duvall. m 1/28/1984 Christine Lee Everitt c 2. Vic S Mary's Epis Ch Andalusia AL 1997-2004. Rotary Intl 1997.

RANDALL SSM, Sarah Archais (Mass) P.O. Box C, Duxbury MA 02331 **Sis Soc Of St Marg Duxbury MA 2010-; Sis Soc Of St Marg 2000-** B Cincinnati OH 1966 d Chandler & Marian. BA Ya 1988; MAT Van 1990; MDiv EDS 2010. D 6/5/2010 Bp Gayle Harris P 1/8/2011 Bp M(Arvil) Thomas Shaw. Dio Haiti Port-au-Prince HT 2011-2013; S Lk's/San Lucas Epis Ch Chelsea MA 2010-2011.

RANDLE, Cameron D (SVa) 6125 Carlos Ave, Los Angeles CA 90028 **S Jas' Ch Accomac VA 2016-; S Geo's Ch Pungoteague Pungoteague VA 2011-** B Mt View MO 1957 s James & Sandra. BA Oral Roberts U 1980; JD U of Tulsa 1987; MDiv Ya Berk 2008. D 1/18/2009 P 9/26/2009 Bp Sergio Carranza-Gomez. m 3/20/1999 Angelica M Garcia c 1. D St Steph Epis Ch Los Angeles CA 2009-2011.

RANDOLPH, Barry Trent (Mich) 231 E Grand Blvd, Detroit MI 48207 B Detroit MI 1962 s Horace & Louise. Total Mnstry Dio Michigan 2002. D 12/16/2001 P 6/29/2002 Bp Wendell Nathaniel Gibbs Jr.

RANDOLPH JR, Henry G (NI) 117 N Lafayette Blvd, South Bend IN 46601 B Richmond VA 1950 s Henry & Morgan. BA S Andrews Coll 1972; MDiv VTS 1977. D 12/6/1978 P 6/6/1979 Bp Robert Poland Atkinson. m 8/19/1972 Anita Adams c 1. Vocations Dir Dio Nthrn Indiana So Bend IN 2002-2016; R S Dav's Epis Ch Elkhart IN 1991-2016; Assoc R S Jas Epis Ch Baton Rouge LA 1986-1991; R S Mary's Ch Kinston NC 1984-1986. Auth, *Var Hymns & Bk Revs*. Hon Cn St Jas Cathd, So Bend IN 2014. vocations@ednin.org

RANEY III, Raymond Raymond (RG) 04 Tano Road, Santa Fe NM 87506 **Transition Off Dio The Rio Grande Albuquerque 2014-, Cn for Dioc Life 2011-, Cmncatn Off 2011-** B Bedford Indiana 1947 s Arthur & Maxine. BA Indiana U 1974; BFA U of New Mex 1992; BAFA U of New Mex 1992; MFA U of New Mex 1995; MDiv Iliff TS 2006. D 5/20/2006 P 12/17/2006 Bp Jeffrey Neil Steenson. m 10/31/1982 Linda Lewis Raney. R Ch Of The H Cross Edgewood NM 2007-2016; P S Bede's Epis Ch Santa Fe NM 2006-2007, D 2006. AAM 2007; ECom 2012. rraney@dioceserg.org

RANK SSP, Andrew Peter Robert (SanD) Po Box 34548, San Diego CA 92163 **Off The Ord of the Hosp of St. Jn of Jerusalem 2008-; Bd Mem Dorcas Hse San Diego CA 2006-; Guardian Fllshp of the Soc of S Paul San Diego CA 1962-** B Des Moines IA 1937 s William & Bessie. D 11/3/1983 P 5/5/1984 Bp Charles Brinkley Morton. Mutual Mnstry Revs Team Dio San Diego San Diego CA 2002-2003; Menber Chapt of St. Paul's Cathd San Diego 2001-2010; Bd Mem S Paul's Sr Hm & Serv San Diego CA 2001-2010; Sunday Pstr Betty Ford Cntr Rancho Mirage CA 1984-1992; Pres Conf of Angl Rel Ord of Amer 1982-1988; Ed St. Paul's Printer mag 1980-2008; R Soc of S Paul San Diego CA 1975-1989; Admin/Pres S Jude Hm Sandy OR 1963-1989; Chapt Cathd Ch Of S Paul San Diego CA 2001-2010. Ed, *S Paul's Printer*, 1980; Ed, *Directory's Conf Rel Life*, 1975. Conf of Angl Rel Ord of Amer 1972; NECAD 1982; Soc of S Paul 1958. Hon Cn S Paul's Cathd 2000; Fell Amer Coll Healthcare Admin 1979.

RANKIN, Annette Reiser (Cal) 10 Old Mill St, Mill Valley CA 94941 **D Ch Of Our Sav Mill Vlly CA 2012-; Instr Epis Sch for Deacons Berkely CA 2010-** B Springfield OH 1951 d Howard & Joanne. BA Beloit Coll 1974; MA Antioch U 1976; Diac Stds The Epis Sch for Deacons 2010. D 12/3/2011 Bp Marc Handley Andrus. c 1.

RANKIN, Deborah Truman (O) 2220 Second St., Cuyahoga Falls OH 44221 B Victoria TX 1948 d Joseph & Frederike. Victoria Coll Victoria TX 1968; BS Baylor U 1970; MA Rice U 1992; Cert Ang Stud Nash 1999. D 6/13/1998 P 6/12/1999 Bp John Henry Smith. c 2. S Ptr's Ch Huntington WV 2013; R S Jn's Epis Ch Cuyahoga Fls OH 2007-2013; The No Cntrl Cluster Buckhannon WV 2003-2004; R S Paul's Ch Weston WV 2001-2007; Chr Ch Point Pleasat WV 1998-2002; Gr Ch Ravenswood WV 1998-2002; Intern S Jn's Ripley WV 1998-2002; River Bend Cluster Pt Pleasant WV 1998-2000. ACPE.

RANKIN, Edward Harris (Oly) 11510 NE 35th Ave, Vancouver WA 98686 **Ret 2000-** B Berkeley CA 1936 s Sheldon & Marion. BA U Pac 1958; BD CDSP 1961; MA Oklahoma St U 1969; MA U of Oregon 1970; DMin SFTS 1989. D 6/25/1961 Bp James Albert Pike P 12/31/1961 Bp Leland Stark. m 3/23/1969 Kara Lynn Rankin c 1. R S Lk's Epis Ch Vancouver WA 1980-2000; R S Steph's Epis Par Portland OR 1973-1980; S Andr's Epis Ch Florence OR 1970-1973; Vic S Mary Ch Gardiner OR 1970-1973; Chapl OK St U 1962-1969; Asst S Andr's Ch Stillwater OK 1962-1969; Cur S Andr And H Comm Ch So Orange NJ 1961-1962. Auth, "Pleasures Forevermore," *The Angl*, 1985. Angl Soc; Associated Parishes. Phi Kappa Phi.

RANKIN, Glenn Edger (Ia) 2206 Frontier Rd, Denison IA 51442 **Co-Chair - Com 1995-; Dioc Ways & Means Com 1994-; Rep Of Provinve Syn 1994-; Instr Of Liturg Dioc Inst For Chr Stds 1992-; Chair Of The Hospice Bd 1990-; Secy For Comp Of Dioc Com 1987-** B Milwaukee WI 1945 s Edger & Janice. BA Carroll Coll 1967; MDiv Nash 1971. D 1/18/1971 P 7/27/1971 Bp Gordon V Smith. c 3. Dnry Vice-Chair 1992-1995; Ecum Ministers Of Iowa Unity Com 1991-1994; Chair Of The Comp Of Dioc Com 1991-1993; Mentor EFM 1991-1993; Vic Trin Ch Carroll IA 1990-2012; Human Needs Com 1989-1992; Chair Of The Crop St Advsry Bd 1989-1991; Crop St Advsry Bd 1988-1991; Chair Of The Mus Cmsn 1987-1994; Trin Ch Denison IA

1975-2012, Vic 1974; Vic H Trin Ch Atlantic IA 1971-1975; P-in-c H Trin Atlantic IA 1971-1975; Vic S Paul's Ch Harlan IA 1971-1975; ADLMC. Associated Parishes, HSEC, AGO.

RANKIN, Jerry Dean (Kan) 406 Hillside St, Abilene KS 67410 **P-in-c S Jn's Ch Abilene KS 2008-** B Manitou Springs CO 1954 s Jack & Sandra. BA Ft Hays St U 1981; MDiv CDSP 1984. D 6/30/1984 Bp John Forsythe Ashby P 1/23/1985 Bp Roger Howard Cilley. m 6/6/1981 Diana Facklam c 3. R S Matt's Ch Enid OK 1996-2004; Ch Of The Epiph Sedan KS 1991-1996; Vic S Matt's Ch Cedar Vale KS 1991; Asst R S Mk's Epis Ch Casper WY 1988-1991; Assoc S Lk's Epis Ch Manchester MO 1986-1988; Cur The Ch of the Gd Shpd Austin TX 1984-1986. jdrankin406@yahoo.com

RANKIN II, William Wright (Cal) 13 Mara Vista Ct, Tiburon CA 94920 **St Johns Epis Ch Ross CA 2005-** B Schenectady NY 1941 s John & Dorothy. BA Duke 1963; BD EDS 1966; PhD Duke 1977; MA Duke 1979. D 6/16/1966 Bp Walter M Higley P 6/16/1967 Bp Ned Cole. m 9/5/1964 Sally Katherine Heller c 2. Assoc Ch Of The Nativ San Rafael CA 1998-2005; Dio California San Francisco CA 1998-2002; Chas Wilson Prof of Chr Ethics EDS of Cambridge MA 1993-1998; Pres/Dn EDS of Cambridge MA 1993-1998; Pres and Dn EDS Cambridge MA 1993-1998; R S Steph's Par Bel Tiburon CA 1983-1993; Assoc R All SS Ch Pasadena CA 1980-1983, Asst 1967-1974; LocTen S Barth's Ch Pittsboro NC 1974-1980; Cur Trin Ch Elmira NY 1966-1967. Auth, "Character Ethics," *A Life of Serv: Jones Laviwa, Refugees, Relief, and AIDS in Rural Malawi*, Montfort Media, 2016; Auth, "Soc Ethics," *Cracking the Monolith*, Crossroads/Doubleday, 1994; Auth, "Profsnl Ethics," *Confidentiality and Cler*, Morehouse Pub, 1990; Auth, "Soc Ethics," *Countdown to Disaster*, Foreward Mvmt, 1982. Bd Overseers, Wellesley Coll Cntr for Wmn 1994-1998; Boston Theol Inst Chair 1996-1998; Intl Bioethics Inst 1990-1993; Renaissance Weekend 1993. 2015 Awd for Global Ldrshp Duke 2015; Distinguished Alum EDS 2014; Vstng Resrch Brocher Fndt, Geneva, CH 2012; Vstng Sci Swiss Tropical Inst, U. Basel, CH 2009; Schlr in Res Rockefeller Fndt, Bellagio, IT 2004.

RANKIN-WILLIAMS, Chris (Cal) Po Box 217, Ross CA 94957 **R St Johns Epis Ch Ross CA 2003-** B New York NY 1968 s Gregory & Daphne. BA Reed Coll 1990; MDiv EDS 1996. D 5/25/1996 Bp George Edmonds Bates P 1/18/1997 Bp Chester Lovelle Talton. m 6/19/1993 Amy C Rankin-Williams c 2. Assoc All SS-By-The-Sea Par Santa Barbara CA 1996-2003. Soc of S Jn the Evang 1996.

RANNA, Claire Dietrich (Cal) **Chr Epis Ch Los Altos CA 2017-** D 6/14/2014 P 12/6/2014 Bp Marc Handley Andrus.

RANNENBERG, Pamela Lamb (RI) 442 Wickford Point Rd, North Kingstown RI 02852 **Dir of Sprtl Care Butter Hosp Providence RI 2004-** B New London CT 1951 d Samuel & Anne. BFA U of Connecticut 1972; MA Old Dominion U 1983; MDiv VTS 1995. D 6/3/1995 P 1/10/1996 Bp Peter J Lee. m 8/27/1972 John Elliott Rannenberg c 2. Cn Dio Rhode Island Providence RI 1999-2004; Chapl S Eliz's Publ Mntl Hlth Serv DC 1996-1999; Asst S Jn's Ch Centreville VA 1995-1996.

RANSOM, Charles Wilfred (O) 716 Coshocton Ave, Mount Vernon OH 43050 B Mount Vernon OH 1938 s Robert & Bess. BA Muskingum Coll 1960; BD Bex Sem 1966. D 6/11/1966 P 12/18/1966 Bp Nelson Marigold Burroughs. m 6/30/1962 Daryl Ransom c 2. S Paul's Ch Mt Vernon OH 1992-1998; R Trin Ch Coshocton OH 1982-1992; S Mk's Epis Ch Wadsworth OH 1974-1978; R S Lk's Epis Ch Niles OH 1969-1973; Cur S Jn's Ch Youngstown OH 1966-1968. Auth, "The Seed Planters," Ransarts, 2000; Auth, "Farm Week: An Alternative To A Smelly Ch Basement," Ransarts, 1999.

RANSOM, Jim (Md) 89 Hilltop Pl, New London NH 03257 **Epis Chapl Epis Hosp Chapl Dartmouth Hitchcock Med Ce 2016-; Mssn Resources Com, Mem Dio New Hampshire Concord NH 2014-** B Norfolk NE 1944 s Clifford & Carolyn. BA U of Nebraska 1967; MDiv GTS 1970. D 6/21/1970 P 12/21/1970 Bp Russell T Rauscher. m 6/19/1976 Deborah Ransom c 2. Int R St. Andr's Ch Hopkinton NH 2014-2016; P-in-c S Mk's Ch Ashland NH 2011-2013; New Cong Mnstrs Dio Maryland Baltimore MD 2000-2005, Eccl Crt 1998-2002, Cn for Congregations and Cler 1989-1997, 1998-2009; R Trin Ch Towson MD 1997-2009; R Ch Of The H Apos Wynnewood PA 1982-1989; Dn Philadelphia Theol Inst 1979-1989; Asst to the R S Paul's Ch Philadelphia PA 1977-1982; Asst to the R/ Int R S Lk's Ch Scranton PA 1976-1977; Chapl S Jn Bapt Sch Mendham NJ 1973-1976; R S Lk's Ch Plattsmouth NE 1970-1972; Bd Mem Well for the Journey Towson MD 2006-2009; Chair Com for the Redevelopment of Chelsea Sq Gnrl Th 2000-2009; Chair beginning Mnstry Together Proj Alb Inst Washing 1996-2002; Trst The GTS New York NY 1993-2009; Bd Mem Epis Cmnty Serv 1987-1989. Fllshp of St. Jn, SSJE 1975.

RANSOM, Lisa Michelle (Vt) 2016 Us Rr 2, Waterbury VT 05676 B Gunnison CO 1968 d Ward & Mary. BA U of Kansas 1991; MDiv Ya Berk 1995. D 6/24/1995 Bp William Edward Smalley P 1/19/1996 Bp Donald Purple Hart. m 1/14/1995 Scott Morgan Baughman c 2. S Jn's In The Mountains Stowe VT 2010; S Dunst's Epis Mssn Waitsfield VT 2002-2009; Dio Vermont Burlington VT 1999-2000; Cur S Matt's Epis Ch Wilton CT 1995-1997.

RAO, Chitra Dasu Sudarshan (Los) 10833 Le Conte Ave, Los Angeles CA 90095 B 1958 d Sudarshan & Saraswathi. M.Div Fuller TS; MDiv Fuller TS; Cert.

in Angl Stds The ETS at Claremont. D 6/7/2014 P 1/17/2015 Bp Joseph Jon Bruno. m 3/27/2004 Roger Cairns-Berteau.

RAPP, Phillip James (WK) 6529 Clifton Rd, Clifton VA 20124 **Pres / CEO Epis Cmnty Serv In Amer Clifton VA 2002-** B Toledo OH 1935 s Phillip & Margaret. BEd U of Toledo 1957; MDiv Bex Sem 1961; MA Bowling Green St U 1970; Untd States-Army War Coll Carlisle PA 1987; W&M Natl Planned Giving Institut 1991. D 6/10/1961 P 12/18/1961 Bp Nelson Marigold Burroughs. m 10/15/1966 Anne L Rapp c 3. Pres & CEO S Fran Acad Inc. 1990-2002; S Fran Cmnty Serv Inc. Salina KS 1988-2002; Chf Chapl Serv-NG Pentagon DC 1984-1988; Off Of Bsh For ArmdF New York NY 1984-1988; St Johns Hm Cleveland OH 1980-1984; Assoc S Andr's Epis Ch Toledo OH 1970-1978; Chapl NG 1962-1991; Vic S Jn The Evang Ch Napoleon OH 1961-1970. Auth, "For Profit & Not for Profit Alliances," *Behavioral Hlth Mgmt*, 1998. Amer Coll of Healthcare Executives 1995-2002; Amer Hosp Assn 1994-2002. Who's Who Among Outstanding Americans 1996; Who's Who Worldwide 1994, 1995, 2000 1995; Legion of Merit US Army 1988; Presidential Awd Lions Intl 1980.

RARDIN, Thomas Michael (Tex) 332 Oklahoma Ave, Hewitt TX 76643 **Asstg P Epis Ch Of The H Sprt Waco TX 2016-** B Akron OH 1952 s Bernard & Roberta. U of Akron 1971; BA Kent St U 1974; MDiv VTS 1977; CPE 1985. D 6/25/1977 Bp John Harris Burt P 2/4/1978 Bp David Keller Leighton Sr. m 9/8/1973 Christine Marie Tostevin c 3. Chf Chapl Serv Cntrl TX Vet Hlth Care System 1996-2012; Chf Chapl VetA Med Cntr Waco TX 1990-1996; Chf Chapl Serv VetA Med Cntr Altoona PA 1985-1990; Chapl Res Geisinger Med Cntr Danville PA 1983-1985; Vic for Deaf Mnstry Dio Cntrl Pennsylvania Harrisburg PA 1982-1985; Vic Ch Of The H Sprt Harrisburg PA 1981-1983; Vic for Deaf Mnstry Dio Maryland Baltimore MD 1979-1981; Asstg P S Tim's Ch Catonsville MD 1977-1979.

RASCHKE, Gerald Wesley (Spr) 2921 Haverford Rd, Springfield IL 62704 **All SS Epis Ch Deltona FL 2003-; D The Cathd Ch Of S Paul Springfield IL 1996-** B Omaha NE 1924 s Otto & Louise. Indiana U; U of Notre Dame. D 12/17/1975 Bp William Cockburn Russell Sheridan. m 5/4/2002 Dorothy May Dennis c 2. Archd Dio Dallas Dallas TX 1994-1996; D Ch Of The Annunc Lewisville TX 1992-1993; D Epis Ch Of The Redeem Irving TX 1976-1996; D The Cathd Ch Of S Jas So Bend IN 1975-1976.

RASCHKE, Vernon Joseph (SD) 625 W Main, Lead SD 57754 B Burke SD 1936 s Herman & Rose. BA S Johns U Collegeville MN 1958; S Johns Sem Collegeville MN 1962; PhD U MN 1972. Rec 5/26/1980 as Priest Bp Walter H Jones. c 2. P Chr Epis Ch Lead SD 2006-2015; R S Thos Epis Ch Sturgis SD 2002-2006; R Trin Epis Ch Winner SD 1999-2002; Dio So Dakota Pierre SD 1999-2001; The Epis Ch of Wichita Falls Wichita Falls TX 1987-1999; P-in-c Trin Ch Henrietta TX 1981-1988; Dio Ft Worth Ft Worth TX 1981-1987; Serv RC Ch 1962-1970. Auth, "Breaks in Adult Sibling Relatns," *Fam Perspective*; Auth, "Dogmatism & Committed & Consensual Religiosity," *Journ for Sci*; Auth, "Post Divorce Adjustment," *Journ of Mar & Fam*. AAMFT 1975-1999.

RASICCI, Michael Dominic (Chi) 222 S Batavia Ave, Batavia IL 60510 **R Calv Epis Ch Batavia IL 2002-; Dn Dio Chicago Chicago IL 2009-, Dioc Coun 2005-** B Akron Ohio 1953 s Sylvester & Dora. AA Lehigh Carbon Cmnty Coll 1973; BA DeSales U 1975; MDiv Cath Theol Un 1980. Rec 10/24/2000 as Priest Bp Bill Persell. m 6/4/1994 Linda K Rasicci. Int Ch Of S Columba Of Iona Hanover Pk IL 2001-2002; P Polish Natl Cath Ch Chicago IL 1994-1997; Rel Ord P RC Ch 1980-1994. CBS 2000; SocMary 2000; SSC 2002.

RASKE, Lynn Keith (Mo) 4916 Jamieson Ave., Apt.2A, Saint Louis MO 63109 **Died 1/27/2017** B Alma MI 1950 s Phillip & Doris. BA Siena Heights U 1976; MDiv SWTS 1982. D 6/26/1982 Bp John Harris Burt P 3/1/1983 Bp Gerald Nicholas Mcallister. c 2. Trin Ch S Jas MO 1994-2003; Non-par 1988-1990; Ch Of The Ascen Pawnee OK 1982-1987; Dio Oklahoma Oklahoma City OK 1982-1987; Vic S Alb's Ch Cushing OK 1982-1987.

RASKOPF, Roger William (LI) 1250 Newport Dr., Oconomowoc WI 53066 B Jamaica NY 1936 s William & Josephine. BA CUNY 1958; Nash 1961; MDiv GTS 1962; PhD S Johns U 1975; Harv 1980. D 4/28/1962 P 12/21/1962 Bp James Pernette DeWolfe. m 9/5/1959 Edythe J DellaCorte c 2. Nash Nashotah WI 2006-2013; Int S Edmunds Ch Milwaukee WI 2006-2008; Int Dn St Paul's Epis Ch Peoria IL 2004-2005; Int Trin-St Jn's Ch Hewlett NY 2002-2003; Int Caroline Ch Of Brookhaven E Setauke NY 2000-2002; Int Gr Epis Ch Utica NY 1999-2000; Int S Andr's Ch Stamford CT 1997-1999; Int S Mary's Ch Ronkonkoma NY 1996-1997; R S Paul's Ch Great Neck NY 1970-1979; Assoc Prof Mercer TS Garden City NY 1968-1979; First R S Jas The Just Franklin Sq NY 1963-1969; P-in-c Trin Elmont NY 1963-1967; Cur S Mk's Ch Jackson Heights NY 1962-1963; D Ch Of The H Cross Brooklyn NY 1961-1962. Kappa Delta Pi 1975; Tchg Fllshp St. Jn's U, NYC 1968.

RASMUS, John Edward (Eau) 5318 Regent St, Madison WI 53705 B Eau Claire WI 1947 s Vernon & Jean. BA U of Wisconsin 1971; MS U of Wisconsin 1978; Nash 1988. D 9/14/1983 P 6/29/1989 Bp William Charles Wantland. m 12/29/1968 Rose Rasmus c 1. Int Zion Epis Ch Oconomowoc WI 2010-2011; R S Paul's Ch Hudson WI 1989-2007. hon Soc Phi Kappa Phi.

R

RASMUS, Paul Alan (SeFla) 3740 Holly Dr, Palm Beach Gardens FL 33410 B Peekskill NY 1947 s Paul & Lillian. BA Florida Intl U 1973; MDiv Sewanee: The U So, TS 1977. D 4/17/1977 P 10/24/1977 Bp James Loughlin Duncan. m 11/15/1987 Brenda Nell Bedwell c 4. R S Andr's Ch Lake Worth FL 2006-2011; Archd - Dioc Deploy Off Dio SE Florida Miami 2002-2004; R S Paul's Ch Key W FL 1994-2002; Assoc S Mk's Ch Palm Bch Garden FL 1988-1993, 1986; Asst The Epis Ch Of The Gd Shpd Tequesta FL 1987; R H Sprt Epis Ch W Palm Bch FL 1979-1986; Cur S Andr's Epis Ch Miami FL 1977-1979. parasmus@aol.com

RASMUSSEN, Cynthia M (Roch) 215 Parkview Dr, Rochester NY 14625 **R S Mk's And S Jn's Epis Ch Rochester NY 2008-** B Honesdale PA 1971 d Robert & Helen. BS Coll Misericordia Dallas PA 1993; MDiv Luth TS 1997; PhD UTS and Presb Sch of Chr 2008. D 6/30/2007 P 4/22/2008 Bp Jack Marston Mckelvey. m 10/30/2015 Mary Ellen Forszt. Prof College Rochester Div Rochester NY 2016, Prof 2009; Epis Catalyst for Urban Mnstry Dio Rochester Henrietta 2014-2016, 2011-2012; Cur S Thos Epis Ch Rochester NY 2007-2008; Chld & Yth Coordntr St Mk's And Sait Jn's Epis Ch 2005-2007.

RASMUSSEN, Jeanne Louise (Az) 520 N Pokegama Ave, Grand Rapids MN 55744 **Assoc S Ptr's Ch Casa Grande AZ 2010-** B Grand Rapids MN 1950 d Jack & Sylvia. D 6/21/2009 P 12/20/2009 Bp James Louis Jelinek. m 8/26/1972 Ronald Lee Rasmussen.

RASMUSSEN, Rik Lorin (NCal) St Paul's Episcopal Church, PO Box 160914, Sacramento CA 95816 **S Matt's Epis Ch Sacramento CA 2015-; Assoc S Paul's Epis Ch Sacramento CA 2013-** B Ogden UT 1959 s Ronald & Ruth. BS U CA 1983; Cert of Angl Stds CDSP 2013. D 6/29/2013 P 5/23/2015 Bp Barry Leigh Beisner. m 10/25/2008 Jon Bruce Marshack.

RASNER, Richard Lewis (Me) 143 State St, Portland ME 04101 B Cincinnati OH 1947 s Louis & Helen. MA U IL 1971; PhD No Wstrn U 1979. D 6/23/2012 Bp Stephen Taylor Lane.

RASNICK, Kenneth Wayne (Mich) B Detroit MI 1960 s Carson & Mary. D 6/14/2014 Bp Wendell Nathaniel Gibbs Jr. m 10/15/1994 Joan Elizabeth Rasnick.

RASNICK, Thomas James (ETenn) 6804 Glenbrook Cir, Knoxville TN 37919 **Cn Pstr S Jn's Epis Cathd Knoxville TN 1998-** B Miami FL 1964 s James & Marilyn. AA Palm Bch Jr Coll 1985; BS Florida St U 1987; MDiv VTS 1992. D 5/28/1992 Bp Calvin Onderdonk Schofield Jr P 12/1/1992 Bp Earl Nicholas Mc Arthur Jr. m 6/17/1989 Cynthia Rasnick c 3. Assoc R S Mich And All Ang Ch Dallas TX 1994-1998; Asst R S Thos Epis Ch And Sch San Antonio TX 1992-1994. trasnick@stjohnscathedral.org

RATCLIFF, Elizabeth Rogers (WLa) B Alexandria LA 1944 D 6/7/2003 P 3/16/2004 Bp D Avid Bruce Macpherson. m 6/18/1966 Robert Ratcliff c 4. Calv Ch Bunkie LA 2009-2014; Trin Epis Ch Natchitoches LA 2004-2006.

RATH, Erin (SD) **D Ch Of The Gd Shpd Sioux Falls SD 2017-** D 6/16/2017 Bp John Tarrant.

RATHBONE, Cristine F (Mass) 138 Tremont St., Boston MA 02111 **The Cathd Ch Of S Paul Boston MA 2009-** B New York NY 1966 d John & Margarita. MDiv Bos TS 2009. D 6/6/2009 Bp M(Arvil) Thomas Shaw. c 2.

RATHBUN JR, Arthur John (Kan) 138 S 8th St, Salina KS 67401 **R S Mk's Ch Blue Rapids KS 2009-; Non-par 1988-** B Erie PA 1936 s Arthur & Bernice. BS Penn 1959; STB GTS 1962. D 6/18/1962 P 6/1/1964 Bp William Crittenden. m 6/6/1987 Theresa Ann Rathbun c 2. Chr Cathd Salina KS 1979-1987; Dio Wstrn Kansas Hutchinson KS 1978-1979; Epis Ch Of The Incarn Salina KS 1977-1979; Chapl Clarion St Coll 1970-1974; Chapl Edinboro St Coll 1966-1974; Vic S Ptr's Ch Waterford PA 1966-1970; Vic S Jn's Ch Kane PA 1964-1966; S Marg's Epis Ch Kane PA 1964-1966; DRE Youthville In Newton 1963-1964; D Gr Ch Lake City PA 1962-1963.

RATHMAN, William E (SC) 251 South Sea Pines Drive, Unit 1924, Hilton Head Island SC 29928 **Ret 1995-** B Middletown OH 1927 s Ernest & Marguerite. BA Ken 1948; JD OH SU 1951; Untd TS 1975. D 6/30/1975 Bp John Mc Gill Krumm. m 11/28/1958 Constance Rathman c 2. Cur The Epis Ch Of The Ascen Middletown OH 1978-1995; Cur Trin Ch Hamilton OH 1977-1978; Cur S Pat's Epis Ch Lebanon OH 1975-1977.

RATLIFF, Ruth Evelyn (Ia) St Luke's Episcopal Church, 2410 Melrose Dr, Cedar Falls IA 50613 **D S Lk's Epis Ch Cedar Falls IA 2013-** B Somerville NJ 1952 d Francis & Evelyn. BA St Olaf Coll 1974; MA U of Iowa 1976; PhD U of Iowa 1988. D 6/8/2013 Bp Alan Scarfe. m 9/11/1982 Jan Clifton Robbins.

RATTERREE, Gretchen Suzanne (At) **Ch Of The Annunc Marietta GA 2016-** D 12/19/2015 P 6/25/2016 Bp Robert Christopher Wright.

RAU, Michael S (Pa) St Mark's Episcopal Church, 111 Oenoke Rdg, New Canaan CT 06840 **Memi Ch Of The H Nativ Jenkintown PA 2015-** B Lansdale PA 1975 s Douglass & Marilyn. BA Montgomery Cnty Cmnty Coll 2000; BA Tem 2000; MDiv GTS 2013; MDiv The GTS 2013. D 6/15/2013 Bp Clifton Daniel III. m 5/29/1999 Melissa L Rau c 3. P S Mk's Ch New Canaan CT 2013-2015. therevmikerau@holynativityrockledge.org

RAULERSON, Aaron D (Ala) 5529 Cedar Mill Dr, Guntersville AL 35976 **Ch Of The Epiph Guntersville AL 2014-** B Augusta GA 1971 s James & Marsha. BA Carson-Newman Coll 1993; MDiv Epis TS of the SW 2001. D 6/2/2001 P 5/18/2002 Bp Philip Menzie Duncan II. m 9/11/1993 Rebecca L Massingill c

3. R H Cross Trussville AL 2007-2014; R Trin Ch Demopolis AL 2006-2007; Coordntr Epis Black Belt Mnstrs 2003-2005; Cur All SS Epis Ch Mobile AL 2001-2003.

RAUSCHER JR, William V. (NJ) 663 N Evergreen Ave, Woodbury NJ 08096 **Ret 1996-; Ret 1996-** B Long Branch NJ 1932 s William & Marie. BS Glassboro St U 1954; BS PDS 1957. D 4/27/1957 P 11/2/1957 Bp Alfred L Banyard. Hon Cn Trin Cathd Trenton NJ 1971; R Chr Ch In Woodbury Woodbury NJ 1960-1996; Vic Sts Steph and Barn Epis Ch Florence NJ 1957-1960; Mem Bd Missions Dio New Jersey Trenton NJ 1978-1979, Trst 1976-1979, Trst of Dioc Fndt 1976-1979, Mem of Cathd Capter 1975-1978, Mem -Bp's Trial Crt 1970-1978, Com Dioc Journ Pub 1968-1975, Dep to Prov Syn 1964-1967, Me 1964-1967, Mem & Secy Mus Cmsn 1964-1965, Mem -Cmsn on Evang 1960-1977. Auth, "Silent Mora: The Story of Louis J. McCord," *Silent Mora: The Story of Louis J. McCord*, 1878 Press, 2014; Auth, "The Death Camp Magicians: A True Story of Holocaust Survivors Werner Reich and Herbert Nivelli," *The Death Camp Magicians: A True Story of Holocaust Survivors Werner Reich and Herbert Nivelli*, 1878 Press, 2014; Auth, "Milbourne Chris: The Man and His Magic," *Milbourne Chris: The Man and His Magic*, 1878 Press, 2012; Auth, "Goebel: The Man w the Magical Mind," *Goebel: The Man w The Magical Mind*, Martinka & Co., 2010; Auth, "Edd Patterson: A Lifetime of Magic and Art," *Edd Patterson: A Lifetime of Magic and Art*, S. S. Adams, 2008; Auth, "Pleasant Nightmares," *Pleasant Nightmares*, S. S. Adams, 2008; Auth, "Rel, Magic and The Supernatural," *Rel, Magic, and The Supernatural*, Mystic Light Press, 2006; Auth, "Magic In Rhyme," *Magic in Rhyme*, 1878 Press, 2003; Auth, "S. S. Adams," *S.S. Adams*, 1878 Press, 2002; Auth, "The Mind Readers: Masters of Deception," *The Mind Readers: Masters of Deception*, Mystic Light Press, 2002; Auth, "The Houdini Code: A Sprt Mystery Solved," *The Houdini Code Mystery: A Sprt Secret Solved*, Magic Words, 2000; Auth, "To Be or Not To Be," *To Be or Not to Be: A Pstr View of Suicide in Today's Wrld*, Xlibris, 2000; Auth, "Servais leRoy: Monarich of Mystery," *Servais LeRoy: Monarch of Mystery*, Magic Words, 1999; Auth, "The Great Raymond: Entertainer of Kings, King of Entertainers," *The Great Raymond: Entertainer of Kings, King of Entertainers Kings-King of Entertainment*, Baldwin, 1996; Auth, "Jn Calvert: Magic & Adventures," *Jn Calvert: Magic & Adventures Around the Wrld*, Claitor, 1987; Auth, "The Case Against Suicide," *The Case Against Suicide*, St Martins, 1981; Auth, "Ch in Frenzy," *Ch In Frenzy*, St Martins, 1980; Auth, "Sprtl Frontier," *The Sprtl Frontier*, Doubleday, 1975; Auth, "Arthur Ford: The Man Who Talked w the Dead," *Arthur Ford: The Man Who Talked w the Dead*, New Amer Libr, 1973. Hon Cn Trin Cathd 1971.

RAVEN, Margaret Hilary (NJ) 324 Edgewood Dr, Toms River NJ 08755 B Liverpool UK 1945 d William & Ruth. BA U of Durham Gb 1967; MEd U of Manchester 1973; MDiv VTS 1995; MDiv Wesley TS 1995. D 6/15/1996 Bp Peter J Lee P 6/14/1997 Bp John Henry Smith. Assoc Chr Ch Toms River Toms River NJ 1999-2000; Trin Epis Ch Martinsburg WV 1996-1999. Auth, "Mangodwoman:Poems," 2000; Auth, "Cmnty Involvement In Hlth Dvlpmt," Wrld Hlth Orgnztn, 1990; Auth, "Strengthening Performance Cmnty Hlth Workers In Primary Hlth Care," Wrld Hlth Orgnztn, 1989; Auth, "Adult Educ Cmnty Proj & Planned Parenthood," Ippf, 1981. Amer Farmland Trust; Int Mnstry Ntwk.

RAVNDAL III, Eric (CFla) 1302 Country Club Oaks Cir, Orlando FL 32804 B Orlando FL 1939 s Eric & Florence. BA Harv 1961; MDiv Nash 1980. D 6/22/1980 P 1/11/1981 Bp William Hopkins Folwell. m 9/26/1964 Sarah B Ravndal c 4. Dio Cntrl Florida Orlando FL 1994-1998, Pres Stndg Com 1996-1998, Stndg Com 1994-1998; R Epis Ch Of The H Sprt Apopka FL 1987-1998; Nash Nashotah WI 1983-1987; Asst S Barn Ch Deland FL 1980-1982.

RAWLINS, P. Allister (LI) 744 Havemeyer Ave, Bronx NY 10473 B 1954 s Charles & Mary. BA Codrington Coll 1980; MA Ford 1984. Trans 3/11/1991. m 12/27/1986 Juliette Charles Charles-Rawlins c 1. R S Geo's Ch Hempstead NY 1999-2016; R S Andr's Ch Bronx NY 1991-1999; Asst to R S Mk's Ch Brooklyn NY 1986-1991; R S Geo Dominica W Indies 1984-1986; Asst S Lk's Epis Ch Bronx NY 1983-1984; Asst Cathd Of St Jn The Div New York NY 1980-1983.

RAWLINSON, John Edward (Cal) 891 Dowling Blvd, San Leandro CA 94577 **Anti-racism Trnr Dio California San Francisco CA 2005-; Mem, Cancionero Exec Com Off of Latino-Hisp Mnstrs New York City 1999-; Sprtl Dir, Curs Sec Dio California San Francisco CA 1989-** B Berkeley CA 1940 s Albert & Iona. BA Humboldt St U 1963; BD CDSP 1970; MA Grad Theol Un 1970; PhD Grad Theol Un 1982. D 6/23/1973 Bp Chauncie Kilmer Myers P 9/1/1974 Bp George Richard Millard. m 8/25/1962 Milene Tackitt c 1. Mem, Racial Recon T/F Dio California San Francisco CA 2010-2012; Mem, Ethnic and Multi-cultural Strategic Plan Com Dio California San Francisco CA 2009-2011; Academia Teologica Latina Instr Dio California San Fransisco CA 2004-2012; Mem, 150th Anniv Com Dio California San Francisco CA 1998-1999; Mem, Cmsn 2000 Dio California San Francisco CA 1996-1999; Coordntr Field Educ Epis Sch for Ds Dio California San Francisco CA 1991-1994, Mem and chairperson 1986-2013, Archv 1986-2006, Cmsn Liturg Renwl 1974-1984, Ethnic Strng Com 2005-2007, Cmsn 2000 1997-1999, Dept of Yth Mnstry 1975-1981; Instr Epis Sch Dio California San

Fransisco CA 1989-1996; Pstr S Jas Ch Oakland CA 1984-2012; Bd Mem Childcare Coordntng Coun of Alameda Cnty 1979-2009; Bd Mem Alameda Cnty Cmnty Food Bank 1979-1988; Field Educ Supvsr CDSP Berkeley CA 1975-1993; Mem, Dept of Yth Mnstry Dio California San Francisco CA 1974-1980; Mem, Com on Non-stipendiary Cler Dio California San Francisco CA 1974-1975; Asst to Vic S Cuth's Epis Ch Oakland CA 1972-1974. Auth, "Congrl Hist: Researching Writing and Enjoying It," 1999; Auth, "Par Archive: Principles Orgnztn & Methods," 1998; "Michellaneous arts," *LivCh.*

RAWSON, William Leighton (Nwk) 10960 Big Canoe, Jasper GA 30143 B Teaneck NJ 1940 s William & Ida. BA Montclair St U 1962; MDiv VTS 1967. D 6/10/1967 Bp Leland Stark P 12/14/1967 Bp George E Rath. m 9/15/1996 Rhonda Stock c 2. R S Andr's Epis Ch Lincoln Pk NJ 1969-1974; Cur S Ptr's Ch Mtn Lks NJ 1967-1969; Ret.

RAY, Andrew M (Pgh) PO Box 38342, Pittsburgh PA 15238 **P-in-c Fox Chap Epis Ch Pittsburgh PA 2008-, 2007-2009, 2007-2009, Asst R 2007-** B Cleveland, OH 1976 s Durwood & Laurie. Nash; BS Grove City Coll 1999; MDiv Fuller TS 2002. D 12/14/2002 Bp Robert William Duncan P 6/21/2003 Bp Joseph Jon Bruno. m 11/12/2005 Julie Ray c 1. Assoc R S Lk's Of The Mountains La Crescenta CA 2003-2007, 2003-2006; Dio Los Angeles Los Angeles CA 2003.

RAY, Douglass E (Colo) 5601 Collins Ave Apt 706, Miami Beach FL 33140 B Greenwich CT 1948 s Edward & Isabel. C. Th. U of Cambridge; BA Wms 1973; Dip Min Stud McGill U 1976; LTh Montreal Inst Montreal QC CA 1976. Trans 9/1/1978 as Priest Bp Morgan Porteus. m 1/13/2007 Melissa Ray c 2. Bd, Epis Ntwk for Stwdshp Epis Ch Cntr New York NY 1999-2003; Bd, Epis Relief and Dvlpmt Epis Ch Cntr New York NY 1999-2003; Colorado Epis Fndt Denver CO 1997-2003; Dio Colorado Denver CO 1988-2008, Pres 1988-2003; S Lk's Par Darien CT 1978-1985; Serv Ch of Can 1974-1978. Auth, "Beacon in the Hills (producer, Dir)," 1993. Outstanding Clergyman Fairfield Cnty Ch 1984. dougray@panaslinzy.com

RAY, Harvey H (Cal) 1354 Primavera Dr E, Palm Springs CA 92264 **Bd Deep Well Ranch 2013-** B Atlanta GA 1947 s Homer & Bernice. BS Valdosta St U 1969; MDiv EDS 1975. D 6/14/1975 Bp Lyman Cunningham Ogilby P 12/20/1975 Bp Jonathan Goodhue Sherman. P-in-c S Mart's Ch Shady Cove OR 2003-2007; P Trin Epis Ch Ashland Ashland OR 2002-2011; Asst S Lk's Ch San Francisco CA 1993-2002; Asst Chr Ch Sausalito CA 1988-1993; Corp Mgmt Stff Nthrn California Presb Hm Inc. San Francisco CA 1980-2001; Asst Ch Of The H Innoc San Francisco CA 1980-1988; Vic All SS Ch Hamlet NC 1978-1979; Asst S Gabr's Ch Hollis NY 1975-1978; The Woodhull Schools Hollis NY 1975-1978; Chapl S Jos's Ch Queens Vlg NY 1975-1977; Bd Ashand Cmnty Hosp 2006-2011; Bd Sthrn Oregon Humane Soc 2003-2005; Ethics Com Dio California San Francisco CA 1991-1993; Bd California Assn of Hm and Serv for the Aging 1990-2000.

RAY, John Sewak (At) 4808 Glenwhite Dr, Duluth GA 30096 B Hyderabad(Sindh) PK 1946 s Chandu & Sarah. BA U of Cbury Christchurch NZ 1970; Dip Regent Coll Vancouver CA 1973; MA Oxf GB 1976. D 8/22/2004 P 3/8/2005 Bp J Neil Alexander. m 7/17/1976 Aqeela Ray c 1. Assoc Chr the King Lilburn GA 2005-2015; P Dio Atlanta Atlanta GA 2005-2015; Exec. Asst The Grapevine Grp Roswell GA 2004; Travel Counslr Amer Express Platinum Travel Serv Norcross GA 2001-2003; Sr VP Sostad And Assoc. Holdrege NE 1998-2000; Exec. VP Haggai Inst For Advncd Ldrshp Atlanta GA 1990-1998; Reg Rep For So Asia Haggai Inst For Advncd Ldrshp Karachi Pakistan 1988-1990; Reg Secy For Cntrl Asia Int'L Fllshp Of Evang Students Karashi Pakistan 1981-1988; Asst. To Gnrl Secy Int'L Fllshp Of Evang. Students Harrow Uk 1979-1981; Yth Worker Epis Dio Iran Isfahan/Teheran Iran 1977-1979; Exec. Secy Pakistan Fllwshp Of Evang Students Karachi Pakistan 1971-1973; Asst. Mstr Karachi Grammar Sch Karashi Pakistan 1970-1971. johnsewakray@aol.com

RAY, Mauldin Alexander (Okla) 1763 E 56th St, Tulsa OK 74105 B Huffman AR 1924 s Thomas & Ella. EdD; Sewanee: The U So, TS. P 11/1/1974 Bp Chilton R Powell. m 8/7/1984 Janet Andersen Ripper c 2. S Jn's Epis Ch Tulsa OK 1978-1992. Kappa Delta Pi; Phi Delta Kappa.

RAY, Michael Fleming (Ct) 830 Whitney Avenue, New Haven CT 06511 **Pres S Thos's Day Sch 1985-** B Corsicana TX 1943 s William & Harriet. BS Steph F Austin St U 1965; MDiv Ya Berk 1969. D 6/18/1969 Bp Charles A Mason P 12/20/1969 Bp Joseph Warren Hutchens. m 1/2/2009 Robert Daniel Harris c 2. R S Thos's Ch New Haven CT 1985-2015; R S Geo's Ch Clifton Pk NY 1978-1985; R S Thos Ch Greenville RI 1971-1978; Asst St Johns Ch W Hartford CT 1969-1971.

RAY, Philip Carroll (NwT) 1608 Monte Vista St, Dalhart TX 79022 B Wichita KS 1943 s Marion & Margaret. BS K SU 1965; DDS U of Missouri Kansas City MO 1969; MS Angelo St U 1991; Cert Theol Stud Epis TS of the SW 2006. D 11/12/2006 P 6/9/2007 Bp C Wallis Ohl. m 3/16/1995 Sarah Otto c 5. S Jas' Epis Ch Dalhart TX 2009-2015. Angl Ord of Preachers, Dominican, Prior 2007.

RAY, Pratik Kumar (RG) D 11/17/2016 Bp James Beattie Magness.

✠ RAY, The Rt Rev Rayford J (NMich) 9922 U 65 Lane, Rapid River MI 49878 B Heidelberg DE 1956 s Corbitt & Gertrude. BA Cameron U 1979; MDiv Nash

1986. D 6/21/1986 Bp Gerald Nicholas Mcallister P 4/10/1987 Bp William Jackson Cox Con 5/21/2011 for NMich. m 6/29/1974 Suzanne Patricia Ray c 1. Bp of Nthrn Michigan Dio Nthrn Michigan Marquette MI 2011, Bp of Nthrn Michigan 2011-, Mnstry Dvlpmt Coordntr 1999-2001, Yth Cmsn 1992-1994; Yth Cmsn 1992-1994; Mnstry Dvlp So Cntrl Reg Manistique MI 1990-2011; Mssn Coun 1988-1990; R Ch Of The Redeem Okmulgee OK 1988-1990; CE Field Team 1987-1989; Mssnr Team 1986-1990; Assoc Mssnr/Cur Green Country Epis Cluster Muskogee OK 1986-1990; Dio Oklahoma Oklahoma City OK 1986-1988. rayfordray@upepiscopal.org

RAY, Suzanne Patricia (NMich) 9922 U 65 Lane, Rapid River MI 49878 **Secy ECW Mnstry Spprt Team 1990-; D Trin Ch Gladstone MI 1990-** B Dearborn MI 1953 d Robert & Elizabeth. Dio Nthrn Michigan D Trng MI; RN Bay De Noc Cmnty Coll 1993. D 9/30/1990 P 6/1/1997 Bp Thomas Kreider Ray. m 6/29/1974 Rayford J Ray.

✠ RAY, The Rt Rev Thomas Kreider (NMich) 250 Partridge Bay Trl, Marquette MI 49855 B Barberton OH 1934 s Donald & Hazel. BA U MI 1956; STB GTS 1959. D 6/20/1959 Bp Benjamin M Washburn P 12/1/1959 Bp Francis W Lickfield Con 8/21/1982 for NMich. m 6/27/1959 Brenda Lee Ray. Asstg Bp Dio Nthrn Michigan Marquette MI 2007-2011, Ret Bp of Nthrn Michigan 1999-, Bp 1982-1999; Asstg Bp Dio Iowa Des Moines IA 2001-2003; R S Lk's Ch Evanston IL 1971-1982; R Geth Epis Ch Marion IN 1964-1971; Vic S Chris's Ch Crown Point IN 1961-1964; Cur S Mk's Ch Grand Rapids MI 1959-1961. Auth, "The Sm Ch: Radical Reformation and Renwl of Mnstry," *ATR*, 1996; "Creating Hospitable Environmnet for Mutual Mnstry," Pub. SPCK London; "Loc Mnstry," *Story Process and Meaning.*

RAY, Wanda Louise (O) 312 Park St, Huron OH 44839 B Gilbert WV 1946 d Alex & Imogene. BA Coll of Charleston 1992; MDiv VTS 1995. D 12/12/1999 P 7/23/2000 Bp Edwin Max Leidel Jr. c 2. R Chr Epis Ch Huron OH 2003-2014; S Jn the Bapt Otter Lake MI 2000-2003; S Jn's Epis Ch Dryden MI 1999-2003; Supt of Wee People Sch Dio Ohio Cleveland 2007-2010; Stndg Com Mem Dio Estrn Michigan Saginaw MI 2001-2003, Dioc Acolyte Coordntr 2000-2003.

RAY, Wayne Allen (Miss) 116 Siowan Ave, Ocean Springs MS 39564 B Owensboro KY 1947 BA Wstrn Kentucky U 1969; MDiv CDSP 1972; PhD OH SU 1981. D 6/29/1972 P 1/1/1973 Bp Charles Gresham Marmion. m 12/21/1984 Susan C Ray c 1. R S Jn's Epis Ch Ocean Sprg MS 1999-2012; Univ. of Virginia S Paul's Memi Charlottesvlle VA 1992-1999; Chapl U VA 1992-1999; AZ St U Dio Arizona Phoenix AZ 1990-1992; Chapl U AZ- St. Tempe ASU AZ 1990-1992; Vic All SS Ch Seymour IN 1988-1990; 1983-1990; Epis Ch of Our Sav Richmond KY 1980-1984; Assoc Trin Ch Covington KY 1977-1980; 1974-1977; Cn Chr Ch Cathd Louisville KY 1972-1974.

RAYBOURN JR, Fred Loren (Neb) 1204 Sunshine Blvd, Bellevue NE 68123 B Carbondale IL 1932 s Fred & Donatila. No Illinois St Teachers Coll Dekalb IL 1953; AA Canal Zone Jr Coll 1957; BS Bradley U 1959; DMagist ETSC 1964. D 5/22/1964 Bp Albert Ervine Swift P 12/8/1964 Bp Reginald Heber Gooden. m 5/31/1967 Susan Raybourn c 2. Par P S Mart of Tours Ch Omaha NE 2003-2007; R S Mart Of Tours Ch Omaha NE 1994-2003; R S Lk's Ch Plattsmouth NE 1990-1992; 1982-1990; Int Cathd Of St Lk Balboa 1980-1981; Int R S Lk's Cathd Ancon Panama 1980-1981; Int San Marcos Ch 1980; Dio Panama 1976-1982; 1973-1976; P-in-c S Simon's Gamboa 1971-1972; R S Andrews Cocoli PCZ 1970-1973; Chapl Gorgas Hosp Ancon PCZ 1965-1973; P-in-c San Jose La Chorrera PCZ 1965-1970; D S Andrews Cocoli PCZ 1964-1965. GAS 1991; P Assoc, Shrine of Our Lady of Walsingham 1991; Soc-Mary 1985; SSC 1991.

RAYBURG-ELLIOTT, Jason Alan (WNY) 128 Pearl St, Buffalo NY 14202 B St Petersburg FL 1980 s Alan & Jacqueline. BA SUNY at Buffalo 2004; MA U of Masschusetts 2011. D 7/10/2010 Bp Michael Garrison. m 5/6/2009 James Rayburg.

RAYE, Janice Marie (Md) 32 Main St, Westernport MD 21562 **Died 7/21/2016** B Keyser WV 1951 d Louie & Norma. D 12/21/2007 Bp John L Rabb. c 2.

RAYLS, John William (WTex) PO Box 6885, San Antonio TX 78209 **Vic Epis Ch Of The Gd Shepard Geo W TX 2012-** B Kokomo IN 1952 s William & Daisy. BS Indiana U 1973; MS St Fran U 1975; MDiv Luther Rice Sem 1985; ABD Capella U 2003. D 4/7/2010 Bp Gary Richard Lillibridge P 10/11/2010 Bp David Mitchell Reed. m 7/20/1974 Susan Rayls c 3. Cn Mssnr for Strategic Dvlpmt Dio W Texas San Antonio TX 2012-2014, 2010; S Bon Ch Comfort TX 2011-2012.

RAYMOND, Patrick (Chi) 647 Dundee Ave, Barrington IL 60010 **Ch Of The Ascen Chicago IL 2016-** B Bakersfield CA 1959 s Robert & Loisjean. BA Wheaton Coll 1981; MDiv GTS 1987. D 3/16/1987 P 9/21/1987 Bp James Winchester Montgomery. m 9/21/1991 Elizabeth Brooke W Raymond c 3. R S Mich's Ch Barrington IL 2011-2015; Int Gr Ch Madison WI 2007-2009; R S Andr's Ch Madison WI 1997-2006; S Dunst's Ch Madison WI 1996-1997; Non-par Dio Chicago Chicago IL 1992-1997; St. Andrews Pentecost Epis Ch Evanston IL 1992-1993; Asst Ch Of Our Sav Chicago IL 1988-1992; Cur S Mk's Barrington IL 1987-1988. patrickrraymond@gmail.com

R

RAYMOND, Seth (Mil) Christ Episcopal Church, 5655 N Lake Dr, Whitefish Bay WI 53217 **Dio Milwaukee Milwaukee WI 2017-** B Lebanon NH 1985 s Bruce & Michelle. BA Bos 2005; BME U CO Boulder 2008; MDiv Duke DS 2012. D 5/4/2012 Bp Robert John O'Neill. m 7/28/2007 Elizabeth K Raymond c 2. Asst Chr Ch Milwaukee WI 2012-2016. hospitalitycenter@diomil.org

RAYMOND, Sue Ann (Ia) Lot 17A, 1771 Golf Course Blvd., Independence IA 50644 **D S Jas Epis Ch Independence IA 2007-** B Independence IA 1939 d Clarence & Arlene. BS TCU 1960; MEd TCU 1963. D 11/6/1999 Bp William Jerry Winterrowd.

RAYSA, Mary G (SO) B Oak park IL 1947 d Richard & Helen. BS Colorado St U 1969; MS Illinois U 1971; Sch for Diac Formation 2013. D 6/29/2013 Bp Thomas Edward Breidenthal.

RAZEE, George Wells (Ct) 234 Essex Mdws, Essex CT 06426 **Ret 1989-** B Milford CT 1924 s George & Edith. AB Dart 1949; STB Ya Berk 1956. D 6/14/1956 P 4/16/1957 Bp Walter H Gray. m 7/13/1957 Nancy G Razee c 3. Dio Connecticut Meriden CT 1984-1989, Consult Lymns Div Dept Yth & Lymns Wk 1966-1983, Com On Evang 1962-1965, Chairman Yth Coun 1959-1961; Berk 1982-1988; S Jn's Epis Ch Bristol CT 1967-1988; R S Ptr's-Trin Ch Thomaston CT 1958-1967; Cur Chr Ch Stratford CT 1956-1958.

RAZIM, Genevieve (Tex) **P Chr Ch Cathd Houston TX 2014-** B Freeport Texas 1969 d Michael & Sharon. BFA U of No Texas 1992; MDiv SMU Perkins 2006. D 6/23/2007 Bp Don Adger Wimberly. m 10/15/1994 Edward A Razim c 2. Trin Epis Ch The Woodlands TX 2010-2014; Palmer Memi Ch Houston TX 2007-2010; Intern St Anne Epis Ch 2005-2006.

RAZZINO, Robin (Va) 1701 N Quaker Ln, Alexandria VA 22302 **The Ch of S Clem Alexandria VA 2016-** B Baltimore MD 1975 d Ted & Barbara. BS Jas Madison U 1997; MS Geo Mason U 2002; MDiv VTS 2008. D 6/14/2008 P 1/24/2009 Bp John Bryson Chane. m 10/29/2010 Brian Edward Razzino c 1. S Thos Epis Ch Mclean VA 2016; Asst to the R The Ch Of The Redeem Beth MD 2008-2016.

REA, Robert Allen (NC) 1226 21st Ave, San Francisco CA 94122 **Non-par 1995-** B Lancaster PA 1943 s Ivan & Marie. BA Franklin & Marshall Coll 1965; MDiv Harvard DS 1987. D 6/11/1988 P 5/29/1989 Bp David Elliot Johnson. Vic Ch Of The Trsfg No Bergen NJ 1994-1995; Soc-St Jn The Evang Cambridge MA 1992-1993, 1988-1989; The Soc Of St Jn The Evang Durham NC 1989-1992; S Jn's Chap Cambridge MA 1988-2014, 1978-1988.

READ, Allison (Ct) 300 Summit St, Hartford CT 06106 **Coll Chapl Trin Chap Hartford CT 2008-** B Point Pleasant NY 1973 BA U of Virginia 1995; MA Yale DS 1997; MDiv Ya Berk 2003. D 3/8/2003 P 9/20/2003 Bp Mark Sean Sisk. m 10/17/1998 James Ebert c 1. Asst Chr Ch Short Hills NJ 2005-2007; P S Jas Ch New York NY 2003-2005; D Chr Ch Bronxville NY 2003.

READ, David Glenn (WTex) 11 Saint Lukes Ln, San Antonio TX 78209 **S Lk's Epis Ch San Antonio TX 2009-** B Winston-Salem NC 1965 s William & Doris. BA Texas St U San Marcos 1988; MDiv VTS 1992. D 6/14/1992 Bp Earl Nicholas Mc Arthur Jr P 12/16/1992 Bp John Herbert MacNaughton. m 6/29/1991 Jacqueline Read c 2. R S Helena's Epis Ch Boerne TX 1998-2009; R S Fran Epis Ch Victoria TX 1995-1998; R S Paul's Ch Brady TX 1992-1995.

READ, Nancy Ann (Nwk) 12 Northfield Ter, Clifton NJ 07013 **D Gr Ch Nutley NJ 2010-;** Hospice RN Homeside Hospice Clark NJ 2007- B Long Island NY 1957 Dip Mountainside Hosp Sch of Nrsng Montclair NJ 1978; Montclair St U 1999; CPE Chr Hosp 2002; Cert EFM 2003; Diac Stds Epis Dio Newark 2003. D 6/5/2004 Bp John Palmer Croneberger. m 11/17/1979 Philip M Read c 2. D Chr Ch Glen Ridge NJ 2004-2009; Archd Dio Newark Newark NJ 2008-2010.

READ II, Philip Daugherty (SwFla) 11698 Pointe Cir, Fort Myers FL 33908 **R S Lk's Ch Ft Myers FL 2002-** B New Smyrna Bch FL 1961 s Philip & Lois. Auburn U 1982; LTh Nash 1995. D 6/12/1995 P 12/21/1995 Bp Jack Leo Iker. R S Andr's Ch Dallas TX 1998-2002; Cur S Alb's Epis Ch Arlington TX 1995-1998; Chapl U Tx Arlington TX 1995-1998. Assn Of Our Lady Of Walsingham 1997; Assn Of The CHS; Bd Trst-Nash 2005; CCU 1995; CBS 1995; Oblate Benedictine Abbey Subiaco Ar 1997; Ord Of S Lk 1995; SocMary 1995; SSC 1998.

REANS, Douglas J (NJ) 512 Sycamore Ter, Cinnaminson NJ 08077 **Vic S Mary's Ch Clementon NJ 2011-** B Wabasha MN 1946 s Aubrey & Bernice. BA U MN 1968; BA U MN 1968; MDiv Bex Sem 1973. D 6/29/1973 P 3/1/1974 Bp Philip Frederick McNairy. m 11/24/2001 Mary Salva c 2. Int S Ptr's Ch Spotswood NJ 2008-2010; R S Andr's Epis Ch Bridgeton NJ 2003-2008; Evergreens Chap Moorestown NJ 1999-2003; Chapl The Evergreens Moorestown NJ 1996-2003; Int S Ptr's Ch Freehold NJ 1995-1996; Int Trin Epis Ch Cranford NJ 1994-1995; Int S Paul's Epis Ch Bound Brook NJ 1993-1994; Int Gr Epis Ch Plainfield NJ 1992-1993; Vic S Cyp's Epis Ch Hackensack NJ 1984-1988; Int Chr Ch Hackensack NJ 1982-1984; Exec Dir Reston Interfaith Reston VA 1978-1982; Prog Dir Fairfax Cnty Cmnty Action Prog 1974-1978; D Dio Minnesota Minneapolis MN 1973-1974. djreans@yahoo.com

REARDIN, Lois Arline (NC) 221 Union St, Cary NC 27511 B West Chester PA 1932 d John & Emma. BS Wm Paterson U 1954; MDiv VTS 1987. D 6/12/1987 P 5/12/1988 Bp Charlie Fuller Mcnutt Jr. c 2. Assoc (post-Ret) S Paul's Epis Ch Cary NC 2004-2016, Assoc 2000-2004; S Jn's Ch Bala Cynwyd PA 1995-1998; Ch Of S Mart-In-The-Fields Philadelphia PA 1995; Assoc R Ch Of The Redeem Bryn Mawr PA 1989-1991; Field Worker Dio Cntrl Pennsylvania Harrisburg PA 1987-1989; D-Intern S Jn's Ch Marietta PA 1987-1988.

REASONER, Rand Lee (Los) 5700 Rudnick Ave, Woodland Hills CA 91367 **Bd Dir Uganda Dvlpmt Initiative Woodland Hills Ca 2013-; Bd Dir Uganda Dvlpmt Initiative 2004-; R Prince Of Peace Epis Ch Woodland Hls CA 1989-; Bd Dir Uganda Dvlpmt Initiative Woodland Hills Ca 2011-** B Los Angeles CA 1954 s Lee & Joy. BA USC 1976; MDiv CDSP 1980. D 6/21/1980 P 4/11/1981 Bp Robert Claflin Rusack. m 11/29/1980 Kathryn A Reasoner c 2. R Trin Par Fillmore CA 1983-1989; Asst All SS-By-The-Sea Par Santa Barbara CA 1981-1983; D Intern/Chapl Dio Los Angeles Los Angeles CA 1980-1981, Dn of Tri Vlly Dnry 2003-2011. Cn Dio Los Angeles 2013. rector@popwh.org

REAT, Lee Anne (SO) 2318 Collins Dr, Worthington OH 43085 **S Jn's Ch Columbus OH 2005-** B Columbus OH 1952 d Albert & Mary. BS Ohio U 1974; MA MI SU 1977; EdD U of Missouri 1987; MDiv Aquinas Coll 1993. D 9/17/1994 Bp Hays H. Rockwell P 5/1/1995 Bp Herbert Thompson Jr. m 8/4/1979 John Bryan Reat c 1. Columbus Comm Mnstrs Columbus OH 1996-2005; Dio Sthrn Ohio Cincinnati OH 1996; Asst R S Pat's Epis Ch Dublin OH 1994-1996.

REBHOLTZ, Brian L (NCal) 79 Denton Rd, Wellesley MA 02482 **P-in-c S Lk's Ch Auburn CA 2015-** B Roseville CA 1984 s David & Deborah. BA U of New Hampshire 2007; MDiv CDSP 2011; MA Grad Theol Un 2011. D 8/30/2011 P 3/26/2012 Bp Vicky Gene Robinson. m 6/5/2010 Catherine Anne Rebholtz c 2. Asst S Andr's Ch Wellesley MA 2011-2015.

RECHTER, Elizabeth I (Los) 2744 Peachtree Rd Nw, Atlanta GA 30305 B Ithaca NY 1960 d Donald & Joan. BS Rutgers The St U of New Jersey 1982; MDiv VTS 1991. D 6/15/1991 Bp Ronald Hayward Haines P 12/1/1991 Bp George Phelps Mellick Belshaw. m 2/5/1983 Jay Rechter c 2. S Mary's Par Laguna Bch CA 2005-2015; Cn Cathd Of S Phil Atlanta GA 1994-2005; Asst Trin Ch Princeton NJ 1991-1994. erechterstillpointca@icloud.com

RECTENWALD, Marion Bridget (SD) 371 New College Dr, Sewanee TN 37375 B Fairmont WV 1949 d James & Helen. BS Wheeling Jesuit U 1971. D 12/27/2002 P 6/6/2003 Bp George Wayne Smith. c 2. Dio So Dakota Pierre SD 2004-2010; S Paul's Epis Ch Sikeston MO 2003-2004.

REDDALL, Jennifer Reddall (NY) 500 E 77th St Apt 1622, New York NY 10162 **P in Charge The Ch Of The Epiph New York NY 2011-, Assoc R 2003-** B Harbor City CA 1975 d Walter & Roberta. BA Ya 1997; MDiv GTS 2002. D 6/29/2002 Bp Robert Marshall Anderson P 1/11/2003 Bp Joseph Jon Bruno. c 1. Cur Ch Of The Epiph Oak Pk CA 2002-2003.

REDDELL, Ronald Kirk (Oly) 910 Harris Ave Unit 408, Bellingham WA 98225 B Everett WA 1948 s Harold & Charlotte. U of St Andrews; AA Skagit Vlly Coll 1970; BA Wstrn Washington U 1972; MDiv Nash 1976. D 7/31/1976 P 6/1/1977 Bp Robert Hume Cochrane. Chapl Whatcom Hospice 1995-2008; Vic Chr Epis Ch Blaine WA 1988-1994; Assoc S Paul Epis Ch Bellingham WA 1986-1988; Chapl Off Of Bsh For ArmdF New York NY 1982-1985; R S Andr's Ch Seattle WA 1979-1981; Assoc Trin Epis Ch Everett WA 1976-1979. Auth, "Liberation Theol & Low Intensity Conflict 86," 1986; Auth, "Bk Revs," 1985; Auth, "Mltry Revs".

REDDIE, Grover Tyrone (Alb) 11192 State Route 9W, Coxsackie NY 12051 B Jamaica 1946 s Caleb & Morgret. BA Untd Theol Coll of W Indies 1997. Trans 11/12/2010 as Priest Bp William Howard Love. m 11/13/1971 Celina V Reddie c 3.

REDDIG, Mike (Cal) 1400 Geary Blvd., #3A, San Francisco CA 94109 B Harvey ND 1946 s Albert & Freda. BA Jamestown Coll 1968; MEd GW 1998; MDiv VTS 2002. Trans 3/20/2003 Bp Peter J Lee. m 7/5/1975 Judith L Reddig c 2. Assoc Cler S Cyp's Ch San Francisco CA 2012-2016; R Chr Epis Ch Great Choptank Par Cambridge MD 2005-2012; Asst R S Ptr's Ch Salisbury MD 2002-2005.

REDDIMALLA, Samuel (NY) 4673 Flatlick Branch Drive, Chantilly VA 20151 B Thadoor IN 1946 s Rajaratnam & Mary. PD Serampore Coll Calcutta IN 1968; BD Untd Theol Coll Bangalore IN 1971; MA Osmania U Hyderabad IN 1977; MTh Asbury TS 1987. Trans 10/9/1999 Bp Rogers Sanders Harris. m 10/23/1974 Dorcas P Reddimalla c 2. S Andr's Ch Beacon NY 2002-2013; P-in-c Dio New York New York NY 2002-2008; R Ch Of The Nativ Maysville KY 1999-2001; P S Martins-In-Fields Summersville WV 1997-1999; Asst Chapl S Aug's Chap Lexington KY 1994-1996; P Ch S Mich The Archangel Lexington KY 1993-1995; Serv Ch of So India 1971-1986.

REDDING, Pamela J (Cal) 2925 Bonifacio Street, Concord CA 94519 B Colorado Springs CO 1950 d Clinton & Dorothy. BA MWC 1972; Cert Shalem Inst Washington DC 1995; MDiv SWTS 1999; DMin 2006. D 7/5/1999 P 1/23/2000 Bp Richard Sui On Chang. R S Mich And All Ang Concord CA 2008-2012; R S Chris-S Paul Epis Ch Detroit MI 2002-2007; Assoc R Par of St Clem Honolulu HI 1999-2002; Campus Mssnr The Epis Ch in Hawaii Honolulu HI 1999-2002; S Andr's Priory Sch Honolulu HI 1999-2001.

REDFIELD, William (CNY) 225 Pelham Rd, Syracuse NY 13214 B Syracuse NY 1948 s William & Jean. BA Trin Hartford CT 1970; MS Bos 1975;

MDiv EDS 1976. D 7/11/1976 P 6/1/1978 Bp Ned Cole. m 5/28/1985 Cathy Dutch. Dio Cntrl New York Liverpool NY 2005; Trin Epis Ch Fayetteville NY 1995-2013, 1994. trinityc@twcny.rr.com

REDMAN, Nolan Bruce (Spok) 3020 E Flintlock Ct, Mead WA 99021 **R St. Andr's Spokane Spokane WA 2003-** B Whittier CA 1939 s Edwin & Thelma. BA Whitworth U 1968; MDiv CDSP 1972. D 12/26/1971 P 7/1/1972 Bp John Raymond Wyatt. m 11/8/2003 Elvira Melendez-Redman c 4. Epis Ch in Almaden San Jose CA 1986-2002; Calv Ch Roslyn WA 1986; Vic Ch Of The Resurr (Chap) So Cle Elum WA 1980-1986; R Gr Ch Ellensburg WA 1975-1986; Vic H Sprt Epis Ch Dover ID 1972-1975; S Mary's Bonners Ferry Bonners Ferr ID 1972-1975.

REDMON, Caroline (Los) 1050 E Ramon Rd Unit 125, Palm Springs CA 92264 B Baltimore MD 1950 d Carroll & Bernice. BS Towson U 1981; MDiv VTS 1987. D 6/20/1987 P 5/14/1988 Bp Albert Theodore Eastman. m 9/17/1999 William Jessie Redmon. Vic S Richard's Epis Ch Skyforest CA 2001-2005; R S Andr's Ch Methuen MA 1999-2001; Assoc Ch Of The Gd Samar San Diego CA 1995-1999; Asst S Jas' Epis Ch Parkton MD 1992-1995; S Jn's Ch Reisterstown MD 1992-1995; Asst Min Emm Ch Baltimore MD 1989-1992; Dio Maryland Baltimore MD 1987-1989; Cur Emm Ch Cumberland MD 1987-1989.

REDMON, William Jessie (Md) 1050 E Ramon Rd Unit 125, Palm Springs CA 92264 **Gr Mssn Moreno Vlly CA 2004-** B Baltimore MD 1932 s John & Myrtle. AA Baltimore Coll of Commerce 1957; BS U of Baltimore 1961; MDiv Bex Sem 1963. D 6/5/1963 P 12/18/1963 Bp Wilburn Camrock Campbell. m 9/17/1999 Caroline Redmon c 3. Assoc Gr Epis Ch Lawr MA 1999-2003; Assoc S Lk's Ch Baltimore MD 1998-1999; Assoc Ch Of S Kath Of Alexandria Baltimore MD 1993-1998; R S Jas' Epis Ch Baltimore MD 1984-1993; S Jas Ch Irvington Baltimore MD 1984-1992; Cur S Mich And All Ang Ch Baltimore MD 1975-1983; R Chr Ch Fairmont WV 1967-1975; Vic Ch Of The Gd Shpd Follansbee WV 1963-1967; Vic Ch of the Gd Shpd WV 1963-1967; Olde S Jn's Ch Colliers WV 1963-1967.

RED OWL, Cordelia (SD) Po Box 354, Porcupine SD 57772 B Kyle SD 1936 d Levi & Sadie. BS Black Hill St U 1958; MS Black Hill St U 1977. D 12/21/1998 P 6/26/2000 Bp Creighton Leland Robertson.

REDPATH, Valerie Jean (NJ) 329 Estate Point Rd, Toms River NJ 08753 **S Jn's Epis Ch Little Silver NJ 2015-** B Brooklyn NY 1950 d Francis & Blanche. BSN Seton Hall U 1972; MDiv GTS 2004. D 6/12/2004 P 1/15/2005 Bp George Edward Councell. m 4/18/1998 Michael Lovell Redpath c 2. R S Jas Ch Long Branch NJ 2007-2015, 2006; Int Ch Of S Mary's By The Sea Pt Pleas Bch NJ 2005. stjohnslittlesilver@verizon.net

REECE, Herbert Anderson (O) 9522 Lincolnwood Dr, Evanston IL 60203 **Ret 1991-** B Elizabeth NJ 1930 s Herbert & Gladys. BS Kent St U 1951; LLB U of Akron 1962; BD EDS 1965. D 6/12/1965 Bp Beverley D Tucker P 2/24/1966 Bp Nelson Marigold Burroughs. m 3/17/1951 Jo Anne Liptak. 1967-1991.

REECE, Jennifer M (Me) 41 Mount Desert St, Bar Harbor ME 04609 B Aberdeen Scotland 1952 d David & Pauline. BA Un Coll 1974; MDiv New Brunswick TS 1987; MDiv New Brunswilk TS 1987; PhD PrTS 2002. D 6/25/2011 P 11/11/2012 Bp Stephen Taylor Lane. S Sav's Par Bar Harbor ME 2014-2015.

REECE, Mark Spencer (SeFla) Iglesia Catedral del Redentor, Calle Beneficencia #18, Madrid 28004 Spain B Hartford CT 1963 s Richard & Loretta. BA Wesl 1985; MA U of York 1987; MTS Harv 1990; MDiv Ya Berk 2011. D 1/26/2011 P 10/2/2011 Bp Leo Frade.

REECE, Nathaniel Treat (Mass) 60 Edward Rd, Raynham MA 02767 B Boston MA 1947 s John & Charlotte. BA U of Pennsylvania 1969; MDiv VTS 1998. Trans 5/7/2002 Bp M(Arvil) Thomas Shaw. Jacksonville Epis HS Jacksonville FL 2008-2009; R Trin Ch Bridgewater MA 2002-2007; Asst R S Ptr's Ch In The Great Vlly Malvern PA 2000-2002.

REECE, Richard Douglas (WVa) 387 Homestead Lane, Romney WV 26757 **Ret 1994-** B Sacramento CA 1931 s Clarence & Evelyn. BA U of Memphis 1961; MDiv Sewanee: The U So, TS 1964. D 6/24/1964 Bp John Vander Horst P 1/6/1965 Bp William Evan Sanders. m 4/26/1989 Linda M Bair. Ther Appalachian Mntl Hlth Prog Elkins WV 1988-1994; Estrn Deanry - Dn Dio W Virginia Charleston WV 1985-1989; Dir Peterkin Conf Cntr Romney WV 1978-1991; S Steph's Ch Romney WV 1978-1990; Peterkin C&C Romney WV 1978-1984; P-in-c Chr Ch Pearisburg VA 1975-1978; 1968-1974; Chapl Sewanee Mltry Acad Sewanee TN 1964-1969; P-in-c S Mk Sewanee TN 1964-1967. Employee of the Year Appalachian Cmnty Hlth Cntr 1991; Psi Chi Memphis St U.

REED, Allan William (Pa) 4270 Biddeford Cir, Doylestown PA 18902 **Died 4/24/2017** B Swanton OH 1929 s John & Nora. BA U of Toledo 1952; MDiv Bex Sem 1955; MA U MI 1961. D 6/18/1955 Bp Nelson Marigold Burroughs P 1/21/1956 Bp Beverley D Tucker. c 3. Ret 1994-2017; Dio New York New York NY 1989-1994; CPE Supvsr S Lk's Hosp NY 1989-1994; S Lk's-Roosevelt Hosp Cntr New York NY 1989-1994; Dir of Pstr Care All SS Hosp Springfield PA 1980-1988; Epis Cmnty Serv Philadelphia PA 1980-1987; S Lk's Epis Hosp Houston TX 1978-1979; Dir CPE S Lk's Hosp Houston TX 1978-1979; CPE Assoc EDS Cambridge MA 1961-1978; Dir of Pstr Care Massachusetts

Gnrl Hosp Boston MA 1961-1977; Vic S Barn' Ch Chelsea MI 1958-1961; Cur Trin Ch Toledo OH 1955-1958; Chapl U of Toledo 1955-1956. Auth, "Problems of Impending Death," *Concerns of the Dying Patient & His Fam.* Dplma Coll Chapl 1976; Life Mem ACPE 1975; NECA 1980. U MI Phi Kappa Phi 1961; U of Toledo Phi Gamma Mu 1952.

REED, Anne L (SO) Diocese of Southern Ohio, 412 Sycamore St., Cincinnati OH 45202 **D Chr Ch - Glendale Cincinnati OH 2017-; D The Soc of the Trsfg Cincinnati OH 2017-; D S Andr's Epis Ch Cincinnati OH 2014-; Chair, TF to Revs Nomination, Election, Trans, Install of PB Dom And Frgn Mssy Soc- Epis Ch Cntr New York NY 2015-, Bd for Transition Mnstry 2010-2015** B Neptune NJ 1956 d William & Ellen. BS Hood Coll 1978; Cert Sewanee: The U So, TS 1984; MTS SWTS 1998. D 6/17/1989 Bp Albert Theodore Eastman. m 9/18/1982 Gifford Edward Blaylock c 1. D Chr Ch Cathd Cincinnati OH 2013-2017; Cn for Mssn Dio Sthrn Ohio Cincinnati OH 2010-2016; D S Lk's Par Kalamazoo MI 2007-2008; Bp's Asst. for Congrl Dev. & Transition Min. Dio Wstrn Michigan Kalamazoo MI 2003-2010; Cohort Fac Bexley Seabury Fed Chicago IL 1999-2012; D S Jas' Epis Ch Baltimore MD 1998-2002; D Cathd Of The Incarn Baltimore MD 1994-1998; Dio Maryland Baltimore MD 1990-1996, 1987-1989; D Imm Epis Ch Glencoe MD 1989-1993. Contrib, "Beginning Mnstry Together," Alb Inst, 2002. NAAD 1987-1996. anne.ctretreats@gmail.com

REED, Bobette P (O) Deer Hill Rr#1, East Hampton CT 06424 **D 1977-** B Cleveland OH 1951 d Robert & Mary. BA Wms 1973; MDiv Harvard DS 1976. D 1/6/1977 Bp John Harris Burt. m 8/22/1980 Jeffrey St.

REED, C Davies (Ind) St. Christopher's Church, 1402 W. Main Street, Carmel IN 46032 **S Fran In The Fields Zionsville IN 2011-** B Bloomington IN 1962 s William & Martha. BA Wabash Coll 1986; MDiv SWTS 2007. D 6/23/2007 Bp Cate Waynick P 9/27/2008 Bp William Edward Smalley. m 6/17/2006 Carol C Rogers. Assoc R S Chris's Epis Ch Carmel IN 2007-2010.

REED, Craig Andrew (Dal) 9714 Lanward Dr, Dallas TX 75238 **Ch Of The H Cross Paris TX 2016-** B Marshall MI 1960 s Clyde & Elizabeth. MDiv Nash 1982; BS SW U Georgetown TX 1982. D 12/27/1989 P 6/28/1990 Bp Clarence Cullam Pope Jr. m 9/4/1982 Karen Reed c 1. Dio Dallas Dallas TX 2006; Pension Fund Mltry New York NY 2006; Spec Mobilization Spprt Plan Washington DC 2006; S Andr's Ch Dallas TX 2004-2016; Ch Of The Incarn Dallas TX 1998-2003; Dio Ft Worth Ft Worth TX 1997-1998; Vic S Anth's Ch Alvarado TX 1997-1998; Ch Of The H Cross Burleson TX 1995-1997; R S Andr's Ch Breckenridge TX 1992-1995; Cur Ch Of The H Apos Ft Worth TX 1990-1991.

✠ REED, The Rt Rev David (Ky) 5226 Moccasin Trl, Louisville KY 40207 B Tulsa OK 1927 s Paul & Bonnie. MDiv VTS 1951; AB Harv 2048. D 7/3/1951 Bp Clinton Simon Quin P 2/14/1952 Bp Reginald Heber Gooden Con 4/25/1964 for Colom. m 4/15/1984 Catherine Luckett c 4. Prov Coordntr, Chapl to Ret Prov IV 2003-2008; Chapl to Ret Cler S Matt's Epis Ch Louisville KY 2000-2013; Exec Secy Global Epis Mssn Ntwk Louisville KY 1998-1999; Asst Bp Dio Connecticut Meriden CT 1994-1995; Chair, PBp's Advsry Comm on Interfaith Rel Epis Ch Cntr New York NY 1992-1997, Asst to Dir of Ovrs Dept 1958-1991; Pres KY Coun Ch 1988-1991; Angl/Orth Theol Consult 1984-1990; Bp of Kentucky Dio Kentucky Louisville KY 1974-1994, Bp Coadj 1972-1974; ARC-USA 1973-1983; Pres Angl Coun Latin Amer 1969-1971; Exec Secy Evang Assn Colom Indns 1968-1971; Trst ETSC 1965-1969; Bp Dio Colombia Bogota 1964-1972; Bp-in-charge Dio Ecuador 1964-1970; Vic S Matt's Epis Ch Rapid City SD 1962-1964; Archd of Colombia Ch in Colombia Bogota: Cali Medellin 1952-1958; D in Charge Ch of the Gd Shpd San Jose Costa Rica 1951-1952; Rgnt Sewanee U So TS Sewanee TN 1977-1981. DD ETSKy Lexington KY 1982; DD U So Sewanee TN 1972; DD VTS Alexandria VA 1964.

✠ REED, The Rt Rev David Mitchell (WTex) P. O. Box 6885, San Antonio TX 78209 **Bp Suffr of W Texas Dio W Texas San Antonio TX 2006-; Bd Mem Texas Conf of Ch Austin Tx 2009-; Trst Epis TS Of The SW Austin TX 2008-** B Brownsville TX 1957 s William & Olive. BJ w/hon U of Texas 1978; MDiv Epis TS of the SW 1983. D 6/12/1983 Bp Stanley Fillmore Hauser P 1/13/1984 Bp Scott Field Bailey Con 8/26/2006 for WTex. m 6/18/1988 Patricia Reed c 2. R S Alb's Ch Harlingen TX 1994-2006, Asst R 1983-1987, Asst R 1983-1987; R S Fran Epis Ch Victoria TX 1987-1994. Bp Elliott Soc 2006. DD Epis TS of the SW 2008. david.reed@dwtx.org

REED, Elizabeth H (Be) 108 N 5th St, Allentown PA 18102 B Allentown PA 1962 d Melvin & Dorothy. BA DeSales U 1984; MA The CUA 1987; MDiv VTS 2009. D 6/6/2009 Bp Peter J Lee P 12/6/2009 Bp Shannon Sherwood Johnston. m 4/20/1996 Jeffrey Jamison Reed c 2. P-in-c Gr Epis Ch Allentown PA 2010-2014.

REED, Harold Vincent (Alb) 1718 Guilderland Ave, Schenectady NY 12306 B Chicago IL 1958 s Harold & Albina. AA Nthrn Virginia Cmnty Coll 1987; BA Geo Mason U 1988; VTS 1989; MDiv Nash 1992. D 12/19/1992 Bp William Charles Wantland P 6/19/1993 Bp Charles Thomas Gaskell. m 10/18/2008 Stephanie Reed. R S Paul's Ch Schenectady NY 1999-2017; S Geo's Epis Ch Schenectady NY 1992-1999. CBS; ESA; Forw In Faith 1999; GAS; SocMary; SSC 1993.

REED SR, James A (WVa) 884 6th Street Hill, Newell WV 26050 **Vic S Matt's Ch Chester WV 1986-** B Chester WV 1934 s Arthur & Mary. TESM. D 6/5/1985 Bp Robert Poland Atkinson P 6/1/1986 Bp William Franklin Carr. m 8/8/1965 Phyllis Jean Carman c 1. Assoc Chr Ch Wellsburg WV 1998-2006; Assoc Olde S Jn's Ch Colliers WV 1998-2006; Upper Hancock Cnty Ministerial Assn.

REED, James Gardner (EC) PO Box 985, Washington DC 27889 **R S Ptr's Epis Ch Washington NC 2017-, P-in-c 2015-2016** B Topeka KS 1954 s Richard & Elizabeth. BS MI SU 1977; MDiv Gordon-Conwell TS 1984. D 6/12/1993 P 12/15/1993 Bp Peter J Lee. c 3. S Paul's Epis Ch Edenton NC 2013-2015; R Ch Of The Mssh Fredericksbrg VA 1995-2013; Vic Ch of the Incarn Mineral VA 1993-1995. BSA.

REED, Jeffrey Bruce (Az) Po Box 42618, Tucson AZ 85733 B 1955 s Robert & Anna. BA New Coll of California; Tcjc Sch of Nrsng Ft Worth TX 1981; MDiv CDSP 2002. D 6/1/2002 P 12/7/2002 Bp William Edwin Swing. Dio Arizona Phoenix AZ 2003-2006; The Edge Chr Campus Cntr San Francisco CA 2002-2003.

REED, Juan Y (Chi) 1617 E 50th Place, Apt 4D, Chicago IL 60615 B Chicago IL 1947 s Earl & Lula. BA H Redeem Coll 1972; MSW Loyola U Chicago 1981; MDiv SWTS 1991; DMin Cath Theol Un at Chicago 2004; DMin Cath Theol Un at Chicago 2004. Rec 7/1/1991 as Priest Bp Frank Tracy Griswold III. S Geo/S Mths Ch Chicago IL 2011-2013; Cathd Of S Jas Chicago IL 2010-2012; S Mart's Ch Chicago IL 1991-2010; Serv RC Ch 1976-1990. juan-reed@att.net

REED, Loreen Hayward Rogers (At) 355 Porter St, Madison GA 30650 **R Ch Of The Medtr Washington GA 2012-** B Jersey City NJ 1944 d Bernard & Doris. Columbia TS; BA Connecticut Coll 1966; MDiv Candler TS Emory U 1997. D 6/7/1997 Bp Onell Asiselo Soto P 12/1/1997 Bp Frank Kellogg Allan. m 6/20/1964 Walter Logan Reed c 3. Actg R St. Greg the Great Epis Ch Athens GA 2012; R The Epis Ch Of The Adv Madison GA 2003-2010; Asst R H Innoc Ch Atlanta GA 2001-2003; Asst S Julian's Epis Ch Douglasville GA 2000; Asst R S Jos's Epis Ch Mcdonough GA 1997-1998.

REED JR, Poulson (Az) 6300 N Central Ave, Phoenix AZ 85012 **R All SS Ch Phoenix AZ 2002-** B Richmond VA 1970 s Poulson & Nancy. BA U of Virginia 1992; MFA U of Utah 1994; MDiv Yale DS 1997. D 6/8/2002 Bp Andrew Donnan Smith P 1/18/2003 Bp William Jerry Winterrowd. m 11/20/2004 Megan Reed c 3. Cn S Jn's Cathd Denver CO 2002-2009.

REED, Richard Wayne (RG) Hc 31 Box 17-B, Las Vegas NM 87701 B Marshalltown IA 1938 s Wayne & Hazel. BA New Mex Highlands U 1964; MS Florida St U 1969. D 8/27/1986 Bp Richard Mitchell Trelease Jr P 6/1/1988 Bp William Davidson. m 1/2/1965 Lucy M Everrett. R S Paul's Peace Ch Las Vegas NM 2001-2010, P 1986-2000; P-in-c H Trin Epis Ch - Mssn Raton NM 1995-2001.

REED, Robert Cooper (NwPa) 105 Waugh Ave Unit 1106, New Wilmington PA 16142 **D Trin Ch New Castle PA 1966-** B New Castle PA 1928 s Jay & Jessie. BS Grove City Coll 1950; DDS U Pgh 1954; DMD U Pgh 1970. D 12/18/1966 Bp William Crittenden. m 6/28/1952 Esther Elizabeth Lindstrom c 4.

REED, Ronald Lind (Kan) 4810 W 67th St, Prairie Village KS 66208 B Ashland KS 1946 s Donald & Lydia. BA U of Oklahoma 1968; Mdiv EDS 1971; BD EDS 1971. D 6/29/1971 P 9/16/1972 Bp Chilton R Powell. m 6/15/1999 Catherine Reed. Vic S Paul's Ch Kansas City KS 2003-2010; R S Jas Ch Wichita KS 1991-2001; Dir of Stwdshp and Dvlpmt Epis Ch Cntr New York NY 1984-1991; Dir Off Stwdshp Educ & Coordntr Ord Process Dio Pennsylvania Philadelphia PA 1982-1984, Yth Mnstry Com Chair 1972-1982, Vice Chair of Stndg Cmsn on Salaries and Pensions 1975-1982; R Chr Ch And S Mich's Philadelphia PA 1975-1982; Asst S Thos' Ch Whitemarsh Ft Washington PA 1971-1974; Bd Mem Epis Cmnty Serv Kansas City MO 2002-2010; Stwdshp Com Dio Kansas Topeka KS 1991-2002. Auth, "The Stewards' Count," The Epis Ch Cntr, 1985. Apos of Stwdshp The Epis Ntwk for Stwdshp at GC 2009.

REED, Stephen K (Ak) 1722 Linden St, Longmont CO 80501 B Watertown NY 1966 s James & Itha. MDiv Epis TS of the SW; Icisf Baltimore MD; BS Utica Coll. D 6/9/2001 P 12/2/2001 Bp William Jerry Winterrowd. m 10/21/1995 Laura J Reed c 2. Vic Prince Of Peace Epis Ch Sterling CO 2003-2010; Cur S Steph's Ch Longmont CO 2001-2003.

REED, Thomas Louis (Pa) 16 Nestlenook Dr, Middleboro MA 02346 B Tulsa OK 1947 s Thomas & Faye. U of Tulsa 1966; BA Oklahoma Bapt U 1969; MDiv SW Bapt TS 1973; Cert Virginia Commonwealth U 1975; Oxf UK 1976. D 5/22/1976 Bp John Alfred Baden P 6/25/1977 Bp Robert Bruce Hall. R St Pauls Ch Philadelphia PA 1982-1992; R Chr Epis Ch Spotsylvania VA 1976-1981; Chapl Med Coll Richmond VA 1974-1975. Biblic Archeological Soc 1970.

REEDER, Thomas Parnell (Fla) 400 San Juan Dr, Ponte Vedra FL 32082 **Assoc Chr Epis Ch Ponte Vedra FL 2013-** B Silver Spring MD 1969 BA U CA 2000; MDiv Sewanee: The U So, TS 2003. D 6/1/2003 Bp Jerry Alban Lamb P 12/7/2003 Bp Stephen Hays Jecko. m 8/11/1990 Deeann Marie Reeder c 2. R Chr Epis Ch Williamsport PA 2005-2013; P-in-c S Mk's Epis Ch Jacksonville FL 2003-2005, Assoc R 2003-2004; D The Epis Dio Nthrn California Sacramento CA 2003; Stndg Com Dio Cntrl Pennsylvania Harrisburg PA 2011-2013.

REEMAN, Karen Baehr (NJ) 69 Broad St, Eatontown NJ 07724 B Danville IL 1956 d George & Melany. MM Chicago Mus Coll 1982; MA Indiana U 1988. D 5/9/2015 Bp William H Stokes. m 3/17/1992 Christopher B Reeman c 2.

REES, Donald Joseph (SJ) 12358 Newport Rd, Ballico CA 95303 **D S Fran' Epis Ch Turlock CA 1996-** B 1925 s Joseph & Susan. D 6/8/1996 Bp David Mercer Schofield. m 2/13/1982 Mary Maddux c 1.

REES, Elizabeth (Va) 1501 River Farm Dr, Alexandria VA 22308 **Assoc R S Aid's Ch Alexandria VA 2007-** B Baltimore MD 1972 d Charles & Patricia. BA Wake Forest U 1994; JD Emory U Atlanta GA 1997; MDiv VTS 2007. D 6/16/2007 Bp Peter J Lee P 12/17/2007 Bp David Colin Jones. m 9/2/2001 Holden Hoofnagle c 2.

REES, Emily Frances (At) Po Box 223, Braselton GA 30517 B Atlanta GA 1946 d Arthur & Emily. D 8/6/2006 Bp J Neil Alexander. c 2.

REESE, Carol Sue (Chi) 1525 W Birchwood Ave, Chicago IL 60626 B St Louis MO 1956 d William & Katharine. BA Georgetown Coll 1978; MDiv Sthrn Bapt TS 1981; MSW U IL 1984; Cert Ang Stud SWTS 2009. D 6/5/2010 P 12/3/2010 Bp Jeff Lee. c 2.

REESE, Donnis Jean (EMich) 200 E Page St, Rose City MI 48654 B Sioux Falls SD 1946 d Daniel & Bernice. BA Sioux Falls U 1977; PhD U of So Dakota 1981; Ecum Theol 1995; Cert in Angl Stds Seabury 2013. D 6/9/2013 P 5/4/2014 Bp Steven Todd Ousley. c 2. D S Andr's Epis Ch Rose City MI 2013-2016.

REESE, Frederic William (Miss) 373 Edenbrook, Brookhaven MO 39601 **Ret 1994-** B Pleasantville NJ 1933 s Franklin & Catherine. BA Merc 1960; MDiv Epis TS in Kentucky 1964. D 5/30/1964 P 12/13/1964 Bp William R Moody. c 2. Assoc Ch Of The Gd Shpd Tomball TX 1999-2003; Vic Ch Of The Redeem Brookhaven MS 1982-1993; Vic Calv Ch Michigan City MS 1978-1982; R Chr Ch Holly Sprg MS 1978-1982; R Ch Of The Gd Samar Knoxville TN 1972-1978; R S Steph Red Sprg NC 1967-1972; R Trin Ch Lumberton NC 1967-1972; R S Thos Ch Beattyville KY 1964-1967.

REESE, Jeannette Ellis (WNC) 45 Spooks Branch Extension, Asheville NC 28804 **D Gr Ch Asheville NC 2009-** B Charleston SC 1945 d Daniel & Anna. BA Queens Coll 1967. D 5/29/1993 Bp Harry Woolston Shipps. m 4/30/1994 Robert Emory Reese c 2. D S Thos Epis Ch Burnsville NC 2007-2008; S Jn's Ch Sylva NC 2006-2007; D S Andr's Ch Darien NC 1999-2004; D S Mk's Ch Brunswick GA 1993-1998.

REESE, John (SwFla) 509 E Twiggs St, Tampa FL 33602 **R S Andr's Epis Ch Tampa FL 2005-** B Passaic NJ 1961 s Arthur & Rose. BA U CO 1986; MDiv VTS 1997. D 6/7/1997 Bp William Jerry Winterrowd P 12/13/1997 Bp David Charles Bowman. m 11/1/1986 Jeanette M Reese c 1. R Trin Epis Ch Fredonia NY 1997-2005.

REESE, John Victor (Ark) 406 W Central Ave, Bentonville AR 72712 B Milwaukee WI 1945 s Harry & Marion. BBA Marq 1968; MSM Cardinal Stritch U 1982; Cert Pstr Stds St Fran Sem 2006. D 6/15/2013 Bp Steven Andrew Miller. m 8/2/1992 Sandra Wilke c 2.

REESE, Judith Foster (WTenn) 800 Rountree Avenue, Kinston NC 28501 **S Mary's Ch Kinston NC 2016-** B Searcy AR 1950 d James & Janie. BS U of Alabama Birmingham 1976; MPH U of Alabama Birmingham 1981; MDiv Memphis TS 1999; Sewanee: The U So, TS 2010. D 1/14/2012 P 7/21/2012 Bp Don Edward Johnson. m 12/9/1989 David Keith Reese c 1. Chr Epis Ch Bowling Green KY 2015-2016; H Trin Epis Ch Fayetteville NC 2014-2015; Dio W Tennessee Memphis 2013-2014; S Elis's Epis Ch Memphis TN 2012-2013. reesejmf@gmail.com

REESE, Mary (EC) 404 E. New Hope Rd., Goldsboro NC 27534 **P-in-c S Andr's Ch Goldsboro NC 2010-; Search and Nomin Com for 8th Bp Dioc Dio E Carolina Kinston NC 2013-, Disciplinary Bd 2011-, COM 2010-, Liturg Cmsn 2009-2011, COM 2009-, Dominican Republic Comp Dio Cmsn 2009-, Comp Dio Com 2008-2011, Trin Cntr Bd Dir 2004-2007** B Brooklyn NY 1946 d William & Mary. BS Cor 1967; MS Syr 1969; MDiv VTS 2008. D 6/14/2008 P 2/21/2009 Bp Clifton Daniel III. c 6.

REESE, Robert Emory (WNC) 45 Spooks Branch Ext, Asheville NC 28804 **Assoc Gr Ch Asheville NC 2010-** B Asheville,NC 1949 s Robert & Ora. BA U So 1971; MDiv VTS 1974; CPE Intern Year Pstr Inst Ft Benning GA 1984; DMin VTS 1998. D 6/22/1974 Bp Matthew George Henry P 6/21/1975 Bp William Gillette Weinhauer. m 4/30/1994 Jeannette Ellis Reese c 2. Int S Thos Epis Ch Burnsville NC 2007-2008; Int S Jn's Ch Sylva NC 2005-2006, P-in-c 1974-2005; S Andr's Ch Darien GA 1999-2004; S Cyp's Ch Darien GA 1999-2004; S Mk's Ch Brunswick GA 1990-1999; Off Of Bsh For ArmdF New York NY 1981-1989; Chapl US-A 1981-1989; Conf Cntr Bd Chairman Dio Georgia Savannah GA 1999-2004, Stndg Com 1999-2003. ACPE 1989-1998. Paul Harris Fell Intl Rotary 2003.

REESE, Thomas Francis (LI) 141 Ascan Ave, Forest Hills NY 11375 **R S Lk's Ch Forest Hills NY 2000-; Dn of Forest Pk Dnry Dio Long Island Garden City NY 2015-, Chairperson of COM 2006-2008, COM 2004-2008, Trst of the Estate 1998-1999; Cnvnr Interfaith Cmnty of Forest Hills New York 2013-** B Bayshore NY 1953 s Thomas & Joan. BA Colg 1975; MDiv EDS 1979; MA The Grad Cntr of CUNY 2011. D 6/2/1979 P 10/18/1980 Bp Wilbur

Emory Hogg Jr. m 11/19/2013 Yin-Wei Liao c 2. R S Ann's Epis Ch Bridge-hampton NY 1992-2000; R Ch Of The H Adv Clinton CT 1988-1992; Assoc R S Paul's Epis Ch Albany NY 1982-1988; Chair of the Rel Dept Doane Stuart Sch 1980-1982; Chapl Doane Stuart Sch Albany NY 1980-1982; Pres of Metropltn Dnry Dio Albany Greenwich NY 1985-1987.

REESON, Geoffrey Douglas (EcuC) Casilla 17-16-95, Quito Ecuador **P-in-c Capellania Mssn 1977-** B Barranquilla CO 1948 s William & Marjory. BS U of The W Indies 1972; MDiv ETSC 1976. D 10/17/1976 P 4/17/1977 Bp William Alfred Franklin. m 5/19/1974 Marta Lidia Revelo c 2. Adv-S Nich Ch Quito 2002-2006; Iglesia Epis Del Ecuador Quito 1987-2002; Iglesia Epis En Colombia Bogota 1978-1987.

REESON, Marta Lidia (EcuC) Casilla 17-16-95, Quito Ecuador B Ecuador 1947 d Segundo & Clementina. Universidad Cntrl del Ecuador; MDiv Seminario Epis del Caribe 1976. D 2/18/2011 Bp Luis Fernando Ruiz Restrepo. m 5/19/1974 Geoffrey Douglas Reeson c 2. Iglesia Epis Del Ecuador Quito 2011.

REEVE, Keith John (NC) 3613 Clifton Ct, Raleigh NC 27604 **Ret 1990-; Ret 1990-** B Ipswich England UK 1930 s Wilfred & Amy. Lic VTS 1967. D 6/29/1967 P 1/6/1968 Bp Thomas H Wright. m 6/5/1954 Carmen Reeve c 5. S Tim's Ch Wilson NC 1989-1990; Chr Ch Rocky Mt NC 1988-1989; Int Dio No Carolina Raleigh NC 1987-1990; Trin Ch Scotland Neck NC 1987-1988; S Mk's Epis Ch Raleigh NC 1970-1986; Asst H Trin Epis Ch Fayetteville NC 1967-1970.

REEVE, Susan Margaret (NCal) 146 Saint Gertrude Ave, Rio Vista CA 94571 **D S Brigid's Epis Ch Rio Vista CA 2004-** B Bishop's Stortford UK 1945 d Leonard & Nellie. BA U of Durham GB 1967; MLS U CA 1976; BA Sch for Deacons 1999. D 11/20/1999 Bp Jerry Alban Lamb. D S Paul's Epis Ch Benicia CA 1999-2004. Assn for Epis Deacons [was NAAD] 1997.

REEVES, Bernice Brysch (WTex) **Partnr In Mnstry Estrn Convoc Kenedy TX 2016-** D 11/29/2015 Bp Gary Richard Lillibridge P 6/14/2016 Bp David Mitchell Reed.

REEVES JR, C(Harles) Edward (Ala) 4015 Knollwood Dr., Birmingham AL 35243 **Died 12/30/2015** B Sandersville GA 1926 s Charles & Pauline. BA Emory U 1949; BD Candler TS Emory U 1952; U So 1961. D 6/11/1961 P 1/13/1962 Bp Randolph R Claiborne. m 3/11/1956 Darline Jackson Grace Darline Jackson c 2. Epis Ch Of The Epiph Leeds AL 2001-2002; Ch Of The Epiph Guntersville AL 2000; Chr Ch Tuscaloosa AL 1998; Ret 1994-2015; Int Dn Cathd Adv 1994-1995; Vice Dn The Cathd Ch Of The Adv Birmingham AL 1988-1995; Dn S Mary's Cathd Memphis TN 1974-1988; R S Paul's Ch Augusta GA 1963-1974; Cn Cathd Of S Phil Atlanta GA 1961-1963.

REEVES, Daniel John (NC) 1737 Hillandale Rd, Durham NC 27705 B Oklahoma City OK 1987 s Donald & Valerie. BA Oklahoma Bapt U 2009; BA Oklahoma Bapt U 2009; MA Duke 2011; MA Duke 2011; Dplma in Angl Stds VTS 2015. D 6/20/2015 Bp Michael B Curry P 12/20/2015 Bp Anne Hodges-Copple. m 11/3/2013 Krysta Marie Marie Gougler Gougler-Reeves. S Lk's Epis Ch Durham NC 2015-2017. djreeves00@gmail.com

REEVES, Diane Delafield (Fla) 13588 Northeast 247th Lane, Box 18, Orange Springs FL 32182 **Vic-unpaid S Andr's Ch Interlachen FL 2000-** B Newton MA 1944 d Gordon & Barbara. D 12/1/1999 P 6/1/2000 Bp Stephen Hays Jecko. m 11/23/1968 Ralph Harold Reeves. standint@windstream.net

REEVES, Frank B (FtW) 2204 Collington Dr, Roanoke TX 76262 B Seattle WA 1942 s Hume & Virginia. BS Texas A&M U 1970; MS Texas A&M U 1971; Lic Sacr Theol Angl TS 1980. D 6/28/1980 Bp Archibald Donald Davies P 11/28/1981 Bp Robert Elwin Terwilliger. m 4/25/1964 Susan Reeves c 2. R S Mart In The Fields Ch Keller TX 1989-2007, Vic 1985-1989; Asst S Chris's Ch And Sch Ft Worth TX 1981-1985; Cur Chr The King Epis Ch Ft Worth TX 1980-1981. Auth, "Perceptual Narrowing as a Function of Peripheral Cue Relevance," *Journ of Peripheral & Motor Skille,* 1971.

REEVES, Jack William (LI) 23 Old Mamaroneck Rd Apt 5R, White Plains NY 10605 B Crawford NE 1940 s Harry & Mildred. BA U of Missouri 1962; BD Nash 1965. D 2/6/1965 P 8/1/1965 Bp Edward Randolph Welles II. R Gr Epis Ch Whitestone NY 1984-2001; R All SS' Epis Ch Long Island City NY 1979-1983; Chr Ch Epis Hudson NY 1975-1979; Vic S Lk's Epis Ch Excelsior Sprg MO 1966-1970; Cur S Paul's Ch Kansas City MO 1965-1966. ESA.

REEVES, Jess L (SeFla) 8619 North Liston Avenue, Kansas City MO 64154 B Pine Bluff AR 1952 s Jess & Elizabeth. BA W&L 1975; MDiv TESM 1987. D 8/24/1987 P 3/1/1988 Bp Bob Gordon Jones. Otey Memi Par Ch Sewanee TN 2013-2015; S Mich And All Ang Savannah GA 2012-2013; Ch Of The Redeem Kansas City MO 2009-2011; S Ptr's Ch Columbia TN 2007-2009; Int S Thos Orange VA 2006-2008; S Thos Epis Ch Orange VA 2006-2007; Assoc for Educ Beth-by-the-Sea Palm Bch FL 1999-2006; The Epis Ch Of Beth-By-The-Sea Palm Bch FL 1999-2004; S Jn's Epis Ch Niantic CT 1998-1999; S Fran Ch Potomac MD 1990-1998; R Ch Of The H Comm Rock Sprg WY 1989-1990; S Geo's Ch Lusk WY 1987-1989. IMN 1995.

REEVES, Robin K (Tex) 523 E 4th St, Tyler TX 75701 **S Geo's Epis Ch Texas City TX 2011-** B Lamesa TX 1962 d Billy & Patricia. BBA U of No Texas 1984; MDiv Epis TS of the SW 2006; MDiv Epis TS of the SW 2006. D 6/24/2006 Bp Don Adger Wimberly P 1/8/2007 Bp Rayford Baines High Jr. Dio

Texas Houston TX 2011; S Lk's Epis Hosp Houston TX 2010-2011; S Jas The Apos Epis Ch Conroe TX 2009-2010; Asst Trin Epis Ch The Woodlands TX 2008-2009; Cur/Asst R Chr Epis Ch Tyler TX 2006-2008.

REEVES JR, William (Va) The Collegiate Schools, Richmond VA 23229 **Headmaster Boys' Sch 1976-** B Southport CT 1934 s William & Elizabeth. BA Ya 1956; MA Harv 1960; Ya Berk 1961; MDiv EDS 1963. D 6/11/1963 Bp Walter H Gray P 4/1/1964 Bp Harry Sherbourne Kennedy. m 2/22/1963 Jane Anne Reeves. S Thos' Ch Richmond VA 2000-2001; Ch Of The Creator Mechanicsvlle VA 1997-1998; S Jn's Ch Richmond VA 1996-1997; All SS Ch Richmond VA 1981-1993; Collgt Schools Richmond VA 1977-1980; Chatham Hall Chatham VA 1971-1977; R Chatham Hall VA 1971-1976; P-in-c S Mk's Ch Honolulu HI 1969-1970; Assoc Vic Waikiki Chap Honolulu HI 1965-1968; Dir Of Admsns Iolani Sch Honolulu HI 1964-1970; S Alb's Chap Honolulu HI 1964-1965; Chair Of The Dept Of Rel Iolani Sch Honolulu HI 1963-1966. Auth, "Sino-Amer Coopration In Med:The Origins Of Hsiang-Ya".

REGAN, Thomas Francis (SD) 708 Sawyer St, Lead SD 57754 B Deadwood SD 1950 s Jack & June. Black Hill St U 1975; EFM Sewanee: The U So, TS 1989; EFM Sewanee: The U So, TS 1995; Niobrara Sum Sem 2000. D 12/15/1991 Bp Craig Barry Anderson. m 8/24/1969 Diana Regan c 2. NAAD.

REGAS, George Frank (Los) 807 Las Palmas Rd., Pasadena CA 91105 **Chair Of The Econ Dvlpmt Corp 1970-** B Knoxville TN 1930 s Frank & Edith. BA U of Tennessee 1953; MDiv EDS 1956; U of Cambridge 1957; Claremont TS 1972; EDS 1992. D 7/25/1956 Bp Theodore N Barth P 6/1/1957 Bp John Vander Horst. m 1/16/1977 Mary McCaslin Regas c 3. 1982-1985; Natl Bte 1971-1976; 1969-1972; R All SS Ch Pasadena CA 1967-1995, 1967-; Peace Advsry Com ECEC 1962-1967; R Gr Epis Ch Nyack NY 1960-1967; P-in-c The Epis Ch Of The Mssh Pulaski TN 1957-1960; Chair Of The Natl Cltn Of Ord Wmn; Regas Inst; Chair - Com Dio Los Angeles Los Angeles CA 1987-1995, Chair - Com 1973-1986; Bp'S Advsry Com On Ch And Race Dio New York New York NY 1963-1964. Auth, "Kiss Yourself & Hug The Wrld". Kilgore Awd & Lectrs For Creative Mnstry; Awd Soc Justice B'Nai B'Rith; Humanitarian Awd La Cnty Pyschol Assn.

REGEN, Catharine Louise Emmert (Tenn) 306 Broadview Dr, Dickson TN 37055 **Ret Dickson TN 2008-** B Indianapolis IN 1931 d James & Bernice. U So; BA Indiana U 1953; MA Van 1955; Sewanee: The U So, TS 1990; MDiv Van 1990. D 6/9/1991 Bp George Lazenby Reynolds Jr P 3/1/1992 Bp William Evan Sanders. m 11/26/1959 Barney Brooks Regen c 2. Co-Cnvnr, NW Convoc Dio Tennessee Nashville TN 1994-1996; Vic Calv Epis Ch Cumberland Furnace TN 1992-2008; S Tim Epis Ch Erin TN 1992-2005. Woodrow Wilson Fllshp Van 1959; Ford Fndt Fllshp Van 1955.

REGISFORD, Sylvanus Hermus Alonzo (SeFla) 7580 Derby Ln, Shakopee MN 55379 B 1941 s David & Myrtle. U Tor; BD Codrington Coll 1965; NMIN Intl Sem 1982; DMin Intl Sem 1983. Trans 1/7/1981 as Priest Bp Calvin Onderdonk Schofield Jr. Ch Of S Chris Ft Lauderdale FL 1981-1998; S Phil's Ch Pompano Bch FL 1981-1998; R Gr Riviere S Lucia 1979-1980; R S Steph's 8 Mile Rock Bahamas 1975-1978. CBS.

REGIST, Antonio Alberto (WTex) 1310 Pecan Valley Dr, Antonio TX 78210 **Mem Epis Dio W- Texas Recon Committe 2009-; Chapl Red Cross San Antonio Texas Vol 2005-** B 1954 s Ernel & Doris. AA Panama Canal/Canal Zone Coll 1980; BS Nova SE U 1982; Cert Centro de Estudios Cristianos de la Iglesia Epis Panama 2000; Cert Centro de Estudios Cristianos de la Iglesia Epis Panama 2000; Cert Epis TS of the SW 2003; MDiv Oblate TS 2005; Cert CPE 2006. Trans 4/24/2008 as Priest Bp Gary Richard Lillibridge. m 7/3/1982 Felmina Regist c 3. R S Phil's Ch San Antonio TX 2009-2012; Chapl Audie L. Murphy Veterans Affrs Hosp San Antonio TX 2008-2009; Stff Cler St. Margarets Epis Ch San Antonio TX 2005-2009; Res Chapl Kerrville VA Hosp San Antonio TX 2005-2006; D- Pstr Santa Fe Epis Ch San Antonio TX 2002-2003; D San Juan Villa Caceres Panama Rep Panama 2000-2001; Rep Dist 1 MEBA (Marine Engr) Washington D.C. 1990-2001; Chairman Comp Dio Com Panama to Ms./Ar./Maine 1988-2000; Ret Chf Engr Untd States Fed Goverment -Panama Canal 1973-1999. Marine Engr- hon Panama Nautical Acad 2001; Fr of the year Altamira Club Panama, Panama 1999.

REHAGEN, Gerry (EMich) 2093 Michaywe Dr, Gaylord MI 49735 B Jefferson City MO 1938 s Henry & Alma. BA Cardinal Glennon Coll 1960; MA Kenrickglennon Sem 1964; S Louis U 1976. Rec 3/14/1987 Bp Donald Maynard Hultstrand. m 5/22/1976 M Donnellan Rehagen c 2. R S Andr's Epis Ch Gaylord MI 1999-2009; P Dio Springfield Springfield IL 1987-1998.

REHBERG, Gloria Irene (RG) 7104 Montano Rd Nw, Albuquerque NM 87120 **D Dio The Rio Grande Albuquerque 1992-, D 1985-1991** B Albuquerque NM 1934 d Leonard & Irene. BA U of New Mex 1982. D 6/26/1985 Bp Richard Mitchell Trelease Jr. m 9/19/1953 Charles Ray Rehberg c 1. D All SS Ch Milan NM 1989-1992. Auth, "Faith & Obedience," Creative Designs, 1998.

✠ **REHBERG, The Rt Rev Dr Gretchen** (Spok) 245 E 13th Ave, 731 E 8th Ave, Spokane WA 99202 B Pullman WA 1964 d Wallace & Margaret. BS U So 1986; PhD U MN 1990; MDiv GTS 2002; D.Min. Wesley TS 2014. D 6/8/2002 P 2/13/2003 Bp Michael Whittington Creighton Con 3/18/2017 for Spok. R Epis Ch of the Nativ Lewiston ID 2006-2017; Asst The Epis Ch Of S Jn The

Bapt York PA 2002-2005; Cn for Reg Mssn Dio Spokane Spokane WA 2011-2017, COM chair 2006-2017; Commitee on Sci, Tech and Faith Exec Coun Appointees New York NY 2009-2012. gretchenr@spokanediocese.org

REHO, James Hughes (SwFla) Lamb Of God Episcopal Church, 19691 Cypress View Dr, Fort Myers FL 33967 **Lamb Of God Epis Ch Ft Myers FL 2013-** B New York City NY 1969 s George & Barbara. BA S Johns U 1990; BS Wag 1994; MA Pr 1996; PhD Pr 2000; MDiv GTS 2008. D 6/14/2008 Bp Clifton Daniel III P 12/20/2008 Bp Leo Frade. m 11/9/1996 Carolanne C Reho. Chapl and Dir of Pstr Care, Deploy, and Formation; Dir of Theol Field Educ The GTS New York NY 2011-2013; Asst Trin Cathd Miami FL 2008-2011. reho@gts.edu

REICH, Jeffrey Walker (Miss) 834 N. 5th Ave, laurel MS 39440 **R S Jn's Ch Laurel MS 2008-** B Rome CA 1972 BS Mississippi St U; MDiv SWTS 2004. D 6/19/2004 P 12/21/2004 Bp Duncan Montgomery Gray III. m 12/13/1997 Catharine Bennett Reich c 3. Vic S Jn's Ch Aberdeen MS 2004-2008.

REICHARD, Bernice Dorothy (Be) P.O. Box 368, Trexlertown PA 18087 **D S Anne's Epis Ch Trexlertown PA 2008-** B Philadelphia PA 1942 d Robert & Dorothy. RN Abington Hosp Sch of Nrsng 1963; BSPA S Jos Coll 1984. D 2/2/2008 Bp Paul Victor Marshall. m 9/18/2004 Ronald Reichard c 3.

REICHEL, Sonya Joan (NCal) **S Fran Epis Ch Fair Oaks CA 2017-** D 8/27/2016 P 3/3/2017 Bp Barry Leigh Beisner.

REICHERT, Elaine Starr Gilmer (Cal) 1605 Vendola Dr, San Rafael CA 94903 B San Jose CA 1948 d Ralph & Lorna. BA California St U 1969; MS California St U 1974; MDiv CDSP 1979. D 12/11/1982 P 12/1/1983 Bp William Edwin Swing. m 10/12/1991 Arthur G Reichert. Asst P S Steph's Par Bel Tiburon CA 2009-2010, 2007; Asst R S Jn's Epis Ch Oakland CA 2007-2011; Vol P S Aid's & S Jn's 1986-1991; Assoc R S Fran Of Assisi Ch Novato CA 1984-1985; Vol The Epis Ch Of S Jn The Evang San Francisco CA 1984-1985; Pstr Assoc S Ptr's Epis Ch San Francisco CA 1982-1983.

REICHMAN, Amy L (Ct) PO Box 698, Sharon CT 06069 **Lic Mstr Soc Worker Professionally Lic -NY St Educ Dept 2013-; D S Jn's Ch New Milford CT 2010-; D Trin Ch Torrington CT 2008-; Assoc. Pstr Counslr Bd Cert -Collegeof Pstr Supervsn & Psych 2007-; D S Andr's Ch Kent CT 2005-** B 1953 MA Hartford Sem 2013; MSW Hunter Coll Silberman Sch of Soc Wk 2013; MA Other 2013; MA Hartford Sem 2014. D 9/17/2005 Bp Andrew Donnan Smith. m 2/15/2009 Constance Cohrt. Vol Serv to Yth Fed of Prot Welf Agencies 2002. reichman.amy@gmail.com

REICHMANN, Jeffrey H (At) 26 Oakwood Ct, Jacksonville Beach FL 32250 B Jamaica NY 1951 s Charles & Jean. BA New Engl Coll 1973; MDiv Nash 1976. D 6/5/1976 P 12/18/1976 Bp Jonathan Goodhue Sherman. m 8/9/1975 Jeanne Reichmann c 3. Vic Ch Of The Gd Shpd Jacksonville FL 2011-2017; H Innoc Ch Atlanta GA 2002-2006; Chapl H Innoc' Epis Sch Atlanta GA 2001-2010; R Chr Ch Babylon NY 1995-2001; Headmaster Beaches Epis Sch Jacksonville Bch FL 1991-1995; S Paul's By-The-Sea Epis Ch Jaxville Bch FL 1991-1995; Chapl Chr Sch & Assoc R Chr Ch Covington LA 1990-1991; Chapl Trin Epis Sch New Orleans LA 1984-1990; Cur Chr Ch Manhasset NY 1976-1984.

REID, Brian S (NwPa) 415 4th Ave, Warren PA 16365 **Stndg Com Dio NW Pennsylvania Erie PA 2013-, Disciplinary Bd Pres 2012-, Secy of Conv 2006-2013, Secy of Conv & Coun 2006-2013, Bp Search Com 2006-2007, Dep to GC 1991-, Dioc Curs Sprtl Dir 1983-1986, COM 1981-2013, Dioc Coun 1978-2013, Const & Cn Com 1977-** B Detroit MI 1948 s Russell & Hulda. BA Wayne 1970; MDiv Nash 1973. D 6/30/1973 Bp H Coleman Mcgehee Jr P 1/18/1974 Bp Archie H Crowley. Int Ch Of Our Sav Dubois PA 2009-2010; Int S Jn's Ch Franklin PA 2007-2008; Int The Lawrencefield Chap Par Wheeling WV 2003-2005; R Trin Memi Ch Warren PA 1996-2004; R S Fran Of Assisi Epis Ch Youngsville PA 1980-1996; Vic Ch Of The H Trin Houtzdale PA 1976-1980; St Laurence Epis Ch Osceola Mills PA 1976-1980; Vic S Albans Highland Pk MI 1974-1976; Cur S Albans Highland Pk MI 1973-1976; Urban Affrs Com Dio Michigan Detroit MI 1974-1976.

REID, Catharine Brannan (Oly) 1123 19th Ave East, Seattle WA 98112 B Bryn Mawr PA 1950 d George & Elsie. AB Smith 1972; MSLS Villanova U 1975; DipHE Trin Bristol Engl 1981; MDiv GTS 1983. D 2/15/2011 P 10/19/2011 Bp Gregory Harold Rickel. P-in-c S Paul's Ch Seattle WA 2015, Assoc 2014-2015; Assoc S Lk's Epis Ch Renton WA 2012-2015; D S Clem's Epis Ch Seattle WA 2011.

REID, Dennis Joseph (Pa) **R S Alb's Epis Ch Reading PA 2017-** D 6/14/2014 Bp Clifton Daniel III.

REID, Franklin Lionel (NY) 1064 E 219th St, Bronx NY 10469 B AI 1959 s Roderick & Felicia. U of The W Indies; BA Codrington Coll 1982. Trans 12/10/1990 Bp Walter Decoster Dennis Jr. m 12/29/1985 Sandra Reid c 2. S Lk's Epis Ch Bronx NY 1990-2010; Serv Ch Of W Indies 1982-1988. OHC.

REID, Gordon (Pa) **R S Clem's Philadelphia PA 2004-** B Hawick Scotland 1943 s William & Elizabeth. MA U of Edinburgh Edinburgh UK 1963; Edinburgh Theol Coll 1964; Cuddesdon Coll 1966; BA Oxf GB 1966; MA Oxf GB 1972. Trans 1/1/2004 Bp Charles Ellsworth Bennison Jr. R S Clements Ch Philadelphia PA 2004-2015; Serv Ch of Engl 1988-2003; Serv Scottish Epis

Ch 1967-1987. "Every Comfort At Golgotha," Tufton Books, 1998; "The Wind from The Stars," Harper Collins, 1992.

REID, Jennie Lou (SeFla) 3840 Alhambra Ct, Coral Gables FL 33134 **Prof & Bd Dioc Sch For Chr Stds 2003-** B Norfolk VA 1945 d Hugh & Marion. BA Duke 1967; MA U NC 1969; EFM 1992; St Georges Coll Jerusalem IL 1998; MDiv VTS 1999. D 6/11/1999 P 1/15/2000 Bp Calvin Onderdonk Schofield Jr. m 12/19/1970 Ralph Benjamine Reid c 3. S Faith's Epis Ch Miami FL 2009-2017; Assoc S Thos Epis Par Miami FL 2004-2008; Trin Cathd Miami FL 2003-2004; Comm On Min Dio SE Florida Miami 2000-2006, Chair -- Comm On Mnstry 2001-2003, Comm On Min 1990-2000, Exec Bd 1983-1989; Asst R S Phil's Ch Coral Gables FL 1999-2002.

REID, Michael Edgar (ECR) 146 12th St, Pacific Grove CA 93950 B Brooklyn NY 1953 s Rupert & Daphne. BA Adel; MA NYU; EdD Tem; MDiv CDSP 2007. D 11/1/2008 P 7/2/2009 Bp Mary Gray-Reeves. m 9/6/2008 William Robnett c 1. Assoc Ch of S Mary's by the Sea Pacific Grove CA 2010-2014, Assoc R for Congrl Dvlpmt 2013-.

REID, M Sue (Oly) 315 Burns Lane, Williamsburg VA 23185 **Chapl to Deacons' Sch Dio Sthrn Virginia 2016-** B Louisville KY 1949 d Stephen & Margaret. Sum Stds Notre Dame; BMus DePauw U 1970; SMM UTS 1972; MDiv VTS 1976. D 6/5/1976 P 6/18/1977 Bp David Reed. Liaison to Epis. students Seattle U Seattle WA 2007-2011; S Mk's Cathd Seattle WA 2004-2007; R S Alb's Ch Indianapolis IN 1996-2004; Cn to Ordnry Dio Indianapolis Indianapolis IN 1988-1997; R Ch Of S Edw Columbus OH 1983-1987; Assoc S Steph's Epis Ch And U Columbus OH 1979-1983; Int S Jn's Ch Louisville KY 1978-1979; Trin Epis Ch Owensboro KY 1977-1978; Dio Kentucky Louisville KY 1976-1977. Auth, "Bk Revs," *Chr Herald*, 1973. AAM 1985-2005; ADLM 1984-1999; EWC 1972.

REID, Paul Dewitt (Pa) 7809 Old York Rd, Elkins Park PA 19027 **P-in-c S Paul's Ch Elkins Pk PA 2011-** B Washington IL 1948 s Paul & Joan. Penn St 1968; Edinburgh U 1976; MDiv Luth TS 2009. D 6/13/2009 P 12/12/2009 Bp Bud Shand. m 12/30/1977 Anne Reid c 2. Washington Memi Chap Vlly Forge PA 2010-2011; Asstg P Washington Memi Chap Vlly Forge PA 2010-2011; Asstg P St. Ptr's Ch in the Great Vlly Malvern PA 2009-2010; Sem/Intern St Dav's Epis Ch Radnor 2006-2009.

REID JR, Raymond W (SeFla) 9825 Diamondback Lane, McKinney TX 75071 B Los Angeles CA 1936 s Raymond & Flory. BA Humboldt St U 1976; MA Epis TS of the SW 1980. D 8/2/1980 P 3/1/1981 Bp Victor Manuel Rivera. m 5/26/1956 Rosalind Reid. R S Matt the Apos Epis Ch Miami FL 1990-2005; R Epis Ch Of Our Sav Placerville CA 1983-1990; S Jas Ch Lindsay CA 1980-1983; Epis Dio San Joaquin Modesto CA 1980-1982. Amer Assn Chr Counslr.

REID OSB, Richard P (NI) 44591 San Rafael Ave, Palm Desert CA 92260 **Ret 1989-** B Denver CO 1921 s William & Ethel. BS Loyola U 1948; SWTS 1986. D 11/23/1953 P 7/29/1954 Bp James Reginald Mallett. Abbot S Greg Abbey 1969-1989; Prior S Greg Abbey 1955-1969. Auth, *Sprt Loose in the Wrld*, Harbor Hse Pu, 1993. S Greg's Abbey, OSB 1948. Hon DD Seabury Wstrn TS 1985.

REID, Richard William (Vt) Po Box 70070, North Dartmouth MA 02747 **Int S Mk's Epis Ch Fall River MA 2001-, R 1969-2000** B Fall River MA 1939 s William & Francis. BA U Roch 1961; MDiv PDS 1964. D 5/23/1964 Bp Allen Webster Brown P 11/28/1964 Bp Charles Bowen Persell Jr. m 12/6/1980 Sondra M Reid c 4. Int S Paul's Epis Ch Westfield NJ 1997-2000; Int S Paul's Ch Norfolk VA 1996-1997; Gr Ch N Attleboro MA 1995-1996; R Imm Ch Bellows Falls VT 1989-1995; Int Emm Ch W Roxbury MA 1988-1989; S Aug And S Mart Ch Boston MA 1979-1988; Dir Case Hse Swansea MA 1974-1980; Dio Massachusetts Boston MA 1974-1980; Asst Trin Ch Potsdam NY 1967-1969; Zion Ch Colton NY 1967-1969; Vic S Paul Ft Covington NY 1964-1966. Acad Par Cler.

REID-LEVY, Schelly (Md) 3002 Holly St, Edgewater MD 21037 B Morgantown WV 1953 d Roberts & Betty. D 6/5/2004 Bp Robert Wilkes Ihloff. m 1/19/1982 Steven Levy.

REIDT, Donna (Vt) 124 Willis Rd, West Charleston VT 05872 **P S Paul's Ch Windsor VT 2014-** B Lowell MA 1948 d Harold & Mary Rose. BA Norwich U 2002; MDiv EDS 2008. D 12/19/2009 P 12/18/2010 Bp Thomas C Ely. m 6/26/1971 James F Reidt c 3. P-in-c St Mary's in The Mountains Epis Wilmington VT 2011-2014; D S Lk's Ch Chester VT 2010.

REILEY, Jennifer B S (Mass) 48 Prospect St, North Andover MA 01845 B Hartford CT 1954 d William & Barbara. Bos; BA Mt Holyoke Coll 1977; MDiv Yale DS 1981; PhD Bos 1986. D 6/13/1981 P 3/1/1982 Bp Arthur Edward Walmsley. Trin Epis Ch Haverhill MA 2007; Edw Hosp Chapl Fndtn Inc Naperville IL 1986-1987; Asst Chapl Mary Hitchcock Memi Hosp Hanover MA 1981-1982.

REIMER, Leslie (Pgh) 5426 Wilkins Ave, Pittsburgh PA 15217 **Assoc Calv Ch Pittsburgh PA 1997-; Dir Sheldon Calv Camp Conneaut OH 1988-** B New Kensington PA 1952 d Charles & Lucetta. BA Dickinson Coll 1974; MDiv GTS 1977. D 10/29/1977 P 12/13/1980 Bp Robert Bracewell Appleyard. Chapl Pittsburgh Chld Hosp Pittsburgh PA 1990-1998; Chapl U Pgh Med Cntr Pittsburgh PA 1983-1990; Chapl Intern U Chicago Hosps Chicago IL 1982-1983; Sheldon Calv Camp Conneaut OH 1981, 1979-1980; Chr Epis Ch Indiana PA 1979-1981; D S Jas Epis Ch Pittsburgh PA 1977-1978; Liturg Asst S Paul's Epis Ch Pittsburgh PA 1986-1998.

REIMER, Susan (RG) 184 Boutwell Ct, Loveland CO 80537 B Aurora CO 1952 d Donald & Alberta. AS N Harris Cmnty Coll 1997; Dio Fond du Lac Deacons Sch 2010; BLS U of Wisconsin OshKosh 2010. D 5/7/2011 Bp Russell Edward Jacobus. m 12/18/1971 Robert Reimer c 2. D All SS Epis Ch Appleton WI 2011-2014.

REIN, Lily A (At) 1105-L Clairemont Ave, Decatur GA 30030 B Memphis TN 1926 d George & Celeste. BA Rhodes Coll 1948; MA Georgia St U 1970. D 10/23/1993 Bp Frank Kellogg Allan. c 2. D Cathd Of S Phil Atlanta GA 1993-1998.

REINECKE, Roderick Laury (NC) 3810 Heritage Dr Rm 104, Burlington NC 27215 **Ret 1997-; Non-par Consult/Counslr Dio No Carolina Burlington 1984-** B Washington DC 1933 s Paul & Esther. BA U NC 1955; MDiv VTS 1958. D 6/29/1958 P 12/30/1958 Bp Edwin A Penick. m 7/9/1976 Ruthmary Ragsdale Wright c 4. Int S Paul's Epis Ch Winston Salem NC 1995-1997; R Ch Of The H Comf Burlington NC 1968-1983; R S Tim's Epis Ch Winston Salem NC 1963-1968; Epis Chapl NC St U-Raleigh Raleigh NC 1958-1963; Vic S Paul's Epis Ch Cary NC 1958-1959. Auth, "Leaving the Pastorate:Staying in Town," *A.I. Monthly Nwsltr*, Alb Inst, 1984; Auth, "In Relatns Column," *City-Cnty mag 1985-1999*. R Emer H Comf, Burlington, NC 1998; Who's Who in Rel Who's Who 1985.

REINERS JR, Alwin (Va) 1600 Westbrook Ave, Richmond VA 23227 **Search Consult Dio Virginia 1998-; Ret 1994-** B Arlington VA 1926 s Alwin & Elizabeth. CUA 1950; LTh VTS 1954. D 5/30/1954 Bp Frederick D Goodwin P 2/25/1955 Bp William Jones Gordon Jr. m 2/5/1955 Joanne M Reiners c 3. R S Paul's Ch Hanover VA 1982-1993; Dir Epis Hm For Chld S Louis MO 1979-1982; Dir Epis Hm for Chld (The Educational Cntr) St. Lou 1979-1982; Natl Netwk Exec Com Cler Assn Dio No Carolina Raleigh NC 1977-1980, Dn Charlotte Cler 1976-1978; R Ch Of The H Comf Charlotte NC 1968-1979; Chair DeptCE Dio Virginia Richmond VA 1966-1967, Exec Bd 1988-1991, Dn of Reg XI 1984-1987, Exec Com Mid-Atlantic Trng Inst 1966-1983, Yth Advsr 1958-1965; P-in-c S Barth's Ch Richmond VA 1961-1968; Asst St Jas Ch Richmond VA 1957-1961; P-in-c S Geo In The Arctic Kotzebue AK 1954-1957.

REINERS, Diane (NY) B Miami FL 1961 d Al & JoAnn. BA NYU 2006; MDiv GTS 2011. D 3/5/2011 P 9/29/2012 Bp Mark Sean Sisk. Cathd Of St Jn The Div New York NY 2011-2015, Asst 2012-; Asst Chapl SUNY Maritime Coll New York NY 2010-2011.

REINHARD, Kathryn Louise (NY) Christ Church, 84 Broadway, New Haven CT 06511 B Oberlin OH 1979 d Donald & Constance. BFA NYU 2001; MDiv Ya Berk 2008. D 3/15/2008 P 9/20/2008 Bp Mark Sean Sisk. Chr Ch New Haven CT 2008-2009.

REINHARDT, Connie (WA) 27 Broad St, Newburyport MA 01950 **S Geo's Ch Glenn Dale MD 2006-** B Long Beach CA 1969 d James & Geraldine. BA Wellesley Coll 1991; MDiv Ya Berk 1995. D 5/9/1998 P 12/5/1998 Bp Douglas Edwin Theuner. m 2/19/2006 Emma Hadley c 1. S Paul's Ch Newburyport MA 2000-2006; Mt Calv Camp Hill PA 1998-1999.

REINHART, Rodney Eugene (Chi) 2508 Walnut St, Blue Island IL 60406 **Died 11/24/2015** B Toledo 1949 s Ralph & Pauline. BA Oakland U 1972; MDiv Bex Sem 1975; Cert Wayne 1978; Cert Int Mnstry Prog 1996. D 12/15/1984 Bp Henry Irving Mayson P 4/12/1986 Bp H Coleman Mcgehee Jr. m 8/14/2015 Alan G Engle. Vic S Jos's And S Aid's Ch Blue Island IL 2011-2015; R S Clem's Ch Harvey IL 2004-2015; Vic St. Jos/St. Aid's Che Blue Island Illinois 2004-2015; S Martha's Ch Detroit MI 2002-2003; Gr Ch Detroit MI 2002; Nativ Epis Ch Bloomfield Township MI 2001; Trin Epis Ch Farmington MI 1999-2001; Trin Epis Ch Monroe MI 1997-1998, 1997, 1997, 1996; S Geo's Epis Ch Warren MI 1994-1995; Supply All SS Ch Detroit MI 1993-1994; Assoc Emm Ch Detroit MI 1988-1994; Asst Pstr S Andr Detroit MI 1985-1987; St Andrews Memi Ch Detroit MI 1985-1987; Asst Pstr S Cyp's Epis Ch Detroit MI 1983-1985; Cur S Mich And All Ang Epis Ch Lincoln Pk MI 1975-1976. "Faith on the Front Line," *A cable TV show*, Chicago St U, 2007; "Lift High The Cross," *A Cable TV show*, Comcast Cable, Plymouth MI, 1998; Auth, "Sprtl Aerobics for the 21st Century," Operation Dome Press, 1996; Auth, "Splinters on the Wind," Operation Dome Press, 1988; Auth, "Twilights of Anth Way Drive," Operation Dome Press, 1988. Bp's Assoc, Chicago 2006; EPF 1980; EUC 1977; People Who Care Mnstrs 1984-2005; The People Who Care Interfaith Fund 1998; Wrld Sabbath of Rel Recon 1998. Cmnty Luminary Awd Detroit Edison and MNA 2003; Gvnr's Publ Serv Awd St of Michigan 2003; Diversity Chanpion Awd Birmingham/Bloomfield Hills MI 2002; Mart Luther King Awd Archdiocese of Detroit 1989; Sprt of Detroit Awd Detroit City Coun 1986; Cert of Merit MI St 1978.

REINHEIMER, John Jay (NH) 227 W 6th St, Port Clinton OH 43452 **Extended Supply S Paul's Ch Bellevue OH 2012-; Int Dio Ohio Cleveland 2007-; Ret 2002-** B Fremont OH 1936 s John & Margaret. BA Hobart and Wm Smith Colleges 1958; BD Bex Sem 1961. D 6/10/1961 Bp Nelson Marigold Burroughs P 12/21/1961 Bp Dudley S Stark. c 4. Vic Ch Of The Mssh No Woodstock NH 1992-2002; Supply P Dio New Hampshire Concord NH 1990-1992; P-in-c S Judes Epis Ch Franklin NH 1982-1989; P-in-c S Mary Penacook NH 1982-1989; Chapl Res MA Gnrl Hosp Boston MA 1973-1974; R S Jn's Ch Clifton Spgs NY 1964-1973; Asst S Thos Epis Ch Rochester NY 1963-1964, Cur 1961-1962. padrejohn@roadrunner.com

REINHEIMER, Philip (NCal) 13948 Gold Country Drive, Penn Valley CA 95945 B Rochester NY 1943 s Frederick & Barbara. BA U Pac 1965; MPA California St U 1986. D 1/12/1975 Bp Chauncie Kilmer Myers P 11/20/1979 Bp John Raymond Wyatt. m 4/1/1967 Vicki R Reinheimer c 3. P Trin Ch Sutter Creek CA 2010; P St Johns Epis Ch Roseville CA 2009-2010; P Emm Epis Ch Grass Vlly CA 2007-2008; Assoc P H Trin Ch Nevada City CA 2000-2009; Assoc P All SS Epis Ch Redding CA 1990-2000; P S Jn The Div Epis Ch Morgan Hill CA 1989-1990, P 1981-1988; P S Jas' Ch Monterey CA 1984-1985, D 1975-1983; Asst All SS Epis Ch Watsonville CA 1976-1990.

REINHOLZ, Andrew C (Va) Epiphany Episcopal Church, 8000 Hermitage Rd, Henrico VA 23228 **Epiph Epis Ch Richmond VA 2016-** B Reading PA 1983 s William & Constance. BA Moravian Coll 2006; MDiv GTS 2012; MDiv The GTS 2012. D 12/21/2012 P 6/30/2013 Bp Paul Victor Marshall. m 1/14/2012 Kimberly Rowles c 1. S Paul's Epis Ch S Clair MI 2016; P S Marg's Ch Emmaus PA 2013-2015; Assoc Dio Bethlehem Bethlehem PA 2012-2014, 2007-2009. areinholz@diobeth.org

REINHOLZ, Kimberly (Va) Christ Church, 205 N 7th St, Stroudsburg PA 18360 **Gr & H Trin Epis Ch Richmond VA 2015-** B Media PA 1981 d Michael & Theresa. BA Tem 2004; MA U of Sussex 2006; MDiv GTS 2013; MDiv The GTS 2013. D 12/21/2012 P 6/30/2013 Bp Paul Victor Marshall. m 1/14/2012 Andrew C Reinholz c 2. Cathd Ch Of The Nativ Bethlehem PA 2013-2015; Chr Ch Reading PA 2008.

REINKEN, Dirk Christian (NJ) 5208 Biltmore Dr, Freehold NJ 07728 **S Ptr's Ch Freehold NJ 2014-** B Anderson SC 1964 s Louis & Mary. BA U of So Carolina 1987; MDiv GTS 1998. D 6/12/1999 P 1/15/2000 Bp Gerry Wolf. m 2/25/2013 Thomas J Hargrove. R S Lk's Ch Trenton NJ 2002-2014; Cur S Lk's Ch Philadelphia PA 1999-2002. Auth, "Archbp Ussher's Proposal For Synodical Govt," *The Angl*, 1998; Auth, "PB For The 21st Century (Bk Revs)," *The Angl*, 1998. OHC, Assoc 1994. rector@stpetersfreehold.org

REISCHMAN, Charles J (Spr) 4767 Redbud Ct, Decatur IL 62526 B Westlake OH 1955 s Paul & Jean. S Marys Sem and U; Walsh U; BA U of Akron 1980; MDiv Epis TS of the SW 1990. D 6/9/1990 Bp James Russell Moodey P 12/1/1990 Bp William Harvey Wolfrum. m 8/5/1989 Gina L Reischman c 3. S Jn's Epis Ch Decatur IL 2008-2011; New Life Epis Ch Littleton CO 2003-2005; Assoc S Lk's Epis Ch Akron OH 1993-2000; Acts 29 Mnstrs Thomasville GA 1991-1993; Ch Of The Trsfg Evergreen CO 1990-1991; Yth Pstr Resurr Sharon OH 1986-1989; Yth Pstr S Mart's Epis Ch Monroeville PA 1983-1986. Auth, "Acts 29 Pub"; Auth, "Focus Renwl News"; Auth, "Charisma". ERM, Ord S Phil-Evang; Joshua Force.

REISHUS, John William (WMich) 5161 E 50 N, Kokomo IN 46901 B Quincy IL 1934 s Harald & Lauretta. BS U of Arizona 1956; PhD Iowa St U 1960; MDiv Nash 1971. D 6/19/1971 Bp Gerald Francis Burrill P 12/20/1971 Bp James Winchester Montgomery. m 4/27/1957 Beverly Reishus. P-in-c Chr Epis Ch Lucketts Leesburg VA 2001-2003; Int Truro Epis Ch Fairfax VA 1999-2001; Asst P-in-c S Jas Ch Potomac MD 1997-1998; Int 1992-1994; Int Chr Ch W River MD 1996-1997; Asst Int R S Tim's Ch Catonsville MD 1995-1996; Int S Andr The Fisherman Epis Mayo MD 1994-1995; S Alb's Mssn N. Muskegon MI 1976-1991; R Dio Wstrn Michigan Kalamazoo MI 1976-1978; Vic Gr Ch Sterling IL 1971-1976; The Ch Of S Anne Morrison IL 1971-1976.

REISNER, Terry Ralph (Dal) **Vic S Paul's Epis Ch Waxahachie TX 2007-** B Toronto Canada 1965 D 6/4/2005 P 4/29/2006 Bp James Monte Stanton. m 4/8/1989 Glenna Clark Reisner c 3. S Phil's Epis Ch Frisco TX 2005-2007; Trin Ch Marshall TX 1992-1999.

REISS, Gerald Anthony (NJ) 1048 Detweiler Ave, Hellertown PA 18055 **Died 1/30/2016** B Bethlehem PA 1932 s Elmer & Anna. BA Leh 1954; MDiv Ya Berk 1960. D 6/1/1960 P 12/1/1960 Bp Frederick Warnecke. m 7/10/1954 Dorothy Spisak c 2. Ret 1995-2016; R S Ptr's Ch Clarksboro NJ 1964-1994; Asst Min Trin Ch Bethlehem PA 1962-1964; Vic Chr Ch Frackville Frackville PA 1960-1962; S Jas Ch Shuykl Haven PA 1960-1962; Dept of Urban Concerns Dio New Jersey Trenton NJ 1976-1984, Dn, Camden-Woodbury Convoc 1974-1977, Secy/Treas, Camden-Woodbury Convoc 1965-1970.

REJOUIS, Mary Kate (Colo) 2700 University Heights Ave, Boulder CO 80302 **R S Aid's Epis Ch Boulder CO 2005-** B Boulder CO 1970 d Jacob & Mary. BA Dart 1993; MDiv SWTS 1997. D 6/14/1997 P 12/20/1997 Bp Douglas Edwin Theuner. m 11/20/2009 Jean Hilaire Rejouis c 2. Vic S Ptr's Ch Basalt CO 2000-2005; P-in-c/Assoc R S Mich And All Ang Ch So Bend IN 1997-2000. rector@saintaidans.org

RELLER, Wilfred Herman (Colo) 71 Aspen Ln, Golden CO 80403 **Chaplin Vista Hospice 2004-; Chapl Boulder Cmnty Hosp in Colorado 1987-** B Old Monroe MO 1939 s William & Coletta. BA Div Word 1963; MDiv Div Word 1967; MA Loyola U 1969. Trans 7/1/1988 Bp William Carl Frey. m 7/28/

1984 Irene Frances Sullivan. Chaplin Heartland Hospice 2003-2004; Chap Of The Resurr Limon CO 1988-2004; Serv Ch of Can 1984-1986; Serv RC Ch 1966-1983.

RELYEA, Michael Johl (NY) 127b east terminal blvd, Atlantic Beach NC 28512 B Faribault MN 1942 s Kenneth & Ruth. BA Lawr 1964; MS USC 1968; MDiv GTS 1973. D 1/27/1974 P 2/15/1975 Bp Philip Frederick McNairy. m 3/21/1970 Maria Magdalena Lemmen c 2. VP Loc 1113 AFSCME New York NY 1996-1998; Investigators' Chapt Chair Loc 1113 AFSCME New York NY 1978-1998; Assoc S Mk's Ch In The Bowery New York NY 1974-2011. "A Comprehensive Guide to the St Mk's Ch in the Bowery Historic Site," St Mk's Ch in the Bowery, 1999. NYC Labor-Rel Cltn 1986.

REMBOLDT, Cherry Ann (SanD) 47535 State Highway 74, Palm Deset CA 92260 B Fargo North Dakota 1952 d William & Meredith. MEd Azusa Pacific U 1994; MEd Azusa Pacific U 1996. D 6/7/2008 Bp Jim Mathes. m 8/13/1972 Henry Remboldt c 1.

REMENTER, Nancy Sandra (CPa) 239 E Market St, Marietta PA 17547 B Medford MA 1944 d Stanley & Jessie. Bucks Cnty Cmnty Coll; Tem; Cert Dio Cntrl PA Sch of Chr Stds 2010. D 10/31/2010 Bp Nathan Dwight Baxter. m 2/8/1964 Francis Rementer c 3.

REMER, Douglas Errick (SwFla) 5231 S Jules Verne Ct, Tampa FL 33611 B Trenton NJ 1948 s Donald & Rose. AB Rutgers Coll 1971; MDiv GTS 1975. D 4/26/1975 Bp Albert Wiencke Van Duzer P 2/5/1976 Bp Ned Cole. m 9/25/1976 Sterling H Hull c 3. Asstg P S Andr's Ch Boca Grande FL 2016-2017; Int R Ch Of The Gd Shpd Cashiers NC 2015-2016; Int R The Epis Ch Of Gd Shpd Asheboro NC 2014-2015; R; Pres & Bd Chair St Jn's Sch St Johns Epis Ch Tampa FL 2003-2013; R; Pres & Bd Chair St Matin's Sch S Mart In The Fields Ch Atlanta GA 1991-2002; R Calv Ch Tarboro NC 1982-1990; Assoc R S Mich's Ch Raleigh NC 1977-1982; Cur Gr Epis Ch Utica NY 1975-1977.

REMINGTON, Melissa E (WVa) 821 Edgewood Dr, Charleston WV 25302 R St Chris Epis Ch Charleston WV 2014-, 2009-2013, Chair of Cmsn on Diversity and Racism 2010-2013 B Bangor ME 1958 d Christopher & Judith. BA U of Massachusetts 1981; MAT Stan 1991; MDiv Bex Sem 2007. D 8/17/2007 P 5/24/2008 Bp Michael Garrison. m 4/2/2016 Edward K Merrit c 3. Assoc R S Mk's Epis Ch Venice FL 2013-2014; Vic S Ptr's Ch Westfield NY 2008-2009. pastormelissa@stchristopherwv.com

REMPPEL, Paulette Evelyn (NY) 52 Brookside Pl, New Rochelle NY 10801 D Ch Of S Simon The Cyrenian New Rochelle NY 2002- B Providence RI 1947 d Patrick & Alice. GTS; Iona Coll 1984. D 5/16/1998 Bp Richard Frank Grein. m 9/4/1993 Alfred R Remppel c 2. D Par of Chr the Redeem Pelham NY 1998-2002.

REMY, Joseph Michel Jean (Hai) 5935 Del Lago Circle, Sunrise FL 33313 B Savanette, Cayes 1943 s Lormestoir & Thernolia. BA Coll of S Pierre HT 1966; BA Coll of S Pierre Haiti 1966; MDiv ETSC 1971; MDiv ETSC, Puerto Rico 1971. D 7/4/1971 P 1/11/1972 Bp Luc Anatole Jacques Garnier. m 7/17/1980 Marie Carmelle Deler c 3. Asst Mssn Sainte Croix 2002-2008; P-in-c Epiph in Port-au-Prince 1998-2002; Asst Mssn Sainte Croix 1993-1998; P-in-c Missions Les Cayes 1977-1993; P-in-c Missions Hinche In Haiti 1972-1977; Dio Haiti Port-au-Prince HT 1971-2008; Asst Annunc Darbonne Haiti 1971-1972. Soc Of S Marg 1971.

RENCHER, Ollie (NC) St Peter's Church, 115 W 7th St, Charlotte NC 28202 R S Ptr's Epis Ch Charlotte NC 2012-; Dioc Liturg Cmsn Dio No Carolina Raleigh NC 2013-; Cmsn on Mus and Liturg Dio W Tennessee Memphis 2011-, Chapl, W Tennessee Haiti Partnership 2009-, COM 2009- B Clarksdale MS 1969 s Varner & Vernice. BA Millsaps Coll 1991; MDiv GTS 2003. D 6/11/2003 P 1/13/2004 Bp Duncan Montgomery Gray III. m 12/18/2010 Ellen R Rencher. Assoc R for Pstr Care and Congrl Dvlpmt Ch Of The H Comm Memphis TN 2008-2012; Asst R/Chapl S Ptr's Ch Oxford MS 2003-2008; Orientation Ldr, Bp's Mssn Corps Dio Mississippi Jackson MS 2006, YA Vocation Com 2004-2007, Bd Mem, Duncan M. Gray Conf Cntr 1992-1995. SSJE 2004.

RENDON OSPINA, Gonzalo Antonio (Colom) Cra 80 No. 53a-78, Medelin Antioquia 99999 Colombia B Rionegro 1957 s Noe & Deyanira. Rec 7/5/1992. m 4/9/2005 Johana Reyes c 1. Iglesia Epis En Colombia Bogota 2006-2009.

RENEGAR, Douglas Mcbane (Ga) 224 Lakefield Rd., Waterloo SC 29384 B Long Island,NY 1948 s Garland & Jeanne. BA Wake Forest U 1970; MA E Carolina U 1974; MDiv VTS 1984. D 6/9/1984 Bp Brice Sidney Sanders P 12/14/1984 Bp A(rthur) Heath Light. m 4/27/2013 Susan Charlene Renegar. R Chr Ch Frederica St Simons Is GA 1992-2004; R S Matt's Epis Ch Darlington SC 1988-1992; R Stras Memi Tazewell VA 1984-1988; The Tazewell Cnty Cluster Of Epis Parishes Tazewell VA 1984-1988; Trin Ch Richlands VA 1984-1988.

RENFREW, William Finch (Mich) 2101 Wellesley Dr, Lansing MI 48911 B Detroit MI 1931 s Charles & Louise. MI SU; AA Lansing Cmnty Coll 1975. D 6/13/1992 Bp R aymond Stewart Wood Jr. m 8/11/1981 Eleanor Nelson Renfrew. D S Paul's Epis Ch Lansing MI 1992-2004. Mi & Intl Police Chapl Assns.

RENGERS, Josiah Daniel (Ala) 109 Woodcrest Circle, Eutaw AL 35462 S Thos Epis Ch Birmingham AL 2015-; R S Steph's Ch Eutaw AL 2011- B Fairmont WV 1983 s Kevin & Joann. BA W Virginia U; MDiv VTS 2011. D 12/4/2010 P 6/14/2011 Bp William Michie Klusmeyer. m 5/22/2010 Katherine

Toshiko Nakamura Rengers c 3. S Lk's Epis Ch Birmingham AL 2013-2015; Dio Alabama Birmingham 2011-2012.

RENICK, Van Taliaferro (SwVa) 170 Mountain Ave, Rocky Mount VA 24151 Ret 1992- B Augusta GA 1930 s Frank & Roberta. BS Oklahoma St U 1952; BD Sewanee: The U So, TS 1967. D 6/18/1967 P 1/1/1968 Bp Albert R Stuart. m 4/25/1952 Kathryn H Renick c 2. R Trin Epis Ch Rocky Mt VA 1971-1992; Cur Chr Ch Martinsville VA 1970-1971; D Chr Epis Ch Cordele GA 1967-1969.

RENN, Wade Allan (Nwk) 558 Highland Ave, Montclair NJ 07043 Collegial Cn Trin And S Phil's Cathd Newark NJ 2008-; P Hse Of Pryr Epis Ch Newark NJ 2006-; Ret 1996- B Freeport NY 1935 s Ralph & Edith. BS Leh 1956; MS Leh 1960; MDiv GTS 1964. D 6/27/1964 P 1/16/1965 Bp Paul Moore Jr. m 2/4/1970 Mary Ann Lewis c 2. S Lk's Epis Ch Montclair NJ 2004-2006; S Andr's Ch Harrington Pk NJ 2002-2004; S Jas' Ch Ridgefield NJ 2000-2002; Int S Andr's Epis Ch Lincoln Pk NJ 1999-2000; Int Gr Epis Ch Westwood NJ 1997-1999; R Gr Ch Nutley NJ 1973-1996; Gr Ch Newark NJ 1969-1970, Cur 1964-1968; ECUSA Mssy Angl Ch in Zambia Zambia 1966-1972.

RENNA, Pamela Stacey (EMich) 123 N Michigan Ave, Saginaw MI 48602 B San Francisco CA 1941 d George & Frances. BA U of Oregon 1963; MA U IL 1965; PhD Br 1971. D 11/8/2009 P 10/20/2012 Bp Steven Todd Ousley. m 6/7/1969 Thomas Julius Renna c 3.

REPLOGLE, Jennifer (Chi) 33 Mercer St, Princeton NJ 08540 St Paul's Epis Ch Peoria IL 2015- B 1982 d David & Rosemary. BA Mississippi Coll 2005; MDiv PrTS 2010; Dip Ang Stud VTS 2011. D 6/18/2011 P 12/16/2011 Bp George Edward Councell. m 6/20/2014 Jonathan R Thomas. Cur Trin Ch Princeton NJ 2011-2014; Epis Election Com Mem Dio New Jersey Trenton NJ 2012-2013. Contributing Auth, "New life I never wanted," Inside Grief, SPCK, 2013. jreplogle@stpaulspeoria.com

REPP, Jeanette Marie (Los) 1648 W 9th St, San Pedro CA 90732 R S Ptr's Par San Pedro CA 2010- B Oakland CA 1961 d Gordon & Nancy. BA U CA 1983; MDiv SWTS 1988; MSW Loyola U 1998. D 12/3/1988 Bp William Edwin Swing P 8/17/1989 Bp Frank Tracy Griswold III. c 2. Assoc S Nich w the H Innoc Ch Elk Grove Vlg IL 2008-2010; Vic Ch Of The Incarn Bloomingdale IL 2004-2008; Int S Giles' Ch Northbrook IL 2003-2004; Assoc S Greg's Epis Ch Deerfield IL 1997-2003; Vic Ch Of The Adv Chicago IL 1989-1997; D Intern Ch of the Adv Chicago IL US 1988-1989. Natl Assoc of Soc Workers 1997-2010.

RESSLER, Richard Alan (SD) St. Paul's Episcopal Church, 309 S. Jackson St., Jackson MI 49201 B Cokato MN 1952 s Harry & Norma. BS U of Wisconsin 1978; MDiv SWTS 1995. D 6/28/1995 Bp James Louis Jelinek P 1/20/1996 Bp Sanford Zangwill Kaye Hampton. m 6/14/1975 Gayle Ann Ressler. S Paul's Epis Ch Jackson MI 2015-2017; Int The Par Of Gd Shpd Epis Ch Wailuku HI 2013-2015; Fr Emm Epis Par Rapid City SD 2008-2013; Dio Oklahoma Oklahoma City OK 2004-2008; R S Jas Epis Ch Oklahoma City OK 2002-2004; Dio Minnesota Minneapolis MN 2001-2002; Chr Ch Austin MN 1995-2000.

RESTREPO CARDONA, Juan Carlos (Colom) Calle 51 # 6-49, Bogota 11116 Colombia Iglesia Epis En Colombia Bogota 2016- B Bogota Colombia 1963 s Jose & Gladys. Lic Filosofia Santo Thos 1986; Psicologo Santo Thos 1986; Lic Teologia Taverciana 1998. Rec 2/7/2009 as Priest Bp Francisco Jose Duque-Gomez. m 1/14/1998 Sonia Jannette Maldonado c 2.

RETAMAL, M Regina (Mass) 59 Lawrence St, Framingham MA 01702 B Parral Chile 1944 d Juan & Regina. Cert Universidad Tecnica del Estada 1977; MRE Gordon-Conwell TS 1988; Cert Instituto Pstr Hispano 1992. D 5/30/1992 P 4/1/1993 Bp David Elliot Johnson. c 2. Iglesia de San Juan Hyde Pk MA 2000-2006; Dio Massachusetts Boston MA 1994-1999; S Paul's Ch Brookline MA 1993-1999; Cltn For Hisp Mnstrs Pepperell MA 1992-1994. FVC; Soc of S Jn the Evang.

RETTGER, John Hubbard (Minn) 65 - 104th Avenue Northwest, Coon Rapids MN 55448 B Ann Arbor MI 1935 s James & Esther. LTh S Chads Coll Regina SK CA 1959; BA U of Connecticut 1961; MDiv The Coll of Emm and S Chad CA 1993; DD U of Emml 2008. Trans 9/3/1964 as Priest Bp Hamilton Hyde Kellogg. m 7/28/1954 Eudora Rettger c 4. Cn Cathd Ch Of S Mk Minneapolis MN 2000-2001; Cn Pstr 2000-2001, Assoc 1994-1997, Hon Cn 1998-; P-in-c S Jas Ch Marshall MN 1999-2000; Int S Mary's Ch S Paul MN 1997-1998; Supply P S Paul's Ch Minneapolis MN 1992-1993; Chapl Integrity Twin Cities MN 1979-1983; R Ch Of The Resurr Minneapolis MN 1968-1992; R S Lk's Ch Willmar MN 1963-1968; R Chr Ch Nokomis Saskatechewan 1959-1963. YMCA Ambassador Awd Emma B. Howe YMCA, Northtown 2015; Hon Cn S Mk Cathd Minneapolis 1997.

RETZLAFF, Georg (USC) 1612 Goldfinch Ln, West Columbia SC 29169 B Köln DE 1946 s Rudolf & Erika. MDiv Universität Bonn DE 1972; Dr. theol. Universität Bern CH 1978. m 12/29/1977 Joy Retzlaff. R All SS Ch Cayce SC 2004-2011; R Ch Of The Redeem Orangeburg SC 2002-2004; Prof Sewanee U So TS Sewanee TN 2001-2002; Prof of Homil U So TS Sewanee 2001-2002; Prof Rel & Philos Voorhees Coll Denmark 1991-2001; Dn of Stds St. Mk's Theol Coll 1987-1991; Prof Exec Coun Appointees New York NY 1984-1991;

Chair Theol Dept Cuttington U Coll 1984-1987; R S Paul's And Resurr Ch Wood Ridge NJ 1980-1984; Asst S Ptr's Ch Beverly MA 1979-1980. Georg Retzlaff, "Paternoster," *The UpsideDown Wrld of the Our Fr*, Authorhouse, 2013; Georg Retzlaff, "Singing the Faith," *Sermon Hymns for Every Sunday*, Authorhouse, 2012; Georg Retzlaff, "Why the Cross?," *Meditations for H Week*, Authorhouse, 2010; Georg Retzlaff, "What Jesus Taught and Why it Matters," *Towards a Chrsnty w no other Fndt but Chr*, Authorhouse, 2010; Georg Retzlaff, "The Other Side," *Hitherto Unpublished Letters by Biblic Heroes*, Authorhouse, 2009; Georg Retzlaff, "Ch Psalter," *The Bk of Psalms for Liturg and Priv Use*, Authorhouse, 2009; Georg Retzlaff, "Die Äussere Erscheinung des Geistlichen im Alltag," *Doctoral Thesis*, Jakob Stämpfli & Cie., Bern, 1978; Georg Retzlaff, "Vorgänge um die alt-katholische Gemeindegründung," *Gedenkschrift*, Kuttruff Publ. Konstanz, 1973.

REUMAN, Eugene Frederic (CFla) 2915 W Henley Ln, Dunnellon FL 34433 **R S Marg's Ch Inverness FL 2001-** B Toledo OH 1950 s Carl & Naomi. AA Cntrl Florida Cmnty Coll 1979; BA S Leo U 1997; MDiv Sewanee: The U So, TS 2001. D 12/8/1990 P 7/1/2001 Bp John Wadsworth Howe. m 9/3/1983 Paula S Reuman. D S Jas Episcoapl Ch 1998-2001; D H Faith Epis Ch Dunnellon FL 1990-1998.

REUSCHLING, Walter Edward (Eas) 108 Oak St, Cambridge MD 21613 **Vic St. Jn's Epis Chap Cambridge MD 2006-; Asst Chapl CAP Westminster MD 1976-** B Baltimore MD 1931 s Walter & Ida. S Marys Sem and U; BEd Towson U 1957; MEd Loyola U 1963. D 2/3/1971 P 11/1/1971 Bp Harry Lee Doll. m 4/25/1957 Kathryn W Reuschling c 3. All Hallow's Ch Snow Hill MD 1995-2002; R H Cross Epis Mssn Stockton CA 1994-2002; Int S Andr's Epis Ch Princess Anne MD 1994-1995; R S Paul's Ch Windsor VT 1988-1994; Int S Mary's Epis Ch Pocomoke City MD 1985-1986; Chapl Wstrn Maryland Coll 1980-1982; DRE, Int P Ch Of S Paul's By The Sea Ocean City MD 1976-1982; Ch Of-Ascen & Prince-Peace Baltimore MD 1974-1977; 1971-1976; Chapl Carroll Cnty Gnrl Hosp.

REUSS, Patricia Ann Osborne (WNC) 133 Liberty Ct, Oak Ridge TN 37830 **Assoc S Steph's Epis Ch Oak Ridge TN 2004-** B Elizabethton TN 1943 d Dana & Georgia. BS Tennessee Tech U 1965; MDiv Ya Berk 1986. D 6/21/1986 P 1/24/1987 Bp George Nelson Hunt III. m 6/15/1968 Robert Julius Reuss c 2. Augusta Discernment Com Dio Georgia Savannah GA 2000-2003; R S Mich's Ch Waynesboro GA 2000-2003; R Ch Of The Mssh Murphy NC 1993-2000; Congrl Mnstry Dio Wstrn No Carolina Asheville NC 1993-2000, Pres, Stndg Com 1999-2000, Stndg Com 1998-2000; Chapl S Eliz's Hm Providence RI 1991-1993; Chapl S Eliz's Hm Providence RI 1989-1993; Asst S Dav's On The Hill Epis Ch Cranston RI 1987-1993; Dioc Coun Dio Rhode Island Providence RI 1990-1993.

REUSS, Robert Julius (WNC) 133 Liberty Ct, Oak Ridge TN 37830 **Assoc P S Steph's Epis Ch Oak Ridge TN 2004-** B Brooklyn NY 1934 s Andrew & Jessie. BA SUNY 1957; MDiv Ya Berk 1960. D 4/23/1960 P 10/29/1960 Bp James Pernette DeWolfe. m 6/15/1968 Patricia Ann Osborne Reuss c 2. Int Trin Ch Statesboro GA 2001-2002; Int Ch Of The Gd Shpd Hayesville NC 1996-1997; Int Ch Of The Incarn Highlands NC 1994-1995; Alum Coun Ya Berk New Haven CT 1984-1991; Par Consult Dio Rhode Island Providence RI 1982-1988, COM 1981-1984, Stndg Com 1981, Coll Wk Cmsn 1974-1980, DeptCE 1965-1973; Trst S Eliz's Hm Providence RI 1980-1984; R S Dav's On The Hill Epis Ch Cranston RI 1971-1994; Asst P Chr Ch Westerly RI 1962-1971; Cur S Jn's Ch Huntington NY 1960-1962.

REVEL, Anna Carter (Ky) 5146 Sunnybrook Dr, Paducah KY 42001 **Ret 2008-; Ret 1990-** B Marion KY 1924 d Thomas & Ruth. BS U of Kentucky 1948; MS U of Wisconsin 1973; Cert Nash 1980; U MN 1983. D 11/28/1981 Bp Charles Thomas Gaskell. D/Asst Gr Ch Paducah KY 1995-2010; D/Asst H Trin Epis Ch In Countryside Clearwater FL 1990-1995; D/Asst Trin Ch Janesville WI 1981-1990. Curs 1978; DAR 2002; Pi Lambda Theta Educ Hon Soc 2002.

REX III, Charles Walton (Chi) 2739 Prairie Ave, Evanston IL 60201 B Orlando FL 1950 s Charles & Samueline. BA VMI 1972. D 2/7/2009 Bp Jeff Lee. m 11/14/1992 Susan Rex c 4.

REX JR, William Moyer (Pa) Rec 6/17/2017 Bp Daniel Gutierrez.

REXFORD, William Nelson (Mich) 7213 Meadow Wood Way, Clarksville MD 21029 **Ret 1984-** B Painesville OH 1934 s Charles & Corene. BA Wayne 1958; MDiv VTS 1969. D 6/28/1969 Bp Richard Stanley Merrill Emrich P 3/1/1970 Bp John Melville Burgess. m 3/12/1955 Barbara Watson c 3. Vic S Matt's Epis Ch Flat Rock MI 1979-1984; Assoc Min S Andr's Epis Ch Livonia MI 1978-1979; Assoc Min S Alfred Lake Orion MI 1974-1978; Asst Min S Jas Epis Ch Birmingham MI 1973-1974; Asst Min S Jn's Ch Royal Oak MI 1970-1973; Cur S Mary's Epis Ch Barnstable MA 1969-1970. Auth, "Lamplight". Natl Assn For The Self- Supporting Active Mnstry.

REYES, Jesus (ECR) P.O. Box 1903, Monterey CA 93942 **Cn for Congrl Growth & Dvlpmt Dio El Camino Real Salinas CA 2008-, BEC 2009-, Dept of Mssn - Cnvnr 2008-; Advsry Bd Mem Credo Inst Inc. Memphis TN 2011-; Disciplianry Bd for Bishops Epis Ch Cntr New York NY 2011-** B MX 1954 s Desiderio & Aurora. BA Seminario Diocesano De Tijuana Tijuana Mx 1976; BA Universidad Iberoamericana Mex City Mx 1982; Dip Ang

Stud VTS 2002. Rec 6/29/2002 as Priest Bp David Colin Jones. m 11/11/2011 Robin Louise Michel Reyes c 1. Ch Planter La Iglesia de Santa Maria Falls Ch VA 2004-2008; Vic San Jose Ch Arlington VA 2002-2005; Stndg Com Mem (elected) Dio Virginia Richmond VA 2004-2007; Alum Assn Exec Coun VTS Alexandria VA 2003-2006. Co-Writer, "Latino and anglo political portraits: lessons from," *Intl Journ of Intercultural Relatns*, Pergamon, 2001. Cltn of Hisp Agencies & Professionals 1991; Communities organized for Relational Power in Action (COPA) 2008; VOICE 2003-2008. jesusreyes@edecr.org

REYES, Juan Pastor (WA) 3001 Wisconsin Ave NW, Washington DC 20016 **S Paul's Epis Ch Paterson NJ 2017-** B 1954 s Telesforo & Andrea. Bachelor in Philos Universidad Autonoma de Santo Domingo 1999; Mstr in Bilingual Educ Universidad Autonoma de Santo Domingo 2004; BA Centro de EStudios Teologelos 2013. D 6/27/2013 P 1/11/2014 Bp Mariann Edgar Budde. m 8/15/2002 Rafaela Cabral c 2. S Jn's Ch Lafayette Sq Washington DC 2014-2015; Dio Washington Washington DC 2013-2015.

REYES PEREZ, Jose R (WMass) 6744 S Kings Hwy, Alexandria VA 22306 **All SS Ch Worcester MA 2016-; Dio Wstrn Massachusetts Springfield 2015-** B Santo Domingo DR 1984 s Ruben & Xiomara. BA Wms; BA Wms 2007; MDiv VTS 2015. D 12/6/2014 P 9/12/2015 Bp Doug Fisher. m 10/27/2016 Mary E Rosendale. S Mk's Ch Alexandria VA 2014-2015.

REYNES, Stephen Alan (Vt) 64 State St, Montpelier VT 05602 B Stamford CT 1946 s Robert & Roberta. BA St Mich's Coll 1967; JD Vermont Law Sch 1979. D 12/12/2015 Bp Thomas C Ely. m 8/17/1991 Janet Tarshis Ancel.

REYNOLDS, Bettye (NCal) 4706 Oakbough Way, Carmichael CA 95608 **D La Mision Hispana El Divino Salvador Sacramento CA 1995-; D St Johns Epis Ch Roseville CA 1992-** B Water Valley MS 1935 d Wayne & Gertrude. Mississippi U For Wmn; BA U of Mississippi 1958; BA California Sch for Deacons 1989. D 9/12/1992 Bp Jerry Alban Lamb. c 3.

REYNOLDS, Bo Daniel (WNY) D 6/3/2017 Bp Sean Walter Rowe.

REYNOLDS JR, Edward Charles (Mich) 2112 Melrose Road, Ann Arbor MI 48104 B Havre de Grace MD 1944 s Edward & Jean. BA U MI 1968; MDiv EDS 1971; JD U of Detroit Mercy 1979. D 7/31/1971 Bp Archie H Crowley P 2/2/1972 Bp Richard Stanley Merrill Emrich. c 2. Dio Michigan Detroit MI 1972; S Matt's Epis Ch Flat Rock MI 1971-1978; Vic St Matt's Ch Flat Rock MI USA 1971-1978; H Fam Epis Ch Midland MI 1971; S Tim Ch Richland MI 1971.

REYNOLDS, Eleanor Francis (Nwk) PO Box 240, Mendham NJ 07945 **Sis Cmnty Of St Jn The Bapt 1998-** B Santa Barbara CA 1948 d Henry & Martha. BA U CA 1970; MDiv Drew U 2006. D 6/7/2008 P 12/13/2008 Bp Mark M Beckwith. P Assoc All SS Ch Millington NJ 2008-2009. Cmnty of St. Jn Bapt 1998.

REYNOLDS V, Elsbery Washington (Haw) 1829 NE Berg Way, Bend OR 97701 **Died 8/29/2015** B Pomona CA 1941 s Christopher & Betty. SWTS; BS OR SU 1964; MDiv CDSP 1967; DMin Claremont TS 1977; Cert Mt San Jacinto Coll 1998. D 6/10/1967 Bp Hal Raymond Gross P 12/10/1967 Bp Harry Sherbourne Kennedy. m 10/21/2000 Illa Reynolds c 2. Vic S Hugh Of Lincoln Mssn Idyllwild CA 2002-2008; R S Jas Epis Ch Kamuela HI 1981-1997; Chapl Ascen Kwajalein Atoll Marshall Islands 1979-1981; Vic Emm Epis Ch Kailua HI 1977-1981; S Andr's Cathd Honolulu HI 1976, 1974-1975; Chapl/ Chair of the Rel Dept S Andr's Priory Honolulu HI 1972-1977; Cur Ch Of The Epiph Honolulu HI 1970-1977; Tchr of Rel Educ S Andr's Priory Honolulu HI 1970-1972; Vic Chr Memi Ch Kilauea HI 1969-1970; St Thos Ch Hanalei HI 1969-1970; Vic S Mich And All Ang Ch Lihue HI 1968-1970; Vic S Lk's Epis Ch Honolulu HI 1967-1968; Asst Dir: Educ, Counslg, Contract Compliance Vlly Restart Hemet. CA 1997-1999; Chapl: Kwajalein, Marshall Islands The Epis Ch in Hawaii Honolulu HI 1979-1981.

REYNOLDS, Frederic William (Roch) 579 Sagamore Ave Unit 84, Portsmouth NH 03801 B New York NY 1950 s Robert & Louise. CPE; BA Hobart and Wm Smith Colleges 1973; MDiv EDS 1978. D 10/28/1978 P 6/1/1979 Bp Robert Rae Spears Jr. m 8/5/1978 Jane P Reynolds c 3. R S Paul's Ch Rochester NY 1995-2014; R S Dav's Epis Ch Kennebunk ME 1986-1995; Assoc S Ptr's by-the-Sea Epis Ch Bay Shore NY 1983-1986; Chapl White Mtn Sch Littleton NH 1981-1983; Trin Epis Ch Watertown NY 1978-1981; Chr Ch Sackets Hbr NY 1978-1979.

REYNOLDS, Gail Ann (Kan) 9119 Dearborn St, Overland Park KS 66207 **D S Paul's Ch Kansas City KS 2007-** B Painesville OH 1938 d Nicholas & Edna. BA OH SU 1960; MA U of Missouri 1972. D 9/9/2000 Bp William Edward Smalley. c 2. D S Thos The Apos Ch Overland Pk KS 2000-2005. Oblate, Ord Of Ben, Mt. St. Scholastica 1996. Archdeacons' Cross Dio Kansas 2010.

REYNOLDS SR, Gordon Armstrong (Me) B Seattle WA 1925 D 4/15/1973 P 5/3/1975 Bp Frederick Barton Wolf. m 9/25/1981 Barbara Ann Reynolds. Ch Of The Mssh Dexter ME 1973-1978.

REYNOLDS, James Ronald (FtW) 3717 Cook Ct, Fort Worth TX 76244 B New Martinsville WV 1949 s Edwin & Janet. BA Northwood U 1997; MDiv Nash 2002. D 6/8/2002 P 12/21/2002 Bp Jack Leo Iker. m 10/16/1969 Linda Lee Dey c 2. R S Mart In The Fields Ch Keller TX 2008-2013, Cur 2002-2008.

REYNOLDS, Joe D (Tex) 145 15th St NE Apt 1006, Atlanta GA 30309 **R S Jas Epis Ch Baton Rouge LA 2016-** B Atlanta GA 1946 s Arthur & Phyllis. BA Georgia St U 1971; MDiv VTS 1974. D 6/15/1974 Bp Milton Legrand Wood P 5/28/1975 Bp Bennett Jones Sims. m 12/26/1965 Elizabeth Childress c 3. Dn Chr Ch Cathd Houston TX 2000-2012; H Innoc Ch Atlanta GA 1990-2000, Asst 1974-1977; Chairnan of the Bd H Innoc' Epis Sch Atlanta GA 1990-2000; R Gr Ch Grand Rapids MI 1982-1990; Chapl US-Army Reserves 1981-1988; Assoc S Fran Ch Potomac MD 1981-1982; R S Jas Ch Eufaula AL 1977-1981. jreynolds@stjamesbr.org

REYNOLDS, Katharine Sylvia (Minn) Loring Green East, 1201 Yale Place #610, Minneapolis MN 55403 B Texas City TX 1933 d Thomas & Edith. BA Penn 1955; MDiv Untd TS PA 1980; Cert EDS 1981. D 12/14/1982 P 6/1/1983 Bp Robert Marshall Anderson. m 11/27/1999 Michael H Schwimmer. Ch Of The Epiph Epis Minneapolis MN 1997; Reynolds Consulting Inc Minneapolis MN 1996-2002; Pstr Counslr Dio Minnesota Minneapolis MN 1987-2002; S Jn's Ch Of Hassan Rogers MN 1987-1988; Non-par 1985-1986; Asst R S Alb's Epis Ch Edina MN 1982-1984.

REYNOLDS, Kay (ETenn) 4017 Sherry Dr, Knoxville TN 37918 **Assoc S Lk's Ch Knoxville TN 2010-** B Shreveport LA 1939 d Irvin & Katherine. BA LSU 1962; MA OH SU 1967; PhD OH SU 1974; MDiv Sewanee: The U So, TS 1989. D 5/31/1989 P 5/1/1990 Bp Duncan Montgomery Gray Jr. S Thos Epis Ch Knoxville TN 2002-2009; Tyson Hse Stdt Fndt Knoxville TN 1995-2000; Dio E Tennessee Knoxville TN 1994-2002; P-in-c S Mich And All Ang Knoxville TN 1994-2002; S Matt's Epis Ch Forest MS 1992-1994; Trin Ch Newton MS 1992-1994; Cur S Paul's Epis Ch Meridian MS 1989-1991. Comt,SCHC 1987.

REYNOLDS, Mary Lou Corbett (Neb) Po Box 921, Ogallala NE 69153 **Died 10/19/2015** B Terrington WY 1936 d John & Clarissa. Nova SE U; BA U of Wyoming 1957; MEd U of Wyoming 1966; MDiv Epis TS of the SW 1995. D 6/22/1995 Bp Bob Gordon Jones P 12/1/1995 Bp James Edward Krotz. m 11/23/2015 Dianna L Fritzler. Vic S Geo's Ch Oshkosh NE 1995-2008; Vic S Paul's Ch Ogallala NE 1995-2008.

REYNOLDS, Max Midgley (WTex) 4485 Medina Hwy, Kerrville TX 78028 **Ret 2002-; Ret 2002-** B Groveton TX 1938 s Clem & Essie. BS Texas A&M U 1961; MDiv Sewanee: The U So, TS 1986. D 2/27/1987 P 10/23/1987 Bp John Herbert MacNaughton. c 3. R S Paul's Ch Brady TX 1998-2002; S Andr's Ch Port Isabel TX 1993-1998; Vic Ch Of Our Sav Aransas Pass TX 1990-1993; Ch Of The Ascen Refugio TX 1990-1993; Epis Ch Of The Gd Shepard Geo W TX 1987-1990; S Mich's Ch Lake Corpus Christi TX 1987-1990; St Mich's Epis Ch Geo W TX 1987-1990. Julian of Norwich 1986.

REYNOLDS, Richard Seaver (Mont) 4530 Asa Trl, Stevensville MT 59870 **P-in-c S Paul's Ch Hamilton MT 2015-; P-in-c S Steph's Epis Ch Stevensville MT 2015-** B El Paso TX 1955 s Thompson & Heather. BA U of Mary Hardin-Baylor 1975; MDiv Brite DS 1979; CTh Epis TS of the SW 1983; DMin Evang Luth Sem Tacoma WA 1995. D 6/11/1983 Bp Robert Elwin Terwilliger P 6/10/1984 Bp Donis Dean Patterson. m 9/8/1978 Victoria Reynolds c 3. Emergency Serv Chapl The Chapl of the Tri-Cities 2010-2013; R S Mary's Par Lompoc CA 2000-2006; Chapl Lompoc Police Dept 2000-2005; Chapl Santa Barbara Sherrif Dept 2000-2005; Chapl Stockton Police Dept 1997-2000; R Epis Ch Of S Anne Stockton CA 1996-2000; R S Fran Ch Heber Sprg AR 1988-1996; Vic S Paul's Epis Ch Waxahachie TX 1985-1988; Cur Epis Ch Of The Ascen Dallas TX 1983-1985; Serv Methodist Ch 1977-1982. Auth, "Marital Violence: A Handbook For Ministers," 1991. Oblate Ord Of S Ben. bitterroot.episcopal. priest@gmail.com

REYNOLDS, Robert Eugene (Cal) 6832 Treeridge Dr, Cincinnati OH 45244 **S Thos Epis Ch Terrace Pk OH 2008-; Cler Assoc Pres Dio California 1995-; Cler Assoc,Pres Dio Oregon 1988-; Dep, GC Dio Spokane 1979-** B Prescott AZ 1937 s Fred & Miriam. BA Arizona St U 1963; MDiv CDSP 1966; DD CDSP 2012. D 6/22/1966 P 12/27/1966 Bp James Walmsley Frederic Carman. m 5/28/1989 Elizabeth W Reynolds c 3. Pres, 2002-04 CDSP Alum/ae Coun 2000-2004; Vice Chair, 2004 CDSP Trst 2000-2004; R S Paul's Epis Ch Walnut Creek CA 1989-2005; Comm. on MinistryChair, Dio Oregon 1984-1988; Comm. on MinistryChair, Dio Oregon 1984-1954; R Chr Ch Par Lake Oswego OR 1979-1989; Stndg Com Dio Spokane 1975-1978; RurD, Snake River Dnry Dio Spokane 1972-1979; R All SS Ch Richland WA 1971-1979; COM Dio Spokane 1971-1975; Assoc S Paul's Epis Ch Salem OR 1966-1971; Epis Chapl Willamette U Salem OR 1966-1971. NNECA 1987. R Emer St. Paul's Epis Ch - Walnut Creek 2006.

REYNOLDS, Roger James (Ore) 18271 SW Ewen Dr, Aloha OR 97003 **D S Gabr Ch Portland OR 2016-** B San Francisco CA 1951 s Robert & Olga. BD DeVry Inst of Techology 1972. D 10/12/1990 Bp Robert Louis Ladehoff. m 10/23/1982 Tammy Ellen Reynolds c 1. Assoc Chapl Gd Samar Hosp Portland OR 1991-1996; D S Barth's Ch Beaverton OR 1990-2016.

REYNOLDS JR, Wallace Averal (CFla) 500 W Stuart St, Bartow FL 33830 B Huntington WV 1945 s Wallace & Betty. BBA Marshall U 1971; Cert VTS 1976; PhD U of Kentucky 1992. D 5/24/1975 P 2/28/1976 Bp Robert Poland Atkinson. m 12/12/1964 Shelia Reynolds c 2. R H Trin Epis Ch Bartow FL

2002-2010; Assoc S Ann's Ch Nashville TN 1992-2002; R S Jas' Epis Ch Lewisburg WV 1981-1987; Int S Ptr's Ch Huntington WV 1979-1981; Assoc Trin Ch Huntington WV 1977-1979; Vic Gr Ch Ravenswood WV 1975-1977. drwalreyn@hotmail.com

REZACH, Karen Beverly (Nwk) 74 Edgewood Pl, Maywood NJ 07607 **Hd Of Middle Sch Kent Place Sch 2000-** B Jersey City NJ 1959 d Eugene & Kyong. BA Wm Paterson U 1981; MDiv Yale DS 1996; EdD Seton Hall U So Orange NJ 2002. D 6/2/2007 Bp Mark M Beckwith. Chr Ch Short Hills NJ 2007-2011.

REZIN, Mary Ellen (Eau) 27042 State Highway 21, Tomah WI 54660 **D S Mary's Epis Ch Tomah WI 2004-** B Sparta WI 1950 d William & Evelyn. ADN Wstrn Tech Coll 1982; BSN U of New York 1994. D 2/7/2004 Bp Keith Whitmore. m 11/9/1976 John Rezin.

RHEA, Pamela Towery (Miss) 318 College St, Columbus MS 39701 B Columbus MS 1959 d Coley & Eltra. BS Mississippi U for Wmn 1992. D 1/9/2010 Bp Duncan Montgomery Gray III. m 11/26/1982 Clyde Rhea c 3. S Paul's Ch Columbus MS 2012-2014.

RHEA, Robert E (Tenn) 1401 Lee Victory Pkwy, Smyrna TN 37167 **Vic All SS Epis Ch Smyrna TN 2016-; Vic Dio Tennessee Nashville TN 2016-** B Idabel OK 1958 s Thomas & Helena. BA Oral Roberts U 1982; MD Oral Roberts U 1986; MA Nash 2014. D 6/6/2015 P 1/30/2016 Bp John Bauerschmidt. m 8/1/1981 Lisa M Rhea c 2.

RHOADES, Mary Ann (Chi) PO Box 494, Dixon IL 61021 B Steubenville OH 1942 d Mike & Marie. D 6/28/2014 Bp John Clark Buchanan. c 2.

RHOADES, Stephen James (USC) Saint James Episcopal Church, 301 Piney Mountain Rd, Greenville SC 29609 **R S Jas Epis Ch Greenville SC 2013-** B Aurora IL 1967 BA U IL 1990; JD Chicago-Kent Coll of Law 2003; MDiv Sewanee: The U So, TS 2007. D 6/2/2007 Bp Bill Persell P 12/6/2007 Bp Mary Gray-Reeves. m 1/7/1995 Anna J Notation-Rhoades c 5. Asst P All SS Ch Of Winter Pk Winter Pk FL 2008-2013; Cur All SS Epis Ch Palo Alto CA 2007-2008.

RHOADS, Robert Louis (Oly) 181 W Maple St, Sequim WA 98382 **R S Lk's Ch Sequim WA 1999-** B Bakersfield CA 1953 s John & Florence. BS U CA 1975; MDiv CDSP 1979. D 6/14/1979 Bp Wesley Frensdorff P 12/1/1979 Bp John Lester Thompson III. m 4/25/1992 Patricia A Rhoads. R S Matt's Ch San Andreas CA 1992-1999; S Jas Epis Par Lincoln CA 1981; St Johns Epis Ch Roseville CA 1979-1992. ERM, Ord Of S Lk.

RHOADS, Tommy L (WTenn) 309 E Baltimore St, Jackson TN 38301 **S Lk's Epis Ch Jackson TN 2014-** B Memphis, TN 1954 s Carl & Tommie. Memphis TS; BA Lambuth Coll 1976; BS Lambuth Coll 1984. D 6/26/2010 Bp Don Edward Johnson. m 5/30/1977 Janice R Rhoads c 1.

RHODENHISER, Imogen Leigh (Mich) 410 Church Rd, Bloomfield Hills MI 48304 **Chr Ch Cranbrook Bloomfield Hills MI 2016-** B Ottawa 1985 d Simon & Daryl. MDiv Duke DS; M.A., hon U of S Andrews 2007; MA, Hons U of St Andrews 2007. D 12/12/2015 P 6/11/2016 Bp Wendell Nathaniel Gibbs Jr. m 5/25/2013 Giles Rhodenhiser.

RHODENHISER, James Cousins (Mich) St. Clare of Assisi Episcopal Church, 2309 Packard Road, Ann Arbor MI 48104 **R S Clare Of Assisi Epis Ch Ann Arbor MI 2003-; Dn, Huron Vlly Dnry Dio Michigan Detroit MI 2014-, Chair, Constitutions and Cn 2005-2006** B Richmond VA 1962 s Oscar & Nancye. BA Duke 1984; MA U of Virginia 1991; MDiv Ya Berk 1992. D 6/13/1992 Bp Robert Poland Atkinson P 12/21/1992 Bp Gethin Benwil Hughes. m 7/31/1993 Jayin Lynn Wavrik c 5. R Epis Ch Of The Gd Shpd Salinas CA 1996-2003; Yth Mssnr Dio Maine Portland ME 1993-1996; Assoc R Trin Epis Ch Portland ME 1993-1996; Asst S Ptr's Epis Ch Del Mar CA 1992-1993; Dn, Salinas Vlly Dnry Dio El Camino Real Salinas CA 2001-2003, Presiding Judge, Eccl Trial Crt 2000-2003. Co-Auth, "What Do We Want To Be?," *The Record*, The Epis Dio Michigan, 2006; Auth, "Mnstry w Yth," *The Outlook*, EvangES, 1996. EvangES. james@saintclarechurch.org

RHODES, Charlotte Dimmick (CFla) 414 Pine St, Titusville FL 32796 B Key West FL 1944 d Arthur & Margaret. The Inst for Chr Stds; AA U of Florida 1964. D 12/10/2011 Bp John Wadsworth Howe. m 8/6/1964 Billy Mikell Rhodes c 2.

RHODES, David Hughes (SanD) 47535 Highway 74, Palm Desert CA 92260 B Washington DC 1942 s David & Isabelle. BS Commerce Rider U 1971. D 2/14/2015 Bp Jim Mathes. m 9/17/1993 Rosemarie Malyzska Gerwien c 3.

RHODES, Diane Lynn (Nwk) 38 Lynn St, Harrington Park NJ 07940 **P-in-c S Andr's Ch Harrington Pk NJ 2008-** B Pittsburgh 1949 d George & Bety. BA U Chi 1971; MBA FD 1982; MDiv Drew U 2004; MDiv Drew U 2004. D 6/11/2005 P 12/17/2005 Bp John Palmer Croneberger. Drew U 1999-2001.

RHODES, Erroll Franklin (Cal) 19 Comly Ave, Greenwich CT 06831 B Japan 1924 s Erroll & Bessie. BA Pepperdine U 1943; PhD U Chi 1948; SWTS 1952; Ya Berk 1968. D 6/1/1953 P 12/8/1953 Bp Henry H Shires. m 6/9/1950 Martha Elizabeth Stowell c 3. Exec Coun Appointees New York NY 1973-1996; Translations Dept ABS New York NY 1968-1996; Prof Rikkyo (S Paul's) U - Japan Tokyo 1954-1967; Mssy To Japan 1953-1968; Instr CDSP 1953-1954; Resrch Asst U Chi 1950-1952; Instr Emory U Atlanta GA 1948-1950. Auth, "Translation from German," *A. A. Fischer: The Text of the OT*, Eerdmans, 2014; Ed,

"Gd News Study Bible," ABS, 2000; Co-Ed, "The Translators To The Rdr: The Original Preface Of The King Jas Version 1611 Revisted," ABS, 1997; Auth, "Translation from German," *E. Würthwein: The Text of the OT*, Eerdmans, 1995; Auth, "Translation from German," *K. Aland: The Text of the NT*, Eerdmans, 1987; Auth, "arts in Biblic Scholarly Pub," *Quarterly Pub and Textbooks*, 1960; Auth, "Annotated List of Armenian NT Manuscripts," Rikkyo (S Paul's) U, 1959. SBL, 1947; Studiorum Novi Testamenti Societas 1954.

RHODES, Judith Louise (Ct) 661 Old Post Rd, Fairfield CT 06824 B Arlington MA 1952 d Robert & Bertha. AB Regis Coll Weston MA 1974; MDiv Harvard DS 1991. D 6/5/1993 P 5/21/1994 Bp Don Edward Johnson. m 7/13/2009 Martha Ellen Hughes. R S Paul's Ch Fairfield CT 2010-2015; R S Mary's Epis Ch Ardmore PA 2002-2010; Emm Ch W Roxbury MA 1996-2002; Chr Ch Needham Hgts MA 1993-1996. Dominican Sis S Cathr; Fllshp Soc Of S Jn The Evang.

RHODES, Margaret Diana Clark (WMo) 1815 NE Independence Ave, Lees Summit MO 64086 **R S Anne's Ch Lees Summit MO 2012-** B Keokuk IA 1984 d John & Colette. BA Drury U 2006; MDiv SWTS 2009. D 12/20/2008 P 6/27/2009 Bp Alan Scarfe. m 8/11/2007 Eric Rhodes. P S Paul's Ch Coun Blfs IA 2009-2012.

RHODES, Matthew Wayne (Va) PO Box 153, Millwood VA 22646 **Cunningham Chap Par Millwood VA 2017-** B Lynchburg VA 1970 s Phillip & Margaret. AA Alabama Sthrn Cmnty Coll 1996; BA U of So Alabama 1998; MDiv VTS 2017. D 6/10/2017 Bp Shannon Sherwood Johnston. m 12/14/1996 Amy Cleveland Breeman-Rhodes c 2.

RHODES, Robert Richard (SO) 9 Harrington Ave., Westwood NJ 07675 **Cn Chr Ch Cathd Cincinnati OH 2014-** B St Louis MO 1968 s Glen & Jude. BFA Fontbonne U 1990; MDiv GTS 2003. D 12/27/2002 P 6/6/2003 Bp George Wayne Smith. m 11/15/1997 Debra G Rhodes. R Gr Epis Ch Westwood NJ 2008-2014; R S Matt's Ch Bogalusa LA 2006-2008; Cur S Mart's Ch Ellisville MO 2003-2006. rrhodes@cccath.org

RHODES, Robert Wayne (Oly) 300 W 8th Street Unit 314, Vancouver WA 98660 **Founding Mem Leaders for Mssn Vancouver WA 2007-** B Seattle WA 1942 s Jewell & Wilma. BA U of Washington 1971; MDiv CDSP 1974. D 7/17/1974 P 7/1/1975 Bp Ivol I Curtis. m 9/15/1962 Rita Rhodes c 3. Ch Of The Gd Shpd Vancouver WA 1978-2006; S Anne's Epis Ch Washougal WA 1976-1979; Res-in-Trng S Lk's Epis Ch Vancouver WA 1974-1976. DD CDSP 2013. bobr42@gmail.com

RHODES, William Chester (Az) 7047 N 28th Dr, Phoenix AZ 85051 **Died 9/2/2015** B Philadelphia PA 1948 s John & Janis. BA Ya 1970; MDiv GTS 1976. D 8/7/1976 Bp Lloyd Edward Gressle P 6/1/1977 Bp Harold Louis Wright. P-in-c S Mary's Epis Ch Phoenix AZ 1999-2003; R Ch Of The Adv Of Chr The King San Francisco CA 1984-1999; Asst S Mk's Ch Mt Kisco NY 1978-1984; Asst S Jn's Ch Larchmont NY 1976-1978. Hon Cn Dio Arizona 2010.

RHYNE, Patty (NC) Christ Church, 1412 Providence Rd, Charlotte NC 28207 **Assoc R Chr Ch Charlotte NC 2012-** B Charlotte NC 1954 d William & Betty. BA Brenau U 1976; MDiv Sewanee: The U So, TS 2006. D 6/24/2006 P 1/24/2007 Bp Dorsey Henderson. m 2/18/2017 Stephen Kale Rhyne c 3. Assoc for Pstr Care S Mich And All Ang Ch Dallas TX 2008-2012; Assoc for Mssn and Outreach Chr Ch Greenville SC 2006-2008. willetp@christchurchcharlotte.org

RICE, Charles Lynvel (Nwk) 618 Quaker Plain Rd, Bangor PA 18013 **P-in-c S Mk's Ch Mendham NJ 2011-** B Chandler OK 1936 s William & Dorothy. BA Baylor U 1959; BD Sthrn Bapt TS 1962; STM UTS 1963; PhD Duke 1967. D 1/16/1988 P 6/4/1988 Bp John Shelby Spong. Trin Epis Ch Mt Pocono PA 2008-2010; S Thos Ch Vernon NJ 2005-2007; Int S Dunst's Epis Ch Succasunna NJ 2001-2003; Int Chr Ch Short Hills NJ 1998-1999; Int S Lk's Ch Hope NJ 1996-1998; Int S Ptr's Ch Morristown NJ 1996-1997, Assoc 1988-1996; Ch Of The Mssh Chester NJ 1987-1988. Auth, *The Embodied Word*, 1990; Auth, *Preaching the Story*, 1980; Auth, *Interp & Imagination*, 1970. Acad Homil 1970. Prof Emer Drew U 2003.

✠ RICE, The Rt Rev David C (SJ) Diocese Of San Joaquin, 1528 Oakdale Rd, Modesto CA 95355 **Epis Dio San Joaquin Modesto CA 2014-** B Lexington NC 1961 s Charles & Wilma. BA Lenoir Rhyne U 1983; MDiv Duke Div 1989; MDiv Duke DS 1989. Trans 2/23/2014 Bp Chester Lovelle Talton. m 10/21/1989 Elizabeth T Rice c 2. bishopdavid@diosanjoaquin.org

RICE, Debra Harsh (WNC) PO Box 2319, Franklin NC 28744 B Columbus OH 1950 d George & Elsie. BS Otterbein U 1971. D 9/22/1980 P 5/1/1981 Bp Robert Shaw Kerr. m 7/10/1971 John David Sayre Rice c 1. R S Jn's Epis Ch Franklin NC 2007-2012; Dir of Chr Formation Ch Of The Gd Shpd Hayesville NC 2006-2007; Chapl Black Mtn Correctional Cntr for Wmn Black Mtn 1999-2004; S Jas Ch Black Mtn NC 1995-1999; St Mary's and St Steph's Epis Ch Morganton NC 1993-1995; S Jn The Bapt Epis Hardwick VT 1990-1991; Stff The Ch Of The H Sprt Lake Forest IL 1986-1988; S Andr's Epis Ch Colchester VT 1984-1985; Dioc Rel Educ Consult Dio Vermont Burlington VT 1980-1983; Assoc S Jas' Epis Ch Black Mtn NC 1999.

RICE, Doreen Ann (Kan) **S Fran Of Assisi Stilwell KS 2016-** D 6/13/2015 P 6/11/2016 Bp Dean E Wolfe.

RICE, Edward G (NH) 37 Harbor Way Unit 13, Wolfeboro NH 03894 B New York NY 1943 s Kurt & Dorothy. BA Trin Hartford CT 1966; MDiv EDS 1971. D 12/16/1972 P 6/16/1974 Bp H Coleman Mcgehee Jr. c 2. Int-R All SS Epis Ch Wolfeboro NH 2012-2014; Int-R S Steph's Ch Ridgefield CT 2011-2012; P-in-c Trin Memi Ch Philadelphia PA 2008-2011; Int-R The Ch Of The H Trin W Chester PA 2005-2008; R S Paul's Ch Dedham MA 1994-2004; R All SS Ch E Lansing MI 1981-1994; Assoc R Chr Ch Dearborn MI 1976-1981; Non-par Common Ground Birmingham MI 1975-1976; Mssnr to Yth Chr Ch Cranbrook Bloomfield Hills MI 1972-1975, Mssnr to Yth 1972-1975; Non-Parochail Action For Boston Cmnty Dvlpmt Boston MA 1968-1972; Chair - Com On Compstn Dio Michigan Detroit MI 1990-1994. Auth, "H Week Lrng Centers"; Auth, "Healthy Chr Communities".

RICE JR, Frank Gracey (Tenn) 4901 Timberhill Dr, Nashville TN 37211 **Died 7/10/2016** B Chattanooga TN 1925 s Frank & Mabel. BA Baylor U 1948; BD Sewanee: The U So, TS 1951; DMin Van 1974. D 8/19/1951 Bp Gerald Francis Burrill P 2/20/1952 Bp Charles A Mason. m 12/30/1954 Isabel J McKay c 2. Ret 1986-2016; Dio Tennessee Nashville TN 1986; Chapl Hosp/Insts Nashville TN 1958-1986; Epis Dvlpmt Corp Nashville TN 1958-1985; P-in-c S Anne's Ch Ft Worth TX 1954-1956; Min in charge S Mart Epis Ch New Boston TX 1951-1953.

RICE, Glenda Ann (Ak) PO Box 1130, Sitka AK 99835 B Scotia CA 1952 d Farrell & Jo Ann. AA U of Alaska SE Sitka 2008. D 5/1/2011 Bp Mark A Lattime. c 3.

RICE, John David Sayre (WNC) 51 North View Circle, Hayesville NC 28904 **St Chapl - NC Ord of S Lk NC 2005-** B Columbus OH 1949 s Earnest & Eleanor. BS U of Vermont 1976; MA U of Vermont 1978; MDiv SWTS 1988. D 6/15/1988 P 12/15/1988 Bp Daniel Lee Swenson. m 7/10/1971 Debra Harsh Rice c 1. R Ch Of The Gd Shpd Hayesville NC 2003-2012; Centurion Hse Asheville NC 2001-2005; R S Jas Ch Black Mtn NC 1993-2001; R S Mk's Epis Ch Newport VT 1988-1993. Ord of S Lk 1998.

RICE JR, John Fay (Va) 240 Old Main St, South Yarmouth MA 02664 B Philadelphia PA 1941 s John & Sonia. BA Rhodes Coll 1963; MDiv SWTS 1968; LEAD Consultants 1980; DMin McCormick TS 1980; Coll of Preachers 1989. D 6/16/1968 Bp John Vander Horst P 5/1/1969 Bp William Evan Sanders. m 5/30/1964 Maxine M Rice c 2. Chapl Hse Of The Redeem New York NY 2011; R Trin Ch Arlington VA 1995-2000; Int S Dav's Epis Mssn Pepperell MA 1995; Cn to the Ordnry Dio Massachusetts Boston MA 1991-1995; R Trin Ch Huntington WV 1987-1991; Dio Tennessee Memphis TN 1983-1991; R S Dav's Epis Ch Nashville TN 1978-1987; Asst Ch Of The H Comm Memphis TN 1975-1978; Vic Ch of the H Apos Collierville TN 1971-1975; Asst Ch Of The Ascen Knoxville TN 1969-1971; Pres, Stndg Com Dio Tennessee Nashville TN 1986-1987, Bd, Mnstry of Recon 1978-1987. Associated Parishes, Liturg Conf 1971-1987.

RICE, Lawrence Allen (NMich) 5526 S Baker Side Rd, Sault Sainte Marie MI 49783 **D S Jas Ch Of Sault S Marie Sault Sainte Marie MI 2006-** B Ogdensburg NY 1938 s Clarence & Violet. D 5/28/2006 Bp James Arthur Kelsey. m 7/2/1960 Catherine Rice c 2.

RICE, Randolf James (ECR) 2534 Dumbarton Ave, San Jose CA 95124 B San Jose CA 1947 s James & Bette. BA U CA 1969; Harv 1970; BD CDSP 1972; JD Hastings Coll of Law 1978. D 6/24/1972 Bp George Richard Millard P 1/6/1973 Bp Clarence Rupert Haden Jr. m 11/26/2013 Robin Nicholas Merrell. Chancllr Dio El Camino Real Salinas CA 1993-1998, Cn Chncllr 1998-, Com 1972-1997; Trin Cathd San Jose CA 1978-1980; Vic Chr Epis Ch Sei Ko Kai San Francisco CA 1975-1978; Cur Calv Epis Ch Santa Cruz CA 1972-1975. Auth, "Var arts Law".

RICE, Rodney Vincent (NY) 914 Adana Road, Pikesville MD 21208 B Winston-Salem NC 1960 s William & Willie. MDiv Yale DS 1987; BA U NC 1993; EdM Harv 1996. D 9/12/1987 P 5/26/1988 Bp Peter J Lee. Assoc S Jas Ch New York NY 1993-1995; R S Andr's Chap At S Andr's Sch 1991-1993; S Andr's Sch Chap Middletown DE 1991-1993; P S Jas' Epis Ch Baltimore MD 1989-1991; S Paul's Ch Richmond VA 1987-1989.

RICE, Sandra Kay (Md) Retired, Frederick MD 21701 **D Dio Maryland Baltimore MD 2000-** B Frederick MD 1945 d Henry & Alice. BA Hood Coll 1995; Sewanee: The U So, TS 2000. D 6/3/2000 Bp Robert Wilkes Ihloff. m 7/21/1963 Wilbur Eugene Rice c 2. Dir of Outreach All SS Ch Frederick MD 2004-2011; Dir of Outreach The Gathering: A Fam Of Faith Epis Ch Walkersville MD 2000-2004; Chapl Assisted Living Ashbury Methodist Vill Gaithersburg MD 1998-2000. Daugters of the King 2001.

RICE, Steven C (NC) 2575 Parkway Dr, Winston Salem NC 27103 **R S Tim's Epis Ch Winston Salem NC 2008-** B Greenwood SC 1979 s Easton & Eleanor. BA Erskine Coll 2000; MDiv Candler TS Emory U 2004; DMin Nash 2013. D 2/5/2005 P 8/6/2005 Bp Henry Irving Louttit. m 10/20/2001 Cherilyn A Rice c 3. D S Mich's Ch Waynesboro GA 2005-2008. Auth, "Catholicity," *Yearning*, Ch Pub, 2013. CBS 2007; Our Lady of Walsingham 2012; Soc of Cath Priests 2009.

RICE, Whitney (Ind) St. David's Episcopal Church, P.O. Box 1798, Nashville IN 47448 **S Fran In The Fields Zionsville IN 2016-; R S Thos Ch Franklin**

IN 2013- B Lee's Summit MO 1982 d Charles & Judith. BA U of Kansas 2005; MDiv Ya Berk 2008. D 6/7/2008 Bp Barry Howe P 1/17/2009 Bp Cate Waynick. R Dio Indianapolis Indianapolis IN 2013-2016; S Dav's Ch Beanblossom Beanblossom IN 2011-2013; Cur Chr Ch Cathd Indianapolis IN 2008-2011; Supervised Mnstry Stdt Chr Ch Redding CT 2007-2008; Supervised Mnstry Stdt S Jn's Ch Guilford CT 2006-2007. rev.whitney.rice@gmail.com

RICE, Winston Edward (La) 512 E Boston St, Covington LA 70433 **Chapl/Exec Dir Maritime Pstr Inst Covington LA 2015-; Asstg P Chr Ch Covington LA 2011-, Assoc R 2008-2015, Asst R 2005-2008, Transitional D 2004-2005; Trst Christwood Ret Cmnty Covington Louisiana 2007-** B Shreveport LA 1946 s Winston & Margaret. JD LSU 1971; Cert Sch for Mnstry Dio Louisiana 2002; Cert The McFarland Inst 2002. D 12/29/2004 Bp Charles Edward Jenkins III P 6/29/2005 Bp James Barrow Brown. m 4/16/1977 Barbara G Gay c 4. Chapl for Gulf Coastal Reg Seamens Ch Inst New York NY 2011-2014; Int Exec Dir of SECC Dio Louisiana New Orleans LA 2010; P-in-c S Matt's Ch Bogalusa LA 2005; Pres Epis Curs in Louisiana New Orleans LA 2001-2003. Mltry and Hospitaller Ord of St. Lazarus of Jerusalem 2008. chapwin@maritimepastoral.org

RICH III, Edward Robins (SwFla) 11315 Linbanks Pl, Tampa FL 33617 B Baltimore MD 1947 s Edward & Carolyn. BA Davis & Elkins Coll 1969; MDiv VTS 1972. D 5/25/1972 P 2/4/1973 Bp David Keller Leighton Sr. m 6/7/1969 Sherry Rich c 3. R St Cathr of Alexandria Epis Ch Temple Terrace FL 2000-2010; Asst S Mary's Par Tampa FL 1998-2000; R Gr Ch Grand Rapids MI 1991-1997; Bd Gvnr Appalachian Peoples Serv Orgnztn 1985-1997; R Chr Epis Ch Of Springfield Springfield OH 1985-1991; Stwdshp Area Rep Off of Stwdshp The Epis Ch 1984-1997; P-in-c New Life Epis Ch Uniontown OH 1982-1984; Dn Akron Cler 1981-1984; Chr Stwdshp Com Dio Ohio 1979-1985; R S Ptr's Ch Akron OH 1976-1985; Asst S Paul's Ch Canton OH 1974-1976; Asst Gd Shephed Ruxton MD 1973-1974. Auth, "The Pearl Of Great Price: A Manual For Par Stwdshp"; Auth, "The Hidden Treasure: Journey In Stwdshp Of Time & Talent".

RICH JR, Ernest Albert (Az) 10625 W White Mountain Rd, Sun City AZ 85351 **Ret 1986-** B Bluefield VA 1922 s Ernest & Alice. BA Ken 1949; VTS 1952. D 6/11/1952 P 12/10/1952 Bp John Thomas Heistand. m 6/21/1952 Ruth W Watt c 5. R S Chris's Ch Sun City AZ 1981-1986; R S Jn's Ch Ellicott City MD 1956-1981; Vic/R S Jas Bedford PA 1952-1956; S Lk's Epis Ch Altoona PA 1952-1956. Auth, *VTS Journ.*

RICH, Michael Glenn (Ala) 408 Church Ave SE, Jacksonville AL 36265 **S Andrews's Epis Ch Birmingham AL 2014-** B Gadsden AL 1961 BD NWU 1984; MS NWU 1985; PhD U of Iowa 2001; MDiv GTS 2006. D 5/31/2006 Bp Marc Handley Andrus P 12/12/2006 Bp Henry Nutt Parsley Jr. R S Lk's Epis Ch Jacksonville AL 2006-2014.

RICH, Nancy Willis (O) 5650 Grace Woods Dr Unit 203, Willoughby OH 44094 **Assoc Trin Cathd Cleveland OH 2002-** B Washington DC 1936 d Howard & Virginia. BA Wstrn Maryland Coll, now McDaniel Coll 1958; MS W Virginia U 1960; CAS GTS 1987; MDiv S Mary Roman CatholicSeminary, Cleveland, OH 1989. D 6/11/1988 Bp James Russell Moodey P 6/3/1989 Bp Arthur Williams Jr. m 8/22/1959 James Chandler Rich c 4. Asst Epis W Side Shared Mnstry Cleveland OH 2001-2002; P-in-c S Mk's Epis Ch Wadsworth OH 1997-2000; "Wmn Together" team; Liturg planner Dayspring Cntr for Sprtlty Wellington OH 1996-2006; Int S Chris's By-The River Gates Mills OH 1996-1997; Int S Phil's Epis Ch Akron OH 1993-1995; S Mk's Ch Cleveland OH 1992; Asst S Paul's Ch Akron OH 1989-1991; Asst Ch Of The Incarn Cleveland OH 1988-1989. nancyw.rich@sbcglobal.net

RICH, Noel David (Minn) 808 Eldo Ln SW, Alexandria MN 56308 **Ret 2007-** B Seattle WA 1942 s Ralph & Lucille. BS Penn 1966; MDiv VTS 1979. D 6/22/1979 Bp David Rea Cochran P 1/5/1980 Bp Samuel B Chilton. m 3/19/1966 Virginia L Rich c 1. R S Jas' Epis Ch Fergus Falls MN 2005-2006; R Emm Epis Ch Alexandria MN 1996-2006; R Chr Ch Madison IN 1987-1996; Asst R S Andr Epis Ch Mentor OH 1983-1987; S Fran By The Sea Ch Kenai AK 1981-1983; P-in-c S Fran-By-The-Sea Kenia AK 1980-1983; P-in-c S Ptr's Ch Seward AK 1980-1983; Mssy Tchr Iglesia Anglicana En Vina Del Mar Vina Del Mar Chile 1979-1980; Truro Epis Ch Fairfax VA 1979-1980. Bd Trst SAMS 1988.

RICH, Susan Chandler (EMich) Grace Episcopal Church, 735 W. Nepessing, Lapeer MI 48446 **R Trin Epis Ch Bay City MI 2016-** B Cleveland OH 1960 d James & Nancy. BS Ohio U 1983; MDiv Epis TS of the SW 2004. D 6/5/2004 Bp Michael Smith P 12/18/2004 Bp Edwin Max Leidel Jr. R Gr Epis Ch Lapeer MI 2010-2016; Mssnr Dio Estrn Michigan Saginaw MI 2009-2012; Dioc Liturg Coordntr 2013-; R S Jn's Epis Ch Dryden MI 2004-2016. revsuerich@gmail.com

RICH, Timothy Thayer (RI) St Luke's Episc Ch, 99 Pierce St, East Greenwich RI 02818 **P S Lk's Epis Ch E Greenwich RI 2012-** B Mount Kisco NY 1962 s Wesley & Joan. BS Geo 1984; U of Maryland 1987; MDiv SWTS 1993. D 6/12/1993 Bp Ronald Hayward Haines P 12/16/1993 Bp Jane Hart Holmes Dixon. c 4. Dio New Hampshire Concord NH 2004-2012; R S Jn's Ch Portsmouth NH 1996-2004; Asst R Chr Epis Ch No Hills Pittsburgh PA 1993-1996; Assoc R Chr Epis Ch Pottstown PA 1993-1996. trich@nhepiscopal.org

RICH, William Warwick (Mass) 333 Ricciuti Drive Unit 1526, Quincy MA 02169 **Sr Assoc for Chr Formation Trin Ch Epis Boston MA 2005-** B Fairmont WV 1953 s Adrian & Marian. BA Wms 1975; MDiv Yale DS 1980; STM UTS 1995; MPhil UTS 2001; PhD UTS 2002. D 4/26/1980 P 5/9/1981 Bp David Keller Leighton Sr. m 9/5/2009 Donald Craig Schiermer. Int S Paul's Ch Doylestown PA 2004-2005; Int Chr Ch Bronxville NY 2003-2004; Int S Dav's Ch Kinnelon NJ 2002-2003; The Ch Of S Lk In The Fields New York NY 2001-2002; Dir Post Ord Trng Dio Maryland Baltimore MD 1992-1994, Dn Diac Formation 1985-1991, Bp's Com on Chr-Jewish Relatns 1988-1998, Liturg and Mus Com 1984-1994; Chapl Goucher Coll 1987-1999; Asst Memi Ch Baltimore MD 1987-1999; R Gr Ch Elkridge MD 1983-1987; Asst S Jn's Ch Reisterstown MD 1980-1983. Auth, "Gr And Imagination," *Journ Of Rel And Hlth*, 2001; Auth, "Var Bk Revs," *Journ of Rel and Hlth.* AAR 2000-2006; SBL 2000-2006. Phi Beta Kappa 1975. wrich@trinitychurchboston.org

RICHARD, Helen Taylor (Ore) 123 Grove St, Lebanon OR 97355 **D S Mart's Ch Lebanon OR 1987-** B Ely NV 1931 d Enoch & Myrna. CDSP; BS Oregon Coll of Educ 1953; MEd OR SU 1963. D 11/1/1987 Bp Robert Louis Ladehoff. m 8/4/1955 John Francis Richard c 2. CHS.

RICHARD, Mary B (WLa) PO Box 1627, Shreveport LA 71165 **R Ch Of The H Cross Shreveport LA 2008-** B Fort Worth TX 1947 d Jack & Elizabeth Mackey. BA U of Texas 1969; Dip Theol Stud The Angl TS 2005. D 6/7/2008 P 3/7/2009 Bp D Avid Bruce Macpherson. m 1/24/1970 Herschel Richard c 3.

RICHARDS, Anne Frances (NY) 150 west end ave apt. 9h, new york NY 10023 **Gr Ch Brooklyn NY 2016-; Int Gr Ch Corona NY 2016-** B Worcester MA 1951 d John & Anne. BA Smith 1973; MA NYU 1980; MDiv GTS 1988. D 12/4/1988 Bp Furman Charles Stough P 6/4/1989 Bp Jose Antonio Ramos. m 5/28/2004 Richard Frank Grein c 2. Sr Asst S Mk's Ch New Canaan CT 2008-2013; Chapl Gr Ch Sch New York New York NY 2004-2008; Chapl Gr Ch Sch New York NY 2004-2008; Sr P Assoc Gr Epis Ch New York NY 2001-2004; Cn Ordnry Dio New York New York NY 1995-2001, COM Chair 1990-1995; Assoc The Ch Of S Lk In The Fields New York NY 1995-2001; Ch Of The Heav Rest New York NY 1995-1996, 1991-1995; Dir Pstr Care Franklin Hosp Med Cntr Vlly Stream NY 1989-1992. Auth, "Cler Sexual Misconduct: Epis & RC Cler," *Predatory Priests, Silenced Victims: The Sexual Abuse Crisis & the Cath Ch*, Analytic Press, 2007. Friends of Julian of Norwich 2001. Bp's Cross Dio New York 2001; Best Sermon Competition (Winner) Epis/Evang Fndt 1994.

RICHARDS, Anne Marie (RI) 7 Cowsill Ln, Newport RI 02840 **R Trin Ch Newport RI 2010-; Ecum Off Dio Rhode Island Providence RI 2013-, Bp's Search Com 2011-2012, Dioc Coun 2010-2012** B Olney MD 1966 d Thomas & Mary. BS Columbia Un Coll Takoma Pk MD 2000; MDiv VTS 2005. D 6/11/2005 P 1/21/2006 Bp John Bryson Chane. m 12/30/1989 Brook Richards c 2. Assoc Trin Ch Princeton NJ 2005-2010.

RICHARDS, Daniel P (Az) 1031 E Sahuaro Dr, Phoenix AZ 85020 **Chr Ch Of The Ascen Paradise Vlly AZ 2015-; P-in-c Ch Of The H Innoc 2005-** B Cleveland MS 1975 s Terry & Judy. BA Grand Canyon U 1997; MDiv CDSP 2003. D 5/24/2003 P 12/13/2003 Bp Robert Reed Shahan. m 2/17/2007 Amy R Richards c 2. Dn (Rural) Dio Wstrn Michigan 2010-2015; Dn - Grand Traverse Dnry Dio Wstrn Michigan Kalamazoo MI 2010-2015; R Gr Epis Ch Traverse City MI 2009-2015; Vic Epis Ch of the H Sprt Phoenix AZ 2008-2009; Vic Dio Arizona Phoenix AZ 2005-2007, COM 2004-2009; Cur Epis Par Of S Mich And All Ang Tucson AZ 2003-2004. Poet, "And We Drown . . .," *Ruah*, Ruah Dominican Soc, 2002. Excellence in Mnstry Schlrshp CDSP 2000. daniel.richards@ccaaz.org

✠ RICHARDS, The Rt Rev David Emrys (SeFla) 625 N Greenway Dr, Coral Gables FL 33134 **Form Bp of Costa Rica Dio Costa Rica 1968-** B Scranton PA 1921 s Emrys & Ida. BA Leh 1942; STB GTS 1945; STD GTS 1952. D 4/7/1945 Bp Frank W Sterrett P 10/1/1945 Bp Reginald Heber Gooden Con 7/19/1951 for Alb. m 6/15/1950 Helen Richards. Epis Ch Cntr New York NY 1978-1988; Coordntr Com Pstr Dvlpmt Ecec 1969-1988; Off Of Pstr Dvlpmt Miami FL 1969-1977; Bp Dio Costa Rica 1967-1968; Bp-in-Charge Dio Nicaragua & Honduras 1967-1968; Bp of Cntrl Amer Dio Cntrl Amer 1957-1967; Suffr Bp Of Alb Dio Albany Greenwich NY 1951-1957, Archd 1950-1951; Asst S Geo's Epis Ch Schenectady NY 1948-1950; P-in-c S Mary The Vrgn Cristobal RP 1945-1948.

RICHARDS, Dennison Sherman (LI) 107-66 Merrick Blvd, Jamaica NY 11433 **R Ch Of S Jas The Less Jamaica NY 2009-** B Castries St Lucia WI 1965 s Quentin & Amy. BA Codrington Coll 1994; Advance CPE Residency Coll of Pstr Supervision and Psych 2000; DD Mstr's Intl Sch of Div 2011. Trans 6/26/2002 Bp Orris George Walker Jr. m 1/7/1995 Fay Moreen Richards c 1. S Paul's Ch Roosevelt NY 2004-2008; Epis Hlth Serv Far Rockaway NY 2003-2008; Dir of Pstr Care/Chapl Bp Chas W Maclean Epis Nrsng Hm Far Rockaway NY 2001-2008; Rel Educ Tchr St. Mk's Day Sch 1346 Pres St Brooklyn NY 1999-2007; Dio Coun Dio Long Island Garden City NY 2008-2011, Bd Dir 2003-2007; Bd Dir Epis Cmnty Serv Long Island 1927 Bay Shore NY

2008-2011. Black Cler Caucus 2002; CPSP Far Rockaway Chapt 2000. DD Masters Intl Sch of Div 2011; Res Chapl Awd Epis Hlth Serv 2000.

RICHARDS, Edward Thomas (CGC) PO Box 7359, Panama City Beach FL 32413 **Vol Cler Kairos of the Emerald Coast 2013-; Visitor Prision Visitation and Spprt Marianna FCI 2013-; Vol Chapl Bay Med Cntr Sacr Heart System 2008-; Vol Chapl Gulf Coast Med Cntr 2008-; Com for Structural Reform Dio Cntrl Gulf Coast Pensacola FL 2013-, Cmsn on Prison Mnstry 2012-** B Providence RI 1944 s Earl & Cathlene. BS Cor 1966; MBA Butler U 1968. D 2/10/2011 Bp Philip Menzie Duncan II. c 4.

RICHARDS, Emily Barr (Pa) 654 N Easton Rd, Glenside PA 19038 **R S Ptr's Ch Glenside PA 2009-; Cathd Chapt Mem Cathd Ch of Our Sav Philadelphia PA 2012-; Dn of Montgomery Deaney Dio Pennsylvania Philadelphia PA 2012-** B Lexington KY 1971 d Garland & Donna. BA U So 1994; MDiv Sewanee: The U So, TS 2002. D 6/8/2002 P 5/20/2003 Bp Stacy F Sauls. m 12/28/1996 Luman Daniel Richards c 1. Asst S Steph's Ch Ridgefield CT 2005-2009; Vic All SS Epis Ch Lexington KY 2005; Vic S Alb's Ch Morehead KY 2002-2005. stpeter654rector@gmail.com

RICHARDS, Erin Kathleen (ND) 301 Main St S, Minot ND 58701 B Montclair NJ 1969 d Paul & Virginia. BS U of No Dakota 1994. D 11/1/2013 P 11/1/2014 Bp Michael Smith. m 8/1/1992 Gregory Richards.

RICHARDS, Fitzroy Ivan (Oly) 12499 Eagle Dr, Burlington WA 98233 **Ret 1998-** B Carapichima Trinidad TT 1926 s Sylvanus & Adora. Dalhousie U; LTh U of Kings Coll Halifax CA 1962. Trans 5/30/1988 Bp Robert Hume Cochrane. m 11/14/1964 Yuklin Clementine Richards c 3. P-in-c Chr Epis Ch Anacortes WA 1992-1998; Vic S Jas Ch Sedro Woolley WA 1988-1990; R S Geo Calgary AB Can 1984-1987; R S Laurence Calgary AB Can 1973-1984; R S Ptr Sicamous BC Can 1968-1972; R S Paul Slocan BC Can 1963-1968; Cur All SS Vernon BC Can 1962-1963.

RICHARDS JR, George Richard (Roch) 18 Haviland Dr, Scotia NY 12302 **Died 5/13/2017** B Scranton PA 1936 s George & Olive. BA Wilkes Coll 1958; STB PDS 1961. D 6/21/1961 P 2/24/1962 Bp Frederick Warnecke. m 6/24/2017 Doris Richards c 1. Non-par 1969-2017; Vic S Mths Epis Ch Rochester NY 1963-1969; Dio Rochester Henrietta 1961-1968; S Jas' Ch Drifton PA 1961-1963.

RICHARDS, Gerald Wayne (Be) 265 Old Mine Rd, Lebanon PA 17042 **Ret 1996-** B Philadelphia PA 1934 s Richard & Margaret. BA Juniata Coll 1956; MDiv Crozer TS 1959; CAS PDS 1960. D 11/18/1961 Bp Andrew Y Tsu P 6/13/1962 Bp Conrad H Gesner. m 10/10/1959 Sue Ann Richards c 3. PA Coun Chs - Del Dio Bethlehem Bethlehem PA 1988-1992; R S Lk's Ch Lebanon PA 1973-1996; R S Mk's Ch Millsboro DE 1966-1973; Gr Epis Ch Madison SD 1961-1966; DeSmet, SD S Steph's Ch DeSmet SD 1961-1966; Vic Trin Howard SD 1961-1966; ExCoun Dio Delaware Wilmington 1970-1973. Angl Soc. Citation for Serv to S Lk's and Lebanon PA Pennsylvania Hse of Representatives 1996.

RICHARDS, Jeffery Martin (O) 2510 Olentangy Dr, Akron OH 44333 **1985-** B Akron OH 1928 s Martin & Mona. BS U of Akron 1951; BD Bex Sem 1959; MA Kent St U 1969. D 6/13/1959 P 12/19/1959 Bp Nelson Marigold Burroughs. P-in-c S Jn's Epis Ch Cuyahoga Fls OH 1984-1985; P-in-c S Andr's Ch Akron OH 1982-1984; Int S Paul's Epis Ch Of E Cleveland Cleveland OH 1967-1968, Cur 1959-1966; P-in-c S Aug's Epis Ch Youngstown OH 1962-1967; Cur Ch Of Our Sav Akron OH 1961-1962.

RICHARDS, Michael Gregory (Los) PO Box 220383, Newhall CA 91322 **Dir Middle Grades Ethics Proj Newhall CA 2007-; Profsnl Advsry Bd Pk Century Sch Los Angeles CA 2002-; Chapl Beverly Hills Police Beverly Hills CA 1992-** B Torrance CA 1947 s Michael & Vera. BA California St U 1968; MDiv GTS 1971; Cert Coll of Fin Plnng 1987; PhD Un Inst & U 2011. D 9/11/1971 P 3/18/1972 Bp Francis E I Bloy. m 8/16/1969 Deborah Elizabeth Saville c 2. Pstr to the Cler Dio Los Angeles Los Angeles CA 2002-2010, Hon Cn Cathd Cntr of St. Paul 2002-, Coordntr - Epis Relief And Dvlpmt 1989-2001, Dioc Coun 1983, Cler Senate 1975-1977; Eductr-in Res S Alb's Epis Ch Los Angeles CA 1998-2002; Trst Pk Century Sch Los Angeles CA 1993-2001; Chapl Campbell Hall Epis Studio City CA 1988-2002; Chapl Campbell Hall Vlly Vlg Ca 1988-2002; Fndr All SS' Sch Beverly Hills CA 1984-2002; R All SS Par Beverly Hills CA 1982-1988; Assoc R S Steph's Par Whittier CA 1971-1973. Auth, "Ethics for YA," *Ethics for YA*, Kazanjian Fndt, 2015; Auth, "When Someone You Know Is Hurting," ZondervanHarper, 1994. St Geo Awd ECUSA 1982.

RICHARDS, Rosalie (Ct) 536 Old Glen Avenue, Berlin NH 03570 B North Platte NE 1949 d Mark & Mary. BA Baylor U 1972; MA U of Texas 1975; MDiv GTS 1981; MSW Col 1992; PhD Univ TX Sch of Publ Hlth 1996. D 6/13/1981 P 3/14/1982 Bp Paul Moore Jr. c 1. Chr Ch Canaan CT 2006-2011; S Lk's Ch Charlestown NH 2004; Un-St. Lk's Epis Ch Claremont NH 2004; Exec Dir New Haven Hm Recovery 1989-1992; Ascen Ch New Haven CT 1984-1989; S Ann's Ch Of Morrisania Bronx NY 1982-1984; Gr Epis Ch Nyack NY 1981-1982. co-Auth, "Alive and Spkng; a Medium Explains the Sprt Wrld to an Epis P," XLibris, 2013; Auth, "Variables Associated w Ethnic Violence and w Nonviolent Response," *Dissertation*, The U of Texas Sch of Publ

Hlth, 1996; Chapt co-Auth, "Homeless Wmn and Feminist Soc Wk Pract.," *Feminist Pract in the 21st Century.*, NASW Press, 1995. Outstanding Wmn of New Haven 1987; Outstanding Wmn of Amer 1983.

RICHARDS, Susan M (Pa) 1074 BROADMOOR RD, BRYN MAWR PA 19010 B Philadelphia PA 1945 d Donald & Mary. BFA Moore Coll of Art & Design Philadelpia PA 1967; MS Neumann Coll Aston PA 1990; MDiv VTS 1994. D 11/12/1994 P 11/1/1995 Bp Allen Lyman Bartlett Jr. m 8/6/1967 John Hartwell Richards. Asst All SS Ch Norristown PA 1999-2004; Incarn H Sacr Epis Ch Drexel Hill PA 1996-1997; The Ch Of The Trin Coatesville PA 1994-1996; P-in-c Incarn-H Sacrement. Soc Of S Marg.

RICHARDS, Tyler Clayton (Ala) 324 Hickory Knl, Birmingham AL 35226 **S Andr's Ch Montevallo AL 2016-** B Scottsboro AL 1984 s Timothy & Beverly. B.A. U of Alabama 2013; M.Div Sewanee: The U So, TS 2016. D 5/14/2016 Bp Santosh K Marray P 12/10/2016 Bp John Mckee Sloan Sr. m 4/23/2016 Colleen Katherine Mikelson. rev.tyler16@gmail.com

RICHARDSON, Carolyn Garrett (SanD) 3515 Lomas Serenas Dr., Escondido CA 92029 **Supply, Tchg, Pstr Care Trin Ch Escondido CA 2011-; Supply Dio San Diego San Diego CA 2007-, Sch For Chr Mnstry - Tchr 2014, Eccl Trial Crt 2008-2011, Bp Com for Study of Open Comm 2006, Bp. Com for Sprtl Direction 2003-2005, Dioc Coun 2001-2004, Sprtl Direction Com 2001-2003, Muhabura Mssn Com 1997-1999, Dioc Coun - Exec Com 1995-1998, Sch For Chr Mnstry - Exec Coun 1995-1997** B Whittier CA 1951 d Owen & Martha. BA California Wstrn U 1973; Cert USIU San Diego CA 1974; MDiv Claremont TS 2001; MA Alliant Intl U 2012. D 6/12/1999 P 8/25/2002 Bp Gethin Benwil Hughes. m 5/25/1974 Kenneth Edward Richardson c 2. MFT Trainee & Intern/Sr Spec No Inland Mntl Hlth Clnc MHS Escondido 2011-2013; Long-term Supply S Anne's Epis Ch Oceanside CA 2010; Chapl & Bereavement Coordntr Hospice of the No Coast Carlsbad CA 2008-2010; Long-term Supply S Hugh Of Lincoln Mssn Idyllwild CA 2008; Tchg Asst. Alliant Intl Univ. 2007-2008; Asst R S Barth's Epis Ch Poway CA 2001-2006; Chapl Eliz Hospice 1999-2000; Chapl Hospice of Sharp HealthCare 1998-1999. "People Can't Be Replaced," *LivCh*, 1996. AAMFT 2007. Dorothy M. Mulac Bk Awd ETS, Claremont 1998.

RICHARDSON, Christopher C (SO) 2151 Dorset Rd., Columbus OH 43221 **S Mk's Epis Ch Columbus OH 2014-** B Columbus OH 1984 s Deryck & Nadya. BS DeVry U 2005; MDiv VTS 2009. D 6/13/2009 P 6/19/2010 Bp Thomas Edward Breidenthal. m 12/6/2014 Sheena L Richardson. S Andr's Ch Dayton OH 2011-2014; S Tim's Epis Ch Cincinnati OH 2009-2011. assistantrector@saintmarkscolumbus.org

RICHARDSON, David Anthony (Az) 3111 Silver Saddle Dr, Lake Havasu City AZ 86406 **R Gr Ch Lake Havasu City AZ 2004-** B Upton Wirral UK 1941 s Cuthbert & Clarice. Soc of the Sacr Mssn 1966. Trans 10/5/2005 Bp Kirk Stevan Smith. m 9/3/1968 Mary Elizabeth Richardson c 2. Gr Epis Ch Lk Havasu City AZ 2005-2012; Assoc St. Phil's in the Hills Tucson AZ 1998-2003; Serv Ch of Engl 1966-1998.

RICHARDSON, Ellen H (Ga) 311 10th St W, Tifton GA 31794 **S Anne's Ch Tifton GA 2014-** B Jacksonville FL 1952 d John & Louise. MDiv EDS; BA Georgia St U 1974; MD Med Coll of Georgia 1987. D 2/9/2008 P 9/27/2008 Bp Henry Irving Louttit. m 8/2/1981 Mark Lewis Richardson c 2. Int P S Paul's On-The-Hill Winchester VA 2013, Assoc P 2010-2012; Int Vic S Lk's Epis Ch Rincon GA 2008-2009. Auth, "H Dying: Stories and Struggles," *Bk*, Ch Pub, 2017. ellen@stannestifton.com

RICHARDSON JR, Grady Wade (Ala) 605 Country Club Dr, Gadsden AL 35901 B New York NY 1938 s Grady & Josephine. BA Birmingham-Sthrn Coll 1961; BD VTS 1968. D 6/14/1968 P 5/18/1969 Bp George Mosley Murray. m 8/29/1964 Virginia G Richardson c 1. P-in-c Calv Ch Oneonta AL 2005-2010; S Phil's Ch Ft Payne AL 1998-2005; R Ch Of The Epiph Tunica MS 1990-1998; Chapl S Mart Pines Birmingham AL 1985-1990; S Martins-In-The-Pines Ret Comm Birmingham AL 1985-1990; Assoc S Mary's-On-The-Highlands Epis Ch Birmingham AL 1978-1985; R S Jas' Epis Ch Alexander City AL 1975-1978; R Gr Ch Cullman AL 1974-1975; Cur Chr Ch Tuscaloosa AL 1968-1970. Contrib, *Living Ch*, 1994; Contrib, *Selected Sermons*, 1990; Auth, *Congressional Record*, 1980; Auth, *Pulpit Dig*, 1974.

RICHARDSON, James David (NCal) 1700 University Ave, Charlottesville VA 22903 **P-in-c Ch Of The Incarn Santa Rosa CA 2015-** B Berkley CA 1953 s David & Margaret. BA U CA 1975; MDiv CDSP 2000. D 6/10/2000 P 1/13/2001 Bp Jerry Alban Lamb. m 5/20/1989 Lori Korleski. R S Paul's Memi Charlottesvlle VA 2008-2015; All Souls Par In Berkeley Berkeley CA 2007-2008; Asst Trin Epis Cathd Sacramento CA 2000-2006. Auth, "The Mem'S Speaker: How Willie Brown Held Cntr Stage In California," *Racial & Ethnic Politics In California*, 1998; Auth, "Willie Brown: A Biography," U CA, 1996; Auth, "California Political Almanac," California Journ Press. Fllshp Of Reconcilliation 2002; Save Hetch Hetchy Soc 1998. revjimr@incarnationsantarosa.org

RICHARDSON, Janet Beverly (Ind) 310 Del Mar Dr, Lady Lake FL 32159 B Rochester NY 1946 d Robert & Betty. BS SUNY 1968; AA Finger Lakes Cmnty Coll 1981; MDiv Earlham Sch of Rel 1993. D 6/24/1992 P 1/17/1993 Bp Edward Witker Jones. m 8/9/1975 Marcus Richardson c 3. Dio Indianapolis In-

R

dianapolis IN 2008-2013, P 2008-; P S Jas Ch New Castle IN 1999-2008; Trin Ch Connersville IN 1999-2003, P 1993-1998, D 1992-1993.

RICHARDSON, Jeffrey Roy (SC) **Vic S Alb's Ch Kingstree SC 2005-; S Steph's Ch S Steph SC 2005-** B Bethesda MD 1955 s Julius & Dorothy. BA Wofford Coll 1977; MDiv Nash 2005. D 6/11/2005 P 12/7/2005 Bp Edward Lloyd Salmon Jr. m 7/4/1981 Patty C Richardson c 4. CBS 2004; SocMary 2003.

RICHARDSON JR, John Dowland (CGC) 19 Gaywood Circle, Birmingham AL 35213 **Sr Pstr St. Ptr's Angl (AMiA) Birmingham AL 2003-** B Tampa FL 1962 s Harold & Betty. BS U of Alabama 1983; MDiv Sewanee: The U So, TS 1993; DMin Trin Evang DS 1999. D 6/5/1993 Bp Furman Charles Stough P 12/11/1993 Bp Robert Oran Miller. m 12/19/2003 Kristen Jane Richardson c 2. H Nativ Epis Ch Panama City FL 1996-2003; Asst. R S Mk's Ch Geneva IL 1994-1996; Cur S Mary's-On-The-Highlands Epis Ch Birmingham AL 1993-1994.

RICHARDSON, John Marshall (WMo) 23405 S Waverly Rd, Spring Hill KS 66083 **D S Ptr's Ch Harrisonville MO 1999-** B Little Rock AR 1949 s William & Elizabeth. BS Missouri Wstrn St U 1973. D 2/14/1998 Bp John Clark Buchanan. m 8/9/1970 Barbara Diane Richardson. Ord Of S Lk.

RICHARDSON, Jon (Pa) 3820 the Oak Rd, Philadelphia PA 19129 **P-in-c H Trin Epis Ch Vlly Stream NY 2014-** B Lake Charles LA 1978 s Charles & Carolyn Ann. BGS LSU 2004; MDiv Drew U 2007. D 6/6/2009 P 12/12/2009 Bp Mark M Beckwith. R Ch Of The Gd Shpd Philadelphia PA 2012-2014; S Paul's Ch In Bergen Jersey City NJ 2010-2012; S Paul's Epis Ch Chatham NJ 2009-2010; Dir of Yth & Fam Mnstry S Ptr's Ch Morristown NJ 2007-2009.

RICHARDSON, Marcia Ann Kelley (Me) 6 Jewett Cove Rd, Westport Is ME 04578 B Natick MA 1939 d Wingate & Marguerite. U of Connecticut 1958; AS Universit of Maine Augusta ME 1989. D 8/29/1998 Bp Chilton Richardson Knudsen. m 6/6/1959 George Dewey Richardson c 4. D S Phil's Ch Wiscasset ME 1998-2000.

RICHARDSON, Mary M (Cal) 5833 College Ave, San Diego CA 92120 **Dio Los Angeles Los Angeles CA 2001-** B Leon MX 1952 d Jose & Yolanda. ETSBH 1999. D 4/26/2002 Bp Joseph Jon Bruno P 2/13/2005 Bp Gethin Benwil Hughes. m 7/11/1997 Scott Eric Richardson. Dio California San Francisco CA 2015; Cathd Ch Of S Paul San Diego CA 2009-2012; Dio San Diego San Diego CA 2003-2008; Epis Chapl Los Angeles CA 2002-2003.

RICHARDSON, Michael Wm (Colo) 16181 Parkside Dr, Parker CO 80134 **R S Matt's Parker CO 2005-** B Portales NM 1957 s William & Bennie. Adams St Coll 1978; BA Metropltn St Coll of Denver 1994; MDiv Epis TS of the SW 1997. D 6/7/1997 P 12/27/1997 Bp William Jerry Winterrowd. m 6/15/1991 Jo Ellen R Randolph c 2. Ch Of Our Sav Colorado Sprg CO 1997-2004. frmichael@smecp.org

RICHARDSON, Susan (Pa) 20 N American St, Philadelphia PA 19106 **Asst Chr Ch Philadelphia Philadelphia PA 2014-, 2006-2010** B Augusta GA 1961 Bachelors of Mus U GA 1983; Masters of Mus Indiana U 1987; PhD Indiana U 1997; MDiv PrTS 2004; CAS VTS 2006. D 6/3/2006 P 12/9/2006 Bp George Edward Councell. c 1. Int S Ptr's Ch Freehold NJ 2012-2014; Gr St Pauls Ch Trenton NJ 2010-2012.

RICHARDSON, W Mark (Cal) Church Divinity School of the Pacific, 2451 Ridge Rd, Berkeley CA 94709 **CDSP Berkeley CA 2010-; Dir Of Prog Cntr For Theol & Natural Sciences 1990-** B Eugene OR 1949 s William & Audrey. BA U of Oregon 1971; MDiv PrTS 1975; PhD Grad Theol Un 1990. D 6/3/1978 P 12/10/1978 Bp Paul Moore Jr. m 6/9/1984 Brenda L Richardson c 2. The GTS New York NY 1999-2010; Trin Educ Fund New York NY 1986-1990; Assoc Dir Trin Inst Brooklyn NY 1986-1990; Trin Par New York NY 1986-1990; Assoc Trin Par Menlo Pk CA 1984-1986, 1982; Cur Ch Of The Ascen New York NY 1978-1981. Stetson Epis Ch Fell. Post-Doc Awd Sir Jn Templeton Fndt.

RICHAUD III, Reynold Hobson (Tenn) P.O. Box 808, Townsend TN 37882 B Midland TX 1950 s Reynold & Elizabeth. BA LSU 1985; MDiv Sewanee: The U So, TS 1993. D 6/12/1993 Bp Robert Jefferson Hargrove Jr P 4/1/1994 Bp Bertram Nelson Herlong. m 8/12/1972 Janet N Richaud c 1. R Trin Ch Clarksville TN 2001-2014; S Matt's Epis Ch Mcminnville TN 1995-2001; Vic S Mich's Epis Ch And U Cookeville TN 1995; D-in-Trng S Geo's Ch Nashville TN 1993-1994; DuBose Conf Cntr Bd Dio Tennessee Nashville TN 2011-2014, COM 2002-2014.

RICHEY, Donald Delose (Ct) 99 Willowbrook Rd, Cromwell CT 06416 **Chr Ch Millville NJ 2005-** B Greenwich CT 1961 s Donald & Diana. D 12/9/2000 Bp Andrew Donnan Smith. m 7/5/1992 Gail Richey c 3. Dio Connecticut Meriden CT 2005-2010.

RICHEY, Leon Eugene (O) 2727 Barrington Dr, Toledo OH 43606 B Dresden OH 1933 s George & Mabel. BA Ohio Wesl 1955; BD Garrett-Evang TS 1959; MDiv Garrett-Evang TS 1972. D 6/17/1967 Bp Nelson Marigold Burroughs P 12/17/1967 Bp John Harris Burt. m 5/29/1955 Mona J Richey c 3. P-in-c S Paul's Ch Oregon OH 1996-2005; Chapl Riverside Hosp Toledo OH 1995-1998; Pstrl Assoc Trin Ch Toledo OH 1993-1995; Int Gr Ch Defiance OH 1990-1992; 1988-1990; R S Mk's Epis Ch Toledo OH 1976-1989; R Gr & S Mary's Cleveland OH 1972-1976; R Gr Ch Cleveland OH 1972-1976; Vic

S Tim's Ch Macedonia OH 1969-1976; Serv Methodist Ch 1956-1967; Plnng Cmsn Dio Ohio Cleveland 1979-1982. Assn S Barn Bro; Intl Ord of S Lk. DD Intl Bible Sem 1984.

RICHMOND III, Allen Pierce (Ak) 2602 Glacier St, Anchorage AK 99508 **Ret 1989-** B Hanover NH 1921 s Allen & Constance. BS U of New Hampshire 1944; MS NYU 1955. D 11/12/1972 P 5/25/1973 Bp William Jones Gordon Jr. m 7/27/1944 Veva P Richmond. Asst S Matt's Epis Ch Fairbanks AK 1979-1989; Asst S Christophers Ch Anchorage AK 1974-1979; Non-par 1972-1973.

RICHMOND, John David (Spr) 4105 S Lafayette Ave, Bartonville IL 61607 **Supply P All SS Ch Morton IL 2006-** B Lincoln NE 1952 s Robert & Mary. BA SMU 1974; MS U IL 1979; MDiv Nash 1985; U IL 1995. D 6/11/1985 P 12/13/1985 Bp Richard Frank Grein. m 8/1/1992 Barbara Ellen Richmond c 1. Chap Of S Jn The Div Champaign IL 2012-2013; Supply P Trin Ch Lincoln IL 2010-2011; S Matt's Epis Ch Bloomington IL 2007-2009; S Paul's Epis Ch Pekin IL 2001-2002; Supply P Dio Texas Houston TX 1995-2001; Supply P Dio Springfield Springfield IL 1994-1995; Chapl Res CPE Meth Hosp Peoria IL 1993-1994; Chr The King Epis Ch Normal IL 1987-1993; Asst S Mich And All Ang Ch Mssn KS 1985-1986; Cur S Thos The Apos Ch Overland Pk KS 1985-1986. Auth, "Hard Times for These Times," *Publ Libraries*, Publ Libr Assn, 2003.

RICHMOND, Seth Gunther (Colo) 460 Prospector Ln, Estes Park CO 80517 **R S Barth's Ch Estes Pk CO 2009-** B Des Moines IA 1960 s Thomas & Joanne. BS Trevecca Nazarene U 1985; Cert Nash 1990; MDiv Trin Evang DS 1990; Cert Norbertine Cntr For Sprtlty 2004. D 6/16/1990 P 12/1/1990 Bp Frank Tracy Griswold III. m 8/12/1989 Sally Carleton Mary Richmond c 1. R S Anne's Epis Ch De Pere WI 2001-2009; R Ch Of The Gd Shpd Rangeley ME 1993-2000; Assoc Trin Epis Ch Oshkosh WI 1990-1993; Dn Dio Fond du Lac Appleton WI 2004-2009, Dioc Coun 2004-2009. Auth, "Power and Authority," *LivCh*, 2000; Auth, "Time of Healing and Hope," *LivCh*, 1996.

RICHMOND, Susan Odenwald (Mass) 197 8th St Apt 801, Charlestown MA 02129 B Saint Paul MN 1949 d Harold & Elaine. BA U NC 1971; MDiv Ya Berk 1996. D 6/1/1996 P 12/7/1996 Bp Richard Frank Grein. m 8/26/1972 Christopher Richmond c 2. Int P S Jas' Epis Ch Cambridge MA 2007-2008; Int P S Andr's Ch Framingham MA 2004-2007; Int P Trin Ch Topsfield MA 2002-2003; Asst Old No Chr Ch Boston MA 2001-2002; Int P S Andr's Ch Brewster NY 1999-2000; Asst S Barn Ch Irvington NY 1996-1999.

RICHNOW, Douglas Wayne (Tex) 4014 Meadow Lake Ln, Houston TX 77027 **Assoc S Jn The Div Houston TX 2003-, Sr. Assoc R 1995-2001** B Pasadena TX 1946 s James & Mary. Doctor of Mnstry Austin Presb TS; BS U of Texas 1970; MDiv VTS 1992; DMin Austin Presb TS 1999. D 6/27/1992 Bp Maurice Manuel Benitez P 1/21/1993 Bp William Jackson Cox. m 8/23/1980 Angela E Epley c 3. R S Lk's Epis Ch Birmingham AL 2001-2003; The Great Cmsn Fndt Houston TX 1994-1995; Assoc R S Matt's Ch Austin TX 1992-1994. Ord of St. Lazarus of Jerusalem 2004.

RICHTER, Amy Elizabeth (Md) St. Anne's Episcopal Church, 199 Duke of Gloucester St, Annapolis MD 21401 **Instr St. Mary's Sem Baltimore MD 2010-; R S Anne's Par Annapolis MD 2009-** B Scarborough ON CA 1966 d George & Patricia. BA Valparaiso U 1987; MTS Harvard DS 1989; MDiv PrTS 1993; CAS GTS 1994; PhD Marq 2010. D 6/4/1994 P 5/27/1995 Bp Allen Lyman Bartlett Jr. m 8/26/1990 Joseph Samuel Pagano. Mssnr for Lifelong Chr Formation Dio Maryland Baltimore MD 2006-2009; R S Paul's Ch Milwaukee WI 2000-2006; Asst R S Chrys's Ch Chicago IL 1995-2000; Asst Min The Epis Ch Of The Adv Kennet Sq PA 1994-1995. Co-Auth, "Love in Flesh and Bone," Wipf and Stock, 2014; Auth, "Enoch and the Gospel of Matt," Wipf and Stock, 2012; Co-Auth, "A Man, A Wmn, a Word of Love," Wipf and Stock, 2012. Enoch Seminar 2013; SBL 2008. arichter@stannes-annapolis.org

RICHTER, Kerlin J (Ore) 399A Himrod St, Brooklyn NY 11237 **Dio Oregon Portland OR 2016-** B Nashville TN 1978 d John & Margaret. BS Tennessee St U 2001; MDiv GTS 2013; MDiv The GTS 2013. D 4/27/2013 Bp Michael Hanley P 12/7/2013 Bp Lawrence C Provenzano. m 6/14/2002 Jordan P Richter c 1. Dio Long Island Garden City NY 2013-2015.

RICHTER JR, William Thompson (Tex) 2929 Woodland Hills Dr, Kingwood TX 77339 **R Ch Of The Gd Shpd Kingwood TX 2015-, 2009-2015** B Greenwood MS 1957 s William & Sherley. BA Millsaps Coll 1979; MS VPI 1986; MDiv Sewanee: The U So, TS 1995. D 6/17/1995 P 3/2/1996 Bp Alfred Marble Jr. m 6/14/2014 Karla K Quinby-Richter c 1. Ch Growth And Evang Cmsn Mem Dio Cntrl Gulf Coast 2005-2007; R S Simon's On The Sound Ft Walton Bch FL 2004-2009; S Andr's Cathd Jackson MS 1995-2004.

RICK II, John William (Ct) 625 S St Andrews Pl, Los Angeles CA 90005 **Asst Soc Of S Marg 1978-** B Saint Louis MO 1941 s John & M Arline. BA Washington U 1965; MBA U of Virginia 1967; MDiv Yale DS 1974. D 6/22/1974 Bp George Leslie Cadigan P 5/1/1975 Bp Joseph Warren Hutchens. Gr Epis Ch Alexandria VA 1996-1997; S Jas Par Los Angeles CA 1994-1995; The Epis Ch Of Beth-By-The-Sea Palm Bch FL 1994; P-in-c S Chris In Nassu 1982-1984; Asst The Ch Of The Adv Boston MA 1979-1980; Cur Chr Ch Greenwich

CT 1974-1975. Omicron Delta Kappa; Outstanding Young Men Amer; Who'S Who In Rel.

RICKARD, Robert Burney (At) 1228 Whitlock Ridge Dr Sw, Marietta GA 30064 **Died 2/18/2016** B Memphis TN 1934 s Carroll & Rubye. BA Rhodes Coll; BD Sewanee: The U So, TS. D 6/24/1959 Bp Theodore N Barth P 6/1/1960 Bp John Vander Horst. m 3/4/1981 Ruth Ann Rickard. S Clem's Epis Ch Canton GA 1989-1996; Asst S Dunst's Epis Ch Atlanta GA 1983-1988; Non-par 1977-1982; Vic S Jas Cumberland Furnace TN 1973-1976; Non-par 1968-1972; Assoc R Ch Of Our Sav Washington DC 1962-1965; Vic Chr Ch Brownsville TN 1960-1962; Cur Chr Ch Cathd Nashville TN 1959-1960. Key To City Washington 1965. wcrickard@gmail.com

RICKARDS JR, Joseph Asher (Ind) Spring Mills, 109 Jamestown Dr, Falling Waters WV 25419 **Ret 1992-** B Raleigh NC 1927 s Joseph & Emily. BS W Virginia U 1950; BD Bex Sem 1959. D 6/11/1959 P 12/19/1959 Bp Wilburn Camrock Campbell. m 3/24/1951 Nancy Rickards c 3. R S Steph's Ch Terre Haute IN 1972-1992; R S Steph's Epis Ch Beckley WV 1960-1972; Asst S Jn's Epis Ch Charleston WV 1959-1960. Fllshp Coll of Preachers 1973.

RICKARDS, Reese Stanley (Eas) 115 Nentego Dr, Fruitland MD 21826 B Johnstown NY 1930 s Harold & Lyle. Chicago Deacons Sch; OH SU; SWTS; Worcester Jr Coll. D 9/16/1972 Bp James Winchester Montgomery. m 10/31/1953 Jean M Rickards c 4. Ret S Alb's Epis Ch Salisbury MD 1993-2000; Asst D Ch Of The H Comm Maywood IL 1989-1992; Asst D S Greg's Epis Ch Deerfield IL 1986-1988; Asst D S Mart's Ch Des Plaines IL 1975-1986; Asst D S Anselm Pk Ridge IL 1972-1975; D Dio Chicago Chicago IL 1972-1974; MC, GC, 2006 Ecusa / Mssn Personl New York NY 2011; Ass't to Bp Dio Easton Easton MD 2002-2005, Cmncatn Off 1995-2002. ECom Assn 1999.

✠ RICKEL, The Rt Rev Gregory Harold (Oly) 3209 42nd Ave SW, Seattle WA 98116 **Bp of Olympia Dio Olympia Seattle 2007-; Bd Trst Epis TS Of The SW Austin TX 2007-** B Omaha NE 1963 s Morris & Linda. BA U of Arkansas 1984; MA U of Arkansas 1987; MA U of Arkansas 1993; MDiv Epis TS of the SW 1996; DMin Sewanee: The U So, TS 2002. D 7/8/1996 P 1/18/1997 Bp Larry Maze Con 9/15/2007 for Oly. m 5/26/1984 Martha R Rickel c 1. R S Jas Ch Austin TX 2001-2007; S Ptr's Ch Conway AR 1996-2001. *Living w Money (included Essay)*, Morehouse, 2002. DD Sem of the SW 2007. GRickel@ecww. org

RICKENBAKER, James Robert (EC) PO Box 275, Stafford VA 22555 **Aquia Ch Stafford VA 2016-** B Spartanburg SC 1989 s Thomas & Matilda. BA Appalachian St; MDiv VTS 2016. D 6/4/2016 Bp Robert Stuart Skirving. m 5/21/2016 Rachel Amelia Rickenbaker.

RICKENBAKER, Rachel Amelia (Va) PO Box 127, Upperville VA 20185 B Montgomery AL 1990 d Dennis & Debra. BS Shenandoah U 2013; BS Shenandoan U 2013; BS Shenandoan U 2013; MDiv VTS 2016. D 6/11/2016 P 12/10/2016 Bp Shannon Sherwood Johnston. m 5/21/2016 James Robert Rickenbaker. rshows08@su.edu

RICKENBAKER, Thomas (EC) Box 548, Edenton NC 27932 B Cheyenne WY 1956 s Arthur & Julia. BA U of So Carolina 1978; MDiv VTS 1983; Certification Ldrshp Acad for New Directions 1984; Certification Int Mnstry Ntwk 2013. D 6/11/1983 P 5/12/1984 Bp William Arthur Beckham. m 6/18/1994 Cynthia Gosnell Rickenbaker c 3. Police Chapl Dio E Carolina Kinston NC 1999-2014, Dn, Albemarle Dnry 2009-2011, COM 2000-2008; R S Paul's Epis Ch Edenton NC 1998-2013; Dio Upper So Carolina Columbia SC 1996-1998, Police Chapl 1996-1998, 1989-1990, Evang Consult 1988-1998, Dioc Coun 1995-1998, Dn Estrn Deanry 1993-1998, Chair Com on Ords 1993-1995, Trst 1991-1992, 1989-1990, Stndg Com 1988, New Ch Growth & Dvlpmt Cmsn 1985-1998, COM 1985-1995, Chair Dioc Yth Mnstrs 1985-1987, Dioc Coun 1985-1987; S Marg's Epis Ch Boiling Spgs SC 1986-1998; No Spartanburg Epis Mssn Boiling Spgs SC 1984-1985; Asst S Chris's Ch Spartanburg SC 1983-1984. Police Chapl Assn 1994-2014.

RICKER, Linda Seay (SVa) D 4/16/2016 Bp Herman Hollerith IV.

RICKER, Mark (Eau) St Andrews Episcopal Church, PO Box 427, Ashland WI 54806 **Epis Ch Of S Jn The Bapt Granby CO 2017-** B Pompton Plains NJ 1955 s Stanley & Claire. BA The King's Coll 1977; AA Cntrl FL Bible Coll 2004; MDiv Nash 2012. D 5/26/2012 Bp Gregory Orrin Brewer P 8/17/2013 Bp William Jay Lambert III. c 4. D-in-c S Andr's Ch Ashland WI 2013-2017, P-in-c 2013-.

RICKERT, David (NCal) **S Mich's Epis Ch Carmichael CA 2016-** D 6/24/2017 Bp Barry Leigh Beisner.

RICKETTS, Linda Harriet (Mass) 12607 Cascade Hls, San Antonio TX 78253 B Haverhill MA 1948 d Kenneth & Mary. BSE U of Arkansas 1970; MDiv VTS 1988. D 6/11/1988 P 12/14/1988 Bp John Thomas Walker. m 9/18/2012 Robert Duane Ferre c 1. Chapl Hope Hospice 2004-2009; Assoc Par Of Chr Ch Andover MA 1998-2004; Dio Wstrn Massachusetts Springfield 1988-1998; Vic S Andr's Ch Turners Fall MA 1988-1998; Assoc S Jas' Ch Greenfield MA 1988-1998.

RICKETTS, Marcia Carole Couey (NwT) 133 Olivias Ct, Tuscola TX 79562 B Mobile AL 1955 d Freddie & Marion. BA Sam Houston St U 1976; BBA Agape

Sem of Jesus Chr 1981. D 10/28/2001 Bp C Wallis Ohl. m 12/18/1976 Robert William Ricketts c 2. D Ch of the Heav Rest Abilene Abilene TX 2001-2006.

RICKETTS, Nancy Lee (Tex) 1500 N Capital of Texas Hwy, Austin TX 78746 **D S Mich's Ch Austin TX 2010-** B Oklahoma City OK 1948 d Lee & Marian. BA Oklahoma St U 1970; JD U of Texas Sch of Law 1973; MDiv Epis TS of the SW 2008. D 6/19/2010 Bp C Andrew Doyle. m 12/30/1972 Philip Ricketts c 1.

RICKEY, David (Cal) 430 29th Ave, San Francisco CA 94131 B Buffalo NY 1946 s John & Dorothy. BA Westminster Coll 1968; MDiv UTS 1972; Cert Blanton-Peale Grad Inst 1977. D 6/12/1971 Bp Leland Stark P 4/8/1972 Bp George E Rath. Chapl Epis Sr Communities Lafayette CA 2005-2013; R S Ptr's Epis Ch San Francisco CA 1997-2013; P-in-c S Paul's And Trin Par Tivoli NY 1993-1995; Non-par 1988-1997; Assoc The Ch of S Ign of Antioch New York NY 1984-1987; P-in-c S Steph's Ch Jersey City NJ 1975-1984; Cur Gr Ch Nutley NJ 1972-1974; S Clem's Ch Hawthorne NJ 1971-1972.

RICO, Bayani Depra (NCal) 2420 Tuolumne St, Vallejo CA 94589 **R Ascen Epis Ch Vallejo CA 2008-; Co-Chair, Cmsn For Intercultural Mnstry The Epis Dio Nthrn California Sacramento CA 2008-** B Bacolod City Phil 1951 s Federico & Merenciana. AA Trin 1969; BTh S Andrews TS 1973; MDiv S Andrews TS 1993. Trans 11/24/2009 Bp Barry Leigh Beisner. m 3/22/1977 Bethsaida Rico c 4.

RIDDICK, Daniel Howison (SwVa) 240 Blackwater Ridge Ln, Glade Hill VA 24092 B Lynchburg VA 1941 s Joseph & Nancy. BA Duke 1963; MD Duke 1967; PhD Duke 1969. D 11/16/1969 Bp Angus Dun P 11/1/1970 Bp William Foreman Creighton. m 6/9/1963 Louisa Riddick c 2. Assoc R Calv Ch Underhill VT 1994-1997; R S Jn's In The Mountains Stowe VT 1986-1991; Asst Trin Epis Ch Collinsville CT 1979-1985; Asst S Jos's Ch Durham NC 1971-1979.

RIDDLE III, Charles Morton (SVa) 1102 Botetourt Gdns Apt B-5, Norfolk VA 23507 B Danville VA 1934 s Charles & Mildred. BA U of Virginia 1957; BD VTS 1963; Sch Cont Educ 1970; London TS 1982; S Georges Coll Jerusalem IL 1982; S Georges Coll Jerusalem IL 1985; DMin VTS 1985. D 6/24/1963 P 6/1/1964 Bp David Shepherd Rose. m 12/12/2009 Patricia L Leake c 3. Ch Of The Epiph Danville VA 2005-2007; Int Epiph Danville VA 2005-2006; Int S Paul's Ch Wilkesboro NC 2003-2004; Int S Andrews on the Sound Wilmington NC 2000-2001; Int The Epis Ch Of Gd Shpd Asheboro NC 1999-2000; Int Ch Of The H Comf Charlotte NC 1997-1999; Int S Mich's Ch Raleigh NC 1995-1997; Int S Jn's Epis Ch Charlotte NC 1994-1995; Int S Paul's Epis Ch Winston Salem NC 1992-1994; Int Chr Ch New Bern NC 1991-1992; R Gr - S Lk's Ch Memphis TN 1986-1991; VTS Alexandria VA 1986-1991; Alt Dep GC 1982-1985; R Estrn Shore Chap Virginia Bch VA 1971-1986; R Calv Ch Tarboro NC 1966-1971; Cur Trin Ch Portsmouth VA 1963-1966; Chair - COM Dio W Tennessee Memphis 1990-1991.

RIDDLE, Hill Carter (La) 1515 Robert St, New Orleans LA 70115 B Danville VA 1936 s Charles & Mildred. BA U of Virginia 1958; MDiv VTS 1964; VTS 1991. D 6/1/1964 Bp George P Gunn P 5/23/1965 Bp David Shepherd Rose. m 8/25/1962 Anne M Riddle c 3. Int S Paul's Ch New Orleans LA 2008; Int R St. Mich and All Ang Ch Dallas TX 2006-2007; Int R St. Augustines Ch Metairie LA 2005-2006; Ch Of The Trsfg Silver Sprg MD 2000-2004; Dep GC Dio Louisiana New Orleans LA 1991-1994, Dep GC 1979-1990; R Trin Ch New Orleans LA 1984-2003; R Chr Epis Ch Roanoke VA 1974-1984; R Ch Of S Jas The Less Ashland VA 1968-1974; Asst to R S Jn's Ch Hampton VA 1964-1968; Exec Bd Dio SW Virginia Roanoke VA 1976-1978; Exec Bd Dio Virginia Richmond VA 1971-1974. "Bloom in Your Season," *Bloom in Your Season*, self, 2004. Hon DD VTS 1991.

RIDDLE, Jennifer Lynne (Ala) 530 Hurst Rd, Odenville AL 35120 **Chapl S Martins-In-The-Pines Ret Comm Birmingham AL 2010-** B Pell City AL 1965 d Frank & Linda. BS Judson Coll 1986; MDiv New Orleans Bapt TS 1990; DAS VTS 2001. D 5/20/2001 P 12/11/2001 Bp Henry Nutt Parsley Jr. Asst R Ch Of The Epiph Guntersville AL 2001-2010.

RIDEOUT, Robert Blanchard (SO) 7121 Muirfield Dr., Dublin OH 43017 **D S Pat's Epis Ch Dublin OH 2009-; Mem, Dioc Coun Dio Sthrn Ohio Cincinnati OH 2014-** B Ithaca NY 1941 s Blanchard & Anne. BA Wesl 1963; MPA Pr 1969. D 6/13/2009 Bp Thomas Edward Breidenthal. m 5/9/1970 Martha S Rideout c 2. On Call Chapl (contingent) Nationwide Chld's Hosp Columbus OH 2007-2011.

RIDER, David M (NY) 424 W End Ave Apt 9c, New York NY 10024 **Pres and Exec Dir Seamens Ch Inst New York NY 2007-** B South Bend IN 1954 s Jack & Catherine. BA Carleton Coll 1977; MDiv UTS 1980; Cert Advncd CPE 1982; Cert Washington Sch of Psych 1988; STM GTS 1989; Cert Harv 1999; STM UTS 2001. D 6/24/1980 P 3/25/1981 Bp Edward Witker Jones. m 5/31/1980 Jacqueline Haines c 2. R All SS Ch Harrison NY 2011-2016; S Mk's Ch New Canaan CT 2004-2007; The CPG New York NY 2003-2015, Sr VP 1992-2002; P-in-c Gr Epis Ch New York NY 2001-2004; Dio New York New York NY 2000-2001; S Mk's Epis Ch Yonkers NY 2000; Pstr Counslg Cntr Oakton VA 1991; Int Ch Of The Ascen Gaithersburg MD 1989-1991; VTS Alexandria VA 1989; Int S Dunst's Epis Ch Beth MD 1988-1989; Assoc

R S Jn's Ch Chevy Chase MD 1982-1987; Asst S Alb's Ch Indianapolis IN 1980-1981. AAPC. Hon Cn Cathd of S Jas 1996. drider@seamenschurch.org

RIDER, Joe (CFla) 400 18th St, E 4, Vero Beach FL 32960 **P-in-c S Simon the Cyrene Ft Pierce FL 2013-** B Fort Worth TX 1948 s Joseph & Jean. B. Sci Texas Wesleyan Coll 1970; Cert GTS 1974; MEd Florida Atlantic U 2000. D 6/5/1974 P 12/7/1974 Bp Theodore H McCrea. R S Jas Cathd Guatemala City Guatemala 1992-1994; Chapl S Edw's Sch Vero Bch FL 1986-1992; R S Jn The Div Epis Ch Burlington WI 1979-1986; Asst S Paul's Ch Milwaukee WI 1978-1979; Assoc Gr Ch Madison WI 1976-1977; Cur S Alb's Epis Ch Arlington TX 1975-1976; Asst S Andr's Ch Grand Prairie TX 1974-1975. joerider@ekit.com

RIDER, Paul G (Minn) 401 S 1st St Unit 610, Minneapolis MN 55401 B Tarrytown NY 1957 s Franklin & Polly. BA U of Arkansas 1981; MA U of Arkansas 1985; MDiv Nash 1989. D 6/29/1989 P 2/1/1990 Bp Craig Barry Anderson. Dio Minnesota Minneapolis MN 2000-2003; R S Jn's Epis Ch Mankato MN 2000-2003; All SS Ch Minot ND 1993-2000; S Jas Epis Ch Belle Fourche SD 1989-1993; R S Thos Epis Ch Sturgis SD 1989-1993. stjohns@hickorytech.net

RIDER, Wm Blake (NY) Episcopal Diocese of New York, 1047 Amsterdam Ave, New York NY 10025 **Cn to the Ordnry Dio New York New York NY 2014-** B Nowata OK 1955 s Will & Norma. BA Oral Roberts U 1978; MDiv VTS 2004. D 6/12/2004 P 12/6/2004 Bp Don Adger Wimberly. R Chr Ch Poughkeepsie NY 2006-2013; Cn Chr Ch Cathd Houston TX 2004-2006. Global Peace and Recon Awd Search for Common Ground 2011; Jn Hines Preaching Awd Virginia Theologial Sem 2006. brider@dioceseny.org

RIDGE, Charles Searls (Oly) 2658 48th Ave SW, Seattle WA 98116 **P Assoc S Paul's Ch Seattle WA 2008-** B Okanogan WA 1936 s Raymond & Estelle. BA Colorado Coll 1958; STB GTS 1961; DMin SMU 1979. D 6/29/1961 Bp William F Lewis P 5/25/1962 Bp John Brooke Mosley. m 2/21/1983 Courtney C Searls-Ridge c 2. P-in-c S Matt Ch Tacoma WA 2010-2012; Bd Dir Chap of S Martha and S Mary of Bethany Seattle WA 1993-1996; R Ch Of The Ascen Seattle WA 1990-2001; Chapl Brookdale Coll Lincroft NJ 1984-1990; R Trin Ch Matawan NJ 1979-1990; Dep GC Dio Dominican Republic 1973-1976; Presdngbp'S Appointee Dio Dominican Republic 1970-1979; PB Appointee Dio The Dominican Republic (Iglesia Epis Dominicana) Gazcue Santo Domingo 1970-1979; Vic Iglesia Epis Epifania Santo Domingo Di 1970-1977; R S Andr's Epis Ch Nogales AZ 1964-1970; Asst Chr Ch Dover DE 1961-1964; Bd Dir Dio Olympia Seattle 1997-2001; Hisp Cmsn Dio New Jersey Trenton NJ 1979-1988. Auth, "Cultural Discernment As Imperative In Mssn: A Proposal," 1979. Benedictine Oblate 2001.

RIDGWAY, George Edward (NCal) 3371 Avington Way, Shasta Lake CA 96019 **Pstr Emer S Barn Ch Mt Shasta CA 2010-, P-in-c 2005-2010; Ret 1995-** B Detroit MI 1930 s George & Virginia. BA U CA 1956; MDiv CDSP 1959. D 6/1/1959 Bp James Albert Pike P 1/2/1960 Bp Henry H Shires. m 4/23/1955 Shirley D Ridgway c 3. Asst All SS Epis Ch Redding CA 2003-2005; Asst Ch Of The Incarn Santa Rosa CA 1996-2003; R S Steph's Epis Ch Sn Luis Obispo CA 1987-1995; R S Tim's Ch Danville CA 1970-1987; S Jas' Ch Monterey CA 1962-1966; Vic S Mths Ch Seaside CA 1962-1963; P-in-c S Mk's Par Crockett CA 1960-1962; Vic S Thos Rodeo CA 1959-1962.

RIDGWAY, Michael Wyndham (ECR) 365 Stowell Ave, Sunnyvale CA 94085 **D S Thos Epis Ch Sunnyvale CA 2010-** B Los Angeles CA 1964 s Robert & Lorelei. BS California St U Sacramento 1994; BD Epis Sch for Deacons 2008; MA San Jose St U 2013. D 11/1/2008 Bp Mary Gray-Reeves. m 10/1/1994 Kari Ridgway c 1. D S Steph's In-The-Field Epis Ch San Jose CA 2008-2009.

RIEBE, Norman W (SanD) 5633 Chalyce Ln, Charlotte NC 28270 **Ret 1995-** B Michigan City IN 1929 s Norman & Gwendolyn. BS U of New Mex 1950; MDiv CDSP 1955; MS Utah St U 1968. D 7/13/1955 P 2/24/1956 Bp C J Kinsolving III. m 12/26/1953 Janice Riebe c 3. Natl Epis Curs 1980-1991; Assoc S Paul's Ch Yuma AZ 1968-2005; S Jn's Epis Ch Logan UT 1962-1968; Prov Dept of Coll Wk Dio Utah Salt Lake City UT 1962-1966; Chairman for Coll Wk Mssy Dist of Utah 1962-1966; The Ch Of The Ascen Denver CO 1958-1962; Secy Bp & Coun Dio Colorado Denver CO 1958-1960; Vic H Trin Epis Ch - Mssn Raton NM 1956-1958; S Jas Epis Ch Taos NM 1955-1958; Asst Ch of the H Faith Santa Fe NM 1955-1956; Sprtl Advsr Angl Curs Dio Arizona Phoenix AZ 1984-1987.

RIEDELL, William George (Cal) 3012 S Fox St, Englewood CO 80110 **Died 8/31/2016** B East Orange NJ 1921 s John & Millicent. Duke 1942; U IL 1948; BA Sch for Deacons 1983. D 6/27/1981 Bp William Edwin Swing. m 6/9/1989 Barbara Anderson. D S Tim's Epis Ch Littleton CO 1998-2016; D All SS Epis Ch San Leandro CA 1993-1998, D 1981-1992; Asst S Clare's Epis Ch Pleasanton CA 1991-1993; Asst Gd Shpd Epis Ch Centennial CO 1986-1990; Chapl Hope Hospice Clerics Wellness Cmsn 2016.

RIEGEL, John Wilfred (Pa) Po Box 288, Bailey Island ME 04003 **Died 10/24/2016** B Boston MA 1926 s John & Marguerite. BBA U MI 1947; MA Harv 1957; PhD Harv 1960; STB Nash 1968. D 1/6/1962 Bp William S Thomas P 12/22/1962 Bp Austin Pardue. m 5/30/1970 Nicole Riegel c 2. Sr Cn All SS' Cathd Milwaukee WI 1966-1967; R Emm Ch Pittsburgh PA 1962-1965.

RIEGEL, Robert Gambrell (USC) 1100 Sumter St, Columbia SC 29201 B New York NY 1930 s Theodore & Mary. BA Wms 1952; STM VTS 1955; LHD Voorhees Coll 1981. D 6/5/1955 Bp Horace W B Donegan P 12/18/1955 Bp Randolph R Claiborne. m 10/30/1983 Keren Riegel. Dn Cntrl Dnry 1995-1996; Cn Mssnr Trin Cathd Columbia SC 1987-1996; Dn 1986-1988; Chapl Furman U Greenville SC 1960-1961; S Jas Epis Ch Greenville SC 1959-1987; Assoc R S Lk's Epis Ch Atlanta GA 1955-1959; Evang Com Dio Upper So Carolina Columbia SC 1989-1992, Dioc Coun 1986-1988, Com 1982-1985, Bp Cmsn On Aging 1980-1981, Dioc Secy 1976-1979, Dioc Trst 1975, Stndg Com 1973-1974, Bp Coun 1967-1972. Auth, "The God Who Will Not Fail You," Trin Cathd, 2001.

RIEGER, Pamela Ann (SanD) **D All Souls' EC San Diego CA 2016-** B 1949 Cert of completion Epis Dio San Diego Sch for Mnstry 2015. D 11/7/2015 Bp Jim Mathes. c 3.

RIERDAN, Pastor Jill (WMass) 128 Main St, Easthampton MA 01027 B Boston MA 1945 d Walter & Dorothy. BA Clark U 1967; MA Clark U 1970; PhD Clark U 1974; MFA Bennington Coll 2000; MDiv Andover Newton TS 2010. D 4/10/2010 P 10/16/2010 Bp Gordon Scruton. P-in-c S Phil's Ch Easthampton MA 2010-2015, R 2010-.

RIETH, Sarah Melissa (NC) 500 East Rhode Island Avenue, Southern Pines NC 28387 **Episc Hm For Ageing Dio Of N C Sthrn Pines NC 2014-; Consult and Trnr Faith Trust Inst Seattle WA 2007-** B Buffalo NY 1951 d William & Martha. Cert in Pstr Counslg Toronto Inst of Human Relatns; BA SUNY at Albany 1972; MDiv Bex Sem 1977; DMin Bex Sem 1994. D 6/4/1977 P 5/13/1978 Bp Harold Barrett Robinson. P-in-c S Andr's Epis Ch Charlotte NC 2010; Mem, Indep Abuse Revs Panel Presb Ch (USA) Louisville KY 2006-2007; Adj Fac Bex Sem 2005-2007; Pstr Counslr and Consult S Ptr's Epis Ch Charlotte NC 2002-2010; Fac Carolina Inst for Clincl Pstr Trng Charlotte 2001-2010; Clincl Consult to Pstr Response Team Dio No Carolina Raleigh NC 2001-2006; Pstr Counslr Methodist Counslg and Consulatation Serv Charlotte NC 2001-2004; Vic Ephphatha Epis Ch Of The Deaf Eggertsville NY 1998-2001; Healing Consult Serv Buffalo NY 1994-1995; Pstr Psych Buffalo NY 1987-2001; Ch Mssn of Help Buffalo NY 1987-1994; P-in-c S Barn Akron NY 1982-1985; Samar Pstr Counslg Cntr Buffalo NY 1981-1987; Asst S Ptr's Epis Ch Buffalo NY 1978-1980; Chair Dioc T/F on Sexual Abuse by Cler Dio Wstrn New York Tonawanda NY 1991-2001. Auth, "My Bro's Keeper: Reflections on Chld Siblings Grief," *In Loss, Illness, and Death: A Dialogue w Theol and Psychol*, Paulist Press, 2010; Auth, "Telling About Brokenheartedness," *Journ of Sprtlty in Mntl Hlth*, 2008; Auth, "Differentiated Solidarity: A Theol of Pstr Supervision," *Journ of Supervision and Trng in Mnstry*, 2001; Auth, "Scriptural Reflections on Deafness and Muteness as Embodied," *Journ of Pstr Theol*, 1993; Auth, "Ignorance is Not a Victimless Crime: The Caring Tchr," *Pstr Psychol*, 1993; Auth, "Adult Survivors: Healed by Faith in Truth," *Action Info*, Alb Inst, 1991; Auth, "The Victimology Handbook," *A New Model for the Treatment of Survivors of Sexual Abuse*, Garland Press, 1990. AAPC 1981; Epis Conf of the Deaf 1998; EWC 1975; Fllshp of St. Jn the Evang 2006; Intl Soc for the Study of Dissociation 1987-2000; No Carolina Fee--Based Practicing Pstr Counslr 2002; Soc of Pstr Theologians 1991. Polly Bond Awd ECom 2000; Distinguished Contribution Awd AAPC, Estrn Reg 1998; Polly Bond Awd ECom 1989. srieth@penickvillage1964.org

RIETMANN, Paul David (Oly) 3615 N Gove St, Tacoma WA 98407 B The Dalles OR 1953 s David & Ruth. BA U CA 1977; MDiv Epis TS of the SW 1981. D 6/24/1981 Bp Leigh Allen Wallace Jr P 6/1/1982 Bp Archibald Donald Davies. m 8/1/2015 Judith Anne Toth. R S Lk's Ch Tacoma WA 1999-2014; Chapl Mntl Hlth Chapl: Submini Tacoma WA 1993-1999; Chapl Annie Wright Sch In Tacoma 1990-1993; R S Matthews Auburn WA 1989-1990; Int Ch Of The H Sprt Vashon WA 1988; Int Ch Of The Gd Shpd Fed Way WA 1987-1988; R S Lk's Ch Mineral Wells TX 1983-1987; Asst Chr Epis Ch Dallas TX 1981-1983.

RIFFEE, Charles Alexander (Va) 1205 W Franklin St, Richmond VA 23220 **S Jas Epis Ch Louisa VA 2014-** B Charleston WV 1986 s Charles & Deborah. BA Cntr Coll 2008; MDiv Ya Berk 2011. D 6/4/2011 Bp William Howard Love P 12/10/2011 Bp Shannon Sherwood Johnston. m 6/18/2011 Yinghao Long. P St Jas Ch Richmond VA 2011-2014. therevriffee@gmail.com

RIGGALL, Daniel John (Me) Po Box 165, Kennebunk ME 04043 B New York NY 1950 s John & Marianne. BA Houghton Coll 1972; MDiv GTS 1978. D 6/3/1978 Bp Albert Wiencke Van Duzer P 12/16/1978 Bp George Phelps Mellick Belshaw. m 12/27/1975 Frances B Riggall. R S Dav's Epis Ch Kennebunk ME 1990-2014; Dn Cathd Ch Of S Paul Burlington VT 1990-1997; R S Ptr's Ch Mtn Lks NJ 1987-1990; R S Paul's Ch Monroe NC 1982-1987; Assoc Chap Of The Cross Chap Hill NC 1980-1982; Cur Chr Ch New Brunswick NJ 1978-1979; Chair, Bp Search Com Dio Maine Portland ME 2005-2007; Dioc Coun Dio Vermont Burlington VT 1991-1997; Cmsn Ce Dio Newark Newark NJ 1987-1990; Chair Dept Mssn Outreach Dio No Carolina Raleigh NC 1984-1987.

RIGGALL, George Gordon (CGC) 3811 Old Shell Rd., Mobile AL 36608 **COO Wilmer Hall 2012-; Stndg Com Dio Cntrl Gulf Coast Pensacola FL 2013-,**

Pres, Stndg Com 2012-2013, Stndg Com 2010-2013 B Hendricks KY 1942 s John & Marianne. BA Gordon Coll 1966; MDiv SWTS 1978. D 6/17/1978 P 5/31/1979 Bp Lyman Cunningham Ogilby. m 12/14/1990 Marguerita Riggall c 2. Wilmer Hall Mobile AL 2012-2014, Bd Chair 2003-2006; R S Paul's Chap Magnolia Sprgs AL 2004-2013; P-in-c Gr Epis Ch Sprg Hill TN 1991-2004; Int S Jas The Less Madison TN 1989-1991; Int S Ann's Ch Nashville TN 1988-1989; R S Tim's Ch Signal Mtn TN 1984-1988; Asst S Geo's Ch Nashville TN 1980-1984; Cur S Jas Ch of Kingsessing Philadelphia PA 1978-1980. Ord of St. Jn of Jerusalem 2012.

RIGGIN, John Harris (CGC) 4051 Old Shell Rd, Mobile AL 36608 **R S Paul's Ch Mobile AL 2001-, Cur 1993-2001, D 1992-** B Little Rock AR 1956 s John & Claudia. Rhodes Coll 1976; BD U of Memphis 1979; MBA U of So Alabama 1986; MDiv Sewanee: The U So, TS 1992. D 6/13/1992 P 5/1/1993 Bp Charles Farmer Duvall. m 8/16/1980 Lauree Riggin c 3. GC Del Dio Cntrl Gulf Coast Pensacola FL 2006, Pres of the Stndg Com 2004-2005, Bd Trst U So, Sewanee 2003-.

RIGGINS, Patricia Readon (WTex) 1310 Pecan Valley Dr, San Antonio TX 78210 **St Fran Epis Ch San Antonio TX 2017-** B Plattsburgh NY 1950 d James & Virginia. AB Sweet Briar Coll 1972; AB Sweet Briar Coll 1972; MBA Tul 1975; MPH Tul 1975; MBA Tul 1975; MPH Tul 1975; MDiv Epis TS of the SW 2009. D 5/29/2009 Bp Jim Mathes P 1/13/2010 Bp Gary Richard Lillibridge. m 11/17/2001 Michael Riggins c 1. P-in-c S Phil's Ch San Antonio TX 2014-2016; Int Trin Ch Victoria TX 2013-2014; Assoc S Andr's Epis Ch Seguin TX 2011-2012; Int The Ch Of The Recon Corpus Christi TX 2010-2011; Asst S Fran By The Lake Canyon Lake TX 2009-2010, D 2009-2010. rectorstphilips.sa@gmail.com

RIGGLE JR, John Field (SwFla) 9267 Sun Isle Dr Ne, Saint Petersburg FL 33702 **Ret 1992-** B Atlanta GA 1934 s John & Louise. BS Georgia Sthrn U 1960; BS Nash 1967. D 6/21/1967 Bp Henry I Louttit P 12/22/1967 Bp William Loftin Hargrave. m 10/11/1975 Jo Ann Riggle c 2. Ch Of The H Cross St Petersburg FL 1974-1991; Cur Cathd Ch Of S Ptr St. Petersburg FL 1967-1974.

RIGGS, Katherine Grace (WTex) 311 W Nottingham Dr Apt 332, San Antonio TX 78209 **Ret 1990-** B Oak Park IL 1925 d John & Frances. BA Vas 1945; MA Col 1947; MDiv Epis TS of the SW 1981. D 6/24/1981 Bp Stanley Fillmore Hauser P 2/2/1982 Bp Scott Field Bailey. c 2. Dioc Rep Kairos prison Mnstry TX 1995-2001; Chapl Wmn's Cbnt Dio W Texas San Antonio TX 1993-1997, Pres Cler Assn 1986-1992; Vic S Fran By The Lake Canyon Lake TX 1983-1989; Dioc Chapl DOK 1982-1988; Asst R S Dav's Epis Ch San Antonio TX 1981-1984. DOK 1977. Hal Brook Perry Awd Epis TS of the SW 2001.

RIGHTMYER, Tom (WNC) 16 Salisbury Dr 7304, Asheville NC 28803 **Ret 2003-** B Lewes DE 1939 s Nelson & Elizabeth. S Andrews Sch Middletown DE 1957; BA JHU 1961; STB GTS 1966; MATheo S Marys Sem & U Baltimore 1972; DMin GTF 1986. D 6/21/1966 P 6/14/1967 Bp Harry Lee Doll. m 9/10/1966 Lucy Oliver c 2. Int Ch of the Advoc Asheville NC 2008; Vic Chap Of The Gd Shpd Ridgeway NC 1997-2001; Mem Moravian-Epis Dialogue 1994-2010; Chapl S Tim's Hale Sch Raleigh NC 1994-1996; Assoc S Phil's Ch Durham NC 1990-2003; Asst GBEC Chap Hill NC 1990-2002; R Ch Of The Redeem Shelby NC 1980-1989; R The Epis Ch Of Gd Shpd Asheboro NC 1974-1980; Vic Copley Par: The Ch Of The Resurr Joppatowne MD 1968-1974; Asst S Anne's Par Annapolis MD 1966-1968; Ecum Chair Dio Wstrn No Carolina Asheville NC 1980-1989; Ecum Chair Dio Maryland Baltimore MD 1970-1974. Auth, "Calendar of the Fulham Papers XLI & XLII," *Angl and Epis Hist 62*, 1993; Auth, "Amer Colonial Angl Cler," in preparation. Assoc, CT 1980; Rotary Intl 1975; Sons of Un Veterans of the Civil War 1988; Sons of the Amer Revolution 1966. Homeless Initiative Bd City of Asheville 2010.

RIIS, Susan (SO) 144884 Harbor Dr E, Thornville OH 43076 B Waterbury CT 1943 d Harold & Hazel. BA U MI 1967; MA U MI 1967. D 2/2/2002 Bp Bill Persell. m 1/2/1984 Thomas Engeman c 1. Trin Ch Highland Pk IL 2002-2011.

RIKER JR, William Chandler (Nwk) 249 Hartshorne Rd, Locust NJ 07760 **Bd Mem So Kent Sch So Kent CT 2010-** B New York NY 1940 s William & Mary. BA U of Oregon 1963; MDiv CDSP 1973. D 4/10/1974 P 11/23/1974 Bp Chauncie Kilmer Myers. m 4/5/1997 Barbara U Carton-Riker c 2. Int S Paul's Epis Ch Morris Plains NJ 2001-2003; Int Chr Ch Glen Ridge NJ 1999-2001; Int S Paul's Ch In Bergen Jersey City NJ 1997-1999; Int S Dunst's Epis Ch Succasunna NJ 1996-1997; Cluster Dep Dio Olympia 1992-1996; Vic S Ben Epis Ch Lacey WA 1989-1996; Fac Dio Olympia TS Seattle WA 1989-1995; R Gr Ch Cincinnati OH 1984-1989; Ch Of The H Sprt Vashon WA 1981-1983; Fac Dio Olympia TS Seattle WA 1979-1984; P-in-c S Aid's Epis Ch Stanwood WA 1978-1979; Chr Epis Ch Anacortes WA 1977-1978; Asst S Ptr's Epis Ch Redwood City CA 1974-1977; Coun Dio Newark Newark NJ 2001-2003, Mem Dioc Coun 2000-2003; COM Dio Sthrn Ohio Cincinnati OH 1985-1988, Deploy Dep 1984-1988, Mem, Comm. on Mnstry 1984-1988; Stwdshp Com Dio Olympia Seattle 1981-1984, Mem Comm. on Mssn 1978-1983; COM Dio California San Francisco CA 1974-1975, Mem Comm. on Mnstry 1974-1975. Pho-

tographer & Ed, "Needlepoint of All SS' Memi," *Needlepoint Proj 2004-2008*, Landmark Trust, 2009; Auth, *Var arts*. williamriker1@juno.com

RILEY, Diane Napolitano (Nwk) **Dir of Advocacy The Cmnty Foodbank of New Jersey 2011-** B Queens NY 1957 D 5/21/2005 Bp John Palmer Croneberger. m 6/1/1985 Elven Riley c 3.

RILEY, Elizabeth Rawlings (Cal) **Assoc Trin Par Menlo Pk CA 2013-** B Palmer AK 1987 d Peter & Kay. BA St Mary's Coll of California 2009; MDiv CDSP 2013; MDiv CDSP 2013. D 6/30/2012 P 8/17/2013 Bp Mark A Lattime. m 1/19/2013 Scott Corbet Riley c 1.

RILEY, George Daniel (NY) 39 Minnesota Ave, Long Beach NY 11561 **Assoc S Jas 1971-** B Cushing OK 1940 s George & Anna. BA Oklahoma Bapt U 1961; MDiv Nash 1968. D 6/7/1969 P 5/1/1971 Bp Horace W B Donegan. Com Of Prot Chapl Jfk Airport 1970-1973.

RILEY, Gregg Les (WLa) 3203 Claiborne Cir, Monroe LA 71201 **P in Res Chr Ch St Jos LA 2013-; Chapl Sheriff's Off 2008-** B Bessemer AL 1947 s Lester & Moselle. AA Arkansas St U 1977; BS U of Kentucky 1979; MDiv Epis TS in Kentucky 1980; STM Nash 2005. D 5/11/1980 P 12/13/1980 Bp Addison Hosea. m 2/11/1969 Carlene Merrick Riley c 2. Cn to the Ordnry Dio Wstrn Louisiana Alexandria LA 2011-2012, Bdgt and Fin Com 2004-2007; R Gr Epis Ch Monroe LA 2002-2010; R Ch Of The Gd Shpd Cedar Hill TX 1998-2002; R Gr Epis Ch Hutchinson KS 1992-1998; Chapl Army NG 1986-2007; R S Jn's Ch Keokuk IA 1986-1992; R All SS Epis Ch Russellville AR 1984-1986; Asst Trin Cathd Davenport IA 1982-1984; P-in-c Chr Ch Ironton OH 1981-1982; Asst Calv Epis Ch Ashland KY 1980-1982; Yth Bd Dio Lexington Lexington 1980-1982; Exec Coun Dio Dallas Dallas TX 1999-2002; Stdng Com Dio Wstrn Kansas Hutchinson KS 1995-1997; Mssn Cmsn Dio Iowa Des Moines IA 1982-1984. Auth, "Chld's prayers," *Bedtime Pryr w Your Chld*, St Fran Acad, 1997. Cmnty of S Mary 1982. Hon Cn Chr Ch Cathd 1997.

RILEY JR, James Foster (Minn) 132 Maj Hornbrook Road, Christchurch Canterbury New Zealand (Aotearoa) B Monett MO 1934 s James & Helen. BA Ken 1956; STB GTS 1959; MDiv GTS 1973. D 9/18/1958 P 3/19/1960 Bp Edward Randolph Welles II. m 5/28/1959 Edith Sevy Riley c 3. Mnstry Enabler Middle Cbury 1997-1999; Archd of Christchurch 1991-1997; R S Lk Evang Christchurch New Zealand 1985-1997; DCE Dio Christchurch 1980-1985; R Heathcote Par Christchurch 1975-1980; R S Nich Ch Minneapolis MN 1966-1975; Cur Chr Epis Ch S Jos MO 1962-1966; D S Paul's Epis Ch Clinton MO 1959-1960.

RILEY, John C (SD) 1333 Jamestown Rd, Williamsburg VA 23185 **Ch Of All Ang Spearfish SD 2016-** B Pinehurst NC 1969 s Wallace & Suzanne. BS Appalachian St U 1992; MDiv VTS 2011. D 6/11/2011 Bp Clifton Daniel III P 1/10/2012 Bp Herman Hollerith IV. m 9/11/1999 Margaret Kate Margaret Kate Berry c 2. Asst S Mart's Epis Ch Williamsburg VA 2011-2016.

RILEY, Mark D (SVa) 3928 Pacific Ave, Virginia Beach VA 23451 **S Jn's Ch Hampton VA 2015-** B Baltimore MD 1966 s Kenneth & Anne. BA Wstrn Maryland Coll 1985; MDiv VTS 2015. D 6/6/2015 P 4/6/2016 Bp Herman Hollerith IV. m 5/13/2006 Laura Sholes Laura Deanne Sholes. Galilee Epis Ch Virginia Bch VA 2015.

RILEY, Reese Milton (Los) 1414 East Grovemont, Santa Ana CA 92705 B Pampa TX 1945 s George & Dorcas. BA Westminster Coll 1968; Harv 1971. D 11/20/1971 P 9/30/1972 Bp Frederick Barton Wolf. m 6/29/1968 Judith V Riley c 2. R S Paul's Epis Ch Tustin CA 1987-2011; R S Paul's Par Lancaster CA 1980-1987; R S Jn's Epis Ch Randolph VT 1976-1980; Res Cn Cathd Ch Of S Lk Portland ME 1972-1976; Vic Chr Ch Gardiner ME 1971-1972. New Engl Trng Inst 1975-1980; OHC 1982. Billing Prize For Publ Spkng Harv 1971; Omicron Delta Kappa Westminster Coll 1968; Phi Alpha Theta Westminster Coll.

RIMASSA, Paul Stephen (NJ) 215 Briner Ln, Hamilton Square NJ 08690 **Trin Ch Rocky Hill NJ 2006-** B Newark NJ 1947 s Joseph & Claire. Rec 11/22/2005 Bp George Edward Councell. m 5/23/2004 Mary St Amour-Rimassa.

RIMER, Kathleen Pakos (Mass) 330 Brookline Ave., Boston MA 02115 B Hyannis MA 1970 d Paul & Patricia. BA Bow 1992; MDiv Harvard DS 1998. D 6/15/2002 P 5/31/2003 Bp M(Arvil) Thomas Shaw. m 6/24/2000 Edward S Rimmer. Int Par Of Chr Ch Andover MA 2003-2004. krimer@bidmc.harvard.edu

RIMKUS, William Allen (Chi) 14755 Eagle Ridge Dr, Homer Glen IL 60491 **D Emm Epis Ch La Grange IL 2002-** B Evergreen Park IL 1942 Illinois Inst of Tech 1961; U IL 1961; Cert Sch of Diac 1987. D 12/26/1987 Bp Frank Tracy Griswold III. m 11/22/1975 Rebekah Rimkus c 5. S Dunst's Epis Ch Westchester IL 1995-2001, 1987-1994; D/Asst St. Dunst of Cbury Winchester IL 1995-2001; Chapl The British Hm Brookfield IL 1987-2004; D/Asst St. Dunstand of Cbury Winchester IL 1987-1994.

RINCON, Virginia M (Me) 121 Margaret St Apt C, South Portland ME 04106 B La Follette TN 1952 d Carlos & Micaela. Lic Houston Tech Inst Form San Jacinto High 1972; BS S Edwards U Austin TX 1993; MDiv EDS 1997. D 12/8/2001 Bp M(Arvil) Thomas Shaw P 9/18/2005 Bp Chilton Richardson Knudsen. c 1. Dio Maine Portland ME 2006-2010; Chr Ch Biddeford ME 2003-2007.

RINEHART, Jim (Be) 108 Arbor Dr, Myerstown PA 17067 **Stndg Com Dio Bethlehem Bethlehem PA 2013-, Dioc Stwdshp Cmsn 2012-, Trst of the Dio**

2011-, Commision on Mnstry 2007-2013; COM - Coordntr Prov III Baltimore MD 2012- B Lima OH 1946 s Claude & Naomi. M.Div Bex; AA S Petersburg Jr Coll 1966; BA U of So Florida 1968; MDiv Bex Sem 1993. D 6/3/1995 Bp Edward Cole Chalfant P 7/13/1996 Bp William George Burrill. m 8/1/1975 Nancy C Rinehart. R Trin Epis Ch Pottsville PA 2007-2015; Chapl Patchogue Fire Dept. Patchogue Vill NY 2003-2007; R S Paul's Ch Patchogue NY 2000-2007; R S Ptr's Epis Ch Bloomfield NY 1996-2000; D S Lk's Ch Fairport NY 1995-1996; Dept of Mnstry Dio Long Island Garden City NY 2005-2007; Dioc Coun Dio Rochester Henrietta 1998-2000.

RINES, Charles Tedford (NCal) 3641 Mari Dr, Lake Elsinore CA 92530 **S Clem's Ch Rancho Cordova CA 2000-; Ret 1999-** B Oakland CA 1933 s Charles & Susan. BA California St U 1958; MDiv Sewanee: The U So, TS 1964. D 6/21/1964 P 12/26/1964 Bp James Albert Pike. m 7/7/1957 Amanda Helen Rines c 3. Int St Steph's Epis Ch Menifee CA 2009-2011; Assoc Vic S Thos Epis Ch Temecula 2002-2009; R Epis Ch Of Our Sav Placerville CA 1992-1998; R Trin Ch Escondido CA 1978-1992; Assoc Cathd Ch Of S Paul San Diego CA 1976-1978; Asst S Ptr's Epis Ch Del Mar CA 1975-1976; R Chr Ch Par Ontario CA 1971-1973; R S Mich The Archangel Par El Segundo CA 1968-1971; Cur All SS Par Long Bch CA 1967-1968; R S Chris's Epis Ch Boulder City NV 1965-1966.

RING, Anthony Richard (Eau) W10601 Pine Rd, Thorp WI 54771 **Chapl Clark Cnty Hlth Care Cntr 1999-** B Eau Claire WI 1937 s Henry & Elvira. D 5/31/2003 Bp Keith Whitmore. m 10/18/1980 Hazel Louise Murrier c 3. Fllshp of S Jn.

RING, Bonnie (Cal) 2011 Carlos Street, Moss Beach CA 94038 **Assoc The Epis Ch Of The Gd Shpd Berkeley CA 2010-** B New York NY 1940 d Richard & Rita. Vas; BA NYU 1962; EdM Bos 1964; UCLA 1966; EdD Bos 1972; MDiv CDSP 1990. D 12/7/1991 P 12/5/1992 Bp William Edwin Swing. Assoc Ch Of The H Fam Fresno CA 2007-2009; Dir, Elder Mnstry St Jn's Epis Ch Oakland CA 2004-2006; S Ambr Epis Ch Foster City CA 2003; S Jn's Epis Ch Oakland CA 2002-2004; Gd Shpd Epis Ch Belmont CA 2002-2003; S Paul's Epis Ch Walnut Creek CA 2002; S Lk's Ch Walnut Creek CA 2001-2002; Assoc Trin Ch San Francisco CA 1995-1999; Assoc S Cuth's Epis Ch Oakland CA 1992-1993. Co-Auth & Co-Ed, "H Relationships And The Authority Of Scripture," Dio California, 2000. APA 1964; California Psychol Assn 1974; Spritiual Dir Intl 1989. Educ Hon Soc Pi Lamda Theta 1965.

RINGLAND, Robin Lynn (Oly) 415 S 18th St, Mount Vernon WA 98274 B Twin Falls ID 1953 d Robert & Jacqueline. BA U CA 1978; MA San Jose St U 1983. D 10/29/2010 Bp Gregory Harold Rickel. m 8/20/1977 Peter Ringland c 2.

RINGLE, Lorena May (Pgh) Christ Episcopal Church, 5910 Babcock Blvd, Pittsburgh PA 15237 **Other Lay Position Chr Epis Ch No Hills Pittsburgh PA 1992-** B Pittsburgh PA 1954 d Charles & Norma. BA Indiana U of Pennsylvania. D 9/19/2015 Bp Dorsey McConnell. m 8/31/1974 William Lawrence Ringle c 2.

RIOS, Austin Keith (Eur) Diocese of Western North Carolina, 900-B Centre Park Dr., Asheville NC 28805 **R S Paul's Within the Walls Rome 2012-** B Webster TX 1977 s Ronald & Cyndy. BA Davidson Coll 1999; MDiv Epis TS of the SW 2003. D 1/15/2005 P 7/16/2005 Bp Porter Taylor. m 7/3/2004 Jill Drzewiwcki Rios c 1. Cn for Spanish-Spkng Mnstrs Dio Wstrn No Carolina Asheville NC 2007-2012; R La Capilla De Santa Maria Hendersonvlle NC 2007-2012; Cur Gr Ch Asheville NC 2005-2007. Transltr (w Gabriela Reyes R, "Spanish Ed of Comp in Transformation," *Comp in Transformation: The Epis Ch's Wrld Mssn in a New Century*, Ch Pub; Contrib, "Mutuality in Mssn: The Tchg of Don Ricardo and his Cats," *The Scripture of their Lives*, Morehouse.

RIOS, Lajunta Michelle (Tex) Trinity Episcopal Church, 5010 N Main St, Baytown TX 77521 **Pstr Care Coordntr St. Jas Hse Baytown TX 2012-; D Trin Epis Ch Baytown TX 2008-** B Abilene TX 1954 d Guy & LaJunta. MA Liberty U 2011. D 2/10/2008 Bp Don Adger Wimberly. m 8/28/1976 James Edward Rios c 2. S Jas Hse Of Baytown Baytown TX 2016.

RIOS QUEVEDO, Jose F (PR) **Died 1/1/2016** B 1934 m 3/9/1980 Iris Rivas Reyes. Dio Puerto Rico Trujillo Alto PR 2004-2006, 1994-2003.

RISARD, Frederick William (SJ) 1541 Bristol Ln, Hanford CA 93230 **Exec Dir St. Fran Merced Respite Inc. 2011-** B Winnemucca NV 1951 s Martin & Alice. BS California St Polytechnic U SLO 1978; MDiv Nash 2004; Fresno Pacific U 2005; Fresno Pacific U 2005; MSW California St U Stanislaus 2013. D 12/10/2005 P 6/11/2006 Bp David Mercer Schofield. Dioc Jubilee Off Epis Dio San Joaquin Modesto CA 2008-2010, Dioc Coun 2008-2011; Dioc Jubilee Off St Nich Epis Ch Atwater CA 2008-2010, Vic 2006-2007.

RISK III, James Lightfoot (Chi) 901 N Delphia Ave, Park Ridge IL 60068 B New York NY 1948 s James & Barbara. BA Hobart and Wm Smith Colleges 1970; MDiv GTS 1975. D 6/14/1975 Bp Quintin Ebenezer Primo Jr P 12/1/1975 Bp James Winchester Montgomery. m 6/21/2008 Paula Allen c 4. Chair, Dioc Strategic Plnng Com Bp Anderson Hse Chicago IL 2003-2004; Exec Dir 2002-2015; Chapl Rush U Med Cntr Chicago IL 2002-2015; Int R S Mary's Ch Pk Ridge IL 2001-2003; Vice Chair to Mssn of Mnstry Dio Chicago 1995-2006; Treas For The Epis Fam Ntwk Natl Ch 1990-2002; Dioc Stndg Com Dio Chicago 1989-1992; Dioc Bd Fin Revs Dio Chicago 1987-1992; Dioc Bdgt Com Dio Chicago 1986-1988; Chair, Dioc Hunger T/F Dio Chicago 1983-1988; R S Giles' Ch Northbrook IL 1982-2001; Assoc Chr Ch Winnetka IL 1978-1982; Asst S Mk's Barrington IL 1975-1978; Dio Chicago Chicago IL 2003-2008. Auth, "Bldg a New Life: A Chapl's Theory Based Case Study of Chronic Illness," *Journ of Hlth Care Chapl*, Taylor and Fran Grp, 2013; Auth, "Sprtl Struggle," *Healing Sprt*, Assn of Profsnl Chapl, 2009; Auth, "Screening for Sprtl Struggle," *Journ of Pstr Care and Counslg*, Journ of Pstr Care and Counslg, 2009; Auth, "Being God's Fam," *Being God's Fam*, Epis Fam Ntwk, 1996. Hon Cn St. Jas Cathd, Dio Chicago 2007.

RITCHIE, Anne Gavin (Va) 1002 Janney's Lane, Alexandria VA 22302 B Coral Gables FL 1949 d Peter & Gertrude. BA Adel 1971; MDiv VTS 1978; DMin SWTS 2005. D 6/24/1978 P 6/7/1979 Bp John Thomas Walker. m 5/19/2012 Gail Elizabeth Collins c 1. R Ch Of The Resurr Alexandria VA 1995-2011; Assoc S Jn's Ch Lafayette Sq Washington DC 1989-1995; Int P Emery Epis Cong Wuerzburg Germany 1987-1988; Assoc S Mk's Ch Washington DC 1978-1986. Co-Auth, "Discussion Plans for So You Think You're Not Rel," *Discussion Plans for So You Think You're Not Rel?*, Alb Inst, 2000; Co-Auth, "What Do I Have Offer?," *What Do I Have to Offer?*, Alb Inst, 1985; Co-Auth, "My Struggle to Be a Caring Person," *My Struggle to Be a Caring Person*, Alb Inst, 1984.

RITCHIE, Harold (Fla) 12013 SW 1st St, Micanopy FL 32667 **P-in-c S Alb's Epis Ch Chiefland FL 2009-; Cler Cont Educ Dio Florida Jacksonville 2003-, Nomin Com 2002-, Yth Cmsn 2002-** B Lancaster PA 1950 s Marion & Dorothea. BA S Leo U 1996; MHS U of Florida 2000; MDiv Sewanee: The U So, TS 2002. D 6/9/2002 P 12/8/2002 Bp Stephen Hays Jecko. m 6/23/1979 Melody Joan Ritchie c 1. Int S Jos's Ch Newberry FL 2009, 2002-2004, Asst 2002-2004; Chapl Ch Of The Incarn Gainesville FL 2006-2007; R S Anne's Epis Ch Keystone Hgts FL 2004-2009. Ord of S Lk's Healing Mnstry 1991.

RITCHIE, Patricia Ritter (Tex) 4090 Delaware St, Beaumont TX 77706 **D S Steph's Ch Beaumont TX 2009-; Bd Dir Ubi Caritas Healing Mnstrs 2009-; Chapl Odyssey Hospice Beaumont Texas 2006-** B Beaumont TX 1950 d James & Betty. BA LSU 1972; The Iona Sch for Mnstry 2009. D 2/22/2009 Bp Don Adger Wimberly. m 4/28/1990 Maurice Ritchie c 1. S Mk's Ch Beaumont TX 2000-2006.

RITCHIE, Robert Joseph (Pa) 7712 Brous Ave, Philadelphia PA 19152 B Philadelphia PA 1948 s Robert & Evelyn. Sch of the Diac Dio PA; BA Tem 1987; FBI Acad 1993; MS S Josephs U 1993. D 10/27/1996 Bp Allen Lyman Bartlett Jr. m 4/28/1973 Charleen Hughes c 2. D Memi Ch Of The H Nativ Jenkintown PA 2003-2007; D Trin Ch Oxford Philadelphia PA 1996-2003.

RITCHIE, Sandra Lawrence (Pgh) 1808 Kent Rd, Pittsburgh PA 15241 B Steubenville OH 1938 RN Ohio Vlly Hosp Sch of Nrsng Steubenville OH 1960; BS K SU 1977; MEd Tem 1983. D 6/14/2003 Bp Robert William Duncan. m 7/11/1964 Richard H Ritchie c 2. S Paul's Epis Ch Pittsburgh PA 2006-2009.

RITCHINGS, Frances Anne (Pa) 36 E Abington Ave, Philadelphia PA 19118 B Baltimore MD 1946 d Edward & Frances. GTS; BA Salisbury U 1968; MA U of Virginia 1970; MLS CUA 1975; MDiv EDS 1987. D 7/11/1987 Bp Ronald Hayward Haines P 2/4/1988 Bp George Nelson Hunt III. m 9/8/2008 Kathryn Hankinson. Ch Of The H Sprt Harleysville PA 1998-2001; Dio Pennsylvania Philadelphia PA 1993-1997; Assoc R S Thos' Ch Whitemarsh Ft Washington PA 1989-1993; Assoc R S Steph's Ch Providence RI 1987-1989. "Establishing the Mssn Ch of the H Sprt," *Journ of the Assn of Angl Mus*, 2004; "Poems," *Windchimes*, 2001. Soc of S Jn the Evang, Soc of S Marg. Salmon Wheaton Prize EDS 1987. bearcuisinenm@comcast.net

RITONIA, Ann M (WA) 680 Racebrook Rd, Orange CT 06477 **S Jn's Ch Ellicott City MD 2017-; R S Ptr's Ch Poolesville MD 2015-** B Boston MA 1957 d Malcolm & Catherine. BA New Engl Conservatory of Mus 1979; MA Webster U 1994; MDiv Wesley TS 2007. D 5/24/2008 P 12/6/2008 Bp Peter J Lee. m 8/16/1986 Michael J Ritonia c 4. Ch Of The Gd Shpd Orange CT 2011-2014; Asst Chr Epis Ch Winchester VA 2008-2011; Asst S Anne's Epis Ch Reston VA 2007-2008.

RITSON, Veronica Merita (Az) 6556 N Villa Manana Dr, Phoenix AZ 85014 B JP 1949 d George & Elizabeth. AA Gateway Cmnty Coll Phoenix AZ 1975; EFM Sewanee: The U So, TS 1993. D 6/5/1993 Bp Robert Reed Shahan. Archd Trin Cathd Phoenix AZ 2000-2015.

RITTER, Christine E (Pa) 1771 Sharpless Rd, Meadowbrook PA 19046 B NJ 1941 d Howard & Eleanor. BA Trenton St Coll 1978; MSW Rutgers The St U of New Jersey 1981; MDiv GTS 1996. D 6/21/1996 P 12/14/1996 Bp Joe Doss. c 2. Dio Pennsylvania Philadelphia PA 2007-2012, Asst to Bp 2006-; Gr Ch Pemberton NJ 2005-2006, 1996-1997; Int Trin Ch Solebury PA 2003-2005; R Ch Of Our Sav Jenkintown PA 1998-2002; Asst S Ptr's Ch In The Great Vlly Malvern PA 1997-1998.

RITTER, Cynthia Anne (Okla) 1604 S Fir Ave, Broken Arrow OK 74012 **Clincl Dir Clarehouse Tulsa OK 2005-** B Mangum OK 1950 d Joe & Doris. RN NWTH Hosp Sch of Nrsng Amarillo TX 1971; BS Langston U 1990; MS U of Oklahoma 1995. D 6/18/2005 Bp Robert Manning Moody. m 4/21/1973 Gordon Jochen Ritter c 3.

RITTER, Kenneth Phillip (Miss) 20 Belvoir Ave, Chattanooga TN 37411 **Trin Ch Natchez MS 2017-; Gr Ch Chattanooga TN 2016-** B New Orleans LA 1961 s Harold & Jeanelle. BA S Jos Sem Coll S Ben LA 1983; M.Div Notre Dame Sem Grad TS 1987; MDiv Notre Dame Sem Grad TS 1987; MHA S Louis U 1993. Rec 4/8/2004 Bp Charles Edward Jenkins III. m 5/29/1993 Juliana M Ritter c 2. Trin Epis Day Sch Natchez MS 2017; Pres & CEO S Jas Place Baton Rouge LA 2011-2015, Pres & CEO 2004-2005, Mem - Bd Dir - CEO 2002-2015; Trin Epis Ch Baton Rouge LA 2005-2011, R - Hd of Sch 2005-2011; P Asst S Marg's Epis Ch Baton Rouge LA 2004; P Asst S Jas Epis Ch Baton Rouge LA 2003-2004; Cler Dep to GC 2012 Dio Louisiana New Orleans LA 2011-2014, Pres - Dioc Stndg Com 2010-2011, Cler Dep to Gnrl Cnovention 2009 2009-2012, Mem - Dioc Exec Bd 2007-2011, Dn - So Baton Rouge Dnry 2006-2014; Mem - Bd Trst Epis HS Baton Rouge Baton Rouge LA 2005-2011. kritter@spiritas-services.com

RITTER, Nathan (LI) 414 E Broad St, Westfield NJ 07090 **S Paul's Epis Ch Westfield NJ 2012-** B St Louis MO 1977 s Alan & Elizabeth. BA Truman St U 2001; MAR Yale DS 2004; MDiv GTS 2010. D 5/29/2010 P 12/3/2010 Bp Wendell Nathaniel Gibbs Jr. m 7/8/2006 Jessica Diane Lambert c 2. S Phil's Ch Brooklyn NY 2011. parishoffice@stpaulswestfield.org

RIVAS, Vidal (WA) Episcopal Church House, Mount Saint Alban, Washington DC 20016 **R S Matt's Epis Ch Hyattsville MD 2008-** B El Salvador 1964 s Antonio & Maria. Rec 1/19/2008 Bp John Bryson Chane. m 11/11/2006 Maria D Rivas c 3. Latino Mssnr Dio Washington Washington DC 2008-2017.

RIVERA, Aristotle C (Cal) PO Box 101, Brentwood CA 94513 **Off Of Bsh For ArmdF New York NY 2013-** B Los Angeles CA 1977 s Efren & Asuncion. BS USMA 1999; MS U of Missouri Rolla 2004; MDiv Ya Berk 2008. D 5/31/2008 Bp William Howard Love P 12/6/2008 Bp Marc Handley Andrus. m 5/6/2005 Roselle p Castro. Area Mssnr/ Vic S Alb's Epis Ch Brentwood CA 2008-2012.

✠ RIVERA, The Rt Rev Bavi Edna (Oly) PO Box 1548, The Dalles OR 97058 B Visalia CA 1946 d Victor & Barbara. BA Wheaton Coll at Norton 1968; MDiv CDSP 1976. D 6/28/1975 Bp Victor Manuel Rivera P 5/5/1979 Bp Chauncie Kilmer Myers Con 1/22/2005 for Oly. m 2/16/1979 Robert Moore c 1. Provsnl Bp of Estrn Oregon Dio Estrn Oregon Cove OR 2009-2016; Bp Suffr Dio Olympia Seattle 2004-2010; R S Aid's Ch San Francisco CA 1994-2004; COM, Chrmn Mnstry Educ & Dvlpmnt, Stndg Com Dio El Camino Real Salinas CA 1985-1992; R S Geo's Ch Salinas CA 1984-1993; COM, Stndg, Yth Mnstry Acad Dio California San Francisco CA 1981-1984; Assoc St Johns Epis Ch Ross CA 1979-1984; Asst S Clare's Epis Ch Pleasanton CA 1977-1979; S Paul's Epis Ch San Rafael CA 1975-1977. Soc of S Fran. DD CDSP 2005. nrivera@episdioeo.org

RIVERA, Jorge Juan (PR) B 1936 m 11/24/2001 Blanca Otaño. Dio Puerto Rico Trujillo Alto PR 2004-2007, 1980-2003, 1973-1979.

RIVERA, Marcos Antonio (CFla) 903 Van Dr, Auburndale FL 33823 **D H Cross Ch Winter Haven FL 1997-; D 1987-; Exec Dir Anchor Hse Mnstry 1974-** B 1939 s Roberto & Pilar. D 3/2/1987 Bp William Hopkins Folwell. m 11/28/1974 Pamela Ann Rivera c 2. Auth, "Touched By The Fr'S Hand".

RIVERA-GEORGESCU, Ana Maria (Alb) St. James Episcopal Church, 14216 NYS RT 9N, Au Sable Forks NY 12912 B New York 1966 d Mariano & Margarita. MMin Nash; BS Empire St Coll 2008; MS Texas Tech U 2010. D 6/1/2013 P 12/15/2013 Bp William Howard Love. m 12/26/1995 Florin Georgescu c 3. S Jas Ch Au Sable Forks NY 2013-2015.

RIVERA PEREZ, Francisco Javier (PR) PO Box 902, Saint Just PR 00978 Puerto Rico **Dio Puerto Rico Trujillo Alto PR 2013-** B Santurce PR 1966 s Ignacio & Maria. Ciencias Religiosas Santo Tomas de Aquino 1992; Maestria en educacion Abierta para adultos 2009; Estudios Anglicanos Seminario San Pedro y San Pablo 2012. Rec 9/21/2013 as Priest Bp David Andres Alvarez-Velazquez. c 2.

RIVERA-RIVERA, Luis Antonio (NY) 550 W 155th St, New York NY 10032 B Puerto Rico 1949 s Luis & Nieves. MA U of Puerto Rico 1976. D 5/16/2015 Bp Andrew Marion Lenow Dietsche. m 5/15/2010 Richard Eugene Johnson c 2.

RIVERA RIVERA, Luis Guillermo (PR) **Chapl Iglesia Epis Puertorriquena S Just PR 2014-; Vic, Mision San Bernabe Iglesia Epis Puertorriquena Bayamon PR 2007-** B Arecibo, PR 1954 s Luis & Josefina. BA Caribbean U 1980; MDiv Seminario San Pedro y San Pablo 1990. D 10/15/1995 P 2/9/1997 Bp David Andres Alvarez-Velazquez. m 3/10/1990 Carmen Zoraida Maldonado Camacho. Dio Puerto Rico Trujillo Alto PR 2004-2015, 1999-2003; Vic, Mision San Judas Tadeo Iglesia Epis Puertorriquena Aibonito PR 1999-2007.

RIVERA-RODRIGUEZ, Angel (PR) **Dio Puerto Rico Trujillo Alto PR 2004-, 2003** B 1962 m 4/27/2013 Abigail Ruiz Diaz.

RIVEROS MAYORGA, Jose Aristodemus (Colom) c/o Diocese of Colombia, Cra 6 No. 49-85 Piso 2, Bogota, BDC Colombia **Iglesia Epis En Colombia Bogota 2016-** B 1965 s Luis. Rec 8/15/2015 as Priest Bp Francisco Jose Duque-Gomez.

RIVERS, Barbara White Batzer (Pa) 378 Paoli Woods, Paoli PA 19301 B Elizabeth NJ 1947 d Reinhold & Marjorie. BA Buc 1969; MS Drexel U 1972; MDiv Estrn Bapt TS 1986. D 6/15/1985 P 5/26/1986 Bp Lyman Cunningham Ogilby. c 2. P-in-c S Christophers Epis Ch Oxford PA 2008-2011; Int S Jas Epis Ch Bristol PA 2007-2008; Int S Jn's Ch Glen Mills PA 2004-2006; Int Memi Ch Of S Lk Philadelphia PA 2003-2004; Int Ch Of The Redeem Bryn Mawr PA 1999-2002; Int Ch Of S Asaph Bala Cynwyd PA 1997-1999; Int The Epis Ch Of The Adv Kennet Sq PA 1996-1997; Int Trin Ch Buckingham PA 1995-1996; Int S Dunstans Ch Blue Bell PA 1994-1995; Int S Jas' Epis Ch Downingtown PA 1992-1994; Int Gr Epiph Ch Philadelphia PA 1990; Asst Ch Of The Mssh Lower Gwynedd PA 1987-1990; Asst Trin Ch Gulph Mills Kng Of Prussia PA 1985-1987. Int Mnstry Ntwk.

RIVERS, David Buchanan (Pa) 148 Heacock Ln, Wyncote PA 19095 **Ret 2004-** B New Haven CT 1937 s Burke & Phyllis. BA Hav 1959; BD EDS 1964. D 6/1/1964 P 3/1/1965 Bp Frederick Warnecke. m 8/5/1961 Elizabeth Lee Rivers c 4. Int H Trin Ch Lansdale PA 2004-2010; R Gloria Dei Ch Philadelphia PA 1972-2004; In-Charge San Esteban San Pedro De Macoris Dominican Republic 1968-1972; Vic S Eliz's Ch Schnecksville PA 1964-1968. Auth, "LivCh," 2001. Swedish Colonial Soc 1973-2004.

RIVERS, John (WNC) 55 Wingspread Dr, Black Mountain NC 28711 B Charleston SC 1931 s Elias & Dorothy. BS Coll of Charleston 1953; BD EDS 1956. D 7/14/1956 P 7/20/1957 Bp Thomas N Carruthers. m 6/23/1956 Jean Rivers c 5. Team Evang Consult Dio Wstrn No Carolina Asheville NC 1988-1991, Sprtl Advsr Curs 1985-1989, 1981-1994, Mssnr to Deaf 1980-; S Dav's Ch Cullowhee NC 1967-1981; Chapl Wstrn Carolina U Cullowhee NC 1967-1980; Asst to the R Chr Ch Cathd Lexington KY 1966-1967; P-in-c All SS Epis Ch Clinton SC 1960-1966; P-in-c All SS Epis Ch Hampton SC 1957-1960; Ch Of The Heav Rest Estill SC 1957-1960; M-in-c Ch Of The H Comm Allendale SC 1956-1957. ECDEF, 1st VP ECD, Ord of S Lk.

RIVERS III, Joseph Tracy (Pa) 2902 Monterey Ct, Springfield PA 19064 **Int S Jas Millcreek DE 2001-** B Buffalo NY 1946 s Joseph & Maxim. BA Harv 1969; MDiv EDS 1975; PhD Duke 1983. D 6/14/1975 P 8/1/1976 Bp Lyman Cunningham Ogilby. m 6/27/1997 Carolyn Draper Rivers. Ch Of The Gd Samar Paoli PA 2011; S Jas Ch Wilmington DE 2001; Int The Ch Of The Ascen Claymont DE 1999-2001; Int Calv Rockdale PA 1998-1999; Resurr Epis Ch Rockdale Aston PA 1998-1999; S Jas Ch Greenridge Aston PA 1995-1997; Dn Brandywine Dnry 1988-1994; R S Andr's Epis Ch Glenmoore PA 1985-1994; Prog Dir Philadelphia Theol Inst 1984-1985; S Giles Ch Upper Darby PA 1978-1985; R S Giles Upper Darby PA 1978-1985; P-in-c S Mk's Epis Ch Roxboro NC 1976-1978; Asst S Jos's Ch Durham NC 1975-1976. Ed, "S Geo Coll Chronicle," 1994; Auth, "Pattern & Process In Early Chr Pilgrimage"; Auth, "Challenge Of Renwl In Inner Suburban Cong". AAR; Conf Angl Theol; SBL.

RIVET, E (Colo) 7102 E Briarwood Dr, Centennial CO 80112 **Chapl Colorado St Veterans Nrsng Hm 2009-; Mssn Partnership Vic S Jn's Epis Ch New Castle CO 2009-** B Providence RI 1946 s Robert & Marguerite. BA Metropltn St Coll of Denver 1973; MA U CO Denver 1979; MDiv SWTS 2004. D 6/12/2004 P 12/18/2004 Bp Robert John O'Neill. m 10/22/1983 Martha Jane Rivet c 2. Vic All SS Epis Ch Battlement Mesa CO 2007-2014; Assoc R Chr's Epis Ch Castle Rock CO 2004-2007; VP of the Bd Dir LIFT UP (Life Interfaith Team for Unemployment And Pvrty 2008-2016; Cler Mem of Stndg Com Dio Colorado Denver CO 2008-2011. Contributing Writer, ""Labyrinths Across the St,"" *Colorado Epis*, Dio Colorado, 2011; Contributing Writer, ""Emerging Mssn Partnerships,"" *Colorado Epis*, Dio Coloorado, 2009. Certifcate Ch Dvlpmt Inst Dio Colorado 2008. ejrivet@stgabriels.org

RIVETTI, Mary Beth (Spok) 1436 Pine Cone Rd Apt 3, Moscow ID 83843 B Great Falls MT 1950 d David & Ellen. BA U CA Santa Barbara 1972; MA U CA Santa Barbara 1974; CPhil U CA Berkeley 1982; MDiv CDSP 2000. D 6/1/2000 P 12/7/2000 Bp Carolyn Tanner Irish. R S Jas Pullman WA 2003-2016; Assoc S Paul's Epis Ch Walnut Creek CA 2000-2003; Dio Utah Salt Lake City UT 1987-1997; Meeting Planner/Events Coordntr Epis Dio Utah Salt Lake City Utah 1987-1997. Participant Preaching Excellence Prog 2000; Grant Rec Soc for the Increase of Mnstry 1999.

RIVOLTA, Agostino Cetrangolo (NJ) 69 Broad St, Eatontown NJ 07724 **P-in-c S Jas Memi Ch Eatontown NJ 2013-** B Carate Italy 1942 s Mario & Canzi. STB CUA 1970; MPhil Drew U 1978; MLS Rutgers The St U of New Jersey 1979. Rec 6/1/2010 as Priest Bp George Edward Councell. m 12/20/1975 Barbara Rivolta.

RIZNER, Andrew Robert (ETenn) 3669 Ivy Way, Sevierville TN 37876 **Died 7/17/2016** B Middletown CT 1926 s Andrew & Georgina. BS U of Florida 1950; STB GTS 1962. D 6/29/1962 Bp Henry I Louttit P 12/29/1962 Bp James Loughlin Duncan. m 2/6/1971 Constance Bufkin. Int Ch Of The Resurr Loudon TN 2002-2003; Int S Jos The Carpenter Sevierville TN 1999-2002; Ret 1995-2016; Liturg Cmsn Dio Cntrl Florida Orlando FL 1985-1986, Chair Campus Mnstry Bd 1984, Dioc Bd 1982-1983, Stndg Com 1978-1981, Stwdshp Chair 1976-1977, Dioc Bd 1990-1992, Stwdshp Chair 1990-1991, Dioc Bd 1988, Chair Fin Cmsn 1985-1986, Dep CG 1985-1986, Dioc Bd 1982-1984, Stndg Com 1978-1988; R S Mary Of The Ang Epis Ch Orlando FL 1973-1995; Cn Cathd Ch Of S Lk Orlando FL 1967-1973; Cur S Steph's Ch Coconut Grove Miami FL 1963-1967; Cur S Jn's Epis Ch Homestead FL 1962-1963. Auth, *Tale of Two Congregations*. Chapl Ord of S Lk 1971; Soc of S Jn the Evang, Assoc 1966. Hon Cn Dio CFla 1995.

R

ROACH, Kenneth Merle (Fla) 92 Atari Rd, Waynesville NC 28786 **Adj Gr in the Mountains Epis Waynesville NC 2012-** B Jacksonville FL 1941 s William & Etheleen. Presb Coll 1966; Jacksonville U 1969; BA U of No Florida 1974; MDiv Sewanee: The U So, TS 1989. D 6/11/1989 P 12/10/1989 Bp Frank S Cerveny. c 2. R S Fran Of Assisi Epis Ch Tallahassee FL 2006-2007; P-in-c S Fran of Assisi Tallahassee FL 2006-2007; R S Lk's Epis Ch Jacksonville FL 1995-2005; R S Paul's Epis Ch Quincy FL 1990-1995; Cur San Jose Epis Ch Jacksonville FL 1989-1990. Acad of Par Cler; OHC.

ROACH, Michelle Mona (CFla) D 1/16/2016 P 7/23/2016 Bp Gregory Orrin Brewer.

ROACH, Robert Eugene (Alb) 8 Brookwood Dr, Clifton Park NY 12065 **D S Geo's Ch Clifton Pk NY 2002-, D 1983-2001** B Barnsdall OK 1923 s Robert & Ella. BS Oklahoma St U 1944. D 6/18/1983 Bp Wilbur Emory Hogg Jr. m 10/19/1979 Susan Rae Roach c 3. D St Fran Mssn Albany NY 2000-2002; Dioc Sprtl Dir Curs Dio Albany Greenwich NY 1988-1990.

ROADMAN, Betsy Johns (NY) 91 Mystic Dr, Ossining NY 10562 **Sprtl Dir Priv Pract Sprtl Direction Ossining 2005-** B Ellwood City PA 1952 d Jay & Sara. BA Clarion U of Pennsylvania 1973; RN Sewickley Vlly Hosp Sch of Nrsng 1980; MDiv UTS 2001. D 3/10/2001 Bp Richard Frank Grein P 9/15/2001 Bp Mark Sean Sisk. m 12/27/1980 Larry Roadman c 2. Co-Pstr for Epis Cong Bedford Hills Correctional Facility Bedford Hills NY 2010-2011; Chapl Phelps Hospice Sleepy Hollow NY 2007-2008; S Aug's Epis Ch Croton Hdsn NY 2007-2008; Int 2005-2006, 2004-2006, Assoc 2004-2005; Cur Chr's Ch Rye NY 2001-2004; Coordntr for EFM, Dio New York Sewanee U So TS Sewanee TN 2004-2012.

ROAF, Phoebe Alison (Va) 2900 Hanes Ave, Richmond VA 23222 **AAEC Pres VTS 2015-; R S Phil's Ch Richmond VA 2011-; Co-Chair, Resolutns Com Dio Virginia 2015-; Dn, Reg XI Dio Virginia 2014-** B Lansing MI 1964 d Clifton & Andree. AB Harv 1986; MPA Pr 1989; JD UALR Bowen Sch of Law 1998; MDiv VTS 2008. D 12/29/2007 P 7/9/2008 Bp Charles Edward Jenkins III. Assoc R Trin Ch New Orleans LA 2008-2011. motherroaf@comcast.net

ROANE, Wilson Kessner (FdL) E2382 Pebble Run Rd, Waupaca WI 54981 **Ret Dio Fond du Lac 2004-; Mem and Pres, Stndg Com Dio Fond du Lac Appleton WI 2009-, Mem, Invstmt Com 2008-, Mem, Stndg Com 2004-2008, Mem, Stndg Com 1996-1998, Mem, Exec Bd 1994-2010** B Evanston IL 1938 s Kearney & C Josephine. BA Ken 1960; MBA U Chi 1964; MDiv Nash 1990. D 12/30/1989 P 7/11/1990 Bp William Louis Stevens. m 12/30/1960 Susan Roane c 3. Int R Intsn Epis Ch Stevens Point WI 2010-2011; Int R S Anne's Epis Ch De Pere WI 2009-2010; Int R Ch Of The H Apos Oneida WI 2007-2008; R S Mk's Ch Waupaca WI 1990-2004, D in Charge 1989-1990; St Olaf's Epis Ch Amherst WI 1989-1990. Sis Of The H Nativ 1990.

ROARK III, Hal (NY) PO Box 350, Granite Springs NY 10527 **Ch Of The Gd Shpd Granite Spgs NY 2016-; Ch Of The Heav Rest New York NY 2015-** B Warwick RI 1965 s Harry & Phyllis. BA Ya 1988; MSW Tul 1993; MDiv Ya Berk 2013. D 4/13/2013 Bp Morris King Thompson Jr P 12/10/2013 Bp Laura Ahrens. m 7/1/1995 Lori Ann Kennedy c 1. Cur S Paul's Ch Riverside CT 2013-2015.

ROBAYO-HIDALGO, Daniel Dario (Va) Emmanuel Episcopal Church, 660 S. Main St., Harrisonburg VA 22801 **R Emm Ch Harrisonburg VA 2009-; Exec Bd Dio Virginia Richmond VA 2017-, Exec Bd 2011-2012, Exec Bd 2011-2012, Chair, Misión Latina Com 2011-, Pres of Stndg Com 2009-2011, Stndg Com 2008-2011, Stndg Com 2007-2009, Misión Latina/Latino Mnstry T/F 2007-, Sprtl Discernment Fac 2006-2011, Sprtl Discernment Fac 2006-2011, Exec Bd 2006-2007, Exec Bd 1998-1999, Bp's Dialogue Grp on Human Sxlty 1997-2003, COM 1990-2006, COM 1990-2006, Asst Hisp Mssnr 1987-1990, Asst Hisp Mssnr 1987-1990, Com On Human Sxlty 1983-1987, Com On Human Sxlty 1983-1987** B Maracaibo VE 1956 s Daniel & Angela. BA Trin Deerfield IL 1983; MDiv VTS 1987. D 6/13/1987 P 4/21/1988 Bp Peter J Lee. m 8/6/2016 Nancy Urrecheaga Urrecheaga Godoy c 3. R Chr Epis Ch Luray VA 2003-2009; S Andr's Ch Burke VA 1999-2003, Assoc R 1999-2003, Assoc R 1988-1991; R Emm Epis Ch Delaplane Delaplane VA 1991-1999; San Marcos Jubilee Com 1988-1990. rector@emmanuelharrisonburg.org

ROBB, George Kerry (SeFla) 521 Rhine Rd, Palm Beach Gardens FL 33410 **Int H Sprt Epis Ch W Palm Bch FL 2017-** B Tampa FL 1936 s Charles & Gladys. BA Stetson U 1958; BD Candler TS Emory U 1961. D 7/28/1967 Bp William Loftin Hargrave P 11/30/1967 Bp Henry I Louttit. m 9/6/1957 Sally T Robb c 3. Int S Ptr's Ch Fernandina Bch FL 2011-2013; Int S Mary's Epis Ch Stuart FL 2009-2011; Int S Paul's Ch Key W FL 2008-2009; Int H Trin Epis Ch Gainesville FL 2006-2007; Int Chr Ch Bradenton FL 2004-2007; R S Mk's Ch Palm Bch Garden FL 1968-2004; Cur S Andr's Ch Lake Worth FL 1967-1968; Conv Secy Dio SEFl 1996-2001; Stndg Com Pres Dio SEFl 1982-1984; Dioc Secy Dio SE Florida Miami 1980-1990, Stndg Com Pres 1974-1976, GC Dep 1973-1991; GC Dep Dio SEFl 1973-1994. Hon Cn Trin Cathd 2000.

ROBB, Stephen (Roch) D 6/3/2017 Bp Prince Grenville Singh.

ROBBINS, Anne Wilson (SO) 10831 Crooked River Rd., #101, Bonita Springs FL 34135 B Chicago IL 1931 d Everett & Bernice. GTS; BA Wells Coll 1953; MEd USC 1968; MDiv Untd TS Dayton OH 1982. D 6/10/1982 P 1/2/1983 Bp William Grant Black. m 6/13/1953 Richard Eugene Robbins c 2. BEC Dio Sthrn Ohio Cincinnati OH 1991-1997, Stndg Com 1997-2002; R S Pat's Epis Ch Dublin OH 1989-2002; R S Dav Vandalia OH 1983-1989; R S Dav Vandalia OH 1983-1989; Asst S Mk's Epis Ch Dayton OH 1982-1983. Auth, *Welcome to Total Mnstry*. ESMA; EWC.

ROBBINS, Buckley (ETenn) 781 Shearer Cove Rd, Chattanooga TN 37405 B Philadelphia PA 1938 s Buckley & Esther. BA U MI 1960; MA U MI 1965; MDiv Sewanee: The U So, TS 1983. D 6/26/1983 P 5/15/1984 Bp William Evan Sanders. m 6/23/1990 Janice M Robbins c 5. Dio E Tennessee Knoxville TN 1991-2008; R S Fran Of Assisi Epis Ch Ooltewah TN 1991-2008; P-in-c S Mary Magd Ch Fayetteville TN 1984-1987; Gr Ch Chattanooga TN 1983-1991; Dio Tennessee Nashville TN 1983-1987. Cmnty of S Mary 1983.

ROBBINS, Charlotte Ann (ND) 3600 25th St. S., Fargo ND 58104 **D Geth Cathd Fargo ND 2007-** B Scottsbluff NE 1939 d Charles & Vada Ardis. BSN U of Nebraska Sch of Nrsng 1961. D 6/22/2007 Bp Michael Smith. m 11/23/1962 James Robbins c 3.

ROBBINS, Herbert John (RG) 104 East Circle Drive, Ruidoso Downs NM 88346 **Ret 2005-** B Hempstead NY 1939 s Herbert & Katharine. BS W Virginia Wesleyan Coll 1969; MDiv S Paul Sem 1972. D 9/15/1978 P 8/6/1979 Bp Richard Mitchell Trelease Jr. m 3/9/1973 Kelly Marie Robbins c 2. R S Paul's Ch Artesia NM 1988-2005, R 1980-1985; Dio The Rio Grande Albuquerque 1985-1988; Dioc Camp Stoney 1985-1987; Cur S Andr's Ch Roswell NM 1979-1980; Asst S Thos A Becket Ch Roswell NM 1978-1979; Serv Methodist Ch 1972-1977. Auth, "Sem Ch Hist".

ROBBINS, Janice M (ETenn) 3425 Alta Vista Dr, Chattanooga TN 37411 **D Ch Of The Gd Shpd Lookout Mtn TN 2009-; S Nich Sch Chattanooga TN 2001-** B Chattanooga TN 1945 BA U of Chattanooga 1967; MS Trevecca Nazarene U 1989. D 6/16/2001 Bp Charles Glenn VonRosenberg. m 6/23/1990 Buckley Robbins c 4.

ROBBINS, Lance (Roch) 1130 Webster Rd, Webster NY 14580 **Dn Dio Rochester Henrietta 2012-; R Ch Of The Gd Shpd Webster NY 1991-** B Chicago IL 1956 s Hiram & Elizabeth. BA Thiel Coll 1978; MDiv SWTS 1982. D 6/5/1982 P 12/18/1982 Bp Donald James Davis. m 7/9/2011 Karyn Robbins c 1. Dioc Coordntr Of Coll Mnstry 1986-1991; Asst R Calv Ch Columbia MO 1986-1991; Vic S Aug Of Cbury Ch Edinboro PA 1982-1985; S Ptr's Ch Waterford PA 1982-1985; Dio NW Pennsylvania Erie PA 1982. ESMHE.

ROBBINS, Mary Elizabeth (Tex) 562 Elkins lk, Huntsville TX 77340 B Lumberton NC 1952 d William & Sybil. D 6/18/2011 P 2/21/2012 Bp C Andrew Doyle. m 7/2/1988 Leonard G Breen c 1.

ROBBINS-COLE, Adrian (Mass) Saint Andrew's Church, 79 Denton Rd, Wellesley MA 02482 **R S Andr's Ch Wellesley MA 2013-** B London ENGLAND 1962 s Eric & Pamela. BS The London Sch of Econ and Political Sci 1984; MA Oxf GB 1992; CAS CDSP 1993; Ripon Coll Cuddesdon Oxford GB 1993; MA Kings Coll London GB 1996. Trans 9/2/2004 Bp Vicky Gene Robinson. m 1/1/1994 Sarah Jane Robbins c 2. R All SS Ch Peterborough NH 2004-2013; Par Mnstry/Area Dn Ch of Engl 1993-2004.

ROBBINS-COLE, Sarah Jane (Mass) 49 Concord St, Peterborough NH 03458 **R S Mich's Epis Ch Holliston MA 2014-** B Des Moines IA 1968 d Henry & Karen. BA U of Vermont 1990; CDSP 1993; MA Oxf GB 1995; MA Kings Coll London 2000. Trans 9/17/2004 as Priest Bp Vicky Gene Robinson. m 1/1/1994 Adrian Cole c 2. All SS Ch Peterborough NH 2006-2013. sarahrobbinscole@yahoo.com

ROBBINS-PENNIMAN, Sylvia Beckman (SwFla) Church of the Good Shepherd, 639 Edgewater Dr, Dunedin FL 34698 **R Ch Of The Gd Shpd Dunedin FL 2010-; Dn, Clearwater Dnry Dio SW Florida Parrish FL 2012-, Dioc Council 2012-, Cmsn on Liturg and Mus 2010-2012, Resolutns Com 2005-2010, Chair, Com on Const and Cn 2004-** B Orange County FL 1954 d Richard & Anne. BA Ken 1976; JD OH SU 1979; Cert Ang Stud Bex Sem 2000; MDiv Trin Luth Sem 2000. D 6/24/2000 P 1/6/2001 Bp Herbert Thompson Jr. m 5/29/1976 Gus Robbins-Penniman c 2. R and Assoc Pstr Lamb Of God Epis Ch Ft Myers FL 2002-2010; Intern All SS Epis Ch New Albany OH 2000-2002; Com on Const and Cn Dio Sthrn Ohio Cincinnati OH 2001-2002, Faith in Life Cmsn 2001-2002, Interfaith & Ecum Relatns Comm. 1996-2002. HSEC 1999-2004. Seidler Awd for Excellence in Systematic Theol Trin Luth Sem 2000; Peters Awd for Ldrshp Trin Luth Sem 1999; Schaaf Awd for Excellence in Ch Hist Trin Luth Sem 1998. beckyrp@churchgoodshepherd.org

ROBERSON, Jason D (SC) **H Cross Faith Memi Epis Ch Pawleys Island SC 2017-** D 5/6/2017 Bp Gladstone Bailey Adams III.

ROBERSON, Mary Moore Mills (USC) 3123 Oakview Rd, Columbia SC 29204 B Greenville SC 1939 d John & Mary. BA Furman U 1985; MDiv GTS 1998. D 6/13/1998 P 5/29/1999 Bp Dorsey Henderson. Assoc S Jn's Epis Ch Columbia SC 2003-2010; Asst R S Ptr's Epis Ch Greenville SC 1999-2003; Chr Epis Ch Lancaster SC 1998-1999.

ROBERT, Mary Christopher (CGC) 551 W Barksdale Dr, Mobile AL 36606 B New Orleans LA 1954 d Frank & Donna. BA Peabody Coll 1975; MDiv Sewanee: The U So, TS 1979; ADN U of Mobile 1982. D 6/18/1979 Bp William F

Gates Jr P 3/19/1983 Bp Charles Farmer Duvall. Asst R All SS Epis Ch Mobile AL 2003-2016, 1996-1997; Asst S Paul's Epis Ch Daphne AL 1982-1986; D S Jn's Epis Cathd Knoxville TN 1979.

ROBERTS, Alice (NH) 2 Moore Rd, Newport NH 03773 **Ch Of The Epiph Newport NH 2014-** B Palo Alto CA 1941 d Herbert & Frances. BA Smith 1962; MDiv EDS 1995. D 4/1/1995 P 5/1/1996 Bp Mary Adelia Rosamond Mcleod. m 8/13/1995 Russell Berry c 4. Chapl Nh St Wmn Prison Goffstown NH 1996-2006.

ROBERTS, Caleb S (Okla) 6400 N Pennsylvania Ave, Nichols Hills OK 73116 **Emm Memi Epis Ch Champaign IL 2017-** B Oklahoma City OK 1988 s Scott & Kimberly. BA Oklahoma St U 2010; MDiv Sem of the SW 2017. D 12/17/2016 Bp Edward Joseph Konieczny P 7/22/2017 Bp Daniel Hayden Martins. m 6/11/2010 Julie Clem c 4.

ROBERTS, Charles Jonathan (SwFla) Calvary Episcopal Church, 1615 First St., Indian Rocks Beach FL 33785 **Calv Ch Indn Rk Bc FL 2013-** B North Carolina 1968 s Charles & Louise. BS No Carolina St U 1990; MS Duke 1998; MDiv Nash 2007. D 6/2/2007 Bp John Bailey Lipscomb P 12/5/2007 Bp Dabney Tyler Smith. m 4/4/1998 Lynne W Watson c 2. Assoc R S Paul's Ch Naples FL 2012-2013; R Gr Epis Ch Monroe LA 2011-2012; R The Epis Ch Of The Gd Shpd Venice FL 2007-2011; Yth Min Ch of the Redeem Sarasota FL 2000-2004; Yth Min First Bapt Ch Hillsborough NC 1995-1997. P, "Gospel in the Digital Age," *The Banner*, The Naples Daily News, 2013; P, "You Are Here," *LivCh*, Living Ch Fndt, 2013; P, "Zion is not above the Apocolypse; It is within it," *The Mssnr*, Nash Sem, 2013. Mich Ramsey Soc 2008.

ROBERTS, George C (Ct) Saint James Episcopal Church, 3 Mountain Rd, Farmington CT 06032 **S Jas Epis Ch Farmington CT 2012-** B Raleigh NC 1963 s Danny & Barbara. BS Campbell U 1986; MFA U of Mississippi 1997; MDiv VTS 2009. D 5/6/2009 P 12/4/2009 Bp Dorsey Henderson. m 6/10/1995 Tracey J Roberts c 4. Cur S Mary's Ch Columbia SC 2009-2012.

ROBERTS, Harold Frederick (Miss) 7417 Falcon Cir., Ocean Springs MS 39564 B Oakville ON CA 1944 s Harold & Jessie. BA Richmond Coll Toronto ON CA 1970; MDiv U Tor CA 1973; York U 1991; DMin SWTS 2008. Trans 3/17/1997 Bp Alfred Marble Jr. m 9/7/1968 Janice Mary Roberts. R The Epis Ch Of The Redeem Biloxi MS 1997-2011; Chapl Metro Toronto Police 1991-1997; Chapl 48th Highlanders of Can - Toronto 1984-1993; Aid de Camp Lieutenant Gvnr of Ontario 1978-1997; Par P Angl Ch of Can - Dio Toronto 1973-1997. P Assoc - The Sis of S Jn the Div - Toron 1973. A Grant of Arms Queen Eliz II 1997; GCLJ(E) Ord of S Lazarus 1993; Can 125 Medal Govt of Can 1992; Hon Cn S Jas Cathd - Toronto 1992; Can Forces Decoration Govt of Can 1983; Queen's Silver Jubilee Medal Govt of Can 1978.

ROBERTS III, Henry Pauling (EC) 260 Houser Road, Blacksburg SC 29702 **Res Chapl 1994-** B Fort Gordon GA 1944 s Henry & Winefred. BBA Georgia Coll GA 1973; MBA Georgia Coll GA 1975; MDiv Sewanee: The U So, TS 1987. D 6/5/1987 Bp Robert Oran Miller P 12/1/1987 Bp Furman Charles Stough. m 8/30/1969 Sarah Roberts. R Chr Ch Eliz City NC 1997-1999; Res Chapl Richmond Memi Hosp Columbia SC 1994-1995; R S Jn's Ch Winnsboro SC 1992-1994; R S Mary's Epis Ch Jasper AL 1987-1992. Auth, "The Twilight's Last Gleaming On Publ Educ," Xlibris Corp, 2008.

ROBERTS, James Beauregard (Miss) 2441 S Shore Dr, Biloxi MS 39532 B Biloxi MS 1941 s Henry & Alma. BA Wm Carey U 1963; MDiv PDS 1966; Amer Bible Inst 1974. D 6/11/1966 P 5/20/1967 Bp John Maury Allin. m 1/26/1962 Pamela M Roberts c 3. R S Mk's Ch Gulfport MS 1969-2013; Vic S Timothys Epis Ch Southaven MS 1968-1969; Cur H Cross Epis Ch Olive Branch MS 1966-1968; H Innoc' Epis Ch Como MS 1966-1968. Outstanding Young Men of Amer; Personalities of the So.

ROBERTS, J Ames Christopher (Mont) PO BOX 2020, Helena MT 59624 **Cn Dio Montana Helena MT 2011-, Dir Dioc Min Formation Prog 1998-2011, Camp Cmsn Chair 1999-2003, COM 1997-1999; Dio Nebraska 2005-** B Hartford CT 1949 s Albert & Audrey. BA Hampden-Sydney Coll 1971; MDiv VTS 1976; MA Duquesne U 1992. D 6/12/1976 P 12/15/1976 Bp David Shepherd Rose. m 9/25/1999 Linda L Roberts c 3. R S Martha's Epis Ch Papillion NE 2003-2009; R Ch Of The Incarn Great Falls MT 1996-2003; The Wheeling Cluster Wheeling WV 1996; Dio W Virginia Charleston WV 1993-1996, Chair BEC 1992-1996, COM 1992-1996; P-in-c S Paul's Ch Wheeling WV 1991-1996; R S Jas' Epis Ch Lewisburg WV 1988-1990; Chapl Boys Hm Covington VA 1986-1987; Chapl Epis Boys Hm Covington VA 1986-1987; R Chr Epis Ch Lancaster SC 1980-1984; Asst S Martins-In-The-Field Columbia SC 1977-1980; P-in-c Emm Ch Mears VA 1976-1977; Stndg Com Dio Nebraska Omaha NE 2004-2009; SCCM Dio Upper So Carolina Columbia SC 1981-1983, Mssn Dvlpmt Committe 1980-1985; COM Dio Sthrn Virginia Newport News VA 1976-1977. mtcto@diomontana.com

ROBERTS, Jason Thomas (WTex) 8642 Cheviot Hts, San Antonio TX 78254 **Vic Ch Of The H Sprt San Antonio TX 2015-, Vic 2009-2015** B Richmond VA 1975 s James & Nancy. BA Jas Madison U 1997; MEd Jas Madison U 1999; MDiv VTS 2003; Cert Virginia Commonwealth U 2006. D 6/14/2003 P 12/20/2003 Bp Peter J Lee. m 1/3/2009 Susannah E Nicholson c 2. Asst/Assoc R Gr & H Trin Epis Ch Richmond VA 2003-2008.

ROBERTS JR, John Bannister Gibson (CFla) 860 Ohlinger Rd, Babson Park FL 33827 B Charleroi PA 1928 s John & Christine. BA Washington and Jefferson U 1950; MDiv PDS 1954. D 6/19/1954 P 12/18/1954 Bp William S Thomas. m 6/14/1952 Fay Kathryn Roberts. S Ann's Epis Ch Wauchula FL 1984-1999; Off Of Bsh For ArmdF New York NY 1959-1969; P-in-c All SS Ch Aliquippa PA 1954-1959; S Lk's Epis Ch Georgetown PA 1954-1959. Legion of Merit USAF 1983; Bronze Star USAF 1970; Meritorious USAF.

ROBERTS, John Charles (NC) **Asst Ch Of S Jn In The Wilderness Flat Rock NC 2017-; Cbury Sch Greensboro NC 2016-** D 6/17/2017 Bp Anne Hodges-Copple.

ROBERTS, Jose (RI) 236 Central Ave, Pawtucket RI 02860 B 1955 s Jose & Carmen. Centro de Estudios Teologicos. D 8/15/1982 P 6/1/1984 Bp Telesforo A Isaac. c 1. S Geo And San Jorge Cntrl Falls RI 2015-2016; Dio Rhode Island Providence RI 2004-2014; Dio Puerto Rico Trujillo Alto PR 2000-2003; Dio The Dominican Republic (Iglesia Epis Dominicana) Gazcue Santo Domingo 1995-2000, 1982-1988; Dio Panama 1988-1990; Vic Iglesia Epis San Andres Santo Domingo Di 1982-1987. ap735@osfn.org

ROBERTS, Judith S (Ind) 342 Red Ash Cir, Englewood FL 34223 **Asst Ch Of The Gd Shpd Punta Gorda FL 2007-** B Nantucket MA 1935 d Albert & Nancy. SWTS; BA Br 1957; MDiv EDS 1957. D 6/23/1995 Bp Edward Witker Jones P 9/15/2002 Bp Cate Waynick. m 8/10/1957 Richard Fred Roberts c 4. Coordntr Dio SE Florida Miami 2005-2008; Asst S Dav's Epis Ch Englewood FL 2003-2007; Asst All SS Ch Seymour IN 2002-2003; D S Paul's Ch Columbus IN 1995-2002; Global Missions Com Dio Indianapolis Indianapolis IN 2000-2003, Stndg Com 1999, Com 1996-1998.

ROBERTS, Katherine Alexander (At) 18 Clarendon Ave, Avondale Estates GA 30002 B New York NY 1942 d Henry & Joan. BA Marymount Manhattan Coll 1972; MDiv Candler TS Emory U 1991; CAS CDSP 1995. D 6/28/1995 Bp James Louis Jelinek P 2/1/1996 Bp Sanford Zangwill Kaye Hampton. c 1. S Barth's Epis Ch Atlanta GA 2002-2012; S Anth's Epis Ch Winder GA 1998-2001; The Epis Ch Of The Nativ Fayetteville GA 1998. Co-Auth, "The Unhealed Wounders," *Restoring the Soul of a Ch*, Liturg Press, 1995. SSAP 2007.

ROBERTS, Kim Elaine (Neb) 2312 J St, Omaha NE 68107 B Omaha NE 1953 d Virgil & Catherine. Clarkson Coll 1984; Iona Sch for Mnstry 2014. D 5/8/2006 Bp Joe Goodwin Burnett P 5/8/2014 Bp Scott Scott Barker. m 11/27/1976 William W Roberts c 1.

ROBERTS, Linda L (Mont) 16404 72nd St, Plattsmouth NE 68048 B Whitehall MT 1946 d Leo & Mary. Montana St U 1969. D 6/11/1991 P 2/1/1996 Bp Charles I Jones III. m 9/25/1999 J Ames Christopher Roberts c 2. S Mary's Epis Ch Blair NE 2004-2006; Dio Montana Helena MT 1997-1999, Mem, Stndg Cmsn 1996-1999, Mem, Cmsn 1991-1996; P Chr Ch Sheridan MT 1996-1999; Epis Mnstry Ennis MT 1995-1996; S Paul's Ch Virginia City MT 1994-1999; Cleric Trin Jeffers MT 1994-1996; S Steph's Ch Billings MT 1991-1994.

ROBERTS III BSG, Malcolm (EC) 520 Taberna Way, New Bern NC 28562 **Vic Peace Epis Ch 2005-** B Camp White OR 1943 s Malcolm & Nancy. AA Mitchell Coll 1964; BA Windham Coll 1966; MDiv VTS 1975. D 6/7/1975 P 12/13/1975 Bp Joseph Warren Hutchens. m 5/13/1972 Mary Roberts c 2. Peace Epis Ch New Bern NC 2006-2010; Chf Dept Mnstry & Pstr Care Walter Reed Walter Reed Army Med Cntr Washington DC 1998-2004; Asst Commandant US-Army Chapl Cntr & Sch Ft Ft Monmouth NJ 1994-1998; Dep Command Chapl TRDOC Ft. Monroe VA 1990-1994; Sr Chapl Clinician Walter Reed Army Med Cntr Washington DC 1987-1990; Asst Corps Chapl H V Corps Frankfurt Germany 1983-1987; Off Of Bsh For ArmdF New York NY 1978-2004; Chapl US-Army 101st Airborne Div BN/Bde 1978-1982; S Jn The Evang Yalesville CT 1975-1978; Cur S Paul's Ch Wallingford CT 1975-1978. Bro of S Greg 1999.

ROBERTS, Mollie (Ala) 3702 Mays Bend Rd., Pell City AL 35128 **S Simon Ptr Ch Pell City AL 2014-** B Orlando FL 1957 d Jo & Marcia. BSBA The U of Cntrl Florida 1978; MBA The U of Cntrl Florida 1993; MDiv Sewanee: The U So, TS 2013; MDiv The TS at The U So 2013. D 6/22/2013 P 2/15/2014 Bp Scott Anson Benhase. c 3. S Paul's Ch Albany GA 2013-2014.

ROBERTS, Patricia Joyce (Ia) 3226 S Clinton St, Sioux City IA 51106 B Sioux City IA 1939 d John & Evelyn. Morningside Coll. D 12/17/1995 Bp Chris Christopher Epting. m 8/20/1960 Vernon Carl Roberts c 2. D Calv Epis Ch Sioux City IA 1995-2015. patriciaroberts@cableone.net

ROBERTS, Patricia Kant (CFla) 35 Willow Dr, Orlando FL 32807 B Mineola NY 1939 d William & Marion. AD Florida Chr U 2005. D 12/9/2006 Bp John Wadsworth Howe. c 8. Swim Coach Ton Enola Swim Club/Colonial Swim Team 1969-1974.

ROBERTS, Paul Benjamin (At) 33 Cross Crk E, Dahlonega GA 30533 **Associating P S Eliz's Epis Ch Dahlonega GA 2012-, R 2002-2012** B Austin TX 1943 s Fowler & Frances. U So 1961; BA SMU 1964; MDiv Ya Berk 1967; DMin Van 1991. D 6/15/1967 P 12/21/1967 Bp William Paul Barnds. m 11/28/1968 Florence Bright c 2. P Assoc Ch of the Resurr Sautee Nacoochee GA 2008-2012, Int 2001-2007; Archd Dio W Virginia Charleston WV 1994-1999; R Trin Ch Huntington WV 1993-2000; R S Mths Ch Nashville TN 1977-1993;

Vic S Thos Epis Ch Knoxville TN 1974-1977; Dio Tennessee Nashville TN 1971-1977; Vic Ch Of Our Sav Gallatin TN 1971-1974; Asst R Gr - S Lk's Ch Memphis TN 1968-1971; Min-In-C S Jas Epis Ch Cumberland Furnace TN 1967-1968. Grad Fllshp Berkely DS 1967; Bromberg Awd SMU 1963; Wilson Fell SMU 1961.

ROBERTS, Peter F (CFla) 5500 N Tropical Trl, Merritt Island FL 32953 **R S Lk's Epis Ch Merritt Island FL 2003-** B Birmingham England 1959 s Jack & Yvonne. BS Nthrn Illinois U 1981; BA U of Leeds Gb 1987; Coll of the Resurr 1988; Untd Coll of the Ascen Selly Oak W Midlands Eng 1991. Trans 9/11/2003 Bp John Wadsworth Howe. m 6/19/1987 Ann Elizabeth Roberts c 3. Vic Serv Ch of Engl Collingham Great Britain (UK) 1995-2001; P-in-c Serv Ch of the W Indies 1991-1995; Cur Serv Ch of Engl Dio Ripon and Leeds Great Br 1988-1991.

ROBERTS, Steven Michael (La) 1613 7th St, New Orleans LA 70115 **Cn Chr Ch Cathd New Orleans LA 2002-** B Glendale CA 1964 s Bryan & Nancy. BS Louisiana Tech U 1987; MDiv SWTS 1996. D 6/8/1996 P 1/12/1997 Bp Robert Jefferson Hargrove Jr. m 6/26/2011 Linda E Bogacki. Assoc R Epis Ch Of The Gd Shpd Lake Chas LA 1999-2002; R Trin Ch Crowley LA 1997-1999; Cur St Mich's Epis Ch Pineville LA 1996-1997.

ROBERTS, Susan Jean (U) 261 S 900 E, Salt Lake City UT 84102 B Elgin IL 1966 d Kenneth & Mabel. BS Wheelock Coll 1988; MDiv CDSP 2005. D 1/22/2015 P 7/22/2015 Bp Scott Byron Hayashi. m 6/2/2010 Robin L James c 1.

ROBERTS, Suzanne Grondin (Me) 143 State St, Portland ME 04101 **Assoc Cathd Ch Of S Lk Portland ME 2013-** B Boston MA 1962 d Leo & Virginia. BS Br 1984; MD and MPH Tul 1989; MDiv Bangor TS 2011. D 6/23/2012 P 3/1/2013 Bp Stephen Taylor Lane. m 4/22/1989 Melville Parker Roberts c 3.

ROBERTS, William Allan (Ida) 1336 E Walker St, Blackfoot ID 83221 **Ret 1995-** B Springfield OH 1933 s Arthur & Lydia. BA Witt 1955; BD CDSP 1958. D 6/14/1958 P 12/9/1958 Bp Henry W Hobson. m 6/9/1957 Lorraine Roberts c 3. Mtn Rivers Epis Cmnty Idaho Falls ID 1991-1995; R Chr Ch Xenia OH 1984-1991; R S Andr's Epis Ch Wshngtn Ct Hs OH 1984-1989; R All SS Epis Ch Portsmouth OH 1977-1984; Assoc The Epis Ch Of The Ascen Middletown OH 1968-1977; Asst S Andr's Ch Meriden CT 1962-1968; Min in charge Gr Ch Pomeroy OH 1958-1962.

ROBERTS, William Bradley (Va) 3737 Seminary Rd, Alexandria VA 22304 **Prof VTS Alexandria VA 2008-** B Greenwood MS 1947 s Roy & Mary. BA Houston Bapt U; M.C.M Sthrn Bapt TS 1976; D.M.A Sthrn Bapt TS 1984. D 11/21/2015 Bp Susan Goff P 5/22/2016 Bp Shannon Sherwood Johnston. m 3/1/2014 David Wesley Hoover c 1. Other Lay Position S Jn's Ch Lafayette Sq Washington DC 2002-2008; Other Lay Position S Phil's In The Hills Tucson AZ 2000-2003. broberts@vts.edu

ROBERTS, William D (Chi) 720 Ambria Drive, Mundelein IL 60060 B Evanston IL 1950 s James & Charlotte. AB Dart 1972; MDiv SWTS 1978. D 6/17/1978 Bp Quintin Ebenezer Primo Jr P 12/16/1978 Bp Walter Cameron Righter. m 3/30/1974 Ingrid C Roberts c 2. R S Greg's Epis Ch Deerfield IL 1988-2015; Asst St. Barth Ch New York NY 1981-1988; Asst Trin Cathd Davenport IA 1978-1981. Auth, "And the Word became Welsh," 2004; Auth, "The Angl Commitment to the Historic Episcopate," *Ecum Trends*, 2000; Auth, "Toward a Luth Anamnesis of the Historic Episcopate," *Ecum Trends*, 1998; Auth, "Two Kinds of Suffering," *LivCh*, 1998; Auth, "Response to the Significance of the ELCA's 1997 Ecum Agenda for the Wider Ch," *Ecum Trends*, 1997; Auth, "A Way to Pray Through the Ch Year Each Week Day by Day," *A Way to Pray Through the Ch Year Each Week Day by Day*, Forw Mvmt Press, 1986.

ROBERTS, William Tudor (Mich) 584 E Walled Lake Dr, Walled Lake MI 48390 **P/Pstr S Anne's Epis Ch Walled Lake MI 2011-, D 2010-2011; Asst for Archv and Hist Dio Michigan Detroit MI 2014-, Chapl of the Dioc Alt-Gld 2014-, Mem of Bp Advsry Com on Total Mnstry 2014-, Mem of the Dioc Stndg Com 2014-, Trst 2011-2014, Cathd Chapt 2010-2013, Cmsn on Const and Cn 2010-2013** B Boston MA 1945 s O Tudor & Jeannette. D 11/3/2010 P 6/21/2011 Bp Wendell Nathaniel Gibbs Jr. m 4/11/1986 Alicia Grajales c 2. Mayor City of Walled Lake Walled Lake MI 1986-2013; Mayor City of Walled Lake Walled Lake MI 1973-1977.

ROBERTSHAW III, Arthur Bentham (Ct) 88 Notch Hill Rd Apt 240, North Branford CT 06471 B Woonsocket RI 1927 s Arthur & Florence. BA Ya 1948; STB Ya Berk 1952. D 6/17/1952 P 12/19/1952 Bp Walter H Gray. R Ch Of The H Adv Clinton CT 1964-1987; P-in-c Ch Of S Jn By The Sea W Haven W Haven CT 1955-1964; Asst St Johns Ch W Hartford CT 1954-1955; Chair Yth Coun Dio Connecticut Meriden CT 1956-1966.

ROBERTSHAW, Michelle Lyn (SwFla) St Andrew's Episcopal Church, PO Box 272, Boca Grande FL 33921 **S Andr's Ch Boca Grande FL 2012-** B Tampa FL 1967 BA U of So Florida 1990; MDiv VTS 2003. D 6/14/2003 P 1/1/2004 Bp John Bailey Lipscomb. Asst R Ch Of The H Fam Chap Hill NC 2006-2012; S Mary Magd Bradenton FL 2005-2006; Asst S Bon Ch Sarasota FL 2003-2005; Lay Chapl + Rel Ed Tchr St. Mary's Epis Ch & Sch 1997-2000.

ROBERTSON, Amanda Kucik (NC) 2701 Park Rd, Charlotte NC 28209 **Assoc R Ch Of The H Comf Charlotte NC 2011-** B Washington DC 1979 d George & Karen. BA U of Virginia 2002; MDiv Ya Berk 2006. D 6/24/2006 P 2/3/2007

Bp Peter J Lee. m 1/24/2015 Terrence Hubert Robertson. Assoc R Ch Of The Incarn New York NY 2006-2011. amandar@holycomforterCharlotte.org

ROBERTSON IV, Ben G. (Miss) The Chapel Of The Cross, 674 Mannsdale Rd, Madison MS 39110 **The Chap Of The Cross Madison MS 2014-** B Louisville KY 1974 s Benjamin & Else. BA Ken 1996; MDiv VTS 2003. D 5/17/2003 P 12/6/2003 Bp Ted Gulick Jr. m 5/25/2002 Ellen Monaghan Robertson c 2. Assoc Calv Ch Memphis TN 2010-2014; R All SS' Epis Ch Gastonia NC 2006-2010; S Matt's Epis Ch Louisville KY 2003-2006.

ROBERTSON, Bruce Edward (NMich) 452 Silver Creek Rd, Marquette MI 49855 B Marquette MI 1951 s Robert & Alberta. D 4/1/1999 Bp Thomas Kreider Ray P 3/5/2000 Bp James Arthur Kelsey.

ROBERTSON, Charles Kevin (Az) 815 2nd Avenue, New York NY 10017 **Distinguished Vstng Prof GTS 2008-; Dom And Frgn Mssy Soc- Epis Ch Cntr New York NY 2007-, Rgstr 2009-2013; Cn to the PBp Epis Ch Cntr New York NY 2007-; Chair, Convening Table on Chr Educ Natl Coun of Ch 2014-; Natl Advsry Bd Mem Cntr for Biblic Stds Ft Washington PA 2011-; Bd Mem Amer Friends of the Angl Cntr in Rome 2008-; Bd Mem ATR Chicago IL 2008-; Advsry Bd Mem Day 1 Atlanta GA 2007-** B El Paso TX 1964 s Francis & Virginia. BA VPI 1985; MDiv VTS 1993; PhD Dur 1999. D 6/19/1993 P 1/6/1994 Bp John Wadsworth Howe. m 5/18/1991 Deborah Ann Robertson c 3. Cn to the Ordnry Dio Arizona Phoenix AZ 2004-2007; R S Steph's Ch Milledgeville GA 1999-2004; Consult/P in Res Ch of Engl 1996-1999; P-in-c S Jn's Ch Melbourne FL 1993-1996; Gvrng Bd Mem Natl Coun of Ch Washington DC 2011-2013; Bd Mem Soc For The Increase Of Mnstry W Hartford CT 2010-2014; Bd Mem The Epis Ntwk for Stwdshp (TENS) 2001-2005. Auth, "BCP: A Sprtl Treasure Chest," SkyLight Paths, 2013; Co-Auth, "Epis Questions, Epis Answers," Ch Pub, 2013; Gnrl Ed, "Stds in Epis and Angl Theol series," Ptr Lang Pub, 2012; Auth, "A Dangerous Dozen: 12 Christians Who Threatened the Status Quo," SkyLIght Paths, 2011; Auth, "Conversations w Scripture: Acts," Morehouse, 2010; Auth, "Transforming Stwdshp," CPI, 2009. Angl Assn of Biblic Scholars 2009; SBL 1997. Commencement Speaker Ming Hua Sem, Hong Kong 2014; Bacclaureate Speaker GTS 2010; Commencement Speaker Sem of the SW 2009; Helping Amer's Yth Honoree White Hse 2005; ECF Fllshp ECF 1998.

ROBERTSON, Claude Richard (Ark) 1605 E Republican Rd, Jacksonville AR 72076 B Moberly MO 1942 BBA SMU 1964; MBA U of Cntrl Arkansas 1975. D 6/3/2006 P 12/9/2006 Bp Larry Maze. c 1.

ROBERTSON JR, Edward Ray (La) 212 Spencer Ave, New Orleans LA 70124 B New Orleans LA 1945 s Edward & Marguerite. BA U of New Orleans 1967; MA U of New Orleans 1969; MDiv Nash 1981. Trans 11/1/2003 Bp Charles Edward Jenkins III. m 6/11/1966 Jeanne Robertson c 2. R S Jn's Epis Ch Thibodaux LA 2005-2011; R S Jude's Epis Ch Niceville FL 2003-2005; R S Mk's Epis Ch Harvey LA 1998-2003; Assoc S Geo's Epis Ch New Orleans LA 1993-1998; Chapl & Chair Dept Rel S Mart's Epis Sch Metairie LA 1990-1998; Gr Ch New Orleans LA 1990-1992; Cn Pstr Chr Ch Cathd New Orleans LA 1989-1990; S Jas Epis Ch Baton Rouge LA 1987-1989, Cur 1981-1984; R Trin Ch Tallulah LA 1984-1987.

ROBERTSON, Frederick W (Kan) 626 E Montclaor St Apt 1D, Springfield MO 65807 **1983-** B Eureka UT 1937 s Stafford & Rose. BA Drury U 1961; MDiv Nash 1974. D 6/24/1974 Bp Arthur Anton Vogel P 12/1/1974 Bp Charles Thomas Gaskell. m 11/23/1960 Charlotte E Robertson. Ch Of The Ascen Neodesha KS 1974-1975; Ch Of The Epiph Independence KS 1974-1975; R S Thos Of Cbury Ch Greendale WI 1974-1975.

ROBERTSON, James Bruce (WMo) 4824 Bell Street, Kansas City MO 64112 **Serv S Mich And All Ang Ch Mssn KS 2012-** B Hot Sprgs AR 1948 s Paul & Myrtle. BA U of Kansas 1970; MA U of Kansas 1972; Cert Pennsylvania Diac Sch 1991; AUD U of Florida 2000; MDiv GTS 2012; MDiv The GTS of the Epis Ch 2012. D 10/9/1993 Bp Allen Lyman Bartlett Jr. m 9/21/2013 Dean L Ennis. Sem Chr Ch Bronxville NY 2011-2012; Serv S Paul's Ch Philadelphia PA 2009-2010, Serv 2001-2008; Serv Cathd Ch Of S Jn Wilmington DE 2006-2009; Serv Gloria Dei Ch Philadelphia PA 1996-1998; Serv S Ptr's Ch Philadelphia PA 1994-1996; Serv Ch Of The H Apos Wynnewood PA 1993-1994. jasbrob@aol.com

ROBERTSON, John (Minn) 38378 Reservation Highway 101, PO Box 369, Morton MN 56270 **Vic Bp Whipple Mssn/St. Cornelia's Ch Lower Sioux Ind 2005-; Dio Minnesota Minneapolis MN 2005-, 1995-1998, Cn Mssnr for Indn Wk 1995-1998, 1993-1994** B Sisseton SD 1952 s Walter & Lorene. Macalester Coll 1977; Minnesota St U Mankato 1984; MDiv SWTS 1993. D 6/19/1993 Bp Robert Marshall Anderson P 12/21/1993 Bp James Louis Jelinek. c 4. Native Mnstrs Off Epis Ch Cntr New York NY 1999-2003; P-in-c Ch Of The Gd Shpd Windom MN 1995-1998; P-in-c S Jas Ch Marshall MN 1994-1995; P-in-c Mazakute Memi Ch S Paul MN 1993-1994.

ROBERTSON, John Brown (EC) St Timothy's Epis Church, 107 Louis St, Greenville NC 27858 **D S Tim's Epis Ch Greenville NC 2015-** B Albuquerque NM 1939 s Alexander & Alice. Colorado Sch of Mines 1961; U of Arizona 1966. D 1/26/2008 Bp Kirk Stevan Smith. m 3/31/1963 Diana Taff Robertson c 4. D Gd Shpd Of The Hills Cave Creek AZ 2008-2014.

ROBERTSON, Josephine (Tex) St John's Kirkland, 105 State St S, Kirkland WA 98033 **S Jn's Ch Kirkland WA 2015-** B Lapeer MI 1977 d Richard & Nancy. BS Wstrn Michigan U 2000; MDiv Epis TS of the SW 2011. D 12/10/2010 P 8/13/2011 Bp Steven Todd Ousley. m 5/12/2011 Timothy Peoples. Assoc S Paul's Ch Waco TX 2012-2014; S Geo's Ch Austin TX 2011-2012.

ROBERTSON, Karen (Suzi) Sue (FtW) 1757 244th Ave NE, Sammamish WA 98074 **Gd Shpd Granbury TX 2015-; Serv Godly Play Intl Trnr 2003-** B Fort Worth TX 1952 d Kenneth & Bertha. BD S Edwards U Austin TX 1982; MA U of St Thos 1984; MDiv Houston Grad TS 2000; DMin SMU 2001. D 10/27/2002 P 5/14/2003 Bp Don Adger Wimberly. m 6/4/1989 Nolen D Holcomb c 1. Vic Gd Samar Epis Ch Sammamish WA 2009-2015; St Jn's Epis Sch Abilene TX 2007-2009; R S Lk The Evang Houston TX 2004-2007; Prof Angl Prov of Tanzania 2003-2004; Prof Exec Coun Appointees New York NY 2003; Assoc Trin Ch Galveston TX 2002-2003; Chr Ch Cathd Houston TX 1998-2000; Serv Methodist Ch 1985-1998; Chair, Cmsn on Schools Dio NW Texas Lubbock TX 2007-2009. Auth, "Windows Into The Sprtlty of Chld," Booksurge Pub, 2006; Auth, "Alexander's Pryr," *Ldr In The Ch Sch Today*, Meth Pub Hse, 2002; Auth, "Recruiting For The New Milennium," *Ldr In The Ch Sch Today*, Meth Pub Hse, 2000; Auth, "Ask, Don't Tell," *Ldr In The Ch Sch Today*, Meth Pub Hse, 2000; Auth, "Brandon's Story," *Ldr In The Ch Sch Today*, Meth Pub Hse, 1999; Auth, "Giving Chld the Light of Chr," *Ldr In The Ch Sch Today*, Meth Pub Hse, 1998; Auth, "The Post Schooling Sunday Sch," *Ldr In The Ch Sch Today*, Meth Pub Hse, 1995; Auth, "How to Chair a Successful Meeting," *Ldr In The Ch Sch Today*, Meth Pub Hse, 1994; Auth, "Latchkey Mnstry: Mssn and Educ," *Tchr mag*, Meth Pub Hse, 1993; Auth, "A Tchr Recruiting Cmpgn that Works," *Ldr In The Ch Sch Today*, Meth Pub Hse, 1992; Auth, "All God's People: A Prog for Persons who are Mentally Retarded," People to People, Carrollton TX, 1987; Auth, "Love Your Neighbor," Yth Mnstry Resource Exch, 1985. Chr Ch Cathd Chapt, Houston TX 2006. Grant Rec Dio Olympia 2011; Grant Rec Trin, Wall St 2005; Grant Rec Dio Texas 2003.

ROBERTSON, Marilyn Sue (Okla) 127 NW 7th St, Oklahoma City OK 73102 **D S Paul's Cathd Oklahoma City OK 2008-** B Oklahoma City OK 1963 d Thomas & Betty. BSN Oklahoma Cntrl St U 1986. D 6/21/2008 Bp Edward Joseph Konieczny.

ROBERTSON, Patricia Rome (Oly) 313 Bromley Place NW, Bainbridge Island WA 98110 **Cler Coach and Mentor Epis Dio Olympia Seattle WA 2014-; Asstg P for Contemplative Mnstrs S Barn Epis Ch Bainbridge Island WA 2014-** B Berwyn IL 1949 d Irvin & Dorothy. BA SUNY 1974; MS U Pgh 1978; MDiv EDS 1986; Cert Seattle U 2007. D 6/13/1987 P 6/6/1988 Bp David Elliot Johnson. m 5/29/1982 George G Robertson c 2. R The Par Of S Mary And S Jude NE Harbor ME 2008-2013; R S Steph's Epis Ch Seattle WA 1997-2007; sabbatical supply Chr Ch Tacoma WA 1996; Vic/R S Ambr Epis Ch Foster City CA 1992-1996; Assoc S Thos Epis Ch Sunnyvale CA 1988-1992; Asst S Mich's Ch Marblehead MA 1987-1988; Dioc Coun Dio Maine Portland ME 2009-2011, Mssn Strtgy Coordntr 2009-2011; Pres, Stndg Com Dio Olympia Seattle 2004-2005; Dioc Coun Dio California San Francisco CA 1993-1995; COM Dio El Camino Real Salinas CA 1989-1992. Auth, "Being Made New," *Congregations*, Alb Inst, 2008; Auth, "Contemplative Ldrshp - Discovering the Wisdom to Lead," *Seattle Theol and Mnstry Revs*, Seattle U, 2008; Auth, "Last Words," *Bklet*, self-Pub, 2007.

ROBESON, Terry Ann (Wyo) 665 Cedar St, Lander WY 82520 **P Trin Ch Lander WY 2006-** B Denver CO 1953 d Alex & Florence. BA U of Nthrn Colorado 1975. D 2/24/2006 P 9/2/2006 Bp Bruce Caldwell. m 7/5/1980 Thomas Ann Robeson c 2.

ROBILLARD, Roger Manuel (Va) 400 S Cedar Ave, Highland Springs VA 23075 B Woonsocket RI 1942 s Raymond & Monique. BTh McGill U 1978; DIT Montreal TS CA 1979. Trans 11/1/1997 Bp Gerry Wolf. Vic Trin Epis Ch Highland Sprg VA 2001-2008; R S Jas Epis Ch At Woonsocket Woonsocket RI 1997-2001; Serv Angl Ch Of Can 1979-1997. Kiwanis 2002-2006; Soc of S Marg 1976.

ROBINSON, Allen Florence (Md) 2729 Moores Valley Dr, Baltimore MD 21209 **R S Jas' Epis Ch Baltimore MD 2002-; R St. Jas Epis Ch Baltimore MD 2002-** B Galveston TX 1970 s Allen & Patricia. BA S Augustines Coll Raleigh NC 1992; MDiv VTS 1995; DMin Fuller TS 2007. D 6/17/1995 Bp Claude Edward Payne P 1/18/1996 Bp Leopoldo Jesus Alard. m 4/20/1996 Allison J Robinson c 3. Assoc Calv Ch Memphis TN 1999-2002; S Dunst's Epis Ch Houston TX 1998-1999; The Great Cmsn Fndt Houston TX 1995-1998; Asst Ch Of The Resurr Houston TX 1995-1997; S Jas Epis Ch Houston TX 1995-1997.

ROBINSON, Carla Lynn (Oly) 15220 Main St, Bellevue WA 98007 **R Ch Of The Ascen Seattle WA 2014-** B Cleveland OH 1958 d Ferdinand & Thelma. BA Concordia Coll 1980; MDiv Concordia TS 1984. D 1/15/2009 Bp Gregory Harold Rickel. All SS Epis Ch Seattle WA 2010-2012; Cler Dio Olympia Seattle 2009, Admin Asst 2005-2009.

ROBINSON, Charles (SVa) 2124 Benomi Dr., Williamsburg VA 23185 **Dio Sthrn Virginia Newport News VA 2016-, Dep GC 2015-, Dn, Convoc Five 2013-2016, Stndg Com 2012-2015, Alt Dep GC 2011-2015, Chair, COM:** Sem Formation 2007-2011 B Ponca City OK 1952 s Charles & Pauline. BBA Natl U 1980; MA Webster U 1982; MDiv Epis TS of the SW 2004. D 6/5/2004 P 12/8/2004 Bp David Conner Bane Jr. m 2/6/1971 Terry L Robinson c 2. Vic Bruton Par Williamsburg VA 2007-2016; R S Jn's Ch Suffolk VA 2004-2007. crobinson@diosova.org

ROBINSON, Charles Edward (U) PO Box 981208, Park City UT 84098 B Houston TX 1955 s Edward & Brenda. H Apos Sem & Coll; BS U of Texas 1978; MDiv Golden Gate Bapt TS 1985; MA San Francisco St U 1987; Cert CD-SP 1988; MBA DeVry U 2004. D 12/3/1988 P 12/1/1989 Bp William Edwin Swing. m 6/1/1985 Bonnie A Brown c 1. Chair - Stwdshp Educ Team Dio Utah Salt Lake City UT 2008-2011, Chair - Cler Compstn T/F 2007-2009, 2004-, Chair - COM 2007-2011; Clincl Dir Phoenix Interfaith Counslg Phoenix AZ 2000-2004; R S Andr's Ch Glendale AZ 1991-1998; Assoc for Fam Mnstrs S Barn On The Desert Scottsdale AZ 1990-1991; Hosp Chapl Hermann Hosp Houston TX 1981-1983; Yth Min So Av Bapt Ch Pasadena TX 1978-1981. AAPC 1998-2004.

ROBINSON, Christopher Mcleod (Miss) 113 S 9th St, Oxford MS 38655 **S Ptr's Ch Oxford MS 2014-** B Tupelo MS 1984 s Joseph & Diane. BA Millsaps Coll 2006; MDiv VTS 2010. D 6/27/2010 P 1/22/2011 Bp Duncan Montgomery Gray III. m 10/5/2012 Whitney Moore Robinson. Par Of The Medtr-Redeem Mccomb MS 2010-2014. chrisrobinson84@gmail.com

ROBINSON, Constance Diane (Eas) 5820 Haven Ct, Rock Hall MD 21661 B Philadelphia PA 1947 d Karl & Constance. BS W Chester U of Pennsylvania 1970; MEd W Chester U of Pennsylvania 1976; MDiv PrTS 1984. D 7/16/2005 P 1/28/2006 Bp Bud Shand. m 9/20/1986 David Gordon Robinson. Chr Ch Worton MD 2006-2007; Emm Epis Ch Chestertown MD 2005-2006.

ROBINSON, Cristopher (WTex) 1621 Santa Monica St, Kingsville TX 78363 B Houston TX 1970 s Allan & Pauline. BS Rice U 1993; MS U of Texas 1995; MDiv Epis TS of the SW 2005. D 7/9/2005 Bp Sylvestre Donato Romero P 1/11/2006 Bp Gary Richard Lillibridge. m 11/18/1995 Kristina Robinson c 2. R St Fran Epis Ch San Antonio TX 2012-2017; R Ch Of The Epiph Kingsville TX 2009-2012; Asst. R S Thos Epis Ch And Sch San Antonio TX 2005-2009; Airport Consult Atac Inc. Sunnyvale CA 1999-2002; Assoc Leigh Fisher Assoc San Mateo CA 1995-1999. crobinson@sfcsa.org

ROBINSON JR, David Gordon (NH) 1035 Lafayette Rd, Portsmouth NH 03801 **Vic Chr Ch Portsmouth NH 2012-; Trin Ch Hampton NH 2012-** B Seaford DE 1953 s David & Erma. BA Salisbury U 1975; MDiv VTS 1979. D 3/6/1982 Bp William Hawley Clark P 3/12/1983 Bp George E Rath. m 5/28/1979 Cynthia L Robinson. Int Ch Of The H Sprt Plymouth NH 2011; Faith Relatns Comm Chair Grtr Nashua HabHum Nashua NH 2006-2011; Ch Of Our Sav Milford NH 2000-2011; R Gr Ch Norwood MA 1986-2000; Asst The Ch Of The H Sprt Orleans MA 1982-1986; Co-Chair, Cler Compstn Com Dio New Hampshire Concord NH 2004-2011, Mem, Dioc Coun 2000-2004. Co-Auth, "w Grateful Hearts," Gr Pub, 1997; Co-Auth, "From Bounden Duty to a Joyful Thing," Gr Pub, 1992. vicarchip@gmail.com

ROBINSON, David Gordon (Eas) 5820 Haven Ct, Rock Hall MD 21661 B Medford MA 1939 s Walter & Miriam. AB Dart 1961; MDiv EDS 1984. D 6/21/1986 P 5/14/1987 Bp George Nelson Hunt III. m 9/20/1986 Constance Diane Robinson c 3. R Chr Ch Worton MD 2004-2007; Chapl, Cbury Fllshp Washington Coll Chestertown MD 2002-2006; Asstg P Chr Ch Cranbrook Bloomfield Hills MI 1987-1999; Chapl, Rel Dept Hd Cranbrook Kingswood Sch Bloomfield Hills MI 1984-2000; Captain, USN (Ret) USN 1961-1989.

ROBINSON, David Kerr (Me) Po Box 7554, Ocean Park ME 04063 **R Trin Ch Saco ME 2006-; Dio Maine Portland ME 2006-** B New York NY 1952 s Irving & Jean. BS S Lawr Canton NY 1974; MDiv Nash 1977. D 6/4/1977 P 12/10/1977 Bp Wilbur Emory Hogg Jr. m 8/17/1974 Patricia Hobson Robinson c 3. Coll Chapl Brockport NY 1986-2006; R S Lk's Ch Brockport NY 1986-2006; Coll Chapl Murray KY 1981-1986; Vic S Jn's Ch Murray KY 1981-1986; Coll Chapl Oneonta NY 1977-1981; Cur S Jas Ch Oneonta NY 1977-1981.

ROBINSON, David Scott (Pa) 603 Misty Hollow Dr, Maple Glen PA 19002 **R S Matt's Ch Maple Glen PA 1985-** B Monterey CA 1953 s George & Virginia. BA Grove City Coll 1975; PrTS 1975; MDiv GTS 1978; STM GTS 1985; CSD Jesuit Cntr For Sprtl Growth Wernersville PA 2003. D 6/9/1978 P 1/25/1979 Bp Dean Theodore Stevenson. m 6/11/1977 Lynn S Smith c 2. R S Jn's Epis Ch Bellefonte PA 1980-1985; Cur Dio Cntrl Pennsylvania Harrisburg PA 1978-1980; S Andr's Ch St Coll PA 1978-1979. rector@saintmattsec.org

ROBINSON, Dorothy Linkous (Tex) 7700 Pleasant Meadow Cir, Austin TX 78731 **Chapl Childrens Hosp Austin TX 1994-** B Blacksburg VA 1940 d Gilbert & Margaret. BS VPI 1962; MDiv Epis TS of the SW 1992. D 3/21/1994 Bp Claude Edward Payne P 12/19/1994 Bp Maurice Manuel Benitez. m 8/23/1963 William Archie Robinson. Asstg P S Jn's Epis Ch Austin TX 1994-1998.

ROBINSON, Franklin Kenneth (Ct) 305 Golden Ginkgo Lane, Salisbury MD 21801 **1972-** B Altadena CA 1929 s Frank & Edna. BA Ya 1951; STM Ya Berk 1954; ThM PrTS 1966; MS The Amer Coll 1966. D 6/2/1954 P 4/1/1955 Bp Walter H Gray. m 9/10/1994 Emilie Wood Robinson c 5. Dir of Pstr Mnstry Chr Ch Greenwich CT 1966-1972; Loc Ten S Mths Epis Ch Rochester NY 1964-1965; P-in-c S Andr's Epis Ch Caledonia NY 1963-1964; Chapl U Roch

R

& U Med Cntr Rochester NY 1960-1965; Serv Ch of PI PI 1956-1960; Cur S Jn's Ch Stamford CT 1954-1956.

ROBINSON, Fredrick Arthur (SwFla) 222 South Palm Avenue, Sarasota FL 34236 **R Ch Of The Redeem Sarasota FL 1994-; Bd Trst Dial Hope 2013-; COM Dio SW Florida 2012-; Chairman, The Cmsn on Liturg & Mus Dio SW Florida Parrish FL 2005-, Dioc Coun 1994-2005; Chairman, External Affrs Com Nash Sem 2002-; Mem, Bd Trst Nash Sem 1998-; Pres of the Bd Resurr Hse Sarasota FL 1995-** B Columbus OH 1951 s Richard & Fredna. BA OH SU 1974; ThM SMU 1978; STM Nash 1982. D 6/26/1982 P 10/26/1982 Bp Archibald Donald Davies. m 6/22/1974 Linda H Robinson c 2. Nomin Com for Bp Coadj Epis Dio SW Florida 2005-2006; Dn Monroe Convoc Dio Wstrn Louisiana Alexandria LA 1990-1994; R Gr Epis Ch Monroe LA 1988-1994; R S Andr's Ch Grand Prairie TX 1984-1988; Cur S Mk's Ch Arlington TX 1982-1984. The Suthers Cntr St. Mart in the Fields, Atlanta GA 2010; Paul Harris Fllshp Rotary Club Intl 2006. FROBINSON@REDEEMERSARASOTA.ORG

ROBINSON, Grant Harris (Minn) 1840 University Ave W Apt 413, Saint Paul MN 55104 **Ret 1990-** B Saint Paul MN 1925 s Donald & Alma. BME U MN 1949; MDiv VTS 1969. D 6/30/1969 P 4/4/1970 Bp Hamilton Hyde Kellogg. m 12/23/1946 Meredith Hatch c 4. P-in-c Ch Of The Redeem Cannon Falls MN 1974-1980; R Ch Of The Nativ Burnsville MN 1971-1990; Vic Ch Of Our Sav Little Falls MN 1969-1971; P-in-c Gr Ch Royalton MN 1969-1971.

ROBINSON JR, Henry Jefferson (Fla) 314 Glen Ridge Ave, 939 Beach Dr. NE Unit 1502, Temple Terrace FL 33617 B Plant City FL 1937 s Henry & Gladys. BMus Stetson U 1961; BA Sthrn Bapt TS 1963; MM U of So Florida 1969; MA U of So Florida 1979; EdD Nova SE U 1985; MDiv GTS 1989. D 6/11/1989 P 12/12/1989 Bp Frank S Cerveny. m 4/26/1975 Patricia V Van Auken c 2. Assoc St Cathr of Alexandria Epis Ch Temple Terrace FL 2006-2014; R S Jas' Epis Ch Lake City FL 1999-2005; Asst S Lk's Epis Ch Live Oak FL 1997-1999; R S Marg's Ch Inverness FL 1990-1993; Asst R S Mich's Ch Gainesville FL 1989-1990. jprobin13@gmail.com

ROBINSON, Janet Rohrbach (Ga) 3565 Bemiss Rd., Valdosta GA 31605 B Selins Grove PA 1924 d Thomas & Hannah. BMusEd Susquehanna U 1946; MM LSU 1975. D 2/12/2009 Bp Henry Irving Louttit. m 3/29/1958 Lavan Robinson.

ROBINSON, Joseph Oliver (Mass) Po Box 1366, Jackson MS 39215 **R Chr Ch Cambridge Cambridge MA 2006-** B Mendenhall MS 1956 s Ned & Willie. BA Delta St U 1978; MDiv Sewanee: The U So, TS 1982. D 5/19/1982 P 2/1/1983 Bp Duncan Montgomery Gray Jr. m 7/29/1978 Diane D Robinson c 2. Dn S Andr's Cathd Jackson MS 1996-2005; Cn S Jn's Cathd Denver CO 1992-1996; R Trin Ch Yazoo City MS 1986-1992; P-in-c S Jn's Ch Aberdeen MS 1982-1986. Auth, "As We Gather To Pray," Ch Hymnal Corp; Auth, "Morning Star Press"; Auth, "Mary," *Jos Huddle Here*. Dio Liturg & Mus Cmsn.

ROBINSON, Katherine Sternberg (Wyo) 2350 S Poplar St, Casper WY 82601 B Philadelphia PA 1948 d Ralph & Marcella. BA U of New Mex 1970; MA U of New Mex 1973; MDiv Iliff TS 2002. D 3/8/2003 P 11/12/2003 Bp Bruce Caldwell. m 11/29/1969 Donald Robinson c 2.

ROBINSON, Linda Gail H Hornbuckle (Ala) 6324 Woodlake Dr., Buford GA 30518 B Attalla AL 1940 d Leonard & Ethel. BS Howard Coll 1962; MDiv Yale DS 1984. D 12/11/1985 P 12/19/1986 Bp Furman Charles Stough. m 8/30/1987 Claud Andrew Robinson. Assoc Ch Of The H Fam Fresno CA 1998-2001; Int All SS Epis Ch Birmingham AL 1989-1990; Int S Fran of Assisi Pelham AL 1988-1989; The Epis Ch Of S Fran Of Assisi Pelham AL 1988-1989; P's Assoc S Fran of Assisi Pelham AL 1986-1988.

ROBINSON, Mark K J (Ct) 82 Shore Rd, Old Lyme CT 06371 **Cn for Mssn S Ann's Epis Ch Old Lyme CT 2009-** B Columbus OH 1958 s Jefferson & Anne. Brooks Sch 1977; ABS Ken 1981; MDiv EDS 1988; Hartford Sem 2009. D 6/4/1988 P 12/3/1988 Bp Edward Cole Chalfant. m 6/27/1987 Eleanor P Perkins c 3. Cn for Mssn Dio Ohio Cleveland 2009-2011; Dio Connecticut Hartford CT 2001-2008; R Calv Ch Stonington CT 1993-2009; R S Fran Ch Potomac MD 1990-1992; Chapl S Andr Sch Bethesa MD 1989-1993; Sch Min S Andr's Epis Sch Potomac MD 1989-1993; Cur S Jn's Ch Georgetown Par Washington DC 1988-1989; R S Jn's Ch Lafayette Sq Washington DC 1988-1989; Stndg Com Dio Connecticut Meriden CT 2003-2007, COM 1996-2009. Ed, *Watch Hill Chap PB*, 1998. Exec Com of the Cbury Cathd's Friends in Am 1995; S.S.J.E. 1988; Uganda Chr U Friends Soc 1998-2003. mkjr@saintannsoldlyme.org

ROBINSON, Michael Eric (Mass) 171 Goddard Ave, Brookline MA 02445 **S Paul's Ch Brookline MA 2016-; The Pk Sch Brookline MA 2013-** B Williamstown MA 1964 s Arthur & Nancy. BS U of Massachusetts 1986; MDiv VTS 1992. D 6/13/1992 Bp Andrew Frederick Wissemann P 12/16/1992 Bp Peter J Lee. m 10/3/1987 Frances Fox Robinson c 3. Lake Forest Country Day Sch Lake Forest IL 2005-2013; S Nich Sch Chattanooga TN 2000-2005, 1999-2000; Upper Sch Hd S Pat's Day Sch Washington DC 1995-1999; S Pat's Epis Day Sch Washington DC 1993-1999; Asst R S Pat's Ch Washington DC 1993-1995; Chapl S Pat's Day Sch Washington DC 1993-1995; Asst R S Mary's Epis Ch

Arlington VA 1992-1993; Asst Convoc of Epis Ch in Europe Paris 1990-1991; Headmaster S Nich Sch Chattanooga TN. Auth, *And a Chld Shall Lead Them: Reflection on the Gift of a Ch Sch*, 1994. Cmnty Cross of Nails; NAES 1994.

ROBINSON, Michael Kevin (Ark) 305 Pointer Trl W, Van Buren AR 72956 **Vic Trin Ch Van Buren AR 2010-, 1991-2010** B Fort Smith AR 1955 s Jerry & Jolea. BA U of Arkansas 1977; MDiv Epis TS of the SW 1986. D 6/28/1986 P 5/23/1987 Bp Herbert Alcorn Donovan Jr. m 7/30/2014 Michelle J Robinson c 4. Gr Ch Siloam Sprg AR 1987-1990; Vic S Thos Ch Springdale AR 1987-1990; Cur Trin Ch Pine Bluff AR 1986-1987.

ROBINSON, Paula (Mo) 123 S 9th St, Columbia MO 65201 B Belfast IE 1950 d Walter & Enis. Dip U of Manchester 1981; MEd U of Manchester 1985; BTh Trin 1994. Trans 3/1/2000. c 1. R Calv Ch Columbia MO 2008-2009; R S Andr's Ch Leonardtown California MD 2000-2008; Serv Ch Of Ireland 1994-2000. Auth, "Restorating Justice: Living The Jubilee," Natl Bible Soc Of Ireland, 1999; Auth, "Crossfire," Dublin And Glendalough Dioceses, 1993; Auth, "A Lent Study," Dublin And Glendalough Dioceses, 1993; Auth, "Guide For FA," Dublin And Glendalough Dioceses, 1993; Auth, "Physical Educ Within Spec Educational Provision- Equality And Entitlement, Equality, Educ," *And Physical Educ*, Falmer Press London, 1993; Auth, "Distance Lrng Courses For Teachers Of Chld w Speech And Lang Disorders," U Of Birmingham Sch Of Educ, 1991; Auth, "Tchg Chld w Physical Disabil," Cassells London, 1989; Auth, "Incontinence," *Profound Rtrdtn And Multiple Impairment*, Chapman And Hall, 1989; Auth, "Spec Educ Spec Schools," *A Dictionary Of Rel Educ*, Scm Press London, 1984. Purser Shortt Liturg Ch Of Ireland Theol Coll 1994; Downes' Theol Ch Of Ireland Theol Coll 1994; Weir, Downes' Oration Ch Of Ireland Theol Coll 1992.

ROBINSON, Sonja Douglas (EC) 1009 Midland Dr, Wilmington NC 28412 B 1939 Ohio Vlly Sch of Nrsng Wheeling WV. D 6/14/2003 Bp Clifton Daniel III. c 2.

ROBINSON, Sybil Clara Frances (Mil) 8301 Old Sauk Rd Apt 321, Middleton WI 53562 **Died 5/20/2016** B ZA 1925 d Archibald & Kathleen. PhD U of Wisconsin 1970. D 6/23/2002 Bp Roger John White. D S Dunst's Ch Madison WI 2002-2016.

✠ **ROBINSON, The Rt Rev Vicky Gene** (NH) Diocese Of New Hampshire, 63 Green St., Washington DC 20005 **Bd Trst Ch Pension Fund New York NY 2003-; SCNC GC- Epis Ch Cntr New York NY 2006-, SCNC 2001-2006, SCNC 1998-2000** B Lexington KY 1947 s Charles & Imogene. BA U So 1969; MDiv GTS 1973. D 6/9/1973 Bp Leland Stark P 12/15/1973 Bp George E Rath Con 11/2/2003 for NH. m 1/1/2010 Mark Andrew c 2. Bp Of New Hampshire Dio New Hampshire Concord NH 2003-2012, Nomin Com for PBp 2001-2003, Dep GC 2000-2003, COM 1981-1987; Cn to the Ordnry Epis Prov Of New Engl Portland ME 1990-2003; Founding Dir Sign of the Dove Retreat Cntr Temple NH 1975-1999; Cur Chr Ch Ridgewood NJ 1973-1975. Auth, "God Believes in Love: Straight Talk about Gay Mar," Alfred Knopf, 2012; Auth, "In the Eye of the Storm: Swept to the Cntr by God," Seabury, 2008; Co-Auth, "Fresh Start: A Resource for Cler and Congregations in Transition," Epis Ch, 2000; Co-Auth, "Epis Guide to Teens for AIDS Prevention," Epis Ch, 1994; Auth, "Bearing Fruit: Resource for Cler Self-Assessment," Cornerstone Fndt, 1992; Auth, "Yth Mnstry in the Age of AIDS," Epis Ch, 1989. DD EDS 2004; DD The GTS 2004. bishopgene9@gmail.com

ROBINSON JR, Virgil Austin Anderson (Chi) 1527 Chapel Ct, Northbrook IL 60062 B New Orleans LA 1938 s Virgil & Myrtle. BS SW U Lafayette LA 1961; Air War Coll 1975; MDiv Oxf GB 1980; S Georges Coll Jerusalem IL 1981; MA Loyola U 1988. Trans 5/16/1986 Bp James Winchester Montgomery. m 1/24/1961 Marilynn Robinson c 2. S Jn's Epis Ch Naperville IL 2004-2006; The Ch Of The H Sprt Lake Forest IL 2004; Int S Lk's Ch Evanston IL 2000-2003; Int S Paul's Ch Milwaukee WI 1998-2000; Int Ch Of S Paul And The Redeem Chicago IL 1996-1998; Int St Paul's Epis Cathd Fond Du Lac WI 1994-1996; Epis Coun At Nthrn Illinois U Sycamore IL 1993-1994; Int Chapl R NWU & S Anselm Pk Ridge IL 1990-1994; S Giles' Ch Northbrook IL 1986-1990; Serv Ch Of Engl 1979-1984.

ROBINSON-COMO, Glenice (Tex) 1111 Texas St, Houston TX 77002 **Pstr Chr Ch Cathd Houston TX 2012-, Chf Admin Off 2010-, The Beacon 2010-; Mssn Search Com Dio Texas Houston TX 2012-, Cmsn on Black Mnstry 2011-; Mem Natl Nomin Com 2012-; Chapl UBE Houston TX 2010-** B Petersburg VA 1959 d Theodore & Ruby. BS Virginia Commonwealth U 1982; MDiv SMU Perkins 2009; Dip Ang Stud Epis TS of the SW 2010. D 6/19/2010 P 1/13/2011 Bp C Andrew Doyle. m 11/2/1991 Paul L Como c 1. Writer, "The Least of These," *Lifting Wmn Voices:Prayers to Change the Wrld*, Morehouse, 2009; Writer, "Meditation," *Yes Jesus Loves Me*, Gd Word Productions, 2003.

ROBISON, Bruce Monroe (Pgh) 5801 Hampton Street, Pittsburgh PA 15206 **Instr MS02 Pittsburgh TS Pittsburgh PA 2002-; R St Andrews Epis Ch Pittsburgh PA 1994-; Dio Pittsburgh Pittsburgh PA 2010-** B Los Angeles CA 1953 s Richard & Mary. BA U CA 1975; MA U CA 1979; MDiv CDSP 1986; DMin Pittsburgh TS 2001. D 6/14/1986 Bp John Lester Thompson III P 1/26/1987 Bp Charlie Fuller Mcnutt Jr. m 5/23/1980 Susan M Johnson c 2. Adj Trin Sch for Mnstry Ambridge PA 2011; R S Paul's Ch Bloomsburg PA

1988-1994; Cur S Andr's Ch St Coll PA 1986-1988. Assoc. CT 1982; Confr. OSB Three Rivers 2006. Phi Beta Kappa 1975. rector@standrewspgh.org

ROBISON, Jeannie (Ala) Church of the Nativity, 208 Eustis Ave SE, Huntsville AL 35801 B Water Valley MS 1942 d James & Myrtis. BA Sanford U 1964; MA U of Alabama 1967. D 10/1/2011 Bp Henry Nutt Parsley Jr.

ROBISON, Sandra L(ee) (Spok) 1407 Thayer Dr, Richland WA 99354 B Seattle WA 1943 d Robert & Willa. Arizona St U 1963. D 2/20/1993 Bp Frank Jeffrey Terry. m 6/8/1963 Thomas John Robison c 3. D All SS Ch Richland WA 1993-1999; Mentor - EFM 1992-1993; Mem, COM Dio Spokane Spokane WA 1994-2000.

ROBLES, Lawrence Arnold (ECR) 651 Broadway, Gilroy CA 95020 **Santa Maria Urban Mnstry 2000-** B Bellflower CA 1956 s Arnold & Rosa. BA California St U 1995; MDiv Amer Bapt Sem of the W 1998. D 9/16/2007 Bp Sylvestre Donato Romero P 3/29/2008 Bp Mary Gray-Reeves. c 2. S Geo's Ch Salinas CA 2012-2016; Santa Maria Urban Mnstry San Jose CA 2009-2011. roblesla@natividadfoundation.org

ROBLES-GARCIA, Daniel (DR) B Bonao DO 1939 s Dionisio & Herminia. U Santa Domingo 1967; MDiv ETSC 1972; MA Universidad Pedro HUreña 1977. D 5/28/1972 P 12/14/1972 Bp Telesforo A Isaac. m 3/30/1968 Maria E Rosario c 2. Asst S Lk's Par Bladensburg MD 2001-2007; Dio Puerto Rico Trujillo Alto PR 1992-1996; Hisp P Dio Washington Washington DC 1986-1999; Mssn San Juan Washington DC 1986-1990; Dio The Dominican Republic (Iglesia Epis Dominicana) Gazcue Santo Domingo 1972-1981; P ofJesus Nazareno,Dom.Rep 1972-1976. Auth, "Vivencia del ministerio anglicano," 2001; Auth, "Ch & Rt In the Dom.Rep.," 1990; Auth, "Dominican Agrarian Rt," 1967.

ROBSON, David John (CPa) 2985 Raintree Rd, York PA 17404 B Toronto ON CA 1955 s John & Brenda. BA U Tor 1978; MDiv The Coll of Emm and S Chad CA 1981; MTh Queens U 1986; MEd Queens U 1996; DMin Luth TS at Gettysburg 2004. Trans 9/1/1999 Bp Michael Whittington Creighton. m 4/28/1984 Dianna Lynn Robson c 1. R S Andr's Epis Ch York PA 2005-2017; Chap Of The Gd Shpd Hawk Run PA 1999-2005; R S Paul's Ch Philipsburg PA 1999-2005; Serv Ch in Can 1981-1999. Auth, "Thinking about Weddings," Angl Bk Cntr: Toronto, 1994.

ROBSON, John Merritt (Neb) 1620 Atlas Ave, Lincoln NE 68521 **Ret 1995-** B Gordon NE 1930 s John & Martha. BS U of Nebraska 1953; MA U Denv 1959; U MN 1966. D 4/26/1991 Bp James Edward Krotz. m 8/26/1951 Kathryn Mae Robson c 3. NAAD 1991.

ROBY JR, Jesse (Mich) 1550 Cherboneau Pl Apt 202, Detroit MI 48207 **Ret 1994-** B Austin TX 1918 s Jesse & Lessie. BS Sam Houston St U 1942; MEd Wayne 1949; Michigan TS 1979. D 6/26/1976 Bp H Coleman Mcgehee Jr. m 8/2/1944 Claudia Josephine Roby c 1. Asst S Jn's Ch Detroit MI 1984-1994; Cler All SS Ch Detroit MI 1976-1983; Non-par 1955-1980. Sacr Ord Of Deacons. Cert Of Merit St Of Michigan 1977.

ROCCOBERTON, Marjorie Ruth Smith (Ct) 82 Shoddy Mill Rd, Bolton CT 06043 **D S Mary's Epis Ch Manchester CT 2013-** B East Orange NJ 1953 d Edward & Ruth. Hartford Sem; Montclair St U 1973; BA Stockton St Coll 1975; MA U of Connecticut 1991; MA U of Hartford 1998. D 6/8/1996 Bp Clarence Nicholas Coleridge. m 12/1/1973 Bartolo Peter Roccoberton c 1. Cn to the Ordnry Dio Connecticut Meriden CT 2000-2012, Pstr Response Coordntr 1999-2000, Pstr Response Coordntr 1999-2000; Psych No E Clincl Ther Willimantic CT 1998-2000; D S Mk's Chap Storrs CT 1996-2000; Primary Psych Wheeler Clnc Plainville CT 1991-1998. AAMFT 1990; CAMFT 1990; NAAD 1996. Kappa Delta Pi 1998.

ROCK, Ian Eleazar (VI) St. George's Episcopal (Anglican) Church, 170 Main Street, Road Town, Miami VI 00801 British Virgin Islands **S Geo Mtyr Ch Tortola 2015-** B Barbados 1958 BA Codrington Coll 1997; MA Codrington Coll 2000; PhD U of Wales, Lampeter 2004. Trans 11/5/2015 Bp Edward Gumbs. m 7/16/1983 Anjella S Rock c 2. ianerock@stg.edotvi.org

ROCK, Jean-Baptiste Kenol (NY) 3061 Bainbridge Ave, Bronx NY 10467 B Gressier Port-au-Prince HT 1958 s Samuel & Vesta. BS Iteh 1985; Seteh Bt 1989. D 7/30/1989 P 2/1/1990 Bp Luc Anatole Jacques Garnier. m 5/23/1992 Thurin Rock c 3. Ch Of The H Nativ Bronx NY 2010; Dio New York New York NY 2008-2009; Dio Haiti Port-au-Prince HT 1989-2006.

ROCK, J Konrad (WK) 706 E 74th Ave, Hutchinson KS 67502 B McPherson KS 1940 s Clayton & Lucille. AA Hutchinson Cmnty Coll 1960; BA U of Kansas 1962; DDS U of Missouri 1966; Cert U of Missouri 1968. D 3/4/1989 Bp John Forsythe Ashby P 3/1/1996 Bp Vernon Edward Strickland. m 6/10/1962 Brenda Elaine Homman. Asst Gr Epis Ch Hutchinson KS 2000-2002; P Dio Wstrn Kansas Hutchinson KS 1996-2007.

ROCK, John Sloane (Minn) PO BOX 1178, Bemidji MN 56619 B White Earth MN 1938 s Reuben & Anna. D 10/29/2005 P 1/20/2007 Bp James Louis Jelinek. m 10/25/1968 Hannchen Rock c 3. Stff Sgt & Gs9 Us Army And Civil Serv 1957-1979.

ROCKABRAND, Walter Ralph (Okla) 7928 Roundrock Rd, Dallas TX 75248 B DeKalb IL 1943 s Charles & Ethel. BS Illinois St U 1965; SWTS 1970. D 6/13/1970 Bp James Winchester Montgomery P 12/1/1970 Bp George R Selway. c 1.

All SS Ch Mcalester OK 1992-1999; Int Adv Crestwood MO 1991-1992; Ch Of The Adv S Louis MO 1991-1992; R S Paul's Epis Ch Sikeston MO 1987-1991; Vic St Aug of Cbury Epis Ch Elkhorn NE 1980-1986; Vic S Steph's Ashland NE 1976-1987; P-in-c S Jn Omaha NE 1975-1976; Dioc Supply P 1972-1975; Vic Nativ In L'Anse L'Anse MI 1970-1972.

ROCKHILL, Cara McKinney (WA) D 11/12/2016 P 6/17/2017 Bp Mariann Edgar Budde.

ROCKMAN, Jane Linda (NJ) 559 Park Ave, Scotch Plains NJ 07076 B Newark NJ 1944 d Joseph & Charlotte. BA Smith 1965; MA NYU 1969; MDiv UTS 1986. D 6/7/1986 P 11/17/1987 Bp Paul Moore Jr. R All SS' Epis Ch Scotch Plains NJ 2000-2015; Cur Ch Of The Ascen New York NY 1989-1999; Epis Ch Cntr New York NY 1986-1987; Pbfwr 1986-1987. Ed, "Peace In Search Of Makers," 1979.

ROCKWELL, Cristine Van Kirk (WMass) 51 Perkins St, Springfield MA 01118 **Ret 2006-; Stwdshp Com 1988-** B Johnson City NY 1948 d Donald & Kathryn. U Neuchalel-Suisse 1969; BS SUNY at Geneseo 1970; MDiv Bex Sem 1988. D 4/1/1990 P 10/1/1990 Bp William George Burrill. m 6/1/1974 Bruce A Rockwell c 1. Asstg Chapl ARK (Chapl at UMass Amherst MA 2000-2004; R S Jn's Ch Clifton Spgs NY 1994-1998; P's Asst Epiph Gates NY 1992-1994; Asst The Ch Of The Epiph Gates NY 1992-1994; D Ch Of The Incarn Penfield NY 1990-1992; Adj & Int Chapl Monroe Cmnty Hosp 1985-1990.

✠ ROCKWELL, The Rt Rev Hays H. (Mo) Po Box 728, West Kingston RI 02892 **Ret Bp of Missouri Dio Missouri S Louis MO 2002-, Bp of Missouri 1991-2002** B Detroit MI 1936 s Walter & Kathryn. Oxf GB; BA Br 1958; BD EDS 1961. D 6/29/1961 Bp Robert Lionne DeWitt P 4/27/1962 Bp John S Higgins Con 3/2/1991 for Mo. m 9/7/1957 Linda Hullinger Rockwell c 4. Chair, Bd Trst Ch Pub Inc 2005-2008; Trst S Lk's Hosp St. Louis MO 1991-2002; Mem, Bd Dir UTS New York NY 1991-1996; Mem, Bd Trst U Roch NY 1981-1991; Mem, Bd Dir UTS New York NY 1978-1987; R S Jas Ch New York NY 1976-1991; CDO Bd The Epis Ch USA 1972-1982; Dn Bex Sem Columbus OH 1971-1976; Bd for Theol Educ The Epis Ch USA 1971-1976; Prot Chapl U Roch NY 1969-1971; Chapl S Geo's Sch Middletown RI 1961-1969. Auth, "Proclamation 2, H Week," *Series C*, Fortress Press, 1979; Auth, *arts, assorted- The New York Times, The St. Louis Post Dispatch, The Chr Century, ATR, etc.*; Auth, "Steal Away," *Steal Away Hm*, Doubleday and Co. Soc of S Jn the Evang 1991. DD U So TS 2000; Doctor of Hmnts S Louis U 1994; DD Epis TS of the SW 1984; DD Ken 1974.

ROCKWELL, Melody Neustrom (Ia) 220 40th St NE, Cedar Rapids IA 52402 **D Chr Ch Cedar Rapids IA 2009-** B Kearney NE 1942 d Willys & Geraldine. BA U of Nebraska at Kearney 1964; MA U of Iowa 1980. D 2/21/2009 Bp Alan Scarfe. m 6/6/1964 Melvin Daniel Rockwell c 3.

ROCKWELL, Raymond Eugene (Alb) D 5/31/2014 Bp William Howard Love.

ROCKWELL III, Reuben L (CGC) 4051 Old Shell Road, Mobile AL 36608 **Cur S Paul's Ch Mobile AL 2008-** B Augusta GA 1980 s Reuben & Gail. AB U GA 2003; MDiv VTS 2007. D 2/3/2007 P 8/18/2007 Bp Henry Irving Louttit. m 7/24/2004 Erin Carroll Rockwell c 2. Vic S Barn Epis Ch Valdosta GA 2007-2008.

ROCKWELL, Sarah (NH) 10 Pond Rd, Derry NH 03038 **S Andr's Ch Manchester NH 2015-** B Geneva IL 1965 d Richard & Jane. BA Smith 1987; MDiv Ya Berk 1993. D 12/1/1996 Bp Chris Christopher Epting P 6/14/1997 Bp Gordon Scruton. m 4/20/2009 Hays Maclean Junkin. Dioc Coun Mem Dio New Hampshire Concord NH 2006-2008; R S Ptr's Epis Ch Londonderry NH 2004-2015; Assoc R Ch Of The Gd Shpd Burke VA 1999-2004; Cur S Andr's Ch Longmeadow MA 1997-1999.

ROCKWOOD, David Alan (Ak) Po Box 23003, Ketchikan AK 99901 B Portland OR 1945 s David & Marjorie. BS OR SU 1968. D 4/7/2008 Bp Rustin Ray Kimsey. m 4/30/1970 Hisako Rockwood c 2.

RODDY, Bonnie Joia (Ore) 266 4th Ave, #601, Salt Lake City UT 84103 B Salt Lake City UT 1933 d James & Margaret. AA Fullerton Coll; U of Utah; BA Chapman U 1962; MCSP Creighton U 1985; MDiv CDSP 1988. D 5/15/1988 P 5/31/1989 Bp George Edmonds Bates. m 6/16/1978 Jack Edward Roddy. Asst All SS Ch Salt Lake City UT 2005-2104, Cur 1988-2004; Dio Oregon Portland OR 1995-2000; Vic S Cathr Of Alexandria Epis Ch Nehalem OR 1995-2000; R S Steph's Baker City OR 1992-1995; Assoc R S Alb's Epis Ch Tucson AZ 1990-1992; Dio Utah Salt Lake City UT 1988-1990. "w Death on My Shoulder," Infinity, 2005.

RODDY, Jack Edward (Ore) 266 4th Ave. Apt 601, Salt Lake City UT 84103 B Carrolton GA 1932 s Seaborn & Julia. D 5/21/1994 Bp Rustin Ray Kimsey. m 6/16/1978 Bonnie Joia Hodgson. D All SS Ch Salt Lake City UT 2005-2010; D S Cathr Of Alexandria Epis Ch Nehalem OR 1995-2000; D S Steph's Baker City OR 1994-2000.

RODENBECK, Benjamin Daniel (Az) Trinity Episcopal Church, PO Box 590, Kingman AZ 86402 B Ft Wayne IN 1974 s Raymond & Mary Elizabeth. D 6/22/2013 Bp Kirk Stevan Smith. m 5/7/2007 Joy Renee Rodenbeck c 1.

RODGERS, Billy Wilson (CFla) 13465 SE 93rd Court Rd, Summerfield FL 34491 **St Mary's 2004-; Ret 1994-** B Erick OK 1932 s Henry & Thelma. BA California St U 1954; MA California St U 1955; BD EDS 1958; ThD GTS

1965. D 6/16/1958 Bp Donald J Campbell P 4/1/1959 Bp Charles Francis Boynton. m 9/15/1951 Helen Irene Rodgers c 3. Prof of NT El Seminario Epis del Caribe - Carolina Puerto Rico 1961-1967; Asst, Spanish Wk S Aug's Ch New York NY 1960-1961; Fell/Tutor S Lk's Epis Ch Metuchen NJ 1958-1960; The GTS New York NY 1958-1960. Auth, "Cristologia: Estudio de La Epistola a Los Hebreos," Centro de Reflexion Teologia, 1993; Auth, "Var arts & Bk Revs".

RODGERS, James Devin Dio Sthrn Ohio Cincinnati OH 2017- D 6/3/2017 Bp Thomas Edward Breidenthal.

RODGERS, Paul Benjamin (Mass) 359 Elm St, Dartmouth MA 02748 B Alexandria VA 1972 s John & Blanche. BA Buc 1994; MDiv TESM 2003. D 6/14/2003 Bp Robert William Duncan P 1/21/2004 Bp Henry W Scriven. m 6/13/1998 Leigh Lauren Rodgers c 1. R S Ptr's Ch Dartmouth MA 2006-2010; Pstr for Yth & YA Trin Ch Tariffville CT 2003-2006; Dio Pittsburgh Pittsburgh PA 2003.

RODGERS, Peter R (Ct) 400 Humphrey St, New Haven CT 06511 **Vic S Andr's In The Highlands Mssn Antelope CA 2009-** B Huntington,NY 1943 s Frederick & Ruth. BLitt Oxf GB; BA Hobart and Wm Smith Colleges 1966; STB GTS 1969. D 6/14/1969 Bp Jonathan Goodhue Sherman P 1/1/1970 Bp Donald J Campbell. m 7/19/1986 Katherine G Rodgers. S Jn's Ch New Haven CT 1979-2003; R Ch Of The Recon Webster MA 1978-1979; Cur H Selpulchure & All SS Cambridge Engl 1976-1977; Non-par 1974-1976; Asst S Jn's Ch Williamstown MA 1969-1974. Auth, "Knowing Jesus".

RODGERS, Stephen M (NY) 14160 SW Teal Blvd. 32 B, Beaverton OR 97008 B Spokane WA 1953 s Walter & Lynne. BA U of Washington 1976; MDiv EDS 1980; MA Portland St Universithy 2003; MA Geo Fox U 2011. D 6/24/1980 Bp Leigh Allen Wallace Jr P 3/4/1981 Bp Paul Moore Jr. c 2. Dio Oregon Portland OR 2016; Ch Of The H Sprt Episco Battle Ground WA 2008-2011; Assoc S Jas Epis Ch Portland OR 2002-2006; Chr Ch Par Lake Oswego OR 1998-1999; Chapl Salisbury Sch Salisbury CT 1988-1995; Chapl Chas Wright Acad Tacoma WA 1985-1988; Asst Ch Of The Heav Rest New York NY 1980-1984.

RODIN, Carol Jane Strandoo (Oly) Christ Episcopal Church, 1216 7th St, Anacortes WA 98221 B Seattle WA 1963 d Orville & Mary Lou. BA Pacific Luth U. D 8/5/2012 P 4/11/2013 Bp Gregory Harold Rickel. m 6/21/1986 Curtis W Rodin c 3.

RODMAN, Edward Willis (Mass) 8 Yorks Rd, Framingham MA 01701 B Indianapolis IN 1942 s Orland & Charllotte. BA Hampton U 1965; BD EDS 1967; LHD S Augustines Coll Raleigh NC 1990. D 6/1/1967 Bp Anson Phelps Stokes Jr P 5/1/1968 Bp Joseph Warren Hutchens. m 1/30/1964 Gladys Rodman c 2. EDS Cambridge MA 2001-2008; Dio Massachusetts Boston MA 1973-2001, Cn Mssnr For Minority Communities 1971-2002; Asst S Paul And S Jas New Haven CT 1967-1971. Auth, "Let There Be Peace Among Us". UBE, EUC, Black Leaders & Dioc Executives.

RODMAN, Janet Laura (EC) 218 Fairway Drive, Washington DC 27889 B NY NY 1955 BA Heidelberg U. D 6/14/2003 Bp Clifton Daniel III. m 2/2/1991 John Douglas Rodman c 2.

RODMAN, Reginald Cary (Ore) 10434 Brackenwood Ln NE, Bainbridge Island WA 98110 B Cambridge MA 1935 s Oliver & Dorothea. BA Marlboro Coll 1957; BD SWTS 1968. D 6/11/1968 Bp Joseph Summerville Minnis P 12/14/1968 Bp Edwin B Thayer. c 3. Int St. Edw's Ch Silverton OR 2004-2009; Vic S Edw's Ch Silverton OR 2004-2008; Southcoast Mssnr Dio Oregon Portland OR 2000-2005, So Coast Mssnr 1999-2004; R Chr Ch Kealakekua HI 1987-1996; Vic S Ambr Epis Ch Boulder CO 1983-1987; Vic S Paul's Epis Ch Cntrl City CO 1980-1983; R Ch Of S Jn Chrys Golden CO 1971-1980; Chapl/Asst S Aid's Epis Ch Boulder CO 1970-1971; Cur S Paul's Epis Ch Lakewood CO 1968-1970.

✠ **RODMAN III, The Rt Rev Samuel S** (NC) 112 Randolph Ave, Milton MA 02186 **Dioc Bp Dio No Carolina Raleigh NC 2017-** B Springfield MA 1959 s Samuel & Mary. BA Bates Coll 1981; MDiv VTS 1987. D 8/22/1987 P 3/19/1988 Bp Andrew Frederick Wissemann Con 7/15/2017 for NC. m 5/26/1985 Deborah N Rodman c 2. Dio Massachusetts Boston MA 2010-2017; R S Mich's Ch Milton MA 1994-2010; Asst R Ch Of The Redeem Chestnut Hill MA 1989-1994; Cur S Thos' Ch Whitemarsh Ft Washington PA 1987-1989; Secy Epis Ch Cntr New York NY 1982-1984. sam.rodman@episdionc.org

RODRIGUES, Theodore Earl (EO) P.O. Box 2206, Sisters OR 97759 **GC Dep-Chair of Del Dio Estrn Oregon Cove OR 2014-, Stndg Com 2014-, GC Dep 2012-2014, Pres of Stndg Com 2007-2008** B Cincinnati OH 1953 s Sherwood & Shirley. BA California St U 1977; MDiv CDSP 1987. D 12/12/1987 P 6/14/1988 Bp David Bell Birney IV. m 5/26/1985 Gayle Rodrigues. R Epis Ch Of The Trsfg Sis OR 2006-2017; Participant Cler Ldrshp Proj 1998-2001; R S Barn Par Portland OR 1993-2006; Vic S Tim's Ch Gridley CA 1987-1993; Dioc Coun Dio Oregon Portland OR 2003-2005, Bd Trst 1996-2002, Dn of Sunset Convoc 1995-2000; Bd Dir Epis Cmnty Servs The Epis Dio Nthrn California Sacramento CA 1988-1992. OHC 1987. therevted@mac.com

RODRIGUEZ, Al (Tex) 2503 Ware Rd, Austin TX 78741 **Assoc R S Jas Ch Austin TX 2014-** B San Antonio TX 1941 s Manuel & Francisca. BBA S Marys U San Antonio TX 1964; BBA S Marys U San Antonio TX 1964;

MA U Pgh 1969; MA U Pgh 1969; MDiv Epis TS of the SW 1996. D 6/22/1996 Bp Claude Edward Payne P 1/12/1997 Bp Leopoldo Jesus Alard. m 4/3/1965 Helen LaVerne Calvin c 2. Adj Fac Epis TS Of The SW Austin TX 2013, Trst 2004-2009; R S Jn's Epis Ch Austin TX 1999-2013; P-in-c Trin Ch Longview TX 1996-1999; Exec Dir El Buen Samaritano Epis Mssn Austin TX 1989-1995; Exec Coun Dio Texas Houston TX 2009-2012, Stndg Commitee, Chair 2002-2005. al.rodriguez@ssw.edu

RODRIGUEZ, Christopher Michael (CFla) 2365 Pine Ave, Vero Beach FL 32960 **R Trin Ch Vero Bch FL 2012-** B Yonkers NY 1968 s Anthony & Susan. BA Penn 1991; MS No Carolina St U 1994; MS No Carolina St U 1996; MDiv TESM 2004. Trans 1/10/2007 Bp George Edward Councell. m 11/2/1996 Kathleen Rodriguez c 3. R Trin Epis Ch Red Bank NJ 2007-2012; Cur All SS Ch Wynnewood PA 2005-2007. Co-Auth, "The Measurement of Orgnztn Citizenship Behavior: Are we expecting too much?," *Journ of Applied Soc Psychol*, Wiley, 1997. crodriguez@trinityvero.org

RODRIGUEZ, Gladys (CFla) 1601 Alafaya Trl, Oviedo FL 32765 B Puerto Rico 1943 d Juan & Miriam. D 1/30/2017 Bp Gregory Orrin Brewer. m 2/25/1986 Victor Rivera c 4.

RODRIGUEZ, Hector Raul (Md) 6960 Sunfleck Row, Columbia MD 21045 **Exec Com Natl Farm Worker Mnstry 2013-; Bd Dir Natl Farm Worker Mnstry 2010-** B Eagle Pass TX 1945 s Salvador & Elisa. BA Pontifical Angelicum U 1968; MDiv Oblate TS 1972; MEd Antioch Coll 1975. Rec 10/4/2009 Bp John L Rabb. m 9/25/1976 Camelia Rodriguez c 3. Ch of the Resurr Dio Maryland Baltimore MD 2010-2011; Latino Mssnr 2009-2011; Lead Organizer Indstrl Areas Fndt 2002-2007; Chr Formation Dir Dio Brownsville 1983-1988; Exec Dir, CSS Archdiocese of Santa Fe 1977-1983; Pstr Archdiocese of San Antonio 1974-1976; Pstr Formation Direc. Oblate TS 1974-1976; Pstr Dio Brownsville 1972-1974. Chr Formation Dir, "Grassroots Ecclesial Communities," *Natl Cath Educ Assn*, NCEA, 1989. Founders Awd Mex Amer Cultural Cntr 1997; Bronze Star US ARMY 1945.

RODRIGUEZ, Isaias Arguello (At) 3004 Mccully Dr NE, Atlanta GA 30345 **Co-ordntr of Hisp Mnstry Prov IV 2006-** B Leon ES 1941 s Erasmo & Felisia. Cert San Juan de la Cruz Burgo de Osma Soria ES 1962; Lic Pontifica Facultas Theol Teresianum Rome IT 1967; Candler TS Emory U 1984; Cert Sewanee: The U So, TS 1984. Rec 1/13/1985 as Deacon Bp Charles Judson Child Jr. m 11/23/1979 Mary Katherine Clawson c 3. Hisp Mssnr Dio Atlanta Atlanta GA 1998-2012, Cn 1998-; Reg Assoc for Hispnaic Minstry Epis Ch Cntr New York NY 1986-1994; S Lk's Epis Ch Atlanta GA 1985-1998. Auth, *Temas de Orientación Prematrimonial*, Forw Mvmt Press, 2000; Auth, *Historia y Reforma de la Iglesia Anglicana*, Forw Mvmt, 1999; Auth, *Reflexiones sobre el Diezmo y la Mayordomía*, Forw Mvmt Press, 1998; Auth, "Temas de un Diario," *El Monte Carmelo*, 1993; Auth, "Yo Creo En El Amor," *Desclée De Brouwer*, 1974.

RODRIGUEZ, Luis Mario (NH) 519 N Douty St, Hanford CA 93230 **Ch Of The H Nativ Honolulu HI 2017-** B 1964 s Luis & Miriam. BA Occ 1986; MA California St U 1993; MTh Oxf St Stephens Hse UK 1999; MA Sch of Psych and Counselling Psychol UK 2008. Trans 12/11/2008 as Priest Bp Jerry Alban Lamb. S Andr's Epis Ch Contoocook NH 2015-2016; R Epis Ch Of The Sav Hanford CA 2008-2015. hanfordrector@gmail.com

RODRIGUEZ, Ramiro (Los) 7540 Passons Blvd, Pico Rivera CA 90660 **Dio Oregon Portland OR 2017-; H Fam Mssn N Hollywood CA 2012-** B MX 1959 s Manuel & Maria. Gnrl Antonio Rosales 1985; Pacific Luth TS 1995. D 6/10/1995 P 1/1/1996 Bp Frederick Houk Borsch. m 9/10/1988 Maria Gloria Cazares Avila c 2. S Barth's Mssn Pico Rivera CA 1996.

RODRIGUEZ ESPINEL, Neptali (Minn) 1524 Summit Ave, Saint Paul MN 55105 **Vic La Mision El Santo Nino Jesus S Paul MN 2010-** B Colombia 1979 s Gustavo & Ana Isabel. Javeriana-ITE PAL 2002; Javeriana-Consolata 2003; seminario 8 anos Inst Misionero San Juan Eudes 2004; Marianum 2004; seminario 8 anos Other 2004. Rec 1/7/2010 as Priest Bp James Louis Jelinek. m 5/16/2007 Rebekah Taylor c 1.

RODRIGUEZ-HOBBS, Joshua (Md) Episcopal Church of the Good Shepherd, 1401 Carrollton Ave, Ruxton MD 21204 **Dio Maryland Baltimore MD 2017-** B Graham TX 1985 s John & Cathy. MDiv Ya Berk; BA Lubbock Chr U 2008. D 6/9/2012 P 12/13/2012 Bp James Scott Mayer. m 6/28/2014 Scott Rodriguez-Hobbs. Ch Of The Gd Shpd Towson MD 2012-2016.

RODRIGUEZ-PADRON, Francisco Manuel (LI) 418 50th St, Brooklyn NY 11220 **P-in-c S Andr's Ch Brooklyn NY 2004-** B Matanzas Cuba 1963 s Agustin & Santa. GTS; U of Matanzas 1985; MDiv Evang TS Matanzas CU 1993. D 3/13/2004 P 9/18/2004 Bp Mark Sean Sisk. All SS' Epis Ch Long Island City NY 2004.

RODRIGUEZ SANCHEZ, Mario Hiram (PR) 1308 Ave Paz Granela, San Juan PR 00921 Puerto Rico **Dio Puerto Rico Trujillo Alto PR 2013-** B Mayaguez PR 1963 s Mario & Maria. MPH Recinto de Ciencias Medicas, UPR 1994; PhD Carlos Albizu 2002; MDiv Seminario San Pedro Y San Pablo 2010. D 11/22/2009 P 6/27/2010 Bp David Andres Alvarez-Velazquez. m 1/7/1989 Carmen Teresa Taboas Sacarello.

RODRIGUEZ-SANJURJO, Jose (CFla) Church of the Incarnation, 1601 Alafaya Trl, Oviedo FL 32765 B Rio Piedras Puerto Rico 1980 s Jose & Ruth. BA Rol 2003; MBA U of Cntrl Florida 2008; MDiv Asbury TS 2013. D 6/8/2013 P 12/21/2013 Bp Gregory Orrin Brewer. m 12/23/2006 Heather Faith Washburn c 1.

RODRIGUEZ-SANTOS, Carlos (Hond) **Dio Honduras San Pedro Sula 2006-** B San Pedro Sula 1952 s Catividad & Ana. D 10/28/2005 Bp Lloyd Emmanuel Allen. m 7/26/1971 Doris Mariela Megia c 4.

RODRIGUEZ-SANTOS, Toribio (NJ) 38 W End Pl, Elizabeth NJ 07202 **Vic San Jose Epis Ch Eliz NJ 2010-** B Dominican Republic 1963 s Ramon & Esperanza. LTh S Thos Aquinas 1994; AA TCI Tech Career Insitute 2008. Rec 4/24/2010 Bp Sylvestre Donato Romero. m 5/9/2001 Tereza Carrion de Rodriguez c 2.

RODRIGUEZ VALLECILLO, Digna Suyapa (Hond) Barrio Zaragoza, Calle De La Shell, Siguatepeque Honduras **Dio Honduras San Pedro Sula 2006-; Iglesia Epis Hondurena San Pedro Sula 2006-** B Villanueva Cortes 1964 d Julio & Eva. Seminario Diocesano. D 10/30/2005 P 7/24/2010 Bp Lloyd Emmanuel Allen. c 3.

RODRIGUEZ-YEJO, Ruben (Del) 1005 Pleasant St, Wilmington DE 19805 **Non-par 1967-** B Guayama PR 1934 s Luis & Ana. BA U of Puerto Rico; MDiv ETSC 1967. D 5/17/1967 P 12/11/1967 Bp Francisco Reus-Froylan. m 11/13/1955 Mary Anne Rodriguez. The Ch Of The Ascen Claymont DE 2007-2014; Chr Ch Christiana Hundred Wilmington DE 1988-1991; Capilla Santa Nombre De Jesus Bani 1986-1988; Dio Puerto Rico Trujillo Alto PR 1967-1979.

ROECK, Gretchen Elizabeth (Minn) 5330 Oliver Ave South, Minneapolis MN 55419 B Chicago IL 1983 d James & Kathryn. BA Denison U 2005; MDiv UTS 2008; Cert Ang Stud GTS 2009. D 6/5/2010 Bp Jeff Lee P 2/17/2011 Bp Brian N Prior. m 5/23/2009 John Jelickman. D Trin Ch Excelsior MN 2010-2013.

ROEGER JR, William Donald (Mo) 419 N 6th St, Hannibal MO 63401 **P-in-c S Jas Epis Ch Griggsville IL 1999-; Ret 1995-** B Camden NJ 1931 s William & Naomi. Drexel U 1952; PDS 1961. D 11/5/1960 P 6/29/1961 Bp Alfred L Banyard. m 5/17/1952 Gwyneth L Jones c 4. Asst St Johns Ch Quincy IL 1995-2002; Conv Plnng & Arrangements Com Dio Missouri S Louis MO 1993-1994, Conv Plnng & Arrangements Com 1988-1989, Pres of the No Convoc 1987-1995; R Trin Ch Hannibal MO 1986-1995; R Chr Ch Ironton OH 1982-1986; R All SS Ch Leonia NJ 1977-1982; R Chr Ch Glen Ridge NJ 1970-1977; R S Jas Trenton NJ 1963-1970; Vic S Andr's Ch Lambertville NJ 1961-1963; Vic H Trin Ch Pennsauken NJ 1960-1961; Archit Cmsn Dio New Jersey Trenton NJ 1953-1969; Bd Missions Dio Newark Newark NJ 1972-1982. wroeger@areatech.com

ROEHL, Cynthia Ann (SwFla) 639 Edgewater Dr, Dunedin FL 34698 B Charleston WVA 1951 d Paul & Virginia. D 6/13/2015 Bp Dabney Tyler Smith. m 8/17/1990 Robert A Roehl c 2.

ROEHNER, Rodney (CFla) 6249 Canal Blvd, New Orleans LA 70214 **R S Paul's Epis Ch New Smyrna Bch FL 2015-** B Philadelphia PA 1971 s Julius & Barbara. MTS Nash; BA- Theol Villanova U. D 6/2/2012 P 12/6/2012 Bp William Howard Love. m 10/20/2002 Carolina Roehner c 2. Cur S Paul's Ch New Orleans LA 2012-2014.

ROESCHLAUB, Robert Friedrich (Ind) 20 Pannatt Hill, Millom, Cumbria LA18 5DB Great Britain (UK) **Ret 1997-** B Melrose Park IL 1939 s George & Elizabeth. BS Pur 1963; STB Ya Berk 1966. D 6/11/1966 P 12/1/1966 Bp John P Craine. c 2. Serv Ch in Engl 1978-1997; Chapl Plainfield Police Dept 1972-1977; R S Mk's Ch Plainfield IN 1970-1977; Cur Trin Ch Indianapolis IN 1966-1970; Stndg Com Dio Indianapolis Indianapolis IN 1974-1976. AAR 1963-1997; CBS 1963; SBL 1963-1997.

ROESKE, Michael Jerome (Mass) 35 Bowdoin St, Boston MA 02114 B Barstow CA 1961 s Jerome & Bevra. BA NWU 1983; MDiv Ya Berk 2000. D 5/27/2001 P 12/8/2001 Bp Keith Whitmore. Trin Ch Houston TX 2011-2014; Ch Of S Jn The Evang Boston MA 2003-2005; St Greg The Tchr Mssn Onalaska WI 2001-2002; Cn Mssnr Dio Eau Claire Eau Claire WI 2000-2002.

ROFF, Lucinda Lee (Ala) 812 5th Ave, Tuscaloosa AL 35401 B Orange NJ 1949 d Ruth. BA Ya 1971; MSW U of Wisconsin 1973; PhD U Denv 1982. D 10/1/2011 Bp Henry Nutt Parsley Jr. m 1/5/1980 David L Klemmack c 2.

ROFINOT, Laurie Ann (Mass) 88 Lexington Ave # 2, Somerville MA 02144 B Cheyenne WY 1956 d N Ensley. BA U MN 1979; MDiv EDS 1986; Certification AAPC 2011. D 6/24/1986 P 12/15/1987 Bp Robert Marshall Anderson. m 8/23/1980 Patrick G Michaels c 1. P-in-c Trin Epis Ch Stoughton MA 2012-2014; Int Pstr Faith Luth Ch Quincy MA 2011-2013; P Assoc All SS Par Brookline MA 2009-2011; Chld/Yth Dir; supply; Field Ed. Dir S Jas' Epis Ch Cambridge MA 2005-2009, 2005-2007, Assoc P 1986-1989; Dio Massachusetts Boston MA 2005, 2003-2004; Prot Chapl Tufts U Epis Chap Medford MA 2003-2005; R S Jn's Ch Charlestown (Boston) Charlestown MA 1996-2003; Asst R S Anne's In The Fields Epis Ch Lincoln MA 1990-1995. Contrib, "Revolutionary Forgiveness: Feminist Reflections On Nic," Orbis, 1987. Am. Assoc. of Pstr Counselors 2011; Assoc - OSA, Bethany 2005; EPF 2000; EWC 1985; MECA Co-Pres 2006-08, Treas 2008-2010 2005; NNECA Bd 2007-08, Ed LEAVEN 2008-09 2007.

ROGAN, Donald Lynn (O) Kenyon College, Box 371, Gambier OH 43022 **Died 9/18/2015** B Staunton VA 1930 s Charles & Jane. BA Morris Harvey Coll 1951; STB GTS 1954; Dplma S Augustines Coll Cbury 1960. D 6/7/1954 Bp Robert E L Strider P 12/15/1954 Bp Wilburn Camrock Campbell. m 8/25/1954 Sarah Larew c 4. Ret 1999-2015; Prof of Rel Ken Gambier OH 1972-1999; Chapl Ken Gambier OH 1965-1999; Chapl Ken Gambier OH 1965-1972; Chapl SS Hilda & Hugh Sch 1964-1965; Assoc Chapl CHS - NYC 1962-1965; Fell and Tutor GTS New York NY 1962-1965; R Trin Ch Morgantown WV 1956-1962; Vic All SS Ch Charleston WV 1954-1956. Auth, *Campus Apocalypse*, Seabury Press, 1969; Ed, *Spkng God's Word*, 1956. DD GTS 2000; DHL Ken/Gambier, OH 1999.

ROGERS, Allan Douglas (SwFla) 4352 Arrow Ave, Sarasota FL 34232 B Summerville SC 1949 s Claude & Pauline. MA U of So Florida 1976. D 1/18/2003 Bp John Bailey Lipscomb. m 7/23/1971 Holly B Rogers c 1.

ROGERS, Annis Elizabeth (Pgh) D 3/4/2017 Bp Dorsey McConnell.

ROGERS, Diana (Ct) 20 Shepherd Ln, Orange CT 06477 **Ch Of The Gd Shpd Orange CT 2015-** B Waynesboro PA 1948 d Gerald & Mary. BA Metropltn St U 2002; Untd TS 2007; MDiv GTS 2008. D 1/25/2008 Bp Keith Whitmore P 10/6/2008 Bp James Louis Jelinek. c 2. P Ch Of The Epiph Durham CT 2014-2015; Int R Chr Ch Austin MN 2010-2011; Coordntr of Vocations Dio Minnesota Minneapolis MN 2002-2007. revdianamrogers@gmail.com

ROGERS, Douglas K (Chi) 412 N Church St, Rockford IL 61103 B Savanna IL 1946 s Ward & Marilyn. BS Sthrn Illinois U 1972. D 2/7/2004 Bp Victor Alfonso Scantlebury. m 4/6/2000 Cheryl J Rogers.

ROGERS III, George M (Alb) 325 East 80th Street, 1D, New York NY 10021 B New York NY 1969 s George & Sylvia. BS Ya 1991; DAS Ya Berk 1995; MDiv Yale DS 1995. D 5/10/1999 P 11/13/1999 Bp Daniel William Herzog. m 7/19/2003 Yun Lee Too. Asst Par of Chr the Redeem Pelham NY 2003-2010; Admin Vic The Ch of S Ign of Antioch New York NY 2002-2003; The GTS New York NY 2001-2003; Asst P S Thos Ch New York NY 2000-2003; Asst Mssns S Paul's Ch Brant Lake NY 1999-2000; Dio Albany Greenwich NY 1999. Dio Albany Theol Cmsn 1999-2004; Grand Lodge of NY - F. and A.M. 2000; Hobart Soc 1995-2003; Yale Club of NYC 1991. Mercer Schlrshp Dio Long Island 1998.

ROGERS, Henry Stanley Fraser (Oly) 4770 116th Ave Se, Bellevue WA 98006 **Ret 1996-** B Port Arthur ON CA 1927 s Henry & Marjorie. BA U of British Columbia Vancouver Bc CA 1950; BCA U of British Columbia Vancouver Bc CA 1952; U of British Columbia Vancouver Bc CA 1952. D 9/29/1975 Bp Ivol I Curtis P 10/18/1979 Bp Robert Hume Cochrane. m 5/9/1953 Helen Rogers. Assoc All SS Ch Bellevue WA 1997-2002; Vic Ch Of Our Sav Monroe WA 1991-1996; Supply Dio Olympia Seattle 1989-1991; P-in-c S Clare of Assisi Epis Ch Snoqualmie WA 1985-1989; Non-par 1975-1985.

ROGERS JR, Jack A (WTenn) 2185 Aztec Dr, Dyersburg TN 38024 **S Anne's Ch Millington TN 2015-** B Macon GA 1957 s Jack & Anne. BA Utc 1994; MDiv Epis TS of the SW 1998. D 6/13/1998 P 2/6/1999 Bp Robert Gould Tharp. m 6/15/1998 Lisa Rogers c 2. S Elis's Epis Ch Memphis TN 2014-2015; S Ptr's Ch Conway AR 2006-2008; S Lk and S Jn's Caruthersvlle MO 2004-2006; S Mary's Epis Ch Dyersburg TN 2003-2006; Asst S Mart Of Tours Epis Ch Chattanooga TN 2000-2003; Asst Vic S Mart's Epis Sch Metairie LA 1999-2000; S Tim's Ch La Place LA 1999-2000; D All SS' Epis Ch Morristown TN 1998-1999.

ROGERS, James Arthur (FtW) 4302 Wynnwood Dr, Wichita Falls TX 76308 B Albuquerque NM 1943 s James & Suzanne. BA U CO 1967; MDiv Nash 1975; AS Midwestern St U 1994. D 6/17/1975 P 12/17/1975 Bp Archibald Donald Davies. m 6/15/1968 Susan M Rogers c 1. Chr's Hm Place Mnstrs Inc. Wichita Falls TX 2003-2004; Asst Ch Of S Jn The Div Burkburnett TX 2002-2004, Int P 1997-2001; S Pat's Ch Bowie TX 1999-2004; Trin Ch Henrietta TX 1999, Int P 1997-1998; Dio Ft Worth Ft Worth TX 1997-2001, P 1992-1997; Co-Dir Chr Hm Place Mnstrs Inc 1992-1997; Ch Of The Gd Shpd Wichita Falls TX 1975-1992.

ROGERS, James Luther (Tenn) 935 Mount Olivet Rd, Columbia TN 38401 B Memphis TN 1946 s Luther & Maggie. BS Lambuth U 1968; MDiv Nash 1971. D 6/27/1971 Bp William F Gates Jr P 4/1/1972 Bp William Evan Sanders. m 6/17/2000 Linda Rogers. Int The Epis Ch Of The Mssh Pulaski TN 2009-2012; P S Mary Magd Ch Fayetteville TN 2002-2008; The Epis Ch Of The Resurr Franklin TN 1989-1995, Vic 1983-1988; Dio Tennessee Nashville TN 1984-1988; Non-par 1979-1983; R S Mart Of Tours Epis Ch Chattanooga TN 1975-1979; Vic S Columba's Epis Ch Bristol TN 1973-1975; D-In-Trng St Jas Epis Ch at Knoxville Knoxville TN 1971-1972; ; Bp Coun; Ch Evang; Dioc Com Of Cler Fam Life.

ROGERS JR, John (Ct) 69 Butternut Ln, Rocky Hill CT 06067 **P Assoc S Andr The Apos Rocky Hill CT 2014-; Ret Dio 2001-; P S Eliz Chap Hartford CT 2001-** B New Haven, CT 1939 s John & Martha. BA Drew U 1960; MDiv GTS 1963; U of Connecticut 1971; VTS 1992. D 6/11/1963 P 2/29/1964 Bp Walter H Gray. m 4/28/1962 Faye Marie Rogers c 2. Sunday Grtr 2003-2010; Chapl Dio Connecticut Meriden CT 1983-2001, Dn 1983-1984; P Trin Ch

R

Wethersfield CT 1975-2001, Asst 1970-1974, P 1963-1966; P Chr Ch Oxford CT 1966-1970. Kappa Pi 1959; Pi Ganna Mu 1959.

ROGERS, John Sanborn (RI) 106 Osprey Dr, Saint Marys GA 31558 **Ret 1999-** B Portland ME 1937 s William & Margaret. BA Mid 1960; MDiv EDS 1963. D 6/8/1963 P 12/15/1963 Bp Oliver L Loring. m 2/4/2005 Laureen Rogers c 3. Int Chr Ch Frederica St Simons Is GA 2009-2010; Int S Mk's Ch Brunswick GA 2008-2011; S Mary's Ch Portsmouth RI 1993-1999; S Geo's Sch Middletown RI 1976-1999; Chapl S Geo's Sch Newport RI 1976-1999; R S Alb's Ch Cape Eliz ME 1969-1976; R S Steph's Epis Ch Bloomfield CT 1965-1969; Chapl Chap Of S Andr Boca Raton FL 1964-1965; Cur S Paul's Ch Holyoke MA 1963-1964. Chapl Emer St. Geo's Sch 2006.

ROGERS, Joy Edith Stevenson (Chi) 65 E. Huron, Chicago IL 60611 B Philadelphia PA 1946 d James & Dolores. BS Penn 1967; BS Penn 1967; AD Lorain Cnty Cmnty Coll 1976; MDiv SWTS 1985; DMin SWTS 1993; DMin SWTS 1993. D 5/31/1985 Bp James Winchester Montgomery P 11/1/1985 Bp Frank Tracy Griswold III. m 9/30/1967 Nathaniel Rogers c 2. Provost Cathd Of S Jas Chicago IL 2007-2014; R S Thos Epis Ch Battle Creek MI 1995-2007; P-in-c Ch Of The H Fam Lake Villa IL 1995; S Lk's Ch Evanston IL 1985-1995. Auth, "Rachel Weeping: Abortion and Jeremiah's God," *Sewanee Theol Revs*, TS, Univ of the So, 1993. Fell, Coll of Preachers Coll of Preachers 1993. joyerogers@me.com

ROGERS, Larry Samuel (Okla) 1310 N Sioux Ave, Claremore OK 74017 B Muskogee OK 1955 s Walter & JoAnn. AAS Regis Coll 1987; BS NE St U 1993; BS Regis Coll 1993; BS Regis Coll 1993. D 8/1/2015 P 3/2/2016 Bp Edward Joseph Konieczny. m 9/17/1987 Susan Lorene Rogers c 2.

ROGERS, Marcus Brayton (Ct) 5601 County Route 30, Granville NY 12832 B New York NY 1934 s Raymond & Marion. BS Cor 1955; STB GTS 1966. D 6/4/1966 P 12/1/1966 Bp Horace W B Donegan. m 6/18/1955 June Q Rogers. Trin Epis Ch Bristol CT 1975-1997; Assoc Grtr Parishes Augusta ME 1967-1968. ERM, Curs, Epis Untd.

ROGERS, Martha C (Ia) 235 Partridge Ave, Marion IA 52302 B Fall River MA 1954 d James & Irene. BS Rhode Island Coll 1976; MS Wstrn Illinois U 1985; MDiv Sewanee: The U So, TS 1997. D 6/13/1997 Bp James Louis Jelinek P 12/15/1997 Bp Creighton Leland Robertson. m 2/13/1982 David G Rogers c 2. R Chr Ch Cedar Rapids IA 2009-2015; Vic Ch of the Resurr Lafayette CO 2007-2009; Vic Santiago Epis Ch 2007-2009; Vic The Epis Ch of the Resurr Boulder CO 2007-2009; R S Alb's Ch Sprt Lake IA 2000-2006; Cn Calv Cathd Sioux Falls SD 1997-2000. Cmnty of S Mary 1996; DOK 2007.

ROGERS, Matthew Arnold (Md) 3100 Monkton Rd, Monkton MD 21111 B Charleston WY 1954 s Lowell & Carroll. MACM St Mary's Ecumerical 2014. D 6/14/2014 Bp Joe Goodwin Burnett P 12/28/2014 Bp Eugene Taylor Sutton. m 9/23/1984 Barbara K Rogers c 2.

ROGERS, Norma Jean (Az) PO Box 4567, Tubac AZ 85646 **Asst R S Phil's In The Hills Tucson AZ 2015-, Affiliated Cler 2011-2015; Ret Ret 2003-** B Gadsden AZ 1937 d Clifford & Ruth. BA Arizona St U 1971; MA Arizona St U 1974; MDiv VTS 1991. D 6/15/1991 P 12/18/1991 Bp Ronald Hayward Haines. m 7/21/1984 John L Rogers c 3. Int Epis Ch Of S Fran-In-The-Vlly Green Vlly AZ 2007-2008, Affiliated Cler 2000-2003; R S Andr's Epis Ch Nogales AZ 1994-2003; Dio Arizona Phoenix AZ 1994; Ch Of S Mary The Vrgn Nixon NV 1992-1994; Vic Dio Nevada Las Vegas 1992-1994; S Mich And All Ang Ch Wadsworth NV 1992-1994; Chapl Beauvoir Sch WDC 1991-1992; Asst to R S Pat's Ch Washington DC 1991-1992. DOK - Chapl 2003.

ROGERS, Page (Ct) 99 Lee Farm Dr, Niantic CT 06357 B Kansas City MO 1953 d George & Suzanne. BA Wheaton Coll at Norton 1976; MDiv Ya Berk 1980. D 12/5/1981 P 6/10/1982 Bp Arthur Edward Walmsley. R S Jn's Epis Ch Niantic CT 1999-2012; Com Chairman Dio Connecticut Meriden CT 1998-2002, Const And Cn 1998-, Excoun 1989-2009, Par Dvlpmt Consult 1984-1997; Vic Chr Epis Ch Middle Haddam CT 1985-1999; Pres Alum Assoc Berk New Haven CT 1985-1987; S Jas Epis Ch Farmington CT 1982-1985. Soc Of S Jn The Evang 1999.

ROGERS, Robert Gerald (La) Po Box 233, Clinton LA 70722 B Baton Rouge LA 1936 s John & Henriette. BA Notre Dame Sem Grad TS 1960; BS Loyola U 1962; MS LSU 1968. Rec 6/1/1981 as Priest Bp James Barrow Brown. m 4/22/1995 Joy Rogers c 2. S Matt's Epis Ch Houma LA 2007-2008; S Andr's Ch Theriot LA 1996-2007; Benedictine Monk S Jos's Abbey S Ben LA 1957-1971.

ROGERS III, Sampson (FtW) 828-28 Avenue North #4, Menomonie WI 54751 B Rockford IL 1929 s Maurice & Jeannette. BA Beloit Coll 1953; LTh SWTS 1957. D 6/15/1957 Bp Charles L Street P 12/21/1957 Bp Gerald Francis Burrill. Asstg Gr Epis Ch Menomonie WI 2002-2011; S Andr's Ch Ashland WI 1987-1990; Non-par 1984-1987; All SS Ch San Diego CA 1983; S Fran Ch Pauma Vlly CA 1982-1983; S Aug's Epis Ch Rhinelander WI 1969-1981; Vic S Bon Plymouth WI 1964-1969; S Paul's Ch Plymouth WI 1964-1969; Cur S Andr's Ch Baltimore MD 1959-1964; Cur S Giles' Ch Northbrook IL 1957-1959; Bec Dio Fond du Lac Appleton WI 1975-1979. Oblate Cmnty Resurr 1968.

ROGERS III, Thomas Sherman (Chi) 1653 West Congress Parkway, Chicago IL 60612 **Bp Anderson Hse Chicago IL 2015-** B Oklahoma City OK 1978 s Thomas & Betty. Oklahoma City U 1998; BA TCU 2000; MDiv SMU Perkins

2004. D 6/4/2005 P 3/25/2006 Bp James Monte Stanton. m 9/21/2013 Jason Mark Sutton. Chapl Dio Maryland Baltimore MD 2011-2015; Assoc R All SS Ch Frederick MD 2006-2011; Cur S Jas Epis Ch Texarkana TX 2005-2006; Chapl Methodist Hlth System Dallas TX 2004-2005. thomas_rogers@rush.edu

ROGERS, Timothy James (Mass) 2920 NE 8th Ter, Apt 101, Wilton Manors FL 33334 **S Jn's Epis Ch Holbrook MA 2014-** B Cambridge MA 1964 s Ernest & Marie. BA Macalester Coll 1995; MDiv CDSP 1998. D 12/2/2000 P 6/2/2001 Bp William Edwin Swing. P-in-c St Margarets and San Francisco de Asis Epis Ch Hialeah FL 2012-2014; P-in-c S Jn's Ch Newtonville MA 2006-2009; R S Ptr's Ch Salem MA 2001-2006; D Trin Par Menlo Pk CA 2000-2001.

ROGERS, Victor (Ct) 111 Whalley Ave, New Haven CT 06511 B 1944 s Grafton & Violet. LTh Codrington Coll; MA Jackson St U; BA Laurentian U; PhD Mississippi St U 1987. m 2/4/1984 Gloria Rogers c 3. R S Lk's Epis Ch New Haven CT 1983-2010; R S Mk's Ch Jackson MS 1974-1983; P-in-c S Jas Sudbury Ontario Can; Cur SS Paul & Phil In Barbados.

ROGERS, William Burns (Tenn) 510 W Main St, Franklin TN 37064 B Springfield TN 1973 s Thad & Carole. BA Sewanee: The U So, TS 1995; BA The U So 1995; MPH U of Alabama 1996; PhD U of Alabama 2005. D 1/25/2014 Bp John Bauerschmidt. m 12/30/2000 Donna D Stokes-Rogers c 1. D S Paul's Ch Franklin TN 2014-2016.

ROGERSON, George William (Ia) 11536 Wild Rose Dr, West Burlington IA 52655 B Eldon IA 1928 s Russell & Beatrice. D 4/7/2001 Bp Chris Christopher Epting. m 1/5/1950 Rita Amelia Rogerson. Par of Chr the Redeem Pelham NY 2007-2008; D Chr Epis Ch Burlington IA 2001-2008.

ROGGE, Joel Jay (WA) 84 County Rd, Ipswich MA 01938 **Non-par 1984-** B New York NY 1934 s Leo & Mollie. JD Col 1958; MDiv EDS 1968; STM Andover Newton TS 1969; ECF 1971; DMin Andover Newton TS 1975; EdD Harv 1976. D 6/29/1968 Bp William Foreman Creighton P 6/29/1969 Bp Frederic Cunningham Lawrence. m 12/27/1959 Maryellen Gongas c 5. Assoc Ascen Memi Ch Ipswich MA 1990-1992; Dir Danvers Pstr Counslg Cntr 1977-1983; Clincal Dir Outpatient Serv No Shore Coun Alcosm Danvers MA 1974-1978; P-in-c S Mart's Epis Ch Fairlee VT 1971; Pstr No St Un Congrl Ch Medford MA 1968-1970. Auth, "Publ Fed Agencies". Diplomate, AAPC, Natl Bd Gvnr; Fell ECF.

ROGINA, Julius M (Nev) 1080 Del Webb Pkwy West, Reno NV 89523 B Zagreb Croatia 1945 s Julius & Maria. BA Filozofski Fakultet Druzbe Isusove Zagreb Croatia 1969; MDiv Jesuit TS 1975; STM Jesuit TS 1976; PhD Grad Theol Un UofCal Berkeley 1981. Rec 6/1/1988 as Priest Bp Stewart Clark Zabriskie. c 3. Stndg Commitee Dio Nevada Las Vegas 2003-2005; P Assoc Trin Epis Ch Reno NV 1988-2012; Serv RC Ch 1974-1978. Auth, "Logotherapy Treatment of Com;icated Grief Syndrom," *Intl Forum of Logotherapy*, Viktor Frankl Inst of Logotherapy, 2010; Auth, "Logotherapy in Clincl Pract," *Psych: Theory & Resrch*, APA, 2008; Auth, "Avoidant Personality Disorders," *Intl Forum of Logotherapy*, Viktor Frankl Insitute of Logotherapy, 2007; Auth, "Gnrl Anxiety Disorders and Logotherapy," *Intl Forum For Logotherapy*, Viktor Frankl Inst of Logotherapy, 2005; Auth, "Treating Nacisistic Personality Disorders," *The Intl Forum for Logotherapy*, Viktor Frankl Inst of Logotherapy, 2004; Auth, "Treating Gnrl Anxiety Disorders," *Intl Forum of Logotherapy*, Viktor Frankl Inst of Logotherapy, 2002; Auth, "On Being Grounded in the Cmnty of Faith," *Desert Ch*, Dio Nevada, 1989; Auth, "Mssn Thoelogy Today," *The Jesuit*, Jesuit Sch fo Theol at Berkeley, 1974. The NNECA 2003.

ROGNAS, Alice Anita (Mont) 713 8th St, Lewiston ID 83501 B Great Falls MT 1940 d Clifford & Doris. Concordia Coll 1959; Estrn Montana Coll 1960; BA U of Montana 1962. D 10/20/2013 Bp James E Waggoner Jr. c 2.

ROHDE, Kay M. (NCal) 1326 East A St., Casper WY 82601 B Eureka CA 1950 d Harold & Marylee. Humboldt St U 1970; BS California St Polytechnic U 1975. D 3/14/1993 P 10/3/1993 Bp Stewart Clark Zabriskie. c 1. S Matt's Epis Ch Sacramento CA 2013-2014; The Epis Dio Nthrn California Sacramento CA 2012-2016; Dio Wyoming Casper 2011-2012, 2007-2010; Int R S Mk's Epis Ch Casper WY 2010-2011; P S Chris's Epis Ch Boulder City NV 1993-2007. CT.

ROHLEDER, Catherine Christine (Kan) B 1972 B.A. Truman St U 1994; M.A. U of Missouri-Columbia 1996; Cert in Presbyteral Stds Bp Kemper Sch for Mnstry 2016. D 12/12/2015 P 7/23/2016 Bp Mike Milliken. m 10/24/2009 Eric G Rohleder c 1.

ROHLEDER, Robert Arthur (Mil) 2409 10th Ave Apt 310, South Milwaukee WI 53172 **Died 1/31/2017** B Milwaukee WI 1931 s Waldemar & Meta. Nash; No Degree Nash 1976; Cert SUNY 1986. D 11/6/1976 Bp Charles Thomas Gaskell. m 2/24/1951 Jane Vernette Rohleder c 2. D S Mk's Ch S Milwaukee WI 1976-2017. SUNY AS 1986.

ROHMAN, Suzannah (Ct) St. Paul's Episcopal Church, 145 Main St., Southington CT 06489 **R S Paul's Ch Southington CT 2009-** B Augusta ME 1973 d James & Marcia. BA Dickinson Coll 1995; MDiv GTS 1999; DMin SWTS 2009. Trans 1/20/2004 Bp Wayne Wright. c 2. Assoc R S Geo's Epis Ch Arlington VA 2003-2009; Asst R S Thos's Par Newark DE 2001-2003; Asst R S Paul's Ch Maumee OH 1999-2001.

ROHRBACH, Marissa S (Ct) St. Andrew's Episcopal Church, 20 Catlin St, Meriden CT 06450 **S Andr's Ch Meriden CT 2014-** B Abington PA 1987 d Paul & Karen. BA The GW 2008; MDiv Ya Berk 2011; STM Yale DS 2012. D 1/14/2012 P 6/9/2012 Bp Charles Ellsworth Bennison Jr. m 11/12/2013 Lynette Adelle Rossano. The Ch Of The H Trin Rittenhouse Philadelphia PA 2012-2014. revmarissa@gmail.com

ROHRER, Glenn E (CGC) 5636 Firestone Dr, Pace FL 32571 **Vic Ch Of The Epiph Crestview FL 2011-** B Columbus OH 1944 s Chester & Bertha. BSW OH SU 1966; MDiv Methodist TS in Ohio 1969; MSW OH SU 1973; PhD OH SU 1979. D 1/8/2011 P 8/20/2011 Bp Philip Menzie Duncan II. m 10/28/1995 Lois Rohrer c 4. H Cross Ch Pensacola FL 2014-2016. Coll of Soc Wk Career Hall of Fame OH SU 2012; Hon Cn Cathd of the Incarn, Garden City, NY 2011; Prof Emer E CArolina U 2006. grohrwer@uwf.edu

ROHRER, Jane Carolyn (Oly) Episcopal Church Of The Holy Cross, 11526 162nd Ave NE, Redmond WA 98052 **Assoc Ch Of The H Cross Redmond WA 2011-** B Faribault MN 1940 d Christian & Lydia. BS U MN 1962; MA U MN 1964; MA Boise St U 1976; PhD Kent St U 1992; MTS SWTS 2005. D 7/12/2008 P 2/21/2009 Bp Dan Thomas Edwards. c 3. Pstr Assoc Trin Epis Ch Reno NV 2008-2010. Auth, "It's not that Simple.," *Sierra Nevada Coll Revs.*, 1999; Joint Auth w Sue Welsch, "The lake Tahoe Watershed Proj: lessons learned about middle Sch females encountering math and Sci," *Roeper Revs*, 1998; Auth, "We interrupt this Prog to show you a bombing: Chld and schools respond to televised war," *Childhood Educ*, 1996; Auth, "Primary Tchr conceptions of giftedness: image, evidence, and nonevidence," *Journ for the Educ of the Gifted*, 1995; Joint Auth, "The impact of portfolio assessment on Tchr classroom activities," *Journ of Tchr Educ*, 1992. Grant Awd Epis EvangES 2005.

ROHRS, John D (SVa) S Andr's Ch Norfolk VA 2009- B Stillwater OK 1976 BA Duke 1999; MDiv Ya Berk 2004. D 6/26/2005 P 2/12/2006 Bp Michael B Curry. m 10/18/2003 Andrea Wigodsky c 3. Asst To The R Chr Epis Ch Raleigh NC 2005-2009.

ROJAS-ARROYO, Sergio (PR) **Dio Puerto Rico Trujillo Alto PR 2004-, 2003** B 1963

ROJAS POVEDA, Jesus A (EC) 737 Delma Grimes Rd, Coats NC 27521 **R Epis Farm Worker Mnstry Dunn NC 2003-** B Columbia South America 1937 Seminario Conciliar. Trans 11/27/2000 Bp Clifton Daniel III. m 12/23/1995 Lucia Duque-Hincapie c 4. Epis Farmworker Mnstry Newton Grove NC 2001-2009.

ROKOS, Michael George (Md) 2203 Mayfield Ave, Baltimore MD 21213 **P-in-c St Marg's Coventry Parkville MD 2004-** B Chicago IL 1946 s George & Dorothea. BA JHU 1968; MDiv VTS 1972; Cert Chas U in Prague 2000. D 5/25/1972 P 2/22/1973 Bp David Keller Leighton Sr. m 11/30/2013 Gene Michael Addis. S Marg's Epis Ch Parkville MD 2004-2013; Deer Creek Par Darlington MD 2003-2004; P-in-c Gr Memi Ch Darlington MD 1994-2003; P-in-c H Commndnt Baltimore MD 1990-1991; Chapl MD St Police 1990-1991; Copley Par: The Ch Of The Resurr Joppatowne MD 1982-1990; Chr Ch Christiana Hundred Wilmington DE 1978-1981; Asst Chr Christiana DE 1978-1981; Asst S Thos' Ch Garrison Forest Owings Mills MD 1974-1978; Asst Ch Of The Ascen Silver Sprg MD 1972-1974. Auth, *Cops & Cults*; Auth, *Cults & the Ch*; Auth, *Identifying & Treating Satanically/Ritually Involved*.

ROLAND, Carla Elena (NY) Church of St Matthew & St Timothy, 26 W 84th St, New York NY 10024 **R The Ch of S Matt And S Tim New York NY 2004-** B Amarillo TX 1971 d Robert & Gloria. MDiv CDSP 2001; MA Grad Theol Un 2001; BS Cor 2004. D 10/13/2002 P 10/5/2003 Bp David Andres Alvarez-Velazquez. Fell ECF 2002.

ROLDAN, Roman D (La) 11621 Ferdinand St, Saint Francisville LA 70775 **R Gr Ch Of W Feliciana St Francisvlle LA 2009-** B Colubmia SA 1966 s Jose & Rosa. BA S Jn Vianney Coll Sem Miami 1989; MSW Rutgers-The St U NEwark NJ 1995; MDiv TESM 2007. D 6/2/2007 Bp John Wadsworth Howe P 12/15/2007 Bp Alan Scarfe. m 6/17/1993 Chris A Roldan c 4. Assoc Trin Cathd Davenport IA 2007-2009; Dep Exec Off Psychotherapeutic Serv of FL 1998-2005; Sprtl Dir, Angola St Prison, Epis Mnstrs Dio Louisiana New Orleans LA 2010-2014, Exec Bd 2010-2013, Partnr in Mssn 2010-2012; COM Dio Iowa Des Moines IA 2008-2009.

ROLES, Elizabeth A (Az) 175 9th Ave # 123, New York NY 10011 **S Barn On The Desert Scottsdale AZ 2014-** B Charleston WV 1970 d Forrest & Emily. BA Tufts U 1992; MDiv Candler TS Emory U 1998; CAS GTS 2006. D 12/21/2005 P 6/25/2006 Bp J Neil Alexander. c 1. Emmaus Hse Epis Ch Atlanta GA 2009-2014; S Mk's Ch Dalton GA 2006-2009.

ROLFE-BOUTWELL, Suzan Jane (Mass) 7588 N Meredith Blvd, Tucson AZ 85741 B New York NY 1945 d David & Helen. BA Harv 1979; MS MIT 1982; MDiv EDS 1987. D 6/13/1987 P 6/4/1988 Bp David Elliot Johnson. m 7/27/1980 Jeffrey Hood Boutwell. S Dav's Epis Mssn Pepperell MA 1991-1992; S Ptr's Ch Beverly MA 1987-1990. Auth, "Harvard Political Revs".

ROLLE, Denrick Ephriam (SeFla) **S Agnes Ch Miami FL 2012-** B Bahamas 1976 s Charles & Theresa. BA Codrington Coll 2002; MPhil U of the W Indies 2012. Trans 12/2/2012 as Priest Bp Leo Frade.

ROLLE, Yolanda Antoinette (Mass) B Nassau Bahamas 1978 d Anthony & Yvonne. BS U of Nebraska 1999; BSEE U of Nebraska 2001; MS U of Nebraska 2002; PhD U of Nebraska 2008; MDiv Yale Berkley DS 2015. D 6/6/2015 Bp Gayle Harris P 1/9/2016 Bp Mariann Edgar Budde. m 3/24/2015 Simone Caroline Ellis.

ROLLINS, Andrew Sloan (La) 640 Carriage Way, Baton Rouge LA 70808 **P Dio Louisiana New Orleans LA 2004-; Chapl S Alb's Chap & Epis U Cntr Baton Rouge LA 2003-** B OH 1963 s Robert & Betsy. BA U So 1987; MDiv VTS 1995. D 6/3/1995 P 1/13/1996 Bp Peter J Lee. m 1/2/1993 Jeanette Randolph Rollins c 5. Assoc R Trin Ch New Orleans LA 1995-2004.

ROLLINS, Belle Frances (WLa) 1001 Berry St, Pineville LA 71360 B Lexington MS 1943 d John & Willie. BA U of Mississippi; MA U of Virginia 1966; MS LSU 1984; MA Loyola U 1996. D 1/12/2002 Bp Robert Jefferson Hargrove Jr. m 8/26/1972 Justin J Rollins. D St Mich's Epis Ch Pineville LA 2007-2008.

ROLLINS, Everette Wayne (Me) 10 Alton St., Portland ME 04103 B South Charleston WV 1956 s Arnold & Janet. BS W Virginia St U 1978; MA Westminster Choir Coll of Rider U 1981; MDiv Methodist TS in Ohio 1997. D 5/26/2004 P 12/11/2004 Bp William Michie Klusmeyer. R S Ptr's Ch Portland ME 2008-2011; Int Ch Of The Gd Shpd Charleston WV 2005-2007.

ROLLINS, John August (Nwk) 11 Fine Road, High Bridge NJ 08829 B Wabasha County MN 1942 s Leonard & Louise. BA Hamline U 1964; U MN 1965; MDiv Drew U 1968; GTS 1969. D 3/26/1969 P 8/3/1969 Bp George E Rath. m 4/21/2015 Janice Ruth Paxton c 2. ECUSA Website Ed Epis Ch Cntr New York NY 1996-2004; Dep GC Dio Newark Newark NJ 1982-2004; R Chr Ch Pompton Lake NJ 1974-2007; Cur Gr Ch Madison NJ 1969-1974. Cmnty of St. Jn Bapt 2012. Bp's Cbury Schlr Dio Newark 1997.

ROLLINS, Roger Burton (Ia) 1551 Franklin St SE Apt. 4002, Grand Rapids MI 49506 **Died 12/1/2016** B Lowell MI 1930 s Ellis & Mary. BA Olivet Nazarene U 1953; BD Garrett-Evang TS 1956. D 10/8/1961 P 6/21/1962 Bp Charles Bennison Sr. m 3/2/2003 Mary Esther Rollins c 2. Ret 1996-2016; Ret Affilliate P S Geo's Epis Ch Dayton OH 1996-2010; Chr Ch Cedar Rapids IA 1986-1995; R S Micheal Cedar Rapids IA 1986-1995; R S Andr's Ch Dayton OH 1967-1986; R S Jn's Epis Ch Cambridge OH 1963-1967; Cur S Lk's Par Kalamazoo MI 1960-1963.

ROLLINSON, John Thomas (RG) 1120 Gidding St, Clovis NM 88101 B Bayonne NJ 1938 s John & Elizabeth. U of Vienna 1959; BA Br 1960; MA Geo 1971; US-A Russian Inst Garmisch-Partenkirchen 1973; MDiv TESM 1985. D 6/8/1985 Bp Alden Moinet Hathaway P 3/23/1986 Bp Victor Manuel Rivera. m 10/15/1977 Shirley Rollinson. Ch Of S Jas The Apos Clovis Curry NM 1992-2006; High Plains Team Mnstry Clovis NM 1992-1993; Asst R S Thos Ch Houston TX 1990-1992; Vic Ch Of The Resurr Clovis Clovis CA 1985-1990; Asst To The Bp Epis Dio San Joaquin Modesto CA 1985-1988. ERM 1992; Forw In Faith/ No Amer 1989; NOEL 1985; SSC 1995. Soc Serv Medal Republic Of Vietnam 1971; Bronze Star US-A 1969; Phi Beta Kappa Br 1960.

ROMACK, Gay Harpster (Az) 609 N Old Litchfield Rd, Litchfield Park AZ 85340 B St. Louis MO 1947 d Rodney & Shirley. BA NWU 1969; MA Asu 2000; MA Claremont TS 2007. D 10/14/2006 Bp Kirk Stevan Smith. m 7/5/1969 John Romack c 1. Dvlpmt Dir W Vlly Fine Arts 2001-2003.

ROMAN, James Michael (NJ) Po Box 77356, West Trenton NJ 08628 **Died 1/1/2017** B Brooklyn NY 1945 s James & Dorothy. BA Rider U 1969. D 4/13/1985 Bp George Phelps Mellick Belshaw. m 10/19/1985 Julia A Steinmetz. Ret 1993-2017; D Trin Cathd Trenton NJ 1985-1993. Ord Of S Lk, SocMary.

ROMANIK, David F (Pa) 230 Pennswood Rd, Bryn Mawr PA 19010 **Ch Of The Redeem Bryn Mawr PA 2014-** B Hartford CT 1985 s Donald & Margaret. BA Bos 2007; MDiv VTS 2011. D 6/11/2011 Bp Laura Ahrens P 1/21/2012 Bp Claude Edward Payne. m 10/9/2011 Sarah Beth Y Romanik c 2. Assoc Ch of the Heav Rest Abilene Abilene TX 2011-2014. dromanik@theredeemer.org

ROMANS, Nicholas J (Chi) 514 S Mountain Road, Mesa AZ 85208 B Los Angeles CA 1955 s Marion & Mary. BA USC 1977; MDiv EDS 1982. Trans 9/21/2006 Bp Kirk Stevan Smith. m 5/8/2014 Rex Lee Romans. Ch Of The Trsfg Palos Pk IL 2012-2016; P-in-c Epis Ch Of The Trsfg Mesa AZ 2007-2012; Int S Steph's Ch Phoenix AZ 2006-2007; Assoc St. Thos of Cbury Long Bch Ca 1996-1999; Serv Ch of Engl 1982-1990.

ROMER, William Miller (NH) 128 Audubon Dr, Acton MA 01720 B Albany NY 1935 s Earle & Helen. BA Br 1957; MDiv EDS 1960. D 5/28/1960 Bp Frederick Lehrle Barry P 12/17/1960 Bp Allen Webster Brown. m 5/20/1983 Molly Hardy c 3. S Jas Epis Ch Laconia NH 2008-2010; R The RathKeale and Kilnaughtin Grp of Parishes Ireland 2003-2008; R The Ch Of The Redeem Rochester NH 2001-2003; Dio New Hampshire Concord NH 1998-2000; Int Specl S Jas Epis Ch At Woonsocket Woonsocket RI 1997; Int Specl Dio Rhode Island Providence RI 1994-1997; Int Specl S Dav's On The Hill Epis Ch Cranston RI 1994-1997; Calv Epis Ch Burnt Hills NY 1992-1994; Ch Of Beth Saratoga Spg NY 1989-1993; Int Spec Dio Albany Greenwich NY 1988; S Lk's Ch Catskill NY 1987-1989; P-in-c S Lk's Troy NY 1970-1971; Chapl S Agnes Sch NY 1967-1970; Vic S Bon Ch Guilderland NY 1965-1970; Asst S Andr's Ch Hanover MA 1964-1965; P-in-c S Mary's Ch Lake Luzerne NY 1960-1964.

R

ROMERIL, Gwendolyn Jane (Be) 26 W Market St, Bethlehem PA 18018 **Dio Bethlehem Bethlehem PA 1988-** B Cornwall NY 1932 d George & Margaret. RN S Johns Epis Hosp New York 1953; MDiv Moravian TS 1981; Cert GTS 1985. D 6/13/1981 P 6/11/1982 Bp Lloyd Edward Gressle. m 11/11/1953 Robert D Romeril c 5. S Andr's Epis Ch Allentown PA 1996-2002; Assoc Trin Ch Easton PA 1988-1995; Cn Pstr Cathd Ch Of The Nativ Bethlehem PA 1980-1988. "Var arts," *The Morning Call, Allentown PA*, 2005; "Womens Uncommon Prayers (Contrib)," Morehouse Pub, 2000.

ROMERO, Silvestre (Mass) **S Ptr's Ch Salem MA 2012-** B GT 1968 s Sylvestre & Evangelina. BS Inst De Bachilerato; BTh Sch for Deacons. Trans 9/15/1999 Bp Frank Jeffrey Terry. m 2/14/1995 Thelma Romero c 2. S Phil's Ch San Jose CA 2003-2012; Dio Spokane Spokane WA 1999-2002; Serv Ch In Cntrl Amer 1996-1999.

✠ ROMERO, The Rt Rev Sylvestre Donato (NJ) 808 W State St, Trenton NJ 08618 Guatemala **Natl Chapl The Ord of DOK 2011-** B Belize ND HN 1944 s Valentine & Cleofa. BA Sem Guatemala 1973; MTh CDSP 1988. Trans 1/13/2005 Bp Frank Tracy Griswold III. m 11/29/1968 Evangelina Romero c 4. Asst Bp of New Jersey Dio New Jersey Trenton NJ 2007-2010; Int Bp Dio El Camino Real Salinas CA 2004-2007, 1992-1993; Bp of Belize Angl Ch of Belize 1994-2004; Asst H Faith Par Inglewood CA 1993; Asst S Phil's Ch San Jose CA 1987-1991; Cn Of The NE Reg Dio Guatemala 1984-1985; P-in-c Todos Los Santos In Gualan 1982-1983; P Dio Guatemala New York NY 1974-1987; R San Esteban 1974-1982. DD CDSP 1998.

ROMERO-GUEVARA, Antonio N (EcuC) Dias De La Madrid 943, Quito Ecuador **Iglesia Epis Del Ecuador Quito 2012-, 1996-2009** B 1954 s Antonio & Olga. D 12/20/1992 Bp Jose Neptali Larrea-Moreno. m 10/1/1977 Maria Elena Zurita c 3.

ROMERO MARTE, Francisco Alfredo (DR) **Dio The Dominican Republic (Iglesia Epis Dominicana) Gazcue Santo Domingo 2010-** B 1949 s Jose & Tonasina. Lic Centro de Estudios Teologicos 2009. D 2/14/2010 P 2/20/2011 Bp Julio Cesar Holguin-Khoury. m 10/9/1983 Teresa Tavarez c 3.

ROMO-GARCIA, Gerardo (Los) 4 Indian Wells Hwy, P, O, Box 139, Amagansett NY 11930 **Dio Long Island Garden City NY 2015-** B Jalisco MX 1966 s Baudelio & Socorro. DAS Seminario De San Andres Mex City Df Mx; Cert Southampton Sch Dist; Cert The Migrant Cntr, St. Fran RC Ch, Manhattan; BTh Universidad Intercontinental Mex City Mx; BA Seminario de Guadalajara 1993; BA Seminario de Aguascalientes 1996. D 5/29/2004 P 1/8/2005 Bp Carlos Touche-Porter. S Hilary's Epis Ch Hesperia CA 2013-2015; Vol Asst Ch of Engl / Dio Birmingham 2012; Bro/Novc The SSF / Eropean Prov 2008-2011; Vic Dio Mex Mex City MOR 2006-2008, Chapl 2005-2008; COM Dio Los Angeles 2014-2015; Hisp Mnstry Coordntr Dio Los Angeles 2014-2015; Offcl for Soc Mnstrs Dio Mex 2004-2008. padregerardoromo@gmail.com

RONALDI, Lynn Petrie (Miss) Episcopal Church Of The Advent, PO Box 366, Sumner MS 38957 **Epis Ch Of The Incarn W Point MS 2015-** B LaGrange IL 1962 d Harry & Jerrianne. BA U of Mississippi 1983; MBA U of Dallas 1987; MDiv U of St Thos TS 2008; DMin Sewanee TS 2015; DMin Sewanee: The U So, TS 2015. D 6/1/2013 P 12/15/2013 Bp Duncan Montgomery Gray III. m 12/30/1983 Thomas Carl Ronaldi c 3. Ch Of The Adv Sumner MS 2013-2015; S Columb's Ch Ridgeland MS 2013; Yth Dir S Paul's Ch Columbus MS 2010-2012.

RONDEAU, Daniel James (SanD) 44910 Calle Placido, La Quinta CA 92253 B Mankato MN 1949 s Richard & Margery. BS U of San Diego 1972; STB Pontifical Gregorian U Rome IT 1975; MS San Diego St U 1983. Rec 2/17/1986 as Priest Bp Charles Brinkley Morton. m 8/6/1980 Carol A Tripoli c 2. Assoc S Marg's Epis Ch Palm Desert CA 1993-2009; Vic S Mary's In The Vlly Ch Ramona CA 1988-1992; Cur S Dav's Epis Ch San Diego CA 1985-1988.

RONKOWITZ, George R (SeFla) 8310 SW 60th Ave, South Miami FL 33143 **Assoc S Andr's Epis Ch Miami FL 2013-** B Teaneck NJ 1946 s Rudolph & Sophia. BA St Bernards Sem Rochester NY 1967; MDiv S Bernards TS and Mnstry 1970; MEd Ford 1976. Rec 12/11/1988 as Priest Bp Jeffery William Rowthorn. m 8/24/2013 Lana Tanca Ronkowitz c 2. R and Sch Headmaster S Jn's Epis Ch Homestead FL 2003-2011; Vic Trin-S Mich's Ch Fairfield CT 1995-2003; Assoc S Ptr's Epis Ch Milford CT 1991-1995; Assoc S Andr's Ch Milford CT 1988-1991. grronk@standrewsmiami.org

RONN, Denise Marie (Ga) 2600 Rolling Hill Dr, Valdosta GA 31602 **S Phil's Ch Hinesville Hinesville GA 2016-; Cert Life Coach Dio Georgia 2014-; Emotional Intelligence Trnr Dio Georgia 2014-; Ch Dvlpmt Trnr Dio Georgia 2013-** B Washington DC 1952 d Robert & Cecilia. BA Pacific Luth U 1976; MA Valdosta St U 1995; Sewanee: The U So, TS 2004; PhD Capella U 2009. D 2/7/2004 P 8/11/2004 Bp Henry Irving Louttit. m 11/13/1971 David Lee Ronn c 2. Vic S Barn Epis Ch Valdosta GA 2008-2016; Sch Counslr Valdosta City Schools Valdosta GA 1999-2009; Sch Counslr Berrian Cnty Schools 1995-1999; Dn of the SW Convoc Dio Georgia Savannah GA 2009-2016.

RONTANI, Aidan A (NCal) **S Jn The Evang Ch Chico CA 2016-** D 6/6/2015 P 8/30/2016 Bp Barry Leigh Beisner.

RONTANI JR, William (NCal) 104 Main St., Wheatland CA 95692 B San Francisco CA 1948 s William & Dorothy. VTS; BA San Jose St U 1971; MDiv CD-

SP 1974; AA Coll of San Mateo 1975. D 6/29/1974 P 5/1/1975 Bp Chauncie Kilmer Myers. c 1. R S Jas Epis Par Lincoln CA 2010-2016, 2006-2010; P-in-c Gr Epis Ch Wheatland CA 2004-2006; Vic S Lk's Mssn Calistoga CA 1995-2006; Non-par Dio California San Francisco CA 1993-1994; R S Chris's Ch San Lorenzo CA 1985-1992, Vic 1975-1984; 1980-1986; Field Educ Supvsr CDSP Berkeley CA. Alum Preaching Prize CDSP 1974.

ROOD JR, Peter H (Los) 702 W Alegria Ave, Sierra Madre CA 91024 **R H Nativ Par Los Angeles CA 2002-** B San Francisco CA 1955 s Peter & Roberta. Pacific Oaks Coll 1991; MDiv Epis TS of the SW 1994. D 6/19/1994 Bp Clarence Rupert Haden Jr P 1/1/1995 Bp Frederick Houk Borsch. m 9/2/1978 Martha S Rood. Ch Of Our Sav Par San Gabr CA 1994-1999.

ROOS, Carl A (Ind) 6920 Mohawk Ln, Indianapolis IN 46260 B Celestine IN 1942 s Harry & Veronica. BS S Meinrad Coll 1964; MTh U Innsbruck AT 1968; MS Indiana U 1977; MS Indiana U 1986; Cert SWTS 1990. Rec 7/1/1990 as Priest Bp Edward Witker Jones. m 10/17/1987 Michelle Kate Roos c 1. R S Jas Ch Vincennes IN 1997-2005; R S Thos' Epis Ch Falls City NE 1992-1997; Assoc Trin Ch Anderson IN 1990-1992; Chapl (Major) Indiana NG 1975-1987.

ROOS, Michelle Kate (Ind) 720 Dr. Martin Luther King Jr St., Indianapolis IN 46202 **Pstr S Phil's Ch Indianapolis IN 2007-** B Indianapolis IN 1955 d Richard & Martha. BS Pur 1980; MDiv SWTS 1995; MA St Meinrad TS 2006. D 6/23/1995 P 2/12/1996 Bp Edward Witker Jones. m 10/17/1987 Carl A Roos c 1. Vic S Geo Epis Ch W Terre Haute IN 1997-2000; Dio Nebraska Omaha NE 1995-1997.

ROOS, Richard John (Ind) 2033 Paradise Oaks Ct, Atlantic Beach FL 32233 B Jasper IN 1945 s Harry & Veronica. BA S Meinrad Coll 1967; STB Gregorian U 1971; MA Indiana U 1974. Rec 6/1/1976 as Deacon Bp John P Craine. m 8/15/2005 Jennifer Roos c 4. R S Phil's Ch Indianapolis IN 1977-2006; Assoc Pstr S Mk's Ch Plainfield IN 1976-1977. *Origines Adamantius*, No Amer Collage, 1971.

ROOSEVELT, Nancy (O) 17100 Van Aken Blvd, Shaker Heights OH 44120 B New York NY 1947 d W Emlen & Arlene. Premier Degree U of Paris-Sorbonne Fr 1967; BA Hollins U 1969; MDiv GTS 1985. D 6/1/1985 Bp George Phelps Mellick Belshaw P 1/5/1986 Bp A(rthur) Heath Light. c 2. R Chr Ch Shaker Heights OH 2000-2004; Cn Dio Rochester Henrietta 1991-1999, Dioc Deploy Off 1987-2000; Dep For Prog Dio SW Virginia Roanoke VA 1987-1991, Chair Com 1986-1987; R E Lee Memi Ch (Epis) Lexington VA 1985-1987; Chapl VMI & W&L Lexington VA 1985-1987; COM Dio Ohio Cleveland 2002-2004; Trst The GTS New York NY 1995-1998. Soc Of S Jn The Evang 1995. nar7747@att.net

ROOSEVELT, Nick (Az) **Assoc S Barn On The Desert Scottsdale AZ 2013-** B Spartanburg SC 1987 s Oliver & Carol. BS Presb Coll 2009; MDiv VTS 2013. D 6/1/2013 P 12/12/2013 Bp W illiam Andrew Waldo. c 1.

ROOT, Diane Eleanor (Vt) 2 Jones Avenue, West Lebanon NH 03784 **Pstr Care Dir Mt. Ascutney Hosp 2004-; Evang Cmsn 1988-; Hosp Mnstry Com 1983-** B Bethesda MD 1953 d Lloyd & Dorothy. BA Colorado Coll 1975; MDiv Andover Newton TS 1982. D 6/5/1982 Bp John Bowen Coburn P 8/1/1983 Bp Morgan Porteus. m 3/1/2012 Margaret Ann Campbell. Vic Ch of Our Sav Killington VT 2011-2012; Three Rivers Reg Mnstry Killington VT 1998-2010; Vic S Lk's Ch Lanesboro MA 1988-1998; Hosp Chapl Grtr Lynn Coun Of Ch 1983-1988; Assoc S Steph's Memi Ch Lynn MA 1983-1988; Dio Massachusetts Boston MA 1982-1983; Asst S Jn's Ch Winthrop MA 1982-1983.

ROPER, Charles Murray (At) 128 River Ridge Ln, Roswell GA 30075 B Atlanta GA 1929 s Robert & Clara. Cert VTS; BS Davidson Coll 1952; MDiv Columbia TS 1955. D 6/1/1956 P 12/1/1956 Bp Randolph R Claiborne. m 8/9/1953 Elizabeth Roper c 6. Cn to Ordnry Dio Atlanta Atlanta GA 1994-1995, Spec Asst To Bp In Dvlpmt Cltn Mnstry 1973-1977, Spec Asst To Bp In Dvlpmt Cltn Mnstry 1973-1976, Exec Bd 1962-1968; S Thos Epis Ch Columbus GA 1978-1995; Vic/R Ch Of The H Cross Decatur GA 1963-1978; Assoc H Trin Par Decatur GA 1958-1963; Vic S Jn's W Point GA 1956-1958. Compsr, "Mass for the Sanctity of Space," Self Pub, 2012; Chas M. Roper, "Mass for the Sanctity of Space," Self Pub, 2012; Auth, "The Wrld, the Flesh and God," Self Pub, 2010.

ROPER, Jeffrey Howard (Kan) 3750 E Douglas Ave, Wichita KS 67208 B Norman OK 1957 s John & Alice. BA U of Kansas 1979; BA Wichita St U 1997; MA Wichita St U 2003; Kansas Sch for Mnstry 2010. D 1/8/2011 Bp Dean E Wolfe. m 12/29/1979 Victoria Roper c 2.

ROPER, John Dee (Kan) 14802 E Willowbend Cir, Wichita KS 67230 **D S Andrews Ch Derby KS 2009-; Dioc D Dio Kansas Topeka KS 2006-** B Oklahoma City OK 1935 s Clay & Hester. BBA Oklahoma St U 1956; LLB Oklahoma St U 1958; MA SMU 1990. D 12/11/1981 Bp Richard Frank Grein. m 3/16/1957 Alice Suzanne Roper c 3. D S Steph's Ch 2005-2006; D S Jn's Ch Wichita KS 1981-2005.

ROPER, Terence Chaus (Pa) 1815 John F Kennedy Blvd Apt 2308, Philadelphia PA 19103 **The Epis Ch Of The Trsfg Dallas TX 2014-, R 1976-1999** B Portsmouth Hampshire UK 1935 s Charles & Mabel. Lon GB 1959; S Bon Coll Warminster GB 1960. Trans 8/6/1965 as Priest Bp Charles A Mason. R The Ch Of The H Trin Rittenhouse Philadelphia PA 1999-2004; R Epis Ch Of The Redeem Irving TX 1973-1976; R Ch Of Our Lady Of Gr Dallas TX 1967-1973;

Asst R The Epis Ch Of S Thos The Apos Dallas TX 1965-1967; Cur S Alb's Epis Ch Arlington TX 1963-1965; Serv Ch of Engl 1960-1963. Bd Trst - EDS, Cambridge, MA` 1963-1998. Dallas AIDS Interfaith Awd 1998.

ROQUE, Christopher Collin (WTex) 3500 N 10th St, Mcallen TX 78501 **S Jas Epis Ch Ft McKavett TX 2008-** B Corpus Christi TX 1970 s Felix & Judy. BA Texas St U San Marcos 1994; MDiv Sewanee: The U So, TS 2005. D 6/13/2005 Bp James Edward Folts P 1/6/2006 Bp Gary Richard Lillibridge. m 3/11/1995 Leticia Ann Roque c 2. R S Jn's Epis Ch Sonora TX 2008-2016; Cur S Jn's Ch McAllen TX 2005-2008.

RORKE, Stephen Ernest (Roch) 6727 Royal Thomas Way, Alexandria VA 22315 **Assoc S Geo's Epis Ch Arlington VA 2011-** B Buffalo NY 1947 s Edward & Alice. BA Trin Hartford CT 1969; MDiv EDS 1975. D 6/29/1975 Bp Robert Rae Spears Jr P 4/20/1977 Bp Harold Barrett Robinson. m 12/16/1971 Jeanne Rorke c 1. Lorton Cmnty Action Cntr Lorton VA 2002-2011; Yth S Ptr's Epis Ch Arlington VA 1998-2002; Arlington Comm Temp Shltr Inc Arlington VA 1997-2001; TACTS Arlington VA 1993-2001; St Fran Cntr Washington DC 1991; Acts Dumfries VA 1990-1991; ACTS Dumfries VA 1985-1991; S Fran Ch Potomac MD 1983-1985; Natl Netwk Runaway & Yth Serv WDC 1977-1982; Dir Compass Hse Buffalo NY 1975-1977; Assoc Epis Ch Hm Buffalo NY 1975-1977. Ed, *Adolescent Abuse & Neglect: Model Progs*, Nat'l Cntr on Chld Abuse & Neglect, 1981; Ed, *Adolescent Maltreatment*, Nat'l Cntr on Chld Abuse and Neglect, 1981; Auth, *Preventing Yth from Running Away*, Dept. of Hlth & Human Serv, 1978; Auth, *Prevention: A Positive Process*, Dept. of Hlth & Human Serv, 1978; Auth, *Manuel for Yth Outreach Projects*; Auth, *Yth Outreach Mnstry*.

ROS, Salvador Patrick (NJ) **R Ch of the Gd Shpd Rahway NJ 2006-** B New York, NY 1956 s Ralph & Maria. BA Cathd Coll of the Immac Concep 1979; MDiv S Josephs Sem Yonkers 1982; MDiv S Josephs Sem Yonkers 1982. Rec 8/18/2001 Bp Julio Cesar Holguin-Khoury. m 4/9/1994 Lisette E Pappaterra c 1. H Comf Ch Rahway NJ 2006-2008; Dio The Dominican Republic (Iglesia Epis Dominicana) Gazcue Santo Domingo 2001-2005.

ROSA, Thomas Phillip (Chi) 121 W Macomb St, Belvidere IL 61008 **Sunday Long Term Supply Trin Epis Ch Aurora IL 2011-; Ret/Affiliating Emm Epis Ch Rockford IL 2009-** B Chicago IL 1942 s Alex & Wanda. U IL 1962; BA Sthrn Illinois U 1966; Ya Berk 1970; MDiv Nash 1971; Cert Int Mnstry Ntwk 2004. D 6/19/1971 Bp Gerald Francis Burrill P 12/18/1971 Bp James Winchester Montgomery. Int S Mk's Ch Evanston IL 2010-2011; Int Emm Epis Ch La Grange IL 2006-2008; Int S Lawr Epis Ch Libertyville IL 2005-2006; Int Epis Ch Of The Atone Chicago IL 2004-2005; Dn Rockford Dnry 1990-1996; R The Epis Ch Of The H Trin Belvidere IL 1974-2001; Asst Ch Of The H Fam Pk Forest IL 1971-1974; Chapt Mem Cathd Of S Jas Chicago IL 1996-1999; Dioc Coun Dio Chicago Chicago IL 1977-1996. AGO 2005. R Emertius H Trin Ch, Belvidere, IL 2008; Dn Emer of Rockford Dnry Dio Chicago 1996.

ROSANAS, Louis Toussaint (Hai) Box 1309, Port-Au-Prince Haiti **Asst La Gonave 1992-; Dio Haiti Port-au-Prince HT 1991-** B Leogane HT 1958 s Lizamene. Cert 1985; Cert Sem 1991. D 9/15/1991 P 4/1/1992 Bp Luc Anatole Jacques Garnier. m 2/23/1995 Erline Rosanas c 4. D S Pierre Mirebalais Haiti 1991-1992.

ROSARIO-CRUZ, Eliacin Rosario 111 NE 80th St, Seattle WA 98115 **S Lk's Epis Ch Vancouver WA 2015-** B Ponce Puerto Rico 1974 s Eliacin & Nydia. BA U de Puerto Rico 1995; MDiv Seattle U TS and Mnstry 2014. P 6/16/2015 Bp Gregory Harold Rickel. m 7/29/2014 Ricci L Kilmer c 4. R S Andr's Ch Seattle WA 2015.

ROSARIO DE LA CRUZ, Juan Antonio (Nwk) 3901 Park Ave, Union City NJ 07087 **Gr Ch Un City NJ 2014-** B San Pedro De Macorís, DR 1964 s German & Maritza. Centro de Estudios Teologicos 1991. D 6/7/1992 P 12/11/1993 Bp Julio Cesar Holguin-Khoury. m 10/30/1992 Reyna Pina De Jesus c 2. Dio The Dominican Republic (Iglesia Epis Dominicana) Gazcue Santo Domingo 1992-2014. gracechurch@outlook.es

ROSE, Ann W (Ore) 7 Saint Johns Rd Apt 30, Cambridge MA 02138 **D S Mary's Epis Ch Eugene OR 1993-** B Portland OR 1943 d Carl & Barbara. BS U of Oregon 1965; BA Lake Erie Coll 1981. D 12/4/1993 Bp Robert Louis Ladehoff.

ROSE, Carol Benson (EO) 2133 N Cajeme Ave, Casa Grande AZ 85222 B Ontario OR 1932 s George & Lillian. D 7/17/1977 P 9/28/1978 Bp William Benjamin Spofford. m 7/20/1967 Laura Lee Shank. Assoc S Ptr's Ch Casa Grande AZ 2005-2013; P S Thos Ch Canyon City OR 1977-1995.

ROSE, Christopher Lee (Ct) 30 Woodland Street Unit 10NP, Hartford CT 06106 B Hartford CT 1953 s Esmond & Anne. BA U of Connecticut 1975; MDiv GTS 1978; STM GTS 1986. D 6/10/1978 P 12/1/1978 Bp Morgan Porteus. m 1/2/2005 Deborah Lee Rose. S Geo's Ch Bolton CT 2013-2014; Pres Of The Stndg Com 1997-1998; Bp Coleridge Del To Chriscon 1993-2000; Dioc Stndg Com 1993-1998; Dn Hartford Dnry 1992-1995; Dioc Liturg Cmsn 1983-1986; Gr Epis Ch Hartford CT 1982-2002; Chapl Connecticut Coll Of Epis Students 1980-1982; S Jas Ch New London CT 1979-1982; Asst S Jn New London CT 1979-1982; Asst S Jn's Epis Par Waterbury CT 1978-1979. Auth, "The Hart-

ford Courant". OHC. Natl Radio Broadcast Awd 88-92; Epis Fndt Top 10 Sermons 91-92; Polly Bond Awd.

ROSE, David D (SwVa) 210 4th St., Radford VA 24141 **Mssnr S Pl Angl Ch Belize 2000-** B Winston-Salem NC 1950 s Norman & Josephine. VTS; BA Lenoir-Rhyne Coll 1974; MDiv Bangor TS 1984. D 6/15/1985 P 3/19/1986 Bp William Gillette Weinhauer. m 2/11/2008 Robin Lynn Rose c 3. R Gr Ch Radford VA 2009-2016; R S Paul's Ch Lancaster NH 2001-2008; Exec Coun Appointees New York NY 2000-2001; Trin Ch Spruce Pine NC 1985-2000.

ROSE, David Jonathan (Ga) St. Anne's Episcopal Church, PO Box 889, Tifton GA 31793 **Vic Dio Georgia Savannah GA 2013-** B Abilene TX 1978 s Gary & Brenda. BA Jas Madison U 2000; MDiv VTS 2011. D 6/18/2011 Bp Michael B Curry P 12/18/2011 Bp Scott Anson Benhase. m 7/31/1999 Amy Hundley Rose c 4. Asst S Anne's Ch Tifton GA 2011-2013; Yth Dir S Tim's Epis Ch Winston Salem NC 2006-2009. frdavid@stlukesrincon.com

ROSE, Edwin Sandford (WTex) Po Box 1943, Fulton TX 78358 **Died 9/30/2016** B Ottawa ON CA 1933 s Edwin & Beatrice. BS Trin Hartford CT 1955; BD VTS 1968. D 6/18/1968 P 3/13/1969 Bp Robert Raymond Brown. m 6/14/1955 Jane Rose c 5. S Ptr's Epis Ch Rockport TX 1996-2002; R S Jn's Ch McAllen TX 1982-1996; R The Epis Ch Of The Adv Alice TX 1976-1982; Asst Ch Of The Gd Shpd Corpus Christi TX 1972-1976; R S Jn's Ch Camden AR 1970-1972; Cur Trin Ch Pine Bluff AR 1968-1970.

ROSE, Josie Rodriguez (NwT) 5539 7th Ave N, Saint Petersburg FL 33710 B Gonzales TX 1943 d Eugenio & Santos. BA U of Texas 1989; MDiv Epis TS of the SW 2003. D 11/30/2002 P 6/7/2003 Bp C Wallis Ohl. c 2. Vic Ch of Santa Maria Virgen Midland TX 2005-2011; Dio NW Texas Lubbock TX 2005-2011; Vic Iglesia Epis de Santa Maria Midland TX 2005-2011; Asst R Ch Of The H Trin Midland TX 2003-2005.

ROSE, Joy Ann (Nwk) Saint Mary's Episcopal Church, 216 Orange Ave, Daytona Beach FL 32114 B Norwalk CT 1944 d Vincent & Anne. BA Syr 1966; MA U of Bridgeport 1980; MA Hartford Sem 1999; Ya Berk 2002; MDiv Ya Berk 2002; DMin VTS 2010. D 7/13/2002 P 1/18/2003 Bp Keith Whitmore. c 2. S Mary's Epis Ch Daytona Bch FL 2013-2014; R S Paul's Epis Ch Piney Waldorf MD 2007-2013; R Emm Ch Harrisonburg VA 2004-2007; Asst Chr Ch Cathd Eau Claire WI 2002-2004; Coun on Collaborative Mnstry Dio Washington Washington DC 2011-2013, Dioc Coun 2009-2013; Cn for CE Dio Eau Claire Eau Claire WI 2003-2004. Auth, "The Ch's Invisible Majority:Active Older Adults," *Doctoral Thesis*, VTS, 2010. The Soc Of S Fran, Third Ord 2000.

ROSE, Leland Gerald (WNY) 602 Crescent Ave, East Aurora NY 14052 **D S Mk's Ch Orchard Pk NY 1998-** B Ithaca NY 1934 s Wayne & Evelyn. BA W Virginia U 1965; MA SUNY 1968. D 9/12/1998 Bp David Charles Bowman. m 8/21/1965 Martha Eileen Darnell c 2. Reg 2 Dir The Intl OSL The Physcn 2009-2015. "Gone w a Pryr," *Sharing mag*, OSL, 2003; "Anointing by Proxy," *Sharing mag*, Ord of St Lk, 2000. Bro of S Andr 1990; Diakoneo 1998; Ord of S Lk 1996.

ROSE, L(oran) A(nson) Paul (WA) 6101 Edsall Rd Apt 508, Alexandria VA 22304 **1986-** B Cleveland OH 1945 s Jerry & Dolores. BA Amer U 1967; MDiv GTS 1972; PhD NYU 1976. D 6/17/1972 Bp William Foreman Creighton P 3/1/1973 Bp Stephen F Bayne Jr. Calv Ch Washington DC 1979-1986; Asst S Paul's Rock Creek Washington DC 1977-1978; Assoc Chr Ch Prince Geo's Par Rockville MD 1974-1976; Chapl Chr Day Sch Rockville MD 1974-1976; Asst Epis Ch of Gr and Resurr E Elmhurst NY 1972-1973.

ROSE, Margaret Rollins (NY) 531 E 72nd St Apt 3c, New York NY 10021 **Ecum Interreligious Dep to the PBp Epis Ch Cntr New York NY 2015-, Dir 2003-2015; Dom And Frgn Mssy Soc- Epis Ch Cntr New York NY 2006-** B CarrolltonGA 1954 d Frank & Ellen. BA Wellesley Coll 1976; Cert Geneva U Geneva NY 1978; MDiv Harvard DS 1979. D 5/30/1981 P 4/18/1982 Bp John Bowen Coburn. m 12/6/2013 William E Curran c 2. Ch Of The Heav Rest New York NY 2013-2014; R S Dunst's Epis Ch Atlanta GA 1992-2003; Int S Barn Ch Falmouth MA 1991-1992; Chr Ch Hyde Pk MA 1989-1991; S Gabr's Epis Ch Marion MA 1988; Coordntr Feminist Liberation Theol Prog EDS Cambridge MA 1987-1989; Ch Of S Jn The Evang Hingham MA 1987; Asst Ch Of S Jn The Evang Boston MA 1983-1986; Stff The Cathd Ch Of S Paul Boston MA 1981-1983; Vic Luth Ch in Germany 1979-1980. mrose@episcopalchurch.org

ROSE, Philip John (Minn) B Minneapolis MN 1960 s James & Jean. CAS CDSP 2012. D 1/24/2013 P 6/27/2013 Bp Brian N Prior. m 8/8/1980 Sheryl Venable Rose c 2.

ROSE, Roger Franklin (Los) 3 Pursuit Apt 109, Aliso Viejo CA 92656 **Asst S Thos' Mssn Hacienda Hgts CA 2005-** B Chicago IL 1926 s Frank & Vivian. BA IL Wesl 1948; MTh Yale DS 1956. D 9/10/1964 P 3/1/1965 Bp Francis E I Bloy. m 2/15/1958 Shirley Jean Reece. Assoc S Gabr's Par Monterey Pk CA 2000-2005; P-in-c H Trin Ch Alhambra CA 1995-2000; Ch Of The H Trin and S Ben Alhambra CA 1994-1998; Vic Ch Of The Epiph Los Angeles CA 1992-1993; P-in-c Trin Epis Par Los Angeles CA 1989-1990; Asst S Steph's Par Whittier CA 1988-1989, Asst 1984-1987; 1982-1984; St Matthews Ch Baldwin Pk CA 1980-1981; Vic S Matt Baldwin Pk CA 1978-1981; Vic Res-

R

urr Montabello CA 1971-1977; Dio Los Angeles Los Angeles CA 1965-1992; Vic S Matt Baldwin Pk CA 1965-1971; Serv Methodist Ch 1956-1963. Ord of Agape and Reconciliation 1973. Blue Key Hon Fraternity 1948.

ROSE, Roland (NwT) 5539 7th Ave. North, St. Petersburg FL 33710 **Died 7/9/2016** B Oklahoma City OK 1939 s Frank & Elena. BA U of No Texas 1962; MEd U of No Texas 1963. D 10/28/2001 Bp C Wallis Ohl. m 5/30/1964 Josie Rodriguez c 2. Iglesia Epis de Santa Maria Midland TX 2005-2016; D Santa Maria Virgen Midland TX 2004-2011; D S Jn's Epis Ch Odessa TX 2001-2004.

ROSE, Shirley Jean (Los) 3 Pursuit # 109, Aliso Viejo CA 92656 B Inglewood CA 1928 d Paul & Ruth. BA U Pac 1951; UTS 1956; MA Claremont TS 1984; ETSBH 1986. D 6/20/1987 P 1/1/1988 Bp Oliver Bailey Garver Jr. m 2/15/1958 Roger Franklin Rose c 3. Assoc S Andr's Luth Ch Whittier CA 2001-2002; Mentor Newly Ord 1998-2000; S Edm's Par San Marino CA 1998-1999; 1994-1995; S Mths' Par Whittier CA 1988-1998, DRE 1979-1987. Auth, "Focus On Galations," *Living The Gd News*, 1989; Auth, "Go In Peace Dio Peace Curric 91". Outstanding Alum Claremaont TS 1994; Hon Cn S Paul Cathd Cntr 1993.

ROSE, William Harrison (SC) 20 Riverview Dr, Beaufort SC 29907 **Ch Of The Heav Rest Estill SC 1999-; Vic Ch Of The H Comm Allendale SC 1999-; Ret 1995-** B New Brunswick NJ 1931 s William & Lucy. U of Kentucky; LTh Epis TS in Kentucky 1963. D 6/1/1963 P 12/1/1963 Bp William R Moody. m 1/28/1961 Beatrice Rose. R The Ch Of The Cross Bluffton SC 1990-1995; So Carolina Charleston SC 1990-1995; R Ch Of The Gd Shpd Columbia SC 1978-1990; R S Jn's Ch Winnsboro SC 1968-1978; R Emm Epis Ch Winchester KY 1963-1968. office@holycomm.org

ROSE-CROSSLEY, Ramona (Vt) 327 University Ave, Sewanee TN 37375 B Philadelphia PA 1935 d William & Vinita. BA Barnard Coll of Col 1957; MS U of Maryland 1963; MDiv Sewanee: The U So, TS 1981. D 2/22/1986 P 4/11/1987 Bp Charles Judson Child Jr. m 2/20/1977 Remington Rose c 2. S Mk's-S Lk's Epis Mssn Fair Haven VT 1999-2003; S Paul's Epis Ch Wells VT 1999-2003; Trin Epis Ch E Poultney VT 1999-2003; Dio Micronesia Tumon Bay GU 1990-1998; Vic The Epis Ch of S Jn the Div Tamuning GU 1990-1998; Vic S Mary Magd Ch Columbus GA 1987-1989; D S Lk's Epis Ch Atlanta GA 1986-1987. Jn Hines Preaching Awd VTS 1999.

ROSE-CROSSLEY, Remington (Vt) **Sprtl Dir for seminarians STUSo 2010-** B New Jersey 1937 s Donald & Maude. BA Trin Hartford CT 1958; MA Pr 1960; PhD Pr 1964; Cert Theol Stud Sewanee: The U So, TS 2005. D 7/16/2005 P 3/30/2006 Bp Thomas C Ely. m 2/20/1977 Ramona Rose-Crossley c 3. Vic SE Tennessee Episc. Mnstry Alto & Monteagle TN 2007-2009.

ROSEN, Elisabeth Payne (Cal) P O Box 1306, Ross CA 94957 **Chapl Kentfield Rehab Hosp Kentfield CA 1990-** B Shreveport LA 1942 d Francis & Ann. BA Hollins U 1964; BD Sch for Deacons 1993. D 6/4/1994 Bp William Edwin Swing. m 5/27/1967 Martin Gerald Rosen c 2. D Ch Of Our Sav Mill Vlly CA 2007-2010; D Chr Ch Sausalito CA 1995-2005; D The Epis Ch Of S Jn The Evang San Francisco CA 1994-1995. Auth, "Hallam's War," *novel (paperback)*, Berkley Books, 2009; Auth, "Hallam's War," *novel (hardcover)*, Unbridled Books, 2008.

ROSENBAUM, Richard Lemoine (Okla) 9804 Cisler Lane, Manassas VA 20111 **EFM Mentor Dio Oklahoma Oklahoma City OK 1995-** B Wellsville OH 1921 s Hazel & Anna. E Carolina U 1958; U of Maryland 1960; BA Tem 1963; Estrn New Mex U 1989. D 6/27/1992 Bp Terence Kelshaw P 6/23/2001 Bp Robert Manning Moody. m 9/10/1984 Mary E Rosenbaum. Assoc S Thos Epis Ch Dallas OR 2008; P-in-c S Hilda's Ch Monmouth OR 2007-2008; P-in-c S Jn's Epis Ch Toledo OR 2005-2007; Assoc All SS' Epis Ch Duncan OK 2004; Assoc S Paul's Ch Clinton OK 2003-2004; Supply P/Chapl Old Post Chap Ft Sill OK 2001-2004; Assoc S Andr's Epis Ch Lawton OK 2001-2004, D 1995-2001; D S Andr's Ch Roswell NM 1992-1995.

ROSENBERG, Elma Joy Van Fossen (SwFla) 125 56th Ave S Apt 314, Saint Petersburg FL 33705 **Ret 2006-** B Northville MI 1948 d Walter & Rosemary. BA Albion Coll 1970; AD S Mary Jr Coll Minneapolis MN 1977. D 6/24/1989 Bp Gerald Francis Burrill. m 9/24/1972 Calvin Lee Ronald Rosenberg. D Cathd Ch Of S Ptr St. Petersburg FL 2001-2006, D 1989-2000; D Dio SW Florida Parrish FL 1999-2001.

ROSENBLUM, Nancy Jo (Alb) 22 Buckingham Dr, Albany NY 12208 **D S Paul's Epis Ch Albany NY 2007-** B Arlington VA 1946 d Owen & Pat. BA SUNY 1968; MA SUNY 1974. D 10/13/1980 Bp Wilbur Emory Hogg Jr. m 8/25/1967 David Alan Rosenblum. Asst S Paul's Ch Troy NY 1997-2006; Dio Albany NY 1996-1997; Cannon Sacrist Cathd of All SS Albany NY 1993-1996; D Cathd Of All SS Albany NY 1988-1993; Com Lay Mnstry Dio Albany NY 1987-1989, Ecum Comm 1986-1999, Secy 1989-1990, Chair COM 1982-1988; Asst S Andr's Epis Ch Albany NY 1980-1988. Amnesty Intl ; Bread for Wrld.

ROSENDAHL, Mary Alvarez (CFla) 1043 Genesee Avenue, Sebastian FL 32958 **R Epis Ch Of The Nativ Port St Lucie FL 2008-** B Camden NJ 1951 d Frank & Celeste. BA Barry U 1994; MDiv Sewanee: The U So, TS 2001. D 5/26/2001 Bp John Wadsworth Howe P 12/9/2001 Bp Stephen Hays Jecko. m 6/17/1972 Michael Rosendahl c 2. Asst R H Trin Epis Ch Melbourne FL 2004-2008;

Asst S Andr's Epis Ch Ft Pierce FL 2003-2004; Assoc R S Mk's Epis Ch Jacksonville FL 2001-2003.

ROSENDALE, Mary E (WMass) **Dio Wstrn Massachusetts Springfield 2016-** B Grand Junction CO 1989 d Edward & Elizabeth. BA Colorado Mesa U 2012. D 6/13/2015 P 6/18/2016 Bp Robert John O'Neill. m 10/27/2016 Jose R Reyes Perez.

ROSENGREN, Linda W (Fla) 5054 Ripple Rush Dr N, Jacksonville FL 32257 **Chapl and Coordntr of Bereavement Serv Wolfson Chld's Hosp Jacksonville FL 2006-** B Charleston SC 1949 d Addie & Ella. BS Winthrop U 1970; MEd Coll of Charleston 1977; Inst for Chr Stds Dio Cntrl Florida 1997. D 12/13/1997 Bp John Wadsworth Howe. m 8/22/1970 Charles Rosengren c 2. Asst to the R Ch Of The Gd Shpd Jacksonville FL 2004-2010; Dir of Chr Formation S Mk's Epis Ch Jacksonville FL 2000-2004; Dir od Chr Formation All SS Ch Of Winter Pk Winter Pk FL 1998-2000; Dio Coordntr of CE Dio Cntrl Florida Orlando FL 1994-1999.

ROSENZWEIG, Edward Charles (Md) 83 Harriman Point Road, Brooklin ME 04616 **Ret 1991-** B Newark NJ 1929 s Edward & Josephine. BA Cntr Coll 1951; MS U of Maryland 1956; PhD U of Maryland 1959; MDiv VTS 1976. D 11/21/1976 Bp Harry Lee Doll P 6/1/1977 Bp David Keller Leighton Sr. m 7/30/1955 Carla H Rosenzweig c 2. 1987-1991; Chapl S Paul's Sch Brooklandville MD 1981-1987; S Paul's Par Baltimore MD 1978-1987; Asst Chapl S Paul's Sch Brooklandville MD 1978-1980; Asst S Jn's Ch Mt Washington Baltimore MD 1976-1978.

ROSERO-NORDALM, Ema (Mass) St Stephen's Episcopal Church, 419 Shawmut Ave, Boston MA 02118 B Tumaco Colombia 1944 d Ezequiel & Ema. BA Concordia U 1972; MA Boston St Coll 1977. D 6/16/2012 Bp M(Arvil) Thomas Shaw. c 1.

ROSHEUVEL, Terrence Winst (NJ) 25 Sunset Ave E, Red Bank NJ 07701 B Charity GY 1944 s John & Ruby. LTh Codrington Coll 1968; MDiv Drew U 1997. Trans 12/1/1981 Bp Albert Wiencke Van Duzer. m 9/18/1971 Maylene Rosheuvel c 3. Dio New Jersey Trenton NJ 1991-1997; Dio New Jersey Trenton NJ 1988-1992; R S Thos Epis Ch Red Bank NJ 1981-2010; Vic S Aid's Wismar 1971-1981; Cur S Geo Cathd Georgetown 1968-1971; Stndg Com Pres Dio New Jersey Trenton NJ 2007-2008, Antiracism Cmsn Pres 2000-2007.

✠ ROSKAM, The Rt Rev Catherine Scimeca (NY) 15502 Friar St, Van Nuys CA 91411 **Dio Los Angeles Los Angeles CA 2013-** B Hempstead NY 1943 d Frank & Elvira. BA Mid 1965; MDiv GTS 1984. D 6/9/1984 Bp James Stuart Wetmore P 12/20/1984 Bp Paul Moore Jr Con 1/27/1996 for NY. m 9/3/1966 Philip Roskam. Ret Bp Suffr of New York Dio New York New York NY 2012, Bp Suffr Of New York 1996-2011; S Thos' Epis Ch Amagansett NY 2009-2011; Dioc Mssnr Dio California San Francisco CA 1991-1995, 1989-1991, Coordntr Cler-In-Trng 1989-1991; P-in-c Ch Of The H Innoc San Francisco CA 1990-1991; Int Ch Of Our Sav Mill Vlly CA 1989-1990; Asst Ch Of The H Apos New York NY 1984-1988; Chapl The GTS New York NY 1984-1986. Soc Of S Jn The Evang 1981. DD GTS 1996. croskam@saintjamesla.org

ROSOLEN, Emil J (SeFla) 100 Ne Mizner Blvd # 1503, Boca Raton FL 33432 **Jas L Duncan Conf Cntr Delray Bch FL 2016-** B Passaic NJ 1948 s Albert & Josephine. BA Thos Edison Coll 1979; MDiv Pontifical Coll Josephinum TS 1987; MPT U of San Francisco 1993; PhD.MIN Austin Presb TS 1996. Rec 3/21/2014 as Priest Bp Leo Frade. P-in-c S Ambr Epis Ch Ft Lauderdale FL 2014-2016. houseofhope@bellsouth.net

ROSOLOWSKI, Robert (Eau) D 10/29/2016 Bp William Jay Lambert III.

ROSS, Anne M (NY) 88 Ridge Rd, Valley Cottage NY 10989 **Adj Prof NYU Silver Sch of Soc Wk 2011-; Psych Dave Schwing Psych 2010-; Mgr Pstr Care and Educ New York Presb Hosp 2008-; Assoc P Gr Epis Ch Nyack NY 1999-** B Star Lake NY 1957 d Kenneth & Anne. BA Dickinson Coll 1979; MDiv UTS 1983; DAS GTS 1997; MSW NYU 2010. D 6/13/1998 P 12/19/1998 Bp Richard Frank Grein. c 2. Epis Ch Cntr New York NY 2013; Dir, Cntr For CPE The Healthcare Chapl 2004-2008; The Healthcare Chapl Inc New York NY 2003-2004, 1999; Dir Of Pstr Care And Educ St. Lk's - Roosvelt Hosp New York NY 2001-2004; Dir Pstr Care & Educ Nyack Hosp Nyack NY 1998-2001; COM Dio New York New York NY 2003-2009. System Centered Ther and Resrch Inst 2002. Acpe Supvsr ACPE 1999.

ROSS, Cleon (SVa) 196 Homeport Ln, Danville VA 24540 **Chr Epis Ch Danville VA 2012-, R 1999-2011, Dn of Convoc 9 2005-; Int S Jn's Epis Ch Halifax VA 2012-** B Portsmouth NH 1946 s John & Mabel. Cert Douglas Hosp 1980; LTh McGill U 1980; Montreal TS CA 1980. Trans 7/1/1983 Bp Frederick Barton Wolf. m 11/15/1969 Pauline T Ross c 2. R All SS Ch So Hill VA 1992-1999; Reg Coun Chair Dio Maine Portland ME 1984-1986; Vic Cntrl Maine Epis Missions Dover-Foxcroft ME 1983-1992; Vic S Aug's Epis Ch Dovr Foxcroft ME 1983-1992; Vic Angl Ch of Can Bay L'Argent Newfoundland 1980-1983; Dn of Convoc 9 Dio Sthrn Virginia Newport News VA 2008-2012, 2005-2008, Dept. of Missions 1994-2004. Auth, "Just Thoughts," *Bk Titled, Just Thoughts*, Morris Pub, 2012; Auth, "Just Thoughts," *Bk, Just Thoughts*, Morris Pub, 2012.

ROSS, David Jeffrey (Cal) Po Box 774, Pinole CA 94564 B Pasadena CA 1954 s Robert & Elizabeth. BA Sch for Deacons 2002. D 12/7/2002 Bp William Edwin Swing. D S Alb's Ch Albany CA 2002-2006.

ROSS, Donna Baldwin (ECR) 3291 Pickwick Ln, Cambria CA 93428 **Assoc S Ben's Par Los Osos CA 2008-** B Los Angeles CA 1940 d DeForest & Mary. BA U CA 1962; MDiv CDSP 1984. D 6/9/1984 P 1/18/1985 Bp William Grant Black. m 6/9/1962 Robert Talman Ross c 3. R S Paul's Ch Cambria CA 1995-2005; R Chr Ch Oberlin OH 1986-1995; Cur R Ptr's Epis Ch Delaware OH 1984-1986; Stndg Com Dio El Camino Real Salinas CA 2002-2005; Stndg Com Dio Ohio Cleveland 1993-1995. Phi Beta Kappa Ucla 1962.

ROSS, Ellen Marie (Neb) 106 Robin Rd, Council Bluffs IA 51503 B Council Bluffs IA 1943 d Robert & Evelyn. Cert Sewanee: The U So, TS 1988. D 5/7/1988 Bp James Daniel Warner. D Trin Cathd Omaha NE 2001-2015; Secy Ch Of The Resurr Omaha NE 1988-1993.

ROSS, George Crawford Lauren (Cal) 19815 Windwood Dr, Woodbridge CA 95258 B Albany NY 1929 s George & Noel. BS NWU 1952; MDiv SWTS 1955. D 6/18/1955 Bp Charles L Street P 12/21/1955 Bp Gerald Francis Burrill. m 2/17/1979 Darlene Sharon Sanderson c 4. Asst S Paul's Epis Ch Walnut Creek CA 2008-2010; Int Chr the Lord Ch Pinole CA 2005-2006; Int S Edm's Epis Ch Pacifica CA 2002-2003; Gr Ch Martinez CA 1978-2001; R Cathd Ch Of S Paul San Diego CA 1974-1978; R S Mk's Ch Milwaukee WI 1967-1974; R Gr Epis Ch Freeport IL 1964-1967; Mssy Japan 1958-1964; Vic S Richard's Ch Chicago IL 1955-1957.

ROSS, George Mark (Minn) Po Box 1231, Cass Lake MN 56633 B White Earth MN 1930 s Mark & Violet. Bemidji St U 1981; MDiv SWTS 1989. D 6/18/1989 P 12/1/1989 Bp Robert Marshall Anderson. Dio Minnesota Minneapolis MN 1989-2001; Vic S Phil's.

ROSS, Jeffrey Austin (Del) 213 W Third St, Lewes DE 19958 **R S Ptr's Ch Lewes DE 2005-** B Chester PA 1965 s James & Janet. BA Millersville U 1987; MS Neumann U Aston PA 1992; MDiv GTS 1998. D 6/20/1998 Bp Charles Ellsworth Bennison Jr P 5/29/1999 Bp Franklin Delton Turner. m 1/18/1992 Sheila M Bravo-Ross c 2. R Emm Ch Quakertown PA 2001-2005; Int Epis Ch At Cornell Ithaca NY 1999-2000; Asst R S Thos' Ch Whitemarsh Ft Washington PA 1998-1999; Yth Coordntr Dio Pennsylvania Philadelphia PA 1991-1995. Auth, "A Model For Dioc Yth Mnstry," *Resource Bk Mnstrs Yth & YA*, 1995; Auth, "Suicide: An Unspoken Fair," *Resource Bk Mnstrs Yth & YA*, 1995; Auth, "The Edge: Boundries And Norms For Yth Prog," *Resource Bk Mnstrs Yth & YA*, 1995.

ROSS, John C (ETenn) 413 Cumberland Ave, Knoxville TN 37902 **Dn S Jn's Epis Cathd Knoxville TN 1985-** B Kansas City MO 1954 s William & Harriet. BS U of Memphis 1976; MDiv Sewanee: The U So, TS 1980. D 6/15/1980 Bp William Evan Sanders P 5/1/1981 Bp William F Gates Jr. m 8/26/1978 Lois Ross c 2. R Ch Of The Redeem Shelbyville TN 1981-1985; D-In-Trng Gr Ch Chattanooga TN 1980-1981.

ROSS, Johnnie (Roch) 283 S Arnold Ave, Prestonsburg KY 41653 **Dio Rochester Henrietta 2016-** B Detroit MI 1957 s Edward & Mary. Berea Coll; EDS; Epis TS in Kentucky; Morehead St U; Prestonsburg Cmnty Coll. D 5/25/1995 P 12/21/1995 Bp Don Adger Wimberly. m 12/15/1991 Kay Hale Ross c 4. S Raphael's Ch Lexington KY 2008-2016; Mssn Dvlp Dio Lexington Lexington 2003-2008, Cn 2000-2009, Dep Gc 2000-2003; S Jas Epis Ch Prestonsburg KY 1999-2005; P-in-c S Davids Ch Pikeville KY 1998-2000. E Kentucky Sci Cntr - Treas/Mem Of The Bd Dir; Floyd Cnty Bd Educ - Chairman/Vice-Chairman/Mem 1998-2002. Big Sandy Reg'S Most Popular Cler Floyd Cnty Times 2003; Admiral Kentucky Natural Resources & Environ Protection Cbnt 2003; Outstanding Young Men Of Amer 1987; St. Geo'S Awd BSA 1987; Colonel Gvnr Off/Commonwealth Of Kentucky 1978; Fac Serv Awd Prestonsburg Cmnty Coll.

ROSS, Nancy J (Cal) 1245 10th Ave E, Seattle WA 98102 **S Mk's Cathd Seattle WA 2017-** B New York 1959 d Joseph & Eileen. BA St Bonaventure U 1980; MFA SUNY Purchase 1997; MDiv CDSP 2014. D 12/5/2015 Bp Chester Lovelle Talton P 6/21/2016 Bp Gregory Harold Rickel. m 8/1/1981 James Patrick Herrmann c 2.

ROSS, Patricia Lynn (Cal) 215 10th Ave, San Francisco CA 94118 B Modesto CA 1951 d Robert & Maxine. BA Sch for Deacons 1995. D 7/22/1995 Bp Jerry Alban Lamb. c 3. D The Epis Ch Of S Jn The Evang San Francisco CA 1996-1998; D Trin Ch Folsom CA 1995-1996. NAAD.

ROSS, Robert (Ct) 91 Miry Brook Rd, Danbury CT 06810 B Winchester MA 1950 s Clinton & Kathryn. ALB Harv 1984; MDiv VTS 1992. D 5/30/1992 P 2/13/1993 Bp David Elliot Johnson. m 1/25/1986 Sarah Hallock Ross c 2. The Par Of Emm Ch Weston CT 2012-2014; S Matt's Epis Ch Wilton CT 2009-2012; Wooster Sch Danbury CT 2005-2012; Dio California San Francisco CA 2002-2006, Exec Coun 2002-2003; R Trin Par Menlo Pk CA 1999-2005; Congrl Stds Adv Comm EDS Cambridge MA 1997-1999; R S Ptr's Ch Osterville MA 1995-1999; Asst to R S Paul's Epis Ch Alexandria VA 1992-1995. "How to Create a Third Serv," *LivCh*, LivCh Fndt, 2007; Auth, "Bldg Up the Ch," *Foward Mvmt*, Forw Mvmt Press, 1996; Auth, "When Your Newcomers Don't Speak Engl," *Congregations*, The Alb Inst, 1994. NAES.

ROSS, Robert Layne (Ala) 2636 River Grand Cir, Vestavia AL 35243 **Ret 1996-** B Covington KY 1928 s Robert & Ruth. BA Samford U 1963; MDiv Sewanee: The U So, TS 1966. D 6/18/1966 Bp Charles C J Carpenter P 4/1/1967 Bp George Mosley Murray. m 7/27/1998 Martha C Ross c 4. Assoc S Mary's-On-The-Highlands Epis Ch Birmingham AL 1996-1998; Assoc The Cathd Ch Of The Adv Birmingham AL 1979-1995; Dir of Outreach Bapt Hlth System Birmingham AL 1975-1996; R H Cross Trussville AL 1969-1979; Dio Alabama Birmingham 1968-1976; R Ch of The Trsfg Birmingham AL 1968-1974; Chapl Marion Inst & Judson Coll Marion AL 1966-1968; S Wilfrid's Ch Marion AL 1966-1968; R St Michaels/H Cross Uniontown AL 1966-1968. Auth, "arts In Var mag". AAPC; Apha; SACEM.

ROSS, Robert William (LI) 225 Surinam St, Punta Gorda FL 33983 **Died 4/14/2017** B Brooklyn NY 1954 s William & Elizabeth. BA Nyack Coll 1981; MDiv Sewanee: The U So, TS 1986. D 6/30/1986 Bp Henry Boyd Hucles III P 2/12/1987 Bp Robert Campbell Witcher Sr. c 1. R Ch Of Chr The King E Meadow NY 1996-2007; Cur Ch Of The Adv Westbury NY 1986-1996. Auth, *S Lk Journ of Theol*, 1987.

ROSS, Rowena Jane (RG) B San Antonio TX 1946 D 7/30/2005 Bp Jeffrey Neil Steenson. m 6/14/1969 Ronald E Ross c 2.

ROSS, Sue Ann (Dal) 2679 Orchid Dr, Richardson TX 75082 **D Epis Ch Of The Ascen Dallas TX 2000-** B Dallas TX 1945 d Clarence & Emma. Lic Angl TS 1999. D 6/3/2000 Bp James Monte Stanton. m 4/28/1971 Lanny Martin Ross c 2. Exec Dir/Chapl Cathd Garden Apartments Dallas TX 2003-2013.

ROSSER SR, James Bernard (At) 2703 Sanibel Ln Se, Smyrna GA 30082 B Savannah GA 1946 s J C & Mildred. BS Florida A&M U 1970; MEd Armstrong Atlantic St U 1980; MDiv GTS 1984. D 6/2/1984 Bp George Paul Reeves P 3/1/1985 Bp Harry Woolston Shipps. m 8/18/1980 Mary Natson c 2. Assoc S Jude's Ch Marietta GA 2007-2013; P-in-c S Mary's 2005-2006; P-in-c S Paul's Epis Ch Atlanta GA 2001-2002; Assoc R for Urban Mssn S Anne's Epis Ch Atlanta GA 1996-1998; Vic The Epis Ch Of S Jn And S Mk Albany GA 1986-1996; Vic Ch Of The Gd Shpd Thomasville GA 1986, D 1984-1985. Co-Auth, "The Afr Frgn Plcy of Secy of St Henry Kissinger," 2007; Co-Auth, "Liberian Politics," *the Portrait by Amer Dplma J. Milton Turner*, 2002; Co-Auth, "Henry Highland Garnet Revisited," *The Journ of Negro Hist*, 1983. OHC 1983.

ROSSI, Kim Elizabeth (WNY) St Stephen's Episcopal Church, PO Box 446, Olean NY 14760 **S Steph's Ch Olean NY 2013-** B Amsterdam NY 1953 d Elmer & Patricia. BS SUNY of Brockport 1979; MSW SUNY Albany Sch of Soc Wk 1987; MDiv Bex Sem 2008; MDiv Bex Sem 2008. D 7/22/2006 P 5/2/2008 Bp Michael Garrison. m 7/14/1995 Owen Kenneth Gould. S Lk's Epis Ch Attica NY 2013.

ROSSO, Patricia Anne (Cal) 716 Hensley Ave # 1, San Bruno CA 94066 **Died 5/2/2017** B Oakland CA 1954 d Richard & Bernice. BA San Francisco St U 1978; BA Sch for Deacons 1992. D 12/6/2003 Bp William Edwin Swing. DOK 2005.

ROTCHFORD, Lisa Marie (Los) 24352 Via Santa Clara, Mission Viejo CA 92692 B Washington DC 1963 d Charles & Monica. BS Syr 1984; MDiv VTS 1991. D 4/18/1991 Bp Robert Poland Atkinson P 1/1/1992 Bp Frederick Houk Borsch. St Jas the Great Epis Ch Newport Bch CA 2001-2003; S Wilfrid Of York Epis Ch Huntington Bch CA 1995-1996; S Jn Chrys Ch Rcho Sta Marg CA 1991-1995.

ROTH, Frank Alwin (Ala) 2310 Skyland Blvd E, Tuscaloosa AL 35405 B Baton Rouge LA 1947 s Walter & Ada. BSF LSU 1970; MS LSU 1972; DF Steph F Austin St U 1983. D 4/25/2004 P 10/23/2004 Bp Larry Maze. m 1/18/1969 Beverly Tye Roth c 3. R S Mths Epis Ch Tuscaloosa AL 2008-2013.

ROTH, Marilyn Lee (EO) 1805 Minnesota St, The Dalles OR 97058 B The Dalles OR 1949 d Keith & Eleanor. Bus Degree Geo Fox U 2001; MA Geo Fox U 2008. D 5/28/2014 Bp Bavi Edna Rivera. m 7/12/1970 Mark Richard Roth c 2.

ROTH, Nancy Leone (O) 330 Morgan St, Oberlin OH 44074 **Assoc Chr Ch Oberlin OH 1999-, 1992-2001; Retreat Conductor 1981-; Fac Credo Inst Inc. Memphis TN 1981-** B New York NY 1936 d Robert & Gertrude. BA Ob 1958; MDiv GTS 1981. D 6/13/1981 Bp Paul Moore Jr P 12/19/1981 Bp James Stuart Wetmore. m 6/20/1959 Robert N Roth c 2. Chapl Spouses of the Bishops of ECUSA 2005-2007; Int S Andr's Epis Ch Elyria OH 1995-1996; Meditation Tchr Manhattan Plaza New York NY 1987-1991; H Sprt Sum Chap W Cornwall CT New York NY 1984-1991; CE Consult Trin Ch Wall St New York NY 1984-1991; Prog Coordntr H Cross Monstry W Pk NY 1984-1986; Trin Par New York NY 1984-1985; The GTS New York NY 1981-1982. Auth, "Sprtlty," *Epis Life*, 2001; Auth, *Invitation to Chr Yoga*, Cowley, 2001; Auth, *New Every Morning: Meditation on Hymns*, Ch Pub Inc, 2000; Auth, *Meditations for Choir Members*, Morehouse Pub, 1999; Auth, "Awake," *My Soul: Meditations on Hymns*, Ch Pub Inc, 1999; Auth, *A Closer Walk: Meditating on Hymns*, Ch Pub Inc, 1998; Auth, *Organic Pryr*, Cowley Press, 1993; Auth, *Praise my Soul: Meditation on Hymns*, Ch Pub, 1991; Auth, *Praying: A Bk for Chld*, Ch Hymnal, 1991; Auth, *The Breath of God*, Cowley Press, 1990; Auth, *A New Chr Yoga*, Cowley Press, 1989; Auth, *We Sing of God: A Hymnal for Chld*, Ch Hymnal, 1989. EPF 1980; Ord of S Helena, Assoc 1977. DD GTS 2010; Bk Awd for Excellence AAR 1994; J Wilson Sutton Prize for hon thesis GTS 1981.

R

ROTH JR, Ralph Carl (Be) Phoebe Berks Village, 9 Reading Dr Apt 242, Wernersville PA 19565 B Philadelphia PA 1936 s Ralph & Pauline. BA Tem 1962; BD TS of The Reformed Epis Ch PA 1962; MDiv PDS 1965. D 6/12/1965 Bp Robert Lionne DeWitt P 12/18/1965 Bp Andrew Y Tsu. c 3. Trin Epis Ch Mt Pocono PA 1967-1998; Cur S Phil in the Fields Oreland PA 1965-1967; Serv Reformed Epis Ch 1962-1964. R Emer Trin Epis Ch 2000; Sr Theol Awd Reformed Epis Sem 1962; OT Exegesis Awd Reformed Epis Sem 1962; Knights Of Pythias Awd Tem 1962.

ROTHAUGE, Arlin John (Ore) 197 Lighthouse Ln, Friday Harbor WA 98250 **SJI Disaster Response Vol Amer Red Cross 2000-** B Eugene OR 1938 s Arvid & Mildred. BA U of Oregon 1961; BA U of Oregon/ NCC 1961; BD Phillips U 1965; PhD U of Glasgow Gb 1968; PhD U of Glasgow, Scotland 1968; DD Ya Berk 1987. D 12/17/1973 Bp James Walmsley Frederic Carman P 12/1/1974 Bp Matthew Paul Bigliardi. m 10/7/1989 Earlene Macneill c 2. Prof Of Congrl Stds Bexley Seabury Fed Chicago IL 1995-2000; Congreg Dvlpmt Epis Ch Cntr New York NY 1981-1994; R All SS Ch Portland OR 1975-1980; Chapl Oregon Epis Schools Portland OR 1974-1975. Auth, "Catechism: The Outline Of The Faith We Profess," Epis Ch Ctr; Auth, "Sizing Up The Cong," Epis Ch Ctr; Auth, "Parallel Dvlpmt," Epis Ch Ctr.

ROTTGERS, Steven Robert (WMo) 3521 NW Winding Woods Drive, Lees Summit MO 64064 **Cn to the Ordnry Dio W Missouri Kansas City MO 2012-** B Fort Thomas KY 1954 s Robert & Wanda. BA No Kentucky St U 1975; MDiv Epis TS in Kentucky 1980; DMin SWTS 2007. D 5/11/1980 Bp Addison Hosea P 12/12/1980 Bp Gray Temple. m 8/2/1979 Mary G Hassenstein c 3. Int S Anne's Ch Lees Summit MO 2011-2012; R Gr Epis Ch Georgetown TX 2007-2011; Corp Chapl Amerex Corp Trussville AL 1999-2006; R H Cross Trussville AL 1997-2006; Dio Michigan Detroit MI 1994-1997; Prof Cleary Bus Coll Ypsilanti Michigan 1989-1995; Chr The King Epis Ch Yorktown VA 1987-1993; Dio Sthrn Virginia Newport News VA 1985-1986; Assoc S Jn's Ch Hampton VA 1982-1985; Assoc S Jn's Ch Florence SC 1980-1981. Auth, "Servnt Ldrshp Workbook," Vervante, 2012; Auth, "Taming the Dragon within Us," Vervante, 2011; Auth, "You Are Not Just a Vol," Vervante, 2010; Auth, "Ripe for the Harvest," Vervante, 2007; Auth, "I am Yours!," *The Entheos Ldr*, Vervante, 2006; Auth, "Rethinking Par Structures: The Quality Questions," Vervante, 2005; Auth, "A Stwdshp Parable," *Outstanding In His Field*, Proctor Pub, 1995; Auth, "Shaping Our Future," *Shaping Our Future*, Cowley Pub, 1995; Auth, "The Entheos Ldr," *Ldrshp for New Apostolic Era*, Vervante, 1993. srottgers@diowestmo.org

ROUFFY, Edward Albert (Colo) 950 SW 21st Ave Apt 402, Portland OR 97205 **Ret 1999-** B New York NY 1936 s Fernand & Deborah. BA U of So Carolina 1958; MDiv Sewanee: The U So, TS 1961. D 6/24/1961 Bp Clarence Alfred Cole P 7/14/1962 Bp Randolph R Claiborne. m 7/1/1961 Virginia Rouffy c 3. R S Jos's Par Buena Pk CA 1992-1999; Int S Paul's Epis Ch Steamboat Sprngs CO 1991-1992; R Chr's Epis Ch Castle Rock CO 1982-1991; R Ch Of The Ascen Salida CO 1969-1982; R Gr Ch Buena Vista CO 1969-1982; Vic S Andr's Ch Cripple Creek CO 1965-1969; S Lk's Ch Westcliffe CO 1965-1969; Cur S Jn's Epis Ch Boulder CO 1963-1965; Cur Chr Ch Macon GA 1961-1963.

ROULETTE, Philip Burwell (Md) 3738 Butler Road, Glyndon MD 21071 **Died 11/7/2015** B Hagerstown MD 1940 s George & Page. BA W&L 1964; MDiv VTS 1967. D 6/20/1967 P 5/1/1968 Bp Harry Lee Doll. m 6/8/1968 Clover Purvis. Chair - Bd Trst Open Gates Clnc 1992-1999; Bd Epis Soc Mnstrs Dio Maryland Baltimore MD 1976-2003; R S Jn's Ch Reisterstown MD 1974-2003; Vic S Chris Epis Ch Linthicum Hts MD 1970-1973; Asst The Ch Of The Redeem Baltimore MD 1967-1970. Auth, "The Baltimore Declaration Of Faith," 1991. Soc Of The Cincinatti, Chapl-Gnrl 1996. Awd Of Recognition Epis Soc Of Ministers of Maryland.

ROUMAS, Peisha Geneva (WMo) 913 E 100th Ter, Kansas City MO 64131 B Maywood CA 1942 D 2/7/2004 Bp Barry Howe. m 9/1/1963 William Stephen Roumas c 3.

ROUNDS, James Arlen (Wyo) PO Box 1194, Laramie WY 82073 B Mountain View WY 1935 s Arlin & Tressa. BSLE U of Wyoming 1959. D 6/6/2015 P 12/18/2015 Bp John Smylie. m 4/30/1966 Ida M Jones c 3.

ROUNDTREE, Ella Louise (NY) 311 Huguenot St, New Rochelle NY 10801 B North Carolina 1952 d DeWitt & Lucille. BS City Coll of New York 1976; MS City Coll of New York 1978. D 5/4/2013 Bp Andrew Marion Lenow Dietsche. m 8/29/1998 Enrique Davis c 1.

ROUNDTREE, Philip (Cal) 60 Martinez Ct, Novato CA 94945 B Freeport NY 1952 s Philip & Mary. PhD Grad Theol Un; BA Ya 1974; MDiv EDS 1979. D 6/23/1979 P 2/18/1980 Bp John Harris Burt. m 6/24/2006 Jodi D Weitz c 3. P-in-c S Steph's Epis Ch Sebastopol CA 2010-2011; Instr CDSP Berkeley CA 1990-1998; R S Fran Of Assisi Ch Novato CA 1982-2010; Asst S Mich And All Ang Par Corona Dl Mar CA 1979-1982.

ROUSE, Albertine (Los) 2500 Honolulu Ave #236, Montrose CA 91020 **Died 12/16/2016** B Laurel MS 1943 d Albert & Myrtle. DMin Fuller TS; BS Alcorn St U 1965; MDiv Duke DS 1996. D 1/27/2002 Bp Chester Lovelle Talton P 9/8/2002 Bp Joseph Jon Bruno. m 10/12/1990 Robert Milton Rouse. Ch Of

The H Comm Gardena CA 2004-2011; Chr The Gd Shpd Par Los Angeles CA 2003-2004.

ROUSE, Charles Ernest (NCal) D 6/6/2015 P 9/8/2016 Bp Barry Leigh Beisner.

ROUSER, John Richard (ETenn) 7555 Ooltewah Georgetown Rd, Ooltewah TN 37363 B Winston-Salem NC 1959 s James & June. Spec Educ Lenoir-Rhyne Coll 1984. D 2/7/2015 Bp George Young III. m 6/25/1988 Gerry Rouser c 2.

ROUSSEAU, Sean Kenneth (Va) St Paul's Episcopal Church, 6750 Fayette St, Haymarket VA 20169 **R S Paul's Ch Haymarket VA 2016-, 2012-2014** B Riverside CA 1968 s Kenneth & Mary. BA S Chas Borromeo Sem 1991; MDiv S Chas Borromeo Sem 1994. Rec 4/3/2011 Bp Shannon Sherwood Johnston. m 7/7/2011 Kerry N Rousseau c 1. P-in-c Dio Virginia Richmond VA 2012-2015, Com on the Diac 2012-; Other Cler Position S Jn's Epis Ch Mc Lean VA 2012; S Ptr's Ch Oak Grove Oak Grove VA 2012; Int Asst R Chr Epis Ch Winchester VA 2011; P-in-c Montross & Washington Par King Geo VA 2011. stpaulsepiscopalhaymarket@gmail.com

ROUSSELL, Chris (SD) Emmanuel Episcopal Church, 717 Quincy St, Rapid City SD 57701 **R Emm Epis Par Rapid City SD 2014-, P-in-c 2013** B Metairie LA 1971 s Francis & Betty. BA LSU 1993; MDiv Notre Dame 2003; MDiv Notre Dame 2003. Rec 9/26/2013 as Priest Bp Edward Stuart Little II. m 4/21/2007 Alison F Roussell. frchris@emmanuelrc.org

ROWAN, Mary Elizabeth (Minn) **Yth Dir S Lk's Epis Ch Hastings MN 2006-** D 6/20/2015 P 6/21/2016 Bp Brian N Prior.

ROWE, Deryl Tobias (Ark) B 1971 D 3/19/2016 P 10/1/2016 Bp Larry Benfield. m 6/27/1998 Natasha Anne Lindsay c 3.

ROWE, Gary Lee (Del) 913 Wilson Road, Wilmington DE 19803 **Cn Dio Delaware Wilmington 2005-, GC Alt Dep 2006-, Stndg Com, Pres 2003-2004, GC Dep 2003-, Stndg Com 2000-2004, GC Alt Dep 2000-, Dioc Coun 1997-2000** B Newport News VA 1955 s Ernest & Dorothy. AB Davidson Coll 1977; MM U Cinc 1979; MDiv EDS 1982. D 6/11/1982 Bp William Grant Black P 2/4/1983 Bp Lyman Cunningham Ogilby. m 10/2/1983 Leslie Acker c 2. R S Dav's Epis Ch Wilmington DE 1996-2005; Assoc R Estrn Shore Chap Virginia Bch VA 1989-1996; R Gr Ch Newport News VA 1984-1988; Asst S Anne's Ch Abington PA 1982-1984; Exec Bd Dio Sthrn Virginia Newport News VA 1987-1988. garyrowe@dioceseofdelaware.org

ROWE, Grayce O'Neill (Va) 1423 E Blue Wash Rd, New River AZ 85087 **P-in-c S Paul's Epis Par Pt Of Rocks MD 2012-** B Huntington NY 1947 d George & Marion. AAS Suffolk Cnty Cmnty Coll 1967; BS SUNY 1974; Duke DS 1993; MDiv GTS 1994. D 6/23/1994 Bp Robert Carroll Johnson Jr P 12/23/1994 Bp Huntington Williams Jr. m 3/5/2011 James Rowe c 3. R S Alb's Epis Ch Annandale VA 2005-2011; Assoc R S Paul's Epis Ch Winston Salem NC 1999-2004; Vic S Mk's Epis Ch Roxboro NC 1994-1998; Fin Fac - CREDO II Credo Inst Inc. Memphis TN 2008-2011.

ROWE, Jacquelyn (NJ) PO Box 326, Pine Beach NJ 08741 B Miami FL 1947 d Albert & Ellen. Ottawa U; U of Nthrn Colorado; BA Pepperdine U 1978; MDiv GTS 1998. D 6/20/1998 Bp John Lewis Said P 12/1/1998 Bp Calvin Onderdonk Schofield Jr. c 2. S Thos Epis Ch Red Bank NJ 2013-2015; Ch Of S Clem Of Rome Belford NJ 2011-2012; Exec Dir of Mnstry Chr Ch Toms River Toms River NJ 2006-2009; R Ch Of The Gd Shpd Mobile AL 2002-2004; Wilmer Hall Mobile AL 2001-2002; R S Geo's Epis Ch Riviera Bch FL 1998-2001. revjrowe@yahoo.com

ROWE, Mary Stone (Mont) B Richmond VA 1947 d James & Elizabeth. D 12/2/1995 P 9/14/2000 Bp Charles I Jones III. m 6/7/1969 Thomas Rowe c 2.

ROWE, Matthew Robert (NwT) Emmanuel Episcopal Church, 3 S Randolph St, San Angelo TX 76903 **R Emm Epis Ch San Angelo TX 2012-; Chapl Cmnty Hospice Batesville MS 2011-; Duncan M. Gray Camp & Conf Cntr Bd Managers Dio Mississippi Jackson MS 2011-, Exec Com 2011-, Exec Com 2011-, GC Alt Dep 2011-** B Bellflower CA 1963 s Robert & Catherine. BS Biola U 1986; MDiv Epis TS of the SW 1993. D 6/12/1993 Bp Chester Lovelle Talton P 12/17/1993 Bp William Harvey Wolfrum. m 10/7/1995 Elizabeth E Rowe c 2. R Ch Of The Nativ Greenwood MS 2006-2012; Assoc R Trin Epis Ch Baton Rouge LA 2005-2006; R S Pat's Ch Zachary LA 2001-2005; R S Chris's Ch Bandera TX 2000-2001; Cur Gr Ch Of W Feliciana St Francisville LA 1997-2000; S Jn Mssn Laurel Hill St Francisville LA 1997-2000; Cur Gr And S Steph's Epis Ch Colorado Sprg CO 1994-1997; Cur S Mk's Epis Ch Durango CO 1993-1994.

ROWE, Michael Gordon (SwFla) 9213 Estero River Cir, Estero FL 33928 **R S Mary's Epis Ch Bonita Sprg FL 2005-** B Manning AB CA 1955 s Thomas & Elizabeth. BA McGill U 1977; MA Oxf GB 1979; MDiv Montreal TS CA 1980; STM McGill U 1983; DMin Sewanee: The U So, 2005. Trans 11/1/1992 as Priest Bp Edward Cole Chalfant. m 7/8/1978 Dianne Calista Rowe c 2. R Ch Of S Thos Camden ME 1992-2005; Actg R Ch Of Bermuda 1991-1992; R Ch Of Can 1980-1991. RECTOR@STMARYSBONITA.ORG

ROWE, Randi Hicks (WNY) 9 Cedar St, Lockport NY 14094 **Instr California U of Mgmt and Sciences 2016-; S Andr's Ch Newfane Burt NY 2016-; S Jn's Ch Wilson NY 2016-; Outreach Spec Jewish Coun for the Aging 2015-** B Richmond Va 1959 d Elmore & Mildred. MS Virginia Commonwealth U 1980; MBA W&M 1988; MACE VTS 2011. D 1/6/2016 P 8/13/2016 Bp Susan Goff. m 3/18/1989 Thomas K Rowe. Ch Of The Resurr Alexandria VA 2015-2016; Other Lay Position S Mk's Ch Highland MD 2011-2013; Other Lay Position S Dunst's Ch Mc Lean VA 2008-2011. saintandrewspriest@gmail.com

ROWE, Richard Charles (NwPa) 706 Wilhelm Rd, Hermitage PA 16148 **Dioc Coun Dio NW Pennsylvania Erie PA 2006-** B Sharon PA 1947 s Walter & Ruth. BS Youngstown St U 1973; MS Youngstown St U 1974; Dioc Sch for Mnstry Titusville PA 2000. D 5/18/2002 P 11/17/2002 Bp Robert Deane Rowley Jr. m 7/6/1968 Patricia Meehan c 2. P-in-c Ch Of The Redeem Hermitage PA 2002-2010. Int Mnstry Ntwk 2002.

ROWE, Richard Charles (WNC) 64 Oak Gate Dr, Hendersonville NC 28739 **Systems Coach, Dept Cong Vitality S Jn's Epis Ch Marion NC 2011-; Dio Wstrn No Carolina Asheville NC 2011-** B Oakland CA 1941 s Ralph & Mary. BA U CA 1963; MDiv EDS 1966; Urban Trng Cntr 1967. D 6/19/1966 Bp James Albert Pike P 10/4/1967 Bp George Richard Millard. m 12/30/1965 Katherine O Rowe. Int S Ptr's Par San Pedro CA 2009-2010; Int Ch Of The Redeem Shelby NC 2005-2009; Int Ch Of The Epiph Laurens SC 2005; Int S Fran of Assisi Chapin SC 2004; Int S Alb's Ch Davidson NC 2002-2003; Cn Dev Mssn/Mnstry Dio Wstrn New York Tonawanda NY 1991-2002; S Annes Ch Mililani HI 1991; Inst For Human Serv Inc Honolulu HI 1989-1991; Vic S Matt's Epis Ch Waimanalo HI 1989-1990; S Steph's Ch Wahiawa HI 1986-1989; R S Ptr's Ch Honolulu HI 1982-1985; S Ambr Epis Ch Foster City CA 1974-1982; Asst S Ptr's Epis Ch Redwood City CA 1971-1973; Vic The Epis Ch Of The Gd Shpd Berkeley CA 1967-1970; Chapl Foster City Dept Of Publ Sfty. Auth, "Prevention Of Chld Abuse: A Manual For Epis Schools"; Auth, "Of Chld Abuse"; Auth, "The Role Of Educators & Caregivers In The Prevention," *Detection & Reporting*.

ROWE, Sandra Jeanne (CFla) PO Box 2206, Breckenridge CO 80424 B Arcadia FL 1946 d Raymond & Ellen. BA Stetson U 1968; MEd Stetson U 1981; EdD U of Cetnral Floriday Orlando FL 1997. D 12/8/1990 Bp John Wadsworth Howe. m 12/30/1967 Gary Robert Rowe c 1. Dir Of Fam Mnstry Epis Ch Of S Jn The Bapt Breckenridge CO 2005-2009; Personl Dir Richland Sch Dist I.

✠ ROWE, The Rt Rev Sean Walter (NwPa) 1870 Henley Pl, Fairview PA 16415 **VTS Alexandria VA 2016-; Dio Bethlehem Bethlehem PA 2014-; Bp of NW Pennsylvania Dio NW Pennsylvania Erie PA 2007-** B Sharon PA 1975 s Richard & Patricia. BA Grove City Coll 1997; MDiv VTS 2000; DD VTS 2009. D 5/27/2000 P 12/2/2000 Bp Robert Deane Rowley Jr Con 9/8/2007 for NwPa. m 9/30/2005 Carly Rowe c 1. R S Jn's Ch Franklin PA 2000-2007. seanwrowe@gmail.com

ROWE-GUIN, Kathy (Va) 5911 Fairview Woods Dr, Fairfax Station VA 22039 **S Marg's Ch Woodbridge VA 2013-** B Dallas TX 1959 d Joseph & Elizabeth. BA Texas Tech U 1981; Tchr Cred Chapman Univerity 1999; MDiv VTS 2011. D 6/4/2011 P 12/10/2011 Bp Shannon Sherwood Johnston. m 6/11/1988 David Guin c 2. S Peters-In-The-Woods Epis Ch Fairfax Sta VA 2011-2013.

ROWELL, Emily Elizabeth (Va) 526 Fontana Dr, Charlottesville VA 22911 **Ch Of S Jn The Bapt Ivy VA 2016-** B Gainesville FL 1988 d William & Carolyn. BA U of Virginia 2010; MDiv Vanderbilt Div 2013. D 5/9/2015 Bp John Mckee Sloan Sr P 12/12/2015 Bp Susan Goff. m 5/14/2011 Daniel Craig Brown. S Mary's Epis Ch Richmond VA 2015-2016; Dio Washington Washington DC 2015.

ROWELL, Ernest Michael (USC) PO Box 847, Ocklawaha FL 32183 **Ret 1998-** B Ocala FL 1944 s Ernest & Dot. BS Florida St U; MDiv Sewanee: The U So, TS. D 6/13/1973 P 6/4/1974 Bp Edward Hamilton West. m 6/3/1972 Amy S Rowell c 2. Int H Trin Epis Ch Fruitland Pk FL 2008-2009; R S Monica's Epis Ch Naples FL 1999; R S Thad Epis Ch Aiken SC 1998, 1985-1997; R S Patricks Ch Albany GA 1978-1985; The Epis Ch Of The Annunc Vidalia GA 1976-1978; Ch Of The Gd Shpd Jacksonville FL 1973-1976.

ROWELL, Rebecca E (Ga) 6329 Frederica Rd, St Simons Island GA 31522 **Chr Ch Frederica St Simons Is GA 2014-** B Moultrie GA 1954 d Lawrence & Earlene. BS U GA 1976; MEd U GA 1977; MPA Georgia Sthrn U 1992. D 11/4/2009 Bp Henry Irving Louttit P 4/23/2015 Bp Scott Anson Benhase. m 5/25/1985 Charles Lamkin.

ROWINS, Charles Howard (Los) 1 Warrenton Rd, Baltimore MD 21210 **Admin JHU Baltimore MD 1995-** B Pasadena CA 1942 s Edward & Lucille. BA U CA 1963; MA GW 1966; MDiv GTS 1969; DMin PrTS 1987. D 6/22/1969 Bp William G Wright P 12/20/1969 Bp Horace W B Donegan. m 6/4/1983 Suzanne M Rowins c 2. P-in-c St Chris By The Sea Gibson Island MD 1997-1999; Headmaster S Jas' Sch Los Angeles CA 1982-1996; Headmaster S Steph's Epis Sch Austin TX 1980-1982; Chapl Kent Sch Kent CT 1971-1980; Asst S Thos Ch New York NY 1969-1971. Auth, *Holding Action: An Understanding of the Ch*, Forw Mvmt Press.

ROWLAND, Kenneth George (Ga) 6463 Cobbham Rd, Appling GA 30802 **P Trin Ch Harlem Harlem GA 2012-** B New York NY 1931 s Edwin & Elizabeth. BS SUNY 1956; MA NYU 1958. D 9/12/2006 P 3/24/2007 Bp Henry Irving Louttit. P Chr Ch Augusta GA 2009-2012; P H Cross Ch Thomson GA 2007-2008.

ROWLAND, Thomas Dayle (RG) St Paul's Episcopal Church, PO Box 949, Truth Or Consequences NM 87901 B Altus Oklahoma 1962 s Thomas & Rober-

ta. BA Atenisi U 1990. Trans 4/12/2013 as Priest Bp Michael Vono. Vic St Pauls Epis Ch Truth Consq NM 2013-2014; Asst P S Alb's Ch El Paso TX 2009-2011; Serv Ch in Prov of Melanesia 1995-2008; Serv Ch in Prov of Melanesia 1995-2008.

ROWLES, Stephen Paul (Va) 9116 Shewsbury Dr, New Kent VA 23124 **R S Ptr's Par New Kent VA 2006-; Pstr Ass't to the R Emm Ch Woodstock VA 2000-** B Halifax VA 1953 s James & Ruth. BA U Rich 1984; MDiv SE Bapt TS 1986; DMin Estrn Bapt TS 1996. D 10/5/2002 P 4/5/2003 Bp Peter J Lee. m 8/8/1981 Cynthia K Rowles. R Beckford Par Woodstock VA 2002-2006; Pstr Ass't to the R Emm Ch Brook Hill Richmond 2002-2003; Reg IX Rep to the Exec Bd Dio Virginia Richmond VA 2013-2016, Dn of Reg IX 2010-2013, Dn of Reg IX 2010-2013. stpeters.rector@gmail.com

ROWLEY, Angela (Ct) Yale New Haven Hospital, 20 York Street, New Haven CT 06510 **Asst S Ptr's Epis Ch Milford CT 2008-; Attending Chapl Yale New Haven Hosp New Haven CT 2008-** B Glasgow Scotland 1946 d John & Margaret. MDiv Ya Berk 2005. D 6/11/2005 Bp Andrew Donnan Smith P 1/28/2006 Bp James Elliot Curry. c 4. P Trin Ch Branford CT 2006-2008; S Jn's Epis Ch Kula HI 2000-2013.

✠ ROWTHORN, The Rt Rev Jeffery William (Ct) 17 Woodland Dr, Salem CT 06420 **Adj Prof Yale and Berkeley Div Schools 2003-; Ret Bp Suffr of Convoc of Ch in Europe Convoc of Epis Ch in Europe Paris 2002-, Bp-in-Charge 1994-2001** B Newport Monmouthshire UK 1934 s Eric & Eileen. BA U of Cambridge 1957; MDiv UTS 1961; Cuddesdon Theolgical Coll 1962; MA U of Cambridge 1962; BLitt Oxf GB 1972. Trans 12/13/1971 as Priest Bp Horace W B Donegan Con 9/19/1987 for Ct. m 11/16/1963 Anne Rowthorn c 3. Bp Suffr Dio Connecticut Meriden CT 1987-1993; Bp Goddard Assoc Prof of Pstr Theol & Wrshp Ya Berk New Haven CT 1973-1987; Assoc Prof Yale DS & Yale Inst. of Sacr Mus 1973-1987; Sum Vic S Mart's Epis Ch Fairlee VT 1969-1980; Chapl, Dn of Instrn, Asst Prof UTS in New York City 1968-1973; Serv Ch of Engl 1962-1968. Auth, "Singing Songs of Expectation," Hope Pub Co, 2007; Auth, "The Wideness of God's Mercy," Morehouse Pub, 2007; Auth, "A New Hymnal for Colleges and Schools," Yale Univ. Press, 1992; Auth, "Laudamus," Yale DS, 1980. Bishops Working for a Just Wrld; Episcopalians for Global Recon 2003; Hymn Soc of No Amer; No Amer Acad of Liturg 1973; Societas Liturgica. Ya Tercentiennial Medal Ya 2001; DD Ya Berk 1987.

ROY, Byron Willard (Roch) 19 Abbotswood Crescent, Penfield NY 14526 **Chapl The Friendly Hm Rochester NY 1992-** B Akron OH 1941 s Bruce & Florence. BA Kent St U 1974; MDiv Bex Sem 1977. D 7/3/1977 Bp Robert Rae Spears Jr P 1/1/1978 Bp John Harris Burt. S Geo's Ch Hilton NY 1978-1992; R S Geo Rochester NY 1978-1991; Cur S Lk And S Simon Cyrene Rochester NY 1978.

ROY JR, Derik Justin Hurd (Alb) 10 W High St, Ballston Spa NY 12020 **R Chr Epis Ch Ballston Spa NY 1994-** B Albany NY 1952 s Derik & Marilyn. BA SUNY 1974; MDiv Nash 1977. D 6/4/1977 Bp Wilbur Emory Hogg Jr P 12/21/1977 Bp Charles Bowen Persell Jr. m 5/19/2007 Catherine Larosa-Roy c 7. Vic S Barth's Epis Ch Mio MI 1981-1994; Vic S Fran Epis Ch Grayling MI 1981-1994; Asst Chr/St Jn's Par Champlain NY 1979-1981; Asst S Steph's Ch Delmar NY 1977-1979.

ROY, Jeffrey A (NJ) 7 Lincoln Ave, Rumson NJ 07760 **Cur S Geo's-By-The-River Rumson NJ 2011-; Chair, Nomin Com Dio New Jersey Trenton NJ 2013-** B Omaha NE 1964 s Virgil & Darlene. BA Bethel U 2006; MDiv GTS 2011. D 7/29/2010 P 6/30/2011 Bp Brian N Prior. m 12/31/1989 Janine R Lamm c 2. jeff@stgeorgesrumson.org

ROY, Robert Royden (Minn) 1289 Galtier St, Saint Paul MN 55117 B White Earth MN 1940 Untd St of the Twin Cities. D 8/24/1999 P 6/3/2000 Bp James Louis Jelinek. m 9/18/1993 Katherine L Masquot c 2.

ROYAL, Dorothy Kaye (Neb) St Mary's Episcopal Church, 116 S 9th St, Nebraska City NE 68410 B Nebraska City NE 1951 d Dale & Dorothy. AA Providence TS 2012. D 11/10/2012 Bp Scott Scott Barker. m 3/5/1983 Franklin Joseph Royal c 6.

ROYALS, Debbie (Az) 7945 N Village Ave, Tucson AZ 85704 **Vic S Geo's Epis Ch Holbrook AZ 2015-; Dio Arizona Phoenix AZ 2014-; The CPG New York NY 2014-; Consult Div Choices 2010-; Fac Credo Inst Inc. Memphis TN 2007-; Chair, Stndg Cmsn on Mssn & Evang GC 2012-; Congrl Dvlp Four Winds Native Amer Cong Sacramento CA 2003-** B Tucson AZ 1953 d Norman & Artemisa. RN U of AZ 1973; BA Prescott Coll 2002; MDiv CDSP 2005; MA CDSP 2006. D 1/16/2005 P 7/16/2005 Bp Mark Lawrence Macdonald. c 2. Asst R Gr St Pauls Epis Ch Tucson AZ 2013-2014; Dir of Dvlpmt Indigenous Theol Trng Inst Minneapolis MN 2011-2012, 2009-2010; P In Charge S Mich's Epis Ch Riverside CA 2011; Supply S Jos Of Arimathea Mssn Yucca Vlly CA 2008-2010; S Mart-In-The-Fields Mssn Twentynine Plms CA 2008-2010; Mssnr for Native Amer Mnstry Dvlpmt Dio Los Angeles Los Angeles CA 2006-2009; Mssnr of Native Amer Mnstry Dvlpmt The Epis Dio Nthrn California Sacramento CA 2005-2007. Auth, "Called to Lead," *First People's Theol Journ*, Indigenous Theol Trng Inst, 2012; Auth, "meditation," *Forw Mvmt Day by Day*, Forw Mvmt, 2012; Proj Design, "The Disciple's PB," *The Disciple's PB*, Indigenous Theol Trng Inst, 2012; Auth/Prod Ed, "How Red Is

R

God?/God is Still Red," *First People's Theol Journ*, Indigenous Theol Trng Inst, 2010; Prod Ed/Auth, "Oklahoma IV 2010 Spec Ed/Recognition/Liturg," *First People's Theol Journ*, Indigenous Theol Trng Inst, 2010; Contributing Auth, "Prayers," *Lifting Wmn Voices*, Moorehouse Press, 2009; Contributing Auth, "Unity in Diversity," *Those Preaching Wmn*, Judson Press, 2008; Prod Ed, "The Gospel in Four Directions," *The Gospel in Four Directions*, Prov VIII Indigenous People's Mnstry Ntwk, 2007; Contributing Auth, "Angl Comm and Homosexuality," *Two Sprt*, Angl Comm, 2007; Auth, "Remembrance, Recognition and Recon," *First People's Theol Journ*, Indigenous Theol Trng Inst, 2006; Auth, "Transformation: Jesus Walked Among Us Too," *First People's Theol Journ*, Indigenous Theol Trng Inst, 2005; Auth, "Creation: The Talking Tree," *First People's Theol Journ*, Indigenous Theol Trng Inst, 2001.

ROYALTY, Beth (At) 901 W Emery St, Dalton GA 30720 **Calv Ch Rochester MN 2017-; R St. Clem's Memi Epis Ch S Paul MN 2007-** B Boston MA 1958 d Robert & Patricia. U So 1978; BS Georgia St U 1986; MDiv Sewanee: The U So, TS 1999. D 6/5/1999 P 2/5/2000 Bp Frank Kellogg Allan. c 1. R S Mk's Ch Dalton GA 2014-2017; R S Clem's Ch S Paul MN 2007-2014; All SS Epis Ch Atlanta GA 1999-2006.

ROZENDAAL, Jay Calvin (Oly) 1134 Finnegan Way # 302, Bellingham WA 98225 **P Assoc S Paul's Ch Seattle WA 2009-** B Holland MI 1962 s John & Ardyce. BMus Westminster Choir Coll of Rider U 1982; MM Cleveland Inst of Mus 1985; MDiv GTS 2002; STM GTS 2005. D 6/29/2002 Bp Sanford Zangwill Kaye Hampton P 1/25/2003 Bp Vincent Waydell Warner. m 11/12/2009 David C Kisling. Vic Chr Epis Ch Blaine WA 2007-2009; Dio New York 2004-2005; The GTS New York NY 2002-2006; The Ch of S Ign of Antioch New York NY 2002; Co-Dir Cntr for Chr Sprtlty New York NY 2001-2006. CHS 2006; Ord of Julian of Norwich 1997-2002. jay.rozendaal@gmail.com

ROZENE, Wendy Anne (Me) 17 Fox Run Rd, Cumberland ME 04021 **D S Ann's Epis Ch Windham Windham ME 2007-; D Dio Maine Portland ME 1990-** B Lawrence MA 1950 d Alfred & Gladys. BS U of Maine 1973; MEd U of New Engl 2004. D 9/13/1990 Bp Edward Cole Chalfant. m 12/22/1973 Richard Arthur Rozene c 3. Bd Trst Bishopswood 1997-2000. NAAD.

ROZO, Oscar A (Mil) 409 S 2nd St, Watertown WI 53094 **S Mk's Ch Beaver Dam WI 2016-** B Bogota Colombia 1984 s Alvaro & Martha. Bus Admin St Aug Coll; BA Edgewood Coll 2009; MDiv VTS 2012. D 4/21/2012 P 10/21/2012 Bp Steven Andrew Miller. m 6/1/2013 Elizabeth B Tester. S Lk's Ch Whitewater WI 2013-2015; S Paul's Ch Watertown WI 2012-2013. rozo.oscar.a@gmail.com

ROZZELLE, Stephen Michael (Nwk) 400 Ramapo Avenue, Pompton Lakes NJ 07442 **P-in-c Chr Ch Pompton Lake NJ 2010-** B Washington DC 1948 s Frederick & Audrey. MDiv PDS 1973; STM NYTS 1981. D 4/28/1973 Bp Alfred L Banyard P 10/27/1973 Bp Albert Wiencke Van Duzer. m 7/5/2008 Maureen Gallivan c 3. R S Mart Mullumbimby Australia 1983-1984; R S Mk's Ch Basking Ridge NJ 1978-2006; St Peters Ch Woodbury Hgts NJ 1975-1976; Vic S Barn Mantua NJ 1974-1978; H Trin Epis Ch Wenonah NJ 1973-1978. Cmnty Of S Jn The Bapt. Humanitarian Of The Year Partnr In Ending Hunger 2003.

RUBEL, Christopher Scott (Los) 250 N Live Oak Ave, Glendora CA 91741 B Long Island NY 1933 s Henry & Dorothy. AA San Bernardino Vlly Coll 1959; BA U of Redlands 1961; BA Claremont TS 1967. D 6/18/1977 P 1/14/1978 Bp Robert Claflin Rusack. m 11/3/1985 Katherine Hauser Rubel c 2. Chapl Citrus Vlly Hlth Partnr 2001-2005; Assoc H Trin Epis Ch Covina CA 2001-2005; Assoc Gr Epis Ch Glendara CA 1979-2000; Chapl Gd Samar Hosp Los Angeles CA 1978-1991; Ther Indn Hill Cnslng Cntr Claremont CA 1972-2007. Auth, *Authentic Being as Model for Mnstry*, 1967. AAMFT; Amer Psych Assn; ACPE; CAMFT; GPASC; Natl Assn for the Self- Supporting Active Mnstry.

RUBIANO-ALVARADO, Raul (CFla) 2851 Afton Cir, Orlando FL 32825 **Assoc S Mary Of The Ang Epis Ch Orlando FL 2005-; D Dio Bogota Bogota Colombia 1983-** B Macheta Cundinamarca CO 1952 s Lucindo & Maria. U Bogota. Rec 4/1/1984 as Priest Bp Bernardo Merino-Botero. m 3/13/1980 Maria Consuelo Garcia Castro c 2. P Iglesia Epis Jesus de Nazaret Orlando FL 2005-2017; P Our Merc Sav Epis Ch Denver CO 2004-2005; Our Merc Sav Mnstrs Denver CO 2004-2005; P Ch Of S Phil And S Jas Denver CO 1998-2004; Iglesia Epis En Colombia Bogota 1995-1998, P 1984-1989; P Dio The Dominican Republic (Iglesia Epis Dominicana) Gazcue Santo Domingo 1990-1995.

RUBIN, Richard Louis (Los) 163 W. 11th St., Claremont CA 91711 **Non-par 1992-** B Pomona CA 1958 s Louis & Catherine. BA Cath U of Louvain 1980; BA U of San Diego 1980; STB Cath U of Louvain 1983. Rec 7/1/1992 as Priest Bp Frederick Houk Borsch. m 4/5/1992 Lauriel Jean Rubin c 3. R Chr Ch Par Ontario CA 1995-2017; S Geo's Ch Riverside CA 1995; Ch Of The Trsfg Arcadia CA 1994-1995; Serv RC Ch 1983-1992.

RUBINSON, Rhonda Joy (NY) 400 W 119th St Apt 11-L, New York NY 10027 **P-in-c Dio New York New York NY 2013-** B Brooklyn NY 1958 d Jacob & Arlene. BA Barnard Coll of Col 1980; MA Col GSAS 1981; MA UTS 1999. D 3/18/2000 P 9/16/2000 Bp Richard Frank Grein. Ch Of The Intsn New York NY 2013; P-in-c S Phil's Ch New York NY 2007-2012; Asst Ch Of The Heav

Rest New York NY 2000-2007. Auth, "Steroid Sprtlty," *Bk*, CreateSpace, 2015; Auth, "Lessons of the Sprt," *Bk*, Mira Pub, 2014. rev.rhondarubinson@gmail.com

RUBRIGHT, Elizabeth Alice Shemet (SwFla) D 6/29/1991 Bp Barbara Clementine Harris.

RUBY, Lorne Dale (Pa) 20 N 2nd St, Columbia PA 17512 B York PA 1937 s Sterling & Martha. BS Millersville U 1959; MS Rutgers The St U of New Jersey 1961; MDiv PDS 1971. D 6/19/1971 P 12/21/1971 Bp Robert Lionne De-Witt. m 9/4/2008 Ernest Dancil. S Phil's Ch New Hope PA 2005-2006; Int Ch Of The Annuniciation Philadelphia PA 2002-2003; Int S Thos The Apos Hollywood Los Angeles CA 2000-2002; P-in-c The Ch Of The Trin Coatesville PA 1999-2000; Int S Jn's Ch Gap PA 1998-1999.

RUCKER, James Cliff (Tex) 203 Ivy Terrace St, Lufkin TX 75901 B Ballinger TX 1952 s Harry & Dorothy. M.A. Baylor U; BA Baylor U 1973; MBA Georgia St U 1978; MDiv Nash 1997. D 6/14/1997 P 12/16/1997 Bp Robert Jefferson Hargrove Jr. m 10/5/1988 Judith Anne Hoover c 3. Dn Dio Texas SE Texas Convoc 2006-2009; R H Trin Epis Ch Port Neches TX 2002-2017; Assoc R Epis Ch Of The Gd Shpd Lake Chas LA 1999-2002; Cn & Dir Hardtner C&C Pollock LA 1998-1999; S Alb's Epis Ch Monroe LA 1997-1998; Cur S Pat's Epis Ch W Monroe LA 1997-1998.

RUDACILLE, Stephen L (SwFla) 2702 Saint Cloud Oaks Dr, Valrico FL 33594 B Winchester VA 1940 s Leonard & Carolyn. BA Lynchburg Coll 1961; BD VTS 1966. D 6/21/1966 P 5/31/1967 Bp Harry Lee Doll. m 6/23/1962 Gayle Paschal c 2. R H Innoc Epis Ch Valrico FL 1976-2005; Assoc R S Ptr's Epis Ch Charlotte NC 1975-1976; Asst R S Thos' Epis Ch St Petersburg FL 1971-1975; Vic Ch Of The Trsfg Braddock Heights MD 1967-1971; Asst S Barth's Ch Baltimore MD 1966-1971.

RUDE, David B (Nwk) 5 Estate Drive, Wantage NJ 07461 **Dir Hse of the Gd Shpd Hacketstown NJ 2015-; Part Time Gr Ch Sterling IL 2007-; P in Charge Ch Of The Gd Shpd Sussex NJ 2013-** B Cooperstown NY 1942 s John & Esther. LTh Epis TS in Kentucky 1976. D 5/16/1976 Bp Addison Hosea P 2/25/1977 Bp Morris Fairchild Arnold. m 1/16/1999 Elizabeth A Swopes c 6. Dir Los Angeles Curs Sec 2001-2006; Vic S Clare Of Assisi Rancho Cucamonga CA 2000-2007; Part Time S Ptr's Par Rialto CA 1997-1998; Part Time S Jos Of Arimathea Mssn Yucca Vlly CA 1995-1997; Part time St Columbas Epis Ch Big Bear City CA 1994-1995; Part Time S Hilary's Epis Ch Hesperia CA 1993-1994; Trin Epis Ch Redlands CA 1990-1993; All SS Epis Ch Riverside CA 1980-1990. frdavidr@aol.com

RUDER, John Williams (Oly) 602 6th St., Castlegar BC V1N2G1 Canada B Albuquerque NM 1949 s John & Mary. BS U of Wisconsin 1971; MDiv Nash 1974. D 4/19/1974 Bp Charles Thomas Gaskell P 12/21/1974 Bp William Hampton Brady. m 5/18/1974 Karen Ruder. Vic S Columba's Epis Ch Kent WA 1996-2009; Serv Ch In Can 1977-1996; Dio Fond du Lac Appleton WI 1974-1977; S Mk's Ch Oconto WI 1974-1977; S Paul's Epis Ch Suamico WI 1974-1977. Theta Alpha Phi.

RUDINOFF, Jan Charles (Haw) 2775 Kanani St, Lihue HI 96766 B Philadelphia PA 1942 s Mortimer & Virginia. BA VMI 1964; MDiv VTS 1972. D 5/27/1972 Bp Robert Bruce Hall P 5/10/1973 Bp John Joseph Meakin Harte. m 3/2/1976 Paula B Rudinoff. Incumbent Serv Angl Ch of Can Nelson BC 2004-2006; Vic Chr Memi Ch Kilauea HI 1982-1984; S Mich And All Ang Ch Lihue HI 1976-2004; Vic St Thos Ch Hanalei HI 1974-1982; Assoc S Phil's In The Hills Tucson AZ 1972-1974. Auth, "Mnstry in Resort Communities," *Alb*, 1988.

RUDOLPH, Patrick Charles (FdL) 1036 Pine Beach Rd, Marinette WI 54143 **Chapl Leesburg Reg Med Cntr 2009-; Chapl Bay Area Med Cntr 2005-; Dio Fond du Lac Appleton WI 2003-; D S Paul's Ch Marinette WI 1996-** B Marinette WI 1940 s Patrick & Dorothy. BA U of Wisconsin 1978. D 9/12/1996 Bp Russell Edward Jacobus. m 1/16/1960 Jacqueline Rudolph c 1. Asst Treas Dio Fond du Lac Appleton WI 2006-2007; Treas S Paul's Ch Marinette WI 1987-2001; Trst Dio Fond du Lac Appleton WI 2004-2007, Fin 1992-2004.

RUEF, John Samuel (SVa) 720 S Main St, Chatham VA 24531 **Died 10/31/2016** B Chicago IL 1927 s John & Leota. BA U Chi 1945; BD SWTS 1950; STM SWTS 1955; ThD Harvard DS 1960. D 5/1/1950 Bp Wallace E Conkling P 1/27/1951 Bp Charles L Street. m 10/11/1951 Jane Margraves Ruef c 4. Emm Epis Ch Chatham VA 1999-2005; R Trin Ch Gretna VA 1999-2005; Ret 1993-2016; Hd Rel Stds Dept Chatham Hall Chatham VA 1985-1993; Dn and Pres Nash Nashotah WI 1974-1985; Assoc S Paul's Memi Charlottesvlle VA 1971-1972; Prof of NT Ya Berk New Haven CT 1960-1971; Asst S Anne's Ch Lowell MA 1959-1960; P-in-c Emm Somerville MA 1957-1959; Asst Instr Bexley Seabury Fed Chicago IL 1954-1956; Vic Ch Of The H Fam Pk Forest IL 1950-1954; Cn Theol Dio Wstrn New York Tonawanda NY 1972-1974, Cn Theol 1972-1974. Auth, "The NT and the Sacraments of the Ch," Self-Pub, 1973; Auth, "Paul's First Letter to Corinth," Penguin Books, 1971; Auth, "Understanding the Gospels," Seabury Press, 1963. Angl Assn of Biblic Sci. DD SWTS 1975.

RUEHLEN, Petroula Kephala (Tex) 3541 Adrienne Ln, Lake Charles LA 70605 **Int S Paul's Epis Ch Orange TX 2012-** B Greece 1938 d Constantinos & Athena. Epis TS of the SW; BA U Thessaliniki 1961; MA LSU 1965. D

5/23/1981 Bp Willis Ryan Henton P 1/19/1991 Bp Robert Jefferson Hargrove Jr. m 9/15/1962 Thomas Ruehlen. Int S Mich And All Ang Lake Chas LA 2015-2016; Int H Trin Epis Ch Sulphur LA 2007-2012; Serv Luth Ch Orange TX 2004-2007; R H Trin Epis Ch Port Neches TX 1992-2001; Ecum Off Dio Wstrn Louisiana Alexandria LA 1991-1992, Lake Chas Convoc D 1981-1990; R Gr Ch Lk Providence LA 1991-1992; Non-par Misc 1981-1990.

RUFFIN, Hunter (SeFla) 8011 Douglas Ave, Dallas TX 75225 **S Mich And All Ang Ch Dallas TX 2015-** B Jackson MS 1980 s Charles & Ellen. BA U of Sthrn Mississippi 2004; MBA Florida Atlantic U 2010; MDiv Epis TS of the SW 2015; MDiv Sem of SW 2015. D 12/20/2014 Bp Leo Frade P 7/11/2015 Bp Rayford Baines High Jr.

RUFFINO, Russell Gabriel (Eur) Corso Cavour, 110, C.P. #81, Orvieto 05018 Italy **Vic Orvieto Epis Mssn 2008-** B Jersey City NJ 1933 s Anthony & Josephie. Lic Sacr Theol Gregorian U 1954; BA Seton Hall U 1954; PhD Gregorian U 1961. Rec 10/27/1990 as Priest Bp George Nelson Hunt III. m 8/1/1970 Barbara Ann Casey c 2. R S Ptr's By The Sea Narragansett RI 1991-2005; Acad Dn Newbury Coll Brookline MA 1990-1991; Asst S Lk's Ch Pawtucket RI 1990-1991; Prog Spec Untd States Govt 1969-1990; Serv RC Ch 1958-1969; Chair, Cler Assn Dio Rhode Island Providence RI 1993-1997. Auth, *Analysis & Critique of BF Skinner*; Ed, *Responsibility of Dissent*. FVC 2003.

RUGGABER, Michael Paul (Nev) D 7/18/2013 P 7/26/2014 Bp Dan Thomas Edwards.

RUGGER, Mildred Susan (NwT) St Andrew's Episcopal Church, 1601 S Georgia St, Amarillo TX 79102 B Spokane WA 1957 d Austin & Arline. BS Faith Bapt Bible Coll 1982; MA U of Nthrn Iowa 1986; Cert in Theol Stds Dio NW Texas Sch of Ord Mnstry 2016. D 1/23/2016 Bp James Scott Mayer. m 12/27/2002 Warren Bruce Stricker.

RUGGLES, Roxanne (Lex) Church of the Nativity, 31 E. Third St, PO Box 3, Maysville KY 41056 **Ch Of The Nativ Maysville KY 2016-; P-in-c Ch Of The Gd Shpd York SC 2014-** B Georgetown OH 1952 d Robert & Shirley. BA Asbury U 1975; MAR Asbury TS 1977; MDiv Epis TS of the SW 2009. D 1/18/2009 Bp Stacy F Sauls P 4/30/2010 Bp Rogers Sanders Harris. c 2. Asst R S Jas Epis Ch Greenville SC 2010-2014; Stwdshp Dir S Dav's Ch Austin TX 2009-2010. motherroxanne@gmail.com

RUGH, Nathan (Los) 1227 4th St, Santa Monica CA 90401 **R S Aug By-The-Sea Par Santa Monica CA 2011-** B Bethlehem PA 1973 s Alex & Lucy. BA U CO 2000; MDiv VTS 2006. D 6/10/2006 P 12/14/2006 Bp Robert John O'Neill. m 6/17/2009 Rebecca C Rugh c 3. Cur Calv Ch Pittsburgh PA 2006-2011. nate. rugh@gmail.com

RUHLE, Kay West (CFla) D 9/10/2016 Bp Gregory Orrin Brewer.

✠ **RUIZ RESTREPO, The Rt Rev Luis Fernando** (DR) Carrera 80 #53 A 78, Medellin Colombia B Medellin CO 1956 s Edildo & Isabel. Simon Bolivar U; Coast Corporetion U Tokyo Jp 1982; BTh S Thos U 1988. D 12/8/1988 P 10/21/1990 Bp Bernardo Merino-Botero Con 8/1/2009 for EcuC. m 9/7/1991 Tania Jaramillo c 2. Bp Dio The Dominican Republic (Iglesia Epis Dominicana) Gazcue Santo Domingo 2012-2014; Iglesia Epis Del Ecuador Quito 2009-2011; Iglesia Epis En Colombia Bogota 2007-2008, 1990-1998; Vic San Lucas 1988-1990.

RUIZ-RIQUER, Cynthia S (FtW) 5910 Black Oak Ln, River Oaks TX 76114 B Lockport NY 1970 d William & Lois. BA,BS U of Rhode Island 1995; MA U of Americas Puebla 1999; MDiv Epis TS Of The SW 2011; MDiv Epis TS of the SW 2011. D 10/23/2012 Bp C Wallis Ohl. m 7/30/1994 Gustavo O Ruiz-Riquer c 3. Iglesia San Francisco de Asis Austin TX 2014.

RUK, Michael (Pa) 10 Chapel Rd, New Hope PA 18938 **R S Phil's Ch New Hope PA 2012-** B Natrona Heights PA 1974 s Raymond & Frances. BA Alleg 1996; MA Duquesne U 1999; MDiv Nash 2003. D 6/14/2003 P 12/21/2003 Bp Robert William Duncan. P-in Charge All SS Epis Ch Levittown PA 2007-2012; R S Paul Ch Levittown PA 2004-2012; Asst P Trin Cathd Pittsburgh PA 2003-2004; Cathd Chapt Cathd Ch of Our Sav Philadelphia PA 2006-2011.

RULE, Alan R (CFla) 216 Orange Ave, Daytona Beach FL 32114 B Beloit WI 1942 s Richard & Gertrude. Nash; U of Wisconsin; Rock Cnty Law Enforcement Acad 1966. D 4/28/1973 Bp Donald H V Hallock P 11/1/1973 Bp Charles Thomas Gaskell. c 3. S Mary's Epis Ch Daytona Bch FL 1982-1998; St Mich & The Ang Ch Platteville WI 1977-1979; Vic S Mich & All Ang Schullsburg WI 1974-1981; S Andr's Epis Ch Monroe WI 1974-1979.

RULE II, John Henry (Okla) 1122 E 20th St, Tulsa OK 74120 **Assoc S Jn's Epis Ch Tulsa OK 2017-, 2005-2006; Assoc S Jn's Epis Ch Tulsa OK 2007-** B Wichita KS 1951 s John & Carol. BA Oklahoma City U 1972; JD U of Texas 1977; MDiv VTS 2005. D 6/25/2005 P 1/7/2006 Bp Robert Manning Moody. m 11/11/1995 Paula Inman c 3. P Ch Of The H Cross Owasso OK 2012-2013. BroSA 1999.

RUMPLE, John G (Ind) 550 University Blvd # 1410, Indianapolis IN 46202 **P S Andr's Epis Ch Greencastle IN 2013-** B Danville IN 1969 s Robert & Shirley. MDiv Emm Chr Sem 1995; MDiv Emm Chr Sem 1995; PhD U of Edinburgh 2009; Dip Ang Stud GTS 2011. D 6/18/2011 P 4/15/2012 Bp Cate Waynick. m 5/14/2011 Christian S Hoffland. D S Mk's Ch Plainfield IN 2011-2013. johnrumple@hotmail.com

RUNDLETT, Brad (Va) St Timothy's Episcopal Church, 432 Van Buren St, Herndon VA 20170 **R S Tim's Ch Herndon VA 1994-** B Atlanta GA 1949 s Brewster & Prudence. BA U GA 1972; MDiv Sewanee: The U So, TS 1981. D 6/13/1981 P 5/15/1982 Bp William Arthur Beckham. m 10/14/1989 Cecile D DeOrnellas c 4. R S Andr The Fisherman Epis Mayo MD 1989-1993; Assoc R S Jas Ch Potomac MD 1984-1989; Vic Epiph Ch Spartanburg SC 1981-1984.

RUNGE, Phillip Diedrich (Ga) 338 Lakeview Dr, Baxley GA 31513 **D S Thos Aquinas Mssn Baxley GA 2009-** B Arrington England 1957 D 5/20/2001 Bp Roger John White. D S Matt's Ch Kenosha WI 2001-2009.

RUNGE, Thomas Leonard (Lex) 7 Court Pl, Newport KY 41071 **D S Paul's Ch Newport KY 2009-** B Covington KY 1945 s Wilfred & Clara. Coll of Mt St Jos 1995. Rec 8/22/2009 Bp Stacy F Sauls. m 10/2/1999 Shelia Runge c 4.

RUNKLE, John Ander (Tenn) St Mary's Sewanee, 770 St. Mary's Lane, Sewanee TN 37375 **Consulting Proj Mgr for the Reconstruction of H Trin Cathd in Port-au-Prince, Haiti Epis Ch Cntr New York NY 2013-, 2011-2012; S Mary's Sewanee Sewanee TN 2013-; Guest Prof Wesley TS Washington DC 2009-; Adj in Aesthetical Theol VTS Alexandria VA 2008-** B Greenville NC 1957 s Charles & Mary. BA Mary Baldwin Coll 1981; BArch U of Tennessee 1984; MDiv Sewanee: The U So, TS 1999. D 6/2/1999 Bp A(rthur) Heath Light P 12/11/1999 Bp Neff Powell. m 7/14/1984 Harriet B Runkle c 1. VTS Alexandria VA 2011; Asst to the R S Mary's Epis Ch Arlington VA 2010-2013; Cathd Conservator Cathd of St Ptr & St Paul Washington DC 2005-2010; Int R Ch Of The Gd Shpd Rocky Mt NC 2003-2004; Assoc R Chr Epis Ch Roanoke VA 1999-2003. Auth, "The Gift," *Stone & Light: A Celebration of a H Place*, The SSJE, 2010; Auth, "Hidden Eternity: Marking A Sacr Space," *Living Stones: Washington Natl Cathd at 100*, Washington Natl Cathd, 2007; Auth, "Bldg and Renovating Ch: Pstr Dimensions of Sacr Space," *Sewanee Theol Revs 49:3*, U So TS, 2006; Ed/Auth, "Searching For Sacr Space," Ch Pub, 2002. Cathd Architects Assn, UK 2006; HSEC 2007. Fell-in-Res U So TS 2004. john.runkle@stmaryssewanee.org

RUNKLE, Robert Scott (Spok) 501 E Wallace Ave, Coeur D Alene ID 83814 **D S Lk's Ch Coeur D Alene ID 2012-** B Washington DC 1936 s Lloyd & Louise. BS Georgia Inst of Tech 1960. D 10/21/2012 Bp James E Waggoner Jr. m 7/12/1992 Mary Beth Jorgensen c 2.

RUNNELS, Stan (WMo) 11 E 40th St, Kansas City MO 64111 **R S Paul's Ch Kansas City MO 2006-** B Hattiesburg MS 1952 s Jessie & Florence. BS Millsaps Coll 1974; MDiv Sewanee: The U So, TS 1983; Harvard DS 2002. D 5/25/1983 Bp Christoph Keller Jr P 2/2/1984 Bp Duncan Montgomery Gray Jr. m 2/16/1980 Mary Guyton Runnels c 3. R S Jn's Ch Laurel MS 1989-2006; R S Steph's Epis Ch Indianola MS 1985-1989; S Mary's Ch Enterprise MS 1983-1985; Vic S Paul's Epis Ch Meridian MS 1983-1985; Trin Ch Newton MS 1983-1985. Chas Merrill Fllshp Harvard Div, Harv 2002.

RUNNER, Paul W (NJ) 370 Main St, Wakefield RI 02879 B Camden NJ 1947 s Edward & Elizabeth. Trenton St Coll 1968; BS Athens St U 1970; MDiv Sewanee: The U So, TS 1988. D 6/11/1988 Bp George Phelps Mellick Belshaw P 1/20/1989 Bp Vincent King Pettit. m 2/8/1969 Karen E Runner c 1. R Ch Of The Ascen Wakefield RI 2010-2014; R Trin Ch Cranston RI 1996-2010; R Ch Of The Atone Laurel Sprg NJ 1991-1996; Asst Trin Ch Moorestown NJ 1988-1990. stsimeons@comcast.net

RUNNING JR, Joseph Martin (EC) 3207 Notting Hill Rd, Fayetteville NC 28311 **H Trin Epis Ch Fayetteville NC 2017-** B Minneapolis MN 1945 s Joseph & Jeanne. BA Langston U 1987; MDiv GTS 2001. D 6/9/2001 Bp David Conner Bane Jr P 12/15/2001 Bp Edwin Max Leidel Jr. m 6/3/1988 Maureen Elizabeth Somers c 3. P-in-c S Paul's Epis Ch Clinton MO 2010-2014; R All SS' Epis Ch Duncan OK 2005-2010; R S Jn's Epis Ch Alma MI 2001-2005.

RUPP, Lawrence Dean (SO) 13 Balsam Acres, New London NH 03257 **Non-par 1966-** B Wauseon OH 1933 s Dewey & Alice. BA Coll of Wooster 1958; MDiv EDS 1961; Bos 1968. D 6/24/1961 Bp Anson Phelps Stokes Jr P 4/19/1962 Bp Roger W Blanchard. m 6/4/1982 Gail Skillings Rupp c 1. Asst Min Emm Epis Ch Wakefield MA 1965-1966; Asst Gr Epis Ch Medford MA 1963-1964; Asst S Paul And S Jas New Haven CT 1962-1963; Asst Emm Ch Boston MA 1961-1962. Faith & Sci Exch, Inst On Rel In An Age Of Sci.

RUPP, Lloyd Gary (Nev) 43 West Pacific Ave, Henderson NV 89015 B Seattle WA 1935 s Lloyd & Beverly. MA CDSP; SFTS; AA Antelope Vlly Coll 1956; BA California St U 1958; BD CDSP 1964; MS CPU 1985; PhD CPU 1987. D 7/22/1964 P 4/1/1965 Bp Clarence Rupert Haden Jr. c 2. R S Tim's Epis Ch Henderson NV 2001-2007; Gr And H Trin Cathd Kansas City MO 1987-2002; Off Of Bsh For ArmdF New York NY 1968-1986; Ch Of The Gd Shpd Orland CA 1966-1968; Vic S Andr's Mssn Corning CA 1966-1968; Vic S Pat's Santa Rosa CA 1964-1966. OHC 1960.

RUPP, Tuesday J (Ct) 2 E 90th St, New York NY 10128 **Ch Of The Heav Rest New York NY 2016-, 2014-2016** B Oregon City 1975 d David & Sara. Cert of Angl Stds Ya Berk; Cert Inst of Sacr Mus; Mstr of Mus Portland St U; MDiv Yale DS. D 1/9/2016 Bp Laura Ahrens. m 9/18/2015 Edgar Benavides. trupp@heavenlyrest.org

RUPPE, David (SO) 25005 SR 26, New Matamoras OH 45767 **Instr in Ethics Washington St Cmnty Coll Marietta OH 2008-** B Rutherfordton NC 1949

R

s James & Ruby. BA Duke 1971; MDiv UTS 1975; PhM Col 1981; PhD Col 1988. D 6/11/1977 Bp Paul Moore Jr P 12/17/1977 Bp Harold Louis Wright. c 3. R S Lk's Ch Marietta OH 2009-2017; Bex Sem Columbus OH 1999-2006; Dn of Angl Acad Dio Sthrn Ohio Cincinnati OH 1999-2004; R Trin Epis Ch Seneca Falls NY 1993-1999; Educ Off Dio Republic of Panama 1991-1992; Exec Coun Appointees New York NY 1991-1992; Vic S Marcos Panama City 1991-1992; S Barth's Ch Pewaukee WI 1988-1991; Asst Prof NT Nash Nashotah WI 1985-1991; The Ch of S Edw The Mtyr New York NY 1985; R Ch Of The Sav Syracuse NY 1981-1983; P The Ch of S Matt And S Tim New York NY 1977-1980; Secy Dio Cntrl New York Liverpool NY 1982-1983.

RUPPE-MELNYK, Glyn Lorraine (Pa) 689 Sugartown Road, Malvern PA 19355 B Camp Lejeune NC 1950 d James & Syble. BA Old Dominion U 1970; MDiv Sewanee: The U So, TS 1992. D 6/27/1992 Bp Henry Irving Mayson P 6/27/1993 Bp R aymond Stewart Wood Jr. m 7/19/1986 Walter William Melnyk c 2. R S Fran-In-The-Fields Malvern PA 2001-2015; R Chr Epis Ch Tarrytown NY 1998-2001; Dioc Examing Chapl Theo Sefl 1996-1998; Dioconate Sch For Chr Stds 1995-1998; R S Jas-In-The-Hills Epis Ch Hollywood FL 1994-1997; Asst R Chr Ch Detroit MI 1992-1994; Consult Sprtl Dir Dio Michigan Detroit MI 1990-1992. Contrib, "Wmn Uncommon Prayers," Morehouse, 2001; Auth, "Feminism Without Illusions," Sewanee Theol Revs, 1992. Cmnty Of S Mary. rectorstfrancisfields@verizon.net

RUSCHMEYER, Henry Cassell (NY) 2929 SE Ocean Blvd Apt M9, Stuart FL 34496 B New York NY 1944 s Henry & Josephine. BA Un Coll Schenectady NY 1966; MEd Bank St Coll of Educ 1973; MDiv GTS 1978; MA NYU 1988. D 6/17/1978 Bp Robert Campbell Witcher Sr P 1/6/1979 Bp Wilbur Emory Hogg Jr. Assoc Ch Of The Redeem Sarasota FL 2002-2003; Asst Chapl Emanuel Sch Wandswoth London 1990-1996; Assoc St. Paul's Ch Knightsbridge London 1989-1996; Asst Ch Of The Gd Shpd New York NY 1983-1989; Cur Ch Of The Ascen New York NY 1981-1983; Assoc S Geo's Ch Clifton Pk NY 1980-1981; Cur S Ptr's Ch Albany NY 1979-1980. Auth, "Chateaugay Lake: The Adirondack Resort Era, 1830-1917," Serbin, 2010.

RUSH, Joyce Anne (Minn) 407 NW 7th St, Brainerd MN 56401 B Elyria OH 1941 d William & Hope. BS Kent St U 1963. D 6/20/2015 P 6/21/2016 Bp Brian N Prior. c 4.

RUSHTON, Joseph (Del) P O BOX 602, Georgetown DE 19947 B Baltimore MD 1955 s John & Gertrude. BA Mt St Marys U 1977; MDiv U of Notre Dame 1980; MSW U of Maryland 1989; Dip Ang Stud VTS 2007. Rec 1/7/2007 as Priest Bp Robert Wilkes Ihloff. m 5/27/2004 Francis Nicholas Codd. R S Paul's Ch Georgetown DE 2011-2017; Int Ch Of The Gd Shpd Towson MD 2011; Int Ch Of The H Comf Luthvle Timon MD 2009-2011; Assoc Trin Ch Towson MD 2007-2009.

RUSK, Michael Frederick (Eur) **Emm Epis Ch Geneva 1201 2017-** Trans 3/31/2017 as Priest Bp Pierre W Whalon.

RUSLING, Julia G (At) 432 Lockwood Ter., Decatur GA 30030 **S Pat's Epis Ch Atlanta GA 2014-** B Rochester NY 1969 d Thomas & Ellen. MDiv Ya Berk; BA Ob. D 9/24/2000 Bp David John Bena P 3/24/2001 Bp Daniel William Herzog. m 6/22/1996 Daniel Jin Lee. Ch Of The Incarn Atlanta GA 2013, 2012-2013; Chr Ch Pittsford Pittsford NY 2005-2006; Calv Epis Ch Burnt Hills NY 2000-2001.

RUSS JR, Frank Dobinson (SC) 1159 Wyndham Rd, Charleston SC 29412 **Chapl Bp Gadsden Epis Ret Cmnty Charleston SC 2007-** B Burgaw NC 1954 s Frank & Barbara. BA U NC 1976; MDiv SE Bapt TS 1981; DAS VTS 1991; E Carolina U 2001. D 6/22/1991 P 12/27/1991 Bp Brice Sidney Sanders. Bp Gadsden Epis Cmnty Charleston SC 2007-2016; The Ch of S Matt And S Tim New York NY 2004-2007; R S Fran Ch Goldsboro NC 1996-2004; Asst To The Bp For Prog & Mnstry Dio E Carolina Kinston NC 1994-1996; R S Christophers Ch Elizabethtown NC 1991-1994.

RUSSELL, Ann Veronica (VI) Box 3066, Sea Cow's Bay, Tortola British Virgin Island VG 1110 British Virgin Islands B Fulham England 1935 d Charles & Claire. BA Hull U; MA Wright St U; Brentwood Teachers Trng Coll 1966. D 6/14/2008 Bp Edward Gumbs. m 11/25/1960 Ronald Russell c 4.

RUSSELL JR, Carl Asa (Me) 9 Perkins Rd, Boothbay Harbor ME 04538 **S Paul's Epis Ch Brighton MI 2006-; Ret 1996-** B Portland ME 1936 s Carl & Ruth. BA Bow 1958; MDiv GTS 1961; Coll of Preachers 1971. D 5/27/1961 P 12/21/1961 Bp Oliver L Loring. m 6/14/1958 Margaret Ellen Street c 4. Chr Ch Shaker Heights OH 2003-2006; S Columba's Epis Ch E Boothbay ME 1997-2000; R S Paul's Ch Darien CT 1992-1996; R Chr Ch Fitchburg MA 1982-1992; Dio Wstrn Massachusetts Springfield 1981-1992; Trin Epis Ch Portland ME 1971-1981; R S Andr's Ch Millinocket ME 1963-1971; Vic S Thos Ch Winn ME 1961-1963.

RUSSELL, Carlton Thrasher (Mass) 27 Abnaki Way, Stockton Springs ME 04981 **Mus Dir/Org St Fran By The Sea Epis Ch Blue Hill ME 2006-; Min of Mus St. Fran by the sea Epis Ch Blue Hill ME 2006-** B Keene NH 1938 s Jay & Nina. BA Amh 1960; Cert AGO 1962; MFA Pr 1962; PhD Pr 1966; MA EDS 1983. D 6/2/1984 Bp John Bowen Coburn P 5/14/1985 Bp Roger W Blanchard. m 8/15/1964 Lorna Smithers Brookes. Ch Of S Thos Camden ME 2005-2006; Assoc Trin Epis Ch Wrentham MA 1985-2005. Auth, w Grateful

Gladness: The Wheaton Organ at 30 CD Rcrdng, Wheaton Coll, 1999; Auth, "sev arts(Ch Mus), anthems," *and Serv settings*. OHC, Assoc.

RUSSELL, Daniel S (NJ) 2365 McAleer Rd, Sewickley PA 15143 **Dio New Jersey Trenton NJ 2016-** B Baltimore MD 1968 s Richard & Patricia. BA Asbury U 1990; MDiv TESM 2001. D 6/15/2002 P 12/22/2002 Bp Robert William Duncan. S Brendan's Epis Ch Franklin Pk PA 2013-2016; Convenor, Interfaith Coun VPI and St U 2010-2011; Bd Mem Vlly Interfaith Chld Care Cntr Christiansburg VA 2004-2006; Assoc R Chr Ch Blacksburg VA 2003-2013, Campus Min at Virginia Tech 2003-2013; Exec Bd Dio SW Virginia Roanoke VA 2004-2007. "Film Revs," *New Dictionary of Chr Apologetics*, InterVarsity Press, 2006. danielscottrussell@gmail.com

RUSSELL, Jack Dempsey (Tex) 800 E Hudson St, Tyler TX 75701 **Ret 1993-** B Corsicana TX 1927 s Jeff & Donia. BS Texas A&M U 1948; BD Epis TS of the SW 1956; MDiv Epis TS of the SW 1971. D 7/6/1956 P 6/29/1957 Bp John Elbridge Hines. c 3. Assoc Chr Epis Ch Tyler TX 2000-2003; R S Geo's Epis Ch Port Arthur TX 1984-1992; CODE 1979-1984; Cn to the Ordnry Dio Dallas Dallas TX 1979-1984; Dep GC 1979-1982; R S Paul's Epis Ch Greenville TX 1969-1979; R S Mths Epis Ch Shreveport LA 1962-1969; R S Mary's Ch Bellville TX 1957-1962; Vic S Dav's Houston TX 1956-1957; Bp' Chapl to Ret Cler Dio Texas Houston TX 1995-2014, Chair of the Div of Coll 1989-1992, Dep to GC 1982, Dep to GC 1979.

RUSSELL, John Alan (WNY) 768 Potomac Ave, Buffalo NY 14209 **Ret 2001-** B Philadelphia PA 1932 s Steuart & Mary. MSW St of New York; BA GW 1956; MDiv Ya Berk 1959; MSW St of New York 1970. D 4/25/1959 P 10/31/1959 Bp Alfred L Banyard. m 6/11/1982 Debra Lee Russell. Vic S Pat's Ch Buffalo NY 2006-2011; Int S Phil's Ch Buffalo NY 2001-2005; R S Jude's Ch Buffalo NY 1992-2000; Ex Coun Com Dio Wstrn New York 1989-1995; Vic S Aid's Ch Alden NY 1987-1992; S Dav's Epis Ch Buffalo NY 1987; Assoc S Jn's Gr Ch Buffalo NY 1984-1987; S Mart In The Fields Grand Island NY 1969-1980; Fndr, Dir Night People Mnstry Buffalo NY 1969-1972; Assoc P Calv Epis Ch Williamsville NY 1967-1969; R S Andr's Epis Ch Lawton OK 1964-1967; Rgnl Dn Sw Ok Dnry 1964-1966; Dn S Fran Boys Hm Salina KS 1962-1964; S Geo's Epis Ch Helmetta NJ 1959-1962; Port. Chapl St Boys Hm Jamesburg NJ 1959-1962. Auth, "Var arts". cl Berkeley Div Sch At Yale 1959.

RUSSELL, Kathleen Sams (Tex) 1823 Montana Sky Drive, Austin TX 78727 **Asst. Prof of Contextual Theol for Mnstry Epis TS of the SW Austin TX 2005-** B Buffalo NY 1947 d Edward & Grace. BA Daemen Coll 1968; MDiv SWTS 1989; D.Min. Austin Presb TS 2012; D.Min. Other 2012. D 6/17/1989 P 12/16/1989 Bp Frank Tracy Griswold III. m 7/15/1972 Michael Bennett Russell c 2. Assoc Prof of Pstr Theol Epis TS Of The SW Austin TX 2005-2016; Cntr for Urban Mnstry San Diego CA 2003-2005; Actg R S Andr's By The Sea Epis Par San Diego CA 2000-2004; Actg R St. Andr's by-the-Sea San Diego CA 2000-2004; Sr Chapl/Mgr of Pstr Care Chld's Natl Med Cntr Washington DC 1989-2000.

RUSSELL, Kenneth Paul (Ore) 5311 Sw Wichita St, Tualatin OR 97062 **D S Fran Of Assisi Epis Wilsonville OR 2008-** B Seattle WA 1960 s Paul & Catherine. BS OR SU 1982; JD L&C 1985. D 9/30/2000 Bp Robert Louis Ladehoff. m 8/14/1982 Cindra Foote c 2. D All SS Ch Hillsboro OR 2007-2008; D Chr Ch Par Lake Oswego OR 2000-2007.

RUSSELL, Margaret Ellen Street (Me) 9 Perkins Rd, Boothbay Harbor ME 04538 B Portland ME USA 1937 d Nathanael & Margaret. Mid; BA U of Sthrn Maine 1976; MA Lesley U 1986; MDiv Ya Berk 1995. D 6/8/1996 P 12/1/1996 Bp Clarence Nicholas Coleridge. m 6/14/1958 Carl Asa Russell c 5. Vic S Columba's Epis Ch E Boothbay ME 1997-2006; Dio Maine Portland ME 1996-2006; S Paul's Ch Darien CT 1996-1997.

RUSSELL, Michael Bennett (Tex) 3112 James St, San Diego CA 92106 B Baltimore MD 1949 s Harry & Avis. BA U of Virginia 1973; MA Chicago TS 1975; MDiv SWTS 1986. D 6/14/1986 Bp James Winchester Montgomery P 12/13/1986 Bp Frank Tracy Griswold III. m 7/15/1972 Kathleen Sams Russell c 2. P The Ch of the Gd Shpd Austin TX 2012-2016; R All Souls' Epis Ch San Diego CA 1999-2012; R Gr Ch Elkridge MD 1989-1999; Ch Of S Paul And The Redeem Chicago IL 1986-1989. Auth, "Greenville: The Non-Un Culture: Sthrn Exposure"; Auth, "Via Media"; Auth, "Political Grief," *An Exploration Of Grieving*. mike@gsaustin.org

RUSSELL, Patricia Griffith (NwT) 1802 Broadway, Lubbock TX 79401 **Sprtl Dir Sprtl Direction Lubbock TX 2014-** B San Angelo TX 1947 d Brandon & Margaret. BA U of Oklahoma 1971; ADN Hartnell Coll 1978; MPA U of Oklahoma 1983; Cert Haden Inst 2014. D 9/20/2008 Bp C Wallis Ohl P 3/28/2009 Bp James Scott Mayer. m 7/30/1988 William F Russell c 4. Chapl Cbury Epis Campus Mnstry at Texas Tech Lubbock TX 2010-2014; Dio NW Texas Lubbock TX 2010-2014. Sprtl Dir Intl 2013.

RUSSELL, Sherrill Ann (WMo) 7110 N State Route 9, Kansas City MO 64152 B Macon MO 1937 d Harold & Shirley. Cntrl Bapt TS; BS U of Cntrl Missouri 1960; MS K SU 1981. D 2/5/2011 Bp Barry Howe. m 1/7/1961 Charles Edward Russell c 3.

RUSSELL, Steven Scott (Eau) B Menomonie WI 1958 s John & Flora. D 10/29/2016 Bp William Jay Lambert III. m 9/20/1997 Kobi Dawn Shaw c 2.

RUSSELL, Susan (Los) 680 Mountain View St, Altadena CA 91001 **Exec Dir All SS Ch Pasadena CA 2002-** B Los Angeles CA 1954 d William & Betty. BA U CA 1976; MDiv Claremont TS 1996. D 6/1/1996 P 1/17/1998 Bp Frederick Houk Borsch. m 6/28/2014 Lori Galloway Kizzia c 2. Asst S Ptr's Par San Pedro CA 1998-2002; S Mk's Par Altadena CA 1997-1998, 1996. srussell@allsaints-pas.org

RUSSELL, Susan Hayden (Mass) 72 Cavendish Circle, Salem MA 01970 **Assoc Chr Ch S Hamilton MA 2013-** B Newton MA 1943 d Jesse & Alice. BA Ob 1965; MDiv SWTS 1998. D 6/20/1998 P 1/23/1999 Bp J Clark Grew II. m 8/3/1968 John Russell c 2. P-in-c Wyman Memi Ch of St Andr Marblehead MA 2008-2011; R All SS Ch Cleveland OH 2000-2008; Asst R S Paul's Epis Ch Medina OH 1998-2000; COM Dio Ohio Cleveland 2007-2008. Ord of S Helena 1971.

RUSSELL, Tracy Johnson (Ct) 89 Lenox St Unit N, New Haven CT 06513 **S Monica's Ch Hartford CT 2015-; Sch Chapl S Thos's Day Sch New Haven CT 2011-; Exec Dir Your Place Yth Cntr 2008-; NED Chapl NANBPWC Inc 2013-** B Indianapolis IN 1969 d Charles & Bonita. BA Mia 1991; MDiv Ya Berk 1995; MA Quinnipiac U 1997. D 6/20/2003 P 7/24/2004 Bp Andrew Donnan Smith. m 3/21/2009 Fitzroy Russell. Sch Chapl S Thos's Ch New Haven CT 2011-2014; Vic S Andr's Ch New Haven CT 2003-2014; Tchr Riverside Educ Acad 2002-2009. Chr Ldrshp Awd Chr Cmnty Cmsn 2013; Oustanding MBA Stdt S Louis U 2012.

RUTENBAR, C Harles Mark (WTenn) 7774 Grand Point Rd., Presque Isle MI 49777 B New Haven CT 1953 s Howard & Jeanne. Dplma Cranbrook Sch Bloomfield Hills MI 1972; BA SMU 1976; MDiv VTS 1980. D 6/11/1980 Bp Arthur Anton Vogel P 12/13/1980 Bp Addison Hosea. m 8/18/1979 Larae Jordan c 2. P-t Asstg Cler Chr Ch Cathd Indianapolis IN 2015-2016; R Ch Of The H Comm Memphis TN 2006-2014; R S Lk's Par Kalamazoo MI 1994-2006; R S Paul's Ch Macon GA 1988-1994; Asst Emm Epis Ch Athens GA 1982-1988; Cur Trin Ch Covington KY 1980-1981; Bp & Coun Dio W Tennessee Memphis 2008-2012; Stndg Com, Pres Dio Wstrn Michigan Kalamazoo MI 2002-2006, Dep GC 2000-2006, Cmsn On Mnstry 1998-2002; Mikell Conf Ctr Bd Dio Atlanta Atlanta GA 1984-1986, Dioc Yth Cmsn 1983-1986; Sprtl Dir Dio Lexington Lexington 1980-1982.

RUTENBAR, Larae Jordan (WMich) 8238 Greengate Cove, Cordova TN 38018 **COM Dio Wstrn Michigan Kalamazoo MI 2003-, Int 1994-2002** B Loup City NE 1954 d Dale & Kathryn. Pacific Luth U 1974; BA Rocky Mtn Coll 1976; MDiv VTS 1980. D 5/31/1980 Bp Jackson Earle Gilliam P 6/1/1982 Bp William Grant Black. m 8/18/1979 C Harles Mark Rutenbar c 2. Trin Ch Indianapolis IN 2014-2016; Emm Epis Ch La Grange IL 2013-2014; S Ptr's Ch Rome GA 2011-2012; Chr Ch Cathd Lexington KY 2010-2011; All SS' Epis Ch Tupelo MS 2007-2008; All SS Ch E Lansing MI 2005-2006; Emm Ch Petoskey MI 2004-2005; Int S Mart Of Tours Epis Ch Kalamazoo MI 2003-2004; P-in-c Epis Ch Of The Gd Shpd Allegan MI 2000-2003; Trin Epis Ch Marshall MI 1999-2000; Trin Ch Niles MI 1997-1999; S Jn's Epis Ch Charlotte MI 1996; S Thos Epis Ch Battle Creek MI 1994-1995; Asst R S Paul's Ch Macon GA 1988-1994; Int The Epis Ch Of The Adv Madison GA 1986-1988; Asst Chapl Chld's Hosp Cincinnati OH 1981-1982; Asst Trin Ch Covington KY 1980-1981; Comp of Dioc Com Dio Atlanta Atlanta GA 1993-1994, Comp of Dioc Com 1988-1992, Supply P 1982-1987.

RUTH, Allen Richard (SwFla) 5210 Pale Moon Dr, Pensacola FL 32507 **D H Sprt Epis Ch Gulf Shores AL 2007-** B New Britain CT 1938 BS USNA 1959; MS U of Washington 1964; MBA City U of Seattle 1982. D 1/18/2003 Bp John Bailey Lipscomb. m 6/3/1959 Ellen Marie Conner c 4. D S Jn's Ch Naples FL 2003-2006.

RUTH, Margaret F (WMo) 402 West 50th #2 South, Kansas City MO 64112 **Died 10/3/2016** B Denver CO 1928 d John & Margaret. BA U of Kansas 1951. D 9/26/1978 Bp Arthur Anton Vogel. c 4. Ret 1996-2016; D S Paul's Ch Kansas City MO 1994-1996, 1978-1993; S Andr's Ch Kansas City MO 1990-1993; D/Stff S Andr's Ch Kansas City MO 1978-1993.

RUTHERFORD, Allen (Ind) 420 Locust Street, Mt. Vernon IN 47620 **R S Jn's Epis Ch Mt Vernon IN 2005-; R St. Jn's Epis Ch Mt. Vernon IN 2005-** B St Paul IN 1962 Cert SWTS 2004; MDiv Chr TS 2005. D 7/17/2004 P 5/22/2005 Bp Cate Waynick. m 6/25/1983 Lydia S Rutherford c 2. Cur H Fam Epis Ch Fishers IN 2004-2007. rutherford317@sbcglobal.net

RUTHERFORD, Ellen C (NJ) 1115 New Pear St, Vineland NJ 08360 **Ch of the Resurr Bridgeton NJ 2014-; P-in-c Epis Shared Mnstry of Cumberland Cnty 2009-; P-in-c Trin Epis Ch Vineland NJ 2009-** B West Chester PA 1956 d Edwin & Nona. BA Duke 1977; MA U Chi 1979; MDiv GTS 1989; MS Pratt Inst 2000. D 6/16/1989 P 12/17/1989 Bp Frank Tracy Griswold III. S Andr's Epis Ch Bridgeton NJ 2009-2014; Incumbent Grtr Par of Gaspe Quebec Can 2006-2009; The Grtr Par of Gaspe Quebec QC 2006-2009; Chr Ch Palmyra NJ 2000-2006; P-in-c Riverfront Epis Team Mnstry Riverside NJ 2000-2006; Vic Riverfront Epis Team Mnstry Riverside NJ 2000-2006; S Steph's Ch Riverside NJ 2000-2006; Chap Of S Jn The Div Tomkins Cove NY 1997-1999; Chr Epis Ch Sparkill NY 1997-1999; Mssnr Dio New York

New York NY 1997-1999; Mssnr Epis Shared Mnstry Of Rockland Tompkins Cove NY 1997-1999; S Paul's Ch Sprg Vlly NY 1997-1999; Trin Epis Ch Garnerville NY 1997-1999; R Thumb Epis Area Mnstry Deford MI 1991-1997; R/Vic Thumb Epis Team Mnstry Cass City MI 1991-1997; Assoc Paris Cluster Chadwicks NY 1989-1991; Assoc Paris Cluster Clinton NY 1989-1991.

RUTHERFORD, Thomas Houston (CFla) 1260 Log Landing Drive, Ocoee FL 34761 **R Ch Of The Mssh Winter Garden FL 1996-** B Memphis TN 1955 s Oliver & Tommie. Marq 1975; BS Middle Tennessee St U 1979; MDiv Sewanee: The U So, TS 1993. D 5/15/1993 Bp William Evan Sanders P 4/17/1994 Bp William Arthur Beckham. m 9/10/2010 Deborah Rosser Rutherford c 3. Int R S Chris's Ch Spartanburg SC 1993-1996; Yth Pstr S Barth's Ch Nashville TN 1979-1990; Stndg Com Dio Cntrl Florida Orlando FL 2012-2013, Stndg Com 2008-2010, COM 2001-. Lifetime Ambassador W Orange ChmbrCom 2014.

RUTHVEN, Carol (Lex) 926 Mason Headley Rd, Lexington KY 40504 B Pembroke, Canada 1958 d Melvin & Amy. BA U of Alberta Edmonton AB CA 1980; MA Queens U Kingston ON CA 1981; PhD Queens U Kingston ON CA 1986; MDiv Sewanee: The U So, TS 2007. D 6/9/2007 P 12/17/2007 Bp Stacy F Sauls. m 6/23/1990 Alan Fryar c 2. S Andr's Ch Lexington KY 2007-2016, R 2007-2016; S Agnes Hse Lexington KY 2007-2008.

RUTHVEN, Scott Alan (RG) 805 Lenox Ave., Las Cruces NM 88005 **R S Andr's Epis Ch Las Cruces NM 2003-** B Los Alamos NM 1955 s William & Lenora. BA Rockmont Coll 1984; MDiv TESM 1988. D 6/11/1988 Bp William Carl Frey P 12/1/1988 Bp Jeffery William Rowthorn. m 7/14/1979 Mary Jo Ruthven c 3. R S Jn's Epis Ch Alamogordo NM 1992-2003; R Ch Of The Ascen Cloudcroft NM 1992; Asst Trin Ch Tariffville CT 1988-1992. SBL.

RUTHY, Rosemary (Eau) D 10/29/2016 Bp William Jay Lambert III.

RUTLAND, Edward Cumpston (Dal) 6106 Sagebrush Ave, Texarkana TX 75503 **Died 8/12/2015** B Houston TX 1926 s James & Margaret. U So 1947; U of Texas 1952; Epis TS of the SW 1955. D 7/1/1955 Bp Clinton Simon Quin P 7/3/1956 Bp Frederick P Goddard. m 6/1/1952 Laura Taylor c 3. Supply S Mk's Ch Hope AR 1995-2000; Int St Mk's Epis Ch Mt Pleasant TX 1993-1995; Ret 1991-2015; All SS Ch Atlanta TX 1991-1993; Vic S Mart Epis Ch New Boston TX 1991-1993; R S Mary's Epis Ch Texarkana TX 1986-1991; Liturg Cmsn Dio Dallas 1975-1978; R S Dav's Ch Denton TX 1973-1986; Dn Tarrant Dnry 1970-1972; R Chr The King Epis Ch Ft Worth TX 1968-1973; Bd Mercy RC Hosp 1963-1968; R Ch Of The Epiph Independence KS 1960-1968; Assoc S Geo's Epis Ch Arlington VA 1958-1960; Mssy S Mk's Ch Gladewater TX 1957-1958; S Jn's Epis Ch Carthage TX 1955-1958; Asst Chr Ch San Aug TX 1955-1957; Mssy S Jn's Cntr San Aug TX 1955-1957; Exec Coun Dio Dallas Dallas TX 1984-1986, Exec Coun 1970-1983. Auth, "Var arts," *LivCh*, 1995; Auth, *The H Mysteries*, Morehouse-Barlow, 1958; Auth, "Var arts," *Epis*. HSEC 1955.

RUTLEDGE, Fleming (NY) 38 Hillandale Rd, Rye Brook NY 10573 B Richmond VA 1937 d John & Alice. BA Sweet Briar Coll 1959; GTS 1975; MDiv UTS 1975. D 6/14/1975 Bp Paul Moore Jr P 1/21/1977 Bp James Stuart Wetmore. m 10/3/1959 Reginald Rutledge c 2. Int S Jn's Ch Salisbury CT 1996-1997; Assoc Gr Epis Ch New York NY 1991-1996; Chr's Ch Rye NY 1975-1981. "Not Ashamed of the Gospel," Eerdmans, 2007; "The Seven Last Words," Eerdmans, 2005; "The Battle for Middle-earth," Eerdmans, 2004; "The Undoing of Death," Eerdmans, 2002; "Help My Unbelief," Eerdmans, 2000; "The Bible and the New York Times," Eerdmans, 1998. DD VTS 1999; Fell Cntr of Theol Inquiry 1997.

RUTLEDGE, Lynn V (Me) 13 Garnet Head Rd, Pembroke ME 04666 **P-in-c S Aidans Ch Machias ME 2014-** B Texarkana AR 1950 EDS; BA U of Houston 1972; Cert Texas A&M U 1991; M.Div. EDS 2014. D 6/19/2004 Bp Chilton Richardson Knudsen P 8/8/2013 Bp Stephen Taylor Lane. m 5/17/2017 Richard Rutledge c 1. D Chr Epis Ch Eastport ME 2013, Assoc 2013-.

RUTLEDGE, Theodore Elsworth (RG) 170 Sunset Ln, Tillamook OR 97141 **Died 12/10/2015** B Puyallup WA 1923 s Keizer & Violet. BA U of Texas 1979; Epis TS of the SW 1982. D 6/24/1982 P 2/18/1983 Bp Richard Mitchell Trelease Jr. c 3. Ret 1988-2015; Asst R All SS Epis Ch El Paso TX 1985-1988, Asst 1982-1984; Mssnr Llano Estacado Ministers 1984-1985; Dio The Rio Grande Albuquerque 1983-1985.

RUTTAN, Karl D (SO) 125 E Broad St, Columbus OH 43215 **S Phil's Ch Columbus OH 2012-** B Detroit MI 1948 s Arden & Marjorie. BA Ken 1970; MDiv Chicago TS 1975; Cert EDS 1975; MEd Duquesne U 1988; PhD Duquesne U 1998. D 6/21/1975 P 5/1/1976 Bp John Harris Burt. m 8/14/1976 Mary C Barkalow c 2. Cn Dio Sthrn Ohio Cincinnati OH 2007-2013; R S Jn's Epis Ch Charleston WV 1994-2006; R Chr Ch Greensburg PA 1984-1994; Exec Coun Appointees New York NY 1980-1983; P-in-c S Mich's Kitwe 1980-1983; Asst S Andr's Epis Ch Elyria OH 1976-1980; Mssnr to YA All SS Par Brookline MA 1975-1976. H Cross 2002. DeRoo Ecum Awd WV Coun of Ch 2006.

RUTTER, Deborah Wood (Va) PO Box 1306, Front Royal VA 22630 **Bd Gvnr S Marg's Sch Tappahannock VA 1991-; Chair, COM Dio Virginia Richmond VA 2011-, Shrine Mont Bd Dir 1998-2011, Exec Bd 1989-1992** B Washington DC 1948 d Jackson & Anne. Certification in Sprtl Direction The Haden Inst; BA W&M 1970; MDiv Pittsburgh TS 1982. D 2/15/1983 Bp Alden

Moinet Hathaway P 1/7/1984 Bp Robert Bruce Hall. m 9/15/1989 George W Rutter c 2. R Calv Epis Ch Front Royal VA 1995-2017; Gr Ch Kilmarnock VA 1992-1995; R Kingston Par Epis Ch Mathews VA 1986-1992; Chapl S Marg's Sch Tappahannock VA 1983-1986, Bd Dir 1996-2012; Chapl S Marg's Sch Tappahannock VA 1983-1986.

RUYAK, Mark (Cal) 5 Weatherly Drive Apt 109, Mill Valley CA 94941 B Pottstown PA 1955 s Joseph & Joanne. BA Penn 1978; MEd Penn 1981; MDiv CDSP 1999. D 4/17/1999 P 1/22/2000 Bp Paul Victor Marshall. Ch Of The Adv Of Chr The King San Francisco CA 2014-2015; Int Ch Of The H Fam Fresno CA 2011-2013; Int S Fran' Epis Ch San Francisco CA 2009-2011; Int Ch Of The Redeem San Rafael CA 2008-2009; Assoc Gr Cathd San Francisco CA 2000-2007; Asst Emm Ch Baltimore MD 1999-2000.

RUYLE, Everett Eugene (At) 1195 Terramont Dr, Roswell GA 30076 **Asst R S Lk's 1980-** B Beatrice NE 1935 s Everett & Naomi. BA U of Florida 1959; BD VTS 1962; PhD Un Grad Sch 1977. D 6/27/1962 P 4/1/1963 Bp Edward Hamilton West. c 3. S Mart In The Fields Ch Atlanta GA 1992-2005; Non-par 1969-1980; Asst R H Trin Epis Ch Gainesville FL 1964-1969; Vic Ch Of The H Comf Cres City FL 1962-1964. Auth, "Making A Life"; Auth, "Team Kit: A Trng Prog For Sm Groups". Tillich Soc.

RYAN SSM, Adele Marie (Mass) 50 Harden Hill Rd, Box C, Duxbury MA 02331 **Superior SSM Boston MA 2011-** B New York NY 1938 d George & Evelyn. BA FD 1960; MA Luth TS Philadelphia 1980; MAR Luth TS Philadelphia 1980; MA Luth TS Philadelphia 1980. D 6/14/1980 P 6/10/1981 Bp Lyman Cunningham Ogilby. Asst Superior SSM Boston MA 2002-2011; Soc Of St Marg Duxbury MA 1996-2010; Superior SSM Boston MA 1990-2002; Dn Wissahickon Dnry Dio Pennsylvania Philadelphia PA 1984-1987, Chair, Sprtl Growth Com 1984-1987; Asst S Lk's Ch Philadelphia PA 1980-1985; Cmsn on the Mnstry Dio Massachusetts Boston MA 1992-1994. "Rel Ord And Congregations 4:Angl," Eerdmans-Brill Encyclopedia Of Chrsnty.

RYAN, Bartholomew Grey (Chi) 2713 6 3/16 Ave, New Auburn WI 54757 B Chicago IL 1950 s Vernon & Barbara. BS Indiana U 1972; MA S Mary 1993; Cert Ang Stud Nash 1995. D 3/22/1995 P 9/1/1995 Bp William Charles Wantland. m 11/4/1972 Barbara B Ryan c 2. Chapl Mnstry Outside the Epis Ch 2007-2013; Trin Ch Muscatine IA 2003-2005; Trin Ch River Falls WI 2000-2003; R S Alb's Ch Superior WI 1995-2000. SSC.

RYAN, David Andrew (RI) 1663 Kensington Pl, The Villages FL 32162 **Died 11/5/2015** B Providence RI 1934 s Edward & Lillian. BA NEU 1957; STB Ya Berk 1960; S Georges Coll Jerusalem IL 1980; Steph Mnstry 2007. D 6/18/1960 P 12/17/1960 Bp John S Higgins. m 6/22/1957 Constance Anita Ryan c 3. Rotary Emer Pawtuxet Vlly Rotary 1997-2015; Ret 1996-2015; Supplemental Benefits Cmsn 1994-2000; Dioc Coun Dio Rhode Island Providence RI 1968-1982; Pres Pawtuxet Vlly Clerics Assn 1968-1971; R The Epis Ch Of S Andr And S Phil Coventry RI 1965-1996; R Ch Of The H Trin Tiverton RI 1962-1965; Cur S Barn Ch Warwick RI 1960-1962.

RYAN, Dennis L (Miss) 3507 Pine St, Pascagoula MS 39567 **R S Jn's Epis Ch Pascagoula MS 2005-** B Biloxi MS 1947 s Adrian & Opal. Mississippi Gulf Coast Cmnty Coll; LTh Sewanee: The U So, TS 1993. D 6/12/1993 Bp Duncan Montgomery Gray Jr P 3/1/1994 Bp Alfred Marble Jr. m 2/21/2009 Susan Kennon Carruth c 3. Assoc S Jn's Epis Ch Pascagoula MS 2000-2013; Trin Ch Hattiesburg MS 1993-2000.

RYAN III, Frances Isabel Sells (Az) 3150 N Winding Brook Rd, Flagstaff AZ 86001 B Weyburn Saskatchewan Canada 1922 d John & Sarah. BA NWU 1943; MS Pur 1970; JD U of Wisconsin 1975; Cert Inst for Chr Stds 1993. D 5/21/1994 Bp Roger John White. c 4. D Ch Of The Epiph Flagstaff AZ 2002-2009; D S Andr's Ch Madison WI 1998-2001, D 1994-1997, D Chr Ch 1995-1997.

RYAN, John Prime (Okla) 3300 NW 61st St, Oklahoma City OK 73112 **Died 9/28/2015** B Lincoln,NE 1932 s Claude & Ida. BA Ken 1954; STB GTS 1957; MTh U Tor 1969; STD Anselmianum Rome IT 1985. D 4/25/1957 Bp Charles Francis Boynton P 10/25/1957 Bp Chilton R Powell. R S Jn's Ch Oklahoma City OK 1988-2003; R Emm Epis Ch Shawnee OK 1982-1988; Exec Asst to Bp Dio Wyoming Casper 1980-1982; Chapl to Cler Dio Los Angeles Los Angeles CA 1977-1980; S Geo's Epis Ch Holbrook AZ 1977; R S Paul's Epis Ch Winslow AZ 1977; Gr St Pauls Epis Ch Tucson AZ 1975-1977; Gr St Pauls Tucson AZ 1975-1977; OHC 1959-1973; Vic S Eliz Nowata OK 1957-1959; Cur S Lk's Epis Ch Bartlesville OK 1957-1959; Chapl U AZ 2015. Auth, *Supernatural Beatitude According to S Albert the Great*; Auth, "The Rational Creatures Natural Appetite for Natural & Supernatural Beatitude Accord," *The Rational Creatures Natural Appetite for Natural & Supernatura*. VP Oklahoma Conf of Ch.

RYAN, Katherine Alice (WNC) 1223 Sea Pines Dr, Aubrey TX 76227 B Dallas,TX 1958 d David & Arden. BS Texas A&M U 1981; MA U of Texas 1984; MDiv Sewanee: The U So, TS 1993; DMin SMU 2000. D 6/12/1993 Bp Robert Jefferson Hargrove Jr P 12/18/1993 Bp James Monte Stanton. c 3. S Paul's Newport AR 2005; Ch Of The H Cross Tryon NC 2003-2004; St Lk's Epis Ch Anth NM 2001-2003; Assoc S Geo's Epis Ch Bradenton FL 2000-2001; S Thos' Epis Ch St Petersburg FL 1999-2000; S Dav's Epis Ch Englewood FL

1996-1999; St Jas Epis Ch and Sch Alexandria LA 1994-1995; Cur S Alb's Epis Ch Monroe LA 1993-1994.

RYAN, Kathryn McCrossen (Tex) 8787 Greenville Ave, Dallas TX 75243 **Cn Dio Texas Houston TX 2014-; Bd Trst; Chair - Governance Epis TS Of The SW Austin TX 2004-** B Raton NM 1964 d Eric & Patricia. BA U So 1986; MDiv Epis TS of the SW 2992. D 6/27/1992 Bp Terence Kelshaw P 6/24/1993 Bp Scott Field Bailey. m 5/20/1989 Timothy D Ryan c 2. R Epis Ch Of The Ascen Dallas TX 1999-2013; Asst S Lk's Epis Ch Mobile AL 1993-1999; Yth Min All SS Epis Ch Austin TX 1992-1993; COM, Chair Dio Cntrl Gulf Coast Pensacola FL 1998-1999. kryan@epicenter.org

RYAN, Matthew Ryan (NwPa) 67 Thomas-Ryan Road, Emporium PA 15834 **P-in-c Emm Epis Ch Emporium PA 2004-; P-in-c Emm Epis Ch Emporium PA 2004-** B Pittsburgh PA 1956 s Joseph & Martha. BA Columbia St U Metaire LA 1997. D 4/20/2002 P 11/17/2002 Bp Robert Deane Rowley Jr. m 6/25/1983 Barbara Williams c 3. Vic S Marg's Epis Ch Kane PA 2002-2004; Vic S Matt's Epis Ch Eldred PA 2002-2004. APMI 1983; SAE 1995.

RYAN, Michael James (WMich) The Church of the Epiphany, 410 Erie Street, South Haven MI 49090 **R The Epis Ch Of The Epiph So Haven MI 2009-; COM Dio Wstrn Michigan Kalamazoo MI 2014-; Addictions Recovery Cmsn Dio Wstrn Michigan Kalamazoo 2012-** B Grand Rapids MN 1962 s Edward & Kathleen. BA S Johns U 1986; MDiv SWTS 2009. D 6/20/2009 Bp Stephen Taylor Lane P 12/20/2009 Bp Robert R Gepert. m 10/20/1990 Susan J Trabucchi. Recovery Mnstrs of the Epis Ch 2007. epiphanysh@gmail.com

RYAN, Michelle Ann (CFla) **S Lk's Ch Louisville KY 2015-** D 5/23/2015 Bp Gregory Orrin Brewer.

RYAN JR, Thomas Francis (SeFla) 3131 Pizzaro Pl, Clermont FL 34715 **Died 9/8/2016** B West Palm Beach FL 1936 s Thomas & Anice. BEd U of Miami 1960; MDiv Yale DS 1972; MA Estrn Illinois U 1977. D 9/11/1971 Bp James Loughlin Duncan P 6/29/1972 Bp Morgan Porteus. m 4/15/1974 Courtenay D Ryan c 3. Assoc S Jas Epis Ch Leesburg FL 2011-2016; P-in-c Corpus Christi Epis Ch Okahumpka FL 2009-2010; Ret 2005-2016; Soc Concerns Off Dio SE Florida Miami 1990-2005, Evang Cmsn 1989-1990, Dioc Bdgt Cmsn 1993-2004, Chair - Cmsn on Soc Concerns 1990-2016, Natl Jubilee Off 1990-2004; R All SS Epis Ch Jensen Bch FL 1988-2004; Evang Off Dio SW Florida Parrish FL 1985-1988, Chair - Cmsn on Evang 1984-1988; R S Barth's Ch St Petersburg FL 1984-1988; Co-Dir Discovery Prog Dio Cntrl Pennsylvania Harrisburg PA 1982-1984, Chapl Berwick Hospita; 1981-1984, Outreach Com 1982-1984; R Chr Ch Berwick PA 1981-1984; Exec Dir Talbot Hm Dio Bethlehem Bethlehem PA 1978-1981, Liturg Cmsn 1979-1981; Assoc S Lk's Ch Lebanon PA 1978-1981; Dio Springfield Springfield IL 1975-1978, Chapl Estrn Illinois Univ. 1975-1978, COM 1976-1978; Liturg; Liturg & Life Trin Epis Ch Mattoon IL 1975-1978; R S Mary Magd Epis Ch Pompano Bch FL 1972-1974; P-in-c S Phil's Ch Pompano Bch FL 1972-1973; Chapl Hartford Gnrl Hosp CT 1971-1972; Chapl Prog Berwick Hosp 2016. Auth, "Dvlpmt Of Self-Death Awareness Scale," Estrn Illinois U; Auth, "arts," *SW Florida Dio Nwspr*; Auth, "Reach Out Column," *The Sthrn Cross*, Dio SW Florida. Who'S Who In Rel 1985.

RYAN, William Wilson (WTenn) 9233 Speerberry Ln, #14101, Cordova TN 38016 B Monroe LA 1958 s Thaddeus & Katherine. BBA SMU 1980; MDiv Sewanee: The U So, TS 1993. D 6/12/1993 P 12/11/1993 Bp Robert Jefferson Hargrove Jr. c 3. S Matt's Ch Covington TN 2010-2012; H Trin Ch Memphis TN 2003-2009; S Mk's Epis Ch Venice FL 1995-2001; Asst R St Jas Epis Ch and Sch Alexandria LA 1994-1995; Cur Gr Epis Ch Monroe LA 1993-1994. w. ryan2109@gmail.com

RYBICKI, Robert (Cal) **Died 9/3/2016** Rec 12/22/2014 as Priest Bp Marc Handley Andrus.

RYDER, Anne Elizabeth (WMass) PO Box 1294, Sheffield MA 01257 B Palo Alto CA 1950 d Oliver & Elizabeth. BS California St U 1982; MDiv VTS 1996; MS Wheelock Coll 1996. D 6/22/1996 P 12/30/1996 Bp Richard Lester Shimpfky. c 1. Chr Epis Ch Sheffield MA 2004-2016; R S Pat's Epis Ch Pagosa Sprg CO 1998-2004; Assoc All SS Ch Carmel CA 1996-1998. Harris Awd VTS 1996. aeryder.50@gmail.com

RYDER SSAP, Barbara Helen (SVa) 12 Spring St, Decatur GA 30030 **Asstg P Ch Of The Epiph Atlanta GA 2006-** B Flint MI 1937 d Orval & Helen. BS Case Wstrn Reserve U 1960; MDiv VTS 1997. D 6/14/1997 Bp Frank Harris Vest Jr P 4/1/1998 Bp Peter J Lee. m 7/11/1959 Craig Anthony Ryder c 2. Chapl Washington Epis Sch Beth MD 2002-2006; Asst S Jn's Ch Centreville VA 1997-2001.

RYERSON, Raymond Willcox (FdL) 1758 Le Brun Rd, De Pere WI 54115 **Died 8/6/2016** B Detroit MI 1932 s Laverne & Edith. BS Wayne 1955; MDiv Nash 1985. D 4/20/1985 P 10/19/1985 Bp William Louis Stevens. m 7/7/1990 Kathleen D Ryerson c 3. P-in-c Ch of the Blessed Sacr Green Bay WI 2011-2013; Int S Mk's Ch Waupaca WI 2004-2005; Int S Ptr's Epis Ch Sheboygan Falls WI 2002-2003; Exec Coun Dio Fond du Lac Appleton WI 2001-2006, Sec Curs Mvmt 1989-1992, Chair, Dioc Bd Trst 2010-2013; Int S Jas Ch Manitowoc WI 2000-2001; P-in-c Chr Ch Green Bay WI 1995-1999; S Bon Plymouth WI

1991-1995; S Paul's Ch Plymouth WI 1991-1995; Vic S Jn's Ch Shawano WI 1985-1991; S Jn's Epis Ch New London WI 1985-1991. NOEL 1988-1996.

RYMER, Lionel Simon (VI) Po Box 7335, St Thomas VI 00801 B Road Town Tortola VI 1936 s Stewart & Maria. MDiv ETSC 1970; MEd U of The Vrgn Islands 1988. D 7/2/1970 P 6/1/1971 Bp Cedric Earl Mills. m 6/29/1961 Riisa T Rymer. S Lk's Ch St Thos VI 1978-2008; Dio Vrgn Islands Charlotte Amalie St Thom VI 1972-1977; Vic S Ursula Ch Cruz Bay St Jn VI 1971-1979. Auth, "S Lk Journ Theol".

S

SAAGER, Rebecca Ann (Lex) 311 Washington St, Frankfort KY 40601 B Buffalo NY 1957 d Stan & Sonia. BS Morehead St U 1979; MS Estrn Kentucky U 1992. D 6/5/2011 Bp Stacy F Sauls. m 5/16/1982 Donald Saager c 2.

SABETTI III, Henry Martin (Eas) 12822 Shrewsbury Church Rd, Kennedyville MD 21645 **R Shrewsbury Par Ch Kennedyville MD 2010-; R Ch of the Trsfg Braddock Heights MD 2004-** B Portland OR 1961 s Henry & Florence. BA Wabash Coll 1984; MSW Indiana U 1986; MDiv VTS 1998. D 6/13/1998 Bp Robert Wilkes Ihloff P 1/30/1999 Bp John L Rabb. m 6/27/2009 Lisa Hartge. Ch Of The Trsfg Braddock Heights MD 2004-2010; S Fran Acad Inc. Ellsworth KS 2002-2003; S Fran Cmnty Serv Inc. Salina KS 2001-2004; Chapl S Fran Acad Inc. Salina KS 2001-2002; S Nich Chap Ellsworth KS 2000-2004; Epis Ch Hm at York Place Inc Columbia SC 2000-2001; Chapl Epis Ch Hm for Chld York SC 2000-2001; Cur Ch Of The H Comf Luthvle Timon MD 1998-2000. Acad of Cert Soc Workers (ACSW); Lic Cert Soc Worker - Clincl (LCSW-C) 1995; NASW 1984.

SABOGAL GUTIERREZ, Diego Fernando (Colom) **Dio The Dominican Republic (Iglesia Epis Dominicana) Gazcue Santo Domingo 2016-** B Palmira 1970 s Gonzalo & Angela. D 6/16/2007 P 5/18/2008 Bp Francisco Jose Duque-Gomez. m 9/20/1996 Doris N Hernandez c 3.

SABOM, William Stephen (At) 1143 Sanden Ferry Dr, Decatur GA 30033 **Clinician The Pstr Inst Columbus GA 2002-** B Houston TX 1942 s William & Felicia. BA Colorado Coll 1964; MDiv VTS 1970; ThM Duke 1974; STD SFTS 1980. D 6/23/1970 Bp Scott Field Bailey. m 11/23/1996 Sharon Ann Mathis c 1. Ed, "Healing a Generation," *J. Am Acad Psychotherapists*, Guiltford Press, 1991; Auth, "The Moral Trauma of the Vietnam Veteran," *Pstr Psychol*, 1990; Auth, "Judgment at Catecka," *Voices*, 1989; Auth, "The Gnostic Wrld of Anorexia Nervosa," *Journ of Psychol & Theol*, 1983; Auth, "Heresy and Pstr Counslg," *J. Pstr Care*, 1980; Auth, "Near-Death Experience: A Revs from Pstr Psychol," *J. Rel and Hlth*, 1979. AAPC 1976.

SABUNE, Petero Aggrey Nkurunziza (NY) 293 Highland Ave, Newark NJ 07104 B Bufumbira Kigezi UG 1952 s Andereya & Ayirini. BA Vas 1977; MDiv UTS 1981. Trans 7/27/1984 Bp James Stuart Wetmore. m 9/4/1978 Maureen Norma Sabune c 4. Epis Ch Cntr New York NY 2010-2012; Vic S Jas Ch New York NY 1998-2004; Dn Trin And S Phil's Cathd Newark NJ 1992-1998; Assoc For Grants Trin Par New York NY 1990-1992; Ch Of The Incarn Jersey City NJ 1987-1990; Dio Newark Newark NJ 1987-1990; R Epis Ch Of SS Jn Paul And S Clem Mt Vernon NY 1982-1987; Cur Gr Ch White Plains NY 1981-1982. CHS; UBE. Cmnty Serv Awd Naacp 1989; Fr of The Year Awd; Cmnty Serv Awd; Mntl Hlth Awd.

SACCAROLA FAVARO, Flavio (EcuC) Apdo 08-01-404, Esmeraldas Ecuador **P Iglesia San Alfonso Ambato 2015-; R Iglesia Santa Maria Esmeraldas Ecuador 2007-; R Dio Ecuador Cntrl Quito Ecuador 1998-; P Dio El Salvador Ambato Tu 1998-** B Venezia, Italia 1946 s Giuseppe & Luigia. BA U Theol & Philos de Latran Titolo Rome IT 1973. Rec 11/1/1997 as Priest Bp Jose Neptali Larrea-Moreno. m 10/16/1992 Catalina Saccarola. Iglesia Epis Del Ecuador Quito 1998-2009; Serv RC Ch 1973-1993.

SACCO, Ronald John (Ind) 374 Shawnee Woods Drive, Bedford IN 47421 **Died 8/12/2015** B Sewickley PA 1944 s John & Margret. MDiv TESM 1987. D 6/4/1988 P 12/1/1988 Bp Alden Moinet Hathaway. m 1/1/2003 Lisa Klein Sacco c 2. S Jn's Epis Ch Bedford IN 1989-2001; S Mk's Ch Johnstown PA 1988-1989; Chapl U Pgh-Johnstown 1988-1989. Bro Of S Andr.

SACHERS, Calvin Stewart (Tex) 145 Lake View Dr, Boerne TX 78006 **Died 1/25/2016** B Richmond VA 1926 s Gustave & Wilhelmina. BA U of Virginia 1950; MDiv Epis TS of the SW 1958. D 6/19/1958 Bp James Parker Clements P 12/1/1959 Bp John Elbridge Hines. m 2/2/1964 Hallie Frances Sachers c 2. Ret 1995-2016; S Thos The Apos Epis Ch Houston TX 1978-1995; R S Thos The Apos Nassau Bay TX 1978-1995; Asst R Chr Epis Ch Charlottesvlle VA 1975-1978; R Buck Mtn Epis Ch Earlysvlle VA 1970-1975; R S Andr's Tyler TX 1967-1969; Cur S Dav's Ch Austin TX 1964-1967; R S Barth's Ch Hempstead TX 1963-1964; Stff Chapl S Lk's Hosp Houston TX 1962-1963; Asst Chapl Texas Mltry Inst In San Antonio 1961-1962; Cur S Mk's Ch Beaumont TX 1960-1961; M-in-c S Jn's Epis Ch Columbus TX 1958-1960.

SACHS, William Lewis (Va) 509 Saint Christophers Road, Richmond VA 23226 **Assoc S Steph's Ch Richmond VA 2014-, Asst 1980-1994; Consult**

Fam Hlth Intl Durham NC 2007-; Dir Cntr for Interfaith Recon Richmond VA 2006- B Richmond VA 1947 s Lewis & Dorothy. BA Baylor U 1969; MDiv Van 1972; STM Yale DS 1973; PhD U Chi 1981. D 5/26/1973 P 5/31/1974 Bp Robert Bruce Hall. m 5/17/1986 Elizabeth Austin Tucker c 1. Fell VTS Alexandria VA 2014-2017, Vstng Prof 2013-2014; Consult Cntr for Amer's First Freedom 2011-2012; Vstng Prof Ya 2006-2007; Dir Of Resrch ECF 2000-2006; VP ECF Inc New York NY 2000-2006; Asst S Lk's Par Darien CT 2000-2006; Consult Cornerstone Proj 1995-2000; R S Matt's Epis Ch Wilton CT 1994-2000; Consult The Lilly Endwmt 1991-1997; Adj Prof UTS-Va U Richmond 1985-1994; Rdr Goe 1984-1990; Fell ECF 1976-1979; Asst S Chrys's Ch Chicago IL 1975-1980; Cur Emm Ch At Brook Hill Richmond VA 1973-1975; Exam Chapl Dio Virginia Richmond VA 1982-1992. Auth, "Sxlty and Anglicanism," *Global Anglicanism in the Wstrn Wrld*, Oxford, 2017; Ed, "Global Anglicanism, 1910 to the Present," *Oxford Hist of Anglicanism, volume 5*, Oxford, 2017; Auth, "Fragmented Lives," Ch Pub, 2016; Auth, "In The Face of Difference," Rowman & Littlefield, 2014; Auth, "A Ch Beyond Belief," Ch Pub, 2014; Auth, "The Emergence of the Angl Comm," *Wiley-Blackwell Guide to the Angl Comm*, Wiley-Blackwell, 2013; Auth, "The Epis Ch in the Twentieth Century," *Encyclopedia of Rel in Amer*, CQ Press, 2010; Auth, "Homosexuality and the Crisis of Anglicanism," Cambridge, 2009; Auth, "Plantations and Missions," *Oxford Guide to the Bookf of Common Pryr*, Oxford, 2006; Auth, "Restoring The Ties That Bind," Ch Pub, 2003; Auth, "The Transformation Of Anglicansim," Cambridge, 1993; Auth, "Of One Body," Westminster/ Jn Knox, 1986; Auth, "Loc Diversity and Interfaith Initiative: Going Global Hits Hm," *Faithful Neighbors*, Ch Pub, 1916. HSEC 1976. Polly Bond Awds For Rel Journalism 1991.

SACQUETY JR, Charles William (Los) 8402 Castilian Dr, Huntington Beach CA 92646 B Detroit MI 1932 s Charles & Lorine. BA U MI 1954; MA U MI 1956; MDiv CDSP 1965. D 6/29/1965 Bp Archie H Crowley P 3/12/1966 Bp Richard Stanley Merrill Emrich. Int Ch of Our Sav San Gabr CA 2007; Int St. Jas Los Angeles CA 2004-2005; Pstr Care All SS Ch Pasadena CA 2001-2003; Archd Dio Los Angeles Los Angeles CA 1998-1999; R S Wilfrid Of York Epis Ch Huntington Bch CA 1978-1998; R The Angl/Epis Ch Of Chr The King Frankfurt am Main 60323 1971-1977; Asst S Mk's Par Glendale CA 1969-1971; Vic Gr Epis Ch Southgate MI 1967-1969; Cur S Dav's Ch Southfield MI 1965-1967. Hon DD CDSP; Hon Cn Dio Los Angeles.

SADLER, Alice Irene (SwFla) 906 S. Orleans Avenue, Tampa FL 33606 **Died 3/3/2016** B Charlotte NC 1949 d James & Florence. BA Erskine Coll 1971; MA U NC 1975; MDiv TESM 2001. D 10/16/2001 P 4/20/2002 Bp John Bailey Lipscomb. Assoc St Johns Epis Ch Tampa FL 2014-2016; Assoc R Trin By The Cove Naples FL 2001-2014. asadler@stjohntampa.org

SAFFORD, Timothy Browning (Pa) 20 N American St, Philadelphia PA 19106 **R Chr Ch Philadelphia Philadelphia PA 1999-** B Pasadena CA 1959 s Henry & Kathryn. BA Claremont McKenna Coll 1981; Cert Ya Berk 1985; MDiv Yale DS 1985. D 6/15/1985 P 1/25/1986 Bp Robert Claflin Rusack. m 5/4/1985 Lynn Annette Karoly c 2. Sr Assoc for Mssn & Outreach All SS Ch Pasadena CA 1988-1999; Cur S Jn's Ch Bridgeport CT 1985-1988. Pstr Theol Cntr for Rel Inquiry, Princeton. 2001; Mikkelsen Preaching Prize St. Jn's Ch, Capitola, CA 2000. tsafford@christchurchphila.org

SAHDER, Michael c (SeFla) D 11/19/2016 P 6/3/2017 Bp Peter David Eaton.

SAID, James T (Ga) 3321 Wheeler Rd, Augusta GA 30909 **S Aug Of Cbury Ch Augusta GA 2016-; Alum Assn Exec Com VTS Alexandria VA 2013-** B Muncie IN 1959 s John & Barbara. BA Indiana U 1981; Masters of Div VTS 2013. D 6/8/2013 Bp Cate Waynick P 1/18/2014 Bp John Lewis Said. m 8/22/1981 Kimberly A Said c 2. S Thos Epis Ch Coll Sta TX 2013-2016. The Ford Chair VTS 2013. fatherjim@knology.net

✠ SAID, The Rt Rev John Lewis (SeFla) 6508 Nw Chugwater Cir, Port Saint Lucie FL 34983 B Marion IN 1932 s Isaac & Vivian. BA Wabash Coll 1955; STB Ya Berk 1958; Ya Berk 1996. D 6/21/1958 P 1/10/1959 Bp Richard Ainslie Kirchhoffer Con 2/25/1995 for SeFla. m 6/11/1955 Barbara Ann Said c 3. Suffr Bp Dio SE Florida Miami 1995-2002, Ret Suffr Bp 2002-; R S Kevin's Epis Ch Opa Locka FL 1987-1994; 1979-1984; S Bern De Clairvaux N Miami Bch FL 1978-1982; S Johns Ch Indianapolis IN 1978; 1969-1977; Mssy Dio Cntrl Brazil 1966-1969; Chapl S Richard Sch Indianapolis IN 1964-1966; Cur Trin Ch Indianapolis IN 1964-1966; R S Mk's Ch Plainfield IN 1960-1964; Cur Gr Ch Muncie IN 1958-1960. Bro of St Andr 1987. Hon DD Berk 1996.

SAIK, Robert (Az) 514 S Mountain Rd, Mesa AZ 85208 **Epis Ch Of The Trsfg Mesa AZ 2013-** B Cincinnati OH 1951 s Richard & Elaine. BS Pur 1973; MBA TCU 1984; MDiv Bex 2013; MDiv Bex Sem 2013. D 6/29/2013 Bp Thomas Edward Breidenthal P 1/19/2014 Bp Kirk Stevan Smith. m 7/22/1977 Janet Lynn Saik c 1. transfiguration rector@gmail.com

SAILER, David Walter (WNC) 3 Oak Leaf Ln, Arden NC 28704 **Assoc Ch Of S Mths Asheville NC 2003-** B Wheeling WV 1941 s Walter & Catherine. BA W Liberty St Coll 1964; MDiv VTS 1967. D 6/12/1967 P 2/24/1968 Bp Wilburn Camrock Campbell. c 3. Int Ch Of The Gd Shpd Tryon NC 2002-2003; Chapl Skyland Fire & Rescue Skyland-Arden NC 1993-1999; R Calv Epis Ch Fletcher NC 1984-1998; Chapl City of Huntington WV Fire Dept 1978-1983; Assoc Trin Ch Huntington WV 1973-1984; Vic S Thos' Epis Ch Weirton WV 1969-1973; Chapl Davis & Elkins Coll Elkins WV 1967-1969; R Gr Epis Ch Elkins WV 1967-1969. Auth, "Hist of Calv, Fletcher, NC," *The Windows of Calv Ch*, 1999. Outstanding Young Men Amer 1976.

SAINTILVER, Margarette (Hai) B 1982 d Gesper & Marthe. Dplma Min Seminaire de Theologie 2011. D 7/29/2012 P 3/13/2014 Bp Jean Zache Duracin. Dio Haiti Port-au-Prince HT 2012-2016.

SAINT JUSTE, Vanel (DR) **Dio The Dominican Republic (Iglesia Epis Dominicana) Gazcue Santo Domingo 2015-** B 1983 s Maneus & Clotide. Licenciado en Teologia Centro de Estudios Teología; Licenciado en Contabilidad Unversidad Nacional Teología. D 2/15/2015 Bp Julio Cesar Holguin-Khoury.

SAINT-PIERRE, Nathanael L B (NY) Haitian Congregation of the Good Samaritan, 661 E 219th St, Bronx NY 10467 **S Aug's Ch New York NY 2012-** B Port-au-Price, Haiti 1963 s Bernardin & Prophite. Dip Cntr Pilote de Formation Propessionelle; Cert Epis TS of the SW 1992; AA Institut Superieu d Electronic 1997. Trans 11/6/2007 Bp Mark Sean Sisk. m 9/27/1986 Karline Bernard c 2. Dio New York New York NY 2007-2012; S Dav's Ch Bronx NY 2007-2012; P-in-c Dio Montreal 2004-2007; Haitian Cong of the Gd Samar Bronx NY 1998-2013.

SAINT ROMAIN, Brad (Tex) 3333 Castle Ave, Waco TX 76710 **R S Fran Par Temple TX 2011-; Convoc Dn Dio Texas Houston TX 2014-** B New Orleans LA 1958 s Joseph & Patsy. BS LSU 1980; MDiv Epis TS of the SW 2003. D 12/28/2002 P 11/17/2003 Bp Charles Edward Jenkins III. m 11/21/1981 Lisa Carlin Terry c 3. Assoc R S Paul's Ch Waco TX 2004-2011; Chr Epis Ch Cedar Pk TX 2004; Chapl Hospice Austin 2003-2004; The Epis Ch of the Gd Shpd,Austin,TX The Ch of the Gd Shpd Austin TX 2003-2004.

SAJNA, Barbara Jean Reiser (FdL) 2100 Ridges Rd., Baileys Harbor WI 54202 B Rhinelander WI 1940 d Max & Dorothy. JD U of Wisconsin 1983; MDiv SMU Perkins 1997. D 6/27/1998 P 5/1/1999 Bp James Monte Stanton. c 3. R S Lk's Epis Ch Sis Bay WI 2004-2012, R 2004-; Cur The Epis Ch Of The Trsfg Dallas TX 2000-2004; Chapl/Asst Ch Of The Gd Shpd Dallas TX 1998-2000.

SAKIN, Charles Robert (NJ) 1812 Rue De La Port Drive, Wall NJ 07719 B Baltimore MD 1943 s Harold & Emma. BA Ge 1965; STB PDS 1968; MTh PrTS 1970; MS Monmouth U 1977. D 4/20/1968 P 10/1/1968 Bp Alfred L Banyard. m 8/26/1967 Katherine Pawlikowski. Assoc Trin Epis Ch Red Bank NJ 1981-1997; P-in-c S Steph's Ch Manchester Twp NJ 1974-1977; Chapl/Instr Admiral Farragut Acad 1970-1973; Cur S Jn's Ch Somerville NJ 1968-1969. Auth, "Its Worth A Laugh".

SAKRISON, David L (U) 280 E 300 S, Moab UT 84532 **P Dio Utah Salt Lake City UT 2010-** B Salida CO 1946 s Linwood & Dorotha. D 6/7/2003 P 5/30/2004 Bp Carolyn Tanner Irish. m 11/23/1974 Melody Lynn Sakrison c 2.

SALAMONE, Robert Emmitt (At) 2490 Orchard Walk, Bogart GA 30622 **R Emm Epis Ch Athens GA 2006-** B Jersey City NJ 1952 s Louis & Eileen. BA Don Bosco Coll 1975; MDiv Immac Concep Sem 1979. Rec 12/21/1999 Bp Bob Johnson. m 8/25/1996 Karen C Salamone. Assoc R S Jas Epis Ch Hendersonville GA 1997-2006; Par Admin S Jas Epis Ch Hendersonvlle NC 1997-1999. rector@emmanuelathens.org

SALAZAR-SOTILLO, Orlando Rafael (Ve) B 1950 D 12/17/1992 P 6/24/1993 Bp Onell Asiselo Soto. m 12/1/1973 Amidalis Teresa de Salazar. Dio Venezuela Caracas 2004-2017.

SALAZAR-VASQUEZ, Jose (Ve) **Dio Venezuela Caracas 2004-** B 1967 D 2/24/2005 Bp Orlando Jesus Guerrero. m 12/28/1990 Pragedes Coromoto Jimenez de Salazar.

SALBADOR, Gus William (Wyo) 2510 Stonebridge Way, Mount Vernon WA 98273 B Lake Charles LA 1929 s Gustave & Anna. BS Steph F Austin St U 1954; DVM Texas A&M U 1958; MDiv The Coll of Emm and S Chad CA 1990. D 11/14/1992 Bp Leo Frade P 9/14/1993 Bp Charles I Jones III. c 2. Cn Dio Wyoming Casper 2001; Int S Matt's Epis Cathd Laramie WY 2000-2001; Vic S Barn Epis Ch Saratoga WY 1998-2000; Vic Iglesia Epis San Geo Roatan Sandy Bay 1992-1998; Iglesia Epis San Pedro de Mar Roatan Is 1992-1998; Dio Montana Helena MT 1992-1997. Cn Cathd El Buen Pstr Sps 1997.

SALCEDO, Federico B (PR) B 1943 s Delio & Alicia. Seminario Sevilla; Universidad Nacional Pedro Henríquez Ureña. m 7/27/1975 Maria Irizarry c 3. Dio The Dominican Republic (Iglesia Epis Dominicana) Gazcue Santo Domingo 2004-2006, 1982-1985; Dio Puerto Rico Trujillo Alto PR 2004, 1985-2003.

SALIK, Lamuel Gill (Dal) 138 Liveoak St, Hereford TX 79045 **Int First Presb Ch 2005-** B Sahiwal Punjab PK 1941 s Feroze & Fazal. LTh Gujranwala TS Pk 1970; BA U of Karachi 1973; GTS 1994; MDiv Faith TS Philadelphia 1997; DRel Faith TS Philadelphia PA 1998. Trans 11/12/1992 Bp George Phelps Mellick Belshaw. m 10/16/1981 Roseline W Salik c 2. R S Jas' Epis Ch Dalhart TX 2006-2009; First Presb Ch Hereford TX 2005-2006; P-in-c S Mk's Epis Ch Plainview TX 2000; R S Thos Epis Ch Hereford TX 1999-2005; Supply Dio New Jersey Trenton NJ 1993-1998; S Lk's Ch Woodstown NJ 1992-1993; Asst S Lk's Epis Ch Metuchen NJ 1989-1991; Asst S Andr's Astoria NY 1982-1989; Serv Ch Of Pakistan 1970-1974. Ed, "Outreach"; Transltr, "A Chr'S Handbook On Communism".

SALINARO, Katherine Ella Mae (Cal) 121 Sheffield, Hercules CA 94547 **D Ch Of The H Trin Richmond CA 2002-, D 2002-** B Saint Louis MO 1936 BA San Francisco St U 1958; BA Sch for Deacons 1984; MA H Name U 1991. D 12/7/1985 Bp William Edwin Swing. c 3. Instr/D Epis Sch For Deacons Berkeley CA 1997-2008; Pstr Counslr For New Directions Chr Counslg Cntr Concord CA 1989-1999. Assn of Epis Deacons 1984; Third Ord SSF 1981.

SALISBURY, Katherine Ann (LI) 157 Montague St, Brooklyn NY 11201 B Washington DC 1977 d Ryan & Ann. BA Col 1999; MA GTS 2014; MA The GTS 2014; MDiv Yale Div 2014; MDiv Yale DS 2014. D 6/7/2014 Bp Lawrence C Provenzano P 6/13/2015 Bp Chilton Richardson Knudsen. m 7/23/2005 Ian Stuart Salisbury c 1. Admin Geo Mercer TS Garden City NY 2015; S Ann And The H Trin Brooklyn NY 2014, Asst 2014-; S Jas Ch New York NY 2005-2011. ksalisbury@stannholytrinity.org

SALLES, Stacy D (Mich) 67640 Van Dyke Rd # 10, Washington MI 48095 **P-in-c Ch Of The Adv Cincinnati OH 2016-; Dn Oakland Dnry Dio MI 2011-; Advsry Bd Whitaker Sch. of Theol Dio MI 2011-** B Owosso MI 1955 d John & Harriett. BS Nthrn St U Aberdeen SD 1978; MDiv SWTS 1999. D 12/21/2002 P 6/25/2003 Bp Wendell Nathaniel Gibbs Jr. c 1. Dn Oakland Dnry Dio MI 2009-2011; R St Paul's Epis Romeo MI 2006-2015; Asst Trin Ch Belleville MI 2003-2006, D 2002-2003.

SALLEY JR, George Bull (Ga) 310 McLaws Street, Savannah GA 31405 **Hon. Assoc The Collgt Ch of St Paul the Apos Savannah GA 2002-; Ret 1999-** B Orangeburg SC 1937 s George & Martha. BS U of So Carolina 1959; MDiv Sewanee: The U So, TS 1973. D 6/26/1973 P 5/30/1974 Bp George Moyer Alexander. m 4/4/1976 Anne B Salley c 2. Asst S Geo's Epis Ch Savannah GA 1999-2001; R S Mich And All Ang Savannah GA 1985-1999; R All SS Ch Cayce SC 1978-1985, Cur 1973-1974; Vic S Alb's Ch Lexington SC 1974-1978; Dioc Coun Dio Georgia Savannah GA 1986-1989.

SALMON JR, Abraham Dickerson (Md) 7351 Willow Rd Apt 2, Frederick MD 21702 **Ret 1993-; Ret 1992-** B Morristown NJ 1930 s Abraham & Audrey. BA Franklin & Marshall Coll 1952; LTh SWTS 1957. D 6/21/1957 Bp Walter M Higley P 6/11/1958 Bp Malcolm E Peabody. c 4. R All SS Ch Frederick MD 1970-1992; R Gr Ch Brunswick MD 1963-1970; Chr Ch Guilford CT 1957-1962.

SALMON, Alan Kent (NJ) 4 Tara Ln, Delran NJ 08075 **Ret 2003-; Hon Cn Trin Cathd Trenton NJ 2015-** B Moorestown NJ 1938 s Walter & Marie. Cert St. Geo's Coll, Jerusalem; Cert U of Madrid 1959; BA Trin Hartford CT 1960; MA Trin Hartford CT 1961; MDiv GTS 1964; DMin Drew U 1989. D 4/25/1964 P 10/31/1964 Bp Alfred L Banyard. Long term supply St. Steph's Mullica Hill NJ 2011-2013; Bd Trst S Mary Hall Doane Acad Burlington NJ 1982-1997; Dn - Burlington Convoc Dio New Jersey Trenton NJ 1978-1981; R Chr Ch Riverton NJ 1970-2003; Vic St Peters Ch Woodbury Hgts NJ 1966-1970; Cur Trin Epis Ch Cranford NJ 1964-1966. Auth, "arts," *Word & Sacr*. Phi Beta Kappa Trin, Hartford, CT 1960.

✠ SALMON JR, The Rt Rev Edward Lloyd (Spr) 9 Westmoreland Place, Saint Louis MO 63108 **Died 6/29/2016** B Natchez MS 1934 s Edward & Helen. BA U So 1956; BD VTS 1960. D 6/24/1960 P 3/1/1961 Bp Robert Raymond Brown Con 2/24/1990 for SC. m 1/26/1972 Louise Salmon c 2. R All SS' Epis Ch Chevy Chase MD 2010-2012; Ret Bp of SC So Carolina Charleston SC 2007-2013, Bp Of SC 1990-2008, 1990-2006; R S Mich & S Geo S Louis MO 1978-1990; S Paul's Ch Fayetteville AR 1967-1978; Vic S Andr's Ch Rogers AR 1960-1963; S Jas Ch Eureka Spgs AR 1960-1963; S Thos Ch Springdale AR 1960-1963; Dn and Pres Nash TS 2012-2016; Epis Dio Washington Epis Visitor 2006-2016; Pres Angl Dig 1965-2016. DD Nash Sem 2007; DD U of thr So 1991; DD VTS 1991.

SALMON JR, John Frederick (Nwk) 195 Woodside Dr, Lumberton NJ 08048 **Ret 1996-; Asstg P Trin Ch Moorestown NJ 1996-** B Camden NJ 1931 s John & Dorothy. BS Rutgers The St U of New Jersey 1953; LTh GTS 1956; MDiv GTS 1958; MEd Rutgers The St U of New Jersey 1965. D 4/28/1956 P 10/27/1956 Bp Alfred L Banyard. m 11/30/1957 Suzanne Virginia Salmon c 3. Ch Of The Adv Newark NJ 1965-1996, R 1965-1996; R Ch Of S Andr The Apos Camden NJ 1957-1965; Vic Ch Of S Clem Of Rome Belford NJ 1957; S Mk's Epis Ch Keansburg NJ 1957; Cur Trin Cathd Trenton NJ 1956-1957; Rgstr The GTS New York NY 1973-1974.

SALMON, Walter Burley Stattmann (At) **Asst The Epis Ch Of Beth-By-The-Sea Palm Bch FL 2015-,** B Natchez MS 1971 s Walter & Myrtis. BA Millsaps Coll 1993; MDiv Ya Berk 1998. D 4/30/2011 Bp Keith Whitmore P 4/6/2013 Bp Robert Christopher Wright. m 10/24/2015 Robert Christopher Jacob Henkel. Chapl Trin Epis Sch Charlotte NC 2013-2015; Cur Ch Of The Redeem Greensboro GA 2013; Tchr The Lovett Sch Atlanta GA 2009-2013. salmon@bbts.org

SALT, Alfred Lewis (Nwk) 4822 Martinique Way, Naples FL 34119 **Asstg P S Mary's Epis Ch Bonita Sprg FL 2013-; Ret (Asstg) Dio SW Florida Sarasota FL 2002-** B Hackensack NJ 1927 s Alfred & Lillian. BA Bishops U QC CA 1949; MA Bishops U QC CA 1951; LST Bishops U QC CA 1954; BD Bishops U QC CA 1960; AMP Harv 1970; DMin GTF 1988. Trans 2/2/1972 as Priest Bp Leland Stark. m 6/18/1949 Elizabeth M Salt c 4. Dir Victorious Mnstrs

744

through Chr Can 1994-2002; Dio Estrn Michigan Saginaw MI 1993-2002; Ret Dio Huron 1993-2001; VP Victorious Mnstrs through Chr 1989-1991; Int'l Bd Dir. Victorious Mnstrs through Chr 1988-1992; Pres S Mart's Hse 1986-1989; Dir Victorious Mnstrs through Chr 1985-1992; Coordntr Victorious Mnstrs through Chr 1983-1985; Comm. on Evang Comm. on Evang 1975-1981; Pres Morris Convoc 1974-1978; Heath Vill 1974-1976; R All SS Ch Millington NJ 1972-1993; Camp Com Chairman Dio Newark Newark NJ 1972-1974; Serv Angl Ch of Can Quebec Can 1951-1972. Auth, "God's Healing Gr," *A COMPASSbook*, BRF, 1995; Auth, "Freedom in Chr Jesus," *Fellows Yearbook 1988*, Wyndham Hill Press, 1988; Auth, "The Nature, Scope," *and Hist of VMTC*, VMTC, 1983; Auth, "Var arts," *Sharing*, OSL. Chapl Ord of S Lk 1980; Comp WSHS/WBHS 2007; Dir VMTC 1981-1992. Marquis Lifetime Achievement Awd Who's Who 2002; Who's Who in Amer 2012; Who's Who in the Wrld 2007; Fell GTF 1988; Hon Cn Dio Quebec 1970.

SALTZGABER, Jan Mcminn (Ga) 225 W Point Dr, Saint Simons Island GA 31522 **D Chr Ch Frederica St Simons Is GA 2001-; Bd, Dir of Spec Projects Intl Seafarers' Cntr 2001-** B Harvey IL 1933 s Merrill & Anna. BA Wayne 1959; MA Wayne 1965; PhD Syr 1974. D 12/19/2001 Bp Henry Irving Louttit. m 6/28/1988 Pauline Elizabeth Jenks.

SALVATIERRA SERIAN, Juan E (EcuC) Apdo 17-11-6165, Quito Ecuador **Vic Catedral de El Senor Quito 1998-** B Empalme Guayas 1966 s Enrique & Humberta. BS Sem Mayor Cristo Sacerdote Colombia CO 1986. Rec 7/1/1996 as Priest Bp Terencio Alfredo Morante-Espana. m 2/16/2003 Zoraida Monserrate Muentes Mora. Iglesia Epis Del Ecuador Quito 1998-2016; Serv RC Ch 1989-1996.

SAM, Albert Abuid Samuel (WNY) 7469 Dysinger Rd, Lockport NY 14094 **Ret 1999-; Ret 1996-** B Dunkirk NY 1938 s Samuel & Mary. SUNY Fredonia 1968; SUNY at Buffalo 1968; U Roch 1968; MDiv Bex Sem 1971. D 1/6/1972 P 7/8/1972 Bp Harold Barrett Robinson. c 4. Ret St. Andr's Epis Ch 2013; St. Jn's Epis Ch Wilson NY 1999-2006; S Jn's Ch Wilson NY 1999; Cn Mssnr Dio Wstrn New York Tonawanda NY 1992-1996; St Mk Epis Ch No Tonawanda NY 1978-1990; Vic S Pat's Ch Buffalo NY 1972-1978.

SAM, Helen (WNY) PO Box 14, Dunkirk NY 14048 B Pomfret NY 1932 d Albert & Nacima. BA SUNY at Buffalo 1980. D 4/14/2009 P 11/8/2009 Bp Michael Garrison.

SAMILIO, Jamie Suzanne (Va) 2455 Gallows Rd, Dunn Loring VA 22027 **Ch Of The H Cross Dunn Loring VA 2015-** B Erie PA 1960 d Coston & Elaine. MACE VTS 2005; MDiv VTS 2015; Angl Stds VTS 2015. D 6/6/2015 Bp Shannon Sherwood Johnston P 12/12/2015 Bp Susan Goff. m 11/21/2013 Sylvia Teresa Saliunas.

SAMMIS, Robert Lyle (Los) B 1959 s John & Elizabeth. D 6/4/2016 Bp Joseph Jon Bruno. m 12/22/1979 Ojeni Panossian c 2.

SAMMONS, Gregory P (O) 4684 Brittany Rd, Toledo OH 43615 B Columbus OH 1950 s James & Dorothy. BA Trin 1972; Harvard DS 1973; MDiv EDS 1976. D 9/25/1976 P 4/23/1977 Bp Alexander D Stewart. m 9/10/1977 Margaret Holt c 2. Transition P in Charge St. Paul's Epis Ch Dayton Ohio 2014-2017; Bd Mem/Chair Coll Mnstry 1997-2007; Dio Ohio 1997-1999; R S Michaels In The Hills Toledo OH 1994-2014; Dioc Liturg Com Dio Michigan 1987-1989; Assoc Chr Ch Grosse Pointe Grosse Pointe Farms MI 1983-1993; R S Phil's Ch Easthampton MA 1978-1983; Asst S Mich's-On-The-Heights Worcester MA 1976-1978; GC Alt Dep Dio Ohio Cleveland 2008-2009, Dn, W Mssn Area 2001-2008, Dioc Coun 2000-2002, Angl Partnerships 1997-2000; Dept of Admin and Fin Dio Wstrn Massachusetts Springfield 1980-1983. Dayton Metro Chapt, Barbershop Harmony Soc of Amer 2014; Rotary Intl of Toledo, Ohio 2008. Phi Beta Kappa Trin, Beta Chapet, Conn. 1971.

SAMMONS, Margaret Holt (O) 208 Lewiston Rd., Kettering OH 45429 B Chicago IL 1948 d James & Joan. BA Wellesley Coll 1971; MDiv EDS 1977; Cert Worcester Pstr Counslg 1978. D 6/5/1977 P 5/19/1978 Bp Charles Bennison Sr. m 9/10/1977 Gregory P Sammons c 2. Co-R S Michaels In The Hills Toledo OH 2003-2014, Assoc 1994-2003; Chr Ch Grosse Pointe Grosse Pointe Farms MI 1984-1993, Assoc 1983-1984; S Jn's Ch Northampton MA 1983, 1980-1983; Int S Lk's Ch Worcester MA 1977-1978; Tchr Peace Corps Vol 1971-1974; S Steph's Ch Spencer IA 1968-1974. Auth, *Declare His Glory: Lenten Study Prog Mssn*, Dio Wstrn Mass., 1979.

SAMPEY, Amanda L (FdL) St James Episcopal Church, 402 2nd St, Mosinee WI 54455 **Assigned D St Jas Epis Ch Mosinee WI 2017-, Assigned D 2011-2016, Appointed D 2011-; Contracted Chapl S Clares Hosp 2012-; Contracted Chapl S Clares Hosp Weston WI 2012-** B Red Bank NJ 1959 d Joseph & Margaret. EFM Cert Sewanee: The U So, TS 2011; EFM Cert U So TS 2011. D 5/7/2011 Bp Russell Edward Jacobus P 12/17/2016 Bp Matthew A Gunter. m 4/6/2005 Dennis Karl Sampey c 3.

SAMPSON, Leon (NAM) PO Box 28, Bluff UT 84512 **Navajoland Area Mssn Farmington NM 2015-** B Monticello 1974 s Mary Rose. AAS Utah Vlly U 2013; D Cert Bishops Collaborative Trng 2014. D 6/14/2014 Bp David Earle Bailey. m 9/3/2011 Madeline Sampson c 3.

SAMPSON, Paula Kathryn (Ak) 4317 Birch Avenue, Terrace V8G 1X2 Canada B Ketchikan AK 1948 d Kenneth & Beatrice. BA U of Washington 1970; MA

H Name U 1991; MDiv PSR 1994; PhD CDSP 2000. D 6/24/1994 P 4/1/1995 Bp Steven Charleston. m 8/3/1996 Ian MacKenzie. R S Phil's Ch Wrangell AK 2009; Serv Angl Ch of Can 1997-2004; S Augustines' Epis Ch Homer AK 1995-1996; D The Epis Ch Of The Gd Shpd Berkeley CA 1994-2004; Pres of The Stndg Com Dio Alaska Fairbanks AK 1988-1989, 1986-1989; Dn Dio Arkansas Little Rock AR 1986-1989; Assoc P Walton Rehab Hosp.

SAMPSON, Timothy Warren (WMass) Via South Maria Di Carvaggio, 5, Pavia 27100 Italy **Died 8/13/2015** B Williamsville NY 1949 s Joseph & Sylvia. BA U of Hartford 1971; MDiv VTS 1976. D 6/16/1976 Bp Alexander D Stewart P 1/26/1977 Bp Harold Barrett Robinson. Asst R S Chris's Ch Chatham MA 1991-1993; Chapl-In-C H Ghost Genova Italy 1989-1991; Asst All S's Milan Italy 1987-1991; Non-par 1978-1987; Cur S Lk's Epis Ch Jamestown NY 1976-1978.

SAMRA, Gordon L (NI) 14823 Waterbrook Rd, Fort Wayne IN 46814 **D Trin Ch Ft Wayne IN 2004-, 2001-2003** B Fort Wayne IN 1943 s Alfred & Gladys. AA S Fran Coll Ft Wayne IN 1986. D 11/30/1995 Bp Francis Campbell Gray. m 7/15/1967 Patricia Anne Samra c 2. Chapl Vstng Nurse & Hospice Hm Ft Wayne IN 2006-2010; Chapl Luth Hosp of Indiana Ft Wayne IN 2004-2005.

SAMS, David Lee (Minn) 203 Aspenwood Drive, Redwood Falls MN 56283 B Sioux City IA 1951 s Leland & Doris. D Formation Prog; BA SW Minnesota St U 1973; MA Minnesota St U Mankato 1996. D 12/27/1984 Bp Robert Marshall Anderson. D S Jn's Epis Ch Mankato MN 2000-2002; D S Jn Worthington MN 1994-1998; D/Asst Bp Whipple Mssn Morton MN 1992-2014, D/Asst 1992-, 1985-1991; D S Ptr's Ch New Ulm MN 1988-1991; D Ch Of The Gd Shpd Windom MN 1984-1985.

SAMS, Jonathan Carter (Mich) 6402 Fredmoor Dr, Troy MI 48098 **Honarary Cn Cathd Ch Of S Paul Detroit MI 2014-** B Charleston SC 1942 s Henry & Carolyn. BA Ob 1963; MDiv Nash 1966. D 6/11/1966 Bp James Winchester Montgomery P 12/17/1966 Bp Gerald Francis Burrill. m 9/4/1999 Nancy I Sams c 6. Assoc Chr Ch Cranbrook Bloomfield Hills MI 2011-2015; Dn Dio Michigan Detroit MI 2002-2005, COM 1996-2001, Total Mnstry Dvlpmt Grp 2000-2004; R S Steph's Ch Troy MI 1991-2011; S Tim's Ch Griffith IN 1983-1991, Yth Dir 1976-1982; S Paul's Epis Ch Munster IN 1977-1982; Assoc S Chris's Ch Crown Point IN 1977-1978; Assoc S Paul Hammond IN 1976-1982; Chapl Lawr Hall Yth Serv 1966-1977; Lawr Hall Sch Chicago IL 1966-1970; Cur Ch Of The Ascen Chicago IL 1966-1967; COM Dio Nthrn Indiana So Bend IN 1985-1988. Auth, "www.theramblingrector.blogspot.com," 2007; Auth, "Fam Album (Poetry)," Bennett, 1993; Auth, "Rambling R (Column)," *Record (Dio Mi Nwspr)*, 1992; Auth, "(Var arts)," *Congregations*, Alb Inst, 1990; Auth, "Chickenbone Lake," Anadromous Press, 1988; Auth, "Reflections Of A Fishing Parson," Abingdon, 1972; Auth, "Angling Theologically," *Field & Stream*, 1970. Living Stones 1984-2000; Soc Of S Jn The Evang 1996.

SAMUEL, Amjad John (Ct) 1361 W Market St, Akron OH 44313 **S Paul's Epis Ch Shelton CT 2014-** B 1971 s John & Shirin. BA Alma Coll 1992; MTS Duke DS 1995. Trans 5/23/2008 Bp James Elliot Curry. m 11/21/2008 Maria Katherine Mitchell-Samuel. Assoc S Paul's Ch Akron OH 2010-2014; Cur/Dir of Chr Formation Calv Ch Stonington CT 2008-2010.

SAMUEL, Daniel (DR) Aptd 764, Santo Domingo Dominican Republic **Vic Iglesia Epis Santa Maria la Virgen Puerto Plata 2008-; Dio The Dominican Republic (Iglesia Epis Dominicana) Gazcue Santo Domingo 1992-** B Leogane HT 1956 s Mathurin & Imanie. BA Centro de Estudios Teologicos 1991; Lic Universidad Autonoma de Santo Domingo 2008. D 6/7/1992 P 12/1/1993 Bp Julio Cesar Holguin-Khoury. m 1/23/1982 Marie Aurianne Rosier c 1. Vic S Gabr Consuelo 2000-2008; Iglesia Epis San Jose Andrés Boca Chica 1994-2000; Iglesia Epis San Tomas Municipio de Gautier Sa 1994-2000; Vic Iglesia Epis San Marcos Haitiana Ft Lauderdale FL 1994-1999; Asst S Andr Santo Domingo Dominican Republic 1993-1994; Asst Sagrada Familia Santo Domingo Dominican Republic 1992-1993; Clero Consejo Latino Americano de Iglesias 1998-2001.

SAMUEL, Jason W (SanD) Saint David's Epis Church, 5050 Milton St, San Diego CA 92110 **P-in-c S Dav's Epis Ch San Diego CA 2014-** B Minden Louisiana 1963 s James & Betty. BA Oral Roberts U 1985; MDiv Nash 1990. D 11/28/1992 P 7/4/1993 Bp Roger John White. R Ch Of The Trsfg Lake S Louis MO 1997-2014; P-in Charge S Andr's Ch Milwaukee WI 1996; R S Dav Of Wales Ch New Berlin WI 1994-1996; Asst S Mk's Ch Milwaukee WI 1992-1993; Crt for trial of Cler Dio Missouri S Louis MO 2012-2015, GC Dep 2012-2015, Dioc Coun 2011-, GC Dep 2009-2012, Stndg Com 2007-2011, GC Dep 2003-2007, GC Cler Dep 2002-2006. Claiming the Blessing Strng Com 2002; EPF 2001; Integrity 1994; NEAC 1999; St. Chas Cnty Soc Justice Soc 2002; The Oasis Missouri 2000. Awd for commitment to Soc justice in our surrounding commities for the outcast St. Chas Cnty Soc Justice Soc 2007; DD St. Paul's Coll, VA 1986. jasonsamuel@earthlink.net

SAMUEL, Pauline Ann (LI) **Other Lay Position S Phil's Ch Brooklyn NY 2013-** D 1/14/2017 Bp Lawrence C Provenzano.

SAMUELS, Robert Marshall (WNY) 201 Saint Francis Dr, Green Bay WI 54301 B Melrose MA 1945 s Robert & Helen. AA Penn Behrend Coll Erie PA 1981;

S

745

MDiv TESM 1988; ThD Slidell Bapt Sem 2000. D 11/30/1988 P 6/17/1989 Bp William Louis Stevens. m 12/14/1968 Sharon L Samuels c 3. Vic S Mary's Ch Salamanca NY 2002-2005; S Mary's Ch Erie PA 2000-2005; R Gr Epis Ch Menomonie WI 2000-2001; H Trin Ch Conrath WI 1998-1999; Our Sav's Phillips WI 1995-1998; R S Kath's Ch Owen WI 1994-1999; S Alb's Epis Ch Marshfield WI 1993; Cur S Anne's Epis Ch De Pere WI 1988-1992.

SAMUELSON, Frank W (CFla) 3901 S Panther Creek Dr, The Woodlands TX 77381 **Epis TS Of The SW Austin TX 2014-** B Munchweiler Germany 1960 s Howard & Irmgard. MDiv The Epis Sem of the SW 2017. D 1/30/2017 Bp Gregory Orrin Brewer. m 5/18/1985 Louise B Louise Booth Bernhardt c 3. fsamuelson@trinitywoodlands.org

SAMUELSON, Louise B (CFla) 2450 River Oaks Blvd, Houston TX 77019 **S Jn The Div Houston TX 2017-; Epis TS Of The SW Austin TX 2014-** B Wilmington DE 1961 d Howard & Martha. MDiv Epis Sem of the SW 2017. D 1/30/2017 Bp Gregory Orrin Brewer. m 5/18/1985 Frank W Samuelson c 3. louisebsamuelson@gmail.com

SANBORN, Calvin (Me) Po Box 823, York Harbor ME 03911 **R S Geo's Epis Ch York ME 2010-, Asst 2002-2004** B Bridgeton ME 1974 s Earl & Patricia. BA S Josephs Coll Standish ME 1996; MDiv EDS 2002. D 6/1/2002 P 11/30/2002 Bp Chilton Richardson Knudsen. m 7/6/2013 Daniel Archibald Summers c 2. R S Matt's Epis Ch Hallowell ME 2005-2010; Dio New York New York NY 2004-2005; Dio Maine Portland ME 2002-2015.

SANBORN, Victoria B M (NY) 3919 Pocahontas Ave, Cincinnati OH 45227 **Exec Com - Com 1986-; Asst Secy For Sthrn Conv 1985-** B Brooklyn NY 1939 d Frederic & Janet. BA Wellesley Coll 1961; BA Oxf GB 1964; MA Oxf GB 1969; MDiv GTS 1982. D 6/2/1979 P 5/1/1980 Bp Paul Moore Jr. Assoc S Jn's Ch New York NY 1997-2000; Dio Sthrn Ohio Cincinnati OH 1985-1989; Vic Chap Of The Nativ Cincinnati OH 1985-1988; Lectr EDS MA 1983-1985; Assoc St. Barth Ch New York NY 1979-1983; Seamens Ch Inst New York NY 1979-1981.

SANCHEZ, Jose D (Tex) 525 NE 15th St, Miami FL 33132 **Vic The Great Cmsn Fndt Houston TX 2017-** B Mexico 1959 s Jesus & Aurora. BA Intercontinental U 1989; BA Universidad Intercontinental 2004. Rec 5/25/2011 Bp Leo Frade. m 12/12/2004 Glenda Reoyo c 2. Ch Of S Nich Pompano Bch FL 2012-2015; Dio SE Florida Miami 2011.

SANCHEZ NAVARRO, Aida Consuelo (Hond) **Novena Provincia Iglesia Epis 2013-; Dio Honduras San Pedro Sula 2006-; Iglesia Epis Hondurena San Pedro Sula 2006-** B Santa Rosa de Coxan 1963 d Sergio & Maria. Universidad Nacional Autonama De Honduras 1988; Programa Diocesano De Educ Teologica 2003. D 10/29/2005 P 11/10/2007 Bp Lloyd Emmanuel Allen. m 1/13/2001 Luis Gustavo Brenes Vaigas c 1. Abogada Unilever 2000-2002.

SANCHEZ NAVARRO, Jose Israel (Hond) **Dio Honduras San Pedro Sula 1998-** B 1964

SANCHEZ NUNEZ, Carlos A (PR) PO Box 327, Manati PR 00674 B 1949 s Leoncio & Norma. BA Universisdad Catolica de PR 1982; Cert Escuela de Estudios Teological Diocesana 1988. D 1/15/1989 Bp Francisco Reus-Froylan P 1/28/1990 Bp David Andres Alvarez-Velazquez. c 3. Dio Nthrn Mex Nuevo Leon 2015-2016; Dio Puerto Rico Trujillo Alto PR 2004-2015, R 1994-2003.

SANCHEZ PUJOL, Augusto Sandino (DR) Santiago #114, Santo Domingo Dominican Republic **Par P Dio The Dominican Republic (Iglesia Epis Dominicana) Gazcue Santo Domingo 1997-** B Bani DO 1953 s Juan & Juana. Coll Epis S Marcos 1975; Centro de Estudios Teologicos 1995. D 6/29/1996 Bp Julio Cesar Holguin-Khoury. m 3/13/1987 Isabel Lantigua.

SANCHEZ-SHABAZZ, Jacqueline Marie (NY) 236 E 31st St, New York NY 10016 B New York NY 1951 d George & Ellen. Med Asst Estrn Tech 1988. D 5/13/2017 Bp Andrew Marion Lenow Dietsche. c 4.

SAND, David Allan (NMich) PO Box 805, Iron Mountain MI 49801 B Iron Mountain, MI 1949 s Bortel & Ruth. BS Nthrn Michigan U 1971; Mutual Mnstry 2010. D 3/29/2010 P 10/3/2010 Bp Thomas Kreider Ray. m 2/16/1974 Lynn Ann Sand c 2.

SAND, Lynn Ann (NMich) PO Box 805, Iron Mountain MI 49801 B Iron Mountain MI 1949 d Robert & Lois. RN Illinois Masonic Hosp Sch of Nrsng 1970; Mutual Mnstry 2010. D 3/29/2010 P 10/3/2010 Bp Thomas Kreider Ray. m 2/16/1974 David Allan Sand c 2.

SANDERS, Edwin Benjamin (Ky) 3812 Burning Bush Rd, Louisville KY 40241 **Ret 2000-** B Marion VA 1938 s Edwin & Elizabeth. BA U of Virginia 1959; BD Drew U 1962. D 12/18/1970 P 4/18/1971 Bp William Henry Marmion. m 12/16/1976 Mary H Sanders. Vic Trin Ch Russellville KY 2005-2008; Sch Chapl/Assistint Ch Of The Gd Shpd Punta Gorda FL 2001-2003; R Calv Ch Louisville KY 1981-2000; Asst S Mary's Cathd Memphis TN 1979-1981; Non-par 1976-1979; R S Eliz's Ch Roanoke VA 1971-1976; Serv Methodist Ch 1962-1970. Phi Beta Kappa U of Virginia 1959.

SANDERS, Harvel Ray (Mo) 110 Walnut Park Dr, Sedalia MO 65301 B Ava MO 1941 s Herbert & Stella. BA U of Missouri 1963; STB EDS 1966. D 6/25/1966 P 1/1/1967 Bp George Leslie Cadigan. m 6/28/2008 Susan Sanders c 2. R Gr Ch Jefferson City MO 1970-2005; R S Paul's Ch S Louis MO 1969-1970; Cur Gr Ch S Louis MO 1966-1969.

SANDERS, Jaime Mw (Ore) 2190 Crest Dr, Lake Oswego OR 97034 **Dio Oregon Portland OR 2015-** B Eugene OR 1956 d David & Barbara. BA U of Oregon 1978; JD Willamette Coll of Law Salem OR 1985; MDiv CDSP 2007. D 6/30/2007 P 1/5/2008 Bp Johncy Itty. m 1/7/1984 Stephen Sanders c 2. S Aid's Epis Ch Portland OR 2014-2015; S Mary's Ch Woodburn OR 2008-2014; S Jn The Evang Ch Portland OR 2008-2013; D All SS Ch Portland OR 2007; Partnr Steel Rives Llp 1985-2002.

SANDERS, James Lemuel (ETenn) 32968 Steelwood Ridge Rd, Loxley AL 36551 **Died 1/7/2016** B Birmingham AL 1931 s Samuel & Nettie. BA Birmingham-Sthrn Coll 1956; VTS 1968. D 6/14/1968 P 3/1/1969 Bp George Mosley Murray. m 10/26/1952 Sara DeLay. Dn S Jn's Epis Cathd Knoxville TN 1980-1997; R S Paul's Ch Selma AL 1971-1980; Vic S Tim's Epis Ch Athens AL 1968-1971. Auth, "Alabama Stwdshp Plan," *Jesus Dollars and Sense.*

SANDERS, Joanne Marie (Cal) Stanford Memorial Church, Stanford University, Stanford CA 94305 **Assoc Dn for Rel Life Stan 2000-** B Buffalo NY 1960 d David & Patricia. D Min Seattle U; BS Grand Canyon U 1982; MS Seattle Pacific U 1990; MDiv CDSP 2000; Cert Seattle U 2010. D 6/3/2000 P 12/2/2000 Bp William Edwin Swing. Yth Dir Trin Par Menlo Pk CA 1995-1997; COM Dio California San Francisco CA 2008-2009. AAR 2008; Assn of Coll and U Rel Affrs 2001; Natl Assn of Coll and U Chapl 2003; Natl Assn of Stdt Personl Administrators 2001. joannesanders@stanford.edu

SANDERS, John Clarke (At) 2744 Peachtree Rd Nw, Atlanta GA 30305 **Died 8/21/2016** B Houston TX 1933 s Carroll & Estelle. BBA Texas 1955; BD Epis TS of the SW 1958; STM VTS 1969. D 6/19/1958 P 6/1/1959 Bp James Parker Clements. m 8/20/2016 Frances Jameson c 3. Dn Cathd Of S Phil Atlanta GA 2001-2016, Dn 1986-1998; R Chr Ch Shaker Heights OH 1975-1986; Dn Cathd Ch Of S Jn Wilmington DE 1970-1975; R S Jas Epis Ch Houston TX 1963-1970; R H Trin Epis Ch Port Neches TX 1960-1963, Vic 1958-1960. Cmnty of the Cross of Nails 1975-1995; Epis Soceity for Cultural and Racial Unity 1963-1972. DD Epis TS of The SW 1993.

SANDERS, Lynn Coggins (NY) St. Bartholomew's Church, 325 Park Avenue, New York NY 10022 **Assoc R St. Barth Ch New York NY 2008-** B Greenville SC 1954 d Woodrow & Ethlyn. BS Furman U 1976; MBA Clemson U 1990; MDiv CDSP 2004. D 3/13/2004 P 9/18/2004 Bp Mark Sean Sisk. Epis Relief and Dvlpmt New York NY 2007-2008; Dir of Ch Relatns Epis Relief and Dvlpmt New York NY 2007-2008; Asst R The Ch of the Gd Shpd Austin TX 2004-2007; Congrl Dvlpmt Com Dio Texas Houston TX 2005-2006, Nomin Com 2004-2007.

SANDERS, Marilyn Mae (CNY) 33092 Bay Ter, Lewes DE 19958 **Mem Title IV T/F II 2010-; Bd Mem Nathan Ntwk 2003-** B Detroit MI 1947 d Robert & Natalie. BS NWU 1969; MDiv Duke DS 1994. D 6/16/2001 P 12/19/2001 Bp Wendell Nathaniel Gibbs Jr. m 7/4/1989 Francis David Sanders c 3. R S Ptr's Ch Bainbridge NY 2008-2012; R S Paul's Epis Ch Albany NY 2006; Int Ch of the Trsfg 2004-2005; Int Epis Ch Of The Trsfg Sis OR 2004-2005; Assoc R Ch Of The Adv Spartanburg SC 2002-2004; Asst to the Int R S Clare Of Assisi Epis Ch Ann Arbor MI 2001-2002.

SANDERS, Megan (NY) 40 Old Mill Rd, Staten Island NY 10306 **S Paul's Ch Pleasant Vlly NY 2015-** B Washington DC 1977 d Frederick & Irene. BA Flagler Coll 1998; MDiv GTS 2007. D 6/14/2007 Bp James Louis Jelinek P 1/12/2008 Bp Richard Lester Shimpfky. m 5/3/2013 Kristin Marie Robyn. S Andr's Epis Ch Staten Island NY 2013-2015; Asstg P S Lk's Epis Ch Montclair NJ 2009-2013; Port Chapl and Tri St Ch Coordntr Seamens Ch Inst New York NY 2008-2013; S Mary's Ch Sparta NJ 2008-2009; Asst R for Yth and Fam Mnstrs S Ptr's Ch Essex Fells NJ 2007-2008; Cpe Res Bapt Hosp Pensacola FL 2003-2004.

SANDERS, Patrick W (Miss) **S Ptr's By The Sea Gulfport MS 2015-** B Vicksburg MS 1975 s Larry & Pamela. U of Mississippi; BD U of Sthrn Mississippi 2003; MDiv Epis TS of the SW 2006; MDiv Epis TS of the SW 2006. D 5/24/2006 Bp Duncan Montgomery Gray Jr P 2/27/2007 Bp Duncan Montgomery Gray III. m 7/31/1999 Jennifer W Sanders c 3. S Timothys Epis Ch Southaven MS 2009-2015; Dio Mississippi Jackson MS 2007-2009; S Jas Ch Greenville MS 2006-2009; St Patricks 1999-2003. sttim199@bellsouth.net

SANDERS, Richard Devon (At) **Dio Atlanta Atlanta GA 2016-** B Tachikawa AB Japan 1971 s Jimmy & Linda. MDiv Candler TS 2015; MDiv Candler TS Emory U 2015. D 12/20/2014 P 6/20/2015 Bp Robert Christopher Wright. m 6/6/1998 Rebekah McKeown Rebekah Baker McKeown c 3. S Gabr's Epis Ch Oakwood GA 2015.

SANDERS, Richard Evan (Ga) 605 Reynolds St, Augusta GA 30901 B Union City TN 1957 s Brice & Nancy. BS Centenary Coll 1979; MDiv VTS 1985; SWTS 2000. D 6/11/1985 P 5/28/1986 Bp Duncan Montgomery Gray Jr. m 10/18/1994 Margaret Juanita Oates c 2. R S Paul's Ch Augusta GA 2002-2014; Assoc R S Geo's Ch Nashville TN 1992-2001; Vic S Jn's Ch Leland MS 1987-1991; Vic S Paul's Ch Leland MS 1987-1991; Cur S Paul's Epis Ch Meridian MS 1985-1987.

SANDERS, Wayne Francis Michael (SanD) 3563 Merrimac Ave, San Diego CA 92117 **Cn for Ecum / Interreligious Affrs Dio San Diego San Diego CA 2005-, Ecum / Interreligious Affrs Off** B Chicago IL 1940 s Edward & Irene.

BA S Mary of the Lake Sem. Rec 8/22/1974 as Priest Bp Robert Munro Wolterstorff. m 4/15/1974 Kathleen Sanders c 2. R Ch Of The Gd Samar San Diego CA 1978-2005; All SS Ch San Diego CA 1974-1978; Headmaster All SS Sch San Diego CA 1974-1978; Chapl USN 1970-1974. wfmsrev@hotmail.com

✠ SANDERS, The Rt Rev William Evan (ETenn) 404 Charlesgate Ct, Nashville TN 37215 B Natchez MS 1919 s Walter & Agnes. BA Van 1942; BD Sewanee: The U So, TS 1945; STM UTS 1946; U So 1959. D 2/18/1945 P 6/11/1946 Bp James M Maxon Con 4/4/1962 for Tenn. m 6/11/2005 Marlin J Sanders c 4. Pres Knox Hsng Partnership 1993-1998; Bd Cora 1990-1996; Econ Justice Com Ecusa 1988-1994; Bp Dio E Tennessee Knoxville TN 1985-1991, Ret Bp Of E Tennessee 1992-; Trst S Andr's/Sewanee Sch 1980-1992; Chair, Dubose Schlrshp Fund U So 1979-1992; Pres Prov IV 1979-1982; GBEC Ecusa 1976-1982; Pres Tennessee Assn Of Ch 1976-1980; Joint Stndg Com On Plnng And Arrangements Ecusa 1973-1985; Regent U So 1973-1979; Chair, Dispatch Of Bus Com HOB 1973-1975; Faith And Ord Com Ncc 1970-1974; Pres Cora 1968-1971; Bd Com On Rel In Appalachia (Cora) 1965-1974; Bd Appalachian Peoples Serv Orgnztn (Apso) 1964-1992; Pres Apso 1964-1967; Bp Coadj Dio Tennessee Nashville TN 1962-1984; Dn S Mary's Cathd Memphis TN 1946-1962; Cur S Paul's Epis Ch Chattanooga TN 1945-1946.

SANDERSON, Dow (SC) 218 Ashley Avenue, Charleston SC 29403 B Montgomery AL 1959 s Henry & Julia. BA Coll of Charleston 1981; MDiv VTS 1986. D 6/15/1986 P 5/10/1987 Bp Christopher FitzSimons Allison. m 5/7/1983 Fiona Sanderson c 2. R Ch Of The H Comm Charleston SC 2001-2017; R Ch Of The Redeem Orangeburg SC 1993-2001; Asst R Ch Of The H Comf Sumter SC 1990-1993; Asst R S Andr's Epis Ch Arlington VA 1989-1990; Vic S Alb's Ch Kingstree SC 1986-1989; Stndg Com (Pres) So Carolina Charleston SC 2005-2008, Exam Chapl 1990-2004.

SANDERSON, Herbert Warren (Alb) 468 Pinewoods Rd, Melrose NY 12121 **Asst Gr Ch Waterford NY 2004-; Asst Gr Ch Waterford NY 2002-** B Brattleboro VT 1931 s Herbert & Elizabeth. BA Bos 1953; MDiv Ya Berk 1959; EdM Bos 1970; PhD SUNY 1973. D 6/20/1959 Bp Anson Phelps Stokes Jr P 12/19/1959 Bp Vedder Van Dyck. m 6/17/2000 Anne Hathaway Sanderson c 3. Int P St Fran Mssn Albany NY 1998-2004; Trin Ch Watervliet NY 1996-1998; Adirondack Mssn Pottersville NY 1996; Ch Of The Ascen Troy NY 1993-1994; Samar Counslg Cntr Schenectady NY 1990; R Ch Of The H Cross Troy NY 1978-1990; Asst Chr Ch Schenectady NY 1972-1978; Chapl Hoosac Sch Hoosick NY 1967-1972; Asst S Ptr's Epis Ch Bennington VT 1965-1967; R S Paul's Epis Ch On The Green Vergennes VT 1961-1965; Chr Ch Island Pond VT 1959-1961; In-c S Ptr's Mssn Lyndonville VT 1959-1961. Amer Assn of Chr Counselors.

SANDERSON, Holladay Worth (Ida) All Saints Episcopal Church, 704 S Latah St, Boise ID 83705 **R All SS Epis Ch Boise ID 2009-; Dep, 2015 GC Dio Idaho Boise ID 2013-, Living Stones Coordntr 2013-, Chair, Liturg Cmsn 2011-2014, Chair, COM 2011-, Dep, 2012 GC 2010-2013, Sexual Ethics Com (Chair) 2010-, COM 2009-** B Raleigh NC 1950 d Hal & Mary. BA U NC 1972; MM E Carolina U 1975; MDiv VTS 2001. D 6/2/2001 P 12/8/2001 Bp James E Waggoner Jr. m 7/2/1984 Stanley M Sanderson. Vic S Andr's Ch Chelan WA 2009; Vic S Paul's Ch Cheney WA 2008-2009; Cn Dio Spokane Spokane WA 2003-2007, Cn for Mnstry Dvlpmt 2006-2009, T/F on Mnstry Dvlpmt, Chair 2005-2006, Living Stones Coordntr 2004-2009, Mssn Imperatives Dvlp 2003-2005, Mssn and Bdgt Com 2003-2005, COM 2002-2009, Sexual Ethics Com (Chair) 2001-2009, Dioc Coun, Mem 2001-2003; R S Mart's Ch Moses Lake WA 2001-2009. hsanderson@q.com

SANDERSON, Joseph Wesley (Ala) Po Box 116, Guntersville AL 35976 **Died 11/9/2015** B Town Creek AL 1934 s Lewis & Etta. LTh SWTS. D Bp Robert Munro Wolterstorff P 5/1/1964 Bp Hamilton Hyde Kellogg. m 9/7/1957 Jan H Harrelson. P-in-c S Barn' Epis Ch Hartselle AL 2004-2015; R Ch Of The Epiph Guntersville AL 1983-1999; S Lk's Epis Ch Jacksonville AL 1978-1983; Trin Ch Wetumpka AL 1976-1978; R S Andr's Ch Marianna AR 1969-1976; Chapl S Chris's At Arkansas St U 1969-1976; Yth Advsr Dio Arkansas Little Rock AR 1966-1967; Vic Trin Par Ch Epis Searcy AR 1965-1967; Vic Emm Epis Ch Alexandria MN 1963-1965.

SANDERSON, Peter O (Ia) 410 Brentwood Dr, Alamogordo NM 88310 **Ret 2000-** B South Shields England UK 1929 s Harold & Doris. BA U of Durham GB 1952; DIT U of Durham GB 1954. Trans 11/1/1991 Bp Chris Christopher Epting. c 3. Int Epis Ch In Lincoln Cnty Ruidoso NM 2008-2009; Trin Cathd Davenport IA 2006-2007, Int 2005-2006; P-in-res Trin Ch Iowa City IA 2000-2002; Vic All SS Epis Ch Storm Lake IA 1991-2000; Serv Scottish Epis Ch 1984-1991; Serv Ch of Engl 1963-1984; Serv Ch of Jamaica 1959-1963; Serv Ch of Engl 1954-1959. RSCM.

SANDFORT, Candace C (Nwk) **S Jn's Epis Ch Montclair NJ 2014-** B Newton MA 1951 d Glen & Eldora. BA U of Virginia 1973; MDiv GTS 2004; STM GTS 2008. D 3/15/2008 P 9/20/2008 Bp Mark Sean Sisk. m 9/24/1972 John M Sandfort c 4. Vic S Paul's Ch Chester NY 2009-2014. rector@stjmontclair.org

SANDLIN, Joseph Allan (At) 1881 Edinburgh Terrace NE, Atlanta GA 30307 **S Barth's Epis Ch Atlanta GA 2016-; GC Dep Convoc of Epis Ch in Europe Paris 2003-, Bd Frgn Parishes 1999-2007, Coun of Advice 1999-2002** B Fort Worth TX 1952 s Bryce & LaVerne. BA SUNY 1976; MMus Hardin-Simmons U 1978; MDiv Candler TS Emory U 1989. D 6/8/1991 P 1/25/1992 Bp Frank Kellogg Allan. m 3/21/1987 Gretchen Elizabeth Nagy c 2. R S Paul's Epis Ch Newnan GA 2011-2016; Assoc R H Trin Par Decatur GA 2007-2011; R The Angl/Epis Ch Of Chr The King Frankfurt am Main 60323 1999-2007; R St Fran By The Sea Epis Ch Blue Hill ME 1994-1999; S Lk's Epis Ch Atlanta GA 1991-1994. Fllshp of St. Jn the Evang 1997. Theta Pi Candler TS 1989; Omicron Delta Kappa Candler TS 1989; Robert W. Woodruff Fell Candler TS 1985. allansandlin@gmail.com

SANDOE, Deirdre Etheridge (WA) 400 Rouen Dr Apt H, Deland FL 32720 B Miami FL 1946 d Earl & Louise. BA U of Tennessee 1990; MDiv VTS 1995. D 6/5/1996 Bp M(Arvil) Thomas Shaw P 6/12/1999 Bp John Wadsworth Howe. Ch Of The H Comf Vienna VA 2002; S Barn Ch Deland FL 1999; D Ch Of The Ascen Silver Sprg MD 1997-2000; D Ch Of S Jn The Evang Boston MA 1995-1997; Chapl Med Cntr At Symmes Arlington MA 1995-1997.

SANDOVAL, Juan (At) 161 Church St NE, Marietta GA 30060 **Cathd Of S Phil Atlanta GA 2016-; Ldr Steph Mnstry 2012-; RN Accelerated Recovery Centers 2010-; RN Gd Samar Hlth and Wellness Cntr Jaspar GA 2010-; Mem, Bp's Bdgt Comm. Dio Atlanta Atlanta GA 2013-** B Phoenix AZ 1947 s Porfino & Lillian. BS Arizona St U 1974; MS Arizona St U 1981; EFM Other 2006; EFM U So EFM 2006; completed D Formation 2011. D 8/6/2011 Bp J Neil Alexander. m 4/18/1994 Elizabeth Anne Sandoval c 4. Malachi's Storehouse S Pat's Epis Ch Atlanta GA 2012-2013; D S Jas Epis Ch Marietta GA 2011-2013. Amer Epis Deacons 2011.

SANDOVAL CROS, Carlos Juan (SeFla) 1000 NW North River Drive #110, Miami FL 33136 **R S Simons Ch Miami FL 1995-; Cn for Hlth Dio SE Florida Miami 2010-** B Puerto Rico 1958 s Lester & Mercedes. Miami-Dade Cmnty Coll; Seminario Epis Teologico Del Ecuador; MD Universidad Catolica Madre Y Maestra 1983; U of Miami 1995. D 12/18/1988 P 5/1/1990 Bp Adrian Delio Caceres-Villavicencio. Int Epis Ch Of The H Fam Miami FL 1994-1995; Assoc Trin Cathd Miami FL 1991-2001, Cathd Cn 2010-; Vic Iglesia Epis Del Ecuador Quito 1990-1991; Vic NE Quito 1989-1991; Tchr TS In The Dio Ecuador 1989-1991. Ed, "Himnos De Vida," 1988; Ed, "Dios Cuida A Su Pueblo," 1988. cjsandoval@bellsouth.net

SANDS, Fred William (SeFla) 300 Sw 29th Ave, Fort Lauderdale FL 33312 **D Ch Of S Chris Ft Lauderdale FL 1995-; S Ambr Epis Ch Ft Lauderdale FL 1995-** B Miami FL 1933 s Charles & Maydon. AA Edw Waters Coll Jacksonville FL 1953; BS Florida A&M U 1958. D 6/12/1995 Bp John Lewis Said. m 6/20/1964 Frances Frandessa Sands c 1. COM, Curs 1995-2000; Curs 1979. Chair, Mnstry On Aging St Chris'S Epis Ch 1994.

SANDWELL-WEISS, Rosa Leah (Az) 8502 N Deer Valley Dr, Tucson AZ 85742 **D S Phil's In The Hills Tucson AZ 2011-** B Columbia MO 1954 d Robert & Rosemary. BA U of Missouri 1975; MA U of Missouri 1977; JD U of Arizona 1984. D 1/29/2011 Bp Kirk Stevan Smith. m 7/5/1980 Karl Sandwell-Weiss c 1.

SANFORD, Carol Webb (WMo) B Springfield MO 1950 GTS; BA Emory U 1972; MDiv CDSP 2005. D 6/4/2005 P 12/3/2005 Bp Barry Howe. m 12/30/1972 Grady H Sanford. Assoc Gr And H Trin Cathd Kansas City MO 2005-2009; Campus Mnstry Coordntr Dio W Missouri Kansas City MO 2005-2006.

SANFORD, Gary Lee (NwT) 1801 Edmund Blvd, San Angelo TX 76901 **Chapl A.S.U. Untd Campus Mnstrs Inc. San Angelo 2008-; Chapl for Untd Campus Mnstrs at Angelo St Uiversity Dio NW Texas Lubbock TX 2008-, Exec Coun 2013-, Exec Coun 2011** B St. John KS 1951 s Charles & Sarah. D 10/29/2006 Bp C Wallis Ohl. m 6/20/1981 Eldra Rosene Sanford c 1. Chapl for Untd Campus Mnstrs Emm Epis Ch San Angelo TX 2006-2012. NAAD / AED 2005; NCMA 2008.

SANG, Clive Oscar (NJ) 205 North Ave, Cranford NJ 07016 **Cn Mssnr for Black Mnstrs Dio New Jersey Trenton NJ 2017-, D 2011-2017** B Kingston Jamaica 1945 s Claudius & Enid. BA NYU 1975; MBA NYU-Stern Grad 1989; MDiv New Brunswick TS 2013. D 5/5/2012 Bp George Edward Councell. m 4/17/2004 Celeste Roberts Sang c 3. trinitycranford@gmail.com

SANGREY, William Frederick (SO) **Chapl Cmnty Care Hospice Wilmington OH 2014-; Chapl Epis Ret Serv Cincinnati OH 2014-** B Houston TX 1965 s Dwight & Patricia. BS Cor 1987; PhD Cor 1994; MDiv Bex Sem 2008. D 6/7/2014 Bp Thomas Edward Breidenthal. m 10/10/1993 Lisa Marie Sweeney c 1.

SANON, Jean-Louis Felix (NY) 2757 Jacob Lane, Douglasville GA 30135 **Ret Dio New York 2007-** B Cazale HT 1940 s Pierre & Quercina. Lic U of Ethnology Port-au-Prince HT 1966; Lic U of Law Port-au-Prince HT 1969; MDiv ETSC 1974; Cert Oxf GB 2001. D 4/28/1974 P 1/30/1975 Bp Luc Anatole Jacques Garnier. m 12/19/1978 Marie M Sanon c 3. Dio New York New York NY 1997-2007; P-in-c Haitian Cong of the Gd Samar Bronx NY 1997-2007; R, St Pierre, Mirebalais Dio Haiti Port-au-Prince HT 1995-1997, P-in-c, St. Simeon, Croix-des-Bouquets 1990-1995, Cathd Admin, Port-au-Prince 1982-1995, La Resurr, Gros-Morne 1975-1982, D, St Sauveur, Cayes 1974-1975; P-in-c St.

S

Pierre Mirebalais Haiti 1995-1996; Admin, H Trin Cathd Epis Ch In Haiti Port-au-Prince HT HT 1982-1990.

SANTANA, Carlos Enrique (DR) **Dio The Dominican Republic (Iglesia Epis Dominicana) Gazcue Santo Domingo 2010-** B 1972 D 2/14/2010 P 2/20/2011 Bp Julio Cesar Holguin-Khoury. m 12/12/2010 Estefanie Garcia de Santana.

SANTANA, Margarita (Md) Apartado 128, San Pedro De Macoris Dominican Republic **Vic Dio Maryland Baltimore MD 2012-** B 1962 d Severiano & Eva. Universidad Autonoma Arquitecta 1987; LTh Centro de Estudios Teologicos 1991. D 3/10/1991 Bp Telesforo A Isaac P 6/1/1992 Bp Julio Cesar Holguin-Khoury. Dio The Dominican Republic (Iglesia Epis Dominicana) Gazcue Santo Domingo 1991-2010. msantana@episcopalmaryland.org

SANTANA-RUIZ, Benjamin (PR) 222 S Palm Ave, Sarasota FL 34236 B 1945 BA Wrld U. D 2/24/1978 P 1/14/1979 Bp Francisco Reus-Froylan. m 2/16/1990 Dielma Santana. Hisp Mnstry Ch Of The Redeem Sarasota FL 2008-2010; Dio Vrgn Islands Charlotte Amalie St Thom VI 2006-2007; S Lk's Ch Brockport NY 2004-2009; All SS Epis Ch Meriden CT 2004-2006; Dio Puerto Rico Trujillo Alto PR 2004, 2002-2003, 1998-2000, 1980-1988, 1978-1979; Dio Wstrn New York Tonawanda NY 2002-2004.

SANTIAGO, Gwen Gettemy (Pgh) 11524 Frankstown Rd, Pittsburgh PA 15235 **Died 9/9/2016** B Greensburg PA 1955 d Russell & Sara. MA U Pgh 1992; MEd California U 1997; MAR TESM 2005; MDiv TESM 2011; MDiv TESM 2011. D 2/18/2012 Bp Kenneth Lester Price P 12/15/2012 Bp Dorsey McConnell. m 8/2/2006 Vicente C Santiago. S Jn's Epis Ch Donora PA 2013-2016; Dio Pittsburgh Pittsburgh PA 2012-2013.

SANTIAGO, Vicente C (Pgh) 132 Sherwood Drive, Greensburg PA 15601 **The Ch Of The Adv Jeannette PA 2012-** B San Juan PR 1944 s Vicente & Lila. MDiv TESM; BS U of Puerto Rico 1967. D 6/12/2004 Bp Robert William Duncan P 12/12/2004 Bp Henry W Scriven. Dio Pittsburgh Pittsburgh PA 2011-2012; S Mk's Ch Johnstown PA 2009-2011; Chapl Heartland Hospice 2006-2009; D S Jas Epis Ch Pittsburgh PA 2004-2006.

SANTIAGO-PADILLA, Gilberto (PR) Carr 187 KM 5.8, Mediana Alta, Loiza PR 00772 Puerto Rico B Rio Piedras PR 1938 s Manuel & Maria. MA Geo Wms; MA Nthrn TS; San Pedro y San Pablo Sem. D 1/20/2013 Bp David Andres Alvarez-Velazquez P 1/24/2015 Bp Wilfrido Ramos-Orench. m 3/31/2007 Alba Lucia Chaparro-Lopez.

SANTIVIAGO-ESPINAL, Maria Isabel (NY) 2453 78th St # 2, East Elmhurst NY 11370 B Asuncion PARAGUAY 1941 d Felipe & Isabel. D 3/18/2000 P 9/16/2000 Bp Richard Frank Grein. S Ann's Ch For The Deaf New York NY 2007-2011; Mision San Juan Bautista Bronx NY 2000-2013; Dio New York New York NY 2000-2009.

SANTOS, Elenito Bravo (NC) 221 Union St, Cary NC 27511 **S Marg's Epis Ch Waxhaw NC 2014-** B Lipa City Philippines 1948 s Demetrio & Magdalena. Theol Maryhill TS 1972; MA St Mary's U 1992; E-MBA Colorado Tech U 2007. Rec 1/12/2014 as Priest Bp Michael B Curry. m 6/6/2000 Annie Albotra Hanner-Santos c 1.

SANTOS-MONTES, Margarita (PR) **Dio Puerto Rico Trujillo Alto PR 2007-** B Ponce 1955 d Justino & Zendoia. BA Pontificia Universidad Catilica 1976; Santisima Trinidad 1994. D 10/15/1995 P 2/11/2007 Bp David Andres Alvarez-Velazquez. m 12/18/1982 Rodriguez Echevarria Efrain.

SANTOS-RIVERA, Carlos (Pa) 3554 N 6th St, Philadelphia PA 19140 B Puerto Rico 1942 s Vicente & Carlina. Mstr Centro Caribeño de Estudios Post-Gradua-do 1971; Mstr Other 1971. Trans 11/21/1986 Bp Lyman Cunningham Ogilby. c 3. Dio Pennsylvania Philadelphia PA 1991-2012; Chr And S Ambr Ch Philadelphia PA 1986-1990; Dio Puerto Rico Trujillo Alto PR 1975-1979.

SANTOSUOSSO, John Edward (SwFla) 4860 Highlands Place Drive, Lakeland FL 33813 **Ret 1998-** B Camden NJ 1939 s John & Mildred. BA Ursinus Coll 1961; MA Clark U 1963; MDiv Louisville Presb TS 1968; PhD U of Florida 1981. D 5/19/1981 Bp William Hopkins Folwell. m 6/15/1968 Janet Ann Beard. D All SS Epis Ch Lakeland FL 1994-1998; D S Ptr's Ch Plant City FL 1986-1994; D S Dav's Epis Ch Lakeland FL 1981-1986; Serv Presb Ch 1968-1970; Prof of Political Sci Florida Sthrn Coll Lakeland FL 1970-2010. Auth, "Can: An Intro for Americans," *Can: An Intro for Americans*, Publish Amer, 2007; Auth, "Shostring Investing Made E-Z," *Shestring Inversting Made E-Z*, Made E-Z Pub, 2000. Frank Lloyd Wright Bldg Conservancy 2012; Frank Lloyd Wright Fndt 2012. Phi Beta Kappa U of Florida 1981.

SANTUCCI, Mark Albert (Ct) 166 Lambtown Rd, Ledyard CT 06339 **P-in-c S Jn's Ch E Hartford CT 2012-** B Bristol CT 1947 s Albert & Martha. BA Lycoming Coll 1969; MS U of Scranton 1972; MDiv GTS 1982. D 6/5/1982 P 12/18/1982 Bp Charlie Fuller Mcnutt Jr. m 8/28/1971 Marlene M Santucci c 2. R S Mk's Ch Mystic CT 1993-2012; R Chr Epis Ch Williamsport PA 1986-1993; Asst St Andrews in the City Epis Ch Harrisburg PA 1983-1986; Dio Cntrl Pennsylvania Harrisburg PA 1982.

SANZO, Maria B (NJ) 318 Huxley Dr, Brick NJ 08723 **S Raphael The Archangel Brick NJ 2016-, D 2003-2009; D/Post to Priesthood St. Geo's at the River Rumson NJ 2006-; Chapl AIDS Spprt Kinship Toms River NJ 2002-; Dioc Coun Dio New Jersey Trenton NJ 2013-, Monmouth/Ocean Convoc Dn 2012-** B Bayonne NJ 1956 d Salvatore & Rose. BA Immaculata

U 1978; MDiv GTS 2010. D 10/21/2000 Bp David Bruce Joslin P 6/19/2010 Bp George Edward Councell. m 12/10/2013 Rita A Micheielli c 1. R Trin Ch Matawan NJ 2011-2016; Asst Ch Of S Mary's By The Sea Pt Pleas Bch NJ 2010-2011; D Trin Ch Asbury Pk NJ 2001-2003; D Chr Ch Toms River Toms River NJ 2000-2001. mariabsanzo@comcast.net

SAPP, Rose Marie (CFla) D 9/10/2016 Bp Gregory Orrin Brewer.

SARAI-CLARK, Wilhelmina Olivia (Spok) 503 E D St, Moscow ID 83843 **Epis Stdt Pstr Common Mnstry At WA SU 1997-; D S Jas Pullman WA 1992-** B Tuskegee Inst AL 1927 d William & Olivia. PhD U of Wisconsin 1970; Cert Dio Spokane TS 1992. D 5/10/1992 Bp Frank Jeffrey Terry. Prof WA SU At Pullman 1965-1992. Auth, "Philos Of Dance As Art For Non-Philosophers"; Auth, "Carnival: A Dance For Two"; Auth, "Isms & Power". NAAD, Sacr Dance Gld.

SARGENT, Arthur Lloyd (Dal) 213 Sierra Ridge Dr, San Marcos TX 78666 **Ret 1998-** B Amarillo TX 1935 s William & Chelsea. BA U of No Texas 1957; STB GTS 1961; MA U of No Texas 1967. D 6/20/1961 Bp Charles A Mason P 12/21/1961 Bp John Joseph Meakin Harte. m 2/9/1957 Jonnie D Sargent c 5. Asst S Jas Epis Ch Taos NM 1999-2002; 1975-1998; Cmnty Consult on Bp Stff Dio Dallas Dallas TX 1973-1975; Chapl U of No Texas 1964-1972; Asst S Mich And All Ang Ch Dallas TX 1961-1963. Auth, "Memi Day," *Preaching Through H Days and Holidays*, Morehouse, 2003.

SARGENT GREEN, Nancy Hunnewell (EO) 18160 Cottonwood Rd Pmb 719, Sunriver OR 97707 **All SS Of The Cascades Epis Ch Bend OR 1998-, 1996, R 1996-; Sr Pstr/R Sunriver Chr Fllshp Sunriver OR 1996-** B Boston MA 1947 d George & Hester. AA Bradford Jr Coll 1967; BA GW 1969; MDiv Andover Newton TS 1977. D 10/15/1977 Bp Morris Fairchild Arnold P 6/3/1978 Bp William Jones Gordon Jr. m 4/28/2007 Roy Donald Green c 2. S Steph's Ch Troy MI 1985-1990, 1984; Int S Jas Ch Grosse Ile MI 1981-1982; Asst Chr Ch Detroit MI 1978-1980; Stndg Com Dio Estrn Oregon Cove OR 2007-2009, Pres, Eccl Crt 2004-2006; Com Dio Michigan Detroit MI 1982-1986.

SARKISSYIAN, Sabi Kamel (Mo) 524 Fox Run Estates Ct, Ballwin MO 63021 B Palestine 1937 s Kamel & Najla. BD Cairo EG 1962. Trans 7/21/2001 Bp Hays H. Rockwell. m 7/5/1970 Feryal S Hawatmeh c 3. Arabic Min S Tim's Epis Ch S Louis MO 2004-2011; Arabic Min Ch Of The Gd Shpd S Louis MO 1999-2004. Cn Emer The Epis Ch of Jerusalem and the M. E. 1997; Cn The Epis Ch of Jerusalem and the M. E. 1983.

SARRAZIN, Victor J (Az) **S Steph's Ch Sierra Vista AZ 2006-** B Montebello CA 1958 BA S Marys Sem 1984; MDiv S Thos Sem 1990. Rec 6/4/2005 Bp Barry Howe. m 8/9/2003 Rhonda R Sarrazin c 3.

SARTIN, Nancy Avera (Ga) 1521 N Patterson St, Valdosta GA 31602 B Macon GA 1957 d Carol & Anne. BSEd Valdosta St U 1979; MA Valdosta St U 1983; EdS Valdosta St U 1984. D 9/11/2010 Bp Scott Anson Benhase. m 4/14/2007 Michael Lee Richardson c 1.

SARTIN, Randall Randall (Fla) 3480 Lakeshore Drive, Tallahassee FL 32312 **R Ch Of The Adv Tallahassee FL 2008-** B New Orleans LA 1955 s Jack & Billie. BS Liberty U 1978; MDiv VTS 1986. D 6/30/1986 P 6/11/1987 Bp Duncan Montgomery Gray Jr. m 12/15/1984 Ute K Sartin c 1. R S Geo's Epis Ch Clarksdale MS 1998-2008; R Ascen Epis Ch Amherst VA 1988-1997; S Mk's Ch Amherst VA 1988-1994; Ch Of The Redeem Greenville MS 1986-1988; P-in-c S Jas Ch Greenville MS 1986-1988; Chair, COM Dio Florida Jacksonville 2010-2013, COM 2009-2013. rsartin@advent-church.org

SASAKI, Norio (Haw) 3252 Charles St, Honolulu HI 96816 **Died 9/8/2015** B Waialua HI 1925 s Nobudane & Yoshi. BA U of Hawaii 1951; MDiv CDSP 1958; Procter Fllshp 1981. D 6/10/1958 Bp Henry W Hobson P 12/10/1958 Bp Harry Sherbourne Kennedy. m 12/8/1951 Florence S Nakagawa c 4. R All Souls Okinawa 1990-1991; Chapl Iolani Sch Honolulu HI 1978-1988; Iolani Sch Honolulu HI 1971-1978; Stff S Eliz's Ch Honolulu HI 1970-1971; Assoc Par of St Clem Honolulu HI 1966-1970; S Alb's Chap Honolulu HI 1958-1988; Vic SS Paul & Jn Kauai HI 1958-1966. Hawaii Cler Assn.

SASSER JR, Howell Crawford (CPa) Saint Paul's Church, PO Box 764, Bloomsburg PA 17815 **S Paul's Ch Bloomsburg PA 2014-** B Tacoma WA 1966 s Howell & Elaine. BA JHU 1988; MPH U of So Carolina 1995; PhD U Pgh 1999; BD Lon GB 2003; Cert Ya Berk 2009; STM Yale DS 2009. D 6/13/2009 Bp Michael B Curry P 4/28/2010 Bp Catherine Scimeca Roskam. m 5/6/2016 James William Strader. S Ptr's Epis Ch Peekskill NY 2012-2013, Int Pstr 2012-2013, P Assoc 2009-2012. Ord of St Jn of Jerusalem 2008. rectorstpauls@gmail.com

SASSMAN, William Arthur (NCal) 7418 Stock Ranch Rd Apt 3305, Citrus Hts CA 95621 **Died 3/25/2016** B Philadelphia PA 1936 s John & Ruth. BS Leh 1958; MTh ETSC 1967; MA Inter Amer U of Puerto Rico 1970; Cert CDSP 1981. D 5/17/1967 P 12/21/1967 Bp Francisco Reus-Froylan. m 7/22/2002 Elizabeth Cano c 3. Speaker Food for the Floor Inc. Coconut Creek 2003-2016; S Fran Epis Ch Fair Oaks CA 1994-2002; Off Of Bsh For ArmdF New York NY 1973-1987; Chapl and Chairman S Andr's Sch Boca Raton FL 1970-1973; Chapl Casa Mar San Juan PR 1967-1970. Auth, "arts," *Interchange*, U.S. AF. Mltry Chapl Assn 1973.

SASSO-CRANDALL, Charles David (NJ) 21 Thistle Avenue, Cape May NJ 08204 **Died 10/1/2015** B Boston MA 1937 s Willis & Dorothy. BS Boston Coll 1959; MDiv GTS 1979. D 6/2/1979 Bp Albert Wiencke Van Duzer P 12/1/1979 Bp George E Rath. m 10/1/2015 Rose Mary Sasso-Crandall c 1. Vic S Mk's Ch Hammonton NJ 1995-2004; Int S Aug's Ch Camden NJ 1993-1995; 1990-1993; Chr Ch Oaklyn NJ 1980-1990; Cur S Ptr's Ch Freehold NJ 1979-1980.

SASSO-CRANDALL, Rose Mary (NJ) 206 Central Ave, Hammonton NJ 08037 **Died 7/18/2016** B Boston MA 1938 d Louis & Josephine. MEd Boston Coll 1960; MDiv GTS 1983; ThM New Brunswick TS 1986. D 6/4/1983 Bp George Phelps Mellick Belshaw P 2/4/1984 Bp Vincent King Pettit. c 2. Vic S Jas Epis Ch Paulsboro NJ 1996-2004; Supply P Chr Ch Oaklyn NJ 1989-1996, R 1984-1988.

SASTRE, Iane M (Ga) 21268 US Highway 17, White Oak GA 31568 **S Athan Ch Brunswick GA 2015-** B Montevideo Uruguay 1953 s Renee & Nenetta. BS Mercy Coll 1981; MA CSUSM 1999; MDiv Sewanee: The U So, TS 2010. D 2/6/2010 Bp Scott Anson Benhase. m 11/16/1995 Lydia W Sastre c 2.

SATERSTROM, Roger Thomas (Tenn) Christ Church Cathedral, 900 Broadway, Nashville TN 37203 B Portage WI 1948 s Thomas & Mary. D 6/4/2016 Bp John Bauerschmidt. m 12/11/1971 Anna Saterstrom c 2.

SATHER, Jerry Earl (SwFla) Psc 47 Box 366, Apo AE 09470 B Libby MT 1958 s Alfred & Gladys. BA U of Montana 1985; MDiv Wstrn Evang Sem 1988; Cert of Angl Stds Nash 2016. D 6/4/2016 P 1/14/2017 Bp Dabney Tyler Smith. m 1/1/1983 Annette M Ludwinski c 3. jerry.sather@us.af.mil

SATO, Judith Ann (Colo) 13741 Windrush dr, Colorado Springs CO 80921 **Ch Of S Mich The Archangel Colorado Spg CO 2013-** B Ventura CA 1952 d Thomas & Bessie. BS Colorado St U 1974; MDiv CDSP 2007. D 6/5/2010 P 1/18/2011 Bp Mary Gray-Reeves. m 9/4/1976 Rodney B Sato c 3. Admin S Steph's In-The-Field Epis Ch San Jose CA 2011-2013.

SATORIUS, Joanna (Los) Po Box 512164, Los Angeles CA 90051 **For Cler Formation and Transitions Mnstry Dio Los Angeles Los Angeles CA 2003-** B Milwaukee WI 1948 d Edwin & Mary. Illinois St U; BFA Stephens Coll 1971; MA U of Iowa 1974; MDiv Claremont TS 1994. D 6/18/1994 Bp Chester Lovelle Talton P 1/14/1995 Bp Frederick Houk Borsch. c 2. R S Geo's Ch Riverside CA 1996-2003; Chapl / CPE Supvsr Loma Linda U Med Cntr Loma Linda CA 1994-1996. DOK; OHC, Assoc.

SATTERLY, Norris Jay (NMich) 132 Henford Ave, Kingsford MI 49802 **D H Trin Ch Iron Mtn MI 2004-** B Charlotte MI 1947 BSW Nthrn Michigan U 1992. D 2/29/2004 Bp James Arthur Kelsey. m 11/19/1967 Hazel Messer c 3. Bronze Star USAF 1968.

SATULA, John A (Mass) 6Schoolhouse Hill Road, Newtown CT 06470 **R S Jas Ch Amesbury MA 2014-** B New York, NY 1980 s Anthony & Deborah. BA Elmira Coll; MDiv GTS 2006; MTh Duke 2007. D 11/30/2006 Bp Gladstone Bailey Adams III P 12/15/2007 Bp Andrew Donnan Smith. Trin Ch Newtown CT 2011-2013; Asst R H Trin Epis Ch Gainesville FL 2009-2011; Asst R S Matt's Epis Ch Wilton CT 2007-2009.

SAUCEDO SICA, Susan Teresa (Nwk) 407 N Broad St, Lansdale PA 19446 **Vic S Greg's Epis Ch Parsippany NJ 2003-** B San Antonio TX 1955 d Melchor & Catherine. BA Concordia U 1978; MDiv GTS 1999. D 5/22/1999 Bp Melchor Saucedo-Mendoza P 2/5/2000 Bp Herbert Alcorn Donovan Jr. m 6/17/1978 David R Sica c 2. Assoc Trin Ch Solebury PA 2002-2003; Assoc R H Trin Ch Lansdale PA 1999-2002. Cmnty Of S Jn The Bapt.

SAUERZOPF, Richard C (Mich) 201 W Shepherd St, Charlotte MI 48813 B Buffalo NY 1967 s Robert & Elizabeth. BA St Jn Fisher Coll 1990; MA U of Albany - SUNY 1993; PhD U of Albany - SUNY 2002; MDiv Bex 2008; MDiv Bex Sem 2008. D 6/13/2009 P 1/23/2010 Bp Wendell Nathaniel Gibbs Jr. S Phil's Ch Beulah MI 2015-2016; S Jn's Epis Ch Charlotte MI 2012-2015.

✠ SAULS, The Rt Rev Stacy F (Lex) 815 Second Ave., New York NY 10017 **Chf Operating Off Dom And Frgn Mssy Soc- Epis Ch Cntr New York NY 2011-; Pres Bd the Amer Com for Kiyosato Educ Exper 2004-** B Atlanta GA 1955 s Kenneth & Joyce. BA Furman U 1977; JD U of Virginia 1980; MDiv GTS 1988; DD GTS 2001; DD Sewanee: The U So, TS 2002; LLM Cardiff U 2009. D 6/11/1988 P 4/6/1989 Bp Frank Kellogg Allan Con 9/30/2000 for Lex. m 8/11/1979 Ginger M Sauls c 2. Epis Ch Cntr New York NY 2011-2016; Form Bp of Lexington Dio Lexington Lexington 2011, Bp of Lexington 2000-2011; Dio Atlanta Atlanta GA 1997-1998, Cler Ldrshp Proj 1994-1997; R S Barth's Epis Ch Atlanta GA 1994-2000; R S Thos Ch Savannah GA 1990-1994; Assoc R S Geo's Epis Ch Griffin GA 1988-1990; Mem Budgetary Funding T/F 2004-2009; Mem Exec Coun Appointees New York NY 2003-2009; Exec Com Forw Mvmt of the Epis Ch Cincinnati OH 2001-2010, Advsry Com 2001-2007; Com on the Resignation of Bishops HOB 2001-2006; Bd Mem Mikell C&C Toccoa GA 1998-2000. *That We May Evermore Dwell in Him and He in Us (w Chas Jenkins)*, Forw Mvmt, 2004.

SAUNDERS, Cora Germaine (At) 607 River Run Dr, Sandy Springs GA 30350 B St Thomas VI 1959 d Clement & Esther. BA Carthage Coll 1982; JD Vermont Law Sch 1989; MDiv Candler TS Emory U 2003. D 11/2/2003 P 1/15/2006 Bp J Neil Alexander. S Mich And All Ang Ch Stone Mtn GA 2006-2009; Legal Counsel to the Cmssnr Crt of the Vrgn Islands 1998-1999.

SAUNDERS, Elizabeth Goodwin (NC) 3029 Mountainbrook Rd, Charlotte NC 28210 **Assoc Chr Ch Charlotte NC 2003-; Assoc R Chr Ch Charlotte NC 1988-** B Winston-Salem NC 1959 d Robert & Caroline. BA U NC 1981; MDiv VTS 1984. D 6/8/1985 Bp Robert Whitridge Estill P 6/1/1986 Bp Calvin Onderdonk Schofield Jr. m 5/24/1981 Timothy Gray Saunders. Cur S Phil's Ch Coral Gables FL 1986-1987.

SAUNDERS, James (NJ) 8113 Rugby St, Philadelphia PA 19150 B Grand Island TC 1945 s Thomas & Catherine. Untd Theol Coll of The W Indies Kingston Jm. D 12/12/1975 Bp The Bishop Of Barbados P 4/4/1976 Bp The Bishop Of Bahamas. m 7/31/1971 Hyacinth Leona Saunders. Par Of Chr The King Willingboro NJ 2002-2013; Dio Pennsylvania Philadelphia PA 1999; Hse Of Pryr Philadelphia PA 1982-1998. leroyrev@gmail.com

SAUNDERS III, Kenneth H (Md) 120 Allegheny Ave, Towson MD 21204 **R Trin Ch Towson MD 2011-** B Portsmouth VA 1967 s Kenneth & Lorraine. Cit Charleston SC 1989; BS U NC Asheville 2003; MDiv Sewanee: The U So, TS 2007. D 6/9/2007 Bp Porter Taylor P 12/21/2007 Bp William O Gregg. m 10/6/1990 Kelly E Everitt c 3. R Chr Epis Ch Cleveland NC 2007-2011. Soc of Cath Priests 2009. The Rev. Jeffrey Lowrance Citizenship Medal Sons of the Amer Revolution 2010. rector@trinitychurchtowson.org

SAUNDERS, Lisa Ann (Tex) 833 W Wisconsin Ave, Milwaukee WI 53233 B Madison WI 1979 d Richard & Susan. BS U of Wisconsin Oshkosh WI 2001; MDiv VTS 2007. D 6/2/2007 P 12/15/2007 Bp Steven Andrew Miller. R S Jas Ch Austin TX 2012-2015; Dio Texas Houston TX 2012; R S Jas Epis Ch Milwaukee WI 2011-2012; Asst R S Jn's Ch Lafayette Sq Washington DC 2007-2011. lisaannsauders@gmail.com

SAUNDERSON, Ann Marie (Oly) 3918 N 24th St, Tacoma WA 98406 **Chapl Franciscan Hlth System Tacoma WA 2001-** B Seattle WA 1946 d Walter & Olive. Linfield Coll 1989; MDiv Seattle U 2005. D 6/24/2006 Bp Vincent Waydell Warner P 2/2/2007 Bp Bavi Edna Rivera. c 2. Assoc Chr Epis Ch Puyallup WA 2007-2010; S Mary's Epis Ch Eugene OR 1989-1996; Chapl U of Oregon Epis Campus Mnstry Eugene 1985-1996.

SAUNKEAH, Bobby Reed (Okla) 110 E 17th St, Ada OK 74820 B Oklahoma City, OK 1954 s Jasper & Dorothy. BS U of Oklahoma 1978. D 6/12/2010 Bp Edward Joseph Konieczny. m 5/24/1985 Peggy Saunkeah c 1.

SAUSSY JR, Hugh (At) 4549 SW24th Ave, Dania FL 33312 **Ret 1994-** B Atlanta GA 1927 s Hugh & Lillian. U So 1947; BA Emory U 1949; BTh PDS 1952; MPA U GA 1970. D 6/11/1952 Bp John Buchman Walthour P 12/16/1952 Bp Edwin A Penick. c 4. Non-par 1967-1994; R H Innoc Ch Atlanta GA 1957-1967; Cn Cathd Of S Phil Atlanta GA 1955-1957; Vic All SS Ch Warner Robins GA 1953-1955; R S Andr's Epis Ch Ft Vlly GA 1952-1955. Epis. Soc for Cultural and Racial Unity 1963-1968.

SAVAGE, Harley Stewart (Tex) 180 CR 222, Bay City TX 77414 B Bay City TX 1931 s Francis & Frances. BBA S Marys U San Antonio TX 1953. D 12/19/1998 Bp Leopoldo Jesus Alard P 8/3/1999 Bp Claude Edward Payne. m 10/12/1951 Jane Kirby. Ret Chr Ch Matagorda TX 1998-2003.

SAVAGE, Jack Laverne (Mich) 1157 E Buckhorn Cir, Sanford MI 48657 **Non-par 1984-** B Vassar MI 1935 s Warren & Thelma. LTh Bex Sem 1968; BA U of Detroit Mercy 1972. D 6/29/1968 P 1/1/1969 Bp Archie H Crowley. S Matt's Epis Ch Flat Rock MI 1984-1985; R S Marg's Ch Hazel Pk MI 1981-1984; Non-par 1974-1980; S Jas Ch Detroit MI 1972-1973; Vic Ch Of The H Sprt Livonia MI 1969-1972; Asst S Andr's Epis Ch Livonia MI 1968-1969.

SAVIDGE, Karen F (WMo) 207 N. 7th, St. Joseph MO 64501 B Marshall MO 1946 d Robert & Tralucia. BS Missouri Wstrn St U 1992; MDiv Yale DS 1995. D 5/10/1995 P 5/1/1996 Bp John Clark Buchanan. m 1/14/1966 George Savidge c 3. R Chr Epis Ch S Jos MO 2007-2011; R All SS Ch Nevada MO 1999-2007; S Andr's Ch Kansas City MO 1998; Dio W Missouri Kansas City MO 1995-1997.

SAVILLE III, John (Los) Po Box 152, Corona CA 92878 B Los Angeles CA 1952 s John & Nellie. BA U of Redlands 1974; MDiv GTS 1982. D 6/19/1982 P 2/5/1983 Bp Robert Claflin Rusack. m 5/1/1976 Kathleen G Saville c 2. R S Jn The Bapt Par Corona CA 1991-2012, R 1985-1990; R S Mary's Par Lompoc CA 1990-1991; Cur Trin Epis Ch Redlands CA 1982-1985.

SAVILLE, Milton (SO) 3580 Shaw Avenue #323, Cincinnati OH 45208 **Ret 1992-** B Kansas City MO 1925 s Virgil & Willie. BA Ken 1948; MDiv EDS 1951. D 6/8/1951 P 2/1/1952 Bp Norman B Nash. Int S Paul's Ch Akron OH 1990-1991; P-in-c S Ptr's Ch Glenside PA 1987; Int Chr Ch Cathd Cincinnati OH 1984-1987, Asst 1983-1984, Asst 1955-1958; St Albans Angl- Epis Ch Tokyo 1977-1982; Exec Coun Appointees New York NY 1973-1982; R S Alb's Tokyo Japan 1973-1982; R 1963-1973; S Jn's Epis Ch Westwood MA 1963-1973; R S Lk's Epis Ch Fall River MA 1958-1963; P-in-c S Paul's Ch Lynnfield Cntr MA 1953-1955; Gr Epis Ch Medford MA 1951-1953.

SAVINO, Bella Jean (Ak) Po Box 70786, Fairbanks AK 99707 **P S Matt's Epis Ch Fairbanks AK 2012-, D 2003-** B Fort Yukon AK 1945 d David & Myra. D 3/17/2002 Bp Mark Lawrence Macdonald P 5/27/2012 Bp Mark A Lattime. m 6/11/1994 Donald Savino.

SAWICKY, Blake A (Colo) The Church of St. Michael & St. George, 6345 Wydown Blvd, St. Louis MO 63105 **S Mich & S Geo S Louis MO 2015-;**

S

Cur S Steph's Ch Providence RI 2013-; S Jas Epis Ch Cincinnati OH 2012- B Marshfield WI 1984 s Jay & Deborah. BA Wheaton Coll 2006; MA U Coll London 2007; MDiv Ya Berk 2011. D 6/4/2011 Bp William Howard Love P 1/21/2012 Bp Robert John O'Neill. S Jn's Cathd Denver CO 2011-2013.

SAWTELLE, Gary Donald (Roch) 2171 Scottsville Rd, Scottsville NY 14546 **Ret 2002-** B Mineola NY 1947 s Donald & Dorothy. BA SUNY 1969; MDiv PDS 1972. D 6/8/1972 P 12/23/1972 Bp Jonathan Goodhue Sherman. m 8/23/1969 Barbara R Sawtelle c 2. Int S Thos Epis Ch Rochester NY 2009-2010, Assoc 2006-2009; Chapl To Ret Cler Dio Rochester Henrietta 2003-2005, Chair Of The Bdgt Com 1994-1995, Chair Of Cont Educ 1989-2002, Com 1989-1995, CE Cmsn 1984-1988, Evang Cmsn 1982-1985, Futures Cmsn 1981-1983; Chair - Com 1994-1995; R Gr Ch Lyons NY 1981-2002; CE Consult Dio Sthrn Virginia Newport News VA 1980-1981, Stwdshp Cmsn 1978-1981; Assoc Old Donation Ch Virginia Bch VA 1976-1981; Cur Gr Epis Ch Massapequa NY 1972-1976.

SAWYER, Anne M (NY) St Mark's Church in the Bowery, 131 E 10th St, New York NY 10003 **Assoc Gunee St. Paul's Epis Ch Tucson AZ 2008-; Imago Dei Middle Sch Tucson AZ 2007-** B Tucson AZ 1964 d Chnelos & Jane. BA U of Arizona 1987; MA U Chi 1993; MDiv Harvard DS 2004. D 2/19/2005 P 9/18/2005 Bp Kirk Stevan Smith. m 12/22/2015 Susan Anderson-Smith. S Andr's Epis Ch Tucson AZ 2008, 2005-2007; Dio Arizona Phoenix AZ 2005-2006. anne@stmarksbowery.org

SAWYER, Frank D (CFla) 210 S Indian River Dr, Fort Pierce FL 34950 **Chapl of Grtr Lisbon Estoril 2016-** B Brantford Canada 1971 s Denzil & Catherine. BA U Tor 1993; MDiv U Tor CA 1997; DMin CDSP 2004. Trans 9/8/1999 Bp William Edwin Swing. m 9/19/1998 Ginnelle Margaret Elliott c 2. S Andr's Epis Acad Ft Pierce FL 2015-2016; Sch Chapl The Ch Of The Gd Shpd Augusta GA 2007-2012; S Matt's Par Sch Pacific Plsds CA 2005-2007; The Par Of S Matt Pacific Plsds CA 2005-2007; Gr Cathd San Francisco CA 1999; Asst Cur St. Clem's Ch Toronto Can 1997-1999. "The Sprtl Life of Boys in an Epis Sch (D.Min. Thesis)," Grad Theol Un Libr, Berkeley, CA, 2004. Coun for Sprtl and Ethical Educ 1999; NAES 1999.

SAWYER, Robert Claremont (NC) Po Box 28024, Raleigh NC 27611 **Ch Of The Gd Shpd Raleigh NC 1996-** B Norfolk VA 1949 s Julian & Dorothy. BA Randolph-Macon Coll 1971; MDiv VTS 1980. D 5/27/1980 P 12/1/1980 Bp Claude Charles Vache. m 4/29/1972 Linda B Sawyer c 2. R S Andr's Ch Richmond VA 1986-1996; Asst Ch Of The Adv Spartanburg SC 1982-1986; Gr Epis Ch Drakes Branch VA 1980-1982; R S Jn's Epis Ch Chase City VA 1980-1982; S Tim's Epis Ch Clarksville VA 1980-1982.

SAWYER, Stanley Whitfield (SVa) 2200 Cape Arbor Dr, Virginia Beach VA 23451 **R All SS' Epis Ch Virginia Bch VA 1981-** B Norfolk VA 1949 s Julian & Dorothy. BS Randolph-Macon Coll 1971; S Georges Coll Jerusalem IL 1975; MDiv VTS 1976; DMin GTF 1993. D 5/26/1976 Bp David Shepherd Rose P 12/13/1976 Bp Claude Charles Vache. m 9/5/1970 Linda Louise Sawyer c 2. Asst Chr And Gr Ch Petersburg VA 1976-1981; Pres of Stndg Com Dio Sthrn Virginia Newport News VA 2008-2009. stansawyer1@verizon.net

SAWYER, Susan Carter (Kan) 1640 Sunflower Rd, Clay Center KS 67432 B Bethesda MD 1950 d William & Mary. AA Bard Coll 1970; MDiv EDS 1985. D 6/1/1985 Bp John Bowen Coburn P 4/29/1986 Bp Andrew Frederick Wissemann. m 11/3/1990 David George Verschelden. R S Paul's Epis Ch Clay Cntr KS 1992-2013; Serv Amer Bapt Ch 1991-1993; Dio Kansas Topeka KS 1991; Chapl KS S U Manhattan KS 1989-1991; Assoc S Paul's Ch Manhattan KS 1989-1990; Dio Wstrn Massachusetts Springfield 1985-1989; Cur S Jn's Ch Northampton MA 1985-1989.

SAWYER HARMON, Cecily Judith (Del) 262 S College Ave, Newark DE 19711 B Bronx, NY 1946 d Samuel & Estelle. MSW Adelphi Sch of Soical Wk 1976; BA Hampton U 1976. D 12/5/2009 Bp Wayne Wright. c 3.

SAXE, Joshua Andrew (WVa) 218 Church St, Lewisburg WV 24901 **P-in-c S Jas' Epis Ch Lewisburg WV 2013-** B Fort Walton Beach FL 1983 s Timothy & Susan. BS W Virginia U 2005; MDiv GTS 2011. D 12/4/2010 P 6/14/2011 Bp William Michie Klusmeyer. m 1/14/2012 Catherine B Saxe c 1. Cur Trin Ch Parkersburg WV 2011-2013.

SAXE, Sarah E (EC) 7302 Us Highway 264 E, Washington NC 27889 **R Zion Epis Ch Washington NC 2016-, P-in-c 2015-2016** B New Bedford MA 1960 d Roger & Janice. BA Boston Coll 1982; MDiv cum laud VTS 2014. D 6/14/2014 Bp Joe Goodwin Burnett P 12/13/2014 Bp Heather E Cook. m 3/23/1990 Thomas King Saxe c 2. priest@zionepiscopal.com

SAXON, Mary-Margaret (Colo) 5527 Harrison Street, Kansas City MO 64110 B New Orleans LA 1941 d James & Mary. RN U of Mobile 1974; MDiv Sewanee: The U So, TS 1988. D 5/2/1988 Bp Leo Frade P 12/1/1988 Bp Frank S Cerveny. S Paul's Epis Ch Lakewood CO 1999-2001; S Jn's Epis Ch Tallahassee FL 1988-1994; Mssy Dio Honduras In San Marcos 1982-1985.

SAXON, Miriam (NC) 2214 Buck Quarter Farm Rd, Hillsborough NC 27278 **S Andr's Ch Haw River NC 2014-; Assoc R Ch Of The Gd Shpd Raleigh NC 2008-** B Baton Rouge LA 1950 d Clarence & Mildred. BA Auburn U 1972; MS Florida St U Tallahassee FL 1974; MA Duke 1985; VTS 2006; MDiv Duke DS 2007. D 5/19/2007 P 12/19/2007 Bp Michael B Curry. m 6/2/1973 John Saxon

c 2. Chapl Res Duke Med Cntr Durham NC 2007-2008; S Matt's Epis Ch Hillsborough NC 2004-2007.

SAXTON II, Carl Millard (Ala) 256 E Church St, Jacksonville FL 32202 B Bristol PA 1976 s Leon & Carol. BA The U of So Florida 2007; MDiv Sewanee: The U So, TS 2014; MDiv The TS at The U So 2014. D 5/22/2014 Bp Rayford Baines High Jr P 12/7/2014 Bp Dorsey Henderson. m 3/29/2004 Laura Elizabeth Saxton. S Jn's Cathd Jacksonville FL 2014-2016.

SAYLOR, Kristin Lee (NY) **S Ptr's Ch Port Chester NY 2015-** D 3/7/2015 P 9/19/2015 Bp Andrew Marion Lenow Dietsche.

SAYLORS, Joann L (Tex) 1225 Texas St, Houston TX 77002 **Cn Dio Texas Houston TX 2017-** B Pittsburgh PA 1968 d Roy & Beryl. BBA U of Texas 1991; BA U of Texas 1991; MDiv Epis TS of the SW 2010. D 6/5/2010 P 5/24/2011 Bp James Monte Stanton. m 4/30/2000 Lawrence C Saylors. Cn for Deploy & Congr Dev Dio W Texas San Antonio TX 2012-2017; Cur Epis Ch Of The Redeem Irving TX 2010-2012. jsaylors@epicenter.org

SCALES, Linda (Ga) 4344 Miller Dr, Evans GA 30809 B Concordia KS 1939 d Paul & Ruth. BS K SU 1960; MS K SU 1978; MEd Bos 1982; EdD Tem 1989. D 4/25/1990 Bp Charles Lovett Keyser. m 6/17/1978 Louie Grady Scales c 2. D Ch Of Our Sav Augusta GA 2002-2009; D S Alb's Epis Ch Augusta GA 2001-2002; D S Paul's Ch Augusta GA 2000-2001; Serv Ch in Germany 1994-2000; D Ft Irwin CA 1992-1994; Serv Ch in Germany 1990-1992. Wmn of Excellence Girls Scouts 2006.

SCALES JR, Louie Grady (Ga) 4344 Miller Drive, Evans GA 30809 B Fayette AL 1947 s Louie & Ruth. BA Birmingham-Sthrn Coll 1969; MDiv Candler TS Emory U 1972; MEd Bos 1982; ThM PrTS 1985. D 10/20/1991 Bp John Mc Gill Krumm P 5/17/1992 Bp Charles Lovett Keyser. m 6/17/1978 Linda Scales c 1. R Ch Of Our Sav Augusta GA 2002-2009; Assoc S Paul's Ch Augusta GA 2000-2002; Off Of Bsh For ArmdF New York NY 1992-2000; Chapl US-Army 1976-2000. Auth, "Poetry, Song & A Theol Tchg," *Mltry Chapl's Revs*, 1987.

SCALES JR, Sherrill (Ct) 568 S Farms Ct, Southington CT 06489 **Died 12/21/2015** B Louisville KY 1924 s Sherrill & Ada. AA U Cinc 1950; BFA Ohio U 1951; MDiv Bex Sem 1957. D 6/2/1957 P 12/2/1957 Bp Henry W Hobson. m 12/21/2015 Joyce Marilyn Higgins c 5. Ret 1993-2015; Dir Risk Mgmt CIC NYC 1990-1993; Pres ECBF NYC 1975-1989; ECBF New York NY 1975-1989; St. Barth Ch New York NY 1975-1977; Ch Of The Gd Shpd Hartford CT 1973-1975; S Jn's Ch E Hartford CT 1968-1975; Gnrl Secy, Dept of Missions & Ch Ext Dio Connecticut Meriden CT 1962-1968; R Calv Ch Suffield CT 1959-1962; Asst S Jas Epis Ch Danbury CT 1958-1959; Asst S Paul's Ch Columbus OH 1957-1958. Auth, *Ch Site & Bldg*, 1982. Hon Cn Dio Connecticut 1967.

SCALIA, Deborah White (La) 10136 Walden Dr, River Ridge LA 70123 **S Mart's Epis Sch Metairie LA 1999-; Dn Of Chr Life St Mart's Epis Sch Metairie LA 1999-** B Wellsboro PA 1951 BA Loyola U 1974. D 9/13/2003 Bp Charles Edward Jenkins III. m 6/1/1974 Salvador S Scalia.

SCALISE, Margaret Mary (Ala) 8816 Old Greensboro Rd Apt 19103, Tuscaloosa AL 35405 B Birmingham AL 1952 d Peter & Frances. BS Birmingham-Sthrn Coll 1974; MD U of Alabama 1978; MDiv Ya Berk 2002. D 6/2/2002 P 12/3/2002 Bp Henry Nutt Parsley Jr. Counslg Mnstry Professionals Tuscaloosa AL 2008-2010; Assoc R Chr Ch Tuscaloosa AL 2002-2009. margaretscalise@bellsouth.net

✠ SCANLAN, The Rt Rev Audrey (CPa) 22 Dyer Ave, Canton CT 06019 **Dio Cntrl Pennsylvania Harrisburg PA 2015-; R St Gabr's Ch E Berlin CT 2006-; Dir. of Spec Needs Mnstry Rhythms of Gr Plainville CT 2004-** B Portchester NY 1958 BA Wheaton Coll at Norton 1980; Cert Cntrl Connecticut St U 1992; MDiv Ya Berk 2003; MDiv Ya Berk 2003; DMin Hartford Sem 2011. D 6/21/2003 P 1/24/2004 Bp Andrew Donnan Smith Con 9/12/2015 for CPa. m 8/11/1984 Glenn Scanlan c 3. Cn for Mssn Collaboration Dio Connecticut Meriden CT 2011-2015, Cn for Mssn Collaboration 2011-; R Ch of our Sav Plainville CT 2006-2011; Cur Trin Ch Torrington CT 2003-2006. Auth, "Rhythms of Gr, Vol 1," *Rhythms of Gr, Vol 1*, Ch Pub, 2010. ascanlan@diocesepca.org

SCANLAN, Paul Joseph (SO) D 6/11/2016 Bp Thomas Edward Breidenthal.

SCANLON, Geoffrey Edward Leyshon (Spr) 2910 E Stone Creek Blvd, Urbana IL 61802 B Dewsbury Yorkshire UK 1944 s John & Edith. Coll Engr Leeds Gb; U of Leeds Gb. D 6/1/1976 P 6/1/1977 Bp The Bishop Of Durham. R Ch Of The H Trin Danville IL 1987-2013; Vic S Dav's Epis Ch Columbia SC 1985-1987; Vic Ch Of The Epiph Laurens SC 1981-1985; Serv Ch Of Engl 1976-1981.

SCANNELL, Alice Updike (Ore) 1500 NE 15th Ave Apt 336, Portland OR 97232 **Sr Resrch Assoc Portland St U Inst on Aging 2009-** B New York NY 1938 d Godfrey & Alice. BA Smith 1960; MRE UTS 1963; Cert Windham Hse 1963; PhD Portland St U 1989. D 5/15/1998 P 12/12/1998 Bp Robert Louis Ladehoff. m 6/13/1964 John Scott Scannell c 2. Vic S Anne's Epis Ch Washougal WA 2004-2010; Chapl S Aidens Place Lake Oswego OR 2000-2004; S Mich And All Ang Ch Portland OR 1998-2004. "Focus Groups Help Congregations Improve Its New Mem Mnstry," *Revs of Rel Resrch*, 2003. Amer Soc on Aging 1985; Assembly of Epis Healthcare Chapl 1999; Assn for Rel Resrch 1990; Assn of Profsnl Chapl 1998; Gerontological Soc of Amer 1985. Fell Coll

S

of Preachers 2002; Woods Fllshp VTS 2002; Post-doctoral Fllshp in Applied Gerontology Gerontological Soc of Amer 1989.

SCANNELL, John Scott (Ore) 1500 NE 15th Ave Apt 336, Portland OR 97232 **R Emer S Mich And All Ang Ch Portland OR 2011-, 2002-2007, R 1979-2007, R 1979-2002; Chapl to Ret Cler Dio Oregon & Prov VIII 2008-; Assoc Trin Epis Cathd Portland OR 2008-** B Mount Vernon NY 1939 s Nicholas & Enid. BA Col 1961; MDiv PDS 1964. D 6/6/1964 P 12/19/1964 Bp Horace W B Donegan. m 6/13/1964 Alice Updike c 2. Int S Paul's Par Oregon City OR 2010-2011; R Ch Of S Thos Bethel CT 1977-1979, Vic 1975-1977; R Chr Ch Waterbury CT 1968-1975; Min in charge Chr Ch Sodus NY 1964-1968; Min in charge S Steph's Ch Wolcott NY 1964-1968; Bd Trst Dio Oregon Portland OR 2004-2007, Dep GC 2000-2006, Stndg Com 1999-2006, Stndg Com 1999-2004, GC Dep/Alt 1998-2006.

SCANTLEBURY, Cecil Alvin (NY) 61 Santuit Pond Rd., Mashpee MA 02649 **Died 8/17/2016** B BB 1931 s Cecil & Elfreda. BA CUNY; DIT Codrington Coll 1955. D 3/1/1955 P 6/1/1955 Bp The Bishop Of Barbados. m 6/25/1960 W Elizabeth Scantlebury c 2. Dio New York New York NY 1997-2003, 1969-1976; S Fran Assisi And S Martha White Plains NY 1976-1996; Asst S Aug's Epis Ch Brooklyn NY 1967-1968; Cur S Andr's Ch New York NY 1963-1967; Serv Ch Of Guyana 1955-1963.

✠ **SCANTLEBURY, The Rt Rev Victor Alfonso** (Chi) 6167 Westwind Rd, Jackson MS 39206 **Int Bp of Cntrl Ecuador Iglesia Epis Del Ecuador Quito 2011-** B Colon PA 1945 s Barclay & Diana. EDS 1972; MDiv ETSC 1973. D 10/29/1973 P 8/6/1974 Bp Lemuel Barnett Shirley Con 3/15/1991 for RP. m 8/11/1973 Marcia Scantlebury c 2. Asst Bp Dio Chicago Chicago IL 2000-2011; R S Mk's Ch Jackson MS 1995-2000; Bp Suffr of Panama Dio Panama 1991-1994; PBFWR 1988-1991; Ecusa 1986-1991; R S Paul Panama City Rp 1985-1991; R St Pauls Ch 1985-1991; Excoun Dio Panama 1985-1989; Cur Iglesia San Juan 1978-1985; Yth Coordntr Prov IX 1977-1986; P-in-c S Jn Villa Caceres Rp 1974-1985; Dio Panama 1973-1994.

SCARBOROUGH, Anjel Lorraine (Md) 2711 Flintridge Ct, Myersville MD 21773 **P-in-c Gr Ch Brunswick MD 2014-, P-in-c 2011-2014; COM Dio Maryland Baltimore MD 2016-, Claggett Cntr Prog Com 2015, Bp's Cmsn on Addiction and Recovery 2015-, Bp's Cmsn on Addiction and Recovery 2015-, Sprtl Advsr to MD Epis Curs 2010-2012, Sprtl Advsr, Maryland Epis Curs 2010-2012** B San Diego CA 1964 d Robert & Earlene. AS Orange Coast Coll Costa Mesa CA 1985; BS California St U Long Bch 1987; MDiv Luth TS 2007. D 6/16/2007 P 2/2/2008 Bp John L Rabb. m 11/18/1988 Stuart K Scarborough c 2. Supply Gr Ch New Mrkt MD 2011; Chapl Hospice of Washington Cnty Hagerstown MD 2009-2011; Asst. R S Mk's Ch Lappans Boonsboro MD 2009; Min of Visitation Calv Meth Ch Frederick MD 2008-2009; Int S Lk's Ch Baltimore MD 2008-2009; R The Gathering: A Fam Of Faith Epis Ch Walkersville MD 2008, D 2007-2008; Owner Computrain LLC Frederick MD 1995-2003. Auth, "We Look for the Resurr of the Dead," *Congregations mag*, The Alb Inst, 2010. DOK 2002; Soc of Cath Priests 2008. NT Schlrshp Luth TS at Gettysburg 2007. rector@gracebrunswick.org

SCARCIA, Steven Angelo (Alb) PO Box 592, Little Falls NY 13365 **R Emm Ch Little Falls NY 1978-** B Peekskill NY 1948 s Angelo & Kathryn. BME Westminster Choir Coll of Rider U 1971; MDiv Nash 1973; DMin Luther Rice TS 1982. D 12/22/1973 Bp Allen Webster Brown P 11/1/1974 Bp Wilbur Emory Hogg Jr. CE Cmsn 1979-1985; Asst Secy Of The Dioc Conv 1978-1979; Liturg Cmsn 1977-1979; Adirondack Mssn Pottersville NY 1974-1978; Trst Dio Albany Greenwich NY 1985-1988.

✠ **SCARFE, The Rt Rev Alan** (Ia) 225 37th St, Des Moines IA 50312 **Bp of Iowa Dio Iowa Des Moines IA 2003-** B Bradford Yorkshire UK 1950 s Norman & Regina. MA Oxf GB 1972; Romanian Orth Institiute Bucuresti RO 1974; Romanian Orth Inst Bucuresti RO 1975; STM GTS 1986; STM GTS 1986. D 6/21/1986 Bp Robert Claflin Rusack P 12/21/1986 Bp Oliver Bailey Garver Jr Con 3/11/2003 for Ia. m 8/23/1975 Donna Scarfe c 4. Mnstry Dio Los Angeles Los Angeles CA 2000-2003, Ecum Off 1995-1998, Cmsn on Ecum 1991-1999; Off Epis Ecum 1996-2003; Chapl Epis/Luth Occ Coll 1991-1997; R S Barn' Epis Ch Los Angeles CA 1990-2003; Assoc R S Columba's Par Camarillo CA 1986-1989. Auth, *Call for Truth- Ch & S in Romania*; Ed/Contrib, *Chrsnty & Marxism*; Auth, "Romanian Orth Ch," *Orth Ch & Politics in 20th Century*. DD GTS 2003. ascarfe@iowaepiscopal.org

SCARFF, Stephen D (Alb) 129 Ledge Hill Rd, Guilford CT 06437 B New York 1966 s William & Erma. MA McGill U 1998; MDiv Ya Berk 2012; CTM U of Cambridge 2012. D 6/1/2013 P 5/11/2015 Bp William Howard Love. Cur S Jn's Ch Beverly MA 2014-2016; St Fran Hosp Hartford CT 2013-2014.

SCARLETT, William George (Md) B 1944

SCARPACE, Ramona (Minn) 2035 Charlton Rd, Sunfish Lake MN 55118 **S Jn In The Wilderness S Paul MN 2017-** B Buffalo NY 1955 d Joseph & Irene. Liberal Arts SUNY at Buffalo 1978; MA Hamline U 1993; MDiv Untd TS 2014. D 12/19/2013 P 6/26/2014 Bp Brian N Prior. m 9/13/2014 Georgianna Smith.

SCHAAL, Richard (CNY) 1504 76th Rd, Berkshire NY 13736 **P St Johns Epis Ch Berkshire NY 2010-** B Erie PA 1947 Formation Prog Dio Cntrl NY; BA Gannon U 1969. D 5/8/2010 P 12/4/2010 Bp Gladstone Bailey Adams III.

SCHACHT, Lawrence Arthur (NY) 525 W End Ave Apt 4-H, New York NY 10024 **Ret 2002-** B Detroit MI 1927 s Edward & Anna. D 5/30/1992 Bp Richard Frank Grein. D The Ch Of The Epiph New York NY 2000-2002; D S Mich's Ch New York NY 1992-1996. NAAD.

SCHADT, Stuart Everett (Va) 6070 Greenway Ct, Manassas VA 20111 **R Trin Ch Manassas VA 1990-** B La Marque TX 1955 s Michel & Marian. BA U of Texas 1976; MDiv VTS 1980. D 6/17/1980 P 3/1/1981 Bp Roger Howard Cilley. m 11/13/1976 Pamela L Schadt c 1. R Gr Epis Ch Houston TX 1983-1990; Asst Trin Ch Galveston TX 1980-1983. Auth, "A Time For Vision".

SCHAEFER III, John (Neb) 7236 County Road 34, Fort Calhoun NE 68023 **R S Andr's Ch Omaha NE 2009-** B Waynesburg PA 1957 s Otto & Rosemary. BS Nthrn Arizona U 1979; MDiv CDSP 1991; DMin SWTS 2004. D 6/15/1991 Bp Frederick Houk Borsch P 12/14/1991 Bp John Stuart Thornton. m 6/17/1989 Margaret Sutherland c 2. Cn Dio Nebraska Omaha NE 2005-2009; S Steph's Ch Grand Island NE 2004-2005; R Ch of Our Sav No Platte NE 1998-2004; Vic Ch Of H Nativ Meridian ID 1993-1995; All SS Epis Ch Boise ID 1991-1993; D Dio Idaho Boise ID 1991-1993. john@standrewsomaha.org

SCHAEFER, Joslyn (WNC) 349 N Haywood St, Waynesville NC 28786 **Gr Ch In The Mountains Waynesville NC 2017-** B Roswell GA 1978 d Jared & Judith. BA Davidson Coll 2000; MTh Edinburgh U 2001; MDiv EDS 2013. D 6/29/2013 Bp Michael B Curry P 1/9/2014 Bp Anne Hodges-Copple. m 5/27/2006 Brian P Schaefer c 2. S Ptr's Epis Ch Charlotte NC 2013-2017. jschaefer@st-peters.org

SCHAEFER, Lee (Ind) 444 South Harbour Drive, Noblesville IN 46062 **R S Mich's Ch Noblesville IN 2007-** B Minneapolis MN 1956 s Philip & June. S Thos Coll Miami FL; AA Normandale Cmnty Coll Bloomington MN 1976; BS S Cloud St U 1978; MDiv VTS 1983; DMin VTS 2005. D 12/6/1983 P 6/1/1985 Bp Robert Marshall Anderson. m 8/18/1984 Alison Schaefer c 2. R S Tim's Epis Ch Kingsport TN 1997-2007; 1994-1996; R Ch Of The Gd Shpd Sioux Falls SD 1992-1997; Cn Geth Cathd Fargo ND 1989-1992; Asst to R Ch Of The Gd Shpd Raleigh NC 1986-1989; Asst to R S Nich Ch Minneapolis MN 1983-1986. *Introducing New Cultures into a Par*, VTS, 2005.

SCHAEFER, Lynette Golderman (Haw) PO Box 1233, Kaunakakai HI 96748 **Chapl Maui Police Dept 2010-** B San Mateo CA 1948 d Philip & Florence. U of New So Wales 1966; BEd U of Hawaii 1971; MDiv CDSP 1976. D 4/25/1977 P 6/29/1978 Bp Edmond Lee Browning. m 12/30/1977 Winthrop S Schaefer c 3. Chapl Hospice Hawaii Molokai 2003-2016; Vic Gr Ch Hoolehua HI 1978-2010; S Ptr's Ch Honolulu HI 1977-1978. HI 1st Lady Awd 1982; Outstanding Young Wmn of Amer 1979.

SCHAEFER, Norma Jane (Chi) 417 N. Beck Road, Lindenhurst IL 60046 B Independence IA 1948 d James & Eleanor. BA NE Illinois U 1990; MDiv SWTS 1994. D 6/18/1994 P 12/17/1994 Bp Frank Tracy Griswold III. m 2/27/1965 Craig Schaefer c 2. The Annunc Of Our Lady Gurnee IL 2011-2013; R The Epis Ch Of S Jas The Less Northfield IL 2003-2010; Assoc The Ch Of The H Sprt Lake Forest IL 1998-2003; Asst to R S Aug's Epis Ch Wilmette IL 1994-1998. CS.JS@COMCAST.NET

SCHAEFER, Philip David (Roch) 47 Brougham Dr, Penfield NY 14526 **P Assoc S Lk And S Simon Cyrene Rochester NY 2011-, P Assoc 2011-; Int Ch Of The Ascen Rochester NY 2000-; Publ Plcy Com Dio Rochester Henrietta 2010-** B Toledo OH 1935 s Philip & Helen. BA Denison U 1957; MDiv Ya Berk 1960; ThM Bex Sem 1973. D 6/11/1960 Bp Beverley D Tucker P 1/21/1961 Bp Nelson Marigold Burroughs. m 9/6/1958 Elsa Anne Brumbaugh c 4. Pstr Care Coordntr Genesee Reg Hm Care Hospice of Rochester Rochester NY 1989-1995; Chapl Epis Ch Hm Rochester NY 1988-1995; Chapl The Chap of the Epis Ch Hm Rochester NY 1988-1995; R Ch Of The Incarn Penfield NY 1974-1987; R Zion Ch Avon NY 1969-1974; R All SS Epis Ch Aliquippa PA 1963-1969; P-in-c S Lk's Epis Ch Georgetown PA 1963-1969; Cur S Jas Ch Painesville OH 1960-1963.

SCHAEFER, John Grant (Oly) 1827 Southeast 18th Place, Renton WA 98055 **Died 11/6/2016** B Washington DC 1929 s William & Lucy. BA U of Washington 1951; Nash 1952; MDiv SWTS 1954. D 6/29/1954 P 6/29/1955 Bp Stephen F Bayne Jr. m 3/4/1984 Loretta Mae LaBranche c 2. Ch Of The Resurr Bellevue WA 2003-2004; S Mich And All Ang Ch Issaquah WA 2002-2016, Int 1999-2001; P-in-c Ch Of The H Cross Redmond WA 2001-2002; Secy Dioc Conv Dio Olympia Seattle 1989-2010, 1968-1988; R S Lk's Epis Ch Renton WA 1959-1994; P Chr Epis Ch Anacortes WA 1956-1959; R S Aug Langley WA 1956-1957; S Steph's Epis Ch Oak Harbor WA 1956-1957; Cur Chr Ch Tacoma WA 1954-1956. Hon Cn St. Mk's Cathd Seattle Wa 2009.

SCHAEFFER, John R (Eas) All Saints Episcopal Church, 3577 McClure Ave, Pittsburgh PA 15212 **S Mary Anne's Epis Ch No E MD 2016-** B New Haven CT 1950 s Francis & Julia. BA U of New Haven 1973; MDiv TESM 2012; MDiv Trin Sch for Mnstry 2012. D 6/2/2012 Bp Kenneth Lester Price P 12/15/2012 Bp Dorsey McConnell. m 11/30/1984 Karen B Schaeffer c 3. All SS Epis

Ch Pittsburgh PA 2014; All SS Epis Ch Brighton Heights Brighton Heights PA 2012-2016. fatherjohn@stmaryanne.org

SCHAEFFER, Susan Edwards (NY) 17 Perkins Ave, Northampton MA 01060 B Oakland CA 1946 d Clarence & Louise. BA Lycoming Coll 1967; MDiv UTS 1980; PhD UTS 1991. D 6/7/1980 P 1/25/1981 Bp Paul Moore Jr. c 2. Dio New York New York NY 1997-2004, Liturg Cmsn 1986-1994, Stndg Com 1992-1996; R S Ptr's Ch Port Chester NY 1992-1996; Assoc The Ch Of S Lk In The Fields New York NY 1980-1992. Auth, "Gospel Of Ptr," 1991; Auth, "SBL Seminar Papers," 1991; Auth, "The Guard At The Tomb". Angl Assn Of Biblic Scholars; SBL.

SCHAFFENBURG, Karl Christian (FdL) 1011 N. 7th St., 103 W. Broad Street, Sheboygan WI 53081 R All SS Chap Elkhart Lake WI 2011-; R Gr Epis Ch Sheboygan WI 2011- B Cleveland OH 1956 s Carlos & Lila. BS U of Mississippi 1980; JD U of Mississippi 1984; MDiv Nash 2006. D 12/17/2005 P 6/24/2006 Bp Russell Edward Jacobus. m 12/23/1986 Elizabeth B Schaffenburg c 2. R Epis Ch Of The Incarn W Point MS 2006-2011; St Paul's Epis Cathd Fond Du Lac WI 2005-2006. Auth, "Irish Evolution and the Politics of Identity," *Orbis: A Journ of Frgn Affrs*, Frgn Plcy Resrch Inst, 2009; Auth, "Russkiy & Rossiiskiy: Russian Natl Identity after Putin," *Orbis: A Journ of Frgn Affrs*, Frgn Plcy Resrch Inst, 2007.

SCHAFFNER, Philip Perry (Minn) 2401 33rd Ave. S, Minneapolis MN 55406 D Dio Minnesota MN 2006- B St Paul MN 1980 s Gregory & Patricia. BA Gri 2001; MPP Harvard Kennedy Sch of Govt 2009. D 6/18/2005 Bp James Louis Jelinek. D St. Geo's Epis Ch St. Louis Pk MN 2005-2007. No Amer Assn of the Diac 2003.

SCHAFROTH, Stephen Louis (EO) 1107 Lewis St, The Dalles OR 97058 GC Dep Dio Estrn Oregon Cove OR 2009- B Ames IA 1949 s Arthur & Alice. D 9/29/1999 Bp Rustin Ray Kimsey. m 5/7/1983 Colleen Schafroth c 1.

SCHAIBLE II, Donald J (Be) Christ and Trinity Parishes, 58 River St, Carbondale PA 18407 R S Anne's Epis Ch Trexlertown PA 2016- B Warren NJ 1963 s Donald & Joan. BA DeSales U 1985; MDiv S Chas Borromeo Sem 1988; MA St Chas 1990; MS U of Scranton 2000. Rec 6/29/2007 Bp Paul Victor Marshall. m 9/17/2005 Sharon P Quinn c 1. R Trin Epis Ch Carbondale PA 2008-2016. rector@stannesepiscopal.net

SCHAITBERGER SSF, Stephen Harold (Minn) 1402 S 8th St, Brainerd MN 56401 B Camp Lejeune NC 1945 s Harold & Betty. BA U MN 1967; MDiv Nash 1970; Command and Gnrl Stff Coll 1980. D 6/29/1970 Bp Hamilton Hyde Kellogg P 2/21/1971 Bp Philip Frederick McNairy. m 12/30/2011 Sharli Lauren Schaitberger. Cn Dio Minnesota Minneapolis MN 1995-2003; R S Paul's Ch Brainerd MN 1980-1995; P-in-c S Jn's Ch Aitkin MN 1980-1986; Chapl US Army NG 1978-2002; R Ch Of The H Comm S Ptr MN 1973-1980; P-in-c H Trin Epis Ch Luverne MN 1971-1973; S Jas Ch Marshall MN 1971-1973; S Paul's Ch Pipestone MN 1971-1973. Soc of S Fran - Tertiary 1986. Bush Fllshp Awd 1994; Chapl, Minnesota Army NG; Commendation,Achievement Medals,Meritorious Serv Medals US-A.

SCHALLER, Joseph G (Pa) 303 W. Lancaster Avenue, Suite 2C, Wayne PA 19087 Asst S Mary's Epis Ch Ardmore PA 2007-; Asst S Gabr's Epis Ch Philadelphia PA 2006- B Rochester NY 1954 s Joseph & Ruby. BA Geo 1978; MDiv Weston Jesuit TS 1981; MA U of Notre Dame 1985; STL Weston Jesuit TS 1989; PsyD Widener U 1999. Rec 6/4/2006 Bp Charles Ellsworth Bennison Jr. m 8/20/2004 Phillip Bennett. drschaller@josephschaller.com

SCHALLER JR, Warren August (Va) 7 Lost Ridge Lane, Galena IL 61036 B Syracuse NY 1937 s Warren & Natalie. BA Ken 1959; MA U MN 1961; STM GTS 1964. D 6/27/1964 Bp Hamilton Hyde Kellogg P 4/1/1965 Bp Philip Frederick McNairy. m 2/11/1961 Patricia A Schaller c 5. P S Mary's Fleeton Reedville VA 2004-2007; Dir Inst For Sprtl Direction 1976-1983; Assoc Truro Epis Ch Fairfax VA 1975-1976; R S Andr's Ch Manchester NH 1971-1973; R Ch Of The H Apos S Paul MN 1967-1971; Vic Epiph Epis Ch S Paul MN 1964-1967; Chapl Hamline U S Paul MN 1964-1967. Auth, "Hist Of The Soc Policies Of The Epis Ch In The 20th Century".

SCHANE, Clifford Edward (Tenn) 1616 Piedmont Ave Ne Apt O9, Atlanta GA 30324 Died 9/11/2016 B Wheeling WV 1937 s Samuel & Helen. BS W Virginia U 1960; MDiv VTS 1964; Ldrshp Acad for New Directions 1977; VTS 1992. D 6/11/1964 P 12/17/1964 Bp Wilburn Camrock Campbell. c 1. Ret 1996-2016; R & Sprtl Dir Otey Memi Par Ch Sewanee TN 1979-1996; Fac U So Sewanee TN 1979-1981; Dn of Reg #15 Dio Virginia Richmond VA 1975-1978; S Anne's Par Scottsville VA 1974-1979; R S Anne's Albemarle Cnty VA 1974-1979; P-in-c Frederick Par Winchester VA 1973-1974; Asst Frederick Par Winchester VA 1972-1973; R Chr Ch Point Pleasat WV 1968-1972; Vic S Jas' Epis Ch Lewisburg WV 1964-1968. OHC - Assoc P 1961.

SCHAPER, Richard L (Cal) 646 Ridgewood Avenue, Mill Valley CA 94941 B Bayshore NY 1945 s Louis & Mary. BA Colg 1967; U Coll Oxford 1968; MTh U Chi 1970; Ya 1971; CFP Golden Gate U 1997; U of San Francisco 1997. Rec 12/7/2002 Bp William Edwin Swing. m 6/18/1983 Anita Ruth Ostrom c 1. Dio California San Francisco CA 2003-2013.

SCHARF, Douglas Frederick (SeFla) 3714 Cystal Dew St, Plant City FL 33567 The Epis Ch Of The Gd Shpd Tequesta FL 2017- B West Islip NY 1979 s Frederick & Carol. BA Florida Gulf Coast U 2001; MDiv VTS 2004. D 6/12/2004 Bp Rogers Sanders Harris P 12/19/2004 Bp John Bailey Lipscomb. m 11/20/1999 Shannon Joy Scharf c 3. R H Innoc Epis Ch Valrico FL 2007-2016; Assoc Ch Of The H Sprt Osprey FL 2004-2007. dscharf04@verizon.net

SCHARF JR, Frederick E (SwFla) 11644 Spindrift Loop, Hudson FL 34667 B Oswego NY 1939 s Frederick & Ruth. BS SUNY 1962; MS SUNY 1972; MDiv VTS 1988. D 6/11/1988 P 12/22/1988 Bp Gerald Francis Burrill. m 4/21/2001 Vera G Scharf c 3. P-in-c S Mart's Epis Ch Hudson FL 2013-2015, Asst 2007-2015; Int The Epis Ch Of The Gd Shpd Venice FL 2006-2007; Vic Lamb Of God Epis Ch Ft Myers FL 1990-1999; Vic St Josephs Ch Ft Myers FL 1990-1999; Cur S Mary's Epis Ch Bonita Sprg FL 1988-1990. fred.scharf@verizon.net

SCHARK, Frederick J (WMich) St Mark Episcopal Church, 27 E Chicago St, Coldwater MI 49036 S Mk's Ch Coldwater MI 2013- B Saginaw MI 1955 s Christian & Flora. MDiv Hur CA; BA Trin IN. D 1/29/2005 P 8/14/2005 Bp Edwin Max Leidel Jr. m 9/22/1997 Kristi T Schark c 1. Trin Epis Ch Lexington MI 2005-2013.

SCHATZ, Stefani S (Cal) 200 Island Ave, Reno NV 89501 Died 7/12/2017 B Dallas TX 1962 d Lawrence & Iva. BA Mills Coll 1984; MDiv EDS 2001. D 6/30/2001 Bp Chester Lovelle Talton P 1/12/2002 Bp Frederick Houk Borsch. m 11/15/2003 Joe F Duggan. Dio California San Francisco CA 2013-2017; R Trin Epis Ch Reno NV 2008-2013; Actg Team R Ch of Engl Gorton Team Mnstry Manchester 2006-2008; Dir Rel Educ All SS Par Brookline MA 2004-2006; Assoc St Cross Epis Ch Hermosa Bch CA 2001-2003; Mem, Stndg Com Dio Nevada Las Vegas 2009-2017. stefanis@diocal.org

SCHAUBLE, Jack (Chi) Po Box 88, Compton IL 61318 B Barrington IL 1934 s Fredrick & Neva. BA Elmhurst Coll 1956; MDiv SWTS 1959; MS U IL 1976; Cert Illinois Vlly Cmnty Coll 2005. D 6/20/1959 P 12/19/1959 Bp Charles L Street. m 5/11/1993 Sandra Jones-Schauble c 3. P-in-c Emm Epis Ch Rockford IL 2006-2007; P-in-c The Epis Ch Of The H Trin Belvidere IL 2004-2005; Int Gr Epis Ch Freeport IL 2001-2003; Int Gr Epis Ch Galena IL 1999-2001; Int Gr Epis Ch New Lenox IL 1998-1999; Int Gr Epis Ch Sheboygan WI 1998; Int S Lk's Ch Dixon IL 1995-1997; Int All SS Epis Ch Appleton WI 1995; Luth Soc Serv Of Illinois Oregon IL 1993-1995; S Jude's Epis Ch Rochelle IL 1986-1990; NW Mil & Nav Acad Lake Geneva WI 1976-1986; Vic S Ann's Ch Woodstock IL 1969-1975; R S Paul's Ch La Salle IL 1962-1969; Cur Ch Of The H Comf Kenilworth IL 1959-1962.

SCHEDA, Claudia (WNY) 54 Linwood Ave, Williamsville NY 14221 S Aid's Ch Alden NY 2015-; P-in-c S Paul's Epis Ch Mayville NY 2012-; Cmpgn Com Chair Epis Partnership for Mssn and Outreach 2011- B Buffalo NY 1965 d Francis & Ruth. BA SUNY at Buffalo 1987; MS Canisus Coll 1989; MDiv GTS 2011. D 4/22/2010 Bp Michael Garrison P 10/8/2011 Bp Ralph William Franklin. m 4/29/1989 Kevin Koczka c 2. Int S Paul's Epis Ch Lewiston NY 2011-2012. Auth, "Reverberation," *The Angl*, The Angl Soc of the US, 2011. churchaldenst.aidans@gmail.com

SCHEEL, William Preston (Ark) 26 Cypress Point, Wimberley TX 78676 B Chicago IL 1936 s Harvey & Mildred. BA U So 1959; BD SWTS 1962; EdD U of Massachusetts 1971. D 6/29/1962 Bp Hamilton Hyde Kellogg P 5/18/1963 Bp Philip Frederick McNairy. m 6/24/1989 Vivian Carol Scheel c 3. Int R S Paul's Epis Ch Dallas TX 2004-2008; Chapl Par Epis Sch Farmers Branch TX 2003-2004; Pres of the Bd Shattuck-S Mary's Sch Faribault MN 1999-2003; Mem Bd Trst Shattuck-St. Mary's Sch Faribault 1998-2004; Assoc Chr Epis Ch Plano TX 1995-2003; Exec Dir SW Assn of Epis Schools Canyon TX 1993-1999; Dio NW Texas Lubbock TX 1988-1990; Hdmstr S Cyp Sch Lufkin TX 1984-1986; Headmaster Berry Acad 1980-1983; Adj Prof Berry Coll 1980-1983; Dio New Jersey Trenton NJ 1977-1980; Headmaster St. Mary's Hall-Doane Acad Burlington NJ 1974-1980; Headmaster Christchurch Sch Christchurch VA 1971-1974; Chapl Shattuck Sch Faribault MN 1967-1969; Asst Dn Shattuck Sch Faribault MN 1966-1969; Asst St Dav's Epis Ch Minnetonka MN 1964-1966; Yth Advsry Coun Dio Minnesota Minneapolis MN 1963-1969; Vic St Jn's Epis Ch Redlake MN 1962-1964. *Var Bk Revs & arts*, 2003. The Rev. A. Dn Calcote Awd SW Assn of Epis Schools 2007; Jn Verdery Awd Nat'l Assn of Epis Schools 2002; Hon Cn Cathd of Our Merc Sav 1967.

SCHEELER, Joseph L (Oly) All Saints Episc Church, 2206 Nw 99th St, Vancouver WA 98665 All SS' Epis Ch Vancouver WA 2016-; Native Amer Mnstry Dio Montana 2005-; Ch Of The Nativ/Elkhorn Cluster Helena MT 2001- B Bryn Mawr PA 1950 BA La Salle U 1976; Mnstry Formation Prog 1999. D 11/10/2001 P 10/8/2002 Bp Charles Lovett Keyser. m 11/26/1983 Mona M Pocha c 3.

SCHEELER, Richard Edward Gerhart (Mil) 1540 S 166th St, New Berlin WI 53151 Property Mgr S Edmunds Ch Milwaukee WI 2012-, D 2000-2012, D 1979-1999; Bp D for Chr Formation Dio Milwaukee Milwaukee WI 2009-, D Formation Sch, Instr 2014-, Lifelong Chr Formation, Mem 2010-2016, D's Coun, chairperson 2010-2014, Chairperson Yth Cmsn 2004-2009, Mem of Yth Cmsn 2004-2009, Gathering(feeding Prog) Exec. Dir 1985-1987,

S

Mem of Yth Cmsn 1982-1989 B Milwaukee WI 1951 s Stanley & Barbara. BA U of Wisconsin-Whitewater 1973; Inst for Chr Stds Dio Sch at Nashotah Ho 1978. D 1/25/1979 Bp Charles Thomas Gaskell. m 6/11/1977 Patty Ann Carney c 3. D S Thos Of Cbury Ch Greendale WI 2008-2009, D 1985-2008; D S Jn Ch/Mision San Juan Milwaukee WI 1990-2000; Bd Dir Inside Outside(prision Mnstry) 1987-1989. Ord of S Vinc 1979. Bp's Shield Bp Dio Milwaukee 2014.

SCHEEPERS, Noble F (Mass) 62 Cedar St, Dedham MA 02026 **Trin Ch Marshfield MA 2015-** B Cape Town South Africa 1953 s Arthur & Ernestine. Lithography Cape Peninsula U of Tech 1975; AFTS Fed TS 1991; Counslg Philipi Trust Coll 2008. Trans 6/12/2012 as Priest Bp M(Arvil) Thomas Shaw. m 10/8/2011 Angela Carolyn Mcconney Scheepers. R Ch Of The Gd Shpd Dedham MA 2012-2015. noble23r@gmail.com

SCHEFF, Tanya Lynn (NI) 600 Franklin St, Michigan City IN 46360 **Trin Ch Michigan City IN 2014-** B Ft Pierce FL 1966 d Jesse & Gloria. BS The U of Memphis 1999; MDiv Nash 2014; MDiv Nash 2014. D 5/24/2014 Bp Gregory Orrin Brewer P 6/5/2015 Bp Edward Stuart Little II. m 11/21/1987 Joseph James Scheff c 3. trinity-church@sbcglobal.net

SCHEIBLE, Anne Clare Elsworth (Minn) 225 5th St Se, Chatfield MN 55923 B Des Moines IA 1942 d John & Katherine. BS Hamline U 1964. D 7/28/1996 Bp Sanford Zangwill Kaye Hampton P 2/15/1997 Bp James Louis Jelinek. m 10/2/1965 James William Scheible. P S Matt's Epis Ch Chatfield MN 1997-2003. Ascp 1964-2003.

SCHEIBLE, **Gordon Kenneth** (SanD) 2151 Bella Vista, Canyon Lake TX 78133 **Prog Consult Addiction Med Serv Berkeley CA 2015-** B San Diego CA 1948 s Walter & Charlotte. BA U of San Diego 1971; MDiv CDSP 1974; Cert Inst of Chrmical Dependency Stds 2007. D 7/7/1974 P 1/25/1975 Bp Robert Munro Wolterstorff. m 2/18/1978 Pamela Ferguson c 3. Int R St. Andr's Epis Ch Seguin TX 2016-2017; Prog Dir The Champion Cntr Lompoc CA 2014-2015; P-in-c S Hugh Of Lincoln Mssn Idyllwild CA 2008-2015; Chem Dependency Counslr/Case Mgr Hemet Vlly Recovery Cntr and Sage Retreat Hemet CA 2008-2014; R The Epis Ch Of The Gd Shpd Hemet CA 1999-2008; Dist Chapl 13th US Coast Guard Dist Seattle WA 1996-1999; Command Chapl USS Amer (CV 1966) Norfolk VA 1992-1995; Regimental Chapl 1st Marine Expeditionary Brigade Kaneohe HI 1989-1992; Serv Sch Command Chapl Naval Trng Cntr Great Lakes IL 1986-1989; Advance Course Stdt Naval Educ & Trng Course Newport RI 1985-1986; Sr Chapl Naval Spprt Activity Naples Italy 1983-1985; Chapl USS Denver (LPD-9) San Diego CA 1980-1983; Chapl Naval Hosp Camp Pendleton CA 1978-1980; Off Of Bsh For ArmdF New York NY 1977-1998; Chapl 3rd Marine Div Okinawa Japan 1977-1978; S Jas By The Sea La Jolla CA 1975-1976; Vice Chairman Cnty of Riverside Bd Mntl Heath 2004-2008. Cmnty of Hope 2015; CBS 1985; Ord of S Lk 1997; OHC - Assoc 1973.

SCHEID, **Daniel S** (EMich) 922 Blanchard Ave, Flint MI 48503 **R S Paul's Epis Ch Flint MI 2015-; Pres of Stndg Com Dio Estrn Michigan Saginaw MI 2016-** B Greenville MI 1965 s Howard & Margaret. BA Aquinas Coll 1990; MDiv SWTS 2006. D 12/17/2005 P 6/24/2006 Bp Robert R Gepert. m 9/12/2009 Kathleen J Scheid c 4. R S Aug Of Cbury Epis Ch Benton Harbor MI 2006-2015. rectoratstpauls@ameritech.net

SCHEIDE, Diana Southwick (NY) PO Box 296, Callicoon NY 12723 **Dio New York New York NY 2014-** B Butler PA 1956 d Russell & Lois. BA Wheaton Coll 1978; MDiv TS Sewanee 2014; MDiv TS Sewanee 2014; MDiv Sewanee: The U So, TS 2014; MDiv The TS at The U So 2014. D 6/20/2014 Bp Robert R Gepert P 1/17/2015 Bp Allen Shin. c 3.

SCHEIDER SSF, **Dave** (Tex) 130 Sobrante Rd Unit 116, Belton TX 76513 **Epis TS Of The SW Austin TX 2013-; Dir CCMV Sem of the SW 2013-; Off Of Bsh For ArmdF New York NY 1999-** B Peoria IL 1957 s Max & Joyce. Doctor of Mnstry Austin Presb TS; BA Columbia Un 1980; MDiv Andrews U 1983; MS Wright St U 1988; MS K SU 1997; Cert Spec Stds Epis TS of the SW 2005; D.Min. Austin Presb TS 2009. D 12/12/1998 P 6/12/1999 Bp David Bruce Joslin. m 8/9/1981 Beverley A Scheider c 3. Chapl (LTC) US-Army 1988-2012; Chapl Kettering Med Cntr Dayton OH 1986-1987. Aamft; Diplomate AAPC 1997. dave.scheider@hotmail.com

SCHELB, Holly Greenmam (NC) 1323 Irving St, Winston Salem NC 27103 B Cortland NY 1955 D 1/8/2005 Bp Michael B Curry. c 2.

SCHELL, Anita Louise (RI) 42 Dearborn St, Newport RI 02840 **Emm Ch Newport RI 2010-, R 2010-; Mem, Stndg Com The Dio Rhode Island 2010-** B Lancaster PA 1957 d Theodore & Anne. BA Br 1979; MDiv GTS 1983; DMin EDS 2009. D 6/10/1983 P 6/14/1984 Bp Charlie Fuller Mcnutt Jr. m 10/25/2013 Stephen Macausland c 2. Chair, Com on the Environ The Dio Vermont VT 2009-2010; Alt Del, Syn Prov One ECUSA 2008-2010; Pres, Stndg Com The Dio Vermont VT 2008-2010; R S Ptr's Epis Ch Bennington VT 2005-2010; S Paul's Ch Philadelphia PA 2001-2005, 1985-1988; Bd Ch Fndt Bd 1991-1995; Assoc Ch Of The H Apos Wynnewood PA 1990-2001; Bd Naes 1989-1993; Asst Chapl Epis Acad Merion PA 1988-2001; The Epis Acad Newtown Sq PA 1988-2001; Dioc Ce Com Dio Pennsylvania Philadelphia PA 1985-2005; Trin Educ Fund New York NY 1984-1985; D-In-Trning Trin Par New York NY

1983-1984; Dio New York New York NY 1983-1985. Outsanding Young Wmn Awd 1985.

SCHELL, Donald J (Cal) 555 De Haro St Ste 330, San Francisco CA 94107 B San Jose CA 1947 s Harold & Nancy. BA S Jn 1968; PrTS 1969; STB GTS 1971; MA U of San Francisco 1992; Coll of Preachers 1999. D 10/11/1971 P 9/23/1972 Bp Stephen F Bayne Jr. m 5/10/1975 Ellen S Schell c 4. Pres All SS Co San Francisco CA 2007-2014; R S Greg Of Nyssa Ch San Francisco CA 1980-2007; Dce Dio Idaho Boise ID 1977-1980, DCE 1973-1976; R S Dav's Epis Ch Caldwell ID 1976-1980; Epis Ch At Yale New Haven CT 1973-1976; Founding Mem, Coordntng Coun Sprtl Dir Intl 1992-1998; Sprtl Curric Dir, Lay Acad Dio California San Francisco CA 1982-1986. Auth, *,My Fr My Daughter: Pilgrims On The Road To Santiago*, Ch Pub Inc, 2000; Ed, "(Pub Ed)," *Connections*, Sprtl Dir Intl , 1994; cont. Auth, "Searching For Sacr Space," Ch Pub Inc; cont. Auth, "What Would jesus Sing," Ch Pub Inc; cont. Auth, "Searching For Sacr Space," Ch Pub Inc; cont. Auth, "What Would jesus Sing," Ch Pub Inc. Associated Parishes Coun 1998; Sprtl Dir Intl 1989-1995. Distingushed Alum The GTS 2004.

SCHELL, Richardson Whitfield (Ct) Kent School, Kent CT 06757 **Sch Headmaster S Jos's Chap at the Kent Sch Kent CT 1981-; Kent Sch Kent CT 1980-** B Evanston IL 1951 s Frank & Carol. BA Harv 1973; MDiv Ya Berk 1976. D 5/24/1976 P 11/1/1976 Bp James Winchester Montgomery. The Ch Of The H Sprt Lake Forest IL 1976-1980.

SCHELLENBERG, Roger Thomas (Va) 5775 Barclay Drive Suite G, Kingstowne VA 22315 B Winchester MA 1958 s Roland & Lydia. BA W&M 1980; MDiv GTS 1984; DMin VTS 2009. D 6/8/1984 P 5/26/1985 Bp Claude Charles Vache. m 10/26/1985 Virginia S Schellenberg c 2. Sr. Pstr Ch Of The Sprt Alexandria VA 2001-2014; Vic Dio Virginia Richmond VA 1997-2000; Dio Wstrn Massachusetts Springfield 1993-1997; S Matt's Ch Worcester MA 1993-1997; R The Par of S Mich's Auburn ME 1987-1993; Asst to the R S Mk's Ch Mt Kisco NY 1985-1987; Asst to the R S Andr's Ch Norfolk VA 1984-1985. Soc of S Jn the Evang 1987.

SCHELLHAMMER, Judith Lynn (Mich) PO Box 287, Onsted MI 49265 B Mineola NY 1951 d Alfred & Marie. BS Hillsdale Coll 2006. D 12/6/2015 P 6/23/2016 Bp Wendell Nathaniel Gibbs Jr. c 3. jschellhammer@hillsdale.edu

SCHELLING, Robert Louis (Colo) 393 Private Road 5730, Jefferson TX 75657 B 1937 s Lovere & Marian. BA Univ of Colorado 1960; MDiv SWTS 1976; BS Colo St Univ-Pueblo 1996. D 6/23/1976 P 12/23/1976 Bp William Carl Frey. m 12/3/1966 Lynda Schelling c 3. Ch Of The Ascen Pueblo CO 1983-1995; S Tim's Epis Ch Rangely CO 1980-1983; S Paul's Ch Blackfoot ID 1978-1979; Interfaith T/F Loveland CO 1976-1977.

SCHELLINGERHOUDT, Elizabeth L (At) 450 Clairmont Ave, Atlanta GA 30030 **P-in-c S Clare's Epis Ch Blairsville GA 2015-** B Cincinnati OH 1960 d Alvin & Lorton. BA Converse Coll 1982; MDiv Candler TS Emory U 2009. D 12/20/2008 P 2/21/2010 Bp J Neil Alexander. m 9/1/1990 Cornelis H Schellingerhoudt c 2. Assoc S Lk's Epis Ch Atlanta GA 2010-2015; S Marg's Ch Carrollton GA 2010; Ch Of The Epiph Atlanta GA 2008-2009.

SCHEMBS, Lois Jean (Nwk) 321 Lamberts Mill Rd, Westfield NJ 07090 B Oceanside NY 1952 d Carl & Kay. BA Hobart and Wm Smith Colleges 1974; MA Suc 1978; MDiv VTS 1981. D 6/24/1981 P 3/1/1982 Bp Edward Witker Jones. m 4/24/1993 Douglas Schembs. Int Gr St Pauls Ch Trenton NJ 2008-2010; S Mart's Ch Maywood NJ 2000-2008, R 2000-2008, Int 1995-1996; Int The Ch Of The Annunc Oradell NJ 1999-2000; Int S Andr's Ch Harrington Pk NJ 1998-1999; Int S Ptr's Ch Mtn Lks NJ 1997-1998; Int S Alb's Ch Oakland NJ 1996-1997; Int All SS Memi Ch Navesink NJ 1993-1995; Assoc S Paul's Epis Ch Westfield NJ 1987-1993; S Jas Epis Ch Bowie MD 1984-1987; The Cathd Ch Of S Paul Des Moines IA 1983-1984; Gr Ch Muncie IN 1981-1983.

SCHENCK, Timothy E (Mass) 172 Main St, Hingham MA 02043 **R Ch Of S Jn The Evang Hingham MA 2009-; Mem Hingham-Hull Rel Leaders Assn 2009-** B Milwaukee WI 1968 s Andrew & Lois. BA Tufts U 1991; MDiv SWTS 2000. D 6/10/2000 P 12/8/2000 Bp John L Rabb. m 3/25/1995 Bryna Rogers c 2. Chair Briarcliff-Ossining Mnstrl Assn 2004-2006; Ed Bd Chair The Epis New Yorker 2003-2007; R All SS' Epis Ch Briarcliff NY 2002-2009; Cur S Paul's Par Baltimore MD 2000-2002; Prov Coun Prov II 2007-2011; Bd Gvnr The Epis Life Philadelphia PA 2007-2011; Dn Epis Dio Of Ny Mid Hudson Regio Boiceville NY 2005-2007. Auth, "Dust Bunnies in the Basket: FInding God in Lent and Easter," Forw Mvmt, 2015; Auth, "Dog in the Manger: Finding God in Christmas Chaos," Forw Mvmt, 2013; Auth, "What Size Are God's Shoes: Kids, Chaos and the Sprtl Life," Morehouse, 2008; Auth, "From Sem to Par: Navigating Your First Cler Job Search," Self, 2001. frtim@stjohns-hingham.org

SCHENEMAN, Mark Allan (CPa) 226 Acre Dr, Carlisle PA 17013 B Washington DC 1948 s William & Jeanne. BA Moravian TS 1970; MDiv GTS 1973; MA Tem 1976; DMin Estrn Bapt TS 1983. D 3/15/1974 P 1/25/1975 Bp Lloyd Edward Gressle. m 8/15/1970 Dorothy Hoshauer c 3. Stndg Com Dio Cntrl Pennsylvania Harrisburg PA 1993-2003, Chair 1990-1999, Dep Gc 1997-2003, Jub Mnstry Off 1991-1996, Fin Com 1987-1990; R S Jn's Epis Ch Carlisle

PA 1986-2015; R S Ptr's Epis Ch Broomall PA 1977-1986; Asst S Anne's Ch Abington PA 1975-1977; Asst S Mary's Epis Ch Ardmore PA 1974-1975; Chair Prog & Bdgt Com Dio Pennsylvania Philadelphia PA 1984-1986, Prog & Bdgt Com 1979-1983. Auth, "Way Of The Cross," Forw Mvmt, 1983. OHC, Assoc 2001. Hon Cn St. Steph's Cathdral, Dio Cntrl PA 1995. mark.a.scheneman@gmail.com

SCHENKEL JR, Robert Downes (Be) 6539 Betsy Ross Cir, Bethlehem PA 18017 **Ret 1996-** B Baltimore MD 1930 s Robert & Caryl. BS W&L 1952; MDiv VTS 1960. D 7/8/1960 Bp Noble C Powell P 5/31/1961 Bp Harry Lee Doll. c 4. P-in-c Dio Bethlehem Bethlehem PA 2005-2009, Dioc Coun 1987-2004; Dn Cathd Ch Of The Nativ Bethlehem PA 1984-1995; R Ch Of The Gd Shpd Nashua NH 1972-1984; Assoc S Andr's Ch Kansas City MO 1968-1972; R S Marg's Ch Annapolis MD 1963-1968; Asst Chr Ch Baltimore MD 1960-1963; Asst Chr Ch Columbia MD 1960-1963. Contrib, *Celebrate.* HSEC 1990.

SCHENONE, Janine L (SanD) 4321 Eastgate Mall, San Diego CA 92121 **Ch Of The Gd Samar San Diego CA 2016-** B San Francisco CA 1962 d Anthony & Ada. BA NWU 1984; MA U CA 1987; MDiv Ya Berk 2012. D 6/16/2012 Bp Barry Leigh Beisner P 1/9/2013 Bp Andrew Marion Lenow Dietsche. c 1. Assoc All SS Ch Pasadena CA 2013-2016.

SCHERCK, Steven H (Alb) P.O. Box 397, Guilderland NY 12084 **R S Bon Ch Guilderland NY 2009-; Great Chapt Representitive Cathd Of All SS Albany NY 2010-** B Morristown NJ 1964 s Edwin & Joan. BS FD Madison 1987; MA Fairfield U 1994; MA Whitefield TS 2005; Lic S Andrews TS 2007; STM S Andrews TS 2008. D 5/31/2008 P 6/13/2009 Bp William Howard Love. m 9/19/1987 Robin L MacDonald c 3.

SCHERER, Anna (SVa) 1830 Kirby Rd, McLean VA 22101 B Austin TX 1982 d Charles & Mary. BA Roa 2003; MDiv VTS 2009. D 6/13/2009 Bp Herman Hollerith IV P 1/9/2010 Bp David Colin Jones. m 1/24/2009 Dave Scherer. Asst R S Dunst's Ch Mc Lean VA 2009-2015.

SCHERER-HOOCK, Joyce Lynn (Mass) Po Box 308, Topsfield MA 01983 **S Andr's Ch Ayer MA 2009-** B Lincoln NE 1954 d Michael & Betty. BA Asbury U 1976; MDiv Gordon-Conwell TS 1980. D 6/11/1988 Bp David Elliot Johnson P 9/17/1989 Bp Barbara Clementine Harris. m 6/21/1980 Robert F Scherer-Hoock. Dir, Sprtl formation S Anne's In The Fields Epis Ch Lincoln MA 2007-2009; P-in-c S Paul's Ch Peabody MA 2004-2007; Trin Ch Topsfield MA 1993-2004; Asst Trin Par Melrose MA 1989-1992; D Gr Ch Salem MA 1988-1989. "Sermon," *Sermons that Wk.* Catechesis of Gd Shpd.

SCHERFF, Holly D (Ia) **Assoc S Jn's Ch Shenandoah IA 2015-** D 12/6/2014 P 6/7/2015 Bp Alan Scarfe.

SCHERM, Mary Cecelia (WMass) 48 Amity Pl, Amherst MA 01002 **R Chr Ch Rochdale MA 2010-; Dn Belmont Chap at S Mk's Sch Southborough MA 2000-** B Larchmont NY 1952 d Albert & Mary. BA Goucher Coll 1974; MDiv EDS 1978; DMin EDS 1992. D 6/3/1978 Bp Paul Moore Jr P 12/31/1978 Bp James Stuart Wetmore. Dio Wstrn Massachusetts Springfield 2010-2017, Intake Off - Title IV, Safe Ch 2012-, Dioc Trst 2011-.

SCHEYER, Joyce (NJ) Church of St John the Evangelist, 189 George Street, New Brunswick NJ 08901 B Fort Dix NJ 1956 d William & Roberta. BA Harv 1978; MS OR SU 1986; PhD U of Nebraska 1998; MDiv EDS 2010. D 6/2/2010 P 1/19/2011 Bp Joe Goodwin Burnett. c 3. P-in-c S Jn The Evang Ch New Brunswick NJ 2014-2017; Min for Yth, Families, and Ch Sch S Lk's Epis Ch Scituate MA 2011-2014; P Intern S Matt's Ch Lincoln NE 2010-2011.

SCHIEFFELIN JR, John Jay (WMass) **Non-par 1971-** B New York NY 1936 s John & Lois. MA U; BA Ya 1959; STB GTS 1962. D 6/22/1962 P 12/1/1962 Bp Robert McConnell Hatch. m 7/15/1973 Lois Shelley Shelly Schieffelin c 3. S Mich's-On-The-Heights Worcester MA 1971; Stff Dio Wstrn Massachusetts Springfield 1970-1971; Vic Ch Of The Nativ Northborough MA 1965-1970; Asst Min S Jas' Ch Greenfield MA 1962-1965.

SCHIEFFLER, Daniel Kent (Ark) 19 Woodberry Rd., Little Rock AR 77212 **R S Mk's Epis Ch Little Rock AR 2008-** B Victoria TX 1955 s Eugene & Lenita. BS U of Arkansas 1977; JD U of Arkansas 1980; MDiv Sewanee: The U So, TS 1999. D 7/10/1999 P 1/15/2000 Bp Larry Maze. m 7/23/1977 Judith Ann Schieffler c 3. Cur S Jn's Epis Ch Ft Smith AR 1999-2008.

SCHIERING, Janet Christine (EO) PO Box 1323, Hood River OR 97031 **Hospice Chapl And Bereavement Coordntr Hospice Of The Gorge 2001-** B Berea OH 1957 d Laird & Eunice. BA Witt 1979; BA Witt 1979; MA Seattle Pacific U 1982; Wstrn Sem 1991; MDiv Wstrn Evang Sem 1994. D 5/22/1994 Bp Rustin Ray Kimsey P 5/9/2006 Bp William O Gregg. m 10/10/1999 David J Hancock. D Our Redeem Luth Ch Elca 2000-2006; D Shpd Of The Hills Luth Ch Elca 1998-2000; Pstr Care Coordntr The Par Of S Mk The Evang Hood River OR 1990-1996. AAPC 1991; Gorge Ecum Mnstrs 1991-1998.

SCHIESLER, Robert Alan (WMich) 30 Kerry Ct, Mechanicsburg PA 17050 **Int S Lk's Epis Ch Mechanicsburg PA 2015-** B Lancaster PA 1949 s Robert & Rita. BA S Marys Sem & U Baltimore 1971; MA S Mary Sem Baltimore MD 1975; MDiv Inter/Met Sem 1977; PhD Pacific Wstrn U 1992. Trans 2/2/2004 Bp John Palmer Croneberger. m 4/12/1997 Mary E Novello. R S Mk's Ch Grand Rapids MI 2007-2015; Dn The Cathd Ch Of S Paul Des Moines

IA 2004-2007; R S Lk's Epis Ch Montclair NJ 1997-2004; R Chr Ch Prince Geo's Par Rockville MD 1996-1997; Ch of St Andrews & St Matthews Wilmington DE 1988-1996; R S Steph's Ch Philadelphia PA 1985-1988; Consult Dioc Dvlpmt Dio Michigan Detroit MI 1982-1985; R Trin Ch Belleville MI 1980-1985; R S Paul's Epis Ch Albany NY 1979-1980; Pres Stndg Com Dio Wstrn Michigan Kalamazoo MI 2011-2015; Exec Coun Mem Dio Newark Newark NJ 2000-2004; GC Del Dio Delaware Wilmington 1991-1996, Pres Stndg Com 1990-1995, Prsident Stndg Com 1989-1994; Chair Anti-Racism Cmsn Dio Pennsylvania Philadelphia PA 1986-1988. Cn of hon Dio Iowa 2006. r.schiesler@comcast.net

SCHIESS, Betty Bone (CNY) 6987 Van Antwerp Dr, Cicero NY 13039 **Ret 1990-** B Cincinnati OH 1923 d Evan & Leah. BA U Cinc 1945; MA Syr 1947; MDiv Colgate Rochester Crozer DS 1972; MDiv CRDS 1972. D 6/25/1972 Bp Ned Cole P 7/29/1974 Bp Daniel Corrigan. m 8/28/1947 William A Schiess. Gr Ch Mex NY 1985-1987; Non-par 1980-1983; Actg Chapl Cor Ithaca NY 1978-1989; Chapl Gr Epis Ch Syracuse NY 1976-1978; Non-par 1972-1974; Gr Ch Baldwinsville NY 1972-1973. Who'S Who Rel; Inducted Natl Wmn'S Hall Fame 94; Who'S Who 98; Who'S Who Of Amer Wmn.

SCHIESZ, Catherine Murdock (Ala) PO Box M, Florence AL 35631 B Nashville TN 1960 d Cecil & Charlotte. BA U So 1982. D 11/3/2012 Bp Santosh K Marray. c 3.

SCHIFF, Paulette Toppin (LI) 217 Tyler Ave, Miller Place NY 11764 **Died 9/17/2016** B Rockville Centre NY 1946 d Arthur & Sophy. BA Muhlenberg Coll 1968; MDiv GTS 1987. D 6/6/1987 Bp Edward Cole Chalfant P 5/14/1988 Bp Allen Lyman Bartlett Jr. m 6/7/1969 Walter Schiff c 1. P-in-c S Paul's Ch Patchogue NY 2009-2011; Int S Jas Epis Ch S Jas NY 2005-2007; Int S Mary's Epis Ch Phoenix AZ 2003-2005; Assoc Gd Shpd Of The Hills Cave Creek AZ 2000-2001; Asstg P Ch Of S Mary The Vrgn New York NY 1997-1999; Int S Ptr's Ch Philadelphia PA 1997-1999; Int Gloria Dei Ch Philadelphia PA 1997; Adj Fac Rosemont Coll Rosemont PA 1996-1997; Asst S Mk's Ch Philadelphia PA 1987-1996.

SCHIFFMAYER, Jeffrey Paul (Tex) 8739 Serenade Ln, Houston TX 77040 B Racine WI 1938 s George & Margaret. BA U of Wisconsin 1961; BD Nash 1964. D 2/22/1964 P 8/1/1964 Bp Donald H V Hallock. m 8/16/1969 Sylvia Schiffmayer c 2. Cullen Memi Chap Houston TX 1997-2004; S Lk's Epis Hosp Houston TX 1997-2004; S Fran Epis Ch Coll Sta TX 1988-1997; Vic S Fran Coll Sta TX 1984-1997; The Great Cmsn Fndt Houston TX 1983-1997; R Ch Of The Redeem Houston TX 1968-1983; Chapl Malosa Sch Kasupe Malawi Afr 1964-1968.

SCHILLING III, Walter Bailey (CFla) 1803 Crane Creek Blvd, Melbourne FL 32940 B Chicago IL 1951 s Walter & Joan. U Freiburg W DE 1972; BA U of Wisconsin 1973; MDiv VTS 1988. D 6/11/1988 Bp James Russell Moodey P 2/1/1989 Bp John Herbert MacNaughton. m 12/31/2004 Kathleen Schilling c 4. R The Centeburry Grp Dhahran 2008-2013; R Hope Epis Ch Melbourne FL 1990-2008; Asst R S Geo Ch San Antonio TX 1988-1990; Stdt VTS 1986-1987; Yth Pstr S Lk's Bath OH 1977-1985.

SCHILLREFF, Kathryn Myrick (SwFla) 278 Sawgrass Ct, Naples FL 34110 **Sprtl Cmnty Advsry Bd Avow Hospice 2011-** B Ann Arbor MI 1946 d Joseph & Barbara. Ball St U; Untd TS; BS Florida St U 1968; MDiv SWTS 1996. D 6/29/1996 P 5/3/1997 Bp Herbert Thompson Jr. m 8/19/1972 Harold Vincent Schillreff c 1. R S Monica's Epis Ch Naples FL 2000-2016; Int Chr Epis Ch Dayton OH 1996-1999; Stndg Com Dio SW Florida Parrish FL 2010-2013, Dn of Naples Dnry 2010-. kschillreff@comcast.net

SCHINDLER, Gary (WNY) 591 E Main St, Springville NY 14141 **P-t Stff Samar Counciling Cntr N. Tonawanda NY 2005-; Vic S Paul's Epis Ch Springville NY 1991-** B Bayshore NY 1956 s Charles & Frances. BS SUNY 1978; MDiv EDS 1983. D 6/19/1983 Bp Harvey D Butterfield P 1/20/1984 Bp Wilbur Emory Hogg Jr. m 8/19/1978 Virginia Lynn Schindler c 3. Samar Pstr Counslg Ctr - Niagara Frontier N. Tonawanda NY 2005-2010; R Epis Untd Mnstry Nanticoke PA 1986-1991; R S Geo's Ch Nanticoke PA 1986-1991; S Mart-In-The-Fields Mtn Top PA 1986-1991; Asst Chr Ch Pittsford Pittsford NY 1983-1986. Soc of S Jn the Evang 1983.

SCHINK, Susan Alma (Nwk) 481 Airmount Avenue, Ramsey NJ 07446 **P-in-c S Clem's Ch Hawthorne NJ 2011-; Assoc S Eliz's Ch Ridgewood NJ 2010-, Assoc for Sprtl Dvlpmt 2003-2010; Mem of Cathd Chapt Dio Newark 2006-** B Paterson NJ 1951 d William & Margaret. BA Colby Coll 1973; MBA Rutgers The St U of New Jersey 1980; MDiv UTS 2003. D 6/7/2003 Bp Rufus T Brome P 12/20/2003 Bp John Palmer Croneberger. Int Asst Chr Ch Short Hills NJ 2010-2011; Int S Agnes Ch Little Falls NJ 2007-2010; Int H Trin Epis Ch Hillsdale NJ 2004-2007; D Trin Epis Ch of Bergen Cnty Allendale NJ 2003-2004; S Mk's Ch Teaneck NJ 2001-2002.

SCHIRMACHER, Michael (Md) 3202 Lake St Apt 2, Houston TX 77098 **CPE Coordntr Md Anderson Cancer Cntr 2000-** B Houston TX 1949 s Grayson & Laura. JHU; BA Amer U 1971; MDiv EDS 1980. D 6/28/1980 P 1/1/1981 Bp David Keller Leighton Sr. S Jas Ch Austin TX 1999; Dir Of Pstr Care Austin St Hosp 1992-2000; Dio Maryland Baltimore MD 1989-1992; Epis Chapl Jn Hopkins Med Institutes 1989-1992; R S Mths' Epis Ch Baltimore MD 1985-1988;

754

Chapl Sprg Grove Baltimore 1982-1984; S Barn Kensington Philadelphia PA 1980-1982. Pstr Care Ntwk For Soc Responsibility; Supvsr ACPE, Fell Coll Of Chapl, AEHC. Robbins Fell 1989.

SCHISLER, Richard Thomas (SO) 2210 Cleveland Ave, Portsmouth OH 45662 **D All SS Epis Ch Portsmouth OH 2002-** B Portsmouth OH 1939 BA Mia 1961; JD U Cinc Coll of Law 1966. D 10/26/2002 Bp Herbert Thompson Jr. m 5/16/1970 Sallie Chellis c 2.

SCHISLER, Sallie Chellis (SO) 2210 Cleveland Ave, Portsmouth OH 45662 **Mem, Bd Bex Sem Columbus OH 2009-** B Huntington WV 1945 d Willard & Marjorie. Cert Epis Dio Sthrn Ohio 2002; Cert Bex Sem 2008. D 10/26/2002 Bp Herbert Thompson Jr P 6/28/2008 Bp Thomas Edward Breidenthal. m 5/16/1970 Richard Thomas Schisler c 2. P-in-c Chr Ch Ironton OH 2010-2017; All SS Epis Ch Portsmouth OH 2002-2010; D Chr Ch Ironton OH 2002-2008.

SCHISSER, Janet (Mo) 1203 Castle Bay Pl, Columbia MO 65203 **D Calv Ch Columbia MO 2015-; PRN Chapl St Mary's Hlth Cntr Mex MO 2014-** B Childress 1943 d William & Mary. EFM Sewanee: The U So, TS; BBA U of Oklahoma 1965. D 6/24/2006 Bp Robert Manning Moody. c 2. D S Matthews Epis Ch Mex MO 2011-2015; D Columbia Hope Ch Columbia MO 2009-2011; D S Mich's Epis Ch Norman OK 2006-2009.

SCHIVELY, John Alrik (NCal) 1441 Marseille Ln, Roseville CA 95747 B San Francisco CA 1934 s Charles & Kalmar. BS U of San Francisco 1956; MDiv CDSP 1960. D 6/26/1960 Bp James Albert Pike P 6/24/1961 Bp George Richard Millard. c 2. Assoc St Johns Epis Ch Roseville CA 2001-2016; Assoc S Fran Epis Ch Fair Oaks CA 1998; R S Matt's Epis Ch Sacramento CA 1986-1998; Ch Of The Redeem Pendleton OR 1983-1986; Gd Samar Epis Ch San Jose CA 1974-1983; R S Jn's Epis Ch Oakland CA 1968-1973; R S Steph's Ch Gilroy CA 1962-1968; Cur Chr Ch Alameda CA 1960-1962; Chapl to the Ret Cler The Epis Dio Nthrn California Sacramento CA 2011-2016. Ord of S Lk.

SCHJONBERG, Mary Frances Frances (Nwk) 407 Seaview Circle, Neptune NJ 07753 **ENS Ed/reporter Epis Ch Cntr New York NY 2005-** B Madison WI 1954 d Conrad & Mildred. BA U of Wisconsin 1975; MDiv CDSP 2000; DD CDSP 2011. D 6/18/2000 P 1/18/2001 Bp Charles I Jones III. Asstg P Chr Ch Epis Shrewsbury NJ 2012-2016; Asstg P Trin Ch Asbury Pk NJ 2005-2012; Asst to the R Chr Ch Short Hills NJ 2000-2005; Mem, Diac Ord Com Dio Newark Newark NJ 2005-2007. Auth, "Theol column," *The Missoulian*, Lee Enterprises, 1997. ECom 2005; Epis Preaching Fndt 2002-2016. DD, h.c. CDSP 2011.

SCHLACHTER, Barbara Jeanne Hartley (Ia) 7 Glenview Knl NE, Iowa City IA 52240 **Died 2/16/2016** B OH 1945 d Charles & Jeanne. BA Ohio Wesl 1967; MA Col 1970; MDiv UTS 1972; DMin Estrn Bapt TS 1988. D 6/9/1973 Bp Paul Moore Jr P 1/20/1977 Bp James Stuart Wetmore. m 8/24/1968 Melvin Harlan Schlachter c 2. Assoc Trin Ch Iowa City IA 2010-2016; Assoc R Chr Ch Cedar Rapids IA 2003-2010; EWC New Era MI 2002; Co-R Trin Epis Ch Troy OH 1987-2002; Co-R S Marg's Ch Staatsburg NY 1982-1987; Asst S Barth's Ch In The Highland White Plains NY 1977-1982. Auth, *How Many Loaves Have You?*. Ch Dvlpmt Bd 1972-1983; Com on Status of Wmn in the Ch 2000-2006; Fndr & 1st Pres EWC 1971-1975; Pres Natl Ntwk of Epis Cler Assn 1992-1998. Phi Beta Kappa Ohio Wesleyan 1967.

SCHLACHTER, Melvin Harlan (Ia) 7 Glenview Knl NE, Iowa City IA 52240 **Bd and Committe Mem Iowa ACLU 2002-; Vol Chapl Iowa City Police Dept 2002-; Chair Iowa River Friends 2002-** B San Pedro CA 1946 s Melvin & Mildred. BA U of Nebraska 1967; MA U of Wisconsin 1968; DIT Oxf GB 1971; MDiv UTS 1972; Shalem Inst for Sprtl Formation Washington DC 1994. D 6/6/1972 Bp Robert Patrick Varley P 12/9/1972 Bp Paul Moore Jr. c 2. Vice Chair, Bd Dir Dio Iowa 2003-2006; R Trin Ch Iowa City IA 2002-2012; Vstng Lectr S Geo Coll Jerusalem 1998-2005; Pstr Counslr Miami Vlly Hosp Dayton OH 1987-2002; Co-R Trin Epis Ch Troy OH 1987-2002; Co-R S Marg's Ch Staatsburg NY 1982-1987; Pstr Counslr Fndt For Rel And Mntl Hlth Briarcliff NY 1975-1981; Chapl Taconic Correctional Facility Bedford Hills NY 1974-1975; Bishops Advsry Com New York NY 1973-1976; Chapl SUNY Purchase NY 1973-1976; Cluster Yonkers NY 1972-1973; Assoc Min San Andres Ch Yonkers NY 1972-1973; Stndg Com Dio Sthrn Ohio Cincinnati OH 1998-2001, 1997-1998, Co-Chair Cler Assn 1990-1996, COM 1988-1989. *Var newpaper/mag essays*. Clincl Cert Intl TA Assn 1976-1980; Fell, AAPC 1976; OHC-Assoc.

SCHLAFER, David John (Mil) 5213 Roosevelt Street, Bethesda MD 20814 **P Assoc (Vol) The Ch Of The Redeem Beth MD 2000-** B Louisville KY 1944 s Frederick & Billie. BA Wheaton Coll 1966; MA Sthrn Illinois U 1969; PhD Sthrn Illinois U 1974; Cert Nash 1984. D 6/28/1980 P 3/1/1985 Bp James Winchester Montgomery. m 6/14/1997 Margaret A Tucker c 2. Assoc Ch of the Redeem Beth MD 2003-2007; Cathd of St Ptr & St Paul Washington DC 2002-2003, 1993-1995; VTS Alexandria VA 2000, 1998, 1996, 1993-1995; Adj Prof of Homil VTS in Alexandria Alexandria VA 1994-2000; Int Dir of Stds Coll of Preachers Washington DC 1994-1996; Vstng Assoc Prof of Pstr Theol TS at U So Sewanee TN 1992-1994; Sewanee U So TS Sewanee TN 1991-1993; Vstng Prof of Homil TS at U So Sewanee TN 1991-1992; Adj

Prof of Homil Seabury-Wstrn Theologial Sem Evanston IL 1990-1991; Nash Nashotah WI 1986-1991; P-in-c St Philips Epis Ch Waukesha WI 1986-1990; Assoc Prof of Homil and Sub-Dn for Acad Affrs Nash Nashotah WI 1984-1991; Dio Chicago Chicago IL 1984-1987; S Lk's Ch Racine WI 1984-1985; Assoc Prof of Philos Trin Deerfield IL 1971-1984. "What's the Shape of Narrative Preaching?," Chalice, 2007; Auth, "Preaching What We Pract: Proclamation and Moral Formation," Morehouse, 2007; "Sermons That Wk (Vol. 5 - 14)," Morehouse, 2006; Auth, "The Shattering Sound of Amazing Gr: Disquieting Tales from St. Jn's Gospel," Cowley, 2006; Auth, "Playing w Fire: Preaching Wk as Kindling Art," Cowley, 2004; Auth, "What Makes This Day Different?: Preaching Gr on Spec Occasions," Cowley, 1998; "Your Way w God's Word: Discovering Your Distinctive Preaching Voice," Cowley, 1995; "Surviving the Sermon: A Guide to Preaching for Those Who Have to Listen," Cowley, 1992.

SCHLEGEL, Stuart Allen (ECR) 3400 Paul Sweet Road, Apt. B-213, Santa Cruz CA 95065 **Asst Epis Ch of St Jn the Bapt Aptos Aptos CA 2004-** B Sewickley PA 1932 s Glenn & Elizabeth. BA U CA 1957; MDiv CDSP 1960; MA U Chi 1965; PhD U Chi 1969. D 5/31/1960 Bp Ivol I Curtis P 1/25/1961 Bp Lyman Cunningham Ogilby. c 2. Asst Calv Epis Ch Santa Cruz CA 1992-2004; R S Lk's Ch Los Gatos CA 1984-1992, Asst 1979-1984; P The Ch Of S Jn The Evang Flossmoor IL 1963-1965; Serv Ch in Philippines 1960-1963. Stuart A. Schlegel, "Same as Name of Pub," *Wisdom From a Rainforest*, U GA Press, 1998; Stuart A. Schlegel, "Same as Name of Pub," *Chld of Tulus: Essays on the Tiruray People*, Giraffe Press, 1994; Stuart A. Schlegel, "Same as Name of Pub," *Tiruray Subsistence*, Ateneo de Manilla U Press, 1979; Stuart A. Schlegel, "Same as Name of Pub," *Tiruray-Engl Lexicion*, U CA Press, 1971; Stuart A. Schlegel, "Same as Name of Pub," *Tiruray Justice: Traditional Tiruray Law and Morality*, U CA Press, 1970. Third Ord of the Soc of S Fran 1997. Lifetime Achievement Awd for Philippine Resrch Anthropological Assn of the Philippines 2002.

SCHLESINGER, Kira (Tenn) 4220 Harding Pike, Nashville TN 37205 **P-in-c The Ch Of The Epiph Lebanon TN 2012-** B Dallas TX 1984 d Kenneth & Karen. BMus Rice U 2007; MDiv Van 2011; MDiv Van 2011. D 6/18/2011 Bp C Andrew Doyle P 4/14/2012 Bp John Bauerschmidt. m 6/7/2008 Joseph John Schlesinger. S Dav's Epis Ch Nashville TN 2011-2013.

SCHLEY JR, Joseph Hastings (FtW) 1300 S Harrison St Apt 1008, Amarillo TX 79101 **R St. Mk's Amarillo TX 2001-; Ret Dio Ft Worth 1999-** B Dallas TX 1939 s Joseph & Jane. U So 1958; BA SMU 1960; JD SMU 1963; S Georges Coll Jerusalem IL 1973; MDiv VTS 1974. D 6/5/1974 P 12/18/1974 Bp Willis Ryan Henton. c 2. Dn Dio Ft Worth Ft Worth TX 1993-1999, 1989-1992; Our Lady Of The Lake Clifton TX 1993-1999; R Ch Of The H Comf Cleburne TX 1987-1989; Dn Dio NW Texas Lubbock TX 1985-1987, 1983-1987, 1974-1976; R S Nich' Epis Ch Midland TX 1979-1987; R S Simons Ch Miami FL 1976-1979; Ch of the Heav Rest Abilene Abilene TX 1974-1976. Auth, "arts," *Living Ch*. Amarillo "Medtr of the Year" Dispute Resolution Ctr. 2005; Midland "Boss of the Year" JCC 1985.

SCHLISMANN, Robert (Neb) 1309 R St, Lincoln NE 68508 **P-in-c Dio Nebraska Omaha NE 2016-** B Chicago IL 1950 s William & Charlotte. BS Illinois St U 1972; MDiv Reformed TS 1987; MDiv Sewanee: The U So, TS 2009. D 10/28/2009 P 5/22/2010 Bp Joe Goodwin Burnett. m 9/19/1974 Carol A Schlismann c 3. R Trin Epis Ch Norfolk NE 2011-2016; Cur S Mk's On The Campus Lincoln NE 2009-2010. sanyu@neb.rr.com

SCHLOSSBERG, Stephen Kenneth Kelley (Alb) 1574 Spring Ave., Wynantskill NY 12198 **R S Jn's Epis Ch Troy NY 2011-** B Minneapolis MN 1963 s Herbert & Teresa. BA Bethel U 1986; MDiv Nash 2007. D 12/7/2006 P 9/30/2007 Bp Keith Lynn Ackerman. m 10/3/1987 Angie K Schlossberg c 5. Asst Zion Epis Ch Oconomowoc WI 2008-2011; Cmncatn Dir Nash Nashotah WI 2007-2011; Truro Epis Ch Fairfax VA 1997-2004.

SCHLOTTERBECK, Marilou Jean (WMich) 12530 Cinder Rd, Beulah MI 49617 **D S Phil's Ch Beulah MI 1994-** B Detroit MI 1946 d Ernest & Mary. EFM 1994. D 8/6/1994 Bp Edward Lewis Lee Jr. m 6/15/1968 Kurt Sand Schlotterbeck c 3.

SCHMALING, Pamela Jane (Oly) 7913 W Golf Course Dr, Blaine WA 98230 B Pomeroy WA 1945 d Lowell & Thelma. Cert Vancouver TS CA 2002. D 8/8/1998 Bp Frank Jeffrey Terry. m 7/5/1990 Jan Charles Schmaling c 1. D S Paul Epis Ch Bellingham WA 2000-2007; S Mich's Epis Ch Yakima WA 1998-2000.

SCHMIDT, Ann W (Ark) 726 Davemar Dr, Saint Louis MO 63123 **Ret 1998-** B Cincinnati OH 1942 d Allen & Elizabeth. BA Mia 1968; MDiv Untd TS Dayton OH 1987. D 8/30/1987 Bp Don Adger Wimberly. m 10/1/1979 Robert Frederick Schmidt. Asst S Matt's Epis Ch Benton AR 1996-1998; Chapl AR Dept Hlth Hospice Team 1993-1995; Asst S Lk's Ch Hot Sprg AR 1992-1995; Chapl Police Cler Team Hamilton Cnty OH 1987-1991; Asst S Andr's Ch Ft Thos KY 1987-1991; Ecum Cmsn Dio Arkansas Little Rock AR 1997-1999. Auth, *Tales of a Wanton Gospeller*, 1994.

SCHMIDT, Carolyn Jean Decker (Minn) PO Box 278, 1633 Croftville Rd, Grand Marais MN 55604 **Asst Sprt of the Wilderness Grand Marais MN 2011-** B Buffalo NY 1952 d James & Marjorie. BA Wells Coll 1974; MDiv VTS 1987.

D 6/24/1987 P 12/1/1987 Bp Robert Marshall Anderson. m 9/23/1976 Milan C Schmidt c 2. Adv Ch Farmington MN 2009-2011; Sprtl Dir Sage Weight and Wellness 2006-2010; Assoc The Epis Cathd Of Our Merc Sav Faribault MN 1997-1998; R Ch Of The H Cross Dundas MN 1994-2005; Vic S Paul's Epis Le Cntr MN 1993-1994; Organizer/P San Jose Obrero Mision Epis Montgomery MN 1990-2011; Calv Ch Waseca MN 1990-1994; Vic S Jn's Epis Ch Janesville MN 1990-1994; Vic S Andrews Epis Ch Waterville MN 1987-1989. RWF, Mn Epis Cleric Assn, Neca.

SCHMIDT, Edward William (Md) 1500 Hilton Ave # 21238, Catonsville MD 21228 **Died 4/8/2017** B Staten Island NY 1939 s Edward & Martha. BA Wag 1960; BD Nash 1963. D 6/11/1963 P 12/21/1963 Bp Horace W B Donegan. All SS Cnvnt Catonsville MD 1981-2004; Chapl All SS Cnvnt 1980-2017; Monk S Greg's Abbey 1978-1979; R Gr Epis Ch Westwood NJ 1973-1978; Tchr S Ptr's Sch Yonkers NY 1970-1973; Chapl Leake & Watts Chld's Hm Yonkers NY 1969-1971; Assoc San Andres Ch Yonkers NY 1969-1970; Vic S Greg's Epis Ch Woodstock NY 1966-1969; Cur Chr Ch Poughkeepsie NY 1964-1966; Cur Par of Chr the Redeem Pelham NY 1963-1964.

SCHMIDT JR, Frederick William (WA) Garrett-Evangelical Theological Seminary, 2121 Sheridan Rd, Evanston IL 60201 **Assoc Prof of Chr Sprtlty Perkins Sch of Theol Sthrn Methodist Univ Dallas TX 2000-; Dir of Sprtl Formation and Angl Stds Perkins TS-SMU 2000-** B Louisville KY 1953 s Frederick & Pauline. BA Asbury U 1975; MDiv Asbury TS 1978; PhD Oxf GB 1986. D 6/11/1993 P 12/1/1993 Bp Charlie Fuller Mcnutt Jr. m 4/18/2009 Natalie Beam Van Kirk c 1. Ch Of The Incarn Dallas TX 2004-2008; S Lk's Epis Ch Dallas TX 2003-2004; S Mich And All Ang Ch Dallas TX 2000; Cn Cathd of St Ptr & St Paul Washington DC 1997-2000; Assoc All SS' Epis Ch Hershey PA 1995-1996; Exec Coun Appointees New York NY 1994-1997; Serv Ch in Jerusalem 1994-1995; Intern St Andrews in the City Epis Ch Harrisburg PA 1993-1994; Serv Methodist Ch 1978-1993. Ed/Contrib, "Conversations w Scripture," Morehouse Pub, 2005; Auth, "What God Wants for Your Life," Harper One, 2005; Auth, "Sofferenza, All ricerca di una riposta," Claudiana, 2004; Auth, "When Suffering Persists," Morehouse Pub, 2001; Auth, "The Changing Face of God," Morehouse Pub, 2000; Auth, "A Still Sm Voice," Syr Press, 1996; Contrib, "44 Minor Entries," *Anchor Bible Dictionary*, Doubleday, 1992. AAR; Angl Assn Biblic Scholars; Cath Biblic Assn; Natl Institutes of Hlth, Pulmonary DSMB (=Data Sfty Mon; New Engl Resrch Inst, Stop II DSMB (=Data Sfty Moni; Soc for the Sci Study of Rel; SBL; The Soc for the Study of Chr Sprtlty. Angus Dun Fellowowship Dio Washington 1999; Class XI, The Cler Ldrshp Proj (CLP) Trin Wallstreet, NY 1999; Serv Recognition Natl Institutes of Hlth 1998; Sr Fell WF Albright Inst of Archeol Resrch 1995; Who's Who in Biblic Stds and Archeol 1993; FW Dillstone Schlrshp Oriel Coll,Oxford 1984; Hall Houghton Schlrshp U of Oxford 1983; Fell Amer Coun on Educ (ACE); Ovrs Resrch Stdt Awd Com of Vice-Chancellors & Principals.

SCHMIDT, Kenneth John (Mass) B Pennsylvania 1952 s Joseph & Thelma. EDS; Kutztown U; MDiv Andover Newton TS 2012. D 6/16/2012 Bp M(Arvil) Thomas Shaw. m 9/20/2012 Vivian Schmidt. D Ecclesia Mnstrs Boston MA 2012-2015.

SCHMIDT, Kenneth L (Cal) 1350 Waller St, San Francisco CA 94117 **R All SS' Ch San Francisco CA 1988-** B Buffalo NY 1946 s Lorenzo & Violet. BA Houghton Coll 1968; MDiv PrTS 1971; PhD PrTS 1980; DMin SFTS 2000. D 6/11/1977 P 3/7/1978 Bp Paul Moore Jr. m 7/9/2008 John Roberts. S Lk's Ch Philadelphia PA 1985-1987; Asst Prof Theol S Jos U Philadelphia PA 1982-1985; Trin Ch Princeton NJ 1980-1982; Chr Ch New Brunswick NJ 1980. SSM 1986.

SCHMIDT, Kevin Lynn (Kan) 15309 W 153rd St, Olathe KS 66062 **S Thos The Apos Ch Overland Pk KS 2009-; S Mk's Ch Lyons KS 2001-; P-in-c SS Mary And Martha Of Bethany Larned KS 2000-** B Larned KS 1964 s Sandy & Vera. BS Sterling Coll 1996. D 1/20/2001 Bp John Forsythe Ashby P 9/15/2001 Bp Vernon Edward Strickland. m 1/14/1995 Lisa Ann Eberle c 2. S Jn's Ch Great Bend KS 2001-2009; P-in-c H Apos Ch Ellsworth KS 2001-2008.

SCHMIDT, Linda Marie (FdL) N2592 State Highway 17, Merrill WI 54452 **D Ch of the Ascen Merrill WI 2003-** B Milwaukee WI 1945 Marq; U of Wisconsin. D 8/30/2003 Bp Russell Edward Jacobus. m 4/20/1968 Earl Schmidt c 6.

SCHMIDT, Norma (Ct) 661 Old Post Rd, Fairfield CT 06824 **Ch Of S Thos Bethel CT 2012-** B Gary IN 1958 d Norman & Phyllis. MA U Chi 1982; MDiv Luth TS 1986; MA Fairfield U 2001. Rec 1/29/2010 Bp Andrew Donnan Smith. m 9/19/1982 David Schmidt c 2. Assoc S Paul's Ch Fairfield CT 2011. pastor. normaschmidt@yahoo.com

SCHMIDT, Richard (CGC) 101 Fairwood Blvd., Fairhope AL 36532 B Louisville KY 1944 s Craig & Betsy. BA Ken 1966; MDiv Van 1970; DMin Wesley TS 1999. D 6/11/1970 P 12/16/1970 Bp Wilburn Camrock Campbell. m 8/17/1968 Pamela H Schmidt c 3. Ed/Dir Forw Mvmt of the Epis Ch Cincinnati OH 2005-2011; Ret 2000-2005; Dio Cntrl Gulf Coast Pensacola FL 1998-2000, Dep GC 1994-2000; R S Paul's Epis Ch Daphne AL 1990-2000; Mng Ed The Epis Life Philadelphia PA 1988-1990; Mng Ed The Epis Inc. Philadelphia 1988-1990; S Ptr's Epis Ch S Louis MO 1982-1988; R Chr Ch Fair-

mont WV 1975-1982; Assoc S Jn's Epis Ch Charleston WV 1971-1975; Emm Ch Moorefield WV 1970-1971; Vic S Steph's Ch Romney WV 1970-1971. Auth, "God Seekers: Twenty Centuries of Chr Spiritualities," Wm B. Eerdmans, 2008; Auth, "A Gracious Rain: A Devotional Commentary on the Prayers of the Ch Year," Ch Pub, 2008; Auth, "Life Lessons from Alpha to Omega," Ch Pub, 2005; Auth, "Praises, Prayers & Curses: Conversations w the Psalms," Forw Mvmt, 2005; Auth, "Glorious Comp: Five Centuries of Angl Sprtlty," Wm. B. Eerdmans, 2002.

SCHMIDT, Wayne Roy (NY) 3 Ashley Dr, Newburgh NY 12550 **R Emer & As-stg P S Geo's Epis Ch Newburgh NY 2006-; Ret 1995-** B Brooklyn NY 1934 s Wainwright & Gertrude. BA Hobart and Wm Smith Colleges 1956; MDiv GTS 1959. D 4/4/1959 P 10/10/1959 Bp James Pernette DeWolfe. m 10/1/1988 Ann Devlin Schmidt c 2. Int Zion Epis Ch Wappingers Falls NY 2004-2005; Asst Zion Epis Ch Wappingers Falls NY 2000-2003; R S Geo's Epis Ch Newburgh NY 1975-1994; Vic S Paul's Ch Pleasant Vlly NY 1964-1973; Asst to the R Ch Of S Jas The Less Scarsdale NY 1960-1964; Cur S Steph's Ch Prt Washington NY 1959-1960; Trst Cathd Of St Jn The Div New York NY 1988-1994; Chair Dioc Liturg Cmsn Dio New York New York NY 1981-1990.

SCHMIDTETTER, Todd T (CFla) **R Epis Ch Of The H Apos Satellite Bch FL 2013-** B Pittsburgh PA 1977 s David & Shirley. BS Charleston Sthrn U 2008; MDiv TESM 2011. D 6/4/2011 Bp Mark Joseph Lawrence P 12/15/2012 Bp Dorsey McConnell. m 4/14/2002 Michelle Schmidtetter c 2. theobrew@yahoo. com

SCHMITT, Barbara Joyce (SO) 115 N 6th St, Hamilton OH 45011 B Cincinnati OH 1960 d Robert & Nancy. D 6/14/2008 Bp Thomas Edward Breidenthal. c 1. Forw Mvmt of the Epis Ch Cincinnati OH 2008-2009.

SCHMITT, Geoffrey (WLa) 3910 Parkway Dr, 1605 Gray Lake Dr, Princeton LA 71067 B Phillipsburg PA 1949 s Robert & Eileen. BS SUNY 1971; MDiv Bex Sem 1978; DMin Gordon-Conwell TS 1995. D 6/17/1978 P 12/18/1978 Bp Alexander D Stewart. m 3/17/2005 Brenda Schmitt. First Luth Ch ELCA Shreveport LA 2009-2010; R S Geo's Ch Bossier City LA 2000-2007; Vic Calv Epis Ch Jacksonville FL 1997-1999; Asst S Marg's Epis Ch Waxhaw NC 1995-1997; R S Chris's Ch Charlotte NC 1990-1995; Vic Ch Of The Resurr Tucson AZ 1985-1990; R Ch Of The Recon Webster MA 1980-1985; Serv Luth Ch 1978-1980. Assn Of Psychol Type.

SCHMITT, Jacqueline (Mass) 31 Ely Dr., Fayetteville NY 13066 **S Matt's Epis Ch Liverpool NY 2017-** B Syracuse NY 1953 d Francis & Dorothy. BA Amer U 1975; MDiv UTS 1980. D 6/21/1980 P 4/11/1981 Bp Ned Cole. c 4. R S Dav's Ch Fayetteville NY 2011-2015, 1980-1982; Vic S Paul's Ch Brockton MA 2005-2011; Assoc Trin Ch Epis Boston MA 2005; Chapl Epis Chapl At Harvard & Radcliffe Cambridge MA 2004-2005; Epis Chapl, Harv Harvard Radcliffe Ch Cambridge MA 2004-2005; Cbury NW Evanston IL 1994-2004; Cn Precentor St Paul's Syracuse Syracuse NY 1992-1994; Vic Emm Ch E Syracuse NY 1990-1992; Paris Cluster Chadwicks NY 1986-1988; Int R S Thos Ch Hamilton NY 1986-1988; Int R Epis Ch Of SS Ptr And Jn Auburn NY 1985-1986; Chapl Columbia/Presb Hosp 1984-1985; Epis Chapl, No Carolina St U Dio No Carolina Raleigh NC 1982-1984; Assoc Dio Cntrl New York Liverpool NY 1980-1982; Chair Coll Wk Cmsn 1988-1994; Ed Plumbline: Journ of MHE 1988-2001. Auth, "The Body and Liturg," *Liturg: Journ*, The Liturg Conf, 2009; Auth, "Sacrifical Adventure," *Deeper Joy*, Ch Pub Inc, 2005; Auth, "Vida Dutton Scudder," *A Heart for the Future*, Ch Pub Inc, 2004; Auth, "Coll Chapl And The Future Of Theol,A New Conversation," *A New Conversation*, Ch Pub Inc, 1999; Auth, "The Epis Ch Welcomes You?,Disorganized Rel," *Disorganized Rel*, Cowley Press, 1998; Auth, "Living Under And Above The Law, Prophet Of Justice," *Prophet Of Life*, Ch Pub Inc, 1997; Ed Bd, "ATR," 1996. ESMHE, Epis W 1980-2004. jacqueline.schmitt@gmail.com

SCHMITZ, Barbara G (CNY) D 6/24/1989 Bp H Coleman Mcgehee Jr P 3/11/1990 Bp R aymond Stewart Wood Jr.

SCHMOETZER, Jane Ellen (Spok) 1940 Thayer Dr., Richland WA 99354 **R All SS Ch Richland WA 2010-** B Fort Bragg NC 1961 d James & Carolyn. BS Pur 1983; MDiv SWTS 2005. D 4/15/2005 P 10/22/2005 Bp Edward Stuart Little II. m 5/28/1983 Bruce E Schmoetzer c 2. Yellowstone Epis Mnstrs Red Lodge MT 2010; Calv Epis Ch Red Lodge MT 2006-2010; Our Sav Epis Joliet MT 2006-2010; S Alb's Epis Ch Laurel MT 2006-2010; S Paul's of the Stillwater Ch Absarokee MT 2006-2010; Vic Dio Montana Helena MT 2006-2009, BEC 2007-2010, VP, Dioc Coun 2007-2010; Cur S Andr's By The Lake Epis Ch Michigan City IN 2005-2006; VP, Dioc Coun Dio Spokane Spokane WA 2013-2015, Dioc Coun 2010-2011. Contrib, "Ordnry Time," St Thursday Press, 2006; Contrib, "A Light Blazes in the Darkness," Cafe Press, 2005. rector@allsaintsrichland.org

SCHNAARE, Anne Elizabeth (WMich) 115 Hart St., Marshall MI 49068 **R Trin Epis Ch Marshall MI 2011-** B Royal Oak MI 1978 d Dexter & Harriet. BA U of Wisconsin-Parkside 2001; MDiv Sewanee: The U So, TS 2009. D 12/20/2008 P 6/27/2009 Bp Russell Edward Jacobus. m 7/14/2001 Matthew R Schnaare c 1. Cur Calv Ch Americus GA 2009-2011.

SCHNABEL, Charles Edward (LI) 143 Lakeside Trail, Ridge NY 11961 **Ret 1998-** B Astoria NY 1936 s John & Gladys. BA CUNY Queens Coll 1958;

MDiv Ya Berk 1961. D 4/8/1961 P 10/28/1961 Bp James Pernette DeWolfe. c 3. Prof Mercer TS Garden City LI 1989-2000; Assoc Prof Theol Mercer TS Garden City LI 1973-1989; Sub-Dn Mercer TS Garden City LI 1973-1977; R Ch Of The Nativ Mineola NY 1963-1998; Instr Mercer TS Garden City LI 1963-1973; Cur H Trin Epis Ch Vlly Stream NY 1961-1963. Angl Theol Conf 1972-1989.

SCHNABL, Emily J (Okla) 4036 Neptune Dr, Oklahoma City OK 73116 **Int S Chris's Ch Midwest City OK 2006-** B Chicago IL 1967 d Ernst & Carile. BA U IL 1988; MA U of Arizona 1991; MDiv SWTS 1999. D 6/11/2000 P 5/8/2001 Bp Peter Hess Beckwith. m 11/10/2001 David Robert Stock. Trin Ch Guthrie OK 2005-2006; Asst R S Geo's Ch Belleville IL 2000-2004. "Christmas Trees Preaching Through H Days & Holidays," Morehoouse, 2003. Phi Beta Kappa 1988. stchristophersmwc@coxinet.net

SCHNACK, Peggy Ellan (Oly) B Norristown PA 1981 BA Coll of St Cathr 2006; BA Coll of St. Cathr 2006; MDiv Sewanee The Sch of the So 2015; MDiv Sewanee: The U So, TS 2015; MDiv The TS at The U So 2015. D 12/13/2014 Bp Gregory Harold Rickel.

SCHNATTERLY, Michael Dean (USC) 5 Mountain Vista Rd, Taylors SC 29687 **P-in-c Ch Of The Gd Shpd Greer SC 2005-** B Hays KS 1955 s Harry & Toya. BA Furman U 1979; MDiv SWTS 1989. D 6/12/1989 Bp William Hopkins Folwell P 12/16/1989 Bp Elliott Lorenz Sorge. m 7/21/1984 Clare Lorelle Inman c 2. R S Fran Ch Greensboro NC 2001-2004; R S Edw The Confessor Mt Dora FL 1996-2001; R Emm Epis Ch Opelika AL 1992-1996; Cur Chr Ch St Michaels Par S Mich MD 1989-1992; Mem of Dioc Exec Coun & Stndg Com Dio Upper So Carolina Columbia SC 2011-2017, Dn, Reedy River Convoc 2006-2008; Mem of Dioc Coun Dio No Carolina Raleigh NC 2003-2004; Sprtl Advsr to Curs Sec Dio Cntrl Florida Orlando FL 1999-2001; Chair of Yth Advsry Coun Dio Easton Easton MD 1990-1992, Exam Chaplin, Liturg 1990-1992. Assoc of Ord Of S Helena 1989. Cotton Memi Awd SWTS 1989; Mem in Mensa Mensa 1980. rector@goodshepherdgreer.org

SCHNAUFER, Dennis Eric (USC) 6 Del Norte Blvd, Greenville SC 29615 B Palestine TX 1945 s Frank & Edith. BA SW U Georgetown TX 1967; VTS 1968; MDiv Epis TS of the SW 1970. D 8/26/1970 Bp James Milton Richardson P 6/28/1971 Bp Scott Field Bailey. m 6/23/1973 Thiela Louise Schnaufer c 1. R S Ptr's Epis Ch Greenville SC 1985-2010; R Chr Epis Ch Dublin GA 1978-1985; Assoc Trin Epis Ch Columbus GA 1974-1978; Gr Epis Ch Georgetown TX 1973-1974; Actg R S Jas' Ch Taylor TX 1973-1974; Chapl SW U Georgetown TX 1973-1974; Vic Ch Of The Gd Shpd Tomball TX 1970-1973.

SCHNEIDER, Charles W (WK) 13702 Stoney Hill Dr, San Antonio TX 67401 **P-in-c S Andr's Epis Ch Liberal KS 2008-; Cn Chr Cathd Salina KS 2002-; Trin Epis Ch Norton KS 1998-; Cdo Dio Wstrn Kansas Hutchinson KS 1997-** B Lewistown IL 1938 s Charles & Hannah. Cert Great Bend Cmnty Coll 1974. D 5/16/1997 P 4/17/1999 Bp Vernon Edward Strickland. m 2/4/2005 LyLith Ann Schneider c 4. P-in-c Epis Ch Of The Incarn Salina KS 2007-2008; S Fran Cmnty Serv Inc. Salina KS 1998-2008.

SCHNEIDER, Edward Nichols (EMich) 7039 W. Saint John Rd., Glendale AZ 85308 **Ret 1989-** B Detroit MI 1926 s Louis & Geraldine. BA U CA 1949; MDiv VTS 1962. D 6/29/1962 Bp Archie H Crowley P 2/1/1963 Bp Robert Lionne DeWitt. c 3. S Jas Epis Ch Birmingham MI 1970-1989; Asst R Trin Ch Swarthmore PA 1967-1970; Vic S Edw The Confessor Epis Ch Clinton Twp MI 1962-1963.

SCHNEIDER, Gregg Alan (NC) 703 Milwaukee Road, Beloit WI 53511 **D S Paul's Epis Ch Beloit WI 2008-** B Green Bay WI 1956 D 6/13/2004 Bp Michael B Curry. m 2/25/1995 Susan Elizabeth Schneider c 2. D The Prince Of Peace Epis Ch 2004-2007.

SCHNEIDER, Judith Irene (Colo) 2187 Canyon Ct W, Grand Junction CO 81503 **D S Matt's Ch Grand Jct CO 2003-; Boec Dio Colorado Denver CO 2005-, D 2002-2004** B Omaha NE 1942 d Lawrence & Irene. Macomb Cmnty Coll; Whitaker TS; AA Colorado Womens Coll 1962; BS New Mex St U 1982. D 6/11/1994 Bp R aymond Stewart Wood Jr. m 5/29/1962 Donald Kenneth Schneider c 3. D Ch Of The Nativ Grand Jct CO 1998-2002; Chapl S Matt's And S Jos's Detroit MI 1996-1998; Co-Fac Chld Bereavement Grp Detroit MI 1994-1998; Vol Chapl Chld's Hosp Detroit MI 1994-1998; D St Paul's Epis Romeo MI 1994-1998.

SCHNEIDER, Marian Helen (Roch) 13 E Water St, Friendship NY 14739 **Vol S Andr's Ch Friendship NY 2004-** B Norwich NY 1943 d John & Clarissa. Mildred Elley Secretarial Coll Albany NY 1962; Bex Sem 2002. D 12/6/2001 P 10/26/2002 Bp Jack Marston Mckelvey. m 11/21/1983 James F Schneider c 2.

SCHNEIDER, Marilyn Butler (Colo) 7900 E Dartmouth Ave Apt 58, Denver CO 80231 **Assoc St Gabr the Archangel Epis Ch Englewood CO 2006-; Asstg P-t St. Gabr the Archangel Cherry Hills Vill CO 2006-** B Pueblo CO 1933 d Howard & Stella. BA U of Nthrn Colorado 1955; MA Indiana U 1966; MA S Thos Sem 1988; MDiv S Thos Sem 1993. D 6/11/1994 P 12/18/1994 Bp William Jerry Winterrowd. c 3. Int, P-in-c St. Mart-in-the-Fields Aurora 2003-2006; S Mart In The Fields Aurora CO 2003-2005; Asstg Chr Epis Ch Denver CO 2003, Assoc R 1995-2002; Int Epiph Epis Ch Denver CO 2001-2002; Int S Thos Epis Ch Denver CO 1999-2001.

SCHNEIDER, Marni Jacqueline (Los) 2972 Cadence Way, Virginia Beach VA 23456 **Vic S Simon's-By-The-Sea Virginia Bch VA 2007-** B Lakewood OH 1942 d Jack & Grace. Pur; BA Loyola U 1982; MDiv CDSP 1986. D 6/21/1986 Bp Robert Claflin Rusack P 12/28/1986 Bp Oliver Bailey Garver Jr. Assoc R S Thos Epis Ch Chesapeake VA 2002-2007; Int S Chris's Epis Ch Portsmouth VA 2002; Int S Jn's Ch Hampton VA 2001; Int S Geo's Epis Ch Laguna Hills CA 1998-2000; Int S Aug By-the-Sea Par Santa Monica CA 1994-1997; Assoc R S Edm's Par San Marino CA 1986-1994.

SCHNEIDER, Matthew (Ala) 2017 6th Ave N, Birmingham AL 35203 **The Cathd Ch Of The Adv Birmingham AL 2014-** B Redwood City CA 1980 s David & Leslie. BA San Francisco St U 2003; MA San Francisco St U 2006; MDiv Ya Berk 2012. D 6/2/2012 Bp Edward Lloyd Salmon Jr. m 9/20/2008 Hawley M Schneider c 3. Assoc All SS Ch Hilton Hd Island SC 2013-2014; Prince Geo Winyah Epis Preschool Georgetown SC 2012-2013.

SCHNEIDER, M P (Vt) 164 Milton Road, Warwick RI 02888 **R S Mary's Epis Par Northfield VT 2010-** B Glocester RI 1952 d Richard & Lois. BS Rhode Island Coll 1974; MA Rhode Island Coll 1980; MDiv GTS 2007. D 3/28/1992 Bp George Nelson Hunt III P 9/25/2010 Bp Gerry Wolf. c 2. D S Steph's Ch Providence RI 1999-2004.

SCHNEIDER, Stephen (Ore) 2427 Ne 17th Ave, Portland OR 97212 B Pasadena CA 1942 s Vance & Madeline. BA Wheaton Coll 1964; MDiv PrTS 1967; CAS GTS 1989. D 7/6/1989 P 1/1/1990 Bp Robert Louis Ladehoff. m 11/14/1970 Ann L Herzog c 2. R Gr Memi Portland OR 1994-2014; Epis Par Of S Jn The Bapt Portland OR 1989-1994; Min To Yth And YA Imm Presb Ch Los Angeles CA 1968-1969.

SCHNEIDER, Thomas Carl (ETenn) 1038 Sparta Hwy, Crossville TN 38572 **S Raphael's Epis Ch Crossville TN 2016-** B Orange CA 1961 s Richard & Carol. BA San Francisco St 1984; BA San Francisco St 1985; MDiv Epis TS Of The SW 2015. D 6/13/2015 Bp Michael Vono P 1/27/2016 Bp George Young III. m 12/17/2005 Sylvia Ann Hewett c 1.

SCHNEIDER, William J (Mass) 276 Riverside Dr Apt 4e, New York NY 10025 **Non-par 1978-** B Cleveland OH 1933 s William & Grace. BA Ya 1955; STM EDS 1958. D 5/30/1958 P 1/1/1959 Bp Nelson Marigold Burroughs. c 3. Epis Chapl At Harvard & Radcliffe Cambridge MA 1963-1978; Chapl Harv Cambridge MA 1963-1978; Asst R E Lee Memi Ch (Epis) Lexington VA 1961-1963; Asst Gr Epis Ch Sandusky OH 1958-1960. Auth, "The Jon Daniels Story".

SCHNITZER, William Lawton (NY) 26 N Manheim Blvd, New Paltz NY 12561 B Newport RI 1933 s Robert & Alice. BA U of Rhode Island 1958; STB Ya Berk 1962; STM UTS 1971. D 6/23/1962 P 12/22/1962 Bp John S Higgins. m 6/14/1958 Carol Ann Schnitzer c 3. S Paul's Ch Pleasant Vlly NY 1996-1997; S Greg's Epis Ch Woodstock NY 1992-1993; Supply P Dio New York New York NY 1985-2003; P-in-c S Paul's Ch Chester NY 1977-1985; Cur S Geo's Epis Ch Newburgh NY 1972-1977; Vic S Aid Patterson NJ 1969-1971; Cur S Paul's Epis Ch Paterson NJ 1968-1969; Cur Ch Of The Gd Shpd Pawtucket RI 1962-1963.

SCHOECK, Lauren M (CPa) 6300 N Central Ave, Phoenix AZ 85012 **P S Jas Ch Lancaster PA 2014-** B Tucson AZ 1986 d Michael & Sandra. BA Arizona St U 2009; MDiv CDSP 2012. D 6/11/2011 P 5/20/2012 Bp Kirk Stevan Smith. m 5/24/2014 Robert Hughes Schoeck. Cur All SS Ch Phoenix AZ 2012-2014.

SCHOECK, Robert Hughes (CPa) 119 N Duke St, Lancaster PA 17602 **D S Jas Ch Lancaster PA 2014-** B Atlanta GA 1982 s Stephen & Patricia. BS Lesley U 2011; MDiv CDSP 2014; MDiv CDSP 2014. D 6/7/2014 Bp M(Arvil) Thomas Shaw P 1/31/2015 Bp Robert R Gepert. m 5/24/2014 Lauren M Lauren Michelle Lenoski.

SCHOENBRUN, Zoila Collier (Cal) 327 San Rafael Ave, Belvedere CA 94920 B Choloma HN 1935 d Zadik & Opal. BA USC 1957; MA CDSP 1980; MDiv CDSP 1985. D 12/7/1985 P 12/6/1986 Bp William Edwin Swing. m 12/18/1955 Richard Lee Schoenbrun c 3. Asst S Steph's Par Bel Tiburon CA 1996-2004.

✠ SCHOFIELD JR, The Rt Rev Calvin Onderdonk (SeFla) 7900 East Dartmouth Ave. # 77, Denver CO 80231 B Delhi NY 1933 s Calvin & Mabel. BA Hobart and Wm Smith Colleges 1959; MDiv Ya Berk 1962; DD Ya Berk 1979; STD Hobart and Wm Smith Colleges 1980; DD Sewanee: The U So, TS 1984. D 6/30/1962 Bp James Loughlin Duncan P 12/31/1962 Bp William Loftin Hargrave Con 3/23/1979 for SeFla. m 8/3/1963 Elaine Schofield c 2. Ret Bp of SE Florida Dio SE Florida Miami 2000-2001, Bp of SE Florida 1979-2000, Dn So Dade Dnry 1972-1976, Dn So Dade Dnry 1972-1976, Yth Advsr Miami Dnry 1964-1972; R S Andr's Epis Ch Miami FL 1964-1978; Chapl USNR 1962-1985; Cur Cathd Ch S Ptr St. Petersburg FL 1962-1964. OHC. DD U So 1984; S.T.B. Hob 1980; D.D. Berk 1979.

SCHOFIELD, Kathlyn Elizabeth (CNY) St Paul's Episcopal Church, 204 Genesee St, Chittenango NY 13037 **Epis Ch Of SS Ptr And Jn Auburn NY 2015-** B Syracuse, NY 1948 d Robert & Kathlyn. BS DYouville Coll 1970; Dioc Formation Prog CNY 2006. D 10/7/2006 P 6/6/2007 Bp Gladstone Bailey Adams III. m 8/31/1970 James Paul Schofield c 3. Trin Epis Ch Fayetteville NY 2013-2015; S Paul's Ch Chittenango NY 2007-2013; Asst Trin Epis Ch 2007.

S

SCHOFIELD, Peter (Alb) 39 Imperial Dr., Niskayuna NY 12309 **P Assoc Chr Ch Schenectady NY 2004-, P's Asst 1980-2004** B Ilford Essex UK 1944 s Thomas & Lilian. BS Rugby UK 1967; MS Rugby UK 1968. D 10/13/1980 Bp Wilbur Emory Hogg Jr P 7/24/2004 Bp Daniel William Herzog. m 5/16/1970 Sylvia T Schofield c 1. Chair, COM Dio Albany Greenwich NY 2008-2014.

SCHOFIELD-BROADBENT, Carrie (CNY) 941 Euclid Ave., Syracuse NY 13210 **Dio Cntrl New York Liverpool NY 2017-** B Syracuse NY 1974 d James & Kathlyn. BA Juniata Coll 1997; MDiv VTS 2003. D 6/28/2003 P 1/3/2004 Bp Gladstone Bailey Adams III. m 6/20/1998 Keith J Schofield-Broadbent c 2. R S Matt's Epis Ch Liverpool NY 2006-2017; Cn St Paul's Syracuse Syracuse NY 2004-2006; S Mk's Ch Candor NY 2003-2004; Cler Asst S Paul's Ch Owego NY 2003-2004; Vic St. Jn' Speedsville NY 2003-2004. carriesb@cnyepiscopal.org

SCHOLER, Linda Carlson (NJ) P O Box 1206, Chincoteague Island VA 23336 B Titusville PA 1946 d John & Marion. MA Georgian Crt Coll 1980; MSS Bryn Mawr Grad Sch Soc Wk 1982; Luth TS 1986; MTh New Brunswick TS 2001. D 6/2/2001 P 1/12/2002 Bp David Bruce Joslin. m 11/29/1986 Frederick R Scholer c 1. S Dav's Ch Cranbury NJ 2007-2008; Asst St. Dav's Carnbury NJ 2006-2008; Assoc P Gr-St. Paul's Mercerville NJ 2004-2006; Calv Epis Ch Flemington NJ 2001-2005. Cmnty St. Jn Bapt-Assoc 1971. Summa Cum Laud New Brunswick Teological Sem 2001.

SCHOMAKER, Kenneth Elmer (Ind) 2030 Chester Blvd IH 7B, Richmond IN 47374 **Ret 2000-** B Pittsburgh PA 1935 s Elmer & Elizabeth. BA Wesl 1957; Mdiv VTS 1960; BD VTS 1960. D 6/13/1960 P 7/6/1961 Bp Walter H Gray. m 10/17/1987 Mary Dianne Hill c 5. Chapl Plainfield Correctional Facility Plainfeld IN 1986-2000; R S Andr's Epis Ch Greencastle IN 1983-1986; Int S Jas Ch Collegeville PA 1981-1982, Asst to R 1979-1980; The Epis Acad Newtown Sq PA 1980-1983; Asst Chapl/Tchr Epis Acad Merion PA 1978-1983; R Gd Shpd Ch Hilltown PA 1974-1978; R Chr Ch And S Mich's Philadelphia PA 1970-1974; Chapl Woodville St Hosp Woodville PA 1968-1969; R Ch Of The Atone Carnegie PA 1963-1970; Cur S Jn's Ch E Hartford CT 1960-1963.

SCHOMBURG, Karen (Spok) Episcopal Diocese Of Spokane, 245 E 13th Ave, Spokane WA 99202 **Cn Dio Spokane Spokane WA 2013-** B Spokane WA 1950 d Hubert & Mary. Angl Immersion CDSP; BA Estrn Washington U 2011; MA Gonzaga 2013. D 6/1/2013 P 6/6/2015 Bp James E Waggoner Jr. m 6/1/1985 Niles B Schomburg c 5. karens@spokanediocese.org

SCHOOLER, William Thomas (Cal) 352 Bay Rd, Atherton CA 94027 **Ret Atherton CA 2009-** B Georgetown SC 1935 s Benjamin & Marion. BA U of So Carolina 1957; MS U of San Francisco 1980; Cert Ang Stud Sch for Deacons 1988. D 12/3/1988 Bp William Edwin Swing. m 3/29/1963 Ruth E Gracy c 1. Chapl Dep't of Veterans Affrs Palo Alto CA 1999-2009; D/Asst Trin Par Menlo Pk CA 1993-2006; Asst S Bede's Epis Ch Menlo Pk CA 1990-1993; Asst Chr Ch Portola Vlly CA 1988-1990. Assembly opf Epis Healthcare Chapl 2000-2009; Mltry Chapl of the US 2000-2009; Natl Assn of Veterans Affrs Chapl 2000-2009.

SCHOONMAKER, Daniel Holt (O) 18426 Winslow Rd, Shaker Heights OH 44122 **R S Hubert's Epis Ch Mentor OH 2000-** B Middletown NY 1959 s Robert & Dorothy. Thunderbird-Mgmt Glendale; BA Rochester Inst of Tech 1981; MA GW 1983; MBA Amer Grad Sch of Intl Mgmt Glendal 1988; MDiv VTS 1996. D Bp Ronald Hayward Haines P 12/14/1996 Bp Robert Reed Shahan. c 3. Int S Paul's Epis Ch Of E Cleveland Cleveland OH 1999-2000; Cur S Anth On The Desert Scottsdale AZ 1996-1998. Auth, "Evang (Chapt)," *Bldg Up The Ch*, Forw Mvmt Press, 1997.

SCHOONMAKER, Lisa Katherine (CPa) 21 S Main St, Lewistown PA 17044 **All SS Epis Ch Riverside CA 2007-** B Schenectady NY 1952 d Harold & Lucille. BMus S Olaf Coll 1975; JD Franklin Pierce Law Cntr 1987; MDiv Va Berk 2004. D 2/12/2005 P 8/27/2005 Bp Keith Whitmore. P-in-c S Mk's Epis Ch Lewistown PA 2007-2010.

SCHRAMM, George T (WVa) Po Box 308, Shepherdstown WV 25443 **R Trin Ch Shepherdstown WV 1983-** B Wheeling WV 1952 s George & Jo. BS Wheeling Jesuit U 1974; MDiv VTS 1977; DMin VTS 1997. D 6/8/1977 P 5/10/1978 Bp Robert Poland Atkinson. m 7/20/1979 Susan Cochran Bailey c 2. Archd Dio W Virginia Charleston WV 1990-1999; Dioc Coun 1980-1989; Com Ecum Rela 1978-1979, Com 2005-; Asst Trin Ch Parkersburg WV 1977-1983. Vol of the Year Hospice of the Panhandle 1998; Outstanding Young Men in Amer 1985.

SCHRAMM, John Eldon (NI) P. O. Box 695, Plymouth IN 46563 B Winona MN 1947 s Eldon & Mary. BA NW Nazarene U 1969; MDiv Nazarene TS 1972; ThM Harvard DS 1981. D 11/26/1978 P 6/5/1979 Bp James Winchester Montgomery. m 7/3/1971 Barbara Jean Schramm c 2. Dio Nthrn Indiana So Bend IN 1985-1991, Liturg Com 1995-1996; R S Thos Epis Ch Plymouth IN 1982-2013; Cur Ch Of The Ascen Chicago IL 1978-1982. Hon Cn Diocesis de Honduras 2000.

SCHRAPLAU, Frederick William (NY) 182 Nixon Avenue, Staten Island NY 10304 **Vic St. Paul's Ch Staten Island NY 2015-; R Emer St. Alb's Ch Staten Island NY 2013-** B Macon GA 1943 s William & Mabel. GTS; BS High Point U 1965; New York Cathd Inst 1978. D 2/18/1978 Bp Harold Louis Wright P 10/25/1978 Bp Paul Moore Jr. m 11/12/2011 James Francis Mitchell. P-in-c S Alb's Epis Ch Staten Island NY 2000-2013, stipendiary 2000-2013; Assoc S Mary's Castleton Staten Island NY 1990-2000; Assoc S Andr's Epis Ch Staten Island NY 1983-1990; S Paul's Ch Staten Island NY 1981-1983, Cur 1978-1979. Soc of the Our Lady of Walsingham 1980.

SCHREIBER, Mary Fiander (WMass) 6 Wall St, Shelburne Falls MA 01370 B Sudbury CA 1941 d Edgar & Grace. RN Greenwich Hosp Sch of Nrsng 1962; BS New Sch U 1988; MDiv Bex Sem 1992. D 5/30/1992 P 9/18/1993 Bp David Bruce Joslin. c 5. P-in-c St Mart's Ch (Epis) Pittsfield MA 2000-2006; Gr Ch Dalton MA 2000; S Lk's Ch Lanesboro MA 2000; R S Paul's Epis Ch Gardner MA 1998-1999; Vic Cathd Of All SS Albany NY 1997-1998; Vic All SS Epis Ch Skowhegan ME 1994-1997; Vic Chr Ch Manlius NY 1993-1994.

SCHREIBER, Michael Nelson (Cal) 162 Hickory St, San Francisco CA 94102 B St Louis MO 1939 s Dalton & Elizabeth. BFA Washington U 1964; AOS California Culinary Acad 1992; Diac Stds The Sch for Deacons 2008. D 6/6/2009 Bp Marc Handley Andrus. m 10/21/1978 Shelley A Schreiber c 3.

SCHREINER, Shawn M (Chi) 5 North 047 Route 83, Bensenville IL 60106 **The Ch Hm At Montgomery Place Chicago IL 2017-** B Greensburg IN 1961 d John & Jean. BA Hanover Coll 1983; MDiv SWTS 1991. D 6/24/1991 P 3/20/1992 Bp Edward Witker Jones. m 8/7/2013 Victoria Garvey. P-in-c Gr Ch Oak Pk IL 2004-2017; Cn Cathd Of S Jas Chicago IL 2002-2004; R S Bede's Epis Ch Bensenville IL 1993-2002; Asst Gr Ch Muncie IN 1991-1993. Auth, "The Rite Place. Kids Do Ch! Adults Do Too!," *The Rite Place. Kids Do Ch! Adults Do Too!*, Ch Pub, 2014. sschreiner2667@gmail.com

SCHRIDER, James Edward (Los) 620 D Street, SE, Washington DC 20003 B Washington DC 1933 s James & Helen. BA Ford 1957; MA Ford 1958; PHL Ford 1959; BTh Wood 1964; ThL Wood 1965; MA U Chi 1968. Rec 5/1/1987 as Priest Bp Oliver Bailey Garver Jr. m 8/30/1971 Fredericka G Schrider c 3. Assoc R S Jas Par Los Angeles CA 1989-1991; Asst S Aug By-The-Sea Par Santa Monica CA 1987-1989. Alb Inst.

SCHRIMSHER, Alyce Marie (Dal) 6132 Yellow Rock Trl, Dallas TX 75248 **D S Barn Ch Garland TX 2001-** B Hillsboro TX 1950 d John & Betty. BA U of Texas Arlington 1972; Lic Angl TS 2000. D 12/19/2001 Bp D Avid Bruce Macpherson. D Ch Of The Epiph Richardson TX 2001-2005. OSL the Physcn 2006; Ord of the DOK 2004.

SCHRODER, Edward Amos (Fla) 15 Hickory Lane, Amelia Island FL 32034 **Pstr Amelia Plantation Chap 2000-** B Hokitika NZ 1941 s Carl & Phyllis. BA U of Cbury Christchurch NZ 1963; ThD U of Durham GB 1966. Trans 12/20/1973 Bp John Melville Burgess. m 3/28/1970 Antoinette B Schroder c 2. Chapl S Mary's Hall San Antonio TX 1990-1994; R Chr Epis Ch San Antonio TX 1986-2000; R Gr Epis Ch Orange Pk FL 1979-1986; Asst to Bp Dio Florida Jacksonville 1976-1979; Chr Ch S Hamilton MA 1974-1976; Dn Gordon Coll Wenham MA 1971-1976; Serv Ch of Engl 1967-1971. Auth, "Why I Believe in Jesus Chr," Amelia Pulpit, 2015; Auth, "Soul Food, Vol.2," Amelia Pulpit, 2014; Auth, "Soul Food, Vol.3," Amelia Pulpit, 2014; Auth, "Soul Food, Vol.4," Amelia Pulpit, 2014; Auth, "Peace of Mind," Amelia Pulpit, 2014; Auth, "God Knows Where They Come From!," Craigs Design & Print Ltd, 2014; Auth, "Why Am I?," Amelia Pulpit, 2013; Auth, "Encouragement in a Wrld of Hurt," Amelia Pulpit, 2013; Auth, "Soul Food Vol.1," Amelia Pulpit, 2013; Auth, "Real Hope," Amelia Island Pub, 2011; Auth, "Solid Love," Amelia Island Pub, 2008; Auth, "Surviving Hurricanes," Amelia Island Pub, 2006; Auth, "Buried Treasure," Amelia Island Pub, 2005; Auth, "Inward Light," Amelia Island Pub, 2003; Auth, "I Will Fear No Evil," 2000; Auth, "Communicating the Gospel w Generation X," 2000; Auth, "The Armor of God," 1999; Auth, "A Vision for the Ch," 1992.

SCHROEDER, Cecelia Carlile (Va) 314 Ayrlee Avenue Nw, Leesburg VA 20176 B Norfolk VA 1978 d John & Amanda. BA TCU 2000; MDiv VTS 2004. D 6/19/2004 Bp Gethin Benwil Hughes P 12/19/2004 Bp Robert Wilkes Ihloff. m 7/21/2003 John Christopher Schroeder c 2. Vic S Gabr's Epis Ch Leesburg VA 2010-2012; Assoc R S Lk's Ch Salisbury NC 2006-2010; Asst R Middleham & S Ptr's Par Lusby MD 2004-2006.

SCHROEDER, Donald John (Spr) 49 Ward Cir, Brunswick ME 04011 **Ret 1990-** B Union City NJ 1927 s Carleton & Ethel. BS Rutgers The St U of New Jersey 1951; MBA NYU 1955; MDiv PDS 1966. D 6/11/1966 Bp Leland Stark P 12/1/1966 Bp George E Rath. Epis Campus Min Estrn Illinois U 1983-1990; Chapl Illinois St Masonic Hm 1983-1990; Dio Springfield Springfield IL 1982-1989; Trin Epis Ch Mattoon IL 1982-1989; Trin Epis Ch Kearny NJ 1982; S Lk's Ch Hope NJ 1981-1982; Newark Epis Coop For Min & Miss Newark NJ 1980; Dept Of Mssn Dio Newark Newark NJ 1973-1975, Secy For The Inter-Faith Com On Aging 1980-1981, Dept Of CSR 1978-1979, Dioc Coun 1975-1977, Evang Com 1973-1974; R S Thos Newark NJ 1969-1980; St Thos Epis Ch Newark NJ 1969-1980; P-in-c Calv Epis Ch Summit NJ 1966-1969.

SCHROEDER, H.B.W. (Va) B Muskegon MI 1947 s Hubert Bernard Walter & Mary. BS MI SU 1972; MA Nash 2009. D 8/2/2014 Bp Shannon Sherwood Johnston P 2/14/2015 Bp Susan Goff. m 10/3/1969 Carol Williams Schroeder c 1.

S

SCHROETER, George Hieronymus (CGC) 500 Spanish Fort Blvd Apt 29, Spanish Fort AL 36527 **Ret 1995-** B Mobile AL 1932 s Herbert & Julia. BA U So 1953; MDiv VTS 1956; MA U of Sthrn Mississippi 1970. D 7/6/1956 Bp Charles C J Carpenter P 5/1/1957 Bp George Mosley Murray. Supply P S Matt's Ch Mobile AL 1980-1995; Vic S Ptr's Ch Jackson AL 1976-1979; Supply P Trin Epis Ch Mobile AL 1965-1975; Cur H Comf Ch Gadsden AL 1964-1965; Vic S Mths Epis Ch Tuscaloosa AL 1962-1964; Vic S Mich's Ch Ozark AL 1957-1962; Ch Of The Epiph Enterprise AL 1956-1957; M-in-c The Epis Ch Of The Nativ Dothan AL 1956-1957; Exam Chapl Dio Alabama Birmingham 1961-1964. Auth, "The Ballad Of Les Mccater," Seabury Press, 1965; Auth, "Perfect Freedom," Seabury Press, 1965.

SCHUBERT, Jill Marie (Minn) 520 N Pokegama Ave, Grand Rapids MN 55744 B Grand Rapids MN 1948 d James & Betty. BA U MN Morris 1969; MSW U Denv 1987. D 12/20/2009 Bp James Louis Jelinek. D Chr Epis Ch Grand Rapids MN 2009-2013.

SCHUBERT, Kevin Lane Johnson (Tex) 3307 Garden Villa Ln, Austin TX 78704 **S Geo's Ch Austin TX 2010-** B Brenham TX 1976 s Charles & Pam. BA Texas St U San Marcos 2000; MDiv Epis TS of the SW 2007. D 6/23/2007 Bp Don Adger Wimberly P 1/22/2008 Bp Dena Arnall Harrison. m 5/1/2004 Heather Schubert c 2. Epis Ts Of The SW Austin TX 2016; Cur S Matt's Ch Austin TX 2007-2010; Dir of Mnstrs, Lay Min St Andr's Epis Ch 2001-2004. co-Auth, "Beyond Contemporary," *Episcorific Issue 2, Fall 2008*, Episcorific, 2008; co-Auth, "2000 Belize Vlly Archeol Field Report, Cayo Dist Belize," *TSU in SM, Anthropology Dept.*, Texas St U, 2001; co-Auth, "Site 41HY37 Excavation of Gnrl Edw Burlesons Cabin San Marcos, TX," *TSU in SM, Cntr for Archeol Stds*, Texas St U, 2001; co-Auth, "1999 Belize Vlly Archeol Field Report, Cayo Dist Belize TSU in SM, Anthropology Dept.," *TSU in SM, Anthropology Dept.*, Texas St U, 2000; co-Auth, illustrator, "1997 The Lower Paleolithic in Oman, Dhofar Reg, Oman Arabian Peninsula," *TSU in SM, Anthropology Dept.*, Texas St U, 1998.

SCHUBERT, Rebecca Malcolm (WMo) 3700 West 83 Terrace, Prairie Village KS 66206 **D All SS Epis Ch Kansas City MO 2006-; Chapl Gr Hospice 2004-** B Bartlesville OK 1943 d Eugene & Ferne. BA U of Missouri 1994; MA U of Missouri 2003; Cert U of Missouri 2003. D 2/4/1995 Bp John Clark Buchanan. m 9/8/1973 Robert Edward Schubert c 4. Chapl S Jos Hlth Cntr 2002-2004; Dir of Sprtl Care Villa S Jos 1999-2002; Dio W Missouri Kansas City MO 1998-1999, Asst to Bp 1997-1998; Chapl Coordntr Heart of Amer Hospice 1996-1997; Chapl Shawnee Mssn Med Ctr 1955-1996. "Best Times," *Bi-Monthly Article*. Assn of Profsnl Chapl 1996; Bd Cert Coll Chapl 1996.

SCHUEDDIG JR, Louis Charles (At) 345 9th St Ne, Atlanta GA 30309 **Pres/Exec Dir Allnce for Chr Media Atlanta GA 2005-; Hon Cn Cathd Of S Phil Atlanta GA 1992-** B Saint Louis MO 1948 s Louis & Beth. BS NWU 1970; MDiv VTS 1973; D.D. VTS 2012. D 6/9/1973 Bp George Leslie Cadigan P 12/8/1973 Bp James Winchester Montgomery. Pres/Exec Dir Epis Media Cntr Inc Atlanta GA 1998-2012; S Mich's Ch Grand Rapids MI 1976-1983; R Dio Wstrn Michigan Kalamazoo MI 1976-1978; Assoc S Aug's Epis Ch Wilmette IL 1973-1976. Auth, "On Being A Godparent," *Epis Life*, 2002; Auth, "No Longer Mainstream," *LivCh*, 2000.

SCHUETZ, Mary (EMich) 3536 West River Road, Sanford MI 48657 B Flint MI 1945 d John & Virginia. MI SU 1964; Saginaw Vlly St U 1985; TS Whitaker TS 1992; Cert SWTS 1996. D 6/13/1992 Bp R aymond Stewart Wood Jr P 12/7/1996 Bp Edwin Max Leidel Jr. m 12/29/1978 James E Schuetz c 1. S Jn's Epis Ch Midland MI 2014-2015; Int Trin Epis Ch Bay City MI 2012; R S Paul's Epis Ch Gladwin MI 2000-2010; Asst S Jn's Epis Ch Saginaw MI 1997-2000; Epis Tri Par Cluster Gladwin MI 1996-1997; R Epis Tri-Par Cluster Midland MI 1996-1997; D Epis Tri-Par Cluster Midland MI 1992-1996.

SCHUILING, Alice Catherine (NMich) 1100 Sunview Dr Apt 201, Saint Johns MI 48879 B Grand Rapids MI 1927 D 10/12/2003 Bp James Arthur Kelsey. m 6/5/1948 Melvin James Schuiling c 3.

SCHULENBERG, George W (ND) 135 Skogmo Blvd, Fergus Falls MN 56537 B Red Wing MN 1938 s Willard & Alta. Macalester Coll 1958; BA Intl Chr Univ Mitaka-shi Hodogaya-Ku Japan 1962; BD EDS 1969; MDiv EDS 1972. D 6/30/1969 Bp Hamilton Hyde Kellogg P 3/8/1970 Bp Philip Frederick McNairy. m 7/22/1962 Etsuko O Schulenberg c 2. Asst to the Bp Dio No Dakota Fargo ND 1990-1992; Asst Dio No Dakota Fargo ND 1990-1992; R Gr Epis Ch Jamestown ND 1988-2001; Reg Vic SE Reg Dio No Dakota Fargo ND 1988-1990; Minnesota Ldrshp Prog Dio Minnesota Minneapolis MN 1983-1988; S Jas' Epis Ch Fergus Falls MN 1975-1983; R Trin Ch Wahpeton ND 1975-1983; Breck Memi Mssn Ponsford MN 1970-1975; S Columba White Earth MN 1970-1975; S Phil Rice Lake MN 1970-1975; Supervising P Samuel Memi Naytahwaush MN 1970-1975; Asst White Earth Reserv Ch MN 1969-1970. Rural Worker's Fllshp 1983-1988.

SCHULENBERG, Michael A (Minn) 715 N High St, Lake City MN 55041 B Red Wing MN 1941 s Willard & Alta. BA Trin Hartford CT 1963; BD EDS 1969. D 6/30/1969 Bp Philip Frederick McNairy P 1/9/1970 Bp Richard Stanley Merrill Emrich. m 9/2/1966 Karen Schulenberg c 2. R H Cross Ch Pensaco-

la FL 1992-2002; R Chr Ch Red Wing MN 1989-1992; R S Mk's Epis Ch Aberdeen SD 1980-1989; S Paul's Epis Ch Flint MI 1969-1980.

SCHULER, Rock Hal (Md) St Andrew The Fisherman Episcopal, PO Box 175, Mayo MD 21106 **S Andr The Fisherman Epis Mayo MD 2012-** B Casper WY 1965 s Harold & De. BS U of Wyoming 1987; MDiv SWTS 1990; DMin SWTS 2002. D 6/25/1990 P 5/30/1991 Bp Bob Gordon Jones. m 11/22/2004 Jennifer Schuler c 2. S Paul's Epis Ch Mt Airy MD 2011-2012; R S Jn's Ch Olney MD 2006-2008; Chr Ch Norcross GA 2004-2006; R H Trin Ch Lansdale PA 1994-2004; Asst S Mk's Epis Ch Casper WY 1991-1994; Vic S Andr's Ch Meeteetse WY 1990-1991; Dioc Fin & Prop Com Dio Wyoming Casper 1998-2000, Stndg Com 1991-1997; Dioc Coun Dio Pennsylvania Philadelphia PA 1997-2000. Auth, "A Living Ch Serving A Living Lord: Mssn And Mnstry In The 21st Century," *Gathering The Next Generation*, Morehouse Pub, 2000; Auth, "The Supplemental Liturg Texts: A Theol Inquiry," *ATR*, 1991. Sylvia Cohen Awd For Cmnty Serv JCRC 1997. rockschuler@hotmail.com

SCHULLER, Christopher David (SwFla) 514 Victoria Ave, Venice CA 90291 B St Louis MO 1959 BA U MI 1983; MDiv EDS 2003. D 6/21/2003 Bp Leo Frade P 1/16/2004 Bp Henry Irving Louttit. m 9/15/1989 Bettina D Schuller c 2. R S Thos' Epis Ch St Petersburg FL 2007-2011; R S Paul's Epis Ch Jesup GA 2003-2007.

SCHULTZ, Alison M (Ore) 5560 Chemin de Vie, Atlanta GA 30342 **Chr Ch Par Lake Oswego OR 2014-** B Akron OH 1958 d Robert & Carol Ann. BS U of Akron 1981; MS U of W Florida 1983; MDiv GTS 2006. D 12/21/2005 P 6/25/2006 Bp J Neil Alexander. m 12/31/1981 Todd A Broadbridge c 2. Assoc H Innoc Ch Atlanta GA 2006-2014.

SCHULTZ, Gregory Allen (FdL) West 7145 County Road U, Plymouth WI 53073 **D S Ptr's Epis Ch Sheboygan Falls WI 1999-** B Sheboygan WI 1949 s Eugene & Cora. DeVry Inst of Techology 1969; Lakeshore Tech 1970. D 8/28/1996 Bp Russell Edward Jacobus. m 10/23/1971 Barbara Ann Susen. D S Paul's Ch Plymouth WI 1996-1999. NAAD.

SCHULTZ, Mark Daniel (NY) B Pomona CA 1975 s Rudiger & Carol. BA UCLA 1997; MFA Col 2000; MDiv Ya Berk 2017. D 3/4/2017 Bp Mary Douglas Glasspool. m 10/6/2012 Erich Harris Erving.

SCHULTZ OHC, Thomas Haines (Cal) St Mary's Retreat House, 505 E. Los Olivos St., Santa Barbara CA 93105 **Chapl Mt Calv Monstry Santa Barbara CA 2008-; Trans to Non-par Dio California 1998-** B Pittsburgh PA 1933 s William & Marian. BA U Pgh 1956; MDiv Nash 1959; MEd Cit 1986; DD CDSP 2006. D 6/13/1959 Bp William S Thomas P 12/19/1959 Bp Austin Pardue. Incarn Priory Berkeley Dio California San Francisco CA 1990-2008; Serv H Sav Priory Guest Hse Pineville SC 1975-1990; Chapl Whitby Hse Dallas TX 1974-1975; Asst Novc Mstr W Pk NY 1972-1974; D Whitby Hse Dallas TX 1968-1972; Asst H Cross Guest Hse W Pk NY 1966-1968; Mssy H Cross Liberia 1964-1966; Monk in Trng H Cross W Pk NY 1959-1964. Auth, *Rosary for Episcopalians*, Incarn Priory Pr, 1992. Amer Counslg Assn 1986; So Carolina Counslg Assn 1986. DD CDSP 2006; MENSA 1984.

SCHULZ, David Allen (Del) 224 N Bayshore Dr, Frederica DE 19946 **Non-par 1988-** B Saint Louis MO 1933 s John & Bertha. BA Pr 1954; MDiv VTS 1960; PhD Washington U 1968. D 2/28/1960 Bp Frederick D Goodwin P 3/1/1961 Bp George Leslie Cadigan. c 1. Aux P Cathd Ch Of S Jn Wilmington DE 1971-1980; Supply P Dio Cntrl Pennsylvania Harrisburg PA 1967-1970; Non-par 1962-1965; Cur Gr Ch S Louis MO 1960-1962. Auth, "The Changing Fam: Its Function & Future"; Auth, "Mar," *The Fam & Personal Fulfillment*.

SCHUNEMAN, Steven Lawrence (Chi) 200 N El Camino Real Spc 179, Oceanside CA 92058 **Owner Always Scene II Video Oceanside CA 2012-; Supply P Supply P Dio San Diego CA 2012-** B Sterling IL 1956 s Robert & Sarah. BA Nthrn Illinois U 1978; MDiv Nash 1982. D 6/19/1982 P 12/18/1982 Bp James Winchester Montgomery. m 9/17/1983 Annette W Schuneman. P-in-c Ch Of The H Nativ Chicago IL 2010-2012; P-in-c S Tim's Ch Griffith IN 2000-2010; Owner Scene II Video Productions Schererville IN 2000-2010; R S Paul's Epis Ch Munster IN 1997-2000; R Trin Ch Niles MI 1987-1997; Asst Trin Ch Milwaukee WI 1984-1987; Vic S Chad Epis Ch Loves Pk IL 1982-1984. Auth, "Epis Radio/Tv Video Welcoming The Newcomer". Dir Epis Radio/Tv Video "8th Commandment"; Dir Epis Radio/Tv Video "Earthen Vessels"; Dir Epis Radio/Tv Video "Welcoming The Newcomer".

SCHUNIOR, Rebecca J (WA) St Mark's Church, 301 A St SE, Washington DC 20003 **S Thos Epis Ch Denver CO 2017-** B Chapel Hill NC 1976 d Charles & Claudia. BA S Johns Coll Annapolis MD 1999; MDiv Candler TS Emory U 2009. D 12/20/2008 P 6/28/2009 Bp J Neil Alexander. m 8/14/2012 Andrew J Baisc. S Mk's Ch Washington DC 2011-2017; Cler Res Chr Ch Alexandria VA 2009-2011.

SCHUSTER III, Franklin Phillip (RG) 28231 Pine Lake St, Edwardsburg MI 49112 B Galveston TX 1954 s Franklin & Bettie. U of Texas; BBA TCU 1977; MDiv SWTS 1984. D 6/26/1984 P 3/5/1985 Bp Richard Mitchell Trelease Jr. m 11/25/1995 Tj Patton. S Jas Epis Ch Taos NM 2007-2013; R Trin Ch Niles MI 1999-2007; R S Andrews Ch Derby KS 1992-1999; Sub-Dn Pro Cathd Epis Ch Of S Clem El Paso TX 1986-1992; S Jn's Cathd Albuquerque NM 1985-1986;

Dio The Rio Grande Albuquerque 1984. Ord Of S Lk. frank.schuster.3@gmail.com

SCHUSTER, Lawrence Arthur (WNY) 10348 2nd St, Dunkirk NY 14048 **Died 3/7/2017** B Chicago IL 1927 s Lawrence & Helen. BS U IL 1950; MDiv Ya Berk 1960. D 5/28/1960 Bp Frederick Lehrle Barry P 12/24/1960 Bp Allen Webster Brown. m 4/28/1951 Mary Patricia Reynolds c 6. P in charge Ch Of S Jn The Bapt Dunkirk NY 1998-2017; R Trin Epis Ch Fredonia NY 1963-1995; Chapl SUNY-Fredonia 1963-1964; Cur Ch Of Beth Saratoga Spg NY 1960-1963.

SCHUSTER WELTNER, Alicia Dawn (At) 2744 Peachtree Rd NW, Atlanta GA 30305 **Cn Dio Atlanta Atlanta GA 2004-** B Rahway NJ 1962 d Allan & Gail. BA Mt Holyoke Coll 1984; MDiv Sewanee: The U So, TS 1995. D 6/10/1995 Bp Frank Kellogg Allan P 12/16/1995 Bp Onell Asiselo Soto. m 8/19/1995 Philip Weltner c 1. Assoc R S Mart In The Fields Ch Atlanta GA 2001-2004; Assoc R & P-in-c H Trin Par Decatur GA 1999-2000; Asst R S Mich And All Ang Ch Stone Mtn GA 1995-1998. "Sermons That Wk Collection," *2003/Morehouse Barlowe*, 2003, 2003. aschusterweltner@episcopalatlanta.org

SCHUTZ, Christine Elizabeth (O) 843 Tarra Oaks Dr, Findlay OH 45840 B Omaha NE 1946 d William & Elizabeth. BA U of Iowa 1968; MDiv Sewanee: The U So, TS 2000. D 6/11/2000 Bp Chris Christopher Epting P 7/26/2001 Bp J Clark Grew II. c 3. Trin Ch Findlay OH 2005-2014; S Paul's Ch Maumee OH 2001-2005; Ch Of The H Comf Monteagle TN 2000-2001.

SCHUYLER, Janice Macfarland (Me) 6 Village Way, Rutland MA 01543 **Died 10/26/2015** B Norwich CT 1942 d Arnold & Lea. Albertus Magnus Coll 1962; BA Ohio Dominican Coll 1967; MA U of Notre Dame 1977; MA Cath Theol Un 1982; Bangor TS 1992. D 12/18/1992 P 8/24/1993 Bp Edward Cole Chalfant. m 4/25/1986 William Kearns Schuyler. Dio Maine Portland ME 2000-2007; Vic S Steph The Mtyr Epis Ch Waterboro Cntr ME 1994-2007; Assoc P S Dav's Epis Ch Kennebunk ME 1993-1995.

SCHUYLER, Philip William (Az) 2010 W San Marcos Blvd, Unit 117, San Marcos CA 92078 **Died 6/12/2017** B Los Angeles CA 1930 s Philip & Helen. BA Stan 1952; BD CDSP 1955. D 6/1/1955 P 2/21/1956 Bp Francis E I Bloy. c 2. Chapl Kindred Rehab Cntr 2010-2017; Pstr Asst S Lk's Ch San Diego CA 2000-2002, Asst to R 1996-1999, Pstr Asst 1995-1996, Pstr Asst 1995; Chapl Yard 2 Donovan St Prison San Diego CA 2000-2001; Chapl Hospice Of The No Coast 1998-2000; Sun Asst S Michaels By-The-Sea Ch Carlsbad CA 1998-1999; Asst to R Trin Ch Escondido CA 1993-1994; Asst to R The Epis Ch Of The Blessed Sacr Placentia CA 1992-1993; Fndr Epis Hsng Mgmnt Corp 1988-1990; Vic Gr Epis Ch Lk Havasu City AZ 1988-1989; R Chr Ch Par Redondo Bch CA 1971-1988; Vic S Mary's Par Lompoc CA 1957-1963; Cur Ch Of The Mssh Santa Ana CA 1955-1957; Fndr Dio Los Angeles Los Angeles CA 1983-1988, Pres Sw Dnry 1977-1982, Chapl Indonesian Refugees 1963-1976. Forw In Faith; PB Soc. Bd Supervisot'S Citation Los Angeles Cnty 1988; Mayor'S Citation For Serv To Srs & Refugees Los Angeles Mayor Tom Bradley 1988; Mayor Barbara Doerr Redondo Bch 1988; Man Of Year Awd Redondo Bch 1978; California Lesgislature Awd California Legislature Gerald Felando.

SCHUYLER, William Kearns (Me) 19 Ridgeway Ave, Sanford ME 04073 B Richmond KY 1945 s Walter & Alene. BA DePauw U 1967; STB GTS 1970. D 6/10/1970 P 12/28/1970 Bp John P Craine. Dio Maine Portland ME 2000-2007; R S Geo's Epis Ch Sanford ME 1993-2007; Ch Of The Gd Shpd Houlton ME 1990-1993; Assoc S Jn's Ch Worthington OH 1988-1990; Non-par 1974-1988; Assoc S Greg's Abbey Three Rivers MI 1970-1974.

SCHWAB, Susan Mary Brophy (Mass) 280 Village St Apt G1, Medway MA 02053 **co-Mssnr S Mk's Ch No Easton MA 2007-; St Johns Ch Taunton MA 2007-** B Urbana IL 1946 d William & Mary. BA Ohio U 1967; MDiv EDS 1987. D 6/2/1990 Bp David Elliot Johnson P 6/7/1991 Bp David Bell Birney IV. Bristol Trin Epis Ch No Easton MA 2014-2016; Bristol Cluster No Easton MA 2014; S Jn The Evang Mansfield MA 2007-2013; Assoc Trin Epis Ch Rockland MA 1999-2001; Supply Dio Massachusetts Boston MA 1992-1999; S Eliz's Ch Sudbury MA 1992-1998; Asst S Paul's Ch Natick MA 1990-1992.

SCHWAB, Wayne Wayne (Nwk) PO Box 294, Hinesburg VT 05461 **Pres and Trnr Mem Mssn Ntwk Inc. Hinesburg 2007-** B Washington DC 1928 s James & Mary. BA Leh 1950; MDiv VTS 1953. D 4/10/1954 P 6/18/1955 Bp Angus Dun. m 10/22/2010 Renate B Parke c 4. P Assoc, Vol Trin Ch Plattsburgh NY 2007-2011; P-in-c S Jn's Ch Essex NY 2000-2002; Supply P St. Jn's Ch Essex NY 1994-1996; Evang Coordntr Epis Ch Cntr New York NY 1975-1993; R S Paul's Ch Montvale NJ 1956-1975; Asst S Paul's Par Washington DC 1954-1956; CE Chair Dio Newark Newark NJ 1964-1975. Auth, "Living the Gospel (Workbook)," *Mem Mssn Ntwk*, Mem Mssn Press, 2010; Ed, "Mem Mssn Nwsltr," *Mem Mssn News*, Mem Mssn Ntwk, Inc, 2003; Auth, "When the Members are the Missionaries," *Mem Mssn Ntwk*, Mem Mssn Press, 2002; Auth, "E-Share," *Evang Off*, Epis Ch Cntr, 1991; Auth, "Proclamation as Offering Story & Choice," *Evang Off*, Epis Ch Cntr, 1988; Auth, "Gdbk. 1: Evang, Ren, Ch Gr Renwl," *Evang Off*, Epis Ch Cntr, 1980; Auth, "Handbook for Evang," *Evang Off*, Epis Ch Cntr, 1979; Auth, "Evang News," *Evang Nwsltr*, Ep. Ch. Cntr, New York, NY, 1975. AAPC 1970-1980. Phi Beta Kappa Leh 1950.

SCHWAHN, Vincent Carl (Los) 117 Avenida San Jeronimo, San Angel, Mexico City 01000 Mexico **St Marks Epis Ch Van Nuys CA 2011-; Dn San Andres Angl Sem Mex City Mx 1997-** B Bismark ND 1959 s Leopold & Geraldine. BTh U of St Thos 1981; MDiv U of St Thos 1987; GTS 1991. D 6/24/1991 P 12/28/1991 Bp Robert Marshall Anderson. m 9/22/2009 Juan J Colin. S Clem's-By-The-Sea Par San Clemente CA 2010-2011; Chr Ch Epis Lomas De Chapultepec 2004-2010; Dio Mex Mex City MOR 1997-2005; Vic Ch Of The Mssh Prairie Island Welch MN 1994-1996; Vic El Santo Nino Jesus S Paul MN 1993-1996; Asst S Paul's On-The-Hill Epis Ch Minneapolis MN 1993-1996; Dio Minnesota Minneapolis MN 1991-1997. vincentkarlschwahn@gmail.com

SCHWARTZ, William Edward (Mil) PO Box 3210, Doha QATAR Qatar **Archd in the Arabian Gulf Dio Cyprus & The Gulf 2009-; R Ch of the Epiph Doha Qatar 2007-; Prov Treas Epis Ch in Jerusalem & the Middle E 2007-; P Exec Coun Appointees New York NY 1993-; Appointed Mssy Epis Ch Cntr New York NY 1993-** B Omaha NE 1952 s John & Patricia. BA Tarkio Coll 1975; Salisbury & Wells Theol Coll Sem Gb 1993. Trans 8/12/1993 as Priest Bp Terence Kelshaw. m 8/21/1976 Edith Louise Schwartz c 4. R Cbury Grp Saudi Arabia 1999-2007; Dio The Rio Grande Albuquerque 1993; Non-par Secy & Treas Dio Cyprus & The Gulf 1989-1999. Off of the British Empire HH Queen Eliz II 2006; Cn, St Chris's Cathd Bahrain Rt Revd G Clive Handford 2006.

SCHWARZ, Robert Carl (SD) 500 S Main Ave, Sioux Falls SD 57104 B Darby PA 1952 s Carl & Virginia. Amer U; Penn; Tem; MDiv Sewanee: The U So, TS 1986. D 5/16/1986 P 11/1/1986 Bp William Cockburn Russell Sheridan. m 6/17/1972 Jeanne L Schwarz c 4. P-in-c Dio So Dakota Pierre SD 2008-2015; Ch Of The Ascen Mt Vernon NY 2007-2008; The Ch of S Ign of Antioch New York NY 2006-2007; Dio New York New York NY 2004-2006, 2002-2004, 2000, 1999; Int S Fran Assisi And S Martha White Plains NY 2004-2006; Int All Souls Ch New York NY 2001-2003; Ground Zero Chapl 2001-2002; Geo Mercer TS Garden City NY 2000; Ch Of The Mssh Lower Gwynedd PA 1998; Mssy Coord Partnership Prg 1996-1997; Exec Coun Appointees New York NY 1996-1997; S Lk's Epis Ch Milwaukee WI 1989-1996; Vic S Clem's Epis Ch Greenville PA 1986-1989. Auth, "Var Poems & arts".

SCHWARZ, Robert Louis (LI) 324 Fairington Dr, Summerville SC 29485 B Jamaica NY 1932 s Louis & Irene. BA Duke 1954; U of Virginia 1970; Cert Mercer TS 1977. D 12/19/1976 Bp Jonathan Goodhue Sherman P 12/17/1977 Bp Robert Campbell Witcher Sr. m 8/28/1954 Barbara Schwarz c 5. Chapl Ret Police Assn Ny St 2000-2003; Geo Mercer TS Garden City NY 2000; Chapl Suffolk Cnty Police Assn 1991-2004; Chapl Sayville Fire Dep'T Sayville NY 1989-2004; R S Ann's Ch Sayville NY 1986-2004; Emm Epis Ch Great River NY 1985-1986; Asst S Ptr's by-the-Sea Epis Ch Bay Shore NY 1977-1979; Asst Chr Ch Babylon NY 1976-1977. FA.

SCHWARZER, Margaret Katherine (Mass) 321 Tappan St Apt 5, Brookline MA 02445 **Assoc R for Adult Formation and Mem S Andr's Ch Wellesley MA 2015-** B Syracuse NY 1963 d Franklin & Harriet. Yale DS; BA Smith 1985; MDiv Ya Berk 1991. D 6/11/1994 Bp Ronald Hayward Haines P 12/1/1994 Bp Joe Doss. c 4. Int Ch Of The Gd Shpd Waban MA 2014-2015; Int Gr Ch Newton MA 2011-2014; Int S Paul's Epis Ch Bedford MA 2010-2011; Int S Mary's Ch Newton Lower Falls MA 2009-2010; Int Par Of Chr Ch Andover MA 2009; Epis Chapl Bos 1997-2008; Dir of Mica Proj Dio Massachusetts Boston MA 1997-2008, 2015-, Trst for the Trst of Donation 2015-, Other Cler Position 1997-2008; Cur Trin Ch Princeton NJ 1994-1997; Co-Pres Massachusetts Epis Cler Assn 2008-2010. Auth, "Essays On The Formation And Mnstry Of Gen X Priests," *Gathering The Next Generation*, Morehouse Pub, 2000; Auth, "Wmn Sermons Series 1 Year A," *The Abingdon Wmn Priesting Annual*, Abingdon Press, 1998; Contrib, "Sermons That Wk Vi," Morehouse Pub, 1997. Best Sermon Competition (1 Of 10 Winners) Epis Evang Fndt 1996.

SCHWEINSBURG JR, Richard Lyle (RI) 46 Fairway Dr, Washington Village, Coventry RI 02816 **Vic S Eliz's Ch Hope Vlly RI 2012-** B Southampton NY 1951 s Richard & Phyllis. BA Ge 1974; MDiv VTS 1977; DMin GTF 1991. D 6/11/1977 Bp Jonathan Goodhue Sherman P 12/17/1977 Bp Robert Campbell Witcher Sr. m 9/3/1977 Jane D Schweinsburg. Supply P Dio Rhode Island Providence RI 2009-2012, Mltry Spprt Chapl 2003-, POC, Mltry Mnstrs 2001-; Assoc S Jos And S Jn Ch Lakewood WA 2008-2009; Prison Chapl, SRC Active Duty Army 2007-2009; Chapl Active Duty Army Germany 2005-2007; P-in-c All SS Epis Ch Heidelberg Germany 2005-2007; Casualty Chapl Active Duty Army 2004-2005; Assoc S Mk's Ch Alexandria VA 2004-2005; AMC Chapl Active Duty Army 2003-2004; Supply P S Mich's-On-The-Heights Worcester MA 2002-2003; R The Epis Ch Of S Andr And S Phil Coventry RI 1998-2001; VP Metropltn Dnry Dio Albany Greenwich NY 1993-1998; R S Paul's Ch Schenectady NY 1988-1998; R Chr Ch Denton MD 1986-1988; R S Paul's Ch Philipsburg PA 1979-1986; S Jn's Epis Ch Lancaster PA 1977-1979; Cur Dio Cntrl Pennsylvania Harrisburg PA 1977-1978; Chapl (Colonel) US Army 1974-2009. Auth, "D.Min Thesis," *A Manual for Acolytes on Video*, GTF, 1991. Angl Soc 1977; Epis Armed Serv Chapl Assn 1977; Mltry Chapl Assn 1977; Soc of S Fran 1977. Humanitarian of Year Animal Protective Fndt Schenectady

Cnty 1995; Amer Red Cross Spec Citation for Exceptional Voluntar Moshannon Vlly Chapt 1986.

SCHWENKE, Carol Flenniken (SwFla) 3000 S Schiller St, Tampa FL 33629 **P Asst Serv Ch of the Ascen Clearwater FL 2001**- B Alexander City AL 1940 d Fred & Lucille. BS U of Tennessee 1962; MS U of Tennessee 1975; MDiv Sewanee: The U So, TS 1985. D 6/22/1985 Bp Emerson Paul Haynes P 4/28/1990 Bp Rogers Sanders Harris. m 11/29/1980 Roger D Schwenke c 3. Ch Pension Fund Benefici 2005; Chapl Lifepath Hospice Tampa FL 2001-2005; Grp Mem Cler Ldrshp Proj Trin Wall St 1998-2001; Cn Gr And H Trin Cathd Kansas City MO 1997-2001; H Innoc Epis Ch Valrico FL 1988-1997; D S Jn's Epis Ch Clearwater FL 1985-1988; Cler Ldrshp Proj Dio W Missouri Kansas City MO 1998-2001; Chair Com on AIDS Mnstry Dio SW Florida Parrish FL 1987-1997.

SCHWENZFEIER, Paul Macleod (Mass) 32 Arlington Rd., Wareham MA 02571 **Ret 2000**- B Lowell MA 1941 s Frederick & Christine. BA Ken 1963; MDiv EDS 1968. D 6/15/1968 P 3/8/1969 Bp John S Higgins. m 1/25/1964 Rita Collar Schwenzfeier c 2. Ch Of Our Sav Somerset MA 1976-2000; R Ch Of The H Sprt Mattapan MA 1976-2000; R Trin Epis Ch Wrentham MA 1969-1976; Asst S Mk's Epis Ch Riverside RI 1968-1969.

SCHWERT, Douglas Peters (WTex) 433 Trojan St, Port Aransas TX 78373 **Vic Trin-By-The-Sea Port Aransas TX 2009-; S Mary's Retreat And Conf Cntr 2002**- B Wellsville NY 1946 s Edward & Virginia. AAS Paul Smiths Coll 1969; BS U Denv 1971; MDiv SWTS 1978. D 6/29/1978 Bp William Hopkins Folwell P 1/5/1979 Bp Charles Bennison Sr. m 12/14/1999 Gerre L Schwert c 2. S Mary's Sewanee Sewanee TN 2002-2008; Incarn Cntr Deep River CT 1996-2002; Incarn Cntr Ivoyton CT 1996-2002; R St Ptr & All SS Epis Ch Kansas City MO 1995-1996; R S Lk's Epis Ch Bartlesville OK 1990-1995; R S Dav's Ch Glenview IL 1985-1990; S Ptr's By-The-Lake Ch Montague MI 1978-1985.

SCHWOYER, Robin Lynn Vanhorn (Pa) 232 American Dr, Richboro PA 18954 B Philadelphia PA 1964 d David & Shirley. BS Drexel U 1987; Cert Pennsylvania Dioc Sch For The Diac 1996; Cert Cntr For Human Integration Philadelphia PA 2003; Cert Cntr of Being - IET Mstr/Instr 2004; Cert Usui Shiki Ryohoh - Reiki Mstr/Tchr 2005; Cert Amer Red Cross Lifeguard/Instr 2007; Cert Yoga - 300 hours 2010. D 9/12/1998 Bp Charles Ellsworth Bennison Jr. m 10/26/1996 Ronald Joseph Schwoyer. Pstr Consult Emm Ch Holmesburg 2004-2005; Cathd D Dio Pennsylvania 2002; D For Yth Mnstry; Growth And Dvlpmt Pennypack Dnry Of The Pa Dio Philadelphia PA 2000-2005; Pennypack Dnry Dio Pennsylvania Philadelphia PA 2000-2003; D The Free Ch Of S Jn Philadelphia PA 1998-2001. NAAD 1998; The Assn For Humanistic Psychol 2003.

SCIAINO, Elizabeth Rauen (NJ) 88 Claremont Rd, Bernardsville NJ 07924 **S Bern's Ch Bernardsville NJ 2015**- B Manchester NH 1977 d Paul & Jane. BA Wesl 1999; MDiv Drew U 2011. D 6/4/2011 P 12/10/2011 Bp Mark M Beckwith. m 7/10/2004 Peter Loftus Sciaino c 2. Assoc Chr Ch Ridgewood NJ 2012-2015; Cur All SS Ch Millington NJ 2011. priest@stbernardsnj.org

SCIME, Michael S (Ind) **D S Alb's Ch Indianapolis IN 2012**- B Buffalo NY 1964 s Sam & Marcia. D Formation Dio Indianapolis - D Formation Prog; EFM Sewanee: The U So, TS; BA Canisius Coll 1986; MPA Indiana U 1988. D 10/22/2011 Bp Cate Waynick. m 5/23/2012 Todd Aaron Kleffman. Dayspring Cntr Indianapolis IN 1993-2005.

SCIPIO, Clarence Tyrone (VI) PO Box 1148, St Thomas VI 00804 B Trinidad 1931 s John & Matilda. D 3/5/2011 Bp Edward Gumbs. m 1/18/1991 Francine Penn-Scipio c 4.

SCISSONS, Antoinette M (EO) 17 Fairview Heights Loop, Burns OR 97720 B Rosebud SD 1944 d Willis & Doris. Portland Cmnty Coll; Cert Vancouver TS CA 2001; MDiv Vancouver TS CA 2002. D 6/24/2000 P 2/17/2001 Bp Robert Louis Ladehoff. c 3. Dio Iowa Des Moines IA 2007-2011; S Andr's Ch Burns OR 2004-2007; S Paul's Indn Mssn Sioux City IA 2004-2007; Dio Oregon Portland OR 2000-2003. ascisns4@live.com

SCOFIELD, Lawrence Frederick (NwPa) 24 W Frederick St, Corry PA 16407 **Int Pstr (P-t) St. Paul Luth Ch 2015**- B NY 1945 s William & Elisabeth. BA Carleton Coll 1967; NYU 1975; MDiv Ya Berk 1986; CAS Ya Berk 1986. D 6/14/1986 Bp Arthur Edward Walmsley P 12/22/1986 Bp Arthur Anton Vogel. m 7/1/1967 Susan M Scofield c 2. P-in-c S Fran Of Assisi Epis Ch Youngsville PA 2013-2014; Dir Corry Area Food Pantry Inc. Corry 2007-2010; Pres Corry Area Food Pantry Inc. Corry 1999-2007; Dioc Coun Mem Dio NWPA 1998-2003; Fire Chapl Stanford Hose Co Corry PA 1996-2013; R Emm Ch Corry PA 1996-2010; Vic S Geo Epis Ch Camdenton MO 1992-1996; Fire Chapl Lake of the Ozarks Mutual Aid Assn Camdenton MO 1988-1996; Cur Chr Epis Ch S Jos MO 1986-1988; Fire Chapl S Jos Fire Dept St. Jos MO 1986-1988; Exam Chapl Dio NW Pennsylvania Erie PA 2004-2010; Sch For Mnstry Coordntr/Dn 1996-2003. Auth, "Asstg Victims: a Theol look at rationale and procedures," *Fire Chapl Inst Trng Manual*, Fed of Fire Chapl, 2004. Fed of Fire Chapl 1987-2014; NNECA 2003-2010.

SCOFIELD, Susan M (NwPa) Nonparochial, 24 W. Frederick St., Corry PA 16407 B St Charles IL 1945 d Harry & Margaret. BA Carleton Coll 1967; U So 1985; Dio Sch for Mnstry 2001. D 11/17/2006 Bp Arthur Williams Jr P 12/21/2007 Bp Sean Walter Rowe. m 7/1/1967 Lawrence Frederick Scofield c 2.

P-in-c S Fran Of Assisi Epis Ch Youngsville PA 2008-2009; Eccl Crt Dio NW Pennsylvania Erie PA 2008-2009.

SCOLARE, Michael Charles (FdL) **R Ch of the Blessed Sacr Green Bay WI 2012**- B St Louis MO 1962 s Charles & Clara. MDiv Trin Evang DS 1997. D 5/7/2011 P 12/3/2011 Bp Russell Edward Jacobus. m 8/22/1987 Kristen Mary Scolare c 4.

SCOOPMIRE, Leslie Barnes (Mo) **Yth Dir Dio Missouri S Louis MO 2017**- B Tulsa Oklahoma 1964 d Cornell & Nina. Mstr of Div Eden TS; Mstr of Arts U of Missouri- St. Louis; Bachelor of Sci U of Tulsa. D 12/16/2016 P 6/29/2017 Bp George Wayne Smith. m 8/6/1988 William James Scoopmire c 3. Soc of Schlr-Priests 2015. leslie@diocesemo.org

SCOTT, Andrew T (Okla) **Cur S Jn's Epis Ch Tulsa OK 2017**- B Auburn CA 1990 s Thomas & Elizabeth. D 12/17/2016 P 7/5/2017 Bp Edward Joseph Konieczny.

SCOTT JR, Benjamin Ives (Minn) 8429 55th St Sw, Byron MN 55920 B Rochester MN 1935 s Benjamin & Jennie. BA NWU 1957; MDiv Nash 1960; NYU 1969. D 6/18/1960 P 5/22/1961 Bp Hamilton Hyde Kellogg. m 7/2/1960 Sarah E Scott c 2. The Epis Cathd Of Our Merc Sav Faribault MN 1997-2001; Dio Minnesota Minneapolis MN 1989-2001, Trst 1978-1984; Trst Gr Memi Ch Wabasha MN 1989-2000; Bexley Seabury Fed Chicago IL 1989-1996; Dn Reg 5 1986-1988; 1978-1982; P-in-c Gr On Pine Island Pine Island MN 1976-1989; Rochester Area 6 Pnt Coord Cncl Rochester MN 1976-1989; Co-ordntr Rochester Area Mnstry Byron MN 1976-1989; S Matt's Epis Ch Chatfield MN 1976-1989; P-in-c S Ptr's Epis Ch Kasson MN 1976-1989; Trin S Chas MN 1976-1989; Dn S Paul Metropltn Reg 7 1971-1974; R S Mary's Ch S Paul MN 1969-1976; S Jn's Ch New York NY 1968-1969; Gr Epis Ch Massapequa NY 1967-1968; Prncpl S Jos Par Sch Queens Vill NY 1964-1967; Vic H Trin Epis Ch Luverne MN 1960-1964. Ed, "Hist of Calv Ch, Rochester," Davies Printing, 2009; Auth, "The 1st Cathd: An Epis Cmnty For Mssn," Mod Printing, 1987; Auth, "Hist of Gr Memi, Wabasha (pamphlet)"; Auth, "Episcopalians In Mn (pamphlet)". Hon Cn Cathd Of Our Merc Sav, Faribault 2000.

SCOTT, Catherine F (Neb) 1903 Pleasantview Ln, Bellevue NE 68005 B Williamsport PA 1952 d Vincent & Hazel. BA Carthage Coll 1973; MDiv SWTS 1977. D 6/28/1977 Bp James Winchester Montgomery P 7/23/1979 Bp William Arthur Dimmick. m 12/14/1974 Robert W Scott c 3. Dn S Mk's Epis Pro-Cathd Hastings NE 2010-2017; Ch Of The H Trin Lincoln NE 2007-2010; Min Dev Coord Dio Nebraska Omaha NE 1997-2007, Dioc Coun 1985-1987; R S Lk's Ch Plattsmouth NE 1997-2007; S Matt's Ch Lincoln NE 1995-1997; Mutual Mnstry Spprt Stff Dio Nthrn Michigan Marquette MI 1988-1994, COM 1982-1993, Dioc Coun 1979-1982; Trin Ch Gladstone MI 1982-1988; Vic Zion Ch Wilson MI 1982-1988; S Pauls Ch Nahma MI 1978-1988; M-in-c S Jn's Ch Munising MI 1978-1980. Soc Of S Fran - Tertiary.

SCOTT, Cathy Ann (Ind) Holy Family Episcopal Church, 11445 Fishers Point Blvd, Fishers IN 46038 **Co-Chair Dioc Anti-Racism Com Dio Indianapolis Indianapolis IN 2014**- B Yokohama Japan 1953 d Francis & Doris. BS Ball St U; BS Ball St U 1976; MSW Indiana U Sch of Soc Wk 1987; MSW Indiana U Sch of Soc Wk 1987; JD Indiana U Sch of Law 2006; JD Indiana U Sch of Law 2006; MTS St Meinrad TS 2014; MTS St Meinrad TS 2015. D 11/3/2012 Bp Cate Waynick. c 1.

SCOTT, David Allan (Va) 3543 SW Ida St, Seattle WA 98126 **Died 1/5/2016** B Providence RI 1936 s Henry & Nora. BA Amh 1958; BD EDS 1961; MA Pr 1965; Tubingen U Tubingen DE 1967; PhD Pr 1968. D 6/24/1961 Bp Robert McConnell Hatch P 12/31/1961 Bp Bravid W Harris. m 10/7/1966 Rosemarie H Hogrebe c 2. Prof Theol & Ethics VTS Alexandria VA 1971-2001; Instr Theol EDS Cambridge MA 1967-1970; Non-par 1964-1966; Mssy S Aug Sch H Cross Mssn Bolahun Liberia 1961-1963. Auth, "Jeremy Taylor & Contemporary Chr Ethics," 1992; Auth, "A Chr Response To Human Sxlty," 1987. Conf Of Angl Theologians 1970-2001; Scholars Engaged w Angl Doctrine 1989-2001.

SCOTT, David Thomas (NwT) Po Box 88, Perryton TX 79070 B Hazel TX 1958 s Boyce & Wanda. W Texas A&M U; BA McMurry U 1980; JD Texas Tech U 1982. D 10/31/1993 P 5/1/1994 Bp Sam Byron Hulsey. m 8/4/1979 Denyce Baucum c 2. S Paul's Epis Ch Dumas TX 2001-2003. St. Geo (BSA) 2004.

SCOTT, Donna Jeanne (Tenn) 404 Siena Drive, Nashville TN 37205 B 1936 d Robert & Virginia. BA SMU 1959; EdS Peabody Coll 1975; Sewanee: The U So, TS 1985; MDiv Van 1985; DMin Wesley Sem Washington DC 1995. D 7/7/1985 P 10/15/1986 Bp George Lazenby Reynolds Jr. m 5/30/2003 John W Eley c 3. S Paul's Ch Franklin TN 1998-2003; P Assoc for Sprtl formation Ch of the Adv Nashville TN 1994-2007; Pstr Counslg (P-t) Ch Of The Adv Nashville TN 1990-1994; S Ann's Ch Nashville TN 1986-1994. Auth, "Caregiver's Bible (NIV) (surrounding material)," Cokesbury, 2008; Co-Auth, "The Eranos Volumes (after C.G. Jung), w Chas E. Scott," *Journ of Rel Stds*, 1983; Ed Asst, "Plato Manuscripts IX-XIII Centuries: A Catalogue," Ya Press, 1960.

SCOTT, Douglas Gordon (Pa) PO Box 1914, Ranchos De Taos NM 87557 **Int R St. Lk the Physcn Epis Ch 2017**- B Philadelphia PA 1949 s Robert & Jean. BA Muskingum Coll 1970; MDiv PDS 1974; STM GTS 1979; MA Penn Coun For Relationships Philadelphia PA 2002; PsyD GTF 2005. D 6/15/1974 P 12/1/1974 Bp Lyman Cunningham Ogilby. m 8/13/1977 Jane Elizabeth Kirkby c

3. R S Mart's Ch Wayne PA 1985-2004; R S Thos Of Cbury Ch Smithtown NY 1980-1984; R Ch Of S Jn The Div Hasbrouck Hts NJ 1977-1980; Cur Ch Of The Atone Tenafly NJ 1975-1977; Dio Pennsylvania Philadelphia PA 1974-1975; Stff Assoc S Mary's Ch Wayne PA 1974-1975. Auth, "There's A War Going On In My Backyard," Ragged Edge Press, 1998; Auth, "Mastering Transitions," Multnomah, 1991.

SCOTT, Edward C (NC) 525 Lake Concord Rd Ne, Concord NC 28025 B Waco TX 1957 s Charles & Ann. BA U NC 1979; MDiv VTS 1986. D 12/14/1986 Bp Robert Whitridge Estill P 12/1/1987 Bp Frank Harris Vest Jr. m 8/18/1984 Noel Elizabeth Rhodes. S Jas Ch Mooresville NC 2006-2012; R All SS' Epis Ch Concord NC 1995-2000; R Trin Ch Mt Airy NC 1989-1995; Asst To The R S Paul's Epis Ch Winston Salem NC 1986-1989.

SCOTT, George Michael (Ga) PO Box 294, Cochran GA 31014 B Raleigh NC 1948 s John & Mary. BA No Carolina St U 1971; MS Georgia St U 1991. D 8/20/2010 Bp Scott Anson Benhase. m 2/20/1999 Nancy Scott c 2.

SCOTT, Horton James (NY) 489 Saint Pauls Pl, Bronx NY 10456 B Freetown, Sierra Leone 1954 s Horton & Cleopatra. BA S Josephs Coll Standish ME 2002; MPS NYTS 2006; MA S Josephs Coll Standish ME 2007. Trans 5/1/2008. c 1. P-in-c S Paul's Ch- Morrisania Bronx NY 2007-2008.

SCOTT, Jack S (WA) 26 Swallow Ct, Falling Waters WV 25419 **Died 4/9/2017** B Roanoke VA 1928 s George & Lucy. BS VPI 1955; BD VTS 1958. D 6/11/1958 P 6/24/1959 Bp William Henry Marmion. c 3. Ret 1994-2017; VTS Alexandria VA 1980-1993; Trst VTS Alexandria VA 1980-1993; R S Jn's Ch Olney MD 1970-1994, 1970-1993; S Andr's Epis Ch Contoocook NH 1965-1970, R 1965-1970; S Thos' Ch Garrison Forest Owings Mills MD 1961-1964, Asst 1961-1964; S Mk's Ch S Paul VA 1958-1961, Vic 1958-1961.

SCOTT JR, James Edward (Tex) 8407 Glenscott St., Houston TX 77061 **Chapl Emer Mnstry to the Port of Houston Houston TX 2001-** B Bay City TX 1935 s James & Fannie. BA Rice U 1957; MDiv Epis TS of the SW 1961. D 7/25/1961 P 2/8/1962 Bp James W Hunter. m 6/2/1957 Carol Ford c 2. S Paul's Ch Houston TX 2006-2007; Int St. Geo's & St. Pat's 2004-2005; S Lk The Evang Houston TX 2001; All SS Epis Ch Hitchcock TX 1996-1999; Vic H Cross Houston TX 1973-1987; Chapl Mnstry to the Port of Houston Houston TX 1972-2001; The Great Cmsn Fndt Houston TX 1972-2001; R S Ptr's Epis Ch Brenham TX 1970-1972; Vic Chr Ch Matagorda TX 1967-1970; S Jn's Epis Ch Palacios TX 1967-1970; R S Geo's Ch Lusk WY 1965-1967; All Souls Ch Kaycee WY 1961-1965; Vic All Souls Edgerton WY 1961-1965; Vic Chr Epis Ch Glenrock WY 1961-1965. Meritorius Serv Awd Houston Intl Seafarers Ctr. 2001; Hal Perry Distinguished Alum Awd Epis TS of the SW 1995.

SCOTT, Jean Pearson (NwT) 1101 Slide Rd., Lubbock TX 79416 B Washington DC d Ivan & Christine. BS U NC 1973; MS U NC 1975; PhD U NC 1979. D 9/20/2008 Bp C Wallis Ohl P 3/27/2009 Bp James Scott Mayer. m 8/12/1973 Gary C Scott c 2.

SCOTT, John Charles (Ala) St Stephens Episcopal Church, PO Box 839, Eutaw AL 35462 B Panama City FL 1938 s Earl & Mildred. BS U of Florida 1962; MDiv Sewanee: The U So, TS 1973; MDiv U So St Lukes Sem 1973. D 6/13/1973 P 5/10/1974 Bp Edward Hamilton West. m 9/5/1959 Sheila Leto Scott c 3. Int R S Agatha's Epis Ch Defuniak Spgs FL 2007-2011; Int R S Lk's Ch Marianna FL 2006-2007; S Barn Ch Lynchburg VA 2000-2003; R Trin Epis Ch Lynchburg VA 2000-2003; R S Nath Ch No Port FL 1990-2000; Cur S Paul's Ch Delray Bch FL 1985-1990; R H Cross Jacksonville FL 1980-1985; S Eliz's Epis Ch Jacksonville FL 1980-1984; Asst Ch Of The Gd Shpd Jacksonville FL 1976-1979; Ch Of The H Comm Hawthorne FL 1973-1976; Vic Dio Florida Jacksonville 1973-1976; Trin Epis Ch Melrose FL 1973-1976. jsscott75@att.net

SCOTT III, John Llewellyn (Alb) 86 Lake Hill Rd, Burnt Hills NY 12027 B Springfield MA 1955 s John & Barbara. BA Bethany Coll 1977; MDiv GTS 1983. D 8/20/1984 Bp Archibald Donald Davies P 6/1/1985 Bp Clarence Cullam Pope Jr. m 7/29/1979 Cynthia Peterson c 4. R Calv Epis Ch Burnt Hills NY 2000-2016; Chr And Zion Par Coun Gilbertsville NY 1996-2000; Dn Susquehanna Dio Albany Greenwich NY 1993-2000, Stndg Com 1997, Dioc Trst 1992-1996, Dioc Coun 1991; Zion Ch Morris NY 1988-1996; Chr Ch Gilbertsville NY 1988-1993; Chapl Bp Davies 1986-1988; Asst S Jn's Ch Ft Worth TX 1986-1988; Asst S Vinc's Cathd Bedford TX 1984-1986.

SCOTT, Keith Elden (RI) 103 Union Ave S, Delmar NY 12054 **P Assoc S Andr's Epis Ch Albany NY 2009-, Int 2000-2009** B Somerset NY 1933 s Ernest & Ruth. BA U Roch 1955; MDiv EDS 1958. D 6/7/1958 Bp Dudley S Stark P 12/14/1958 Bp Roger W Blanchard. m 6/24/1967 Mary P White c 3. P-in-c St Fran Mssn Albany NY 2003-2005; Int Gr Epis Ch Norwalk CT 1999; Int Gr Ch Millbrook NY 1997-1999; Int S Paul's Ch Southington CT 1996-1997; P-in-c Chr Ch Coxsackie NY 1987-1991; R S Ptr's By The Sea Narragansett RI 1969-1978; Assoc Gr Ch In Providence Providence RI 1964-1969; M-in-c S Andr's Epis Ch Cincinnati OH 1961-1964; Asst Chr Epis Ch Of Springfield Springfield OH 1958-1961.

SCOTT, Marshall Stuart (WMo) 1256 W 72nd Ter, Kansas City MO 64114 **St Lk's Chap Kansas City MO 2011-, 1994-2004; Chapl S Lk's So Hosp Overland Pk KS 1998-** B Knoxville TN 1955 s James & Jane. BA U of Tennessee

1976; MDiv Sewanee: The U So, TS 1980. D 3/25/1981 Bp William Evan Sanders P 10/11/1981 Bp William F Gates Jr. m 7/16/1988 Karen L Woods c 2. St Lk's So Chap Overland Pk KS 1994-2011; Assoc Chapl 1994-2001; Henry Ford Cont Care Harper Woods MI 1992-1993; Dio Michigan Detroit MI 1989-1994; Chapl Henry Ford Hosp & Cont Care Detroit MI 1989-1994; Advoc Hlth Care Oak Brook IL 1987-1988; Chapl-in-Res Luth Gnrl Hosp Pk Ridge IL 1987-1988; Chapl Barth Hse Epis Cntr Memphis TN 1984-1987; Dio W Tennessee Memphis 1984-1987; Asst S Jn's Epis Ch Memphis TN 1981-1984; Chapl Res Chld's Memi at Grant Hospitals Chicago IL 1980-1981. Auth, *Caregiver Journ*; Auth, *Journ of Pstr Care*; Auth, *S Lk's Journ of Theol*. Assembly of Epis Healthcare Chapl 1991; Assoc, OHC 1979. mscott@saint-lukes.org

SCOTT, Matthew Rhoades (NwPa) 209 West St, Warren PA 16365 **Vic Trin Memi Ch Warren PA 2010-** B Sliver Spring MD 1975 s Jerry & Brenda. BA U of Connecticut 1997; BS U of Connecticut 1999; MDiv VTS 2007. D 6/9/2007 Bp Andrew Donnan Smith P 12/17/2007 Bp David Colin Jones. m 6/22/2002 Nancy Sue Scott c 2. Assoc R Ch Of The Gd Shpd Burke VA 2007-2010.

SCOTT, Nolie Edward (ETenn) 12026 Pine Cove Dr, Soddy Daisy TN 37379 B Blountsville AL 1939 s Lee & Alma. BS U of Alabama 1962; PhD Pur 1968. D 6/16/2001 Bp Charles Glenn VonRosenberg. m 6/21/1969 Susan Elizabeth McGaghie c 2. D S Alb's Epis Ch Hixson TN 2001-2009.

SCOTT, Norma J (Nev) Po Box 750, Hawthorne NV 89415 **R H Trin 2004-; S Philips-in-the-Desert Hawthorne NV 1992-** B Chico CA 1928 d William & Ruth. D 12/15/1991 P 6/28/1992 Bp Stewart Clark Zabriskie. m 9/25/1954 James Scott.

SCOTT, Peggy King (La) 607 E Main St, New Roads LA 70760 **P-in-c S Mary's Ch Morganza LA 2010-; S Paul's/H Trin New Roads LA 2010-** B Andalusia AL 1949 d William & Johnnie Ruth. BA Samford U 1971; MA Florida St U 1974; MDiv Wycliffe Coll Toronto CA 2009; MDiv Wycliffe Coll/Univ of Toronto/CA 2009. D 12/27/2008 Bp Charles Edward Jenkins III P 7/17/2010 Bp Morris King Thompson Jr. c 2. Dir, Pstr Care Gr Ch Of W Feliciana St Francisvlle LA 2010.

SCOTT, Rebecca Jean (Oly) B Long Beach CA 1943 D 6/25/2005 Bp Vincent Waydell Warner.

SCOTT, Richard Hervey (Oly) 4885 NW Chad Ct, Silverdale WA 98383 **P-in-c St Steph's Epis Ch Oak Harbor WA 2012-** B Seattle WA 1939 s Clayton & Virginia. BA Estrn Washington U 1990; MDiv CDSP 1993. D 5/29/1993 Bp Frank Jeffrey Terry P 1/4/1994 Bp Vincent Waydell Warner. m 7/27/1963 Margaret L Scott c 2. Dir Of Corp. Dio Olympia Seattle 1998-2004, Stndg Com 1996-1999; Vic S Antony Of Egypt Silverdale WA 1993-2007; Dioc Coun Dio Spokane Spokane WA 1987-1988. Chart Property Casualty Underwriters 1989.

SCOTT II, Robert Alfred (Okla) B Shreveport LA 1947 s Robert & Agnes. BA U of Arkansas 1970; MBA U of Arkansas Grad Sch of Bus 1971; Iona Sch of Formation 2017. D 6/30/2017 Bp Edward Joseph Konieczny. m 7/19/1969 Jann Gillespie Jann Torrance Gillespie c 2.

SCOTT, Robert W (Neb) 13054 Thomas Drive, Bellevue NE 68005 **R S Jn Megaunee MI 1989-; Secy 1985-; 1979-** B Omaha NE 1950 s William & Jane. BS K SU 1972; MDiv SWTS 1977. D 6/15/1977 Bp James Daniel Warner P 1/1/1978 Bp James Winchester Montgomery. m 12/14/1974 Catherine F Scott c 3. Ch Of The H Sprt Bellevue NE 1994-2007; Gr Ch Ishpeming MI 1989-1994; R S Jn's Ch Negaunee MI 1989-1994; So Cntrl Reg Manistique MI 1989; Vic Trin Ch Gladstone MI 1982-1988; Dio Nthrn Michigan Marquette MI 1978-1988; S Alb's Ch Manistique MI 1978-1982; Vic S Jude's Ch Curtis MI 1978-1982; Asst St. Andrews Pentecost Epis Ch Evanston IL 1977-1978; Liturg Cmsn Dio Nebraska Omaha NE 1995-1996.

SCOTT, Roger Timothy (Az) D 6/14/1968 P 5/25/1969 Bp John Maury Allin.

SCOTT, Sheila Maria (Mil) 4700 W. Deer Run Dr # 103, Brown Deer WI 53223 B Pankota Romania 1955 d Arpad & Aniko. BSN Marian Coll 1993; MSN U of Phoenix 2007. D 8/28/2010 Bp James Scott Mayer.

SCOTT, Shelby Hudson (Okla) 9119 S 89th E Ave, Broken Arrow OK 74133 **R S Pat's Epis Ch Broken Arrow OK 2000-** B Duncan OK 1963 s George & Ellen. BS SW Oklahoma St U 1984; MDiv SWTS 1990. D 6/23/1990 Bp Robert Manning Moody P 12/23/1990 Bp Francis Campbell Gray. m 5/7/2011 Rebecca Scott c 2. Dio Oklahoma Oklahoma City OK 1996-1999; S Jn Of The Cross Bristol IN 1990-1996. frshelby@saint-patricks.com

SCOTT, Thomas Crawford Hunt (WMich) 2327 park place #2, evanston IL 60201 B Pittsburgh PA 1950 s Walter & Nancy. BA U Pgh 1976; MA MI SU 1978; MDiv EDS 1981; Cert Pittsburgh Pstr Inst Intern 1983; DMin Drew U 1990. D 6/11/1981 P 12/12/1981 Bp Robert Bracewell Appleyard. m 6/10/1978 Dorothy F Scott c 2. R S Paul's Ch Muskegon MI 2008-2013; Dn Evanston Dnry 1999-2002; Dn Evanston Dnry 1992-1994; R S Mk's Ch Evanston IL 1990-2008; R S Andr's Epis Ch Lincoln Pk NJ 1985-1989; Cur Calv Ch Pittsburgh PA 1981-1985. Soc Of S Jn The Evang 1981; Soc of Cath Priests 2014. Cler Grant The Lilly Fndt 2002. tchscott@aol.com

SCOTT JR, William Tayloe (Cal) 95 Winfield St, San Francisco CA 94110 **Vic S Cyp's Ch San Francisco CA 2009-** B Harrisonburg VA 1979 s William & Rebecca. BA Simons Rock Coll of Bard 2000; MDiv VTS 2004. D 6/26/2004 P 1/10/2005 Bp Peter J Lee. m 10/14/2008 Matthew Chayt. Dio California San

S

Francisco CA 2011; Assoc Gr Cathd San Francisco CA 2006-2010; Assoc S Jn's Epis Ch Mc Lean VA 2004-2006.

SCOTT-HAMBLEN, Shane (NY) 1 Chestnut St, Cold Spring NY 10516 **Mem Liturg Cmsn 2005-; Mem Bdgt/Fin Com 2004-; Mem Dioc Coun 2003-; Chapl Cold Sprg Fire Dep'T 2002-; Reg Dn No Hudson Dnry 2002-; R S Mary's Ch Cold Sprg NY 2002-** B Lawrenceburg IN 1966 s Jerry & Linda. ThD GTS; BMus Webster U 1989; S Louis U 1991; STB Pontifical U of S Thos Aquinas Angelicum IT 1994; MA Pontifical U of St Thos Aquinas 1995; STL Pontifical U of St Thos Aquinas 1996. Rec 12/18/1999 Bp Cate Waynick. c 3. S Paul's Epis Ch Evansville IN 1999-2002; Serv Ch Of Engl 1996-2002. Auth, "Martha's Old Mistake," *LivCh*, 2003.

SCOTTO, Vincent Francis (SwFla) 23465 Harborview Rd Apt634, Port Charlotte FL 33980 B New York NY 1948 s Frank & Vivian. BFA New York Inst of Tech 1970; LTh CDSP 1974. D 6/8/1974 Bp Paul Moore Jr P 12/21/1974 Bp Harold Louis Wright. m 10/15/2005 Kathleen Scotto c 2. Dn Dio SW Florida Parrish FL 1995-2000, Dioc Coun 1990-1994, Epis Nomntns Com 1987-1989; R Ch Of The Gd Shpd Punta Gorda FL 1986-2010; Chapl Yates Cnty Correctional Facility Penn Yan NY 1981-1983; Vic S Mk's Epis Ch Penn Yan NY 1979-1986; S Lk's Ch Branchport NY 1979-1981; Asst Gr Epis Ch Nyack NY 1977-1979; Cur Zion Epis Ch Wappingers Falls NY 1974-1976. Amer. Soc on Aging 1998; ISL 1995; Int Mnstry Ntwk 1999; RWF 1979; Soc. for Study of Myth & Tradition 1998; Via Media 2004.

SCRANTON, Susan Lee (Los) 1420 E Foothill Blvd, Glendora CA 91741 **R Gr Epis Ch Glendora CA 1997-** B Monterey Park CA 1954 d James & Marilyn. BMus USC 1976; MM USC 1978; Fuller TS 1992; MDiv VTS 1994. D 6/11/1994 Bp Chester Lovelle Talton P 1/1/1995 Bp Frederick Houk Borsch. Asst S Ptr's Par San Pedro CA 1994-1997.

SCRIBNER, Jean Mary (Neb) 1725 Old Haywood Rd., Asheville NC 28806 B Appleton WI 1944 d Charles & Mary. BMus U of Wisconsin 1969; MMus U of Washington 1973; MDiv SWTS 1983. D 1/23/1987 P 11/24/1987 Bp Rustin Ray Kimsey. Beatrice Cmnty Hosp Beatrice NE 1997-2006; Supply Dio Oregon Portland OR 1990-1995; Sr Stff Chapl Legacy Gd Samar Hosp Portland OR 1990-1995; Ch of the Medtr Harbert MI 1988-1990; R S Aug Of Cbury Epis Ch Benton Harbor MI 1988-1989; Pstr Asst Methodist Ch 1984-1988. Auth, "Wmn Uncommon Prayers," Morehouse Pub, 2000. AAPC, Par Assoc 1992; Assembly Of Epis Healthcare Chapl, Past Pres 2004-2007; Assn of Profsnl Chapl, Bd-Cert Chapl 1992.

SCRIVEN, Elizabeth A (Mo) 2309 Packard St, Ann Arbor MI 48104 **Chapl Dio Missouri S Louis MO 2015-** B Cleveland OH 1980 d Peter & Laurel. BA Smith 2003; MDiv SWTS 2007. D 6/9/2007 Bp Mark Hollingsworth Jr P 10/18/2008 Bp David Charles Bowman. Assoc S Clare Of Assisi Epis Ch Ann Arbor MI 2008-2015. beth@rockwellhouse.org

SCRIVENER, William Eugene (SO) 7193 Foxview Dr, Cincinnati OH 45230 **Hon Cn Chr Ch Cathd 2005-; Chair Cincinnati Chld's Hosp Bio-Ethics Com 2011-** B Munich West Germany 1947 s Wayne & Helen. BA Leh 1969; MDiv ETS 1973. D 6/9/1973 Bp Joseph Warren Hutchens P 2/1/1974 Bp Morgan Porteus. m 6/14/1975 Luvenia Pace c 3. Sr Dir Pstr Care Chld's Hosp Med Cntr Cincinnati OH 1990-2015; Dir Pstr Care Stamford Hosp Stamford CT 1983-1990; Chapl Coordntr Cpe Chld Memi Hosp Grant Hosp Chicago IL 1981-1983; Zion Epis Ch N Branford CT 1977-1981; Cur Gr Epis Ch Norwalk CT 1973-1975; Pres ACPE 2009-2010; Chair ACPE Certification Cmsn 2000-2002; Com On Oversight & Exam Dio Connecticut Meriden CT 1984-1990, Asst To Dir Ordinands Trng Prog 1977-1983. Contrib, "Bioethics Educ In A Pediatric Med Cntr," 2000. ACPE Supvsr 1980; Assn Of Profsnl Chapl, Bd Cert Chapl 1985-2017.

SCRUGGS JR, Charles Perry (ETenn) 540 Bryant Rd, Chattanooga TN 37405 B Jacksonville FL 1949 s Charles & Eleanor. BA Florida St U 1971; MDiv VTS 1974. D 6/4/1974 Bp Edward Hamilton West P 5/4/1975 Bp Frank S Cerveny. m 5/23/1998 Sue E Scruggs c 2. Assoc Ch Of The Gd Shpd Lookout Mtn TN 1994-2004; Ch Of The Gd Shpd Raleigh NC 1990-1993; Chapl ETSU-Dio E TN Johnson City TN 1987-1990; Epis U Mnstry Johnson City TN 1987-1990; Vic S Mk's Epis Ch Troy AL 1983-1987; H Innoc Ch Atlanta GA 1977-1983; H Innoc' Epis Sch Atlanta GA 1977-1979; Asst Ch Of The Adv Tallahassee FL 1974-1977.

SCRUTCHINS, Arthur Paul (Okla) Holland Hall School, 5666 E 81st St, Tulsa OK 74137 **Holland Hall Sch Tulsa OK 2005-; Upper Sch Chapl Holland Hall Tulsa OK 2005-** B Oklahoma City OK 1956 s James & Glenda. Cert of Rel Stds Sch of Iona; BA Oklahoma Bapt U 1980; EFM Sewanee: The U So, TS 1987. D 7/1/1987 Bp William Jackson Cox P 5/19/2014 Bp Edward Joseph Konieczny. m 3/13/2004 Ramona Carole Scrutchins c 2. Dio Oklahoma Oklahoma City OK 2010, 2009, 2008, Mem of Dioc Bdgt Com 2010-, Chair of Oklahoma Cmsn of Epis Schools 2008-; Emm Epis Ch Shawnee OK 1999-2005; Chapl Shawnee Police OK 1989-2005. Auth, "Friend of Crime Fighters," *LivCh*. ascrutchins@hollandhall.org

✠ SCRUTON, The Rt Rev Gordon (WMass) 40 Carriage Hill Dr, Wethersfield CT 06109 **Bp Protector Third Ord SSF 2003-** B Rochester NH 1947 s Paul & Marjorie. BA Barrington Coll 1968; ThM Bos 1971. D 6/5/1971 Bp John S Higgins P 1/30/1972 Bp Frederick Hesley Belden Con 10/12/1996 for WMass. m 6/15/1968 Rebecca Polley Scruton c 2. Ret Bp of Wstrn Massachusetts Dio Wstrn Massachusetts Springfield 2012, Bp of Wstrn Massachusetts 1996-2012, Cong Dvlmnt Comm 1987-1996, EFM Coordntr 1984-1986, Chair, Sp Life Comm 1979-1987, Dn, N. Berk Dnry 1979-1981; Mem Stndg Cmsn on Rel. Ord & Communities 2009-2012; Mem SCWM 2006-2009; Mem Stndg Commision on Stwdshp & Dvlpmt 2000-2006; Superior Fllshp of the Way of the Cross 1986-1996; R S Fran Ch Holden MA 1981-1996; R Gr Ch Dalton MA 1977-1981; Asst S Paul's Ch N Kingstown RI 1975-1977; Asst S Mk's Epis Ch Riverside RI 1971-1975; COM Dio Rhode Island Providence RI 1974-1977, Evang Comm 1973-1976. Auth, "Pstr's Sp Life," *New Engl Ch Resource Handbook*, 1980; Auth, "arts," *Living Ch*. FVC 1973. gpscruton@gmail.com

SCULLY, Edward Anthony (SwFla) 311 Irwin Ave, Albion MI 49224 **P-in-c S Eliz's Epis Ch Zephyrhills FL 2009-** B San Francisco CA 1940 s Edward & Bernice. BA U of San Francisco 1973; MA U of San Francisco 1975; MDiv EDS 1987. Trans 12/1/1989. m 11/21/1981 Susan Scully c 2. Dio Wstrn Michigan Kalamazoo MI 1999-2002; R S Jas' Epis Ch Of Albion Albion MI 1994-2009; S Jn's Ch Fremont MI 1989-1994; R S Mk's Ch Newaygo MI 1989-1990; Serv Angl Ch Of Can 1987-1989. Acad Par Cleric; Amer Acad Mnstry; Associated Parishes; ADLMC; Conf Of S Ben; Life Mem Of Amer Assn For Respiratory Care; Liturg Conf; No Amer Catechumenal Con; No Amer Forum On Catechumenate; Ord Of S Lk. Outstanding Young Man Of Amer.

SCUPHOLME, Anne (SeFla) 1990 English Oaks Cir N, Charlottesville VA 22911 **D St. Paul's Memi Ch 2004-** B Whitby UK 1942 d Albert & Kathleen. BA Florida Intl U 1986; MA U of Miami 1989. D 9/11/1998 Bp Calvin Onderdonk Schofield Jr. D Trin Cathd Miami FL 1998-2000; D Blue Ridge Mtn. ACNM; ACOG; APHA; NAAD.

SEABURY, Scott Hamor (WMass) 10 Rawlings Brook Rd, Suffield CT 06078 B New York NY 1952 s Raymond & Helen. BA U of Massachusetts 1974; MDiv Ya Berk 1983. D 9/18/1983 P 4/1/1984 Bp Alexander D Stewart. m 4/10/1976 Linda Williams c 1. Chr Formation Mssnr S Chris's Ch Fairview Chicopee MA 2008-2016; Dio Wstrn Massachusetts Springfield 2003-2007, 2000-2002, 1983-1999, Secy of Conv & Dioc Coun 2012-, 2008-2011; Asst R S Dav's Ch Feeding Hills MA 2000-2002; R All SS Ch So Hadley MA 1993-1999; R S Barn And All SS Ch Springfield MA 1986-1993; Asst S Paul's Ch Holyoke MA 1983-1986.

SEADALE, Vincent Gerald (Mass) **S Andr's Ch Edgartown MA 2009-** B Brooklyn NY 1960 s Vincent & Joyce. BA Colg 1982; JD U of Connecticut 1988; MDiv Ya Berk 2004. D 6/12/2004 Bp Andrew Donnan Smith P 2/24/2005 Bp Samuel Johnson Howard. m 5/28/1983 Colleen M Seadale c 3. R The Epis Ch of The Redeem Jacksonville FL 2007-2009; Chr Epis Ch Ponte Vedra FL 2005-2007.

✠ SEAGE, The Rt Rev Brian (Miss) 106 Vinson Cv, Madison MS 39110 **Bp of Mississippi Dio Mississippi Jackson MS 2014-** B Thousand Oaks CA 1963 s Richard & Mary Ann. BA Pepperdine U 1986; MDiv Epis TS of the SW 1997. D 6/21/1997 Bp Chester Lovelle Talton P 1/17/1998 Bp Frederick Houk Borsch Con 9/27/2014 for Miss. m 10/14/1995 Kyle Dice c 2. R S Columb's Ch Ridgeland MS 2005-2014; R S Thos Epis Ch Diamondhead MS 1997-2005; Dir Yth Mnstry S Patricks Ch And Day Sch Thousand Oaks CA 1990-1994. brseage@dioms.org

SEAGE, Kyle Dice (Miss) 106 Vinson Cv, Madison MS 39110 **P-in-c S Phil's Ch Jackson MS 2010-** B Topeka KS 1966 d Joseph & Patricia. BA U So 1988; MDiv Epis TS of the SW 1996. D 6/22/1996 P 4/22/1997 Bp Alfred Marble Jr. m 10/14/1995 Brian Seage c 2. All SS Ch Inverness MS 2009-2010; Dio Mississippi Jackson MS 2005-2008, Dvlpmt Dir 2005-; Int Chr Ch Bay S Louis MS 2003-2005; Devlp Dir S Fran Acad Picayune MS 2000-2002; S Fran Cmnty Serv Inc. Salina KS 2000-2002; Assoc R S Jn's Epis Ch Pascagoula MS 1997-2000.

SEAGLE, Teresa Ryan (Fla) 301 Brooks Cir E, Jacksonville FL 32211 **P Jacksonville Epis HS Jacksonville FL 2013-** B Decatur IL 1966 d Charles & Barbara. BA U of No Florida 1990; MEd U of No Florida 1999; MDiv Sewanee: The U So, TS 2008. D 6/1/2008 Bp Samuel Johnson Howard. m 11/20/2010 Keith Thomas Seagle. S Paul's Epis Ch Jacksonville FL 2011-2013; R S Fran Of Assisi Epis Ch Tallahassee FL 2008-2011.

SEAL, Chris Houston (NCal) 201 Nevada St, Nevada City CA 95959 **R H Trin Ch Nevada City CA 1994-** B Long Beach CA 1950 s William & Betty. AB Occ 1972; MDiv CDSP 1981. D 6/21/1981 P 1/10/1982 Bp Robert Claflin Rusack. m 1/7/1983 Gae Seal c 4. R of Etton w Helpston Ch of Engl 1988-1994; Vic Chr The King Quincy CA 1983-1988; Cur S Mk's Par Glendale CA 1981-1983; Dn, Sierra Reg Dnry The Epis Dio Nthrn California Sacramento CA 2011-2013, Chair, Congrl Dvlpmt T/F 2000-2007, Dioc Coun 1996-2010. Auth, "Post Reformation Monuments," *Monuments in Cambridgeshire Ch 1530-1994*, Paul Watkins Pub., 1997. Assoc Alum Nash 1997; Oblate Benedictine Camaldolese Ord (RC) 1985. Hon Cn, St. Ptr's Cathd Dio Kinkiizi, Uganda 2008; Colonel Aide De Camp St of Tennessee 1992.

SEALES, Hea Suk (Ala) **H Trin Epis Ch Auburn AL 2017-** D 5/24/2015 Bp Santosh K Marray.

SEALS, William Frederick (CFla) 23 Surrey Run, Hendersonville NC 28791 B Miami OK 1939 s Denver & Louise. BS Oklahoma St U 1961. D 6/12/1995 Bp John Lewis Said. m 7/10/1983 Treva Lynn Seals c 2. D Gloria Dei Epis Ch Cocoa FL 1996-2003; S Jas Epis Ch Hendersonvlle NC 1996-2002; Chapl Henderson Cnty Sheriffs Dept 1995-1996; D S Jas The Fisherman Islamorada FL 1995-1996.

SEAMAN, Kelly S (NH) 52 Gould Rd, New London NH 03257 **S Andr's Ch New London NH 2015-** B Aberdeen MD 1963 d Lorna. AB Davidson Coll 1985; MA U of Virginia 1987; Cert of Angl Stds CDSP 2015. D 6/6/2015 P 12/21/2015 Bp A Robert Hirschfeld. m 7/28/1990 David M Seaman c 3. Epis Hosp Chapl Hanover NH 2015-2016; S Thos Ch Hanover NH 2015-2016.

SEAMAN, Martha Lee (Az) 7419 E Palm Ln, Scottsdale AZ 85257 B Dearborn MI 1952 d Allen & Janet. BA MI SU 1974; JD Wayne 1977. D 10/9/2004 Bp Robert Reed Shahan. c 2. D Epis Ch Of The Trsfg Mesa AZ 2007-2014.

SEAMANS, Timothy Joseph Sommer (At) **Epis HS Alexandria VA 2017-; H Innoc' Epis Sch Atlanta GA 2016-** D 12/19/2015 P 6/25/2016 Bp Robert Christopher Wright.

SEARLE, S Elizabeth (Nwk) 200 W 79th St Apt 14-P, New York NY 10024 B Wichita KS 1947 d Oscar & Maxine. BA Wichita St U 1976; JD Harv 1979; MDiv EDS 1998. D 6/13/1998 P 12/19/1998 Bp Richard Frank Grein. Chr Ch Ridgewood NJ 2006-2010; S Jn's Ch New City NY 2004-2005; Assoc Chr Ch Bronxville NY 2000-2004; Asst R All SS Ch New York NY 1998-2000.

SEARS III, Albert Nelson (Mass) 98 Ridgewood Dr, Rocky Hill CT 06067 **Asst S Paul Cathd 1971-** B Brockton MA 1941 s Albert & Beulah. BA Estrn Nazarene Coll 1964; MDiv Ya Berk 1969. D 5/26/1971 Bp John Melville Burgess P 5/1/1972 Bp Morris Fairchild Arnold. Ch Of Our Sav Middleboro MA 2001-2004; Dio Massachusetts Boston MA 1973-1976.

SEARS, Barbara (Md) 7030 Upland Ridge Dr, Adamstown MD 21710 B Orange NJ 1925 d Ralf & Mary. Swarthmore Coll 1945; BS NYU 1949. D 6/3/1989 Bp Alden Moinet Hathaway. m 11/28/1953 Kenneth Avard Brown c 3. D S Jas Epis Ch Mt Airy MD 2009-2011; D-At-Lg 1998-2000; Chapl Franklin Cnty Sheriff's Dept 1995-1998; D/Asst Otey Memi Par Ch Sewanee TN 1990-1993; Asst S Thos' Epis Ch Canonsburg PA 1989-1990. Cmnty S Mary 96-; NAAD.

SEARS, Barbara Anne (Md) 1000 Weller Cir Apt 221, Westminster MD 21158 **D Ch Of The Ascen Westminster MD 2012-** B Baltimore MD 1946 d Earl & Margaret. BA Wstrn Maryland Coll 1966; MA Morgan St U 1971; EFM Sewanee: The U So, TS 1994. D 6/10/1995 Bp Charles Lindsay Longest. m 10/11/1969 William Norman Sears. D S Jas Epis Ch Mt Airy MD 2009-2012; D Geo Ch Hampstead MD 2001-2009; D S Jas Ch Monkton MD 1998-2001; Chapl Carroll Hosp Cntr Westminster MD 1995-2010; D Ch Of The Trsfg Braddock Heights MD 1995-1998. NAAD 1995.

SEARS, Gwen W (WMass) 235 Walker St. Apt. 162, Lenox MA 01240 **D S Steph's Ch Pittsfield MA 1981-** B Rhinebeck NY 1928 d Clarence & Helen. AA Virginia Intermont Coll 1947. D 10/9/1982 Bp Alexander D Stewart. m 6/5/1948 Noel Sears c 4. Ret.

SEATON, Anne Christine (Az) 168 W Arizona St, Holbrook AZ 86025 B Concordia KS 1958 d Gerald & Anna. BSN Marymount Coll 1981; MSN Ft Hays St U 2004; MDiv Nash 2015. D 6/7/2014 P 12/16/2014 Bp Kirk Stevan Smith. m 9/17/1998 Robert Deane Seaton. P-in-c S Geo's Epis Ch Holbrook AZ 2014-2015.

SEATON, Robert Deane (WK) 137 Aspen Rd, Salina KS 67401 **D Chr Cathd Salina KS 2001-** B Iola KS 1949 s Deane & Martha. BA U of Kansas 1971; MD U of Kansas 1978. D 11/30/2001 Bp Vernon Edward Strickland P 3/1/2003 Bp James Marshall Adams Jr. m 9/17/1998 Anne Christine Seaton.

SEATVET, John (WK) St Cornelius Episcopal Church, 200 W Spruce St, Dodge City KS 67801 B Ft. Campbell KY 1954 s Lloyd & Dana. MMin Nash; BA U of Wisconsin - Milwaukee. D 12/12/2015 P 9/3/2016 Bp Mike Milliken. m 12/31/1999 Jeanette L Seatvet c 2.

SEAVER, Maurice Blanchard (WNC) 3500 Carmel Rd, Charlotte NC 28226 **Asst To Vic S Mary 1976-** B Johnson City TN 1927 s Wiley & Barbara. Astc 1948; No Carolina St U 1949. D 6/12/1976 Bp William Gillette Weinhauer. m 2/4/1949 Bobbie Nell Brown c 2.

SEAVEY, Suzanne E (ETenn) 135 Fountainhead Ct, Lenoir City TN 37772 B Houston TX 1946 d Albert & Bernice. BA U GA 1968; MDiv SWTS 1990. D 6/16/1990 P 12/15/1990 Bp Frank Tracy Griswold III. Ch Of The Resurr Loudon TN 2002-2006; Asst R Ch Of The Ascen Hickory NC 1999-2002; H Sprt Ch Indianapolis IN 1995-1999; Dio Indianapolis Indianapolis IN 1995, Vic New Ch Dvlpment 1995-1999; Int S Ambr Ch Chicago Hts IL 1993-1995; Int Gr Epis Ch New Lenox IL 1992; S Chas Ch St. Chas IL 1990-1992; Assoc St. Chas Epis Ch St. Chas IL 1990-1992.

SEAY, Donald Robert (CFla) 247 N Main St #14, Dousman WI 53118 **Hon R St. Jn's Chrys Delafield WI 1999-; Ret 1991-** B Lebanon OH 1926 s Curtis & Anna. BA U of Kentucky 1950; MDiv Nash 1976. D 5/15/1976 Bp Quintin Ebenezer Primo Jr P 11/1/1976 Bp James Winchester Montgomery. m 3/17/1948 Carol Powell c 3. R S Fran Of Assisi Epis Ch Lake Placid FL 1986-1991;

Assoc R Gr Epis Ch Of Ocala Ocala FL 1983-1986; Ch Of The Resurr Blue Sprg MO 1978-1983; Dio W Missouri Kansas City MO 1978-1983; Vic S Mich's Epis Ch Independence MO 1978-1982; Gr Ch Sterling IL 1976-1978; Vic The Ch Of S Anne Morrison IL 1976-1978. CHS Ord of S Fran, Cath C.

SEBRO, Jacqueline Marie (ECR) 815 Sycamore Canyon Rd, Paso Robles CA 93446 **Dir Loaves & Fishes Paso Robles CA 1995-; D-In-Res S Jas Ch Paso Robles CA 1994-** B San Bernardino CA 1956 d William & Barbara. BS California St Polytechnic U 1978; MA Epis TS of the SW 1993; Cert California Sch for Deacons 1994. D 7/9/1994 Bp Matthew Paul Bigliardi.

SECAUR, Stephen Charles (Mil) 435 SOM Center Rd., Mayfield Village OH 44143 **S Barth's Ch Cleveland OH 2012-; P-in-c St. Jn's Cntr TX/Chr Ch. 2011-** B Lincoln NE 1944 s Charles & Frances. MDiv SWTS 1981. D 6/29/1981 P 12/29/1981 Bp Robert Marshall Anderson. m 3/15/1969 Nancy K Secaur. P-in-c S Paul's Woodville TX 2004-2011; P-in-c S Lk's Ch Whitewater WI 1999-2004; R Trin Ch Baraboo WI 1993-1999; Vic S Steph's Ch Mt Carmel PA 1990-1993; R H Trin Epis Ch Shamokin PA 1988-1993; Assoc Ch Of Our Sav Akron OH 1987-1988; R S Mk's Epis Ch Wadsworth OH 1984-1986; P-in-c Chr Ch Duluth MN 1981-1984; R S Andr's Ch Cloquet MN 1981-1984. OHC. frstephen.saintbartohio@gmail.com

SECOR, Neale Alan (Pa) 4 Appletree Ct, Philadelphia PA 19106 B Peekskill NY 1934 s Allen & Edith. Amer U 1955; BA Drew U 1956; JD U Chi 1959; MDiv UTS 1966; The New Sch 1980. D 6/11/1966 P 12/10/1966 Bp Horace W B Donegan. m 9/17/2011 Ricardo A Liriano c 2. Sum P in charge Ch Of The Redeem Longport NJ 1997-2000; Shattuck-S Mary's Sch Faribault MN 1996; Dir Seaman's Ch Inst Philadelphia Philadelphia PA 1985-1997; Dir Seamens Ch Inst Philadelphia PA 1985-1996; Port Mssr Seaman's Ch Inst NY & NJ Port Newark NJ 1980-1984; Port Newark Dir Seamens Ch Inst New York NY 1980-1984; R S Mary's Manhattanville Epis Ch New York NY 1976-1980; YA Min Glide Fndt San Francisco CA 1964-1965; Yth Min Methodist Ch 1964-1965; Pstr Untd Ch of Chr Crested Butte CO 1963; Co-Chair, Cler Disciplinary Comm. Dio Pennsylvania Philadelphia PA 2010-2011; Judge of Elctns City of Philadelphia Philadelphia PA 2009-2012; Bd Dir Cetana Chld's Fndt Princeton NJ 2007-2010; Bd Dir Wrld Trade Assn. Philadelphia PA 1993-1996; Chair, Dioc Property Comm. Dio New York New York NY 1970-1972. Auth, "Brief for a Homosexual Ethic," *The Same Sex*, Pilgrim Press, 1967; Co-Auth, "Taxation of Ch Property," *Law and Rel*, Seabury Press, 1965. Man-of-the-Year Wrld Trade Assn 1996.

SEDDON, Anne Christine (Ct) 4 Maybury Rd, Suffield CT 06078 B Dorchester MA 1946 d Ejnar & Anne. BA S Marys Coll So Bend IN 1968; MDiv Maryknoll TS 1983. D 6/14/1986 P 12/27/1986 Bp Arthur Edward Walmsley. m 6/29/1968 John Seddon c 3. R Ch Of The Gd Shpd Shelton CT 1989-1997; Guesthouse Dir H Cross Monstry W Pk NY 1986-1989; H Cross Monstry W Pk NY 1986-1988. SBL, AAR.

SEDDON, Matthew T (Tex) St. John's Episcopal Church, 11201 Parkfield Drive, Austin TX 78758 **S Jn's Epis Ch Austin TX 2014-** B Ithaca NY 1968 s Thomas & Jeanette. BA U Chi 1990; PhD U Chi 1998; MDiv CDSP 2012; MDiv CDSP 2012. D 6/9/2012 P 12/15/2012 Bp Scott Byron Hayashi. m 8/15/1998 Heather K Stettler c 1. Dio Utah Salt Lake City UT 2012-2014. Phi Beta Kappa Phi Beta Kappa 1990. revmatt@austinstjohns.org

SEDGWICK, Roger Stephen (O) 647 Reid Ave, Lorain OH 44052 B Melrose Park IL 1946 s Roger & Virginia. BA Lawr 1967; STB GTS 1970. D 6/13/1970 Bp James Winchester Montgomery P 12/17/1970 Bp William Jones Gordon Jr. m 8/30/1991 Carol M Sedgwick c 1. Ch Of The Gd Shpd Lyndhurst OH 2009-2012; R Ch Of The Redeem Lorain OH 2000-2009; Epis W Side Shared Mnstry Cleveland OH 1994-2000; S Mk's Ch Cleveland OH 1994-1998; Int Trin Ch Excelsior MN 1992-1993; Int Trin Ch Anoka MN 1990-1992; Dio Minnesota Minneapolis MN 1987-1988; S Barth's Epis Ch Bemidji MN 1983-1990; Int Chr Ch Hackensack NJ 1982-1983; Vic SS Mary And Mk Epis Ch Oakes ND 1977-1980; St Marks Ch Oakes ND 1977-1980; Gd Shpd Lakota ND 1975-1977; Dio Alaska Fairbanks AK 1970-1973; P-in-c S Mk's Ch Nenana AK 1970-1973. RWF Pres 1987-1990.

SEDLACEK, Carol Westerberg (Ore) 2103 Desiree Pl, Lebanon OR 97355 **Cn for Chr and Ldrshp Formation Dio Oregon Portland OR 2016-, Mssnr for Camping and Yth Mnstry 2013-2016, 2005-2013** B Astoria OR 1966 d Robert & Grace. BS OR SU 1990; MDiv VTS 1994. D 5/28/1994 P 11/29/1994 Bp Robert Louis Ladehoff. m 4/20/1996 Wes Sedlacek. Assoc R S Mart's Ch Lebanon OR 2002-2014; S Fran Ch Sweet Hm OR 2002-2007; The Epis Ch Of The Gd Samar Corvallis OR 2002-2005; Assoc R The Ch of the Gd Shpd Austin TX 1999-2002; Assoc R S Barth's Ch Beaverton OR 1994-1999.

SEDLACEK, Wes (Ore) 2103 Desiree Pl, Lebanon OR 97355 **Chapl Samar Lebanon Cmnty Hosp Lebanon OR 2012-; Chapl Samar Albany Gnrl Hosp Albany OR 2005-; Chapl Samar Albany Gnrl Hosp Albany OR 2005-** B Oregon City OR 1971 s Lawrence & Janice. BA U of Portland 1993; MDiv Epis TS of the SW 2002. D 6/19/2002 P 12/28/2002 Bp Robert Louis Ladehoff. m 4/20/1996 Carol Westerberg. Asst The Epis Ch Of The Gd Samar Corvallis OR 2002-2005; Dio Oregon Portland OR 1994-1999, GC Dep 2013-2016, GC Dep 2010-2013, GC Dep 2007-2010, GC Dep 2004-2007, COM 2003-2008,

S

Dioc Coun 1995-1997, Yth Mnstry Cmsn 1994-1997. Bd Cert Chapl Assn of Profsnl Chapl 2010. wsedlacek@samhealth.org

SEDWICK, Katherine L (Oly) 5128 40th Avenue South, Minneapolis MN 55417 **R S Mich And All Ang Ch Issaquah WA 2013-; R St. Lk's Epis Ch Minneapolis MN 2007-** B St Louis MO 1961 d Eldred & Ann. BA U of Washington 1998; MDiv Seattle U 2002. D 6/28/2003 P 1/17/2004 Bp Sanford Zangwill Kaye Hampton. m 4/14/1984 John Michael Sedwick c 2. S Lk's Ch Minneapolis MN 2006-2013; Trin Par Seattle WA 2003-2006; CoChair of COM Dio Minnesota Minneapolis MN 2006-2011. "Reporting on AAC in Plano," *The Voice*, Dio Olympia, 2003.

SEEBECK, William Bernard (NY) 23 Randolph Pl., Unit 204, Northampton MA 01060 **Died 12/13/2015** B San Francisco CA 1950 s John & Margaret. Manhattan Coll 1970; Ford 1972. D 6/29/1990 Bp Richard Frank Grein. m 10/5/1985 Joan Elizabeth Seebeck c 2. New York Dioc Coun 1992-1993; Vice-Chair Westchester Shore IPC 1991-1993; D Trin S Paul's Epis New Rochelle NY 1990-2015. NAAD.

SEEBER, Laurian (Vt) 47 Shadow Lang Berlin, Barre VT 05641 **Vic S Dunst's Epis Mssn Waitsfield VT 2011-** B Cambridge MA 1938 d Robert & Dorothea. BA U of Kansas 1959; MA U NC 1963; PhD U NC 1973; MA EDS 1978. D 11/16/1992 P 6/13/1993 Bp Daniel Lee Swenson. Asst to the R Chr Ch Montpelier VT 2000-2009; Pstr Assoc S Ptr's Ch Port Chester NY 1999-2000; Pstr Assoc S Barn Ch Ardsley NY 1996-1998; Loc P S Paul's Ch Canaan VT 1993-1996.

SEEFELDT, Scott Allen (Mil) **Zion Epis Ch Oconomowoc WI 2016-** B Wausau WI 1975 s Charles & Ann. BD U of Wisconsin 1999; MDiv Nash 2007. D 6/2/2007 P 12/8/2007 Bp Steven Andrew Miller. m 11/13/1999 Stephanie L Seefeldt c 4. R Trin Ch Baraboo WI 2009-2016; Asst S Mich's Epis Ch Racine WI 2007-2009; Camus Stff Worker Intervarsity Chr Fllshp 1999-2004.

SEEGER, Elisabeth Ann (Oly) 4467 S. 172nd St., SeaTac WA 98188 B Buffalo NY 1945 d Willard & Patricia. BA U of Washington 1971; MDiv CDSP 1991. D 6/18/1991 P 2/13/1992 Bp Vincent Waydell Warner. R S Eliz's Ch Seattle WA 2013-2014, 2005-2006; Int Chr Epis Ch Puyallup WA 2005; R St Ptr's Epis Par Seattle WA 2002-2005; R S Paul's Epis Ch Sacramento CA 1994-2002; Vic H Fam of Jesus Cambodian Seattle WA 1992-1994; Vic H Fam of Jesus Epis Ch Tacoma WA 1992-1993; Assoc S Paul Epis Ch Bellingham WA 1991. Celtic Cross Soc.

SEEGER, Sue Fisher (Mass) 28 Seagrave Rd, Cambridge MA 02140 B Natick MA 1939 d Alvan & Florence. BA Mid 1961; EdM Harv 1987; Massachusetts Diac Formation Prog 2005. D 6/3/2006 Bp M(Arvil) Thomas Shaw. D S Jn's Ch Charlestown (Boston) Charlestown MA 2007-2012; D Chr Ch Cambridge Cambridge MA 2006-2007; Prog Mgr, Textbook Ed Ginn And Co 1963-1986.

SEEKINS, Sheila Anne (Me) D 6/14/2014 P 5/6/2017 Bp Stephen Taylor Lane.

SEELEY, Janet Lynne (Wyo) D 6/11/2014 P 2/14/2015 Bp John Smylie.

SEELEY JR, Walt (Wyo) 2024 Rolling Hills Road, Kemmerer WY 83101 **S Jn's Ch Green River WY 2017-; P S Jas Ch Kemmerer WY 2000-** B Charleston SC 1955 s Walter & Alma. BS U of Wyoming 1981. D 5/16/2000 P 12/6/2000 Bp Bruce Caldwell. m 8/6/1977 Janet Lynne Seeley c 2. Mnstry Dvlp Dio Wyoming Casper 2010-2016. seeley@hamsfork.net

SEELY, Shirley Ann (EMich) 3201 Gratiot Ave, Port Huron MI 48060 **Assoc S Paul's Epis Ch Port Huron MI 2008-** B Bay City MI 1935 d Russell & Laura. RN Sparrow Hosp 1956. D 6/7/2008 P 12/13/2008 Bp Steven Todd Ousley. c 4.

SEELYE FOREST, Elizabeth Jane (Mich) 14191 Ivanhoe Dr Apt 3, Sterling Heights MI 48312 B 1948 D 6/20/2001 Bp Wendell Nathaniel Gibbs Jr. m 5/20/2001 Raymond Forest c 1. D S Steph's Ch Troy MI 2001-2012.

SEFCHICK, Frank Stephen (Be) 1498 Quakake Rd, Weatherly PA 18255 B Chester PA 1949 s Frank & Justine. BS Tem 1973; PharmD Broadmore U 2001. D 9/21/1994 P 9/19/1995 Bp James Michael Mark Dyer. c 2. S Mart-In-The-Fields Mtn Top PA 2003-2007; .

SEFTON, Kate (NCal) D 8/13/2016 Bp Barry Leigh Beisner.

SEGAL, D(anna) Joy (Pa) 916 South Swanson Street, Philadelphia PA 19147 **R Gloria Dei Ch Philadelphia PA 2006-; Dioc Coun Mem Dio Pennsylvania Philadelphia PA 2011-, Dioc Consult Team co-chair 2008-, Stndg Com Mem 2007-2011, Dn of Southwark Dnry 2007-2010** B Peru IN 1949 d Daniel & Erlene. BA Tem 1998; MDiv GTS 2001. D 6/23/2001 P 6/1/2002 Bp Charles Ellsworth Bennison Jr. m 9/11/1982 Alan J Segal. R Trin Ch Buckingham PA 2003-2006; Asst R Ch Of The Mssh Lower Gwynedd PA 2001-2003; Treas Ch Trng Dss Hse Bd 2006-2012.

SEGER, David L (NI) 13259 Hisega Dr, Rapid City SD 57702 **Com on Dispatch of Bus Stff HOB 2009-; Consult HOB Off of Pstr Care 2000-** B Mason City IA 1938 s Joe & Beulah. BA U of Iowa 1960; MDiv Nash 1972; MEd LSU 1983; MEd LSU 1983. D 8/8/1971 P 9/21/1972 Bp Walter H Jones. m 2/11/1961 Nancy Roberts c 3. Int R S Bon Preschool Sarasota FL 2015-2016; Int R Trin Epis Ch Baton Rouge LA 2013-2014; Int R S Lk's Ch Baton Rouge LA 2012-2013, Int R 2012-2013, Asst P 1976-1983, Asst P 1974-1983; JSCN GC 2006-2009; Int R Emm Epis Par Rapid City SD 2006-2008; Stndg Cmsn on Mssn and Evang GC 1999-2006; Coordntr of Wrshp GC 1994-2009; SCER GC 1994-1997; Cn to theOrdinary Dio Nthrn Indiana So Bend IN 1991-2006;

Dir of Admssns Nash Nashotah WI 1987-1991; Asst Dir - CDO Epis Ch Cntr New York NY 1984-1987; Asst Secy - GC Exec & Secy Off New York NY 1983-1984; Chair of Dept. of Rel Epis HS Baton Rouge Baton Rouge LA 1974-1983; P-in-c H Trin Epis Ch Luverne MN 1972-1974; All SS Sch, Souix Falls - Hd of Sch Dio So Dakota Pierre SD 1972-1974. CODE 1991-2007. DD Nash 2014.

SEGER, Nikki Elizabeth Louise (Mich) **S Mich's Epis Ch Lansing MI 2014-** B Laramie WY 1962 d David & Nancy. BA LSU 1984; MA The U of Iowa 1990; MDiv Bexley-Seabury 2014; MDiv Bexley-Seabury 2014. D 6/14/2014 P 12/13/2014 Bp Wendell Nathaniel Gibbs Jr. m 11/25/2013 Jennifer R Rangel.

SEGERBRECHT, Stephen Louis (Kan) 1715 Prestwick Dr, Lawrence KS 66047 **D Trin Ch Lawr KS 2006-** B 1955 s Brian & Margaret. BA U of Kansas 1977; MD U of Kansas 1980. D 6/3/2006 Bp Dean E Wolfe. m 5/3/1980 Lynn Segerbrecht c 2.

SEIBERT, Joanna Johnson (Ark) 27 River Ridge Rd, Little Rock AR 72227 **D Trin Cathd 2005-** B Richmond VA 1942 d James & Florence. BA U NC 1964; MD U of Tennessee 1968; LA U of Iowa 1973. D 4/28/2001 Bp Larry Maze. m 10/18/1969 Robert Walstrom Seibert c 3. D Trin Cathd Little Rock AR 2007-2011; D S Marg's Epis Ch Little Rock AR 2001-2005. Ed, "Surrounded By A Cloud Of Witnesses," Rose Pub, 1994; Auth, "Var arts, LivCh, Workbook Of ECW Of Arkansas," *And Arkansas Epis*, 1988. Recognition Of The Diac Mnstry In The Tradtiion Of St Steph Naad 2003.

SEIBERT, Thomas E (Colo) 145 W 5th St, Delta CO 81416 **R S Lk's Epis Ch Delta CO 2009-** B Chicago IL 1949 s John & Mary. St JohnSeminary 1975; BA Marq Milwaukee 2006; Cert Ang Stud SWTS 2008. Rec 5/1/2009 Bp Victor Alfonso Scantlebury.

SEIDMAN, Kimberly Anne (NwT) Holy Comforter Episcopal Church, PO Box 412, Broomfield CO 80038 **Vic Ch Of The H Comf Broomfield CO 2010-; Faith and Ord Cmsn Natl Coun Of Ch New York NY 2012-; COM Dio Colorado Denver CO 2011-** B Austin, TX 1977 d Sheila. BA Abilene Chr U 1999; MDiv Candler TS Emory U 2003; Dip Ang Stud VTS 2008. D 1/8/2008 P 6/26/2008 Bp C Wallis Ohl. m 7/5/2003 Raj Chitikila. Cler Res Chr Ch Alexandria VA 2008-2010.

SEIFERT, Cynthia (Tenn) 5041 English Village Dr, Nashville TN 37211 **Vic S Anselm's Epis Ch Nashville TN 2013-** B Decatur GA 1971 d Clarence & Gwendolyn. BA Presb Coll 1993; MDiv TESM 2004. D 6/5/2005 P 4/29/2006 Bp Bertram Nelson Herlong. m 10/20/2009 John Seifert c 1. Asst R Ch Of The Gd Shpd Brentwood TN 2007-2012; Int R S Phil's Ch Nashville TN 2006-2007; Asst to R/Campus Min S Paul's Epis Ch Murfreesboro TN 2005-2006; Chapl Res Veteran's Hosp Murfreesboro TN 2004-2006; Yth Dir S Barth's Ch Nashville TN 1996-2003; Yth Dir Ch Of Our Sav Glenshaw PA 1994-1996.

SEIFERT, Robert Joseph (ECR) 161 Palo Verde Ter, Santa Cruz CA 95060 **Admin Vic S Lk's Epis Ch Jolon CA 2008-** B Paris AR 1941 s Leonard & Mary. BA San Jose St U 1967; MA San Jose St U 1968; Doctorand U of Bucharest 1969; BTS California Sch for Deacons 1982; Coll of Preachers 1995; STM Jesuit TS 1996; S Vladimirs Orth TS 1997. D 9/23/1984 Bp Charles Shannon Mallory. c 2. Chapl Santa Cruz Cnty Jail Santa Cruz CA 1999-2009; D S Tim's Epis Ch Mtn View CA 1997-2008; D S Lk's Ch Los Gatos CA 1992-1997; D S Geo's Ch Salinas CA 1989-1992; D S Lk's Ch Hollister CA 1988-1989; Dioc Admin Dio El Camino Real Salinas CA 1985-1988; Dioc Admin Epis Ch of St Jn the Bapt Aptos Aptos CA 1985-1988; S Jas' Ch Monterey CA 1984-1985, D 1984-1985. vicarjolon@gmail.com

SEIFERT, Sarah Lavonne (Kan) 14301 S Blackbob Rd, Olathe KS 66062 B Kansas City KS 1944 d Oscar & Margaret. BA U of Kansas 1966; MA EDS 2012. D 1/5/2013 P 8/24/2013 Bp Dean E Wolfe. m 5/3/1980 David Paul Seifert c 1.

SEILER, Jeffrey Hamilton (Va) 4003 St Erics Turn, Williamsburg VA 23185 B Boston MA 1950 s Peter & Marilyn. AA Mitchell Coll 1971; BA Framingham St Coll 1979; MDiv Gordon-Conwell TS 1982; CAS VTS 1986. D 6/4/1986 Bp John Bowen Coburn P 10/4/1986 Bp Peter J Lee. m 6/18/1977 Jennie Delzell Seiler c 4. Command Chapl Naval Weapons Sta Yorktown VA 2009-2011; Dep Command Chapl Naval Med Cntr Portsmouth VA 2007-2009; Stdt Naval Med Cntr Portsmouth VA 2006-2007; Grp & Command Chapl USS ENTERPRISE (CVN 65) Norfolk VA 2004-2006; Grp Chapl COMPHIBGRU THREE San Diego CA 2001-2004; Chapl MCB Camp Lejeune NC 1997-2001; Command Chapl USS MISSISSIPPI (CGN40) Norfolk VA 1995-1997; Chapl 2D Marine Div Camp Lejeune NC 1992-1995; Chapl US Navy Off Of Bsh For ArmdF New York NY 1989-2011; Chapl Naval Air Sta Barbers Point HI 1989-1992; Assoc R S Marg's Ch Woodbridge VA 1986-1989. AAPC 1981-1985; APA 2007; ACPE 1981.

SEILER, Michael E (Los) 300 W Ocean Blvd Apt 6203, Long Beach CA 90802 B Redwood City California 1961 s Fred & Lorraine. BA Pepperdine U 1982; Cert Ya Berk 1997; MDiv Yale DS 1997. D 6/14/1997 P 1/11/1998 Bp Frederick Houk Borsch. Mng Assoc R The Par Of S Matt Pacific Plsds CA 2001-2016; Cur S Mk's Ch Philadelphia PA 1997-2001. Fllshp of S Jn 1997.

S

SEILER, Robert Stuart (Va) 4810 Stuart Ave, Richmond VA 23226 **Died 9/20/2016** B San Francisco CA 1919 s Charles & Louise. VTS 1952. D 6/6/1952 Bp Frederick D Goodwin P 6/1/1953 Bp Robert Fisher Gibson Jr. c 3. Ret 1989-2016; Shepherds Cntr Richmond VA 1984; Dio Virginia Richmond VA 1983-1984; M-in-c Mssh Highland Sprg VA 1952-1955.

SEILER-DUBAY, Noreen (WA) 1510 Oakview Dr, Silver Spring MD 20903 **Stff Chapl for Indep Living Asbury Methodist Vill Cont Care Ret Communit 2016-** B New York NY 1956 d Carl & Regis. BA Villanova U 1978; MA CUA 1980; MDiv VTS 1990; CAS (Certif. Adv. Stds) Loyola U 2015. D 6/9/1990 P 12/18/1990 Bp Ronald Hayward Haines. m 5/17/2017 Charles F Dubay c 2. All Faith Epis Ch Charlotte Hall MD 2014-2016; Int S Chris's Ch New Carrollton MD 2012-2014; Int Asst H Trin Epis Ch Bowie MD 2012; Supply P Dio Washington Washington DC 2011-2012, Com on Const and Cn 2013-, Transition Com in Bp's Election 2010-2011; R S Matt's Epis Ch Hyattsville MD 2001-2011; Int Chr Epis Ch Clinton MD 1999-2001; Int Nativ Epis Ch Temple Hills MD 1998-1999; Int S Dav's Par Washington DC 1995-1996; Assoc R Chr Ch Capitol Hill Washington DC 1990-1995; Chapl H Cross Hosp Silver Sprg MD 1983-1984; Admin St. Steph & the Incarn Ch Washington DC 1980-1983. ACPE 1989-1993.

SEILS, Donald Davis (Colo) 5749 N Stetson Ct, Parker CO 80134 **NECC Rep Epis Curs Mnstry Aurora CO 2012-, Sec 2008-** B Rochester NY 1948 s Edward & Arlene. BA U of Houston 1974; MDiv VTS 1979. D 7/10/1979 P 8/6/1980 Bp Roger Howard Cilley. m 4/25/1987 Allison Klefke Seils c 2. Int Chr Epis Ch Denver CO 2011-2013; Int S Phil In-The-Field Sedalia CO 2010; Calv Ch Golden CO 2004; P-in-c H Apos Epis Ch Englewood CO 2000; Assoc Ch Of The Trsfg Evergreen CO 1997-1998; Vic S Eliz's Epis Ch Brighton CO 1990-1996; Vic S Andr's Epis Ch Ft Lupton CO 1990-1993; Vic S Matt's Parker CO 1989-1990; Asst R S Paul's Ch Leavenworth KS 1986-1989; R H Trin Carrizo Sprg TX 1984-1986; Non-par 1982-1983; Cur Gr Epis Ch Hutchinson KS 1980-1982; Vic S Matthews & S Jas Beaumont TX 1979-1980; St Jas Ch Houston TX 1979-1980; St Matthews Ch Beaumont TX 1979-1980; The Great Cmsn Fndt Houston TX 1979-1980; ; Chapl Lamar U.

SEIPEL, James Russell (Los) 25769 Player Dr, Valencia CA 91355 **Assigned P Chr The King A Jubilee Mnstry Palmdale CA 2006-** B Buffalo NY 1942 s Edson & Frances. BA San Diego St U 1965; STB GTS 1968. D 9/7/1968 P 3/9/1969 Bp Francis E I Bloy. m 11/15/1986 Elizabeth C Seipel c 2. Int S Paul's Par Lancaster CA 1993-1996; S Steph's Epis Ch Valencia CA 1974-1984; Cur St Cross Epis Ch Hermosa Bch CA 1968-1974.

SEIPP, Vivian (NY) 39 Cumberland Rd, Fishkill NY 12524 B New York NY 1928 d Peter & Ursula. AAS Dutchess Cmnty Coll Poughkeepsie NY 1985; EFM Sewanee: The U So, TS 1991. D 5/30/1992 Bp Richard Frank Grein. m 5/4/1952 Charles John Seipp c 4. D Trin Ch Fishkill NY 1992-2004.

SEITER, Claudia D (U) 540 W 2350 S, Brigham City UT 84302 **Assoc Dio Utah Salt Lake City UT 2008-, COM 2010-, Dioc Coun Mem 2006-2009, Strategic Plnng Com 2003-2006** B Colorado Springs CO 1952 d Robert & Eloie. MS Weber St U 1980; MS Indiana U 1986; MA Harv 1991. D 11/30/2000 P 6/24/2001 Bp Carolyn Tanner Irish. m 6/24/1988 David Michael Seiter c 4. Assoc Ch Of The Gd Shpd Ogden UT 2001-2008.

SEITZ, Christopher R (Dal) Wycliffe College, University Of Toronto, Toronto ON M5S 1H7 Canada **P Asst St Matthews Angl Ch Toronto Ontario 2007-; Wycliffe Coll Toronto ON 2007-; Resrch Prof Wycliffe Coll Toronto Ontario 2007-; Pres Angl Comm Inst Beaumont TX 2003-** B Blowing Rock NC 1954 s Thomas & Mary. BA U NC 1976; MA VTS 1979; STM Yale DS 1981; MA Ya 1982; PhD Ya 1986. D 6/22/1980 P 1/11/1981 Bp William Hopkins Folwell. m 12/19/2009 Jeanne Elizabeth New-Seitz. Cbury Hse Dallas TX 2015; Cn Theol Dio Dallas Dallas TX 2012-2014, Cn 2012-; P Assoc Ch Of The Incarn Dallas TX 2008-2012; The Angl Comm Inst Inc Beaumont TX 2008-2012; Prof Of The OT And Theol Stds U Of S Andr 1998-2007; Asst S Paul's Ch Fairfield CT 1991-1992; Prof Of OT Ya 1987-1979; Assoc Ch Of Our Sav Jenkintown PA 1985-1986; Asst Prof Of The OT Luth Sem PA 1984-1987; Asst Chr Ch New Haven CT 1981-1984; Com Dio Connecticut Meriden CT 1992-1993. Auth, "Joel: Intnl Theol Commentary," Bloomsbury, 2016; Auth, "Colossians," Brazos Press, 2014; Auth, "The Character of Chr Scripture," Baker Acad, 2011; Auth, "Goodly Fllshp of the Prophets," Baker Acad, 2009; Auth, "Prophecy and Hermeneutics," Baker Acad, 2007; Auth, "Isaiah 40-66," Abingdon Press, 2001; Auth, "Figured Out," Westminster Jn Knox, 2001; Auth, "Seven Lasting Words," Westminster Jn Knox, 2001; Auth, "Word Without End," Eerdmans, 1998; Auth, "Isaiah 1-39," Westminster Jn Knox, 1993; Auth, "Zion's Final Destiny," Fortress, 1991; Auth, "Theol In Conflict," Walter de Gruyter, 1989. Amer Theol Soc 1995; Angl Comm Inst 1997; SBL 1980; Soc of OT Study 1998. Fell Alexander von Humboldt 2011; Fell Cntr of Theol Inquiry 2005; Grant Rec The Henry Luce III Fndt 1999; Fell Alexander von Humboldt 1992; Fell ECF 1983.

SEITZ, Mark Ellis (WVa) PO Box 508, Wheeling WV 26003 **R S Matt's Ch Wheeling WV 1995-; Stndg Com - Mem & Pres Dio W Virginia Charleston WV 2010-, GC - Alt 2006-2010, GC - Dep 2003-2006, Stndg Com - Mem & Pres 2001-2005, GC - Dep 2000-2003, GC - Alt 1997-2000, Stndg Com**

- Mem 1996-2000, Archd 1991-1997 B Huntington WV 1956 s Thomas & Mary. BA U NC 1978; MDiv Epis TS of the SW 1983. D 6/11/1983 P 2/1/1984 Bp Emerson Paul Haynes. m 1/12/1985 Kathleen Seitz c 2. S Andr's Ch Oak Hill WV 1990-1995; Mssnr The New River Epis Mnstry Pratt WV 1990-1995; Vic S Paul's Epis Ch Woodville TX 1986-1990; The Great Cmsn Fndt Houston TX 1986-1990; Asst Ch Of The Gd Shpd Tomball TX 1985-1986; Cur S Andr's Epis Ch Sprg Hill FL 1983-1985.

SEITZ, Phil (EMich) 3003 Mill Station Road, Hale MI 48739 **P-in-c S Mk's Epis Ch Atlanta MI 2012-; Chair Mssn T/F Dio Estrn Michigan 2004-; Stndg Com Dio Estrn Michigan Saginaw MI 2008-, Chair, Mssn T/F 2004-, GC Dep 2004-** B Lima OH 1939 s Carl & Miriam. BS OH SU 1962; MS MI SU 1978; Cert Theol Stud SWTS 2002. D 11/2/2002 P 5/24/2003 Bp Edwin Max Leidel Jr. m 11/4/1960 Phyllis Seitz c 3. R Trin Epis Ch W Branch MI 2003-2011; R Gr Epis Ch Standish MI 2002-2007.

SEITZ JR, Thomas Comstock (CFla) 221 S 4th St, Lake Wales FL 33853 **R The Epis Ch Of The Gd Shpd Lake Wales FL 1997-** B Blowing Rock NC 1952 s Thomas & Mary. BA U NC 1974; MDiv VTS 1977. D 6/8/1977 P 6/15/1978 Bp Robert Poland Atkinson. m 5/20/1978 Anna P Seitz c 3. R S Paul's Epis Ch Lansing MI 1992-1997; Dn Monongahela Deanry Dio W Virginia Charleston WV 1984-1992; R Chr Ch Clarksburg WV 1981-1992; Ch Of The Gd Shpd Burke VA 1978-1981; S Steph's Epis Ch Beckley WV 1977-1978; Dn SW Dnry Dio Cntrl Florida Orlando FL 2005-2008.

SEITZ SR, Thomas Comstock (CFla) 2565 Salzburg Loop, Winter Haven FL 33884 **Died 1/2/2017** B Springfield OH 1928 s William & Florence. BA Ken 1949; MDiv Bex Sem 1951; MA Wstrn Carolina U 1971. D 6/27/1951 P 6/4/1952 Bp Matthew George Henry. m 6/16/1951 Janet Seitz c 4. Ret 1993-2017; Dn SW Dnry 1988-1992; R S Jn's Ch Huntington WV 1981-1993; S Mk's Cathd Shreveport LA 1978-1981; Headmaster St Mk's Ch Shreveport LA 1977-1981; S Paul's Sch Clearwater FL 1976-1978; Asst Headmaster St Jn's Sch Clearwater FL 1976-1977; Chr Sch Arden NC 1967-1976; Chapl Teachr Chr Sch Arden NC 1967-1976; R Chr Ch Fairmont WV 1959-1967; R S Ptr's Ch Huntington WV 1955-1958; P-in-c S Lk's Ch Boone NC 1951-1955; P-in-c S Mary Of The Hills Epis Par Blowing Rock NC 1951-1955; P-in-c S Mary's Beaver Creek NC 1951-1955; Stndg Com Dio W Virginia Charleston WV 1986-1989, Exec Coun 1957-1985.

SELDEN, Elizabeth Ann (Minn) 6212 Crest Ln, Edina MN 55436 **Ret 1988-** B Tacoma WA 1920 BA Mills Coll 1941. D 10/23/1978 Bp Robert Marshall Anderson. D/Asst S Steph The Mtyr Ch Minneapolis MN 1978-1988.

SELES, Deborah Galante (SanD) 1172 Woodriver Dr, Twin Falls ID 83301 **S Marg's Epis Ch Palm Desert CA 2016-; Dioc Coun, Cler at Lg Dio Idaho Boise ID 2010-** B Chicago IL 1951 d Sebastian & Donna. BA Quincy Coll 1974; MSW U IL 1979; MDiv SWTS 2002. D 6/15/2002 P 12/21/2002 Bp Bill Persell. R Ch Of The Ascen Twin Falls ID 2010-2016; S Richard's Ch Chicago IL 2009-2010; Int S Phil's Epis Palatine IL 2008-2009; Chapl Bp Anderson Hse Chicago IL 2006-2010; Long Term Supply Ch Of S Columba Of Iona Hanover Pk IL 2006-2007; L'Arche Chicago Chicago IL 2002-2005; L'Arche Chicago Cicero IL 2002-2005; Assoc S Chris's Epis Ch Oak Pk IL 2002; Mem, Bp's T/F on Tentmaker Mnstrs Dio Chicago Chicago IL 2007-2010, Founding Chair T/F on Disabil 2001-2007. Auth, "2 Reasons," *101 Reasons To Be Epis*, Morehouse Pub, 2003; Auth, "The Risk Of Meeting Chr," *Living Pulpit*, 2002. W.T. Tayolr Stephenson Awd In Theol Seabury 2001; H.N. Moss Bk Awd Seabury 2001.

SELF, Deborah Davis (SwFla) **P S Giles Ch Pinellas Pk FL 2014-** B Ann Arbor MI 1953 BS MI SU 1975; MDiv TS 2004; MDiv Sewanee: The U So, TS 2004. D 4/17/2004 P 11/20/2004 Bp Leo Frade. m 4/3/1992 David L Self c 2. Chap Of S Andr Boca Raton FL 2010-2012; S Greg's Ch Boca Raton FL 2004-2010.

SELFE-VERRONE, Ann Christine (NY) Chapel of St. Francis, 3621 Brunswick Ave., Los Angeles CA 90039 **Vic S Ann's Ch For The Deaf 2005-** B Lock Haven PA 1960 d John & Catherine. BA Gallaudet U; GTS 2004. D 6/12/2004 Bp Henry Nutt Parsley Jr P 12/18/2004 Bp Catherine Scimeca Roskam. m 9/16/2006 Alexander Joseph Verrone. Supply P Epis Chap Of S Fran Los Angeles CA 2007-2012; Dio Los Angeles Los Angeles CA 2007-2008; Vic S Ann's Ch For The Deaf New York NY 2003-2007.

SELL, James William Henry (SVa) 239 Duke St Unit 207, Norfolk VA 23510 **Trin Ch Portsmouth VA 2014-** B Charleston,WV 1942 s James & Helen. BA W Virginia U 1964; MDiv VTS 1969. D 6/11/1969 P 12/19/1969 Bp Wilburn Camrock Campbell. m 8/31/1968 Ellen D Major c 2. Int Trin Ch On The Green New Haven CT 2009-2011; Int Trin Ch Princeton NJ 2007-2009; Int St Martins-In-The-Field Ch Severna Pk MD 2006; R Chr and S Lk's Epis Ch Norfolk VA 1990-2005; Archd Dio Newark Newark NJ 1985-1990; R S Mary's Ch Sparta NJ 1980-1985; Vts Alum VTS Alexandria VA 1980-1983; R S Jas' Epis Ch Lewisburg WV 1978-1980; S Thos Epis Ch Wht Sphr Spgs WV 1972-1977; Vic Chr Memi Ch Williamstown WV 1970-1972; Vic S Martins-In-Fields Summersville WV 1969-1970. Auth, "The Face in the Jar," 2017; Auth, "Lrng to Live," 2015.

SELLERS, Robert (Tex) 1401 S PALMETTO AVE, APT 207, DAYTONA BEACH FL 32114 B Fayetteville AR 1937 s Robert & Mary. BA Ya 1958; MA Oxf GB 1962; MDiv CDSP 1963; Oxf GB 1998. D 6/19/1963 P 5/5/1964

S

Bp John Elbridge Hines. c 2. Serv Ch in Bahamas 1998-2002; R Ch Of St Philips Matt Town 1998-2000; R S Steph's Ch Liberty TX 1990-1997; Coordntr Chapl Polly Ryon Hosp Richmond TX 1982-1988; S Mk's Epis Ch Richmond TX 1981-1990; The Great Cmsn Fndt Houston TX 1981-1985; Fam Pstr Missouri City Episcopalians 1980-1981; Hd of Hist Dept S Thos Ch Houston TX 1970-1979; Chapl-Intern S Lk Hosp Houston TX 1969-1970; R S Paul's Ch Kilgore TX 1965-1969; Asst S Jn The Div Houston TX 1963-1965. Auth, "Revs," *FIDES ET HISTORIA*.

SELLERY, David (LI) PO Box 393, Salisbury CT 06068 **S Jn's Ch Salisbury CT 2014-; Dir Of Dvlpmt Settlement Hsng Fund 2002-** B Norwood MA 1966 s Stephen & Priscilla. BA U of Connecticut 1989; MDiv GTS 1992. D 6/13/1992 Bp Arthur Edward Walmsley P 1/9/1993 Bp Robert Gould Tharp. m 1/4/2003 Jane M Muir c 4. Dio Long Island Garden City NY 2013-2014; S Ptr's by-the-Sea Epis Ch Bay Shore NY 2007-2013; Asst St Jn's Ch Cold Sprg Harbor NY 2005-2007; Asst Chr Ch Bronxville NY 2001-2005; P-in-c S Barth's Ch In The Highland White Plains NY 1999-2001; Cur S Thos Ch New York NY 1995-1999; Cur S Mart Of Tours Epis Ch Chattanooga TN 1993-1994; Cur S Paul's Epis Ch Kingsport TN 1992-1993; Ecum Cmsn Dio New York New York NY 1996-2002; Ecum Off Dio E Tennessee Knoxville TN 1994-1995. Auth, "The Challenge Of Evang," *Acts 29*, 1992; Auth, "The Hist Episcopate Obstacle & Opportunity For Ch Unity? 92," *Ecum Trends*, 1992; Auth, "Triadic Vs. Trinitarian: A Battle For The Gospel," *The Angl*, 1992. The Most Venerable Ord Of S Jn Of Jerusalem - Sub-Chapl 1996. Ord Of Civil Merit Hse Of Savoy 1998.

SELL-LEE, William Merle (WA) 965 Winslow Way E Unit 103, Bainbridge Island WA 98110 **Ret 1998-; Memi Ch Baltimore MD 1985-** B Santa Maria CA 1936 s Merle & Vivian. BS California St Polytechnic U 1962; (Spec Ord Prog) CDSP 1975. D 2/26/1974 Bp Chauncie Kilmer Myers P 5/21/1975 Bp George Richard Millard. m 5/1/1979 Sandra Sell-Lee c 4. R S Lk's Ch Sequim WA 1989-1998; Int S Mich And All Ang Ch Issaquah WA 1987-1989; Int Epiph Par of Seattle Seattle WA 1985-1986; Int Trin Par Seattle WA 1983-1984; Asstg P, Int R S Barn Epis Ch Bainbridge Island WA 1979-1983; Asstg D, P Epis Ch in Almaden San Jose CA 1974-1979.

SELLS, Jeffery Edward (Oly) Po Box 3090, Salt Lake City UT 84110 **Non-par 1983-** B Pueblo CO 1945 s Bob & Pauline. BS U of New Mex 1967; MDiv CDSP 1972. D 8/31/1972 P 8/1/1973 Bp Richard Mitchell Trelease Jr. m 7/24/2013 Elaine F Sells c 2. The Ch Of S Dav Of Wales Shelton WA 2003-2009; Cathd Ch Of S Mk Salt Lake City UT 1997-2003; Dio Utah Salt Lake City UT 1997-2001; R S Steph's Baker City OR 1976-1982; Trin Epis Ch Reno NV 1975-1976; Dio The Rio Grande Albuquerque 1972-1974; .

SELLS, Patti (Oly) **D St Chris's Ch - A Fed Cong Olympia WA 2012-** B 1949 D 6/14/2001 Bp Carolyn Tanner Irish. c 3. Dio Olympia Seattle 2010-2011, 2006-2008, jubilee Off 2011; D The Ch Of S Dav Of Wales Shelton WA 2008-2010, 2004; D Cathd Ch Of S Mk Salt Lake City UT 1996-2003.

SELNICK, Thomas Conrad (O) 5040 Wright Terrace, Skokie IL 60077 B Bay Village OH 1957 s William & Barbara. BA JHU 1979; MDiv EDS 1983; MS Case Wstrn Reserve U 1997. D 6/11/1983 P 12/1/1983 Bp William Grant Black. m 6/16/1984 Elizabeth A Eaton c 2. Bexley Seabury Fed Chicago IL 2014-2016; R S Chris's By-The River Gates Mills OH 2003-2013; Int R S Paul's Epis Ch Medina OH 2001-2003; R S Ptr's Epis Ch Ashtabula OH 1990-1999; Organizing Pstr S Andr's Ch Pickerington OH 1987-1990; Asst R S Alb's Epis Ch Of Bexley Columbus OH 1983-1986; GC Dep Dio Ohio Cleveland 2009. Auth, "Hosting A 12 Step Grp In Your Ch".

SELVAGE, Dan (CPa) 102 Faust Cir, Bellefonte PA 16823 **P-in-c S Paul's Ch Lock Haven PA 2012-; Penn St U Dio Cntrl Pennsylvania Harrisburg PA 2009-, Chair, Dioc BEC 2010-, Mem, Dioc Liturg and Mus Cmsn 1993-** B Philipsburg PA 1949 s William & Morrell. BA Mansfield U of Pennsylvania 1972; MDiv GTS 1975. D 6/14/1975 P 12/20/1975 Bp Donald James Davis. Chapl Epis Campus Mnstry at Penn St U 2009-2012; R S Jn's Epis Ch Bellefonte PA 1991-2009; Archd Dio NW Pennsylvania Erie PA 1984-1990; Vic S Mary's Ch Erie PA 1979-1982; Vic Ch Of The H Cross No E PA 1975-1984; Chapl/Admin S Barn Hse PA 1975-1977. CBS 1982; NNECA 1994. Cn St. Steph's Cathd, Harrisburg, PA 2008; Archd (honoris causa) Dio NW Pennsylvania 1990.

SELVEY, Mark F (Neb) 3310 16th Ave, Omaha NE 68022 **Dn Dio Nebraska Omaha NE 2014-; R S Fran Epis Ch Scottsbluff NE 2013-** B Columbus NE 1955 s Richard & Janet. AS Coll of S Mary 1977; BA Chadron St Coll 1995; MDiv Iliff TS 2006. D 5/18/2006 P 2/15/2007 Bp Joe Goodwin Burnett. m 12/31/1991 Jill M Selvey c 5. R St Aug of Cbury Epis Ch Elkhorn NE 2008-2013; Cur S Martha's Epis Ch Papillion NE 2006-2008. frmarks@me.com

SELZER, David Owen (WNY) 4 Phylis St, NEPEAN ON K2J 1V2 Canada **Exec Archd Dio Ottawa Ottawa ON 2010-, Co-Incumbent 2008-2010; Ret Epis Ch 2009-** B Portsmouth VA 1951 s Christian & Betty. BA U of Kentucky 1972; MDiv Nash 1976. D 6/5/1976 P 6/8/1977 Bp David Reed. m 11/24/1985 Ann Miller c 2. Prof Bex Sem Columbus OH 2001-2009; R The Epis Ch Of The Gd Shpd Buffalo NY 1995-2008; Chapl U Epis Cntr Minneapolis MN

1984-1995; Assoc S Matt's Epis Ch Louisville KY 1976-1984. EPF 1989; Ord of S Helena, Assoc 1988.

SEMES, Robert Louis (Ore) 1354 Primavera Drive E, Palm Springs CA 92264 B Miami FL 1941 s Louis & Aretta. BA Belhaven Coll 1962; Nash 1965; MA U of Virginia 1968; ABD Rutgers The St U of New Jersey 1971; MDiv EDS 1976; Harv 1976. D 6/12/1976 P 12/21/1976 Bp William Gillette Weinhauer. P S Marg's Epis Ch Palm Desert CA 2011-2012; P Trin Epis Ch Ashland Ashland OR 2004-2005; Prof Epis Sch For Deacons Berkeley CA 1994; P Ch Of The Adv Of Chr The King San Francisco CA 1992-1996; Mgr, Epis Bookstore Epis Sch for Deacons 1991-1994; Int S Jn's Epis Ch Oakland CA 1991-1992; Assoc S Matt's Epis Ch San Mateo CA 1989-1991; Asst S Fran' Epis Ch San Francisco CA 1987-1989; Admin Grad Theol Un 1983-1986; P Chr Ch Sausalito CA 1983-1985; P S Lk's Ch San Francisco CA 1981-1982; P Trin Ch San Francisco CA 1980-1981; R Ch Of The Epiph Newton NC 1977-1979; Asst S Thos Ch Mamaroneck NY 1976-1977; Dn - San Francisco Dnry Dio California San Francisco CA 1992-1993, Mem - Resolutns Com - Dioc Conv 1987-1995. Auth, "A Ch Grows in the Desert: A Hist of the Epis Ch of St. Paul in the Desert, 1939-2014," 2015; Auth, "Hawai'i's H War: Engl Bp Staley Amer Congregationalists and the Hawaiian Monarchs 1860-1870," The Hawaiian Journ of Hist, 2000; Auth, "What is a D in the Epis Ch?," The Sch for Deacons (Dio California), 1993; Auth, "Of These Stones: A Hist Sketch of the Ch of S Matt San Mateo California 1865-1990," St. Matt's Epis Ch San Mateo California, 1990; Auth, "A Hse of Pryr for All People: A Short Hist of St. Fran' Epis Ch San Francisco California," St. Fran' Epis Ch San Francisco California, 1987. Resrch Grant HSEC 1998.

SEMON, Kenneth J (RG) 311 E. Palace Avenue, Santa Fe NM 87501 **Died 7/28/2016** B Milwaukee WI 1945 s Milton & Joyce. BA U of Wisconsin 1968; PhD U of Washington 1971; MDiv SWTS 1980. D 6/14/1980 Bp Quintin Ebenezer Primo Jr P 12/13/1980 Bp James Winchester Montgomery. m 12/7/1973 Caroline C Semon c 4. R Ch of the H Faith Santa Fe NM 2007-2016; R Chr Ch Of The Ascen Paradise Vlly AZ 1999-2007; R S Mich & S Geo S Louis MO 1991-1997; R S Fran On The Hill El Paso TX 1985-1991; R St Jn's Epis Ch of Sturgis Sturgis MI 1981-1985; Cur The Ch Of The H Sprt Lake Forest IL 1980-1981; Cn for Ecum Affrs Dio The Rio Grande Albuquerque 2014-2016, Pres of the Stndg Com 2013-2016, Bd of Exam Chapl 2011-2016, Stndg Com 2011-2016, Bd Dir Epis Chars 1987-2011; Stndg Com Dio Missouri S Louis MO 1994-1997, Com 1992-1993. "Var arts & Revs In Living Ch Rg Epis Other Journ". Engl Spkng Un 2000-2004; OSB, Oblate 1989.

SEMON-SCOTT, Deborah Anne (Mich) 3 N Broad St, Hillsdale MI 49242 B Grand Rapids MI 1952 d Donald & Virginia. AA Grand Rapids Cmnty Coll 1973; BS Grand Vlly St U 1975; MDiv SWTS 1979. D 6/16/1979 P 4/1/1980 Bp H Coleman Mcgehee Jr. m 8/9/1980 Leonard Harry Scott c 3. S Chris-S Paul Epis Ch Detroit MI 2009-2015; S Ptr's Epis Ch Hillsdale MI 2001-2006; S Mk's Ch Coldwater MI 1999-2001. sarah@stchristopherstpaulepiscopal.org

SEMPARI, Izabella Lilli D 6/10/2017 Bp Marc Handley Andrus.

SENECHAL, Roger (WMass) 7601 Harper Road, Joelton TN 37080 **P Assoc S Geo's Ch Nashville TN 2007-** B Leominster MA 1944 s Edward & Simonne. BA Marist Coll 1967; MDiv Weston Jesuit TS 1974; ThM Harvard DS 1980. Rec 7/1/1984 as Deacon Bp Philip Alan Smith. m 9/4/1978 Diana Senechal c 1. R S Thos Epis Ch Auburn MA 1988-2007; Assoc Chr Ch Exeter NH 1985-1988; Cur RC Ch 1967-1977. Fllshp of the Way of the Cross 1991. roger.senechal@stgeorgesnashville.org

SENEY, Robert William (Miss) 14165 Denver West Cricle #3407, Lakewood CO 80401 B Springfield MO 1938 s Alvia & Inez. BA U of Missouri 1960; MDiv Nash 1965; Cert Texas Tech U 1974; EdD U of Houston 1987. D 6/20/1965 P 12/21/1965 Bp Chilton R Powell. m 6/1/1972 Judith Arlene Stockton c 1. P-in-c S Paul's Ch Mancos CO 2009-2014; Ch Of The Ascen Brooksville MS 1996-2006; Visting P Ch Of The Nativ Macon MS 1996-2006; Vic Cassady Sch Oklahoma City OK 1976-1979; Headmaster Bp Noland Epis Day Sch Lake Chas LA 1973-1976; Headmaster Epis Ch Of The Gd Shpd Lake Chas LA 1973-1976; Headmaster S Chris's Epis Ch Lubbock TX 1970-1973; Cur Gr Epis Ch Ponca City OK 1968-1970; Vic S Mk's Ch Blackwell OK 1966-1968; Cur S Paul's Ch Clinton OK 1965-1966. Auth, "Adv: A Time for Prepration - A Time for Reneal," same, Parsons Porch, 2017; Auth, "Books, Books, More Books," Tchg for High Potential, Natl Assn for Gifted Chld, 2014; Auth, "Revs for Young Readers," Columbus Comercial Dispatch, Comercial Dispatch, 2006; Auth, "Plnng the Lrng Environ," Methods and Materials for Tchg the Gifted (2001), Prufrock Press, 2005; Auth, "The Process Skills and the Gifted Chld," Methods and Materials for Tchg the Gifted (2001) ``, Prufrock Press, 2005; Auth, "About Books," Twice Exceptional Nwsltr, 2ENewsletter. Colorado Acad of Educatiors of the Gifted, Talented and Creative 2008; Colorado Assn for Gifted and Talented 2006; MS Assn for Gifted Chld 1992-2006; Natl Assn of Gifted Chld 1982; Natl Conf for Gvnr's Schools 1992; Phi Delta Kappa 1958-1960; Texas Assn for Gifted Chld 1978; Wrld Coun for Gifted Chld 1985. Prof Emer Mississippi U for Wmn 2006; Jim Brey and Lil Press Awd for Life Time Contribution to Gift Natl Conf of Gvnr's Schools 2006; Heritage Who's

S

Who 2005; Who's Who in Amer Educ 2005 2005; Pres's Awd Texas Assn for Gifted and Talented 1996. rwseney@muw.edu

SENUTA, Lisa Ann (Chi) 550 Sunset Ridge Rd, Northfield IL 60093 **The Epis Ch Of S Jas The Less Northfield IL 2012-** B Kansas City MO 1972 d Glen & Carol. MDiv Epis TS of the SW; BA K SU. D 3/17/2001 P 10/16/2001 Bp William Edward Smalley. m 7/31/1994 Chad K Senuta c 2. Assoc S Mich And All Ang Ch Mssn KS 2003-2011; Cur S Thos The Apos Ch Overland Pk KS 2001-2003.

SENYONI, Christian (ND) Grace Episcopal Church, 405 2nd Ave NE, Jamestown ND 58401 **Int Dio No Dakota Fargo ND 2014-; Int Gr Epis Ch Jamestown ND 2014-** B Kinshasa (DRC) 1971 s Athanase & Cecile. Lic in Theol Cornerstone Coll 2002; MA Wheaton Coll 2008; MDiv Nash 2013. D 12/20/2012 P 7/6/2013 Bp Michael Smith. m 12/16/2000 Josephine Uwayezu c 3. christian.senyoni@gmail.com

SERACUSE, Linda Kay (Tex) Po Box 559, Conroe TX 77305 B Denver CO 1945 d Frebert & Addie. BA Colorado Coll 1966; Cert Epis TS of the SW 1991; MDiv Iliff TS 1991. D 6/15/1991 P 1/25/1992 Bp William Jerry Winterrowd. c 3. S Jas The Apos Epis Ch Conroe TX 2001-2009; Gr And S Steph's Epis Ch Colorado Sprg CO 1992-2001; Dir CE Consult S Paul's Epis Ch Lakewood CO 1991-2001.

SERAS, Barbara (Md) 67 River Bend Park, Lancaster PA 17602 **S Jn's Epis Ch Lancaster PA 2015-; Co-ordinator Prov III ECUSA Lancaster PA 2004-; Prov III Baltimore MD 2004-** B Carlisle PA 1951 d Peter & Anna. BA Chatham Coll 1973; JD Penn St Dickinson Sch of Law 1978; MDiv SWTS 1992. D 6/13/1992 P 5/19/1993 Bp Albert Theodore Eastman. Assoc R S Jas Ch Lancaster PA 2012-2014; R S Mary's Epis Ch Woodlawn Gwynn Oak MD 2005-2011; R St Mary the Vrgn Ch Baltimore MD 2005-2011; R S Mk's Ch Highland MD 1997-2002; Asst to R Chr Ch Columbia MD 1992-1997; Assoc Epis Soc Ministy Baltimore MD 1988-1990. Ord of S Helena. Fell Coll of Preachers Washington DC 2002.

SERDAHL, Dennis Lee (Ark) 831 Northpointe Dr, Mountain Home AR 72653 B Des Moines IA 1933 s Emil & Frances. BS U IL 1956; MDiv Ken 1964. D 6/13/1964 P 12/1/1964 Bp Nelson Marigold Burroughs. m 10/19/1958 Margot Serdahl c 3. Vic S Andr's Ch Mtn Hm AR 1992-1998; R S Simon Cyrenne Rio Rancho NM 1991-1992; Cn Mssnr Dio The Rio Grande Albuquerque 1990-1991; Ch Of The Redeem Pendleton OR 1987-1990; St Paul's/San Pablo Epis Ch Salinas CA 1976-1987; Dio El Camino Real Salinas CA 1975-1976; Par Contracts Consult 1969-1974, Dn, Deanry VII 1966-1968, Dn, Dnry VII 1966-1976; Cur S Jn's Ch Youngstown OH 1964-1966.

SERFES, Patricia May (Me) 2524 Casa Dr, New Port Richey FL 34655 B Lapeer MI 1933 d Dewey & Helen. Maine Diac Formation Prog 1983. D 1/7/1984 Bp Frederick Barton Wolf. m 3/4/1955 Harry Frank Serfes c 3. D All SS Ch Tarpon Spgs FL 1996-2013; D S Lk's Ch Land O Lakes FL 1993-1995; D H Trin Epis Ch In Countryside Clearwater FL 1992-1993; D S Mart's Epis Ch Hudson FL 1991-1992; D, Cleric-in-Charge Ch Of The H Sprt Portland ME 1989-1990; D S Steph The Mtyr Epis Ch Waterboro Cntr ME 1987-1989; D Chr Ch Biddeford ME 1984-1987; Chapl Maine Correctional Cntr Windham 1983-1991. DOK 1996; ECW 1996; Sis of Charity 1984.

SERIO, Robert Andrew (Ala) Church of the Nativity, 208 Eustis Ave Se, Huntsville AL 35801 **D Ch Of The Nativ Epis Huntsville AL 2016-** B Washington DC 1951 s Andrew & Susie. BS U of Alabama 1973; MD UAB Sch of Med 1976. D 10/1/2016 Bp John Mckee Sloan Sr. m 3/18/1978 Margaret Baldwin Serio c 3. bserio@nativity-hsv.org

SERMON, William Todd (Colo) 1612 E Custer St, Laramie WY 82070 **R S Andr's Ch Cripple Creek CO 2000-** B Kansas City MO 1933 s William & Martha. BA Colorado Coll 1955; The Coll of Emm and S Chad CA 1999. D 4/17/1995 P 11/17/1995 Bp Bob Gordon Jones. m 6/29/1980 Kristine Utterback. R Gr Epis Ch Chadron NE 2006-2013. EFM Mentor.

SERPA-ORDONEZ, Pedro Abel (EcuC) Casilla Postal 533, Riobamba Ecuador **Vic San Gabr Riobamba Ecuador 1990-** B Canar EC 1932 s Abel & Mercedes. Sem 1987. D 3/14/1987 P 12/1/1988 Bp Adrian Delio Caceres-Villavicencio. Iglesia Epis Del Ecuador Quito 1993-2004; Iglesia San Gabr Riobamba 1988-2004; R Iglesia San Gabr Riobamba Ecuador 1988-2004; R Sagrada Familia Cuenca Ecuador 1988-1989.

SERRA-LIMA, Federico (Alb) 28 Harrington Lane, Old Chatham NY 12136 B Buenos Aires AR 1929 s Federico & Elena. BS Col 1963; MA NYU 1965; PhD NYU 1971; Cert GTS 1981. D 6/19/1982 P 12/21/1982 Bp Wilbur Emory Hogg Jr. m 3/17/1974 Margaret Serra-Lima. Trin Ch Ashland Ashland NY 1996-1997; S Jn's Ch Cohoes NY 1994-1996; S Lk's Ch Chatham NY 1987-1992; COM Dio Albany Greenwich NY 1982-1988; S Paul's Ch Franklin NY 1982-1986. Auth, "The Buddhist Influence," *LivCh*, 2009; Auth, "PB Revs in Theory and Reality," *LivCh*, 2006; Auth, "Beyond Christmas Day," *LivCh*, 1988. SSC 2000. Fell NEH 1979; Founders' Day Awd NYU 1972; Woodrow Wilson Fell 1963; Phi Beta Kappa 1963.

SERRANO POREDA, Nelson Evelio (Colom) c/o Diocese of Colombia, Cra 6 No. 49-85 Piso 2, Bogota, BDC Colombia B 1987 s Jesus & Esperanza. Seminario Mayor De Bogota 2009; Universidad Militar Nueva Granada 2010; Uni-

versidad Nacional De Colombia 2015. D 7/25/2015 Bp Francisco Jose Duque-Gomez.

SERVAIS, Jean Neal (Okla) PO Box 165, Coalgate OK 74538 B Hugo OK 1942 s Jean & Pearl. BS E Cntrl St 1965; BiVocational P Iona Sch of Mnstry 2013. D 6/15/2013 P 1/12/2014 Bp Edward Joseph Konieczny. m 8/6/2012 Svetlana Servais c 2.

SERVELLON, Maria Filomena (NY) 30 Pine Grove Avenue, 20 Carroll Street, Poughkeepsie, Kingston NY 12401 **Ch Of The H Cross Kingston NY 2012-; Dio New York New York NY 2012-, 2011-2012; Vic Mision San Juan Bautista Bronx NY 2011-** B El Progreso Honduras 1949 d Alfonso & Julia. BA Autonomous U of Honduras 1978; MDiv GTS 2006. D 3/11/2006 P 9/15/2007 Bp Mark Sean Sisk. c 1. Supply Iglesia San Juan Bautista 2009-2011; Asst Ch Of The Medtr Bronx NY 2008.

SERVETAS, Linda Anne (Alb) 16 Dean St, Deposit NY 13754 **D Chr Ch Deposit NY 2002-** B Miami FL 1943 d William & Evelyn. Bangor TS; Paterson St Teachers Coll; Rutgers The St U of New Jersey. D 6/1/2002 Bp David John Bena. m 1/6/1973 Nickolas Servetas.

SERVETAS, Nickolas (Alb) 16 Dean St, Deposit NY 13754 B South Berwick ME 1941 s Nickolas & Mildred. MA Bangor TS 1992. D 7/8/1992 Bp Edward Cole Chalfant P 5/1/1993 Bp David Standish Ball. m 1/6/1973 Linda Anne Servetas c 1. Chr Ch Deposit NY 1995-2013; S Paul's Ch Bloomville NY 1995-1998; Chr Ch Walton NY 1993-1998.

SESSIONS, Judy Karen (WTex) 2910 Treasure Hills Blvd Apt B, Harlingen TX 78550 B Idabel OK 1944 d Joseph & Alene. BA Colorado Coll 1966; GTS 1990; MDiv Epis TS of the SW 1991; Grad Theol Un 1994. D 6/22/1991 P 1/4/1992 Bp Robert Manning Moody. Long Term Supply All SS Epis Ch San Benito TX 2009-2014; Assoc R S Alb's Ch Harlingen TX 2000-2009; Assoc St Lk's Epis Ch Anth NM 1998-2000; Assoc Gr St Pauls Epis Ch Tucson AZ 1994-1997. Phi Beta Kappa The Colorado Coll 1966.

SESSIONS, Marcia Andrews (RI) 15 Hattie Ave, Greenville RI 02828 **Non-par Epis Dio Rhode Island Providence RI 1995-** B Providence RI 1953 d Henry & Carolyn. BS Barrington Coll 1975; MLS U of Rhode Island 1982; MDiv VTS 1991. D 6/22/1991 P 1/4/1992 Bp George Nelson Hunt III. R S Thos Ch Greenville RI 1994-1995; Pohick Epis Ch Lorton VA 1991-1994. Epis Ntwk for Animal Welf 2006.

SESSUM, Robert Lee (Lex) 12000 Diamond Creek Rd Apt 102, Raleigh NC 27614 **Mem Bd fo the Archv of the Epis Ch 2012-2018; Mem Bd Archv Dom And Frgn Mssy Soc- Epis Ch Cntr New York NY 2012-2018, Stndg Com on the Structure of the the Ch 2009-2015, Chair, Intl Concerns Com of Exec Coun 2000-2003, Exec Coun 1997-2003, Stndg Com on Angl and Intl Peace w Justice 1991-1997, Dep to Gnrl Conventioni 1985-2015; Mem of the Bd Driectors Kanuga Conf Cntr Hendersonville NC 2012-2018** B Memphis TN 1943 s William & Elaine. BA Rhodes Coll 1965; MDiv VTS 1970. D 7/5/1970 Bp John Vander Horst P 4/24/1971 Bp William F Gates Jr. m 7/8/1967 Donna Snyder c 1. R Ch Of The Gd Shpd Lexington KY 1994-2010; R All SS' Epis Ch Concord NC 1979-1993; Assoc R Chr Epis Ch Raleigh NC 1974-1979; Vican Ch Of The Nativ Ft Oglethorp GA 1972-1974; D; Asistant to the R S Paul's Epis Ch Chattanooga TN 1970-1972; Fin Com Dio Lexington Lexington 2015-2016, Exec Com 2006-2009, Lexington Cler Convenor 1996-2009, Ecum Off 1994-1997; Pres Prov IV Jackson MS 2003-2009; Mem of the Admin and Fin Com Angl Consultative Coun London Engl 2002-2009; Treas, No Amer Reg Com St Geo's Coll Jerusalem 1992-2005. Paul Harris Fell Concord Rotary 1993; Sr Man of the Year Concord Jaycees 1984; Outstanding Young Citizen ChmbrCom 1973.

SETMEYER, Robert Charles (Chi) 711 S River Rd Apt 508, Des Plaines IL 60016 B Hammond IN 1946 s Charles & Eleanore. BS DePaul U 1972; BS Nash 1975. D 6/14/1975 P 12/13/1975 Bp James Winchester Montgomery. m 11/26/1983 Joyce A Setmeyer c 2. R S Mart's Ch Des Plaines IL 1978-2007; Cur Ch Of The Redeem Elgin IL 1975-1978; Advsr Yth Elgin Dnry Dio Chicago Chicago IL 1974-1978. Graduated on Dn's List DePaul U 1972.

SETTLES, Russell Lee (NC) 9118 Kings Canyon Dr, Charlotte NC 28210 B Cheyanne WY 1954 s George & Ruth. Brenau U; Spartanburg Methodist Coll; U GA; Cert No Carolina Diac Prog 1999. D 6/12/1999 Bp James Gary Gloster. m 5/20/1995 Tammy Maria Helms. D S Jn's Epis Ch Charlotte NC 1999-2000; D S Andr's Epis Ch Charlotte NC 1998-2004.

SETZER, Stephen F (Del) 5100 Ross Ave, Dallas TX 75206 B Lenoir NC 1985 s Robert & Audrey. BH Pensacola Chr Coll 2008; CGS Dallas TS 2009; MDiv Wycliffe Coll 2013; MDiv Wycliffe Coll Toronto CA 2013. D 6/15/2013 Bp Paul Emil Lambert. m 5/23/2015 Yoana Sampayo. Chr Ch Christiana Hundred Wilmington DE 2015, Assoc 2015-; S Matt's Cathd Dallas TX 2013-2015. ssetzer@christchurchde.org

SEUFERT, Carmen Rae (Roch) 103 Williams St, Newark NY 14513 **R NE Partnr in Epis Mnstry NY 2004-** B Kansas City MO 1946 d George & Carmen. BS SUNY 1986; MDiv Bex Sem 1994. D 12/9/1995 P 9/14/1996 Bp David Charles Bowman. m 5/22/1965 Dwight Robert Seufert. Gr Ch Lyons NY 2009-2013; S Jn's Ch Sodus NY 2004-2013; S Mk's Ch Newark NY 2004-2013; R S Pat's Ch Buffalo NY 2000-2004; P-in-c S Paul's Ch Holley NY 1996-2000.

SEVAYEGA, Reginald Delano (HB) 4701 Belfiore Rd, Warrensville Heights OH 44128 **Non-par 1973-** B Harrisburg PA 1937 s William & Thelma. BS JCU 1962; MDiv Evang Luth TS 1970; MA U Pgh 1974; PhD U Pgh 1975. D 6/19/1968 P 12/1/1968 Bp John Harris Burt. c 1. S Aug's Epis Ch Youngstown OH 1968-1973. Auth, "Mobility & Rigid Body Transport"; Auth, "La Filosofia De La Vida Capitalista Y La Lucha Para Libertad".

SEVER, Cynthia A (Spr) 3390 Lyell Rd, Rochester NY 14606 **S Paul's and Trin Chap Alton IL 2016-** B Blue Island IL 1959 d Raymond & Marilyn. BA U IL 1981; AAS Parkland Coll Champaign IL 1983; MDiv Bex Sem 2000. D 6/1/2002 P 12/14/2002 Bp Jack Marston Mckelvey. m 5/29/1982 Byron R Sever c 1. R Gr Ch Lockport NY 2012-2016; Chr Ch Albion NY 2009-2012; Asst R Chr Ch Pittsford Pittsford NY 2007-2008; Yth Mssnr Dio Rochester Henrietta 2004-2007; Cur S Mk's And S Jn's Epis Ch Rochester NY 2002-2004. cindysever210@gmail.com

SEVICK, Gerald (Tex) 3901 S. Panther Creek, The Woodlands TX 77381 **R Trin Epis Ch The Woodlands TX 2007-** B Bryan TX 1954 s Thomas & Doris. BA Baylor U 1977; Grad Sch of Soc Wk-Arlington Arlington TX 1982; MDiv SWTS 1987; DMin Sem of the So 2009; DMin Sem of the So 2009. D 7/25/1987 Bp Clarence Cullam Pope Jr P 5/21/1988 Bp Donis Dean Patterson. m 7/24/1982 Donna K Sevick c 4. R S Anne's Epis Ch Desoto TX 1990-2007; Asst P Epis Ch Of The Ascen Dallas TX 1987-1989. Auth, "Sacrificial Servnt," *LivCh (September 30)*, 2001; Auth, "Embracing The Cntr," *LivCh (February 14)*, 1999; Auth, "A Season Of Pryr For The Healing Of Hunger & Pvrty"; Auth, "Meditation On Matt 5:42," *Roots Of Hope*. Professed Tertiary Of The Soc Of S Fran 1983.

SEVILLE, John C (Chi) 802 Foxdale Ave, Winnetka IL 60093 B Pittsburgh PA 1943 s David & Katherine. BA Ups 1967; MDiv PDS 1970. D 6/28/1970 P 3/1/1971 Bp Dean Theodore Stevenson. m 8/18/1984 Cindee Ruth Clark c 1. Int Trin Epis Ch Reno NV 2013-2015; S Paul's Ch Manhattan KS 2012-2013; Int S Paul's Ch Charlottesville VA 2011-2012; Int R The Memi Ch Of The Gd Shpd Parkersburg WV 2009-2010; Dio W Virginia Charleston WV 2008-2009; S Jas' Epis Ch Lewisburg WV 2008; S Ptr's Ch Salisbury MD 2007-2008; Int Chr Epis Ch Winchester VA 2006-2007; Int Trin Ch Highland Pk IL 2004-2005; Int S Geo's Ch Fredericksburg VA 2003-2004; Int Ch Of The Trsfg Palos Pk IL 2001-2003; Int S Hilary's Ch Prospect Hts IL 1999-2001; S Jn's Epis Ch Mt Prospect IL 1997-1999; Int Ch Of Our Sav Chicago IL 1995-1997; Int Gr Epis Ch Freeport IL 1994-1995; S Mk's Ch Geneva IL 1993-1994; P-in-c S Chrys's Ch Chicago IL 1993; Int S Mk's Barrington IL 1991-1993; Int Chr Ch Waukegan IL 1989-1991; Int Gr Ch Oak Pk IL 1988-1989; Int P-in-c S Pat's Franklin Pk IL 1986-1988; 1982-1985; Dn Dio Connecticut Meriden CT 1980-1981, Exec Coun 1979-1980, Sub-Dn of New Haven Dnry 1978-1979; R Ch of the H Sprt W Haven CT 1977-1981; Vic St Jas Epis Ch Exch PA 1972-1977; R S Jas Ch Muncy PA 1971-1977; Dio Cntrl Pennsylvania Harrisburg PA 1970-1971; D-Intern S Jas Ch Lancaster PA 1970-1971; D-Intern S Thos Ch Lancaster PA 1970-1971. Auth, *Be of Gd Cheer*.

SEVILLE, Joseph Yates (CPa) 1405 Wedgewood Way, Mechanicsburg PA 17050 **Assoc The Epis Ch Of S Jn The Bapt York PA 2010-** B Pittsburgh PA 1948 s David & Katharine. BA Tem 1970; MDiv Yale DS 1973; MPA Penn 1981. D 6/8/1973 P 3/23/1974 Bp Dean Theodore Stevenson. m 8/21/1971 Linda Seville. St Andrews in the City Epis Ch Harrisburg PA 2002-2010; Cn Ordnry Dio Cntrl Pennsylvania Harrisburg PA 1996-2010, Yth Cmsn 1975-1983; R S Thos The Apos Ch Overland Pk KS 1989-1996; R Chr Epis Ch Great Choptank Par Cambridge MD 1983-1989; R S Lk's Epis Ch Mt Joy PA 1979-1983; R S Jn's Epis Ch Bellefonte PA 1974-1979; Intrn S Lk's Epis Ch Altoona PA 1973-1974; Asst Ecum Off Dio Kansas Topeka KS 1991-1996; Stwdshp Dept Dio Easton Easton MD 1984-1989. Auth, "The Epis Dio Cntrl Pennsylvania As A Systems Model: A Case Study".

SEWARD, Barbara J (Minn) Trinity Episcopal Church, 322 2nd St, Excelsior MN 55331 **S Bride's Epis Ch Oregon IL 2015-** B Lawrenceville VA 1965 d Milton. BS Fayetteville St U 1995; MS The JHU 2003; MDiv Estrn Mennonite Sem 2011; Angl Stds VTS 2013. D 6/8/2013 Bp Shannon Sherwood Johnston P 12/14/2013 Bp Brian N Prior. c 1. Trin Ch Excelsior MN 2013-2014. revbarbj@gmail.com

SEWELL, Edith (Haw) 1212 Punahou #2504, Honolulu HI 96826 **D S Andr's Cathd 1990-** B Atlanta GA 1931 d Frank & Margaret. Agnes Scott Coll; BA U NC 1953; MA U of Hawaii 1974; Dio Hawaii Diac Prog Ord HI 1985. D 7/18/1985 Bp Edmond Lee Browning. m 4/8/1989 Robert Barr Husselrath. D- in - Res-Vol S Barth's Epis Ch Poway CA 1998-2004; D S Eliz's Ch Honolulu HI 1985-1990. Hawaii Epis Cleric Assn.

SEWELL, John Wayne (WTenn) 53 Shepherd Ln, Memphis TN 38117 **R S Jn's Epis Ch Memphis TN 2003-; R S Jn's Epis Ch Memphis TN 2002-** B Lester AL 1951 s Neil & Doris. BS U of No Alabama 1974; MDiv Asbury TS 1979; Cert SWTS 1981. D 5/30/1981 P 12/1/1981 Bp Furman Charles Stough. m 5/23/1987 Marilyn Sewell. R The Chap Of The Cross Madison MS 1989-2002; Assoc R S Lk's Epis Ch Birmingham AL 1987-1989; R Chr Epis Ch Albertville AL 1981-1987; S Phil's Ch Ft Payne AL 1981-1982.

SEXTON, Jessica Elaine (Md) 1401 Carrollton Ave, Baltimore MD 21204 **Ch Of The Gd Shpd Towson MD 2016-** B Baltimore MD 1986 d William & Judy. BA Notre Dame of Maryland U 2008; MDiv Yale DS 2011; Angl Stds Cert VTS 2016. D 1/16/2016 Bp Chilton Richardson Knudsen P 9/29/2016 Bp Eugene Taylor Sutton.

SEXTON, Patricia Mary (USC) 1001 12th St, Cayce SC 29033 **R All SS Ch Cayce SC 2011-** B Buffalo NY 1951 d Allen & Audrey. BA SUNY at Buffalo 1973; JD Case Wstrn Reserve U 1976; MDiv VTS 2011. D 6/4/2011 Bp William Jerry Winterrowd P 12/9/2011 Bp Robert John O'Neill. c 2.

SEXTON, Timothy Wayne (Haw) PO Box 181, Des Moines NM 88418 **part time H Trin Epis Ch - Mssn Raton NM 2011-** B South Charleston WV 1948 s Buford & Wanda. U of So Florida 1970; BS U of Cntrl Florida 1978; MDiv Nash 1983. D 3/1/1976 P 6/21/1983 Bp William Hopkins Folwell. m 8/1/1997 Barbara J Metzker c 6. Chapl Ambercare Hospice Raton NM 2012-2015; Provost S Andr's Cathd Honolulu HI 2004-2010, Cn 2004-2007; Cn Chr Epis Ch Anacortes WA 2000-2003; Cn S Jas Ch Sedro Woolley WA 1999-2003; R/Cn Mssnr S Paul's Epis Ch Mt Vernon WA 1997-2004; Cn Dio Utah Salt Lake City UT 1989-1996; R Ch of Our Sav No Platte NE 1986-1989; P-in-c S Aidans Ch Hartford WI 1984-1986, In-c 1982-1983, D-in-c 1980-1981; Yth Dir Dio Milwaukee Milwaukee WI 1983-1986; Asst S Mart's Ch Milwaukee WI 1983-1984; D S Mary Of The Ang Epis Ch Orlando FL 1978-1980; D S Chris's Ch Orlando FL 1976-1978; D Chr The King Epis Ch Orlando FL 1976.

SEYMOUR, John Jack David (Chi) 1631 N Tripp Ave, Chicago IL 60639 **Re-Vive Cntr for Hsng and Healing Chicago IL 2010-; D Ch Of S Paul And The Redeem Chicago IL 2004-** B Springfield IL 1952 s John & Loretta. IL Wesl 1972; BA U IL 1975; MDiv Chicago TS 2011. D 9/19/1994 Bp Peter Hess Beckwith. m 9/4/1976 Janis Joy Gomien c 2. D The Cathd Ch Of S Paul Springfield IL 1994-2002; Dir, Sch for Deacons Dio Chicago Chicago IL 2009-2014. jseymour@revivecenter.org

SEYMOUR, Marlyne Joyce (Mil) 862 No. Sandy Lane, Elkhorn WI 53121 **D Chr Epis Ch Of Delavan Delavan WI 1991-** B Madison WI 1932 d Arthur & Agnes. U of Wisconsin 1952. D 10/21/1989 Bp Roger John White. m 7/13/1957 William Lester Seymour. S Jn In The Wilderness Elkhorn WI 1989-1991. DOK 1986; NAAD 1989; Ord of Julian of Norwich 1988.

SGRO, Anthony Huston (At) **Headmaster Rabun Gap-Nacoochee Sch 2011-; D S Jas Epis Ch Clayton GA 2011-** B Norfolk VA 1965 s Joseph & Beverly. BA VPI 1989; MPA VPI 1992; EdD U of Pennsylvania 2006; Diac Stds Diac Formation Inst- Dio Virginia 2011. D 12/13/2011 Bp Keith Whitmore. m 7/24/2004 Faulkner Bagley Elizabeth Bourne Faulkner Bagley c 3. Asst Headmaster Woodberry Forest Sch 1999-2011. asgro@rabungap.org

SHACKELFORD, Lynn Clark (Okla) 404 Washington Avenue, Sand Springs OK 74063 **PT Vic St. Matt Epis Ch Sand Sprg OK 2014-** B Nashville TN 1946 s Clarence & Grace. BA Van 1967; JD Nashville Sch of Law 1977; MDiv Epis TS of the SW 1994. D 6/24/1994 Bp Edward Witker Jones P 12/23/1994 Bp John Forsythe Ashby. m 4/20/1974 Jane Shackelford c 4. Dn Dio Oklahoma Oklahoma City OK 2012-2013, Dioc Intake Off 2014-, Founding Dn, Iona TS 2012-2013, Chair, BEC 2009-, Dioc Coun 2003-2004, Dn, Tulsa Reg 2000-2003, Justice, Eccl Crt 1999-2003, BEC - Exam in H Scripture 1995-; Bd Mem OK Coun of Ch Oklahoma City 2007-2009; Epis Sem of the SW Bd Trst Austin 2005-2010; R Emm Epis Ch Shawnee OK 2004-2010; R S Matt's Ch Sand Sprg OK 2002-2004; Chapl Sand Sprg Police Dept Sand Sprg OK 1999-2004; Chapl Oklahoma DOK Tulsa OK 1997-2000; Bd Mem Interfaith Allnce Tulsa OK 1996-2004; R S Lk's Epis Ch Scott City KS 1994-1995. Auth, "Rel column," *Countrywide News & Shawnee Sun, Tecumseh, OK*, 2009; Auth, "Rel column," *Shawnee News-Star, Shawnee, OK*, 2005; Auth, "Rel column," *Sand Sprg Ldr, Sand Sprg, OK*, 1997. CHS 1997; Ecum Soc of BVM 2008; Soc of Cath Priests 2012; The Queen's Engl Soc 2015. Wm Wiseman Awd Interfaith Allnce of Tulsa, OK 2004.

SHACKLEFORD, Richard Neal (LI) Timber Ridge, 711 John Green Rd, Jonesborough TN 37659 **R S Tim's Epis Ch Kingsport TN 2008-; Dio E Tennessee Knoxville TN 2008-** B LaGrange MO 1940 s Benjamin & Oma. BA U Denv 1964; MA U of Nthrn Colorado 1974; Oxf GB/ S Sstephen's Hse 1985. Trans 2/1/1989 Bp William Carl Frey. m 4/19/2017 Belen Hugh Kendall. R S Bon Epis Ch Lindenhurst NY 2005; Licebsed to Officiate Dioceses of E Tennessee 1996-2005; 1992-1996; S Jn's Cathd Denver CO 1988-1992; Serv Ch of Engl 1986-1988. sttimothyskpt@embarqmail.com

SHACKLETT JR, Richard L (Kan) 6535 Maple Dr, Mission KS 66202 B Wichita KS 1927 s Richard & Kay. BA Friends U 1950; BD EDS 1954; MS U of Utah 1973. D 6/11/1954 Bp Goodrich R Fenner P 6/20/1960 Bp James W Hunter. m 10/12/1957 Ela E Shacklett. P-in-c Experimental Mnstry Kansas City MO 1966-1971; Assoc Gr And H Trin Cathd Kansas City MO 1964-1966; R All SS Ch Wheatland WY 1962-1964; R S Paul's Epis Ch Dixon WY 1960-1961; 1956-1960.

SHADLE, Jennifer L (WTex) B Bryan TX 1948 d Charles & Mareta. BM Sam Houston St U 1970; MA Sam Houston St U 1976; PhD S Louis U 1992. D 6/13/2015 P 6/18/2016 Bp Robert John O'Neill. jennifer.shadle@ssw.edu

SHADOW, Burton Alexander (FtW) 3540 Manderly Place, Fort Worth TX 76109 **Bilingual Elem. Tchr Ft Worth Indep Sch Dist 2006-2036** B Fort Lauderdale FL 1963 s Roger & Waltraut. BA Ramapo St Coll 1986; MSW Ford 1988; MDiv NYTS 1998; STM Nash 2000. D 4/24/2000 P 11/18/2000 Bp Jack Leo Iker. m 4/24/1993 Ingrid L Shadow c 2. S Jn's Ch Ft Worth TX 2000-2006; Cur Dio Ft Worth Ft Worth TX 2000-2002. Auth, "The Dio Responds to the Changing Nbrhd," *Forw in Mssn*, 2001; Auth, "Hisp Ordinands Need Cmnty," *LivCh*, 2001. CCU 2001.

SHAEFER III, Harry Frederick (Mich) 407 Highland Ave., Johnson City TN 37604 **Extended Supply P S Thos Ch Elizabethton TN 2010-** B Brooklyn NY 1939 s Harry & Dorothea. BA Ob 1961; GTS 1963; BD UTS 1964; Estrn Michigan U 1976; DMin Ecum TS 1992; Wayne 2009. D 6/13/1964 P 12/14/1964 Bp Nelson Marigold Burroughs. m 3/17/1974 Marjorie Moore c 4. Supply during R's sabbatical Ch Of The Incarn Pittsfield Twp Ann Arbor MI 2005; Ret 1998-2007; Cathd Ch Of S Paul Detroit MI 1998-1999; R S Jas' Epis Ch Dexter MI 1978-1991; Assoc S Clem's Epis Ch Inkster MI 1969-1977; Cur Par Of S Jas Ch Keene NH 1966-1969; S Jn's Ch Walpole NH 1966-1969; S Ptr Drewsville NH 1966-1969; Cur Ch Of The Ascen Mt Vernon NY 1964-1966. Auth, "First Thessalonians: The Hidden Hist of the Pauline Ch," Kephalos Pub LLC, 2013.

SHAEFER, Susan A (Mich) 1605 E. Stadium Blvd., Ann Arbor MI 48104 **Vic S Jn's Ch Clinton MI 2012-** B Ann Arbor MI 1978 d Jeanne. BA U MI 2000; MDiv SWTS 2005. D 12/18/2004 P 7/2/2005 Bp Wendell Nathaniel Gibbs Jr. m 6/8/2002 Harry Luke Shaefer c 1. Assoc P S Jn's Ch Plymouth MI 2009-2011; Mssnr for Yth & YA Dio Michigan Detroit MI 2007-2008; Cur S Paul's Epis Ch Lansing MI 2005-2007. NAECED 2009.

SHAFER, Gail Ann (Mich) D 6/10/2017 Bp Wendell Nathaniel Gibbs Jr.

SHAFER, Lee Franklin (Ala) 5 Booger Holw, Anniston AL 36207 **R Gr Ch Anniston AL 2008-** B Gasden AL 1961 d Denson & Virginia. BS U of Alabama 1984; STM Nash 2003; DMin Sewanee: The U So, TS 2012. D 9/18/2001 P 4/17/2002 Bp Henry Irving Louttit. m 8/26/2004 Thomas Shafer c 2. S Jn's Epis Ch Tallahassee FL 2006-2008; Chr Ch Valdosta GA 2003-2006. gracerector@cableone.net

SHAFER, Linda Jean (Mich) 151 N Main St, Brooklyn MI 49230 B Batavia NY 1943 d George & Jean. D 6/14/2014 Bp Wendell Nathaniel Gibbs Jr. m 9/14/1985 Jerry L Shafer.

SHAFER, Michael Gales (NY) 21 Decker Road, Stanfordville NY 12581 B New York NY 1941 s Judson & Helene. BA Bard Coll 1966; STB Ya Berk 1969. D 6/7/1969 P 12/1/1969 Bp Horace W B Donegan. m 6/17/1967 Johanna M Shafer c 2. P-in-c Ch Of The Regeneration Pine Plains NY 2000-2013; P-in-c S Lk's Ch Chatham NY 1995-1999; Trin Ch Watervliet NY 1989-1995; Assoc S Ptr's Ch Albany NY 1986-1988; R S Jn Lewisboro NY 1971-1986; S Jn's Ch So Salem NY 1971-1986; Cur H Trin Epis Ch Vlly Stream NY 1969-1971. *Old Values for a New Generation*, Vantage Press, 2002.

SHAFER, Samuel H (RG) 630 66th St, Oakland CA 94609 B Denver CO 1939 s Samuel & Fern. BA U CO 1963; MDiv Iliff TS 1982. D 9/1/2001 P 9/5/2002 Bp Terence Kelshaw. m 12/11/1965 Joanna Shafer c 3. Asst R Chr The King Epis Ch Santa Barbara CA 2002-2004; Asst for Mssn & Outreach St Jas the Great Epis Ch Newport Bch CA 1982-1989.

SHAFFER, Brian Keith (Mich) Cathedral Church of St. Paul, Detroit MI 48201 **D Cathd Ch Of S Paul Detroit MI 2015-; D Trin Ch Columbus OH 1997-** B Kittanning PA 1973 s William & Beverly. MTS Angl Inst/St Albans 1998. D 10/1/2013 Bp Thomas Edward Breidenthal. bshaffer@detroitcathedral.org

SHAFFER, Charles Omer (Md) 7200 3rd Ave, Cot. C119, Eldersburg MD 21784 **Assoc S Andr's Epis Ch Glenwood MD 2013-; Ret 1991-** B Madisonville KY 1933 s Marion & Nannie. BA Transylvania U 1956; MDiv Epis TS in Kentucky 1971. D 5/29/1971 Bp William R Moody P 6/23/1972 Bp Addison Hosea. Int Ch Of The Mssh Baltimore MD 1993; R Harriet Chap Catoctin Epis Par Thurmont MD 1975-1991; Asst to R S Tim's Ch Catonsville MD 1972-1975. Elected to Mem Maryland Sr Citizens Hall of Fame 2008.

SHAFFER, Dallas Bertrand (WVa) 1415 Cornell St, Keyser WV 26726 B Northfork WV 1933 s Carl & Hazel. VTS; BA U Rich 1954; MA W Virginia U 1961; PhD W Virginia U 1966. D 6/14/1997 P 6/13/1998 Bp John Henry Smith. m 10/15/1960 Jennie Mae Lininger. R Hampshire Hardy Yoke 1997-2000.

SHAFFER, Dee (Ga) 299 Ga Episcopal Conference Ctr Rd, Waverly GA 31565 **S Paul's Epis Ch Jesup GA 2013-; Chapl Heartland Hospice Brunswick Georgia 2010-; Vic Ch of Our Sav at Honey Creek Waverly GA 2008-** B Pittsburgh PA 1954 d Richard & Jean. BA Queens U 1976; Tchr Cert Armstrong Atlantic St U 1995; MDiv Asbury TS 2007. D 9/25/2008 P 6/18/2009 Bp Henry Irving Louttit. m 9/3/1987 Michael Richard Shaffer c 2. Asst Chr Ch Frederica St Simons Is GA 2013-2014, 2010-2013; Int St Richard's Of Chichester Epis Mssn Jekyll Island GA 2012-2013; Prog Dir Georgia Epis Conf Cntr At Honey Creek Waverly GA 2009-2010.

SHAFFER, James M (WMo) PO Box 2714, Friday Harbor WA 98250 B Sugar Creek MO 1956 s James & Phyllis. BS SMU 1978; Juris Doctor The U of Missouri Kansas City Sch of Law 1981; Juris Doctor The U of Missouri¿Kansas City Sch of Law 1981; Juris Doctor UMKC Sch of Law 1981; Juris Doctor

UMKC Sch of Law 1981; Angl Stds Bp Kemper Sch for Mnstry 2014. D 2/5/2000 Bp Barry Howe P 4/26/2014 Bp Martin Scott Field. m 1/1/1991 Sally Wood c 2.

SHAFFER, John Alfred (CNY) 162 W 3rd St, Oswego NY 13126 B York PA 1951 s Lester & Mildred. BA W Virginia Wesleyan Coll 1973; MA U of Wisconsin 1975; MDiv Nash 1992. D 6/13/1992 P 6/11/1993 Bp John Henry Smith. m 8/5/1972 Barbara A Ammerman c 2. R Gr Ch Baldwinsville NY 1996-2003; Asst; P-in-c S Matt's Ch Wheeling WV 1992-1996; Dir of Arts Programming SUNY Oswego Oswego NY 2012-2017; Dn, Nthrn Allnce Dist Dio Cntrl New York Liverpool NY 2000-2003. Auth, "Winifred's Well," Cold Tree Press, 2008; Auth, "Mystery," *LivCh*, LivCh Fndt, 2006.

✠ SHAHAN, The Rt Rev Robert Reed (Az) 10175 S North Lake Ave, Olathe KS 66061 B Elkhart KS 1939 s John & Freda. BS U of Kansas 1961; MBA MI SU 1967; MDiv Nash 1973; PhD NWU 1979; SWTS 1994. D 5/19/1973 P 11/24/1973 Bp Charles Bennison Sr Con 10/3/1992 for Az. m 8/11/1963 Mary Carol Shahan. Bp Of Az Dio Arizona Phoenix AZ 1992-2004; Dn Gr Cathd Topeka KS 1985-1992, Dn 1984-1992; Pres Fam Cnslng Serv Of Aiken SC 1983-1984; Pres Mead Hall Epis Sch Aiken SC 1981-1984; R S Thad Epis Ch Aiken SC 1981-1984; Vic S Fran Epis Ch Chicago IL 1976-1981; Bexley Seabury Fed Chicago IL 1975-1981; Vic S Alb's Mssn N. Muskegon MI 1973-1975. Hon DD SWTS.

SHAHINIAN, Katharine Anne (Md) St Martin's In The Field, 375 Benfield Rd, Severna Park MD 21146 B Baltimore MD 1953 d William & Helen. BA Coll of Notre Dame 1986; MA Coll of Notre Dame 1990. D 6/1/2013 Bp Joe Goodwin Burnett. m 6/20/2003 George C Shahinian c 1.

SHAIN-HENDRICKS, Christy A (Colo) Po Box 10000, Silverthorne CO 80498 **Ch Of The Ascen Pueblo CO 2016-** B Waco TX 1956 d Rox & Nancy. BA U CO 1995; MDiv Iliff TS 1999. D 6/5/1999 P 12/11/1999 Bp William Jerry Winterrowd. m 7/21/1979 Glenn Arthur Hendricks c 3. Int Emm Ch Houston TX 2015-2016; R Epis Ch Of S Jn The Bapt Breckenridge CO 2006-2014; Dio Colorado Denver CO 2005-2013; P-in-c Ch Of The H Sprt Colorado Spg CO 2004-2006; S Ben Epis Ch La Veta CO 2002-2004; Ch Of S Ptr The Apos Pueblo CO 1999-2001. Dok. J Spangler Awd For Excellence In Rel And Psychol Iliff TS 1999.

SHAKESPEARE, Lyndon (WA) 543 Beulah Rd NE, Vienna VA 22180 **Ch Of The H Comf Vienna VA 2016-** B Gosford New South Wales AU 1972 s Leslie & Rosslyn. BA Wheaton Coll 1995; MDiv VTS 2002; PhD Archbp's Examination in Theol 2015. D 6/8/2002 Bp Barry Howe P 12/8/2002 Bp James Winchester Montgomery. m 1/4/1997 Amie F Shakespeare c 3. Int S Anselm's Ch Shoreham NY 2015-2016; S Fran Epis Ch Great Falls VA 2014-2015; S Paul's Par Washington DC 2013-2014; Dir of Prog and Mnstry Cathd of St Ptr & St Paul Washington DC 2011-2013; R All SS Memi Ch Navesink NJ 2006-2011; Asst to R Chr Ch Georgetown Washington DC 2002-2006. Soc of Schlr-Priests 2013. Pstr Study Proj Louisville Inst 2010; Promising Schlr ECF 2005.

SHALLCROSS, Lexa Herries (Be) 150 Elm St, Emmaus PA 18049 B Philadelphia PA 1946 d Herbert & Elizabeth. BA Douglass Coll 1968; MS Rutgers The St U of New Jersey 1971; MDiv GTS 1987. D 5/30/1987 P 2/7/1988 Bp James Michael Mark Dyer. m 11/23/1968 Domenick J Billera c 1. R S Marg's Ch Emmaus PA 1989-2010; P-in-c Chr Ch Forest City PA 1987-1989; P-in-c Trin Epis Ch Carbondale PA 1987-1989.

SHAMBAUGH, Benjamin Albert (Me) 143 State St, Portland ME 04101 **Advsry Bd Mem St Eliz's Essentials Pantry/Jubilee Cntr Portland 2015-; Chair, then Dep GC Dep Dio Maine 2012-; Mem, then Pres Stndg Com Dio Maine 2011-; Bd Mem Preble St Resource Cntr Portland Maine 2009-; Dn Cathd Ch Of S Lk Portland ME 2005-** B Washington DC 1963 s George & Katherine. BA NWU 1985; Codrington Coll 1987; MDiv GTS 1988; DMin SWTS 2005. D 6/18/1988 P 12/16/1988 Bp Frank Tracy Griswold III. m 8/19/1989 Shari G Shambaugh c 2. Bd Mem The Rel Cltn Against Discrimination Portland 2008-2013; Adj Fac Bangor TS Portland Maine 2007-2012; Bd Mem Afr Palms USA Olney Maryland 1995-2005; R S Jn's Ch Olney MD 1995-2005; Bd Chair St. Jn's Epis Sch Olney Maryland 1995-2005; Chapl Washington Natl Cathd Washington DC 1995-2005; Cn The Amer Cathd of the H Trin Paris 75008 1991-1995; Cur The Ch Of The H Sprt Lake Forest IL 1988-1991. Auth, "The Epis Ch Is Or The Epis Ch Are," *LivCh*, 2002; Auth, "A Call To Curacy," *Gathering The Next Generation*, 2000; Auth, "Are We An Epis Or A Congrl Ch?," *LivCh*, 1999. No Amer Cathd Deans 2005; Washington Epis Cler Assn 1995-2005. Founders Awd Integrity Maine 2013; Bd Mem of the Year Preble St 2013. bs.shambaugh@gmail.com

SHAMEL, Andrew (Cal) 55 Monument Cir Ste 600, Indianapolis IN 46204 B Abington PA 1982 s Louis & Cynthia. AB Dart 2005; MDiv CDSP 2010; MA CDSP/GTU 2011. D 6/19/2010 P 4/9/2011 Bp Jim Mathes. Stanford Cbury Fndt Palo Alto CA 2013-2017; Chr Ch Cathd Indianapolis IN 2011-2013. andys@cccindy.org

SHAMHART, Lewis Roper (LI) 510 W 46th St Apt 621, New York NY 10036 **Died 7/30/2017** B Johnson City TN 1926 s Paul & Emily. BA W&L 1948; MDiv VTS 1951; GTS 1957. P 12/21/1951 Bp Henry D Phillips. 1994-2017; Chair of the Dept of Mssn 1994-2017; Archd for Multicultural Ministers Dio

Long Island Garden City NY 1994-1998, Liturg Cmsn 1967-1993, BEC 1962-1980, Pres of Epis Assn 1961-1966; S Dav's Epis Ch Cambria Heights NY 1991; Archd of Queens 1984-1993; Chair of the Com on Liturg & Ch Mus 1981-1984; Chair of the Com on Ch Archit 1980-1981; 1972-1977; R S Mk's Ch Jackson Heights NY 1960-1991; Chapl BSA in Long Island 1960-1984; Chapl BSA in New York 1958-1960; Assoc Ch Of The Heav Rest New York NY 1957-1960; Asst Chr And S Steph's Ch New York NY 1956-1957; Asst Gr Ch Madison NJ 1955-1956; Asst S Jn's Epis Ch Wytheville VA 1953-1955; R S Thos Epis Christiansbrg VA 1951-1953. Oblate Ord of S Ben 1998. Hon Cn Cathd of the Incarn 1998.

SHAMO, Vincent (Los) 3225 Hollypark Dr Apt 4, Inglewood CA 90305 **St Mary in Palms Los Angeles CA 2005-** B Teshie Accra 1954 LTh S Nich Theol Coll Cape Coast GH. Trans 4/27/2004 Bp Joseph Jon Bruno. m 9/21/1991 Florence K Shamo c 3. Dio Los Angeles Los Angeles CA 2004-2010; S Jas Par Los Angeles CA 2003-2004; Chapl Cbury Irvine Fndt U CA Irvine.

SHAN, Becky King-Chu (ECR) 450 Old San francisco Rd Apt A110, Sunnyvale CA 94086 B CN 1937 d Luen-Li & Pui-Chun. Cert Grantham Teachers Trng Coll 1958; Evening Sch of High Chinese Stds 1965; UTS Hong Kong 1968. D 3/27/1993 P 11/6/1993 Bp Richard Lester Shimpfky. c 2. Dio El Camino Real Salinas CA 2000-2007; Vic H Light Chinese Cong Campbell CA 1995-2003; Asst S Thos Epis Ch Sunnyvale CA 1993-1994.

SHANAHAN, Thomazine Weinstein (CPa) 4426 Reservoir Rd Nw, Washington DC 20007 B Miami Beach FL 1944 d Jerome & Thomazine. BA Penn 1965; MA GW 1978; MDiv VTS 1990. D 6/9/1990 P 1/1/1991 Bp Ronald Hayward Haines. c 1. Dio Cntrl Pennsylvania Harrisburg PA 1998-2007; Asst S Pat's Ch Washington DC 1996-1998; Asst Chr Ch Georgetown Washington DC 1990-1996.

✠ **SHAND, The Rt Rev Bud** (Eas) 208 Somerset Ct, Queenstown MD 21658 **Epis VIsitor Epis Carmel of S Teresa 2014-; Hon Bd Chair VTS Alexandria VA 2009-, Trst 2003-2009; Mem HOB 2003-** B New York NY 1946 s Jean & Mary. BA Canaan Coll 1969; MDiv PDS 1972; MA VTS 1999; DD VTS 2003. D 4/22/1972 P 10/28/1972 Bp Alfred L Banyard Con 1/25/2003 for Eas. m 8/3/1974 Lynne Stevens Shand c 2. Dio Easton Easton MD 2003-2014, Committe on CE and Stwdshp 1979-1991, Dioc Coun and Stndg Com 1977-1987, Camp Wright Com 1976-1985, GC Dep 2000-2003, Stndg Com, Pres 1998-2001, GC Dep 1982-1994, Dioc Coun 1978-1997; Bp of Easton Trin Cathd Easton MD 2003-2014; R Chr Ch Par Kent Island Stevensville MD 1989-2002; R S Mary Anne's Epis Ch No E MD 1975-1989; Asst Gr Ch Merchantville NJ 1972-1975; Chairman of the Bd Trst VTS 2009-2017. DD VTS 2003. budlynne83@yahoo.com

SHAND III, William Munro (WA) PO Box 326, Saluda NC 28773 B Columbia SC 1950 s William & Evelyn. BA U of So Carolina 1971; MA U of So Carolina 1977; MDiv VTS 1981. D 6/13/1981 Bp William Arthur Beckham P 5/15/1982 Bp Maurice Manuel Benitez. m 5/26/1979 Jennifer Benitez c 2. R S Fran Ch Potomac MD 1987-2015; R S Paul's Epis Ch Prnc Frederck MD 1983-1987; Vic Calv Ch Pauline SC 1981-1983; COM Dio Washington Washington DC 2000-2006. Auth, "arts," *Angl Dig*, Angl Dig, 2011; Auth, "From There He Will Come To Judge," *Exploring & Proclaiming The Apos' Creed*, Eerdman's, 2004; Auth, "Sing Praise to God," *Hymns from Amer*, Oxf Press, 2003. wmshand@gmail.com

SHANDS III, Alfred Rives (Ky) 8915 Highway 329, Crestwood KY 40014 B Washington DC 1928 s Alfred & Elizabeth. BA Pr 1950; BD VTS 1954. D 6/20/1954 Bp Arthur R Mc Kinstry P 5/1/1955 Bp John Brooke Mosley. m 9/1/1967 Mary Shands. Vic S Jn's Ch Harbor Spgs MI 1985-1999; Vic S Clem's Ch Louisville KY 1976-1991; Non-par 1969-1976; Vic S Aug's Epis Ch Washington DC 1960-1969; Assoc Ch Of The Adv Louisville KY 1958-1960; Rep Study Liturg Mvmt In Eur Cathd Cathd Of St Jn The Div New York NY 1956-1957; Cur Calv Epis Ch Hillcrest Wilmington DE 1954-1956. Auth, "Liturg Mvmt & Loc Ch," *How & Why*.

SHANDS, Harriet Goodrich (WNC) 21 Chestnut Ridge Road, Pisgah Forest NC 28768 **P-in-c S Paul's Ch Edneyville NC 2009-** B Madison WI 1940 d Ruebush & Elizabeth. Cottey Coll 1960; BA U of Wisconsin 1963; Nash 1987; MDiv SWTS 1989; Dip SWTS 1997; Dip SWTS 2011. D 8/12/1989 Bp Thomas Kreider Ray P 5/19/1990 Bp Roger John White. m 5/4/2006 Francis Sheahan. P-in-c St. Paul's Epis Ch Edneyville NC USA 2009-2016; Vic S Andr's Epis Ch Monroe WI 1997; R S Paul's Epis Ch Beloit WI 1996-2002; Ch Of The Epiph Centerville IA 1993-1995; Gr Ch Albia IA 1993-1995; Vic S Andr's Ch Chariton IA 1993-1995; Dio Iowa Des Moines IA 1990-1995, COM; Liturg & Wrshp Com; Mision San Miguel Milwaukee WI 1989-1990; Asst S Dunst's Ch Madison WI 1989-1990; Stndg Com Dio Milwaukee Milwaukee WI 2000-2002. Professed OA 1994.

SHANE, Janette (Mo) Trinity Episcopal Church, PO Box 652, Kirksville MO 63501 **Ch Of The H Fam Pk Forest IL 2016-** B Louisville KY 1954 BA Rhodes Coll 1976; JD Wm Mitchell Coll of Law 1987; MDiv CDSP 2006. D 6/13/2008 P 12/6/2008 Bp Marc Handley Andrus. Vic Trin Epis Ch Kirksville MO 2010-2016; Assoc S Anne's Ch Fremont CA 2008-2010. holyfamilyparkforestpriest@gmail.com

SHANK, Jason Nathaniel (NwPa) **Dio NW Pennsylvania Erie PA 2016-** B Hagerstown MD 1985 d David & Cindy. BA Mssh Coll 2007; MDiv Wesley TS 2011. D 12/15/2016 P 6/25/2017 Bp Sean Walter Rowe. m 7/20/2013 Erin L Betz-Shank.

SHANK, Michael Joseph (Alb) 87 E Main St, Sidney NY 13838 **Ret 2006-; S Marg's Ch Margaretville NY 2006-; Vic S Mary's Ch Downsville NY 2006-; Chapl Broome Developmental Cntr Dickinson NY 2003-** B Abington PA 1940 s Charles & Mildred. BA W&L 1963; MDiv PDS 1966. D 6/11/1966 P 12/20/1966 Bp Robert Lionne DeWitt. m 8/5/2000 Carol E Waverly-Shank. Dn Susquehanna 2004-2007; Chr Ch Gilbertsville NY 2004-2006; Vic S Paul's Ch Franklin NY 2000-2004; S Paul's Ch Sidney NY 2000-2004; Vic S Paul's Ch Sydney NY 2000-2004; R Gr Ch Waterford NY 1994-1999; Chapl Bellmawr Fire Co Bellmawr NJ 1989-1994; Vic S Lk's Ch Westville NJ 1987-1994; Vic H Sprt Bellmawr NJ 1987-1993; DRC Dio New Jersey Trenton NJ 1986-1991; R H Trin Ch Collingswood NJ 1982-1987; Cur Gr Ch Merchantville NJ 1979-1982; Assoc Chapl Holmesburg Prison Philadelphia PA 1977-1979; Asst S Mary's Epis Ch Philadelphia PA 1976-1979; Asst Resurr Epis Ch Rockdale Aston PA 1975-1978; R S Aidans Ch Cheltenham PA 1969-1975; Ch Of Our Sav Jenkintown PA 1967-1969; Cantar Ch Of S Asaph Bala Cynwyd PA 1967-1969; Cur Trin Ch Oxford Philadelphia PA 1966-1967; Bdgt Com Dio New Jersey Trenton NJ 1992-1993, Dn, Camden Convoc 1986-1991, Dept of CSR 1983-1992, Dept of CE 1980-1985; Com on Democratic Process Dio Pennsylvania Philadelphia PA 1970-1977.

SHANK, Nancy (CPa) 111 Pine St, Danville PA 17821 **Chr Memi Epis Ch Danville PA 2009-** B South Bend IN 1955 d Donald & Rosemary. BS Nyack Coll 1978; MDiv SWTS 1987. Trans 9/9/1991 Bp Frank Tracy Griswold III. R Gr Ch Chanute KS 2003-2009; All Ang Ch Des Moines IA 1995-2003; Dio Iowa Des Moines IA 1995-2003; Vic S Jn's Ch Shenandoah IA 1995-2003; S Jn's Epis Ch Glenwood IA 1995-2003; R Trin Epis Par Waterloo IA 1993-1995; Neosho Vlly Epis Cluster Chanute KS 1991-1993; Int Neosho Vlly Reg Mnstry Chanute KS 1991-1993; S Barth's Ch Wichita KS 1990-1991; S Jas Ch Wichita KS 1990-1991; Int Emm Epis Ch Rockford IL 1989-1990; Dio Chicago Chicago IL 1988-1989; S Paul's Ch Kankakee IL 1987.

SHANKLES, Jeffrey Scott (Va) 6800A Columbia Pike, Annandale VA 22003 **Asst R S Alb's Epis Ch Annandale VA 2005-; D S Steph's Boise ID 1988-** B Anchorage AK 1960 s Troy & Velta. BA Geo Fox U 2002; MDiv VTS 2005. D 1/31/1998 Bp John Stuart Thornton P 9/28/2005 Bp Harry Brown Bainbridge III. m 10/28/1983 Katheryn Wettstein c 2. jshankles@stalbansva.og

SHANKS, Estelle (Nev) PO Box 98, Austin NV 89310 B Reno NV 1924 d Matthew & Charlotte. D 4/5/1988 P 10/1/1988 Bp Stewart Clark Zabriskie. m 2/15/1986 John Shanks c 3.

SHANKS, Margaret Ruth (Lex) 367 Stratford Dr, Lexington KY 40503 **Ch Of The Resurr Nicholasville KY 2015-** B Ashland KY 1952 d George & Jean. BD U of Kentucky 1976; BS U of Kentucky 1990. D 6/9/2001 Bp Stacy F Sauls. Epis Ch of Our Sav Richmond KY 2014-2015; P-in-c Dio Lexington Lexington 2010-2013; S Agnes Hse Lexington KY 2005-2008. margaretshanks@twc.com

SHANKS OHC, Stephen Ray (Ala) 112-C King Valley Rd, Pelham AL 35124 **S Andr's Ch Montevallo AL 2004-** B San Antonio TX 1956 s Leroy & Jane. D 10/30/2004 Bp Marc Handley Andrus. m 8/6/1977 Vickie Lynn Shanks c 1. EPF 1975; OHC 2002.

SHANLEY-ROBERTS, Eileen (Chi) 326 N Martin Luther King Jr Ave, Waukegan IL 60085 **Chapl Homer Darringer Post of the AmL Gurnee IL 2008-; R Chr Ch Waukegan IL 2007-, Dn, Waukegan Dnry 2011-; Dn, Waukegan Dnry Dio Chicago Chicago IL 2011-, Hlth Ins sub-Com 2009-, Dioc Coun 2008-2012, Dioc Coun Representatve 2008-2011** B Freemont NB 1967 d Donald & Helen. BA U of Notre Dame 1989; MA U of Notre Dame 1994; MDiv EDS 2004. D 10/25/2003 Bp Herbert Thompson Jr P 6/19/2004 Bp Kenneth Lester Price. m 2/2/1991 Ross Alan Shanley-Roberts c 2. Asst The Ch Of Ascen And H Trin Cincinnati OH 2004-2007; Prog Dir Campus Mnstry Cntr Mia Oxford 1998-2001; Instr Ch Hist and Scripture Marian HS Mishawaka IN 1994-1996. Epis Environ Ntwk 2006; Natl Epis Historians and Archivists 2009; SCHC 2005. Mnstry Fell Fund for Theol Educ 2001.

SHANNON JR, Carl Steen (Tex) 102 Pecan Grv Apt 121, Houston TX 77077 B Wharton TX 1932 s Carl & Leonora. BA SMU 1955; MDiv Epis TS of the SW 1958. D 6/27/1958 Bp James Parker Clements P 6/25/1959 Bp John Elbridge Hines. m 6/6/1956 Carolyn Jo Shannon. R S Ptr's Epis Ch Brenham TX 1993-1996; Stndg Com Dio Mex 1990-1993; R Chr Ch Epis Lomas De Chapultepec 1985-1993; R Chr Ch In Mex City 1985-1993; R S Andr's Epis Ch Pearland TX 1982-1985; R The Ch Of Dearborn MI 1970-1976; R Ch Of The Ascen Houston TX 1966-1970; H Trin Epis Ch Austin TX 1965-1966; P-in-c S Mk's Ch Austin TX 1965-1966; Cur San Andres Mayaguez Puerto Rico 1964-1965; P-in-c San Pablo Arecibo Puerto Rico 1963-1964; Vic S Steph's Ch Huntsville TX 1960-1962; Vic S Dav's Houston TX 1958-1959.

SHANNON, Carolyn Louise (Nev) 2366 Aqua Vista Ave, Henderson NV 89014 B Portland OR 1941 d Isaac & Ellen. BS Linfield Coll 1964. D 10/25/1992 Bp Stewart Clark Zabriskie. m 7/2/1971 Jack Vernon Shannon. D Dio Nevada Las Vegas 1992-2011. NAAD.

SHANNON SR, Himie-Budu (O) 988 Carlone Place, South Euclid OH 44121 **Died 2/2/2016** B Monrovia Liberia 1954 s Jonathan & Albertha. Cert Natl Police Acad 1974; BA S Augustines Coll Raleigh NC 1980; MDiv VTS 1984; MSW UCONN Connecticut 2003. Trans 12/2/1993 Bp Frank Harris Vest Jr. m 9/28/1985 Madia Richardson c 3. R S Andr's Ch Cleveland OH 2009-2016; R S Monica's Ch Hartford CT 1994-2005; Vic Chr Epis Ch Halifax VA 1991-1994; Vic Gd Shpd 1984-1990. Bro Of S Andr 1984.

SHANNON, James (Pa) 112 Lansdowne Ct, Lansdowne PA 19050 **Philadelphia Theol Inst Philadelphia PA 1992-** B Easton PA 1946 s Thomas & Marjorie. BA FD 1968; MDiv PDS 1973. D 6/9/1973 Bp Leland Stark P 12/16/1973 Bp Robert Lionne DeWitt. Int Ch Of The Epiph Royersford PA 2007-2009; EDS Cambridge MA 2007-2008; Cn Residentiayr / Sub Dn Cathd Ch of Our Sav Philadelphia PA 2003-2007; Cathd Chap Dio Pennsylvania Philadelphia PA 2001-2003; R Chr Epis Ch Bensalem PA 1992-2003; Trin Ch Princeton NJ 1992; R St Pauls Ch Philadelphia PA 1978-1981; Asst Chr Ch Philadelphia Philadelphia PA 1973-1977. Assoc Sis S Margeret 1998; S Geo Soc 1975.

SHANNON SSF, James Michael (ND) 319 S 5th St, Grand Forks ND 58201 **Dioc Coun Dio No Dakota 2011-; Com Dio No Dakota 2004-; R S Paul's Epis Ch Grand Forks ND 2003-** B Winfield KS 1950 s Donald & Helen. Cov Coll Lookout Mtn GA; BA LeTourneau U 1972; MDiv Cov TS S Louis 1976; DMin Grad Theol Un 1982. D 9/18/1998 P 3/19/1999 Bp Andrew Fairfield. m 8/3/1970 Ruth L Shannon c 5. Stndg Com Dio No Dakota 2005-2007; NDCCR Dio No Dakota 2004-2009; Com Dio Wstrn Kansas Hutchinson KS 2000-2003; R S Andr's Epis Ch Liberal KS 1999-2003.

SHANNON, Marvin Boyd (FtW) Po Box 5555, Laguna Park TX 76644 B Fort Worth TX 1948 s Marvin & Martha. ABS Dallas Inst of Mortuary Sci Dallas TX 1971; BBA TCU 1974; MDiv Nash 1998. D 6/27/1998 P 1/6/1999 Bp Jack Leo Iker. m 6/27/1969 Mary E Shannon c 2. All SS' Epis Ch Ft Worth TX 2008-2013; Dio Ft Worth Ft Worth TX 2004-2008; Vic S Mary's Epis Ch 2004-2008; Vic Our Lady Of The Lake Clifton TX 2002-2003; S Alb's Epis Ch Arlington TX 1998-2002.

SHANNON II, Robert Lloyd (Roch) 17 Uncle Bens Way, Orleans MA 02653 **The Cmnty Of Jesus Inc Orleans MA 1991-; Cmnty of Jesus Orleans MA 1988-** B JP 1953 s Robert & Norma. BA Hobart and Wm Smith Colleges 1974; MDiv Gordon-Conwell TS 1977; Cert EDS 1988; PhD CUA 2008. D 1/6/1988 P 6/29/1988 Bp William George Burrill. m 8/24/1974 Mary Jane Shannon c 4. Serv Presb Ch 1977-1987.

SHAON, Gerald E (Cal) 911 Main St Unit 2908, Kansas City MO 64105 **D/Par Admin St. Mary's Epis Ch Kansas City MO 2006-** B Kansas City MO 1940 s Claude & Rosa. BS U of Cntrl Missouri 1964; BA California Sch for Deacons 1994. D 12/3/1994 Bp William Edwin Swing. Dio California Stndg Com San Francisco 1999-2002; Gr Cathd San Francisco CA 1994-2005. St. Stehpen's Awd NAAD 2000; St. Steph's Awd Dio California Sch for Deacons 1994. gerrys1207@yahoo.com

SHAPTON, Eleanor (Spok) 240 Maringo Rd, Ephrata WA 98823 B Los Angeles CA 1948 d Edward & Aileen. BA U CA 1971; MLS USC 1973; MDiv CDSP 1982. D 11/4/1984 P 5/1/1985 Bp Wesley Frensdorff. Dio Spokane Spokane WA 2001-2005, Dioc Coun 1991-1994; Vic S Dunst's Epis Ch Grand Coulee WA 1990-2000; S Jn The Bapt Epis Ch Ephrata WA 1990-2000; Vic St Dunstans Ch Electric City WA 1990-2000; All SS Epis Ch Las Vegas NV 1988-1990; Dio Nevada Las Vegas 1988-1990; Assoc S Chris's Epis Ch Boulder City NV 1987-1990; Assoc S Matt's Ch Las Vegas NV 1985-1990; Prot Chapl U Cntr Of Rel & Life Las Vegas Nv 1982-1990. Rev Ellie Shapton Day Nv S 1988.

SHARP, Carolyn Jackson (Ct) Yale Divinity School, 409 Prospect St., New Haven CT 06511 **D St Thos Epis Ch 2011-; Prof Ya New Haven CT 2000-** B Hartford CT 1963 d Thomas & Sarah. BA Wesl 1985; MAR Yale DS 1994; PhD Ya 2000. D 6/11/2011 Bp Laura Ahrens P 4/21/2012 Bp James Elliot Curry. m 6/10/1989 Leo Lensing c 2. Cur S Andr's Ch New Haven CT 2011-2012.

SHARP, James L (ETenn) 135 Scenic Shores Dr, Dandridge TN 37725 **Ch Of The Annunc Newport TN 2016-** B Helena AR 1947 s Homer & Helen. E Tennessee St U; EFM Sewanee: The U So, TS; AS Columbia St Cmnty Coll Columbia TN 1972; BS U of Memphis 1974. D 6/14/1997 Bp Robert Gould Tharp P 12/13/2016 Bp George Young III. m 2/27/2004 Virginia Gale Ganther. D All SS.

SHARP, Jeffrey Robert (Oly) 205 East 96th St, Tacoma WA 98445 B Long Island NY 1950 s Robert & Marion. BA U of So Florida 1972; MDiv Sthrn Sem 1975; PhD Sthrn Sem 1979. D 12/13/2014 P 6/16/2015 Bp Gregory Harold Rickel. m 5/23/1969 Constance Booth c 2. Ch Of The H Apos Bellevue WA 2015-2017; Ch Of The Resurr Bellevue WA 2015-2017.

SHARP CSF, Lynne (Roch) PO Box 249, Hammondsport NY 14840 **Dio Rochester Henrietta 2016-; R S Jas Ch Hammondsport NY 2014-** B Rochester NY 1954 BA SUNY at Brockport 1982; MEd SUNY at Brockport 1984; MDiv CDSP 2008. D 6/13/2008 P 12/6/2008 Bp Marc Handley Andrus. c 2. Ch Of The Gd Shpd Savona NY 2014-2016; Assoc S Paul's Epis Ch Burlingame CA 2011-2013; Asst Gr Cathd San Francisco CA 2010-2011; Asst S Aid's Ch San Francisco CA 2008-2010.

SHARP, Virginia Gale (ETenn) PO Box 1780, Dandridge TN 37725 B Troy NY 1959 d Howard & Angela. MDiv Sewanee: The U So, TS; BS Florida Atlantic U 1986; BA Florida Atlantic U 1991; Dioc SE Florida Sch For Chr Stds FL 1998. D 9/11/1998 Bp Calvin Onderdonk Schofield Jr P 12/13/2016 Bp George Young III. c 2. D S Jos's Epis Ch Boynton Bch FL 1998-2000.

SHARP, Wesley Eric (Ala) 700 Rinehart Rd, Lake Mary FL 32746 **H Cross Trussville AL 2016-** B Ft Payne AL 1979 s William & Darleen. MDiv Reformed TS 2007; MDiv Reformed TS 2007; Cert Ang Stud Nash Sem 2010; Cert Ang Stud Nash Sem 2010. D 6/11/2011 Bp Hugo Luis Pina-Lopez P 12/17/2011 Bp John Wadsworth Howe. m 8/9/2003 Alison K Kittrell c 3. Asst S Ptr's Epis Ch Lake Mary FL 2011-2016.

SHARPE ACF, Sheila Gast (Del) 65 East Stephen Drive, Newark DE 19713 **D Imm Ch Highlands Wilmington DE 2010-; Transition Com, Dio Delaware Prov III Baltimore MD 2017-, Coun 2011-2017** B Glen Ridge, NJ 1941 d Raymond & Helen. BA U of Delaware 1964; MS Neumann U 2001; Dip Luth TS 2009. D 12/5/2009 Bp Wayne Wright. m 8/6/1966 Richard Arden Sharpe c 3. D S Alb's Ch Wilmington DE 2009-2010. Assn of Epis Deacons 1999.

SHARPE, Virginia Edna (CFla) 210 Fallen Timber Trl, Deland FL 32724 B Chicago IL 1935 d Phillip & Edna. BEd U of Miami 1956; MEd Florida Atlantic U 1970; 1975; EdD U of Florida 1988. D 6/15/1975 Bp William Hopkins Folwell. c 1. S Barn Ch Deland FL 1996-2005, 1975-1995; The Ch Of The H Presence Deland FL 1988-1996. Who's Who in Educ 2007; Who's Who in Amer Wmn.

SHARPTON, Larry (Ala) 8501 Olde Gate, Montgomery AL 36116 **Dept Of CE 1993-; Kairos Dist Bd 1990-; Sprtl Dir Of The Happ 1987-** B Denver CO 1943 s Clarence & Barbara. BA U of Alabama 1965; MDiv Sewanee: The U So, TS 1982. D 6/5/1982 P 12/1/1982 Bp Furman Charles Stough. m 7/22/1967 Patricia Sharpton c 5. P-in-c Epis Ch Of The Epiph Tallassee AL 2007-2011; Supply P S Matthews In The Pines Seale AL 1999-2007; P-in-c Trin Un Spgs Montgomery AL 1996-1998; Assoc Ch Of The H Comf Montgomery AL 1990-1999; Dio Alabama Birmingham 1989-1999; R H Cross Trussville AL 1987-1989; Birmingham Epis Campus Mnstrs Birmingham AL 1984-1986; R S Jn's Ch Birmingham AL 1984-1986; Cur Chr Ch Tuscaloosa AL 1982-1984.

SHARROW, Charles (WTex) 960 Toledo Dr, Brownsville TX 78526 **Dio W Texas San Antonio TX 2007-; Vic S Paul's Epis Ch Brownsville TX 2004-** B Saint Paul MN 1950 s Clarence & Lucille. 2 years and transfer Stout St U 1970; BS Minnesota St U Mankato 1972; MDiv Epis TS of the SW 1994. D 6/29/1994 Bp James Louis Jelinek P 1/6/1995 Bp James Edward Folts. m 5/11/1973 Ruthanne Sharrow c 3. Asst R Ch Of The Adv Brownsville TX 1994-2004. pastor@sanpablobr.org

SHATAGIN, Theodore Ivan (Vt) Po Box 1807, Ardmore OK 73402 **Hoosac Sch Hoosick NY 1972-; Non-par 1969-; All SS' Epis Ch S Burlington VT 1969-** B Detroit MI 1939 s John & Helen. BA Earlham Coll 1960; U MI 1961; BD Yale DS 1964. D 12/14/1966 Bp Wilburn Camrock Campbell P 11/1/1967 Bp Harvey D Butterfield. m 6/28/1969 Betsy Bucklin Shatagin c 1. Asst To The R & Prog Dir S Ptr's Epis Ch Bennington VT 1967-1969; Asst S Andr's Ch Beckley WV 1966-1967; S Steph's Epis Ch Beckley WV 1966-1967.

SHATTUCK JR, Gardiner Humphrey (RI) 190 North St, Warwick RI 02886 B Boston MA 1947 s Gardiner & Mary. BA Br 1970; MDiv GTS 1975; MA Harv 1981; PhD Harv 1985. D 6/10/1975 P 12/20/1975 Bp John Melville Burgess. m 1/8/1983 Cynthia Logan c 1. P-in-c Ch Of The Gd Shpd Pawtucket RI 2009-2013; P Assoc S Steph's Ch Providence RI 2004-2009; Supply P Dio Rhode Island Providence RI 1990-2004; R Ch Of The Ascen Cranston RI 1986-1990; Int Epiph Par Walpole MA 1985-1986; Libr Asst Harvard DS Cambridge MA 1981-1985; Supply P Dio Massachusetts Boston MA 1978-1985; Grad Stdt Harv Canbridge MA 1978-1985; Asst All SS' Epis Ch Belmont MA 1975-1978. Auth, "This Great Day of Suffering: Redeeming Memories of the Civil War," Angl and Epis Hist, 2012; Auth, "Weeping over Jerusalem: Anglicans and Refugee Relief in the Middle E," Angl and Epis Hist, 2011; Auth, "True Israelites: Chas Thorley Bridgeman and Angl Missions in Palestine," Angl and Epis Hist, 2008; Co-Auth, "The Episcopalians," Praeger, 2004; Co-Auth, "The Episcopalians (pbk)," Ch Publ, 2004; Auth, "Episcopalians & Race," Univ Press Ky, 2000; Co-Auth, "Encyclopedia of Amer Relig Hist," Facts on File, 1996; Auth, "A Shield & Hiding Place," Mercer Univ Pr, 1987. Advsry Ed, Angl & Epis Hist 2004; Strng Comm, Afr Amer Epis Hist Collection 2004.

SHAUBACH, Sheila Kathryn (SJ) Po Box 164, Raymond CA 93653 B Bakersfield CA 1935 d Frances & Martha. San Joaquin Schools For Mnstry. D 12/13/2003 Bp David Mercer Schofield. c 4.

SHAVER, Ellen M (Me) 139 High Head Rd, Harpswell ME 04079 B Detroit MI 1941 d Lawrence & Jean. BPS Pace U 1978; BD Pace U 1978; MDiv Yale DS 1981. D 6/16/1981 P 2/1/1982 Bp Paul Moore Jr. m 2/1/1961 Alan M Shaver. Assoc S Paul's Ch Brunswick ME 1998-1999, Int 1996-1997; Dio New York New York NY 1990-1995, Cn To The Ordnry For Deploy 1990-1995; R S Jn's Ch Tuckahoe Yonkers NY 1983-1989; Cur S Jn's Ch Larchmont NY 1981-1983.

SHAVER, John (Minn) 3448 Rum River Dr, Anoka MN 55303 B 1939 s John & Caroline. BA U MN 1962; MA U MN 1967; MDiv Nash 1975. D 4/26/1975

S

P 11/1/1975 Bp Charles Thomas Gaskell. m 7/11/1962 Virginia Ann Shaver. Assoc Mssh Epis Ch S Paul MN 2002-2006; P-in-c S Mary's Basswood Grove Hastings MN 1995-2000; S Jn's Epis Ch Mankato MN 1994-1995; St Dav's Epis Ch Minnetonka MN 1990-1992; Trin Ch Anoka MN 1982-1990; Crt Chapl Dio Milwaukee Milwaukee WI 1978-1982; Cur S Jas Epis Ch Milwaukee WI 1975-1977.

SHAVER, Stephen Richard (Oly) B Denison TX 1981 s Mark & Sara. BA Emory U 2003; MDiv GTS 2007. D 12/21/2006 P 7/1/2007 Bp J Neil Alexander. m 5/27/2007 Julia Shaver c 1. All Souls Par In Berkeley Berkeley CA 2015; CDSP Berkeley CA 2013, 2013, Doctoral Stds 2012-2016; Asstg P S Mk's Par Berkeley CA 2012-2015; Int Assoc Ch of the Apos Seattle WA 2012; Supply P S Lk's Epis Ch Seattle WA 2012; Chapl Providence Hospice of Snohomish Cnty Everett WA 2011-2013; Supply P S Phil Ch Marysville WA 2011-2012; Assoc S Steph's Epis Ch Seattle WA 2010-2011; P Assoc S Paul's Ch Seattle WA 2009-2011; Chapl Res Harborview/UW Med Centers Seattle WA 2009-2010; Assoc Epis Ch Of The Ascen Dallas TX 2007-2009; Mem, Liturg and Arts Cmsn Dio Olympia Seattle 2010-2012. Auth, "The Word Made Flesh: Toward a Sacramental Theol of Lang," *Proceedings of the No Amer Acad of Liturg*, 2014; Auth, "O Oriens: Reassessing Eastward Eucharistic Celebration for Renewed Liturg," *ATR*, 2012. Soc of Cath Priests 2010. Bogard Fllshp CDSP 2015; Newhall Fllshp Grad Theol Un 2014.

SHAVER, Thomas Ronald (SO) 25 State Rd 13 Apt H8, Saint Johns FL 32259 **P Assoc St Pat's Epis Ch S Johns FL 2011-** B Evanston IL 1934 s Clarence & Hazel. BA Mia 1955; JD Stan 1960; MDiv CDSP 1986. D 6/21/1986 Bp Robert Claflin Rusack P 1/10/1987 Bp Oliver Bailey Garver Jr. m 9/5/1959 Marylin Ann Shaver c 3. Permanent Supply P S Lk Ch Cincinnati OH 2003-2010; Int S Andr's Epis Ch Cincinnati OH 2000-2001; Int S Mk's Epis Ch Columbus OH 1998-1999; Int Calv Ch Cincinnati OH 1998; R All SS Ch Cincinnati OH 1989-1997; Assoc S Mich and All Ang Epis Ch Studio City CA 1988-1989; Assoc Trin Epis Ch Orange CA 1986-1988. OHC 1987. Meritorious hon Awd Untd States St Dept 1965; Phi Beta Kappa Iota of Ohio, Miami Uniiversity 1955.

SHAW, Adrianna S (Kan) St Philip's Episcopal Church, 302 E. General Stewart Way, Hinesville GA 31314 B Aberdeen WA 1974 d William & Diane. BA Pacific Luth U 1997; MDiv Epis TS Of The SW 2012; MDiv Epis TS of the SW 2012. D 6/2/2012 P 1/5/2013 Bp Dean E Wolfe. m 9/2/2000 Scott A Shaw c 2. S Andr's Ch Burke VA 2016-2017; S Phil's Ch Hinesville Hinesville GA 2014-2016; S Richard's Of Round Rock Round Rock TX 2013.

SHAW, Jane Alison (Cal) 110 California St, San Francisco CA 94111 **Stan Stanford CA 2014-** B Peterborough England 1963 d Jack & Joyce. BA Oxf GB 1985; MDiv Harvard DS 1988; PhD U CA 1994. Trans 10/19/2010 as Priest Bp Marc Handley Andrus. m 10/27/2010 Sarah Ogilvie. Dn Gr Cathd San Francisco CA 2010-2014.

SHAW, Margaret Elizabeth (Alb) 10215 Carriage Dr, Plymouth IN 46563 **Chapl St. Jos Reg Med. Ctr Plymouth IN 1998-** B Albert Lea MN 1947 d Richard & Alice. Associated Mennonite Biblic Sem; BA Cornell Coll 1969; MS Indiana U 1985. D 6/9/2006 P 1/12/2007 Bp Edward Stuart Little II. c 2. S Jn's Ch Essex NY 2009-2014; P-in-c S Eliz's Epis Ch Culver IN 2007-2009.

SHAW, Martini (Pa) 6361 Lancaster Ave, Philadelphia PA 19151 **R The Afr Epis Ch Of S Thos Philadelphia PA 2003-** B Detroit MI 1959 s Melton & Joyce. BA Wayne 1983; BS Wayne 1983; MDiv McCormick TS 1988; CAS SWTS 1988; DMin GTF 2008. D 6/18/1988 P 12/18/1988 Bp Frank Tracy Griswold III. R Ch Of S Thos Chicago IL 1990-2003; Cur The Ch Of S Jn The Evang Flossmoor IL 1988-1989.

SHAW, Philip Algie (Az) Trinity Episcopal Church, P.O. Box 590, Kingman AZ 86402 **Trin Epis Ch Kingman AZ 2015-, 2007-2009** B Camden SC 1950 s Algie & Vera. BLA Mississippi St U 1977; Dip Ang Stud Epis TS of the SW 2007. D 6/23/2007 P 2/2/2008 Bp Kirk Stevan Smith. m 7/4/1970 Beverly Shaw c 1. Vic Dio Arizona Phoenix AZ 2010-2015.

SHAW, Robert Clyde (Mil) 46 New Cross N, Asheville NC 28805 **Non-par 1977-** B Saint Louis IL 1932 s Clyde & Eugenia. BA U of Wisconsin 1954; BD Nash 1957; STM Nash 1960; MA U of Wisconsin 1962; PhD U of Wisconsin 1967; MS U of Wisconsin 1980. D 4/27/1957 P 11/1/1957 Bp Donald H V Hallock. m 9/7/1977 Janet Nadina Shaw. R S Andr's Ch Madison WI 1960-1977; Vic S Fran Ch Menomonee Falls WI 1957-1960.

SHAW, Samuel Gates (Ala) 4112 Abingdon Ln, Birmingham AL 35243 B Birmingham AL 1946 s Samuel & Anne. BA W&L 1968; MDiv GTS 1981. D 3/24/1981 P 10/1/1981 Bp Furman Charles Stough. m 5/22/1993 Margaret Rafield Smith c 2. Chr Ch Fairfield AL 1999-2013; Assoc The Cathd Ch Of The Adv Birmingham AL 1995-1997; S Andr's Ch Montevallo AL 1991-1993; S Andrews's Epis Ch Birmingham AL 1981-1983; Gr Ch Birmingham AL 1981-1982. christchurchfairfield@gmail.com

SHAW, Timothy Joel (CFla) 901 Thompson Cir Nw, Winter Haven FL 33881 **P-in-c St Alb's of Auburndale Inc Auburndale FL 2013-** B Springfield OH 1945 s Delmas & Rheba. BA S Leo U 1980; MDiv SWTS 1983. D 6/24/1983 Bp William Hopkins Folwell P 1/10/1984 Bp Calvin Onderdonk Schofield Jr. c 2. R S Paul's Ch Winter Haven FL 1998-2011; R Ch Of Our Sav Okeechobee

FL 1985-1998; Cur All SS Epis Ch Jensen Bch FL 1983-1985. Soc H Cross 1993; SocMary 1993. Hon Cn Dioceses Negros Oriental 1994.

SHAW, Warren Ervin (Pa) 1029 Bristlecone Ln, Charlottesville VA 22911 **Ret 1998-** B Philadelphia PA 1933 s Ervin & Esther. BA Tem 1955; MDiv Tem 1958. D 6/9/1962 P 12/15/1962 Bp Joseph Gillespie Armstrong. m 10/13/1956 Shirley Shaw c 3. Int Emm Ch Rapidan VA 2002-2003; S Paul's Ch Chester PA 1962-1998; Serv Methodist Ch 1957-1961. Forw in Faith 1994.

SHEARER, Donald Robert (Nwk) 156 Mountain Dr, Greentown PA 18426 **Team Mnstry Chr Ch Indn Orchard PA 2006-; Supply P Dio Bethlehem 2003-** B Sydney NSW AU 1938 s Robert & Enid. S Johns Coll Morpeth NSW 1962. Trans 4/1/1970 as Priest Bp Robert Lionne DeWitt. m 8/16/2014 James David Lloyd. Int Vic S Jn's Ch Passaic NJ 2004-2006; Cathd Chapt Trin And S Phil's Cathd Newark NJ 1996-1998, Cathd Chapt 1986-1995; Dept of Missions Dio Newark Newark NJ 1990-1996, Pres So Essex Convoc 1983-1989; Chapl Cbury Vill W Orange NJ 1985-2002; R All SS Ch Orange NJ 1982-2002; Chapl Passaic Cnty Cmnty Coll 1978-1982; Pres Paterson Epis Mssn 1977-1980; R Ch Of The H Comm Paterson NJ 1975-1982; Dioc Liturg Cmsn Dio Pennsylvania Philadelphia PA 1973-1975; Asst S Anne's Ch Abington PA 1971-1975; Dir Mus Vlly Forge Yth Conf 1968-1984; Cur S Clements Ch Philadelphia PA 1968-1970; Cur Serv Angl Ch of Australia 1962-1968. CBS 1963; GAS 1963; P Assoc C.S.J.B. 1986; P Assoc O.L.W. 1964. Cbury Schlolarship Awd Dio Newark 1986.

SHEARER, Robert L (Nwk) 2077 Center Ave Apt 20A, Fort Lee NJ 07024 **Int Chr Ch So Amboy NJ 2004-** B Sunnyside WA 1936 s Maynard & Aileen. CDSP; AB Whitman Coll 1958; MDiv GTS 1960. D 6/20/1960 Bp John Joseph Meakin Harte P 12/11/1960 Bp Charles A Mason. c 3. P-in-c S Paul's Ch Englewood NJ 2009-2014; Int S Ptr's Ch Morristown NJ 2007-2009; Int Chr Epis Ch Tarrytown NY 2006-2007; Int Chr Ch New Brunswick NJ 2004-2006; Int S Ptr's Ch Medford NJ 2003-2004; Int Chr Ch Toms River Toms River NJ 2001-2002; Int Gr Epis Ch Plainfield NJ 1999-2001; Int S Ambr Epis Ch New York NY 1997-1998; Int S Phil's Ch New York NY 1996-1998; P-in-c Ch Of The H Trin Pawling NY 1989-1995; Archd Dio Rhode Island Providence RI 1981-1986; Dio California San Francisco CA 1980-1981; Montgomery St Cntr 1971-1980; Prof CDSP Berkeley CA 1969-1971; Vic S Barth Burney CA 1968-1969; Vic St Bartholomews Ch Burney CA 1968-1969; Vic S Mich's Ch Anderson CA 1965-1969; Asst S Lk's Ch Louisville KY 1962-1965; Chapl U of Louisville KY 1962-1965; S Jas Ch Pewee Vlly KY 1962-1963; Vic Ch Of The Epiph Dallas TX 1960-1961; Ch Of The Incarn Dallas TX 1960-1961. Auth, *One-Minute Liturg*, H Trin Press, 1995; Auth, *Affirmative Action Bk*; Auth, *Mysticism & Rel*. Mastery Fndt Trst 1983-1993.

SHEARS, Sidney Herbert (SanD) 4166 Clubhouse Rd, Lompoc CA 93436 **Ret 1975-** B Rochester NY 1913 s Sidney & Florence. BA Syr 1938; MDiv Colgate Rochester Crozer DS 1942; MDiv CRDS 1942; MA Col 1950; CDSP 1964. D 9/10/1964 P 3/10/1965 Bp Francis E I Bloy. m 4/17/1972 Ethna Shears. R S Paul In The Desert Palm Sprg CA 1968-1975; Asst Min Ch Of Our Sav Par San Gabr CA 1964-1968; Chapl (Capt) USN 1942-1963; Serv Methodist Ch 1941-1964.

SHEAY, Virginia M (NJ) 12 Glenwood Ln, Stockton NJ 08559 **Assoc Trin Ch Solebury PA 2002-** B Whitehouse NJ 1939 d George & Edna. BMus Westminster Choir Coll of Rider U 1962; MDiv GTS 1975; PrTS 1975; STM NYTS 1983; DMin Drew U 1992; Cert Cler Ldrshp Proj The Epis Ch Fundation 1995. D 4/26/1975 Bp Albert Wiencke Van Duzer P 4/30/1977 Bp George Phelps Mellick Belshaw. m 9/22/1962 Ronald J Sheay c 3. R S Lk's Ch Trenton NJ 1983-2001; Chapl Rider U Lawrenceville NJ 1979-2001; Asst S Matt's Ch Pennington NJ 1975-1983; Chair, Congrl Dvlpmt Com Dio New Jersey Trenton NJ 2001-2007, Prov II Crt Revs 1990, GC Dep 1988-2003, Dept of Missions 1987-1990; Dom And Frgn Mssy Soc- Epis Ch Cntr New York NY 1994-2000; Exec Coun Mem Prov II 1994-2000. Auth, "Developing a Mnstry of Evang Through Hosp at S Lk's," 1992. Hon Cn Cn to the Cathd 2009.

SHECTER, Teri Ann (Colo) 2461 F 1/4 Road #231, Grand Junction CO 81505 **D Ch Of The Nativ Grand Jct CO 2004-; Reg D Dio Colorado Denver CO 2002-** B New Haven CT 1955 d Frederick & Majorie. MA U CO. D 11/9/2002 Bp William Jerry Winterrowd. m 6/27/1998 William Dale Page.

SHEEHAN JR, David (Del) 3401 Greenbriar Ln, West Grove PA 19390 **Ret 1995-** B Philadelphia PA 1931 s David & Mary. BS U of Delaware 1954; BD VTS 1959. D 10/3/1959 P 10/8/1960 Bp John Brooke Mosley. m 8/20/1960 Charlotte Rode c 2. R Calv Epis Ch Hillcrest Wilmington DE 1975-1995; Vic S Nich' Epis Ch Newark DE 1964-1974; Cur Ch of St Andrews & St Matthews Wilmington DE 1959-1963; Chr Ch Delaware City DE 1959-1961.

SHEEHAN, John Thomas (Va) 512 Duff Rd Ne, Leesburg VA 20176 **R Ch of Our Redeem Aldie VA 2006-; D Ch Of Our Redeem Aldie VA 2001-** B Springfield MA 1947 s John & Irene. BS La Salle U; MDiv TESM 2001. D 6/23/2001 P 12/29/2001 Bp Peter J Lee. m 6/23/1979 Denise Ann Sheehan c 3. Evang Fllshp - USA 1999.

SHEEN RODRIGUEZ, Juan Enrique (DR) **Dio The Dominican Republic (Iglesia Epis Dominicana) Gazcue Santo Domingo 2015-** B Dominican Republic 1950 s Jose & Juana. Doctor en Odontologia Universidad Autonoima de Santo

773

Domingo 1980; Licenciado en Teologia Centro de Estudios Teologicos 2013. D 2/16/2014 P 2/15/2015 Bp Julio Cesar Holguin-Khoury. m 6/11/1983 Elida A Paulino Peralta c 1.

SHEETZ, David Allan (Cal) 250 Baldwin Ave Apt 303, San Mateo CA 94401 **Assoc Chr Ch Portola Vlly CA 2010-, Dir Mus & Lit 1999-2006** B Detroit MI 1946 s Harold & Doris. Ripon Coll Cuddesdon Oxford GB; BA Wayne 1971; MA Stan 1974; MDiv CDSP 1993. D 6/3/1995 P 6/1/1996 Bp William Edwin Swing. Assoc S Bede's Epis Ch Menlo Pk CA 2013-2014, Assoc 2007-, Int 1995; Dir Mus All SS Epis Ch Palo Alto CA 1997-1998; Int S Paul's Epis Ch Burlingame CA 1997; Int S Fran' Epis Ch San Francisco CA 1996; Assoc Chr Epis Ch Los Altos CA 1995-2008.

SHEFFIELD III, Earl J (Tex) 325 Apache Run Road, Wallisville TX 77597 B Galveston TX 1939 s Earl & Madelyne. AA Alvin Coll 1958; BA U of Texas 1961; MDiv Epis TS of the SW 1968; BS Lamar U 1979. D 6/12/1968 Bp James Milton Richardson P 5/1/1969 Bp Frederick P Goddard. m 6/20/1964 Renee F Sheffield c 3. P-in-c Trin Ch Winnie TX 2001-2005; Chapl S Jas Hse Baytown TX 2000-2004; Asst R Cullen Memi Chap Houston TX 1999-2000; S Jas Epis Ch Houston TX 1999-2000; S Lk's Epis Hosp Houston TX 1999-2000; Chapl SFASU Nacogdoches TX 1996-1999; Chr Ch San Aug TX 1994-1999; P-in-c S Jn's Epis Ch Cntr TX 1994-1999; R S Mk's Epis Ch Richmond TX 1990-1994, Asst 1983-1990; Asst Ch Of The H Trin Midland TX 1976-1977; Chapl Lamar U Beaumont TX 1971-1976; P-in-c S Matt's Beaumont TX 1971-1976; St Matthews Ch Beaumont TX 1971-1976; The Great Cmsn Fndt Houston TX 1968-2004; Vic S Mk's Ch Gladewater TX 1968-1971; S Mich And All Ang' Epis Ch Longview TX 1968-1971.

SHEFFIELD, John Joseph (Tex) PO Box 12615, San Antonio TX 78212 **Fndr Deep River Mnstrs TX 2001-** B Albuquerque NM 1949 s Bordeau & Mary. BA U of Houston 1976; MTh SMU 1981; CTh Epis TS of the SW 1992; DMin SWTS 2001. D 6/27/1992 Bp Maurice Manuel Benitez P 1/1/1993 Bp William Jackson Cox. m 7/13/1974 Anna Marie Sheffield c 2. S Chris's Epis Ch Austin TX 1992-2001; The Great Cmsn Fndt Houston TX 1992-1995. "The Genesis Seed," Imago Pub, 2008; "Under Healing Wings," Imago Pub, 2005; "God's healing River," Imago Pub, 2003.

SHEFFIELD, Sharon (Los) 10354 Downey Ave, Downey CA 90241 B Long Beach CA 1965 d John & Luella. AB Occ 1987; MDiv Bloy Hse/Claremont TS 2012; MDiv ETSBH 2012. D 6/16/2012 Bp Diane Jardine Bruce P 1/12/2013 Bp Joseph Jon Bruno. m 6/26/2004 Michael David Sheffield. S Mk's Par Downey CA 2013-2017.

SHEHANE, Mary Kathryn (Oly) 9416 1st Ave Ne Apt 408, Seattle WA 98115 **D Ch Of The Ascen Seattle WA 2011-** B Shreveport LA 1947 d Guy & Kathryn. Cntrl Washington U; Cert Dioc TS 1993. D 6/24/1995 Bp Vincent Waydell Warner. c 2. Dio Olympia Seattle 2001-2012; D S Mk's Cathd Seattle WA 2001-2011; Chr Ch Seattle WA 1997-2000. NAAD.

SHELBY, Franck Stuart (Tex) Saint Richard's Episcopal Church, 1420 E Palm Valley Blvd, Round Rock TX 78664 **R S Richard's Of Round Rock Round Rock TX 2011-** B Mobile AL 1975 s Franck & Glenda. BA Samford U 1997; MDiv VTS 2005. D 6/4/2005 P 6/10/2006 Bp Philip Menzie Duncan II. m 6/1/2002 Crista Joy McKinney c 4. Assoc S Mart's Epis Ch Houston TX 2007-2011; Cur S Jas Ch Fairhope AL 2005-2007; Ch Planter Epis Ch Of The Apos Daphne AL 1998-2002; Dir of Chld's and Yth Mnstry S Jn's Ch Monroeville AL 1998-1999. stuart@saintrichards.org

SHELBY, Jason B (Miss) 106 Sharkey Ave, Clarksdale MS 38614 **S Geo's Epis Ch Clarksdale MS 2010-** B Fort Wayne IN 1977 s Stephen & Barbara. BA Indiana U 2003; MDiv Sewanee: The U So, TS 2007. D 12/21/2006 P 9/11/2007 Bp Edward Stuart Little II. m 10/3/2008 Sarah A Shelby c 1. S Columb's Ch Ridgeland MS 2008-2010; S Mart's Epis Sch Metairie LA 2007-2008.

SHELDON, Carren (NCal) 1500 State Street, Santa Barbara CA 93101 **Ch Of S Mart Davis CA 2016-** B California 1961 d Warren & Carolyn. MDiv CDSP 2012; MDiv CDSP 2012. D 6/29/2013 P 1/4/2014 Bp Barry Leigh Beisner. c 1. Trin Epis Ch Santa Barbara CA 2014-2016; Assoc for Families, Chld and Yth Gr Cathd San Francisco CA 2013-2014, 2008-2013. csheldon@trinitysb.org

SHELDON, Jaclyn Struff (Ct) 85 Holmes Rd, East Lyme CT 06333 **S Paul's Epis Ch Willimantic CT 2009-** B Manchester CT 1952 d John & Barbara. BS U of Bridgeport 1977; MDiv Ya Berk 1996. D 6/14/1997 P 5/1/1998 Bp Clarence Nicholas Coleridge. m 7/29/1978 William Phelps Sheldon c 2. Vic S Jas Ch Preston CT 2000-2008; Vic All SS Ch Ivoryton CT 1998-2000; Incarn Cntr Deep River CT 1997-2000. office@stpaulswillimantic.org

SHELDON III, Joseph Victor (Spr) 1220 Uss Daniel Boone Ave, Kings Bay GA 31547 **Baltimore Intl Seafarers' Cntr Inc Baltimore MD 2007-; Dn, Baton Rouge Dnry Dio Louisiana 2004-; Chapl Untd States Naval Reserve 1990-** B Charlotte NC 1960 s Joseph & Martha. BS LSU 1982; MDiv TESM 1989. D 6/10/1989 P 4/1/1990 Bp Herbert Alcorn Donovan Jr. Spec Mobilization Spprt Plan Washington DC 2007-2012; Pension Fund Mltry New York NY 2007-2008; R S Marg's Epis Ch Baton Rouge LA 1995-2007; Cn Pstr Chr Ch Cathd New Orleans LA 1992-1995; Asst to R Chr Epis Ch Little Rock AR 1990-1992; Dio Arkansas Little Rock AR 1990; Intern/Cur Trin Ch Van Buren

AR 1989. Evang Fllshp In The Angl Comm 1989; Mustard Seed Orphanage - Bd Mem 1992.

SHELDON, Karen Sears (Vt) 86 S Main St, Hanover NH 03755 **Ret 1999-** B Grand Rapids MI 1937 d Philip & Esther. BA U MI 1960; MA U MI 1964. D 7/11/1979 P 5/24/1980 Bp Robert Shaw Kerr. m 2/8/1964 Richard Robert Sheldon c 4. R S Jn The Bapt Epis Hardwick VT 1992-1999; Assoc S Thos Ch Hanover NH 1988-1991; R S Mart's Epis Ch 1984-1987; S Mart's Epis Ch Fairlee VT 1984-1987; Asst S Paul's Epis Ch White Riv Jct VT 1981-1983; Instr Dio Vermont Burlington VT 1980-1994. Auth, "Navigating In The Divine-Milieu," *Teilhard Revs*.

SHELDON, Patricia Lu (Neb) 3818 N 211th St, Elkhorn NE 68022 **D St Aug of Cbury Epis Ch Elkhorn NE 1997-** B Washington DC 1940 d Frank & Lucille. BS U of Maryland 1962; BS San Jose Chr Coll 1989; AAS Metropltn Cmnty Coll Omaha NE 1993. D 12/1/1997 Bp James Edward Krotz. m 5/20/1967 Laurence Francis Sheldon c 3. DOK 2000; OSL 2008. Wmn Mnstry Honored Wmn Dio Nebraska 2009.

SHELDON, Peggy Ann (SeFla) 2000 Sw Racquet Club Dr, Palm City FL 34990 **Sprtl Dir Dio SE Florida Miami 1995-** B Webster NY 1927 d Carroll & Dorothy. Michigan TS 1975; GTS 1977; Shalem Inst for Sprtl Formation Washington DC 1994. D 8/20/1977 Bp Henry Irving Mayson P 9/29/1978 Bp H Coleman Mcgehee Jr. m 9/11/1947 Howard Walter Sheldon c 5. S Mary's Epis Ch Stuart FL 1999-2013; P-in-c S Monica's Ch Stuart FL 1994-1996; Asst S Lk's Epis Ch Stuart FL 1988-1991; Asst Hong Kong & Macao China 1980-1985; Chapl S Jn Angl Cathd 1980-1985; Asst S Mich's Ch Grand Rapids MI 1978-1980.

SHELDON, Raymond S (Oly) 1075 Alexander Pl Ne, Bainbridge Island WA 98110 **Vic Faith Ch Kingston WA 2004-** B Glendale AZ 1944 s Edward & Nina. BA NYU 1969; MBA Loyola Coll 1975. D 6/26/2004 Bp Vincent Waydell Warner P 7/25/2009 Bp Gregory Harold Rickel. m 11/28/1969 Jere J Allen c 3.

SHELDON, Terry Lynn (CNY) 21 White St, Clark Mills NY 13321 **Supply All SS Ch Utica NY 2009-, Assoc 1985-2008; R S Mk's Ch Clark Mills NY 2002-; R S Geo's Epis Ch Chadwicks NY 1995-** B Hudson NY 1937 s Gerald & Mildred. BS Syr 1959; Sewanee: The U So, TS 1983. D 6/8/1985 P 5/20/1986 Bp O'Kelley Whitaker. m 9/5/1959 Mary Anne Seeger c 3. Chapl CAP 1988-1993. Chapl, "Var arts 2006-2011," *The Empire St Patriot*, Sons of the Amer Revolution. OHC 1984. Chapl of the Year New York St CAP 1991. tlmas@roadrunner.com

SHELL, Lawrence S (NMich) 201 E. Ridge St., Marquette MI 49855 B De Kalb IL 1963 s Lawrence & Leona. BA NWU 1987. D 5/27/2007 Bp James Arthur Kelsey.

SHELLITO, John Ellis (Va) St George's Church, 915 N Oakland St, Arlington VA 22203 **Assoc R S Geo's Epis Ch Arlington VA 2013-** B Boston MA 1984 s Paul & Barbara. AB Dart 2008; MDiv UTS 2012. D 5/21/2012 P 12/30/2012 Bp Vicky Gene Robinson. m 1/1/2011 Haley Bolin. CPE Chapl Residency Stdt Alta Bates Summit Med Cntr Berkeley CA 2012-2013. The Maxwell Fllshp, for a graduating M.Div Stdt who shows promise of excellence in future Serv to the Par Mnstry Given by Auburn Sem at the discretion of the UTS Fac Com 2012; Indiana Cnty Civic Ldr of the Year nominee Indiana Cnty Serv Orgnztn 2009.

SHELLY, Marshall Keith (NJ) 505 Main St, Spotswood NJ 08884 **R S Ptr's Ch Spotswood NJ 2010-** B East Lansing MI 1967 s Robert & Ann. U of Aberdeen Aberdeen GB 1988; BA Ken 1989; MDiv GTS 1994; Cert Int Mnstry Ntwk 2004. D 6/17/1994 P 6/17/1995 Bp Herbert Thompson Jr. m 10/28/2000 Laura B Shelly. Int R Trin Ch Matawan NJ 2009-2010; R/Hd of Sch Trin Ch Solebury PA 2005-2009; Int R S Andr's Epis Ch New Providence NJ 2003-2005; Assoc R Gr Ch Madison NJ 1998-2003; Assoc R Trin Ch Newport RI 1995-1998; Assoc R S Steph's Epis Ch And U Columbus OH 1994-1995. Blogger, "newministrynewpaths.blogspot.com," *1995 to present*, self. Seymour Prize: Gk GTS 1994; Extemporaneous Preaching GTS 1994.

SHELTON, Benson Eldridge (Va) 9220 Georgetown Pike, Great Falls VA 22066 **S Steph's Epis Ch Culpeper VA 2014-** B Langley VA 1981 s Matthew & Susan. AAS Pat Henry Cmnty Coll 2003; BS Radford U 2005; MDiv VTS 2010. D 9/29/2010 P 4/2/2011 Bp Neff Powell. m 7/14/2012 Adrianne Katrina Shelton c 1. Asst R S Fran Epis Ch Great Falls VA 2010-2014; D-in-c S Paul's Ch Martinsville VA 2010.

SHELTON, Edna S (Mich) 18270 Northlawn St, Detroit MI 48221 B Tyrone PA 1937 d James & Edna. RN Lewistown Hosp Sch 1958; Siena Coll 1988; Whitaker TS 1993. D 6/12/1993 Bp R aymond Stewart Wood Jr. m 10/27/1962 Bobby Leonard Shelton c 3. D S Pat's Epis Ch Madison Hts MI 2000-2010; D S Martha's Ch Detroit MI 1993-2000.

SHELTON, Joan Adams (CNY) 2126 Connecticut Ave Nw Apt 49, Washington DC 20008 B Ithaca NY 1932 d John & Alice. BA Vas 1954; MEd Leh 1979; MDiv Moravian TS 1979. D 6/17/1976 P 3/29/1979 Bp Lloyd Edward Gressle. Supply Dio Long Island Garden City NY 1999-2002; Fac Dio Haiti Port-au-Prince HT 1996-1999; Vic S Jas Ch Cleveland NY 1991-1996; Vic S Paul's Ch Chittenango NY 1991-1996; Calv Ch Syracuse NY 1989-1990; Int Calv Ch Syracuse NY 1989-1990; R S Paul's Ch Portsmouth RI 1986-1989; Chr Ch Stroudsburg PA 1985-1986; S Mk's Epis Ch Moscow PA 1985; S Dunstans Ch

Blue Bell PA 1983-1984; Int Dio Bethlehem Bethlehem PA 1982-1986; S Alb's Epis Ch Reading PA 1981-1983; Int S Alb Reading PA 1980-1982; Chapl St Hosp Allentown PA 1976-1978. Auth, "Stone Turning Into Star," Panlist, 1986. Tertiary Of The Soc Of S Fran. scl Moravian TS 1979; Phi Beta Kappa 1954.

SHELTON, Linda Ross (Tex) 3507 Plumb St, Houston TX 77005 **D Palmer Memi Ch Houston TX 2007-** B Bartlesville OK 1952 d Jack & Charlotte. BA U of Texas 1973; Iona Sch for Mnstry-- Dio Texas 2007. D 2/9/2007 Bp Don Adger Wimberly. m 11/9/1974 Thomas Shelton c 2.

SHEMATEK, Jon Paul (Md) 9120 Frederick Rd, Ellicott City MD 21042 B Sewickley PA 1946 s Matthew & Ann. BA Bos 1968; MD U Pgh 1972. D 6/17/1989 Bp Albert Theodore Eastman. m 7/5/1969 Eleanor Ann Shematek c 2. Maryland Cler Assn; D Chr The King.

SHEMAYEV, Roman Aeired (Mil) 3528 Valley Ridge Rd, Middleton WI 53562 B Saint Petersburg Russia 1972 s Vyacheslav & Tatyana. Herzen St Pedagogical U of Russia 1993; MDiv Aquinas Inst of Theol 2000. Rec 9/11/2005 Bp Steven Andrew Miller. m 4/12/2002 Kara McCarty. Assoc R Gr Ch Madison WI 2005-2007. Comp of St. Lk-OSB 2007.

SHEPARD, Alfred Hugh (Colo) 3013 Taos Meadows Dr NE, Rio Rancho NM 87144 B Denver CO 1932 s John & Mary. BA U CO 1957; Dio Colorado Bishops TS CO 1982; Cert Nash 1984. D 6/2/1982 Bp William Carl Frey P 6/17/1984 Bp William Harvey Wolfrum. c 4. Assoc Ch of St. Phil & St. Jas Denver CO 2008-2011; Chapl Hospice of St. Jn Lakewood CO 2004-2008; Cur The Epis Par of S Greg Littleton CO 1996-2004; Vic S Mths Epis Ch Monument CO 1991-1993; S Marks Ch Eau Claire WI 1988-1991; Vic S Phil's Ch Turtle Lake WI 1988-1991; Coun On Mssn Strtgy Dio Eau Claire Eau Claire WI 1988-1990; S Barn Ch Clear Lake WI 1984-1991; Vic S Mk Barron WI 1984-1990; Vic Ch Of S Thos And S Jn New Richmond WI 1984-1988; Asst Ch Of S Phil And S Jas Denver CO 1982-1984. Ed, "Herald".

SHEPARD, Diane Elise Rucker (Pgh) 1155 Brintell St, Pittsburgh PA 15201 B Washington DC 1941 d Leslie & Doris. BA W&M 1963; MA U CA 1972; MDiv Pittsburgh TS 1984; MS Chatham U 2011. D 6/2/1984 P 12/13/1984 Bp Alden Moinet Hathaway. m 8/24/1963 Paul Shepard c 2. P The Ch Of The Redeem Pittsburgh PA 2012-2013; P Calv Ch Pittsburgh PA 2007-2011; R S Steph's Epis Ch Pittsburgh PA 1992-2006; Assoc R St Andrews Epis Ch Pittsburgh PA 1984-1991.

SHEPARD, Kenneth (Neb) D 8/6/1979 P 5/9/1980 Bp Richard Mitchell Trelease Jr.

SHEPARD, Margaret Smith (CGC) 1608 Baker Ct, Panama City FL 32401 B Birmingham AL 1940 d Robert & Jimmie. BA Birmingham-Sthrn Coll 1962; Cert U of Alabama 1964; MDiv Sewanee: The U So, TS 1994; DMin Wesley TS 2009. D 5/21/1994 P 12/3/1994 Bp Robert Oran Miller. m 8/21/1964 William Scott Shepard c 2. S Andr's Epis Ch Panama City FL 2011-2012; S Jn The Evang Robertsdale AL 2006-2009; H Sprt Epis Ch Gulf Shores AL 2005-2006; R Gr Epis Ch Pike Road AL 2002-2004; Bd Mem Jubilee Cntr 2002-2004; Stndg COM All SS' Ch Sthrn Shores NC 1997-2001; R S Andr's Ch Montevallo AL 1994-1996; Bd Mem Epis Place 1992-1996; Stndg Com Dio Cntrl Gulf Coast Pensacola FL 2013-2016, Peace and Justice Cmsn 2013-2014, Camp Beckwith Bd 2012-2015; Dio E Carolina Kinston NC 1997-2001. Auth, "Called to Serve in Cmnty; Transforming a Par Vitality Through Intentionality and Pract," 2009; Auth, "Birmingham, Oh Birmingham," *Tracings*, STUSo, 1994. Dn of the Albemarle Dio E Carolina 1998; Biblia Hebrica STUSo 1994.

SHEPHERD, Angela Fontessa (Md) Episcopal Diocese of Maryland, 4 E University Pkwy, Baltimore MD 21218 **Sutton Scholars Com Chairperson Dio Maryland Baltimore MD 2015-, Title IV Intake Off 2011-, Cn for Mssn 2010-, Truth and Recon Cmsn 2010-, GC Dep, 2009, 2006, 2003 2003-2012, Stndg Com 2003-2007, COM 2000-2005; Trst Chesapeake Bay Trust Annapolis MD 2013-; Exec Coun Com on Racism Dom And Frgn Mssy Soc-Epis Ch Cntr New York NY 2012-, Disciplinary Bd for Bishops 2011-** B Louisville KY 1960 d Thomas & Anna. BBA Austin Peay St U 1983; MA Webster U 1988; MDiv SWTS 1996; DMin McCormick TS 2014. D 6/22/1996 Bp Ted Gulick Jr P 12/21/1996 Bp Arthur Williams Jr. c 1. Ex-officio St. Phil's Fam Life Cntr Inc Annapolis 2000-2010; R S Phil's Ch Annapolis MD 1999-2010; Vic S Aug's Epis Ch Youngstown OH 1996-1999; Dioc Coun Dio Ohio Cleveland 1997-1999. Auth, "Sharing the Cup," *Maryland Ch News*, Dio Maryland, 2006; Auth, "At A Vigil for Dom Violence," *Wmn Uncommon Prayers*, Morehouse Pub, 2000. DOK 1994. ML King Peace Maker Awd Anne Arundel Co. Black Cler Assoc. 2003; Field Prize for Homil SWTS 1996. ashepherd@episcopalmaryland.org

SHEPHERD, Burton Hale (WTex) 185 Towerview Dr Apt 1101, Saint Augustine FL 32092 **Ret 1990-** B Kansas City KS 1927 s Orin & Mary. BA Wstrn St Coll of Colorado 1952; MDiv Epis TS of the SW 1981. D 6/23/1981 Bp Scott Field Bailey P 1/20/1982 Bp Stanley Fillmore Hauser. m 7/9/1950 Mildred Shepherd c 2. R Ch Of The Epiph Kingsville TX 1983-1989; P-in-c S Fran By The Lake Canyon Lake TX 1982; Asst S Mk's Ch San Marcos TX 1981-1982; USN 1945-1978; Exec Coun Dio W Texas San Antonio TX 1983-1990.

SHEPHERD, Karlyn Ann (RG) 22 Bowersville Rd, Algodones NM 87001 B Washington DC 1944 d Henry & Barbara. BA California St U. D 7/31/1990 Bp

Charles I Jones III. m 4/4/1974 Gordon Shepherd c 3. D S Mich And All Ang Ch Albuquerque NM 1999-2004.

SHEPHERD, Nancy Delane (At) 1100 Pine Valley Road, Griffin GA 30224 **R S Geo's Epis Ch Griffin GA 2005-** B McKinney TX 1953 d Richard & Velta. BA Austin Coll 1974; MA Austin Coll 1975; MDiv SMU Perkins 1989; DAS VTS 1993. D 6/5/1993 P 12/15/1993 Bp A(rthur) Heath Light. m 6/30/1995 William Henry Shepherd c 1. R S Andr's Ch Milford CT 1996-2005; Assoc R S Matt's Ch Maple Glen PA 1993-1996; S Jn's Ch Lynchburg VA 1989-1992.

SHEPHERD, Nancy Hamilton (Mass) 172 Harvard Rd, Stow MA 01775 B Brooklyn NY 1931 d Peter & Nancy. BA Mid 1953; MEd Bos 1975; MDiv Bex Sem 1981. D 5/30/1981 Bp John Bowen Coburn P 6/1/1982 Bp Roger W Blanchard. m 8/15/1953 Thomas R Shepherd c 4. Dn Of Concord River Dnry Dio Massachusetts Boston MA 1996-1999, Chair - Prison Min Comm 1990-1995, Co-Chair Of Pstr Outreach Cmsn 1987-1990, Co-Chair Of Par Dvlpmt Com 1983-1989; R Trin Chap Shirley MA 1984-2002, Asst 1981-1982. Ma Epis Cleric Assn.

SHEPHERD, Richard Golder (NY) **Ret 1993-; EME 1976-** B Syracuse NY 1927 s Thomas & Elsbeth. BFA Cor 1949; STB Ya Berk 1956; STM Yale DS 1957. D 6/1/1956 P 12/18/1956 Bp Horace W B Donegan. c 2. Interfaith Counslg Cntr Exec Com 1983-1992; Exec Com 1978-1980; R Trin Ch Saugerties NY 1960-1992; P-in-c Ch Of The Epiph Southbury CT 1956-1960; Chapl Trng Sch Southbury CT 1956-1960; Asst Instr Of Homil Ya Berk New Haven CT 1956-1958; Instr Of Biblic Stds Ulster Acad; Liturg Cmsn Dio New York New York NY 1973-1983.

SHEPHERD, Stephen Gregory (Va) 6019 Hibbling Ave, Springfield VA 22150 **R S Dunst's Ch Mc Lean VA 2005-** B Denville NJ 1960 s Dennis & Ivy. BS NYU 1982; MDiv VTS 2002. D 6/15/2002 P 12/18/2002 Bp Peter J Lee. m 7/18/1987 Tami Shepherd. Asst S Barn Ch Annandale VA 2002-2005. office@ stdunstans.net

SHEPHERD, Thomas Charles (Mass) 6600 Ne 22nd Way Apt 2323, Fort Lauderdale FL 33308 **Ret 2000-; Friends of Prisoners 1983-** B Toledo OH 1938 s Wayne & Virginia. BA U of Toledo 1960; MDiv Bex Sem 1963. D 6/15/1963 P 12/21/1963 Bp Nelson Marigold Burroughs. S Columba Epis Ch Marathon FL 2006-2007; Int St Marg's 2005-2006; R Chr Ch Epis Harwich Port MA 1982-2000; R S Andr's Ch Walden NY 1973-1982; 1971-1972; Chapl S Steph's Sch Rome Italy 1969-1970; Chapl Trin Sch Pawling NY 1965-1969; Asst S Andr's Epis Ch Toledo OH 1963-1965; Dioc Coun Dio New York New York NY 1979-1981. Auth, "Ministering to Ex-Offenders," *Wit*, 1985.

SHEPHERD, Thomas E (WMo) 1107 Saratoga Drive, Euless TX 76040 B Jackson TN 1936 s Earle & Loaraine. BS U of Louisville 1969; MS U of Louisville 1973; MDiv Sewanee: The U So, TS 1980. D 6/21/1980 P 1/10/1982 Bp David Reed. m 12/30/1958 Anna Shepherd c 4. R S Aug's Ch Kansas City MO 1999-2004; R S Matt's Epis Ch Delray Bch FL 1990-1999; Dio W Tennessee Memphis 1987-1990, Bp & Coun Bd; Cmsn on Evang & Racism; Emm Epis Cntr Bd; Sprtl Dir for Curs 1985-2000; R Emm Ch Memphis TN 1985-1990; Ch Of Our Merc Sav Louisville KY 1981-1985; Dio Kentucky Louisville KY 1980-1981; D S Geo's Epis Ch Louisville KY 1980-1981; Stndg Com; Dio W Missouri Kansas City MO 2003-2004; COM; Soc Concerns Commision; Dioc Nwsltr Bd; Bd Truistees, St. Andr's Sch, Boca Raton Dio SE Florida Miami 1992-1998. EUC 1980-1990; OHC 1980; UBE 1980-2004. Bp's Shield Bp of W Missouri 2004; Annual Awd for Meritorious & Faithful Serv for Establis UBE 1993.

SHEPHERD JR, William Henry (At) 1100 Pine Valley Rd, Griffin GA 30224 B Indianapolis IN 1957 s William & Joycelyn. BA U GA 1979; MDiv Ya Berk 1982; PhD Emory U 1994; MLIS Valdosta St U 2008. D 10/28/1982 P 5/25/1983 Bp Edward Witker Jones. m 6/30/1995 Nancy Delane Layton. Dir of Angl Stds Candler TS Emory U 2010-2012; Int S Jn's Ch Bridgeport CT 2003-2005; Int S Ptr's Epis Ch Cheshire CT 2002-2003; Int Gr And S Ptr's Epis Ch Hamden CT 1999-2001; Int Chr Ch Avon CT 1998-1999; Prof Geo Mercer TS Garden City NY 1996-2000; Int S Lk's Ch Katonah NY 1996-1998; Int Emm Ch Quakertown PA 1995-1996; Int S Geo's Ch Pennsville NJ 1994-1995; Asst Prof Homil VTS Alexandria VA 1991-1993; Asst S Cathr's Epis Ch Marietta GA 1989-1991; Assoc S Paul's Epis Ch Indianapolis IN 1984-1986; Asst S Chris's Epis Ch Carmel IN 1982-1983. Auth, "Without a Net," CSS, 2004; Auth, "If a Sermon Falls in The Forest: Preaching Resurection Texts," CSS, 2003; Auth, "No Deed Grtr than a Word," CSS, 1998; Auth, "Narrative Function of H Sprt in Lk-Acts," Scholars Press, 1994.

SHEPHERD, William John (Pa) 110 W Johnson St, Philadelphia PA 19144 B Philadelphia PA 1929 s John & May. BS Tem 1957; STM PDS 1960. D 5/14/1960 Bp Joseph Gillespie Armstrong P 11/1/1960 Bp Albert Ervine Swift. m 2/18/1969 Dolores R Shepherd. Cathd Ch Of Our Sav Philadelphia PA 1997-1999; Int S Lk's Ch Philadelphia PA 1995-1997, Asst 1984-1994; Nonpar 1967-1984; Vic S Geo S Barn Ch Philadelphia PA 1960-1961.

SHEPIC, Charlotte Louise (Colo) 14031 W Exposition Dr, Lakewood CO 80228 **Com Mem Sprtl Direction Colorado Denver Colorado 2014-** B Elkhart KS 1954 d Robert & Ida. BA Knox Coll 1976; Cert Barnes Bus Coll 1985; D Formation Prog 1997; Certification Sursum Corda 2005. D 11/8/1997

Bp William Jerry Winterrowd. m 9/20/1980 John Shepic c 1. D S Paul's Epis Ch Lakewood CO 2001-2015; Admin Asst to the COM Dio Colorado Denver CO 1998-2005; D S Martha's Epis Ch Westminster CO 1998-2000; D S Eliz's Epis Ch Brighton CO 1997-1998.

SHEPLER, Dawn (Colo) D 6/10/2017 Bp Robert John O'Neill.

SHEPLEY, Joseph (Ct) 65 Grey Rock Road, Southbury CT 06488 **R S Paul's Ch Brookfield CT 2012-, P-in-c 2009-2012, Assoc 2007-2009; Prog and Bdgt Com Dio Connecticut Meriden CT 2010-, Stwdshp Com 2009-2015** B Saint Louis MO 1970 s Joseph & Carolyn. BS Bradley U 1992; MDiv TESM 1996. D 6/8/1996 Bp John Clark Buchanan P 12/14/1996 Bp Sanford Zangwill Kaye Hampton. m 8/20/1994 Tara Shepley c 3. Outreach/Urban Mssnr Epis Dio New York 2002-2006; Cur S Thos Ch New York NY 1999-2002; Cur S Mary's Ch Lakewood WA 1996-1999.

SHEPPARD, Dale Eugene (WVa) 1051 Walker Road, Follansbee WV 26037 **Mssnr Brooke-Hancock Epis Mnstrs 2006-** B Parkersburg WV 1948 s Dale & Irene. BS Ohio Vlly Coll 2001; MDiv Bex 2006; MDiv Bex Sem 2006. D 12/10/2005 P 6/10/2006 Bp William Michie Klusmeyer. m 10/29/1968 Janice Sheppard c 3. Mssnr Brooke-Hancock Cluster Weirton WV 2006-2015; Prod Tech G.E. Plastics 1971-2003.

SHEPPARD, Patricia (Fla) 919 San Fernando St., Fernandina Beach FL 32034 B Cleveland OH 1949 d Irvin & Margaret. MDiv CDSP 2001. D 1/6/2002 Bp Jerry Alban Lamb P 7/13/2002 Bp J Clark Grew II. m 9/11/2005 Don A Robbins c 1. S Fran Of Assisi Epis Ch Tallahassee FL 2011-2012; Bethany Ch Hilliard FL 2007-2008; S Ptr's Fernandina Bch FL 2006-2012; R Ch of the H Sprt Charlestown RI 2004-2006; Ch Of The H Sprt Charlestown RI 2004-2005; S Jn's Epis Ch Bowling Green OH 2002-2004.

SHEPPARD, Ricardo Wayne (NJ) S Alb's Epis Ch New Brunswick NJ 2016- B Trinidad and Tobago 1966 s Valentine & Norma. Masters of Div PrTS; Dplma of Angl Stds Sewanee: The U So, TS; Bachelors of Sci The Coll of New Rochelle. D 6/1/2016 P 12/10/2016 Bp William H Stokes. c 4. revsheppard@ stalbansnewbrunswick.org

SHERARD, Susan (NC) 402 West Smith Street, 4J, Greensboro NC 27401 B Vicksburg MS 1949 d James & Florence. BA Lake Forest Coll 1971; MA Sangamon St U 1974; MDiv GTS 1985. D 6/15/1985 P 1/18/1986 Bp William Gillette Weinhauer. m 11/11/2000 Thomas James Panek. H Trin Epis Ch Greensboro NC 2013-2016; S Dav's Epis Ch Laurinburg NC 2004-2005; Chair COM Dio Wstrn No Carolina Asheville NC 1995-2000, Dn Asheville Deanry 1990-1993, COM 1987-1995, 1987-1989; Epis Ch Of The H Sprt Mars Hill NC 1985-2000. susan@holy-trinity.com

SHERER, Valori (WNC) 506 W Sumter St, Shelby NC 28150 B Perth Amboy NJ 1958 d Edward & Manuela. AA Cnty Coll of Morris 1978; BA Rutgers The St U of New Jersey 1984; MDiv Sewanee: The U So, TS 2005. D 2/5/2005 P 9/7/2005 Bp Henry Irving Louttit. m 4/16/1988 Steven T Sherer c 3. R Ch Of The Redeem Shelby NC 2009-2016; R S Mary's Epis Ch Cadillac MI 2007-2009; Cur S Paul's Epis Ch St Jos MI 2005-2007. vmsherer@gmail.com

SHERFICK, Kenneth L (WMich) 1517 Emoriland Blvd, Knoxville TN 37917 **Ret 1998-** B Washington IN 1936 s Kenneth & Edith. BA Franklin Coll 1962; BD ETS Cambridge MA 1965. D 6/14/1965 P 12/20/1965 Bp John P Craine. m 8/16/1983 Kathleen English c 5. Chapl Cmnty Hlth Cntr 1988-1998; R S Mk's Ch Coldwater MI 1984-1998; Chapl Ball St U Muncie IN 1968-1984; R Gr Ch Muncie IN 1968-1984; Cur Chr Ch Cathd Indianapolis IN 1965-1968; Dep GC Dio Wstrn Michigan Kalamazoo MI 1991-1993, Stndg Com 1990-1998, Bps Search Com 1988-1989; Dep GC Dio Indianapolis Indianapolis IN 1979-1982, Pres Stndg Com 1978-1980.

SHERIDAN, Dennis Arnol (Los) 242 E Alvarado St, Pomona CA 91767 B Bogalusa LA 1953 s Lawrence & Melba. BA LSU 1975; MEd LSU 1978; MRE SW Bapt TS 1982; EDD SW Bapt TS 1987; PhD U CA, Los Angeles 1997; Cert of Angl Stds ETS 2014. D 12/20/2014 Bp Joseph Jon Bruno. c 2.

SHERIDAN-CAMPBELL, Laura M (SanD) 6540 Ambrosia Ln Apt 1128, Carlsbad CA 92011 **Vic H Cross Epis Ch Carlsbad CA 2010-; COM Dio San Diego San Diego CA 2011-** B Des Moines IA 1964 d Harold & Patricia. Wartburg Coll 1984; BA U of Iowa 1987; MS Iowa St U 1990; MDiv Ya Berk 1993; DMin CDSP 2010. D 5/19/1993 P 3/1/1994 Bp Chris Christopher Epting. m 6/5/2010 Jerry Lynn Campbell. S Jn's Epis Ch Odessa TX 1996-2008, Chapl 1996-2008; Cur The Cathd Ch Of S Paul Des Moines IA 1993-1996; Tchg Asst CDSP Berkeley CA 2008-2010; Stndg Com Dio NW Texas Lubbock TX 2006-2008, GC Cler Dep 2004-2006, GC Cler Dep Alt. 2001-2003.

SHERMAN, Andrew James (SeFla) 245 NE 2nd St., Boca Raton FL 33432 **R S Greg's Ch Boca Raton FL 2005-; Bd, Epis Chars 2008-, Dn, So Palm Bch Dnry 2006-2010** B Rockville Center NY 1962 s Harry & Joan. BA Amer U 1984; MA U of Virginia 1992; MDiv VTS 1992. D 6/23/1992 Bp John Wadsworth Howe P 2/20/1993 Bp Charlie Fuller Mcnutt Jr. m 8/18/2005 Anita Sarah Cherian c 2. Adj Fac Gettysburg Luth Sem 2003-2005; R The Memi Ch Of The Prince Of Peace Gettysburg PA 1995-2005; S Jn's Epis Ch Carlisle PA 1992-1995. co-Auth, "I Believe," *Cnfrmtn Prog*, Ldr Resources, 2006.

SHERMAN, Clark Michael (Mont) 5 W Olive St, Bozeman MT 59715 **Reg Cn Dio Montana Helena MT 2005-; R S Jas Ch Bozeman MT 1997-** B Ancon PA 1957 s Louis & Mildred. BD How 1979; MA Steph F Austin St U 1984; MDiv Iliff TS 1991; S Thos Sem 1992; DPS Evang Chr U Monroe LA 2001. D 6/12/1993 P 12/18/1993 Bp William Jerry Winterrowd. m 12/29/1978 Jamie D Sherman c 3. Vic S Pat's Epis Ch Pagosa Sprg CO 1993-1997.

SHERMAN, Elizabeth Ann (Cal) St. Francis Episcopal Church, San Francisco CA 94127 **R S Fran' Epis Ch San Francisco CA 2011-; Chapl Br And Rhode Island Sch Of Design 2004-** B Dallas TX 1955 d Wilbur & LaRue. BA U of Texas 1977; MDiv GTS 1981. D 6/7/1982 Bp Brice Sidney Sanders P 4/9/1983 Bp John Shelby Spong. P-in-c S Dav's On The Hill Epis Ch Cranston RI 2008-2011; Brown and RISD Dio Rhode Island Providence RI 2004-2008; Vic St Fran Epis Ch Coventry RI 1998-2008; Chapl Austin Hospice 1992-1997; Asst For Ce Trin Par New York NY 1985-1990; Cur Chr Ch Ridgewood NJ 1982-1985.

SHERMAN, Guy Charles (Oly) 12527 Roosevelt Way NE Apt 405, Seattle WA 98125 B Tenino WA 1940 s Robert & Elsie. BA U of Puget Sound 1964; MDiv CDSP 1973. D 11/10/1973 Bp Ivol I Curtis P 5/9/1980 Bp Robert Hume Cochrane. c 2. Int S Paul's Epis Ch Bremerton WA 2009-2010; Int Chr Epis Ch Puyallup WA 2005-2007; Int St Jn's Epis Ch of Sturgis Sturgis MI 2003-2004; Int Ch Of The H Trin Midland TX 2002-2003; Int Chr Ch Eureka CA 2000-2002; Convenor of Reg Advsry Coun CDSP Berkeley CA 1990-1993; Vic S Aid's Epis Ch Stanwood WA 1988-1998; Dio Olympia Seattle WA 1987-1988, 1980-1983; Assoc Trin Epis Ch Everett WA 1976-1988; Asst Chr Ch Seattle WA 1973-1974.

SHERMAN JR, Levering Bartine (Me) 130 Cedar St, Bangor ME 04401 B Charlotte NC 1946 s Levering & Elizabeth. BA U NC 1969; Pr 1971; MDiv EDS 1973; MA U NC 1984. D 11/4/1973 P 6/8/1974 Bp Matthew George Henry. m 3/5/2011 Ann Livingston Holland c 3. P-in-c S Andr's Ch Millinocket ME 2014-2015, 2012-2014; P-in-c S Thos Ch Winn ME 2012-2014; Vic S Mart's Epis Ch Palmyra ME 2006-2012; P Dio Maine Portland ME 2000-2014, Dep, GC 2009-, Chair, Tech + Environ Comms 1993-2008; Vic All SS Epis Ch Skowhegan ME 1997-2012; Other Position Maine St Libr Augusta ME 1997-2006; Other Position Media Producer Univ of Maine System Augusta ME 1992-1997; Vic S Barn Ch Augusta Augusta ME 1989-1997; R Ch of S Mths Asheville NC 1973-1975; Cler Rep Dom Violence T/F Somerset ME 2008-2012. Auth, *Like an Ever-Rolling Stream: Sm Ch in Maine*, Maine PBS, 1991; Auth, *Pokin' Fun: The Tradition of Maine Humor*, Maine PBS, 1991. Maine Broadcasters Assn Awd of Excellence 1990; Who's Who in Amer Colleges and Universities 1972.

SHERMAN, Russell E (WTex) 202 Primera Dr, San Antonio TX 78212 **Bereavement Mgr Benevolent Hospice San Antonio TX 2008-** B Oceanside NY 1949 s Robert & Martha. JYA Amer U of Beirut, Lebanon 1970; BA Ken 1972; MDiv Sewanee: The U So, TS 1985. D 6/16/1985 Bp Frank S Cerveny P 5/1/1986 Bp Allen Lyman Bartlett Jr. m 12/27/1975 Kathleen Sherman c 3. Res Bapt Med System San Antonio TX 2011-2012; Chapl VITAS Hospice San Antonio TX 2003-2008; Assoc Chr Epis Ch San Antonio TX 1997-2003; R S Johns Ch Indianapolis IN 1995-1997; Asst Ch Of The Gd Samar Paoli PA 1985-1995. ERM; Episcopalians Untd; Ord Of S Lk; Ord Of S Mary.

SHERMAN, Walter (Ind) 5023 N. Pennsylvania St, Indianapolis IN 46205 **Exec Coun Dio Indianapolis Indianapolis IN 2006-** B Newark OH 1952 s Gail & Florence. BA Muskingum Coll 1974; Lic Universite de Nice France 1976; MDiv GTS 1982. D 6/6/1982 P 5/31/1983 Bp William Grant Black. m 1/6/2012 Richard T Vaughan. S Alb's Ch Indianapolis IN 2005-2010, R 2005-; S Jude's Epis Ch Fenton MI 2004; Dn Dio Michigan Detroit MI 1999-2004, Stndg Com 1997-2001, COM 1996-2000, Cathd Chapt 1994-1998, Cler Ldrshp Proj 1994-1997, Prov V Educational Unit Prog 1994-1996; S Paul's Epis Ch Brighton MI 1994-2004; Bd Dir Dio Michigan Whitaker TS 1994-1996; Dn Dio Indianapolis SW Dnry IN 1991-1993; Bd Dir NEAC 1987-1993; Trin Ch Lawrenceburg IN 1987-1993, Vic 1986-1993; S Lk Ch Cincinnati OH 1986-1987; Non-par 1984-1986; Dio Sthrn Ohio Cincinnati OH 1984-1985; Cur The Ch Of Ascen And H Trin Cincinnati OH 1982-1984; Stndg Com Dio Indianapolis Indianapolis IN 1988-1992.

SHERRER, Wayne Calvin (Be) 150 Elm Street, Emmaus PA 18049 **S Ptr's Ch Mt Arlington NJ 2014-** B Phillipsburg NJ 1951 s August & Lois. BA Immac Heart Coll 1980; MDiv McCormick TS 1986. D 2/2/2009 Bp John Palmer Croneberger P 9/29/2009 Bp Paul Victor Marshall. m 4/9/1994 Mildred Evangeline Sherrer c 2. P-in-c S Marg's Ch Emmaus PA 2010-2013; Assoc Trin Ch Easton PA 2009-2010; D S Geo's Epis Ch Hellertown PA 2009.

SHERRILL, Christopher Ralph (NJ) P.O. Box 45, Southport ME 04576 B Warm Sprgs GA 1935 s Ralph & Edith. BA Geneva Coll 1960; BD Yale DS 1965. D 6/19/1965 Bp William S Thomas P 12/18/1965 Bp Austin Pardue. m 8/13/1960 H Leigh Sherrill c 3. Assoc Trin Ch Princeton NJ 1992-2001; Assoc The Ch Of The Epiph Washington DC 1988-1992; R Chr Ch Wm And Mary Newburg MD 1986-1988; Asst All Souls Memi Epis Ch Washington DC 1984-1986; R S Matt Seat Pleasant MD 1979-1980; Int St Matthews Ch Bowie MD 1979-1980; R S Pat's Ch Washington DC 1972-1979; R S Alb's Ch Daniel-

S

son CT 1969-1972; Assoc Chr Epis Ch S Jos MO 1966-1969; P-In-C S Geo's Jefferson Boro PA 1965-1966. EvangES 1995-2001.

SHERRILL II, Edmund Knox (NH) Church Farm School, 1001 E Lincoln Hwy, Exton PA 19341 **Hd of Sch CFS The Sch At Ch Farm Exton PA 2009-; NAES New York NY 2006-; Hd Chapl St. Mk's Sch Southborough MA 2003-; Bd Dir Natl Assoc Of Epis Schools- Epis Ch New York NY 2005-** B Dickinson ND 1956 s Franklin & Mary. BA Macalester Coll 1979; MDiv Ya Berk 1983. D 6/28/1985 P 5/1/1986 Bp Philip Alan Smith. m 8/18/1979 Elizabeth Roberts Sherrill c 3. Chapl St. Mk's Sch of Southborough Inc. Southborough MA 2003-2009; Int R S Andr's-In-The-Vlly Tamworth NH 2003; Headmaster/Vic Dio Micronesia Tumon Bay GU 1998-2002; Vic/Hdmstr S Jn's Epis Ch & Sch Guam 1998-2002; COM Dio New Hampshire Concord NH 1992-1998; Chalpain S Paul's Sch Concord NH 1991-1998, 1990-1998, Chapl 1985-1986; Dn of Chap S Paul's Sch Concord NH 1990-1998; Chapl Wooster Sch Danbury CT 1986-1990; Chapl Wooster Sch Danbury CT 1986-1990; Assoc R H Cross Epis Ch Weare NH 1984-1986; Mstr Tchr S Paul's Sch Concord NH 1983-1986.

SHERRILL JR, George (SO) 906 Main St Apt 412, Cincinnati OH 45202 **P-in-c Indn Hill Ch Cincinnati OH 2016-** B Atlanta GA 1966 s George & Claire. BA Wofford Coll 1989; MDiv VTS 2006. D 12/10/2005 P 6/10/2006 Bp William Michie Klusmeyer. m 12/29/2011 Karen F Flynt c 3. Chr Ch Clarksburg WV 2008-2012; S Tim's In The Vlly Hurricane WV 2006-2008. gsherrill@indianhillchurch.org

SHERRILL, Joan (NC) D 1/24/2015 Bp Anne Hodges-Copple.

SHERRILL, Karen F (SO) St. John's Episcopal Church, 3000 Washington Blvd, Huntington WV 25705 B Radford VA 1959 d James & Linda. BA E Carolina U 1982; MDiv GTS 2006. D 6/24/2006 P 1/20/2007 Bp Dorsey Henderson. m 12/29/2011 George Sherrill c 1. S Jn's Ch Huntington WV 2008-2012; S Alb's Ch Lexington SC 2006-2008; Chapl Spartanburg Reg Hosp 2002-2003.

SHERROUSE, Wanda Gail (CFla) 121 W 18th St, Sanford FL 32771 B Toledo OH 1952 AS Valencia Cmnty Coll. D 12/13/2003 Bp John Wadsworth Howe. c 2. D H Cross Epis Ch Sanford FL 2003-2004.

SHERWIN, Lawrence Alan (Vt) 54 E State St, Montpelier VT 05602 B Bennington VT 1939 s Leo & Margaret. BA U of Vermont 1962; MA EDS 1968. D 6/15/1968 P 12/1/1968 Bp Harvey D Butterfield. c 3. R S Jas Epis Ch Arlington VT 1970-1974; Cur Cathd Ch Of S Paul Burlington VT 1968-1970.

SHERWOOD, Robert Leon (Mass) 165 Main St, Buzzards Bay MA 02532 **Assoc. Campus Mnstry Chapl Massachusetts Maritime Acad Buzzards' Bay MA. 2014-; D S Ptr's Ch On The Canal Buzzards Bay MA 2013-** B Urbana OH 1942 s Leon & Martha. BS OH SU 1971; MBA U of Dayton 1974. D 6/22/2013 Bp M(Arvil) Thomas Shaw. m 9/1/1962 Nancy Jean Bonner c 1.

SHERWOOD, Zalmon Omar (Mich) PO Box 1342, Arcadia FL 34265 **Investigator St of Florida Dept of Chld and Families 2013-** B Geneva OH 1956 s Zalmon & Janet. BA Hiram Coll 1979; MDiv EDS 1984; MA New Engl Conservatory of Mus 1984. D 6/30/1984 Bp James Russell Moodey P 6/22/1985 Bp Robert Whitridge Estill. Soc Worker Florida Sheriffs Yth Ranch Parrish FL 2005-2013; Chapl Ionia Maximum Correctional Facility Ionia MI 1993-1997; Exec Dir St. Jas Colony Beaver Island MI 1990-1993; Cur S Paul's Epis Ch Jackson MI 1986-1990; Cur Emm Par Epis Ch Sthrn Pines NC 1984-1985. Auth, "Equal Rites: Liberating Wrshp For Lesbians & Gay Men," Westminster, 1990; Auth, "Kairos- Confessions Of A Gay P," Alyson, 1986.

SHEVLIN, James Charles (CFla) Saint Paul's Church, 25 River St, Sidney NY 13838 **R Ch Of Our Sav Okeechobee FL 2015-; Dn Dio Albany Susquehanna Dnry 2010-; Mem Dioc Cmsn of Mnstry Albany NY 2006-; Mem Dioc Trst Albany NY 2006-; R St. Paul's Episciopal Ch Sidney NY 2004-; P S Paul's Ch Sidney NY 2003-** B Johnson City NY 1949 s John & Margaret. Dip Ang Stud TESM 2008. D 1/12/2003 Bp David John Bena P 12/15/2007 Bp William Howard Love. m 1/26/1991 Jean Marie Shevlin c 7.

SHEW, Debbie (At) 3627 Shadowood Pkwy Se, Atlanta GA 30339 B Fort Dix NJ 1960 d Richard & Martha. BA Davidson Coll 1982; MEd Georgia St U 1985; Pyschological Stds Inst For Chr Counslg 1985; MDiv GTS 1994. D 6/4/1994 P 12/1/1994 Bp Frank Kellogg Allan. m 7/17/2003 David S Shew c 2. The Ch Of S Matt Snellville GA 2013-2014; Dio Atlanta Atlanta GA 1999-2012; H Innoc Ch Atlanta GA 1994-1999.

SHEWMAKER, David Paul (NCal) St Paul's Episcopal Ch, 220 E. Macken, Crescent City CA 95531 B St Joseph MO 1945 s Marion & Carolyn. BA U of Missouri 1969; MA U of Missouri 1971; CAS CDSP 2007; CAS CDSP 2007. D 9/7/2007 P 4/12/2008 Bp Barry Leigh Beisner. m 11/29/1986 Alicia Shewmaker c 2. P-in-c S Paul's Mssn Cres City CA 2008-2017; Branch Mgr Apria Healthcare 1978-2005.

SHIELD, Catherine Ann (Kan) 13420 E Harry St, Wichita KS 67230 **D S Jude's Ch Wellington KS 2007-** B Abilene TX 1946 d Dixon & Mary. BS U of Oklahoma 1968; Masters of Div S Paul TS 2009. D 10/26/1990 Bp William Edward Smalley. m 8/31/1966 Charles Franklin Shield c 3. D S Andr's Epis Ch Emporia KS 2004-2006; D S Jas Ch Wichita KS 1993-2006; D S Chris's 1990-1993. NAAD.

SHIELDS, James Mark (Md) 6153 Waiting Spg, Columbia MD 21045 B Pittsburgh PA 1931 s James & Mary. BA U of Maryland 1965; BD ETS 1968. D 6/29/1968 Bp William S Thomas P 12/21/1968 Bp Robert Bracewell Appleyard. m 12/22/1955 Seiko Shields c 1. Int R St. Alb's Angl-Epis Ch Tokyo Japan 2004-2005; Int R St. Mk's-On-the-Hill Pikesville MD 2002-2004; R Chr Ch Columbia MD 1979-1999; R Ch Of The Adv Pittsburgh PA 1970-1979; D-in-c Ch Of The Gd Shpd Pittsburgh PA 1968-1969.

SHIELDS, John (NC) 520 Summit St, Winston Salem NC 27101 B Winston-Salem NC 1938 s John & Myrtle. U NC; VTS; Wake Forest U; BA Guilford Coll 1960. D 4/25/1985 P 4/25/1986 Bp Robert Whitridge Estill. c 3. Int S Paul's Ch Wilkesboro NC 2012-2014; Int Ch Of The H Comf Charlotte NC 2009-2010; S Paul's Epis Ch Winston Salem NC 1997-2009; Chr Ch Walnut Cove NC 1986-1996; Vic S Eliz Epis Ch King NC 1986-1996; Asst S Tim's Epis Ch Winston Salem NC 1985-1986.

SHIELDS, John W (WNC) 2508 Amity Ave, Gastonia NC 28054 **Ch Of The Trsfg Bat Cave NC 2014-** B Asheville NC 1977 BS No Carolina St U 1999; MDiv Sewanee: The U So, TS 2003. D 5/31/2003 P 12/4/2003 Bp Bob Johnson. m 12/30/2000 Laura G Shields c 4. Gr Ch Asheville NC 2012-2014; S Columba's Epis Ch E Boothbay ME 2009-2011; Ch Of S Andr's In The Pines Pinedale WY 2004-2009; S Mk's Ch Gastonia NC 2003-2004.

SHIELDS, Richard Edward (Haw) 1330 1st Ave Apt 424, New York NY 10021 **Supply P The Epis Ch in Hawaii Honolulu HI 2006-, Supply P 2006-** B Beacon NY 1952 s Roger & Kathleen. BS Creighton U 1974; LTh SWTS 1979; MA U of Nebraska 1983; PharmD U IL 1996. D 5/21/1979 Bp Quintin Ebenezer Primo Jr P 11/30/1979 Bp James Daniel Warner. m 5/23/2017 Kevin Kaipo William Sasan. Supply P Dio Georgia Savannah GA 2003-2005; Supply P Dio W Virginia Charleston WV 1997-2003; Supply Cler Dio Massachusetts Boston MA 1990-1997; Novc, SSJE S Jn's Chap Cambridge MA 1989-2014; Soc-St Jn The Evang Cambridge MA 1989-1990; Int All SS Epis Ch Boise ID 1988-1989; Mssy Exec Coun Appointees New York NY 1987-1988; Vic Iglesia Buen Pstr San Pedro Sula Hond 1987-1988; Vic Iglesia Espiritu Santo Tela Hond 1986-1987; Supply P Dio Nebraska Omaha NE 1985-1986; R S Phil Omaha NE 1984-1985; Chapl S Monica Hm Lincoln NE 1983-1986; Chr Ch Cntrl City NE 1981-1983; R S Johns Ch Albion NE 1981-1983; Cur S Andr's Ch Omaha NE 1979-1980. Soc of St Jn the Evang 1989-1990.

SHIER, Marshall Wayne (Los) 1348 E Wilshire Ave, Fullerton CA 92831 B Port Angeles WA 1944 s Lloyd & Frances. BA Seattle U 1966; MLS U CA 1969; Cert U CA 1970; ETSBH 1975; MA Claremont TS 1976. D 6/19/1976 P 1/15/1977 Bp Robert Claflin Rusack. m 5/8/2012 Melvin Duane Steadman. S Andr's Par Fullerton CA 1976-2009.

SHIER, Nancy Katherine (Los) 224 Bradbury Dr, San Gabriel CA 91775 B Pasadena CA 1938 d Cyril & Katherine. BA Stan 1960; MA California St U 1974; MA California St U 1987; MDiv Claremont TS 2000. D 10/21/2001 Bp Frederick Houk Borsch P 11/23/2002 Bp Chester Lovelle Talton. c 2. Ch Of Our Sav Par San Gabr CA 2003-2010; Imm Mssn El Monte CA 2001-2003.

SHIER, Pamela C (WVa) 164 Mason Ridge Rd, Mount Morris PA 15349 **Mem Compass Rose Soc 2011-; Assoc P Ch of the Epiph Doha Qatar 2008-; P-in-c Prince Of Peace Salem Salem WV 1999-; P-in-c Prince Of Peace Salem WV 1999-** B Plainfield NJ 1952 d Leon & Joan. BS Cor 1975; MDiv EDS 1979. D 6/23/1979 P 6/24/1980 Bp Ned Cole. m 12/29/1973 David Shier. Assoc, Prot Ch in Oman Dio Cyprus and the Gulf Muscat Oman 2001-2006; 1990-1999; Fell Coll of Chapls 1982-1990; COM Dio W Virginia Charleston WV 1982-1990, 1980-1990; Dir of Chapl Serv W Virginia U Hospitals Morgantown WV 1980-1990; S Thos a Becket Epis Ch Morgantown WV 1980-1988; D S Andr's Ch Ann Arbor MI 1979-1980; Chapl Res U MI-Ann Arbor MI 1979-1980. Compass Rose Soc 2011. Prof Serv Awd Coll of Chapl 1990.

SHIFLET JR, William Ray (Md) 4520 Cornflower Ct, Ellicott City MD 21043 **Part Time CPG 2006-** B Roanoke VA 1947 s William & Rachel. AA Ferrum Coll 1967; BS VPI 1969; MDiv VTS 1972; DMin Hartford Sem 1980. D 6/9/1972 Bp William Henry Marmion P 12/13/1972 Bp Philip Alan Smith. m 8/26/1967 Mary L Shiflet c 2. VTS Alexandria VA 2006-2008, Trst 1991-2013; R S Jn's Ch Ellicott City MD 1987-2005; R Trin Ch Branford CT 1980-1987; Assoc Trin Epis Ch Southport CT 1976-1980; Asst Chr Epis Ch Roanoke VA 1972-1976. Branford Citizen Of The Year 1986.

SHIGAKI, Jerry Moritsune (Oly) 6963 California Ave Sw Unit 102, Seattle WA 98136 B Seattle WA 1946 s George & Yasuko. BA U of Washington 1968; MSW U of Washington 1975; MDiv SWTS 2000. D 6/24/2000 P 1/13/2001 Bp Sanford Zangwill Kaye Hampton. c 1. Dio Olympia Seattle 2000-2010; Mssnr for Ethnic Mnstry S Ben Epis Ch Lacey WA 2000-2002.

SHIGAKI, Pauline Yuri (Oly) B Cleveland OH 1945 d Seigo & Mitsuko. BA U of Washington 1978. D 11/9/2013 Bp Gregory Harold Rickel. m 1/8/1966 John M Shigaki c 3.

SHIKE, Charles Wesley (Nwk) 601 Kappock St Apt 1F, Bronx NY 10463 **Pstr Psychoanalyst 1962-** B Hope NJ 1924 s Charles & Virginia. BA Swarthmore Coll 1948; MDiv VTS 1951; Robbins Fell 1963; Cert Natl Psychol Assn For Psychoanalysis 1967; DMin Andover Newton TS 1974. D 6/16/1951 P 6/1/

S

1952 Bp Angus Dun. m 7/17/2003 Soomintra Rai Shike c 2. The Ch of S Matt And S Tim New York NY 1994-1998; S Paul's Ch Montvale NJ 1963-1965; Inst of Pstr Counslg Inc. 1960-1963; Chapl Res St Hosp Greystone Pk NJ 1960-1963; Dio Newark Newark NJ 1960-1961, Dept Of Chr Soc Relatns 1960-1961, Advsr For The Newark Archdnry 1958-1960, Bd Yth Consulting Serv 1957-1962, Dept Of Missions 1957-1958, Dept Of CE 1954-1959; R S Thos Ch Lyndhurst NJ 1953-1960; Advsr Of NW Chr Yth Coun Dio Washington Washington DC 1952-1953, Dept Of CE 1951-1953; S Alb's Par Washington DC 1951-1953. AAPC, AAMFC; Amer Assn Play Ther; Chair Bd Exam Natl Assn Advancement Psychol 1996. Robbins Fell 1960; Dip Aapc.

SHILEY, Ed (Pa) 145 West Springfield Road, Springfield PA 19064 **Chapl Springfield EMT Springfield PA 2009-** B Winchester VA 1944 s Earl & Vada. BA Westminster Choir Coll of Rider U 1966; MDiv EDS 1997. D 7/12/1997 Bp Arthur Williams Jr P 1/1/1998 Bp J Clark Grew II. m 8/21/1976 Kim A Shiley c 2. Shiley, E. Edw Ch Of The Redeem Springfield PA 2004-2016; R S Ptr's Epis Ch Broomall PA 2000-2004; R S Jas Epis Ch Boardman OH 1997-2000; Ch Fndt Bd Dio Pennsylvania Philadelphia PA 2009-2012, Dn of Delaware Dnry 2008-2011, Salaries and Pennsions 2007-2008, Dioc Coun 2002-2011. eeshiley3@verizon.net

✠ SHIN, The Rt Rev Allen (NY) Episcopal Diocese of New York, 1047 Amsterdam Ave, New York NY 10025 **Bp Suffragon of New York Dio New York New York NY 2014-** B Seoul KR 1956 s Kyung & Chu. SWTS 1995; MDiv GTS 1996; STM GTS 2001; Oxf GB 2001. D 6/15/1996 Bp Frank Tracy Griswold III P 12/7/1996 Bp Richard Frank Grein Con 5/17/2014 for NY. m 5/25/1991 Clara H Mun. R S Jn's Ch Huntington NY 2010-2014; Chapl/Theol Tutor Keble Coll Oxf UK 2005-2010; Asst All SS Ch Marg St. London 2003-2005; Cur Ch Of S Mary The Vrgn New York NY 1999-2001, Asst 1996-1999; Asst Congreg Mnstrs Epis Ch Cntr New York NY 1996-1999. bpshin@dioceseny.org

SHINN, Richard Emerson (Mich) 6710 Little Hemlock St, Stanwood MI 49346 **Died 7/7/2017** B Brooklyn MI 1927 s Emerson & Marian. BA MI SU 1951; BD Bex Sem 1962. D 7/1/1962 Bp Archie H Crowley P 1/24/1963 Bp Robert Lionne DeWitt. m 6/25/1966 Marlene Edna Shinn c 3. Supply P S Jn's Ch Mt Pleasant MI 1999-2000; P-in-c Chr The King Epis Ch Taylor MI 1993-1996; Ret 1991-2017; R S Thos Ch Trenton MI 1975-1991; Asst to Bp for Admin and Fin Dio Michigan Detroit MI 1973-1975, Asst Exec Dir Admin 1968-1973, Asst Exec Dir of Admin 1968-1973; Vic Gr Epis Ch Southgate MI 1965-1968; Vic St Margarets Harbor Bch MI 1963-1965; D in Charge S Paul's Epis Ch Bad Axe MI 1962-1963.

SHIPMAN, Bruce MacDonald (Ct) 241 Monument St Apt 6, Groton CT 06340 **P-in-c H Trin Ch Oaxaca Mex 2016-; VP of the Bd Epis Ch At Yale New Haven CT 2000-** B Minneapolis MN 1941 s Harold & Lois. BA Carleton Coll 1963; BA Oxf GB 1965; MDiv GTS 1968. D 6/8/1968 P 12/21/1968 Bp Horace W B Donegan. P in charge Epis Ch at Yale 2013-2014; Vic Ch Of The H Adv Clinton CT 2006-2011; Vic All SS Ch Ivoryton CT 2000-2005; R Chr Ch Roxbury CT 1981-2000; Assoc Chr And H Trin Ch Westport CT 1973-1981; Asst All SS Ch Bayside NY 1970-1972; Cur S Ptr's Ch Port Chester NY 1968-1970; Bd Mem, Chld's Mssn S Paul And S Jas New Haven CT 2000-2008; Mem COM Dio Connecticut Meriden CT 1992-1999, COM 1991-1996, Mem Dioc Exec Com 1990-1999, Mem, Camp Washington Bd Dir 1990-1999, Chair, Bd Managers, Camp Washington 1990-1996, Dioc Exec Com Mem 1986-1998. Letter to the Ed, "Are Liberal Christians Becoming Rare?," *The New York Times*, New York Times Fndt, 2012; "Misc. arts," *The Day*, New London Day Trust, 2006; Auth, "Why I Am Going To Hebron," *Gd News*, Dio CT Nwspr, 2002; "Misc. Bk Revs," *Gd News*, Dio CT Nwspr, 2001; "Misc. arts," *LivCh*, Living Ch Fndt, 1999. Polly Bond Awd ECom 1996; Phi Beta Kappa Wesl 1985.

SHIPMAN, Josh (Colo) **S Lk's Epis Ch Altoona PA 2015-** B Selmer TN 1982 s Michael & Rhonda. BA U of Mississippi 2004; MA Colorado U 2009; MA U CO, Denver 2009; MA Colorado U 2010; MA U CO, Denver 2010; MDiv Epis TS Of The SW 2015; MDiv Epis TS of the SW 2015. D 6/14/2014 P 6/13/2015 Bp Robert John O'Neill. m 8/12/2008 Timothy O'Neal. rector@stlukesaltoona.org

SHIPP, Mary Jane Mccoy (Mont) 120 Antelope Dr, Dillon MT 59725 **Ret 2001-** B Greenville SC 1939 d Henry & Lucile. Mstr of Sacr Mus UTS; BA Furman U 1961; GTS 1984. D 6/7/1992 P 12/21/1992 Bp Charles I Jones III. m 5/31/1967 Clifford M Shipp c 3. Supply P Dio Montana Helena MT 2010-2011, 2003-2008, 1999-2000; S Jas Ch Bozeman MT 2010-2011, 2001, 1992-1998; R St Jas Epis Ch Dillon MT 2009. Assoc: OSH 1979.

SHIPPEE, Richard C (RI) 3330 E Main St Lot 109, Mesa AZ 85213 B Pawtucket RI 1949 s Elmer & Virginia. BA Colby Coll 1971; MDiv UTS 1974; STM Nash 1978; CG Jung Inst 1982. D 6/14/1975 P 1/1/1977 Bp Frederick Hesley Belden. m 8/16/1969 Cathy Lynn Shippee c 2. SS Matt and Mk Barrington RI 2012-2013; S Mk's Epis Ch Riverside RI 2009-2011; S Ptr's By The Sea Narragansett RI 2007-2008; S Mart's Ch Pawtucket RI 2006; S Jn's Ch Ashton RI 2005-2006; S Paul's Ch Pawtucket RI 1982-1984, 1979, Cur 1976-1979. Auth, "The Cloud Of Unknowing".

SHIPPEN II, Joseph J (At) PO Box 1213, Griffin GA 30224 **Epis Chapl Georgia Diagnostic Prison Jackson GA 2008-** B Atlanta GA 1977 s Benjamin & Josephine. BSE Merc 2002; BS Presb Coll 2002; MDiv GTS 2006. D 12/21/2005 P 7/29/2006 Bp J Neil Alexander. m 7/20/2003 Suzanne Elizabeth Hobby-Shippen c 2. Chr Ch Macon GA 2012-2017; R S Jas Ch Macon GA 2009-2012; Int S Fran Ch Macon GA 2009; Asst S Jas Epis Ch Marietta GA 2006-2008.

SHIPPEN, Sallie Elliot (Cal) 756 14th Way Sw, Edmonds WA 98020 **Ret 1995-** B Philadelphia PA 1935 d Robert & Frances. BA Portland St U 1978; MDiv CDSP 1982. D 6/23/1982 Bp Matthew Paul Bigliardi P 6/29/1983 Bp Rustin Ray Kimsey. c 3. CDSP Berkeley CA 1994-1996; R S Jn's Epis Ch Oakland CA 1992-1995; CDSP Berkeley CA 1989-1992; Dep GC Dio Oregon 1988-1991; Dep GC Dio Oregon 1985-1988; R Gr Epis Ch Astoria OR 1984-1992; Asst Epis Par Of S Jn The Bapt Portland OR 1982-1984.

SHIPPEY, Edgar Elijah (Ore) 940 N Dean St, Coquille OR 97423 B Poteau, OK 1937 s William & Elizabeth. BA U of Arkansas 1959; BD Epis TS of the SW 1962. D 6/14/1962 P 6/1/1963 Bp Robert Raymond Brown. m 7/18/1987 Christina Shippey c 3. Dio Oregon Portland OR 1996-2009, Chapl to Ret Cler-So Coast 2010-; R H Trin Epis Ch Ukiah CA 1987-1996; Non-par 1979-1987; The California Wind Chld Novato CA 1979-1981; Asst S Fran Of Assisi Ch Novato CA 1977-1979; Non-par 1970-1977; Asst Trin Cathd Little Rock AR 1964-1970; Vic S Jas Ch Eureka Spgs AR 1962-1964; S Thos Ch Springdale AR 1962-1964; Asst To Chapl U Of Arkansas 1962-1964. Auth, "The Flower & The Flag," 1978; Auth, "A Sprtl Drama," 1976; Auth, "A Folksong Life Of Chr," 1966.

✠ SHIPPS, The Rt Rev Harry Woolston (Ga) 95 Skidaway Island Park Rd Unit 20, Savannah GA 31411 **Died 11/17/2016** B Trenton NJ 1926 s Harry & Ruth. New York St Maritime Acad Ft Schuyler NY 1946; GD Sewanee: The U So, TS 1958. D 5/20/1958 Bp Albert R Stuart P 1/17/1959 Bp Alfred L Banyard Con 1/6/1984 for Ga. m 5/16/1953 Louise Huntington Shipps c 4. Bp in Res The Collgt Ch of St Paul the Apos Savannah GA 2000-2016; Ret Bp of Georgia Dio Georgia Savannah GA 1995-2016, Bp Of Georgia 1985-1994, Bp Coadj 1984, Dn Augusta Convoc 1977-1984, Chair COM 1977-1983, Pres | Stndg Com 1974-1976, Chair Ecum Cmsn 1970-1978, Stndg Com 1967-1971; Dio Dallas Dallas TX 1995-1999; R S Alb's Epis Ch Augusta GA 1970-1983; R H Apos Savannah GA 1967-1970, Vic 1963-1967; P in C for St Johns The Epis Ch Of S Jn And S Mk Albany GA 1958-1963, R for St Marks 1958-1963. *arts in Ecum and Hist Journ*, 2003. Compas Rose Soc 1997; Ord of S Jn of Jerusalem 1996; OHC (Assoc) 1956. Hon DD STUSo 1986.

SHIRES, Robert A (SeFla) 10860 Tamoron Ln, Boca Raton FL 33498 B Ronceverte WY 1944 s Charles & Birdie. BA W Virginia U 1966; MDiv Gordon-Conwell TS 1969; DMin PrTS 1983. D 9/19/2004 P 4/23/2005 Bp James Hamilton Ottley. m 12/31/1993 Beth L Shires c 1. P-in-c Epis Ch Of The Adv Palm City FL 2009-2016; Zion Evang Luth Ch Deerfield Bch FL 2008-2009; S Mk The Evang Ft Lauderdale FL 2005-2008.

SHIREY, William Carrol (Colo) 277 Old Man Mountain Ln, Estes Park CO 80517 **Died 9/14/2016** B Chickasha OK 1929 s George & Lovell. BA U of Oklahoma 1954; JD U of Oklahoma 1956; MDiv SWTS 1964. D 6/18/1964 P 12/18/1964 Bp Theodore H McCrea. m 6/24/1956 Shirley L Shirey c 2. Asstg P S Barth's Ch Estes Pk CO 2001-2016, Int 1996-2000; Ret 1990-2016; Dept Of Missions Dallas TX 1986-1990; S Chas The Mtyr Daingerfield TX 1986-1990; S Dav's Ch Gilmer TX 1986-1990; Vic St Mk's Epis Ch Mt Pleasant TX 1986-1990; R S Andr's Epis Ch Lawton OK 1971-1986; R S Barth's Arlington TX 1969-1971; Vic S Barth's Arlington TX 1965-1969; Cur S Vinc's Hurst TX 1964-1965; Chapl (Col) US Army ARNG 1946-1989; Chair Prov VII Mssn Cler Conf Dio Oklahoma Oklahoma City OK 1972-1989. Legion of Merit U. S. Army 1989; Combat Infantry Man's Badge U. S. Army 1951.

SHIRLEY, Diana Frangoulis (SO) 664 Glacier Pass, Westerville OH 43081 B Newton MA 1944 d John & Florence. BS Bos 1966; MEd Rivier Coll Nashua NH 1991. D 5/13/2006 Bp Kenneth Lester Price. m 4/15/1966 Fredric C Shirley c 2. Bex Sem Columbus OH 2013-2014.

SHIRLEY, Fredric C (SO) 664 Glacier Pass, Westerville OH 43081 **D Ch Of S Edw Columbus OH 2011-** B Boston MA 1941 s Fredric & Ethel. BS Bentley Coll 1966; MS SUNY 1970; Angl Acad 2006. D 5/13/2006 Bp Kenneth Lester Price. m 4/15/1966 Diana Frangoulis c 2. D S Matt's Epis Ch Westerville OH 2008-2011; D for 3 Ch cluster Ch Of The Epiph Urbana OH 2006-2008; Bus Tech Consult Nationwide Ins 1996-2004.

SHIRLEY, Mike (Mass) 28 Amherst St, Lawrence MA 01843 **Int Exec Dir Communities Together Inc. Lawr MA 2017-** B New London NH 1941 s Morison & Lillian. BA Bos 1963; STB Ya Berk 1966. D 6/25/1966 Bp Anson Phelps Stokes Jr P 5/25/1967 Bp Frederic Cunningham Lawrence. m 10/27/1988 Edna Marie Shirley c 2. Pres Communities Together Inc. Lawr MA 2012-2014; R S Jas Ch Amesbury MA 1986-2006; Int S Jn's Ch Winthrop MA 1985-1986; R S Andr's Ch Belmont MA 1975-1985; Asst Par Of The Mssh Auburndale MA 1972-1975; Asst S Jn's Ch Newtonville MA 1972-1975; Asst Chr Ch Manhasset NY 1968-1971; Cur S Paul's Ch Brockton MA 1966-1968; Chapl to Ret Cler Dio Massachusetts Boston MA 2007-2013. Mng Ed, "Issues," The Consult, 2000. EPF 1982; Heifer Intl 1967; Lawr Rotary Club, Pres

S

2012-2013; Merrimack Vlly Proj 1995; Rotary Intl 1969. Paul Harris Fllw 2015.

SHIRLEY, Sarah A (WA) 5 Laguna St Unit 302, Fort Walton Beach FL 32548 **Sprtl Dir Futurehope Advisors 2012-; Chapl Florida Air NG Jacksonville FL 2006-** B Cambridge MA 1960 d Robert & Mary. BA Webster U 1991; MDiv Claremont TS 1997; MAS Air U 2011. D 4/20/1997 P 12/29/1997 Bp Stewart Clark Zabriskie. Chapl Res Alvin C. York VA Med Cntr Murfreesboro TN 2011-2012; Chapl Spec Mobilization Spprt Plan Washington DC 2008-2011; Pension Fund Mltry New York NY 2008-2009; R S Mary's Epis Ch Andalusia AL 2008; Mltry Saves Dir Consumer Fed of Amer Washington DC 2006-2011; Chapl Off Of Bsh For ArmdF New York NY 2001-2006; Chapl USAF Untd States 2001-2006; Chapl St Teresa Of Avila Desert Cathd Flagstaff AZ 1997-2001; Chapl S Teresa's Cathd Las Vegas NV 1997-2000; Chapl (Relief Duty) Sunrise Hosp and Med Cntr Las Vegas NV 1995-2011; Chapl Interfaith AIDS Mnstry Las Vegas NV 1994-1997; Pstr Wesley Meth Ch No Las Vegas NV 1993-1995. AAR 2012; Amer Assn of Suicidology 2016; ACPE 2009; Assn of Profsnl Chapl 2010; EPF 2005; Epis Publ Plcy Ntwk 2005; EWC 2001; Mltry Chapl Assn 2010; Natl Assn of VA Chapl 2011; Soc for the Sci Study of Rel 2016. revsarah@mac.com

SHIRLEY, Sylvia Kirkland (Okla) St John's Episcopal Church, 5201 N Brookline Ave, Oklahoma City OK 73112 **Vic Chr Memi Epis Ch El Reno OK 2011-** B Glasgow Scotland 1948 d Thomas & Margaret. BS Oklahoma Bapt U 1971; MDiv Epis TS of the SW 2005. D 6/23/2007 Bp Robert Manning Moody P 6/28/2011 Bp Edward Joseph Konieczny. c 1.

SHIROTA, Andrew Kunihito (Mich) 4700 Lowe Rd, Louisville KY 40220 **R S Paul's Ch Louisville KY 2014-** B Tokyo Japan 1973 s Kunihiko & Kimi. BS City U of Seattle 2001; MDiv SWTS 2009. D 4/17/2009 Bp Gregory Harold Rickel P 11/17/2009 Bp Bavi Edna Rivera. Asst R All SS Ch E Lansing MI 2011-2014; Hon Assoc All SS Angl Ch Windsor Ontario 2011; S Ben Epis Ch Lacey WA 2010, Assoc Vic 2009-2010. fr.shirota@gmail.com

SHISLER, Sara Lynn (Md) 480 Olinda Rd, Makawao HI 96768 B Calvert County MD 1982 d Michael & Joan. Doctor of Mnstry EDS; BA Elon U 2004; MDiv Yale DS 2008; STM Yale DS 2009. D 6/19/2010 Bp John L Rabb P 1/29/2011 Bp Eugene Taylor Sutton. m 10/20/2012 Heather E Goff. Asst Trin Ch Towson MD 2014-2015; Asst P Cathd Of The Incarn Baltimore MD 2010-2017.

SHIVES, Beverly Mason (SeFla) 159 Biscayne Ave, Tampa FL 33606 **Chapl Baycare Hlth System 2002-** B Winston-Salem NC 1929 s Raymond & Ruby. Sthrn Tech Inst Orlando FL 1951; BFA Art Inst of Atlanta 1960; Georgia Inst of Tech 1962; Dio SE Florida Sch For Mnstry FL 1990; CPE Tampa Gnrl Hosp 1998. D 2/11/1990 Bp Calvin Onderdonk Schofield Jr. m 11/12/1983 Pamela Von Stroh Smith c 5. Outrch Com S Jn's Tampa FL 1998-2005; St Johns Epis Ch Tampa FL 1996-2002; Dio Property & Loan Com Dio SE Florida Miami 1991-1994, Serv 1990-, Dioc Stwshp Cmsn 1987-1989; Dioc Convnt Dio SW Florida Parrish FL 1999-2000. Epis Conf Of The Deaf Of The Epis Ch In The 1990. Fell Ecdec.

SHIVES, Robert Edward (WVa) D 6/3/2017 Bp Mark A Van Koevering.

SHOBE, Melody W (RI) 2407 Cranston St., Cranston RI 02920 B Little Rock AR 1981 d Robert & Mary. BA Tufts U 2003; MDiv VTS 2006. D 6/24/2006 Bp Peter J Lee P 1/18/2007 Bp Don Adger Wimberly. m 5/21/2005 Robert Casey Shobe. Forw Mvmt of the Epis Ch Cincinnati OH 2014-2017; Assoc Emm Epis Ch Cumberland RI 2011-2014; Assoc Chr Ch In Lonsdale Lincoln RI 2008-2011; Asst S Thos The Apos Epis Ch Houston TX 2006-2008.

SHOBE, Robert Casey (Dal) 14115 Hillcrest Road, Dallas TX 75254 **The Epis Ch Of The Trsfg Dallas TX 2014-; Mem of Bp Search Transition Com Dio Rhode Island Providence RI 2011-, Chair of 2015 Strategic Needs T/F 2010-, Chair of Congrl Dvlpmt Cmsn 2010-** B Richmond VA 1978 s Michael & Susan. The U of Texas Sch of Law; BA U of Texas 2000; MDiv VTS 2006. D 6/24/2006 P 1/18/2007 Bp Don Adger Wimberly. m 5/21/2005 Melody W Wilson c 2. R S Ptr's By The Sea Narragansett RI 2008-2014; Cur Chr Ch Cathd Houston TX 2006-2008.

SHOBERG, Warren E (SD) 3316 E 28th St, Sioux Falls SD 57103 B Rapid City SD 1941 s Walfred & Ethel. BA Augustana Coll 1963; MM U of So Dakota 1983. D 9/29/1981 P 9/29/1982 Bp Walter H Jones. Int S Mich And All Ang' Ch Denver CO 2012-2013; Int 2009, Int 2008; Vic Ch Of The H Apos Sioux Falls SD 1983-2007; P-in-c H Trin Epis Ch Luverne MN 1982-1985; Dn, Estrn Dnry Dio So Dakota Pierre SD 2004-2007, Chair, Cmsn on Liturg, Mus, et al 2000-2007. Cn of the Ord of S Ben 1996; CBS 1984; FIF/NA 1990; GAS 1987; P Assoc Shrine Our Lady of Walsingham 1995; SocMary 1988; SSC 1987.

SHOCKLEY, Stephanie Elizabeth (NJ) 316 E 88th St, New York NY 10128 **Prog Dir, New York Intern Prog S Mary's Manhattanville Epis Ch New York NY 2012-; Chapl Hlth Care Chapl 2010-** B Stratford, NJ 1974 d Thomas & Elizabeth. BA MWC 1997; MDiv GTS 2009. D 5/16/2009 Bp Sylvestre Donato Romero P 6/19/2010 Bp George Edward Councell. m 11/30/2002 Daniel Aaron Shockley.

SHODA, David Brian (WVa) 108 S Washington St, Berkeley Springs WV 25411 B Bluefield WV 1956 s Robert & Margaret. BA Wheeling Jesuit U 1979; MDiv St. Mary's Sem and U 1987. Rec 9/10/2014 as Priest Bp William Michie Klusmeyer. Other Lay Position S Mk's Epis Ch Berkeley Spg WV 2013-2014.

SHOEMAKE, Daniel O (Ga) 4346 Ridge Rd, Buford GA 30519 **Assoc S Mary And S Martha Ch Buford GA 2017-** B St Louis Park MN 1985 s Curtis & Nancy. BA U MN 2012; MDiv Candler TS 2015. D 6/26/2014 P 6/20/2015 Bp Brian N Prior. m 6/22/2015 Nicolette E Paso c 3. Chr Ch Valdosta GA 2015-2016. dshoemake@maryandmarthabuford.org

SHOEMAKER, Adam (NC) The Episcopal Church of the Holy Comforter, 320 East Davis Street, Burlington NC 27215 B 1979 s Thomas & Jamie. BS Bos 2001; MDiv Harvard DS 2005; Cert Ang Stud Gnrl Sem 2007; Cert Ang Stud GTS 2007. D 6/2/2007 P 1/12/2008 Bp M(Arvil) Thomas Shaw. m 5/31/2008 Courtney D Shoemaker c 3. R Ch Of The H Comf Burlington NC 2011-2017; Asst R Par Of Chr Ch Andover MA 2007-2011. adam712@gmail.com

SHOEMAKER, Courtney D (NC) 1019 E Willowbrook Drive, Burlington NC 27215 B Nashville TN 1965 d Hugh & Jan. BA Dickinson Coll 1997; MDiv GTS 2008. D 6/7/2008 Bp M(Arvil) Thomas Shaw P 1/10/2009 Bp Roy Frederick Cederholm Jr. m 5/31/2008 Adam Shoemaker c 1. Lutherans Episcopalians and Friends Elon NC 2013-2017; S Andr's Ch Haw River NC 2012-2013; Asst S Steph's Memi Ch Lynn MA 2008-2011.

SHOEMAKER, Eric Wayne (WA) 8795 Lowell Road, Pomfret MD 20675 **D Chr Ch Port Tobacco Paris La Plata MD 2003-** B Muncy PA 1947 s Clyde & Edith. BA W&M 1972; MS Virginia Commonwealth U 1978; VTS 2003. D 9/1/2001 Bp Leo Frade. m 9/15/1979 Joan Louise Shoemaker c 1. D Chr Ch Durham Par Nanjemoy MD 2002-2003; D S Jn's Epis Ch Homestead FL 2001-2002. S Greg'S Abbey - Confrator 2003. Mem Phi Kappa Phi 1978.

SHOEMAKER, Hetty Stephanie Condon (RI) 96 Washington St, Newport RI 02840 B Fulton NY 1940 d Donald & Hetty. BA Bryn 1962; MDiv EDS 1996. D 3/16/1991 Bp George Nelson Hunt III P 6/15/1996 Bp Gerry Wolf. m 6/30/1962 Charles P Shoemaker c 3. Int Emm Ch Newport RI 2008-2010; R S Jn The Div Ch Saunderstown RI 2001-2007; Assoc S Columba's Chap Middletown RI 1996-2000; D S Matt's Par Of Jamestown Jamestown RI 1991-1994.

SHOEMAKER, Jack G (Haw) 3045 Fir Tree Dr Se, Salem OR 97317 **Died 7/29/2016** B Lancaster PA 1929 s Allison & Florence. MDiv VTS 1954; BA Washington Coll 1954. D 12/18/1954 Bp Angus Dun P 12/5/1955 Bp Charles Francis Hall. m 3/18/1983 Roxanne Hutchison c 5. Ret 1996-2016; Chapl Mid Pacific Inst Honolulu HI 1994-1996; Emm Epis Ch Kailua HI 1981-1994; Chapl Punahou Sch Honolulu HI 1980-1994; Chapl Asheville Sch Asheville NC 1977-1980; Ashville Sch Inc Asheville NC 1977-1980; Chapl Arden Sch Arden NC 1976-1977; Chr Sch Arden NC 1976-1977; Chapl Trin Sch Orlando FL 1974-1975; Chapl Belmont Chap at S Mk's Sch Southborough MA 1965-1974; R S Lk's Epis Ch Seaford DE 1962-1965; Assoc Cn Cathd of St Ptr & St Paul Washington DC 1961-1962; Mstr Sacr Stds S Paul's Ch Concord NH 1954-1956; Chair NH BEC Dio New Hampshire Concord NH 1959-1961. Auth, *For Heaven's Sake! (Collection of Poems)*, 2007.

SHOEMAKER, Patricia Ross Pittman (NC) 22 Mayflower Ln, Lexington NC 27295 **D Dio No Carolina Raleigh NC 1988-** B Southampton County VA 1939 d Robert & Frances. BD Med Coll of Virginia 1961; MS U NC 1979. D 10/2/1988 Bp Robert Whitridge Estill. m 8/1/1964 John Bruce Shoemaker c 2. NAAD.

SHOFSTALL, Sarah J (O) Saint Barnabas Church, 468 Bradley Rd, Bay Village OH 44140 **S Barn Ch Bay Vill OH 2012-; Fac CREDO 2006-; Convenor/Mem Deploy Mnstry Conf 2000-** B Presque Isle ME 1951 d Jack & Iris. BS U of Nebraska 1973; JD U of Nebraska 1979; GTS 1990. D 5/7/1988 Bp James Daniel Warner P 8/11/1990 Bp James Edward Krotz. Cn Dio Wstrn Massachusetts Springfield 1997-2012; R Gr Ch Amherst MA 1997-2000; Dio Iowa Des Moines IA 1994-1997; Gr Ch Boone IA 1994-1997; Chapl Iowa St U Ames IA 1994-1997; Assoc S Lk's Ch Kearney NE 1988-1999. The SCHC 1987. sshofstall@yahoo.com

SHOLANDER, Mark Earl (CFla) 907 Oakway Dr, Auburndale FL 33823 **R Chr the Redeem Ch Manassas VA 2007-** B Detroit MI 1954 s Carl & Beatrice. BA U MI 1974; MPA U MI 1985; MDiv TESM 2000. D 5/27/2000 P 12/9/2000 Bp John Wadsworth Howe. m 6/30/1979 Cynthia Mae Sholander c 3. R St Alb's of Auburndale Inc Auburndale FL 2002-2006; Asst All SS Ch Of Winter Pk Winter Pk FL 2000-2002.

SHOLTY JR, Henry Edward (Dal) 5942 Abrams Rd # 209, Dallas TX 75231 **Non-par 1988-; Bd Dir Epis Cler Assn Dallas TX 1987-; Instr In CE Angl TS Dallas TX 1983-** B Dallas TX 1942 s Henry & Melba. BA U of No Texas 1964; U of Dallas 1966; BD Nash 1970. D 6/18/1970 Bp Theodore H McCrea P 1/1/1971 Bp Stanley Hamilton Atkins. m 1/25/1964 Mary Janet Sholty c 2. Asst To The Dn S Matt's Cathd Dallas TX 1982-1987; LocTen Ch Of The H Cross Dallas TX 1982; Strng Com In Camp Crucis 1980-1982; Cur S Dav's Ch Garland TX 1979-1981; Supply P In The Mnstry Of Dallas 1976-1979; BEC Dio Eau Claire Eau Claire WI 1971-1973, 1970-1972; Vic Our Sav Lugerville WI 1970-1976; Exec Coun Our Sav's Phillips WI 1970-1976; S Marg's Epis Ch Pk Falls WI 1970-1976. Ed, "Convocare 88-". NNECA.

SHORT, James Healy (Colo) 797 Tower Hill Rd., Appomattox VA 24522 B Pittsburgh PA 1933 s Leo & Elizabeth. BA U of Dayton 1955; U of Fribourg

779

S

Ch 1963; MA Ford 1964; Cert Lumen Vitae Brussels 1964. Rec 2/1/1978 as Priest Bp William Carl Frey. m 6/28/1970 Barbara Short c 5. Asst S Jn's Ch Portsmouth VA 2002-2005; R The Ch Of The Ascen Denver CO 1980-2001; Dio Colorado Denver CO 1978-1979; DRE St Mary's RC Ch Ridgefield Conn. 1969-1975. Dir of Prod, "Living the Gd News Curric," 1977. SocMary 1950-1970.

SHORT, James Ritchie (SJ) Casanova & ocean, Carmel CA 93921 B 1951 s Margaret. MDiv CDSP; MDiv CDSP; BA Lebanon Vlly Coll; Nasd Series 6-80; Series 7 63-98 Lutcf 94; Cert Wycliffe Hall of Oxf. D 6/4/1977 P 6/16/1978 Bp Victor Manuel Rivera. c 1. Ch Of The Epiph Corcoran CA 1997-2000; S Phil's Ch Coalinga CA 1997-2000; Epis Dio San Joaquin Modesto CA 1979-1981; S Columba Ch Fresno CA 1977-1979. Auth, "Is Universal Life A Plan For All Seasons?," 1990; Auth, "Less Thunder More Lightning," 1989. Natl Assn For The Self- Supporting Active Mnstry.

SHORT, Molly (NC) 290 Quintard Rd, Sewanee TN 37375 **S Andr's-Sewanee Sch Sewanee TN 2015-** B Augusta GA 1988 d Thomas & Laura. BS in Earth and Environ Sciences Furman U 2011; MDiv Duke DS 2014; DAS The TS at Sewanee 2015. D 6/20/2015 Bp Michael B Curry P 1/23/2016 Bp Anne Hodges-Copple. m 12/28/2013 Michael Kelly Short. mollyshort@sasweb.org

SHORTELL, Bruce Mallard (At) PO Box 1293, Flowery Branch GA 30542 **Ret 1998-** B Pittsburgh PA 1934 s John & Lillian. BS Moravian TS 1956; MDiv VTS 1964. D 6/20/1964 P 3/27/1965 Bp Frederick Warnecke. m 7/10/2006 Carolyn P Fairchild c 3. Cn Pstr Cathd Of S Phil Atlanta GA 1981-1998; P-in-c S Steph's Ch Harrington DE 1973-1981; P-in-c S Ptr's Epis Ch Tunkhannock PA 1964-1973. EvangES.

SHORTES, Stephen Edward (NCal) 2883 Coloma St, Placerville CA 95667 **D Epis Ch Of Our Sav Placerville CA 1999-** B Fort Worth TX 1944 s Louis & Betty. BS California St U Sacramento 1967; BA Sch for Deacons 1999. D 7/24/1999 Bp Jerry Alban Lamb. m 9/5/1980 Leslyn Marlene Meyers.

SHORTRIDGE, Delores J (Nev) 973 S. Fulton St., Denver CO 80247 B Oklahoma City OK 1944 d Leon & Mary. BS U of Cntrl Oklahoma 1967; MDiv Iliff TS 2005. D 1/9/2005 P 1/7/2006 Bp Katharine Jefferts Schori. m 11/26/1968 Earl Wade Shortridge c 4. Ch Of S Ptr The Apos Pueblo CO 2010-2011; Our Merc Sav Epis Ch Denver CO 2008-2010; Our Merc Sav Mnstrs Denver CO 2006-2009.

SHORTT, Mary J (EMich) P.O. Box 151, West Branch MI 48661 **Bereavement Coordntr hospice advantage W Branch MI 2013-; S Eliz's Epis Ch Roscommon MI 2011-** B West Branch 1960 d Lee & Beverly. BA Saginaw Vlly St U 1983; MDiv VTS 1989; BSW Saginaw Vlly St U 1997. D 10/16/1999 P 7/22/2000 Bp Edwin Max Leidel Jr. Assoc S Barth's Epis Ch Mio MI 2011-2014; S Andrews-By-The-Lake Epis Ch Harrisville MI 2011-2012; Chapl Heartland Hospice W Branch MI 2005-2012; R S Paul's Ch Fremont OH 2004-2006; P-in-c Calv Epis Ch Hillman MI 2001-2004; P-in-c Gr Epis Ch Lachine MI 2001-2003; Assoc Chr Epis Ch E Tawas MI 2000-2001; Assoc Lakeshore Epis Area Parishes Oscoda MI 1999-2001; Chapl Ascen Hlth 1999-2000.

SHOUCAIR, James Douglas (Pgh) 130 Westchester Dr, Pittsburgh PA 15215 **R Chr Epis Ch No Hills Pittsburgh PA 2002-** B Kingston Jamaica West Indies 1958 s Elias & Nellie. BA Bos 1979; JD Ford Sch of Law 1982; MDiv TESM 1998. D 6/20/1998 P 1/8/1999 Bp Robert William Duncan. m 2/22/1980 Sandra Leigh Shoucair c 4. Cn Pstr/P-in-c Trin Cathd Pittsburgh PA 1999-2002; Asst Ch Of The Nativ Pittsburgh PA 1998-1999; Com on Const and Cn Dio Pittsburgh Pittsburgh PA 2008-2010, Secy to Conv 2008-, Ecum Off 2007-2008, BEC for the Priesthood 2003-.

SHOULAK, Jim (Minn) 20475 County Road 10, Corcoran MN 55340 **D All SS Epis Indn Mssn Minneapolis MN 2014-** B Manitowoc WI 1958 s Eugene & Margaret. AA Anoka-Ramsey Cmnty Coll 2007; MA Untd TS 2010. D 7/29/2010 Bp Brian N Prior. m 9/14/1984 Judith Shoulak c 3. Singer-Songwriter, "Stayin' Focused CD," Cedar Lodge Mus, 2012.

SHOULDERS, David Ira (Ind) 3415 Windham Lake Place, Indianapolis IN 46214 B Detroit MI 1941 s Charles & Frances. BA Indiana U 1969; MS Penn 1970; MDiv VTS 1975. D 6/6/1975 P 3/1/1976 Bp Dean Theodore Stevenson. m 9/6/1969 Ruth Shoulders c 2. Cn Pstr Chr Ch Cathd Indianapolis IN 2000-2006; S Paul's Epis Ch Indianapolis IN 1996-2001; R Chr Ch Waukegan IL 1991-1996; Cn to the Ordnry Dio Indianapolis Indianapolis IN 1986-1991; Vic S Johns Ch Indianapolis IN 1979-1986; Gd Shpd Montoursville PA 1976-1979; Ch Of Our Sav Montoursville PA 1976-1978; M-in-c Our Sav & Gd Shpd Montoursville PA 1976-1978; Asst R Dio Cntrl Pennsylvania Harrisburg PA 1976-1977, 1975-1976; S Jn's Epis Ch Lancaster PA 1975-1976. Listening Hearts Mnstrs 1994-2008. Cn Emer Chr Ch Cathd, Indianapolis 2006; Mayor's Awd 96 Mayor of Waukegan, Illinois 1996; Phi Beta Kappa Indiana U 1969.

SHOWERS, David G (Md) Middleham & St. Peter Ep. Parish, PO Box 277, Lusby MD 20657 **R Middleham & S Ptr's Par Lusby MD 2008-** B Battle Creek MI 1949 s Gordon & Luella. MA Asbury U 1971; MDiv Asbury TS 1974; GTS 2005. D 10/29/2005 Bp Robert Wilkes Ihloff P 5/7/2006 Bp John L Rabb. m

6/15/2013 Bruce C Calvin. S Lk's Ch Baltimore MD 2006-2008; Vic Ch Of S Paul The Apos Baltimore MD 2005-2007. office@middlehamandstpeters.org

SHOWS, William Derek (NC) 1077 Fearrington Post, Pittsboro NC 27312 **P Assoc S Steph's Ch Durham NC 1992-, Int 1989-1991, Int 1985-1988** B Soso MS 1936 s William & Mitchell. BA U IL 1957; MA U IL 1958; U of Heidelberg DE 1960; PhD Duke 1967; Cert Ang Stud GTS 1982. D 6/29/1982 P 6/24/1983 Bp Robert Whitridge Estill. m 5/18/1974 Priscilla Walker Shows c 4. Sabbatical Prof The GTS New York NY 1999-2000; 1990-1992; 1987-1988; Asst S Mk's Epis Ch Raleigh NC 1982-1984. Auth, "A Psychol Theory of Later Years-CG Jung," *GeroPsychology*, 1977; Auth, "Psychol Differentiation & the A-B Dimension:A Dyadic Interaction Hyposthesis," *Genetic Psychol Monographs*. Amer Psychoanalytical Assn 1988-2008; APA 1968; CG Jung Soc 1983; NC Psychoanalytical Soc; NC Psychol Assn 1968.

SHOWS CAFFEY, Elizabeth Kristen (At) 634 W Peachtree St NW, Atlanta GA 30308 **Assoc S Lk's Epis Ch Atlanta GA 2015-** B Zurich Switzerland 1976 d William. Bow 1996; BA Duke 1998; MDiv GTS 2005. D 6/26/2005 P 3/11/2006 Bp Michael B Curry. c 1. Assoc R All SS Epis Ch Atlanta GA 2007-2014; Ch Of The H Trin New York NY 2005-2006; Geo W So Ch of Advoc Philadelphia PA 2004-2006; Chap Of The Cross Chap Hill NC 1999-2002. elizabeth@stlukesatlanta.org

SHRIVER, Domingo Frances (WMich) 301 N James St, Ludington MI 49431 **Emanuel Evang Luth Ch Ludington MI 2013-; Gr Epis Ch Of Ludington Ludington MI 2013-** B York PA 1965 s Joseph & Frances. BA Sprg Arbor U 2001; MDiv VTS 2005. D 1/29/2005 P 10/15/2005 Bp Robert R Gepert. m 5/9/1997 Paula Marie Shriver c 6. R Ch Of The Resurr Hopewell Jct NY 2007-2013; Assoc P S Mk's Ch Grand Rapids MI 2005-2007.

SHRIVER JR, Frederick Hardman (NY) 37 W. 12th Street, Apt. 4K, New York NY 10011 B Parkersburg WV 1932 s Frederick & Evelyn. BA Harv 1954; STB GTS 1960; PhD U of Cambridge 1967. D 6/10/1960 P 12/1/1960 Bp Wilburn Camrock Campbell. m 9/23/1961 Susan C Shriver c 2. Prof The GTS New York NY 1971-1998, Tutor 1962-1964; Fell ECF 1964-1967; Asst Trin Ch Morgantown WV 1960-1962. Auth, "Engl Hist Revs"; Auth, "The Study Of Anglicanism".

SHUART, Robert Stephen (NwPa) Po Box 368, South Harwich MA 02661 B Englewood NJ 1943 s Herman & Audrey. BA Thiel Coll 1966; Westminster Coll 1966; MDiv Ya Berk 1969. D 6/23/1969 P 12/19/1970 Bp William Crittenden. c 3. R S Lk's Epis Ch Smethport PA 2003-2004; R S Jn's Ch Kane PA 1995-2004, Vic 1969-1977; Non-par 1978-1991; Vic S Marg's Epis Ch Kane PA 1969-1976. stephen.shuart@verizon.net

SHUCKER II, Courtney A (U) 203 Palmer St, Salida CO 81201 B Fort Lauderdale FL 1946 s Courtney & Geraldine. U of Redlands 1968; MDiv CDSP 1996. D 11/21/1996 P 5/18/1997 Bp Stewart Clark Zabriskie. Ascen S Matt's Ch Price UT 1998-2006; P Ch Of The H Trin E Carbon UT 1998-2006; Assoc Dio Utah Salt Lake City UT 1998-2006; P-in-c Gr-St Fran Cmnty Ch Lovelock NV 1998; Dio Nevada Las Vegas 1996-1998. Assn of Angl Mus 1976-1997.

SHUFORD, Carlton Lamont (Ga) 131 Avondale Dr, Augusta GA 30907 **P-in-c Gr Epis Ch Sandersville GA 2010-** B Atlanta GA 1948 s Charles & Louise. BLA U GA 1974; MDiv Erskine TS 2008. D 3/1/1990 Bp Harry Woolston Shipps P 4/3/2008 Bp Henry Irving Louttit. m 9/12/1970 Kathleen Mackaye Shuford c 3. Assoc P Ch Of Our Sav Augusta GA 2008-2010, D 1990-2008.

SHUFORD, Sheila Cathcart (Nwk) 12 Sorman Ter, Randolph NJ 07869 **Chaplintern Greystone Pk Psych Hosp 2003-** B NYC NY 1935 d James & Elizabeth. D 6/3/2006 Bp John Palmer Croneberger. m 8/27/1960 Sydney Shuford c 1.

SHULDA, David Leroy (Ore) 2139 Berwin Ln, Eugene OR 97404 B New Britain CT 1927 s Charles & Elizabeth. Teachers Coll of Connecticut. D 2/1/1984 Bp Matthew Paul Bigliardi. m 4/24/1954 Anne Laura Lutynski c 1. D Ch Of S Jn The Div Springfield OR 1984-2010.

SHUMAKER, John Hilton (SJ) 1317 Gold Hunter Rd, San Andreas CA 95249 **Gold Country Mssnr The Dio San Joaquin 2011-; P-in-c S Matt's Ch San Andreas CA 2010-, R 2001-2005; Bd Mem Calaveras Cnty Salvation Army Serv Unit 2002-** B Pittsburgh PA 1947 s John & Laverne. Dplma The Salvation Army Sch for Off Trng 1967; AA Cmnty Coll of Allegheny Cnty Pittsburgh PA 1970; BA U Pgh 1971; MDiv Nash 1975. D 10/25/1975 Bp Robert Bracewell Appleyard P 6/2/1976 Bp James Winchester Montgomery. Dioc Liturg The Dio San Joaquin 2009-2013; Cler Mem Stndg Com 2008-2013; Dn Delta Dnry Dioces of San Joaquin 2008-2010; Adj Prof San Joaquin Delta Coll Stockton California 2004-2009; Mem, Nwsltr Ed, Tail Twister San Andreas 49er Lions Club 2001-2015; Mnstrs Coun of Urban Mssn 1999-2000; Amer Red Cross Steubenville OH 1998-1999; R S Paul's Ch Steubenville OH 1993-2001; R S Rocco's Ch Youngstown OH 1986-1993; R The Ch Of The Adv Jeannette PA 1980-1985; Pres Algoma Mnstrl Assn Algoma WI 1978-1979; Ch Of S Agnes By The Lake Algoma WI 1977-1980; Vic Ch of the Precious Blood Gardner WI 1977-1980; Cur Gr Ch Oak Pk IL 1975-1977; Stndg Com Epis Dio San Joaquin Modesto CA 2008-2013; Dioc Coun Dio Ohio Cleveland 1995-1996; Dioc Coun Dio Pittsburgh Pittsburgh PA 1982-1983; Chair, T&C Cmsn Dio

Fond du Lac Appleton WI 1977-1980; Sec., Ad Hoc Hisp Cmsn Dio Chicago Chicago IL 1976-1977. CBS; GAS; SocOLW.

SHUMARD, James Bradley (Ga) 140 Mercer Rd, Savannah GA 31411 **S Mk's Epis Ch Casper WY 2015-** B Fort Belvoir VA 1951 s Gordon & Mary. BA Rhodes Coll 1974; MDiv Candler TS Emory U 1985; DMin EDS 2010. D 6/7/1997 Bp Onell Asiselo Soto P 12/13/1997 Bp Frank Kellogg Allan. m 4/5/1986 Maureen H Sumard c 2. R S Mich's Ch Waynesboro GA 2010-2015; Consult for CE All SS Epis Ch Thomasville GA 2010; Temporary Asst. S Ptr's Epis Ch Savannah GA 2009; R S Fran Of The Islands Epis Ch Savannah GA 2001-2009; R S Alb's Ch Elberton GA 1998-2001; S Andr's Ch Hartwell GA 1998-2001; Asst R Gr Epis Ch Gainesville GA 1997-1998.

SHUMATE, Jonathan Kale Gavin (Ore) D 11/12/2016 P 6/1/2017 Bp Michael Hanley.

SIBERINE, Katherine Harmon (Chi) 1704 Ne 43rd Ave, Portland OR 97213 B Summit NJ 1989 d Raymond & Susan. BA U of Wisconsin 2011; MDiv VTS 2016. D 12/19/2015 P 7/21/2016 Bp Jeff Lee. m 6/7/2016 Zachary Charles Harmon.

SIBLEY, David C (LI) 54 George St, Manhasset NY 11030 **R Chr Ch Manhasset NY 2014-** B Camden SC 1985 s Mark & Denilynn. BS Furman U 2007; MS Furman U 2008; MDiv GTS 2011. D 6/4/2011 Bp W illiam Andrew Waldo P 12/10/2011 Bp Lawrence C Provenzano. m 10/1/2016 Emily Sarah Larsen. Ch Of S Mary The Vrgn New York NY 2012-2014; Asstg P Dio Long Island Garden City NY 2012-2014, Alt Dep to GC 2016-, Chair, Com on Cn 2016-, Mem, Stndg Com 2016-, Mem, Com on Cn 2014-2016; P-in-c S Jn's Epis Ch Ft Hamilton Brooklyn NY 2011-2014. dsibley@christchurchmanhasset.org

SICHANGI, Nicholas Nyongesa (Eas) Trans 12/31/2013 Bp Santosh K Marray.

SICKELS, Peter L (Ia) 4814 Amesbury Ct, Davenport IA 52807 B Dayton OH 1946 s William & Shirley. Golden Gate Bapt TS; BA Denison U 1968; MDiv Nash 1984. D 6/7/1986 P 10/1/1987 Bp William Edwin Swing. c 2. Chr Epis Ch Clinton IA 2011-2016; Zion Luth Ch Princeton IA 2003-2011; Shpd Of The Cross Luth Ch Muscatine IA 2002; First Luth Ch Moline IL 2001-2002; Trin Cathd Davenport IA 1990-1999; Vic S Paul's Ch Durant IA 1986-1990; Chapl U of Iowa Hospial In Iowa City 1985-1986. Curs Amer Farmland Trust.

SICKLER, Brenda Pamela (WMo) 5 E 337th Rd, Humansville MO 65674 **D S Alb's In The Ozarks Ch Bolivar MO 1999-** B Hove Sussex UK 1935 d Basil & Laura. D 2/13/1999 Bp Barry Howe. m 3/2/1958 Kenneth Lynch Sickler.

SICKLES, Clarence William (Nwk) 68 Heath Village, Hackettstown NJ 07840 B Harrison NJ 1921 s John & Mary. BA Col 1945; STB GTS 1951; MEd Col 1972; MDiv GTS 1976. D 5/23/1948 P 11/30/1948 Bp Benjamin M Washburn. m 2/11/1950 Jean Sickles c 8. Asst Pstr S Jn's Ch Dover NJ 1993-1995; Assoc Chr Ch Short Hills NJ 1990-1991; R H Fam W Bangor ME 1988-1990; Heath Vill Ret Cmnty Hackettstown NJ 1965-1983; Vic S Jas' Epis Ch Hackettstown NJ 1953-1965; Vic Chr Ch Stanhope NJ 1953-1955; S Ptr's Ch Mt Arlington NJ 1953-1955; Cur Chr Ch New Brunswick NJ 1951-1953; Epis Chapl Rutger's U New Brunswick NJ 1951-1953; Vic Ch Of The Atone Fair Lawn NJ 1949-1951; Cur S Mary's Ch Sparta NJ 1948-1949. Pres ESMA 1974-1976. DD GTS 1976.

SIDEBOTHAM, John Nelson (EC) 16 W Fayetteville St, Wrightsville Beach NC 28480 **Forw Mvmt of the Epis Ch Cincinnati OH 2013-; S Jas Par Wilmington NC 2013-** B Bronxville NY 1954 s John & Grace. BA Trin 1976; MDiv UTS 1989. D 12/10/1989 P 6/24/1990 Bp George Nelson Hunt III. m 4/20/1985 Frances D Murchison c 2. R The Ch Of The H Sprt Lake Forest IL 2004-2013; Vic St. Barth Ch New York NY 1999-2004; S Lk's Epis Ch Durham NC 1995-1998; Assoc S Columba's Ch Washington DC 1991-1995; Asst S Mart's Ch Providence RI 1989-1991.

SIDERIUS, Donna-Mae Amy (SVa) 3 Mizzen Cir, Hampton VA 23664 **Conf Ldr CREDO Inst Inc 2002-** B Winnipeg MT CA 1948 d Stewart & Donna. BTh McGill U 1981; STM GTS 1997. Trans 2/1/1990 Bp Claude Charles Vache. m 7/5/1969 John Siderius c 2. R S Jn's Ch Hampton VA 2003-2011, Asst R 1990-2002; Cn Dio Sthrn Virginia Newport News VA 1995-2002; Serv Ch Of Can 1985-1990.

SIDES, Serena Wille (WA) 620 G St SE, Washington DC 20003 **Chr Ch Capitol Hill Washington DC 2017-** B Washington DC 1970 d Roland & Barbara. D 11/12/2016 P 6/17/2017 Bp Mariann Edgar Budde. m 3/12/2005 John Michael Sides c 2.

SIEFFERMAN, Norman Clyde (Va) 609 Shaw Ct, Fredericksburg VA 22405 **Ret 1997-** B Cincinnati OH 1934 s Floyd & Phyllis. BA Merc 1958; MDiv Epis TS of the SW 1961; Emory U 1982. D 6/1/1961 P 7/1/1962 Bp Randolph R Claiborne. m 6/20/1954 Sara Siefferman c 2. R The Epis Ch-King Geo Co King Geo VA 1982-1998; R Emm Ch King Geo VA 1982-1997; 1976-1984; Trin Epis Ch Columbus GA 1964-1979; Vic St Mary's Atlanta GA 1961-1964; Vic S Aug Forest Pk GA 1961-1962. Auth, Camb Press, 1980; Auth, Camb Press, 1980; Auth, U So--Sewanee, 1975; Auth, *A Study of Prospon in Nestorius' Bazaar of Heracleides.* Intl Herder Soc.

SIEGEL II, Carl De Haven (WMo) 1405 Boyce Ave, Baltimore MD 21204 **Nonpar 1987-** B Kansas City MO 1955 s Carl & Ruth. BA U So 1978; MDiv GTS 1982; PhD California Sch of Profsnl Psychol 1990. D 6/21/1982 P 12/1/1982

Bp Arthur Anton Vogel. m 5/26/1984 Katherine Tucker Smith. Gr And H Trin Cathd Kansas City MO 1982-1986.

SIEGENTHALER, David John (Mass) 54 Concord Ave Apt 102, Cambridge MA 02138 **Ret 1995-** B Buffalo NY 1926 s Gottlieb & Agatha. BA Franklin & Marshall Coll 1947; BD Yale DS 1950; MA Ya 1952; EDS 1995. D 6/25/1955 P 1/21/1956 Bp Norman B Nash. c 4. Tutor Hist EDS Cambridge MA 1969-1995; R Ch Of S Jn The Evang Duxbury MA 1957-1968; Cur Emm Ch Boston MA 1955-1957.

SIEGFRIEDT, Karen (NCal) 170 Verdon St, Morro Bay CA 93442 B Boston MA 1954 d Karle & Faye. AS U of Indianapolis 1973; BA U of Massachusetts 1977; MS U of San Francisco 1986; MDiv CDSP 1992. D 6/6/1992 P 6/5/1993 Bp William Edwin Swing. m 1/17/2014 Stephanie Jesse Sherman. R Trin Ch Sutter Creek CA 2010-2017; R Ch Of S Jude The Apos Cupertino CA 1998-2010; Assoc S Lk's Ch Los Gatos CA 1994-1998; P-in-c S Barth's Epis Ch Livermore CA 1993; Assoc Ch Of The H Innoc San Francisco CA 1992-1993. Auth, "Prize Sermon," *Sermons That Wk*, 1995. rector@trinitysuttercreek.org

SIEGMUND, Mary Kay (Kan) 3 Ne 83rd Ter, Kansas City MO 64118 **P-in-c S Lk's Epis Ch Shawnee KS 2014-** B Kansas City MO 1953 d John & Agnes. MDiv MidWestern Bapt TS 1995; Cert Epis TS of the SW 1998. D 6/6/1998 Bp Barry Howe P 12/1/1998 Bp John Clark Buchanan. m 12/27/1979 Mark Steven Siegmund c 2. P-in-c S Matt's Epis Ch Newton KS 2010-2014; Dio Kansas Topeka KS 2006-2009; Asst Ch Of The Gd Shpd Nashua NH 2001-2006; Vic S Jn's Ch Kansas City MO 1998-2001. oficeslshawnee@gmail.com

SIENER, George Richard (NH) 6 Whippoorwill Ln, Exeter NH 03833 B New York NY 1937 s George & Frances. BA U of Bridgeport 1959; MDiv Ya Berk 1962; VTS 1982; DD (honoris causa) Ya Berk 1996. D 6/1/1962 Bp Walter H Gray P 3/16/1963 Bp Joseph Warren Hutchens. m 6/10/1961 Sheila Day Siener. Asst S Jn's Ch Portsmouth NH 2002-2003; Asst Ch Of The Gd Shpd Nashua NH 1998-2002; R Chr Ch Exeter NH 1975-1997; R S Dav's Ch Gales Ferry CT 1964-1975; Cur S Jn's Ch Stamford CT 1962-1964; GC Del Dio New Hampshire Concord NH 1985-1988. Fllshp of the Way of the Cross 1966.

SIERACKI, Emily K (Ida) 518 N 8th Street, Boise ID 83702 **Cn S Mich's Cathd Boise ID 2014-** B Washington DC 1981 d Paul & Connie. BA Barnard Coll of Col 2003; MDiv UTS 2007; MDiv UTS 2007. D 3/10/2007 P 9/15/2007 Bp Mark Sean Sisk. m 9/8/2014 Andrew F Van Hise. Chr And H Trin Ch Westport CT 2013-2014; Asst to the R Gr Epis Ch Nyack NY 2007-2012.

SIERRA, Federico (Los) 425 N Stoneman Ave Apt A, Alhambra CA 91801 B Mexico 1951 s Luis & Julia. BA Natl U of Mex 1974; MS ITAM 1983; BTh St Andrews Sem Mex City 2000. Trans 1/7/2005 Bp Joseph Jon Bruno. S Thos Of Cbury Par Long Bch CA 2012-2014; St Mary in Palms Los Angeles CA 2012; Assoc St Marks Epis Ch Van Nuys CA 2008-2011; Vic Ch Of The Ascen Tujunga CA 2005-2008; Dn Dio Cuernavaca 2004; Vic Dio Mex Mex City MOR 2000-2004; Povincial Treas Angl Ch of Mex 1996-2004.

SIERRA, Frank (WMo) 2718 Alabama Ct, Joplin MO 64804 **R S Phil's Ch Joplin MO 2005-** B Morenci AZ 1955 s Demecio & Natalia. U of Arizona 1974; AA Phoenix Coll Phoenix AZ 1976; MDiv Nash 1990. D 6/9/1990 Bp William Harvey Wolfrum P 12/14/1990 Bp John Herbert MacNaughton. m 9/12/1980 Deborah Sierra c 2. Cntrl Convoc Partnership In Mssn San Antonio TX 2003-2005; Cn Ch Of The H Cross San Antonio TX 2003-2004; Trin Ch San Antonio TX 2003-2004; R S Steph's Epis Ch San Antonio TX 1992-2003; R Gr Ch Weslaco TX 1990-1992.

SIERRA, Jose De Jesus (NC) Iglesia Episcopal Puertorriquena, PO Box 902, Saint Just PR 00978 Puerto Rico B Bucaramanga Colombia 1957 s Jose & Maria. Rec 7/8/2008 as Priest Bp David Andres Alvarez-Velazquez. m 7/8/2006 Olga M Rodriguez Santos c 1. Iglesia El Buen Pstr Durham NC 2012-2015; Dio Puerto Rico Trujillo Alto PR 2009-2012.

SIERRA ECHEVERRY, Gabriel Alcides (Colom) Parroquia La Anunciacion, El Bagre, Apartado Aereo 52964, Bogota Colombia **Vic San Francisco De Asis 1987-** B Caracoli Antioquia CO 1950 s Pedro & Maria. Lic 1984. D 2/28/1986 P 1/1/1987 Bp Bernardo Merino-Botero. m 4/17/1986 Luz Marina Ramirez Ramirez Torres. Iglesia Epis En Colombia Bogota 1986-2005.

SIFFORD, Thomas Andrew (Ark) 74 Sierra Dr, Hot Springs Village AR 71909 **Ret 1997-** B Benbrook TX 1929 s Thomas & Novice. BA U of Texas 1968; Angl TS 1975. D 9/15/1975 Bp Archibald Donald Davies P 9/29/1976 Bp Robert Elwin Terwilliger. c 3. Vic H H Trin Epis Ch Hot Sprg AR 1986-1997; S Alb's Epis Ch Arlington TX 1985; Dio Ft Worth Ft Worth TX 1984; S Greg's Epis Ch Mansfield TX 1983; Cur S Mich's Ch Richland Hills Ft Worth TX 1975-1982.

SIGAFOOS, Richard Vaughn (Colo) 131 31 Rd, Grand Junction CO 81503 B Omaha NE 1940 s Rolland & Mary. BA U CO 1967. D 12/29/1991 Bp William Harvey Wolfrum P 6/1/1992 Bp William Jerry Winterrowd. m 8/7/1965 Gretchen L Sigafoos c 2. R Ch Of The Nativ Grand Jct CO 1993-2005; Stndg Com Dio Colorado Denver CO 2000-2005.

SIGAMONEY, Christopher (LI) B 1952 s Christopher. BD UNITEED Theol Coll BANGALORE INDIA 1981; DMin NYTS 1996; DMin NYTS 2002. m 5/28/1982 Freeda Sigamoney c 1. P Ch Of Chr The King E Meadow NY 2009-2013; Assoc S Bede's Epis Ch Syosset NY 2009-2013; Chapl Interfaith

S

781

Med Cntr Brooklyn NY 2004-2011; Chapl Epis Hlth Serv Far Rockaway NY 2003-2004; Chapl Bp HUCLES Nrsng Hm BROOKLYN NY 1998-1999.

SIGLER, James (NCal) P.O. Box 467, Wimberley TX 78676 B Corpus Christi TX 1941 s Robert & Myrtle. BA U So 1963; MDiv VTS 1967. D 6/23/1967 Bp Everett H Jones P 1/4/1968 Bp Richard Earl Dicus. m 1/1/1991 Shelley G Sigler c 2. Dioc Coun The Epis Dio Nthrn California Sacramento CA 1994-1996, Pres Cler Assn 1992-1996; R Emm Epis Ch Grass Vlly CA 1991-2006; R All SS' Epis Ch Duncan OK 1986-1991; Assoc S Geo's Epis Ch Schenectady NY 1985-1986; Dn Sthrn Deanry Dio Dallas Dallas TX 1976-1985; Vic S Alb's Ch Hubbard TX 1975-1983; R S Jn's Epis Ch Corsicana TX 1972-1985; Assoc S Dav's Epis Ch San Antonio TX 1968-1972; Assoc S Thos And S Mart's Ch Crp Christi TX 1967-1968; Dioc Coun Dio Oklahoma Oklahoma City OK 1988-1991.

SIGLER JR, Richard Eugene (NC) 930 Walker Ave, Greensboro NC 27403 B Miami FL 1973 s Richard & Katherine. BM U NC, Greensboro 1997. D 1/28/2017 Bp Anne Hodges-Copple. m 6/13/1997 Helen Hunt Helen Kathleen Hunt c 2.

SIGLOH, Jane Engleby (SwVa) 4068 Garth Rd, Crozet VA 22932 B Houston TX 1934 d Thomas & Kate. BA Sweet Briar Coll 1956; MA Hollins U 1975; MDiv Ya Berk 1987. D 6/10/1989 Bp Arthur Edward Walmsley P 3/31/1990 Bp Jeffery William Rowthorn. m 4/14/1979 Dennis Boyde Sigloh. Chapl of Spouses HOB 1999-2000; R Emm Ch Staunton VA 1992-1998; Cur S Matt's Epis Ch Wilton CT 1989-1991; COM Dio SW Virginia Roanoke VA 1995-1996. "Like Trees Walking," Cowley, 2007; Contrib, *Sermons that Wk*, 1991; Auth, *More Sermons That Wk 1992 & 1995*. OSH 1988. Prchng Excellence Awd Epis Evang Fndt 1991.

SIGNORE, Richard S (WMass) 19 Briggs Ave., Bourne MA 02532 B Newton MA 1952 s Frank & Ethel. BA Boston Coll 1974; MDiv GTS 1977; ThM New Brunswick TS 1986. D 6/4/1977 Bp Albert Wiencke Van Duzer P 12/11/1977 Bp George Phelps Mellick Belshaw. m 7/25/1977 Nina Signore c 2. The Chap Of All SS Leominster MA 2011-2013; S Ptr's Ch On The Canal Buzzards Bay MA 1988-2004; R S Mths Ch Hamilton NJ 1982-1988; Dio New Jersey Trenton NJ 1978-1981; Vic Trin Epis Ch Vincentown NJ 1978-1981, Asst 1977.

SIGNORELLI, Barry M (NY) 278 Monmouth St Apt 4-L, Jersey City NJ 07302 B 1958 s John & Lois. BFA Webster U 1981; MDiv GTS 1987. D 6/13/1987 Bp Paul Moore Jr P 12/1/1987 Bp Richard Beamon Martin. m 3/4/2004 Bruce E Parker. The Ch Of The Sav Denville NJ 2013; P S Paul's Ch In Bergen Jersey City NJ 2012-2013; Ch Of The H Apos New York NY 1999-2009, 1998-1999, 1990-1998; Asst S Jn's Ch Brooklyn NY 1988-1990; 1987-1988; The Ch Hymnal Corp New York NY 1987. Auth, "The Dream Realized," *Washington Dc Natl Cathd*, 1990; Auth, "Our Journey," *GC*, 1988. Integrity.

SILAS, Berkman (Ak) Saint Barnabas Church, Minto AK 99758 **Died 10/5/2015** B Old Minto AK 1922 s Louis & Susan. D 5/13/1972 P 1/1/1974 Bp William Jones Gordon Jr. m 3/24/1944 Sarah Silas. Serv S Barn 1973-2015.

SILBAUGH, Morgan Collins (Cal) 914 Mountain Meadows Cir, Ashland OR 97520 B Lancaster OH 1935 s Hugh & Charlotte. BA Amh 1957; MA Cor 1958; BD EDS 1963. D 6/8/1963 P 6/13/1964 Bp Walter M Higley. m 2/12/1977 Charlotte V Silbaugh c 3. S Lk's Ch Grants Pass OR 2017; Assoc Trin Epis Ch Ashland Ashland OR 2005-2009; Stndg Com Dio California San Francisco CA 1996-1998, Dep Prov Syn 1993-1996; R Chr Epis Ch Los Altos CA 1990-2000; Stndg Com Dio Cntrl New York Liverpool NY 1989-1990, VIM Funding Com Chair 1985-1990, Mssy-in-c St. Jn'sPhoenix, New York 1963-1984; Trin Epis Ch Watertown NY 1985-1990; R Chr Ch Manlius NY 1968-1984; Assoc S Thos' Epis Ch Syracuse NY 1966-1968; Fresh Start Fac Dio Oregon 2010-2016. Planned PArenthood of Sthrn Oregon 2013. Fayetteville-Manlius Rotary Citizen of Dist Rotary 1984; Vill of Manlius Citizen Recogniton Awd Vill of Manlius New York 1979.

SILBEREIS, Richard M (Ct) 155 Wyllys St, Hartford CT 06106 B Dayton OH 1951 s Charles & Julie. BA The Athenaeum of Ohio 1973; BA U Cinc 1980; MDiv CDSP 1987. D 6/27/1987 P 1/1/1988 Bp Oliver Bailey Garver Jr. m 6/29/1980 Helen Elaine Scalzo c 2. Serv Ch Of The Gd Shpd Hartford CT 1995-2008; R S Clare Mint Hill NC 1991-1995; S Clare's Ch Matthews NC 1991-1995; Asst Min S Andr's Ch Saratoga CA 1988-1991; Chr Ch Alameda CA 1988, 1987-1988; Chapl Thompson Chld's Hm.

SILCOX JR, James Heyward (Va) Wicomico Parish Church, PO Box 70, Wicomico Church VA 22579 **Wicomico Par Ch Wicomico Ch VA 2012-; Assoc S Paul's Ch Augusta GA 2006-** B Charleston SC 1950 BS USMA 1972; MA U of Wisconsin 1980; MDiv Sewanee: The U So, TS 2005. D 4/17/2005 Bp Leo Frade P 10/18/2005 Bp Henry Irving Louttit. m 11/18/1972 Jane Anne Thornley c 3. Cur S Paul's Ch Augusta GA 2005-2012. elisalive@aol.com

SILIDES JR, George Constantine (Los) 830 W Bonita Ave, Claremont CA 91711 **S Ambr Par Claremont CA 2012-** B Fairbanks AK 1955 s George & Mary. BEd U of Arizona 1977; MDiv GTS 1986. D 6/14/1986 Bp George Phelps Mellick Belshaw P 6/6/1987 Bp William Edwin Swing. m 12/21/1997 Hunter P Silides c 4. R The Ch Of The H Trin Juneau AK 2004-2012; Exec Coun Appointees New York NY 2002-2008; Dvlpmt Off Dio Alaska Fairbanks AK 2002-2007, 1998-2004; Reg Vic Appointed Mssy of TEC Ft Yukon Fairbanks

2000-2004; Co-Vic S Steph's Ch Ft Yukon AK 1998-2002; co-Vic Vol for Mssn Ft Yukon AK 1998-2000; S Paul's Day Sch Of Oakland Oakland CA 1989-1998; Chapl St. Paul's Epis Sch Oakland CA 1989-1998; Chair of the Dept of Yth Mnstry Dio California San Francisco CA 1987-1996; Cur S Matt's Epis Ch San Mateo CA 1986-1989. revsilides@gmail.com

SILIDES, Hunter P (Los) 411 Gold St, Juneau AK 99801 B New York NY 1963 d John & Sarah. BA Wesl 1968; MDiv CDSP 1992. D 12/5/1992 P 12/4/1993 Bp William Edwin Swing. m 12/21/1997 George Constantine Silides c 4. The Ch Of The H Trin Juneau AK 2008-2009; Exec Coun Appointees New York NY 2002-2008; Fairbanks Luth Ch Fairbanks AK 2002-2003; Vic S Mk's Ch Nenana AK 2001-2004; Appointed Mssy Appointed Mssy DFMS Dio Alaska AK 2000-2008; Dio Alaska Fairbanks AK 1998-2002; Co-Vic/Appointed Mssy S Steph's Ch Ft Yukon AK 1998-2001; Chapl Cathd Sch For Boys 1993-1998; Minor Cn Gr Cathd 1993-1998; Trin Par Menlo Pk CA 1993.

SILK-WRIGHT, Margaret E (CFla) 1813 Palo Alto Ave, Lady Lake FL 32159 **P-in-c S Steph's Epis Ch Ocala FL 2011-** B Pontiac MI 1938 d Albert & Margaret. AA Dupage Glen Ellyn IL 1978; BS Geo Wms 1980; MDiv SWTS 1985. D 9/21/1985 Bp James Winchester Montgomery P 4/1/1986 Bp Frank Tracy Griswold III. c 5. P-in-c Ch Of The Adv Dunnellon FL 2008-2009; Vic S Fran Of Assisi Ch Bushnell FL 2003; Assoc S Geo Epis Ch The Villages FL 1997-2003; Vic Calv Epis Ch Sioux City IA 1990-1996; Dio So Dakota Pierre SD 1990-1996; S Geo's Epis Ch Le Mars IA 1990-1996; S Paul's Epis Ch Vermillion SD 1990-1996; Assoc S Jn's Ch Plymouth MI 1987-1990; Emm Ch Petoskey MI 1986-1987. Int Mnstry Ntwk. wright4u@comcast.net

SILLA, SuzeAnne Marie (NI) Diocese of Northern Indiana, 117 N Lafayette Blvd, South Bend IN 46601 B Roscoe NY 1943 d Harold & Iola. BA Miami-Dade Cmnty Coll 1981; Cert U So 1998. D 5/8/1984 P 7/11/1998 Bp Calvin Onderdonk Schofield Jr. c 4. Cn to the Ordnry Dio Nthrn Indiana So Bend IN 2007-2015; Dio Milwaukee Milwaukee WI 2003-2007; Dio SE Florida Miami 2003, 1992-2002, Chair - Com 1986-1988; S Mary Magd Epis Ch Pompano Bch FL 2003; Asst St Margarets and San Francisco de Asis Epis Ch Hialeah FL 1992-2003; Asst Epis Ch Of The H Fam Miami FL 1984-1992. canon@ednin.org

SILTON, Margaret Kanze (NC) PO Box 608, Wake Forest NC 27588 **D S Johns Epis Ch Wake Forest NC 2012-** B White Plains NY 1954 d Edward & Joyce. BA Binghamton U 1976; MA Duke 1977; MDiv Duke DS 2005. D 6/14/2008 Bp Michael B Curry. m 3/12/1977 Andrew Silton c 3. D Chap Of The Cross Chap Hill NC 2010-2012; D S Jos's Ch Durham NC 2008-2010.

SILVA-GONZALEZ, Alvaro (PR) **Dio Puerto Rico Trujillo Alto PR 2016-** B Colombia 1961 s Julio & Natividad. MDiv Seminario San Pio 1987; MTh Seminario San Pio X 1987; Maestria en Consejeria Profesional Universidad Interamericana 2012; Delineante Liceo Arte Y Techologia 2012. Rec 1/24/2015 as Priest Bp Wilfrido Ramos-Orench. m 4/3/2010 Daisy M Leon Rios.

SILVER, Deborah Lee (At) 3005 St James Pl, Grovetown GA 30813 B Aberdeen WA 1953 BS Manchester Coll 1978; MDiv Bethany TS 1983; DMin Columbia Sem 1996. D 12/19/1998 P 6/23/1999 Bp Henry Irving Louttit. m 1/27/1990 Bill Deneke. Asst H Trin Par Decatur GA 2000-2010; Min Of Pstr Care Dio Georgia. Auth, "A Feminist," *Trinitarian Model Of Pstr Care & Counslg w Wmn*. AAPC.

SILVER, Gay (Fla) 14557 Basilham Ln, Jacksonville FL 32258 **Cn to the Ordnry Dio Florida Jacksonville FL 2004-** B New York NY 1942 d Charles & Emma. BA Mercy Coll 1967; MDiv GTS 1997. D 6/21/1997 P 6/20/1998 Bp Robert Carroll Johnson Jr. c 2. Dio Florida Jacksonville 2004-2009; Assoc Trin Par New York NY 2000-2004; Asst Vic S Pat's Epis Ch Mooresville NC 1997-2000.

SILVERSTRIM, Elaine Margaret (CPa) 110 Dry Run Rd., Coudersport PA 16915 **Ret. - P-in-c Potter Cnty Epis Mnstry Coudersport PA 2007-** B Sidney NY 1946 d John & Ruby. BS Albany St U 1976; MA U of Scranton 1988; MDiv GTS 1991. D 6/8/1991 P 2/5/1992 Bp James Michael Mark Dyer. m 2/8/1969 Leland Silverstrim c 5. Lead Supply Ch Of Our Sav Montoursville PA 2009; R Chr Ch Coudersport PA 2002-2006; Vic Trin Ch Renovo PA 1996-2002; Chapl Mont Hospice Norristown PA 1995-1996; Vic Trin Ch Boothwyn PA 1993-1995; P-in-res Cathd Ch Of The Nativ Bethlehem PA 1992-1993; Dio Bethlehem Bethlehem PA 1991-1993. Sis of St. Marg 1995.

SIMEONE, Richard John (Mass) 203 Pemberton St Unit 3, Cambridge MA 02140 **Assoc S Jn's Ch Charlestown (Boston) Charlestown MA 2013-; EFM Co-Coordntr Dio Massachusetts Boston MA 2010-, Eccl Trial Crt Judge 1997-2003** B Harrisburg PA 1941 s Ernest & Frances. AB Br 1963; MDiv GTS 1966. D 6/15/1966 Bp John Thomas Heistand P 12/17/1966 Bp Thaddeus F Zielinski. m 11/23/1986 Lyn G Gillespie c 3. R S Jn's Epis Ch Gloucester MA 1997-2010; Dioc Mus Cmsn Dio Connecticut Meriden CT 1994-1997; R Trin Epis Ch Collinsville CT 1978-1997; Liturg Cmsn Dio Maine Portland ME 1970-1978; Vic All SS Epis Ch Skowhegan ME 1968-1978; S Mart's Epis Ch Palmyra ME 1968-1978; Cur S Mths Epis Ch E Aurora NY 1966-1968. Assoc of the OHC 1990. sim6366@gmail.com

SIMMONDS, Richard Frank (Ak) Po Box 58041, Minto AK 99758 **Died 9/5/2016** B Troy NY 1931 s Raymond & Charlotte. BA Ken 1953; STB Ya Berk

1956. D 5/27/1956 Bp Frederick Lehrle Barry P 12/1/1956 Bp William Jones Gordon Jr. m 6/1/1962 Pauline Joyce Simmonds c 2. Dio Alaska Fairbanks AK 1992; Ret 1991-2016; R S Matt's Epis Ch Fairbanks AK 1990-1991, P 1970-1987; S Fran By The Sea Ch Kenai AK 1985-1988; Asst S Jn's Epis Ch Troy NY 1967-1970; Vic S Lk's Troy AK 1967-1970; P-in-c S Matt's Ch Beaver AK 1962-1967; P-in-c S Barn Ch Minto AK 1956-1962.

SIMMONS, C Douglas (Ark) 1558 N Stable Ave, Fayetteville AR 72703 **Died 9/26/2015** B Ypsilanti MI 1937 s Carl & Dortha. BS Estrn Michigan U 1960; MDiv VTS 1965; DMin VTS 1984. D 6/29/1965 Bp Chauncie Kilmer Myers P 2/5/1966 Bp Archie H Crowley. m 6/27/1959 Nina Seddon c 2. Dio Arkansas Little Rock AR 1995-2001; Assoc R S Paul's Ch Fayetteville AR 1995-2000; P Gd Shpd Epis Ch Silver Sprg MD 1991-1995; Dn Asheville Dnry 1987-1990; Int Dio Washington Washington DC 1986-1990; R Trin Epis Ch Asheville NC 1984-1991; R Chr Epis Ch Of Springfield Springfield OH 1976-1984; Assoc S Paul's Ch Kansas City MO 1972-1976; Asst S Steph The Mtyr Ch Minneapolis MN 1970-1972; Assoc Chr Ch Mex City Mex 1966-1970; Vic S Alfred Lake Orion MI 1965-1966; Chair of Cont Ed. Com for Cler Dio Wstrn No Carolina Asheville NC 1982-1991. Auth, "Bk-The Joshua Chronicles," Red Lead Press, 2010; Auth, "Bk-The Joshua Chronicles," Red Lead Press, 2010.

SIMMONS, Charles Winston (NY) St Andrew's Church, 781 Castle Hill Ave, Bronx NY 10473 **Dio New York New York NY 2013-** B Nassau Bahamas 1962 s Edgar & Harriet. BA Codrington Coll 1994; BBA Loyola U 1997; MBA Loyola U 1998. Trans 4/23/2012 as Priest Bp Mark Sean Sisk. m 1/27/2001 Sheryl Simmons c 1. S Andr's Ch Bronx NY 2012-2013.

SIMMONS, David (Mil) 808 S East Ave, Waukesha WI 63186 **Ecum Off St Mths Epis Ch Waukesha WI 2008-; Bd Secy EDEO Ft Myers FL 2015-, Bd Mem 2011-2015; Stndg Com Dio Milwaukee Milwaukee WI 2014-, Ecum Off 2008-** B Lawrence KY 1970 s Herbert & Judy. BA Wstrn Kentucky U 1992; MDiv VTS 2001. D 6/3/2001 P 1/12/2002 Bp Ted Gulick Jr. m 6/27/1992 Dawn M Simmons c 2. Chapl Murray St U Murray KY 2003-2007; R S Jn's Ch Murray KY 2003-2007; Cur S Matt's Epis Ch Louisville KY 2001-2003; Dep to Gnrl Assembly Natl Coun Of Ch New York NY 2010-2011. Ord of Julian of Norwich 2006.

SIMMONS, David Clark (NMich) 5976 Whitney 19.8 Blvd, Gladstone MI 49837 B Minneapolis MN 1941 s Bert & Dortha. BBA U of Iowa 1964. D 8/21/1992 P 2/21/1993 Bp Thomas Kreider Ray. m 9/24/1966 Mary Rose Simmons.

SIMMONS, Elizabeth (Ak) PO Box 1668, Kodiak AK 99615 B Tokyo Japan 1957 d Ronald & Helene. BA U NC 1980; MDiv GTS 1994. D 6/18/1994 Bp Brice Sidney Sanders P 1/18/1995 Bp David Charles Bowman. S Matt's Epis Ch Fairbanks AK 2016-2017; S Jas The Fisherman Kodiak AK 2014-2016; Int S Lk's Epis Ch Jamestown NY 2012-2014; R S Lk's Ch Racine WI 2009-2012; Asst S Jn's Epis Ch Boulder CO 2008-2009; Vic Ch Of The Apos Oro Vlly AZ 2006-2008; R S Steph's Ch Phoenix AZ 1999-2006; Assoc S Phil's In The Hills Tucson AZ 1996-1999; Asst R Trin Epis Ch Buffalo NY 1994-1996.

SIMMONS, Harriet (Miss) 4911 Country Club Dr, Meridian MS 39305 B Yazoo City MS 1947 d Darrington & Werdna. Millsaps Coll 1966; BA U of Mississippi 1968; MA Mississippi Coll 1973; New Orleans Bapt TS 1989. D 2/22/1992 Bp Duncan Montgomery Gray Jr P 5/21/2000 Bp Alfred Marble Jr. m 3/23/1968 William Simmons c 2. Vic S Fran Of Assisi Ch Philadelphia MS 2001-2011; S Mary's Ch Enterprise MS 2001-2011, P 2000-2001; D S Paul's Epis Ch Meridian MS 1992-2000. NAAD.

SIMMONS, Harriette J (At) Saint Paul'S Church, 605 Reynolds Street On The Riverwalk, Augusta GA 30901 B Macon GA 1942 d Russell & Elizabeth. BA Wesleyan Coll 1964; MDiv Candler TS Emory U 1994. D 6/10/1995 P 12/16/1995 Bp Frank Kellogg Allan. c 3. Int R Chr Ch Macon GA 2008-2014, 1995-2002; S Jas Epis Ch Port Gibson MS 2008; S Aug Of Cbury Ch Augusta GA 2005-2008; S Paul's Ch Augusta GA 2002-2004. Rotary Club 1996-2003. Outstanding Alum Wesleyan Coll 1996.

SIMMONS, Kenneth William (Minn) 11 Kellogg Blvd E Apt 715, Saint Paul MN 55101 **Bd Examinnig Chapl 1969-** B Ponca City OK 1935 s Lyle & Karolyn. BA U of Tulsa 1958; MDiv Epis TS of the SW 1963. D 6/29/1963 P 5/20/1964 Bp Hamilton Hyde Kellogg. m 6/29/1975 Barbara Ann Langer c 2. Non-par 1985-1999; 1980-1982; Dn S Paul Reg 1980-1982; 1974-1976; U Epis Cntr 1971-1973; Chair of the Dept of Higher Educ 1970-1974; Bp and Coun 1969-1971; R Gd Shpd At Sunfish Lake Sunfish Lake MN 1966-1983; S Anne's Epis Ch S Paul MN 1966-1983; Gr Ch Pine Island MN 1963-1966.

SIMMONS, Mary Rose (NMich) 5976 Whitney 19.8 Blvd, Gladstone MI 49837 B South Bend IN 1942 d William & Rose. BA Marygrove Coll 1964. D 5/27/2001 Bp James Arthur Kelsey. m 9/24/1966 David Clark Simmons.

SIMMONS, Ned Allen (Ga) 109 Flint River Circle, Quitman GA 31643 **D S Jas Epis Ch Quitman GA 1992-** B Ambrose GA 1923 s Charlie & Maggie. BS U GA 1945; MS Florida St U 1950. D 3/4/1990 Bp Harry Woolston Shipps. c 2. Chapl Presb Nrsng Hm 1995-2001.

SIMMONS IV, Tom (Va) 1807 Hungary Rd, Richmond VA 23228 **R S Ptr's Epis Ch Purcellville VA 2002-** B Denver CO 1967 s Thomas & Blair. BA Jas Madison U 1989; MDiv Westminster TS 1993; VTS 1998. D 6/13/1998 P 4/20/

1999 Bp Peter J Lee. m 2/25/1995 Tait N Simmons c 5. All SS Ch Richmond VA 1998-2002.

SIMMONS, Walter Clippinger (Md) 514 Limerick Cir. Unit 201, Lutherville Timonium MD 21093 **Ret 2003-** B Cincinnati OH 1940 s Benjamin & Virginia. BA Mia 1964; MA U Pac 1967; MDiv EDS 1972. D 7/16/1972 P 6/3/1973 Bp John Raymond Wyatt. R S Marg's Epis Ch Parkville MD 1994-2003; Vic S Steph's Elwood IN 1993-1994; S Paul's Epis Ch Indianapolis IN 1991-1993; Jub Off Dio Rhode Island Providence RI 1987-1990; R Ch Of The Mssh Providence RI 1981-1990; Chr Epis Ch Anacortes WA 1980-1981; Assoc S Lk's Ch Tacoma WA 1975-1980; Chapl Chas Wright Acad Tacoma WA 1975-1976; Chapl Chas Wright Acad Tacoma WA 1974-1975; Chapl S Geo Sch Spokane WA 1972-1974; Cur S Dav's Ch Spokane WA 1972-1973; COM Dio Indianapolis Indianapolis IN 1991-1993. *Var arts*, 2003. Providence 1 in 350 Ldrshp Awards City of Providence 1986.

SIMMONS, Warren Reginald (SeFla) 4971 Summerswell Ln, Southport NC 28461 **R S Aid's Epis Ch Milton GA 2017-** B Marion SC 1965 s Warren & Fannie. BSBA Cit 1987; MDiv Duke DS 2009; Post Grad Dplma-Angl Stds VTS 2010. D 5/30/2015 P 11/21/2015 Bp Leo Frade. m 7/30/2005 Kimberly Louise Simmons c 2. S Phil's Ch Southport NC 2016-2017; Trin Ch Washington DC 2015-2016. fr.reginald@staidans.com

SIMON JR, Ken (SanD) 6556 Park Ridge Boulevard, San Diego CA 92120 B Paterson NJ 1974 s Kenneth & Daisy. BA U of San Diego 1996; MDiv Fuller TS 2004; CAS CDSP 2009. D 6/27/2009 P 12/19/2009 Bp Jim Mathes. S Michaels By-The-Sea Ch Carlsbad CA 2014-2017; P S Dunst's Epis Ch San Diego CA 2009-2014; D Chr Ch Coronado CA 2009.

SIMONIAN, Marlene Jenny (RI) 1346 Creek Nine Dr, North Port FL 34290 B Providence RI 1942 d Pasquale & Anastasia. Rhode Island Sch for Deacons 1988. D 6/23/1990 Bp George Nelson Hunt III. m 2/29/1972 Robert Martin Simonian c 2. D St. Jas Epis/Angl Ch Port Charlotte FL 2003-2007; D Ch Of The Gd Shpd Punta Gorda FL 1998-2003; D St Mich & Gr Ch Rumford RI 1994-1998; Chapl Zambarano Hosp RI 1993-1998; D S Mk's Ch Warren RI 1990-1994; Stndg Com Dio Rhode Island Providence RI 1984-1988.

SIMONS, Daniel J (NY) 74 Trinity Pl, New York NY 10006 **P for Liturg, Hosp & Pilgrimage Trin Par New York NY 2008-** B Land O'Lakes WI 1964 s James & Lois. BA Wheaton Coll 1987; MDiv VTS 1994. D 6/18/1994 Bp Frank Tracy Griswold III P 12/18/1994 Bp John Clark Buchanan. m 8/8/2008 Francisco Javier Galito-Cava. All SS Co San Francisco CA 2004-2008; Bro S Jn's Chap Cambridge MA 1998-2014; Rel SSJE Cambridge MA 1998-2004; Bro Soc-St Jn The Evang Cambridge MA 1998-2004; Cn Pstr Cathd Ch Of S Steph Harrisburg PA 1995-1998; P S Paul's Ch Leavenworth KS 1994-1995.

SIMONS, James Burdette (Pgh) 731 Laurel Dr, Ligonier PA 15658 **Dio Pittsburgh Pittsburgh PA 2000-, Cathd Dn Search Com 1999, Chair - Com 1997-1998; R S Michaels Of The Vlly Epis Ch Ligonier PA 1988-** B Sewickley PA 1957 s Stephen & Dolly. BS Alleg 1980; MDiv TESM 1985; DMin TESM 2007. D 6/8/1985 P 12/19/1985 Bp Alden Moinet Hathaway. c 3. Asst R S Mart's Epis Ch Monroeville PA 1985-1988.

SIMONSEN, Douglas C (Oly) P.O. Box 1974, Anacortes WA 98221 **P-in-c The Epis Par of St Dav Friday Harbor WA 2008-** B Flint MI 1949 BS Michigan Tech U 1977; MTS Seattle U 1994; CAS CDSP 1996. D 6/28/1997 P 6/20/1998 Bp Vincent Waydell Warner. m 10/6/1978 Cynthia S Simonsen c 2. Reg Mssnr Dio Spokane Spokane WA 2004-2005; P-in-c H Trin Epis Ch Sunnyside WA 2004-2005; Vic S Hilda's - S Pat's Epis Ch Edmonds WA 2000-2002; Assoc Gr Ch Bainbridge Island WA 1997-2000.

SIMOPOULOS, Nicole M (Haw) 563 Kamoku St, Honolulu HI 96826 **Iolani Sch Honolulu HI 2013-** B San Francisco CA 1973 BA Stan 1995; MDiv Amer Bapt Sem of the W 2000; MDiv Amer Bapt Sem of the W 2000; MA Grad Theol Un 2002. D 5/27/2003 Bp Robert Louis Ladehoff P 1/3/2004 Bp Johncy Itty. c 1. Lower Sch Chapl Cathd of St Ptr & St Paul Washington DC 2009-2013; Asst to the R Gr Memi Portland OR 2005-2008; Dio Oregon Portland OR 2003-2005; Cur Epis Par Of S Jn The Bapt Portland OR 2003-2005; Chapl Oregon Epis Sch Portland OR 2002-2009.

SIMPSON, Cynthia (WA) Christ Episcopal School, 107 S Washington St, Rockville MD 20850 **Asst to the R Chr Ch Prince Geo's Par Rockville MD 2007-; Chr Epis Sch Rockville MD 2007-** B Alexandria, VA 1958 d Omer & Mary Adelle. BA Baylor U 1981; MDiv Sthrn Bapt TS 1985; Dip VTS 2005. D 6/9/2007 P 1/19/2008 Bp John Bryson Chane. c 1. S Ptr's Ch Poolesville MD 1999-2007. csimpson@cesrockville.org

SIMPSON, Dawn Marie (Colo) Po Box 291, Monte Vista CO 81144 **Cur S Thos The Apos Alamosa CO 2003-** B Pekin IL 1961 d William & MaryLou. BS Adams St Coll 1989; MTh Trin TS 2009. D 7/19/2003 Bp William Jerry Winterrowd P 1/29/2004 Bp Robert John O'Neill. m 5/1/1990 Grant Simpson c 3. Epis Mssn of the San Luis Vlly Alamosa CO 2008-2009; P-t S Thos The Apos Epis Ch Alamosa CO 2003-2009.

SIMPSON, Elizabeth Bass (Mo) St Matthew's Episcopal Church, 1100 Grove St, Mexico MO 65265 B Tupelo MS 1948 d Dorothy. Certifacate Dioc Epis Sch for Mnstry; BA U of Memphis. D 11/20/2015 Bp George Wayne Smith. m 12/27/1967 Waits Andrew Simpson c 2.

SIMPSON, Geoffrey Sedgwick (Mil) The Laurels, Queen Street, Yetminster, Dorset DT9 6LLGB Great Britain (UK) B South Milwaukee WI 1932 s Alexander & Helen. BA Ham 1954; STB GTS 1957; MA U of Wisconsin 1966; PhD U of Cambridge 1973. D 6/1/1957 P 12/1/1957 Bp Donald H V Hallock. m 8/18/1971 Mary Simpson c 2. Serv Ch of Engl 1976-2002; Asst Chapl S Steph's Ch Racine WI 1963-1966; Vic S Barth's Ch Pewaukee WI 1958-1962; Cur Chr Ch Milwaukee WI 1957-1958.

SIMPSON, Geoffrey Stewart (Pa) Church Of The Good Samaritan, 212 W Lancaster Ave, Paoli PA 19301 **S Thos Ch Houston TX 2017-; Assoc Cler Ch Of The Gd Samar Paoli PA 2010-; Chapl Woodberry Forest Sch 1993-** B Norfolk VA 1964 s John & Gret. Coll of Wooster; BA Trin 1987; MDiv TESM 1993. D 6/12/1993 Bp Arthur Edward Walmsley P 12/15/1993 Bp Peter J Lee. Bd Trst Fllshp of Christians in universities and Schools 2001-2007; Dio Virginia Richmond VA; Yth Mnstry Gr Epis Ch Trumbull CT 1985-1990.

SIMPSON JR, John Patrick (Pa) 244 Woodbine Ave, Narberth PA 19072 B Philadelphia PA 1939 s John & Charlotte. BS Tem 1961; MDiv VTS 1968. D 6/8/1968 P 3/8/1969 Bp Robert Lionne DeWitt. m 7/29/1999 Robert E Crook c 3. Long-term Supply St Ptr's Germantown Philadelphia 2004-2005; Long-term Supply S Barth's Ch Philadelphia PA 1992-2002; Chapl Frankford Hosp Philadelphia PA 1980-2005; R S Mths Ch Philadelphia PA 1977-1980; Res Dir S Fran Girls' Hm Loudonville NY 1975-1977; S Fran Cmnty Serv Inc. Salina KS 1970-1977; Long-term Supply H Apos Ch Ellsworth KS 1970-1975; Res Dir S Fran Boys' Hm Ellsworth KS 1970-1975; Cur Ch Of The Gd Samar Paoli PA 1968-1970. AAPC; Coll of Chapl.

SIMPSON, Richard Edmund (LI) 754 Main St, Islip NY 11751 **Dn Atlantic Dnry Dio Long island 2008-; Sprtl Dir Curs Secratariat 2008-; R S Mk's Ch Islip NY 2001-** B Port Huron MI 1954 s Jorma & Lois. BA MI SU 1976; MDiv Epis TS of the SW 1981. D 6/30/1981 Bp Henry Irving Mayson P 5/1/1982 Bp H Coleman Mcgehee Jr. m 7/26/1980 Janet Simpson c 1. No E Cler Rep Natl Epis Curs Com 2010-2012; Bd Mem, Vice Chair Geo Mercer Jr. TS Garden city NY 2001-2007; JPIC Team Prov VI Prov 6 USA IA 1995-2001; Dioc Human Needs Com Dio Iowa IA 1993-1995; Cler Fam Proj IA 1990-1993; R Trin Ch Muscatine IA 1988-2001; Cn Trin Cathd Davenport IA 1985-1988; Vic S Paul's Ch Durant IA 1983-1985; Asst S Phil's Epis Ch Rochester MI 1981-1983; Dn of the Atlantic Dnry Dio Long Island Garden City NY 2006-2007, Secratary of Conv 2002-2005; Dioc Jub Off Dio Iowa Des Moines IA 1990-1993, Dioc Mus & Liturg Cmsn 1989-1992. CBS; Tertiary of the Soc of S Fran 1991; Treas Gnrl C.B.S. 1993.

SIMPSON, Richard Michael (WMass) 88 Highland St, Holden MA 01520 **Cn to the Ordnry Dio Wstrn Massachusetts Springfield 2013-, Chair, Bp Search Com 2011-2013, Mem of Dioc Coun 2004-2011, Chair, COM 2006-2010; Lectr in Theol Assumption Coll Worcester MA 2005-; R S Fran Ch Holden MA 1998-** B Honesdale PA 1963 s Ernest & Margaret. U of St Andrews 1984; BA Geo 1985; MDiv Drew U 1988; ThM PrTS 1990; DMin Columbia TS 2005. D 6/12/1993 Bp Arthur Edward Walmsley P 2/5/1994 Bp Clarence Nicholas Coleridge. m 5/25/1986 Elizabeth H MacMahon c 2. Assoc R Chr And H Trin Ch Westport CT 1993-1998; Serv as Pstr Meth Ch 1988-1993; Police Chapl (Vol) Town of Holden MA 2005-2013. Contrib, "Homiletical Notes (two volumes)," *Feasting on the Word*, Westminister/Jn Knox Press, 2011. rsimpson@diocesema.org

SIMPSON, Richard Roy (RI) 7009 SE 117th Pl., Portland OR 97266 **Assoc S Jn The Evang Ch Portland OR 2010-** B Seattle WA 1943 s Floyd & Elsie. BA U of Hawaii 1966; BD CDSP 1969. D 6/10/1969 P 12/1/1969 Bp Edwin Lani Hanchett. m 8/28/1965 Cynthia K Simpson. R S Dav's On The Hill Epis Ch Cranston RI 1997-2001; Chapl S Fran Cmnty Serv Inc. Salina KS 1994-1997; R Trin Ch Sonoma CA 1987-1994; R S Pauls Epis Ch The Dalles OR 1981-1987; R S Jn's Ch Hermiston OR 1977-1981; R S Andr's Epis Ch Mccall ID 1976-1977; R Ch Of H Nativ Meridian ID 1975-1977; R Ch Of The Redeem Salmon ID 1973-1975; Vic S Andr's Cathd Honolulu HI 1971-1972; Vic S Thos Kauai HI 1970-1971; Asst Ch Of The Epiph Honolulu HI 1969-1970.

SIMPSON, Sallie O'Keef (NC) 1725 N New Hope Rd, Raleigh NC 27604 B Raleigh NC 1948 d Herbert & Margaret. BS U NC 1970; MBA Appalachain St U 1993. D 1/25/2014 Bp Anne Hodges-Copple. c 2.

SIMPSON, Ward Howard (SD) 500 South Main Ave, Sioux Falls SD 57104 **Dn Calv Cathd Sioux Falls SD 2009-; GC Dep Dio So Dakota Pierre SD 2012-** B Faribault MN 1962 s Charles & Alma. BS Minnesota St U Mankato 1984; MDiv Nash 1991. D 6/24/1991 Bp Robert Marshall Anderson P 12/27/1991 Bp William Charles Wantland. m 12/10/1983 Barbara Annette Simpson c 3. Mem Stndg Cmsn on Const and Cn 2004-2009; R S Andr's Ch Ashland WI 1995-2009; S Alb's Ch Spooner WI 1991-1995; Vic S Steph's Shell Lake WI 1991-1995; GC Dep Dio Eau Claire Eau Claire WI 2009, GC Dep 2003, GC Dep 1997. dean.simpson@calvarycathedral.net

SIMRILL, Spenser Davenport (At) 4945 Dupont Ave S, Minneapolis MN 55419 B Charlotte NC 1948 s Frank & Francis. BA Hampden-Sydney Coll 1970; MA U of Louisiana 1974; MDiv Louisville Presb TS 1978; Cert GTS 1979; DMin Louisville Presb TS 1989. D 6/25/1979 P 6/1/1980 Bp David Reed. m 9/2/1972 Stuart Davenport Simrill c 2. Dn Cathd Ch Of S Mk Minneapolis MN

2002-2012; R S Lk's Epis Ch Atlanta GA 1992-2002; R The Ch Of Ascen And H Trin Cincinnati OH 1986-1992; P-in-c Chr Ch Cathd Louisville KY 1986, D-In-Res 1979-1985; Prov Iv CE Strng Com YA Natl Ch 1980-1982; Dio Kentucky Louisville KY 1979-1980, Com 1985-1986. Advsry Bd, Angl Observer To The Untd Nations 2003; Bd Mem, Endowed Parishes Consortium Of The Epis Ch 2001-2004. Prchr Awd Gnrl Theolgical Sem 1979; Mayors Distinguished Citizens Awd 85; Archdio Louisville Peace & Justice Awd 85.

SIMS, Carol Carruthers (SVa) 3929 Ocean Cut Lane, Virginia Beach VA 23451 B Charlottesville VA 1938 d Thomas & Mabel. BA U NC 1972; MEd U of Virginia 1975; EdS U of Virginia 1979; Mnstry Formation Prog 1997. D 6/21/1997 P 12/20/1997 Bp Charles I Jones III. c 3. Pstr Asst Ch Of The Epiph Norfolk VA 2008-2010; Assoc Galilee Epis Ch Virginia Bch VA 2007-2009; Upper Yellowstone Epis Ch Livingston MT 2007; Asst Epis Ch of the Upper Yellowstone MT 2006-2007; All SS in Big Sky Big Sky MT 2004-2007; Dio Montana Helena MT 2001-2002; R S Jas Ch Lewistown MT 1997-2001. Auth, "Emotional Responses Of Cancer Diagnosis," *Coping*, 1995; Auth, "Travesty In Palestine," *The Middle E Journ*, 1990.

SIMS, Elizabeth Erringer (Cal) 1700 Santa Clara Ave, Alameda CA 94501 B Dallas TX 1961 d Orville & Elizabeth. BA U CA San Diego 1984; MPH U CA Berkeley 1996; BD The Sch for Deacons 2011. D 12/3/2011 Bp Marc Handley Andrus. m 2/6/2009 Steven Morgan Sims c 2.

SIMS, Gregory Brian (Chi) 4233 Ahlstrand Dr, Rockford IL 61101 B Linton IN 1947 s George & Marjory. BA U IL 1969; MDiv Nash 1972. D 5/20/1972 Bp Albert A Chambers P 12/2/1972 Bp Albert William Hillestad. R Emm Epis Ch Rockford IL 1990-2002; Cn Res S Jn's Cathd Albuquerque NM 1987-1990; R Sprt of Gr Luth Epis Ch W Bloomfield MI 1982-1986; R S Thos Epis Ch Plymouth IN 1976-1981; R S Ptr's By-The-Lake Ch Montague MI 1973-1976; Cur Emm Memi Epis Ch Champaign IL 1972-1973. Cn Res St. Jn's Cathd, Albuquerque, NM 1988.

SIMS, Gregory Knox (Cal) Po Box 1, Boonville CA 95415 **Fac/Psychol Coll of San Mateo Temple U U U C Berkeley 1965-** B Moline IL 1933 s Wilbert & Mary. BA U CA 1955; BD CDSP 1960; MA Stan 1964; PhD Stan 1971. D 6/13/1960 P 3/3/1961 Bp Francis E I Bloy. m 8/27/1965 Clarissa H Sims c 4. Assoc R&Asst Epis.Chaplln, Stanford U. All SS Epis Ch Palo Alto CA 1962-1964; Asst Rect/P in Charge: Dn, Day Sch S Ptr's Par San Pedro CA 1960-1962. Co-Auth, "Treating Sprtl Disorders: Promoting Sprtl Recovery," Hlth Acc Pr, 2001. Commencement Speaker U Ca-Berk 1973.

SIMS, Kenneth Harry (SeFla) 3970 Nw 188th St, Opa Locka FL 33055 B Miami FL 1942 s James & Leola. EdD Nova SE U; BS Florida A&M U 1966; MS Florida Atlantic U 1980. D 6/16/2001 Bp John Lewis Said. m 6/21/1986 Gwendolyn Tynes.

SIMS, Mark Howard (SeFla) 1165 Ne 105th St, Miami Shores FL 33138 **S Mary Magd Epis Ch Pompano Bch FL 2003-; Chapl Epis Aids Mnstry 2001-** B Lakeland FL 1957 s Howard & Violet. BA U of Florida 1979; MDiv Epis TS of the SW 2000. D 6/14/2000 Bp John Lewis Said P 12/15/2000 Bp Leo Frade. m 9/10/2003 Gail Haldeman Sims c 1. Trin Cathd Miami FL 2000-2003. Comission On Mnstry. revmarksims@mac.com

SIMS, Richard Osborn (Nev) 24 Elysium Dr, Ely NV 89301 **P S Barth's Ch Ely NV 2000-** B Ely NV 1952 s Philip & Marilyn. Educ Dynamics Inst; Utah Tech Coll. D 4/2/2000 Bp John Stuart Thornton P 11/18/2000 Bp George Nelson Hunt III. m 1/7/1975 Shelba Sims.

SIMS, Ronald Frank (Wyo) 200 Country Brook Dr Apt 2427, Keller TX 76248 **Sprtl Dir Wyoming Angl Curs Sec 1976-; Vice-Pres of Trst E Wyoming Cmnty Coll 1973-** B Ogden UT 1929 s Frank & Elna. BA U of Wyoming 1963; BD CDSP 1966. P 12/1/1966 Bp James W Hunter. m 8/12/1949 Shirley D Sims c 3. S Matt's Epis Cathd Laramie WY 1986-1992; R Ch Of S Thos Rawlins WY 1977-1986; Dir of the Estrn Area Mnstry 1973-1975; Dep GC 1970-1973; R All SS Epis Ch Torrington WY 1968-1976; R Ch Of Our Sav Hartville WY 1968-1975; S Barn Epis Ch Saratoga WY 1966-1968; Vic S Jas Ch Encampment WY 1966-1968.

SIMSON, John Everett (Mass) 4773 Abargo St, Woodland Hills CA 91364 B Hamilton OH 1958 s Everett & Mimi. BA U CA 1984; MDiv GTS 1993; DMin CDSP 2008. D 6/26/1993 P 5/14/1994 Bp Richard Lester Shimpfky. m 9/13/1986 Suzanne M Simson c 1. R S Anne's Ch Lowell MA 1996-2003; Cur Ch Of S Jn The Evang Hingham MA 1994-1996. Dioc Coun 2001-2002; Exec Com Epis City Mssn 1997-2003.

SINCLAIR, Barbara Louise (Chi) St James Episcopal Church, 425 E MacArthur Ave, Lewistown IL 61542 **S Jas Epis Ch Lewistown IL 2013-** B Pekin IL 1945 d Harold & Grace. BA Wstrn IL U 1968. D 2/2/2013 Bp John Clark Buchanan. c 1.

SINCLAIR, Elisabeth Anne (Mil) 7110 N State Route 9, Kansas City MO 64152 **Ch Of The Redeem Kansas City MO 2015-** B Milwaukee WI 1974 d Paul & Lisa. BA Bethel Sem 1996; MDiv Bethel Sem 2011; Angl Stds VTS 2015. D 6/13/2015 P 1/30/2016 Bp Steven Andrew Miller. m 4/16/2016 Bryan William Spoon.

SINCLAIR, Gregory Lynn (NwT) 801 Ross Ave, Abilene TX 79605 B Geneva IL 1944 s Edward & Virginia. BAS Abilene Chr U 1995; MEd Hardin-Simmons U 2003. D 11/6/1988 Bp Sam Byron Hulsey. m 8/28/1968 Mary-Margaret Sinclair c 1. D Gr Ch Muskogee OK 2007-2013; D S Mk's Epis Ch Abilene TX 2000-2007, D 1988-1999; D S Steph's Ch Sweetwater TX 1996-1999. Ord Of S Lk The Physcn 2001.

SINCLAIR, Nancy Park (Los) 502 Hawk Ln, Fountain Valley CA 92708 B New Orleans LA 1945 D 1/31/2004 P 1/22/2005 Bp Joseph Jon Bruno. m 6/10/1967 Donald M Sinclair c 2. Vic S Theo Of Cbury Par Seal Bch CA 2006-2014; S Mk's Par Downey CA 2004-2005.

SINCLAIR, Roderick Doig (SwVa) Wcbr 250 Pantops Mountain Rd, Apt. 131, Charlottesville VA 22911 **Ret 1996-** B Nassau BS 1931 s Thomas & Dorothy. BA U of Virginia 1953; LLB U of Virginia 1958; MDiv VTS 1966. D 6/11/1966 Bp Robert Fisher Gibson Jr P 12/10/1966 Bp David Shepherd Rose. m 2/27/1954 Louise Sinclair c 3. Chr Ch Blacksburg VA 1992-1996; Chapl Va Tech Blacksburg VA 1988-1996; Chapl Radford U Radford VA 1988-1992; Dio SW Virginia Roanoke VA 1988-1991; Hollins Coll Roanoke VA 1981-1987; Chapl S Dunst's: The Epis Ch at Auburn U Auburn AL 1975-1981; Co-Chapl S Paul's Memi Charlottesvlle VA 1968-1971; Assoc Min S Geo's Epis Ch Arlington VA 1966-1968. Auth, "Epis Life, Jubilee," *Plumline*. Cltn For Justice 1970; Cuba Proj 1980-1988; Fllshp Recon 1980-1988; Virginia Inter-Faith Cntr For Publ Plcy 1996-2005.

SINCLAIR, Scott Gambrill (Cal) 663 Coventry Rd, Kensington CA 94707 **Non-par 1991-** B Baltimore MD 1950 s James & Pauline. BA JHU 1971; MA JHU 1972; MDiv CDSP 1976; PhD Grad Theol Un 1986. D 6/26/1976 Bp Chauncie Kilmer Myers P 5/19/1977 Bp Chilton R Powell. Tutor Codrington Coll S Jn Barbados 1987-1991; Ch Of The Ascen Burlingame CA 1977-1978; Vic Ascen Burlingame CA 1976-1978; S Andr's Epis Ch San Bruno CA 1976-1977. Auth, "A Saintudy Guide To S Paul'S Letter To The Romans," Bibal Press, 2000; Auth, "A Study Guide To Mk'S Gospel," Bibal Press, 1996; Auth, "The Road And The Truth: The Ed Of Jn'S Gospel," Bibal, 1994; Auth, "Revelation: A Bk For The Rest Of Us," Bibal Press, 1992; Auth, "Jesus Chr According To S Paul," Bibal Press, 1988.

SINGER, Allen Michael (EC) 800 Rountree St., Kinston NC 28501 **Ch Of The Servnt Wilmington NC 2016-** B Waynesboro PA 1955 s Edward & Barbara. BA Morris Harvey Coll 1977; MDiv Nash 1980. D 6/13/1980 P 12/20/1980 Bp Dean Theodore Stevenson. m 8/26/1978 Teresa Belcher Singer c 1. R S Mary's Ch Kinston NC 1999-2016; Chapl VetA 1993-1999; R S Lk's Epis Ch Altoona PA 1984-1999; Dept Ch Growth Dio Cntrl Pennsylvania Harrisburg PA 1981-1995; Trin Ch Jersey Shore PA 1981; P-in-c All SS Epis Ch Williamsport PA 1980-1984; Chair COM Dio E Carolina Kinston NC 1999-2005.

SINGER, Susanna Jane (Cal) 1233 Howard Street #714, San Francisco CA 94103 **Assoc Prof of Mnstry Dvlpmt CDSP Berkeley CA 2005-** B London England UK 1957 d Kenneth & Doris. MA U of Cambridge 1979; MDiv CDSP 1989; PhD Boston Coll 2008. D 12/8/1990 P 12/7/1991 Bp William Edwin Swing. m 9/19/1981 David William Singer c 1. Asst All SS Par Brookline MA 2002-2005; Educ Crdntr All SS' Ch San Francisco CA 1997-2002; Dio California San Francisco CA 1997-2002; Cn Liturg Gr Cathd San Francisco CA 1991-1996.

SINGER-HEDLUND, Sylvia Marly (SJ) 416 S Regent St, Stockton CA 95204 **Died 5/22/2016** B Cambridge MA 1933 d Bauer & Eleanor. BA U CA 1955; MA U CA 1960; MDiv CDSP 1983; DMin SFTS 1992. D 7/17/1983 Bp Victor Manuel Rivera. m 5/27/1989 Richard James Hedlund c 2. Non-par 1996-2016; Int Epis Ch Of S Anne Stockton CA 1995-1996; St Laurences Ch Stockton CA 1984-1989; Epis Dio San Joaquin Modesto CA 1983-1989; Vic S Lawr Mssn 1983-1989. OHC.

✠ SINGH, The Rt Rev Prince Grenville (Roch) 4 Cathedral Oaks, Fairport NY 14450 **Bp of Rochester Dio Rochester Henrietta 2008-** B Nergercoil Jamil Nadu IN 1962 s Yesudian & Ida. Drew U; BD Un Biblic Sem Pune Mr IN 1989; ThM UTS Richmond 1994; MTh PrTS 1995. Trans 4/18/2000 Bp John Palmer Croneberger Con 5/31/2008 for Roch. m 10/18/1991 Jebaroja Singh c 2. R S Alb's Ch Oakland NJ 2000-2008. prince@episcopaldioceseofrochester.org

SINGH, Simon Peter (Chi) 261 W Army Trail Rd, Bloomingdale IL 60108 **First Asian Ch Bloomingdale IL 2009-** B Allahabad, India 1950 s Khushal & Indira. GTh Allahabad Bible Sem 1973; MA Narmada Mahavidayla 1976. Trans 11/20/2009 as Deacon Bp Jeff Lee. m 5/14/1980 Deepa Singh c 4.

SINGLETON, Jill (Nwk) **Other Lay Position All SS Epis Day Sch Hoboken NJ 2004-** D.

SINGLETON, Lester Brian (Fla) 18120 Southeast 59 Street, Micanopy FL 32667 **Vic Ch Of The H Comm Hawthorne FL 1998-** B Miami FL 1942 s Jack & Edith. Luth TS at Chicago; BA U Chi 1964; MDiv cl SWTS 1967. D 6/17/1967 Bp James Winchester Montgomery P 12/16/1967 Bp Gerald Francis Burrill. m 6/25/1983 Addie L Singleton. S Matthews Ch Mayo FL 1989-1990; Vic Ch Of The Medtr Micanopy FL 1988-2006; Vic S Barn Epis Ch Williston FL 1988-1996; Pryr and Praise Com Dio Milwaukee Milwaukee WI 1975-1979; R S Steph's Ch Racine WI 1970-1979; Cur Emm Epis Ch La Grange IL 1967-1970. Auth, "Bk Revs," *Living Ch*. Cmnty of S Mary, SBL 1966.

SINGLETON, Richard Oliver (Mich) 1520 W River Rd, Scottsville VA 24590 **Vic S Jn's Columbia Columbia VA 2008-** B Pontiac MI 1939 s William &

Lydia. BA MI SU 1961; MA MI SU 1962; MDiv EDS 1965. D 6/29/1965 P 4/1/1966 Bp Richard Stanley Merrill Emrich. m 6/18/1960 Sharron Loretta Singleton c 2. Exec Dir Metropltn Chr Coun: Detroit Wndsor Detroit MI 1998-2006; Dn Cathd Of S Jn Providence RI 1986-1998; Dio Rhode Island Providence RI 1986-1998, Ecum Off 1986-1998; R S Aid's Ch Ann Arbor MI 1968-1986; Asst Min S Andr's Ch Ann Arbor MI 1966-1976; Cur S Mich And All Ang Epis Ch Lincoln Pk MI 1965-1966; Ecum Off Dio Michigan Detroit MI 1976-1986. Auth, *Last Words of Resurrected Chr*, S Mary's Press, 1998; Auth, *One Person Exhibit-Photographs*; Auth, *The Radiant Call-Folk Hymns*. Coll of Preachers; Ord of S Lk 1995.

SINISI, Gabriel Arcangelo (Az) 17025 W Aberdeen Dr, Surprise AZ 85374 **R Ch of the Adv Sun City AZ 2005-** B Englewood NJ 1947 s Joseph & Marie. Cert Seton Hall NYU Fairleigh Dickinson Univ 1970; MD U of Guadalajara Guadalajara Jalisco MX 1974; MDiv Sewanee: The U So, TS 1997. D 5/31/1997 Bp Jack Marston Mckelvey P 12/6/1997 Bp John Shelby Spong. m 3/1/1990 Mary B Sinisi c 3. R Ch Of The Adv Sun City W AZ 2006-2015; S Chris's By-The-Sea Epis Ch Key Biscayne FL 1999-2005; R Ch Of The H Sprt Verona NJ 1997-1999. Third Ord, Soc of S Fran 1995. Stdt Body Pres The STUSo 1996. gabesinisi@msn.com

SINK, Thomas Leslie (NJ) Po Box 3010, Pt Pleasant NJ 08742 B Philadelphia PA 1944 s Thomas & Eleanor. MA FD; BA Eliz 1965; STB PDS 1968; PrTS 1969. D 4/20/1968 P 10/1/1968 Bp Alfred L Banyard. m 8/19/1968 Martha Ziegler. P-in-c S Elis's Ortley Bch Mnchstr Twp NJ 1988-1992; Non-par 1984-1987; P-in-c S Raphael The Archangel Brick NJ 1982-1983; Non-par 1969-1981; Asst Chr Ch Toms River Toms River NJ 1968-1969; Int S Lk.

SINNING, Thomas John (Minn) 1517 Rosewood Cir, Alexandria MN 56308 **D Emm Epis Ch Alexandria MN 1987-** B Canton SD 1949 s Thomas & Leona. U of So Dakota. D 10/25/1987 Bp Robert Marshall Anderson. m 8/14/1971 Mary Ann Sinning c 3.

SINNOTT, Lynn (Roch) 2842 Hawks Rd, Wellsville NY 14895 B Philadelphia PA 1947 d Clarence & Stella. BL Elizabethtown Coll 1997; MDiv GTS 2000; DMin Drew U 2008. D 6/9/2000 P 1/10/2001 Bp Michael Whittington Creighton. m 12/19/1970 Peter S Sinnott c 3. Procter Conf Cntr London OH 2016; P-in-c Chr Ch Xenia OH 2013-2017; Int Ch Of The Ascen Bradford PA 2008-2009; R Zion Epis Ch Palmyra NY 2002-2008; Dio Cntrl Pennsylvania Harrisburg PA 2000-2013; Founding Mssnr Gleam Williamsport PA 2000-2001; Chapl Chapl Res 1992-1994.

SINTIM, Hector (NC) 1925 waters DR, Raleigh NC 27610 **P in charge S Steph's Epis Ch Winston Salem NC 2009-** B Ghana 1962 s George & Olivia. LTh St Nich TS 1989; MDiv Shaw DS 2001; MDiv Shaw DS 2001; PhD Trin TS 2005. Trans 10/4/2005 Bp Michael B Curry. c 3. Asst R S Ambroses Ch Raleigh NC 2006-2008; Dioc Coun Dio No Carolina Raleigh NC 2010-2013, Dioc Coun -Mem 2009-2013, Sprtl Advsr 2009-2011.

SIPE, Robert Billie (Ore) 59048 Whitetail Ave., Saint Helens OR 97051 B Weiser ID 1948 s Billie & Margaret. BS U of Idaho 1976; MDiv CDSP 2001. D 5/20/2001 P 12/14/2001 Bp Harry Brown Bainbridge III. m 6/8/1968 Martha W Sipe c 2. Vic Chr Ch S Helens OR 2001-2013.

SIPES, David Sheldon (O) 446 Shepard Rd, Mansfield OH 44907 B Shelby OH 1935 s Irvin & Eleanor. BA Bowling Green St U 1958; BD Bex Sem 1961. D 6/1/1960 P 12/10/1961 Bp Nelson Marigold Burroughs. m 8/27/1960 Margaret L Sipes c 4. Gr Epis Ch Mansfield OH 1961-1998.

SIPPLE, Peter Warren (Pa) 45 Bay View Avenue, Cornwall on Hudson NY 12520 B Cleveland OH 1939 s Elmer & Alice. BA Ya 1962; MA Harv 1964; PhD U CA 1968; MA Grad Theol Un 1969. D 6/9/1973 P 6/1/1974 Bp John Melville Burgess. m 7/18/1964 Margaret Sipple c 2. R Ch Of The Redeem Bryn Mawr PA 2005-2009, 2000-2001, Int R 2000-2001; S Paul's Ch Philadelphia PA 2004; Int S Paul's Epis Ch Philadelphia PA 2003-2004; Epis Cmnty Serv Philadelphia PA 2002-2003, 2001-2002; Dir of Dvlpmt Epis Cmnty Serv Philadelphia PA 2001-2003; Ya Berk New Haven CT 1999-2000; Dir of Dvlpmt Yale DS New Haven CT 1998-2000; Oregon Epis Sch Portland OR 1975-1982; Headmaster Oregon Epis Sch Portland OR 1974-1982. Auth, "Separatism, Assimilation & Interaction: Case of Urban Schools," *NAES Journ*; Auth, "Another Look at Stdt Freedom," *NAES Journ*. Pres, NAES 1981-1984. DD CDSP 2006.

SIRCY, Micheal John (SwFla) D 12/10/2011 Bp Dabney Tyler Smith.

SIRIANI, Laura Eustis (Los) 1221 Wass St, Tustin CA 92780 **Other Lay Position S Paul's Epis Ch Tustin CA 2014-** B Greenville MS 1947 d Harold & Doris. BS Miss U for Wmn 1970; Diac Stds Bloy Hse 2017. D 5/21/2017 Bp Diane Jardine Bruce. m 5/27/1971 Bruce Siriani c 2. Laura@stpauls.org

SIROTA, Victoria R (NY) Cathedral Church of St John the Divine, 1047 Amsterdam Ave, New York NY 10025 **S Jn's Ch Getty Sq Yonkers NY 2016-; Bd Mem Global Wmn Fund 2013-; Chair, Com for a Solitary Dio New York New York NY 2010-** B Oceanside NY 1949 d Henry & Ruth. BMus Ob 1971; MMus Bos 1975; DMA Bos 1981; MDiv Harvard DS 1992. D 6/5/1993 P 9/17/1994 Bp David Elliot Johnson. m 12/21/1969 Robert B Sirota c 2. Cn Pstr and Vic Cathd Of St Jn The Div New York NY 2007-2016; Asst Min Cathd Ch of St. Jn the Div New York NY 2006-2007; Vic Ch Of The H Nativ Baltimore MD

1996-2005; Asst. Prof of Ch Mus Ya Berk New Haven CT 1992-1995; Mssn Strtgy Com Dio Maryland Baltimore MD 2001-2005, Dioc Coun 1997-2000. Auth, "Preaching to the Choir: Claiming the Role of Sacr Mus," Ch Pub, 2006; Auth, "Four Sermons," *The Journ of the AAM*, AAM, 2005; Auth, "From the Chapl (Columns)," *The Amer Org*, AGO, 2000; Auth, "An Exploration of Mus as Theol," *Sacr Imagination: The Arts and Theol Educ*, Theol Educ, 1994. Ord of Urban Missioners 2000; Soc of S Marg 1996. Ecum Serv Awd Cntrl MD Ecum Coun 2002; Excellence in Arts Newington-Cropsey Fndt 2002; Outstanding Ord Mnstry Bp's Awd, Dio MD 2001; Excellence in Tchg Ecum Inst of Theol 1999. vsirota@stjohndivine.org

SISK JR, Edwin Kerr (Ark) 9649 Reeder Pl, Overland Park KS 66214 **Ret 1996-; Ret 1996-** B Detroit MI 1930 s Edwin & Grace. BA MI SU 1955; MDiv Bex Sem 1969. D 6/28/1969 Bp Richard Stanley Merrill Emrich P 1/3/1970 Bp Archie H Crowley. m 3/26/1955 Barbara Sisk c 3. Int S Thos Ch Springdale AR 2002-2004; Int S Jn's Epis Ch Alma MI 2000-2001; Div Of Evang And Ch Growth Dio Arkansas Little Rock AR 1988-1990; S Theo's Epis Ch Bella Vista AR 1986-1996; Chapl S Lk's Hosp Kansas City MO 1981-1982; St Lk's So Chap Overland Pk KS 1981-1982; Dio W Missouri Kansas City MO 1980-1986; Vic S Mich's Epis Ch Independence MO 1980-1986; R Chr Ch Lima OH 1976-1980; Chapl All SS Sch Sioux Falls SD 1971-1973; Cn Calv Cathd Sioux Falls SD 1970-1976; Asst Min All SS Epis Ch Pontiac MI 1969-1970; Stndg Com Dio So Dakota Pierre SD 1973-1974.

✠ SISK, The Rt Rev Mark Sean (NY) PO Box 53, Jefferson NY 12093 B Takoma Park MD 1942 s Robert & Alma. BS U of Maryland 1964; STB GTS 1967; DD GTS 1985; DD GTS 1998; DCL SWTS 1998. D 6/24/1967 Bp William Foreman Creighton P 12/24/1967 Bp Alfred L Banyard Con 4/25/1998 for NY. m 8/31/1963 Karen L Sisk c 3. Bp of New York Dio New York New York NY 1998-2013, 1977-1984; Dn Bexley Seabury Fed Chicago IL 1984-1998; R S Jn's Epis Ch Kingston NY 1973-1977; Asst Chr Ch Bronxville NY 1970-1973; Cur Chr Ch New Brunswick NJ 1967-1969. Soc of S Fran 1967. DL Seabury-Wstrn TS 1998; DD The GTS 1985; Hon Cn Cathd S Jn Div NYC 1977. marksisk@att.net

SISK, Robert Buchanan (Mont) Rr 1 Box 241, Wilsall MT 59086 **D 1973-** B Waterloo IA 1943 s Clyde & Matilda. BA U of Iowa 1965; BD CDSP 1969. D 6/28/1969 P 1/29/1970 Bp Gordon V Smith. m 2/6/1981 Carol K Sisk c 1. Dio Iowa Des Moines IA 1973, 1972, 1971; Cur S Andr's Ch Des Moines IA 1969-1971.

SISSON, Duane (Cal) 2973 California St, Oakland CA 94602 **Asst S Alb's Ch Albany CA 2011-** B Waterloo IA 1938 s Ralph & Cheryl. BA Sioux Falls Coll 1960; MDiv Amer Bapt Sem of the W 1965; Cert California St U 1986; CDSP 1987. D 6/3/1989 P 6/5/1990 Bp William Edwin Swing. m 11/19/2009 Burt Kessler c 2. R S Giles Ch Moraga CA 2001-2010; The Epis Ch Of S Jn The Evang San Francisco CA 2000-2001; Int Ch Of The H Fam Fresno CA 1999-2000; Int S Fran' Epis Ch San Francisco CA 1999; S Anselm's Epis Ch Lafayette CA 1997-1998; Chr Ch Alameda CA 1995-1997; P-in-c S Jn's Epis Ch Oakland CA 1990.

SISSON, Penny Ray (Miss) 414 Turnberry Cir, Oxford MS 38655 **D S Ptr's Ch Oxford MS 2001-** B Alexandria LA 1942 d Henry & Fern. BA U of Mississippi 1964; MA U of Mississippi 1980. D 1/6/2001 Bp Alfred Marble Jr. m 12/27/1964 Edward Sisson.

SITTON, Gary William (Colo) 7695 Quitman St, Westminster CO 80030 B Los Angeles CA 1938 s Boyd & Wilhelmina. AA Pierce Jr Coll 1958; BA California St U Los Angeles 1961; MDiv CDSP 1964. D 9/10/1964 P 3/1/1965 Bp Francis E I Bloy. c 4. S Andr's Epis Ch Ft Lupton CO 1995-2015; Assoc S Thos Epis Ch Denver CO 1992; Dio Colorado Denver CO 1987-1992; Vic S Martha's Epis Ch Westminster CO 1983-1987; P Intsn Epis Ch Denver CO 1981-1982; R S Mk's-In-The-Vlly Epis Los Olivos CA 1966-1976; Cur Gr Epis Ch Glendora CA 1965-1966; Cur S Jude's Epis Par Burbank CA 1964-1965.

SITTS, C Joseph (CFla) 271 New Waterford Pl, Longwood FL 32779 B Ilion NY 1942 s Clifton & Alice. BA Syr 1964; STM Ya Berk 1968. D 6/1/1968 P 12/7/1968 Bp Charles Bowen Persell Jr. m 9/7/1968 Margaret L Jones c 3. Dio Cntrl Florida Orlando FL 1999-2008, Sheriff Chapl 1994-2009, Com 1986-1998, Dir 1984-1985, Police Chapl 1982-1983, Chair 1980-1981; R Epis Ch Of The Resurr Longwood FL 1992-2008; Dio Ohio Cleveland 1982-1992; Chr Epis Ch Warren OH 1977-1993; R S Steph's Ch Schenectady NY 1970-1977; P Ch Of The H Sprt Schenevus NY 1968-1970; S Jas Ch Oneonta NY 1968-1970. Auth, "Var Article".

SIVE, Marian Mae (Alb) PO Box 41, Burnt Hills NY 12027 **Dio Albany Greenwich NY 2014-; Admin Calv Epis Ch Burnt Hills NY 2004-** B Sidney NY 1959 d Walter & Lettie. AAS SUNY Coll of Agriculture and Tech 1979. D 5/31/2014 Bp William Howard Love. m 11/20/1982 Alfred David Sive.

SIVLEY, John Stephen (CPa) 869E Rhue Haus Ln, Hummelstown PA 17036 **Asstg P Cathd Ch Of S Steph Harrisburg PA 2011-; Ther Riegler Shienvold and Assoc Harrisburg PA 2007-** B Memphis TN 1953 s John & Martha. BA Jas Madison U 1974; MDiv Sewanee: The U So, TS 1981; MSW Norfolk St U Norfolk VA 1990. D 6/27/1981 P 4/24/1982 Bp David Keller Leighton Sr. c 1. P Assoc All SS' Epis Ch Hershey PA 1999-2010; Sr Clincl Soc

Worker Philhaven/Lebanon Lebanon PA 1995-2007; Ther Cntr for Chld and Fam Serv Hampton VA 1992-1995; Ther Navy Fam Serv Norfolk VA 1992; P Assoc Chr and S Lk's Epis Ch Norfolk VA 1990-1995; Asst R Ch Of The Gd Shpd Norfolk VA 1982-1987; Cur S Anne's Par Annapolis MD 1981-1982; Mem, Stndg Com Dio Cntrl Pennsylvania Harrisburg PA 2008-2011, Stannding Com 2008-2011, Partnr In Mssn Commision 2006-, Chair, Sprtlty Commision 2004-2008, Mem Partnr in Mssn Cmsn Chair, Casa Dia Proj 2004-. Auth, *Confirmed to Serve.*

SIVRET, David Otis (Me) 46 Oak Lane, Alexander ME 04694 B Augusta ME 1955 s Robert & Hope. BA Bangor TS 1988; MDiv Bangor TS 1998; BD SUNY 1998. D 6/4/1988 P 12/17/1988 Bp Edward Cole Chalfant. m 9/28/1982 Sherry Sivret c 5. S Anne's Ch Calais ME 2006-2010, 2004-2005, R 2004, 2003-2004; Chr Epis Ch Eastport ME 2006, 2004-2005, 2003-2004; Off Of Bsh For ArmdF New York NY 2005; Pension Fund Mltry New York NY 2004-2005; Dio Maine Portland ME 2000-2010; Asst R S Matt's Epis Ch Hallowell ME 1998-2003, Asst 1988-1989; R Chr Ch Coxsackie NY 1995-1998; S Judes Epis Ch Franklin NH 1989-1995; Vic S Jude's Ch Franklin NH 1989-1995; R Trin Epis Ch Tilton NH 1989-1995. SocMary 1989.

SIWEK, Peter Christopher (Chi) 733 Hayes Ave, Oak Park IL 60302 B Jersey City NJ 1972 s Christopher & Barbara. BA U of Notre Dame 1995; MDiv SWTS 2002. D 6/15/2002 P 12/21/2002 Bp Bill Persell. m 1/1/2000 Juan A Perez c 2. Gr Ch Oak Pk IL 2016-2017; P Ch Of The Adv Chicago IL 2009-2015; Vic Cathd Of S Jas Chicago IL 2002-2008.

SIX, George (Los) PO Box 235, Horse Shoe NC 28742 **Mem, Strng Com Mtn Peoples Assembly 2014-; Exec Dir Henderson Cnty NAACP 2012-** B Lyons KS 1934 s Henderson & Helen. BS U of Kansas 1963; BS U of Kansas 1964; MDiv Bex Sem 1967; Cert Cbury Ecum Sch 1983; Cert Amer Mgmt Assn NY 1986; Cert Amer Mgmt Assn NY 1986. D 7/1/1967 P 12/1/1967 Bp Gordon V Smith. m 6/10/1955 Irene C Six c 3. Int and Supply Duties Dio Wstrn No Carolina Asheville NC 1999-2009; Vic Chr The King A Jubilee Mnstry Palmdale CA 1995-1999; Int Ch Of The Epiph Oak Pk CA 1994; Mssnr Dio Los Angeles Los Angeles CA 1993-1994; R The Par Of S Matt Pacific Plsds CA 1991-1992; R and Hd Mstr S Phil's Ch Coral Gables FL 1984-1991; CODE 1980-1983; Archd Dio Arizona Phoenix AZ 1980-1983, Mem, Dioc Coun 1980-1983, Chair, Dioc Missions 1976-1979; Area Dn Colorado River Mnstry 1977-1980; R S Paul's Ch Yuma AZ 1977-1980; Sprtl Dir, Curs 1970-1988; R Trin Ch Muscatine IA 1969-1977; P-in-c S Alb's Ch Sprt Lake IA 1967-1969; Trst Bex Sem Columbus OH 1986-1997; Dep, GC Dio Iowa Des Moines IA 1976, Chr Comm Bp Search, Dioc Coun 1973.

SIZE, Patricia Barrett (Mil) 2215 Commonwealth Ave, Madison WI 53726 B Camden New Jersey 1945 d John & Mary. BS U of Pennsylvania 1970; MS U of Wisconsin 1978; MDiv SWTS 2000. D 5/20/2000 P 12/2/2000 Bp Roger John White. m 12/30/1972 Timothy Size c 4. Gr Ch Madison WI 2004-2010; Assoc R S Andr's Ch Madison WI 2000-2003.

SKAGGS, Richard Lee (WVa) 1410 Chapline St, Wheeling WV 26003 **Bd Mem Chld's Hm of Wheeling Bd. of Dir 2013-; Bd Mem Sandscrest Fndt Inc Wheeling WV 2013-; Bd Mem Faith in Action Caregivers Bd. of Dir 2010-; Asst S Matt's Ch Wheeling WV 2007-; Chair of Cmsn on Sprtlty Dio W Virginia Charleston WV 2008-** B Wheeling WV 1947 s William & Dorothy. BA W Liberty St Coll 1970; MA Wheeling Jesuit U 1990. D 6/11/1991 Bp John Henry Smith P 9/14/2004 Bp William Michie Klusmeyer. P St. Jn's Chap 1991-2017.

SKALA, Kira (Va) 241 Signal Ridge Ln, Winchester VA 22603 B Middletown NY 1963 d Robert & Elizabeth. BS Shenandoah U 1985; MDiv VTS 2001. D 6/23/2001 P 12/28/2001 Bp Peter J Lee. m 7/29/2006 Timothy Skinner c 1. R Emm Epis Ch Delaplane Delaplane VA 2003-2009; Asst R Emm Ch Middleburg VA 2001-2003.

SKALESKI, Elizabeth Harris (Ct) **S Jn's Ch Stamford CT 2009-** B Norwalk CT 1956 d Arthur & Norine. BMus Wstrn Connecticut St U 1985. D 9/12/2009 Bp Andrew Donnan Smith. m 9/21/1985 Robert A Skaleski c 3.

SKAU, Laurie Jean (Minn) 6727 France Ave N, Brooklyn Center MN 55429 **Chapl Presb Hm In Lake Minnetonka 1991-** B Duluth MN 1953 d Vernon & Ethel. S Lk Sch 1977; BA Coll of St Scholastica 1980; MDiv Bex Sem 1985. D 6/24/1985 P 7/1/1986 Bp Robert Marshall Anderson. Presb Hm Of Minnesota St Paul MN 1992-1995; Coordntr Of The Aids Mnstry Dio Minnesota Minneapolis MN 1990-1991; R H Trin Intl Falls MN 1986-1989; Chapl Intern U Chi Med Cntr Chicago IL 1985-1986. ACPE.

SKAUG, Jon (Az) B 1940 BSEd U of Nebraska 1963. D 1/23/2010 Bp Kirk Stevan Smith. m 7/24/1980 Catherine Nourie-Skaug c 3.

SKEATES, Winifred June (NH) 270 Stark Hwy N, Dunbarton NH 03046 B Worcester MA 1958 d Ernest & Nancy. BA Bates Coll 1981; MTS Harvard DS 1985. D 6/6/2015 P 12/12/2015 Bp A Robert Hirschfeld. c 1. Vic H Cross Epis Ch Weare NH 2016-2017; Ch Of S Jn The Evang Dunbarton NH 2015-2017.

SKEITH, Paul (Tex) SoCo Episcopal Community, 1502 Eva St, Austin TX 78704 B New York NY 1972 s Francis & Mary. M.P.AFF Lyndon B. Johnson Sch of Publ Affrs; Dplma The Iona Sch for Mnstry; BA U of Pennsylvania; J.D

U of Texas Sch of Law. D 6/25/2016 Bp C Andrew Doyle. m 12/11/1999 Minerva Camarena Skeith c 2.

SKELLEN, Bonnie Jean (NwPa) 425 E Main St, Ridgway PA 15853 B Rochester NY 1946 d Robert & Shirley. D 1/27/1996 Bp Robert Deane Rowley Jr. c 2. Gr Epis Ch Ridgway PA 2006-2007, D 1996-.

SKELLY, Herbert Cope (Mass) 40 Woodland Way, Eastham MA 02642 **Ret 2000-** B Dover NH 1935 s Alexander & Mary. BA U of New Hampshire 1957; MDiv EDS 1961. D 6/15/1961 P 12/16/1961 Bp Charles Francis Hall. m 8/26/1961 Margaret Conant Sheldon c 3. The Ch Of The H Sprt Orleans MA 1987-1993; Int Ch Of The Gd Shpd Clinton MA 1986-1988; Asst S Jn's Ch Worcester MA 1984-1986; Supply P Dio Wstrn Massachusetts Springfield 1971-1984; Vic Trin Ch N Scituate RI 1964-1970; Vic S Chris's Ch Plaistow NH 1963-1964; Cur Ch Of The Gd Shpd Nashua NH 1961-1963. Auth, "An Adv Event," Morehouse-Barlow.

SKIDMORE, Joanne Louise (FdL) 2389 Penny Lane, Sister Bay WI 54234 **Mem, Dioc Transition Team Dio Fond du Lac Appleton WI 2017-, Mem, Cmsn on Congrl Vitality 2015-2017** B Schenectady NY 1950 d Burton & Marjorie. Montana St U; San Jose St U; SWTS; BA WA SU 1973; MA Chapman U 1976; MDiv SWTS 1998. D 6/27/1998 Bp Charles I Jones III P 1/17/1999 Bp Frank Tracy Griswold III. m 7/8/1972 David P Skidmore c 1. P-in-c S Jn The Div Epis Ch Burlington WI 2001-2013; Asst P St Mths Epis Ch Waukesha WI 1998-2000; Chair, Cmsn on Mssn and Dvlpmt Dio Milwaukee Milwaukee WI 2009-2012.

SKIFFINGTON, Steven Wayne (NCal) Trinity Cathedral, 2620 Capitol Ave, Sacramento CA 95816 **Cathd D Trin Epis Cathd Sacramento CA 2013-; Cmsn on Intercultural Mnstrs The Epis Dio Nthrn California Sacramento CA 2010-** B Oakland CA 1946 s John & Rita. MA Calif. St Univ., Sacramento 1997; BDS Epis Sch for Deacons 2013; BDS Epis Sch for Deacons 2013. D 6/8/2013 Bp Barry Leigh Beisner. m 8/21/2008 Nelson Conolly Lucas c 2. deaconskiff@gmail.com

SKILLICORN, Gerald Amos (WMo) 2207 Conrad Way, Somerset NJ 08873 B Watsonville CA 1930 s Walter & Thelma. B.A. U CA-Berkeley 1953; STB GTS 1956. D 7/1/1956 P 1/12/1957 Bp Karl M Block. m 5/16/1969 Melisande Skillicorn. S Paul's Epis Ch Lees Summit MO 1990-1995; R Ch Of The Epiph Kirkwood S Louis MO 1987-1989; R S Paul's Epis Ch St Jos MI 1981-1987; Asst S Hilary's Ch Prospect Hts IL 1976-1980; Non-par 1970-1975; Asst All SS Epis Ch San Leandro CA 1962-1965; R S Fran' Epis Ch Turlock CA 1958-1962; Cur The Epis Ch Of S Mary The Vrgn San Francisco CA 1956-1958.

SKILLINGS, Thomas (Cal) 1104 Mills Ave, Burlingame CA 94010 **R S Paul's Epis Ch Burlingame CA 2002-** B Greenbrae CA 1959 s Thomas & Helen. Diablo Vlly Coll 1983; BA California St U 1986; MDiv Ya Berk 1989. D 6/3/1989 P 6/9/1990 Bp William Edwin Swing. m 1/4/1992 Julie Ann Graham c 1. S Mich And All Ang Concord CA 1993-2002; Assoc R S Paul's Epis Ch Walnut Creek CA 1989-1993.

✠ SKILTON, The Rt Rev William Jones (DR) 4969 Parkside Dr, North Charleston SC 29405 **Bp Asst Epis Ch In Dominican Republic 2008-** B Havana CU 1940 s William & Blandina. BS Cit 1962; LTh Sewanee: The U So, TS 1965; U So 1999. D 7/10/1965 Bp Gray Temple P 1/26/1966 Bp Paul Axtell Kellogg Con 3/2/1996 for SC. m 2/4/2017 Deborah Causey c 2. Bp Suffr So Carolina Charleston SC 1996-2006, Bp Coun 1991-1995, Stndg Com 1988-1990, Bp Coun 1982-1985, Bp Coun 1978-1980, Bp Coun 1973-1976, Campus Min 1972-1976, Mem, Dioc Coun 1991-1994, Mem, Stndg Com 1988-1991; R S Thos Epis Ch N Charleston SC 1988-1996; Vic/Chapl Epifania Centro de Estudios Teologicos Dominican Republic 1985-1988; R H Trin Epis Ch Charleston SC 1976-1985; The Ch Of The Cross Bluffton SC 1972-1973; Vic, Sch Dir Todos los Santos Ch and Sch La Romana D.R. 1965-1972; Mem, Exec Coun Dio The Dominican Republic (Iglesia Epis Dominicana) Gazcue Santo Domingo 1965-1972. DD Cit, the Mltry Coll of SC 2006; Doctor in Div U So, Sewanee, Tenn. 2001.

SKINNER, Beatrice (SD) B Bullhead SD 1936 d Michael & Olivia. D 6/22/2007 Bp Creighton Leland Robertson.

SKINNER, Jean Mary (CNY) 40 Faxton St, Utica NY 13501 B 1945 d Ralph & Virginia. BS SUNY 1977. D 11/19/2005 Bp Gladstone Bailey Adams III.

SKINNER, Susan (Mo) 400 Mark Dr, Saint Louis MO 63122 B Lexington KY 1941 AB Transylvania U 1962; MEd U of Missouri 1976; MDiv Eden TS 1979. D 6/7/1980 Bp Morris Fairchild Arnold P 6/11/1981 Bp John Bowen Coburn. c 1. Int Ch Of The Gd Shpd S Louis MO 2010-2011; Int S Mart's Ch Ellisville MO 2007-2010; Int S Matt's Epis Ch Warson Woods Kirkwood MO 2005-2006; Cn Chr Ch Cathd S Louis MO 2004-2005; Epis City Mssn St Louis MO 2002-2006; Epis City Mssn St. Louis MO 2002-2006; P-in-c S Jn's Ch W Point VA 2001-2002; R Emm Epis Ch Webster Groves MO 1996-2001; R Emm Epis Ch S Louis MO 1981-2001; Assoc Emm Epis Ch Webster Groves MO 1981-1996; GC; ST. Comm. St of The Ch Dom And Frgn Mssy Soc-Epis Ch Cntr New York NY 1997, GC; PB&F;Ex. Com 1994-1997, GC; Dispatch of Bus 1984-2013; Chair; COM Dio Missouri S Louis MO 1995-1997,

Com to Elect a Bp 1990-1991, Pres, Stndg Com 1987-1988, Pres, Stndg Com 1986-1987, Dep, GC 1984-2003. scskinner@charter.net

✠ SKIRVING, The Rt Rev Robert Stuart (EC) Episcopal Diocese of East Carolina, PO Box 1336, Kinston NC 28503 B Windsor Ontario Canada 1960 s Archibald & Anne. Cert SWTS; BA U of Waterloo 1982; MDiv Hur CA 1986. Trans 1/1/2005 Bp Edwin Max Leidel Jr Con 11/8/2014 for EC. m 10/4/1986 Sandra F Skirving c 2. Dio E Carolina Kinston NC 2014, Bp 2014-; R S Jn's Epis Ch Midland MI 2004-2014; P/R Serv Angl Ch of Can 1986-2004; Dn Dio Estrn Michigan Saginaw MI 2011-2014. DD The U So 2015. rskirving@diocese-eastcarolina.org

SKOGLUND, Lars David Jacob (Mil) D 6/11/2016 Bp Steven Andrew Miller.

SKORNIK, Andria (Chi) St Andrew's Episcopal Church, 1125 Franklin St, Downers Grove IL 60515 **Emm Epis Ch Rockford IL 2014-** B Wichita KS 1983 d Raymond & Janet. BA Warner Pacific Coll; BA U of Oregon 2008; MDiv U Chi DS 2011. D 11/27/2011 P 10/18/2012 Bp Jeff Lee. m 6/24/2006 Jordan E Skornik c 1. Cur S Andr's Ch Downers Grove IL 2012-2014.

SKRAMSTAD, Dawn Marie (Alb) St. Mary's Church, P.O. Box 211, Lake Luzerne NY 12846 B Corinth NY 1956 D 6/11/2005 Bp Daniel William Herzog. m 10/8/2004 Lawrence Skramstad c 2.

SKUTCH, Patrick J (Chi) 306 S Prospect Ave, Park Ridge IL 60068 **S Mary's Ch Pk Ridge IL 2015-** B Savannah GA 1979 s Janison & Marie. BA U GA 2002; MDiv GTS 2005. D 12/21/2004 P 7/31/2005 Bp J Neil Alexander. m 6/8/2002 Bonny E Skutch c 2. Chr Ch Bay S Louis MS 2009-2015; S Mart In The Fields Ch Atlanta GA 2005-2009.

SKYLES, Benjamin Henry (Tex) 2110 Canyon Lake Dr, Deer Park TX 77536 B Des Moines IA 1934 s Jack & Bernice. BA U of Texas 1955; BD Epis TS of the SW 1958; MA U of Houston 1974. D 6/1/1958 Bp Frederick P Goddard P 6/10/1959 Bp James Parker Clements. m 8/5/2006 Mary Wood c 5. S Ptr's Ch Pasadena TX 1964-1999; Assoc S Mk's Ch Beaumont TX 1961-1964; Min in charge S Thos' Epis Ch Rockdale TX 1958-1961; Stndg Com Dio Texas Houston TX 1983-1986, ExCoun 1969-1982. Auth, *Alive Now*; Auth, "arts," *Epis*; Auth, *From the Belly of the Great Fish*; Auth, *Tell Us of the Morning*. Distinguished Alum Awd Epis Sem of the SW 2006; DD Epis TS of the SW 1983; Rel Serv Awd Natl Conf Ch & Jews.

SLABACH, Brock Allen (WMo) 16808 S State Route D, Belton MO 64012 B Topeka KS 1960 s Kenneth & Lois. D 11/4/2016 Bp Martin Scott Field.

SLACK, James Cooper Simmons (Dal) 1019 Sassafras Lane, Niles MO 49120 **R S Matt's 1995-** B St Louis MO 1937 s Morris & Dorthy. BA Earlham Coll 1959; LTh SWTS 1964. D 6/27/1964 Bp Hamilton Hyde Kellogg P 4/9/1965 Bp Philip Frederick McNairy. m 8/31/1963 Karen M Slack c 3. S Chas The Mtyr Daingerfield TX 1998; R S Dav's Ch Gilmer TX 1998; St Mk's Epis Ch Mt Pleasant TX 1997-2007; S Matthews Epis Ch Mex MO 1994-1997; S Phil's Ch Circleville OH 1977-1994; Bi Par Mnstry Addyston OH 1972-1976; R Tri-Par Mnstry W Cincinnati OH 1972-1976; Vic S Jn Minneapolis MN 1966-1972; Vic S Jn Olivia MN 1966-1972; Vic S Columba White Earth MN 1964-1966.

SLACK, Sean C (Pa) St Paul's Church, 89 Pinewood Dr, Levittown PA 19054 **All SS Epis Ch Levittown PA 2012-; P-in-c S Paul Ch Levittown PA 2012-** B Doylestown PA 1972 s Paul & Barbara. MA U of Notre Dame 1994; MDiv EDS 2010. D 6/9/2012 Bp Charles Ellsworth Bennison Jr P 1/12/2013 Bp Edward Lewis Lee Jr.

SLADE, Debra Katherine Ann (Ct) 503 Old Long Ridge Rd, Stamford CT 06903 **Dir of Sprtl Care Norwalk Hosp Norwalk CT 2011-; Asst S Fran Ch Stamford CT 2009-** B 1957 d Donald & Evelyn. BA U of Manitoba 1978; MA U of Manitoba 1981; BA Oxf GB 1983; MA Oxf GB 1998; Cert Ang Stud Ya Berk 2008; MDiv Yale DS 2008. D 6/13/2009 Bp Andrew Donnan Smith P 1/2/2010 Bp James Elliot Curry. m 3/14/1986 Peter Kent c 2.

SLADE, Kara Nicole (NC) Saint David's Episcopal Church, PO Box 334, Laurinburg NC 28353 **Grad Asst Duke Durham NC 2013-; Bp's Advsry Com on Med Ethics Dio No Carolina Raleigh NC 2014-; Bd Dir Soc of Schlr-Priests 2014-** B Pensacola FL 1972 d Philip & Nancy. BSE Duke 1994; BSE Duke 1994; MS Duke 1996; MDiv Duke 2000; PhD Duke 2000; MDiv Duke DS 2012. D 11/24/2012 Bp Philip Menzie Duncan II P 7/1/2013 Bp Michael B Curry. Vic S Dav's Epis Ch Laurinburg NC 2014-2016. Soc of Schlr-Priests 2014. kara.slade@duke.edu

SLAKEY, Anne Elisa Margaret (Ida) 110 N. 10th St., Payette ID 83661 **Assoc S Paul's Epis Ch Sacramento CA 2111-; D St Marys Ch Elk Grove Sacramento CA 2002-** B Annapolis MD 1964 d Thomas & Marion. BA S Johns Coll Santa Fe NM 1988; MA Iowa St U 1993; MDiv CDSP 2002. D 11/16/2002 Bp Roger John White P 9/29/2003 Bp Gethin Benwil Hughes. S Jas Ch Payette ID 2008-2010; S Thos Ch Canyon City OR 2006; S Matt's Epis Ch Ontario OR 2005-2008.

SLANE, Christopher DuTeil (Neb) **Emm Epis Ch S Louis MO 2017-** D 4/27/2014 Bp Scott Scott Barker.

SLANE, Melanie W (Mo) 3737 Seminary Rd, Alexandria VA 22304 **Emm Epis Ch S Louis MO 2014-** B St. Louis MO 1986 d Stephen & Lisa. BSBA The U of Missouri; MDiv VTS 2013. D 12/21/2012 P 6/21/2013 Bp George Wayne

Smith. m 9/2/2012 Christopher DuTeil Slane. The Ch Of The Epiph Washington DC 2013-2014.

SLANGER, George Comfort (ND) 8435 207th St. W., Lakeville MN 55044 B Big Timber MT 1937 s Benjamin & Josephine. BS Montana St U 1959; MA San Francisco St U 1965; PhD U of Washington 1976. D 10/8/2000 P 5/21/2001 Bp Andrew Fairfield. m 11/28/1980 Joanne Mary Slanger c 4.

SLATER, Amy A (Fla) **Assoc S Mary's Epis Ch Arlington VA 2017-** B Jacksonville FL 1964 d T Edward & Patricia. BA U of Florida 1985; MDiv VTS 2014. D 12/8/2013 P 6/15/2014 Bp Samuel Johnson Howard. m 5/10/1986 Thomas F Slater c 2. Assoc Chr Epis Ch Ponte Vedra FL 2016-2017; Chapl Dio Florida Jacksonville 2014-2016. amy.slater@stmarysarlington.org

SLATER, Chadwick M (WVa) 200 Duhring St, Bluefield WV 24701 **Chr Ch Bluefield WV 2013-; Ecum Off Dio W Virginia Charleston WV 2014-** B Charleston WV 1982 s Larry & Rigenia. BA W Virginia Wesleyan Coll 2004; MDiv Bex 2013; MDiv Bex Sem 2013. D 12/19/2012 P 8/24/2013 Bp William Michie Klusmeyer. m 4/9/2005 Jennifer L Slater c 2.

SLATER, Joan (NMich) PO Box100, Mackinac Island MI 49757 B 1955 D 2/7/2001 P 8/12/2001 Bp James Arthur Kelsey.

SLATER, Jo Ann Kennedy (Mich) 5416 Parkgrove Rd, Ann Arbor MI 48103 **R S Lk's Epis Ch Ypsilanti MI 2006-, P-in-c 2001-2006** B Indianapolis IN 1953 d John & Mary. BA Pur 1974; MA DePaul U 1975; DMin Chicago TS 1990; JD U MI 2001. D 6/19/1993 P 12/18/1994 Bp R aymond Stewart Wood Jr. Asst S Andr's Ch Ann Arbor MI 1995-1998; Asst Dio Michigan Detroit MI 1993-1994, Asst 1993-1994, Asst 1992-1993, Trst 2010-. AAR; ABA; Coll for Theol Soc; SBL.

SLATER, Michael (Nev) 7900 Pueblo Drive, Stagecoach NV 89429 **Co-Chair Natl Assn of InterChurch & Interfaith Families 1996-** B Romford England 1942 City of London Coll 1970; DIT ETSBH 2003; MDiv Claremont TS 2006. D 7/16/2005 Bp Joseph Jon Bruno. m 4/12/1986 Barbara Slater. Epis Outreach-Silver Sprg, Stagecoach, & Dayton NV Dio Nevada Las Vegas 2010-2011; Ad Hoc Ecum & Interreligious Off 2009-; D S Paul's Ch Virginia City NV 2009; D S Jn The Div Epis Ch Costa Mesa CA 2005-2007.

SLATER, Sarah Elizabeth (WA) **Chapl S Andr's Epis Sch Potomac MD 2015-** B Phoenix AZ 1961 d Robert & Favour. BA U of Arizona 1982; BA U of Arizona 1982; MS Syr 1983; MS Syr 1983; MSW Syr 1994; MSW Syr 1994; MDiv, Angl Cert Ya Berk 2014; MDiv, Angl Cert Yale DS/Berkely DS 2014. D 12/7/2013 P 6/14/2014 Bp Mariann Edgar Budde.

SLATER, Scott Gerald (Md) 4 East University Parkway, Baltimore MD 21218 **Dio Maryland Baltimore MD 2010-** B Long Beach CA 1960 s Gerald & Helen. BLA U of Florida 1981; MACE VTS 1992; MDiv VTS 1992; DMin Columbia TS 2000. D 6/20/1992 P John Wadsworth Howe P 1/7/1993 Bp James Barrow Brown. m 10/12/1985 Rebecca M Slater c 2. Cn to the Ordnry Ch Of The Gd Shpd Towson MD 2010; VTS Alexandria VA 2001, 1998; Assoc S Columba's Ch Washington DC 1996-2001; Assoc S Lk's Epis Ch Birmingham AL 1993-1996; Chapl S Mart's Epis Sch Metairie LA 1992-1993; Root Grp Coordntr Dio Cntrl Florida Orlando FL 1983-1985; Yth Min H Trin Epis Ch Melbourne FL 1985-1989. Contributing Ed, "Epis Curric for Yth," Morehouse, 1996; Auth, "Shopping for the Rt Ch," *Living On,* Living Ch, 1995; Auth, "Antique Bible Proves Popular Among Chld...," *Epis Tchr,* VTS, 1993; Contrib, "Epis Chld Curric," Morehouse, 1992. Maryland Epis Cler Assn 2003-2009; Washington Epis Cler Assn 1996-2000. sslater@episcopalmaryland.org

SLAUGHTER, Susan (FtW) 1612 Boardwalk Ct, Arlington TX 76011 **D S Lk's In The Meadow Epis Ch Ft Worth TX 2009-, R 2009-** B St. Louis MO 1942 d Max & Mary. BA Sam Houston St U 1975; MEd U of No Texas 1981; Cert Angl TS 2002. D 10/12/2002 Bp Jack Leo Iker P 11/15/2009 Bp Ted Gulick Jr. c 4.

S

SLAUSON, Holley B (NY) 75 de Maio Dr Apt B12, Milford CT 06460 **Par of St Paul's Ch Norwalk Norwalk CT 1998-** B Norwalk CT 1942 s Holley & Frances. BA Wstrn Connecticut St U 1971; MDiv GTS 1977. D 3/19/1977 P 5/19/1978 Bp Morgan Porteus. R S Anne's Ch Washingtonville NY 1984-1987, R 1982-1987, Vic 1977-1982; Epis. Comm Of Cntrl Orange Goshen NY 1979-1983; S Dav's Ch Highland Mls NY 1979-1982; St Johns Ch W Hartford CT 1977-1979.

SLAWNWHITE, Virginia Ann (NH) Po Box 433, Portsmouth NH 03802 **Chapl Wentworth-Douglass Hosp Dover NH 1997-** B Lynn MA 1941 d Clifford & Vera. D 11/1/1997 Bp Douglas Edwin Theuner. m 5/7/1961 Stephen C Slawnwhite. D The Ch Of The Redeem Rochester NH 1998-2000.

SLAWSON III, H Thomas (Md) 3695 Rogers Avenue, Ellicott City MD 21043 **Nave Chapl Washington Natl Cathd 2013-; R S Ptr's Epis Ch Ellicott City MD 2012-** B Memphis TN 1955 s Henry & Marion. BA U of Tennessee 1978; MDiv SWTS 1985. D 6/30/1985 P 5/11/1986 Bp William Evan Sanders. m 11/1/2013 Sonja Darlene Wells c 2. R S Phil's Ch Jackson MS 1996-2010; Assoc S Paul's Epis Ch Meridian MS 1991-1996; Vic H Innoc' Epis Ch Como MS 1986-1991; Ch Of The Epiph Tunica MS 1986-1989; D-In-Trng Gr Ch Chattanooga TN 1985-1986. tom@stpetersec.org

SLAY, Pearlean Boykin (Ala) D 10/1/2016 Bp John Mckee Sloan Sr.

SLAYMAKER, Lorraine P (Ark) 1112 Alcoa Rd, Benton AR 72015 **P-in-c Gr Ch Pine Bluff AR 2015-; Vic S Matt's Epis Ch Benton AR 2008-** B Hartford CT 1956 d Fred & Phyllis. BS U of Connecticut 1978; BS Montana St U 1990; MDiv Epis TS of the SW 1999. D 5/29/1999 Bp Charles I Jones III P 2/2/2000 Bp Larry Maze. m 5/16/1981 William D Slaymaker c 2. Cur S Lk's Ch Hot Sprg AR 1999-2003.

SLAYTER, Malcolm Franklin (NwT) 2809 Moss Ave, Midland TX 79705 **Ret 1984-; Cmsn on Mininstry Epis Ch in Guam Guam 1978-** B Boston MA 1920 s John & Helen. BA Omaha U 1957; MA Omaha U 1959; MA S Marys Sem and U Baltimore MD 1973; DMin GTF 1988. D 1/15/1975 Bp Paul Saneaki Nakamura P 12/1/1976 Bp Benito C Cabanban. m 9/3/1962 Fumiko O Slayter c 4. Assoc S Nich Epis Ch Midland TX 1980-1984; S Nich' Epis Ch Midland TX 1980-1983; Dio Micronesia Tumon Bay GU 1977-1980; Chapl S Jn Preparatory Sch Agana Guam 1977-1980; Brent Intl Sch 1976-1977; Chapl Brent Intl Sch Baguio City Philippines 1976-1977; Asst All Souls Epis Ch Okinawa Japan 1975-1976. Auth, "The Role of an AF Tactical Hosp in Med Air Evacuation," *ArmdF Med Journ.*

SLEMMER, Amy Whitcomb (Mass) D 6/3/2017 Bp Gayle Harris.

SLEMP, Dennett Clinton (SVa) 11001 Ashburn Rd, North Chesterfield VA 23235 **Pstr Counslr Assoc Stff VA Inst Pstr Care Richmond VA 1992-** B Washington DC 1932 s Patton & Dorothy. BA JHU 1957; MDiv VTS 1961; Inst of Rel Houston TX 1967; STM Epis TS of the SW 1968. D 6/26/1961 P 6/27/1962 Bp William Henry Marmion. m 6/22/1957 Mary Slemp c 2. F-t Stff VA Inst Pstr Care Richmond VA 1973-1992; Virginia Inst Of Pstr Care Richmond VA 1973-1991; Assoc Stff VA Inst Pstr Care Richmond VA 1970-1973; Vic Epis Ch Of Our Sav Midlothian VA 1968-1973; Vic Par Botetourt Cnty VA 1962-1966. Diplomate AAPC 1970.

SLENSKI, Mary (Ind) 5256 Central Ave., Indianapolis IN 46220 **Int Gr Ch Oak Pk IL 2017-; Pres Int Mnstrs of Epis Ch 2015-; Stndg Com Dio Indianapolis Indianapolis IN 2014-** B Detroit MI 1958 d Joseph & Judith. BSE U of Florida 1980; MBA Wright St U 1990; MDiv EDS 2008. D 6/14/2008 P 6/20/2009 Bp Thomas Edward Breidenthal. m 11/8/1980 George Slenski c 2. Int Ch Of The Nativ Indianapolis IN 2014-2016; Int S Steph's Ch Terre Haute IN 2013-2014; Sabbatical Supply Trin Ch Lawrenceburg IN 2012; Asst to the R Chr Epis Ch Dayton OH 2010-2012, Asst 2010, 2010-; S Paul's Epis Ch New Albany IN 2010-2012; Monthly supply P S Paul's Epis Ch Greenville OH 2010; Asst S Mk's Epis Ch Dayton OH 2008-2010; Advsry Commmittee on Compstn and Resources Dio Sthrn Ohio Cincinnati OH 2008-2012. Int Mnstry Ntwk 2010. rev.maryslenski@gmail.com

SLIGH, John Lewis (SeFla) 2422 W Stroud Ave, Tampa FL 33629 **Non-par 1987-** B Washington DC 1951 s John & Norma. Juilliard Sch 1970; BA U GA 1974; MDiv Nash 1977. D 2/14/1977 Bp George Paul Reeves P 10/1/1978 Bp William Carl Frey. Cur S Benedicts Ch Ft Lauderdale FL 1985-1987; P-in-c S Lk's Epis Ch Ft Collins CO 1980-1983, Cur 1978-1979; Nash Nashotah WI 1977-1978; Tchr'S Asst Nash WI 1977-1978.

SLOAN III OJN, Carey Erastus (O) 2390 N Orchard Rd NE, Bolivar OH 44612 B Atlanta GA 1940 s Carey & Mildred. BA Duke 1962; MDiv VTS 1965; DMin IAPS 1984. D 6/29/1965 P 6/29/1966 Bp Thomas Augustus Fraser Jr. m 9/26/1981 Katherine L Sloan c 2. R S Mk's Ch Canton OH 1976-2007; R S Paul's Ch Henderson KY 1967-1976; S Lk's Ch Salisbury NC 1966-1967; R S Matt Ch Salisbury NC 1966-1967; D-in-C S Jn's Ch Battleboro NC 1965-1966; S Mich's Ch Tarboro NC 1965-1966. Auth, *The Secret of the Rose,* St Marks, 1993; Auth, *The Meaning of a Secular Soc,* St Marks, 1992; Auth, *If We Could Talk to the Animals,* St Marks, 1991; Auth, *How to Improve Your Score,* St Marks, 1989; Auth, *Use of Humor in Par Ch,* 1985. Ord of Julian of Norwich 1988. R Emer St Marks Epis Ch, Canton OH 2008.

SLOAN, Ellen Margaret (SwFla) St. Michael & All Angels, 2304 Periwinkle Way, Sanibel FL 33957 **R Ch Of S Mich And All Ang Sanibel FL 2009-; Chair of COM Dio SW Florida Parrish FL 2011-** B New Bedford MA 1950 d William & Rosemary. BS Plymouth St U 1972; MA Dart 1977; PhD U of Connecticut 1996; MDiv GTS 2002. D 6/1/2002 Bp Rufus T Brome P 12/7/2002 Bp John Palmer Croneberger. m 12/26/1993 Ralph Edward Sloan c 2. Chapl/Dn of Cmnty The GTS New York NY 2005-2009, Bd Trst 2013-2015; Assoc Chr Ch Ridgewood NJ 2002-2004; Prof/Grad Sch U of Connecticut 1993-1998; Dir/Accreditation New Engl Assoc. of Schools/Colleges 1985-1993; ESL Amer Sch of The Hague 1982-1985; ESL Escuela Bella Vista Venezuela 1980-1982. Auth, "Strategies for Fostering Partnerships Between Educators and Hlth Professionals," *Boundary Crossings,* Jossey-Bass, 1997; Auth, "Interns as legitimate Participants in the Cmnty of Pract," *Journ of Sch Ldrshp,* Technomic, 1996. Cmsn on Wmn 2000-2009; Pine Manor Improvement Assoc. 2012; SIM 2012; ZONTA Intl 2010. rector@saintmichaels-sanibel.org

✠ SLOAN SR, The Rt Rev John Mckee (Ala) 521 North 20th Street, Birmingham AL 35203 **Bp of Alabama Dio Alabama Birmingham 2012-, Bp Suffr of Alabama 2007-2012, Stndg Com 1999-2003, Dioc Coun 1995-1998** B Vicksburg MS 1955 s Richard & Mary. BA Mississippi St U 1976; MDiv Sewanee: The U So, TS 1981. D 5/16/1981 P 5/29/1982 Bp Duncan Montgomery Gray Jr Con 1/12/2008 for Ala. m 10/3/1987 Tina B Sloan c 2. R St Thos Epis Ch

Huntsville AL 1993-2007; Asst S Ptr's Ch Oxford MS 1990-1993; All SS Epis Ch Grenada MS 1987-1990; Vic Epis Ch Of The Incarn W Point MS 1983-1986; Cur H Cross Epis Ch Olive Branch MS 1981-1983; Exec Com Dio Mississippi Jackson MS 1985-1989, Gray Cntr Bd 1973-1977. ksloan@dioala. org

SLOAN, Richard D (NY) 90 Gilbert Road, Ho-Ho-Kus NJ 07423 **Col Dio New York New York NY 1993-** B Weymouth MA 1948 s Walter & Ruth. BA Rutgers The St U of New Jersey 1970; MDiv PDS 1973; JD Pace U 1979. D 5/11/1974 Bp Frederick Hesley Belden P 11/16/1974 Bp George E Rath. m 9/7/1974 Carolyn K Kennedy c 2. Int S Steph's Ch Armonk NY 2008-2009; R Gr Epis Ch Monroe NY 1988-1994; Asst S Eliz's Ch Ridgewood NJ 1977-1981; Cur S Paul's Ch Pawtucket RI 1974-1976. Gld of S Ives 1997; Soc of the Magi 2000. Bp's Cross Dio New York 2001.

SLOAN, Stan Jude (Chi) 2313 N Kedzie Blvd # 2, Chicago IL 60647 B Guthrie OK 1963 s Bob & Mary. BS Oklahoma St U 1985; MDiv U of S Mary of the Lake Mundelein Sem 1991; MA Weston Jesuit TS 1992. Rec 6/1/1997 as Priest Bp Frank Tracy Griswold III. ReVive Cntr for Hsng and Healing Chicago IL 1998-2000; Vic S Geo/S Mths Ch Chicago IL 1997-1999; Epis Chars And Cmnty Serv (Eccs) Chicago IL 1997-1998. Chicago Cltn For The Homeless Bd; Ecum Coun; Westhaven Dvlpmt Bd.

SLOAN, Susan Pullen (Ala) 821 Baylor Drive, Huntsville AL 35802 **R S Steph's Epis Ch Huntsville AL 2005-; Stndg Com Dio Alabama Birmingham 2013-** B Mobile AL 1949 d Milton & Ernestine. BS U of Alabama 1989; MDiv Sewanee: The U So, TS 1996. D 1/13/1996 P 7/20/1996 Bp Robert Oran Miller. m 3/22/1969 Thomas D Sloan c 2. S Mk's Ch Birmingham AL 2004; Int Gd Shpd Decatur AL 2002-2003; Assoc R S Lk's Epis Ch Birmingham AL 1999-2002; Cn The Cathd Ch Of The Adv Birmingham AL 1996-1999; Trst Sewanee U So TS Sewanee TN 2008-2013. "Epis Chld's Curric," Morehouse. Dioc Coun 2002-2004; Prog Com Kanuga Conf Cntr 2001-2004; SOT Alum Com 2000-2008; Sewanee Alum Coun 2000-2004; Stndg Com 2005-2008; Stndg Com of Dio 1997-2000; Trst, U So 2009-2013. Lowery Serv Awd SOT Sewanee 1996.

SLOCOMBE, Iris Ruth (Mich) APDO Postal 673, Ajijic Jalisco 45920 Mexico **Ret 1995-** B Goodmayes UK 1928 d John & Milla. SRN Poole Gnrl Sch of Nrsng Poole GB 1958; Neath U Sch of Nrsng 1960; MA U of Oklahoma 1962; MDiv Sewanee: The U So, TS 1983. D 5/15/1983 Bp Furman Charles Stough P 5/10/1984 Bp Claude Charles Vache. m 3/27/1948 Albert E Slocombe c 3. Serv Angl Ch of Mex 1995-2005; R Gr Ch Mt Clemens MI 1989-1995; Assoc R S Jn's Epis Ch Memphis TN 1987-1989; Asst R Estrn Shore Chap Virginia Bch VA 1983-1987. Auth, "Adam's Song," *S Lk Journ*, 1983. Altrusa Wmn of the Year - Memphis Altrusa Intl 1989.

SLOCUM, Robert Boak (Lex) PO Box 2505, Danville KY 40423 **Med Prog Coordinatory U of Kentucky 2016-; Narrative Med Prog Coordntr U of Kentucky HealthCare 2015-** B Macon GA 1952 s James & Sara. BA Van 1974; JD Van 1977; MDiv Nash 1986; DMin Sewanee: The U So, TS 1992; PhD Marq 1997. D 6/21/1986 P 5/2/1987 Bp James Barrow Brown. m 4/22/2007 Victoria Slocum c 3. Fac U of Kentucky 2015-2016; Asstg P S Raphael's Ch Lexington KY 2014-2016; R Trin Epis Ch Danville KY 2007-2010; P-in-c Ch Of The H Comm Lake Geneva WI 1993-2002; Chapl (P.T.) VetA 1993-1998; R St Philips Epis Ch Waukesha WI 1991-1992; S Andr's Ch Clinton LA 1987-1991; Vic S Pat's Ch Zachary LA 1987-1991; D-in-Trng Trin Ch New Orleans LA 1986-1987; Ecum Off Dio Lexington Lexington 2009-2011; Dispatch of Bus for Dioc Conv Dio Milwaukee Milwaukee WI 2001-2002. Auth, "The Angl Imagination: Portraits and Sketches of Mod Angl Theologians," Ashgate Pub, Ltd./Routledge (Taylor & Fran Grp), 2015; Auth, "Seeing & Believing, Reflections for Faith, A Devotional Journ," Forw Mvmt, 2013; Co-Ed, "A Point of Balance, The Weight and Measure of Anglicanism," Morehouse Pub/Cbury Press, 2012; Auth, "Light in a Burning-Glass, A Systematic Presentation of the Theol of Austin Farrer," Un.of So. Carolina Press, 2007; Ed, "A Heart for the Future, Writings on the Chr Hope," Ch Publishing, Inc, 2004; Co-Ed, "Discovering Common Mssn; Lutherns & Episcopalians together," Ch Publishing, Inc, 2003; Co-Ed, "To Hear Celestial Harmonies, Essays on Wit of Jas DeKoven and The DeKoven Cntr," Forw Mvmt, 2002; Ed, "Engaging the Sprt, Essays on the Life and Theol of the H Sprt," Ch Pub, Inc, 2001; Co-Ed, "An Epis Dictionary of the Ch," Ch Pub, Inc, 2000; Auth, "The Theol of Wm Porcher DuBose: Life, Mvmt, and Being," Un. of So. Carolina Press, 2000; Ed, "A New Conversation, Essays on the Future of Theol and the Epis Ch," Ch Pub, Inc, 1999; Ed, "Prophet of Justice, Prophet of Life, Essays on Wm Stringfellow," Ch Pub, Inc/Wipf & Stock Pub, 1997; Co-Ed, "Documents of Witness, A Hist of the Epis Ch, 1782-1985," Ch Pub, Inc, 1994.

SLONE, Remington (Fla) 400 San Juan Dr., Ponte Vedra Beach FL 32082 **Assoc Chr Epis Ch Ponte Vedra FL 2013-; Vocare Strng Com Dio Georgia Savannah GA 2012-, Gnrl Ord Exam Rdr 2011-** B Tyler TX 1982 s Thomas & Debra Lynn. AB U GA 2008; MDiv GTS 2011. D 2/11/2011 P 8/20/2011 Bp Scott Anson Benhase. m 5/19/2007 Maria L Gullickson c 3. Asst S Ptr's Epis Ch Savannah GA 2011-2013.

SLOVAK, Anita M (Az) Christ The King Episcopal Church, 2800 W Ina Rd, Tucson AZ 85741 **Chr The King Ch Tucson AZ 2016-** B Johnstown PA 1958 d George & Anna. BA U Pgh 1979; MS U of Texas 1983; MDiv SMU Perkins 2006. D 1/26/2008 P 10/11/2008 Bp James Monte Stanton. m 6/27/1998 Johnny V Slovak c 2. R All SS' Epis Ch Duncan OK 2011-2016; Chapl Cbury Epis Sch Desoto TX 2010-2011; Asst S Nich Ch Flower Mound TX 2010-2011; Cur Ch Of The Gd Shpd Dallas TX 2008-2010; DCE Ch Of The Epiph Richardson TX 2004-2008; Par Mgr S Phil's Epis Ch Frisco TX 2002-2003; Chair - Chr Formation Cmsn Dio Dallas Dallas TX 2006-2011. mtranita@ctktucson.org

SLUSHER, Montie Bearl (Ak) 1133 Park Dr., Fairbanks AK 99709 **D S Matt's Epis Ch Fairbanks AK 1990-** B Billings MT 1935 s Earl & Myrtle. BS Rocky Mtn Coll 1962; Iliff TS 1964; MAT L&C 1978. D 6/4/1985 Bp Barbara Clementine Harris. m 11/22/1975 Lynn Locke c 4.

SLUSS, Mark (Mo) 2918 Victor St, Saint Louis MO 63104 **D Dss Anne Hse (Epis Serv Corp) 2014-** B Columbus OH 1965 s Roger & Barbara. AA Jefferson Coll 1985; BS Missouri St U 1988. D 2/7/2007 Bp George Wayne Smith.

SMALL, Timothy Keesey (CPa) 370 Spring Hill Ln, Columbia PA 17512 **P Hope Epis Ch Manheim PA 2009-** B York PA 1955 s George & Catherine. BA Juniata Coll 1977; MDiv VTS 1982. D 6/5/1982 P 12/17/1982 Bp Charlie Fuller Mcnutt Jr. m 8/20/1977 Betsy Righter Small. S Lk's Epis Ch Mechanicsburg PA 2008, 2001-2008; Int H Trin Epis Ch Shamokin PA 1999-2000; R S Paul's Ch Manheim PA 1989-1998; Vic S Edw Columbia PA 1984-1989; S Edw's Epis Ch Lancaster PA 1983-1989; Asst S Edw Landisville PA 1982-1983; Dio Cntrl Pennsylvania Harrisburg PA 1982.

SMALL, William David (Alb) 451 State Route 86, Paul Smiths NY 12970 **Died 4/23/2017** B Albany NY 1934 s William & Helen. BA SUNY 1957; MDiv Va Berk 1960. D 5/28/1960 Bp Frederick Lehrle Barry P 12/18/1960 Bp Allen Webster Brown. m 11/11/2007 Darleen E Small c 5. Ret 1996-2017; Ret 1996-2017; S Jn's Ch Johnstown NY 1977-1996; Headmaster Doane Stuart Sch Albany NY 1971-1977, Chapl 1964-1970; Headmaster St. Agnes Sch Albany NY 1971-1976; Chapl SUNY Albany NY 1965-1970; Vic S Bon Ch Guilderland NY 1962-1965; Cur S Andr's Epis Ch Albany NY 1960-1962.

SMALLEY, H Bud (Ida) 5170 Leonard Rd, Pocatello ID 83204 B Ashland OH 1951 s Harold & Florence. Cert Idaho St U 1986. D 12/8/1996 P 6/14/1997 Bp John Stuart Thornton. m 5/26/1976 Ann Flatt. S Jn's Epis Ch Amer Fls ID 1997-2009; Trin Epis Ch Pocatello ID 1997-2002.

SMALLEY, Nancy T (Dal) 416 Victorian Dr, Waxahachie TX 75165 **Mltry Chapl CAP 2001-** B Ardmore OK 1949 d John & Jane. BFA SMU 1971; MA U of Texas 1975; STL Angl TS 1989; MS Texas A&M U 1990; Cert Theol Stud Epis TS of the SW 1996. D 4/2/1997 P 5/5/1998 Bp James Monte Stanton. m 5/19/1973 Tom Edward Smalley c 2. Int Epis Ch Of The Ascen Dallas TX 2014-2015; Int The Epis Ch Of S Thos The Apos Dallas TX 2013-2014; Int S Anne's Epis Ch Desoto TX 2008-2009; Int Epis Ch Of The Redeem Irving TX 2002-2004; Supply S Mart's Ch Lancaster TX 2001-2002; Cur S Lk's Epis Ch Dallas TX 1997-2001. CT.

SMALLEY, Richard Craig (Ala) 2017 6th Avenue North, Birmingham AL 35203 **Cn for CE The Cathd Ch Of The Adv Birmingham AL 2006-** B Orlando FL 1968 s Richard & Barbara. BA Cit 1990; MDiv VTS 1995. D 5/28/1995 P 12/16/1995 Bp Edward Lloyd Salmon Jr. m 5/28/1992 Paula H Smalley c 3. R Epis Ch Of The Ascen Birmingham AL 2001-2006; LocTen Trin Epis Ch The Woodlands TX 2000-2001; Assoc Ch Of The H Cross Sullivans Island SC 1997-2000; Chapl S Alb's Ch Cit SC 1996-1997; Cur Cathd Of S Lk And S Paul Charleston SC 1995-1997. Chairman Dept Coll Mnstry; Dioc Eccl Crt; Sprtl Dir, Happ Of So Carolina.

SMALLEY, Stephen Mark (Pgh) 210 Strawberry Circle, Cranberry Township PA 16066 B Washington DC 1953 s Robert & Ruth. BA McDaniel Coll 1975; MDiv Garrett-Evang TS 1978; DMin Drew U 2005. D 1/25/1992 P 8/1/1992 Bp David Mercer Schofield. m 6/28/1975 Kristin P Peterson c 2. Dio Pittsburgh Pittsburgh PA 2011-2012; R S Barn Ch Brackenridge PA 1999-2011; R Aug Par Chesapeake City MD 1995-1999; Off Of Bsh For ArmdF New York NY 1992-1995; Chapl U. S. AF Active Duty 1983-1995; Assoc Pstr First Meth Ch Charlottesville VA 1978-1992; Pstr So Fluvanna Charge Palymra VA 1978-1981; Dioc Coun Dio Easton Easton MD 1996-1999; Bd Dir, Secy of Bd Allegheny Vlly Assn of Ch 1929-2010.

✠ SMALLEY OSB, The Rt Rev William Edward (Ind) 13809 E 186th St, Noblesville IN 46060 **P-in-c Trin Ch Anderson IN 2007-** B New Brunswick NJ 1940 s August & Emma. BA Leh 1962; STM EDS 1965; MS Tem 1970; DMin Wesley TS 1987. D 6/26/1965 P 3/5/1966 Bp Frederick Warnecke Con 12/8/1989 for Kan. m 9/12/1964 Carole Kuhns c 2. Int S Paul's Ch Columbus IN 2005-2006; Ret Bp of Kansas Dio Kansas Topeka KS 2004-2014, Bp of Kansas 1989-2003; R Ch Of The Ascen Gaithersburg MD 1980-1989; R Epis Mnstry Un Palmerton PA 1975-1980; R S Jn's Epis Ch Palmerton PA 1975-1980; R All SS Epis Ch Lehighton PA 1967-1975; Vic S Mart-In-The-Fields Mtn Top PA 1965-1967; Pres PB's Coun of Advice 1994-2003; Pres Prov VII of Epis Ch 1994-2002; VP Ch Deploy Bd 1994-2000; Mem PB Nomin Comm. 1994-1997; COM Dio Washington Washington DC 1988-1989; Dep GC Dio Bethlehem

Bethlehem PA 1976-1979, ExCoun 1969-1975. Auth, "Reg Mnstrs," *The Sm Ch Nwsltr*, 1994. Oblate Ord of S Ben 1998. Omicron Delta Kappa Leh 1962.

SMALLWOOD, Richard Lewis (Nev) 4709 S Nellis Blvd, Las Vegas NV 89121 B Washington DC 1946 s Lewis & Dorothy. BS Bapt Coll at Charleston 1980; ERM U So TS 2010; EFM U So TS 2010. D 5/4/2014 P 12/20/2014 Bp Dan Thomas Edwards. m 6/16/1966 Jeanne Lorraine Padgett Smallwood c 2.

SMART JR, James Hudson (NwT) 1826 Elmwood Dr, Abilene TX 79605 **Assoc S Mk's Epis Ch Abilene TX 2011-; R S Mk's Ch Abilene TX 2004-** B Abilene TX 1948 s Hudson & Martha. BS McMurry U 1970; JD Texas Tech U 1973. D 5/8/2004 P 11/20/2004 Bp C Wallis Ohl. m 10/8/1977 Patricia Smart.

SMART, John A (Pa) 5100 N Northridge Cir, Tucson AZ 85718 **Vic S Paul's Ch Tombstone AZ 2013-** B McKeesport PA 1934 s William & Jean. BA Indiana St U 1957; STB Ya Berk 1961. D 7/17/1961 Bp Austin Pardue P 12/9/1961 Bp William S Thomas. c 1. R S Mich's Ch Coolidge AZ 2003-2006; R S Alb's Epis Ch Wickenburg AZ 1996-2000; Dio Pennsylvania Philadelphia PA 1985-1986; R The Ch Of The H Trin Rittenhouse Philadelphia PA 1984-1996; R S Mart's Ch Wayne PA 1977-1984; R Trin Ch Solebury PA 1968-1977; Cur Ch Of The Redeem Springfield PA 1963-1968; Cur S Paul's Epis Ch Westfield NJ 1961-1963.

SMART, John Dennis (At) 442 Euclid Terrace N.E., Atlanta GA 30307 B Waco TX 1940 s Noble & Ruth. BA Baylor U 1963; MA U of Texas 1972; MDiv VTS 1978. D 6/13/1978 Bp Roger Howard Cilley P 6/1/1979 Bp James Milton Richardson. c 2. Ch Of The H Cross Decatur GA 1994-2002; Gd Shpd Epis Ch Austell GA 1992-1993; Dio Atlanta Atlanta GA 1991, Dn of Macon Dnry 1986-1990; R All SS Ch Warner Robins GA 1984-1991; Assoc Trin Ch Longview TX 1980-1984; Chr Ch Jefferson TX 1978-1980; Vic S Paul's Ch Leigh TX 1978-1980; S Paul's Ch Marshall TX 1978-1980; St Pauls Ch 1978-1980.

SMART, Lula Grace (Pa) 147 7th Ave, Folsom PA 19033 B Limon CR 1951 d Rudolph & Adina. BA Universidad Autonomus De Centro Amererica 1987; MDiv GTS 1997; Doctor of Mnstry How Sch of Div 2009; Doctor of Mnstry Other 2009. D 6/21/1997 Bp Allen Lyman Bartlett Jr P 5/30/1998 Bp Franklin Delton Turner. R Calv Ch Germantown Philadelphia PA 1998-2013; The Afr Epis Ch Of S Thos Philadelphia PA 1997-1998.

SMEDLEY IV, Walter (Chi) Saint Chrysostom's Church, 1424 N Dearborn St, Chicago IL 60610 **S Chrys's Ch Chicago IL 2013-** B Pennsylvania 1974 s Walter & Kathleen. BA Wms 1996; Earlham Sch of Rel 1999; MDiv Ya Berk 2002. D 6/22/2002 P 5/31/2003 Bp Charles Ellsworth Bennison Jr. m 10/17/2004 Loraine Freeman Smedley c 2. R Ch Of The H Cross Dunn Loring VA 2005-2013; Asst Chr Ch Philadelphia Philadelphia PA 2002-2005.

SMELSER, Todd Dudley (At) 1358 E Rock Springs Rd Ne, Atlanta GA 30306 **Pstr Care Assoc Cathd Of S Phil Atlanta GA 2008-, Cn for Pstr Care & Wrshp 2002-2008** B Richmond IN 1948 s Wayne & Marie. BA Earlham Coll 1970; MDiv Andover Newton TS 1974. D 6/8/1974 P 11/30/1974 Bp John P Craine. m 10/4/2014 James Michael Gerhart. Assoc S Pat's Epis Ch Atlanta GA 2002; Int S Geo's Epis Ch Maplewood NJ 1999-2001; Dn Cathd Of S Jas Chicago IL 1992-1999; R S Jn The Bapt Epis Ch Minneapolis MN 1983-1992; Regent 2 Of New York Pleasantville NY 1981-1983; S Alb's Epis Ch Ft Wayne IN 1980-1981; Trin Ch Ft Wayne IN 1974-1979; Litur Cmsn Dio Minnesota Minneapolis MN 1983-1989.

SMERCINA, Eugene Edward (O) 4307 Cleveland Rd E, Huron OH 44839 B Cleveland OH 1933 s Edward & Helen. BA Kent St U 1955; BD Bex Sem 1959; MA Bowling Green St U 1969; GTS 1985. D 6/13/1959 P 12/21/1959 Bp Nelson Marigold Burroughs. m 5/23/1981 Susanne Smercina. Chr Epis Ch Huron OH 1966-2001; Vic S Matt's Ch Ashland OH 1959-1966. stpaulepiscopal@frontier.com

SMIRAGLIA, Richard Paul (Pa) 340 Fitzwater Street, Philadelphia PA 19147 B New York NY 1952 s Sylvio & Marcia. BA L&C 1973; MLS Indiana U 1974; PhD U Chi 1992; MDiv GTS 1997. D 6/21/1997 Bp Allen Lyman Bartlett Jr P 6/13/1998 Bp Charles Ellsworth Bennison Jr. m 5/31/2008 James Bradford Young. S Chris's Ch Milwaukee WI 2016-2017; The Ch Of The H Trin Rittenhouse Philadelphia PA 2007-2012; R S Phil Memi Ch Philadelphia PA 2002-2006; P-in-c S Mk's Ch Philadelphia PA 2000-2001; Asst S Mary's Ch Hamilton Vill Philadelphia PA 1999-2000; Asst Trin Memi Ch Philadelphia PA 1997-1998.

SMITH, Aaron William (Fla) 4775 Godwin Ave, Jacksonville FL 32210 **Dio Florida Jacksonville 2017-** B Sudbury Ontario Canada 1979 s Jerry & Marjorie. S.T.M. GTS; BA McMaster U 2003; MA Sewanee: The U So, TS 2007. D 1/23/2012 P 9/7/2012 Bp John Bauerschmidt. m 10/11/2008 Meredith Nicole Smith c 2. S Paul's Chap Magnolia Sprgs AL 2013-2017; Asst S Matt's Ch Maple Glen PA 2012-2013. asmith@diocesefl.org

SMITH, Aidan (Alb) TESM Ambridge PA 2015- D 3/28/2015 P 10/30/2015 Bp William Howard Love.

SMITH, A Lan Bruce (SO) 627 Yaronia Dr N, Columbus OH 43214 **Bd Dir Bexley-Seabury Sem Chicago IL 2014-; Bd Dir Epis Ret Hm Inc. Cincinnti OH 2014-** B Newark NJ 1951 s Alan & Emilie. BA Ithaca Coll 1973; MDiv Drew U 1996; MTS Methodist TS in Ohio 1999. D 6/24/2000 P 1/6/2001 Bp

Herbert Thompson Jr. m 6/26/1982 Susan Warrener Smith. P-in-c Trin Ch Mc Arthur OH 2012-2015; Assoc S Mk's Epis Ch Columbus OH 2000-2012; Fin Cmsn Dio Sthrn Ohio Cincinnati OH 2012-2014. revabs0630@gmail.com

SMITH JR, Alfred Hersey (Los) 9566 Vervain St, San Diego CA 92129 **Died 12/26/2015** B San Rafael CA 1934 s Alfred & Susie. BA U So 1956; BD CDSP 1959; DMin VTS 1988. D 7/30/1959 P 2/29/1960 Bp William Jones Gordon Jr. m 6/3/1961 Stephanie S Harms c 2. P in Res - Vol S Barth's Epis Ch Poway CA 2006; S Columba's Par Camarillo CA 1970-1999; R S Tim's Epis Ch Apple Vlly CA 1966-1970; Asst S Fran' Par Palos Verdes Estates CA 1964-1966; Vic S Tim's Ch Tanacross AK 1962-1964; Vic S Matt's Ch Beaver AK 1960-1962; Vic S Andr's Ch Stevens Vlg AK 1959-1960. Auth, "Call To Excellence," Foward Mvmt Pub, 1992; Auth, "Dvlpmt Of The Vstry Of S Columba'S Ch," 1988. OHC.

SMITH, Aloha Lee (Los) 5848 Tower Rd, Riverside CA 92506 B Spokane WA 1942 d Edward & Chloe. BA U CO 1964; Cert Rutgers The St U of New Jersey 1982; BTh McGill U 1986; STM McGill U 1987; MDiv Montreal TS CA 1988; DMin Sewanee: The U So, TS 1997. D 10/1/1988 P 5/14/1989 Bp Reginald Hollis. m 12/26/1972 Roberts Cameron Smith c 2. Assoc S Mich's Epis Ch Riverside CA 2007-2008; P-in-c S Fran Of Assisi Par Sn Bernrdno CA 2002-2006; Assoc Trin Epis Ch Redlands CA 1998-2002; Serv Angl Ch of Can 1989-1998. Chapl Ord of S Lk - Co-Dir Reg VII 1990; EFM Mentor 1994; Ord of S Helena 1980.

SMITH, Andrea (Ct) 16 Clam Shell Alley, P.O. Box 412, Vinalhaven ME 04863 B Greenwich CT 1943 d Andrew & Gail. BA Syr 1970; MDiv EDS 1980. D 6/13/1981 P 3/17/1982 Bp Arthur Edward Walmsley. m 8/19/1972 John Howard Hale c 2. Chapl Bridgeport Cmnty Mntl Hlth Cntr 1994-2002; Chapl Fairfield Hills Hosp 1984-1994; S Jas's Ch W Hartford CT 1981-1984; Asst St Jas Epis Ch Hartford CT 1981-1984. AAPC 1994; Assocation of Profsnl Chapl 1988. Proclamation of Dedicated Efforts in Response to September 11th Gvnr Jn Rowland 2002.

✠ SMITH, The Rt Rev Andrew Donnan (Ct) 106 Vista Way, Bloomfield CT 06002 B Albany NY 1944 s Frederick & Grace. BA Trin Hartford CT 1965; BD EDS 1968; DD Ya Berk 2000. D 6/11/1968 P 3/22/1969 Bp Walter H Gray Con 5/4/1996 for Ct. m 6/12/1971 Kate T Smith c 2. Asst Bp Dio New York New York NY 2010-2013; Bp Dioc Dio Connecticut Meriden CT 2000-2010, Bp Suffr 1996-2000, Hartford Dnry 1987-1991; Bp of Connecticut All SS Chap Hartford CT 1999-2010; R S Mary's Epis Ch Manchester CT 1985-1996; R S Mich's Ch Naugatuck CT 1976-1985; Asst S Jn's Epis Par Waterbury CT 1971-1976; Cur Trin Epis Ch Hartford CT 1968-1971. Chapl Hartford Chapt Comp H Cross 1993-1995; Soc For The Increase Of Mnstry 1989.

SMITH, Anne Largent (NCal) 9085 Calvine Rd., Sacramento CA 95829 **P-in-c St Marys Ch Elk Grove Sacramento CA 2014-** B Pennsylvania 1975 d Jorg & Elizabeth. U of Maryland; BA Pepperdine U 1997; MDiv CDSP 2010. D 6/5/2010 Bp Marc Handley Andrus P 12/11/2010 Bp Jerry Alban Lamb. m 1/3/1998 Keith Smith c 2. P-in-c S Jn's Epis Ch Stockton CA 2015; Asst S Jn The Bapt Lodi CA 2011-2013. reverendannesmith@gmail.com

SMITH, Ann-Lining (Cal) 7261 Mesa Dr, Aptos CA 95003 B Florence AL 1949 d Lewis & Nancy. CDSP; Intl Ministers Ntwk; BA U of Alabama 1971; MDiv Amer Bapt Sem of the W 1976. D 1/6/1980 Bp Chauncie Kilmer Myers P 3/1/1981 Bp William Edwin Swing. All SS Epis Ch Watsonville CA 1997-1999; S Mths Ch Seaside CA 1996-1997; Int Epis Ch Of The Gd Shpd Salinas CA 1995-1996; Pres Of The Stndg Com 1994-1995; Bd Trst Gr Cathd 1994-1995; Dio California San Francisco CA 1992-1993; 1991-1995; Com On Cn 1985-1996; Dept Of Stwdshp 1985-1995; Vic Ch Of The H Fam Fresno CA 1984-1992; Dep Vic S Clare's Epis Ch Pleasanton CA 1983-1984; Supervising Chapl San Francisco Gnrl Hosp CA 1982-1985; Int Ch Of The Incarn San Francisco CA 1982-1983, Cur 1980-1982. Auth, "Reverend Ms Evelyn Morgan Jones," *I Love You*.

SMITH, Ann Robb (Pa) 816 Castlefinn Ln, Bryn Mawr PA 19010 B Philadelphia PA 1928 d Henry & Gertrude. BA U of Pennsylvania 1950; MDiv Luth TS at Gettysburg 1991. D 6/16/1990 Bp Allen Lyman Bartlett Jr P 6/15/1991 Bp Barbara Clementine Harris. m 7/1/1950 Kaighn Smith c 3. Chapl Hosp of the U of Pennsylvania Philadelphia PA 2002-2004; Dn Wissahickon Deanry Dio Pennsylvania Philadelphia PA 1995-1998; Geo W So Ch of Advoc Philadelphia PA 1991-1997; Chapl Res Presb Med Cntr Philadelphia PA 1990-1991. Auth, "El Salvador: A People Crucified," *Wit mag*, 1988; Auth, "Nicaragua: A People Longing for Peace," *Wit mag*, 1988. Quality of Life Awd Founders Bank 2002; Marg Bailey Speer Awd The Shipley Sch 2001.

SMITH, Arthur Wells (CNY) 341 Main St, Oneida NY 13421 **P-in-c S Jn's Epis Ch Oneida NY 2014-** B Syracuse NY 1948 s Arthur & Marietta. BA Hob 1971; MDiv Colgate Rochester Crozer DS 2013; MDiv Colgate Rochester Crozier DS 2013. D 12/7/2013 P 8/13/2014 Bp Gladstone Bailey Adams III. m 11/27/1988 Gale Susan LaPlante c 4. stjohnsoneida@verizon.net

SMITH, Barbara Joan (U) c/o Episcopal Carmel of Saint Teresa, 123 Little New York Rd, Rising Sun MD 21911 **Carmelite Nun Epis Carmel of S Teresa 2017-** B Vancouver CA 1935 d Clair & Wanda. BA U of British Columbia Vancouver BC CA 1957; MDiv Vancouver TS CA 1988. D 6/13/1987 Bp Arthur

Edward Walmsley P 3/17/1989 Bp George Edmonds Bates. P-in-c S Geo's Ch Cordova AK 2002-2009; R S Paul's Epis Ch Vernal UT 1996-2002; Dio Utah Salt Lake City UT 1993-2002; S Fran Ch Moab UT 1993-1996, R 1989-1992; D S Faith Vancouver Bc Can 1987-1988. srbarbaraocd@gmail.com

SMITH, Bardwell Leith (Minn) 104 Maple St, Northfield MN 55057 B Springfield MA 1925 s Winthrop & Gertrude. BA Ya 1950; BD Yale DS 1953; MA Ya 1957; PhD Ya 1964; Harv 1965; London U 1972; Kyoto U 1986. D 6/13/1954 P 12/1/1954 Bp Horace W B Donegan. m 8/19/1961 Charlotte McCorkingdale Smith c 5. Prof Carleton Coll Northfield MN 1960-1995; Asst Chapl Yale U CT 1957-1960; Cur Trin Ch Highland Pk IL 1954-1956. Auth, *The City as a Sacr Cntr: Essays on 6 Asian Contexts*, E.J. Brill (Netherlands), 1987; Auth, *Essays on Gupta Culture*, Motilal Banarsidass, 1983; Co-Ed/Contrib, "Warlords," *Artists, Warlords & Commoners: Japan in 16th Century*, U Press of Hawaii, 1981; Auth/Ed, *Rel and Legitimation of Power in Sri Lanka*, Anima Press, 1978; Ed/Contrib, *Hinduism: New Essays in Hist of Rel*, E.J. Brill, 1976; Auth/Ed, *Unsui: Diary of Zen Monastic Life*, U Press of Hawaii, 1973. AAR 1960; Amer Soc for the Study of Rel 1982; Assn for Asian Stds 1962. Pres Amer Soc for the Study of Rel 1996; Resrch Grant Natl Endowmt for the Hmnts (NEH) 1991; Fulbright Resrch Grant (Japan) Fulbright 1986; Resrch Fllshp Amer Coun Learned Socs 1972.

SMITH JR, Ben Huddleston (Md) 1401 Carrollton Ave, Baltimore MD 21204 B Richmond VA 1932 s Ben & Katherine. PhD U NC 1962; Cert GTS 1982. D 5/21/1982 P 5/1/1983 Bp A(rthur) Heath Light. Assoc Cathd Of The Incarn Baltimore MD 2000-2001; R Ch Of The Gd Shpd Towson MD 1985-1999; Asst Chr Ch Alexandria VA 1982-1984.

SMITH, Bert Orville (At) 841 Kings Grant Dr NW, Atlanta GA 30318 **D Ch Of The H Comf Atlanta GA 2006-** B Atlanta GA 1948 s Bert & Yancey. D 8/6/2006 Bp J Neil Alexander. m 5/15/2007 Patricia Smith.

SMITH, Betty Lorraine (NMich) 8114 Trout Lake Rd, Naubinway MI 49762 B Epoufette MI 1933 d Mack & Mary. D 10/13/2002 Bp James Arthur Kelsey. c 2.

SMITH, Bill (Ore) 17320 Quaker Ln Apt B21, Sandy Spring MD 20860 B Paterson NJ 1933 s Edward & Lilliam. CDSP; BS NEU 1956; MS U of Vermont 1964; VTS 1980. D 9/20/1970 Bp George Richard Millard P 11/6/1972 Bp Chauncie Kilmer Myers. m 8/25/1956 Janet M Jellison c 4. Vic S Tim's Ch Brookings OR 2000-2003; Vic S Anth Of The Desert Desert Hot Sprg CA 1988-1995; Vic S Tim's Ch San Diego CA 1988-1995; R S Jn's Ch Indio CA 1985-1988; Vic S Clare's Epis Ch Pleasanton CA 1975-1985; 1971-1972.

SMITH, Bobby (Chi) 217 Houston St, Ripon WI 54971 **S Fran Cmnty Serv Inc. Salina KS 2014-** B Cocoa Beach FL 1971 s Richard & Julia. BA Estrn Illinois U 1994; MA Webster U 2003; MA Nash 2009. D 6/29/2010 P 1/15/2011 Bp Russell Edward Jacobus. m 11/19/1994 Angela Smith c 4. Lasalle Cnty Epis Mnstry Ottawa IL 2011-2014. rns31794@gmail.com

SMITH, Bonnie (EC) 501 S Harding Dr Apt 1002, Goldsboro NC 27534 **P-in-c Ch Of The H Innoc Seven Sprg NC 2008-; R S Aug's Epis Ch Kinston NC 1991-** B Washington DC 1957 d John & Edith. BA Converse Coll 1979; MDiv Yale DS 1983. D 6/11/1983 P 5/12/1984 Bp William Arthur Beckham. c 2. Liturg Cmsn Dio E Carolina Kinston NC 2007-2011, 1995-2003, Chair, COM 1992-1995; Vic Ch Of The H Comm Allendale SC 1984-1989; Vic Ch Of The Heav Rest Estill SC 1983-1989; Vic All SS Epis Ch Hampton SC 1983-1986; Dioc Coun So Carolina Charleston SC 1987-1989. Career Achievement Awd 86 Converse Coll 1986; Outstndng Yng Wmn Amer 1984.

SMITH, Bradford Ray (NC) 116 S Church St, PO Box 293, Monroe NC 28111 **R S Paul's Ch Monroe NC 2009-; Bd Trst (Univ. of the So) Dio No Carolina Raleigh NC 2011-; Sewanee U So TS Sewanee TN 2011-** B Lexington KY 1970 s Donald & Faith. BA W&M 1992; PhD U of Tennessee 1998; MDiv Sewanee: The U So, TS 2003. D 5/31/2003 P 1/31/2004 Bp Charles Glenn VonRosenberg. m 12/30/1994 Deborah Ann Gold. Adj Prof Emory Univeristy Candler TS 2008; Assoc R The Ch Of S Matt Snellville GA 2005-2009; Supply S Fran' Ch Norris TN 2005; Asst R S Andr's Ch Maryville TN 2003-2005; New Beginnings, Sprtl Dir Dio Atlanta Atlanta GA 2008, Bp's Congrl Consult Com 2007-2009, Cmsn on Educ 2005-2009; Co-Fndr/Co-Dir, Cmsn on Bioethics Dio E Tennessee Knoxville TN 2004-2005. "Rel Elements in Healing," *The Hlth Care Profsnl as Friend and Healer: Bldg on the Wk of Edm D. Pellegrino*, Geo Press, 2000; "Re-establishing Connections Between Bioethics & Chrsnty: Narratives & Virtues in Caring for a Chr Patient," U of Tennessee, Knoxville, 1998. Fllshp of S Jn 2002-2005; Oblate (St. Greg's Abbey) 2005. Woods Ldrshp Awd U So TS 2002.

SMITH, Brian Eliot (Fla) 655 W Jefferson St, Tallahassee FL 32304 **Chapl Epis U Cntr Tallahassee FL 2015-** B Michigan City IN 1978 s Timothy & Barbara. BS U of New Hampshire 2001; MDiv VTS 2007. D 12/20/2006 P 6/29/2007 Bp George Wayne Smith. m 5/28/2012 Bethany B Haynes c 1. R Ch of the H Trin 2012-2015; Cur Ch of the Apos 2011; Asst R Trin Epis Ch St Aug FL 2007-2009. fb@rugehall.org

SMITH, Bruce (Cal) 14 Ardmore Ct, Pleasant Hill CA 94523 **Stndg Com Dio California 2008-; R Ch Of The Resurr Pleasant Hil CA 1987-** B Washington DC 1950 s Richard & Mary. BA U CA Berkeley 1972; MDiv PSR 1979. D 6/

28/1980 P 7/1/1981 Bp William Edwin Swing. m 4/27/1980 Deborah Dee Holderness. Chair Of The Dept Of Campus Mnstry 1994-1998; Com 1994-1996; Com 1986-1989; 1983-1985; S Steph's Epis Ch Orinda CA 1982-1987; S Andr's Ch St Coll PA 1980-1982; Cur S Andr's St Coll PA 1980-1982; Pres Stndg Com Dio California San Francisco CA 2011-2012.

SMITH, Carol Diane (Minn) 1211 Jackson Ave, Detroit Lakes MN 56501 **R S Columba White Earth MN 2007-** B Cass Lake MN 1958 d Harold & Joyce. D 10/29/2005 P 1/20/2007 Bp James Louis Jelinek. m 8/6/1976 Richard Smith c 2. ECCIM 2003; MCIW 1997.

SMITH, Carol Kay Huston (Mil) 4522 Aztec Trail, Fitchburg WI 53711 **D Gr Ch Madison WI 2008-** B Washington DC 1942 d Carl & Lucy. BME Florida St U 1964; MA Florida St U 1970. D 3/28/1987 Bp Roger John White. m 8/16/1965 Stephen Wesley Smith. D S Lk's Ch Racine WI 2000-2008; D S Mich's Epis Ch Racine WI 1987-2000.

SMITH, Carter Austin (CFla) 2499 N Westmoreland Dr, Orlando FL 32804 **S Mich's Ch Orlando FL 2011-** B Washington DC 1945 s Hule & Marjorie. BA Golden Gate U 1974. D 12/5/2009 Bp Leo Frade. m 5/7/2011 Mia Cunningham c 1.

SMITH, Cathleen Anne (WNY) 410 N Main St, Jamestown NY 14701 **Chapl Hospice Chautauqua Cnty 2005-; D S Lk's Epis Ch Jamestown NY 2005-** B Jamestown NY 1957 d Norman & Theresa. AAS Jamestown Cmnty Coll 1989; BS Ashford U 2009. D 6/19/2005 Bp Michael Garrison. m 9/26/2010 Matthew Lee Smith.

SMITH, Cecilia Mary Babcock (Tex) PO Box 2247, Austin TX 78768 **Safe Ch Min Dio Texas Houston TX 2008-, Supply P 2007-2008, Stndg Com 2004-2007, Exec Bd 1999-2004, GC Dep 2005-2010, Stndg Com 2004-2007** B Buffalo NY 1942 d Donald & Mary. BA Vas 1964; MA U of Texas 1970; MDiv Epis TS of the SW 1990; ThM S Mary U San Antonio TX 1990. D 6/16/1990 Bp Maurice Manuel Benitez P 1/1/1991 Bp Anselmo Carral-Solar. m 10/30/1964 Virgil Raymond Smith c 3. S Andr's Ch Bryan TX 2007; R S Ptr's Epis Ch Brenham TX 1997-2007; Assoc R S Dav's Ch Austin TX 1994-1997, Asst 1990-1991.

SMITH, Channing (ECR) 13601 Saratoga Avenue, Saratoga CA 95070 **R S Andr's Ch Saratoga CA 2009-** B Niskayuna NY 1966 s Channing & Elizabeth. BA Ken 1988; MDiv GTS 1992. D 7/25/1992 P 5/15/1993 Bp Herbert Thompson Jr. m 5/25/1991 Mary Richards Smith. Stndg Com Pres Dio California San Francisco CA 2006-2007; R Trsfg Epis Ch San Mateo CA 1997-2009; Treas/Secy of Alum The GTS New York NY 1995-1996; Chair of the Dioc Steward Com 1994-1997; The Ch of the Redeem Cincinnati OH 1992-1997.

SMITH, Charles Howard (Az) 807 W Toledo St, Chandler AZ 85225 **R S Matt's Ch 1979-** B Detroit MI 1932 s Charles & Ethel. BBA SMU 1954; MDiv CDSP 1964. D 6/20/1964 Bp John Joseph Meakin Harte P 12/1/1964 Bp Harry Sherbourne Kennedy. m 10/29/1955 Betty Smith. Chapl Banner Hospice Chapl 1997-2009; Dioc Coun Dio Arizona Phoenix AZ 1984; Chair Of Dioc Strtgy Com 1981-1983; S Matt's Ch Chandler AZ 1980-1997, 1975-1979; R S Jn's Epis Ch Stockton CA 1970-1975; 1970-1973; R S Tim's Ch Aiea HI 1969-1970; Vic S Barn On Ewa Bch Ewa Bch HI 1968-1969; Vic H Innoc' Epis Ch Lahaina HI 1964-1968; Dioc Coun The Epis Ch in Hawaii Honolulu HI 1968-1970.

SMITH, Charles J St Michael and All Angels, 6408 Bridgewood Rd, Columbia SC 29206 **S Mich And All Ang' Columbia SC 2016-; Trin Ch Portsmouth VA 2014-** B Roanoke VA 1982 s Andre & Pammy. BA Hampden-Sydney Coll 2005; MDiv VTS 2011. D 6/18/2011 Bp Herman Hollerith IV P 1/14/2012 Bp William Andrew Waldo. m 7/15/2006 Christina R Smith. D S Matt's Epis Ch Spartanburg SC 2011-2014. charles.jeremy.smith@gmail.com

SMITH, Charles L (Ak) PO Box 3346, Odessa TX 79760 **Chapl Chld's Hm & Berkley Sch 1980-** B Fort Worth TX 1950 s James & Francis. BA Austin Coll 1973; MDiv Nash 1979. D 5/13/1979 Bp Addison Hosea P 12/14/1979 Bp Emerson Paul Haynes. m 5/19/1978 Casey Smith. S Jn's Epis Ch Odessa TX 2009-2010; S Fran Ch Tampa FL 1981-1983; S Chris's Ch Tampa FL 1980-1981; Cur S Steph's Ch New Prt Rchy FL 1979-1980.

SMITH, Charles Rodney (Tex) 156 Fairacres Ln, Sewanee TN 37375 B 1938 s William & Elsa. BS Tusculum Coll 1960; MEd Mississippi Coll 1967; MDiv Sewanee: The U So, TS 1971. D 5/30/1971 P 5/1/1972 Bp John Maury Allin. m 12/26/1992 Annette C Cacioppo c 3. H Sprt Epis Sch Houston TX 1996-2000; H Sprt Epis Ch Houston TX 1994-1996; Cbury Epis Sch Desoto TX 1992-1994; Fndr/Headmaster Cbury Epis Sch Duncanville TX 1991-1994; S Clem's Epis Par Sch El Paso TX 1981-1992; Headmaster Par Sch El Paso TX 1981-1991; Assoc Pro Cathd Epis Ch Of S Clem El Paso TX 1981-1991; Fndr/Headmaster Epis Sch Of Acadiana Cade In La 1977-1981; Epis Sch Of Acadiana Inc. Cade LA 1976-1981; Headmaster Ascen Sch LA 1976-1977; Asst Headmaster Trin Sch New Orleans LA 1974-1976; Trin Epis Sch New Orleans LA 1973-1976; Prncpl S Andr's Upper Sch Jackson MS 1971-1974. Auth, "Sci arts".

SMITH, Charles Stuart (Alb) 45 Pierrepont Ave., Potsdam NY 13676 **Chapl Bare Hill Correctional Malone NY 2001-** B Boston MA 1955 s David & Janet. BA Coll of Wooster 1979; MDiv GTS 1990. D 6/9/1990 Bp Arthur Edward Walmsley P 5/1/1991 Bp Clarence Nicholas Coleridge. m 12/27/1986

S

Elaina Marie Smith c 2. P-in-c The St Lawr Team Ministr Waddington NY 1998-2001; R Ch Of The H Trin Greenport NY 1993-1997; Asst S Mk's Ch Islip NY 1991-1993; Asst Gr Epis Ch Norwalk CT 1990-1991.

SMITH, Christopher Atkins (Alb) 12 Main St., Hagaman NY 12086 B Waterbury CT 1947 s James & Julie. BA U of Connecticut 1969; MDiv GTS 1979. D 7/18/1979 P 6/7/1980 Bp Morgan Porteus. m 9/15/1973 Maria Smith c 1. R S Ann's Ch Amsterdam NY 1990-2011; Vic S Paul's Ch Plainfield CT 1983-1990; Cur Chr Ch Stratford CT 1979-1983.

SMITH, Claude (Mass) 160 River Street, Norwell MA 02061 B Boston MA 1933 s Claude & Elizabeth. BA Pr 1954; Yale DS 1954; STB EDS 1957; PhD Harv 1964. D 6/22/1957 Bp Anson Phelps Stokes Jr P 12/21/1957 Bp Donald B Aldrich. m 9/7/1957 Elizabeth Scoville Smith c 4. The Par Of S Chrys's Quincy MA 1998-2005; Adj Fac Seabury Wstrn TS Evanston IL 1997-2004; Assoc S Andr's Ch Hanover MA 1993-1997; Assoc S Mk's Barrington IL 1986-1993; 1965-1985; R S Andr's Epis Ch Contoocook NH 1962-1964; Asst S Andr's Ch Wellesley MA 1961-1962, Cur 1957-1960; P-in-c S Paul's Epis Ch Bedford MA 1959-1960. Auth, "Jonathan Edwards & the Way of Ideas," *Harvard Theol Revs*, Harv Press Vol. 59, #2., 1966. 1954.

SMITH, Claudia L (Me) 810 Morgan Bay Rd, Blue Hill ME 04614 **R St Fran By The Sea Epis Ch Blue Hill ME 2007-; Grants Revs Com Dio Maine Portland ME 2011-, Chair, Cmsn on Congrl Life 2010-, Dioc Coun 2010-** B New York NY 1949 d John & Florence. AA Chr Coll 1970; BS SE Oklahoma St U 1973; MDiv Sewanee: The U So, TS 2005. D 6/11/2005 P 12/17/2005 Bp Robert John O'Neill. c 1. Vic S Ben Epis Ch La Veta CO 2005-2007.

SMITH, Coleen Haas (Mil) **Chapl - Pstr Counslg Gd Shephard Hostpital Barrington IL 2005-** B 1948 BA DePaul U 2003; MA Loyola U 2006. D 2/4/2005 Bp Victor Alfonso Scantlebury. m 3/14/1999 James Robert Smith c 1. D S Paul's Ch Milwaukee WI 2008-2011.

SMITH III, Colton Mumford (SC) 1 Bishop Gadsden Way Apt 346, Charleston SC 29412 **Ret 2001-** B Vicksburg MS 1935 s Colton & Alice. BA U So 1958; STB GTS 1961; DMin Sewanee: The U So, TS 1980. D 6/17/1961 Bp Duncan Montgomery Gray P 12/20/1961 Bp John Maury Allin. m 11/11/1961 Angela P K Smith c 3. R Ch Of Our Sav Johns Island SC 1991-2001; Cn Dio Mississippi Jackson MS 1984-1991; R S Phil's Ch Jackson MS 1981-1984; Stff Coventry Cathd Engl 1973-1974; R All SS Ch Jackson MS 1969-1981; Ch Of The Ascen Hattiesburg MS 1965-1969; Vic S Steph's Ch Columbia MS 1965-1969; Chapl U Sthrn MS-Hattiesburg 1965-1969; Vic Par Of The Medtr-Redeem Mccomb MS 1962-1965; Cur S Jas Ch Jackson MS 1961-1962. Auth, *A Period of Adjustment & Growth: A Study of the Epis Dio Mississippi*; Auth, *A Position Paper on Ord of Wmn to the Priesthood & the Epis Ch*; Auth, *Intrnernship for Deacons & 1st Year P*.

SMITH, Craig Faulkner (Vt) 5167 Shelburne Road, Shelburne VT 05482 **Dio Vermont Burlington VT 2014-** B Springfield VT 1954 s Alexander & Janet. BA U of Vermont 1980; MDiv GTS 1983. D 5/21/1983 P 11/1/1983 Bp Robert Shaw Kerr. m 12/29/1979 Candace R Smith c 2. H Trin Epis Ch Swanton VT 2015; R Trin Ch Shelburne VT 1998-2013; Ch Of The Gd Shpd Barre VT 1984-1998; Cur Chr Ch Montpelier VT 1983-1984.

SMITH JR, Curruth Russell (WNC) 670 Run Away Rdg, Clyde NC 28721 **Died 4/21/2017** B Birmingham AL 1931 s Curruth & Cecile. BS U of Alabama 1953; MD U of Alabama Sch of Med 1956; Dio Cntrl Florida Inst Chr Stds FL 1992. D 11/7/1992 Bp John Wadsworth Howe. m 6/27/1953 Barbara Bates Smith c 3. D S Andr's Epis Ch Canton NC 1996-2017; D S Dav's Epis Ch Lakeland FL 1992-1995.

✠ **SMITH, The Rt Rev Dr Dabney Tyler** (SwFla) The Diocese of Southwest Florida, 8005 25th Street East, Parrish FL 34219 **Bp of SW Florida Dio SW Florida Parrish FL 2007-; Exec Coun ECEC 2015-** B Brownwood TX 1953 s Dorsey & Dorothy. AA Santa Fe Cmnty Coll 1975; BA U of So Florida 1980; MDiv Nash 1987; DMin SWTS 1999. D 6/23/1987 P 12/28/1987 Bp William Hopkins Folwell Con 3/10/2007 for SwFla. m 6/23/2013 Mary Wallis Smith c 3. R Trin Ch New Orleans LA 2005-2007; R H Trin Epis Ch Melbourne FL 1998-2005; R S Mich And All Ang Ch So Bend IN 1989-1998; Asst Gr Epis Ch Inc Port Orange FL 1987-1989; Finalist for PBp The Epis Ch 2015; Vice-Pres Prov IV 2012-2015; Plnng Com HOB 2010-2012; Fac for New Bishops & Spouses Conf Coll for Bishops 2009-2011. DD Seabury-Wstrn 2008; DD Sewanee 2008; DD Nash 2007. dsmith@episcopalswfl.org

SMITH, Dale Leroy (Los) 10451 Jordan Parkway, Hopewell VA 23860 B Glendale CA 1942 s Carlyle & Beryl. BA Los Angeles Pacific Los Angeles CA 1964; MDiv SWTS 1971. D 7/11/1971 P 7/1/1972 Bp John Joseph Meakin Harte. m 4/12/2012 Frances Batte-Hardenbergh Smith c 3. All SS Par Long Bch CA 2003-2004; S Barth's Mssn Pico Rivera CA 1999-2003; P-in-c Imm Mssn El Monte CA 1997-1998; Assoc St Steph Epis Ch Los Angeles CA 1985-1995; Assoc S Jas' Par So Pasadena CA 1980-1984; St Elizabeths Mssn Phoenix AZ 1976-1979, 1972; Dio Arizona Phoenix AZ 1972-1976, 1971-1972; Vic S Eliz's Phoenix AZ 1971-1979.

SMITH, David Grant (Roch) St. Mark's Episcopal Church, P.O. Box 424, Penn Yan NY 14527 B Saginaw MI 1962 BA Olivet Nazarene U 1983; MDiv Bex Sem 1999; MDiv Colgate Rochester DS / Bex Sem 1999. D 6/30/2007 P 4/

12/2008 Bp Jack Marston Mckelvey. Dio Maryland Baltimore MD 2015-2016; P-in-c S Mk's Epis Ch Penn Yan NY 2008-2014; D S Lk's Ch Fairport NY 2007-2008.

SMITH, David Gregory (Mont) 5 W Olive St, Bozeman MT 59715 **S Jas Ch Bozeman MT 2016-; Mntl Hlth Ther D Greg Smith MA LCPC LMHC 2002-** B Butte, MT 1965 s David & Sherrie. Bachelor of Arts Carroll Coll 1987; Bachelor Pontifical Gregorian U 1990; Lic Pontifical Gregorian U 1992; Mstr of arts Seattle U 2002. Rec 11/22/2015 as Priest Bp Charles Franklin Brookhart Jr. m 8/20/2015 Kenneth Eugene Spencer. frdgsmith@gmail.com

SMITH, David Hayes (Va) 800 Chatham Hall Cir., Chatham VA 24531 **Chapl Woodberry Forest Sch 2010-** B Roanoke VA 1952 s W R & Helen. BA S Andrews Presb Coll 1974; DMin UTS 1979. D 11/14/2008 Bp John Clark Buchanan P 6/2/2009 Bp Herman Hollerith IV. m 7/19/1990 Jane Smith c 2. Chatham Hall Chatham VA 2009-2010; Emm Epis Ch Chatham VA 2009-2010; Chapl Chatham Hall Sch 2002-2010.

SMITH, David Lester (WNY) 5448 Broadway St, Lancaster NY 14086 B Buffalo NY 1944 s Raymond & Dorothy. EFM Sewanee: The U So, TS 1995; EFM U So TS 1995. D 4/9/2011 Bp Michael Garrison. m 12/16/2006 Laurie T Smith c 2.

SMITH, Dennis Lee (USC) B Chester SC 1936 s John & Beulah. BA U of So Carolina 1963; MDiv VTS 1963; PhD U of So Carolina 1978. D 6/29/1966 P 7/2/1967 Bp John Adams Pinckney. m 3/18/1978 Shirley Ann Hanson-Smith c 1. S Matt's Epis Ch Spartanburg SC 1993-2001; Asst To Bp Dio Wstrn No Carolina Asheville NC 1986-1989; Non-par 1983-1985; Cn To Ordnry Dio Upper So Carolina Columbia SC 1979-1982, 1971-1982; P-in-c S Fran of Assisi Chapin SC 1979-1980; Chapl U Sc-Columbia 1971-1979; Dce Chr Ch Greenville SC 1967-1971; Cur Gr Epis Ch Camden SC 1966-1967.

SMITH, Donald Hedges (Roch) 2492 Keystone Lake Drive, Cape Coral FL 33909 **Ret 1990-; Ret 1985-** B Cambridge NY 1925 s Richard & Margaret. BA Ya 1949; MDiv Bex Sem 1971. D 6/19/1971 Bp John Mc Gill Krumm P 12/18/1971 Bp Robert Rae Spears Jr. c 4. Serv Angl Ch of the Bahamas 1978-1989; S Thos Epis Ch Rochester NY 1975-1980; Serv Angl Ch of the Bahamas 1972-1975; Asst Ch Of The Incarn Penfield NY 1971-1972.

SMITH III, Donald M (Ala) 860 N Section St, Fairhope AL 36532 **Gr Ch Sheffield AL 2016-; Chairman of the Allied Arts Com Dio Cntrl Gulf Coast Pensacola FL 2013-, Dioc Fin Com 2011-; Bd Mem Beckwith C&C Fairhope AL 2009-** B Memphis TN 1969 s Donald & Martha. BBA U of Mississippi 1991; MDiv Epis TS of the SW 2007. D 6/2/2007 P 12/8/2007 Bp Don Edward Johnson. m 12/28/1991 Lloyd Early Smith c 2. S Jas Ch Fairhope AL 2008-2016; All SS Epis Ch Memphis TN 2007-2008; DCE St Jn's Epis Ch 2001-2004. frdon@bellsouth.net

SMITH, Don Leland (Oly) 8989 S Pine Dr, Beulah CO 81023 **Ret 1995-** B Portland OR 1935 s Clarence & Ola. BTh NW Chr Coll Eugene OR 1958; BA U of Oregon 1958; BD PSR 1963. D 6/23/1963 Bp James Albert Pike P 6/1/1964 Bp George Richard Millard. m 6/29/1963 Patricia Smith c 2. S Paul's Epis Ch Mt Vernon WA 1982-1995; R S Fran Of Assisi Ch Novato CA 1972-1982; Vic S Edm's Epis Ch Pacifica CA 1966-1972; Cur Trin Par Menlo Pk CA 1963-1966.

SMITH, Doris Graf (At) 11210 Wooten Lake Rd, Kennesaw GA 30144 B Atlanta GA 1946 d George & Jennie. BS U GA 1968; MDiv Candler TS Emory U 1984. D 6/9/1984 P 5/1/1985 Bp Charles Judson Child Jr. c 2. Weekend Sprtl Dir New Beginnings 2004-2005; R Chr Epis Ch Kennesaw GA 2002-2014; Sprtl Dir Atlanta Epis Curs Cmnty Atlanta GA 2001-2005; Int Asst H Innoc Ch Atlanta GA 2000-2001; Cn for Adult Educ Cathd Of S Phil Atlanta GA 1994-1999; Int Asst S Mich And All Ang Ch Stone Mtn GA 1993-1994; R Ch Of The Ascen Cartersville GA 1989-1993; Asst R S Cathr's Epis Ch Marietta GA 1984-1989; Bd Gvnr Mikell C&C 2002; Cmsn on Higher Educ Dio Atlanta Atlanta GA 2007-2011, Schlrshp Com 2007-, Chair, Centennial Celebration Com 2005-2007, Stwdshp Cmsn/Fin Com 2003-2004, COM 1997-2002, Exec Com 1986-1991, Mus and Liturg Cmsn.

SMITH, Douglas Cameron (CPa) 21 Cornell Dr, Hanover PA 17331 B Providence RI 1951 s Donald & Gladys. BA Br 1974; MDiv Andover Newton TS 1987. D 6/13/1987 P 5/1/1988 Bp Don Edward Johnson. m 8/9/1975 Beth Smith c 4. All SS Ch Hanover PA 2004-2017; R Chr Ch Cooperstown NY 1989-2004; Asst R Gr Ch N Attleboro MA 1987-1989.

SMITH, Dr. Smith (SO) 333 S. Drexel Avenue, Bexley OH 43209 **Ch Of The Nativ Indianapolis IN 2017-** B Fort Benning GA 1947 d Richard & Ruth. BA Wake Forest U 1969; MTS Candler TS Emory U 1985; U of Notre Dame 1992; PhD Grad Theol Un 2002. D 8/12/1995 Bp Steven Charleston P 5/4/1996 Bp Herbert Thompson Jr. S Alb's Epis Ch Of Bexley Columbus OH 2012-2016; Supply Chr Ch St. Jos MO 2011; Prof S Paul TS Kansas City MO 2007-2010; Asst S Paul's Ch Kansas City MO 2004-2010; Chapl S Andr's Sch Saratoga CA 2001-2003; S Mk's Par Berkeley CA 1997-1999; S Mary's Ch Anchorage AK 1996-1997, Yth Dir 1995. Auth, "Caring Liturgies," Fortress, 2012; Auth, "Rituals of Separation," *Liturg*, The Liturg Conf, 2012; Auth, "Chr Ritualizing and the Baptismal Process," Wipf and Stock, 2011; Auth, "Preaching commentaries," *Feasting on the Word*, 2008; Auth, "Healing Rituals," *Liturg*, The Liturg Conf, 2007; Auth, "Stranger at The Table," *Benedictines*, 2004; Auth,

"Mo Earth, Absorber, Chr," *SS Today*, 1992; Auth, "Cnfrmtn," *Mnstry Dvlpmt Journ*, 1986. Acad of Homil 2003-2010; No Amer Acad of Liturg 2000; Oblate Ord of S Ben 1992; Societas Liturg 1999. Res Schlr Collegeville Resrch Inst 2007. rector@stalbansbexley.org

SMITH, Duane Andre (Lex) 110 Chestnut Ct, Berea KY 40403 **R S Hubert's Ch Lexington KY 2012-** B Cherokee OK 1957 s Norval & Nedra. BA Wm Penn U 1980; MDiv Earlham Sch of Rel 1983; MDiv Other 1983; MDiv Other 1983; ThM Harvard DS 1986; AM Harv 1991; PhD Harv 1994. D 1/18/2009 P 8/19/2009 Bp Stacy F Sauls. c 2. St. Hubert's Dio Lexington Lexington 2010-2012. duane.smith@berea.edu

SMITH, Edward D (CFla) 1210 Locust St, Saint Louis MO 63103 B Jacksonville FL 1956 s Willard & Gertrude. BA U of Cntrl Florida 1978; MDiv Nash 1981; DMin SWTS 2001. D 6/21/1981 P 1/17/1982 Bp William Hopkins Folwell. m 7/1/1978 Evelyn M Smith c 2. Cn to the Ordnry Dio Missouri S Louis MO 2003-2015; R S Tim's Epis Ch W Des Moines IA 1996-2002; R S Chris's Ch Kailua HI 1988-1996; S Matt's Epis Ch Orlando FL 1987-1988; Emm Ch Orlando FL 1982-1986; Cur S Sebastian's By The Sea Melbourne Bch FL 1981-1982. edsmith@diocesemo.org

SMITH, Edwin Ball (FdL) 1060 S Westhaven Dr, Oshkosh WI 54904 **Assoc S Thos Ch Menasha WI 2004-** B Milwaukee WI 1937 s Alanson & Mary. BS Carroll Coll 1961; Indiana U 1961; PhD Kent St U 1965; DMin GTF 2000; EdD GTF 2007. D 10/18/1983 Bp William Louis Stevens P 9/7/1996 Bp Russell Edward Jacobus. m 8/27/1960 Joan Williamson. Int R S Thos Ch Menasha WI 2009-2010, Int 2001-2008; Int S Anne's Epis Ch De Pere WI 2000-2001; Int Trin Epis Ch Oshkosh WI 1997-1998, Asst 1983-1996; Asst All SS Epis Ch Appleton WI 1986-1996.

SMITH, Edwin Earl St Clair (Pa) 154 Locksley Rd, Glen Mills PA 19342 **Ret 1997-** B Chicago IL 1930 s Neal & Mary. BS U IL 1953; BD SWTS 1956; MA Marq 1970; STM SWTS 1970. D 6/18/1956 Bp Charles L Street P 12/21/1956 Bp Gerald Francis Burrill. m 1/25/1958 Alma Smith. P-in-c Calv St Aug Epis Ch Philadelphia PA 1997-2003; R S Mk's Ch Wilmington NC 1991-1997; S Mary Epis Ch Chester PA 1989-1990; S Andr's Ch Bronx NY 1986-1988; Assoc R The Afr Epis Ch Of S Thos Philadelphia PA 1984-1986; Chapl Cheyney St Coll PA 1979-1984; Dio Pennsylvania Philadelphia PA 1979-1984; Vic S Monica's Ch Stuart FL 1974-1978; Instr Of Rel Stds U Of Sthrn Florida In Tampa 1972-1979; Cn/Urban Vic All SS' Cathd Milwaukee WI 1969-1972; R S Cyp's Ch San Francisco CA 1966-1969; Chapl/Instr S Aug's Coll Raleigh NC 1964-1966; Vic H Cross Morgan Pk IL 1958-1964; Cur H Cross Morgan Pk IL 1957-1958; Cur S Jas' Epis Ch Baltimore MD 1957-1958; Cur Ch Of S Thos Chicago IL 1956-1957. Auth, "Living Ch". Soc Of S Jn The Evang.

SMITH JR, Elton Osman (WNY) 4101 Cathedral Ave Nw Apt 817, Washington DC 20016 **Asst R St Jas' Ch Potomac. 2005-; Dn-Emer St. Paul's Cathd Buffalo 1994-** B Springfield MO 1929 s Elton & Mary. BA Drury U 1950; Bossey Ecum Inst 1955; MDiv GTS 1956; Sewanee: The U So, TS 1961; VTS 1982. D 6/21/1956 P 12/22/1956 Bp Edward Randolph Welles II. Asst. R S Jas Ch Potomac MD 2005-2011; Int Gr Ch Washington DC 2003-2004; Cn Cathd of St Ptr & St Paul Washington DC 1994; Dn S Paul's Cathd Buffalo NY 1968-1994; R S Geo's Ch Kansas City MO 1962-1968; R S Paul's Epis Ch Lees Summit MO 1959-1962, Vic 1956-1958. Co-Ed, *Manual for Everymem Canvasses*. Doctor of Div inity D.D. Drury U 1999; Doctor of Laws LL.D D'Youville Coll, Buffalo, N.Y. 1994; DD D.D. GTS 1981.

SMITH JR, Frank Warner (Neb) 2303 Elk, Beatrice NE 68310 **D Chr Ch Epis Beatrice NE 1999-** B Omaha NE 1922 s Frank & Donna. BS U of Nebraska 1948. D 8/10/1999 Bp James Edward Krotz. m 12/2/1946 Verna Julene Vickers.

SMITH, Gail S (Mass) 35 Skyline Drive, Chatham MA 02633 B Buffalo NY 1949 d Elmer & Mary. BA Towson U 1985; MDiv VTS 1993. D 6/12/1993 Bp Albert Theodore Eastman P 5/14/1994 Bp Charles Lindsay Longest. m 6/1/1968 David M Smith c 2. Asst S Chris's Ch Chatham MA 2007-2013; Serv Ch of the Netherlands 2003-2005; Serv Ch of Engl 2000-2007; S Jn's Ch Ellicott City MD 1993-1999.

SMITH, Geoffrey T (NH) 400 E 58th St Apt 3c, New York NY 10022 **Dom And Frgn Mssy Soc- Epis Ch Cntr New York NY 2017-; Epis Ch Cntr New York NY 2017-; D Par Of S Jas Ch Keene NH 2015-** B New Britain CT 1956 s Leander & Beverly. BA U of Connecticut 1978; MBA DePaul U 1981; Sch for Deacons 1996. D 2/3/1996 Bp Frank Tracy Griswold III. m 10/6/1979 Gerri L Hibbard c 2. Archd Ch Of S Jn The Evang Hingham MA 2012-2014; Archd Dio Massachusetts Boston MA 2011-2014, Archd 2011-2014, Archd, Deploy and Pstr Care 2011-2014; D Old No Chr Ch Boston MA 2008-2011; D Trin Epis Ch Portland ME 2003-2008; D Cathd Of S Jas Chicago IL 2000-2002; D S Greg's Epis Ch Deerfield IL 1996-2000; Safe Ch Trng Coordntr Dio Maine Portland ME 2003-2008. Recognition in the Tradition of St. Steph No Amer Assn of the Diac 2007. gsmith@episcopalchurch.org

SMITH III, George Dresser (Chi) 792 Forest Ave, Glen Ellyn IL 60137 **R S Mk's Epis Ch Glen Ellyn IL 2006-; R St. Mk's Glen Ellyn IL 2006-; Bd Dir Bp Anderson Hse Chicago IL 2010-** B Chicago IL 1963 s George & Rosemarie. BA Wesl 1985; MBA NWU 1992; MDiv SWTS 2003. D 6/21/2003 P 12/20/

2003 Bp Bill Persell. m 6/29/1991 Cecilia L Lad c 3. Assoc Chr Ch Winnetka IL 2005-2006; Chr Ch Winnetka IL 2003-2006; Bd Dir Epis Chars And Cmnty Serv (Eccs) Chicago IL 2009-2014; COM Dio Chicago Chicago IL 2008-2013. Cert Mstr Police Chapl Intl Conf of Police Chapl 2012; Phi Beta Kappa Wesl 1985.

✠ **SMITH, The Rt Rev George Wayne** (Mo) 823 Carillon Ct, Saint Louis MO 63141 **Bp of Missouri Dio Missouri S Louis MO 2002-** B Abilene TX 1955 s George & Hilda. BA Baylor U 1975; MA Baylor U 1978; MDiv Nash 1981; Dmin Sewanee: The U So, TS 1993. D 6/12/1981 P 6/11/1982 Bp Sam Byron Hulsey Con 3/2/2002 for Mo. m 5/21/1977 Debra Lynn Morris c 3. R S Andr's Ch Des Moines IA 1989-2002; R Emm Ch Hastings MI 1983-1989; The Epis Ch Of The Gd Shpd Brownfield TX 1981-1983; Dio NW Texas Lubbock TX 1981; Vic S Chris's Epis Ch Lubbock TX 1981. Auth, "Admirable Simplicity," Ch Pub Inc, 1996. bishop@diocesemo.org

SMITH, Georgianna (Minn) B 1959 d Robert & Janice. D 6/21/2016 Bp Brian N Prior. m 9/13/2014 Ramona Scarpace. deacong@saintannesmn.org

SMITH, Glenn Colyer (Chi) 754 Main St, Islip NY 11751 **Ret 1994-; Ret 1986-** B Oak Park IL 1924 s Frank & Ada. AA Evanston Coll Inst Evanston IL 1948; BD Loyola U 1951; MS CUA 1955; MDiv CUA 1955; DMin Trin Evang DS 1981. D 6/18/1971 Bp Gerald Francis Burrill P 2/15/1972 Bp James Winchester Montgomery. Asst Emm Epis Ch Rockford IL 1986-1994; R Ch Of S Jn Chrys Delafield WI 1972-1978; Cur S Dav's Epis Ch Aurora IL 1971-1972. Auth, "Cath Pastors Manual For Evang," Tyndall Hse; Auth, "Evang In The 80s," Tyndall Hse; Auth, "Evangelizing Adults," Tyndall Hse; Auth, "Evangelizing Yth," Tyndall Hse; Auth, "Evangelizing Blacks," Tyndall Hse; Ed, "Cath Living Bible," Tyndall Hse; Auth, "11 Manuals For Evang," Apostolic Mininstries.

SMITH, Graham Michael (Chi) St George's College Jerusalem, PO Box 1248, Jerusalem ISRAEL OR 91000 **Dn St. Geo's Coll Jerusalem 2011-** B Winnipeg MT CA 1948 s Norman & Ann. BA Ford 1970; MDiv EDS 1974; DMin VTS 1997. D 6/8/1974 Bp Paul Moore Jr P 1/25/1975 Bp Harold Louis Wright. m 5/5/1973 Sharon Smith c 1. R S Dav's Ch Glenview IL 1992-2011; R Ch Of The Gd Shpd Lyndhurst OH 1977-1992; Asst S Ptr's Epis Ch Lakewood OH 1974-1977. Auth, "Doctoral Thesis," *Servnt Ldrshp in the Par*, VTS, 1997.

SMITH, Gregory Louis (SC) 314 Grove Street, Charleston SC 29403 **D St Fran Epis Ch Charleston SC 2014-** B Denver CO 1947 s Robert & Janet. BS Colorado St U 1970. D 9/4/1999 Bp Edward Lloyd Salmon Jr. m 5/14/2011 Marilyn Smith c 2. Mgr Pstr Care Roper/St. Fran Hosp Charleston SC 2009-2011; D S Steph's Epis Ch Charleston SC 2007-2014; D St Andr's Mssn Charleston SC 2004-2007; D Epis Ch of the Gd Shpd Charleston SC 1999-2004.

SMITH, H Alan (CNY) 2891 Oran Delphi Rd, Manlius NY 13104 B 1940 BA Hobart and Wm Smith Colleges 1964; STB PDS 1969. D 6/7/1969 Bp William Elwood Sterling P 12/1/1969 Bp John Harris Burt. m 6/28/1969 Louise Harrington Smith. Archd And Cn To The Ordnry Dio Cntrl New York Liverpool NY 1988-2004; S Paul's Ch Watertown NY 1979-1987; S Andr's Ch New Berlin NY 1971-1979; S Matt's Ch So New Berlin NY 1971-1979; Cur S Chris's By-The River Gates Mills OH 1969-1971.

SMITH JR, Harmon Lee (NC) 3510 Randolph Rd, Durham NC 27705 B Ellisville MS 1930 s Harmon & Mary. BA Millsaps Coll 1952; BD Duke 1955; PhD Duke 1962. D 2/24/1972 P 6/24/1972 Bp Thomas Augustus Fraser Jr. m 8/21/1951 Bettye Watkins. Vic S Mk's Epis Ch Roxboro NC 1992-2014; Int S Tit Epis Ch Durham NC 1991-1992, Int 1987-1990, LocTen 1979-1986, LocTen 1974-1978; LocTen S Paul's Epis Ch Smithfield NC 1983-1984. Auth, *Where Two or Three are Gathered: Liturg & the Moral Life*, Pilgrim, 1995; Auth, *Profsnl Ethics and Primary Care Med*, Duke, 1986; Auth, *The Promiscuous Teenager*, Chas C. Thos, 1974; Auth, *Ethics and the New Med*, Abingdon, 1970; Auth, *The Chr and his Decisions*, Abingdon, 1969; Auth, *Var arts*. Amer Assn of Theol Schools - Fell 1968; Cooper Fndt for Neurologic Resrch and Educ - Fello 1968; Gurney Harris Kearns Fndt - Fell 1961; Lilly Fndt - Fell 1959; Mary Duke Biddle Fndt - Fell 1967; Natl Hmnts Cntr - Fell 1982; S Barn' Hosp - The Bronx, NY - Resrch Fell 1973. DSA of Merit Amer Heart Assn 1980.

SMITH, Harold Vaughn (Ind) 8328 Hawes Ct, Indianapolis IN 46256 B Muncie IN 1935 s Norman & Beatrice. BD Ball St U Teachers Coll 1962; MA Ball St U 1966; Estrn Kentucky U 1979; DMus Ball St U 1981; MDiv Epis TS in Kentucky 1987. D 7/13/1988 P 2/18/1989 Bp James Daniel Warner. m 6/26/1976 Christine M Smith c 2. P-in-c Trin Ch Connersville IN 2004-2008; Mem Dio Indianapolis Mssn Stategy Cmsn 2007-2009; Mem Dio Indianapolis Cmsn on Wrshp 1996-2000; Bd Proj Help 1995-2003; Vic S Ptr's Ch Lebanon IN 1995-2003; Adj Prof Estrn Wyoming Coll 1993-1995; R All SS Epis Ch Torrington WY 1991-1995; Bd Hse of the Trsfg Bayard NE 1991-1995; S Mk's Ch Creighton NE 1988-1991; Vic S Ptr's Ch Neligh NE 1988-1991. Natl Assn of Teachers of Singing 1974-2013.

SMITH, H Gregory (Pa) 5421 Germantown Ave, Philadelphia PA 19144 B Chicago IL 1951 s Harold & Mable. BS Bradley U 1974. D 6/14/1980 Bp Quintin Ebenezer Primo Jr P 12/1/1980 Bp James Winchester Montgomery. S Lk's Ch Philadelphia PA 1997-2015; R Ch Of The H Redeem Denver CO

S

1993-1997; Vic S Tim's Decatur GA 1990-1993; R S Lk And S Simon Cyrene Rochester NY 1985-1990; Ch Of The H Cross Chicago IL 1981-1985; Asst S Edm's Epis Ch Chicago IL 1980.

SMITH, Hilary Borbon (Va) 4924 Bethlehem Rd., Richmond VA 23230 **Ch Of The H Comf Richmond VA 2013-** B Washington DC 1968 d David & Rosemary. BA U Rich 1990; MA U of Leicester 1993; PhD U of Virginia 1997; MDiv VTS 2000. D 6/24/2000 P 2/6/2001 Bp Peter J Lee. R S Paul's On-The-Hill Winchester VA 2003-2012; Assoc R Ch Of S Jas The Less Ashland VA 2002-2003; Asst R S Paul's Ch Richmond VA 2000-2002. hilary@hoco.org

SMITH, H Mark (Mass) 10 Linda Lane, #2-8, Dorchester MA 02125 **Dio Massachusetts Boston MA 2014-, D, Yth Mnstrs Off 2010-2014, D, Boston Chinese Mnstry 2006-2010; D, Ch of the H Sprt Ch Of The H Sprt Mattapan MA 2013-** B Bellefonte PA 1956 s Mearle & Trudie. BA Buc 1978; MA Emerson Coll 1985. D 6/3/2006 Bp M(Arvil) Thomas Shaw. m 10/20/2013 David Cline. D S Jn's Epis Ch Holbrook MA 2011-2013; YouthReach Prog Mgr Massachusetts Cultural Coun Boston MA 1996-2014; Mem, Bd Dir Barbara C. Harris Camp & Conf Cntr 2012-2014. hmsmith@diomass.org

SMITH, Howard Louis (Alb) 970 State St., Schenectady NY 12307 **D Chr Ch Schenectady NY 2008-** B Derby CT 1972 s Leroy & Beverly. AA Hudson Vlly Cmnty Coll 1992. D 5/10/2008 Bp William Howard Love. m 10/4/1997 Sheila Smith c 3.

SMITH, Jacob Andrew (NY) 61 Gramercy Park N APT 7, 209 E 16th St, New York NY 10003 **Calv and St Geo New York NY 2007-** B Monument Valley UT 1976 s David & Mary. BA U of Arizona 2000; MDiv TESM 2006. D 6/4/2006 Bp Jim Mathes P 12/2/2006 Bp Egbert Don Taylor. m 8/4/2001 Melina Luna Smith c 2. S Paul's Ch Yuma AZ 2000-2003. revjacob@gmail.com

SMITH, Jacqueline Kay (Oly) 6208 83rd St Sw, Lakewood WA 98499 **Tchr of Spec Educ Auburn Sch Dist Auburn WA 1997-** B Hemet CA 1933 d Raymond & Ruby. California St U; Heritage U; U of Puget Sound; U of San Diego; BA USC 1954; MA USC 1961; Tchr Cred U CA 1976. D 6/25/2005 Bp Vincent Waydell Warner. c 3. Adult Educ Kauai HI 1996-1997; Dept. Chair of Spec Ed Cntr Unified Sch Dist Antelope CA 1987-1993.

SMITH, James Albert (Az) 8228 E Mohawk Ln, Scottsdale AZ 85255 B 1925 D 10/5/2002 Bp Robert Reed Shahan. m 12/29/1995 Diane Campbell c 2.

SMITH, James Clare (Be) 302 Pine St, Ashland PA 17921 **R H Apos St Clair PA 2000-; P No Par Epis Ch St. Clair PA 1999-** B Reading PA 1932 s Dorothy. D 9/25/1999 P 3/15/2000 Bp Paul Victor Marshall. m 11/11/1955 Lois Joan Batdorf.

SMITH, James Drinard (SVa) 3235 Sherwood Ridge Dr, Powhatan VA 23139 **Trst Boys Hm Inc. Covington VA 2010-; Fac Sthrn Virginia Sch for Mnstry Formation 2007-; Consult COM Dio SW Virginia Roanoke VA 1992-, Chair Evang Cmsn 1990-, Sprtl Advsr 1990-, Cmsn on Alco Use and Abuse 1989-, Educ Consortium 1989-, Exec Bd/Prog Com 1990-1994, Consult 1986-; Mentor EFM 1987-; Bd Mem Torch Club Richmond VA 2015-** B Richmond VA 1936 s George & Elizabeth. BA U Rich 1959; BD VTS 1962; MDiv VTS 1970; Fell Coll of Preachers Natl Cathd 1971; VTS 1984; EFM Sewanee: The U So, TS 2001. D 6/9/1962 P 6/1/1963 Bp Robert Fisher Gibson Jr. m 6/9/1959 Geraldine Hoffman Smith c 2. Int S Mich's Ch Richmond VA 2012; P-in-c S Steph's Ch Petersburg VA 2003-2011; Bd Managers Chairman, Dir Pres Chanco on the Jas Conf Cntr 1999-2008; Chr Ch Amelia Ct Hs VA 1997-2003; Emm Epis Ch Powhatan VA 1997-2003; R S Jas Ch Cartersville VA 1997-2002; Dn So Richmond Convoc Dio Sthrn Virginia Newport News VA 1997-1999, ExCoun 1984-1996, 1984-1985, Prog Design Team 1981-1983, Cmsn on Alco Use and Abuse 1980-1985, Cmsn on Alco Use and Abuse 1980, Curs Sprtl Advsr 1976-1979, Curs Sprtl Advsr 1976-1979, Inst Ldr 1975, Sch of Mnstry Romation Fac 2003-2008, Exec Bd 1998-2001, Exec Bd, Convoc Dn 1984-1985; Dn Roanoke Convoc 1993-1994; R S Eliz's Ch Roanoke VA 1989-1997; Int S Steph's Epis Ch Forest VA 1989; Int S Thos' Epis Ch Abingdon VA 1987-1989; Int S Jas Ch Roanoke VA 1986-1987; Int Gr Ch Lewiston NC 1985-1986; S Mk's Ch Roxobel NC 1985-1986; R S Chris's Epis Ch Portsmouth VA 1974-1985; Cn Assoc Cathd Of S Paul Erie PA 1970-1974; Assoc Trin Ch Manassas VA 1968-1970; Vic S Geo Pine Grove VA 1965-1968; R Chr Epis Ch Luray VA 1962-1968; Vic S Paul Ingham VA 1962-1968; Trst Boys Hm Covington VA 2007-2013; Assoc to Dn Dio NW Pennsylvania Erie PA 1970-1974; Yth Advsr to Dio Dio Virginia Richmond VA 1966-1970. SWECA 1989-1990. Personalities of the So 1975; Who's Who in Rel 1975.

SMITH JR, James Owen (EC) 113 S Woodlawn Ave, Greenville NC 27858 **D 1988-** B Bessemer AL 1949 s James & Mary. Auburn U 1970; BS U of Alabama 1973; MA U of Mississippi 1975; PhD U of Mississippi 1980. D 2/11/1988 Bp Brice Sidney Sanders. m 8/10/1974 Sylvia Dianne Smith c 1.

SMITH, James Ross (NY) 145 W 46th St #4, New York NY 10036 **Cur Ch Of S Mary The Vrgn New York NY 2007-, Asstg P 2004-2007, Asst 2001-2003, Asstg P 1998-1999** B North Tonawanda NY 1951 s William & Ann. BA Cor 1973; MFA Cor 1977; MDiv UTS 1987; STM Ya Berk 1989; MPhil Ya 1993. D 6/10/1989 Bp Paul Moore Jr P 12/9/1989 Bp Richard Frank Grein. m 6/22/2012 Jose A Vidal. Asstg P Chr Ch New Haven CT 1989-1996. ECF Fllshp. Fell ECF 1989.

SMITH, Jane Gravlee (WNC) 40 Wildwood Ave., Asheville NC 28804 B Birmingham AL 1936 d William & Lula. BS Wstrn Carolina U 1977; MDiv Sewanee: The U So, TS 1994. D 6/5/1994 P 12/10/1994 Bp Bob Johnson. c 1. Int S Jn's Ch Asheville NC 2006-2007; Cn to the Ordnry Dio Wstrn No Carolina Asheville NC 2001-2005, 1994-2005; Sewanee U So TS Sewanee TN 1998-2000; Gr Ch Asheville NC 1994-2001. S Mary's Cnvnt Sewanee.

SMITH, Jean (Ia) Saint Timothy's Epscopal Church, 1020 24th St, West des Moines IA 50266 **D S Tim's Epis Ch W Des Moines IA 2013-; Outside Coun Mem Wmn at the Well UMC Mitchellville Iowa 2016-; Bd Chair Cntr for Soc Mnstry Des Moines Iowa 2015-; Bd Chair The FreeStore Des Moines Iowa 2011-; Treas Iowa Rel Media Serv Des Moines Iowa 2002-** B Syracuse NY 1947 d John & Elizabeth. AB Cor 1969. D 5/18/2013 Bp Alan Scarfe. m 9/13/1969 William Herbert Smith c 4. deacon@sttimothysiowa.org

SMITH, Jean Ann (Ind) 6033 Gladden Dr, Indianapolis IN 46220 **S Phil's Ch Indianapolis IN 2007-; P S Alb's Ch Indianapolis IN 1998-** B Indianapolis IN 1943 d William & Ann. BA Butler U 1965; MDiv Chr TS 1999. D 6/24/1997 Bp Edward Witker Jones P 7/5/1998 Bp Cate Waynick. Theta Phi Chr TS 1997.

SMITH, Jean Reinhart (NJ) 58 Jenny Ln, Brattleboro VT 05301 **Assoc S Mich's Epis Ch Brattleboro VT 2008-** B Saint Louis MO 1942 d John & Elizabeth. BS NWU 1964; MDiv CDSP 1980; CDSP 1995. D 6/28/1980 Bp William Edwin Swing P 5/1/1981 Bp George Phelps Mellick Belshaw. m 6/15/1964 Peter T Smith c 2. Exec Dir Seamens Ch Inst New York NY 2003-2007, Dir Of Seafarers' Serv 1990-1995; Trin Ch Princeton NJ 1980-1990. DD CDSP 1998.

SMITH, Jeffry Bradford (SJ) 10 St Theresa'S Avenue, W Roxbury MA 02132 Great Britain (UK) **Cur S Paul 1985-** B Inglewood CA 1956 s Roger & Marguerite. Ripon Coll Cuddesdon Oxford Gb; BA Pitzer Coll 1982; MDiv CDSP 1985. D 2/22/1986 P 4/1/1987 Bp Victor Manuel Rivera. m 12/10/1977 Barbara H Smith. S Paul's Epis Ch Visalia CA 1986.

SMITH, Jerry W (Fla) 4800 Belmont Park Ter, Nashville TN 37215 **P-in-c H Comf Epis Ch Tallahassee FL 2016-** B Bracebridge Ontario CA 1951 s Clarence & Elaine. BA U of Wstrn Ontario CA 1973; MDiv Hur CA 1976; DMin Trin Evang DS 1995; MEd Nipissing U No Bay ON CA 2002. Trans 1/1/2005 as Priest Bp Bertram Nelson Herlong. m 5/30/1953 Betty Jean Smith c 3. R S Barth's Ch Nashville TN 2005-2016; Actg Acad Dn TESM Ambridge PA 2004-2005; Assoc Prof of Pstr Theol TESM Ambridge PA 2001-2005; Serv in the Angl Ch of Can 1976-2001.

SMITH, Jesse George (FtW) 2825 Winterhaven Dr, Hurst TX 76054 **Chapl Baylor All SS Med Cntr Ft Worth TX 2005-** B Poolville TX 1932 s Burcus & Stella. BA Baylor U 1953; BS U of New Mex 1960; MDiv Nash 1987. D 12/23/1987 P 6/23/1988 Bp Clarence Cullam Pope Jr. m 5/30/1953 Betty Jean Smith c 3. Int S Mich's Ch Richland Hills Ft Worth TX 2000-2001; Asst S Mart In The Fields Ch Keller TX 1997-2000; R S Lk's In The Meadow Epis Ch Ft Worth TX 1995-1997; S Anth's Ch Alvarado TX 1993-1995; Dio Ft Worth Ft Worth TX 1992; Assoc R S Steph's Epis Ch Hurst TX 1988-1991.

SMITH, Jessica (Oly) St Anne's Episcopal Church, 2350 Main St, Washougal WA 98671 **S Anne's Epis Ch Washougal WA 2012-** B Chester PA 1982 d Christopher & Iona. BA Goddard Coll 2005; MDiv Epis TS Of The SW 2012; MDiv Epis TS of the SW 2012. D 1/17/2012 P 7/17/2012 Bp Gregory Harold Rickel. m 8/27/2016 Drakar Abbah Druella.

SMITH IV, Jess Wayne (Wyo) 33 Windy Ridge Rd, Laramie WY 82070 B Denver CO 1947 s Jess & Virginia. Colorado Sch of Mines 1970. D 6/3/1997 P 12/13/1997 Bp Stewart Clark Zabriskie. m 7/26/1969 Leigh Ann Wailes c 2. Dio Wyoming Casper 2012-2014.

SMITH, Jethroe Larrie (At) 46 S Main St, Wadley GA 30477 B Millen GA 1944 s Elder & Ethel. BBA Georgia St U 1969; MDiv VTS 1973; Franciscan U of Steubenville 1981; U So 1981; Sch Pstr Care 1983. D 12/19/1973 Bp Bennett Jones Sims P 6/1/1974 Bp R aymond Stewart Wood Jr. m 11/8/2003 Janet R Clifton c 2. Dir S Jn's Day Sch W Point GA 1980-2006; Mentor Theol Educ By Ext 1979-1983; Exec Com Epis Dio Atlanta 1979-1980; Exec Bd Epis Dio Atlanta 1978-1990; Dn Chattanooga Vlly Conv 1978-1981; Dept Of Cong Dvlpmt Epis Dio Atlanta 1977-1985; S Jn's W Point GA 1975-2006; Asst S Mich And All Ang Ch Stone Mtn GA 1974-1975; Chapl Lorter Yth Cntr 1972-1973.

SMITH, Joan (Ky) 1077 Merrick Dr, Lexington KY 40502 B Beckley WV 1948 d John & Dorothy. BA Randolph-Macon Wmn's Coll 1971; MDiv VTS 1971. D 6/2/1982 P 6/1/1983 Bp Robert Poland Atkinson. Admin Dio Lexington Lexington 2015-2016; Int Ch Of The Gd Shpd Lexington KY 2014-2015, 1999-2000; Cn to the Ordnry Dio Kentucky Louisville KY 2007-2013; Int S Paul's Ch Henderson KY 2006-2007; P-in-c S Phil's Ch Harrodsburg KY 2004-2005; Int Ch Of The Adv Louisville KY 2003-2004; Int S Paul's Ch Louisville KY 2002-2003; Int S Raphael's Ch Lexington KY 2000-2002; Trin Epis Ch Danville KY 1999; Int Ch Of The Nativ Maysville KY 1998-1999; Ch S Mich The Archangel Lexington KY 1998-1999; 1995-1998; Assoc The Ch of the Redeem Cincinnati OH 1990-1995; P-in-c S Pat's Epis Ch Lebanon OH 1987-1990; Asst Chr Ch Cathd Cincinnati OH 1983-1987; Dio W Virginia Charleston WV 1982-1983; D Trin Ch Huntington WV 1982-1983; Cler Dio

Sthrn Ohio Cincinnati OH 1983-1994; Trst VTS Alexandria VA 1981-1985. jasmithrve@gmail.com

SMITH, John Cutrer (NY) 45 E 85th St, New York NY 10028 **Non-par 1959-** B Clarksdale MS 1924 s Edward & Blanche. U of Virginia 1948; STB GTS 1954; Cert Amer Fndt of Rel & Psych 1958; STM UTS 1962. D 6/4/1954 Bp Frederick D Goodwin P 12/18/1954 Bp James Pernette DeWolfe. Asst S Ann And The H Trin Brooklyn NY 1958-1959, Cur 1954-1957. AAPC.

SMITH, John Ferris (Mass) Box 3064, Wellfleet MA 02667 **P-in-c Chap Of S Jas The Fisherman Wellfleet MA 2000-** B Flint MI 1934 s Joseph & Agnes. BA U MI 1956; MDiv EDS 1959. D 6/27/1959 Bp Archie H Crowley P 1/21/1960 Bp Richard Stanley Merrill Emrich. c 2. Gvrng Bd NAES 1991-1994; Chapl S Jn's Chap Groton MA 1978-2000; Chapl Dio Massachusetts Boston MA 1961-1978; Cur S Chris-S Paul Epis Ch Detroit MI 1959-1961. Auth, "Cycle of Pryr for Epis Schools, 2nd Ed," NAES, 2008; Auth, *Living Forw: Reflections on Reaching A Certain Age*, Sorin Books, 2003; Auth, *Raising a Gd Kid*, Sorin Books, 2002; Auth, "Cycle of Pryr," *NAES*, NAES, 1991; Auth, *The Bush Still Burns*, Sheed Andrews and McMeel, 1978.

SMITH, John Harmon (SVa) 1741 Stratford View Dr, Blacksburg VA 24060 **Ret 1990-; 1968-** B Newport News VA 1924 s Charles & Susie. BS VPI 1948; BD Epis TS in Kentucky 1960. D 6/8/1960 P 12/17/1960 Bp William R Moody. c 2. Cur S Paul's Epis Ch Salem VA 2003-2006; Trin Ch Shepherdstown WV 1999-2006; Emm Ch Glenmore Buckingham VA 1986-1989; Emm Ch Scottsville VA 1976-1989; S Anne's Ch Appomattox VA 1976-1989; Dio Sthrn Virginia Newport News VA 1976-1978; Vic Hickory Neck Ch Toano VA 1969-1975; Vic Dio SE Florida Miami 1966-1967; Vic S Lukes Managua Nicaragua 1965-1966; Vic Iglesia Epis Espiritu Santo Tela 1962-1965; Vic Ch S Mich The Archangel Lexington KY 1960-1962.

SMITH, John Moffett (Va) 3000 S Randolph St Apt 284, Arlington VA 22206 B Bluefield WV 1936 s Clyde & Margaret. BA Duke 1959; MDiv VTS 1982. D 6/13/1962 P 12/19/1962 Bp Wilburn Camrock Campbell. m 8/18/1962 Eleanor Harrison Boothe Smith c 3. R S Jas' Epis Ch Leesburg VA 1975-1998; Assoc Chr Ch Charlotte NC 1974-1975; Chapl Epis HS Alexandria VA 1968-1974; Chapl Epis HS Alexandria VA 1968-1974; Assoc Chr Ch Exeter NH 1964-1968; Asst Trin Ch Morgantown WV 1962-1964. Auth, "Upholding Mar," 1988.

SMITH, John Perry (Fla) 256 E Church St, Jacksonville FL 32202 B Knoxville TN 1944 s John & Yuma. BA GW 1971; MA U of Oklahoma 1977; STM VTS 2003. D 2/29/1988 Bp William Davidson P 6/25/2002 Bp Robert Wilkes Ihloff. m 11/20/2010 Lisbeth Lynn Smith c 2. Cn S Jn's Cathd Jacksonville FL 2008-2013; Ch Of S Marks On The Hill Pikesville MD 2004; Emm Ch Baltimore MD 2002-2004; D Cathd Of The Incarn Baltimore MD 1999-2001; Nonpar 1996-1998; Assoc S Ptr's Epis Ch Ellicott City MD 1995-1996; Int Ch Of The Ascen And S Agnes Washington DC 1993-1994; Assoc Cathd Ch Of S Mk Minneapolis MN 1989-1993; Assoc SS Martha And Mary Epis Ch S Paul MN 1988-1989.

SMITH, John Peterson (WLa) 1904 Jasmine Dr, Opelousas LA 70570 B Carlsbad NM 1943 s Joe & Helen. BA TCU 1966; MDiv SWTS 1969. D 6/18/1969 Bp Charles A Mason P 1/1/1970 Bp William Paul Barnds. m 12/27/2014 Jennifer Reed. R Ch Of The Epiph Opelousas LA 1990-2015; R Gr Ch Lk Providence LA 1987-1990; S Paul's Ch Mc Gehee AR 1978; R Emm Ch Lake Vill AR 1976-1987; R S Thos Ch Ennis TX 1971-1976; Cur All SS' Epis Ch Ft Worth TX 1969-1971.

SMITH JR, John Robert (Az) 602 N Wilmot Rd, Tucson AZ 85711 B National City CA 1949 s John & Florence. BA S Thos 1971; STB Gregorian U 1974. Rec 11/1/1983 as Priest Bp Robert Hume Cochrane. m 6/26/2010 Teresa A Smith c 3. R Epis Par Of S Mich And All Ang Tucson AZ 1995-2015; R S Mich's Ch Coolidge AZ 1987-1995; Assoc S Paul's Ch Seattle WA 1983-1987; Assoc Pstr Ch of the Assumption Bellingham WA 1978-1980; Assoc Pstr St. Fran of Assisi Burien WA 1975-1978; COM Dio Arizona Phoenix AZ 1989-1994. EPF; SocMary.

SMITH, John Thomas (Md) 1204 Maple Ave, Annapolis MD 21401 B Philadelphia PA 1942 s Arthur & Laura. BS Penn 1972; MDiv Epis TS of the SW 1996. D 12/15/1996 P 7/11/1997 Bp John Stuart Thornton. m 8/21/2010 Sue Smith c 2. R S Lk's Ch Annapolis MD 2002-2010; P-in-c S Jas Ch Payette ID 1997-2002, D 1996-2002.

SMITH, Joseph Kershaw (Pa) 101 Shelton Dr, Spartanburg SC 29307 **S Mary's Ch Wayne PA 2014-; GC Dep Dio Upper So Carolina Columbia SC 2011-, Dioc Stndg Com 2010-2013, Bp's Election Transition Com 2010-2012, Bp's Transiton Com 2009-2010, Dioc Exec Com 2009-; Bd Dir Homeworks of Amer 2008-** B Columbia SC 1965 s Robert & Margaret. BA Coll of Charleston 1987; MDiv Sewanee: The U So, TS 2007. D 5/26/2007 P 2/2/2008 Bp Dorsey Henderson. m 7/2/1998 Sharon B Smith c 3. Vic S Chris's Ch Spartanburg SC 2009-2014; Asst S Matt's Epis Ch Spartanburg SC 2007-2008; Yth Dir S Jn's Epis Ch Columbia SC 1993-2004. Gathering of Leaders 2011.

SMITH, Juanita Dawn (Wyo) 15 S Tschirgi St, Sheridan WY 82801 B Hot Springs SD 1960 d Earle & Carmen. D 8/9/2014 Bp John Smylie. m 5/6/1991 Kurt Henry Eisenach c 2.

SMITH, Julie Honig (Ore) 335 SE 8th Ave, Hillsboro OR 97123 **Chapl Assoc Legacy Gd Samar Med Cntr 2016-; Sprtl Care Coordntr Tuality Health-Care 2014-; Mssnr for Ch Dvlpmt Dio Oregon Portland 2007-; Assoc S Jn the Bapt Portland OR 2005-** B Saint Louis MO 1952 d Harry & Ellen. BSW S Louis U 1974; MSW S Louis U 1979; Seattle U TS & Mnstry 1999; M.Div. CDSP 2000. D 6/24/2000 Bp Sanford Zangwill Kaye Hampton P 1/13/2001 Bp Vincent Waydell Warner. m 10/22/1994 Thomas Martin Smith. Vic S Bede's Ch Forest Grove OR 2005-2014; S Mk's Ch Yreka CA 2004-2005; S Barn Ch Mt Shasta CA 2002-2005; Vic All SS Epis Ch Redding CA 2002-2003; Assoc R S Barn Epis Ch Bainbridge Island WA 2000-2002. AAPC; CHS. julie.smith@tuality.org

SMITH, Karen (Ore) St John the Baptist, 100 S French St, Breckenridge CO 80424 **Dio Oregon Portland OR 2016-; Trin Ch Kremmling CO 2013-** B St Albans NY 1953 d Edward & Nellie. BS SUNY 1975; MA U CO 1993; MDiv Iliff TS 2013. D 1/26/2013 P 8/3/2013 Bp Robert John O'Neill. m 12/31/1980 James S Smith c 3. Vic Epis Ch Of S Jn The Bapt Breckenridge CO 2013-2015.

SMITH, Kathryn Barr (Ala) St Stephen's Episcopal Church, 3775 Crosshaven Dr, Vestavia AL 35223 **Dir of Pstr Care S Martins-In-The-Pines Ret Comm Birmingham AL 1986-** B Shreveport LA 1947 d Arthur & Martha. BM Westminster Choir Coll 1969. D 11/2/2002 Bp Henry Nutt Parsley Jr. m 9/13/1969 David John Smith c 2. D S Steph's Epis Ch Birmingham AL 2012-2013.

SMITH, Kent Clarke (Ct) 112 Sconset Ln, Guilford CT 06437 **P Affiliate Chr Ch New Haven CT 2004-** B Teaneck NJ 1937 s William & Dorothy. AB Pr 1959; MA Ya 1961; PhD Ya 1970; Cert EDS 1982. D 6/9/1984 P 4/13/1985 Bp Arthur Edward Walmsley. m 3/21/1970 Margaret W Williams c 2. GOE Rdr GBEC 2003-2011; R Chr Ch Redding CT 1986-2003; Cur Trin Ch Newtown CT 1984-1986; Ch Missions Pub Corp Bd Dio Connecticut Meriden CT 2004-2013, Coordntr D Trng Prog 1999-2005, Com on Pstr Oversight and Examination 1989-1995, Dioc Exec Coun 1989-1992, Archv Com 1987-2013. Auth, "arts & Revs In Chinese Hist". The Fllshp of S Jn 1985. Phi Beta Kappa 1959.

SMITH, Kermit Wade (WMo) PO Box 634, Kimberling City KS 65086 **Ret 1997-** B Bedford OH 1932 s Reuben & Blanche. BA SMU 1953; MTh SMU 1956. D 12/18/1966 P 7/3/1968 Bp Chilton R Powell. c 2. Vic S Mk's Epis Ch Kimberling City MO 2000-2007; Chapl Samar Hlth Serv Corvallis OR 1987-1997; The Coll of Chapl Schaumburg IL 1980-1985; Chapl Resrch & Med Cntr Overland Pk MO 1970-1980; Chapl Resrch Med Cntr Kansas City MO 1970-1980; Asst S Andr's Epis Ch Lawton OK 1966-1968; Pstr The Methodist Ch KS 1956-1963. (Clergycompanion) Worker Sis/Brothers Of The H Sprt 1975; Assn Of Profsnl Chapl 1969. The Bp's Shield Dio W Missouri 2009.

SMITH, Kerry Jon (Md) 6097 Franklin Gibson Rd, Tracys Landing MD 20779 **Archd S Jas' Par Lothian MD 2011-; Archd Dio Maryland Baltimore MD 2006-** B Brockton MA 1948 s John & Lorraine. BS USNA 1970; MBA Geo Mason U 1982; EFM Sewanee: The U So, TS 2000. D 6/10/2000 Bp Robert Wilkes Ihloff. m 12/6/1980 Arlinda Richard. D All SS Epis Par Sunderland MD 2003-2008; D Chr Ch W River MD 2000-2003.

SMITH, Kevin Corbin (Oly) 507 Mcgraw St, Seattle WA 98109 **S Clem's Epis Ch Seattle WA 2015-** B Yonkers NY 1956 s Vernard & Helen. BA Pacific Luth U 1979; MDiv GTS 1991. D 6/27/1992 P 4/1/1993 Bp Vincent Waydell Warner. S Geo Epis Ch Maple Vlly WA 2009-2010; S Andr's Ch Seattle WA 2004-2006; S Catherines Ch Enumclaw WA 1995-2003.

SMITH, Kirby (Los) 27802 El Lazo Rd., Laguna Niguel CA 92677 **Assoc S Lk's Of The Mountains La Crescenta CA 2015-, 2009-2011** B Mt Clemens MI 1954 s Wayne & Evelyn. BA Van 1976; MBA U of San Diego 1983; MDiv Claremont TS 2009. D 6/7/2008 P 1/10/2009 Bp Joseph Jon Bruno. m 9/19/2008 Clifford Chally. Vic Faith Epis Ch Laguna Niguel CA 2011-2015; S Geo's Par La Can CA 2010-2011; Asst The Ch Of The Ascen Sierra Madre CA 2008-2009; The Gooden Cntr Pasadena CA 1998-2005. Soc of Cath Priests 2010. kirby@stlukeslacrescenta.org

✠ SMITH, The Rt Rev Dr Kirk Stevan (Az) 114 W Roosevelt St, Phoenix AZ 85003 **Bp of Arizona Dio Arizona Phoenix AZ 2004-** B Soap Lake WA 1951 s Richard & Harriet. BA L&C 1973; MDiv Ya Berk 1979; MA Cor 1983; PhD Cor 1983. D 6/23/1979 Bp Joseph Thomas Heistand P 1/1/1980 Bp Morgan Porteus Con 4/24/2004 for Az. m 5/23/1998 Laura Fisher Smith c 1. R S Jas Par Los Angeles CA 1991-2004; R S Ann's Epis Ch Old Lyme CT 1984-1991; Assoc R St Johns Ch W Hartford CT 1979-1984. Auth, *Foundations of Chr Faith*; Auth, "Pope," *Teachers & Canonists*; Auth, *Thos Netter of Walden An Engl Conciliarist*. DD Berkely DS 2006. bishop@azdiocese.org

SMITH, Kristy K (Ia) 4339 W Sawmill Ct, Castle Rock CO 80109 B Davenport IA 1950 d Robert & Mary. BFA U of Iowa 1973; MDiv SWTS 1986. D 5/30/1986 P 12/3/1986 Bp Walter Cameron Righter. m 6/1/1974 David Edwin Smith c 2. S Andr's Ch Des Moines IA 2002-2003; Reg Vic S Matt's-By-The-Bridge Epis Ch Iowa Falls IA 1998-1999; Cler Fam Cmsn Dio Iowa Des Moines IA 1990-1993, Stndg Com 1992-1995, Bd Dir Dio 1986-1991; R S Mk's Epis Ch Des Moines IA 1989-1996; Asst to R The Cathd Ch Of S Paul Des Moines IA 1986-1989.

SMITH, Larry Phillip (Dal) 17236 Lechlade Lane, Dallas TX 75252 B Columbus OH 1941 s Phillip & Joanna. Mar 1968; BA W Liberty St Coll 1974; MDiv Nash 1977. D 6/8/1977 P 4/10/1978 Bp Robert Poland Atkinson. m 7/8/1967 Patricia A Smith c 2. Ch Of The Incarn Dallas TX 1997-2007; R Trin Ch Milwaukee WI 1982-1997; R Trin Ch Arkansas City KS 1978-1981; D-In-Trng Chr Ch Fairmont WV 1977-1978.

SMITH, Leslie Carl (NJ) 153 Seamans Rd, New London NH 03257 B Montague MA 1939 s Leslie & Janis. BA Suffolk U 1961; Bos 1965; MDiv VTS 1969. D 6/21/1969 Bp Anson Phelps Stokes Jr P 5/1/1970 Bp John Melville Burgess. m 8/13/1960 Lois K Dougherty c 5. Int Trin Epis Ch Southport CT 2013-2015; Assoc R S Lk's Par Darien CT 2011-2012; R Calv Ch Stonington CT 2009-2011; R Chr Ch Short Hills NJ 2007-2009; R Trin Ch Princeton NJ 1991-2006; Archd Dio Newark Newark NJ 1986-1990; R Chr Ch Glen Ridge NJ 1979-1986; Assoc R The Ch Of The Epiph Washington DC 1972-1979; Asst Min and McLean Hosp Chapl All SS' Epis Ch Belmont MA 1969-1972; Chapl Mclean Hosp Belmont MA 1969-1972. DD VTS 2005; Polly Bond Journalism Awds Epis Pub 1990; Polly Bond Journalism Awds Epis Pub 1988.

SMITH, Letitia Lee (NC) 2725 Wilshire Ave. S.W., Roanoke VA 24015 **Ret 2004-** B Washington DC 1952 d Henry & Virginia. BA Mid 1975; MA Iliff TS 1978; MDiv Iliff TS 1981; Syr 1997; CAS Epis TS of the SW 1999; Int Mnstry Prog 2000. D 6/7/1999 P 12/18/1999 Bp Robert Jefferson Hargrove Jr. m 3/22/1994 Ralph Bradley Laycock. Vic S Barn' Ch Greensboro NC 2003-2004; Ch of the Epiph Rumford RI 2001; St Mich & Gr Ch Rumford RI 2001; Int S Alb's Ch Wilmington DE 2000; The Ch Of The H Trin Rittenhouse Philadelphia PA 1999-2000; Serv Meth Ch 1978-1998. Auth, "Wmn and Adult Educ: An Analysis of Perspectives in Major Journ," *Adult Educ Quarterly*, 1994.

SMITH, Linda Becker (Nev) St Paul's Episcopal Church, PO Box 737, Sparks NV 89432 B Phoenix AZ 1946 d William & Phyllis. BS Arizona St U; MA U of Nevada. D 6/23/2012 Bp Dan Thomas Edwards. c 4.

SMITH, Lisa White (Minn) 4900 Nathan Lane, Plymouth MN 55442 **R Ch Of The Epiph Epis Minneapolis MN 2011-** B Ardmore OK 1957 d Otis & Nita. Oklahoma St U; BS Marymount Coll 1979; MDiv SWTS 1992. D 6/13/1992 P 1/6/1993 Bp Robert Manning Moody. m 5/24/1980 Michael Smith c 3. Dio Minnesota Minneapolis MN 1997-2011; Vic Samuel Memi Naytahwaush MN 1994-1997; Cur St Phil's Epis Ch Ardmore OK 1992-1994.

SMITH, Lizabeth Patterson (Nwk) 653 Courtney Hollow Lane, Madison VA 22727 B Bellefonte PA 1946 d Ralph & Mary. BA Maryville Coll 1968; MSW SUNY at Buffalo 1996. D 1/11/2003 Bp Michael Garrison. m 4/6/1969 Stuart Hardie Smith c 3. Asst Chapl S Clem's Ch Hawthorne NJ 2003-2011; The Epis Acad Newtown Sq PA 2003-2005.

SMITH, Lora Alison (Alb) 531 County Route 59, Potsdam NY 13676 **D Trin Ch Potsdam NY 2003-** B Warren OH 1959 D 6/29/2003 Bp Daniel William Herzog. m 8/25/1984 David Alan Smith c 3.

SMITH III, L(Ouis) Murdock (NC) St. Martin's Church, 1510 E. Seventh Street, Charlotte NC 28204 **Sec HOD 2003-; Dn Dio No Carolina Raleigh NC 2009-, Dioc Coun Mem 2004-2007, COM 2001-2008** B Raleigh NC 1948 s Louis & Susanne. BA Swarthmore Coll 1972; MDiv Epis TS of the SW 1982; MS U of Tennessee 1989; STM GTS 1990; PhD U of Tennessee 1994. D 6/16/1982 P 6/11/1983 Bp Robert Whitridge Estill. m 2/1/1975 Linda Van Tassel Smith c 3. R S Mart's Epis Ch Charlotte NC 1999-2013; Par Of S Jas Ch Keene NH 1995-1999; Int Trin Epis Ch Gatlinburg TN 1992-1993; Asst Ch Of The Ascen Knoxville TN 1986-1988; R S Alb's Epis Ch Hixson TN 1984-1986; Asst S Mary's Epis Ch High Point NC 1982-1983. Auth, "Var Theol & Counslg arts". AAMFT 1992; Ord Of S Lk 1986-1994; OHC 1982.

SMITH, Manning Lee (Md) PO Box 2157, Mountain Lake Park MD 21550 B Winston-Salem NC 1943 s Charles & Martha. BA Wake Forest U 1964; MDiv VTS 1968; MA Marshall U 1977; EdD U of Maryland 1989. D 6/11/1968 P 12/18/1968 Bp Wilburn Camrock Campbell. m 6/14/1969 Katharine L Smith c 2. R S Jas Epis Ch Westernport MD 2000-2007; Dn of Students Garrett Coll 1986-2000; R S Matt's Par Oakland MD 1974-1986; S Jas Ch Charleston WV 1971-1974; St Chris Epis Ch Charleston WV 1971-1974; Chapl W Virginia St Coll Inst WV 1971-1974; Asst Calv Epis Ch Ashland KY 1970-1971; Vic Emm Ch Moorefield WV 1968-1970. ACA 1977; NBCC 1983.

SMITH, Marc D (Mo) 4520 Lucas and Hunt Rd, Saint Louis MO 63121 **Vic Ch Of The Ascen S Louis MO 2011-; Borard of Trst, Epis Presb Hlth Trust Dio Missouri S Louis MO 2012-** B Cody WY 1949 s Albert & Eddyth. BS U of Missouri 1971; MDiv Luth TS 1975; PhD S Louis U 1979; Cert CDSP 2010. D 12/23/2010 P 6/24/2011 Bp George Wayne Smith. m 12/17/1977 Mary E Lee c 1. Auth, "For the Common Gd," *Trst mag*, Amer Hosp Assn, 2010; Co-Auth, "Best Practices in Hosp and Hlth System Governance," Missouri Hosp Assn, 2005; Auth, "Resrch: Reflection on Achilles' Heel, Magic Bullets and Routine Complications," *Anatomy of a Merger: BJC Hlth System*, Hlth Admin Press, 1997; Auth, "Missions, Margins and the Multitudes," *Anatomy of a Merger: BJC Hlth System*, Hlth Admin Press, 1997; Auth, "Creating a Clincl Resrch Framework for the Latvian Partnership," *Commonwealth*, 1996; Auth, "Cert of Need Regulation: Seeking Common Ground," *Hlth Systems Revs*, 1996; Ed, "BJC Hlth System: Anatomy of a Merger," Hosp Resrch and Education-

al Trust, 1995; Co-Auth, "Governance in Integrated Delivery Systems: Serving the Publ's Interest," *Frontiers of Hlth Serv Mgmt*, 1995; Co-Auth, "Transplantation and the Medicare End-Stage Renal Disease Prog," *New Engl Journ of Med*, 1988; Co-Auth, "The Hlth Ins Experience and Status of Missouri Renal Transplant Recipients," *Missouri Med*, 1987; Co-Auth, "Depressive Symptomatology and Treatment in Patients w End-Stage Renal Disease," *Psychol Med*, 1987; Co-Auth, "Living-Related Kidney Donors: A Multicenter Study of Donor Educ, Socioeconomic Status and Rehab," *Amer Journ of Kidney Diseases*, 1986; Co-Auth, "An Assessment of the Soc Networks of Patients Receiving Maintenance Ther for End-Stage Renal Disease," *Perspectives*, 1986; Auth, "An Integrated Thanatology Curric for a Grad Prog in Hlth Serv Admin," *The Thanatology Curric for Schools of Med, Nrsng, and Related Hlth Professions*, Col Press, 1986; Co-Auth, "Does Soc Spprt Determine the Treatment Setting for Hemodialysis Patients?," *Amer Journ of Kidney Diseases*, 1985; Co-Auth, "Geographic Access to Hlth Care Serv: The Case of Maintenance Hemodialysis," *Amer Journ of Kidney Diseases*, 1985; Co-Auth, "Diagnosis of Depression in Patients w End-Stage Renal Disease: Comparative Analysis," *The Amer Journ of Med*, 1985; Co-Auth, "Treatment Bias in the Mgmt of End-Stage Renal Disease," *Amer Journ of Kidney Diseases*, 1983; Co-Auth, "The Quality of Maintenance Ther for End-Stage Renal Disease: A Revs of Soc Adjustment and Rehab," *Evaltn & the Hlth Professions*, 1983; Co-Auth, "Pretreatment Intervention in the Mgmt of End-Stage Renal Disease," *Dialysis & Transplantation*, 1982; Co-Auth, "Pretreatment Depression in End-Stage Renal Disease," *The Lancet*, 1982; Co-Auth, "Instrn in Ethics in Schools of Pharmacy," *Amer Journ of Pharmaceutical Educ*, 1981; Auth, "Mediating Structures in the Regionalization of an Inpatient Pediatric System," *System Sci in Hlth Care*, Pergamon Press, 1981; Co-Auth, "Characteristics of Death Educ Curric in Amer Med Schools," *Journ of Med Educ*, 1980. Wm Coolidge Awd Cross Currents 2013; HOD Medal HOD 2012; Grant Rec Lilly Fndt for Cler Renwl 2012; DSA SE Missouri Hosp 2009; DSA Missouri Hosp Assn 2008; Distinquished Alum Awd Yale Univerity 2007; Frank R. Bradley Endowed Lectr Washington U Sch of Med 2006; Carden Awd Berry Coll 2004; Regent's Awd Amer Coll of Healthcare Executives 2002; Outstanding Tchr Awd Washington U Sch of Med 1985.

SMITH, Mark (Pa) 1904 Walnut St, Philadelphia PA 19103 **Ch Of S Jn The Evang Essington PA 2016-; S Paul's Ch Chester PA 2016-; The Ch Of The H Trin Rittenhouse Philadelphia PA 2014-** B Newton, MA 1965 BA The Curtis Inst of Mus 1987; BA U of Pennsylvania 1988; MDiv Candler TS Emory U 2006. D 12/21/2005 P 6/28/2006 Bp J Neil Alexander. m 6/4/1994 Wendy Wood Smith c 2. R S Lk's Epis Ch Mechanicsburg PA 2008-2013; Assoc S Paul's Ch Macon GA 2006-2008; Bassoonist Atlanta Symphony Orchestra 1990-2005.

SMITH, Martin L (WA) 429 N St SW Apt S306, Washington DC 20024 B Bury Lancashire UK 1947 s Edward & Pamela. BA Oxf GB 1968; Ripon Coll Cuddesdon 1970; MA Oxf GB 1971. Trans 11/5/1981 Bp Morris Fairchild Arnold. Assoc S Columba's Ch Washington DC 2007-2012; Adj Assoc S Columba's Washington DC 2005-2006; Superior SSJE 1992-2001; S Jn's Chap Cambridge MA 1981-2014; Mem SSJE 1981-2002; Soc-St Jn The Evang Cambridge MA 1981-2002; Asst Superior SSJE 1981-1989; Serv Ch of Engl 1970-1981. Co-Auth, "Go In Peace: The Art of Hearing Confessions," Ch Pub, 2012; Auth, "Love Set Free," Ch Pub, 2012; Auth, "Compass and Stars," Ch Pub, 2007; Auth, "A Season for the Sprt," Cowley Pub, 1991; Auth, "The Word Is Very Near You," Cowley Pub, 1989; Auth, "Recon: Preparing for Confession in the Epis Ch," Cowley Pub, 1985.

SMITH, Mary Jo (Vt) 973 Route 106, Reading VT 05062 B Fort Monmouth NJ 1943 d John & Constance. BA S Norbert Coll De Pere WI 1970. D 4/13/1985 Bp George Phelps Mellick Belshaw. m 6/27/1970 Channing Leslie Smith c 2. D S Barth's Ch Cherry Hill NJ 1985-2000.

SMITH, Melissa M (NC) 84 Broadway, New Haven CT 06511 B Nashville TN 1972 d Gilbert & Mary Jane. BA Trin 1995; MDiv UTS 2003; CAS CDSP 2008. D 6/28/2008 Bp Alfred Marble Jr P 5/15/2009 Bp Michael B Curry. m 10/12/2002 Edwin D Williamson c 2. S Aug's Chap Nashville TN 2010-2017; D Chr Ch New Haven CT 2008-2010.

SMITH JR, Merle Edwin (Ia) 715 W 7th St S, Newton IA 50208 **Vocational D S Steph's Ch Newton IA 2001-** B Des Moines IA 1955 D 4/7/2001 Bp Chris Christopher Epting. m 4/6/1991 Jana Illingworth.

✠ SMITH, The Rt Rev Michael (ND) Po Box 8, Naytahwaush MN 56566 **Bp of No Dakota Dio No Dakota Fargo ND 2004-** B Purcell OK 1955 s Harold & Nora. BS Oklahoma St U 1977; BA Marymount Coll 1980; MSK U of Oklahoma 1985; MDiv SWTS 1991. D 6/22/1991 P 1/18/1992 Bp Robert Manning Moody Con 5/8/2004 for ND. m 5/24/1980 Lisa White Smith c 5. Dn Geth Cathd Fargo ND 2011-2013; Vic S Columba White Earth MN 1997-2004; Vic Breck Memi Mssn Ponsford MN 1994-1997; Samuel Memi Naytahwaush MN 1994-1997; Chapl Oak Hall Epis Sch Ardmore OK 1991-1994; Cur St Phil's Epis Ch Ardmore OK 1991-1994. bpnodak@aol.com

SMITH, Michael Allen (Az) 2800 W Ina Rd, Tucson AZ 85741 **Assoc Ch Of S Matt Tucson AZ 2013-; R Chr the King Epis Ch Tucson AZ 2004-** B Las Cruces NM 1963 s William & Martha. Van 1982; BA U of Texas 1984; MDiv

VTS 1994. D 6/25/1994 Bp James Monte Stanton P 2/25/1995 Bp Sam Byron Hulsey. m 8/13/1994 Tamara Kim Hainline c 1. R Chr The King Ch Tucson AZ 2004-2012; Dio NW Texas Lubbock TX 1994-2004; Chapl Dio NW Texas Lubbock TX 1994-2004; Assoc Emm Epis Ch San Angelo TX 1994-2004; Emm Epis Ch San Angelo TX 1994-2003. Auth, "Burning Questions for God," *Sermons That Wk IX*, Morehouse Pub, 2000; Auth, "Creation's Praise of God: A Reading of Aug's Cosmology," hon *Thesis*, VTS, 1994.

SMITH, Michael John (SO) B Cincinnati OH 1947 s Jack & Dorothy. EdD No Cntrl U; BA Mt S Mary Sem Cincinatti OH 1969; MDiv Mt S Mary Sem Cincinatti OH 1973; MREd Loyola U 1978; MA Mt S Mary Sem Cincinatti OH 1988; EdD No Cntrl U 2012. Rec 6/4/2014 as Priest Bp Thomas Edward Breidenthal. m 5/2/2009 James Michael Newman. Asst The Ch of the Redeem Cincinnati OH 2015, P-in-c 2015-.

SMITH, Michael W (SC) 218 Ashley Ave., Charleston SC 29403 **Chapl Pinelands Grp Hm 2010-; D Ch Of The H Comm Charleston SC 2006-** B Charleston SC 1949 s Vernon & Gwendolyn. AS Trident Tech Coll 1972; MAR Luth Theol Sthrn Sem 2006; MAR Other 2006; STM Luth Theol Sthrn Sem 2012; STM Other 2012; STM Other 2012. D 10/12/2006 Bp Edward Lloyd Salmon Jr. m 3/24/1996 Eleanor Smith c 2. Chapl Carolina Yth Dvlpmt Cntr 2006-2009; Chapl Res Roper S Fran Hospitals 2004-2005.

SMITH, Miles Miles (Va) Grace Church, PO Box 43, 5607 Gordonsville Rd, Keswick VA 22947 **R Gr Ch Keswick VA 2013-** B Charlotte NC 1956 s Herman & Connie. BA Duke 1978; MDiv Duke DS 1981. D 6/4/2001 P 4/27/2002 Bp Bob Johnson. c 1. P-in-c Ch Of The Epiph Newton NC 2012-2013; P-in-c S Lk's Epis Ch Lincolnton NC 2008-2013; Spprt Serv Supvsr Hospice of Haywood Reg Med Cntr 2006-2008; Cur S Mary's Ch Asheville NC 2002-2003; Elder The Meth Ch 1981-1997. gmiles@gracekeswick.org

SMITH, Mitchell T (La) 1329 Jackson Ave, New Orleans LA 70130 **Trin Ch New Orleans LA 2011-** B Oconomowoc WI 1981 s Edward & Evelyn. BA Wstrn Illinois U 2003; SWTS 2006. D 12/17/2005 P 7/1/2006 Bp Alan Scarfe. m 6/21/2003 Denise M Smith c 2. Trin Epis Par Waterloo IA 2006-2011. msmith@trinitynola.com

SMITH, Molly Dale (NJ) 805 Timber Ln., Nashville TN 37215 **P Assoc S Dav's Epis Ch Nashville TN 2009-; Fac Serv Int Mnstry Ntwk 2004-; Fac Int Mnstry Ntwk 2003-** B Rochester NY 1945 d William & Corinne. BA Hollins U 1967; MTS Candler TS Emory U 1990; MDiv SWTS 1993; DMin S Paul TS 2000. D 6/5/1993 P 12/6/1993 Bp John Clark Buchanan. m 3/18/1967 Richard Smith c 3. S Ptr's Epis Ch Peekskill NY 2006-2007; Int R All SS Epis Ch Jacksonville FL 2003-2006; Int R All SS Ch Millington NJ 2003, Int R 2000-2002; Chr Ch Three Bridges NJ 2002; Int S Thos Ch Alexandria Pittstown NJ 2000; Int Chr Ch Ridgewood NJ 1999-2000; Asstg P S Lk's Ch Gladstone NJ 1999; Int S Paul's Epis Ch Morris Plains NJ 1998-1999; Dio W Missouri Kansas City MO 1994-1998. Ed, "Transitional Mnstry: Time of Opportunity," Ch Pub, 2009.

SMITH, Myrl Elden (O) 4541 Gilhouse Rd, Toledo OH 43623 B Circleville OH 1938 s Myrl & Helen. BS Witt 1960; MDiv EDS 1964. D 6/13/1964 P 12/19/1964 Bp Roger W Blanchard. c 4. R Trin Ch Findlay OH 1979-2004; R S Paul Epis Ch Norwalk OH 1972-1979; Vic S Matt's Ch Ashland OH 1966-1972; Asst S Phil's Ch Columbus OH 1964-1966.

SMITH, Nancy Metze (SwFla) 13011 Sandy Key Bend, Apt 1, North Fort Myers FL 33903 **D All Souls Epis Ch No Ft Myers FL 2010-; D Ch Of The Epiph Cape Coral FL 2005-** B Charleston SC 1939 d Hugo & Irene. D 6/18/2005 Bp John Bailey Lipscomb. c 2. "UN's Millennium Dvlpmt Goal," *The Sthrn Cross*, Dio SW FL, 2006; "A Pryr from the Beacon of H.O.P.E.," *Pine Island Eagle*, The Breeze Pub., 2005. OSL 2008; Steph Min Ldr 2008.

SMITH, Nancy Spencer (Mass) 29 W Cedar St, Boston MA 02108 B Boston MA 1941 d Carlton & Helen. BA Connecticut Coll 1963; JD Bos 1966; MDiv EDS 1991. D 6/5/1993 P 6/1/1994 Bp Don Edward Johnson. m 3/10/1984 Geoffrey Welles Smith. The Epis Ch Of S Jn The Bapt Sanbornville NH 1993-1994.

SMITH, Nora (NY) 11 N. Broadway, Irvington NY 10533 B New York NY 1957 d Robert & Jean. BA Brandeis U 1981; MDiv Ya Berk 2007. D 3/10/2007 P 9/15/2007 Bp Mark Sean Sisk. R S Barn Ch Irvington NY 2009-2017; Assoc Ch Of The Intsn New York NY 2007-2009; Dio New York New York NY 2007-2009.

SMITH, Paul Bruce (Ak) 9631 Noaya, Eagle River AK 99577 **Chapl Kodiak Police Dept 1984-** B Wheeling WV 1947 s Charles & Catherine. BA W Liberty St Coll 1980; MDiv VTS 1984. D 6/6/1984 P 4/15/1985 Bp Robert Poland Atkinson. R H Sprt Epis Ch Eagle River AK 2010-2015; S Jas The Fisherman Kodiak AK 2008-2010, P-in-c 2008-2010, R 1993-1998; S Mk's Epis Ch Berkeley Spg WV 1985-1993; Cur Trin Ch Huntington WV 1984-1985. Natl Inst Of Ethics 2001.

SMITH, Paul Weeghman (Ky) 3724 Hillsdale Rd, Louisville KY 40222 **Ret 1994-** B Richmond IN 1935 s Paul & Dessolyn. BA MI SU 1957. D 11/19/1976 P 4/25/1978 Bp William Cockburn Russell Sheridan. m 6/25/1961 Susan Smith c 4. Non-Stipendiary S Mk's Epis Ch Louisville KY 1994-2000; R S Ptr's Epis Ch Louisville KY 1986-1994; Non-stip S Geo Ch Berne IN 1983-1985; Assoc Trin Ch Ft Wayne IN 1982-1985.

SMITH, Perry Michael (WA) 15 Charles Plz Apt 2307, Baltimore MD 21201 **Ret 1994-** B Springfield MO 1937 s Perry & Marian. BA Harv 1959; STB Ya Berk 1962; U Chi 1966. D 4/24/1962 P 11/8/1962 Bp Edward Randolph Welles II. R Ch Of The Ascen And S Agnes Washington DC 1985-1994; Vic Ch of the H Name Dolton IL 1977-1985; Dir - Coll Wk Dept Dio Wstrn New York Tonawanda NY 1966-1972; Chapl SUNY In Buffalo 1966-1972; Asst S Lk's Ch Evanston IL 1963-1966; Chapl Missouri Vlly Coll In Marshall 1962-1963; P-in-c S Paul Carrollton MO 1962-1963; Vic Trin Epis Ch Marshall MO 1962-1963; Commision on Mnstry Dio Washington Washington DC 1987-1992. Auth, "Cfm:A Confrontation"; Auth, "Last Rites," Scribners; Auth, "For Jeff," Dell. CCU; ECM.

SMITH, P(hilip) Kingsley (Md) 8339 Carrbridge Cir, Towson MD 21204 **Ret 1996-** B Toronto CA 1929 s Frank & Amy. BA Amh 1950; MDiv VTS 1956; Coll of Preachers 1984. D 7/5/1956 P 4/12/1957 Bp Noble C Powell. m 11/17/1951 Mary E Smith c 4. P-in-c Imm Epis Ch Glencoe MD 2008-2012; Asst Ch Of The Gd Shpd Towson MD 2004-2007; Asst Gd Shpd Towson MD 2004-2007; Int Ch Of The Redemp Baltimore MD 2002-2003; Int Sherwood Epis Ch Cockeysville MD 1999-2001; S Geo's Ch Perryman MD 1996-1998; Trin Ch Towson MD 1956-1995; Chapl USNR 1955-1976; Hstgr Dio Maryland Baltimore MD 1996-2015, 1988-1995. Auth, *Towson Under God*, Baltimore Cnty Libr, 1976. Natl Epis Historians & Archivists 1996; SBL 1957.

SMITH, Ralph (NY) 219 Old Franklin Grove Dr Apt 6-A, Chapel Hill NC 27514 **S Paul's Ch- Morrisania Bronx NY 2003-; Ret 1997-** B Inman SC 1932 s Hubert & Hulda. BA CUNY 1966; MDiv GTS 1969; STM NYTS 1976. D 6/7/1969 P 12/20/1969 Bp Horace W B Donegan. m 9/7/1991 Susannah Rankin Smith c 3. S Andr's Ch Bronx NY 2003-2005; Int S Andr's Epis Ch Bronx NY 2003-2005; Int Ch Of S Jn The Div Hasbrouck Hts NJ 1994-1996; S Ptr's Ch Rochelle Pk NJ 1994; Int Chr Ch Hackensack NJ 1993-1994; Int Chr Ch Hackensack NJ 1993-1994; Vic Ch Of The Trsfg No Bergen NJ 1990-1993; Ch Of The H Comm Paterson NJ 1990; S Mart Ch Detroit MI 1987-1990; R S Mart's Ch Detroit MI 1987-1989; P-in-c Chr Ch Marlboro NY 1985-1987; Chr Ch Marlboro NY 1977-1987; R S Thos Epis Ch New Windsor NY 1971-1985; Ch Of S Thos Detroit MI 1971-1984; Dio New York New York NY 1969-1976; Asst S Paul's Epis Ch Bronx NY 1969-1971. ralphsmith4@yahoo.com

SMITH JR, Ralph Wood (ETenn) Po Box 476, Mountain Home TN 37684 **Ret 1989-** B Bluefield WV 1926 s Ralph & Gladys. BS Davidson Coll 1947; MDiv VTS 1950. D 7/25/1950 Bp Robert E L Strider P 7/21/1951 Bp Wilburn Camrock Campbell. m 5/28/1977 Jeanne B Smith c 1. S Jn's Ch Mart TN 1985-1989; Chapl U Tn Mart TN 1985-1989; Dio W Tennessee Memphis 1985-1988; R S Anne's Ch Millington TN 1980-1984; Chapl Veta Psych Hosp 1977-1980; R Ch Of The Ascen Lafayette LA 1966-1967; R S Tim's Epis Ch Kingsport TN 1960-1966; Chapl W&L Vmi Lexington VA 1956-1960; R S Andr's On The Sound Ch Wilmington NC 1953-1956; R Chr Ch Wellsburg WV 1951-1953. CH. Soc for Coll Wk 1955-1960.

SMITH, Raymond Robert (Colo) 23321 E Dry Creek Cir, Aurora CO 80016 **Ret 1989-** B Columbus OH 1921 s Raymond & Clara. Carnegie Inst of Tech 1944; FD 1964; BS U CO 1968; MDiv Nash 1978. D 6/29/1978 P 2/14/1979 Bp William Carl Frey. m 10/22/2006 Maryan Sneed c 3. Assoc S Lk's Ch Denver CO 1996-1997, Int 1991-1995; R S Greg's Ch Littleton CO 1984-1989; The Epis Par of S Greg Littleton CO 1979-1989; Dio Colorado Denver CO 1978-1979; H Apos Epis Ch Englewood CO 1978-1979.

SMITH, Richard Byron (NC) 6 Natchez Court, Greensboro NC 27455 **Ret 1987-** B Newport News VA 1927 s Charles & Susie. U of Tennessee 1956; Epis TS in Kentucky 1961; CR Lang Sch 1965. D 6/11/1961 P 12/17/1961 Bp William R Moody. m 9/5/1953 Mary B Smith c 3. Asst S Jn's Ch Hampton VA 1987-1989; R Ch Of The Adv Enfield NC 1984-1987; P-in-c S Jn's Ch Battleboro NC 1984-1987; R S Geo's Epis Ch Newport News VA 1968-1984; Asst S Fran All SS Managua Nic 1966-1968; Asst Chr Epis Ch Warren OH 1963-1965; R S Jn the Evang Dayton KY 1961-1963.

SMITH, Richard Leslie (Cal) 226 Clinton Park, San Francisco CA 94103 **P Assoc The Epis Ch Of S Jn The Evang San Francisco CA 2001-** B Seattle WA 1950 s Leslie & Margaret. MDiv Loyola U 1979; PhD Greaduate Theol Un Berkeley CA 1993. Rec 6/2/2001 Bp William Edwin Swing. m 6/17/2000 Robby C K Tan.

SMITH JR, Richard Winton (Pa) 305 E 83rd St Apt 4g, New York NY 10028 B Wyandotte MI 1939 s Richard & Alicia. MDiv EDS; BA MI SU 1961. D 6/29/1965 Bp Chauncie Kilmer Myers P 1/1/1966 Bp Richard Stanley Merrill Emrich. m 6/24/1978 Mildred Smith c 3. H Innoc S Paul's Ch Philadelphia PA 1994-1999; Evang Stff Dio Michigan Detroit MI 1990-2002, 1987-1994; R Gr Ch Mt Clemens MI 1977-1987; R S Lk's Epis Ch Allen Pk MI 1971-1977; Cur S Paul's Epis Ch Flint MI 1965-1969.

SMITH JR, Robert Adrian (Me) 35 Prospect St, Caribou ME 04736 **Vic S Anne's Ch Blaine ME 1991-** B Augusta ME 1945 s Robert & Barbara. BS Aroostook St Teachers Coll 1967; MA U of Maine 1968; MDiv Bangor TS 1991; DMin Bangor TS 1997. D 6/10/1991 P 12/14/1991 Bp Edward Cole Chalfant. m 10/4/1969 Thelma Jean Smith c 2. Dio Maine Portland ME 2000-2012; R Aroostook Epis Cluster Caribou ME 1991-2012; Ch Of The Adv Limestone ME 1991; S

S

Jn's Ch Presque Isle ME 1991; S Lk's Ch Caribou ME 1991; S Paul's Ch Ft Fairfield ME 1991.

SMITH, Robert Angus (WMich) 212 Courtland St, Dowagiac MI 49047 **Ret 1998-** B Chicago IL 1933 s James & Lora. BA Lawr 1955; BD Nash 1958; MA U of Wisconsin 1975; STM Nash 1979; Ldrshp Acad for New Directions 1983; DMin GTF 1986. D 3/22/1958 P 10/4/1958 Bp William Hampton Brady. R S Paul's Epis Ch Dowagiac MI 1988-1998; Del Prov Vic Syn Dio Nthrn Michigan Marquette MI 1978-1986, Dioc Coun 1981-1984, Chair Ecum Rel Com 1979-1987, COM 1978-1988, Chair Com Memis & Resolutns 1978-1987, Hunger Cmsn 1978-1980, Human Sxlty Com 1977; R Gr Epis Ch Menominee MI 1976-1988; Gr Ch Madison WI 1974-1976; Vic S Mk's Ch Oconto WI 1971-1974; Vic S Paul's Epis Ch Suamico WI 1960-1974; Asst S Bon Chilton WI 1958-1960; Asst S Paul's Ch Plymouth WI 1958-1960; Com on Wrshp Dio Wstrn Michigan Kalamazoo MI 1992-2004, Ecum Rela Com 1991; ExCoun Dio Fond du Lac Appleton WI 1972-1974, ExCoun 1965-1971.

SMITH, Robert Clarke (Pa) 2033 Bainbridge St, Philadelphia PA 19146 **Int S Andr's Epis Ch Glenmoore PA 2015-** B Sioux Center IA 1940 s Alfred & Elizabeth. BA U of Iowa 1962; MA U Chi 1963; Luth TS 2000; MDiv GTS 2001. D 6/23/2001 P 6/1/2002 Bp Charles Ellsworth Bennison Jr. m 8/27/1983 Lorene E Cary c 3. S Paul's Ch Doylestown PA 2017-2004, 2017-, Asst 2001-2004; Int S Mary's Ch Wayne PA 2013-2014; Bd Trst Epis Cmnty Serv 2010-2012; Dn Dio Pennsylvania Philadelphia PA 2008-2010; R Ch Of The Gd Shpd Philadelphia PA 2004-2012.

SMITH, Robert E (Mich) 22326 Cherry Hill St, Dearborn MI 48124 **Epis D Sprt of Hope Epis/Luth Ch Detroit MI 2006-; Trin Ch Detroit MI 1996-** B Detroit MI 1944 s Edward & Marion. BA Wayne 1973; Cert Whitaker TS 1994. D 9/28/1996 Bp R aymond Stewart Wood Jr. m 8/24/1968 Sharon Smith c 3. Chr Ch Dearborn MI 2001-2011; D Chr Ch Detroit MI 1996-2000. NAAD 1997. Meritorious Serv Medal U.S. AF 1995.

SMITH, Robert Kennedy (CFla) 3224 Carleton Circle East, Lakeland FL 33803 B Clarksburg WV 1949 s Gerald & Betty. DMin RTS Orlando in Progress; BA W Virginia U 1975; MDiv VTS 1988. D 6/1/1988 Bp Robert Poland Atkinson P 6/1/1989 Bp William Franklin Carr. m 11/8/1968 Deborah M Smith c 2. R S Dav's Epis Ch Lakeland FL 1999-2012; Trin Ch Vero Bch FL 1990-1998; S Jn Wheeling WV 1990-1991; S Lk's Ch Wheeling WV 1990-1991; Assoc S Paul's Ch Wheeling WV 1990-1991; The Wheeling Cluster Wheeling WV 1989-1990; D-in-Trng S Matt's Ch Wheeling WV 1988-1989. Amer Assn Chr Counslrs.

SMITH, Robert Russell (Eas) 35 Spruance Ct, Elkton MD 21921 B Englewood NJ 1947 s James & Viola. BA Amer U in Cairo 1970; MDiv GTS 1976. D 6/5/1975 P 12/11/1976 Bp George E Rath. m 5/24/1975 Susan D'Antonio. R S Mk's Epis Ch Perryville MD 2006-2010; R Ch Of The H Comm Norwood NJ 1995-2006; Chr Edu Com Dio Newark Newark NJ 1995-1998; R S Jas' Ch Indn Hd MD 1981-1994; Asst Gr St Pauls Epis Ch Tucson AZ 1980-1981; Cur Par of Chr the Redeem Pelham NY 1976-1979. Auth, "Full length Drama," *The Inquiry: A New Look at the Death of Jesus*, 2011; Auth, "Chancel Comedies," *Bad Ideas About God*, 2002; Auth, "Chancel Comedies," *Talent Show*, 1996; Auth, "Tomb KV5: Is Underground Tomb for Sons of Ramses II a Coptic Monstry?," *Coptic Ch Revs*, 1995; Auth, "Chancel Drama," *Kiss of Peace*, 1985; Auth, "Chancel Comedies, All In The One Fam (Adam and Eve," *Cain and Abel)*; Auth, "Chancel Comedies," *I Dissed My Boss w His Own Dough- A Chancel Comedy on Stwdshp*; Auth, "Chancel Comedies, Henry VIII vs Mart Luther," *Next on Theologically Incorrect*; Auth, "Chancel Comedies," *Parents Who Forgive Prodigals for Anything Next on Horrendo*; Auth, "Chancel Comedies," *The Temptation Zone*. Fllshp Of Merry Christians 2002; WECA 1981-1994.

SMITH, Roberts Cameron (Los) B Charlotte NC 1941 s David & Carol. BA U of Vermont 1968; MDiv CDSP 1972; DMin Sewanee: The U So, TS 1997. D 11/1/1974 Bp Harvey D Butterfield P 5/23/1975 Bp Robert Shaw Kerr. m 12/26/1972 Aloha Lee Von Glan c 2. Curs Sec Mem Dio Los Angeles Los Angeles CA 2001-2005; R S Mich's Epis Ch Riverside CA 1998-2008; Serv Angl Ch of Can 1983-1998; Cmsn on Lay Mnstry Dio New Jersey Trenton NJ 1980-1982, Curs Sec Mem 1979-1981; R S Jn The Evang Ch New Brunswick NJ 1979-1982; Asst/Assoc S Lk's Ch Gladstone NJ 1976-1979; Exec Coun Appointees New York NY 1976; Curs Sec Mem Dio Vermont Burlington VT 1975-1976; H Trin Epis Ch Swanton VT 1975-1976; DCN-Cur/Vic NW Area Mnstry St. Albans VT 1974-1976. OSL the Physcn 1976.

SMITH, Robin (Pa) 107 Allison Rd, Oreland PA 19075 B Vancouver WA 1951 d Bernard & Elaine. BA Rosary Coll River Forest IL 1973; MDiv GTS 1982; STM GTS 1983. D 6/5/1982 Bp Albert Wiencke Van Duzer P 12/21/1982 Bp George Phelps Mellick Belshaw. c 2. R S Phil in the Fields Oreland PA 2012-2016; S Jn's Ch Clinton MI 2008-2012; P-in-c S Ptr's Ch Tecumseh MI 2008-2012; Chapl Forks Cmnty Hosp 2005-2008; Dio New York New York NY 1997-2001; R S Andr's Ch Walden NY 1992-2000; R St Fran of Assisi Montgomery NY 1992-1996; Ch Of S Clem Of Rome Belford NJ 1991-1992; Vic Ch Of The Trsfg Rome GA 1986-1990.

SMITH, Robin Penman (Dal) 2712 E Aspen CT, Plano TX 75075 **P-in-c Trin Epis Ch Dallas TX 2010-** B Hamilton ON CA 1939 s Harold & Ruth. BA Gordon Coll 1965; MDiv Ya Berk 1969; DMin Fuller TS 1989. D 6/21/1969 Bp

Anson Phelps Stokes Jr P 5/31/1970 Bp John Melville Burgess. m 8/26/1965 Diana Smith c 2. Int S Ptr's Ch Mc Kinney TX 2009-2010; R Ch Of The Apos Coppell TX 1990-2009; Vic Dept Of Missions Dallas TX 1989-1990; R Trin Ch Covington KY 1983-1989; R S Steph's Epis Ch Mckeesport PA 1980-1983; Assoc S Barth's Ch Nashville TN 1977-1979; R Ch Of The Gd Shpd Watertown MA 1971-1977; Cur The Par Of S Chrys's Quincy MA 1969-1971. Auth, "7 Keys to a Working Faith," *Chr Life mag*, 1993; Auth, "Leading Christians To Chr: Evangelizing The Ch," Morehouse, 1989. CBS; Oblate Ord Of S Ben 1997.

SMITH, Roger Stilman (Me) 70 Country Club Rd, Manchester ME 04351 B Norwood MA 1928 s Edward & Gladys. BA Colg 1950; MDiv Ya Berk 1953; DMin Hartford Sem 1985. D 6/15/1953 P 3/30/1954 Bp Oliver L Loring. m 6/6/1953 Edna Smith c 2. Int S Jas Ch Old Town ME 1992-1993; Int Ch Of S Jas The Less Scarsdale NY 1991; Vic S Andr's Ch Winthrop ME 1986-1990; St Andrews Mssn Augusta ME 1986-1990; Cathd Ch Of S Lk Portland ME 1977-1982; P-in-c S Andr's Winthrop ME 1965-1977; R S Mk's Ch Augusta ME 1965-1977; Chapl ARAMCO Cmntys Saudi Arabia 1960-1964; P-in-c S Anne's Mars Hill ME 1955-1960; R S Paul's Ft Fairfield ME 1955-1960; Vic Ch Of The Gd Shpd Rangeley ME 1953-1955. Contrib, *Ecology & Chr Responsibility*, 1975. Comp CCN.

SMITH, Roger W (SC) 15 Newpoint Rd, Beaufort SC 29907 **P in Charge St. Marks Epis Ch Port Royal SC 2003-; Ret 1993-** B Jackson MI 1928 s Hugh & Genevieve. BA U MI 1949; STB EDS 1954; Coll of Preachers 1965; Oxf GB 1971; MA Trin Hartford CT 1972. D 6/20/1954 P 12/21/1954 Bp Albert Ervine Swift. m 5/30/1953 Headley Hall Smith c 4. Assoc All SS Ch Hilton Hd Island SC 1995-2003; R Par Ch of St. Helena Beaufort SC 1984-1993; R Ch Of The H Sprt Wayland MA 1976-1984; Dn Cathd of Chr the King Kalamazoo MI 1975-1976; Dio Wstrn Michigan Kalamazoo MI 1975-1976; R S Jas Epis Ch Farmington CT 1961-1975; R S Jn's Ch Christiansted St Croix VI 1957-1960; Vic S Andr's Ch St Thos VI 1956-1957; Headmaster All SS Sch S Thos VI 1955-1957; All SS Cathd Sch St Thos VI 1954-1957; Cur All SS Epis Ch S Thos VI 1954-1957. OHC 1964.

SMITH, Ron (Tex) 1403 Preston Ave, Austin TX 78703 B Kansas City MO 1947 s J Neil & Frances. BA U of Kansas 1970; MA U of Kansas 1974; MDiv Epis TS of the SW 1975; MBA U of Texas 1983; MA U of Texas 1992. D 7/13/1986 P 6/15/1988 Bp Thomas Kreider Ray. m 6/1/1969 Anna Kay Smith c 1. S Dav's Ch Austin TX 1992-2012; Dio Nthrn Michigan Marquette MI 1986-2001.

SMITH, Rose Ann (NwT) 3500 Barclay Dr, Amarillo TX 79109 B Santa Fe NM 1938 d William & Rosaamond. Dplma NW Texas Hosp Nrsng Sch 1973; Cert U of Texas 1979; BSN W Texas St U 1983; MSN W Texas A&M U 1993. D 11/6/1988 Bp Sam Byron Hulsey. m 11/18/1968 William Burnam Smith c 3. D S Ptr's Epis Ch Amarillo TX 1993-2003; D S Thos Epis Ch Hereford TX 1988-1993.

SMITH, Samuel Earl (Cal) 2673 Alder St, Eugene OR 97405 B Long Beach CA 1936 s Samuel & Myrtle. BA U CA 1959; MDiv GTS 1962; MS U of Oregon 1971. D 6/24/1962 Bp James Albert Pike P 3/1/1963 Bp George Richard Millard. m 9/5/1964 Elizabeth Smith c 2. Non-par 1964-1970; Cur S Paul's Epis Ch Walnut Creek CA 1962-1964.

SMITH, Samuel J (WMass) 1047 Amsterdam Ave, New York NY 10025 **Dio Wstrn Massachusetts Springfield 2015-** B Corpus Christi TX 1962 s Jerry & Betty. BMus SW U 1985; MS Indiana U 1987; MDiv GTS 2009. D 6/20/2009 P 2/4/2010 Bp Cate Waynick. m 2/2/2012 Donald R Temples. S Mich's Ch New York NY 2013-2015; H Trin Epis Ch Inwood New York NY 2012-2013; Dir of Prog Epis Chars of the Dio NY New York NY 2011-2013; Asstg P Cathd Of St Jn The Div New York NY 2010-2011; Dir of Cmncatn Trin Ch Indianapolis IN 2002-2006.

SMITH, Sarah K (EC) 917 Gordon Woods Rd, Wilmington NC 28411 **S Andr's On The Sound Ch Wilmington NC 2016-** B 1984 M Div Duke DS 2016. D 6/4/2016 P 12/17/2016 Bp Robert Stuart Skirving. sarah@saots.org

SMITH, Stanley James (O) 249 E 7th St, New York NY 10009 **Non-par 1970-** B Memphis TN 1943 s Stanley & Grayson. BA U of Tennessee 1965; BD EDS 1970. D 9/23/1970 P 5/31/1971 Bp John Harris Burt.

SMITH, Stephen (Tex) 3310 Nathanael Rd., Greensboro NC 27408 B Belville IL 1951 s Sanford & Ann. BA Campbell U 1974; MDiv TESM 1979; DPS St Johns Coll Nottingham Engl 1980. D 11/30/1980 P 8/1/1981 Bp Robert Bracewell Appleyard. Part Time P-in-c S Matt's Epis Ch Kernersville NC 2011-2014, P-in-c 2011-; Part Time Vic Ch Of The H Sprt Greensboro NC 2009-2017, Part Time - Regular Supply 2009-, Mssy Vic 2012-; Int S Paul's Par Oregon City OR 2004-2005; Cert Ldr, Ldrshp Trng for Men New Warrior Trng Adventure The ManKind Proj 1999-2002; Transitional/Conflict Mgmt Consult Dio Oregon Portland OR 1997-2005, Int/Supply 1995-1997; Prncpl Coach Sacr Space Inc. Exec Coaching Serv 1996-2006; Int R/Supply Dio Olympia Seattle 1995-1998; Exec Dir Recovery Works Inc. Houston 1992-1996; Asst S Jn The Div Houston TX 1986-1992; Coll Chapl Chap of the Incarn U of F. Gainesville 1983-1986; Coll Chapl Dio Florida Jacksonville 1983-1986; P-in-c S Paul's Cathd Victoria Seychelles 1981-1983; Asst. Sta Mgr FEBA RADIO Angl Mssn

S

Seychelles 1980-1981; Regular Supply P - Epis Ch of the H Sprt, GSO, NC Dio No Carolina Raleigh NC 2009-2012. Natl Assn of Christians in Recovery 1989-1995; NECAD 1989-1997; Wiconi Fndt 1992-1992.

SMITH, Stephen Bradley (SO) 7121 Muirfield Dr., Dublin OH 43017 **R S Pat's Epis Ch Dublin OH 2003-** B Lansing MI 1957 s Wallace & Anna. BS Ohio U 1979; Untd TS 1984; MDiv Sewanee: The U So, TS 1988; DMin TS 2013; DMin Sewanee: The U So, TS 2013. D 6/18/1988 P 4/25/1989 Bp William Grant Black. m 7/11/1981 Jan Smith c 2. R Chr Ch Epis Hudson OH 1996-2003; R Ch Of The Redeem Lorain OH 1990-1996; Asst Chr Ch Cathd Cincinnati OH 1988-1990. Auth, "Saving Salvation: the Amazing Evolution of Gr," Morehouse, 2005; Auth, "When Scandal Strikes," *Living Ch*, 1993; Auth, "From Outreach Proj to Cmnty Action Agcy," *The Wk You Give Us to Do*, Seabury, 1985. CT 1992. Best Sermon Competition: 2nd Place Epis Evang Fndt 1991; Woods Ldrshp Awd TS Sewanee 1986.

SMITH, Stephen H (Dal) B Fort Worth Texas 1946 MDiv Nash; BMEd TCU. D 6/20/1971 P 12/26/1971 Bp Archibald Donald Davies. m 5/15/1992 Nancy J Seaberry. Dio Ft Worth Ft Worth TX 1986-1992; Ch Of The Gd Samar Dallas TX 1972-1980.

SMITH, Stephen John Stanyon (WNY) 100 Beard Ave, Buffalo NY 14214 B London UK 1949 s Peter & Margaret. BA U of Sussex 1981; MSOC.Sci U of Birmingham Birmingham Gb 1983; Cert Theol Stud Westcott Hse Cambridge GB 1985; PhD St U New York at Buffalo 2015. Trans 3/1/1994 Bp Creighton Leland Robertson. m 6/25/1994 Sarah Wallace Buxton. P Assoc S Andr's Ch Buffalo NY 2008-2012; Ph.D Stdt SUNY at Buffalo 2004-2015; Cn Pstr S Paul's Cathd Buffalo NY 1998-2004; Asst All SS Ch Ivoryton CT 1995-1998; Assoc S Jn's Epis Ch Essex CT 1995-1998; Pstr Assoc Annand Prog Yale DS 1995-1998; Chapl Servicemaster Rehab CT 1995-1997; Mssnr Rosebud Epis Mssn Mssn SD 1991-1994; Assoc Mssn P Cheyenne River Reserv Epis Missions 1989-1991; Serv Ch Of Engl 1985-1989; Ecum Interfaith Off Dio Wstrn New York Tonawanda NY 2000-2004. Auth, "One Sunday In January," *Epis Life*, 1998. The Angl Comm Compass Rose Soc 2013.

SMITH, Stephen Richard (Cal) **S Simons Ch Arlington Hts IL 2016-** B San Francisco 1984 s Bruce & Deborah. Mstr of Div VTS 2016. D 6/11/2016 Bp Marc Handley Andrus. stephen@saintsimons.org

SMITH, Stephen Vaughn (Mass) 32 Popponesset Ave, Mashpee MA 02649 B Dayton OH 1954 s Burton & Audrey. BA Macalester Coll 1976; PrTS 1978; MDiv EDS 1981. D 6/29/1981 P 1/6/1982 Bp Robert Marshall Anderson. m 8/25/1979 Jeannette Hanlon c 3. R S Mary's Epis Ch Barnstable MA 2004-2011; R S Jn's Epis Ch Westwood MA 1989-2004; Ch Of The Redeem Chestnut Hill MA 1984-1989; Asst S Chris's Epis Ch S Paul MN 1981-1984. Auth, "Blinding Glory," *Desert Call*, Sprtl Life Inst, 2008. Soc Of S Jn The Evang, Epis Soc For Min; Soc Of S Jn The Evang, ESMHE.

SMITH, Steven Ronald (Eur) Church of the Ascension, Seybothstrasse 4, 81545 Munich Germany **R Ch of the Ascen Munich 2009-** B Salt Lake City UT 1961 s Ronald & Ellen. BA U of Utah 1985; JD Bos 1989; STM GTS 2003; MDiv Yale DS 2003. D 6/29/2002 Bp Chester Lovelle Talton P 1/11/2003 Bp Joseph Jon Bruno. c 2. Mssn Consult Trin Par New York NY 2007-2009; Assoc R for Mssn S Jas Ch New York NY 2004-2007; Ch Of The H Trin New York NY 2002-2004.

SMITH, Stuart Hardie (Nwk) 653 Courtney Hollow Ln, Madison VA 22727 **S Geo's Ch Stanley VA 2012-** B Miami FL 1948 s William & Helen. BA Maryville Coll 1971; MDiv VTS 1986. D 6/14/1986 P 3/21/1987 Bp William Gillette Weinhauer. m 4/6/1969 Lizabeth Patterson Smith c 3. S Steph's Epis Ch Culpeper VA 2013-2014; Dio Newark Newark NJ 2007-2010; R S Clem's Ch Hawthorne NJ 2003-2011; S Aid's Ch Alden NY 2003, 1996-2000; Fin Com Dio Wstrn New York Tonawanda NY 2000-2002; Int Ch Of S Jn The Bapt Dunkirk NY 1994-1996; R St Mk Epis Ch No Tonawanda NY 1991-1993; R Ch Of The Resurr Loudon TN 1989-1990; Cmsn on Mssns Dio Virginia Richmond VA 1988-1989; Farnham Ch No Farnham Par Farnham VA 1986-1989; R S Jn's Ch Warsaw VA 1986-1989; Stwdshp Cmsn Dio Newark Newark NJ 2005-2010, Bp Search Com 2005-2006, Mnstry Consultants 2004-2011; Dept Mssn Dio E Tennessee Knoxville TN 1989-1991.

SMITH, Susannah Rankin (NY) 219 Old Franklin Grove Dr, Chapel Hill NC 27514 **Sprtl Dir Self-employed Chap Hill NC 2011-; Consult, Retreat Ldr Inspirited Ldrshp Inc 2005-** B Atlanta GA 1939 d James & Margaret. BA Van 1961; MDiv UTS 1989. D 6/3/1989 P 12/16/1989 Bp John Shelby Spong. m 9/7/1991 Ralph Smith c 3. Assoc R S Jas Ch New York NY 1997-2004; R S Ptr's Ch Clifton NJ 1992-1997; Int R The Ch Of The Sav Denville NJ 1992; Locum Tenans Ch Of The Gd Shpd Ft Lee NJ 1991-1992; Int R Ch Of The Incarn Jersey City NJ 1990-1991; Int Vic S Jn Jersey City NJ 1990-1991; Bergen Hill Mssnr Dio Newark Newark NJ 1989-1991; Cler Ethics Com 1995-1997, Mem, Cmsn on Mssn 1990-1997; CREDO Fac The CPG New York NY 2005-2011; Reg Rep for Cornerstone Porject The ECF Champaign IL 1995-1997. Pub, "Writings on Ch Ldrshp," *Inspirited Ldrshp*, self.

SMITH, Susan Sims (Ark) 1809 Canal Pointe, Little Rock AR 72202 B Jonesboro AR 1950 d Charles & Kakie. BA Rhodes Coll 1972; MS U of Arkansas 1974; Cert Theol Stud Epis TS of the SW 1998. D 8/29/1998 P 3/13/1999 Bp Larry Maze. m 10/29/1979 George Smith c 3. Dio Arkansas Little Rock AR 2001-2007, Dir of Off of Tchg & Evang 2000-2007; Cur Trin Cathd Little Rock AR 1998-2000.

SMITH, Taylor Magavern (Md) 3608 Horned Owl Ct, Ellicott City MD 21042 **R S Mk's Ch Highland MD 2012-** B Buffalo NY 1965 s Philip & Julie. BA Duke 1987; MDiv VTS 1996. D 5/29/1996 P 12/7/1996 Bp Bob Johnson. m 6/22/1996 Katherine Phillips Smith c 2. R Gr Ch Elkridge MD 2000-2012; Assoc R S Alb's Ch Hickory NC 1997-2000; Asst for Mnstry w Chld and Yth Trin Epis Ch Asheville NC 1996-1997; Dio Wstrn No Carolina Asheville NC 1996. stmarksec@yahoo.com

SMITH, Ted William (Tex) PO Box 10357, Liberty TX 77575 **R S Steph's Ch Liberty TX 2010-** B Zanesville OH 1955 s William & Margaret. BTS S Michaels Coll 2005; MDiv S Michaels Coll 2008; MDiv S Michaels Coll 2008; Cert of Completion Iona Sch for Mnstry 2011. D 6/19/2010 P 12/21/2010 Bp C Andrew Doyle. m 9/11/1975 Kathryn F Smith c 3.

SMITH, Thee (At) 3530 Fairlane Dr NW, Atlanta GA 30331 **P Assoc Cathd Of S Phil Atlanta GA 2001-; Rel Dept. Fac Emory U Atlanta GA 1987-** B Athens GA 1951 s W Harold & Josephine. BA St Johns Coll Annapolis MD 1975; MTS VTS 1977; PhD Grad Theol Un 1987. D 6/9/2001 Bp Robert Gould Tharp P 11/12/2002 Bp J Neil Alexander. c 1. Contributing Auth, "Vengeance Is Never Enough: Alternative Visions of Justice," *Roads to Recon: Conflict & Dialogue in the Twenty-First Century*, M.E. Sharpe Pub, 2005; Contributing Auth, "Working the Spirits: The Will to Transformation in Afr Amer Vernacular Art," *Souls Grown Deep: Afr Amer Vernacular Art. Vol. 2*, Tinwood Books, 2001; Contributing Auth, "Howard Thurman," *Handbook of Chr Theologians*, Abingdon, 1996; Auth, "Conjuring Culture: Biblic Formations Of Black Amer," *Conjuring Culture: Biblic Formations of Black Amer*, Oxf Press, 1994; Auth & Co-Ed, "King & the Quest to Cure Racism," *Curing Violence: Essays on René Girard*, Polebridge Press, 1994; Auth, "From Cure Of Souls To Curing Culture: The Prospect For Ritual Ldrshp In The Black Rel Tradition," *Virginia Sem Journ*, VTS, 1993; Contributing Auth, "THe Sprtlty of Afro-Amer Traditions," *Chr Sprtlty: Post-Reformation & Mod*, Crossroad, 1989. AAR 1987; Colloquium on Violence & Rel 1990; Cmnty of the Cross of Nails 2001-2011. R Emer St. Paul's Epis Ch 2009; Bk Awd for Excellence AAR 1994. thee.smith@emory.edu

SMITH, Thomas A (Dal) Trans 9/13/2016 as Priest Bp George Robinson Sumner Jr.

SMITH, Thomas Eugene (EMich) P.O. Box 86, Dryden MI 48428 B Dennison OH 1955 s Dwane & Norma. BS OH SU 1978; MS Michigan St 1995. D 9/13/2008 Bp Steven Todd Ousley. m 11/20/1982 Marie Smith c 2. D S Jn's Epis Ch Dryden MI 2008-2014.

SMITH, Thomas Gibson (Chi) 118 Tanglewood Dr, Elk Grove Village IL 60007 B Columbus OH 1939 s Ralph & Frances. BS OH SU 1961; SWTS 1973. D 1/12/1974 Bp James Winchester Montgomery. c 3. D Asst Calv Ch Lombard IL 2003-2011; Asst Ch Of Our Sav Elmhurst IL 1999-2002; Asst One In Chr Ch Prospect Heights IL 1997-1999; Trst-Bp & Trst Dio Chicago Chicago IL 1990-2005, Trst Dioc Cler Relief Soc 1988-2002, Mem Dioc Audit Com 2000-; D Asst S Nich w the H Innoc Ch Elk Grove Vlg IL 1974-2002. NASSAM; NAAD.

SMITH JR, Thomas Parshall (NY) 225 W 99th St, New York NY 10025 B Tallahassee FL 1955 s Thomas & Jean. BS Florida St U 1979; MDiv SWTS 1996. D 8/24/1996 P 4/19/1997 Bp Frank Tracy Griswold III. Asst Pstr S Mich's Ch New York NY 1997-2000.

SMITH JR, Thomas Richard (Va) 1500 Westbrook Ct Apt 3142, Richmond VA 23227 **Ret 1992-** B Quincy FL 1932 s Thomas & Christine. BA U of Florida 1954; BD VTS 1957; UTS 1963. D 7/1/1957 P 3/1/1958 Bp Edward Hamilton West. R The Fork Ch Doswell VA 1987-1992; Assoc St Jas Ch Richmond VA 1983-1987; Int Par Ch of St. Helena Beaufort SC 1982-1983; R S Aug's Epis Ch Washington DC 1973-1977; Res Cn Cathd Ch Of S Lk Portland ME 1969-1973; Assoc St. Barth Ch New York NY 1964-1968; Assoc S Thos Epis Ch Terrace Pk OH 1960-1962. Auth, ""The Rituals of Death" My Wk w Death Row Inmate," *The Virginia Epis*, Dio Virginia, 1991.

SMITH, Timothy Clarke (Cal) 2325 Union St, San Francisco CA 94123 B Cleveland OH 1944 s Milton & Martha. AB Pr 1966; JD/MBA Col 1971; BA Sch for Deacons 2015. D 6/13/2015 Bp Marc Handley Andrus. m 10/28/1972 Ilia Salomone-Smith c 2.

SMITH, Travis H (Tex) Holy Comforter Episcopal Church, 227 S Chenango PO BOX 786, Angleton TX 77515 **Ch Of The H Comf Angleton TX 2014-** B Bryan TX 1975 s Harry & Nancy. Angl Stds Epis TS Of The SW; Angl Stds Epis TS of the SW; MA Grand Canyon U 1999; MDiv Baylor U Truett TS 2002. D 6/16/2012 Bp C Andrew Doyle. m 9/13/2003 Suzanne Gail Weidner c 3. Cur S Mk's Ch Austin TX 2012-2014. Ldrshp Angleton Angleton Chmbr-Com 2017.

SMITH, Travis K (Md) St. Michael's Episcopal Church, 1520 Canterbury Rd., Raleigh NC 27608 **P-in-c Gr Ch Elkridge MD 2013-** B Edmonds WA 1977 s Kerry & Sharon. MDiv GTS 2005. D 6/25/2005 P 1/14/2006 Bp Vincent Waydell Warner. m 8/11/2002 Aleta Skaanland-Smith c 3. All SS Ch Loveland CO

SMITH, [continued] 2010-2013; Assoc R of Emerging Mnstrs S Mich's Ch Raleigh NC 2007-2010; Ch of the Apos Seattle WA 2006-2007; Chapl S Alb's Ch Edmonds WA 2003-2004, 2000-2002. graceelkridge@gmail.com

SMITH, Twila J (Be) 2451 Ridge Rd, Berkeley CA 94709 **P The Epis Ch Of The Medtr Allentown PA 2014-** B Oklahoma City OK 1961 d Wayne & Mona Jean. BA U of Oklahoma 1985; MEd U of Oklahoma 1992; MDiv CDSP 2014; MDiv CDSP 2014. D 1/24/2014 P 8/2/2014 Bp Edward Joseph Konieczny. Admin Asst S Jn's Ch Norman OK 2007-2011.

SMITH, Vickie Mitchel (Ark) 601 Brookside Dr Apt 12, Little Rock AR 72205 B Decatur IN 1958 BA LSU. Trans 2/1/2004 Bp Charles Edward Jenkins III. c 2. Cur S Mk's Epis Ch Little Rock AR 2003-2005.

SMITH, Vicki Lovely (Kan) 10104 Sorrills Creek Lane, Raleigh NC 27614 **S Dav's Epis Ch Topeka KS 2017-** B Portland ME 1957 d Thurber & Carla. BA U of Maine 1979; MDiv Ya Berk 1984; DMin McCormick TS 2002. D 6/2/1984 P 12/8/1984 Bp Frederick Barton Wolf. m 8/28/1983 Kevin Smith. S Johns Epis Ch Wake Forest NC 2011-2016; R S Thos Epis Ch Reidsville NC 2008-2011; Int S Phil's Ch Durham NC 2006-2007; R S Mk's Epis Ch Columbus OH 1999-2006; R S Jn's Epis Ch Cuyahoga Fls OH 1993-1999; Assoc S Dav's Ch Wayne PA 1990-1993; Assoc S Ptr's Epis Ch Amarillo TX 1988-1990; Int Ch Of The Annunc Bridgeview IL 1986-1988.

SMITH, Walter E (At) 3750 Peachtree Rd.NE, Atlanta GA 30319 **All SS Epis Ch Atlanta GA 2007-, Asst 1964-2006** B Jacksonville,FL 1932 s Walter & Elizabeth. Emory U; Georgia St U; BA W&L 1954; MDiv VTS 1957. D 6/27/1957 P 4/1/1958 Bp Edward Hamilton West. c 3. Camp Mikell Bd 1966-1969; Asst H Trin Epis Ch Gainesville FL 1961-1964; P-in-c: Vic S Fran Of Assisi Gulf Breeze FL 1957-1961; COM Dio Atlanta Atlanta GA 1972-1982, Pstr Ther 1969-1971, Exec Coun 1965-1968. "Bk Revs," *Int'l Journ Grp Psych*, AGPA, 1983; Auth, *Portrait of Atlanta*, Seabury Press, 1969; Auth, *Yth Mnstry Notebook*, Seabury Press, 1969. Amer Assn for Mar and Fam Ther 1972; Amer Grp Psych Assn 1971. Fell Amer Grp Psych Ass 1983.

SMITH III, Walter Frederick (RG) 10328, Albuquerque NM 87114 B Trenton NJ 1943 s Walter & Marion. BA MacMurray Coll 1966; MDiv PDS 1970. D 4/11/1970 P 10/1/1970 Bp Alfred L Banyard. m 11/13/1971 Elizabeth Smith c 2. R S Fran Ch Rio Rancho NM 1994-2005; Pres Nm Chapl Assn Dio The Rio Grande Albuquerque 1990-1992, 1989; Chapl Dept Pstr Care S Jos Hlthcare System Albuquerque NM 1984-1994; R S Jn's Epis Ch Alamogordo NM 1980-1984; R Ch Of The H Sprt Lebanon NJ 1973-1980; Cur S Jn's Ch Somerville NJ 1970-1973. Fell Coll of Chapl 1989.

SMITH, Wendy M (ECR) 4061 Sutherland Dr, Palo Alto CA 94303 B Bloomington IL 1946 d Martin & Joan. BA Scripps Coll 1968; MTS Harvard DS 1970; PhD U of Washington 1977. D 5/10/1975 Bp James Walmsley Frederic Carman P 2/9/1977 Bp Robert Hume Cochrane. m 1/3/2013 Troy W Barbee c 1. Epis Ch Almaden Dio El Camino Real Salinas CA 2015, Exam Chapl, Chair 2003-2013, Dir of Corp 2003-2007, Chair, Dioc Coun 1999-2003, Dep, GC 1999-2003, Exam Chapl 1998-2003; Dio Oregon Portland OR 2014; R S Thos Epis Ch Sunnyvale CA 1996-2013; Assoc R Chr Epis Ch Los Altos CA 1990-1996; All SS Epis Ch Palo Alto CA 1990, Asst 1989-1990, 1989; Int Trin Par Menlo Pk CA 1987-1988; Int Ch Of S Jude The Apos Cupertino CA 1986-1987; Int S Clare's Epis Ch Pleasanton CA 1986; Mem of the Bd Untd Campus Chr Mnstry Bd 1980-1985; Assoc/Asst Dn Memi Ch at Stan Stanford CA 1974-1985; Exam Chapl Dio California San Francisco CA 1992-1996, COM 1989-1996.

SMITH, Wesley Wesley (At) 210 Willie Six Road, Sewanee TN 37375 **Exec Coun and Bd Dio Atlanta Atlanta GA 2006-** B Savannah GA 1953 s Joseph & Velma. BA Trevecca Nazarene U 1975; MDiv Van 1985; DMin Sewanee: The U So, TS 2004. D 12/19/1998 Bp Vincent Waydell Warner P 6/19/1999 Bp Sanford Zangwill Kaye Hampton. m 6/21/1996 Shirley Kristina Smith c 3. Int S Paul's Ch Franklin TN 2014-2015; S Jn's Ch Roanoke VA 2013-2014; Sr Chapl Dover AFB Off Of Bsh For ArmdF New York NY 2010-2013, 1999-2010; S Mk's Epis Ch Lagrange GA 2009; R Chr Ch Macon GA 2003-2009; S Dav's Epis Ch Topeka KS 2000-2003; S Mary's Ch Lakewood WA 1998-2000; Chapl US Army Chapl 1987-2013; Pstr Serv Meth Ch 1976-1988; Stndg Com/Trst Dio Kansas Topeka KS 2001-2003. OSL the Physcn 2000. Bronze Star US Army. weskey@stpaulsfranklin.com

SMITH, Whitney B (Ind) 2020 Bundy Ave, New Castle IN 47362 **Vic Dio Indianapolis Indianapolis IN 2017-, 2016-2017** B Cincinnati OH 1956 s Lawrance & Ruby. BA Indiana U 1978; MDiv Bexley-Seabury 2015; MDiv Bexley-Seabury 2015. D 1/24/2015 P 1/31/2016 Bp Cate Waynick. S Paul's Epis Ch Gas City IN 2016-2017; S Mary's Epis Ch Martinsville IN 2016; Trin Ch Indianapolis IN 2016. whitinindy@hotmail.com

SMITH, WillaMarie Eileen (CFla) 381 N Lincoln St, Daytona Beach FL 32114 B New York NY 1943 d JeRoyd & Portia. AA Daytona St Coll 2012. D 9/27/2014 Bp Gregory Orrin Brewer. c 3.

SMITH, William Charles (NwT) St Matthew's Episcopal Church, 727 W Browning Ave, Pampa TX 79065 B Lubbock TX 1955 s Alfred & Patricia. D 6/8/2013 P 12/18/2013 Bp James Scott Mayer. m 6/5/1981 Karen W Smith c 3. ecc123@sbcglobal.net

SMITH, William Herbert (WMich) 2073 SE North Blackwell Dr, Port St Lucie FL 34952 B Surrey England 1934 s Donald & Muriel. S Aidans Birkenhead Engl 1964; Dip Lon GB 1964. Rec 4/5/1997 Bp Edward Lewis Lee Jr Trans 4/5/1997. m 6/2/1972 Paula Ann Marie Smith c 7. P-in-c H Faith Epis Ch Port St Lucie FL 2008-2012, Int 2002-2008; Int S Mary's Epis Ch Cadillac MI 1995-2000.

SMITH, William Herman (Cal) 3001 Veazey Ter Nw, Washington DC 20008 **Non-par 1962-** B Centerville IA 1930 s Herman & Mildred. BA Wesl 1952; BD SMU 1955. D 3/12/1960 Bp Gordon V Smith P 10/29/1960 Bp George Richard Millard. m 6/18/1950 Mary Lou Smith c 3. Assoc R S Ptr's Epis Ch Redwood City CA 1960-1962; Serv Methodist Ch 1955-1959.

SMITH, William Louis (Md) 24 Lake Drive, Bel Air MD 21014 **P Assoc Emm Ch Bel Air MD 2015-** B Baltimore MD 1943 s William & Grace. BS Cit 1965; STM PDS 1968. D 6/18/1968 P 6/3/1969 Bp Harry Lee Doll. R S Mary's Ch Abingdon MD 1972-2011; Asst All SS Ch Frederick MD 1970-1972; Asst Epiph Ch Dulaney Vlly Luthvle Timon MD 1968-1970.

SMITH III, William Paul (Fla) PO Box 1005, Hilliard FL 32046 **P-in-c Bethany Ch Hilliard FL 2008-** B 1944 s William & Gereldina. MDiv Iliff TS; MDiv Iliff TS; ABS Pfeiffer. D 6/2/1982 P 10/18/1982 Bp William Carl Frey. m 3/23/1968 Martha Josephine Smith c 1. S Eliz's Epis Ch Jacksonville FL 2011-2016; Dio Florida Jacksonville 2010-2011; P-in-c Gr Epis Ch Florence KY 2004-2007; S Alb's Ch Superior WI 2001-2003; S Paul's Epis Ch Goodland KS 1992-2000. Auth, "Older Elem"; Auth, "Fllshp Times".

SMITH, Willie James (Nwk) **R Trin Ch Cliffside Pk NJ 2005-; D St. Jn The Div Hawbnouck Hights NJ 2004-** B New York NY 1953 s Jessie & Sarah. BA S Josephs Coll 1976; MS Ford 1986; Cert Natl Psychol Assn For Psychoanalysis 1999; MDiv GTS 2004. D 6/12/2004 Bp Martin Gough Townsend P 1/8/2005 Bp John Palmer Croneberger. Who'S Who In Amer Colleges 1976.

SMITH, Winston Teal (Pa) **S Anne's Ch Abington PA 2017-** D 6/11/2016 Bp Clifton Daniel III P 12/10/2016 Bp Daniel Gutierrez.

SMITH-ALLEN, Serita Verner (EO) Po Box 186, Union OR 97883 B Jefferson City MO 1948 d Henry & Louise. AA Mesa Cmnty Coll 1985; BA Arizona St U 1987; MDiv CDSP 1992. D 6/3/1995 P 6/4/1996 Bp William Edwin Swing. m 8/1/1997 John F Allen c 7. S Ptr's Ch La Grande OR 1999-2003; St Johns Epis Ch Ross CA 1996-1999; S Steph's Epis Ch Orinda CA 1995-1996.

SMITH BOOTH, Rebecca Lee (Tex) Trinity Episcopal Church, 5010 N Main St, Baytown TX 77521 **Cur Trin Epis Ch Baytown TX 2013-** B Carthage Tunisia 1965 d Virgil & Cecilia. BS The U So, Sewanee 1987; BS The U So, Sewanee 1987; MDiv VTS 2013; MDiv VTS 2013. D 6/15/2013 P 1/30/2014 Bp C Andrew Doyle. m 12/27/2014 Christopher Russell Booth. S Dunst's Epis Ch Houston TX 2002-2007; Bd Mem Camp Allen Navasota TX 1998-2000; Happ Lay Dir Dio Texas Houston TX 1992-1994. beccy@trinitybaytown.org

SMITH-CRIDDLE, Linda C (O) 19 Pent Road, Madison CT 06443 B Philadelphia PA 1936 d Joseph & Kathryn. BA Colby Coll 1958; MDiv Winebrenner TS 1980; MA Bowling Green St U 1996; DMin GTF 1996; PhD GTF 2000. D 6/28/1980 P 1/26/1981 Bp John Harris Burt. m 12/25/1987 Arthur Hawthorne Criddle c 4. Vic S Johns Mssn Temperance MI 1987-1993; Assoc S Paul's Ch Oregon OH 1981-1984; Chapl Riverside Hosp Toledo OH 1979-1980; Dep GC Dio Ohio Cleveland 1979-1982. Auth, *Shaping Access to Hosp Ethics Committees*. APC 1980; APC Bioethics Com 1998-2001; AEHC 1980; ACPE 1980.

SMITHDEAL JR, Foss Tyra (NC) 8050 Ravenwood Ln, Stanley NC 28164 **D S Mk's Epis Ch Huntersville NC 2012-; Penick Vill Ret Hm 2005-** B Winston-Salem NC 1943 s Foss & Lucia. High Point U. D 6/13/2004 Bp Michael B Curry. m 3/18/1989 Debra Lavern Jacobs c 6. D S Mart's Epis Ch Charlotte NC 2004-2014.

SMITHER, Gertrude Gaston (Dal) 7900 Lovers Ln, Dallas TX 75225 **Died 10/19/2016** B Dallas TX 1937 d John & Sallie. Sweet Briar Coll 1957; BA U of Texas 1959; MDiv Epis TS of the SW 1985. D 10/13/1990 P 4/28/1991 Bp William Elwood Sterling. c 4. Assoc S Chris's Ch Dallas TX 2004-2007; Excoun Dio Dallas Dallas TX 1997-2000, Stndg Com 2000-2016, Mssnr 1997-1999, Dir Hosp Chapl 1992-1996; S Matt's Cathd Dallas TX 1992-1997; Wm Temple Epis Ctr Galveston TX 1990-1992; S Vincents Epis Hse Galveston TX 1987-1989; Chapl Wm Temple Fndt Galveston TX 1985-1992. Assembly Of Epis Hospitals Chapl 1987; Assn Of Profsnl Chapl 1987; Dok 1994; Ord Of S Lk 1988.

SMITHERMAN, Gene (ETenn) 211 Brookwood Dr, Chattanooga TN 37411 B Birmingham AL 1947 s Erskine & Eva. BA Van 1970; JD U of Alabama 1974; MDiv Sewanee: The U So, TS 1996. D 6/29/1996 P 3/15/1997 Bp Robert Gould Tharp. m 12/19/1971 Suzanne Nichols Smitherman c 2. Gr Ch Chattanooga TN 2002-2010; S Chris's Ch Kingsport TN 1997-2002; All SS' Epis Ch Morristown TN 1996-1997.

SMITHERMAN, Suzanne Nichols (ETenn) 1108 Meadow Ln, Kingsport TN 37663 B Chattanooga TN 1952 d Nicholas & Caroline. BD U of Alabama 1974; MDiv Sewanee: The U So, TS 1996. P 3/1/1997 Bp Robert Gould Tharp. m 12/19/1971 Gene Smitherman c 2. Assoc R S Paul's Epis Ch Chattanooga TN 2005-2014; Chr Ch Epis S Pittsburg TN 2003-2004; S Paul's Epis Ch Kingsport TN 1997-2002; All SS' Epis Ch Morristown TN 1996-1997.

SMITH GRAHAM, Shirley Elizabeth (Va) 5000 Pouncey Tract Rd, Glen Allen VA 23059 **R Chr Ch Glen Allen VA 2015-** B Mountain View CA 1968 BA California St U 1989; MDiv VTS 2002. D 6/1/2002 P 12/18/2002 Bp Jerry Alban Lamb. m 8/5/2001 Earnest N Graham c 1. R S Mart's Epis Ch Williamsburg VA 2007-2015; Chr Ch Alexandria VA 2002-2007; Assoc R The Ch Of The Epiph Washington DC 2002-2003. Auth, "The Unlikely Chosen," *The Unlikely Chosen*, Ch Pub, 2008. The Chas And Janet Harris Awd Virginia Sem 2002. s. smithgraham@christchurchrichmond.com

SMITHGRAYBEAL, Felicia Marie (Colo) 8738 Triple Crown Dr., Frederick CO 80504 **Vic St Brigit Epis Ch Frederick CO 2009-** B Ruston LA 1967 d Charles & Karen. BA U of Cntrl Florida 1989; MDiv VTS 2002. D 6/8/2002 P 1/11/2003 Bp William Jerry Winterrowd. m 3/15/1997 Lyle Graybeal. Cur S Mary Magd Ch Boulder CO 2002-2008.

SMITH-KURTZ, Mary Bonnagean (WMich) 7280 Deepwater Point Rd, Williamsburg MI 49690 **D Dio Wstrn Michigan Kalamazoo MI 1992-** B Laredo TX 1944 d Richard & Mary. Pediatric Nurse Practioner; AS NW Michigan Coll 1964; RN NW Michigan Coll 1966; MI SU 1967. D 5/2/1992 Bp Edward Lewis Lee Jr. m 11/4/1967 William Kurtz c 3. Auth, "Post-Traumatic Therap," *Post-Traumatic Ther & Victims Of Violence*. Fllshp Merry Christmas, Associated Parishes, Diakoneo.

SMITH-MORAN, Barbara Putney (Mass) 93 Anson Road, Concord MA 01742 **Bd Mem Soc of Ord Scientists 2014-** B Richmond VA 1945 d Maynard & Mary. BA Randolph-Macon Coll 1967; BA Randolph-Macon Wmn's Coll 1967; MAT JHU 1969; MA Harv 1974; MDiv EDS 1989; DMin CDSP 2009. D 6/3/1989 P 5/8/1990 Bp David Elliot Johnson. m 11/30/1974 James Michael Moran c 2. R Gr Ch Everett MA 2007-2015; Int P Chr Ch Cambridge Cambridge MA 2004-2005, 1990-1992; Boston Theol Inst Newton Cntr MA 2002-2003, 1997-1998, Asst 1990-2000; Int Trin Chap Shirley MA 2002-2003; Asst Grad Theol Un Berkeley CA 2000-2002; Asst The Ch Of The Gd Shpd Acton MA 2000-2001; Int S Jn's Epis Ch Westwood MA 1996; Chapl Framingham St Coll Framingham MA 1993-1995; Int S Andr's Ch Framingham MA 1992-1995, 1991-1992; Chapl Lesley Coll Cambridge MA 1989-1993; Sci & Rel Prog Dir Boston Theol Inst Newton Cntr MA; Wrdn, No Amer Prov Soc of Ord Scientists 2010-2014; Co-chair, Exec. Cncl Cmte Sci, Tech & Faith Ecusa / Mssn Personl New York NY 1997-2005. Auth, "Preformationist Theory: Its Persistent influence," *Bulletin*, Soc of Ord Scientists, 2006; Auth, "Bldg Victim Awareness into Ch Websites," *Wit*, 2006; Contributing Auth, "A Catechism of Creation: An Epis Understanding," ECUSA, 2005; Prncpl Auth, "The Sci of Sexual Behavior in Humans and Other Animals: A Resource for the Ch," Dioc. of Massachusetts, 2005; Auth, "Strategies for Bldg a Ch Based Allnce," *Reshape*, Sexual Assault Cltn, 2005; Auth, "The Evolutionary Past & Future of God," *God for the 21st Century*, Templeton Press, 2000; Auth, "Soul at Wk: Reflections on Sprtlty of Working," St. Mary's Press, 1999; Co-Ed, "Consumption, Population & Sustanability," Island Press, 1999; Ed, "Proceedings of Forum on Human Genetic Enhancement," Dioc. of Massachusetts, 1998; Ed, "Journ of Faith & Sci Exch, 1997-2001," Boston Theol Inst., 1997. Dio Mass EWC 1986-1993; Epis Ch Ntwk for Sci, Tech & Faith 1994-2005; ECom 2000-2006; EPF 2003; Mass. Cler Assn 1989; Soc of Ord Scientists 1992. The Genesis Awd for Sci and Rel Episc. Ch. Ntwk for Sci, Tech & Faith 2007; Polly Bond Awd ECom 2006; Polly Bond Awd ECom 2001; Team Tchg Grant Louisville Inst 1996.

SMITS, Hilary Jerome (CPa) 631 Colonial Ave, York PA 17403 **Died 5/5/2016** B DePere WI 1931 s Irvin & Agnes. BA S Norbert Coll De Pere WI 1953; MA U of Notre Dame 1961. Rec 4/1/1983 as Priest Bp Emerson Paul Haynes. m 7/16/1975 Doris Lerew. S Lk's Epis Ch Mt Joy PA 1996-2000; R S Jn's Ch Marietta PA 1995-1999; Chr Ch Coudersport PA 1994-1996; R S Jas Bedford PA 1990-1993; R Chr Epis Ch Pulaski VA 1985-1990; S Wlfd's Epis Ch Sarasota FL 1983-1984; Serv RC Ch 1956-1974; Norbertine Ord 1949-1971. Auth, "The Mass In Progress," S Norbert Abbey Press, 1965.

SMODELL, George (CFla) 2394 Lakes of Melbourne Dr, Melbourne FL 32904 **D S Sebastian's By The Sea Melbourne Bch FL 1989-** B Albany NY 1928 s John & Thelma. Brevard Cmnty Coll; Inst for Chr Stds. D 10/28/1989 Bp John Wadsworth Howe. m 9/24/1956 Donna Smodell. NAAD.

SMOKE, Joan Claire (Ind) Trinity Episcopal Church, 60 S Dorset Rd, Troy OH 45373 **P-in-c Trin Epis Ch Troy OH 2014-** B Boston MA 1944 d Edwin & Mary. U of Wisconsin; BS Indiana St U 1966; Garrett-Evang TS 1968; MEd U of Wisconsin 1980; D Formation Prog 1998. D 6/27/1998 Bp Russell Edward Jacobus P 2/11/2006 Bp Steven Andrew Miller. R H Cross Epis Ch Wisconsis Dells WI 2007-2013. NAAD; Oblate Ord of S Ben. hlysmk@gmail.com

SMOLKO, Regis Joseph (Pgh) 2365 Mcaleer Rd, Sewickley PA 15143 B Colver PA 1951 s Stephen & Mary. Rec 12/17/2016 as Priest Bp Dorsey McConnell. m 6/3/2014 Kenneth Ray Parsons.

SMUCKER III, John Reed (Mich) 108 N Quaker Ln, Alexandria VA 22304 **Ret 1984-** B Kansas City MO 1928 s John & Dorothy. BS Swarthmore Coll 1952; MDiv VTS 1958. D 6/13/1958 Bp Frederick D Goodwin P 5/29/1959 Bp Richard Stanley Merrill Emrich. m 6/28/1958 Louisa Dawson c 2. Vic S

Barn' Ch Chelsea MI 1962-1966; S Columba Ch Detroit MI 1958-1961; Asst St. Columba Ch Detroit MI 1958-1961. Soc of the Anchor Cross (BPFWR).

SMULLEN, Thelma Alice (Md) 15708 Bradford Drive, Laurel MD 20707 **Cler Assoc S Barth's Ch Baltimore MD 2007-; Transition Consult Dio Maryland Baltimore MD 2007-, Fresh Start Team 2006-2014, Dioc Coun 1992-2006** B Baltimore MD 1943 d Oswald & Marion. BA Washington Coll 1964; MDiv VTS 1984. D 6/9/1984 P 12/15/1984 Bp John Thomas Walker. m 6/12/1965 John Alfred Smullen c 2. Int S Geo's Ch Glenn Dale MD 2004-2005; Int Chr Ch Par Kent Island Stevensville MD 2003-2004; Int S Marg's Ch Annapolis MD 2002; Int The Ch Of The Redeem Baltimore MD 2000-2001; R The Ch Of The H Apos Halethorpe MD 1989-2000; Int Gr Ch Washington DC 1988-1989; Int The Ch Of The Ascen Lexingtn Pk MD 1987-1988; Int Ch Of The Ascen Silver Sprg MD 1986-1987. Fell Coll of Preachers 1994.

✠ SMYLIE, The Rt Rev John (Wyo) 123 S Durbin St, Casper WY 82601 **Bp of Wyoming Dio Wyoming Casper 2010-** B Baltimore MD 1952 s Charles & Marguerette. BA Syr 1975; MDiv EDS 1981. D 6/12/1982 P 12/15/1982 Bp John Shelby Spong Con 7/31/2010 for Wyo. m 1/25/2003 Jill L Smylie c 5. R S Mk's Epis Ch Casper WY 2007-2010; Dn Cathd Of S Jn The Evang Spokane WA 1998-2005; R Trin Epis Ch Hamburg NY 1989-1998; Assoc Calv Epis Ch Summit NJ 1987-1989; Assoc Chr Ch Ridgewood NJ 1985-1987; R S Lk's Ch Hope NJ 1982-1984. Auth, "Chr Parenting"; Auth, "Treasure," *Audio Rcrdng*; Auth, "Forw In Faith," *Audio Rcrdng*; Auth, "Love Rise," *CD*; Auth, "The Other Side Of Day," *Record Album*. Soc Of S Jn The Evang 1979. bishopsmylie@wyomingdiocese.org

SMYTH, Margaret Emma Ferrell (NJ) 53 Mulberry St, Medford NJ 08055 **D S Mart-In-The-Fields Lumberton NJ 1998-** B Camden NJ 1943 d Robert & Elizabeth. Burlington Cnty Coll 1995; D Formation Prog 1998. D 10/31/1998 Bp Joe Doss. m 4/20/1963 Tyson Smyth Robert Smyth. Oblate OHF.

SMYTH, William E (NC) PO Box 615, Columbia NC 27925 **P-in-c S Andr's Ch Columbia NC 2011-** B Greensboro NC 1947 s Thomas & Julia. BA Davidson Coll 1969; MA Mid 1973; MDiv GTS 1980. D 6/7/1980 Bp Paul Moore Jr P 12/21/1980 Bp Thomas Augustus Fraser Jr. m 12/28/1991 Frances W Wilson c 2. Vic S Lk's Ch Tarboro NC 1994-2010; R Calv Ch Tarboro NC 1992-2010; R All SS Ch Roanoke Rapids NC 1983-1992; Cmnty Worker S Jas Ch New York NY 1980-1982.

SMYTHE JR, Colville Nathaniel (Los) 2103 Hill Ave, Altadena CA 91001 **Asstg St. Edm's Ch San Marino CA 2008-; Dio Los Angeles Los Angeles CA 2007-** B Los Angeles CA 1943 s Colville & Pauline. BA U CA Riverside 1965; Cert U CA Riverside 1967; STB GTS 1971. D 9/11/1971 P 5/27/1972 Bp Francis E I Bloy. m 1/14/1989 Sylvia D Smythe. Adj Prof or Engl Citrus Cmnty Coll 2007-2013; R S Mk's Par Altadena CA 1995-2007; R S Andr's Ch Ben Lomond CA 1988-1995; Assoc R Ch Of The Mssh Santa Ana CA 1984-1988; Assoc S Mths' Par Whittier CA 1978-1984; Lang Instr Perkins Sch for the Blind 1974-1978; Cur S Lk's Of The Mountains La Crescenta CA 1972-1974; Cur S Steph's Ch Phoenix AZ 1971-1972. Auth, "'Nelson Captures Stockholm,'" *The Nelson Dispatch*, The Nelson Soc, 2016; Auth, "'Adventures in Tchg,'" *The Vintage Voice*, The Ch Pesion Fund, 2012. The Nelson Soc 1997-2017.

SMYTHE, Sally Lee (ND) 301 Main St S, Minot ND 58701 B Monterey CA 1945 d Burwell & Mildred. BS U of Maryland 1983. D 7/23/2010 Bp Michael Smith. c 2.

SNAPP, J(Ames) Russell (Ark) **Cn Trin Cathd Little Rock AR 2016-, 2010-2015** B Newport AR 1959 s James & Marianne. BA U So 1981; AA Harv 1982; PhD Harv 1988; MDiv GTS 2004. D 12/27/2003 P 6/29/2004 Bp Larry Maze. Gr - S Lk's Ch Memphis TN 2015; Int S Jn's Epis Ch Helena AR 2013-2014; All SS Epis Ch Paragould AR 2013; Dio Arkansas Little Rock AR 2013; R S Paul's Newport AR 2006-2010; Gr Ch Siloam Sprg AR 2004-2006. "Jn Stuart And The Struggle For Empire On The Sthrn Frontier," LSU Press, 1996. rsnapp@trinitylittlerock.org

SNARE, Pamela Porter (Tenn) 1024 Chicamauga Ave, Nashville TN 37206 **Cn to the Ordnry Dio Tennessee Nashville TN 2007-** B Winston-Salem NC 1953 d Ivil & Leona. BA U NC 1975; MDiv Duke DS 1979; Cert Ang Stud GTS 1983. D 5/28/1983 P 6/9/1984 Bp Robert Whitridge Estill. m 6/5/1999 Gerald Snare. Cur Chr Ch Covington LA 1997-2007; Int H Trin Epis Ch Greensboro NC 1995-1997; Int Chr Epis Ch Cleveland NC 1992-1993; Int Ch Of The Nativ Raleigh NC 1991; Asst to R S Tim's Epis Ch Winston Salem NC 1983-1987; Min WNCC Methodist Fllshp Ch 1979-1981. psnare@edtn.org

SNEARY, Jerry (WTex) 164 Fox Rdg, Canyon Lake TX 78133 B Hardtner KS 1943 s Edward & Alice. BA U NC 1965; BD SMU 1968. D 6/25/1983 P 1/7/1984 Bp Gerald Nicholas Mcallister. m 6/17/1995 Martha A Sneary c 5. R S Fran By The Lake Canyon Lake TX 2002-2009; R S Jas' Epis Ch Dalhart TX 1995-2001; Vic S Jn's Epis Ch Woodward OK 1991-1995; Dio Oklahoma Oklahoma City OK 1983-1995; Vic S Steph's Alva Alva OK 1981-1995.

SNELL, Carol Burkey (CPa) 182D Dew Drop Rd, York PA 17402 **D / Par Admin St. Andr's Epis Ch 2004-; D S Andr's Epis Ch York PA 1988-** B Old Washington OH 1942 d John & Evelyn. OH SU; Cert of Graduation Dioc Sch of Chr Stds 1988. D 6/10/1988 Bp Charlie Fuller Mcnutt Jr. m 1/6/1962 Harry H Snell c 3. Archd Dio Cntrl Pennsylvania Harrisburg PA 1997-2004, 1990,

S

Archd Emer 2011-; Corp. Dir of Chapl Serv Geo M Ldr Fam Corp Country Meadow 1991-1999; Chapl Hershey Med Cntr - Penn St U Pk PA 1985-1988; Exec Dir Hospice of York York PA 1980-1983. NAAD 1988.

SNELLING, Kathryn Sue (Ak) PO Box 1130, Sitka AK 99835 B Sitka AK 1950 d Robert & Donna. D 1/18/2006 Bp Mark Lawrence Macdonald. m 9/27/1969 Jerry Wayne Snelling c 1.

SNEVE, Paul (SD) 12 Linden Ave, Vermillion SD 57069 Archd Dio So Dakota Pierre SD 1999- B Cedar Rapids IA 1961 s Vance & Virginia. BFA U of So Dakota 1983; MDiv Vancouver TS CA 1999. D 12/21/1998 P 6/27/1999 Bp Creighton Leland Robertson. m 1/1/1994 Tally K Salisbury c 3. Vic S Matt's Epis Ch Rapid City SD 1999-2013. Contributing Auth, "Monday, March 6," *Lenten Meditations 2017*, Epis Relief & Dvlpmt, 2017; Contributing Poet, "Cedar Breaks, Iyeska & Two Wmn," *I Walked by the River; Scurfpea Poetry Anthology, Vol. 7*, Scurfpea Pub, 2016; Contributing Auth, "Exegesis," *First Peoples Theol Journ; Native Voices; A Tchg Series, Vol. 7, No. 1*, Indigenous Theol Trng Inst, 2014; Contributing Auth, "Anamnesis in the Lakota Lang and Lakota Concepts of Time and Matter," *The ATR*, The ATR, 2013; Contributing Auth, "Afterword," *First Peoples Theol Journ; God is Still Red, Vol. 5, No. 1*, Indigenous Theol Trng Inst, 2010; Contributing Auth, "Black Elk as Pauline Prophet," *First Peoples Theol Journ; Remembering God, Vol. 1, No. 3*, Indigenous Theol Trng Inst, 2005. paul.diocese@midconetwork.com

SNICKENBERGER, Patricia Wolcott (Chi) 179 School Street, Libertyville IL 60048 R S Lawr Epis Ch Libertyville IL 2007-; Bd Trst Lake Cnty Haven 2011- B Geneva IL 1953 d Oliver & Leota. BA Drake U 1974; MSW U IL 1976; MDiv SWTS 1999. D 6/12/1999 Bp David Bruce Joslin P 2/2/2000 Bp Bill Persell. m 5/14/1983 Thomas W Snickenberger c 3. Chr Ch Winnetka IL 1999-2006; Bd Trst Epis Chars And Cmnty Serv (Eccs) Chicago IL 2011-2017; COM Dio Chicago Chicago IL 2004-2010. Auth, "Where Do You Stand?," *Sermons That Wk XIII*, Morehouse, 2005; Auth, "All SS' Day," *The Chorister*, 2002. Henry Benjamin Whipple Schlr Seabury Wstrn TS 1999.

SNIDER II, Michael Elsworth (Fla) St Patrick's Episcopal Church, 1532 Stratford Ct, Saint Johns FL 32259 P-in-c S Paul's Fed Point E Palatka FL 2015- B Canton OH 1974 s Michael & Carol. BA Mt Un Coll 1998; MDiv Sewanee: The U So, TS 2005; STM St Lukes TS 2006. D 9/27/2006 Bp Porter Taylor P 10/23/2007 Bp William Michie Klusmeyer. m 9/23/2000 Penelope J Snider c 4. S Paul's Epis Ch Jacksonville FL 2015-2016; Dio Florida Jacksonville 2014; R St Pat's Epis Ch S Johns FL 2012-2013; R Chr Ch Bluefield WV 2007-2012.

SNIDER, Stephen B (Pa) 10527 W Albany St, Boise ID 83704 Ret 2006- B Iowa City IA 1948 s John & Wilma. BA U So 1970; MDiv SWTS 1974. D 6/17/1974 P 12/20/1974 Bp Walter Cameron Righter. m 6/14/1974 Irene C Kale c 2. P-t Incarn H Sacr Epis Ch Drexel Hill PA 2013; Full-time All SS Ch Philadelphia PA 2010-2012; P-t Nevil Memi Ch Of S Geo Ardmore PA 2008-2009; P-t The Ch Of The H Comf Drexel Hill PA 2008; P-t Asst Ch Of The Redeem Bryn Mawr PA 2006-2007; Full-time Ch Of The H Apos Wynnewood PA 1991-2006. Integrity 1994.

SNIECIENSKI, Ed (Los) 908 N AVENUE 65, LOS ANGELES CA 90042 D The Ch Of The Ascen Sierra Madre CA 2012- B New York NY 1948 s Thomas & Maria. California St U; ETSBH; BA S Fran Coll Brooklyn NY 1971. D 1/14/2005 Bp Joseph Jon Bruno. Cn Dio Los Angeles Los Angeles CA 2005-2011. No Amer Assn of Deacons 2003. deaconed@gmail.com

SNIFFEN, Ernest Timothy (Me) P0 Box 368, Readfield ME 04355 B Newport News VA 1944 s Harold & Anna. BA Trin Hartford CT 1966; MDiv EDS 1971; BS U of New Engl Biddeford 1986. D 6/19/1971 P 6/1/1972 Bp David Shepherd Rose. m 4/21/1972 Luvia Sniffen c 3. Int S Andr's Ch Winthrop ME 1991-1992; P-in-c S Paul's Ch Ft Fairfield ME 1979-1984; S Anne's Ch Blaine ME 1979-1980; Asst All SS Ch Richmond VA 1978-1979; Chapl Med Coll VA Hosp Richmond 1977-1978; S Jas Ch Tanana AK 1972-1977; Mssy Dist Of Alaska New York NY 1972-1974; D-in-trng Galilee Epis Ch Virginia Bch VA 1971-1972.

SNIFFEN, Michael Thomas (LI) 520 Clinton Ave, Brooklyn NY 11238 Dn Cathd Of The Incarn Garden City NY 2015-; Luce Fell Cntr for Chrsnty in Global Contexts 2011-; Mem Drew TS Alum Bd 2011-; VP Epis Response to AIDS 2008-; Tchg Asst Drew TS Madison NJ 2006- B Glen Cove NY 1980 s Robert & Diane. BA W Virginia Wesleyan Coll 2002; MDiv Drew U 2005; PhD Drew U 2013. D 9/15/2007 P 3/29/2008 Bp Mark M Beckwith. m 10/14/2010 Joanna M Yoho. P-in-c The Ch Of S Lk and S Matt Brooklyn NY 2010-2015; Cur S Jn's Of Lattingtown Locust Vlly NY 2007-2010; Asst S Ptr's Ch Essex Fells NJ 2006-2007; Yth Dir S Ptr's Ch Mtn Lks NJ 2005-2006. Epis Preaching Excellence Prog 2005-2005; No Amer Acad of Liturg 2008; The Amer Acad of Homil 2011; The AAR 2006. msniffen@incarnationgc.org

SNIVELY, Candace Foley (NC) D S Paul's Epis Ch Cary NC 2005- B Boston MA 1945 d Paul & Helen. Penn 1965; Barry U 1990; BA Meredith Coll 2001. D 5/16/2005 Bp Michael B Curry. m 6/25/1965 Craig Snively c 2.

SNODGRASS, A Bowie (NY) 60 Knollwood Road, Short Hills NJ 07078 Chr Ch Short Hills NJ 2016- B Manhattan NY 1977 d Thomas & Mary. BA Vas 1997; MDiv UTS 2003; Angl Stds Dplma GTS 2015; STM GTS 2016. D 3/5/2016 Bp Allen Shin P 10/15/2016 Bp Andrew Marion Lenow Dietsche. m 9/

25/2007 Palliath George Mathew c 1. Chr Ch Glen Ridge NJ 2016; Calv and St Geo New York NY 2015-2016; Other Lay Position S Jas Ch New York NY 2012-2014. bsnodrgrass@christchurchshorthills.org

SNODGRASS, Cynthia Jean (SO) 5146 SW 9th Lane, Gainesville FL 32607 B Iowa City Iowa 1950 d William & Lila. BA Syr 1976; MA Syr 1979; MDiv Bex Sem 1985; PhD Univ of Stirling - Scotland 2008. D 12/17/1988 P 7/20/1989 Bp William Grant Black. m 6/22/1985 Patrick Leroy Scully. Dir/Mgr No Cntrl Hospice VNHSC - Vernon CT 1999-2006; Chapl to Int Dir No Cntrl Hospice Vernon CT 1999-2006; Chapl Hospice VNA - Washington DC 1996-1998; Chapl Hospice of the Rapidan - Culpeper VA 1995-1996; Dir Sacr Sound Inst 1994-2013; Cbury Crt Dayton OH 1993, Chapl 1991-1992; Chapl Canterybury Crt W Carrollton OH 1991-1993; Asst P S Geo's Epis Ch Dayton OH 1990-1992; Chapl Hospice of Dayton - Dayton OH 1987-1990. Auth, "The Sonic Thread," *The Sonic Thread*, Paraview Press, 2000. AAR 2005-2013; Assn of Profsnl Chapl 1983-2013.

SNODGRASS, Galen D (WMo) 3317 N 103rd Ct, Kansas City KS 66109 R Ch Of The Gd Shpd Kansas City MO 2015-, P-in-c 2014-2015 B St. Joseph MO 1957 s David & Effie. BS U of Missouri; MS Pittsburg St U 2001. D 2/7/2004 Bp Barry Howe P 4/26/2014 Bp Martin Scott Field. m 9/1/1979 Kimberly Ann Surber c 4.

SNODGRASS, Thomas James (PR) 705 Gladstone Ave, Baltimore MD 21210 P-in-c St. Jn's Epis Ch Havre de Gr MD 2013- B Chicago IL 1947 s Thomas & Jeanne. BA Lawr 1970; Cert GTS 1976; MDiv UTS 1977. D 10/4/1975 Bp Paul Moore Jr P 5/28/1976 Bp Harold Louis Wright. m 7/1/1995 Patricia E Parsley c 7. Chapl 2017 Natl Boy Scout Jamboree 2017; Co-Fndr & Vic Dio Puerto Rico Centro Espiritu Santo Aibonito 2006-2012; R S Steph's Ch Olean NY 1990-2006; R Chr Ch Cathd Cincinnati OH 1986-1990; R Hse Of Pryr Epis Ch Newark NJ 1984-1986; Hisp Chapl Essex Cnty Jail Newark NJ 1984-1984; Assoc S Ann's Ch Of Morrisania Bronx NY 1978-1980; Cur Gr Ch White Plains NY 1976-1978; D Chr Ch Bronxville NY 1975-1976; Pres, Stndg Com Dio Wstrn New York Tonawanda NY 2001-2005, Co-Chair, Comp Dio WNY & Puerto Rico 2000-2006, Dn, Cattaraugus Dnry 1998-2006, Dir, Dioc Sleep Away Camp 1994-2004; Co-Fndr & Pres Genesis Hse Olean NY 1995-2005; Bd Mem Coll of Preachers Washington DC 1987-1990; Co-Fndr & Pres Apos Hse Newark NJ 1984-1986; Pres & VP Ch and City Conf 1983-1991. The Soc of S Jn the Evang 1974. Ecum Awd OLEAN Assn of Ch 2005; Intl Fell Col 1974. tjamessnodgrass@gmail.com

SNOOK, Susan Brown (Az) 3116 NW 21st St, Oklahoma City OK 73107 Bd Mem Exec Coun The Epis Ch 2012-; Dep 2009, 2012 GC 2008-; Fndr, Bd Mem The Acts 8 Moment 2012- B Neubrucke Germany 1962 d James & Glenda. BA Rice U 1983; MA Rice U 1985; MBA Rice U 1985; MDiv CDSP 2003. D 5/24/2003 P 12/13/2003 Bp Robert Reed Shahan. m 12/24/1983 Thomas Dykes Snook c 2. Ch Planter/R Epis Ch of the Nativ Scottsdale AZ 2010-2017; Assoc R S Anth On The Desert Scottsdale AZ 2004-2006; Dioc Coun, Mem Dio Arizona Phoenix AZ 2003-2004, Congrl Spprt Com, Mem 2011-2013, Chap Rock Conf Cntr, Chair of Bd 2006-2009; Cur S Ptr's Ch Litchfield Pk AZ 2003-2004; Bd Mem The Epis Ntwk for Stwdshp 2005-2012. Auth, "God Gave the Growth: Ch Planting in the Epis Ch," Ch Pub, Inc., 2015. canonsusan@epiok.org

SNOW, George Richard (WLa) 151 Washakie Dr, Evanston WY 82930 S Tim's Ch Alexandria LA 2014-; P S Paul's Epis Ch Evanston WY 2002- B Evanston WY 1969 s George & Sharyl. BS U of Wyoming 1993. D 11/7/2001 P 5/9/2002 Bp Bruce Caldwell. m 4/22/1995 Nikki Lyn Snow c 5.

SNOW, Peter David (Oly) 927 36th Ave, Seattle WA 98122 Ret 2001- B Chadwell Heath Essex UK 1937 s Arther & Ena. BA U of Cambridge 1962; MA U of Cambridge 1965. Trans 1/1/1968. m 11/30/1991 Elizabeth Spencer Robertson c 3. P-in-c S Hilda's - S Pat's Epis Ch Edmonds WA 2002-2003; R Ch Of The H Cross Redmond WA 1991-2001, P-in-c 1988-1990; Asst R Ch Of The Resurr Bellevue WA 1983-1986; R S Jn's Epis Ch Jackson WY 1975-1981; Yth Cn Mssnr Dio Los Angeles Los Angeles CA 1971-1975; Asst All SS-By-The-Sea Par Santa Barbara CA 1967-1971; Serv Ch Of Engl 1964-1967. Auth, "Jesus: Man, Not Myth," *Bk*, Bk Pub's Ntwk, 2010.

SNOW, Robert Gerald (Neb) Po Box 407052, Fort Lauderdale FL 33340 D S Matt & Corrections Dept 1985- B Great Falls MT 1943 s Gerald & Alice. BA U of Nebraska 1966. D 11/8/1985 Bp James Daniel Warner. m 9/22/1963 Ellen Fay Snow. Dio Nebraska Omaha NE 1999-2012; SAMS Ambridge PA 1994-1999.

SNYDER, Albert Eric (Be) 290 Conklin St, Farmingdale NY 11735 Ret 1994- B Glendale CA 1925 s Roy & Margaret. BA Occ 1945; BD UTS 1949; MS Col 1957. D 10/9/1957 P 6/24/1958 Bp Horace W B Donegan. c 5. R Calv Ch Tamaqua PA 1987-1994; R S Jas' Ch Drifton PA 1987-1992; Int Chr Ch Towanda PA 1985-1987; Int Chr Ch Forest City PA 1983-1985; Trin Epis Ch Carbondale PA 1983-1985; Asst Gr Ch White Plains NY 1959-1963; Cur S Mich's Ch New York NY 1957-1959.

SNYDER, Albert Llwyd (WTex) 527 Sonnet Dr, San Antonio TX 78216 Died 8/17/2016 B Muskogee OK 1938 s Llwyd & Helen. Wichita St U; BD U of Nebraska 1975; MDiv Epis TS of the SW 1984. D 1/22/1985 P 7/22/1985 Bp

Stanley Fillmore Hauser. c 2. Assoc St Andr's Epis Ch 2003-2016; Dio W Texas San Antonio TX 1987-2003; Vic Ch Of The H Cross San Antonio TX 1985-2003; Santa Fe Epis Mssn San Antonio TX 1985-1987.

SNYDER, Belinda Ann Wright (WTenn) 539 Cherry Rd, Memphis TN 38117 **Chapl Memphis TS 2004-; Chr Epis Ch Forrest City AR 2002-; Gr Ch Wynne AR 2002-** B Saint Louis MO 1947 d Horace & Audrey. BA U of Tennessee 1969; MA U of Memphis 1972; MA Memphis TS 1996; MDiv Memphis TS 1998; U of Wales at Lampeter 1998; GTS 2000; DMin Sewanee 2012. D 3/15/2002 P 9/10/2002 Bp Larry Maze. c 3. All SS Epis Ch Memphis TN 2009-2014; Dio Arkansas Little Rock AR 2003-2009; Ch Of The Gd Shpd Forrest City AR 2002-2004; P Calv Epis Ch Osceola AR 2002-2003; S Steph's Ch Blytheville AR 2002-2003; Cmncatn Off Dio W Tennessee Memphis 1986-1990. Assoc - Cmnty of S Mary, Sewanee 1995; Coun for Wmn Mnstrs 1986; DOK/Dio Chapl 1997; ECom 1986-1991; HSEC 2001; Natl Epis Historians and Archivists (NEHA) 2001. MHE Bd Dio W Tennessee 2007; Bd Trst Natl Epis Historians and Archivists 2007; Chair, Transition Com Dio Arkansas 2006; Chapl DOK Dio W Tennessee 2006; Natl Pres EWHP 2005.

SNYDER, David L (NJ) St. Andrew's Episcopal Church, 121 High Street, Mt. Holly NJ 08060 **S Andr's Ch Mt Holly NJ 2015-** B Lansdale PA 1950 s Richard & Margaret. BS Lock Haven U 1972; MDiv Sthrn Bapt TS 1985; DMin Bangor TS 1997. Rec 2/24/2008 Bp George Edward Councell. m 8/18/1973 Susan L Rosenberry c 4. P Ch Of The Gd Shpd Pitman NJ 2014-2015; Assoc S Lk's Ch Gladstone NJ 2011; P-in-c Ch Of The Atone Laurel Sprg NJ 2010-2011; The Evergreens Moorestown NJ 2010.

SNYDER, George Lewis (SO) **D S Mk's Epis Ch Dayton OH 2011-** B Troy OH 1947 s Clarence & Isabelle. Sch for the Deaconate; BA Wilmington Coll 1969; MEd Wright St U 1981. D 10/20/2001 Bp Herbert Thompson Jr. c 1.

SNYDER, Judith Urso (Be) 4621 Ashley Ln, Bethlehem PA 18017 B Reading PA 1948 d Frank & Martha. BS Bloomsburg U of Pennsylvania 1970; Moravian TS 1991; MDiv GTS 1992. D 3/8/1992 P 11/23/1992 Bp James Michael Mark Dyer. c 1. S Anne's Epis Ch Trexlertown PA 2004-2013, D / Intern 1992-1993; Vic S Brigid's Ch Nazareth PA 1999-2003; Asst R H Trin Ch Lansdale PA 1998-1999; Asst Chapl Epis Acad Merion PA 1996-1998; The Epis Acad Newtown Sq PA 1996-1998; Trin Ch Bethlehem PA 1996; Int S Ptr's Epis Ch Hazleton PA 1993-1995; Dio Bethlehem Bethlehem PA 1992-1993.

SNYDER, Larry Alan (Chi) 240 S 4th St, Warsaw IL 62379 **P-in-c S Jn's Ch Keokuk IA 2007-; Vic S Paul's Ch Warsaw IL 2007-; Dioc Coun Dio Quincy Peoria IL 2011-; Hm Hlth Advsry Bd Keokuk Area Hosp Keokuk IA 2011-; Bd Dir Warsaw Ambulance Squad Warsaw IL 2011-** B York PA 1947 s Earl & Marjorie. BS Millersville U 1968; MDiv PDS 1972. D 6/24/1972 Bp Robert Lionne DeWitt P 1/20/1973 Bp Lyman Cunningham Ogilby. m 5/25/1968 Karen L Snyder c 2. R S Lk's Ch In The Cnty Of Buck Newtown PA 1986-2007; Asst R Washington Memi Chap Vlly Forge PA 1982-1986; Nonpar 1978-1982; R Trin Ch Coshocton OH 1975-1977; Asst Chr Ch Epis Hudson OH 1972-1975. SSC 1977. stjohnskeokukiowa@gmail.com

SNYDER, Paul Leech (Okla) PO Box 10722, Midwest City OK 73140 B Oklahoma City OK 1949 s Byron & Kathrine. D 6/19/2010 Bp Edward Joseph Konieczny. m 8/5/1978 Marry Snyder c 2.

SNYDER, Philip L (Dal) 2220 Susan Cir, Plano TX 75074 **D Trin Epis Ch Dallas TX 2010-** B Maysville CA 1962 s Albert & Karen. BS U of Texas 1990; LM Angl TS 2004. D 6/5/2004 Bp James Monte Stanton. m 9/25/1987 Beverly Snyder c 2. D S Jas Ch Dallas TX 2004-2010.

SNYDER, Philip Wiseman (CNY) 248 Buckfield Dr, Lititz PA 17543 B Albany NY 1947 s Willis & Margaret. BA Franklin & Marshall Coll 1968; BD EDS 1971. D 6/5/1971 Bp Allen Webster Brown P 12/4/1971 Bp Charles Bowen Persell Jr. m 9/18/1971 Kluane Baier c 3. R S Jn's Ch Ithaca NY 1988-2012; R Chr Epis Ch Burlington IA 1985-1988; Dn No Adirondack Dnry 1981-1984; R The Ch of St Lk The Beloved Physcn Saranac Lake NY 1974-1984; Cur S Geo's Epis Ch Schenectady NY 1971-1974; Stndg Com Dio Cntrl New York Liverpool NY 1993-2000; Trst Dio Albany Greenwich NY 1978-1984. Auth, "River Trips, Revelations, and Old Trees," Morehouse- Barlow, 2000.

SNYDER, Richard (NAM) PO Box 22771, Carson City NV 89721 **Chapl Nevada Law Enforcement Off' Memi 2015-; Assoc S Mich And All Ang Ch Wadsworth NV 2012-; Chapl Warm Sprg Correctional Cntr Carson City NV 2012-; Sr Correspondent Epis Journ 2011-** B Bakersfield CA 1946 s David & Margaret. AA Bakersfield Cmnty Coll 1966; BA San Jose St U 1968; MDiv CDSP 2004. D 1/9/2005 Bp Katharine Jefferts Schori P 9/1/2005 Bp Carolyn Tanner Irish. m 10/4/1992 Debra McDonald. Chapl Nevada St Assembly 2015; P-in-c Ch Of Coventry Cross Minden NV 2013-2014; Consult (P-t) San Juan Mssn Farmington NM 2011; Treas and Admin Navajoland Area Mssn Farmington NM 2008-2011; S Christophers Ch Bluff UT 2008-2009; Reg Mnstry Dvlp S Mary Of-The-Moonlight Oljato UT 2008-2009; Utah Reg Bluff NM 2008-2009; Cmncatn Dir Dio Utah Salt Lake City UT 2005-2007; P-in-c S Mich's Ch Brigham City UT 2004-2008; Stndg Cmsn on Cmncatn and Info Tech Epis Ch Cntr New York NY 2009-2014. Auth, "Wovoka: The Paiute Prophet," *Nevadans: The Sprt of the Silver St*, Nevada Pub, 2014; Auth, "Pancakes and Prayers," *Epis Journ*, Epis Journ, 2013; Auth, "Rhythm and Balan-

ce," FMP, 2007; Auth, "Richard's Poor Almanac," *Dioc Dialogue*, Dio Utah, 2007. ECom 1978-2012; NAAD 2008-2013. Polly Bond Gnrl Excellence Awd-Journalism ECom 1986; Polly Bond Gnrl Excellence Awd-Photography ECom 1984.

SNYDER, Robert Paul (Ind) 3221 - 29th, Bedford IN 47421 **Ret 1988-** B Princeton IN 1923 s Charles & Della. MA Indiana St U; BA Wabash Coll 1946; EdS Indiana U 1956. D 12/19/1970 Bp John P Craine. c 4. D-in-c S Jn's Ch Washington IN 1981-1983; Cur S Jn's Epis Ch Bedford IN 1970-1988.

SNYDER, Sharon Boublitz (Eas) 12842 Fox Ridge Ct, Bishopville MD 21813 **Vol Coastal Hospice Breavement Team 2017-; D The Ch Of The H Sprt Ocean City MD 2015-** B Baltimore MD 1942 d John & Ethel. BA MWC 1965; MS Madison U 1969; MA Loyola of New Orleans 1990. D 6/18/2011 Bp Herman Hollerith IV. m 9/26/2014 John Snyder c 1.

SNYDER, Susanna Jane (Mass) 99 Brattle St, Cambridge MA 02138 B Hertford UK 1978 d Michael & Mary. BA Emml 2000; Queens Fndt 2004; MA Emml 2005; PhD U of Birminghan 2009. Trans 8/24/2011 Bp M(Arvil) Thomas Shaw. m 10/16/2012 Michael A Barnes. EDS Cambridge MA 2011-2013.

SNYDER, William Delpharo (O) 4920 Woodview Rd, Ravenna OH 44266 **D Gr Ch Ravenna OH 1997-** B Charlestown WV 1943 s Oliver & Merlin. D 11/13/1992 Bp James Russell Moodey. m 5/16/1965 Marsha A Snyder c 2.

SOARD II, John Robert (Tex) 207 Bob O Link Ln, Wharton TX 77488 **R S Thos Ch Wharton TX 2012-** B Houston TX 1980 s Robert & Susan. BA Baylor U 2002; MDiv Epis TS of the SW 2011. D 6/18/2011 P 1/15/2012 Bp C Andrew Doyle. m 3/8/2003 Claire B Soard c 4. Cur Trin Epis Ch Baytown TX 2011-2012.

SOBOL, Walter (O) 4627 Indian Ridge Rd, Sylvania OH 43560 **Ret 1993-** B Malden MA 1935 s Demasus & Margaret. BA Tufts U 1957; BD EDS 1960. D 6/18/1960 Bp Anson Phelps Stokes Jr P 12/1/1960 Bp Frederick Warnecke. R Trin Ch Toledo OH 1987-1993; R S Lk's Epis Ch Montclair NJ 1981-1987; R All SS Ch Chelmsford MA 1975-1981; R S Mk's Ch Foxborough MA 1968-1974; R Trin Epis Ch Weymouth MA 1963-1968; Asst S Steph's Epis Ch Wilkes Barre PA 1960-1963. Auth, "Chr Century".

SODERGREN, Oscar Frederick (Alb) 9 Pinewood Dr, Scotia NY 12302 **Died 9/16/2016** B Whitefield NH 1922 s Oscar & Hazel. BA RPI 1956; MS Un Coll Schenectady NY 1971. D 10/13/1980 Bp Wilbur Emory Hogg Jr P 7/1/1998 Bp Daniel William Herzog. m 8/12/1944 Doris Edna Best. P Asst Calv Epis Ch Burnt Hills NY 2000-2016; P-in-c All SS Ch Round Lake NY 1998-2002, D-In-C 1990-1997, Asst 1986-1989; Non-par 1993-1998; Asst Treas Dio Albany Greenwich NY 1991-1998, Admin Trsts 1987-1998; Asst Ch Of Beth Saratoga Spg NY 1980-1986.

SOJWAL, Imlijungla (NY) 201 W 72nd St Apt 15e, New York NY 10023 **Trin Ch Tariffville CT 2017-** B Mokokchung India 1965 d Limatemjen & Lanlila. BD Un Biblic Sem 1990; MS Ford 2001; STM GTS 2005. D 3/11/2006 P 9/23/2006 Bp Mark Sean Sisk. m 1/5/1990 Milind Sojwal c 2. P Ch Of The Div Love Montrose NY 2014-2016; Int Gr Ch Millbrook NY 2013-2014; All Souls Ch New York NY 2011-2012; Epis Ch Of Our Sav New York NY 2007-2009; Prog Assoc Wrld Vision 2001-2002.

SOJWAL, Milind (NY) 16 All Saints Rd, Princeton NJ 08540 B Nagpur Maharashtra IN 1960 s Bhaskar & Manorama. BA Madras Chr Coll 1982; Symbiosis Inst 1984; BD Un Biblic Sem Pune Mr IN 1989; MTh PrTS 1995. Trans 7/1/1998 Bp Joe Doss. m 1/5/1990 Imlijungla Lima c 2. R All Ang' Ch New York NY 2000-2017; Asst R Ch Of The Redeem Bryn Mawr PA 1999-2000; All SS Ch Princeton NJ 1998-1999. msojwal@gmail.com

SOL, Brenda (SanD) 8011 Douglas Ave, Dallas TX 75225 **R The Epis Ch Of S Andr Encinitas CA 2014-** B Wolf Point MT 1961 BS Montana St U 1986; MA Antioch U 1998; MDiv VTS 2012. D 1/17/2012 P 8/1/2012 Bp Gregory Harold Rickel. S Mich And All Ang Ch Dallas TX 2012-2014. rector@standrewsepiscopal.org

SOLA, Geri Ely (Eau) 6579 W Center Dr, Hurley WI 54534 **R Ch Of The Trsfg Ironwood MI 1998-** B South Haven MI 1944 d Franklin & Cleone. MS Wstrn Michigan U 1971. D 11/12/1997 P 5/31/1998 Bp Thomas Kreider Ray. m 7/21/1972 John Raymond Sola.

SOLAK, Ketlen A (Del) 913 Wilson Rd, Wilmington DE 19803 **P-in-c Dio Delaware Wilmington 2014-** B Haiti 1961 BA CUA 1983; MA CUA 1988; MDiv VTS 2005. D 6/18/2005 P 12/21/2005 Bp Peter J Lee. m 4/23/1988 Scott J Solak. Assoc R S Lk's Ch Alexandria VA 2005-2014; D S Mary's Epis Ch Arlington VA 2005. bcmrector@comcast.net

SOLANG SR, Eduardo Pecdasen (NPhi) **Died 4/7/2016** B 1938 m 6/24/1971 Helen Solang. Dio Nthrn Philippines 1975-1993.

SOLBAK, Mary Martha (CPa) 1001 E. Oregon Rd, Lititz PA 17543 B Lancaster PA 1941 d Robert & Catherine. BA Lake Erie Coll 1963; Cert U of Pennsylvania 1964; Cert Dioc Sch of Chr Stds Harrisburg PA 1987; Cert Pennsylvania U Hosp Chapl 1988; MA Lancaster TS 2002. D 6/16/1989 Bp Charlie Fuller Mcnutt Jr. m 2/4/1967 Arne Solbak c 3. Arch D Dio Cntrl Pennsylvania Harrisburg PA 2003-2015, COM 2008-, Stndg Com 2002-2007; Cur S Jas Ch Lancaster PA 1989-2006; Tchr, Bp Hall Jubilee Sch Epis Ch Dom and Frgn Missions Hong Kong 1964-1966. Bd, Dioc Sch of Chr Stds 2003-2012; Bd, Epis

S

Gardens, Thompsontown 1993-2000; Bd, Epis Hm, Shippensburg 1990-2016; Cmsn on Liturg and Ch Mus 1996-2012; NAAD, Life Mem 1990; VP ESMA 1993-2001. Bp's Lifetime Awd for Distinguished Mnstry Dio Cntrl Pennsylvania 2013; Distinguished Alum Lake Erie Coll 2005; Alum of the year Lancaster Country Day Sch 1990.

SOLDWEDEL, Erik Gustav (Nwk) 31 Mulberry St, Newark NJ 07102 **S Paul's Epis Ch Paterson NJ 2017-; D of the Hosp Chr Hosp Jersey City NJ 2009-** B Ridgewood NJ 1958 s Warren & Solveig. Newark TS; Ramapo Coll of NJ. D 12/15/2007 Bp Mark M Beckwith. m 12/30/1989 Linda Aprile-Soldwedel. Prog Dir Dio Newark Newark NJ 2010-2016.

SOLIBA, Ignacio C (NLuz) **Died 3/29/2016** B 1944 D 6/17/1973 P 2/4/1974 Bp Edward G Longid. Dio Nthrn Luzon Tabuk 1986-1993; Dio Nthrn Philippines 1975-1985.

SOLLER, Robin (NH) 23 Old Bristol Rd, New Hampton NH 03256 **R Trin Ch Meredith NH 1995-** B Cambridge MA 1958 d Julian & Gisela Elisabeth. BA Hobart and Wm Smith Colleges 1980; MEd U of Maine 1985; MDiv VTS 1989. D 6/10/1989 P 1/30/1990 Bp Edward Cole Chalfant. m 11/4/2000 Jon Mark Soller. Cur Trin Ch Ft Wayne IN 1992-1995; Cur Zion Epis Ch Wappingers Falls NY 1989-1992.

SOLOMON, Dana Lee (Colo) St Stephen's Episcopal Church, 1303 S Bross Ln, Longmont CO 80501 **Asst S Steph's Ch Longmont CO 2012-** B Denver CO 1957 d Ronald & Judith. BA U of Nthrn Colorado 1981; MDiv Illif TS 2009. D 6/6/2009 P 6/16/2012 Bp Robert John O'Neill.

SOLON JR, Robert Francis (Md) 1301 S Charles St, Baltimore MD 21230 **Fin Admin Chr Ch Glen Ridge NJ 2014-; Fin Admin Nrsry Sch at Chr Ch Glen Ridge NJ 2014-; Treas/Bd Mem Cross Roads Camp and Retreat Cntr Port Murray NJ 2008-; Treas Epis Response to AIDS New York NY 2007-** B Grand Rapids MI 1967 s Robert & Joanie. BA Capital U 1988; MBA Anderson U 1999; MDiv GTS 2006. D 6/24/2006 P 2/3/2007 Bp Cate Waynick. S Andr's Epis Ch Staten Island NY 2015-2016; Fin Admin S Ptr's Ch Clifton NJ 2014; R Ch Of The Adv Baltimore MD 2013-2014; Vic S Thos Ch Vernon NJ 2008-2011; Trin Ch Bayonne NJ 2006-2008; Windmill Allnce Inc. Bayonne NJ 2006-2008; Windmill Allnce Inc. Bayonne NJ 2006-2007. Fllshp of St. Jn 2002.

SOLON, Terry Tim (Wyo) 3251 Acacia Dr, Cheyenne WY 82001 **Ret 2000-** B Elyria OH 1934 s Howard & Marjorie. BA Hiram Coll 1956; BD Bex Sem 1959; MDiv Bex Sem 1971. P 3/1/1961 Bp William Crittenden. c 4. R S Chris's Ch Cheyenne WY 1987-2000; Non-par 1981-1987; S Steph's Ch Casper WY 1967-1981; Vic Chr Ch - Epis Newcastle WY 1963-1967; Vic Ch Of The Epiph Grove City PA 1960-1963; Vic S Edm Mercer PA 1960-1962. Auth, "Pre-Marital Inventory And Related Materials," Bess Assoc., 1972. Soc Justice Advoc Wyoming Assn Of Ch 2003.

SOLTER, Katrina Howard (WA) St Patrick's Episcopal Church, 4700 Whitehaven Pkwy NW, Washington DC 20007 **S Pat's Ch Washington DC 2014-; Advncd Stds Chapl S Paul's Sch Concord NH 2008-; Yth T/F Dio New Hampshire Concord NH 2012-, Cler Dvlpmt Grp 2011-** B Cambridge MA 1970 d Richard & Josephine. BA Coll of Wooster 1994; MDiv Andover - Newton TS 2011; MDiv Andover Newton TS 2011. D 1/11/2012 P 9/5/2012 Bp Vicky Gene Robinson. m 3/15/1997 Thomas W Solter c 3. S Andr's Epis Ch Contoocook NH 2012-2013. solterk@stpatrickschurch.org

SOLTYS, Jacqueline Rebecca (Chi) 65 E Huron St, Chicago IL 60611 B Boston MA 1964 d John & Florence. B.A. Wesl 1985; M.Phil. Ya 1990; M.A. Ya 1990; Ph.D. Ya 1994. D 12/19/2015 P 7/9/2016 Bp Jeff Lee. m 6/6/1992 Stuart Douglas Henderson c 2. Cur Cathd Of S Jas Chicago IL 2016-2017. jsoltys@saintjamescathderal.org

SOMERS, David Wayne (CFla) 5873 N Dean Rd, Orlando FL 32817 **S Matt's Epis Ch Orlando FL 2010-** B Fremont MI 1959 s Wayne & Susan. Nash; BA Oral Roberts U 1981; U of Cntrl Florida 1993. D 12/11/2010 Bp John Wadsworth Howe. m 4/25/1987 Patricia Somers c 3.

SOMERS, Faye Veronica (SeFla) 2707 NW 37th St, Boca Raton FL 33434 **D Chap Of S Andr Boca Raton FL 2011-; Lower Sch Chapl S Andrews Sch Boca Raton Florida 2007-** B Jamaica West Indies 1953 d Edna. BS York U 1974; MA Natl U 1991; Dioc Sch for Chr Stds 2009. D 4/8/2011 Bp Leo Frade. c 3. faye.somers@saintandrews.net

SOMERVILLE II, Ben Leonidas (Az) 542 Raymond Dr, Sierra Vista AZ 85635 B Savannah GA 1940 s Ben & Edna. BS W Virginia U 1962; MDiv Sewanee: The U So, TS 1968. D 6/29/1968 Bp Milton Legrand Wood P 5/17/1969 Bp Randolph R Claiborne. m 8/15/1959 Mary Anne Somerville c 2. R S Steph's Ch Sierra Vista AZ 1999-2005; R Gr Epis Ch Canton NY 1989-1999; P-in-c Trin Chap Morley Canton NY 1989-1999; P-in-c Trin Morely NY 1989-1999; Dio Maryland Baltimore MD 1988-1989, 1974-1976; Ch Of The H Cov Baltimore MD 1987-1989; P-in-c Ch of the H Commandment Baltimore MD 1987-1989; Ch Of-Ascen & Prince-Peace Baltimore MD 1986-1987; R Ch of the Ascen and Prince of Peace Baltimore MD 1985-1987; Dio Wyoming Casper 1983-1985; Trin Epis Ch Hartford CT 1980-1983; Assoc Trinty Harford CT 1980-1983; S Lk's Ch Annapolis MD 1979-1980; EFM Mentor ; EFM Trnr Sewanee U So TS Sewanee TN 1976-1996; Vic S Andr The Fisherman Epis Mayo MD 1975-1980; Campus Min Ecum Campus Mnstry Baltimore MD 1973-1975;

Asst St Martins-In-The-Field Ch Severna Pk MD 1970-1973; Vic Calv Cornelia GA 1968-1970; Vic Gr-Calv Epis Ch Clarkesville GA 1968-1970. Auth, *Var Journ arts.*

SOMERVILLE, David James (Ga) 128 King Cotton Rd, Brunswick GA 31525 B Yonkers NY 1943 s Robert & Elizabeth. MS LIU; BA Bos 1967; STB PDS 1969. D 4/19/1969 P 10/1/1969 Bp Alfred L Banyard. m 6/22/1996 Sherry Somerville c 1. Int S Paul's Epis Ch Jesup GA 2002-2003; Chr Ch Middletown NJ 1995-2008; Off Of Bsh For ArmdF New York NY 1976-1995; Reserve Chapl US-A NG 1973-1978; S Barth's Ch Cherry Hill NJ 1972-1976; Dio New Jersey Trenton NJ 1970-1973; Vic The Ch Of The Gd Shpd Berlin NJ 1969-1973.

SOMES, Norman F (ECR) 85 Anna Laura Rd., 85 Anna Laura Drive, Jacksonville OR 97530 B Romford Essex England 1936 s Norman & Mary. BS Lon GB 1957; MS Lon GB 1962; PhD Lon GB 1964; PMD Harv 1976; MDiv CDSP 1988. D 6/4/1988 P 6/3/1989 Bp William Edwin Swing. m 3/8/1958 Patricia Lilian Somes c 3. R S Barn Ch Arroyo Grande CA 1992-2005; Assoc Ch of S Mary's by the Sea Pacific Grove CA 1988-1992; Chair Cler Dio El Camino Real Salinas CA 1993-1994, Dioc Coun 1992. Auth, "So, you really want Ch growth. A handbook for Epis Ch rectors.," Jacksonville Press, 2011.

SOMMER, Robert Lane (ECR) All Saints Church/Cristo Rey, 437 Rogers Ave, Watsonville CA 95076 B Englewood NJ 1966 s Frederick & Wilma. BS Van 1988; BDS Epis Sch for Deacons 2011. D 10/22/2011 Bp Mary Gray-Reeves.

SOMMER, Susan Lemmon (Chi) 2410 Glenview Rd, Glenview IL 60025 **R S Dav's Ch Glenview IL 2013-; Subdean & Cn Pstr Gr & H Trin Cathd Kansas City MO 2005-** B Ann Arbor MI 1956 d Robert & Kay. BA Cntrl Michigan U 1977; MDiv SWTS 1993. D 6/24/1993 Bp Robert Marshall Anderson P 1/6/1994 Bp William Walter Wiedrich. m 1/14/1979 Rick Sommer c 1. Gr And H Trin Cathd Kansas City MO 2005-2013; Vic Gr Epis Ch New Lenox IL 1999-2005; Asst R Emm Epis Ch La Grange IL 1994-1999; Dir Stdts Servs Bexley Seabury Fed Chicago IL 1993-1994; Asst R The Annunc Of Our Lady Gurnee IL 1993-1994. "Actg ourselves into Thinking Rt," Preaching as Prophetic calling Sermons that Wk XII, 2004.

SOMODEVILLA, Rene Francisco (Dal) 4018 S Lakewood Dr, Memphis TN 38128 **Cn to the Ordnry Dio W TN Memphis TN 2004-** B Havana CU 1946 s Santiago & Elvira. BA Midwestern U 1969; MSW U of Texas 1972; Lic Sacr Theol Angl TS 1984. D 6/16/1984 P 1/23/1985 Bp Donis Dean Patterson. m 5/9/1992 Nancy Ann Somodevilla c 4. Asst S Andr's Epis Ch Collierville TN 2010-2013; Dio W Tennessee Memphis 2004-2010; R S Elis's Epis Ch Memphis TN 1997-2004; R S Barn Ch Garland TX 1986-1997; Cur Epis Ch Of The Ascen Dallas TX 1984-1986.

SONDEREGGER, Kathrine Ann (Va) 669 Weybridge St # 5753, Middlebury VT 05753 **Prof Of Theol VTS Alexandria VA 2002-** B Marquette MI 1950 d Richard & Marion. D 8/13/2000 Bp Mary Adelia Rosamond Mcleod. D S Steph's Ch Middlebury VT 2000-2002; Prof Of Rel Mid 1987-2002.

SONLEY, Joseph (Hai) **Dio Haiti Port-au-Prince HT 2009-** B Lascahobas Haiti 1974 s Emma. BA Faculti de Droit de Port-A-Prince 2001; BA Seminaire de Theol Haiti 2010; MA VTS 2012. D 11/1/2009 P 6/29/2010 Bp Jean Zache Duracin. m 7/26/2012 Yvrance Rondeau.

SONNEN, Jon Anton (Tex) 4403 Seneca St, Pasadena TX 77504 B Houston TX 1936 s Louis & Waldene. BA SMU 1959; MA SMU 1965; MDiv Epis TS of the SW 1974. D 6/16/1974 Bp James Milton Richardson P 6/1/1975 Bp Scott Field Bailey. m 12/28/1957 Marilyn Sonnen c 3. S Barn Epis Ch Houston TX 1990-1999; Vic S Jn's Epis Ch Silsbee TX 1988-1990; Other Cler Position The Great Cmsn Fndt Houston TX 1988-1990; S Thos Ch Houston TX 1987-1988; R S Barth's Ch Hempstead TX 1978-1987; Vic Adv Stafford TX 1974-1978; All SS Epis Ch Stafford TX 1974-1978. Auth, "Concept Of Duty In Plato & Kant," 1964. CBS, ECM; NOEL.

SONNESYN, Roger Earl (Minn) B 1949 D 6/24/1980 Bp Robert Marshall Anderson. m 2/3/1979 Patricia Margaret Sonnesyn. Supply P S Andr's Epis Ch Minneapolis MN 2008-2013; S Catherines Ch Enumclaw WA 1987-1989; S Jas Epis Ch Kent WA 1984-1986; Exec Coun Appointees New York NY 1980-1984.

SOPER JR, Leroy Dilmore (At) 514 E. NewJersey Ave Apt. 5125, Southern Pines NC 28387 B Brownsville TX 1921 s Leroy & Valentine. BA Cit 1943; MDiv Sewanee: The U So, TS 1959. D 6/1/1959 Bp William Francis Moses P 12/24/1959 Bp Henry I Louttit. c 4. Assoc Gr And S Steph's Epis Ch Colorado Sprg CO 2009-2010, Chapl 1998-2008; Int Ch Of S Mich The Archangel Colorado Spg CO 1997-1998; Int Ch Of The Ascen Pueblo CO 1996-1997; Int Par of St Clem Honolulu HI 1993-1994; Vic S Jude's Hawaiian Ocean View Ocean View HI 1991-1993; R The Epis Ch Of The Adv Madison GA 1987-1989; Dio Cntrl Florida Orlando FL 1968-1970; R H Cross Epis Ch Sanford FL 1964-1986; R S Mary Of The Ang Epis Ch Orlando FL 1959-1964.

SOPER, Robert Arthur (WTex) 300 Hollywood Dr, Edinburg TX 78539 B Fort Benning GA 1940 s Leroy & Jeanette. BS Georgia Inst of Tech 1963; MDiv Epis TS of the SW 1968; MEd U of Texas Pan Amer 1975; U of Texas 1980. D 7/25/1968 P 1/29/1969 Bp Richard Earl Dicus. m 6/8/1982 Julia Ava Soper c 3. S Steph's Epis Sch Austin TX 1978-1980; Vic Redeem Mercedes TX

1973-1974; Chapl Pan Amer U Edinburg TX 1968-1974; Vic S Matt's Ch Edinburg TX 1968-1974.

SORENSEN, John Thomas (Pa) 576 Concord Road, Glen Mills PA 19342 **R S Jn's Ch Glen Mills PA 2006-; Dioc Mssn Plnng Cmsn Dio Pennsylvania Philadelphia PA 2009-, Dioc Coun 2007-** B East Orange NJ 1952 s William & Julanne. AA Cape Cod Cmnty Coll 1978; AB Boston Coll 1982; MDiv VTS 1985; DMin SWTS 2004. D 6/4/1986 Bp John Bowen Coburn P 6/1/1987 Bp Ronald Hayward Haines. m 5/19/1984 Jeannine M Sorensen c 2. Trst Dio Albany Greenwich NY 2000-2004, RurD, Nthrn Adirondacks 1998-2005; COM Dio NW Texas Lubbock TX 1998-1999; Adj Prof SUNY Plattsburgh 1997-2005; R Trin Ch Plattsburgh NY 1991-2006; Ch Of The H Trin Midland TX 1987-1990; Chapl Trin Sch Of Midland Inc. Midland TX 1987-1990; Ass't Chapl St Steph Sch Alexandria VA 1986-1987. Auth, "Bk Revs/arts," 2003. Albany Via Media 2003-2006; Fndr Alexandria Christmas In April 1985-1987. Dn, Nthrn Adirondack Dnry Dio Albany 1999.

SORENSEN, Lael (Me) St Peter's Episcopal Church, 11 White St, Rockland ME 04841 **R S Ptr's Ch Rockland ME 2015-; Chapl Gr Epis Day Sch Kensington MD 2010-** B Berkeley, CA 1957 d Harry & Barbara. BA Rutgers The St U of New Jersey 1979; MA U MI 1984; MDiv Ya Berk 2010. D 6/19/2010 Bp Stephen Taylor Lane P 1/22/2011 Bp John Bryson Chane. m 12/10/2012 Katherine C Adams. Gr Epis Ch Silver Sprg MD 2010-2013. rector. stpetersrockland@gmail.com

SORENSEN, Richard Todd (Nev) 1580 G St, Sparks NV 89431 **P S Steph's Epis Ch Reno NV 1997-** B Reno NV 1950 s Alfred & Jo Ann. BA U of Nevada at Reno 1979. D 9/6/1996 P 5/17/1997 Bp Stewart Clark Zabriskie. m 1/12/1980 Ellen Easton.

SORENSEN, Todd Wallace (Colo) 6653 W Chatfield Ave, Littleton CO 80128 **R The Epis Par of S Greg Littleton CO 1990-** B Minneapolis MN 1951 s Neil & Nancy. BA Arizona St U 1974; MDiv CDSP 1975. D 6/24/1979 Bp Joseph Thomas Heistand P 5/25/1980 Bp George R Selway. m 6/26/2004 Barbara J Hartmann c 3. Vic S Thos Epis Ch Temecula CA 1985-1990; Assoc The Epis Ch Of The Gd Shpd Hemet CA 1985-1988; Asst St Jas the Great Epis Ch Newport Bch CA 1982-1985; Cur Chr Ch Of The Ascen Paradise Vlly AZ 1979-1982; Eccl Crt Dio Colorado Denver CO 2009-2011; Camps & Conferences (Chair final year) Dio Arizona Phoenix AZ 1980-1982.

SORENSON, James Ronald (EMich) 226 W Nicolet Blvd, Marquette MI 49855 B Marquette MI 1940 s Leslie & Eva. Bex Sem; TS Dio Michigan; BA Alma Coll 1962; SWTS 1972. D 7/24/1972 Bp H Coleman Mcgehee Jr P 11/24/1973 Bp Archie H Crowley. c 3. Reg Mssnr S Jn's Epis Ch Sand Point MI 2002-2005, P-in-c 1977-2001; COM Dio Estrn Michigan Saginaw MI 1996-2000, Stndg Com 1994-1996; R S Matt's Epis Ch Saginaw MI 1993-2005; P-in-c S Andrews-By-The-Lake Epis Ch Harrisville MI 1992-1993; Nthrn Convoc Dio Michigan Detroit MI 1988-1992, COM 1985-1987, SW Convoc 1975-1984; R Chr Epis Ch E Tawas MI 1985-1993; S Paul's Epis Ch Bad Axe MI 1977-1985; The Epis Ch In Huron Cnty Bad Axe MI 1977-1985; P-in-c S Marg's Epis Ch Harbor Bch MI 1977-1984; Vic S Andr's Ch Jackson MI 1974-1985; R Chr Ch Pleasant Lake MI 1974-1977; Cur S Lk's Epis Ch Rogers City MI 1972-1973; Cur Trin Epis Ch Alpena MI 1972-1973. R Emer St. Matt's Saginaw, MI 2005.

SORENSON, Suzanne Marie (EMich) 226 W Nicolet Blvd, Marquette MI 49855 **Died 2/28/2016** B Saginaw MI 1940 D 11/24/2001 Bp Edwin Max Leidel Jr. m 5/22/2004 James Ronald Sorenson c 2. D S Jn's Epis Ch Saginaw MI 2002-2004.

SOREY, Gene Christine (Fla) 4304 Redtail Hawk Dr, Jacksonville FL 32257 **Chapl OSL 1997-** B Washington DC 1946 d Daniel & Gene. Cert Sewanee: The U So, TS 1995; BS Jacksonville U 2000. D 9/17/1995 Bp Stephen Hays Jecko. Chapl/Rel Educ Tchr San Jose Epis Day Sch Jacksonville FL 2000-2010; COM San Jose Epis Ch Jacksonville FL 1999-2010, D 1995-2010; Dio Florida Jacksonville 1999-2003. Chapl, Ord Of S Lukes; NAES; NCA; Natl hon Soc; NAAD; SocMary. revchris@comcast.net

SORVILLO, August Louis (CFla) 90 Bridgewater Ln, Ormond Beach FL 32174 B Youngstown OH 1938 s August & Louise. Youngstown St U 1958; LTh Nash 1973; DMin Pittsburgh TS 1992. D 5/26/1973 P 12/7/1973 Bp William Hopkins Folwell. m 6/23/1962 Shirley Sorvillo c 3. R S Jas Epis Ch Ormond Bch FL 1982-2003; Vic Gloria Dei Epis Ch Cocoa FL 1975-1982; Cur S Barn Ch Deland FL 1973-1975.

SORVILLO SR, James August (CFla) 9101 Palm Tree Dr., Windermere FL 34786 **R Epis Ch Of The Ascen Orlando FL 2003-** B Miami FL 1963 s August & Shirley. D Min. Sewanee: The U So, TS; AA Daytona Bch Cmnty Coll 1985; BA U of Cntrl Florida 1987; MDiv Sewanee: The U So, TS 2000. D 5/27/2000 P 12/9/2000 Bp John Wadsworth Howe. m 6/25/1988 Debra J Apicella c 2. Int Dir Epis Counslg Cntr 2014-2015; Asst H Trin Epis Ch Melbourne FL 2000-2003. rector@ascension-orlando.org

SOSA, Gary Rafael (NAM) Po Box 216, Bluff UT 84512 **D Utah Reg 1991-** B San Francisco CA 1954 s Hugo & Marie. BS Bethany Coll 1976. D 6/16/1991 Bp Steven Tsosie Plummer Sr. m 8/24/1974 Linda Ann Higley.

SO-SCHOOS, Alistair (Md) All Hallows' Parish, P.O.Box 235, Davidsonville MD 21035 **R All Hallows Par So River Edgewater MD 2008-** B Shijiazhuang

China 1976 s Sze-Man & Monica. BS Amer U 1998; MS Geo 2000; MDiv VTS 2005. D 6/11/2005 P 1/21/2006 Bp John Bryson Chane. m 8/27/2011 Daniel Schoos. Assoc R S Mart's-In-The-Field Day Sch Severna Pk MD 2005-2008; St Martins-In-The-Field Ch Severna Pk MD 2005-2008. Soc of Cath Priests 2010; Soc of Ord Scientists 2010.

SOSNOWSKI, Frederick Skinner (SC) 2426 Sea Island Yacht Club Rd, Wadmalaw Island SC 29487 **Ret 1994-** B Charleston SC 1925 s John & Eliza. BA U of So Carolina 1951; MDiv VTS 1955. D 6/16/1955 P 7/1/1956 Bp Thomas N Carruthers. m 5/29/1982 Polly Sanford. Dioc Rep PorterGaud Sch Bd Trst 1998-2002; Asst Epis Ch of the Gd Shpd Charleston SC 1994-1997; S Jas Ch Charleston SC 1990-1994; Dir: Pstr Counslg Ctr So Carolina Charleston SC 1977-1994, Dio Coun 1971-1976; Atone Ch Walterboro SC 1975-1977; R S Jude's Epis Ch Walterboro SC 1975-1977; Asst S Phil's Ch Charleston SC 1968-1975; R S Matt's Ch Henderson TX 1957-1959; Asst Trin Cathd Columbia SC 1955-1957.

SOSNOWSKI, John W (NJ) 808 W State St, Trenton NJ 08618 **Chr Epis Ch Villanova PA 2016-** B Torrington CT 1954 s Edward & Mary. AA S Thos Coll 1974; BA S Mary Seminar Coll 1976; BA S Mary Sem Coll 1976; MDiv S Marys Sem and U 1979; MA Sthrn Connecticut St U 1986. Rec 6/1/1995 as Priest Bp Clarence Nicholas Coleridge. m 9/16/1989 Cynthia B Sosnowski c 2. Cn to the Ordnry Dio New Jersey Trenton NJ 2012-2016, Cnvnr of Vitality / Viability T/F 2013-, Rt Onward Visioning Com 2007-2012, Dn of Atlantic Convoc 2006-2009; R S Mary's Epis Ch Stone Harbor NJ 1997-2012; Supply Dio Connecticut Meriden CT 1995-1997; Pstr RC Ch 1979-1988; Founding Mem Mustard Seed of Cape May Cnty Stone Harbor NJ 2008-2012; Bd Mem Vol in Med Cape May Crt Hse NJ 2005-2010. Amer Assn of Mar & Fam Ther 1986; Connecticut Lic Mar & Fam Ther 1989. jsosnowski@dioceseofnj.org

SOTELO, Fabio A (At) St Bede's Episcopal Church, 2601 Henderson Mill Rd NE, Atlanta GA 30345 **Hisp Mssnr Dio Atlanta Atlanta GA 2012-; S Bede's Ch Atlanta GA 2012-** B Saboya Colombia 1964 s Pablo & Maria. MA S Thos Aquinas 1993; MD Mt S Mary's 1999. Rec 5/27/2012 as Priest Bp J Neil Alexander. m 10/30/2011 Claudia P Sotelo c 3.

SOTELO, George Salinas (Az) 13685 N Balancing Rock Dr, Oro Valley AZ 85755 B Adrian MI 1949 s Jose & Marta. Sch for Deacons; BD Wm Tyndale Coll 1975; Cert Ang Stud CDSP 1993. D 6/5/1993 P 12/1/1993 Bp William Edwin Swing. m 5/17/2014 Stephen L Mcelroy. Dio Arizona Phoenix AZ 2011, 2006-2011; R S Andr's Epis Ch Tucson AZ 2006-2011; Dio California San Francisco CA 1994-2005; Ch Of The H Trin Richmond CA 1993-2003; S Aid's Ch San Francisco CA 1993-1994; The Epis Ch Of S Jn The Evang San Francisco CA 1993-1994; Non-par 1993.

SOTO, Luis Fernando (DR) B San Jose Costa R CA 1950 s Enrique & Maria. Cert Cntrl Sem Cr 1976; Cert Gregorian U 1978; Cert Angelicum U 1980. Rec 7/1/1985. m 3/19/1985 Guiselle Soto. Dio The Dominican Republic (Iglesia Epis Dominicana) Gazcue Santo Domingo 1986-1988. Soc Recon & Agape.

✠ SOTO, The Rt Rev Onell Asiselo (Ala) 3350 Torremolinos Ave, Doral FL 33178 **Died 8/5/2015** B 1932 s Juan & Maria. BA U of Havana Cu 1956; STM Sewanee: The U So, TS 1964. D 6/29/1964 Bp George Mosley Murray P 8/18/1965 Bp David Reed Con 7/11/1987 for Ve. m 7/4/1960 Nina Ulloa. Asst Dio Alabama Birmingham 1999-2001; Asst Bp Dio Atlanta Atlanta GA 1995-1999; VP Resurr AIDS Ecum Mnstry Dio Venezuela 1993-1995; Bp of Venezuela Dio Venezuela 1987-1995; VP CRISEV Chr-Jewish Orgnztn for Venezuela Dio Venezuela 1987-1995; Anglicanos 1984-1995; Mssn Info & Educ Off ECEC Epis Ch Cntr New York NY 1978-1987; Prov IX New York NY 1971-1977; P-in-c S Nich Ch Quito Ecuador 1965-1971; Asst S Steph's Epis Ch San Antonio TX 1964-1965. ECom. DD TS U So 1988; Ord of Simon Bolivar Pres of Venezuela.

SOTOMAYOR, Ricardo S (Tex) B 1942 s Antonio & Maria. MDiv Lateranensis U IT 1969. Rec 6/14/1995 Bp Claude Edward Payne. m 7/17/2003 Angelina Sotomayor c 2. S Paul's Ch Houston TX 1997-2002; The Great Cmsn Fndt Houston TX 1995-2007; Vic Mssn De La Santa Cruz Houston TX 1995-2006. Angl Stds The TS/The U So 1995.

SOUCEK, Paul (Nwk) B 1939 D 7/1/1973 P 6/8/1974 Bp George E Rath. m 10/13/1966 Paula Novakova.

SOUDER, Diane J (Az) Po Box 1077, Winter Park FL 32790 B Miami FL 1941 d H Lloyd & Frances. BA U of Florida 1963; MDiv GTS 1992. D 6/29/1992 Bp Calvin Onderdonk Schofield Jr P 1/1/1993 Bp Jane Hart Holmes Dixon. c 1. P Sprtl Dir/Supply P Dio CF 2001-2013; Chapl Westminster Care of Delaney Pk Orlando FL 2001-2004; P-in-c Cong Ahwatukee Foothills Phoenix AZ 1999-2000; Chapl RTA Hospice Phoenix AZ 1999; S Lk's At The Mtn Phoenix AZ 1999, 1995-1996; Assoc Ch Of The Epiph Tempe AZ 1996-1998; Asst S Pat's Ch Washington DC 1992-1993.

SOUGHERS, Tara Kathleen (Mass) 23 Horseshoe Dr., Plainville MA 02762 **Doctoral Stdt Bos TS 2009-** B Indianapolis IN 1961 d Richard & Peggy. BS New Mex Tech 1981; MA Rice U 1985; MDiv VTS 1990. D 6/17/1990 P 1/9/1991 Bp Don Adger Wimberly. m 7/18/1981 Michael Hans Helmuth Dehn c 2. Epis Ch Of S Thos Taunton MA 2016-2017; Epiph Par Walpole

S

MA 2016; R Trin Epis Ch Wrentham MA 2005-2009; Bp's Coun, Exec Coun Dio Connecticut Meriden CT 2001-2003; R Trin Ch Portland CT 2000-2004; Lead R, Tri-Cnty Cluster Dio Cntrl New York Liverpool NY 1995-2000, Dioc Counc 1994-2000; R Calv Ch Homer NY 1992-2000; S Matt's Ch Moravia NY 1992-2000; Tri-Cnty Cluster Glen Aubrey NY 1992-2000; All SS Ch Salt Lake City UT 1991-1992; Dio Utah Salt Lake City UT 1990-1991. Auth, "Treasures of Darkness: Finding God When Hope Is Hidden," Abingdon Press, 2009; Auth, "Fleeing God: Fear, Call and the Bk of Jonah," Cowley/Rowman & Littlefield, 2007; Auth, "Falling In Love w God: Passion, Pryr and the Song of Songs," Cowley, 2005; Auth, "To Equip the SS (Curric)," Privately distributed.

SOUKUP, Patricia Marie (RG) 3700 Parsifal St NE, Albuquerque NM 87111 **Other Dio The Rio Grande Albuquerque 2014-; D S Mk's On The Mesa Epis Ch Albuquerque NM 2012-** B Albuquerque NM 1963 d Richard & Carol. BA U of New Mex 1986; MA U of New Mex 1994; Ext Prog of TESM 2006. D 10/21/2006 Bp Jeffrey Neil Steenson. m 5/2/1987 Michael Scott Soukup. D S Jn's Cathd Albuquerque NM 2007-2012; D S Mary's Epis Ch Albuquerque NM 2006-2007, Verger 2003-2006; Verger St. Jn's Epis Cathd Albuquerque NM 1998-2003. psoukup@dioceserg.org

SOULE, Judith Christine (Spok) 625 C St, Cheney WA 99004 **S Paul's Ch Cheney WA 2012-, Cmnty P 2009-** B Los Angeles CA 1937 d Charles & Maydean. BS U of Montana 1991; MS Estrn Washington U 1993; Dioc Theol Prog 2008. D 12/21/2002 P 11/15/2008 Bp James E Waggoner Jr. c 6.

SOULE, Patrick Ross (WTex) 13026 Leopard St, Corpus Christi TX 78410 **Texas Mltry Inst San Antonio TX 2017-** B Pontiac MI 1974 s Douglas & Sandra. BSBA Tennessee Tech U 1997; MDiv TESM 2007. D 6/2/2007 P 4/12/2008 Bp John Bauerschmidt. m 6/19/1999 Cassandra B Soule c 3. S Helena's Epis Ch Boerne TX 2013-2016; Vic S Andr's Epis Ch Corpus Christi TX 2009-2013; S Phil's Ch Nashville TN 2008-2009, 2007-2008; Sr Tech Analyst Willis No Amer 1997-2004.

SOULIS, Cameron J (WA) National Cathedral School, 3612 Woodley Rd, NW, Washington DC 20016 **Cathd of St Ptr & St Paul Washington DC 2014-** B Boston MA 1964 d Wilbur & Jane May. BA Hood Coll 1986; M.Div. VTS 2014. D 12/7/2013 P 6/14/2014 Bp Mariann Edgar Budde. m 5/17/2014 Michael John Salmon. csoulis@cathedral.org

SOUTH, Lynn Crisco (Haw) 100 Kulanihakoi St, Kihei HI 96753 B Charlotte NC 1950 d John & Carolyn. D 11/2/2013 Bp Robert Leroy Fitzpatrick. c 1.

SOUTHALL, Jennifer Lea (Miss) 3921 Oakridge Dr, Jackson MS 39216 **S Jas Ch Jackson MS 2015-; Other Lay Position Dio Mississippi Jackson MS 2012-** B Vicksburg MS 1970 d Robert & Nell. BA U of Mississippi 1992; MA Mississippi St U 1996; MDiv VTS 2015. D 6/13/2015 P 1/16/2016 Bp Brian Seage.

SOUTHERLAND, Thomas Rudolph (SO) 10555 Montgomery Rd., Apt 32, Cincinnati OH 45242 B Stonega VA 1937 s James & Thelma. Sthrn Ohio D Acad London OH; U Cinc OH. D 6/23/2007 Bp Thomas Edward Breidenthal. m 10/6/1958 Barbara Southerland c 4. Computer Spec Us Govt 1961-1998.

SOUTHERN JR, John Carlton (WNC) 42 Alclare Ct, Asheville NC 28804 **Died 2/23/2017** B Winston-Salem NC 1946 s John & Mary. GTS 1972; BA U NC 1973. D 6/8/1974 P 6/14/1975 Bp William Gillette Weinhauer. S Lk's Epis Ch Lincolnton NC 2006-2008; S Mk's Ch Gastonia NC 2004-2005; Ch Of The Gd Shpd Rocky Mt NC 2004; Int S Lk's Ch Boone NC 2002-2004; Ch Of The Gd Shpd Cashiers NC 2001-2002; S Lk's Ch Salisbury NC 1999-2000; Par Of The H Comm Glendale Sprg NC 1998-1999; Trin Epis Ch Asheville NC 1992-1998; P Dio Wstrn No Carolina Asheville NC 1986-1990; Ch Of The Redeem Asheville NC 1981-1986; Asst R S Mary's Ch Asheville NC 1977-1980; Vic S Mich's Ch Baton Rouge LA 1975-1977; Chapl Sthrn U Baton Rouge LA 1975-1977; Vic Trin Ch Kings Mtn NC 1974-1975.

SOUTHWICK, Susan Bowman (Ala) D 10/1/2016 Bp John Mckee Sloan Sr.

SOUZA, Raymond Manuel (EC) 846 Wide Waters, Bath NC 27808 B Richmond VA 1955 s Raymond & Violet. BA W&M 1979; MDiv Epis TS of the SW 1998. D 6/13/1998 Bp Frank Harris Vest Jr P 12/12/1998 Bp Joe Doss. m 12/19/1992 Heidi E Souza. R S Thos' Epis Ch Bath NC 2001-2009; Asst Trin Ch Moorestown NJ 1998-2001.

SOWAH, Constance Kate (Minn) 4180 Lexington Ave S, Eagan MN 55123 B Accra Ghana West Africa 1954 d Abraham & Phyllis. BSC U MN 2006; Dplma Sewanee: The U So, TS 2013; Dplma U So TS 2013; D Shared Mnstry Team 2014. D 6/26/2014 P 6/20/2015 Bp Brian N Prior. c 1.

SOWAN, Michael George (Alb) Box 1185, Street Sacrement Lane, Bolton Landing NY 12814 **Ret 2003-; Ret 2003-** B Potsdam NY 1939 s George & Rose. BA Hobart and Wm Smith Colleges 1961; STB PDS 1966. D 6/11/1966 P 12/19/1966 Bp Allen Webster Brown. m 7/22/1973 Nancy Jutiva Sowan c 1. R Ch Of S Sacrement Bolton Landing NY 1995-2003; R S Paul's Ch Kansas City KS 1980-1995; R S Steph's Ch Billings MT 1973-1980; Cur S Ptr's Cathd Helena MT 1970-1973; R H Cross Ft Plain NY 1967-1970; P The Ch Of The Gd Shpd Canajoharie NY 1967-1970; Cur S Mich Albany NY 1966-1967; Stndg Com Dio Montana Helena MT 1973-1980.

SOWARDS, William Michael (Pa) St James Episcopal Church, 3768 Germantown Pike, Collegeville PA 19426 **S Jas Ch Collegeville PA 2013-** B

Portsmouth VA 1960 s Billy & Ina. BA U of No Florida 1997; MEd U of No Florida 2000; MDiv VTS 2007. D 5/27/2007 P 12/9/2007 Bp Samuel Johnson Howard. m 6/20/1981 Sonya K Sonya Kay Nutter c 2. Epis U Cntr Tallahassee FL 2012; P-in-c S Paul's Epis Ch Quincy FL 2008-2012; Dio Florida Jacksonville 2007-2011.

SOWERS, Susan R (CGC) 3200 N 12th Ave, Pensacola FL 32503 **Assoc R S Chris's Ch Pensacola FL 2010-** B Frankfurt, Germany 1960 d William & Mary. BS USMA 1982; MS U of Washington 1991; MS US Army War Coll 2003; MDiv VTS 2010. D 6/5/2010 Bp Shannon Sherwood Johnston P 12/18/2010 Bp Philip Menzie Duncan II. m 7/22/2015 Donna Van Van Winkle. Assoc S Andr's Cathd Honolulu HI 2013-2015. susan@scpen.org

SOWINSKI, Charles Paul (Az) 6300 N Central Ave, Phoenix AZ 85012 B Chicago IL 1956 s Robert & Maryann. Philos Our Lady of Ang Franciscan Sem 1987. D 6/7/2014 Bp Kirk Stevan Smith.

SOX, Harold D (Cal) 20 The Vineyard, Richmond, Surrey TW 10 6 AN Great Britain (UK) **Died 8/28/2016** B Hickory NC 1936 s Samuel & Nellie. BA U NC 1958; MDiv UTS 1960; VTS 1961. D 6/10/1961 P 12/1/1961 Bp Leland Stark. m 10/24/2014 Virtus Allison Offermann. Serv Ch in Engl 1982-2016; Chapl Campbell Hall Sch No Hollywood CA 1981-1982; Campbell Hall Vlly Vlg CA 1981-1982; Serv Ch in Engl 1974-1980; Minor Cn Gr Cathd San Francisco CA 1971-1974; Chapl Cathd Sch San Francisco CA 1970-1974; Chapl Trin Sch New York NY 1964-1970; Chapl Cranbrook Sch Bloomfield Hills MI 1963-1964; Asst S Jas Ch Montclair NJ 1961-1963. Auth, "Pere Dav," *Pere Dav*, Sessions of York, 2009; Auth, "Jn Woolman," *Jn Woolman*, Sessions of York, 2003; Auth, "Quaker Plant Hunters," *Quaker Plant Hunters*, Sessions of York, 2003; Auth, "Bachelors of Art," *Bachelors of Art*, Fourth Estate, 1991; Auth, "Unmasking the Forger," *Unmasking the Forger*, Geo Allen and Unwin, 1987; Auth, "Relics and Shrines," *Relics and Shrines*, Geo Allen and Unwin, 1985; Auth, "Gospel of Barn," *Gospel of Barn*, Geo Allen and Unwin, 1984; Auth, "Image on the Shroud," *Image on the Shroud*, Geo Allen and Unwin, 1981; Auth, "File on the Shroud," *File on the Shroud*, Hodder and Stoughton, 1978. Rel Soc of Friends 1996.

SOYARS, Jonathan E (Chi) 115 West Seventh Street, Charlotte NC 28202 **S Mart's Epis Ch Charlotte NC 2015-** B Onondaga NY 1981 s Richard & Elaine. PhD U Chi; BA Wheaton Coll 2003; MDiv PrTS 2007; ThM PrTS 2008; MA U Chi 2013. D 12/15/2013 Bp Chris Christopher Epting P 11/16/2014 Bp Anne Hodges-Copple. m 8/16/2003 Johanna Gill Soyars c 2. Asstg P S Ptr's Epis Ch Charlotte NC 2014-2015.

SPACCARELLI, Cara Elizabeth (WA) 620 G St SE, Washington DC 20003 **R Chr Ch Capitol Hill Washington DC 2010-** B Cincinnati OH 1980 d John & Janeth. BA Carleton Coll 2002; MDiv Epis TS of the SW 2006. D 6/8/2006 P 12/21/2006 Bp James Louis Jelinek. m 1/3/2004 Michael Christopher Lawyer c 2. Cn Cathd Ch Of S Mk Minneapolis MN 2006-2010.

SPAETH, Colleen Grayce (NJ) 247 Merion Ave, Haddonfield NJ 08033 **D S Barth's Ch Cherry Hill NJ 1998-** B Trenton NJ 1950 d Jos & Margaret. Rutgers The St U of New Jersey; AA Burlington Cnty Coll 1985. D 10/31/1998 Bp Joe Doss. m 10/10/1992 David Charles Spaeth.

SPAFFORD, Donald Wick (Dal) 5903 Bonnard Dr, Dallas TX 75230 B Pampa TX 1935 s Perry & Ebba. D 8/26/1972 P 3/15/1973 Bp William Jones Gordon Jr. c 2. Chapl Dio Dallas Dallas TX 2013-2014; Assoc S Lk's Epis Ch Dallas TX 2005-2014; Assoc S Mich And All Ang Ch Dallas TX 1997-2005. dws3536@aol.com

SPAGNA, Amy L (Va) Christ Church, 7 Elm St, Westerly RI 02891 **Chr Ch Westerly RI 2015-** B Troy NY 1976 d George & Sylvia. BA Randolph-Macon Coll 1998; Dplma of Angl Stds Ya Berk 2012; MDiv Yale DS 2012. D 6/9/2012 P 12/15/2012 Bp Shannon Sherwood Johnston. Cur Trin Ch Bethlehem PA 2012-2015. RSCM 2012. mother_amy@christchurchwesterly.org

SPAID, William John (WMich) 2008 Hudson Ave, Kalamazoo MI 49008 **Cn To The Ordnry Dio Wstrn Michigan Kalamazoo MI 2003-; Assoc The Par Ch Of Chr The King Kalamazoo MI 2003-** B Lorain OH 1953 s John & Phyllis. BS Frostburg St U 1975; MEd Frostburg St U 1977; MDiv Nash 1986. D 9/6/1986 Bp Albert Theodore Eastman P 3/21/1987 Bp Howard Samuel Meeks. c 2. Conf Asst CREDO Memphis TN 2000-2002; R S Mart of Tours Epis Ch Kalamazoo MI 1986-2002; Org/Chrmstr S Thos Of Cbury Ch Greendale WI 1983-1986; Dep GC- Epis Ch Cntr New York NY 2015. wspaid@edwm.org

SPAINHOUR, John Robert (Vt) 4616 McClelland Dr, Unit 203, Wilmington NC 28405 **H Trin Epis Ch Swanton VT 2015-; elected to Dioc Exec Coun The Epis Dio E Carolina Kinston N.C. 2012-; CE Resource Ntwk lay Mem The Dio SC Charleston SC 1986-** B Morganton NC 1956 s William & Mary. BA The Coll of Charleston 1978; MEd Cit 1984; MDiv TESM 1992. D 6/4/1992 P 12/12/1992 Bp Edward Lloyd Salmon Jr. c 2. P-in-c Ch Of The Adv Williamston NC 2013-2015; Assoc to the R S Jas Par Wilmington NC 2009-2013; Par P S Christophers Ch Elizabethtown NC 2006-2009; R S Chris's Epis Ch Elizabethtown NC 2005-2009; Mem and then Pres of Ecclesiatical Crt The Dio SC Charleston SC 2000-2002; Mem of Dioc Coun The Dio SC Charleston SC 1999-2002; Mem and then Pres of Dioc Stndg Com The Dio SC Charleston SC 1999-2001; Cler/Spouse Conf Com The Dio SC Charleston SC 1993-2000;

Cler and later Hd Sprtl Dir SC Curs Charleston SC 1993-1994; P So Carolina Charleston SC 1992-2006; R S Jn's Ch Charleston SC 1992-2002; Transitional D-in-c (6 mos) and then R S Jn's Epis Ch Oakland Charleston SC 1992-2002; LayTeacher/Stff of Dioc Conf The Dio SC Charleston SC 1987-1989; Lay vestryman-in-charge of CE Trin Epis Ch Pinopolis SC 1984-1986. Cursillos in Chrsnty 1981; Kairos 1986; The Bro of S Andr 1989; The OSL 1987.

SPALDING, Kirsten Snow (Cal) 333 Ellen Dr, San Rafael CA 94903 **P Ch Of The Nativ San Rafael CA 2015-** B New Bedford MA 1963 d Edward & Emma. BA Yale Coll 1984; JD Hastings Coll of Law 1990; MDiv CDSP 2012; MDiv CDSP 2012. D 12/7/2013 P 6/14/2014 Bp Marc Handley Andrus. m 7/6/1997 Joseph Wh Lough c 2. kss@well.com

SPANGENBERG, Carol (WMich) 1612 Stoney Point Dr, Lansing MI 48917 **Asst to R S Dav's Ch Lansing MI 2012-; Pstr Care Stff Hayes Green Breech Hosp Charlotte MI 1997-** B Detroit MI 1941 d William & Mary. BA MI SU 1964; MA MI SU 1974; EdS MI SU 1978; DMin Gnrl Theol Fndt-Notre Dame U 1989. D 9/12/1983 Bp William Jones Gordon Jr P 6/1/1990 Bp Henry Irving Mayson. m 7/27/1963 David Spangenberg c 3. R S Jn's Epis Ch Charlotte MI 1997-2010; D S Paul's Epis Ch Lansing MI 1983-1990; Pstr Care Stff Sparrow Hosp Lansing MI 1980-1993. Auth, *Cultural Journalism*; Auth, *Fells Yearbk.*

SPANGENBERG, Ronald Wesley (SVa) 6085 River Crest, Norfolk VA 23505 **Contract Epis Chapl Chap of the Centurion Ft Monroe VA 2006-** B Washington DC 1931 s Wesley & Jessie. BS U of Maryland 1954; MDiv Epis TS of the SW 1960; EdD Indiana U 1970. D 7/7/1960 Bp Everett H Jones P 1/25/1961 Bp Richard Earl Dicus. m 5/30/1958 Dorothy Spangenberg c 1. R 2000-2005; Vic Chr The King Epis Ch Yorktown VA 1997-2003; Vic 1997-2000; 1967-1997; P-in-c Epiph Little Rock AR 1965-1966; P-in-c S Steph's Epis Ch Jacksonville AR 1964-1966; Cur Chr Epis Ch Little Rock AR 1962-1966; Vic Ch Of The Ascen Refugio TX 1960-1962. Auth, "Human Factors in Design of Carrels"; Auth, "Structural Coherence in Pictorial & Verbal Displays," *Journ of Educational Psychol.* Ch Hisorical Soc 1964; Ord of S Lk 1965.

SPANGLER, DeLiza (WNY) 128 Pearl St, Buffalo NY 14202 **COM Dio Wstrn New York Tonawanda NY 2007-** B Clinton MO 1953 d Robert & Nancy. BA Lindenwood U 1975; PrTS 1976; MDiv GTS 1978; JD Willamette U 1985. D 5/21/1978 P 5/18/1979 Bp William Augustus Jones Jr. m 1/30/2009 Luanne Bauer. Dn S Paul's Cathd Buffalo NY 2006-2014; Cler Comp Cmsn Dio Wstrn Michigan Kalamazoo MI 1996-1997, Dioc Wrshp Cmsn. Chair 1996-2002; R S Paul's Epis Ch St Jos MI 1995-2005; S Phil's Ch Wrangell AK 1991-1995, 1989, Assoc 1985-1988, Co-R 1979-1982; Asst S Paul's Epis Ch Salem OR 1982-1985; Dio Alaska Fairbanks AK 1979-1982, Dioc Coun 1993-1994; S Andr's Epis Ch Petersburg AK 1979-1982; Asst Gr Ch Jamaica NY 1978-1979. Doctor of Humane Letters Lindenwood U 2012.

SPANGLER, Haywood B (Va) 1205 Swan Lake Dr Apt 303, Charlottesville VA 22902 **Dir of Educ Ldrshp Metro Richmond 2011-; Bd Mem/Governance Chair Ptr Paul Dvlpmt Cntr Of The Epis Ch Richmond VA 2006-** B Danville VA 1971 s John & Bes. BA U NC 1993; MDiv Yale DS 1996; PhD U of Virginia 2003. D 9/6/1997 P 3/14/1998 Bp Bob Johnson. R S Barth's Ch Richmond VA 2004-2011; P-in-c Mcilhany Par Charlottesville VA 2001-2003; Int Chr Epis Ch Luray VA 2000-2001; Int S Paul's Memi Charlottesville VA 1999; D S Lk's Epis Ch Asheville NC 1997-1998. Inventor, "Spangler Ethical Reasoning Assessment," *Self-scoring preference survey*, Auth holds the copyright, 2009.

SPANGLER, Robert Joseph (Okla) 7 Strathmore Dr, Arden NC 28704 **Ret 1992-** B Ash Grove MO 1927 s John & Vada. BA U of Kansas 1950; U of Missouri 1952; MA Ft Hays St U 1962; MDiv CDSP 1968. D 4/25/1968 P 12/21/1968 Bp William Davidson. m 9/3/1950 Linda Spangler c 3. Assoc S Jn's Epis Ch Tulsa OK 1980-1992; Chair DeptCE Dio Oklahoma Oklahoma City OK 1976-1978, Bp Coun 1976-1977, Chair Dept CE 1988-1991, Curs Strng Com 1986-1987, Bd VOOM 1979-1985, Dep GC 1970-1978; R S Mary's Ch Edmond OK 1974-1980; Asst Gr Epis Ch Hutchinson KS 1973-1975; P-in-c S Steph's Ch Guymon OK 1969-1973; S Tim's Epis Ch Hugoton KS 1969-1973; Vic S Jn's Ch Ulysses KS 1968-1973. Auth, "Hist of the Hays Daily News," *Ft Hays Stds*, Ft Hays St Coll, 1962. Preaching Awd CDSP 1968; Sigma Delta Chi 1951.

SPANN, Paul Ronald (Mich) 2971 Iroquois St, Detroit MI 48214 **Chr Ch Grosse Pointe Grosse Pointe Farms MI 2014-, Dir, Chr Ch Sprtlty Cntr 2003-** B Ann Arbor MI 1943 s Paul & Ruth. BA Kalamazoo Coll 1965; U Roch 1966; MDiv EDS 1970; Emory U 1987; Cert PRH-Inst Intl Poitiers FR 1998. D 6/29/1970 Bp Archie H Crowley P 1/16/1971 Bp Richard Stanley Merrill Emrich. m 1/4/1976 Jacqueline Graves c 2. Adj Fac Ecum TS Detroit MI 2004-2012; Sprtlty Fac CREDO Inst 2002-2017; Assoc R Chr Ch Cranbrook Bloomfield Hills MI 1998-2002; R Ch Of The Mssh Detroit MI 1971-1996; Econ Justice Cmsn Dio Michigan Detroit MI 1993-2005, Stndg Com 1992-1995, Exam Chapl in Issues in Contemporary Soc 1988-1992. Auth, "Chapt 11: Mustard Tree Co-op," *Making Hsng Happen*, Chalice Press, 2006; Auth, "Another Point of View," *Sermons That Wk XIII*, Morehouse, 2005; Auth, "Preaching Jesus to Urban Teens," *Wit*, Wit, 1996; Auth, "Recon and Race,"

Sojourners, Sojourners, 1990; Auth, "Cmnty and Identity," *Sojourners*, Sojourners, 1990; Auth, "Liturg and Justice," *Liturg*, No Amer Liturg Conf, 1989. Chr Cmnty Dvlpmt Assn, Un of Black Epi 1989; Inst Personnalite et Relatns Humaines 1998; Sprtl Dir Intl 2007; UBE 1973. Thompson Lecture in Rel Kalamazoo Coll 2001; Alum of the Year Kalamazoo Coll 1999; Hon Cn Cathd S Paul 1993; 1st McGehee Fund Cmnty Builder of Year 93 Schiffman Fndt and Econ. Justice Cmsn, Dio. of Mich 1993.

SPANNAGEL JR, Lawrence Elden (NwT) 676 E Willowbrook Dr, Meridian ID 83646 B Memphis TX 1943 s Lawrence & Sula. D 4/23/1972 P 11/26/1972 Bp William Jones Gordon Jr. c 3. Int S Ptr's Epis Ch Amarillo TX 2007-2008; Dio NW Texas Lubbock TX 2004-2008; Mssnr Panhandle Reg Mssnr 2004-2008; S Ptr's Epis Ch Borger TX 2000-2003; R S Lk's Epis Ch Wenatchee WA 1997-2000; R Chr Ch Anchorage AK 1994-1996; Int H Sprt Epis Ch Eagle River AK 1992-1993; S Dunst's Epis Ch Carmel CA 1989-1990; S Mary's Ch Anchorage AK 1974-1989.

SPANNAUS, Timothy Wise (Mich) 27786 Rainbow Cir, Lathrup Village MI 48076 **D S Jn's Ch Royal Oak MI 2006-; Advsry Bd Cntr for Chr Stds Winnipeg MB Can 2016-; CALL Advsry Bd CDSP Berkeley CA 2016-; COM Dio Michigan Detroit MI 2015-; Whitaker Inst Advsry Com 2014-** B Seattle, WA 1946 s Ruben & Olive. BS U IL - Urbana 1968; MS U IL - Urbana 1973; PhD Wayne - Detroit 1981. Rec 6/10/2016 Bp Wendell Nathaniel Gibbs Jr. m 10/31/1992 Collette Pariseau c 2. Assn for Epis Deacons 2013. Servnt Ldr Awd Dio Michigan 2014. deacon@stjohnro.org

SPANUTIUS, Warren Frederick (WTex) 505 Coral Pl, Corpus Christi TX 78411 **Died 9/3/2016** B Bethlehem PA 1928 s Edward & Marion. BS U of Alabama 1952. D 8/19/1967 Bp Milton Legrand Wood P 11/3/1974 Bp Harold Cornelius Gosnell. m 3/29/1947 Audrey Mae Sandlin. Ret 1995-2016; Int Gr Ch Port Lavaca TX 1994-1995; Vic S Thos And S Mart's Ch Crp Christi TX 1986-1993; Asst All SS Epis Ch Corpus Christi TX 1982-1987, D 1967-1981; EME Dio W Texas San Antonio TX 1976-1982.

✠ **SPARKS, The Rt Rev Dr Doug** (NI) 624 Park Ave, South Bend IN 46616 **Bp Dio Nthrn Indiana So Bend IN 2016-; Treas Dio Minnesota Minneapolis MN 2012-, Joint Stndg Com on Prog, Bdgt and Fin 2011-2013, Fin Com 2008-, Dep to GC 2007-, Reg Dn / Dioc Coun 1996-2012; Fin Com Rochester Publ Schools 2012-** B Saint Louis MO 1956 s Lenn & Myrtress. BA S Mary's Sem Coll 1980; MDiv DeAndreis Sem 1984; CAS SWTS 1989; DMin SWTS 1993; Cert SWTS 2003. Rec 6/4/1989 as Priest Bp William Augustus Jones Jr Con 6/25/2016 for NI. m 12/28/1988 Dana W Sparks c 3. R S Lk's Epis Ch Rochester MN 2004-2016; Dn Wellington Cathd of St. Paul New Zealand (Aotearoa) 2003-2004; R St Mths Epis Ch Waukesha WI 1995-2002; R S Lk's Epis Ch Whitewater WI 1990-1994; Asst S Greg's Epis Ch Deerfield IL 1989-1990; Serv RC Ch 1983-1988; Dep to GC Dio Milwaukee Milwaukee WI 1998-2001, Congrl Dvlpmt - Chairperson 1997-2002, Reg Dn / Mem of Dioc Coun 1996-2000, COM 1995-1999, Catechumenal Cmsn - Chairperson 1995-1997, Liturg and Mus Cmsn 1992-1994. bishop.sparks@ednin.org

SPARKS JR, Noy Leon (CFla) Cathedral Church of St Luke, 130 N Magnolia Ave, Orlando FL 32801 **S Mary's Ch Hamilton TX 2017-** B Ft Worth TX 1950 s Noy & Ruby. BA The Criswell Coll 1982; MA Reformed TS 2003. D 5/26/2012 P 12/1/2012 Bp Gregory Orrin Brewer. m 1/25/1969 Lynda Sparks c 3. All SS' Epis Sch Of Ft Worth Ft Worth TX 2016-2017; Chr Ch Longwood FL 2014-2016; Cathd Ch Of S Lk Orlando FL 2014-2015. noyjrtsfl@aol.com

SPARROW, Kevin H (Mass) 45 Yerxa Rd Unit 307, Cambridge MA 02140 **Chr Ch Cambridge Cambridge MA 2015-; S Jas Epis Ch Teele Sq Somerville MA 2014-** B Warner Robins GA 1974 s John & Ann. BA U So 1996; MDiv Harvard DS 2000; MDiv Harvard DS 2000; Cert Angl Stds CDSP 2010. D 6/2/2012 P 12/1/2012 Bp Marc Handley Andrus. m 12/27/2013 Eric Mauldin Westby. Trsfg Epis Ch San Mateo CA 2013-2014.

SPAULDING, Mark Alan (Cal) 19179 Center St, Castro Valley CA 94546 **R H Cross Epis Ch Castro Vlly CA 2003-** B Richmond CA 1958 s Glenn & Mary. BA California St U 1987; MDiv Yale DS 1990. D 6/9/1990 P 6/8/1991 Bp William Edwin Swing. m 8/9/1986 Susan T Spaulding c 2. Chapl Untd States Navel Hosp 29 Palms CA 2000-2003; Off Of Bsh For ArmdF New York NY 1998-2003; Chapl 3rd Battalion 7th Marines USN 1998-2000; Assoc S Tim's Ch Danville CA 1990-1998; Yth Min And Pstr Asst. S Tim's Epis Ch Fairfield CA 1988-1990; Dir Of Yth Mnstrs S Paul's Epis Ch Walnut Creek CA 1980-1985.

SPEAR, Leslie Edward (WTex) 4222 State Hwy. 7 West, Crockett TX 75835 **Vic S Lk's Epis Ch TX 2007-** B Corpus Christi TX 1947 s Everett & Dorothy. Angl TS 1985; BA Steph F Austin St U 1989; MDiv Epis TS of the SW 1993. Trans 1/1/2004 Bp Creighton Leland Robertson. m 3/26/2004 Tanya Y Bartlett-Spear c 5. S Lk's Ch Cypress Mill TX 2007-2008; Gr Ch Weslaco TX 2004-2006; R Gr Epis Ch TX 2004-2006; Mnisose Cluster Sioux Falls SD 2002-2003; Chr Ch Chamberlain SD 2001-2004; Chr Epis Ch Ft Thompson SD 2001-2004; H Comf Epis Ch Lower Brule SD 2001-2004; S Alb's Epis Ch Porcupine SD 2001-2004; St Jn the Bapt Epis Ch Pukwana SD 2001-2004.

SPEARE-HARDY II, Benjamin E K (SO) 5301 Free Pike, Trotwood OH 45426 **R S Marg's Ch Dayton OH 2000-** B Monrovia LR 1958 s Benjamin &

Theresa. BS S Augustines Coll Raleigh NC 1983; MDiv VTS 1990. D 6/13/1992 Bp Robert Poland Atkinson P 12/16/1992 Bp Peter J Lee. S Mary Magd Ch Columbus GA 1994-1999; Christchurch Sch Christchurch VA 1992-1994; Chapl Chr Ch Sch VA 1990-1994. Auth, "Epis Chld Curric"; Auth, "Out From The Shameful Past," *Pstr Forum*. Prince Hall Free And Accepted Masons. Cmnty Serv Awd Negro Bus & Profsnl Wmn Club, Inc 1998; Resolution For Cmnty Serv Relatns City Coun Of Columbus Ga 1997.

SPEAR-JONES, Michael W (SVa) 12 Milnor Terrace, Crossville TN 38558 B Muncie IN 1952 s William & Dorothy. BA U So 1974; MDiv Nash 1978. D 6/4/1978 P 12/12/1978 Bp James Loughlin Duncan. m 10/12/2003 Gwen V Spear-Jones c 1. Cn for Transition Mnstry and Cler Dvlpmt Dio Sthrn Virginia Newport News VA 2010-2016; R S Thos Epis Ch Chesapeake VA 1995-2010; Assoc R Bruton Par Williamsburg VA 1988-1995; Cn for Educ and Yth Mnstrs Dio SE Florida Miami 1981-1988; Cur H Trin Epis Ch W Palm Bch FL 1978-1981. Auth, "A Living Hope," *RC Hymnal*, 1988; Auth, "Personal Reflections (Poem)," *The Nashotah Revs*, Nash, 1978; Auth, "Selected Poetry," *Mtn Sum (Anthology 1972-74)*, Sewanee Press, 1974. AP 1978-1995. mspear.jones@gmail.com

SPEARS, Melanie Lea (Minn) 3543 22nd Ave S, Minneapolis MN 55407 B Minneapolis MN 1957 d James & Phyllis. BA Macalester Coll 1980; MDiv SWTS 1991. D 12/16/1992 P 6/1/1993 Bp Robert Marshall Anderson. m 8/14/1976 George L Spears. P-in-c All SS Epis Indn Mssn Minneapolis MN 1992-2003; Dio Minnesota Minneapolis MN 1992-2003.

SPECK-EWER, Nathan Stewart (Ct) **Vic S Dunst's Epis Ch Largo FL 2013-; Chapl S Steph's Epis Sch Bradenton FL 2011-** D 6/8/2002 Bp Andrew Donnan Smith P 2/22/2003 Bp Wilfrido Ramos-Orench.

SPEEKS, Mark William (NY) 267 Humphrey St # 3, New Haven CT 06511 **Regimental Chapl 71 City of London Yeomanry Signal Regiment 2010-; Asst P St Ptr's Belsize Pk & St Sav's Chalk Farm London 2010-** B Northampton UK 1962 s John & Rita. BA U of Exeter Gb 1982; MS Oxf GB 1983; MDiv Yale DS 2002. D 3/16/2002 P 9/21/2002 Bp Mark Sean Sisk. Asst P St Botolph's Ch Aldgate City of London 2008-2010; Asst P St Jas Ch & St Mary's Ch Kilburn London 2004-2008; Asst S Alb's Epis Ch Los Angeles CA 2002-2003.

SPEER, James D (Ct) 63 Clyde Ave, Waterbury CT 06708 B Pasadena CA 1950 s Donald & Barbara. Westchester Inst; BA U of Puget Sound 1973; MDiv Vancouver TS CA 1979; CG Jung Inst 2001. Trans 12/15/1993 Bp William Charles Wantland. c 2. S Ptr's Epis Ch Oxford CT 2009-2012; R S Paul's Ch Camden Wyoming DE 2005-2006; Dio Minnesota Minneapolis MN 2002-2005; Vic S Antipas Ch Redby MN 2002; S Jn-In-The-Wilderness Red Lake MN 2002; Mnstry In Europe 2000-2001; R Par Of Liscomb-Port Bickerten Nova Scotia 1999-2000; R Five Point Par Of All SS-By-Sea (5 Yoked Par) 1995-1999; Vic Ch of the Gd Shpd 1993-1994; The Epis Ch In Navajoland Coun Farmington NM 1993-1994; R/Vic Ch Of Can 1979-1993. Minnesota Jung Assn 2002-2004; N.A.A.P. 2007.

SPEER, Richard T (WTex) 800 S. Inediana Ave, 800 S. Indiana Ave, Weslaco TX 78596 **Coastal Bend Partnr in Mnstry Corpus Christi TX 2017-** B New York NY 1945 s James & Irene. BA U of Texas 1968; MDiv Epis TS of the SW 1986. D 6/15/1986 P 6/13/1987 Bp Donis Dean Patterson. m 8/20/1972 Laura Speer c 3. R Gr Ch Weslaco TX 2008-2016; R Ch Of The Epiph Kingsville TX 1999-2008; Vic S Andr's Epis Ch Corpus Christi TX 1993-1999; R The Epis Ch Of The Adv Alice TX 1989-1993; Asst R For Yth Ch Of The Epiph Richardson TX 1987-1989; Cur H Trin Epis Ch Garland TX 1986-1987.

SPEER, Robert Hazlett (Md) 5732 Cross Country Blvd, Baltimore MD 21209 B Kalispell MT 1939 s Robert & Mary. BA Montana St U 1961; MDiv SWTS 1964; MS Ford 1977; MA CUA 1990. D 6/21/1964 P 1/25/1965 Bp Chandler W Sterling. c 3. Gr And S Ptr's Ch Baltimore MD 1998-2011; S Paul's Par Baltimore MD 1991-1993; Ch Of S Paul The Apos Baltimore MD 1990; Vic S Tim's Ch Frederick MD 1987-1989; Off Of Bsh For ArmdF New York NY 1967-1987; Kent Sch Kent CT 1966-1967; Asst S Jos's Chap at the Kent Sch Kent CT 1966-1967; Cur Chr Ch Las Vegas NV 1964-1966. Auth, *Letters from Jim*.

SPEER, William Roth (NJ) 2000 Miller Ave #12, Millville NJ 08332 B Baltimore MD 1936 s William & Josephine. BA U Rich 1959; STM PDS 1962; MSW Rutgers The St U of New Jersey 1990. D 6/26/1962 Bp Noble C Powell P 4/1/1963 Bp Harry Lee Doll. c 2. Chapl New Jersey Veterans Memi Hm Vineland NJ 1996-2002; Assoc Trin Epis Ch Vineland NJ 1988-2001; P & Hse Parent S Jude's Ranch for Chld Boulder City NV 1983-1984; Assoc Par Of Chr The King Willingboro NJ 1980-1983; Vic Trin Ch Debran NJ 1974-1977; Trin Ch Riverside NJ 1974-1977; Asst S Jas Ch New London CT 1968-1970; Asst Chr And H Trin Ch Westport CT 1967-1968; Vic Ch Of The Trsfg Braddock Heights MD 1963-1967; S Anne's Epis Ch Smithsburg MD 1963-1966; Asst Vic Ch Of The Resurr Baltimore MD 1962-1963; Asst H Evang Baltimore MD 1962-1963. Mercy of God Cmnty 1999.

SPEIR, Edmund Lawrence (Ida) D 12/21/2014 P 6/21/2015 Bp Brian James Thom.

SPEIR, Susan Elizabeth (Ida) **R S Lk's Epis Ch Idaho Falls ID 2008-; COM Dio Idaho Boise ID 2009-** D 6/10/2000 Bp William Jerry Winterrowd P 12/9/2000 Bp James Gary Gloster.

SPELLER, Lydia Agnew (EMich) Grace Church, 1213 6th St, Port Huron MI 48060 **Int Gr Epis Ch Port Huron MI 2013-; Dep General Conv 2009-; Dep GC 2006-; GOE Rdr 2002-; Dep GC 2000-** B New York NY 1954 d Seth & Mary. AB Bryn 1975; DPhil Oxf GB 1980; STM GTS 1987. D 10/31/1987 P 5/1/1988 Bp James Michael Mark Dyer. m 8/20/1977 John L Speller c 2. Int Ch Of The H Sprt Missoula MT 2010-2011; R S Mk's Ch S Louis MO 1993-2010; Assoc R Chr Ch Reading PA 1988-1993, 1987-1988; A; Chair - COM Dio Missouri S Louis MO 2001-2006. Auth, "The Empty Womb," *The C Mnstry*, 1993; Auth, "A Note on Eusebius of Vercelli," *JTS*, 1985; Auth, "New Light on the Photinians," *JTS*, 1983. interim@graceporthuron.net

SPELLERS, Stephanie (LI) 82 Commonwealth Ave Apt 2, Boston MA 02116 **Epis Ch Cntr New York NY 2016-** B Frankfort KY 1971 BA Wake Forest U 1993; MA Harvard DS 1996; MDiv EDS 2004. D 6/4/2005 P 1/7/2006 Bp M(Arvil) Thomas Shaw. The GTS New York NY 2014-2015; Cn Dio Long Island Garden City NY 2012-2015; The CPG New York NY 2010-2013; Cox Fell & Radical Welcome Mssnr The Cathd Ch Of S Paul Boston MA 2005-2012.

SPELLMAN, Lynne (Ark) 1219 W Lakeridge Dr, Fayetteville AR 72703 **P S Paul's Ch Fayetteville AR 2000-** B Omaha NE 1948 d Robert & Marjorie. BA Sthrn Illinois U 1969; MA U IL 1973; PhD U IL 1977; Dip Ang Stud GTS 1999. D 4/24/1999 P 12/11/1999 Bp Larry Maze. m 3/20/1973 James Spellman. Philos Prof U of Arkansas 1977-2014. Auth, "Unbolting the Dark, a Memoir: On Turning Inward in Search of God," Hamilton Books (Rowman & Littlefield), 2011; Auth, "Origen On The Images And Mediating Activities Of The Logos," *Journ Of Neoplatonic Stds*, 1999; Auth, "Substance And Separation In Aristotle," Cambridge U Press, 1995. Amer Philos Assn 1977-2014; No Amer Patristics Soc 2001-2002; Soc Of Ancient Gk Philos 1977-2014; Soc Of Chr Philosophers 1987-2014. Vstng Fell, Lucy Cavendish Coll, Camb 1990.

SPELLMAN, Robert Garland Windsor (Ct) 322 Seabury Dr, Bloomfield CT 06002 B Cleveland OH 1921 s Frank & Agnes. Wstrn Reserve U 1942; BA U Sask CA 1946; Wstrn Reserve U 1948; LTh Emml Saskatoon CA 2046. Trans 4/16/1950 as Deacon Bp Frederick G Budlong. Par Admin S Thos's Ch New Haven CT 1975-1986, 1960-1970; Chapl S Thos's Day Sch New Haven CT 1975-1986; Vic S Ptr's Ch Plymouth CT 1974-1975; Vic Trin Ch Northfield CT 1972-1975; Trin Ch Torrington CT 1972-1975; All SS Epis Ch Oakville CT 1972-1974; Cur Ch Of The Mssh Baltimore MD 1970-1972; R Ch of the Ascen Munich 1956-1960; S Steph's Ch Pittsfield MA 1951-1956; Cur S Ptr's Ch Springfield MA 1951; Cur Ch Of The H Trin Middletown CT 1948-1951; Serv Angl Ch of Can 1946-1948. Auth, "Ebenezer Landon & Some of His Descendants," 1962.

SPELMAN, Harold James (HB) **Asst Resurr 1970-** B Chicago IL 1923 s William & Helen. BA U Chi 1946; JD U Chi 1948. D 5/23/1970 Bp James Winchester Montgomery. m 6/14/1947 Joanne Adams c 2. Auth, "Var Legal Journ".

SPELMAN, Katherine C (Chi) 20 N American St, Philadelphia PA 19106 **All SS Ch Wstrn Sprgs IL 2014-** B New York NY 1984 d John & Rosalie. BA U Chi 2006; Dip Ang Stud Ya Berk 2011; MDiv Yale DS 2011; MDiv Yale DS 2011. D 6/4/2011 Bp Jeff Lee P 1/14/2012 Bp Charles Ellsworth Bennison Jr. Chr Ch Philadelphia Philadelphia PA 2011-2014. kates.spam@gmail.com

SPENCER, Adam P (Chi) D 6/17/2017 Bp Jeff Lee.

SPENCER, Allison D (LI) 12706 Se Pinehurst Ct, Hobe Sound FL 33455 **Supply P S Monica's Ch Stuart FL 1996-; Ret 1995-** B Glen Cove NY 1931 d Nelson & Mary. AA SUNY 1980; Mercer TS 1982; BS Clayton U 1989. D 6/13/1983 Bp Robert Campbell Witcher Sr P 6/13/1989 Bp Orris George Walker Jr. c 3. R Chr Ch Babylon NY 1989-1994, D 1983-1989.

SPENCER JR, Arthur James (LI) 12706 Se Pinehurst Ct, Hobe Sound FL 33455 **Died 8/25/2016** B Floral Park NY 1927 s Arthur & Mildred. BA Adel 1949; Mercer TS 1981. D 6/1/1981 Bp Robert Campbell Witcher Sr P 6/1/1988 Bp Orris George Walker Jr. m 4/18/1953 Allison D Disbrow c 3. Supply P S Monica's Ch Stuart FL 1996-2016; Ret 1994-2016; D/Asst S Thos Of Cbury Ch Smithtown NY 1981-1988.

SPENCER, Bonnie S (Colo) 3006 S Holly Pl, Denver CO 80222 **Cn S Jn's Cathd Denver CO 2017-** B New York NY 1961 d Peter & Carol. BA U Colo 1983; MDiv GTS 1999. D 6/5/1999 P 12/12/1999 Bp William Jerry Winterrowd. m 9/10/2014 Catherine E Anderson. R S Paul's Epis Ch Ft Collins CO 2009-2015; R Ch Of Our Sav Somerset MA 2005-2009; Asst R Gd Shpd Epis Ch Centennial CO 1999-2005. bonnie@sjcathedral.org

SPENCER, Carol (Miss) 1623 Acadia Ct., Jackson MS 39211 B New Orleans LA 1947 d Clayton & Doris. BA Centenary Coll 1969; MA Loyola U 1994. D 1/4/1997 Bp Alfred Marble Jr. m 5/30/2009 Robert Spencer c 2. D S Andr's Cathd Jackson MS 2009-2013; D S Ptr's By The Sea Gulfport MS 2006-2008; Dio Mississippi Jackson MS 2004-2008; D Gr Epis Ch Canton MS 2000-2009; D The Chap Of The Cross Madison MS 1997-1998. Trin Cleric Ldrshp Proj; Alpha Sigma Nu; Fndr's Awd MS Rel Ldrshp Conf.

SPENCER, Cindy (ECR) 15163 N Cutler Dr, Tucson AZ 85739 B Minneapolis MN 1943 d John & Dorothy. BA U MN 1964; MBA Golden Gate U 1986;

MDiv GTS 1990. D 6/2/1990 Bp Charles Shannon Mallory P 4/13/1991 Bp Robert Deane Rowley Jr. Int S Mich's Ch Coolidge AZ 2010; S Paul's Epis Ch Elk Rapids MI 2002-2003; Int Gr Epis Ch Kingston PA 2001-2002; Int St. Jas Epis Ch Paso Robles CA 2000-2001; S Jas Ch Paso Robles CA 2000; S Paul's Ch Cambria CA 2000; Dio El Camino Real Salinas CA 1995-1998, Chair of Cmsn on Hisp Mnstry 1985-1994, COM 1994-1998; Vic Ch Of S Jos Milpitas CA 1993-1999; R S Jn's Ch Kane PA 1990-1993; Hisp Mnstry Cmsn Prov VIII 1986-1987; ; BEC Dio NW Pennsylvania Erie PA 1991-1993.

SPENCER, Dorothy Jane (NMich) PO Box 302, Manistique MI 49854 B Saint Johns MI 1946 d Robert & Dorothy. B.S Cntrl Michigan U 1968; M.A Cntrl Michigan U 1969. D 7/13/2014 Bp Rayford J Ray. m 12/31/1982 Robert Paul Spencer c 3.

SPENCER, James Scott (CFla) 4220 Saxon Dr, New Smyrna Beach FL 32169 **R S Ptr The Fisherman Epis Ch New Smyrna FL 2003-** B Glenridge NJ 1950 s William & Barbara. BS Davis & Elkins Coll 1973; ThM Gordon-Conwell TS 1978; MDiv PrTS 1980. D 5/14/1989 P 11/1/1989 Bp William Hopkins Folwell. m 2/28/1995 Sally Wells Spencer c 1. R S Simon's On The Sound Ft Walton Bch FL 1998-2003; Assoc R All SS Ch Of Winter Pk Winter Pk FL 1989-1998, 1982-1989. frjim@stpetersnet.net

SPENCER, Leon P (NC) 6005 Starboard Dr, Greensboro NC 27410 B Roanoke Rapids NC 1943 s Leon & Jane. BA Wake Forest U 1965; MA Indiana U 1967; PhD Syr 1975; MDiv VTS 1989. D 6/6/1989 P 12/8/1989 Bp Robert Oran Miller. m 8/8/1998 Karen O Olson c 2. Lectr St Aug TS Dio Botswana 2013-2016; Adj Fac Wake Forest U DS Winston-Salem NC 2007-2015; Dio No Carolina Raleigh NC 2004-2009, Chart Com on Hist and Archv 2010-2014, BEC 2009-2014, BEC 2009-, Botswana Comp Link Com 2008-; Dn Dio No Carolina Sch of Mnstry Greensboro NC 2004-2009; Washington Off On Afr Washington DC 1998-2004; Exec Dir Washington Off on Afr Washington DC 1998-2004; Grtr Birmingham Mnstrs Birmingham AL 1997-1998; Assoc S Lk's Epis Ch Birmingham AL 1997-1998; Faith in Cmnty Coordntr Grtr Birmingham Mnstrs Birmingham AL 1996-1998; Exec Coun Appointees New York NY 1994-1996; Dn of Stds, Trin Ch in Kenya Nairobi Kenya 1992-1996; R S Lk's Ch Brighton Brookeville MD 1991-1992; Chapl Samar Mnstry of Grtr Washington Washington DC 1990-1992; Intern on So Afr issues Epis Ch Off of Govt Relatns Washington Washington D 1989-1990; Washington Off Of The Epis Ch Washington DC 1989-1990. Auth, "Toward an Afr Ch in Mozambique," Mzuni Press, 2013; Auth, "Theol Educ in the Angl Comm," *Blackwell Comp to the Angl Comm*, Blackwell, 2013; Auth, "Not Yet There: Seminaries and the Challenge of Partnership," *Intl Bulletin of Mssy Resrch*, 2010; Producer, "Toward a Mssy Dio," *Sch of Mnstry Par DVDs*, Dio No Carolina, 2009; Producer, "Toward a Theol of partnership," *Sch of Mnstry Par DVDs*, Dio No Carolina, 2008; Interviewee and producer, "Reflections on Chr formation," *Sch of Mnstry Par DVDs*, Dio No Carolina, 2008; Producer, "Conversations about the Kingdom of God," *Sch of Mnstry Par DVDs*, Dio No Carolina, 2008; Auth, "Mssn and Mnstry through the Millennium Dvlpmt Goals," *Sch of Mnstry Par Stds*, Dio No Carolina, 2006; Auth, "Strengthening Chr ethical discourse: Conversations about societal issues," *Sch of Mnstry Par Stds*, Dio No Carolina, 2006; Auth, "Toward Solidarity/Struggle in So Afr: A Congregational Resource for Understanding the Ch's Witness," Epis Ch Cntr, 1990; Auth, "Ch and St in Colonial Afr," *Journ of Ch and St*, 1989; Auth, "Sthrn Afr in `Context: The Challenge of Grassroots Theol Educ," *Virginia Sem Journ*, 1989; Auth, "Radical Discipleship and the Afr Ch," *Communities of Faith and Radical Discipleship*, Merc Press, 1986; Auth, "Chrsnty and Colonial Protest," *Journ of Rel in Afr*, 1982. DD VTS 2005.

SPENCER, Michael Edwin (NH) 325 Pleasant Street, Concord NH 03301 **P-in-c S Jn's Epis Ch Fishers Island NY 2008-; Dn of Chap and Rel Life S Paul's Sch Concord NH 2007-; Dn of Chap and Rel Life St. Paul's Sch Concord NH 2007-** B New Bedford MA 1971 s Edwin & Izabel. STM Ya Berk; BA Coll of the H Cross 1993; MDiv Yale DS 1998; Cert Ang Stud Ya Berk 2004. D 6/12/2004 P 1/16/2005 Bp Andrew Donnan Smith. m 7/22/1995 Amy Cofone Spencer c 2. Asst P S Jn's Epis Par Waterbury CT 2004-2007. Auth, "A New Pentecost: Epis Schools and the Future of Anglicanism," *NAES Connections*, NAES, 2009; Auth, "Morning has Broken," *Alum Horae*, St. Paul's Sch, 2008; Auth, "To the No and to the So: Tayeb Salih and encounters w the other," *Wrld Rel Nwsltr*, Coun for Sprtl and Ethical Educ, 2007; Auth, "Taft: Rel and Sprtl Life," *Taft Alum Bulletin*, The Taft Sch, 2003; co-Auth, "Applied Ethics," *Applied Ethics*, Coun for Sprtl and Ethical Educ, 1999; Auth, "The Price," *Theol Today*, Theol Today, 1998. Forw Mvmt 2007; NAES 2007.

SPENCER, Orval James (Neb) 6700 Tamerson Ct, Raleigh NC 27612 **Ret 1991-** B Virden MT CANADA 1929 s Edward & Edith. BA U of Manitoba 1950; LTh S Jn CA 1954. Trans 6/1/1957 Bp Howard R Brinker. c 2. R S Matt's Ch Allnce NE 1961-1991; P-in-c S Jn's Ch Valentine NE 1957-1961; Serv Ch Of Can 1952-1957; Ex Coun Dio Nebraska Omaha NE 1959-1973.

SPENCER, Patricia Ann (CFla) 851 Village Lake Dr S, Deland FL 32724 B Tallahassee FL 1948 Wesleyan Coll. D 12/14/2002 Bp John Wadsworth Howe. c 1. D S Barn Ch Deland FL 2002-2010.

SPENCER, Peter Levalley (RI) 107 Green Hill Ave, Wakefield RI 02879 **Asst S Jn The Evang Ch Newport RI 2008-; St Eliz Cmnty E Greenwich RI 2008-; Ret RI 2001-** B Providence RI 1938 s Lee & Mary. BA Br 1960; STB GTS 1965; Cert EDS 1994. D 6/1/1965 P 2/12/1966 Bp John S Higgins. m 5/4/1961 Eugenia Bruno Spencer c 4. Dn Narragansett Deanry Dio Rhode Island Providence RI 1982-1985, Pres Stndg Com 1998-1999, Stndg Com 1995-1997, Chair Evang Com 1992-1994, Stndg Com 1986-1991, Dn Narragansett Deanry 1982-1985, Sprtl Dir Intern 1980-1981, Chair Evang Com 1978-1979, Dioc Coun 1976-1977, Evang Com 1971-1978, Evang Com 1971-1975, Dioc Coun 1971-1974, Deptce 1969-1970, Dept Mssn 1967-1968; Cn Cathd Of S Jn Providence RI 1972-2001; Secy Old Narragansett Ch 1971-2001; R S Paul's Ch N Kingstown RI 1967-2001; Cur S Paul's Ch Pawtucket RI 1965-1967.

SPENCER, Richard William (NY) 4 Hemlock Rd, Hartsdale NY 10530 **D S Barn Ch Ardsley NY 1999-** B Yonkers NY 1952 s Thomas & Evelyn. BS Emerson Coll 1974. D 5/16/1998 Bp Richard Frank Grein. m 9/11/1982 Susan Anne Spencer c 2. Trin Epis Ch Ossining NY 2006-2013; D S Andr's Epis Ch Hartsdale NY 1998-2006. "Epis New Yorker Advsry Bd," 2006.

SPENCER, Robert (Miss) 1623 Acadia Court, Jackson MS 39211 **D S Mk's Ch Jackson MS 2008-; Exec Dir Stewpot Cmnty Serv Jackson MS 2003-; D The Chap Of The Cross Madison MS 2003-** B Greenwood MS 1947 s Benjamin & Mary. BA U of Mississippi 1970; JD U of Mississippi 1974. D 1/4/2003 Bp Alfred Marble Jr. m 5/30/2009 Carol Borne c 2. NAAD 2002.

SPENCER, Robert Dennis (Wyo) 4508 Cottage Ln, Cheyenne WY 82001 B Warren PA 1939 s Robert & Marguerite. Mar 1962; VTS 1972; Dplma Acad for Pstr Ed 1996. D 1/29/1972 Bp Robert Bruce Hall P 9/9/1972 Bp Gray Temple. m 9/10/1965 Eleanor Gaye Spencer c 2. Chapl Coordntr Sweetwater Co. Hosp Rock Sprg WY 2012-2013; Res Supplly P Ch Of The H Comm Rock Sprg WY 2007-2013; S Mk's Ch Cheyenne WY 1997; Dir of Pstr Serv Cheyenne Reg Med Cntr Cheyenne WY 1996-2003; Res Chapl SC St Hosp 1994-1996; Mtn Rivers Epis Cmnty Idaho Falls ID 1989-1991; P-in-c Ch Of The Redeem Salmon ID 1988-1991; Dio Idaho Boise ID 1988-1989; Estrn Idaho Pstr Care Idaho Falls ID 1985-1994; R Trin Epis Ch Pocatello ID 1981-1985; Assoc Ch Of The Adv Spartanburg SC 1978-1981; Coordntr Yth Mnstrs Dio Upper So Carolina Columbia SC 1978-1981; Asst Ch Of The H Comf Sumter SC 1974-1999; R Ch Of The Cross Columbia SC 1974-1978; Chapl Heathwood Hall Sch Columbia SC 1974-1978; Chapl Coll Chapl Spartanburg SC; Chapl to Ret Cler Dio Wyoming Casper 2005-2013, Dioc Coun 2000-2005; Bd Mem & Chair Equality St Plcy Cntr Casper WY 2002-2013; Mntl Hlth Advsry Coun WY Mntl Hlth Dept Cheyenne WY 1998-2013; Bd Mem Wyoming Equality Cheyenne WY 1998-2013. Auth, "Aids- The Pstr Perspective"; Auth, "Trng Manual For Hosp Chapl". AEHC; Assn Of Profsnl Chapl 1985-2015.

SPENCER, Robert Paul (NMich) PO Box 302, Manistique MI 49854 B Inglewood CA 1946 s William & Claudiafae. BA U of Las Vegas 1968; BS U of Las Vegas 1982. D 1/8/2014 P 7/13/2014 Bp Rayford J Ray. m 12/31/1982 Dorothy Jane Sawyer c 2.

SPENCER, Ronald Dwight (WMo) Po Box 197, Angel Fire NM 87710 B Oakland CA 1934 s Dwight & Aubrey. BA U CA 1958; MDiv CDSP 1963. D 1/26/1963 Bp George Richard Millard P 7/27/1963 Bp Richard Ainslie Kirchhoffer. c 2. Chapl ST Lukes Hosp 1989-2000; R Chr the King El Paso TX 1983-1989; Chapl US Army 1963-1982. Comp, Worker Sis And Worker Brothers Of The H Spiri 1993. spencerdssj@comcast.net

SPENCER, Warren Dove (NJ) 68 Hull Ave, Freehold NJ 07728 **D S Ptr 1985-** B Brooklyn NY 1941 s Samuel & Marion. D 4/13/1985 Bp George Phelps Mellick Belshaw. m 8/19/1967 Susan Lewis.

SPEROPULOS IV, PETER J (CFla) D 9/10/2016 P 4/1/2017 Bp Gregory Orrin Brewer.

SPERRY, Rebecca Lynne (Chi) 2056 Vermont St, Blue Island IL 60406 **D S Jos's And S Aid's Ch Blue Island IL 1991-** B Blue Island IL 1953 d Thomas & Margaret. Moraine Vlly Cmnty Coll Palos Hills IL 1975; U IL 1981; Chicago Deacons Sch 1991. D 12/7/1991 Bp Frank Tracy Griswold III. Liturg Cmsn Dio Chicago Chicago IL 1994-2000.

SPICER JR, Clyde Allen (Md) 724 Morningside Dr, Towson MD 21204 **Chapl to Cler and Cler Families (FOCUS) Dio Maryland Baltimore MD 2010-; Chairman of the Bd Trst Bp Claggett Cntr Adamstown MD 1999-** B Baltimore MD 1937 s Clyde & Mildred. BA McDaniel Coll 1959; BD VTS 1962; STD McDaniel Coll 1981. D 6/26/1962 Bp Harry Lee Doll P 4/9/1963 Bp Noble C Powell. m 6/13/1964 Gwendolyn N Spicer. Assoc R Ch Of The H Comf Luthvle Timon MD 1998-2010; R S Geo's Ch Perryman MD 1998-2000; The Ch Of The Nativ Cedarcroft Baltimore MD 1984-1998; Secy of the Cmsn KCER 1973-1979; Admin Asst To Bp Of Easton Dio Easton Easton MD 1972-1983, Secy of the Dioc Coun 1972-1983, Dir of Camp Wright 1965-1983; Dn Trin Cathd Easton MD 1972-1983; R Emm Epis Ch Chestertown MD 1968-1972; R Chr Ch Denton MD 1965-1968; Asst R Emm Ch Baltimore MD 1963-1965; Asst S Jn's Ch Relay Baltimore MD 1962-1963. S.T.D Dr. Of Sacr Theol Wstrn Maryland Coll 1982.

SPICER, John M (WMo) St. Andrews Episcopal Church, 6401 Wornall Terrace, Kansas City MO 64113 **R S Andr's Ch Kansas City MO 2005-** B Springfield

MO 1965 s Holt & Marion. BA SW Missouri St U 1986; MDiv Epis TS of the SW 2002. D 6/8/2002 P 12/7/2002 Bp Barry Howe. m 8/11/1990 Ann E Spicer c 2. Vic Ch Of The Gd Shpd Springfield MO 2002-2005; Dio W Missouri Kansas City MO 2002-2005. Pstr Study Prog Grant Louisville Inst 2014. frjohn@standrewkc.org

SPICER, John Tildsley (Fla) 25 Eyrie Dr, Crawfordville FL 32327 B Washington DC 1952 s Donald & Mary. Earlham Coll 1971; BA W&L 1974; MDiv GTS 1978. D 6/16/1978 P 2/24/1979 Bp William Henry Marmion. c 2. R S Teresa Of Avila Crawfordville FL 2003-2008; Vic All SS Epis Ch Brighton Heights Brighton Heights PA 2000-2003; Int S Chris's Epis Ch Mars PA 1999-2000; Chr Epis Ch Indiana PA 1998-1999; S Thos Ch In The Fields Gibsonia PA 1985-1998; R S Thos Epis Ch Pittsburgh PA 1985-1998; Reg Dir Dio Wstrn No Carolina Asheville NC 1983-1985; R S Andr Ch Mt Holly NC 1983-1985; Cur Chr Ch Blacksburg VA 1978-1983.

SPICER, Stephen L (Tex) 304 E Stockbridge St, Eagle Lake TX 77434 **Chr Ch Eagle Lake TX 2015-** B Craig CO 1968 s William & Linda. BS U of Wisconsin; MDiv Sewanee: The U So, TS 2014; MDiv The TS at The U So 2014. D 8/3/2013 P 6/14/2014 Bp Robert John O'Neill. m 1/30/1999 Amy M Spicer c 4. Trin Ch Houston TX 2014-2015.

SPIEGEL, Phyllis (SO) 120 Cherry Ln, Christiansburg VA 24073 **R S Anne Epis Ch W Chester OH 2015-; R S Thos Epis Christiansbrg VA 2006-, P-in-c 2004-2015** B Roanoke VA 1966 d Wm & Margaret Peggy. BA Emory and Henry Coll 1984; MDiv VTS 2004. D 4/13/2004 P 10/15/2004 Bp Neff Powell. c 1. GC Dep Dio SW Virginia Roanoke VA 2009-2011, 2009-2010, 2005-2008; Owner For The Birds Inc. Blacksburg VA 1990-2001; Field Exec Hornets' Nest Girl Scout Coun Charlotte NC 1990; Tchr Chemuswa Secondary Sch Chemuswa Kenya 1989.

SPIERS, Linda Mitchell (Ct) 3 Whirling Dun, Canton CT 06019 **Alt for Jvnl Revs Bd Town of Canton CT 2014-; Canton Hsng Authority Town of Canton CT 2012-; Bd Mem Soc For The Increase Of Mnstry W Hartford CT 2011-; Title IV Disciplinary Bd Dio Connecticut Meriden CT 2010-** B Washington DC 1945 d Carl & Margaret. BS MWC 1966; MBA U Rich 1990; MDiv Ya Berk 2000. D 6/10/2000 Bp Andrew Donnan Smith P 1/20/2001 Bp James Elliot Curry. R Trin Epis Ch Collinsville CT 2004-2017; Part time Chapl Capital Cmnty Coll Hartford CT 2002-2004; Assoc Chr Ch Cathd Hartford CT 2000-2004. lindaspiers@aol.com

SPIGNER, Charles Bailey (Va) 10355 Spencer Trail Pl, Ashland VA 23005 B Columbia SC 1951 s Adolphus & Henrietta Geddes Bailey. U So; BA U of So Carolina 1977; MDiv VTS 1985. D 6/8/1985 P 5/10/1986 Bp William Arthur Beckham. m 2/26/2011 Elizabeth Page c 2. Imm Ch Mechanicsvlle VA 2015-2017; Trin Epis Ch Highland Sprg VA 2013-2015, 2013; S Marg's Ch Woodbridge VA 2012-2013; Chapl and Pstr Counslr Capital Hospice Falls Ch VA 2004-2012; P in Res S Andr's Epis Ch Arlington VA 2004-2006; Int S Barn Ch Annandale VA 1999-2000; The Epis Ch-King Geo Co King Geo VA 1998-1999; Assoc R Ch Of The H Comf Vienna VA 1996-1998; Int S Mary's Ch Columbia SC 1995-1996; Assoc R S Martins-In-The-Field Columbia SC 1987-1995; Vic Ch Of The Epiph Laurens SC 1985-1987; DCE S Mich And All Ang' Columbia SC 1980-1982; Dir of Chr St. Mich and All Ang Columbia SC 1980-1982. cbspigner@gmail.com

SPINA, Frank Anthony (Oly) 414 W Newell St, Seattle WA 98119 **Assoc S Marg's Epis Ch Bellevue WA 1998-** B Long Beach CA 1943 s Frank & Mary. BA Greenville Coll 1965; MDiv Asbury TS 1968; MA U MI 1970; PhD U MI 1977. D 6/26/1999 P 1/23/2000 Bp Vincent Waydell Warner. m 12/17/1994 JoEllen Watson. Serv Free Meth Ch 1971-1999.

SPINELLA, Linda Jean (NH) 270 Stark Hwy N, Dunbarton NH 03046 B Arlington MA 1956 d William & Evelyn. BA Gordan Coll 1978; MDiv Harvard DS 2010. D 4/6/2013 P 10/12/2013 Bp A Robert Hirschfeld. m 8/24/1991 Frank P Spinella c 1. Ch Of S Jn The Evang Dunbarton NH 2013-2015.

SPINILLO GRZYWA, Jonathan Michael (Minn) D 6/27/2017 Bp Brian N Prior.

SPLINTER, John Theodore (FdL) 4332 W Rotamer Rd, Janesville WI 53546 **Ret 1998-** B Watertown WI 1941 s Herbert & Elizabeth. BS U of Wisconsin 1963; BD Nash 1966. D 3/5/1966 P 9/13/1966 Bp Donald H V Hallock. m 6/25/1966 Barbara A Schaefer c 2. Vic S Jn's Epis Ch Sparta WI 2000-2004; Natl Epis Curs Com 1997-2000; Vic Ch Of The H Apos Oneida WI 1994-1998; Dio Fond du Lac Appleton WI 1994-1995; Ch Of S Jn The Bapt Wausau WI 1993-1994; R S Alb's Epis Ch Marshfield WI 1976-1993; Vic S Barn Epis Ch Tomahawk WI 1972-1976; St Ambr Epis Ch Antigo WI 1972-1976; Vic S Hugh of Lincoln Ch Greendale WI 1969-1972; R, (Cur 66-68) Imm Ch Racine WI 1966-1969. Hon Cn Dio Fond du Lac 1998.

✠ SPONG, The Rt Rev John Shelby (Nwk) 24 Puddingstone Rd, Morris Plains NJ 07950 **Vstng Lectr Harvard DS Cambridge MA 2006-; Vstng Lectr U Pac Stockton CA 2003-; Fac Grad Theol Un Berkeley CA 2000-; Wm Belden Noble Lectr Harv Cambridge MA 2000-** B Charlotte NC 1931 s John & Doolie. BA U NC 1952; MDiv VTS 1955. D 6/24/1955 Bp Richard Henry Baker P 12/28/1955 Bp Edwin A Penick Con 6/12/1976 for Nwk. m 1/1/1990 Christine M Spong c 3. Bp of Newark Dio Newark Newark NJ 1978-2000, Bp Coadj 1976-1978; Mem, Exec Coun ECUSA 1973-1976; R S Paul's Ch Richmond VA 1969-1976; R S Jn's Ch Lynchburg VA 1965-1969; Mem, Bd Dir Kanuga Conferences 1961-1965; Calv Ch Tarboro NC 1957-1965; S Lk's Ch Tarboro NC 1957-1965; St Marys Epis Ch Speed NC 1957-1965; R S Jos's Ch Durham NC 1955-1957; Mem, Stndg Com Dio Virginia Richmond VA 1973-1976, Dep to GC 1969-1973; Pres, Stndg Com Dio SW Virginia Roanoke VA 1966-1969; Mem, Exec Coun Dio No Carolina Raleigh NC 1959-1962, Chair, Evang Cmsn 1958-1959. Auth, "Re-Claiming the Bible for a Non-Rel Wrld," 2011; Auth, "Eternal Life: A New Vision," 2009; Auth, "Jesus for the Non-Rel," 2007; Auth, "The Sins of Scripture: Exposing the Bible's Texts of Hate to Reveal the God of Love," 2005; Columnist, "Columnist," *WaterfrontMedia.com*, 2002; Auth, "A New Chrsnty For a New Wrld," 2001; Auth, "Columnist," *BeliefNet.com*, 2000; Auth, "Here I Stand: My Struggle for a Chrsnty of Integrity," *Love and Equality*, 2000; Auth, "The Bp's Voice: Essays Compiled and Edited by Christine Mary Spong," 1999; Auth, "Why Chrsnty Must Change or Die: A Bp Speaks to Believers in Exile," 1998; Auth, "Liberating the Gospels: Reading the Bible w Jewish Eyes," 1996; Auth, "Ressurection: Myth or Reality," 1994; Auth, "b of A Wmn," 1992; Auth, "Rescuing the Bible from Fundamentalism," 1991; Auth, "Living in Sin? A Bp Rethinks Human Sxlty," 1988; Auth, "Beyond Moralism," 1985; Auth, "Into the Whirwind, The Future of The Ch," 1983; Auth, "The Easter Moment," 1980; Auth, "The Living Commandments," 1977; Auth, "Life Approaches Death," 1976; Auth, "Dialogue In Search of Jewish Chr Understanding," 1975; Auth, "Christpower," 1975; Auth, "This Hebr Lord," 1974; Auth, "Honest Pryr," 1973. Dav Friedrich Strauss Soc 2002; Jesus Seminar 1988. Portrait commissioned and placed in Hall of Prophets at the Mart Luther King, Jr. Chap for Civil Rts Ldrshp Morehouse Coll 2010; Faithful Servnt Prisoners for Chr 2010; DHL Drew U 2009; DHL Leh 2006; DHL U NC 2006; DHL Holmes Inst 2002; DHL Muhlenberg Coll 1998; Jn A T Robinson Awd for Theol Integrity Jesus Seminar 1996; Quatercentenary Schlr Camb 1992; Awd ACLU of NJ 1988; DD VTS 1977; DD S Paul's Coll Lawrenceville VA 1976; Phi Beta Kappa 1952.

SPOON, Bryan William D 6/10/2017 Bp Shannon Sherwood Johnston.

SPOOR, Cornelia P (NJ) Po Box 624, Roosevelt NJ 08555 **Died 2/22/2017** B Niagara Falls NY 1952 d K Franklin & Margaret. BA Rutgers The St U of New Jersey 1987; MS Rutgers The St U of New Jersey 1993; Cert New Jersey Cntr For Fam Stds 1999. D 9/21/2001 Bp David Bruce Joslin. c 2. D Trin Ch Princeton NJ 2002-2004.

SPORS, Daniel Paul (Mil) **S Ptr's Epis Ch Arlington VA 2016-** D 6/11/2016 Bp Steven Andrew Miller.

SPRAGUE, James W (Los) PO Box 303, Santa Barbara CA 93102 **S Mk's Epis Sch Downey CA 2014-** B Aurora IL 1948 s Theodore & Janet. BA Hobart and Wm Smith Colleges 1970; MDiv GTS 1979. D 6/23/1979 P 12/21/1979 Bp Frederick Barton Wolf. m 6/21/2008 Ann Bradbury c 4. S Andr's Epis Ch Ojai CA 2016; S Patricks Ch And Day Sch Thousand Oaks CA 2016; S Mk's Par Downey CA 2014-2015; S Paul's Epis Ch Ventura CA 2011-2013; Transitional R S Mths' Par Whittier CA 2009-2011; Chapl & Dn of Rel Life S Mart's Epis Sch Metairie LA 1998-2005; Chapl S Jas Sch 1994-1998; Chapl & Dept Hd St Jas Sch Hagerstown MD 1994-1998; Chapl Trin Pawling Sch Pawling NY 1992-1994; Transitional P S Lk's Ch Hudson MA 1992-1993; Chapl S Mk Sch Southboro MA 1988-1992; Chapl & Dept Hd St. Mk's Sch of Southborough Inc. Southborough MA 1988-1990; Chapl S Mk Sch Dallas TX 1984-1988; Chapl & Tchr S Marks Sch Of Texas Dallas TX 1984-1988; S Mart's Epis Ch Palmyra ME 1979-1982; Vic All SS Epis Ch Skowhegan ME 1979-1980.

SPRAGUE, Minka Shura (La) 703 Audubon Trce, New Orleans LA 70121 **Dio Louisiana New Orleans LA 2013-** B Kansas City MO 1944 d Daniel & Mary. BA U MN 1966; MA GTS 1978; ThD GTS 1985. D 12/8/1986 Bp Paul Moore Jr P 5/1/2006 Bp Duncan Montgomery Gray III. c 2. Vic Ch Of The H Sprt New Orleans LA 2013-2016; Epis Ch Of The H Sprt In Baton Rouge Baton Rouge LA 2013-2016; Assoc R S Jas Ch Jackson MS 2003-2013, D 2003-2006; D Cathd Of St Jn The Div New York NY 1988-1997; Prof NT & Biblic Langs NYTS 1987-2003; Adj Fac UTS NYC 1986-1988; D for Educ Ch Of The H Trin New York NY 1985-1988; Post-Doctoral Fell Cntr Congreg Stds 1985-1986; Asst Dir Cont Educ The GTS New York NY 1977-1980. Auth, "One to Watch, One to Pray," *One to Watch, One to Pray*, Ch Pub, 2004; Auth, "Praying from the Free Throw Line - For Now," *Praying from the Free-Throw Line -- For Now*, Ch Pub, 1999.

SPRATT, George Clifford (Kan) 828 Center St, Fulton MO 65251 **Ret 1992-** B Los Angeles CA 1929 s George & Jean. BA Macalester Coll 1952; MDiv Bec 1955. D 6/29/1955 Bp Hamilton Hyde Kellogg P 12/21/1955 Bp Stephen E Keeler. m 8/3/1957 Mary L Sommers c 3. Asst S Mich And All Ang Ch Mssn KS 1983-1991; Asst S Andr's Ch Kansas City MO 1974-1983; Asst Chr Ch Overland Pk KS 1967-1974; R Gr Memi Ch Wabasha MN 1963-1967; Tchr & Asst S Jn in Robertsport Liberia 1961-1963; Supt Bromley Mssn in Liberia 1959-1961; P-in-c All SS Ch Northfield MN 1957-1958; P-in-c Ch Of The H Cross Dundas MN 1956-1958; P-in-c S Pat's Epis Ch Bloomington MN 1956-1957; In-charge Gilfillan Memi Chap Squaw Lake MN 1955-1956.

S

SPRICK, Lynne Ann (Minn) 110 S Oak St, Lake City MN 55041 B Lake City MN 1949 d Frank & Bernetta. Practical Nurse Rochester Vocational 1982. D 6/20/2015 Bp Brian N Prior. m 12/18/1982 Roger Willard Sprick c 2.

SPRINGER, Alice E (Dal) 1410 S Goliad St Apt 2007, Rockwall TX 75087 **Non-par 1972-** B Beeville TX 1937 d James & Jewel. BS U of Texas 1961; MA SWTS 1968. D 6/23/1968 Bp Charles A Mason. m 9/27/1969 Robert Harris Springer c 1. Stff S Jas Epis Ch Texarkana TX 1968-1970.

SPRINGER, David R (Alb) 12 Shannon Ct, West Sand Lake NY 12196 B Baltimore MD 1946 Amh 1968; PDS 1973. D 6/9/1973 Bp Paul Moore Jr P 12/15/1973 Bp William Henry Mead. c 2. Ch Of The H Cross Troy NY 1991-1999; Vic Ch Of The H Trin Brookville PA 1985-1991; S Barn Ch Bay Vill OH 1981-1984; Dio Bethlehem Bethlehem PA 1981; Assoc AP Allentown PA 1976-1980; The Epis Ch Of The Medtr Allentown PA 1976-1980; Dio Delaware Wilmington 1975-1976; S Jas Epis Ch Newport Newport DE 1975-1976; Asst Imm Ch Highlands Wilmington DE 1974-1975.

SPRINGER, Lloyd Livingstone (NY) 1358 E Normandy Blvd, Deltona FL 32725 **Died 1/31/2016** B BB 1930 s Oscar & Olive. GOE Codrington Coll 1963; STM NYTS 1975; Cert Acad of Gerontology Educ & Dvlpmt 1981; MA NYU 1982. D 1/6/1971 P 12/8/1971 Bp Horace W B Donegan. c 1. R S Edm's Ch Bronx NY 1973-2000; Non-par 1972-1973; Asst S Mart's Ch New York NY 1971-1972. S Edm's Appreciation Awd From Vstry And Servers 1983; Bronx Borough Pres Cmnty Serv Awd; Mt Hope Cmnty Awd For Cmnty Serv; Honoraryored Citizen Of The St Of New York; Citation From City Of New York, Borough Of The Bronx For Excellent Cmnty Wk; Cert Of Merit From Dio New York; Aliens Citizen Awd Emmigrant Bank.

SPRINGER, Nancy (WTex) St John's Episcopal Church, 2500 N 10th St, McAllen TX 78501 **S Alb's Ch Harlingen TX 2016-** B Nuremberg Germany 1967 d Marlin & Sylvia. BA The U of Texas in San Antonio 1993; MDiv Wycliffe Coll 2012; MDiv Wycliffe Coll 2012; MDiv Wycliffe Coll Toronto CA 2012; MDiv Wycliffe Coll Toronto CA 2012. D 6/11/2012 Bp David Mitchell Reed P 12/13/2012 Bp Gary Richard Lillibridge. c 1. S Jn's Ch McAllen TX 2012-2016.

SPRINGER, Susan Woodward (Colo) St John's Episcopal Church, 1419 Pine St, Boulder CO 80302 **R S Jn's Epis Ch Boulder CO 2012-** B Ridgewood NJ 1958 d William & Edith. Mid 1977; U of Sthrn Maine-Portland 1978; MDiv Sewanee: The U So, TS 2009. D 3/21/2009 Bp Brian James Thom P 12/1/2009 Bp Carolyn Tanner Irish. R Dio Utah Salt Lake City UT 2009-2012; S Thos Epis Ch Sun Vlly ID 2003-2006. Epis Preaching Fndt, BOD 2011. sspringer@stjohnsboulder.org

SPROAT, Jim (WTex) 2109 Sawdust Rd Apt 27102, Spring TX 77380 B Grand Rapids MI 1947 s Robert & Jeanne. BS Tarleton St U 1970; MEd Texas A&M U 1974; MDiv Epis TS of the SW 1979. D 7/3/1979 P 6/3/1980 Bp Roger Howard Cilley. c 4. R Trin Ch Jct TX 2006-2013; Vic Calv Ch Menard TX 2005-2013; Chapl Austin Coll Sherman TX 1999-2004; R S Steph's Epis Ch Sherman TX 1999-2004; Chapl Sam Houston St Univ Huntsville TX 1990-1999; Chapl Texas Dept Of Corrections Huntsville TX 1990-1999; Vic H Innoc' Epis Ch Madisonville TX 1990-1991; Vic All SS Ch Baytown TX 1983-1990; Chapl Lee Coll Baytown TX 1983-1990; The Great Cmsn Fndt Houston TX 1979-1999; Chapl Prairie View A&M Univ Prairie View TX 1979-1983; S Fran Of Assisi Epis Prairie View TX 1979-1983; Dioc Com On Scouting Dio Texas Houston TX 1987-1999; Cler Pstr Care Com 1984-1999. CBS 1965; ESA 1988; The Loyal Ord of the Purple Suspender 1993. Silver Beaver SHAC - BSA 1999; Vigil hon OA - BSA 1995; St Geo Awd - BSA PECUSA 1987.

SPROUL, James Renfro (EC) 881 Lakeside Dr., Lenoir City TN 37772 **S Fran by the Sea Bogue Banks Salter Path NC 2004-** B Williamsburg,KY 1935 s Harvey & Ruth. BA U of Tennessee 1957; MDiv Ya Berk 1960; DMin Van 1973. D 2/16/1978 P 6/9/1979 Bp William Gillette Weinhauer. c 2. Int Chr Ch Eliz City NC 1995-1997; Int S Fran Ch Goldsboro NC 1994-1995; Int S Jas Par Wilmington NC 1993-1994; Int Trin Epis Ch Seneca Falls NY 1990-1992; Dio Tennessee Nashville TN 1988-1990; Int Sis of St Mary Sewanee TN 1988-1990; Int S Paul's Ch Franklin TN 1987-1988; Assoc S Andr's Epis Ch Tampa FL 1985-1987; R Ch Of The Epiph Newton NC 1980-1985; Calv Epis Ch Fletcher NC 1979-1980. Auth, "A New Ecum Mnstry," *Campus Mnstry Bulletin (Winter)*, 1971; Auth, "The New Creation," *The Pulpit (September)*, 1966. Danforth Fllshp Grant Danforth Fndt 1966. auraw@earthlink.net

SPROUSE, Herbert Warren (CPa) The Memorial Church of the Prince of Peace, 20 W. High St, Gettysburg PA 17325 **The Memi Ch Of The Prince Of Peace Gettysburg PA 2013-** B Charlottesville VA 1954 s William & Catharine. DMin EDS; BMus Ithaca Coll 1976; MBA Yale Sch of Mgmt 1979; MMus Yale Sch of Mus 1979; MDiv EDS 2009. D 10/31/2009 P 5/11/2010 Bp Vicky Gene Robinson. Cur S Paul's Ch Concord NH 2010-2013. rector@gettysburgepiscopal.org

SPRUHAN, John Halsey (SD) 720 Diamond Road, Salem VA 24153 **Vol Virgina Veteran's Care Cntr 2012-** B Detroit MI 1950 s John & Beatrice. BS U MI 1972; MDiv No Pk TS 1978; Cert SWTS 1980. D 6/14/1980 Bp Quintin Ebenezer Primo Jr P 12/13/1980 Bp James Winchester Montgomery. m 5/20/

1972 Judy Bennett Judd c 2. Supervising P Ch Of The H Sprt Ideal SD 2008; Calv Epis Ch Okreek SD 2004-2010; Vic Gr Epis Ch Soldier's Creek SD 2004-2010; Supervising P/Vic Trin Epis Ch Mssn SD 2004-2010; Supervising P/Vic Ch of Jesus Rosebud SD 1998-2010; H Innoc Epis Ch Parmelee SD 1998-2010; S Paul's Ch Norris SD 1998-2010; S Thos Ch Corn Creek SD 1998-2010; Supervising P/Vic Rosebud Epis Mssn Mssn SD 1997-2010; Vic St Cyprians Ch Chicago IL 1981-1998; Dn, Rosebud Dnry Dio So Dakota Pierre SD 2007-2010, Ecum Off 2001-2010; Dn, Chicago W Dnry Dio Chicago Chicago IL 1995-1999, Chair Hunger Cmsn 1985-1998. HSEC 2010. Freeman Awd for Merit Sewanee: The U So, TS 2010; Champion for Chld hon Roll So Dakota Voices for Chld 2009; Phil Marquard Hunger Awd Grtr Chicago Food Depositiry 1996; Hunger Fighter of the Year Ch Fed of Grtr Chicago 1992; Outstanding Young Citizen Chicago Jr ChmbrCom & Industry 1984.

SPRUHAN, Judy Bennett (SD) 720 Diamond Rd, Salem VA 24153 **Supply P Dio SW Virginia 2011-; Par Nurse St Paul's Salem VA 2011-; Dioc Liaison for Hlth Mnstrs Dio SW Virginia Roanoke VA 2012-; Faith Cmnty Nurse/Hlth Mnstrs St Paul's Epis Ch Salem VA 2011-** B Northville MI 1951 d William & Helen. Judson Coll 1970; Dplma Cook Cnty Sch of Nrsng Chicago IL 1976; BS No Pk U 1986; MS No Pk U 1996. D 12/2/1989 Bp Frank Tracy Griswold III P 6/25/2000 Bp Creighton Leland Robertson. m 5/20/1972 John Halsey Spruhan c 2. P Ch Of Jesus Rosebud SD 2000-2010; P H Innoc Epis Ch Parmelee SD 2000-2010; P Rosebud Epis Mssn Mssn SD 2000-2010; Par Nurse St Cyp's Chicago IL 1995-1997; D St Cyprians Ch Chicago IL 1989-1997. Faith Cmnty Nurse, "Monthly Hlth arts," *Connections*, Dio SW Virginia; Faith Cmnty Nurse, "Monthly Hlth arts," *Connections*, Dio SW Virginia. Hlth Mnstrs Assocation 2011.

SPRUILL, Robert Leigh (Tenn) 5825 Robert E Lee Dr, Nashville TN 37215 **Dio Tennessee Nashville TN 2007-; U So Sewanee TN 2006-; R S Geo's Ch Nashville TN 2005-; Epis Search Com Dio Tennessee Nashville TN 2006-** B Richmond VA 1963 s Joseph & Cora. BA U NC 1988; MDiv Sewanee: The U So, TS 1996. D 6/15/1996 P 1/7/1997 Bp Peter J Lee. m 10/28/1989 Susalee C Spruill c 3. R S Mk's Epis Ch Jacksonville FL 2001-2005; S Lk's Epis Ch Birmingham AL 1998-2001; Asst R St Jas Ch Richmond VA 1996-1998.

SPRUILL JR, William Arthur (Fla) 4107 Marquette Ave, Jacksonville FL 32210 **Ret 1995-; Ret 1994-** B Miami FL 1931 s William & Elizabeth. BA U So 1953; MA Col 1956; BD VTS 1968. D 6/26/1968 Bp C J Kinsolving III P 12/27/1968 Bp Albert Ervine Swift. m 2/27/1960 Charlotte Spruill c 3. Rep Fl Coun Chs Dio Florida Jacksonville 1976-1994, Asst To Bp 1975; Asst Min S Paul's Ch Delray Bch FL 1968-1975. Ccn. Dsa 1995.

SPULNIK, Frederick Joseph (RI) 4873 Collwood Blvd unit B, San Diego CA 92115 B Boise ID 1941 s Joseph & Helen. AA Boise St U 1961; BA U of Portland 1963; MDiv GTS 1966. D 6/26/1966 Bp Norman L Foote P 1/6/1967 Bp Charles Waldo MacLean. R S Matt's Par Of Jamestown Jamestown RI 1983-2004; R S Andr's Ch New Bedford MA 1973-1983; Assoc Ascen Memi Ch Ipswich MA 1968-1973; Cur S Lk's Ch E Hampton NY 1966-1968.

SPURGIN, Joyce M (Okla) 516 McLish St, Ardmore OK 73401 **D St Phil's Epis Ch Ardmore OK 2014-** B Dallas TX 1948 d Earl & Effie. BSN TCU 1971; MS U of Oklahoma 1980; Cert Iona Sch for Mnstry 2014. D 6/20/2014 Bp Edward Joseph Konieczny. c 1.

SPURLOCK, Michael Douglas (NY) Saint Thomas Church, 1 W. 53rd St., New York NY 10019 **Cur S Thos Ch New York NY 2010-** B Knoxville TN 1968 s Michael & Edna. BFA U of Tennessee 1993; MDiv Nash 2007. D 6/2/2007 P 12/8/2007 Bp John Bauerschmidt. m 12/18/1997 Aimee M Spurlock c 2. Vic All SS Epis Ch Smyrna TN 2007-2010.

SPURLOCK, Paul Allan (Colo) 10000 E Yale Ave Apt 4, 10000 E. Yale Ave Apt43, Denver CO 80231 B Denver CO 1940 s Granderson & Addie. BS Metropltn St Coll of Denver 1975; MDiv Iliff TS 1989. D 2/2/2002 P 8/6/2002 Bp William Jerry Winterrowd. m 7/20/2001 Saundra Spurlock c 2. S Thos Epis Ch Denver CO 2001-2007.

SQUIER, Timothy J (Chi) 500 East Depot Street, Antioch IL 60002 B Indianapolis IN 1971 s Larry & Susan. BA TCU 1993; MDiv Chr TS 1996; BA Briar Cliff U 2003; CAS SWTS 2004; MTS SWTS 2005. D 12/18/2004 P 10/2/2005 Bp Alan Scarfe. m 1/11/2003 Kristal J Squier c 4. R S Ign Of Antioch Ch Antioch IL 2008-2017; Asstg P S Mk's Ch Evanston IL 2006-2007; Int Asstg P Cbury Hse Evanston IL 2005-2006.

SQUIRE, James Richard (Pa) Episcopal Academy, 1785 Bishop White Dr, Newtown Square PA 19073 **Chapl The Epis Acad Newtown Sq PA 1978-** B Conshohocken PA 1945 s Walter & Harryanna. BS W Chester U of Pennsylvania 1967; MDiv Ya Berk 1970; ThM Duke 1971. D 6/6/1970 P 1/30/1971 Bp Robert Lionne DeWitt. m 12/20/1969 Vicki G Squire c 4. H Apos And Medtr Philadelphia PA 1980; The Epis Acad Newtown Sq PA 1978-2016; Asst Trin Ch Swarthmore PA 1971-1978; Chapl-Intern Duke Med Cntr Durham NC 1970-1971.

SQUIRE JR, Willard Searle (CFla) 748 Hammond Pl, The Villages FL 32162 B Detroit MI 1938 s Willard & Mary. BS U of Nebraska 1972; MAJ Wichita St U 1978; MDiv Sewanee: The U So, TS 1985. D 6/29/1985 Bp George Lazenby Reynolds Jr P 1/5/1986 Bp William Evan Sanders. m 9/17/1959 Margaret

V Squire c 6. Assoc S Geo Epis Ch The Villages FL 2008-2012; Chr Epis Ch Tracy City TN 2001-2002; Int R S Lk's Ch Cleveland TN 2001-2002, Cur 1985-1987; R Ch Of The Adv Nashville TN 1997-2000; Asst Ch Of The Ascen Hickory NC 1997; Partnr for Dvlpmt Dio Haiti Port-au-Prince HT 1993-1996; Cn Dio E Tennessee Knoxville TN 1991-1996; R S Tim's Epis Ch Kingsport TN 1987-1991. SSM 1994.

SRAMEK JR, Tom (Ore) PO Box 8834, Medford OR 97501 **S Mk's Epis Ch Medford NY 2016-** B Pittsburgh PA 1968 s Thomas & Suzanne. BA Humboldt St U 1990; MDiv VTS 1995. D 12/2/1995 Bp William Edwin Swing P 12/21/1996 Bp Franklin Delton Turner. m 8/1/1992 Elizabeth A Bell c 2. R Gd Samar Epis Ch San Jose CA 2009-2016; Vic S Alb's Epis Ch Albany OR 2002-2009; P Assoc for Yth S Ambr Epis Ch Foster City CA 2001-2002; Chapl Cbury at Hayward St Univ Hayward CA 2000-2002; Int Vic S Chris's Ch San Lorenzo CA 2000-2001; Assoc R S Paul's Epis Ch Burlingame CA 1997-2000; Asst/Cur The Ch Of The H Trin W Chester PA 1995-1997; GC, 1st Cler Alt Dio El Camino Real Salinas CA 2013-2016, Mem, Stndg Com 2010-2016. Auth, "Who Will Lead the Ch? (PB profiles)," *LivCh*, Living Ch Fndt, 2015; Auth, "Out of the Darkness," *LivCh*, Living Ch Fndt, 2007; Auth, "PB Profile - Jefferts Schori," *LivCh*, Living Ch Fndt, 2006; Auth, "PB Profile - Parsley," *LivCh*, Living Ch Fndt, 2006; Auth, "The Quadrilateral: Our Only Unity?," *LivCh*, Living Ch Fndt, 2002. Gathering the Next Generation (GTNG) 1998; Pi Gamma Mu 1990; Psy Chi (Psychol) 1990. rector@stmarks-medford.org

SSERWADDA, Emmanuel (NY) 69 Georgia Ave, Bronxville NY 10708 B Masaka UG 1956 s Issachar & Margaret. BA Buwalasi Teachers Inst 1976; Cert Bp Tucker Theol Coll Mukono Ug 1979; BD Bp Tucker Theol Coll Mukono Ug 1981; Cert Mercer TS 1991. Trans 5/1/1989 Bp Orris George Walker Jr. m 12/3/1983 Harriet Sserwadda c 3. Epis Ch Cntr New York NY 2005-2010; Dio New York New York NY 2000-2002; R Ch Of The Ascen Mt Vernon NY 1998-2007; Bd Gvnr Long Island Coun Of Ch 1994-1998; R Ch Of The Mssh Cntrl Islip NY 1993-1998; S Phil's Ch Brooklyn NY 1989-1993; Asst S Phil's Ch Brooklyn NY 1989-1992; Serv Ch Of Uganda 1979-1989. Li Curs; UBE.

STABLER-TIPPETT, Joycelyn D (Miss) St Stephen's Episcopal Church, 1300 Church St, Columbia MS 39429 **Trin Ch Mt Airy NC 2017-** B Greenville AL 1954 d Lemuel & Gloria. BS Troy St U 1976; MA U of Alabama - Birmingham 1982; PhD U of Sthrn Mississippi 2002; MDiv Sewanee: The U So, TS 2013; MDiv The TS at The U So 2013. D 6/1/2013 P 12/11/2013 Bp Duncan Montgomery Gray III. m 9/23/2006 Robert Thomas Tippett c 2. S Steph's Ch Columbia MS 2013-2017.

STACEY, Caroline Mary (NY) 487 Hudson St, New York NY 10014 **R The Ch Of S Lk In The Fields New York NY 2005-; Chair, Dioc Campus Mnstry Bd Dio New York New York NY 2010-, Dioc Assessment Revs Bd 2010-** B Chelmsford England UK 1963 d Michael & Barbara. MA U of St Andrews 1986; MDiv Ya Berk 1990. D 6/9/1990 P 2/17/1991 Bp Arthur Edward Walmsley. m 6/4/2007 Scott D Askegard. R All SS Ch E Lansing MI 1996-2005; Assoc R Trin Ch On The Green New Haven CT 1992-1996; Asst Trin Par New York NY 1990-1992; Bd Trst Ya Berk New Haven CT 2006-2010; Stndg Committe: Mem and Pres Dio Michigan Detroit MI 2002-2005, Area Dn 2000-2004; Mus Cmsn Dio Connecticut Meriden CT. Auth, "Justification by Faith in the 2 Books of Homilies," *ATR*, 2001; Auth, "Bloy As Mentor," *Journ of Rel & Intellectual Life*, 1985. Rdr. Gnrl Ord Examinations 2000; Fell, Coll of Preachers 1999.

STACK JR, Gene AJ (SO) 541 2nd Ave, Gallipolis OH 45631 **Assoc S Ptr's Ch Gallipolis OH 2015-** B Athens OH 1981 s Gene & Robin. BA Ohio U 2006; MDiv Bex Sem 2015. D 6/6/2015 P 6/4/2016 Bp Thomas Edward Breidenthal. m 5/27/2015 Steven Wei-Ming Huang.

STACKHOUSE, Marcia K (Colo) 3432 Vallejo St, Denver CO 80211 B Kalamazoo MI 1940 d Gordon & Helen. BA Loretto Heights Coll 1988. D 6/29/1988 Bp William Carl Frey. m 6/4/1960 Robert Arnold Stackhouse c 3. Our Merc Sav Epis Ch Denver CO 2006-2012; Our Merc Sav Mnstrs Denver CO 2006-2012; Asst Epis Ch Of S Ptr And S Mary Denver CO 2003-2005; S Lk's Ch Denver CO 1994-2006; Dir Of Diac Formation Dio Colorado Denver CO 1990-2006; Pstr Asst The Ch Of The Ascen Denver CO 1988-1990. NAAD 1987; NAAD, Bd Mem 2001-2003.

STACY, Charles Herrick (Los) 1509 Eucalyptus Dr, Solvang CA 93463 B Berkeley CA 1944 s Clarence & Eleanor. BA U CA 1966; BD CDSP 1969; MS California St U 1973. D 6/28/1969 Bp Chauncie Kilmer Myers P 1/10/1970 Bp George Richard Millard. m 6/15/1968 Shirley M Stacy c 2. R S Mk's-In-The-Vlly Epis Los Olivos CA 1976-2008; Asst All SS Ch Carmel CA 1973-1976; Vic S Barn Ch San Francisco CA 1971-1973; Cur S Fran' Epis Ch San Francisco CA 1969-1971.

STADEL, Jerold Russell (SwFla) 1014 Pinegrove Dr, Brandon FL 33511 B Buffalo NY 1943 s Russell & Kathryn. BA S Lawr Canton NY 1965; STB Ya Berk 1968. D 6/22/1968 Bp Harold Barrett Robinson P 12/22/1968 Bp Dudley B McNeil. m 8/19/1967 Anne Saunders c 1. Asst S Andr's Epis Ch Tampa FL 2008-2016; Chapl Jn Knox Vill C.C.R.C. Tampa 2005-2007; Bp's Cn to Cler and their Families Dio SW Florida Parrish FL 2002-2016, Chapl to

Ret Cler, Spouses and Surviving Spouses 1998-2016, Dir/D Trng 1985-1992, Chair Pstr Care Cmsn 1982-1998, Chair of Fam Com 1980-1981, Secy of Aging Com 1974-1979; Coordntr of Chapl to Ret Cler C.P.G. 2000-2003; St Cathr of Alexandria Epis Ch Temple Terrace FL 1970-1993; Cur S Mths Epis Ch E Aurora NY 1968-1970. ESMA 1974-1992.

STAFFORD, Gil (Az) **P-in-c S Ptr's Ch Litchfield Pk AZ 2017-; Vic Dio Arizona Phoenix AZ 2015-** B Cheyenne OK 1953 s Finis & Loretta. BS Arizona St U 1976; MA Arizona St U 1979; PhD Trin Theol 1998; DMin SWTS 2005. D 6/18/2005 P 12/17/2005 Bp Kirk Stevan Smith. m 11/22/1971 Catherine Ann Stafford c 2. Chapl Epis Campus Mnstrs at ASU Tempe AZ 2015; Vic S Aug's Epis Ch Tempe AZ 2006-2015. Auth, "Wisdom Walking: Pilgrimage as a Way of LIfe," Ch Pub, 2017; Auth, "When Ldrshp And Sprtl Direction Meet," Rowman and Littlefield, 2014; Contrib, "Meeting God Day by Day," Forw Mvmt, 2014; Contrib, "Seeking God Day by Day," Forw Mvmt, 2013; Contrib, "Sharing the Pract," *Zealot Bk Revs*, The Acad of Par Cler, 2013; Contrib, "Sharing the Pract," *Dream or Nightmare*, The Acad of Par Cler, 2012; Contrib, "The Coll Campus as a Web of Sociality," *Transforming Campus Life*, Ptr Lang, 2001. OHC 2007. gstafford3@gmail.com

STAFFORD, Robert Holmes (NY) 401 S El Cielo Rd Apt 71, Palm Springs CA 92262 B Minneapolis MN 1947 s Edward & Betty. BA U MN 1968; MDiv Nash 1971; Cert U MN 1978; STM GTS 1979. D 6/29/1971 P 3/12/1972 Bp Philip Frederick McNairy. S Thos Ch New York NY 2004-2010, Asst 1985-1991; Dir MP AIDS Proj Manhattan Plaza Assoc New York NY 1994-2004; Chapl Manhattan Plaza AIDS Proj New York NY 1992-1994; Adj Prof The GTS New York NY 1985-1991; Chapl Morningside Hse Nrsng Hm Bronx NY 1982-1984; R S Paul's Epis Ch Owatonna MN 1980-1982; Ther Fam Renweal Treatment Cntr Minneapolis MN 1979-1980; Ther Fam Renwl Treatment Cntr Minneapolis MN 1976-1978; Chapl/Ther S Mary's Treatment Cntr Minneapolis MN 1973-1975; Cur S Mich & All Ang Ch Monticello MN 1971-1973.

STAFFORD, William Sutherland (Fla) 4316 Hampshire Pl, San Jose CA 95136 B San Francisco CA 1947 s Chase & Harriette. BA Stan 1969; MA Ya 1972; PhD Ya 1975. D 5/2/1981 P 1/17/1982 Bp Robert Bruce Hall. m 6/7/1969 Barbara M Stafford c 5. Dn Sewanee U So TS Sewanee TN 2005-2012; Dn The TS The U So Sewanee 2005-2012; Prof of Ch Hist The TS The U So Sewanee 2005-2012; Assoc Dn VTS Alexandria VA 1997-2004, Asst Prof Ch Hist 1976-1996; S Chris's Ch Springfield VA 1981. Auth, "Disordered Loves: Healing the Seven Deadly Sins," Cowley, 1994; Auth, "The Eve of the Reformation: Bp Jn Fisher 1509," *Hist mag of the Prot Epis Ch of the USA*, 1985; Auth, "Domesticating the Cler:The Inception of the Reformation in Strasbourg," Scholars Press, 1976. Amer Soc of Ch Hist 1976; Cath Hist Soc 1982. DD VTS 2005; Phi Beta Kappa Stan 1969.

STAFFORD-WHITTAKER, William Paul (WA) **Par of St Monica & St Jas Washington DC 2015-** B Manchester United Kingdom 1969 s Ernest & Jean. Dplma Mnstrl Theol Chichester Theol Coll 1994. Trans 6/3/2015 as Priest Bp Mariann Edgar Budde.

STAGGS, Katresia Anne (Ark) 501 S Phoenix Ave, Russellville AR 72801 B Little Rock AR 1948 d Thomas & Wanda. Iona Initiative Sem of the SW. D 8/8/2015 Bp Larry Benfield. m 7/1/1982 Roy Joe Staggs c 2.

STAHL, Daryl Wayne (RI) 91 Pratt St, providence RI 02906 **Ret 2000-** B Huron SD 1935 s Edward & Gwendolyn. BA Hur CA 1957; BD EDS 1960. D 6/24/1960 P 12/28/1960 Bp Conrad H Gesner. m 9/2/1960 Elizabeth Ann Stahl c 3. R S Jn's Ch Barrington RI 1990-2000; R S Thos' Epis Ch Sioux City IA 1976-1990; Asst S Mk's Ch New Britain CT 1969-1976; Vic All SS Ponca Creek SD 1960-1969; Ch Of The Incarn Greg SD 1960-1969; Vic S Andr's Ch Bonesteel SD 1960-1969.

STAIR, Adrian (Mass) 51 Longmeadow Dr, Amherst MA 01002 B Port Chester NY 1944 d Gobin & Julia. BA Antioch Coll 1967; MSW CUNY 1990; MDiv EDS 2003. D 6/7/2003 P 6/5/2004 Bp M(Arvil) Thomas Shaw. R Emm Ch Braintree MA 2005-2008; Asst Bristol Cluster No Easton MA 2004-2005.

STALEY, Mary (Va) PO Box 482, Put In Bay OH 43456 **P-in-c S Paul's Epis Ch Put In Bay OH 2010-** B 1955 d Harlow & V. BA Iowa St U 1977; MA Webster U 1995; MDiv VTS 2005. D 6/18/2005 Bp Peter J Lee P 12/21/2005 Bp David Colin Jones. Asst R Ch Of Our Sav Charlottesvlle VA 2006-2010; Asst Vic S Patricks Ch Falls Ch VA 2005.

STALLER, Margaretmary B (Cal) 4821 Wolf Way, Concord CA 94521 **Chapl Heartland Hospice Concord CA 2000-; Chapl Contra Costa Hospice Pleasant Hill CA 1984-; Oncology Chapl Jn Muir Hosp Walnut Creek CA 1984-** B Buffalo NY 1933 d George & Kathleen. AA Burlington Cnty Coll 1981; BA Sch for Deacons 1984. D 12/7/1985 Bp William Edwin Swing. m 6/26/1954 Thomas Owen Staller. Gr Ch Martinez CA 2003-2004; S Lk's Ch Walnut Creek CA 1999-2000, 1992-1994; Chapl So Jersey Hospice Vineland NJ 1994-1997; D Trin Epis Ch Vineland NJ 1994-1997; Liturg D Gr Cathd San Francisco CA 1986-1992. NAAD, ACPE, AEHC; NAAD, ACPE, AEHC.

STALLINGS, Buddy Monroe (NY) 435 E 52nd Street, Apt 10A2, New York NY 10022 B Houston MS 1953 s Floyd & Christine. BA Mississippi Coll 1975; MA U of Tennessee 1976; MDiv GTS 1992. D 5/30/1992 P 5/1/1993 Bp Alfred

Marble Jr. c 1. R St. Barth Ch New York NY 2013-2015, Vic 2008-2013; R Ch Of The Ascen Staten Island NY 2002-2008; S Jas Ch Jackson MS 1992-2001. stallingsbuddy@gmail.com

STAMBAUGH, Doran Bartlett (SanD) PO Box 127, Carlsbad CA 92018 **P-in-c S Michaels By-The-Sea Ch Carlsbad CA 2011-, Cur 2005-** B Cooperstown NY 1974 BA Wheaton Coll 1996; MDiv Nash 2005. D 1/25/2005 P 8/6/2005 Bp Keith Lynn Ackerman. m 8/23/1997 Therese M Stambaugh c 3. SSC 2006.

STAMM, George (Eau) 13497 45th Ave, Chippewa Falls WI 54729 B Syracuse NY 1942 s George & Roberta. BA Waynesburg Coll 1966; MDiv Nash 1970; Cert Hazelden Treatment Cntr 1981. D 2/28/1970 P 11/28/1970 Bp Stanley Hamilton Atkins. m 10/7/1995 Cynthia Stamm c 6. Chr Ch Chippewa Fls WI 2000-2008; S Simeon's Ch Chippewa Falls WI 2000-2008; Chapl/Counslr L. E Phillips Treatment Cntr Chippewa Falls WI 1977-1999; S Barn Ch Clear Lake WI 1970-1977; S Phil's Ch Turtle Lake WI 1970-1977.

ST AMOUR III, Frank S (Eas) 51 N Main St, Mullica Hill NJ 08062 **R S Paul's Par Kent Chestertown MD 2016-; R S Steph's Ch Mullica Hill NJ 2013-** B Philadelphia PA 1958 s Frank & Doris. BA St Johns Coll Annapolis MD 1980; BD U of Wales GB 1983. Trans 4/8/1988 Bp John Thomas Walker. m 6/1/1985 Susan M St Amour. Trin Epis Old Swedes Ch Swedesboro NJ 2013-2016; R S Steph's Epis Ch Whitehall PA 2008-2013; R S Steph's Epis Ch Hurst TX 2002-2008; Assoc R All SS Epis Ch Lakeland FL 1997-2002; Int Ch Of S Mich And All Ang Berwyn IL 1996-1997; R Chr Ch Joliet IL 1994-1996; Chapl Army NG 1992-2004; R S Alb's Ch Silver Creek NY 1992-1994; R Ch Of S Jn The Bapt Dunkirk NY 1989-1994; Asst Chr Ch Par Kensington MD 1987-1989; Serv Cont Ch 1985-1987; Asst. Cur Ch in Wales 1983-1985; COM Dio Bethlehem Bethlehem PA 2010-2013. SocMary 1990; SSC 1998. rector@stpaulkent.org

STANDIFORD, Sarah Euphemia (Md) **Died 4/17/2016** B 1929

STANFORD, Bill (FtW) 3550 SW Loop 820, Fort Worth TX 76133 **R S Chris's Ch And Sch Ft Worth TX 2000-; Chairperson Cmsn of Epis Schools 2016-** B Houston TX 1954 s Wilbur & Ruth. BA Tarleton St U 1980; MDiv Nash 1987. D 7/25/1987 P 2/2/1988 Bp Clarence Cullam Pope Jr. m 12/26/2015 Serin Yates Stanford c 3. Gd Shpd Granbury TX 1998-2000; P-in-c S Jos's Epis Ch Grand Prairie TX 1997-1999; Cur/Co-Admin Of Sch S Andr's Ch Grand Prairie TX 1994-1997, Cur 1987-1989; Dio Ft Worth Ft Worth TX 1989-1992, Ecum Off 2016-, Other Cler Position 1989-1992; Vic S Pat's Ch Bowie TX 1989-1992; Vic Trin Ch Henrietta TX 1989-1992. Auth, "Unthrown Stone (Poem)," *Living Ch*, 1990.

STANFORD, David Dewitt (Chi) 2705 Armfield Road, Hillsborough NC 27278 B Battle Creek MI 1949 s Freeman & Nelle. BA JHU 1971; MDiv VTS 1980. D 6/21/1980 Bp John Thomas Walker P 1/4/1981 Bp A(rthur) Heath Light. m 6/20/2014 Althea Kintanar c 1. Hospice Chapl NorthShore U Hlth Systems 2012-2015; Asst S Edm's Epis Ch Chicago IL 2010-2015; Lawr Hall Sch Chicago IL 1996-2010; Chapl Lawr Hall Yth Serv 1996-2010; R Ch Of S Paul And The Redeem Chicago IL 1989-1996; Assoc for Campus Mnstry Chap Of The Cross Chap Hill NC 1983-1989; Asst Chr Epis Ch Roanoke VA 1980-1983; P Assoc S Matt's Epis Ch Hillsborough NC 2015-2017; Asstg Cler St. Paul-by-the-Lake 2015; Asstg Cler Cathd Of S Jas Chicago IL 2008-2015. AEHC 1997; Assn of Profsnl Chapl 1998-2017.

STANFORD, Donna Lynn (WMo) 100 E Red Bridge Rd, Kansas City MO 64114 B St Joseph MO 1951 d Richard & Alice. Bachelor of Arts U of Missouri at Kansas City 1973; juris doctor U of Missouri at Kansas City 1978; Cert Bp Kemper Sch for Mnstry 2014. D 11/7/2014 Bp Martin Scott Field. c 1.

STANFORD, Ian M (Ore) **Chr Ch Par Lake Oswego OR 2017-** D 6/18/2016 P 1/28/2017 Bp Michael Hanley.

STANFORD, Virginia Francene (Md) 10901 Farrier Rd, Frederick MD 21701 **R Trin Ch Long Green MD 2007-, Int 2005-2006** B Memphis TN 1953 d Carl & Jean. BS U of Memphis 1973; MD U of Tennessee 1976; MDiv VTS 1993; CAS Ecumenical Inst St Marys Sem Baltimore MD 2007. D 6/19/1993 P 5/21/1994 Bp Don Adger Wimberly. m 2/15/2017 Virginia Ann Boyd. R Harriet Chap Catoctin Epis Par Thurmont MD 1997-2005; Assoc S Jn's Ch Lynchburg VA 1993-1997; COM Dio Maryland Baltimore MD 2004-2010, Dioc Coun 1998-2004. Alpha Omega Alpha Honoraryor Soc 1974.

STANGER, Mark E. (Cal) 124 Panorama Dr, San Francisco CA 94131 **Assoc Pstr Gr Cathd San Francisco CA 1997-** B Berwyn IL 1951 s Edward & Dolores. BA S Johns U 1973; MDiv S Johns U 1978; Patristic Inst Augustinianum 1984. Rec 6/6/1992 Bp William Edwin Swing. m 11/11/2009 Mark A Johnson. non-stipendiary Cler Ch Of The Adv Of Chr The King San Francisco CA 1992-1997. Contrib, "Lent responsorial psalm exegetical commentaries," *Feasting on the Word, Year B vol 2*, Westminster Jn Knox, 2008; Contrib, "Pictures," *Preaching as Pstr Caring: Sermons that Wk XIII*, Morehouse, 2005.

STANLEY, Anne Grant (Me) Po Box 63, Paris ME 04271 B Newton MA 1941 d George & Jane. BA Wellesley Coll 1963; MA Oakland U 1988; MDiv EDS 1994. D 6/11/1994 P 12/21/1994 Bp Douglas Edwin Theuner. m 11/26/1965 David Stanley c 3. Dio Maine Portland ME 2000-2011; R Chr Ch Norway ME 1998-2011; Asst Gr Ch Manchester NH 1994-1998.

STANLEY, Arthur Patrick (Ia) 10 Knights Ct, Frome Somerset BA 11 1JD England Great Britain (UK) **Ret 1994-** B Kilmacthomas Ireland 1932 s Charles & Violet. ThD Trin Dublin IE 1954; BA Trin Dublin IE 1954; MA Trin Dublin IE 1963. Trans 12/1/1988 Bp Walter Cameron Righter. m 8/15/1983 Jessie Stanley c 2. P-in-c All Ang Ch Des Moines IA 1988-1994; P-in-c S Jn's Ch Shenandoah IA 1988-1994; Chapl British Army 1958-1983; Serv Ch of Ireland 1955-1958. Auth, "Var arts," *Royal Army Chapl Dept Journ*, 1981; Auth, *Var Arts Royal Army Chapl Dept Journ 71-81*. Hon Chapl Britannic Majesty's Forces 1983.

STANLEY, E Bevan (Ct) 25 South St, PO Box 248, Litchfield CT 06759 **Dep GC Dio Newark Newark NJ 2006-, Dioc Coun 2001-2005; Conciliator Dio Connecticut Meriden CT 2012-, Dioc Coun 1986-1992** B Abington PA 1951 s Edward & Alice. BA Chart Oak St Coll 1981; MDiv Ya Berk 1983; DMin Hartford Sem 2003. D 6/11/1983 P 2/7/1984 Bp Arthur Edward Walmsley. m 11/25/1972 Alinda Horn c 2. R S Mich's Ch Litchfield CT 2015, P-in-c 2015-, P-in-c 2012-2014; Int Chr Ch Bethany CT 2011-2012; Int Ch Of The Gd Shpd Orange CT 2008-2011; Bd Trst Ya Berk New Haven CT 2002-2006; R Chr Ch Short Hills NJ 1999-2007; R Gr And S Ptr's Epis Ch Hamden CT 1995-1999, Vic 1990-1995; Dep GC Dio Connecticut 1991-1999; Consult & Trnr Dio Connecticut 1986-2000; Vic S Ptr's Ch Hamden CT 1984-1999; Cur Chr Ch New Haven CT 1983-1984. Auth, "Organizing the Cong: The Use of Communityt Organizing Techniques in the Trng of Congrl Leaders," UMI Dissertaion Serv, 2003. CDI Trainers 1999. rector@stmichaels-litchfield.org

STANLEY BSG, Gordon John (Chi) 340 W Diversey Pkwy, Chicago IL 60657 B Indianapolis IN 1946 s George & Doris. BA Pur 1972; MA U of San Diego 1976. D 2/5/2000 Bp Bill Persell. D S Ptr's Epis Ch Chicago IL 2000-2013.

STANLEY, James Martin (NI) 320 Franklin St, Geneva IL 60134 **S Phil's Epis Palatine IL 2016-** B Cleveland OH 1965 s John & Marjorie. BS Moody Bible Inst; Dplma Cmncatn Moody Bible Inst; MMin Nash 2013. D 2/14/2014 P 9/7/2014 Bp Edward Stuart Little II. m 8/6/1988 Carrie LeAnn Stanley c 1. S Mk's Ch Geneva IL 2014. jsojourner1@gmail.com

STANLEY JR, John Hiram (FtW) 4105 Hartwood Dr, Fort Worth TX 76109 B Chicago IL 1938 s John & Pauline. BA Denison U 1960; BD SWTS 1963. D 6/15/1963 Bp James Winchester Montgomery P 12/1/1963 Bp Gerald Francis Burrill. m 8/13/1960 Lynne Stanley. Trin Epis Ch Ft Worth TX 1975-1998; Ex-ec Asst To The Bp Of Nebraska Dio Nebraska Omaha NE 1973-1975; Cn Trin Cathd Omaha NE 1970-1972; Vic S Mich's Ch Grand Rapids MI 1966-1970; Cur S Aug's Epis Ch Wilmette IL 1963-1966.

STANLEY, Lauren Regina (SD) PO Box 256, Mission SD 57555 **P-in-c Dio So Dakota Pierre SD 2013-; P-in-c S Paul's Ch Norris SD 2013-** B Kirkwood MO 1960 d James & Marione. AA S Petersburg Jr Coll 1980; BA Marq 1982; MDiv VTS 1997; DMin VTS 2013. D 6/14/1997 P 4/21/1998 Bp Peter J Lee. Consult Mssn Consult 2010-2013; Appointed Mssy Epis Ch Haiti 2009-2010; Exec Coun Appointees New York NY 2008-2010, Mssy, Sudan 2005-2009, Mssy, Haiti 2005-2007; Appointed Mssy Epis Ch Sudan 2005-2009; Assoc S Alb's Epis Ch Annandale VA 2001-2005; R Gr Epis Ch Allentown PA 2000-2001; Assoc Trin Ch Arlington VA 1999-2000; Assoc Ch Of The Gd Shpd Burke VA 1997-1999. "Handbook for Short-Term Mssn," Dio Virginia, 2003; *Nwspr Column*, McClatchey/Tribune News Serv, 1994.

STANLEY, Marjorie Jean (Spok) 255 W Shore Ln, Sandpoint ID 83864 **Asstg P H Sprt Epis Ch Dover ID 2002-** B Ashland WI 1928 d Harold & Ruth. BA U of Wisconsin 1949; MA Indiana U 1950; PhD Indiana U 1953; Brite DS 1986; MDiv SWTS 1988. D 12/13/1997 P 7/11/1998 Bp Frank Jeffrey Terry. c 2. Supply P S Mary's Bonners Ferry Bonners Ferr ID 2008-2013; Assoc S Dav's Ch Spokane WA 1998-2002. Auth, "The Irwin Guide To Investing In Emerging Markets," Irwin, 1995; Auth, "Ethical Issues In Emerging Fin Markets," *Emerging Global Bus Ethics*, Quorum, 1994; Auth, "Multinational Capital Budgemultinational Capital Bdgt, Emerging Markets & Mng Agcy: A Proposal For Ethically Constrain," 1993; Auth, "Capital Bdgt In Countries w Less Developed Capital Markets: Fin & Ethical Issues," *Bus Fin In Less Deveioped Capital Markets*, Greenwood, 1992; Auth, "Ethical Perspective On The Frgn Direct Invstmt Decisions," *Journ Of Bus Ethics Volume 9 #1*, 1990; Auth, "The Frgn Direct Invstmt Decisions & Job Export As Ethical Dilemma For Multinational Corp," *Ethics And The Multinational Enterprise*, U Press, 1986. Beta Gamma Sigma; Sigma Delta Pi; Theta Phi. Phi Kappa Phi 1949.

STANLEY, Mark (Md) Old St. Paul's Church, 309 Cathedral Street, Baltimore MD 21201 **S Paul's Par Baltimore MD 2004-; R S Paul's Sch Brooklandville MD 2004-** B Evanston IL 1964 s John & Lynne. MA U of Texas 1986; MDiv CDSP 1990. D 6/9/1990 P 6/8/1991 Bp William Edwin Swing. m 7/22/1989 Mary Stanley c 2. R Chr Ch Sausalito CA 1994-2004; Cur All SS Epis Ch Palo Alto CA 1990-1994; Chair of Mssn Strtgy Grp Dio Maryland Baltimore MD 1999-2000. Phi Beta Kappa 1986.

STANLEY, Mary (Md) Old St. Paul's Church, 309 Cathedral St., Baltimore MD 21201 **Assoc R S Paul's Par Baltimore MD 2006-** B Houston TX 1964 d George & Jane. BS Texas A&M U 1987; MDiv CDSP 1997. D 6/7/1997 P 12/1/1997 Bp William Edwin Swing. m 7/22/1989 Mark Stanley c 2. Ch Of Our Sav Mill Vlly CA 2002; Asst Ch Of The Resurr Pleasant Hil CA 1997-1999. Auth, "Yth Mnstry Acad Manual". mary@osp1692.org

S

STANLEY, Stephen Ranson (SwVa) St. Mark's Episcopaql Church, 111 South Roanoke St. P.O. Box 277, Fincastle VA 24090 **Dioc Liturg And Mus Cmsn 1988-** B Asheville NC 1949 s Sherburn & Helen. AA Gulf Coast Cmnty Coll 1970; BS U of W Florida 1972; MS U of Florida 1978; MDiv VTS 1982. D 6/26/1982 Bp Clarence Edward Hobgood P 2/1/1983 Bp Maurice Manuel Benitez. m 6/20/1981 Jacqueline Hamilton Stanley c 1. P Mssnr S Mk's Ch Fincastle VA 2011-2015; Assoc R Chr Epis Ch Roanoke VA 2003-2011; Assoc Chap Of The Cross Chap Hill NC 1990-2003; Epis Chapl U NC 1990-2003; R All SS' Epis Ch Gastonia NC 1987-1990; The Great Cmsn Fndt Houston TX 1985; Epis Chapl Baylor U Baylor TX 1982-1987; Assoc S Paul's Ch Waco TX 1982-1987. Auth, "Discovering Genesis 25-50," *Guideposts Hm Biblic Stds*, 1988; Auth, "Discovering Lk," *Guideposts Hm Biblic Stds*, 1985. Cross Of Nails 1990; Iona Cmnty 2010. srstanley@cox.net

STANLEY, William S (At) **St Cross Epis Ch Hermosa Bch CA 2017-** B Washington DC 1989 s Mitchell & Kathleen. BA The TS at The U So; BA Sewanee: The U So, TS 2012; BA The U So 2012; BA The U So 2012; MDiv Ya Berk 2015. D 12/20/2014 P 6/20/2015 Bp Robert Christopher Wright. H Innoc Ch Atlanta GA 2015-2017. Omicron Delta Kappa 2011.

STANSBERY, Marylen Wilkins (Mo) 2 Warson Ln, Saint Louis MO 63124 B Kansas City MO 1935 D 4/30/1998 Bp Hays H. Rockwell. m 12/24/1987 Gary Lee Stansbery c 3.

STANTON JR, Barclay Reynolds (Eas) 24447 94th St S, Kent WA 98030 B Primos PA 1938 s Barclay & Louise. BA Wms 1961; MDiv VTS 1966. D 6/29/1966 Bp Allen J Miller P 6/1/1967 Bp George Alfred Taylor. m 6/19/1971 Barbara L Stanton c 2. S Matt Ch Tacoma WA 1990-2001; R All SS Ch Wstrn Sprgs IL 1985-1989; All SS Ch Brookland PA 1976-1984; R Chr Ch Coudersport PA 1976-1984; Asst Chr Ch S Ptr's Par Easton MD 1975-1976; Chapl Groton Sch Groton MA 1969-1971; Asst Chr Epis Ch Great Choptank Par Cambridge MD 1967-1969; Cur Emm Epis Ch Chestertown MD 1966-1967.

STANTON, James Malcom (Ind) 321 Market St, Jeffersonville IN 47130 B New Albany 1952 s Charles & Emma. BS U of Indianapolis 1975; MS Indiana U SE 1981; MST Indiana U SE 1986. D 10/23/2015 Bp Cate Waynick. m 12/29/1979 Katherine King c 1.

✠ STANTON, The Rt Rev James Monte (Dal) 1630 N Garrett Ave, Dallas TX 75206 B Atchison KS 1946 s Jewell & Dorothy. BA Chapman U 1968; DMin Sthrn California TS 1975; Cert CDSP 1977; Sewanee: The U So, TS 1994; Nash 1996; CDSP 2009. D 6/18/1977 Bp Robert Claflin Rusack P 10/23/1977 Bp Victor Manuel Rivera Con 3/6/1993 for Dal. m 12/29/1968 Diane Hanson. Bp of Dallas Dio Dallas Dallas TX 1993-2014; R S Mk's Par Glendale CA 1987-1992; R S Lk's Epis Ch Cedar Falls IA 1982-1987; Vic S Steph's Ch Stockton CA 1977-1981; Chair of Wrld Mssn Cmsn Epis Dio San Joaquin Modesto CA 1979-1981. jmsdallas@edod.org

STANTON, John Frank (Nwk) 7900 Harbor Island Dr Apt 1501, North Bay Village FL 33141 **Assoc Trin Cathd Miami FL 2011-** B Orange,NJ 1936 s Vernon & Emily. BA Ham 1958; MDiv GTS 1962; MBA Wag 1976. D 10/6/1962 Bp Leland Stark P 4/6/1963 Bp Donald MacAdie. m 5/20/2006 Nora Stanton c 3. Int R S Jas The Fisherman Islamorada FL 2008-2011; Assoc P Trin Cathd 2005-2007; Vic S Matt's Ch Paramus NJ 1998-2004, P 1994-1996; Int R Chr Ch Teaneck NJ 1997-1998; Int R Ch Of The H Sprt Verona NJ 1996; Int R Chr Ch Belleville NJ 1991-1992; Vic S Gabr Milton NJ 1986-1990; Supply P Dio Newark Newark NJ 1985-1986; Cur Chr Ch Hackensack NJ 1971-1985, Asst 1962-1970; R Trin Ch Hoboken NJ 1965-1971. stantonjf@gmail.com

STANTON, John Robert (At) 4906 Sulky Dr Apt 204, Richmond VA 23228 **Epis Ch Of Our Sav Midlothian VA 2004-; Our Sav VA 2004-; Ret 1998-** B Macon GA 1922 s Clarence & Florence. BA Merc 1949; MDiv VTS 1953. D 6/24/1953 P 1/6/1954 Bp Henry D Phillips. c 1. Int Trin Epis Ch Highland Sprg VA 1999-2001; Chapl Psych Hosp Riverdale GA 1993-1998; R S Aug Of Cbury Morrow GA 1983-1993; S Barth's Epis Ch Atlanta GA 1982-1983; S Steph's Ch Newport News VA 1961-1981; R Mssh Highland Sprg VA 1956-1960; R Trin Epis Ch Rocky Mt VA 1953-1956. AFP 1975-1990.

STANTON, Sarah Morningstar (EO) 4701 7th Ave. SW Unit 303, Olympia WA 98502 B Abilene KS 1945 d Fillepe & Shirley. BA Mt Mary Coll 1966; MEd U of New Hampshire 1972; MDiv CDSP 1987. D 12/5/1987 P 12/3/1988 Bp William Edwin Swing. c 2. R S Ptr's Ch La Grande OR 2003-2009; R S Steph's Epis Ch Latonia KY 1993-2003; Chapl S Eliz's Med Cntr Covington KY 1992-1993; Chapl Mt St U-Bozeman 1989-1992; Asst S Jas Ch Bozeman MT 1989-1992; Cur S Jn's Epis Ch Oakland CA 1988-1989. Auth, "Two Bk Revs," *ATR*, 2002. Soc Of S Fran - Tertiary 1984-2002.

STANTON, William B (Colo) 7157 High St, Frederick CO 80504 **Ch Of The H Comf Broomfield CO 2016-** B Denver CO 1964 s Douglas & Naomi. BA U of Nthrn Colorado 1987; JD U Denv, Coll of Law 1990; MDiv Ilif TS 2016; MDiv Ilif TS 2016; MDiv Iliff TS 2016. D 6/13/2015 P 6/18/2016 Bp Robert John O'Neill. m 4/15/2015 Charles Robert Mason.

STANWISE, Ralph Joseph Francis (Chi) 2608 N Kingston Dr, Peoria IL 61604 **Dio Quincy Peoria IL 1994-** B Brooklyn NY 1943 s Ralph & Dorothy. BA U Denv 1965; MDiv Nash 1969; MA U of Wisconsin 1972. D 6/14/1969 P 12/20/1969 Bp Jonathan Goodhue Sherman. m 6/23/1973 Lynda J Stanwise c

1. Cn St Paul's Epis Ch Peoria IL 1994-2007; R S Jn's Ch Ogdensburg NY 1990-1993; R Gr Epis Ch Menomonie WI 1977-1990; P-in-c S Aidans Ch Hartford WI 1973-1977; S Ptr's Ch Northlake WI 1973-1977; Cur Chr Ch Babylon NY 1969-1973; Stndg Com Dio Eau Claire Eau Claire WI 1979-1990. Mem Phi Alpha Theta 1965; Mem Phi Beta Kappa 1965.

STANWOOD, Thomas Reid (Ore) 1638 Boca Ratan Dr, Lake Oswego OR 97034 **Died 3/15/2016** B Boston MA 1939 s William & Elisabeth. BA Un Coll Schenectady NY 1961. D 10/4/2003 Bp Johncy Itty. D Chr Ch Par Lake Oswego OR 2003-2016.

STAPLES, Ann McDonald (Pgh) Po Box 1, Marion Center PA 15759 **Coal Cnty Hang-Out Yth Cntr No Cambria PA 1996-; Ch of SS Thos and Lk Patton PA 1993-; D S Thos Ch Nthrn Cambria PA 1993-** B San Antonio TX 1931 d Aubrey & Doris. PhD Indiana U; BA SMU 1952; MA SMU 1953. D 6/22/1984 Bp Alden Moinet Hathaway. m 8/27/1967 James Staples c 6. D All SS Epis Ch Verona PA 1989-1991; D S Alb's Epis Ch Murrysville PA 1984-1993; Chapl Fam Hospice Indiana Cnty.

STAPLETON JR, Jack (Colo) 4222 W. 22nd Street Road, Greeley CO 80634 **R Trin Ch Greeley CO 2008-, P-in-c 2003-** B Lexington KY 1952 s Jack & Freda. BA Transylvania U 1974; MDiv Epis TS in Kentucky 1978. D 5/14/1978 P 12/17/1978 Bp Addison Hosea. m 6/23/1979 Dorie Ann Hucal. Assoc Chr Epis Ch Denver CO 2001-2003; Asst Epiph Epis Ch Denver CO 1999-2001; Adj Instr Colorado Chr U Lakewood CO 1997-2002; R Ch Of The Trsfg Evergreen CO 1989-1997; Assoc S Thos's Par Newark DE 1983-1989; Asst Ch Of The Gd Shpd Lexington KY 1981-1983; Vic S Alb's Ch Morehead KY 1979-1981. Cmnty of Aid and Hilda 1994; Third Ord, SSF 1974-1994. frjack@trinitygreeley. org

STARBUCK, Elizabeth (Ct) 88 N Main St, PO Box 983, Kent CT 06757 B Orange NJ 1958 d Leroy & Elizabeth. BA Pepperdine U 1981; MDiv Fuller TS 1985; CTh Epis TS of the SW 1993. D 6/23/1993 Bp William Elwood Sterling P 3/1/1994 Bp Claude Edward Payne. m 7/20/2002 Peter Shephard Starbuck c 2. S Mich And All Ang Par Corona Dl Mar CA 2012; Vic S Paul's Epis Ch Bantam CT 2006-2008; Kent Sch Kent CT 2001-2004; Chapl S Jos's Chap at the Kent Sch Kent CT 2001-2004; Chapl S Andr's Chap S Andrews TN 1999-2001; S Andr's-Sewanee Sch Sewanee TN 1999-2001; Assoc R H Sprt Epis Ch Houston TX 1994-1999; Asst to R S Fran Ch Houston TX 1993-1994; Chapl S Fran Day Sch Houston TX 1993-1994.

STARK, Gregory (O) D 6/1/2017 Bp Mark Hollingsworth Jr.

STARKES, Lionel Alfonso (Nev) Po Box 50763, Henderson NV 89016 **S Matt's Ch Las Vegas NV 1993-** B Greenville FL 1945 s Lester & Katie. BA Sthrn Illinois U 1975; MS Sthrn Illinois U 1984. D 4/4/1993 P 11/23/1998 Bp Stewart Clark Zabriskie. P Dio Nevada Las Vegas 1993-1998. stmatts@embarqmail. com

STARKWEATHER, Betty (ND) 679 Lehigh Dr., Merced CA 95348 B Gardenville PA 1932 d Franklin & Elsie. BA Wheaton Coll 1954; MS New York St U 1957. D 10/8/1999 P 4/23/2000 Bp Andrew Fairfield. m 8/20/1955 David Starkweather c 4.

STARR, Charles Michael (Pgh) 4048 Circle Dr, Bakerstown PA 15007 **Chapl Shadyside Hosp 1986-** B Syracuse NY 1951 s Nicholas & Florence. BA Wadhams Hall Sem Coll 1973; MA CUA 1976; DMin Pittsburgh TS 1996. Rec 10/22/1984 as Priest Bp Walter Cameron Righter. m 12/9/1990 Paulette Miriam Baer. Chapl S Lk Reg Med Cntr 1983-1986. Auth, "Dio Pittsburgh Bk Of Daily Pryr 90". Coll Chapl Pa Soc, Chapl Hosp Assn, AEHC, ACPE.

STARR, Chris (At) Church of the Atonement (Episcopal), 4945 High Point Road, Sandy Springs GA 30342 **S Jas Epis Ch of Greeneville Greeneville TN 2016-** B Atlanta GA 1952 s David & Margaret. S Marys Sem & U Baltimore; BA S Marys Sem & U Baltimore 1975; MDiv S Vinc De Paul Reg Sem Boynton Bch 1980. Rec 12/12/1993 as Priest Bp Frank Kellogg Allan. m 12/15/1984 Cecilia Kathy Wright-Starr c 1. R Ch Of The Atone Sandy Sprg GA 2008-2015, Assoc 1993-2000; Major Gift Off Epis Relief and Dvlpmt Atlanta GA 2007-2008; Epis Relief and Dvlpmt New York NY 2007-2008; Chf Exec Off Natl Kidney Fndt Atlanta GA 1995-2007; Exec Dir Henry W. Grady Fndt Atlanta GA 1992-1995; Dir of Dvlpmt Winship Cancer Cntr Emory Univ. Atlanta 1989-1991; VP Lehfeldt & Assoc Atlanta GA 1985-1989; Natl Kidney Disease Educ Prog Natl Inst of Hlth Beth MD 2003-2004. Sr. Ed, "Kidney Disease in Georgia, 2005, The People at Risk, The Power to Prevent," *Kidney Disease in Georgia, 2005, The People at Risk, The Power to Prevent*, Georgia Dept of Publ Hlth, 2005. Chas T. Weber Awd Natl Kidney Fndt Profsnl Stff Assn 2003; Bd Chairman The Hamlin Sch 1978.

STARR III, David H (Los) 6884 Burnside Dr, San Jose CA 95120 B Atlanta GA 1944 s David & Margaret. BS Georgia Inst of Tech 1968; MBA USC 1973; MDiv CDSP 2005. D 6/4/2005 P 12/3/2005 Bp William Edwin Swing. m 10/4/2008 Shelley Booth c 2. Chr Epis Ch Los Altos CA 2015-2016; Vic S Jn's Par Sn Bernrdno CA 2006-2015; Assoc R St Steph Epis Ch Los Angeles CA 2006; Dioc Coun Mem Dio Los Angeles Los Angeles CA 2009-2011. Fran Toy Multicultural Mnstry Awd CDSP 2005.

STARR, Mark Lowell (CGC) 41 Olympic Blvd, Port Townsend WA 98368 B Long Beach CA 1946 s Perry & Gayle. BA San Diego St U 1969; MDiv PrTS

1972; MA U CA 1976; CPhil U CA 1978; PhD U CA 1988. D 6/11/1981 P 12/1/1981 Bp Robert Munro Wolterstorff. m 3/25/1996 Barbara Starr c 2. S Matt's Ch Mobile AL 2004-2008; S Ptr's Ch Jackson AL 1997-2002; R Ch Of S Mart Davis CA 1983-1988; Cur S Ptr's Epis Ch Del Mar CA 1981-1983. Dawson Tchr of the Year Sprg Hill Coll 1996; Vstng Fell Epis TS of the SW 1987; Dissertation Fllshp U of CA 1979; Fllshp Natl Endwmt for Hmnts 1975.

STARR, Nancy Barnard (Mil) 76 Grange Road, Mount Eden, Auckland NZ 1024 New Zealand (Aotearoa) B Baton Rouge LA 1953 d John & Doris. BA U Roch 1975; MA U of Iowa 1978; MDiv Duke DS 1993; CAS CDSP 1994. D 1/14/1995 P 7/16/1995 Bp Roger John White. m 5/10/1976 Richard Granville Starr c 3. S Ambr Epis Ch Foster City CA 1995; D S Ambr Dio California 1994-1995.

STARR, Therese Ann (Okla) PO Box 759, Eufaula OK 74432 **D Trin Ch Eufaula OK 2011-** B St. Louis MO 1963 d John & Mary. BS S Louis U 1984. D 6/18/2011 Bp Edward Joseph Konieczny. m 4/18/1998 Morris Starr.

STARR, William Frederic (NY) 36 South Rd, Chilmark MA 02535 **Died 2/11/2017** B New Haven CT 1933 s William & Janet. BA Ya 1955; STB GTS 1958; STM GTS 1965; PhD Col 1983. D 6/11/1958 P 1/1/1960 Bp Walter H Gray. m 12/14/1974 Susan Lee Strane. Dio New York New York NY 1983-1994; Bishops Advsry Com New York NY 1973-1982; Epis Campus Min Col New York NY 1965-2002; R Gr Ch Dalton MA 1960-1964; Trin Ch On The Green New Haven CT 1958-1960; Cur Trin Ch Hartford CT 1958-1960. Auth, *Never Trust a God Over 30*. ESMHE, Epis U.

STASSER, Nina (U) 2225 S Jasmine St Unit 310, Denver CO 80222 B Goodland KS 1942 d Cecil & Phyllis. BA Colorado St U 1963; Metropltn St Coll of Denver 1982; Loretto Heights Coll 1983; U of Nthrn Colorado 1985; Adams St Coll 1991; MDiv Iliff TS 1998. D 6/6/1998 P 12/12/1998 Bp William Jerry Winterrowd. m 12/16/1962 Richard Victor Stasser c 3. Chapl DOK Dio Arizona 2013-2015; Asstg P Chr The King Ch Tucson AZ 2011-2016, Affiliate, Ret 2010-2011; St Gabr the Archangel Epis Ch Englewood CO 2007-2009; Dio Utah Salt Lake City UT 2004-2008; R S Paul's Epis Ch Vernal UT 2004-2007; S Barn Ch Glenwood Spgs CO 1999-2004; Cur Epis Ch Of S Jn The Bapt Granby CO 1998-1999; Mssn Partnership Dvlpmt and Trng Dio Colorado Denver CO 2007-2010, Coordntr Of Mutual Mnstry 1999-2006. The Ord of the DOK 2003.

STATER, Catherine J (CFla) 319 W Wisconsin Ave, Deland FL 32720 B Sparta IL 1938 d John & Nina. BGS U of Maryland 1980. D 12/11/2010 Bp John Wadsworth Howe. m 1/4/1995 Dennis L Weir.

STATEZNI, Gregory George (SJ) 7000 College Ave Apt 21, Bakersfield CA 93306 **D Quest- Real People- Real Answers- Real Ch Bakersfield CA 1997-** B Schenectady NY 1947 s George & Lenamae. BA Sonoma St U 1977; Cert Untd States Intl U 1985. D 6/14/1997 Bp David Mercer Schofield. m 1/19/1980 Deborah Lee Statezni c 4.

STATHERS JR, Birk Smith (SeFla) 208 N Lee St, Lewisburg WV 24901 **Died 5/17/2017** B Clarksburg WV 1936 s Birk & Margaret. BS U of Pennsylvania 1958; MDiv GTS 1963. D 6/5/1963 P 12/18/1963 Bp Wilburn Camrock Campbell. c 3. Chr Ch Bluefield WV 2006-2007; Int S Greg's Ch Boca Raton FL 2004-2005; Int S Thos Epis Ch Wht Sphr Spgs WV 2002-2004; Int Trin Ch Huntington WV 2000-2001; Int S Thad Epis Ch Aiken SC 1997-1998; Int Chr Ch Greenville SC 1995-1997; Int S Jn's Ch Ogdensburg NY 1994-1995; Int S Jn's Epis Ch Clearwater FL 1993-1994; Int Chr Ch Clarksburg WV 1992-1993; Int S Paul's Ch Wilkesboro NC 1990-1992; R S Matt the Apos Epis Ch Miami FL 1977-1989; Assoc Ch Of The Resurr Miami FL 1973-1977; Supply P Dio W Virginia Charleston WV 1965-1969; Vic S Tim & S Dav Nitro WV 1963-1965; Exec Bd Dio SE Florida Miami 1983-1986. Soc of S Jn the Evang 1990.

STAYNER, David (Ct) 28 Myra Rd, Hamden CT 06517 **The Rev Dr S Ptr's Epis Ch Cheshire CT 2006-; Psychol Ya 1994-** B 1951 Ya Berk; BA Duquesne U 1988; MS Mumbai U New York City 1993; PhD Mumbai U New York City 1994. D 6/21/2003 P 12/20/2003 Bp Andrew Donnan Smith. m 8/15/1987 Sandra Hardyman Stayner c 1. Gr And S Ptr's Epis Ch Hamden CT 2005.

STAYNER, Sandra Hardyman (Ct) 39 Pleasant Drive, Cheshire CT 06410 **The Rev S Ptr's Epis Ch Cheshire CT 2003-** B Bristol England UK 1953 d William & Sheila. Cert Bedford Coll 1974; Yale DS 1988; MDiv Ya Berk 1990. D 6/2/1990 P 1/26/1991 Bp Alden Moinet Hathaway. m 8/15/1987 David Stayner c 1. Ya Berk New Haven CT 1999-2003; Chr Ch Greenwich CT 1990-1999; R St. Ptr's Epis Ch Cheshire CT.

STAYTON, Darrell Lynn (Ark) PO Box 726, Stuttgart AR 72160 **Vic St. Peters Epis Ch DeValls Bluff AR. 2010-; Vic S Alb's Ch Stuttgart AR 2008-** B Pine Bluff AR 1952 s Max & Rosa Mae. BA U of Arkansas 1978; JD U of Arkansas Sch of Law 1982; Nash 2007; The Prot Epis TS 2008. D 6/7/2008 P 12/7/2008 Bp Larry Benfield. m 2/17/1979 Roberta Susan Stayton c 4.

ST CLAIR, Melinda Lee (Mont) Saint Luke's Church, 119 N 33rd St, Billings MT 59101 **R S Lk's Ch Billings MT 2016-** B Worland WY 1958 d Darrell & Molly. BS U of Wyoming 1985; MS U of Wyoming 1988; MDiv VTS 2001. D 6/2/2001 P 12/12/2001 Bp James E Waggoner Jr. R All SS Epis Ch El Paso TX 2010-2016; P S Jas Epis Ch Brewster WA 2002-2008; R S Andr's Ch Chelan WA 2001-2008; Dn, Wenatchee Dnry Dio Spokane Spokane WA

2005-2008, Stndg Com 2004-2007, Dio. Cmsn on Theol Educ 2001-2008, Dioc Coun 2001-2005. rector@stlukesbillings.org

ST CLAIRE II, Elbert Kyle (Pa) 1650 Franklin Dr, Furlong PA 18925 B Bryn Mawr PA 1945 s Elbert & Barbara. BA Hav 1968; MDiv EDS 1971; STM Yale DS 1974; MBA Tem 1982. D 6/18/1971 P 1/14/1972 Bp Robert Lionne DeWitt. m 3/24/1973 Teresa W St Claire c 2. Int Ch Of The Incarn Morrisville PA 2010-2011; Vic S Phil's Ch New Hope PA 1983-2005; Chr Ch And S Mich's Philadelphia PA 1982; Dio Pennsylvania Philadelphia PA 1981-1998, Dioc Addiction Recovery Cmsn 1981-1989; St Pauls Ch Philadelphia PA 1981; R H Trin Ch Lansdale PA 1976-1980; Stff Cler S Mk's Ch New Canaan CT 1974-1976; P-in-c S Jn's Ch New Haven CT 1973-1974; Asst Epis Acad Philadelphia PA 1971-1973; Asst The Epis Acad Newtown Sq PA 1971-1973. Soc of S Jn the Evang (Fllshp Mem).

STEADMAN, David Wilton (NCal) 756 Robinson Rd, Sebastopol CA 95472 **Died 3/11/2017** B Honolulu HI 1936 s Alva & Martha. BA Harv 1960; MA Harv 1961; MA U CA 1966; PhD Pr 1974; MA CDSP 2002; Cert Sch for Deacons 2003. D 10/16/2004 Bp Jerry Alban Lamb. c 3.

STEADMAN, Larry Kenneth (WK) 705 W 31st Ave, Hutchinson KS 67502 **Assoc Gr Epis Ch Hutchinson KS 2006-** B Hays KS 1936 s Charles & Vivian. AA Los Angeles Vlly Coll 1961. D 2/24/2001 Bp Vernon Edward Strickland P 12/21/2002 Bp James Marshall Adams Jr. m 7/14/1973 Diane M Steadman c 5. Vic S Thos Ch Garden City KS 2001-2006.

STEADMAN, Marguerite Alexandra (Me) 3116 O St Nw, Washington DC 20007 **S Jn's Ch Bangor ME 2007-** B Toronto ON CA 1969 d Richard & Mary. BA Br 1991; MDiv GTS 1997. Trans 10/7/2003 Bp Mark Sean Sisk. m 6/24/2001 Eric C H Steadman c 2. Asst Chr Ch Georgetown Washington DC 1997-2007.

STEAGALL, Patricia V (Ore) PO Box 1266, Manzanita OR 97130 **Assoc for Spanish-Lang Mnstry The Kaleidoscope Inst 2011-; S Cathr Of Alexandria Epis Ch Nehalem OR 2008-; Anti-Racism Mnstrs Fac Prov VIII San Diego CA 2015-; Cmsn to End Racism and Anti-Racism Trnr Dio Oregon Portland OR 2008-** B Mexico City Mexico 1962 d William & Consuelo. BA Trin U San Antonio 1985; MDiv Epis TS of the SW 2004. D 6/11/2004 Bp Joseph Jon Bruno P 1/14/2006 Bp Frank Tracy Griswold III. m 9/23/1989 Jerry Millard c 2. H Cross Epis Ch Boring OR 2008-2013; Chapl St. Vinc's Hosp Portland OR 2007-2008; S Wilfrid Of York Epis Ch Huntington Bch CA 2005-2007; Prov VIII Rep to the Anti-Racism Com Exec Coun Appointees New York NY 2012-2015; Dioc Coun Rep Dio Oregon 2009-2015.

STEARNS, Fellow Clair (ECR) Po Box 2789, Saratoga CA 95070 **Assoc S Andr's Ch Saratoga CA 1974-** B San Jose CA 1939 s Elwin & Bertha. U CA 1964. D 1/2/1972 P 5/1/1975 Bp Chauncie Kilmer Myers. m 9/21/1963 Molly Mattewson Wool.

STEARNS, H Joanne (SO) 5380 Dovetree Blvd. Apt 10, Moraine OH 45439 B Detroit MI 1938 d John & Kathryn. BA Aquinas Coll 1984; MDiv CDSP 1984. D 6/8/1985 P 6/7/1986 Bp William Edwin Swing. c 1. Ret Affilliate P S Geo's Epis Ch Dayton OH 2006-2010; Chapl Fairborn Police Dept OH 1998-2001; R S Chris's Ch Fairborn OH 1993-2005; Asst to R S Phil's Ch Durham NC 1989-1993; Assoc R Ch Of The H Nativ Honolulu HI 1986-1989; D Ch Of The Resurr Pleasant Hil CA 1985-1986; Dioc Coun Dio Sthrn Ohio Cincinnati OH 1995-1998.

STEARNS, Samuel D (RG) 3705 Utah St Ne, Albuquerque NM 87110 **D S Mary's Epis Ch Albuquerque NM 1997-** B Seattle WA 1930 s Samuel & Constance. BS Stan 1953; MS U of New Mex 1962; Ds U of New Mex 1962. D 11/21/1997 Bp Terence Kelshaw. m 6/19/1993 Mary Esther Stearns. D Epis Ch Of The Epiph Socorro NM 1998-2005.

STEBBINS JR, George Griswold (CFla) 1219 Augustine Dr, The Villages-Lady Lake FL 32159 **Died 2/9/2016** B Madison WI 1930 s George & Berenice. BA U of Wisconsin 1952; MD U of Wisconsin 1955; Amer Bd Surgery 1965; FACS Amer Coll of Surgeons 1967; Amer Coll of Emergency Physicians 1988. D 6/15/1975 Bp William Hopkins Folwell. m 8/3/1951 Alice Ruth Stebbins c 4. S Geo Epis Ch The Villages FL 1998-2016; Asst D S Geo's Epis Ch The Villages FL 1998-2016; Asst Ch of the Resurr Sautee Nacoochee GA 1997-1998; Asst Gr-Calv Epis Ch Clarkesville GA 1988-1997; Asst H Cross Ch Winter Haven FL 1975-1988. Auth, "Med arts". Assn Mltry Surgeons; Chr Med Soc; FGBM-FI; NAAD; Ord of S Lk.

STEBBINS, Martha E (NC) **R S Tim's Ch Wilson NC 2010-; Dioc Chr Formation Com Dio No Carolina Raleigh NC 2011-** B Fort Belvoir VA 1960 DVM No Carolina St U Coll of Veterinary Medici 1987; MPH U NC Sch of Publ Hlth 1991; PhD No Carolina St U Coll of Veterinary Medici 1994; MDiv Epis TS of the SW 2005. D 6/26/2005 P 12/28/2005 Bp Michael B Curry. m 7/2/1993 Robert W Grudier c 1. P All SS Ch Hamlet NC 2005-2010; Assoc S Dav's Epis Ch Laurinburg NC 2005-2010; Cluster Mssnr Sandhills Cluster Carthage NC 2005-2010.

STEBER, Gary David (NC) 406 Lorimer Road, Box 970, Davidson NC 28036 B Mobile AL 1937 s David & Sydney. BS U So 1959; MA Ya 1964; MDiv Sewanee: The U So, TS 1979. D 6/6/1979 P 4/27/1980 Bp George Mosley Murray. m 7/24/1982 Linda Gay Steber c 2. Int S Paul's Ch Monroe NC 2009-2010; S

Alb's Ch Davidson NC 1994-2002; S Lk's Ch Salisbury NC 1992-1994; R S Mths Epis Ch Tuscaloosa AL 1987-1992; Vic The Ch Of The Redeem Mobile AL 1982-1987; Cur All SS Epis Ch Mobile AL 1980-1982; Cur The Epis Ch Of The Nativ Dothan AL 1979-1980; Cur S Paul's Ch Mobile AL 1979; Par Dvlpmt Com Dio Alabama Birmingham 1990-1992; Stndg Com Dio Cntrl Gulf Coast Pensacola FL 1985-1987.

STEBINGER, Peter A R (Ct) 615 Bethmour Rd, Bethany CT 06524 **Missional P S Paul's Epis Ch Bantam CT 2015-; Chapl/EMT CT-1 Disaster Med Assis Team Hartford CT 2006-; Bd Mem WIKS NGO - Nairobi Kenya 2006-; Dioc Disaster Coordntr - ER&D Dio Connecticut Meriden CT 2011-** B London England UK 1954 s Arnold & Jean. BA Bow 1976; MDiv Yale DS 1980; MA U of Connecticut 1997. D 6/14/1980 Bp Morgan Porteus P 2/26/1981 Bp Arthur Edward Walmsley. m 6/5/1976 Caron Stebinger c 2. Missional P S Andr's Ch Milford CT 2013-2014; Hospice Chapl VNS of Connecticut 2012-2015; Chapl Hartford Hosp Hartford CT 2011-2017; Adj Fac, D. Min. Prog Bexley Seabury Fed Chicago IL 2002-2007; R Chr Ch Bethany CT 1982-2011; Field Educ Supvsr Yale DS New Haven CT 1982-2011; Cur S Jn's Epis Par Waterbury CT 1980-1982; Pstr Counslr S Raphael Hosp New Haven CT 1979-1981. Auth, "Congrl Paths to Holiness," Forw Mvmt, 2000; Auth, "Faith, Focus & Ldrshp," Forw Mvmt, 1990; Auth, "Var arts". Assoc of Profsnl Chapl 2012; IC-ISF 1995. Hon Cn Schlr Chr Ch Cathd 1998; Resrch Grant ECF 1994.

STECH, Ernest William (Mich) 20500 W Old US Highway 12, Chelsea MI 48118 **P S Barn' Ch Chelsea MI 2010-** B Denver CO 1961 s Ernest & Cynthia. BS Ferris St U 1983; MS Estrn Michigan U 2004. D 1/30/2010 P 11/20/2010 Bp Wendell Nathaniel Gibbs Jr. m 11/8/1986 Margaret Stech c 2.

STECKER IV, Rick (NH) Box 293, New London NH 03257 **Degree Advsry Bd Boston Grad Sch of Psychoanalysis Brookline MA. USA 2016-; P Assoc Emm Ch Boston MA 2014-** B Fairmont WV 1946 s Frederick & Virginia. BA U So 1968; BA U So 1968; MDiv VTS 1972; Proctor Schlr EDS 1984; D.Min. Bangor TS 1994; Ya 2007; Psya.D. Boston Grad Sch of Psychoanalysis 2008; Psya.D. Boston Grad Sch of Psychoanalysis 2008; Fell Sewanee: The U So, TS 2008; Sewanee: The U So, TS 2008. D 6/17/1972 Bp John Mc Gill Krumm P 12/18/1972 Bp Lyman Cunningham Ogilby. m 8/28/1971 Ann Page Stecker c 1. Adj Assoc Prof Colby-Sawyer Coll 1995-2011; Vol for Mssn Dio Vrgn Islands Charlotte Amalie St Thom VI 1995-1996; R S Andr's Ch New London NH 1979-2002; Emm Par Epis Ch Sthrn Pines NC 1977-1979; Asst All SS Ch Wynnewood PA 1972-1977; Chair Bd Trst of the Boston Grad Sch of Psychoanal 2010-2016; Mem Bd Trst of the Boston Grad Sch of Psychoanal 1999-2016. Ed, "I Win,We Lose: The New Soc Darwinism and the Death of Love," *The Writings of The Rev. Jn H. Snow*, Wipf & Stock, 2015; Auth, "The Podium, the Pulpit, and the Republicans: How Presidential Candidates Use Rel Langguage in Amer Politics," Praeger, 2011; Auth, "Var arts," *Epis, Living Ch, Cornerstone Proj, Clio's Psyche*.

STECKLINE, Donna Louise (Alb) P.O. Box 345, Gilbertsville NY 13776 **Chr Ch Gilbertsville NY 2013-; Chapl Hospice & Palliative Care of Chenango Cnty 2008-** B Norwich NY 1961 d John & Ann. AAS SUNY - Cobleskill 1981. D 5/10/2008 Bp William Howard Love. m 7/14/1990 Kevin Steckline c 2. S Steph's Ch Delmar NY 2002-2004.

STEDMAN, David Algernon (WNY) Po Box 7488, St Thomas VI 00801 B Mandeville JM 1941 s Algernon & Enid. S Peters Theol Coll 1965. Trans 8/1/1988 Bp Egbert Don Taylor. St Pauls Ch-Sea Cow Bay Sea Cows Bay 1998-2006; Vic S Paul's Epis/Angl Ch 1988-2006; Dio Vrgn Islands Charlotte Amalie St Thom VI 1988-1997; Serv Ch In Jamaica 1965-1981.

STEED, John Griffith (NJ) 11b Portsmouth St, Whiting NJ 08759 B Dayton OH 1942 s James & Marion. BA OH SU 1964; MA OH SU 1965; MDiv GTS 1971; BA No Carolina Wesleyan Coll 1987; MA No Carolina Cntrl U 1993. D 6/26/1971 P 5/30/1972 Bp Robert Fisher Gibson Jr. m 12/19/1965 Mary Lou Steed c 1. R S Steph's Ch Manchester Twp NJ 1999-2004; R Trin Ch Scotland Neck NC 1993-1998; Supply P Ch Of The Epiph Rocky Mt NC 1991-1993; Chr Ch Rocky Mt NC 1989-1993; R Chr Ch Rocky Mtn NC 1989-1993; R S Jos's Ch Durham NC 1975-1989; Assoc S Tim's Ch Wilson NC 1972-1975; Cur S Steph's Epis Ch Culpeper VA 1971-1972. CT.

STEED, Ronald Scott (Ct) 95 Route 2a, Preston CT 06365 B San Diego CA 1959 s Vedder & Charleen. BSEE Cit 1981; Mstr Engr Mgt Old Dominion U 2004. D 1/28/2017 Bp Ian Theodore Douglas. m 8/20/1983 Roxanne Kirby Steed c 2.

STEEDMAN SANBORN, Marda Leigh (Oly) Diocese of Olympia, 1551 10th Ave E, Seattle WA 98102 **Secy Of Conv Dio Olympia Seattle 2011-** B Chelsea MA 1951 d Allen & Marguerite. Cert Olympia TS; BA U of Washington 1972; MEd U of Washington minor in Speech 1974; EdD Seattle U minor in Theol Stds 1991. D 1/27/1992 P 11/22/1996 Bp Vincent Waydell Warner. m 8/27/1988 Douglas C Sanborn c 1. R S Jas Epis Ch Kent WA 1997-2014; P S Mk's Cathd Seattle WA 1992-1997. Auth, "Coping w Stress: The Kindergarten Fndt," 1991. msanborn@ecww.org

STEELE, Christopher Andrew (Dal) 11122 Midway Rd, Dallas TX 75229 **S Mary's Epis Ch And Sch Irving TX 2015-** B Nashville TN 1972 s Edward & Carol. BA U of Alabama 1994; MDiv Mundelein Sem 2000. Rec 7/16/2014 Bp Paul Emil Lambert. m 3/16/2007 Concepcion Piloto. Ch Of The Gd Shpd Dallas TX 2015; Int S Lk's Epis Ch Dallas TX 2015. csteele12@gmail.com

STEELE, Christopher Candace (Oly) 7747 31st Ave Sw, Seattle WA 98126 **Non-par 1989-** B Meeker CO 1952 d Volney & Joan. Colgate Rochester Crozer DS; CRDS; GTS; U So 1975; CDSP 1979. D 7/22/1979 P 1/1/1980 Bp Jackson Earle Gilliam. S Clem's Epis Ch Seattle WA 2005-2008; S Catherines Ch Enumclaw WA 2004-2005; S Andr's Epis Ch Tacoma WA 2002; Trin Ch Houston TX 2000-2001; S Fran Ch Houston TX 1999-2000; S Lk's Epis Hosp Houston TX 1986-1989; Chapl S Lk's Epis Hosp Houston TX 1986-1989; Palmer Memi Ch Houston TX 1984-1985; The Epis Ch Of The Gd Shpd Berkeley CA 1983-1984; Ch Of The H Sprt Missoula MT 1979-1980. Auth, "Aids In Tx: Facing The Crisis". Associated Parishes, Cmnty Of Cross Nails Coventry Engl. Arthur Lichtenberger Fllshp 1976; Assoc Dir Legis & Plcy, Hlth Law Plcy Inst U Houston 95; Helen Farabee Fell 90-93; No Amer Mnstrl Fell 76-79.

STEELE, Gary Ross (Ak) 2708 W 65th Ave, Anchorage AK 99502 **Int Gloria Dei Luth Ch 2013-; Supply P Dio Alaska Fairbanks AK 2002-** B Anchorage AK 1962 s Ira & Ione. BA Mid Amer Chr U 1984; MDiv Sthrn Bapt TS 1991. D 10/18/1999 P 3/26/2000 Bp Mark Lawrence Macdonald. m 4/30/1988 Treva Rene Steele c 2. Int St. Mk Luth Chruch Anchorage AK 2009-2011; Int Amazing Gr Luth Ch 2008; Chr Ch Anchorage AK 2000-2002; P-in-c S Mary's Ch Anchorage AK 2000-2001; Serv Amer And Sthrn Bapt 1992-1999; Serv Two Non-Denominational Ch 1984-1988.

STEELE, James Logan (Chi) 317 Goold Park Dr, Morris IL 60450 **R S Thos Ch Morris IL 1971-** B Chicago IL 1944 s Fred & Edith. BA U Chi 1965; MDiv GTS 1968. D 6/15/1968 Bp James Winchester Montgomery P 12/21/1968 Bp Gerald Francis Burrill. Dn Kankakee Dnry 2000-2006; Pres Chicago CCU 1996-2005; Dn Kankakee Dnry 1990-1996; BACAM Dio Chicago Chicago IL 1973-1986, Dioc Coun 1972-1978, Dioc Coun 2000-2003, Dioc Coun 1990-1999, COM 1976-1989; Vic Gr Ch Sterling IL 1968-1971; The Ch Of S Anne Morrison IL 1968-1971; Del to GC - Dep 1994 & 1997 Alt. 200 Dio Chicago. Auth, *arts Ch Pub*. CCU; CBS; SOM; SSC.

STEELE, Kelly Ann (Ga) **GOE Exam Chapl COM Savannah GA 2015-** B Oakdale PA 1991 d William & Sandra. BA Duquesne U 2012; MDiv Duke DS 2015. D 11/14/2015 P 5/21/2016 Bp Scott Anson Benhase. m 5/3/2014 Guillermo Alejandro Arboleda. AAR 2012. scl Duke DS 2015.

STEELE, Lawrence Jay (Los) 490 E Indian School Ln, Banning CA 92220 **D S Alb's Epis Ch Yucaipa CA 2007-; Asstg S Alb's Mssn Yucaipa CA 2007-; Police Chapl Banning Police Dept 2005-; Asstg Gr Epis Ch 2002-** B Kansas City KS 1939 s John & Ruth. MS USC 1972; ETSBH 1998. D 10/30/1999 Bp Chester Lovelle Talton. c 2. Asstg S Agnes Mssn Banning CA 1989-2002.

STEELE, Nancy J (EMich) PO Box 452, Chesaning MI 48616 B Flint MI 1947 d Keith & Victoria. BS MI SU 1969. D 8/17/2007 P 2/23/2008 Bp Steven Todd Ousley. m 11/22/1969 Jonathan Steele c 2. P S Albans Epis Ch Bay City MI 2012-2013.

STEELE, Robert Emanuel (Nwk) 250 Kawaihae St Apt 1b, Honolulu HI 96825 **Non-par 1970-** B Mobile AL 1943 s Rollie & Minnie. BA Morehouse Coll 1965; MDiv EDS 1968; MPH Ya 1971; MS Ya 1974; PhD Ya 1975. D 11/30/1968 Bp George E Rath. m 6/6/1967 Jean Elizabeth Acker c 1. Auth, "Suicide In The Black Cmnty". Assn of Yale Alum Gvrng Bd 2003-2006; Assn of Yale Alum in Publ Hlth, Pres 2000-2004; EDS Bd Trst 2008; Sigma Xi 1975; Yale Art Gallery Gvrng Bd 2003. Benny Lifetime Alum Awd Morehouse Coll 2016; Dr. Anna Julia Hayward Cooper hon Awd UBE 2016; Afr Amer Art Lifetime Achievement Awd Howard Univerity 2012; Yale Medal Yale Univerity 2012; Distinquished Alum Awd Yale Univerity 2007; Outstanding Donor EDS 2006; Man of the Year Morehouse Coll 1995.

STEELE, Sean William (Tex) St. Isidore Episcopal, 3901 S Panther Creek Dr, The Woodlands TX 77381 **Cur Trin Epis Ch The Woodlands TX 2012-** B Omaha NE 1979 s William & Irene. BBA U of Texas Austin 2001; MA Creighton U 2005; MDiv Epis TS of the SW 2012. D 6/16/2012 P 5/8/2013 Bp C Andrew Doyle. m 10/12/2002 Rebecca Nancy Steele c 3. sean@isidores.org

STEEN, James James (Chi) 749 Holland St, Saugatuck MI 49453 B Tulsa OK 1944 s Sidney & Flora. BA W&L 1966; MDiv GTS 1969. D 6/29/1969 Bp Chilton R Powell P 12/27/1969 Bp Frederick Warren Putnam. m 11/26/2011 Thomas Chesrown c 1. Dir of Mnstrs Dio Chicago Chicago IL 2011-2016, Bp's Dep for Congregations and Admin 2011; R Ch Of S Paul And The Redeem Chicago IL 1998-2010; P-in-c S Mk's Ch Washington DC 1996-1998; Exec Dir Prism Parishes Inc Washington DC 1995-1996; Pres Gts Alum The GTS New York NY 1992-1996; R S Pat's Ch Washington DC 1979-1994; Assoc The Ch Of S Lk In The Fields New York NY 1976-1979; Trin Par New York NY 1975-1976; Assoc Trin Ch Princeton NJ 1972-1975; Cur S Thos Epis Ch Medina WA 1970-1972; Cur S Dunst's Ch Tulsa OK 1969-1970; The ECF Champaign IL 1969-1970; Chapl U Tulsa 1969-1970.

STEEVER JR, Raymond George Edward (Los) Route 1, Box 109, Pullman WA 99163 **D S Paul's Epis Ch Ventura CA 2007-; Asst S Jas 1980-** B Dallas TX 1943 s Raymond & Ruth. BS WA SU 1965. D 12/13/1980 Bp Leigh Allen Wallace Jr. m 7/6/1968 F Rebecca Cohen c 2.

STEEVES, Joan Altpeter (Colo) 6337 Deframe Way, Arvada CO 80004 B Plymouth MA 1935 d Leland & Mabel. BA U of Massachusetts 1957; Bishops Inst for Diac Formation 1992. D 10/24/1992 Bp William Jerry Winterrowd. m 9/8/1956 Carl Richard Steeves c 3. D The Ch Of Chr The King (Epis) Arvada CO 1992-2010. NAAD 1992.

STEEVES, Timothy (Pa) 409 E Lancaster Ave, Downingtown PA 19335 **R S Jas' Epis Ch Downington PA 2005-; Chapl (LtCol) US-A 1975-** B Chelsea MA 1945 s Frederick & Zona. MA Bos; MS Col; New York Psychoanalytic Soc and Inst; BA U of Massachusetts; MDiv VTS. D 6/9/1973 Bp John Melville Burgess P 12/1/1973 Bp William Hopkins Folwell. m 7/21/1984 Deborah M Steeves c 4. R S Jas' Epis Ch Downingtown PA 2005-2013; Assoc R S Thos' Ch Whitemarsh Ft Washington PA 2000-2005; Bdgt Com Dio Virginia Richmond VA 1995-1997, T/F on Sexual Misconduct in Pstr Care 1994-2000, Ecum Cmsn 1993-1995; Montross & Washington Par King Geo VA 1990-2000; S Jas Ch Montross VA 1990-2000; R S Ptr's Ch Oak Grove Oak Grove VA 1990-2000; Chapl Connecticut Hospice Branford CT 1984-1987; Asst R Trin Ch Branford CT 1984-1985; R S Jas' Ch New Haven CT 1983-1984; Trin Ch On The Green New Haven CT 1978-1981; Pstr Hlth U Ch 1975-1978; Cur S Jas Epis Ch Ormond Bch FL 1973-1975. Auth, "arts & Bk Revs," 2003. ACSW; Mltry Chapl Assn.

STEFANIK, Alfred Thomas (Vt) 49 Raintree Circle, Palm Coast FL 32164 **Asst S Thos Flagler Cnty Palm Coast FL 2014-** B Copaigue NY 1939 s Alfred & Julia. BA Cathd Coll of the Immac Concep 1961; STB CUA 1965; MA S Michaels Coll Vermont 1970. Rec 8/15/1977 as Deacon Bp Robert Shaw Kerr. m 10/3/1969 Claire H Stefanik c 2. Vol Chapl Copley Hosp Morrisville VT 2009-2014; S Jn's In The Mountains Stowe VT 2009-2010; S Jn The Bapt Epis Hardwick VT 2007-2009; Int Gr Ch Vineyard Haven MA 2004-2006; P-in-c H Innoc' Epis Ch Lahaina HI 2002-2004; R Trin Epis Ch Roslyn NY 1996-2002; R Trin Ch Shelburne VT 1988-1996; Campus Min Dio Vermont Burlington VT 1987-1988, Chapl to Ret Cler and Spouses/Partnr 2008-2010; Vic Trin Milton VT 1984-1987; Chapl Epis/Luth Campus Mnstry NE Syndod LCA & ELCA 1983-1988; Campus Min Cathd Ch Of S Paul Burlington VT 1983-1987; R S Fran Mssn Johnson VT 1977-1983; Cur RC Dio Rockville Cntr Rockville Cn-tr 1964-1969. Auth, "Short Changing Our Yth," *Epis Life*, 1988; Auth, "Copycat Sam: Developing Ties w A Spec Chld," Human Sciences Press NYC, 1982; Auth, "Grandma'S Halloween," Burlington Free Press VT, 1978; Auth, "Bread Making On The Rise," *New York Times*, 1975; Auth, "Striped Bass Out Back," *E Coast Fisherman*, 1970. astefanik@cfl.rr.com

STEFFENHAGEN, Leverne Richard (WNY) 9705 Niagara Falls Blvd Apt 19, Niagara Falls NY 14304 **Non-par 1989-** B Cheektowaga NY 1932 s Louis & Regina. D 6/9/1984 Bp Harold Barrett Robinson. Asst to R St Mk Epis Ch No Tonawanda NY 1984-1989.

STEFFENSEN, Leslie N (Va) Grace Episcopal Church, 3601 Russell Rd, Alexandria VA 22305 **Epis Ch Cntr New York NY 2017-** B Bartow FL 1967 d Charles & Rhona Charlotte. BA The JHU 1988; MTS VTS 2006; MDiv VTS 2012. D 6/2/2012 Bp Ted Gulick Jr P 12/15/2012 Bp Shannon Sherwood Johnston. m 10/2/1989 Kirk A Steffensen c 3. Gr Epis Ch Alexandria VA 2012-2017.

STEFKO, Nadia M (Chi) 3857 N Kostner Ave, Chicago IL 60641 **Assoc Chr Ch Winnetka IL 2016-** B Pittsburgh PA 1982 d Daniel & Mary Ann. D 6/20/2015 P 4/9/2016 Bp Jeff Lee. m 1/2/2010 Stephen Thorngate c 2. nadia@christchurchwinnetka.org

STEGELMANN, Dawn M (Ct) 651 Pequot Ave, Southport CT 06890 **S Lk's Par Darien CT 2015-; Sprtl Dir, Annand Prog Ya Berk New Haven CT 2011-** B Moline IL 1961 d Larry & Julie. BA Hillsdale Coll 1983; MDiv Ya Berk 2008. D 6/14/2008 Bp Andrew Donnan Smith P 2/7/2009 Bp James Elliot Curry. c 3. Assoc Trin Epis Ch Southport CT 2008-2015. dawn.stegelmann@saintlukesdarien.org

STEIDL, Gerald Scobie (CFla) 127 E Cottesmore Cir, Longwood FL 32779 **D H Trin Epis Ch Fruitland Pk FL 2013-; D Epis Ch Of The H Sprt Apopka FL 1997-** B Cincinnati OH 1942 s Nelson & Alice. Mia; U Cinc; AA Seminole Cmnty Coll 1996; Inst for Chr Stds Dio Cntrl Florida 1997. D 12/13/1997 Bp John Wadsworth Howe. m 7/16/1966 Susan Richter Steidl c 3. HabHum- Pres; Honduras Med Missions; Prison Mnstry, Chapl & Kairos.

STEIG, George Terrance (Oly) 5241 12th Ave Ne, Seattle WA 98105 **Asst S Andr's Ch Seattle WA 2000-** B Longview MA 1948 s George & Margaret. BA S Thos Coll Kenmore WA 1970; STB Pontifical U of S Thos Aquinas Angelicum IT 1973; MA Gregorian U 1974; MEd U of Puget Sound 1983. Rec 6/22/1989 as Priest Bp Robert Hume Cochrane. m 8/16/1980 Theresa Lee Forhan c 2.

STEILBERG, Isabel Fourqurean (SVa) 221 34th St, Newport News VA 23607 **Stndg Commitee Dio Sthrn Virginia Newport News VA 2000-, 1994-1997, Mssn & Mnstry Fndt 1998-, Chair Dept Outreach Mnstrs 1994-1997** B 1941 d Henry & Lightfoot. Duke 1960; BA U NC 1962; MA Virginia Commonwealth U 1981; MDiv VTS 1992. D 6/7/1992 P 12/19/1992 Bp Frank Harris Vest Jr. m 9/22/1962 Robert Steilberg. R S Paul's Ch Newport News VA 1996-2013; Vic Chr King Poquoson VA 1994-1996; Chr The King Epis Ch Yorktown VA 1994-1996; S Andr's Epis Ch Newport News VA 1992-1994.

STEIN, Edward Lee (Tex) 717 Sage Rd, Houston TX 77056 B Houston TX 1947 s Edward & Laura. BA U So 1969; MDiv VTS 1972. D 6/28/1972 Bp Frederick P Goddard P 6/1/1973 Bp James Milton Richardson. Cn Precentor Chr Ch Cathd Houston TX 2000-2013; The Great Cmsn Fndt Houston TX 1996-2000; Asst S Bede Epis Ch Houston TX 1972-1999; S Mart's Epis Ch Houston TX 1972-1996.

STEINBACH, Frederick Leo (Ia) PO Box 838, Chariton IA 50049 **Vic S Andr's Ch Chariton IA 2014-** B 1949 s Louis & Gay. B.S U of Nthrn Iowa 1973; M.S Mankato St 1980; MS Mankato St 1980; Ed.S U of Wyoming 1994; Wartburg TS 2013; TEEM Wartburg TS 2013. D 12/7/2013 P 7/6/2014 Bp Alan Scarfe. m 5/24/1997 Sherry Pauline Toombs c 4.

STEINER IV, John (Md) 7474 Washington Blvd, Elkridge MD 21075 B Washington DC 1947 s John & Blanche. BS VMI 1969; MS U of Florida 1977; MDiv GTS 1988. D 5/28/1988 P 12/1/1988 Bp James Michael Mark Dyer. m 9/3/1972 Carolyn Steiner c 2. R Trin Ch Waterloo Elkridge MD 1993-2013; Asst R Ch Of The Gd Shpd Towson MD 1990-1993; P Gr Epis Ch Allentown PA 1988-1990.

STEINER, Scott A (Mich) B 1975 s Robert & Henrietta. Bexley-Seabury; B.A. Sacr Heart Major Sem 1999; A.A.S. Henry Ford Coll 2007. D 12/12/2015 P 6/11/2016 Bp Wendell Nathaniel Gibbs Jr. m 8/6/2013 Mary K Weise c 2. S Jn's Ch Royal Oak MI 2016-2017.

STEINFELD, John Wilfred (Nev) 915 Gear St, Reno NV 89503 **S Nich Mssn Tahoe City CA 2007-** B Philadelphia PA 1933 s Hans & Irma. BA U CO 1955; MDiv SWTS 1967. D 6/5/1967 P 12/21/1967 Bp Joseph Summerville Minnis. c 2. Trin Epis Ch Reno NV 1993-2000; Chr The King Quincy CA 1991-2001; Vic S Cuth's Epis Ch Oakland CA 1971-1974; Assoc S Mk's Epis Ch Palo Alto CA 1969-1971; S Andr's Epis Ch Ft Lupton CO 1967-1969; Vic S Eliz's Epis Ch Brighton CO 1967-1969.

STEINHAUER, Roger Kent (Roch) 25 Chadbourne Rd, Rochester NY 14618 **Non-par 1978-** B 1935 s William & Charlotte. BA Amh 1956; BD UTS 1959. D 6/13/1959 P 3/1/1960 Bp Nelson Marigold Burroughs. m 1/5/1974 Maryanne Hamilton c 2. Dept Of Chr Soc Relatns 1963-1967; P-in-c The Epis Ch of The Redeem Jacksonville FL 1962-1967; Actg Chapl Florida St U 1961-1962; Epis U Cntr Tallahassee FL 1959-1962; Assoc Chapl Florida St U 1959-1961.

STEINHAUSER, Elizabeth (Mass) 419 Shawmut Ave., Boston MA 02118 **Yth Dir S Steph's Epis Ch Boston MA 2008-** B New York, NY 1967 d Richard & Elizabeth. BA Colg 1989; MDiv Harvard DS 1996; Cert Ang Stud EDS 2007. D 6/7/2008 Bp M(Arvil) Thomas Shaw P 1/10/2009 Bp Roy Frederick Cederholm Jr. m 6/3/2004 Cora Roelofs c 1.

STELK, Lincoln Frank (NY) 241 Bluff Rd, Yarmouth ME 04096 **Ret 1998-** B Chicago IL 1934 s Lincoln & Anna. BA Ohio Wesl 1956; BD EDS 1964. D 6/27/1964 Bp Paul Moore Jr P 1/16/1965 Bp William Foreman Creighton. m 6/17/1960 Virginia Jo Horn c 3. R S Mary's Ch Mohegan Lake NY 1987-1998; Int S Tim's Ch Macedonia OH 1986-1987; R Harcourt Par Gambier OH 1977-1986; Chapl Ken Gambier OH 1977-1984; Chapl Ken Gambier OH 1977-1984; R Dio Sthrn Ohio Cincinnati OH 1976-1977, Mem, Dioc Coun 1971-1977, Mem, Liturg Cmsn 1967-1974; R S Ptr's Epis Ch Delaware OH 1966-1977; Dept CSR Dio Ohio Cleveland 1978-1984. BD Bex 1982.

STELLE, Eric Arthur (Oly) 7701 Skansie Ave, Gig Harbor WA 98335 **Rev S Jn's Epis Ch Gig Harbor WA 2011-** B Vallejo CA 1971 s David & Rosalind. BA U CA Los Angeles 1994; MDiv Other 2002; MDiv Other 2002; MDiv Regent Coll 2002; DAS Other 2009; DAS Sewanee: The U So, TS 2009. D 5/19/2009 P 12/18/2009 Bp Henry Nutt Parsley Jr. m 8/18/2001 Cynthia Tidwell Stelle c 2. Reverend All SS Epis Ch Birmingham AL 2009-2011.

STELLMAN, Jill (Alb) Episcopal Diocese Of Albany, 580 Burton Rd, Greenwich NY 12834 **S Jn's Ch Richfld Spgs NY 2016-; Chr Ch Herkimer NY 2013-; Cmncatn and Tech Off Dio Albany Greenwich NY 2012-** B Chicago IL 1966 BA NE Illinois U 1995; MBA Baylor U 1998; MS De Paul U 2004; MDiv Nash 2012. D 6/2/2012 P 1/5/2013 Bp William Howard Love. m 5/18/1996 Paul Michael Androski. Asstg P Cathd Of All SS Albany NY 2012-2013. jstellman@albanydiocese.org

STELZ, Patricia A (NH) 466 Summit House, West Chester PA 19382 **Died 2/21/2016** B Mt Vernon NY 1948 d Ernest & Catherine. BA U of New Hampshire 1991; MSW Bos 1997; MDiv Bos TS 1997; CTh EDS 2004. D 6/11/2005 P 12/17/2005 Bp Vicky Gene Robinson. m 5/15/2010 Edward G Rice c 2. Dio Massachusetts Boston MA 2015-2016; S Dunstans Epis Ch Dover MA 2014-2015; Int S Mich's Epis Ch Holliston MA 2013-2016; Int All SS Epis Ch Oakville CT 2011-2012; Assoc The Ch Of The H Trin W Chester PA 2005-2011; Yth Dir Dio New Hampshire Concord NH 2000-2005; Anti-Racism Cmsn Dio Pennsylvania Philadelphia PA 2006-2010.

STEN, Pamela V (WMich) 605 W 4th St Apt 2, Buchanan MI 49107 B Towanda PA 1951 d Michael & Mary. BS Penn 1972; MDiv SWTS 2002. D 6/8/2002 Bp Edward Lewis Lee Jr P 12/21/2002 Bp Bill Persell. c 2. P-in-c Trin Ch Niles MI 2013-2015; R S Paul's Epis Ch St Jos MI 2007-2013; Asst R S Dav's Ch Glenview IL 2002-2007.

STENNER, David Anthony (Md) 203 E Chatsworth Ave, Reisterstown MD 21136 **Congrl Dvlpmt Com Dio Maryland Baltimore MD 2006-** B Oakland CA 1949 s Donald & Evelyn. AA Chabot Coll 1969; BA S Marys Coll Moraga

CA 1984; MDiv TESM 1988; DMin SWTS 2005. D 9/17/1988 P 3/17/1989 Bp John Lester Thompson III. m 6/17/1972 Janet C Stenner c 3. Dio Maryland Baltimore MD 2006-2008; R All SS Epis Ch Reisterstown MD 1998-2015; Chapl Fortuna Police Dept Fortuna CA 1995-1998; Vic S Fran Ch Fortuna CA 1988-1998; Exec Com Capital Funds Cmpgn The Epis Dio Nthrn California Sacramento CA 1995-1997, Bp's Search Com 1990-1994. allsaints_church@verizon.net

STENNETTE, Lloyd Roland (SeFla) PO Box 11383, Miami FL 33101 B Limon 1936 s Ridley & Emeline. BA Colegio Nocturno De Limon Cr 1964; Centro de Estudios Teologicos 1967; Epis TS of the SW 1983. D 7/10/1966 P 7/1/1968 Bp David Emrys Richards. m 1/25/1969 Doris Ritchie Watts Stennette. Ch Of S Andr The Apos Camden NJ 1990-1997; Dio New York New York NY 1986-1989; Mision San Pablo New York NY 1986-1989; S Ann's Ch Of Morrisania Bronx NY 1986; R S Jos The Workman Cienequito Limon Costa Rica 1976-1981; R S Mk Limon Costa Rica 1971-1975; St Marks Ch 1969-1976; P-in-c H Sprt In Tela-Atlantida Tela-Atlantida Honduras 1968-1969; Dio Costa Rica San Jose 1966-1976. Auth, "Stations Of The Cross In Spanish".

STENNING, Gordon J (RI) 36 Brant Rd, Portsmouth RI 02871 Ret 1995- B Providence RI 1930 s John & Ethel. BA Br 1952; STB Other 1955. D 6/24/1955 P 3/24/1956 Bp John S Higgins. m 6/28/1952 Barbara Stenning c 2. Pres Bible & Common PB Soc. 1992-1996; VP and Secy The CPG New York NY 1988-1995; Natl Exec Coun 1987-1989; Pres Prov 1 Prov One 1984-1986; Dep - Rhode Island GC 1964-1988; Chair, Exec Com Seaman's Ch Inst Newport RI 1960-1986; Del Prov 1 Prov One 1959-1986; R S Mary's Ch Portsmouth RI 1957-1988; Cur S Paul's Ch Pawtucket RI 1955-1957; Chair Exec Com Ovrs Mssns Dio Rhode Island Providence RI 1983-1988, Dioc Coun 1970-1982, Dn Aquidnock Deanry 1969, 1958-1968. Portsmouth Citizen of the Year 1980.

STEPHENS, Jeff (U) 2141 Horizon View Dr, St George UT 84790 B Los Angeles CA 1933 s Jefferson & Sallie. BA California St U 1955; MDiv CDSP 1958; MA U of San Francisco 1978. D 6/2/1958 Bp Francis E I Bloy P 12/7/1958 Bp Harry Sherbourne Kennedy. m 6/10/1989 Peggy Ann Stephens c 3. Exec Dir Cmsn on Schools Dio Los Angeles Los Angeles CA 2001-2009; Assoc S Geo's Par La Can CA 1995-1999; Headmaster Chandler Sch 1979-2001; Cathd Sch For Boys San Francisco CA 1972-1979; Headmaster Cathd Sch For Boys San Francisco CA 1972-1979; Chapl (Captain) US-A 1966-1969; Cur Trin Par Menlo Pk CA 1962-1966; Vic S Jn Waiokoa HI 1958-1960.

STEPHENS, Josh (SVa) Bruton Parish Episcopal Church, PO Box 3520, Williamsburg VA 23187 **Assoc R for Fam Mnstry Bruton Par Williamsburg VA 2016-; Other Lay Position S Andr's Ch Norfolk VA 2011-** B Jacksonville Beach FL 1985 s Henry & Deborah. BA Milligan Coll 2008; M.Div. Sewanee: The U So, TS 2016. D 6/11/2016 P 12/17/2016 Bp Herman Hollerith IV. m 5/16/2009 Rosanna Patrice Couture. jstephens@brutonparish.org

STEPHENS, Paul Jeffery (Miss) P. O. Box 1358, Tupelo MS 38802 **Dio Mississippi Jackson MS 2017-** B Starkville MS 1956 s Caril & Lois. BS Mississippi St U 1978; JD U of Mississippi 1983; MDiv Sewanee: The U So, TS 2002. D 6/15/2002 Bp Alfred Marble Jr P 1/5/2003 Bp Duncan Montgomery Gray III. m 6/23/1979 Martha Jane Stephens c 2. R All SS' Epis Ch Tupelo MS 2009-2016; Int Ch of the H Apos Collierville TN 2008; Int S Jn's Ch Laurel MS 2007-2008; Hd of Sch Coast Epis Sch Long Bch MS 2004-2007; Coast Epis Schools Inc Long Bch MS 2004-2007; Cur/Sch Chapl Trin Ch Natchez MS 2002-2004. pstephens@dioms.org

STEPHENS, Stephen Daniel (RG) Rec 5/3/2017 as Priest Bp Michael Vono.

STEPHENS, Thomas Lee (Okla) 1560 SE Pecan Place, Bartlesville OK 74003 B Boca Raton FL 1945 s Thomas & Rose. BA Oklahoma Bapt U 1969; MDiv MidWestern Bapt TS 1972; DMin MidWestern Bapt TS 1976; Angl TS 1991. D 6/27/1992 Bp Maurice Manuel Benitez P 2/2/1993 Bp William Jackson Cox. m 12/17/1988 Lynda D Stephens c 3. T/F On Recon Dio Oklahoma Oklahoma City OK 2002-2003, Dioc Coun 1997-2001, Dioc Coun 2002-2003; R S Lk's Epis Ch Bartlesville OK 1997-2017; Asst Chr Epis Ch Tyler TX 1992-1996.

STEPHENS, Wyatt E (Mil) 1538 N 58th St, Milwaukee WI 53208 **Ret Dio Milwaukee Milwaukee WI 1996-, Cn for Parishes 1988-1996** B Sulphur OK 1933 s Ira & Julia. BA U of Oklahoma 1958; MS U of Oklahoma 1960; PhD U of Oklahoma 1963; MA Nash 1979. D 9/1/1979 P 3/1/1980 Bp Albert William Hillestad. m 8/23/1953 Dixie L Stephens c 4. R Ch Of The H Comm Lake Geneva WI 1980-1988; Asst Trin Ch Milwaukee WI 1979-1980.

STEPHENSON, Amanda C (NC) **S Mary's Epis Ch High Point NC 2016-** D 6/4/2016 P 12/10/2016 Bp John Bauerschmidt.

STEPHENSON, John William (Kan) Rr 1 Box 190, Riverton KS 66770 B 1946 s John & Thelma. AS Missouri Sthrn St U 1974; BA Missouri Sthrn St U 1975. D 5/12/1988 P 11/1/1988 Bp Richard Frank Grein. m 8/15/1965 Norma Geraldine Stephenson c 2. P S Mary's Epis Ch Galena KS 1988-2004; SE Convoc Bd Ft Scott KS 1988-1991.

STEPHENSON, Michael (Okla) 3621 24th Ave SE Apt 3, Norman OK 73071 **R St Phil's Epis Ch Ardmore OK 2017-** B Joplin MO 1952 BA Tul 1974; MBA Washington U 1979; MDiv Chicago TS 2008. D 6/23/2007 Bp Robert Manning Moody P 1/26/2008 Bp Bill Persell. c 2. Cn Dio Oklahoma Oklahoma City OK 2013-2017; Int R S Andr's Ch Stillwater OK 2011-2013; Assoc Chapl

NW Memi Hosp Chicago IL 2008-2011; Cn for Dvlpmt Dio Chicago Chicago IL 2007-2011; Asstg P S Andr Ch Grayslake IL 2005-2011.

STEPHENSON, Randolph (WA) 4 Jeb Stuart Ct, Rockville MD 20854 B Savannah GA 1946 s Randolph & Kathleen. Geo; Armstrong Atlantic St U 1966; BA U GA 1968; Hofstra U 1973; MDiv VTS 1975. D 6/5/1976 Bp Jonathan Goodhue Sherman P 4/1/1977 Bp Reginald Heber Gooden. c 2. Middleham & S Ptr's Par Lusby MD 2008-2014; Int Chr Ch S Jn's Par Accokeek MD 1998-2001; P-in-c Trin Epis Par Hughesville MD 1995-1998; P-in-c S Mary's Chap Ridge Ridge MD 1993-1994; Vic S Geo's Ch Glenn Dale MD 1982-1988; S Alb's Chap & Epis U Cntr Baton Rouge LA 1982, 1979-1980; Asst S Mk's Cathd Shreveport LA 1976-1978. Washington Epis Cleric Assn.

STEPHENSON-DIAZ, Lark (SanD) 1023 Iris Ct, Carlsbad CA 92011 B Vallejo CA 1962 d John & Katherine. BA U of Portland 1984; MDiv Ya Berk 1988. D 6/22/1988 P 1/5/1989 Bp Robert Louis Ladehoff. m 5/27/1995 Roberto Domingo Diaz. S Alb's Epis Ch El Cajon CA 2011-2013; S Ptr's Epis Ch Del Mar CA 2005-2010; S Marg Of Scotland Par San Juan Capo CA 1995-2005; Asst S Tim's Ch San Diego CA 1995-1998; Assoc S Jas Par Los Angeles CA 1991-1994; Assoc S Jn The Evang Ch Portland OR 1988-1991.

STER, David (CPa) 1363 Princeton Rd, Mechanicsburg PA 17050 **D S Lk's Epis Ch Mechanicsburg PA 1999-** B Cleveland OH 1953 s August & Lona. AA U of Maryland 1981. D 6/11/1999 Bp Michael Whittington Creighton. m 2/26/1977 Patricia Pearce.

STERCHI, Margaret (NJ) 11 North Ave., Wilmington DE 19804 **R S Jn The Evang Ch Blackwood NJ 2006-** B Silver City NM 1951 d Robert & Louise. BS U of New Mex 1974; MDiv Epis TS of the SW 2001. D 6/9/2001 Bp D Avid Bruce Macpherson P 5/11/2002 Bp James Monte Stanton. Asst All SS and St Georges Ch Rehoboth Bch DE 2003-2006; Cn Cathd Ch Of S Jn Wilmington DE 2001-2003; Dn of Camden Convoc Dio New Jersey Trenton NJ 2014-2017, Pres of Disciplinary Bd 2013-2014, Mem of Stndg Cmsn for Cler Compstn 2011-2017, Mem of Wmn Cmsn 2009-2016, Mem of Nomin Com 2008-2015.

STERKEN, Janet Leigh (Eau) 322 N. Water St., Sparta WI 54656 B Harvard IL 1968 d Wayne & Linda. BS Mt Senario Coll 1990; MA Bridgewater St Coll 2000. D 11/21/2008 Bp Mark Lawrence Macdonald.

STERLING III, Edward Arthur (Oly) 3762 Palisades Pl W, University Place WA 98466 **Asst S Andr's Epis Ch Tacoma WA 1986-** B Grandfield OK 1921 s Edward & Mary. BS Texas A&M U 1942; MDiv Epis TS of the SW 1957. D 6/19/1957 Bp John Elbridge Hines P 6/18/1958 Bp Frederick P Goddard. c 4. P S Catherines Ch Enumclaw WA 1980-1986; LocTen Chr Epis Ch Puyallup WA 1978-1979; S Mary's Ch Lakewood WA 1977-1978; Chapl (LtCol) USA 1959-1975; Off Of Bsh For ArmdF New York NY 1959-1975; M-in-c S Mary's Ch W Columbia TX 1957-1959; Dioc Coun Dio Olympia Seattle 2004-2007, Stwdshp Cmsn 1981-2003.

STERLING, Franklin Mills (Cal) 1707 Gouldin Rd., Oakland CA 94611 **D S Jn's Epis Ch Oakland CA 2008-** B Ridley Park PA 1932 s Allan & Mary. BS Ohio U 1960; MBA Golden Gate U 1981; Epis Sch For Deacons 2007. D 12/1/2007 Bp Marc Handley Andrus. m 5/28/1977 Marion Coles Sterling c 3.

STERLING, Leslie Katherin (Mass) St. Bartholomew's Church, 239 Harvard Street, Cambridge MA 02139 **P-in-c S Barth's Epis Ch Cambridge MA 2009-** B Washington DC 1957 d Mack & Barbarajean. ABS Harv 1979; Cert St Elizabeths Med Cntr 1999; MDiv EDS 2001. D 6/2/2001 Bp Barbara Clementine Harris P 6/8/2002 Bp M(Arvil) Thomas Shaw. Pres, Massachusetts Chapt UBE 2011-1996; Asst R All SS Par Brookline MA 2001-2009. UBE 2000.

STERN, Linda Sue (Okla) 516 Mclish St, Ardmore OK 73401 B Columbus NE 1952 d James & Marcia. BSN U of Oklahoma 1974; MDiv S Paul TS 1995; Angl Stds Cert Iona Sch for Mnstry 2015. D 2/1/2016 P 10/29/2016 Bp Edward Joseph Konieczny. c 3.

STERNE, Colleen Kathryn (Los) Trinity Episcopal Church, 1500 State St, Santa Barbara CA 93101 B Santa Monica CA 1958 d Lynn & Mildred. No degree Epis Theologica Sem in Sthrn California; BA U CA, Santa Barbara 1980; Juris Doctor Santa Barbara Coll of LA 1988. D 6/3/2006 P 1/6/2007 Bp Joseph Jon Bruno. m 2/7/1981 James Bernhard Sterne.

STERNE, Martha Packer (At) 805 Mount Vernon Hwy NW, Atlanta GA 30327 B Alexandria LA 1947 d James & Anna. BA Van 1970; MEd Georgia St U 1983; MDiv Candler TS Emory U 1988. D 6/11/1988 P 4/1/1989 Bp Frank Kellogg Allan. m 6/20/1970 Carroll P Sterne c 2. Assoc H Innoc Ch Atlanta GA 2007-2013; S Andr's Ch Maryville TN 1997-2007; All SS Epis Ch Atlanta GA 1988-1997. "Earthly Gd," OSL, 2003. Theta Pi.

STERRY, Steven Chapin (Los) Anglican Church of the Epiphany, 5151 Cordova Rd,, La Mirada CA 90638 **Asstg P Angl Ch of the Epiph 2016-; Foundor and Spnsr Califoria Inst for Men Chino: Veterans in Prison 2016-; Co-Fndr and Spnsr California Inst for Wmn Corona: Veterans in Prison 2013-; Founding Mem/Dir of Educ Untd States Conf of Chapl 2011-; Affiliate Stff Mem Campus Crusade for Chr Mltry Mnstry 2010-** B Los Angeles CA 1942 s Charles & Eva. BS U CA 1965; MBA U CA 1972; Talbot TS 2009; MA Biola U Sch of Apologetics 2013. D 1/24/2009 Bp Chester Lovelle Talton. c 1. Int P Chr the King Reformed Epis Ch 2014-2015; Dioc Coun Alt Dio Los Angeles

Los Angeles CA 2011-2014. Beta Gamma Sigma Natl hon Soc 1972. Graduation mcl Biola U Sch of Apologetics 2013. sgvec@juno.com

STEUER, Lawrence William (Alb) 343 Pettis Rd, Gansevoort NY 12831 B Portland OR 1926 s Lawrence & Beneatha. BA U of Washington 1949. D 12/19/1981 Bp Wilbur Emory Hogg Jr. m 12/23/1945 Mary Elizabeth Steuer c 2. D The Ch Of The Mssh Glens Falls NY 1995-2005; D /Asst S Tim's Ch Westford NY 1989-1995; D /Asst Ch Of Beth Saratoga Spg NY 1981-1989.

STEVENS JR, Arthur Grant (WMass) 904B West Victoria St, Santa Barbara CA 93101 B Washington DC 1941 s Arthur & Frances. BA Cntr Coll 1963; MA U of Kentucky 1965; PhD U MI 1970; MDiv CDSP 1987. D 6/6/1987 Bp Don Adger Wimberly P 6/3/1988 Bp Charles Shannon Mallory. m 6/11/1983 Judy Stevens. Int S Jas Ch Paso Robles CA 1992-1993; Asstg Cler S Ben's Par Los Osos CA 1989-1999; S Tim's Epis Ch Mtn View CA 1988; Dioc Sprtl Dir Dio El Camino Real Salinas CA 1988-1991. "Abundant Living For Christians: Making Decisions In Ch And Fam," Xulon Press, 2005. Ord Of H Cross.

STEVENS JR, Ernest Lee (Az) 7002 Volar Dr, Cheyenne WY 82009 **Died 8/16/2015** B Contoocook NH 1925 s Ernest & Marguarita. BA U of New Hampshire 1950; MDiv EDS 1957; US-A Chapl Sch 1970; AAS Rio Salado Coll 1990; MA Ottawa U 2002. D 6/29/1957 Bp Charles Francis Hall P 5/27/1960 Bp Richard Stanley Merrill Emrich. m 8/26/1989 Dorothy B Barnett. Chr Ch Of The Ascen Paradise Vlly AZ 1993-1997; P-in-c S Paul's Ch Phoenix AZ 1993; Vic Epiph On The Desert Gila Bend AZ 1992-1994; Int S Jn The Bapt Globe AZ 1990; Asst S Steph's Ch Phoenix AZ 1987-1990; Vic All SS Epis Ch Safford AZ 1980-1982; R SS Phil And Jas Morenci AZ 1977-1987; Chapl US-A 1962-1977; Off Of Bsh For ArmdF New York NY 1962-1969; Chapl US-A-Arizona NG 1961-1962; R S Steph's Epis Ch Douglas AZ 1960-1962; Cathd Ch Of S Paul Detroit MI 1959-1960; Cur Chr Ch Dearborn MI 1957-1959. Phi Kappa Phi UNH 2049; MA - High hon Ottawa U 2003; Bronze Star US Army 1972; hon Grad US Army Chapl Sch 1970.

STEVENS, George Read (Mass) St. John's Church, P.O. Box 5610, Beverly MA 01915 **S Mary's Ch Newton Lower Falls MA 2010-** B NC 1976 s Hugh & Marilyn. BA U Rich 1999; MDiv GTS 2006. D 6/3/2006 Bp Michael B Curry P 1/12/2008 Bp M(Arvil) Thomas Shaw. m 10/12/2002 Margaret H Stevens c 2. Yth Min S Paul's Epis Ch Winston Salem NC 2000-2003; S Jn's Ch Beverly MA 1996-2010.

STEVENS III, Halsey (Ct) 63 Route 81, Killingworth CT 06419 **P-in-c Chr Ch Avon CT 2008-; Ret 2000-** B Hartford CT 1939 s Halsey & Margaret. BA Nasson Coll 1962; MDiv Ya Berk 1965. D 6/14/1965 Bp Walter H Gray P 12/18/1965 Bp Joseph Warren Hutchens. m 6/13/1964 Betsey Burr Stevens c 2. Trin Ch Portland CT 2004-2007; P-in-c Chr Ch W Haven CT 2000-2004; Ch of the H Sprt W Haven CT 2000; R S Paul's Ch Pawtucket RI 1993-2000; R S Mary's Ch Portsmouth RI 1990-1993; R Trin Ch Uppr Marlboro MD 1982-1990; Vic S Andr The Apos Rocky Hill CT 1969-1982; Dio Connecticut Meriden CT 1965-1981; Vic Ch Of The Epiph Southbury CT 1965-1969.

STEVENS, Judy (WMass) 904B W Victoria St, Santa Barbara CA 93101 **Nonstipendiary P Trin Epis Ch Santa Barbara CA 2005-** B Columbus OH 1939 d William & Mary. BA Smith 1961; MA Col 1963; PhD Col 1967; MDiv CDSP 1987. D 6/6/1987 Bp Don Adger Wimberly P 6/3/1988 Bp Charles Shannon Mallory. m 6/11/1983 Arthur Grant Stevens. Dio Wstrn Massachusetts Springfield 1999-2004; R S Jn's Ch Northampton MA 1999-2004; Chapl to Epis students Smith Northampton MA 1999-2004; S Ben's Par Los Osos CA 1989-1999; Cur All SS Epis Ch Palo Alto CA 1987-1989; 1961-1984; Dioc Coun Mem Dio El Camino Real Salinas CA 1991-1994, Alternate Dep to GC 1991-, Epis Search Com 1989-1990, Bdgt Com 1988-1992. Auth, *Conv Decisions and Voting Records*, Brookings, 1973; Auth, *The Conventional Problem*, Brookings, 1972; Auth, *Voting for Pres*, Brookings, 1970; Auth, *Congr and Urban Problems*, Brookings, 1969. Assoc of the H Cross 1983. Bp's Excellence Awd Dioc Conv 1992.

STEVENS, Karl Peter Bush (SO) Saint Stephen's Episcopal Church, 30 W Woodruff Ave, Columbus OH 43210 B Albion MI 1971 BA Ken; M-Div SWTS 2003. D 6/12/2003 P 1/19/2004 Bp James Louis Jelinek. m 8/17/1997 Amy B Stevens c 1. Mssnr for Campus Mnstry Dio Sthrn Ohio Cincinnati OH 2012-2016; S Paul's Ch Mt Vernon OH 2010-2012, P-in-c 2009-; Dio Ohio Cleveland 2003-2010; Chapl Ken Gambier OH 2003-2010.

STEVENS, M(errill) Richard (EO) St Pauls Episcopal Church, 1805 Minnesota St, The Dalles OR 97058 **S Pauls Epis Ch The Dalles OR 2016-; Vic Utah Reg Bluff NM 2011-; S Christophers Ch Bluff UT 2009-; S Jn The Baptizer Montezuma Creek UT 2009-; Vic S Mary Of-The-Moonlight Oljato UT 2009-; Vic, SE Reg Gd Shpd Mssn Navajo Area Mssn Ft Defiance 2007-; Pres, Stndg Com The Epis Ch In Navajoland Coun Farmington NM 2011-** B Sewanee TN 1947 s Merrill & Walli. BA St Johns Coll Annapolis MD 1969; JD U of Arizona 1985; MDiv CDSP 1995; PhD Grad Theol Un 2003. D 10/13/2001 P 5/16/2004 Bp Mark Lawrence Macdonald. m 7/4/1983 Willie E Hulce c 1. Navajoland Area Mssn Farmington NM 2007-2015; Cler Assoc The Epis Ch Of The Gd Shpd Berkeley CA 2001-2007. Auth, "Burning for the Other," *Bk*, VDM Verlag Dr Mueller, 2009. redstevensgsm@gmail.com

STEVENS, Nancy (Roch) The Church of the Epiphany, 3285 Buffalo Rd, Rochester NY 14624 **P-in-c Ephphatha Mssn For The Deaf Gates NY 2010-; Epis SeniorLife Communities 2001-** B Rochester NY 1950 d Robert & Jane. Beloit Coll 1971; BSN Case Wstrn Reserve U 1973; U of Dallas 1989; MDiv Bex Sem 1993. D 11/22/1993 P 5/28/1994 Bp William George Burrill. m 9/1/1995 David Lee Williams c 4. R The Ch Of The Epiph Gates NY 1999-2014; Asst to the R S Jas' Ch Batavia NY 1993-1999. Assoc, OSH 1991.

STEVENS, Patricia D (At) P.O. Box 155, Johnston SC 29832 B Cincinnati OH 1949 d Andrew & Marguerite. BA Manhattanville Coll 1971; JD U of Connecticut 1974; MDiv Ya Berk 1989. D 6/10/1989 P 12/1/1989 Bp Arthur Edward Walmsley. c 1. Ch Of The Ridge Trenton SC 2009-2010; S Pat's Epis Ch Atlanta GA 2003-2007; Ch Of The Epiph Atlanta GA 2001-2003; Pstr Asst Chr Ch Cathd Hartford CT 1995-1996; Chr Ch Cathd Houston TX 1994-1995; Vic Zion Epis Ch N Branford CT 1991-1993; Asst R S Jas's Ch W Hartford CT 1989-1991; Res-In-Trng Georgia Assoc Pstr Counslr.

STEVENS JR, Rob (NH) 1113 Macon Ave, Pittsburgh PA 15218 **R S Jn's Ch Portsmouth NH 2005-** B Orlando FL 1968 s Robert. BS Florida St U 1991; MDiv SWTS 2001. m 1/1/1994 Jennifer Ellsworth Stevens. Cur Calv Ch Pittsburgh PA 2001-2005. rectorsjc@gmail.com

STEVENS, Robert Ellsworth (CFla) 2346 Colfax Ter., Evanston IL 60201 B Baltimore MD 1937 s O Ellsworth & Lillian. U of Baltimore 1956; BA Maryville Coll 1959; MDiv Columbia TS 1972. D 9/5/1976 P 3/1/1978 Bp William Hopkins Folwell. m 9/7/1962 Elizabeth Jane Stevens c 2. Chapl Bexley Seabury Fed Chicago IL 1993-2001; Emm Ch Orlando FL 1987-1998; S Steph's Ch Lakeland FL 1978-1987; S Lk The Evang Ch Mulberry FL 1978.

STEVENS, Scott J (Ct) PO Box 151, Hampton CT 06247 **D Gr Epis Ch Yantic CT 2017-** B Concord NH 1955 s Robert & Patricia. BA U of New Hampshire 1977; MA U of Connecticut 1980. D 12/1/1990 Bp Arthur Edward Walmsley. m 6/16/1979 Jodie Vail Stevens c 2. D S Paul's Ch Plainfield CT 2005-2017; D S Paul's Ch Windham CT 1990-2005. Auth, "Pstr Care of Sexual Offenders," *Diakoneo*, NAAD, 2002. Assn of Epis Deacons 1992.

STEVENS III, Walter Alexander (Haw) P.O. Box 207, Kapaau HI 96755 B Petersburg VA 1946 s Walter & Ida. BA Col 1967; MDiv EDS 2000. D 6/22/2000 P 3/25/2001 Bp Richard Sui On Chang. m 7/26/1998 Kathleen Kagimoto c 1. S Steph's Ch Wahiawa HI 2007-2011; Vic Kohala Epis Mssn Kapaau HI 2002-2005; S Paul's Ch Kohala Mssn Kapaau HI 2002-2004; Assoc R For Chld & Yth Calv Epis Ch Kaneohe HI 2001; St Jn the Bapt Epis Ch Waianae HI 2000-2001.

STEVENS, William Clair (PR) B 1935 m 7/25/1959 Gretchen Engler.

STEVENS-HUMMON, Rebecca M (Tenn) 2902 Overlook Dr, Nashville TN 37212 B Milford CT 1963 d Gladstone & Anne. BA U So 1985; MDiv Van 1990; Cert Sewanee: The U So, TS 1991. D 6/9/1991 Bp George Lazenby Reynolds Jr. m 10/8/1988 Marcus S Hummon c 4. S Aug's Chap Nashville TN 2010, Chapl 2010-; Dio Tennessee Nashville TN 1994-2009, D-In-Trng 1991-1993; The Epis Ch Of The Resurr Franklin TN 1993-1994. Narpm.

STEVENSON, Ann (NH) P O Box 743, 18 High St, North Berwick ME 03906 B Edinburgh Scotland GB 1948 d Ivar & Ann. BA Champlain Coll 1967; MDiv Louisville Presb TS 1987; GTS 1990. D 6/3/1990 P 5/1/1991 Bp David Reed. m 1/1/1995 Wendel William Meyer c 2. Pstr Affiliate Emm Chap Manchester MA 2003-2009; Pstr Affiliate S Jn's Ch Beverly MA 2003-2009; Assoc R S Jn's Ch Portsmouth NH 2000-2003; Assoc R of Pstr Care Trin Ch Epis Boston MA 1997-2000; Sr Assoc Ch Of The Redeem Bryn Mawr PA 1991-1997; D S Phil's Ch Garrison NY 1990-1991. SCHC (ME), Chapl 2002.

STEVENSON, Anne B (Tenn) 216 chestnut hill, Nashville TN 37215 B Jackson MS 1939 d Charles & Octavia. BA Agnes Scott Coll 1961; BA U of Louvain 1982; MA U of Louvain 1983; STB U of Louvain 1983. D 6/24/1983 Bp John Mc Gill Krumm P 9/1/1984 Bp Robert Bracewell Appleyard. c 3. Cn Chr Ch Cathd Nashville TN 1989-2011; Asst S Jas Ch Jackson MS 1985-1989; Chapl S Andr's Sch Jackson MS 1984-1989; Assoc H Trin Pro-Cathd & All SS Waterloo Belgium 1983-1984.

STEVENSON, Carolyn Eve (NH) 231 Main St, Salem NH 03079 **R S Dav's Ch Salem NH 2005-; COM Dio New Hampshire Concord NH 2009-, Cler Dvlpmt 2007-, Cnvnr of Sthrn Convoc 2007-** B Youngstown OH 1954 d James & Joan. BS Kent St U 1976; MDiv Ya Berk 1987. D 2/14/1987 Bp Arthur Edward Walmsley P 12/22/2001 Bp Douglas Edwin Theuner. m 11/13/2009 Cynthia T Morse. Asst S Matt's Ch Goffstown NH 2001-2004; Sprtl Care & Bereavement Coordntr Cmnty Hlth & Hospice NH 2000-2005; Non-par Soc Justice for Wmn MA 1992-2000; Chapl Mansfield Trng Sch CT 1988-1992; Asst S Mk's Ch Mystic CT 1987; Incarn Cntr Deep River CT 1976-1985. Tertiary Of The Soc Of S Fran 1992.

STEVENSON, E Mark (La) 14909 Lone Spring Dr, Little Elm TX 75068 **Epis Ch Cntr New York NY 2013-; Dio Louisiana 2005-; Bd Mem Epis Relief & Dvlpmt 2012-** B Savannah GA 1964 s Philip & Helen. BS U IL 1986; MDiv Nash 2000. D 12/29/1999 P 8/5/2000 Bp Charles Edward Jenkins III. m 1/14/1995 Joyce Owen Stevenson. Cn to the Ordnry Dio Louisiana New Orleans LA 2005-2013; R Ch Of The Gd Shpd Maitland FL 2004-2005; R The Ch Of The Annunc New Orleans LA 2000-2004. mstevenson@episcopalchurch.org

S

STEVENSON, Frank Beaumont (SO) School Lane, Stanton Saint John, Oxford OX33 1ET Great Britain (UK) **Serv Ch in Engl 1969-** B Cincinnati OH 1939 s Howard & Laura. BA Duke 1961; BD EDS 1964. D 6/13/1964 P 12/1/1964 Bp Roger W Blanchard. Serv Dio Zambia 1966-1969; Epis Ch Cntr New York NY 1966-1968; Ch Of S Edw Columbus OH 1964-1966. Auth, "Dementia & Rel," *Degenerative Neurological Disease in the Elderly*; Auth, "An Application of Grp Analytic Principals in Pstr Trng for Cler," *Groeps Psychol.* Hon Cn Chr Ch Cathd, Oxford 1998.

STEVENSON, Frederic George (CPa) 890 Mccosh St, Hanover PA 17331 B Bethlehem PA 1947 s Dean & Doris. BA Leh 1969; MDiv PDS 1972. D 5/27/1972 P 2/1/1973 Bp Dean Theodore Stevenson. m 8/22/1970 Mary Stevenson c 1. Dio Cntrl Pennsylvania Harrisburg PA 2008-2010; Assoc S Andr's Epis Ch York PA 1998-2009, Asst 1997-; The Epis Ch Of S Jn The Bapt York PA 1974-1997; R All SS Ch Hanover PA 1974-1994; Non-par 1972-1974. fatherfredstevenson@yahoo.com

STEVENSON, Janis Jordan (Mich) 430 Nicolet St, Walled Lake MI 48390 **P S Anne's Epis Ch Walled Lake MI 2011-** B Sebring FL 1934 d Harold & Leona. Th Cert Dio Michigan 2010. D 11/3/2010 P 6/21/2011 Bp Wendell Nathaniel Gibbs Jr. c 3.

STEVENSON, R(ichard) Hugh (NCal) 610 Los Alamos Rd, Santa Rosa CA 95409 B London UK 1945 s Arthur & Olivia. BA U of Exeter GB 1968; Westcott Hse Cambridge 1970; DMin Bex Sem 1984. Trans 10/1/1980 as Priest Bp Robert Rae Spears Jr. m 11/18/1972 Angela Bea Stevenson c 2. Int Sprg Lake Vill 2014; R S Patricks Ch Kenwood CA 1991-2013; R S Lk's Ch Fairport NY 1981-1991; Other ClerRector Dio Rochester Rochester NY 1980-1981; P-in-c S Steph's Stanley Hong Kong 1977-1980; Sr Chapl & Int St Jn's Cathd Hong Kong 1974-1980; Serv Ch of Engl 1970-1974; Dist Dn The Epis Dio Nthrn California Sacramento CA 1998-1999; COM Dio Rochester Henrietta 1985-1991, Dioc Coun 1982-1985.

STEVENSON, Thomas Edward (Ore) PO Box 29, Alsea OR 97324 **1988-** B Antioch CA 1940 s John & Marian. BA U of Oregon 1963; MDiv GTS 1967. D 7/21/1967 P 2/13/1968 Bp William Jones Gordon Jr. m 4/4/1964 Gwendolyn Frances Stevenson c 2. R S Matt's Epis Ch Ontario OR 1973-1988; P-in-c Gd Shpd Huslia AK 1969-1973; Assoc R S Ptr's By-The-Sea Sitka AK 1967-1969.

STEVENS-TAYLOR, Sally Hodges (Az) PO Box 65840, Tucson AZ 85728 B Tucson AZ 1952 d Paul & Mary Louise. BS U of Arizona 1980. D 1/23/2010 Bp Kirk Stevan Smith. c 3.

STEVICK, Daniel Bush (Pa) 600 E Cathedral Rd Apt D203, Philadelphia PA 19128 **R Gr Ch Hulmeville PA 1969-** B Elyria OH 1927 s Harlie & Lois. BA Wheaton Coll 1950; STB Tem 1953; STM Tem 1956; U of Cambridge 1965; Fell Inst Ecuminical & Cultural Resrch 1970. D 6/13/1953 P 12/1/1953 Bp Joseph Gillespie Armstrong. c 2. EDS Cambridge MA 1974-1989; Vic All SS Ch Fallsington PA 1965-1969; Prof of Liturg and Homil PDS Philadelphia PA 1959-1965; Prof of Liturg and Homil EDS Cambridge MA 1957-1966; All SS Epis Ch Levittown PA 1953-1959; Gr Epis Ch Hulmeville PA 1953-1954. Auth, "The Altar's Fire: An Intro to Chas Wesley's Hymns on the Lord's Supper," Epworth, Engl, 2005; "By Water and the Word: The Scriptures of Baptism," Ch Pub, 1997; "To Confirm or To Receive?," *Baptism and Mnstry: Liturg Stds I*, Ch Hymnal Corp., 1994; "The Crafting of Liturg: A Guide for Preparers," Ch Hymnal Corp., 1990; "A Matter of Taste: 1 Ptr 2:3," *Revs for Rel, Vol. 47, No.4.*, 1988; "Baptismal Moments: Baptismal Meanings," Ch Hymnal Corp., 1987; "The Sprtlty of BCP," *Angl Sprtlty*, Morehouse-Barlow, 1982; "Lang in Wrshp: Reflections on a Crisis," Seabury Press, 1970; "Civil Disobedience and the Chr," Seabury Press, 1965; "Cn Law: A Handbook," Seabury Press, 1965; "Beyond Fundamentalism," Jn Knox Press, 1964. Pres No Amer Acad of Liturg 1976; STD Gnrl Sem, NY 1971; Mem Drafting Com on Chr Initiation SLC 1970.

STEWART, Audrey (Mass) Parish of the Epiphany, 70 Church St, Winchester NJ 01890 B Newburyport MA 1981 d William & Roni. BA Wheelock Coll 2003; MDiv VTS 2012. D 6/2/2012 Bp Gayle Harris P 1/13/2013 Bp M(Arvil) Thomas Shaw. m 8/14/2015 Christopher James Stewart. S Dunstans Epis Ch Dover MA 2015-2016; Asst Par Of The Epiph Winchester MA 2012-2015.

STEWART, Barbara (Los) 1014 Presidio Drive, Costa Mesa CA 92626 B Berkeley CA 1946 d Frederick & Phyllis. BA U CA 1968; PhD U CA 1973; MDiv ETSBH 1992. D 6/13/1992 Bp Chester Lovelle Talton P 1/9/1993 Bp Frederick Houk Borsch. c 2. R S Jn The Div Epis Ch Costa Mesa CA 2002-2013, P-in-c 2001; Assoc S Fran' Par Palos Verdes Estates CA 1995-2001; Asst S Aug By-The-Sea Par Santa Monica CA 1992-1995.

STEWART, Bonnie (Ore) Saint Michael And All Angels Church, 1704 NE 43rd Ave, Portland OR 97213 **S Mich And All Ang Ch Portland OR 2015-** B Berkeley CA 1951 d Robert & Joanne. Diablo Vlly Coll; Merritt Coll; Diac Stds Epis Sch for Deacons 2012. D 12/1/2012 Bp Marc Handley Andrus. H Cross Epis Ch Castro Vlly CA 2013-2014.

STEWART, Caroline Rinehart (Md) 4024 Stewart Rd, Stevenson MD 21153 **Assoc The Ch Of The Redeem Baltimore MD 2011-, 2009-2010** B Charlottesville VA 1948 Dip Ang Stud VTS; BA Converse Coll 1970; MEd U of Virginia 1971; MA Loyola Coll 2002. D 6/24/2006 Bp John L Rabb P 1/6/2007

Bp Robert Wilkes Ihloff. m 10/20/1973 William Stewart c 2. S Jn's Ch Reisterstown MD 2010; Asst R S Andr's Epis Ch Glenwood MD 2006-2008; Chapl St. Paul's Sch For Girls 2002-2005.

STEWART, Carol Wendt (Roch) 3074 O'Donnell Rd, Wellsville NY 14895 **P-in-c S Jn's Ch Wellsville NY 2014-** B 1949 BS Clarkson U 1971; MEd Canisius Coll 1985. D 2/14/2009 P 10/10/2009 Bp Prince Grenville Singh. m 12/19/1970 Gilbert Stewart. Dio Rochester Henrietta 2015-2016.

STEWART, Charles Neil (CNY) PO Box 62, Skaneateles NY 13152 **D S Jas Ch Skaneateles NY 2016-; Asst Chapl Upstate U Hosp 2015-** B Albany NY 1945 MDiv Colgate Rochester Crozer DS; PhD U IL at Urbana-Champaign 1974; MBA U Roch 1997. D 6/25/2016 Bp Gladstone Bailey Adams III. m 10/15/2000 Pamela Jean Olson. Mem, Dioc Bd Cntrl New York Liverpool NY 2010-2013; Dep/Alt Dep, GC 2009, 2012 2007-2013. cnstewart@verizon.net

STEWART JR, Claude York (WNC) 409-D Cane Creek Rd, Sylva NC 28779 **Died 12/13/2015** B Knoxville TN 1940 s Claude & Anne. BS Carson-Newman Coll 1962; STB Harvard DS 1966; ThD Harvard DS 1980; CAS GTS 1987. D 7/11/1987 P 1/1/1988 Bp William Gillette Weinhauer. m 10/14/1997 Christ D Stewart c 2. S Alb's Epis Ch Hixson TN 2007-2008; S Fran' Ch Norris TN 2005-2006; Ch Of The Mssh Murphy NC 2004-2005, 2000-2001; Int S Agnes Epis Ch Franklin NC 2002-2003; Epis Ch Of The H Sprt Mars Hill NC 2002; S Jn's Epis Ch Marion NC 1999-2000; Epis Ch Of S Ptr's By The Lake Denver NC 1991-1995; S Jn's Ch Sylva NC 1988-1998; Cur Ch Of The H Cross Tryon NC 1987; Asst Prof Of Rel And Philos Maryville Coll In Tennesee 1971-1978. AAR, Centr For Ethics & Soc Plcy.

STEWART, Clifford Thomas (Ore) Po Box 447, Lake Oswego OR 97034 B Edmonton AB CA 1920 s Clifford & Florence. BA Willamette U 1947; Cntr for Diac Mnstry 1989. D 7/18/1989 Bp Hal Raymond Gross. m 9/14/1963 Eleanor Mae Stewart c 2. D Chr Ch Par Lake Oswego OR 1999-2000; D S Fran Of Assisi Epis Wilsonville OR 1989-1998. NAAD. Gave Opening Pryr On 10/4/1994 Untd States Senate 1994.

STEWART, Daniel R (Oly) 322 Aoloa St Apt 1101, Kailua HI 96734 **Tchr Iolani Sch Honolulu HI 1988-** B Seattle WA 1943 s Daniel & Margaret. BA U of Washington 1965; STB ATC 1969; MA Salve Regina U 1988; MA U of Hawaii 1995. D 8/6/1969 P 5/16/1970 Bp Ivol I Curtis. m 4/29/1967 Maryanne J Stewart. S Alb's Chap Honolulu HI 1988-2008; Off Of Bsh For ArmdF New York NY 1980-1988; Assoc S Lk's Epis Ch Seattle WA 1969-1980. Auth, "S Andr'S Cross".

STEWART, Duke Summerlin (Ga) 701 Gaskin Ave N, Douglas GA 31533 **Dir Pro S&S Productions 2005-** B Columbus GA 1955 s Jack & Virginia. Emory U 1975; BS U GA 1977; MDiv Sthrn Sem 1980; CAS VTS 1998. D 7/1/1998 P 1/9/1999 Bp Henry Irving Louttit. m 3/30/1991 Diane Stewart c 3. Pstr S Andr's Epis Ch Douglas GA 1998-2002.

STEWART, James Allen (Wyo) St Mark's Episcopal Church, 1908 Central Ave, Cheyenne WY 82001 **S Chris's Ch Cheyenne WY 2016-; D S Mk's Ch Cheyenne WY 2012-** B Wheatland WY 1961 s George & Roberta. Advncd Angl Cert Sem of Pacific. D 6/16/2012 P 5/16/2015 Bp John Smylie. m 3/17/1988 Sylvia Gail Stewart c 4.

STEWART, James Macgregor (NC) D 6/21/2014 Bp Anne Hodges-Copple P 1/16/2015 Bp D Avid Bruce Macpherson.

STEWART, Jane Louise (Ia) 912 20th Ave., Coralville IA 52241 B Searcy AR 1956 d Robert & Louise. BA Rhodes Coll 1979; MDiv UTS Richmond 1982. D 7/26/2009 P 1/31/2010 Bp Alan Scarfe. m 6/5/2009 Linda Kroon c 2.

STEWART, John Bruce (Va) 4327 Ravensworth Rd Apt 210, Annandale VA 22003 **Goodwin Hse Incorporated Alexandria VA 2007-; Dir of Chapl Serv Goodwin Hse Ret Cmnty Alexandria VA 2007-; Adj Fac Oral Interp of Scripture VTS Alexandria VA 2003-; Adj Fac Liturg Dance Wesley TS Washington DC 1996-; Cntr For Liturg And The Arts Annandale VA 1989-; Fndr/Dir Cntr for Liturg and the Arts Annandale VA 1981-** B Schenectady NY 1951 s James & Rose. BA cl Hobart and Wm Smith Colleges 1973; MDiv VTS 1978. D 6/10/1978 Bp John Shelby Spong P 6/22/1979 Bp Robert Bruce Hall. Arts & Rel Forum Chair Washington Theol Consortium Washington DC 1982-1992; Cur S Alb's Epis Ch Annandale VA 1978-1980; Dio Sthrn Virginia Newport News VA 1982-2000; Dio SW Virginia Roanoke VA 1982-2000; Encounter Mus & Sprtl Dir Dio Virginia Richmond VA 1982-2000, Liturg Cmsn 1982-1987. "Hope for the Future," 2005; "Living the Image," 1983; "Never Give Up," 1981. ADLMC; CE Ntwk; EPF; OHC CCL.

STEWART JR, John Plummer (Ala) St Matthias Episc Church, 2310 Skyland Blvd E, Tuscaloosa AL 35405 B Charlotte NC 1951 s John & Fay. D 10/1/2016 Bp John Mckee Sloan Sr. c 3. Dept of Mnstry and Outreach Dio Alabama Birmingham 2017, Mem, Cmsn on Race Relatns 2017-.

STEWART, Kevin Paul (Mil) 4722 N 104th St, Wauwatosa WI 53225 **Dio Milwaukee Milwaukee WI 2014-; Mnstry Dir Hope St Mnstrs Milwaukee WI 2008-; D Trin Ch Milwaukee WI 2007-** B Akron OH 1957 s Paul & Betty. D 6/2/2007 Bp Steven Andrew Miller. m 7/6/1991 Melanie Stewart. Ord of Julian of Norwich 2009.

STEWART, Leslie (Dal) PO Box 292365, Lewisville TX 75029 **Dio Dallas Dallas TX 2016**- B Creve Coeur MO 1973 d Curtis & Ruth. BS Embry-Riddle Aeronautical U 1997; Physiology Off Flight Trng USAF Sch of Aerospace Med 2000; Aerospace Physiology Cert USAF Sch of Aerospace Med 2001; MDiv SMU - Perkins TS 2014. D 6/14/2014 P 5/9/2015 Bp Paul Emil Lambert. m 9/11/1993 Michael Dean Stewart c 1. D Ch Of The Annunc Lewisville TX 2014-2016. lesliestewart17@gmail.com

STEWART, Matthew Wellington (Mass) 11 W. Grove St., Middleboro MA 02346 **Ch of the H Sprt Fall River MA 2008**- B Boston MA 1974 D 6/4/2005 P 1/7/2006 Bp M(Arvil) Thomas Shaw. m 8/20/2005 Natasha Staatz c 2. Ch Of The Ascen Fall River MA 2008; S Steph's Memi Ch Lynn MA 2005-2008.

STEWART, Natalie Ann (ECR) PO Box 515, Aromas CA 95004 B Carmel CA 1945 d Hampton & Margaret. BA USC 1967; Cert Ang Stud Sch for Deacons 1995. D 6/11/1996 Bp Richard Lester Shimpfky. D All SS Ch Carmel CA 1998-2005; D S Mths Ch Seaside CA 1996-1998; Chair, Diocesean Corp Dio El Camino Real Salinas CA 1999-2001.

STEWART, Natasha (Mass) 407 Rochester St, Fall River MA 02720 **R Trin Ch Bridgewater MA 2011-, P-in-c 2008**- B Milwaukee WI 1978 d William & Christina. BA U NC 2001; MDiv GTS 2005. D 5/28/2005 Bp Porter Taylor P 1/7/2006 Bp Roy Frederick Cederholm Jr. m 8/20/2005 Matthew Wellington Stewart c 1. Asst R Par Of The Epiph Winchester MA 2006-2008; Asst for Chld, Yth and Families S Mich's Ch Marblehead MA 2005-2006.

STEWART, Pamela Fay (Colo) 126 W 2nd Ave, Denver CO 80223 B Minneapolis MN 1958 d Thomas & Shirley. RN Asbury Hospice Sch of Nrsng 1978; RN Asbury Hospice Sch of Nrsng 1978; RN Asbury Hosp Sch of Nrsng 1978; PA U of No Dakota Sch of Med 1996. D 6/13/2015 Bp Robert John O'Neill.

STEWART, Ralph Roderick (Oly) 23 Turtle Rock Ct, New Paltz NY 12561 **Ret 1995**- B Huron SD 1933 s Clarence & Julia. BA Carleton Coll 1954; STB GTS 1957; STM SWTS 1962. D 6/19/1957 P 12/21/1957 Bp Conrad H Gesner. c 3. Archit Com Dio Olympia Seattle 1981-1986, Dioc Counc 1995-1998, Chapl Loc Chapt Integrity 1987-1994, Cathd Chapt 1986, Ex Chapt 1985, Ecum Com on Bp 1984, Bd Cler Assn 1983, Bp Com CE 1981-1984, Bd Dir TS 1981-1982; R S Jn The Bapt Epis Ch Seattle WA 1980-1995; R All SS Epis Ch Appleton WI 1970-1980; P-in-c S Fran Ch Menomonee Falls WI 1962-1970; Assoc S Lk's Ch Evanston IL 1961-1962; Asst Cathd Of S Jas Chicago IL 1960-1962; Vic H Trin Epis Ch Geneseo IL 1957-1960; S Mary's Epis Ch Webster SD 1957-1960; ExCoun Dio Fond du Lac Appleton WI 1973-1974; Chair Com Ch Mus Dio Milwaukee Milwaukee WI 1963-1970. Auth, "A Christological Experiment," *The Amer Ch Quarterly*, 1963.

STEWART, Sarah C (WA) **S Jas Ch New York NY 2015**- D 11/8/2014 P 6/13/2015 Bp Mariann Edgar Budde.

STEWART JR, William Owen (Ga) PO Box 1171, Leesburg GA 31763 **Assoc Chr Epis Ch Cordele GA 2003**- B Americus GA 1948 s William & Patsy. Florida St U; U of The So Sch of Theo Sewanee; BA Valdosta St U 1995. D 11/29/2001 P 6/29/2004 Bp Henry Irving Louttit. m 7/16/1976 Ann Sharon c 3. Dn The Epis Ch Of S Jn And S Mk Albany GA 2009-2014; Int The Epis Ch Of The Annunc Vidalia GA 2008-2009; S Steph's Lee Cnty Leesburg GA 2003-2007.

STEWART-SICKING, Joseph (Md) 8890 McGaw Rd, Columbia MD 21045 **Asst Prof of Pstr Counslg Loyola U Maryland Baltimore MD 2007**- B Cincinnati OH 1973 s James & Angela. BS Xavier U 1995; EdD U Cinc 2002; CAS VTS 2003; MTS VTS 2008. D 6/23/2007 Bp Kenneth Lester Price P 6/28/2008 Bp Thomas Edward Breidenthal. m 5/10/1997 Megan Elizabeth Stewart-Sicking c 1. Adj Fac VTS Alexandria VA 2003-2009. Auth, "Joy that is complete," *All shall be well: Stories from CREDO*, Ch, 2009; Auth, "Resrch Methodology," *Chrsnty for the rest of us: How the Nbrhd Ch is revitalizing the faith*, HarperOne, 2006.

STEWART-SICKING, Megan Elizabeth (Md) 1509 Glencoe Rd, Glencoe MD 21152 **R Imm Epis Ch Glencoe MD 2010-; Co-chair, Conv Plnng Com Dio Maryland Baltimore MD 2011**- B Cincinnati OH 1975 BA Xavier U 1998; MDiv VTS 2003. D 10/26/2002 P 6/21/2003 Bp Herbert Thompson Jr. m 5/10/1997 Joseph Stewart-Sicking c 1. Assoc R Ch Of The Gd Shpd Burke VA 2004-2009; Trin Ch Columbus OH 2003-2004; Dir of Yth Mnstrs Dio Sthrn Ohio Cincinnati OH 1998-2000, Com on Agenda and Dispatch of Bus 2003-2004, Com on Agenda and Dispatch of Bus 1998-2000. megan@immanuelglencoe.org

STEWMAN, Kerry Jo (O) Po Box 366274, Bonita Springs FL 34136 B Springfield OH 1948 d Joe & Martha. U of Memphis 1969; BA Middle Tennessee St U 1981; MDiv Ya Berk 1988. D 6/1/1988 Bp Robert Poland Atkinson P 6/1/1989 Bp William Franklin Carr. m 11/26/1982 Zev William David Rosenberg c 3. Assoc Iona Hope Epis Ch Ft Myers FL 2011-2015; Vic New Life Epis Ch Uniontown OH 1995-1997; S Ptr's Ch Akron OH 1992-1995; P-in-c S Ptr's Epis Ch Akron OH 1992-1995; Ch Of The Gd Shpd Dallas TX 1991-1992, 1990-1991; Cur S Jn's Epis Ch Charleston WV 1988-1989.

ST GEORGE, David (Nwk) 8 Binney Rd, Old Lyme CT 06371 **Ret 1990**- B Montclair NJ 1925 s Lee & Pattie. DMin Drew U; BA U of Pennsylvania 1952; BD EDS 1955; Coll of Preachers 1960; STM PrTS 1968. D 7/1/1955 Bp Benjamin M Washburn P 2/1/1956 Bp Lane W Barton. c 6. Supply Dio Connecticut

Meriden CT 1994-2003; Int S Jas Ch Montclair NJ 1993-1994; Int S Geo's Epis Ch Maplewood NJ 1992-1993; Int Chr Ch Short Hills NJ 1991-1992, P-in-c 1958-1990; R S Ptr's Ch Essex Fells NJ 1971-1990; R All SS Ch Millington NJ 1964-1971; S Simon By-The-Sea Summit NJ 1958-1978; Ch of Our Sav Sum Lake OR 1955-1958; P-in-c S Lk's Ch Lakeview OR 1955-1958. Auth, "Pulpit Dig".

ST. GERMAIN, Beverly Anne Lavallee (Vt) Three Cathedral Square 3A, Burlington VT 05401 B Burlington VT 1933 d Romeo & Eva. D 9/21/1988 Bp Daniel Lee Swenson. m 3/17/1952 Kenneth Paul St Germain c 1. D Cathd Ch Of S Paul Burlington VT 1988-1998; Chapl/Perp D Burlington Hosp 1988-1996.

ST GERMAIN JR, Kenneth Paul (SO) 2151 Dorset Rd, Columbus OH 43221 **R S Mk's Epis Ch Columbus OH 2007**- B Burlington VT 1965 s Kenneth & Beverly. BA U of Vermont 1987; MDiv Yale DS 1990. D 8/24/1990 Bp Daniel Lee Swenson P 6/21/1991 Bp John Henry Smith. P-in-c S Mary's Ch Waynesville OH 2006-2007; Assoc R S Geo's Epis Ch Dayton OH 1993-2007; Cur S Jn's Ch Huntington WV 1990-1993. Wilcott Calkins Prchng Awd.

ST GERMAIN-ILER III, Robert (Ala) 347 South Central Ave., Alexander City AL 35010 **R S Jas' Epis Ch Alexander City AL 2012-; Dn, Convoc of E Alabama Dio Alabama Birmingham 2013-, Dioc Coun 2009-2012, Dioc Hd Sprtl Dir, Curs 2009-, Cmsn on Hisp Mnstrs 2002-2004; Bd Mem Tallapoosa Chr Crises Cntr Alexander City AL 2012**- B Glendale CA 1957 s Robert & Lorraine. AA Snead St Coll 2001; BA Athens St U 2003; MDiv Sewanee: The U So, TS 2006. D 5/24/2006 Bp Marc Handley Andrus P 12/12/2006 Bp Henry Nutt Parsley Jr. m 10/6/1990 Elizabeth A St Germain-Iler c 3. R S Columba-In-The-Cove Owens X Rds AL 2006-2012; Bd Mem Care Cntr New Hope AL 2006-2012.

STICHWEH, Michael Terry (CFla) 410 Meridian Street, Apt 604, Indianapolis IN 46204 **Ret 1995**- B Dayton OH 1940 s Carl & Catherine. BD EDS; BS Mia 1962. D 6/4/1966 P 12/17/1966 Bp Horace W B Donegan. S Mths Epis Ch Clermont FL 1996-1997; S Mary Of The Ang Epis Ch Orlando FL 1995-1996; S Gabr's Ch Hollis NY 1973-1995; The Woodhull Schools Hollis NY 1973-1995; Asst Min Ch Of The Incarn New York NY 1966-1972. Phi Beta Kappa.

STICKLEY, David (Cal) 101 Gold Mine Dr, San Francisco CA 94131 **Archd Dio California San Francisco CA 2016-; Epis Sch For Deacons Berkeley CA 2015-; Sojourn Multifaith Chapl San Francisco CA 2014-; D S Aid's Ch San Francisco CA 2009**- B Binghamton, NY 1963 s Karl & Jean. BS Ithaca Coll 1985; Diac Stds Sch for Deacons 2005. D 6/6/2009 Bp Marc Handley Andrus. Ch Of The H Innoc San Francisco CA 2009-2015; The Epis Ch Of S Jn The Evang San Francisco CA 2009-2014. david.stickley@sfdph.org

STICKNEY, James (Cal) 1324 Devonshire Ct, El Cerrito CA 94530 B San Francisco CA 1945 s Robert & Mary. BA Gonzaga U 1969; MDiv Jesuit TS 1975; STM Jesuit TS 1976. Rec 10/1/1982 as Priest Bp William Edwin Swing. m 10/4/1997 Joan J Stickney. Int S Jn The Bapt Lodi CA 2011-2013; P-in-c S Paul's Epis Ch Modesto CA 2009-2011, P-in-c 2009-2010; Int Ch Of The H Fam Fresno CA 2008-2009; Int Epis Ch Of The Sav Hanford CA 2008; Int St. Jn's Epis Ch Clayton CA 2006-2008; R S Alb's Ch Albany CA 1986-2006; Asst S Mk's Epis Ch Palo Alto CA 1984-1986; Asst Gd Shpd Epis Ch Belmont CA 1982-1984; Chair/Cnvnr Dio California San Francisco CA 2003-2007, Dioc Coun 1999-2003. Auth, "Splitting Your Dio: Can You Afford It?," *LivCh*, LivCh, 2008; Auth, "A Hist of Camp Galilee, Nevada: 1920 - 2000," Camp Galilee Fndt, 2001.

STICKNEY, Jane Burr (Ct) 14 Lone Pine Trl, Higganum CT 06441 B Bridgeport CT 1947 d Horace & Rita. BA Drew U 1968; Cert Moray Hse Coll of Educ Edinburgh Gb 1969; MEd Boston U 1971; STM GTS 1987. D 6/13/1987 P 11/17/1987 Bp Arthur Edward Walmsley. m 5/23/1970 David A Stickney. Vic S Jn's Ch Guilford CT 1997-2009; Middlesex Area Cluster Mnstry Higganum CT 1996-1997, 1987-1989; Ch Of The H Trin Middletown CT 1987-1996; Middlesex Cluster Mnstry 1986-1997; Serv UCC 1972-1986.

STICKNEY, Joyce Erwin (Los) 28211 Pacific Coast Hwy, Malibu CA 90265 **R S Aid's Epis Ch Malibu CA 2005**- B Boston MA 1970 d Robert & Nanette. BA Ob 1992; MDiv Fuller TS 1995; CAS CDSP 1998; D.Min. Fuller TS 2012. D 6/6/1998 Bp Chester Lovelle Talton P 9/9/1999 Bp Frederick Houk Borsch. c 2. Assoc S Aug By-The-Sea Par Santa Monica CA 2000-2005; Assoc S Edm's Par San Marino CA 1998-2000; Assoc For Yth And Fam Mnstrs S Geo's Par La Can CA 1992-1995.

STIEFEL, Jennifer H (NH) 30 Holiday Drive #341, Dover NH 03820 B Boston MA 1944 d Kilby & Elizabeth. BA Rad/Harv 1966; MDiv Nash 1978; MPhil UTS 1993; PhD UTS 2000. D 5/29/1985 Bp William Carl Frey. m 12/6/1969 Robert Earl Stiefel. D Chr Ch Portsmouth NH 1991-2002; 1985-1991; Dir Epis Inst Dio Colorado Denver CO 1980-1987, COM 1981-1987; Dioc Coun Dio New Hampshire Concord NH 1994-1995. Auth, "Wmn Deacons in 1 Tim: a Linguistic & Literary look at 'Wmn likewise' (1 Tim 3:11)," *NT Stds Volume 41*, 1995; Auth, "Scripture Background," *Living the Gd News, Inc.*; Auth, "Scripture Background," *Living the Gd News, Inc..* AAR 1992-2002; NAACP 1993; No Amer Assn for Diac 1985; SBL 1988-2002. Rel Schlr SBL 1996; Fllshp ECF 1987. jstiefel1@comcast.net

STIEFEL, Robert Earl (NH) 30 Holiday Dr Unit 341, Dover NH 03820 **P Dio New Hampshire Concord NH 2002-, Committe for Election and Consecration of a Bp 2002-2004, Cont Educ of the Cler (Chair) 1998-2004, COM 1994-2000, GC Dep 1993-1997; Res Chapl Maple Suites Indep Living Ret Cmnty 2012-** B Baltimore MD 1941 s Earl & Gertrude. BA Ob 1963; PhD Harv 1970; MDiv Nash 1978. D 6/17/1978 Bp Lyman Cunningham Ogilby P 2/26/1979 Bp William Carl Frey. m 12/6/1969 Jennifer H Smith. Dir, Fellowships Off U of New Hampshire Durham NH 2005-2011; Instr in Hmnts U of New Hampshire Durham NH 1992-2013; R Chr Ch Portsmouth NH 1991-2001; R Trin Ch Asbury Pk NJ 1988-1991; R The Ch Of Chr The King (Epis) Arvada CO 1980-1988; Asst to Bp Dio Colorado Denver CO 1978-1980, Exam Chapl 1981-1988; Asst. Prof. of German Hav Haverford PA 1969-1975; Res Asst. to the Sr Tutor Lowell Hse Harv 1966-1969; Pres's Cmsn on GLTBQ Affrs U of New Hampshire 2002-2005. Auth, "At the Loss of a Pet or Other Animal: A Serv of Grieving and Thanksgiving," *nhepiscopal.org*, 1997; Auth, "Preaching to All the People," *ATR*, 1991; Auth, "Transfiguraton and Transformation in Dante's Div Comedy," *Nashotah Revs*, 1976; Auth, "Heine's Ballet Scenarios," *Germanic Revs*, 1969. Amer Assn for Psychol Type 1984-2001; AAPC 1985-2011; Integrity, USA 1994; OSB - Confrator 1963-1984; OSB - Life Oblate 1984. Awd for Racial and Rel Harmony B'nai B'rith and Temple Israel, Portsmouth, NH 2000; Fell Coll of Preachers 1986.

STIEGLER, Mark A (Roch) 3835 Oneill Rd, Lima NY 14485 B Flushing NY 1941 s George & Edna. BFA SUNY 1966; MDiv Bex Sem 2002. D 6/1/2002 P 3/22/2003 Bp Jack Marston Mckelvey. m 9/19/2002 Shirley Stiegler c 2. R Zion Ch Avon NY 2003-2012; Dio Rochester Henrietta 2002-2003; Cur Gr Ch Lyons NY 2002-2003.

STIEPER, John Richard (Chi) 7 Fernwood Dr, Barrington IL 60010 **Ret 2000-** B Chicago IL 1935 s Elmer & Margaret. BA DePauw U 1957; Cert U of Montpelier Montpelier FR 1958; MDiv Ya Berk 1961. D 10/20/1961 Bp Gerald Francis Burrill P 4/1/1962 Bp Charles L Street. c 2. R Ch Of S Columba Of Iona Hanover Pk IL 1964-2000; Admin. Dir S Leonards Oratory Chicago IL 1963-1964; Cur Ch Of S Paul And The Redeem Chicago IL 1961-1963; Dioc Coun Dio Chicago Chicago IL 1979-1984. SSC 1972.

STIFLER, Linnea (WMich) 2010 Nichols Rd, Kalamazoo MI 49004 B Kalamazoo MI 1949 d Robert & Ruth. MEd Aquinas Coll 1999; MDiv Earlham Sch of Rel 2012; MDiv Earlham Sch of Rel 2012; Angl Dplma Seabury Wstrn 2012. D 12/15/2012 P 6/22/2013 Bp Robert R Gepert. m 10/6/1974 Michael Edward Stifler c 3. S Mart Of Tours Epis Ch Kalamazoo MI 2013-2017.

STILES, Katherine Mitchell (Me) 99 Brattle St, Cambridge MA 02138 **Sr Advsr to Prog Tutu Inst for Pryr and Pilgrimage 2004-; Pstr Care and Sprtl Direction EDS Cambridge MA 2003-; Clincl Soc Worker; U Hlth Serv Harv Cambridge MA. 2001-; Psych and Sprtl Direction Priv Pract Cambridge MA. 1986-; Psych and Sprtl Direction Priv Pract Cambridge MA. 1977-** B Salem MA 1952 B.A. Smith 1973; MSW Case Wstrn Reserve U 1977; MDiv EDS 2003. D 6/14/2003 P 12/20/2003 Bp Chilton Richardson Knudsen. c 1.

STILES-RANDAK, Susan (RI) Peace Dale Estates, 1223 Saugatucket Rd Apt A102, Peace Dale RI 02879 B Chicago IL 1940 d Arthur & Mary. Salem Coll Winston-Salem NC 1960; Providence Coll 1988; MDiv Andover Newton TS 1992. D 1/27/1996 Bp Morgan Porteus P 5/24/1997 Bp Gerry Wolf. c 1. Ch Of The H Sprt Charlestown RI 2005-2008, Int Vic 2005-2008; Int Emm Epis Ch Cumberland RI 2003-2005; P-in-c Chr Epis Ch Tarrytown NY 2001-2003; Int Ch Of The Ascen Wakefield RI 2000-2009; Int S Thos Ch Hanover NH 2000-2001; Int Ch Of The H Sprt Plymouth NH 1999-2000; Int S Jn The Evang Yalesville CT 1998-1999; Int S Mart's Ch Providence RI 1997-1998; S Jn The Div Ch Saunderstown RI 1996-1997; S Paul's Ch N Kingstown RI 1996.

STILL, Kimberly L. (Fla) 919 San Fernando St, Fernandina Beach FL 32034 **Assoc The Epis Ch Of Beth-By-The-Sea Palm Bch FL 2014-** B Springfield IL 1960 d Samuel & Rosita. BD OR SU 1985; MBA Loyola Coll 1995; MDiv Sewanee: The U So, TS 2007; MDiv Sewanee: The U So, TS 2007. D 5/27/2007 P 12/9/2007 Bp Samuel Johnson Howard. S Ptr's Ch Poolesville MD 2013-2014; S Marg's-Hibernia Epis Ch Fleming Island FL 2009-2012; S Ptr's Ch Fernandina Bch FL 2007-2009.

STILLINGS, Eugene Nelson (Eau) 1220 East St, Baraboo WI 53913 **Died 12/6/2015** B London OH 1919 s Carl & Cora. BS OH SU 1942; MS OH SU 1947; Cert Bex Sem 1957. D 6/15/1957 Bp John P Craine P 12/21/1957 Bp Richard Ainslie Kirchhoffer. c 5. Ret 1984-2015; Int Dio Eau Claire Eau Claire WI 1984-2002, Cn-Mssy 1976-1984; Dio Fond du Lac Appleton WI 1984-2002; Int Dio Milwaukee Milwaukee WI 1984-2002; Our Sav's Phillips WI 1982-1984; S Kath's Ch Owen WI 1982-1984; S Marg's Epis Ch Pk Falls WI 1982-1984; St Marys Ch Medford WI 1982-1984; Cn-Mssy S Mary In Medford WI 1978-1984; R S Jas Epis Ch Milwaukee WI 1969-1976; Assoc R Gr Ch Madison WI 1965-1969; R S Andr's Epis Ch Greencastle IN 1959-1965; Vic S Lk's Epis Ch Shelbyville IN 1957-1959.

STILLINGS, Kyle David (WTenn) St. Elisabeth's Episcopal Church, 6033 Old Brownsville Rd, Memphis TN 38135 **S Elis's Epis Ch Memphis TN 2015-; Exec Dir Wm Temple Epis Ctr Galveston TX 2008-** B Seattle WA 1979 s David & Donna. BA U of Washington 2001; MDiv VTS 2007. D 1/26/2008 P 12/11/2008 Bp Gregory Harold Rickel. m 1/2/2012 Ines G Grevel c 2. Chapl Epis U Cntr Tallahassee FL 2012-2015; The Wm Temple Fndt Galveston TX 2008-2012.

STILLMAN, Ann Allen (CNY) 2239 Gridley Paige Rd, Deansboro NY 13328 **D Gr Epis Ch Waterville NY 2006-** B Utica NY 1931 d Albert & Lillian. BS NWU 1953; MS U of Wisconsin 1979; Bex Sem 2005. D 10/7/2006 P 6/27/2007 Bp Gladstone Bailey Adams III. c 4. Dept Chairperson New Hartford HS 1978-1994.

STIMPSON, Peter K (NJ) 220 W Kilbride, Williamsburg VA 23188 **P-in-c H Trin Ch Sprg Lake NJ 2003-** B White Plains NY 1946 s Charles & Ina. AA Mater Christi Sem Albany NY 1966; BA U S Paul Ottawa ON CA 1968; BA U of Ottawa 1968; STB U S Paul Ottawa ON CA 1971; BTh U of Ottawa 1971; MTh S Paul U Ottawa CA 1972; MSW SUNY 1977. Rec 6/2/1983 as Priest Bp Wilbur Emory Hogg Jr. m 8/14/2005 Laurene P Orcutt c 2. Bd Trst The Carrier Clnc Belle Mead NJ 2007-2010; Trin Counslg Serv Princeton NJ 1989-2014; Dir Trin Counslg Serv Princeton NJ 1989-2014; P-in-c All SS Ch Round Lake NY 1985-1987; Dir Epis Counslg Serv Albany NY 1977-1989; Chair, Pstr Response Team Dio New Jersey Trenton NJ 2005-2014, Nominee, Election for Bp 2003, Mem, Anti-Racism Cmsn 2002-2008, Chair, Deputation to GC 2001-2003, Mem, Stndg Com 1998-2001, Chair, Deputation to GC 1998-2000, Mem, Dioc Coun 1994-1997, Chair, Wellness Com 1993-1998; Chair Com on Mar & Fam Dio Albany Greenwich NY 1986-1989, Chair, Com on Mar and the Fam 1986-1989, Dep, Deputation to GC 1986-1989, Mem, Stndg Com 1986-1989. Auth, "Personal Advice Column," *US 1*, 2011; Auth, "MAP TO HAPPINESS: Straightforward Advice on Everyday Issues," *Self-Help Bk*, iUniverse, 2008; Auth, "Personal Advice Column," *Town Topic*, 1996; Auth, "Personal Advice Column," *Via Media*, Dio New Jersey, 1990; Auth, "Sectarian Agencies," *Encyclopedia of Soc Wk*, 1986; Auth, "Personal Advice Column," *The Albany Epis*, Dio Albany, 1983. AAMFT 1981; Dplma Amer Bd Exams in Clincl Soc Wk 1988; Dplma NASW 1987. Soc Worker of the Year Awd SUNY 1992; Bp's Awd for Distinguished Serv Dio Albany 1989.

STINE, Stephen Blaine (Tex) 1220 Quirby Lane, Tyler TX 75701 **Hon Chapl Smith Cnty Commissioners Crt Tyler Texas 2007-; Hon Chapl Texas Hse of Representatives Austin Texas 2007-; D Chr Epis Ch Tyler TX 1998-** B Midland TX 1951 s Edward & Katherine. BS Texas Tech U 1972; Dplma Rutgers The St U of New Jersey 1980; Cert Theol Stud Prchr Lewis Sch of Mnstry 1985; EFM Sewanee: The U So, TS 1990; MA The U of Memphis 1996; PhD The U of Memphis 2007. D 8/24/1986 Bp Richard Mitchell Trelease Jr. m 2/4/1999 Laurie Margaret Dowell c 1. D Chr Ch Memphis TN 1992-1998; Chapl St. Aloysis AIDS Hospice Memphis Tennessee 1992-1995; D Ch of the H Apos Collierville TN 1990-1992; D Calv Ch Memphis TN 1987-1990; Imm Epis Ch La Grange TN 1987-1990; D St Lk's Epis Ch Anth NM 1986-1987; Secy of the Hisp Mnstry Cmsn Dio The Rio Grande Albuquerque 1985-1987. Auth, "Hist of WHER Radio in Memphis," *Papers of W Tennessee Hist Soc*, W Tennessee Hist Soc, 2000. Assn for Epis Deacons 2011.

STINGLEY, Elizabeth Anne (Los) 12880 Riverview Drive, 8821 SVL Box, Victorville CA 92395 **Chapl Victor Vlly Global Med Cntr VIctorville CA 2010-** B Los Angeles CA 1938 d Harry & Mary. BS Lebanon Vlly Coll 1976; MDiv CDSP 1990. D 6/16/1990 P 1/12/1991 Bp Frederick Houk Borsch. c 2. Vic S Hilary's Epis Ch Hesperia CA 1992-2009; Assoc S Paul's Par Lancaster CA 1991-1992.

STINNETT, Roger Allen (WMo) 804 Wendy Ln, Carthage MO 64836 **Ret 2003-** B Joplin MO 1942 s Jack & Meta. Dioc Sch for Mnstry; Other; AA SW Bapt U 1962; BS Pittsburg St U 1964; MS Pittsburg St U 1968; Trng Sch In Theol MO 1972. D 12/7/1991 P 6/7/1992 Bp John Clark Buchanan. m 11/30/1963 Sherrie Lynne Stinnett c 2. Vic (Ret) S Steph's Ch Monett MO 2003-2005; S Jn's Ch Springfield MO 2000-2002, R 2000-2002, 1997-1998; Chapl Freeman Hosp Joplin MO 1998-2000; S Phil's Ch Joplin MO 1996-1997, P-in-c 1994-1996, 1994-1995, Assoc 1994, Asst 1992-1994, D 1991-1992. Auth, "Joplin: A Pictorial Hist," 1981. The Bishops Shield Bp Barry R. Howe, Dio W - Mo 2002.

STINSON, Marian (Ct) 84 Ledgewood Dr, Glastonbury CT 06033 B Minneapolis MN 1951 d Malcolm & Loraine. BSW USC 1973; MS USC 1974; MDiv CDSP 1991. D 6/15/1991 Bp Frederick Houk Borsch P 2/16/1992 Bp William Edwin Swing. m 5/25/1991 William Hardwick c 2. P-in-c S Lk's Ch So Glastonbury CT 2006-2016; St Gabr's Ch E Berlin CT 2004-2006; P-in-c Trin Epis Ch Collinsville CT 2000-2004; St Columbas Epis Ch Big Bear City CA 1995-2000; S Paul's Epis Ch San Rafael CA 1993-1995; S Steph's Par Bel Tiburon CA 1992-1993, 1991.

STINSON, Richard Lyon (Pgh) 191 Ashby Ln, Front Royal VA 22630 B New York NY 1938 s Dwight & Doris. BA Hob 1960; MDiv EDS 1963; STM Sewanee: The U So, TS 1969; Cert Amer U 1974; DMin How 1976. D 6/8/1963 P 12/21/1963 Bp Leland Stark. m 12/28/1960 Anne M Freudenberg c 3. Supply Plus Chr Ch Millwood VA 2015-2017; Dep/Chapl Indiana Cnty PA Coroner's Off 2009-2013; Vic Ch of SS Thos and Lk Patton PA 2007-2009; Chapl Pennsylvania St Police 2002-2011; Asst St Pauls Epis Ch Oaks PA 2001-2005; R Washington Memi Chap Vlly Forge PA 1992-2000; Adj Prof VTS Alexandria VA 1983; Chapl (Col) Virginia NG VA 1971-1991; R S Jas' Epis Ch Mt Vernon

VA 1970-1992; Chapl US-A 1967-1970; Assoc Vic Gd Shpd Mssn (Navajo) Ft. Defiance AZ 1966-1967; R S Lk's Ch Hope NJ 1963-1966. Assoc, Cmnty of St. Jn Bapt 1965; Assoc, OHC 1965; Fllshp Contemplative Pryr 1970-2004; Intl Conf Of Police Chapl, Life Mem 1984; Ord S Lazarus Of Jerusalem 1984; Sub-Chapl Ord S Jn 1996. Silver Pat Henry Awd For Patriotic Serv Mltry Ord Of The Wrld Wars 1998; Brigadier Gnrl St Of Virginia 1992; LJ McConnel Awd For Outstanding Serv As Police Chapl Inst Of Indstrl And Commercial Mnstrs 1983; Life Saving Awd Of Merit Amer Red Cross 1969. annestinson1@centurylink.net

STIPE, Nickie Maxine (Ak) 280 Northern Ave Apt 10-A, Avondale Estates GA 30002 B Hereford TX 1960 d Paul & Frances. Emory U; BS Oklahoma Panhandle St U 1983; MDiv Ya Berk 1993; STM Ya Berk 1994. D 8/24/1993 Bp Sam Byron Hulsey. Non-par. AAR; SBL.

STISCIA, Alfred Ronald (CPa) 5092 Riverfront Dr, Bradenton FL 34208 B Upland PA 1942 s Alfred & Elizabeth. BA Dickinson Coll 1964; STB GTS 1967. D 6/1/1967 P 12/1/1967 Bp Dean Theodore Stevenson. R St Andrews in the City Epis Ch Harrisburg PA 1973-2007; Vic S Mich And All Ang Ch Middletown PA 1968-1973; Cur S Jn's Epis Ch Carlisle PA 1967-1968.

STITT, David Watson (WLa) 713 Circle C, Hastings NE 68901 **Ret 2005-; Ret 2001-** B Hastings NE 1938 s William & Agnes. BSinBA U of Nebraska 1960; MDiv Trin Theol Coll, Singapore 1985; DMiss TESM 2005. Trans 9/1/1989 as Priest Bp William Harvey Wolfrum. m 4/18/1958 Darlene G Stitt c 2. Ch Of The Incarn Alexandria LA 1999-2005; H Sprt Episc. Ch Epis Ch Of The H Sprt Lafayette LA 1999-2000; R Gr Epis Ch Chadron NE 1993-1999; R Epis Ch Of The Trsfg Vail CO 1989-1993; Serv Ch of Singapore 1982-1989. Auth, "Cov - Martoma Ch," *India - Kerala St*, 1989. p.mdavid@windstream.net

STIVERS, Donald Austin (Los) 5023 Calle Tania, Santa Barbara CA 93111 **Ret 1991-** B Geneva NY 1924 s Clinton & Laura. BA Hobart and Wm Smith Colleges 1948; BD SWTS 1951; S Augustines Coll Cbury GB 1967; MTh Colgate Rochester Crozer DS 1972; MTh CRDS 1972. D 6/11/1951 P 12/21/1951 Bp Dudley S Stark. m 9/10/1960 Florence Stivers c 2. Vic Chr The King Epis Ch Santa Barbara CA 1983-1991; R S Chris's Epis Ch Boulder City NV 1979-1982; R All SS Angl Ch Rochester NY 1953-1979; Cur S Thos Epis Ch Rochester NY 1951-1953. Phi Beta Kappa Hob, Geneva, NY 2048; Polly Bond Awd-Photography ECom 1984; Henry Benjamin Whipple Schlr Seabury-Wstrn, Evanston, IL 1951; Challes Palmerston Anderson Schlr Seabury-Wstrn, Evanston, IL 1950.

ST JOHN, Andrew Reginald (NY) 1 E 29th St, New York NY 10016 B Melbourne Australia 1944 s Reginald & Lillian. LLB U of Melbourne 1966; Australian Coll of Theol 1971; STM GTS 1984. Trans 2/2/2006 Bp Mark Sean Sisk. R Ch Of The Trsfg New York NY 2006-2016; Int Ch Of The H Trin New York NY 2003-2005; Serv Angl Ch of Australia 1971-2001. DD GTS, New York 1995.

ST JOHNS, Ernest Keys (RG) 1002 N Robert St, Ludington MI 49431 **Ret Assoc S Mary's Epis Ch Albuquerque NM 2001-; 1993-** B Pontiac MI 1927 s Harrison & Bessie. Ya Berk; GW; BA Grand Vlly St U; Wayne. D 6/28/1959 P 6/29/1960 Bp Richard Stanley Merrill Emrich. m 12/24/1969 Rosemary E St Johns c 2. Supply P Dio Wstrn Michigan Kalamazoo MI 1993-1997, Int 1986-1990, Vic 1977-1978; Rgstr S Geo's Coll Jerusalem IL 1992-1993; R S Andr's Ch Big Rapids MI 1980-1985; Ch of the Medtr Harbert MI 1977-1980; Non-par 1965-1976; Cur S Paul's Epis Ch St Jos MI 1962-1965; Vic S Paul's Epis Ch Elk Rapids MI 1960-1962; P-in-c S Sebaldus Bellaire MI 1960-1962; Cur S Tim's Ch Detroit MI 1959-1960; Rgstr; Vol in Mssn St Geo's Coll Jerusalem 1992-1993.

ST LOUIS, JN Michelin (Hai) **Dio Haiti Port-au-Prince HT 2009-** B Thomazeau Haiti 1978 s Martin & Marie. BTh Seminaire de Theologie EEH 2007. D 11/1/2009 P 6/29/2010 Bp Jean Zache Duracin.

ST LOUIS, June Allison (Ct) Virginia Theological Seminary, 3737 Seminary Road, Alexandria VA 22304 **Dir of Field Educ and the Second Three Years Prog VTS Alexandria VA 2010-** B Trinidad WEST INDIES 1959 d Lawrence & Ivy. BA How 1985; MS How 1988; PhD How 1991; MDiv VTS 2000. D 6/10/2000 Bp Ronald Hayward Haines P 1/13/2001 Bp Jane Hart Holmes Dixon. Cn Vic Chr Ch Cathd Hartford CT 2005-2010; Asst to R Ch Of Our Sav Silver Sprg MD 2000-2004. Prof Nissim Levy Undergraduate Resrch Awd How 1984; Phi Beta Kappa How 1984. astlouis@vts.edu

ST LOUIS, Leslie (WA) 13106 Annapolis Rd, Bowie MD 20720 **R H Trin Epis Ch Bowie MD 2008-** B Wiesbaden Germany 1960 d Terence & Lydia. BS U of New Mex 1985; MDiv Sewanee: The U So, TS 2004. D 5/29/2004 P 1/8/2005 Bp Charles Glenn VonRosenberg. Asst S Paul's Ch Rochester NY 2004-2008.

ST LOUIS, Samuel (Hai) **Dio Haiti Port-au-Prince HT 1999-** B 1966 D. m 4/18/2006 Guerling Julmiste Saint Louis c 3.

STOCK, David Robert (Okla) 4036 Neptune Dr, Oklahoma City OK 73116 **R S Jn's Ch Oklahoma City OK 2005-** B Logan UT 1964 s Reed & Janet. BS Utah St U 1988; MDiv CDSP 2000. D 6/1/2000 P 1/25/2001 Bp Carolyn Tanner Irish. m 11/10/2001 Emily J Schnabl. Asst S Ptr's Epis Ch S Louis MO 2000-2005.

STOCKARD, Matthew Easter (EC) Po Box 1336, Kinston NC 28503 **Fac CREDO Memphis TN 2010-; Cn Ordnry Dio E Carolina Kinston NC 2000-** B Greensboro NC 1955 s Ben & Elizabeth. BA U NC 1977; MA U NC 1980; MDiv Sewanee: The U So, TS 1986. D 12/7/1986 Bp Robert Whitridge Estill P 12/13/1987 Bp Frank Harris Vest Jr. m 2/28/1981 Lisa Stockard. R S Paul's Ch Beaufort NC 1989-1999; S Tim's Ch Wilson NC 1987-1989. mstockard@diocese-eastcarolina.org

STOCKSDALE, Robert (Ct) 183 Pin Oak Dr, Southington CT 06489 **Int Gr Ch Newington CT 2012-** B Jacksonville FL 1942 s William & Ena. PhD Arizona Pharmaceutical Assn 1986; MDiv Bex Sem 1991. D 6/8/1991 Bp Joseph Thomas Heistand P 12/1/1991 Bp William George Burrill. m 6/14/2003 Roberta Stocksdale c 3. Supply S Mart's Ch Hartford CT 2012; Supply S Paul's Epis Ch Shelton CT 2012; R S Andr's Ch Meriden CT 2003-2011; R Ch Of The Gd Shpd Sioux Falls SD 1998-2003; R St Mk Epis Ch No Tonawanda NY 1994-1998, Asst 1991-1992; Dir Of Hosp Chapl Childern's Hosp Buffalo NY 1992-1998; Asst Ch Of The Ascen Buffalo NY 1992-1994; Dio Wstrn New York Tonawanda NY 1992-1994; Stff Chapl Childern's Hosp Buffalo NY 1991-1994; Stff Chapl Strong Memi Hosp Rochester NY 1989-1991. ACPE 1998; Emiss 1993.

STOCKTON, James Vernon (Tex) 16306 Ascent Cove, Pflugerville TX 78660 B Saint Louis MO 1958 s Vernon & Martha. BA Abilene Chr U 1992; MDiv Harvard DS 1996; CITS Epis TS of the SW 1999. D 8/28/1999 Bp Claude Edward Payne P 8/30/2000 Bp Don Adger Wimberly. m 6/26/1988 Lee Elena Stockton c 3. Chapl Dio Texas Houston TX 2013-2015; R Ch Of The Resurr Austin TX 2001-2013; Asst R S Steph's Epis Ch Houston TX 1999-2001.

STOCKTON, Marietta Grace (WK) 406 W. Kingman Ave., Lakin KS 67860 B Cherokee OK 1939 d Nora Belle. D 11/9/2002 P 10/11/2003 Bp James Marshall Adams Jr.

STOCKWELL-TANGEMAN, Carolyn Lee (WMo) 5618 Wyandotte St, Kansas City MO 64113 B Elmhurst IL 1945 d Clifford & Helen. U of Missouri 1968; U of Pennsylvania 1968; W Missouri Sch of Mnstry 1993. D 1/23/1993 Bp John Clark Buchanan. m 6/4/1987 John Theodore Tangeman c 1. D Gr And H Trin Cathd Kansas City MO 1993-2000.

STODDARD, Gary David (Colo) B 1955 D 6/18/2016 Bp Robert John O'Neill. m 12/27/1977 Rachelle Paulich c 3. CBS 2012; GAS 2012; SocMary 2008.

STODDART, David Michael (Va) Church of Our Saviour, 1165 Rio Road East, Charlottesville VA 22901 **R Ch Of Our Sav Charlottesvlle VA 2005-** B Port Chester NY 1961 s James & Deborah. BA Harv 1983; MDiv GTS 1989. D 7/1/1989 P 1/27/1990 Bp George Nelson Hunt III. m 6/19/1993 Lori Ann Stoddart c 2. R S Lk's Ch Worcester MA 1994-2005; Assoc Chr Ch Westerly RI 1989-1994. Fllshp of S Jn.

STODGHILL, Dawnell S (WLa) St Thomas Episcopal Church, 3706 Bon Aire Drive, Monroe LA 71203 **Iglesia Epis La Esperanza de Familias Unidas Monroe LA 2017-; P in Res S Thos' Ch Monroe LA 2007-** B Butte MT 1966 d Donald & Ruth. BA U of Montana 1989; MDiv CDSP 1996. D 4/28/2007 P 12/1/2007 Bp D Avid Bruce Macpherson. m 1/7/1995 Thomas Whitfield Stodghill c 2.

STODGHILL, Marion W (Ky) Norton Hospital, Chaplain, 200 E. Chesnut Street, Louisville KY 40202 **Chapl Norton Healthcare Louisville KY 2001-; P Norton Healthcare Louisville KY 2001-** B Baltimore MD 1959 d William & Susan. BA U MI 1981; MDiv Ya Berk 1984. D 6/10/1984 P 5/1/1985 Bp David Reed. c 1. S Mk's Epis Ch Louisville KY 2015-2016; Resurr Ch Louisville KY 2010; H Trin Ch Brandenburg KY 2006-2007; S Jas Ch Shelbyville KY 2005-2006; S Paul's Epis Ch New Albany IN 2005, 2004; St Andr's Ch Louisville KY 1997-2001; St Dav's Epis Ch Minnetonka MN 1993-1996; Cathd Ch Of S Mk Minneapolis MN 1989-1990; Asst R S Pat's Ch Washington DC 1987-1989; Cur S Paul's Ch Kansas City MO 1985-1987; D-In-Res S Fran In The Fields Harrods Creek KY 1984-1985.

STODGHILL III, Thomas Whitfield (WLa) 3435 Westminster Avenue, Monroe LA 71201 **R S Alb's Epis Ch Monroe LA 2011-** B Winnsboro LA 1958 s Thomas & Mary. BA LSU 1982; MDiv CDSP 1996. D 6/1/1996 P 6/7/1997 Bp William Edwin Swing. m 1/7/1995 Dawnell S Stodghill c 2. R S Andr's Epis Ch Mer Rouge LA 2000-2011; Vic Ch Of The Redeem Oak Ridge LA 2000; Asst S Paul's Epis Ch Walnut Creek CA 1998-2000; Asst S Paul's Epis Ch Benicia CA 1996-1998. wsodghill@aol.com

STOESSEL, Andrew James (Mass) 36 Cornell St, Roslindale MA 02131 **P-in-c S Mich's Ch Marblehead MA 2002-** B Santa Monica CA 1954 s James & Deborah. BA U of Massachusetts 1980; MDiv EDS 1998. D 6/2/2001 Bp Barbara Clementine Harris P 6/8/2002 Bp M(Arvil) Thomas Shaw. m 8/30/1997 Susan Mary Wythe. Asst R S Steph's Ch Cohasset MA 2001-2002.

STOFFREGEN, Diana Lynn Jacobson (Spok) 5609 S Custer Street, Spokane WA 99223 B Colfax WA 1946 d Edward & Afton. Gonzaga U; BA Estrn Washington U 1991; MDiv CDSP 1994. D 1/14/1995 P 6/4/1995 Bp Frank Jeffrey Terry. m 3/8/1969 Robert Eric Stoffregen c 3. CDSP Berkeley CA 1999-2000; Cathd Of S Jn The Evang Spokane WA 1997-1998. Angl Wrld; EWHP; Soc for Study of Chr Sprtlty.

STOFFREGEN, Megan Amy (Spok) 5609 S Custer Rd, Spokane WA 99223 B Spokane WA 1971 d Robert & Diana. BA U of Puget Sound 1993; MA Gonzaga U 1994; MDiv CDSP 1999. D 5/29/1999 Bp Leigh Allen Wallace Jr P 12/18/1999 Bp Douglas Edwin Theuner. CDSP Berkeley CA 2002; Asst Ch Of The Gd Shpd Nashua NH 1999-2001.

STOKES, Grant Anthony (SVa) Christ and St Luke's Epis Church, 560 W Olney Rd, Norfolk VA 23507 **Asst Chr and S Lk's Epis Ch Norfolk VA 2013-** B Green SC 1976 s James & Cathy. BS Gardner-Webb U 2009; MDiv Sewanee: The U So, TS 2013; MDiv The TS at The U So 2013. D 12/15/2012 P 9/14/2013 Bp Porter Taylor.

✠ **STOKES, The Rt Rev William H** (NJ) Episcopal Diocese Of New Jersey, 808 W State St, Trenton NJ 08618 **Dioc Bp Dio New Jersey Trenton NJ 2013-; Mem Bd Trst The GTS New York NY 2014-** B Manhassett NY 1957 s Richard & Jean. D.D. (Honorus Causa) GTS; BA Manhattan Coll 1987; MDiv GTS 1990. D 6/22/1990 P 4/27/1991 Bp Orris George Walker Jr P 12/3/2013 for NJ. m 4/3/1976 Susan Stokes c 4. Exam Chapl Dio SE Florida 2011-2013; Dn Dio SE Florida Miami FL 2003-2006; R S Paul's Ch Delray Bch FL 1999-2013; Assoc The Epis Ch Of Beth-By-The-Sea Palm Bch FL 1995-1998; Cur Gr Epis Ch Massapequa NY 1990-1994; Bd Epis Chars of SE Florida Dio SE Florida Miami 2006-2012, Mem of Exec Bd 2000-2005, Cmsn on Educ 1996-2002. Bp of Newark Preaching Prize GTS 1990; Seymour Prize Best Extemporaneous Preaching 90 GTS 1990. wstokes@dioceseofnj.org

STOMSKI, William Leonard (Nev) 3300B S Seacrest Blvd, Boynton Beach FL 33435 **Trin Epis Ch Reno NV 2015-; Dir Dn of Dioc Sch of Chr Stds 2011-** B Pittsfield MA 1952 s Bernard & Helen. BS Arizona St U 1974; MDiv Luth TS 1978; MA U of Notre Dame 1986; DMin VTS 2012. Rec 8/15/2005 as Priest Bp Leo Frade. S Jos's Epis Sch Inc. Boynton Bch FL 2011-2015; S Jos's Epis Ch Boynton Bch FL 2005-2015.

STONE, Carey Don (Ark) 112 Traveler Ln, Maumelle AR 72113 **R S Lk's Epis Ch N Little Rock AR 2011-; Bd Mem for The Arkansas Hse of Pryr Dio Arkansas Little Rock AR 2010-** B 1963 s Lero & Wilma. BMus Arkansas St U 1986; MRC Arkansas St U 1992; MDiv VTS 2005. D 12/21/2004 P 7/22/2005 Bp Larry Maze. Assoc. R S Mk's Epis Ch Little Rock AR 2005-2011. Geo Herbert Soc 2003-2005; Phillips Brooks Soc 2008; Sem Hill Soc 2010. Fell of Engl Poets Many Rivers Pub 2011.

STONE, David Lynn (HB) 940 Channing Way, Berkeley CA 94710 **non-stipendiary P Assoc All Souls Par In Berkeley Berkeley CA 2007-; Ret 1998-** B Santa Monica CA 1930 s Stanley & Ruth. BA Reed Coll 1957; BD CDSP 1960. D 6/22/1960 P 2/1/1961 Bp James Walmsley Frederic Carman. m 1/9/1960 Carol Christopher Kelton Drake c 4. Vic S Lk's Epis Ch Idaho Falls ID 1965-1967; Vic S Lk's Ch Weiser ID 1961-1965; Asst All SS Ch Portland OR 1960-1961.

STONE, Dean Putnam (Kan) 9201 West 82nd Street, Overland Park KS 66204 B Chicago IL 1923 s George & Mildred. BS California Inst of Tech 1946. D 12/19/1976 P 6/24/1977 Bp Otis Charles. m 9/1/1951 Harriet Marie Stone c 4. Asst St Ptr & All SS Epis Ch Kansas City MO 1986-1990; Associated P S Mich And All Ang Ch Mssn KS 1977-2008; Sac D Cathd Ch Of S Mk Salt Lake City UT 1976-1977.

STONE, John Curtis (NJ) 40-B Center St, Highlands NJ 07732 **Ret 2001-** B Jacksonville FL 1938 s Pebble & Mildred. BA Davidson Coll 1960; STB GTS 1963; STM GTS 1993. D 6/29/1963 P 6/29/1964 Bp Richard Henry Baker. m 6/5/1965 Mary Ruth Stone c 2. Vic S Jas Ch Long Branch NJ 1998-2001; Ch Of The H Sprt Tuckerton NJ 1995-1998; Dio New Jersey Trenton NJ 1995-1998; S Aug's Epis Ch Asbury Pk NJ 1995-1998; Int S Mk's Epis Ch Keansburg NJ 1995-1998; S Lk's Ch Gladstone NJ 1994-1995; Non-par 1992-1993; Vic Ch Of The Incarn W Milford NJ 1986-1992; Vic S Gabr's Ch 1986-1989; Mineral Area Reg Coun De Soto MO 1981-1986; Vic Mineral Area Reg Mnstry Desoto MO 1981-1986; R Emm Epis Ch Chatham VA 1975-1981; S Jn's Ch Gretna VA 1975-1981; Trin Ch Gretna VA 1975-1981; P-in-c All SS Ch Hamlet NC 1968-1972; P-in-c S Dav's Epis Ch Laurinburg NC 1968-1972; Vic All SS Epis Ch Charlotte NC 1965-1968; Vic S Andr's Ch 1963-1965; Com Const & Cns Dio Sthrn Virginia Newport News VA 1976-1981. Auth, "Pryr In Post-Mod Theol". Intgerim Mnstrs Ntwk; RWF.

STONE JR, Lewis Seymour (NH) 11 Governor Sq, Peterborough NH 03458 B Danbury CT 1937 s Lewis & Elaine. BBA Texas Tech U 1959; STB Ya Berk 1962; DMin Bos 1988. D 6/23/1962 P 12/23/1962 Bp John S Higgins. m 4/26/1980 Eve Stone. R All SS Ch Peterborough NH 1971-2001; R S Dav's On The Hill Epis Ch Cranston RI 1964-1971; Cur All SS' Memi Ch Providence RI 1962-1964.

STONE, Mary Ruth (NJ) 40 - B Center St, Highlands NJ 07732 **Ret 2003-** B Winston-Salem NC 1936 d Paul & Mary. BA U NC 1958; MSW U NC 1961; MDiv GTS 1990. D 10/27/1990 Bp John Shelby Spong P 5/1/1991 Bp Jack Marston Mckelvey. m 6/5/1965 John Curtis Stone c 2. Chapl Compassionate Care Hospice Clifton NJ 2000-2003; Int Ch of the Gd Shpd Rahway NJ 1999-2001; Int All SS Epis Ch Lakewood NJ 1998-1999; Chapl Riverview Rgnl Cancer Cntr Red Bank 1993-1998; Res Chapl Chr Hosp Jersey City NJ 1991-1992; Asst S Paul's Epis Ch Paterson NJ 1990-1991. Assn Of Profsnl Chapl; Cert Grief Ther In Assn For Death Educ &; Coll Of Chapl.

STONE, Matt (Colo) D 6/10/2017 Bp Robert John O'Neill.

STONE, Michael D (Tex) 18300 Upper Bay Rd, Houston TX 77058 **R S Thos The Apos Epis Ch Houston TX 2015-** B Lexington KY 1979 s Freddie & Dinah. BS Gardner-Webb U 2001; White Sch of Div 2001; MDiv Emory U 2003; MDiv Emory U 2003. D 4/20/2013 Bp Jim Mathes. m 5/30/2004 Rebecca Joy Andrews c 2. Chr Ch Coronado CA 2012-2013. rector@sttaec.org

STONE, Michael Lee (SVa) 12120 Diamond Hill Dr, Midlothian VA 23113 **R Chr Ch Amelia Ct Hs VA 2017-; Chair, Dispatch of Bus Dio Coun Dio Sthrn Virginia Newport News VA 2006-** B Texarkana AR 1951 s Hilliard & Peggy. BA U of Texas 1974; AKC Kings Coll Lon 1977; MDiv Epis TS of the SW 1978. D 6/25/1978 Bp Robert Elwin Terwilliger P 6/22/1979 Bp Archibald Donald Davies. m 5/31/1982 Virginia L Ayoub c 1. R Manakin Epis Ch Midlothian VA 2004-2015; Assoc The Ch Of The Redeem Baltimore MD 1990-2004; Vic H Apos Albuquerque NM 1983-1990; Assoc R S Mk's On The Mesa Epis Ch Albuquerque NM 1981-1982; Camp Stoney Santa Fe NM 1980-1985; Actg Headmaster St. Lk's Par Sch La Un NM 1979-1980; Cur St Lk's Epis Ch Anth NM 1978-1980.

STONE, Sandra Elizabeth (Lex) 3416 Crooked Creek Rd, Carlisle KY 40311 **St Martha's Epis Ch Lexington KY 2012-; Exec Dir Cedar Hill Retreat Cntr Inc. 2005-** B Charleston WV 1956 d Richard & Evelyn. BA Morehead St U 1978; MDiv GTS 1999. D 2/28/1999 Bp Don Adger Wimberly P 8/29/1999 Bp Ted Gulick Jr. m 6/13/1981 Timothy Terrell Durbin c 1. Adv Ch Cynthiana KY 2005-2010; Assoc R Ch S Mich The Archangel Lexington KY 1999-2005; Stndg Com Dio Lexington Lexington 2008-2011, Bdgt Com 2006-2007, long range Plnng Com for Dio 2003, Exec Coun 2000-2003.

STONE, Thomas Michael (Chi) 3601 N North St, Peoria IL 61604 B Peoria IL 1948 s Virgil & Opal. MDiv Luth TS 2006. D 6/14/2008 Bp Keith Lynn Ackerman P 8/21/2009 Bp John Clark Buchanan. m 8/8/1970 Penelope Jane Stone c 1. Dio Chicago Chicago IL 2013; S Jn's Epis Ch Kewanee IL 2012-2016; Cn to the Ordnry Dio Quincy Peoria IL 2011-2013; Gr Epis Ch Galesburg IL 2009-2012. fatherstone@att.net

STONER, D Scott (Mil) 2017 E. Olive St., Milwaukee WI 53211 **Exec Dir Samar Fam Wellness Fndt 2008-** B Pittsburgh PA 1955 s David & Muriel. BA U of Wisconsin 1977; MDiv SWTS 1981; DMin Chicago TS 1985. D 5/30/1981 P 12/1/1981 Bp Charles Thomas Gaskell. m 8/6/1977 Holly H Stoner c 3. S Paul's Ch Milwaukee WI 2016; S Chris's Ch Milwaukee WI 2001-2008, R 2001-2008, Int 2000; Int Zion Epis Ch Oconomowoc WI 2000-2001; Int Chr Ch Milwaukee WI 2000; Int S Mk's Ch Milwaukee WI 1998-1999; Int Trin Ch Milwaukee WI 1997-1998; Pstr Counslr Chicago IL 1981-1986; Asst S Matt's Ch Evanston IL 1981-1983. Auth, "Your Living Compass: Living Well in Thought, Word, and Deed," Ch Pub, Inc., 2014; Creator, "Living Compass Faith & Wellness Prog," *Faith & Wellness*, Living Compass Mnstry, 2010. Amer. Assoc. Mar & Fam Ther 2008; AAPC 1985.

STONER, Suzanne (Ark) **Cur S Paul's Ch Fayetteville AR 2006-** B McKeesport PA 1955 d Robert & Jacquelyn. Cert ETSBH 2004; Cert SWTS 2005. D 1/8/2006 P 6/10/2006 Bp Larry Maze. m 11/23/1983 William Elliott West c 6.

STONESIFER, John DeWitt (WA) 3603 Gleneagles Dr Apt 3c, Silver Spring MD 20906 **The Ch Of The H Sprt Lake Forest IL 2017-; Fac Int Mnstry Ntwk Baltimore MD 2006-** B Alexandria VA 1958 s Joseph & Jean. BA Clemson U 1980; MDiv VTS 1984; MBA Templeton Inst Nassau BS 1995; DMin Louisville Presb TS 2015. D 6/23/1984 Bp Peter J Lee P 12/21/1984 Bp Emerson Paul Haynes. m 6/2/1984 Susan Lee Meachum c 2. Chr Ch Columbia MD 2016-2017; Int R S Mary Magd Ch Silver Sprg MD 2015-2016; S Mk's Epis Ch Louisville KY 2013-2015; St Annes Epis Ch Middletown DE 2012-2013; Int R Imm Ch On The Green New Castle DE 2011-2012; Int R Gr Epis Ch Utica NY 2010-2011; Int R Trin Ch Morgantown WV 2008-2010; Int R S Jn's Ch Huntington WV 2007-2008; Int R S Barth's Ch Gaithersburg MD 2005-2007; Int R S Mary's Epis Ch Woodlawn Gwynn Oak MD 2004-2005; Int Dir PC Buckingham's Choice Adamstown MD 2003-2004; All SS' Epis Ch Chevy Chase MD 2000-2003, Assoc 1997; Vic H Sprt Epis Ch Germantown MD 1999-2003; Chapl Trin-Pawling Sch Pawling NY 1997-1999; S Paul's Epis Par Pt Of Rocks MD 1996-1997, 1993-1994; Chr Ch Prince Geo's Par Rockville MD 1994, 1992; Chapl Washington Epis Sch Beth MD 1990-1997; Assoc R S Fran Ch Potomac MD 1988-1990; R S Andr's Epis Ch Princess Anne MD 1986-1988; Asst S Jn's Ch Naples FL 1984-1986; Bp Search Com Dio Washington Washington DC 2000-2001. Auth, "Chld of Abraham," Rockshire Press, 1998; Auth, "Putting a Sm Indep Sch on the Map," Thesis, 1995. Boardmember - NECA 2016; Priesident- Int Ministies in the Epis Ch 2012-2014. Templeton Fell Theol Coll of the Bahamas 1995.

STOPFEL, Barry Lee (Nwk) RD1 Box 146, Mifflinburg PA 17844 **P-in-c St Anne's Epis Ch Conway SC 2014-** B Harrisburg PA 1947 s Marlin & Carolyn. BS Bos 1969; MA Col 1972; MDiv UTS 1988. D 9/30/1990 Bp Walter Cameron Righter P 9/1/1991 Bp John Shelby Spong. Unitarian/Universalist Cong Northumberlnd PA 2000-2002; S Geo's Epis Ch Maplewood NJ 1993-1999; Ch Of The Atone Tenafly NJ 1990-1993; Dir Of Bp Anand'S Chr Resource Cntr Dio Newark Newark NJ 1988-1989.

S

STOPPEL, Gerald Corwin (WMich) PO Box 65, Saugatuck MI 49453 **R All SS Ch Saugatuck MI 1990-** B Rochester MN 1952 s Fabian & Eleanore. BA Morningside Coll 1973; MDiv Duke DS 1976; Cert Nash 1985; PhD Columbia Pacific U 1993. Trans 1/1/1990 Bp Edward Lewis Lee Jr. m 8/19/2000 Patricia Dewey. Vic S Jn's Ch Marlinton WV 1988-1990; Serv Ch of Can 1986-1988. "Living Words," *Cowley,* 2004; Auth, "Road to Resurr," *Cowley,* 2003. Soc of S Jn the Evang.

STOREY, Wayne Alton (CNY) 311 S Massey St, Watertown NY 13601 B Potsdam NY 1938 s Burton & Beatrice. Cntrl New York Dio Formation Prog w Bex 2007. D 10/7/2006 P 6/16/2007 Bp Gladstone Bailey Adams III. m 6/25/1960 Elizabeth C Storey c 2. Assoc All SS Ch Tarpon Spgs FL 2013, Assoc 2012-2013, Assoc 2010-2012, Asst 2010-2011, Asst 2009-2010, Assoc 2009-2010, Asst 2008-2009, Assoc 2008-2009, Assoc 2007-2008; S Jn's Ch Black River NY 2013, 2012-2013, 2011-2012, Supply 2011-, 2010-2011, Asst 2010, Asst 2009; Assoc S Paul's Ch Watertown NY 2009, Assoc 2008-2009, Assoc 2007.

STORM, Astrid J (NY) 19 Kent Street, Beacon NY 12508 **Ch Of S Jas The Less Scarsdale NY 2016-** B Fort Riley KS 1975 d Roger & Sarah. BA Wheaton Coll 1997; MDiv Ya Berk 2001. D 10/28/2000 P 6/23/2001 Bp Herbert Thompson Jr. m Andrew Wood c 2. Vic Ch Of S Nich On The Hudson New Hamburg NY 2007-2016; Ed Bd Epis New Yorker Dio New York New York NY 2007-2011, Adjustment Bd 2015-, COM 2011-; Cur Gr Epis Ch New York NY 2004-2006; S Lk's Par Darien CT 2004; Asst S Jn's Ch Worthington OH 2001-2004. "Blogger," *Huffington Post;* "Contrib," *Slate mag.* astridstorm@gmail.com

STORM, David Anderson (Oly) 2611 Broadway E, Seattle WA 98102 **Died 3/11/2016** B Seattle WA 1928 s Jerome & Dorothy. BA Whitman Coll 1950; MDiv VTS 1965. D 6/20/1965 P 6/24/1966 Bp Russell S Hubbard. Asstg P S Steph's Epis Ch Seattle WA 1995-2016; Ret 1993-2016; All SS' Epis Ch Hershey PA 1993-2013; Trng And Constation Serv Dio Olympia Seattle 1974-1990, Dioc Evaltn Com 1974-1980, Dioc Ce Cmsn 1968-1978, Dioc Coun 1978-1982; R S Andrews Epis Ch Port Angeles WA 1972-1993; Vic S Hilda's - S Pat's Epis Ch Edmonds WA 1967-1972; Asst/Cur S Steph's Epis Ch Spokane WA 1965-1967.

STORMENT, J(ohn) Douglas (WTex) 1635 Thrush Court Cir, San Antonio TX 78248 B Bartlesville OK 1942 s Joseph & Waltha. BS U of Tulsa 1964; MDiv Melodyland TS 1978; CTh Epis TS of the SW 1986; CTh Epis TS of the SW 1986. D 6/17/1986 Bp Stanley Fillmore Hauser P 12/20/1986 Bp Scott Field Bailey. m 12/18/1965 Marilyn Storment c 2. R St Fran Epis Ch San Antonio TX 1998-2006; S Mk's Ch Crp Christi TX 1987-1998; Dio W Texas San Antonio TX 1986.

STORMER, Eugene Allen (Spr) 825 Lorraine Ave, Springfield IL 62704 B Alton IL 1942 s Walter & Helen. Dioc Sem of the Immac Concep; BA S Mary of the Lake Sem 1964; MA U of S Mary of the Lake 1968; STB U of S Mary of the Lake Mundelein Sem 1968; MSW S Louis U 1973. Rec 2/9/1986 as Priest Bp Donald James Parsons. m 5/8/1972 Janet Stormer c 2. Dio Springfield Springfield IL 2005-2010, Cn Pstr 2004-2013, Dioc Coun 2002-2011; Part Time S Thos Epis Ch Glen Carbon IL 2005-2010; Int S Barn Ch Havana IL 2003-2004; Dio Springfield Springfield IL 2002-2008; Dio Springfield Springfield IL 2001-2005; Int S Andr's Ch Carbondale IL 2001-2002; Int S Jn's Epis Ch Decatur IL 1999-2001; Supply Cler S Lk's Ch Springfield IL 1998-1999; Int Dio Quincy Peoria IL 1996-2000; S Matt's Epis Ch Bloomington IL 1996-1998; P-in-c S Jas Epis Ch Griggsville IL 1986-1990.

STORY, Mark Denslow (Okla) 1701 Mission Rd, Edmond OK 73034 **R S Mary's Ch Edmond OK 2002-** B Dallas TX 1955 s William & Verda. BA Augustana Coll 1978; MDiv SWTS 1983; DMin SMU 2005. D 6/4/1983 Bp Conrad H Gesner P 12/11/1983 Bp Charles Bennison Sr. m 6/21/1980 Susan H Story c 3. R/Hdmstr Epis Ch Of The Redeem Irving TX 1992-2002; R Gr Epis Ch Traverse City MI 1986-1991; Asst S Lk's Par Kalamazoo MI 1983-1986.

STOUDEMIRE, Stewart Mcbryde (WNC) 950 - 36th Avenue Circle Northeast, Hickory NC 28601 B Rock Hill SC 1941 s George & Margaret. BS No Carolina St U 1965. D 5/25/1986 Bp William Gillette Weinhauer. m 8/8/1964 Cornelia Mcaulay Stoudemire c 2. D S Alb's Ch Hickory NC 1986-2009.

STOUT, Arla Jeanne (Mich) 204 Sunnyside Ave, Cameron WI 54822 B Bisbee ND 1934 d C W & Florence. S Lukes Hosp Sch of Nrsng Fargo ND 1953; Bismarck St Coll 1986. D 6/29/1995 Bp William Charles Wantland. m 1/14/1956 James Stout c 3. Dioc Admnstr Dio Eau Claire Eau Claire WI 1995-2006; D Gr Ch Rice Lake WI 1995. NAAD 1995.

STOUT, David Alan (Haw) St. James' Church, PO Box 278, Kamuela HI 96743 **R S Jas Epis Ch Kamuela HI 2013-, P-in-c 2011-2013** B Kendallville IN 1967 s Jerry & Linda. AS Vincennes U 1987; BS Ball St U 1989; Cbury Cathd 1995; MDiv Duke DS 1996. D 4/9/1997 P 10/18/1997 Bp Clifton Daniel III. m 12/14/2013 Bobby Greer Clement. R Trin Ch Asbury Pk NJ 2004-2011; Assoc R St. Barth Ch New York NY 2000-2004; Cur S Paul's Ch Beaufort NC 1997-2000; Sem in Res Cbury Cathd Cbury Untd Kingdom 1995-1996; Sem Intern S Fran Ch Goldsboro NC 1994-1995; Campus Mnstry Stff Res Duke Univ. Epis Stdt Cntr Durham NC 1990-1991; Ball St Campus Mnstry Stff Res Serv

Meth Ch Muncie IN 1989-1990; Yth Min at Selma UMC Serv Meth Ch Selma IN 1988-1989. SSJE - Assoc 1990.

STOUTE, Barclay Lenardo (LI) 28 Fallon Ct, Elmont NY 11003 B BB 1954 s Seth & Clarice. DIT Codrington Coll 1978; GTS 1980; BA U of The W Indies 1980. Trans 4/25/1989 Bp Drexel Gomez. m 7/20/1985 Marcia W Stoute c 1. R Ch Of SS Steph And Mart Brooklyn NY 1989-2006; Asst P Ch Of S Thos Brooklyn NY 1986-1988; Serv Ch of Barbados 1980-1986; Dn No Brooklyn NY. Black Cleric Caucus, OHC.

STOUT-KOPP OJN, Ronnie T (Nwk) 50 Brams Hill Dr, Mahwah NJ 07430 **H Trin Epis Ch Hillsdale NJ 2016-; Adj Drew U-Adj Prof Med Hmnts 2011-** B Jersey City NJ 1958 d Edward & Veronica. BA Montclair St U 1980; MDiv GTS 2000; STM GTS 2002; Doctor of Arts & Letters Drew U 2010. D 6/12/2004 Bp John L Rabb P 12/18/2004 Bp John Palmer Croneberger. m 4/25/1986 David A Kopp. P in Charge S Gabr's Ch Oak Ridge NJ 2012-2013; P in Charge All SS Ch Bergenfield NJ 2010-2011; LocTen Ch Of The Gd Shpd Ringwood NJ 2007-2012; Curs: Sprtl Dir Dio Newark 2005-2006; Asst to R Chr Ch Pompton Lake NJ 2004-2006; Chair: Sprtl Formation Cmsn Dio Newark Newark NJ 2007-2009.

STOWE, Barbara E (Mass) 33 Washington St, Topsfield MA 01983 B Lynn MA 1942 d Chester & Margaret. RN Beverly Hosp Sch of Nrsng 1963; BS Emml 1987. D 10/6/2001 Bp M(Arvil) Thomas Shaw. c 4. D S Ptr's Ch Beverly MA 2001-2006.

STOWE, David Andrew (NJ) Pine Run Community, 777 Ferry Rd, Doylestown PA 18901 **Ret 1996-** B New Brunswick NJ 1930 s Walter & Katherine. BA Dart 1953; STB GTS 1956. D 4/28/1956 P 10/27/1956 Bp Alfred L Banyard. m 9/6/1956 Priscilla Stowe c 2. R S Jn's Ch Somerville NJ 1965-1996; Cn Cathd Of All SS Albany NY 1959-1965; Vic The Ch Of The Gd Shpd Acton MA 1958-1959; Cur H Trin Ch Collingswood NJ 1956-1958. Epis Ch Hist Soc 2005.

STOWE, Howard Timothy Wheeler (NY) 79 Ne 93rd St, Miami Shores FL 33138 B Danbury CT 1943 s Howard & Marjorie. BA W Virginia Wesleyan Coll 1966; STM Ya Berk 1969; CSD GTS 1974. D 6/6/1970 P 12/19/1970 Bp Horace W B Donegan. m 11/9/2011 Anthony P Lee Loy. P-in-c S Steph's Ch Coconut Grove Miami FL 2001-2002, Assoc 1996-2013; Chapl S Steph's Epis Day Sch Miami FL 1996-2002; R The Ch of S Ign of Antioch New York NY 1977-1995, Cur 1973-1977; Bp's Asst Cathd Of St Jn The Div New York NY 1971-1973; Ed Dio New York New York NY 1970-1971; Serv- Natl Yth Dir, USA & Can Armenia Orth Ch in USA and Can 1969-1970. CHS - P Assoc 1995; CBS 1970; GAS 1970. Knights' Chapl Ord of S Jn of Jerusalem 1979.

STOWELL, Philip W (NJ) 929 E Laddoos Ave, San Tan Valley AZ 85140 **IRB Bd Coriell Inst for Med Resarch Camden NJ 2000-** B Chicago IL 1945 s Frank & Marie. AB Pr 1967; MDiv EDS 1970. D 6/10/1970 Bp John Henry Esquirol P 2/27/1971 Bp Joseph Warren Hutchens. m 11/8/1986 Susan M Mann c 1. Firefighter & Chapl Moorestown Fire Dept Moorestown NJ 2002-2015; Bd Trustes The Evergreens Moorestown NJ 1996-2008; R Trin Ch Moorestown NJ 1995-2015; R S Barth's Ch In The Highland White Plains NY 1990-1995; Assoc R S Phil's In The Hills Tucson AZ 1988-1990; Assoc S Mary's Epis Ch Manchester CT 1986-1988; R S Jn's Ch Ellicott City MD 1983-1985; R Chr Ch Avon CT 1972-1983; Asst to R S Ptr's Epis Ch Cheshire CT 1970-1972; Dn, Burlington Convoc Dio New Jersey Trenton NJ 2009-2012, Chair, Benefits Com 2000-2015, Vice Chair Proctor Fndt 2000-2015, Chair Pension Com 1996-2009; Chair Com on Chr Initiation Dio Maryland Baltimore MD 1983-1985. philip.stowell@aol.com

STOY, Carol Berry (NJ) 221 Herrontown Rd, Princeton NJ 08540 B New York NY 1922 d Samuel & Carolyn. BS CUNY 1943; Polytech Inst of Brooklyn 1945; D Formation Prog 1980. D 4/13/1985 Bp George Phelps Mellick Belshaw. m 4/2/1949 William S Stoy c 2. Archd Dio New Jersey Trenton NJ 1999-2005; Cler Asst Trin Ch Princeton NJ 1985-2006. S Steph's Awd NAAD 1997.

ST PIERRE, Joanne Madelyn (EMich) PO Box 217, Otter Lake MI 48464 B Warren MI 1940 d Robert & Cecilia. D 3/21/2009 Bp Steven Todd Ousley. m 6/11/1971 Joseph Jean Denis St Pierre c 3.

STRADER-SASSER, James William (CPa) 120 E Market St, Danville PA 17821 **Chr Memi Epis Ch Danville PA 2017-** B Tucson AZ 1957 s William & Bette. BA U of Arizona 1980; MA GW 1997; MDiv EDS 2003. D 5/27/2006 P 12/2/2006 Bp Kirk Stevan Smith. m 5/6/2016 Howell Crawford Sasser. S Andr's Epis Ch Lewisburg PA 2016-2017; R S Jas Epis Ch Cincinnati OH 2011-2015; Cur S Geo's-By-The-River Rumson NJ 2008-2011; Fac Axia Coll 2006-2015; Chapl Epis Campus Mnstry - U of Arizona Tucson AZ 2006-2008; Cmsn on Congrl Life Dio Sthrn Ohio Cincinnati OH 2013-2015, Dioc Restructuring T/F 2013-2014; Stdt Cler Ldrshp Prog 2012-2014; Com on Congrl Life Dio New Jersey Trenton NJ 2010-2011. cmecjim@ptd.net

STRAHAN, Linda C (RI) 103 Kay St, Newport RI 02840 B Council Bluffs IA 1945 d Charles & Helen. BA Stan 1967; MA U CA 1968; PhD U CA 1976; MDiv VTS 1979. D 6/23/1979 P 5/1/1980 Bp Robert Bruce Hall. Dio Rhode Island Providence RI 2012-2013; Asst Emm Ch Newport RI 1988-1991; Int S Dav's Ch Gales Ferry CT 1987-1988; Ch of the Epiph Rumford RI 1986; St

S

Mich & Gr Ch Rumford RI 1986; Asst S Mart's Ch Providence RI 1983-1985; Asst Ch Of The Redeem Chestnut Hill MA 1979-1983. Auth, "Intro To Alan Of Lille'S Bk On The Plaint Of Nature". EvangES, OHC.

STRAIN, William Henry (Nwk) 4 Acacia Dr, Boynton Beach FL 33436 **Died 11/9/2016** B East Orange NJ 1928 s William & Ethel. BA Hobart and Wm Smith Colleges 1953; Pr 1954; MDiv GTS 1957. D 6/15/1957 P 12/21/1957 Bp Benjamin M Washburn. m 5/17/1997 Phyllis Lloyd Smith c 2. Ret 1993-2016; R Calv Epis Ch Summit NJ 1968-1993; Vic S Mich's Epis Ch Wayne NJ 1957-1968; Stndg Com Dio Newark Newark NJ 1971-1979; Chapl Wayne Police Dept Wayne NJ 1958-1968. Phi Beta Kappa Hob 1953.

STRAINGE JR, Roy Thomas (SeFla) 6025 Verde Trl S, Boca Raton FL 33433 B New Haven CT 1924 s Roy & Cornelia. BA U So 1945; STB GTS 1948. D 6/11/1948 Bp Henry I Louttit P 5/14/1949 Bp Wallace J Gardner. Int S Jas-In-The-Hills Epis Ch Hollywood FL 1998-1999; Asst S Jn's Ch Hollywood FL 1968-1986; Non-par 1950-1968; Cur H Trin Epis Ch W Palm Bch FL 1948-1949; S Geo's Epis Ch Riviera Bch FL 1948-1949.

STRALEY, Benjamin P (Ct) **Other Lay Position Prot Epis Cathd Fndt Washington DC 2012-** D 6/10/2017 Bp Laura Ahrens.

STRAND, Jon Carl (Mass) Po Box 238, Natick MA 01760 **P-in-c S Paul's Ch Natick MA 1998-** B Winfield KS 1964 s James & Carolyn. BA Wichita St U 1988; MDiv Ya Berk 1992; Cert Ya 1992. D 8/20/1992 Bp William Edward Smalley P 6/1/1993 Bp Edward Cole Chalfant. m 6/18/1994 Elizabeth Anderson Strand c 2. Cathd Ch Of S Lk Portland ME 1992-1998.

STRANDE, Dana (Minn) 7305 Afton Rd, Woodbury MN 55125 **Ch Of The Nativ Burnsville MN 2015-** B Benson MN 1965 d Richard & Karen. BA The Coll of St. Scholastica 1997; Cert in Ch Bus Admin U of S Thos 2008. D 6/26/2014 P 6/20/2015 Bp Brian N Prior. m 1/6/2001 Michael Michael Strande c 2. Ch Of The H Apos S Paul Mn 2015; Chr Ch S Paul MN 2014-2015, 2003-2014; Par Life Min Chr Epis Ch 2003-2014.

STRANDLUND, Daniel P (Ala) 113 Madison Ave, Montgomery AL 36104 **S Jn's Ch Montgomery AL 2015-; Other Lay Position S Steph's Epis Ch Birmingham AL 2009-** B Jacksonville FL 1984 s William & Claudia. BA Birmingham- Sthrn Coll 2006; BA Birmingham-Sthrn Coll 2006; MDiv Epis TS Of The SW 2015; MDiv Sem of the SW 2015. D 5/30/2015 Bp Santosh K Marray P 12/12/2015 Bp John Mckee Sloan Sr. m 10/9/2010 Lucy B Bridgers. danielstelizabeth@gmail.com

STRANE, Steven Roberts (SanD) 4489 Caminito Cuarzo, San Diego CA 92117 **Assoc S Jas By The Sea La Jolla CA 2011-** B Bethesda MD 1949 s John & Doris. BA California St U, Northridge 1971; Tchr Cred San Diego St U 1974; MDiv VTS 1978. D 6/12/1978 P 12/16/1978 Bp Robert Munro Wolterstorff. m 4/14/1973 Jane H Smith c 1. R S Tim's Ch Danville CA 1988-2010; P-in-c All Souls' Epis Ch San Diego CA 1979-1987; Cur S Paul In The Desert Palm Sprg CA 1978-1979.

STRANG, Ruth Hancock (Mich) 504 Prospect St, Howell MI 48843 B Bridgeport CT 1923 d Robert & Ruth. BA Wellesley Coll 1944; MD New York Med Coll 1949; Ecum TS 1992; MDiv SWTS 1993. D 6/19/1993 P 9/14/1994 Bp Raymond Stewart Wood Jr. P-in-c S Jn's Ch Howell MI 1994-2009; Asstg D S Aid's Ch Ann Arbor MI 1993-1994. SCHC 1984.

STRANGE, Phillip Ross (Los) PO Box 3144, Wrightwood CA 92397 **Supply P Dio Los Angeles Los Angeles CA 1998-, Dn, Dnry 2 1997-2004, 2004-, 1998-2003** B Ardmore OK 1941 s Oscar & Laura. BA Rice U 1962; MDiv GTS 1965; SMU 1973; U of New Mex 1990. D 6/18/1965 P 12/21/1965 Bp Charles A Mason. m 5/27/1967 Susan G Green c 3. Asst Chr Ch Par Ontario CA 2004-2017; R S Paul's Par Lancaster CA 1996-2003; R S Mich's Epis Ch Riverside CA 1990-1996; Int S Thos Of Cbury Epis Ch Albuquerque NM 1989-1990; Vic S Chad's Epis Ch Albuquerque NM 1988-1990; Sub-Dn Dallas Dnry E Dio Dallas Dallas TX 1974-1978; R S Jas Ch Dallas TX 1973-1980; Dir Stds Cathd Cntr for Cont Educ S Matt's Cathd Dallas TX 1971-1973, Asst to Dn 1966-1970; Asst S Mk's Ch Irving TX 1968-1971; Vic S Barn Ch Garland TX 1965-1966. Associated Parishes for Liturg & Mssn 1975-1993.

STRASBURGER, Frank C (NJ) 27 Tidal Run Lane, Brunswick ME 04011 B Baltimore MD 1945 s Charles & Janet. BA Pr 1967; MA JHU 1971; MDiv EDS 1980. D 4/26/1980 P 11/1/1980 Bp David Keller Leighton Sr. m 11/27/1982 Caroline Strasburger c 3. Int S Andr's Ch Newcastle ME 2008-2010; Founding Pres Princeton in Afr 2000-2005; Assoc Trin Ch Princeton NJ 1999-2007; Pres Med Educ for So Afr Blacks 1997-1999; Chapl Epis Ch at Pr Princeton NJ 1986-1997; Epis Chapl Pr NJ 1986-1997; Cn The Amer Cathd of the H Trin Paris 75008 1984-1986; Asst S Mk's Ch New Canaan CT 1981-1984; D S Lk's Ch Katonah NY 1980-1981. Auth, "Growing Up: Limiting Adolescence in a Wrld Desperate for Adults," Friesen Press, 2012; Auth, "Why the Angl Comm Matters," Forw Mvmt, 2008; Auth, "Honoring hon," *Princeton Alum Weekly*, 1995; Auth, "Can Princeton Act Morally?," *The Nassau Weekly*, 1991; Auth, "Qui Est L'Etranger?," *Sens*, 1985; Auth, "Keeping the Faith: The Challenge of the Ch Sch," *NAES Journ*, 1980.

STRASBURGER, Roy W (ECR) 175 S Garden Way Apt 120, Eugene OR 97401 **Ret 1991-** B Temple TX 1928 s Roy & Aileen. BS Texas St U San Marcos 1949; MDiv VTS 1952; DMin VTS 1977. D 7/1/1952 P 1/25/1953

Bp Everett H Jones. c 2. VTS Alexandria VA 1985-1988; Alum Exec Com VTS Alexandria VA 1985-1988; Stndg Com Dio El Camino Real Salinas CA 1983-1988, Dep, GC 1982-1988, Election Process Com 1979-1981; R S Andr's Ch Saratoga CA 1957-1991; Dir of Rel Activities S Mary's Hall San Antonio TX 1955-1957; Cur S Mk's Epis Ch San Antonio TX 1952-1955; Trst CDSP Berkeley CA 1983-1987.

STRASSER, Gabor (Va) 18525 Bear Creek Ter, Leesburg VA 20176 **Non-par 1992-** B Budapest HU 1929 s Rezso & Theresa. BD SUNY 1953; MS SUNY 1959; PMD Harv 1968; MDiv VTS 1992. D 6/13/1992 Bp Robert Poland Atkinson P 12/1/1992 Bp Peter J Lee. m 2/2/1978 Joka Strasser c 2. S Marg's Ch Woodbridge VA 1992-1993.

STRATFORD, Jane (Cal) 66 Saint Stephens Dr, Orinda CA 94563 **Assoc S Steph's Epis Ch Orinda CA 2015-; Cur S Jn's Epis Ch Clayton CA 2013-** B Epsom UK 1960 d Herbert & Pamela. BSC Cardiff U 1982; Cert Seattle U 2008; MDiv CDSP 2011; MDiv CDSP 2011. D 12/1/2012 P 6/8/2013 Bp Marc Handley Andrus. c 3. Admin Dio California San Francisco CA 2013-2015. jane@ststephensorinda.org

STRATTON, Jonathan Robert (Mo) 1210 Locust St, Saint Louis MO 63103 **R Trin Ch S Louis MO 2015-** B Olny IL 1984 s Richard & Marcia. STM Sewanee: The U So, TS; STM U So TS; BA Estrn Illinois U 2008; MDiv Eden TS 2011. D 6/6/2012 P 1/6/2013 Bp George Wayne Smith. m 9/10/2005 Susan E Stratton c 2. Dio Missouri S Louis MO 2012-2015. jon@trinityepiscopal.net

STRAUB, Gregory (Eas) 1920 S Ocean Dr Apt 1004, Fort Lauderdale FL 33316 B Irvington NJ 1948 s Stephen & Dorothy. BA Dickinson Coll 1970; MDiv PDS 1973; DMin Drew U 1990. D 6/8/1973 P 3/30/1974 Bp Dean Theodore Stevenson. Exec Off and Secy of the GC Epis Ch Cntr New York NY 2005-2012; R Emm Epis Ch Chestertown MD 1976-2005; Cur S Thos Ch Lancaster PA 1973-1975; Trst EDS Cambridge MA 2004-2010; Stndg Com Dio Easton Easton MD 2001-2005, Bp Search Com Chair 2001-2002, Comp Dio Chair 1988-1990, GC Dep 1985-2003, Exec Coun Secy 1985-1993, Secy of Dioc Conv 1983-2006. HSEC 2003; NEHA 1983. DD EDS 2013; Bp's Cross Dio Easton 2012; HOD Medal HOD 2012; Hon Cn Dio Los Angeles 2009.

STRAUGHN, Richard Daniel (SwFla) 373 Corson Ln, Cape May NJ 08204 **Ret 1996-** B Sea Isle City NJ 1947 s Richard & Lina. BA Lycoming Coll 1969; MDiv PDS 1972. D 4/22/1972 P 10/28/1972 Bp Alfred L Banyard. m 9/20/2008 Lawrence Canter c 2. Vic S Chad's Ch Tampa FL 1989-1996; Ch Of The H Sprt Tuckerton NJ 1988-1989; Assoc The Ch Of S Uriel The Archangel Sea Girt NJ 1983-1988; Vic Ch Of S Jn-In-The-Wilderness Gibbsboro NJ 1973-1983.

STRAUSS, Arlen Richard (CNY) 109 Glenside Rd, Ithaca NY 14850 **Supply P Chr Epis Ch Willard NY 2003-; Assoc S Jn's Ch Ithaca NY 1980-** B Canton PA 1933 s James & Helen. BA Ithaca Coll 1955. D 6/23/1979 P 6/7/1980 Bp Ned Cole.

STRAVERS, Cynthia A (NY) 2 E 90th St, New York NY 10128 **Ch Of The Heav Rest New York NY 2014-** B Grand Rapids MI 1956 d Gordon & Jeanne. BS Wstrn Michigan U 1992; MA Wstrn Michigan U 1995; MDiv GTS 2009. D 6/20/2009 Bp Wendell Nathaniel Gibbs Jr P 1/9/2010 Bp Laura Ahrens. m 4/6/1998 Richard Lee Stravers c 3. Asst to the P Par of St Paul's Ch Norwalk Norwalk CT 2009-2014; S Lk's Par Kalamazoo MI 1997-2007.

STRAVERS, Richard Lee (WMich) Po Box 56, Richland MI 49083 **Exec Dir Open Doors Kalamazoo Kalamazoo Michigan 1999-** B Grand Rapids MI 1952 s Dick & Ruth. BA Calvin Coll 1976; MDiv GTS 1987. D 12/6/1986 P 6/11/1987 Bp Howard Samuel Meeks. m 4/6/1998 Cynthia A Stravers c 3. S Tim Ch Richland MI 1988-1999; S Lk's Par Kalamazoo MI 1986-1988.

STRAWBRIDGE, Jennifer R (Va) Keble College, Parks Road, Oxford OX1 3PG Great Britain (UK) **Resrch Lectr Keble Coll U of Oxford Oxford UK 2013-; Chapl & Fell Keble Coll U of Oxford Oxford UK 2010-; Chapl to Coll of Bishops (2015) Ch Of Engl London 2015-; Dioc Vocations Advsr Dio Oxford No Hinksey OXFORD 2011-; Secy of Advowsons Keble Coll U of Oxford (UK) 2010-** B Pittsburgh PA 1978 d Craig & Susan. BA W&L 2001; MST Oxf 2002; DAS Ya Berk 2004; MDiv Yale DS 2004; MA Oxf 2010; PhD Oxf 2013; PhD Oxf 2014; PhD Oxf 2014. D 6/11/2004 P 12/15/2004 Bp Neff Powell. Assoc R S Mary's Epis Ch Arlington VA 2005-2009; Chapl Res Bridgeport Hosp Dept Of Pstr Care Bridgeport CT 2004-2005; Chr Ch New Haven CT 2004-2005; Cmsn on Wrld Mssn (Chair, 2008-2009) Dio Virginia Richmond VA 2006-2009. Auth, "A Sch of Paul? Pauline Texts in Early Chr Schooltext Papyri," *A Chapt in: Ancient Educ and Early Chrsnty*, T&T Clark, 2015; Co-Auth, "The Songs We Used to Sing: Hymn 'Traditions' and Reception in Pauline Letters," *Journ for the Study of the NT*, 2015; Auth, "A Cmnty of Interp: The Use of 1 Corinthians 2.6-16 by Early Christians," *Studia Patristica*, Peeters Press, 2013; Auth, "How present is Romans in early Chr Sch exercises: Is P.Lond.Lit 207 mislabelled?," *Oxford Resrch Archive Journ*, Oxf Press, 2011; Auth, "The Word of the Cross: Mssn, Power and the Theol of Ldrshp," *ATR*, 2009. Gathering of Leaders 2006; SBL 2012. Phi Beta Kappa 2000.

STREEPY, Robert Shawn (Kan) 10700 W 53rd St, Shawnee KS 66203 **S Aid's Ch Olathe KS 2013-** B Cheyenne WY 1952 BA U of Kansas 1973; JD U of Kansas 1976; Kansas Sch of Mnstry 2003. D 9/27/2003 Bp William Edward Smalley P 6/6/2009 Bp Dean E Wolfe. m 4/25/1982 Marcia Kathleen Streepy c 2. D S Lk's Epis Ch Shawnee KS 2011-2013; Gr Ch Chanute KS 2009-2011. staidansolathe@sbcglobal.net

STREET III, Claude Parke (Colo) 35 KILDEER Rd, Hamden CT 06517 B Nashville TN 1934 s Claude & Elisabeth. BA Van 1952; BD Yale DS 1960; U So 1962; Coll of Preachers 1976; S Georges Coll Jerusalem IL 1982; DMin PrTS 1986. D 3/3/1963 P 7/3/1963 Bp Charles Gresham Marmion. m 7/30/2000 Eleanor Lee McGee-Street c 3. S Lk's Ch Westcliffe CO 2001-2002; Ret 1997-2011; Bad Wound's Sta Mart SD 1991-1996; Ch Of The Adv Pine Ridge SD 1991-1996; Ch Of The Epiph Pine Ridge SD 1991-1996; Ch of the Mssh Mssn Sioux Falls SD 1991-1996; Mssnr Dio So Dakota Pierre SD 1991-1996; H Cross Epis Ch Pine Ridge SD 1991-1996; S Alb's Epis Ch Porcupine SD 1991-1996; S Andr's Epis Ch Wakpamni Lake SD 1991-1996; S Jn's Epis Ch Pine Ridge SD 1991-1996; S Julia's Epis Ch Porcupine SD 1991-1996; S Katharine's Ch Mart SD 1991-1996; S Mich's Ch Batesland SD 1991-1996; Vic S Ptr's Epis Ch Oglala SD 1991-1996; S Thos Ch Porcupine SD 1991-1996; R S Aug's Epis Ch Washington DC 1978-1991; Assoc S Marg's Ch Washington DC 1966-1978; Cn Chr Ch Cathd Louisville KY 1963-1966; Weca Bd Dio Washington Washington DC 1984-1988, Chair Par Intrnshp Prog 1979-1983, Weca Bd 1973-1978.

STREET, Terry Terriell (WTenn) 210 Walnut Trace Dr, Cordova TN 38018 **R S Phil Ch Memphis TN 2008-; Bp and Coun Dio W Tennessee Memphis 2008-** B Memphis TN 1955 s Conway & Elois. BA U of Memphis 1978; MA U of Memphis 1984; MDiv TS 2006; MDiv Sewanee: The U So, TS 2006; MDiv Sewanee: The U So, TS 2006; MDiv Sewanee: The U So, TS 2006. D 8/5/2006 Bp Don Edward Johnson. m 7/16/1983 Edith Brown Street c 2. S Jn's Epis Ch Memphis TN 2006-2008; Psychol Self 1985-2003. OHC Assoc 2000.

STREETER, Chris (Roch) 36 S Main St, Pittsford NY 14534 **R Ch Of The Incarn Penfield NY 2014-** B Newton NJ 1980 s Michael & Denise. BMus Eastman Sch of Mus 2003; MDiv VTS 2009. D 6/6/2009 Bp Prince Grenville Singh P 12/12/2009 Bp Jack Marston Mckelvey. m 7/9/2011 Jennifer Streeter c 2. Gr Ch Scottsville NY 2012-2014; Chr Ch Pittsford Pittsford NY 2009-2012.

STREEVER, Hilary Brandt (Va) St. James's Episcopal Church, 1205 W. Franklin Street, Richmond VA 23220 **Assoc St Jas Ch Richmond VA 2015-** B Richmond VA 1983 d John & Rebecca. BS Virginia Tech 2005; BA Virginia Tech 2005; MDiv Ya Berk 2012. D 6/2/2012 P 12/15/2012 Bp Neff Powell. m 4/12/2013 David L Streever. P-in-c S Thos' Epis Ch Abingdon VA 2012-2015. hstreever@doers.org

STREIFF, Suzanne (Oly) 305 Burma Rd, Castle Rock WA 98611 **D S Matt Ch Castle Rock WA 2004-** B Kelso WA 1937 d Stanley & Mina V. D 2/28/2004 Bp Sanford Zangwill Kaye Hampton. m 6/11/1960 Donald Edward Streiff c 3.

STREIT JR, Jep (Mass) 41 Ackers Ave Apt 2, Brookline MA 02445 B Washington DC 1951 s John & Ann. BA Dickinson Coll 1973; MDiv EDS 1978. D 6/18/1978 Bp Morris Fairchild Arnold P 5/13/1979 Bp John Bowen Coburn. m 7/17/2004 Susan McCandless-Knight c 3. Dn The Cathd Ch Of S Paul Boston MA 2001-2017, 1995-2017, Dn 1995-2000; U Chapl- Bos Dio Massachusetts Boston MA 1984-2000; Asst The Ch Of Our Redeem Lexington MA 1978-1984. "Big Questions Worthy Dreams," *ATR*, 2002. ESMHE; Soc of S Jn the Evang.

STREUFERT, Nancy Stimac (NCal) 625 15th St, Eureka CA 95501 **Assoc P Chr Ch Eureka CA 2015-; P Assoc S Alb's Ch Arcata CA 2015-** B Davenport IA 1950 d Emil & June. BS U of Iowa 1972; Bachelor of Sci U of Iowa 1972; BS U of CA 1981; Bachelor of Sci U of CA 1981; JD U of W LA Sch of Law 2001; Juris Doctor U of W LA Sch of Law 2001; Mstr of Arts in Mnstry Nash 2014; MA Nash 2014. D 6/28/2014 P 1/31/2015 Bp Barry Leigh Beisner. m 9/25/1987 Richard C Streufert.

STRIBLING, Anna Jones (Va) 4540 Carrington Rd, Markham VA 22643 **Ret 2000-** B Winchester VA 1939 d James & Anna. BS U Rich 1961; MDiv VTS 1982. D 6/9/1982 Bp David Henry Lewis Jr P 5/28/1983 Bp Robert Bruce Hall. m 7/1/1961 William C Stribling c 3. Dn, Reg III Dio Virginia Richmond VA 1994-1998, Nomin Com for Bp Suffr 1992-1993, Chair, CE Com 1991, Pres, Stndg Com 1986-1988, Peace Cmsn 1983-1993; R S Jn's Epis Ch Arlington VA 1989-2000; Assoc Ch Of The H Comf Vienna VA 1985-1989; Asst S Jas' Epis Ch Warrenton VA 1982-1984; Trnr and Field Supvsr VTS Alexandria VA 1993-1998.

STRIBLING, Emily B (WA) 4621 Laverock Pl NW, WASHINGTON DC 20007 **Trin Ch Castine ME 2015-, Assoc 2013-** B Washington DC 1947 d E Taylor & Mary. BA Sarah Lawr Coll 1968; MDiv GTS 2002. D 6/9/2007 P 1/19/2008 Bp John Bryson Chane. m 9/13/2002 Robert M Stribling c 2. S Andr And S Jn Epis Ch SW Hbr ME 2010-2011; Cathd of St Ptr & St Paul Washington DC 2007-2009; Prof Uesley TS Washington DC 1999-2004; The Ch Of The Epiph New York NY 1992-1994.

STRIBLING JR, Jess Hawkins (Va) 1 Colley Ave Apt 600, Apt 600, Norfolk VA 23510 B Chicago IL 1937 s Jess & Antoinette. BA U NC 1959; BD VTS 1962; STM VTS 1973; JD GW 1974. D 6/16/1962 P 12/22/1962 Bp William Foreman Creighton. m 6/6/1959 Miriam Love McLaughlin c 1. Asst S Geo's Epis Ch Arlington VA 1986-2001; Assoc S Mich's Epis Ch Arlington VA 1982-1986; R S Ptr's Epis Ch Arlington VA 1967-1974; R Ch Of The As-

cen Silver Sprg MD 1964-1966; Asst The Ch Of The Epiph Washington DC 1962-1964.

STRICKER, David Walter (USC) 1028 Kinsey Dr. SE, Huntsville AL 35803 **Died 1/26/2017** B Pittsburgh PA 1939 s Joseph & Margaret. BA Otterbein U 1965; MDiv PDS 1968. D 5/25/1968 Bp William S Thomas P 12/21/1968 Bp Robert Bracewell Appleyard. c 3. Vic S Barn Ch Dillon SC 2001-2007; St Thos Epis Ch Huntsville AL 2000-2017; Off Of Bsh For ArmdF New York NY 1982-2001; Chapl US-A 1982-2001; Cntrl Sussex Cltn Georgetown DE 1975-1982; S Mk's Ch Millsboro DE 1975-1982; P-in-c Ch Of The Gd Samar Mckeesport PA 1968-1975; Ch Of The Trsfg Clairton PA 1968-1975.

STRICKLAND, Harold Somerset (Ark) 610 Northwest K, Bentonville AR 72712 **Died 9/16/2016** B Kansas City MO 1921 s Frank & Edith. BA U of Kansas 1947; BD Sewanee: The U So, TS 1950. D 6/18/1950 P 12/18/1950 Bp Edward Randolph Welles II. m 6/19/1950 Mary Ellen Strickland. Ret 1985-2016; Vic Gr Ch Siloam Sprg AR 1981-1985; S Theo's Epis Ch Bella Vista AR 1981-1985; Coll Field Des Moines IA 1972-1980; S Lk's Epis Ch Cedar Falls IA 1970-1981; R S Paul's Ch Leavenworth KS 1962-1970; Vic S Mart-In-The-Fields Edwardsville KS 1957-1962; P-in-c S Lk's Epis Ch Excelsior Sprg MO 1950-1956.

✠ STRICKLAND, The Rt Rev Vernon Edward (WK) 665 N Desmet Ave, Buffalo WY 82834 B Holopaw FL 1938 s Vernon & Edna. BA Carson-Newman Coll 1967; Candler TS Emory U 1969; MDiv VTS 1970. D 6/24/1970 Bp Edward Hamilton West P 4/16/1971 Bp George Mosley Murray Con 10/25/1994 for WK. m 5/22/1965 Mary Joyce Strickland c 1. Asstg Bp Of Wyoming Dio Wyoming Casper 2002-2012, Archd of Wy 1990-1995, Chair Com 1987-1989; Bp Of Wstrn Kansas Dio Wstrn Kansas Hutchinson KS 1995-2002; R S Lk's Epis Ch Buffalo WY 1985-1989; Archd Ch Of S Jas The Apos Clovis Curry NM 1983-1985; R S Jas Epis Ch Dillon MT 1982-1983; Archd Dio The Rio Grande Albuquerque 1980-1982; R S Dav's Epis Ch Lakeland FL 1977-1979; Asst S Mich's Ch Orlando FL 1973-1977; R S Lk's Epis Ch Live Oak FL 1971-1973; Vic S Agatha's Epis Ch Defuniak Spgs FL 1970-1971; Chair Prog Cmsn Dio Cntrl Florida Orlando FL 1973-1979.

STRICKLAND, Virginia Lisbeth (Cal) 14 Lagunitas Rd, Ross CA 94957 **St Johns Epis Ch Ross CA 2015-** B Houston TX 1978 d Larry & Kristin. BA U NC 2001; MDiv Yale DS 2006. D 6/4/2011 P 12/11/2011 Bp Pierre W Whalon. Asst Ch Of The Incarn New York NY 2011-2015; Dir of Yth and YA Mnstrs Amer Ch in Paris 2006-2011.

STRICKLAND JR, William Earl (Alb) 4 Avery Place, Clifton Park NY 12065 **S Paul's Epis Ch Greenwich NY 2012-; Cur Gr Ch Waterford NY 2008-** B Oxford MS 1958 s William & Jane. BA U of Mississippi 1980; MA U of Texas 1982; JD Amer U 1988; MA Nash 2008. D 5/31/2008 P 12/6/2008 Bp William Howard Love. m 7/12/2003 Elizabeth McFarland c 2.

STRICKLIN, Paul (USC) 6408 Bridgewood Rd., Columbia SC 29206 B Birmingham AL 1952 s Elmer & Marcella. Cert Walker Coll 1972; BS U of Alabama 1974; MDiv VTS 1978. D 6/12/1978 P 12/12/1978 Bp Furman Charles Stough. m 5/14/1977 Kathrine Stricklin c 2. R S Mich And All Ang' Columbia SC 2008-2013; R Calv Epis Ch Cleveland MS 2004-2008; Sr Chapl Epis Sch Of Dallas Dallas TX 1997-2004; Asst R Ch Of The Gd Shpd Dallas TX 1992-1997; Chapl Gd Shpd Epis Sch Dallas TX 1992-1997; Chr Sch Arden NC 1989-1992; Chapl Chr Sch Arden NC 1989-1992; R S Geo's Epis Ch Summerville SC 1986-1989; Chapl S Ptr's Ch Oxford MS 1984-1986; Dio Alabama Birmingham 1983-1984; Asst R All SS Epis Ch Birmingham AL 1980-1984; Cur S Paul's Ch Selma AL 1978-1980. Cris 1989-2004; NAES 1989-2004; Saes 1992-2004. paulestricklin@gmail.com

STRID, Paul Eric (Cal) 3115 W Meadow Dr SW, Albuquerque NM 87121 **Assoc S Mich And All Ang Ch Albuquerque NM 2007-** B Fresno CA 1946 s Paul & Hallie. BA Pomona Coll 1968; MDiv Amer Bapt Sem of the W 1972; U CA 1974; CDSP 1988; CDSP 2006. D 12/2/1989 P 12/1/1990 Bp William Edwin Swing. Vic S Cuth's Epis Ch Oakland CA 1995-2003; Int S Aid's Ch San Francisco CA 1993-1994; Int S Ptr's Epis Ch Redwood City CA 1992-1993; D S Alb's Ch Albany CA 1989-1990. Associated Parishes, OHC, No Amer As. pstrid505@mac.com

STRIDIRON, Andrea Renee (Roch) 2000 Highland Ave, Rochester NY 14618 **Secy to the Conv Dio Rochester Henrietta 2016-** B Philadelphia PA 1953 s Clifton & Theresa. Cert Bex Sem; Masters SUNY Brockport; B.S. W Chester St Coll. D 5/2/2009 Bp Prince Grenville Singh.

STRIMER, Peter (Oly) 863 E Gwinn Place, Seattle WA 98102 B Delaware OH 1954 s Robert & Jane. BA Duke 1976; MSW U of Connecticut 1980; MDiv Yale DS 1980; PhD OH SU 1994. D 9/7/1980 P 3/15/1981 Bp William Grant Black. m 7/29/1995 Eleanor W Mcfarland. R S Andr's Ch Seattle WA 2006-2014; Cmncatn Mssnr Dio Olympia Seattle 2003-2006; Cn for Urban Wk S Mk's Cathd Seattle WA 1995-2003; Co-Pstr Third Av Cmnty Churc Columbus OH 1994-1995; Vic S Jn's Ch Columbus OH 1991-1995; The Hunger Ntwk Columbus OH 1984-1988; Trin Ch Columbus OH 1981-1985.

STRING, Jansen Edward (Md) 2900 Dunleer Rd, Baltimore MD 21222 **R S Geo's And S Matthews Ch Dundalk MD 1994-** B Cleveland OH 1952 s Ralph & Barbara. BA U of Wisconsin 1974; MDiv EDS 1983; MS Loyola Coll 2000.

S

D 6/25/1983 Bp John Harris Burt P 6/1/1984 Bp Frank S Cerveny. m 5/27/1995 Constance String c 4. R Gd Samar Epis Ch Orange Pk FL 1991-1994; S Eliz's Epis Ch Jacksonville FL 1986-1991; Dio Florida Jacksonville 1985-1986; Cur Ch Of The Gd Shpd Jacksonville FL 1983-1985; Cur Ch Of The H Cross Tryon NC 1983.

STRINGER, Pamela (EC) 111 N King St, Bath NC 27808 **R H Trin Epis Ch Hampstead NC 2000-** B Oak Park IL 1947 d Warner & Barara. BD U of Florida 1969; MA U of Alabama 1973; MDiv SWTS 1984. D 6/24/1984 Bp William F Gates Jr P 4/21/1985 Bp William Evan Sanders. Int S Thos' Epis Ch Bath NC 1999-2000; S Paul's Epis Ch Clinton NC 1997-1999; Cn Mssnr Chr Ch Cathd Indianapolis IN 1991-1996, P 1985-1986; S Steph's Epis Ch Oak Ridge TN 1984-1991.

STRINGER, Stacy (Tex) 4613 Highway 3, Dickinson TX 77539 **R H Trin Epis Ch Dickinson TX 2010-; Dn of Galveston Convoc Dio Texas Houston TX 2011-** B New York 1958 d Francis & Patricia. BA SUNY at Plattsburgh; MDiv Epis TS of the SW 2008. D 6/28/2008 Bp Don Adger Wimberly P 2/7/2009 Bp C Andrew Doyle. m 11/30/1985 Stephen Stringer. Asst R Trin Ch Houston TX 2008-2010. OSH (Epis) 2010.

STRINGFELLOW III, Howard (Be) 333 Wyandotte St., Bethlehem PA 18015 **Ch Of The Gd Shpd Scranton PA 2015-** B Fort Huachuca AZ 1952 s Howard & Jean. BA Van 1974; MA Wake Forest U 1976; MDiv GTS 1986. D 10/4/1986 Bp William Arthur Beckham P 5/31/1987 Bp Michael Eric Marshall. m 5/19/1984 Carolyne E Stringfellow. Archd Dio Bethlehem Bethlehem PA 2005-2014; R S Lk's Ch Scranton PA 1993-2004; Cur S Thos Ch New York NY 1986-1993; Ecum Cmsn Dio New York New York NY 1990-1993.

STRIZAK, Jenna (At) Holy Trinity Parish, 515 E Ponce de Leon Ave, Decatur GA 30030 **H Trin Par Decatur GA 2012-** B Bayshore NY 1981 d Michael & Cynthia. BA Hampshire Coll 2003; MDiv Candler TS Emory U 2011. D 6/9/2012 Bp J Neil Alexander P 1/12/2013 Bp Robert Christopher Wright. strizak@htparish.com

STROBEL JR, Henry Willis (Tex) 2701 Bellefontaine St Apt B32, Houston TX 77025 **Asst S Bede Epis Ch Houston TX 2000-; P Assoc Palmer Memi Ch Houston TX 1972-** B Charleston SC 1943 s Henry & Madge. BS Coll of Charleston 1964; PhD U NC 1968; Michigan TS 1972. D 2/20/1971 Bp Richard Stanley Merrill Emrich P 6/9/1979 Bp James Milton Richardson. m 6/15/1968 Josephine Northup. Epis Hlth Chars 1998-2002; Cur S Aid's Ch Ann Arbor MI 1971-1972. Auth, "Recombinant Dna Tech & The Relatns Of Humanity To God"; Auth, "S Lk Journ Of Theol". ESMHE. Sigma Xi.

STROBEL, Pam Owen (NY) 123 Henry St, Greenwich CT 06830 B Chicago IL 1949 d Alfred & Marjorie. Grad Sch of Rel Ford; Syr 1968; NEU 1969; CUNY 1984; BA SUNY 1995; MDiv GTS 1998. D 6/13/1998 P 12/19/1998 Bp Richard Frank Grein. c 1. S Barn Ch Ardsley NY 2013-2015; Trin Ch Torrington CT 2012; Exec Coun Appointees New York NY 2011; Sr Assoc to the R Chr Ch Greenwich CT 2000-2011; Gr Epis Ch Port Jervis NY 2000; Dio New York New York NY 1998-2000; S Jas' Ch Goshen NY 1998-2000.

STROH, Nancy Marshall (Pa) 3440 Norwood Pl, Holland PA 18966 B Wilmington DE 1938 d Alva & Jessie. BA Drew U 1960; MEd Goucher Coll 1961; GTS 1987; MA Luth TS 1988. D 6/11/1988 P 5/27/1989 Bp Allen Lyman Bartlett Jr. c 2. P-in-c Ch Of The Redemp Southampton PA 2007-2010; Vic Ch Of The H Nativ Wrightstown PA 1991-2006; Int Trin Ch Gulph Mills Kng Of Prussia PA 1990-1991; Asst R S Andr's Ch Yardley PA 1988-1990; Cathd Chapt Dio Pennsylvania Philadelphia PA 1995-2001.

STROHL, Patrick Francis (CPa) 113 S Broad St, Mechanicsburg PA 17055 **Bd Dir Ecum Hm of Harrisburg 2009-; Chair-Prison Mnstry Cmsn Dio Cntrl Pennsylvania Harrisburg PA 2004-, Chapl to the Bp 2007-2010; Treas/BOD The Epis Hm of Shhippensburg 2004-; Treas/BOD St. Steph Epis Sch Harrisburg PA 2003-; D Cathd Ch Of S Steph Harrisburg PA 2010-** B Chicago IL 1943 s Peter & Pearl. BS U of Cntrl Florida 1975; Cert Dioc Sch of Chr Stds 2005. D 11/19/2005 Bp Michael Whittington Creighton. m 6/1/1996 Sandra Strohl c 2. D S Benedicts Epis Ch New Freedom PA 2005-2007. Assoc. of Epis Deacons 2005; Cler Assoc. of Cntrl PA- 2005; Cler Assoc. of Cntrl PA-Sec'y 2005-2010; NNECA Bd Dir 2008; NNECA Bd Dir-Past Pres 2011; NNECA Bd Dir-Pres 2010-2011.

STROHM, Ralph William (WVa) 2248 Adams Ave, Huntington WV 25704 **R S Simon's Ch Buffalo NY 2000-** B Muscatine IA 1944 s Ralph & Ferris. BBA U of Iowa 1967; Cert U of Iowa 1969; MA Nthrn Arizona U 1975; JD U of Iowa 1978; MDiv Bex Sem 1990. D 1/30/1991 P 10/1/1991 Bp William George Burrill. c 3. S Ptr's Ch Huntington WV 2009-2011; Int Gr Ch Lockport NY 2000-2000; R Ch of the Incarn Penfield NY 1994-1999; Ch Of The Incarn Penfield NY 1992-1999; Int Ch of the Incarn Penfield NY 1992-1994; The Ch Of The Epiph Gates NY 1991-1992; Asst Ch of the Epiph Rochester NY 1990-1992. Bex Soc 1987-1990; Soc of S Jn the Evang 2004.

STROM, Aune Juanita (Mo) St Andrew's By the Lake Episcopal, PO Box 8766, Michigan City IN 46361 **R Chr Ch Rolla MO 2009-** B Renton Washington 1952 d Erick & Elsi. BA Whitworth U 1975; MA Fuller TS 1979; PhD Fuller TS 1981; SWTS 2005. D 10/7/2007 P 4/9/2008 Bp Edward Stuart Little II. m 8/7/1987 Jon E Threlkeld. S Andr's By The Lake Epis Ch Michigan City IN 2007-2009; Assoc for Chr Formation St Thos Epis Ch 2001-2003.

STROMBERG, Matthew Roy (Alb) **S Geo's Epis Ch Schenectady NY 2016-** D 5/31/2014 P 12/6/2014 Bp William Howard Love.

STROMWELL, Gloria Regina (Md) 126 E. Liberty St., Oakland MD 21550 **D S Matt's Par Oakland MD 2008-** B Minneapolis MN 1939 d Charles & Esther. D 7/5/2008 P 6/27/2009 Bp John L Rabb. m 12/26/1959 Stephen W Stromwell c 2.

STRONG, Anne Lorraine (Az) PO Box 65840, Tucson AZ 85728 B Chicago IL 1945 d Langdon & Lorraine. D 1/23/2010 Bp Kirk Stevan Smith. c 3.

STRONG, Daniel Robert (WMass) 17 Exeter Dr, Auburn MA 01501 B Winthrop MA 1949 s William & Roberta. BA Wstrn Connecticut St U 1979; MDiv GTS 1982. D 6/5/1982 Bp Paul Moore Jr P 3/25/1983 Bp James Stuart Wetmore. m 11/14/1981 Nancy Baillie Strong c 1. P-in-c S Jn's Ch Worcester MA 2002-2006; Dio Wstrn Massachusetts Springfield 2000-2005; Int Trin Epis Ch Milford MA 2000-2002; Dio New York New York NY 1996-2000; S Dav's Ch Highland Mls NY 1985-2000; P-in-c S Paul's Ch Chester NY 1985-2000; Epis. Comm Of Cntrl Orange Goshen NY 1985-1995; Cur Chr Ch Of Ramapo Suffern NY 1982-1984; Vic Chr Epis Ch Sparkill NY 1982-1984; Pstr Orange Cnty Hm 1996-2005. Ord Of S Lk.

STRONG, Elizabeth Anne (Minn) 2200 Minnehaha Ave E, Saint Paul MN 55119 B St Louis MO 1936 d Hans & Mary. BS Metropltn St U 1991. D 6/20/2015 Bp Brian N Prior. m 9/1/1957 Doyle Lemmard Strong c 4.

STRONG III, Maurice LeRoy (Chi) 26 E Stonegate Dr, Prospect Heights IL 60070 **Vic Ch Of The Incarn Bloomingdale IL 2009-** B Washington DC 1960 s Maurice & Nancy. BS Pur 1987; MDiv SWTS 1992; MS NWU 2006; DMin SWTS 2013. D 6/13/1992 Bp Joseph Thomas Heistand P 12/1/1992 Bp Frank Tracy Griswold III. m 6/16/1984 Kimberly Strong c 2. Dir NASSAM 2013-2015; Asst S Lawr Epis Ch Libertyville IL 2004-2008; Assoc S Greg's Epis Ch Deerfield IL 1993. DMin Thesis, "Tentmakers: Changing the Variables in the Equation of Econ Viability for Congregations in the Dio Chicago," *DMin Thesis*, SWTS, 2013. AOC Hall of Fame Inductee Accociation of Old Crows 2003; Fredrick Clifton Grant Prize in NT SWTS 1992. fr.marc_coi@hotmail.com

STRONG, Nancy Baillie (WMass) 17 Exeter Dr, Auburn MA 01501 **R S Matt's Ch Worcester MA 2000-; Chair, COM Dio Wstrn Massachusetts Springfield 2010-, Mem, Dioc Coun 2007-, Mem, BEC 2003-2010** B Chester PA 1954 d Craig & Nancy. BA Lebanon Vlly Coll 1976; MDiv GTS 1983. D 6/11/1983 Bp Lyman Cunningham Ogilby P 11/10/1984 Bp Walter Decoster Dennis Jr. m 11/14/1981 Daniel Robert Strong c 3. Dio New York New York NY 1997-2000; Pstr Ch Of The Gd Shpd Newburgh NY 1993-2000; Hudson Vlly Mnstrs New Windsor NY 1990-1996; P-in-c Ch Of The Gd Shpd Greenwood Lake NY 1988-1989; Asst S Steph's Ch Pearl River NY 1983-1985. Auth, "Poetry," *Wmn Uncommon Prayers*, Morehouse Pub, 2000.

STROO, Eric Edward (Oly) 111 NE 80th St, Seattle WA 98115 B Flushing NY 1954 s Hans & Mary. BA Ken 1976; MA U of Texas at Arlington 1981; MA Seattle U 2009. D 11/9/2013 Bp Gregory Harold Rickel. c 2.

STROTHEIDE, Cassandra Jo (Colo) 19210 E Stanford Dr, Aurora CO 80015 **Asst The Ch Of The Ascen Denver CO 2010-; Exec Com- High Plains Reg Dio Colorado Denver CO 2009-** B Ossining NY 1949 d Charles & Patricia. BS Colorado St U 1971; MDiv Epis TS of the SW 2005. D 6/11/2005 P 12/17/2005 Bp Robert John O'Neill. m 4/7/1972 Larry L Strotheide c 2. P-in-c All SS Epis Ch Denver CO 2007-2008; S Matt's Parker CO 2005-2007, Asst 2005-2007.

STROUD, Daniel (Pa) PO Box 247, Ft Washington PA 19034 **Asst S Thos' Ch Whitemarsh Ft Washington PA 2014-** B Jacksonville NC 1985 s Joseph & Rhonda. BA The TS at The U So 2007; BA U So 2007; BA U So 2007; MDiv VTS 2014. D 6/7/2014 Bp Peter J Lee P 12/13/2014 Bp Clifton Daniel III. m 10/12/2013 Lara Stroud c 1.

STROUD, Lara (Pa) PO Box 247, Fort Washington PA 19034 **Asst S Thos' Ch Whitemarsh Ft Washington PA 2014-** B Birminghan AL 1983 d James & Susanne. BM Appalachian St U 2007; MDiv VTS 2012. D 4/15/2012 P 11/11/2012 Bp Scott Scott Barker. m 10/12/2013 Daniel Stroud. All SS and St Georges Ch Rehoboth Bch DE 2013-2014; All SS Epis Ch Omaha NE 2012-2013. motherlara@gmail.com

STROUD, Nancy Webb (WMass) 64 Westwood Dr, Westfield MA 01085 **R Ch Of The Atone Westfield MA 2009-; Dio Wstrn Massachusetts Springfield 2009-, Stndg Com, Pres 2016-, COM 2013-, Dep to GC 78 and 79 2013-, Stndg Com 2013-, Del to Prov I 2012-** B Bryn Mawr PA 1957 d Stuart & Julia. BA U of Virginia 1979; Luth TS 2004; MDiv GTS 2005. D 6/4/2005 P 12/17/2005 Bp Charles Ellsworth Bennison Jr. m 8/20/1983 William D Stroud c 3. Bd Trst Epis Cmnty Serv Philadelphia PA 2006-2009; S Ptr's Ch In The Great Vlly Malvern PA 2006-2009; S Paul's Ch Philadelphia PA 2005-2006. rector@atonementwestfield.net

STROUD, Robert L (WNC) B 1940 D. m 4/11/1960 Earlene Stroud.

STROUP, Susan Louise (Oly) **D S Paul's Epis Ch Bremerton WA 2004-** B Kellogg ID 1962 BA Evergreen St Coll 2002. D 6/26/2004 Bp Sanford Zangwill Kaye Hampton.

STROUT, Shawn Owen (WA) 2430 K St Nw, Washington DC 20037 **S Paul's Par Washington DC 2016-** B Claremont NH 1971 s Merle & Muriel. BA Pensacola Chr Coll 1993; MA Webster U 1998; MA Liberty U 2008; MDiv VTS 2012. D 6/2/2012 P 1/26/2013 Bp Mariann Edgar Budde. Ch Of The Ascen And S Agnes Washington DC 2014-2016; Par of St Monica & St Jas Washington DC 2014; Asst R Chr Ch Par Kensington MD 2012-2014. strout@stpauls-kst.com

STRUBEL, Gary Francis (Alb) 457 3rd St, Troy NY 12180 **All SS Ch Hoosick Falls NY 2011-, 2005-2008** B Troy NY 1968 BA SUNY 1993; MLS SUNY 1996; MA St Bernards TS And Mnstry Rochester NY 2004. D 6/12/2004 Bp Daniel William Herzog P 1/15/2005 Bp David John Bena. m 9/14/1996 Tina Krstine Strubel c 2. D S Paul's Ch Troy NY 2004-2005.

STRUBLE, Kenneth Charles (At) 4076 Riverdale Rd., Toccoa GA 30577 **Dir Dio Atlanta Atlanta GA 2002-; Exec Dir Mikell C&C Toccoa GA 2002-** B Toccoa GA 1962 s Robert & Peggy. BA U GA 1987; MDiv GTS 1993; MA Georgia Sch of Profsnl Psychol Atlanta GA 2000. D 6/5/1993 P 12/1/1993 Bp Frank Kellogg Allan. m 12/30/1989 Melanie Gearing Struble c 3. Asst R S Dav's Ch Roswell GA 1993-2002.

STUART JR, Calvin Truesdale Biddison (Mo) 5008 Bischoff Ave, Saint Louis MO 63110 **Ret 1998-** B Saint Louis MO 1937 s Calvin & Cynthia. BS Washington U 1961; MDiv EDS 1964. D 6/1/1964 P 12/4/1964 Bp George Leslie Cadigan. c 3. 1971-1998; Asst Ch Of The Ascen S Louis MO 1964-1965.

STUART, Charles Moore (EMich) 821 Adams St, Saginaw MI 48602 **Ret 1993-** B Grand Rapids MI 1928 s James & Margaret. BA Ya 1950; BD EDS 1956; Coll of Preachers 1970; DMin VTS 1983. D 6/23/1956 P 12/23/1956 Bp Dudley B McNeil. m 6/28/1958 Judith A Stuart c 4. Archd Reg I Dio Estrn Michigan Saginaw MI 1986-1992; R S Jn's Epis Ch Saginaw MI 1967-1993; Cathd Chapt Dio Michigan Detroit MI 1966-1969, Exec Coun 1965-1967, Chair, Fin Com 1966-1967; R Trin Epis Ch Monroe MI 1962-1967; S Jn's Ch Mt Pleasant MI 1958-1962; Asst Gr Epis Ch Traverse City MI 1956-1958; Chair, Dept CSR Dio Wstrn Michigan Kalamazoo MI 1958-1962.

STUART, Judith Lynne (Mass) PO Box 789, Chatham MA 02633 **Dio Massachusetts Boston MA 2006-** B Boston MA 1955 d Robert & Carol. BS NEU 1981; MEd Boston Coll 1982; MDiv EDS 2001. D 5/9/2002 P 11/3/2002 Bp Edwin Max Leidel Jr. m 6/7/1975 William J Stuart c 2. Ch Of The Redeem Chestnut Hill MA 2003-2006; Asst S Christophers Epis Ch Grand Blanc MI 2002-2003.

STUART, Lawrence Earl (Mich) 3901 Cheyenne Rd, Richmond VA 23235 **Vic S Jn's Ch Chesaning MI 1969-; Cur Calv Memi Epis Ch Saginaw MI 1968-** B Schenectady NY 1931 s Clifford & Thelma. Michigan TS 1968. D 3/28/1968 Bp Archie H Crowley P 9/1/1976 Bp H Coleman Mcgehee Jr. m 12/27/1949 Lilia Elizabeth Tipaldi. Asst Ch Of The Gd Shpd Richmond VA 1995-2006.

STUART, Marianne D(esmarais) (Ala) 249 Arch St, Philadelphia PA 19106 B Springfield MA 1951 d Camille & Marjorie. U of Alabama; NW Connecticut Cmnty Coll Winsted CT 1971; MacMurray Coll 1973; Bp St 1976. D 5/26/1994 Bp Calvin Onderdonk Schofield Jr P 10/1/1995 Bp John Lewis Said. c 9. S Jn's Epis Deaf Ch Birmingham AL 2006-2017; Dio Pennsylvania Philadelphia PA 2001-2006; All Souls Ch For The Deaf Philadelphia PA 2001; Mssnr w The Deaf Dio Wstrn No Carolina Asheville NC 1997-2001. Epis Conf Of The Deaf Of The Epis Ch In The USA.

STUART, Mark (Los) 2260 N Cahuenga Blvd # 507, Los Angeles CA 90068 **P-in-c H Trin Epis Ch Covina CA 2013-; Asst S Thos The Apos Hollywood Los Angeles CA 2013-, Assoc 2002-2010; Chair, Stwdshp and Dvlpmt Dio Los Angeles Los Angeles CA 2007-** B Hutchinson KS 1951 s Donald & Eunice. BA San Francisco St U 1974; MDiv Nash 1979. D 6/30/1979 Bp Chauncie Kilmer Myers P 4/12/1980 Bp William Edwin Swing. Int Ch Of The Mssh Santa Ana CA 2011-2013; Int S Aug By-The-Sea Par Santa Monica CA 2010-2011; Dir of Dvlpmt Torrance - So Bay YMCA California 2003-2005; Dir of Dvlpmt YWCA San Gabr Vlly California 2002-2003; Assoc Trin Epis Ch Mobile AL 1993-2000; Wilmer Hall Mobile AL 1990-2001; Assoc R Trin Ch Atchison KS 1989-1990; Vic Ch Of The Trsfg Bennington KS 1986-1989; S Fran Cmnty Serv Inc. Salina KS 1981-1990; Cur Calv Epis Ch Santa Cruz CA 1979-1981; Com Dio California San Francisco CA 1979-1980; Com Dio Wstrn Kansas Hutchinson KS 1982-1984. Auth, "Grief Transformed," Paige Press, 2010. fathermark@holytrinitycovina.com

STUART IV, Mose Wadsworth (Ala) D 6/3/2017 Bp John Mckee Sloan Sr.

STUART, Toni Freeman (NCal) 4881 8th St, Carpinteria CA 93013 **Asst S Mich's U Mssn Isla Vista CA 2005-** B Bakersfield CA 1937 d Jack & Elinor. MA Epis St at Claremont; BA Stan 1959; MA Claremont TS 1989. D 6/10/1989 P 1/13/1990 Bp Frederick Houk Borsch. c 3. R S Matt's Epis Ch Sacramento CA 2000-2005; Vic Epis Chap Of S Fran Los Angeles CA 1993-2000; Int S Thos' Mssn Hacienda Hgts CA 1993; Asst S Paul's Pomona Pomona CA 1991-1993; Assoc All SS Par Los Angeles CA 1989-1991. Co-Ed, "The Last Great Bch Town Revs," Lulu, 2009; Auth, "Adventures Of The Soul," 2000. Immac Heart Cmnty 1998. Polly Bond Awd Epis Cmncatn 1995.

STUBBS, John Derek (WNY) 33 Linwood Avenue, Whitinsville MA 01588 **Vic S Jn's Ch Millville MA 2012-; R Trin Epis Ch Whitinsville MA 2011-** B Johannesburg ZA 1952 s Derek & Margaret. BTh U of So Afr ZA 1980; MDiv GTS 1983; STM UTS 1984; Organisational Dvlpmt 1988; Microsoft Access Visual Basic 1995; Myers Briggs Type Indicator 1995; ThD U of So Afr ZA 1999. Trans 4/2/1985 as Priest Bp Paul Moore Jr. m 5/28/2009 Barbara Stubbs c 3. Int S Mary's Castleton Staten Island NY 2008-2010; Dir Angl Hse of Stds Pietermaritzburg So Afr 2006-2008; Dn Dio Grahamstown 1999-2008; Dn Cathd of Ss. Mich & Geo Grahamstown So Afr 1999-2006; Dn Dio Cape Town 1995-1999; Asst Exec Coun Appointees New York NY 1991-1995; Asst Ch Of The Heav Rest New York NY 1986-1991; Asst Heav Rest New York City NY 1986-1991; Asst Chr Ch Of Ramapo Suffern NY 1985-1986. Auth, "Dinazade: Tell Me Your Story," *Online Pub: johnderekstubbs.com*, Online Pub: johnderekstubbs.com, 2013; Auth, Unpublished, 2005; Auth, "A Certain Wmn Raised Her Voice: The Use of Grammatical Structure and the Origins of Texts.," *Neotestamentica 36(1-2) 2002, page 21 37. Festschrift for Prof Jn Suggit*, U of Kwa-Zulu Natal, 2002; Auth, "Synoptic Hist and Style Through Syntax," *Doctoral Dissertation*, U of So Afr, 1999; Auth, *The Ord Process in the Dio Capetown*, The Angl Dio Cape Town, 1998; Auth, "Popo Molefe," *Witness mag*, 1990; Auth, *Prov Yth Mnstry Manual*, The Angl Ch of So Afr, 1978. NT Soc of So Afr; SBL. Hon Cn Dio Grahamstown, So Afr 2006; Citation of Mnstry So Afr Cmnty in the USA 1991.

STUBE, Peter B (Pa) 125 Timothy Circle, Wayne PA 19087 **P-in-c S Mary's Epis Ch Stone Harbor NJ 2016-** B Gloucester MA 1951 s Edwin & Barbara. U NC 1971; BA Columbia Intl U 1973; Estrn Nazarene Coll 1975; MDiv VTS 1979; DMin VTS 1990. D 6/30/1979 Bp David Keller Leighton Sr P 1/6/1980 Bp Jackson Earle Gilliam. m 6/22/1974 Rachael O Stube c 3. Exec Dir Seamens Ch Inst Philadelphia PA 2013-2016; Dn of Trin Dnry Dio E Carolina 2011-2013; Cn Theol Dio E Carolina 2004-2013; Chairman of Recon Cmsn Dio E Carolina 2004-2006; R Chr Ch New Bern NC 2003-2013; Dn Dio Pennsylvania Philadelphia PA 1999-2003, Liturg Cmsn 1992-1998; R Ch Of The Redeem Springfield PA 1990-2003; Assoc S Jude's Ch Marietta GA 1986-1990; R Ch Of The Gd Shpd Forrest City AR 1983-1986; Dio Oklahoma Oklahoma City OK 1981-1983; Vic Ch Of The H Cross Owasso OK 1981-1982; Cur S Lk's Ch Billings MT 1979-1981; Pres of the Stndg Com Dio E Carolina Kinston NC 2009-2010, Exec Coun 2007-2010, Cn Theol 2006-2013, GC Dep 2006-2012. Auth, *Preparing a Grp for Servnt Ldrshp: An Experiment in Mssn/ Cov*. Soc of S Fran - Tertiary 1987. Liberty hon Awd Craven Cnty NAACP 2007. peter.stube@gmail.com

STUBER, Richard Leonard (Wyo) 1320 Landon Ave, Yakima WA 98902 B Wapato WA 1933 s Leonard & Fern. Lic Vancouver TS CA 1971. Trans 8/27/1978 Bp Bob Gordon Jones. m 4/18/1958 Mary Ann Stuber c 4. S Mk's Epis Ch Casper WY 1978-1980; Serv Ch Of Can 1971-1978.

STUCKEY, Ross W (WMo) 1654 E Cardinal St, Springfield MO 65804 **Mem, Dept of Congrl Dvlpmt/Urban & Suburban Dio W Missouri Kansas City MO 2004-, Pres, Stndg Com 1999-2000, Mem, Stndg Com 1996-2000, Dep, GC 1992-2004, Ecum Off 1992-, Chair, Cler Compstn Com 1991-2000, Mem, COM 1990-1996** B Monticello AR 1938 s Monroe & Helen. Arkansas A&M Coll; SW-at-Memphis; St. Petersburg St U, Russia; U of Maryland; BA U of Arkansas 1962; MDiv VTS 1976. D 5/22/1976 Bp John Alfred Baden P 3/12/1977 Bp Christoph Keller Jr. m 6/1/1996 Paula B Stuckey c 3. R S Jas' Ch Springfield MO 1990-2008; Assoc Gr Ch Carthage MO 1986-1989; R S Jn's Ch Harrison AR 1982-1985; Vic Ch Of The Gd Shpd Forrest City AR 1978-1982; Gr Ch Wynne AR 1978-1982; Vic S Jas Ch Magnolia AR 1976-1978; S Mary's Epis Ch El Dorado AR 1976-1978; Dn, NW Convoc Dio Arkansas Little Rock AR 1984, Mem, Ecum Cmsn 1984, Mem, Exec Coun 1981-1984, Chair, Liturg & Mus Cmsn 1981-1983, Mem, Liturg & Mus Cmsn 1977-1983.

STUDDIFORD, Linton (Me) 124 Bunganuc Rd, Brunswick ME 04011 B New York NY 1941 s Andrew & Marjorie. BA Pr 1963; MA U of Pennsylvania 1966; MDiv Bangor TS 1985; DMin Bangor TS 1997. D 6/29/1980 P 3/1/1985 Bp Frederick Barton Wolf. m 4/3/1963 Bonnie Studdiford c 2. S Phil's Ch Wiscasset ME 2009-2011; Cn to the Ordnry Dio Maine Portland ME 1999-2008, Dep, GC 2009-2011, Dep, GC 2006-2008, Dep, GC 2003-2005, Dep, GC 2000-2002, Dep, GC 1997-1999, Pres, Stndg Com 1994-1997, Dep, GC 1994-1996; R S Alb's Ch Cape Eliz ME 1992-1999; R S Geo's Epis Ch Sanford ME 1985-1992; Vic All SS Epis Ch Skowhegan ME 1985, Asst 1980-1982. Soc of S Jn the Evang.

STUDENNY, Ronald Roman (Dal) 977 W Highway 243, Canton TX 75103 **S Justin's Canton TX 2011-** B Queens NY 1961 s Raymond & Eleanor. Dip Min Stud Stanton Cntr for Mnstry Formation 2011. D 6/11/2011 P 12/10/2011 Bp James Monte Stanton. m 12/14/1991 Pamela Dorris Studenny c 4.

STUDLEY, Carolyn Kay Mary (Minn) 614 N Old Litchfield Rd, Litchfield Park AZ 85340 **Wrld Mssn Com Dio Arizona Phoenix AZ 2006-, Sudanese Connection 2004-** B Duluth MN 1931 d Orien & Helen. S Lukes Sch of Nrsng 1953; BS Bemidji St U 1983; Cert Kino Inst Phoenix AZ 2002. D 10/25/1987 Bp Robert Marshall Anderson. c 3.

STUDLEY, Richard E (Minn) 9817 W. Pinecrest Dr, Sun City AZ 85351 B Brockton MA 1932 s John & Sarah. BS Bryant U 1957; MA U of San Francisco 2004. D 10/25/1987 Bp Robert Marshall Anderson. m 12/27/1955 Carolyn

Mary Sudley. D Ch Of The Adv Sun City W AZ 2010-2013; D S Christophers Epis Ch Peoria AZ 2000-2007; S Ptr's Ch Litchfield Pk AZ 2000-2007; D The Par of St Paul's Epis Ch Duluth MN 1987-2000. Ord of S Lk.

STUDWELL, Catheen Mildred (Nwk) B Passaic NJ 1963 d Robert & Marie. D 12/10/2016 P 6/10/2017 Bp Mark M Beckwith. m 9/12/1981 Jay Norman Studwell c 2.

STUHLMAN, Byron David (CNY) PO Box 74, Round Pond ME 04564 B Dayton OH 1941 s Byron & Margaret. BA Ya 1963; STB GTS 1966; PhD Duke 1991. D 6/11/1966 Bp Walter H Gray P 3/1/1967 Bp John Henry Esquirol. m 6/28/1968 Hester K Stuhlman c 1. Chair, Dioceasn Cmsn on Liturg & Mus Dio Cntrl New York Liverpool NY 1998-2007; R Gr Epis Ch Waterville NY 1997-2007; Emm Ch Norwich NY 1996-1997; Chenango Cluster Norwich NY 1996; Assoc S Jas' Ch Clinton NY 1992-2001; Non-par 1988-1992; R S Thos Of Cbury Sherman CT 1977-1988; Chair, Liturg Cmsn Dio Connecticut Meriden CT 1972-1985; R S Mk's Ch Bridgewater CT 1971-1988; Cur Chr Ch Cathd Hartford CT 1966-1971. Auth, "The Initiatory Process in the Byzantine Tradition," Gorgias Press, 2009; Auth, "A Gd and Joyful Thing," Ch Pub, Inc, 2000; Auth, "Occasions of Gr," Ch Publshing, Inc, 1995; Auth, "Redeeming the Time," Ch Pub, Inc, 1992; Auth, "Eucharistic Celebration 1789-1979," Ch Pub, 1988; Auth, "PB Rubrics Expanded," Ch Pub, Inc, 1987. ADLMC, Societas Liturgica 1976-1992.

STUHLMANN, Robert (Ct) 2000 Main St, Stratford CT 06615 B Boston MA 1943 s Robert & Phyllis. BA Hobart and Wm Smith Colleges 1966; MDiv ETS-BH 1970. D 11/6/1971 Bp John Melville Burgess P 12/14/1976 Bp John Bowen Coburn. m 5/31/2003 Jean Guenther c 2. Chr Ch Stratford CT 1996-2010; Cathd Ch of Our Sav Philadelphia PA 1995-1996; Urban Coordntr Dio Connecticut Meriden CT 1987-1996; Dio New Jersey Trenton NJ 1987-1994; S Jn's Ch Jamaica Plain MA 1984-1986; Ch Of Our Sav Boston MA 1979-1985; P-in-c Our Sav Roslindale MA 1979-1984. Auth, "Dorchester Argus Citizen". Nj Epis Cleric Assn.

STUMP, Celeste Smith (Los) 330 E 16th St, Upland CA 91784 B New Orlens LA 1956 d James & Armantine. BA Loyola U New Orleans 1978; MPA U of Arizona 1984; Cert Diac Stud ETSBH 2010. D 5/23/2010 Bp Chester Lovelle Talton. m 9/28/1990 Scott Stump c 2.

STUMP, Derald William (CPa) 106 S Outer Dr, State College PA 16801 **Ret 2001-; Res Chapl SCI 1982-** B Des Moines IA 1930 s Joseph & Leah. Cert University of Pennsylvania; BA Drake U 1953; MDiv EDS 1959; Harv 1959; U So 1963; MEd Penn 1968; EdD Penn 1979. D 6/29/1959 P 5/28/1960 Bp Gordon V Smith. m 6/5/1957 Jean Conway Stump. R S Mk's Epis Ch Lewistown PA 1999-2001; Cnvnr Altoona Convoc Dio Cntrl Pennsylvania Harrisburg PA 1997-1999, 1989-1991, Mem Eccl Trial Crt 1988-1991, Chair Dept MHE 1974-1982, Secy 1973, COM 1971-1972, Bd Profnl Dvlpmt Mnstry 1970, Ex-Coun 1967-1971; Assoc R S Andr's Ch St Coll PA 1997-1999, P 1963-1996; Chapl CFS The Sch At Ch Farm Exton PA 1982-1983; Chapl Penn St U U Pk PA 1965-1982; Dioc Mssy Dio Iowa Des Moines IA 1960-1963; Cur The Cathd Ch Of S Paul Des Moines IA 1959-1960. Contrib, *The Gospel According to ES-PN: Saviours and Sinners*, 2003; Auth, *Nile Kinnick: The Man & The Legend*, Univ of iowa press, 1975. ESMHE 1969-1982. Homilist, Ord of Deacons The Epis Dio Pennsylvania 2011; Vision Awd Nevada Cler Assn 2010; Who's Who in Cmnty Serv Who's Who 1997; Who's Who in Amer Rel Who's Who 1996; Who's Who in Amer Rel Who's Who 1996.

STURGEON, Mary Sue (Neb) 5176 S 149th Ct, Omaha NE 68137 B Bedford IN 1940 d Grant & Maxine. D 11/8/1985 Bp James Daniel Warner. m 9/4/1993 William John Kouth c 3. D All SS Epis Ch Omaha NE 1985-2007.

STURGEON, Stephen C (U) 85 E 100 N, Logan UT 84321 **Vic S Jn's Epis Ch Logan UT 2014-, D 2010-2014; P Dio Utah Salt Lake City UT 2012-** B Berkeley, CA 1967 s Jack & Jack. BA Gri 1990; PhD U CO 1998; Cert Utah Mnstry Formation Progran 2009. D 6/12/2010 Bp Carolyn Tanner Irish P 2/15/2014 Bp Scott Byron Hayashi. m 7/25/1998 Stacy Sturgeon c 1. Epis Cmnty Serv Inc Salt Lake City UT 2011-2012.

STURGES, Harriette Horsey (WA) 3001 Wisconsin Ave NW, Washington DC 20016 **Dio No Carolina Raleigh NC 1990-** B Savannah GA 1944 d Richard & Harriette. BA Sweet Briar Coll 1966; MTS Duke 1989; Sch for Deacons in NC 1990. D 6/9/1990 Bp Robert Whitridge Estill. m 9/3/1966 Conrad Sturges c 2. D S Cyp's Ch Oxford NC 2012-2015; D and Coordntr of Chld's Mnstrs S Alb's Par Washington DC 2007-2011; D and Coordntr of Chld's Mnstrs S Phil's Ch Durham NC 2001-2007; D Duke Epis Cntr Durham NC 1992-1997; D Sprtl Dir S Paul's Ch Louisburg NC 1990-1993. NAAD 1990; Soc Comp of the H Cross 1986.

STURGES, Kathleen McAuliffe (Va) 3134 Mollifield Lane, Charlottesville VA 22911 **Ch Of S Jn The Bapt Ivy VA 2001-; Asst Ch Of Our Sav Charlottesvlle VA 1996-** B Walnut Creek CA 1968 d John & Kathryn. BA Seattle Pacific U 1991; MDiv Ya Berk 1996. D 6/22/1996 Bp Vincent Waydell Warner P 1/7/1997 Bp Peter J Lee. c 3. Vic Dio Virginia Richmond VA 2001-2016.

STURGESS, Amber D (Cal) 6208 Sutter Ave, Richmond CA 94804 **All SS Ch Carmel CA 2016-** B Tulia TX 1962 d Larry & Phyllis. BA Texas Tech U 1984; MA Texas Tech U 1989; MTS Perkins TS, SMU 1996; MA SMU Perkins 1996;

CAS Cdsp Berkeley 2005; C.A.S. CDSP 2005. D 10/16/2004 P 9/7/2005 Bp C Wallis Ohl. S Steph's Epis Ch Sn Luis Obispo CA 2014-2015; S Geo's Epis Ch Antioch CA 2007-2013; CDSP Berkeley CA 2006-2007; Asst S Cuth's Epis Ch Oakland CA 2005-2006.

STURGIS, Janet Elizabeth (Neb) Po Box 2285, Kearney NE 68848 B Mount Holly NJ 1943 d Malcolm & Ann. BA U of Missouri 1965; MDiv VTS 1984. D 5/26/1984 Bp Walter Cameron Righter P 12/18/1984 Bp William Foreman Creighton. m 10/28/1967 Terry Elsberry c 2. Chapl Epis Ch At Cornell Ithaca NY 2001-2003; R S Lk's Ch Kearney NE 1999-2001; Int Chr Ch Fairmont WV 1997-1999; S Jas The Apos Epis Ch Tempe AZ 1993-1995; Int S Mich's Ch Naugatuck CT 1992-1993; Int Chr Ch Oxford CT 1990-1992; Int S Jn's Epis Ch Bristol CT 1989-1990; Chr Ch Greenwich CT 1986-1989; S Fran Ch Potomac MD 1986; Zion Epis Ch Chas Town WV 1985-1986; Chapl Intrn S Eliz's Hosp Wdc 1984-1985. Ees.

STURNI, Gary Kristan (WTenn) 6922 Great Oaks Rd, Germantown TN 38138 **Co-Fndr, Natl Ntwk Coordntr Epis Cmnty Serv of Amer Clifton VA 2000-** B Newark NJ 1946 s Albert & Kathryn. BA California St U Sacramento 1967; BD CDSP 1970; MA Grad Theol Un 1970; DMin SFTS 1987; Cert W&M 2000. D 6/29/1970 Bp Clarence Rupert Haden Jr P 5/1/1971 Bp Edward McNair. m 12/28/1976 Cynthia C Sturni c 3. R S Geo's Ch Germantown TN 2004-2013; Ch Of The Mssh Lower Gwynedd PA 2003-2004; Int Ch of the Mssh Gwynedd PA 2002-2004; The Ch Of Ascen And H Trin Cincinnati OH 2001-2003; H Trin Epis Ch Oxford OH 1997; S Fran Cmnty Serv Inc. Salina KS 1993-2003; Natl Chapl, VP Level St. Fran Acad Inc. Hamilton 1993-2002; R Trin Ch Hamilton OH 1988-1993; Sr Assoc S Andr's Ch Saratoga CA 1985-1988; Sierra RurD 1981-1983; Founding P-in-c Chr The King Quincy CA 1978-1980; Chapl California St U in Chico 1974-1985; R S Jn The Evang Ch Chico CA 1974-1985; Vic S Lk's Mssn Calistoga CA 1972-1974; Cur Chr Ch Eureka CA 1970-1972; Chair of the Funding Com Dio Sthrn Ohio Cincinnati OH 1988-2003. Auth, "Producer Hisp Mnstry in Prov VIII," *Hisp Mnstry in ECR videos*.

STURTEVANT, Henry Hobson (NY) 484 W 43rd St Apt 33-H, New York NY 10036 B Portland ME 1945 s Peter & Katharine. BFA Bos 1967; BD EDS 1971. D 7/24/1971 P 4/27/1972 Bp Henry W Hobson. S Andr's Ch Oceanside NY 1995-2010; S Clem's Ch New York NY 1975-1980; Asst Indn Hill Ch Cincinnati OH 1971-1972.

STUTLER, Jamie (At) 1029 Wellesley Crest Dr, Woodstock GA 30189 **R S Clem's Epis Ch Canton GA 2004-** B Charleston SC 1956 s Warren & Joan. GW 1975; BA U So 1979; JD Mississippi Coll 1986; MDiv Sewanee: The U So, TS 1999. D 6/6/1999 P 12/12/1999 Bp Edward Lloyd Salmon Jr. m 11/23/2008 Melissa Lynn Stutler c 4. Vic S Alb's Ch Kingstree SC 1999-2004; Vic S Steph's Ch S Steph SC 1999-2004.

SUAREZ, Eva Noemi (WA) 335 E 116th St Apt 3, New York NY 10029 **Trin Par New York NY 2015-** B 1991 d Rafael & Carole. M.S.W Silberman Sch of Soc Wk at Hunter Coll; M.Div UTS; B.A Col 2013. D 11/21/2015 P 6/17/2017 Bp Mariann Edgar Budde. esuarez@trinitywallstreet.org

SUAREZ ELLES, Jose Armando (Colom) Cr 3 Sur # 11-A-02, Malambo AT-LANTICO Colombia B Cartagena Bolivar 1968 s Jose & Acela. Lic Pontificio Universidad Jaucnana; Seminario Mal De Cristo; Seminario Prov De Cartogena. D 10/14/2006 Bp Francisco Jose Duque-Gomez. m 12/30/2005 Carmen Cecilia Kammerer Herrera c 1.

SUCRE-CORDOVA, Guillermo Antonio (Ve) B 1941 D 7/24/1997 Bp Orlando Jesus Guerrero. m 1/17/1960 Audilia Ramona Hernandez. Dio Venezuela Caracas 2003-2013.

SUELLAU, Nancy Shebs (Fla) St Catherines Episcopal Church, 4758 Shelby Ave, Jacksonville FL 32210 **Assoc S Mk's Epis Ch Jacksonville FL 2015-; Chair of Dispatch of Bus, Dioc Conv 2012 Dio Florida Jacksonville 2012-, Alt Deligate to Natl Conv 2012 2011-, Mem of the Eccl Crt 2010-2012, Dioc Congreational Emergency Response Team Mem 2009-, ECW Chapl 2009-, Congrl Dvlpmt Com 2008-2013** B Tallahassee FL 1954 d Robert & Mary. BA Florida St U 1975; MS Flordia St U 1976; BSN Florida St U 1983; MDiv TESM 2007. D 5/27/2007 P 12/9/2007 Bp Samuel Johnson Howard. c 2. R S Cathr's Ch Jacksonville FL 2007-2015. d the King 2000.

SUGENO, David Senkichi (Tex) **R Trin Epis Ch Marble Falls TX 2009-** B 1965 s Frank. BA Connecticut Coll 1987; MA Texas A&M U 2000; MDiv Epis TS of the SW 2006. D 6/24/2006 Bp Don Adger Wimberly P 1/20/2007 Bp Dena Arnall Harrison. m 4/17/1999 Amy S Sugeno c 1. Asst S Jas The Apos Epis Ch Conroe TX 2006-2009.

SUHAR, John Charles (SwFla) 771 34th Ave N, Saint Petersburg FL 33704 **P-in-c S Thos' Epis Ch St Petersburg FL 2011-, Assoc R 2005-2016** B Weisbaden GERMANY 1950 s Walter & Yvonne. U of Missouri Columbia Whiteman Afb MO; BS USAF Acad 1972; JD U of Miami 1978; MA Pepperdine U Homestead Afb FL 1981; MDiv VTS 2005. D 6/18/2005 P 12/18/2005 Bp John Bailey Lipscomb. m 6/23/1973 Barbara Lynn Van Eaton c 2. Res Chapl Tampa Gnrl Hosp Tampa FL 2001-2002; Intern Chapl Tampa Gnrl Hosp Tampa FL 2001; Off U.S. AF 1972-1998.

S

SUHR, Esther Jean (Mont) 2584 Mt Hwy 284, Townsend MT 59644 **Cn 9 P S Jn's Ch/Elkhorn Cluster Townsend MT 2006-** B Billings MT 1960 d Louis & Olive. D 9/18/2005 P 7/29/2006 Bp Charles Franklin Brookhart Jr.

SUIT, Marvin Wilson (Lex) 440 Fountain Avenue, Flemingsburg KY 41041 B Maysville KY 1933 s Perry & Mary. BS U of Kentucky 1955; JD U of Kentucky 1957; Lic Epis TS in Kentucky 1988. D 6/12/1988 P 4/1/1992 Bp Don Adger Wimberly. m 6/8/1956 Nancy Calhoun Suit. P-in-c S Alb's Ch Morehead KY 2000-2004; Vic S Fran' Epis Ch Flemingsburg KY 1992-2000. NAAD; Tertiary of the Soc of S Fran.

SUITTER, Andrew M (Mo) 1210 Locust St, Saint Louis MO 63103 **Cur S Aug's Epis Ch Wilmette IL 2017-** B Augusta ME 1982 s Peter & Lori Jean. D 12/16/2016 P 6/29/2017 Bp George Wayne Smith. Ch Of The Gd Shpd S Louis MO 2016-2017.

SULERUD, Mary (Md) 1222 Berry St, Baltimore MD 21211 **Int R All Hallows Ch 2017-** B Richmond VA 1951 d Leo & Gene. BS S Cloud St U 1973; MDiv VTS 1988. D 6/23/1988 Bp Robert Marshall Anderson P 5/5/1989 Bp Peter J Lee. m 12/6/1975 Peder A Sulerud c 1. Int R Emm Epis Ch 2016-2017; P S Steph's Ch Richmond VA 2014-2016; Int S Thos' Ch Richmond VA 2013-2014; Imm Ch-On-The-Hill Alexandria VA 2012-2013; Cn Cathd of St Ptr & St Paul Washington DC 2011-2012; Int Precentor Washington Natl Cthd Washington DC 2004-2005; Cn Dio Washington Washington DC 2003-2011, Cn for Stwdshp 2002-2011; R Ch Of The Ascen Silver Sprg MD 1995-2002; Asst Gr Epis Ch Alexandria VA 1988-1995. EDOW Coun 1998-2002; EDOW Fin Com Chair 1999-2002; GBEC 2002-2009; WECA Bd Mem 1999-2003.

SULLIVAN, Ann Mary (NCal) 5850 Crestmoor Dr, Paradise CA 95969 **R Ch Of S Nich Paradise CA 2006-; Asst S Tim's 1998-** B San Jose CA 1957 d Eugene & Yvonne. California St U; BS San Diego St U 1980; MS Santa Clara U 1987; MDiv CDSP 1997. D 6/27/1998 P 2/1/1999 Bp Richard Lester Shimpfky. m 10/6/2001 Linn J Brownmiller c 3. Gd Samar Epis Ch San Jose CA 2001-2006; S Mk's Epis Ch Santa Clara CA 1999-2000. revannstnick@gmail.com

SULLIVAN, Bernadette Marie (LI) Po Box 243, Hampton Bays NY 11946 B Bronx NY 1948 d John & Helen. BA SUNY 1992; MDiv GTS 1997. D 6/28/1997 Bp Rodney Rae Michel P 3/1/1998 Bp Orris George Walker Jr. c 4. R S Mary's Ch Hampton Bays NY 2000-2012; Asst S Jn's Of Lattingtown Locust Vlly NY 1997-2000.

SULLIVAN, Bradley Joseph (Tex) 3003 Memorial Ct Apt 2405, Houston TX 77007 B 1978 BS U of Texas 2000; MDiv VTS 2005. D 6/11/2005 P 12/17/2005 Bp Don Adger Wimberly. m 5/22/2004 Kristin Louise Sullivan c 3. S Mk's Ch Bay City TX 2012-2016; Asst To The R Emm Ch Houston TX 2005-2012.

SULLIVAN, Brian Christopher (At) 3361 Clubland Drive, Marietta GA 30068 **R St Ben's Epis Ch Smyrna GA 2010-** B White Plains NY 1971 s Gary & Margaret. BFA U GA 1993; MDiv GTS 1997. D 6/7/1997 Bp Onell Asiselo Soto P 12/1/1997 Bp Frank Kellogg Allan. m 5/20/2000 Mindy Sullivan c 3. R Ch Of The Incarn Highlands NC 2004-2010; Assoc S Anne's Epis Ch Atlanta GA 2000-2004; Asst S Ptr's Ch Rome GA 1997-2000.

SULLIVAN, David Andrew (Alb) P.O. Box 146, Elizabethtown NY 12932 B Plattsburgh NY 1949 s Francis & Virginia. MA Nash 2010. D 5/10/2008 P 12/19/2010 Bp William Howard Love. m 7/8/1972 Roberta Sullivan c 1. D Vic Ch Of The Gd Shpd Elizabethtown NY 2008-2010.

SULLIVAN, Elmer Lindsley (NJ) 13 Llanfair Ln, Ewing NJ 08618 **Ret Ret 1995-** B Philadelphia PA 1930 s Robert & Marion. AB Dart 1952; STB GTS 1955; MTh PrTS 1978. D 4/30/1955 P 11/5/1955 Bp Alfred L Banyard. m 2/4/1967 Jean Carhart Sullivan c 2. Int S Mich's Ch Trenton NJ 1991-1994; Admin Asst to the Bp Dio New Jersey Trenton NJ 1983-1989, Urban Coordntr 1978-1983, Dept Mssns 1962-1977, BEC 1957-1961; R S Lk's Ch Trenton NJ 1974-1983, R 1955-1967, Vic 1955-1962; Assoc Chr Ch and S Aug's Eliz NJ 1973-1974; R S Aug's Eliz NJ 1967-1973. Phi Beta Kappa 1951.

SULLIVAN, Herbert Patrick (Mich) 1400 Northwood Rd, Austin TX 78703 B Detroit MI 1932 s Herbert & Gertrude. BD/MA U Chi 1956; MLitt Banares Hindu U 1959; PhD U of Durham Gb 1960; JD U of Tx 1990. D 6/25/1955 Bp Richard Stanley Merrill Emrich P 6/17/1956 Bp Archie H Crowley. m 6/24/1960 Joyce Ann Sullivan c 2. Prof. Rel. & Dn of Fac Vassar Coll Poughkeepsie NY 1970-1988; Non-par Dio New York 1970-1986; Asst S Tit Epis Ch Durham NC 1967-1970, P-in-c 1960-1966; Serv Ch of No India 1964-1965; Prof Rel Duke Durham NC 1960-1970; Serv Ch In Engl 1956-1960; Asst Ch Of The H Cross Chicago IL 1955-1956. Auth, "Numerous books, monographs & arts". Life Fell, Royal Asiatic Soc 1964. Rel Ldrshp Awd Maine Coun of Ch 1999; ACLS Fell 1976; Guggenheim Fell 1974; D. Litt. U of Delhi 1972; Ford Fnd Fellowow 1971; Ford Fnd Fell 1968; Fulbright Fell 1965; Fulbright Fell 1962; Spalding Fell Oxf 1959.

SULLIVAN, Judith A (Pa) Philadelphia Episcopal Cathedral, 3723 Chestnut Street, Philadelphia PA 19104 **Dn Cathd Ch of Our Sav Philadelphia PA 2010-, Cn Res 2004-2007; Bd Mem Epis Cmnty Serv Kansas City MO 2009-** B New Haven CT 1956 d William & Muriel. BA Wellesley Coll 1978; MDiv GTS 2004. D 6/19/2004 P 12/18/2004 Bp Charles Ellsworth Bennison Jr. c 2. Assoc Ch Of The Redeem Bryn Mawr PA 2007-2010.

SULLIVAN, Karen Sue Racer (Ind) 1770 N. Layman Ave., Indianapolis IN 46218 **D S Phil's Ch Indianapolis IN 2008-; Dioc Jubiliee Off Dio Indianapolis Indianapolis IN 2015-, COM 2011-, Dir of LEV Trng 2008-2013, Coun on the Diac 2005-** B Hartford City IN 1955 d Donald & Joan. U of Nevada at Las Vegas 1979; D Formation Prog 2005; BA St Mary-of-the-Woods Coll 2009. D 6/18/2005 Bp Cate Waynick. m 6/9/1975 Sean Kevin Sullivan c 3. Assn of Epis Deacons 2005.

SULLIVAN, Kristin Louise (Tex) **S Mk's Epis Sch Houston TX 2016-** B PA 1978 d Roger & Sandra. BA Jas Madison U; MDiv VTS. D 6/26/2004 P 1/10/2005 Bp Peter J Lee. m 5/22/2004 Bradley Joseph Sullivan c 3. Ch Of The Epiph Houston TX 2010-2012; Palmer Memi Ch Houston TX 2005-2010; Asst S Mary's Epis Ch Arlington VA 2004-2005.

SULLIVAN, Margaret L (SwFla) 513 Nassau St S, Venice FL 34285 **S Mk's Epis Ch Venice FL 2016-** B Highland Park IL 1963 d Joseph & Carole. BS U of Dayton 1985; MDiv VTS 2016. D 12/5/2015 P 7/9/2016 Bp Dabney Tyler Smith. c 2. maggiesullivan@stmarksvenice.com

SULLIVAN, Mark Campbell (Del) 463 Nicole Ct, Smyrna DE 19977 B Springfield MA 1949 s Edward & Dorothy. AB Ken 1971; MDiv VTS 1974. D 6/16/1974 P 1/1/1975 Bp Alexander D Stewart. m 2/16/1985 Jane Sullivan. R S Ptr's Ch Smyrna DE 1999-2011; Assoc S Ptr's Ch Salisbury MD 1997-1999; Cn for Mnstry Dvlpmt Dio Easton Easton MD 1994-1997; Dn Trin Cathd Easton MD 1984-1994; Int Gr Epis Ch Trumbull CT 1983-1984; Prog Dir Natl Inst for Lay Trng New York NY 1982-1984; Co-R S Andr's Epis Ch Lincoln Pk NJ 1981-1982; Emm Epis Ch Stamford CT 1979-1981; Vic Imm Epis Ch Stanford CT 1979-1981; Asst S Paul's Ch Riverside CT 1975-1979; Asst S Jn's Ch Williamstown MA 1974-1975. Auth, "Contributing Ed," *Mnstry Dvlpmt Journ.*

SULLIVAN, Maryalice (Mass) 104 N Washington St, North Attleboro MA 02760 **P-in-c All SS' Memi Ch Providence RI 2017-** B Bronx NY 1947 d Robert & Mary. Cert Manchester Cmnty Coll 1984; BA Estrn Connecticut St U 1986; MDiv Ya Berk 1990. D 9/23/1990 P 10/10/1991 Bp Arthur Edward Walmsley. m 7/22/1967 John L Sullivan c 4. Ch of the Epiph Rumford RI 2015; R Gr Ch N Attleboro MA 1997-2014; No Cntrl Reg Mnstry Enfield CT 1993-1997; Asst Calv Epis Ch Summit NJ 1991-1992. Auth, "Chld Advoc Awareness 1995," *Cltn Chld.* Soc of St Jn the Evang 1991.

SULLIVAN, Mary Bea (Ala) D 5/10/2014 Bp John Mckee Sloan Sr P 11/22/2014 Bp Santosh K Marray.

SULLIVAN, Mary Patricia (NMich) 201 E Ridge St, Marquette MI 49855 B E Grand Rapids MI 1951 d Robert & Margaret. BMus Wstrn Michigan U 1973. D 12/15/2013 Bp Rayford J Ray. c 2.

SULLIVAN JR, Matthew Robert (SeFla) 8144 Bridgewater Ct Apt C, West Palm Beach FL 33406 **Exec VP, Electrical Contractor Sullivan Electric And Pump Inc Lake Worth FL 1984-** B 1945 D 6/3/2006 Bp Leo Frade. m 6/18/1966 Linda Frances Sullivan c 3.

SULLIVAN, Michael Radford (At) 805 Mount Vernon Highway NW, Atlanta GA 30328 **Kanuga Confererences Inc Hendersonvlle NC 2016-; H Innoc' Epis Sch Atlanta GA 2009-; Regent Sewanee U So TS Sewanee TN 2011-** B Seneca SC 1966 s Leland & Patricia. BA Wofford Coll 1989; JD U of So Carolina 1995; MDiv Sewanee: The U So, TS 2000. D 9/23/2000 P 6/8/2001 Bp Dorsey Henderson. m 5/18/1991 Page Poston Sullivan c 2. R H Innoc Ch Atlanta GA 2009-2016; R S Jn's Ch Lynchburg VA 2005-2009; Cn For Mssn Trin Cathd Columbia SC 2002-2005; Asst R Ch Of The Adv Spartanburg SC 2000-2002; Exec Coun Dio SW Virginia Roanoke VA 2008-2009; Stndg Com and Exec Coun Dio Upper So Carolina Columbia SC 2003-2005. Auth, "Windows into the Light," Morehouse, 2008; Auth, "Windows into the Soul," Morehouse, 2006. Woods Ldrshp Awd U So 1998; Ord Of The Coif U Of SC 1994; Law Revs U Of SC 1993; AmL Awd Wofford Coll 1989; Phi Beta Kappa Wofford Coll 1988.

SULLIVAN, Paul David (Mass) 138 Tremont St., Boston MA 02111 **D Veterans Mnstry 2009-** B Waltham MA 1946 s Paul & Margaret. BS Boston St Coll 1974. D 6/6/2009 Bp M(Arvil) Thomas Shaw. m 4/8/1972 Patricia Sullivan c 3. D Ch Of The Adv Medfield MA 2009-2012.

SULLIVAN, Peggy (NY) P.O. Box 708, Walden NY 12586 B Highland Park, IL 1953 BA Natl Coll of Educ 1976; MA Hartford Sem 2000; ThM EDS 2005. D 6/11/2005 P 1/14/2006 Bp Andrew Donnan Smith. m 6/26/1976 Peter Bland Sullivan c 2. Dio New York New York NY 2009-2016; S Andr's Ch Walden NY 2009-2013; Int S Paul's Ch Woodbury CT 2008-2009; Asst S Jas Ch Glastonbury CT 2005-2008.

SULLIVAN JR, Robert Edmund (NJ) 3450 Wild Oak Bay Blvd, Apt 138, Bradenton FL 34210 **Ret 1997-; Asst S Jas Ch Long Branch NJ 1971-** B Philadelphia PA 1925 s Robert & Marion. BA Pr 1949; MDiv PDS 1952; Institut Catholique De Paris 1959. D 6/14/1952 Bp Alfred L Banyard P 12/20/1952 Bp Wallace J Gardner. P-in-res Chr Ch In Woodbury Woodbury NJ 1998-2009; R S Jn The Evang Ch Blackwood NJ 1972-1997; OHC Mssn Liberia 1964-1971; Novc OHC 1959-1964; Vic S Jas Epis Ch Paulsboro NJ 1952-1958; St Peters Ch Woodbury Hgts NJ 1952-1958; Pres Camden-Woodbury Cler Dio New Jersey Trenton NJ 1979-1981, Missions Bd 1974-1978. office@christchurch.woodburynj.org

S

SULLIVAN, Rosemari Gaughan (Va) 402 Virginia Avenue, Alexandria VA 22302 B ScrantonPA 1946 d John & Margaret. BA CUA 1973; MS CUA 1974; MDiv VTS 1985; DMin Wesley TS 2009. D 6/22/1985 P 3/29/1986 Bp Peter J Lee. m 11/24/1973 Edmund Sullivan c 2. Epis Ch Cntr New York NY 2010-2011, 1998-2005, Exec Off-Secy of GC 1998-2005; R S Paul's Rock Creek Washington DC 2006-2011; VTS Alexandria VA 2005-2006; Dir of Alum VTS Alexandria VA 2005-2006; Exec Off and Secy The GC of The Epis Ch 1998-2005; R The Ch of S Clem Alexandria VA 1987-1998; Assoc R Gr Epis Ch Alexandria VA 1985-1987. "Web Homilies," *Natl Cath Reporter Online*, Natl Cath Reporter, 1998; Auth, "No Ordnry Time: The Season After Pentecost at S Clem," *Liturg*, 1996. Oblate Ord of S Ben 1997. DD VTS 2005; Untd Way Serv Awd Untd Way Alexandria 1996.

SULLIVAN-CLIFTON, Sonia (CFla) 5873 N Dean Rd, Orlando FL 32817 **Tchr Trin Preparatory Sch 2011-; R S Matt's Epis Ch Orlando FL 2010-** B Savannah GA 1963 d George & Carole. BBA Valdosta St U 1984; MBA Valdosta St U 1988; MDiv Sewanee: The U So, TS 1993. D 5/29/1993 P 12/19/1993 Bp Harry Woolston Shipps. m 6/14/2003 Steve Clifton c 2. Sum Camp Dir Georgia Epis Conf Cntr At Honey Creek Waverly GA 2010-2011; Chapl Trin Preparatory Sch Of Florida Winter Pk FL 2004-2011; Assoc R Chr The King Epis Ch Orlando FL 2003-2010; Vic Ch Of The Gd Shpd Swainsboro GA 1993-2003; Vic Epis Ch Of S Mary Magd Louisville GA 1993-1995; Happ Natl Com 1990-2000; Stndg Com Dio Georgia Savannah GA 1999-2003, Diocesean Coun 1996-1999, Yth Coord 1995-2003. stmatthewsorlando@gmail.com

SUMMERFIELD, Leroy James (WNC) 5365 Pine Ridge Dr, Connellys Springs NC 28612 B Akron OH 1933 s LeRoy & Emily. BA Bob Jones U 1956; MDiv New Orleans Bapt TS 1962; Advncd CPE 1970; BSW Livingstone Coll 1979; DMin NYTS 1989. D 12/23/1978 P 6/1/1979 Bp William Gillette Weinhauer. m 6/17/1960 Joan Patten Summerfield c 3. P-in-c S Steph's Epis Ch Morganton NC 1998-1999, P 1978-1981; Sr Chapl Mid Hudson Psych Cntr 1993-1995; P S Ptr's Ch Millbrook NY 1983-1984; Chapl Harlem Vlly Psychiatic Cntr Wingdale NY 1981-1993; Chapl Broughton Hosp Morganton NC 1968-1981. Assn Mntl Hlth Chapl, Assembly of Epis Hospi 1972; New York Counsel of Ch 1981-1995. Off of the Year Elks 2012; Colonel U.S.Army 2010.

SUMMEROUR, William W (WNC) 233 Deep Ford Fls, Lake Toxaway NC 28747 B Jackson MS 1950 s Tom & Margaret. MDiv Sewanee: The U So, TS 2007; MDiv Sewanee: The U So, TS 2007. D 12/30/2006 Bp Charles Edward Jenkins III P 7/25/2007 Bp Porter Taylor. m 6/9/1973 Carroll Summerour c 3. Assoc R Ch Of The Gd Shpd Cashiers NC 2007-2013.

SUMMERS, Charles Raymond (Ia) 936 Grayson Dr. Apt. 329, Springfield MA 01119 **Ret 1995-** B Philadelphia PA 1930 s Clifford & Rose. BA Ursinus Coll 1952; ThB PDS 1955; MDiv EDS 1980; MEd U of Pennsylvania 1981. D 5/21/1955 P 12/3/1955 Bp Oliver J Hart. c 1. P-in-c S Barn And All SS Ch Springfield MA 2000-2015; Int S Jas' Ch Greenfield MA 1998-1999; Int Ch Of The Atone Westfield MA 1997-1998; Int Trin Epis Par Waterloo IA 1996; Int Intsn Epis Ch Stevens Point WI 1995-1996; Liturg & Mus Com Dio Iowa Des Moines IA 1990-1995, Educ Cmsn 1988-1995; S Paul's Ch Marshalltown IA 1988-1995; S Mk's Ch Hammonton NJ 1984-1987; S Mary's Ch Burlington NJ 1982-1983; S Mart's Ch Bridgewater NJ 1981-1982; Dioc Fndt Dio New Jersey Trenton NJ 1978-1981, Csr 1977-1987, Corp Relief Of Widows & Orphans 1975-1987; R Gr Ch Pemberton NJ 1966-1980; R S Andr Plainfield NJ 1958-1966; Asst S Chrys's Ch Chicago IL 1955-1958.

SUMMERS, Joseph Holmes (Mich) 1435 South Blvd, Ann Arbor MI 48104 **Oasis Mnstry Ann Arbor MI 2008-; Vic Ch Of The Incarn Pittsfield Twp Ann Arbor MI 1987-** B Hartford CT 1955 s Joseph & UT. BA U MI 1977; MDiv Ya Berk 1987; MA U MI 1994. D 6/27/1987 P 6/27/1988 Bp H Coleman Mcgehee Jr. m 4/28/1990 Donna Susan Ainsworth. "Peace In Israel," Wit, 1998; "Unpacking Anti-Racism," Wit, 1998; "The End Of The Age Of The U.S.," Wit, 1992; "The Lessons Of Counter Terrorism," Wit, 1986. Distinguished Cmnty Serv Awd St Of Michigan Allnce For The Mentally Ill 1993; Distinguished Cmnty Serv Awd Washtenaw Cnty Allnce For Mentally Ill 1992; Cmnty Serv Recognition Awd Washtenaw Cmnty Coll 1991.

SUMMERS, Ronald Wayne (Lex) 777 Liberty Ridge Ln, Lexington KY 40509 **Dn, Cathd Of St. Geo the Mtyr Dio Lexington Lexington 2009-** B Lexington KY 1937 s Horace & Geneva. BA U of Kentucky 1962; MDiv Epis TS in Kentucky 1975; Evang Bible Coll 1975; DMin Lexington TS 1986. D 3/19/1976 P 8/15/1976 Bp Addison Hosea. c 1. Int R Ch Of The H Trin Georgetown KY 2014-2015; Int R Chr Epis Ch Harlan KY 2014, P-in-c 2013; R S Andr's Ch Ft Thos KY 1984-2009; R S Raphael's Ch Lexington KY 1976-1984. Auth, *Daily Guide to Devotions*, Standard Pub. Assn ComT; Ord of S Lk. r.summers777@twc.com

SUMMERSON, Stephen Lyn (Me) PO Box 8, Presque Isle ME 04769 **Aroostook Epis Cluster Caribou ME 2007-; D S Jn's Ch Presque Isle ME 2007-** B Millinocket ME 1951 s Frank & Katherine. AS Nthrn Maine Cmnty Coll 1972; BA Husson U 1974. D 8/4/2007 Bp Chilton Richardson Knudsen. m 4/16/1994 Teresa Summerson c 1.

SUMMERVILLE, Stephen Claude (HB) **Non-par 1969-** B Wichita KS 1941 s Herbert & Beulah. LTh SWTS; BA Wichita St U. D 1/18/1968 Bp George

R Selway. Chapl Nthrn Michicgan U 1968-1969; Vic S Jas Marquette MI 1968-1969; Asst R S Paul's Ch Marquette MI 1968-1969.

SUMNER JR, Edwin Roberts (NJ) 8 Heath Vlg, Hackettstown NJ 07840 **Ret 1996-** B Moorestown NJ 1931 s Edwin & Margaret. BA Dart 1952; STB GTS 1957; MDiv GTS 1972; ThM PrTS 1985. D 4/27/1957 P 11/2/1957 Bp Alfred L Banyard. m 12/30/1995 Carol A Sumner c 3. R Calv Epis Ch Flemington NJ 1969-1996; R S Lk's Ch Woodstown NJ 1963-1969, Vic 1959-1962; S Steph's Ch Mullica Hill NJ 1959-1962; Cur Trin Cathd Trenton NJ 1957-1958; Chair, Evang Cmsn Dio New Jersey Trenton NJ 1983-1986, Secy, Cmsn on Mus 1964-1982. Chapl 1975; Ord of S Lk 1975; OHC 1957.

✠ SUMNER JR, The Rt Rev George Robinson (Dal) 20 Queens Park Crescent West, Toronto ON M5S 2W2 Canada **Bp Dio Dallas Dallas TX 2015-** B Springfield MA 1955 s George & Audrey. BA Harv 1977; MDiv Yale DS 1981; PhD Ya 1994. Trans 12/8/2003 Bp Gordon Scruton Con 11/14/2015 for Dal. m 5/24/1980 Stephanie A Hodgkins c 2. Wycliffe Coll Toronto ON 1999-2003; R Trin Ch Geneva NY 1995-2002, 1995-1999; Asst Assabet Cluster 1994-1995; S Lk's Ch Hudson MA 1994-1995; Dio Wstrn Massachusetts Springfield 1994, 1984-1986; Middlesex Area Cluster Mnstry Higganum CT 1992-1993; Dio Connecticut Meriden CT 1991-1993, Mssnr Middlesex Cluster Mnstry 1991-1993; Non-par 1989-1991; Vic Navajoland Area Mssn Farmington NM 1986-1989; The Epis Ch In Navajoland Coun Farmington NM 1986-1989; Cur S Matt's Ch Worcester MA 1984-1986; Non-par 1981-1984; Exec Coun Appointees New York NY 1981-1984; Tutor S Phil's Theol Coll In Kongwa Tanzania 1981-1984. Auth, "Reclaiming Faith"; Auth, "Rule Of Faith". Co-Ed Sead. Phi Beta Kappa; Grad Fell Ecf. gsumner@edod.org

SUMNERS III, Charles Abram (WTex) 115 Northwood Dr., Cuero TX 77954 **Gr Ch Cuero TX 2016-** B Austin TX 1941 s Charles & Virginia. BA SW U Georgetown TX 1964; MDiv VTS 1967. D 6/27/1967 Bp Scott Field Bailey P 5/1/1968 Bp John Elbridge Hines. m 3/17/2000 Robin Sumners c 2. Dio W Texas San Antonio TX 1987-2000; R S Phil's Ch Beeville TX 1983-1999; S Helena's Epis Ch Boerne TX 1983; Epis TV Ntwk New York NY 1979-1983; Dir of Cmncatn St. Barth Ch New York NY 1978-1980; S Lk's Epis Ch Atlanta GA 1972-1978; Asst S Jn Beth MD 1970-1972.

SUNDARA, John Deepak (Dal) 3966 Mckinney Ave, Dallas TX 75204 **Cur Ch Of The Incarn Dallas TX 2017-** B Chennai India 1985 s Benjamin & Christina. BSC U of British Columbia 2007; MDiv Wycliffe Coll 2016. D 1/6/2017 Bp George Robinson Sumner Jr. m 4/5/2013 Naomi Sundara c 1. jsundara@incarnation.org

SUNDERLAND, Douglas Clark (Wyo) 18 Manning Rd, Cody WY 82414 **Assoc Cler Chr Ch Cody WY 2002-** B Morristown NJ 1953 d Hovey & Aline. BA Trin Hartford CT 1975; MSW U of Washington 1980. D 9/17/2001 P 4/26/2002 Bp Bruce Caldwell. m 6/23/1984 Gale Sunderland c 2.

SUNDERLAND, Edward (NY) 310 E 49th St Apt 10C, New York NY 10017 **Cmnty Mnstry St. Barth Ch New York NY 2010-** B Pittsburgh PA 1957 s James & Margaret. BA Grove City Coll 1978; MDiv SWTS 1985; MSW Arizona St U 1998. D 6/29/1985 Bp Donald James Davis P 1/25/1986 Bp Wesley Frensdorff. m 10/31/2013 Victor Madrid Villanueva. Spanish Mnstry Cathd Of St Jn The Div New York NY 2009-2010, Asst 2007-2009, Asst 1998-2003; Clincl Coordntr Common Ground New York NY 2006-2010; Spanish Mnstry Gr Ch White Plains NY 2006-2007; P S Simon's Ch Staten Island NY 2003-2006; Sr Soc Worker Col Med Cntr New York NY 2002-2006; Soc Worker Montifiore Med Cntr Bronx NY 2001-2002; Prog Off Open Socety Inst New York NY 1998-2000; Dioc Mssnr Iglesia Epis De San Pablo Phoenix AZ 1991-1998; R Ch Of The Epiph Los Angeles CA 1988-1991; Arizona St U S Aug's Epis Ch Tempe AZ 1985-1988; Mem, Dioc Coun Dio Arizona Phoenix AZ 1996-1998, Mem, COM 1994-1998. edward@crossroadsnyc.org

SUNDERLAND JR, Edwin Sherwood Stowell (Me) 115 Williams St, Providence RI 02906 **Ret 1991-** B New York NY 1926 s Edwin & Dorothy. BA Harv 1949; JD Harv 1952; MDiv CDSP 1957; U of Cambridge 1960; CUA 1982. D 6/30/1957 P 1/11/1958 Bp Karl M Block. m 7/28/1991 Phyllis Choumenkovitch c 2. VTS Alexandria VA 1983-1988; Cn The Cathd Ch Of S Paul Boston MA 1975-1979; Lectr Cn Law The GTS New York NY 1972-1980; R S Jn's Ch Newtonville MA 1968-1971; Asst S Ptr's Epis Ch Cambridge MA 1966-1968; Asst S Paul's Ch Dedham MA 1965-1966; Ch Of The Gd Shpd Dedham MA 1964-1965; R Ch of the Gd Shpd Boston MA 1964-1965; R S Eliz's Ch Sudbury MA 1961-1964; Serv Ch in Engl 1960-1961; Cur S Lk's Ch San Francisco CA 1957-1958. Auth, *Dibdin & the Engl Establishment*, 1995; Auth, "arts," *Angl & Epis Hist*. SEAD 1994-2006.

SUNDERLAND, Melanie (O) 1103 Castleton Rd, Cleveland Heights OH 44121 **Dir of Sprtl Care Luth Chapl Serv/Ahuja Med Ctr Beachwood OH 2011-** B Salt Lake City UT 1956 d John & Jean. BS U IL 1984; MA NYU 1992; MDiv VTS 2001. D 7/11/2002 P 5/15/2003 Bp Carolyn Tanner Irish. m 10/1/2006 Christina Rouse c 1. S Phil's Epis Ch Akron OH 2015-2017; S Andr's Epis Ch Elyria OH 2012-2013; Luth Chapl Serv Cleveland OH 2011-2012, 2003-2007; Assoc Cler Chr Ch Shaker Heights OH 2010-2015; Stff Chapl Cleveland Clnc Cleveland OH 2007-2011; Dir of Pstr Care Luth Chapl Serv/Luth Hosp Cleve-

S

land OH 2003-2007; Cur Dio Utah Salt Lake City UT 2002-2003; Chapl Res S Mk's Hosp Salt Lake City UT 1996-1997. sunderm@ccf.org

SUNDIN, Chad Ludwig (Az) 1735 S College Ave, Tempe AZ 85281 **Epis Campus Mnstrs at ASU Tempe AZ 2015-; S Aug's Epis Ch Tempe AZ 2014-** B St Charles IL 1975 s William & Charlotte. BA Lynchburg Coll 1998. D 6/7/2014 P 6/13/2015 Bp Kirk Stevan Smith. m 1/2/1999 Jana Patrice Burns c 3.

SUPIN, Charles Robert (Nev) 554 East Landing Ridge Circle, Jefferson NC 28640 B Brooklyn NY 1933 s Louis & Eleanor. BA Adel 1955; STB Ya Berk 1960; MFA U of Nevada at Las Vegas 1993. D 4/23/1960 P 10/1/1960 Bp James Pernette DeWolfe. m 12/26/1959 Benita Supin c 2. All SS Epis Ch Las Vegas NV 1974-1979; P Trin-St Jn's Ch Hewlett NY 1960-1974; Gr Epis Ch Massapequa NY 1960-1962; Non-par. Auth, "Beyond Pledging"; Auth, "Dennis"; Auth, "Undertow".

SURGEON, Ornoldo A (SeFla) 20011 Nw 39th Ct, Miami Gardens FL 33055 B Panama City PA 1937 s Pete & Rosalia. Miami-Dade Cmnty Coll; Our Lady of Carmen 1954. D 6/12/1995 Bp John Lewis Said P 9/30/2006 Bp Leo Frade. m 2/3/1960 Diana E Surgeon c 2. D Ch Of The Atone Ft Lauderdale FL 2002-2008; D Ch Of The H Comf Miami FL 2002-2003.

SURINER, Noreen Priscilla (WMass) PO Box 464, Middlefield MA 01243 **S Lk's Ch Lanesboro MA 2014-** B Northampton MA 1947 d Wayne & Priscilla. BA Berkshire Chr Coll 1969; MEd Amer Intl Coll 1974; MDiv VTS 1976; S Georges Coll Jerusalem IL 1988; Cert Sewanee: The U So, TS 2004. D 6/13/1976 P 3/12/1977 Bp Alexander D Stewart. Int All SS Ch So Hadley MA 2008-2009; Int S Jn's Ch Northampton MA 2007-2008; Stndg Com Secy Dio Cntrl New York Liverpool NY 2005, 2003-2004; R Trin Memi Ch Binghamton NY 1995-2007; R Epis Ch Of Chr The King Baltimore MD 1982-1995; Assoc The Ch Of The Redeem Baltimore MD 1980-1982; P-in-c S Columba's Ch Washington DC 1979-1980; Yth Min 1976-1977; Bd Trst The CPG New York NY 1990-2002; Alum Bd VTS Alexandria VA 1988-1991; Dioc Coun Dio Maryland Baltimore MD 1986-1988. Auth, "Surviving Mnstry From Wmn Perspective," *Surviving Mnstry*, 1990. NNECA 1989; Paul Harris Fndt 1999-2007; Rotary 1998-2007.

SURUDA, Teresa Ann (NJ) 58 Ravine Dr, Matawan NJ 07747 B Jersey City NJ 1941 d John & Helen. BA Caldwell Coll 1968; MA Trenton St Coll 1974. D 10/21/2000 Bp David Bruce Joslin. D Trin Ch Matawan NJ 2000-2010.

SUTCLIFFE, David (Alb) 75 Willett St. Apt. 41, Albany NY 12210 **R S Lk's Ch Catskill NY 2013-; St Marg's Cntr for Chld, Bd Dir Dio Albany 2007-** B Pawtucket RI 1948 s Kenneth & Thelma. BA Hobart and Wm Smith Colleges 1970; MDiv GTS 1975. D 5/15/1976 Bp Morris Fairchild Arnold P 11/16/1976 Bp Robert Poland Atkinson. m 6/29/1974 Paula H Sutcliffe c 3. Int The Ch of St Lk The Beloved Physcn Saranac Lake NY 2005-2007; Int S Christophers Ch W Palm Bch FL 2004-2005; Int Ch Of The H Redeem Lake Worth FL 2003; Chapl Recovery Mnstrs Dio Louisiana 2002-2003; Curs Mvmt, Sec Dio Louisiana 2000-2003; R Gr Ch New Orleans LA 2000-2003; Vic Ch Of The Gd Shpd Ft Defiance AZ 1996-2000; Chair Mnstry Formation Navajoland 1996-2000; Sprtl Dir Curs Mvmt Dio Milwaukee 1992-1995; R S Fran Ch Menomonee Falls WI 1985-1996; Chair Of The Dioc Evang Com Dio Milwaukee 1983-1992; Bd Missions Dio Milwaukee 1983-1985; Dn Nashotah Dnry 1983-1985; Com For The Election Of Bp Dio Milwaukee 1983-1984; S Dav Of Wales Ch New Berlin WI 1980-1985; Vic St Philips Epis Ch Waukesha WI 1980-1985; CE Cmsn Dio W Virginia 1978-1980; Vic All Souls' Epis Ch Daniels WV 1977-1980; Asst S Matt's Ch Wheeling WV 1976-1977. Auth, "Var arts on Chr Iniation and Formation," *Var*, Var, 1990. Assoc, Ord of St Mary 2007; Int Mnstry Ntwk 2004; The Cmnty of the Cross of Nails 1996.

SUTER, Vernon L (SanD) 30329 Keith Ave, Cathedral City CA 92234 B Phoenix AZ 1931 s Harold & Nellie. Cert The Wm Glasser Inst; Arizona St U 1950; CPE 1979; MDiv Untd TS 1981; BA California Coast U 2000. D 4/13/1980 Bp Robert Marshall Anderson P 5/9/1983 Bp Charles Brinkley Morton. m 6/16/1973 Bonnie L Suter. Assoc S Paul In The Desert Palm Sprg CA 1990-2012; Chapl SSP 1986-1989; Assoc S Marg's Epis Ch Palm Desert CA 1985-1989, 1983-1984; S Jn's Ch Indio CA 1984-1985.

SUTHERLAND, Alan (Okla) 18417 Black Bear Trail, Norman OK 73072 B 1955 s Donald & Alma. Greystoke Coll; CTh Salisbury & Wells Theol Coll Sem GB 1980. Trans 9/13/1984 Bp Charles Judson Child Jr. m 4/29/2006 Judith Sutherland c 2. R S Mich's Epis Ch Norman OK 2010-2014; R S Jn's Ch Versailles KY 2004-2009; R Emm Epis Ch Winchester KY 1995-2004; R All SS Epis Ch Russellville AR 1987-1995; Asst R S Mart In The Fields Ch Atlanta GA 1983-1987; P Ch of Engl 1980-1983.

SUTHERLAND, Linda Ann (FtW) 830 County Road 109, Hamilton TX 76531 **D S Mary's Ch Hamilton TX 2009-** B Fresno CA 1941 d Milton & Muriel. BA San Francisco St U 1966; Dplma St Lukes Sch of Nrsng 1966; Cert St Andrews Coll for Diac 1983. D 11/11/1983 Bp Edmond Lee Browning. m 6/17/1988 Neal Sutherland.

SUTHERLAND, Mark R (RI) St Martin of Tours, 50 Orchard Ave, Providence RI 02906 **R S Mart's Ch Providence RI 2014-; Cn Pstr Trin Cathd Phoenix AZ 2013-, Int Dn 2012-2013, Cn Pstr 2010-2014, Pstr Care & Counslg 2009-2010; Bp's Advsr, COM Dio Rhode Island Providence RI 2014-** B

Christchurch New Zealand 1955 s Frank & Ann. LLB U of Cbury 1977; Oxford Cert Theol Ripon Coll Cuddesdon GB 1985; MA Lon GB 1995; MA U of E London 2004. Trans 11/23/2010 as Priest Bp Kirk Stevan Smith. m 12/11/2013 Alvin Julian Marcetti. Chapl Res Banner Gd Samar Med Cntr 2009-2010; Bp's Advsr, COM Dio Arizona Phoenix AZ 2009-2014. Auth, "Contribution of Chapl in the Psych Setting," *A Handbook for Psych Trainees*, Royal Coll of Psychiatrists, 2008; Co-Auth, "Mntl Hlth-care: the ultimate context for Sprtl and Pstr Educ," *Sprtl Care in Mntl Hlth*, Jessica Kingsley Press, 2007; Auth, "Care in a Rapidly Changing Culture," *Contact - interdisciplinary Journ of Pstr Stds*, vol 154, 2005; Auth, "Developing a Transpersonal Approach to Pstr Counselling," *British Journ of Gdnc and Counselling*, Vol 29 No 4, 2001; Auth, "Towards Dialogue: an exploration of Relatns between Rel and Psych," *Blackwell Rdr in Pstr Theoloy*, Blackwell Pub, 2000; Auth, "The Stff Spprt Grp as a Monitor for Wk Related Stress," *Occupational Stress*, Stanley Thornes, 1998; Auth, "Mntl Hlth or Life Crisis," *Psych and Rel*, Routledge, London, 1996. Assn for Pstr Supervision and Educ 2008-2015; British Assn for Counselling 1990-2008; Coll of Hlth Care Chapl UK 1990-2008; The Revs Club 2015; UK Bd for Hosp Chaplainy 2007-2009; Untd Kingdom Coun for Psych 2004-2008. mark@stmartinsprov.org

SUTHERLAND, Melody (Eas) 219 Somerset Rd, Stevensville MD 21666 **D Chr Ch Par Kent Island Stevensville MD 2001-; Stff/Chapl Shore Hlth System 1999-** B Kalamazoo MI 1948 d Harold & Charlotte. Cert Dio Easton Sch For Total Mnstry Easton MD. D 9/15/2001 Bp Martin Gough Townsend. m 1/24/1970 Donald K Sutherland c 3. Assn CPE 2000.

SUTHERS, Derwent Albert (At) 1178 Circulo Canario, Rio Rico AZ 85648 **Asstg P S Andr's Epis Ch Nogales AZ 2011-** B Columbus OH 1931 s Albert & Ruth. BA Ob 1952; BD CDSP 1955. D 6/25/1955 P 12/24/1955 Bp Richard Stanley Merrill Emrich. Assoc R S Mart In The Fields Ch Atlanta GA 1998-2003; S Dav's Barneveld NY 1989-1997; Utica Area Coop Mnstry Whitesboro NY 1988; Assoc Gr Epis Ch Utica NY 1986-1989; Non-par 1968-1986; Serv Ch Of Brazil 1965-1968; R S Kath's Ch Williamston MI 1962-1965, Vic 1955-1961. The Suthers Cntr St. Mart in the Fields, Atlanta GA 2010; cl Wabash Coll 1973.

SUTOR, Jack Thomas (Va) PO Box 120, Hanover VA 23069 **Mem Dio Com on Par Giving 2012-; R S Paul's Ch Hanover VA 2004-; Dir Bloomfiled Fndt 2015-; Mem Dio Com on Par Giving 2011-** B Lynchburg VA 1945 s Jack & Jane. BA U of Virginia 1969; JD U Rich 1978; MDiv VTS 1990. D 6/2/1990 P 2/6/1991 Bp Peter J Lee. c 1. R S Paul's Ch Hanover VA 2004-2015; Int Emm Ch Harrisonburg VA 2003-2004; Int Emm Ch Harrisonburg VA 2003-2004; R Trin Ch Martinsburg VA 1993-2003; R Trin Epis Ch Martinsburg WV 1993-2003; Asst to R S Geo's Ch Fredericksburg VA 1990-1993. Ldrshp Awd Bex Sem 2012; Mem Breadloaf Writers Conf 2000; Gvnr's Awd, Virginia 1987; Acad of Amer Poets 1969.

SUTTERFIELD, Ragan K (Ark) **S Marg's Epis Ch Little Rock AR 2016-** D 3/19/2016 P 10/1/2016 Bp Larry Benfield.

SUTTON, Christine Marie (Be) PO Box 198, Lehman PA 18627 **D Prince Of Peace Epis Ch Dallas PA 2014-** B Kingston PA 1950 d Emery & Cornelia. Register Nurse Dplma Prog Mercy Hosp Sch for Nrsng 1971. D 12/21/2009 Bp Paul Victor Marshall. m 4/3/1971 David Sutton c 3.

✠ SUTTON, The Rt Rev Eugene Taylor (Md) 4 East University Parkway, Baltimore MD 21218 **Bp of Maryland Dio Maryland Baltimore MD 2008-; Co-Cnvnr Bishops Untd Against Gun Violence 2013-; Chair Presb-Epis Dialogue 2009-; Mem, Bd Trst The GTS New York NY 2009-** B Washington DC 1954 s James & Aleen. PrTS; BA Hope Coll 1976; MDiv Wstrn TS 1981. D 10/19/1995 P 4/27/1996 Bp Joe Doss Con 6/28/2008 for Md. m 6/19/1999 Sonya S Subbayya c 4. Cn Pstr Cathd of St Ptr & St Paul Washington DC 2000-2008; Assoc R S Columba's Ch Washington DC 1998-2000; P-in-c S Mary's Epis Ch Foggy Bottom Washington DC 1997-1998; P-in-c S Marg's Ch Washington DC 1996-1997; Dio New Jersey Trenton NJ 1995-1996; Asst To Bp S Mich's Ch Trenton NJ 1995-1996; Asst Prof Van DS 1992-1995; Asst Prof New Brunswick TS 1989-1992. Auth, "Afr Amer Sprtlty," *The Diversity Of Centering Pryr*, Continuum, 1999; Auth, "More Will Be Given," *Sermons That Wk*; Auth, "Nobodies," *Sermons That Wk*. Epis EvangES; Epis Homil Consult; Fndr Contemplative Outreach Metropltn Washington; Global Epis Mssn Ntwk. Distinguished Alum Awd Hope Coll 2003. esutton@episcopalmaryland.org

SUTTON, John D (Cal) 1045 Neilson St, Albany CA 94706 **R S Anselm's Epis Ch Lafayette CA 1998-** B Oakland CA 1956 s Charles & Anne. BA U CA 1979; MBA Golden Gate U 1986; MS Golden Gate U 1987; MDiv CDSP 1995. D 6/3/1995 P 6/1/1996 Bp William Edwin Swing. m 4/8/1989 Elizabeth Ann Sutton c 1. Assoc S Paul's Epis Ch Walnut Creek CA 1995-1998.

SUTTON, Norma Sarah (Chi) **Asst S Ptr's Epis Ch Chicago IL 2007-; Prof of Theol Bibliography No Pk TS Chicago Illinois 1979-** B Three Rivers MI 1946 d Elmore & Wilma. BS Goshen Coll 1968; MDiv Associated Mennonite Biblic Sem 1976; MA U of Notre Dame 1978; MA Emory U 1979; Cert SWTS 2004. D 6/18/2005 P 12/17/2005 Bp Bill Persell. Intern S Jn's Epis Ch Chicago IL 2003-2004. Sutton, Norma, "Arise for it is Day: The Jn Day Imprints and the Engl Reformation, 1545-1559," *Journ of Rel & Theol Info*, 1993; Sut-

833

S

ton, Norma, "A Gift ot the Ch," *The Mennonite*, 1991; Sutton, Norma, "God's Gr in My Life," *Cov Comp*, 1984; Sutton, Norma, "Simplicity: The Call and the Challenge," *Cov Comp*, 1983; Sutton, Norma, "To the Glory of God," *Cov Quarterly*, 1982; Sutton, Norma, "The Influence of Radical Pietism on Russian Mennonites," *Cov Quarterly*, 1980; Auth, *Var arts*.

SUTTON, Sharon Laverne (NJ) St Stephen's Episcopal Church, 324 Bridgeboro St, Riverside NJ 08075 **S Lk's Ch Gladstone NJ 2016-; D S Steph's Ch Riverside NJ 2008-** B Charleston SC 1952 d Roy & Isabelle. BA New Jersey City U 1995. D 6/9/2007 Bp George Edward Councell.

SVOBODA-BARBER, Helen (NC) c/o St. Luke's Episcopal Church, 1737 Hillandale Rd, Durham NC 27705 B Abiline KS 1969 d Charles & Betty. Doctor of Mnstry Austin Presb TS; BA U of Kansas 1991; MDiv Epis TS of the SW 1998. D 2/9/1998 P 9/12/1998 Bp William Edward Smalley. m 11/25/2000 Shawn R A Barber c 2. S Lk's Epis Ch Durham NC 2014, R 2014-; Dir, Bd Sprtl & Rel Life Ken 2012-2014; R Harcourt Par Gambier OH 2004-2014; Asst Pstr through Called to Common Mssn H Cross Luth Ch Overland Pk KS 2001-2004; Chapl Kansas Hse of Representatives Topeka KS 1999-2001; Cn Gr Cathd Topeka KS 1998-2001; Stndg Cmsn on Lifeline Chr Formation GC 2013-2015; Epis Cmnty Serv Dvlpmt Coun Dio Ohio Cleveland 2012-2014, Dioc Coun 2011-2014, Const and Cn Com 2009-2011, Chair, Chr Formation Com 2008-2009; Bd Mem, Personel Com Interchurch Soc Serv 2005-2014; Bd Dir Hollis Retreat Cntr 2002-2004; BEC Dio Kansas Topeka KS 2001-2004, Pres, NW Convoc 1999-2001, Coll Wk Com 1990-1996; Coun of Advice to the Pres of the HOD GC 2000-2006; Dep and Alt GC 1999-2006; Bd Mem and Secy Topeka Cntr for Peace and Justice 1999-2001. rector@stlukesdurham.org

SWAIN, Barry Edward Bailey (NY) Church of the Resurrection, 119 East 74th Street, New York NY 10021 **R Ch Of The Resurr New York NY 2001-** B New York NY 1959 BA Alleg 1981; MA McMaster U 1982; MDiv GTS 1986. D 12/16/1987 P 6/29/1988 Bp Robert Campbell Witcher Sr. R S Clements Ch Philadelphia PA 1992-2001, Cur 1988-2001; Cur Ch Of S Mary The Vrgn New York NY 1988.

SWAIN, Storm (NY) **Assist. Prof. of Pstr Care & Theol; Dir of Angl Stds The Luth TS Philadelphia PA 2009-** B 1965 d Roger & Rhondda. BTh U of Otago/Knox Theol Hall 1992; Cert Ashburn Hall Educ and Resrch Fndt 1996; STM UTS 1999; Cert Blanton Peale Grad Inst 2004; MPhil UTS 2004; PhD UTS 2009. Trans 7/31/2004 Bp Mark Sean Sisk. m 9/18/2004 Stephen Riker Harding c 1. Asst P Gr Ch Bronx NY 2007-2010; Assoc P The Ch of S Ign of Antioch New York NY 2007-2009; Cn Pstr Cathd Of St Jn The Div New York NY 2005-2007, Cn Pstr 2002-2007, Asst P 2000-2002; Psych Res Blanton-Peale Counslg Cntr 2000-2004; Assoc St Paul's Cathd Dunedin New Zealand 1999-2000; Assoc St Ptr's Ch Caversham Dunedin 1995-1998; Chapl To Mntl Hlth Serv Cpe Supvsr Hosp Chapl' Coun Dunedin New Zealand 1994-2000. Bk, "Trauma & Transformation at Ground Zero: A Pstr Theol," Fortress Press, 2011; Article, "The T. Mort. Chapl at Ground Zero: Presence and Privilege on H Ground," *Journ of Rel and Hlth: Volume 50, Issue 3*, 2011; Article, "From Ground Zero to Ground Zero: Looking at One Disaster in the Light of Another," *Plainviews*, The Healthcare Chapl, NY, 2011; Article, "Ten Days Before Christmas 2001," *Journ of Rel and Hlth: Volume 41, Issue 1*, 2002. AAR 2009. Cmnty Serv Awd Blanton Peale Grad Inst 2003; Wmn Awd U of Otago, New Zealand 1992; U Bookshop Prize in Theol U of Otago, New Zealand 1991.

SWAN, Clinton E (Ak) Po Box 50037, Kivalina AK 99750 B Kivalina AK 1914 s David & Regina. D 4/23/1972 P 12/1/1972 Bp William Jones Gordon Jr. m 1/21/1935 Charlotte Swan.

SWAN, Craig R (RI) 72 Central St, Narragansett RI 02882 **S Ptr's By The Sea Narragansett RI 2015-** B Hartford CT 1962 s Leslie & Beverly. BS S Lawr Canton NY 1984; MDiv Ya Berk 1988. Trans 10/23/2003 Bp M(Arvil) Thomas Shaw. m 6/28/1986 Maureen Ellen Winters-Swan c 2. R S Lk's Epis Ch Camillus NY 2003-2015; Asst R Ch Of The Redeem Chestnut Hill MA 2000-2003; Soc Worker/Supvsr Dept of Chld and Families St of Connecticut 1989-2000. Niles Awd St. Lawr 1984.

SWAN, Richard A (Spr) P.O. Box 1513, Decatur IL 62525 **R S Jn's Epis Ch Decatur IL 2011-** B Cleveland OH 1948 s Harold & Dorothy. BBA U Cinc 1971; MBA U of Dayton 1986; MDiv Nash 1995. Trans 3/10/2004 Bp J Clark Grew II. m 1/4/1969 Mary Ann Swan c 2. Cn Mssnr Dio Springfield Springfield IL 2004-2011, 1996-1998, Pres, Stndg Com 2008-2009, Coun 2004-; Prison Chapl Dio Ohio Cleveland 1998-2004; Prison Chapl Marion Correctional Inst Marion OH 1998-2004; Assoc Assoc Cnvnt of Trsfg. Blessed Sacr 1994; SocMary 96 1996.

SWANLUND, Callie E (Pa) 8000 Saint Martins Ln, Philadelphia PA 19118 **Assoc Chr Epis Ch Raleigh NC 2015-; COM Dio Pennsylvania Philadelphia PA 2013-, Liturg Cmsn 2011-** B Normal IL 1982 d Randall & Courtenay. BS Illinois St U 2005; MDiv CDSP 2008. D 6/5/2010 Bp Jeff Lee P 1/22/2011 Bp Charles Ellsworth Bennison Jr. m 9/4/2005 Phillip Joseph Augustine Fackler c 1. Assoc for Formation & Fam Mnstry Ch Of S Mart-In-The-Fields Philadelphia PA 2011-2015; Int Asst. Min Chr Ch Philadelphia Philadelphia PA 2010-2011; Com on the Status of Wmn Exec Coun Appointees New York NY 2006-2009. cswanlund@christchurchraleigh.org

SWANN, Albert Henry (ETenn) 4515 Glennora Drive, Walland TN 37886 **R S Paul's Ch 2006-; Vic S Paul's Ch 2006-** B Dandridge TN 1936 s Henry & Irene. BS Carson-Newman Coll 1958; MS U of Mississippi 1963; EdD U of Mississippi 1967; Emmanual Sch of Rel Johnson City TN 1983; U So 1985. D 7/7/1985 P 6/8/1986 Bp William Evan Sanders. m 4/7/1979 Sharon Guinn c 4. R Ch Of The Gd Shpd Knoxville TN 1988-2006; Asst S Jn's Epis Ch Johnson City TN 1987-1988, D 1985-1986; LocTen S Tim's Epis Ch Kingsport TN 1986-1987.

SWANN, Catherine Williams (Va) 387 Harbor Drive, Reedville VA 22539 **Fac Crusillo Dio of Sthrn Virginia 1985-** B Nashville TN 1945 d Peyton & Elbert. BA Converse Coll 1967; Cert Sewanee: The U So, TS 1992; MDiv VTS 1999. D 6/12/1999 Bp David Conner Bane Jr P 12/11/1999 Bp Donald Purple Hart. m 8/5/1967 Robert Rudd Swann c 2. Chapl D Sch for the Dio Virginia and Sthrn Virgi 2014-2016; Fac Fresh Start Dio of Virginia 2006-2016; R Cople Par Hague VA 2005-2013; Fac Fresh Start Dio of Sthrn Virginia 2003-2004; Assoc S Andr's Ch Norfolk VA 1999-2004; Chapl Deacons' Sch Dios of VA and SVA Richmond & Williamsburg 2014-2016; Transition Com for Bp. Coadj Dio Virginia Richmond VA 2006-2008, Com on Const and Cn 2006, Fresh Start Facillitator 2006-; Secy of Stndg Com Dio Sthrn Virginia Newport News VA 2002-2003, Stndg Com 2000-2003, Liturg Cmsn 1999-2004. NECA 2001-2004; SoVECA 2001-2004. choirman45@yahoo.com

SWANN, Stephen Barham (Dal) 4223 Ridge Rd, Dallas TX 75229 **R Epis Sch Dallas TX 1974-** B Longview TX 1944 s Robert & Jane. BA NE St U 1967; SMU 1968; BD CDSP 1970. D 6/18/1970 Bp Theodore H McCrea P 12/20/1970 Bp Archibald Donald Davies. m 4/7/1998 Carolyn C Swann c 2. Epis Sch Of Dallas Dallas TX 1975-1995; Asst S Mich And All Ang Ch Dallas TX 1971-1974; Cur S Vinc's Euless TX 1970-1971. Ord of S Jn of Jerusalem.

SWANN, Stuart Alan (Los) 1560 S Fredrica Ave, Clearwater FL 33756 **St Columbas Epis Ch Big Bear City CA 2014-** B Atlanta GA 1953 s Conon & Nancy. BS Florida St U 1975; MSW U NC 1979; MDiv VTS 1992. D 6/13/1992 Bp Robert Poland Atkinson P 12/1/1992 Bp Peter J Lee. c 2. S Alb's Epis Ch St Petersburg FL 2010-2012; P-in-c S Dunst's Epis Ch Largo FL 2010-2012; R S Jn's Epis Ch Brooksville FL 2008-2010; Vic S Matt's Epis Ch Sterling VA 1995-1999; Asst S Anne's Epis Ch Reston VA 1992-1995. stuswann@outlook.com

SWANNER-MONTGOMERY, Rhoda J (Tex) Saint Thomas Episcopal Church, 906 George Bush Dr, College Station TX 77840 **Died 10/25/2015** B Washington DC 1962 d Joe & Regina. BA Baylor U 1983; MDiv Epis TS of the SW 2001; DMin SWTS 2009. D 6/16/2001 P 6/20/2002 Bp Claude Edward Payne. m 4/6/2002 Robert H Montgomery. S Thos Epis Ch Coll Sta TX 2010-2015; Cn Chr Ch Cathd Houston TX 2008-2010; LocTen The Epis Ch of the Gd Shpd Austin TX 2007-2008; Asst The Ch of the Gd Shpd Austin TX 2001-2008.

SWANSON, George Gaines (Nwk) 349 Seawall Rd, Manset ME 04679 B San Francisco CA 1933 s Walter & Leta. AB Harv 1955; STB GTS 1958. D 6/29/1958 Bp Henry H Shires P 6/11/1959 Bp James Albert Pike. Heights Hudson Proj Hoboken NJ 1979-1984; R Ch of the Ascen Jersey City NJ 1977-1993; R St Georges Ch Kansas City MO 1968-1977; P in Charge Angl Congregations around Francistown Botswana 1965-1966; R S Phil's Ch Coalinga CA 1960-1968; Cur Trin Par Menlo Pk CA 1958-1960. Auth, "A Folk Opera," *Natural Causes Killed Victor*, eBook, 2012; Auth, "Ten Reasons to Find Another Ch," *Or At Least Rattle the Pstr's Cage*, Wipf and Stock, 2012; Auth, "Are Cler Necessary?," eBook, 2011; Pub, "Wmn & H Ord," The Propers, Kansas City MO, 1974; Auth, "The Propers," The Propers, Kansas City, MO, 1972; Auth, "Setswana Through Pictures," Self Pub in Francistown, Botswana, 1966. Maine Prisoners' Advocacy Cltn 2010; Natl Rel Cmpgn Against Torture 2009; Oblate Of Concep Abbey 1975; Sis Of The Trsfg 1958.

SWANSON, Geraldine Ann (NY) 250 Greeley Ave, Staten Island NY 10306 **Diocesean ERD Rep Dio New York New York NY 2007-** B Bronx NY 1949 d John & Florence. BA Hunter Coll CUNY NYC, NY 1971; MEd Richmond Coll CUNY 1975; MA GTS 2008. D 4/26/1997 Bp Richard Frank Grein. m 12/9/1972 Robert Steven Swanson c 4. D Chr Ch New Brighton Staten Island NY 2010-2017; D Ch Of The Ascen Staten Island NY 2007-2010; D S Clem's Ch New York NY 2001-2006; D The Ch Of S Steph Staten Island NY 1999-2000; D S Andr's Epis Ch Staten Island NY 1997-1999. Auth, "Dss Susan Trevor Knapp," *Epis New Yorker*, Dio NY, 2011; Auth, "Reflections on a Flawed Past," *The Epis New Yorker*, Dio NY, 2010; Auth, ""Be Thour my Vision..."A Reflection," *Diakoneo*, NAAD, 2005; Auth, "Feetwashing/Servanthood/Boarders," *Diakoneo*, 2002; Auth, "Deacons And The Mssn Field," *Diakoneo*, 2001; Auth, "Dss," *Diakoneo*, 2000. Cmnty Serv Awd New York St Untd Teachers 1998.

SWANSON OJN, John-Julian (Mil) 450 Sunnyslope Dr Apt 305, Hartland WI 53029 **Monk The Ord of Julian of Norwich Waukesha WI 1985-** B Green Bay WI 1932 s Clifford & Mildred. BA cl Carleton Coll 1954; MDiv Nash 1957. D 2/2/1957 P 8/9/1957 Bp William Hampton Brady. P-in-c S Mk's Ch S Milwaukee WI 1988-1995; R Ch Of The Resurr Norwich CT 1981-1988; Dir Soc Serv Inst Norwich CT 1979-1981; Adj Prof Univ. of RI/Hampshire Coll 1977-1979; Co-Proprietor KennebunkBookPort Kennebuck-

S

port ME 1974-1977; Sem of the Streets Trin Par New York NY 1970-1974; R Chr Ch Portsmouth NH 1960-1970; Vic Ch Of S Mary Of The Snows Eagle River WI 1957-1960. Auth, "non-fiction," *Letters to Jacob: Mostly About Pryr*, Paraclete Press, 2016; Auth, "non-fiction," *Elements of Offering*, Nashotah Press, 2015; Auth, "Poetry," *Eyes Have I That See*, Paraclete Press, 2015; Auth, "non-fiction," *The Complete Cloud of Unknowing*, Paraclete Press, 2015; Auth, "non-fiction," *The Pract and Power of Priesthood*, Nashotah Press, 2015; Auth, "non-fiction," *The Complete Intro to the Devout Life*, Paraclete Press, 2013; Auth, "non-fiction," *The Complete Imitation of Chr*, Paraclete Press, 2012; Auth, "non-fiction," *Revelations of Div Love*, Paraclete Press, 2011; Co-Auth, "non-fiction," *Love's Trin: A Comp to Julian of Norwich*, Liturg Press, 2009; Auth, "non-fiction," *Stars in a Dark Wrld*, Outskirts Press, 2009; Auth, "non-fiction," *The Complete Julian of Norwich*, Paraclete Press, 2009; Auth, "fiction," *Tales of the Golden Castle*, Julian Press, 1990; Auth, "non-fiction," *A Lesson of Love: The Revelations of Julian of Norwich*, Walker/iUniverse, 1989.

SWANSON, Karen (ECR) Saint Andrew's Episcopal Church, 1600 Santa Lucia Ave, San Bruno CA 94066 B Fairbault MN 1956 d Henning & Ruth. BA S Olaf Coll 1978; MDiv CDSP 1983. D 6/29/1983 Bp Robert Marshall Anderson P 6/1/1984 Bp Edmond Lee Browning. m 2/4/1984 David Yasuhide Ota c 1. P All SS Epis Ch San Leandro CA 2014-2015; S Ambr Epis Ch Foster City CA 2013; S Andr's Ch Saratoga CA 2010-2013; Int S Andr's Epis Ch San Bruno CA 1999-2010; S Matt's Epis Ch San Mateo CA 1997-1998; Dio Hawaii Honolulu HI 1994-1997; S Andr's Cathd Honolulu HI 1992-1997, Cn Pstr 1985-1986, Yth Mnstry 1984-1985; Cnvnr Cler The Epis Ch in Hawaii Honolulu HI 1990-1992, Dioc Coun 1988-1990; R Ch Of The Epiph Honolulu HI 1986-1991; S Andr's Priory Sch Honolulu HI 1985-1986; Chapl S Andr's Priory Sch Honolulu HI 1983-1986.

SWANSON, Kenneth Banford (At) 1015 Old Roswell Rd, Roswell GA 30076 **R S Dav's Ch Roswell GA 2010-** B Minneapolis MN 1948 s Neil & Helen. BA U of Wisconsin 1972; MDiv Fuller TS 1976; PhD U of Edinburgh Gb 1979. D 6/13/1981 Bp James Stuart Wetmore P 12/18/1981 Bp Walter Decoster Dennis Jr. m 4/28/2012 Darlene Jamerson Price c 1. Dn Chr Ch Cathd Nashville TN 1997-2007; R Gr Ch Millbrook NY 1987-1997, Sr Cur 1982-1987; Gr Opportunity Proj 1982-1987; Gr Epis Ch New York NY 1982-1987; St. Barth Ch New York NY 1981-1982. Auth, "Uncommon Pryr: Approaching Intimacy w God". swanson510@gmail.com

SWANSON, Richard Alden (Cal) 3101 Peninsula Rd Apt 301, Oxnard CA 93035 **Asst S Paul's Epis Ch Ventura CA 2013-** B Saint Paul MN 1939 s John & Ruth. BBA U MI 1961; MDiv EDS 1964; MA Ball St U 1974; EdD USC 1980. D 6/29/1964 Bp Archie H Crowley P 1/25/1965 Bp Richard Stanley Merrill Emrich. m 6/8/1963 Janice Rae Swanson c 2. Asst Ch Of The Incarn Santa Rosa CA 2004-2011; R All SS Epis Ch San Leandro CA 1987-2001; Chapl (LtC) USAF San Antonio TX 1983-1987; Chapl USAF San Francisco CA 1981-1983; Chapl USAF Keflavik Iceland 1980-1981; Chapl USAF San Francisco CA 1976-1980; Chapl USAF Madrid Spain 1972-1976; Chapl USAF WDC 1970-1972; Chapl USAF U-Tapaeo Thailand 1969-1970; Chapl Off Of Bsh For ArmdF New York NY 1966-1987; Chapl USAF Biloxi MS 1966-1969; Chair, Assessment Appeals Dio California San Francisco CA 1997-2001. Auth, "Sexual Knowlege and Attitudes of Theol Students," 1980.

SWANSON, Richard Reif (Vt) PO Box 1175, Stowe VT 05672 **R S Jn's In The Mountains Stowe VT 2010-** B Saint Paul MN 1970 s William & Helen. AA U of Montana 1993; BA California St U 1995; MDiv SWTS 2000. D 6/24/2000 P 1/6/2001 Bp Frederick Houk Borsch. m 7/14/2012 Timothy Darwin Heath-Swanson. R S Paul's Epis Ch Dowagiac MI 2006-2010; Assoc For Yth And Fam Mnstrs S Ptr's Ch Morristown NJ 2002-2006; Cur S Mk's-In-The-Vlly Epis Los Olivos CA 2000-2001.

SWARR, J Peter (WMass) 1 Porter Rd, East Longmeadow MA 01028 **Dn of Hampden Dnry Dio Wstrn Massachusetts Springfield 2017-; R S Mk's Epis Ch E Longmeadow MA 2009-** B Biddeford Maine 1979 s James & Martha. BA Wheaton Coll 2002; MDiv VTS 2006. D 6/25/2006 P 2/24/2007 Bp Chilton Richardson Knudsen. m 6/21/2002 Angela T Swarr c 2. Assoc Int Chr Ch Cathd Springfield MA 2013; Assoc R S Jn's Ch Plymouth MI 2006-2009. Harris Awd VTS 2006. rector@stmarksma.org

SWARTHOUT, James Edward (Chi) 10275 N. River Rd, Barrington Hills IL 60102 **Rosecrance Behavioral Hlth Cler Congrl Coordntr 2012-** B HIghland Park IL 1954 s James & Theresa. BA Wstrn Illinois U 1980; MDiv S Marys Sem and U 1986; MSW Loyola U 1996. Rec 1/17/2002 as Priest Bp Bill Persell. m 7/11/1998 Claudia Swarthout. Samar Counslg Cntr Barrington IL 2011-2012; R S Paul's Ch Mchenry IL 2007-2012, Int 2007-2011, 2002-2003; S Greg's Epis Ch Deerfield IL 2006-2007; R S Jas Ch Dundee IL 2003-2006. "Keeping the Faith," *NW Herald.*

SWARTSFAGER, Ames Kent (LI) 1022 Marine Dr Ne Unit 2, Olympia WA 98501 **Ch Of The Annunc Lewisville TX 1997-; Ret 1991-** B New York NY 1938 s Vernon & Grace. BA San Francisco St U 1961; BD CDSP 1964; Advncd CPE and Actg CPE Supervis 1977. D 6/21/1964 Bp James Albert Pike P 12/22/1964 Bp David Emrys Richards. m 7/26/1958 Judith A Swartsfager c 3. Serv Ch In Colombia 1994-1995; Trin Ch Cali 1994-1995; Chapl Reg Chapl

Adminstr Mid Atlantic Reg 1989-1991; Chapl Fed Corrcntl Inst Terminal Is CA 1979-1988; Chapl Ft Worth - 1975-1979; Chapl Fed Corrctional Inst Tallahasee 1970-1975; Gr Ch Middletown NY 1968-1969, Assoc 1968-1969; Serv Ch In Honduras 1965-1967. Auth, "Involving Fam & Cmnty In Rehabilitating Offenders". Chapl Of The Year U.S. Bureau Of Prisons 1989.

SWARTZENTRUBER, A Orley (NJ) 309 Bridgeboro Rd Apt 22, Moorestown NJ 08057 B Buenos Aires AR 1926 s Amos & Edna. BA Goshen Coll 1948; BD Goshen Biblic Sem 1951; MA Pr 1963; PhD Pr 1970. D 5/14/1963 P 9/1/1963 Bp Allen Webster Brown. m 9/8/1950 Jane Swartzentruber c 4. R All SS Ch Princeton NJ 1968-1993; Asst Headmaster & Chapl S Agnes Sch Albany NY 1964-1966; Chapl Darrow Sch New Lebanon NY 1962-1964.

SWAYZE, Marie Zealor (Pa) 540 Lowell St, Wakefield MA 01880 **Supply/ Bridge/Int Dio Massachusetts Boston MA 2016-; Chapl Emer St. Jas Epis Sch Philadelphia PA 2014-** B Bryn Mawr PA 1943 d Murray & Marie. BS Trin Washington DC 1965; MS W Chester U of Pennsylvania 1985; MDiv GTS 1993; MDiv Luth TS Philadelphila PA 1993. D 6/13/1992 P 6/12/1993 Bp Allen Lyman Bartlett Jr. c 2. Chapl St. Jas Epis Sch Phila. PA 2011-2013; Asstg P S Mk's Ch Philadelphia PA 2009-2015, Asstg P 2006-2015, Int 1996-1997; Asstg P All SS Ch Norristown PA 2006-2009; PreSchool Dir Chr Ch Media PA 2004-2006; Co-Fndr 'The Clnc' Phoenixville PA 2003-2013; R S Ptr's Ch Phoenixville PA 1998-2004; Int S Andr's Ch Yardley PA 1997-1998; Int St Pauls Epis Ch Oaks PA 1994-1995; Ch Sch Dir. S Mary's Epis Ch Ardmore PA 1993; Chapl Hosp of The U of Pennsylvania 1992-1993; Trans D S Jas' Epis Ch Downingtown PA 1992-1993; Hosp Chapl U Of Pennsylvania Philadelphia PA 1993-1994. AAUW, Lifetime Mem 1971. Sem Awd ABS 1989. revmarieswayze@gmail.com

SWEENEY, Craig Chandler (Be) 2411 SW 35th Ter, Topeka KS 66611 B Baltimore MD 1951 s John & Virginia. MBA U Denv; BA U Denv 1973; JD U Denv 1978; MDiv VTS 2001. D 3/17/2001 P 9/29/2001 Bp William Edward Smalley. m 8/25/1973 Robin Jo Roy c 3. R Ch Of The Epiph Glenburn Clarks Summit PA 2006-2013; Gr Epis Ch Winfield KS 2001-2006; R Trin Ch Arkansas City KS 2001-2006.

SWEENEY, David Cameron (Ore) 503 N Holladay Dr, Seaside OR 97138 **R Calv Ch Seaside OR 1992-** B Seattle WA 1956 s Donald & Margaret. BS NWU 1979; MDiv VTS 1984. D 6/16/1984 Bp Quintin Ebenezer Primo Jr P 6/24/1985 Bp James Winchester Montgomery. Vic S Chris's Ch Port Orford OR 1992-1999; S Jn-By-The-Sea Epis Ch Bandon OR 1992-1999; All SS Ch Hamlet NC 1987-1992; R Ch Of The Mssh Rockingham NC 1987-1992; Asst S Mary's Epis Ch High Point NC 1984-1987; R Calv, Seaside, Oregon Dio Oregon Portland OR 1999.

SWEENEY, Joseph Francis (NJ) 25 Quail Hollow Drive, Westampton NJ 08060 **Chapl Cooper U Hosp 2010-; Chapl Hampton Behavior Hlth Cntr 2010-; Chapl Masonic Hospice Serv 2010-** B Flushing NY 1939 s Joseph & Clara. Diac Stds Sch for Deacons 2010. D 5/16/2009 Bp Sylvestre Donato Romero. m 5/11/1985 Lynn Sweeney c 3. D Gr Ch Pemberton NJ 2009-2010.

SWEENEY, Meghan T (Mass) All Saints' Episcopal Church, 121 N Main St, Attleboro MA 02703 **D-in-c All SS Epis Ch Attleboro MA 2012-; Assoc Prof of the Pract Boston Coll 2006-; Mem, Dioc Coun Dio Massachusetts Boston MA 2013-, Mem, Dioc Resolutns Com 2010-2015** B New York NY 1971 d Wilson & Therese. BA Coll of the H Cross 1993; MDiv Harvard DS 1999; PhD Emory U 2007; Cert EDS 2011. D 6/2/2012 Bp Gayle Harris P 1/12/2013 Bp M(Arvil) Thomas Shaw. m 12/2/2006 Margaret E Lias. Bd Mem Attleboro Area Coun of Ch 2013-2017. meghantsweeney@gmail.com

SWEENEY, Sylvia A (Los) Bloy House The Episcopal Theological School At Claremont, 1325 N College Ave, Claremont CA 91711 **Assoc S Mk's Par Altadena CA 2012-; Dn and Pres Bloy Hse Claremont CA 2009-** B Fort Sill OK 1955 d James & Lieselotte. BS Florida St U 1975; MS Florida St U 1980; MDiv SWTS 1985; PhD CDSP 2007. D 6/15/1985 Bp Frank S Cerveny P 2/1/1986 Bp Charles I Jones III. m 3/10/1985 John Robert Honeychurch c 1. Assoc R S Jas Ch Fremont CA 2005-2008; Mentor P Dept Of Missions San Francisco CA 2001-2003; Co-R S Lk's Epis Ch Idaho Falls ID 1992-2001; Vic H Trin Epis Ch Troy MT 1988-1992; Co-Vic S Lk's Ch Libby MT 1987-1992; Dioc Yth Circuit Rider Dio Montana Helena MT 1985-1986; Mem GC T/F on Mar 2013-2016; Dioc BEC Dio California San Francisco CA 2006-2008, Mnstry Dvlpmt Off 2003-2005; Chair of COM Dio Idaho Boise ID 1997-2001. Auth, "Future Directions in Liturg Dvlpmt," *ATR Vol. 95 #3*, ATR, 2013; Ed, "Female Images of God in Chr Wrshp," *Ptr Lang Liturg Stds Series*, Ptr Lang Pub, 2013; Contrib, "Redemp," *On Sacr Ground: Jewish and Chr Cler Reflect on Transformative Passages from the Five Books of Moses*, Blackbird Books, 2012; Auth, "Baptism as the Gateway to Epis Liturg Renwl," *Liturg: The St of Liturg Renwl*, The Liturg Conf, 2011; Ed, "Embodying the Femine in the Dances of the Wrld's Rel," *Ptr Lang Liturg Stds Series*, Ptr Lang Pub, 2011; Auth, "Discussion Guide," *Chr Holiness and HumanSexuality*, Chicago Consult, 2009; Auth, "An Ecofeminist Perspective on Ash Wednesday and Lent," *Ptr Lang Amer U Stds Series*, Ptr Lang Pub, 2009. No Amer Acad of Liturg 2007. Bogard Fell CDSP 2006. ssweeney@cst.edu

S

SWEENY, Thomas Edward (NJ) 102 New St, Egg Harbor Township NJ 08234 **D Ch Of S Mk And All SS Absecon Absecon NJ 2002-** B New Rochell NY 1942 D 9/21/2002 Bp David Bruce Joslin. m 8/6/1960 Bari Colleen Green c 3.

SWEET, Fran Maciver (Cal) Po Box 1384, Alameda CA 94501 B Tucson AZ 1940 d Robert & Clemence. San Francisco City Coll 1960; Foothill Coll 1970; BA San Francisco St U 1977; BTh California Sch for Deacons 1989. D 6/8/1991 Bp William Edwin Swing. m 7/12/1980 Allen Alexander Sweet c 4. D Chr Ch Alameda CA 2002-2004; D H Cross Epis Ch Castro Vlly CA 1998-2002; Dir Chld'S Mnstrs All SS Epis Ch Palo Alto CA 1996-1998; S Patricks Ch And Day Sch Thousand Oaks CA 1993-1995; D S Anne's Ch Fremont CA 1991-1992; Chapl S Rose Hosp Haywood CA 1989-1992. NAAD 1984.

SWEET, Portia Ann (Tex) 1656 Blalock Rd, Houston TX 77080 **D S Chris's Ch Houston TX 2015-** B Charleston WV 1939 d William & Mary. Sr. Profsnl in HR (Cert) HR Certification Inst; BA U of Houston 1973; Cert Coll of Ins 2012; Cert Iona Sch for Mnstry 2012. D 6/16/2012 Bp C Andrew Doyle. c 2. D St Andrews Epis Ch Houston TX 2012-2015; Chapl Houston Hospice Patient Care Unit 2010-2015. Natl hon Soc in Psychol - Psi Chi 1972-1973; Soc for Human Resource Mgmt 1990-2000. portia@stchrishouston.org

SWEIGERT, Cynthia (Pgh) 5700 Forbes Ave, Pittsburgh PA 15217 B Minneapolis MN 1952 d Edgerton & Roxanne. BA U MN 1975; MDiv GTS 1978. D 6/24/1978 Bp Robert Marshall Anderson P 12/1/1980 Bp Philip Frederick McNairy. m 11/12/1994 Dan Keith Sweigert. S Jn's Ch S Cloud MN 2014-2016; R The Ch Of The Redeem Pittsburgh PA 1995-2012; Buffalo Area Metro Mnstrs Inc Buffalo NY 1993-1994; Cn S Paul's Cathd Buffalo NY 1989-1992; S Jn's Ch Youngstown OH 1985-1989; Assoc Chr And S Steph's Ch New York NY 1980-1986; Trin Epis Ch Roslyn NY 1978-1979.

SWENSON, Richard Clive (Minn) **P-in-c Gr Ch Tecumseh Nebraska City NE 2006-** B Ann Arbor MI 1947 JD Creighton U 1978; MA Creighton U 2004. D 5/20/2004 P 12/16/2004 Bp Joe Goodwin Burnett.

SWESEY, Jean Elizabeth (Minn) 1008 Transit Ave, Roseville MN 55113 B Minneapolis MN 1935 d Thomas & Marjorie. BA U MN 1958; BA U MN 1978. D 1/25/1984 Bp Robert Marshall Anderson. m 11/22/1958 John Frank Swesey c 2. D S Nich Ch Minneapolis MN 1992-2001; D Ch of the Resurr S Lk Pk MN 1985-1992; S Mk's Ch Annandale MN 1985-1992; D S Chris's Epis Ch S Paul MN 1984-1985.

SWETMAN, Margarita O (Nwk) 2528 Palmer Ave, New Orleans LA 70118 B Sucre BO 1938 d Maximo & Concpcion. BA U of Sthrn Mississippi 1966; MA Tul 1971; MDiv CDSP 1997. D 6/21/1997 P 1/1/1998 Bp Frederick Houk Borsch. Gr Ch Un City NJ 2002-2004; Epis Chapl Los Angeles CA 2000-2001; Asst St Johns Pro-Cathd Los Angeles CA 1997-1999. Curs.

SWIEDLER, Anne Elizabeth (At) 5625 Mill Glen Ct, Atlanta GA 30338 **Asst to the R for Pstr Care and Sprtl Form S Dav's Ch Roswell GA 2003-; Assoc R S Dav's Ch Roswell GA 2002-** B 1950 d William & Eleanor. BA U of New Hampshire 1982; MDiv Candler TS Emory U 2001. D 6/8/2002 P 1/25/2003 Bp J Neil Alexander. c 2.

SWIFT, Daniel Willard (Los) 24874 Olive Tree Ln, Los Altos CA 94024 B Long Beach CA 1940 s Howard & Jessella. BA U CA 1965; MDiv Nash 1970. D 9/12/1970 Bp Francis E I Bloy P 3/27/1971 Bp Victor Manuel Rivera. S Matt's Epis Ch San Mateo CA 1984-1985; Trin Epis Ch Santa Barbara CA 1976-1977, 1973-1974, 1973; Corp Of The Cathd Ch Of St Paul Los Angeles CA 1973; Asst All SS Par Long Bch CA 1970-1972.

SWIFT, John Kohler (WMo) 6 Hunter Dr, Guilford CT 06437 **CPE Supvsr Partnr In CPE Hartford CT 2008-** B Hartford CT 1939 s Donald & Marion. BA Hav 1961; RelD TS at Claremont CA 1969. Trans 6/1/1985 Bp Arthur Edward Walmsley. m 11/24/1983 Elizabeth A Swift. Dir, Sprtl Wellness St Lk's Chap Kansas City MO 1999-2005; Sr VP Pstr Educ Healthcare Chapl Nyc 1994-1999; Dir Pstr Care Hartford Hosp Hartford CT 1984-1994. ACPE, Coll Chaplai 1984; Assn of Profsnl Chapl 1984.

SWIFT, Steve Albert (Md) 8403 Nunley Dr Apt E, Parkville MD 21234 B Dennison TX 1946 s Robert & Mary. BA U of Kansas 1968; MDiv GTS 1972. D 6/18/1972 Bp Albert Ervine Swift P 6/1/1973 Bp Stephen F Bayne Jr. m 9/2/1985 Amy Swift c 2. Ch Of The Mssh Baltimore MD 2008-2009; Chr Ch Fairmont WV 2003-2008; Ch Of The Gd Shpd Dunedin FL 2002-2003; Int S Chris's Epis Ch Carmel IN 2000-2002; S Andr Epis Ch Kokomo IN 1999-2000; R Gr Ch Brunswick MD 1996-1999; Chapl S Pat's Ch Washington DC 1995-1996; Chapl S Pat's Washington DC 1995-1996; Chapl S Anne Sch Alexandria VA 1992-1995; Int S Aid's Epis Ch Boulder CO 1991-1992; Vic S Mary Magd Ch Boulder CO 1990-1991; Vic H Cross Epis Mssn Sterling CO 1985-1987; Assoc Calv Ch Columbia MO 1978-1985; R S Jn's Ch Durant OK 1977-1978; Cur Chr Chr Epis Ch Denver CO 1974-1977; The Ch Of Chr The King (Epis) Arvada CO 1974-1977; Cur Holyrood Ch New York NY 1972-1974. Phi Beta Kappa; Phi Beta Kappa.

SWINDELL, Kay Howard (EC) 1514 Clifton Rd, Jacksonville NC 28540 B Rocky Mount NC 1951 d Walter & Maxine. AA Louisburg Coll 1971. D 6/20/1992 Bp Huntington Williams Jr. m 2/16/1985 Robert Temple Swindell c 2. S Anne's Epis Ch Jacksonville NC 2010, Dir of Lay Mnstry 2003-2009, D 1992-2002.

SWINDLE, Frank Moody (NwT) 649 Hwy 577, Pioneer LA 71266 B Bastrop LA 1943 s Moody & Elaine. BA NE Louisiana U 1965; MDiv Sewanee: The U So, TS 1973; DMin Sewanee: The U So, TS 1996. D 6/18/1973 P 5/12/1974 Bp Robert B Gooden. m 11/29/1963 Gloria Swindle c 1. Int S Jn's Epis Ch Odessa TX 2010-2011; S Nich' Epis Ch Midland TX 2005-2007; Int S Phil's Ch Joplin MO 2001-2003; Int S Paul's Par Kent Chestertown MD 2001; Int Chr Epis Ch Little Rock AR 1999-2000; Int S Ptr's Epis Ch Amarillo TX 1996-1999; Vic All SS Ch Colorado City TX 1986-1996; S Steph's Ch Sweetwater TX 1986-1996; R Tri SS Cluster Sweetwater TX 1986-1996; Cur Gr Epis Ch Monroe LA 1981-1986; Cur Epis Ch Of The Gd Shpd Lake Chas LA 1978-1980; Vic Leonidas Polk Meml Epis Mssn Leesville LA 1976-1978; Trin Epis Ch Deridder LA 1976-1978; Cur S Paul's Ch New Orleans LA 1973-1976.

SWINEHART, Bruce Howard (Colo) 1404 Orchard Ave, Boulder CO 80304 **S Mary Magd Ch Boulder CO 2016-** B Berkeley CA 1957 s Howard & Elizabeth. BA Bow 1980; MA U CO 1984; MDiv CDSP 2009. D 6/6/2009 Bp Robert John O'Neill P 12/21/2009 Bp Stacy F Sauls. m 8/22/1987 Daphne Chellos. P-in-c S Jas Epis Ch Wheat Ridge CO 2013-2016; P-in-c S Pat Ch Somerset KY 2009-2012.

SWINEHART JR, Charles Henry (Mich) 1615 Ridgewood Dr, East Lansing MI 48823 **Chair or co-chair Epis Dio Michigan Disabil Awareness Com 2003-** B Cleveland OH 1940 s Charles & Rosemary. BA U So 1962; MDiv VTS 1965. D 6/29/1965 Bp Chauncie Kilmer Myers P 1/3/1966 Bp George R Selway. m 4/30/1966 Carol Y Swinehart c 3. Vic S Andr's Ch Jackson MI 2000-2010; 1992-1995; R S Steph's Ch Hamburg MI 1988-1992; Supply P 1976-1988; Asst Trin Epis Ch Bay City MI 1974-1976; Vic S Alb's Ch Manistique MI 1969-1973; S Pauls Ch Nahma MI 1969-1973; Vic Ch Of The Ascen Ontonagon MI 1965-1969; S Marks Ch Ewen MI 1965-1969. Advoc of the Year Epilepsy Fndt of Amer 1997.

✠ SWING, The Rt Rev William Edwin (Cal) 105 Pepper Ave., Burlingame CA 94010 **Pres and Fndr Untd Rel Initiative 1996-** B Huntington WV 1936 s William & Elsie. BA Ken 1958; BD VTS 1961; VTS 1980; Ken 1981; LHD U of San Francisco 2005; Churc h DS of the Pacific 2008; LHD U of Palo Alto 2009. D 6/11/1961 P 12/1/1961 Bp Wilburn Camrock Campbell Con 9/29/1979 for Cal. m 10/7/1961 Mary T Swing c 2. Bp of California Dio California San Francisco CA 1979-2006; R S Columba's Ch Washington DC 1969-1979; Vic S Matt's Ch Chester WV 1963-1968; S Thos' Epis Ch Weirton WV 1963-1968; Asst S Matt's Ch Wheeling WV 1961-1963. "A Swing w A Crosier," Epis Dio California, 1999; "The Coming Untd Rel," Conexus Press, 1998; "Bldg Wisdom'S Hse (Co-Authored w Rabbi Steph Pearce Jn Schlegel S.J. And Bonnie Menes Kahn," Addison Wesley Longman, 1997. DD Ch Div. Sch of the Pacific 2007; Doctor of Humane Letters U of San Francisco 2005; DD Ken 1980; DD VTS 1980.

SWINNEA, Stephanie Lavenia (Okla) 510 S 15th St, Mcalester OK 74501 **R All SS Ch Mcalester OK 2007-** B Oklahoma 1951 d Myron & Stella. BS Texas Womans U 1973; MDiv Epis TS of the SW 2005. D 6/25/2005 P 1/7/2006 Bp Robert Manning Moody. m 2/23/1973 Billy Samuel Swinnea c 4. Cur Dio Oklahoma Oklahoma OK 2005-2007; S Lk's Epis Ch Bartlesville OK 2005-2007. "I, Pat, A Sinner," Aaron Allgood Books, 1999. DOK 2005. allsaintsmembers@att.net

SWINSKI, Grace Elaine (RI) B 1958 d Frederick & Ruth. D 6/11/2016 Bp W Nicholas Knisely Jr. m 4/21/1991 Joseph John Swinski c 2.

SWITZ, Robert (Cal) 1189 W Park View Pl, Mount Pleasant SC 29466 **P-in-c The Ch Of The Epiph Summerville SC 2009-, 1999-2009** B Upper Darby PA 1936 s Louis & Margaret. BS Villanova U 1960; BD VTS 1968. D 6/21/1968 Bp James Loughlin Duncan P 1/1/1969 Bp William Loftin Hargrave. m 7/1/1981 Cheryl D Switz c 3. Trin Ch San Francisco CA 1997-1999; R Gd Samar San Francisco CA 1982-1984; Indn Epis Mnstry San Francisco CA 1982-1983; Assoc Gr Cathd San Francisco CA 1980-1982; R S Greg's Ch Boca Raton FL 1974-1980; Chapl (Major) US-AR 1970-1987; Vic H Sacr W Hollywood FL 1970-1974; Instnl Chapl So And SE Florida 1968-1970; Asst Trin Cathd Miami FL 1968-1970.

SWITZER, John Benton (Miss) **Cur S Jn's Epis Ch Ocean Sprg MS 2017-; Ecum Off Dio Mississippi 2015-** D 6/10/2017 Bp Brian Seage.

SWONGER, Timothy Lee (Nev) 1560 Jamielinn Ln Unit 103, Las Vegas NV 89110 **P S Thos Ch Las Vegas NV 1997-** B Los Vegas NV 1955 s Verna. D 6/22/1997 P 12/1/1997 Bp Stewart Clark Zabriskie.

SWOPE, Bob (Ak) D 9/12/1973 Bp Matthew George Henry P 4/1/1974 Bp William Gillette Weinhauer.

SWORD OHC, Carl Richard (NY) 200 East 33rd St, Apt # 14-J, New York NY 10016 **Psychoanalyst/Psych Psychoanalyst Priv Pract 1979-; P H Cross Monstry W Pk NY 1973-** B Bath PA 1931 s Rodgelio & Hilda. K SU; Marymount Coll; BS Penn 1958; MDiv EDS 1962; MC Arizona St U 1972; Cert Westchester Inst 1982. D 6/16/1962 Bp William S Thomas P 12/22/1962 Bp Austin Pardue. CEO S Fran Hm Albany NY 1972-1973; Soc Worker S Fran Boys Hm Bavaria KS 1964-1970; Asst Trin Epis Ch Washington PA 1963-1964; In-c S Thos' Epis Ch Canonsburg PA 1962-1964; P-in-c S Geo's

Ch Waynesburg PA 1962-1963. Dio Gld Pstr Psychologists 1983; OHC: Life Professed 1973.

SY, Jonathan J (Los) 21202 Spurney Ln, Huntington Beach CA 92646 B Cebu, Philippines 1956 s Priscilo & Maria Corazon. BS Chem Engr U of San Carlos 1979; MDiv SWTS 2010. D 6/12/2010 Bp Diane Jardine Bruce P 1/8/2011 Bp Mary Douglas Glasspool. Assoc S Lk's At The Mtn Phoenix AZ 2013-2014; Supply Cler Ch Of The H Trin and S Ben Alhambra CA 2011-2012; Assoc S Jn The Div Epis Ch Costa Mesa CA 2010-2011; Counslr Serenity Life Counslg 2010.

SYDNOR JR, Charles Raymond (Va) 175 Rogue Point Ln, Heathsville VA 22473 B Kinsale VA 1944 s Charles & Mary. BA U Rich 1966; MDiv VTS 1970. D 6/20/1970 P 5/15/1971 Bp Philip Alan Smith. c 1. S Geo's Ch Fredericksburg VA 1973-2003; D S Matt's Epis Ch Sterling VA 1970-1973.

SYEDULLAH, Masud Ibn (NY) 35 Circle Dr, Hyde Park NY 12538 **Epis-Muslim Relatns Com Dio New York 2013-; Dir Roots & Branches: Prog for Sprtl Growth 1997-; Epis-Muslim Relatns Com Dio New York New York NY 2015-, COM 2014-, Ecum and Interfaith Cmsn 2014-, Chair, Epis Muslim Relatns Com 2008-2011, Sprtl Dir, Happ 2006-2008, Pres Stndg Com 2005-2006, Mem Stndg Com 2002-2006, Mem, Epis-Muslim Relatns Com 1998-2011, Cmsn on Liturg and Mus 1992-2002, Mem, Ecum & Interfaith Cmsn 1991-2011; External Relatns Off Third Ord SSF Prov of the Americas 2013-** B Saint Louis MO 1948 s Masud & Alice. BMusEd Oral Roberts U 1971; MMus U CO 1974; MDiv SWTS 1979. D 6/16/1979 P 4/14/1980 Bp Gerald Nicholas Mcallister. m 7/16/1971 Janice Mae Taylor c 2. Assoc R for Adult Chr Formation, and Liturg Ch of the H Faith Santa Fe NM 2011-2012; Chair, Epis-Muslim Relatns Com Dio New York 2008-2011; Stndg Com Pres Dio New York 2005-2006; Stndg Com Mem Dio New York 2002-2006; Min Prov Third Ord Prov of the Americas Soc of St Fran 2002-2005; Min Prov Third Ord Soceity of St Fran Prov of the Americas 2002-2005; Vic Ch Of The Atone Bronx NY 1998-2011; Ecum and Interfaith Cmsn Dio New York 1991-2011; Mem, Epis-Muslim Relatns Com Dio New York 1991-2011; Assoc for Wrshp and Educ Mnstrs Trin Par New York NY 1990-1996; Assoc for Adult Educ and Liturg Chr Ch Cathd Cincinnati OH 1988-1990; Prov Chapl Third Ord Soc of S Fran Prov of the Americ 1985-1988; Vic S Aid's Epis Ch Tulsa OK 1981-1988, Assoc 1979-1981; Sprtl Dir, Happ Dio Oklahoma Oklahoma City OK 1979-1988; Chapl & Hd of Rel and Psychol Holland Hall Sch Tulsa OK 1979-1981; Min Prov Third Ord Soc of St Fran Prov of the Americas 2002-2005; Prov Chapl Third Ord Soc of S Fran Prov of the Americas 1985-1988. Third Ord, Soc of S Fran 1979; UBE 1988.

SYKES, Robert (Pa) 102 Woodland Dr, Lansdale PA 19446 **Died 5/23/2017** B Philadelphia PA 1931 s Joseph & Rebecca. BS Tem 1954; STB PDS 1957; MA U of Pennsylvania 1980; Cert Montgomery Cnty Cmnty Coll 1983; AA Montgomery Cnty Cmnty Coll 1984. D 4/27/1957 P 11/1/1957 Bp Alfred L Banyard. m 9/11/1954 Mary Hehn Sykes c 4. Ret 1991-2017; 1979-1991; R Memi Ch Of The H Nativ Jenkintown PA 1969-1979; Vic The Ch Of The Gd Shpd Berlin NJ 1960-1969; Cur Chr Ch In Woodbury Woodbury NJ 1957-1960.

SYLER, Gregory Charles (WA) St George Church, PO Box 30, Valley Lee MD 20692 **R St Georges Ch Leonardtown MD 2007-** B Chicago IL 1975 s Earl & Dorothy. BA S Xavier U Chicago 1993; MDiv U Chi DS 2000; DAS VTS 2005. D 6/18/2005 P 12/17/2005 Bp Bill Persell. m 10/29/2016 Iman L G Syler c 1. Cur Ch Of Our Sav Chicago IL 2005-2007; Theol Tchr Mo Mcauley HS Chicago IL 2000-2004.

SYLVESTER, Kay (Los) **Prog Dir S Paul's Epis Ch Tustin CA 2005-; D Ch Of The H Innoc San Francisco CA 2004-; Every Voice Ntwk San Francisco CA 2004-; Prog Dir Every Voice Ntwk San Francisco CA 2004-** B Durango CO 1959 d John & Roma. BA Ft Lewis Coll 1981; MDiv CDSP 2003. D 6/19/2004 Bp Chester Lovelle Talton P 1/22/2005 Bp Joseph Jon Bruno. m 6/28/2014 Cynthia Katherine Case. kay@stpauls.org

SYMINGTON, Ann Pritzlaff (Los) 4450 E Camelback Rd, Phoenix AZ 85018 B Milwaukee WI 1952 d John & Mary. BA Scripps Coll 1974; Cert San Francisco St U 1975. D 10/5/2002 Bp Robert Reed Shahan. m 2/7/1976 J Symington c 3. D S Barn On The Desert Scottsdale AZ 2002-2005.

SYMINGTON, Sidney S (ECR) 545 Shasta Ave, Morro Bay CA 93442 **R S Ptr's By-The-Sea Epis Ch Morro Bay CA 2013-** B St Louis MO 1956 BA Ya 1978; MFA NYU 1984; MDiv Ya Berk 2004. D 6/6/2009 P 2/13/2010 Bp Prince Grenville Singh. c 4. Assoc S Ptr's Epis Ch Henrietta NY 2009-2011.

SYMONDS, John W (Pa) 321 W Chestnut St, Lancaster PA 17603 **S Jas' Epis Ch Downington PA 2015-** B Lancaster PA 1967 s Gordon & Carole. BS Rutgers The St U of New Jersey 1990; MDiv Lancaster TS 2007; DAS Epis TS of the SW 2008. D 6/7/2008 P 2/18/2009 Bp Nathan Dwight Baxter. m 9/10/2010 Kimberly Dawn Symonds c 2. P-in-c S Mary's Epis Ch Blair NE 2010-2015; S Jas Ch Lancaster PA 2009-2010.

SYMONS, Frederic Russell (NCal) 5301 Whitney Ave, Carmichael CA 95608 **Assoc St Paul's Sacramento 2006-** B Sussex NJ 1947 s Harold & Mary. BA San Diego St U 1971; MDiv CDSP 1974. D 7/25/1974 P 5/31/1975 Bp Wesley Frensdorff. m 10/28/2007 Haviland Anne Symons c 1. Assoc S Paul's Epis Ch Sacramento CA 2013; Vic S Andr's In The Highlands Mssn Antelope CA

1995-2003; Vic Dio El Camino Real Salinas CA 1990-1993, Asst 1987-1990; S Jn's Chap Monterey CA 1988-1990; Asst S Jn Del Monte CA 1987-1990; Nonpar 1986-1987; Cur S Matt's Epis Ch San Mateo CA 1980-1985; Ch Mus Cmsn Epis Dio San Joaquin Modesto CA 1978-1980, Ch Growth Cmsn 1977-1980; R S Phil's Ch Coalinga CA 1976-1980; Cur Chr Ch Alameda CA 1974-1975. Dn SE Dnry 2000-2003; Eccl Crt 1997-2000.

SYNAN, Thomas Norbert Justin (WMass) Church Of The Heavenly Rest, 2 E 90th St, New York NY 10128 **Dio Wstrn Massachusetts Springfield 2013-; Hon Chapl New York City Fire Dept 2008-; Mem, Advsry Bd Hlth Advocates for Older People 2004-; Mem, Fam Selection Com HabHum New York City 2003-; Cler Liaison New York City Police Dept 2003-; Chapl New York Fire-Flag 2003-; Bd Mem HabHum New York City 2002-** B New York NY 1961 s William & Catherine. BS U of Pennsylvania 1983; JD Geo 1989; MDiv Ya Berk 2000. D 3/18/2000 P 9/16/2000 Bp Richard Frank Grein. Chair, Fam Selection Com HabHum New York City 2005-2011; Assoc P Ch Of The Heav Rest New York NY 2000-2013; Com to Elect a Bp Dio New York New York NY 2010-2011, Advsry Com, Epis Chars of New York 2010-, Chair, Soc Concerns Cmsn 2010-, Dioc Coun 2010-, Indaba Team 2010-, Strng Com for the Carpenter's Kids Prog 2010-, COM 2006-. Ord of St.Jn of Jerusalem 1990.

SZACHARA, Joell Beth (CNY) 3415 Havenbrook Dr Apt 104, Kingwood TX 77339 **S Steph's Ch New Hartford NY 2007-** B Binghamton NY 1967 d Bernard & Shea. AA SUNY 1987; BA S Jn Fisher Coll 1990; MDiv VTS 1997. D 6/11/1997 Bp David Bruce Joslin P 5/1/1998 Bp Claude Edward Payne. Dio Cntrl New York Liverpool NY 2008; S Jn's Ch Marcellus NY 2006; S Thos' Epis Ch Syracuse NY 2005-2006; All SS Ch Frederick MD 1999-2005; Ch Of The Gd Shpd Kingwood TX 1997-1999. ststephens4u@juno.com

SZARKE, Christopher J (Me) St Margarets Episcopal Church, 95 Court St, Belfast ME 04915 **S Marg's Ch Belfast ME 2015-** B St Cloud MN 1964 s Jame & Patricia. BA St Cloud St U 1987; MA H Names Coll 1996; MDiv Candler TS Emory U 2013; MDiv Candler TS at Emory U 2013. D 5/22/2013 P 12/21/2013 Bp Robert Christopher Wright. Epis Ch Of SS Ptr And Jn Auburn NY 2014.

SZOBOTA, Nick (Md) 230 Owensville Rd, West River MD 20778 **R Chr Ch W River MD 2011-; Chair, Sprtl Care Advsry Commitee Anne Arundel Med Cntr Annapolis MD 2012-; Chair, Liturg and Mus Com Dio Maryland Baltimore MD 2012-** B Bridgeport CT 1979 s Stephen & Heidi. BA Drew U 2001; MDiv GTS 2005. D 6/11/2005 Bp John Palmer Croneberger P 12/21/2005 Bp David Colin Jones. Assoc R S Jn's Ch Ellicott City MD 2007-2011; Cler Res Chr Ch Alexandria VA 2005-2007. Maryland Epis Curs 2012. ccwrnick@comcast.net

SZOKE, Robyn J (CPa) 6 Kitszell Dr, Carlisle PA 17015 **Dio Cntrl Pennsylvania Harrisburg PA 2010-** B SyracuseNY 1950 d Robert & Lela. BA Austin Coll; BS W Chester U of Pennsylvania 1972; MEd Leh 1984; MDiv Moravian TS 1988; STM GTS 1989. D 5/28/1988 P 1/17/1989 Bp James Michael Mark Dyer. m 3/8/2013 Philip W Coolidge. S Jn's Epis Ch Carlisle PA 2004-2011; Sff Off For Chldrn'S Mnstrys And Chrstn Ed Epis Ch Cntr New York NY 1999-2004; Dio Pennsylvania Philadelphia PA 1995-1999; Asst Chr Epis Ch Pottstown PA 1990-1995; Trin Epis Ch Pottsville PA 1990-1995; Assoc S Steph's Epis Ch Wilkes Barre PA 1989-1990; Asst The Epis Ch Of The Medtr Allentown PA 1988-1989. Jn Hus Awd Moravian TS.

SZOST, Lois Anne Whitcomb (NY) 57 Goodwin Rd, Stanfordville NY 12581 **D St Thos Ch Amenia NY 1998-** B Wilton NH 1930 d Leon & Nancy. D 5/16/1998 Bp Richard Frank Grein.

SZYMANSKI, Michael Stephen (WNY) 21 Modern Ave, Lackawanna NY 14218 B Buffalo NY 1949 s Stanley & Irene. D 12/11/1999 Bp Michael Garrison. m 12/9/1972 Jane Wall.

SZYMANSKI SSF, Walter (Pgh) 334 Main St, Pittsburgh PA 15201 **Asst Calv Ch Pittsburgh PA 1997-; Lic Supply P Dio Pittsburgh Pittsburgh PA 1995-** B Pittsburgh PA 1939 s Walter & Helen. Dplma US Army Signal Corp 1958; BA S Vinc Sem Latrobe PA 1964; MDiv S Bernards TS and Mnstry 1970; ThM St Bernards Sem Rochester NY 1971; DMin Colgate Rochester Crozer DS 1979; DMin CRDS 1979; Dplma Alleg 1998. Rec 6/1/1973 as Priest Bp Robert Rae Spears Jr. m 1/1/1984 Paul Marocco. S Paul's Ch Monongahela PA 1994-1995; Int Mnstry Shpd Wellness Cmnty Pittsburgh PA 1993-1997; Dio Rochester Henrietta 1984-1993; R Calv S Andr's Rochester NY 1979-1993; Calv/St Andr's Par Rochester NY 1979-1993; Asst S Lk And S Simon Cyrene Rochester NY 1976-1979; Asst S Thos Epis Ch Rochester NY 1972-1975. Auth, "Blessings of Same Gender Relationshps," Integrity Pub, 1982; Auth, "As We Believe God," Integrity Pub, 1982; Auth, "Fam Mnstry in a Homophile Cmnty," Integrity Pub, 1981; Auth, "Clincl Implications in Human Relatns," Integrity Pub, 1979. Angl Soc of S Fran 2002; Intl Assn of Cert Chem Addiction Couns 2001; Life Mem, Amer Assn for Mar and Fam Thera 1973. LifeTime Serv to The Gay and Lesbian Cmnty Interfaith Alliances For Gay Lesbian and Bisexual Persons 1995; Cn for Spec Mnstrs Epis Dio Rochester 1979.

S

T

TABB, Stewart M (SVa) 405 Talbot Hall Rd, Norfolk VA 23505 **Ch Of The Ascen Norfolk VA 2015-; R St. Julian's Epis Chuch Douglasville GA 2003-** B Charlottesville VA 1959 d Waller & Anthony. BA Davidson Coll 1982; MDiv CDSP 1999. D 12/5/1998 P 6/5/1999 Bp Stewart Clark Zabriskie. H Trin Epis Ch Greensboro NC 2013-2015; S Julian's Epis Ch Douglasville GA 2003-2013; Asst R S Tim's Ch Herndon VA 2000-2003; Reg Vic Dio Nevada Las Vegas 1999-2000.

TABER II, Kenneth William (SwFla) 200 College Ave NE, Grand Rapids MI 49503 B Pasadena CA 1938 s Kenneth & Alice. BA Dart 1960; MDiv VTS 1963; Virginia Commonwealth U 1972; MSW Wstrn Michigan U 1992. D 7/15/1963 Bp Noble C Powell P 6/12/1964 Bp Harry Lee Doll. m 12/30/1988 Cornelia M Taber c 3. S Phil's Epis Ch Grand Rapids MI 2008-2009; R S Mich's Ch Grand Rapids MI 2002-2007; Ch of the H Sprt Belmont MI 1995-2000; Int S Andr's Ch Big Rapids MI 1992-1994; 1985-1992; R Chr Ch Stratford CT 1974-1985; Chapl (Capt) VA NG 1969-1971; Vic Ch Of The Creator Mechanicsvlle VA 1967-1974; Asst H Trin Epis Ch Greensboro NC 1965-1967; Asst S Thos Baltimore MD 1963-1965; ExCoun Dio Connecticut Meriden CT 1980-1985. "Sacrifice of Praise and Thanksgiving," *St. Mich's Ch*, 2007; Auth, "Outplacement: An Idea Whose Time Has Come," *Connections - WMU*, 1995; Auth, "ISMS: Use of Narrative in Healing Racism," *Institutes For Healing Racism Trng*, 1994. Intl TA Assn 1965; NASW 1962; USATransactional Analysis Assoc. 2006. Counslr Natl Bd Cert Counselors 1996; Career Counslr Natl Bd Cert Counselors 1996; Lic Clincl Soc Worker St of Michigan 1996; Career Mgmt Fell Intl Career Certification Inst 1995; Developmenr Spec NTL 1965. kta4careers@gmail.com

TABER-HAMILTON, Nigel (Oly) PO Box 11, Freeland WA 98249 **R S Augustines In-The-Woods Epis Par Freeland WA 2000-; Bd Mem, Faith Action Ntwk Dio Olympia Seattle 2009-, Ecum and Inter-Rel Off 2007-2016** B London UK 1953 s Kenneth & Kathleen. BA U of Wales Bangor 1975; BA U of Birmingham GB 1976; MDiv Queens Coll 1977; Cert CDSP 1978; DMin SFTS 2012. Trans 8/29/1979 Bp William Edwin Swing. m 5/1/1993 Rachel K Taber. Vic All SS Ch Seymour IN 1994-2000; Assoc Trin Epis Ch Bloomington IN 1992-1994; Int R S Steph's Epis Ch New Harmony IN 1991-1992; Int R S Jn's Epis Ch Crawfordsvlle IN 1990-1991; Int R S Jn's Epis Ch Bedford IN 1988-1989; Assoc S Mk's Par Berkeley CA 1979-1981; Serv Ch in Engl 1978-1979; Cmsn on Mssn Strtgy Dio Indianapolis Indianapolis IN 1997-2000, Cmsn on Stwdshp 1997-2000, COM 1984-1999. writer, "The Reformation Continues," *Epis Voice*, Dio Olympia, 2005; writer, "The Windsor Report: a critical Revs," *Epis Voice*, Dio Olympia, 2004. Associated Parishes 1997. Polly Bond Awd of Merit, ECom/The Reformation Continues 2006; Polly Bond Awd of Excellence, ECom/The Windsor Report 2005; WCC Ecum Fell WCC 1977. rector@whidbey.com

TABER-HAMILTON, Rachel K (Oly) 333 High St, Freeland WA 98249 **R Trin Epis Ch Everett WA 2011-; Com on Indigenous Mnstrs Exec Coun Appointees New York NY 2009-** B Cleveland Heights OH 1963 d Julian & LaVene. BA SUNY; MA U Alaska Fairbanks 1988; PhD Indiana U 1991; MDiv Loyola U Chicago 1994. D 6/28/2003 P 2/14/2004 Bp Vincent Waydell Warner. m 5/1/1993 Nigel Harris. Dir Pstr Care MaineGeneral Med Cntr 2008-2011; St Steph's Epis Ch Oak Harbor WA 2007-2008; R St. Steph Epis Ch Oak Harbor 2006-2008; Coordnr Pstr Care 2001-2008; Assoc S Augustines In-The-Woods Epis Par; Dioc Coun Dio Olympia Seattle 2006-2008, First Nations Com, Chair 2004-2008. Auth, "The Necessity of Native Amer Autonomy for Successful Partnerships," *ATR*, Seabury Wstrn, 2010. Assn of Profsnl Chapl (APC) 2000. Polly Bond Awd ECom 2004; Polly Bond Awd ECom 2004; Bd Cert Chapl Assn of Profsnl Chapl 2001.

TABOR, Henry Caleb Coleman (NC) 408 Granville St., Oxford NC 27565 **S Andr's Ch Haw River NC 2016-; Vic S Cyp's Ch Oxford NC 2015-** B Durham NC 1987 s Larry & Amanda. BA Elon U 2009; MDiv Candler Sch of Div, Emory U 2013; COC VTS 2013. D 6/20/2015 Bp Michael B Curry P 12/20/2015 Bp Anne Hodges-Copple. m 10/10/2015 Logan Michael Brackett.

TACHAU, Charles Brandeis (Ky) 1080 Baxter Ave Apt 1, Louisville KY 40204 **Died 5/16/2016** B Louisville KY 1922 s Charles & Jean. Swarthmore Coll 1942; MDiv VTS 1963; JD U of Louisville 2048. D 6/18/1963 P 1/27/1964 Bp Charles Gresham Marmion. Ret 1989-2016; Archd Dio Kentucky Louisville KY 1986-1989, BEC 1968-1972; S Geo's Epis Ch Louisville KY 1975-1985; Vic S Andr's Ch Glasgow KY 1963-1965; Chapl Wstrn Kentucky St Coll Bowling Green KY 1963-1965.

TACKKETT, Antoinette Vance (Kan) 613 Elm St, Coffeyville KS 67337 **COM Dio Kansas Topeka KS 2012-** B Kansas City MO 1947 d Roy & June. BA U of Missouri 1968; MS Pittsburg St U Pittsburg KS 1990; Cert Kansas Sch For Mnstry Topeka KS 2011. D 6/5/2010 P 1/8/2011 Bp Dean E Wolfe. m 5/15/1990 Dale Tackkett c 8. Vic S Paul's Epis Ch Coffeyville KS 2012-2015, Vic 2012-, Assoc 2011. PEO 1979; Rotary Intl 2012.

TADKEN, Neil Alan (Los) 122 S. California Ave., Monrovia CA 91016 **S Lk's Epis Ch Monrovia CA 2013-; Prog Grp on GLBT Mnstrs Dio Los Angeles Los Angeles CA 2011-, Prog Grp on HIV/AIDS Mnstrs 2005-2011, Dnry 3 Treas 2005-** B New York NY 1960 s Donavan & Ellen. BA Occ 1983; MFA Cor 1985; MDiv ETSBH 2004. D 6/11/2005 Bp Chester Lovelle Talton P 1/14/2006 Bp Joseph Jon Bruno. m 7/11/2008 Frank A Slesinski. S Jn's Ch Indio CA 2013; Assoc R for Pstr Care S Jas Par Los Angeles CA 2005-2012; D St Jas the Great Epis Ch Newport Bch CA 2005-2006; Dir ACTION: AIDS CareTeams in our Neighborhoods 2004-2005; Bd Dir Epis Urban Intern Prog Los Angeles CA 2006-2010. Presidents Awd for Acad Excellence Claremont TS 2004; Ribbon of Hope Awd Acad of Television Art and Sciences 1997. revntadken@me.com

TAFLINGER, Mary (Ind) 5553 Leumas Rd, Cincinnati OH 45239 **Vic Trin Ch Lawrenceburg IN 1996-** B Findlay OH 1958 d Donald & Bette. BA Mia 1980; MDiv Harvard DS 1986. D 6/20/1987 P 5/1/1988 Bp William Grant Black. m 9/7/1991 Christopher Meshot c 1. R S Jn's Epis Ch Crawfordsvlle IN 1990-1995; S Alb's Epis Ch Of Bexley Columbus OH 1987-1990.

TAFOYA, Stacey T (Colo) 315 Leyden St, Denver CO 80220 **R Epiph Epis Ch Denver CO 2002-** B Denver CO 1970 s Timothy & Martha. BA Colorado Chr U 1992; MDiv Epis TS of the SW 2000. D 6/10/2000 P 12/10/2000 Bp William Jerry Winterrowd. m 7/11/1998 Sarah E Tafoya c 5. Cur The Ch Of Chr The King (Epis) Arvada CO 2000-2002. SS Alb & Sergius 2001; Soc Of S Mary 2001.

TAFT JR, Paul Eberhart (Tex) 5504 Andover Dr, Tyler TX 75707 B Houston TX 1939 s Paul & Harriet. BA Van 1961; MDiv VTS 1967. D 6/27/1967 Bp James Milton Richardson P 5/30/1968 Bp Scott Field Bailey. m 9/10/1960 Lucy Akerman c 3. All SS Epis Sch Tyler TX 2003-2007; R S Steph's Ch Liberty TX 1998-2003; S Jn's Epis Ch Austin TX 1992-1998; The Great Cmsn Fndt Houston TX 1992-1994; Non-par 1992; R S Alb's Epis Ch Waco TX 1979-1992; R H Trin Epis Ch Dickinson TX 1972-1979; Vic Chr Epis Ch Mexia Mexia TX 1968-1972; Vic S Mths Waco TX 1968-1972; Cur Chr Ch Cathd Houston TX 1967-1968.

TAGGART, Mary (NCal) D 6/10/2017 Bp Barry Leigh Beisner.

TAIT, Charles William Stuart (WA) PO Box 25541, Seattle WA 98165 **Died 2/13/2017** B Boston MA 1923 s Charles & Jennie. BA Harv 1947; BD VTS 1961. D 6/17/1961 Bp William Foreman Creighton P 6/9/1962 Bp Stephen F Bayne Jr. c 1. Ret 1988-2017; Salisbury Sch Salisbury CT 1971-1987; Salisbury Sch Dio Connecticut Meriden CT 1968-1987; Asst S Andr's Ch Wellesley MA 1964-1966; Serv Ch of Engl 1961-1962.

TAKACS, Erika (Pa) Saint Mark's Church, 1625 Locust St, Philadelphia PA 19103 **P S Mk's Ch Philadelphia PA 2011-** B West Chester PA 1973 d Frank & Norma. BS W Chester U of Pennsylvania 1995; MM Westminster Choir Coll Princeton NJ 1998; MDiv VTS 2007. D 12/15/2007 Bp Franklin Delton Turner P 6/26/2008 Bp C Wallis Ohl. m 8/2/2016 Daniel Shapiro. Chr Ch Alexandria VA 2009-2011, Cler Res 2007-2011.

TAKES WAR BONNETT, Ray Lee (SD) 840 Spruce St Lot 38, Rapid City SD 57701 **D 1988-** B Pine Ridge SD 1955 s Leo & Sophia. MDiv Sewanee: The U So, TS 1988. D 6/19/1988 Bp Craig Barry Anderson. m 1/4/1975 Delores Annette Broken Rope.

TALBERT, Thomas Keith (CGC) 701 N Pine St, Foley AL 36535 **R S Paul's Ch Foley AL 2001-** B Columbus GA 1955 s Thomas & Joyce. BS U of Alabama 1977; MDiv Sewanee: The U So, TS 1994. D 6/4/1994 P 2/1/1995 Bp Charles Farmer Duvall. m 3/12/1978 Carol Lynn Talbert c 2. S Paul's Epis Ch Daphne AL 1994-2001, Assoc 1994-2000.

TALBIRD JR, John D (ETenn) 3184 Waterfront Drive, Chattanooga TN 37419 **Mssnr Epis Cmsn of SE Tennessee Chattanooga TN 2008-** B Macon GA 1940 s John & Sara. BA U GA 1962; MDiv VTS 1965. D 6/26/1965 P 3/19/1966 Bp Randolph R Claiborne. m 6/26/1976 Mary Misiewicz c 5. Ch Of The Gd Shpd Lookout Mtn TN 1982-2006; Assoc Ch of the Gd Shpd Lookout Mtn TN 1982-1984; Ch Of The Incarn Gainesville FL 1967-1982; Dio Florida Jacksonville 1967-1982; Assoc Chapl Epis U Cntr Tallahassee FL 1967-1969; Asst S Lk's Epis Ch Atlanta GA 1965-1967. Auth, "The In Hse Critic," *Living Ch*, LivCh Fndt, Inc., 1977.

TALBOT, Jarod C D 6/3/2017 Bp Thomas Edward Breidenthal.

TALBOTT, John Thayer (WA) 8 Ledge Road, Old Saybrook CT 06475 **Cur St Ann's Old Lyme CT 2004-** B New York NY 1939 s Harold & Margaret. AS Odessa Coll 1964; BA U of Alabama 1983; MDiv Van 1985; CAS Sewanee: The U So, TS 1986. D 6/28/1986 P 2/8/1987 Bp George Lazenby Reynolds Jr. m 6/26/1965 Anne Insolving Talbott c 3. Assoc S Ann's Epis Ch Old Lyme CT 2000-2010; R S Aug's Epis Ch Washington DC 1992-2004; R Ch Of The Redeem Shelbyville TN 1986-1992; Min Serv Chr Ch (DofC) Cookeville TN 1981-1986. Auth, *Chr Wrshp: A Study Guide for Disciples.*

TALCOTT, Barbara Geer (NH) St. Mark's School, 25 Marlboro Rd., Southborough MA 01772 **Chapl & Chair, Rel Dept St Mk's Sch Southborough MA 2009-; S Paul's Sch Concord NH 2008-** B Boston MA 1961 d Hooker & Jane. BA Pr 1983; MBA Stan 1988; MTS Harvard DS 2003. D 6/25/2008 P 2/4/

2009 Bp Vicky Gene Robinson. m 12/3/1983 Douglas C Borchard c 3. Interfaith Chapl S Paul's Sch Concord NH 2008-2009.

TALIAFERRO, Bob (Mo) St. Paul's Episcopal Church, 1010 N Main St, Sikeston MO 63801 **S Paul's Epis Ch Sikeston MO 2016-** B Greensboro NC 1956 s Richard & Esther. AAS Oklahoma St U 1994; BA U of Cntrl Oklahoma 1996; MDiv Epis TS of the SW 1999. D 6/26/1999 P 12/21/1999 Bp Robert Manning Moody. m 11/3/1984 Margaret W Taliaferro c 3. R S Ptr's Epis Ch Amarillo TX 2009-2015; R S Ptr's Ch Tulsa OK 2001-2009; S Jn's Ch Norman OK 1999-2001; Cur S Jn's Ch Oklahoma City OK 1999-2000. frbobt@aol.com

TALK IV, John Gordon (NC) 304 S Ridge St, Southern Pines NC 28387 **Emm Par Epis Ch Sthrn Pines NC 2015-** B Dallas TX 1964 s John & Clarice. BA Centenary Coll. D 10/26/2002 P 6/21/2003 Bp Herbert Thompson Jr. m 8/30/2006 Shelly S Saff c 5. R Chr Ch Detroit MI 2009-2015; R Epis Ch Of The Epiph Wilbraham MA 2006-2009; Chapl Epis Ret Serv Cincinnati OH 2003-2006.

TALLANT, Greg (At) 3285 Kensington Road, Avondale Estates GA 30002 **R H Trin Par Decatur GA 2012-** B Cumming GA 1969 s Jimmy & Constance. BA Presb Coll 1991; No Georgia Coll and St U 1993; MDiv GTS 2007. D 12/21/2006 P 7/14/2007 Bp J Neil Alexander. m 11/16/1996 Emily George Tallant c 2. Assoc R S Ptr's Ch Rome GA 2007-2012.

TALLEVAST, William Dalton (CPa) University Med Ctr Dept of Pastoral Care, 1501 N Campbell Ave, Tucson AZ 85724 **Adj Fac Inst Of Rel Houston TX 1979-; Coordntr Of CPE H Sprt Hosp 1977-; Non-par 1972-** B Asheville NC 1941 s William & Irene. BA U NC 1965; BD VTS 1968; Duke 1970. D 6/17/1968 P 12/1/1968 Bp Matthew George Henry. c 1. Epis Pstr Counslg Cntr 1974-1975; Chapl Med Coll At Virginia Hosp In Richmond 1971-1973; P-in-c S Jn's Lousia VA 1971-1972; P-in-c S Lk's Ch Mineral Wells TX 1971-1972; Pstr Counslr Durham Mntl Hlth Clnc NC 1970-1971; Asst S Phil's Ch Durham NC 1970-1971; D S Andr's Ch Mt Holly NJ 1968-1970. Auth, "Eschatolgoy & Self-Integratn". AAPC, ACPE.

TALLMAN, Samuel Vose (WNC) St Mary of the Hills Church, PO Box 14, Blowing Rock NC 28605 **Cn Cathd Ch Of S Ptr St. Petersburg FL 2012-; Cur S Mary Of The Hills Epis Par Blowing Rock NC 2012-; Trst The GTS New York NY 2017-; Bd Pres Valle Crucis Conf Cntr Valle Crucis NC 2016-, Dir 2013-2016** B Richmond VA 1947 s Samuel & Stanley. BA Davidson Coll 1969; MBA U of Virginia 1971; MDiv GTS 2012. D 12/17/2011 P 6/23/2012 Bp Porter Taylor. m 2/14/2013 Michael Thomas Zuravel. Fllshp of St. Jn the Evang 2002. sam@stmaryofthehills.org

✠ TALTON, The Rt Rev Chester Lovelle (Los) 1528 Oakdale Road, Modesto CA 95355 B Eldorado AR 1941 s Chester & Mae. BS California St U 1965; BD CDSP 1970. D 6/27/1970 P 2/1/1971 Bp Chauncie Kilmer Myers Con 1/26/1991 for Los. m 5/25/2007 April G Talton. Provsnl Bp Epis Dio San Joaquin Modesto CA 2011-2014; Bp Suffr Dio Los Angeles Los Angeles CA 1991-2010, 1990-1991; R S Phil's Ch New York NY 1985-1990; Trin Educ Fund New York NY 1981-1985; Mssn Off Trin Par New York NY 1981-1985; Dio Minnesota Minneapolis MN 1980-1981; R S Phil's Ch S Paul MN 1976-1981; Ch Of The H Cross Chicago IL 1973-1976; All SS Ch Carmel CA 1971-1973; The Epis Ch Of The Gd Shpd Berkeley CA 1970-1971. DD CDSP 1992. cktalton@sbcglobal.net

TAMKE, Stephen C (LI) D 1/14/2017 Bp Lawrence C Provenzano.

TAMMEARU, Deborah Gibson (NY) 1047 Amsterdam Avenue, New York NY 10025 **Transition Mnstry Dio New York New York NY 1998-** B Passaic NJ 1947 d Charles & Sophia. BS FD 1970; MDiv GTS 1982. D 6/24/1982 Bp Richard Mitchell Trelease Jr P 2/1/1983 Bp Walter Decoster Dennis Jr. R S Thos Ch Mamaroneck NY 1994-2012; Wstrn Dutchess Mnstry Wappingers Falls NY 1985-1994; Cur Zion Epis Ch Wappingers Falls NY 1982-1984; New York Trng Sch For Dss. dtammearu@dioceseny.org

TAN, Wee Chung (Minn) B 1930 Trans 4/9/1973 Bp Philip Frederick McNairy.

TANABE, Irene (Haw) 1041 10th Ave, Honolulu HI 96816 **R Ch Of The Epiph Honolulu HI 2014-** B Tokyo Japan 1951 d Shinichiro & Toshiko. BA Wstrn Washington U 1977; JD U CO Sch of Law 1985; CDSP 2011. D 2/15/2011 Bp Gregory Harold Rickel. m 7/7/2001 Michael Burnap c 1. Assoc S Steph's Epis Ch Seattle WA 2013-2014; Cur S Mk's Cathd Seattle WA 2011-2013.

TAN CRETI, Michael J (Neb) 2051 N 94th St, Omaha NE 68134 B Carroll IA 1940 s Marcus & Irene. BA Dart 1962; MDiv Ya Berk 1967; Aquinas Inst of Theol 1980. D 6/22/1967 P 12/1/1967 Bp Gordon V Smith. m 6/3/1967 Jane Tan Creti. All SS Epis Ch Omaha NE 1977-2005; S Jn's Epis Ch Dubuque IA 1974-1977; S Paul's Epis Ch Grinnell IA 1969-1973; R All SS Ch.

TANG, Chris (Md) 3118 Cape Hill Ct, Hampstead MD 21074 **R Ch Of The H Comf Luthvle Timon MD 2011-, Cur 1996-1998** B Washington DC 1966 s Douglas & Karen. BA U of Maryland 1989; MDiv VTS 1996. D 6/15/1996 P 1/1/1997 Bp Robert Wilkes Ihloff. m 7/14/2013 Monica Marie Butta. R S Geo Ch Hampstead MD 1998-2011.

TANKERSLEY, Rebecca (Dal) 9845 Mccree Rd, Dallas TX 75238 **S Jas Ch Dallas TX 2015-** B Boston MA 1969 d Richard & Sara. BA U MI 1992; JD U MI Law 1995; MDiv Perkins TS 2015; MDiv SMU Perkins 2015. D 6/14/2014 P 4/11/2015 Bp Paul Emil Lambert. m 11/13/1999 Scott C Tankersley

c 3. D St Aug of Hippo Epis Ch Dallas TX 2014-2015. Auth, "Bass to Gr," *edod.org*, Epis Dio Dallas, 2015; Auth, "The Lives of Mâr Yahbh-Allâhâ and Rabban Sâwma," *The Perkins Stdt Journ*, Perkins TS at SMU, 2012. Perkins Prothro Fell Perkins TS at SMU 2014; Paul W. Qullian Awd in Homil Perkins TS at SMU 2014; Chas C. Selecman Awd in NT Gk Perkins TS at SMU 2013. rtankersley@stjamesdallas.com

TANNER, Michael Abbott (At) **Vic Ch Of The H Comf Atlanta GA 2006-** B Pascagoula MS 1948 s Abbott & Mary. AA Florida Coll 1968; AB U of Alabama 1973; JD U of Alabama Sch of Law 1976; MDiv Candler TS Emory U 2005; DMin Sewanee: The U So, TS 2013. D 12/21/2005 P 7/26/2006 Bp J Neil Alexander. m 6/2/1970 Cozette D Tanner c 5. Dio Atlanta Atlanta GA 2006-2014, Dn, N. Atlanta Convoc 2012-2014, Mem, Exec Bd 2007-2008.

TANTIMONACO, Daniel Frank (Az) 307 N Mogollon Trail, Payson AZ 85541 **Chapl Payson Reg Med Cntr Payson AZ 2008-; R S Paul's Ch Payson AZ 2006-** B Bridgeport CT 1953 s Anthony & Florence. Dip Epis TS of the SW 2005. D 4/17/2005 Bp Leo Frade P 11/5/2005 Bp Kirk Stevan Smith. m 9/25/1993 Roberta H Tantimonaco c 2. Cn Assoc. - Trin Cathd Dio Arizona Phoenix AZ 2005-2006.

TAPLEY, William Clark (WTex) 1604 W Kansas Ave, Midland TX 79701 **Ret 1996-** B Rochester NY 1930 s Iaian & Ethel. BA U Roch 1955; MA Col 1957; MDiv Bex Sem 1971; Ldrshp Acad for New Directions 1984; CPE 1986. D 6/12/1971 P 12/1/1971 Bp Harold Barrett Robinson. m 6/26/1961 Joyce E Tapley c 2. R Ch Of The Redeem Eagle Pass TX 1994-1996; Vic H Trin Carrizo Sprg TX 1994-1996; Vic S Jas Ch Monahans TX 1987-1994; Chapl Cedar Vale Cntr Cedar Vale KS 1986-1987; Chapl Prairie View Newton KS 1985-1986; 1981-1983; Ch Of The Epiph Sedan KS 1980-1985; R Dio Kansas Topeka KS 1980-1985; S Matt's Ch Cedar Vale KS 1980-1985; Vic SS Mary And Martha Of Bethany Larned KS 1977-1980; Convoc Secy 1977-1979; Pittsburgh Cathd Chapt 1975-1977; R All SS Ch Aliquippa PA 1975-1977; Asst Dn Trng Prog Min Barnesboro PA 1974-1975; P-in-c Ch of SS Thos and Lk Patton PA 1972-1975; Chapl Cresson & Ebensburg Schools For The Retarded 1972-1975; P-in-c S Thos Barnesboro PA 1972-1975; S Mk's Ch Johnstown PA 1972-1974; Chapl/Housemaster S Jas Sch Faribault MN 1971-1972; Com Dio Wstrn Kansas Hutchinson KS 1977-1980. Auth, "Happily Ever After Is No Accident: Premarital & Mar Counslg Prog"; Auth, "Finding Serenity: Sprtlty For Recovery". ERM. Rossiter Schlr 1981.

TAPPE, Elizabeth Peden (Fla) 2935 Tidewater St, Fernandina Beach FL 32034 B Hickory NC 1951 d James & Ann. AA S Marys Jr Coll Raleigh NC 1971; BA U NC 1973; MDiv VTS 1977. D 6/25/1977 P 5/6/1978 Bp William Gillette Weinhauer. c 2. R S Ptr's Ch Fernandina Bch FL 1998-2005; Stndg Com, Stndg Com Chair; Exec Coun (ex officio) Dio Florida Jacksonville 1998-2002, Int Assoc, Epis HS in Jacksonville, FL 1996-1997, Com on St of the Ch, and Chair; Com on Mnstry, Eccl Crt 1989-1996; R S Cathr's Ch Jacksonville FL 1997-1998; R Ch Of The Gd Shpd Jacksonville FL 1990-1996; Stndg Com, Bp Coadj Search Com, Com Trans Episcopate Dio Wstrn No Carolina Asheville NC 1987-1989, COM, Eccles Crt 1983-1986; R S Jn's Ch Asheville NC 1983-1989; Exec Coun Dio Connecticut Meriden CT 1981-1982, Deacons' Trng Prog; Epis Soc Serv, Com V COM 1977-1980; R S Mich's Ch Naugatuck CT 1980-1982; R S Andr's Ch Meriden CT 1979-1980, P-in-c 1978-1980, R 1978, Cur 1977-1978; Ya Berk New Haven CT 1978-1980.

TARBET JR, Bob (Tex) 121 Goliad St., Mc Gregor TX 76657 **Died 4/21/2016** B Dallas TX 1938 s Robert & Lula. BS USMA 1962; MDiv Epis TS of the SW 1973; MBA SMU 1984. D 1/3/1974 Bp James Milton Richardson P 12/14/1974 Bp Scott Field Bailey. m 7/28/1962 Beverly Bragg Tarbet c 2. 1998-2016; R Trin Epis Ch Marble Falls TX 1993-1997; Vic S Lk's Epis Ch Lindale TX 1992-1993; Other Cler Position The Great Cmsn Fndt Houston TX 1991-1993; 1990-1991; Chapl Off Of Bsh For ArmdF New York NY 1977-1991; Chapl US-Army 1977-1989; Chr Ch Matagorda TX 1974-1976; S Jn's Epis Ch Palacios TX 1974-1976; 2016.

TARBOX, Janet Ellen (USC) 318 Palmer Dr, Lexington SC 29072 B Lafayette IN 1953 d Gurdon & Milver. BA U of So Carolina 1975; MEd U of So Carolina 1978; MDiv VTS 1992. D 12/12/1992 P 6/12/1993 Bp William Arthur Beckham. Vic Ch Of The Ridge Trenton SC 2001-2008; Assoc S Thos' Ch Whitemarsh Ft Washington PA 1997-2000; Asst S Jas Par Wilmington NC 1995-1997; Asst Gr Epis Ch Camden SC 1992-1995.

TARDIFF, Richard A (Haw) PO Box 545, Kealakekua HI 96750 B Bangor ME 1952 s Raymond & Eleanor. B.S. U of Maine 1974; MDiv CDSP 2005; MEd U of Hawaii 2005; EdD U of Sarasota Orange CA 2005. D 11/27/2004 P 6/18/2005 Bp Mark Lawrence Macdonald. m 6/30/1979 Pamela S Vanwechel. R Chr Ch Kealakekua HI 2010-2017; R S Andr And S Jn Epis Ch SW Hbr ME 2006-2010; Educ Outreach Mgr Alaska Sealife Cntr 2006-2007; Assoc S Christophers Ch Anchorage AK 2005-2006.

TARPLEE JR, Cornelius (Nwk) 1405 Duncan St., Key West FL 33040 B Charles Town WV 1944 s Cornelius & Priscilla. BA Ob 1967; MA U of Wisconsin 1968; MDiv VTS 1980. D 6/14/1980 Bp Arnold M Lewis P 12/17/1980 Bp Ned Cole. m 2/1/1987 Judith Anne Baldwin c 3. R S Steph's Ch Millburn NJ

1992-2009; Vic Ch Of S Jn The Evang Dunbarton NH 1986-1992; Vic H Cross Epis Ch Weare NH 1986-1992; R S Thos Ch Hamilton NY 1980-1986.

TARPLEY, Kent W (SwVa) 375 East Pine St, Wytheville VA 24382 B Elgin IL 1949 s Kenneth & Vera. BA Trin Hartford CT 1971; MDiv SWTS 1974; MSW Loyola U 1981; Cert Shalem Sprtl Gdnc Prog 1996; Cert Ch Dvlpmt Inst 2003. D 6/8/1974 Bp Quintin Ebenezer Primo Jr P 12/21/1974 Bp James Winchester Montgomery. m 5/12/1979 Laura J Tarpley c 2. R S Jn's Epis Ch Wytheville VA 2008-2015; Curs Sprtl Advsr Dio Maine Portland ME 1997-2008; Curs Sprtl Advsr S Marg's Ch Belfast ME 1997-2008; Chapl Deacons Sch Dio Chicago Chicago IL 1995-1997; R S Paul's Ch Kankakee IL 1992-1997; Dn Lakeshore Deanry Dio Fond du Lac Appleton WI 1987-1991; R S Ptr's Epis Ch Sheboygan Falls WI 1985-1992; Asst S Lk's Ch Evanston IL 1978-1985; Monk S Greg Abbey Three Rivers MI 1976-1978; Asst The Epis Ch Of S Jas The Less Northfield IL 1974-1976; Exec Bd Dio SW Virginia Roanoke VA 2011-2014. Conf Of S Ben 1978; Soc Of S Jn The Evang 1998.

✠ **TARRANT, The Rt Rev John** (SD) 500 South Main Ave, Sioux Falls SD 57104 **Bp Dio So Dakota Pierre SD 2009-** B Kansas City MO 1952 s Robert & Leticia. BA MI SU 1974; MDiv VTS 1983. D 6/11/1983 Bp Charles Bennison Sr P 2/11/1984 Bp Alexander D Stewart Con 10/31/2009 for SD. m 6/29/1990 Patricia J Tarrant c 2. R Trin Epis Ch Pierre SD 2005-2009; Dio Wstrn Massachusetts Springfield 1996-2005; P Grtr Waterbury Mnstry Waterbury CT 1991-1996; Asst S Paul's Ch Holyoke MA 1989-1991; R S Paul's Epis Ch Stockbridge MA 1985-1991; S Paul's Epis Ch Gardner MA 1985-1989; Cur Ch Of The Atone Westfield MA 1983-1985. bishop.diocese@midcontwork.com

TARRANT, Paul John (RI) 39 Jeffrey Street, Edinburgh EH1 1DH Great Britain (UK) **Serving Scottish Epis Ch 1996-** B Barton-on-Sea UK 1957 BA U of Birmingham Birmingham Gb 1981; Chichester Theol Coll 1982. Trans 3/1/1990. Vic S Andr's By The Sea Little Compton RI 1995-1996; Bp Coadj Nomin Com Dio Rhode Island 1993-1994; Liturg & Mus Com Dio Massachusetts Boston MA 1991-1994; R Epis Ch Of S Thos Taunton MA 1990-1994; Serv Ch Of Engl 1982-1990; Birmingham U Theol Soc 1978-1979.

TARSIS, George Michael (O) 399 Jefferson Ave, Barberton OH 44203 B Chicago IL 1949 s George & Agnus. BBA U of Kentucky 1972; MBA U of Kentucky 1973; MDiv Epis TS in Kentucky 1985. D 6/1/1985 Bp Addison Hosea P 3/16/1986 Bp Don Adger Wimberly. m 1/8/1972 Mary K Tarsis c 2. R S Andr's Ch Barberton OH 2000-2011; R Trin Epis Ch Norfolk NE 1993-2000; Adv Ch Cynthiana KY 1985-1993.

TARTT JR, Jo Cowin (WA) 2727 34th Pl Nw, Washington DC 20007 **Nonpar 1982-** B Birmingham AL 1941 s Jo & Dorothy. BA W&L 1965; MDiv VTS 1969. D 6/6/1969 Bp George Mosley Murray P 6/1/1970 Bp William Foreman Creighton. m 1/11/1993 Judith W Tartt c 2. Gr Ch Washington DC 1971-1981; R Gr Georgetown MD 1971-1981; Asst Min S Mk's Ch Washington DC 1969-1971.

TARVER, Brian Michael (Tex) 14301 Stuebner Airline Rd, Houston TX 77069 **S Dunst's Epis Ch Houston TX 2015-** B Ft Worth TX 1985 s Lawrence & Holly. BFA U of No Texas 2009; MDiv Epis TS Of The SW 2015. D 6/20/2015 P 1/31/2016 Bp C Andrew Doyle. m 1/15/2010 Anna Tarver c 2.

TARWATER, Thomas William (ECR) 610 Le Point St, Arroyo Grande CA 93420 **D S Steph's Epis Ch Sn Luis Obispo CA 1992-; Chapl San Luis Obispo Cnty Sheriff Dept. San Luis Obispo CA 1992-** B Pasadena CA 1928 s Thomas & Alice. AA Pasadena City Coll 1955; BA California Sch for Deacons 1992. D 6/27/1992 Bp Richard Lester Shimpfky. m 6/5/2004 Patricia Myers c 4. Asst Chapl Atascadero St Hosp Atascadero CA 1994-2011; Chapl Vol California Men's Colony Prison San Luis Obispo CA 1992-2000; Chapl San Luis Obispo Cnty Jail 1988-2000; Chapl San Luis Obispo Cnty Gnrl Hosp 1987-1999. San Luis Obispo Cnty Publ Sfty Chapl Assn 1992.

TASY, Beverly Ann Moore (RG) St Christopher's Episcopal Church, 207 E Permian Dr, Hobbs NM 88240 **S Chris's Epis Ch Hobbs NM 2016-** B Utica NY 1956 d Catherine. BA Keuka Coll 1978; MDiv VTS 1985. D 6/8/1985 P 5/1/1989 Bp O'Kelley Whitaker. m 7/10/1982 Alexander Stephen Tasy. All SS Epis Ch Toledo OH 2006-2016; Gr In The Desert Epis Ch Las Vegas NV 2004; R S Clem's Epis Ch Inkster MI 1996-2004; Dir Of Campus Mnstry Dio Wstrn New York Tonawanda NY 1994-1996; Asst R All SS Epis Ch Pontiac MI 1990-1993. tasyb@stchristopherhobbs.com

TATE, Donald Steven (At) 201 Ellen Ct, Warner Robins GA 31088 B Chicago IL 1956 s Byron & Mildred. BA No Cntrl Coll 1979; MS Geo Wms 1982; PhD U IL 1988; MDiv Sewanee: The U So, TS 2002. D 4/5/2002 P 11/1/2002 Bp Creighton Leland Robertson. m 7/16/1994 Ruth Newman Tate c 1. R S Andr's Epis Ch Ft Vlly GA 2003-2015; Vic S Mary's Epis Ch Montezuma GA 2003-2014; Asst St Jas Epis Ch Sewanee TN 2002-2003. Ord of Julian of Norwich 1990.

TATE, Mary Katherine (Del) 18 Olive Ave, Rehoboth Beach DE 19971 B New York NY 1961 d Edward & Lucretia. BA Emory and Henry Coll 1983; MEd U of So Florida 1987; Luth TS at Gettysburg 2000. D 6/23/2001 Bp Charles Ellsworth Bennison Jr. m 5/24/2011 Sandra White c 1. Assoc for Fam Mnstrs S Ptr's Ch Lewes DE 2010-2012; Yth/YA/Higher Ed Dir Dio SW Florida

Parrish FL 2002-2009; Yth Coordntr The Epis Ch Of The Adv Kennet Sq PA 2001-2002, Yth Min 1996-2001.

TATE, Robert Lee (Pa) 7209 Lincoln Dr., Philadelphia PA 19119 **Assoc Cathd Ch of Our Sav Philadelphia PA 2010-; Search/Discernment Consult Dio Pennsylvania Philadelphia PA 2008-** B New York NY 1950 s Robert & Constance. BA Pr 1972; MDiv Ya Berk 1976. D 6/9/1979 P 3/29/1980 Bp Morgan Porteus. m 8/7/1977 Ann Greene c 2. R Ch Of S Mart-In-The-Fields Philadelphia PA 1995-2009; R Chr Ch Capitol Hill Washington DC 1984-1995; Asst Cathd Ch Of The Nativ Bethlehem PA 1980-1984; Chapl Wooster Sch Danbury CT 1979-1980. Epis Ch & Visual Arts Bd 1999; Epis Cler Assoc. of PA 1995; Int Mnstry Ntwk 2007.

TATE, Ruth Newman (At) 201 Ellen Ct, Warner Robins GA 31088 B Shattuck OK 1954 d Floyd & Erwina. BA Oklahoma City U 1976; MS U of Oklahoma 1978; PhD U of Oklahoma 1984; MDiv Sewanee: The U So, TS 2003. D 4/25/2003 Bp Creighton Leland Robertson P 2/29/2004 Bp J Neil Alexander. m 7/16/1994 Donald Steven Tate c 1. Assoc R S Andr's Epis Ch Ft Vlly GA 2003-2015; Assoc R S Mary's Epis Ch Montezuma GA 2003-2014. DOK 2002.

TATEM, Catherine Leigh (Roch) St Peter's Episcopal Church, 3825 E Henrietta Rd, Henrietta NY 14467 **R S Ptr's Epis Ch Henrietta NY 2012-** B Pittsfield MA 1961 d William & Sandra. BA Franklin & Marshall Coll 1983; MDiv Sewanee: The U So, TS 2008. D 6/7/2008 P 12/14/2008 Bp Duncan Montgomery Gray III. S Steph's Ch Columbia MS 2008-2012; P-in-c S Eliz's Mssn Collins MS 2008-2010. Auth, "Recon," *Recon and Healing*, The Epis Preaching Fndt, 2007; Bk Revs, "Ladies Aux," *Tuesday Morning*, Rev. Dr. Susanna Metz, 2007. Bp Leopoldo Alard Prize for Excellence in Liturg Readin U So TS 2008.

TATEM, Sandra Lou (Alb) 39 Greyledge Dr, Loudonville NY 12211 **D S Jn's Epis Ch Troy NY 2006-** B Johnson City NY 1932 d Charles & Ella. AA SUNY 1955. D 6/10/2006 Bp Daniel William Herzog. m 2/4/1956 William Arthur Tatem c 3.

TATEM, William Arthur (Alb) 39 Graystone Rd, Loudonville NY 12211 **D Trin Ch Watervliet NY 2006-** B 1932 s Frank & Margaret. BS Alfred U 1954; MS Alfred U 1962. D 6/10/2006 Bp Daniel William Herzog. m 2/4/1956 Sandra Lou Tatem c 3.

TATLIAN, Edward Anthony (CFla) 6400 N Socrum Loop Rd, Lakeland FL 33809 B Brooklyn NY 1937 s Charlies & Rose. Rec 10/22/2015 as Deacon Bp Gregory Orrin Brewer. m 5/20/2000 JoAnn Cronin Tatlian c 3.

TATLOCK, Alan Ralph (Alb) 2938 Birchton Rd, Ballston Spa NY 12020 B Amsterdam NY 1939 s Ralph & Irene. BS USNA 1964; MS Un Coll Schenectady NY 1974. D 10/10/1994 Bp David Standish Ball. m 1/18/1986 Jane Elizabeth Tatlock c 4. D Asst Calv Epis Ch Burnt Hills NY 1994-2009.

TATRO, Marie A (LI) St Gabriel's Episcopal Church, 331 Hawthorne St, Brooklyn NY 11225 **Vic Dio Long Island Garden City NY 2017-** B Westfield MA 1961 d Albert & Frances. BA Amh 1984; Juris Doctorate The CUNY 1991; MDiv GTS 2013; MDiv The GTS 2013. D 6/1/2013 P 12/7/2013 Bp Lawrence C Provenzano. m 8/21/2009 Meghan Faux c 4. S Gabr's Ch Brooklyn NY 2013-2015. mtatro@dioceseli.org

TATTERSALL, Elizabeth Russell (Nev) 1048 Wisteria Dr., Minden NV 89423 **P Ch Of Coventry Cross Minden NV 2012-, 2011-; Secy Stndg Com Dio Nevada NV 2006-; Chapl CAP NV 2002-; Chapl CAP NV 2001-** B Palo Alto CA 1961 d Richard & Ann. BA Stan 1984; PhD U of Nevada at Reno 2006. D 9/6/1996 P 3/15/1997 Bp Stewart Clark Zabriskie. m 4/3/1993 Stewart Tattersall. Cred Com GC Dep NV 2003-2006; P S Jn's In The Wilderness Ch Glenbrook NV 1996-2010. Mltry Chapl Assn 2003; Soc of Ord Scientists 2015.

TAUBE, Kimberly Lynn (WMo) 524 4th St, Boonville MO 65233 B Columbia MO 1968 d Barry & Linda. D 5/3/2014 Bp Martin Scott Field. m 5/22/1993 Gregory Paul Taube c 2.

TAUPIER, Linda (WMass) D 6/10/2017 Bp Doug Fisher.

TAVERNETTI, Suzanne (ECR) 7021 Timber Trail Loop, El Dorado Hills CA 95762 B Salinas CA 1938 d Loran & Olga. BA California Sch for Deacons 1989. D 6/24/1989 Bp Charles Shannon Mallory. m 6/6/1964 David E Tavernetti c 3. D In Charge S Lk's Ch Jolon CA 1993-2003; S Matt's Ch San Ardo CA 1993-1997; Asst S Mk's Ch King City CA 1989-1992. NAAD 1989.

TAVOLARO, Dante A (RI) D 6/3/2017 Bp W Nicholas Knisely Jr.

TAYEBWA, Onesmus OT (Los) 5700 Rudnick Ave, Woodland Hills CA 91367 **Prince Of Peace Epis Ch Woodland Hls CA 2013-** B Uganda 1962 s Christopher & Apophia. BA Afr Bible Coll; Dplma Theol BP McAllister Sem 1992; MACE Nairobi Intl U 2005. Trans 10/28/2014 as Priest Bp Joseph Jon Bruno. m 6/8/1998 Norah Tumuheirwe c 3.

TAYLOR, A(lice) Susan (NJ) 13 Forsythia Ct, Marlton NJ 08053 B Great Barrington MA 1938 d Bernherd & Irma. D 4/13/1985 Bp George Phelps Mellick Belshaw. m 9/10/1960 Wilber N Taylor c 3. D Ch Of The Div Love Montrose NY 1993-2004; Gr Ch In Haddonfield Haddonfield NJ 1990-1992, Par Secy 1967-1969.

TAYLOR, Andrea Maija St Davids Church, 205 Old Main St, South Yarmouth MA 02664 **R S Dav's Epis Ch S Yarmouth MA 2016-** B Milwaukee WI 1967 d John & Bettie. BA Pr 1988; MDiv Harvard DS 1994. D 6/4/1994 P 4/29/1995 Bp J Clark Grew II. m 6/16/1990 Jonathan B Taylor c 2. Assoc S Bon Ch Sarasota FL 2007-2016; DCE The Ch Of Our Redeem Lexington MA 1998-2007; Asst To The R S Ptr's Ch Beverly MA 1997-1998; Asst Min All SS' Epis Ch Belmont MA 1994-1997. andi1@rcn.com

TAYLOR, Arnold Godfrey (WA) 507 3rd St SE, Washington DC 20003 **R Emer Chr Ch Durham Par Nanjemoy MD 2000-, R 1971-1993; Ret Epis Ch 1993-** B Providence RI 1925 s Leander & Viola. BA Pacific U 1951; MDiv VTS 1968. D 6/29/1968 P 6/5/1969 Bp William Foreman Creighton. m 7/3/1954 Lilian B Taylor c 3. Mem Inter-racial T/F 1975-1977; Asst Chr Epis Ch Clinton MD 1968-1971; News Photographer Washington Evening Star 1951-1965; Dioc Coun Dio Washington Washington DC 1981-1983. Washington DC Epis Cler Assn 1968.

TAYLOR, Barbara Brown (At) PO Box 1030, Clarkesville GA 30523 **Butman Prof of Rel & Philos Piedmont Coll Demorest GA 1998-** B Lafayette IN 1951 d Earl & Rebecca. BA Emory U 1973; MDiv Ya Berk 1976. D 6/11/1983 P 5/1/1984 Bp Charles Judson Child Jr. m 11/20/1982 Ernest E Taylor, Jr c 2. R Gr-Calv Epis Ch Clarkesville GA 1992-1997; All SS Epis Ch Atlanta GA 1983-1992; Asst Dir of Dvlpmt Yale TS New Haven CT 1981-1982; Asst to Dn Candler TS Atlanta GA 1976-1981. Auth, *Leaving Ch*, HarperSanFrancisco, 2006; Auth, *The Seeds of Heaven*, Westminster Jn Knox, 2004. Hon DD U So 2005; Hon DD SWTS 2002; Hon DD VTS 2001; Hon DD Berk 1997.

TAYLOR, Brenda M (CPa) 4284 Beaufort Hunt Dr, Harrisburg PA 17110 **D S Phil's Ch Columbus OH 1995-** B Harrisburg PA 1942 d Patrick & Beulah. D 10/28/1995 Bp Herbert Thompson Jr. m 11/22/2002 Antonio Kelly. Epis Ch Of The Resurr Longwood FL 2004-2012.

TAYLOR, Brian Clark (Chi) 1401 Los Arboles Avenue Northwest, Albuquerque NM 87107 **Fac CREDO Inst 2005-** B Sacramento CA 1951 s William & Marylou. BA Goddard Coll 1973; MA Goddard Coll 1975; MDiv CDSP 1981. D 6/27/1981 P 5/30/1982 Bp William Edwin Swing. m 12/30/1978 Susanna H Taylor c 2. R S Mich And All Ang Ch Albuquerque NM 1983-2013; Asst Gr Cathd San Francisco CA 1981-1983; Chair T/F on the Study of Mar 2012-2015; Mem Coun of Advice to the Pres of the HOD 2006-2009. Auth, "Becoming Human," Cowley Pub, 2005; Auth, "Becoming Chr," Cowley Pub, 2002; Auth, "Setting the Gospel Free," Continuum Pub, 1996; Auth, "Sprtlty for Everyday Living," Liturg Press, 1989. Hon Doctorate of Div CDSP 2004. bctaylor@me.com

TAYLOR, Bruce W (VI) The Valley, Box 65, Virgin Gorda VI VG1150 B McKinney TX 1947 s Willard & Nadia. BA Wstrn St Coll of Colorado 1969; MS Our Lady of the Lake U 1974; MDiv Epis TS of the SW 1985. D 6/13/1985 Bp Donis Dean Patterson P 2/24/1986 Bp John Herbert MacNaughton. m 2/24/2001 Nancy Taylor c 6. St Mary the Vrgn Ch Vrgn Gorda VG 1150 1995-1998; Ch Of The Resurr Windcrest TX 1990-1991; Gr Ch Cuero TX 1989; Chr Epis Ch San Antonio TX 1985-1988. Associated Parishes.

TAYLOR, Carlene Holder (Ga) D 6/22/2013 Bp Scott Anson Benhase.

TAYLOR, Charles Dean (At) 1600 Southmont Dr, Dalton GA 30720 **Int The Ch Of Our Sav Atlanta GA 2017-** B Auburn AL 1955 s Bobby & Celia. BA U So 1978; MDiv VTS 1984. D 7/8/1984 Bp William Evan Sanders P 4/1/1985 Bp William F Gates Jr. c 3. S Cathr's Epis Ch Marietta GA 2015-2017; Ch Of Our Sav Jacksonville FL 2014-2015; Gr Epis Ch Gainesville GA 2012-2013; Int S Bon Ch Sarasota FL 2011-2012; S Jas Epis Ch Marietta GA 2010-2011; R S Mk's Ch Dalton GA 1990-2010; Assoc S Fran In The Fields Harrods Creek KY 1987-1990; D Ch Of The Adv Nashville TN 1984-1987. deantaylor1955@gmail.com

TAYLOR, Charles Gary (CNY) 40 South Main, PO Box 370, New Berlin NY 13411 **Died 4/16/2016** B Barnesboro PA 1951 s Charles & Lois. BA U Pgh 1972; MDiv Bex Sem 1979. D 6/9/1979 P 12/1/1979 Bp Robert Bracewell Appleyard. m 1/1/1972 Donna Lee Taylor c 2. Emm Ch Norwich NY 2009-2016; S Andr's Ch New Berlin NY 1985-2016; S Matt's Ch So New Berlin NY 1985-2016; S Mk's Ch Johnstown PA 1981; S Thos Ch Nthrn Cambria PA 1980-1985; Ch of SS Thos and Lk Patton PA 1980-1981; Vic S Thos Barnesboro PA 1979-1985.

TAYLOR, Charles Henry (WNC) 84 Keasler Rd, Asheville NC 28805 B Lockport NY 1939 s Henry & Mildred. BS SUNY 1962; STM PDS 1967; MA S Thos U Miami FL 1990. D 6/17/1967 P 12/21/1967 Bp Lauriston L Scaife. m 1/7/1990 Sheila Taylor c 2. R S Jn's Ch Asheville NC 1990-2005; Vic S Mich's Ch SW Ranches FL 1987-1990; R Ch Of The H Redeem Lake Worth FL 1984-1987; R Zion Epis Ch Palmyra NY 1975-1984; R St Johns Epis Youngstown NY 1969-1975; Cur Gr Ch Merchantville NJ 1967-1969.

TAYLOR, Charles Wellington (Cal) 3518 CJ Barney Dr NE Apt T2, Washington DC 20018 **Died 7/3/2016** B Dayton OH 1937 s Charles & Georgia. BA W Virginia U 1958; MDiv Bex Sem 1967; DMin Wesley TS 1979. D 6/17/1967 P 12/1/1967 Bp Roger W Blanchard. c 4. Asst S Steph's Par Bel Tiburon CA 1998; Prof Of Pstr Theol CDSP CA 1987-2016; S Clare's Epis Ch Pleasanton CA 1985; Prof CDSP Berkeley CA 1978-1998; Assoc Prof Of Pstr Theol CDSP CA 1978-1987; R Ch Of The H Comf Washington DC 1971-1978; Chapl How Washington DC 1970-1971; ECEC 1968-1969; Chapl OH SU Columbus OH 1967-1968; Asst S Steph's Epis Ch And U Columbus OH 1967-1968. Auth, "Premarital Gdnc," Fortress Press, 1999; Auth, "The Skilled Pstr," Fortress Press, 1991.

TAYLOR, Cynthia nan (Ga) 973 Hunting Horn Way W, Evans GA 30809 **H Comf Ch Martinez GA 2006-; R Ch of the H Comf Martinez GA 1999-** B Indianapolis IN 1955 d Robert & Janice. BA U of So Carolina 1977; MDiv VTS 1986; DMin Sewanee: The U So, TS 2007. D 6/15/1986 P 5/15/1987 Bp Christopher FitzSimons Allison. S Paul's Ch Augusta GA 1991-2006; Cn The Amer Cathd of the H Trin Paris 75008 1988-1991; All SS Ch Florence SC 1986-1988; Asst All SS Florence SC 1986-1988.

TAYLOR, David Edwin (SwVa) PO Box 527, Rocky Mount VA 24151 **Trin Epis Ch Rocky Mt VA 2013-** B Carbondale IL 1965 s Robert & Ruby. BA Sthrn Illinois U 1988; MDiv Midwestern TS 1998; Nash 1999. D 2/27/1999 P 10/18/1999 Bp Keith Lynn Ackerman. m 7/16/1988 Angela D Taylor c 4. R S Paul's Ch Lancaster NH 2011-2013; R S Andr's Ch Carbondale IL 2003-2008; R S Barn Ch Havana IL 2000-2003; Cur S Lk's Ch In The Cnty Of Buck Newtown PA 1999-2000.

TAYLOR, David Kenneth (Nwk) 124 Franklin Ct, Flemington NJ 08822 **1999-; 1996-** B Trenton NJ 1942 s Earl & Anne. BA W Maryland Coll 1964; MDiv PDS 1967; MA Univ of Pennsylvania 1970; Ph.D. Ford 1982. D 4/22/1967 P 10/1/1967 Bp Alfred L Banyard. m 12/30/1995 S Christine Jochem. Assoc P Trin Cathd Trenton NJ 1987-1996; 1976-1987; R S Geo's Ch Pennsville NJ 1974-1976; R Sts Steph and Barn Epis Ch Florence NJ 1970-1974; Cur H Apos Epis Ch Trenton NJ 1967-1970. Auth, *God & Being in Thought of Austin Farrer*, 1991. Cath Theol Soc of Amer 1994; Soc of Chr Philosophers 1986. Phi Beta Kappa; Hon Cn 93 Trin Cathd.

TAYLOR, Edgar Garland (La) 1716 Soniat St, New Orleans LA 70115 **Trin Ch New Orleans LA 2014-** B Pittsburgh PA 1965 s Edgar & Guion. BA Ya 1987; EdM Harvard Grad Sch of Educ 1991; MDiv VTS 2011. D 6/11/2011 Bp Laura Ahrens P 1/20/2012 Bp Wayne Wright. m 8/10/1991 Karen Taylor c 3. S Anne's Epis Sch Middletown DE 2011-2014. gtaylor@trinitynola.com

TAYLOR, Edward Norman (Mich) 80 Wellesley Street East #904, Toronto M4Y 2B5 Canada B Hamilton ON CA 1943 s Russell & Joan. LTh U Tor 1972. D 5/1/1972 P 1/1/1973 Bp The Bishop Of Saskatoon. m 8/27/1966 Beverley Dawn Taylor c 3. All SS Ch Prudenville MI 1979-1982; Trin Ch Emmetsburg IA 1976-1979; Serv Ch Of Can 1972-1975.

TAYLOR, George Williamson (NY) 311 Huguenot St, New Rochelle NY 10801 **Dio New York New York NY 2015-** B 1965 s Williamson & Monica. BA U of Massachusetts 1989; MDiv Andrews U 2006; MDiv Andrews U 2006; Angl Stds GTS 2012. D 3/7/2015 P 9/19/2015 Bp Andrew Marion Lenow Dietsche. m 6/24/1998 Josephine Taylor c 2.

TAYLOR, Gloria Atkinson (NI) 1809 Holly Ln, Munster IN 46321 B New York NY 1929 d Walter & Margaret. Dioc Sch of Faith & Mnstry So Bend IN 1989. D 6/12/1989 Bp Francis Campbell Gray. m 2/23/1947 Frederic Edward Taylor. Trin Ch Michigan City IN 1989-2011; Dio Nthrn Indiana So Bend IN 1989-1999; AIDS Coordntr S Paul's Epis Ch Munster IN 1989-1993. NAAD; Sacr Ord of Deacons.

TAYLOR, Gordon Kevin (Los) 6503 Stone Crest Way, Whittier CA 90601 **Died 9/18/2016** B Dublin IE 1938 s Benjamin & Florence. GOE Ch of Ireland Theol 1973. Trans 8/1/1982. Asst S Mths' Par Whittier CA 2012-2016; Ret 2004-2016; Asst S Marg's Epis Ch So Gate CA 2004-2011; P-in-c S Geo's Mssn Hawthorne CA 1999-2001; R S Mich The Archangel Par El Segundo CA 1994-2004; S Jn's Mssn La Verne CA 1994; R St. Mk's Downey CA 1984-1994; S Mk's Par Downey CA 1984-1993; S Wilfrid Of York Epis Ch Huntington Bch CA 1982-1984; Cur S Lk Belfast Ireland 1973-1976.

TAYLOR, Gregory Blackwell (Va) 250 Pantops Mountain Rd. Apt. 5407, Charlottesville VA 22911 **Non-par 1967-** B Cleveland OH 1930 s Blackwell & Helen. BA Ya 1952; JD Harv 1957; MDiv VTS 1963. D 6/15/1963 P 12/1/1963 Bp Nelson Marigold Burroughs. m 9/8/1956 Anne Barbour Taylor c 2. Chapl Colleges & Universities Cleveland OH 1963-1967.

TAYLOR, James Delane (CFla) 10 Fox Cliff Way, Ormond Beach FL 32174 B Nashville GA 1946 s John & Mary. BS Florida St U 1969; MDiv Nash 1983. D 6/24/1983 P 1/10/1984 Bp William Hopkins Folwell. m 3/12/1969 Glenda Taylor c 1. R S Mary's Epis Ch Daytona Bch FL 2001-2012; R S Steph's Ch Lakeland FL 1988-2000; Cur/Assoc S Jas Epis Ch Ormond Bch FL 1983-1988. Life Mem Bro of S Andr, Ord of S Lk 1998; Life Mem OSL 1999.

TAYLOR JR, James Edward (SC) 1150 East Montague Ave., North Charleston SC 29405 **R S Thos Epis Ch N Charleston SC 2003-; Treas So Carolina Charleston SC 2013-, Stwdshp Chair 2011-2012** B Wilmington NC 1960 s James & Ellen. BA U NC Wilmington 1988; MDiv VTS 1992; DMIN VTS 2014. D 6/20/1992 Bp Huntington Williams Jr P 12/22/1992 Bp Brice Sidney Sanders. Assoc R S Jn's Epis Ch Fayetteville NC 1999-2003; R Gr Ch Whiteville NC 1996-1999; R Emm Ch Farmville NC 1992-1994.

TAYLOR, James Maurice (Pa) 160 Marvin Rd, Elkins Park PA 19027 **Ch Of S Mart-In-The-Fields Philadelphia PA 2012-; Kindergarten Tchr Wyncote Elem Sch Wyncote PA 2008-** B Washington DC 1966 s Volney & Janise. BA Emory and Henry Coll 1988; MDiv VTS 1994; MA La Salle U 2007; Cert La Salle U 2011. D 6/11/1994 P 12/14/1994 Bp Peter J Lee. m 8/31/2002 Douglas K Alderfer. First Grade Tchr Myers Elem Sch Elkins Pk PA 2005-2008; R Gr

Epiph Ch Philadelphia PA 1998-2005; Asst Chr Ch Philadelphia Philadelphia PA 1994-1998.

✠ **TAYLOR, The Rt Rev John Harvey** (Los) 19968 Paseo Luis, Yorba Linda CA 92886 **Bp Coadj Dio Los Angeles Los Angeles CA 2017-; Vic St. Jn Chrys Ch And Sch 2004-** B Detroit MI 1954 s Harvey & Jean. BA U CA 1980; MDiv Claremont TS 2003. D 6/7/2003 P 1/24/2004 Bp Joseph Jon Bruno Con 7/8/2017 for Los. m 7/6/2002 Kathy OConnor c 3. Vic S Jn Chrys Ch Rcho Sta Marg CA 2004-2017; Asst S Andr's Par Fullerton CA 2003-2004. "Patterns Of Abuse," Wynwood Press, 1989. Hon Cn Dio Los Angeles 2008. jtaylor@ladiocese.org

TAYLOR, Josephine A (SVa) 3100 Shore Dr Apt 625, Virginia Beach VA 23451 **S Aid's Ch Virginia Bch VA 2005-** B Richmond VA 1933 d Robert & Josephine. BA Rich 1954; MA Tul 1965; MDiv VTS 1982. D 6/23/1984 Bp Peter J Lee P 5/11/1985 Bp David Henry Lewis Jr. c 1. Assoc Chr and S Lk's Epis Ch Norfolk VA 2008-2012; Int S Aid's Epis Ch Virginia Bch VA 2005-2007; Par Assoc Chr and S Lk's Ch Norfolk VA 2004-2005; Int Hungars Par Machipongo VA 2002-2004; Int Abingdon Epis Ch White Marsh VA 2001-2002; Ch Of The Epiph Norfolk VA 2000-2001; Int The Epis Ch Of The Adv Norfolk VA 1999-2000; Int S Geo's Epis Ch Newport News VA 1998-1999; Int All SS Epis Ch Reisterstown MD 1996-1998; S Geo Ch Hampstead MD 1987-1996; Asst R S Paul's Ch Wallingford CT 1984-1987; COM Dio Maryland Baltimore MD 1995-1997, Dioc Coun 1990-1994.

TAYLOR, LeBaron (SwVa) P.O. Box 709, Covington VA 24426 **R Emm Ch Covington VA 2008-** B Mobile AL 1939 s Herbert & Lucille. BS Alabama St U 1961; MDiv Claremont TS 1990; CAS VTS 1995. D 6/3/1995 P 12/9/1995 Bp Robert Jefferson Hargrove Jr. c 1. S Steph's Epis Ch Winston Salem NC 2003-2007; S Eliz Epis Ch King NC 2003-2005; S Aug's Coll Raleigh NC 2001-2003; S Thos Ch Minneapolis MN 1997-1998; D Ch Of The H Cross Shreveport LA 1995-1997; Pstr Methodist La & CA 1988-1994.

TAYLOR, Linda Sue (ECR) 1809 Palo Santo Dr, Campbell CA 95008 **Mem, Bd Dir Shires Memi Cntr San Jose CA 2009-** B Fort Worth TX 1943 d Elmo & Irma. BD San Jose St U 1977; MS U CA 1981; MBA San Jose St U 1991; MDiv CDSP 1999. D 6/26/1999 P 1/22/2000 Bp Richard Lester Shimpfky. c 2. R S Mk's Epis Ch Santa Clara 2001-2014; Assoc Trin Cathd San Jose CA 2000-2001; D S Andr's Ch Saratoga CA 1999-2000; VP, Bd Trst Dio El Camino Real Salinas CA 2012-2013, Title IV Intake Off 2011-, Mem, Bd Trst 2010-2013, Pres, Stndg Com 2007-2008, Secy, Stndg Com 2005-2007, Mem, COM 2001-2005.

TAYLOR, Lloyd Hopeton (LI) 13304 109th Ave, South Ozone Park NY 11420 B 1942 s Isaac & Henrietta. DIT Untd Theol Coll of The W Indies Kingston Jm 1974; BA U of The W Indies 1974; BBA CUNY 1989. D 6/29/1974 P 1/1/1975 Bp The Bishop Of Belize. m 1/19/2005 Yvette V Taylor c 2. R S Jn's Ch So Ozone Pk NY 1983-2014; Dn Forest Pk Dnry.

TAYLOR, Margaret Anne (Ala) Po Box 361352, Birmingham AL 35236 B Pasadena CA 1945 d James & Luada. BA Colorado Coll 1967; MA Fairfield U 1982; MDiv GTS 1990. D 6/23/1990 P 1/2/1991 Bp George Nelson Hunt III. The Epis Ch of the H Apos Hoover AL 1995-2011; Par Dvlpmt Dio Alabama Birmingham 1994-1998, 1994-1995, Evang Com 1991-1994, COM, Chair 1999-, Chair T/F Human Sxlty 1991-1993; Asst R Ch Of The Nativ Epis Huntsville AL 1990-1994; Alum Exec Com The GTS New York NY 1998-2003.

TAYLOR, Marjorie B (Mich) St. John's Episcopal Church, 26998 Woodward Ave, Royal Oak MI 48067 **S Jn's Ch Royal Oak MI 2014-** B Buckhannon WV 1965 d John & Martha. BA Nthrn Arizona U 1989; MDiv SWTS 2010. D 6/5/2010 Bp Robert John O'Neill P 1/29/2011 Bp Wendell Nathaniel Gibbs Jr. m 8/13/1994 Mark A Miliotto c 2. Assoc Chr Ch Cranbrook Bloomfield Hills MI 2010-2014. bethtaylor@stjohnro.org

TAYLOR, Mary Ann Demetsenaere (Me) 83 Indian Hill Ln, Frankfort ME 04438 **P-in-c, Part Time S Fran By The Sea 2005-** B Newark NY 1936 d Achiel & Emma. BA Coll of New Rochelle 1958; S Bonaventure U 1966; U Roch 1974; MDiv Bex Sem 1987. D 11/17/1988 P 5/18/1989 Bp William George Burrill. S Jas Ch Old Town ME 2005; R S Jn's Epis Ch Honeoye Falls NY 1989-1994; Cmncatn Off Dio Rochester Henrietta 1988-1989. EWC, ADLMC, Associated Parishes.

TAYLOR, Norman Dennis (Oly) 4218 Montgomery Place, Mount Vernon WA 98274 B Evanston IL 1948 s Bernard & Joy. ADN Everett Cmnty Coll 1977; AA Skagit Vlly Coll 1977; Cert Dioc TS 1994. D 7/7/2001 Bp Vincent Waydell Warner. m 3/13/1971 Mary Ann Krahe c 1. Steph Mnstry Awd NAAD 2007.

TAYLOR, Patricia Lois (Oly) 75 E Lynn St Apt 104, Seattle WA 98102 B Vancouver BC CA 1932 d William & Winifred. EdD U of British Columbia Vancouver Bc CA 1953; ADN Shoreline Cmnty Coll 1975; Cert Olympia TS 1977. D 6/30/1984 Bp Robert Hume Cochrane P 11/22/1996 Bp Vincent Waydell Warner. m 3/27/1953 James Vinton Taylor. Fac Dio Olympia Dioc Sch Of Mnstry & Theol 2004-2009; Ch In The Wrld Cmsn Dio Olympia Seattle 2000-2001, Bd 1993-1999, Hosp Chapl Coordntr 1986-1992; All SS Epis Ch Seattle WA 1996-2001; D S Geo's Ch Seattle WA 1992-1995; Cath Chapt S Mk's Cathd Seattle WA 1991-1994; Trin Par Seattle WA 1986-1991; Cler Res

Epiph Par of Seattle Seattle WA 1984-1986. Wmn Of Light Awd Homeless Wmn Cltn, Seattle 2000.

TAYLOR, Paul N. (WMass) 34 Boylston Cir., Shrewsbury MA 01545 B Brighton MA 1943 s David & Erna. BA MacMurray Coll 1965; BD Yale DS 1968; STM Yale DS 1970; Tubingen Universitat 1974; PhD U of Iowa 1979. D 6/22/1968 Bp Anson Phelps Stokes Jr P 5/1/1969 Bp Joseph Warren Hutchens. m 6/29/1987 Andrea Taylor c 2. R Trin Epis Ch Shrewsbury MA 1988-2007; Ch Of S Jn The Evang Duxbury MA 1984-1987; Asst Prof Of Philos & Rel Iowa St U 1975-1983; Non-par 1971-1983; Asst S Jn's Ch No Haven CT 1968-1970.

TAYLOR JR, Phil (WTex) 2086 Grand Loop, Boerne TX 78006 **Died 6/28/2017** B Philadelphia PA 1945 s Philip & Jeanette. Leh 1964; BS Parsons Coll 1967; MDiv PDS 1972; DMin McCormick TS 1987. D 6/6/1970 Bp Robert Lionne DeWitt P 6/23/1971 Bp Harold Cornelius Gosnell. m 6/20/1970 Helen Taylor c 3. R S Andr's Ch Port Isabel TX 1999-2010; Calv Ch Menard TX 1994-1999; Vic Trin Ch Jct TX 1994-1999; Vic All SS Epis Ch Pleasanton TX 1993-1994; S Mths Devine TX 1993-1994; Assoc S Dav's Epis Ch San Antonio TX 1978-1993; P-in-c Ch Of Our Sav Aransas Pass TX 1974-1978; Trin-By-The-Sea Port Aransas TX 1974-1978; Asst S Lk's Epis Ch San Antonio TX 1971-1974; Chapl Intern Bryan Memi Hosp Lincoln NE 1970-1971.

TAYLOR, Phyllis Gertrude (Pa) 401 Central Ave, Cheltenham PA 19012 B Fort Erie ON CA 1944 d Garnet & Beatrice. BA U Tor 1967; BD Melbourne Coll of Div 1971. D 6/15/1985 P 5/31/1986 Bp Lyman Cunningham Ogilby. m 9/10/1966 John M Taylor. Trin Ch Oxford Philadelphia PA 1995-2007; Int S Thos' Ch Whitemarsh Ft Washington PA 1993-1995; Int S Ptr's Ch Glenside PA 1992-1993; Int Trin Ch 1990-1991; Cur Trin Ch 1987-1990; Chapl Wissahickon Hoispice 1987-1990; P-Intern Ch Of The Mssh Lower Gwynedd PA 1985-1987. Auth, "Epis Evang Fndt Best Sermon Competition Winner 93," *Grand Winner 94.* Soc of S Jn the Div. Best Sermon Competion Grand Winner Epis Evang Fndt 1994; Best Sermon Competition Winner, 1993 Epis Evang Fndt 1993.

✠ TAYLOR, The Rt Rev Porter (WNC) 44 Ravenwood Dr, Fletcher NC 28732 B Rock Hill SC 1950 s Richard & Sarah. BA U NC 1972; MA U of So Carolina 1974; PhD Emory U 1983; MDiv Sewanee: The U So, TS 1993. D 6/6/1993 Bp William Evan Sanders P 4/13/1994 Bp Bertram Nelson Herlong Con 9/18/2004 for WNC. m 5/13/1972 Jo Abbott Taylor c 2. Bp of Wstrn No Carolina Dio Wstrn No Carolina Asheville NC 2004-2016; R S Greg The Great Athens GA 1996-2004; Asst S Paul's Ch Franklin TN 1993-1996. Auth, "To Dream As God Dreams," Green Berry Press, 2000. portertaylor80@gmail.com

TAYLOR, Ralph Douglas (Az) St Philips in the Hills, PO Box 65840, Tucson AZ 85728 B Niagra Fall NY 1945 s Ralph & Ruth Ann. BSPA U of Arizona 1978. D 1/26/2008 Bp Kirk Stevan Smith. c 9.

TAYLOR JR, Raymond George (NC) 461 Pemaquid Harbor Rd, Pemaquid ME 04558 B New Brighton PA 1939 s Raymond & Florence. BS Buc 1959; BD EDS 1962; MS U of Pennsylvania 1964; EdD U of Pennsylvania 1966; MPA Penn 1977; MBA U of Sthrn Maine 1986; PhD GTF 1996. D 6/9/1962 Bp Joseph Gillespie Armstrong P 3/2/1963 Bp Andrew Y Tsu. m 6/1/1959 Christine Mary Morton c 2. R Ch of Engl St Geo Malaga 2010-2011; R Ch of Engl St Geo Malaga 2004-2006; S Thos Ch Oriental NC 1997-1990; Assoc S Paul's Epis Ch Smithfield NC 1987-1990; Prof No Carolina St U 1986-2011; Vic S Mary's Ch Warwick RI 1970-1977; Cur S Mart-in-theFields Chestnut Hill PA 1962-1966. Intellectual Benefit to Soc Amer Mensa 2011; Edelman Laureate Internat'l Forum Oprtns Resrch and Mgmt Sciences 2007.

TAYLOR, Richard Louis (WLa) 108 Jason Ln, Natchitoches LA 71457 **LocTen S Paul's Ch Winnfield LA 2002-; Ret 1998-** B Corbin KY 1933 s Bryan & Sarah. BA Piedmont Coll 1959; MA E Carolina U 1962; MDiv Sewanee: The U So, TS 1975. D 6/11/1975 P 12/22/1975 Bp Christoph Keller Jr. m 1/28/1966 Marilyn Taylor c 5. Int Chr Memi Ch Mansfield LA 2000-2001; Int S Tim's Ch Alexandria LA 1998-1999; R Trin Epis Ch Natchitoches LA 1982-1998; R Ch Of The H Comf Angleton TX 1980-1982; R S Andr's Ch Marianna AR 1975-1980. Paul Harris Fllshp Rotary Club Intl 2006; Fell, Univ Va The Asia Soc 1964.

TAYLOR, Robert (NC) 813 Darby Street, Raleigh NC 27610 **S Ambroses Ch Raleigh NC 2012-** B Henderson NC 1977 s Robert & Levonia. BS No Carolina St U 2000; MS Stan 2002; MDiv GTS 2009. D 5/6/2009 Bp Dorsey Henderson P 11/21/2009 Bp James Monte Stanton. Mssnr S Mich And All Ang Ch Dallas TX 2009-2012. jtaylor@stambroseraleigh.org

TAYLOR, Robert C (USC) 511 Roper Mtn Rd, Greenville SC 29615 **Pstr All SS' Quilmes 1981-; Int S Jn's Jersey City 1981-** B Brooklyn NY 1945 s Mortimer & Constance. LTh Gregorian U; MS Rutgers The St U of New Jersey. Rec 2/5/1981 Bp Robert Campbell Witcher Sr. m 1/24/1989 Margaret Taylor. Dio Upper So Carolina Columbia SC 2014-2017, 2007-2014; Trin Ch Paterson NJ 1986; Exec Coun Appointees New York NY 1981-1984; Serv RC Ch 1971-1974.

TAYLOR, Robert E (Ct) 4 Harbor View Drive, Essex CT 06426 B Bridgeport CT 1943 s Lewis & Anna. BA U of Bridgeport 1966; MDiv Ya Berk 1969. D 6/11/1969 P 12/12/1969 Bp John Henry Esquirol. m 6/15/1968 Judith Taylor. R

T

S Paul's Ch Riverside CT 1992-2007; R S Mk's Ch Mystic CT 1983-1992; Dio Connecticut Meriden CT 1974-1983; S Mk's Chap Storrs CT 1974-1983; Chapl U CT 1974-1983; Vic S Jas' Ch New Haven CT 1971-1974; Cur S Andr's Ch Meriden CT 1969-1971.

TAYLOR, Robert Stuart (SeFla) 3325 E. Community Dr., Jupiter FL 33458 B Providence RI 1950 s James & Elizabeth. BA U of Rhode Island 1972; MDiv EDS 1976. D 6/11/1976 P 12/16/1976 Bp Frederick Hesley Belden. m 10/7/1978 Marlene J Taylor c 3. Dn No Palm Bch Deanry Dio SE Florida Miami 1993-1996; R The Epis Ch Of The Gd Shpd Tequesta FL 1989-2015; R Trin Epis Ch Wrentham MA 1983-1989; Asst S Mart's Ch Providence RI 1979-1983; Cur S Jn's Ch Barrington RI 1976-1979.

TAYLOR, Robert Vincent (Oly) 32508 W Kelly Road, Benton City WA 99320 **Chair & Pres Desmond Tutu Peace Fndt 2013-** B Cape Town ZA 1958 s Donald & Elizabeth. BA Rhodes U Grahamstown Za 1979; MDiv UTS 1984. D 12/18/1983 Bp Paul Moore Jr P 6/18/1984 Bp Walter Decoster Dennis Jr. m 5/25/2014 Gerald Dwight Smith. Dn S Mk's Cathd Seattle WA 1999-2009; R S Ptr's Epis Ch Peekskill NY 1988-1999; Int Trin S Paul's Epis New Rochelle NY 1987-1988; Int Ch Of S Mary The Vrgn Chappaqua NY 1986-1987; Asst Gr Ch White Plains NY 1983-1986. Auth, "A New Way to Be Human," New Page Books, 2012; Commentator, "arts," *Fox News*; Blogger, "arts," *Huffington Post*; Auth, "arts," *Washington Post*.

TAYLOR, Robin (WA) 7 Potomac Ave, Indian Head MD 20640 **S Jas' Ch Indn Hd MD 2017-** B Havre de Grace MD 1955 d Brady & Mabel. BS JHU 1977; MDiv VTS 2011. D 6/4/2011 Bp Eugene Taylor Sutton P 12/18/2011 Bp Robert Leroy Fitzpatrick. m 4/21/1979 David Hugh Taylor c 3. All SS Ch Kapaa HI 2012; Vic Chr Memi Ch Kilauea HI 2011-2017. rector.st.james.indianhead@gmail.com

TAYLOR, Ronald Brent (WNC) 7545 Sarah Dr., Denver NC 28037 **Chapl US-AF Aux (CAP) 2011-; R Epis Ch Of S Ptr's By The Lake Denver NC 1996-** B Gastonia NC 1958 s Ray & Mima. BA Wingate U 1980; MDiv Sewanee: The U So, TS 1992; DMin Sewanee: The U So, TS 2006. D 6/6/1992 P 5/1/1993 Bp Bob Johnson. m 6/2/1984 Karen Taylor c 2. Asst S Jn's Epis Ch Columbia SC 1992-1996.

TAYLOR, Scott Clay (Los) 504 N Camden Dr, Beverly Hills CA 90210 **All SS Par Beverly Hills CA 2015-** B Waukesha WI 1961 s Don & Carol. BS NWU 1984; MBA Cor 1990; MAT Fuller TS 2016. D 12/20/2014 Bp Joseph Jon Bruno. c 2.

TAYLOR, Stanley Richard (HB) 157 Patrick Crescent, Essex N8M 1X2 Canada **Non-par 1978-** B Windsor ON CA 1940 s Stanley & Margaret. Electronics Inst Detroit MI 1962; LTh Hur CA 1968; BA U of Windsor 1976; BEd U of Windsor 1977. D 5/1/1968 Bp The Bishop Of Huron. m 6/1/1968 Karen Eileen Taylor. R Ascen Essex Ontario 1970-1978; Serv Ch Of Can 1968-1970. Auth, "Neither Bond Nor Free".

TAYLOR, Stefanie Elizabeth (At) 3110 Ashford Dunwoody Rd NE, Atlanta GA 30319 **S Mart's Epis Sch Atlanta GA 2013-** B Denver CO 1983 d Erich & Lizabeth. BA U of So Carolina 2007; MDiv GTS 2011. D 12/18/2010 P 8/13/2011 Bp Porter Taylor. m 8/15/2009 Arthur Taylor. Cur St Johns Epis Ch Tampa FL 2011-2013.

TAYLOR, Susan (Me) St John's Episcopal Church, 4 Prospect Ave, Randolph VT 05060 **S Andr's Ch Winthrop ME 2017-** B Pensacola FL 1961 d Cecil & Brenda. BFA Maine Coll of Art 1993; MDiv EDS 2013. D 5/31/2013 P 12/14/2013 Bp Thomas C Ely. m 8/30/1991 James Wilson Taylor c 2. R S Jn's Epis Ch Randolph VT 2013-2017. rev.taylor@stjohnsrandolphvt.org

TAYLOR, Sylvester O'Neale (LI) 485 Linwood St, Brooklyn NY 11208 **P in charge S Barn Epis Ch Brooklyn NY 2000-** B BB 1959 s Vernon & Alicia. BS SUNY 1994; MDiv GTS 1996. D 9/15/1997 Bp Orris George Walker Jr P 5/2/1998 Bp Rodney Rae Michel. m 5/26/1990 Jocelyn G Taylor c 2. S Phil's Ch Brooklyn NY 1997-2000.

TAYLOR, Terrence Alexander (SeFla) 20822 San Simeon Way Apt. 109, Miami FL 33179 **R Ch Of The Trsfg Opa Locka FL 2012-** B Miami FL 1966 s Hilton & Mary. BS Florida St U 1988; MPA Florida Intl U 1992; Dip Ang Stud Ya Berk 2003; MDiv Yale DS 2003. D 6/21/2003 P 12/20/2003 Bp Leo Frade. S Agnes Ch Miami FL 2010-2012; S Kevin's Epis Ch Opa Locka FL 2010-2012; S Christophers Ch W Palm Bch FL 2006-2009; P-in-c St. Chris's Epis Ch W Palm Bch FL 2006-2009; Mem, Grad Soc Coun Berk @ Yale New Haven CT 2005-2009; Cn for Yth and YA Mnstry Dio SE Florida Miami 2003-2006, Chairperson, Cmsn on Ant-Racism 1995-2000; Bd Mem, 2001-05, 2007-Present EUC; Life Mem UBE. terrence.taylor@aya.yale.edu

TAYLOR, Terry Ray (O) 1108 Secretariat Dr W, Danville KY 40422 B Evansville IN 1940 s William & Violet. BA Kentucky Wesleyan Coll 1963; MDiv Epis TS in Kentucky 1968. D 5/25/1968 P 12/1/1968 Bp William R Moody. m 5/29/1965 Mary L Jeffers. P Trin Epis Ch Danville KY 2001; R S Barth's Ch Cleveland OH 1984-2001; Chapl Penick Hm Sthrn Pine NC 1982-1984; The Bp Edwin A Penick Vill Sthrn Pines NC 1982-1984; All Souls Ch Ansonville NC 1974-1982; Calv Ch Wadesboro NC 1974-1982; P-in-c All Souls Ansonville NC 1974-1981; P-in-c Ch Of The Mssh Mayodan NC 1970-1974; Vic S Alb's Ch Morehead KY 1968-1970.

TAYLOR, Thomas Herbert (NCal) 14234 N Newcastle Dr, Sun City AZ 85351 B Salem OR 1939 s James & Lois. California St U 1959; BA U of Oregon 1962; DMD U of Oregon 1967; Cert California Sch for Deacons 1980. D 6/19/1982 Bp William Edwin Swing P 2/1/1984 Bp George Clinton Harris. m 9/23/1978 Gloria Irene Taylor. Vic S Paul's Mssn Cres City CA 2004; The Epis Dio Nthrn California Sacramento CA 1999-2004; R Ch Of The H Apos Hilo HI 1989-1999; Vic S Augustines' Epis Ch Homer AK 1984-1989. Auth, "Healed From Depression," *Sharing mag*, 1985. Ord Of S Lk 1986.

TAYLOR JR, Timus Gayle (Tenn) 4715 Harding Pike, Nashville TN 37205 **P Assoc S Geo's Ch Nashville TN 1998-, 1995-1997** B Paducah KY 1935 s Timus & Virginia. BA Van 1956; Cntrl Coll of Ang Comm Cbury Engl 1957; Yale DS 1958; U of Louisville KY 1960; DMin VTS 1963. D 6/27/1964 P 1/9/1965 Bp Paul Moore Jr. m 2/9/1957 Mary Ready Taylor c 2. Sthrn Dnry Team Dio Springfield Springfield IL 1988-1990; S Mart's-In-The-Fields Mayfield KY 1986-1987; P S Paul's Ch Hickman KY 1986-1987; S Ptr's of the Lakes Gilbertsville KY 1986-1987; Trin Epis Ch Fulton KY 1986-1987; R Gr Ch 1981-1985; P S Jas Epis Ch Dahlgren IL 1980-1981; P S Steph's Ch Harrisburg IL 1980-1981; Paducah Coop Mnstry Paducah KY 1975-1976; Gr Ch Paducah KY 1973-1985; Int Gr Epis Ch Paris TN 1971-1975; Asst All SS Par Beverly Hills CA 1967-1970; Vic S Phil's Epis Ch Aquasco MD 1965-1967; Dioc Mssnr Dio Washington Washington DC 1964-1967. "Selected Sermons and Occasional Writings," 2001. Natioanl Cathd Assn; NOEL.

TAYLOR, Walter Hamilton (Tex) Po Box 2126, Lenox MA 01240 **Ret 1999-** B Cincinnati OH 1938 s Robert & Margaret. BA Ken 1960; MDiv VTS 1963; Ya Berk 1988. D 6/15/1963 P 12/1/1963 Bp Roger W Blanchard. m 6/18/1960 Mary Taylor c 2. Dn Chr Ch Cathd Houston TX 1992-1998; R S Lk's Par Darien CT 1977-1992; R Trin Ch Columbus OH 1969-1977; P-in-c H Trin Epis Ch Oxford OH 1966-1969; Asst Chr Ch Cathd Cincinnati OH 1963-1966. Auth, "Faces," *Voices & the Lord*, 1986. Ord of S Lk.

TAYLOR JR, Willard Seymour (EC) 245 Mcdonald Church Rd, Rockingham NC 28379 B Charlotte NC 1936 s Willard & Frances. BA U NC 1959; BD VTS 1962. D 4/29/1963 Bp Richard Henry Baker P 2/1/1964 Bp Thomas H Wright. m 5/4/1997 Margaret R Taylor. Int Chr Ch Albemarle NC 1998-1999; S Steph's Epis Ch Erwin NC 1992-1997; S Jas The Fisherman Epis Ch Shallotte NC 1969-1998; P-in-c S Phil's Ch Southport NC 1969-1998; D Emm Ch Farmville NC 1963-1964.

TAYLOR JR, William Brown (SVa) 4025 Reese Dr S, Portsmouth VA 23703 **R S Jn's Ch Hopewell VA 2007-** B Wheeling WV 1957 s William & Susan. BA Old Dominion U 1981; MDiv VTS 1986. D 6/6/1987 P 4/30/1988 Bp Claude Charles Vache. m 12/18/2004 Kathryn Taylor c 1. Exec Dir Dio Sthrn Virginia Newport News VA 2002-2007, 1992-2002, Dir Yth Mnstrs 1992-2002; R Ch Of The Epiph Norfolk VA 1989-1992; Asst Ch Of The Ascen Norfolk VA 1987-1989.

TAYLOR III, William John (FtW) 2814 Waterford Dr, Irving TX 75063 **Died 7/6/2017** B Cleveland OH 1943 s William & Mildred. BA Cor 1964; JD U of Virginia 1967; MDiv UTS 1984; Cert GTS 1985. D 8/9/1986 Bp Quintin Ebenezer Primo Jr P 4/1/1988 Bp Donis Dean Patterson. m 10/7/1989 Jillian S Taylor. Trin Epis Ch Ft Worth TX 2004-2009; Epis Ch Of The Ascen Dallas TX 2002-2004; Epis Cntr For Renwl Dallas TX 2001-2002; R S Steph's Epis Ch Hurst TX 1992-2001; Cur S Alb's Epis Ch Arlington TX 1988-1992; Cur S Lk's Epis Ch Dallas TX 1987. Travelling Fllshp Uts.

TAYLOR, Williamson Sylvanus (NY) 29 Drake St, Mount Vernon NY 10550 B Freetown LK 1942 s George & Marie. BA Forah Bay Coll of Dur 1969; MEd How 1975; MA How 1977; STM Bos TS 1984; ThD Bos 1989. Trans 3/1/1994 Bp Calvin Onderdonk Schofield Jr. m 11/7/1970 Monica B Taylor c 1. Dio New York New York NY 2002-2014; Cn For Congrl Dvlpmt S Jos's Ch Bronx NY 2002-2013; R S Andr's Epis Ch Of Hollywood Hollywood FL 1994-2002; S Anne's Epis Ch Hallandale Bch FL 1994-2002; Assoc P The Cathd Ch Of S Paul Boston MA 1990-1993; Supply P Dio Massachusetts Boston MA 1983-1993; Serv Ch Of Sierra Leone In W Afr 1980-1983. AAR; Hallandale Ministral Allnce; SBL.

TAYLOR LYMAN, Susan May (SD) 325 N Plum St, Vermillion SD 57069 B Sioux Falls SD 1943 d Harry & Pauline. Heidelberg TS Vermillion SD; MDiv Niobrara Sum Sem; No Amer Bapt Sem; BD U of So Dakota Vermillion SD 1989. D 6/22/2007 Bp Creighton Leland Robertson. m 11/21/1998 Samuel Kenneth Lyman c 4.

TCHAMALA, Theodore K (Md) 6515 Loch Raven Blvd., Baltimore MD 21239 B 1945 s Moise & Madeleine. BTh Jn XXIII Sem 1972; MA Sorbonne 1976; PhD U of Montreal 1986. Trans 3/20/2008 Bp John L Rabb. m 8/30/1979 Anne Tchamala c 3. S Andr's Ch Baltimore MD 2007-2012.

TEAGUE, Charles Steven (Mil) 337 Marley Was, Fuquay Varina NC 27526 **S Dav's Epis Ch Laurinburg NC 2017-; Dn, Metro Milwaukee Convoc Dio Milwaukee Milwaukee WI 2009-** B Hickory NC 1950 s Charles & Adelaide. BA U NC 1972; MDiv Sthrn Bapt TS 1975; Cert Wake Forest U 1982; DMin SE Bapt TS 1983; DAS VTS 2000. D 6/24/2000 P 12/30/2000 Bp Clifton Daniel III. m 5/28/1988 Karen Teague c 2. R S Paul's Ch Milwaukee WI 2007-2016; R Ch S Mich The Archangel Lexington KY 2004-2007; Assoc S Jas

Par Wilmington NC 2000-2004; Chapl/Bereavement and Sprtl Care Hm Hlth and Hospice 1998-1999; Dn, Lower Cape Fear Dnry Dio E Carolina Kinston NC 2001-2003. Writer, "Re-imaging the Ch's Image," *Doctor of Mnstry Dissertation*, SEBTS, 1983. Soc of Schlr Priests 2015. DD Hampden Sydney Coll, Hampden Sydney, VA 1986.

TEASLEY, Robin (SVa) 11406 Glenmont Road, North Chesterfield VA 23236 **P Chr Ch Glen Allen VA 2015-** B Richmond VA 1958 d Robinet & Jane. BA Catawba Coll 1979; MDiv UTS 2010; Dip Ang Stud VTS 2011. D 6/18/2011 P 2/15/2012 Bp Herman Hollerith IV. m 11/24/1979 Paul W Teasley c 3. S Lk's Ch Blackstone VA 2012-2015; D Ch Of The Redeem Midlothian VA 2011. r. teasley@christchurchrichmond.com

TEDERSTROM, John Patton (Ky) 1007 Hess Ln, Louisville KY 40217 B Pittsburgh PA 1938 s Albert & Roberta. Wk on degree suspended Indiana U; BA Pr 1960; MDiv CDSP 1964. D 6/20/1964 Bp Conrad H Gesner P 12/19/1964 Bp Austin Pardue. m 6/21/2012 Mark Anthony Cannon c 5. Int S Geo's Epis Ch Louisville KY 1999-2001, Int 1987-1989; Supply P Dio Kentucky Louisville KY 1996-1999, Supply P 1994, Supply P 1989-1991, Supply P 1983-1985; Int Ch Of Our Merc Sav Louisville KY 1995-1996; Int Ch Of The Adv Louisville KY 1992; Epis Chapl U of Louisville 1991-1992; R S Jn's Ch Louisville KY 1980-1983; Int Ch Of Our Sav Middleboro MA 1979-1980; Chapl H Trin Ch Nice France 1979-1980; P-in-c Amer Mnstry In The Riviera 1975-1979; R Ch of S Aug of Cbury 65189 Wiesbaden 1972-1975; R S Jas Epis Ch Firenze 50123 1967-1972; Reserv Mnstrs Dio So Dakota Pierre SD 1964-1967; Dep GC Convoc of Epis Ch in Europe Paris 1979, Alt Dep GC 1976, Dep GC 1973, Convoc Secretaty1971-1979 1971-1979. Hon Mem Royal British Legion 1979; Phi Beta Kappa 1960.

TEDESCO, Robert Lincoln (Va) 407 Russell Ave Apt 605, Gaithersburg MD 20877 **Ret 2002-** B Hartford CT 1927 s Nicholas & Mary. BA U of Connecticut 1951; MS Trin Hartford CT 1959; MDiv VTS 1985. D 8/30/1985 Bp David Henry Lewis Jr P 5/31/1986 Bp Peter J Lee. m 11/7/1953 Dorothy G Tedesco c 4. Par Assoc Olivet Epis Ch Alexandria VA 1992-2000, P 1992-, Int 1990-1992, Cur 1985-1986; Dio Virginia Richmond VA 1989-1990; Assoc S Tim's Ch Herndon VA 1986-1989. "Tech arts on Nuclear Power," 1957. ANS 1972-1982.

TEDESCO, William Nicholas (Ct) 20 Erickson Way, South Yarmouth MA 02664 **Ret 1988-** B Hartford CT 1924 s Nicholas & Mary. MA Trin Hartford CT; BA U of Hartford; MDiv VTS. D 6/8/1974 P 12/21/1974 Bp Joseph Warren Hutchens. c 4. R Trin Ch Seymour CT 1977-1988; Cur All SS Epis Ch Oakville CT 1974-1977; Cur Chr Ch Par Epis Watertown CT 1974-1977.

TEED, Lee B (SanD) 4860 Circle Dr, San Diego CA 92116 B Mount Kisco NY 1940 d George & Phyllis. BA U CA 1967; MA Untd States Intl U 1975; MDiv CDSP 1990. D 6/16/1990 P 12/15/1990 Bp Charles Brinkley Morton. Cathd Ch Of S Paul San Diego CA 1994-2005; Cur The Epis Ch Of S Andr Encinitas CA 1990-1992. Ord Of H Cross.

TEETS, James C (SeFla) 1140 Cason Ln, Murfreesboro TN 37128 **Ch of the H Cross Murfreesboro TN 2017-** B Orlando FL 1962 s Frank & Sue. B.B.A Stetson U 1984; MDiv Sewanee: The U So 2017. D 11/19/2016 P 6/3/2017 Bp Peter David Eaton. m 6/5/1993 Sharon R Teets c 2.

TEETZ, Margaret Lou-Sarah (Alb) Christ Church, 970 State St, Schenectady NY 12307 B Cleveland OH 1942 d William & Florence. BA Albion Coll 1964. D 11/6/2013 Bp William Howard Love. c 2.

TELZLAFF, Tyler J (Lex) **Epis Ch of Our Sav Richmond KY 2016-, 2015-2016** B Watertown, NY 1983 s Richard & Karen. Bachelors St. Bonaventure 2006; M.Div EDS 2012. D 4/9/2016 Bp Terry Allen White P 10/15/2016 Bp Bruce Caldwell. m 6/12/2013 Chana Chana Joy Winger. Auth, "Easter Day C: The Unlikely Evanglist," *Mod Metanoia*, Rev. Marshall Jolly, 2016; Auth, "The Miracles of the everyday," *Patheos*, Rev. Jennifer Woodruff-Tait, 2015. tjatecos@gmail.com

TEMBECKJIAN, Renee Melanie (CNY) 4782 Hyde Rd, Manlius NY 13104 **Trin Epis Ch Fayetteville NY 2015-, 2013** B New York NY 1955 d Edward & Arpine. MS SUNY Coll at Oswego 1983; PhD Syr 1992; Dioc Formation Prog 2009. D 6/29/2009 P 1/9/2010 Bp Gladstone Bailey Adams III. m 7/10/1988 Thomas Zino c 2. Dio Cntrl New York Liverpool NY 2015, 2011-2015.

TEMME, Louis H (Pa) Church Of The Advent, 12 Byberry Rd, Hatboro PA 19040 B Philadelphia PA 1944 s Louis & Rose. BS Drexel U 1967; CPE St Lukes Hosp Houston Texas 1969; MDiv PDS 1970; MS S Johns U 1972; Cert Credo Conf Roslyn VA 2004. D 6/6/1970 P 12/1/1970 Bp Robert Lionne DeWitt. m 4/5/1975 Kathryn M Rosse c 2. Int R Ch Of The Adv Hatboro PA 2013-2014; Int R S Mary's Ch Hamilton Vill Philadelphia PA 2012-2013; Int R Ch Of S Mart-In-The-Fields Philadelphia PA 2009-2011; Int R Washington Memi Chap Vlly Forge PA 2007-2009; Int R Trin Ch Swarthmore PA 2005-2007; R Trin Memi Ch Philadelphia PA 1972-2005; Asst R Chr Ch Oyster Bay NY 1970-1972; Title IV Intake Off Dio Pennsylvania Philadelphia PA 2012-2017, Pres Stndg Com 1994-2000, Pres Stndg Com 1991-2000, Cnvnr Cler Profsnl Assn (PRIDE) 1979-1983; Wintershelter/Communicare Bd Dir Cmnty Outreach Partnership Philadelphia PA 1984-2005; Pres, Bd Dir Trin Playgroup 1973-1978. Achievement Awd Dio Pennsylvania 2000; Fllshp Cont Educ VTS 1986.

TEMPLE, Charles Sloan (NY) 1 E 29th St, New York NY 10016 B Indianapolis IN 1950 s Charles & Mary. BA Rhode Island Coll 1976; MDiv GTS 1979. D 6/2/1979 Bp Frederick Hesley Belden P 12/13/1979 Bp John S Higgins. Ch Of The Trsfg New York NY 1982-1997; Cur S Jn's Ch Barrington RI 1979-1982.

TEMPLE, Gordon Clarence (ETenn) 6808 Levi Rd, Hixson TN 37343 B Knoxville TN 1934 s Clarence & Julia. BD U of Tennessee 1954; BD Auburn U 1959; MDiv Sewanee: The U So, TS 1986; VTS 1995. D 6/22/1986 P 5/1/1987 Bp William Evan Sanders. m 6/6/1958 Haven J Temple. Int S Mart Of Tours Epis Ch Chattanooga TN 2003-2011; Int S Tim's Ch Signal Mtn TN 2002-2003; Int Gr Ch Chattanooga TN 2001-2002; Int All SS Epis Ch Columbia Falls MT 1999-2001, R 1992-1998; Asst R Ch Of The Ascen Knoxville TN 1998-1999, Int 1996-1997, Assoc 1986-1987; R S Matt's Ch Columbia Fls MT 1993-1996. Prov Coordntr, ESMA, Chapl Ord Of S Lk.

TEMPLE JR, Gray (At) 10685 Bell Rd, Duluth GA 30097 B Washington DC 1941 s Gray & Maria. Schlr Gottingen U DE 1964; BA U NC 1965; BD VTS 1968. D 6/17/1968 P 12/18/1968 Bp Matthew George Henry. m 8/28/1966 Jean Temple c 2. R S Pat's Epis Ch Atlanta GA 1975-2006; Vic S Lk's Ch Boone NC 1968-1975. Auth, "The Molten Soul," Ch Pub Inc, 2001; Auth, "When God Happens," Ch Pub Inc, 2001; Auth, "52 Ways To Help Homeless People," 1991; Auth, "5 Sermons," *Selected Sermons*. Hon Cn S Lk Cathd 1985.

TEMPLE, Palmer Collier (At) 1883 Wycliff Rd Nw, Atlanta GA 30309 **Dir Of Pstr Care Chld's Grant Hospitals Chicago IL 1970-** B Nashville TN 1934 s Thomas & Margaret. BA Van 1957; MDiv Candler TS Emory U 1960. D 2/18/1976 Bp James Winchester Montgomery P 6/1/1976 Bp Quintin Ebenezer Primo Jr. m 12/21/1968 Helen Elizabeth Temple c 2. Serv, Trng and Counslg Cntr S Lk's Epis Ch Atlanta GA 1981-1994; St Lukes Trng & Coun.Ctr Atlanta GA 1981-1994; S Tim's Decatur GA 1978-1980; Chapl Georgia Mntl Hlth Inst Atlanta GA 1967-1970; Methodist Pstr Perry & Prairie Vill KS 1962-1967. Auth, "Chld in Hospitals: A Matter of Life, Death and Lrng," *Chicago Tribune mag*, 1975; Auth, "Var arts," *Journ on Pstr Care*.

TEMPLEMAN, Mark Alan (Mass) 60 Monument Avenue, Swampscott MA 01907 **R The Ch Of The H Name Swampscott MA 2006-** B Fayetteville NC 1968 s Bruce & Jane. BA Wright St U 1999; MA TESM 2002. D 10/20/2001 P 6/1/2002 Bp Herbert Thompson Jr. m 10/22/1995 Jennifer M Templeman c 3. Chr Ch Frederica St Simons Is GA 2004-2006; Stff P Chr Ch St. Simons Island GA 2004-2006; Cur S Lk's Ch Marietta OH 2002-2003. Auth, "A Distant Shore," *A Distant Shore*, Idyllwood Press, 2002; Auth, "Candle in an Ocean," *Candle in an Ocean*, Idyllwood Press, 1999. St. Lk the Physcn 2004. Mike Henning Preaching Prize Mike Henning Memi Preaching Schlrshp 2000.

TEMPLETON, Gary Lynn (Okla) 903 N Primrose St, Duncan OK 73533 **D All SS' Epis Ch Duncan OK 1987-** B Bartlesville OK 1947 s Henry & Catherine. BS Oklahoma St U 1974. D 8/24/1987 Bp Gerald Nicholas Mcallister. m 9/30/1978 Ellen Louise Templeton.

TEMPLETON, John (At) 274 Hershey Lane, Clayton GA 30525 B Memphis TN 1938 s Loyd & Virginia. BA Rhodes Coll 1962; MDiv Sewanee: The U So, TS 1969; MSW U GA 1989. D 6/29/1969 P 6/1/1970 Bp John Adams Pinckney. m 10/15/2015 John M Siegel c 3. R S Paul's Ch Macon GA 1977-1988; R Chr the King Pawleys Island SC 1971-1977; Asst S Jn's Epis Ch Columbia SC 1969-1971.

TEMPLETON, Patricia Dale (At) 4393 Garmon Road NW, Atlanta GA 30327 **R S Dunst's Epis Ch Atlanta GA 2004-** B Houston TX 1956 d Robert & Lena. BA U GA 1978; MDiv Sewanee: The U So, TS 1994. D 5/29/1994 Bp Bertram Nelson Herlong P 5/25/1995 Bp Robert Gould Tharp. m 12/29/1996 Joseph E Monti c 1. Chapl Hospice of Chattanooga 2002-2004; Assoc R S Tim's Ch Signal Mtn TN 1995-2002; Assoc R Ch Of The Ascen Knoxville TN 1994-1995. Auth, "Runaway Bunnies -- and Believers," *Sermons That Wk XIV*, Morehouse, 2006; Auth, "Sanctifying What Has Been Desecrated," *Sermons That Wk XIII*, Morehouse, 2005; Auth, "A Reason For Wounds In A Risen Body," *Sermons That Wk IX*, Morehouse, 2000. Pres, Stndg Com Dio Atlanta 2010; Pres, Stndg Com Dio E Tennessee 2000.

TENCH, Jack Marvin (Oly) 1919 NE Ridgewood Ct, Poulsbo WA 98370 B Chicago IL 1938 s Marvin & Ruth. BA Colorado Coll 1960; STB GTS 1964. D 6/13/1964 Bp James Winchester Montgomery P 12/19/1964 Bp Gerald Francis Burrill. m 4/3/1970 Joan B Tench c 3. R S Lk's Epis Ch Seattle WA 1991-2000; R St Steph's Epis Ch Oak Harbor WA 1981-1991; Exec Coun Appointees New York NY 1979-1981; R Buen Pstr and San Andres Epis Ch San Pedro Sula 1979-1980; R Ch Of The Resurr Bellevue WA 1971-1979; R Ch of the Resurr Bellevue WA 1971-1979; Cur S Eliz's Seahurst NJ 1968-1971; Vic S Jas Guatemala City Guatemala 1966-1968; Cur S Jn's Epis Ch Mt Prospect IL 1964-1966.

TENDICK, James Ross (U) 1780 Plateau Cir, Moab UT 84532 **Vic Mision de San Francisco Moab UT 2007-** B Long Beach CA 1948 s Cullen & Sylvia. CDSP 1988; MDiv CDSP 2000. D 6/4/1988 Bp William Edwin Swing P 5/13/1989 Bp George Edmonds Bates. m 8/5/1978 Marcia Tendick c 3. Dio Utah Salt Lake City UT 1996-2011; R S Fran Ch Moab UT 1996-2006; Assoc S Jas Salt Lake City UT 1992-1996; S Jas Epis Ch Midvale UT 1989-1996; Cur S Jas Salt Lake City UT 1989-1992.

T

✠ **TENNIS, The Rt Rev Cabell** (Oly) 725 9th Ave, Apt. 904, Seattle WA 98104 B Hampton VA 1932 s Calvin & Francis. BA W&M 1954; BA W&M 1954; JD W&M 1956; JD W&M Marshall-Wythe Law 1956; MDiv VTS 1964. D 6/1/1964 P 12/19/1964 Bp George P Gunn Con 11/8/1986 for Del. m 8/21/1954 Hyde Southall Tennis c 4. Bp Dio Delaware Wilmington 1986-1997; Dn S Mk's Cathd Seattle WA 1972-1986; Assoc Trin Epis Ch Buffalo NY 1965-1969; Asst S Jn's Ch Portsmouth VA 1964-1965; ExCoun Dio Olympia Seattle 1972-1975; ExCoun Dio Wstrn New York Tonawanda NY 1969-1972. Assn For Conflict Resolution. Hon DD VTS 1987. cabellhyde@gmail.com

TENNISON, George Nelson (La) 401 Magnolia Ln, Mandeville LA 70471 **P-in-c All SS Epis Ch Ponchatoula LA 2015-; Supply P Dio Louisiana New Orleans LA 2014-, Sprtl Dir for Curs 2012-** B New Orleans LA 1944 s George & Elise. U of New Orleans; BS Lamar U 1967; Sch for Mnstry Dio Louisiana 2003. D 12/30/2006 P 6/30/2007 Bp Charles Edward Jenkins III. m 6/10/1977 Martha Ann North c 1. P-in-c S Matt's Ch Bogalusa LA 2011-2013; Cur S Mich's Epis Ch Mandeville LA 2006-2011.

TENNY, Claire Mary (Chi) Po Box 426, Vails Gate NY 12584 **Novc Cnvnt of St. Helena Vails Gate NY 2006-** B New York NY 1959 d Fred & Claire. MD Albany Med Coll 1983; BS Un Coll Schenectady NY 1983; MDiv Sewanee: The U So, TS 2002. D 6/8/2002 P 12/8/2002 Bp William Jerry Winterrowd. Cathd Of St Jn The Div New York NY 2007-2009; R S Andr Ch Grayslake IL 2003-2006; Assoc for Campus Mnstry S Alb's Ch Davidson NC 2002-2003.

TEPAVCHEVICH, Kathie Elaine (Chi) 6588 Shabbona Rd, Indian Head Park IL 60525 **D Ch Of The H Nativ Clarendon Hls IL 2001-** B Springfield IL 1953 d Harvey & Nancy. Natl-Louis U; BA Quincy Coll 1975. D 2/15/1997 Bp Frank Tracy Griswold III. m 11/23/1974 Thomas Tepavchevich. D Emm Epis Ch La Grange IL 1997-2002.

TEPE, Donald James (EMich) 3226 Meadowview Ln, Saginaw MI 48601 **Ret 1993-** B Chicago IL 1929 s James & Ruth. BS NWU 1954; BD Garrett-Evang TS 1957; SWTS 1961; MSW U MI 1973. D 6/20/1961 P 12/26/1961 Bp Charles Bennison Sr. c 2. P in charge Calv Memi Epis Ch Saginaw MI 1995-2010, P-in-c 1976-1994; 1988-1995; R S Jas' Epis Ch Of Albion Albion MI 1969-1973; Vic S Alb's Mssn N. Muskegon MI 1966-1969; Cur Gr Ch Grand Rapids MI 1961-1966.

TERHUNE, Jason Scott (Tenn) **P-in-c S Mary Magd Ch Fayetteville TN 2016-** D 6/6/2015 P 12/7/2015 Bp John Bauerschmidt.

TERHUNE JR, Robert Dawbarn (Tex) 2605A Spring Ln, Austin TX 78703 **1971-** B New Haven CT 1932 s Robert & Josephine. BA Ya 1953; STB Ya Berk 1958; MA U of Houston 1976. D 6/22/1958 Bp Henry I Louttit P 12/22/1958 Bp William Francis Moses. m 4/16/1955 Lorna Terhune c 4. Chapl in Res S Lk's Hosp Houston TX 1969-1971; Chapl Ft Logan Mntl Hlth Cntr Littleton CO 1968-1969; Vic S Mk's Ch Palm Bch Garden FL 1963-1968; Cur Ch Of The Resurr Miami FL 1961-1963; P-in-c S Dunst's Epis Ch Largo FL 1958-1961; S Giles Ch Pinellas Pk FL 1958-1960. SocMary 1998.

TERRILL, Bob (Kan) 3524 Sw Willow Brook Ln, Topeka KS 66614 B Brookfield MO 1936 s Curtis & Esther. Bus Admin U of Kansas 1958; MDiv SWTS 1961. D 6/11/1961 P 12/1/1961 Bp Edward Clark Turner. m 6/10/1989 Judith Ann Franke c 2. Provost Gr Cathd Topeka KS 1997-2000; R Chr Epis Ch S Jos MO 1988-2000; Ch Of The Resurr Blue Sprg MO 1984-1988; Dio W Missouri Kansas City MO 1984-1988; Ch Of Our Sav Colorado Sprg CO 1982-1983; P-in-c S Lk's Ch Westcliffe CO 1978-1982; Trin Ch Trinidad CO 1978-1982; R S Mk's Epis Ch Glen Ellyn IL 1972-1978; Vic S Barth's Ch Wichita KS 1971-1972; R S Chris's Epis Ch Wichita KS 1968-1972; R Trin Ch Arkansas City KS 1964-1968; Vic S Barn Coun Grove KS 1962-1964; Vic S Lk's Ch Wamego KS 1961-1964. Epis Cleric Assn. terrillrj@icloud.com

TERRY, Andrew Bennett (Va) 2209 E Grace St, Richmond VA 23223 **S Ptr's Epis Ch Richmond VA 2015-** B Richmond VA 1982 s Roy & Jane. BA W&M 2004; Post Grad Cert Ripon Coll - Cuddesdon 2008; MDiv VTS 2012. D 6/9/2012 P 12/15/2012 Bp Shannon Sherwood Johnston. c 1. Richmond Hill Richmond VA 2012-2015.

TERRY, Eleanor Applewhite (Mass) 193 Salem St, Boston MA 02113 **Old No Chr Ch Boston MA 2013-** B New Haven CT 1969 d Philip & Harriet. BA Smith 1991; MDiv Ya Berk 1997. D 6/8/2002 P 5/24/2003 Bp Andrew Donnan Smith. m 7/3/1999 Bronson E Terry c 3. Secy of Conv Dio Connecticut Meriden CT 2007-2012; Vic S Paul's Ch Plainfield CT 2005-2012; Assoc R S Ptr And Paul Epis Ch Portland OR 2003-2005; Min Of Sprtlty And Aging S Paul And S Jas New Haven CT 1998-2002. revellie@oldnorth.com

TERRY, Mildred Carlson (SwFla) 4071 Center Pointe Pl, Sarasota FL 34233 **D S Wlfd's 1996-** B Chicago IL 1925 d Svenn & Esther. BA U Chi 1945; Chicago St U 1954; MA S Xavier Coll 1969; Cert Inst for Chr Stds 1987. D 9/2/1987 Bp William Hopkins Folwell. m 7/16/1945 Joseph Garside Terry c 3. D S Marg Of Scotland Epis Ch Sarasota FL 1989-2000; D St Alb's of Auburndale Inc Auburndale FL 1987-1989; Chapl Gd Shpd Hospice Polk Cnty FL 1985-1989. Dok.

TERRY, Susan Preston (Kan) 3209 W 25th St, Lawrence KS 66047 **Campus Mssnr Dio Kansas KS 2007-; Int S Aug's Epis Ch 2004-** B Fort Benning GA 1947 d James & Wilma. BA S Mary 1971; MDiv Epis TS in Kentucky 1986. D 11/8/1986 Bp Don Adger Wimberly P 5/23/1987 Bp Joseph Thomas Heistand. c 4. Dio Kansas Topeka KS 2007-2012; H Cross Ch Thomson GA 2001-2003; Chapl The Ch Of The Gd Shpd Augusta GA 1988-2007; S Greg HS Tucson AZ 1987-1988; Chapl S Greg HS Tucson AZ 1986-1988.

TERRY, Teresa F (Del) D 11/12/2016 P 6/17/2017 Bp Mariann Edgar Budde.

TERRY, William Hutchinson (La) 626 Congress St., New Orleans LA 70117 **Bd Mem New Orleans Musicians Clnc 2008-; Chairman Oportunidades - Laitno Outreach 2007-; Chairman St. Anna's Mobile Med Unit 2005-; R S Anna's Ch New Orleans LA 2003-** B New Orleans LA 1951 s Arthur & Betty. BA Tul 1978; MPS Loyola U 2002; MDiv Nash 2003. D 12/28/2002 P 7/20/2003 Bp Charles Edward Jenkins III. m 7/30/1983 Victoria L Terry c 3. Chapl Recovery Mnstrs of Dio Louisiana 2009-2011; P-in-c gr Ch New Orleans LA 2008-2010; , Missions Com Epis Dio Louisiana 2003-2005; Chair, Hobgood Fund for Servnt Mnstry Dio Los Angeles Los Angeles CA 2007-2009. Auth, "A Cmnty Within Communities," *Loc News Paper*, 2011. Our Lady of Walsingham P Assoc 2006; Soc of Cath Priests 2009-2011. Mart Luther King Jazz Awd Irvin Mayfield and New Orleans Jazz Orchestra 2010; Alpha Sigma Nu Jesuit hon Soc 2000.

TESCHNER, David Hall (SVa) 31 Belmead St, Petersburg VA 23805 B Natick MA 1951 s Douglass & Mary. BA U of Rhode Island 1977; MDiv VTS 1986. D 6/21/1986 P 3/22/1987 Bp George Nelson Hunt III. m 12/30/2000 Juanita Watts Teschner. R Chr And Gr Ch Petersburg VA 1990-2016; Chapl St. Catharine's Sch 1989-1990; Asst to R S Steph's Ch Richmond VA 1986-1990. dtesch31@gmail.com

TESI, Elizabeth A B (WA) 6701 Wisconsin Ave, Chevy Chase MD 20815 **S Jn's Ch Chevy Chase MD 2015-** B Hartford CT 1979 d Robert & Kathleen. BA Wells Coll 2001; MDiv VTS 2004; MS Virginia Commonwealth U 2007. D 6/12/2004 P 4/14/2005 Bp Andrew Donnan Smith. m 5/11/2007 Martin G Tesi. Int Ch Of The H Cross Dunn Loring VA 2013-2015; Dio Oregon Portland OR 2011-2013, COM, Ord 2011-; Asst S Mary's Epis Ch Eugene OR 2011-2013; Chapl Hartford Hosp Hartford CT 2007-2011; P-in-c Ch Of The Epiph Southbury CT 2007-2010; Int Vic Ch Of Our Sav Montpelier VA 2006-2007; Chapl Res Virginia Commonweath Univ Hlth System 2006-2007; Asst R Trin Ch Arlington VA 2004-2006. Assn of Profsnl Chapl 2010.

TESKA, William Jay (Minn) 940 Franklin Terrace, Apt. 409, Minneapolis MN 55406 B Minneapolis MN 1942 s Roy & Alice. BA Dart 1964; STB Ya Berk 1968. D 10/7/1968 Bp Hamilton Hyde Kellogg P 6/1/1969 Bp Philip Frederick McNairy. The OTCG Tucson AZ 2000-2003; Chapl Tuller Sch Tucson AZ 2000-2003; Dio Minnesota Minneapolis MN 1999; R S Paul's On-The-Hill Epis Ch Minneapolis MN 1991-1999; R Par Of The H Trin And S Anskar Minneapolis MN 1984-1989; P-in-c Epiph Epis Ch S Paul MN 1981-1984; Epis Par Of S Mich And All Ang Tucson AZ 1980-1981; Assoc Chapl U Epis Cntr Minneapolis MN 1968-1980; Mstr of Sacr Stds Groton Sch Groton MA 1966-1967.

TESS, Mike (Mil) 124 Dewey St, Sun Prairie WI 53590 B Manitowoc WI 1964 s Clayton & Nancy. BA S Johns U 1987; MDiv U of S Mary of the Lake Mundelein Sem 1991; Iliff TS 1998. Rec 5/9/1998 as Priest Bp William Jerry Winterrowd. m 5/9/1998 Heidi A Tess c 4. Vic Ch Of The Gd Shpd Sun Prairie WI 2010-2016; Dio Milwaukee Milwaukee WI 2007-2009; P-in-c S Aidans Ch Hartford WI 2001-2007.

TESSMAN, Michael J R (Ct) 289 Balsam Rd, South Kingstown RI 02879 **Founding Co-Dir Alpha & Omega Mnstrs: Consulting/Coaching 2013-** B Saint Paul MN 1948 s Roger & Jean. AB U Chi 1970; MDiv Yale DS 1973; Cert WCC-Geneva 1987; Cert GTS 1997; DMin GTF 1998. D 6/12/1976 P 4/3/1977 Bp Joseph Warren Hutchens. m 7/21/1974 Carol E Davidson c 2. Int R S Jn's Epis Ch Niantic CT 2012-2014; P-in-c Ch Of The H Sprt Charlestown RI 2008-2012; Int R S Jn's Ch Washington CT 2007-2008; Int R S Monica's Ch Hartford CT 2006-2007; Int R S Jn's Ch New Haven CT 2003-2005; Dn of Students Nash Nashotah WI 2001-2003; Dir of the Boone Porter Inst Nash Sem WI 1999-2002; Dir of Field Educ Nash Sem WI 1997-2003; Pstr Theol Nash Nashotah WI 1997-2003; R Imm S Jas Par Derby CT 1991-1997; Vic S Mk's Ch Waterbury CT 1988-1991; Cmsn on Human Sxlty Dio Connecticut Meriden CT 1985-1989, Stndg Com 1989-1992; R Trin Epis Ch Trumbull CT 1981-1988; Vic S Jn The Evang Yalesville CT 1979-1981; Vic S Paul's Ch Wallingford CT 1979-1981; Cur Ch Of The H Trin Middletown CT 1976-1979; Ecum Off Dio Milwaukee Milwaukee WI 1999-2002. Auth, "Is Mar All the Same?," *LivCh*, Living Ch Fdn., 2012; Auth, "Bk Revs," *LivCh*, LivCh, 2001; Auth, "Remembering Henri Nouwen," *LivCh*, LivCh, 2000; Auth, "The Legacy of Roland Allen," *Missiology for the 21st Century*, GTF, 1998; Auth, "Getting Little at Christmas," *LivCh*, LivCh, 1998; Auth, "The Ch's Responsibility to Homosexual Persons," *Karatana Papers*, Karatana, Inc, 1981. ACPE 1998-2003; Karatana Cmnty 1972; Theol of Institutions Proj (STW) 1998-2008. Fell GTF 1998; Fell Rockefeller Brothers Fndt 1970.

TESTA, Dennis Arthur (Md) 302 Homewood Rd, Linthicum MD 21090 B Laurelton,NY 1945 s Vincent & Rosalie. BA Adams St Coll 1969; MDiv GTS 1973. D 6/16/1973 P 9/22/1973 Bp Jonathan Goodhue Sherman. m 8/23/1969 Margaret Testa c 2. S Alb's Epis Ch Glen Burnie MD 1981-2004; Copley Par: The Ch Of The Resurr Joppatowne MD 1978-1981; Dio Nthrn Michigan Mar-

T

quette MI 1974-1977; S Alb's Ch Manistique MI 1974-1977; S Jn's Ch Munising MI 1974-1977; Vic-In-C S Mich Suncook NH 1973-1974.

TESTER, Elizabeth B (Mil) **Dio Milwaukee Milwaukee WI 2016-; S Paul's Ch Watertown WI 2013-** B Boone NC 1979 d James & Helen. Philos and Rel Appalachian St U 2007; Mstr of Div VTS 2013. D 12/15/2012 P 8/31/2013 Bp Porter Taylor. m 6/1/2013 Oscar A Rozo. Ch Of The Ascen Hickory NC 2008-2010.

TESTER, Helen Whitener (Miss) 743 Milwaukee Rd, Beloit WI 53511 **S Paul's Epis Ch Beloit WI 2015-** B Hickory NC 1950 d Thomas & Sophie. BA Lenoir-Rhyne Coll 1973; MA Appalachian St U 1983; DMin VTS 2011. D 1/15/2000 Bp Alfred Marble Jr P 1/22/2005 Bp Duncan Montgomery Gray III. m 6/1/1996 Charles K(amper) Floyd c 2. R The Epis Ch Of The Medtr Meridian MS 2007-2015; H Trin Ch Crystal Sprg MS 2002-2006; Dir Chapl Hospice Ministers Ridgeland MS 1996-2000; Asst to the Bp Dio Wstrn No Carolina 1990-1991. Mississippi Soc For Lic Mar & Fam Therapists 2000. Included In "50 Leading Bus Wmn For 2000" Mississippi Bus Intl 2000.

TESTIN, Joan Marie (RI) Emmanuel Episcopal Church, 120 Nate Whipple Hwy, Cumberland RI 02864 **R Emm Epis Ch Cumberland RI 2013-** B Pittsburgh PA 1961 d Robert & Jeanette. BA W&M 1983; Cert VTS 2009; MDiv Luth TS 2010. D 6/12/2010 P 12/18/2010 Bp Bud Shand. m 2/8/2013 Barbara Kay Mooney. Cur Emm Epis Ch Chestertown MD 2010-2013; Mus Dir Waldron Mercy Acad 1988-2006; Tchr Walsingham Acad 1983-1988.

TETER, Jane (Be) 1728 Butztown Rd Apt A4, Bethlehem PA 18017 **Died 1/17/2017** B Schenectady NY 1937 d Thomas & Esther. Hobart and Wm Smith Colleges 1956; Cert Moravian TS 1983; Cert Moravian TS 1985. D 9/7/1983 P 11/1/1984 Bp James Michael Mark Dyer. m 2/16/2017 Lloyd E Teter c 5. Vic S Brigid's Ch Nazareth PA 1995-2001; Cn Dio Bethlehem Bethlehem PA 1994-2009, Cn for Mnstrs 2006-2010; The Welcome Place Bethlehem PA 1993; Int Chr Ch Stroudsburg PA 1991-1992; Asst Trin Ch Bethlehem PA 1987-1990; Int S Marg's Ch Emmaus PA 1984-1985, Asst 1983-1984. jteter@diobeth.org

TETRAULT, David Joseph (SVa) 22501 Cypress Point Road, Williamsburg VA 23185 B Kankakee IL 1941 s Omer & Eloise. BA S Jos Rensselaer IN 1962; DMin S Marys Sem & U Baltimore 1986. D 6/23/1973 Bp William Foreman Creighton P 12/23/1973 Bp David Shepherd Rose. m 10/11/1977 Georgia A Prescott c 2. Int S Cyp's Epis Ch Hampton VA 2012-2014; Int S Geo's Epis Ch Newport News VA 2011-2012; Chapl Ringling Bros & Barnum & Bailey Circus 1994-2006; Volntr Pstr Care Mnstry Advsr Bruton Par Williamsburg VA 1987-1996; deaf Mnstry Dio Virginia Richmond VA 1983-1987; Int Gr Ch Newport News VA 1982; Dir Epis Deaf Mnstrs 1979-1987; Asst S Paul's Ch Richmond VA 1977-1980. Epis Conf of the Deaf of the Epis Ch in the 1977-1987.

TETRAULT, Joanne Russell (Md) B Baltimore MD 1964 d Thomas & Elizabeth. M.A., Sprtl and Pstr Care Loyola U Maryland; Post-Grad Dplma in Angl Stds VTS. D 1/15/2017 Bp Chilton Richardson Knudsen. m 9/17/1994 Joseph Bernard Tetrault.

TETZ, William Edward (Mich) 5127 Richmond Ave # 118, Houston TX 77056 **Vic S Paul 1974-** B Pittsburgh PA 1944 s Edward & Elizabeth. BA Hillsdale Coll; MDiv Hur CA. D 6/15/1974 P 3/15/1975 Bp H Coleman Mcgehee Jr. m 6/26/1964 Kathleen Tetz c 2.

TETZLAFF, Chana (Lex) Emmanuel Episcopal Church, 2410 Lexington Rd, Winchester KY 40391 **Yth Dir S Matt's Epis Ch Sacramento CA 2006-** B Paradise CA 1984 d Nordon & Christine. AA Sierra Coll 2004; BA U CA, Davis CA 2006; MDiv VTS 2013. D 6/29/2013 Bp Barry Leigh Beisner P 3/6/2014 Bp Doug Hahn. m 6/12/2013 Tyler J Telzlaff. Emm Epis Ch Winchester KY 2013-2017.

THABET, David George (WVa) 1305 15th St, Huntington WV 25701 **Ret 2000-** B Spencer WV 1938 s George & Martha. LTh Epis TS in Kentucky 1968. D 6/11/1968 P 12/18/1968 Bp Wilburn Camrock Campbell. m 11/17/1957 Edna L Thabet c 3. All SS Ch Charleston WV 2001-2006; R Chr Epis Ch Spotsylvania VA 1991-1999; R S Ptr's Ch Huntington WV 1986-1991; Chapl Reynalds Memi Hosp Glendale WV 1973-1985; R Trin Ch Moundsville WV 1973-1985; R H Trin Ch Logan WV 1968-1973. "Nueden," Xulon Press, 2008.

THACKER II, James Robert (SwVa) 207 Lookout Point Dr., Osprey FL 34229 B Buckhannon WV 1940 s James & Katherine. BA W Virginia St U 1963; M.Div. Nash 1966; MSW CUA 1976. D 6/3/1966 P 12/1/1966 Bp Wilburn Camrock Campbell. m 8/15/1970 Maria Martin Thacker c 3. R S Alb's Tokyo Japan 2000-2004; R St. Markis Bermuda 1992-2000; Chr Epis Ch Roanoke VA 1985-1992; R Gr Memi Ch Lynchburg VA 1979-1985; S Mk's Ch Westhampton Bch NY 1977-1978; S Andr's-On-The-Mt Harpers Ferry WV 1972-1977; S Lk's Ch Wheeling WV 1968-1971; R S Paul's Ch Martins Ferry OH 1968-1971; Trin Ch Bellaire OH 1968-1971.

THADEN, Tim Robert (Colo) 780 Devinney Ct, Golden CO 80401 **R Ch Of S Jn Chrys Golden CO 2006-** B Denver CO 1952 s Robert & Imogene. AA Front Range Cmnty Coll 1997; BA Metropltn St Coll of Denver 1999; MDiv Epis TS of the SW 2004. D 6/12/2004 P 12/18/2004 Bp Robert John O'Neill. m 9/17/1983 Katherine H Thaden c 3. Mssnr, Front Range Reg of the Dio

Colorado Dio Colorado Denver CO 2010-2017; Vic Trin Ch Kremmling CO 2004-2006; Exec Coun Mem Colorado Coun of Ch Denver CO 2009-2012; Ecum Off of the Dio Colorado Dio Colorado Denver CO 2009-2012, Exec Com, Colorado Coun of Ch 2009-2012. trthaden@msn.com

THAMES, David Blake (Tex) 4419 Taney Ave No 202, Alexandria VA 22304 B San Antonio TX 1962 s Clendon & Mary. BS U of Texas 1985; MDiv VTS 1992; MS Duquesne U 2011. D 6/27/1992 P 2/1/1993 Bp Maurice Manuel Benitez. c 1. R S Mk's Ch Beaumont TX 2000-2002; Camp Allen Navasota TX 1996-2000; R S Mary's Epis Ch Cypress TX 1994-1996; Asst R S Paul's Ch Waco TX 1992-1994. Sead.

THAO, Choua May (Minn) 2200 Minnehaha Ave E, Saint Paul MN 55119 B Nan Yau Laos 1967 d Cheng & Vang. Med Asst Bryan and Stratton 1992. D 6/20/2015 Bp Brian N Prior. m 10/5/1985 Chay Lee c 4.

THAO, Thomas (Minn) D 6/20/2015 P 6/21/2016 Bp Brian N Prior.

THARAKAN, Angeline H (Ark) 501 S Phoenix Ave, Russellville AR 72801 B IL 1967 d Leslie & Alice. Sewanee TS; BS Illinois St U 1989; MDiv Estrn Bapt TS 1996. D 10/16/2010 P 5/7/2011 Bp Larry Benfield. m 6/8/2003 Jos C Tharakan c 2. Assoc All SS Epis Ch Russellville AR 2011-2014.

THARAKAN, Jos C (Ark) 158 Dawn Cir., Russellville AR 72802 **R All SS Epis Ch Russellville AR 2007-** B Nemmini India 1964 s Chakkunni & Rosy. BA U of Delhi 1988; BA Calv Philos Coll 1991; MDiv St Fran Theol 1995; BEd U of Bhopal 1996. Rec 7/18/2006 Bp Larry Maze. m 6/8/2003 Angeline H Tharakan c 2. Mssy Chapl Chr Ch Mena AR 2006-2007; Dio Arkansas Little Rock AR 2006-2007, Mem of Exec Coun 2009-2012, Mem of COM 2008-2014; Chapl Res Jefferson Reg Med Cntr 2003-2004; Chapl Res Christus Santa Rosa Healthcare 2001-2003; Mem of COM Dio Arkansas Little Rock AR US 2009-2014.

THATCHER, Anne C (Pa) 8000 Saint Martins Ln, Philadelphia PA 19118 **Aux Chapl Welsh Soc of Philadelphia 2017-; Ch Of S Mart-In-The-Fields Philadelphia PA 2015-** B Denver CO 1974 d George & Jaqueline. B.A Whitman Coll 1997; M.Ed Wstrn Washington U 2005; Dipl. Angl Stds Ya Berk 2014; MDIV Yale DS 2014. D 10/19/2014 P 6/6/2015 Bp James E Waggoner Jr. Assoc Ch Of The Mssh Santa Ana CA 2014-2015. athatcher@stmartinec.org

THAYER, Andrew Richard (Ala) 1329 Jackson Ave, Church of the Ascension, Montgomery AL 36104 **R Ch Of The Ascen Montgomery AL 2014-** B Austin TX 1968 s Gilbert & Ann. D. Phil. (Cand.) Oxf GB; BFA U of Texas; MDiv Sewanee: The U So, TS 2004. D 6/26/2004 P 1/6/2005 Bp James Edward Folts. m 6/4/1994 Kelsey M Thayer c 3. S Barth's Ch Corpus Christi TX 2006-2009; S Mk's Epis Ch San Antonio TX 2004-2006. Optime Merens Sewanee 2004. andythay@gmail.com

THAYER JR, Charles Cleveland (FdL) 1409 W Dow Rummel St, Apt 114, Sioux Falls SD 57104 **Died 4/21/2017** B Abingdon VA 1931 s Charles & Margaret. BA Emory and Henry Coll 1953; MDiv Drew U 1956; Nash 1964; U MN 1971. D 12/17/1958 P 12/21/1959 Bp William Henry Marmion. m 6/29/1956 Evelyn Thayer c 1. S Thos' Epis Ch Abingdon VA 1987-2006; R S Aug's Epis Ch Rhinelander WI 1981-1987; S Mart's Epis Ch Fairmont MN 1972-1981; Gd Shpd Blue Earth MN 1972-1976; Chapl The Epis Cathd Of Our Merc Sav Faribault MN 1969-1972; Sub-Dn Cathd Ch Of S Mk Minneapolis MN 1965-1969; Vic S Marks Ch and Gr Hse-on-Mt. S Paul VA 1961-1965; S Mk's Ch S Paul VA 1961-1965; Cur S Jn's Ch Roanoke VA 1957-1961. Angl Soc; Anglicans for Life; Assoc. Sis of H Nativ; CCU; Confraternal Ord of S Ben; CBS; Curs; Ord of St. Vinc; P Assoc. Shrine of Our Lady; Soc. King Chas Mtyr; SocMary. Who's Who Rel 1977.

THAYER, Evan L (Mass) 15 Elko St # 2135, Brighton MA 02135 **S Aug And S Mart Ch Boston MA 2005-** B Baton Rouge LA 1961 BA LSU. D 6/7/2003 P 6/5/2004 Bp M(Arvil) Thomas Shaw. staugustine1@verizon.net

THAYER II, Frederick William (SanD) 12103 Caminito Corriente, San Diego CA 92128 B Quincy MA 1949 s Donald & Corinne. BA Colg 1971; MDiv EDS 1975. D 6/10/1975 Bp John Melville Burgess P 5/2/1976 Bp Robert Rae Spears Jr. m 8/31/1974 Ann Marie Thayer. R S Barth's Epis Ch Poway CA 2006-2013; R Calv Ch Columbia MO 1998-2006; R S Lk's Ch Forest Hills NY 1986-1998; R S Lk's Ch Sea Cliff NY 1980-1986; S Ann's Ch Sayville NY 1977-1980; Asst The Ch Of The Epiph Gates NY 1975-1977; Dioc Exec Coun Dio San Diego San Diego CA 2010-2013, Mem Epis Cmnty Serv Bd 2008-2010; Pres Stndg Com Dio Missouri S Louis MO 2004-2005, Dep to GC 2001-2004, VP Corp 2001-2004; Mem Epis Hlth Serv Bd Dio Long Island Garden City NY 1988-1998.

THAYER, Judith Ann (Ia) 912 20th Ave, Coralville IA 52241 B 1941 d Arthur & Helen. BA U of Iowa 1963; MA U of Iowa 1976. D 12/6/2014 Bp Alan Scarfe. m 9/1/1991 David Lewis Thayer c 3.

THAYER, Steven Allen (NJ) Po Box 440, Jamison PA 18929 **Non-par 1975-** B Berlin NH 1948 s Wendall & Mary. BA Iowa Wesleyan Coll 1970; MDiv PDS 1973. D 4/28/1973 Bp Alfred L Banyard P 10/27/1973 Bp Albert Wiencke Van Duzer. Cur S Jn's Ch Somerville NJ 1973-1975.

THEODORE, Margaret Bessie (Alb) P.O. BOX 446, Potsdam NY 13676 **D Trin Ch Potsdam NY 2011-; Chapl Canton Potsdam Hosp Potsdam NY 2004-; Mem CANTON POTSDAM Hosp Sprtl CARE Com POTSDAM 2003-; Mem Canton Potsdam Hosp Sprtl Care Cmtte Potsdam NY 2003-; Mem**

T

D'S Coun ALBANY Dio 2003-; Mem Deacons' Coun Dio Albany 2003- B Watertown NY 1941 d Peter & Bessie. BS SUNY at Oswego 1966. D 6/29/2003 Bp Daniel William Herzog. m 6/25/1966 Chris James Theodore c 4. Mem Norwood Mnstrl Assoc Norwood NY 2008-2010; D Vic S Phil's Ch Norwood NY 2007-2010; Exec Bd Helping Hands of Potsdam Inc. Potsdam NY 2004-2011; Fac/Tchr PRISON Mnstry BIBLE STUDY MALONE NY 2002-2009; Fac/Tchr Prison Mnstry Bible Study Malone NY 2002-2009. DOK 2003; OSL'S 1991.

THEODORE, Pamela Hillis (Dal) 6055 Walnut Hill Cir, Dallas TX 75230 **Adj P S Mich and All Ang Ch Dallas TX 2004-** B Little Rock AR 1946 d Charles & Polly. BS SMU 1978; MDiv SMU Perkins 1997. D 6/27/1998 P 5/23/1999 Bp James Monte Stanton. m 7/3/1973 Douglas Brent Theodore. Assoc S Mich And All Ang Ch Dallas TX 2009-2015, 2006-2007, Asst R 1998-2004; Chair, Cmsn on Chld & Violence Dio Dallas Dallas TX 1999-2004, Mem, Chr Formation Cmsn 1997-1999.

THEUS SR, James Graves (WLa) 6291 Old Baton Rouge Hwy, Alexandria LA 71302 B Monroe LA 1944 s John & Louise. BA LSU; MDiv Sewanee: The U So, TS 1967. D 6/23/1970 P 4/1/1971 Bp Iveson Batchelor Noland. m 12/29/1982 Caroline Theus c 3. Ch Of The Gd Shpd Cashiers NC 2006, 2005, 2004, 1998-2003; Ch Of The Incarn Highlands NC 2005, 2002-2004, 1998-2002; Calv Ch Bunkie LA 1991-2007; S Jn's Ch Oakdale LA 1983-1986; R S Tim's Ch Alexandria LA 1974-1983; Vic Ch Of The Incarn Amite LA 1971-1974; Chapl So Estrn Louisiana U 1971-1974; Cur Ch Of The Redeem Ruston LA 1970-1971.

THEW, Richard H (EO) Po Box 125, Cove OR 97824 B Long Beach CA 1940 s Henry & Imogene. Oregon Tech Inst 1959; BA Estrn Oregon U 1965; MDiv EDS 1970. D 8/12/1970 P 8/1/1971 Bp William Benjamin Spofford. m 8/31/1968 Kathy Jane Thew c 1. Asst S Ptr's Ch La Grande OR 1981-2002; Chapl Estrn Oregon St Coll 1975-1978; Dio Estrn Oregon Cove OR 1970-1982; Vic S Thos Ch Canyon City OR 1970-1975. thewre@coveoregon.com

THEW FORRESTER, Kevin Lee (NMich) 402 Harrison St, Marquette MI 49855 **Mnstry Dvlp S Jn's Ch Negaunee MI 2008-; S Paul's Ch Marquette MI 2007-** B Monroe MI 1957 s Joseph & Patricia. BA U of St Thos 1980; MA CUA 1984; PhD CUA 1992; MA CDSP 1993. D 6/19/1993 Bp R aymond Stewart Wood Jr P 5/27/1994 Bp Robert Louis Ladehoff. m 11/5/1984 Rise Fay Thew Forrester c 2. Mnstry Dvlpmt Coordntr Dio Nthrn Michigan Marquette MI 2001-2006; Dio Estrn Oregon Cove OR 1997-2001; S Alb's Epis Ch Redmond OR 1997-2001; S Andr's Epis Ch Prineville OR 1997-2001; Co Mssnr S Mk's Epis and Gd Shpd Luth Madras OR 1997-2001; Dio Oregon Portland OR 1996-1997; Vic Four Winds Cmnty Portland OR 1995-1998; S Mich And All Ang Ch Portland OR 1993-1997. Auth, "My Heart is a Raging Volcano of Love for You," LeaderResources, 2011; Auth, "Holding Beauty in My Soul's Arms," LeaderResources, 2011; Auth, "I Have Called You Friends," Ch Pub, 2003; Auth, "Ldrshp And Mnstry Within A Cmnty Of Equals," InterCultural Mnstry Dvlpmt, 1997. kevingtf@gmail.com

THEW FORRESTER, Rise Fay (NMich) 402 Harrison St, Marquette MI 49855 **Mnstry Dvlp So Cntrl Reg Manistique MI 2011-; Mnstry Dvlp Estrn Reg-Dio No. Michigan Sault Ste. Marie MI 2008-** B Hillsboro OR 1964 d Henry & Ann. BS U of Oregon 1986; MDiv CDSP 1993. D 6/10/1993 P 1/22/1994 Bp Robert Louis Ladehoff. m 11/5/1984 Kevin Lee Thew Forrester c 2. Dio Nthrn Michigan Marquette MI 2008-2011, 2001-2003; Mssnr Ch Of S Jas The Less Marquette MI 2001-2003; Mssnr S Thos Ch Canyon City OR 2000-2001; Mssnr Dio Estrn Oregon Cove OR 1997-2001; S Alb's Epis Ch Redmond OR 1997-2001; S Andr's Epis Ch Prineville OR 1997-2001; Co-Mssnr S Mk's Epis and Gd Shpd Luth Madras OR 1997-2001; Dio Oregon Portland OR 1994-1997; Vic S Andr's Ch Portland OR 1994-1997; Chapl Legacy Gd Samar Hosp Portland OR 1993-1994; Assoc S Jn The Evang Ch Portland OR 1993-1994. risetf@gmail.com

THIBODAUX, Louise Ruprecht (Ala) B New York NY 1944 BA Mt Holyoke Coll 1966; MA USC 1969; PhD U of Alabama 2002. D 11/2/2002 Bp Marc Handley Andrus. m 6/23/1973 Paul Thibodaux. S Thos Epis Ch Birmingham AL 2015; D Dio Alabama Birmingham 2005-2015.

THIBODEAUX, James L (Oly) 7904 Manzanita Dr. NW, Olympia WA 98502 **St Chris's Ch - A Fed Cong Olympia WA 2014-; Pres Cler Assn of the Dio Olympia 2017-; Advsry Bd Mem Camp Mich Lacey WA 2016-; Chapl OSF OSF (Epis) 2010-** B Los Gatos CA 1977 s James & Judy. BA Westmont Coll 2000; MDiv Luth TS at Philadelphia 2006; STM GTS 2007. D 3/25/2007 Bp Paul Victor Marshall P 5/18/2008 Bp Bavi Edna Rivera. m 7/28/2001 Annaka G Gustafson Annaka Alane c 2. R St Ptr's Epis Par Seattle WA 2008-2014; Dioc Coun Dio Olympia Seattle 2012-2014; GC Alt 2011-2012, Safeguarding God's Chld Trnr 2011-, Epis Asian-Amer Com 2008-2010. james.thibodeaux@gmail.com

THIEL, Spencer Edwin (Chi) 12407 S 82nd Ave, Palos Park IL 60464 **Died 10/31/2016** B Oak Park IL 1940 s Edwin & Margaret. BA NWU 1962; STM GTS 1965; STM SWTS 1970. D 6/12/1965 Bp Gerald Francis Burrill P 12/18/1965 Bp James Winchester Montgomery. P-in-c S Chris's Ch Crown Point IN 2002-2016; Vic Santa Teresa Chicago IL 1994-1995; P-in-C Santa Teresa

Chicago IL 1992-1994; P-in-C S Aid Blue Island IL 1973-1974; S Jos's And S Aid's Ch Blue Island IL 1970-2001; R S Jos Chicago IL 1970-1973; Cur Trin Ch Highland Pk IL 1967-1970; Cur S Greg's Epis Ch Deerfield IL 1965-1967. Hisp Affrs Cmsn; Int Mnstry Ntwk 2000; Spanish-Spkng Priests Assn. stchristophercp@juno.com

THIELE, William C (Nwk) 215 Lafayette Ave., Passaic NJ 07055 **R S Jn's Ch Passaic NJ 2007-** B Detroit MI 1942 s Richard & Clara. BS Pur 1965; MDiv GTS 2004. D 6/12/2004 P 12/19/2004 Bp George Edward Councell. m 4/26/1986 Marilyn M Schaefer c 3. Cur S Paul's Epis Ch Westfield NJ 2004-2006.

THIERING, Barry Bernard (WTex) 2404 W Riviera Dr, Cedar Park TX 78613 **Chapl Robinson Creek Hospice Austin TX 2008-** B Sydney NSW AU 1930 s Bernard & Pearl. ThL Moore Theol Coll Sydney 1954; BA U of Sydney 1954; Dip Rel Educ Melbourne Coll of Div 1956; MA U of Sydney 1967; DMin SFTS 1983. Trans 6/10/1992 as Priest Bp John Herbert MacNaughton. m 9/5/1981 Linda Carol Wukasch c 5. P / Prchr Food for the Poor Inc Coconut Creek FL 2000-2010; P-in-c Emm Epis Ch Lockhart TX 1992-2000; S Eliz's Epis Ch Buda TX 1992-1994; Lectr St. Fran Angl Coll (Sem) Brisbane Qld 1986-1989; Asst Chapl St. Paul's Sch Bald Hills Brisbane Qld 1986-1989; Sch Chapl Cranbrook Sch Sydney NSW 1959-1986; R St. Stephens Mitagong NSW 1956-1959. Auth, *The Bk of Howlers*, Kangaroo Press, 1985; Auth, *Australian Ch*, Ure Smith, 1979; Auth and Co-Ed, *Towards Understanding (series of textbooks)*, Westbooks, 1974; Co-Auth, *Some Trust in Chariots*, Westbooks, 1973; Auth, *A Guide to Me & You*, Fam Life Mvmt of Australia, 1967. Mem of the Australian Coll of Educ 1988; Mem of the Australian Coll of Educ 1968.

THIGPEN III, William Mccord (At) 5152 Patriot Dr, Stone Mountain GA 30087 B Atlanta GA 1955 s William & Doris. BS Oral Roberts U 1978; BA Oral Roberts U 1978; MDiv GTS 1983. D 6/25/1983 Bp Gerald Nicholas Mcallister P 5/26/1984 Bp William Jackson Cox. m 6/28/2013 John Paul Lavier c 3. R S Barth's Epis Ch Atlanta GA 2002-2016; Trin Epis Par Los Angeles CA 1990-2002; Tchr S Jas Sch Los Angeles CA 1990-1991; R S Jas' Sch Los Angeles CA 1990-1991; Asst R S Jas Par Los Angeles CA 1988-1990; Trin Ch Tulsa OK 1983-1988; Dep GC 2012 Dio Atlanta Atlanta GA 2011-2013, Stndg Com 2011-2013. Auth, "Let your heart sing!," *Pathways*, Dio Atlanta, 2008; Auth, "Out in Sprt," *Edge Sprtlty Column*, Edge mag, 1994.

THIM, Paul Russell (At) 697 Densley Dr., Decatur GA 30033 **Primary Counslr Metro Atlanta Recovery Residences Inc. 2008-** B New Haven CT 1946 s John & Mary. BA Swarthmore Coll 1968; MDiv Candler TS Emory U 1972. D 10/23/1974 P 6/2/1975 Bp Bennett Jones Sims. m 1/24/1981 Alexandra Thim c 2. Cov Cmnty Inc Atlanta GA 2004-2006; Cov Cmnty Inc. 2004-2006; Assoc R - Chr Soc Mnstrs All SS Epis Ch Atlanta GA 1997-2004, Asst 1974-1981; S Barth's Epis Ch Atlanta GA 1996-2007; S Lk's Epis Ch Atlanta GA 1995-1997; St Lukes Trng & Coun.Ctr Atlanta GA 1995-1997; Epis Ch Of The H Fam Jasper GA 1994; Ch Of The Ascen Cartersville GA 1992-1994; Dio Wstrn Massachusetts Springfield 1987-1992; R S Jn's Ch Worcester MA 1987-1992; S Augustines Ch S Louis MO 1981-1987; P S Paul's Ch S Louis MO 1981-1987; Dio Missouri S Louis MO 1981-1982.

THOBER, Ellie Thober (Neb) 4718 18th St, Columbus NE 68601 B San Pedro CA 1943 d Melvin & Mildred. Dip Bp Clarkson Sch of Nrsng 1969; BA Doane Coll 1990; MDiv VTS 2004. D 6/18/2004 P 12/19/2004 Bp Joe Goodwin Burnett. c 3. R Gr Ch Par -Epis Columbus NE 2010-2016; Exec Cmsn Dio Nebraska Omaha NE 2007-2010, Ins Com 2010-, 2004-2010; R Ch of Our Sav No Platte NE 2006-2010; Cur S Andr's Ch Omaha NE 2004-2006.

THOENI, Thomas Andrew (SwFla) 302 Carey St, Plant City FL 33563 **R S Ptr's Ch Plant City FL 2003-** B Ocala FL 1962 s John & Martha. BD U of Florida 1988; MDiv SWTS 1994; DMin SWTS 2012. D 6/18/1994 P 12/21/1994 Bp Stephen Hays Jecko. m 12/28/1996 Quincey B Thoeni c 2. Asst Chr Epis Ch Pensacola FL 1997-2003; S Paul's Ch Albany GA 1994-1997.

THOM, Ashley Jane Squier (Chi) 3626 N. Francisco Ave., Chicago IL 60618 B Burlington VT 1965 d Kenley & Susan. BA Stan 1988; MDiv Harvard DS 1993; CAS Nash 1998. D 6/10/1998 P 12/17/1998 Bp Roger John White. m 7/31/1993 Winfield Scott Thom. P All SS Epis Ch Chicago IL 2000-2002; Dio Milwaukee Milwaukee WI 1998; Cur Trin Ch Janesville WI 1998.

✠ **THOM, The Rt Rev Brian James** (Ida) 1858 W. Judith Lane, Boise ID 83705 **Bp of Idaho Dio Idaho Boise ID 2008-; Epis Visitor Brothers of St Jn the Evang Freeland WA 2016-** B Portland OR 1955 s Arnold & Rose. BS OR SU 1980; MDiv CDSP 1987. D 6/24/1987 P 3/25/1988 Bp Robert Louis Ladehoff Con 10/11/2008 for Ida. m 1/30/2010 Ardele R Hanson c 2. R Ch Of The Ascen Twin Falls ID 1991-2008; Asst R S Marg's Epis Ch Palm Desert CA 1989-1991; Cur Epis Par Of S Jn The Bapt Portland OR 1987-1989. D. Div (Honoris Causa) CDSP 2014. bthom@idahodiocese.org

THOM, Dave (Az) 540 Atchison Lane, Wickenburg AZ 85390 **Chapl Fed Bureau of Investigation (FBI) Phoenix AZ 2006-** B Chicago IL 1944 s Franklin & Annabelle. Maryknoll TS 1965; BA Seattle U 1966; Arizona St U 1982; CAS Sewanee: The U So, TS 1999; STM Sewanee: The U So, TS 2004. Rec 11/24/1996 as Deacon Bp Bertram Nelson Herlong. c 4. R S Alb's Epis Ch Wickenburg AZ 2006-2008; Int Ch Of The Adv Sun City W AZ 2005; R Ch Of The Epiph Tunica MS 1999-2004; D S Clem's Epis Ch Clemmons NC 1998-1999;

T

S Jn's Epis Ch Mt Juliet TN 1997-1998; D The Ch Of The Epiph Lebanon TN 1997-1998; D S Phil's Ch Nashville TN 1997; D RC Ch 1980-1996.

THOM, Kenneth Stow (Eas) 3849 Sirman Dr, Snow Hill MD 21863 B Philadelphia PA 1937 s William & Catherine. BS Drexel U 1960; MDiv VTS 2001. D 5/19/2001 Bp Martin Gough Townsend P 11/18/2001 Bp Charles Lindsay Longest. m 7/4/1958 Arlene McElhaney c 2. P-in-c All Hallow's Ch Snow Hill MD 2003-2009; Asst R Ch Of S Paul's By The Sea Ocean City MD 2001-2002.

THOMAS, Adam P (Ct) 15 Pearl St, Mystic CT 06355 **S Mk's Ch Mystic CT 2014-** B Portland ME 1983 s William & Edna. BA U So 2005; MDiv VTS 2008. D 12/15/2007 P 6/14/2008 Bp William Michie Klusmeyer. m 2/12/2011 Leah E Thomas c 2. S Steph's Ch Cohasset MA 2010-2014; Trin Epis Ch Martinsburg WV 2008-2010. Auth, "Unusual Gospel for Unusual People," Abingdon Press, 2014; Auth, "Letters from Ruby," Abingdon Press, 2013; Auth, "Who is Jesus?," *Converge Bible Study Series*, Abingdon Press, 2013; Auth, "Digital Disciple," Abingdon Press, 2011; Auth, "Living by the Word," *The Chr Century*, 2010. rector@stmarksmystic.org

THOMAS, Allisyn Lorna (SanD) St. Paul's Cathedral, 2728 Sixth Avenue, San Diego CA 92103 **Dio San Diego San Diego CA 2013-; Sub-Dn St. Paul's Cathd San Diego CA 2007-; Cn for Sprtl Formation St. Paul's Cathd San Diego CA 2002-** B Berkeley CA 1953 d Geoffrey & Lorna. BA Wstrn St U Coll of Law 1982; JD Wstrn St U Coll of Law 1982; ETSBH 1996; MDiv GTS 2000. D 6/10/2000 P 12/14/2000 Bp Gethin Benwil Hughes. m 12/22/1999 John A Thomas. Cn Cathd Ch Of S Paul San Diego CA 2002-2013; Assoc Pstr S Jn's Epis Ch Chula Vista CA 2000-2002. Juris Prudence Awd Wstrn St U Coll of Law. athomas@edsd.org

THOMAS JR, Arthur Robert (Ak) Po Box 1872, Seward AK 99664 **R S Ptr's Ch Seward AK 2013-, R 2000-2008; Instr Alaska Maritime Trng Cntr Seward AK 2008-** B Seattle WA 1957 s Arthur & Joanne. BA Chapman U 1993; MA Salve Regina U 2000; MDiv Vancouver TS CA 2006. D 12/21/1999 Bp Drexel Gomez P 8/6/2000 Bp Mark Lawrence Macdonald. Dio Alaska Stndg Com 2004-2008; Chapl Sprg Creek Correctional Cntr Seward AK 2003-2008; Var USCG 1976-2000.

THOMAS JR CSM, Benjamin A (ETenn) Sewanee U So TS Sewanee TN 2016- D 2/11/2017 Bp George Young III.

THOMAS, Benjamin Randall (WK) 402 S 8th St, Salina KS 67401 **S Fran Cmnty Serv Inc. Salina KS 2016-** B Fresno 1974 s Bobby & Rhonda. BS U of Oklahoma 1997; BA U of Oklahoma 1997; MA CU- Boulder Boulder CO 2000; MDiv GTS 2007; MDiv GTS 2007; Th.D GTS 2011. D 6/9/2007 P 12/8/2007 Bp Robert John O'Neill. m 3/22/2002 Holly Ann Thomas c 4. Chr Cathd Salina KS 2010-2016; Gr Epis Ch New York NY 2008-2010; Property Mgr 2000-2004. Auth, "An Angl Hermeneutic of the Trsfg," Ptr Lang, 2013; Auth, "Priests and Bishops in Bede's Ecclesiology: the use of 'sacerdos' through the Historia," *Ecclesiology*, Brill, 2010; Auth, "Chr Hope and Liturg Ord in 1 Clem 40-44," *Internationale Kirchliche Zeitschrift*, Stampfli Publikationen AG, 2008.

THOMAS, Bethany (Colo) 1221 Illinois St. Apt 2A, Golden CO 80401 **D Calv Ch Golden CO 1998-, 1997, 1989-1995** B Lansing MI 1950 d William & Beverly. AA Grand Rapids Cmnty Coll 1970; BA Wstrn Michigan U 1972; U MI 1975; S Thos Sem 1987. D 9/21/1988 Bp William Harvey Wolfrum P. c 4.

THOMAS, Cheeramattathu John (Tex) 301 Eagle Lakes Dr, Friendswood TX 77546 B Punnaveli Kerala IN 1925 s Cheeramattathu & Mariam. BA S Berchmans Coll Changanacherry IN 1946; BD Govt Teachers Coll 1949; BD Untd Theol Coll Serampore U Bangalore IN 1955; MA Andover Newton TS 1966. Trans 8/1/1996 Bp Claude Edward Payne. m 6/9/1955 Mary Abraham. Mssy S Steph's Ch Liberty TX 1997-1998; R Adv Dio TX 1990-1993; P S Thos Ch Houston TX 1988-1989; Serv Ch Of Engl 1965-1983; Chapl Osl League City TX. Auth, "The Mssy Task Of Our Csi Members In No Amer," Csi Coun Of No Amer, 1998; Auth, "A Short Hist Of The First Hundred Years Of The Par Ch Of S Jn The Evang Great Sutton 1879-1979," Dio Chester, 1979; Auth, "Some Thoughts On Adv And Christmas," Eastham Par Ch, 1972.

THOMAS, David R (Nwk) 7740 LIGUTHOUSE COVE DR., PORT HOPE MI 48468 B Highland Park MI 1942 s Evan & Monima. BA Detroit Inst of Tech 1965; S Davids Coll Lampeter GB 1966; MDiv CDSP 1968; MA Montclair St U 1981; EdS Seton Hall U 1984. D 6/29/1968 Bp Archie H Crowley P 3/1/1969 Bp Richard Stanley Merrill Emrich. m 7/28/1979 Daphne Florence Thomas c 4. P-in-c S Paul's Epis Ch Bad Axe MI 2010-2014; Long Term Int Chr Ch Harrison NJ 2000-2010; Supply P Chr Ch Harrison NJ 2000-2010; S Cyp's Epis Ch Hackensack NJ 1991-2000; Int and Suooly Dio Newark NJ 1974-1991; S Jn's Ch Passaic NJ 1972-1974; Calv Ch Tamaqua PA 1970-1972; R S Phil's Summit Hill PA 1970-1972; R Trin And S Phil's Epis Ch Lansford PA 1970-1972; Vic S Anne's Epis Ch Trexlertown PA 1969-1970; Cur The Ch Of The Redeem Southfield MI 1968-1969.

THOMAS, Douglas Earl (WTex) 2722 Old Ranch Rd, San Antonio TX 78217 B Corpus Christi TX 1944 s Jesse & Gertrude. BA Texas A&M U Kingsville 1971; MDiv Epis TS of the SW 1974. D 6/6/1974 Bp Richard Earl Dicus P 12/7/1974 Bp Harold Cornelius Gosnell. m 2/14/1970 Pamela Thomas c 1. Epis Ch Of The Mssh Gonzales TX 1993-1995; R The Mssh Epis Ch Gonzales TX 1993-1995; R Gr Ch Port Lavaca TX 1988-1993; Asst R / Sch Chapl S Geo

Ch San Antonio TX 1985-1988; R St Chris's By-the-Sea Epis Ch Portland TX 1983-1985; S Chris's By The Sea Portland TX 1978-1985; Vic St Chris's By-the-Sea Epis Ch Portland TX 1978-1983; H Comf Sinton TX 1978-1980; Asst R S Lk's Epis Ch San Antonio TX 1976-1978; R Ch Of The Annunc Luling TX 1974-1976.

THOMAS, Douglas Paul (NwT) 602 Meander St, Abilene TX 79602 **Ch of the Heav Rest Abilene Abilene TX 2016-** B Brownwood TX 1947 s Carlos & Anita. BA California Bapt Coll 1969; PhD Untd States Intl U 1981; Cert Dio NW Texas Sch of Ord Mnstry 2016. D 12/12/2015 P 6/23/2016 Bp James Scott Mayer. m 12/19/1970 Deanna Kay Thomas c 1.

THOMAS, Elaine Ellis (Va) St. Paul's Memorial Church, 1700 University Avenue, Charlottesville VA 22903 **S Paul's Memi Charlottesvlle VA 2014-** B Kinston NC 1960 d Leland & Diane. BA Estrn U 1999; MDiv Ya Berk 2013. D 6/2/2013 P 4/29/2014 Bp Nathan Dwight Baxter. m 10/1/1999 Timothy Ivan Thomas c 2. Cur S Edw's Epis Ch Lancaster PA 2014. elaine.thomas@stpaulsmemorialchurch.org

THOMAS JR, Frederick S (Md) 707 Park Ave, Baltimore MD 21201 **Died 5/26/2016** B Erwin NC 1948 s Fredrick & Elizabeth. MDiv GTS; BA U So. D 5/31/1973 Bp Addison Hosea P 12/1/1973 Bp David Keller Leighton Sr. Asst Gr And S Ptr's Ch Baltimore MD 1977-2016; Asst S Mich's Ch New York NY 1975-1976; Asst Mt Calv Ch Baltimore MD 1973-1975. CCU, ECM, Cath League, Epis Syn Amer.

THOMAS, Jaime Alfredo (Dal) P.O. Box 15, Fort Ord CA 93941 B Consuelo DO 1943 s John & Helena. BA Inter Amer U of Puerto Rico 1969; MDiv ETSC 1974. D 8/18/1974 Bp Telesforo A Isaac P 6/1/1977 Bp Francisco Reus-Froylan. c 2. Asst St Paul's/San Pablo Epis Ch Salinas CA 1999-2003; Off Of Bsh For ArmdF New York NY 1978-1993; Asst Sagrada Familia in Puerto Rico 1976-1978; Dio The Dominican Republic (Iglesia Epis Dominicana) Gazcue Santo Domingo 1974-1976.

THOMAS JR, James Morris (ECR) 18402 Yale Court, Somoma CA 95476 **P-in-c Trin Ch Sonoma CA 2011-; Assoc to the R S Andr's Epis Ch Saratoga CA 2003-** B Sedalia MO 1940 s James & Thelma. BS Drury U 1963; MS Estrn Washington U 1970; PhD Oklahoma St U 1973; MDiv VTS 2001. D 6/23/2001 Bp Robert Manning Moody P 1/31/2002 Bp Richard Lester Shimpfky. m 1/1/1981 Sara Thomas c 2. S Andr's Ch Saratoga CA 2004-2010; Dio El Camino Real Salinas CA 2002-2003; Cn to the Ordnry Dio El Camino Real Seaside CA 2002-2003; Assoc P S Tim's Epis Ch Mtn View CA 2001-2002; S Tim's Epis Ch Mtn View CA 2001. "The Seven Steps to Personal Power: Creating Opportunities Within," Hlth Cmncatn, Inc., 1993; "arts & Bk chapters re. Mntl Hlth issues".

THOMAS, John Alfred (Va) 3800 Powell Ln Apt 813, Falls Church VA 22041 B Dubuque IA 1933 s Gailen & Martha. MA Aquinas Inst of Theol 1959; MA Aquinas Inst of Theol 1960; STD U of S Thos Rome It 1962. Rec 5/13/1976 as Deacon Bp Robert Bruce Hall. m 9/7/1968 Helene C Garrett. Int Ch Of The H Cross Dunn Loring VA 1999-2001; Asst S Jas' Epis Ch Warrenton VA 1991-1997; Asst S Alb's Epis Ch Annandale VA 1976-1991. Ed, "Reconsiderations". CHS 1983.

THOMAS, John Harvey (Mass) Po Box 536, Sandwich MA 02563 **Died 11/18/2016** B Camden ME 1928 s George & Frances. BS U of Maine 1950; MDiv EDS 1959; DMin VTS 1987. D 6/1/1959 Bp Anson Phelps Stokes Jr P 1/17/1960 Bp Frederic Cunningham Lawrence. c 5. Ret 1993-2016; R S Jn's Ch Sandwich MA 1993, M-in-c 1959-1968. Auth, *Thesis Mnstry w Men in a Sm Town*.

THOMAS, John Paul (Dal) 739 Middale Rd, Duncanville TX 75116 **Consult Wycliffe Bible Translators Orlando FL 1982-** B Seattle WA 1952 s Robert & Aileen. BS U of Washington 1974; MDiv Gordon-Conwell TS 1982; MA U of No Dakota 1992. D 10/18/2008 Bp James Monte Stanton. m 12/19/1981 Barbara Perch c 2. Field Rep Kellermann Fndt 2014-2017. bophame@gmail.com

THOMAS, John Taliaferro (Ga) 290 Quintard Rd, Sewanee TN 37375 **Frederica Acad St Simons Island GA 2017-; Headmaster St. Andr's-Sewanee Sch Sewanee TN 2008-** B Wilmington OH 1966 s Emory & Frances. BA U So 1988; MDiv VTS 1993. D 6/12/1993 Bp Peter J Lee P 2/10/1994 Bp Charles Farmer Duvall. m 2/20/1993 Janice M Thomas c 2. Chr Ch Frederica St Simons Is GA 2016-2017; P S Andr's-Sewanee Sch Sewanee TN 2008-2016; S Andr's Epis Sch Potomac MD 2002-2008; S Columba's Ch Washington DC 2002-2007; Chapl S Andrews Epis Sch Potomac MD 1999-2008; Assoc R S Lk's Epis Ch Atlanta GA 1996-1999; Asst R Chr Epis Ch Pensacola FL 1993-1996.

THOMAS, John Walter Riddle (ETenn) 4530 Joack Ln, Hixson TN 37343 **Died 10/12/2015** B Richard City TN 1929 s Walter & Bennie. BMus U of Chattanooga 1951; STB PDS 1960. D 7/3/1960 P 4/25/1961 Bp John Vander Horst. m 4/25/1962 Elizabeth Carleton Etter c 1. Assoc S Ptr's Ch Chattanooga TN 1998-2010; Ret 1995-2015; Vic S Mk's Ch Copperhill TN 1992-1995; R Trin Epis Ch Gatlinburg TN 1986-1992; R Ch Of The H Cross Sullivans Island SC 1984-1986; R S Paul's Ch Bennettsville SC 1972-1984; Vic S Lk's Epis Ch Honolulu HI 1970-1971; Vic H Cross Malaekahana HI 1967-1970; Chapl S Andr's Priory Sch 1967-1970; P-in-c S Barn Ch Tullahoma TN 1962-1967; S Bede's Epis Ch Manchester TN 1962-1965; Vic S Elis's Epis Ch Memphis TN 1960-1962; Vic S Eliz's Mssn 1960-1962; S Mary's Cathrdral 1960-1962.

THOMAS, Jonathan R (Chi) 1864 Post Rd, Darien CT 06820 **St Paul's Epis Ch Peoria IL 2015-** B Fredericksburg VA 1981 s Janes & Robin. BA U of Virginia 2004; MDiv PrTS 2010; Dip Ang Stud VTS 2011. D 6/18/2011 P 12/16/2011 Bp George Edward Councell. m 6/20/2014 Jennifer Replogle. S Lk's Par Darien CT 2011-2015.

THOMAS, Joshua (Oly) 505 Alexander Ave, Durham NC 27705 **Exec Dir Kids4Peace Intl 2010-** B Kingston PA 1977 s Jay & Dorothy. AB Dart 2000; MDiv UTS 2005; PhD (cand) Candler TS Emory U 2014. D 6/1/2007 P 1/20/2008 Bp Vicky Gene Robinson. Asst S Mk's Ch Washington DC 2015; Dioc Stff Dio Olympia Seattle 2011-2013; Int Pstr Ch of the Apos Seattle WA 2011-2012; Lectr Bos TS 2009-2010; Bos Dio Massachusetts Boston MA 2009-2010; Dio New Hampshire Concord NH 2008-2010; Asstg P S Andr's Ch New London NH 2008-2010; Dir of Yth & YA Mnstry S Barth's Epis Ch Atlanta GA 2007-2008.

THOMAS, Kathryn L (NI) 10010 Aurora Pl, Fort Wayne IN 46804 **R Gr Epis Ch Ft Wayne IN 2008-** B Lakewood OH 1951 d Leo & Ruth. BS Kent St U 1973; MA St Meinrad TS 1988; MDiv Chr TS 2001. D 2/15/2004 P 10/3/2004 Bp Cate Waynick. m 10/14/1972 David S Thomas c 3. Assoc R S Paul's Epis Ch Indianapolis IN 2004-2008; Dir. of CE S Chris's Epis Ch Carmel IN 1992-2003; Tchr, Rel Stds Cathd HS 1990-2003; DRE St. Paul's Cath Ch Tell City IN U.S.A 1983-1989. kthomas@gracefwi.comcastbiz.net

THOMAS, Kathryn Pauline (Va) 214 Church St, Madison VA 22727 B Ft Clayton Panama 1951 d Ovel & Pauline. BA and MT Mary Baldwin Coll 1976; Diac Formation Inst 2012. D 2/23/2013 Bp Shannon Sherwood Johnston. m 7/24/1970 John Robert Thomas c 5.

THOMAS, Keila Carpenter (Lex) 145 E 5th St, Morehead KY 40351 **P-in-c S Alb's Ch Morehead KY 2013-, 2012-2014; M-in-c Dio Lexington Lexington 2012-** B Lexington KY 1951 d Ralph & Alice. Melodyland TS; Masters of Sci U of Kentucky 1980; Doctorate U of Kentucky 1984; Cert SWTS 2012. D 6/30/2012 Bp Chilton Richardson Knudsen P 1/5/2013 Bp Doug Hahn. m 1/1/1985 John Charles Thomas c 2. keilacarpenterthomas@gmail.com

THOMAS, Kenneth Dana (Ct) 5 Bassett St Apt B10, West Haven CT 06516 **Ret 1991-; Atndg P Chr Ch New Haven CT 1991-** B Bridgeport CT 1927 s Kenneth & Bessie. BA Trin Hartford CT 1952; STB GTS 1955. D 6/14/1955 P 5/26/1956 Bp Walter H Gray. R S Jn's Epis Ch Essex CT 1964-1991; St Pauls Mssn of the Deaf W Hartford CT 1958-1964; P-in-c St. Paul's Epis Ch Hartford CT 1958-1964; Cur Trin Epis Ch Hartford CT 1955-1958.

THOMAS, Laughton (Fla) 516 Howard Ave, Tallahassee FL 32310 B Buffalo NY 1945 s Laughton & Ormah. BS SUNY 1973; MDiv GTS 1978. D 6/3/1978 P 12/1/1978 Bp Albert Wiencke Van Duzer. m 6/16/2012 Sharon Sams Thomas. S Mich And All Ang Ch Tallahassee FL 2003-2013; S Paul's Coll Lawrenceville VA 1993-2002; Chapl S Paul's Coll 1989-2002; Vic S Paul's Memi Chap Lawrenceville VA 1989-2002; Chapl USNR (Ret) 1989-1998; S Alb's Epis Ch New Brunswick NJ 1979-1989; Asst S Mk's Ch Plainfield NJ 1978.

THOMAS, Leonard Everett (EC) 916 Lord Granville Dr., Morehead City NC 28557 **R S Fran by the Sea Bogue Banks Salter Path NC 2008-** B Gastonia NC 1943 s Leonard & Thelma. MDiv SE Bapt TS 1968; ThM SE Bapt TS 1975; DMin SE Bapt TS 1977; BA Mars Hill Coll 1995; PhD GTF 2000. D 1/27/1978 P 5/30/1978 Bp Hunley Agee Elebash. R The Epis Ch Of Gd Shpd Asheboro NC 2000-2008; R S Lk's Epis Ch Lincolnton NC 1983-2000; S Jn's Epis Ch Fayetteville NC 1978-1982. AAMFC; AAPC; Natl Allnce Of Familly Life Incorporated.

THOMAS, Margaret (ECR) 1084 Paseo Guebabi, Rio Rico AZ 85648 **S Phil's Ch San Jose CA 2014-; Mem, Border Issues/Immigration Prog Grp Dio Arizona Phoenix AZ 2006-, Mem, Hisp Mnstry Prog Grp 2006-, ERD Dioc Rep 2005-** B Sonora CA 1947 d Leon & Catherine. BA Bryn 1968; Cert Universidad de San Cristobal de Huamanga Ayacucho PE 1969; MA Washington U 1972; MDiv CDSP 1995. D 6/9/1995 Bp Robert Louis Ladehoff P 12/20/1995 Bp James Louis Jelinek. San Pablo Iglesia Anglicana de Mex Guanajuato 2012-2014; Dio Arizona Phoenix AZ 2004-2006; R S Andr's Epis Ch Nogales AZ 2003-2012; Supvsr/Team Mentor Sprt of the Lakes Total Mnstry Team Hermantown MN 2002-2003; Assoc R The Par of St Paul's Epis Ch Duluth MN 1995-2003; Ombudsperson & Mem, Bd Trst CDSP Berkeley CA 1994-1995; Serv on Immigration and Hisp Commissions Ecum Mnstrs of Oregon Portland OR 1984-1992; Dir D Formation Prog Dio Minnesota Minneapolis MN 1999-2001, Liturg & Mus Cmsn 1996-2000. "The Legacy of Enmegahbowh," *The Great Minnesota Welcome, 74th GC*, The Epis Dio Minnesota, 2003. MinnECA 1996-2003; NNECA 1996. Louise Hunderup Awd/Rel Educ Ecum Mnstrs of Oregon 1993.

THOMAS, Margaret Ann (Me) 297 Wardwell Point Rd, Penobscot ME 04476 B Cleveland OH 1945 d Frank & Marie. BA Albion Coll 1967; MA MI SU 1969; PhD MI SU 1981; Bangor TS 1995; MDiv GTS 1997. D 8/16/1997 Bp Frederick Barton Wolf P 6/6/1998 Bp Chilton Richardson Knudsen. m 9/14/1978 James Blake Thomas. P-in-c Trin Ch Castine ME 2011-2014, P Assoc

2003-; Coordntr of Angl Stds Bangor TS & Dio Maine 2002-2010; Sprtl Ed Advsr FaithLinks Chicago IL 2001-2003; Coordntr of D Formation Prog Dio Maine Portland ME 1999-2010; St Fran By The Sea Epis Ch Blue Hill ME 1997-1999. SSM / Assoc 2002.

THOMAS, Margaret Warren (Minn) 9426 Congdon Blvd, Duluth MN 55804 B Ann Arbor MI 1936 d Edward & Wava. SWTS; BA U MI 1958; MA U MI 1982; MDiv Untd TS of the Twin Cities 1997. D 6/13/1997 P 12/15/1997 Bp James Louis Jelinek. m 11/29/1958 Nelson Allen Thomas c 3. The Par of St Paul's Epis Ch Duluth MN 2010, Asst 2006-2009; S Edw's Ch Duluth MN 2004-2006, 1999-2003, 1998.

THOMAS, Marilu James (Va) B Atlanta GA 1957 d Clarence & Rose. Rec 2/1/2017 as Priest Bp Shannon Sherwood Johnston. m 6/19/1982 Stuart C Thomas c 2. Other Lay Position Chr Epis Ch Charlottesvlle VA 2014-2017. marilu@christchurchcville.org

THOMAS, Megan Evans (NJ) 16 All Saints Rd, Princeton NJ 08540 **S Lk's Ch Trenton NJ 2014-** B Newport News VA 1957 d Lowell & Judith. AB Dart 1979; JD U of Pennsylvania Law Sch 1989; MDiv GTS 2014; MDiv The GTS 2014. D 6/8/2013 Bp George Edward Councell. m 9/27/2014 Thomas Bodenberg c 4. met1283@aol.com

THOMAS, Michael Jon (WNY) 703 W Ferry St Apt C9, Buffalo NY 14222 **1993-** B Auburn NY 1939 s Joseph & Janice. BA Cntrl Wesleyan Coll Cntrl SC 1966; Bex Sem 1968; CDSP 1969. D 6/21/1969 P 1/3/1970 Bp Lauriston L Scaife. m 2/12/2011 Katrina P Thomas. P-in-c S Mich's Epis Ch Oakfield NY 1984-1992; 1972-1983; Cur Gr Ch Lockport NY 1969-1971.

THOMAS, Micki-Ann (Alb) PO Box 29, Greenwich NY 12834 B Barton VT 1948 d Thomas & Alice. LPN Sthrn Adirondack Ed Ctr 1983; AS Nrsng Adirondack Cmnty Coll 1989. D 5/10/2008 Bp William Howard Love. m 7/2/1966 Ronald Lucien Thomas c 3.

THOMAS, Patricia Menne (EC) 136 Saint Andrews Cir, New Bern NC 28562 B Evanston IL 1936 d Wilbur & Kathryn. BA U CA 1958; MDiv VTS 1979; DMin VTS 1988. D 6/15/1979 P 4/13/1980 Bp Dean Theodore Stevenson. m 8/16/1958 Hoben Thomas c 2. Ch Of The H Innoc Seven Sprg NC 2004-2007; Asst S Paul's Epis Ch Greenville NC 2003-2005; R Chr Ch New Bern NC 1999-2002; VTS Alexandria VA 1998, Liturg Instr 1996, 1989-1994; Cn Precentor Cathd of St Ptr & St Paul Washington DC 1996-1999; Cn to Ordnry Dio Washington Washington DC 1992-1996; Assoc R S Columba's Ch Washington DC 1984-1992; Vic S Jn's Epis Ch Huntingdon PA 1980-1984; Field Wkr Dio Cntrl Pennsylvania Harrisburg PA 1979-1984; Chapl Epis Mnstry Penn St U PA 1979-1980. Auth, *Identification & Trng of Baptismal Sponsors in a Par Setting*, 1988.[1]Fllshp Contemplative Pryr, WECA 1980-1986.

THOMAS, Peter Glyn (Tex) 831 Walker Stone Dr Apt 104, Cary NC 27513 B Detroit MI 1938 s Glyn & Marion. BA U So 1960; MDiv VTS 1963; DMin Candler TS Emory U 1993. D 6/29/1963 P 6/29/1964 Bp Richard Henry Baker. m 11/28/1964 Carolyn M McLoud c 2. Dir Pstr Care and Mssn Outreach S Mart's Epis Ch Houston TX 1996-2004; Adj Prof Beeson Sch of Div Birmingham AL 1993-1995; Cn Dir Pstr Care & Prog The Cathd Ch Of The Adv Birmingham AL 1989-1996; R S Paul's Ch Augusta GA 1981-1989; S Lk's Epis Ch Atlanta GA 1976-1981, Asst 1970-1976; Dir St Lukes Trng & Coun.Ctr Atlanta GA 1976-1981; Assoc Ch Of The H Comm Memphis TN 1966-1970; Cur Ch Of The H Comf Charlotte NC 1963-1966; Bd Trst Sewanee U So TS Sewanee TN 1986-1988. Clincl Pstr Eductr, "CPE Supvsr," *Lay Pstr Educ in the Urban Par: A Methodology of Recon for Practical Theol*, Emory U, 1993. Cert Supvsr, Assoc. of CPE 1976-2013; Clincl Mem For AAMFT 1976-2013; Ldrshp, Georgia 1981-1987. cmtpgt@gmail.com

THOMAS JR, Phillip Langston (La) 1318 Washington Ave, New Orleans LA 70130 **Died 3/15/2017** B Erwin NC 1934 s Phillip & Rose. U NC 1957; LTh Epis TS in Kentucky 1968; MS Estrn Kentucky U 1971; MDiv Epis TS in Kentucky 1971. D 5/25/1968 P 12/15/1968 Bp William R Moody. c 2. Ret 1994-2017; Non-par 1988-1994; S Mary's Ch Franklin LA 1985-1988; The Dept Of Missions Danville KY 1984-1985; Cn Mssny Cathd Of S Geo The Mtyr Lexington KY 1982-1985; S Aug's Chap Lexington KY 1981-1983; R Chr Ch Slidell LA 1975-1981; Chapl Se La Mntl Hosp 1975-1981; Fndr Chr In Hai 1972-1981; R S Phil's Ch Brevard NC 1971-1975; Vic S Phil's Ch Harrodsburg KY 1967-1970; Chapl Police Lexington KY 1966-1971; Pres Dio Cler Dio Lexington Lexington 1982-1984, Chair Dept Coll Wk 1981, Pres Dio Cler 1969-1980.

THOMAS, Rachel Woodall (Ct) 155 Essex St, Deep River CT 06417 **Dio Connecticut Meriden CT 2017-** B Atlanta GA 1955 d Robert & Matilda. BA W&M 1977; MA Wheaton Coll 1981; MA Ya Berk 1991; DMin Hartford Sem 2007. D 6/8/1991 P 12/1/1991 Bp Arthur Edward Walmsley. m 1/6/2001 Eric J Thomas. Int S Dav's Ch Gales Ferry CT 2014-2017, 2012; Int S Mk's Ch Mystic CT 2012-2014; R S Steph's Ch E Haddam CT 2006-2010, 1996-2006; Mssnr Middlesex Area Cluster Mnstry Higganum CT 1991-1996; Asst Epis Ch At Yale New Haven CT 1987-1989; Asst Dir Epis Camp & Confernce Cntr Ivoryton CT 1983-1987; Admin Coordntr A Chr Mnstry in the Natl Parks in New York City 1981-1983. Fresh Sprg Retreats 2012.

T

THOMAS, Robert Leroy (WVa) 401 11th Ave, Huntington WV 25701 **Died 9/7/2016** B Williamsburg VA 1925 s Minor & Grace. BA Bridgewater Coll 1947; MDiv VTS 1950. D 6/29/1950 P 4/25/1951 Bp Henry D Phillips. c 3. Ret 1987-2016; Asst Chr Ch Ironton OH 1987-2013; R Trin Ch Huntington WV 1965-1987; Dce Dio SW Virginia Roanoke VA 1960-1965; R Chr Ch Blacksburg VA 1955-1960; R Gd Shpd Splashdam VA 1950-1955.

THOMAS CSF, Robert William (NC) 413 Dogwood Creek Pl, Fuquay Varina NC 27526 **Chapl Dio No Carolina 2016-; D S Tim's Ch Wilson NC 2015-; Mem, Soc Action Com Dio No Carolina 2013-; Secy, Raleigh Epis Campus Mnstry Dio No Carolina 2012-** B Philadelphia PA 1950 s Harold & Rosemarie. BA Rutgers The St U of New Jersey 1972; ME Rutgers The St U of New Jersey 1986; Dio NJ D Formation Prog 1998. D 10/31/1998 Bp Joe Doss. m 8/6/1983 Cynthia Grace Scott c 2. Mem, Election Com Dio No Carolina 2010-2013; D S Mk's Epis Ch Raleigh NC 2010-2013; Sprtl Advsr, NC Curs Sec Dio No Carolina 2010-2012; D S Paul's Epis Ch Smithfield NC 2008-2010; D The Epis Ch Of The H Comm Fair Haven NJ 2006-2008; D S Dav's Ch Cranbury NJ 2001-2006; D Coun Dio New Jersey Trenton NJ 1999-2001; D Trin Cathd Trenton NJ 1998-2001. Auth, "Prov II: New Jersey," *Diakoneo*, NAAD, 2002; Auth, "Deacons Search Hidden Windows," *Via Media*, Dio NJ, 2002; Auth, "Liturg Crown Fest," *Via Media*, Dio NJ, 2002. Assn for Epis Deacons 1996; forma 2004.

THOMAS, Samuel Sutter (SeFla) 135 W Crescent Dr, Clewiston FL 33440 B Philadelphia PA 1941 s Samuel & Cecile. LTh SWTS 1966; MEd Florida Atlantic U 1971; MDiv SWTS 1975; PhD U of Miami 1975; Cert U of Paris-Sorbonne FR 1985; Cert Universite de Strassbourg 1986. D 6/29/1966 Bp James Loughlin Duncan P 1/5/1967 Bp William Loftin Hargrave. c 1. R S Mart's Ch Clewiston FL 2000-2006, R 2000-, 1976-1977; Int Ch Of S Chris Ft Lauderdale FL 1998-2000; Int S Phil's Ch Pompano Bch FL 1998-2000; Int Ch Of The Atone Ft Lauderdale FL 1994-1998; S Fran Cmnty Serv Inc. Salina KS 1993; P, Reg Dn Ch in Can 1980-1993; Asst S Matt the Apos Epis Ch Miami FL 1972-1975; Vic H Faith Ft Pierce FL 1969-1972; Cur All SS Epis Ch Lakeland FL 1966-1969. Auth, "weekly arts," *Clewiston News*, 2000-present, 2000; Auth, "Val d'Or Star," *Northland mag*, (1980-1989), 1980; Auth, "Auth & Emot Indep-Clrgy Cnslrs & Perceived Effectiveness," *Ph. D. Dissertation*, Univ of Miami, Coral Gables, FL, 1975; Auth, "Denial as Psychol Mechanism among Alcoholics". Amer Orthopsychiatic Assn 1981; Amer Psychol Assoc 1977; AEHC 1983; Can Register of Hlth Serv Providers in Psychol 1986; Florida Psychol Assoc 1977; Intl Conf of Police Chapl 2001; St and Prov Boards of Examiners in Psychol 1999. Pres Rotary Club 2003; Fell Amer Orthopsychiatric Assn 1988.

THOMAS, Sherry Hardwick (Va) 386 N Anna Dr, Louisa VA 23093 B Cincinnati OH 1949 d Coy & Louise. Vas 1968; BA U Cinc 1971; MDiv VTS 1989. D 6/10/1989 P 3/24/1990 Bp Peter J Lee. c 3. Int Trin Epis Ch Charlottesvlle VA 2008-2009; R S Jas Epis Ch Louisa VA 1998-2005; Assoc R Ch Of The Gd Shpd Burke VA 1994-1998; S Phil's Ch Cincinnati OH 1994; Dir Yth Mnstrs Dio Sthrn Ohio Cincinnati OH 1991-1993; Asst to R Gr Ch Silver Sprg MD 1989-1991; S Dav's Par Washington DC 1989-1991; Gr Epis Ch Silver Sprg MD 1989-1990.

THOMAS, Teresa Ann Collingwood (Ak) PO Box 76, Fort Yukon AK 99740 **D S Steph's Ch Ft Yukon AK 1990-** B Newton Abbot Devon UK 1936 d Ivan & Mary. U of Alaska; U NC; MA S Andrews U 1960. D 6/29/1990 Bp George Clinton Harris. m 9/1/1967 John Thomas c 2. Cler-in-Charge S Jn's Epis Ch Eagle AK 2001-2005.

THOMAS, Timothy Bosworth (SeFla) 3434 N Oceanshore Blvd, Flagler Beach FL 32136 B Portland IN 1950 s William & Marjorie. Wstrn Michigan U; BA Indiana U 1972; MDiv SWTS 1980. D 5/25/1980 Bp Charles Ellsworth Bennison Jr P 12/1/1980 Bp James Winchester Montgomery. m 5/31/1980 Marguerite Thomas c 1. Com Biomedical Ethics Com 2005-2011; Chapl Exch Club of Pompano Bch 2002-2011; R Ch Of S Nich Pompano Bch FL 1993-2011; Assoc R Trin Ch New Orleans LA 1985-1993; Assoc R S Fran Ch Potomac MD 1983-1984; Asst to R Ch Of Our Sav Chicago IL 1980-1983; Chair, Cler Assistance Prog Dio SE Florida Miami 2007-2011, Mnstry Discernment Assoc 1998-2011, Bp Cmsn - Vice Chair 1996-2006, COM - Chair 1996-2006, COM 1995-2005. Auth, "Bldg a Zuckermann Clavichord VI," *Boston Clavichord Soc*, Boston Clavichord Soc, 2016.

THOMAS, Trevor Emrys George (Nwk) 90 Rossini Road, Westerly RI 02891 **Ret 1989-** B Cardiff Wales GB 1925 s Philip & Sarah. BA S Davids Coll Lampeter GB 1948; GOE S Davids Coll Lampeter GB 1950. D 3/24/1951 P 10/27/1951 Bp Benjamin M Washburn. c 3. Pres Bd Trst Gd Shpd Hse Hackettstown NJ 1975-1989; Archd Dio Newark Newark NJ 1969-1974; R Ch Of The H Innoc W Orange NJ 1952-1989, Vic 1951-1952, R Emer 1989-.

THOMAS, Valerie Bricker (Fla) 244 Ashley Lake Dr, Melrose FL 32666 B Olswinford Worchester UK 1944 d Gerald & Audrey. D 9/14/1997 Bp Stephen Hays Jecko. m 2/15/1986 Wallace Fitzgerald Thomas. D S Mk's Ch Palatka FL 2000-2002; D S Mich's Ch Gainesville FL 1998-2000; D Ch Of The Medtr Micanopy FL 1997-1998.

THOMAS, Victor J (Tex) 3129 Southmore Blvd, Houston TX 77004 **S Jas Epis Ch Houston TX 2009-** B Oakland CA 1966 s Albert & Rachel. BA New Coll of California 1994; MDiv CDSP 1997. D 6/21/1997 Bp Richard Lester Shimpfky P 5/1/1998 Bp Michael Whittington Creighton. m 12/17/1994 Nicole Jessica Thomas c 3. R S Paul's Epis Ch Harrisburg PA 2002-2008; Assoc R S Jas Ch Lancaster PA 1997-2002.

THOMAS, Wayland Eugene (Md) 55 Brooklyn Hts Rd, Thomaston ME 04861 B Peckville PA 1940 s Wayland & Mildred. BS Tem 1965; MDiv Yale DS 1972. D 6/24/1972 P 1/5/1973 Bp Harold Barrett Robinson. m 6/18/1988 Judith E Larabee c 3. Prog Outreach Dir Salvation Army - Annapolis Corps 1992-1994; Dir Annapolis Area Mnstrs - Homeless Shltr 1991-1992; Asstg P Memi Ch Baltimore MD 1989-1994; Fin Dir Quarter Way Hse - Alco/drug Rehab 1989-1990; R S Barn Ch Rumford ME 1984-1988; S Andr's Ch Millinocket ME 1982-1984; R St Mk Epis Ch No Tonawanda NY 1974-1978; Cur S Mk's Ch Orchard Pk NY 1972-1974. waylandet@msn.com

THOMAS, William Carl (NJ) Christ Church, 90 Kings Hwy, Middletown NJ 07748 **Chr Ch Middletown NJ 2015-; Ecum Off Dio W Virginia 2008-** B Mount Kisco NY 1952 s Samuel & Dorothy. BS Bos 1985; Mstr of Div Nash 1989; MDiv Nash 1989; Doctor of Mnstry VTS 2014. D 6/17/1989 Bp Orris George Walker Jr P 12/20/1989 Bp Robert Campbell Witcher Sr. m 1/13/1973 Edna M Parsons c 2. Chr Ch New Bern NC 2013-2015; S Ptr's Ch Huntington WV 2013; Stndg Com Dio W Virginia 2004-2006; R S Matt's Ch Charleston WV 2003-2012; R S Mths Epis Ch Tuscaloosa AL 1995-2003; R S Mk's Ch Warren RI 1991-1994; Chapl US-AR 1990-1996; Chapl/Consult PBFWR New York NY 1990-1992; Assoc S Ann's Ch Sayville NY 1989-1991. Auth, "Deep Ch," *LivCh*, LivCh Fndt, 2002; Auth, *Giving the Increase:Supporting God's Wk in the Wrld*, Dio Long Island, 1994; Auth, *Putting Powerful Prchng in the Pulpit*, Preaching Excellency Fndt, 1989; Auth, "Living Our Baptismal Cov-The Milwaukee Process," *Video Producer & Workbook Ed / Dio Milwaukee*, 1989. williamcarlthomas@gmail.com

THOMAS, William Steven (SeFla) 14445 Horseshoe Trce, Wellington FL 33414 **R S Dav's-In-The-Pines Epis Ch W Palm Bch FL 1991-** B Augusta GA 1955 s William & Jean. BA Transylvania U 1976; BTh Chichester Theol Coll 1981; STM Sewanee: The U So, TS 1990. D 6/13/1981 P 3/28/1982 Bp Addison Hosea. m 5/28/2005 Erin Burke c 4. Inst Dio SE Florida Miami 1988-1990; Chapl Chap Of S Andr Boca Raton FL 1986-1991; S Andew's Sch Boca Raton FL 1986-1991; Cur S Mk The Evang Ft Lauderdale FL 1984-1986; Mus Cmsn Dio Rhode Island Providence RI 1982-1984; Cur S Mich's Ch Bristol RI 1981-1984. AAM.

THOMAS, William Tuley (Mo) 7846 Gannon Ave, Saint Louis MO 63130 **Nonpar 1971-** B Louisville KY 1931 s Vincent & Mary. BA U of Louisiana 1954; BD VTS 1957; DMin Eden TS 1971. D 6/20/1957 P 12/1/1957 Bp Charles Gresham Marmion. m 8/13/1984 Kathleen M Standley. Vic S Tim Chesterfield MO 1961-1966; S Jn's Ch Murray KY 1957-1961; P-in-c S Mart's-In-The-Fields Mayfield KY 1957-1961.

THOMASON, Clayton Leslie (Chi) 42 Ashland Ave, River Forest IL 60305 **Assoc Gr Ch Oak Pk IL 2007-; Bisop Anderson Prof of Rel & Ethics in Med Rush U Med Cntr Chicago IL 2006-, Chair, Dept. of Rel, Hlth & Human Values 2006-; COM Dio Chicago Chicago IL 2011-; Trst Ya Berk New Haven CT 2003-** B Los Angeles CA 1959 s James & Lois. AA Simons Rock Coll of Bard 1979; BA U CA 1980; JD USC 1987; MDiv Ya Berk 1994. D 6/15/1994 Bp Oliver Bailey Garver Jr P 1/14/1995 Bp Frederick Houk Borsch. m 6/6/1992 Mary Hope Griffin. Chair, BEC All SS Ch E Lansing MI 2000-2003; P-in-c S Paul's Epis Ch Lansing MI 1999; Assoc S Jas Par Los Angeles CA 1994-1998; Working Grp on Bioethics Dom And Frgn Mssy Soc- Epis Ch Cntr New York NY 2005; Dio Michigan Detroit MI 2000-2006; Trst Gd Samar Hosp Los Angeles CA 1998-1999; Dioc Coun, COM, Dnry Coun Dio Los Angeles Los Angeles CA 1994-1998. Fitchett G,Thomason C,Lyndes K, "What Hlth Care Chapl Think about Quality Improvement.," *Hastings Cntr Report*; Nov-Dec, 2008; Thomason C, Brody H., "Inclusive Sprtlty.," *Journ of Fam Pract 48(2):21-22 (Feb.)*, 1999. Ascpe, EFM, Epis Evang Fndt. Convoc Prchr Ya Berk 2005; Bp Garver Cler Dvlpmt Awd Dio Los Angeles 1997; Preaching Excellence Prog Epis Evang Fndt 1993. clayton_thomason@rush.edu

THOMASON, Steven (Oly) 1245 10th Avenue East, Seattle WA 98102 **Dn and R S Mk's Cathd Seattle WA 2012-** B Little Rock AR 1965 s Robert & Mary. BS U So 1987; MD U of Arkansas 1991; Diplomate Amer Bd Fam Med 1994; MDiv Epis TS of the SW 2004; Diplomate Amer Bd Hospice and Palliative Med 2010. D 12/27/2003 P 6/26/2004 Bp Larry Maze. m 8/3/1985 Katherine M Thomason c 2. P Assoc S Paul's Ch Fayetteville AR 2009-2012; Chf Med Off Cir of Life Hospice 2007-2011; Cn Mssnr Dio Arkansas Little Rock AR 2005-2008; R S Thos Ch Springdale AR 2004-2008.

THOMPSON, Barkley Stuart (Tex) 1117 Texas St, Houston TX 77002 **Dn Chr Ch Cathd Houston TX 2013-** B Paragould AR 1972 BA Hendrix Coll 1995; MA U Chi 1998; MDiv Epis TS of the SW 2003. D 6/28/2003 P 1/10/2004 Bp Don Edward Johnson. m 6/10/1995 Jill B Thompson c 2. R S Jn's Ch Roanoke VA 2007-2013; R Ch of the H Apos Collierville TN 2003-2007. Auth, "Elements of Gr," *Elements of Gr*, Trin Books, 2013; *Conciliar Authority*, LivCh,

T

2004; *The Barber Shop and Sabbath Time*, Ratherview, 2001; *The Melting Pot Overturned: Preparing the Ch for a Multicultural Soc*, Ratherview, 2001; *Toward a Christology of Purpose: The Early Royce and the Incarn*, Amer Journ of Philos and Theol, 2000.

THOMPSON, Carla Eva (Va) 322 N Alfred St, Alexandria VA 22314 B Kenosha WI 1948 d Carl & Olga. BA U of Wisconsin 1970; MDiv VTS 1997. D 6/14/1997 P 3/11/1998 Bp Peter J Lee. Ch Of The Trsfg Silver Sprg MD 2006-2008; Meade Memi Epis Ch Alexandria VA 1999-2006; Asst Trin Ch Arlington VA 1997-1998.

THOMPSON, Catherine M (Dal) Episcopal Church of the Annunciation, 602 N. Old Orchard Lane, Lewisville TX 75077 **R Ch Of The Annunc Lewisville TX 2014-; Alum Interviewer and Coll Fair Rep Vas Poughkeepsie NY 1994-** B Dallas TX 1971 d Michael & Donna. BA Vas 1993; MDiv VTS 2000. D 6/3/2000 P 5/23/2001 Bp D Avid Bruce Macpherson. m 10/23/1993 Mark Anthony Thompson c 2. R Trin Epis Ch Natchitoches LA 2006-2014; Assoc R S Phil's Epis Ch Frisco TX 2002-2006; Dir of Yth Mnstrs S Anne's Epis Ch Desoto TX 2000-2002; Mem, Transition Com for Bp Dio Dallas Dallas TX 2014-2015, Sum Camping Dn, Camp All SS 2014-; Mem Friends of the Natchitoches Par Libr 2012-2014; Mem, Dioc Cmsn on Liturg and Mus Dio Wstrn Louisiana Alexandria LA 2011-2014, Mem, Elctns Com for Bp 2011-2012, Mem, Dioc Cmsn on Sum Camping 2010-2014, First Cler Alt to GC 2009, Sprtl Dir for Curs 2007-2014, Dn of the Alexandria Convoc 2007-2010, Chair, Missions Com 2007-2009, Mem, Dioc Coun 2006-2009; VP and Mem, Bd Dir DOVES Inc. Natchitoches LA 2010-2014; Asst Ldr Girl Scouts Troop #462 Natchitoches 2009-2014; Mem of Critical Response Team Sthrn Law Enforcement Fndt LA 2007-2014; Mem Natchitoches Min. Allnce/Comm. Partnr Natchitoches LA 2006-2014; Mem and Form VP Parents at the Lab Sch (PTA) Natchitoches LA 2006-2014; Mem of the AAEC VTS Alexandria VA 2000-2001. mtrcatherine@annunciationlewisville.org

THOMPSON, Chris Christopher (WVa) Church of the Holy Communion, 218 Ashley Ave, Charleston SC 29403 **Vic Greenbrier Monroe Epis Mnstry Wht Sphr Spgs WV 2011-** B Portsmouth OH 1953 s Charles & Judith. CREDO I; CREDO II; BA W Liberty U 1975; MDiv VTS 1979; VTS 1995. D 6/6/1979 P 6/4/1980 Bp Robert Poland Atkinson. m 11/22/1980 Mary Jo Brown c 1. Dn Sthrn Dnry - W Virginia 2013-2014; Int S Steph's Epis Ch Beckley WV 2010-2011; R Estrn Shore Chap Virginia Bch VA 2005-2010; Dn S Petersburg Dnry - SW Florida 1997-2003; R S Thos' Epis Ch St Petersburg FL 1996-2005; Chapl (LtCol) USAFR 1996-2003; Dn Scioto Vlly Dnry - Sthrn Ohio 1995-1996; Chapl (Major) Ohio Air NG 1987-1996; R All SS Epis Ch Portsmouth OH 1986-1996; Dn OH Vlly Dnry - W Virginia 1985-1986; Chapl (Captain) W Virginia Army NG 1982-1987; Vic S Jn's Ripley WV 1980-1986; D S Jn's Ch Huntington WV 1979-1980; Chapl Virginia Bch Police Dept 2008-2010; Chapl Cbury Sch of Florida St. Petersburg 2002-2005; Chapl Portsmouth Ohio Police Dept 1987-1996; Yth Coordntr Dio W Virginia Charleston WV 1981-1985. NNECA 2003-2010. Distinguished Serv Medallion Bp Suffr of Chaplaincies 2004.

THOMPSON, Claud Adelbert (Mil) 5030 Vista View Crescent, Nanaimo BC V9V 1L6 Canada **Died 7/3/2017** B Milwaukee WI 1933 s Claud & Emily. BA Ripon Coll Ripon WI 1955; MA Col 1960; BD SWTS 1964; PhD U of Wisconsin 1970. D 6/1/1964 P 12/1/1964 Bp William Hampton Brady. m 8/31/1968 Phyllis Ann Kuhn c 1. Fell ECF 1968-1970; Non-par 1967-2017; Asst St Fran Hse Madison WI 1966-1968; Asst All SS Epis Ch Appleton WI 1964-1966; Chapl Lawr Appleton WI 1964-1966. Auth, "Doctrine and Discipline of Divorce, A Bibliographical Study," *Transactions of the Cambridge Bibliographical Soc*, Camb Libr, 1977; Auth, "Trinities in Piers Plowman," *Mosaic*, U of Manitoba Press, 1976; Auth, "'Coded' Signatures: A Printer's Clue...," *Papers of the Bibliographical Soc of Amer*, The Soc, 1974; Auth, "Spenser's 'Many Faire Pourtraicts, and Many a Faire Feate," *Stds in Engl Lit*, Jn Hopkins Press, 1972; Auth, "Rhetorical Madness: An Ideal in the 'Phaedrus,'" *Quarterly Journ of Speech*, Speech Assn of Amer, 1969; Auth, "'That Two-Handed Engine' Will Smite: Time Will Have a Stop," *Stds in Philology*, U NC Press, 1962.

THOMPSON, Danielle L (Ala) 1910 12th Ave S, Birmingham AL 35205 **S Mary's-On-The-Highlands Epis Ch Birmingham AL 2015-** B Iowa City IA 1980 d Steven & Barbara. BA Lipscomb U 2001; MDiv Van 2006; Cert Ang Stud Sewanee: The U So, TS 2010; STM Sewanee: The U So, TS 2011. D 6/5/2010 P 12/13/2010 Bp John Bauerschmidt. m 6/21/2003 Joshua B Davis c 2. Epis Ch Cntr New York NY 2014; The GTS New York NY 2013-2014; Assoc S Chrys's Ch Chicago IL 2010-2013; Chapl St. Thos Hosp Nashville TN 2007-2009.

THOMPSON, David Frank Ora (USC) 622 Stanton Dr, North Augusta SC 29841 B Cumberland MD 1951 s Guy & Audrey. BA Salisbury U 1973; MDiv GTS 1976; STM GTS 1985. D 6/4/1976 P 4/16/1977 Bp David Keller Leighton Sr. m 8/16/1975 Virginia Gaiser c 4. R S Barth's Ch No Augusta SC 1985-2015; Tutor The GTS New York NY 1983-1985; R S Mths' Epis Ch Baltimore MD 1978-1983; Cur S Marg's Ch Annapolis MD 1976-1978. churchoftheridge@gmail.com

THOMPSON, David James (Dal) 417 Olive St, Texarkana TX 75501 **S Jas Epis Ch Texarkana TX 2016-** B Norman OK 1984 s Gary & Deborah. M. Reg and City Plnng U of Oklahoma; BS U of Oklahoma; MDiv Wycliffe Coll. D 1/2/2016 P 7/2/2016 Bp Edward Joseph Konieczny. m 8/8/2009 Heather M Thompson c 3. dthompson@saintjamestxk.org

THOMPSON, David Joel (Colo) 360 Scrub Oak Cir, Monument CO 80132 B Waterloo IA 1950 s Wayne & Carol. BA Colorado St U 1974; MDiv GTS 1979; MA U Denv 1984; U CO 1996. D 10/28/1982 P 1/1/1985 Bp William Harvey Wolfrum. Prince Of Peace Epis Ch Sterling CO 2011-2012; Vic S Paul's Epis Ch Lamar CO 2000-2006; Int Ch Of The Ascen Salida CO 1997-1999; Int S Barn Ch Glenwood Spgs CO 1991-1992; Vic S Dav Of The Hills Epis Ch Woodland Pk CO 1988-1991; Cur Gr And S Steph's Epis Ch Colorado Sprg CO 1986-1988; P-in-c Ch Of S Mich The Archangel Colorado Spg CO 1985-1986; Chapl Colorado Coll Colorado Sprg CO 1982-1984. ESMA.

THOMPSON, Donald Frederick (Ct) 11 Lenox Ave, Norwalk CT 06854 **Asstg Cler S Lk's Par Darien CT 2003-** B Winnipeg Manitoba CA 1944 s Donald & Lillian. BA U of Manitoba 1965; MTS Harvard DS 1968; MA Harvard DS 1968; PhD McGill U 1981; DD S Johns Coll Winnipeg Mn CA 1996; DCT Montreal Dioc Theol Coll CA 2001; DCT Montreal TS CA 2001; DST Thorneloe U CA 2008. Trans 4/19/2002 Bp Andrew Donnan Smith. m 6/15/1968 Susan Smith c 2. Gnrl Secy Colleges & Universities of the Angl Comm New York NY 2001-2011; Pres & Vice-Chncllr Thorneloe U Sudbury Ontario Can 1991-2001; Dir Of Acad Stds Cntr For Chr Stds Toronto Can 1982-1991; Dir of Stds Montreal Dioc Theol Coll - McGill Univ 1971-1982; Asst R S Geo's Ch Montreal Can 1970-1971. Co-Auth, "Reply Of The Angl-RC Dialogue Of Can To The Vatican Response To The Final Report Of The Angl-RC Intl Comm," 1993; Co-Auth, "Initiation Into Chr: Ecum Reflections And Common Tchg On Preparation For Baptism," Wood Lake Books/ Novallis, 1992; Auth, "Ch And Culture: An Analytic Structure For The Relatns," *Arc: The Journ Of The Fac Of Rel Stds*, Mcgill U, 1991; Auth, "Whose Chld Is This?," Toronto, 1990; Auth, "Lonergan And Educating For Mnstry: A Construction, Method: A Journ Of Lonergan Stds, Vol. 8," *No. 12*, 1990; Auth, "A Theol Reflection On Chr Values And 'Surrogacy,'" *Surrogacy: The Report Of Angl T/F On Surrogate Motherhood*, Angl Ch Of Can, 1989; Auth, "Pstr Care Of Interchurch Families, One In Chr, Vol. 24," *No.3*, 1988; Ed/ Co-Auth, "Violence Against Wmn: Taskforce Report To Gnrl Syn 1986 Of The Angl Ch Of Can," Toronto, Angl Bk Cntr, 1987; Auth, "Coalitions As Vehicles For Unity: The Can Experience.," *Oecumenisme/ Ecum #86*, 1987; Auth, "Experiential Theol: Fad Or Fndt?," *Justice As Mssn: An Agenda For The Ch*, Toronto, Trin Press, 1984. Amer Assn Of Rel 1980; Can Theol Soc 1980.

THOMPSON, Ed (La) 5500 St. Claude Avenue, New Orleans LA 70119 B Maryland County Liberia 1962 s John & Blaa-Hedoo. AS Tubman Coll of Tech 1984; BTh Cuttington U 1988; Cert Intl Sch of Evang 1992; MDiv Nash 2000. Trans 11/27/2002 Bp Roger John White. m 5/7/1994 Vashti J Thompson c 4. R All Souls Ch and Cntr New Orleans LA 2017, 2012-2017; S Lk's Ch New Orleans LA 2014-2015; R S Paul's Epis Angl Ch Frederiksted St Croix VI 2004-2012; P-in-c S Mart's Ch Milwaukee WI 2002-2004; Chr Ch Milwaukee WI 2002; Asst Vic S Andr's Epis Ch Brown Deer WI 1999-2000; COM Dio Milwaukee Milwaukee WI 2003-2004. Rotary Intl 1997-2004. Stdt Ldrshp Awd Cuttington U Coll 1988.

THOMPSON, Edgar Andrew (Colo) 971 E Lone Pine Road, Pahrump NV 89048 **Ret 1995-** B White Plains NY 1930 s Herbert & Vera. BA U CO 1956; BD Nash 1959; MDiv Nash 1960; Beth Hosp 1983. D 6/29/1959 P 2/2/1960 Bp Joseph Summerville Minnis. m 8/31/1979 Roberta R Thompson c 3. Rgnl P Mssnr Ch Of The H Sprt Bullhead City AZ 1996-1999; Chapl Dept Corrections CO St Dio Colorado 1983-1995; CPE Beth Hosp Denver CO 1982-1983; R All SS Epis Ch Torrington WY 1980-1982; Cur All SS Epis Ch Denver CO 1979; Vic St Andr Epis & H Cross Luth Ch La Junta CO 1978; R S Steph's Ch Longmont CO 1965-1977; Cur S Paul's Epis Ch Lakewood CO 1961-1965; Vic/R S Andr's Ch Manitou Sprg CO 1959-1961. Auth, "Chapl in Corrections," *Corrections Today*, 1989; Auth, "Jennifer Wants to Speak, Lord," *Beth Bulletin*, 1983. Amer Correctional Assn 1985-1995; RACA 1997.

THOMPSON, Edward (Cal) 1714 Santa Clara Ave, Alameda CA 94501 B Bethesda MD 1963 s Edward & Lynn. BA Wms 1985; U MI 1992; MDiv CDSP 1995. D 6/8/1996 Bp R aymond Stewart Wood Jr P 6/1/1997 Bp William Edwin Swing. m 10/2/2004 Mary Ann Kimura. The Epis Ch Of S Mary The Vrgn San Francisco CA 2016; Ch Of The H Comf Vienna VA 2013; Long-Term Int R Chr Ch Alameda CA 2002-2009; Chr Epis Ch Sei Ko Kai San Francisco CA 1997-2002; Asst to R Trin Par Menlo Pk CA 1996-1997, 1995-1996.

THOMPSON, Elena M (Ga) PO Box 1167, Baxley GA 31515 **Pstr St. Thos Aquinas Baxley GA 2006-** B Glen Ridge NJ 1952 d Stuart & Dorothy. BA Duke 1974; MA U of Florida 1975; MDiv Sewanee: The U So, TS 1982; PhD U of Texas 1988. D 8/3/2002 P 2/24/2003 Bp Henry Irving Louttit. Asst The Collgt Ch of St Paul the Apos Savannah GA 2010-2013; S Paul's Epis Ch Jesup GA 2007-2008; S Thos Aquinas Mssn Baxley GA 2006-2010; Ch Of The H Nativ St Simons Is GA 2003-2006; Int H Nativ St. Simons Island GA 2003-2006; S Aug Of Cbury Ch Augusta GA 2002-2003.

T

THOMPSON JR, Fred Edward (SC) 2138 Allandale Plantation Rd, Wadmalaw Island SC 29487 **S Mich's Epis Ch Charleston SC 2005-** B Charleston SC 1966 s Fred & Lois. BA Newberry Coll 1988; MA Luth TS 1995. D 9/10/2005 Bp Edward Lloyd Salmon Jr P 1/17/2016 Bp Charles Glenn VonRosenberg. m 7/1/1989 Alicia Anderson Thompson.

THOMPSON, Fred Leonard (NC) 538 Furth Ln, Southern Pines NC 28387 **Assoc S Mary Magd Ch Troy NC 2008-; Ret 1995-** B Charlotte NC 1928 s Leonard & Amelia. BS Cit 1951; Cert VTS 1984. D 6/16/1984 P 6/30/1985 Bp Robert Whitridge Estill. m 6/16/1951 Lena Miller c 2. All Souls Ch Ansonville NC 1990-1995; R Calv Ch Wadesboro NC 1990-1995; Asst Emm Par Epis Ch Sthrn Pines NC 1984-1990.

THOMPSON, Helen Plemmons (At) 91 Wylde Wood Dr, McDonough GA 30253 B Buncome County NC 1937 d Merlin & Ruby. D 8/6/2006 Bp J Neil Alexander. c 3. S Jos's Epis Ch Mcdonough GA 2006-2009.

THOMPSON III, Henry Lawrence (SC) 2310 Meadow Vue Dr, Moon Township PA 15108 **Dn of Doctoral Stds TESM Ambridge PA 2001-; Assoc Prof TESM Ambridge PA 1999-** B Toledo OH 1953 s Henry & Charlotte. BA Denison U 1975; BA Trin Bristol GB 1978; MDiv GTS 1979; Cert Estrn Bapt TS 1984; DMin TESM 2001. D 6/23/1979 P 5/24/1980 Bp John Harris Burt. m 6/28/1975 Mary Thompson c 3. SCLM 2003-2009; TESM Ambridge PA 1997-2009; Dio Connecticut Meriden CT 1986-1993, Reg Dn 1986-1989; Gr Epis Ch Trumbull CT 1985-1997; Asst R Ch Of The Gd Samar Paoli PA 1979-1985. Auth, "Sprtl Journeys," *MV Alum mag*, 2007; Auth, "Common Wrshp Lectionary," *ATR*, 2002; Auth, "Feast of the Wrld's Redemp," *Living Ch*, 2001; Auth, "Personality Type & Evang," *New Engl Ch Life*, 1987. Assn of Psychol Type 1987; FOCUS, Bd 1994-1996; Fllshp of Witness / EFAC USA Bd 1985; St Mk's Day Care Bd 1995-1997.

THOMPSON SR, Howard Dale (Alb) 140 Foster Rd, North Lawrence VA 12967 B Salem OR 1941 s Robert & Grace. D 6/11/2005 Bp Daniel William Herzog. m 2/2/1963 Geraldine Vina Bissell-Thompson c 6. D Chr Ch Morristown NY 2005-2008.

THOMPSON, James Calvin (SVa) 2003 Camelia Cir, Midlothian VA 23112 **Ret 1992-** B South San Gabriel CA 1932 s John & Mary. BA U of Redlands 1953; MA USC 1956; MTh Claremont TS 1959; Cert GTS 1964. D 9/10/1964 P 3/11/1965 Bp Francis E I Bloy. m 8/28/1954 Lois A Thompson c 2. Asst Ch Of The Redeem Midlothian VA 1998-2008; Spec Asst in Mnstry Dio Caledonia Angl Ch of Can Can 1994-1997; P-in-c So Peace Par in the Dio Caledonia 1994-1997; Mnstry Spprt Dio Caledonia Angl Ch of Can Can 1992-1994; R S Jn's Par Porterville CA 1977-1992; Epis Dio San Joaquin Modesto CA 1969-1977; S Tim's Ch Bp CA 1969-1977; Vic Trin Memi Epis Ch Lone Pine CA 1969-1970; Vic S Geo's Ch Riverside CA 1964-1969; Chapl U CA 1964-1969; Serv Untd Ch 1955-1964. Auth, *Notes on Catechism*, Morehouse, 1979.

THOMPSON, James E (SJ) 3930 SE 162nd Ave Spc 22, Portland OR 97236 B Roseburg OR 1947 s Wilbur & Louise. NW Chr Coll Eugene OR 1974. D 11/16/1975 Bp Matthew Paul Bigliardi P 6/1/1994 Bp Robert Louis Ladehoff. c 3. S Lk's Epis Ch Gresham OR 2002-2007; Cn Ordnry Epis Dio San Joaquin Modesto CA 1998-2002; S Jas Epis Cathd Fresno CA 1994-1998; Admin S Steph's Epis Par Portland OR 1987-1990; Asst S Matt's Epis Ch Portland OR 1981-1983; Asst to Bp of Ore Dio Oregon Portland OR 1979-1983; Asst S Ptr And Paul Epis Ch Portland OR 1979-1981; Asst S Mk's Ch Myrtle Point OR 1977-1979; Asst S Geo Porland OR 1975-1979. Cmnty of Chr Fam Mnstry 2004. Hon Cn Dio Oregon 1987.

THOMPSON, Jerry A. (Neb) St. Mark's on the Campus Episcopal Church, Lincoln NE 68508 **R S Mk's On The Campus Lincoln NE 2005-** B Warren OH 1960 s Dean & Mary. BA Coll of Wooster 1982; MA Indiana U 1985; MDiv Chr TS 1989; CAS SWTS 1990; DMin SWTS 1994. D 6/24/1990 P 5/1/1991 Bp Edward Witker Jones. m 6/26/1982 Carol Lynn Thompson c 2. Int S Johns Ch Indianapolis IN 2004-2005; S Tim's Ch Indianapolis IN 2004-2005; Cn Chr Ch Cathd Indianapolis IN 1998-2004; R S Matt's Epis Ch Brecksville OH 1992-1997; Trin Epis Ch Bloomington IN 1990-1991. Theta Phi 1988. Alumni Awd Chr TS 1989; Theta Phi Chr TS 1988; Fac Awd Chr TS 1988; Shelton Awd Chr TS 1987; Phi Beta Kappa Coll Of Wooster 1982; Eta Sigma Phi Coll Of Wooster 1980. smoc.rector@stmarks-episcopal.org

THOMPSON, John E (Roch) 21 Main Street, Geneseo NY 14454 **St Peters Memi Ch Dansville NY 2016-; Dn Dio Rochester Henrietta 2013-, SW Dist Cler Rep to Dioc Coun 2011-2013** B Sumter SC 1977 s E & Gail. Bachelors The U of Tennessee at Knoxville 1998; Masters TS 2004; Masters Sewanee: The U So, TS 2004. D 12/21/2004 P 8/20/2005 Bp J Neil Alexander. c 1. Emm Epis Ch La Grange IL 2014-2016; R S Mich's Epis Ch Geneseo NY 2011-2014; Assoc S Jas' Epis Ch Warrenton VA 2009-2011; Chapl ArmdF and Fed Ministires New York NY 2005-2009; D Ch Of The H Cross Decatur GA 2004-2005; Chapl Res Emory Cntr for Pstr Serv 2003-2005. priest@stpetesdansville.org

THOMPSON, John Francis (CFla) 90 E Jinnita St, Hernando FL 34442 **D S Marg's Ch Inverness FL 1997-** B Chaptico MD 1933 s Alton & Margaret. BS U of Maryland 1960; MS U of Maryland 1964; PhD MI SU 1966. D 8/25/1984 Bp Charles Thomas Gaskell. m 8/19/1967 Janet M Thompson c 2. D Chr Ch

Epis Madison WI 1994-1996; D S Andr's Ch Madison WI 1990-1993; D Gr Ch Madison WI 1984-1990.

THOMPSON, John Kell (Oly) 21630 102nd Ln SW, Vashon WA 98070 B Pittsburgh PA 1943 s Gordon & Ruth. BA Muskingum Coll 1966; MS San Diego St U 1970; PhD U of Arizona 1972; CDSP 1991. D 6/18/1991 P 12/21/1991 Bp Vincent Waydell Warner. m 6/13/1965 Joan W Thompson c 2. R Ch Of The H Sprt Vashon WA 1994-2008; Assoc to Prog Dvlpmt S Thos Epis Ch Medina WA 1991-1994; Stndg Com Dio Olympia Seattle 1993-1996.

THOMPSON, John Paul (Alb) PO Box 180, Copake Falls NY 12517 **R S Jn In-The-Wilderness Copake Falls NY 2008-** B Milwaukee WI 1958 BA Cardinal Stritch U 1982; MA Franciscan U of Steubenville 1987; MDiv Sewanee: The U So, TS 2005. D 6/5/2005 Bp Samuel Johnson Howard P 12/13/2005 Bp Henry Nutt Parsley Jr. S Mths Epis Ch Tuscaloosa AL 2006-2008; Chr The Redeem Ch Montgomery AL 2005-2006.

THOMPSON, Karen Elizabeth (EMich) 18890 Fireside Hwy, Presque Isle MI 49777 B Detroit MI 1950 d Rudolph & Eugenia. BA Oakland U 1972; CTh Whitaker TS 1989. D 6/24/1989 Bp H Coleman Mcgehee Jr. m 6/2/1979 Jack Thompson c 2. D Asst Trin Epis Ch Alpena MI 2001-2011; Asst S Ptr's Ch Detroit MI 1997-2000; Asst S Gabr's Epis Ch Eastpointe MI 1989-1997. Auth, "Reflections On Jail Mnstry," *Diakoneo*, Naad, 1999; Auth, "Day w Dad," *The Record*, 1999. Epis Cler Assn Of Michigan 1991; Michigan Chapl Assn 1999; NAAD 1989.

THOMPSON, Kenneth David (Ky) 1768 Plum Ridge Rd, Taylorsville KY 40071 **Ret 1998-** B Lexington KY 1926 s Elmer & Beulah. D 12/21/1963 P 3/2/1969 Bp Charles Gresham Marmion. m 9/27/1947 Phyllis Burton Valleau. S Lk's Ch Louisville KY 2004-2013; Int S Jas Ch Shelbyville KY 1999-2002; Int Ch Of The Ascen Bardstown KY 1986-1998; Int S Alb's Epis Ch Louisville KY 1980-1986; S Thos Epis Ch Louisville KY 1980-1986; Cn Chr Ch Cathd Louisville KY 1974-1984, Stff 1963-1973; Vic S Ptr's Epis Ch Louisville KY 1971-1974; Asst S Paul's Ch Louisville KY 1965-1971; S Geo's Epis Ch Louisville KY 1964-1965. Auth, *Beyond the Double Night*, Buggy Whip Press, 1996; Auth, *Bless This Desk*, Abingdon Press, 1976.

THOMPSON, Lori Lee L (ETenn) 590 Walthour Rd, Savannah GA 31410 **Trin Epis Ch Chocowinity NC 2017-** B Palo Alto CA 1960 d Harold & Darlene. BA U Ca 1982; JD Pepperdine U 1985; MDiv Sewanee: The U So, TS 2013; MDiv The TS at The U So 2013. D 11/24/2012 Bp Philip Menzie Duncan II P 10/4/2013 Bp Scott Anson Benhase. m 9/13/1980 Bruce Charles Fehr c 2. Ch Of The Nativ Ft Oglethorp GA 2016-2017; Assoc S Fran Of The Islands Epis Ch Savannah GA 2013-2015.

THOMPSON, Marisa Tabizon (Neb) 9320 Blondo St, Omaha NE 68134 **R All SS Epis Ch Omaha NE 2015-** B Albany OR 1976 d Daniel & Marjorie. BA U of Oregon 1998; Cert Ang Stud Ya Berk 2004; MDiv Yale DS 2004. D 5/30/2009 P 1/16/2010 Bp Sanford Zangwill Kaye Hampton. m 7/4/2005 Joseph P Thompson c 2. Asst Ch Of The H Comf Burlington NC 2012-2015; S Mary's Epis Ch Eugene OR 2010-2012, D 2009-2012; Chapl Epis Campus Mnstry Eugene OR 2008-2012; Natl Bd Dir Girl Scouts of the USA New York NY 2005-2011.

THOMPSON, Mark A (Minn) 700 Douglas Ave Apt 907, Minneapolis MN 55403 **Vic S Paul's On-The-Hill Epis Ch 2005-** B Anaheim CA 1961 s Elliot & Betty. BA Castleton St Coll 1989; MDiv SWTS 1992. D 6/11/1992 P 12/21/1992 Bp Daniel Lee Swenson. Vic S Paul's On-The-Hill Epis Ch Minneapolis MN 2005-2015; P-in-c SS Martha And Mary Epis Ch S Paul MN 2000-2005; Int Ch Of The Epiph Epis Minneapolis MN 1999-2000; Int St Geo's Epis Ch Minneapolis MN 1997-1999; Assoc S Anne's Epis Ch Warsaw IN 1992-1997; Vic All SS Ch Syracuse IN 1992-1995. Associated Parishes; Int Mnstry Ntwk. Presidential Schlrshp Castleton St Coll 1988; Steel Fllshp 88.

THOMPSON, M Dion (Md) 1208 John St, Baltimore MD 21217 **Int Gr Memi Ch Darlington MD 2016-** B Los Angeles CA 1956 AA California St U 1979; MFA USC 1982; MDiv GTS 2007. D 6/16/2007 P 1/26/2008 Bp John L Rabb. m 2/15/1986 Jean E Thompson c 1. S Andr's Ch Baltimore MD 2013; R Ch Of The H Cov Baltimore MD 2007-2016.

THOMPSON, Michael Bruce (EC) Dashwood House, Sidgwick Avenue, Cambridge CB3 9DA Great Britain (UK) **Vice-Prncpl Ridley Hall Cambridge UK 1995-; Serv Ch of Engl Cambridge and Nottingham UK 1988-** B Goldsboro NC 1953 No Carolina St U 1973; BA U NC 1975; MTh Dallas TS 1979; VTS 1980; PhD U of Cambridge 1988. D 8/16/1980 Bp Hunley Agee Elebash P 2/1/1981 Bp Brice Sidney Sanders. m 5/26/1979 Susanne Thompson. Lectr in NT St Jn's Coll Bramcote Nottingham 1988-1995; Asst R Chr Ch New Bern NC 1980-1983. Co-Ed, "Arianism: Is Jesus Chr Div and Eternal or Was He Created?," *Heresies and How to Avoid Them, ed B Quash and M Ward*, SPCK, 2007; Auth, "When Should We Divide?," Grove Books Ltd, 2004; Auth, "The New Perspective on Paul," Grove Books Ltd, 2002; "Transforming Gr: A Study of 2 Corinthians," Bible Reading Fllshp, 1998; "A Vision for the Ch," T & T Clark, 1997; "The H Internet: Cmncatn Between Ch in the First Chr Generation," *The Gospels for All Christians, ed R Bauckham*, Eerdmans, 1997; "Stumbling Block, Strong and Weak, Tchg/Paraenesis, Tradition," *Dictionary of Paul & His Letters, ed R P Mart et al*, InterVarsity Press, 1993; "Clothed w Chr:

The Example & Tchg of Jesus in Romans 12-15.13," JSOT Press, 1991. Inst for Biblic Resrch 1991; SBL 1983; Tyndale Fllshp 1985.

THOMPSON, Michael King (NC) 103 Sheffield Rd, Williamsburg VA 23188 **Ret 2002-** B Staten Island NY 1942 s William & Beatrice. BA Randolph-Macon Coll 1964; MDiv VTS 1967; ConEd Fell VTS 1977; Coll of Preachers 1984; Cert Int Mnstry Prog 1993; MS Radford U 1993. D 6/10/1967 P 6/15/1968 Bp Robert Fisher Gibson Jr. m 1/27/1968 Elizabeth Johanna Van Wert Thompson c 3. Major Gifts Dir Thompson Chld's Hm Charlotte NC 2000-2002; Spec Gifts Dir Wingate U Wingate N.C. 1996-2000; Assoc S Jn's Epis Ch Charlotte NC 1996-1999; Supply P Dio SW Virginia Roanoke VA 1994-1995, Liturg Cmsn Chair 1974-1993, Ecum Cmsn Chair 1985-1991, Three time Pres of Stndg Com 1980-1991; P-in-c Chr Ch Blacksburg VA 1992-1994; R Gr Ch Radford VA 1972-1991; Asst Chr Epis Ch Winchester VA 1968-1972; Asst S Chris's Ch Springfield VA 1967-1968; Instr & Asst Chapl S Steven's Sch Alexandria VA 1967-1968.

THOMPSON III, Morris King (Miss) 3831 35th Ave, Meridian MS 39305 **The Epis Ch Of The Medtr Meridian MS 2016-; S Paul's Ch Columbus MS 2015-; Other Lay Position Dio Mississippi Jackson MS 2012-** B Ashland KY 1987 s Morris & Rebecca. BA Mississippi St U 2010; MDiv VTS 2015. D 6/13/2015 P 1/16/2016 Bp Brian Seage. m 8/21/2010 Emily Nunnelee Thompson c 1.

✠ THOMPSON JR, The Rt Rev Morris King (La) 1623 7th Street, New Orleans LA 70115 **Bp of Louisiana Dio Louisiana New Orleans LA 2010-** B Cleveland MS 1955 s Morris & Jean. BS Mississippi St U 1980; MDiv Sthrn Bapt TS 1983. D 12/2/1990 P 6/9/1991 Bp Don Adger Wimberly Con 5/10/2010 for La. m 6/5/1982 Rebecca Roper Thompson c 2. Dn & R Chr Ch Cathd Lexington KY 1997-2010; Assoc S Jas Ch Jackson MS 1992-1997; Assoc Calv Epis Ch Ashland KY 1991-1992. DD U So, Sewanee 2010. mthompson@edola.org

THOMPSON, Owen C (NY) Grace Church, 130 1st Ave, Nyack NY 10960 **R Gr Epis Ch Nyack NY 2013-; S Lk's Ch Trin Par Beth MD 2005-** B Brooklyn NY 1971 s Herbert. BA Hobart and Wm Smith Colleges. D 10/26/2002 P 6/21/2003 Bp Herbert Thompson Jr. m 8/6/2000 Jonna Thompson c 2. Trin-St Jn's Ch Hewlett NY 2005-2013; Cur S Mk's Ch Islip NY 2003-2005. othompson@gracechurchnyack.org

THOMPSON, Paul Mason (Vt) 4323 Main Street, Rt 6A, Cummaquid MA 02637 **Int Assoc S Ptr's Ch Osterville MA 2002-; Ret 1998-** B Spartanburg SC 1935 s Paul & Byrd. BA Rhodes Coll 1958; STB EDS 1962; Oxf GB 1967. D 7/2/1962 P 5/21/1963 Bp Duncan Montgomery Gray. m 2/9/1963 Sallie M Thompson c 2. R S Mich's Epis Ch Brattleboro VT 1974-1998; Vic S Jas Epis Ch Bowie MD 1968-1974; Vic Allentown Rd Proj Oxon Hill MD 1967-1968; Vic Ch Of The Redeem Greenville MS 1963-1966; S Jn's Ch Leland MS 1963-1966; S Jas Ch Greenville MS 1963-1965; P-in-c S Steph's Ch Columbia MS 1962-1963.

THOMPSON, Peggy Reid (ECR) 451 Vivienne Dr, Watsonville CA 95076 B Washington DC 1938 d Vernon & Lillian. BA Sch for Deacons 1987. D 6/26/1987 Bp Charles Shannon Mallory. m 12/28/1966 Gene E Thompson. D S Geo's Ch Salinas CA 1999-2001; Chapl Monterey Cnty Jail 1992-2003; D Calv Epis Ch Santa Cruz CA 1992-1999; D S Phil The Apos Scotts Vlly CA 1987-1992; Chapl Santa Cruz Cnty Jails 1987-1992. NAAD.

THOMPSON, Peter D (Ct) 60 East Ave, Norwalk CT 06851 **Par of St Paul's Ch Norwalk Norwalk CT 2015-** B Washington DC 1990 s Douglas & Carol. BA Col 2012; MDiv Yale DS 2015. D 11/8/2014 Bp Mariann Edgar Budde P 5/14/2015 Bp Ian Theodore Douglas.

THOMPSON, Robert Gaston (Colo) 3377 Mill Vista Rd Unit 3612, Highlands Ranch CO 80129 **Ret Epis Ch 2005-** B Powell WY 1938 s Herbert & Dorritt. BA U of Nthrn Colorado 1960; US-A Chapl Sch 1966; MDiv CDSP 1967. D 6/21/1967 P 12/21/1967 Bp James W Hunter. m 6/30/1960 Ivajean Thompson c 2. Chapl S Anne Epis Sch 1995-2005; Chapl S Anne's Epis Sch Denver CO 1995-2005; R H Apos Epis Ch Englewood CO 1994-1995; Dioc Stndg Com Dio Colorado 1989-1991; Dn, Metro So Dnry Dio Colorado 1987-1991; R S Jos's Ch Lakewood CO 1982-1991; S Fran Of Assisi Colorado Spg CO 1977-1982; Vic S Fran Assisi CO Sprgs CO 1976-1982; Dioc Exec Coun Dio Colorado 1976-1978; Dioc Camps and Conf Com Dio Colorado 1972-1976; Dioc Educ Com Dio Colorado 1971-1976; Gr And S Steph's Epis Ch Colorado Sprg CO 1971-1976; Dio Wyoming 1969-1971; R S Andr's Ch Basin WY 1967-1971. Who's Who in Rel 1975.

THOMPSON, Robert Wildan (Ky) 1206 Maple Ln, Anchorage KY 40223 **Mntl Hlth Chapl Veterans Affrs Med Cntr Louisville KY 2008-** B Salem OR 1951 s George & Marjorie. MDiv Emm Chr Sem 1983; MS Abilene Chr U 1993; ThM Brite DS 2008; DMin Brite DS 2011; DMin Brite DS 2011. D 5/29/2010 P 2/5/2011 Bp William Michie Klusmeyer. m 5/27/2000 Pamala Thompson c 3. Asst S Lk's Ch Louisville KY 2010-2015. Amer Assn for Mar & Fam Ther 1995; AAPC 2000. opa.thompson@gmail.com

THOMPSON, Roderick James Marcellus (Cal) 601 Van Ness Ave Apt 123, San Francisco CA 94102 **Assoc Ch Of The Adv Of Chr The King San Francisco CA 2002-** B Twickenham UK 1957 s James & Nina. BS Lon GB 1978; MS Portland St U 1982; MDiv CDSP 1993. D 7/4/1993 P 6/25/1994 Bp William George Burrill. Vic S Cyp's Ch San Francisco CA 1999-2002; Assoc Ch Of The H Innoc San Francisco CA 1994-1999; Assoc S Steph's Epis Par Portland OR 1993-1994. "Liber Precum Publicarum: The 1979 Bk of Common Pryr in Latin," The Laud Liturg Press, 2008.

THOMPSON, Scott A (Tex) Holy Cross Episc Church, 5653 W. River Park Dr., Sugar Land TX 77479 **R H Cross Epis Ch Sugar Land TX 2008-** B Richmond CA 1963 s Harry & Carole. BA Gr TS Pleasant Hill CA 1986; MTh Dallas TS 1991; Cert Nash 1999. D 6/5/1999 P 10/24/1999 Bp Russell Edward Jacobus. m 7/21/1990 Linda S Thompson c 1. Vic St Jas Epis Ch Mosinee WI 1999-2008.

THOMPSON SR, Stephen Lafoia (ETenn) 134 Iris Pl, Newport TN 37821 **D Annunc San Diego CA 1991-** B Kingsport TN 1950 s Lafoia & Edith. BS E Tennessee St U 1972; MA E Tennessee St U 1976; EdS E Tennessee St U 1986. D 6/24/1991 Bp Robert Gould Tharp. c 2. Ch Of The Gd Samar San Diego CA 2013-2014; D / Dir - Chr Formation Ch Of The Gd Shpd Knoxville TN 2002-2006.

THOMPSON, Sue (Cal) St Edmund's Episcopal Church, PO Box 688, Pacifica CA 94044 B New Haven CT 1951 d Lawrence & Patricia. BS U GA 1973; MEd U GA 1974; Candler TS Emory U 1996; MDiv CDSP 1999. D 5/13/2000 P 11/28/2000 Bp Richard Lester Shimpfky. m 7/8/2008 Kristin Stina Pope c 2. Vic S Edm's Epis Ch Pacifica CA 2003-2015; Instr Epis Sch For Deacons Berkeley CA 2002-2010; Chr Ed Coord Dio California San Francisco CA 2002-2003, Stndg Com 2010-, Stndg Com 2010-, Dioc Coun Pres 2006-2007, Dioc Coun 2004-2007, COM of All the Baptised 2003-2007, Dept of Faith Formation 2000-2008; Chld's Prog Coord S Thos Epis Ch Sunnyvale CA 2002; P-in-c Chr Ch Alameda CA 2001-2002, Assoc for Educ 2000-2002; Prog Coordntr Jerusalem Hse Atlanta GA 1991-1994. revweaver@gmail.com

THOMPSON, Tommy Alan (Pa) St. Andrew's Church, West Vincent, 7 Saint Andrews Ln, Glenmoore PA 19343 **S Andr's Epis Ch Glenmoore PA 2016-; S Thos' Ch Whitemarsh Ft Washington PA 2012-** B Nashville TN 1980 s Jerry & Diana. MDiv Asbury TS 2007; B.A. Trevecca Nazarene U 2007; Post-Grad Dplma in Angl Stds VTS 2016. D 6/11/2016 Bp Clifton Daniel III P 12/11/2016 Bp Daniel Gutierrez. m 7/30/2000 Leslie Ross Thompson c 2. Soc of Cath Priests 2017. fathertommy@outlook.com

THOMPSON, Walter Douglas (NCal) 1431 S St, Eureka CA 95501 **Ret Ret 2000-** B Pine Ridge OR 1939 s Walter & Alta. BS Sthrn Oregon U 1961; MDiv CDSP 1964; VTS 1990. D 6/29/1964 P 1/25/1965 Bp James Walmsley Frederic Carman. m 1/21/1962 Hannell Thompson c 3. Int S Alb's Ch Arcata CA 2006-2007; Mem Bp's Search and Nomination Comm. Nthrn CA 2004-2006; Dn NW Deanry The Epis Dio Nthrn California Sacramento CA 1997-2002, Dn 1987-; R Chr Ch Eureka CA 1982-2000; R S Paul's Ch Klamath Fall OR 1976-1982; R Epis Ch Of S Anne Stockton CA 1972-1976; Chapl U Pac Stockton CA 1972-1975; Cur Calv Epis Ch Santa Cruz CA 1970-1972; S Andr's Epis Ch Florence OR 1966-1970; Vic S Mary Ch Gardiner OR 1966-1970; Cur S Matt's Epis Ch Portland OR 1964-1966. ComT; NNECA; NoCCA, Pres 1999-2000.

THOMPSON, Wanda Jean (Me) 1375 Forest Ave. Apt. H14, Portland ME 04103 **D St.Geo's Epis Sanford Maine 2009-; Aroostook Epis Cluster Caribou ME 2002-** B Jeffersonville IN 1938 d Frank & Dorothy. Luth Hosp Sch of Nrsng Moline IL 1959; BS Unity Coll Unity ME 1978. D 4/13/2002 Bp Chilton Richardson Knudsen. c 1. D Cathd Ch Of S Lk Portland ME 2007-2009; D S Paul's Ch Ft Fairfield ME 2002-2005.

THOMPSON, Warren Norvell (CFla) Po Box 1606, Winter Haven FL 33882 **P S Lk The Evang Ch Mulberry FL 2010-; Ret 1992-** B Ladysmith WI 1922 s Eben & Lydia. BS U of Wisconsin 1947; MDiv Nash 1964. D 4/25/1964 P 12/21/1964 Bp Donald H V Hallock. Int S Fran Of Assisi Epis Ch Lake Placid FL 1998; Int S Paul's Ch Winter Haven FL 1990-1991, Cur 1978-1989; Vic Chr Ch Longwood FL 1966-1976; Cur S Barn Ch Deland FL 1965-1966; Asst S Matt's Epis Ch Minneapolis MN 1964-1965.

THOMPSON, Zachary R (At) 805 Mt Vernon Hwy NW, Atlanta GA 30327 B Cincinnati OH 1982 s Michael & Carmen. BA Piedmont Coll 2006; MDiv Candler TS Emory U 2011. D 12/18/2010 P 6/26/2011 Bp J Neil Alexander. m 5/31/2009 Amy C Thompson c 2. The Ch Of Our Sav Atlanta GA 2014-2017; H Innoc Ch Atlanta GA 2012-2014; S Jas Ch Cedartown GA 2011-2012. Soc of Cath Priests 2011. zachary42@gmail.com

THOMPSON DE MEJIA, Kara Ann (Hond) Spring Garden, Islas De La Bahia, Roatan Honduras **Dio Honduras San Pedro Sula 2006-; Iglesia Epis Hondurena San Pedro Sula 2006-** B New Brunswick Canada 1974 d Gordon & Bell. BA S Stephens U. D 10/29/2005 Bp Lloyd Emmanuel Allen. m 1/19/2002 Nelson Yovany Mejia c 2.

THOMPSON-QUARTEY SSM, John John 109 Brookcrest Dr, Marietta GA 30068 **Cn Dio Atlanta Atlanta GA 2014-** B Ghana W. Africa 1961 s George & Beatrice. Montclair St U 1990; BS Rutgers The St U of New Jersey 1993; MDiv GTS 1997. D 5/31/1997 Bp John Shelby Spong P 12/13/1997 Bp Jack Marston Mckelvey. m 6/26/1993 Jerlyn Paula Fitzpatrick c 3. R Ch Of S Mary's By The Sea Pt Pleas Bch NJ 2005-2014; Chapl St. Paul's Sch Concord NH 1999-2005; Asst Chr Ch Ridgewood NJ 1997-1999. EvangES 2007-2010; SSM 1987; UBE 1997. jthompsonquartey@episcopalatlanta.org

THOMPSON-UBERUAGA, William (Ida) 518 N 8th St, Boise ID 83702 B Boise ID 1943 s William & Rosa Maria. MDiv St Thos 1969; STM St Mary's Sem and U 1970; PhD St Mich's U Tor 1973. Rec 7/11/2015 as Priest Bp Brian James Thom. m 8/7/1976 Patricia Kobielus Thompson c 2.

THOMSEN, William Robert (WNC) 299 Locust Grove Rd, Weaverville NC 28787 B Greenwich CT 1933 s William & Elizabeth. ASME Norwalk St Tech Coll 1963. D 10/27/1990 Bp David Elliot Johnson. m 10/18/1986 Brenda England c 4. D Epis Ch Of The H Sprt Mars Hill NC 2002-2011; S Thos Epis Ch Burnsville NC 1994-2006.

THOMSON, Jacqueline (Va) 9405 Shouse Dr, Vienna VA 22182 **Pres, Stndg Com Dio Virginia Richmond VA 2013-, Mem, Stndg Com 2011-, Exec Bd 2008-2011, Chair, Cmsn on the Prevention of Sexual Misconduct 2006-2011, ember, Cmsn on the Prevention of Sexual Misconduct 2000-2011; Colloquy Mentor VTS Alexandria VA 2000-** B Boston MA 1948 d Charles & Carolyn. BA Simmons Coll 1970; U of Maryland 1971; MDiv VTS 1998. D 6/13/1998 P 4/15/1999 Bp Peter J Lee. m 5/16/1970 Bernard Melchoir Thomson c 4. Sr Assoc R S Anne's Epis Ch Reston VA 2007-2013, Asst R 2000-2006; Cur S Alb's Epis Ch Annandale VA 1998-2000. contributer, "sermon for 9/11," *Gd Prchr - online*, Lectionary Homil, 2011.

THOMSON, James (Okla) 501 S Cincinnati Ave, Tulsa OK 74103 B Methil Fife Scotland 1939 s Walter & Agnes. LTh S Andrews Coll Melrose Gb 1963; Cert Theol Stud Epis TS of the SW 1989. Rec 6/1/1989 as Priest Bp James Russell Moodey. c 1. Assoc Trin Ch Tulsa OK 1995-2005; R S Matt's Ch Enid OK 1990-1995; Cur All Souls Epis Ch Oklahoma City OK 1989-1990; Serv RC Ch In Scotland 1963-1983.

THOMSON, Malcolm Davis (WMich) B 1929 D 6/4/1955 P 12/8/1955 Bp Dudley B McNeil.

THOMSON, Richard Dwight (Los) 714 Osprey Ct, Mount Pleasant SC 29464 **Died 7/18/2016** B Minneapolis MN 1928 s Dwight & Katheryn. AMS U MN 1948; Cert CDSP 1962. D 6/29/1962 P 12/19/1962 Bp Richard S Watson. m 4/18/1982 Marylou Thomson c 4. Vic S Jas Santee Ch Mc Clellanville SC 1993-2006; Ret 1992-2016; R H Trin Epis Ch Covina CA 1974-1992; R S Paul's Epis Ch Tustin CA 1971-1974; Assoc Cathd Ch Of S Paul San Diego CA 1966-1971; Cur Ch of S Mary's by the Sea Pacific Grove CA 1964-1965; Vic S Paul's Epis Ch Vernal UT 1962-1964.

THOMSON, Ronald Reed (RG) 733 Lakeway Dr, El Paso TX 79932 **Supply P Dio Texas Houston TX 1997-** B Coffeyville KS 1932 s Samuel & Lena. BBA Texas A&I U 1954; BD Epis TS of the SW 1963. D 6/28/1963 Bp Richard Earl Dicus P 1/5/1964 Bp Everett H Jones. m 12/20/1952 Doris Thomson c 3. Team Mem Partnr in Mnstry San Antonio TX 2006-2007; Int S Mk's On The Mesa Epis Ch Albuquerque NM 2001-2002; Int/Team Mem Epis Ch of Lincoln Cnty Ruidoso NM 2000-2005; Chapl to the Bp Dio The Rio Grande Albuquerque 1998-2000, Supply P 1997-, Stndg Com 1974-1997, GC Dep 1978-2003; Int S Thos A Becket Ch Roswell NM 1997-1998; Pres Epis Chars 1989-1995; R/ Provost Pro Cathd Epis Ch Of S Clem El Paso TX 1972-1996; R S Jn's Ch New Braunfels TX 1966-1972; Asst Ch Of The Gd Shpd Corpus Christi TX 1963-1966.

THON, Susan Cecelia (WA) 34 Wellesley Circle, Glen Echo MD 20812 B Baltimore MD 1947 d Robert & Evelyn. BA Cor 1969; JD Cor 1975; MDiv GTS 1989. D 6/10/1989 Bp Paul Moore Jr P 12/9/1989 Bp Richard Frank Grein. m 10/22/2011 Claude Peter Magrath c 4. R The Ch Of The Redeem Beth MD 1994-2013; Asst The Ch Of The Redeem Baltimore MD 1989-1994. "Signs," *Preaching from Psalms, Oracles, and Parables*, Morehouse Pub, 2006; "Risks in Spkng Out--or Not," *Preaching as Prophetic Calling*, Morehouse Pub, 2004. EvangES 2003-2010.

THOR, Margaret Carlson (Minn) 60 Kent St, Saint Paul MN 55102 B Topeka KS 1961 d Nicholas & Beatryce. BA U CA 1984. D 6/26/2014 Bp Brian N Prior. m 1/21/1989 Eric Joel Thor c 2.

THOR, Peter Chianeng (Minn) 2200 Minnehaha Ave E, Saint Paul MN 55119 B 1963 s Ga & My. AA Inver Hills Cmnty Coll; BS Natl Coll. D 6/20/2015 P 6/21/2016 Bp Brian N Prior. m 5/13/1993 Mai Xiong Thor c 5.

THORME, Trisha Ann (NJ) 1040 Yardville Allentown Rd, Trenton NJ 08620 B Stanford CT 1967 d John & Nan. BA Yale Coll 1989; MA Cor 1994. D 5/9/2015 Bp William H Stokes. m 5/1/1993 John Edward Meier c 1.

THORNBERG, Anne (EC) 3321 Rustburg Dr, Fayetteville NC 28303 B Des Moines IA 1981 d David & Nancy. BA U NC 2004; MDiv GTS 2010. D 6/12/2010 Bp Clifton Daniel III P 12/16/2010 Bp Vicky Gene Robinson. m 5/23/2009 Jeff Thornberg. Cur Chr Ch Exeter NH 2010-2012.

THORNBERG, Jeff (EC) 1601 Raeford Rd, Fayetteville NC 28305 **R H Trin Epis Ch Fayetteville NC 2015-** B Phoenix AZ 1982 s Douglas & Susan. MDiv GTS; BA U of Texas 2005. D 6/3/2008 P 12/12/2008 Bp Vicky Gene Robinson. m 5/23/2009 Anne Thornberg c 2. Vic S Paul's Epis Ch Indianapolis IN 2012-2015; S Jn's Ch Portsmouth NH 2008-2012.

THORNE, Joyce Terrill (RI) 670 Weeden Street, Pawtucket RI 02860 **D S Lk's Ch Pawtucket RI 2011-; Mem of Cmsn on Fin Epis Dio Rhode Island 2013-** B Cambridge MA 1942 d George & Virginia. D 5/22/2010 Bp Gerry Wolf. c 1.

THORNELL, Kwasi (Cal) 1525 Casino Cir, Silver Spring MD 20906 B Tuskegee AL 1944 s Harold & Mabel. BA Alma Coll 1967; MDiv EDS 1972; DMin EDS 2004. D 6/29/1972 Bp Richard Stanley Merrill Emrich P 3/31/1973 Bp John Thomas Walker. m 5/11/1996 Linda B Thornell. Chr Ch Cathd Cincinnati OH 2000-2004, Cn Vic 2000-2004; R S Phil's Ch Columbus OH 1996-2000; Asst R Calv Ch Washington DC 1993-1995; Cathd of St Ptr & St Paul Washington DC 1985-1993; Cn Washington Natl Cathd Washington DC 1985-1993; S Steph's Ch S Louis MO 1983-1985; Dio Missouri S Louis MO 1978-1983; Alexander Crummell Cntr Highland Pk MI 1977-1978; Dir and Min Alexander Crummell Cntr for Wrshp and Lrng Highland 1974-1978; S Matt's And S Jos's Detroit MI 1974-1976; Asst Ch Of The Intsn New York NY 1973-1974; Assoc Gr Ch Detroit MI 1972-1973. Auth, *Encore*. ktimani@yahoo.com

THORNTON, Corey Todd (Haw) PSC 473 Box 10, FPO AP 96349 Japan B Milwaukee OR 1975 s Robert & Esther. BA Oral Roberts U 1997; MDiv Oral Roberts U 2000. D 10/28/2011 P 6/22/2012 Bp Robert Leroy Fitzpatrick. m 5/24/1997 Sarah Elizabeth Thornton c 3.

THORNTON, Daniel Ingram (Ala) 1402 Prier Dr, Marion AL 36756 B Florence AL 1943 s Melton & Mabel. BA U So 1965; MA U of Alabama 1967; PhD U of Alabama 1975; DMin Sewanee: The U So, TS 2004. D 12/21/1993 P 6/24/1994 Bp Robert Oran Miller. m 4/3/1969 Mary Goodloe Yarbrough c 2. R S Wilfrid's Ch Marion AL 2006-2015; Pstr 1994-1996; Epis Black Belt Mnstry Greensboro AL 1997-2005; Pstr S Paul's Ch Carlowville AL 1996-2005; Pstr S Jn's Ch Forkland AL 1994-2005; Trin Ch Demopolis AL 1993-2000; Pstr S Paul's Ch Greensboro AL 1993-1999.

✠ THORNTON, The Rt Rev John Stuart (Ida) 323 W Jefferson St Apt 204, Boise ID 83702 B Somonauk IL 1932 s Andrew & Gertrude. BA Indiana U 1954; MDiv SFTS 1962; CDSP 1995; Albertson Coll 1996. D 6/19/1962 P 12/19/1962 Bp James W Hunter Con 9/1/1990 for Ida. 6/9/1978 Janylee Thornton. Asst to the R S Mary's Epis Ch Eugene OR 2005-2010; Sabbatical Dn Geth Cathd 2005; Transitional R S Barn On The Desert Scottsdale AZ 2002-2005; Asstg Bp Dio Spokane Spokane WA 1999-2000; Ret Bp of Idaho Dio Idaho Boise ID 1998-1999, Bp of Idaho 1990-1998; Vic Ch Of Chr The King On The Santiam Stayton OR 1982-1990; R S Steph's Par Bel Tiburon CA 1969-1982; R Chr Ch Sausalito CA 1964-1968; Asst S Ptr's Epis Ch Sheridan WY 1962-1964. DD Albertson Coll 1996; DD CDSP 1995; Phi Beta Kappa Indiana U 1954.

THORNTON, Norman Edward (Del) Box 2805, Northfield MA 01360 **Tchr Rel Stds Northfield Mt Herman Sch 1977-** B Winchester MA 1948 s Norman & Ruth. BA Hobart and Wm Smith Colleges 1970; MDiv Harvard DS 1977; Cert Amer U in Cairo 1987; MA U of Massachusetts 2000. D 6/18/1977 P 12/20/1978 Bp William Hawley Clark. m 9/16/1972 Gretchen Krull.

THORNTON, Theresa Joan (SO) 10345 Montgomery Rd, Cincinnati OH 45242 **Epis Cmnty Serv Fndt Cincinnati OH 2015-; H Trin Ch Cincinnati OH 2011-** B Brooklyn NY 1950 d Pasquale & Elodia. U Cinc; BFA SUNY Albany 1972; MDiv Bex Sem 2008; MDiv Bex Sem 2008. D 6/14/2008 P 6/20/2009 Bp Thomas Edward Breidenthal. m 8/23/1980 James L Thornton c 2. S Barn Epis Ch Cincinnati OH 2008-2011.

THORP, Steven Tanner (Spr) 1717 Park Haven Dr, Champaign IL 61820 **P-in-c S Andr's Ch Paris IL 2000-; D Ch Of S Chris Rantoul IL 1997-** B Westerly RI 1948 s Ira & Audrey. BA U of Rhode Island 1970; MDiv SWTS 1978; BS NWU 1982. D 6/1/1997 Bp Peter Hess Beckwith. m 7/12/1980 Jael Cronk.

THORPE, John A (Dal) 2117 North 4th Ave East, Newton IA 50208 **P S Jn's Epis Ch Dallas TX 2014-** B Tulsa OK 1977 s Robert & Christine. BMus Oral Roberts U 2002; BA Oral Roberts Universtiy 2002; MDiv Ya Berk 2005. D 6/11/2005 Bp Daniel William Herzog P 12/21/2005 Bp David John Bena. m 12/29/2001 Beth N Thorpe c 2. R S Steph's Ch Newton IA 2008-2014; Assoc R S Ptr's Ch Albany NY 2007-2008; Cur 2005-2006; Sem Intern S Ptr's Epis Ch Milford CT 2004-2005.

THORPE, Mary Brennan (Va) 110 W Franklin Street, Richmond VA 23220 **Dio Virginia Richmond VA 2014-** B Elizabeth NJ 1952 d Joseph & Ann. DMin Columbia TS; BA New Jersey City U 1973; MME U of Hartford 1976; MDiv VTS 2009. D 6/6/2009 Bp Peter J Lee P 12/6/2009 Bp Shannon Sherwood Johnston. m 10/12/1997 Douglas M Thorpe c 3. R Epiph Epis Ch Richmond VA 2010-2014; Int S Gabr's Epis Ch Leesburg VA 2009-2010. mthorpe@thediocese.net

THORSTAD, Anita Fortino (SeFla) 951 De Soto Rd Apt 330, Boca Raton FL 33432 **D S Greg's Ch Boca Raton FL 2006-** B Norristown PA 1941 Dioc Sch For Chr Stds Dio SE F 2005. D 1/21/2006 Bp Leo Frade. c 2. Proj Coordntr Food For The Poor 1999-2009.

THRALL, Barbara (WMass) 19 Hadley St Apt D12, South Hadley MA 01075 B Chicago IL 1951 d Frederick & Catherine. BA Loyola U 1974; MRE Loyola U 1979; MDiv GTS 1986. D 6/7/1986 P 12/14/1986 Bp Paul Moore Jr. m 6/29/1974 Edward Anthony Farrell c 1. R S Paul's Ch Holyoke MA 2007-2017; R All SS Epis Ch Littleton NH 1990-2007; Asst Chr And S Steph's Ch New York NY 1986-1990.

THREADGILL, Nancy (Pgh) 335 Locust St, Johnstown PA 15901 **P-in-c S Mk's Ch Johnstown PA 2014-** B Honolulu HI 1950 d Walter & Selena. BS

MI SU 1972; MS MI SU 1978; BSN U of Wisconsin 1987; MDiv SWTS 2006. D 6/3/2006 P 4/28/2007 Bp Philip Menzie Duncan II. R Ch Of The Gd Shpd Mobile AL 2008-2014; Cur S Lk's Epis Ch Mobile AL 2006-2008.

THROOP, John R (FdL) PO Box 29, Adams NY 13605 **R S Ptr's Epis Ch Sheboygan Falls WI 2016-; Zion Ch Pierrepont Manor NY 2013-** B Evanston IL 1956 s Robert & Catherine. BA U Chi 1978; MDiv Sewanee: The U So, TS 1981; DMin Fuller TS 1995; None Sabbatical 2013; Sabbatical 2913. D 6/3/1981 Bp Quintin Ebenezer Primo Jr P 12/4/1981 Bp James Winchester Montgomery. m 12/31/1993 Cindy J Ford c 2. R Emm Ch Adams NY 2013-2015; P-in-c Trin Ch Portsmouth VA 2009-2012; Asst Lasalle Cnty Epis Mnstry Ottawa IL 2007-2009; Int S Geo's Ch Macomb IL 2006; Vic Chr Ch (Limestone) Hanna City IL 1996-2005; Chapl Proctor Endwmt Hm 1996-2002; Chapl Chillicothe Fire Dept 1994-1996; Pres Summit Plnng Grp (Self-employed) 1993-2009; Vic S Fran Epis Ch Chillicothe IL 1989-1996; Episcopalians Untd 1987-1989; Asst S Paul's Ch Akron OH 1987-1989; Assoc Chr Ch Shaker Heights OH 1986-1987; R Ch Of The Medtr Chicago IL 1983-1985; Cur S Simons Ch Arlington Hts IL 1981-1983; Mem Peoria IL Race Relatns Cmsn 1994-1999. Auth, Dav C Cook Pub Co, 1988; Auth, "Shape Up From The Inside Out," Tyndale Hse, 1986; Auth, "Your Ch"; Auth, "Wrshp Leaders"; Auth, "arts," *Chrsnty Today*; Auth, "Bk Revs," *Living Ch*; Auth, "Bk Revs," *Pub Weekly*. Amer Red Cross Bd Mem 1993-2000; Bd Source 1998-2007; Cntrl IL Friends of People w AIDS 1994-2002; Chr Mgmt Assn 1996-2005; City Cler Fllshp 1981; City of Portsmouth VA/ADA Cmsn 2010-2012; Grtr Peoria Mass Transit Dist/Trst 2000-2004; Jubilee Coll St Historic Site 1994-2004; Title IV Bd 2011-2013.

THRUMSTON, Richard Emmons (SanD) 3642 Armstrong St, San Diego CA 92111 **Ret 1984-** B Chicago IL 1922 s Richard & Patience. BA Ripon Coll Ripon WI 1947; LTh SWTS 1950; U MN 1958. D 4/11/1950 P 10/28/1950 Bp Harwood Sturtevant. m 11/5/1987 Edith Johnson c 3. R Calv Ch Hyannis NE 1981-1984; P S Jos's Ch Mullen NE 1981-1984; Int S Jn's Ch Broken Bow NE 1981; R S Andr's By The Sea Epis Par San Diego CA 1969-1978; R Chr Ch Cn City CO 1962-1969; Cn Chancllr Gr And H Trin Cathd Kansas City MO 1959-1962; R S Matt's Ch S Paul MN 1955-1959; R S Aug's Epis Ch Rhinelander WI 1952-1955; R S Paul's Ch Plymouth WI 1950-1952. Auth, "arts," *Chr Challenge*; Auth, "arts," *Living Ch*.

THULLBERY, Marion Francis (NC) Durham Va Medical Center, 508 Fulton St, Durham NC 27705 **CPE Supvsr/Chapl VA Med Cntr Durham NC 2009-; Dio No Carolina Raleigh NC 2002-** B Lake Wales FL 1954 d Alfred & Betty. BA Erskine Coll 1976; MDiv TESM 1984; PhD GTF 2008. D 12/21/1985 P 9/15/1986 Bp William Hopkins Folwell. m 9/2/2012 Sally Harbold. Dir Dept. of Pstr Care & Educ Jn Umsted Hosp Butner NC 1999-2009; Vic S Paul's Epis Ch Smithfield NC 1998-2000; ACPE Supvsr Trng Residency UNC Hosp Chap Hill NC 1994-1997; Asst All SS Epis Ch Deltona FL 1990-1992; Vic Hope Epis Ch Melbourne FL 1987-1990; Cur S Richard's Ch Winter Pk FL 1986-1987.

THURSTON, Anthony Charles (Ore) 39 Greenridge Ct, Lake Oswego OR 97035 B Holland MI 1940 s Judson & Kathryn. BA Butler U 1966; STM Ya Berk 1969; New Sch U 1969; NYU 1969. D 6/13/1969 Bp John P Craine P 12/1/1969 Bp Horace W B Donegan. m 1/30/1965 Christine A Thurston c 2. P-in-c S Jn The Evang Ch Portland OR 2009-2012, Int 2003-2004; Int S Matt's Epis Ch Eugene OR 2007-2008; Exec Dir Oregon Hlth Action Cmpgn 2006-2008; Int Dn Trin Epis Cathd Sacramento CA 2005-2006; Dn Trin Epis Cathd Portland OR 1991-2003; Cn Dio Milwaukee Milwaukee WI 1986-1991; Cn Epis Hm Mgt Milwaukee WI 1986-1991; R S Paul's Ch Milwaukee WI 1981-1986; R Chr Ch Rochester NY 1977-1981; Cn Cathd Ch Of S Mk Minneapolis MN 1974-1977; Assoc Chr Ch Cathd Indianapolis IN 1971-1972; Bd Trst Dio Oregon Portland OR 2006-2012. Chas Berwind Awd Big Brothers/Big Sis 1971; Watson Fllshp Berk 1969.

THWEATT III, Richmond Fitzgerald (WLa) 7109 Woodridge Ave, Oklahoma City OK 73132 B Norman OK 1939 s Richmond & Viola. BA U of Oklahoma 1961; MDiv SWTS 1964; VTS 1985. D 6/20/1964 P 2/2/1965 Bp Chilton R Powell. m 6/27/1964 Josephine E Edwards c 2. R Leonidas Polk Memi Epis Mssn Leesville LA 1998-2006; Trin Epis Ch Deridder LA 1998-2006; Supply P Chr Epis Ch S Jos MO 1997-1998; Int S Paul's Epis Ch Lees Summit MO 1995-1996; Asst S Mich's Epis Ch Independence MO 1994-1998; Trin Epis Ch Marshall MO 1992; Dio W Missouri Kansas City MO 1987-1991; Vic S Mary's Epis Ch Kansas City MO 1987-1990; Int Chr Epis Ch Charlevoix MI 1986-1987; R Trin Epis Ch Grand Ledge MI 1969-1986; S Mk's Ch Hugo OK 1968; Dioc Yth Camps 1965-1996; Vic S Lk The Beloved Physcn Idabel OK 1965-1969; Cur Gr Ch Muskogee OK 1964-1965; Vic St Philips Muskogee OK 1964-1965; Sec Dioc Conv Dio Wstrn Michigan Kalamazoo MI 1986-1987, Sprtl Dir Happ 1979-1985, 1977-1978. Auth, *40 Days and 40 Nights- The Flood of '93*.

THWING, Robert C (Ak) Po Box 91943, Anchorage AK 99509 **Asst S Mary's Ch Anchorage AK 1973-** B Seattle WA 1934 s Samuel & Marianne. BA U of Washington. D 11/26/1972 P 5/1/1973 Bp William Jones Gordon Jr. m 6/19/1955 Georgia Bigelow. Assoc S Geo's Ch Cordova AK 1974-1980. Who'S Who In Rel 1977.

TIAPULA, Imo Siufanua (Haw) Po Box 2030, Pago Pago AS 96799 **Asst All SS In Wstrn Samoa 1978-** B Laulii 1938 s Mamea & Salavao. BA Simpson Coll 1970; MEd Brigham Young U 1975. D 6/26/1971 Bp Chauncie Kilmer Myers P 1/6/1974 Bp Edwin Lani Hanchett. m 7/27/1970 Sandra Tiapula c 1. Evang Tchr Trng Assn.

TIBBETTS, Catherine Johnson (Va) The Falls Chruch Episcopal, 225 E. Broad Street, Falls Church VA 22046 **Chr Epis Ch Luray VA 2014-; Int P-in-c The Falls Ch Epis Falls Ch VA 2012-, Vic 2012-, Asst 2008-2013** B Jacksonville FL 1951 d James & Elizabeth. BS U NC 1973; MPH U Pgh 1977; MDiv VTS 2008. D 5/24/2008 P 12/14/2008 Bp Peter J Lee. m 4/7/1984 Clark Tibbetts c 2.

TIBBETTS, Ronald Creighton (Mass) 9 Cooney Ave, Plainville MA 02762 **D All SS Epis Ch Attleboro MA 2009-, D 2010-** B Newton MA 1953 s Harmon & Carol. D 10/6/2001 Bp M(Arvil) Thomas Shaw. m 2/22/1974 Victoria A Tibbetts c 1. Nbrhd Action Inc Boston MA 2002-2009.

TICHENOR, Liz (Cal) All Souls Episcopal Parish, 2220 Cedar St, Berkeley CA 94709 **Assoc All Souls Par In Berkeley Berkeley CA 2014-** B Lebanon NH 1985 d David & Susan. AB Dart 2007; MDiv CDSP 2012; MDiv CDSP 2012; MA CDSP 2013. D 5/21/2012 P 12/4/2012 Bp Vicky Gene Robinson. m 6/27/2009 Jesse Tichenor c 2. Galilee Epis Camp & Conf Cntr Inc. Glenbrook NV 2013-2014, 2012; Asst Trin Epis Ch Reno NV 2013-2014; CDSP Berkeley CA 2013. liz@allsoulsparish.org

TICKNOR, Patricia Horan (WMo) 12270 N New Dawn Ave, Oro Valley AZ 85755 **Chapl Casa de la Luz Hospice Tucson Az. 2007-** B Indianapolis IN 1939 d Frederick & Mary. Ottawa U; U of Kansas; W Missouri Sch of Mnstry. D 1/18/1992 Bp John Clark Buchanan. m 2/7/1958 Brian L Ticknor. S Andr's Ch Kansas City MO 1993-2007.

TICKNOR, William Howard Correa (Md) 5757 Solomons Island Rd, Lothian MD 20711 **R S Jas' Par Lothian MD 1973-; R S Mk's Chap Deale Deale MD 1973-** B Baltimore MD 1946 s William & Elizabeth. BS Towson U 1968; MDiv PDS 1971. D 6/22/1971 Bp Harry Lee Doll P 2/5/1972 Bp David Keller Leighton Sr. m 4/20/1979 Pamela Crandell Ticknor c 4. Asst Epiph Ch Dulaney Vlly Luthvle Timon MD 1971-1973.

TIDWELL, Janet Ruth (At) 582 Walnut St, Macon GA 31201 B Detroit MI 1942 d George & Erma. BS Wayne 1965. D 8/6/2011 Bp J Neil Alexander. c 2.

TIDY, John Hylton (SeFla) 4025 Pine Tree Dr, Miami Beach FL 33140 **R All Souls' Epis Ch Miami Bch FL 2006-** B Chatham UK 1948 s Derek & Helen. AKC Kings Coll London 1971. Trans 6/26/2007 Bp Leo Frade. m 4/12/2008 Jill Louise Baker c 3.

TIEDERMAN, Nancy Jo Copass (Oly) 920 Cherry Ave NE, Bainbridge IS WA 98110 **Asstg P S Barn Epis Ch Bainbridge Island WA 2011-** B Seattle WA 1940 d Mike & Lucile. BA Stan 1962; MDiv Chr TS 1990. D 9/21/1982 P 7/11/1992 Bp Edward Witker Jones. m 6/29/1963 William G Tiederman c 3. R The Epis Par of St Dav Friday Harbor WA 2002-2008; Chapl Ch Of The Incarn Gainesville FL 1996-2002; Dio Florida Jacksonville 1996-2002; Chapl Epis U Cntr U FL Gainseville 1996-2002; Vic St Marys Epis Ch Palatka FL 1995-1996; Asst Chapl Epis U Cntr U FL Gainseville 1993-1995; Asst Chapl Gd Shpd Campus Mnstry Pur 1992-1993. Theta Phi. Theta Phi Hon Soc.

TIEGS, Karen Sara Bretl (Ore) All Saints' Episcopal Church, 3847 Terracina Dr., Riverside CA 92506 B Portland OR 1976 d Robert & Diana. BA Linfield Coll 1999; MDiv CDSP 2007. D 6/30/2007 Bp Johncy Itty P 3/29/2008 Bp Sergio Carranza-Gomez. m 7/7/2007 Peter Greg Tiegs. All SS Ch Hillsboro OR 2010-2015; Cur All SS Epis Ch Riverside CA 2007-2009.

TIELKING, Claudia Gould (WA) 6533 Mulroy Street, Mc Lean VA 22101 **Exec Dir Mid-Atlantic Epis Schools Assn 2011-; Bd Mem S Andr's Epis Sch Potomac MD 2001-** B Manhassett NY 1961 d Gerald & Sue. BA Connecticut Coll 1983; MDiv VTS 1990. D 6/9/1990 P 12/15/1990 Bp Ronald Hayward Haines. m 9/21/2002 Nathan Edward Tielking c 2. Beauvoir Sch Cathd of St Ptr & St Paul Washington DC 1993-2014; S Albans Sch Prot Epis Cathd Fndt Washington DC 1992; Asst R Ch Of Our Sav Silver Sprg MD 1990-1992.

TIERNEY, Bridget Katherine (La) 114 N Pine St, New Lenox IL 60451 **Chr Ch Cathd New Orleans LA 2013-; Vic Gr New Lenox 2007-** B Geneva IL 1948 d Lawrence & Dorothy. BS Xavier U; MDiv SWTS 2003. D 10/26/2002 P 6/21/2003 Bp Herbert Thompson Jr. m 11/28/2009 John Joseph Nicastro c 3. Gr Epis Ch New Lenox IL 2007-2010; Int S Jn's Ch Worthington OH 2006; S Jas Epis Ch Columbus OH 2005-2006; P-in-c Trin Epis Ch Troy OH 2003-2005.

TIERNEY, Dennis Stanley (Oly) 6973 Island Center Rd NE, Bainbridge Island WA 98110 B Los Angeles CA 1946 s Stanley & Laurel. BA U IL 1968; MA NE Illinois U 1974; PhD Claremont Grad Schl 1979; MDiv CDSP 2002. D 6/1/2002 P 12/7/2002 Bp William Edwin Swing. m 11/24/1978 Grace Elinor Grant. P S Barn Epis Ch Bainbridge Island WA 2007-2016; P S Bede's Epis Ch Menlo Pk CA 2002-2007. dtierney@stbbi.org

TIERNEY III, Peter George (RI) PO Box 491, Little Compton RI 02837 **S Jas Epis Ch At Woonsocket Woonsocket RI 2015-** B Geneva NY 1977 s Peter & Susan. MDiv Ya Berk 2006; STM Ya Berk 2007; BA Hobart and Wm Smith Colleges 2007. D 6/30/2007 P 2/25/2008 Bp Jack Marston Mckelvey. m 8/11/2007 Veronica Mary Tierney. R S Andr's By The Sea Little Compton RI 2010-2015; Cur Chr Ch Needham Hgts MA 2007-2010.

TIERNEY, Philip Joseph (RI) 1412 Providence Rd, Charlotte NC 28207 B Boston MA 1950 s John & Ethel. DMin Bos; BA Gordon Coll 1972; S Jn Coll GB 1974; MDiv VTS 1976. D 6/9/1976 Bp Morris Fairchild Arnold P 5/11/1977 Bp William Henry Marmion. m 7/9/1988 Sandra T Tierney c 1. S Paul's Ch N Kingstown RI 2004-2010; R Chr Ch Charlotte NC 1998-2004; R Trin Par Menlo Pk CA 1988-1998; The Par Of S Chrys's Quincy MA 1987-1988; Int Rectorates 1985-1989; Ch Of The Ascen Pittsburgh PA 1980-1984; Chapl Foxcroft Sch Middleburg VA 1979-1980; Mentor VTS Alexandria VA 1979-1980; Assoc S Chris's Ch Springfield VA 1978-1980; Chr Ch Blacksburg VA 1976-1978; Chapl Virgina Tech St U In Blacksburg 1976-1978; Chapl Geo Washington DC 1975-1976; Chair - Com Dio California San Francisco CA 1989-1998; Chair - Com Dio Pittsburgh Pittsburgh PA 1982-1984. Clincal Theol Assn.

TIERNEY, Veronica Mary (RI) St. George's School, PO Box 1910, Newport RI 02840 **Chr Ch In Lonsdale Lincoln RI 2016-; Asst Chapl S Geo's Sch Middletown RI 2010-** B Victoria BC Canada 1973 d Barrie & Rosemary. BA Clark U 1995; MDiv Ya Berk 2007. D 6/9/2007 P 5/31/2008 Bp Joseph Jon Bruno. m 8/11/2007 Peter George Tierney. The Ch Of The H Cross Middletown RI 2013-2015; P Assoc Trin Par of Newton Cntr Newton Cntr MA 2007-2010.

TIFF II, Richard Olin (Los) B Arcadia CA 1969 D 6/11/2005 Bp Chester Lovelle Talton P 1/14/2006 Bp Joseph Jon Bruno. Off Of Bsh For ArmdF New York NY 2005-2008; S Marg Of Scotland Par San Juan Capo CA 2005-2008; S Mary's Par Lompoc CA 1998-2004; Ch Of The Epiph San Carlos CA 1998-2002.

TIFFANY, Roger Lyman (Mich) 941 Damon Dr, Medina OH 44256 **Ret 1985-** B Hartford CT 1923 s Wallace & Marjorie. BA Br 1948; BD EDS 1951; MLS Kent St U 1975. D 5/30/1951 Bp William A Lawrence P 6/1/1952 Bp Granville G Bennett. c 3. Vic S Mk's Epis Ch Marine City MI 1977-1984; R S Thos' Epis Ch Port Clinton OH 1958-1975; R Trin Epis Ch Collinsville CT 1955-1958; Asst Gr Ch In Providence Providence RI 1951-1955.

TIFFANY, Susan Jean (NI) 53720 Ironwood Rd, South Bend IN 46635 **Ch Of The Redeem Lorain OH 2017-; S Paul's Ch Akron OH 2016-** B Hartford CT 1956 d Roger & Persis. BA Mt Un Coll 1978; MDiv TESM 2011; MDiv TESM 2011. D 2/14/2014 P 9/26/2014 Bp Edward Stuart Little II.

TIGHE, Maureen (Ore) 1001 B-Ne 90th Ave, Portland OR 97220 **Trin Epis Cathd Portland OR 1997-** B Minneapolis MN 1933 d William & Josephine. BA U MN 1957; MFA Mills Coll 1978; MDiv CDSP 1996. D 6/30/1996 P 4/6/1997 Bp Robert Louis Ladehoff. c 2. P Assoc Legacy Gd Samar Hosp Portland OR 1997-2005. Assembly Of Epis Hosp Chapl 1996; Assn Of Profsnl Chapl 1996-2007.

TILDEN, George Bruce (NCal) B 1939 D 6/23/1963 Bp James Albert Pike P 12/19/1970 Bp Clarence Rupert Haden Jr. m 6/10/1961 Sandra Percy.

TILDEN, Roger (Md) 8089 Harmony Rd, Denton MD 21629 B Brooklyn NY 1940 s Earle & Margaret. BA Hobart and Wm Smith Colleges 1962; STB Ya Berk 1965; STM UTS 1968; DMin S Mary Sem/U Baltimore 1982. D 6/19/1965 P 12/21/1965 Bp Jonathan Goodhue Sherman. c 2. R S Paul's Ch Trappe MD 2001-2004; R S Mich And All Ang Ch Baltimore MD 2000-2001; S Jas Epis Ch Birmingham MI 1986-1999; R S Lk's Ch Alexandria VA 1983-1986; R S Paul's Ch Petersburg VA 1978-1983; R Ch Of S Marks On The Hill Pikesville MD 1975-1978; Chapl Riviera France 1973-1974; Cn Res H Trin Cathd Paris France 1970-1973; Assoc S Lk's Ch E Hampton NY 1968-1970; Asst S Mk's Ch Islip NY 1965-1967. Fell Coll Of Preachers 1992.

TILING, Robert Henry (Chi) 1691 Campos Dr., The Villages FL 32162 **Dn Cathd H Trin Manila Philippines 1996-** B Saint Paul,MN 1945 s Henry & Elizabeth. BA U MN 1968; MA Penn 1971; MDiv Nash 1985. D 6/24/1985 Bp Robert Marshall Anderson P 1/1/1986 Bp William Charles Wantland. m 6/7/1969 Carla Gwen Tiling. Brent Intl Sch 2000-2006; Ch Of The H Trin 1996-2000; R Gr Epis Ch Galesburg IL 1992-1996; Our Sav's Phillips WI 1989-1992; S Marg's Epis Ch Pk Falls WI 1989-1992; S Kath's Ch Owen WI 1985-1992; Ecum Relatns Dio Cntrl Philippines. Auth, "7 Hist arts For Mn Hist Soc".

TILLER, Monte Jackson (SeFla) 6409 Lantana Pines Dr, Lantana FL 33462 B Louisville KY 1942 s Armand & Mona. MDiv Louisville Presb TS 1982; SWTS 1982; Sfcts 1993. D 8/30/1979 P 11/4/1980 Bp David Reed. m 5/21/1994 Susan A Tiller c 1. R Ch Of The H Redeem Lake Worth FL 1994-2002; Int S Mary Magd Epis Ch Pompano Bch FL 1992-1994; Non-par 1986-1991; Vic Ch Of The Resurr W Chicago IL 1982-1985; S Lk's Ch Louisville KY 1980-1982; D S Andr's Ch Louisville KY 1979-1980.

TILLEY, David James (La) 12636 E Robin Hood Dr, Baton Rouge LA 70815 B Jersey City NJ 1939 s Louis & Mary. BA LSU 1961; MDiv Sewanee: The U So, TS 1970. D 6/25/1970 P 4/1/1971 Bp Iveson Batchelor Noland. m 9/1/1962 Carole L Tilley c 3. Epis Ch Of The H Sprt In Baton Rouge Baton Rouge LA 1988-1990; Vic S Tim's Ch La Place LA 1981-1984; Non-par 1979-1980; S Aug's Ch Baton Rouge LA 1971-1979; Cur Epis Ch Of The Gd Shpd Lake Chas LA 1970-1971. ERM, Curs, Fa.

TILLITT, Jay Lanning (LI) 1021 N University St, Redlands CA 92374 **Nonpar 1978-** B San Bernardino CA 1941 s Harley & Sylvia. BA U of Redlands

1963; Nash 1967. D 7/25/1968 Bp Joseph Summerville Minnis P 12/1/1969 Bp Jonathan Goodhue Sherman. R All SS' Epis Ch Long Island City NY 1975-1978; Cur Chr Ch Epis Hudson NY 1973-1975; Cur S Jn's Ch Brooklyn NY 1969-1973; Cur S Andr's Ch Stamford CT 1968-1969. Cltn Of The Apolistic Mnstry; Tertiary Of The Soc Of S Fran.

TILLMAN, Ann Marie (WNY) 24 Maple Rd, East Aurora NY 14052 **R S Mths Epis Ch E Aurora NY 2012-** B Fairbanks AK 1959 d Perry & Jean. BS Cor 1998; MDiv GTS 2008. D 6/14/2008 Bp Gladstone Bailey Adams III P 2/21/2009 Bp Egbert Don Taylor. m 10/20/1990 Jason L A Alford c 2. Cur Caroline Ch Of Brookhaven E Setauke NY 2008-2012; Pstr Assoc Ch Of The Atone Bronx NY 2008; Cler Collegiality Team Dio Wstrn New York Tonawanda NY 2013-2016, Wrshp Cmsn 2013-, Dioc Coun 2012-2015. CHS-Assoc 1987. stmatthiasrector@gmail.com

TILLMAN, Christine Wylie (WMich) 3828 Cook Ct. S.W., Wyoming MI 49519 B Grand Rapids MI 1951 d Robert & Peggyann. BA Wstrn Michigan U 1974. D 5/3/1986 Bp Howard Samuel Meeks. m 9/13/1974 Brian Gerard Tillman c 2. Archd Dio Wstrn Michigan Kalamazoo MI 2012-2013, Dioc D for Yth and Chld 2008-2014; Stff H Trin Epis Ch Wyoming MI 1986-1995. NAAD.

TILLMAN, Jane Guion (WMass) **P Assoc S Paul's Epis Ch Stockbridge MA 2016-** B Chapel Hill NC 1961 d Rollie & Mary. AB U NC 1983; MDiv Duke 1987; MDiv Duke 1987; PhD U of Tennessee 1995. D 12/14/2013 P 6/14/2014 Bp Doug Fisher.

TILLOTSON, Ellen Louise (Ct) 38 Fair St, Guilford CT 06437 **Supply P and Consult Dio Connecticut Meriden CT 2011-, COM 2008-, Stndg Com 2006-2011, COM 1987-2006** B Bismarck ND 1957 d William & Doris. BA U of No Dakota 1979; MDiv GTS 1983; STM Yale DS 2014. D 7/10/1983 P 2/14/1984 Bp Harold Anthony Hopkins Jr. m 8/7/1999 Frank Miller Turner. S Jn's Epis Ch Bristol CT 2014-2016; R Trin Ch Torrington CT 1992-2011; Assoc Trin Ch On The Green New Haven CT 1983-1992; Alum/ae Exec Commitee Pres The GTS New York NY 2006-2009; Mem SCMD 2001-2006. Auth, 1985. Paul Harris Fell Rotary Intl 2006. ellentillotson@me.com

TILSON, Alan Russell (Kan) 711 W 47th St, Kansas City MO 64112 B Maryville MO 1949 s Billy & Clarice. BA Washburn U 1975; MDiv Nash 1984. D 6/29/1984 P 1/1/1985 Bp John Forsythe Ashby. c 3. R S Paul's Ch Kansas City KS 1997-2003; Ch Of The Cov Jct City KS 1997; Ch Of The Nativ Burnsville MN 1992-1996; R Ch Of The H Comm S Ptr MN 1986-1991; P-in-c S Ptr's Ch New Ulm MN 1986-1991; P-in-c Ch Of The Trsfg Bennington KS 1984-1986; S Fran Cmnty Serv Inc. Salina KS 1984-1986.

TILSON, Brent Edward (Spok) St Martin's Episcopal Church, 416 E Nelson Rd, Moses Lake WA 98837 B Seattle WA 1959 s Clarence & Mildred. D 10/18/2015 P 6/11/2016 Bp James E Waggoner Jr. m 6/25/2005 Kathleen McDonald c 2.

TILSON JR, Hugh Arval (NC) 3819 Jones Ferry Rd, Chapel Hill NC 27516 **Natl Prog Dir U.S. Environ Protection Agcy 1989-** B Plainview TX 1946 BS Texas Tech U 1968; PhD U MN 1972. D 6/3/2006 Bp Michael B Curry. m 9/4/1981 Gaylia Harry.

TIMMERMAN, Melissa Roen (SC) 484 Lymington Rd, Severna Park MD 21146 B Los Angeles CA 1957 d John & Patricia. D 6/5/2004 Bp Robert Wilkes Ihloff. m 5/21/1983 Robert Joseph Timmerman c 2. D H Cross Faith Memi Epis Ch Pawleys Island SC 2008-2013; D Gr Ch Elkridge MD 2005-2008; S Mary's Outreach Cntr Baltimore MD 2004-2005.

TINDALL, Byron Cheney (SC) 102 Fir Court Unit 1260, Waleska GA 30183 **P Assoc Epis Ch Of The H Fam Jasper GA 2008-** B Atlanta GA 1941 s James & Gladys. W&M 1961; BA Emory and Henry Coll 1965; Cert Sewanee: The U So, TS 1979. D 6/17/1978 P 6/1/1979 Bp Ned Cole. m 3/16/1963 Anne Talbot c 3. Chr Ch Denmark SC 1992-2006; Vic Chr Epis Ch Denmark SC 1985-2006; Supply Cler So Carolina Charleston SC 1983-1984; Non-par Headwaters Field Boonville NY 1978-1982.

TINKLEPAUGH, John R (Pa) 400 Walnut Lane, North East MD 21901 **P-in-c S Clemets Massey MD 2007-** B Binghamton NY 1936 s Joseph & Pearl. BA The Kings Coll Briarcliff Manor NY 1960; MDiv Denver Sem 1964; VTS 1974; DMin Lancaster TS 1995. D 6/23/1974 P 11/10/1974 Bp Robert Rae Spears Jr. m 1/2/1981 Carole N Nunamaker c 4. S Paul's Ch Plymouth WI 2007-2010; R Ch Of S Jude And The Nativ Lafayette Hill PA 1985-2006; Ch Of Our Sav Jenkintown PA 1985; Int Dio Pennsylvania Philadelphia PA 1983-1985; R Ch Of S Andr And S Monica Philadelphia PA 1982-1983; Ch Of The Gd Shpd Savona NY 1980-1981; S Jas Ch Hammondsport NY 1980-1981; Chapl VetA Hosp Bath NY 1979-1982; L'Eglise Epis au Rwanda New York NY 1978-1980; Mssy Epis Ch to Rwanda 1978-1979; Asst Min S Paul's Ch Rochester NY 1974-1978.

TINNON, Becky (Haw) 98-939 Moanalua Rd, Aiea HI 96701 B New Castle PA 1961 d Edward & Mardelle. BA Olivet Nazarene U 1984; MRE Nazarene TS Kansas City MO 1987; MDiv Nazarene TS 1997. D 1/6/2008 P 6/28/2008 Bp Philip Menzie Duncan II. m 10/26/1985 Michael Scott Tinnon c 2. Int H Faith Par Inglewood CA 2014-2015; S Tim's Ch Aiea HI 2011-2013; Ch Of The Epiph Crestview FL 2011; Cur S Simon's On The Sound Ft Walton Bch FL 2008-2011.

TINNON, Michael Scott (Haw) 98-939 Moanalua Rd, Aiea HI 96701 **The Epis Ch Of The Blessed Sacr Placentia CA 2017-** B Lexington KY 1950 s Lloyd & Carolyn. BA U of Kentucky 1982; MDiv Nazarene TS 1987; DMin Asbury TS 2001. D 1/6/2008 P 6/28/2008 Bp Philip Menzie Duncan II. m 10/26/1985 Becky Tinnon c 3. Peace in Chr Ch Eliz CO 2016; P S Tim's Ch Aiea HI 2011-2013. fathermiketinnon@gmail.com

TINSLEY JR, Fred Haley (WLa) 3535 Santa Fe St Unit 41, Corpus Christi TX 78411 B Pampa TX 1948 s Fred & Juanita. BS U of Oklahoma 1972; MDiv Sewanee: The U So, TS 1982. D 6/24/1982 P 2/21/1983 Bp Sam Byron Hulsey. m 6/6/1969 Judy Kay Watkins c 2. R St Jas Epis Ch and Sch Alexandria LA 2003-2014; R S Matt's Epis Ch Houma LA 1996-2003; R Ch Of The H Cross W Memphis AR 1992-1996; Asst S Andr's Epis Ch Amarillo TX 1988-1992; All SS Epis Sch Lubbock TX 1987-1988; H Cross Lubbock TX 1987-1988; Vic H Cross Lubbock TX 1987-1988; Vic Gr Ch Vernon TX 1984-1987; Vic Trin Ch Quanah TX 1984-1987; Cur Ch Of The H Trin Midland TX 1982-1984.

TIPPETT, Michael R (Minn) 2202 Lexington Parkway South, Saint Paul MN 55105 **P-in-c S Paul's Epis Ch Owatonna MN 2002-** B Kilwinning Scotland GB 1954 s Ronald & Jessie. Oxf GB 1976; BA Royal Mltry Acad 1978; PSC British Army Stff Coll 1985; MDiv Ya Berk 1994. D 6/11/1994 Bp Clarence Nicholas Coleridge P 3/1/1995 Bp Sanford Zangwill Kaye Hampton. m 5/28/1989 Krista W Tippett c 2. Geth Ch Minneapolis MN 2000-2001; Int S Jn The Evang S Paul MN 1996-2000, Assoc 1994-1995.

TIPTON, Harry Steadman (CGC) 129 Camellot Ct, Crestview FL 32539 B Knoxville TN 1937 s Harry & Henrietta. BS LSU 1960; MTh SWTS 1965. D 6/26/1965 Bp Iveson Batchelor Noland P 5/1/1966 Bp Girault M Jones. Ch Of The Epiph Crestview FL 1991-1998; P-in-c S Monica's Cantonment FL 1990-1991; Off Of Bsh For ArmdF New York NY 1969-1990; Vic Calv Ch Bunkie LA 1965-1969; Vic H Comfort Lecompte LA 1965-1969. ECM, ERM, Bro Of S Andr. Commendation Medal 3rd Oak Leaf Cluster; Meritorious Serv Medal Af.

TIPTON, Tommy (USC) 1029 Old Plantation Dr, Pawleys Island SC 29585 B Rutherforton NC 1952 s Alvin & Edith. AA S Leo U 1988; MDiv Sewanee: The U So, TS 1991. D 6/24/1991 P 6/1/1992 Bp Edward Lloyd Salmon Jr. c 1. Dio Upper So Carolina Columbia SC 2011; R H Cross Faith Memi Epis Ch Pawleys Island SC 1999-2011; Prince Geo Winyah Epis Preschool Georgetown SC 1991-1999; Asst to R Prince Geo Winyah Epis Ch Georgetown SC 1991-1999.

TIPTON-ZILE, Cynthia (Md) 4500 C Dunton Ter, Perry Hall MD 21128 **Died 1/13/2017** B Rome GA 1950 d James & Ethel. EFM 1995; Maryland TS 1995. D 6/10/1995 Bp Charles Lindsay Longest P 12/20/2003 Bp Robert Wilkes Ihloff. m 1/10/2009 Eric Neil Zile. R S Alb's Epis Ch Glen Burnie MD 2006-2012; R Ch Of The Ascen Middle River MD 1999-2006; Cathd Of The Incarn Baltimore MD 1999-2000; Chapl Res Johns Hopkins Hosp 1998-1999; D H Cross Ch St MD 1995-1998; Prog and Bdgt Com Dio Maryland Baltimore MD 2005-2011, Dioc Coun 1999-2005, Bp's Search Com 1997-1998, Eccl Crt 1996-1999.

TIRADO, Hernan (Colom) B 1930 D 9/7/1974 P 2/13/1976 Bp William Alfred Franklin. m 9/8/1971 Amparo Cardon. Iglesia Epis En Colombia Bogota 1974-1980.

TIRADO, Vincent (SeFla) 18601 Sw 210th St, Miami FL 33187 B Puerto Rico 1943 s Vincent & Recci. D 7/25/2003 Bp Leo Frade. m 5/3/1964 Delia Tirado c 3. Aircraft Pilot U.S. Customs/Homeland Defense 1976-1996.

TIRRELL, Charles David (Tex) 9701 Meyer Forest Dr Apt 12112, Houston TX 77096 B Phillipsburg NJ 1935 s Matthew & Ruth. BA Villanova U 1958; MTh Augustinian Coll 1962; MA CUA 1966. Rec 12/1/1998 as Priest Bp Claude Edward Payne. m 9/2/1978 Brenda P Tirrell c 2. S Mk's Ch Houston TX 2002-2005; S Steph's Epis Ch Houston TX 2002; Asst Emm Ch Houston TX 2000-2001; Vic Lord Of The St Epis Mssn Ch Houston TX 1999-2000. Cert Pstr Addictions Counslr; Lic Psychol.

TIRRELL, John Alden (Cal) Box 456, Athens 125 Greece **Non-par 1959-** B Chicago IL 1932 s Henry & Dorothy. BA Stan 1955; BTh VTS 1958; Phillips U 1959. D 6/24/1958 P 6/1/1961 Bp James Albert Pike.

TISDALE JR, William Alfred (Ct) 27 Church St, Stonington CT 06378 **R Calv Ch Stonington CT 2010-; Dn--Seabury Dnry Dio Connecticut Meriden CT 2013-, Fresh Start Co-Ldr 2013-, Com on Deacons 2010-** B Sumter SC 1953 s William & Lottie. BA Wofford Coll 1975; BA Wofford Coll 1975; DMin UTS 1979; STM GTS 1999. D 6/13/2009 Bp Andrew Donnan Smith P 1/16/2010 Bp James Elliot Curry. m 12/28/1974 Leonora Tisdale c 2. Assoc Dn Ya Berk New Haven CT 2010; Assoc.Dn/Dir of Angl Ya Berk 2009-2010; Chr Ch New Haven CT 2009-2010.

TISDELLE, Celeste (Fla) St. Mary's Episcopal Church, 400 St. Johns Ave, Green Cove Springs FL 32043 **P-in-c S Mary's Epis Ch Green Cv Spg FL 2009-** B Key West FL 1951 d Jacob & Rosemary. BA U of Florida 1974; MDiv Sewanee: The U So, TS 2003. D 6/8/2003 P 12/7/2003 Bp Stephen Hays Jecko. m 5/14/1977 Achille Carlisle Tisdelle c 3. Chapl to Day Sch Gr Epis Ch Orange Pk FL 2006-2009; Cn for Pstr Care & Chapl to Cathd Fndt S Jn's Cathd Jacksonville FL 2004-2006; Chapl to Day Sch S Andr's Ch Jacksonville FL 2003-2004.

TITCOMB, Cecily Johnson (SeFla) 141 S. County rd, Palm Beach FL 33480 B Saint Paul MN 1947 d Donald & Marjorie. BS Barry U; Briarcliffe Coll; Wms. D 11/7/2004 Bp Leo Frade. m 8/16/1969 Edward Rodman Titcomb c 4. D The Epis Ch Of Beth-By-The-Sea Palm Bch FL 2005-2010, D 1979-. Doctorate of Humane letters Cazenovia Coll 2012; Chapl Legislature of the St of Kansas 1998.

TITTLE, Darlene Anne Duryea (Nwk) 11 Overhill Dr, Budd Lake NJ 07828 B Orange NJ 1943 d Norman & Viola. BA Glassboro St U 1966; MA Virginia Tech U 1973; MDiv VTS 1981; DMin Wesley Sem 1993; DMin Wesley TS 1993. D 6/13/1981 P 12/1/1981 Bp Robert Bruce Hall. m 7/18/1976 Richard L Tittle. R Chr Ch Budd Lake NJ 2004-2008; P-in-c S Steph's Ch S Louis MO 1999-2003; H Sprt Epis Ch Germantown MD 1986-1999; All SS' Epis Ch Chevy Chase MD 1981-1986; Asst S Chris's Ch Springfield VA 1980-1981; Asst Chr Ch Columbia MD 1976-1979. Auth, "A Handful Of Quiet"; Auth, "The Sprtl Ldrshp Of The Epis Ch"; Auth, "We Are One In The Sprt".

TITUS, Bessie Charlotte (Ak) B Fairbanks AK 1955 D 9/3/2000 P 4/8/2001 Bp Mark Lawrence Macdonald.

TITUS, Fred David (Ia) St. Thomas' Episcopal Church, 710 N. Main St., Garden City KS 67846 B North Platte NE 1942 s Fred & Kathleen. LTh Epis TS in Kentucky 1978. D 5/26/1978 P 3/1/1979 Bp Walter Cameron Righter. m 11/13/1967 Charleen Titus. Calv Epis Ch Sioux City IA 1984-1988; S Geo's Epis Ch Le Mars IA 1984-1985; Dio Iowa Des Moines IA 1978-2007; S Andr's Ch Des Moines IA 1978-1984.

TITUS, John Clark (At) 5428 Park Cir, Stone Mountain GA 30083 **Archd Dio Atlanta 2004-** B Philadelphia PA 1940 s George & Clare. BA Pr 1962; MA GW 1972. D 10/23/1993 Bp Frank Kellogg Allan. m 5/4/1968 Mary Louise Ann Toal. D S Mich And All Ang Ch Stone Mtn GA 1992-2014.

TITUS, Luke (Ak) Saint Barnabas Mission, Minto AK 99758 **Vic S Barn Mssn 1976-; 1974-** B Tenana AK 1941 s Robert & Elsie. Cook Chr Trng Sch. D 7/14/1971 P 1/1/1972 Bp William Jones Gordon Jr. m 5/21/1969 Alice Lee Titus c 1. Navajoland Area Mssn Farmington NM 1978-1979; Dio Alaska Fairbanks AK 1971-1978. Auth, "Epis".

TITUS, Nancy Espenshade (NC) 1739 Berwickshire Cir, Raleigh NC 27615 B Washington DC 1940 d Paul & Irene. BSN Duke 1962; MS Boston Coll 1964; Dio No Carolina 1995; Cert Haden Inst 2009. D 1/6/1996 Bp Huntington Williams Jr. c 3. D Epis Campus Mnstry No Carolina St U Raleigh NC 2010-2012; Nurse Urban Mnstrs of Wake Co./Open Door Clnc 2008-2013; D Ch Of The Nativ Raleigh NC 2000-2009; D S Paul's Epis Ch Smithfield NC 1996-1999; Nurse Hospice of Wake Cnty 1988-2005. DOK 1984.

TJELTVEIT, Maria Washington Eddy (Be) 124 S Madison St, Allentown PA 18102 **R The Epis Ch Of The Medtr Allentown PA 1999-** B Sapporo JP 1959 d Elizabeth. BA Swarthmore Coll 1981; MDiv Ya Berk 1986. D 6/11/1986 P 6/12/1987 Bp Robert Poland Atkinson. m 4/5/1997 Alan Charles Tjeltvelt. R S Andr's Ch Harrington Pk NJ 1994-1998; Asst R S Jn's Epis Ch Richmond VA 1988-1994; S Paul's Epis Ch Alexandria VA 1988-1994; Asst R S Matt's Ch Charleston WV 1986-1988.

TJOFLAT, Marie Elizabeth (Fla) 1255 Peachtree St, Jacksonville FL 32207 **Dio Florida Jacksonville 2011-** B Jacksonville FL 1960 d Gerald & Sarah. BA Jacksonville U 1984; MA USC 1993; Dip Ang Stud Ya Berk 2011; MDiv Yale DS 2011. D 12/5/2010 P 6/19/2011 Bp Samuel Johnson Howard. Asst St Fran in the Field Ponte Vedra FL 2011-2012; intern Chr Ch Redding Ridge CT 2010-2011. St Georges Coll Awd Ya Berk 2011; Oliver Ellsworth Daggett Schlrshp Yale DS 2011; Chas S. Mersick Prize Yale DS 2011.

TLUCEK, Laddie Raymond (Okla) 1509 Nw 198th St, Edmond OK 73003 B Nampa ID 1945 s Louis & Helen. BA U of Idaho 1966; U of Utah 1968; MDiv CDSP 1971; MEd Albertson Coll 1979. D 6/25/1971 P 12/28/1971 Bp John Joseph Meakin Harte. m 7/7/1973 Andrea Tlucek c 2. Assoc All Souls Epis Ch Oklahoma City OK 2000-2010; R S Paul's Epis Ch Grand Forks ND 1996-2000; R S Lk's Epis Ch Wenatchee WA 1982-1996; Vic S Geo's Ch Seattle WA 1979-1982; R S Jas Epis Ch Midvale UT 1974-1979; R S Mary's Ch Emmett ID 1972-1974; Cur Gd Shpd Of The Hills Cave Creek AZ 1971-1972; S Steph's Ch Phoenix AZ 1971-1972.

TOALSTER, Rebecca D (CFla) 311 11th St, Ambridge PA 15003 B Lakeland FL 1984 d Steven & Linda. AA Polk Cmnty Coll; BA U of So Florida 2007; MDiv TESM 2011. D 6/11/2011 Bp Hugo Luis Pina-Lopez P 4/7/2013 Bp Gregory Orrin Brewer. TESM Ambridge PA 2011-2013.

TOBERMAN, Harold Frederick (Ark) 329 Colony Green Dr, Bloomingdale IL 60108 **Lic Dio Chicago 2013-; D S Lawr Epis Ch Libertyville IL 2013-; Non-par Dio Arkansas 2000-** B Chicago IL 1950 s Harold & Lorraine. BA No Cntrl Coll 1972; MBA Loyola U 1978; Cert 1987. D 12/26/1987 Bp Frank Tracy Griswold III. m 7/3/1971 Linda Marie Toberman c 3. D S Mk's Ch W Frankfort IL 2013-2014; Lic Dio Springfield 2011-2015; D S Jas Chap Marion Marion IL 2011-2013; D Emm Ch Lake Vill AR 2000-2006; D Ch Of The Incarn Bloomingdale IL 1987-1999. NAAD 1988.

TOBIAS, Gwendolyn (SeFla) 3300A S. Seacrest Blvd., Boynton Beach FL 33435 **Assoc P S Jos's Epis Ch Boynton Bch FL 2011-** B Milwaukee WI 1954 d James & Beverley. MDiv VTS 2008. D 12/22/2007 P 7/1/2008 Bp Leo Frade.

857

T

c 3. Dir of Wrshp Cathd of St Ptr & St Paul Washington DC 2008-2011, Assoc for Liturg 2008-2010; Lay Chapl and Tchr S Jos's Epis Sch 1995-2005; Chld and Yth Min S Jos's Epis Ch 1993-1996. revwendy@srtjoesweb.org

TOBIN, Barbara Kinzer (Pa) D 6/17/2017 Bp Daniel Gutierrez.

TOBIN, Florence Lane (Roch) PO Box 304, Corning NY 14830 **Supply P Lic Dio Cntrl New York Ch 2012-; Supply P Dio Rochester NY Epis Ch 2009-; Apportnmt T/F Dio Rochester Henrietta 2011-, GC Alt Dep 2011-, Safe Ch Trnr 2011-, Anti Racism Com Trnr 2008-, Dioc Coun 2008-, Oasis Rochester 2008-** B Oak Bluffs MA 1939 d Elizabeth & Elizabeth. BA Bennington Coll 1961; MA GTS 2002; Providence Coll Grad Rel Stds 2003; CPE St Annes Hosp 2003. D 4/20/2008 Bp Jack Marston Mckelvey P 11/22/2008 Bp Prince Grenville Singh. c 2. Long Term Supply S Matt's Epis Ch Horseheads NY 2011-2012; Supply Pstr Our Sav Luth Ch Horseheads NY 2009-2010; P in Charge Chr Corning NY 2009, Asst P 2008-2011; Dir Pstr Care Guthrie/Corning Hosp Corning NY 2005-2009; Chapl St Anne's Hosp Fall River MA 2002-2003. Integrity USA 2007; Integrity USA Dioc Organizer 2011; Ord of St Lk the Physcn 1990; Recovery Mnstrs Natl Bd 2004-2010; Recovery Mnstrs of the Epis Ch 2003.

TOBIN JR, Robert Wallace (Mass) Po Box 113, Sunset ME 04683 B Austin TX 1936 s Robert & Frances. BA U of Texas 1957; MDiv Epis TS of the SW 1960; CAS Harv 1977; EdD Harv 1980. D 6/13/1960 P 12/21/1960 Bp George Henry Quarterman. m 6/3/1958 Maurine M Tobin c 5. R Chr Ch Cambridge Cambridge MA 1987-2004; Headmaster All SS Epis Sch Lubbock TX 1981-1987; Int Gr Ch Salem MA 1978-1979; Int S Mk's Ch Westford MA 1976-1977; VP Bos 1973-1976; Hedmaster Cbury Sch 1966-1973; Vic S Ptr's Epis Ch Borger TX 1960-1966. "How Long O Lord," Cowley, 2003. Morris Arnold Awd Epis City Mssn-Boston 2005.

TOBIN, Roger Martin (SeFla) 5690 N Kendall Dr, Miami FL 33156 **Dir Miami Area Pstr Serv So Miami Florida 2010-** B Minneapolis MN 1951 s John & Barbara. BA Hobart and Wm Smith Colleges 1972; MDiv EDS 1977; MS Barry U 1998. D 7/3/1977 P 6/3/1978 Bp Robert Rae Spears Jr. m 9/11/1971 Janis Tobin c 2. S Thos Epis Par Sch Coral Gables FL 1987-2003; S Thos Epis Par Miami FL 1986-2009; R S Steph's Epis Ch Pittsburgh PA 1981-1986; Asst S Thos Epis Ch Rochester NY 1977-1981. Auth, "Eds Quarterly"; Auth, "Living Ch".

TOBOLA, Cynthia Pruet (Tex) PO Box 895, Palacios TX 77465 B San Angelo TX 1947 d Royce & Mary. Texas Tech U 1969; MBA U of Houston 1987; Iona Sch for Mnstry 2009. D 6/20/2009 Bp C Andrew Doyle P 12/21/2009 Bp Rayford Baines High Jr. m 8/4/1984 Logic Tobola c 4.

TODARO, Alicia Butler (Alb) St Paul's Church, 58 3rd St, Troy NY 12180 B 1955 Dio Albany D Formation; BA Russel Sage Coll 1981; PhD RPI 1988. D 5/10/2008 Bp William Howard Love. m 5/15/1982 Mark Todaro c 1. DCNALICIA@STPAULSTROY.ORG

TODD, Charles E (Ga) St Paul Episcopal Church, 1802 Abercorn St, Savannah GA 31401 **Dio Georgia Savannah GA 2016-; Vic The Collgt Ch of St Paul the Apos Savannah GA 2013-** B Madison IN 1969 s John & Kathryn. BA Indiana U 1990; MDiv SWTS 1993. D 6/30/2012 P 12/30/2012 Bp Scott Anson Benhase.

TODD, Christopher Howard (SeFla) 30243 Coconut Hwy, Big Pine Key FL 33043 **R S Fran-In-The-Keys Episcop Big Pine Key FL 2002-** B St. Louis MO 1954 s William & Phyllis. BA Wheaton Coll 1977. D 6/16/2002 P 12/21/2002 Bp Leo Frade. m 10/7/1978 Julia Elaine Buryn c 2. "Superheroes of the Faith," The Net, Epis Dio SE Florida, 2007; "Sherlock Holmes as Literary Chr Figure," The Baker St Journ, Ford Press, 1985.

TODD, Edward Pearson (Eur) 18 Hall Pond Lane, Copake NY 11516 Afghanistan **Non-par 1991-** B Cleveland OH 1945 s Donald & Marjorie. BA Harv 1967; MDiv GTS 1970. D 6/21/1970 P 12/1/1970 Bp Frederick Barton Wolf. m 5/24/2004 Charles B Matlock c 3. R S Paul Within-The-Walls Rome Italy 1986-1991; R S Paul's Within the Walls Rome 1986-1991; Int The Ch Of Our Redeem Lexington MA 1984-1985; Exec Coun Appointees New York NY 1972-1984; Serv The Epis Ch in Jerusalem and the Middle E 1972-1983; All SS Epis Ch Skowhegan ME 1970-1972; S Hugh Ch Lincoln ME 1970-1972; M-in-c S Thos Ch Winn ME 1970-1972.

TODD, James Converse (NC) B Concord, MA 1975 s Conrad & Harriet. Bachelor of Arts Duke 1998. D 2/20/2016 Bp Anne Hodges-Copple. m 8/5/2006 Ann Marie Mccaig c 4.

TODD, Michael P (SwFla) 1620 Boathouse Cir, GR 208, Sarasota FL 34231 **R Ch Of The H Sprt Osprey FL 2011-** B Lake Wales FL 1974 s Russell & Carol. BS U of So Flordia 1997; MDiv TESM 2004. D 5/22/2004 Bp John Wadsworth Howe P 2/13/2005 Bp Gethin Benwil Hughes. Asst S Paul's Ch Yuma AZ 2008-2011. OSL 2005.

TODD, Richard Alfred (Minn) 38378 Glacier Dr, North Branch MN 55056 **Mntl Hlth Profsnl Minnosota Adult and Teen Challenge 2017-; D Epis. Ch. of St. Jn in the Wilderness White Bear Lake MN 2005-** B Duluth MN 1960 s Richard & Carol. BA U MN 1982; MA U MN 1992. D 6/12/2003 Bp James Louis Jelinek. m 6/7/1986 Jill Wobbe c 2. D Epis Ch of the Resurr Sprg Lake Pk MN 2003-2005; Clincl Psychol Dept of Corrections Chisago MN 1991-2017.

TODD JR, Samuel Rutherford (Tex) 2423 Mcclendon St, Houston TX 77030 **Ret 2002-** B Columbia SC 1940 s Samuel & Jane. BA Harv 1962; MDiv UTS 1966. D 12/27/1965 Bp Horace W B Donegan P 7/9/1966 Bp Charles Francis Boynton. c 4. Assoc R Palmer Memi Ch Houston TX 1996-2002; Ch Of Recon San Antonio TX 1979-1996; R The Ch of Recon San Antonio TX 1979-1996; Assoc Chr Epis Ch San Antonio TX 1976-1979; Instr Theol S Steph Sch Austin TX 1972-1976; S Steph's Epis Sch Austin TX 1972-1976; Dir Stds Marg Hall Sch Zapopan Mex 1971-1972; Asst Calv and St Geo New York NY 1966-1971. Auth, An Intro to Chrsnty: a First Millennium Fndt for Third Millennium Thinkers, Brocton Pub Co, 2000; Contributing Ed, Dio W Texas News; Contributing Ed, The Texas Epis.

TOEBBEN, Warren B (Ore) **S Paul's Ch Milwaukee WI 2017-; S Mary's Epis Ch Eugene OR 2014-** D 6/21/2014 P 12/20/2014 Bp Michael Hanley.

TOELLER-NOVAK, Thomas (WMich) 555 Michigan Ave, Holland MI 49423 **Epis Ch Of The Gd Shpd Allegan MI 2011-** B Muskegon MI 1940 s Leo & Mary. BA Athenaeum 1961; STB Pontifical Gregorian U Rome IT 1963; STL Pontificia U Gregoriana Rome It 1965. Rec 11/1/1984 as Priest Bp Howard Samuel Meeks. m 6/30/1976 Deirdre Toeller-Novak. Int S Paul's Epis Ch St Jos MI 2006-2007; R Gr Ch Holland MI 1990-2005; Int Gr Ch Grand Rapids MI 1990, Asst R 1985-1987; Res P S Mk's Ch Grand Rapids MI 1984-1985.

TOFANI, Ann Lael (Spr) 427 W 4th St, Mount Carmel IL 62863 **Vic S Mary's Ch Robinson IL 2013-, D 2010-** B Milwaukee WI 1939 d Halsey & Lois. BA U of Evansville 1973. D 6/11/2000 Bp Peter Hess Beckwith P 11/20/2012 Bp Edward Stuart Little II. D Ch Of S Jn The Bapt Mt Carmel IL 2000-2009. aht19@frontier.com

TOFFEY, Judith E (Ct) 41 Cannon Ridge Dr, Watertown CT 06795 B Waterbury CT 1946 d Herbert & Julie. BA U of Massachusetts 1972; MS Bos 1976; MDiv EDS 1987. D 6/11/1988 Bp David Elliot Johnson P 5/1/1989 Bp Barbara Clementine Harris. S Mich's Ch Naugatuck CT 2011-2012; Chr Ch Waterbury CT 2009-2011; S Paul's Ch Southington CT 2007-2009; S Mary's Epis Ch Manchester CT 2006; Trin Epis Ch Trumbull CT 2002-2005; Exec Coun Appointees New York NY 2002; All SS Epis Ch Oakville CT 1992-2000; Cur Gr Ch New Bedford MA 1988-1992.

TOIA, Frank Phillip (Pa) 2127 Kriebel Rd, Lansdale PA 19446 B Sewickley PA 1937 s Thomas & Helen. BA Duke 1959; MDiv PDS 1962; U of Pennsylvania 1971; Estrn Pennsylvania Psych Inst 1972. D 6/16/1962 Bp William S Thomas P 12/16/1962 Bp Harry Sherbourne Kennedy. m 11/17/1985 Linda Toia c 4. Asstg P Ch Of S Mart-In-The-Fields Philadelphia PA 1999; Gd Shpd Ch Hilltown PA 1979-1999; Ch Of The Mssh Lower Gwynedd PA 1972-1979; Vic Ch Of S Jn The Evang Philadelphia PA 1971-1972; Vic Epiph Santo Domingo Dominican Republic 1966-1970; Cur All SS In Naha Okinawa 1962-1965.

TOLA, Elaine M (NC) B Raleigh NC 1967 d Peter & Anne. BA U NC 1990; Cert U NC 2006; MDiv Duke DS 2014. D 1/24/2015 Bp Anne Hodges-Copple.

TOLAND, Paula (WMass) 270 Main St, Oxford MA 01540 **Dio Wstrn Massachusetts Springfield 2017-** B Worcester MA 1961 d Walter & Ruth. BA Clark U 1983; MS Capella U 2003; MDiv EDS 2013. D 6/22/2013 P 1/4/2014 Bp M(Arvil) Thomas Shaw. m 10/29/1983 Ronald Gene Toland c 3. S Jn's Epis Ch Franklin MA 2013-2016. RevPaulaToland@comcast.net

TOLAND JR, William Leslie (Spr) Po Box 3161, Springfield IL 62708 **Ret 1996-** B Macomb IL 1928 s William & Winifred. BS Wstrn Illinois U 1950; LTh Bex Sem 1955; MA Bradley U 1957. D 6/2/1955 P 12/6/1955 Bp William L Essex. m 8/25/1962 Rosemary Kathryn Gahwiler. S Laurence Epis Ch Effingham IL 1987-1990; Non-par 1970-1996; Assoc Chr Ch Springfield IL 1965-1970; Vic Trin Epis Ch Mattoon IL 1960-1965; Asst S Jn's Epis Ch Decatur IL 1958-1960; Assoc S Jas Epis Ch Lewistown IL 1955-1958; S Ptr's Ch Canton IL 1955-1958; Chair Dio Springfield Springfield IL 1963-2000, Chair 1957-1962. Mltry Chapl Assn; OHC.

TOLES, John F (Okla) 518 W Randolph Ave, Enid OK 73701 **R S Matt's Ch Enid OK 2015-** B Bastrop LA 1964 s Donal & Elizabeth. BBA Steph F Austin St U 1989; Masters of Div Nash 2004; Doctorate of Mnstry Nash 2012. D 9/14/2004 P 5/5/2005 Bp Charles Franklin Brookhart Jr. R S Lk's Ch Billings MT 2013-2015; S Marks Pintler Cluster Anaconda MT 2010-2013; D Dio Montana Helena MT 2004-2009; BEC Dio Oklahoma Oklahoma City OK 2015, COM 2015-. fr.john.toles@me.com

TOLL, Richard Kellogg (Ore) 1707 Se Courtney Rd, P.O. Box 220112, Milwaukie OR 97269 B Pecos TX 1939 s Richard & Francis. BBA Texas Tech U 1962; MDiv CDSP 1967; DMin VTS 1985. D 6/29/1967 Bp C J Kinsolving III P 1/10/1968 Bp James Walmsley Frederic Carman. m 9/1/1962 Wanda Elaine Toll c 2. Pres Cler Assn Dio Olympia Seattle 1990-1992, 1981-2003, Pres Cler Assn 1981-1983; R S Jn The Evang Ch Portland OR 1984-2003; Cn Pstr S Mk's Cathd Seattle WA 1976-1984; Pres Stndg Com Dio Estrn Oregon Cove OR 1973-1976, Dioc Coun 1972-1976; R S Steph's Baker City OR 1971-1976; Chapl Res Emm Hosp Portland OR 1970-1971; Assoc Gr Memi Portland OR 1967-1970; Pres Stndg Com Dio Oregon Portland OR 1991-1993; Bd Trst CDSP Berkeley CA 1979-1991. DD CDSP 2001; Hon Cn Dio Olympia 1984.

TOLLEFSON, Jane Jill Carol (Minn) 2700 Canby Ct, Northfield MN 55057 B Weymouth MA 1946 d Arthur & Ruth. Emerson Coll. D 6/17/2001 Bp James

Louis Jelinek. m 6/26/1965 Rolf H Tollefson c 4. D All SS Ch Northfield MN 2007-2013; D La Mision El Santo Nino Jesus S Paul MN 2004-2007; D The Epis Cathd Of Our Merc Sav Faribault MN 2001-2003. Third Ord Franciscan 2000.

TOLLETT, Mitchell Joseph (Tex) St. Francis Episcopal Church, 3232, Tyler TX 75701 **S Fran Epis Ch Tyler TX 2014-** B Houston TX 1968 s HJ & Joann. Computer Engr Tech U of Houston 1995; MDiv Epis TS Of The SW 2012; MDiv Epis TS of the SW 2012. D 6/16/2012 Bp C Andrew Doyle. m 8/7/1999 Camille Tollett c 1. Cur Chr Epis Ch Temple TX 2012-2013. rector@stfrancistyler.org

TOLLEY, John Charles (Cal) 594 Los Altos Drive, Chula Vista CA 91914 B Cleveland OH 1935 s James & May. BBA Baldwin-Wallace Coll Berea Ohio 1961; Cert Dio of California Dioc Sch for Mnstrs San Fran 1980; BA California Sch for Deacons 1983; Cert CDSP Berkeley CA 1988. D 4/12/1981 P 12/3/1988 Bp William Edwin Swing. m 6/15/1959 Sarah Jane Tolley c 2. S Jn's Epis Ch Chula Vista CA 2001-2015; Pstr Assoc S Paul's Epis Ch Walnut Creek CA 1995-2001, 1986-1987; S Mich And All Ang Concord CA 1992-1995; S Clem's Ch Berkeley CA 1991-1992; Pstr Assoc S Jn's Epis Ch Clayton CA 1989-1991; Bay Area Seafarers' Serv Oakland CA 1988-1992; Port Chapl Bay Area Seafarers Serv Oakland CA 1986-1991; Field Educ Supvsr CDSP Berkeley CA 1985-1986. Cmnty Serv Awd Contra Costa Cnty, CA 1986.

TOLLISON, Ann Black (Va) PO Box 100, Gum Spring VA 23065 B Spartanburg SC 1945 d Sam & Nancy. BA Queens Coll 1968; MDiv Sewanee: The U So, TS 1988. D 6/11/1988 P 5/20/1989 Bp William Arthur Beckham. m 11/1/2015 Henry Ernest Tollison c 3. R S Jas Epis Ch Louisa VA 2007-2012; P-in-c St. Jas Epis Ch Louisa VA 2006-2007; The Virginia Shpd's Stff Richmond VA 2003-2011; The Shpd Stff Inc Sarasota 2000-2003; Asst R S Fran Ch Greenville SC 1989-1999; D S Fran Epis Ch Greenville SC 1988-1989.

TOLLISON JR, Henry Ernest (USC) 105 Freeport Dr, Greenville SC 29615 B Greenville SC 1937 s Henry & Mary. BS Clemson U 1959; MDiv Sewanee: The U So, TS 1969. D 6/29/1969 P 6/24/1970 Bp John Adams Pinckney. m 11/1/2015 Ann Black Tollison. R S Fran Ch Greenville SC 1977-2001; Ch Of The Incarn Gaffney SC 1972-1977; Chapl Converse & Wofford Colleges Spartenburg SC 1972-1977; Dio Upper So Carolina Columbia SC 1972-1977; Asst S Martins-In-The-Field Columbia SC 1970-1972; Asst Gr Epis Ch Anderson SC 1969-1970. churchofepiphany@hotmail.com

TOLLIVER, Lisa (Ky) 7504 Westport Rd, Louisville KY 40222 **S Lk's Chap Louisville KY 2014-** B Bristol TN 1967 d L Earl & Edwinna. MS U of Kentucky; SWTS 2010; MDiv Lexington TS 2011. D 6/19/2010 P 12/20/2010 Bp Stacy F Sauls. m 10/29/2015 Teresa Ann Wood. Dio Lexington Lexington 2012; S Alb's Ch Morehead KY 2010-2012.

TOLLIVER, Richard (Chi) 4729 S. Drexel Blvd, Chicago IL 60615 B Springfield OH 1945 s Kenneth & Evelyn. BA Mia 1967; MA Bos 1971; MDiv EDS 1971; PhD How 1983; MA Bos 1986. D 6/5/1971 P 12/18/1971 Bp Horace W B Donegan. Gilead Mgmt Co Chicago IL 2004-2017; S Edm's Redevelopment Corp Chicago IL 1993-2017; R S Edm's Epis Ch Chicago IL 1989-2017; R S Tim's Epis Ch Washington DC 1977-1984; R S Cyp's Ch Boston MA 1972-1976; Asst S Phil's Ch New York NY 1971-1972. DD SWTS 1997; Distinguished Achievement Medal 1996.

TOLZMANN, Lee Ann (Ct) Episcopal Church in Connecticut, 219 Pratt Street, Meriden CT 06450 **Dio Connecticut Meriden CT 2015-** B New York NY 1955 d Leslie & Ann. BA Dart 1977; MDiv GTS 2001. D 6/9/2001 Bp Robert Wilkes Ihloff P 12/9/2001 Bp John L Rabb. m 6/19/1976 David C Tolzmann c 2. R S Paul's Ch Riverside CT 2008-2015; R Ch Of The Mssh Baltimore MD 2003-2008; Asst to the R S Andr's Epis Ch Glenwood MD 2001-2003. latolzmann@episcopalct.org

TOMAINE, Jane A (Nwk) 349 Short Dr, Mountainside NJ 07092 **Retreat Ldr St. Ben's Toolbox Mnstrs 2008-** B Milwaukee WI 1947 d Stanley & Cecelia. BA Cornell Coll 1969; MA OH SU 1971; MDiv Drew U 1995; DMin Drew U 2004. D 6/3/1995 Bp Jack Marston Mckelvey P 12/9/1995 Bp John Shelby Spong. m 7/27/1991 John J Tomaine. R S Ptr's Epis Ch Livingston NJ 1995-2008. *St. Ben's Toolbox: The Nuts and Bolts of Everyday Benedictine Living*, Morehouse Pub, 2005. SCHS - Chapl New York Chapt 2006-2008.

TOMBAUGH, Richard Franklin (Ct) 58 Terry Rd, Hartford CT 06105 B Syracuse NY 1932 s John & Mary. BA Pr 1954; MA Col 1956; STB GTS 1958; ThD GTS 1964. D 6/14/1958 Bp Charles L Street P 12/14/1958 Bp Gerald Francis Burrill. m 1/31/1959 Sandra Tombaugh c 3. P in charge Chr Ch Waterbury 2011-2015; Assoc St Paul's on the Green Norwalk CT 2005-2011; Exec Secy GBEC Hartford CT 2001-2010; Cn to he Ordnry Dio Connecticut Meriden CT 1986-1998; Mssnr Middlesex Area Cluster Mnstry CT 1985-1987; P-in-c H Cross Fairview Heights Fairview Heights IL 1981-1985; P-in-c Mineral Area Reg Mnstry MO 1980-1981; Exectuive Dir Arts And Educ Coun Of St Louis S Louis MO 1978-1982; Chapl to Colleges and Universities in S Louis Dio Missouri S Louis MO 1970-1976; Team Mnstry Trin Ch S Louis MO 1969-1970, P-in-c 1967-1968; Asst The Ch of S Ign of Antioch New York NY 1960-1964; Cur Gr Epis Ch Hinsdale IL 1958-1960; Chairman of the Bd Soc For The Increase Of Mnstry W Hartford CT 2010-2013. Auth, "Ecclesial Impatience: A Response to the Windsor Report," *Conversations in Rel and Theol*, Blackwell, 2005. ESCRU 1964-1980; ESMHE 1964-1986; The Epis Majority 2006-2010. The Bp's Awd for Ch and Cmnty Dio Connecticut 1998.

TOMCZAK, Beth Lynn (WMich) 321 N Main St, Three Rivers MI 49093 B Three Rivers MI 1959 d Elwin & Beverly. Dav Oakahater Sch for Deacons 2008. D 6/21/2008 Bp Robert R Gepert. c 2.

TOMEI, Gail R (Pa) Church Of The Ascension, 406 W 2nd Ave, Parkesburg PA 19365 **P in Charge Dio Pennsylvania Philadelphia PA 2013-** B Minneapolis MN 1946 d Orem & Jean. BA Denver U 1968; MTS VTS 1995; MDiv VTS 2004. D 6/12/2004 P 1/8/2005 Bp Rogers Sanders Harris. m 6/11/1988 Anthony J Tomei. Ch Of The Ascen Parkesburg PA 2013-2016; Supply Cler Dio Cntrl Pennsylvania Harrisburg PA 2009-2013; Assoc S Jn's Ch Marietta PA 2009-2013; Assoc S Mary's Epis Ch Bonita Sprg FL 2006-2009; Chapl Hospice Naples FL 2004-2006; Dir of Pstr Care S Jn's Ch Naples FL 2000-2003. ascensionpriest@verizon.net

TOMLIN, Kyle R (Va) 6769 Ridge Ave # A, Philadelphia PA 19128 **Ch Of The Mssh Fredericksbrg VA 2015-** B Elmer NJ 1975 s Earl & Sharon. BA Richard Stockton Coll 1997; MDiv TESM 2009. D 12/12/2009 P 6/21/2010 Bp William Howard Love. m 4/12/2003 Holly M Tomlin c 1. R S Alb's Ch Roxborough Philadelphia PA 2010-2015.

TOMLINSON, Diane B (EC) **S Thos' Epis Ch Bath NC 2014-** B Royal Oak Michigan 1960 BBA Walsh Coll 2002; MDiv Hur CA 2006. D 6/6/2006 P 12/9/2006 Bp Wendell Nathaniel Gibbs Jr. m 8/18/1984 Mark C Tomlinson c 1. R S Andr's Ch Waterford MI 2010-2013; Assoc Emm Ch Baltimore MD 2008-2010; Cur Nativ Epis Ch Bloomfield Township MI 2006-2007.

TOMLINSON, Liz (Va) 3439 Payne St, Falls Church VA 22041 **S Paul's Ch Bailey's Crossroads Falls Ch VA 2014-** B Champaign-Urbana IL 1947 d Robert & Elizabeth. BA Wake Forest U 1969; MSW Virginia Commonwealth U 1991; MDiv VTS 2014. D 2/22/2014 Bp Susan Goff P 9/13/2014 Bp Shannon Sherwood Johnston. c 3. Dio Virginia Richmond VA 2014. tomlinson@stpaulsbxr.org

TOMLINSON, Ruth Marie (Neb) 5704 North 159th St, Omaha NE 68116 B Culver City, CA 1948 d Kenneth & Rosemary. BA California St U 1970; MA California St U 1973; MDiv Claremont TS 2000. D 6/3/2000 Bp Joseph Jon Bruno P 1/6/2001 Bp Frederick Houk Borsch. c 2. S Dav Of Wales Epis Ch Lincoln NE 2011-2014; R Trin Epis Ch Norfolk NE 2004-2010; Assoc Vic S Jn Chrys Ch Rcho Sta Marg CA 2000-2004; S Marg's Epis Sch San Juan Capo CA 1979-1987. DOK 2006. Participant, Sum Collegium VTS 2007; Pres's Awd, Highest Grade Point Average Claremont TS 2000.

TOMLINSON III, Samuel Alexander (Miss) 28 Homochitto St, Natchez MS 39120 B Natchez MS 1935 s Samuel & Jane. BA Millsaps Coll 1958; MDiv GTS 1961. D 6/9/1961 Bp Duncan Montgomery Gray Jr P 12/20/1961 Bp John Maury Allin. m 6/24/1989 Susanne K Tomlinson c 1. Asstg P Trin Ch Natchez MS 1998-2002; Vic S Jas Epis Ch Port Gibson MS 1988-1997; S Fran Of Assisi Ch Philadelphia MS 1986-1988; Vic S Matt's Epis Ch Kosciusko MS 1986-1988; Vic S Eliz's Mssn Collins MS 1976-1986; Non-par 1974-1976; Cur Trin Ch Pine Bluff AR 1970-1974; Tchr All SS Epis Sch Vicksburg MS 1969-1970; Vic The Chap Of The Cross Madison MS 1965-1969; R Gr Epis Ch Canton MS 1964-1969; P-in-c S Paul's Epis Ch Corinth MS 1961-1964.

TOMMASEO, Ellis (LI) B Trieste Italy 1972 s Filippo & Natalia. BA Seminario Vescoville 1994; BA Seminario Vescoville 1998; BA/MS Universita Hegustuai 2005. Rec 6/11/2016 as Priest Bp Gerry Wolf. m 9/23/2010 Maria Jeanette Tommaseo c 2.

TOMOSO, John Hau'oli (Haw) 51 Kuula St, Kahului HI 96732 **Pacific Hlth Mnstry On-Call Chapl Maui Memi Med Cntr 2016-; Assoc P The Par Of Gd Shpd Epis Ch Wailuku HI 2016-** B Wailuku HI 1953 s Constantine & Winona. BA Coll of St. Thos 1975; MSW U of Hawai'i at Manoa 1975; 3 Year Iona Initiative Curric Waiolaihui'ia Dioc Prog 2015; 3 Year Iona Initiative Curric Waiolaihui'ia Dioc Prog 2015. D 10/23/2015 P 7/30/2016 Bp Robert Leroy Fitzpatrick. m 7/9/1977 Susan D Brabeck c 2. Acad of Cert Soc Workers (ACSW) 1980; Royal Ord of Kamehameha The First 2001; Soc of Cath Priests (SCP) 2017.

TOMPKIN, William Frederick (O) 307 Portage Trail East, Cuyahoga Falls OH 44221 **S Jn's Epis Ch Cuyahoga Fls OH 2000-, D 1992-1999** B Cuyahoga Falls OH 1932 s James & Winifred. U of Akron. D 11/13/1992 Bp James Russell Moodey. m 6/9/1951 Betty Jean Fairhurst c 5. D/Adj Chapl Childern's Hosp Akron OH 2000-2002; S Paul's Ch Canton OH 1995-2000.

TOMPKINS JR, Douglas Gordon (Pa) 310 S Chester Rd, Swarthmore PA 19081 **R Chr Ch Epis Ridley Pk PA 2000-** B Newport RI 1954 s Douglas & Nancy. BA U of Wisconsin 1977; MDiv GTS 1981; Dip CG Jung Inst of NY 2007. D 6/12/1981 P 12/16/1981 Bp William Charles Wantland. m 12/27/1980 Joyce Laura Ulrich Tompkins c 3. R Chr Ch Milwaukee WI 1992-2000; R S Paul's Ch In Nantucket Nantucket MA 1986-1992; Asst Chr Ch Short Hills NJ 1982-1986; Cur S Mary's Ch Pk Ridge IL 1981-1982. rector@christchurchridleypark.org

TOMPKINS III, George Johnson (SC) 90 Fieldfare Way, Charleston SC 29414 **Died 11/17/2015** B Lexington VA 1951 s George & Jeanne. U of Edinburgh GB 1972; BA U of Virginia 1973; MAR Yale DS 1975; MDiv GTS 1976; DMin

T

Sewanee: The U So, TS 1990. D 6/12/1976 P 3/12/1977 Bp Joseph Warren Hutchens. c 2. R Emer S Andr's Par Ch Charleston SC 2006-2015; R St Andr's Mssn Charleston SC 1987-2006; R S Thos' Ch Windsor NC 1982-1987; Cur Bruton Par Williamsburg VA 1978-1981; Cur S Jas Ch New London CT 1976-1978.

TOMPKINS, Joyce Laura Ulrich (Pa) 310 S Chester Rd, Swarthmore PA 19081 **Assoc Trin Ch Swarthmore PA 2008-, 2000-2006; Partnr in Mnstry - Swarthmore Coll Swarthmore PA 2006-; Chapl Swarthmore Coll Swarthmore PA 2004-** B Morristown NJ 1955 d Henry & Ada. BA Cor 1977; Ds Ya Berk 1980; MDiv GTS 1982. D 6/12/1982 P 12/14/1982 Bp John Shelby Spong. m 12/27/1980 Douglas Gordon Tompkins. Chr Ch Milwaukee WI 1992-1999; S Paul's Ch In Nantucket Nantucket MA 1988-1992; Asst Chr Ch Short Hills NJ 1985-1986; Assoc R S Paul's Epis Ch Morris Plains NJ 1982-1985.

TOMTER, Patrick Austin (Oly) PO Box 10785, Portland OR 97296 **Hon Cn Trin Epis Cathd Portland OR 1995-** B Long Beach CA 1938 s Austin & Jessie. BA Occ 1960; MDiv CDSP 1964; Cert U of So Florida 1986. D 9/10/1964 P 3/11/1965 Bp Francis E I Bloy. m 7/7/1961 Evelyn J Tomter c 3. Dir Sprtl Care Legacy Gd Samar Hosp Portland OR 1994-2010; Archd Dio Olympia Seattle 1990-1994, 1969-1972, U of W Campus Min 1969-1972, Dep to GC (4) 1982-1990, Stndg Com (Pres, 1982) 1979-1983, Yth Dir 1970-1972; R Chr Ch Tacoma WA 1976-1990; R S Eliz's Ch Seattle WA 1972-1976; Assoc S Steph's Epis Ch Longview WA 1968-1969; Vic Epiph Epis Ch Santa Maria 1966-1968; Cur S Mk's Par Altadena CA 1964-1966; Alum/ae Coun CDSP Berkeley CA 2003-2009; Chair, COM Dio Oregon Portland OR 1997-2001; Evang Coordntr Prov VIII 1987-1992.

TONEY, Martha Ann (CFla) D 9/27/2014 Bp Gregory Orrin Brewer.

TONGE, Samuel Davis (Ga) 1023 Woods Road, Waycross GA 31501 B Macon GA 1947 s Jack & Eloise. Furman U 1965; U GA 1968; OD Sthrn Coll of Optometry Memphis TN 1972; MDiv ETSBH 1985; MDiv Epis TS 1985; MRE S Meinrad TS 1985; DMin SWTS 2000. D 4/27/1985 P 1/24/1986 Bp Harry Woolston Shipps. m 8/2/1975 Sharon Tonge c 5. R Gr Ch Waycross GA 1988-2011; Vic S Matt's Epis Ch Fitzgerald GA 1985-1987; Pres, Stndg Com Dio Georgia Savannah GA 2006-2007, Stndg Com 2004-2007, Dep to GC 1997, Dioc Curs Sp. Dir 1996-1999, Convoc Dn 1994-2010, Stndg Com 1992-1995. *Var arts, Angl Dig*, 2004.

TONGUE, Mary Jane (Md) 203 Star Pointe Ct Unit 3d, Abingdon MD 21009 B Baltimore MD 1937 d Paul & Mary. Bon Secours Sch of Nrsng 1958; MD D Formation Prog 1997. D 6/14/1997 Bp Charles Lindsay Longest. m 4/3/1976 Noble T Tongue. D Copley Par Gunpowder Hundred: The Ch Of The Resurrect.

TONSMEIRE SR, Louis Edward (At) 224 Trammell St, Calhoun GA 30701 B Mobile AL 1933 s Arthur & Marie. BA Sprg Hill Coll 1954; MDiv Sewanee: The U So, TS 1957. D 7/17/1957 P 5/1/1958 Bp Charles C J Carpenter. m 12/5/1957 Sarah B Tonsmeire c 2. R S Tim's Epis Ch Calhoun GA 1994; R S Thaddaeus' Epis Ch Chattanooga TN 1990-1994; R The Epis Ch Of S Ptr And S Paul Marietta GA 1982-1989; Dio Atlanta Atlanta GA 1981; R Ch Of The Ascen Cartersville GA 1965-1981; S Andr's Epis Ch Sylacauga AL 1960-1965; Vic S Mary's Epis Ch Childersburg AL 1960-1965; Cur All SS Epis Ch Birmingham AL 1957-1960.

TONTONOZ, David Costa (Eas) 5211 Dove Point Ln, Salisbury MD 21801 B Saint Louis MO 1939 s John & Nellie. BS Coll of the H Cross 1961; BD EDS 1966; DMin Andover Newton TS 1973. D 6/22/1966 P 12/21/1966 Bp Robert McConnell Hatch. c 3. R S Ptr's Ch Salisbury MD 1988-2007; Gr Epis Ch Lawr MA 1984-1988; R S Dav's Epis Ch Wilmington DE 1975-1983; R Trin Epis Ch Milford MA 1967-1975; Cur H Trin Epis Ch Southbridge MA 1966-1967; Pres of Stndg Com Dio Easton Dio Easton Easton MD 1992-1995. Auth, "arts," *Bro Of S Andr*; Auth, "arts," *New Life*. AAPC 1973.

TOOF, Jan Jarred (CNY) 2006 Manchester Rd, Wheaton IL 60187 B Highland Park IL 1938 s Frederick & Yvonne. BA Lake Forest Coll 1960; MDiv SWTS 1963; MBA Keller Chicago IL 1983. D 6/15/1963 Bp James Winchester Montgomery P 12/14/1963 Bp Gerald Francis Burrill. m 6/23/1962 Norma Merrett c 1. Int S Jn's Epis Ch Chicago IL 1995-1996, Asstg 1993-1995; Other Cler Positions Var 1968-1993; Vic Bp Huntington Chap Smithville Flats NY 1965-1968; R Gr Ch Guilford NY 1965-1968; Cur Gr Ch Oak Pk IL 1963-1965. Soc of S Mary 1963. jantoof@gmail.com

TOOKEY, Carol (NAM) PO Box 436, Aztec NM 87410 **Chapl, Bereavement Counslr NW New Mex Hospice 2009-** B Rangely CO 1955 d George & Carol. AD San Juan Coll Farmington NM 1984; Cert Prchr Lewis Sch of Mnstry 1985; BSW New Mex St U 1992; MS New Mex Highlands U 1994; MDiv Vancouver TS CA 2007. D 2/29/1988 Bp William Davidson P 5/1/1999 Bp Chris Christopher Epting. m 8/23/1975 Leslie Spencer Lundquist. N.M.R. Vic, Admin Navajoland Area Mssn Farmington NM 2007-2008; All SS Farmington NM 2001-2007; Asst Trin Cluster Harlan IA 1999-2001; D Trin Cluster Harlan IA 1994-1999; D S Paul's Peace Ch Las Vegas NM 1992-1994; D S Andr's Epis Ch Las Cruces NM 1990-1992; D St Johns Epis Ch Farmington NM 1988-1990. Tertiary of the Soc of S Fran 1979.

TOOMEY, David C (NY) PO Box 1467, Norwich VT 05055 B New York NY 1950 s Arthur & Ruth. BA Bos 1972; MDiv Bex Sem 1976; PhD Rhodes U 1998. D 6/8/1976 P 4/1/1977 Bp Morris Fairchild Arnold. m 8/19/1978 Lindsey C Toomey c 3. Diocese of Grahamstown, So Afr Exec Coun Appointees New York NY 1996-2000; R Chr Ch Poughkeepsie NY 1985-1993; R S Jn's Ch Winthrop MA 1980-1985; Asst All SS Ch Chelmsford MA 1979-1980; Asst S Anne's Ch Lowell MA 1977-1978; Asst S Matt And The Redeem Epis Ch Boston MA 1976-1977. Auth, "Grades and Standards Regimes in Sthrn Afr," *USAID Monograph Series*, USAID, 2000; Auth, USAID, 1997; Auth, "Bus Dvlpmt through Interfirm Linkages," *Econ Revs*, USAID, 1994; Auth, "Litany In Memi Of Dr Ml King Jr," Rossiter Schlr, 1983.

TOONE, Susan Krueger (U) 1579 S State St, Clearfield UT 84015 **Assoc Epis Cmnty Serv Inc Salt Lake City UT 2010-, 1999-2009** B Oklahoma City TX 1949 d William & Harriett. Dip Theol Stud Epis TS of the SW 2010. D 6/12/2010 Bp Carolyn Tanner Irish P 6/18/2011 Bp Scott Byron Hayashi. m 10/5/2013 Matthew N Toone c 2. Asst S Paul's Ch Salt Lake City UT 2011-2012.

TORNQUIST, Frances C (Cal) 2748 Wemberly Dr, Belmont CA 94002 B Shawnee OK 1942 d Jack & Frances. BA Westminster Coll 1964; MDiv CDSP 1989. D 6/3/1989 P 6/1/1990 Bp William Edwin Swing. m 9/7/1963 John W Tornquist c 1. Gr Cathd San Francisco CA 1990-2006; Asst S Bede's Epis Ch Menlo Pk CA 1989-1990. DD CDSP 2007.

TORO, Arthur N (Los) 135 Loden Pl, Jackson MS 39209 **Vic Ch Of The H Comm Gardena CA 2012-** B Kenya 1950 s Hamuel & Josephine. Dip Kagumo Coll 1977; BA Daystar U 1996; MDiv Reformed TS 2005. Trans 1/29/2009 Bp Duncan Montgomery Gray III. m 7/6/1974 Jane W Ndungu c 5. arthurtoro@yahoo.com

TORO, Suzanne Frances Rosemary (NY) 70 Clinton St, Cornwall NY 12518 **R S Jn's Ch Cornwall NY 2013-** B Miami, FL 1962 d Anthony & Shirlie. BMus U Tor 1986; Dplma Amer Mus & Dramatic Acad 1989; MDiv GTS 2010. D 3/13/2010 P 9/25/2010 Bp Mark Sean Sisk. Assoc P Ch Of The H Apos New York NY 2010-2012. perzanne.toro@gmail.com

TORRES, Juan Antonio (PR) B 1944 s Juan & Juana. m 12/1/1967 Eneida Martinez c 3. Dio Puerto Rico Trujillo Alto PR 2004-2009, 2000-2003, 1996-1998.

TORRES, Julio Orlando (NY) 232 E 11th St # 3, New York NY 10003 B San Salvador El Salvador EC 1946 s Julio & Margoth. Baldwin-Wallace Coll; Cntrl Amer U; BA SUNY 1978; MDiv EDS 1982; MA Drew U 1996. D 10/4/1982 P 6/25/1983 Bp John Harris Burt. m 10/2/1999 Maria Torres c 4. S Mk's Ch In The Bowery New York NY 2000-2006; The Ch of S Matt And S Tim New York NY 1996-2000; R Gr Ch White Plains NY 1994-1999; Int The Ch of S Edw The Mtyr New York NY 1985-1986; Hisp Epis Cntr San Andres Ch Yonkers NY 1985; Assoc S Ann's Ch Of Morrisania Bronx NY 1984-1985. Auth, "Face To Face w A Crucified People"; Auth, "La Eucaristia".

TORRES, Michele Angier (Mass) 103 Harvard Ave, Medford MA 02155 B La Jolla CA 1966 d John & Carolyn. BA Stan 1989; MDiv EDS 1995; MA Lesley U 1996. D 6/24/1995 P 6/1/1996 Bp Richard Lester Shimpfky. Gr Ch Everett MA 2004-2006; S Jn's Epis Ch Westwood MA 1998-2007; Asst S Steph's Epis Ch Boston MA 1996-1998.

TORRES BAYAS, Jose Javier (Cal) Guerrero #589, Tuxtepec Mexico **Vic Ch Of The H Trin Richmond CA 2012-, Vic 2005-2009; Vic Ascen Puyo Pastaza 1966-** B Bolivar EC 1964 s Jorge & Libia. Pontifical Cath U of Ecuador 1990; ETSBH 1995; Epis TS 1995. Rec 5/28/1995 as Priest Bp Jose Neptali Larrea-Moreno. m 5/28/1991 Laura Dahik c 1. Vic Dio California San Francisco CA 2010-2011; Dio SE Mex 2004, 2002; Vic Iglesia Epis Del Ecuador Quito 1996-2001.

TORRES FUENTES, Pascual Pedro (Hond) Apdo 16, Puerto Cortes Honduras **Vic Iglesia Epis San Juan Bautista Puerto Cortes 1991-; Dio Honduras San Pedro Sula 1989-** B San Pedro Sula Cortes HN 1959 s Carlos & Ziola. Lic Universidad Nacional Autonoma De Honduras 1981; Sewanee: The U So, TS 1987; MA Epis TS of the SW 1989. D 10/6/1989 P 3/1/1991 Bp Leo Frade. m 12/19/1992 Elizabeth Perdomo-Caceres.

TORRES MARTINEZ, Wilfrido Oswaldo (EcuC) Convencion Y Solanda 056, Guaranda Ecuador **D El Salvador Ambato 1992-** B Pelileo Tuaguarahua 1946 s Abel & Maria. Universidad Catolica; Sem Mayor San Jose 1977. Trans 12/1/1992 Bp Jose Neptali Larrea-Moreno. m 11/6/2002 Irma Pilar Salazar Ramos c 4. Iglesia Epis Del Ecuador Quito 2003-2009.

TORREY, Bruce (Ct) 187 Dewitt Rd, Accord NY 12404 **Cler Speaker Food for the Poor 2017-; Trin Ch Canaseraga NY 1989-** B Mineola NY 1956 s Robert & Barbara. BA SUNY 1978; MDiv SWTS 1981. D 6/1/1981 P 12/6/1981 Bp Robert Campbell Witcher Sr. m 4/30/1995 Kathleen M Torrey c 5. S Jn's Ch E Windsor CT 1998-2012; Chr Epis Ch Hornell NY 1989-1998; R St Peters Memi Ch Dansville NY 1989-1998; Tri-Par Mnstry Hornell NY 1989-1998; R H Trin Epis Ch Vlly Stream NY 1984-1989; Cur S Ann's Ch Sayville NY 1981-1984.

TORREY, Dorothy Ellen (NCal) 901 Lincoln Rd Apt 40, Yuba City CA 95991 B Buffalo NY 1947 d Henry & Dorothy. MS San Francisco St U 1992; BS Wstrn Connecticut St U 1992; MDiv CDSP 2001. D 6/23/2001 P 2/16/2002 Bp Richard Lester Shimpfky. S Fran Epis Ch San Jose CA 2011-2012; S Aug Of

Cbury Rocklin CA 2011; R S Jn's Epis Ch Marysville CA 2006-2010; Asst S Mich's Epis Ch Carmichael CA 2001-2006. dori.torrey@gmail.com

TORVEND, Samuel Edward (Oly) 15 Roy St, Seattle WA 98109 **Chr Ch Tacoma WA 2015-** B Longview WA 1951 s Elmer & Alice. MDiv Wartburg TS 1975; MA Aquinas Inst 1980; PhD S Louis U 1990; AB Pacific Luth U 1993. Rec 2/15/2009 Bp Gregory Harold Rickel. Assoc for Adult Educ S Paul's Ch Seattle WA 2009-2015.

TOTHILL, Marlene Grey (NwT) 19 Winchester Ct, Midland TX 79705 **Non-par 1992-** B Birmingham AL 1930 d Aaron & Florence. BS W Chester U of Pennsylvania 1952; MA U of Texas 1979; MDiv Epis TS of the SW 1985. D 6/15/1985 P 5/1/1986 Bp Gerald Nicholas Mcallister. m 1/19/1968 Richard Tothill c 2. Asst S Chad's Epis Ch Albuquerque NM 2002-2004; Int S Chris's Epis Ch El Paso TX 1991, Asst R 1987-1989; Res Chapl Midland Memi Hosp Midland TX 1986-1987; Cur S Jn's Epis Ch Tulsa OK 1985-1986.

TOTMAN, Glenn Parker (CGC) 122 County Road 268, Enterprise AL 36330 B Apalachicola FL 1937 s Donald & Sybil. BA U So 1960; VTS 1963; MBA U of So Alabama 1981. D 6/24/1963 P 3/1/1964 Bp Edward Hamilton West. m 6/1/1979 Nancy Totman. Ch Of The Epiph Enterprise AL 1997-2003; S Mk's Ch Chattahooche FL 1989-1991; S Paul's Epis Ch Quincy FL 1983-1989; S Jn The Evang Robertsdale AL 1973-1978; S Paul's Ch Foley AL 1973-1978; Asst Chr Epis Ch Pensacola FL 1969-1973; Chapl (Captain) US-A 1966-1969; Vic Ch Of The Ascen Carrabelle FL 1965-1966; Vic Bethany Ch Hilliard FL 1963-1965; S Jas Ch Macclenny FL 1963-1965.

TOTTEN, Julia Kay (Spok) PO Box 15, Florence OR 97439 B Columbia MS 1945 d Kenneth & Sarach. BS L&C 1985; MS Whitworth U 1988. D 5/23/2009 Bp Bavi Edna Rivera. m 9/29/1984 William Robert Totten c 3.

TOTTEN, William Robert (Spok) PO Box 15, Florence OR 97439 **Pomeroy Meth Ch Pomeroy WA 2014-; P-in-c S Ptr's Ch Pomeroy WA 2014-** B Helena MT 1949 s William & Shirley. BS U of Idaho 1971; MBA U of Idaho 1972; MDiv CDSP 2009. D 5/23/2009 Bp Bavi Edna Rivera P 12/15/2009 Bp Sanford Zangwill Kaye Hampton. m 9/29/1984 Julia Kay Totten c 2. Vic S Andr's Epis Ch Florence OR 2009-2012.

TOTTEY JR, Alfred George (CNY) 7385 Norton Ave, Clinton NY 13323 B Ithaca NY 1938 s Alfred & Edna. BA Duke 1959; CPE 1961; MDiv EDS 1962; Coll of Preachers 1970. D 6/18/1962 P 6/22/1963 Bp Walter M Higley. c 2. Non-par 1984-2002; Calv Ch Homer NY 1975-1984; Pres Rome Conf of Ch Rome NY 1969-1971; Assoc Zion Ch Rome NY 1968-1971; Pres Coun of Ch Chittenango NY 1965-1967; D S Paul's Ch Chittenango NY 1962-1963; Mem, Dioc Coun Dio Cntrl New York Liverpool NY 1975-1977, Prov Yth Liaison 1971-1973, Chair Of The Yth Cmsn 1967-1974.

TOUCHSTONE, G Russell (Los) 1069 S Gramercy Pl, Los Angeles CA 90019 **Chapl LACounty+USC Med Cntr Los Angeles CA 2002-** B Los Angeles CA 1932 s Grady & Geraldine. USC 1954; Wells Theol Coll 1965. Trans 1/1/1970 as Priest Bp Horace W B Donegan. m 6/4/1964 Terri Lavonne Touchstone c 1. Int S Fran Mssn Norwalk CA 2004; Int S Marg's Epis Ch So Gate CA 2002-2004, Int 1995-1998; Int Epis Chap Of S Fran Los Angeles CA 2001; Int Cathd Cong Los Angeles CA 2000, Asst 1973; Asst S Thos The Apos Hollywood Los Angeles CA 1990-1994; Int S Clem's Mssn Huntington Pk CA 1988; Asst Trin Epis Par Los Angeles CA 1986-1988; Assoc H Fam Mssn N Hollywood CA 1985; Assoc Iglesia Epis De La Magdalena Mssn Glendale CA 1985; Cmsn on Racism and Discrimination Gr Epis Ch Glendora CA 1984; Asst All SS Par Beverly Hills CA 1980-1983; Asst Chr The Gd Shpd Par Los Angeles CA 1974-1976; Res Chapl S Monica's Hm Roxbury MA 1971-1972; Admin Asst ACU Pelham Manor NY 1970-1971; Cur Chap of S Chris - Trin Par New York NY 1969-1970; Serv Ch of Engl 1965-1968; Dio Los Angeles Los Angeles CA 1984-1988. Cmnty of the Servnt of the Will of God; SSC. daddyrussell@juno.com

TOURANGEAU, Edward J (Ind) 260 Elm Ct, Troy VA 22974 B Syracuse NY 1945 s Donald & Ruth. BA U of Utah 1967; MDiv Nash 1970. D 6/24/1970 Bp Richard S Watson P 12/21/1970 Bp Donald H V Hallock. m 7/14/1967 Patricia Ann Searle c 1. R St Johns Epis Ch Lafayette IN 1991-2010; R Emm Epis Ch Great River NY 1987-1990; Dio Quincy Peoria IL 1981-1987, 1976; Cn St Paul's Epis Ch Peoria IL 1980-1987; Vic H Trin Epis Ch Geneseo IL 1977-1979; Vic S Mk's Epis Ch Silvis IL 1975-1979; Vic Ch Of S Chris Rantoul IL 1972-1975; Cur S Mk's Ch Milwaukee WI 1970-1972.

TOURNOUX, Gregory Allen (Spr) 2056 Cherry Road, Springfield IL 62704 **Adj Prof Erskine TS Due W SC 2006-; R Chr Ch Springfield IL 2005-** B Canton OH 1958 s Richard & Marilyn. BS Slippery Rock U 1982; MDiv VTS 1988; DMin Trin TS IN 1997; DRS Trin TS IN 2010. D 6/11/1988 Bp James Russell Moodey P 5/9/1989 Bp Peter J Lee. m 8/30/1986 Nada Tournoux c 4. R Chr Epis Ch Owosso MI 1991-2004; Assoc S Paul's Epis Ch Winston Salem NC 1989-1991; Cur S Paul's Ch Haymarket VA 1988-1989; COM Dio Springfield 2005-2006; Bp's Search Com, Dn Diocse of Estrn Michigan 1992-1995; Exec Coun, Com on New Congregations Dio Michigan 1991-1992; Evang & Renwl Cmsn, Cler Exec Comm Dio No Carolina 1989-1990; Cler, Conf on Renwl Dio Virginia 1988-1989. Auth, "Evangelizing Postmodern Pre-Christians Through Holistic Cells & Liturg Celebration," *Evangelizing Postmodern Pre-Christians*

Through Holistic Cells & Liturg Celebration, Trin Press, 2012; Auth, "What Will the Thriving Epis Ch of the Future Look Like?," *LivCh*, 1999; Auth, "A Modest Proposal," *Pro Fide*. Fllshp of Chr Athletes 1977. christchurch1@sbcglobal.net

TOVEN, Kenneth H (Minn) 1505 13th Street N., Princeton MN 55371 **Asst H Trin Epis Ch Elk River MN 2014-; Total Mnstry Advsr Chr Epis Ch Grand Rapids MN 2007-** B Grand Rapids MN 1951 s Harold & Marion. BA Coll of St Scholastica 1976; MDiv SWTS 1980. D 6/24/1980 P 12/1/1980 Bp Robert Marshall Anderson. m 1/15/1972 Pamela Jean Toven. P-in-c S Jas Ch Marshall MN 2003-2006; R Ch Of The Resurr Minneapolis MN 1992-2001; Int Ch Of The Nativ Burnsville MN 1990-1991; Int S Chris's Epis Ch S Paul MN 1989-1990; P-in-c S Mich & All Ang No S Paul MN 1985-1989; Asst Ch Of The Ascen Stillwater MN 1980-1984.

TOWERS, Arlen Reginald (Cal) 43 Wildwood Pl, El Cerrito CA 94530 **Ret 1993-; 1971-** B San Antonio TX 1929 s Harold & Bonnie. BA S Mary U 1960; MDiv CDSP 1964; MEd U of Texas 1971. D 6/30/1964 Bp Richard Earl Dicus P 1/1/1965 Bp Everett H Jones. m 4/10/1953 Dione Darling Towers c 1. Supply P Dio California San Francisco CA 1971-1993; S Mk's Par Berkeley CA 1971-1993; Vic Ch Of The Resurr Windcrest TX 1968-1970; R S Andr's Epis Ch Seguin TX 1966-1968; Vic S Dav Hondo TX 1964-1966; Vic S Chris's Ch Bandera TX 1964-1965.

TOWERS, Paul (Be) St Paul's Church, 276 Church St, Montrose PA 18801 B 1948 BS Vlly Forge Chr Coll 1978; MDiv Drew U 1983; DMin VTS 2001. D 7/3/2007 P 1/16/2010 Bp Gladstone Bailey Adams III. m 7/2/1977 Marian L Towers. S Paul's Ch Montrose PA 2012-2016; R S Lk's Epis Ch Altoona PA 2010-2011.

TOWERS, Richard A (CNY) St John's Episcopal Church, 210 N Cayuga St, Ithaca NY 14850 Korea (South) **Epis Sch Of Dallas Dallas TX 2015-** B Rochester NY 1969 s Sherwood & Terry. BA Houghton Coll 1992; MDiv Bex Sem 1997. D 10/9/1999 Bp William George Burrill P 6/26/2000 Bp Jack Marston Mckelvey. m 8/28/1993 Rupa Barbara Towers. R S Jn's Ch Ithaca NY 2012-2015; S Marks Sch Of Texas Dallas TX 2008-2011; Bexley Seabury Fed Chicago IL 2005-2008; The Epis Ch of S Jn the Div Tamuning GU 2003-2005; S Paul's Ch Rochester NY 2001-2002.

TOWLER, Lewis Wilson (Mich) 1711 Pontiac Trl, Ann Arbor MI 48105 **Asst S Andr's Ch Ann Arbor MI 2008-; Ret 1997-** B Cincinnati OH 1925 s John & Dorothy. BA U MI 1950; U of Heidelberg DE 1951; UTS 1952; MA U MI 1952; BD VTS 1955; STM GTS 1966. D 7/17/1955 P 1/24/1956 Bp Richard Stanley Merrill Emrich. c 3. Asst S Jn's Ch Plymouth MI 2000-2005; Assoc S Paul's Ch N Kingstown RI 1989-1997; Asst S Aug's Ch New York NY 1987-1989; Assoc R All Ang' Ch New York NY 1984-1987; Vic S Jn's Ch Chesaning MI 1980-1984; Cbury MI SU E Lansing MI 1978-1980; Asst Chapl MSU E Lansing MI 1978-1980; Assoc R Chr Ch Cranbrook Bloomfield Hills MI 1973-1978; Asst Cathd Of St Jn The Div New York NY 1964-1971; Fac Gnrl Sem New York NY 1963-1973; Fac The GTS New York NY 1963-1973; Asst Chr Ch Bronxville NY 1963-1964; R 62-63 S Matt's Epis Ch Saginaw MI 1957-1962; Cur All SS Epis Ch Pontiac MI 1955-1957; US Navy 1943-1946. Auth, "arts," *Living Ch*; Auth, "Bk," *Planned Cont CE for Cler & Laity*. ActorsEquity Asscn. 1987.

TOWNE, Jane Clapp (ND) 1111 N 1st St Apt 10, Bismarck ND 58501 B Detroit MI 1927 d Frederick & Hazel. Mia 1945; BA Carleton Coll 1948. D 11/23/2001 Bp Andrew Fairfield. m 6/27/1953 Roy Towne c 3.

TOWNER, Paul Eugene (Nev) 1090 War Eagle Dr N, Colorado Springs CO 80919 **Ret 1997-** B Denver CO 1932 s Reginald & Lorraine. BA Colorado Coll 1954; STB Ya Berk 1957. D 6/24/1957 P 1/6/1958 Bp Joseph Summerville Minnis. Rep to CDM Prov VIII 1982-1991; Stndg Com Dio Nevada Las Vegas 1971-1991, Chair - COM 1968-1996, DioCoun 1967-1990; S Paul's Epis Ch Sparks NV 1966-1997; H Trin Epis Ch Fallon NV 1964-1966; S Philips-in-the-Desert Hawthorne NV 1964-1966; Vic Gr And S Steph's Epis Ch Colorado Sprg CO 1957-1964.

TOWNER, Philip Haines (NY) 552 W End Ave, New York NY 10024 B St Paul MN 1953 s Earl & Martha. BA NWU 1978; MA Trin DS 1981; PhD U of Aberdeen 1984. D 3/2/2013 P 9/7/2013 Bp Andrew Marion Lenow Dietsche. m 5/25/2008 Kathleen Mary Towner c 2. ABS New York NY 2013.

TOWNER, Robert Arthur (Mo) 38 N Fountain St, Cape Girardeau MO 63701 **Instr SE Missouri St U Cape Girardeau MO 2002-** B Portsmouth VA 1949 s Robert & Nancy. BA Trin Hartford CT 1973; MDiv SWTS 1977. D 6/18/1977 Bp Quintin Ebenezer Primo Jr P 12/1/1977 Bp James Winchester Montgomery. m 8/19/1973 Helen Iuich Towner c 1. S Paul's Epis Ch Sikeston MO 2006-2008; R Chr Ch Cape Girardeau MO 2001-2012; S Jn's Ch Mason City IA 1987-2001; Vic S Paul's Epis Ch Grinnell IA 1980-1987; Chapl Gri Grinnell IA 1977-1980; Cur S Giles' Ch Northbrook IL 1977-1980. LAND 1986; Mssnr to Sudan 2006; NECAD 1980; RACA, Past Pres & Direct 1979.

TOWNES III, Henry C (Chi) 12219 S 86th Ave, Palos Park IL 60464 **D Trsfg In Palas Pk 1987-** B Beech Grove IN 1937 s Henry & Ruth. BA Indiana U 1960. D 12/26/1987 Bp Frank Tracy Griswold III. m 11/12/1964 Margaret G Townes c 3.

TOWNLEY JR, Rick (NJ) 43 Delaware Ave, Lambertville NJ 08530 **Died 7/22/ 2017** B Elizabeth NJ 1948 s Richard & Eleanor. BA Drew U 1970; MDiv VTS 1973. D 6/9/1973 P 1/1/1974 Bp Leland Stark. m 7/3/2010 Laura M Townley. S Andr's Ch Lambertville NJ 1989-2017; Vic S Thos Ch Alexandria Pittstown NJ 1976-1983; Chap Of St Thos Of Alexandria Annandale NJ 1976-1982; Cur S Lk's Epis Ch Metuchen NJ 1973-1975. Auth, "Final Report Progress Report"; Auth, "Food For The Journey"; Auth, "Who In The Wrld?".

TOWNSEND, Bowman (Tex) 2205 Matterhorn Ln, Austin TX 78704 B Knoxville TN 1956 BS U of Tennessee 1979; MDiv Epis TS of the SW 2003; MAC S Edwards U Austin TX 2008. D 5/31/2003 Bp Charles Glenn Von-Rosenberg P 1/17/2004 Bp Don Adger Wimberly. m 10/27/1984 Elizabeth Lee Townsend c 2. Epis TS Of The SW Austin TX 2016; R S Chris's Epis Ch Austin TX 2006-2016; R S Richard's Ch Of Round Rock Round Rock TX 2004-2006, R 2003-2006. btownsend@jacksonsjoberg.com

TOWNSEND, Craig D (NY) 445 Degraw St, Brooklyn NY 11217 B Syracuse NY 1955 s Terry & Sara. BA Br 1978; MDiv EDS 1982; PhD Harv 1998. D 6/19/1982 Bp O'Kelley Whitaker P 5/26/1983 Bp Ned Cole. m 8/21/1982 Catherine N Fuerst c 2. Vic S Jas Ch New York NY 1997-2016; Engl Tchr S Ann's Sch Brooklyn NY 1994-1997; Asstg P S Phil's Ch New York NY 1994-1997; Chapl Trin Sch New York NY 1987-1990; Assoc S Ann And The H Trin Brooklyn NY 1984-1987; Asst Chr Ch Cranbrook Bloomfield Hills MI 1982-1984. Auth, "Faith in Their Own Color: Black Episcopalians in Antebellum New York City," Col Press, 2005; Auth, "Episcopalians and Race in New York City's Anti-Abolitionist Riots of 1834: The Case of Ptr Williams and Benjamin Onderdonk," *Angl and Epis Hist*, 2003. HSEC. Fllshp ECF 1991.

TOWNSEND, John Tolson (Mass) 40 Washington St, Newton MA 02458 **Prof EDS Cambridge MA 1994-, 1974-1993; Lectr on Jewish Stds Harvard DS Cambridge MA 1994-; Ret 1993-** B Halifax NS CA 1927 s William & Olley. AB Br 1949; LTh U Tor CA 1952; STM Harvard DS 1953; ThD Harvard DS 1959. D 6/14/1952 P 12/21/1952 Bp Granville G Bennett. m 6/13/1956 Mary V Townsend c 2. Instr/Assoc. prof. Philadelphia Div. Sch Philadelphia PA 1960-1974; In-c H Nativ Johnston RI 1959-1960; Min in charge S Barth Cranston RI 1959-1960; P-in-c Ch Of The Gd Shpd Fairhaven MA 1955-1957; Cur Ch Of The Mssh Providence RI 1953-1954; Min in charge S Barth Cranston RI 1952-1953. Auth, "Midrash Tanhuma (Buber)," *vol. 3*, KTAV, 2003; Auth, "Midrash Tanhuma (Buber)," *vol. 2*, KTAV, 1991; Auth, "Midrash Tanhuma (Buber)," *vol. 1*, KTAV, 1989; Auth, *A Liturg Interp of the Passion of Jesus Chr in Narrative Formation (2nd ed.)*, NCCJ, 1985; Contrib, *Antisemitism & the Foundations of Chrsnty*; Auth, *Date of Lk-Acts*; Auth, *Study of Judaism I & II*; Auth, *The Gospel of Jn & the Jews*. Assn Jewish Stds 1978; Chr Schlrshp Grp on Chr-Jewish Relatns 1969; Chr Schlrshp Grp on Chr-Jewish Relatns, Chai 1983-1984; Natl Assn of Professors of Hebr 1995; SBL 1956.

✠ TOWNSEND, The Rt Rev Martin Gough (Eas) HC 86 Box 48 C-1, Springfield WV 26763 **Ret Bp of Easton Dio Easton Easton MD 2001-, Bp of Easton 1992-2001** B Cambridge England UK 1943 s Frederick & Beatrice. BA Hobart and Wm Smith Colleges 1965; MDiv VTS 1968; DMin VTS 2000; DD VTS 2003. D 6/20/1968 P 5/26/1969 Bp Ned Cole Con 11/23/1992 for Eas. m 8/22/ 1964 Barbara Townsend. P-in-c Emm Ch Keyser WV 2008-2011; Int R Trin Ch Upperville VA 2005-2007; Asst Bp Dio Newark Newark NJ 2004; Int The Ch of the Redeem Cincinnati OH 2001-2003; VTS Alexandria VA 2001; R Chr Ch Blacksburg VA 1987-1992; R S Mary's Chap Ridge Ridge MD 1977-1987; R S Chris's Ch New Carrollton MD 1971-1977; Bec Dio Cntrl New York Liverpool NY 1969-1971; Asst St Paul's Syracuse Syracuse NY 1968-1971; Chair Stndg Cmsn on Ch in Sm Communities 1997-2000. Auth, "Breathed into Flame," *collected writings*, Trin Par, 2007. DD VTS 1993.

TOWNSEND III, Thomas Pinckney (Ga) Ch Of The H Nativ St Simons Is GA 2017- B Greenville, SC 1963 s Thomas & Lucie. NDTS Sewanee: The U So, TS; BS Bus Cit 1985. D 5/14/2016 P 11/16/2016 Bp Scott Anson Benhase. m 3/3/2012 Laura Andrews c 3. tptownsend3@icloud.com

TOWSON, Louis Albert (CFla) 348 Sherwood Ave, Satellite Beach FL 32937 **Vic S Jas Ch Macclenny FL 2008-** B Miami,FL 1947 s Harry & Julia. BS Florida St U 1969; MDiv VTS 1973. D 6/13/1973 P 5/9/1974 Bp Edward Hamilton West. m 2/4/1995 Susan Ann Towson. R Epis Ch Of The H Apos Satellite Bch FL 1980-2005; Asst H Trin Epis Ch Melbourne FL 1977-1979; Bethany Ch Hilliard FL 1976-1977; S Geo Epis Ch Jacksonville FL 1975-1977; S Ptr's Ch Fernandina Bch FL 1975-1977; Ch Of The Medtr Micanopy FL 1974-1976; P-in-c S Barn Epis Ch Williston FL 1974-1976; Dio Florida Jacksonville 1973-1977. Auth, "How To Run A Com Or Orgnztn: A Manual For Ch Leaders," Resource Pub, Inc., 2000; Auth, "The Effective Ch Com: A Mem'S Handbook," Resource Pub, Inc., 2000.

TOY, Fran Yee (Cal) 4151 Laguna Ave, Oakland CA 94602 **Assoc S Jn's Epis Ch Oakland CA 2012-; Sprtlty Fac Credo Inst Inc. Memphis TN 2000-; China Friendship Com Dio CA 1993-** B Oakland CA 1934 d Joe & Bertha. BA U CA 1956; MA U of San Francisco 1977; MDiv CDSP 1984. D 6/9/ 1984 P 6/8/1985 Bp William Edwin Swing. m 8/5/1956 Arthur Chun Toy c 2. Pres Epis Asiamerica Mnstry Coun 2003-2009; Fac CREDO 1999-2005; Sesquicentennial Com Dio 1996-1999; Ch Deploy Bd 1994-2000; Exec Coun

For the GC 1991-1997; Dir Of Alum/ae and Stdt Affrs CDSP Berkeley CA 1991-1996, AlumCoordinator 1987-1990; Int R Ch Of The Resurr Pleasant Hil CA 1986-1987; Int R Chr Ch Alameda CA 1986; Vol Assoc Epis Ch Of Our Sav Oakland CA 1985-2011; COM Dio CA 1985-1987; Dept of Stwdshp Dio CA 1985-1987; Int R True Sunshine Par San Francisco CA 1984-1985. Auth, "Cutting Through the Double Blind," *Daughters of Sarah*, 1989. Bd Dir EWC 1985-1987; EAM Advocates 1997; Epis Asiamerica Mnstry 1973; Exec Bd EWHP 1985-1988; Fdr Coun of Wmn Mnstrs 1983-2003. DD CDSP 1996.

TRACHE, Robert G (SeFla) 1750 East Oakland Park Blvd, Fort Lauderdale FL 33334 **Hd of Sch S Mk The Evang Ft Lauderdale FL 2008-** B Newburgh NY 1947 s Gustave & Ida. BA GW 1969; MA GW 1973; MDiv Harvard DS 1977. D 6/4/1977 Bp Robert Bruce Hall P 1/1/1978 Bp Hunley Agee Elebash. m 4/4/2002 Eliza Robinson Ragsdale c 2. R Par Of The Epiph Winchester MA 2005-2008; Corpus Christi Metro Mnstrs Corpus Christi TX 2004-2005; Chf Operating Off Great Vlly Cntr Modesto CA 2000-2004; Dio Atlanta Atlanta GA 2000; R St Jas Ch Richmond VA 1994-2000; R Imm Ch-On-The-Hill Alexandria VA 1984-1994; R S Eliz's Ch Sudbury MA 1980-1984; Fac in Philos & Rel Departments No Carolina U in Wilmington 1977-1980; Asst S Jn's Epis Ch Wilmington NC 1977-1979. Auth, *Opening Day*.

TRACHMAN, Michael David (Okla) 2213 Galaxy Dr, Altus OK 73521 **D S Paul's Ch Altus OK 2004-** B Malden MA 1940 AA Wstrn Oklahoma St Coll. D 6/19/2004 Bp Robert Manning Moody. m 7/6/1979 Linda Long c 4.

TRACY, Dick Blaylock (Kan) 3020 Oxford Cir, Lawrence KS 66049 **D Trin Ch Lawr KS 2000-** B Bushton KS 1936 s Henry & Lucy. BS U of Kansas 1958; MS U of Kansas 1965; PhD U of Kansas 1966. D 9/9/2000 Bp William Edward Smalley. m 5/29/1964 Rita Vanessa Tracy.

TRACY, Edward J. (SVa) 600 Talbot Hall Rd, Norfolk VA 23505 **Cn for Admin Dio Sthrn Virginia Newport News VA 2011-, Cn for Admin 2011-** B Manhattan NY 1952 s Edward & Clare. BA U of Albuquerque 1974; MDiv VTS 1995; MDiv VTS 1995. D 7/1/1995 Bp Terence Kelshaw P 1/25/1996 Bp David Charles Bowman. m 6/29/1985 Lee Ann Tracy. R Ch Of S Jas The Less Ashland VA 2007-2011; R 2007-2011; R Johns Memi Epis Ch Farmville VA 1998-2007, R 1998-2007; Asst Calv Epis Ch Williamsville NY 1995-1998, Asst R 1995-1998. etracy@diosova.org

TRACY, Paul John (NI) 1025 Park Pl Apt 159, Mishawaka IN 46545 B Caldwell ID 1932 s Walter & Lottie. BA U of Idaho 1958; BD CDSP 1961; MA U of Notre Dame 1985. D 6/12/1961 P 12/16/1961 Bp Norman L Foote. Asst S Dav's Epis Ch Elkhart IN 1995-1996; R S Paul's Ch Mishawaka IN 1986-1995; P-in-c S Ptr's Ch Rensselaer IN 1981-1986; S Lk's Ch Weiser ID 1979-1981; R S Jas Ch Payette ID 1971-1981; Cn S Mich's Cathd Boise ID 1969-1971; P-in-c Ch Of The Epiph Arco ID 1964-1969; Ch Of The Redeem Salmon ID 1964-1969; Vic Gd Shpd Ft Hall ID 1961-1964. Auth, "Chr Initiation Complete In Baptism? A Cont Question For Anglicans"; Auth, "The 4th Day". Angl Soc, SocMary.

TRACY, Rita Vanessa (Kan) 3020 Oxford Cir, Lawrence KS 66049 **D Trin Ch Lawr KS 2000-** B Leavenworth KS 1938 d Wilbert & Evelyn. BD U of Kansas 1960; MS Ohio U 1972; MS U of Kansas 1982. D 9/9/2000 Bp William Edward Smalley. m 5/29/1964 Dick Blaylock Tracy.

TRAFFORD, Edward John (RI) 45 Rotary Dr, West Warwick RI 02893 B Providence RI 1944 s Harold & Catherine. BS Bryant U 1978; MA Rhode Island Coll 1993. D 4/5/1986 Bp George Nelson Hunt III. m 10/29/1966 Susanne Trafford c 2. D All SS' Memi Ch Providence RI 2001-2008; Serv Gr Ch In Providence Providence RI 1993-2000; Archd for Diac 1991-1996; D Dio Rhode Island Providence RI 1986-1991.

TRAFTON, Clark Wright (Cal) 875 S Nueva Vista Dr, Palm Springs CA 92264 **S Marg's Epis Ch Palm Desert CA 2005-** B Marathon IA 1935 s Rex & Myrtle. BS Iowa St U 1955; MS Iowa St U 1957; MDiv CDSP 1960; Cert Westchester Inst 1978. D 6/15/1960 P 12/17/1960 Bp Gordon V Smith. m 6/20/2008 Lewis Kerman. Int S Mk's Ch Jackson Heights NY 2002-2005; Int S Geo's Epis Ch Maplewood NJ 2000-2002; Chapl Vill Nrsng Hm 1998-2003; P-in-c S Mk's Ch In The Bowery New York NY 1997-2000; Chapl S Jn's Ch New York NY 1996-2000; Vic Trin Ch Winterset IA 1963-1965; Vic H Trin Atlantic IA 1963-1965; Vic S Paul Epis Ch Creston IA 1960-1965. Amer Psych Assn, Diplomate 2000-2006; Natl Assn for the Advancement of Psychoanalysis 1979-2006; OHC 1965-1992. DD CDSP 1984.

TRAGER, Jane (O) 222 Eastern Heights Blvd, Elyria OH 44035 B New Haven CT 1943 d George & Sadie. MA St U of NY Buffalo. D 11/12/2010 Bp Mark Hollingsworth Jr.

TRAIL, Shirley Ethel (WNY) 42 Haller Ave, Buffalo NY 14211 B Buffalo NY 1945 BA SUNY. D 3/1/1986 Bp Harold Barrett Robinson.

TRAINOR, Helen C (WA) Legal Aid & Justice Center, 1000 Preston Ave. Ste A, Charlottesville VA 22903 B Boston MA 1949 d Irving & Anne. BA Smith 1971; JD Suffolk U 1976. D 6/16/2002 Bp Leo Frade. Dio Massachusetts Boston MA 2013-2014; Chr Ch Par Plymouth MA 2012-2014; S Columba's Ch Washington DC 2004-2007; D Chr Ch Prince Geo's Par Rockville MD 2002-2008.

T

TRAINOR, Mary Patricia (Los) 10925 Valley Home Ave, Whittier CA 90603 **S Jos's Par Buena Pk CA 2016-** B Bell CA 1945 d Robert & Della. BS California St Polytechnic U 1969; MDiv Epis TS of the SW 2005. D 6/11/2005 P 1/14/2006 Bp Joseph Jon Bruno. P in Charge under Spec circumstances St. Steph's Par Whittier CA 2006-2007; D S Steph's Par Whittier CA 2005-2016.

TRAINOR, Mary Stoddard (FdL) E942 Whispering Pines Rd, Waupaca WI 54981 **Fin Com Dio Fond du Lac Appleton WI 2013-** B Milwaukee WI 1950 d Frederick & Annette. BS U IL 1972; MS U IL 1974; PhD U CA 1979; TESM 2000; TESM 2006. D 2/21/1998 Bp Terence Kelshaw P 5/23/2009 Bp Russell Edward Jacobus. m 2/21/1987 Robert James Trainor c 3. Vic S Jn's Ch Shawano WI 2011-2015; Asst Intsn Epis Ch Stevens Point WI 2004-2011; D S Fran On The Hill El Paso TX 2002-2004; Dir, CE S Mk's On The Mesa Epis Ch Albuquerque NM 1999-2002; D Trin On The Hill Epis Ch Los Alamos NM 1998-1999. Auth, "Var arts," *Profsnl Journ in Educ, biology, educational Tech.* Bp's Cross Dio Fond du Lac 2010.

TRAINOR, Robert James (FdL) E942 Whispering Pines Rd, Waupaca WI 54981 **Dep, GC Dio Fond du Lac Appleton WI 2011-, VP, Exec Coun 2009-2012, Dn, Wisconsin River Dnry 2006-2012; Sci, Tech and Faith Exec Coun Appointees New York NY 2013-** B Bell CA 1944 s Robert & Della. BS California St Polytechnic U 1966; MS U CA 1970; PhD U CA 1974; TESM 2002; MDiv Trin TS Newburgh IN 2002. D 2/21/1998 P 3/16/1999 Bp Terence Kelshaw. m 2/21/1987 Mary Stoddard c 3. R Intsn Epis Ch Stevens Point WI 2004-2010; R S Fran On The Hill El Paso TX 2002-2004; Assoc R S Mk's On The Mesa Epis Ch Albuquerque NM 1999-2002; D Trin On The Hill Epis Ch Los Alamos NM 1997-1999. Auth, "Waverly's Universe, a Novel," UpNorth Press, 2012; Auth, "Grasp: Making Sense of Sci and Sprtlty," UpNorth Press, 2010; Auth, "60 arts," *Profsnl Physics Journ.*

TRAKEL, Debra Lynn (Mil) N81 W13442 Golfway Drive, Menomonee Falls WI 53051 **Pres, Disciplinary Bd Dio Milwaukee Milwaukee WI 2012-, Asst to Bp for Pstr Care 1996-1999, 2015-, Exec Coun 2004-2007, Stndg Com 2002-2004, Cler Misconduct Case Mgr 1995-2007; Fam Medtr St of Wisconsin 2009-** B Madison WI 1953 d Donald & Arlene. Trauma Cert U of Wisconsin; BA Mt Mary Coll 1975; MSW U of Wisconsin 1981; MDiv SWTS 1995; Certification Int Mnstry Ntwk 1997; Mediation Cert U of Wisconsin 2010. D 2/2/1995 P 9/9/1995 Bp Roger John White. R S Chris's Ch Milwaukee WI 2010-2015; R S Jas Epis Ch Milwaukee WI 1999-2010; P-in-c H Cross Epis Ch Wisconsin Dells WI 1997-1999; Assoc Chapl St Fran Hse Madison WI 1995; Com on Sexual Exploitation Dom And Frgn Mssy Soc- Epis Ch Cntr New York NY 2000-2003. EWC 1995; Mem Natl Com on Sexual Exploitation 2000-2003; Nathan Ntwk 2002; OSH--Assoc Mem 1995. Soc Worker of the Year NASW-WI 2009; Jonathan Myrick Daniels Fell EDS 1994; Natl Fell Fund for Theol Educ 1992.

TRAMBLEY, Adam Thomas (NwPa) 343 Forker Blvd, Sharon PA 16146 **R S Jn's Epis Ch Sharon PA 2009-; Fac, Strategic Plnng Process Dio NW Pennsylvania Erie PA 2011-, Pres, Stndg Com 2010-, Dep to GC 2006-2009** B Erie PA 1971 s Gerald & Marlene. AB Harv 1994; MDiv VTS 2004. D 10/25/2003 P 6/12/2004 Bp Robert Deane Rowley Jr. m 12/21/1996 Jane Trambley c 2. R Trin Memi Ch Warren PA 2004-2009. Soc for Biblic Lit 2003.

TRAMEL, Stephanie M (Ia) 2300 Bancroft Way, Berkeley CA 94704 B Davenport IO 1967 d Frederick & Ann Janette. AB Bryn 1989; MA U of Iowa 1994; MDiv CDSP 2000. D 6/10/2000 P 1/7/2001 Bp Chris Christopher Epting. m 6/30/2006 James Russell Tramel c 1. S Paul's Ch Oakland CA 2017; Ch Of S Jude The Apos Cupertino CA 2015-2016; S Jas Ch Fremont CA 2013-2014; All SS Epis Ch San Leandro CA 2011-2013; Sabbatical Int Assoc R Trsfg Epis Ch San Mateo CA 2008.

TRAMMELL, Robert William (Okla) St. Augustine Of Canterbury, 14700 N. May Ave., Oklahoma City OK 73134 **Vol D S Aug Of Cbury Oklahoma City OK 2007-** B Siloam Springs AR 1952 s Bobby & Edna. BA Cntrl St U 1979; MA U of Oklahoma 1986. D 6/16/2007 Bp Robert Manning Moody. m 4/19/1974 Linda Trammell c 3.

TRAN, Catherine Caroline (Colo) 6556 High Dr., Morrison CO 80465 **Co Pstr Gr Ch Buena Vista CO 2014-, 2012-2014, 2011-2012, 2011, 2011** B North Babylon NY 1959 d Louis & Caroline. U CO 1979; MDiv S Thos Sem 1994; MA S Thos Sem 1995; Cert Sprtl Direction Shalem Inst Washington DC 1998. D 6/11/1994 P 1/14/1995 Bp William Jerry Winterrowd. m 8/18/1979 Tam Tran c 2. S Tim's Epis Ch Littleton CO 2014; R Ch Of The Trsfg Evergreen CO 1998-2009. Auth, "Sprtl Discovery: a Method for Discernment in Sm Groups and Congregations," Alb, 2015.

TRAPANI, Kathleen (Cal) 30 Greenridge Pl, Danville CA 94506 **Ch Of The Resurr Pleasant Hil CA 2015-** B San Jose CA 1957 d Joseph & Alice. BA U CA 1979; MBA U CA 1987; MDiv CDSP 2001. D 12/2/2000 P 6/2/2001 Bp William Edwin Swing. m 5/31/1980 Thomas A Trapani c 4. S Paul's Epis Ch Walnut Creek CA 2013; Int S Tim's Ch Danville CA 2002-2013. Phi Beta Kappa 1979.

TRAPP, Grace J (SwVa) PO Box 328, Harpswell ME 04079 B Milwaukee WI 1950 d Eugene & Grace. BS U of Wisconsin 1973; MDiv SWTS 1976; MEd Natl-Louis U 1996. D 5/1/1976 Bp Charles Thomas Gaskell P 12/19/1979 Bp

A(rthur) Heath Light. Dir Pstr Care S Lk's Hosp Racine WI 1986-1987, Chapl 1976-1979; Asstg P S Lk's Ch Evanston IL 1983-2003; Chapl Rush-Presb-St Lk's Hoapital Chicago 1981-1983; COM Dio SW Virginia Roanoke VA 1979-1981; Asstg P Emm Ch Staunton VA 1979-1981; Stuart Hall Staunton VA 1979-1981; Spec Mnstry Com Dio Milwaukee Milwaukee WI 1976-1979, Spec Mnstry Cmsn 1977-1979. Rec Wmn's Bd Prize SWTS 1976.

TRAPP, James E. (NY) PO Box 40697, Portland OR 97240 **Non-par 1984-** B Paducah KY 1946 s Ralph & Mary. BMusEd NWU 1968; MDiv Nash 1971. D 6/19/1971 Bp Gerald Francis Burrill P 12/18/1971 Bp James Winchester Montgomery. m 9/16/2005 John L Keating c 1. Assoc R Ch Of The Intsn New York NY 1979-1984; Asst Chr Ch Fitchburg MA 1977-1979; Yth Dir Dio Sthrn Ohio Cincinnati OH 1974-1977; Cur Trin Epis Ch Wheaton IL 1971-1974.

TRAQUAIR, Megan Mcclure (Az) 10222 South 44th Lane, Laveen AZ 85339 **Cn Dio Arizona Phoenix AZ 2013-** B Pasadena CA 1962 d Malcolm & Patricia. BA Pomona Coll 1985; MDiv SWTS 1991. D 6/15/1991 P 1/11/1992 Bp Frederick Houk Borsch. m 8/24/1985 Philip S Smittle c 2. Vic Ch Of The Apos Oro Vlly AZ 2008-2013; S Phil's In The Hills Tucson AZ 2002-2008; R Geth Epis Ch Marion IN 1997-2002; S Jn Of The Cross Bristol IN 1994-1996; Asst to R S Mich And All Ang Par Corona Dl Mar CA 1991-1993. megan@azdiocese. org

TRASK III, Robert Palmer (EMich) 13 Circle Ave, Wheaton IL 60187 B Boston MA 1947 s Robert & Hazel. BA Gordon Coll 1969; MDiv TESM 1983. D 6/19/1983 P 5/20/1984 Bp John Forsythe Ashby. m 2/17/1973 Margaret S Trask c 5. Ret Gr Epis Ch Port Huron MI 1998-2012; R S Alb's Epis Ch Mc Cook NE 1987-1998; Vic S Eliz's Ch Russell KS 1985-1987; H Apos Ch Ellsworth KS 1983-1987; Vic S Mk's Ch Lyons KS 1983-1985; COM Dio Nebraska Omaha NE 1989-1998.

TRAVERSE, Alfred (CPa) 1245 Westerly Pkwy Apt 59, State College PA 16801 **Died 9/15/2015** B P.E.I. Canada 1925 s Alfred & Pearle. SB Harv 1946; Cert in botany Camb 1947; AM Harv 1948; PhD Harv 1951; MDiv Epis TS of the SW 1965; Cert in botany Camb 2047. D 6/1/1965 Bp James Milton Richardson P 5/1/1966 Bp Scott Field Bailey. m 6/30/1951 Elizabeth Jane Insley c 4. Ret 1988-2015; Non-par 1982-1987; Asst Chr Old Cath Ch Zurich Switzerland 1980-1981; Vic S Jn's Epis Ch Huntingdon PA 1976-1980; Cur S Paul's Ch Philipsburg PA 1966-1975; Cur S Matt's Ch Austin TX 1965-1966. Auth, "more than 100 arts, beginning in 1950n," Var Sci Journ, 2013; "Paleopalynology," *Second Ed (Topics in Geobiology)*, Springer; 2nd Ed, 2008; Ed, "Sedimentation of Organic Particles," *Bk in Geological Series*, Cambridge Univ. Press, 1994; Auth, "Paleopalynology," *First Ed*, Unwin-Hyman, 1988. CBS. Cert of Appreciation St Coll, PA, Tree Cmsn 2009; Hon Mem Awd Amer Assn Strat. Palynol. 2005; Excellence in Educ Medal Amer Assn Strat. Palynol. 2002; Crspndg Mem Senckenberg Naturforschende Gesellschaft 1992; Indn Int Gold Medal In Palaeobotany 91-92 1991; Phi Beta Kappa 1950.

TRAVIS, Doug (Tex) 9701 Shadows Ct, Granbury TX 76049 **Dn & Pres Emer Epis TS Of The SW Austin TX 2013-, Dn & Pres 2007-2013** B San Antonio TX 1953 s Murray & Jane. BA Trin U San Antonio 1975; MATS McCormick TS 1977; MA U Chi 1980; STM GTS 1994; DMin SMU 2000; DD GTS 2008. D 6/13/1987 P 5/1/1988 Bp Donis Dean Patterson. m 8/16/1975 Pamela Jean Travis c 2. S Mich And All Ang Ch Dallas TX 2015-2016; Cn for Formation Dio The Rio Grande Albuquerque 2013-2015; R Trin Epis Ch The Woodlands TX 2001-2006; Bd Trst The U So Sewanee TN 2000-2001; S Jas Ch Dallas TX 1992-2001; Cn S Matt's Cathd Dallas TX 1989-1991; Dn The Angl TS Dallas TX 1987-1991; Cur Epis Ch Of The Redeem Irving TX 1987-1989; COM Dio Texas Houston TX 2003-2006, Exec Coun 2003-2006; COM Dio Dallas Dallas TX 1994-2001, Exec Coun 1992-1995. DD GTS 2008; Phi Beta Kappa.

TRAVIS, Kathleen Ann (Ia) 3120 E 24th St, Des Moines IA 50317 **P-in-c S Mk's Epis Ch Des Moines IA 2015-** B Fort Wayne IN 1958 d Joseph & Junine. BS Tri-St U 1980; PhD OH SU 1988; MDiv Luther Sem 2015; MDiv Luther Sem 2015. D 12/6/2014 P 6/6/2015 Bp Alan Scarfe. kathleen_travis@msn.com

TRAVIS, Michelle Halsall (Mont) 1821 Westlake Dr Apt 124, Austin TX 78746 **Non-par 1990-** B Jackson MS 1947 d Archibald & Amy. BA Rice U 1971; MS Rice U 1977; MDiv Epis TS of the SW 1985. D 5/23/1985 P 12/1/1985 Bp Jackson Earle Gilliam. m 11/16/1984 Arthur Edwin Travis. Asst R S Mk's Ch Austin TX 1987-1989; Asst R S Dav's Epis Ch San Antonio TX 1985-1986.

TRAVIS, R. Carroll (CFla) 2103 Indian River Dr, Cocoa FL 32922 B Williamson WV 1940 s Robert & Nell. BA Col 1962; STB GTS 1967; MA Rhode Island Coll 1984. D 6/17/1967 P 12/21/1967 Bp Jonathan Goodhue Sherman. c 3. R Ch Of S Dav's By The Sea Cocoa Bch FL 1998-2008; R Trin Ch Rochester NY 1983-1998; R All SS Epis Ch Attleboro MA 1978-1983; R Gr Ch In The Mountains Waynesville NC 1970-1978; Cur S Steph's Ch Prt Washington NY 1967-1970. Auth, "Discovering the Treasure Within," Maple Creek Media, 2011; Auth, "Cmnty Meditations On The Stations Of The Cross," Ldr Resources Inc., 2003.

TRAVIS, Robert P. (RI) 326 Kenyon Avenue, Wakefield RI 02879 **Ch Of The Ascen Wakefield RI 2015-; Sr Trnr J2A Ldr Resources Leeds MA 2001-** B Waynesville NC 1976 s R. & Karen. BA Col 1998; MDiv Sewanee: The U So, TS 2006. D 5/27/2006 P 12/16/2006 Bp John Wadsworth Howe. m 2/8/2003

Jacqueline H Camm c 3. Assoc Ch Of The Ascen Knoxville TN 2008-2015; Chapl - CPE Res Florida Hosp Orlando FL 2007-2008; Asst R S Mich's Ch Orlando FL 2006-2007; Dir of Yth Mnstry S Steph's Ch Prt Washington NY 1999-2003. Ch Club of New York 2001-2004. ABS CE Prize STUSo 2006. fatherrobtravis@gmail.com

TRAVIS, Sherry Margaret (Miss) 1365 Sweetwater Dr, Brentwood TN 37027 B Jackson MS 1948 d Loyd & Margaret. LSU 1968; BA Belhaven Coll 1971; MEd Mississippi St U 1978; MDiv VTS 1992. D 6/20/1992 Bp Duncan Montgomery Gray Jr P 11/30/1993 Bp Alfred Marble Jr. Cn for Pstr Care S Andr's Cathd Jackson MS 2006-2012; Epis Chapl Jacksonville St U 1999-2006; R S Lk's Epis Ch Jacksonville AL 1999-2006; Asst R St Thos Epis Ch Huntsville AL 1996-1999; Asst R Ch of the H Trin Vicksburg MS 1992-1996. Cler Ldrshp Proj 2001; HabHum - Bd Mem 1997-1999.

TRAYLOR, Thomas Wallace (Cal) 1801 Jackson St Apt 4, San Francisco CA 94109 **Pstr Assoc All SS' Ch San Francisco CA 2003-; Hospice Chapl Kaiser Permanente Med Cntr Hayward CA 2000-** B Atlanta GA 1950 s Herbert & Eva. BA Emory U 1972; MDiv Sthrn Bapt TS 1975; MSW U of Louisville 1986. D 12/6/2003 P 6/5/2004 Bp William Edwin Swing.

TRAYNHAM, Warner Raymond (Los) 6125 Alviso Ave, Los Angeles CA 90043 **Asst S Alb's Epis Ch Los Angeles CA 2006-; Ret 2001-** B Baltimore MD 1936 s Hezekiah & Virginia. BA Dart 1957; Oxf GB 1958; BD VTS 1961. D 7/6/1961 P 4/4/1962 Bp Noble C Powell. m 1/23/1965 Jocelyn P Traynham c 4. R St Johns Pro-Cathd Los Angeles CA 1983-2001; Dn of Tucker Fndt Dart 1974-1983; Dir Black Stds Boston TS 1972-1974; R S Cyp's Ch Boston MA 1967-1972; Assoc Chapl Harvard Coll Cambridge MA 1965-1967; Vic S Phil's Ch Annapolis MD 1962-1965; Asst S Jas' Epis Ch Baltimore MD 1961-1962; Dep GC Dio Los Angeles Los Angeles CA 1988-2000. Auth, "Chr Faith in Black & White," Parameter Press. Paul Harris Fell Rotary Intl 2009; Cn Dio LA 1996; Phi Beta Kappa Dartmouth Phi Beta Kappa 1957.

TREADWELL II, Richard Allen (Ore) 1916 NE Gibbs Circle, McMinnville OR 97128 **Died 9/1/2016** B Portland OR 1938 s Richard & Eva. BS OR SU 1961; MDiv CDSP 1964. D 6/29/1964 Bp James Walmsley Frederic Carman P 12/30/1964 Bp William Jones Gordon Jr. m 3/24/1962 Shirley Vaughan Treadwell c 3. Dio Oregon Portland OR 2000-2006, Epis Chars Bd 1991-1994; Natl Bd Mar Encounter Epis Expression 1978-1981; R S Barn Par McMinnville OR 1976-2005; R S Jas Epis Ch Taos NM 1970-1976; P-in-c S Andr's Ch Stevens Vlg AK 1966-1970; S Matt's Ch Beaver AK 1966-1970; P-in-c S Jn's Epis Ch Eagle AK 1964-1966; P-in-c S Paul's Ch Eagle Town AK 1964-1966; H Trin Ch Cir AK 1964-1965; S Steph's Ch Ft Yukon AK 1964-1965. OHC 1960.

TREADWELL III, William Charles (Tex) 11704 Via Grande Dr, Austin TX 78739 **R S Dav's Ch Austin TX 2016-** B Rock Hill SC 1960 s William & Louise. BA Geo 1983; MDiv Sewanee: The U So, TS 1989. D 6/17/1989 P 5/31/1990 Bp Donis Dean Patterson. m 6/8/1985 Christine Lynn Treadwell c 3. R S Paul's Ch Waco TX 2004-2016; R S Ptr's Ch Mc Kinney TX 1993-2004; Chapl S Mich Sch Dallas TX 1991-1993; Cur S Mich And All Ang Ch Dallas TX 1989-1993. Auth, "Earth Lent"; Auth, "Adoption".

TREANOR, Susan Mary (Be) B Bronx NY 1945 d William & Anne. BA Mercy Coll; MSW NYU; MDiv GTS 2009. D 2/6/2016 P 9/24/2016 Bp Sean Walter Rowe.

TREES, Thomas H (CFla) 1616 Sterns Dr, Leesburg FL 34748 **S Jas Epis Ch Leesburg FL 2014-** B Washington DC 1968 s Heino & Annabelle. BA U of Virginia 1991; MDiv Regent U 1997; STM Cranmer Theol Hse 2000. D 11/30/2002 Bp David John Bena P 5/31/2003 Bp Daniel William Herzog. m 3/23/1997 Kathleen Q Trees c 6. Assoc Ch Of The Ascen Lafayette LA 2009-2013; R St Augustines Ch Ilion NY 2002-2009; COM Dio Albany Greenwich NY 2008-2009, Dioc Coun 2003-2009. frtrees@stjames-leesburg.org

TREGARTHEN, Doran Woodrow (Los) 27625 Summerfield Ln, San Juan Capistrano CA 92675 **Died 8/5/2015** B San Pedro CA 1919 s Harold & Alice. BA U CA 1942; MEd U CA 1954; MA Claremont TS 1988. D 6/25/1988 Bp Frederick Houk Borsch P 1/7/1989 Bp Oliver Bailey Garver Jr. m 12/21/1942 Ethel Mae Geabhart. Asst S Marg Of Scotland Par San Juan Capo CA 1988-2015. Auth, *Tchg in the Elem Sch*; Auth, *Who Are the Poor?*.

TREGO, Randall (Tex) 3106 Heritage Creek Oaks, Houston TX 77008 **S Dunst's Epis Ch Houston TX 2014-; Chapl Cullen Memi Chap Houston TX 2002-** B Lancaster PA 1953 s Earl & Elsie. BA Gordon Coll 1976; MDiv VTS 1987. D 6/13/1987 Bp David Elliot Johnson P 5/6/1988 Bp Cabell Tennis. m 5/20/1978 Lois Anne Trego c 2. Dio Texas Houston TX 2011-2014; S Lk's Epis Hosp Houston TX 2001-2011; The Great Cmsn Fndt Houston TX 2001; Assoc S Jn The Div Houston TX 1989-2001; Cur Chr Ch Christiana Hundred Wilmington DE 1987-1989.

TREHERNE-THOMAS, Rhoda Margaret (NY) 10 Bay Street Lndg Apt 6L, Staten Island NY 10301 **Assoc S Jn's Ch Staten Island NY 2003-; Chapl Staten Island U Hosp 2000-** B Mumbles Wales GB 1927 d Francis & Margaretta. BA Smith 1948; MA Col 1951; MDiv UTS 1980. D 6/7/1980 P 12/7/1980 Bp Paul Moore Jr. Supply P S Paul's Ch Staten Island NY 2008-2015; P-in-c S Simon's Ch Staten Island NY 1994-1999; Asst S Ptr's Ch Bronx NY 1993-1997, Asst 1980-1984; Asst Par of Chr the Redeem Pelham NY 1992-1994, Assoc

1988-1991; Int Chr Epis Ch Tarrytown NY 1990-1991; P-in-c S Jos's Ch Bronx NY 1986-1988; Consult Epis Ch Cntr New York NY 1985-1988; Int Chapl Morningside Hse Bronx NY 1984-1985; Chapl Calv Hosp Bronx NY 1980-1990; Sis Cmnty of St Mary 1960-1967; Mssy Ang Dioc of Jerusalem & the Middle E 1952-1960. CSM 1982.

TREI, Rosemary (Dal) 5923 Royal Ln, Dallas TX 75230 **Archd Dio Dallas Dallas TX 2013-** B Long Beach CA 1944 d Ralph & Julia. BA H Names U 1966; Tchr Cred San Diego St U 1967; Dplma Stanton Cntr for Mnstry Formation 2008. D 6/6/2009 Bp James Monte Stanton. m 6/24/1967 Charles A Trei c 3. D S Lk's Epis Ch Dallas TX 2009-2016; Rgstr of Stanton Cntr S Matt's Cathd Dallas TX 2009-2014.

TREJO-BARAHONA, Oscar (Hond) B 1961 P 3/5/2005 Bp Lloyd Emmanuel Allen. m 4/16/1993 Filomena Chicas Romero c 3. Dio Honduras San Pedro Sula 1998-2015.

TRELEASE, Murray Lincoln (Oly) 343 Eagles Roost Ln, Lopez Island WA 98261 B Kansas City MO 1929 s Richard & Ruth. BA U of Kansas 1952; MDiv CDSP 1959. D 6/1/1959 Bp John Brooke Mosley P 12/9/1959 Bp William Jones Gordon Jr. m 4/8/1961 Mariette G Trelease. Vic Gr Ch Lopez Island WA 2000-2002, P-in-c 1992-1993; Dio Olympia Seattle 1993-1994; R/ Headmaster S Paul's Ch Kansas City MO 1980-1992; R S Paul's Ch Milwaukee WI 1972-1980; Cn P S Mk's Cathd Seattle WA 1967-1971; Vic S Steph's Ch Ft Yukon AK 1964-1967; Yukon Vlly Mssnr Dio Alaska Fairbanks AK 1959-1967. Auth, "Dying Among Alaskan Indians"; Auth, "Death The Final Stage Of Growth"; Auth, "Dioc Nwspr Series Aunt Clara's Famous Ironing Bd Lectures".

TREMAINE, Gordon Hyde (Fla) 100 Ne 1st St, Gainesville FL 32601 B New York NY 1954 s A Robert & Shirley. BA Dickinson Coll 1976; MDiv VTS 1981. D 6/13/1981 P 12/1/1981 Bp John Shelby Spong. c 2. R H Trin Epis Ch Gainesville FL 2002-2006; R S Ptr's Ch Essex Fells NJ 1991-2002; R S Steph's Ch Millburn NJ 1984-1991; Cur Calv Epis Ch Summit NJ 1981-1984.

TREMBATH, Jack Graham (Mich) 939 Chippewa St, Mount Clemens MI 48043 **D S Mich's Ch Grosse Pointe MI 1987-; Chair Com Affirmative Aging Dio Michigan Detroit MI 1998-, Pres D Coun 1995-1997** B Windsor ON CA 1922 s John & Theresa. Amer Coll of Life Underwriters 1969; Whitaker TS 1976. D 12/10/1976 Bp Henry Irving Mayson. m 4/27/1946 Redina Josephine Trembath c 3. S Edw The Confessor Epis Ch Clinton Twp MI 1986-1987; Chapl Macomb Cnty Jail Mt Clemens MI 1977-1993; Gr Ch Mt Clemens MI 1976-1986.

TREMMEL, Marcia Ann (SwFla) 11588 57th Street Cir. E., Parrish FL 34219 **Bd Mem Help2Home Inc. 2013-** B Orlando FL 1948 d Louis & Sylvia. Masters in Mnstry Nash; BA U of So Florida 1969; MBA U of So Florida 1992; BS U of So Florida 1996. D 6/12/2004 Bp Rogers Sanders Harris P 12/14/2016 Bp Dabney Tyler Smith. m 4/13/1968 Allan Tremmel c 2. D S Mary Magd Bradenton FL 2007-2014; D S Mary's Epis Ch Palmetto FL 2005-2006; D S Wlfd's Epis Ch Sarasota FL 2004-2005; Mem, COM Dio SW Florida Parrish FL 2011-2013, COM 2011-, Safeguarding God's Chld Admin 2008-, Deacons' Coun Mem 2006-2009. stwilfredepiscopal@gmail.com

TREPPA, Joyce Lynn (Mich) 1150 Tarpon Center Dr. #503, Venice FL 34285 **D S Mk's Epis Ch Venice FL 2012-** B Detroit MI 1949 d Elmer & Marjorie. BS Estrn Michigan U 1988; Whitaker TS 2001. D 6/16/2001 Bp Wendell Nathaniel Gibbs Jr. m 8/8/1981 Jonathan Carl Campbell. D All SS Epis Ch Pontiac MI 2011; Hospice Chapl St. Jn Hospice Clinton Twp. 2007-2011; Chapl Integrated Hlth Serv Hospice 2002-2007; D Chr Ch Detroit MI 2001-2009; Chapl Heartland Hospice Southfield MI 1999-2002. NAAD 2001.

TREVATHAN, W Illiam Andre (Ky) 1 Franklin Town Blvd Apt 1515, Philadelphia PA 19103 B Little Rock AR 1931 s William & Martha. BA U So 1953; STB GTS 1956; U of Puerto Rico 1983. D 6/17/1956 Bp Charles Gresham Marmion P 12/17/1956 Bp Horace W B Donegan. m 6/2/1985 Carol A Altland c 3. Epis Chapl Murray St U KY 1986-1997; Vic S Jn's Ch Murray KY 1986-1996; Int Purhas Coun Epis Ch Paducah KY 1985-1986; Admin Asst To Bp 1980-1985; Archd Of Nthrn Puerto Rico 1980-1985; Asst Dio Puerto Rico Trujillo Alto PR 1977-1979, 1971-1973, P-in-c 1962-1973; Dioc Mssnr 1975-1985; Chapl S Lk's Hosp Ponce Puerto Rico 1965-1972; Vic S Paul In Arecibo Puerto Rico 1964-1965; Vic S Ptr & S Paul Bayamon Puerto Rico 1962-1964; Asst Trin Par New York NY 1958-1962; Asst Chapl Ch Of The Incarn New York NY 1956-1958; Ret; Dept Of CSR Dio Kentucky Louisville KY 1987-2002. Iglesia Epis Puertorrique, "Ritos Autorizados," *Ritos Autorizados*, Iglesia Epis Puertorriqueña, 1983. Cmnty Of S Mary 1986-2006.

TREVER, Stephen Cecil (Cal) 2300 Bancroft Way, Berkeley CA 94704 **S Anne's Ch Fremont CA 2017-** B Atlanta GA 1974 s James & Mary. BA U of W Florida 1997; MDiv Yale DS 2000; MDiv Yale DS 2000; Angl Stds VTS 2013. D 6/22/2013 P 1/4/2014 Bp M(Arvil) Thomas Shaw. m 6/14/2003 Lisa S Trever c 1. S Mk's Par Berkeley CA 2014-2016; CE Dir Gr Epis Ch Medford MA 2011-2012. sctrever@gmail.com

TREWHELLA, Charles Keith (Ore) 19691 Nw Meadow Lake Rd, Yamhill OR 97148 B Eureka CA 1928 s William & Erlene. BA U of Portland 1953; ATC 1969. D 6/24/1969 P 3/7/1970 Bp James Walmsley Frederic Carman. Bp Of

Oregon Fndt Portland OR 1989-1993; Legacy Gd Samar Hosp Portland OR 1969-1989. AEHC 1969.

TREZEVANT, Margaret Anne (Cal) 1755 Clay St, San Francisco CA 94109 **Ch Of Our Sav Mill Vlly CA 2016-** B Travis A.F.B., CA 1950 d Lee & Mayme. BA San Francisco St U 1985; BA San Francisco St U 1985; MS U CA - San Francisco 1994; MS U CA - San Francisco 1994; BDS Epis Sch for Deacons 2009; BDS Sch for Deacons 2009. D 6/6/2009 Bp Marc Handley Andrus. m 3/26/1983 Richard Gray Trezevant c 1. Instr Epis Sch for Deacons 2012-2014; Sojourn Multifaith Chapl San Francisco CA 2010-2011; D All SS' Ch San Francisco CA 2009-2013. Assn of Epis Deacons 2006.

TRIGG, Joseph (WA) Po Box 760, La Plata MD 20646 B Henderson KY 1949 s George & Jean. VTS; BA Rice U 1971; MA U Chi 1974; PhD U Chi 1978. D 6/15/1984 P 5/1/1985 Bp David Reed. m 6/12/1983 Joy E Scheidt c 2. VTS Alexandria VA 2006, 2003-2004, 2002, 2001, 1998, 1996, 1991-1992, 1987-1989; R Chr Ch Port Tobacco Paris La Plata MD 1993-2013; S Patricks Ch Falls Ch VA 1986-1993; Gr Ch Paducah KY 1984-1986. Auth, "Message of the Fathers of the Ch: Volume 9," *Biblic Interp*; Auth, *Of One Body: Renwl Movements in the Ch*; Auth, *Origen (Early Chr Fathers)*. No Amer Patristic Soc. Phi Beta Kappa Rice U 1971.

TRIGLETH, John Paul (Mil) S3919A Highway 12, Baraboo WI 53913 B Vandalia IL 1941 s Irwin & Mary. BD U of Wisconsin 1986. D 1/13/2001 Bp Roger John White. m 11/2/1963 Margaret Bertha Vander. D Trin Ch Baraboo WI 2001-2009.

TRILLOS, Alejandra (NY) Iglesia San Andres, 22 Post St, Yonkers NY 10705 **Dio New York New York NY 2016-; CE Dir The Ch of S Edw The Mtyr New York NY 2008-** B Colombia 1974 d Alonso & Graciela. MDiv UTS 2008; Angl Stds GTS 2012. D 6/2/2012 P 12/8/2012 Bp Lawrence C Provenzano. m 2/14/2014 Walter L Grote. P-in-c Dio Long Island Garden City NY 2014-2016, 2014; S Jn's Ch Huntington NY 2012-2014.

TRIMBLE, James Armstrong (Pa) 326 S Third St, Philadelphia PA 19106 **Ret 1997-** B Philadelphia PA 1931 s James & Ella. BA U of Pennsylvania 1953; BD VTS 1956. D 6/1/1956 Bp Joseph Gillespie Armstrong P 1/25/1957 Bp Oliver J Hart. m 12/26/1996 Gail H Trimble c 3. R Chr Ch Philadelphia Philadelphia PA 1978-1998; Chapl The Epis Acad Merion PA 1963-1978; The Epis Acad Newtown Sq PA 1963-1977; July R S Chris Sum Chap Winter Harbor ME 1961-2010; Vic Ch Of The Redemp Southampton PA 1958-1960; Cur Gr Ch Mt Airy PA 1956-1958. Auth, "Var arts," *Var Epis Pub*. DD VTS 1989.

TRIMBLE, Jim Edward (USC) 102 Monroe Rd, Spartanburg SC 29307 **S Chris's Ch Spartanburg SC 2015-** B Louisville KY 1967 s Robert & Ursula. BS Murray St U 1990; MDiv Epis TS of the SW 2005. D 6/4/2005 P 12/10/2005 Bp Ted Gulick Jr. m 9/18/1999 Sarah P Peoples c 1. R S Jas Ch Pewee Vlly KY 2009-2015; Assoc S Matt's Epis Ch Louisville KY 2007-2009; R S Mary's Ch Madisonville KY 2005-2007. Writer, "Jump...Or You'll Get Pushed," *Place Gives Rise to Sprt: Writers on Louisville*, Fleur de Lis Press, 2001. jim.trimble@gmail.com

TRIMBLE, Sarah M (Va) 3401 Chantarene Dr, Pensacola FL 32507 B Saint Paul BR 1940 d Prudencio & Sarah. BA Florida St U 1962; MDiv VTS 1989. D 6/10/1989 Bp Peter J Lee P 3/3/1990 Bp Robert Poland Atkinson. m 6/26/1965 Henry Leland Trimble c 2. R The Fork Ch Doswell VA 1993-1997; Int Epis Ch Of Leeds Par Markham VA 1992-1993; Asst R S Jas' Epis Ch Warrenton VA 1989-1991.

TRIPLETT, Laurie Ann (RG) D 6/4/2016 Bp Michael Vono.

TRIPP, Arthur Davis (RG) Po Box 398, Raton NM 87740 B San Antonio TX 1932 s Arthur & Anna. BS NE St U 1955; MDiv Epis TS of the SW 1959. D 5/20/1959 P 11/30/1959 Bp Chilton R Powell. m 1/21/1977 Nilah Tripp c 3. Vic H Trin Epis Ch - Mssn Raton NM 2001-2009; Dn Dioc Sch for Mnstry 1996-2008; Asst The Epis Ch In Lincoln Cnty Chap Of 1995-2000; R S Chris's Epis Ch El Paso TX 1992-1996; Dn S Jas Cathd Guatemala City Gua 1982-1991; Exec Coun Appointees New York NY 1977-1992; Archd Dio Nicaragua Managua Nicaragua 1976-1982; R S Aid's Epis Ch Tulsa OK 1967-1976; Chair Dept Mssn Dio Oklahoma Oklahoma City OK 1959-1976.

TRIPP, Roy (SC) PO Box 761, Port Royal SC 29935 **St Mk's Epis Ch Port Royal SC 2017-** B Bangor ME 1954 s Claivoy & Lillian. MDiv CDSP 1996. D 6/22/1996 P 5/1/1997 Bp Vincent Waydell Warner. m 9/16/1982 Lizbeth Ann Tripp. R Ch Of S Jn The Evang Duxbury MA 2007-2017; R S Alb's Ch Wilmington DE 2001-2007; S Clare of Assisi Epis Ch Snoqualmie WA 1998-2001; Trin Epis Ch Everett WA 1997-1998. OHC.

TRIPP, Thomas Norman (WNY) 354 Burroughs Dr, Amherst NY 14226 B Buffalo NY 1947 s Norman & Betty. BS SUNY at Buffalo 1968; MS SUNY at Buffalo 1973. D 11/17/2007 Bp Michael Garrison. m 1/23/1971 Lois Jean Tripp c 3.

TRIPSES, Kathleen Ruth McDowell (Ia) 2844 NW Northcreek Circle, Ankeny IA 50023 **D S Anne's By The Fields Ankeny IA 2001-** B Eagle Grove IA 1932 d C Leroy & M Helene. BS Iowa St U 1954; Drake U 1972. D 4/7/2001 Bp Chris Christopher Epting. m 6/20/1954 Richard Tripses c 4. OSL the Physcn 2001; Third Ord, SSF 1985.

TRISKA, Patricia Ilene (Ia) 1009 Parkway Dr Apt 7, Boone IA 50036 **Died 1/20/2017** B Prescott AZ 1931 d John & Thelma. RN Des Moines Cmnty Coll Des Moines IA 1989; EFM Sewanee: The U So, TS 1993. D 5/25/1995 Bp Chris Christopher Epting. c 2. D Gr Ch Boone IA 1995-2014; Camps & Conf Cntr Boone IA 1977-1987.

TRISTRAM SSJE, Geoffrey Robert (Mass) 980 Memorial Dr, Cambridge MA 02138 **S Jn's Chap Cambridge MA 2008-, 2002-2007; Soc-St Jn The Evang Cambridge MA 2002-** B Cardiff UK 1953 s Frank & Patricia. BA U of Cambridge 1978; Westcott Hse Cambridge 1979; MA U of Cambridge 1981. Trans 3/13/2002 Bp M(Arvil) Thomas Shaw. Serv Ch of Engl 1979-1999.

TRIVELY, Tim (SwFla) 4 Gatehouse Ct, Asheville NC 28803 **1989-** B Lincoln NE 1937 s Ilo & Maxine. BS Clemson U 1960; MDiv Sewanee: The U So, TS 1963. D 6/29/1963 P 6/1/1964 Bp Richard Henry Baker. m 8/26/1961 Elizabeth Anne Wells c 2. Acts Of The Apos Mssn St Petersburg FL 1990-1997; Dio SW Florida Parrish FL 1988-1989; S Andr's Epis Ch Tampa FL 1983-1988; R S Jas Epis Ch Lenoir NC 1967-1983; R Trin Ch Scotland Neck NC 1964-1967; M-in-c Ch Of The Gd Shpd Rocky Mt NC 1963-1964.

TROEGER, Thomas Henry (Colo) 56 Hickory Rd, Woodbridge CT 06525 B Suffern NY 1945 s Henry & Lorena. BA Ya 1967; BD Colgate Rochester Crozer DS 1970; BD CRDS 1970; STD Dickinson Coll 1993. D 6/5/1999 P 12/5/1999 Bp William Jerry Winterrowd. m 6/25/1967 Merle Butler Troeger.

TROGDON, Denise A (Va) 1700 Wainwright Dr, Reston VA 20190 **Ch Of The H Cross Dunn Loring VA 2015-** B England 1959 d Floyd & Berenice. BA W&M 1980; MSW Virginia Commonwealth U 1988; MDiv VTS 2008. D 5/24/2008 P 12/14/2008 Bp Peter J Lee. c 2. S Lk's Par Darien CT 2012-2015; Assoc R Fam Mnstrs S Anne's Epis Ch Reston VA 2008-2012.

TRONCALE, John E (NJ) 301 Meadows Dr, Forest VA 24551 **Chapl Gr Lodge Lynchburg VA 2006-; Chapl Rusk & Pratt Alzheimer's Adult Care Lynchburg VA 2000-; Chapl Rusk & Pratt Residential Adult Care Lynchburg VA 1997-** B Elizabeth NJ 1946 s Pellegrino & Ninfa. BA Kean U 1980; MDiv GTS 1983. D 6/4/1983 P 12/1/1983 Bp George Phelps Mellick Belshaw. c 4. Chapl Rehab Cntr Lynchburg VA 1998-2007; Vic Chr Ch Millville NJ 1991-1994; S Lk's Ch Woodstown NJ 1987-1990; S Paul's Ch Camden NJ 1984-1987; Ch Of Our Sav Camden NJ 1983-1987; Asst Ch of Our Sav Camden NJ 1983-1987; S Wilfrid's Ch Camden NJ 1983. "His Mysterious Ways," *Guideposts*.

TROTTER, Scott (Ark) 1121 W Pecan, Blytheville AR 72315 **Calv Epis Ch Osceola AR 2014-; S Steph's Ch Blytheville AR 2010-; Mssnr E Arkansas Epis Ministres W Memphis AR 2006-** B Atlanta GA 1953 DMin Memphis TS; AA Oxford Coll of Emory U 1972; BA Emory U 1975; MDiv Sewanee: The U So, TS 1994. D 6/4/1994 P 12/10/1994 Bp Frank Kellogg Allan. c 2. S Ptr's Epis Ch Bon Secour AL 2008-2010; R Ch Of The H Cross W Memphis AR 2001-2007; Mssnr New River Cluster Oak Hill WV 1996-2001; The New River Epis Mnstry Pratt WV 1996-2001; Vic Epis Ch Of The H Fam Jasper GA 1994-1996. frscott94@gmail.com

TROUTMAN-MILLER, Jana Lee (Mil) 1840 N Prospect Ave, Milwaukee WI 53202 **S Jn's on The Lake Milwaukee WI 2014-** B Macomb IL 1974 d Jerry & Janice. BA Wstrn Illinois U 1996; MA Lincoln Chr Sem 2000; Angl Stds Bexley Seabury 2014. D 3/15/2014 P 9/4/2014 Bp Steven Andrew Miller. m 8/4/2006 Randolph Alan Miller.

TROW, Chester John (CFla) **D Gr Epis Ch Of Ocala Ocala FL 2015-** B Cambridge MA 1946 JD Florida St U; BSBA and MA U of Florida. D 9/12/2015 Bp Gregory Orrin Brewer. m 5/17/1994 Barbara J Trow c 1.

TROWBRIDGE, Dustin E (NY) St George's Church, 105 Grand St, Newburgh NY 12550 **S Geo's Epis Ch Newburgh NY 2012-** B Glen Dale WV 1976 s Ronald & Patricia. BA Ya 1998; BA Ya 1998; MA Indiana U 2005; MPA Indiana U 2005; MDiv GTS 2009. D 6/20/2009 Bp Cate Waynick P 1/9/2010 Bp Wayne Wright. m 10/17/2014 John Cleveland Howell. S Thos Epis Ch New Windsor NY 2012-2014; Assoc R Trin Par Wilmington DE 2009-2012.

TRUAX, Heidi M (Ct) 31 Hilltop Rd, Sharon CT 06069 **R Trin Ch Lakeville CT 2009-** B Santa Ana CA 1955 d Fred & Bette. BA UC Santa Barbara 1979; MDiv Ya Berk 2004. D 6/11/2005 P 1/28/2006 Bp Andrew Donnan Smith. c 4. Asst. P Epis Dio Honduras Tegucigalpa 2008-2009; Cur Trin Epis Ch Southport CT 2005-2008.

TRUBY, Laura (Ore) 14221 Livesay Rd, Oregon City OR 97045 **R All SS Ch Portland OR 2012-** B Evanston IL 1947 d Keith & Marilynn. BA Cornell Coll 1969; MDiv S Paul TS 1972. D 6/10/2000 P 12/9/2000 Bp Edward Lewis Lee Jr. m 5/16/1971 Thomas Lavern Truby c 2. S Jas Chr Lincoln City OR 2010-2011; Int Montavilla Meth Ch Portland OR 2007-2009; Int Chr Epis Ch Owosso MI 2004-2006; Trin Epis Ch Flushing MI 2004; Ch Of The Redeem Elgin IL 2003; Cur, Asst to the R S Thos Epis Ch Battle Creek MI 2000-2001; Pstr Schoolcraft Meth Ch Schoolcraft MI 1992-1998; Pstr Coloma Meth Ch Coloma MI 1987-1992; Pstr Faith Meth Ch Bridgeman MI 1985-1986; Assoc Min First Meth Ch Des Plaines MI 1978-1981; Pstr Bethel Meth Ch Chicago IL 1975-1977.

TRUE, Jerry Erwin (WMass) 2612 Brightside Ct, Cape Coral FL 33991 B Fulton NY 1939 s Lisle & Marjorie. BLS Amer Intl Coll 1976; MDiv GTS 1979. D

T

6/1/1979 P 12/8/1979 Bp Alexander D Stewart. m 12/28/2015 David C Melrose. P-in-c Gr Ch Chicopee MA 2007-2011; R S Lk's Epis Ch Attica NY 1983-2005; Asst S Mich's-On-The-Heights Worcester MA 1979-1983; Yth Cmsn Dio Wstrn Massachusetts Springfield 1979-1982; Pres Stndg Com Dio Wstrn New York Tonawanda NY 2000-2002, Dioc Coun 1987-1999. Affirming Angl Catholicism Of No Amer 1995. jerry5185@aol.com

TRUE, Timothy E (SanD) 1550 S 14th Ave, Yuma AZ 85364 **S Paul's Ch Yuma AZ 2015-** B Oxnard CA 1968 s Daniel & Cheryl. AB U CA 1993; MDiv Sewanee: The U So, TS 2013; MDiv The TS at The U So 2013. D 12/28/2012 Bp Gary Richard Lillibridge P 7/7/2013 Bp David Mitchell Reed. m 9/11/1993 Holly K Robinson c 5. S Lk's Epis Ch San Antonio TX 2013-2015; Trst, TMI - The Epis Sch of Texas Dio W Texas San Antonio TX 2014-2015, Mem, Cmsn for Liturg and Mus 2013-2015. rectorstpaulsyuma@gmail.com

TRUELOVE, Kenneth Elwood (WA) 508 S Mckinley Ave, Champaign IL 61821 **Int S Laurence Epis Ch Effingham IL 2000-; S Mary's Ch Robinson IL 2000-** B Terre Haute IN 1939 s Herman & Flora. BA DePauw U 1961; BD SMU 1964; PDS 1970. D 6/6/1970 P 3/31/1971 Bp Robert Lionne DeWitt. m 5/29/1963 Theresa Truelove. S Andr's Ch Paris IL 2005-2006; Trin Epis Ch Mattoon IL 2004-2011, 1995-1998; S Andr's Ch Livingston MT 2002-2003; Chr Ch Cape Girardeau MO 1998-1999; Dio Springfield Springfield IL 1995-1998; Trin Ch S Chas MO 1994-1995; Non-par 1982-1993; Dio Washington Washington DC 1974-1983; R Emm Washington DC 1974-1982; Asst S Jas The Less Philadelphia PA 1972-1974; Non-par 1970-1972.

TRUIETT SR, Melvin Edward (Md) 2322 Ivy Ave, Baltimore MD 21214 **Asst S Jas' Epis Ch Baltimore MD 2013-; Ret 2001-** B Baltimore MD 1936 s Melvin & Edna. U of Baltimore. D 6/26/1983 Bp David Keller Leighton Sr P 6/1/1994 Bp Robert Manning Moody. m 7/20/1963 Alice G Truiett c 3. Int Ch Of The H Cov Baltimore MD 2002-2007; R Epis Ch Of The Redeem Oklahoma City OK 1994-2001, Asst 1988-1990; Asst S Paul's Cathd Oklahoma City OK 1991-1993; P-in-c H Fam Ch Langston OK 1989-1994; Asst S Steph's Epis Ch Winston Salem NC 1986-1988; Asst S Anne In Winston Salem NC 1985-1988; D Gr And S Ptr's Ch Baltimore MD 1983-1984.

TRUITT, Ann Harris (Va) 1132 N Ivanhoe St, Arlington VA 22205 B Burlington NC 1958 d James & Janie. BS U NC at Greensboro 1981; BS U NC at Greensboro 1981; MS The Amer U 1984; MTS Wesley TS 2010. D 6/8/2013 P 12/14/2013 Bp Shannon Sherwood Johnston. m 7/19/2014 Mary Catherine Miller. D Ch Of The Resurr Alexandria VA 2013-2014.

TRUJILLO NIETO, Jose David (EcuC) B Quito Ecuador 1950 s Jose & Laura. D 2/18/2011 Bp Luis Fernando Ruiz Restrepo. m 11/24/2006 Lidia Santos. Iglesia Epis Del Ecuador Quito 2011-2015.

TRULL, Charles Scott (NJ) 327 s juniper st, Philadelphia PA 19107 **Dioc Bd Revs 1990-; Dn Monmouth Convoc 1990-; Persident of Pstr Care Com NOHS 1983-; R S Mary-by-the-Sea 1979-** B New Brunswick NJ 1941 s George & Sarah. BA U NC 1965; MDiv UTS 1977. D 6/11/1977 Bp Paul Moore Jr P 12/1/1977 Bp Harold Louis Wright. c 3. Chr Ch Riverton NJ 2003-2005; Ch Of S Mary's By The Sea Pt Pleas Bch NJ 1979-2003; Cur Ch Of The Atone Tenafly NJ 1977-1979. Soc of S Jn the Evang 1977.

TRUMBLE JR, John Louis (O) 51 Walnut St, Tiffin OH 44883 B Martin SD 1950 s John & Florence. BA W Virginia Wesleyan Coll 1980; MDiv VTS 1983. D 6/1/1983 P 4/1/1984 Bp Robert Poland Atkinson. m 5/26/1979 Rebecca Trumble c 2. Old Trin Epis Ch Tiffin OH 2000-2007; Trin Epis Shared Mnstry Tiffin OH 1995-2007; Mssnr No Cntrl Cluster 1990-1995; The No Cntrl Cluster Buckhannon WV 1990-1995; Gr Epis Ch Elkins WV 1986-1990; Cur S Mart-In-The-Fields Summerville WV 1983-1986; S Martins-In-Fields Summersville WV 1983-1986.

TRUMBLE, Jordan E (WVa) D 6/3/2017 Bp Mark A Van Koevering.

TRUMBORE, Frederick Rhue (Va) xxxxxxxxxxxx, delete all of above address, Woodstock VA 22664 B Wilkes-Barre PA 1934 s Frederick & Leah. BA Leh 1956; MDiv PDS 1960; Cert Ldrshp Acad for New Directions 1987. D 6/16/1960 P 12/1/1960 Bp Frederick Warnecke. m 11/5/1960 Jean Killam Trumbore c 2. Int Meade Memi Epis Ch White Post VA 2003-2004; Int Emm Ch Woodstock VA 2001-2003; S Andr's Ch Mt Jackson VA 2001-2003; Dio Virginia Richmond VA 1996-1999; Chr Epis Ch Luray VA 1984-1999; Ch Of Our Sav Okeechobee FL 1969-1984; Vic Ch Of The H Chld Ormond Bch FL 1964-1969; Vic S Mich's Of The Intsn Ft Lauderdale FL 1962-1964; P-in-c S Geo's Epis Ch Olyphant PA 1960-1962. LAND, RWF; Phi Alpha Theta (Natl Hist Soc) 1956.

TRUSCOTT, Nancy Jean Baldwin (Alb) 10 Orchard Street, Delhi NY 13753 **D S Jn's Ch Delhi NY 2003-** B Rockville Centre NY 1945 d Raymond & Jean. SUNY; BS SUNY 1968. D 1/18/2003 Bp David John Bena. m 7/20/1968 David Winston Truscott c 3. Dioc Coun Mem Dio Albany Greenwich NY 2005-2010. Ord of the DOK 2004.

TRUTNER, Thomas Kirk (Cal) 22 Cedar Lane, Orinda CA 94563 **Ret 2004-** B Oakland CA 1935 s Herman & Everlyn. BA U CA 1958; MDiv PrTS 1961. D 6/19/1982 P 12/1/1982 Bp William Edwin Swing. m 4/5/2002 Roxanna Trutner c 3. S Steph's Epis Ch Orinda CA 1991-2004, P 1983-; Serv Presb Ch 1967-1970; Ecum Guest Pstr In Hamburg 1965-1966; Serv Presb Ch 1961-1965.

TRYGAR SR, Earl P (Be) RR 2, Box 2229, Moscow PA 18444 **R S Mk's Epis Ch Moscow PA 2003-** B Scranton,PA 1951 s Walter & Beverly. Kutztown U; Penn. D 4/6/2002 P 10/6/2002 Bp Paul Victor Marshall. m 12/19/1970 Mary Helen Shorten c 2. Asst S Lk's Ch Scranton PA 2002-2003.

TRYTTEN, Patricia Shoemaker (Oly) 310 N K St, Tacoma WA 98403 **Asst S Matthews Auburn WA 2012-** B Philadelphia PA 1943 d William & Elizabeth. BA Parsons Coll 1964; MDiv CDSP 1995. D 6/24/1995 P 1/1/1996 Bp Richard Lester Shimpfky. P-in-c Chr Ch Tacoma WA 1997-2008; Int S Andr's Ch Ben Lomond CA 1995-1997.

TSAI, Ching-Yi (Tai) **Dio Taiwan Taipei 2014-** B Taiwan 1964 d Kun-Tse & Chang. D 8/23/2014 Bp Jung-Hsin Lai. m 11/12/1994 Kuang-Yu Wang c 2.

TSOU, Tsai-Hsin (Tai) 1 F #5 Ln 348 Lishan St, Neihu Dist, Taipei 11450 Taiwan **Dio Taiwan Taipei 2010-** B Yilan County Taiwan 1976 AE St Jn's U 1997; RSB Fu Jen Cath U 2009. D 7/31/2010 P 1/6/2012 Bp Jung-Hsin Lai. m 7/19/2003 Li-Chun Hsu.

TUBBS, James Collin (Tenn) 5256 Village Trce, Nashville TN 37211 **Ret 2004-** B Chattanooga TN 1940 s Eugene & Delphi. BS U of Tennessee 1976; MDiv Sewanee: The U So, TS 1981. D 6/21/1981 Bp William F Gates Jr P 4/21/1982 Bp William Evan Sanders. m 4/22/1960 Carole Elizabeth Tubbs c 2. R S Mths Ch Nashville TN 1998-2004; Dio E Tennessee Knoxville TN 1986-1998; Vic S Jos The Carpenter Sevierville TN 1986-1998; S Jn's Epis Cathd Knoxville TN 1981-1985.

TUBBS, Suzanne Freeman (Tex) 604 Tryon Ct, Tyler TX 75703 B Dallas TX 1944 d Linton & Martha. BA SMU 1966; MEd U of No Texas 1982; MDiv Sewanee: The U So, TS 1999. D 10/6/1991 Bp Joseph Thomas Heistand P 6/18/1999 Bp Henry Irving Louttit. m 8/6/1977 Michael Tubbs c 4. S Fran Epis Ch Tyler TX 2005-2010; S Paul's Ch Macon GA 2003-2004; Assoc R S Pat's Epis Ch Atlanta GA 2002-2003; Vic S Jn's Epis Ch Bainbridge GA 1999-2002; Dir Of Sprtl Dio Arizona Phoenix AZ 1994-1996; D Gr St Pauls Epis Ch Tucson AZ 1991-1996.

TUCHOLS, Franklin Joseph (Ct) 661 Old Post Rd, Fairfield CT 06824 B Buffalo NY 1945 s Franklin & Florance. MA CUA 1971; MDiv St Jn Vianney Sem 1971; MSW SUNY 1985. Rec 8/20/2013 as Priest Bp Ian Theodore Douglas. m 3/27/2010 Robert Valle.

TUCK, Michael G (WMass) 114 George St, Providence RI 02906 **Dio Wstrn Massachusetts Springfield 2012-** B Bryn Mawr PA 1977 s Ralph & Mary. AB Br 1999; MA Coll of the Resurr 2009. D 7/4/2009 Bp Stephen Platten. m 8/20/2005 Annemarie Haftl c 2. Brown/RISD Chapl Dio Rhode Island Providence RI 2009-2012; Brown/RISD Chapl S Steph's Ch Providence RI 2009-2012. fr. michael.tuck@gmail.com

TUCKER, Alice Elizabeth (Tex) 2900 Bunny Run, Austin TX 78746 B Bomi Hills LR 1958 d James & Marjory. BA Swarthmore Coll 1980; MDiv VTS 1987. D 6/11/1987 Bp Gordon Taliaferro Charlton P 6/1/1988 Bp Anselmo Carral-Solar. c 1. S Steph's Epis Sch Austin TX 1993-2008; Assoc R S Thos The Apos Epis Ch Houston TX 1988-1993; DRE S Steph's Epis Ch Houston TX 1982-1984.

TUCKER, Douglas Jon (Tex) 2 Barque Ln., Galveston TX 77554 B Cedar Rapids IA 1942 s Robert & Dorothy. BS U of Nebraska 1965; MS GW 1976; MDiv Sewanee: The U So, TS 1980. D 6/7/1980 Bp Walter Cameron Righter P 6/25/1981 Bp Maurice Manuel Benitez. m 4/13/1968 Cheryl Tucker c 3. Int Gr Ch Galveston TX 2011-2012; Int S Geo's Epis Ch Texas City TX 2011; Hosp Chapl U of Texas Med Branch Galveston TX 2010; Int H Trin Epis Ch Dickinson TX 2008-2010; R S Cyp's Ch Lufkin TX 2004-2008; Assoc S Jn The Div Houston TX 2001-2004; Dio Texas Houston TX 1999-2008, Epis Fndt 1990-1998; R S Alb's Epis Ch Waco TX 1993-2001; R Chr Ch Nacogdoches TX 1983-1992; Asst S Chris's Ch League City TX 1981-1983; Asst Chapl Sewanee U So TS Sewanee TN 1980-1981.

TUCKER, Elizabeth (CFla) 1020 Keyes Ave, Winter Park FL 32789 **D All SS Ch Of Winter Pk Winter Pk FL 2006-** B Teaneck NJ 1956 d Peter & Jean. D 12/9/2006 Bp John Wadsworth Howe. m 11/22/1980 John W Tucker c 2.

TUCKER, Gene Richard (CPa) 212 Penn Street, Huntingdon PA 16652 **S Jn's Epis Ch Huntingdon PA 2015-; P-in-c S Jn's Ch Centralia IL 2008-** B David City NE 1947 s Jesse & Clara. BA Eastman Sch of Mus 1969; MDiv VTS 2004. D 6/29/2004 P 3/12/2005 Bp Peter Hess Beckwith. m 10/17/1981 Deborah K Tucker c 2. The Cathd Ch Of S Paul Springfield IL 2014-2015; R Trin Ch Mt Vernon IL 2007-2014; Asst Hale Dnry Team Mnstry 2004-2007; Dn Estrn Dnry 2009-2013; COM Dio Springfield 2006-2012; Secy Dio Springfield 2005-2013. Mem Pi Kappa Lambda Mus hon Soc 1969. friartuck3@yahoo.com

TUCKER, James M (NJ) 130 Prince St., Bordentown NJ 08505 **D-in-c Chr Ch Bordentown NJ 2008-** B Long Branch NJ 1974 s James & Caroline. BA Elon U 1997; MDiv VTS 2008. D 6/7/2008 Bp George Edward Councell P 12/7/2008 Bp Sylvestre Donato Romero. m 7/2/2010 Doan H Tucker.

TUCKER, James Thomas (Tex) 107 Oakstone Dr., Chapel Hill NC 27514 B Alexandria VA 1952 BA U of Texas 1974; MDiv VTS 1981. D 6/18/1981 P 2/1/1982 Bp Maurice Manuel Benitez. m 6/10/1978 Virginia Moyer Tucker c 2. R Ch Of The Epiph Houston TX 1996-2013; Chapl S Lk's Epis Hosp Houston TX

1996; Asst Palmer Memi Ch Houston TX 1986-1995; Asst S Ptr's Ch Pasadena TX 1982-1986; none none.

TUCKER, Jared Horton (Los) 3227 N Rancho La Carlota Rd, Covina CA 91724 **Died 3/21/2017** B San Francisco CA 1930 s Hyman & Gertrude. BA Whittier Coll 1953; MD U CA 1958. D 11/1/1995 Bp Chester Lovelle Talton. m 1/28/1956 Marilyn Elaine Tucker c 2. Assoc S Barn' Par Pasadena CA 2011; D H Trin Epis Ch Covina CA 1999-2017; D S Jn's Mssn La Verne CA 1997-2000.

TUCKER, Jennifer Lynn (U) D 6/10/2006 Bp Carolyn Tanner Irish P 8/31/2007 Bp Victor Alfonso Scantlebury.

TUCKER, Julia (SVa) 901 Poquoson Cir, Virginia Beach VA 23452 B Norfolk VA 1931 d William & Nell. BA Salem Coll Winston-Salem NC 1953; MA Oklahoma St U 1980. D 1/18/1997 Bp Frank Harris Vest Jr. D S Fran Ch Virginia Bch VA 1997-2002.

TUCKER, Kenneth Merrill (USC) 1502 Greenville Street, Abbeville SC 29620 **Ret 1997-** B Arlington MA 1931 s William & Doris. BS Franklin & Marshall Coll 1953; MDiv Ya Berk 1969. D 6/10/1969 Bp Charles Francis Hall P 12/19/1969 Bp William Henry Marmion. m 2/5/1977 Mary E Martin c 3. Int S Jn's Epis Ch Wilmington NC 2007-2008; Vic Trin Ch Abbeville SC 1994-1997, Actg Vic 2010-2012; Vic S Mich And All Ang' Epis Ch Sonora CA 1990-1994; Vic Episcpoal Ch Of Groveland Groveland CA 1990-1992; P-in-c S Andr's Epis Ch Greenville SC 1988-1989; R Ch Of The Mssh Murphy NC 1986-1988; Vic Gr Ch Mohawk NY 1980-1984; Vic Chr W Burlington NY 1979-1986; R S Jas Epis Ch Westernport MD 1978-1979; Asst S Tim's Ch Catonsville MD 1975-1977; R S Geo's Ch Maynard MA 1972-1975; Cur S Mths Epis Ch E Aurora NY 1971-1972; Vic S Mk's Ch S Paul VA 1969-1971.

TUCKER, Martha D (Pa) **Assoc S Dav's Ch Wayne PA 2014-** D 6/14/2014 Bp Clifton Daniel III.

TUCKER-GRAY, Lisa (Mich) 4225 Walden Dr, Ann Arbor MI 48105 **P S Jn's Ch Plymouth MI 2013-** B Munich Germany 1962 d Whitmore & Svea. DMin SWTS; BA Ohio Wesl 1984; MDiv CDSP 2003. D 12/18/2004 P 7/2/2005 Bp Wendell Nathaniel Gibbs Jr. m 11/9/2012 Kim A Tucker-Gray c 1. S Jn the Bapt Otter Lake MI 2013; Dio Michigan Detroit MI 2006-2013, Cn to the Ordnry 2003-2013; D Nativ Epis Ch Bloomfield Township MI 2005. lisaannegray@me.com

TUCKER-PARSONS, Martha L (ETenn) 8321 Georgetown Bay Dr, Ooltewah TN 37363 **R S Fran Of Assisi Epis Ch Ooltewah TN 2009-** B Knoxville TN 1955 BA U So 1977; MDiv TS 2002; MDiv Sewanee: The U So, TS 2002. D 5/25/2002 P 1/25/2003 Bp Charles Glenn VonRosenberg. c 2. Gr Ch Chattanooga TN 2006-2009; Chapl Hospice of Chattanooga Chattanooga TN 2004-2009; Chapl Memi Hosp Chattanooga TN 2004; Cur St Jas Epis Ch at Knoxville Knoxville TN 2002-2004. rectorsf@comcast.net

TUDELA, Mary Elizabeth (Chi) 4364 Hardy Street, Lihue HI 96766 **Exec Dir Samar Counslg Cntr 2007-; Trst Dio Chicago Chicago IL 2013-** B Ponce Puerto Rico 1954 d Ramon & Edith. BA U IL 1976; MBA Illinois Inst of Tech 1988; MDiv SWTS 2004; Cert FaithBridge 2010; Cert FaithBridge 2010. D 6/19/2004 Bp Bill Persell P 1/19/2005 Bp Victor Alfonso Scantlebury. c 2. Int S Ann's Ch Woodstock IL 2011; Int S Mk's Barrington IL 2008; S Mich's Ch Barrington IL 2007-2008, Assoc 2004-2006. Auth, "Walking My Faith," Trafford, 2011. Wmn of Achievement Honoree Anti-Defamation League 1999.

TUDOR, Richard Beresford (Mo) 3106 Aberdeen Dr, Florissant MO 63033 B Little Rock AR 1942 s Robert & Emily. BA U of Kansas 1966; MDiv CDSP 1971; DMin Eden 1996. D 6/24/1971 Bp George T Masuda P 5/3/1972 Bp John Harris Burt. m 6/22/1974 Elizabeth A Tudor c 4. R S Barn Ch Florissant MO 1989-2008; S Mich's and All Ang' Ch Cartwright ND 1976-1989; Vic S Ptr's Epis Ch Williston ND 1974-1989; Cur S Paul's Ch Akron OH 1971-1973; Plnng Com Dio Missouri S Louis MO 1997-2000, Dept Congrl Dev. 1990-1996, Chair COM 1980-1989. Auth, "The Challenge of Change," *Living Ch*, 2009; Auth, "The Empty Stocking," *Angl Dig*, 2008; Auth, "Feeling the Sqeeze," *Living Ch*, 2007; Auth, "A Long Series of Revolutions," *Angl Dig*, 2005; Auth, "How Firm a Fndt," *Living Ch*, 2005; Auth, "Mar in the Wrong Aisle," *Living Ch*, 2003; Auth, "The Flow Goes On," *Living Ch*, 1990. Unit Mnstry Team of the Year US-A 1989.

TUDOR, William Ellis (Ind) 3021 94th Ave E, Edgewood WA 98371 **Pres Advocates for Immigrants in Detention 2016-; Assoc Chr Ch Tacoma WA 1996-** B Iowa City IA 1931 s Hugh & Eugenie. BA U of Puget Sound 1955; MA U of Iowa 1956; BD CDSP 1959. D 6/29/1959 Bp Stephen F Bayne Jr P 6/11/1960 Bp William F Lewis. m 6/9/1956 Jean Tudor c 2. Cn Pstr Chr Ch Cathd Indianapolis IN 1983-1996; Assoc R Chr Ch Grosse Pointe Grosse Pointe Farms MI 1978-1983; R Gr Ch Newport News VA 1969-1978; Mssnr Ch In Colombia 1962-1969; Cur S Mk's Cathd Seattle WA 1959-1962. Auth, "Theo's Tricks," *Theo's Tricks*, GrecoPress, 2013.

TUDOR-FOLEY, Hugh (Ct) 3168 Dona Sofia Dr, Studio City CA 91604 **Mem, Cler Educ Com Dio San Diego San Diego CA 2007-** B Wharton TX 1940 s Edred & Aileen. BA U of Houston 1972; MA Fairfield U 1988; MDiv Ya Berk 1991. D 2/23/1992 P 10/31/1992 Bp Clarence Nicholas Coleridge. m 3/5/1978 Rebecca Tudor-Foley. Int R The Epis Ch Of The Gd Shpd Hemet CA 2008-2010; Int R S Paul's Ch Yuma AZ 2007-2008; Int R S Jn's Ch Stamford

CT 2006-2007; Chapl Silver Hill Hosp New Canaan CT 2006-2007; Int R All SS Memi Ch Navesink NJ 2004-2005; Int R Trin Ch Rutland VT 2002-2004; Asst R Chr Ch Greenwich CT 1995-2002; Assoc R St. Barth Ch New York NY 1993-1995; Cur Gr Epis Ch Norwalk CT 1992-1993; DRE S Lk's Par Darien CT 1990-1991. Auth, "Video," *A Gift of Hope*, Miami Proj to Cure Paralysis; Auth, "Video," *Formation in Cmnty*, Berkeley at Yale; Auth, "Video Inst of Bp Andr Smith," *Video Consecration of Bp Jas Curry & Wilfredo Ramos-Orenz*, Dio Connecticut. Assn of Profsnl Chapl 2006; Inerim Mnstry Ntwk 2002; Int Mnstry Ntwk 2001; NAEMS 2006; OHC 1998; Pres Greenwich Fllshp Cler 1999-2002; RACA 2001. Peer Evaltn AIBS SPARS 2011; Peer Evaltn SAMHSA 2011. frhugh@allsaintssfl.org

TUELL IV, Henry Offord (Mont) **Dio New York New York NY 2017-; The GTS New York NY 2014-** D 3/7/2017 Bp Charles Franklin Brookhart Jr.

TUFF, Roy Wynn (SwFla) 401 W. Henry St, Punta Gorda FL 33950 **R Ch Of The Gd Shpd Punta Gorda FL 2010-; Chapl Gd Shpd Schools 2010-** B Hays KS 1962 s Robert & Judy. BA Florida Gulf Coast U 2000; MDiv Sewanee: The U So, TS 2003. D 6/14/2003 P 12/20/2003 Bp John Bailey Lipscomb. m 7/13/1985 Maria Renee Tuff c 3. Supply Cler Dio SW Florida 2009-2010; Chapl S Steph's Epis Sch Bradenton FL 2003-2010; Chr Ch Bradenton FL 2003-2009. tuffroy@gmail.com

TULIS, Edward (CNY) B 1931 D 6/22/1957 Bp Anson Phelps Stokes Jr P 1/18/1958 Bp Frederic Cunningham Lawrence. m 8/30/1952 Roselyn Johnson.

TULL, Sandra Ann (Fla) 1021 Oxford Dr, Saint Augustine FL 32084 **P prison Mnstry Dio FL Jacksonville 2000-; co-chair Cmsn on prison and Related Mnstry Dio FL 2014-** B Plattsburg NY 1943 d Henry & Dorothy. RN U of Miami 1965; BS S Josephs Coll No Windham ME 1985; MA Norwich U 1987; Dio FL Sch of Angl Stds 2002; Dio FL Sch of Angl Stds 2003; Dio Fl Sch of Angl Stds 2004. D 11/9/2004 P 5/10/2005 Bp Samuel Johnson Howard. m 1/28/1967 John Tull c 2. Asst The Epis Ch of The Redeem Jacksonville FL 2013-2015; Asst Ch Of The Nativ Jacksonville FL 2008-2010; P-in-c Ch Of The Epiph Jacksonville FL 2007-2013; chair Cmsn on Prison and Realted Mnstry 2006-2009; Eccl Crt Mem Dio Florida Jacksonville 2006-2008, Chair, Cmsn on Prison Mnstry 2005-2011, Prison Mnstry 2004-.

TULLER, Stuart (Va) 2132 Owls Cove Ln, Reston VA 20191 B Great Barrington MA 1935 s Stuart & Mary. New Coll, U of Edinburgh, Scotland; BA Amh 1957; MDiv VTS 1960. D 6/4/1960 P 6/1/1961 Bp Robert McConnell Hatch. m 6/20/1959 Ann Worthington Howard c 3. R S Chris's Ch Springfield VA 1965-1971; Vic All SS Ch Hanover PA 1963-1965; Cur S Matt's Ch Bedford NY 1960-1963.

TULLY, Coleen Marie (Minn) 101 N 5th St, Marshall MN 56258 B Menomonie WI 1957 d James & Sally Rae. U of WI 1989. D 6/12/2005 Bp Daniel Lee Swenson P 12/11/2005 Bp James Louis Jelinek. m 4/12/1990 Steven Thomsen c 4.

TULLY, William M (NY) 1810 Loma St, Santa Barbara CA 93103 B Glendale CA 1947 s Andrew & Leah. BA Occ 1968; MS Col 1969; MDiv GTS 1974. D 3/24/1974 Bp Harold Louis Wright P 9/29/1974 Bp Paul Moore Jr. m 6/16/1968 Jane W Tully c 2. R St. Barth Ch New York NY 1994-2012; R S Columba's Ch Washington DC 1980-1994; Assoc S Fran Ch Potomac MD 1976-1980; Cur The Ch Of The Epiph New York NY 1974-1976.

TUMMINIO HANSEN, Danielle (Ct) 12 Quincy Ave, Quincy MA 02169 **Epis TS Of The SW Austin TX 2016-** B Manhattan NY 1981 d Gregory & Marguerite. BA Ya 2003; MDiv Ya Berk 2006; MDiv Ya Berk 2006; STM Ya Berk 2008; STM Ya Berk 2008; PhD Bos 2012. D 6/12/2010 Bp Ian Theodore Douglas P 1/15/2011 Bp Laura Ahrens. m 9/4/2010 Eric T Hansen c 1. Groton Sch Groton MA 2015-2016; The Ch Of Our Redeem Lexington MA 2012-2013; S Anne's In The Fields Epis Ch Lincoln MA 2012; Chr Ch Quincy MA 2011.

TUNKLE, Paul Dennis (Md) 200 Common Rd, Dresden ME 04342 B New York NY 1950 s Samuel & Sophie. BS-cl U of Maine 1981; MDiv-cl GTS 1984; DMin Drew U 1993. D 6/2/1984 Bp Frederick Barton Wolf P 6/1/1985 Bp Robert Whitridge Estill. m 2/28/1972 Judith Elaine Tunkle c 2. S Phil's Ch Wiscasset ME 2014-2016; R The Ch Of The Redeem Baltimore MD 2001-2014; R St Jas Epis Ch and Sch Alexandria LA 1993-2001; R H Trin Ch So River NJ 1988-1993; Asst S Lk's Ch Salisbury NC 1984-1987; COM Dio Maryland Baltimore MD 2012-2014; Pres - Stndg Com Dio Wstrn Louisiana Alexandria LA 1998-2000, Chair - COM 1995-1997. OHC 1983.

TUNNELL, Janet A (SwFla) St Thomas Episcopal Church, 1200 Snell Isle Blvd NE, St Petersburg FL 33704 **All SS Ch Tarpon Spgs FL 2017-** B Chicago IL 1974 d William & Karen. Illinois St U; BS U of So Florida 1998; MDiv Epis TS Of The SW 2013; MDiv Epis TS of the SW 2013. D 12/8/2012 P 6/29/2013 Bp Dabney Tyler Smith. m 5/20/2000 Michael E Tunnell. Asst S Thos' Epis Ch St Petersburg FL 2013-2016.

TUNNEY, Elisabeth Ellerich (LI) **Dio Long Island Garden City NY 2014-; P-in-c S Paul's Ch Patchogue NY 2011-** B New York NY 1956 d Joseph & Lillian. BA Smith 1978; MBA Wstrn New Engl Coll 1990; MDiv GTS 2011. D 3/19/2011 Bp Gordon Scruton P 9/25/2011 Bp Lawrence C Provenzano. Soc for the Comp of the H Cross 2006. liz.tunney@gmail.com

T

TUOHY, James Fidelis (Ala) 3842 11th Ave S, Birmingham AL 35222 B Thurles IE 1937 s Denis & Bridget. MDiv All Hallows Coll 1961; BA U of Alabama 1971; DMin Van 1978. Rec 12/1/1980 as Priest Bp Furman Charles Stough. m 10/16/1970 Elizabeth H Tuohy c 2. R S Andr's Ch Montevallo AL 1999; S Mich And All Ang Anniston AL 1992-1999; Assoc S Andrews's Epis Ch Birmingham AL 1980-1992; Chapl U of Alabama in Birmingham 1980-1992; Asst RC Ch 1961-1970.

TURBERG, Judith Evelyn (Az) 100 S Laura Ln, Casa Grande AZ 85194 **Rgstr/ Chapl ETS at Claremont Claremont CA 2002-** B Glen Cove NY 1945 d Joseph & Evelyn. BA NWU 1967; MS Adel 1975; USC 1977; MDiv ETSBH 1998. D 6/13/1998 Bp Robert Marshall Anderson P 1/9/1999 Bp Frederick Houk Borsch. Vic S Ptr's Ch Casa Grande AZ 2011-2013; Bloy Hse Claremont CA 2002-2011; Asst/Assoc S Ambr Par Claremont CA 2000-2002; S Thos' Mssn Hacienda Hgts CA 1999; D S Mich And All Ang Par Corona Dl Mar CA 1998-1999.

TURBEVILLE, Keith (Dal) P.O. Box 292, Buda TX 78610 **R H Trin Ch Rockwall TX 2014-** B Charleston SC 1966 s Norman & Sandra. BS SUNY 1991; The Prot Epis TS 2005; MDiv Epis TS of the SW 2008. D 5/24/2008 Bp Peter J Lee P 12/4/2008 Bp Gary Richard Lillibridge. m 4/27/1991 Karen Turbeville c 3. Assoc Chr Ch Greenville SC 2011-2014; Vic S Eliz's Epis Ch Buda TX 2008-2011; Dir of Yth and Fam Mnstry S Jas' Epis Ch Leesburg VA 2002-2005.

TURCZYN, Jeffrey Robert (NY) 40 Running Hill Road, Scarborough ME 04074 B Bronx NY 1945 s Steve & Maria. BA Villanova U 1968; STB CUA 1971; STL CUA 1972; MS Col 1988. Rec 6/24/1995 as Priest Bp Walter Decoster Dennis Jr. m 10/10/1987 Kathleen Scott. Trin Ch Saugerties NY 1998-2013; Dio New York New York NY 1998-2008; Asstg P S Mich's Ch New York NY 1995-1997; Serv RC Ch 1971-1987.

TURK, Davette Lois (Fla) 8256 Wallingford Hills Ln, Jacksonville FL 32256 B Asbury Park NJ 1935 d David & Regina. GTS; BA Villanova U 1960; MA La Salle U 1985. D 6/16/1985 P 12/15/1985 Bp Frank S Cerveny. Int R The Epis Ch of The Redeem Jacksonville FL 2007, Asst R 1986-1989; Fresh Mnstrs Jacksonville FL 1998-2004; Assoc R All SS Epis Ch Jacksonville FL 1989-1997.

TURMO, Joel Lee (WMich) 9798 E BC Ave, Richland MI 49083 **R S Tim Ch Richland MI 2012-; Dioc Concil Dio Wstrn Michigan Kalamazoo MI 2013-** B Carson City MI 1969 s David & Hazel. BS Cntrl Michigan U 1995; MS Wstrn Michigan U 1998; MDiv TS 2008; MDiv Sewanee: The U So, TS 2008. D 12/22/2007 P 6/28/2008 Bp Russell Edward Jacobus. m 5/7/1995 Melissa B Turmo c 2. Dnry Yth Coordntr S Greg's Ch Boca Raton FL 2008-2012; Dio SE Florida Miami 2008-2012.

TURNAGE, Benjamin Whitfield (Ala) 1124 Lakeview Crescent, Birmingham AL 35205 B Charleston,SC 1945 s Benjamin & Alexandra. BS Charleston Sthrn U 1971; MS Clemson U 1973; MDiv VTS 1976. D 6/18/1976 P 1/1/1977 Bp Gray Temple. m 3/24/1984 Melissa R Turnage c 2. R Trin Ch Long Green MD 1988-2004; Chr Ch Macon GA 1985-1988; R Ch Of The Epiph Atlanta GA 1980-1984; Asst S Phil's Ch Charleston SC 1977-1980; Asst S Lk's Epis Ch Hilton Hd Island SC 1976-1977. benjamint035@gmail.com

TURNAGE, Richard Wentworth (SC) 1920 Rimsdale Dr, Myrtle Beach SC 29575 B Hartsville SC 1929 s Louis & Vivian. BS Davidson Coll 1950. D 9/14/1997 Bp Edward Lloyd Salmon Jr. m 3/22/1952 Joan McIver Turnage. The Epis Ch Of The Resurr Myrtle Bch SC 1999; Pstr Care Cler All SS 1997-1999.

TURNBULL, Henry George (RI) 6465 River Birchfield Rd, Jamesville NY 13078 **Died 12/31/2016** B Providence RI 1931 s Henry & Esther. BA Br 1953; BD Nash 1960. D 6/23/1956 P 3/1/1957 Bp John S Higgins. Ret 1992-2016; R S Jn The Evang Ch Newport RI 1960-1991; Cur Trin Ch Newport RI 1957-1960; Cur S Jn's Ch Barrington RI 1956-1957.

TURNBULL, Malcolm Edward (Va) 13342 Beachcrest Dr, Chesterfield VA 23832 B Asheville NC 1937 s Arthur & Betty. BA U of Virginia 1958; MDiv VTS 1970. D 5/28/1970 Bp Philip Alan Smith P 12/13/1970 Bp Edwin Lani Hanchett. m 7/1/1960 Nell J Turnbull c 2. R S Barth's Ch Richmond VA 1977-2002; Chapl Virginia Epis Sch Lynchburg VA 1976-1977; Asst R Bruton Par Williamsburg VA 1973-1976; Chapl W&M in Virginia 1973-1976; Vic Emm Epis Ch Kailua HI 1971-1973; Asst R Ch Of The H Nativ Honolulu HI 1970-1971; Dn, Reg XII Dio Virginia Richmond VA 1980-1984. AAPC 1989-2013.

TURNER, Alice Camp (WNY) 90 South Dr, Lackawanna NY 14218 B Buffalo NY 1940 d Russell & Grace. AAS Erie Cmnty Coll 1960. D 6/11/1983 Bp Harold Barrett Robinson. m 10/1/1960 Richard Howard Turner c 4. D S Dav's Epis Ch Buffalo NY 1989-2006; S Thos Ch Buffalo NY 1983-1989.

TURNER, Alicia Beth (WNC) 900 Centre Park Dr # B, Asheville NC 28805 **S Thos Epis Ch Burnsville NC 2016-** B Raleigh NC 1962 d George & Alice. BA Carson-Newman Coll 1984; MDiv SE Bapt TS 1989. D 5/29/2004 Bp Robert Carroll Johnson Jr P 5/15/2005 Bp Porter Taylor. Mssnr for Adult Vocation Dio Wstrn No Carolina Asheville NC 2010-2015, 2004-2005; Assoc Ch Of The H Cross Valle Crucis NC 2005-2009. strector@gmail.com

TURNER, Amy (CFla) 1100 Sam Perry Blvd, Fredericksburg VA 22401 **H Trin Epis Acad Melbourne FL 2016-; Vauters Ch Loretto VA 2015-** B Winchester VA 1982 d Philip & Barbara. AB Washington U 2004; MDiv VTS 2010; MEd U of Mary Washington 2012. D 1/9/2010 P 1/8/2011 Bp William Michie Klusmeyer. m 7/10/2010 William Turner. Hanover w Brunswick Par - S Jn King Geo VA 2016; S Ptr's Port Royal Port Royal VA 2013-2014; CPE Res Mary Washington Hosp 2010-2011. Auth, "Nurturing a Fragile Faith: An Intersection of Rel Communities and the Mentally Handicapped," VTS, 2010.

TURNER, Anne (Va) 5814 19th St N, Arlington VA 22205 **S Tim's Ch Herndon VA 2016-** B Springfield OH 1971 d Michael & Linnea. BA W&M 1993; MA Shakespeare Inst U of Birgmingham 1996; MDiv Ya Berk 2003. D 6/14/2003 Bp Jun Bryson Chane P 12/22/2003 Bp Allen Lyman Bartlett Jr. m 5/30/1998 Stephen Baldwin Watts c 2. Emm Ch Middleburg VA 2016; Asst S Mary's Epis Ch Arlington VA 2009-2016; Assoc Gr Ch Amherst MA 2008; Asst R Gr Epis Ch Alexandria VA 2003-2007.

TURNER, Arlie Raymond (RG) 397 Old Offen PO Rd, Traphill NC 28685 B Huntington WV 1939 s Carl & Pauline. BA Marshall U 1967; MA Marshall U 1971; MDiv VTS 1985. D 6/5/1985 Bp Robert Poland Atkinson P 12/19/1985 Bp William Franklin Carr. m 8/2/1963 Cora Dean Turner c 2. P-in-c Ch Of The H Sprt Gallup NM 2005-2007; R H Sprt Epis Ch El Paso TX 1996-2005; Assoc S Matt's Ch Charleston WV 1992-1996; R S Tim's In The Vlly Hurricane WV 1985-1991. padrepete39@hotmail.com

TURNER, Bonnie L (NMich) 510 E Park Dr, Peshtigo WI 54157 **Non-par 1994-; Gr Epis Ch Menominee MI 1994-** B Escanaba MI 1947 BS U of Wisconsin 1973; MA Viterbo U 1994. D 3/17/1994 P 10/1/1994 Bp Thomas Kreider Ray. m 6/10/1967 John Turner.

TURNER, Brian William (CFla) 1204 Foxridge Pl, Melbourne FL 32940 **Epis Ch of the Blessed Redeem Palm Bay FL 2017-** B Columbus OH 1980 s James & Victoria. BA OH SU 2003; MDiv VTS 2010. D 6/12/2010 Bp Thomas Edward Breidenthal P 1/8/2011 Bp William Michie Klusmeyer. m 7/10/2010 Amy Turner. Int S Paul's Owens King Geo VA 2013-2016; Chapl Trin Ch Fredericksbrg VA 2013-2014, Asst R 2010-2013; Chapl UMW Cbury Campus Mnstry 2010-2014. Auth, "Pro Christo Per Ecclesiam: A Hist of Coll Mnstry in the Epis Ch," 2010. revbrianwturner@gmail.com

TURNER, Carl Francis (NY) 1 W 53rd St, New York NY 10019 **R S Thos Ch New York NY 2014-** B Kingston-upon-Hull UK 1960 s Albert & Vera. BA St Chad's Coll U of Durham 1981; PG Cert in Theol St Steph's Hse 1985; MTh Westminster Coll, Oxford 1999. Trans 9/13/2014 as Priest Bp Andrew Marion Lenow Dietsche. m 8/18/1990 Alison J Cooper c 3. rector@saintthomaschurch.org

TURNER, Carlton Barry (ECR) 891 Vista Del Brisa, San Luis Obispo CA 93405 **Assoc S Ben's Par Los Osos CA 2014-** B Sutherland NE 1947 s Roy & Joyce. BA U CA San Diego 1970; MDiv Fuller TS 1979; MDiv CDSP 1980. D 10/23/1980 P 4/27/1981 Bp John Lester Thompson III. m 8/16/1980 Ruth Ann Turner c 2. Stwdshp Chair Dio El Camino Real Salinas CA 2002-2012, Stwdshp Cmsn 1997-; R S Steph's Epis Ch Sn Luis Obispo CA 1996-2014; Stwdshp Chair The Epis Dio Nthrn California Sacramento CA 1986-1996; R S Paul's Epis Ch Oroville CA 1985-1996; P-in-c Emm Ch Coos Bay OR 1984-1985; Assoc Chr Ch Par Lake Oswego OR 1983-1984; Asst S Mary's Epis Ch Napa CA 1980-1982.

TURNER JR, Claude Sylvester (SVa) 118 Little John Rd, Williamsburg VA 23185 **Died 10/12/2016** B Martinsville VA 1932 s Claude & Amy. BS Georgia Inst of Tech 1956; MDiv Sewanee: The U So, TS 1969. D 6/24/1969 P 6/29/1970 Bp George P Gunn. m 2/6/2005 Mollie Douglas c 3. Int S Jas Epis Ch Portsmouth VA 1991-1992; Int Emm Ch Franklin VA 1989-1991; Assoc Chr and S Lk's Epis Ch Norfolk VA 1988-1989; Presenter; Unit & Natl Bd Mem EME 1981-1992; R Gr Ch Yorktown Yorktown VA 1976-1988; P S Paul's Ch Petersburg VA 1974-1976; R S Jn's Ch Petersburg VA 1971-1976; Asst S Mich's Ch Richmond VA 1969-1971; Vstng Com Sewanee U So TS Sewanee TN 2007-2010.

TURNER, Clay Howard (USC) 2285 Armstrong Creek Road, Marion NC 28752 B Mobile AL 1938 s Henry & Mary. BA SMU 1961; MDiv Duke DS 1964; ThM Duke 1965; Cert Ang Stud EDS 1966; DMin PrTS 1992. D 6/29/1966 P 6/1/1967 Bp Thomas Augustus Fraser Jr. m 9/1/1961 Jane Rollins Turner c 3. R Ch Of The Adv Spartanburg SC 1990-2004; R S Jn's Ch Roanoke VA 1975-1990; R Trin Epis Ch Statesville NC 1969-1975; Chr Ch Rocky Mt NC 1966-1969; D-in-c S Jn's Ch Battleboro NC 1966-1969; Chair of Exam Chapl Dio SW Virginia Roanoke VA 1981-1990. "The Potter's Wheel," *Selected Sermons through the Cycle of the Liturg Year*, The Reprint Co, 2006. Amer Assn for Mariage and Fam Ther 1973; AAPC 1970; Assn for Couples in Mar Enrichment.

TURNER, Diana Serene (NCal) 605 Tahoe Island Dr., South Lake Tahoe CA 96150 B Sacramento CA 1960 d Robert & Gail. Fuller TS; AS Umpqua Cmnty Coll 1982. D 11/9/1997 P 10/1/1998 Bp Stewart Clark Zabriskie. m 9/20/1991 Teddy Nathan Turner c 2. Assoc Trin Epis Cathd Sacramento CA 2015-2017; Assoc S Andr's In The Highlands Mssn Antelope CA 2006-2015;

Assoc S Geo's Ch Carmichael CA 2001-2006; P S Alb's Epis Ch Yerington NV 1997-2002. pastordianahlc@gmail.com

TURNER, Donald Lee (CNY) PO Box 865, Barnegat Light NJ 08006 **Vic S Ptr's At The Light Epis Barnegat Light NJ 2005-** B Indianapolis IN 1938 s Vance & Thelma. Georgetown Coll 1957; BA Butler U 1961; MDiv CRDS 1965; CTh SWTS 1984. D 6/16/1985 Bp Frank Tracy Griswold III P 10/18/1985 Bp Allen Webster Brown. m 4/21/1978 Candace R Turner c 4. R Trin Epis Ch Watertown NY 1991-2004; Vic Trin Ch River Falls WI 1987-1991; P-in-c S Mich's Ch Barrington IL 1986-1987, Cur 1985; Serv Untd Ch of Chr 1965-1976; Pres, Dioc Bd, Dio CNY Dio Cntrl New York Liverpool NY 1999-2001, Mem, Long Range Plnng, Dio CNY 1997-2004, Mem, Dioc Bd 1997-2001, Dn, No Country Dist 1994-2004; Dn, Star Prairie Dnry, Dio Eau Claire Dio Eau Claire Eau Claire WI 1988-1991. Ed, "Wrshp," *A Bk of Wrshp for the Healing Mnstry*, Orrville Press, 1971; Ed, "Wrshp," *A Bk of Wrshp: Comm and Antecommunion*, Orrville Press, 1970. Cath Fllshp Epis Ch 1985; Ord of S Lk 1969-1977; SocMary 1987. frdlt@outlook.com

TURNER, Elizabeth Holder (Del) 125 Gull Pt, Millsboro DE 19966 B Wilmington DE 1930 d William & Eleanor. D 1/12/1980 Bp John Mc Gill Krumm. c 3. D All SS and St Georges Ch Rehoboth Bch DE 1996-2001, 1995-1999; Asst S Geo's Chap Lewes DE 1996-2001; Dio Delaware Wilmington 1988-2001; Asst S Mk's Ch Millsboro DE 1988-1990; D'S Asst S Mart-In-The-Field In Shelbyville 1988-1990; Non-par 1984-1986; D'S Asst Gd Shpd Cincinnati OH 1980-1983; Ch Of Gd Shpd Cincinnati OH 1980-1982.

TURNER, Elizabeth Zarelli (Tex) 9520 Anchusa TRL, Austin TX 78736 B Tacoma WA 1953 d Albert & Georgina. BA Seattle Pacific U 1976; MA Ya Berk 1978; MDiv GTS 1984. D 6/30/1984 Bp Robert Hume Cochrane P 2/2/1985 Bp William Grant Black. m 5/25/1986 Philip Williams Turner c 1. R S Mk's Ch Austin TX 2005-2017, Asst R 1999-2004; Assoc St. Mk's Ch 2005-2008; All SS Ch Atlanta TX 1997-1999; Assoc All SS Epis Ch Austin TX 1997-1999; Asst Dir of Admssns Yale DS New Haven CT 1995-1997; Ya Berk New Haven CT 1994-1997; Assoc S Jas Ch New York NY 1988-1991; Epis Ch Cntr New York NY 1986-1988; Asst Ecum Off All Ang' Ch New York NY 1986-1987; Asst to R The Ch of the Redeem Cincinnati OH 1984-1986. Auth, "Men & Wmn: Sexual Ethics In Turbulent Times"; Auth, "Implications Of The Gospel"; Auth, "Study Guide For Luth- Epis Dialogue Document"; Auth, "Love," *Mar & Friendship*.

TURNER SR, Eric Wood (CFla) 4581 Bellaluna Dr., West Melbourne FL 32904 **R S Jn's Ch Melbourne FL 2004-; Stndg Com Dio Cntrl Florida Orlando FL 2010-, Chair, Chr Formation Cmsn 2009-, Dn of SE Dnry 2007-2010** B Pittsburgh PA 1958 s Russell & Frances. W Virginia U 1977; BS Alleg 1980; MDiv TESM 1988. D 6/4/1988 P 4/1/1989 Bp Alden Moinet Hathaway. m 12/15/1984 Charlene S Turner c 2. R S Paul's Epis Ch Shelton CT 2001-2004; Vic Chr Ch Three Bridges NJ 1994-2001; Dio New Jersey Trenton NJ 1994-1996; Asst R S Matt's Ch Richmond VA 1988-1994. Ord of S Lk. Phi Beta Kappa.

TURNER, Irvin D (Minn) 37688 Tulaby Lake Rd, Waubun MN 56589 **Non-par/ Sabbatical 1/4 time Vic Trin Epis & Prebyterian Ch 2011-; owner Peaceful BAy Enterprises 2004-** B White Earth MN 1943 s Robert & Blanche. 1982; BS Minnesota St U Moorhead 1982; MDiv SWTS 1985. D 8/3/1985 P 2/13/1986 Bp Robert Marshall Anderson. m 2/27/1965 Mary M Turner c 3. Chapl Epis Cmnty Serv Bemidji MN 2005-2006; Indigenous Theol Trng Inst Oklahoma City OK 1999-2000; Indegenous Theol Trng Inst. 1997-2000; Vic Dio Minnesota Minneapolis MN 1985-1998; Breck Memi Mssn Ponsford MN 1985-1994; D Samuel Memi Naytahwaush MN 1985-1994. Auth, "Blood, Bone & Sprt," *First Peoples Theol Journ*, ITTI, 2010; Auth, "I Put My Back To It," *First Peoples Theol Journ*, ITTI, 2006; Auth, "The Way (Poem)," *First Peoples Theol Journ*, ITTI, 2006; Auth, "Meeting Jesus Again," *First Peoples Theol Journ*, ITTI, 2005; Auth, "Native Sprtl Realities (Poem),*" First Peoples Theol Journ*, ITTI, 2005; Auth, "Traditional Native Amer And Chr Sprtlty: A Dialogue," *First Peoples Theol Journ*, ITTI, 2002; Auth, "Creation," *First Peoples Theol Journ*, Indigenous Theol Trng Inst (ITTI), 2001; Auth, "A Warrior w A Pen," *Stories Migrating Hm*, Loon Feather Press, 1999. 2006 Chld's Ldrshp Awd The Sheltering Arms Fndt 2006.

TURNER, James Scott (Colo) St. Paul's Episcopal Church, P.O. Box 770722, Steamboat Springs CO 80477 **Pres of the Stndg Com Dio Colorado Denver CO 2014-** B Lubbock TX 1954 s Kenneth & Golda. BA Texas Tech U 1976; MDiv Sewanee: The U So, TS 1980. D 6/21/1980 Bp Willis Ryan Henton P 6/20/1981 Bp Sam Byron Hulsey. m 11/1/1996 JoAnne Modesitt Grace c 2. P-in-c S Paul's Epis Ch Steamboat Sprngs CO 2009-2017; All SS Ch Loveland CO 2007-2009, Assoc 2000-2003; Outreach Spokesman Cross Intl Pmpano Bch FL 2007-2009; P-in-c S Alb's Ch Windsor CO 2004-2007; R The Ch Of Chr The King (Epis) Arvada CO 1988-1994; Assoc Trin Ch Galveston TX 1984-1988; S Jn The Bapt Epis Clarendon TX 1980-1984; Vic Dio NW Texas Lubbock TX 1980-1981; S Matt's Ch Pampa TX 1980-1981. EPF 1979. frscott@steamboatstpauls.org

TURNER, John Edward (Haw) 19446 N. 110th Lane, Sun City AZ 85373 B Tulsa OK 1952 s William & Dixie. Loc Trng for P Dioc Inst of Hawawi'i. D 3/4/

2000 P 7/14/2001 Bp Richard Sui On Chang. S Jude's Hawaiian Ocean View Ocean View HI 2004-2006, P 2001-2003.

TURNER, Linnea (Va) 5701 Hunton Wood Dr, Broad Run VA 20137 B Washington DC 1946 d George & Lucille. BA Duke 1968; MA Wright St U 1975; MDiv VTS 1989. D 6/10/1989 Bp Peter J Lee P 3/15/1990 Bp Robert Poland Atkinson. m 9/2/1967 Michael V Turner c 2. Chair, Cmsn on Wrld Mssn Dio Virginia Richmond VA 2000-2003; R Epis Ch Of Leeds Par Markham VA 1993-2010, Int 1991-2010; Assoc All SS' Epis Ch Chevy Chase MD 1992-1993; Asst S Patricks Ch Falls Ch VA 1989-1991. Busmn of the Year in the Area of Serv Fauquier Cnty Bus & Profsnl Wmn Club 2000.

TURNER, Maurice Edgar (Cal) 4222 Churchill Drive, Pleasanton CA 94588 B Manchester England UK 1932 s Edward & Emily. BS Royal Tech Coll Salford Gb 1956; MDiv CDSP 1973. D 6/24/1972 Bp Chauncie Kilmer Myers P 12/1/1972 Bp Sumner Walters. c 3. S Clare's Epis Ch Pleasanton CA 1986-2003; Assoc R S Steph's Epis Ch Orinda CA 1979-1986; R Redeem And Hope Epis Ch Delano CA 1976-1978; S Mich And All Ang Concord CA 1974-1976; Asst Ch Of The H Trin Richmond CA 1972-1973.

TURNER, Melvin Eugene (Minn) 4759 Shellbark Rd, Owings Mills MD 21117 **Died 8/25/2016** B Grimes County TX 1936 s Oliver & Essie. Nthrn Bapt TS 1959; VTS 1977. D 6/24/1978 P 3/18/1979 Bp John Thomas Walker. m 1/10/1959 Margaret A Turner c 3. Assoc All SS Epis Ch Reisterstown MD 2004-2016; S Phil's Ch S Paul MN 1990-2001; R Dio MN S Phil's Ch St Paul MN 1990-2001; S Phil's Chap Baden Brandywine MD 1978-1990; R Dio Washington S Phil's Ch MD 1978-1990. Outstanding Cler of the Year 1988.

TURNER, Mollie Douglas (SVa) 77 Chestnut St Unit 201, Tryon NC 28782 **Assoc Ch Of The H Cross Tryon NC 2017-** B Ticonderoga NY 1948 d Benjamin & Mary. BA Agnes Scott Coll 1970; MDiv Candler TS Emory U 1994. D 6/4/1994 P 12/10/1994 Bp Frank Kellogg Allan. c 3. P Assoc Abingdon Epis Ch White Marsh VA 2013-2014; P-in-c Bruton Par Williamsburg VA 2008-2009, Assoc R 2000-2010; Vic S Jas Epis Ch Clayton GA 1996-2000; Asst R Gr Epis Ch Gainesville GA 1994-1996; Pres of Stndg Com Dio Sthrn Virginia Newport News VA 2009-2010, Stndg Com 2007-2010, Exec Bd & Dn of Jamestown Convoc 2002-2009. Contrib, "Commentaries on Psalms," *Feasting on the Word (Year B, Vol. 3)*, Westminster Jn Knox, 2009. Theta Phi hon Fraternity Candler TS 1994. mollie@holycrosstryon.org

TURNER, Peter Knight (NJ) PO Box 1134, Hillburn NY 10931 **Died 6/11/2016** B Rockford IL 1935 s William & Marion. BA Wms 1957; MBA NYU 1971; Cert Merc 1978. D 6/3/1978 P 12/1/1978 Bp Albert Wiencke Van Duzer. c 2. Extended Supply Ch Of The Gd Shpd Greenwood Lake NY 2008-2016; S Lk's Ch Beacon NY 2006; Chr Ch Of Ramapo Suffern NY 2005-2008; S Mk's Epis Ch Yonkers NY 2004; Gr Epis Ch Monroe NY 2001-2007; Dio New York New York NY 2001-2003; S Andr's Ch Schenectady NY 2000; S Paul's Epis Ch Greenwich NY 1999-2000; P-in-c S Lk's Ch Catskill NY 1998-1999; S Steph's Ch Schenectady NY 1998; S Jn In-The-Wilderness Copake Falls NY 1997-1998; Gr Epis Ch Port Jervis NY 1995-1996; Tri-Cnty Epis Area Mnstry Monticello NY 1995; Assoc Gr Ch Middletown NY 1990-1994; Assoc S Mary's-In-Tuxedo Tuxedo Pk NY 1989-1990; S Mk's Ch Hammonton NJ 1988-1989; Vic Trin Ch Eliz NJ 1981-1988; Cur All SS' Epis Ch Scotch Plains NJ 1978-1981.

TURNER, Philippa Anne (NY) 2 E 90th St, New York NY 10128 B London UK 1964 d Amedee & Deborah. BA U of Durham GB 1986; MDiv Ya Berk 1988. D 7/9/1994 P 2/16/1995 Bp Richard Frank Grein. Ch Of The Heav Rest New York NY 1995-2008, Assoc 1995-; Chapl S Jas Ch New York NY 1992-1995; Hosp Chapl Hosp Chapl Inc. New York NY 1990-1995. Coll of Chapl 1991; Secy AEHC 1991. Hon Doctorate Ursinus Coll 2002.

TURNER III, Philip Williams (Tex) 9520 Anchusa Trl, Austin TX 78736 **Ret 1998-** B Winchester VA 1935 s Philip & Constance. BA W&L 1958; BD VTS 1961; Oxon 1965; MA Pr 1973; PhD Pr 1978. D 6/17/1961 P 12/1/1961 Bp Angus Dun. m 5/25/1986 Elizabeth Zarelli c 4. Int Ch Of The Incarn Dallas TX 2007-2008; Int Dn Epis TS Of The SW Austin TX 2005-2007, 1974-1979; Dn Ya Berk 1991-1998; S Alb's Epis Ch St Petersburg FL 1991-1998; All Ang' Ch New York NY 1986-1987; Fac The GTS New York NY 1980-1991; Fac ETSSw TX 1974-1979; Fac Makerere Coll 1966-1971; Fac Bp Tucker Coll 1962-1966; Mssy Uganda 1961-1971. Auth, "The Fate of Comm"; Auth, "Sex Money and Power"; Auth, "Crossroads Ave For Meeting"; Auth, "Men & Wmn: Sexual Ethics In Turbulent Times"; Auth, "The Crisis Of Moral Tchg In The Epis Ch". Hon Doctorate Ya Berk; Hon Doctorate Epis TS of the SW; Hon Doctorate VTS.

TURNER, Robert (NJ) 525 Pleasant Ave, Piscataway NJ 08854 **Congrl Dvlpmt Dio New Jersey Trenton NJ 2006-, Stwdshp commision 2004-2008, D 2002-, Com on Diac 1994-2001, 1985-1993, Dept of CSR 1985-1988** B Newark NJ 1938 s Major & Ruth. BS Bloomfield Coll 1979. D 1/25/1975 Bp George E Rath. m 5/28/1965 Dolores Letitia Turner c 4. Dio New Jersey Trenton NJ 2005-2008; Congrl Dvlpmt Dio New Jersey Trenton NJ 2004-2005; D Ch Of The H Trin New York NY 1999-2002; D S Mk's Ch Plainfield NJ 1992-1999; Asst S Fran Ch Dunellen NJ 1982-1992.

TURNER, Saundra Lee (Ga) 2104 Amberley Pass, Evans GA 30809 **D Ch Of Our Sav Augusta GA 2006-; Archd Dio Georgia Savannah GA 2014-** B Milford DE 1947 d James & Elsie. Dplma Washington Hosp Centr 1968; BA Amer U 1972; MS Cath Univ 1974; EdD U GA 1990; Post Masters FNP Georgia Sthrn U 1994. D 5/31/2006 Bp Henry Irving Louttit. Assoc. Dn Georgia Rgnts U 1987-2015.

TURNER, Sharon Richey (Dal) 6728 Mayer Road, La Grange TX 78945 B Beaumont TX 1942 d James & Emma. BFA U of Texas 1964; MEd U of Houston 1975; MDiv Epis TS of the SW 1987; DMin Austin Presb TS 2007. D 6/8/1987 Bp Anselmo Carral-Solar P 5/11/1988 Bp Maurice Manuel Benitez. m 9/4/1965 Michael Lucian Turner c 2. P-in-c S Jn's Epis Ch Columbus TX 2008-2013; Supply P Partnr-in-Mnstry-E Dio W Texas 2006-2016; Asstg Cler Ch of the Trsfg Dallas Texas 2004-2007; Assoc R S Mich And All Ang Ch Dallas TX 1994-2002; Assoc R H Sprt Epis Ch Houston TX 1987-1994; Asst Ch Of The Gd Shpd Tomball TX 1987. Auth, "The Lesson and the Arts," *Lectionary*, 2000. Sis of Belle Coeur 2013. sharyn.richey.artist@gmail.com

TURNER, Stephen Deree (EC) 16 Gregg Way, Fort Rucker AL 36362 **Chapl Ft Rucker AL 1997-** B Atlanta GA 1953 s Trevor & Lois. BA U of Virginia 1975; MDiv Candler TS Emory U 1978; DMin Candler TS Emory U 1988. D 9/12/1993 Bp Charles Lovett Keyser P 3/1/1994 Bp Claude Charles Vache. m 6/6/1982 Loura Dale Hardesty c 1. Off Of Bsh For ArmdF New York NY 1994-2001; Chapl US-A Camp Zama In Japan 1993-1994; Serv Meth Ch 1976-1992.

TURNER III, Thomas (WTex) 200 N. Wright Streed, Alice TX 78332 B Norfolk VA 1945 s Thomas & Maudine. BA Emory and Henry Coll 1974; JD St Marys and U Sch of Law 1978; Cert Iona Sch for Mnstry 2010. D 6/24/2010 Bp Gary Richard Lillibridge. m 10/8/1966 Darlene Turner c 2. The Epis Ch Of The Adv Alice TX 2011-2017; D S Mk's Ch Crp Christi TX 2010-2011. Bp Elliott Soc 2013. aliceadvent@sbcglobal.net

TURNER, Timothy Jay (WTex) 120 Herweck Dr, San Antonio TX 78213 B San Antonio TX 1950 s Marion & Margaret. BA U of Houston 1972; MDiv Oblate TS 1979; CTh Epis TS of the SW 1991; MBA U of Texas San Antonio 1999. Rec 6/10/1991 as Priest Bp John Herbert MacNaughton. m 8/2/1986 Elizabeth Kimmell Turner. Epis Dio W Texas San Antonio TX 1997-2011; R Trin Ch San Antonio TX 1993-1997; Asst S Jn's Ch McAllen TX 1991-1993; Var Serv Oblatos de Mex Oaxaca and Distrito Fed Mex 1977-1983. Auth, "Loc Govt e-Disclosure & Comparisons: Equipping Deliberative Democracy for the 21st Century," U Press of Amer, 2005; Auth, "Welcoming the Baptized: Angl Hosp within the Ecum Enterprise," Grove Books Ltd., 1996. Texas Bus Hall of Fame Schlrshp Texas Bus Hall of Fame 1999.

TURNER JR, William Joseph (CNY) 2 Ridgefield Pl, Biltmore Forest NC 28803 **Ret 1991-** B Milwaukee WI 1926 s William & Dorothy. BA Carroll Coll 1947; MA U of Wisconsin 1950; STB Ya Berk 1956. D 6/3/1956 P 12/1/1956 Bp Horace W B Donegan. m 6/30/1954 Barbara Turner c 2. S Fran Of Assisi Cherokee NC 2004-2006; Vic Gr Ch Mex NY 1991-1994; R S Matt's Epis Ch Liverpool NY 1983-1991; R S Jn's Epis Ch Gloucester MA 1975-1983; Assoc S Andr's Ch Wellesley MA 1966-1975; Chapl Wellesley Coll Wellesley MA 1966-1975; Cn Chncllr S Paul's Cathd Buffalo NY 1962-1966; Cur S Simon's Ch Buffalo NY 1956-1958.

TURNER-JONES, Nancy Marie (SO) 318 E. 4th St., Cincinnati OH 45202 **P-in-c S Barn Epis Ch Cincinnati OH 2014-; Bd, Trsfg Sprtlty Cntr Dio Sthrn Ohio Cincinnati OH 2012-, Chair, Liturg & Mus Cmsn 2012-** B 1954 d Theodore & Gertrude. BA Mia 1988; MA Cincinnati Conservatory of Mus Cincinnati 1991; MDiv Lexington TS 1995; DMin Sewanee: The U So, TS 1999. D 12/16/2000 P 9/6/2001 Bp Stacy F Sauls. m 7/21/2001 Larry Paul Jones c 3. Int Ch Of The Epiph Guntersville AL 2013-2014; Dn's Cn Chr Ch Cathd Cincinnati OH 2008-2014; Int The Epis Ch Of The Ascen Middletown OH 2007-2008; R S Dav's Ch Southfield MI 2004-2007; Asst S Jas Epis Ch Birmingham MI 2002-2004; Prof Sewanee U So TS Sewanee TN 2002; Asst Ch Of The Ascen Frankfort KY 2001-2002; D Chr Ch Cathd Lexington KY 2000-2001. Essay, "Shaping the Reformation:Reflecting on Luther and cranmer:," *Simul Iustus et Peccator: Essays in hon of Donald S. Armentrout*, the TS, 2003; Dictionary, "Contrib," *An Epis Dictionary of the Ch*, Ch Pub, 1999; Hymnal Comp, "Contrib," *Chalice Hymnal Wrshp Leaders' Comp*, Chalice Press, 1998; Article, "Adv:A Serv of Lessons and Carols," *Lexington Theol Quarterly*, Lexington TS, 1998; Article, "The Chalice Hymnal: Broken Bread-One Body," *The Hymn*, The Hymn, 1997.

TURNEY, Nancy J (O) 1632 Hilltown Pike, Hilltown PA 18927 B Carlsbad NM 1944 d Hardin & Ina. BA W&M 1966; MA hours minus thesis New Mex Highlands U 1971; MFA U Denv 1973; Phd. hours minus orals/thesis Wayne 1977; MDiv SWTS 1993. D 6/5/1993 Bp James Russell Moodey P 1/18/1994 Bp Arthur Williams Jr. m 5/29/1977 Wayne Scott Turney c 1. P-in-c Gd Shpd Ch Hilltown PA 2006-2013; R S Andr Epis Ch Mentor OH 1998-2006; Assoc S Paul's Epis Ch Cleveland OH 1996-1998; Asst S Ptr's Epis Ch Lakewood OH 1993-1996. revharp@verizon.net

TURRELL, James Fielding (Be) School of Theology, U. of the South, 335 Tennessee Ave, Sewanee TN 37383 **Prof Sewanee U So TS Sewanee TN 2014-,** assoc. prof. 2008-2014, asst. prof. 2002-; Mem SCLM 2015-; Theol participant Theol Com HOB 2012- B Tunkhannock PA 1970 s James & Susan. BA Ya 1991; MDiv Ya Berk 1996; MA Van 1999; PhD Van 2002. D 6/8/1996 Bp James Michael Mark Dyer P 12/21/1996 Bp Paul Victor Marshall. m 5/1/2004 Jennie Goodrum c 1. stated supply P Trin Ch Clarksville TN 2000-2001; stated supply P S Jn's Epis Ch Mt Juliet TN 1999-2000; Res Intern The Cathd Ch Of S Jas So Bend IN 1996-1998. Auth, "Celebrating the Rites of Initiation," Ch Pub, 2013; Auth, "Angl Theologies of the Euch," *Comp to the Euch in the Reformation*, Brill, 2013; Auth, "Angl Liturg Practices," *Comp to the Euch in the Reformation*, Brill, 2013; Auth, "Richard Baxter's Attempt to Rehabilitate Cnfrmtn," *Studia Liturgica*, 2011; Auth, "A Dim Mirror: Archbp Rowan Williams's Reflections on the 2009 GC," *ATR*, 2010; Auth, "Uniformity and Common Pryr," *Comp to Richard Hooker*, Brill, 2008; Auth, "P and People in the Angl Tradition," *Sewanee Theol Revs*, 2008; Auth, "Muddying the Waters of Baptism: Theol Com's Report on Baptism, Cnfrmtn, and Chr Initiation," *ATR*, 2006; Auth, "Catechisms," *Oxford Guide to BCP*, Oxford Univ. Press, 2006; Auth, "Until Such Time as He Be Confirmed: Laudians and Cnfrmtn," *Seventeenth Century*, 2005; Auth, "The Ritual Of Royal Healing: Scrofula, Liturg And Politics," *Angl And Epis Hist*, 1999. Amer Soc Of Ch Hist 2000; No Amer Acad of Liturg 2005. Doctoral Fell ECF 2001. jturrell@sewanee.edu

TURRIE, Anne Elizabeth (RG) PO Box 2427, Mesilla Park NM 88047 B Marion IN 1946 d William & Carolyn. BA U CO 1970; MA Ball St U 1972; Dip Trin Sem 2009. D 9/19/2009 Bp William Carl Frey. m 6/5/1971 Stephen Turrie. D S Jas' Epis Ch Las Cruces NM 2009-2012.

TURTON, Neil Christopher (NJ) 509 Lake Ave, Bay Head NJ 08742 **Fac Fresh Start Trenton NJ 2008-** B Manchester GB 1945 s Alan & Helen. Oxf GB 1979. Trans 3/14/2002 Bp David Bruce Joslin. m 7/7/1979 Wendy W Turton c 2. R All SS Ch Bay Hd NJ 2002-2014.

TUSKEN, Mark Anthony (Chi) 327 S 4th St, Geneva IL 60134 **R S Mk's Ch Geneva IL 1994-** B Lansing MI 1956 s Roger & Margaret. BA Van 1978; MDiv TESM 1981; DMin GTF 1999. D 10/11/1981 P 5/4/1982 Bp Bob Gordon Jones. m 2/3/2007 Peggy Tusken c 1. Chapl (Capt) Al Air Ng 187th Tactical Fighter Grp 1990-1994; R Chr The Redeem Ch Montgomery AL 1986-1994; Asst R S Jn's Ch Huntingdon Vlly PA 1983-1986; Cur S Mk's Epis Ch Casper WY 1981-1983.

TUTASIG TENORIO, Digna Mercedes (Eur) B Quito Ecuador 1960 d Luis & Maria. D 10/14/2012 P 12/12/2015 Bp Pierre W Whalon. m 11/13/1983 Luis Fernando Paredes c 1.

TUTON, Dan (RG) 8409 La Ventura Ct NW, Albuquerque NM 87120 **R Hope in the Desert Eps Ch 2007-; Asst R All SS Epis Ch Reisterstown MD 2004-** B Nebraska City NE 1955 BS U CA 1978; MS California St U Sacramento 1986; MDiv TESM 2003. D 6/21/2003 P 1/24/2004 Bp Terence Kelshaw. m 6/7/1986 Michele Lynn Hathaway Tuton c 4. Asst All SS Epis Ch Reisterstown MD 2003-2007.

TUTTLE, Jonathan D (Ga) 2425 Cherry Laurel Ln, Albany GA 31705 **The Epis Ch Of S Jn And S Mk Albany GA 2015-** B Columbus OH 1987 BA Milligan Coll 2010; MDiv Duke DS 2015. D 10/18/2015 P 8/6/2016 Bp Scott Anson Benhase. m 7/24/2010 Lindsey N Tuttle c 1.

TUTTLE, Margaret Constance (Nwk) 19 Oberlin St, Maplewood NJ 07040 **Pstr Mnstrs Mgr Cedar Crest Vill Ret Cmnty Pomptin Plains NJ 2001-** B Brooklyn NY 1954 d Edward & Josephine. BS NYU 1975; MA NYU 1978; MDiv Drew U 1999. D 6/1/2002 P 12/14/2002 Bp John Palmer Croneberger.

TUTTLE, Peggy Elaine Wills (Minn) 4603 Bontia Dr, Palm Beach Gardens FL 33418 **Bp's Disciplinary Com Mem Dom And Frgn Mssy Soc- Epis Ch Cntr New York NY 2012-** B Fort Worth TX 1940 d Marvin & Mabel. MDiv VTS 1995; BS Natl-Louis U 1996. D 10/16/1996 P 5/1/1997 Bp James Louis Jelinek. m 1/24/1976 Jon F Tuttle c 2. S Jn The Evang S Paul MN 2010-2011; S Mart's By The Lake Epis Minnetonka Bch MN 2009-2010, 2008; The Par of St Paul's Epis Ch Duluth MN 2005-2006; St Dav's Epis Ch Minnetonka MN 2004, 2000-2002; Dio Minnesota Minneapolis MN 1999-2003; Adv Ch Farmington MN 1998; Asst S Jos's Ch Lakewood CO 1997-1998.

TUTU, Mpho A (WA) 3001 Park Center Dr Apt 1119, Alexandria VA 22302 B London England 1963 d Desmond. D 6/7/2003 Bp Gordon Scruton P 1/17/2004 Bp Desmond Mpilo Tutu. m 12/31/1993 Joseph Charles Tutu c 1. Chr Ch Alexandria VA 2003-2006.

TUTU, Nontombi Naomi (Tenn) B Krugersdorp - South Africa 1960 BA Berea Coll; MA U of Kentucky; Angl Stds Dplma VTS. D 6/3/2017 Bp John Bauerschmidt. c 3. tutun@bellsouth.net

TUYISHIME, Emmanuel (SO) Dio Sthrn Ohio Cincinnati OH 2017- D 6/3/2017 Bp Thomas Edward Breidenthal.

TWEEDALE, David Lee (Colo) 423 E Thunderbird Dr, Fort Collins CO 80525 **Assoc Pstr S Alb's Ch Windsor CO 2002-** B Denver CO 1946 s Gilbert & Evelyn. BA Minnesota St U Moorhead 1989. D 7/31/2002 P 2/26/2003 Bp William Jerry Winterrowd. m 2/4/1996 Weltha Ann McGraw.

TWEEDIE, William Duane (Tex) 301 E 8th St, Austin TX 78701 **Vic Ch Of The Resurr Austin TX 2013-** B Milford CT 1976 s William & Andrea. Texas St U 2001; MDiv Epis TS of the SW 2009. D 6/20/2009 P 1/5/2010 Bp C Andrew

Doyle. m 10/19/2002 Laura Jayne Tweede c 2. Assoc S Dav's Ch Austin TX 2011-2013; Cur Dio Texas Houston TX 2010-2011; Cur S Paul's Ch Waco TX 2009; Yth Dir Chr Ch Cathd Houston TX 2004-2006; Yth Dir S Mk's Ch Houston TX 2002-2004.

TWEEDY, Jeanette Elizabeth (NY) PO Box 172, Peacham VT 05862 B Kingston NY 1950 d Oliver & Helen. Eisenhower Coll 1970; BS Green Mtn Coll 1981; MDiv Bex Sem 1991. D 6/22/1991 Bp O'Kelley Whitaker P 5/5/1992 Bp David Bruce Joslin. c 1. Dio New York New York NY 2010-2012; Cn Dio Vermont Burlington VT 2002-2010; S Andr's Epis Ch St Johnsbury VT 1999-2001; R S Mary's Epis Ch Hillsboro OH 1993-1998; D Intern Of The Chenango Cluster Of Ch Dio Cntrl New York Liverpool NY 1991-1993.

TWELVES, Paul Douglass (RI) 341 Spinnaker Lane, Bristol RI 02809 **S Mich's Ch Bristol RI 2008-** B Philadelphia PA 1929 s John & Rachel. BS Tem 1951; MDiv EDS 1954. D 5/29/1954 Bp Oliver J Hart P 12/7/1954 Bp Norman B Nash. m 9/30/1989 Joy W Wassell c 3. Int Ch Of The Mssh Providence RI 2000-2002; Int S Paul's Ch Portsmouth RI 1998-2000; Int S Mart's Ch Providence RI 1997-1998; Int S Alb's Ch N Providence RI 1995-1997; Int Gr Ch Amherst MA 1994-1995; Int S Matt's Ch Bedford NY 1993-1994; Int S Paul's Ch Kansas City MO 1992-1993; Int S Jn's Ch Lynchburg VA 1991-1992; Int S Geo's Epis Ch Dayton OH 1989-1991; Int S Steph's Epis Ch And U Columbus OH 1988-1989; Int S Alb's Ch Syracuse NY 1987-1988; R S Ptr's Ch Glenside PA 1975-1986; R All SS Ch Chelmsford MA 1954-1975.

TWENTYMAN JR, Donald Graham (Ia) 107 24th St, Spirit Lake IA 51360 B Rochester MN 1941 s Donald & Gwendolyn. AB U Chi 1964; Epis Dio Minnesota 1982. D 12/2/1982 Bp William Arthur Dimmick. m 6/27/1998 Mary B Twentyman c 2. D S Mk's Epis Ch Mesa AZ 2010-2015; D S Alb's Ch Sprt Lake IA 1998-2015; D Gr Memi Ch Wabasha MN 1996-1998; D/Mentor S Matt's Epis Ch Chatfield MN 1993-1996; D Calv Ch Rochester MN 1982-1993. Assn for Epis Deacons 1980.

TWIGGS, Frances R (Spok) 428 King St, Wenatchee WA 98801 **R S Lk's Epis Ch Wenatchee WA 2015-; Chapl Res VA New York Harbor Healthcare System 2012-** B Kingsport TN 1960 d Henry & Joan. BSW E Tennessee St U 1982; MDiv GTS 2002. D 10/20/2001 P 6/1/2002 Bp Herbert Thompson Jr. Int S Alb's Epis Ch Staten Island NY 2014-2015; R S Jn's Ch New City NY 2005-2011; S Anne Epis Ch W Chester OH 2005; Ch Of The Gd Samar Amelia OH 2004-2005; Int Ch of the Gd Samar Cincinnati OH 2004-2005; Cur The Ch of the Redeem Cincinnati OH 2002-2004. rectorstlukeswenatchee@nwi.net

TWINAMAANI, Benjamin Bamwangiraki (SwFla) 9533 Pebble Glen Ave, Tampa FL 33647 **R Gr Ch Tampa FL 2005-** B Kabale Uganda 1961 s Ishamaeil & Faith. BDiv Bp Tucker Theol Coll Mukono Ug 1990; MTh Dallas TS 2000; PhD Candidate U of So Florida 2011. Trans 11/18/2004 Bp John Bailey Lipscomb. m 8/22/1998 Camilla Judith Twinamaani c 3. Tampa Dnry Rep Dioc Coun Dio SW Florida 2005-2010; Mem HIV/AIDS Cmsn Dio Dallas 1994-1995; Mem Intl. Students Advsry Coun Dallas Theol. Sem 1993-1995; Liaison to Media/Kampala City Organs Decade of Evang Prov Team Uganda 1991-1992; Founding Mem Angl Fllshp Choir Prov Off Uganda 1984-1992. Auth, "Faithful Locally, Prayerful Globally: Par Mnstry in the new Angl Disorder," *Fulcrum: Renewing the Evang Cntr UK*, LivCh mag, 2010; Auth, "Preparing for Lambeth 2008: Praying, Hoping and Working for Angl Faith and Ord," *Angl Comm Inst Website*, Angl Comm Inst, 2007; Auth, "How Amer Anglicans Think and Act: A Primer for the Global So.," *Angl Comm Inst Website*, Angl Comm Inst, 2007; Auth, "Let's Keep It Real," *LivCh mag*, LivCh mag, 1999; Auth, "The Hermeneutical Aspects of Proper Biblic Names and their Impact on Bible Translation for Afr," *unpublished Masters Thesis*, Dallas TS, 1999. Angl Comm Partnr Cler 2010; Angl Evang Soc 2005. Honorable Mem The Natl Scholars hon Soc 2007.

TWISS, Ian (Mich) Trinity Episcopal Church, 11575 Belleville Road, Belleville MI 48111 **P Trin Ch Belleville MI 2014-** B Canberra Australia 1971 s Robert & Helen. AB Pr 1994; MFA U MI 1997; MDiv SWTS 2007. D 12/16/2006 P 6/23/2007 Bp Wendell Nathaniel Gibbs Jr. m 8/13/1994 Nancy R Twiss c 3. Par R H Faith Ch Saline MI 2007-2014; Asst Dir/Lectr/Tchr/Admin U MI 1997-2005; Dn of the Huron Vlly Dnry Dio Michigan Detroit MI 2009-2014. rector@trinitybell.com

TWO BEARS, Neil V (ND) Po Box 685, Fort Yates ND 58538 **S Jas Ch Ft Yates ND 2003-; D S Lk's Ch Ft Yates ND 2003-** B Cannon Ball ND 1929 D 6/12/2003 P 12/13/2003 Bp Andrew Fairfield.

TWO BULLS, Robert G (U) Po Box 168, Hermosa SD 57744 B Pine Ridge SD 1934 s Peter & Martha. Dakota Ldrshp Prog; DLP Niobrara Sum Sem. D 6/25/1978 P 6/1/1980 Bp Walter H Jones. c 5. P Dio Utah Salt Lake City UT 1996-1998, 1993-1995; P S Eliz's Ch Whiterocks UT 1996-1998; P Dio So Dakota Pierre SD 1995-1996, 1995, 1983-1993; R S Matt's Epis Ch Rapid City SD 1986-1993; Dn Pine Ridge Reg 1983-1986; R Chr Ch Red Shirt Table SD 1980-1986.

TWO BULLS, Robert W (Los) 3317 33rd Ave S, Minneapolis MN 55406 **Vic All SS Epis Indn Mssn Minneapolis MN 2006-; Dir, Dept Of Indn Mnstrs Dio Minnesota Minneapolis MN 2006-** B Rapid City SD 1963 s Robert & Delores. BS U of Maryland 1996; MDiv GTS 2000. D 6/1/2000 Bp Carolyn Tan-

ner Irish P 1/6/2001 Bp Frederick Houk Borsch. m 6/26/1990 Ritchie R Two Bulls c 2. Prog Off For Native Amer Mnstrs Dio Los Angeles Los Angeles CA 2003-2006; Assoc R S Geo's Par La Can CA 2000-2003.

TWO BULLS, Twilla R (SD) D 6/24/2017 Bp John Tarrant.

TWO HAWK, Webster Aaron (SD) 604 East Missouri Avenue, Fort Pierre SD 57532 B White River SD 1930 s Albert & Annie. BS U of So Dakota 1952; BD Bex Sem 1957. D 6/29/1957 P 2/3/1958 Bp Conrad H Gesner. m 8/29/1996 Marjorie F Two Hawk c 1. Non-par (Lv of absence) 1968-1982; Dir S Eliz Mssn Hm Wakpala SD 1962-1968; P-in-c S Ptr's Ch Lake Andes SD 1957-1962. DD Hur 1972.

TWOMEY, Patrick Timothy (FdL) 415 E Spring St, Appleton WI 54911 B Saint Clair Shores MI 1960 s James & Irene. BA Albion Coll 1981; MDiv SWTS 1986. D 6/28/1986 Bp Henry Irving Mayson P 1/6/1987 Bp H Coleman Mcgehee Jr. m 7/18/1981 M Catherine Catherine Twomey c 2. R All SS Epis Ch Appleton WI 1995-2015; S Lk's Ch Dixon IL 1990-1995; Asst Trin Epis Ch Oshkosh WI 1986-1990.

TWYMAN, Thomas Wellwirth (CNY) 122 Metropolitan Ave, Ashland MA 01721 B Jackson MI 1938 s Wilford & Karolina. BA Mia 1960; BD VTS 1965; MS Bos 1978; Cert Boston Grad Sch of Psychoanalysis 1992. D 6/12/1965 Bp Leland Stark P 2/1/1966 Bp John S Higgins. m 8/22/1964 Jean Marie Twyman c 1. Trin Ch Claremont NH 1985-1986; Non-par 1971-1985; R Emm Ch E Syracuse NY 1967-1971; Cur S Jn's Ch Barrington RI 1965-1967.

TYLER, Lera Patrick (WTex) 116 US Highway 87, Comfort TX 78013 B Henderson TX 1948 d Clifton & Cecile. BA SW U 1971; MA U of New Orleans 1986; MAPM Epis TS of the SW 2005; MAPM Sem of the SW 2005; DAS Epis TS of the SW 2009; DAS Sem of the SW 2009. D 1/14/2009 Bp Gary Richard Lillibridge P 8/6/2009 Bp David Mitchell Reed. c 2. S Bon Ch Comfort TX 2012-2016; Asst R S Thos Epis Ch And Sch San Antonio TX 2009-2012.

TYLER, Pamela Hawes (Los) 1101 Witt Road, Taos NM 87471 **S Jas Epis Ch Taos NM 2010-** B Ankara TURKEY 1948 d Morgan & Norma. BA Florida St U 1970; JD U of Florida 1986; MDiv Ya Berk 1995. D 6/10/2000 Bp Joseph Jon Bruno P 1/6/2001 Bp Frederick Houk Borsch. Dio Los Angeles Los Angeles CA 2005-2009; S Geo's Epis Ch Laguna Hills CA 2000-2005. Vice Chncllr Of Dio Dio Los Angeles 2004.

TYLER SMITH, Virginia Stewart (Roch) 11 Episcopal Ave, Honeoye Falls NY 14472 **R S Jn's Epis Ch Honeoye Falls NY 2015-** B Boston MA 1967 d James & Jane. BA U Roch 1989; MDiv Harvard DS 1994; MDiv Harvard DS 1994; MDiv Harvard DS 1994. D 5/13/2015 P 11/20/2015 Bp Prince Grenville Singh. m 10/5/2013 Bradford Kent Smith. vtyler231@gmail.com

TYNDALL, Constance Flanigan (WMo) 4239 E Valley Rd, Springfield MO 65809 B Carthage MO 1936 d John & Minerva. W Missouri Sch for Mnstry; U of Missouri 1957; SW Missouri St U 1990. D 5/12/1991 Bp John Clark Buchanan. m 8/23/1957 Brent Vincent Tyndall c 3. D S Jas' Ch Springfield MO 1991-2011; Dep GC Dio W Missouri Kansas City MO 1998-2006, Chair - Cmnty of Deacons 1995-1997. Bp's Shield Dio W Missouri 2010; Steph Awd NAAD 2010; Omicron Delta Kappa 1989.

TYNDALL, Jeremy Hamilton (Ore) The Rectory, 55 Cove Road, Farnborough Hants GU140EX Great Britain (UK) **Team R, Cove Ch of Engl Guildford Dio 2008-** B Sutton Surrey UK 1955 s Francis & Peggy. BTh U of Nottingham/St Johns 1981; CEFACS Birmingham 1998; MPhil U of Birmingham GB 2001. Trans 10/1/2001 Bp Robert Louis Ladehoff. m 3/5/1994 Susan Marie Knight c 4. S Thos' Epis Ch Eugene OR 2002-2008, R St Thos Eugene, Dn of Cntrl Convoc 2001; Serv full time Par Mnstry Ch of Engl 1981-2001; Dn of Cntrl Covocation Dio Oregon Portland OR 2006-2008.

TYO JR, Charles Hart (Roch) 16 Elmwood Ave, Friendship NY 14739 B Potsdam NY 1944 D 12/8/2001 P 10/26/2002 Bp Jack Marston Mckelvey. m 8/14/1965 Bonnie Pratt c 3.

TYON, Agnes Lucille (SD) Po Box 282, Pine Ridge SD 57770 **Died 10/3/2015** B Pine Ridge SD 1933 d William & Elsie. Black Hill St U; TS - Native Sch of Mnstrs Vancouver B. D 10/12/1993 Bp Harold Stephen Jones P 10/17/1997 Bp Creighton Leland Robertson. m 4/25/1952 Eugene G Tyon.

TYON, Benjamin Ruben (SD) Po Box 14, Pine Ridge SD 57770 **Vic H Cross 1987-** B Pine Ridge SD 1934 s George & Sarah. BS Chadron St Coll 1957; MS Black Hill St U 1976. D 6/29/1980 Bp William Augustus Jones Jr P 11/1/1984 Bp Craig Barry Anderson. m 6/3/1957 Clementine E Tyon c 1. Dio So Dakota Pierre SD 1987-2004.

TYREE, James Scott (Okla) 235 W Duffy St, Norman OK 73069 B Janesville WI 1966 s Eugene & Alyce. BA U of Oklahoma 1995; Graduated Iona Sch of Cler Formation 2017. D 6/30/2017 Bp Edward Joseph Konieczny. c 3.

TYREE, Richard Douglas (SwVa) 132 Lincoln St, Holyoke MA 01040 **Died 6/29/2016** B Lynch Sta VA 1925 s Charles & Anne. VPI 1947; LTh VTS 1961. D 6/1/1961 P 6/3/1992 Bp William Henry Marmion. m 7/11/1980 Linda E Eggleston. Int S Lk's Ch Springfield MA 1998-2000; Ret 1990-2016; Exec Coun Appointees New York NY 1983-1990; Mssy Tutor S Jn Sch Mssn Kokise 1983-1990; Archd Dio SW Virginia Roanoke VA 1969-1983; R Gr Memi Ch Lynchburg VA 1964-1969; Vic Gr Massies Mill VA 1961-1964; Vic Trin Ch Arlington VA 1961-1964.

T

TYREE-CUEVAS, Susan McCorkle (Oly) 1804 Pointe Woodworth Dr NE, Tacoma WA 98422 B Lexington VA 1949 d William & Lula. BFA Virginia Commonwealth U 1971; MDiv VTS 1986. D 6/18/1988 P 4/18/1989 Bp Peter J Lee. m 9/13/1992 Charles L Cuevas. R S Matt Ch Tacoma WA 2003-2010; Int Ch Of The Ascen Seattle WA 2002; Dio Virginia Richmond VA 1999-2001; Mssnr/Ch Planter So Riding Ch Loudon Cnty VA 1999-2001; Assoc R S Dunst's Ch Mc Lean VA 1988-1999.

TYRIVER, Marcia Rivenburg (NCal) 255 Ba Wood Ln, Janesville WI 53545 B 1940 d Charles & Esther. BA Lawr 1962; MA U IL Champaign-Urbana IL 1965. D 6/2/2007 Bp Steven Andrew Miller. c 2. D Trin Ch Janesville WI 2007-2009; Assoc Chld'S Libr Hedberg Publ Libr 1985-2005.

TYSON, Lynda (Ct) 10 Evarts Lane, Madison CT 06443 B Lorain OH 1955 BS The OH SU 1977; MDiv Ya Berk 2005; DMin EDS 2015. D 6/11/2005 P 12/17/2005 Bp Chilton Richardson Knudsen. m 2/14/1986 Charles R Tyson. Ya Berk New Haven CT 2015-2016; Assoc R S Jn's Ch Beverly MA 2011-2013; Sr. Assoc R S Lk's Par Darien CT 2007-2010; PLSE Mssnr Epis Ch Cntr New York NY 2006-2007; Epis PLSE Coordntr The AEC New York NY 2005-2006. Auth, "Feelings in the Bible: Tools for Rel Ldrshp Educ," *Journ of Rel Ldrshp*, Acad of Rel Ldrshp, 2014.

TYSON, Stephen Alfred (Ore) 370 Market Ave., Coos Bay OR 97420 **Dn Sthrn Convoc Dio Oregon Portland OR 2010-** B Portland OR 1949 s Alfred & Caroline. BA Dart 1971; GTS 1972; MDiv CDSP 1974. D 7/26/1974 P 6/8/1975 Bp Matthew Paul Bigliardi. m 6/26/1971 Celeste Anne Kaye. R Emm Ch Coos Bay OR 2001-2013, 1974-1977, Cur 1974-1977; R S Jn's Epis Ch Marysville CA 1989-2001; Vic S Hilda's Ch Monmouth OR 1978-1981; S Thos Epis Ch Dallas OR 1977-1988.

TZENG, Wen-Bin (Tai) No. 7 Lane 105, Section 1, Hang Chow South Road, Taipei Taiwan **Dio Taiwan Taipei 2002-** B Zhanghua TW 1974 s Tzeng & Guo. MA Inst of Rel Sci; BA Fujen Cath U 2001. D 1/25/2002 P 8/24/2002 Bp Jung-Hsin Lai. m 11/30/2002 Ming-Chin Ming Yang c 1.

U

UBIERA, Ramon (NJ) 207 Summit Avenue Apt 1, Newark NJ 07104 **Dio New Jersey Trenton NJ 2014-** B San Pedro de Macoris DO 1973 s Ramon & Maribel. BA S Stephens Sch 1993; Cntr For Theol Educ 1998. D 4/10/1999 P 5/13/2000 Bp Julio Cesar Holguin-Khoury. m 3/1/2014 Fedia Reynoso c 3. Vic All SS Epis Ch Lakewood NJ 2012-2014; Nuestra Senora De Guadalupe Waukegan IL 2011-2012; Dio The Dominican Republic (Iglesia Epis Dominicana) Gazcue Santo Domingo 1999-2010; P Iglesia Epis San Felipe Apostol Santo Domingo Norte 1999-2010.

UDELL, George Morris Edson (Tex) 1436 Daventry Dr, DeSoto TX 75115 **P S Anne's Epis Ch Desoto TX 2005-** B Providence RI 1931 s George & Alice. BA U of New Mex 1957; CDSP 1960. D 6/1/1960 P 12/1/1960 Bp C J Kinsolving III. m 12/18/1955 Rosemary Udell c 3. Asst Ch Of The Gd Shpd Cedar Hill TX 2002-2004; R Chr Ch Jefferson TX 1998-2001; R S Fran Par Temple TX 1977-1996; The Great Cmsn Fndt Houston TX 1971-1977; Assoc S Paul's Ch Waco TX 1969-1977; Asst Pro Cathd Epis Ch Of S Clem El Paso TX 1966-1969; Vic S Mich's Ch Tucumcari NM 1963-1966.

UEDA, Ajuko Lois Kaleikea (Haw) Rikkyo University, 1-2-26, Kitano, Niizashi, Saitama Japan **Chapl Rikkyo U Tokyo Japan 2003-** B Kawasaki JP 1956 d Ryoji & Teruko. BA Musashino Musica Academia Tokyo JP 1978; BD Tokyo Cntrl TS 1985; MDiv CDSP 1994. D 5/31/2001 P 5/25/2002 Bp Richard Sui On Chang. m 11/3/1986 Noriaki Simon Peter Ueda. D/P S Jn's By The Sea Kaneohe HI 2001-2003; CE Dir S Mk's Ch Honolulu HI 1996-1999; Hosp Chapl Pacific Hlth Mnstry Honolulu HI 1996-1998; Japanese Lang Mssnr The Epis Ch in Hawaii Honolulu HI 1994-2003; Serv The Angl Ch of Japan 1985-1986.

UFFELMAN, Stephen Paul (EO) 915 Ne Crest Dr, Prineville OR 97754 **P S Andr's Epis Ch Prineville OR 1996-** B Portland OR 1946 s Richard & Rae. BS OR SU 1969. D 4/22/1995 P 8/1/1996 Bp Rustin Ray Kimsey. m 6/15/1968 Janet Fuller c 1.

UFFMAN, Craig David (Roch) 2000 Highland Avenue, Rochester NY 14618 B Baton Rouge LA 1960 s Kenneth & Grace. BS USNA 1982; MDiv Duke DS 2008. D 8/28/2009 P 2/28/2010 Bp Edward Stuart Little II. m 8/21/1982 Claudia Schaedel Uffman c 3. S Thos Epis Ch Rochester NY 2010-2015; S Anne's Epis Ch Warsaw IN 2009-2010.

UHLIK, Charles R (WMo) 2641 E Southern Hills Blvd, Springfield MO 65804 **Gr Ch Paducah KY 2015-** B 1963 s Delbert & Norma. BA U of St Thos 1987; MDiv U of S Mary of the Lake Mundelein Sem 1991. Rec 6/4/2005 as Priest Bp Barry Howe. m 5/26/2000 Susan K Uhlik c 3. R S Jas' Ch Springfield MO 2010-2015; R Chr Ch Red Wing MN 2006-2010; Asst to the P Redeem Epis Ch 2003; Chapl Asst. U.S. Army Reserve Washington D.C. 1985-1990; Chapl Asst. U.S. Army Reserve Washington D.C. 1984-1989. BroSA 2012.

UITTI, Aaron Leopold (At) 124 Commercial Ave, East Palatka FL 32131 B Hancock MI 1937 s William & Julia. BA NW Coll 1959; MDiv Concordia TS 1965; STM Concordia TS 1972. D 6/16/1985 P 12/15/1985 Bp Frank S Cerveny. m 12/18/1983 Penelope Uitti. R S Paul's Fed Point E Palatka FL 2011-2013; R The Epis Ch Of S Ptr And S Paul Marietta GA 1993-2007; Cn S Jn's Cathd Jacksonville FL 1988-1993; Assoc All SS Epis Ch Jacksonville FL 1985-1988. SBL 1964.

ULLMAN, Richard L (O) 241 S 6th St Apt 2408, Philadelphia PA 19106 **Ret 2001-** B Wilmington DE 1939 s Emanuel & Jacqueline. BA Amh 1961; BD EDS 1966. D 9/17/1966 Bp John Brooke Mosley P 3/18/1967 Bp Frederick Warnecke. m 10/18/1980 Margaret E Espenschied c 3. R Trin Ch Toledo OH 1993-2001; Int Galilee Epis Ch Virginia Bch VA 1992-1993; Int Ch Of The Gd Shpd Raleigh NC 1992; Archd Dio Sthrn Ohio Cincinnati OH 1989-1991; Reg Exec Miami Vlly Epis Coun Dayton OH 1980-1988; R Ch Of The Redeem Springfield PA 1971-1980; R S Paul's Ch Camden Wyoming DE 1968-1971; Asst S Lk's Ch Scranton PA 1966-1968. Auth, "Choosing to Serve," CDO, 1991; Auth, "Called to Wk Together," Off for Mnstry Dvlpmt, 1983; Auth, "Var arts," *Action Info*, Alb Institue; Auth, "Var arts," *Leaven*, NNECA; Auth, "Var sermons," *Selected Sermons*. Fell Alb Inst 1983.

ULLMANN, Clair Filbert (Eur) B Baytown TX 1944 d Bryson & Steppie. STB U of Leuven 1994; Angl Stds VTS 1995. Trans 6/30/2002 Bp Pierre W Whalon. m 3/7/1969 Hans Rainer Ullmann c 4.

ULRICH, Stephanie Lyn (Neb) 9302 Blondo St., Omaha NE 68134 **Hlth Min All SS Epis Ch Omaha NE 2008-** B Ortonville MN 1951 d Donald & Terrel. Dplma Bp Clarkson Sch of Nrsng 1972; Dio Nebraska Sprtl Direction 2005. D 6/22/2008 Bp Joe Goodwin Burnett. m 7/15/1972 Frederick Joseph Ulrich c 1. Auth, "Natl Epis Hlth Minisries," *Hlth Mnstry in the Loc Cong*, 815- Natl Ch, 2011.

UMEOFIA, Christian Chinedu (NC) Po Box 1333, Goldsboro NC 27533 B Nnewi NG 1958 s Edwin & Jannet. Jackson St U; Langston U; BA Cntrl St U 1984; MA Epis TS of the SW 1987. Trans 5/1/1996 Bp Brice Sidney Sanders. m 8/1/1984 Faith C Umeofia c 3. S Andr's Ch Goldsboro NC 1995-1998.

UMPHLETT, David Alton (NC) 108 W. Farriss Ave., High Point NC 27262 **Chapl Grtr Greensboro Chapt AGO 2011-; Bd Mem Hospice of the Piedmont 2011-; Mem Chap Bd Visitors High Point U 2010-; R S Mary's Epis Ch High Point NC 2009-; Liturg Off Dio No Carolina Raleigh NC 2013-, Mem, Swindell Speakers Fund 2011-, Alt Dep (4th), The 77th GC 2010-, Mem, Fair Share Appeals Bd 2010-, Mem, Liturg Cmsn 2010-; Mem, Bd Trst Kanuga Conferernces Inc Hendersonvlle NC 2012-** B Norfolk VA 1977 s Mack & Martha. BMus U NC 2000; MDiv VTS 2004. D 6/19/2004 P 12/21/2004 Bp Clifton Daniel III. m 6/28/2003 Lorinda H Umphlett c 2. R Gr Epis Ch Plymouth NC 2004-2009; S Lk's/S Anne's Epis Ch Roper NC 2004-2009; Mem, Chap for the Ages Com VTS Alexandria VA 2010-2012; Dep, The 76th GC Dio E Carolina Kinston NC 2007-2009, Chair, Liturg Cmsn 2005-2009, Chair, Cmsn of Coll Students and YA 2004-2008. AP 2004-2007.

UNDERHILL, Robin (Los) Tigh Ban, Hightae, Lockerbie DG-11 1JN Great Britain (UK) B Birmingham UK 1931 s Walter & Mabel. CIB NWU 1971; DBS ETSBH 1985; DIT ETSBH 1987; AA Marymount Coll 1988; BS Woodbury U 1991; MA ETSBH 1992. D 6/12/1993 Bp Chester Lovelle Talton P 1/15/1994 Bp Frederick Houk Borsch. c 1. Secy Mssn to Seafarers Scotland 2005-2010; Serv Scottish Epis Ch 2001-2004; Int S Simon's Par San Fernando CA 1998-2000; Port Chapl Ports of Los Angeles & Long Bch CA 1993-1998; Chapl Seamens Ch Inst Of Los Angeles San Pedro CA 1993-1998; Pstr Care Asst All SS Par Beverly Hills CA 1992-1994. Mssn to Seafarers 1993; No Amer Maritime Ministers Assn 1993-1998.

UNDERHILL, Scott Andrew (Alb) 912 Route 146, Clifton Park NY 12065 **D S Geo's Ch Clifton Pk NY 2009-** B Schenectady NY 1969 s Jack & Martha. BS SUNY at Buffalo 1991; MS SUNY at Buffalo 1993. D 5/30/2009 Bp William Howard Love. m 2/5/1994 Lynne M Underhill c 3.

UNDERHILL, William Dudley (WA) 25 Nottingham Dr, Kingston MA 02364 **Ret 1998-** B Boston MA 1931 s Frank & Marion. BA Wesl 1953; BD UTS 1956; Cert EDS 1963; Cert S Georges Coll Jerusalem IL 1986. D 6/23/1956 P 1/13/1957 Bp Norman B Nash. m 7/20/1991 Sandra R Underhill c 2. S Andr's Ch Hanover MA 2005-2007; Search Consult Dio Massachusetts 2004-2007; Int Trin Ch Bridgewater MA 2001-2002; R Chr Epis Ch Clinton MD 1991-1998; Int S Andr's Ch Ayer MA 1989-1991; Int S Jn's Ch Stamford CT 1988-1989; S Dav's Epis Mssn Pepperell MA 1987-1988; Sem Field Educ Supvsr EDS Cambridge MA 1974-1978; R The Par Of S Chrys's Quincy MA 1969-1987; R Trin Epis Ch Wrentham MA 1959-1969; Cur Trin Par Melrose MA 1956-1959. Co-Auth, "Alco," *I Can Take It or Lv It*, Foreward Mvmt Press. Alb Inst 1990-1998; Washington DC Epis Cleric Assn 1991-1998; Washington DC Fllshp of St. Jn 1998. Norman B Nash Fell Dio Massachusetts 1985.

UNDERWOOD, Bonnie Gordy (At) **Epis Ch Of The H Sprt Cumming GA 2015-** B Abbeville LA 1957 d John & Beatrice. BA U of Texas 1980; MDiv Sewanee: The U So, TS 2015. D 12/20/2014 P 6/20/2015 Bp Robert Christopher Wright. m 3/18/1989 Jesse Robert Underwood c 5.

UNDERWOOD, Deborah Ann (Okla) 501 S. Cincinnati Ave., Tulsa OK 74103 B Hollywood CA 1957 d Norman & Betty. D 6/21/2008 Bp Edward Joseph Konieczny. m 3/20/1981 Michael Underwood c 4.

872

UNDERWOOD, Robert Franklin (CPa) 4109 Cochise Ter, Sarasota FL 34233 **Ret 1989-** B Mount Carmel PA 1929 s Lewis & Florence. BA Dickinson Coll 1951; MDiv GTS 1961. D 6/13/1961 P 2/24/1962 Bp Frederick Warnecke. m 5/12/1962 Lois Ann Underwood c 3. Assoc All SS' Epis Ch Hershey PA 1987-1989; Non-par 1973-1986; Vic All SS Ch Selinsgrove PA 1969-1973; Vic S Mk's Epis Ch Northumberlnd PA 1969-1973; R Chr Ch New Brighton PA 1966-1969; R S Dav Scranton 1961-1966; Vic S Jn The Bapt Scranton PA 1961-1966.

UPCHURCH, Stanley Ray (Okla) 617 Leaning Elm Dr, Norman OK 73071 **D S Tim's Epis Ch Pauls Vlly OK 2001-** B Ardmore OK 1946 s Stanley & Eva. BS U of Oklahoma 1979. D 6/30/1990 Bp Robert Manning Moody. m 5/2/1969 Carol Jo Upchurch c 1. Dio Oklahoma Oklahoma City OK 2007-2010, Archv 1992-; D S Jn's Ch Norman OK 1990-2010. Natl Epis Historians and Archv 1990. Cn Jn Davis Awd Natl Epis Historians and Archv 2000.

UPHAM, Judith Elizabeth (FtW) 9805 Livingston Rd, Fort Washington MD 20744 **Asst S Alb's Epis Ch Arlington TX 2011-** B Tulsa OK 1942 d John & Marion. BA Rad 1964; MDiv EDS 1967; MSW Washington U 1972. D 12/6/1975 P 1/1/1977 Bp William Augustus Jones Jr. S Mk's Ch Candor NY 2004-2007; St Johns Epis Ch Berkshire NY 2004-2007; All SS Ch Fulton NY 2002-2003; Int S Phil's Ch San Jose CA 1999-2002; S Barth's Ch Gaithersburg MD 1997-1998; Int S Jas' Ch Indn Hd MD 1995-1996; Int Chr Ch Durham Par Nanjemoy MD 1993-1995; Syracuse Urban Cluster Syracuse NY 1989-1991; Gr Epis Ch Syracuse NY 1979-1989; Asst Chapl Chr Hosp NE/NW S Louis MO 1978-1979; Dio Missouri S Louis MO 1977-1978; LocTen S Steph's Ch S Louis MO 1977-1978; D S Mk's Ch S Louis MO 1975-1976.

UPTON, David Hugh (USC) 206 W Prentiss Ave, Greenville SC 29605 **Ret 2007-** B Fayetteville NC 1947 s Richard & Hazel. Das Goethe Institut; Middlebury Lang Sch; BA U NC - Chap Hill 1969; MDiv VTS 1973. D 6/23/1973 Bp Thomas Augustus Fraser Jr P 3/1/1974 Bp Philip Frederick McNairy. R S Andr's Epis Ch Greenville SC 1997-2007, Int R 1996-1997; Sr Chapl Chr Ch Epis Sch Greenville SC 1996-1997; Chr Ch Preschool Greenville SC 1996-1997; Virginia Epis Sch Lynchburg VA 1987-1996; Chapl Virginia Epis Sch Lynchburg VA 1987-1996; Ch Of The Gd Shpd Greer SC 1981-1987; Chapl Chr Ch Epis Sch Greenville SC 1975-1982; Chr Ch Greenville SC 1975-1981; Chapl, Shattuck S Mary's Sch Faribault MN 1973-1975. Hon Cn Cathd Of Our Merc Sav 1975.

UPTON, Thomas Lee (Neb) 14017 Washington St, Omaha NE 68137 **Mem, Bdgt Com Dio Nebraska Omaha NE 2004-** B Omaha NE 1944 s Carl & Nancy. BS U of Nebraska 1967; MBA Creighton U at Omaha 1974. D 4/8/1989 Bp James Daniel Warner. m 11/18/1966 Jane Evelyn Upton c 2. D S Andr's Ch Omaha NE 2005-2013, D 1989-2004; D H Fam Epis Ch Omaha NE 2002-2005.

URANG, Gunnar (Vt) Po Box 306, Norwich VT 05055 **Ret 1994-** B Staten Island NY 1929 s Olai & Anna. MA U Chi 1951; PhD U Chi 1969. D 6/9/1984 P 12/1/1984 Bp Robert Shaw Kerr. m 6/21/1971 Sarah Horton c 2. R Geth Ch Proctorsville VT 1986-1994; R S Mk's Ch Springfield VT 1986-1994; Asst Trin Ch Rutland VT 1984-1986. "An Inquirer's Guide to Chr Believing," Wilf and Stock, 2005; "Chas Williams & JRRTolkien," SCM Press, 1971; Auth, "Shadows Of Heaven, Rel & Fantasy In The Writings Of Cs Lewis," Pilgrim Press, 1970.

URBAN JR, Percy Linwood (Pa) The Quadrangle # 2301, 3300 Darby Road, Haverford PA 19041 **Ret 1986-** B Philadelphia PA 1924 s Percy & Mary. BA Pr 1946; STB GTS 1948; STM GTS 1954; ThD GTS 1959. D 5/28/1948 P 12/16/1948 Bp Frederick G Budlong. m 6/16/1951 Ann C Coward c 3. Inst. to Prof Swarthmore Coll Swarthmore PA 1957-1986; Chapl Leake & Watts Chld's Hm Yonkers NY 1953-1957; P-in-c S Ptr's Ch New York NY 1950-1953; Stff Chr Ch Cathd Hartford CT 1948-1950; Vic S Andr Hartford CT 1948-1950. Auth, "A Short Hist Of Chr Thought (Revised & Enlarged)," Oxf Press, 1995; Auth, "Willam Of Ockams Theol Ethics," *Franciscan Stds*, Annual, 1973; Auth, "Was Luther A Thoroughgoing Determinist?," *Journ Of Theol Stds (April)*, 1971. AAR; Amer Philos Assn; Conf Angl Theologians. Phi Beta Kappa 1946.

URBANEK, Virginia (Me) P.O. Box 455, Houlton ME 04730 **Ch Of The Gd Shpd Houlton ME 2011-** B Merrill WI 1946 d Gerard & Arline. AA Concordia Jr Coll 1966; BA Valparaiso U 1969. D 6/29/2008 Bp Chilton Richardson Knudsen P 3/21/2009 Bp Stephen Taylor Lane. c 2. S Thos Ch Winn ME 2009-2011.

URE III, Lincoln Richard (U) 80 S 300 E, Salt Lake City UT 84111 **Died 6/10/2016** B Salt Lake City UT 1947 s Lincoln & Betty. BA U of Utah 1970; MDiv GTS 1974. D 6/16/1974 P 12/22/1974 Bp Otis Charles. m 8/30/1969 Maureen O'Hara c 1. Chapl Epis Cmnty Serv Inc Salt Lake City UT 1991-2016; Dir of Pstr Care and CPE Supvsr S Mk Pstr Care Cntr Inc. Salt Lake City UT 1991-2016; P-in-c S Lk's Epis Ch Pk City UT 1980-1990; Chapl S Mk's Hosp Salt Lake City UT 1976-1991; St Marks Hosp Salt Lake City UT 1976-1991; D-In-Trng Ch Of The Gd Shpd Ogden UT 1974-1975; Chapl Res So Carolina St Hosp Salt Lake City UT 1972-1973. ACPE 1983.

URINOSKI, Ann Kathryne (Del) PO Box 3510, Wilmington DE 19807 **Chr Ch Christiana Hundred Wilmington DE 2017-** B Plainfield NJ 1986 d William & Kirby. Bachelor of Arts U of Delaware 2010; Mstr of Div GTS 2016.

D 12/16/2015 P 6/18/2016 Bp William H Stokes. S Mk's Ch Basking Ridge NJ 2015-2016. aurinoski@christchurchde.org

URMSON-TAYLOR, Ralph (Okla) 47a Via Porta Perlici PG, Assisi OK 06081 Italy B Rochdale England 1928 s Ralph & Lucy. BD Kelham Theol Coll 1956; MA U of Tulsa 1972; Manchester Coll 1974. Trans 5/1/1967 as Priest Bp Chilton R Powell. Holland Hall Sch Tulsa OK 1980-1993; Trin Ch Tulsa OK 1977-1993, Asst P 1962-1965; P-in-c S Bede's Ch Westport OK 1971-1973; Chapl Holland Hall Sch Tulsa OK 1965-1993; Serv Ch of Engl 1956-1962.

URQUIDI, Ashley Elizabeth (Md) 4449 N Witchduck Rd, Virginia Beach VA 23455 **Asst Old Donation Ch Virginia Bch VA 2015-** B Harrisburg PA 1987 MDiv Epis TS Of The SW 2015; BA Hood Coll 2015. D 1/10/2015 Bp Eugene Taylor Sutton P 7/14/2015 Bp Herman Hollerith IV. m 12/17/2011 Benjamin Paul Urquidi c 2. aurquidi@olddonation.org

USHER JR, Guy Randolph (Eau) 303 S Hollybrook Dr, Chillicothe IL 61523 **Int R S Paul's Ch Hudson WI 2007-** B Hayward WI 1971 s Guy & Evelyn. MDiv Nash; BA Estrn Illinois U 1993; MA Estrn Illinois U 1994. D 12/21/1996 P 6/1/1997 Bp William Charles Wantland. S Kath's Ch Owen WI 2000-2007; Vic S Fran Epis Ch Chillicothe IL 1997-2000.

UZOMECHINA, Gideon (NJ) 600 Cleveland Avenue, Plainfield NJ 07060 **Mem, Dioc Coun Dio New Jersey Trenton NJ 2013-, Mem, Bd Missions 2012-, Mem, Mssn to the Imprisoned 2011-; Bible Study/Pstr Counslg Vol Garden St Yth Correctional Facility Yardville NJ 2011-** B Nigeria 1975 s Charles & Juliana. Dplma Bp Crowther Coll of Theol 2001; Dplma Other 2001; Dplma U of Jos 2001; Bachelor of Educ Nnamdi Azikiwe U 2006; Cert St. Geo's Coll, Jerusalem 2008; Cert Robert Wood Johnson U Hosp 2010; Mstr of Arts Liberty U 2012; Mstr of Arts Other 2012; D. Min Afr Theol Educ Ntwk 2013; D. Min Other 2013. Trans 10/13/2011 as Priest Bp George Edward Councell. m 4/12/2004 Nkeiruka Ernestina Uzomechina c 3. Gr Epis Ch Plainfield NJ 2014-2017; Assoc S Ptr's Ch Freehold NJ 2009-2010; P-in-c S Alb's Epis Ch New Brunswick NJ 2002-2014. The Soc of Cath Priests (SCP) 2009. Fell, Chr Theologians and Philosophers (FCTP) Afr Theol Educ Ntwk 2013; Phi Beta Kappa Hob, Geneva, NY 1948.

UZUETA JR, Luis (Ak) 1392 Benshoof Dr, North Pole AK 99705 **Died 1/4/2016** B Deming NM 1947 s Luis & Anita. BA New Mex Highlands U 1970; MDiv Nash 1977. D 6/4/1977 P 12/1/1977 Bp James Daniel Warner. m 3/19/1970 Lona Claire Uzueta. S Jude's Epis Ch No Pole AK 2004-2016; Dio Alaska Fairbanks AK 1991-2000; Vic S Mk's Ch Gordon NE 1980-1991; Vic S Mary's Ch: Holly Rushville NE 1980-1991; Asst S Matt's Ch Lincoln NE 1977-1980; P-in-c S Steph Ashland NE 1977-1980; P-in-c Trin Memi Epis Ch Crete NE 1977-1980. Auth, "Soup in the Sandhills," *Jubilee Journ*, Jub. SocMary 1976.

V

VACA TAPIA, Harold Alexander (EcuC) Calle Calderon entre Argentina y Chile, Tulcan Carchi Ecuador B Tulca 1979 s Victor & Bertha. Sin Titulo S.M. Nuestra Senora de la Esperanza; Licenciado Educacion Basica Universidad Tecnica del Norte. D 6/29/2012 Bp Victor Alfonso Scantlebury. m 4/12/2003 Maira Tatiana Bolanos Huertas c 1. Iglesia Epis Del Ecuador Quito 2012-2017.

VACCARO, Anthony Joseph (Chi) Church of Our Saviour, 530 W Fullerton Pkwy, Chicago IL 60614 **Ch Of Our Sav Chicago IL 2015-** B Brooklyn NY 1960 s Ralph & Carolyn. BS Boston Coll 1982; MD Bos Sch 1989; MDiv Garrett Evang Theol 2012; MDiv Garrett-Evang TS 2012. D 6/8/2013 P 12/14/2013 Bp Jeff Lee. m 8/2/2014 Giovanni Battista Colucci. Asstg P Cathd Of S Jas Chicago IL 2013-2014, Asstg D 2013.

VADERS, Nancy Johnson (NC) St Anne's Episc Ch, 2690 Fairlawn Dr, Winston Salem NC 27106 B Houston TX 1980 d Charles & Susan. BA U of Tennessee 2002; MDiv Duke DS 2006. D 2/18/2012 Bp Michael B Curry. m 7/6/2003 Mark Jennings Vaders c 1.

VAFIS, John Symon (NCal) PO Box 1044, Colusa CA 95932 **P S Steph's Epis Ch Colusa CA 2005-** B Detroit MI 1938 s Symon & Annie. BA Stan 1960; MA U Pgh 1965. D 5/15/2005 P 11/20/2005 Bp Jerry Alban Lamb. m 3/28/1960 Patricia Vafis c 1.

VAGGIONE OHC, Richard Paul (Cal) 1601 Oxford St, Berkeley CA 94709 **Professed OHC 1980-** B San Jose CA 1945 s Roger & Evelyn. BA Santa Clara U 1966; BA Cath U of Louvain 1969; STB GTS 1970; STM GTS 1970; PhD Oxf GB 1976. D 6/27/1970 Bp Chauncie Kilmer Myers P 2/1/1971 Bp Jonathan Goodhue Sherman. H Cross Monstry W Pk NY 2005-2006; All Souls Par In Berkeley Berkeley CA 1992-1993; Int S Ambr Epis Ch Foster City CA 1991-1992; Int S Clem's Ch Berkeley CA 1989-1990; R S Mths Angl Ch In Toronto Ontario Can 1985-1989; S Dav's Epis Ch Castleton NY 1982-1984; Ch Of The Epiph Corcoran CA 1979-1980; Asst P S Jas Epis Ch Scarborough ME 1977-1978; Int S Jn's Epis Ch Clayton CA 1976-1977; Asst S Alb-The-Mtyr Oxford Engl 1973-1976; Lectr In Medieval Latin The GTS New York NY 1971-1972; Cur S Lk's Ch E Hampton NY 1970-1971. Auth, "Over All Asia?";

V

Auth, "Journ Of Biblic Lit"; Auth, "Theo Of Mapsuestia'S Contra Eunomium". SBL.

VAGUENER, Martha (SwFla) 3105 Short Leaf St, Zephyrhills FL 33543 **Asstg Cler St. Mk's Ch Tampa 2011**- B Boston MA 1945 d Hugo & Mary. MA Providence Coll; BA Bos 1967; MEd Salem St Coll Salem MA 1971; MA Providence Coll 1978; MDiv EDS 1985; Cert Boston Coll 2004. D 7/13/1985 P 1/26/1986 Bp George Nelson Hunt III. S Eliz's Epis Ch Zephyrhills FL 2004-2010; R S Paul's Ch Peabody MA 1998-2004; Vic S Jn's Ch Millville MA 1988-1998; Asst Chr Ch In Lonsdale Lincoln RI 1987-1988; Dio Rhode Island Providence RI 1985-1987; Mssy Kenya 1985-1987; Cncl Dn, Tampa Dnry Dio SW Florida 2007-2009; Cncl Dn, Worcester Dnry Dio Wstrn Massachusetts 1995-1998. AAUW 1990; Assn of Psychol Type 1984-2010; Catechesis of the Gd Shpd 2007; MECA 1999; NECCA 1999.

VAIL, Jean Parker (Chi) 305 Sutherland Ct, Durham NC 27712 **Assoc S Matt's Epis Ch Hillsborough NC 1999**- B Santa Barbara CA 1932 d Henry & Emily. BA Wellesley Coll 1954; MDiv SWTS 1985; DMin SWTS 1993. D 9/20/1985 Bp James Winchester Montgomery P 5/24/1986 Bp Frank Tracy Griswold III. m 12/29/1956 Thomas Peale Vail c 3. Int S Mart's By The Lake Epis Minnetonka Bch MN 1996-1998; Bexley Seabury Fed Chicago IL 1994-1998; Cathd Ch Of S Mk Minneapolis MN 1994-1996; Int S Helena's Ch Burr Ridge IL 1993; Provost Cathd Of S Jas Chicago IL 1990-1991; Int S Elis's Ch Glencoe IL 1989-1990; Assoc S Andr's Ch Downers Grove IL 1987-1989; D All SS Ch Wstrn Sprgs IL 1985-1986. Auth, "In the Name of GOD," Chap Hill Press, 2004. BEC- Dioc Of NC 2004; Chapl: Soc. of Comp of H Cross 2000. Hon Cn Cathd of S Jas Chicago 1998.

VALANDRA, Linda Beth (SD) 410 University Ave, Hot Springs SD 57747 B Burnet TX 1953 d Thomas & Marion. D 6/11/2005 Bp Creighton Leland Robertson. c 1.

VALANTASIS, Richard L (Mo) 17 Wildflower Way, Santa Fe NM 87506 **Prof of Ascetical Theol Candler TS Emory Unviersity Atlanta 2006-; Assoc Prof Theol Stds S Louis U S Louis MO 1992**- B Canton OH 1946 s Louis & Irene. BA Hope Coll 1968; EDS 1972; MTh Harvard DS 1982; ThD Harvard DS 1988. D 6/9/1973 P 3/1/1974 Bp John Melville Burgess. m 6/10/1973 Janet Valantasis. Cn Theol Dio The Rio Grande Albuquerque 2011-2012; Prof of NT & Chr Origins Iliff TS 1999-2006; Dir of Ministers Stds Harvard DS Cambridge MA 1990-1992; Ch Of S Jn The Evang Boston MA 1987-1992; R S Jn's Ch Winthrop MA 1975-1978; Cur S Paul's Ch Natick MA 1974-1975. "Beliefnet Guide to Gnosticism and Other Vanished Christianities," Doubleday, 2006; "The New Q: Translation and Commentary," T & T Clark, 2005; "Centuries of Holiness," Continuum, 2005; "Rel of Late Antiquity in Pract," Pr Press, 2000; "The Gospel of Thos," *NT Readings*, Routledge, 1997; Auth, "Asceticism," Oxf Press, 1995; Auth, "Third Century Sprtl Guides," *Harvard Dissertations in Rel*, Fortress Perss, 1991. AAR; SBL. Woodrow Wilson Fell 1968.

VALCOURT, Theodore Philippe-Francois (CGC) 401 Live Oak Ave, Pensacola FL 32507 **Battalion Chapl Off Of Bsh For ArmdF 2008-; Off Of Bsh For ArmdF New York NY 2007**- B Savannah GA 1965 s Arthur & Dorothy. BA Morris Brown Coll 1989; MPH Savannah St U 1991; MDiv Interdenominational Theol Cntr 1995; MS Troy U 2004. D 2/17/2007 P 7/28/2007 Bp Philip Menzie Duncan II. m 5/20/1995 Rosalyn Valcourt c 3.

VALDEMA, Pierre-Henry (Hai) Eglise Sainte Trinite, Rue Mgr Guilloux, Box 1309, Port-Au-Prince Haiti **R S Pierre In Mirebabais 1980**- B 1951 s Charles & Alda. Coll Philadelphie Degre Secondary 73; Theol Etude Theologique. D 7/29/1979 P 5/1/1980 Bp Luc Anatole Jacques Garnier. m 9/6/1984 Marie Carmel Germain Valdema c 3. Dio Haiti Port-au-Prince HT 1979-2017.

VALDERRAMA SANABRIA, Juan Pablo (Colom) c/o Diocese of Colombia, Cra 6 No. 49-85 Piso 2, Bogota, BDC Colombia **Iglesia Epis En Colombia Bogota 2016**- B 1971 s Juan & Luz. Piesbitero Mayor de San Jose 1997; Licenciado enTedogio Universidad Javeriana 1999; Licenciado enTedogio U of Javerrana 1999; Licenciado enTedogio U of Javerrana 1999; Especialista Bioctica Universidad Javeriana 2001. D 12/6/1996 P 12/6/1997 Bp Francisco Jose Duque-Gomez. m 7/15/2006 Katty Zorayda Diaz Gomez c 1.

VALDES, Fernando Joaquin (Los) **St Johns Pro-Cathd Los Angeles CA 2016**- B Los Angeles CA 1965 s Fernando & Maria. D 11/1/2015 Bp Joseph Jon Bruno. c 1.

VALDES, Paul Anthony (NC) 8105 Summit Springs Ct, Browns Summit NC 27214 **Died 8/26/2015** B New York NY 1939 s Paul & Roslyn. BA Greensboro Coll. D 6/26/2005 Bp Michael B Curry. m 5/4/1974 June Swanston-Valdes c 6.

VALDEZ, Pedro A (Micr) 826 Howard St, Carthage MO 64836 B Guatemala City GT 1943 s Pedro & Clotilde. Esciela De Comercio Guatemala; U Mariano Galvez De Guatemala Gt; BA Sem Santotomas Apostol Gt 1980; Lic Theol U Luteran of The El Salvador CA Sv 1997. D 7/4/1980 P 10/1/1981 Bp Anselmo Carral-Solar. m 8/8/1968 Lilia Valdez. Dio W Missouri Kansas City MO 2000-2008; Vic Iglesia San Marcos 1996-1999; Vic Catedral Santiago Apostol Guatemala 1990-1995; Vic San Juan Bautista Guatemala 1984-1989; Dio Guatemala New York NY 1980-1999.

VALENTINE III, A Wilson (Ak) 924 C St, Juneau AK 99801 **Chair Of Const And Cn 1995**- B Richmond VA 1952 s Allen & Dora. Chris Newport U 1972; BA U of Alaska 1977; MDiv Bex Sem 1991. D 5/9/1991 Bp George Clinton Harris P 8/1/1992 Bp Steven Charleston. m 6/2/1982 Priscilla Harris. The Ch Of The H Trin Juneau AK 2012; S Phil's Ch Wrangell AK 2011-2017; Presiding Judge Eccl Crt Dio Alaska Fairbanks AK 1995-2001; R S Brendan's Epis Ch Juneau AK 1993-2000; Asst Trin Ch Rochester NY 1991-1992. Gvnr'S Awd For Heroism St Of Alaska 1984. akpriest03@gci.net

VALENTINE, Darcy Adrian (Minn) 615 Vermillion St, Hastings MN 55033 **CE Dir S Lk's Epis Ch Hastings MN 2010**- B De Smet SD 1965 s Rodney & Marlene. BA Augustana Coll 1987. D 6/20/2015 Bp Brian N Prior. m 7/30/1998 Lisa Marie Valentine c 3.

VALENTINE JR, John Carney (WVa) 206 E 2nd St, Weston WV 26452 **R S Paul's Ch Weston WV 2008**- B Logan WV 1955 s John & Norma. MDiv S Marys Sem and U 1985. Rec 5/3/2008 Bp William Michie Klusmeyer. m 12/30/2000 Bertha Valentine c 2.

VALENTINE, Peggy Lee (NwT) St Mark's Episcopal Church, 3150 Vogel St, Abilene TX 79603 **D S Mk's Epis Ch Abilene TX 2007**- B Corning NY 1946 d Robert & Florence. BS Fredonia St Univ of NY 1968; MA Hardin-Simmons U 1985. D 10/31/2007 Bp C Wallis Ohl. m 4/7/1973 Gary Valentine c 2. DOK 2006.

VALENTINE, Ronald Andrew (Chi) St James the Less Episcopal Church, 550 Sunset Ridge Rd, Northfield IL 60093 B Chicago IL 1942 s Andrew & Dorothy. BS NWU 1965; MBA NWU 1968. D 1/19/2008 Bp Victor Alfonso Scantlebury. m 11/21/1980 Deborah Valentine c 4. The Epis Ch Of S Jas The Less Northfield IL 2008-2014, 2004-2007; Mem Bp's T/F on the Diac 2013-2014; Mem Faith based T/F- Kellogg/ NW Univ. 2012-2014; co- chair D's Coun of Dio Chicago 2011-2013; Mem, Advsry Coun Elder Abuse- No Shore 2008-2014; Trst Trst Bp Anderson Hse 2007-2015; Dir Dir Porchlight Counslg Serv 2005-2014. Kellogg Exec Schlr Kellogg Sch of Mgmt, NW Univ. 2012; Fulbright-Hays Schlr US Dept of Educ 2011.

VALENTINE DAVIS, Melinda R (Mil) **S Jas Ch W Bend WI 2016**- B Waterloo IA 1978 d Melvin & Linda. BA U of Nthrn Iowa 2000; MDiv Sewanee U of So TS 2016. D 12/12/2015 P 8/6/2016 Bp Alan Scarfe. m 6/10/2000 Kevin C Davis c 3. mothermindystjames@gmail.com

VALIATH, Abraham J (Be) 365 Lafayette Ave., Palmerton PA 18071 B Mylapra India 1944 s Thomas & Sarah. BD Leonard Theol Coll 1969; MA Mysore U 1989; MTh Serampore U IN 1997. Trans 6/1/2008 Bp Paul Victor Marshall. c 2. R S Jn's Epis Ch Palmerton PA 2008-2016; Assoc S Andr's Epis Ch Allentown PA 2007-2008.

VALLE, Jose Francisco (WA) 1700 Powder Mill Rd, Silver Spring MD 20903 **Ch Of Our Sav Silver Sprg MD 2015**- B Zacatecoluca La Paz El Salvador 1971 s Jose & Maria. Rec 2/28/2015 as Priest Bp Mariann Edgar Budde. m 10/19/2013 Margoth Lourdes Orellana c 2.

VALLE-PLAZA, Juan Nelson (EcuC) Casilla 0901-5250, Guayaquil Ecuador B Penipe EC 1963 s Carlos & Rosa. U of Loja; Epis TS 1997. D 7/14/1996 P 3/1/1998 Bp Terencio Alfredo Morante-Espana. m 1/6/1993 Mireya Valle-Plaza. Litoral Dio Ecuador Guayaquil 1997-2001.

VALOVICH, Stephen Anthony (SeFla) 3395 Burns Rd, Palm Beach Gardens FL 33410 B Gary IN 1944 s Joseph & Rose. D 11/23/2013 Bp Leo Frade. m 4/12/1998 Linda Laurenzo Valovich.

VAN, Maron Ines (Ore) 4435 Fox Hollow Rd, Eugene OR 97405 **D Ch Of The Resurr Eugene OR 1988**- B North Bend OR 1936 d Earl & Evelyn. U of Oregon. D 1/9/1988 Bp Robert Louis Ladehoff. m 6/22/1957 Maurice Allen Van c 4.

VAN ANTWERPEN, Alanna Mary (NH) 214 Main St, Nashua NH 03060 **Asst Ch Of The Gd Shpd Nashua NH 2010**- B Danbury CT 1975 d Thomas & Maureen. BA S Anselm Coll 1997; MDiv Jesuit TS 2007; Cert Ang Stud CDSP 2008. D 7/1/2010 P 1/6/2011 Bp Vicky Gene Robinson. m 6/23/2007 Franklin Van Antwerpen c 1.

VAN ATTA, Ralph Sherwood (Pa) 6505 Tabor Ave Apt 5116, Philadelphia PA 19111 **Died 8/13/2016** B Binghamton NY 1919 s Ralph & Jessie. BS SUNY 1944; BD Ya Berk 1949. D 6/18/1949 Bp Walter M Higley P 11/1/1950 Bp Malcolm E Peabody. Asst Emm Holmesburg Philadelphia PA 1989-1991; Ret 1985-2016; Int All SS Ch Rhawnhurst Philadelphia PA 1984-1985; Ret 1981-2016; Ch Of The Gd Shpd Philadelphia PA 1980-1981; The Ch Of Emm And The Gd Shpd Philadelphia PA 1980-1981; H Apos And Medtr Philadelphia PA 1978-1979; Non-par 1976-1984; Dn Convoc Dio Pennsylvania Philadelphia PA 1962-1964; R S Paul's Ch Philadelphia PA 1957-1975; Asst S Barth's Ch Baltimore MD 1955-1957; Chr Epis Ch Willard NY 1951-1954; Mssnr Ch Of The Epiph Trumansburg NY 1951-1954; Chapl Willard S Hosp 1951-1954; Asst Chenango Cnty Missions Norwich NY 1949-1951.

VANAUKER, Margaret Elizabeth (Md) 225 Bowie Trl, Lusby MD 20657 **D All SS Epis Par Sunderland MD 2008**- B Youngstown OH 1945 d Earl & Gladys. BA Youngstown St U 1968; MLa JHU 1977; MA S Mary Sem Ecuminical Inst Baltimore MD 1994. D 6/12/1993 Bp Albert Theodore Eastman. m 12/20/1968 Joseph William Van Auker c 2. D Middleham & S Ptr's Par Lusby MD 2001-2008; D Chr Ch Columbia MD 1999-2001; D Ch Of Engl Dio Ripon 1996-1998; D S Andr's Ch Pasadena MD 1993-1995. NAAD.

VANBAARS, Sven Layne (Va) PO Box 146, Gloucester VA 23061 **R Abingdon Epis Ch White Marsh VA 2010-** B Portsmouth VA 1962 s Frans & Jacquelyn. Un-PSCE; AA Craven Cmnty Coll 1983; BA E Carolina U 1985; MPA E Carolina U 1988; MDiv VTS 2008. D 5/24/2008 P 12/6/2008 Bp Peter J Lee. m 8/3/1991 Jennifer Warfel. Asst S Mart's Epis Ch Williamsburg VA 2008-2010; Dir of Stwdshp and Dvlpmt Dio Virginia Richmond VA 2000-2006.

VAN BEVEREN, Eugene Charles (Neb) 3041 SW Isaac Ave, Pendleton OR 97801 **Lic Dio Estrn Oregon Cove OR 2008-; Ret 2002-** B Hood River OR 1935 s Henry & Mary. BA Mt Ang Abbey 1958; BS Estrn Oregon U 1973. Rec 6/1/1981 as Priest Bp Rustin Ray Kimsey. m 7/28/1973 Charlanne E Van Beveren c 3. P-in-c S Jn's Ch Valentine NE 2006-2007; P-in-c Calv Ch Okreek SD 2003-2006; P-in-c Ch of the H Sprt Ideal SD 2003-2005; R Trin Epis Ch 2002-2005; Vic Ch Of The Incarn Greg SD 2002-2003; Vic Ch Of The Resurr (Chap) So Cle Elum WA 1991-2002; R Gr Ch Ellensburg WA 1991-2002; Dio Oregon Portland OR 1988-1991; S Chris's Ch Port Orford OR 1984-1988; S Jn-By-The-Sea Epis Ch Bandon OR 1984-1988; S Matt's Epis Ch Gold Bch OR 1984-1988; P-in-c S Andr's Epis Ch Prineville OR 1980-1983; Serv RC Ch 1962-1973.

VAN BRUNT, Thomas Harvey (SO) 534 Chapel Road, Amelia OH 45102 **Long Term Supply St. Mary Magd Maineville Ohio 2013-; Supply P Dio Sthrn Ohio 2008-** B Willard OH USA 1943 s Percy & Emma. BA OH SU 1966; MA OH SU 1968; PhD Indiana U 1976; MDiv Sewanee: The U So, TS 1986. D 6/7/1986 P 12/7/1986 Bp Don Adger Wimberly. m 6/14/1969 Nancye Eileen Knowles c 2. Int S Aug's Epis Ch Danville IN 2009-2011; Soc Worker/Case Mgr Life Point Solutions Amelia Ohio 2008-2013; Vic Ch Of The Gd Samar Amelia OH 2005-2008; R S Ptr's Epis Ch Delaware OH 1996-2005; Dn Wstrn Convoc Dio Upper So Carolina Columbia SC 1993-1996; R Ch Of The Resurr Greenwood SC 1990-1996; S Alb's Ch Morehead KY 1986-1990; Vic S Fran' Epis Ch Flemingsburg KY 1986-1990. CT 1986. Fell in Res Univ of the So 2008; Fllshp Coll Of Preachers Coll of Preachers 1996.

VANBUREN, Andrew David (Roch) 32 East Main Street, Clifton Springs NY 14432 **P-in-c S Jn's Ch Clifton Spgs NY 2015-** B Akron OH 1987 s George & Christine. Angl Stds Cert Bexley-Seabury Fed; BA Swarthmore Coll 2010; MDiv Colgate Rochester Crozer 2015. D 5/13/2015 P 11/22/2015 Bp Prince Grenville Singh.

VAN BUREN, Robert Barrett (Los) 15524 Pintura Dr, Hacienda Heights CA 91745 **Dioc Supply P Dio Los Angeles LA CA USA 2014-; P Asstg/Chapl S Jn's Mssn La Verne CA 2014-, D Asstg/Chapl 2008-2014** B Norwalk CA 1960 s Robert & Muriel. BA California St U, Fullerton 1989; MDiv GTS 2005. D 11/1/2005 P 8/16/2014 Bp Joseph Jon Bruno. m 11/19/1988 Penelope Baxter c 1. Stff Clincl Chapl Pomona Vlly Hosp Med Cntr Pomona CA 2015-2017; D/Cur S Jas' Par So Pasadena CA 2007-2008; D/Cur Dio Los Angeles Los Angeles CA 2006-2007; D/Cur The Ch Of The Ascen Sierra Madre CA 2005-2006.

VANCE, Craig Douglas (Haw) 2140 Main St, Wailuku HI 96793 **P-in-c The Par Of Gd Shpd Epis Ch Wailuku HI 2016-** B Regina,Sask. Canada 1958 s Frederick & Donna. BA U of Regina 1982; Dplma C.S. Regent Coll 1987; MDiv Vancouver TS 2003. Trans 5/26/2016 as Priest Bp Robert Leroy Fitzpatrick. c 2. pastor@goodshepherdmaui.org

VANCE, Marcus Patrick (Ind) 2651 California St., Columubus IN 47201 **R S Paul's Ch Columbus IN 2006-** B Versailles KY 1962 s Henry & Patricia. BS Estrn Kentucky U 1986; BS Estrn Kentucky U 1987; MDiv Sewanee: The U So, TS 1997. D 8/23/1997 P 3/20/1998 Bp Don Adger Wimberly. m 5/8/1993 Leticia Lynn Christison c 3. Assoc R H Trin Epis Ch Melbourne FL 1999-2006; Cn Assoc Gr And H Trin Cathd Kansas City MO 1997-1999; Yth Dir S Jn's Ch Versailles KY 1990-1993. fr.marc.vance@gmail.com

VANCE, Timothy Keith (SwVa) PO Box 344, Sewanee TN 37375 B Norwalk CA 1958 s Dennis & Donna. BA OR SU 1981; MDiv Yale DS 1986; Sewanee: The U So, TS 1997; Sewanee: The U So, TS 2008. D 5/25/1989 Bp William Hopkins Folwell P 11/30/1989 Bp Charles I Jones III. m 9/1/2010 Sherry Vance c 2. R S Paul's Epis Ch Salem VA 1999-2006; R S Matthews Auburn WA 1992-1999; Vic S Jas Ch Lewistown MT 1989-1992; Chapl Trin Preparatory Sch Of Florida Winter Pk FL 1986-1989. Auth, "Fly Fishing And Par Mnstry," *LivCh*, 2003; Auth, "Advice For Search Committees," *LivCh*.

VANCE, William Walter (CFla) 26 Willow Dr, Orlando FL 32807 **Chr The King Epis Ch Orlando FL 2010-** B Goshen NY 1951 s Walter & Vivian. MA Amer Grad U; BS Excelsior U 1989. D 12/11/2010 Bp John Wadsworth Howe. m 10/23/1971 Sue Vance c 2.

VANCOOTEN-WEBSTER, Jennifer Elizabeth (LI) 286-88 7th Ave, Brooklyn NY 11215 B Guyana South America 1954 d George & Gladys. Cuny Brooklyn Coll; Mercer TS; B.A Cuny Brooklyn Coll 2003; M.A CUNY Brooklyn Coll 2007. D 6/7/2014 Bp Lawrence C Provenzano. m 12/27/1986 Philip Webster c 3.

VAN CULIN JR, Samuel (WA) 3900 Watson Place, NW #5D-B, Washington DC 20016 **Res Cn Washington Natl Cathd 2002-; Ret 1994-** B Honolulu HI 1930 s Samuel & Susie. VTS; BA Pr 1952; BD VTS 1955. D 6/3/1955 Bp Frederick D Goodwin P 11/30/1955 Bp Harry Sherbourne Kennedy. P Ch Of Engl 1994-2001; Gnrl Secy Angl Consultative Coun London Engl 1983-1995; Secy Angl Primates Meeting 1982-1994; Wrld Mssn Off Epis Ch Cntr New York NY 1961-1982; Gnrl Secy Laymen Intl Washington DC 1960-1961; Asst R S Jn's Ch Georgetown Par Washington DC 1958-1960; Cur S Andr's Cathd Honolulu HI 1955-1956. Hon Cn Cbury Cathd; Hon Cn Ibadan Cathd; Hon Cn Prov Of So Afr; Hon Cn S Andrews Cathd, Hawaii; Res Cn Washington Natl Cathd.

VAN CULIN, T(homas) Andrew K. (Mich) 61 Grosse Pointe Blvd., Grosse Pointe Farms MI 48236 **R Chr Ch Grosse Pointe Grosse Pointe Farms MI 2013-; July R S Chris Sum Chap Winter Harbor ME 2011-** B Honolulu HI 1973 s Thomas & Sarah. BA Davidson Coll 1995; MDiv EDS 1999. D 7/18/1999 P 3/5/2000 Bp Richard Sui On Chang. m 1/9/2004 Jessica L Van Culin c 2. Sub-Dn S Jn's Cathd Denver CO 2009-2013; Assoc for Chr Formation The Epis Ch Of Beth-By-The-Sea Palm Bch FL 2005-2009; R S Dav Of The Hills Epis Ch Woodland Pk CO 2003-2005, P-in-c 2001-2002; Chapl Serv at Memi Hosp Colorado Sprg CO 2001-2002; Cur S Jas Epis Ch Kamuela HI 1999-2001; Yth Dir W Hawaii Yth Mnstry Kamuela HI 1999-2001; Yth Min Chr Ch Kealakekua HI 1999-2001; Kohala Epis Mssn Kapaau HI 1999-2001. dvanculin@christchurchgp.org

VAN CULIN, Thomas Meyers (Haw) 2578-F Pacific Heights Rd, Honolulu HI 96813 B Honolulu HI 1938 s Samuel & Susie. AA Barstow Cmnty Coll 1964; BS California St U 1966; MDiv CDSP 1990. D 9/1/1991 P 3/15/1992 Bp Donald Purple Hart. m 12/20/1992 Ernestina M Wiiliams-Van Culin c 1. S Lk's Epis Ch Honolulu HI 2007-2010; Dn Winward Deanry The Epis Ch in Hawaii Honolulu HI 1996-1998; S Matt's Epis Ch Waimanalo HI 1993-2007; Chf Chapl 9 Hi St Prisons 1990-1993. Ka Papa Anaina Hawaii, O Kristo.

VANDAGRIFF, Mary Cordelia (Ala) 220 S Wood Rd, Homewood AL 35209 B Manhattan KS 1931 d William & Tacy. MA U of Alabama. D 10/30/2004 Bp Henry Nutt Parsley Jr. c 4.

VAN DEN BLINK, Arie Johannes (Be) 315 W Washington Ave, Elmira NY 14901 **P-in-c S Paul's Ch Troy PA 2010-; Chapl Gnrl CT Cincinnati. OH 2002-** B Mojowarno Java ID 1934 s Jan & Tine. BA Trin Hartford CT 1955; BD Yale DS 1962; PhD PrTS 1972. D 7/19/1993 P 1/22/1994 Bp William George Burrill. m 6/30/1956 Katherine van den Blink c 3. Int Gr Epis Ch Elmira NY 2009; Pres AAPC Fairfax VA 1998-2000; Prof of Ascetical & Pstr Theol Bex Sem Columbus OH 1993-2006. "Alle malen zal ik wenen: traumaverwerking en spiritualiteit," *Psyche en Geloof*, Boekencentrum Uitgevers, 2005; "Late Vocation: A Personal Reflection," *The Angl Cath*, Affirming Angl Catholicism, 2004; "Grp Sprtl Direction in Sem," *The Lived Experience of Grp Sprtl Direction*, Paulist Press, 2003; Auth, "Pastorale Counslg en Spiritualiteit," *Deel 2-60 Geestelijke Volksgezondheid*, KSGV, Tilburg, 2002; "Thoughts on the Trsfg," *The Angl Cath*, Affirming Angl Catholicism, 2002; Auth, "Reflections on Sprtlty in Angl Theol Educ," *ATR*, ATR, 1999; Auth, "Trauma Reactivation in Pstr Counslg," *Amer Journ of Pstr Counslg*, Haworth Press, 1998; Auth, "Seeking God: The Way of the Sprt: Some Reflections on Sprtlty and Pstr," *Journ of Pstr Theol*, Soc of Pstr Theol, 1995. Affirming Angl Catholicism 1996; AAPC 1972; Soc Pstr Theol 1990. Pres AAPC 1998; Sr Choice Awd/Outstanding Fac Mem Bex and CRDS 1998; Distingushed Contribution Awd AAPC Estrn Reg 1997.

VANDERAU JR, Robert Julian (RI) 2305 Edgewater Drive, Apt 1718, Orlando FL 32804 **P Assoc S Richard's Ch Winter Pk FL 2012-, P-in-c 2010-2011** B Columbus OH 1945 s Robert & Margaret. BS OH SU 1968; MDiv VTS 1976. D 6/10/1976 P 12/17/1976 Bp John Mc Gill Krumm. Cn to the Ordnry Dio Rhode Island Providence RI 2005-2007; R Ch Of The Ascen Cranston RI 1994-2005; Cn Precentor Cathd Ch Of S Lk Orlando FL 1982-1994; Asst to the R Ch Of The Gd Shpd Jacksonville FL 1980-1982; Cur Chr Ch Prince Geo's Par Rockville MD 1976-1980. AAM 1997; ADLMC 1986-2001; CODE 2005-2013.

VANDERCOOK, Peter John (Chi) 616 8th Ave Apt 201, Monroe WI 53566 **Ret 1995-** B Derby CT 1935 s Willard & Margaret. BA Ya 1956; STB Ya Berk 1959. D 6/11/1959 P 5/27/1960 Bp Walter H Gray. Vic The Ch Of The H Innoc Hoffman Schaumburg IL 1970-1995; Vic S Chad Epis Ch Loves Pk IL 1964-1970; Cur S Lk's Ch Evanston IL 1962-1964; Cur S Jn's Ch Stamford CT 1959-1962.

VANDERCOOK, Ross Allan (Mich) 9900 N Meridian Rd, Pleasant Lake MI 49272 B Detroit MI 1949 s Edsall & Naomi. BA MI SU 1971; MA Wayne 1975; EdS Cntrl Michigan U 1983. D 11/11/2010 P 7/2/2011 Bp Wendell Nathaniel Gibbs Jr. m 6/16/1973 Susan Elizabeth Vandercook c 2.

VANDERCOOK, Susan Elizabeth (Mich) 9900 N Meridian Rd, Pleasant Lake MI 49272 B Tucson AZ 1949 d Raymond & Betty. BA MI SU 1970; JD Wayne 1975. D 11/11/2010 P 7/2/2011 Bp Wendell Nathaniel Gibbs Jr. m 6/16/1973 Ross Allan Vandercook c 2.

VAN DER HIEL, Rudolph J (CPa) 156 Jones Road, RR 1, Comp 5, Parry Sound ON P2A 2W7 Canada **P-t R S Andr's Ch Tioga PA 2013-** B Philadelphia PA 1940 s Peter & Johanna. BA Susquahanna U 1963; JD Tem 1966; MDiv Bex Sem 1984. D 6/8/1984 P 5/1/1985 Bp Charlie Fuller Mcnutt Jr. m 6/6/1964 M Lynne van der Hiel c 4. P-t Incumbent Par of Muskoka Lakes Dio Algoma Can 2005-2013; R Trin Wellsboro PA 1991-2005; S Jas Ch Mansfield PA 1985-2005; (Pres 2001-2003) EAM 1985-2003; Assoc P, Nthrn Tier Cluster Mnstry Dio Cntrl Pennsylvania PA 1985-1991; S Paul's Ch Wellsboro PA

V

1984-1985; D-in-c Trin Antrim PW 1984-1985; Dep, GC Dio Cntrl Pennsylvania; Dio Cntrl Pennsylvania Harrisburg PA; Const and Cn Com, Chair Dio Algoma Sault Ste Marie ON 2007-2015; Pres, Stndg Com Dio Cntrl Pennsylvania Harrisburg PA 2001-2002. Auth, "Rudolph J. van der Hiel," *A Night in the Tioga Cnty Jail*. Mansfield Min, PA Coun Ch 1984-2005; W Muskoka Mnstrl Assn 2005. Pearl Jones Awd for Serv to Appalachia Cmsn on Rel in Appalachian. 1994; 1993 Outstanding Citizen Mansfield Area ChmbrCom 1993; Outstanding Serv to Law Enforcement Awd Tioga Cnty Law Enforcement Off Assn 1979.

VANDER LEE, Jerome Neal (SD) 500 S Main Ave, Sioux Falls SD 57104 B Rock Rapids IA 1962 s Norman & Ruby. BA NW Coll 1985; MA Sioux Falls Sem 2005. D 4/22/2015 Bp John Tarrant. m 9/2/2004 Nancy Wise-Vander Lee c 2.

VANDERMARK, Roy James (Alb) 825 Covered Bridge Rd, Unadilla NY 13849 **Vic S Tim's Ch Westford NY 2013-, D Vic in Charge 2008-2013** B Sidney NY 1947 s Fredrick & Pauline. D 6/12/2004 Bp Daniel William Herzog. c 3. D S Matt's Ch Unadilla NY 2004-2008. Gd Neighbor Awd Unadilla Chamber if Commerce 1999; Fireman of the year Otsego Cnty 1998.

VANDERMEER, Leigh A (Chi) 19760 W Woodmere Ter, Antioch IL 60002 B Harvard IL 1958 d Matthew & Beverley. BS Wstrn Illinois U 1981; MDiv SWTS 2005. D 6/18/2005 P 12/17/2005 Bp Bill Persell. c 2. P S Greg's Epis Ch Deerfield IL 2012-2013; Samar Interfaith Naperville IL 2012; Int Cbury NW Evanston IL 2009-2011; Assoc S Mich's Ch Barrington IL 2005-2009. vmeer@aol.com

VANDERSLICE, Thomas Arthur (NH) 22 Stratham Grn, Stratham NH 03885 **S Andr's Ch Manchester NH 2000-; Ret 1993-** B Chicago IL 1928 s Thomas & Maria. BA Ripon Coll Ripon WI 1951; MDiv GTS 1954. D 6/2/1954 P 12/21/1954 Bp Gerald Francis Burrill. m 2/23/1957 Marion Vanderslice c 2. Int Trin Ch Hampton NH 2008-2009; Int S Andr's Ch Manchester NH 2003-2006; Int Ch Of The Trsfg Derry NH 2000-2003; Int S Geo's Epis Ch York ME 1999-2000; Int S Geo's Ch Durham NH 1995-1998; R The Ch Of S Jn The Evang Flossmoor IL 1978-1993, Cur 1954-1957; R S Mk's Ch Geneva IL 1966-1978; Vic S Ann's Ch Woodstock IL 1961-1966; Assoc Trin Epis Ch Cranford NJ 1960-1961; R S Mart's Ch Chicago IL 1957-1959.

VANDERVEEN, Peter Todd (Pa) 230 Pennswood Rd, Bryn Mawr PA 19010 **Bd Mem GBEC 2012-; R Ch Of The Redeem Bryn Mawr PA 2009-** B Detroit MI 1961 s Edward & Dawn. BA Calvin Coll 1983; MDiv Ya Berk 1986. D 6/10/1989 P 2/24/1990 Bp Arthur Edward Walmsley. m 7/21/1990 Patricia W Bennett. R S Ann's Epis Ch Old Lyme CT 1995-2009; Assoc S Chris's Ch Chatham MA 1993-1995; Cur Trin Ch Branford CT 1989-1993. "Ethics and the Ch," *New Engl Watershed*, 2006. Assoc of Angl Musicians 2002.

VAN DERVOORT, Virginia Ann (Tenn) 1106 Chickering Park Dr, Nashville TN 37215 B Indianapolis IN 1941 d Edward & Virginia. U of Wisconsin 1959; RN Jas Ward Thorne Sch of Nrsng 1963; BA Stephens Coll 1975; MDiv Van 1983; Cert Epis TS of the SW 1995. D 6/24/1995 Bp Chester Lovelle Talton P 1/13/1996 Bp Frederick Houk Borsch. m 3/27/1965 Robert Lordner Van Dervoort c 2. Assoc S Paul's Ch Franklin TN 1998-2012; P Assoc Epis Ch of the Redeem-Irving Texas 1996-1998; D Epis Ch Of The Redeem Irving TX 1995-1996. Cross Wind Retreat Cntr (Bd) 2000-2004; ECW; EWC(Bd Mem) 1985; Pstr Counslg Cntr of TN (Bd Mem) 1999-2012. hon in Ethics Vanderbilt DS 1983; hon in the field Educ Vanderbilt DS 1983.

VANDER WEL, Brian (WA) Christ Church, 600 Farmington Rd W, Accokeek MD 20607 **R Chr Ch S Jn's Par Accokeek MD 2007-** B Battlecreek MI 1967 s Norman & Lois. BA Calvin Coll 1990; MDiv w hon TESM 1999. D 6/12/1999 P 12/15/1999 Bp Robert William Duncan. m 12/17/1993 Elizabeth Page Bogard Vander Wel. Workgroup Mem The Proj on Lived Theol Workgroup 2002-2004; Asst Chr Epis Ch Charlottesvlle VA 2001-2006; Dio Pittsburgh Pittsburgh PA 2001, Exam Chapl in Ch Hist for Deaconal Ord 2000-2001, BEC for the Vocational Diac in Ch Hist 2000, Liason for PA Epis Publ Plcy Ntwk 1999-2001; Int S Chris's Epis Ch Mars PA 2000; Asst Ch Of The Nativ Pittsburgh PA 1999-2000; Bd Mem Racial Recon Cmsn Charlottesville VA 2005-2006; Workgroup Mem The Proj on Lived Theol Charllottesville VA 2002-2004; Asst to the Dir Faith Tech Pittsburgh PA 2001; Temporary Asstg P Trin Cathd Pittsburgh PA 2001.

VAN DE STEEG, Franklin Exford (Minn) PO Box 155, Hastings MN 55033 **P S Lk's Epis Ch Hastings MN 2010-** B Sauk Centre, MN 1942 s Marenius & Lorrayne. D 6/24/2009 P 1/9/2010 Bp James Louis Jelinek. m 4/24/1965 Lynette Van De Steeg c 1.

VAN DEUSEN, Robert Reed (CPa) 205 King St, Northumberland PA 17857 **R Chr Ch Milton PA 2009-; S Mk's Epis Ch Northumberlnd PA 2004-; R St Mk Northumberland 2004-** B Scranton PA 1947 s Lawrence & Louise. Thiel Coll 1968; BA Franklin Coll 1971; MDiv Sewanee: The U So, TS 1997. D 6/14/1997 Bp Rogers Sanders Harris P 6/12/1999 Bp John Bailey Lipscomb. m 7/14/2001 Mary Jean Van Deusen c 3. R S Matt's Epis Ch Sunbury PA 2004-2008; R Chr Ch River Forest IL 2001-2004; Ch Of The Redeem Cairo IL 1999-2001; Team Min Dio Springfield Springfield IL 1999-2001; S Jas Chap Marion Marion IL 1999-2001; S Mk's Ch W Frankfort IL 1999-2001; Assoc P S Steph's Ch Harrisburg IL 1999-2001.

VAN DEUSEN, Robert Wayne (Mil) 9360 West Terra Court, Milwaukee WI 53224 B Goshen NY 1951 s Robert & Jeanne. BA Hartwick Coll 1973; MDiv Nash 1976. D 8/5/1977 Bp Albert William Hillestad P 6/7/1978 Bp James Winchester Montgomery. R S Ptr's Ch Milwaukee WI 1991-2009; R S Andr's Ch Kenosha WI 1985-1991; Vic S Mary's Epis Ch Cadillac MI 1981-1985; Lawr Hall Sch Chicago IL 1979-1981; Chapl Lawr Hall Boys Sch Chicago IL 1978-1981.

VANDEVELDER, Frank Radcliff (Va) 12191 Clipper Dr Apt 110, Woodbridge VA 22192 B Jackson MI 1928 s Peter & Myra. BA Pasadena Coll 1951; MA Pasadena Coll 1953; MDiv VTS 1963; PhD Drew U 1967; Ecumencial Inst Tantur 1977. D 6/15/1963 Bp Robert Fisher Gibson Jr P 12/21/1963 Bp Leland Stark. c 4. P Assoc Trin Ch Fredericksbrg VA 2004-2010; P Assoc S Steph's Epis Ch Oak Ridge TN 1998-2003; Prof Biblic Languages & Theol VTS Alexandria VA 1974-1994; Prof Biblic Stds Seminario San Andres Mex D.F. Mex 1966-1969; Asst to the R Chr Epis Ch E Orange NJ 1963-1966. Auth, "The Biblic Journey of Faith," *Biblic Journey of Faith: The Road of the Sojourner*, Fortress Press, 1988. SBL 1969-1994. Fell ECF ECF 1968; Fell ECF ECF 1967.

VAN DEVENTER, Arthur Reed (Roch) 53 Winding Rd, Rochester NY 14618 **Ret 1989-** B Rochester NY 1934 s Philip & Emily. BA Hobart and Wm Smith Colleges 1955; BD Bex Sem 1958; MDiv Bex Sem 1974; CTh VTS 1978; Cert Ldrshp Acad for New Directions 1985. D 6/7/1958 P 12/19/1958 Bp Dudley S Stark. m 6/20/1959 Abigail B Van Deventer c 4. R S Jas Epis Ch Hibbing MN 1973-1988; Assoc S Ptr's Epis Ch Ashtabula OH 1969-1973; Vic S Lk's Epis Ch Bath OH 1965-1969; R Chr Epis Ch Huron OH 1960-1965; Cur S Mk's And S Jn's Epis Ch Rochester NY 1958-1960. SSC 1999. R Emer S Jas' Ch, Hibbing, MN 1995.

VANDEVENTER, Heather Ann (Va) 118 N Washington St, Alexandria VA 22314 **Assoc Chr Ch Alexandria VA 2011-; Asst Chapl The Epis HS Alexandria VA 2008-** B Hazelton PA 1972 d James & Joan. BA Ya 1994; MDiv SWTS 1998. D 3/25/1998 Bp Carolyn Tanner Irish P 10/21/1998 Bp Herbert Alcorn Donovan Jr. m 10/16/1999 David Timothy Gortner c 2. Epis HS Alexandria VA 2008-2011; Assoc R S Aug's Epis Ch Wilmette IL 2003-2004; Asst R 1998-2002.

VAN DINE JR, John Henry (Nwk) St John's Church of Boonton, 226 Cornelia St, Boonton NJ 07005 B Dover NJ 1952 s John & Bernice. D 12/12/2015 Bp Mark M Beckwith. m 8/17/1974 Elizabeth Ann Alloco c 3.

VANDIVORT JR, Paul M (Mo) 12366 Federal Dr, Des Peres MO 63131 **Nonpar 1968-** B Cape Girardeau MO 1940 s Paul & Ida. Gri 1960; BA SE Missouri St U 1963; MDiv VTS 1968; MD U of Missouri 1977. D 6/22/1968 P 5/1/1974 Bp George Leslie Cadigan. m 5/20/1971 Linda Minna Kilsheimer.

VAN DOOREN, John David (Chi) 5749 N Kenmore Ave, Chicago IL 60660 **Ch Of The Trsfg New York NY 2017-** B Hendersonville NC 1959 s Peter & Sarah. BA U NC 1982; MDiv VTS 1987. D 11/1/1989 Bp Brice Sidney Sanders P 5/31/1990 Bp James Winchester Montgomery. m 5/17/2017 Gary Wayne Norcross. R Epis Ch Of The Atone Chicago IL 2005-2017; R All Souls Memi Epis Ch Washington DC 1992-2005, Cur 1989-1990; St Martins-In-The-Field Ch Severna Pk MD 1991-1992; Chapl Epis Hm Washington DC 1990-1992. GAS; SocMary.

VANDOREN JR, Robert Lawson (WTenn) 5097 Greenway Cv, Memphis TN 38117 B Columbia SC 1944 s Robert & Elizabeth. BA U So 1966; MDiv Memphis TS 2007. D 10/28/2000 Bp James Malone Coleman P 5/22/2004 Bp Don Edward Johnson. m 12/29/2007 Pamela VanDoren. Assoc S Jn's Epis Ch Memphis TN 2002-2016. rvandoren@stjohnsmemphis.org

VAN DUFFELEN, Marilyn (Ia) PO Box 895, Sioux City IA 51102 **Dio Iowa Des Moines IA 2017-** B Toronto, Ontario, Canada 1960 d Jaap & Elisabeth. Trans 1/16/2017 as Priest Bp Alan Scarfe. stpaulsscia@msn.com

VAN DUSEN, David Buick (Mass) 3905 N Old Sabino Canyon Road, Tucson AZ 85750 **Ret 1991-** B Detroit MI 1929 s Charles & Catherine. BA Pr 1951; STM VTS 1957; STM Bos 1964. D 6/30/1957 P 1/1/1958 Bp Richard Stanley Merrill Emrich. m 11/17/2006 Margaret MCE Matter c 6. P-in-c S Brendan's Epis Ch Deer Isle ME 1991-1993; R S Ptr's Ch Weston MA 1976-1991; R Chr Ch Greensburg PA 1972-1976; Assoc Ch Of The Redeem Bryn Mawr PA 1968-1972; Chapl Bolles Sch Jacksonville FL 1967-1968; Asst Trin Ch Epis Boston MA 1963-1967; Asst S Jas Epis Ch Birmingham MI 1960-1963; Vic S Dunst's Epis Ch Davison MI 1957-1959; Dioc Coun Dio Massachusetts Boston MA 1981-1984.

VAN DYKE, Bude (Ala) Po Box 824, Sewanee TN 37375 **Sprtl Dir Sewanee U So TS Sewanee TN 2001-** B Jackson TN 1953 s Robert & Clara. MDiv Sewanee: The U So, TS 1999; DMin Sewanee: The U So, TS 2003. D 2/24/2000 P 9/10/2000 Bp Henry Nutt Parsley Jr. m 6/15/1974 Pamela Kay Van Dyke. Vic S Matt's Epis Ch Mcminnville TN 2011-2015; Chapl S Andr's-Sewanee Sch Sewanee TN 2001-2014. Auth, "Paul's Letter to Philemon: and appeal above and beyond the law," *Sewanee Theol Revs*, The TS, 1998. Fire Keeper Oklahoma IV Consult 2010.

VAN EENWYK, John Richter (Roch) P. O. Box 1961, Olympia WA 98507 **S Ben Epis Ch Lacey WA 1999-** B Sodus NY 1946 s John & Dorothy. BA Colg

1967; STB EDS 1970; Propadeuticum CG Jung Inst Zurich 1977; Dplma CG Jung Inst Chicago 1981; PhD U Chi 1981. D 6/19/1970 Bp Archie H Crowley P 12/19/1970 Bp Robert Rae Spears Jr. m 6/5/1970 Juliet Schneller c 2. Assoc S Jn's Epis Ch Olympia WA 1992-1999; Assoc Ch Of Our Sav Chicago IL 1977-1992; Epis Ch Of The Atone Chicago IL 1977-1992; P-in-c Balaclava-Shiloah Cure Jamaica WI 1971-1972; Chapl S Anne Sch Arlington Heights MA 1970-1971. Auth, "Clincl Chaos: The Strange Attractors of Childhood Trauma," Inner City Books, 2013; Auth, "Archetypes and Strange Attractors: The Chaotic Wrld of Symbols," Inner City Books, 1997; Auth, "Journ arts," *Var.* NASSAM 1985. Alum Humanitarian Awd Colg 2009; Lifetime Acievement Awd Thurston Cnty Human Rts Cmsn 2008; Soc Issues Awd Washington St Psychol Assn 2008; Serval Awd Long Island Inst of Mntl Hlth 1985; Robbins Fllshp EDS 1974; Tchg Fllshp Harv 1970.

VAN ES, Kenneth (Eau) 2603 Yorktown Ct, Eau Claire WI 54703 **D Chr Ch Cathd Eau Claire WI 1998-** B Milwaukee WI 1950 s Kenneth & June. BA U of Wisconsin 1972. D 4/18/1998 Bp William Charles Wantland. m 7/31/1982 Rebecca Olivia Laverne Haltner.

VANG, Marshall Jacob (Alb) 88 Circular St Apt1, Saratoga Springs NY 12866 **Int Ch Of Beth Saratoga Spg NY 2012-; Trst Nash Nashotah WI 1988-** B Corning NY 1947 s Norman & Lucretia. BA Ken 1970; MDiv GTS 1974. D 4/25/1974 P 10/28/1974 Bp Robert Rae Spears Jr. P-in-c Ch Of The H Cross Warrensburg NY 2011; Dn Cathd Of All SS Albany NY 1998-2010; R S Geo's Epis Ch Schenectady NY 1987-1998; R S Anth Of Padua Ch Hackensack NJ 1977-1986; Cur Gr Epis Ch Westwood NJ 1974-1977. CBS 1974; GAS 1977; SocMary 1977. deano192010@gmail.com

VANG, Toua (Minn) 2200 Minnehaha Ave E, Saint Paul MN 55119 **Dio Minnesota Minneapolis MN 2014-** B Laos 1966 s Paul & Mary. MDiv VTS 2013. D 6/28/2012 P 6/27/2013 Bp Brian N Prior. m 10/24/1994 Joua Xiong c 4.

VAN GORDEN SR, Schuyler Humphrey (Eau) 120 10th Ave, Eau Claire WI 54703 **Ret 1993-** B Osseo WI 1918 s Clyde & Elsie. BS U of Wisconsin; MS U of Wisconsin 1972. D 8/10/1982 Bp William Charles Wantland. m 9/18/1937 Eileen Henrietta LaMay c 4. D Chr Ch Cathd Eau Claire WI 1982-1993.

VAN GULDEN, Sarah Ann (Mass) 74 S Common St, Lynn MA 01902 **S Steph's Memi Ch Lynn MA 2014-** B Cincinnatti OH 1982 d David & Marcia. BA Connecticut Coll 2004; MDiv EDS 2007. D 6/7/2014 Bp M(Arvil) Thomas Shaw P 1/10/2015 Bp Alan Gates. m 8/7/2010 Derek Peter van Gulden. svangulden@ststephenslynn.org

VAN HOOK, Peter (U) PO Box 17972, Salt Lake City UT 84117 **P-in-c S Mary's Ch Provo UT 2011-** B Los Angeles CA 1947 s James & Elizabeth. BS L&C 1969; MDiv CDSP 1972; PhD U of Utah 1995. D 7/16/1972 P 2/1/1973 Bp Victor Manuel Rivera. m 3/8/1969 Carole Marie Morris c 3. Int R Ch Of The Gd Shpd Ogden UT 2009-2011; Fresh Start, Fac & Mentor Dio Utah Salt Lake City UT 2009, Supply 2003-2008, 2001, Supply 1995, 1993-1994, 1993, COM 1992-1995, 1988-1990, Transitioinal Mnstrs in The Epis Ch, Bd 2010-2014, Stndg Com; Pres, 2011-13 2010-2013, Mutual Mnstry Revs Team, Consult 2010-2012, Dioc Coordntr, PBFWR 1995-2002; Int R S Jn's Epis Ch Logan UT 2008-2010; Int Pstr Shpd of the Mountains ELC Pk City UT 2007-2008; Int Gr Epis Ch St Geo UT 2005-2006; Disaster Response Consult Ch Wrld Serv Elkhart IN 2002-2003; R All SS Ch Salt Lake City UT 1981-1993; R S Mary's Ch Emmett ID 1975-1981; Vic St Raphael's Epis Ch Oakhurst CA 1974-1975; Epis Dio San Joaquin Modesto CA 1972-1975; Chapl Bakersfield St Coll - CA 1972-1974; Asst to Bp of San Joaquin S Paul's Ch Bakersfield CA 1972-1974; Ecum Off Dio Idaho Boise ID 1979-1981, Stndg Com, Secy 1977-1981. Auth, "[Var]," *Intl Encyclopedia of Publ Plcy & Admin*, 1985; Auth, "Using an Ethics Matrix in an MPA Prog," *Journ of Publ Admin*, 1985. Int Mnstrs in The Epis Ch (TMEC) 2005; Int Mnstry Ntwk (IMN) 2005; Stonefly Soc of the Wasatch 1995. Mem Pi Alpha Alpha 1993. pastor@stmarysprovo.org

VAN HOOSER, Jack Boyd (WMich) 801 Vanosdale Rd Apt 511, Knoxville TN 37909 **Died 5/22/2016** B Chattanooga TN 1928 s Hoskins & Ruth. BBA U of Tennessee 1950; BBA U of Tennessee at Chattanooga 1950; BD CDSP 1958; ThD Harvard DS 1963. D 6/22/1958 Bp John Vander Horst P 4/25/1959 Bp Theodore N Barth. m 8/19/1955 Mary Taliaferro c 5. Ret 1994-2016; Search Com For Bp Coadj Dio Wstrn Michigan Kalamazoo MI 1983-1984, Gnrl Bd Examnng Chapl 1989-1994, 1984-1988, Resolutns Com 1983-1987, Chair Com For Diac 1982-1983; R S Thos Epis Ch Battle Creek MI 1982-1993; P-in-c S Elis's Ch Glencoe IL 1977-1978; Sub-Dn Bexley Seabury Fed Chicago IL 1975-1982, Full Prof OT 1973-1974, Assoc Prof OT 1969-1982; Prof Epis Sem Sao Paulo Brazil 1964-1965; Assoc S Paul's Angican Ch Sao Paulo Brazil 1962-1965; Asst Instr OT EDS Cambridge MA 1960-1962; Asst The Ch Of Our Redeem Lexington MA 1959-1962; Evang & Renwl Cmsn Dio Chicago Chicago IL 1981-1982. Auth, "arts & Revs". OHC 1974.

VAN HORN, Richard Scott (Los) 3050 Motor Ave, Los Angeles CA 90064 **Pres Emer Mntl Hlth Amer of Los Angeles Long Bch CA 2009-; Asst S Mary's Epis Ch Los Angeles CA 1981-, Urban Assoc 1967-1968; Chair Bd Dir Mntl Hlth Amer Natl 2014-; Mntl Hlth Serv Oversight and Accountability Com St of California 2009-** B Arcadia CA 1939 s Harlan & Evelyn. BA Harv 1961; MDiv GTS 1965. D 9/16/1965 P 3/1/1966 Bp Francis E I Bloy. m 2/2/1986 Kay Miriam Van Horn c 1. Pres and CEO Mntl Hlth Amer of Los Angeles Long Bch CA 1980-2009; Cn Mssnr For Plnng Dio Los Angeles Los Angeles CA 1974-1980, Cathd Corp 1988-2005, Stndg Com 1984-1988, COM 1981-1984; Sch Dir The Par Ch Of S Lk Long Bch CA 1971-1974; R S Barn' Epis Ch Los Angeles CA 1968-1970; Cur St Marks Epis Ch Van Nuys CA 1965-1967; Chair-elect Bd Dir Mntl Hlth Amer Natl 2012-2014; Vice-chair, Bd Dir Mntl Hlth Amer Natl 2009-2012; Mem, Bd Dir Natl Coun on Behavioral Hlth 2008-2014. Cn of the Dio Dio Los Angeles 1980. rvanhorn@mhala.org

VAN HORNE, Beverly (Mo) 11907 Bardmont Drive, Saint Louis MO 63126 **Assoc Trin Ch S Louis MO 2012-** B Columbia SC 1947 d George & Barbara. Dioc Sch for Mnstry; BA Randolph-Macon Wmn's Coll 1969; CDSP 1970. D 12/22/2004 P 6/24/2005 Bp George Wayne Smith. m 6/12/1970 Peter Van Horne c 2. Int Dn The Epis Sch for Mnstry 2010-2012; P-in-c Trin Ch De Soto MO 2005-2010.

VAN HORNE, Peter (Mo) 11907 Bardmont Dr, Saint Louis MO 63126 B Caldwell ID 1944 s Robert & Elizabeth. BA U of Idaho 1967; MDiv CDSP 1970; MA Grad Theol Un 1970; DMin SWTS 2001. D 6/24/1970 P 12/19/1970 Bp Norman L Foote. m 6/12/1970 Beverly Dew c 2. Int R S Mk's Ch S Louis MO 2011-2012; Int R Trin Epis Ch Kirksville MO 2009-2010; Instr Epis Sch for Mnstry Dio Missouri S Louis MO 2002-2007, Conv Secy 2005-2009, Stndg Com 2004-2008; Vic All SS Epis Ch Farmington MO 2001-2009; Vic Emm Epis Ch Kailua HI 1995-2001; Cn The Epis Ch in Hawaii Honolulu HI 1986-1995, Ch Hist Instr Diac Prog 1983-1994, Stwdshp Com 1995, Dioc Coun 1981-1984, Dioc Coun 1977-1979; R Ch Of The Epiph Honolulu HI 1978-1986; R S Jn's Epis Ch Kula HI 1976-1978; Chapl CA St U 1972-1973; Cur All SS Epis Ch Boise ID 1970-1971. Auth, *ATR.* CODE - Pres 1987-1996.

VAN HUSS, Teri Hewett (SJ) PO Box 7446, Visalia CA 93290 B 1953 d William & Nancy. Cert in Diac Stds The Sch for Deacons 2014. D 6/28/2014 Bp David C Rice. m 6/12/2001 Thomas Manuel Van Huss c 3. vanhess@pacbell.net

VANI, Benedict Sele (CFla) 2341 Port Malabar Blvd Ne, Palm Bay FL 32905 **Ret 1994-** B Glima LR 1932 s Baysama & Christian. Cert Cuttington U 1967; Cert Bird S Coler Memi Hosp 1975; Lic Epis TS in Kentucky 1975. D 1/6/1976 P 1/6/1977 Bp George Daniel Browne. c 4. Dio Liberia Monrovia 1976-1982.

VAN KIRK, Andrew D (Dal) 6400 McKinney Ranch Parkway, McKinney TX 75070 **St Andrews Ch McKinney TX 2013-; Assoc R Epis Ch Of The Ascen Dallas TX 2012-, Cur 2010-2013** B Chicago IL 1982 s Mark & Natalie. BA Duke 2004; MDiv PrTS 2008; ThM PrTS 2009. D 5/2/2010 Bp George Edward Councell P 1/6/2011 Bp James Monte Stanton. m 1/3/2009 Stephanie M Van Kirk c 3. Convoc Chair (Estrn Convoc) Dio Dallas Dallas TX 2013, Nomin Com Mem 2012-2014, Stanton Cntr Fac 2011-. andrewv@standrewsonline.net

VAN KIRK, Natalie Beam (Chi) 22W415 Butterfield Rd, Glen Ellyn IL 60137 **R S Barn' Epis Ch Glen Ellyn IL 2015-; Adj Instr Inst of Pstr Stds Loyola U Chicago 2014-** B Baltimore MD 1956 d Roger & Joanna. BS Duke 1978; MTS SMU Perkins 2000. D 5/24/2003 P 11/29/2003 Bp James Monte Stanton. m 4/18/2009 Frederick William Schmidt c 3. Vic Ch Of The Gd Samar Dallas TX 2010-2013; Cn for Cler Formation Dio Dallas TX 2004-2006, Fac, Exam Chapl 2005-2006, Cn Mssnr for Cler Formation 2004-2006, COM 2004-2006; Cn Theol S Matt's Cathd Dallas TX 2003-2008; Adj Fac Perkins TS SMU Dallas 2000-2012; Rdr GBEC 2006-2013. Auth, ""Gr for the Present Moment: The Cn of Sacraments,"" *Cncl Theism: A Proposal for Theol and the Ch*, Eerdmans, 2008; Auth, ""Imagining Theol: The Cn of Images,"" *Cncl Theism: A Proposal for Theol and the Ch*, Eerdmans, 2008; Ed, Auth, *Cncl Theism: A Proposal for Theol and the Ch*, Eerdmans, 2008; Auth, ""Finding One's Way through the Maze of Lang: Rhetorical Usages that Add Meaning in S Bern's Style(s),"" *Cistercian Stds Quarterly, volume 42.1 2007*, Gethsemani Abbey, Trappist KY, 2007; Auth, ""The Difference Between Catching Butterflies and the Mysteries of God,"" *Preaching Psalms, Oracles, and Parables, Sermons that Wk, vol. 14, ed. Roger Ailing and Dav J. Schlafer*, Morehouse Pub, 2006. AAR 2000; Soc for Biblic Lit 2007; Soc for the Study of Anglicanism 2005; Soc for the Study of Chr Sprtlty 2004; Soc of Cath Priests 2010; Sprtl Dir Intl 2000. SHUBERT M. OGDEN Fllshp FOR Acad EXCELLENCE IN Theol SMU 2004; ALBERT C. OUTLER Awd FOR EXCELLENCE IN Theol Perkins TS 1998; Dn'S ACHIEVEMENT Awd Schlrshp Perkins TS 1998; ANGIER B. DUKE Schlr Duke 1974. nvankirk@saint-barnabas.net

VAN KLAVEREN, Dina Els (Md) 1216 Seminole Dr, Arnold MD 21012 **R S Andr's Epis Ch Glenwood MD 2009-** B Pomona, CA 1973 BA Whittier Coll 1995; MS U of Rhode Island 1997; MDiv CDSP 2006, MDiv CDSP 2006. D 6/24/2006 Bp John L Rabb P 1/6/2007 Bp Robert Wilkes Ihloff. m 6/27/1998 David Stimler c 2. S Marg's Ch Annapolis MD 2006-2009; Higher Educ Admin Maryland Inst Coll Of Art 1997-2003.

VAN KOEVERING, Helen Elizabeth (WVa) B St Albans UK 1960 d Terence & Joan. Trans 1/6/2017 as Priest Bp William Michie Klusmeyer. m 1/11/1991 Mark A Van Koevering c 3.

✠ VAN KOEVERING, The Rt Rev Mark A (WVa) 1608 Virginia St E, Charleston WV 25311 **Dio W Virginia Charleston WV 2016-** B Grand Rapids, MI 1957 s Robert & Norma. Bachelors of Sci MI SU 1979; Masters of Sci MI SU 1985;

Bachelors of Arts (Honours) Trin, U of Bristol 1999. Trans 2/9/2016 Bp William Michie Klusmeyer. m 1/11/1991 Helen Elizabeth Van Koevering c 3. Fell Rockefeller Fndt 1987. mvankoevering@wvdiocese.org

VAN KUIKEN, Ali (NJ) 100 Sullivan Way, Trenton NJ 08628 **S Lk's Ch Trenton NJ 2015-** B Grand Rapids MI 1987 d John & Patricia. BA Mssh Coll 2009; MDiv PrTS 2013; Dplma of Angl Stds The GTS 2015. D 6/3/2015 P 12/19/2015 Bp William H Stokes. m 9/6/2010 Scott Todd Steed Van Kuiken.

VAN LIEW, Christina (LI) **P-in-c Epis Ch of The Resurr Williston Pk NY 2006-** B Glen Ridge NJ 1950 d Willard & Vicki. BS Bos 1975; MDiv GTS 2004. D 9/28/2004 P 2/5/2005 Bp Johncy Itty. c 2. Cur St Jn's Ch Cold Sprg Harbor NY 2004-2005.

VANN, Deborah Louise (CFla) 380 Royal Palm Dr, Melbourne FL 32935 **R Hope Epis Ch Melbourne FL 2009-** B Melbourne FL 1954 d Russell & Charlotte. MS Florida St U 1982; MDiv Sewanee: The U So, TS 2004. D 5/22/2004 P 1/30/2005 Bp John Wadsworth Howe. m 2/2/1985 John M Campbell c 2. S Aug Of Cbury Epis Ch Vero Bch FL 2007-2008; Asst Ch of Our Sav Palm Bay FL 2005-2007.

VANN, Tim E (Ia) 6651 Park Crest Dr, Papillion NE 68133 B Mitchell SD 1949 s Walter & Phyllis. BA U of Texas 1974; MDiv Sewanee: The U So, TS 1977; MBA U of So Dakota 1989. D 6/26/1977 P 1/6/1978 Bp Walter H Jones. m 5/31/1980 Cindy Schlosser. Dio Iowa Des Moines IA 2004-2008; S Martha's Epis Ch Papillion NE 2002-2003; S Lk's Ch Plattsmouth NE 1996-1997; Cn Dio Nebraska Omaha NE 1991-2004; Int Trin Cathd Omaha NE 1990-1991; Calv Epis Ch Sioux City IA 1989-1990; Int S Geo's Epis Ch Le Mars IA 1989-1990; Dio So Dakota Pierre SD 1988-1990; Ch Of Our Most Merc Sav Santee NE 1988-1989; Int S Paul's Epis Ch Vermillion SD 1988-1989; Int S Paul's Ch Brookings SD 1987-1988; R Ch Of The Gd Shpd Sioux Falls SD 1983-1986; Asst Emm Epis Par Rapid City SD 1980-1983; R Chr Epis Ch Gettysburg SD 1977-1980; S Jas Epis Ch Mobridge SD 1977-1980.

VAN NIEL, Noah (Mass) 172 Main St, Hingham MA 02043 **Ch Of S Jn The Evang Hingham MA 2015-** B Boston MA 1986 s Anthony & Maureen. D 6/6/2015 Bp Gayle Harris P 12/19/2015 Bp Alan Gates. m 9/5/2009 Melinda B Van Niel.

VANO, Mary Foster (Ark) 20900 Chenal Pkwy, Little Rock AR 72223 **R S Marg's Epis Ch Little Rock AR 2011-; COM Dio Arkansas Little Rock AR 2012-** B Andrews Air Force Base 1976 d Robert & Robbie. BA TCU 1999; MDiv Epis TS of the SW 2003. D 5/18/2003 P 11/15/2003 Bp Gethin Benwil Hughes. m 8/7/1999 Stephen T Vano c 2. Assoc P S Dav's Ch Austin TX 2003-2011; COM Dio Texas Houston TX 2005-2011. Gathering of Leaders 2008. mvano@stmargaretschurch.org

VAN OSS SR, Earl T (U) 737 East Center, Orem UT 84057 **Asst S Marv 1982-** B Sherwood ND 1913 s Ingbrighd & Magli. BS U of Montana 1934. D 6/13/1976 Bp Otis Charles. m 6/18/1975 Nadine Johnson. Asst The Epis Ch Of The Gd Shpd Hemet CA 1976-1982; Asst S Marv 1976-1979.

VAN OSS, William Joseph (Minn) 1710 E Superior St, Duluth MN 55812 **R The Par of St Paul's Epis Ch Duluth MN 2006-** B Green Bay WI 1964 s Arnold & Jean. BA U of St Thos 1986; MDiv U of S Mary of the Lake Mundelein Sem 1991; CAS SWTS 2000. Rec 5/1/2000 as Priest Bp James Louis Jelinek. m 6/24/1996 Susan M Van Oss c 1. R All SS Ch Northfield MN 2004-2006, 2000-2003; Serv RC Ch 1991-1996.

VANOVER, Debra A (Haw) 25 Hiatt St, Lebanon OR 97355 **Mng Chapl Samar Lebanon Cmnty Hosp Lebanon OR 2003-** B La Grande OR 1952 d Ralph & Arbelyn. BA Victoria U Wellington NZ 1973; MA Fuller TS 1983; Vancouver TS CA 1995. D 7/22/1996 Bp George Clinton Harris P 1/1/1998 Bp Mark Lawrence Macdonald. c 2. P Ch Of The H Nativ Honolulu HI 2013-2016; Samar Lebanon Hosp Lebanon OR 2003-2012; R S Jas The Fisherman Kodiak AK 1998-2002; Asst S Ptr's By-The-Sea Sitka AK 1997-1998; Chapl Vancouver Hosp Vancouver British Columbia 1995-1997. Assn of Epis Chapl 2002.

VAN PARYS, Cynthia Leigh (NI) 1464 Glenlake Dr, South Bend IN 46614 **D S Mich And All Ang Ch So Bend IN 1996-** B Dowagiac MI 1957 d Timothy & Susan. D 10/16/1996 Bp Francis Campbell Gray. m 5/6/1978 Randy Michael VanParys.

VAN PLETZEN-RANDS BSG, Blane Frederik (WNY) Five Eighteen Belle Square, 323 State St, La Crosse WI 54601 **Epis Rel The Comp of Our Lady of Walsingham - OLW 2008-; Chapl Gundersen Luth La Crosse WI 2017-** B Zimbabwe 1960 s George & Helen. BA Weber St U 1985; MA Utah St U 1988; MDiv GTS 2010. D 6/12/2010 Bp Carolyn Tanner Irish P 12/18/2010 Bp Michael Garrison. m 7/21/2007 Scott Rands c 1. Friar and R Trin Epis Ch Hamburg NY 2012-2017; Cn S Paul's Cathd Buffalo NY 2010-2011.

VAN SANT, Mark Richard (NJ) 27 Tocci Ave, Monmouth Beach NJ 07750 B Elizabeth NJ 1956 s John & Lovey. BA Glassboro St Coll 1979; MDiv Nash 1983. D 6/4/1983 Bp George Phelps Mellick Belshaw P 12/6/1983 Bp Albert Wiencke Van Duzer. m 9/27/1997 Sandra S Segrest c 2. R S Jn's Epis Ch Little Silver NJ 1987-2013; Cur S Mary's Ch Haddon Heights NJ 1983-1987.

VAN SANT, Paul Albion (NJ) 38 Anne Dr, Tabernacle NJ 08088 **R S Steph's Ch Manchester Twp NJ 2006-** B Philadelphia PA 1954 s John & Lovey. BA Rutgers The St U of New Jersey 1984; MDiv Nash 1988; ThM New Brunswick

TS 1995. D 6/11/1988 Bp George Phelps Mellick Belshaw P 2/24/1989 Bp Vincent King Pettit. m 9/29/1979 Priscilla L Van Sant c 5. The Ch Of The Gd Shpd Berlin NJ 1990-2006; Asst Camden Team Ministers Camden NJ 1988-1990; S Paul's Ch Camden NJ 1988-1990; Fin & Bdgt Com Dio New Jersey Trenton NJ 1996-1999. Auth, "The Person Concept In Monkeys"; Auth, "Journ Of Experimental Psychol: Animal Behaviour Processes". CBS, GAS; Dioconate Chapl Dok.

VAN SCOYOC, Gardner Warren (Va) 5928 Lomack Ct, Alexandria VA 22312 **Ret 1997-** B Portland OR 1930 s Melwood & Beth. Lic in Nrsng Hm Administor Virginia 71; AA Keystone Jr Coll 1952; BA Leh 1954; STM VTS 1958; GW 1966; Cert Virginia Commonwealth U 1971. D 6/13/1958 Bp Frederick D Goodwin P 6/27/1959 Bp Robert Fisher Gibson Jr. m 6/26/1954 Nancy Jean Van Scoyoc c 4. Exec Dir Dio Va Hms Dio Virginia Richmond VA 1970-1973; Exec Secy Dept CSR 1963-1969; Westminster-Cbury Richmond VA 1965-1978; D-in-c Emm Ch Rapidan VA 1958-1959. Auth, "Life Care: A Long Term Solution?," Amer Assoc of Hm for Aging, 1977. ESMA 1967. DSA Amer Assn Hms & Serv for the Aging 1992.

VAN SICKLE, Kathleen (Cal) 555 Pierce St Apt 340e, Albany CA 94706 **D S Alb's Ch Albany CA 2007-** B Grayling MI 1952 d Chester & Marion. BA Oakland U 1975; MDiv CDSP 1986; MS U CA 1992. D 6/10/1986 Bp John Lester Thompson III. CDSP Berkeley CA 2004; The Epis Ch Of The Gd Shpd Berkeley CA 1997-2007, Events Coordntr 1987-1991; Gr Cathd San Francisco CA 1987-1990; D S Paul's Epis Ch Sacramento CA 1986-1987.

VAN SICLEN, John Remsen (Me) PO Box 523, Damariscotta ME 04543 B New York NY 1949 s John & Mary. BA Hobart and Wm Smith Colleges 1973; MDiv EDS 1977; DMin Bangor TS 1994. D 6/11/1977 Bp Jonathan Goodhue Sherman P 1/24/1978 Bp John Harris Burt. m 7/5/1980 Pamela S Van Siclen c 1. P-in-c S Giles Ch Jefferson ME 2008-2011; Int Chr Ch In Lonsdale Lincoln RI 2005-2006; R S Mich's Ch Bristol RI 1999-2005; R S Paul's Epis Ch White Riv Jct VT 1990-1999; Int All SS Epis Ch Littleton NH 1990; R S Eliz's Ch Sudbury MA 1986-1990; R Ch Of The Adv Pittsburgh PA 1980-1986; Cur S Ptr's Epis Ch Lakewood OH 1977-1980. Fllshp of St. Jn 2007. Hon Cn S Jn's Cathd 1999.

VAN SLYKE, Charlotte Sturgis (Ala) B Portsmouth NH 1946 d Raymond & Eleanor. Dplma St Vincents Sch of Nrsng 1965; BS U of Alabama Birmingham 1989; MA U of Alabama Birmingham 1991. D 10/1/2011 Bp Henry Nutt Parsley Jr. m 5/7/2011 Larry Van Slyke c 2.

VANUCCI, Anthony Joseph (Pa) 9700 Entrada Pl. N.W., Albuquerque NM 87114 B Philadelphia PA 1941 s Anthony & Blanche. STL S Marys Sem & U Baltimore; STB S Marys Sem and U 1968; MEd Coll of New Jersey 1979. Rec 1/1/1997 as Priest Bp Allen Lyman Bartlett Jr. m 8/12/1972 Anna Vanucci c 1. R S Jas Epis Ch Bristol PA 2000-2007; R Ch of Our Sav Somerset MA 1997-2000; Vic Ch Of The Redeem Bensalem PA 1994-1997; Serv RC Ch 1967-1972.

VAN VALKENBURGH, William Burton (WMich) 6632 W. South Lake Gage Dr., Angola IN 46703 **Ret 1969-** B Deer Creek OK 1926 s Alvin & Osie. BS U of Oklahoma 1950; MS Garrett Biblic Inst 1953; NWU 1954; Drew U 1963. D 11/28/1962 Bp Donald MacAdie P 4/6/1963 Bp Leland Stark. m 9/9/1950 Marilyn Joan Van Valkenburgh c 3. Asst S Mich Cascade MI 1970-1972; P-in-c S Ptr's Ch Clifton NJ 1966-1969; Cur Ch Of The Redeem Morristown NJ 1963-1966; Serv-Coll Pstr Methodist Ch 1952-1961. Wmich Epis Cleric Assn 1970. Danforth Grant 1963.

VANVLIET-PULLIN, Dana Mae (SVa) St Peter's Episc Church, 224 S Military Hwy, Norfolk VA 23502 B Easton PA 1954 d Frederick & Eleanor. Grad Sch for Mnstry Formation 2010. D 6/9/2012 Bp Herman Hollerith IV. m 10/26/2010 Kevin Wade Pullin c 2.

VAN WALTEROP, Norman Phillip (SJ) 2716 C Sherwood Ave, Modesto CA 95350 **Died 4/24/2016** B Davenport IA 1928 s William & Adeline. BS U of Iowa 1954; MA U of Iowa 1958; MDiv CDSP 1963. D 6/22/1963 P 12/21/1963 Bp Sumner Walters. P S Dunstans Epis Ch Modesto CA 1963-1966.

VAN WASSENHOVE, Mark (Ind) 10202 Winlee Court, Indianapolis IN 46236 **S Mary's Epis Ch Martinsville IN 2016-** B Kewanee IL 1958 s Leonard & Betty. BA U of Notre Dame 1980; MDiv Jesuit TS 1988; MC U of Phoenix 1997. Rec 10/25/2000 as Priest Bp Robert Reed Shahan. m 3/5/1994 Kimberly A Van Wassenhove c 2. R S Matt's Ch Indianapolis IN 2005-2016; Assoc S Barn On The Desert Scottsdale AZ 2000-2005.

VAN WELY, Richard Francis (Ct) 223 Weaver St Apt 20D, Greenwich CT 06831 **Ret 2002-** B Albany NY 1936 s Richard & Myrtle. BA Siena Coll 1960; STB Ya Berk 1962; STM Yale DS 1972. D 6/16/1962 P 12/16/1962 Bp Allen Webster Brown. m 12/14/1957 Judith L Van Wely c 4. R S Barn Epis Ch Greenwich CT 1976-2002; Asst Chapl Yale Med Sch New Haven CT 1975-1982; Vic S Andr's Ch Northford CT 1971-1976; Vic Zion Epis Ch N Branford CT 1969-1976; R Gr Epis Ch Canton NY 1965-1969; R S Andr's Epis Ch Albany NY 1962-1965.

VAN ZANDT, Jane Whitbeck (NH) 58 Hanson Rd, Chester NH 03036 **Non-stip Gr Ch Manchester NH 2000-; Cler Dvlpmt Com Dio New Hampshire Concord NH 2009-, Cler Dvlpmt Com 2008-** B Boston MA 1942 d Earl

& Genevieve. BSN Bos 1963; MDiv EDS 1981. D 6/5/1982 Bp John Bowen Coburn P 9/24/1983 Bp Edward Randolph Welles II. m 9/19/1987 W Allan Knight. Assoc Cathd Of The Incarn Baltimore MD 1995-1999; Chapl Baltimore Cnty Police & Fire Baltimore MD 1992-2000; Asst All SS Par Brookline MA 1985-1986; AIDS Mnstry Dio Massachusetts Boston MA 1984-1991; Chapl S Barn' Gld for Nurses Boston MA 1980-1985; Chair, AIDS Mnstry Dio Maryland Baltimore MD 1991-1999. Auth, "Revolutionary Forgiveness," Orbis Press, 1987; Auth, "Close-up: Cory's Legacy," *Wit*, 1986. EPF Exec Bd 1994-1997; EWC 1979; Integrity 1979; NEAC 1990.

VAN ZANDT, Polk (Tenn) Saint Paul's Episcopal Church, 116 N Academy St, Murfreesboro TN 37130 **R S Paul's Epis Ch Murfreesboro TN 2008-** B Greenville MS 1952 s Thomas & Virginia. BA U So 1974; MDiv Sewanee: The U So, TS 1994. D 5/21/1994 P 12/3/1994 Bp Alfred Marble Jr. m 5/31/1975 Mary Josephine Pratt c 3. R S Paul's Ch Selma AL 2000-2008; R Epis Ch Of The Incarn W Point MS 1994-2000.

VAN ZANTEN JR, Peter Eric (Oly) 1111 Archwood Dr. SW #442, Olympia WA 98502 **P-in-c S Germains Epis Ch Hoodsport WA 2012-; P In Charge St. Germain Epis Ch Hoodsport WA 2012-** B Minneapolis MN 1932 s Peter & Hilda. BA U MN 1961; MDiv SWTS 1963. D 6/27/1964 Bp Hamilton Hyde Kellogg P 4/1/1965 Bp Philip Frederick McNairy. Vic St Chris's Ch - A Fed Cong Olympia WA 1992-1999; S Matthews Auburn WA 1990-1991; S Paul's Epis Ch Lees Summit MO 1988-1989; Ch Of The Redeem Kansas City MO 1988; S Mich & S Geo S Louis MO 1978-1981; Asst Chr Epis Ch S Jos MO 1976-1978; Gr Ch Carthage MO 1972-1976; S Jn Worthington MN 1968-1973; H Trin Epis Ch Luverne MN 1968-1970; Vic S Paul's Ch Pipestone MN 1968-1970; Epis Cmnty Servs Bd Dio Minnesota Minneapolis MN 1965-1968; Vic S Lk's Ch Detroit Lakes MN 1964-1968; Vic St. Jn's Epis Ch Worthington MN 1960-1970.

VARAS, Dwayne Anthony (Ga) 3901 Davis Blvd, Naples FL 34104 **S Thos Epis Ch Thomasville GA 2014-** B Tampa FL 1966 s Antonio & Rose Marie. Rec 6/6/2009 as Priest Bp Dabney Tyler Smith. m 1/17/2010 Elizabeth P Varas c 2. S Jas Epis Ch Ormond Bch FL 2012-2013; Asst R S Paul's Ch Naples FL 2009-2012.

VARDEMANN, Brady Jodoka (Mont) 556 S Rodney St, Helena MT 59601 B Breckenridge TX 1943 d Armour & Midge. D 2/27/1999 P 9/4/1999 Bp Charles I Jones III. Montana Assn of Ch Helena MT 2005-2008; Dio Montana Helena MT 2000-2005, Dioc Deploy Off 1999-; Int S Fran Epis Ch Great Falls MT 1999-2000.

VARELA SOLORZANO, Marco Antonio (Hond) Colonia La Sabana, Samparo Sula Honduras **Dio Honduras San Pedro Sula 2006-** B Yuscaran el Paraiso 1974 s Maximo & Catalina. D 10/28/2005 P 10/16/2010 Bp Lloyd Emmanuel Allen. m 10/18/1997 Suyapa Marisala Ardon c 3.

VARELA ZUNIGA, Nery Yolanda (Hond) Colonia Los Robles, Atlantida, Ceiba 31105 Honduras **Dio Honduras San Pedro Sula 2006-; Iglesia Epis Hondurena San Pedro Sula 2006-** B Tegucigalpa M.D.C. 1979 d Ramon & Albertina. Programa Diocesano Educ Teologica 2003. D 10/29/2005 Bp Lloyd Emmanuel Allen. m 9/4/2002 Javier Armando Sierra Figueroa c 2.

VARGHESE, Winnie Sara (NY) 464 Riverside Drive. Apt. 41, New York NY 10027 **Trin Par New York NY 2015-; R S Mk's Ch In The Bowery New York NY 2012-, P-in-c 2009-2015** B Dallas TX 1972 d Cherian & Leelamma. BA SMU 1994; MDiv UTS 1999. D 6/19/1999 Bp Chester Lovelle Talton P 1/8/2000 Bp Frederick Houk Borsch. m Elizabeth Anne Toledo c 2. Chapl Dio Los Angeles Los Angeles CA 2002-2009; Columbia Univ Chapl Dio New York New York NY 2002-2009; Asst to the R Cbury Westwood Fndt Los Angeles CA 1999-2002; S Alb's Epis Ch Los Angeles CA 1999-2002.

VARNER, Joshua H (Ga) Diocese of Georgia, 611 E Bay St, Savannah GA 31401 **Vic Dio Georgia Savannah GA 2012-** B Durham NC 1975 s Grant & Vivian. BA U So 1997; MTS Harvard DS 1999; MDiv VTS 2001. D 6/23/2001 Bp Michael B Curry P 5/18/2002 Bp James Gary Gloster. m 6/19/1999 Elizabeth A Varner c 2. Asst to the R H Trin Epis Ch Greensboro NC 2004-2011; Asst to the R S Lk's Epis Ch Durham NC 2001-2004. stpatrickspooler@gmail.com

VARNUM, Benedict J (Neb) 285 S 208th St, Elkhorn NE 68022 **R St Aug of Cbury Epis Ch Elkhorn NE 2015-** B Shawnee Mission KS 1984 s Ralph & Gaile. BA U Chi 2006; SWTS 2009; MDiv U Chi DS 2010; MDiv U Chi DS 2010; CPE Chapl's Residency Rush U Med Cntr 2011; CPE Chapl's Residency Rush U Med Cntr 2012. D 11/1/2011 Bp Jeff Lee P 5/9/2012 Bp Dean E Wolfe. Asst R S Thos The Apos Ch Overland Pk KS 2011-2015; Chapl Res (Neurosurgery) Rush U Med Cntr Chicago IL 2010-2013. rector@sainta.net

VASQUEZ, Irineo M (Az) Saint Andrew's Church, 6300 W Camelback Rd, Glendale AZ 85301 **Cn Dio Arizona Phoenix AZ 2014-; S Andr's Ch Glendale AZ 2012-** B Guatemala 1964 s Prudencio & Lugarda. BA S Thos PETED Guatemala 1986; St Andrews Sem Mex City 1992; BA Jacob Arbens Sch Guatemala 1995. D 6/6/1986 P 11/1/1988 Bp Armando Roman Guerra Soria. m 4/28/1984 Marie E Vasquez c 3. Vic S Geo's Mssn Hawthorne CA 2001-2012; Dio Guatemala New York NY 1990-1995; D in Charge (San Pablo-Guatemala) 1986-1987. The OSL 2007.

VASQUEZ, Jaime Armando (Hond) IMS SAP Dept 215. PO Box 523900, Miami FL 33152 Honduras B 1972 s Amelia. GTS 2002. D 3/11/2007 Bp Lloyd Emmanuel Allen. c 3. D Iglesia La Trinidad Santa Barbara 2010-2015; D Iglesia San Juan Bautista Puerto Cortes 2004-2009; Lead Pstr Iglesia La Epifania Villanueva Cortes 1999-2003.

VASQUEZ, Martha Sylvia Ovalle (Cal) 8002 Grissom Crst, San Antonio TX 78251 B San Antonio TX 1952 d Joe & Celia. None San Antonio Coll; MTS Oblate TS 1991; MDiv Epis TS of the SW 1995. D 6/4/1995 Bp John Herbert MacNaughton P 12/7/1995 Bp James Edward Folts. c 1. Asstg Cler S Paul's Epis Ch San Antonio TX 2017-1996, 2017-, Asst R 1995-1996; R S Paul's Epis Ch Walnut Creek CA 2006-2016; Cn for Congrl Dvlpmt Dio New York New York NY 2003-2006; Vic S Dav's Ch Highland Mls NY 2003-2006; Assoc R Trin Par Wilmington DE 2000-2003; Vic All SS Epis Ch Pleasanton TX 1997-2000; Epis Ch Of The Gd Shepard Geo W TX 1997-2000. "Spkng the Word," *Sermons that Wk XII*, Morehouse Pub, 2004; Auth, "A Bean Taco and a Cup of Coffee," *Sermons that Wk*, Morehouse Pub, 1997. DOK 1995; EHWP 1992; EWC 1995. canonvasquez@yahoo.com

VASQUEZ, Oscar Arturo (SwFla) 2153 46th Ter SW Apt B, Naples FL 34116 **Vic S Barn 1985-** B Jocotan Chiquimula GT 1932 s Manuel & Gloria. San Jose Inter-Dioconate Sem 1957; BA Pstr Inst Rome It 1964. Rec 11/1/1980 as Priest Bp Hugo Luis Pina-Lopez. m 2/28/1970 Rosani Vasquez c 2. St Barn Bookstore Immokalee FL 1987-1991; Dio Cntrl Florida Orlando FL 1984-1985; Vic Iglesia La Esperanza Orlando FL 1984-1985; Dio Honduras San Pedro Sula 1980-1981.

VASQUEZ, Otto Rene (Los) D 6/3/2017 Bp Diane Jardine Bruce.

VASQUEZ SANCHEZ, Vicente Oswaldo (Hond) **Dio Honduras San Pedro Sula 2000-** B 1969 m 7/9/1999 Rosa Maria Lavaire-Guzman c 2.

VASQUEZ-VERA, Gladys Elisa (EcuC) Ulloa 213 Y Carriba Apdo 17-02-5304, Quito Ecuador **Iglesia Epis Del Ecuador Quito 2004-, 1996-2001; Vic Iglesia del Buen Pstr Quito 1988-** B Guayaquil EC 1958 d Alfonso & Elisa. Colegio Bachiller; Seminario-Bachiller En Teologia 4 Yrs; Teologia Anglicana. D 12/18/1988 P 12/1/1992 Bp Jose Neptali Larrea-Moreno. m 12/16/1994 Felicisimo Navas c 1. Dio SE Mex 2001-2004.

VAUGHAN, Jesse L (NCal) 5801 River Oak Way, Carmichael CA 95608 **Assoc Trin Epis Cathd Sacramento CA 1991-** B Emporia VA 1947 s Douglas & Elizabeth. BS Hampton U 1969; MDiv EDS 1973; CAS Harv 1976. D 6/23/1973 Bp Robert Lionne DeWitt P 3/2/1974 Bp Morris Fairchild Arnold. P-in-c S Mich's Epis Day Sch Carmichael CA 1993-2013, 1993-2012, Headmaster 1981-1989; Assist Hd of Sch All SS' Epis Day Sch Carmel CA 1979-1981; Assoc S Dunst's Epis Ch Carmel CA 1979-1980; P-in-c S Mths Ch Seaside CA 1977-1979; Cur Par Of Chr Ch Andover MA 1975-1977; Asst to Chapl Phil Acad Andover MA 1971-1975. Auth, *Sprtl Crisis & The Young.*

VAUGHAN, John (CFla) 3295 Timucua Cir, Orlando FL 32837 B IE 1957 s John & Eileen. BA S Jn Waterford 1981; MTh S Jn Waterford 1984. D 2/18/1996 P 6/1/1996 Bp John Wadsworth Howe. m 6/22/1991 Rebecca Vaughan. S Jos Epis Ch Orlando FL 1998-2005; S Paul's Ch Winter Haven FL 1996-1998; Dio Cntrl Florida Orlando FL 1996-1997; Asst Pstr S Kevin's Miami FL 1985-1990.

VAUGHAN, Denise C (WMo) 4116 Paint Rock Dr, Austin TX 78731 **The Epis Ch Of The Annunc Vidalia GA 2015-** B Utica NY 1954 d Daniel & Florence. BA U of So Florida 1976; MDiv Epis TS of the SW 2008. D 6/14/1997 Bp Rogers Sanders Harris P 2/22/2009 Bp Dena Arnall Harrison. c 1. R Gr Epis Ch Chillicothe MO 2010-2015; The Ch of the Gd Shpd Austin TX 2008-2010; Sem Epis TS Of The SW 2005-2008; D S Dav's Epis Ch Englewood FL 2003-2005; D S Jas Epis Ch Pt Charlotte FL 2000-2002; D S Nath Ch No Port FL 1997-2000.

VAUGHN, James Barry (Nev) Saint Alban's Church, 429 Cloudland Dr, Birmingham AL 35226 **Chr Ch Las Vegas NV 2013-; R S Jn's In The Prairies Ch Forkland AL 2000-; S Steph's Ch Eutaw AL 2000-** B Mobile AL 1955 s Henry & Vera. BA Harv 1978; MDiv Yale DS 1982; PhD U of St Andrews 1990. D 10/14/1992 P 4/17/1993 Bp Robert Oran Miller. S Alb's Ch Hoover AL 2007-2013; S Lk's Epis Ch Jacksonville AL 2006; R S Ptr's Ch Germantown Philadelphia PA 2000-2004; S Matt's Epis Ch San Mateo CA 1999-2000; S Ptr's Epis Ch Redwood City CA 1998-1999; Pstr S Wilfrid's Ch Marion AL 1997-1998; Epis Black Belt Mnstry Greensboro AL 1993-1998; Asst Epis Ch Of The Epiph Leeds AL 1992-1993. Auth, "In A New Light," *Sermon In Libr Of Distinctive Preaching*, 1996. AAM. Best Sermon Competition Runner-Up Epis Evang Fndt.

VAUGHN, Jessie Harriet (NwT) 3303 Bacon St, Vernon TX 76384 **Died 2/17/2016** B Waterloo NY 1941 d Thomas & Jessie. Hobart and Wm Smith Colleges. D 10/27/2002 Bp C Wallis Ohl. c 4. "The D's Charge (a poem)," *Invoking the Muse*, Watermark Press, 2004.

VAUGHN, Peter Hancock (Ct) 36 Main St, Ellington CT 06029 **D H Trin Epis Ch Enfield CT 2008-** B Los Angeles CA 1937 s Milton & Gladys. BA U of Hartford 1965; MBA U of Connecticut 1973. D 6/9/1990 Bp Arthur Edward Walmsley. m 11/23/1957 Sally Anne Vaughn c 3. D S Andr's Epis Ch

V

Enfield CT 1996-2008; D S Jn's Epis Ch Vernon Rock Vernon Rockville CT 1990-1997.

VAUGHN, Robert Joseph (SeFla) D 12/23/1990 Bp Calvin Onderdonk Schofield Jr.

VAUGHN, S Chadwick (At) St Bede's Episcopal Church, 2601 Henderson Mill Rd NE, Atlanta GA 30345 **R S Bede's Ch Atlanta GA 2012-; Trst Epis TS Of The SW Austin TX 2016-, Pres of the Alum Strng Com 2011-2012; Dn of E Atlanta Convoc Dio Atlanta Atlanta GA 2015-, Exec Bd 2011-2012, Dioc Cmncatn Cmsn 2010-2014, Dn of the Macon Convoc 2010-2012** B Atlanta GA 1973 s Steven & Alice. BA Oglethorpe U 1997; MDiv Epis TS of the SW 2006. D 12/21/2005 P 6/25/2006 Bp J Neil Alexander. m 7/22/2000 Amanda Elizabeth Smith. R S Fran Ch Macon GA 2009-2012; Assoc S Dav's Ch Austin TX 2006-2009; Exec Asst to the Dn Cathd Of S Phil Atlanta GA 2000-2003; Dioc Liturg Cmsn Dio Texas Houston TX 2008-2009. Gathering of Leaders 2008. cvaughn@stbedes.org

VAZQUEZ-GELI, Jose R (PR) B 1928 D P. m 7/28/1951 Zenaida Busigo. Dio Puerto Rico Trujillo Alto PR 1997-2002.

VAZQUEZ-JUAREZ, Patricia Ellen (Tex) 1534 Milam St, Columbus TX 78934 B Philadelphia PA 1954 d Thomas & Margaret. BA Neumann Coll Aston PA 1995; MDiv VTS 1997. D 10/11/1997 Bp Charles Bennison Sr P 6/13/1998 Bp John Henry Smith. m 6/26/2009 Jose Luis Vasquez-Juarez c 3. S Lk's Epis Hosp Houston TX 2008-2009; R S Jn's Epis Ch Columbus TX 2004-2008; S Matt's Ch Wheeling WV 2000-2004; S Ptr's Ch Huntington WV 1999-2000; Cur S Matt's Ch Charleston WV 1997-1999.

VEACH, Deborah Joan (Ind) 215 N. 7th St., Terre Haute IN 47807 B Terre Haute IN 1953 d Jack & Joanna. AA Indiana St U 1989. D 10/26/2008 Bp Cate Waynick. m 6/19/1987 Alan Veach c 4.

VEAL, David Lee (NwT) 3026 54th St Apt 410, Lubbock TX 79413 **Ret 2001-; Dep to GC Dio W Texas San Antonio TX 1979-, COM 1973-1983, Cn 1973-1980; Del to WCC Assembly, Harare, Zimbabwe Dom And Frgn Mssy Soc- Epis Ch Cntr New York NY 1998-, SCER 1994-2000, Angl - RC Dialogue USA 1992-1998** B Knoxville TN 1938 s Edward & Ida. BA U of Alabama 1960; MDiv Sewanee: The U So, TS 1971; DMin PrTS 1988. D 6/10/1971 P 12/15/1971 Bp Furman Charles Stough. m 8/11/1967 Sue E McGough c 2. Vic S Lk's Epis Ch Levelland TX 2008-2014; Int S Chris's Epis Ch Lubbock TX 2005-2008; Int S Barn' Epis Ch Of Odessa Odessa TX 2002-2003; Trst Sewanee U So TS Sewanee TN 1994-1997, Trst 1983-1993, Trst 1994-1997, Trst 1983-1986; U So TS Sewanee TN 1994-1997; Cn Dio NW Texas Lubbock TX 1987-2001, Dep to GC 2000-, Dep to GC 1997-, Dep to GC 1994-, Dep to GC 1991-, Dep to GC 1988-; U So TS Sewanee TN 1983-1986; R Ch Of The Resurr Windcrest TX 1980-1987; Dir W Texas Epis Campus Mnstrs 1973-1975; Chapl (LtCol) US-AR 1971-1985; R S Steph's Ch Eutaw AL 1971-1973; Pres EDEO Ft Myers FL 2007-2010; Trst Epis TS Of The SW Austin TX 1976-1978; Ecum Off Dio Alabama Birmingham 1971-1973. Auth, "Calendar of SS," Forw Mvmt Press, 2004; Auth, "The Moravians," Forw Mvmt Press, 1999; Auth, "An Esssential Unity," Morehouse Pub, 1997; Contrib, "Lesser Feasts and Fasts," *Lesser Feasts and Fasts*, Ch Pub, Inc, 1980; Auth, "SS Galore," Forw Mvmt Press, 1971. CODE 1975-2001; Epis Dioc Ecum & Interreligous Off 1976-2011; No Amer Acad of Eumenists 1988-2000. DuBose Awd for Serv U So TS 2006.

VEALE, David Scott (Vt) 8 Bishop St, Saint Albans VT 05478 B Ridgefield NJ 1962 s Stewart & Nancy. BA The Coll of New Jersey 1984; Diac Stds Epis Sch for Deacons 2000; MTS Nash 2006. D 12/16/2000 Bp Richard Lester Shimpfky P 9/2/2006 Bp Keith Lynn Ackerman. m 11/21/1999 Donna Lynn Veale c 3. R S Lk's Ch S Albans VT 2010-2015; R Gr Ch Un City NJ 2008-2010; D S Fran Ch Alta IL 2005-2006; D Ch of St. Anth of Padua Hackensack NJ 2003-2004; D S Andr's Ch Ben Lomond CA 2000-2002. SSC 2007.

VEALE, Donald Meier (Ore) 5346 Don Miguel Dr, Carlsbad CA 92010 B Saint Louis MO 1931 s Donald & Emma. BA U Pgh 1954; MDiv PDS 1958. D 6/30/1958 Bp Thaddeus F Zielinski P 6/17/1959 Bp Lauriston L Scaife. m 8/20/1973 Barbara M Veale c 2. S Matt's Epis Ch Gold Bch OR 1994-2003, Vic 1991-1993; Ret 1994-1996; Dio Oregon Portland OR 1991-1993; S Tim's Ch Brookings OR 1991-1993; Int St Cross Epis Ch Hermosa Bch CA 1990-1991; Int H Faith Par Inglewood CA 1989-1990; Int S Fran' Par Palos Verdes Estates CA 1987-1988; All SS Epis Ch Verona PA 1978-1987; S Paul's Ch Monongahela PA 1977; R All SS Ch Rosedale PA 1976-1986; Vic Ch Of The H Sprt Erie PA 1972-1974; Vic S Jn Erie PA 1966-1971; Chapl Edinboro St Coll (PA) 1962-1966; Vic S Ptr's Ch Waterford PA 1962-1966; Vic Calv Epis Ch Williamsville NY 1958-1962.

VEALE JR, Erwin Olin (Ga) 3120 Exeter Rd, Augusta GA 30909 **S Mich's Ch Waynesboro GA 2016-; P-in-c H Cross Ch Thomson GA 2013-, Vic 1995-1997** B Savannah GA 1958 s Erwin & Gloria. BS U GA 1980; MDiv Sthrn Bapt TS 1985; DAS Sewanee: The U So, TS 1995. D 6/1/1994 Bp Harry Woolston Shipps P 3/14/1996 Bp Henry Irving Louttit. m 12/28/1991 Virginia Corinne Veale c 2. Asst S Paul's Ch Augusta GA 2013, 2000-2004; The Ch Of The Gd Shpd Augusta GA 2006-2013; Chapl Georgia Rgnts Med Cntr 1997-2014; Chapl Walton Rehab Hosp 1988-1994. Chapt Contrib, "Psy-

chosocial and Sprtl Needs of the Chld and Fam," *Palliative Care for Infants, Chld and Adolescents*, The JHU Press, 2004. Assn of Profsnl Chapl 1989-2015. church3430@bellsouth.net

VEINOT, William Paul (Ct) 327 Orchard St, Rocky Hill CT 06067 **Chapl Rocky Hill CT Fire Dept 2008-; R S Andr The Apos Rocky Hill CT 1991-** B Winchester MA 1954 s Richard & Ellen. AAS Paul Smiths Coll 1975; MDiv Bangor TS 1987; BS SUNY 1987; STM Yale DS 1988; DMin Gordon-Conwell TS 2003. D 6/4/1988 P 5/1/1989 Bp Edward Cole Chalfant. m 8/26/1989 Wendy Veinot c 3. Cur S Jn's Ch Larchmont NY 1988-1991.

VEINTIMILLA, Carlos (EcuC) Brisas De Santay Mz G, V 30, Duran Ecuador **P-in-c S Mich 1981-** B Guayaquil EC 1938 s Luis & Maria. Seminario De San Andres Mex City Df Mx 1973. D 10/22/1972 Bp Jose Guadalupe Saucedo P 6/30/1973 Bp Adrian Delio Caceres-Villavicencio. m 3/3/1984 Juanita Veintimilla c 2. P-in-c Iglesia Cristo Rey Guayaquil Gu 2000-2003; P-in-c Iglesia de la Transfiguracion Guayaquil Gu 1995-2003; Litoral Dio Ecuador Guayaquil 1986-2003; P-in-c S Jas In Jerusalem Quito 1977-1980; Iglesia Epis Del Ecuador Quito 1973-1994; P-in-c 1912 Apos 1973-1976. Scroll Of Friendship 1962.

VEIT JR, Richard Fred (Wyo) 7711 Hawthorne Dr, Cheyenne WY 82009 **R S Mk's Ch Cheyenne WY 2005-** B Bronxville NY 1967 s Richard & Betty. BA U CO 1989; MDiv VTS 1998. D 6/5/1999 P 12/1/1999 Bp William Jerry Winterrowd. m 2/23/2002 Caroline C Veit c 2. Asst S Marg's Ch Woodbridge VA 2000-2005; Asst All SS Ch Loveland CO 1999-2000. Young Men's Literary Club of Cheyenne 2007.

VELA, Debra Smith (Dal) D 6/4/2016 Bp George Robinson Sumner Jr.

VELARDE, Inez Jean (NAM) St Luke's-in-the-Desert, PO Box 720, Farmington NM 87499 B 1951 d Paul & Grace. D 6/24/2012 P 7/27/2013 Bp David Earle Bailey. m 9/29/1979 Gilbert Velarde c 1. Navajoland Area Mssn Farmington NM 2012-2016, 1974-2012; Other Lay Position S Lk's In The Desert Farmington NM 1975-2016.

VELASQUEZ BORJAS, Gladis Margarita (Hond) Aldea Santa Cruz, Tegucigalpa, Tegucigalpa M.D.C. FM 15023 Honduras **Dio Honduras San Pedro Sula 2006-; Iglesia Epis Hondurena San Pedro Sula 2006-** B Villa de San Francisco F.M. 1961 d Carlos & Margarita. DIT Seminario Diocesano. D 10/29/2005 Bp Lloyd Emmanuel Allen. c 3.

VELAZQUEZ-MORALES, Juan Alberto (PR) **Archd Dio Puerto Rico S Just PR 2014-** B Ponce, PR 1952 s Francisco & Lydia. Asociado Universidad de Puerto Rico 1973; Certificado en Teologia Seminario Epis Del Caribe 1978. D 2/24/1978 P 10/21/1979 Bp Francisco Reus-Froylan. c 3. Archd Dio Puerto Rico Trujillo Alto PR 2004-2012, 1980-2001, 1978-1979; Sprtl Advsr San Lucas Hospice Ponce PR 1986-2004. padrejvelazquez@episcopalpr.org

VELEZ-RIVERA, Daniel (Va) 11625 Vantage Hill Road, Unit 11C, Reston VA 20190 **Bd Mem Epis Serv Corps 2013-; Vic S Gabr's Epis Ch Leesburg VA 2012-; Trst, Hisp Schlrshp Trust Fund Dom and Frgn Mssn Soc New York NY 2009-; Dn's Advsry Bd Bos TS 2012-** B New York NY 1960 s Máximo & Socorro. BSIE NEU 1983; MSW Bos 2005; MDiv Bos TS 2006. D 6/3/2006 Bp M(Arvil) Thomas Shaw P 1/6/2007 Bp Gayle Harris. m 5/20/2004 Theodore Gallagher. Consult Hisp Mnstrs Dom And Frgn Mssy Soc- Epis Ch Cntr New York NY 2012, Personal Rep Pres. Hse Deputies Stndg Cmsn Mssn & Evang 2012-; Consult Hisp Mnstrs Epis Ch Cntr New York NY 2012; Int S Mich And All Ang Ch Baltimore MD 2012; Co-P in Charge S Ptr's Ch Salem MA 2009-2011; Urban Res/Cur Gr Ch Salem MA 2006-2009. Essay, "Will you respect the dignity of every human being?: A Latino perspective on same-gender blessing," *Encouraging Conversation Resources for Talking about Same-Sex Blessings*, Ch Pub, Inc., 2013; Essay, "Will you respect the dignity of every human being?: A Latino perspective on same-gender blessing.," *Encouraging Conversation: Resources for Talking About Same-Sex Blessings*, Ch Pub, 2013; Article, "Transforming Lives, Tranforming Communities: The Mnstry of Presence," *The ATR*, ATR, 2011; Essay, "Lay Wmn and Dss in Puerto Rico: the legacy of Catalina Olivieri Rivera," *Deeper Joy: Lay Wmn And Vocation in the 20th Century Epis Ch*, Ch Pub, Inc., 2005. Distinguished Alum Awd Bos TS 2009; Transformational Mnstry Fell ECF 2007.

VELEZ-VELAZQUEZ, Carlos (PR) **Dio Puerto Rico Trujillo Alto PR 2016-** B Caguas 1961 s Enrique & Bonifacia. D 9/19/2015 P 5/28/2016 Bp Wilfrido Ramos-Orench.

VELLA, Joan Christine (WNC) 147 Sourwood Road, State Road NC 28676 B New York NY 1936 d Vincent & Catherine. BA Meredith Coll 1986; MTS Washington Theol Un 1988; MA Washington Theol Un 1988; MDiv Sewanee: The U So, TS 1997; DMin Hood TS 2007. D 6/21/1997 P 6/20/1998 Bp Robert Carroll Johnson Jr. Int S Tim's Ch Wilson NC 2008-2010, Int R 2008-2010, Asst 1997-2000; Int Gr Ch In The Mountains Waynesville NC 2007-2008; Int Ch Of The Epiph Newton NC 2005-2007; R Yadkin Vlly Cluster Salisbury NC 2004-2005; Vic Galloway Memi Chap Elkin NC 2000-2003; Asst P S Mk's Ch Wilson NC 1997-2000.

VELLA JR, Joseph Agius (SwFla) 125 Lamara Way Ne, Saint Petersburg FL 33704 B Beaufort SC 1948 s Joseph & Mary. U Grenoble Fr 1967; U So 1970; BA U of So Carolina 1984; MDiv TESM 1988. P 5/1/1989 Bp Plinio L Simoes.

m 9/9/1978 Judith Vella. St Josephs Ch Ft Myers FL 1999-2000; Ch Of The H Cross St Petersburg FL 1998-1999; Dio Arkansas Little Rock AR 1995-1997; Ch Of The Annunc Cordova TN 1994-1995; R All SS Ch Cayce SC 1992-1994; D S Jn's Ch Charleston SC 1988-1989.

VELLOM, Lee Sherwin (Az) 1741 North Camino Rebecca, Nogales AZ 85621 B Pasadena CA 1932 s Ralph & Dorothy. BA U CA 1954; BA Sch for Deacons 1984. D 12/3/1988 Bp William Edwin Swing. m 4/11/1953 James Fitzsimmons c 1. D S Andr's Epis Ch Nogales AZ 1996-2013; D S Jn's Epis Ch Oakland CA 1994-1996; D All SS Epis Ch San Leandro CA 1989-1993. NAAD 1983. Life Regent Natl Eagle Scout Assn 1980.

VELLOM, Timothy John (WTex) 15919 Colton Wl, San Antonio TX 78247 **R S Matt's Epis Ch Universal City TX 1999-** B New London CT 1958 s Lee & James. BA U So 1980; MDiv TESM 1985. D 6/20/1985 Bp Scott Field Bailey P 1/1/1986 Bp Stanley Fillmore Hauser. m 1/3/1981 Ann R Vellom c 2. S Jas Epis Ch Del Rio TX 1993-1999; R Trin Epis Ch Edna TX 1992-1993, Vic 1988-1991; Asst All SS Epis Ch Corpus Christi TX 1985-1988.

VELTHUIZEN, Teunisje (NI) 608 Cushing St, South Bend IN 46616 B Ermelo NL 1944 d Teunis & Aartje. BA Hope Coll 1966; MRE Wstrn TS 1977; MDiv GTS 1985; CSD GTS 1996. D 6/8/1985 P 12/1/1985 Bp Howard Samuel Meeks. R Ch Of The H Trin So Bend IN 1991-2007; Int S Paul's Epis Ch Jackson MI 1991; Int Ch Of The Resurr Battle Creek MI 1989-1990; Vic S Steph's Epis Ch Plainwell MI 1985-1989. Ord Of Julian Of Norwich, Oblate 1998.

VENABLE, Charles Wallace (Ala) D 10/1/2016 Bp John Mckee Sloan Sr.

VENEZIA, Deborah L (CFla) 7725 Indian Ridge Trail South, Kissimmee FL 34747 B Morristown NJ 1956 d Michael & Alice. BS FD 1979; MA Rutgers The St U of New Jersey 1992; MDiv Drew U 2004. D 6/12/2004 Bp Martin Gough Townsend P 12/18/2004 Bp John Palmer Croneberger. m 7/31/1982 Ralph Venezia. Vic S Jos Epis Ch Orlando FL 2007-2012; Int S Jn's Epis Ch Boonton NJ 2005-2007; D S Geo's Epis Ch Maplewood NJ 2004-2005.

VENKATESH, Catherine Richardson (WMass) 281 Renfrew St, Arlington MA 02476 **Lic Supply P Dio Massachusetts Boston MA 2007-, Lic supply P 2007-** B Lancaster PA 1966 d Jonathan & Alice. BA Wms 1988; Dplma U of Warwick 1989; MS U of Washington 1993; MDiv CDSP 1998. D 6/20/1998 Bp Vincent Waydell Warner P 1/9/1999 Bp Edward Lewis Lee Jr. m 11/11/2006 Venkatesh Natarajan c 1. Int S Jn's Ch Newtonville MA 2009; Mem, Congrl Dvlpmt Grants Team Gr Ch Great Barrington MA 2002-2006; Int S Paul's Epis Ch Elk Rapids MI 2001-2002; Assoc R Gr Epis Ch Traverse City MI 1998-2001; Dio Wstrn Massachusetts Springfield 2002-2006. Auth, "Jos'S Cross," *Preaching Through The Year Of Matt: Sermons That Wk X*, Morehouse, 2001; Auth, "The Wounds Of The Risen Chr," *Preaching Through The Year Of Mk: Sermons That Wk Viii*, Morehouse Pub, 1999; Auth, "Hope For All Creation: Seeds For A Chr Enviromental Ethic," *Millenium 3*, 1997. Phi Beta Kappa Wms 1988.

VENTRIS, Margaret Pyre (Los) 72348 Larrea Ave, Twentynine Palms CA 92277 **S Mart-In-The-Fields Mssn Twentynine Plms CA 2011-** B Tucson AZ 1949 d Jackman & Jane. Bloy Hse/CST; BS San Diego St U. D 6/4/2011 P 12/17/2011 Bp Joseph Jon Bruno. m 4/27/1968 Kenneth Ventris c 2.

VERBECK III, Guido Fridolin (WLa) 4741 Crescent Dr, Shreveport LA 71106 **Chapl Shreveport Fire Dept 2010-** B Syracuse NY 1940 s Guido & Dorothea. BA Marq 1965; MDiv VTS 1983; VTS 1994. D 6/10/1983 P 5/18/1984 Bp Charles Farmer Duvall. c 2. R S Paul's Epis Ch Shreveport LA 1996-2011; R S Alb's Epis Ch Monroe LA 1992-1996; Cur S Paul's Ch Mobile AL 1983-1990; Chapl BSA 1979-2011; Dep, GC Dio Wstrn Louisiana Alexandria LA 2000-2012, Chair Camp Hardtner Cmsn 1996-2005. Auth, "Funny Things Happen On The Way To The Altar". R Emer St. Paul's Epis Ch 2017; Ord of St. Geo BSA 2004. frguido@bellsouth.net

VERDAASDONK, Henry Joseph (Alb) 34 Spencer Blvd, Coxsackie NY 12051 **D S Lk's Ch Catskill NY 2003-** B Coxsackie NY 1935 s Jacobus & Maria. D 1/25/2003 Bp David John Bena. m 4/13/1958 Joyce Danetta Verdaasdonk c 3.

VERDI, Barry Ellis (Los) 12571 Kagel Canyon Rd, Sylmar CA 91342 B Los Angeles CA 1937 s Vaughn & Edith. BA San Jose St U 1959; MDiv CDSP 1962; MA San Jose St U 1969. D 6/29/1962 P 1/1/1963 Bp Gordon V Smith. m 7/9/1986 Vicenta Verdi. Asst S Nich Par Encino CA 2002; H Fam Mssn N Hollywood CA 1987-2002; Assoc S Simon's Par San Fernando CA 1983-1986; R S Jn's Epis Ch Clayton CA 1977-1981; Urban Assoc Trin Cathd San Jose CA 1973-1976, Urban Assoc 1966-1972; Vic S Lawr Campbell CA 1970-1972; P-in-c All SS Epis Ch Palo Alto CA 1969-1970; Vic Trin Ch Denison IA 1962-1965; Vic Trin Mapleton IA 1962-1965. Auth, "The Pk". Melchizedek Assn. Nosotros Pres Awd For Contrib To Hisp Cause 1990.

VERELL, Gary Archer (SeFla) 917 E Ridge Village Dr, Miami FL 33157 **Ret 1998-** B Richmond VA 1933 s Emmett & Nena. BA Catawba Coll 1956; MDiv PDS 1959; CTP U NC 1983. D 9/19/1959 P 3/26/1960 Bp Richard Henry Baker. m 12/28/1959 Phyllis Mead Verell c 2. S Faith's Epis Ch Miami FL 1989-1998; H Apos Ch Ellsworth KS 1982-1989; Chapl & Prog Dir S Fran Cmnty Serv Inc. Salina KS 1982-1989; S Nich Chap Ellsworth KS 1982-1989; Ch Of S Andr And S Monica Philadelphia PA 1980-1981; R All SS Ch Norristown PA 1976-1978; R Emm Ch Covington VA 1969-1976; R S Thos Epis Ch

Reidsville NC 1962-1969; Min In Charge Calv Burlington NC 1959-1962; Min in charge S Andr's Ch Haw River NC 1959-1962; Stndg Com Dio SE Florida Miami 1996-1998; Stndg Com Dio Wstrn Kansas Hutchinson KS 1984-1989; Stndg Com Dio SW Virginia Roanoke VA 1971-1976.

VERGARA, Winfred Bagao (LI) 40-11 68th Street #2, Woodside NY 11377 **H Trin Epis Ch Hicksville NY 2016-; P-in-c S Jas Ch Elmhust NY 2013-; Mssnr, Asiamerica Mnstrs Epis Ch Cntr New York NY 2004-** B Pili Ajuy Iloilo PH 1950 s Aureo & Clarita. BA Trin U of Asia PH 1973; MDiv S Andrews TS Manila PH 1978; ThM SE Asia Grad Sch Sg 1983; DMin SFTS 1990; DD CDSP 2007. Rec 1/1/1993 as Priest Bp Richard Lester Shimpfky. m 1/27/1979 Angela Cornel Vergara. Dio Long Island Garden City NY 2013-2016; P-in-c St. Mich & All Ang Seaford New York 2011-2013; Asian Mssnr Dio El Camino Real Salinas CA 1993-2004; Founding Vic H Fam Epis Ch San Jose CA 1991-2004; Assoc S Phil's Ch San Jose CA 1988-1991; Mssy P Angl Ch In Singapore Singapore 1980-1986; Par P Philippine Independentt Ch Metro-Manila . Philippines 1978-1980. Auth, "Being Epis," The Epis Ch, 2011; Auth, "Catholicity and Brief Hist of the Epis Ch in the Philippines," The Epis Ch, 2010; Auth, "Evang, Mssn, Globalization," The Epis Ch, 2009; Auth, "Mainstreaming: Asians in ECUSA," *Epis Books & Resources*, The Epis Ch, 2006; Auth, "Milkfish In Brackish Water," *Filipino Mnstry In Amer Context*, Sunrise Pub, 1992; Auth, "Filipino Immigration And Theol Of Versatility," *Pacific Theol Revs*, SFTS, San Anselmo, California, 1990; Auth, "The Contextual Theol Of Kosuke Koyama," SEAGST, Singapore, 1989; Auth, "Dynamics Of Rel Revolution," SFTS, San Anselmo, California, 1989; Auth, "Theol Of The People:Aglipayan Challenge," SATS, Quezon City, Philippines, 1972. Alpha Phi Omega 1970; Epis Asiamerica Mnstry 1990; Filipino Amer Coun 1986-1995. Oustanding Alum Trin U of Asia 2009; DD, honoris causa CDSP 2007; Cn To Asian Cultures Epis Dio El Camino Real 2000. wvergara@episcopalchurch.org

VERGARA GRUESO, Edison (Colom) Carrera 6 No 49-85, Piso 2, Bogota Colombia B Buenaventura Colombia 1960 s Jesus & Anatilde. Theol Cristo Sacerdote 1994; UT choco 2003. D 6/16/2007 P 10/18/2008 Bp Francisco Jose Duque-Gomez. m 9/9/1995 Ambrosina Cordona-Renteria c 2.

VERHAEGHE, Ronald Edward (WMo) 4401 Wornall Rd, Kansas City MO 64111 **Chr Ch Warrensburg MO 2016-** B Saint Louis MO 1962 s Donald & Frances. BS Rockhurst Coll 1987; MDiv S Mary's of the Lake 1992; MDiv S Mary's of the Lake 1992. Rec 10/27/2011 Bp Martin Scott Field. m 5/21/2016 Jeffrey Young Bennett. Chapl St Lk's So Chap Overland Pk KS 2012-2017; St Lk's Chap Kansas City MO 2011-2012. verhaegheron@aol.com

VERNON, Valerie Veronica (SeFla) Po Box 22462, West Palm Beach FL 33416 B Montego Bay Jamaica 1951 AA Northwood U. D 7/26/2003 Bp Leo Frade. c 2.

VERRET, Joan Claire (CFla) 220 E Palm Dr, Lakeland FL 33803 **D S Dav's Epis Ch Lakeland FL 2012-; Chapl Camp Wingmann Avon Pk FL 2006-; Chapl Third Ord Soc of S Fran 1990-; Bd Dir Camp Wingmann Avon Pk FL 1995-** B Youngstown OH 1935 d Frederick & Ida. Dplma S Josephs Hosp of Nrsng Reading PA 1956; BA S Leo U 1979; Cert Inst for Chr Stds Florida 1989. D 12/8/1990 Bp John Wadsworth Howe. c 4. D S Steph's Ch Lakeland FL 1997-2002; Chapl Cmnty of the SS of Lazarus Lakeland FL 1992-1995; Chapl Corps Lakeland Police Dept FL 1992-1995; Dir Pstr Care All SS Epis Ch Lakeland FL 1990-1996. Anglical Fllshp of Pryr; NAAD. Rec of Steph Awd Dio Cntrl Florida 1999.

VERRETTE, Sallie Cheavens (Ia) St. Paul's Episcopal Church, 6th & State., Grinnell IA 50112 **S Paul's Epis Ch Grinnell IA 2007-** B El Paso TX 1932 d John & Erid. BA Willamette U 1954; MSW U of Iowa 1982. D 12/16/2006 P 6/16/2007 Bp Alan Scarfe. m 1/14/1956 Victor Verrette c 3.

VERSHURE, Claude Edward (SD) 25413 He Sapa Trail, Custer SD 57730 **R S Lk's Ch Hot Sprg SD 2005-; Vic S Lk's Ch Hot Sprg SD 2005-** B Bemidji MN 1946 s Clarence & Arlotte. AA Hibbing Cmnty Coll 1972; BS Minnesota St U Moorhead 1976; Niobrara Sum Sem 1996; Other 1996. D 6/12/2000 P 7/23/2005 Bp Creighton Leland Robertson. m 6/12/1971 Dorothy Susan Vershure c 2.

VERVYNCK, Jennifer R (Oly) 290 Oak Shore Dr, Port Townsend WA 98368 B Honolulu HI 1947 d George & Anna. Wstrn Washington U 1967; BA U of Washington 1968; Cert in Theol Stds ETSBH 1988. D 6/4/1988 Bp Charles Brinkley Morton. m 7/20/1968 Brian D Vervynck c 3. Hd of Sch S Jn's Epis Ch Chula Vista CA 2011, Par Asst and Sch Chapl 2010-2011; Cn to the Ordnry for Mnstry Dvlpmt Dio San Diego San Diego CA 1996-2010, Cn Congrl Dev., Deploy, and Formation 1996-; Int Asst S Barth's Epis Ch Poway CA 1996-1997; Chapl Epis Cmnty Serv Natl City CA 1995; D in Charge S Anne's Epis Ch Oceanside CA 1995; D All SS Ch Vista CA 1988-1994. jennyvervynck@gmail.com

VESGA-ARDILA, Ramon (Ve) B 1950 D 5/17/2002 Bp Orlando Jesus Guerrero. Dio Venezuela Caracas 2004-2015.

VEST, Douglas Carter (Los) 250 Pantops Mountain Rd Apt 327, Charlottesville VA 22911 **Ret 1989-** B Covington KY 1920 s Hugh & Geraldine. U Cinc 1942; MS USNA 1945; MS JHU 1953; MDiv EDS 1966; MA Duquesne U 1982. D 9/1/1966 P 3/11/1967 Bp Francis E I Bloy. m 12/11/1982 Norvene Foster c 2.

Asst Epis Ch Of S Fran-In-The-Vlly Green Vlly AZ 2007-2010; Asst S Mk's Par Altadena CA 2002-2007; Asst Ch Of The Ang Pasadena CA 1997-2001; Asst Gr Epis Ch Glendora CA 1990-1997; Cn Mssnr for Mnstry Dio Los Angeles Los Angeles CA 1982-1989; Assoc All SS Ch Pasadena CA 1975-1981; Vic Epis Ch Of S Andr And S Chas Granada Hills CA 1968-1975; Chapl San Fernando Vlly St U Los Angeles CA 1968-1975; Asst S Andr's Par Fullerton CA 1966-1968. Auth, "Life's Flow," 48-hour Books, 2014; Auth, "Pathways to Self," Cedar Creek Books, 2012; Auth, "A Second Helping," Cedar Creek Books, 2010; Auth, "Churchianity Lite," Xulon Press, 2007; Auth, "Entering the Mystery," Xulon Press, 2006; Auth, "Hm for the Heart," Xulon Press, 2005; Auth, "Deep Treasures from Retreat," Source Books, 2003; Contrib, "Sprtl formation Bible (4 Books)," Zonderven, 1999; Auth, "On Pilgrimage," Cowley Press, 1998; Auth, "Luminous Island," Source Books, 1996; Auth, "Sauntering into Holiness," Source books, 1995; Auth, "Why Stress Keeps Returning," Loyola, 1991. Oblate Ord of S Ben 1989.

VETTEL-BECKER, Richard A (Cal) 706 Tabriz Dr, Billings MT 59105 **D/Mgr Dss Med Cntr 1992-** B Fort Belvoir VA 1955 s Arthur & June. GTS; BA Evangel U 1977; MDiv Gordon-Conwell TS 1981. D 6/1/1992 P 7/22/1993 Bp Charles I Jones III. m 12/16/1978 Cynthia Dawne Hutchinson. Trin Ch San Francisco CA 2003-2004; P Calv Epis Ch Roundup MT 1994-2006; Serv Deconesses Med Cntr 1981-1987. ACPE; ACPE.

VIA, John Albert (At) 8340 Main St., Port Republic VA 24471 B Gorman TX 1937 s Albert & Hallie. BA Baylor U 1959; MA Mississippi St U 1961; PhD U IL 1968. D 5/16/1976 P 6/1/1977 Bp Addison Hosea. m 9/9/1989 Alison Hardwick c 2. R S Alb's Ch Elberton GA 2004-2006; R Ch Of The Medtr Washington GA 1990-2006; R Ch Of The Redeem Greensboro GA 1990-2003; Assoc H Trin Par Decatur GA 1982-1986; D S Bede's Ch Atlanta GA 1976-2006. Auth, *Milton's Antiprelatical Tracts: The Poet Speaks in Prose*, Milton Stds V; Auth, *Milton's The Passion: A Successful Failure*, Milton Quarterly; Auth, *The Rhythm of Regenerate Experience*, Renaissance Papers.

VICENS, Leigh Christiana (Mil) Religion, Philosophy, & Classics Dept., Augustana College, 2001 S Summit Ave, Sioux Falls SD 57197 **Asst Prof of Philos Augustana Coll Sioux Falls SD 2012-** B Boston MA 1981 d Guillermo & Martha. BA Dart 2004; MA U of Wisconsin 2006; MDiv VTS 2009; PhD U of Wisconsin 2012. D 6/6/2009 Bp Steven Andrew Miller. P S Andr's Ch Madison WI 2010-2012, D 2009-2012.

VICKERS, David (Colo) 8119 M 68, Indian River MI 49749 **S Mk's Epis Ch Marine City MI 2017-** B Detroit MI 1947 s Robert & Dorothy. AA Macomb Cmnty Coll 1968; BA Estrn Michigan U 1971; MA Estrn Michigan U 1971; DMA U CO 1979; MDiv Epis TS of the SW 1999. D 6/5/1999 P 12/18/1999 Bp William Jerry Winterrowd. m 7/1/1981 Barbara Ruth Vickers. R S Jn's Epis Ch Ouray CO 2011-2016, R 2011-; S Andr's Epis Ch Gaylord MI 2010-2011; Dn Dio Estrn Michigan Saginaw MI 2002-2011, Dn-Nthrn Convoc 2000-2011; Trsfg Epis Ch Indn River MI 2000-2011; The Ch Of Chr The King (Epis) Arvada CO 1999-2000.

VICKERY JR, Robby (Tex) St. Michael's Episcopal Church, 1500 N. Capital of Texas Highway, Austin TX 78746 B Lubbock TX 1951 s Robert & Norma. BS Rice U 1973; MDiv VTS 1976. D 6/17/1976 P 6/22/1977 Bp Roger Howard Cilley. m 5/25/1973 Debra Ann Gil c 3. R S Mich's Ch Austin TX 1990-2017; P-in-c S Mart's Epis Ch Copperas Cove TX 1983-1988; R S Chris's Ch Killeen TX 1979-1990; Chr Ch Cathd Houston TX 1979; Asst S Mart's Epis Ch Houston TX 1976-1979. EvangES 1977.

VIDAL, Gene Vance (Az) Po Box 13647, Phoenix AZ 85002 **Vic S Alb's Coop Par Hamilton New Zealand 1981-** B Washington DC 1942 s Eugene & Katherine. BA U of Arizona 1963; BD VTS 1966; MA U of Arizona 1971. D 6/22/1966 P 12/1/1966 Bp John Joseph Meakin Harte. m 6/7/1966 Mary Vidal. Dio Maryland Baltimore MD 2003-2004; Asst S Mich's Ch Coolidge AZ 1978-1981; All SS Epis Ch Stafford TX 1974-1978; Vic SS Phil And Jas Morenci AZ 1974-1978; Int S Andr's Epis Ch Nogales AZ 1971-1974; Asst Gr St Pauls Epis Ch Tucson AZ 1968-1969; Asst S Phil's In The Hills Tucson AZ 1967-1968; Vic Chr Ch Florence AZ 1966-1967; Vic S Phil Eloy AZ 1966-1967.

VIDMAR, Mary Burton (WMass) 18018 Avondale Ave, Lake Milton OH 44429 **long term supply S Steph's Ch E Liverpool OH 2011-, long term supply 2011-; S Jas Epis Ch Boardman OH 2010-, Ret P Assoc 2010-** B Toledo OH 1938 d Burton & Florence. BA Mary Manse Coll 1966; MDiv U of Notre Dame 1987; CATS SWTS 2000. D 6/24/2000 P 1/6/2001 Bp Herbert Thompson Jr. c 2. Chr Memi Ch No Brookfield MA 2004-2010; R Dio Wstrn Massachusetts Springfield 2004-2010; P Dvlp H Fam Episc Fllshp Harrison OH 2000-2004; P-in-c S Lk Ch Cincinnati OH 2000-2004. Fllshp of the Way of the Cross 2005.

VIE, Diane E (SwVa) 3536 Willow Lawn, Lynchburg VA 24503 **S Paul's Epis Ch Lynchburg VA 2015-** B Pittsburgh PA 1966 d David & Barbara. BS Estrn Illinois U 1988; MDiv VTS 2007. D 6/2/2007 Bp Bill Persell P 12/8/2007 Bp William Michie Klusmeyer. m 6/19/1993 Todd M Vie c 1. Asst to the R S Jn's Ch Lynchburg VA 2007-2015; Casualty Claims Analyst Liberty Mutual 1988-2004.

VIE, Todd M (SwVa) 3536 Willow Lawn Dr, Lynchburg VA 24503 **Assoc S Paul's Epis Ch Lynchburg VA 2007-** B St Louis MO 1963 s Richard & Joan. U of Missouri; BD No Cntrl Coll 1987; MDiv VTS 2007. D 6/2/2007 Bp Bill Persell P 12/8/2007 Bp William Michie Klusmeyer. m 6/19/1993 Diane E Diane E Edwards c 1.

VIECHWEG, Edrice Veronica (Ct) 503 Old Long Ridge Rd, Stamford CT 06903 B 1952 d Eric & Helen. BS Sacr Heart U 1992; MBA Sacr Heart U 1994. D 9/15/2007 Bp Andrew Donnan Smith. m 12/28/1985 Trevor Viechweg c 2.

VIEL, Brian John (WK) 800 W. 32nd Ave., Hutchinson KS 67502 **S Mk's Ch Lyons KS 2015-, Vic 2015-; Vol Chapl Hutchinson Correctional Facility Hutchinson Kansas 2011-** B Los Angeles CA 1949 s Andrew & Lynne. AA Ft Scott Cmnty Coll 1980; BS Wichita St U 1982; MS Pittsburg St U 1989; Ed.S Pittsburg St U 1992. D 3/15/2008 P 1/10/2009 Bp James Marshall Adams Jr. m 5/1/1987 Mary June Grant c 2. Assoc Gr Epis Ch Hutchinson KS 2011-2015; S Jn's Mltry Sch Salina KS 2009-2011. bviel@cox.net

VIERECK, Alexis (Mass) B 1946 D 12/1/1974 Bp John Melville Burgess P 12/6/1975 Bp Morris Fairchild Arnold. m 11/18/1972 Deborah Howard.

VIGGIANNO, Alyse Elizabeth (Pgh) D 6/4/2016 Bp Dorsey McConnell.

VIGGIANO, Robert Peter (Tex) 241 Yorktown Ct, Malvern PA 19355 **Asstg Cler St. Jn's Epis Ch Compass PA 2015-; Supply Cler Dio Pennsylvania 2013-** B Ridgewood NJ 1958 s Victor & Dorothy. BA Alleg 1980; MA Shippensburg U 1993; MDiv Epis TS of the SW 1999. D 6/11/1999 P 1/15/2000 Bp Michael Whittington Creighton. m 12/27/1997 Karen Viggiano c 1. Asstg Cler S Mk's Ch Austin TX 2011; Asstg Cler St. Richard's Epis Ch Round Rock TX 2010-2011; The Great Cmsn Fndt Houston TX 2007; R S Jas' Epis Ch La Grange TX 2001-2005; Cur The Epis Ch Of S Jn The Bapt York PA 1999-2001.

VIGIL, Vaughn (Md) B Elizabeth NJ 1962 s Noris. Masters U of Maryland U Coll 2014. D 6/11/2016 Bp Eugene Taylor Sutton. D Dio Maryland Baltimore MD 2016, D at Memi Epis Ch 2016-.

VIL, Jean Madoche (Hai) PO Box 407139, C/O Lynx Air, Fort Lauderdale FL 33340 Haiti **P-in-c Dio Haiti Port-au-Prince HT 2002-** B Port-au-Prince Haiti 1974 s Jean & Josélia. Dplma Epis U of Haiti 1999. D P 7/28/2002 Bp Jean Zache Duracin. m 12/18/2008 Ketia Dorvilas c 1.

VILAR MENDEZ, Jose Francisco (PR) **Dio Puerto Rico Trujillo Alto PR 2014-, 2009-2011, 2007-2008** B Mayaguez PR 1957 s Ildefonso & Gladys. Maestria en Divinidad San Pedro y San Pablo 2007; BA Metropolitana 2008. D 8/27/2006 P 11/28/2007 Bp David Andres Alvarez-Velazquez. m 4/13/1984 Wanda Raquel Fussa Bonilla c 3.

VILAR-SANTIAGO, Jose E (PR) 3735 Lancewood Pl, Delray Beach FL 33445 B Fajardo Puerto Rico 1937 s José & Irene. M.Div Ya Berk 1962; M.Div Ya Berk 1962; Stm Centro Caribeño de Estudios Postgraduados 1976; Stm Other 1976; Adventuras, Locura y Travesuras De Los Hijos Del Cura 2015. D 6/23/1962 P 1/5/1963 Bp Albert Ervine Swift. m 10/18/1962 Elizabeth A Holmes c 3. Chapl to Ret Cler Dio Puerto Rico Trujillo Alto PR 2004-2005, Var Missions 1987-2003, Mssn Cler 1977-1979, Dioc Off- Pstr Asst, Hosp Chapl, etc. 1962-1973; Incarn Par Mssn San Juan Washington DC 1981-1986; Fac Epis Sem Of The Caribbean Carolina PR 1973-1975. EPF 1981.

VILAR-SANTIAGO, Miguel E (Md) PO Box 264, Brooklanville MD 21022 **Asst (Ret) Los Tres Santos Reyes MD 2007-** B Juana Diaz PR 1940 s Jose & Irene. BA U of Puerto Rico 1964; MDiv ETSC 1967; STM Centro Estudios Caribbean 1973. Trans 6/1/1990 Bp Albert Theodore Eastman. m 10/24/1970 Barbara R Vilar c 3. Dio Puerto Rico Trujillo Alto PR 2004, 1996-2003, 1980-1988, 1971-1979; Serv Ch of Puerto Rico PR 1995-2004; Dio Maryland Baltimore MD 1990-1995; Hisp Mssnr 1989-1995; Hisp Mssn Baltimore MD 1990-1995; Vic Santos Evangelistas MD 1989-1995; Serv Ch of Puerto Rico PR 1967-1989.

VILAS, Franklin Edward (Nwk) 18 Greylawn Dr, Lakewood NJ 08701 **Ret 2000-** B New York NY 1934 s Franklin & Annis. BA Ya 1956; BD VTS 1959; STM Andover Newton TS 1971; DMin NYTS 1978. D 6/11/1959 Bp Walter H Gray P 3/19/1960 Bp John Henry Esquirol. m 6/3/1958 Joyce H Vilas c 2. S Mk's Ch Basking Ridge NJ 2008-2009; S Lk's Ch Gladstone NJ 2005-2007; Int Dir SCI Port Newark Intl NJ 2003; All SS Ch Bay Hd NJ 2001-2002; R S Paul's Epis Ch Chatham NJ 1991-2000; Exec Dir Wainwright Hse Conf Cntr Rye NY 1985-1991; Wainwright Hse Rye NY 1985-1991; Dio Connecticut Meriden CT 1981-1985; S Ann And The H Trin Brooklyn NY 1976-1981; P-in-c Trin Par New York NY 1973-1976; R S Jn's Ch Beverly MA 1964-1973; Cur S Mk's Ch New Canaan CT 1959-1964. Auth, "Teilhard and Jung: A Cosmic and Psychic Convergence," *Teilhard Stds Number 56*, Amer Teilhard Assn, 2008.

VILLACIS MACIAS, Carlos Emilio (EcuL) **Litoral Dio Ecuador Guayaquil 2015-** B La Libertad 1983 s Carlos & Colombia. D 10/11/2014 Bp Terencio Alfredo Morante-Espana. m 9/15/2007 Janeth Del Rocio Pilay Quirumbay c 3.

VILLAGOMEZA, Christian G (SwFla) 1119 Dockside Dr, Lutz FL 33559 **Vic S Chad's Ch Tampa FL 2003-; Chapl Intl Seafarers Mssn of Tampa Bay Tampa FL 2000-** B Cotabato Philippines 1958 s Cesar & Winifreda. AA Trin of Quezon City Ph 1978; BTh St Andrews TS Quezon City Ph 1982; MDiv S

Andrews TS Manila PH 1990. Trans 12/21/2005 Bp John Bailey Lipscomb. m 10/26/1983 Liwliwa S Villagomeza c 3.

VILLALOBOS, Fabian (Dal) Christ Episcopal Church 534 W Tenth street, Dallas TX 75208 **R Chr Epis Ch Dallas TX 2012-** B Bogota Colombia 1977 s German & Luz. STB Pontifical Lateran U 2002; MA Regina Apostolorum Pontifical U 2008; LST Salesian Pontifical U 2008. Rec 4/3/2012 as Priest Bp James Monte Stanton. m 12/26/2009 Deeann Villalobos.

VILLAMARIN-GUTIERREZ, Washington Rigoberto (EcuC) Calle Hernando Sarmiento, N 39-54 Y Portete, Setor El Batan Quito Ecuador **Iglesia Epis Del Ecuador Quito 2009-** B Quito Ecuador 1959 s Angel & Rosa. D 10/15/2000 Bp Jose Neptali Larrea-Moreno P 5/30/2009 Bp Wilfrido Ramos-Orench. m 11/20/1990 Angelica Ortiz c 3.

VILLARREAL, Arthur Wells (At) **D Chr Ch Macon GA 2013-** B Houston TX 1962 s Eugene & Gloria. ABA Gainesville St Coll 1986; BBA No GA Coll and St U 1988; BDS The Sch for Deacons 2011. D 8/6/2011 Bp J Neil Alexander. m 12/4/2013 Ben Reid Wells.

VILLEMUER-DRENTH, Lauren Anne (NC) 321 S Cleveland Rd, Lexington KY 40515 **S Paul's Epis Ch Winston Salem NC 2015-** B Inglewood CA 1961 d Philip & Nancy. AAS U of Houston 1988; RN Alvin Coll 1991; Formation Prog Cntrl New York w Bex 2005. D 11/19/2005 Bp Gladstone Bailey Adams III. c 3. D Ch Of The Gd Shpd Lexington KY 2006-2013; D St. Matt's Epis Ch Horseheads NY 2005-2006. lvillemuer-drenth@stpauls-ws.org

VILORD, Charles Louis (SwFla) **D Dio SW Florida Parrish FL 1974-** B Suffern NY 1932 s Charles & Evelyn. D 12/21/1974 Bp Emerson Paul Haynes. m 8/4/1955 Elizabeth A Russell.

VINAL, K N (CFla) 5700 Trinity Prep Ln, Winter Park FL 32792 **Assoc S Matt's Epis Ch Orlando FL 2014-; Trin Preparatory Sch Of Florida Winter Pk FL 2000-** B Jacksonville FL 1960 s Nelson & Doris. Bachelors of Sci U of Florida 1983; M-Div TS 1995; M-Div Sewanee: The U So, 1995. D 6/11/1995 Bp Stephen Hays Jecko P 12/16/1995 Bp Don Adger Wimberly. m 10/21/1989 Laura Vinal c 2.

VINAS-PLASENCIA, Aquilino Manuel (CFla) 31 S Forsyth Rd, Orlando FL 32807 **Died 5/28/2017** B 1928 s Felix & Victoria. Epis TS of the SW; BTh Los Pinos Nuevos Sem Cuba 1954; BD Instituto de Segunda Ensenanza 1960; BD UTS 1960; Institucion Nacional de Comercio 1964; Nova SE U 1979. Trans 8/25/1967 as Priest Bp Walter C Klein. c 5. Hisp Mssnr Mision Hispana el Espiritu Santo Orlando FL 2006-2017; Hisp Mssnr S Chris's Ch Orlando FL 2002-2017; Assoc Hisp Mssnr Chr The King Epis Ch Orlando FL 1997-2001, Cur 1967-1996; Hisp Mssnr Santa Maria de los Angeles Orlando FL 1997-2000; Assoc Cathd Ch Of S Lk Orlando FL 1984-1995; Vic La Esperanza 1978-1986; Dio Cntrl Florida Orlando FL 1974-1989; Serv Ch of Cuba 1960-1967. "Obras y Promesas de Dios"; "Senderos de Fe"; Auth, "Mi Vida in El Campo"; Auth, "Albores De La Esperanza". hon a Quien hon merece Iglesia Santa Maria de los Angeles 2004; Reconocimento por labor Iglesia San Cristobal 2003; Honoring por Job in Hisp Mssn Cristo el Rey, Jerusalem 2001; Certificado de Apreciasin Cristo el Rey, Jerusalem.

VINCE, Gail Lynne (EMich) 449 Irons Park Dr, West Branch MI 48661 B Detroit MI 1935 d George & Kathryne. BA U MI 1956; Cert U CA 1959; MDiv SWTS 1991. D 6/21/1991 Bp Henry Irving Mayson P 9/12/1992 Bp Raymond Stewart Wood Jr. m 2/12/1966 Robert E Vince c 1. P-in-c S Andr's Epis Ch Rose City MI 2004-2013; Dio Estrn Michigan Saginaw MI 2003; R Trin Epis Ch W Branch MI 1994-2002; Asst Journey of Faith Epis Ch Dearborn MI 1993-1995; Dio Michigan Detroit MI 1991-1992; Asst S Andr's Ch Waterford MI 1991-1992. Evang Educational Soc; OCCA.

VINCENT, Janet (NY) St Columba's Church, 4201 Albemarle St NW, Washington DC 20016 B Yonkers NY 1955 d Frederick & Louise. BA Manhattanville Coll 1978; MDiv GTS 1983. D 6/4/1983 P 1/8/1984 Bp Paul Moore Jr. R S Columba's Ch Washington DC 2006-2014; R Gr Ch White Plains NY 1997-2006; Pres Gr Cmnty Cntr 1997-2006; Santa Rosa Mssn at Gr Ch White Plains NY 1997-2006; R S Jn's Epis Ch Kingston NY 1988-1997; Supvsr/Lectr, Cntr for Xian Sprtlty The GTS New York NY 1986-1990; Assoc R Gr Epis Ch Nyack NY 1983-1988; CREDO Fac The CPG New York NY 1999-2007; Chair, COM Dio New York New York NY 1996-2000; Ulster Cler Dn 1989-1995. Contrib, "Ground Zero Journ," *Virginia Sem Journ*, Virginia Sem, 2013; Contrib, "Geo Herbert as Mentor," *Gnrl Sem Journ*, Gnrl Sem, 1998; Contrib, "Voice of the Shepherdess," Sheed and Ward, 1996.

VINCENT-ALEXANDER, Samantha Ann (SVa) 431 Massachusetts Ave., Norfolk VA 23508 **S Jn's Ch Hampton VA 2013-** B Bethesda MD 1977 d William & Jan. BA Ge 1999; MDiv PrTS 2004; Dip VTS 2005. D 12/3/2005 P 6/24/2006 Bp Gladstone Bailey Adams III. m 5/20/2006 Conor Matthew Alexander c 1. Asst to the R Ch Of The Ascen Norfolk VA 2005-2013. samanthavincent@hotmail.com

VINE, Walter James (Mil) 2655 N Grant Blvd, Milwaukee WI 53210 B Milwaukee WI 1946 s Pembroke & Mabel. MA Chicago Med Sch Chicago IL; AS Milwaukee Area Tech Coll; BS U of St Fran. D 5/9/1998 Bp Roger John White. m 8/29/1970 Sharon Rae Vine c 4.

VINSON, Donald Keith (WVa) 1701 Crestmont Dr, Huntington WV 25701 B Gadsden AL 1949 s Laurence & Opha. BA U of Alabama 1971; MA U of Alabama 1978; MDiv GTS 1987. D 6/11/1987 P 12/17/1987 Bp Furman Charles Stough. m 8/21/1971 Linda F Frost c 2. Cn for Mssn and Transitions Dio W Virginia Charleston WV 2007-2015; R S Jn's Ch Huntington WV 1994-2007; R S Mk's Epis Ch Perryville MD 1990-1994; Assoc R S Lk's Epis Ch Birmingham AL 1987-1990.

VINSON, Richard Lee (Pa) Holy Nativity Church, 5286 Kalanianaole Highway, Honolulu HI 96821 **Trin Ch Solebury PA 2012-** B Winchester VA 1955 s Freeland & Elizabeth. BA W Virginia Wesleyan Coll 1978; MDiv Wesley TS 1981; Cert VTS 1986; Cert VTS 1986. D 6/14/1986 P 12/1/1986 Bp John Thomas Walker. m 11/19/1983 Ellen L Vinson c 2. R Ch Of The H Nativ Honolulu HI 2006-2012; Dn Calv Cathd Sioux Falls SD 2002-2006; S Andr's Cathd Honolulu HI 2001-2002, Int Pstr 2001-2002; Int S Jn's Ch Hampton VA 1999-2000; R Emm Epis Ch Hampton VA 1994-1999; Chapl Westminster Cbury Virginia Bch VA 1989-1994; Asst Chr Ch Prince Geo's Par Rockville MD 1986-1989; Serv Meth Ch 1979-1982.

VIOLA, Carmen Joseph (NJ) 51 N Main St, Mullica Hill NJ 08062 B Philadelphia PA 1960 s Carmen & Mary. BA Tem 1982; MS St Joes U 1995; The Sch For Deacons 2009. D 5/16/2009 Bp Sylvestre Donato Romero. m 12/13/2003 Rachelle DeSha Viener c 2.

VIOLA, Harry Alexander (WNC) Po Box 1046, Hendersonville NC 28793 **Assoc Ch Of S Jn In The Wilderness Flat Rock NC 2005-** B Concord NC 1940 s George & Blanche. BA Lenoir-Rhyne Coll 1962; STB GTS 1965; Lenoir-Rhyne Coll 1993. D 6/24/1965 P 6/18/1966 Bp Matthew George Henry. m 4/25/1970 Anne Viola c 1. R S Jas Epis Ch Hendersonvlle NC 1974-2002; Assoc The Cathd Of All Souls Asheville NC 1968-1974; P-in-c S Steph's Epis Ch Morganton NC 1966-1967; M-in-c S Gabr's Ch Rutherdforton NC 1965-1966. Dd Lenior Rhyne Coll 1993.

VISCONTI, Richard Dennis (LI) 1 Dyke Rd, Setauket NY 11733 **R Caroline Ch Of Brookhaven E Setauke NY 2002-** B New York NY 1954 s Michael & Mimi. SUNY 1974; BS CUNY 1976; MDiv Sacr Heart TS Hales Corners 1980; CTh Epis TS of the SW 1985; DMin Pittsburgh TS 1994. Rec 10/27/1985 as Priest Bp Joseph Thomas Heistand. m 12/31/1985 Janna Visconti c 2. Mem and EDEIO Rep ARCUSA New York NY 2005-2008; Prov II Coordntr for Ecum Relatns Epis Ch USA New York NY 2004-2008; R S Mich's Epis Ch Carmichael CA 1995-2002; R S Mary's Ch Charleroi PA 1990-1995; Asst S Matt's Ch Bedford NY 1985-1990; Stff Chapl Scottsdale AZ Memi Hosp Scottsdale AZ 1982-1984; The Eccl Trial Crt Dio Long Island Garden City NY 2010-2012, Ecum Off 2002-; Ecum Off The Epis Dio Nthrn California Sacramento CA 1996-2002; Chair Nomin Com Dio Pittsburgh Pittsburgh PA 1991-1995. Auth, "Grief Mnstry: A Ch's Response To Those Who Mourn," Pittsburgh TS Press, 1994. ACPE 1980; Ord of S Lk - Chapl 1992; Ord of St. Vinc 1990; Soc of Cath Priests in the USA 2012. Hon Cn Dio Long Island 2014.

VISGER, James Robert (Neb) 610 Sycamore Dr, Lincoln NE 68510 B Minneapolis MN 1940 s Harry & Mina. D 11/8/1985 Bp James Daniel Warner. m 7/16/1960 Merry Rue Lindgren c 2. D Ch Of The H Trin Lincoln NE 1992-2013; D S Dav Of Wales Epis Ch Lincoln NE 1985-1992; Chapl S Monica Halfway Hm Lincoln NE 1985-1992.

VISMINAS, Christine Elizabeth (Pgh) 70 Dennison Ave, Framingham MA 01702 **Non-par 1986-** B Summit NJ 1953 d Anthony & Roberta. BA Duquesne U 1977; MA Pittsburgh TS 1980. D 12/11/1982 Bp Robert Bracewell Appleyard P 9/1/1983 Bp Alden Moinet Hathaway. m 5/1/1974 Steven Debolt Clark. Pstr Assoc The Ch Of The Redeem Pittsburgh PA 1982-1986.

VITET, Kino (Alb) 1417 Union St, Brooklyn NY 11213 **P-in-c S Mk's Ch Brooklyn NY 2015-, 2011-2012** B 1977 s Samuel & Sybil. BS Leh 1999; MA Ford 2002; MDiv Ya Berk 2011. D 6/4/2011 P 2/2/2012 Bp William Howard Love. m 9/16/2006 Elsie Poisson-Vitet c 3. S Jos's Ch Queens Vlg NY 2012-2015; Dio Long Island Garden City NY 2012.

VIVIAN, Tim (SJ) 10105 Mountaingate Ln, Bakersfield CA 93311 **Vic St Paul's Epis Ch Bakersfield CA 2008-** B Austin TX 1951 s Jerrold & Louise. BA U CA 1973; MA California St Polytechnic U 1974; MA U CA 1981; PhD U CA 1985; MDiv CDSP 1988; Yale DS 1988. D 6/25/1988 Bp Frederick Houk Borsch P 12/1/1988 Bp Edward Witker Jones. m 7/20/1985 Miriam Lynn Vivian. Int S Andr's Epis Ch Ojai CA 1994-1995; Cur S Andr's Ch Meriden CT 1988-2000. Co-Auth, "The H Workshop of Virtue: The Life of S Jn the Little," Cistercian, 2010; Co-Auth, "Mk the Monk: Counsels on the Sprtl Life," St. Vladimir's, 2009; Ed, "Becoming Fire: Through the Year w the Desert Fathers and Mothers," Cistercian, 2009; Co-Auth, "Witness to Holiness: Abba Daniel of Scetis," Cistercian, 2008; Auth, "Words to Live By: Journeys in Ancient and Mod Monasticism," Cistercian, 2005; Auth, "S Macarius the Spiritbearer," St. Vladimir's, 2004; Auth, "Four Desert Fathers," St. Vladimir's, 2004; Co-Auth, "The Life of Antony," Cistercian, 2003; Co-Auth, "The Life of the Jura Fathers," Cistercian, 2000; Auth, "Paphnutius: Histories of the Monks of Upper Egypt and the Life of Onnophrius," *rev.ed.*, Cistercian, 2000; Auth, "Journeying into God: Seven Early Monastic Lives," Fortress, 1996; Co-Auth, "The Life of S Geo of Choziba and The Miracles of the Most H Mo of God at Choziba,"

V

ISP, 1994; Auth, "Paphnutius: Histories of the Monks of Upper Egypt and the Life of Onnophrius," Cistercian, 1993; Co-Auth, "Two Coptic Homilies Attributed to S Ptr of Alexandria," Opus dei Copti manoscritti litterari, 1993; Auth, "S Ptr Of Alexandria: Bp & Mtyr," Fortress Press, 1988. Fac Resrch Awd CSU Bakersfield 2008; Annual Awaard S Shenouda the Archimandrite Coptic Soc 2005.

VIZCAINO, Roberto (EcuC) Jose Herboso 271, Cdla, La Flo, Quito Ecuador **Mssy Nthrn Missions 1973-** B Guayaquil EC 1933 s German & Amanda. D 5/18/1975 Bp Adrian Delio Caceres-Villavicencio. m 3/8/1951 Abigail Vizcaino. Iglesia Epis Del Ecuador Quito 1975-1977; Pstr Evang 1969-1971. Auth, "Rebeldia Juvenil".

VOCELKA, Craig Robert (Oly) PO Box 1362, Poulsbo WA 98370 **Faith Ch Kingston WA 2016-; P S Antony Of Egypt Silverdale WA 2012-; COM Dio Olympia Seattle 2015-, Liturg and Arts Cmsn 2013-2016** B Houston TX 1952 s Frank & Elaine. Cert Texas Heart Inst U of Texas; BA U of St Thos 1981; None Dominican Sch of Phil and Theol 1984; MDiv Seattle U 2012. D 1/17/2012 P 8/1/2012 Bp Gregory Harold Rickel. m 6/27/1987 Victoria Fields-Vocelka.

VOELKER, Sharon L (EMich) St Alban's, 105 S Erie St, Bay City MI 48706 **S Albans Epis Ch Bay City MI 2013-, P-in-c 2013-, Transitional D 2012-2013** B Saginaw MI 1944 d Richard & Irene. Coppage-Gordon Sch for Mnstry 2012. D 10/20/2012 P 4/20/2013 Bp Steven Todd Ousley. Transitional D S Jn's Epis Ch Saginaw MI 2012.

VOETS, Keith A (LI) Church Of Saint Alban The Martyr, 11642 Farmers Blvd, Saint Albans NY 11412 **Ch Of S Alb The Mtyr S Albans NY 2016-** B Hartford CT 1979 s Gregory & Judith. BA Chart Oak St Coll 2004; MDiv GTS 2012. D 6/9/2012 Bp James Elliot Curry P 12/15/2012 Bp Ian Theodore Douglas. m 5/21/2016 Kevin L Morris. S Barn Ch Irvington NY 2014-2016; S Jn's Epis Ch Essex CT 2012-2014; Asst R S Paul And S Jas New Haven CT 2012-2013; Conv Plnng Com Dio Connecticut Meriden CT 2013-2014, COM 2012-2016. Soc of Cath Priests 2015.

VOGEL, Caroline (ETenn) 425 N Cedar Bluff Rd, Knoxville TN 37923 **D Ch Of The Gd Samar Knoxville TN 2011-** B Knoxville TN 1976 d Howard & Lynn. MS U of Tennessee; BA DePauw U 1998; MDiv Harvard DS 2007. D 1/15/2011 Bp Charles Glenn VonRosenberg P 12/3/2011 Bp George Young III. m 7/9/2005 Charles Brown c 2.

VOGELE, Nancy AG (NH) 97 Victory Cir, White River Junction VT 05001 **Our Sav Luth Ch Campus Mnstry Haover NH 2017-** B Hinsdale IL 1963 d Robert & Ruth. BA Dart 1985; MDiv Ya Berk 1993; DMin EDS 1999. D 8/6/1993 P 2/12/1994 Bp Douglas Edwin Theuner. R S Paul's Epis Ch White Riv Jct VT 2001-2012; S Matt's Ch Goffstown NH 1998-2001; Asst S Paul's Ch Concord NH 1993-1997. Auth, "Conversion And Cmnty," *Gathering The Next Generation: Essays On The Formation And Mnstry Of Generation X Priests*, Morehouse Pub, 2000. Ord Of S Helena, Assoc 1998.

VOGEL-POLIZZI, Virginia Margaret (WMass) D 12/10/2016 P 6/17/2017 Bp Doug Fisher.

VOGT JR, Charles Melvin (Minn) 5216 Meadow Rdg, Edina MN 55439 **Died 2/20/2017** B Tiffin OH 1932 s Charles & Mabel. BA Ken 1955; MDiv Bex Sem 1958; Coll of Preachers 1960; Ya Berk 1964; Coventry Cathd & Epis TS Edinburg 1964; Coll of Preachers 1966; Study USSR 1986; U MN 1990. D 5/30/1958 Bp Nelson Marigold Burroughs P 12/6/1958 Bp Beverley D Tucker. m 6/13/1955 Jean F Vogt c 3. Ret 1998-2017; Hon Cn Cathd Ch Of S Mk Minneapolis MN 1997-2012; R S Alb's Epis Ch Edina MN 1973-1997; R Ch Of The Incarn Great Falls MT 1968-1973; R Emm Epis Ch Stamford CT 1965-1968; R S Jas' Ch New Haven CT 1961-1965; Asst S Ptr's Epis Ch Ashtabula OH 1958-1961. Auth, "Covenent Document, Epis & RC Ch in Mnstry," 1996; Auth, "Natl Proj - Gd Life in Light of the Chr Gospel".

VOIEN, Lucinda H (Los) 1645 W 9th St # 2, San Pedro CA 90732 B Whittier CA 1954 d James & Guelda. AB U CA Los Angeles 1976; CPhil U CA Los Angeles 1985; MDiv CDSP 2009. D 6/6/2009 Bp Sergio Carranza-Gomez P 1/9/2010 Bp Chester Lovelle Talton. m 10/17/1975 Chris Steven Voien c 2. S Ptr's Par San Pedro CA 2009-2015. lvoien@whittier.edu

VOLKMANN, Jan Elizabeth (NY) 60 Pine Hill Park, Valatie NY 12184 **S Paul's Ch Kinderhook NY 2006-** B Peekskill NY 1942 d Edward & Marjorie. D 5/15/1999 Bp Richard Frank Grein. m 9/22/1962 Peter Francis Volkmann c 1. Exec Dir-Noontime Meals S Ptr's Epis Ch Peekskill NY 2001-2006; D S Ptr's Epis Ch Peekskill NY 2000-2006.

VOLLAND, Mary Catherine (RG) 1601 S Saint Francis Dr, Santa Fe NM 87505 **S Bede's Epis Ch Santa Fe NM 2014-** B Buffalo NY 1954 d Edward & Lucy. MDiv Iliff TS 2006. D 7/8/2008 Bp James Louis Jelinek P 1/10/2009 Bp Robert John O'Neill. m 3/1/2014 Margaret M Thompson. Asst P S Thos Epis Ch Denver CO 2009-2013; D S Bede Epis Ch Denver CO 2008-2009.

VOLLKOMMER, Marsha Merritt (Chi) Grace Episcopal Church, 309 Hill St, Galena IL 61036 B Lake City IA 1948 d Robert & Marylou. Iowa St U; BS U of Delaware 1971; Angl Cert SWTS 2011; MDiv Wartburg TS 2012. D 9/22/2012 P 5/25/2013 Bp Chris Christopher Epting. m 4/12/1969 Robert Joseph Vollkommer c 3.

VOLPE, Gina (Chi) 9300 S. Pleasant Ave, Rectory, Chicago IL 60643 **Dio Chicago Chicago IL 2005-** B Chicago IL 1963 d Micheal & Mary. BA S Mary of the Woods Coll 1985; MA Illinois St U 1989; MDiv SWTS 1993; Cert Rush U 2004. D 6/17/1995 P 12/16/1995 Bp Frank Tracy Griswold III. R Ch Of The H Nativ Chicago IL 2015, R 2015-, P-in-c 2013-2015; Int R Ch Of The H Fam Pk Forest IL 2011-2013; P in Charge St. Hilary Epis Ch 2008-2009; Fac Coach-Quality Partnr Collaborative Natl Hospice and Palliative Care Orgnztn Washington 2007-2011; Chapl/Clincl Mgr Midwest Palliative & Hospice CareCenter Glenview IL 2004-2011; Long Term Supply H Trin 2004-2005; Ch Of The Redeem Elgin IL 2000-2003; Ch Of The H Comm Maywood IL 1996-1998; Asst Ch Of The H Nativ Clarendon Hls IL 1995-1996; Chapl Vitas Innovative Hospice Care Lombard IL 1994-2004; Bd Dir The Ch Hm At Montgomery Place Chicago IL 2013-2014; Search Com for Bp of Chicago Dio Chicago Chicago IL 2005-2007. Contrib, "Mus at the End of Life: Easing the Pain and Preparing the Passage," Prager, 2010; Contrib, "We Can Do it!," Natl Hospice and Palliative Care Orgnztn, 2008; Contrib, "Faithful Living, Faithful Dying," *Angl Reflections of End of Life*, Morehouse, 2000. Assembly of Epis Healthcare Chapl 1994-2011; Natl Hospice and Palliative Care Orgnztn 2005-2011; Soc of Cath Priests 2013. Fndr's Awd - Hospice Chapl of the Year Vitas Healthcare Corp 2001; Loc Awd - Chapl of the Year - Chicago NW Vitas Healthcare Corp 2000. 95revgina@gmail.com

VOLQUEZ-PEREZ, Huascar Emilio (PR) Mision Episcopal Cristo Rey, 24 Calle Palmeras, Salinas PR 00751 **Dio Puerto Rico Trujillo Alto PR 2015-** B Duverge Republica Dominicana 1975 s Evaristo & Servia. BA Universidad Cntrl de Bayamon 2005; MA Centro de Estudios Avanzados de Puerto Rico y el Caribe 2014; MDiv San Pedro Y San Pablo Seminario 2015; Certification IS-TEPA Instituto Superior Teologico 2016. D 9/19/2015 P 10/8/2016 Bp Wilfrido Ramos-Orench. m 1/29/2016 Elisa Villegas Borges c 4.

VON DREELE, James Davison (Pa) 27107 Valley Run Dr., Wilmington DE 19810 **Cn for Seafarer Mnstry Dio Pennsylvania Philadelphia PA 2010-** B Minneapolis MN 1946 s Carl & Helen. BA Drew U 1968; MDiv Ya Berk 1971. D 6/12/1971 Bp Leland Stark P 12/18/1971 Bp George E Rath. m 1/20/1968 Elizabeth A Von Dreele c 2. Exec Dir Seamens Ch Inst Philadelphia PA 1996-2012; R S Matt's Epis Ch Homestead PA 1976-1996; R Ch Of S Jn The Div Hasbrouck Hts NJ 1973-1976; Asst Trin And S Phil's Cathd Newark NJ 1971-1972. No Amer Maritime Mnstry Assn - Pres 2002-2006.

VON GONTEN, Kevin P (LI) 11571 Ruby Ct., Ellendale DE 19941 B Brooklyn NY 1949 s Joseph & Marion. BA S Fran Coll Brooklyn NY 1979; AM Ford 1982; STM GTS 1987. D 6/8/1987 P 12/19/1987 Bp Robert Campbell Witcher Sr. m 12/11/2010 Christine Marie Federico. Vic Ch Of S Jn The Bapt Ctr Moriches NY 2004-2014; Sabbatical Lv Dio Long Island Garden City NY 2003-2004; Sabbatical Lv Dio Long Island Garden City NY 2003, Pres Bd Mgr Camp DeWolfe 2001-2002, 1999-2001, Chair, Dept of Mssn 1996-2000, VP, Bd Managers Camp DeWolfe 1996-1998, Trst of the Estate Belonging to the Dio Long Island 1995-1998, Chair, Dioc Conv Arrangements Com 1994-1997, Dioc Epis AIDS Cmsn 1992-1996, Dept of Bdgt 1992-1995, Secy of the Conv 1991-1999, Secy, Dioc Coun 1991-1999, Chair, Dioc Cmsn on Liturg and Mus 1990-1999, Dir, Exploration of Mnstry Prog 1989-1999, Trst of the Estate Belonging to the Dio Long Island 1985-1998; Prof of Liturg Geo Mercer TS Garden City NY 1994-2000, Prof of Liturg 1994-2000; Vic All Souls Ch Stony Brook NY 1989-2001; Prof Liturgcs Geo Mercer TS Garden City NY 1989-2000; Assoc R S Steph's Ch Prt Washington NY 1987-1989; Asst to the R S Greg's Epis Ch Parsippany NJ 1985-1987; Adj Assoc Prof S Fran Coll Brklyn NY 1982-1987; Pres Bd Managers Camp DeWolfe 1998-2000. Auth, "The Great Vigil of Easter," *Tidings mag*, Dio Long Island, 1988. AAR 1980; Associated Parishes 1994; Coll Theol Soc 1980; FASNY 1997; New York Assn of Fire Chapl 1995; No Amer Assn for Catechumenate (Life Mem) 1996. Franciscan Sprt Awd St. Fran Coll 1987; Theta Alpha Kappa Theta Alpha Kappa 1984. stpcamden@verizon.net

VON GRABOW, Richard Henri (NCal) 580 Cooper Dr, Benicia CA 94510 **D Ascen Epis Ch Vallejo CA 2008-, D 2002-2007; D, Non-par Dio Nthrn California 2004-** B Oak Park IL 1932 s Henri & May. BA Ball St U 1955; MA Ball St U 1958; Cert Stan 1963; DMA USC 1972; BTh Sch for Deacons 2000. D 3/3/2002 Bp Jerry Alban Lamb. m 6/4/1955 Joan von Grabow c 2. D H Fam Epis Ch Rohnert Pk CA 2007-2008. Pub/Ed, *Mus Pub (Carillon)*, Amer Carillon Mus Editions, 1984. Gld Of Carillonners in No Amer 1973; Ord of S Lk 2001. Pi Kappa Lambda (Natl Mus hon Soc) Ball St U, Muncie IN 1955.

VONGSANIT, Sam Chanpheng (SJ) 709 N Jackson Ave, Fresno CA 93702 B Sayaburi Laos 1964 s Bounthan & Khong. BA GTS 2005. D 12/20/1997 P 6/1/1998 Bp David Mercer Schofield. m 5/10/1986 Tankhai Tankhai Vongsanit c 4. S Mart Of Tours Epis Ch Fresno CA 1998-2012.

VON HAAREN, Barbara Elizabeth (Minn) 1862 W 6th St, Red Wing MN 55066 **D Chr Ch Red Wing MN 2007-; D Chr Ch Old Frontenac 1988-** B Saint Petersburg FL 1941 d Weldon & Verla. U MN. D 4/3/1986 Bp Robert Marshall Anderson. m 2/27/1971 Peter Wolfgang Von Haaren c 2. D S Mk's Ch Lake City MN 1986-1988.

VON HAAREN, Erika Shivers (Az) 6715 N Mockingbird Ln, Scottsdale AZ 85253 **Assoc for Mssn Mnstrs S Barn On The Desert Scottsdale AZ 2015-, Assoc for Mssn Mnstrs 2006-2015; Stndg Com Dio Arizona Phoenix AZ 2008-** B Wabasha MN 1977 d Peter & Barbara. BA U MN 2001; MDiv GTS 2006. D 6/8/2006 Bp James Louis Jelinek P 12/9/2006 Bp Kirk Stevan Smith. m 11/30/2007 Alexander Christopher Shivers c 3.

VON NESSEN, Wayne Howard (HB) C/O Howard Von Nessen, Route 1, Box 240, Arlington VT 05250 **Died 6/14/2016** B New York NY 1942 s Howard & Dorothy. BA Muhlenberg Coll 1964; MDiv PDS 1968. D 5/25/1968 Bp Frederick Warnecke P 12/1/1968 Bp John Harris Burt. m 12/8/1975 Carol Von Nessen c 2. Vic S Mart 1970-2016; R Gr Epis Ch Of Ludington Ludington MI 1969-1970; Cur Chr Epis Ch Warren OH 1968-1970.

✠ VONO, The Rt Rev Michael (RG) Episcopal Diocese of the Rio Grande, 4304 Carlisle Blvd NE, Albuquerque NM 87107 **R Dio The Rio Grande Albuquerque 1992-** B Providence RI 1948 s Anthony & Lucy. BA Our Lady of Providence 1972; MA CUA 1974; VTS 1976; DMin Hartford Sem 1986. D 6/26/1976 Bp William Foreman Creighton P 2/12/1977 Bp Alexander D Stewart Con 10/22/2010 for RG. R S Paul's Within the Walls Rome 1992-2010; Res Chapl McLean Hosp Washington D.C 1991-1992; R Chr Ch Rochdale MA 1980-1992; Cur All SS Ch Worcester MA 1976-1980. bp.michael@dioceserg.org

VON RAUTENKRANZ, Sue (WA) The Episcopal Diocese of Washington, Mount St. Alban, Washington DC 20016 **Dio Washington Washington DC 2016-, COM 2014-2017, T/F on the Diac 2013-2016** B Evanston IL 1956 d Carter & Patricia. BS Marian Coll 1978; Dio Minnesota D Trng 1992; U MN 1997; Cert PrTS 2006. D 11/14/1992 Bp Sanford Zangwill Kaye Hampton. Chr Formation Coordntr S Dunst's Epis Ch Beth MD 2012-2017; D S Paul's Ch Plymouth WI 2011-2012; Dio Upper So Carolina Columbia SC 2011, Cn for Ldrshp Dvlpmt, Formation and Liturg 2001-2011, Cn for Ldrshp Dvlpmt, Formation and Liturg 2001-2010, The Bp Gravatt Cntr Bd 2003-2010; D Trin Cathd Columbia SC 2002-2009; Int Off Mgr Sheltering Arms Fndt Minneapolis MN 2000-2001; Exec Admin to Episcopate Dio Minnesota Minneapolis MN 1997-2000, Yth Bd 1985-1997, Bp's Advsry Com for Liturg & Mus 1992-1997; Yth Mnstry S Anne's Epis Ch S Paul MN 1995-1997; D For Yth Mnstry S Clem's Ch S Paul MN 1995-1997; Asst Chapl Epis Cntr In The U MN-Minneapolis 1992-1994; Min To Chld And Yth S Jn In The Wilderness S Paul MN 1985-1995; DRE Ch Of The Ascen Stillwater MN 1985-1986; Yth Min Gr Epis Ch Sheboygan WI 1978-1985; Bd Trst Heathwood Hall Epis Sch Columbia SC 2006-2010; Yth Mnstry Advsry Bd Dio Fond du Lac Appleton WI 1980-1985. Auth, "Epis Yth Event Develops Leaders Among Yth," *The Epis Tchr*, Cntr for the Mnstry of Tchg, VTS, 2011; Auth, "Giving Your Heart Away: Some Thoughts on the Baptismal Cov," *Crosswalk*, Dio Upper So Carolina, 2008; Auth, "A Journey of Transitions," *Resource Bk for Mnstrs w Yth and YA*, The Epis Ch, 1995. Forma 2010. archdeacon@edow.org

VON ROESCHLAUB, Warren K (LI) 4 Cornwall Ln, Port Washington NY 11050 **VP Trst of the Dio Long Island 2010-** B Mineola NY 1938 s Warren & Elsbeth. BA LIU 1974; Cert The Geo Mercer Jr TS Garden City NY 1975; STM GTS 1991. D 6/11/1977 Bp Jonathan Goodhue Sherman P 12/17/1977 Bp Robert Campbell Witcher Sr. m 4/2/1962 Priscilla A Von Roeschlaub c 2. Vice-Pres, Trst Trst of the Dio Long Island Garden City NY 1997-2005; Trst Soc for Promoting Chr Knowledge/USA Sewanee TN 1994-2007; Trst (Cler VP) SCI New York NY Ctr 1991-2007; Chapl Lions Club NY 1988-1989; Chapl Manhasset Bay Yacht Club Port Washington NY 1987-1988; Chapl Manhasset Bay Sportsmen's Club Port Washington NY 1980-2010; S Steph's Ch Prt Washington NY 1978-2010; Co-Fndr EME New York NY 1969-1974; Russia Com Dio New York New York NY 1997-2001; Dep, GC Dio Long Island Garden City NY 1991-1992, Secy, Dioc Conv 1986-1989, Dn, No Nassau Dnry 1985-1988, Racial Justice Com 1985-1988, Dept of Missions 1984-1985. Auth, "arts," *Ch of Ireland Gazette*; Auth, "arts," *Living Ch*; Auth, "arts," *Port Washington News*; Auth, "arts," *Tidings*. Compass Rose Soc 2000; Port Washington Cler Assn 1980.

✠ VONROSENBERG, The Rt Rev Charles Glenn (ETenn) 132 Beresford Creek St., Daniel Island SC 29492 B Fayetteville NC 1947 s Charles & Frances. U So; BA U NC 1969; MDiv VTS 1974. D 6/29/1974 P 3/20/1975 Bp Hunley Agee Elebash Con 2/27/1999 for ETenn. m 6/2/1973 Ann Vonrosenberg c 2. Provsnl Bp So Carolina Charleston SC 2013-2016; Ret Bp of E Tennessee Dio E Tennessee Knoxville TN 2011, Bp of E Tennessee 1999-2011; R S Jas Par Wilmington NC 1994-1999, 1994-1998, Assoc 1977-1979; R St. Jas Epis Ch Wilmington NC 1994-1999; Cn to the Ordnry Dio Upper So Carolina Columbia SC 1989-1994, COM 1984-1986; R Ch Of The Resurr Greenwood SC 1983-1989; R S Paul's Ch Beaufort NC 1979-1983; Asst S Jas Epis Ch Marietta GA 1976-1977; R S Jas Epis Ch Belhaven NC 1974-1976; Vic S Jn's Ch Belhaven NC 1974-1976; S Mary's Ch Belhaven NC 1974-1976; Vic S Matt Yeatsville NC 1974-1976; Exec Coun Dio E Carolina Kinston NC 1980-1983; Exec Coun Dio Atlanta Atlanta GA 1976-1977. Auth, *Journ of Pstr Care*. DD U So TS 2000; DD VTS 1999. info@episcopalchurchsc.org

VON WRANGEL, Carola (Tenn) Church of the Advent, 5501 Franklin Pike, Nashville TN 37220 B Feldkirch AT 1948 d Claus & Margaret. JD Seattle U 1979; MDiv Fuller TS 1989; DAS TESM 1999. D 3/24/2000 P 9/30/2000 Bp Daniel William Herzog. Ch Of The Adv Nashville TN 2012-2014; The Angl/Epis Ch Of Chr The King Frankfurt am Main 60323 2008-2012; S Mary's Ch Lakewood WA 2007-2008; Dio Albany Greenwich NY 2005-2007; Gr Ch Waterford NY 2001-2007; S Jas Ch Oneonta NY 2001.

VOORHEES, Cynthia Evans (Los) 1308 Santiago Dr., Newport Beach CA 92660 **Asstg S Phil's Par Los Angeles CA 2013-** B Youngston OH 1954 d Elwyn & Elizabeth. BA California St U 1978; Cert Theol Stud ETSBH 2002. D 6/19/2004 P 1/22/2005 Bp Joseph Jon Bruno. m 3/21/1987 Robert W Voorhees c 1. Dio Los Angeles Los Angeles CA 2015; Vic St Jas the Great Epis Ch Newport Bch CA 2014-2015; Nonstipendiary Asstg St Johns Pro-Cathd Los Angeles CA 2006-2012; Asst S Jn's Epis Ch Los Angeles CA 2006-2007; Asst S Mich And All Ang Par Corona Dl Mar CA 2004-2005. Soc of Cath Priests 2010. cindy@voorheesdesign.com

VOORHEES JR, Edwin H (O) 115 Washington St., St. Augustine FL 32084 **Vic S Cyp's St Aug FL 2008-** B Montreal QC CA 1944 s Edwin & Mildred. BS Methodist U 1966; MA DePauw U 1968; MDiv VTS 1975. D 6/24/1975 Bp Hunley Agee Elebash P 6/12/1976 Bp Thomas Augustus Fraser Jr. m 9/1/1990 Caren S Goldman c 2. P-in-c S Jn's Ch Northampton MA 2004-2007; R S Mk's Epis Ch Toledo OH 1989-2004; R S Johns Epis Ch Wake Forest NC 1983-1989; R All SS Ch Alexandria VA 1978-1983; Asst S Fran Ch Greensboro NC 1975-1978. Co-Auth, "Across The Threshold, Into the Questions," Morehouse Pub, 2008. stcypriansted@aol.com

VOORHEES, James Martin (SD) HC 30 Box 151, Belle Fourche SD 57717 B Sturgis SD 1934 s James & Bertha. EFM. D 10/2/1994 Bp Creighton Leland Robertson. m 8/31/1952 Myrtle Alice Voorhees.

VOORHEES, Jonathan Andrew (Va) 1700 University Ave, Charlottesville VA 22903 **Kent Sch Kent CT 2004-; Upper Sch Chapl S Mk's Sch Salt Lake City UT 1993-** B Turlock CA 1966 s Albert & Nedra. USMA 1984; BA U CA 1989; GTS 1990; MDiv CDSP 1992; Chapl Off Basic Course 1994. D 6/27/1992 Bp Richard Lester Shimpfky P 5/1/1993 Bp George Edmonds Bates. m 6/27/1998 Amy Meyer Voorhees. Assoc R S Paul's Memi Charlottesvlle VA 1999-2004; Dio Utah Salt Lake City UT 1994-1996; Rowland Hall/S Mk's Sch Salt Lake City UT 1994-1996; St Marks Sch Salt Lake City UT 1993-1994; Assoc P Cathd Ch Of S Mk Salt Lake City UT 1992-1994; Upper Sch Chapl Oregon Epis Sch.

VORKINK II, Peter (NH) 20 Main St, Exeter NH 03833 **Chair, Rel Dept Phillips Exeter Acad Exeter NH 2014-; Instr in Rel Phillips Exeter Acad Exeter NH 1972-** B Plainfield NJ 1943 s Francois & Janice. BA Ya 1965; MDiv UTS 1968; BD UTS 1968; MA Harv 1978; PhD Harv 2015. D 6/24/1972 Bp Robert Lionne DeWitt P 4/15/1973 Bp Charles Francis Hall. m 6/8/1968 Gaye Vorkink c 1. Instr Hokkaido Intl Sch Sapporo Japan 2003-2004; Instr S Jos Int'L Sch - Yokohama Japan 1990-1991; Chair, Rel Dept Phillips Exeter Acad Exeter NH 1985-1990; Asst Sch Min Phillips Exeter Acad Exeter NH 1972-1976. Ed, "Bonhoeffer In A Wrld Come Of Age," Fortress Press, 1968.

VOSBURGH, Linda Ann (Colo) PO Box 1023, Broomfield CO 80038 B Baltimore MD 1945 d Gilbert & Barbara. BS Mia 1964; MAT U Denv 1977. D 11/17/2007 Bp Robert John O'Neill. m 6/24/1995 Arthur L Douglas.

VOTAW, Al (SC) 657 Wampler Dr, Charleston SC 29412 **P-in-c Epis Ch of the Gd Shpd Summerville SC 2013-; Chapl to Ret Cler So Carolina Charleston SC 2013-, Chapl to Ret Cler, Spuses and Survivors 2013-; Trst Bp Gadsden Ret Cmnty 2012-; Patient Vol Odyssey Hospice Inc 2011-** B Newcastle-upon-Tyne England 1939 s Verling & Elizabeth. W&L 1959; BS Indiana U 1961; MDiv VTS 1964. D 6/13/1964 P 12/12/1964 Bp Roger W Blanchard. c 3. R Trin Epis Ch Southport CT 1989-2003; Assoc Chr Ch Greenwich CT 1983-1989; S Jn's Ch Portsmouth NH 1982; Trin Ch Hampton NH 1980-1982; Dio New Hampshire Concord NH 1975-1982; Chr Ch Exeter NH 1975-1980; S Jn's Ch Worthington OH 1967-1970; Asst S Thos Epis Ch Terrace Pk OH 1964-1967. Beta Gamma Sigma 1961.

VOUGA, Anne Fontaine (Ky) St Thomas Episcopal Church, 9616 Westport Road, Louisville KY 40241 **S Andr's Ch Louisville KY 2015-** B Houston TX 1961 d William & Anne. BA U So 1982; LInstitut Prot de Theologie Montpellier France 1986; MA The U of Louisville 1997; Cert Ang Stud VTS 2007; MDiv Louisville Presb TS 2008. D 12/21/2007 P 6/21/2008 Bp Ted Gulick Jr. c 3. R S Thos Epis Ch Louisville KY 2011-2015; S Paul's Ch Henderson KY 2010-2011; Asst S Mk's Epis Ch Louisville KY 2008-2010; Eccl Crt Dio Kentucky Louisville KY 2008-2011, COM 2008-. Auth, "L'eglise Reformee de France," *The Presb Outlook*, Vol. 173, No. 40, 1991; Auth, "Presb Missions& Louisville Blacks: The Early Years," *Filson Club Hist Quarterly, Vol 58, No. 3*, 1984.

VOYLE, Robert J (Ore) 24965 Nw Pederson Rd, Hillsboro OR 97124 B Hamilton NZ 1952 s Wilfred & Margaret. BS U of Auckland Nz 1976; BD S Jn Theol Coll 1980; MS California St U 1988; PsyD Fuller TS 1994. Trans 8/1/1986 Bp Oliver Bailey Garver Jr. m 1/24/1987 Kim M Voyle. Trin Epis Cathd Portland OR 2002-2004; All SS-By-The-Sea Par Santa Barbara CA 2001-2002; S Paul's

Epis Ch Santa Paula CA 2000-2001; All SS Par Beverly Hills CA 1996-1997; S Mich's U Mssn Isla Vista CA 1996, 1990-1991; P-in-c S Nich Par Encino CA 1993-1995; P-in-c All SS Epis Ch Oxnard CA 1991-1992; Non-par 1988-1990; Assoc R S Jos's Par Buena Pk CA 1986-1988, Pstr'S Asst 1984-1986; Serv Ch Of New Zealand 1979-1981; Int Mnstry Spec & Consult. Auth, "Assessing Skills & Discerning Calls". Int Mnstry Ntwk.

VOYSEY, Stephen Otte (Mass) 1 Colpitts Road, Weston MA 02493 B Evanston IL 1950 s Frank & Betty. BA U of Pennsylvania 1972; MA Rutgers The St U of New Jersey 1973; MDiv EDS 1977. D 6/4/1977 Bp Quintin Ebenezer Primo Jr P 12/3/1977 Bp James Winchester Montgomery. m 1/19/2001 Amanda F Barnum c 2. R S Ptr's Ch Weston MA 2006-2016; R S Mk's Ch Mt Kisco NY 1996-2006; Dio New York New York NY 1990-1996, 1982-1989; R S Paul's Ch Pleasant Vlly NY 1983-1996; Cur S Andr's Epis Ch Staten Island NY 1980-1983; Cur Trin Epis Ch Wheaton IL 1977-1979. Jas Arthur Muller Prize Hist EDS 1977; Pi Gamma Mu 1972.

VROON, Daron Jon (At) 939 James Burgess Road, Suwanee GA 30024 S Jas Epis Ch Marietta GA 2012-; Mem of Cmsn on Liturg Dio Atlanta Atlanta GA 2011- B East Lansing MI 1979 s Anton & June. BS Hope Coll 2001; PhD Georgia Inst of Tech 2007; MDiv GTS 2010. D 12/19/2009 Bp J Neil Alexander. m 9/11/2004 Julie Williamson Vroon c 3. S Columba Epis Ch Suwanee GA 2010-2012.

VRYHOF SSJE, David B (Mass) 980 Memorial Dr, Cambridge MA 02138 Novc Guardian SSJE Cambridge MA 2011-; Bro SSJE Cambridge MA 1995-; Soc-St Jn The Evang Cambridge MA 1995- B Grand Rapids MI 1951 s Wesley & Frances. BA Calvin Coll 1973; MA Gallaudet U 1975; Duke 1992; MDiv GTS 1993. D 5/30/1993 Bp Huntington Williams Jr P 8/20/1994 Bp R aymond Stewart Wood Jr. Asst. Superior SSJE Cambridge MA 2007-2013; Novc Guardian SSJE Cambridge MA 2000-2004; S Jn's Chap Cambridge MA 1995-2014; Dio Michigan Detroit MI 1993-1994; S Columba Ch Detroit MI 1993-1994; Bro Soc of S Jn the Evang (SSJE) Cambridge MA 1985-1991.

VUKICH, Dawn Elizabeth (Los) 26391 Bodega Ln, Mission Viejo CA 92691 B Burbank CA 1960 d Martin & Carol. BA Biola U 1992; MDiv Talbot TS 2004. Trans 4/27/2010 Bp Joseph Jon Bruno.

VUKMANIC, Paula (Los) 2200 Via Rosa, Palos Verdes Estates CA 90274 Appointed Mem Dioc COM 2012-; Assoc R S Fran' Par Palos Verdes Estates CA 2010-; Appointed Mem Dioc Commision on Mnstry 2012- B Torrance CA 1949 d Frank & Mary. BFA Mt St Marys Coll Los Angeles CA 1976; MMin Seattle U 1987; MDiv ETSBH 2009. D 6/6/2009 P 1/9/2010 Bp Sergio Carranza-Gomez. Chapl The Cbury 2009-2010. paula.vukmanic@stfrancispalosverdes.org

VUONO, Reverend Deacon Dorothy (Del) 19337 Fleatown Rd, Lincoln DE 19960 Sitter Bayhealth Hosp 2015-; D All SS Epis Ch Delmar DE 2012- B Bayonne NJ 1945 d Vincent & Irene. AA Brookdale CC. D 12/5/2009 Bp Wayne Wright. m 8/19/1978 Joseph Vuono c 3.

W

WACASTER, David C (WA) 2711 Parkway Pl, Cheverly MD 20785 R Gd Shpd Epis Ch Silver Sprg MD 2010- B Eugene OR 1970 s Cecil & Harriet. BA U So 1992; MDiv VTS 2004. D 6/12/2004 P 1/22/2005 Bp John Bryson Chane. Asst S Lk's Ch Trin Par Beth MD 2005-2010; Cur S Thos' Par Washington DC 2004-2005. rector@gsecmd.org

WACHNER, Emily J (NY) 74 Trinity Pl, New York NY 10006 The GTS New York NY 2015- B Indianapolis IN 1982 d Edward & Penny. BA Washington U 2004; Ya Berk 2009. D 12/15/2008 P 6/27/2009 Bp George Wayne Smith. m 10/19/2012 Julian J Wachner. Trin Par New York NY 2011-2015; S Tim's Epis Ch S Louis MO 2009-2011.

WACOME, Karen Ann Halvorsen (Ia) 415 3rd St Nw, Orange City IA 51041 Ch of the Sav Orange City IA 2007- B Elizabeth NJ 1952 d Henry & Blanche. BA Kings Coll Wilkes-Barre PA 1974; MA Ya Berk 1991; CAS CDSP 1994; PhD Grad Theol Un 2005. D 3/23/1996 P 12/7/1996 Bp Chris Christopher Epting. m 8/24/1974 Donald Henry Wacome. Dio Iowa Des Moines IA 2006-2007; S Geo's Epis Ch Le Mars IA 1998-2005. Aabs; SBL. Schlrshp: Excellence In Mnstry CDSP 1994. wacome@frontiernet.net

WADDELL, Clayton Burbank (SeFla) 141 S County Rd, Palm Beach FL 33480 D The Epis Ch Of Beth-By-The-Sea Palm Bch FL 2007- B Sarasota FL 1961 s Wallace & Harriett. BA U of Florida 1983. D 5/6/2007 Bp Leo Frade. m 8/11/1990 Jacqueline Waddell c 2.

WADDELL, Jonathan H (Ala) 5014 Lakeshore Dr, Pell City AL 35128 D Gr Ch Birmingham AL 2000- B Centerville MS 1941 s Howard & Annie. BA Wm Carey U 1963; MTh New Orleans Bapt TS 1967; MRE New Orleans Bapt TS 1968; DEd New Orleans Bapt TS 1972. D 4/17/1991 P 9/1/1991 Bp Robert Oran Miller. m 11/24/1995 Lexa Magnus. Corp Dir Pstr Cnslng Bapt Med Cntr Birmingham AL 1991-1994; Serv Bapt Ch 1965-1977. Auth, "The Use Of Rel

Lang In Pstr Counslg". ACPE; Dplma AAPC. Who'S Who In The So And SW 1993; Who'S Who In Rel 1975; Outstanding Young Men Of Amer 1972.

WADDELL, Thomas Robert (Va) 5911 Edsall Rd Ph 5, Alexandria VA 22304 B Wheeling WV 1940 s Robert & Geneva. BA Bethany Coll 1962; BD Bex Sem 1965; Colgate Rochester Crozer DS 1974; CRDS 1974; MS Syr 1981; Cert GW 1990. D 11/27/1965 P 11/27/1966 Bp Nelson Marigold Burroughs. Supply P Dio Virginia Richmond VA 1981-2001; R S Mary's Epis Ch Gowanda NY 1974-1979; Vic S Barn Akron NY 1973-1974; Chapl S Jn's Hm Painesville OH 1969-1973; R S Jas Ch Painesville OH 1967-1973.

WADDINGHAM, Gary Brian (Mont) 119 N 33rd St, Billings MT 59101 Cn Dio Montana Helena MT 2005- B Helena MT 1950 s Marvin & Betty. BS Montana St U 1972; MDiv Epis TS of the SW 1975; Emory U 1981. D 6/30/1975 P 7/3/1976 Bp Jackson Earle Gilliam. c 3. R S Lk's Ch Billings MT 1994-2013; Vic S Andr's Ch Meeetetse WY 1992-1994; R S Andr's Ch Basin WY 1981-1994; P/Cn Cathd Of S Phil Atlanta GA 1976-1981; Pres Stndg Com Dio Wyoming Casper 1987-1988. Auth, "Literary Sources Reveal Buying Power of Drachma," Celator; Auth, "Numismatic Evidence of a Benevolent Semitic Goddess," Celator.

WADDLE, Helen Ann (Okla) PO Box 12402, Oklahoma City OK 73157 B Oklahoma City 1950 d William & Leona. D 6/19/1999 Bp Robert Manning Moody. c 2. Gr Ch Epis Yukon OK 2004-2007.

WADE, Carol Lynn (Lex) Christ Church Cathedral, 166 Market St, Lexington KY 40507 Chr Ch Cathd Lexington KY 2011- B 1955 MDiv Ya Berk. D 6/7/2003 P 1/24/2004 Bp Chester Lovelle Talton. Cathd of St Ptr & St Paul Washington DC 2004-2010; Assoc Chr Ch New Haven CT 2003-2004.

WADE, Elizabeth Ann Till (Ky) 1110 Fairview St, Lee MA 01238 B Montgomery AL 1947 d David & Dorothy. BA Huntingdon Coll 1969; Mstr's Study Auburn U 1971; Louisville Presb TS 1997; MDiv GTS 1998. D 5/31/1998 P 1/9/1999 Bp Ted Gulick Jr. m 6/19/1971 James Calhoun Wade c 2. Dio Wstrn Massachusetts Springfield 2015; Int S Paul's Epis Ch Stockbridge MA 2015; R Gr Ch Paducah KY 2005-2014; R Ch Of Our Merc Sav Louisville KY 2000-2005; Asst S Mk's Epis Ch Louisville KY 1998-2000; Asst Chr Ch Cathd Louisville KY 1998-1999; Trst & Coun Dio Kentucky Louisville KY 2009-2011, GC Dep 2005-2011. Auth, "God Of The Night," Wmn Uncommon Prayers, Morehouse Pub, 2000; Auth, "Pryr For A Vstry," Wmn Uncommon Prayers, Morehouse Pub, 2000. Bell Awd For Excellence In Biblic Stds Louisville Presb Sem 1996; Presidential Schlr Louisville Presb Sem 1995.

WADE, Francis Howard (WA) 4800 Fillmore Ave #1452, Alexandria VA 22311 B Clarksburg WV 1941 s William & Eleanor. BA Cit 1963; BD VTS 1966; DMin VTS 1981. D 6/3/1966 P 12/21/1966 Bp Wilburn Camrock Campbell. c 2. Int Cathd of St Ptr & St Paul Washington DC 2012; R S Alb's Par Washington DC 1983-2005; R The Memi Ch Of The Gd Shpd Parkersburg WV 1972-1983; R St Chris Epis Ch Charleston WV 1968-1972; S Andr's-On-The-Mt Harpers Ferry WV 1966-1968; Cur Zion Epis Ch Chas Town WV 1966-1968. Auth, "Transforming Scripture," Ch Pub, 2008; Auth, "The Art of being Together," Forw Mvmt, 2005; Auth, "Rites of Our Passage," Posterity Press, 2002; Auth, "Comp Along the Way," Posterity Press, 1996; Auth, "Beyond the Ordnry in the Kingdom of God," Forw Mvmt, 1991. DD VTS 2013; Hon Cn The Bp of Los Angeles 2011.

WADE, J Merrill (Tex) 11561 Cedarcliffe Dr, Austin TX 78750 R S Matt's Ch Austin TX 2002-; Great Cmsn Fndt of Texas Dio Texas Houston TX 2014-, Epis Fndt of Texas 2013-, Com on the Diac 2004-2008 B Tampa FL 1954 s John & Charlotte. BBA U of Texas 1976; MDiv GTS 1989. D 5/12/1989 P 4/18/1990 Bp Duncan Montgomery Gray Jr. m 6/2/1990 Crystal Wade c 2. R S Paul's Epis Ch Meridian MS 1997-2002; Vic S Patricks Epis Ch Long Bch MS 1992-1997; Cur Ch of the H Trin Vicksburg MS 1989-1992; Bd Trst S Steph's Epis Sch Austin TX 2007-2013.

WADE SR, Joseph Alfred (NY) 108 Horsley Dr, Hampton VA 23666 Died 5/9/2016 B Port Limon Province Limon CR 1927 s Ishmael & Matilda. BA SUNY; S Aug Coll Cbury Gb 1964; CUNY 1969; Col 1969. D 9/29/1953 P 9/1/1954 Bp Robert B Gooden. c 1. Ret 1992-2016; Ret 1992-2016; S Johns Epis Hosp Far Rockaway NY 1986-1992; Chapl St Lk's Hosp New York NY 1979-2016; S Lk's Cnvnt Av New York NY 1979-1992; S Lk's-Roosevelt Hosp Cntr New York NY 1975-1986; Dio New York New York NY 1969-1986; Vic Gr Epis Ch New York NY 1967-1982; Asst S Ann's Ch Of Morrisania Bronx NY 1964-1967; P-in-c S Jn Bapt Puerto Cortes Honduras 1961-1964; Vic S Mary Siquirres Cr 1953-1960; Asst S Aug's Ch Oakland CA 1952-1953. AEHC.

WADE, Karin Elizabeth (Mass) Po Box 372, Rockport MA 01966 R S Mary's Epis Ch Rockport MA 1994- B North Kingstown RI 1951 d Carl & Bertha. BA Amer U 1974; MDiv Nash 1989. D 6/14/1989 Bp Charles Lee Burgreen P 12/6/1989 Bp Bob Gordon Jones. Dioc Coun Dio Massachusetts Boston MA 1995-1999, Exec Comm 1995-1999, Cathd Chapt 1996-1999; R All SS Ch Wheatland WY 1989-1994; Vic Ch Of Our Sav Hartville WY 1989-1994; Stndg Com Dio Wyoming Casper 1990-1994. Soc for the Increase of Mnstry - Exec Com 1999; Third Ord of the Soc of S Fran 1988.

WADE, Mary Macsherry (Miss) 2681 Lake Cir, Jackson MS 39211 B Watertown NY 1951 d Richard & Mary. BA Skidmore Coll 1975; MDiv EDS 1979.

W

D 6/23/1979 P 5/1/1980 Bp Ned Cole. S Phil's Ch Jackson MS 2005; S Andr's Cathd Jackson MS 1980-1997; D-In-Trng All SS Par Brookline MA 1979-1980. Inst Servnt Leadrshp. Humanitarian Of Year 95; City & Canonty Spec Serv Hon Citation; Rel Ldrshp Wmns Awd.

WADE, Stephen Hamel (Va) 132 N Jay St, Middleburg VA 20117 **Retreat Dir, Ecum Ignatian Retreat Team H Trin Cath Ch Washington DC 2010-; Adj Retreat Dir Bon Secours Retreat Cntr Marriottville MD 2005-** B Saint Louis MO 1945 s Leo & Hermoine. BA Denison U 1967; MDiv Yale DS 1970; MA Col 1974; Cert Sprtl Dir Weston Jesuit TS 1993; Certification Loyola Hse Guelph Ontario 2002; Certification Oxf GB 2002. D 6/10/1970 Bp John Henry Esquirol P 1/25/1971 Bp Joseph Warren Hutchens. m 9/4/1993 Mary S Huske c 3. Chair, Dioc Com on Discernment Dio Virginia Richmond VA 2006-2013; R Imm Ch-On-The-Hill Alexandria VA 1995-2006; Sr Assoc R S Chrys's Ch Chicago IL 1994-1995; Assoc R Trin Ch Epis Boston MA 1985-1994; R Trin Ch Torrington CT 1977-1985; Assoc R Chr Ch Greenwich CT 1975-1977; Asst R S Mich's Ch New York NY 1970-1975. Auth, "Parade: A Photographic Record of the Thanksgiving Day Parade, Charlotte, No Carolina," Blurb.com, 2015; Auth, "A Prchr's Tale," Blurb.com, 2015; Auth, "Some Reflections on Retreats in the Ignatian Tradition," *Bridges*, Bon Secours Sprtl Cntr, 2007; Auth, "Ask The Fundraising Profsnl In Your Cong To Help," *The Ch Fundraising Nwsltr*, Stevenson Pub, Inc., 2000; Auth, "Look Before Leaping Into That Next Real Estate Gift," *The Major Gifts Report*, Stevenson Pub, 1999; Auth, "Bk Revs: A Practical Guide To Cmnty Mnstry," *VTS Journ*, 1996; Auth, "Sprtl And Moral Educ: Grappling w Diversity," *Choate Rosemary Hall mag*, 1993; Auth, "Epistemology And Models In Rel Tchg," *The Journ Of The Rel Educ Assn US & Can*, 1975. First Place, Photography Loudoun Cnty Arbor Day Com 2015.

WADE, Suzanne (Mass) 75 Cold Spring Rd, Westford MA 01886 **P-in-c S Mk's Ch Westford MA 2011-** B Beverly MA 1969 d Richard & Marian. BA NEU 1991; MDiv EDS 2010. D 6/25/2011 P 1/14/2012 Bp M(Arvil) Thomas Shaw. m 9/7/1991 Richard Wade c 2. suzanne@rswade.net

WADE, William St Clair (Tenn) 1 Casey Road, East Kingston NH 03827 B Brooklyn NY 1943 s David & Ann. BA U So 1965; MDiv VTS 1968. D 6/29/1968 Bp Thomas H Wright P 1/6/1969 Bp Hunley Agee Elebash. m 6/23/1973 Joan A Wade c 2. S Andr's-Sewanee Sch Sewanee TN 1981-2008; Cathd of St Ptr & St Paul Washington DC 1978-1981; S Paul's Sch Concord NH 1973-1977; Asst Chr Ch Exeter NH 1971-1973; Asst S Jn's Epis Ch Fayetteville NC 1968-1971. "No Srings Attached," 2008; Auth, "What is Rel?," 1979. Ruth Jenkins Awd Natl Assocation of Epis Schools 2000; DD U So 1989.

WAFER-CROSS, Melissa Lee (NwT) 3502 47th St, Lubbock TX 79413 **D S Chris's Epis Ch Lubbock TX 1999-** B El Paso TX 1948 d William & Katherine. BA Texas Tech U 1970; MA Texas Tech U 1996. D 10/29/1999 Bp C Wallis Ohl. m 8/3/1979 David Dyer Cross c 1.

WAFF, Kay Childers (SwVa) 314 N Bridge St, Bedford VA 24523 B Oklahoma City OK 1943 d Clem & Cathryn. AA St Marys JR Coll 1963; BA U NC 1965. D 2/14/2003 Bp Neff Powell. m 7/29/1966 John Waff c 4.

WAFF, William Dubard Razz (Mil) 2443 Lawson Blvd., Gurnee IL 60031 **Dir of Pstr Care, Ethics and Interp Svcs Vista Heatlh Waukegan IL 2001-; P Assoc S Lk's Ch Evanston IL 1984-** B Memphis TN 1954 s William & Dorothy. BMus U of Mississippi 1976; N/A VMI 1976; MDiv SWTS 1983; DMin GTF 1997; MSS US-A War Coll 2001. D 6/11/1983 P 5/13/1984 Bp William Arthur Beckham. m 5/23/1992 Kathleen C Busby. Chmn, Army Reserve Forces Plcy Cmttee Major Gnrl US Army Reserve 2014-2015; HQDA Dep G-1 Major Gnrl US Army Reserve 2013-2015; CG, 99th RSC Major Gnrl US Army Reserve 2010-2013; Dir of Pstr Care & Ethics S Lk's Hosp Racine WI 1985-2002; Columbia Epis Inst Mnstry Ch Of The Gd Shpd Columbia SC 1983; CPE Res NW Memi Hosp Chicago IL 1983; Chapl Evanston Hosp Evanston IL 1982-1983; Major Gnrl US Army Reserve 2010-2015. AEHC 1986; Assn of Prof Chapl 1987; ACPE 1983; Chapl S Jn Bapt SMOTJ 1997; Natl Chapl- SMOTJ 2000-2002; OHC 1980; Ord of St. Lazarus 2001. DSM w/1 OLC US Army 2015; Humanitarian Serv Medal (Sandy) Dept of Defense 2013; DSM US Army 2013; Legion of Merit w/1OLC US Army 2010; Legion of Merit US Army 2008; Meritorious Svc Medal w/4 OLC US Army 2005; Ord of the H Sprt SMOTJ 2002; DSA Assn of Prof Chapl 1998; Awd for Outstanding Serv Bp for Chaplaincies 1998; Distinguished Chapl Awd Wis Chapl Comm 1998; Citation of Achievement Amer Prot Hlth Assn 1991; Joint Svc Com Medal US Army 1980.

WAFLER, Donald Samuel (Minn) 628 1st St Se, Faribault MN 55021 **Ret 1992-** B Alliance OH 1916 s William & Ida. Manchester Coll 1936; BA No Cntrl Coll 1939; U MN 1968. D 1/29/1979 Bp Robert Marshall Anderson. m 4/16/1943 Helen Margaret Hoyt c 2. Assoc The Epis Cathd Of Our Merc Sav Faribault MN 1979-1990. Auth, "Relatns Of Speech To The Rdr". Sr Citizens Of Faribault.

WAGAMAN, Stanley Warner (Az) Episc Ch Of St Francis In The Valley, 600 S La Canada Dr, Green Valley AZ 85614 B Grinnell IA 1953 s Willard & Phyllis. AA Ellsworth Cmnty Coll 1973; (3)Assoc Degrees Cmnty Coll of Denver

1982; BS Wstrn Oregon U 2004. D 6/22/2013 Bp Kirk Stevan Smith. m 12/17/2005 Dawn Gunderson c 2.

WAGAR, Catherine (Los) The Episcopal Church of St. Philip the Evangelist, 2800 Stanford Street, South Los Angeles CA 90011 **Mem Dio Los Angeles - Deacons' Coun 2013-; Assoc. Chapl - On Call Olive View UCLA Med Cntr 2013-** B Saginaw MI 1948 d Wayne & Lorene. AB Br 1970; CPhil Wright Inst Los Angeles 1985; Cert Theol Stud ETSBH 2008. D 1/24/2009 Bp Chester Lovelle Talton. m 5/19/1991 Bruce Rankin. Co-Fac Dio Los Angeles - Deacons' Seminar 2011-2016; Chapl PRISM Restorative Justice Mnstry 2009-2013; Interfaith Refugee & Immigration Serv (IRIS) Dio Los Angeles Los Angeles CA 2009; Trst ETS at Claremont/Bloy Hse 2007-2011.

WAGEMAN, Carole Allcroft (Vt) 173 Hollow Road, North Ferrisburgh VT 05473 **Co-chaplin to Ret Cler Dio Vermont Burlington VT 2015-, Conv Prog Chair 2014, Safer Ch Trng 2012-, Alt Del 2009 Conv 2008-, Alt Eccl Crt 2007-, Co-chair, COM 2003-2013** B Paterson NJ 1948 d Harry & Vera. BA Jas Madison U 1970; New Brunswick TS NJ 1972; MA UTS 1974; Cert EDS 2003. D 5/29/2003 P 12/20/2003 Bp Thomas C Ely. m 5/17/1975 Edwin J Wageman c 3. Chapl Vstng Nurses Assn 2015-2016; Int R S Lk's Ch Chester VT 2012-2014; Asst R Trin Ch Shelburne VT 2003-2012. Auth, "The Light Shines Through: Our Stories Are God's Story," *The Light Shines Through: Our Stories Are God's Story*, Ch Pub, Inc., 2017; Auth, "Inviting the Light: Monthly Reflections," *The Mtn: Bi-monthly Nwsltr*, The Epis Ch in Vermont, 2016; Auth, "Baptismal Mnstry in Vermont," *Baptismal Mnstry in Vermont*, Dioc Report, 2003.

WAGENSEIL JR, Robert Arthur (SwFla) 1700 Patlin Cir S, Largo FL 33770 B Jamaica NY 1954 s Robert & Marie. Friedrich-Wilhelms Universitaet; BA Leh 1976; MDiv Nash 1980. D 6/7/1980 P 5/2/1981 Bp Robert Campbell Witcher Sr. m 8/12/1978 Patricia T Wagenseil. P Calv Ch Indn Rk Bc FL 1995-2013; Chapl Pinellas Suncoast Fire and Rescue 1995-2013; Archd Dio Long Island Garden City NY 1992-1995; R All SS' Epis Ch Long Island City NY 1984-1995; Cur S Mary's Ch Ronkonkoma NY 1983-1984; Cur S Lk's Ch Forest Hills NY 1981-1983. Life Mem Indn Rocks Profsnl Firefighters Loc 3206 2013; Citizen of the Year Rotary Club of Indn Rocks Bch 2011; Vol Fireman of the Year Pinellas Suncoast Fire and Rescue 2005.

WAGENSELLER, Joseph Paul (Ct) 6 Clifford Ln, Westport CT 06880 **Assoc. Prof. Grad. Dept. Psychol Teachers Coll New York NY 2001-; Pres Temenos Inst Westport CT 1976-** B Portage WI 1939 s Wayne & Mary. BA Elizabethtown Coll 1961; MDiv GTS 1964; DMin Andover Newton TS 1975; CG Jung Inst 1975. D 6/22/1964 Bp John Thomas Heistand P 11/5/1965 Bp Robert Fisher Gibson Jr. m 10/3/1970 Virginia F Wagenseller c 3. Pres Jung Inst New York NY 2003-2005; Bd Jung Inst New York NY 2001-2005; VP Jung Inst New York NY 1994-1996; Pres Jung Fndt New York NY 1992-1993; Bd Jung Fndt New York NY 1988-1994; Assoc Prof Pratt Inst Brooklyn NY 1974-1979; Dir Mead Counslg Cntr Greenwich CT 1974-1976; S Andr's Ch Stamford CT 1973; Asst S Mk's Ch New Canaan CT 1966-1970; Asst S Paul's Ch Richmond VA 1964-1966. Auth, "The Archetype of Vocation," *Protestantism and Jungian Psychol*, New Falcon Pub, Tempe, AZ, 1995; Auth, "Sprtl Renwl at Midlife," *Journ of Rel and Hlth*.

✠ **WAGGONER, The Rt Rev James E** (Spok) 8028 N Pamela St, Spokane WA 99208 B Ironton OH 1947 s James & Vera. BA Marshall U 1973; MDiv VTS 1979; VTS 1985; DMin VTS 1999. D 6/6/1979 P 6/4/1980 Bp Robert Poland Atkinson Con 10/21/2000 for Spok. m 6/22/1967 Gloria J Henshaw c 2. Bp of Spokane Dio Spokane Spokane WA 2000-2017; Cn to the Ordnry Dio W Virginia Charleston WV 1992-2000; R Trin Epis Ch Martinsburg WV 1985-1991; R S Ptr's Ch Huntington WV 1981-1985; Calv Ch Montgomery WV 1979-1981; R Ch Of The Gd Shpd Hansford WV 1979-1981. DD VTS 2001. bpjimw8@gmail.com

WAGGONER JR, Janet Cuff (FtW) 2724 Stone Oak Drive, Fort Worth TX 76109 **Cn to the Ordnry / Transition Mnstry Off Dio Ft Worth Ft Worth TX 2013-; Advsr - Title IV Disciplinary Processes Epis Ch Cntr New York NY 2012-; Bd Mem WIKS-Nambale USA Inc. 2012-** B The Dalles OR 1967 d Thomas & Peggy. BA Willamette U 1989; MDiv Ya Berk 2001. D 6/17/2001 Bp Robert Louis Ladehoff P 2/2/2002 Bp Andrew Donnan Smith. m 10/12/1996 Edward F Waggoner c 2. Rejoice Luth Ch Coppell TX 2012-2013; Int Pstr Rejoice Luth Ch Coppell TX 2012-2013; R S Paul's Epis Ch Shelton CT 2006-2012; Asst R S Matt's Epis Ch Wilton CT 2003-2006; Assoc R S Lk's Par Darien CT 2001-2003; Corporator Birmingham Hlth Grp / Umbrella Shltr 2011-2012; B&D Exec Coun Dio Connecticut Meriden CT 2009-2012, Advsr - Title IV Disciplinary Processes 2007-2012, Bp's Convoc for Pryr 2002-2011; Pres Shelton Cler Assn 2008-2009. Alb Inst 2005; ConnECA 2008-2012; Int Mnstry Ntwk 2012; Nneca 2002; SCHC 1998; Sprtl Dir Intl 2007. Lux et Veritas Awd Yale DS 2012; Kentucky Colonel Kentucky Gvnr 2008; DD Ya Berk 2004; Cn St. Matt's Cathd,Dallas,Texas 2003; Thos Philips Memi - excellence in Liturg Ya Berk 2001; Henry Hallam Tweedy Prize - Pstr Ldrshp Yale DS 2001; mcl Yale DS 2001; Mary Cady Tew Prize - scholastic excellence Yale DS 2000; Preaching Excellence Prog Yale DS 1999. janet.waggoner@edfw.org

W

WAGGONER, Leigh F (Colo) 110. W. North St., Cortez CO 81321 **R S Barn Of The Vlly Cortez CO 2011-** B Huntington WV 1946 d James & Phyllis. BS TCU 1968; MDiv SWTS 2003; DMin SWTS 2010. D 8/15/1997 Bp William Charles Wantland P 5/10/2003 Bp Keith Whitmore. m 9/28/1991 W Waggoner c 4. P-in-c S Jn's Epis Ch Sparta WI 2004-2010; D S Alb's Ch Spooner WI 1997-2000. rector@stbarnabascortez.org

WAGNER, Barbara Jean (WMich) 2430 Greenbriar, Harbor Springs MI 49740 **Ret Michigan 2010-** B Allegan MI 1941 d James & Laura. BA MI SU 1967; MA Cntrl Michigan U 1975; CTh Whitaker TS 1988. D 4/29/1989 Bp H Coleman Mcgehee Jr. m 3/22/1969 Richard F Wagner c 3. Archd Epis Dio Wstrn Michigan 2004-2006; D Chr Epis Ch Charlevoix MI 2002-2009; D Emm Ch Petoskey MI 1999-2002; D S Jn's Epis Ch Alma MI 1989-1998.

WAGNER, Beth Anne (CFla) PO Box 1115, Apo AP 96555 **D Epis Ch Of The Ascen Orlando FL 2001-, D 1993-2000** B Watertown NY 1955 d David & Gail. BA SUNY 1977; AOS Mohawk Vlly Cmnty Coll 1983; Cert Inst For Chr Stds 1992. D 12/18/1993 Bp John Wadsworth Howe. m 8/23/1975 David Wagner c 2. Serv S Ptr's Medford NJ 1998-2001.

WAGNER, Dan (USC) **S Aug Of Cbury Aiken SC 2017-** D 6/7/2014 Bp W illiam Andrew Waldo P 1/10/2015 Bp Philip Menzie Duncan II.

WAGNER, David W (At) 465 Clifton Rd NE, Atlanta GA 30307 **H Innoc' Epis Sch Atlanta GA 2016-** B Atlanta GA 1981 s Jack & Nancy. BA Presb Coll 2003; MDiv GTS 2011. D 12/18/2010 P 6/26/2011 Bp J Neil Alexander. m 8/14/2010 Kathleen Wagner. P S Lk's Epis Ch Atlanta GA 2014-2016; Asst S Martins-In-The-Field Columbia SC 2011-2014. david.wagner@hies.org

WAGNER, John C (Be) 1070 Oakhurst Drive, Slatington PA 18080 **R Epis Par Of S Mk And S Jn Jim Thorpe PA 2008-** B Lewistown PA 1947 s Max & Betty. TS Mary Immac Sem; BS Penn 1974; MS Villanova U 1976. D 6/1/1986 P 12/10/1988 Bp James Michael Mark Dyer. m 12/20/1969 Nancy Elizabeth Wagner c 3. S Mk's Epis Ch Moscow PA 2002-2003; Asst S Steph's Ch Whitehall PA 1986-2005. Intl Ord Of S Lk.

WAGNER, Mary M (Ia) **Trin Ch Ottumwa IA 2017-; Dir of Cmncatn Dio Iowa Des Moines IA 2016-** D 12/6/2014 P 6/21/2015 Bp Alan Scarfe.

WAGNER, Mary Scott (Mass) 54 Robert Rd, Marblehead MA 01945 **C&C Bd Pres Dio Massachusetts Boston MA 2011-, Const and Cn Com Chair 2009-, 2004-2008** B Bristol TN 1963 d Michael & Carole. BA Carson-Newman Coll 1985; JD Van 1989; MDiv Harvard DS 1999. D 12/19/1998 P 12/4/1999 Bp M(Arvil) Thomas Shaw. m 8/5/1989 James Gray Wagner. R Ch Of The Gd Shpd Reading MA 2010-2016; R Wyman Memi Ch of St Andr Marblehead MA 2006-2008; R All SS Epis Ch of the No Shore Inc Danvers MA 2000-2006; Asst Par Of The Epiph Winchester MA 1999-2000.

WAGNER, Ralph Fellows (Ak) Po Box 1502, Palmer AK 99645 **Died 11/24/2016** B Pittsburgh PA 1928 s Frank & Ruth. BA Penn 1950; MDiv Nash 1957; Duquesne U 1970. D 6/1/1957 Bp Austin Pardue P 12/1/1957 Bp William S Thomas. m 8/13/1949 Dorothy R Wagner c 4. Vic S Barth's Ch Palmer AK 1991-1994; All SS' Epis Ch Anchorage AK 1990; New Life Epis Ch Uniontown OH 1989; Chapl (Colonel) (Ret) US-AR (Retierd 1988) 1988-2016; Chf Cleveland OH 1975-1988; ArmdF and Fed Ministres New York NY 1971-1988; R S Thos Memi Epis Ch Oakmont PA 1970-1971; Cn Trin Cathd Pittsburgh PA 1966-1970; Chapl (Colonel) US-A 1963-1988; R The Ch Of The Adv Jeannette PA 1957-1963.

WAGNER, Richard Alden (Los) 40562 Via Amapola, Murrieta CA 92562 **Ret 2000-** B Fitchburg MA 1937 s Herbert & Sigrid. BA Tufts U 1959; MA Auburn U at Montgomery 1971; MDiv SWTS 1984. D 5/11/1984 Bp Richard Frank Grein P 11/18/1984 Bp James Winchester Montgomery. m 9/9/1959 Joan Lillian Watt c 3. Vic S Alb's Epis Ch Yucaipa CA 2001-2013; R All SS Ch Vista CA 1996-2001; R The Annunc Of Our Lady Gurnee IL 1990-1996; Vic S Hugh Of Lincoln Epis Ch Elgin IL 1987-1990; Cur Trin Epis Ch Wheaton IL 1984-1986.

WAGNER, Sharon Lavonne (Cal) 1921 Hemlock Dr, Oakley CA 94561 B San Francisco CA 1946 d Howard & Elizabeth. BA California St U 1968; BA Sch for Deacons 1986. D 12/3/1988 Bp William Edwin Swing. m 6/12/1971 Fred Jay Wagner c 3. D S Geo's Epis Ch Antioch CA 1988-2002.

WAGNER, Wm Beau (Me) St Matthew's Episcopal Church, PO Box 879, Lisbon ME 04250 **R S Matt's Epis Ch Lisbon Falls ME 2007-** B Flushing NY 1955 s William & Janet. BA Bos 1976; JD Geo 1980; MS Geo 1984; MDiv Allnce TS 2007. D 6/9/2007 P 12/10/2007 Bp William Howard Love. m 11/25/1995 Debra Ryba c 1. pastorbeau@gwi.net

WAGNER-PIZZA, Ken E (CPa) 1206 Faxon Parkway, Williamsport PA 17701 **R Trin Epis Ch Williamsport PA 2008-** B West Rockhill PA 1969 s Kenneth & Martha. BS Elizabethtown Coll 1991; Luth TS at Gettysburg 1999; MDiv VTS 2002. D 6/21/2003 P 12/20/2003 Bp Charles Ellsworth Bennison Jr. m 10/16/1993 Rebecca J Wagner-Pizza c 2. Dn Dio Pennsylvania Delaware Dnry PA 2006-2008; P-in-c Ch Of S Jn The Evang Essington PA 2003-2008.

WAGNER SHERER, Kara Marie (Chi) 3857 N. Kostner Ave, Chicago IL 60641 **R S Jn's Epis Ch Chicago IL 2005-; Co-Chair of Congregations Cmsn Dio Chicago Chicago IL 2014-, Exec Bd, Prov V 2012-2014, Mem of Congregations Cmsn 2011-2014, Dn of Chicago W Dnry 2009-2014** B El-lensburg WA 1969 d Curtis & Margret. BA S Olaf Coll 1991; MDiv SWTS 2003. D 6/21/2003 P 12/20/2003 Bp Bill Persell. m 6/12/1993 John William Sherer c 2. Asst R Ch Of S Paul And The Redeem Chicago IL 2003-2005; Yth Dir St Geo's Epis Ch Minneapolis MN 1992-1993. Sprtlty, "Many Paths: Reflections on a Chr Journy," *Many Paths: Reflections on a Chr Journy*, self, 2014; Liturg, "All God's People Give Thanks: An Ord for Celebrating the H Euch w the Full Inclusion of Chld," *Open: Journ for Associated Parishes for Liturg & Mssn*, Associated Parishes for Liturg & Mssn, 2004. rector@stjohnschicago.com

WAGNON, William S (WA) 9225 Crestview Dr, Indianapolis IN 46240 B Birmingham AL 1963 s William & Nancy. BA Amer U 1985; MDiv Ya Berk 1993. D 6/12/1993 Bp Ronald Hayward Haines P 1/1/1994 Bp Morgan Porteus. m 5/29/1993 Verity Jones c 1. Affiliate/Supply S Geo Epis Ch W Terre Haute IN 1999-2000; Affiliate/Supply S Steph's Ch Terre Haute IN 1998-1999; P-in-c S Andr's Ch Paris IL 1997-1998; Assoc St Johns Ch W Hartford CT 1993-1997.

WAHL, Eugene Richard (Colo) 4400 Wellington Rd, Boulder CO 80301 **Physical Sci Natl Climatic Data Cntr (NOAA) Boulder CO 2008-** B National City CA 1954 s John & Lillian. BA San Diego St U 1977; MA San Diego St U 1982; MDiv CDSP 1988; PhD U MN 2002. D 6/4/1988 Bp Charles Brinkley Morton P 11/1/1989 Bp William Edwin Swing. m 9/17/1988 Barbara A Dumke. Ch of the Gd Shpd Colorado Spg CO 2008-2012; Asst Prof Alfred U Environ Stds Dept. Alfred NY 2004-2008; Adj Grad Prof. St. Mary-of-the-Woods Coll St. Mary-of-the-Woods IN 2003-2012; Postdoctoral Fell Natl Cntr for Atmospheric Resrch Boulder CO 2002-2004; Trin Ch Anoka MN 1997-2000; Supply S Mich & All Ang Ch Monticello MN 1993-1997; Asst St Johns Epis Ch Ross CA 1989-1992; D S Tim's Ch Danville CA 1988-1989; Lectr San Diego St U Econ Dept 1983-1985; Econ City of San Diego Fin Mgmt Dept 1980-1983; Dio Minnesota Minneapolis MN 1993-1996. Auth, "On the Implications of Ecology for Incarn: Triangle Theol," *Sustaining Creation*, Angl Prov of W. Australia, 2002; Auth, "Country Cur'S Diary Gives Clues To An Environmntl Sprtly," *Soundings*, Epis Dio Minn, 1994; Auth, "The Rel Value Of Biodiversity," *Ecojustice Quarterly*, 1993. EPF 1982. Global Peacemakers Awd The Rumi Forum 2011; Fndr's Medal Berea Coll 2010; Phi Beta Kappa San Diego St U 1977.

WAHL, Hughes Edward (Md) 5010 Marina Cove Dr Apt 203, Naples FL 34112 **Chapl Hospice Norh VA 1996-** B Pittsburgh PA 1942 s Carl & Margaret. BS Alderson-Broaddus Coll 1964; MDiv How 1995. D 6/17/1989 Bp Albert Theodore Eastman. m 11/26/1977 Deborah Fallon Wahl c 4. D S Andr The Fisherman Epis Mayo MD 1991-1996; D S Jas' Par Lothian MD 1989-1991. Untd States Naval Reserves - Lieutenant 1964; Eagle Scout BSA 1957.

WAHLGREN, Matthew David (O) 206 N Park Ave, Fremont OH 43420 **S Paul's Ch Fremont OH 2017-** B Toledo OH 1983 s David & Judith. BA Moody Bible Inst 2007; MDiv No Pk Sem 2015. D 2/4/2017 Bp Bill Persell. m 9/25/2010 Melanie Ann Wahlgren c 3.

WAID, Anna Neil Magruder (Del) 301 Woodlawn Rd, Wilmington DE 19803 B Greenwood MS 1945 d Douglas & Marjorie. BA LSU 1966; MA Jacksonville U 1972; MA Luth TS 1984. D 6/16/1984 P 6/11/1985 Bp Lyman Cunningham Ogilby. m 4/30/1968 William Waid c 2. R Gr Epis Ch Wilmington DE 1999-2010; Vic The Ch Of The Trin Coatesville PA 1994-1999; Int The Ch Of The H Comf Drexel Hill PA 1994; S Mary's Ch Hamilton Vill Philadelphia PA 1993-1994; S Mary's Epis Ch Philadelphia PA 1993-1994; Int Trin Ch Boothwyn PA 1990-1992; Asst The Ch Of The H Trin W Chester PA 1984-1990.

WAINWRIGHT, Philip (Pgh) 326 Maple Terrace, Pittsburgh PA 15211 B Hastings England UK 1945 s Charles & Doris. BD U of New Mex 1981; MTh Lon GB 1984; PhD U of Kent at Cbury 2011. D 1/27/1986 P 2/12/1987 Bp Richard Mitchell Trelease Jr. m 8/27/1988 Thekla S Wainwright c 6. Campus Min Dio Pittsburgh Pittsburgh PA 2012-2016, Co-ordinator for Campus Mnstry 2011-2016; Assoc St Andrews Epis Ch Pittsburgh PA 2011-2013; R S Ptr's Epis Ch Brentwood Pittsburgh PA 1999-2010; Cople Par Hague VA 1996-1999; R Nomini Ch Mt Holly Hague VA 1996-1999; S Jas Ch Tidwells Hague VA 1996-1999; Yeocomico Ch Tucker Hill Hague VA 1996-1999; S Jn's Epis Par Johns Island SC 1995-1996; R Ch of the H Faith Santa Fe NM 1988-1995, D-In-Trng 1986-1987. Ed, "Epis Evang Journ," 1994. Alcuin Club 1989; Barn Proj 2008; EFAC USA 1994; Ecclesiological Soc 1990.

WAINWRIGHT, Robert F (PR) **Died 4/1/2017** B 1949 m 12/26/1992 Carmen Wainwright. Dio Puerto Rico Trujillo Alto PR 2004-2013, 1992-2003.

WAINWRIGHT-MAKS, Laurence Christopher (Miss) 105 N Montgomery St, Starkville MS 39759 **Ch Of The Resurr Starkville MS 2014-** B Augusta GA 1983 s Stephen & Sarah. BA U of Sthrn Mississippi 2006; MDiv Epis TS Of The SW 2014; MDiv Epis TS of the SW 2014. D 10/1/2014 Bp Duncan Montgomery Gray III P 4/22/2015 Bp Brian Seage.

WAIT III, Benjamin Wofford (CFla) 962 Ocean Blvd, Atlantic Beach FL 32233 **Asst S Andr's Epis Ch Ft. Pierce FL 2006-** B Tampa FL 1934 s Benjamin & Martha. BS U of Florida 1957; MA Sewanee: The U So, TS 1997; DMin Sewanee: The U So, TS 2006. D 6/15/1975 Bp William Hopkins Folwell P 5/1/1997 Bp Stephen Hays Jecko. m 8/24/1957 Shirleen Sasser Wait. Cn Dio Florida Jacksonville 1997-2006; Asst Epis Ch Of The H Sprt Tallahassee FL 1990-1995; Asst Epis U Cntr Tallahassee FL 1982-1990; Asst Gr Epis Ch

W

Inc Port Orange FL 1981-1982; Asst S Paul's Epis Ch New Smyrna Bch FL 1976-1980; Asst S Mary Of The Ang Epis Ch Orlando FL 1975-1976. Angl Frontier Missions 2000; FA Natl Bd; Five Talents Intl 2001.

WAIT, Curtis C (Colo) 228 S Jefferson Ave, Louisville CO 80027 B Ann Arbor MI 1963 BS U CO 1988; MDiv Sewanee: The U So, TS 2004. D 6/12/2004 P 12/18/2004 Bp Robert John O'Neill. m 6/9/1984 Anne Margaret Wait c 2. Assoc R Intsn Epis Ch Denver CO 2007-2016; Vic The Epis Ch of the Resurr Boulder CO 2004-2006.

WAIT, Roger Lee (Neb) 3711 A St, Lincoln NE 68510 **Wrdn S Mk's on the Campus Lincoln NE 1984-** B Comstock NE 1934 s Elvin & Marian. BA U of Nebraska 1964; Cert EFM 1989; CDTP SE Cmnty Coll Lincoln NE 1992. D 11/8/1985 Bp James Daniel Warner. m 5/9/1987 Phyllis Wait. JPIC Team Dio Nebraska Omaha NE 1997-2000; D S Mk's On The Campus Lincoln NE 1985-2006, Bp's Com 1981-1984. ACLU 2003; NAAD 1986; The Planetary Soc 2002-2003. valedictoriam Teachers Coll HS 1952.

WAJDA, Kathryn Annemarie Reardon (Md) 1505 Sherbrook Rd, Lutherville Timonium MD 21093 B Methuen MA 1945 d William & Bertha. BS U of New Hampshire 1967; MS U of Maine 1982; MDiv EDS 1984; DMin SWTS 2004. D 5/21/1985 Bp Philip Alan Smith P 3/9/1986 Bp Albert Theodore Eastman. m 9/16/1967 Michael Wajda c 2. Bd Mem Episcocpal Hsng Corp Baltimore MD 2000-2016; R Epiph Ch Dulaney Vlly Luthvle Timon MD 1998-2016, Int 1996-1997; R Dio Maryland Baltimore MD 1998-2000; S Jn's Ch Ellicott City MD 1985-1996. EWC.

WAJNERT, Theresa Altmix (Nwk) PO Box 37, Calistoga CA 94515 B Denver CO 1948 d Richard & Harriet. Drew U; BA Albertus Magnus Coll 1970; MDiv Yale DS 1974; Grad Theol Un 1983; all but dissertation (ABD) Drew U 1988; Drew U 1988; MS (expected 2016) Hawthorn U 2016. D 6/29/1974 P 2/1/1977 Bp Chauncie Kilmer Myers. m 1/2/1982 Thomas C Wajnert c 4. Ch Of The Redeem Morristown NJ 1990-2004; Asst Ch of S Jn on the Mtn Bernardsville NJ 1984-1990; S Bern's Ch Bernardsville NJ 1984-1990; S Aid's Ch San Francisco CA 1980-1984, 1977-1979; Asst Trin Cathd San Jose CA 1975-1976; Asst S Andr's Ch Saratoga CA 1974-1975.

WAKABAYASHI, Allen Mitsuo (Spr) D 6/22/2017 Bp Daniel Hayden Martins.

WAKEEN, Teresa Mary (Mich) 4800 Woodward Ave, Detroit MI 48201 B Port Huron MI 1961 d James & Lydia. BA MI SU 1983; MDiv CDSP 2016. D 12/10/2016 P 6/10/2017 Bp Wendell Nathaniel Gibbs Jr. c 3. Other Lay Position Dio Michigan Detroit MI 2003-2006.

WAKELEE-LYNCH, Julia (Cal) 1501 Washington Avenue, Albany CA 94706 **R S Alb's Ch Albany CA 2009-** B Ventura CA 1965 BA Occ 1983; MDiv CDSP 2003; MA Grad Theol Un 2003. D 6/28/2003 P 1/24/2004 Bp Joseph Jon Bruno. c 1. Int R Ch Of The Epiph San Carlos CA 2008-2009; Assoc The Par Ch Of S Lk Long Bch CA 2004-2008; D/Asstg P S Jas Epis Ch San Francisco CA 2003-2004. EPF 2000.

WAKELY, Nancy Kay (Okla) PO Box 2088, Norman OK 73070 B Norman OK 1949 d Vernon & Betty. D 6/16/2007 Bp Robert Manning Moody. m 11/4/1983 Thomas Martin Wakely c 2.

WAKEMAN, Nancy Ann (Md) **Mentor, Exploring Baptismal Mnstry Dio Maryland Baltimore MD 2011-** B Ephrata PA 1955 d Robert & Lorraine. D 6/4/2011 Bp Eugene Taylor Sutton. m 6/18/1994 Timothy Wakeman c 4.

WAKITSCH, Randal John (Chi) 503 W Jackson St, Woodstock IL 60098 **P The Epis Ch Of The H Trin Belvidere IL 2015-** B Waukegan IL 1963 s Gerald & Marcella. BA Loras Coll 1985; MDiv St Mary Sem and U 1989; MDiv St Mary Sem and U 1989. Rec 2/5/2012 as Priest Bp Chris Christopher Epting. m 8/16/2004 Julie Ann Monroe. trinitybelvidere@gmail.com

WALBERG, Elsa Phyllis (Mass) PO Box 245, Danville VT 05828 **Ret 1991-** B Weehawken NJ 1925 d George & Sophie. BA CUNY 1949; MA NYU 1956; MDiv EDS 1962. D 2/19/1972 P 2/19/1977 Bp John Melville Burgess. Assoc S Andr's Epis Ch St Johnsbury VT 1995-2004; Supply P Dio Vermont Burlington VT 1992-2004; Sprtl Direction Com 1999-2001; Assoc S Ptr's Mssn Lyndonville VT 1992-1994; T/F on Environ Dio Massachusetts Boston MA 1988-1991, 1981-1983; R S Paul's Epis Ch Bedford MA 1983-1991; Assoc R S Andr's Ch Wellesley MA 1977-1983; Ecum Mnstry To Older Persons Brookline MA 1974-1977; Mssnr Ecum Mnstry to Older Persons Brookline MA 1973-1977; Asst Trin Par Melrose MA 1962-1973. Ed, *Voices*, 2006; Auth, "Consider the Heavens," *NorthStar Monthly*, 1991; Auth, "Consider the Heavens," *monthly column*, 1991. EWC 1975-1990; SCHC 1974. Procter Fllshp EDS 1973.

WALCOTT, Robert (O) 2173 W 7th St, Cleveland OH 44113 **1994-** B Boston MA 1942 s Robert & Rosamond. BA Coll of Wooster 1964; MDiv CDSP 1967; MA OH SU 1972. D 6/19/1968 P 12/24/1968 Bp John Harris Burt. m 9/3/1966 Diane Walcott c 1. H Trin Ch Lisbon OH 2005; S Aug's Epis Ch Youngstown OH 1993-1996; S Rocco's Ch Youngstown OH 1993-1995; Vic New Life Epis Ch Uniontown OH 1991-1993; R Ch Of The Trsfg Buffalo NY 1988-1991; P-in-c S Mart In The Fields Grand Island NY 1986-1987; Assoc S Lk's Ch Brockport NY 1981-1985; Assoc Chr Ch Oberlin OH 1979-1981, Assoc 1975-1978; 1977-1978; P-in-c S Jas Epis Ch Wooster OH 1972-1973; 1970-1972; Cur S Mart's Ch Chagrin Fall OH 1968-1970. EPF 1968-2009. Marquis Who's Who

in Amer; Marquis Who's Who in Healthcure; Marquis Who's Who in the Midwest.

WALDEN, Jan (Mass) 110 Dean St., Unit #37, Taunton MA 02780 **S Jn The Evang Mansfield MA 2006-, 2006-; S Mk's Ch No Easton MA 2006-, 2006-; St Johns Ch Taunton MA 2006-, 2006-** B New London CT 1956 d David & Cynthia. BA Chart Oak St Coll 1991; MDiv Ya Berk 1995; STM Ya Berk 1996. D 6/8/1996 Bp Clarence Nicholas Coleridge P 1/25/1997 Bp Andrew Donnan Smith. Area Mssnr Bristol Cluster No Easton MA 2006-2016; Middlesex Area Cluster Mnstry Higganum CT 1996-2006; Ch Of The Epiph Durham CT 1996-2006; Co-Mssnr Emm Ch Killingworth CT 1996-2006; S Andr's Ch Northford CT 1996-2006; S Jas Epis Ch Higganum CT 1996-2006; S Paul's Ch Westbrook CT 1996-2006.

WALDEN, Robert Eugene (Haw) 46-290 Ikiiki St, Kaneohe HI 96744 **Died 4/10/2017** B Paragould AR 1938 s Clifton & Vivian. BA Hendrix Coll 1959; MS USC 1972; MDiv CDSP 1977. D 8/31/1977 P 4/4/1978 Bp Edmond Lee Browning. c 4. Int Gr Ch Hoolehua HI 2012-2013; Ret 2003-2017; R Dio Okinawa 1997-2003; Chapl Mahelona Hospice 1987-1997; Dioc Coun The Epis Ch in Hawaii Honolulu HI 1981-2010; R All SS Ch Kapaa HI 1979-1997; Vic Chr Memi Ch Kilauea HI 1979-1981; Assoc Ch Of The H Nativ Honolulu HI 1977-1979. Auth, "Impact Of Asian-Amer Culture On Chr Wrshp," 1976. SSF 1976-1988.

WALDIE, Nanette Marie (Oly) 4228 Factoria Blvd SE, Bellevue WA 98006 B Denver CO 1956 d Donald & Therese. MPM Seattle U 1990; AS CDSP 2006; MDiv Seattle U 2007; MDiv Seattle U 2007. D 1/15/2009 P 7/31/2009 Bp Gregory Harold Rickel. m 9/1/1979 Ian Spencer Waldie c 2. Ch Of Our Sav Monroe WA 2014-2016.

WALDING, Jennifer Maureen (Minn) 4180 Lexington Ave S, Eagan MN 55123 **Other Lay Position U Epis Ch Minneapolis MN 2004-** B Sioux City IA 1960 d Edward & Claire. BA Iowa St U 1986. D 6/26/2014 P 6/20/2015 Bp Brian N Prior. c 1.

WALDO JR, Mark E (Ala) 311 Lindsey Road, Coosada AL 36020 **R S Mich And All Ang Millbrook AL 2005-; COM Dio Alabama Birmingham 2015-, Com on Diac Formation 2012-** B Houston TX 1956 s Mark & Anne. BA Transylvania U 1979; MDiv VTS 1988. D 6/18/1988 P 4/25/1989 Bp Peter J Lee. m 5/16/2009 Mitzi Waldo c 4. Asst S Patricks Ch Falls Ch VA 2001-2005; R S Alb's Epis Ch Murrysville PA 1993-1998; Asst to R S Geo's Epis Ch Arlington VA 1988-1993. mark@stmichaelandallangels.com

WALDO SR, Mark Edward (Ala) 2046 Hazel Hedge Ln, Montgomery AL 36106 **R Emer Ch Of The Ascen Montgomery AL 2007-, 1961-1989; Ret 1989-** B Fort Monroe VA 1926 s George & Annie. BA W&M 1948; MDiv VTS 1951; VTS 1969; Hampden-Sydney Coll 1983. D 6/24/1951 P 3/25/1952 Bp Middleton S Barnwell. m 6/5/1950 Anne Waldo c 6. Locten Gd Shpd Ch Montgomery AL 1989-1996; S Paul's (Carlowville) Carlowville AL 1989-1996; S Paul's Epis Ch Lowndesboro AL 1989-1996; Excoun Dio Alabama Birmingham 1972-1973, Dep Gc 1969-1973, Pres 1982-1984, Stndg Com 1980-1981, Chair Deptce 1978-1979, Com 1971-1977, Chair Dept Stwdshp & Evang 1966-1970, Excoun 1964-1965; Cn Pstr Chr Ch Cathd Houston TX 1956-1961; Asst Secy Dio Georgia Savannah GA 1953-1955, Exec Coun 1954-1956; Vic S Andr's Epis Ch Douglas GA 1951-1956; S Matt's Epis Ch Fitzgerald GA 1951-1956. Omicron Delta Kappa 1948; Phi Beta Kappa 1947.

✠ **WALDO, The Rt Rev W illiam Andrew** (USC) 847 Kilbourne Rd, Columbia SC 29205 **Mem Bishops Untd Against Gun Violence 2016-; Citizen Advsry Com Mem Columbia Police Dept Columbia SC 2015-; Bp of Upper So Carolina Dio Upper So Carolina Columbia SC 2010-; Partnr Bp Fllshp of SC Bishops (Ecum - Epis Polities) 2010-** B Douglas GA 1953 s Mark & Anne. BA Whittier Coll 1975; MA New Engl Conservatory of Mus 1980; MDiv Sewanee: The U So, TS 1988. D 6/25/1988 P 4/19/1989 Bp Douglas Edwin Theuner Con 5/22/2010 for USC. m 6/13/1981 Mary H Halverson c 3. R Trin Ch Excelsior MN 1994-2010; R S Mk's Epis Ch Lagrange GA 1990-1994; Cur Gr Ch Manchester NH 1988-1990. Auth, "Baptism and Euch: Challenges," *OPEN*, Associated Parishes, 2000. D.Div. Hon. STUSo 2011. awaldo8@edusc.org

WALDON, Mark W. (Nwk) 2 Marble Ct Apt 1, Clifton NJ 07013 **EfM Coordntr Dio Newark Newark NJ 2011-, Chair Evang Consults 1987-2002** B Ocala FL 1944 s Albert & Mildren. BA Davidson Coll 1966; MDiv Candler TS Emory U 1969; Cert VTS 1970. D 6/24/1970 P 9/29/1971 Bp Edward Hamilton West. R Chr Ch Totowa NJ 1985-2012; Vic Bethany Ch Hilliard FL 1980-1984; Vic S Mart Jacksonville FL 1980-1984; S Eliz's Epis Ch Jacksonville FL 1980; S Mary's Epis Ch Madison FL 1979; Locem Tenens H Comf Epis Ch Tallahassee FL 1971-1972; Vic Dio Florida Jacksonville 1970-1984; Chr Ch Monticello FL 1970-1979. Auth, "Article," *The Epis*, 1983. Theta Phi. Theta Phi.

WALDON JR., Raymond J (U) 412 Shelby Springs Farms, Calera AL 35040 **S Paul's Ch Waco TX 2017-** B Shreveport LA 1956 s Raymond & Marilyn. BA Louisiana Tech U 1978; Lousiana St U Law Sch 1982; MDiv VTS 1995; Trin Newbury 2003. D 6/3/1995 P 12/3/1995 Bp Robert Jefferson Hargrove Jr. m 9/9/1978 Lisa F Waldon c 2. Dn Cathd Ch Of S Mk Salt Lake City UT 2011-2017; P-in-c S Ptr's Epis Ch Talladega AL 2008-2011; H Cross Ch Pensacola FL 2003-2007; R Gr Epis Ch Camden SC 1998-2003; R/ Yoked- added

1998 S Alb's Epis Ch Monroe LA 1997-1998; R S Pat's Epis Ch W Monroe LA 1995-1998. Interview, "Ch," *Pensacola Journnal*, Pensacola Journ, 2003; Auth, "What Christmas Means," *Camden Chronicle*, Camden Chronicle, 2001; Ed, "Dio Upper So Carolina Customary," *Bp's Customary*, Dio, 2000; Interview, "NBC Nightly Newiths w Tom Brokaw," *NBC*, NBC, 2000; Auth, "Stories On Rel And Ethics," *KNOE-TV*, KNOE TV 1995-1998, 1998; Rel Correspondence, "Nightly News," *KNOE-TV 1995-1998*, KNOE-TV 1995-1998, 1998; Auth, "Assisted Suicide," *Epis Life*, 1996. Bd Mem Birdell Fund 1999-2003; Bd Mem Hospice 1999-2003; Bd Mem Mnstrl Assn 1998-2003; Servnt Of Chr Priory-Oblate 2001; York Place Advsry 2001-2003. rwaldon@stmarkscathedral-ut.org

WALDRON, Susan G (Alb) 107 State St., Albany NY 12207 **Assoc S Ptr's Ch Albany NY 2012-, 2008-2011, Cur 2008-2011; Dio Albany Greenwich NY 2011-; Great Cathd Chapt Mem Cathd Of All SS Albany NY 2009-** B Albany NY 1966 d George & Carol. AS SUNY Empire St Coll Saratoga 2002; BS SUNY Empire St Coll Saratoga 2003; MDiv Nash 2008. D 5/31/2008 P 12/21/2008 Bp William Howard Love. c 1. COM Mem S Mary's Ch Lake Luzerne NY 2011-2012. DOK 2004.

WALDRON, Teresa Jane (Cal) 920 Oak St, Lafayette CA 94549 B Oakland CA 1953 d William & Emma. BA U CA Davis 1976; MLIS U CA Berkeley 1987; MDiv CDSP 2003. D 6/21/2003 P 3/6/2004 Bp Jerry Alban Lamb. m 1/16/2015 Samuel Peregrine Waldron. S Jas Ch Oakland CA 2016-2017; Chapl Kaiser Hosp San Rafael CA 2011-2016; Int S Giles Ch Moraga CA 2010-2011; Chapl Alta Bates Summit Med Cntr Berkeley CA 2009-2010; Asst Trin Ch Folsom CA 2005-2009; Yth Dir The Epis Dio Nthrn California Sacramento CA 2003-2006; Asst S Matt's Epis Ch Sacramento CA 2003-2005.

WALDROP, Charlotte Macon Egerton (USC) 137 Summerwood Way, Aiken SC 29803 B Louisburg NC 1937 d Frank & Pattie. BA U NC Asheville 1976; MDiv Duke DS 1986; Cert VTS 1986. D 6/14/1986 P 12/17/1986 Bp William Gillette Weinhauer. c 2. P Asstg S Thad Epis Ch Aiken SC 2006-2007; Vic All SS Ch Beech Island SC 2002-2010; Hospice Chapl Luth Hm of So Carolina 2001-2002; Assoc R S Martins-In-The-Field Columbia SC 1999-2001, P-in-c 1998-1999, Assoc R 1995-1997; R Ch Of The Gd Shpd Hayesville NC 1986-1995; Int D Trin Ch Arlington VA 1986; Del, Prov IV Wmn Conf Dio Wstrn No Carolina Asheville NC 1998, Dn Wstrn Deanry 1993-1998, Mem Stwdshp 1990-1995, Mem Liturg Cmsn 1989-1995.

WALK, Everett Prichard (SwFla) 8700 State Road 72, Sarasota FL 34241 B Washington DC 1949 s Everett & Sybil. BA Laf 1972; MDiv VTS 1977. D 6/2/1977 Bp Lloyd Edward Gressle P 12/18/1977 Bp Frank S Cerveny. m 7/16/1977 Deborah W Wood c 1. R S Marg Of Scotland Epis Ch Sarasota FL 1991-2015; Cn Pstr Cathd Ch Of S Lk Orlando FL 1986-1991; S Jn's Epis Ch Tallahassee FL 1977-1985. Ord Of S Lk.

WALKER, Aurilla Kay (Neb) B Alliance NE 1949 D 12/13/2004 P 6/13/2005 Bp Joe Goodwin Burnett. c 2.

WALKER, Charles Henry (SD) 304 1st St, Wilmot SD 57279 B Pierre SD 1946 s William & Marjorie. None Dakota Ldrshp; None DeVry Inst of Techology; None U of So Dakota; Hlth Admin Presentation Coll Aberdeen SD 2002. D 11/5/1988 Bp Craig Barry Anderson. m 11/9/1965 Betty Anne Koan c 3. Presentation Coll Bus Club 2001-2002; Class Pres Presentation Coll 2002; Deans List Presentation Coll 2002; Pres'S List Presentation Coll 2001.

WALKER, David Bruce (Spok) 127 E 12th Ave, Spokane WA 99202 B Sacramento CA 1956 s Samuel & Elizabeth. BS Natl U 1991. D 6/11/2005 Bp James E Waggoner Jr. m 4/18/1981 Julia L Walker c 2.

WALKER, David Charles (Los) 6072 Avenida De Castillo, Long Beach CA 90803 B Washington DC 1938 s Edwin & Frances. BA IL Wesl 1960; SMM UTS 1965; MDiv GTS 1973. D 6/9/1973 Bp Paul Moore Jr P 5/9/1974 Bp Ned Cole. m 2/11/2015 Nam Thanh Nguyen. Gd Samar Hosp Los Angeles CA 1991-2003; Chapl and Dir of Pstr Care Gd Samar Hosp Los Angeles CA 1991-2003; Int S Lk's Epis Ch Monrovia CA 1990; All SS Par Beverly Hills CA 1985-1990; Assoc All Souls' Epis Ch San Diego CA 1980-1985; R S Phil's Ch Brooklyn NY 1976-1980; Fac The GTS New York NY 1973-1976. Auth, "Hymn tune: Gnrl Sem," *The Hymnal 1982*, Ch Pub, 1982; Auth, "Hymn tune: Point Loma," *The Hymnal 1982*, Ch Pub, 1982.

WALKER, Edwin Montague (SwFla) 1532 Vantage Pointe, Mount Pleasant SC 29464 **Chapl Charleston Port & Seafarers' Soc 2006-; Ret 1999-** B Yonkers NY 1933 s Harold & Gladys. BEE RPI 1954; MSEE Georgia Inst of Tech 1956; MDiv VTS 1961; MA Van 1973. D 7/6/1961 Bp Noble C Powell P 6/22/1962 Bp Harry Lee Doll. m 6/29/1957 Margaret B Blackman c 3. Supply Ch Of The Redeem Pineville SC 2001-2008; S Dav's Epis Ch Englewood FL 1991-1999; Mem Natl Epis Curs Com 1987-1989; S Mk's Epis Ch Charleston SC 1982-1991; Asst S Mich's Epis Ch Charleston SC 1980-1981; Assoc Chr Epis Ch Mt Pleasant SC 1978-1980; Supply P So Carolina Charleston SC 1973-1978; P-in-c S Jas Cumberland Furnace TN 1972-1973; P-in-c S Andr's Epis Ch New Johnsonville TN 1971-1972; P-in-c H Sprt Springfield TN 1969-1971; Proyecto Educativo Epis Barranquilla Colombia 1965-1969; Vic S Jn The Evang Ch Barranquilla Colombia 1965-1969; P-in-c Our Sav Cargagena Colombia 1965-1966; Vic S Nich Quito Ecuador 1964-1965; Mssy Dio Costa Rica 1963-1964; Chapl BroSA MD 1962-1963;

Cur S Dav's Ch Baltimore MD 1961-1963. Auth, "Urbanism & the Adaptation of Migrants," *So Atlantic Urban Stds Vol 2*, U of So Carolina Press, 1978; Auth, "Urbanism and the Adaptation of Migrants," *So Atlantic Urban Stds Vol 2*, U of So Carolina Press, 1978.

WALKER, Elizabeth Ann (WVa) 3343 Davis Stuart Road, Fairlea WV 24902 **Chapl Fed Bureau of Prisons Fed Prison Camp Alderson WV 1996-; Ed The Dayspring - Dio WV Nwspr Charleston WV 1989-** B Clifton Forge VA 1957 d Weymouth & Betty. BD Concord U 1979; MDiv VTS 1987. D 5/30/1987 Bp Robert Poland Atkinson P 5/21/1988 Bp William Franklin Carr. Off Of Bsh For ArmdF New York NY 1996-2014; Dio W Virginia Charleston WV 1996-2010, Stndg Com 1992-1997; Vic Gr Ch Ravenswood WV 1993-1996; R S Jn's Ripley WV 1988-1996; D-in-Trng Chr Ch Bluefield WV 1987-1988.

WALKER, Frederick Wyclif (SVa) 140 Tynes St, Suffolk VA 23434 **R S Jas Epis Ch Portsmouth VA 2015-** B Liberia 1961 s Frederick & Maggie. INC Cuttington U 1990; BD S Nich Theol Coll Cape Coast GH 1993; BD S Johns Coll of theo 1995; MTh U Cape Coast 1998; Dplma Virginia Sem 2006; Wesley TS 2007. Trans 4/26/2010 as Priest Bp Herman Hollerith IV. m 5/30/1992 Salome Walker c 4. R S Mk's Ch Suffolk VA 2010-2017. Hon Cn Dio Cape Coast, Ghana 2011.

WALKER JR, Harold William (SeFla) St Thomas Episcopal Parish, 5690 N Kendall Dr, Coral Gables FL 33156 **S Phil's Ch Brevard NC 2016-; Asst P S Thos Epis Par Miami FL 2011-** B Cincinnati OH 1946 s Harold & Claire. BA W&L 1968; JD W&L 1971; MDiv Florida Cntr for Theol Stds 2009. D 12/21/2010 P 6/24/2011 Bp Leo Frade. m 6/29/1968 Laura C Walker c 3.

WALKER, James Arvie (NwT) **Vic S Lk's Epis Ch Levelland TX 2016-** D 12/12/2015 P 6/21/2016 Bp James Scott Mayer.

WALKER, James Lee (Los) 4114 South Norton Ave, Los Angeles CA 90008 **P St Johns Pro-Cathd Los Angeles CA 2008-** B Houston TX 1948 s James & Myrtle. BA U of Texas 1971; MDiv GTS 1973. D 6/11/1973 P 12/13/1973 Bp Theodore H McCrea. R Chr The Gd Shpd Par Los Angeles CA 1999-2003; Chr Ch Greenwich CT 1989-1999; Dio Ft Worth Ft Worth TX 1982-1985; Vic S Mart In The Fields Ch Keller TX 1982-1985; Asst S Cybi Holyhead Wales Uk 1980-1982; S Elis Ch Ft Worth TX 1976-1980; Vic S Eliz's Ft Worth TX 1976-1980; Cur S Chris's Ch And Sch Ft Worth TX 1974-1976; Intern Trin Ch Easton PA 1973-1974.

WALKER, Janice Ficke (WNC) 2709 Pleasant Run Dr, Richmond VA 23233 B Davenport IA 1935 d Parker & Lucile. BA Carleton Coll 1957; MDiv SWTS 1979. D 6/16/1980 Bp James Winchester Montgomery P 2/24/1981 Bp Quintin Ebenezer Primo Jr. c 1. Assoc The Cathd Of All Souls Asheville NC 1998-2006; Assoc R S Mary Epis Ch Crystal Lake IL 1992-1995; Assoc R S Mk's Barrington IL 1988-1991, Asst 1979-1987; Chapl Gd Shpd Hosp Barrington IL 1985-1988; Chapl Luth Gnrl Hosp Pk Ridge IL 1982-1985; Chapl Advoc Hlth Care Oak Brook IL 1982-1984.

WALKER III, John Edward (LI) 64 S Country Rd, Bellport NY 11713 **Died 4/13/2017** B New York NY 1948 s Edward & Jane. AA Queensborough Cmnty Coll 1969; BA CUNY 1971; MDiv Nash 1974. D 6/15/1974 P 12/1/1974 Bp Jonathan Goodhue Sherman. m 6/6/1978 Judith Durking c 1. Stndg Com Dio Long Island Garden City NY 2006-2011, Epis Hlth Serv 1988-1991, Ecum Relatns Com 1981-1986, Hstgr 2003-2017, Mercer Bd Mem 2000-2002, Stwdshp Com Chair 1998-1999, Dioc Coun 1988-1989, Peace Com 1985-1997, Cler Conf Com 1981-1984; Dn Great So Bay Dnry 1997-2017; R Chr Ch Bellport NY 1995-2015; Deploy Advsry Grp Dio Pennsylvania Philadelphia PA 1994-1995, Stwdshp Com 1992-1994; Chapl Aston Police Dept 1992-1994; S Jas Ch Greenridge Aston PA 1991-1994; R S Jas Epis Ch S Jas NY 1991-1994; Dn Peconic Dnry 1987-1991; Exec Com Archdeanery In Suffolk 1984-1991; Instr In LayR Course Mercer TS Garden City NY 1981-1984; R Ch Of The H Trin Greenport NY 1980-1991; Chapl BSA 1980-1990; Chapl Greenport Fire Dept 1980-1984; Asst S Mk's Ch Islip NY 1978-1980; Cur Ch Of The Trsfg Freeport NY 1977-1978; S Geo's Par Flushing NY 1976; Asst S Mary's Hosp Flushing NY 1975-1977; Asst Ch Of The H Apos Oneida WI 1974-1975. Rotarian Of The Year 1982. xchurchbellport@verizon.net

WALKER, Lynell (NCal) 2380 Wyda Way, Sacramento CA 95825 **P-in-c S Paul's Epis Ch Sacramento CA 2005-; S Mich's Epis Day Sch Carmichael CA 2004-; P-in-c St. Paul's Epis Ch Sacramento CA 2004-; Cn for Sprtl Formation Trin Epis Cathd Sacramento CA 2003-, Cn for Sprtl Formation 1999-2003; Chapl S Mich's Epis Sch Carmichael CA 2000-** B Whttier CA 1948 d Edgar & Francella. MDiv CDSP 1996. D 10/11/1998 P 5/25/1999 Bp Jerry Alban Lamb. m 10/7/2016 Patricia Ann Park c 3. S Mich's Epis Ch Carmichael CA 2001-2003; Chapl S Mich's Epis Sch 1998-1999.

WALKER, Mary Lu (Okla) 620 E Logan Ave, Guthrie OK 73044 **Died 12/1/2016** B Berlin NH 1934 d Richard & Lucia. BA Hood Coll 1956; MA U of Texas 1971; MA U of Texas 1974; MDiv Epis TS of the SW 1987. D 5/26/1996 Bp Sam Byron Hulsey P 11/25/1996 Bp Robert Manning Moody. m 10/23/2000 Thomas Tanner Walker c 2. R Trin Ch Guthrie OK 2003-2005; Vic at Trin Ch Guthrie, OK Dio Oklahoma Oklahoma City OK 1996-2002; Chapl Res Meth Hosp Lubbock 1994-1996; Ch Of The Resurr Austin TX 1987-1994.

W

WALKER, Michelle I (NI) Calumet Episcopal Ministry Partnership, 1101 Park Dr, Munster IN 46321 **Admin Dio Nthrn Indiana So Bend IN 2016-; P Calumet Mnstry Partnership Munster IN 2014-** B Reed City MI 1972 d Carleton & Sandra. BS Ferris St U 1994; MA U of Notre Dame 2011. D 4/18/2012 P 11/30/2012 Bp Edward Stuart Little II. m 7/5/1997 Joseph W Walker c 2. Fam Life Mnstry Pstr S Andr's Epis Ch Valparaiso IN 2012-2013. revmiw12@gmail.com

WALKER, Noble Ray (WTenn) 6855 Branch Rd, Olive Branch MS 38654 B Milan/Atwood TN 1940 s John & Frances. BA Rhodes Coll 1962; MA U of Iowa 1963; STB GTS 1968; MS U of Memphis 1981. D 6/15/1968 Bp John Vander Horst P 5/6/1969 Bp William F Gates Jr. c 1. H Cross Epis Ch Olive Branch MS 1989-2007; Dio W Tennessee Memphis 1983-1985; Vic Bp Otey Memi Ch Memphis TN 1980-1986; Dio Tennessee Nashville TN 1980-1982; Assoc S Jn's Epis Ch Memphis TN 1975-1980; P-in-c S Jas The Less Madison TN 1971-1975; Asst Gr Ch Chattanooga TN 1969-1971. Auth, "Washington Journ," *The Unicorn*, Gts_Ny, 1969; Auth, "O Tempus O Mores," *The Unicorn*, Gts-Ny, 1968; Auth, "Versos Del Sendero," *The Unicorn*, Gts-Ny, 1968.

WALKER, Paul Edward (Ia) 510 Columbia St, Burlington IA 52601 B Taylor PA 1951 s Harold & Doris. BA Marywood U 1978; MS Marywood U 1981; MDiv Bex Sem 1986. D 6/1/1986 P 1/24/1987 Bp James Michael Mark Dyer. m 7/10/2004 Randy Lee Webster c 2. R S Paul's Ch Montrose PA 2009-2012; Co-Cnvnr (Dn) Dist 7 Dio Newark Newark NJ 2003-2009, Trnr for Lay Eucharistic Ministers and Hm Visitors 2003-2009, Mem, Bd Dioc Ward Herbert Fund 1999-2009; Vic Chr Ch Belleville NJ 1999-2009; Treas, AIDS Resource Ctr Dio Newark Newark NJ 1999-2006; Chair of the Dioc AIDS T/F Dio Rochester Henrietta 1998-1999, Chair, Dioc Dept of Soc Mnstry 1998-1999, RurD 1993-1999, Vice Moderator of the Dioc Coun 1993-1999, Chair of the Dept for Soc Mnstry 1990-1992; Chapl Rochester Inst Tech 1996-1999; Gr Ch Scottsville NY 1988-1999; R S Andr's Epis Ch Caledonia NY 1988-1999; Chair of the Dioc AIDS T/F Dio Wstrn Massachusetts Springfield 1986-1988, Cur 1986-1988. ChmbrCom (Vice-Pres) 1999-2006; Rotary (Past-Pres) 1999-2009; Suburban Essex Cnty Chamber of Commerse, VP 2006-2009.

WALKER, Paul Nelson (Va) 100 W Jefferson St, Charlottesville VA 22902 **R Chr Epis Ch Charlottesvlle VA 2004-, 1995-2001** B Richmond VA 1964 s Randolph & Lovey. BA U of Virginia 1986; MDiv VTS 1995. D 6/3/1995 P 1/1/1996 Bp Peter J Lee. m 6/14/1986 Christie Lynn Walker c 3. Cn for Par Life; Chapl to Day Sch 2001-2004; The Cathd Ch Of The Adv Birmingham AL 2001-2004. *Sermons For Chr Ch*, Legacy Word Pub, 2001.

WALKER, Peggy (WNC) 824 Arabella St, New Orleans LA 70115 **Intern The Mc Farland Inst For Cler And Congrl Care 2002-** B Alexandria LA 1951 d William & Jane. BA LSU 1973; MA Tul 1982; MA Tul 1983; MDiv Sewanee: The U So, TS 1992. D 6/13/1992 P 12/19/1992 Bp James Barrow Brown. m 8/30/1997 Francis Marion Covington King c 1. S Jn's Epis Ch Marion NC 2010-2011; Dio Louisiana New Orleans LA 2005-2008; S Paul's Ch New Orleans LA 2001-2002, R Prtem 2001-2002, 1995-1998, Assoc R 1995-1998, Asst R 1992-1994; Assoc R Chr Ch Covington LA 1994-1995.

WALKER, Robert Lynn (NY) B Anna IL 1929 D 6/11/1958 P 12/17/1958 Bp Gordon V Smith.

WALKER, Roger D (Mich) PO Box 8101, Louisville KY 40257 **Chr Ch Elizabethtown KY 2016-; H Trin Ch Brandenburg KY 2016-; Supply P S Mich's Epis Ch Lansing MI 2013-** B Henderson KY 1947 s Leonard & Mary. BA U of Evansville 1969; MSSW U of Louisville 1985; MDiv SWTS 2009. D 6/11/2011 P 12/10/2011 Bp Wendell Nathaniel Gibbs Jr. Mnstry Dvlp Dio Michigan Detroit MI 2011-2012; Cur S Paul's Epis Ch Brighton MI 2011-2012; Mnstry Dvlp Dio Michigan (Lay Position) 2009-2011. fr.rwalker@gmail.com

WALKER, Samuel Clevenger (WA) Zach Fowler Road, Box 8, Chaptico MD 20621 B Bryn Mawr PA 1943 s Danforth & Dorothy. BA Ups 1965; MDiv PDS 1968; STM Yale DS 1977; DMin GTF 1993. D 6/8/1968 Bp Robert Lionne DeWitt P 12/1/1968 Bp Jonathan Goodhue Sherman. m 8/24/1968 Alice E Walker c 2. P-in-c Chr Ch Chaptico MD 1991-2002; R Emm Par Epis Ch Sthrn Pines NC 1983-1991; R S Jn's Ch Bridgeport CT 1978-1983; Asst Chr Ch Greenwich CT 1973-1978; Cur All SS Ch Great Neck NY 1968-1969. Auth, "Natl Observer". Tosf, AAPC, ACPE, CHS. Outstanding Young Men Amer 1977; Who'S Who Rel Amer 78; Polly Bond Awd Excellence Rel Jornalism 94 Epis Cmncatns Assn.

WALKER, Scott D (CFla) 3-6-25 Shiba-Koen, Minato-ku, Tokyo Japan 105-0011 Japan **S Agnes Ch Sebring FL 2013-** B Memphis TN 1967 s Tolbert & Jerri. BA SMU 1989; MBA Baylor U 2002; MA Nash 2008. D 10/28/2008 P 6/29/2009 Bp William Howard Love. m 3/8/1994 Akemi Sato Walker c 1. St Albans Angl- Epis Ch Tokyo 2010-2012.

WALKER, Stacy (Chi) 910 Normal Road, DeKalb IL 60115 **S Chas Ch St. Chas IL 2017-; Dn of the Rockford Deaney Dio Chicago Chicago IL 2012-** B Kansas City MO 1974 d Grover & Janet. BS MI SU 1997; MDiv Epis TS of the SW 2006. D 12/18/2005 P 8/5/2006 Bp Edwin Max Leidel Jr. m 7/29/2000 Richard A Frontjes c 2. R S Paul's Ch Dekalb IL 2010-2017; Asst S Edm's Epis Ch Chicago IL 2009-2010; R S Albans Epis Ch Bay City MI 2006-2009; Del of the Epis Del to the Untd Nations Cmsn on the Status of Wmn #59 Dom And Frgn Mssy Soc- Epis Ch Cntr New York NY 2014-2015. stacywalker059@gmail.com

WALKER, Stephen Bruce (WNC) 520 Main St, Highlands NC 28741 B Spartanburg SC 1953 s Lemuel & Betty. BS U of So Carolina 1975; DMD Med U of So Carolina 1981; MDiv Sewanee: The U So, TS 1997. D 6/14/1997 P 5/9/1998 Bp Dorsey Henderson. m 8/25/1979 Susie Young Walker c 3. R Ch Of The Incarn Highlands NC 2012-2016; R Gr Ch Morganton NC 2002-2012; Assoc R S Paul's Ch Augusta GA 1999-2002; Asst R S Barth's Ch No Augusta SC 1997-1999. sbwalker1979@gmail.com

WALKER, Susan Kennard (WA) 1317 G St NW, Washington DC 20005 **Res Serv Dir St Mary's Crt Sr Hsng Washington DC US 2013-** B Nashville TN 1951 d Dewitt & Mabel. M.A Geo Peabody Coll; BA Geo Peabody Coll; MTS Washington Theoligical Sem. D 9/22/2012 Bp Mariann Edgar Budde. m 6/21/2008 Carl E Scheffey c 2. S Mary Crt Hsng Corp Washington DC 2013-2014; The Ch Of The Epiph Washington DC 2012, 1999-2012. stmaryscourtlease@spm.net

WALKER, Terrence Alaric (SVa) PO Box 753, Lawrenceville VA 23868 **All SS Ch So Hill VA 2014-; Trin Ch So Hill VA 2014-, 2007-2009** B Pittsburgh PA 1966 s Edwin & Annie. BS Jas Madison U 1988; MA Norfolk St U Norfolk VA 1990; MDiv Epis TS of the SW 1993; EdD GTF 2000. D 6/5/1993 Bp O'Kelley Whitaker P 5/21/1994 Bp William Elwood Sterling. S Andr's Epis Ch Lawrenceville VA 2012-2013, 2012; S Mk's Ch Bracey VA 2012; S Paul's Coll Lawrenceville VA 2002-2011; S Lk The Evang Houston TX 1993-2000. Auth, "The Educational Theol of Jas Solomon Russell," *Proceedings of the Midwest Philos of Educ Soc*, MPES, 1997.

WALKER, Thomas Cecil (NC) 2933 Wycliffe Rd, Raleigh NC 27607 **1972-** B McCaysville GA 1939 s Henry & Laura. BA U NC 1962; MDiv EDS 1965; PGCS U NC 1976; PGCS U of Tennessee 1979. D 6/29/1965 Bp Thomas Augustus Fraser Jr P 12/1/1967 Bp William Moultrie Moore Jr. Asst R S Mich's Ch Raleigh NC 1965-1971.

WALKER, William Ray (CPa) St. Paul's Episcopal Church, P.O. Box 170, Philipsburg PA 16866 B Hawk Run PA 1939 s Raymond & Sarah. BS Lock Haven U 1961; MEd U of Pennsylvania 1965; Cert Sch Chr Stds PA 1996. D 11/9/1996 P 2/17/2002 Bp Michael Whittington Creighton. m 11/24/1974 Alice Walker c 1. S Paul's Ch Philipsburg PA 2006-2011; D St Laurence Epis Ch Osceola Mills PA 1999-2002.

WALKER, William Royce (Wyo) 157 Pleasant Valley Rd, Hartville WY 82215 **P Ch Of Our Sav Hartville WY 2004-** B Hartville WY 1938 s Albert & Violet. D 3/12/2004 P 12/18/2004 Bp Bruce Caldwell. m 10/11/1959 Nina Mae Walker c 3.

WALKER-SPRAGUE, Patricia Shields (Cal) 5653 Merriewood Dr, Oakland CA 94611 **P S Mk's Par Berkeley CA 1997-** B San Jose CA 1934 d Kenneth & Elizabeth. Rad 1952; BA U CA 1955; MBA City U of Seattle 1984; MDiv CDSP 1997. D 10/28/1989 Bp Robert Hume Cochrane P 12/6/1997 Bp William Edwin Swing. non-stipendiary P Assoc All Souls Par In Berkeley Berkeley CA 1998-2012; Non-par 1994-1997; Chapl Harborview Med Cntr Seattle WA 1989-1994; D S Paul's Ch Seattle WA 1989-1994. NAAD.

WALKLEY, Richard Nelson (Ga) 918 E Ridge Village Dr, Cutler Bay FL 33157 **Ret 1991-** B Chattanooga TN 1929 s Richard & Dorothy. BS U of Memphis 1952; GD Sewanee: The U So, TS 1955. D 7/2/1955 P 6/29/1956 Bp John Vander Horst. c 1. Int S Jn's Epis Ch Homestead FL 1990-1991, Int 1986-1987; Int Emm Epis Ch Hampton VA 1989-1990; Int S Steph's Ch Coconut Grove Miami FL 1987-1989; S Lk's Epis Hawkinsville GA 1982-1986; 1977-1982; Asst S Thos Epis Ch Thomasville GA 1972-1977; Asst S Jas Epis Ch Baton Rouge LA 1969-1972; Ch Of The Incarn Amite LA 1967-1969; Vic S Fran Ch Denham Spgs LA 1967-1969; R Trin Ch Demopolis AL 1962-1967; Vic S Tim's Ch Tanacross AK 1959-1962; Min in charge S Mary Magd Ch Fayetteville TN 1955-1959.

WALL, Anne Fuller (ECR) 535 Torrey Pine Pl, Arroyo Grande CA 93420 **S Steph's Epis Ch Sn Luis Obispo CA 2007-** B Chicago IL 1946 d Douglas & Ruth. BA Stan 1969; BA Sch for Deacons 1998. D 6/3/2000 Bp William Edwin Swing. m 7/8/1967 James Curtis Wall c 2. S Mk's Epis Ch Palo Alto CA 2004-2006; S Bede's Epis Ch Menlo Pk CA 2000-2008; Chapl Epis Chapl at Stan Hosp Stanfor 2000-2004; Mem/ COM Dio California San Francisco CA 2000-2007.

WALL, Daniel S (NC) **Ch Of The Ascen At Fork Advance NC 2017-; S Clem's Epis Ch Clemmons NC 2016-** B High Point NC 1952 s Hubert & Betty. BA High Point U 1974; MDiv Duke DS 1978. D 6/20/2015 Bp Michael B Curry P 12/20/2015 Bp Anne Hodges-Copple. father.dan@danswall.com

WALL, Henry Pickett (USC) 5220 Clemson Ave, Columbia SC 29206 B Columbia SC 1982 s Henry & Allison. BS Johnson and Wales 2008; MDiv GTS 2013; MDiv The GTS 2013. D 6/15/2013 P 2/20/2014 Bp Steven Andrew Miller. m 5/15/2008 Lee A Wall c 2. S Martins-In-The-Field Columbia SC 2015-2017; S Jn's Mltry Acad Delafield WI 2013-2015.

WALL JR, John Furman (Spr) 507 Hanover St, Fredericksburg VA 22401 B Boise ID 1931 s John & Helen. BS USMA 1956; MS Pr 1961; PhD Cor 1973; JD GW 1982; MA VTS 1995. D 9/19/1994 P 4/25/1995 Bp Peter Hess Beck-

W

with. m 6/30/1956 Suzanne J Wall c 3. P-in-c S Ptr's Port Royal Port Royal VA 2005-2009; P-in-c Cople Par Hague VA 1999-2003; Nomini Ch Mt Holly Hague VA 1999-2003; P-in-c S Jas Ch Tidwells Hague VA 1999-2003; Yeo-comico Ch Tucker Hill Hague VA 1999-2003; P-in-c S Alb's Epis Ch Olney IL 1994-1999; S Mary's Ch Robinson IL 1994-1999. "Numerous Sci And En-gr Treatises," 2003. Asce 1975; Crawford Cnty Ministral Assn 1994-1999; Dc Bar Assn 1985; Richland Cnty Ministral Assn 1994-1999; Soc Of The Cicinnati 1975. Fell Asce; Fell Same.

WALL, John N (NC) English Dept Of Box 8105, NC State University, Raleigh NC 27695 **Prof NC St U 1973-; P Assoc S Mk's Epis Ch Raleigh NC 1973-** B Wadesboro NC 1945 s John & Frances. BA U NC 1967; MA Duke 1969; MDiv EDS 1972; PhD Harv 1973. D 6/24/1972 P 6/1/1974 Bp Thomas Augustus Fraser Jr. m 8/22/1970 Terry Cobb Wall c 2. Int S Chris's Epis Ch Garner NC 1975; Cur S Jn's Chap Cambridge MA 1972-1973. Auth, "Virtual Paul's Cross Proj," *vpcp.chass.ncsu.edu*, NC St U, 2013; Auth, "A Dictionary for Episco-palians," Cowley, 2000; Auth, "A New Dictionary for Episcopalians," Harper-Collins, 1990; Auth, "Transformations of the Word," Univ of Georgia Press, 1988; Auth, "Geo Herbert: Engl Works," Paulist Press, 1980. Phi Beta Kappa 1966. Who's Who in the Wrld Marquis 2013; Fell Natl Hmnts Cntr 2013; Dig-ital Hmnts Grant Natl Endwmt for the Hmnts 2011; Holladay Medal NC St U 2003; Vstng Fell Wolfson Coll, Cambridge 2003; Fell Natl Hmnts Cntr 1980; Fell Mellon Fndt 1975; Acad hon Phi Kappa Phi 1972.

WALL, Richard David (WA) 2430 K Street NW, Washington DC 20037 **S Paul's Par Washington DC 2015-** B Wordsley England 1978 s Richard & Shirley. BA Oxf GB 1999; Dip St Stephens Hse Oxford 2002; MA Oxf GB 2004. Trans 7/24/2006 as Priest Bp Charles Ellsworth Bennison Jr. R S Andr's Ch St Coll PA 2009-2015; Cur S Clements Ch Philadelphia PA 2005-2009; Serv Ch of Engl 2002-2005. wall@stpauls-kst.org

WALL, Sean (Ore) 2201 SW Vermont St, Portland OR 97219 **S Barn Par Port-land OR 2013-** B Fairfield CA 1967 s John & Susan Jane. BS U of Idaho 1989; MDiv CDSP 2013; MDiv CDSP 2013. D 7/6/2013 P 1/4/2014 Bp Michael Han-ley. m 5/20/1989 Melissa Susan Wall c 4. Chr Ch Par Lake Oswego OR 2013.

WALLACE, Arland Lee (Kan) 8021 W 21st St N, Wichita KS 67205 B Spring-field MO 1952 s Ted & Mildred. Assoc Sch of Radiologic Tech 1973; Assoc Sch of Radiologic Tech 1973; Bp Kemper Sch of Mnstry 2015. D 6/13/2015 Bp Dean E Wolfe.

WALLACE, Gene Richard (Los) 1775 Wilson Ave, Upland CA 91784 B Fall River MA 1948 s Irving & Dolores. BA Bridgewater Coll 1970; MA EDS 1984; PsyD California Grad Inst 2008. D 5/28/1983 Bp John Bowen Coburn P 5/1/1984 Bp John Melville Burgess. Mng Dir Cntr for Process Stds: Process and Faith 2013-2014; R Ch Of The Trsfg Arcadia CA 1995-2008; R S Geo's Ch Riverside CA 1986-1995; Assoc R S Mich And All Ang Par Corona Dl Mar CA 1984-1986; D S Paul's Ch Brockton MA 1983-1984. wallace.gene48@gmail.com

WALLACE, Hugh J (SC) 10172 Ocean Hwy, Pawleys Island SC 29585 **Calv Ch Americus GA 2015-** B Albany GA 1956 s William & Lucy. BA Lenoir-Rhyne Coll 1979; MDiv Luth Theol Sthrn Sem 1984. D 6/7/2007 P 12/13/2007 Bp Ed-ward Lloyd Salmon Jr. m 6/3/1978 Stephanie Stout Wallace c 4. P Assoc Chr the King Pawleys Island SC 2009-2012.

WALLACE JR, James Edward (ETenn) Po Box 3073, Montgomery AL 36109 **R S Mart Of Tours Epis Ch Chattanooga TN 2011-** B Pittsburgh PA 1953 s James & Marian. BA SUNY 1975; MDiv VTS 1981. D 6/10/1981 Bp Harold Barrett Robinson P 12/1/1981 Bp Furman Charles Stough. R All SS Ch Mont-gomery AL 1996-2011; S Paul's Ch Kansas City MO 1995-1996; Assoc S Jn's Ch Montgomery AL 1991-1994; Ch Of The Resurr Rainbow City AL 1983-1991; Cur S Lk's Epis Ch Birmingham AL 1981-1983. EDEO 1998.

WALLACE, John Bruce (EMich) 5845 Berry Lane, Indian River MI 49749 **Tchg Chapl Healthcare Chapl Mnstry Assn 2003-; Chapl Cheboygan Cnty Sher-rif 1995-; Dir of Pstr Care Cheboygan Memi Hosp Cheboygan MI 1992-** B MI 1934 s John & Cecilia. Lawr Tech U; U MI; EFM Sewanee: The U So, TS 1996; BSW Madonna U 2003. D 10/1/1995 Bp H Coleman Mcgehee Jr. m 8/10/1996 Mary Lynn Kraywinkel. D Trsfg Epis Ch Indn River MI 1995-2006.

WALLACE, John Robert (Pa) 736 11th Ave, Prospect Park PA 19076 **Mem Dio of the Cntrl Gulf Coast Cmsn on Yth Mnstry 2004-; R St. Mary's Epsico-pal Ch Mi ton 2004-** B Wilmington DE 1953 s William & Frances. BA U of W Florida 1976; MDiv Epis TS of the SW 2003. D 1/18/2003 P 9/9/2004 Bp Wayne Wright. m 7/4/1992 Patricia A Wallace c 2. S Jas Epis Ch Prospect Pk PA 2012-2016; Memi Ch Of The H Nativ Jenkintown PA 2009-2011; S Mary's Epis Ch Milton FL 2004-2009; S Mich's Ch Austin TX 2003-2004; Chapl So Austin Hosp Austin TX 2003-2004. Assoc SHN 2002.

WALLACE, Kathryn McLaughlin (NCal) 4308 Wood St, Dunsmuir CA 96025 B Houston TX 1944 d James & Josephine. BA Sch for Deacons 2014. D 6/14/2014 Bp Barry Leigh Beisner. c 2.

WALLACE, Lance S (SwFla) 5250 Championship Cup Ln, Spring Hill FL 34609 **R S Andr's Epis Ch Sprg Hill FL 2013-; Stndg Com Dio SW Florida Parrish FL 2014-** B Minneapolis MN 1953 s Benjamin & Ilene. MTS Re-formed TS 2007; Cert Ang Stud Nash 2010; Cert Ang Stud Nash 2010. D 6/5/

2010 P 12/7/2010 Bp John Wadsworth Howe. m 5/23/2003 Diane L Wallace. P Ch Of The Redeem Sarasota FL 2010-2013. fr.lwallace@gmail.com

WALLACE, Martha Ellen (WA) 530 SW Cove Pt, Depoe Bay OR 97341 B Steubenville OH 1948 d John & Ona. BA VPI 1971; JD Suffolk Law Sch 1976; MS MIT 1983; MDiv SWTS 1999. D 6/26/1999 P 6/22/2000 Bp R aymond Stewart Wood Jr. m 1/4/1986 Dennis C White. Emm Epis Ch Alexandria MN 2011-2013; Emm Epis Ch Alexandria VA 2011-2013; Gr Ch Washington DC 2011; Int Chr Ch Capitol Hill Washington DC 2008-2010; Int S Andr's Epis Ch Coll Pk MD 2007-2008; Assoc R S Paul's Epis Ch Piney Waldorf MD 2006-2007; S Clare Of Assisi Epis Ch Ann Arbor MI 2004-2006; Asst Chr Ch Grosse Pointe Grosse Pointe Farms MI 2002-2004; All SS Epis Ch Pontiac MI 2000-2002. Alfred P Sloan Fell MIT 1982. girlpriestwhalecove@gmail.com

WALLACE, Peter Marsden (At) 2920 Landrum Education Dr, Oakwood GA 30566 **Epis Media Cntr Inc Atlanta GA 2017-, 2001-2014; S Gabr's Epis Ch Oakwood GA 2016-** B Parkersburg WV 1954 s Aldred & Margaret. BA Marshall U 1976; ThM Dallas TS 1984; Angl Stds Candler TS Emory U 2013. D 12/21/2013 P 6/21/2014 Bp Robert Christopher Wright. m 8/23/2014 Daniel Scott Le c 2. S Paul's Epis Ch Newnan GA 2014-2016. Auth, "Getting to Know Jesus (Again)," *Bk*, Ch Pub, 2017; Auth, "The Passionate Jesus," *Bk*, SkyLight Paths, 2012; Auth, "Connected," *Bk*, Ch Pub, 2010; Auth, "Living Loved," *Bk*, Ch Pub, 2008. pwallace@day1.org

WALLACE, Robert Edgar (FdL) 2140 Bonnycastle Ave Apt 9B, Louisville KY 40205 **R S Mths' Manitowish Waters Cong Manitowish Waters WI 1993-** B Osceola IA 1957 s Robert & Betty. BA Morningside Coll 1980; MDiv SWTS 1984. D 5/21/1984 Bp Walter Cameron Righter P 3/29/1985 Bp Gerald Nicholas Mcallister. m 6/15/2017 William Lloyd Bippus. R S Mths Minocqua WI 1990-2014; Asst To Dn S Paul's Epis Cathd Fond Du Lac WI 1986-1989; Cur S Lk's Epis Ch Ada OK 1984-1986; Vic S Tim's Epis Ch Pauls Vlly OK 1984-1986; Trst Bexley Seabury Fed Chicago IL 1994-1996. Conf Of The Blessed Sacrement - Gnrl Secy 1983; SHN - Assoc 1983.

WALLACE, Sean M (NY) 119 E 74th St, New York NY 10021 **Cur Ch Of The Resurr New York NY 2009-** B Ft Smith AR 1966 s James & Martha. BMus Jn Br 1989; MM Eastman Sch of Mus 1993; DMus MI SU 2000; MDiv GTS 2009. D 12/27/2008 Bp Charles Edward Jenkins III P 7/24/2009 Bp Herbert Alcorn Donovan Jr. m 8/5/1989 Marcia Wallace c 2.

WALLACE, Tanya R (WMass) 7 Woodbridge St, South Hadley MA 01075 **R All SS Ch So Hadley MA 2009-; Dio Wstrn Massachusetts Springfield 2009-** B Montague MA 1972 BA Mt Holyoke Coll 1994; MDiv UTS 2000. D 6/10/2000 P 12/16/2000 Bp John Palmer Croneberger. m 11/19/1999 Kathleen West c 1. Cn Cathd Ch Of S Paul Burlington VT 2002-2009; Cur Ch Of The Ascen New York NY 2000-2002. "Abraham and Isaac Revisited," Out in the Mountains, 2003; "The Face in the Mirror," St. Lk's Revs, 1999. EWC 1996; OSH - Assoc 1997.

WALLACE, Thomas (Tex) 407 E 22nd Ave, Belton TX 76513 B Houston TX 1946 s Howard & Lois. BA U of Texas at Austin 1969; MDiv VTS 1972. D 6/28/1972 Bp Frederick P Goddard P 6/20/1973 Bp James Milton Richardson. m 11/26/1970 Patricia Ann Skutca c 2. S Lk's Epis Ch Salado TX 1998-2006; Dioc Depatment of Cmncatn Mem Dio Texas Houston TX 1992-1995, Dn of the Cntrl Convoc 1996-1998, Texas Epis Ed Bd Mem 1991-1995, Dioc Exec Bd Mem 1989-1992, Dioc Day Sch Cmsn Mem 1988-2000, Dioc Dept. of CE Mem 1981-1990; R S Mary's Ch Bellville TX 1981-1998; Assoc R S Mk's Ch Beau-mont TX 1974-1981; Vic S Lk's Ch Livingston TX 1972-1974; Vic S Paul's Epis Ch Woodville TX 1972-1974.

WALLACE, William Lewis (Los) 1448 15th St Ste 203, Santa Monica CA 90404 **Asst The Par Of S Matt Pacific Plsds CA 1983-; Non-par 1976-** B Santa Monica CA 1939 s Maurice & Deane. BA California St U Northridge 1962; MDiv CDSP 1965; MA Peabody Coll 1972; PhD Peabody Coll 1978. D 9/1/1965 Bp Robert Claflin Rusack P 6/15/1966 Bp Francis E I Bloy. m 7/23/1960 Sarah Wallace. Asst S Phil's Epis Ch Laurel MD 2002-2003; Asst Prof Fuller TS Pasadena CA 1976-1983; Asst S Geo's Ch Nashville TN 1973-1975; P-in-c Ch Of The H Trin Nashville TN 1971-1973; Asst S Mart-In-The-Fields Par Winnetka CA 1966-1968; Cur S Mk's Par Glendale CA 1965-1966. APA 1978; California Psychol Assn 1976; Los Angeles Cnty Psychol Assn 1992. Hlth Plcy Fell APA 2002; Pres Ca Psych Assn 1999; Pres Los Angeles Cnty Psych Assn 1995.

WALLACE-WILLIAMS, Joseph Anthony (WTenn) Grace - St Lukes Episcopal Church, 1720 Peabody Ave, Memphis TN 38104 B New Orleans LA 1984 s John & Lora. BGS Nicholls St U 2008; MDiv Sewanee: The U So, TS 2012; MDiv The TS at The U So 2012. D 12/17/2011 P 6/23/2012 Bp Morris King Thompson Jr. Gr - S Lk's Ch Memphis TN 2012-2014.

WALLENS, Michael Gary (Tex) 510 North 2nd St., Alpine TX 79830 **Chapl St. Steph's Sch Austin TX 2009-** B Chicago IL 1950 s Richard & Barbara. BS U So 1972; MDiv GTS 1978. D 6/17/1978 Bp Quintin Ebenezer Primo Jr P 12/16/1978 Bp James Winchester Montgomery. m 1/20/1973 Susan Patricia Wal-lens c 2. Epis Ch Of The Redeem Irving TX 2014-2016; Cbury Epis Sch Des-oto TX 2013-2016; S Mart In The Fields Ch Keller TX 2013-2014; Chapl Epis Sch Of Dallas Dallas TX 2012-2013; S Steph's Epis Sch Austin TX 2009-2012;

Int S Thos' Ch Garrison Forest Owings Mills MD 2007-2009; Trin Ch Towson MD 2004-2005; Epis Ch Of Chr The King Baltimore MD 2004; Int Old St. Paul's Baltimore MD 2003-2004; Int S Paul's Par Baltimore MD 2002-2004; S Paul's Sch Brooklandville MD 1998-2007; Chapl S Paul's Sch MD 1998-2007; Hd Chapl H Innoc Ch (Epis Sch) Atlanta GA 1994-1998; H Innoc Ch Atlanta GA 1994-1998; H Innoc' Epis Sch Atlanta GA 1994-1998; S Marg Of Scotland Par San Juan Capo CA 1991-1994; Chapl St. Marg Epis Sch San Juan Capistrano CA 1991-1994; Chapl The S Mich Sch Dallas TX 1988-1991; S Mich And All Ang Ch Dallas TX 1982-1991; Dio Chicago Chicago IL 1981-1982; St Cyprians Ch Chicago IL 1980-1981; S Mary Magd Villa Pk IL 1978-1979. michaelwallens@gmail.com

WALLER, Clifford Scott (WTex) Po Box 12349, San Antonio TX 78212 B El Paso TX 1935 s Clifford & Ona. BA Trin U San Antonio 1957; MDiv EDS 1960. D 7/7/1960 Bp Everett H Jones P 1/25/1961 Bp Donald J Campbell. m 8/25/1956 Elizabeth S Waller c 2. Int S Dav's Epis Ch San Antonio TX 1997-1998; Assoc R S Phil's Ch San Antonio TX 1990-1996; Dio W Texas San Antonio TX 1987-1989, Headmaster, Texas Mltry Inst 1987-1989, 1980-1983, Instnl Chapl Of W Texas 1962-1966; Epis Ch Cntr New York NY 1983-1985; Ch Of The H Sprt San Antonio TX 1981-1983; P-in-c Santa Fe Epis Mssn San Antonio TX 1966-1979; S Mk's Epis Ch San Antonio TX 1962-1966. Auth, "Human Sxlty: A Chr Perspective". Worker Sis/Brothers Of The H Sprt, Comp; Wtex Cleric Assn. DD Epis Sem of the SW 1986.

WALLER, Ryan C (Dal) B 1982 D 1/6/2017 Bp George Robinson Sumner Jr. m 12/29/2016 Caroline R Waller c 2.

WALLER, Stephen Jay (Dal) 8108 Crowberry Lane, Irving TX 75063 B Shreveport LA 1946 s Morgan & Elizabeth. BA W&L 1969; MDiv GTS 1972. D 6/9/1972 Bp Reginald Heber Gooden P 2/24/1973 Bp Iveson Batchelor Noland. R The Epis Ch Of S Thos The Apos Dallas TX 1989-2012; R S Tim's Ch Milwaukee WI 1981-1989; Vic S Alb's Epis Ch Monroe LA 1977-1981; Cur Trin Epis Ch Baton Rouge LA 1973-1977; Cur Ch Of The Redeem Ruston LA 1973; Cur S Lk's Chap Grambling LA 1973; Dio Louisiana New Orleans LA 1972-1973; Asst Chapl Louisiana Tech U Ruston LA 1972-1973. Bk, "Our Souls in Silence Wait," PDQ Press, Dallas. Soc of S Fran - Tertiary 1983.

WALLEY, Kent R (NJ) 182 Main St, P.O. Box 605, Gladstone NJ 07934 **R S Lk's Ch Gladstone NJ 2008-** B Pittsburgh PA 1961 s Richard & Mary. BD U MI 1983; MDiv TESM 1999; DMIN Fuller TS 2012. D 6/12/1999 Bp Robert William Duncan P 1/30/2000 Bp Edward Lloyd Salmon Jr. m 6/6/1987 Joy Walley c 2. Assoc R S Lk's Epis Ch Hilton Hd Island SC 1999-2007.

WALLEY, Seth Martin (Miss) 113 S 9th St, Oxford MS 38655 **Assoc S Jas Ch Jackson MS 2013-; Mssnr St. Steph's Epis Ch Batesville MS 2011-; Chapl The Epis Ch at Ole Miss 2011-** B Ocean Springs MS 1986 s Glennis & Sally. BBA The U of Mississippi 2008; MDiv VTS 2011. D 6/4/2011 P 1/22/2012 Bp Duncan Montgomery Gray III. m 4/16/2016 Jessica Lynn Douglas. S Ptr's Ch Oxford MS 2011-2013.

WALLING II, Albert Clinton (Tex) 8406 Lofty Ln, Round Rock TX 78681 **Died 1/5/2017** B Fort Lauderdale FL 1925 s Jacob & Nora. U San Luis Potosi Mx 1945; BA Trin U San Antonio 1948; MDiv EDS 1953; Harv 1963; SMU 1972; STM Sewanee: The U So, TS 1973; Van 1975; DMin Sewanee: The U So, TS 1977. D 7/15/1953 P 1/25/1954 Bp Everett H Jones. m 12/26/1964 Carroll W Walling c 2. H Sprt Epis Ch Houston TX 1982; R S Alb's Ch Houston TX 1977-1982; Assoc R S Mk's Ch Houston TX 1974-1977; Chair Strng Com S Mk's Sr Citizen's Cntr Houston TX 1974-1977; U So 1972-1974; R Epis Ch Of The Ascen Dallas TX 1971-1974; R Ch Of The Gd Shpd Terrell TX 1966-1971; Epis Chapl Terrell St Hosp Terrell TX 1966-1971; Assoc S Jn's Ch Ft Worth TX 1964-1966; Vic S Nich Ft Worth TX 1961-1964; Ch Of The H Fam Mc Kinney TX 1960-1961; Prncpl S Sav Sch Mckinney TX 1960-1961; Asst R S Dav's Ch Austin TX 1954-1960; D All SS Epis Ch Pleasanton TX 1953-1954; Epis Ch Of The Gd Shepard Geo W TX 1953-1954. Auth, "Battle Memories in the Lone Star Star St," *Clan Chisholm Journ*, 1975; Auth, "The Puritan Concept of God in Cov w Engl as Seen in the Founding of Jamestowne VA," *Thesis*, U So, 1973. Ch Hist Soc; Rel Speech Assn. Dep to Prov Syn Dio Dallas 1970; Trst U So Dio Dallas 1968.

WALLING, Ann Boult (Tenn) 6501 Pennywell Dr, Nashville TN 37205 B Nashville TN 1939 d Reber & Olivia. BA Van 1962; MA Scaritt Coll 1977; Diac Trng SC 1997; Sewanee: The U So, TS 2000. D 9/14/1997 Bp Edward Lloyd Salmon Jr P 10/4/2000 Bp Bertram Nelson Herlong. m 7/19/1975 Clarence Dallas Walling c 4. Asst S Dav's Epis Ch Nashville TN 2000-2009; D All SS Ch Hilton Hd Island SC 1997-2000. EWC; Interfaith Allnce; NAAD. Bp Gray Temple Human Relatns Awd Dio So Carolina 1984.

WALLING, Carolyn M (U) B London UK 1947 d Alfred & Kathleen. Dartington 1968; Rolle Coll U 1969; MDiv EDS 1987. D 12/14/1986 P 6/1/1987 Bp Otis Charles. m 8/4/1972 Brian Walling. Cur S Mary Angl Battersea Engl 1991-1994; Chapl Gulf Dhahran 1988-1990; Asst Cbury Grp Dio Cyprus & Gulf Dhahran 1987-1988; Bp'S Cur-In-Charge Calv Par; Chapl Sligo Grammar Sch.

WALLING, Charles Edward (Miss) 4394 E Falcon Dr, Fayetteville AR 72701 **Asst S Paul's Ch Fayetteville AR 2000-** B West Keansburg NJ 1937 s Alfred & Edna. MTh PDS 1962; BA U of Nthrn Colorado 1962. D 4/28/1962 P 10/27/1962 Bp Alfred L Banyard. m 7/14/2014 Betty L Wright-Walling c 3. R S Jn's Ch Aberdeen MS 1995-2000; R S Jn's Ch Harrison AR 1987-1995; Epis Campus Mnstry Dio W Missouri Kansas City MO 1984-1987; R S Barn Epis Ch Denton TX 1975-1984; R S Mths Ch Hamilton NJ 1969-1975; R S Lk's Ch Westville NJ 1965-1969; Vic Our Sav Cheesequake NJ 1962-1965.

WALLINGFORD, Katharine Tapers (Tex) 6221 Main St, Houston TX 77030 **Asstg P Palmer Memi Ch Houston TX 2006-, Assoc 2003-2006** B Tallahassee FL 1940 d John & Alma. BA Randolph-Macon Wmn's Coll 1962; JD Harv 1965; PhD Rice U 1984. D 6/21/2003 P 1/21/2004 Bp Don Adger Wimberly. m 7/22/1966 John Rufus Wallingford c 2. Auth, "Robert Lowell's Lang of the Self," Univ. of No Carolina Press, 1988.

WALLIS, Benjamin E (Pa) Church of the Epiphany, 115 Jefferson Ave, Danville VA 24541 **Incarn H Sacr Epis Ch Drexel Hill PA 2013-; The Ch Of The H Comf Drexel Hill PA 2013-** B Chambersburg, PA 1983 s David & Ruth. BA Estrn U 2006; MDiv GTS 2012; MDiv The GTS 2012. D 6/9/2012 Bp Charles Ellsworth Bennison Jr P 1/12/2013 Bp Edward Lewis Lee Jr. m 8/5/2006 Cori L Wallis c 1. Ch Of The Epiph Danville VA 2012-2013. fatherben@ihschurch.org

WALLIS, Hugh W (Colo) 1005 S Gilpin St, Denver CO 80209 B Denver CO 1942 s Hugh & Clarissa. BA U of Pennsylvania 1965; BD Nash 1968. D 6/11/1968 Bp Joseph Summerville Minnis P 12/1/1968 Bp Edwin B Thayer. Dio Colorado Denver CO 1973-1980; S Andr's Epis Ch Ft Lupton CO 1973-1980; P-in-c S Eliz's Epis Ch Brighton CO 1973-1980; Cur Epis Ch Of S Ptr And S Mary Denver CO 1971-1973; Cur The Ch Of The Ascen Denver CO 1969-1971; Cur S Gabr The Archangel Englewood NJ 1968-1969.

WALLIS, James Howard (Nev) 2528 Silverton Drive, Las Vegas NV 89134 **Assoc Gr In The Desert Epis Ch Las Vegas NV 2002-; Prof Coll of Sthrn Nevada 1996-; Adj Prof U of Nevada Las Vegas 1996-** B Pontiac MI 1943 s Olis & Opal. BA Wayne 1968; MA Wayne 1976; MDiv EDS 1981; MA Claremont Grad U 1988; PhD Claremont Grad U 1993. D 6/13/1981 P 6/13/1982 Bp H Coleman Mcgehee Jr. m 12/23/2016 Soon Bock Moon Wallis. R S Mk's Ch Detroit MI 1989-1994; Asstg S Mk's Epis Ch Upland CA 1985-1989; Asst R S Chris-S Paul Epis Ch Detroit MI 1982-1985; Asst Ch Of The Resurr Ecorse MI 1981-1982; Mnstry Dvlpmt Cmsn, Mem Dio Nevada Las Vegas 2011-2014, Supply P 1998-2011. Auth, "The Interfaith Coun of Sthrn Nevada and the Interreligious Dialogue," *Far-W Amer Culture Assn*, 2010; Auth, "Irving Greenberg's Contribution to Holocaust Stds," *Far-W Amer Culture Asso.*, 2005; Auth, "L.L. Langer's Contribution to Holocaust Stds," *Far-W Amer Culture Asso.*, 2004; Auth, "The Holocaust: Theodicy and Anti-Theodicy," *Far-W Amer Culture Assn*, 2003; Auth, "Rel Responses to the Holocaust," *Far-W Amer Culture Assn*, 2001; Auth, "Rel in Amer Today," *Far-W Amer Culture Assn*, 2000; Auth, "Post-Holocaust Chrsnty," U Press of Amer, Inc, 1997. AAR 1985; Amer Philos Assn 1985; Cntr for Process Stds 1985; Interfaith Coun of Sthrn Nevada 2002; SBL 1985. Fllshp - Seminar in Jeruselam Natl Conf of Chr and Jews, (NY,NY) 1987; Gr Schlrshp Claremont Grad U 1986.

WALLNER, Frank (Pa) 404 Levering Mill Rd., Bala Cynwyd PA 19004 **Vic S Dav's Ch Philadelphia PA 2011-; R S Jn's Ch Bala Cynwyd PA 2008-** B New York NY 1946 s Frank & Jean. SWTS; BS U of Scranton 1968; MS SUNY 1972; EdM Col 1982; MDiv GTS 1986. D 6/7/1986 P 1/15/1987 Bp Paul Moore Jr. c 1. R Ch Of The H Cross Kingston NY 1990-2008; Cur Gr Ch Middletown NY 1986-1990.

WALLNER, Ludwig John (Alb) 11631 Scenic Hills Blvd., Hudson FL 34667 B New York NY 1941 s Ludwig & Antonette. AAS Orange Cnty Cmnty Coll 1961; BS SUNY 1964; MS SUNY 1967; CAS SUNY 1972; EdD Highland U Athens TN 1982. D 1/4/2003 Bp Daniel William Herzog. m 12/19/1964 Carolyn Elizabeth Wallner c 2. D S Jn's Epis Ch Brooksville FL 2013-2015; D S Andr's Epis Ch Sprg Hill FL 2008-2012; D S Mary's Ch Lake Luzerne NY 2004-2007; D The Ch Of The Mssh Glens Falls NY 2003-2005.

WALLS, Alfonso S (Los) 9324 Capobella, Aliso Viejo CA 92656 B Mexico City MX 1975 s Lourdes. BA S Ambr U Davenport IA 2000; MDiv SWTS 2006. D 6/3/2006 Bp Joseph Jon Bruno. Asst S Clem's-By-The-Sea Par San Clemente CA 2006.

WALMER, Corey Ann (Me) St Luke's Episcopal Church, PO Box 249, Farmington ME 04938 **Bd Deacons Dio Maine Portland ME 2014-** B Pueblo CO 1959 d Allen & Mary Jane. Bus Gnrl Stds U of Maine at Farmington 2001; Bachelor's Gnrl Stds U of Maine at Farmington 2001; MSW U of Maine 2004; Cert. Advncd Study Smith 2011. D 6/29/2013 Bp Stephen Taylor Lane. m 7/9/1980 Robert Timothy Walmer c 2.

WALMER, Robert Timothy (Me) 368 Knowlton Corner Rd, Farmington ME 04938 **Dio Maine Portland ME 1997-; S Lk's Ch Farmington ME 1997-** B Beloit KS 1950 s Paul & Crystal. BA U of Sthrn Colorado 1972; MDiv VTS 1984. D 6/16/1984 P 12/1/1984 Bp William Carl Frey. m 7/9/1980 Corey Ann Griffith c 2. S Alb's Ch Worland WY 1986-1997; S Alb's Ch Windsor CO 1986-1996; Vic S Mk's Ch Craig CO 1984-1986.

WALMISLEY, Andrew John (Haw) Po Box 625, Point Reyes Station CA 94956 B Fareham Hants UK 1955 s Raymond & Elaine. BA U of Exeter Gb 1975;

Bourguiba Sch 1976; U of Cambridge 1978; MA San Francisco St U 1990. Trans 11/1/1981. m 6/17/2008 Jonathan Walter Allen c 2. Assoc S Jn's Epis Ch Kula HI 2007-2012; Seabury Hall Makawao HI 2007-2012; R All Souls Par In Berkeley Berkeley CA 1997-2007; R S Ptr's Epis Ch Redwood City CA 1993-1997; Chapl Trin Par New York NY 1990-1993; Trin Sch New York NY 1990-1993; Chapl S Matt's Epis Ch San Mateo CA 1986-1990; Asst The Epis Ch Of S Mary The Vrgn San Francisco CA 1983-1986; Asst Chr Ch Portola Vlly CA 1981-1983; Serv Ch Of Engl 1978-1981.

✠ WALMSLEY, The Rt Rev Arthur Edward (Ct) 644 Old County Rd, Deering NH 03244 B New Bedford MA 1928 s Harry & Elizabeth. BA Trin Hartford CT 1948; MDiv EDS 1951; DHum New Engl Coll 1972; Ya Berk 1980; Trin Hartford CT 1982. D 6/8/1951 Bp Norman B Nash P 5/1/1952 Bp Arthur C Lichtenberger Con 10/27/1979 for Ct. m 12/29/1954 Roberta Brownell Walmsley c 2. Bp Of Connecticut Dio Connecticut Meriden CT 1981-1993, Bp Coadj 1979-1981; R S Paul And S Jas New Haven CT 1974-1979; Dep to R Trin Par New York NY 1972-1974; Gnrl Secy MA Coun of Ch 1969-1972; P-in-c Gr Ch Amherst MA 1968-1969; Assoc Dir Dep't of Chr Soc Relatns 1958-1968; Ch Of The Ascen S Louis MO 1953-1955; Trin Ch S Louis MO 1953-1955; R H Apos S Louis MO 1952-1953; Cur H Apos S Louis MO 1951-1952; BEC Dio Missouri S Louis MO 1953-1958. Auth, *Ch In a Soc of Abundance*. Pi Gamma Mu; Phi Beta Kappa.

WALMSLEY, John W (CFla) 367 Jaybee Ave, Davenport FL 33897 B England 1937 s George & Kathleen. BA Wycliffe Hall Oxford 1968; MA Hiju U 1972; PLD Hiju U 1980. Trans 4/23/2007 Bp John Wadsworth Howe. m 6/27/1997 Patricia Ann Walmsley c 2. S Mk's Epis Ch Haines City FL 2007-2009.

WALN, William W (WK) D Gr Epis Ch Hutchinson KS 2015- B Valentine, NE 1969 s Clarence & Carol. BA-Orgnztn Ldrshp Ft Hays St U 2005; Bp Kemper Sch for Mnstry 2015. D 12/12/2015 P 12/10/2016 Bp Mike Milliken. m 6/5/1993 Michelle M Denaeyer c 3.

WALPOLE, Lisa Calhoun (SC) 464 Golf Dr, Georgetown SC 29440 Archd So Carolina Charleston SC 2013-, 1999-2003; Vic Gr Ch Cathd Charleston SC 2009- B Charleston SC 1968 BA Clemson U 1990; MDiv Sewanee: The U So, TS 2005. D 6/25/2005 P 12/17/2005 Bp Edward Lloyd Salmon Jr. Asst H Cross Faith Memi Epis Ch Pawleys Island SC 2005-2008.

WALSER, Gay Craggs (WNY) 119 N Ellicott St, Williamsville NY 14221 Ret 2003- B Colon Panama 1937 d Hugh & Gay. Dioc Prog; Katharine Gibbs Sch. D 6/9/1984 Bp Harold Barrett Robinson. c 5. D Calv Epis Ch Williamsville NY 1993-2003; Pstr's Asst S Mk's Ch Buffalo NY 1984-1990.

WALSH, Eileen Patricia (SVa) 519 W 20th St Apt 303, Norfolk VA 23517 R S Chris's Epis Ch Portsmouth VA 2005- B Bristol PA 1959 d William & Virginia. BS Bloomsburg U of Pennsylvania 1981; MDiv GTS 2002. D 6/15/2002 P 1/6/2003 Bp David Conner Bane Jr. Ch Of The Ascen Norfolk VA 2002-2005.

WALSH, Lora (Ark) 617 N Mount Olive St, Siloam Springs AR 72761 S Paul's Ch Fayetteville AR 2012- B 1978 d James & Carol. BA Pepperdine U 2000; Cert SWTS 2009; PhD NWU 2010. D 6/4/2011 P 12/10/2011 Bp Jeff Lee. m 5/30/2009 Joshua Smith. Gr Ch Siloam Sprg AR 2013-2016; Epis Chars And Cmnty Serv (Eccs) Chicago IL 2011-2012. lorawalsh@gmail.com

WALSH, Paul David (Ida) 1565 E 10th N, Mountain Home ID 83647 D S Jas Ch Mtn Hm ID 1998- B Saint Paul MN 1964 s Gregory & Carolyn. D 10/31/1998 Bp John Stuart Thornton. m 8/28/1987 Dale Skeen.

WALSH, Peter F (Ct) 111 Oenoke Rdg, New Canaan CT 06840 R S Mk's Ch New Canaan CT 2008- B Buffalo NY 1959 s Frederick & Breffny. BA Harv 1983; MDiv Ya Berk 1992. D 6/11/1994 P 12/10/1994 Bp Richard Frank Grein. m 10/4/1986 Jennifer W Walsh c 5. R All SS Ch Phoenix AZ 2003-2008; Assoc S Paul's Epis Ch Cleveland OH 1996-2003; Kent Sch Kent CT 1994-1996; Chapl Kent Sch Kent CT 1992-1997. Assoc, SSJE 1992.

WALSH, Ruth Dimock (Va) 16640 Harwood Oaks Ct Apt 101, Dumfries VA 22026 B Greenwich CT 1941 d Thomas & Mabel. BA Amer U 1980; MDiv VTS 1991. D 12/10/1991 Bp Peter J Lee P 6/1/1992 Bp Robert Poland Atkinson. Goodwin Hse Incorporated Alexandria VA 1998-2008; Int All SS Ch Alexandria VA 1996-1998; S Jas' Epis Ch Mt Vernon VA 1995-1996; Int S Jas Alexandria VA 1994-1996; Assoc R S Mk's Ch Alexandria VA 1991-1992. Dok.

WALSH-MINOR, Gina (SwFla) 1A Hamilton Avenue, Cranford NJ 07016 B Manhattan NY 1950 d Albert & Marguerite. BA Florida Atlantic U 1974; MEd U of Miami 1976; EdD U of Miami 1997; MDiv GTS 2003. D 6/21/2003 Bp Leo Frade P 1/17/2004 Bp George Edward Councell. c 4. S Alfred's Epis Ch Palm Harbor FL 2015-2017; R Trin Epis Ch Cranford NJ 2008-2015; Int S Jas Ch Long Branch NJ 2007; Vic Ch Of S Clem Of Rome Belford NJ 2004-2007; Vic S Mary'The Vrgn Epis Ch Keyport NJ 2004-2006; Vic S Mary's Ch Keyport NJ 2004-2006.

WALSTON, Gerald Wayne (Fla) 1718 Oakbreeze Ln, Jacksonville Beach FL 32250 B Sasakwa OK 1938 s Kenneth & Eunice. AA Jacksonville Jr Coll Jackson TN 1976; LTh Sewanee: The U So, TS 1979. D 6/5/1979 P 12/18/1979 Bp Frank S Cerveny. c 3. R Resurr Epis Ch Jacksonville FL 2005-2011; R Resurr Jacksonville FL 2005-2009; Vic Resurr Jacksonville FL 2005-2009; Assoc Chr

Epis Ch Ponte Vedra FL 1987-2004, Asst 1979-1981; R S Lk's Epis Ch Jacksonville FL 1981-1987. Cmnty Of S Mary 1979.

WALTER, Andrew Wallace (WA) Grace Episcopal Church, 1607 Grace Church Rd, Silver Spring MD 20910 R Gr Epis Ch Silver Sprg MD 2011- B Tarrytown NY 1963 s John & Christine. BA Buc 1986; MDiv GTS 2007. D 3/10/2007 P 9/15/2007 Bp Mark Sean Sisk. m 9/6/1986 Susan Walter c 3. Assoc R S Lk's Par Darien CT 2007-2011.

WALTER, Aran Evan (FdL) St Thomas Episcopal Church, 226 Washington St, Menasha WI 54952 Assoc S Thos Ch Menasha WI 2013-, 1998-2012 B Green Bay WI 1972 s Anthony & Jennifer. Jesus St. Geo's Coll - Jerusalem; BA Lawr 1995; MAME-YM TESM 1998; MAME-YM TESM 1998. D 12/15/2012 P 6/22/2013 Bp Russell Edward Jacobus. m 7/15/1995 Shannon Leigh Townsend c 4. Writer, "Chr Ethics from Hollywood? Captain Amer: Civil War," *Chr Ethics from Hollywood? Captain Amer: Civil War*, www.buildfaith.org, 2016; Writer, "Film Sch, for Sunday Sch," *Film Sch, for Sunday Sch*, www.buildfaith.org, 2016. aranwalter@gmail.com

WALTER, Cynthia Byers (WVa) PO Box 4063, Table Rock Lane, Wheeling WV 26003 R The Lawrencefield Chap Par Wheeling WV 2006- B Winchester MA 1955 d William & Dorothy. Doctor of Mnstry VTS; BA U of Virginia 1977; MDiv VTS 2003. D 6/14/2003 P 12/20/2003 Bp Peter J Lee. m 5/21/1977 Richard William Walter c 2. COM Dio W Virginia Charleston WV 2011-2014, Dn, Nthrn Reg 2011-2014, Sandscrest Bd 2010-2016, Chair, BEC 2010-; Asst R/Dre Chr Ch Par Kensington MD 2003-2006. Auth, "How Fostering Sprtl Pract Builds Sprtl Confidence," *Doctoral Thesis*, Unpublished, 2017. Dudley Prize VTS 2003; Phi Beta Kappa U of Virginia 1977. info@lawrencefield.comcastbiz.net

WALTER, Francis Xavier (Ala) 100 Rattlesnake Spring Ln, Sewanee TN 37375 Ret 2000- B Mobile AL 1932 s Francis & Martha. BA Sprg Hill Coll 1954; MDiv Sewanee: The U So, TS 1957. D 7/17/1957 Bp Charles C J Carpenter P 6/24/1958 Bp George Mosley Murray. m 6/11/1977 Faye Sisson Walter c 2. Assoc The Epis Ch Of S Fran Of Assisi Pelham AL 2000-2003; R S Andrews's Epis Ch Birmingham AL 1985-1999, Assoc 1974-1985; S Andr's Fndt Birmingham AL 1974-1985; Dio Alabama Birmingham 1973-1977, 1971-1972; Dir Selma Interreligious Proj Tuscaloosa AL 1965-1974; P-in-c Gr Ch Van Vorst Jersey City NJ 1963-1965; Vic H Apos Savannah GA 1961-1963; R S Jas Ch Eufaula AL 1959-1961; Fell & Tutor The GTS New York NY 1957-1959. Auth, *The Naval Battle of Mobile Bay*, Prester Meridian Press, 1993; Auth, "Une Presence en Alabama," *Periodique Trimestriel: Publie par la Communante de Taize*.

WALTER II, George Avery (Ore) 77287 S Ash Rd, Stanfield OR 97875 Vic S Matt's Epis Ch Gold Bch OR 2012- B Wenatchee WA 1948 s Willard & Lois. BA Wstrn Washington U 1971; MDiv Sewanee: The U So, TS 2001. D 5/12/2001 Bp William Harvey Wolfrum P 11/13/2001 Bp Mark Lawrence Macdonald. m 9/26/1980 Norma Walter. R S Andr's Epis Ch Polson MT 2008-2012; R S Jn's Ch Hermiston OR 2004-2008; R S Brendan's Epis Ch Juneau AK 2001-2004.

WALTER, Kathy Marie (SwFla) 2638 Pinewood Dr, Dunedin FL 34698 P-in-c S Jn's Epis Ch Clearwater FL 2014- B Philadelphia PA 1955 d Lothar & Rose. BA La Salle U 1977; MEd Tem Philadelphia PA 1982; MDiv GTS 2007. D 6/9/2007 Bp Charles Ellsworth Bennison Jr P 12/15/2007 Bp Franklin Delton Turner. m 8/16/1975 Gerard M Boone c 3. R Ch Of S Jude And The Nativ Lafayette Hill PA 2007-2014; Sch Psychol Sch Dist of Philadelphia 1986-2006.

WALTER, Verne Leroy (FdL) 12660 Red Chestnut Ln SPC 47, Sonora CA 95370 B San Francisco CA 1945 s Verne & Mary. AA Modesto Jr Coll 1966; BS Chapman U 1996; MDiv Nash 1999. D 6/19/1999 P 12/21/1999 Bp David Mercer Schofield. m 5/22/1966 Ruth Foster c 2. R S Alb's Epis Ch Marshfield WI 2005-2009; Cur S Michaels By-The-Sea Ch Carlsbad CA 1999-2005. vernelwalter@yahoo.com

WALTERS, Delores Marie (ND) PO Box 214, Fort Yates ND 58538 B Wakpala SD 1941 d John & Sophia. D 6/9/2007 Bp Michael Smith. m 8/22/1959 Ronald Walters c 6.

WALTERS, Fred Ashmore (USC) 1001 12th St, Cayce SC 29033 B Greenville SC 1951 s James & Mary Frances. BS U of So Carolina 1975; JD U of So Carolina 1978. D 1/31/2009 Bp Dorsey Henderson. m 11/8/1975 Connie B Walters c 1.

WALTERS, Gloria Louise (Okla) St Mark Episcopal Church, 800 S 3rd St, Hugo OK 74743 B Durant OK 1947 d George & Elizabeth. BMus U of Houston 1970; Mstr of Behavior Stds SE Oklahoma St U 1979; PhD Texas Wmn's U 1983; MDiv Perkins - SMU 1992; MDiv SMU Perkins 1992. D 10/12/2013 P 6/20/2014 Bp Edward Joseph Konieczny.

WALTERS, Jennifer Louise (Mich) 100 Laurel Hill Rd, Westhampton MA 01027 Dn of Rel Life Smith Northampton MA 2001-; Int Dir, Cntr for Cmnty Collaboration Smith Northampton MA 2013-; Co-Dir, Wmn Narratives Proj Smith Northampton MA 2008- B Buffalo NY 1960 d Terrence & Sonia. BA Marq 1982; MA Boston Coll 1985; DMin EDS 1990; MA MI SU 1994. D 6/19/1993 P 8/18/1994 Bp R aymond Stewart Wood Jr. m 2/19/2010 Celeste E Whiting c 3. Actg Vic S Jn's Ch Ashfield MA 2014; Epis Stdt Fndt

Ann Arbor MI 2000-2001; Assoc Chapl Epis Stdt Mnstry of the U MI Ann 2000-2001; Vic Ch Of The Incarn Pittsfield Twp Ann Arbor MI 1993-2000. Auth, "Stdt Rel Orgnztn and the Publ U," *The Transformation of Campus Life: Sprtlty and Rel Pluralism in Stdt Affrs*, Ptr Lang Pub, 2001; Co-Auth, "Evaluating the use of culture in HIV/AIDS educational materials," *AIDS Educ and Prevention Journ*, Guilford, 1994; Co-Auth, "HIV Risk Assessment and Pre- and Post-Test Counslg: A Primary Care Approach," *Curric*, MI SU, 1994; Co-Auth, "Psychosocial care of HIV-infected persons," *Mntl Hlth Aspects of HIV/AIDS: Curric Modules*, U MI, 1992; Auth, "Case study: Chr Sci, the Govt, and the clash over Sprtl healing, first commentary," *Med Hmnts Report*, MI SU, 1991. AAR 1989; Assn for Conflict Resolution 1999; Phi Kappa Phi 1994.

WALTERS, Joshua David (Roch) Christ Church, 36 S Main St, Pittsford NY 14534 **R Chr Ch Pittsford Pittsford NY 2012-** B Evansville IN 1976 s David & Betty. BA Indiana U 1999; MDiv GTS 2006. D 6/24/2006 P 1/20/2007 Bp Cate Waynick. m 5/24/2003 Emily M Blecksmith c 2. R Gr Epis Ch Massapequa NY 2009-2012; Assoc R Chr Ch Winnetka IL 2006-2009. Alum/Alum Awd for Hist GTS 2006. josh@christchurchpittsford.com

WALTERS, Karen Graf (SVa) 150 Bella Vista Terrace, Unit D, No Venice FL 34275 B Pensacola FL 1945 d Edward & Elouise. BFA Nthrn Illinois U 1979; MDiv VTS 1982; MS Loyola U 1985. D 1/4/1986 P 9/1/1986 Bp Barry Valentine. m 4/24/2015 Susan E Rector. R S Dav's Epis Ch No Chesterfield VA 1991-1996; Int S Mary's Ch Baltimore MD 1989-1991; Int The Ch Of The H Apos Halethorpe MD 1988-1989; Asst R Emm Ch Baltimore MD 1986-1988; Asst Copley Par: The Ch Of The Resurr Joppatowne MD 1985-1986.

WALTERS, Lawrence Robert (Mich) 11179 Delight Creek Rd, Fishers IN 46038 B Newton KS 1948 s Cecil & Volneese. U of Kansas 1971; BA Boise St U 1989; MDiv Sewanee: The U So, TS 1992; DMin SWTS 2006. D 2/2/1992 P 8/2/1992 Bp John Stuart Thornton. m 8/5/1972 Teresa A Walters c 1. R S Paul's Epis Ch Jackson MI 2000-2014; Assoc S Andr's Ch Kansas City MO 1998-2000; R S Mary's Ch W Columbia TX 1994-1998; Assoc & Org/Choir S Chris's Ch Houston TX 1992-1994.

WALTERS, Robert Carroll (WMass) 17 Briarwood Circle, Worcester MA 01606 **Chapl Jail Cuyahoga Cnty OH 1961-** B Indianapolis IN 1935 s Wallace & Carol. BA Butler U 1956; STB Harvard DS 1959; GTS 1960; MA U of Massachusetts 1970; CAGS Clark U 1992. D 6/11/1960 P 12/1/1960 Bp John P Craine. c 2. S Mich's Ch Marblehead MA 1998; Asst S Mich's-On-The-Heights Worcester MA 1986-1998; Non-par 1967-1986; Vic Chr Ch Rochdale MA 1966-1967; Vic S Paul's Ch Ft Benton MT 1961-1966; Cur Ch Of Our Sav Akron OH 1960-1961. None.

WALTERS, Roxanne S (Cal) 1217 Skycrest Dr Apt 3, Walnut Creek CA 94595 B Morristown NJ 1943 d Walter & Laura. BS California St U Sacramento 1975; BTh Sch for Deacons 1985. D 12/7/1985 Bp William Edwin Swing. m 6/28/1992 Sumner Francis Dudley Walters c 2.

WALTERS, Scott (Ark) **Calv Ch Memphis TN 2017-** B Norwalk CT 1967 s James & Lynda. BA Jn Br 1990; MDiv VTS 2005. D 1/18/2005 P 7/16/2005 Bp Larry Maze. m 12/18/1993 Roberta A Walters c 2. R Chr Epis Ch Little Rock AR 2005-2017. Harris Awd VTS 2005.

WALTERS JR, Sumner Francis Dudley (Cal) 1217 Skycrest Dr Apt 3, Walnut Creek CA 94595 B Fort Scott KS 1924 s Sumner & Evelyn. MA Stan 1949; BA Stan 1949; PhD Oxf GB 1956. D 6/8/1952 Bp The Bishop Of Croydon P 12/26/1952 Bp Sumner Walters. m 6/28/1992 Roxanne S Walters c 4. Chapl - Hospice Nthrn California 1996-2003; Vic S Andr's Ch Oakland CA 1991-1995; S Ambr Epis Ch Foster City CA 1982-1991; Ret 1980-1982; Stndg Comm. Dio Olympia Seattle 1975-1979, R 1966-1979, R 1966-1975; R S Lk's Epis Ch Vancouver WA 1966-1979; Headmaster San Rafael Acad - Dio. of CA 1961-1966; Ldrshp Trnr - Dept. of Chr Ed. Epis Ch Cntr New York NY 1956-1961; R The Par Of S Mk The Evang Hood River OR 1952-1956; Eccumentical Off Dio California San Francisco CA 1996-1995, Exam Chapl 1982-1995. Auth, *The Dvlpmt of Theol Educ C of E and ECUSA 1900-1950*.

WALTERS, William Harry (USC) 1109 W Woodmont Dr, Lancaster SC 29720 B Indianapolis IN 1941 s Harry & Alice. BA Milligan Coll 1965; GTS 1968; MDiv Chr TS 1969. D 8/23/1968 Bp Henry I Louttit P 5/23/1970 Bp William Hopkins Folwell. m 1/23/1968 Dana Walters c 2. R Chr Epis Ch Lancaster SC 1985-2006; R H Trin Epis Ch Fruitland Pk FL 1982-1985; Vic S Fran Of Assisi Epis Ch Lake Placid FL 1976-1982; Ch Of The Gd Shpd Maitland FL 1976; Cur 1975-1976; Asst Chr The King Epis Ch Orlando FL 1972-1975; Cur All SS Epis Ch Lakeland FL 1969-1972; Dioc Curs Coun Dio Upper So Carolina Columbia SC 1995-1997.

WALTERS MALONE, Sandra A (VI) c/o St George's Episcopal Church, PO Box 28 Main St, Road Town, Tortola British Virgin Islands VG1110 British Virgin Islands **St Pauls Ch-Sea Cow Bay Sea Cows Bay 2014-** B Barbados 1957 d Everton & Wilma. Dplma U of the Kingston; CAS CDSP 2013. D 6/14/2008 P 3/6/2010 Bp Edward Gumbs. m 8/21/1993 Meade Wilbur Malone c 2.

WALTERS-PACE, Jill A (NwT) 1601 S Georgia St, Amarillo TX 79102 **S Andr's Epis Ch Amarillo TX 2016-, D 2015-2016** B Tulsa OK 1965 d George & Kaye. B.A. Austin Coll 1987; Ph.D. U of No Texas 1994; Cert of Theol Stds

NW Texas Sch of Ord Mnstry 2016. D 12/12/2015 P 6/26/2016 Bp James Scott Mayer. m 6/4/1988 Robert F Pace c 1. jwalters@standrewsamarillo.org

WALTHALL, Charles Leroy (Eas) 224 NE 30th Street, Wilton Manors FL 33334 **Cath Chpl Cathd of St Ptr & St Paul Washington DC 2004-** B Kansas City MO 1943 s Albert & Naomi. BA SUNY 1965; MM CUA 1969; DMA CUA 1981; MDiv VTS 2001; DMin Sewanee: The U So, TS 2010. D 6/29/2002 P 6/8/2003 Bp Peter Hess Beckwith. R All Faith Chap Miles River Par Easton MD 2005-2012; Ch Of The Redeem Cairo IL 2002-2004; Dio Springfield Springfield IL 2002-2004; D/Assoc P S Jas Chap Marion Marion IL 2002-2004; S Jas Epis Ch Dahlgren IL 2002-2004; S Mk's Ch W Frankfort IL 2002-2004; P S Steph's Ch Harrisburg IL 2001-2004. Auth, "Portraits of Johann Joachim Quantz," *Early Mus*, Oxf Press, 1986. Cmnty of St Mary Assoc 2006; SSJE friends of 1995. Magan cl SUNY Buffalo 1965.

WALTHER, Aileen Dianne Pallister (CFla) 753 Creekwater Ter Apt 101, Lake Mary FL 32746 B London England UK 1950 d Mervyn & Ellen. AA Lansing Cmnty Coll 1971; BA MI SU 1976; CTh Whitaker TS 1990; Cert Ang Stud TESM 2000. D 6/21/1991 Bp Henry Irving Mayson. m 8/23/1986 Patrick Bogart Walther. D Epis Ch Of The Resurr Longwood FL 1992-1994. Auth, "Writing Your Life Story w God As Your Guide," 2003; Auth, "Journ Writing," *LivCh*, 1997.

WALTMAN, Lynne Marie (FtW) All Saints Episcopal Church, 5001 Crestline Rd, Fort Worth TX 76107 **Admin All SS' Epis Ch Ft Worth TX 2004-** B Lake Forest, IL 1952 d John & Marie. MA, Biomedical Cmncatn Univ. of Texas Hlth Sci Cntr at Dallas; MBA U of Oklahoma, Ext. in Dhahran, Saudi Arabia; BA VPI and St U; Mstr of Mnstry Nash 2010; M. Div. Equivalent Brite DS 2016. D 1/15/2016 Bp James Scott Mayer P 9/14/2016 Bp Sam Byron Hulsey. m 7/24/1976 William Dewitt Waltman c 2. mthwaltman@asecfw.org

WALTON, Billy R (Miss) 608 W Jefferson St, Tupelo MS 38804 B Jackson MS 1961 s Billy & Catherine. BS Mississippi St U 1983; DO W Virginia Sch of Osteopathic Med 1988; Dplma Theol Lon 2009. D 1/11/2014 Bp Duncan Montgomery Gray III. m 11/1/2002 Robin Walton c 3.

WALTON, Carol Leighann (Nev) 234 Scotgrove St, Henderson NV 89074 **S Tim's Epis Ch Henderson NV 2015-** B Bellefonte PA 1954 MDiv CDSP 2004. D 10/10/2003 P 10/30/2004 Bp Katharine Jefferts Schori. c 1. P-in-c All SS Epis Ch Las Vegas NV 2012-2015; Cler Intern Chr Ch Epis Las Vegas Nevada 2010-2012; Sr Chapl Broward correctional Inst Ft. Lauderdale FL 2007-2009; Stff Chapl Mart Correctional Inst Indiantown FL 2005-2007.

WALTON SSF, Dunstan (LI) Po Box 399, Mount Sinai NY 11766 **Died 6/26/2016** B Winchendon MA 1922 s Wendell & Dorothy. BA S Anselm Coll 1947; Mercer TS 1955. D 11/5/1955 P 7/7/1956 Bp James Pernette DeWolfe. P-in-c St. Aug Trinidad 2002-2006; P-in-c St. Agnes Trinidad 2001-2002; P-in-c St. Crisp Trinidad 2000-2001; Int Gd Shpd Trinidad 1997-2000; Int Chap 0r:15; Asst Ch Of S Thos Brooklyn NY 1990-1994; Int S Steph Trinidad & Tobago 1989-1990; Int Ch Of The Trsfg Freeport NY 1987-1988; Int S Ann's Ch Sayville NY 1985-1986; SSF 1955-1984. Auth, *Little Chronicle*; Auth, *St. Anns Correspondent*; Auth, *Trsfgs New Life*; Auth, *W Indies Fran News*. Curs; Ord of S Lk.

WALTON JR, Harry Edwin (Mass) 100 Park Terrace Dr Apt 143, Stoneham MA 02180 **Trin Epis Ch Stoughton MA 2014-** B Philadelphia PA 1957 s Harry & Mary. MDiv EDS 2014. D 6/7/2014 Bp M(Arvil) Thomas Shaw P 1/10/2015 Bp Alan Gates. c 1. Benefits and Compstn Com Mem Dio Massachusetts 2017; Chair, Elctns Com Dio Massachusetts 2011-2016. The J. Norman Hall Prize EDS 2014; The Wm H. Lincoln Prize EDS 2013. clergy@trinitystoughton.com

WALTON, Hugh (Ind) 8480 Craig St Apt 5, Indianapolis IN 46250 **Died 4/20/2016** B Birmingham England UK 1925 s Harry & Elinor. Lon GB 1948; PE Indiana Soc of Profsnl Engr 1964. D 4/16/1978 P 12/1/1978 Bp Edward Witker Jones. m 9/3/1949 Kathleen Mary Walton c 3. Assoc Ch Of The Nativ Indianapolis IN 1993-2013; R Trin Ch Connersville IN 1978-1993. Natl Epis Curs 1981.

WALTON, James Brooke (Pa) 919 Tennis Ave, Maple Glen PA 19002 **Asst S Matt's Ch Maple Glen PA 2015-, 2014-2015** B Bethlehem PA 1970 s Terrence & Diane. BA Muhlenberg Coll 1993; MDiv CDSP 2014; MDiv CDSP 2014. D 6/14/2014 P 1/17/2015 Bp Clifton Daniel III. c 1. jay@saintmattsec.org

WALTON, Joy Edemy (Del) 2550 Kensington Gdns Unit 103, Ellicott City MD 21043 B Baltimore MD 1943 d J(Ames) & Ella. BA Untd States Intl U 1964; MS Old Dominion U - Norfolk VA 1979; MDiv GTS 1994. D 5/28/1994 P 3/11/1995 Bp Frank Harris Vest Jr. c 2. PRN Assoc Chapl Howard Cnty Gnrl Hosp 2012-2016; Chapl S Andr's Sch Chap Middletown DE 2005-2010; R S Cyp's Epis Ch Hampton VA 1998-2005; P-t Vic Mssn of the H Sprt Norfolk VA 1995-1996; Cur Old Donation Ch Virginia Bch VA 1994-1998. AAPC 1999-2004; Mem of Sthrn Virginia Cler Assn 2000-2005; Ord of S Helena (Assoc) 1995.

WALTON, Lori Ann (Cal) 7688 Shady Hollow Dr, Newark CA 94560 **R S Jas Ch Fremont CA 2010-** B San Francisco CA 1967 d Richard & Patricia. BA New Coll of California 1999; MDiv CDSP 2004. D 6/5/2004 P 12/4/2004 Bp

William Edwin Swing. m 5/28/2011 Ronald Larson c 1. Assoc R S Mk's Epis Ch Palo Alto CA 2007-2010; All SS Epis Ch Palo Alto CA 2006-2007; S Alb's Epis Ch Brentwood CA 2005.

WALTON, Macon Brantley (SVa) 202 Ridgeland Dr, Smithfield VA 23430 **Ret 1996-; Vic Brandon Epis Ch Disputanta VA 1996-; Chr Ch Waverly VA 1996-** B Richmond VA 1932 s Percy & Anne. BA VMI 1955; MDiv VTS 1958. D 6/1/1958 P 6/1/1959 Bp Frederick D Goodwin. Int The Epis Ch Of The Adv Norfolk VA 1992-1995; Cntrl Mecklenburg Cure Chase City VA 1990-1992; Int S Tim's Epis Ch Clarksville VA 1990-1991; Int H Trin Prot Epis Ch Onancock VA 1989-1990; R Chr Epis Ch Smithfield VA 1967-1988; Assoc Ch Of The Ascen Norfolk VA 1966-1967; Asst Galilee Epis Ch Virginia Bch VA 1962-1966; R S Asaph's Par Ch Bowling Green VA 1958-1962; S Ptr's Port Royal Port Royal VA 1958-1962; R Vawter Ch Loretto VA 1958-1962.

WALTON, Mary Fish (Md) 1810 Park Ave, Richmond VA 23220 B Birmingham AL 1948 d Bruce & Virginia. VPI; BA Colorado Womens Coll 1969. D 7/9/1994 Bp Robert Manning Moody. m 6/8/1969 Daniel Robert Walton c 2. D S Paul's Par Baltimore MD 2000-2008. SCHC.

WALTON, Regina Laba (Mass) Parish Of The Good Shepherd, 1671 Beacon St, Waban MA 02468 **Gr Ch Newton MA 2014-** B Pompton Plains NJ 1978 d Michael & Jacqueline. PhD Bos; BA Hampshire Coll 2000; MDiv Harvard DS 2003. D 6/2/2007 P 1/12/2008 Bp M(Arvil) Thomas Shaw. m 7/12/2003 Christopher L Walton c 2. S Ptr's Ch Weston MA 2013-2014; Asst R Ch Of The Gd Shpd Waban MA 2007-2013; Tchg Fell Bos 2006-2013; Dir of Chld's Mnstrs Trin Ch Concord MA 2003-2006. Bk reviewer, "Bk Revs: The Web of Friendship: Nich Ferrar and Little Gidding by Joyce Ransome," *ATR vol. 93 no. 4*, 2011. Fllshp of St. Jn (SSJE) 2004; Massachusetts Epis Cler Assn 2009. Doctoral Fell ECF 2005.

WALTON JR, Richard Lindsley (WNC) PO Box 1866, Sparta NC 28675 **S Giles Chap Deerfield Asheville NC 2015-** B Washington DC 1966 s Richard & Sally. BA Gordon Coll 1991; MTS Duke 1997; MDiv VTS 1999. D 12/17/1999 Bp Peter J Lee P 6/17/2000 Bp Martin Gough Townsend. m 8/17/1996 Nancy Dixon Walton c 2. Reverend Chr Epis Ch Sparta NC 2010-2015; Asst S Jn's Epis Ch Tallahassee FL 2008-2009; Int Dir Angl Theol Inst Belmopan Belize 2002-2006; Exec Coun Appointees New York NY 2002-2006; Asst R S Ptr's Ch Salisbury MD 1999-2002. "Witness in Sudan," *The Chr Century*, 2008; "Fear of God and Darwin," *newsweek.washingtonpost.com*, 2008; "Liberating Mssn," *Epis Life*, 2007; "Div Can Make Faith Stronger," *Tallahassee Democrat*, 2007.

WALTON, Robert Harris (WMich) 2186 Tamarack Dr, Okemos MI 48864 B Bay City MI 1933 s John & Gladys. BA Cntrl Michigan U 1955; MDiv Bex Sem 1958; MA MI SU 1973. D 6/29/1958 Bp Archie H Crowley P 5/25/1960 Bp Lane W Barton. m 6/25/1960 Julia Ann Walton c 3. Trin Epis Ch Grand Ledge MI 1986-1988; Supply P Dio Wstrn Michigan Kalamazoo MI 1984-2002; S Jn's Epis Ch Charlotte MI 1975-1984; Asst Min S Mich's Epis Ch Lansing MI 1970-1974; Asst S Paul's Epis Ch Lansing MI 1968-1970; Min in charge Trin Ch Fostoria OH 1963-1968; Chapl Toledo St Hosp Toledo OH 1960-1963; S Steph's Ch Wyandotte MI 1958-1959.

WALTON, Sandra Lee (Colo) 10751 W 69th Ave, Arvada CO 80004 B Milwaukee WI 1950 d Gerhardt & Lillian. AA Front Range Cmnty Coll 1984; BA Metropltn St Coll of Denver 1995. D 5/27/1987 Bp William Harvey Wolfrum. m 10/19/1968 Ray Allen Walton c 3. Chapl Chld's Hosp Denver CO 1987-1992.

WALTZ, Bill (Colo) 207 Rainbow Acres Lane, PO Box 21, Gunnison CO 81230 **Linked Mnstry w Gd Samar in Gunnison, CO All SS Of The Mtn Epis Chap Crested Butte CO 2007-; Vic Ch Of The Gd Samar Gunnison CO 2007-** B Decatur IL 1947 s Harry & Lazora. BA U of Iowa 1969; MDiv CDSP 1973. D 10/23/1973 P 1/1/1976 Bp Walter Cameron Righter. m 3/6/1982 Rhonda Renee Knoche c 2. Int S Barn Ch Glenwood Spgs CO 2006-2007; S Barn Par Portland OR 1988-1991; Chair On Const And Cn Com 1982-1986; Chair On Idaho Evang Com 1982-1984; Gr Epis Ch Glenns Ferry ID 1982-1984; R S Jas Ch Mtn Hm ID 1981-1987; Vic S Fran No Liberty IA 1977-1981; Asst S Mich's Cedar Rapids IA 1976-1977; Dio Iowa Des Moines IA 1974; Vic Gr Epis Ch Chas City IA 1973-1974; S Andr's Ch Waverly IA 1973-1974. bill.waltz@gmail.com

WALWORTH, Diana Lynn (Mich) PO Box 287, Onsted MI 49265 **P S Mich And All Ang Brooklyn MI 2011-, Other Lay Position 2004-2011** B Toledo OH 1962 d Ervin & Bonnie. U of Toledo; Whitaker TS Dio Michigan. D 10/27/2010 P 5/24/2011 Bp Wendell Nathaniel Gibbs Jr. c 3.

WALWORTH, James Curtis (LI) 443 River Rd Ste 210, Highland Park NJ 08904 **Ret 1992-** B Wilmette IL 1926 s Jesse & Lela. BA Ripon Coll Ripon WI 1948; Lic GTS 1956. D 6/18/1956 Bp Charles L Street P 12/17/1956 Bp Horace W B Donegan. m 7/9/1960 Dorothy E Walworth c 3. Asst S Paul's Epis Ch Willimantic CT 1995-2002; Chapl S Johns Epis Hosp Far Rockaway NY 1985-1991; Chapl Bp Davies Cntr Inc Hurst TX 1981-1985; Chapl Baylor All SS Med Cntr Ft Worth TX 1968-1985; S Lk's-Roosevelt Hosp Cntr New York NY 1962-1968, 1959-1961; Int R for El Campo and Palacios Dio Texas Houston TX 1962; S Jn's Epis Ch Palacios TX 1962; St Lukes Ch El Campo TX

1962; S Lk's Epis Hosp Houston TX 1961-1962; Cur S Ptr's Epis Ch Peekskill NY 1957-1959; Cur Chr's Ch Rye NY 1956-1957. Auth, "A Way to Light a Ch," *LivCh*, 1989. AEHC 1961; Assn of Profsnl Chapl 1965.

WALWORTH, Roy Chancellor (Wyo) 216 Southridge Rd, Evanston WY 82930 B Bremerton WA 1941 s Chancellor & Frieda. U of Puget Sound 1965; BS WA SU 1980; MDiv The Coll of Emm and S Chad CA 1992. D 5/4/1992 P 1/25/1993 Bp Bob Gordon Jones. m 5/19/1973 Antoinette M Walworth c 2. Mnstry Dvlp Dio Wyoming Casper 1992-2008; Vic S Paul's Epis Ch Evanston WY 1992-1997. rwalw@allwest.net

WAMPLER, Dean Delos (Alb) 5 Union St Apt 3, Schenectady NY 12305 **Died 5/8/2017** B Chanute KS 1923 s Charles & Lillys. BS U of Kansas 1947; LTh SWTS 1953; MDiv SWTS 1954. D 6/14/1953 Bp Frederick Lehrle Barry P 12/21/1953 Bp David Emrys Richards. Asst P S Geo's Epis Ch Schenectady NY 1993-2011; Exec Coun Dio Albany Greenwich NY 1960-1987, Dep to GC 1973-1985; Admin Barry Hse Conf Cntr Brant Lake NY 1959-1993; Adirondack Mssn Pottersville NY 1959-1991; P S Paul's Ch Brant Lake NY 1959-1991; P-in-c Gr Chap Stamford NY 1953-1959; P-in-c S Paul's Ch Bloomville NY 1953-1959; S Ptr's Ch Stamford NY 1953-1959. Oblate Soc of S Jn the Evang. Hon Cn All SS Cathd 1975.

WAMSLEY, Shawn Earl (Pa) Diocese Of Pennsylvania, 3717 Chestnut St Ste 300, Philadelphia PA 19104 **Dio Pennsylvania Philadelphia PA 2016-** B Albuquerque NM 1978 s Steven & Ruth. BA Evangel U 2001; MS SW Assemblies of God U 2003; MDiv Liberty Bapt TS 2010. D 6/21/2014 P 5/23/2015 Bp Michael Vono. m 12/19/1997 Miriam L Griffith c 3. CE Dir S Jn's Cathd Albuquerque NM 2013-2014. swamsley@diopa.org

WAN, Sze-Kar (Mass) 87 Herrick Rd, Newton Center MA 02459 **Jn Norris Prof Of NT Interp Andover Newton TS 1990-** B 1954 s Chai-Lai & Chiu-Ying. MDiv Gordon-Conwell TS 1982; ThD Harvard DS 1992. D 6/4/2005 Bp M(Arvil) Thomas Shaw P 1/6/2007 Bp Gayle Harris. m 8/24/1996 Maria Mak.

WANAMAKER, Katherine Elizabeth (Minn) 615 Vermillion St, Hastings MN 55033 B Albany GA 1963 d Walter & Grace. BS Concordia; BS Concordia 2004; BS Concordia 2004; BS Concordia U 2004. D 6/20/2015 P 6/21/2016 Bp Brian N Prior. m 9/2/1989 Thomas Charles Wanamaker.

WANCURA, Paul Forsyth (LI) Po Box 641, Shelter Island Heights NY 11965 **Ret 2000-** B Brooklyn NY 1930 s Frank & Mary. BA CUNY 1952; MBA Col 1954; MDiv GTS 1960. D 4/23/1960 P 10/28/1960 Bp James Pernette De-Wolfe. R Caroline Ch Of Brookhaven E Setauke NY 1974-2000; Hon Cn Cathd Of The Incarn Garden City NY 1968; Archd Dio Long Island Garden City NY 1966-1974; R Ch Of The Ascen Greenpoint Brooklyn NY 1960-1966.

WAND, Thomas C (Pa) 31 Kleyona Ave, Phoenixville PA 19460 **Ret 2003-** B Denver CO 1948 s Robert & Lois. AB Col 1970; MDiv EDS 1973; MBA RPI 1982; Coll of Preachers 1987; Int Mnstry Trng 1996. D 6/9/1973 Bp Paul Moore Jr P 12/9/1973 Bp William Jones Gordon Jr. m 10/8/1977 Marlene Haines c 2. Int R S Mary's Epis Ch Ardmore PA 2011-2012; Chapl Caring Hospice Serv Ft. Washington PA 2004-2010; Oprtns Mgr Talley Mgmt Co Mt Royal NJ 2003-2004; Interims Dio Pennsylvania Philadelphia PA 2002-2003, Fin and Property Com 2006-2011, Cmsn on Cler Compstn and Employee Benefits 1992-2012; Int R S Paul's Epis Ch Indianapolis IN 2000-2002; Int R S Mk's Ch Philadelphia PA 1999-2000; Dn (Int) Trin Cathd Trenton NJ 1997-1999; R S Ptr's Ch Phoenixville PA 1991-1997; R S Mary's Epis Ch Albuquerque NM 1989-1991; R S Matt Albuquerque NM 1984-1989; S Tim's Ch San Diego CA 1978-1984; R St Jas Epis Ch Hartford CT 1978-1984; Assoc Gr Ch Manchester NH 1976-1978; Vic Gd Shpd Huslia AK 1973-1976; Chair Liturg & Mus Cmsn Dio The Rio Grande Albuquerque 1987-1989; Bd Chair St. Mart's Hosp Cntr 1986-1989. Natl Treas Natl Epis Cler Assn 1986-1992. resurrectionpriest@verizon.net

WANDALL, Frederick Summerson (Va) Green Spring Village, 7416 Spring Village Dr Apt 116, Springfield VA 22150 B Camden NJ 1930 s Frederick & Thelma. BA Wesl 1953; MDiv GTS 1956; U of Pennsylvania 1958; MLitt Oxf GB 1961. D 4/28/1956 P 10/27/1956 Bp Alfred L Banyard. c 2. Cler Assoc Truro Epis Ch Fairfax VA 1992-2009; Asst S Andr's Epis Ch Arlington VA 1990-1991; Tchr Geo Mason U 1989-1990; Ch Of The Gd Shpd Burke VA 1977-1978; Asst Gr Epis Ch Alexandria VA 1972-1975; P-in-c S Mary's Epis Ch Arlington VA 1971-1972; Asst Chapl, Tchr St Steph Sch Alexandria VA 1969-1989; P-in-c Ch Of The Gd Shpd Staunton VA 1968-1969; Chapl Stuart Hall Staunton VA 1967-1969; Chapl Stuart Hall Staunton VA 1967-1969; Vic S Andr's Epis Ch New Paltz NY 1963-1967; Asst Gr Epis Ch Nyack NY 1961-1963; Chapl Chr Ch Oxford Engl 1959-1960; Asst Chr Ch In Woodbury Woodbury NJ 1956-1957. Auth, "Chas Williams," *Minor British Novelists*. Phi Beta Kappa 1953.

WANG, Kathleen Marie (Me) PO Box 158, East Waterboro ME 04030 **Mem of COM Dio Maine Portland ME 2011-, Cler Del to Prov I Syn 2010-, Mar Study Grp 2009-, Mem of Mssn Strtgy Study Grp 2009-** B Taipei Taiwan ROC 1960 d Jesse & Meda Marie. AB Smith 1981; MDiv Ya Berk 1984. D 6/14/2008 Bp Chilton Richardson Knudsen P 12/14/2008 Bp Stephen Taylor Lane. m 6/6/2004 Susan Elizabeth Tennant c 1. Vic S Steph The Mtyr Epis Ch Waterboro Cntr ME 2008-2014; DCE S Jn's Ch Beverly MA 1999-2002.

WANSTALL, Donald Penton (CFla) 719 Cobblestone Drive, Ormond Beach FL 32174 **Died 8/22/2016** B Wilmington DE 1930 s James & Anne. Inst for Chr Stds; U of Delaware. D 6/29/1983 Bp William Hopkins Folwell. m 11/16/1948 Nancy Ruth Wanstall c 4. D S Mary's Epis Ch Daytona Bch FL 2000-2016; S Jas Epis Ch Ormond Bch FL 1983-2000. BroSA; OSL; Steph Mnstry.

WANTLAND, David C (NC) D 6/17/2017 Bp Anne Hodges-Copple.

WAPLE, Gary (WVa) RR 2 Box 243, Lewisburg WV 24901 **Ret 2001-** B Arlington VA 1946 s George & Catherine. Hagerstown Jr Coll 1967; Riverview Hosp Sch Red Bank NJ 1971; Epis TS in Kentucky 1990. D 6/11/1991 Bp John Henry Smith. m 9/11/1980 Carol Ann Waple c 1. D Chap on the Mt Showshoe WV 1995-2000; D Ch Of The Incarn Ronceverte WV 1995-2000; Emm Ch Wht Sphr Spgs WV 1995-2000; S Jn's Ch Marlinton WV 1995-2000; S Thos Epis Ch Wht Sphr Spgs WV 1995-2000; D S Jas' Epis Ch Lewisburg WV 1991-1994. NAAD 1990. S Steph's Awd NAAD 1997.

WARD, Barbara Pyle (Ida) 450 W Highway 30, Burley ID 83318 **D Calv Epis Ch Jerome ID 2010-; D St Matthews Epis Ch Rupert ID 2006-** B Chicago IL 1947 d Ronald & Beatrice. BA DePauw U 1969; MEd Indiana U 1974; SPED Indiana U 1975. D 2/2/1997 Bp John Stuart Thornton. m 8/8/1985 Thomas Ward.

WARD, Edwin Michael (Va) 8 Governors Ln, Hilton Head SC 29928 B Richmond VA 1927 s Varney & Virginia. BA Emory U 1950; MDiv VTS 1955. D 6/3/1955 Bp Frederick D Goodwin P 12/15/1955 Bp George Mosley Murray. m 12/29/1954 Allein Ward c 2. Assoc R S Lk's Epis Ch Hilton Hd Island SC 1993-2001; Hdmstr S Steph Sch Alexandria VA 1981-1990; Headmaster Salisbury Sch (Epis) Salisbury CT 1965-1981; Salisbury Sch Salisbury CT 1965-1981; Chapl S Mk's Sch Southborough MA 1959-1965; Vic S Mk's Epis Ch Troy AL 1955-1959. Pres NAES 1973.

WARD, Elizabeth Howe (Chi) 79 Meadow Hill Rd, Barrington IL 60010 B Oak Park IL 1940 d John & Marion. IL Wesl 1960; BA Lake Forest Coll 1984; MDiv SWTS 1993. D 3/21/1996 P 9/21/1996 Bp William Walter Wiedrich. m 9/7/1963 John Arthur Ward c 3. Asst S Mk's Barrington IL 2000-2004; S Giles' Ch Northbrook IL 1996-1999.

WARD, Eugene Lee (Ky) 6877 Green Meadow Cir, Louisville KY 40207 **Ret 2001-; P-in-c S Andr's Ch Glasgow KY 2001-, Int 1989-2000** B Detroit MI 1934 s Stewart & Anna. S Jos Rensselaer IN 1953; BA S Meinrad Coll 1956; STB S Meinrad TS 1961. Rec 6/3/1988 as Priest Bp James Daniel Warner. m 6/28/1968 Jan W Ward c 2. Dio Kentucky Louisville KY 1993-1999; Calv Ch Louisville KY 1993-1997; Asst S Andr's Ch Louisville KY 1993-1997; Barren River Area Coun Louisville KY 1991-1993; Int Area Min Chr The King Columbia KY 1989-1992; S Jas Ch Franklin KY 1989-1992; Trin Ch Russellville KY 1989-1992; S Lk's Ch Kearney NE 1988-1989; Serv RC Ch 1954-1968.

WARD, Geoffrey F (FdL) 29 Foothills Way, Bloomfield CT 06002 **S Chris's Ch Milwaukee WI 2017-; Assoc Chr Ch Cathd Hartford CT 2007-** B Utica NY 1960 s Roger & Haroldbelle. BA Viterbo U 1982; MFA Trin U San Antonio 1984; MTS SWTS 2006. D 12/22/2007 P 1/3/2009 Bp Russell Edward Jacobus. m 5/22/2010 Valerie Ward c 6. P-in-c Dio Fond du Lac Appleton WI 2014-2016; P-in-c S Fran Epis Ch Eagle River WI 2014-2016.

WARD JR, George (Md) **Died 9/26/2016** B 1935 m 1/9/1988 Janice Wheeler.

WARD JR, Herbert Arthur (Nev) 112 Wyoming St, Boulder City NV 89005 **Ret 2000-** B Jackson MS 1937 s Herbert & Frances. BA Millsaps Coll 1958; STM GTS 1961; Nash 1990. D 6/16/1961 Bp Duncan Montgomery Gray P 12/1/1961 Bp John Maury Allin. m 3/28/1978 Nancy Ruth Ward. S Jude Gd Shpd Campus 1989-1991; Natl Pres & Ceo S Jude's Chld's Ranch 1970-2000; Chapl Sis Of Charity 1970-1980; Headmaster S Geo's Sch New Orleans LA 1968-1970; Cur S Geo's Epis Ch New Orleans LA 1965-1970; P-in-c S Chris's Wiggins MS 1962-1965; Vic S Patricks Epis Ch Long Bch MS 1962-1965; S Mk's Ch Gulfport MS 1961-1965; Cur S Ptr's By The Sea Gulfport MS 1961-1963.

WARD, Horace (SeFla) 18501 Nw 7th Ave, Miami FL 33169 **R Epis Ch Of The H Fam Miami FL 1995-** B Kingston JM 1955 s Horace & Myrtle. MDiv Luth Theol Sthrn Sem; LTh Untd Theol Coll of The W Indies Kingston Jm 1977; Untd Theol Coll of The W Indies Kingston Jm 1977. D 6/19/1977 P 4/1/1978 Bp The Bishop Of Jamaica. m 12/16/1978 Marcia Ward c 3. Vic Ch Of The Gd Shpd Sumter SC 1990-1995; Cn In Res Trin And S Phil's Cathd Newark NJ 1984-1990; Asst R Chr Ch Shaker Heights OH 1981-1984; Cur S Andr's In Kingston Jamaica W Indies 1977-1980.

WARD, James (Cal) 202 El Prado Ave., San Rafael CA 94903 B San Francisco CA 1947 s Herbert & Margery. BA Ya 1969; MDiv Yale DS 1974. D 6/29/1974 P 5/1/1975 Bp Chauncie Kilmer Myers. m 10/20/1979 Janet Erikson c 3. R S Steph's Par Bel Tiburon CA 1994-2010; Prof of Field Educaton CDSP Berkeley CA 1985-1986; R S Cuth's Epis Ch Oakland CA 1981-1994; Assoc S Steph's Epis Ch Orinda CA 1977-1981; Assoc S Andr's Ch Saratoga CA 1974-1977. Auth, "Cracking the Prison Cultural Code," Colloquium on Violence and Rel, 2010; Auth, Dio California, 1989. NNECA.

WARD, Jeremiah (Tex) 43 N High Oaks Cir, Spring TX 77380 **Ret 1999-** B Wharton TX 1948 s Jeremiah & Lucie. BS Lamar U 1970; MDiv VTS 1978. D 6/23/1978 Bp James Milton Richardson P 7/1/1979 Bp Roger Howard Cilley. m 12/11/1992 Linda Ward c 3. Asstg R S Jas The Apos Epis Ch Conroe TX 2002-2011; Assoc Cleric Trin Epis Ch The Woodlands TX 1999-2002; Dn Of Cntrl Convoc Dio Texas Houston TX 1988-1999, Dept Of CE 1985-1999; R & Exec Dir Camp Allen Dioc C&C 1985-1999; Camp Allen Navasota TX 1985-1996; Int S Dunst's Epis Ch Houston TX 1984; Secy E Harris Convoc 1982-1999; Chr Emphasis Com Houston Metro Ymca 1982-1984; Bd Ethics Reverand Kelsey Seybold Fndt 1981-1999; Asst Palmer Memi Ch Houston TX 1980-1984; Vic S Cuth's Epis Ch Houston TX 1978-1980; The Great Cmsn Fndt Houston TX 1978-1980.

WARD, Karen Marie (Oly) 4272 Fremont Ave N, Seattle WA 98103 **S Andr's Ch Portland OR 2013-** B Cleveland OH 1961 d James & Barbara. Rec 8/22/2009 Bp Gregory Harold Rickel. Ch of the Apos Seattle WA 2009-2011.

WARD, Katherine Lydia (Cal) 10370 Greenview Dr, Oakland CA 94605 B New Orleans LA 1934 d Johnny & Corella. BA Jackson St U 1956; MA California St U 1969; EdD Nova SE U 1981; MDiv CDSP 1994; CDSP 2005. D 6/4/1994 P 6/1/1995 Bp William Edwin Swing. c 4. R S Aug's Ch Oakland CA 1996-2004; Asst Dio California San Francisco CA 1996-2001; S Fran' Epis Ch San Francisco CA 1996; Asst S Steph's Par Bel Tiburon CA 1995; Non-par. Auth, "...and A Heaping Cup of God's Love," Mod Profiles of an Ancient Faith, Epis Dio California, 2001; Auth, "Begin w The Tchr," The Montclarian, 1981. Epis Mnstry To Convalescent Hosps 1990; UBE 1994.

WARD, Mary Christine Mollie (Spr) 1104 N Roosevelt Ave, Bloomington IL 61701 **Mgr, Sprtl Care & CPE Advoc BroMenn Med Cntr Normal IL 2011-** B Stuttgart Germany 1967 d Curtis & Christine. BA U of Oklahoma 1989; MDiv SWTS 2002. D 6/15/2002 P 12/21/2002 Bp Bill Persell. m 6/17/1989 Gregory Shaw c 2. Chapl Supvsr BroMenn Healthcare Normal IL 2008-2010; Supervisory Res BroMenn Healthcare Normal IL 2004-2007; S Matt's Epis Ch Bloomington IL 2002-2007; Chapl Res BroMenn Healthcare Normal IL 2002-2003. Contrib, "Power and the Supervisory Relatns,"Courageous Conversations: the Tchg and Lrng of Pstr Supervision, U Press of Amer, 2010. CHS (Assoc) 1998; EPF 1989. ACPE Theory Paper of the Year Journ of Reflective Pract 2009.

WARD, Meredyth W (WMass) 35 Somerset St, Worcester MA 01609 **Dio Wstrn Massachusetts Springfield 2014-, Pres, Stndg Com 2009-, VP, Dioc Coun 2009-, GC Dep 2006-2012** B Springfield MA 1955 d Robert & Jeanne. BA Coll of the H Cross 1977; MDiv Jesuit TS 1981; CAS CDSP 2001. D 6/16/2001 P 12/15/2001 Bp Gordon Scruton. m 9/17/1983 Matthew Oliver Ward c 2. P-in-c Epis Ch Of The Epiph Wilbraham MA 2009-2013; R Chr Ch Rochdale MA 2001-2013.

WARD, Patrick Carroll (Mass) 147 Concord Rd, Lincoln MA 01773 **Trin Ch Epis Boston MA 2011-** B Stoneham MA 1964 s Henry & Theresa. BA Br 1987; MDiv Ya Berk 2008. D 6/7/2008 Bp M(Arvil) Thomas Shaw. Asst R S Anne's In The Fields Epis Ch Lincoln MA 2008-2011.

WARD JR, Patrick John (NY) 75A Prospect Ave, Ossining NY 10562 B Philadelphia PA 1951 s Patrick & Rosemary. BA Wheaton Coll 1977; MDiv Nash 1980; MFT Sthrn Connecticut St U 1989. D 6/14/1980 Bp Quintin Ebenezer Primo Jr P 12/21/1980 Bp Edward Clark Turner. m 8/11/1979 Barbara L Todisco c 2. Int Chr Ch Riverdale Bronx NY 2012-2014; Int S Mk's Ch Westhampton Bch NY 2010-2012; Int Ch Of The Gd Shpd Granite Spgs NY 2008-2009; R S Mary's Ch Of Scarborough Briarcliff NY 2006-2008; Int S Jas' Epis Ch Parkton MD 2005-2006; Int Chr Ch Forest Hill MD 2003-2004; R Ch Of The Gd Shpd Dunedin FL 1999-2002; Vic S Steph's Ch W Vlly City UT 1995-1999; Vic S Peters-In-The-Woods Epis Ch Fairfax Sta VA 1990-1995; R Chr Ch Oxford CT 1983-1990; Cur S Dav's Epis Ch Topeka KS 1980-1983.

WARD, Richard Philip (Spok) 1841 Fairmount Blvd, Eugene OR 97403 **P-t Vic St. Paul's Epis Chuch Tombstone AZ 2013-** B Medford OR 1945 s Lloyd & Elise. BS Pacific U 1967; MDiv CDSP 1982. D 7/15/1982 P 3/20/1983 Bp Edmond Lee Browning. m 4/2/1966 Dona Ward c 2. R S Tim's Epis Ch Yakima WA 1999-2009; R The Ch Of The H Trin Juneau AK 1995-1999; Asst R Chr Ch Coronado CA 1990-1995; Assoc R S Chris's Epis Ch Lubbock TX 1984-1990; S Andr's Cathd Honolulu HI 1982-1984; The Epis Ch in Hawaii Honolulu HI 1982-1983; Yth Coordntr Dio NW Texas Lubbock TX 1985-1990.

WARD IV, Samuel Mortimer (Los) 2524 Chapala St, Santa Barbara CA 93105 B New York NY 1937 s Samuel & Marion. BA Heidelberg U 1961; MDiv CDSP 1964. D 6/21/1964 Bp James Albert Pike P 3/11/1965 Bp Francis E I Bloy. m 2/7/1981 Alessandra Ward c 4. Int S Mk's-In-The-Vlly Epis Los Olivos CA 2008-2009; Int St. Fran Ch Palos Verdes Estates CA 2007-2008; Int S Mary's Par Lompoc CA 2006-2007; Int St. Marys Ch Lompoc CA 2006-2007; Fac Int Mnstry Ntwk Baltimore MD 2002-2013; Int S Jas' Par So Pasadena CA 2001-2002; Int St. Jas Ch So Pasadena 2001-2002; Int S Patricks Ch And Day Sch Thousand Oaks CA 1998-2001; Int S Tim's Epis Ch S Louis MO 1998; Int S Ptr's Epis Ch S Louis MO 1997-1998; Int St. Ptr's Ch Ladue MO 1997-1998; Int S Mart-In-The-Fields Par Winnetka CA 1995-1996; Int Chr The King A Jubilee Mnstry Palmdale CA 1994-1995; R Trin Epis Ch Santa Barbara CA 1986-1994; Coordntr Wrshp GC 1985-1988; Transition Spec Dio Los Angeles Los Angeles CA 1981-2013, 2003-, Comm. Liturg & Mus (chair) 1976-1988; Vic S Fran Of Assisi Epis Ch Simi Vlly CA 1980-1986; R S Barth's Epis Ch Poway CA 1967-1980; Asst R H Trin Epis Ch Covina CA 1966-1967; Cur S

W

Mary's Par Laguna Bch CA 1964-1966; Dioc Coun, Comm. Liturg & Mus Dio San Diego San Diego CA 1974-1976. Alb Inst 2002; Conf. Ord of S Ben 1965; Fresh Start Fac 2009; Int Mnstry Ntwk Fac 2002; TMEC 1997.

WARD, Suzanne Lynn (SJ) 1934 S Santa Fe Ave, Visalia CA 93292 **St Pauls Epis Fllshp Visalia CA 2013-** B Weiser ID 1952 d Thomas & Lois. Cert California St U 1977; BA U of Montana 1995; Cert California St U 1997; MDiv Mennonite Brethren Biblic Sem 2009. D 6/14/1997 Bp David Mercer Schofield P 6/27/2009 Bp Jerry Alban Lamb. m 9/2/1978 Jonathan L J Ward c 2. D S Paul's Epis Ch Visalia CA 1997-2008; Bd Mem Tulare-Kings Cnty Homeless Allnce 2015-2017; Pres of Stndg Com Epis Dio San Joaquin Modesto CA 2014-2015.

WARD JR, Tom (Tenn) Po Box 3270, Sewanee TN 37375 B Meridian MS 1945 s Thomas & Carolyn. BA U So 1967; MA Oxf GB 1969; MDiv VTS 1975. D 5/31/1975 P 5/31/1976 Bp Duncan Montgomery Gray Jr. m 5/19/1974 Margaret Nagley Ward c 1. Chapl Sewanee U So TS Sewanee TN 1994-2005; R Chr Ch Cathd Nashville TN 1981-1994; R All SS Epis Ch Grenada MS 1977-1981; Asst Trin Ch Hattiesburg MS 1975-1977.

WARD, Valerie K (Los) PO Box 1868, Santa Maria CA 93456 B Fort Sam Houston TX 1949 d Peter & Phyllis. Cert of Diac Stds Bloy Hse The ETS At Claremont; BS Fran Marion 1972. D 1/5/2014 Bp Joseph Jon Bruno. c 1.

WARDE, Erin J (Dal) 14115 Hillcrest Rd, Dallas TX 75254 **Assoc The Epis Ch Of The Trsfg Dallas TX 2015-** B Montgomery AL 1987 d Peter & Gwendolyn Claire. BS Troy U 2009; MDiv Epis TS Of The SW 2012; MDiv Epis TS of the SW 2012. D 12/21/2011 P 8/3/2012 Bp Philip Menzie Duncan II. Cur S Paul's Ch Waco TX 2012-2015. ewarde@transfiguration.net

WARDER, Oran Edward (Va) 228 S Pitt St, Alexandria VA 22314 **R S Paul's Epis Ch Alexandria VA 1999-** B Philippi WV 1961 s Joseph & Mary. BA Marshall U 1984; MA Marshall U 1985; MDiv VTS 1988. D 6/1/1988 Bp Robert Poland Atkinson P 6/1/1989 Bp William Franklin Carr. m 1/17/2010 Barbara Califf Warder c 3. VTS Alexandria VA 2011, 2006, 2004, 2003, 2002; Cn To Ordnry Dio Delaware Wilmington 1993-1999; Assoc S Phil's Epis Ch Laurel MD 1990-1993; Asst Trin Ch Huntington WV 1988-1990.

WARE, Anita Faye (WNC) 1201 S New Hope Rd, Gastonia NC 28054 B North Carolina 1965 d Michael & Shirley. D 1/23/2010 Bp Porter Taylor. D All SS' Epis Ch Gastonia NC 2010-2016.

WARE, David James (Md) 5603 N Charles St, Baltimore MD 21210 **The Ch Of The Redeem Baltimore MD 2015-** B Oak Ridge TN 1962 s Kenneth & Mary. BA Ya 1984; MA S Johns Coll Santa Fe NM 1991; MDiv GTS 1995. D 6/17/1995 Bp Jane Hart Holmes Dixon P 1/6/1996 Bp Ronald Hayward Haines. m 10/7/1989 Sarah Adams Hoover c 1. R St Jn's Ch Cold Sprg Harbor NY 2007-2015; Hd of Upper Sch Cathd of St Ptr & St Paul Washington DC 2001-2007; Hd of Upper Sch S Alb's Sch Washington DC 2001-2007; Assoc Trin Par Wilmington DE 1997-2001; Assoc Chr Ch Ridgewood NJ 1995-1997. dware@redeemeronline.com

WARE, Jordan H (FtW) All Saints' Episcopal Church, 5001 Crestline Rd, Fort Worth TX 76107 **Assoc All SS' Epis Ch Ft Worth TX 2013-; Chair, COM Dio Ft Worth Ft Worth TX 2015-** B Dallas Texas 1985 d Mark & Virginia. BA U of Texas 2007; MDiv Ya Berk 2013. D 12/21/2012 P 7/9/2013 Bp Rayford Baines High Jr. m 6/22/2013 Derek Kevin Ware. Auth, "The Ultimate Quest: A Geek's Guide to (the Epis) Ch," Ch Pub, 2017. mthware@asecfw.org

WAREHAM, George Ludwig (NwPa) 3111 Pearl Dr, New Castle PA 16105 **Ret 2004-** B Furstenfeldbrook W. Germany 1956 s Samuel & Clara. BA Thiel Coll 1989; MDiv TESM 1993. D 10/30/1993 P 5/1/1994 Bp Robert Deane Rowley Jr. m Agatha S Littlefield c 1. R Trin Ch New Castle PA 2001-2003; Dir - Yth Comm. Assoc Dio NW Pennsylvania Erie PA 1994-2001; S Jn's Epis Ch Sharon PA 1994-2001. Ord Of S Lk.

WAREING, Robert Edgar (Tex) 3122 Red Maple Dr, Friendswood TX 77546 B Corsicana TX 1947 s Edgar & Betty. BS Texas A&M U 1969; MDiv VTS 1981. D 6/17/1981 Bp Roger Howard Cilley P 2/25/1982 Bp Maurice Manuel Benitez. m 8/15/1970 Patricia Wareing. R All SS Epis Ch Stafford TX 1999-2008; R Ch Of The Gd Shpd Friendswood TX 1990-1999; Chr Epis Ch Cedar Pk TX 1986-1990; Chr Epis Ch Cedar Pk TX 1986-1990; Vic Chr Leander TX 1985-1990; The Great Cmsn Fndt Houston TX 1985-1990; Cur S Matt's Ch Austin TX 1981-1985.

WARFEL, John B (NY) 17 Crescent Pl, Middletown NY 10940 B Cheverly MD 1958 s George & Patricia. BS Geo 1980; MDiv CDSP 1993. D 6/5/1993 P 12/4/1993 Bp William Edwin Swing. m 6/17/2010 Thomas Peter Mollicone. R Gr Ch Middletown NY 1998-2016; Chr Ch Las Vegas NV 1993-1998. "The Ultimate Conclusion to Every Question," *Sermons That Wk XIV*, Morehouse, 2006.

WARFIELD JR, Edward Snowden (Md) 7200 Third Ave Apt C-036, Sykesville MD 21784 **Died 3/18/2016** B Baltimore MD 1933 s Edward & Betty. BA JHU 1956; MDiv VTS 1962. D 6/26/1962 Bp Harry Lee Doll P 4/10/1963 Bp Noble C Powell. m 10/19/1973 Mary Rex Keener c 4. Assoc S Barth's Ch Baltimore MD 2003-2016, Assoc 1995-1996; Ret St Bartholomews Epis Baltimore MD 1995-2016; Ch Of S Marks On The Hill Pikesville MD 1987-1991; Assoc S Mk-on-the Hill Baltimore MD 1986-1993; P Ch Of The Mssh Baltimore

MD 1969-1986; R Ascen Middle River MD 1963-1967; Cur H Trin Essex MD 1962-1963.

WARFILED, Sara D 6/10/2017 Bp Marc Handley Andrus.

WARING, J(ames) Donald (NY) 802 Broadway, New York NY 10003 **R Gr Epis Ch New York NY 2004-; Trst Epis Chars of the Dio NY New York NY 2011-; Trst Gr Ch Sch New York New York NY 2004-** B Orange NJ 1962 s James & Virginia. BA U of Sioux Falls 1984; MDiv GTS 1989. D 6/24/1989 Bp H Coleman Mcgehee Jr P 4/21/1990 Bp R aymond Stewart Wood Jr. m 12/30/1995 Stacie Anne Soule c 2. Dn Dio Sthrn Ohio Cincinnati OH 1998-2004; R S Thos Epis Ch Terrace Pk OH 1995-2004; Int R Chr Ch Cranbrook Bloomfield Hills MI 1993-1995, Assoc R 1989-1995. Auth, "Best Sermons 4"; Auth, "Sermons That Wk Iii"; Auth, "Sermons That Wk Vi". dwaring@gracechurchnyc.org

WARLEY, Dianne Goodwin (Ct) 73 Ayers Point Rd, Old Saybrook CT 06475 **Assoc S Jn's Epis Ch Niantic CT 2013-** B Milton MA 1943 D 12/9/2000 Bp Andrew Donnan Smith. m 5/23/1964 Edward Rogers Warley c 2.

WARNE II, William Thomas (CPa) 197 Urie Ave., Lake Winola PA 18625 B Scranton, PA 1941 s Thomas & Edna. BA Hobart and Wm Smith Colleges 1963; STB/MDiv PDS 1966; Cert VTS 1979. D 6/18/1966 P 3/18/1967 Bp Frederick Warnecke. m 5/23/1964 Frances Louise DeMartino c 3. P in Res Ch Of The Gd Shpd Scranton PA 2005-2009, Supply P 2005; R Ch of the Nativ-St Steph Newport PA 1974-2004; D/P-in-c Calv Epis Ch Wilkes-Barre PA 1966-1969; Pres, Bd Trst Epis Commons Inc. Newport 1990-2004; Pres, Bd Trst Epis Gardens Inc. Thompsontown 1985-2004; Chair Of Plnng Com Dio Cntrl Pennsylvania Harrisburg PA 1977-1983. Harrisburg Cler, Dio Cntrl PA 1974-2004; Newport Min 1974-2004. Hon Cn S Steph's Cathd 1991; Eleanor Henschen Memi Awd For Vol Serv Tri-Cnty MHA 1981.

WARNE III, William Thomas (Oly) 2915 SE 173rd Ct, Vancouver WA 98683 **R Ch Of The Gd Shpd Vancouver WA 2008-** B Wilkes-Barre PA 1967 s William & Frances. Dplma U of Kent Cbury UK 1988; BA Hobart and Wm Smith Colleges 1989; California St U Northridge 1992; MDiv Sewanee: The U So, TS 1997; DMin SWTS 2003. D 6/6/1997 P 2/21/1998 Bp Michael Whittington Creighton. m 6/24/1994 Saran R Warne c 3. R S Jn's Epis Ch Huntingdon PA 1997-2008. Druid Soc of Hob 1988; Soc of S Jn the Evang 1997. tomw@goodshepherdvancouver.org

WARNECKE JR, Frederick John (NC) 3017 Lake Forest Dr, Greensboro NC 27408 **Int Vic S Paul's Epis Ch Thomasville NC 2002-** B Ridgewood NJ 1933 s Frederick & Edith. BA Leh 1955; MDiv VTS 1958. D 5/30/1958 Bp Benjamin M Washburn P 5/1/1959 Bp Frederick Warnecke. m 6/21/1958 Abigail B Warnecke c 2. S Fran Ch Greensboro NC 1985-1999; R S Jas Ch Montclair NJ 1971-1985; R Emm Ch At Brook Hill Richmond VA 1961-1971; In-Charge S Ptr's Par Ch New Kent VA 1958-1961; In-Charge S Tim's Richmond VA 1958-1961. Confrerie De La Chaine Des Rotisseurs 2001; Confrerie Des Chevaliers Du Tastevin 1981. Commandeur Confrerie Des Chevaliers Du Tastevin 2003; Chevalier Confrerie Des Chevaliers Du Tastevin 1981; Phi Beta Kappa 1955; Chevalier Du Taste Vin.

WARNER, Anthony Francis (Md) 2434 Cape Horn Rd, Hampstead MD 21074 **S Geo Ch Hampstead MD 2011-** B Danville PA 1943 s Anthony & Theophilia. Cath U; Geo Washington Unversity; BSIE Penn 1954. Rec 6/7/2011 as Deacon Bp Eugene Taylor Sutton. m 11/23/1957 Sheila Warner c 3.

WARNER, Christopher Scott (At) 1315 Cove Ave, Sullivans Island SC 29482 **R S Chris Camp & Conf Cntr Johns Island SC 2007-** B Pueblo CO 1969 s Donald & Ellen. BA U NC 1991; MDiv TESM 2000. D 6/10/2000 Bp Robert William Duncan P 1/16/2001 Bp Robert Gould Tharp. m 10/23/1993 Catherine Dixon Warner c 3. Ch Of The H Cross Sullivans Island SC 2011-2013, Assoc 2007-2010, Assoc 2002-2007; S Chris C&C Johns Island SC 2007-2010; Cur Trin Epis Ch Columbus GA 2000-2002.

WARNER, Dale Alford (Fla) 2736 NW 77th Blvd Apt #152, Gainesville FL 32606 **Ret 1997-** B Toledo OH 1927 s Charles & Alma. BS U of Florida 1949; PhD U of Florida 1953; MDiv Sewanee: The U So, TS 1987. D 6/14/1987 Bp Frank S Cerveny P 2/2/1988 Bp William Hopkins Folwell. m 8/15/1948 Lempi Fredericka Warner c 4. P-in-c S Mich's Ch Gainesville FL 2007-2008; Vic Trin Epis Ch Melrose FL 1990-1997; Asst Epis Ch Of The Resurr Longwood FL 1987-1990. Phi Beta Kappa U of Florida 1952.

WARNER, David Maxwell (Va) 8206 Chamberlayne Rd, Richmond VA 23227 **Died 1/1/2017** B Denver CO 1931 s Maxwell & Ethel. BA U Denv 1952; LTh SWTS 1955. D 6/29/1955 P 1/25/1956 Bp Joseph Summerville Minnis. m 11/26/1994 Penelope G Warner c 5. Int S Paul's Owens King Geo VA 2002-2004; Int S Dav's Ch Aylett VA 2000-2001; Int Aquia Ch Stafford VA 1996-1998; Ret 1994-2017; Serv Ch of Engl 1994-1995; P-in-c Emm Ch At Brook Hill Richmond VA 1994; R Chr Ascen Ch Richmond VA 1974-1994; 1971-1974; R Ch Of The Gd Shpd Ogden UT 1959-1971; S Paul's Epis Ch Vernal UT 1957-1959; Vic S Tim's Epis Ch Rangely CO 1957-1959; Chapl Fitzsimmons Hosp Aurora CO 1956-1967; Vic 1956-1957; The Ch Of Chr The King (Epis) Arvada CO 1956-1957; Vic S Martha's Epis Ch Westminster CO 1955-1957.

WARNER, Deborah (Mass) Church of the Messiah, 13 Church St, Woods Hole MA 02543 **R Ch Of The Mssh Woods Hole MA 2008-, P-in-c 2005-** B

New York NY 1951 d Wolcott & Eloise. BA Salem Coll Winston-Salem NC 1974; MDiv UTS 1980. D 6/5/1982 Bp Paul Moore Jr P 4/16/1983 Bp Walter Decoster Dennis Jr. R S Dunstans Epis Ch Dover MA 1990-2005; Epis Ch Of S Thos Taunton MA 1987-1990; Ch Of S Jn The Evang Hingham MA 1984-1987; Asst Chr Ch Riverdale Bronx NY 1982-1984; Chapl Res Hosp Chapl Inc NYC 1980-1981; Co-Chair Cler Fam Ntwk Dio Massachusetts Boston MA 1990-1993, Co-Chair Cler Fam Ntwk 1990-1993, COM 1986-1992, COM 1986-1989. Auth, "Bk Revs," *ATR*. Massachusetts Epis Cler Assiciation 1984.

WARNER, Donald Emil (Neb) 422 W 2nd St # 1026, Grand Island NE 68801 B Waverly NE 1922 s Arthur & Ruth. BS U of Nebraska 1947. D 11/8/1985 Bp James Daniel Warner. m 4/5/1947 Elizabeth Ann Kouanda c 3. D Epis Ch Of S Fran-In-The-Vlly Green Vlly AZ 1991-1992; D S Steph's Ch Grand Island NE 1985-2012.

WARNER, Donald Nelson (Colo) 6961 S. Cherokee St., Littleton CO 80120 B Dallas TX 1935 s Nelson & Margaret. BA Tarkio Coll 1957; MSM Sthrn Bapt TS 1960; MDiv Nash 1973. D 3/19/1973 Bp William Hopkins Folwell P 9/21/1973 Bp William Carl Frey. c 2. Inerim Min of Mus S Jn's Cathd Jacksonville FL 2006-2007; R S Tim's Epis Ch Littleton CO 1988-2003, Assoc 1976-1987, Cur 1973-1976; Chair Mus ; Liturg Com 1978-1986; R S Mk's Epis Ch Durango CO 1977-1988; Ex Coun & Stndg Com Dio Colorado Denver CO 1980-1988; Chair Liturg & Mus Com Dio Colorado 1978-1986. Compsr, "3 Mus Settings Of Rite 2". AGO 2007; Integrity 1995.

WARNER, Janet Avery (EO) 444 NW Apollo Rd, Prineville OR 97754 **D, Non-Stipendiary S Andr's Epis Ch Prineville OR 2002-** B Washington DC 1955 d Edward & Mary Jane. Estrn Oregon U 1975. D 5/1/2002 Bp William O Gregg. m 9/21/1975 Daniel Warner c 2.

WARNER, John Seawright (Ga) 2211 Dartmouth Rd, Augusta GA 30904 **D S Aug Of Cbury Ch Augusta GA 2002-** B New Haven CT 1952 s George & Patricia. BA NE Louisiana U 1974; MS NE Louisiana U 1977; MBA Augusta St U 1989. D 7/9/2002 Bp Henry Irving Louttit. m 3/31/1979 Marsha Sue Warner c 1.

WARNER, Katherine Wakefield (SwFla) PO Box 272, Boca Grande FL 33921 **Com 1988-; Asst S Lk's Chap Of The Epis Hm 1987-** B Louisville KY 1941 d George & Gladys. BA Sarah Lawr Coll 1966; MDiv GTS 1986. D 6/24/1986 P 10/1/1987 Bp David Reed. m 4/27/1974 Lawrence Askew Warner c 4. Assoc S Andr's Ch Boca Grande FL 2004-2012; S Lk's Chap Louisville KY 1994-1997; Liturg Cmsn 1987-1991; 1987-1990; D-In-Res S Andr's Ch Louisville KY 1986-1987. cappy@iglou.com

WARNER, Keithly R (At) P.O. Box 468, Christiansted VI 00821 B 1937 s Rufus & Ruby. ETSC; Inter Amer U of Puerto Rico. D 6/11/1971 P 5/1/1972 Bp Dean Theodore Stevenson. R S Jn's Ch Christiansted St Croix VI 1994-1997; S Aug's Epis Ch St Petersburg FL 1989-1994; Ch Of Beth Saratoga Spg NY 1986-1988; Chapl Jersey City St Coll 1980-1985; Ch Of The Incarn Jersey City NJ 1977-1985; Calv Ch Charleston SC 1976; R Ch Of S Simon The Cyrenian New Rochelle NY 1972-1976. SSC.

WARNER, Kevin C (SwFla) 622 Tanana Fall Drive, Ruskin FL 33570 **S Jn The Div Epis Ch Sun City Cntr FL 2014-** B Fort Wayne IN 1957 s Roger & Carol. BA Olivet Coll 1980; MDiv VTS 1985. D 6/29/1985 Bp H Coleman Mcgehee Jr P 2/22/1986 Bp William Arthur Beckham. m 8/9/1980 Susan E Warner c 4. R S Dunst's Epis Ch San Diego CA 2009-2014; R Sprt of Gr Luth Epis Ch W Bloomfield MI 1994-2009; R S Kath's Ch Williamston MI 1988-1994; Asst R Gr Epis Ch Anderson SC 1985-1988. 3ontanana@gmail.com

WARNER JR, Richard Wright (EC) 835 Calabash Rd. NW, Calabash NC 28467 B New Castle PA 1938 s Richard & Emily. BA Westminster Coll 1961; MEd SUNY 1966; EdD SUNY 1969; Auburn U 1978; Cert Theol Stud VTS 1984. D 5/29/1984 P 12/5/1984 Bp Brice Sidney Sanders. m 10/15/1989 Frances B Warner c 3. R S Jas The Fisherman Epis Ch Shallotte NC 1989-2003; R S Paul's Epis Ch Wilmington NC 1988-1989; R S Thos' Epis Ch Ahoskie NC 1985-1988; Asst S Steph's Ch Goldsboro NC 1984-1985. Auth, "Grp Counslg: Theory And Process," Rand Mcnally, 1976; Auth, "Counslg: Theory & Process," Allyn And Bacon/Houghton/Mifflin. DSA Amer Personl And Gdnc 1980; Alum Prof Auburn U 1978. frwarner@atmc.net

WARNER, Suzanne McCarroll (Ky) 1265 Bassett Ave, Louisville KY 40204 B Little Rock AR 1936 d John & Willma. BA Rhodes Coll 1957; JD U of Louisville 1977; MA Presb TS 2008; MA Sewanee: The U So, TS 2010. D 12/21/2009 P 7/8/2010 Bp Ted Gulick Jr. c 3.

✠ WARNER, The Rt Rev Vincent Waydell (Oly) Po Box 12126, Seattle WA 98102 B Roanoke VA 1940 s Vincent & Virginia. Lic VTS 1971; VTS 1990. D 6/4/1971 P 12/1/1971 Bp William Henry Marmion Con 7/8/1989 for Oly. m 2/8/2004 Shen Yu Warner c 1. Ret Bp of Olympia Dio Olympia Seattle 2007, 1989-2007; R S Andr's Ch Wellesley MA 1983-1989; Archd Dio Maine Portland ME 1980-1983; R S Ptr's Ch Osterville MA 1976-1980; Asst Chr Ch Grosse Pointe Grosse Pointe Farms MI 1974-1976; Asst S Jn's Ch Roanoke VA 1971-1974.

WARNKE, James William (Nwk) 680 Albin St, Teaneck NJ 07666 B Plattsburg NY 1947 s Ernest & Ruth. BA Ford 1969; MA Manhattan Coll 1974; MS Ford

1978; DAS GTS 1996. D 6/1/1996 Bp John Shelby Spong P 12/1/1997 Bp Jack Marston Mckelvey. m 12/28/1969 Marie Jones c 2. Assoc S Paul's Ch Englewood NJ 1999-2009; S Mk's Ch Teaneck NJ 1996-1999. Auth, "Becoming An Everyday Mystic," Abbey Press, 1990.

WARNOCK, James Howard (NI) 2365 N Miller Ave, Marion IN 46952 **R Geth Epis Ch Marion IN 2002-; Dioc Coun Dio Nthrn Indiana So Bend IN 2010-, Stndg Com 2005-2011, COM 2004-** B San Francisco CA 1951 s Howard & Dorothy. MCS Regent Coll Vancouver BC 1984; PhD U of Washington 1989; Dip Ang Stud Nash 1998. D 9/6/1998 P 3/13/1999 Bp Keith Lynn Ackerman. m 9/10/1976 Kresha Richman Warnock c 2. Adj Fac Taylor U 2010-2015; Asst All SS Par Long Bch CA 1999-2002. Amer Hist Assn; Conf On Faith & Hist.

WARREN III, Allan Bevier (Mass) 30 Brimmer St, Boston MA 02108 **R The Ch Of The Adv Boston MA 1999-, Asst to the R 1990-1993** B Charlottsville VA 1947 s Allan & Claudia. STB GTS; BA Pr. D 6/25/1972 Bp John Adams Pinckney P 3/31/1973 Bp George Moyer Alexander. R Ch Of The Resurr New York NY 1993-1999; R Ch Of The Gd Shpd Waban MA 1984-1990; Cn The Amer Cathd of the H Trin Paris 75008 1981-1984; Cur Ch Of The Trsfg New York NY 1974-1981; All SS Epis Ch Clinton SC 1972-1974; Vic Ch Of The Epiph Laurens SC 1972-1974.

WARREN, Annika Laurin (Ct) 31 Woodland St, Hartford CT 06105 B Hartford CT 1959 d Hubbard & Annie. BS S Augustines Coll Raleigh NC 1981; MDiv VTS 1984. D 6/9/1984 Bp Arthur Edward Walmsley P 2/1/1985 Bp Clarence Nicholas Coleridge. m 7/11/1987 Mozallen McFadden. S Monica's Ch Hartford CT 1990-1993; Chapl Weaver HS Hartford CT 1987-1990; Chr Ch Cathd Hartford CT 1984-1987.

WARREN, Daniel (Me) 730 Mere Point Rd, Brunswick ME 04011 **The Par of S Mich's Auburn ME 2014-** B New York NY 1948 s George & Dorothy. BA Ya 1970; MDiv EDS 1977. D 6/11/1977 Bp Paul Moore Jr P 6/7/1978 Bp John Harris Burt. m 9/18/1976 Margaret L Warren c 2. S Paul's Ch Brunswick ME 1998-2011; R Gr Ch In Providence Providence RI 1982-1998; Dio Rhode Island Providence RI 1982-1985; Ch Of The H Trin New York NY 1979-1982; Assoc H Trin Epis Ch Inwood New York NY 1979-1982; S Michaels In The Hills Toledo OH 1977-1979. Auth, "Var arts," 2003. Fellowowship, Coll Of Preachers 1995.

WARREN, George Henry (WMass) 12 Walnut Hill Rd, Pascoag RI 02859 B Pawtucket RI 1945 s James & Anna. BA U of Rhode Island 1967; MDiv PDS 1971. D 6/5/1971 P 12/11/1971 Bp John S Higgins. m 12/9/2010 Annette Remington-Klein. P-inc S Mk's Ch Warwick RI 2003-2008; P-inc S Jn's Ch Millville MA 1998-2003; Non-par 1992-2001; Pstr Counslr S Camillus Hospice 1992-2001; P-inc S Jn's Epis Ch Sutton MA 1992-1995; Dio Wstrn Massachusetts Springfield 2003-2003; R Trin Epis Ch Milford MA 1975-1992; Cur S Barn Ch Warwick RI 1971-1974. Ord Of S Camillus (RC) 2001.

WARREN JR, Hallie DeLesslin (ETenn) 1021 Meadow Lake Rd, Chattanooga TN 37415 **Ret 1993-** B Camden SC 1928 s Hallie & Elnora. BA U of So Carolina 1950; MDiv Sewanee: The U So, TS 1953; SSAS Ya 1959. D 6/25/1953 P 3/1/1954 Bp Thomas N Carruthers. m 7/16/1949 Martha C Warren c 4. Int Ch Of The Nativ Ft Oglethorp GA 1996-1998; R S Ptr's Ch Chattanooga TN 1964-1993; R Gr Ch Waycross GA 1957-1964; Asst R S Paul's Epis Ch Chattanooga TN 1956-1957; S Alb's Ch Kingstree SC 1953-1956; Min In Charge S Steph's Ch S Steph SC 1953-1956.

WARREN, Harold Robert (Colo) 6625 Holyoke Ct, Fort Collins CO 80525 **Asst Chr's Epis Ch Castle Rock CO 2016-** B Needham MA 1948 s Robert & Agnes. BA U of So Florida 1970; MA U of So Florida 1972; MDiv Sewanee: The U So, TS 1975; DMin Columbia TS 1990. D 6/11/1975 Bp William Loftin Hargrave P 12/19/1975 Bp Emerson Paul Haynes. m 6/5/1971 Judith M Ackerman c 2. R S Lk's Epis Ch Ft Collins CO 2000-2011; R S Tim's Epis Ch Lake Jackson TX 1996-2000; R The Epis Ch Of The Gd Shpd Lake Wales FL 1989-1996; R S Sebastian's By The Sea Melbourne Bch FL 1983-1988; R S Mary's Epis Ch Palmetto FL 1977-1983; Cur S Bede's Ch St. Petersburg FL 1975-1977; Cmsn on the Mnstry Dio Colorado Denver CO 2005-2008, Bp's T/F on Human Sxlty 2003-2005; Mem of the Bp Quin Fndt Dio Texas Houston TX 1998-2000; Dn of the SW Dnry Dio Cntrl Florida Orlando FL 1994-1996, Mem of the Crt of Array 1993-1995; Chairman of the Educ Com Dio SW Florida Parrish FL 1982-1983, Cmsn on the Mnstry 1979-1981. Auth, *Personality Factors & Sprtl Styles (Thesis)*. Faithful Alum Awd Univ of the So 1999.

WARREN, Heather Anne (NC) 170 Reas Ford Rd, Earlysville VA 22936 B Bellshill, Scotland 1959 d James & Marjorie. BA Cor 1981; BA Oxf GB 1984; MDiv Candler TS Emory U 1985; PhD The JHU 1992. D 12/19/2009 P 6/26/2010 Bp Michael B Curry. c 2.

WARREN, J Lewis (Neb) 309 N 167th Plz Apt 5, Omaha NE 68118 B Texas City TX 1941 s James & Sidney. BA SMU 1964; MA U of Oregon 1966; MTS SWTS 1977; PhD OH SU 1979; DMin GTF 1994. D 6/14/1977 P 12/21/1977 Bp Charles Thomas Gaskell. m 8/29/1964 Rose Lee Christe c 1. R S Fran Epis Ch Scottsbluff NE 1983-2001; R Ch of St Jn the Evang Wisconsin Rapids WI 1979-1982; Asst Trin Ch Milwaukee WI 1977-1979; Eccl Crt Dio Nebraska Omaha NE 1990-1992; Stndg Com Dio Fond du Lac Appleton WI

1980-1982. Auth, "Var arts". Dplma APA; Ocampr; Ordo Constantini Magni; SHN. elias1941@gmail.com

WARREN, John Wells (Ala) 1347 Shelton Mill Rd, Auburn AL 36830 **P-in-c Epis Ch Of The Epiph Tallassee AL 2013-; P-in-c S Matt's in-the-Pines Epis Ch Seale AL 2006-; Chapl Dio Alabama Birmingham 1999-; Chapl S Dunst's: The Epis Ch at Auburn U Auburn AL 1999-** B Bryan TX 1952 s William & Carolyn. BA Auburn U 1974; MEd Auburn U 1979; U of Alabama 1986; Cert Sewanee: The U So, TS 1992; DMin Sewanee: The U So, TS 2004. D 1/13/1996 P 7/20/1996 Bp Robert Oran Miller. m 11/17/2009 Laura Leigh Williamson c 2. S Matthews In The Pines Seale AL 2009-2010; Vic Emm Epis Ch Auburn AL 2005-2006; Emm Epis Ch Opelika AL 2005-2006; H Trin Epis Ch Auburn AL 2000-2003; Vic S Mich's Epis Ch Fayette AL 1996-1999. The HSEC 2004. Phi Kappa Phi hon Soc Auburn U 1989; Phi Delta Kappa Educ Hon Auburn U 1980; Sigma Tau Delta Engl Hon Auburn U 1974.

WARREN, Joseph Palmer (Ala) 2017 6th Ave N, Birmingham AL 35203 B Mobile AL 1946 s Claude & Esther. BA U of Alabama 1970; MDiv VTS 1990. D 6/2/1990 P 4/10/1991 Bp Charles Farmer Duvall. m 9/7/1968 Susan L Warren. Dir Pstr Care The Cathd Ch Of The Adv Birmingham AL 1996-2012; S Mary's Fleeton Reedville VA 1991-1996; R S Steph's Ch Heathsville VA 1991-1996; D The Epis Ch Of The Nativ Dothan AL 1990-1991. Auth, *Restoring the Broken Image*, 2001. Dioc Coun of Alabama 2000.

WARREN, Matthew Douglas (NCal) Christ the King Episcopal Church, 545 Lawrence St, Quincy CA 95971 **H Sprt Mssn Lake Almanor CA 2015-; Vic Chr The King Quincy CA 2013-** B Tuscon AZ 1979 s Douglas & Leslie. AB Occ 2001; Ya Berk 2004; Yale DS 2004. D 10/13/2012 P 5/4/2013 Bp Barry Leigh Beisner. m 7/24/2004 Kristy Marie Warren c 2. Prog Mgr YAYA Dio California San Francisco CA 2005-2006.

WARREN, Penelope Sandra Muehl (Minn) 3124 Utah Ave N, Crystal MN 55427 B Milwaukee WI 1946 d Earl & Luella. BS U of Wisconsin 1969; MS Illinois St U 1974; PhD Pur 1978; MDiv CDSP 1986. D 6/4/1988 P 6/1/1989 Bp William Edwin Swing. m 9/21/1968 Richard Lynn Warren. Assoc Ch Of The H Innoc San Francisco CA 2000-2004; Sr P Assoc The Epis Ch Of S Jn The Evang San Francisco CA 1994-2000, 1991-1993; Asst R Ch Of The Incarn San Francisco CA 1988-1990; Counslr San Francisco St U CA 1977-1988.

WARREN JR, Ralph (SeFla) 223 East Tall Oaks Circle, Palm Beach Gardens FL 33410 **Chplin, Rtd Cler & surviving spouses Dio SE Florida 2009-; August R S Chris Sum Chap Winter Harbor ME 2009-; Trst ECBF 1990-** B New York NY 1940 s Ralph & Virginia. BA Trin 1962; STM Ya Berk 1965; Dip Pstr Stud U of Birmingham GB 1966; Ya Berk 1989. D 6/12/1965 P 12/17/1966 Bp Horace W B Donegan. m 12/5/1998 Roselle Warren c 2. Dio SE Florida 2000-2002; Dio SE Florida 1996-1998; Trst & Chairman Alb Inst Beth MD 1990-2000; R The Epis Ch Of Beth-By-The-Sea Palm Bch FL 1982-2009; R S Paul's Epis Ch Pittsburgh PA 1977-1982; P-in-c S Jas Ch New York NY 1976, Asst 1966-1977. Chapl Most Venerable Ord Hosp of S Jn in Jerusal 1978. Chapl Most Venerable Ord Hosp of S Jn 1983.

WARREN, Randall Richard (WMich) 247 W Lovell St, Kalamazoo MI 49007 **P-in-c S Lk's Par Kalamazoo MI 2011-** B Fort Lauderdale FL 1961 s Richard & Veneta. BA Milligan Coll 1983; MDiv SWTS 1986; ACPE Chr Hosp Oak Lawn IL 1987; CG Jung Inst 1992; DMin GTF 1997. D 6/17/1989 P 12/16/1989 Bp Frank Tracy Griswold III. T/F Mem Title IV T/F II: On Educ 2009-2012; Vic Chr The King Ch Lansing IL 1999-2007; Dir, Off of Pstr Care Dio Chicago Chicago IL 1998-2011; Mssnr Trin Epis Ch Lansing IL 1996-1998; P-in-c Ch Of The H Comm Maywood IL 1995-1996; Cler Team Mem Gr Ch Oak Pk IL 1992-1994; P-in-c H Trin Ch Skokie IL 1991-1992; Pstr Care Instr Sch for Deacons Dio Chicago IL 1990-2003; Chapl Vitas Innovative Hospice Care Lombard IL 1990-1997; Cur Ch Of Our Sav Elmhurst IL 1989-1990. Auth, "Incarnating Ch: The Liturg Redesign of a Sm Mssn Cong," *God's Friends*, St. Greg of Nyssa, 2004; Auth, "Contrib to," *Enriching Our Wrshp 2*, Ch Pub, 2000; Auth, "Connecting Themes through Liturg Seasons," *Open*, Associated Parishes, 1999; Auth, "Trsfg after the Bomb," *Pilgrimage mag*, Pilgrimage Press, 1998. The Nathan Newtork 2004-2011.

WARREN, Robert James (Eur) Christ Church, 8 rue d Bon Pasteur, Clermont-Ferrand 63000 France **Chr Ch Clermont-Ferrand France Royat 63130 2012-** B Vancouver BC 1958 s James & Joan. BTh McGill U 1982; MDiv Montreal Dioc Theol Coll 1984; MTh U of Edinburgh 2011. Trans 7/1/2012 Bp Pierre W Whalon. m 4/19/2008 Caireen Ailsa Warren c 1.

WARREN, Thomas Paine Hopfengardner (EC) 800 Rountree Ave, Kinston NC 28501 **S Mary's Ch Kinston NC 2011-** B Cheverly MD 1981 s George & Sandra. BS USCG Acad 2003; MDiv Duke DS 2011; MDiv Duke DS 2011. D 6/11/2011 P 2/11/2012 Bp Clifton Daniel III. m 5/30/2004 Holly Alisha Carraway Warren c 1.

WARREN, Victoria Daniel (Nev) 1776 Us Highway 50, Glenbrook NV 89413 **R S Jn's In The Wilderness Ch Glenbrook NV 2015-, P-in-c 2012-2015, 2011; Chairman Mnstry Dvlpmt Cmsn Dio Nevada Las Vegas 2013-, Mem Cmsn on Ord and Licensing 2012-** B Monroe OK 1947 d Robert & Bonnie. BA Notre Dame Coll Belmont CA 1971; CTS CDSP 2005; CTS CDSP 2005.

D 10/24/2008 P 6/27/2009 Bp Dan Thomas Edwards. m 10/2/2010 Ronald Lee Warren c 3. Assoc S Ptr's Epis Ch Carson City NV 2009-2011.

WARREN-BROWN, Judith Anne (CFla) D 5/26/2012 Bp Gregory Orrin Brewer.

WARRINGTON, James Malcolm (Nwk) 2849 Meadow Ln, Falls Church VA 22042 B Boston MA 1926 s Lester & Helen. BA VMI 1950; BD Sewanee: The U So, TS 1960; MBA FD 1966. D 6/28/1960 Bp Frederick D Goodwin P 7/1/1961 Bp Samuel B Chilton. Off Of Bsh For ArmdF New York NY 1966-1977; Asst Ch Of The Atone Tenafly NJ 1963-1964; Cur S Jn's Epis Ch Mc Lean VA 1960-1963.

WARTHAN, Frank Avery (Chi) 298 S Harrison Ave, Kankakee IL 60901 B Dinwiddie County VA 1938 s Linwood & Elizabeth. BS Marymount Coll 1972. D 10/5/1975 P 4/10/1976 Bp William Davidson. m 7/5/1980 Toni Warthan. R S Paul's Ch Kankakee IL 1999-2009; St Philips Epis Ch Waukesha WI 1995-1998; Non-par Dio Milwaukee Milwaukee WI 1988-1999; Dio Wstrn Kansas Hutchinson KS 1983-1988; Vic S Mk's Ch Med Ldg KS 1983-1988, Assoc 1979-1982; Assoc S Thos Ch Garden City KS 1981-1982; Chr Ch Kingman KS 1979-1988; Gr Ch Anth KS 1979-1988; S Fran Cmnty Serv Inc. Salina KS 1975-1977.

WARWICK, Charles C (Be) PO Box 406, New Milford PA 18834 **S Steph's Epis Ch Wilkes Barre PA 2016-; The Epis Ch Of S Clem And S Ptr Wilkes Barre PA 2016-; S Andr's Ch Nanticoke PA 2014-** B Hazleton PA 1959 s Charles & Doris. BA Kings Coll 1982. D 11/1/2011 P 5/18/2012 Bp Paul Victor Marshall. m 10/19/1985 Patty K Warwick c 1. S Steph's Ch Whitehall PA 2013-2014; S Mk's New Milford PA 2011-2013.

WARWICK, Eilene Robinson (Miss) 25 Twelve Oaks Dr, Madison MS 39110 B Jackson MS 1931 d Carroll & Jane. BA Belhaven Coll 1956; MA Mississippi Coll 1973; EFM Sewanee: The U So, TS 1997. D 1/15/2000 Bp Alfred Marble Jr. m 1/10/1953 Charles Warwick c 3. Bd Mem Recovery Mnstrs of the Epis Ch 2002-2006; Recovery Mnstry Dio Mississippi Jackson MS 2000-2003. Recovery Mnstrs of the Epis Ch 1998.

WARWICK-SABINO, Debra Ann (NCal) 1405 Kentucky St, Fairfield CA 94533 **R Epis Ch Of Our Sav Placerville CA 2014-; Title IV Coordntr The Epis Dio Nthrn California Sacramento CA 2010-, Safe Ch Coordntr 2003-** B Detroit MI 1952 d William & Nancy. BS Estrn Michigan U; MA PSR; MDiv PSR 1993; MA PSR 1994. D 10/18/1998 P 5/16/1999 Bp Jerry Alban Lamb. m 11/12/1993 Robert Lewis Sabino c 5. R Gr Epis Ch Fairfield CA 2004-2014; Asst R Ch Of S Mart Davis CA 1999-2004; Asst Cur Trin Epis Ch Reno NV 1998-1999. Coll of Chapl.

WAS, Brent (Ore) 120 Main St, Amesbury MA 01913 **R Ch Of The Resurr Eugene OR 2011-** B Bad Kreuznach Germany 1971 s Robert & Barbara. BA Carnegie Mellon U 1993; MDiv Harvard DS 2005; DMin EDS 2010. D 1/8/2011 P 6/25/2011 Bp M(Arvil) Thomas Shaw. m 8/26/2006 Windy Marie Dayton c 2. Cur S Jas Ch Amesbury MA 2011-2013; S Jn's Chap Cambridge MA 2006-2015; Soc-St Jn The Evang Cambridge MA 2006-2011.

WASDYKE, Wesley Roger (NH) 6569 The Masters Ave, Lakewood Ranch FL 34202 **Gr Ch Manchester NH 1980-** B Passaic NJ 1942 s Bernard & Cecelia. Intern 76-77/ Res 77-79 UVM Burlington VT; BA Hope Coll 1964; MDiv EDS 1969; MD Washington U St. Louis 1976; Cert Amer Bd Anesth 1981. D 6/21/1969 Bp Anson Phelps Stokes Jr P 1/5/1970 Bp Roger W Blanchard. m 7/20/1968 Cynthia Spinney c 2. Asst S Bon Ch Sarasota FL 2006-2010; P-in-c S Mary Magd Bradenton FL 2003-2005; Asst S Mich & S Geo S Louis MO 1975-1976; Asst Ch Of The H Comm S Louis MO 1972-1973; Asst Chr Ch Cathd Cincinnati OH 1969-1972; COM Dio New Hampshire Concord NH 1994-2000.

WASHAM JR, Charles W (Lex) 2734 Chancellor Drive, Suite 202, Crestview Hills KY 41017 **Dir Dio Lexington Lexington 1994-, Chairman of COM 2003-2005, Bp's Consult and Pstr Counslr for Cler 2001-2011** B Oceanside CA 1952 s Charles & Sherry. BA Coll of Idaho 1974; Duke 1975; MDiv VTS 1977; CPE Residency Epis TS of the SW 1978; Advncd CPE 1981; Emory U 1983; MEd Georgia St U 1984; Psychoanalytic Cert Seabury Inst for Psych 1987; DMin GTF at Notre Dame 1989; MSW U of Kentucky 1998. D 6/18/1977 Bp Hunley Agee Elebash P 1/15/1978 Bp John Harris Burt. m 7/6/1989 Constance J Washam c 1. P-in-c Ch Of The H Trin Georgetown KY 2005-2006; Assoc Ch Of The Gd Shpd Lexington KY 1994; Pstr Psych Gr And S Steph's Epis Ch Colorado Sprg CO 1992-1993; Dn and Chapl Heathwood Hall Epis Sch Columbia SC 1989-1991; Pstr Psych S Anne's Epis Ch Atlanta GA 1984-1989; Dn of Students Pace Acad Atlanta GA 1983-1984; Chapl S Andew's Sch Boca Raton FL 1980-1982; Asst S Tim's Epis Ch Massillon OH 1979-1980; Asst Chapl S Steph's Epis Sch Austin TX 1978-1979; Cur S Jn's Ch Youngstown OH 1977-1978. Amer Acad of Psychotherapists 1990; Amer Assn of Mar and Fam Ther 1984; AAPC 1984; Amer Grp Psych Assn 1984; ACPE 1983; Natl Cert Grp Psychotherapists 1998. DD Sem of the SW 2012; Awd of Merit The Can Ch Press 2012; Fell AAMFT 2010; Kentucky Colonel Kentucky Gvnr 2008; DD Berk 2007; Fell AAPC 1998.

WASHBURN, Elizabeth Lane (WMass) D 6/10/2017 Bp Doug Fisher.

WASHINGTON, Derek Wayne (Eau) 931 Leroy Ct, River Falls WI 54022 B Sumter SC 1960 s Will & Mary. BD U of No Florida 1990; MDiv TESM 1996.

D 6/13/1996 P 12/8/1996 Bp Stephen Hays Jecko. m 11/12/1994 Dorothy A McGinnis c 3. Dio Eau Claire Eau Claire WI 2012-2014; S Paul's Ch Hudson WI 2005-2007; Angl Frontier Missions Richmond VA 2000-2005; Serv Ch In Nepal 2000-2003; Asst Ch Of The Adv Tallahassee FL 1996-2000. Auth, "Album: Passion In The Dark," In-To-Me-See Mus, 2003; Auth, "Album: The Shpd'S Heart," In-To-Me-See Mus, 2000; Auth, "We Shall Be Like Him (Album)," In-To-Me-See Mus. Soc For The Preservation And Encouragement Of The Barbershop Quartet 1973.

WASHINGTON SR, Emery (Mo) 1267 Mohave Dr, Saint Louis MO 63132 **Died 9/21/2015** B Palestine AR 1935 s Booker & Fannie. BA Philander Smith 1957; MDiv VTS 1961; Eden TS 2002. D 7/20/1961 P 6/14/1962 Bp Robert Raymond Brown. m 10/1/1965 Alice Marie Bogard c 3. R All SS Ch S Louis MO 1983-2001; Emm Ch Memphis TN 1977-1983; Dio Tennessee Nashville TN 1976; S Mich's Epis Ch Little Rock AR 1974-1976; Ecum Off & Cn Mssn Dio Arkansas Little Rock AR 1971-1976; Chapl Grtr Little Rock Instns Higher Lrng 1971-1976; P-in-c Chr Epis Ch Forrest City AR 1962-1971; Min in charge S Andr Pine Bluff AR 1961-1966. Congregations Allied for Cmnty Dvlpmt 1999; Dep to Six Gnrl Conventions 1969; Metropltn Ch Untd 1999; NAACP 1965; Natl Concerns Cmsn 2000-2003; Natl Coun on Soc & Spec Mnstrs 1985-1991; UBE 1965; Urban League 1988. Bp's Awd for Outstanding Serv Dio Missouri 2001; Citizen's Awd Human Serv Corp 2001; A Salute to Black Men Alpha Kappa Alpha-Alpha Nu Cp. 1996; Publ Serv Awd- Ldrshp Alpha Phi Alpha 1996; Serv Awd Mart Luther King, Jr. St Com 1995; Literacy Awd Alpha Kappa Alpha-Gamma Cp. 1990; Serv Awd S Louis Black Pages 1985; Amer Outstanding Cleric Dio Ark Ldrshp Dio Arkansas 1970.

WASHINGTON, Joyce D (NY) 657 E 222nd St, Bronx NY 10467 **D S Phil's Ch New York NY 1998-** B Norfolk VA 1927 d Amos & Mattie. Bank St Coll of Educ; BA VTS 1950; MA Hampton U 1963. D 5/16/1998 Bp Richard Frank Grein. m 12/22/1967 Booker T Washington. NAAD.

WASHINGTON, Lynne E (Va) 8076 Crown Colony Pkwy, Mechanicsville VA 23116 **Ch Of The Incarn Atlanta GA 2015-** B Washington DC 1962 d John & Margaret. Franklin U 1984; MDiv GTS 1997; BS S Paul Coll 1997. D 3/18/1997 Bp Frank Harris Vest Jr P 9/27/1997 Bp David Conner Bane Jr. m 8/27/1995 Larry Hancock Washington c 3. Ptr Paul Dvlpmt Cntr Of The Epis Ch Richmond VA 2006-2011; Dio Virginia Richmond VA 1999-2006, Asst to Bp for Outreach & Witness 1998-2006; S Mths Epis Ch Midlothian VA 1996-1998; S Mich's Ch Richmond VA 1996-1998.

WASINGER, Doug (Wyo) 513 E Hart St, Buffalo WY 82834 **S Lk's Epis Ch Buffalo WY 2012-** B San Francisco CA 1969 s Harold & Anita. BA Ft Lewis Coll 1992; MDiv Epis TS of the SW 2003. D 6/26/2003 P 1/13/2004 Bp Bruce Caldwell. m 1/1/2000 Kellie Marie Wasinger c 3. Mnstry Dvlp Dio Wyoming Casper 2003-2011.

WASTLER, Mark William (Md) 1415 Foxwood Ct, Annapolis MD 21409 **S Paul's Ch Sharpsburg MD 2010-** B Gettysburg PA 1967 s Clarence & Frances. BA Mssh Coll 1992; MDiv EDS 1999. D 6/12/1999 P 12/4/1999 Bp Robert Wilkes Ihloff. S Marg's Ch Annapolis MD 2003-2008; Par Of The Epiph Winchester MA 1999-2003.

WASZCZAK, Brigid (Az) St Matthew's Episcopal Church, 9071 E Old Spanish Trail, Tucson AZ 85710 **D Ch Of S Matt Tucson AZ 2015-; Sprtl Dir Sprtl Direction Tucson AZ 2012-; Bd Mem AZ Fndt for Contemporary Theol Scottsdale AZ 2016-** B Pittsburgh PA 1948 d James & Winifred. D Ord D Stds; AA Carlow U 1968; BA W Virginia U 1970. D 5/5/2012 Bp Kirk Stevan Smith. m 5/23/1970 John Paul Waszczak c 4. Assn of Epis Deacons 2012; Sprtl Dir Intl 2005. brigie@hotmail.com

WATAN, Jay Sapaen (Cal) 900 Edgewater Blvd, Foster City CA 94404 **Battalion Chapl w the 445th Civil Affrs Battalion, U U.S. Army Reserves in Mtn View CA. 2017-; Yth Min & Chapl S Ambr Epis Ch Foster City CA 2006-** B San Francisco CA 1971 s Pedro & Dolores. BA San Francisco St U 1996; MDiv CDSP 2007. D 6/3/2006 Bp William Edwin Swing P 6/2/2007 Bp Marc Handley Andrus. m 7/8/2000 Lilian Bulahao-Watan c 1. Yth Min Ch Of The Epiph San Carlos CA 2002-2005; Conf Coordntr Epis Asiamerica Mnstry New York NY 1996-1999; Yth Min H Chld At S Mart Epis Ch Daly City CA 1993-1996.

WATERS, Elliott Michael (Pa) 325 Cameron Station Blvd, Alexandria VA 22304 **Asstg P Trin Ch Arlington VA 2013-** B Crisfield MD 1947 s Grover & Ella. BS Morgan St U 1969; MS USC 1980; MDiv VTS 2001. D 6/23/2001 P 12/29/2001 Bp Peter J Lee. m 8/31/1968 Barbara H Waters. Ch Of The Annunciation Philadelphia PA 2004-2012; Ch Of The H Cross Dunn Loring VA 2003-2004; S Paul's Epis Ch Alexandria VA 2001-2003.

WATERS, Margaret Hunkin (Tex) 4902 Ridge Oak Dr, Austin TX 78731 B Cleveland OH 1946 BA Stan; MDiv Epis TS of the SW 2000. D 10/19/2002 P 7/5/2003 Bp Don Adger Wimberly. m 12/22/1991 John Bennet Waters c 4. R S Alb's Epis Ch Austin Austin TX 2005-2014; Assoc S Dav's Ch Austin TX 2002-2005.

WATERS, Sonia E (Nwk) 369 Sand Shore Rd, Budd Lake NJ 07828 B Sussex 1972 d Anthony & Marilyn. BA Wheaton Coll 1994; MDiv GTS 2005. D 6/11/2005 Bp Chester Lovelle Talton P 4/1/2006 Bp Joseph Jon Bruno. m 5/2/2008

John A Mennell. P-in-c Chr Ch Budd Lake NJ 2009-2014; Asst Gr Ch Brooklyn NY 2005-2008.

WATERSONG, Auburn Lynn (Vt) Christ Episcopal Church, 64 State St, Montpelier VT 05602 B Syracuse NY 1967 d William & Brenda. BA Earlham Coll 1991; MDiv EDS 2012. D 6/17/2012 P 12/22/2012 Bp Thomas C Ely. Chr Ch Montpelier VT 2013-2015.

WATKINS, Gilbert Harold (WVa) 2721 Riverside Dr, Saint Albans WV 25177 **R St Mk's Epis Ch St Albans WV 1993-** B Birmingham England UK 1930 s Herbert & Belle. Mercer TS 1973; Ya Berk 1974. D 6/10/1974 Bp Robert Poland Atkinson P 12/1/1974 Bp Wilburn Camrock Campbell. m 8/18/1951 Monica Watkins c 4. Part Time S Ptr's Ch Huntington WV 1999-2009; Archd Dio W Virginia Charleston WV 1991-1994; Vacancy Consult 1990-1993; 1985-1989; Convoc Dn 1985-1989; 1985-1987; Pres 1980-1982; R S Mk's Epis Ch St Albans WV 1978-1993; 1978-1982; Del Prov III 1976-1979; R S Pauls Epis Ch Williamson WV 1974-1978; P-in-c St Ptr's Epis Ch Huntington WV.

WATKINS, Jane Hill (CGC) 10100 Hillview Dr Apt 2311, Pensacola FL 32514 B Kansas City MO 1946 d Ralph & Jane. BA SMU 1964; STL GTS 1986; Cert Theol Stud Epis TS of the SW 1989. D 6/17/1989 P 5/19/1990 Bp Donis Dean Patterson. m 7/27/1970 John Watkins c 2. H Trin Epis Ch Pensacola FL 2003-2011; S Matt's Cathd Dallas TX 1999-2003; Int S Mary's Epis Ch Texarkana TX 1997-1998; Vic S Ptr's By The Lake Ch The Colony TX 1993-1997; Epis Sch Of Dallas Dallas TX 1991-1993; Chapl Epis Sch Dallas TX 1989-1993. Tertiary Of The Soc Of S Fran 1994.

WATKINS, Laurel Josephine (Okla) 210 E 9th St, Bartlesville OK 74003 **CE Dir S Lk's Epis Ch Bartlesville OK 2012-** B Corvallis OR 1948 d Norman & Evelyn. BA OR SU 1970; MHd U of Kansas 1981; Certification Iona Sch of Mnstry 2013. D 6/15/2013 Bp Edward Joseph Konieczny. m 1/1/1994 Michael Mack Watkins c 3.

WATKINS, Leeanne Ingeborg (Minn) 1895 Laurel Ave, Saint Paul MN 55104 **R S Mary's Ch S Paul MN 1998-** B Great Falls MT 1966 d Bruce & Ardelle. BA U of Montana 1990; MDiv CDSP 1993. D 7/19/1993 Bp Charles I Jones III P 1/29/1994 Bp Sanford Zangwill Kaye Hampton. m 7/8/2009 David Harold Dorn c 1. Assoc R Ch Of The Ascen Stillwater MN 1993-1998.

WATKINS, Linda King (CPa) 407 Greenwood St, Mont Alto PA 17237 **R S Mary's Epis Ch Waynesboro PA 2006-** B Dayton OH 1956 d Cameron & Jeanne. BA SUNY 1979; MA MI SU 1981; MDiv GTS 1997. D 6/21/1997 Bp Frank Tracy Griswold III P 1/7/1998 Bp David Bruce Joslin. m 9/3/2000 Kenneth G Watkins. Vic S Ann's Ch Afton NY 1999-2006; S Ptr's Ch Bainbridge NY 1999-2006; Assoc Shared Epis Mnstry Watertown NY 1997-1999; Shared Mnstry Of Nthrn NY Brownville NY 1997-1999. Third Ord Soc of S Fran 1994.

WATKINS, LindaMay (SO) 20 W 1st St, Dayton OH 45402 B Cincinnati OH 1954 d Jean. D 6/6/2015 Bp Thomas Edward Breidenthal. c 5.

WATKINS, Lucien Alexander (SwFla) 1545 54th Ave S, Saint Petersburg FL 33705 **D S Barth's Ch St Petersburg FL 2011-** B AG 1938 s Lissue & Doreen. D 6/12/1999 Bp John Bailey Lipscomb. m 11/19/1983 Barbara Dianne Wiltshire. Archd S Thos' Epis Ch St Petersburg FL 1999-2011.

WATKINS, Michael Mack (Okla) 210 E 9th St, Bartlesville OK 74003 B Okmulgee OK 1948 s Richard & Clara. BS U of Kansas 1971; D Cert Iona Sch of Formation 2015. D 8/1/2015 Bp Edward Joseph Konieczny. m 1/1/1994 Laurel Josephine Watkins c 1.

WATKINS JR, Tommie Lee (Ala) **Cbury Chap and Coll Cntr Tuscaloosa AL 2016-** D 5/13/2016 Bp Santosh K Marray P 11/11/2016 Bp John Mckee Sloan Sr.

WATROUS, Janet Couper (NC) 415 S Boylan Ave, Raleigh NC 27603 B New York NY 1950 d Joseph & Katharine. Kirkland Coll 1970; BA U of E Anglia Norwich Gb 1972; MDiv EDS 1977. D 6/16/1977 P 6/22/1978 Bp Ned Cole. m 5/14/1977 Robert Charles Kochersberger Jr c 2. Int Epis Ch Of SS Ptr And Jn Auburn NY 2014-2015; Chr Ch Binghamton NY 2011-2013; S Paul's Ch Montrose PA 2009; St Elizabeths Epis Ch Apex NC 2007-2008, R 2006-2007, Assoc R 2004-2005, Assoc R 2004-2005; All SS Ch Frederick MD 2006; Int Emm Par Epis Ch Sthrn Pines NC 2005-2006; Dio No Carolina Raleigh NC 2001-2003, Dir New Congrl Dvlpmt 2001-2002; Int S Andr's Ch Greensboro NC 1999-2000; R S Mart's Epis Ch Charlotte NC 1998-1999; Ch Of The Gd Shpd Raleigh NC 1994-1998; Chapl S Mary's Coll Raleigh NC 1985-1994; P-in-c Gr Epis Ch Elmira NY 1984-1985; S Fran' Ch Norris TN 1984, P-in-c 1983-1984; P-in-c Chr Ch Wellsburg NY 1981-1983; Gr Ch Waverly NY 1981-1983; P-in-c Gr Epis Ch Cortland NY 1979-1980; Serv Methodist Ch 1977-1979. Bd Nceca 1994; Bd/ Pres EWHP 1992-1998. Wmn Of Achievement Awd 1978. revjanw@gmail.com

WATSON, Amanda Jane Price (NwT) 701 Amarillo St, Abilene TX 79602 **Ch of the Heav Rest Abilene Abilene TX 2016-** B 1944 d Karl & Bobbie. D 9/25/2010 P 6/23/2016 Bp James Scott Mayer. m 12/20/1968 Thomas Wheeler Watson c 3. awatson@heavenlyrestabilene.org

WATSON JR, Clyde M (Va) B Atlanta GA 1926 D 6/21/1958 Bp Robert E Gribbin P 12/22/1958 Bp Randolph R Claiborne. m 2/9/1952 Gloria F Watson.

WATSON, George Stennis (WTenn) 1319 Cheyenne Dr., Richardson TX 75080 B Tupelo MS 1953 s George & Ethel. BA Millsaps Coll 1975; MDiv Harvard

DS 1979; Cert GTS 1980; MA U of Mississippi 1996; PhD U of Mississippi 1999. D 6/7/1980 P 5/1/1981 Bp Duncan Montgomery Gray Jr. m 3/12/2012 Barbara Craft Watson. Assoc Chr Ch Seattle WA 2007-2012; CPE Res, Supvsr-in-Trng, and Chapl Methodist Hospitals of Memphis TN 1989-1993; Non-par Dioceses of Mississippi W Tennessee and Olympia 1988-2012; Ch Of The H Comm Memphis TN 1988-1989; Chapl Ms U For Wmn Columbus MS 1982-1988; Vic The Epis Ch Of The Gd Shpd Columbus MS 1982-1988; Cur Ch of the H Trin Vicksburg MS 1980-1982.

WATSON, Jack Lee (Fla) 23 Cameo Drive, Flat Rock NC 28731 **Ret 1997-** B Cedar Key FL 1935 s Joseph & Verona. BS Florida St U 1957; U So 1961. D 6/14/1961 P 4/1/1962 Bp Edward Hamilton West. m 7/29/1972 Tari B Watson c 1. Chr Ch Cedar Key FL 2000-2007; S Alb's Epis Ch Chiefland FL 1990-1997; 1989-2002; R S Paul's Ch Edneyville NC 1980-1989; Vic Ch Of The Epiph Laurens SC 1975-1980; Ch Of The Gd Shpd Hayesville NC 1967-1975; P-in-c Ch Of The Mssh Murphy NC 1967-1975; P-in-c S Barn Murphy NC 1967-1970; M-in-c S Mk's Ch Chattahooche FL 1961-1967.

WATSON, James Darrell (Tex) 1101 Tiffany Ln, Longview TX 75604 **Prof Of Engl Letourneau U 1992-** B Vancouver WA 1945 s Boyd & Frances. BA U of Texas 1972; ThM Dallas TS 1977; EdD Texas A&M U 1981. D 6/24/2006 Bp Don Adger Wimberly P 1/27/2007 Bp Rayford Baines High Jr. m 8/24/1968 Sarah Watson c 4.

WATSON, Janice McKee (Haw) Episcopal Church in Micronesia, 911 N Marine Corps Dr, Tamuning GU 96913 Guam B Beaumont TX 1949 d William & Eugenia. BA Tarleton St U 1975; MA Tarleton St U 1979; Diac Iona Sch for Mnstry 2008. D 2/10/2008 Bp Don Adger Wimberly. m 7/26/1979 Thomas Richard Watson c 1.

WATSON JR, Joel Joel (LI) 3216 Kensington Ave, Richmond VA 23221 B Toronto ON CA 1944 s Shelley & Alice. Randolph-Macon Coll 1963; BA Frederick Coll Portsmouth VA 1967; Mercer TS 1973. D 6/26/1976 Bp Chauncie Kilmer Myers P 6/11/1977 Bp Chilton R Powell. m 9/5/1981 Margaret H Hambly. Dio Oregon Portland OR 2000-2002; Vic S Mart's Ch Shady Cove OR 1996-2003; Non-par 1991-1995; Assoc Ch Of The Incarn Santa Rosa CA 1989-1990; Non-par 1983-1989; R Ch Of The Ascen Greenpoint Brooklyn NY 1981-1982; Tutor The GTS New York NY 1979-1983; Asst Ch Of The H Innoc San Francisco CA 1976-1977; Epis Chapl City Prison & Gnrl Hosp San Francisco CA 1975-1978. Auth, "The Reverend Geo Young & His Descendents 1749-1962".

WATSON III, John R (NwT) 2700 W 16th Ave Apt 314, Amarillo TX 79102 **Died 12/5/2015** B Haskell TX 1942 s John & Rosa. BA U of Texas 1970; MDiv Epis TS of the SW 1987. D 6/17/1987 Bp Anselmo Carral-Solar P 4/1/1988 Bp Gordon Taliaferro Charlton. m 11/26/1966 Lesley M Schumacher. Dio NW Texas Lubbock TX 2007; S Ptr's Epis Ch Amarillo TX 1999-2007; Trin Ch Potsdam NY 1995-1999; R H Trin Epis Ch Thermopolis WY 1990-1995; Asst Calv Epis Ch Richmond TX 1987-1989.

WATSON, Karen Elizabeth (Neb) 925 S. 84th St., Omaha NE 68114 **P S Eliz's Ch Holdrege NE 2011-; COM Dio Nebraska Omaha NE 2011-, Global Mssn Com 2011-** B Omaha NE 1946 d Louis & Elizabeth. BS U of Nebraska 1971; MA Creighton U 2005; Cert Ang Stud CDSP 2009. D 10/28/2009 P 5/6/2010 Bp Joe Goodwin Burnett. c 3. Cur S Andr's Ch Omaha NE 2009-2010.

WATSON, Margaret H (SD) 503 Main St., Eagle Butte SD 57625 **P-in-c Dio So Dakota Pierre SD 2012-** B Berkeley CA 1956 d Alvin & Joan. BA Sonoma St U 1991; MA U of Delaware Winterthur 1993; MDiv CDSP 2003. D 4/26/2003 Bp Robert Louis Ladehoff P 11/15/2003 Bp Gethin Benwil Hughes. m 9/5/1981 Joel Joel Watson. R S Mk's Ch Richmond VA 2005-2012; Asst R For CE & Formation S Marg's Epis Ch Palm Desert CA 2003-2005. Scholarships Soc For The Increase Of Mnstry 2001. cheyenneriverepiscopal@gmail.com

WATSON, Martha (Nev) St Peter's, 3695 Rogers Ave, Ellicott City MD 21043 **Ch Of S Marks On The Hill Pikesville MD 2017-** B Dallas TX 1941 d William & Fayette. BA Rice U; PhD U of Texas; MA U of Texas 1966; MDiv Wesley TS 2011. D 10/8/2011 Bp Dan Thomas Edwards P 4/11/2012 Bp Mariann Edgar Budde. m 12/26/1993 George Watson c 2. S Barn Epis Ch Sykesville MD 2014-2016.

WATSON, Richard Avery (SVa) 9 Westwood Drive, East Haddam CT 06469 B Hartford CT 1937 s Arthur & Helen. BA Dart 1959; MDiv Gordon-Conwell TS 1983; DMin Wesley TS 1999. P 1/22/1989 Bp Douglas Edwin Theuner. m 12/13/1986 Susan Watson c 3. Int Calv Ch Bath Par Mc Kenney VA 2000-2003; Int Ch of the Gd Shpd Mc Kenney VA 2000-2003; R Chr Ch Xenia OH 1993-2000; Par Of S Jas Ch Keene NH 1992; Monadnock Pstrl Cnslng Serv Keene NH 1990-1993; Assoc Ch of Cntrl Afr 1987-1989.

WATSON, Robert William (Ct) 52 Missionary Rd # 22, Cromwell CT 06416 **P St Gabr's Ch E Berlin CT 2001-; Assoc Ch of Our Sav Plainville CT 2000-; Ret 1994-** B Greenwich CT 1930 s Robert & Jessie. BA U of New Hampshire 1953; MDiv Ya Berk 1956; DMin S Marys Sem & U Baltimore 1986. D 6/14/1956 P 6/14/1957 Bp Walter H Gray. c 3. R S Chris Epis Ch Linthicum Hts MD 1974-1994; R Bp Seabury Ch Groton CT 1965-1974; R H Trin Epis Ch Enfield CT 1958-1965; S Jn's Ch Stamford CT 1956-1958; Vic S Lk's Par Darien CT 1956-1958.

WATSON, Suzanne E (SanD) 5 Rainey Ln, Westport CT 06880 **First Alt to GC Dio San Diego San Diego CA 2011-** B Burbank CA 1962 d Park & Maureen. BS U CA 1985; MA California St Polytechnic U 1991; MDiv CDSP 2002. D 6/22/2002 P 3/29/2003 Bp Richard Lester Shimpfky. c 4. P-in-c S Dav's Epis Ch San Diego CA 2010-2012; Stff Off For Congr Dvlpmt-Sm Mem Ch Epis Ch Cntr New York NY 2006-2010; Assoc S Dunst's Epis Ch Carmel CA 2003-2004. Auth, "Article," *ATR*, 2009; Auth, "Creative Models of Sacramental Ldrshp," Epis Books & Resources, 2008; Auth, "Sm Ch Growth Strtgy Handbook," Epis Books & Resources, 2007. Seal of the Angl Dio the Waikato Angl Dio the Waikato, New Zealand 2004.

WATSON, Wendy (NCal) 990 Mee Lane, St Helena CA 94574 B Berkeley CA 1948 d James & Margaret. BA U CA 1970; MDiv VTS 1983. D 6/25/1983 Bp William Edwin Swing S 5/11/1984 Bp Lyman Cunningham Ogilby. S Lk's Ch Woodland CA 2007-2015; Int S Paul's Epis Ch Walnut Creek CA 2005-2006; Int S Paul's Epis Ch Benicia CA 2003-2005; Int H Faith Par Inglewood CA 2001-2003; Assoc S Wilfrid Of York Epis Ch Huntington Bch CA 1997-2001; Ch Of The Mssh Santa Ana CA 1993-1997; Dio Los Angeles Los Angeles CA 1992; R Ascen Tujunga CA 1990-1993; Ch Of The Ascen Tujunga CA 1990-1991; Asst Chr Ch Philadelphia Philadelphia PA 1989; Asst to R Ch Of The Redeem Bryn Mawr PA 1983-1988.

WATSON III, William John (SwVa) PO Box 3123, Lynchburg VA 24503 **R S Jn's Ch Lynchburg VA 2010-** B Woodbury NJ 1951 s William & Elisabeth. BA U of Virginia 1973; MEd U of Virginia 1975; MD Estrn Virginia Med Sch Norfolk VA 1979; MDiv VTS 2003. D 2/15/2003 P 8/15/2003 Bp Ted Gulick Jr. m 5/25/1974 Sallie Turner Watson c 3. Mem, Stndg Com Dio Kentucky Louisville KY 2007-2009; Mem, Trst and Coun Dio Kentucky Louisville KY 2004-2006; R Gr Ch Hopkinsville KY 2003-2010; Pres of Stndg Com Dio Kentucky Louisville KY 2009, Pres, Stndg Com 2008-. Harris Awd VTS 2003.

WATSON EPTING, Susanne K (Ia) 86 Broadmoor Ln, Iowa City IA 52245 B Muscatine IA 1949 d Stanley & Bettie. U of Iowa 1970; BS U MN 1975; MA U of Iowa 1989. D 11/4/1989 Bp Chris Christopher Epting. m 11/9/2001 Chris Christopher Epting c 2. Exec Dir Assn for Epis Deacons 2004-2013; Dir Assocation for Epis Deacons Bettendorf IA 2003-2013; Cn to the Ordnry Dio Iowa Des Moines IA 1996-2001; Dir Inst for Chr Stds 1991-1996; Proclaiming Educ for All Exec & Secy Off New York NY 2004-2008; Theol Educ in the Angl Comm Dio Cbury London 2004-2007. Auth, "Unexpected Consequences: The Diac Rewnewed," *Bk*, Morehouse Pub, 2014; Auth, "Beijing Circles," *Resource Guide*, Epis Ch Cntr, 2006; Auth, "Hannah Rose," *Wmn Uncommon Prayers*, Morehouse Pub, 2000; Auth, "Formation of Ministering Christians," *(monograph)*, NAAD, 1999. Assn for Epis Deacons (Form NAAD) 1995; Convenor, Living Stories Dioc Partnership 1998-2000; Pres, NAAD 1999-2001. Isabel Turner Human Rts Awd 1996.

WATT, Gilbert Merwin (Pgh) 396 Woodlands Dr, Verona PA 15147 **Ret 1985-** B IN 1921 s James & Shirley. BA Washington and Jefferson U 1942; Wstrn TS 1948; Bex Sem 1949. D 6/15/1949 P 12/1/1949 Bp Austin Pardue. c 2. S Paul's Ch Monongahela PA 1984-1985; R S Dav's Bethel Pk PA 1959-1984; S Dav's Epis Ch Peters Township PA 1951-1984; M-in-c Trin Patton PA 1949-1951.

WATT, Jacqueline Tyndale (At) 605 Dunwoody Chace Ne, Atlanta GA 30328 B Asheville NC 1935 d Bill & Katherine. Candler TS Emory U; BS Sewanee: The U So, TS; BS U GA 1957. D 10/23/1993 Bp J Neil Alexander. m 9/14/1957 John F Watt c 4. H Innoc Ch Atlanta GA 2007-2008, D 1993-2009; Chapl Childrens Hlth Care Of Atlanta @ Scottish Rite 1988-2005. Apc; Assn Death Educ & Counslg; ACPE.

WATT, James Henry (Tex) Rr 6 Box 88-E, Mission TX 78574 B Houston TX 1935 s James & Eleanor. BA Rice U 1957; BD Epis TS of the SW 1960. D 6/28/1960 P 5/1/1961 Bp Frederick P Goddard. R S Jn's Epis Ch Columbus TX 1963-1978; Vic S Jas' Epis Ch La Grange TX 1963-1968, R 1960-1962; Calv Epis Ch Bastrop TX 1960-1963. Auth, "Sacrifice Of Glory".

WATT, Tim (Az) 3737 Seminary Rd, Alexandria VA 22304 **S Jn's Ch Georgetown Par Washington DC 2017-** B Mountain Home ID 1974 s James & Carole. Mstr VTS; Bachelor of Arts Boise St U 1998; Mstr Nthrn Arizona U 2010. D 6/11/2016 P 5/25/2017 Bp Kirk Stevan Smith. m 7/31/1999 Tanya C Losack. Golden Key hon Soc 2008-2010. timothy.j.watt@gmail.com

WATTON, Sharon L (Mich) PoBox 80643, Rochester MI 48308 B Detroit MI 1945 d Richard & Jeanne. Whitaker TS 2000. D 6/16/2001 Bp Wendell Nathaniel Gibbs Jr. c 3. D Emerita Cathd Ch Of S Paul Detroit MI 2012, D-in-Res 2010-2012; Fin Admin S Jn's Ch Royal Oak MI 2011-2015; D S Phil's Epis Ch Rochester MI 2006-2009; D Cathd Ch Of St. Paul Detroit MI 2003-2005; Dio Michigan Detroit MI 2001-2009; D Sprt of Gr Luth Epis Ch W Bloomfield MI 2001-2007. N.A.A.D. 2001; OHC 2001. sharonwatton@stjohnro.org

WATTS, Charles Melvin (O) 4113 West State Street, Route 73, Wilmington OH 45177 **Chr Epis Ch Dayton OH 2006-; Mem Chr Ch 2003-; Non-par 1990-** B Mattoon IL 1948 s Garland & Betty. BS Mississippi St U 1972; MDiv Sewanee: The U So, TS 1977; Securities Exch Cmsn 1990; AAM Coll for Fin Plnng 2002; CRPC Coll for Fin Plnng 2004. D 6/4/1978 P 1/4/1980 Bp Duncan Montgomery Gray Jr. m 5/29/1969 Mary Watts c 1. S Fran Epis Ch Springboro OH 1990-2009; R S Paul Epis Ch Norwalk OH 1983-1990; Vic S Lk and S Jn's

W

Caruthersvlle MO 1981-1983; Asst S Lk's Ch Brandon MS 1979-1981; S Ptr's By The Lake Brandon MS 1979-1981; D S Jas Ch Jackson MS 1978-1979. Rotary Intl Paul Harris Fell.

WATTS, Janice Diane (Az) St. Andrew's Episcopal Church, 6300 W. Camelback Rd., Glendale AZ 85301 **Asstg P S Andr's Ch Glendale AZ 2013-** B Oakland CA 1950 d Richard & Mary. BA U of W Florida 1988; MDiv SWTS 2007. D 12/12/2009 P 6/13/2010 Bp Jeff Lee. m 6/10/1971 Patrick Watts c 2. Assoc for Pstr Care All SS Of The Desert Epis Ch Sun City AZ 2010-2013; Reverend All SS Ch Wstrn Sprgs IL 2009-2010.

WATTS, Marilyn Ruth (Haw) 1525 Wilder Ave Apt 304, Honolulu HI 96822 **Vic St Jn the Bapt Epis Ch Waianae HI 1988-** B Denver CO 1946 d Charles & Carolyn. BA Col 1971; MEd U of Hawaii 1975; MDiv SFTS 1977. D 2/14/1988 P 6/24/1988 Bp Donald Purple Hart. m 12/21/1974 John Norris. Serv Untd Ch Of Chr 1976-1978. CHS.

WATTS, Robert William (Dal) 113 Summer View Ln, Pottsboro TX 75076 **Died 7/7/2017** B Pontiac MI 1937 s Joseph & Dorothy. AA Oakland Cmnty Coll MI 1975; Whitaker TS 1993. D 10/27/1993 Bp James Monte Stanton. m 9/22/1956 Judith Ann Watts c 3. D S Lk's Ch Denison TX 1993-2000.

WATTS, Sharon Lee Jones (Md) 4 E University Pkwy, Baltimore MD 21218 **Gr Ch New Mrkt MD 2013-** B Baltimore MD 1952 d Robert & Nancy. BSN U of Maryland 1974; MDiv VTS 2013. D 1/19/2013 Bp Joe Goodwin Burnett P 10/8/2013 Bp Eugene Taylor Sutton. m 4/23/1975 Heber E Watts c 1. gracechurchoffice@comcast.net

WATTS, Timothy Joe (At) **R S Mary And S Martha Ch Buford GA 2007-** B Munich FRG 1960 BS Troy U 1984; MPA U of W Florida 1994; MDiv Epis TS of the SW 2004. D 6/12/2004 P 5/14/2005 Bp Philip Menzie Duncan II. m 11/1/1991 Alyce Stansill Watts c 2. Int S Jude's Epis Ch Niceville FL 2005-2006; S Jn The Evang Robertsdale AL 2004-2005.

WATTS JR, William Joseph (WMass) 19 Pleasant St, Chicopee MA 01013 **P-in-c S Lk's Ch Woodsville NH 2007-** B Boston MA 1943 s William & Berthe. BA U of Virginia 1965; MDiv EDS 1976. Trans 4/1/1981 Bp John Bowen Coburn. m 6/8/1967 Noreen Watts. R Gr Ch Chicopee MA 1988-2006; R Ch Of The H Trin Marlborough MA 1981-1987; R S Anth's Newfoundland Can 1978-1980; Asst Par Of Channel Porte Aux Basques Newfoundland Can 1976-1978. grekwall@earthlink.net

WAUTERS JR, Will (Los) 1722 Timber Oak, San Antonio TX 78232 **Vic Santa Fe Epis Mssn San Antonio TX 2012-, Vic 1991-1996** B Long Branch NJ 1949 s John & Mary. BA Stan 1971; MDiv CDSP 1980. D 6/28/1980 P 5/29/1981 Bp William Edwin Swing. m 6/26/1976 Anna Guerra-Wauters c 2. Vic Ch Of The Epiph Los Angeles CA 2002-2008, Asst 1980-2002; Asst Trin Cathd Trenton NJ 1997-2003; Chapl Lawrenceville Sch Lawrenceville NJ 1996-2002; Dio W Texas San Antonio TX 1991-1996; Vic Ch Of The Gd Samar San Francisco CA 1985-1991; Gd Samar Cmnty Cntr San Francisco 1985-1991; Vic Iglesia Epis Del Buen Samaritano San Francisco CA 1985-1991; ACTS/VIM Newark NJ 1983-1984; Vic S Jn Jersey City NJ 1982-1984; Dio Newark Newark NJ 1982-1983; R S Jn & S Stephens Jersey City NJ 1981-1983; Dn , Dnry 4 Dio Los Angeles Los Angeles CA 2005-2009. Contrib, *Shocking Violence*, 2000.

WAVE, John Erford (CGC) 3615 Phillips Ln, Panama City FL 32404 **Int S Jas' Epis Ch Port S Joe FL 2006-** B Manistee MI 1934 s Hjalmar & Bessie. BS Florida St U 1957; MS Florida St U 1963; MDiv Sewanee: The U So, TS 1967. D 6/29/1967 P 6/26/1968 Bp Edward Hamilton West. m 8/31/1955 Mary J Wave c 3. Int P for Pstr Care H Nativ Epis Ch Panama City FL 2004-2005; Int S Jas' Epis Ch Port St Joe FL 2001-2002; Supply P Trin Ch Apalachicola FL 1999-2000; S Andr's Epis Ch Panama City FL 1994-1998; Ch Of The Epiph Crestview FL 1986-1989; Supply P S Agatha's Epis Ch Defuniak Spgs FL 1986-1989; R S Agnes Epis Ch Franklin NC 1980-1984; R S Jude Valparisio FL 1968-1980; S Jude's Epis Ch Niceville FL 1968-1980; D-in-trng S Paul's By-The-Sea Epis Ch Jaxville Bch FL 1967-1968.

WAWERU, Christine Gatheni (LI) 215 Forward Support Battalion, Battalion & 74th St, Fort Hood TX 76544 B New York 1965 m 12/3/1988 David G Waweru c 2. Off Of Bsh For ArmdF New York NY 2003-2011.

WAWERU, David G (LI) 2142 Modoc Dr, Harker Heights TX 76548 **Off Of Bsh For ArmdF New York NY 1994-** B Kiambu KE 1959 s Francis & Esther. Cert Bp Kariuki Bible Coll/U Nairobi Rel & T 1987; BD S Paul Theol Coll 1989; MTh PrTS 1993. Trans 9/27/1994 Bp Orris George Walker Jr. m 12/3/1988 Christine Gatheni Waweru. Chapl / First Lieutenant US-A Ft Hood TX 1994-1998; P-in-c S Mk's Jersey City NJ 1993-1994; P-in-c S Steph's Ch Jersey City NJ 1993-1994; Asst to R S Mk's Ch W Orange NJ 1992-1994; Serv Ch of Kenya 1988-1992.

WAY, Harry L (Az) 4102 W Union Hills Dr, Glendale AZ 85308 B Long Beach CA 1948 s Wallace & Mary. BA Phillips U 1970; MDiv Epis TS of the SW 1973. D 6/16/1973 Bp Chilton R Powell P 12/1/1973 Bp Frederick Warren Putnam. m 12/26/1970 Patricia Way c 2. S Jn The Bapt Epis Ch Glendale AZ 2001-2010, R 2001-2010; R Ch Of S Thos Rawlins WY 1993-2001; R St Andr Epis & H Cross Luth Ch La Junta CO 1986-1993; R S Jas' Epis Ch Fergus Falls MN 1984-1985; Trin Ch Wahpeton ND 1984-1985; Dio Montana Helena MT 1980-1984; Dir, Rel Educ MT 1980-1984; Dio Oklahoma Oklahoma City

OK 1977-1980; Trin Ch Guthrie OK 1974-1976; Cur S Geo Oklahoma City OK 1973-1974; St Georges Ch Oklahoma City OK 1973-1974.

WAY, Jacob Edson (NwT) 2807 42nd St., Lubbock TX 79413 **P-in-c The Epis Ch Of S Mary The Vrgn Big Sprg TX 2016-** B Chicago IL 1947 s Jacob & Amelia. BA Beloit Coll 1968; MA U Tor ON CA 1971; PhD U Tor ON CA 1978; MDiv Epis TS of the SW 2008. D 1/8/2008 P 6/28/2008 Bp C Wallis Ohl. m 9/6/1969 Jean Chappell Jean Ellwood Chappell c 3. R S Chris's Epis Ch Lubbock TX 2008-2015.

WAY, Michael (NJ) 503 Asbury Ave, Asbury Park NJ 07712 **R Trin Ch Asbury Pk NJ 2015-** B Chillicothe OH 1959 s David & Wanda. BA Mia 1981; MDiv Bex Sem 2010. D 6/13/2009 P 6/19/2010 Bp Thomas Edward Breidenthal. P Chr Ch Red Wing MN 2011-2015; All SS Epis Ch New Albany OH 2010-2011. frmichael@trinitynj.com

WAY, Peter Trosdal (Va) **P Chr Epis Ch Brandy Sta VA 2012-** B Jacksonville FL 1936 s Thomas & Beverley. Gri; U of Virginia; VTS. D 5/27/1972 Bp Robert Bruce Hall P 5/1/1973 Bp Robert Fisher Gibson Jr. m 1/25/1964 Elizabeth Way c 4. Assoc R S Anne's Par Scottsville VA 2013-2011, 1973-1977; R Gr Ch Bremo Bluff VA 1977-1978. pteway@embarqmail.com

WAY SSJE, Russell (Mass) 6969 11 Mile Rd NE, Rockford MI 49341 **Ret 1986-; Serv Gvnr King - early 1970's Gvnr's Com for Chld and Fam Boston MA 1970-** B Sydney Mines Nova Scotia CA. 1924 s John & Rachel. BA U Tor 1951; LTh U Tor 1953; U Tor 1953; BD Gnrl Syn of Can Wycliffe Coll Toronto ON CA 1955; STM Bos 1956. Trans 6/1/1957 as Priest Bp Norman B Nash. c 3. Assoc Old No Chr Ch Boston MA 1982-1985; R S Jas' Epis Ch Cambridge MA 1961-1982; Serv Pres Jn F. Kennedy Allnce For Progress Washington D. C. 1960-1963; R All SS Ch Stoneham MA 1957-1961; Serv Ch in Engl St.Phillips Ch Cambridge 1956-1957; R Trin Epis Ch Weymouth MA 1955-1956; Cur Ch of Can St. Barn Ch Toronto 1953-1955; Serv Ch of Can Baddeck Nova Scotia 1947-1953; Serv and helped found Ch Ch of Can Mac Neils Mills Prince Edw Island 1947-1953. Phillips Brooks Club 1957-1986.

WAYLAND, David Frazee (Va) 1342 Allister Green, Charlottesville VA 22901 B Charlottesville VA 1935 s George & Norman. BA U of Virginia 1959; MDiv VTS 1962; Fell Coll of Preachers 1991; Coll of Preachers 1991. D 6/9/1962 Bp Robert Fisher Gibson Jr P 6/1/1963 Bp Samuel B Chilton. m 7/4/1964 Virginia Ruth Peck c 4. Chapl Westminster Cbury of the Blue Ridge Charlottesville VA 1997-2006; Ch Of S Jn The Bapt Ivy VA 1997-2000; Vic H Cross Ch Afton VA 1997-2000; Int S Jas Epis Ch Louisa VA 1996-1997; Int Cople Par Hague VA 1995-1996; Int Gr Ch Keswick VA 1993-1995; Int S Mich's Ch Colonial Heights VA 1993, Int R 1992-1993; Coordntr Joint Epis Metropltn Mnstry 1988-1992; Vic S Paul's Ch Martins Ferry OH 1988-1992; Bd Mem Apso 1980-1985; R S Cathr's Epis Ch Marietta GA 1977-1988; Assoc R Trin Ch Covington KY 1971-1977; R Trin Epis Ch Rocky Mt VA 1968-1971; R Buck Mtn Epis Ch Earlysville VA 1963-1968; Int Asst Ch Of Our Sav Charlottesvlle VA 1962-2012; P-in-c Gd Shpd-of-the-Hills Boonesville VA 1962-1968. Auth, "Making A Difference: Effective Preaching For Soc Change," *Fell Coll Of Preachers*, COP, 1991; Auth, "Plnng For Liturg," *Aware*, 1979. dwayland35@gmail.com

WAYMAN, Teresa Lachmann (WVa) 3085 Sycamore Run Road, Glenville WV 26351 **P S Mk's Ch Glenville WV 2001-, D 1999-2000** B Cincinnati OH 1954 d Francis & Vella. Dio W Virginia. D 9/9/1999 Bp John Henry Smith P 9/20/2001 Bp Claude Charles Vache. m 6/10/1978 Paul Hartmann c 2.

WAYNE, David Boyd (NY) Po Box 271, Rowe MA 01367 **Ret 1992-** B Burbank CA 1931 s John & Grace. BA U Pac 1953; STB GTS 1961. D 6/11/1961 P 12/16/1961 Bp Horace W B Donegan. c 2. R S Aug's Epis Ch Croton Hdsn NY 1976-1992; Dio New York New York NY 1973-1976; Chapl Calv Hosp Bronx NY 1970-1973; Calv Hosp Bronx NY 1970-1973; R S Simeon's Ch Bronx NY 1967-1976; R S Edm's Ch Bronx NY 1964-1970; Cur The Ch Of The Epiph New York NY 1961-1964. Auth, "Behind Cranmer's Offertory Rubrics: The Offering of the People in the Mass Before the Reformation," *ATR*, 1969. R Emer S Aug's Epis Ch, Croton-on-Hudson, NY 1997.

✠ WAYNICK, The Rt Rev Cate (Ind) 5537 Woodacre Ct., Indianapolis IN 46234 **Gvnr Angl Cntr in Rome 2013-; Pres Disciplinary Bd - HOB 2012-; Mem GC Spec Com 25 2000-** B Jackson MI 1948 d Sevedus & Janet. Cntrl Michigan U; BA Madonna U 1981; MDiv St Johns Prov Sem Plymouth MI 1985; D D honoris causa GTS 1998; D D honoris causa GTS 1999. D 6/29/1985 P 10/19/1986 Bp H Coleman Mcgehee Jr Con 6/7/1997 for Ind. m 11/28/1968 Larry Wade Waynick c 2. Bp of Indianapolis Dio Indianapolis Indianapolis IN 1997-2017; R All SS Epis Ch Pontiac MI 1993-1997; Assoc R Chr Ch Cranbrook Bloomfield Hills MI 1985-1993; Asst Secy HOB 2007-2012; Chair GC T/F to Revise Title IV 2001-2006; Mem Stndg Com on Constitution and Canonss 1997-2003. Contrib, "Pryr Included In," *Uncommon Pryr*, 2000. DD GTS 1998; Frances Willard Awd For Outstanding Accomplishment Alpha Phi. hob929@aol.com

WEATHERFORD, David William (SanD) 10835 Gabacho Dr, San Diego CA 92124 B Los Angeles CA 1928 s David & Clara. BA Occ 1950; PrTS 1952; STB GTS 1959; Cert Chicago Urban Trng Cntr 1967; USC 1970. D 6/16/1958 Bp Donald J Campbell P 2/1/1959 Bp Francis E I Bloy. m 6/27/1959 Regina K

W

Weatherford c 5. Asst S Eliz's Epis Ch San Diego CA 1976-1988; Asst Cathd Ch Of S Paul San Diego CA 1971-1976, Cur 1958-1970; Vic S Andr's Epis Ch Ojai CA 1960-1967.

WEATHERHOLT, Anne Orwig (Md) 19 West High Street, Hancock MD 21750 **R S Mk's Ch Lappans Boonsboro MD 1994-; Secy of Conv Dio Maryland Baltimore MD 2011-** B Lansing MI 1952 d James & Katharine. Berea Coll 1970; BA S Olaf Coll 1973; MDiv VTS 1978. D 5/14/1978 Bp Addison Hosea P 2/3/1980 Bp David Keller Leighton Sr. m 12/27/1980 Floyd Allan Weatherholt c 2. Asst All SS Ch Frederick MD 1983-1993; Chapl Hood Coll Frederick MD 1979-1983; Chapl S Aug's Chap Lexington KY 1978-1979. Contributig Auth, "Wisdom Found: Stories of Wmn Transfigured by Faith," Forw Mvmt, 2011; Auth, "Breaking the Silence: The Ch Responds to Dom Violence," Ch Pub, 2008; Auth, "Eleven Little Lies," *Tract*, Forw Mvmt, 2007; Auth, "Pregnancy and Priesthood," *Alb Inst*, Alb Inst, 1985; Auth, "Epis Chld's Curric," *Intermediate Level*, Living the Gd News, 1983; Auth, "New Approaches to Counslg Battered Wmn," *Nwsltr*, Alb Inst, 1979. DOK 2003. rector@stmarkslappans.org

WEATHERHOLT JR, Floyd Allan (Md) 2 E High Street, Hancock MD 21750 **Vol Chapl Maryland St Police 1994-; R S Thos' Par Hancock MD 1980-; COM Dio Maryland Baltimore MD 2011-, Dioc Coun 1984-2011, Par Intern Supvsr 1984-** B Cumberland MD 1948 s Floyd & Elizabeth. AA Allegany Coll of Maryland 1969; BA Frostburg St U 1972; MDiv VTS 1975; Coll of Preachers 1982. D 5/28/1975 P 2/15/1976 Bp David Keller Leighton Sr. m 12/27/1980 Anne Orwig c 2. Field Educ Supvsr VTS 1990-1993; S Jn's Par Hagerstown MD 1977-1979; Epiph Ch Dulaney Vlly Luthvle Timon MD 1975-1977. BroSA 2000. Bp's Awd for Outstanding Ord Mnstry Epis Dio Maryland 2005; Outstanding Young Man Of Amer 1980. stthomashancock@aol.com

WEATHERLY, Beverly Kay Hill (WA) 44078 Saint Andrews Church Rd, California MD 20619 **R S Andr's Ch Leonardtown California MD 2010-** B Indiana PA 1950 d Hal & Mildred. Drew U; BS OH SU 1972; MDiv PrTS 1984; Cert GTS 1985. D 6/14/1986 Bp George Phelps Mellick Belshaw P 1/1/1987 Bp Vincent King Pettit. m 4/12/1986 John Weatherly. Int S Andr's Epis Ch Arlington VA 2005-2009; Assoc Chr Ch Alexandria VA 1995-2005; Assoc S Lk's Par Darien CT 1993-1995; Assoc S Andr's On The Sound Ch Wilmington NC 1991-1992; P Exec Coun Appointees New York NY 1987-1990; Mssy Dio Brasilia In Brazil 1987-1989; Cur Chr Ch Trenton NJ 1986-1987; Cur S Matt's Ch Pennington NJ 1986-1987.

WEATHERLY, Joe (Tenn) 885 Spring Valley Rd, Cookeville TN 38501 B Selma AL 1949 s Joseph & Elizabeth. M. Div Sewanee: The U So, TS; BS Engr Georgia Inst of Tech 1972. D 6/8/1996 P 5/17/1997 Bp Dorsey Henderson. m 3/1/1975 Louise M Milner c 5. R S Mich's Epis Ch And U Cookeville TN 2003-2016; Asst S Jn's Epis Ch Columbia SC 2000-2003; Cur S Mich And All Ang' Columbia SC 1996-2000. joeweatherlyof@gmail.com

WEATHERLY, John (Va) 8441 Porter Ln, Alexandria VA 22308 **R S Mk's Ch Alexandria VA 2007-, 1997-2006; Chapl US-Army 1988-; Exec Coun, Dn, Bdgt Com Dio Virginia 2011-** B Bethlehem PA 1951 s Bruce & Margaret. BA U So 1973; MA Duke 1974; MDiv Yale DS 1981; ThM New Brunswick TS 1995. D 6/6/1981 Bp Albert Wiencke Van Duzer P 12/10/1981 Bp George Phelps Mellick Belshaw. m 4/12/1986 Beverly Kay Hill Weatherly c 3. Chapl Spec Mobilization Spprt Plan Washington DC 2005-2007; P-in-c S Barn Epis Ch Temple Hills MD 1995-1997; Assoc S Lk's Par Darien CT 1993-1995; R H Trin Epis Ch Hampstead NC 1989-1992; Mssy to Brasilia, Brasil Epis Ch Cntr New York NY 1987-1989; R S Andr's Ch Trenton NJ 1982-1987; Vic Chr Ch Trenton NJ 1981-1987; Dio New Jersey Trenton NJ 1981; ExCoun/Farmwkrs Mnstry/COM Dio E Carolina Kinston NC 1989-1992. EUC 2004; NECA 1997. The Bp's Cross The Bp of New York 2011; Colonel U.S.Army 2010.

WEATHERLY, Robert H (Miss) 1414 Chambers St, Vicksburg MS 39180 **Chap Of The Cross Rolling Fork MS 2011-; D All SS Epis Sch Vicksburg MS 2003-; All SS' Epis Sch Vicksburg MS 2003-** B Ripley MS 1946 s Ernest & Grace. BS Mississippi St U 1968. D 1/4/2003 Bp Alfred Marble Jr. m 12/27/1969 Danella C Weatherly c 2.

WEATHERWAX, Elizabeth May (Pgh) 402 Royal Ct, Pittsburgh PA 15234 B Pittsburgh PA 1935 d Nicholas & Joy. BS Chatham Coll 1957; VTS 1981. D 6/4/1980 P 6/1/1981 Bp Robert Poland Atkinson. m 6/28/1958 David Eugene Weatherwax. Par Visitor S Paul's Epis Ch Pittsburgh PA 1987-2011; Vic Prince Of Peace Salem Salem WV 1981-1987; Asst S Barn Bridgeport WV 1980-1981.

WEAVER III, David England (Chi) 3835 Johnson Ave, Western Springs IL 60558 B Chicago IL 1940 s David & Phyllis. BA Ripon Coll Ripon WI 1962; MDiv GTS 1965; MA NWU 1969; DMin Chicago TS 1996; MS Natl-Louis U 1999. D 6/12/1965 Bp James Winchester Montgomery P 12/18/1965 Bp Gerald Francis Burrill. m 7/2/1966 Sally Weaver c 3. R Emm Epis Ch La Grange IL 1987-2006; S Paul's On-The-Hill Epis Ch Minneapolis MN 1986-1987; S Paul's Ch Minneapolis MN 1986, Int R 1983-1985; Int S Phil's Ch S Paul MN 1981-1983; S Pat Minneapolis MN 1979-1981; Int St. Ptr's Ch Bloomington MN 1979-1981; Ch Of The H Nativ Clarendon Hls IL 1975-1979; Asst to R S

Mart's Ch Des Plaines IL 1970-1975; Cur Gr Epis Ch Hinsdale IL 1965-1966. APA 1999; Natl Fire Chapl Assn 1990-2000.

WEAVER, Eric James (LI) 8 Oceanside Ct, Northport NY 11768 **Supply P Dio Long Island 2009-** B Purley Surrey UK 1938 s Edward & Cecily. AB Pr 1958; MDiv GTS 1961; MS CUNY 1968; PD Hofstra U 1973; EdD Hofstra U 1980. D 4/8/1961 P 5/19/1962 Bp James Pernette DeWolfe. m 8/19/1973 Joyce Lynn McKean c 4. Int R Trin Ch Northport NY 2006-2009, Int R 1999-2009, Asst R 1966-1999; Asst to the R Gr Ch Huntington Sta NY 1963-1966; Asst to the R Ch Of S Jas The Less Jamaica NY 1963; Dio Long Island Garden City NY 1963; Counslg Clin. Intern Cntrl Islip St Hosp 1962; Chapl, Aux Police Suffolk Cnty Ny Suffolk Cnty Aux Police 1961-1970; Vic Ch Of The Mssh Cntrl Islip NY 1961-1963; Vic S Mich And All Ang Gordon Hts NY 1961-1963; Vic St Mich And All Ang Ch Medford NY 1961-1963. Auth, "Spec Educ Needs Perceived by Teachers and Administrators," *U MICROFILMS*, HOFSTRA U, 1980; Auth, "Ocular, Manual & Podiatric Dominance in a Severely Retarded Adolescent Population," *Adolescent Population Monographs*, U Pub, 1968; Auth, "Rudolf Bultmann & Mod Biblic Study Monograph," GTS, 1961. Ord Of H Cross P Assoc 1956. Proclamation Northport Ecum Lay Coun 2010; R Emer Trin Ch 2009; Trin Cross Trin Ch 2009; Proclamation New York St Senate 1998; Proclamation Suffolk Cnty Legislature 1998; Proclamation New York St Senate 1986; Fell AAMD 1979; Phi Delta Kappa Hofstra U 1973.

WEAVER, Evelyn Jean (SD) 2018 13th Ave, Belle Fourche SD 57717 **Paraprofessional Belle Fourche HS 2003-** B 1945 D 6/11/2005 P 2/12/2006 Bp Creighton Leland Robertson. m 7/19/1963 Ivan Michael Weaver c 2.

WEAVER, Ivan Michael (SD) **Log Deck Optr Pope And Talbot 1983-** B 1942 D 6/11/2005 Bp Creighton Leland Robertson. m 7/19/1963 Evelyn Jean Weaver c 2.

WEAVER, Joseph Clyde (WA) 703 Winged Foot Drive, Aiken SC 29803 **Ret 1993-** B Irwin PA 1928 s Clyde & Retta. BD Epis TS in Kentucky 1967; MA Duquesne U 1971; MDiv Epis TS in Kentucky 1971; PhD Walden U Naples FL 1984. D 6/10/1967 Bp William S Thomas P 12/17/1967 Bp Austin Pardue. m 2/26/1983 Louise D Weaver c 2. R S Andrews Lenordtown MD 1984-1993; S Andr's Ch Leonardtown California MD 1984-1992; R S Mk's Ch Marco Island FL 1973-1983; Assoc Ch Of The Gd Shpd Dunedin FL 1971-1973; D/Vic S Geo Jefferson Boro PA 1967-1971.

WEAVER, Lorne Edward (Los) 1725 Partridge Ave., Upland CA 91784 B Lancaster PA 1944 s Lester & Mary. BA Gordon Coll 1969; Harvard DS 1970; STM Gordon-Conwell TS 1972; MA U of Washington 1974; MDiv Fuller TS 1976; Claremont TS 1979. D 6/23/1979 P 1/12/1980 Bp Robert Claflin Rusack. c 3. Int S Alb's Epis Ch Los Angeles CA 2002-2004; Int St. Lk's Epis Ch Long Bch CA 2001; Int S Ptr's Par Santa Maria CA 1999-2001; Int Trin Epis Ch Orange CA 1997-1999; Int S Geo's Mssn Hawthorne CA 1994-1997; R S Lk's Epis Ch Monrovia CA 1990-1993; Assoc S Geo's Epis Ch Laguna Hills CA 1988-1990; Vic St Andr Epis Ch Irvine CA 1981-1987; Asst S Patricks Ch And Day Sch Thousand Oaks CA 1979-1981; Asst All SS Ch Pasadena CA 1975-1979. Auth, "Psalms 90, 91, and 92: Ancient Israel's Legacy of Trusting Yahweh," *Psalms Stds*, Wipf and Stock, 2013; Auth, "Ancient Israel's Legacy of Trusting Yahweh," Wipf and Stock, 2012.

WEAVER, Robert Crew (O) 2553 Derbyshire Rd, Cleveland Heights OH 44106 **Ret 2003-** B Clarksburg WV 1938 s Karl & Marian. BA Denison U 1960; MDiv SWTS 1965. D 6/12/1965 Bp James Winchester Montgomery P 12/18/1965 Bp Gerald Francis Burrill. m 5/23/1992 Gertrude Adelia Bauer c 2. Dn - Cleveland E Dnry Dio Ohio Cleveland 1989-1990, Dn, Cleveland E 1989-1990, Dioc Coun 1986-1989; R S Alb Epis Ch Cleveland OH 1987-2003; R Ch Of The Incarn Cleveland OH 1981-1987; Urban Vic of Chicago Dio Chicago Chicago IL 1967-1968, Urban Vic - Taylor Hm / Stateway Gardens 1965-1966.

WEAVER, Roger Warren (Minn) Po Box 820, Tower MN 55790 B Muskegon MI 1940 s Chester & Leona. BS U of Wisconsin 1962; Chicago Urban Trng Cntr 1967; MDiv SWTS 1967. D 6/1/1967 Bp Richard Stanley Merrill Emrich P 3/8/1968 Bp Archie H Crowley. m 8/11/1962 Kathleen Patti Weaver c 1. R S Mary's Ch Ely MN 1980-2001; R S Paul's Ch Virginia MN 1980-2001; S Jn's Ch Eveleth MN 1980-1981; Chr Ch Frontenac MN 1973-1980; Gr Memi Ch Wabasha MN 1973-1980; R S Mk's Ch Lake City MN 1973-1980; Asst Trin Cathd Davenport IA 1970-1973; P-in-c S Mich And All Ang Brooklyn MI 1967-1970.

WEAVER, Sally Sykes (Mo) 2575 Sunrise Dr, Eureka MO 63025 **Vic S Fran Epis Ch Eureka MO 2010-** B Saint Louis MO 1953 d William & Winifred. BA Washington U 1975; MLA Washington U 1993; MDiv Eden TS 2005. D 12/22/2004 P 6/24/2005 Bp George Wayne Smith. m 1/3/2004 Anthony Weaver. Int S Jn The Evang Ch Elkhart IN 2008-2009; Assoc S Mart's Ch Ellisville MO 2006-2008; Epis City Mssn St Louis MO 2006-2007, 2005; Exec Dir Epis City Mssn St. Louis MO 2006-2007; Gr Ch S Louis MO 2005-2006; Chapl Epis City Mssn St. Louis MO 2002-2005; Bd Dir Doorways St. Louis MO 2010-2014.

WEAVER, Shahar Caren (Chi) 3801 S Wabash Ave, Chicago IL 60653 B Chicago IL 1947 d Carey & Alfrieda. BFA How 1990; MDiv SWTS 2005. D 2/11/2015 P 6/16/2016 Bp Jeff Lee.

W

WEBB II, Alexander Henderson (WTenn) 4645 Walnut Grove Rd, Memphis TN 38117 **Ch Of The H Comm Memphis TN 2013-** B Framingham MA 1983 s Alexander & Ruth. AB Ham 2010; MDiv VTS 2010. D 3/13/2010 P 9/25/2010 Bp Mark Sean Sisk. Epis Ch Cntr New York NY 2013-2015, GC Off 2005-2007, Liturg Consult for the GC 2008-2015; Assoc to R for Outreach & Liturg S Jn's Ch Roanoke VA 2010-2013. Auth, "Stndg Commissions in the Twenty-First Century: A Case for Reform," *Journ of Epis Ch Cn Law*, VTS, 2010. Phi Beta Kappa 2010. swebb@holycommunion.org

WEBB, **Anne Slade Newbegin** (NH) 43 Thorndike Pond Rd., Jaffrey NH 03452 **P-in-c S Fran Chap Marlborough Marlborough NH 2011-** B Ciudad Trujillo DO 1944 d Robert & Katharine. BA Hollins U 1966; MDiv ETS 1969. D 7/17/1976 P 3/12/1977 Bp Philip Alan Smith. m 6/7/1969 Richard Cassius Lee Webb c 2. R S Mk's Ch Springfield VT 1994-2003; Co-R Ch Of The H Sprt Wayland MA 1985-1992; Int S Matt's Ch Goffstown NH 1983-1985; Vic S Michaels Ch Suncook NH 1979-1982; Asst Gr Ch Manchester NH 1978-1979.

WEBB, **Benjamin S** (Ia) 511 W 12th St, Cedar Falls IA 50613 **All S's Epis Ch Indianola IA 2016-; Mem ECUSA Comm. on Corp. Soc Responsibility 2007-** B Davenport IA 1954 s William & Mary. BS Iowa St U 1978; MDiv CD-SP 1993; MA Grad Theol Un 1993. D 3/30/1993 P 1/6/1996 Bp Chris Christopher Epting. c 4. P-in-c Chr Ch Cedar Rapids IA 2014-2016; Dio Iowa Des Moines IA 2014-2015, 2009-2010; Int Trin Ch Iowa City IA 2012-2014; Int S Paul's Ch Coun Blfs IA 2012; Int S Mk's Epis Ch Ft Dodge IA 2011-2012; Int S Lk's Ch Des Moines IA 2011; R S Lk's Epis Ch Cedar Falls IA 1996-2009; Non-par The Regeneration Proj 1993-1996. Auth, "Fugitive Faith:Conversations Sprtlty, Environ," & *Cmnty Renwl*, Orbis Books, 1998.

WEBB, **Estelle C** (Ct) 1651 Dickson Ave Apt 124, Scranton PA 18509 B Philadelphia PA 1945 MDiv GTS 2000; Cert Cntr for Sprtlty and Justice CSPJ 2001; STM GTS 2001. D 10/18/1996 P 5/30/1997 Bp Paul Victor Marshall. c 2. Assoc Trin Ch On The Green New Haven CT 2001-2010; Admin Vic The Ch of S Ign of Antioch New York NY 2000-2001; Asst Gr Epis Ch Honesdale PA 1996-1998. Revs, "Living Hope: A Practical Theol of Hope for the Dying," *Revs in Rel & Theol*, Blackwell, 2008; Revs, "Crowded Canvas: Faith in the Making," *Revs in Rel & Theol*, Blackwell, 2007. Soc of Cath Priests 2009; Sprtl Dir Intl 2001.

WEBB, **Fain Murphey** (Nwk) P.O. Box 336, Columbia NJ 07832 **P in Res S Dunst's Epis Ch Succasunna NJ 2015-** B Chattanooga TN 1946 d Reid & Valeria. BA Van 1968; MDiv GTS 1992; STM GTS 1993. D 6/12/1993 Bp George Phelps Mellick Belshaw P 12/1/1993 Bp Joe Doss. m 7/6/1968 John Webb c 4. Vic Ch Of The Gd Shpd Sussex NJ 1996-2011; S Paul's Epis Ch Bound Brook NJ 1993-1996; Gr Epis Ch Plainfield NJ 1993-1994. CSJB 2006.

WEBB, Frieda Van Baalen (WNY) 3360 McKinley Parkway, Buffalo NY 14219 **Vic Ch Of The H Comm Lake View NY 2010-, Vic 2010-** B Buffalo NY 1943 d Joseph & Sheila. BA Hobart and Wm Smith Colleges 1975; MDiv Bex Sem 2006. D 12/20/2003 P 4/15/2007 Bp Michael Garrison. c 2. Assoc S Mths Epis Ch E Aurora NY 2008-2010, 1985-1989; Assoc S Dav's Epis Ch Buffalo NY 2003-2007.

WEBB JR, James Wilson (Miss) 309 E Parkway Dr, Indianola MS 38751 B Durham NC 1946 s James & Anna. BA U of Mississippi 1968; Sewanee: The U So, TS 2000; MDiv Sewanee: The U So, TS 2000. D 8/30/2000 P 3/18/2001 Bp Duncan Montgomery Gray III. m 8/25/1968 Marsha Cole. All SS Ch Inverness MS 2012-2014; R S Steph's Epis Ch Indianola MS 2005-2013; Vic S Jas Epis Ch Port Gibson MS 2000-2005. Griffin Awd for Study in the H Land 2000.

WEBB III, Joseph (Va) 4074 Thorngate Dr, Williamsburg VA 23188 **Ret 2004-** B Bryn Mawr PA 1938 s Vernon & Emily. BA Valdosta St U 1961; MDiv VTS 1964; Coll of Preachers 1981. D 6/13/1964 Bp Robert Lionne DeWitt P 3/20/1965 Bp Randolph R Claiborne. m 9/2/1961 Toni S Webb c 3. R S Dunst's Ch Mc Lean VA 1988-2004; Ch Of The H Comf Luthvle Timon MD 1977-1988; Trin Ch Towson MD 1969-1976; Cur Chr Ch Macon GA 1964-1969. R Emer St. Dunst's Ch, McLean VA 2005.

WEBB III SSJE, Joseph Baxtar (Eau) 6101 Bannocks Dr., San Antonio TX 78239 **Lic P Dio W Texas Lic Cler Supply P 2015-; Asstg P S Paul's Epis Ch San Antonio TX 2015-** B Sturgeon Bay WI 1945 s Joseph & Gloria. CPE ACPE; BA Milton Coll 1969; MDiv NWU 1973; MA U of Wisconsin 1987; Nash 1988; DMin GTF 1991; CGSC Command and Gnrl Stff Coll 1998. D 3/19/1988 P 9/24/1988 Bp William Charles Wantland. m 4/4/1998 Victoria Sue Summy c 2. Supply P, Lic Dio Texas TX 2005-2013; Pstr Assoc Gr Epis Ch Georgetown TX 2005-2010; Instr IONA Sch for Mnstry 2004-2009; Asstg P Chr Ch Par La Crosse WI 2003-2005, Asstg P 1988-2002; Int Gr Epis Ch Menomonie WI 2001-2002; Int Trin Ch Baraboo WI 2000; Int S Jn's Epis Ch Sparta WI 1991-1994; Pstr Counslr Luth Hosp La Crosse WI 1988-1999; Pstr Counslr Gundersen Luth Med Cntr La Crosse WI 1980-2004; Chapl Mayo Clnc/Meth Hosp Rochester MN 1979-1980; Chapl US-Army Chapl Corps 1975-2004. Auth, *PTSD: Diagnosis & Treatment*, US Army, 1991; Auth, *Creative Use of Loneliness & Separation*, Gundersen Luth.Med.Ctr., 1986; Auth, "Calling in the Hosp," *Rel and Sprtlty*, Gundersen Luth.Med.Ctr., 1982. Amer. Assoc. Past. Counselors 1980-2004; Amer.Orthopsychiatric Assn. 1981-2004; SSJE Assoc 2005. Var U.S.Army Medals/Awards U.S. Army/DOD 2004.

WEBB, Pamela Connor (Va) 8221 Old Mill Lane, Williamsburg VA 23188 B New Orleans LA 1948 d John & Jane. BEd U of Mississippi 1970; MDiv VTS 1994. D 5/28/1994 P 12/3/1994 Bp Frank Harris Vest Jr. m 6/8/1996 Robert Daniel Webb c 3. S Geo's Ch Fredericksburg VA 2013-2014; Int Emm Epis Ch Greenwood VA 2012-2013; Int Emm Ch At Brook Hill Richmond VA 2011-2012; Int Ch Of The H Comf Burlington NC 2010-2011; Int S Paul's Ch Wilkesboro NC 2009-2010; Dir. Alum Affrs and Ch Relatns Virginia Theol Semiary Alexandria VA 2006-2009; VTS Alexandria VA 2006-2009; R S Jn's Epis Ch Richmond VA 2000-2006; Chr Epis Ch Smithfield VA 1996-2000; R S Lk's Historic Shrine Smithfield VA 1996-2000; Asst S Andr's Epis Ch Newport News VA 1995-1996.

WEBB, **Richard Cassius Lee** (NH) 43 Thorndike Pond Rd., Jaffrey NH 03452 **P-in-c S Fran Chap Marlborough Marlborough NH 2010-; Ret 2003-** B Concord NH 1945 s Charles & Ann. AB Harv 1967; BD EDS 1970. D 6/24/1970 P 1/16/1971 Bp Charles Francis Hall. m 6/7/1969 Anne Slade Newbegin c 2. S Lk's Ch Charlestown NH 1993-2003; Un-St. Lk's Epis Ch Claremont NH 1993-2003; Co-R Ch Of The H Sprt Wayland MA 1985-1992; S Chris's Ch Hampstead NH 1974-1985; Vic S Chris's Ch Plaistow NH 1974-1985; Cur S Thos Ch Hanover NH 1970-1974; Chair Dioc Liturg Cmsn Dio New Hampshire Concord NH 1974-1980.

WEBB, Robert Joseph (Ind) 721 W Main St, Madison IN 47250 **1976-** B Franklin PA 1937 s William & Elinor. ABS Wabash Coll 1959; MDiv VTS 1962. D 6/16/1962 P 12/1/1962 Bp John P Craine. m 11/10/1987 Marjorie Ann Webb c 3. Asst S Ptr's Ch Lebanon IN 1976-1978; 1974-1975; Asst S Mich's Ch Noblesville IN 1972-1975; 1971-1972; Asst All SS Ch Seymour IN 1970-1972; R S Jn's Epis Ch Crawfordsvlle IN 1967-1969; Chapl U of Oklahoma 1963-1967; Cur Chap Of The Gd Shpd W Lafayette IN 1962-1963; Assoc Chapl Pur IN 1962-1963.

WEBB, Ross Allan (USC) 2534 Shiland Dr, Rock Hill SC 29732 B Westchester NS CA 1923 s William & Permilla. BA Acadia U 1949; MA U Pgh 1951; PhD U Pgh 1956. D 11/26/1961 Bp William R Moody P 12/19/1981 Bp William Arthur Beckham. m 6/19/1954 Ruth Evangeline Keil. Asst S Paul's Epis Ch Ft Mill SC 1973-1979; Asst Ch Of The Gd Shpd York SC 1971-1973; Asst Ch Of Our Sav Rock Hill SC 1967-1971; Asst Chr Ch Cathd Lexington KY 1961-1967. Auth, "The Torch Is Passed," Baak, 2002; Auth, "Var Works". Distinguished Prof 1977; Omicron Delta Kappa; Phi Beta Kappa.

WEBB, **William Charles** (WNY) 29 Grove St, Angola NY 14006 **S Simon's Ch Buffalo NY 2016-; Chapl Buffalo Fire Dept 1991-** B Norwich NY 1950 s Charles & Doris. BA U Roch 1973; MDiv Bex Sem 1976. D 7/3/1977 P 9/10/1979 Bp Robert Rae Spears Jr. S Paul's Ch Holley NY 2009-2011; S Jude's Ch Buffalo NY 2001-2006; Int S Pat's Ch Buffalo NY 2000; Trin Epis Ch Hamburg NY 1998-1999, 1984-1989; Int S Phil's Ch Buffalo NY 1995-1998; Dio Wstrn New York Tonawanda NY 1993-1994; S Paul's Epis Ch Lewiston NY 1993, P-in-c 1992-1993; P-in-c S Jn's Ch Wilson NY 1991-1992; S Mary's Epis Ch Gowanda NY 1990-1991, Int 1989-1990; Int S Ptr's Ch Westfield NY 1989-1990; Ch Of The H Comm Lake View NY 1984-1989; Assoc Team Mnstrs Epis Tri-Par Mnstry Dansville NY 1984; S Jn's Ch Canandaigua NY 1977-1979. Kairos; New Directions Ne; Ny Assn Firefighters Chapl.

WEBBER, Ann (Mich) 850 Timberline Dr, Rochester Hills MI 48309 **Ch Of The H Cross Novi MI 2010-** B St. Andrews Jamaica 1949 D 12/20/2003 P 6/26/2004 Bp Wendell Nathaniel Gibbs Jr. m 7/11/1970 Paul K Webber c 3. S Jn's Ch Westland MI 2008-2009; S Phil And S Steph Epis Ch Detroit MI 2008; Trin Ch Toledo OH 2006-2007; S Jn's Ch Royal Oak MI 2004-2006.

WEBBER, Bruce Milton (NJ) 19105 35th Avenue, Apt. J, Flushing NY 11358 **Psych Priv Pract NY NY 1997-** B Woodbury NJ 1953 s Edward & Doris. BMus U Roch 1975; MDiv GTS 1978; ThM PrTS 1986; MSW Ford 1997; NCPsyA Inst for Mod Psychoanalysis 2002. D 6/3/1978 Bp Albert Wiencke Van Duzer P 12/1/1978 Bp George Phelps Mellick Belshaw. S Jas Ch New York NY 1997; Int S Clem's Ch New York NY 1995-1996; Int S Andr's Epis Ch Staten Island NY 1994-1995; Int The Ch Of S Lk In The Fields New York NY 1992-1993; Asst Trin Ch Princeton NJ 1986-1992; R H Apos Epis Ch Trenton NJ 1982-1986; Cur Gr Ch Madison NJ 1980-1982; Cur Ch Of S Mary's By The Sea Pt Pleas Bch NJ 1978-1979.

WEBBER, **Christopher L** (Ct) 1601 19th Avenue, San Francisco CA 94122 **Pstr Assoc Ch Of The Incarn San Francisco CA 2013-; Ret Ret 1994-** B Cuba NY 1932 s Roy & Hortense. Coll of Preachers; AB Pr 1953; STB GTS 1956; STM GTS 1963; DD GTS 2006; DD GTS 2009. D 4/7/1956 Bp James Pernette DeWolfe P 10/20/1956 Bp Jonathan Goodhue Sherman. m 4/7/1958 Margaret Elisabeth Rose c 4. Vic S Paul's Epis Ch Bantam CT 2009-2013; R Chr Ch Canaan CT 1995-2006; Bd Trst The GTS New York NY 1985-1991, Tutor and Fell 1956-1958, Trst 1985-1991; R Chr Ch Bronxville NY 1972-1994; R St. Alb's Ch Tokyo Japan 1966-1972; R Chr Epis Ch Lynbrook NY 1960-1966; R Ch Of The Ascen Greenpoint Brooklyn NY 1957-1960; Trst Cathd Of St Jn The Div New York NY 1978-1987. Auth, "Give Me Liberty: Speeches and Speakers that Shaped Amer Hist," Pegasus, 2014; Auth, "Dear Friends: Letters of St. Paul to Christians in Amer," Yucca Press, 2014; Auth, "The Beowulf Trilogy," CreateSpace, 2012; Auth, "Amer to the Backbone," Pegasus, 2011; Auth,

W

"Welcome to Chr Faith," Morehouse, 2011; Auth, "Beyond Beowulf," iUniverse, 2008; Auth, "A Bk of Vigils," Ch Publ., 2002; Auth, "Hymns from the Bible 2000," Gemini Press, 2000; Auth, "Welcome to the Epis Ch," Morehouse, 1999; Auth, "Finding Hm," Cowley, 1997; Auth, "Re-inventing Mar," Morehouse, 1994; Auth, "A Vstry Handbook," Morehouse, 1991; Auth, "A New Metrical Psalter," Ch Publ., 1987. DD GTS 2006.

WEBBER, Michael Basquin (NY) Po Box 121, Paradox NY 12858 **Chr Ch Pottersville NY 1996-; Ch Of The Gd Shpd Brant Lake NY 1996-; Asst S Andr's Ch Schroon Lake NY 1996-; S Barbara's Ch Newcomb NY 1996-; S Chris's Ch No Creek NY 1996-; S Paul's Ch Brant Lake NY 1996-** B Cuba NY 1934 s Roy & Hortense. BA Trin Hartford CT 1956; GTS 1961; STB PDS 1962. D 4/28/1962 Bp James Pernette DeWolfe P 11/3/1962 Bp Charles Waldo MacLean. m 9/9/1961 Katherine L Webber c 3. R Zion Epis Ch Wappingers Falls NY 1978-1996; R S Ptr's Ch Port Chester NY 1975-1978, Cur 1967-1968; Vic S Cuth's Epis Ch Selden NY 1968-1975; R S Jn Mk Tsumeb SW Afr 1962-1967.

WEBER, Claudia Jo (ECR) 443 Alberto Way Unit B221, Los Gatos CA 95032 **Archd Dio El Camino Real Salinas CA 2012-, Bd Trst 2011-2016** B Crestline OH 1939 d Merl & Anne. AB Vas 1961; MA California St U 1976; CTS CDSP 2000; BTS Sch for Deacons 2002. D 5/31/2003 Bp Richard Lester Shimpfky. m 7/15/2008 Mary K Morrison c 2. D S Lk's Ch Atascadero CA 2008-2013; Fac, Dn of Chap Epis Sch For Deacons Berkeley CA 2005-2015; Mem Dir Assn for Epis Deacons 2003-2016; D S Lk's Ch Los Gatos CA 2003-2008; Admin Asst Sojourn Chapl Dio California San Francisco 2003-2008; Vol Supvsr GC 2015 2015; Vol Supvsr GC 2012 2012; Stndg Com The Epis Dio Nthrn California Sacramento CA 1985-1989. Assn for Epis Deacons, Life Mem 1985. Bp's Cross Dio El Camino Real 2016.

WEBER, Dean A. (Nwk) 81 Highwood Ave, Tenafly NJ 07670 **Trst Dio Newark 2012-; P-in-c All SS Ch Leonia NJ 2002-** B Chicago IL 1952 s William & Patricia. BA Col 1974; JD Rutgers The St U of New Jersey 1987; MDiv UTS 2002. D 6/1/2002 P 12/1/2002 Bp John Palmer Croneberger. m 5/31/1986 Lynne Bleich Weber. Chncllr Dio Newark Newark NJ 2002-2004, Ecum and Interfaith Cmsn 2002-.

WEBER, Lynne Bleich (Nwk) 81 Highwood Ave, Tenafly NJ 07670 **R Ch Of The Atone Tenafly NJ 2000-** B Jersey City NJ 1957 d Theodore & Dorothy. BA Houghton Coll 1979; MDiv UTS 1993. D 6/5/1993 Bp John Shelby Spong P 5/21/1994 Bp Jack Marston Mckelvey. m 5/31/1986 Dean A. Weber. Prov Syn Dio Newark Newark NJ 1998-2000, Chair Womens Cmsn 1996-1998; Assoc S Eliz's Ch Ridgewood NJ 1993-2000. CHS 1991.

WEBER-JOHNSON, Jered Paul (Minn) 3001 Wisconsin Ave NW, Washington DC 20016 **S Jn The Evang S Paul MN 2011-** B Bemidji MN 1980 s David & Pauline. BS Greenville Coll 2002; MDiv GTS 2009. D 4/17/2009 Bp Gregory Harold Rickel. m 5/31/2002 Erin R Weber c 2. S Alb's Par Washington DC 2009-2011.

WEBSTER, Alan K (WVa) 36 Norwood Rd, Charleston WV 25314 **P-in-c S Matt's Ch Charleston WV 2017-** B Alamance NC 1956 s Jessie & Bessie. BA Lynchburg Coll 1978; RN Lynchburg Gnrl Hosp Sch of Nrsng 1991; MDiv VTS 1998. D 6/12/1998 P 12/7/1998 Bp Neff Powell. m 11/29/1980 Carol J Webster c 2. R S Jn's Epis Ch Waynesboro VA 2003-2017; Vic S Ptr's Ch Altavista VA 1999-2003; Chapl Westminster-Cbury Of Lynchburg Lynchburg VA 1998-2003; Chapl Westminster-Cbury VA 1998-2003.

WEBSTER, Alice Elizabeth (EC) 12903 Saint Georges Ln NW, Mount Savage MD 21545 B Baltimore MD 1936 d John & Alice. BA Frostburg St U 1988. D 11/2/2003 P 5/15/2004 Bp John L Rabb.

WEBSTER, Daniel J (Md) 5204 Downing Rd, Baltimore MD 21212 **Cn for Evang & Mnstry Dvlpmt Dio Maryland Baltimore MD 2010-** B Grand Island NE 1948 s James & Lillian. Creighton U 1967; BA U of San Diego 1970; MS Col 1973; MDiv Epis TS of the SW 1996. D 5/25/1996 Bp George Edmonds Bates P 2/8/1997 Bp Carolyn Tanner Irish. m 11/5/2011 Meredith Gould c 2. Dio New York New York NY 2008-2009; Cn St Fran of Assisi Montgomery NY 2008-2009; Natl Coun Of Ch New York NY 2006-2007; Dir Of Media Relatns Natl Coun Of Ch New York NY 2006-2007; Dir of Cmncatn Dio Utah Salt Lake City UT 2001-2006, Media Advsr 1996-1998; R Chr Ch Alameda CA 1999-2001; Int Vic S Jn's Epis Ch Logan UT 1998-2011; Media Advsr Dio California San Francisco CA 1998-1999; All SS Ch Salt Lake City UT 1996-1998. Auth, "Barack Obama - Powered by Hope," *Search/A Ch of Ireland Journ*, Ch of Ireland, 2009; Auth, "Media shun mainstream Ch' message," *Rel News Serv*, 2006; Auth, "Honoring Young Peacemakers," *Wit*, Epis Ch Pub Co., 2005; Auth, "Power, Money, Control...It's the Ch," *Search/A Ch of Ireland Journ*, Ch of Ireland, 2004; Auth, "Praying your labels: One response to globalization," *Wit*, Epis Ch Pub Co., 2004; Auth, "Preaching Peace In Wartime," *Epis News Serv*, The Epis Ch, 2003; Auth, "Terry Waite Urges Ch To Be Voice For Peace," *Epis News Serv*, The Epis Ch, 2003; Auth, "Hard Hearts, Minds On Faith's Frontline," *Salt Lake Tribune*, Media News Grp, 2002; Auth, "Get Facts Straight Before Calling U.S. Chr Nation," *Salt Lake Tribune*, Media News Grp, 2002; Auth, "Challenge Voices For War," *Wit*, Epis Ch Pub Co., 2002. ECom

1996; EPF 2002; Fllshp of Recon 2004. Polly Bond Awd Of Excellence-Ed, Nwspr Below 12000 Ci ECom 2002. dwebster@episcopalmaryland.org

WEBSTER, Edwin Crowe (La) 895 Will Brown Rd, Eros LA 71238 **Ret 1988-** B Fond du Lac WI 1925 s Edwin & MaryEva. BA Ripon Coll Ripon WI 1949; MA U of Wisconsin 1950; BD Nash 1953. D 2/8/1953 Bp Harwood Sturtevant P 10/4/1953 Bp Reginald Heber Gooden. m 6/15/1948 Carol J Webster c 6. R S Jn's Ch Kenner LA 1982-1988; P Chr Ch St Jos LA 1977-1982; Gr Ch S Jos LA 1977-1982; Cathd Of St Lk Balboa 1971-1977; Dn Cathd of St. Lk Ancon Panama 1969-1977; Archd Chr Ch Colon Panama 1968-1969; Archd St. Marg Margarita Panama 1958-1967; Archd St. Geo Almirante Panama 1953-1957. Auth, "A Rhetorical Study of Isaiah 66," *JSOT*, 1986; Auth, "Strophic Patterns in Job," *JSOT*, 1983; Auth, "Pattern in the Fourth Gospel," *Art & Meaning*, Sheffield U., 1982; Auth, "Defense of Portobelo," *FSU*, 1970. SBL 1951.

WEBSTER, Kiah S (USC) 11540 Ferguson Rd, Dallas TX 75228 B Grand Prairie TX 1980 d Toni. BA Van 2003; MDiv Epis TS of the SW 2006. D 5/14/2005 Bp Herbert Thompson Jr P 6/24/2006 Bp Kenneth Lester Price. m 8/21/2004 Phillip Webster c 4. S Mary's Ch Columbia SC 2015; Dio Dallas Dallas TX 2010-2012; Assoc S Paul's On The Plains Epis Ch Lubbock TX 2009-2010; Asst R S Geo's Epis Ch Dayton OH 2007-2009; P-in-c S Paul's Ch Chillicothe OH 2006-2007.

WEBSTER, Pamela Ball (Minn) 435 Sunset Rd, Ely MN 55731 B Toronto Canada 1931 d Allen & Mary. BA Wellesley Coll 1954; EdM Harv 1955. D 10/12/2009 Bp James Louis Jelinek P 6/27/2010 Bp Brian N Prior. m 8/27/1978 Peter W Davis c 4.

WEBSTER II, Phillip (USC) St Mary's Church, 170 Saint Andrews Rd, Columbia SC 29210 B Chillicothe OH 1971 s Phillip & Elsie. BA Pontifical Coll Josephinum 1993; MA Pontifical Coll Josephinum 1995; JCL The CUA Washington DC 2001; MDiv Bex Sem 2008. D 6/23/2007 P 6/28/2008 Bp Thomas Edward Breidenthal. m 8/21/2004 Kiah S Webster c 4. R S Mary's Ch Columbia SC 2012-2016; Vic Dio Dallas Dallas TX 2010-2012; Chapl Dio NW Texas Lubbock TX 2009-2010; Asst R S Fran Epis Ch Springboro OH 2008-2009; Asst R S Geo's Epis Ch Dayton OH 2007-2008; Dir Of Yth Mnstry St Matthews Epis Ch 2004-2006.

WEBSTER, Randy Lee (Ia) 510 Columbia St, Burlington IA 52601 **Min of Faith and Wrshp First Presb Ch Bulington Iowa 2014-** B Burlington IA 1957 d Shirley & Shirley. BA Coe Coll 1982; BA Coe Coll 1982; MDiv Bex Sem 1996; MDiv Bex Sem 1996. D 10/15/2005 P 4/22/2006 Bp John Palmer Croneberger. m 7/10/2004 Paul Edward Walker. P Chr Ch Susquehanna PA 2010-2014; P S Mk's New Milford PA 2010-2011; Chr Ch Belleville NJ 2006-2009; Gr Ch Newark NJ 2000-2009; Cantor and Org Mssh Luth Ch Bulington Iowa 2012-2014.

WEBSTER, Richmond Rudolphus (Ala) 202 Gordon Dr Se, Decatur AL 35601 **S Lk's Epis Ch Birmingham AL 2004-** B Clanton AL 1962 s Rufus & Barbara. U of Montevallo 1981; Huntingdon Coll 1983; BA Auburn U Montgomery 1993; MDiv VTS 1997. D 6/11/1997 Bp Robert Oran Miller P 12/17/1997 Bp Henry Nutt Parsley Jr. m 8/12/1988 Ellen Webster c 2. R S Jn's Ch Decatur AL 1999-2004; Chapl H Cross Sch 1998-1999; Cur S Jn's Ch Montgomery AL 1997-1999. "Snapshots of Hope," Morehouse, 2005.

WEBSTER, Thomas (NC) 2906 Ridge Rd Nw, Wilson NC 27896 B Minneapolis MN 1949 s Herbert & Patricia. BS U Pgh 1971; BSW York U-Toronto 1974; MBA U of Manitoba 1990; LTh Montreal Dioc Theol Coll, Quebec 1993; MS Grand Canyon U 2011; MS Grand Canyon U 2012. Trans 2/1/2001 Bp Michael B Curry. m 8/31/1974 Jane Suzanne Webster c 2. Ch Of The Epiph Rocky Mt NC 2011-2012; Vic St Marys Epis Ch Speed NC 2010-2014; Ch Of The Adv Enfield NC 2006-2010; San Jose Mssn Smithfield NC 2006; Int All SS Ch Roanoke Rapids NC 2004-2005; Vic San Jose Mssn 2002-2006; E Reg Mnstry Tarboro NC 2002-2004; P Mssnr, E Reg Mnstry Dio No Carolina Raleigh NC 2001-2004, 2001-2002. thwebster146@yahoo.com

WEBSTER, Valerie Minton (Mont) 311 S 3rd Ave, Bozeman MT 59715 B New Haven CT 1958 d Dwight & Marian. BA Mid 1982; Montana Mnstry Formation Prog 2004; Cert Epis TS of the SW 2005. D 9/18/2005 P 6/10/2006 Bp Charles Franklin Brookhart Jr. m 6/24/1986 James G Webster c 3. Asst All SS in Big Sky Big Sky MT 2015; S Jas Ch Bozeman MT 2008-2009; P-in-c Geth Ch Manhattan MT 2006-2008, D-in-c 2005-2006; Asstg Cleric St Jas' Epis Ch Bozeman MT 2005-2007. Ord of S Lk 2003.

WEBSTER II, W Raymond (Chi) 51 Pine Grove, Amherst MA 01002 B Chelsea MA 1945 s Warren & Mildred. BA Pr 1967; Mdiv EDS 1970. D 6/20/1970 P 12/15/1970 Bp John Melville Burgess. m 6/30/1970 Eleanor Eve Webster c 2. R S Chrys's Ch Chicago IL 1993-2012; R S Ptr's Ch Osterville MA 1981-1993; Assoc S Jas Ch New York NY 1977-1981; Supplement Accounts Boston MA 1976; R Trin Epis Ch Weymouth MA 1972-1977; Asst Chr Ch Needham Hgts MA 1970-1972. Dio Chicago Stndg Com 1997-2000; Stndg Com, Pres 2000-2000.

WEDDERBURN, Derrick Hexford (NJ) Broadway & Royden, Cadmen NJ 08104 B Westmoreland Jama CA 1950 s Chester & Myrtle. Untd Theol Coll of The W Indies Kingston Jm; BA U of The W Indies 1980. D 7/6/1980 P 7/26/1981 Bp The Bishop Of Jamaica. m 12/29/1972 Madge S Wedderburn c 1.

S Mk's At The Crossing Ch Williamstown NJ 2012-2017; S Mary's Epis Ch Pleasantville NJ 2008-2011; S Aug's Ch Camden NJ 1995-2005; S Mary's Epis Ch Phoenix AZ 1993-1995; Serv Ch Of Jamaica 1980-1992. Auth, "Fest Of The Palms Brochure".

WEDDLE, Karl G (ETenn) 313 Twinbrook Dr, Danville KY 40422 **Non-par 1984**- B Lincoln County KY 1936 s Carl & Helen. BA Estrn Kentucky U 1960; MDiv SWTS 1968; MS U of Tennessee 1976; PhD U of Tennessee 1981. D 6/15/1968 Bp William F Gates Jr P 5/1/1969 Bp John Vander Horst. c 3. Ch Of The Gd Shpd Knoxville TN 1971-1983; D-In-Trng Calv Ch Memphis TN 1968-1969.

WEDGWOOD-GREENHOW, Stephen John Francis (NwT) 15804 Alameda Dr, Bowie MD 20716 B Maryport England UK 1957 s Colin & Jean. MA U of Cambridge 1978; BA U of Manchester 1982; MTh U of Edinburgh Edinburgh GB 1984. Trans 1/1/1991 as Priest Bp John Lester Thompson III. m 5/10/2010 Myrna Wedgwood-Greenhow. Ch Of The H Trin Midland TX 2010-2013; S Thos Epis Ch Sturgis SD 2006-2010; S Jas Of Jerusalem Epis Ch Yuba City CA 2004-2005; The Epis Dio Nthrn California Sacramento CA 1998-2003, 1995-1996; Int Trin Ch Sonoma CA 1994-1995; Int S Paul's Epis Ch Sacramento CA 1992-1994; S Mich's Epis Ch Carmichael CA 1990-1992; Serv S Lk's Meth Ch Midland TX 1986-1988; Serv Ch of Engl 1984-1986.

WEEDON, Sarah Lipscomb (Pa) 150 E Lincoln St, Shamokin PA 17872 **H Trin Epis Ch Shamokin PA 2015**- B New York NY 1956 d Hugh & Barbara. BA Hiram Coll 1978; MS Newmann U 2005; MDiv The TS at The U So 2015. D 6/13/2015 P 1/16/2016 Bp Clifton Daniel III. c 3. sarahlweedon13@gmail.com

WEEKS, Ann Gammon (ETenn) **D for Outreach S Paul's Epis Ch Chattanooga TN 2009**- B Chattanooga TN 1946 d Wirt & Brooke. BS U of Tennessee 1968. D 12/8/2007 Bp Charles Glenn VonRosenberg. m 1/21/1978 WIlliam Bradley Weeks c 2.

WEEKS, Arianne R (Md) 1405 Boyce Ave, Towson MD 21204 **R Ch Of The Gd Shpd Towson MD 2011**- B New Yok City NY 1970 d John & Dianne. BMus New Engl Conservatory of Mus 1992; MDiv GTS 2008. D 3/15/2008 P 9/20/2008 Bp Mark Sean Sisk. c 1. Assoc S Phil's Ch Durham NC 2008-2011; Cler Disciplinary Bd Dio No Carolina Raleigh NC 2011. kchalmers@goodshepherd-towson.org

WEEKS, Jo Ann (Los) 23446 Swan St, Moreno Valley CA 92557 B Vernon TX 1939 d Thomas & Eva. BA Wiley Coll 1960; MA Atlanta U Atlanta GA 1964; ETSBH 1988; MDiv CDSP 1990. D 6/16/1990 P 1/12/1991 Bp Frederick Houk Borsch. m 5/25/1963 Stanton Allen Weeks c 2. Vic Gr Mssn Moreno Vlly CA 1992-2011, P-in-c 1992-; Assoc All SS Epis Ch Riverside CA 1990-1992. Chapl OSL the Physcn 2003; Dioc Chapl Ord of the DOK 1994; Ord of DOK 1976; OSL the Physcn 2003. weeksj@msn.com

WEEKS, Lawrence Biddle (Me) 12 Catherine St, Portland ME 04102 **R Trin Epis Ch Portland ME 2002-; Dio Maine Portland ME 1996**- B Houston TX 1948 s William & Thelma. BA Harv 1972; JD U of Arizona 1975; MDiv CDSP 1996. D 6/15/1996 P 12/1/1996 Bp Robert Reed Shahan. m 12/19/1997 Marcia Abbott Weeks c 2. Chr Ch Florence AZ 1996-2002; Reg Mssnr Dio Arizona Phoenix AZ 1996-2002; R S Mich's Ch Coolidge AZ 1996-2002; S Ptr's Ch Casa Grande AZ 1996-2002. rector@trinitychurchportland.org

WEEKS, WIlliam Bradley (ETenn) Grace Episcopal Church, 20 Belvoir Ave, Chattanooga TN 37411 B Chattanooga TN 1949 s William & Elizabeth. BA U So 1971; JD U of Tennessee 1975. D 12/8/2007 Bp Charles Glenn VonRosenberg. m 1/21/1978 Ann Gammon Weeks c 2.

WEEKS WULF, Marta Joan (SeFla) 7350 SW 162nd Street, Palmetto Bay FL 33157 **Bd Trst U of Miami Miami FL 2007**- B Buenos Aires AR 1930 d Frederick & Anne. Beloit Coll 1949; BA Stan 1951; MDiv Epis TS of the SW 1991. D 11/30/1991 P 6/5/1992 Bp Calvin Onderdonk Schofield Jr. m 9/1/2008 Karleton B Wulf c 3. Asst S Andr's Epis Ch Miami FL 2007-2010, Asst 2000-2006; Dir SE Florida Epis Fndt 2002-2003; Advsry Bd Cntr for Sxlty and Rel 1997-2007; Asst S Jas Epis Ch Midvale UT 1994-1995; P-at-Lg Dio SE Florida Miami 1992-2007, 1992-1993; Chapl Jackson Memi Hosp Miami FL 1992-1993. Auth, "Our Lord was Baptized, You Know," iuniverse, 2007. Dame, Ord S Jn of Jerusalem 1994. Hon Cn Trin Cathd, Miami Fl 2008; Hon DD Episc. Theol Sem. of the SW 2006.

WEGER, Rohani Ann (SeFla) 1225 Texas St, Houston TX 77002 **S Simons Ch Miami FL 2000**- B Tanjung Indonesia 1965 d Dale & Alice. BA Wheaton Coll 1987; MDiv Epis TS of the SW 2007. D 12/27/2008 Bp Leo Frade P 1/23/2010 Bp Dena Arnall Harrison. m 7/11/1993 Hans Thomas Weger c 1. Dio Texas Houston TX 2011-2012; The Great Cmsn Fndt Houston TX 2011-2012.

WEGLARZ, Eileen E (NY) 98 Stewart Ave, Eastchester NY 10709 B Reading PA 1948 d Ralph & Fannie. Penn; Lic VTS 2002. D 6/8/2002 Bp Michael Whittington Creighton P 12/8/2002 Bp David John Bena. P Chr Ch Epis Hudson NY 2014, P 2014-; S Jn's Ch New Rochelle NY 2014; Int Chr Ch Warwick NY 2012; R S Mk's Ch Mt Kisco NY 2008-2012; R S Jn's Ch Essex NY 2002-2008; Assessment Revs Bd Mem Dio New York New York NY 2009-2012; Dioc Missions Coordntr Dio Albany Greenwich NY 2003-2008.

WEGMAN, Jay D (NY) Cathedral Station, Box 1111, New York NY 10025 B Estherville IA 1964 s Jerry & Rochelle. BA U MN 1989; MDiv GTS 1993;

STM Yale DS 1995; Cert Col 2002. D 6/24/1993 Bp Robert Marshall Anderson P 2/5/1994 Bp James Louis Jelinek. m 8/29/2008 Stephen Anthony Facey. Lectr The GTS New York NY 2002-2003; Cathd Of St Jn The Div New York NY 1993-2003; Com Dio New York New York NY 1997-2003. AAR 1995. Vilar Fell The Kennedy Cntr 2003.

WEHMILLER, Paula Jean Lawrence (Pa) 612 Ogden Ave., Swarthmore PA 19081 **Consult, Sprtl Dir, Retreat Ldr Non-par 1999**- B Nashville TN 1946 d Charles & Margaret. BA Swarthmore Coll 1967; MS Bank St Coll of Educ 1971; MDiv GTS 1997. D 6/21/1997 Bp Allen Lyman Bartlett Jr P 6/27/1998 Bp Charles Ellsworth Bennison Jr. m 9/2/1967 John Frederick Wehmiller c 2. Pstr Bp'S Stff Dio Pennsylvania Philadelphia PA 1998-1999, 1997-1999, Asst To Bp Coadj 1997-1998; Elected by GC to the Bd Trst The GTS New York NY 2004-2007; Ecum Bd Benedictine Wmn of Madison 1999-2006; The SLC of the Epis Ch The GC of the Epis Ch 1983-1986. Auth, "Spkng the Truth in Love," *A Sermon Preached on the Feast of Blessed Absalon Jones*, Philadelphia Cathd, 2012; Auth, "Spkng the Truth in Love, A Sermon Preached on the Feast of Blessed Absalom Jones," *An Occasional Paper for the Philadelphia Cathd*, self-Pub, 2012; Auth, "A Gathering Of Gifts: A Journey Bk," Ch Pub, Inc., 2002; Auth, "Mister Rogers: Keeper of the Dream(Chapt)," *Mister Rogers Nbrhd: Chld, Television and Fred Rogers*, U Pgh Press, 1996; Auth, "When the Walls Come Tumbling Down (Chapt)," *Shifting Histories: Transforming Schools for Soc Change*, Harvard Educ Revs, 1995; Auth, "Face To Face: Lessons Learned On The Tchg Journey," *A Tyson-Mason Occasional Paper*, Friends' Coun On Educ, 1992; Auth, "When The Walls Come Tumbling Down," *Harvard Educational Revs*, Harvard Educational Revs, 1992; Auth, "The Miracle of the Bread Dough Rising," *A Tyson-Mason Occasional Paper*, Friends' Coun on Educ, 1986; Auth, "The Miracle Of The Bread Dough Rising," *Indep Sch Journ*, Natl Assn of Indep Schools, 1986. EPF 1997; SSM - Assoc 1999; UBE 1997. Ecum Awd Benedictine Wmn of Madison 2007.

WEHNER, Paul B (Tex) 7327 Timberlake Dr, Sugar Land TX 77479 **R Calv Epis Ch Richmond TX 2011**- B Austin TX 1948 s Sterling & Elizabeth. Epis TS of the SW; BD U of Texas 1971; MBA SMU 1972; MDiv Epis TS of the SW 2001. D 6/16/2001 Bp Claude Edward Payne P 6/18/2002 Bp Don Adger Wimberly. m 9/6/1969 Sherry S Wehner c 2. Gr Ch Galveston TX 2003-2011; Locum Tenons S Steph's Ch Beaumont TX 2001-2003.

WEHRS SR, John Martin (SanD) 4062 Varona St, San Diego CA 92106 **R Chr Ch by the Sea Puerto Vallarta Jalisco Mx 2000-2018** B Chicago IL 1940 s Raymond & Florence. BA U of St Thos 1962; CTh ETSBH 1988; MDiv CDSP 1990. D 7/7/1991 Bp John Lester Thompson III P 12/11/1993 Bp Jerry Alban Lamb. m 6/2/1980 Shirley Kay Schiltz c 4. Dio San Diego San Diego CA 2003-2005, Dioc Liaison Mnstrs for Mex 2000-, Corp Dir 1998-2009, Dioc Coun 1996-1998; S Columba's Epis Ch Santee CA 1999-2001; Vic S Anth Of The Desert Desert Hot Sprg CA 1996-1998; All SS Epis Ch Brawley CA 1994-1996; Asst S Steph's Epis Ch Sebastopol CA 1992-1993; Asst Ch Of The Incarn Santa Rosa CA 1991-1992.

WEI, Fei-jan Elizabeth (Tai) 114 Fuhe Rd 6FL, Yunghe City Taipei 23449 Taiwan **P-in-c Gd Shpd Taipei Taiwan 1997**- B 1947 d Chao-Chun & Jui-Lan. BA Fu-Jen Cath U 1997. D 5/30/1993 P 9/1/1997 Bp John Chih-Tsung Chien. m 12/25/1966 Te-pei Peter Chen c 2. Dio Taiwan Taipei 2009-2012, 1997-2001.

WEICKER, Harold H (Cal) 220 N Zapata Hwy #11-1014, Laredo TX 78043 **Died 1/31/2017** B New York NY 1934 s Lowell & Mary. CDSP; BA Ya 1956; MDiv CDSP 1965; DMin of Creation Sprtlty 2000. D 6/20/1965 Bp James Albert Pike P 12/1/1965 Bp Horace W B Donegan. m 1/24/1975 Carolyn M Weicker c 5. S Paul's Epis Ch San Rafael CA 2003-2017; Non-par 1992-2001; Chr Ch Windsor CA 1988-1992; Vic Chr Ch Santa Rosa CA 1987-1992; The Epis Dio Nthrn California Sacramento CA 1987; Asst S Aug's Epis Ch Tempe AZ 1984-1987; S Jn's Cathd Albuquerque NM 1973-1975; Asst The Ch of S Edw The Mtyr New York NY 1968-1972; R S Ptr's Epis Ch Monroe CT 1967-1968; Cn Mssnr Trin Cathd Phoenix AZ 1966-1967; Asst S Clem's Ch Berkeley CA 1965-1966. The Soc of the Anchor The PBp 1992.

WEIDMAN, Hal (SD) 910 Soo San Dr, Rapid City SD 57702 **S Andr's Epis Ch Rapid City SD 2016**- B Birmingham AL 1957 BS Auburn U 1980; MPH U of Alabama Birmingham 1987; MDiv Sewanee: The U So, TS 2002. D 6/8/2002 Bp Jerry Alban Lamb P 12/15/2002 Bp Henry Nutt Parsley Jr. m 11/19/2005 Sara M Mixon c 2. R S Paul's Ch Macon GA 2010-2015; R S Jn's W Point GA 2007-2010; Assoc S Ptr's Epis Ch Talladega AL 2002-2003; Mem, Appleton Fam Mnstrs Dio Atlanta Atlanta GA 2011-2017. Soc of Cath Priests 2013. st.andrew57@yahoo.com

WEIDNER, David Jeffery (Fla) 128 Bilbao Dr, Saint Augustine FL 32086 **R Trin Epis Ch S Aug FL 2004-; R Trin Epis Ch St Aug FL 2004**- B Canonsburg PA 1959 s Thomas & Ora. BS U Pgh 1981; MDiv TESM 1986; DMin Gordon-Conwell TS 1998. D 6/8/1986 Bp Alden Moinet Hathaway P 4/9/1987 Bp Claude Charles Vache. m 7/25/1981 Susan Jane Henderson c 2. R S Chris's By The Sea Portland TX 1996-2004; Mssn Com Dio W Texas San Antonio TX 1996-2002; R Epis Ch Of Our Sav Midlothian VA 1989-1996; Assoc The Epis

907

Ch Of The Mssh Chesapeake VA 1986-1989; Mem, Dioc Coun Dio Florida Jacksonville 2004-2007. Bro of S Andr 2004; Ord of S Lk 1996.

WEIERBACH, Cornelia Miller (Va) 5613 23rd St N, Arlington VA 22205 **Ch Of The Sprt Alexandria VA 2015-** B Bad Cannstatt, Germany 1955 d Robert & Cornelia. BA S Johns Coll Annapolis MD 1977; MA GW 1983; MDiv VTS 2010. D 6/5/2010 P 12/11/2010 Bp Shannon Sherwood Johnston. m 11/10/1990 Robert Weierbach c 2. Int All SS Ch Alexandria VA 2013-2014; S Barn Ch Annandale VA 2013; Int Imm Ch-On-The-Hill Alexandria VA 2012, 2011; Int Trin Ch Arlington VA 2011.

WEIHER, Joie Muir Clee (Va) 7057 Blackwell Rd, Warrenton VA 20187 B Houston TX 1976 BA U of Houston 1999; MDiv VTS 2005. D 6/11/2005 Bp Don Adger Wimberly P 12/21/2005 Bp Peter J Lee. m 1/8/2000 Jesse C Weiher. Ch Of The H Cross Dunn Loring VA 2011-2012; R S Lk's Ch Remington VA 2007-2011; Cur Trin Ch Upperville VA 2005-2006.

WEIKERT, Robert Curtis (Mich) 4212 Wylie Rd, Dexter MI 48130 **Chapl Mt Carmel Mercy Hosp Detroit MI 1975-** B Rochester NY 1943 s Raymond & Ruth. AA Concordia Jr Coll 1963; BA Concordia Sr Coll 1965; MDiv Concordia TS 1969. P 2/1/1977 Bp H Coleman Mcgehee Jr. m 8/9/1969 Joanne Kay Bolinski. Serv Luth Ch 1969-1975.

WEIL, Louis (Cal) 2451 Ridge Rd, Berkeley CA 94709 B Houston TX 1935 s Ralph & Alma. Std 72; BA SMU 1956; MA Harv 1958; STB GTS 1961; Cath U of Paris 1966. D 6/20/1961 Bp Charles A Mason P 1/1/1962 Bp John Joseph Meakin Harte. CDSP Berkeley CA 1988-2007; SLC 1985-1991; Nash Nashotah WI 1971-1988; Prof In The Grad Prog Of Theol La Salle RC Coll Philadelphia PA 1967-1972; Cn S Jn's Cathd San Juan Puerto Rico 1966-1968; P-in-c San Barlolome Bartolo Puerto Rico 1962-1964; Cur San Barlolome Bartolo Puerto Rico 1961-1962; Societas Liturgica. Auth, "Liturg For Living"; Auth, "Sacraments & Liturg".

WEILER, Matthew Gordon Beck (CFla) 3538 Lenox Rd, Birmingham AL 35213 B Milwaukee WI 1970 s Gordon & Lois. BS U of Cntrl Florida 1992; MA U of Florida 1995; DAS Ya Berk 2001; MDiv Yale DS 2001. D 5/26/2001 Bp John Wadsworth Howe P 11/30/2001 Bp Frank Tracy Griswold III. m 12/17/1995 Janna Weiler. Asst The Cathd Ch Of The Adv Birmingham AL 2004-2005; Int Ch Of The Resurr Hopewell Jct NY 2003-2004; Cur Ch Of S Mary The Vrgn New York NY 2001-2003.

WEILER, William Leon (Va) 5908 9th St N, Arlington VA 22205 B Philadelphia PA 1936 s Harry & Bertha. BD Reformed Epis Sem 1961; BA U of Pennsylvania 1961; Cert PDS 1962; PhD Hebr Un Coll 1971. D 6/9/1962 Bp Oliver J Hart P 12/1/1962 Bp Joseph Gillespie Armstrong. m 9/10/1960 Carol Ruth Weiler c 3. Assoc R S Mich's Epis Ch Arlington VA 1998-2000; Luth TS Columbia SC 1994-1997; Luth Theo Sthrn Sem Columbia SC 1993-1996; Ch Of The Gd Shpd Lexington KY 1992-1993; Dir of Dvlpmt Nash Nashotah WI 1989-1991; S Ptr's Epis Ch Arlington VA 1989; Epis Ch Cntr New York NY 1979-1989; Dir Epis Ch Cntr Washington Off Washington 1979-1989; S Geo's Epis Ch Arlington VA 1979-1981; Natl Coun Of Ch New York NY 1974-1979; Exec Dir, Off of Chr-Jewish Relatns Natl Coun of Ch New York NY 1974-1979; 1967-1971; R Ch Of S Jn The Evang Essington PA 1964-1967; Cur H Apos And Medtr Philadelphia PA 1962-1963. AAR. Fell ECF 1967.

WEINBERG, Richard M (WA) St. Margaret's Episcopal Church, 1830 Connecticut Ave NW, Washington DC 20009 **Dio Washington Washington DC 2017-; S Marg's Ch Washington DC 2017-; Other Lay Position Prot Epis Cathd Fndt Washington DC 2010-** B Fairfax VA 1980 s Richard & Karen. Mstr of Div Candler TS, Emory U; Mstr of Arts Geo Mason U; Bachelor of Mus Peabody Conservatory, JHU. D 11/12/2016 P 6/17/2017 Bp Mariann Edgar Budde.

WEINER, Margaret Yoder (Ia) 2525 Patricia Dr, Urbandale IA 50322 B Washington DC 1940 d Samuel & Jete. BA Duke 1963; MA Penn 1968; PhD Penn 1975; MDiv SWTS 1987. D 6/13/1987 P 12/19/1987 Bp Walter Cameron Righter. m 9/22/2002 Jerry Weiner. supply P, Mnstry Dvlpmt Team Coach S Paul Epis Ch Creston IA 2005-2010; Vic S Jas Epis Ch Oskaloosa IA 1990-2002; Vic Trin Ch Ottumwa IA 1987-2002; Asst to Bp (Vol) Dio Iowa Des Moines IA 2008-2012. Whipple Schlr SWTS 1987; Anderson Schlr SWTS 1986.

WEINER, Mary Lou (Ida) 4933 W View Dr, Meridian ID 83642 **D S Mich's Cathd Boise ID 1991-** B Deer Lodge MT 1941 d Ralph & Marjorie. BS U of Washington 1965; Rad 1969; MS U of Washington 1978; MA NW Nazarere U 2007. D 10/4/1991 Bp John Stuart Thornton. m 8/20/1989 Morton Alan Weiner. Coordntr Ecum Soup Kitchen 1991-2000. "Response to a Call," *Love Among Us*, 2009; "Demons Amongst Us/Sermon," *Prchr's mag*, Nazarere Pub Hse, 2007. Diac Mnstry In Tradition Of S Steph Naad 2001.

WEINER TOMPKINS, Rebecca (NY) 145 W 46th St, New York NY 10036 **D Ch Of S Mary The Vrgn New York NY 2009-** B Cleveland OH d Jack & Gloria. PhD Grad Cntr - CUNY; BA UCSB 1974; MFA Goddard Coll 1981; D Formation Prog and EFM 2009. D 5/2/2009 Bp Mark Sean Sisk. c 2.

WEINREICH, Gabriel (Mich) 2116 Silver Maples Drive, Chelsea MI 48118 **Ret 1996-** B Vilna PL 1928 s Max & Regina. BA Col 1948; MA Col 1949; PhD Col 1954. D 6/29/1985 P 1/1/1986 Bp H Coleman Mcgehee Jr. c 5. R S Steph's Ch

Hamburg MI 1993-1996; Non-par 1990-1993; Adj Min S Clare Of Assisi Epis Ch Ann Arbor MI 1985-1990. Auth, "Confessions of a Jewish P," *Bk*, The Pilgrim Press, 2005.

WEIR, Daniel Sargent (WNY) 337 NH 16A, Intervale NH 03845 **Assoc Trin Ch Topsfield MA 2012-; Ret 2010-** B Ithaca NY 1946 s Charles & Gertrude. BA U of Massachusetts 1969; MDiv EDS 1972; Oxf GB 1973; Cert Hartford Sem 1991. D 9/17/1972 P 10/21/1973 Bp Alexander D Stewart. m 5/20/1972 Janette M Weir c 2. R S Mths Epis Ch E Aurora NY 2001-2010; Int Ch Of The H Comm Lake View NY 2000-2001; Trin Epis Ch Buffalo NY 1993-1999; Int Calv Epis Ch Williamsville NY 1991-1993; Convenor Cler Assn Dio Wstrn New York Tonawanda NY 1991-1993, Cmsn on Racism 1989-1991, BEC 1988-1992, Dep for Outreach Mnstrs 1988-1991; BEC Dio Wstrn Massachusetts Springfield 1986-1988, Dep GC 1982-1988, 1973-1988; R H Trin Epis Ch Southbridge MA 1979-1988; H Trin Ch Chesapeake VA 1979-1986; R Trin Epis Ch Ware MA 1976-1979; P-in-c S Mart's Ch Pittsfield MA 1974-1976; Asst S Steph's Ch Pittsfield MA 1973-1976; Exec Dir Erie Cnty Cmsn on Homelessness Buffalo NY 1993-1999. EPF 1972. Hon Cn S Paul's Cathd 1988.

WEIR, Silas Michael (Colo) 4009 Histead Way, Evergreen CO 80439 B Chicago IL 1939 s Homer & Mildred. BS NWU 1961; MA U MI 1969; MA Iliff TS 1997; MDiv Iliff TS 2000. D 11/9/2002 Bp William Jerry Winterrowd. m 9/27/1959 Eunice Elizabeth Weir c 3. Par of St Paul's Ch Norwalk Norwalk CT 2005-2008; Ch Of The Trsfg Evergreen CO 2005-2006, 2003-2005.

WEISE, John Winfred Thorburn (WVa) Po Box 1642, Parkersburg WV 26102 **Com 1981-** B Philadelphia PA 1931 s George & Georgia. BS Salisbury U 1959; MDiv Nash 1962; Epis TS in Kentucky 1983; DMin GTF 1992. D 6/9/1962 Bp Oliver J Hart P 12/1/1962 Bp Joseph Gillespie Armstrong. S Steph's Epis Ch Beckley WV 2002-2003; Chr Ch Clarksburg WV 2001-2002; Int Zion Epis Ch Chas Town WV 1999-2001; Int S Mary's Epis Ch Pocomoke City MD 1998-1999; S Ptr's Ch Huntington WV 1997; Trin Ch Parkersburg WV 1994-1997; S Mk's Epis Ch St Albans WV 1993-1994; Int Peterkin Conf Cntr 1992-1993; Pres Stndg Com 1978-1980; Calv Epis Ch Ashland KY 1974-1992; P-in-c Chr Ch Ironton OH 1974-1982; R S Steph's Epis Ch Cincinnati OH 1968-1974; Chapl Stout St U 1966-1968; Cn To Bp Dio Eau Claire Eau Claire WI 1965-1968; Cur S Paul's Ch Albany GA 1964-1965; Yth Cmsn 1962-1964; Libr PDS PA 1962-1964; Cur S Clements Ch Philadelphia PA 1962-1964. Auth, "arts Ch Pub".

WEISER, Samuel Ivan (RG) 848 Camino De Levante, Santa Fe NM 87501 **Hon Asst S Thos Ch New York NY 2000-, Hon Asst 1989-1999** B New York NY 1935 BA U Chi 1957; MA U Tor 1960; MA Oxf GB 1967. D 10/12/1962 Bp James Winchester Montgomery P 4/20/1963 Bp The Bishop Of Quebec. m 1/18/1967 Antoinette Weiser c 3. Vic S Thos the Apos Santa Fe NM 2001-2006; Int Ch of the H Faith Santa Fe NM 1995-1996; 1973-1987; R Ch Of The Epiph Tempe AZ 1966-1973; Vic S Tim's Ch Fairfield CT 1965-1966; Asst S Paul's Ch Fairfield CT 1964-1966; Cur Chr Ch Winnetka IL 1962-1964. Phi Beta Kappa.

WEISS, Charles Sumner (Del) PO Box, Dover DE 19903 **R Chr Ch Dover DE 2015-** B Pittsburgh PA 1961 s Charles & Mary. BA Witt 1983; MS Drexel U 1986; MDiv VTS 1997. D 6/21/1997 Bp Alden Moinet Hathaway P 1/17/1998 Bp Robert William Duncan. m 3/5/1988 Martha A Hill c 2. R S Thos' Epis Ch Canonsburg PA 2007-2015; Chapl St. Edm's Acad Pittsburgh PA 2002-2009; Asst Chr Ch Christiana Hundred Wilmington DE 1997-2002. office@christchurchdover.org

WEISS, Edward Allen (CFla) 200 Nw 3rd St, Okeechobee FL 34972 **Mem Eccl Trial Crt Dio Cntrl Florida FL 2007-; Mem COM Dio Cntrl Florida FL 2003-; R Ch Of Our Sav Okeechobee FL 2000-** B Paterson NJ 1935 s George & Florence. BA Drew U 1955; MCP U of Nuevo Leon Monterey MX 1967; MD U NC 1972; Cert Inst for Chr Stds Florida 1991; DMin Drew U 1996. D 12/14/1991 P 11/1/1996 Bp John Wadsworth Howe. m 7/6/1974 JoAnne Weiss c 2. Dn SE Dnry Dio Cntrl Fl FL 2004-2007; P-in-c Emm Ch Orlando FL 1998-2000; Asst S Marg's Ch Inverness FL 1996-1998; Mem Curs Cmsn Dio Cntrl Florida FL 1995-2000; Mem Dioc Bd Dio Cntrl Florida FL 1991-2006. Acad of Par Cler 2001; All Mltry & Med Societies 1966; Ord St. Ben (O) 1985.

WEISS, James Michael Egan (Mass) Dept of Theology, Boston College, Chestnut Hill MA 02467 **Consult on Rel Plimoth Plantation 2009-; Asst Boston Coll Campus Mnstry Chestnut Hill MA 2006-; Prof;CapstoneVocationalSeminarsDirector;FulbrightAdvser Boston Coll Dept of Theol 1979-** B Chicago IL 1946 s Walter & Mary. BA Loyola U 1967; MA U Chi 1970; PhD U Chi 1979; EDS 1996; Ludwig-Maximilian U Munich 1997. D 6/7/1997 P 5/30/1998 Bp M(Arvil) Thomas Shaw. Asst Emm Ch Boston MA 2001-2006; Assoc S Mary's Epis Ch Boston MA 1997-2006; Chair, Forum for Faith & the Future Dio Massachusetts Boston MA 1983-1986. Auth, "Humanist Biography in Renaissance Italy & Reformation Germany," Ashgate, 2010; Auth, "Humanism, Renaissance, Oxford Encyclopedia Of The Reformation," 1996; Auth, "Var Scholarly arts Renaissance & Reformation Hist," 1979. Soc For The Study Of Chr Sprtlty 2001; Sprtl Dir Intl 2002. Waldron Tchg Awd Boston Coll Undergraduate Govt. 2007.

WEISS, Louise Lindecamp (RG) 3900 Trinity Dr, Los Alamos NM 87544 **Asstg P Trin On The Hill Epis Ch Los Alamos NM 2008-** B Sandusky OH 1949 d Charles & Margery. BA Thos Edison St Coll 2005; DCS TESM 2008. D 6/7/2008 P 12/13/2008 Bp William Carl Frey. m 7/24/1969 Douglas Weiss c 1.

WEISSMAN, Stephen Edward (Mo) 434 Gorman Bridge Rd, Asheville NC 28806 **P Assoc S Mary's Ch Asheville NC 2007-, P Assoc 2007-** B Cincinnati OH 1940 s Frederick & Margot. BA Ken 1962; Kelham Theol Coll 1964; MDiv EDS 1965; BS OH SU 1968; Cert Int Trng Course 2012. D 6/26/1965 P 1/8/1966 Bp Roger W Blanchard. m 6/22/2006 Gary George Ross-Reynolds c 5. Fell in Res S Paul's Par Washington DC 2013, Fell in Res 2012-2013; Mssn P No Convoc Partnership MO 1995-2000; Mutual Mnstry P No Convoc Palmyra MO 1995-2000; Vic S Steph's Ch S Louis MO 1991-1995; Vic S Paul's Ch Windham CT 1990-1991; Jub Min Dio Springfield Springfield IL 1985-1990; R S Andr's Epis Ch Edwardsville IL 1975-1990; Chapl Sthrn IL U-Edwardsville 1975-1986; Cur S Phil's Ch Columbus OH 1966-1968; Cur S Edw Columbus OH 1965-1966. Auth, *Word & Wit*.

WEITZEL, Mark Augustin (Los) 1020 N. Brand Blvd., Glendale CA 91202 B Los Angeles CA 1962 s Harlan & Jane. BA U CA 1984; U of Kansas 1986; MDiv GTS 1989. D 9/16/1989 Bp Oliver Bailey Garver Jr P 3/24/1990 Bp Frederick Houk Borsch. m 6/20/1992 Shelley L Filip c 2. Int S Mk's Par Glendale CA 1993, R 1993-, Assoc 1991-; Asst S Mart-In-The-Fields Par Winnetka CA 1990-1991; Chapl Dio Los Angeles Los Angeles CA 1989-1990. maw1@me.com

WELCH, Elizabeth Jean (Cal) Sojourn Chaplain, San Fransico General Hospital, San Fransico CA 94110 **Sojourn Multifaith Chapl San Francisco CA 2008-** B Colorado Springs CO 1978 d Rock & Jean. BA S Olaf Coll 2000; MDiv CD-SP 2004. D 6/13/2008 P 12/6/2008 Bp Marc Handley Andrus. All SS' Ch San Francisco CA 2008-2013.

WELCH, George Truman (Mass) 1692 Beacon St, Waban MA 02468 **Chair Com Dio Massachusetts Boston MA 1994-** B Montgomery AL 1946 s George & Jean. BA U of Alabama 1968; MDiv GTS 1974. D 6/17/1974 P 10/5/1974 Bp Furman Charles Stough. R Ch Of The Gd Shpd Waban MA 1991-2014; H Trin Epis Ch Hot Sprg AR 1985; Assoc S Mk's Epis Ch Little Rock AR 1982-1991; Asst S Mart's Epis Ch Metairie LA 1979-1982; Asst All SS Epis Ch Birmingham AL 1974-1979. Auth, "Var arts".

WELCH, Jimmy Dean (Okla) 4250 W Houston St, Broken Arrow OK 74012 B Detroit MI 1958 s James. BA.DNF Oklahoma St U 1982; Acad Stds Iona Sch of Formation 2015. D 8/1/2015 Bp Edward Joseph Konieczny. m 12/8/2000 Cynthia Mina Weller c 2.

WELCH, Lauren Marie (Md) 7 Overpark Ct, Baltimore MD 21234 **Past-Pres Associatin for Epis Deacons 2017-; D for Mssn Dio Maryland Baltimore MD 2013-, Archd for D Formation 2006-2012, Liaison for Justice and Peace 1996-2006, Mem Truth and Recon Cmsn 2011-, Sprtl Advsr, Epis Serv Corps 2011-, Mem COM 2006-2012, Mem Commisson on Mnstry 1990-1999; Mem Ord of Urban Missioners 2000-** B Fairmont WV 1947 d Leo & Martha. AA Potomac St Coll 1967; BS W Virginia U 1969. D 6/17/1989 Bp Albert Theodore Eastman. c 1. Pres Assn for Epis Deacons 2015-2017; VP/Pres Elect Assn for Epis Deacons 2013-2015; Mem Bd Dir Assn for Epis Deacons 2011-2013; D The Ch Of The Nativ Cedarcroft Baltimore MD 1992-1996; D Ch Of The Guardian Ang Baltimore MD 1989-1992. Assn for Epis Deacons 1996.

WELDON JR, James A (Ga) 4800 Old Dawson Rd, Albany GA 31721 **Ch Of The Gd Shpd Waban MA 2016-; R S Patricks Ch Albany GA 2009-** B Griffin GA 1978 s James & Marilyn. BBA U GA 2000; MDiv Merc 2007; STM GTS 2009. D 7/2/2008 P 2/11/2009 Bp Henry Irving Louttit. m 9/23/2006 Alison Sarrat Weldon c 2. Asst Gr Epis Ch New York NY 2008-2009; Lay Cur King Of Peace Kingsland GA 2007-2008. SW Georgia 40 under 40 The Albany Herald 2012; Liggett Schlr Chr TS 2001.

WELDON, Jonathan Naylor (Oly) 415 S. Garden Street, Bellingham WA 98225 **R S Paul Epis Ch Bellingham WA 2010-, Cn Mssnr 2008-; Dioc Coun Dio Olympia Seattle 2010-, Personl Com 2010-** B Portland OR 1954 s Herbert & Olive. BA U of Oregon 1980; MDiv GTS 1989. D 6/18/1989 P 2/1/1990 Bp Robert Louis Ladehoff. m 5/31/1980 Sharon Lee Weldon c 2. Cn to the Ordnry Dio Oregon Portland OR 2004-2008, Stndg Com Pres 2003-2004, Stndg Com 2000-2004, COM 1989-2005; R Ch Of The Resurr Eugene OR 1991-2004; Cur S Mk's Epis Par Medford OR 1989-1991.

WELDY JR, Robert Lee (Cal) PO Box 430, Inverness CA 94937 B Savannah GA 1957 s Robert & Joyce. BA Armstrong Atlantic St U 1980; MS Valdesta St Coll 1985; PhD Columba Pacific 1989; STM Nash 2006; STM Nash 2006. D 10/11/2005 P 5/21/2006 Bp Mark Lawrence Macdonald. m 12/18/2000 Candace Weldy. S Columba's Ch Inverness CA 2011-2016.

WELIN, Amy Doyle (Ct) 58 Brookfield Rd, Seymour CT 06483 B Hackensack NJ 1957 d Francis & AnnMarie. BA Chestnut Hill Coll 1979; MA Ford 1981; MDiv Ya Berk 2004. D 6/12/2004 Bp Andrew Donnan Smith P 1/15/2005 Bp Wilfrido Ramos-Orench. m 10/11/2003 Gregory William Welin c 4. S Paul's Ch Fairfield CT 2016-2017; P-in-c S Jn's Epis Par Waterbury CT 2012-2016;

Int Trin Ch Torrington CT 2011-2012; P-in-c Chr Ch Ansonia CT 2006-2011; Cur S Paul's Ch Riverside CT 2004-2006.

WELIN, Gregory William (Ct) 58 Brookfield Rd, Seymour CT 06483 B New Haven CT 1961 s Leonard & Mary. BA Gordon Coll 1983; MDiv Gordon-Conwell TS 1989; STM Ya Berk 1991; CAS Ya Berk 1991; DMin Hartford Sem 2012. D 6/13/1992 Bp Arthur Edward Walmsley P 1/15/1994 Bp Clarence Nicholas Coleridge. m 10/11/2003 Amy Doyle. P-in-c S Paul's Ch Woodbury CT 2012-2017; P-in-c S Jn's Ch New Milford CT 2009-2012; Int Trin Ch Seymour CT 2008-2009; Vic Trin-S Mich's Ch Fairfield CT 2004-2008; Asst R S Mk's Ch New Britain CT 1996-2003; Cur S Jas Ch New London CT 1993-1996; Stndg Com Dio Connecticut Meriden CT 2010-2015.

WELLER, Edie (Oly) 8216 14th Ave Ne, Seattle WA 98115 B Winchester VA 1953 BS U of Wisconsin. D 6/28/2003 P 1/17/2004 Bp Vincent Waydell Warner. m 12/29/1973 Albert John Weller c 2. R Ch Of The Resurr Bellevue WA 2008-2015; Cur Trin Epis Ch Everett WA 2003-2006.

WELLER, Gordon Frederick (Mich) 218 Ottawa St., Lansing MI 48933 B Utica NY 1947 s Grant & Mary. AA Hudson Vlly Cmnty Coll 1968; BA Johnson St Coll 1970; MDiv Bex Sem 1973; DMin Drew U 1994. D 6/9/1973 P 12/15/1973 Bp Charles Bowen Persell Jr. m 7/18/1970 Linda Jo Weller c 2. R S Paul's Epis Ch Lansing MI 1999-2012; R S Jn's Ch Mt Pleasant MI 1987-1999; Asst S Jas Epis Ch Birmingham MI 1976-1986; Asst S Jn's Ch Massena NY 1973-1976; P S Paul's Ch Waddington NY 1973-1976.

WELLER, Gretchen Kay (WMich) 435 SOM Center Road, Mayfield Village OH 44143 **R S Barth Epis Ch Mayfield Vill OH 2002-** B Springfield OH 1944 d Harry & Gretchen. BS OH SU 1988; MDiv Ya Berk 1993. D 6/24/1996 P 2/21/1997 Bp Edward Witker Jones. c 1. Emm Ch Hastings MI 2009-2013; S Barth's Ch Cleveland OH 2002-2009; R S Alb's Ch Sussex WI 2000-2002; Assoc S Jn's Ch Lynchburg VA 1998-2000; Int Asst S Steph's Ch Ridgefield CT 1997-1998; Cur Chr Ch Cathd Indianapolis IN 1996-1997. DOK 2000. graceepiscopalchurch@live.com

WELLER JR, Thomas Carroll (CGC) 2300 W Beach Dr, Panama City FL 32401 **Assoc H Nativ Epis Ch Panama City FL 2009-, Assoc 2003-2004, Assoc 1999-2000; Vic St.Thos Epis Ch Laguna Bch FL 2004-** B Panama City FL 1935 s Thomas & Louise. BS U of Florida 1957; MBA U MI 1963; US Naval War Coll Newport RI 1969; Cert Luth TS at Gettysburg 1984. D 6/10/1983 P 3/1/1984 Bp Charlie Fuller Mcnutt Jr. m 6/29/1957 Linda Noble Weller c 4. Vic S Thos By The Sea Panama City Bch FL 2004-2009; Chapl & Tchr H Nativ Epis Sch Panama City FL 2002-2008; Assoc H Nativ Epis Ch Panama City FL 2002-2004; Int Gr Epis Ch Panama City Bch FL 2000-2001; Vic Trin Ch Apalachicola FL 1984-1998; Cur Mt Calv Camp Hill PA 1983-1984.

WELLES JR, George H (Mass) 810 Monterrosa Dr., Myrtle Beach SC 29572 B Norwood MA 1935 s George & Flora. BA Wms 1957; MDiv VTS 1964; Cert of Acheivement EDS 2000; Cert of Achievement EDS 2000. D 6/20/1964 Bp Anson Phelps Stokes Jr P 1/16/1965 Bp William Foreman Creighton. m 6/6/1958 Annie M Welles c 8. Stndg Com Dio Massachusetts Boston MA 2008-2010, Dn of So Shore Dnry 2005-2010, Bdgt Com Chairman 2002-2008, Convenor Dist 1916 1985-1986; R Ch Of Our Sav Milton MA 1999-2011; The Ch Of S Mary Of The Harbor Provincetown MA 1989-1997; S Mary's Epis Ch Barnstable MA 1986-1989; Nrsng Hm Coordntr Cape Cod Coun of Ch Barnstable MA 1983-1986; Asst Min S Dav's Epis Ch S Yarmouth MA 1983-1986; Exec Dir Cntr City Ch Hartford CT 1978-1982; Urban Mnstry Com Chairman Dio Connecticut Meriden CT 1978-1982; Part Time Asst S Monica's Ch Hartford CT 1972-1982; Soc Serv Capitol Reg Conf of Ch Hartford CT 1971-1978; Min/Tchr Westledge Sch Simsbury CT 1969-1971; Part Time Asst S Alb's Ch Simsbury CT 1967-1971; Min/Tchr Westminster Sch Simsbury CT 1966-1969; Asst Min The Ch Of The Epiph Washington DC 1964-1966; Tchr & Coach Noble & Grenough Sch Dedham MA 1957-1961. Florence Sabin Distinguished Alum Awd Vermont Acad,Saxtons River,VT 2003.

WELLES, Hope Virginia (Mo) 4455 Atlantic Blvd, Jacksonville FL 32207 B Toledo OH 1981 D 12/21/2007 P 6/21/2008 Bp George Wayne Smith. m 1/18/2008 Luke Jernagan. Jacksonville Epis HS Jacksonville FL 2009-2013.

WELLFORD, Eleanor L (Va) 510 S Gaskins Rd, Richmond VA 23238 B Richmond VA 1953 d Maynard & Mary. BA Hollins U 1975; MBA Virginia Commonwealth U 1977; MDiv UTS Richmond 2005. D 6/24/2006 P 2/3/2007 Bp Peter J Lee. m 6/24/1978 Ten Eyck T Wellford c 3. Assoc R S Mary's Epis Ch Richmond VA 2007-2015; Chapl Westminster Cbury Richmond VA 2006-2007; S Andr's Ch Richmond VA 2005-2006.

WELLNER, Robert Harry (Ct) 4750 Welby Drive, P.O. Box 142, Schnecksville PA 18078 **Ret 1988-** B Brooklyn NY 1928 s Robert & Harriet. BA Leh 1952; MDiv Ya Berk 1955. D 4/16/1955 P 11/5/1955 Bp James Pernette DeWolfe. m 12/27/2003 Ruth S Wellner c 2. Supply P Trin And S Phil's Epis Ch Lansford PA 1991-2011; R S Jn's Epis Ch Vernon Rock Vernon Rockville CT 1969-1988; Chapl Ch Hm 1963-1987; R St Jas Epis Ch Hartford CT 1961-1969; R Chr Ch Towanda PA 1957-1961; Asst Trin Ch Ft Wayne IN 1956-1957; Vic S Alb's Ch Brooklyn NY 1955-1956. Educ Awd Rockville ChmbrCom 1981.

W

WELLS, Ben Reid (At) St. Francis Episcopal Church, 432 Forest Hill Road, Macon GA 31210 **R S Fran Ch Macon GA 2013-, Asst 2011-2012, R 2011-** B Frenchburg KY 1959 s William & Edith. BS U of Kentucky 1981; MS U of Kentucky 1982; MDiv CDSP 2011. D 12/18/2010 P 8/27/2011 Bp J Neil Alexander. m 12/4/2013 Arthur Wells Villarreal.

WELLS, Charlotte E (EO) 241 Se 2nd St, Pendleton OR 97801 **Ch Of The Redeem Pendleton OR 2015-** B Plainfield NJ 1957 d Charles & Margaret. BS Kean U 1995; MDiv GTS 2008. D 6/7/2008 Bp George Edward Councell P 12/10/2008 Bp Sanford Zangwill Kaye Hampton. m 7/11/1998 Donald J Wells. S Mart's Ch Lebanon OR 2014-2015; Asst to the R/Yth Min S Barth's Ch Beaverton OR 2008-2012. rector.pendletonepiscopal@gmail.com

WELLS, David L (Spr) Cathedral of St. Paul the Apostle, 815 S Second Street, Springfield IL 62704 B Chicago IL 1950 s George & Virginia. LLB LaSalle U 1979; BS Elmhurst Coll 1993; MS Lewis U 1996; MAMin Nashotah TS 2015. D 5/1/2015 P 5/14/2016 Bp Daniel Hayden Martins. m 10/7/2013 Mary Ellen Richter. Ch Of The Incarn Dallas TX 2015. davidwells99@yahoo.com

WELLS, Dorothy Sanders (WTenn) St. George's Episcopal Church, 2425 S. Germantown Road, Germantown TN 38138 **R S Geo's Ch Germantown TN 2015-, P-in-c 2013-2015; Stndg Com Dio W Tennessee Memphis 2016-, The Bp and Coun -- Secy 2013-2016, Secy to Dioc Conv 2013-, The Bp and Coun 2012-2016, Asst Secy to Dioc Conv 2012-2013, Co-Chair, Anti-Racism Cmsn 2012-, Chapl -- ECW 2011-** B Mobile AL 1961 d Elbert & Willie Lee. BA Rhodes Coll 1982; JD U of Memphis Cecil C. Humphreys Sch of Law 1993; MDiv Memphia TS 2012. D 6/2/2012 P 12/15/2012 Bp Don Edward Johnson. m 12/15/1990 Herbert Wells c 2. Ch of the H Apos Collierville TN 2012-2013; Mem, Bd Trst St. Mary's Epis Sch (Memphis TN) 2007-2013. Auth, "Blog," *Mo Dorothy's Musings*, http://dorothywsmusings.blogspot.com/. Algernon Sydney Sullivan Awd for Serv Rhodes Coll 2015; Distinguished Alum Rhodes Coll 2011. dorothy@stgeorgesgermantown.org

WELLS, Edgar Fisher (NY) 400 W 43rd St Apt V V, New York NY 10036 **Ret 1998-** B New York NY 1930 s Edgar & Isabelle. BA Br 1954; MDiv Nash 1960; Marq 1969. D 1/28/1960 P 8/9/1960 Bp William Hampton Brady. Evang Com Dio New York New York NY 1980-1985, Sprtl Dir | Curs 1980-1982; R Ch Of S Mary The Vrgn New York NY 1979-1998; Chapl, Estrn Prov The CSM Peekskill NY 1979-1994; R Annunc of Our Lady Epis Ch Waukegan IL 1976-1979; Alum Wrdn Nash Nashotah WI 1974-1979; The Annunc Of Our Lady Gurnee IL 1965-1979; Vic Annunc Our Lady Waukegan IL 1965-1976; Asst S Ptr's Ch Bronx NY 1963-1965; Vic S Paul's Ch Plymouth WI 1961-1963; S Bon Plymouth WI 1960-1963. Affirming Catholicism 1990; Pres, CCU, Dio New York 1983-1984. Hon DD GTS 1998.

WELLS, Jane Ely (Minn) 105 S Cedar St, Oberlin OH 44074 B Lexington KY 1939 d Fordyce & Dikka. BA Ob 1961; MA U IL 1962; MEd Kent St U 1980. D 11/13/2004 Bp Mark Hollingsworth Jr. m 12/28/1962 Charles F Wells c 2. S Andr's Epis Ch Elyria OH 2005-2011.

WELLS, Jason (NH) 18 Kimball St, Pembroke NH 03275 **Vic Gr Epis Ch Concord NH 2007-; Chair Dioc Cmsn on Evang 2010-** B Dallas TX 1979 s John & Diane. BS SMU 2001; BS SMU 2001; MDiv PrTS 2004. D 9/18/2004 P 4/9/2005 Bp Vicky Gene Robinson. m 12/5/2009 Courtney Eschbach Eschbach-Wells c 1. Cur Gr Ch Manchester NH 2004-2007; Dep GC 2015; Alt GC 2012. Soc of Cath Priests 2013. Champion for Chld Concord Sch Dist 2014. office@graceeastconcord.org

WELLS SR, John T (Tex) 14043 Horseshoe Cir, Woodway TX 76712 **Chapl Police Dept Waco Texas 2003-** B Harmony KY 1941 s Jack & Eila. BS Estrn Kentucky U 1964; MA Equivalent Army War Coll 1984; MS Shippensburg U Shippensburg PA 1984; MDiv Epis TS of the SW 1998. D 11/7/1998 Bp Leopoldo Jesus Alard P 8/8/1999 Bp Claude Edward Payne. m 10/24/1981 Su T Han c 3. R Epis Ch Of The H Sprt Waco TX 2003-2013; Vic S Paul's Epis Ch Woodville TX 2000-2003; R Trin Epis Ch Jasper TX 1998-2003. Pres's Vol Serv Awd - Gold Corp for Natl & Cmnty Serv 2016.

WELLS, Lloyd Francis (At) 335 Forest Heights Dr, Athens GA 30606 B Woodstock VA 1942 s Lloyd & Rose. BA U of Delaware 1965; BD EDS 1968; MS Atlanta U Atlanta GA 1974. D 9/21/1968 Bp John Brooke Mosley P 3/1/1969 Bp William Henry Mead. m 2/17/1979 Patricia J Peterson c 2. S Mary And S Martha Ch Buford GA 2001-2003; Vic S Anth's Epis Ch Winder GA 1990-1997; Int S Chrys Douglasville GA 1989-1990; S Julian's Epis Ch Douglasville GA 1989-1990; Cathd Of S Phil Atlanta GA 1984-1988; S Martha's Epis Ch Bethany Bch DE 1968-1971; Vic S Martins-In-The-Fields Wilmington DE 1968-1971.

WELLS, Lynwood Daves (SwVa) Po Box 4103, Martinsville VA 24115 **Ret 1996-** B Danville VA 1926 s Jabe & Claudine. BS VPI 1951; MDiv VTS 1986. D 5/14/1987 P 11/14/1987 Bp William Franklin Carr. m 6/11/1977 Anna Bowe Lester c 3. Int S Thos Epis Ch Wht Sphr Spgs WV 1994-1995; Int S Jas' Epis Ch Lewisburg WV 1990-1991; Vic All SS Ch Un WV 1987-1996; Ch Of The Incarn Ronceverte WV 1987-1994.

WELLS, Mary Beth (SeFla) 231 Spring Hill Dr, Gordonsville VA 22942 **D Chr Epis Ch Gordonsville VA 2009-** B Dallas TX 1936 d Owen & Ruth. BA Syr 1958; MA Tufts U 1964; MEd Tufts U 1975; MA S Vinc De Paul Reg Sem

Boynton Bch 2005. D 5/4/2002 Bp John Lewis Said. c 2. S Paul's Ch Delray Bch FL 2002-2007. Auth, "Parents And Creativity In Young Chld," *Journ Of Mar And Fam Living*, 1966. Acpe 1999; Apa 1973; Apc 1999; SDI 2000.

WELLS, Robert Louis (Tex) 9302 Sunlake Dr, Pearland TX 77584 B Alexandria LA 1939 s Charles & Marie. BA LSU 1961; BD Golden Gate Bapt TS 1965; MDiv Golden Gate Bapt TS 1971. D 11/19/1990 P 6/4/1991 Bp Sam Byron Hulsey. m 4/3/1983 Carol Wells c 3. Pstr Care Assoc S Fran Ch Houston TX 2011-2012; Asstg P for Pstr Care S Dunst's Epis Ch Houston TX 2009-2011; Dir, The Cmnty of Hope S Lk's Epis Hosp Houston TX 2002-2009; Asstg P Trin Ch Galveston TX 1996-2002; The Great Cmsn Fndt Houston TX 1995-2002; Exec Dir Wm Temple Epis Ctr Galveston TX 1995-1996; Asst R S Paul's Ch Waco TX 1991-1995, Cbury Chapl 1991-1995. AAPC 1981-1993; Assn of Psychol Type 1988-2001; Lambda Chi Alpha Fraternity 1958; Masons: Jas H. Lockwood Lodge #1343, Waco, TX 1993; Masons: Oliver Lodge #084, Alexandria, La 1961; Natl Assn of Eagle Scouts; Scottish Rite of Freemasonry, Waco, TX 1993; York Rite Masonic Bodies, Alexandria, La 1961. Par Min's Fell The Fund for Theol Educ, Inc. 1975.

WELLS JR, Roy Draydon (Ala) 3608 Montclair Rd, Birmingham AL 35213 B Tuskegee AL 1935 s Roy & Pollie. BA Birmingham-Sthrn Coll 1957; BD Van 1960; PhD Van 1969. D 5/26/1999 P 5/23/2000 Bp Henry Nutt Parsley Jr. m 2/15/1957 Laura Elizabeth Stephenson. R S Andrews's Epis Ch Birmingham AL 2011. Auth, "Var arts," 2003. Aabs; SBL.

WELLS, William Edward (Los) 202 Avenida Aragon, San Clemente CA 92672 **Newport Harbor Luth Ch Newport Bch CA 2013-; Chapl in Res S Clem's-By-The-Sea Par San Clemente CA 2009-** B Santa Ana CA 1963 s Richard & Nancy. BMus Biola U 1987; MDiv Claremont TS 2007; Dplma ETSBH 2007. D 6/6/2009 Bp Sergio Carranza-Gomez P 1/9/2010 Bp Chester Lovelle Talton.

WELLS JR, William Smith (Va) 6914 West Grace Street, Richmond VA 23226 **Ret 2007-** B Durham NC 1941 s William & Margaret. BA U NC 1963; MDiv EDS 1968. D 6/28/1968 P 6/1/1969 Bp Thomas Augustus Fraser Jr. m 8/8/1964 Marion Wells c 4. S Cathr's Sch Richmond VA 2000-2007; P-in-c S Mart's Ch Doswell VA 1996-2002; Chapl St. Cathr's Sch Richmond VA 1994-2007; R Ch Of The H Comf Richmond VA 1987-1994; S Anne's Ch Winston Salem NC 1978-1987; Chapl Wake Forest U In Winston Salem NC 1978-1987; Assoc S Jn's Ch Roanoke VA 1975-1978; Epis Chapl No Carolina St U At Raleigh 1971-1975; Asst S Phil & Tit Durham NC 1968-1970.

WELLS MILLER, Tracy (ECR) The Episcopal Church of St. John the Baptist, PO Box 188, Aptos CA 95001 **Epis Ch of St Jn the Bapt Aptos Aptos CA 2017-** B Columbia SC 1981 BA Furman U 2003; MTS Harvard DS 2006; MDiv Sewanee: The U So, TS 2012. D 12/17/2011 P 6/24/2012 Bp J Neil Alexander. m 7/30/2009 Thomasjohn Miller. S Cuth's Epis Ch Oakland CA 2016-2017; Assoc P S Paul's Ch Franklin TN 2012-2015. Freeman Awd for Merit Sewanee: The U So, TS 2010. mtrtracy@gmail.com

WELSAND, Randy Arthur (Minn) 1928 38th St S, St Cloud MN 56301 B Duluth MN 1953 s Arthur & Joyce. BA U MN Duluth 1991. D 4/6/2002 Bp Frederick Warren Putnam P 10/6/2002 Bp Daniel Lee Swenson. m 7/8/1978 Maren Kay Welsand c 1.

WELSH, Clement William (WA) 16 N. Cherry Grove Ave., Annapolis MD 21401 **Died 6/10/2017** B Oakmont PA 1913 s James & Ada. BA Harv 1934; UTS 1935; BD EDS 1937; PhD Harv 1958; STD Ken 1960. D 2/15/1939 P 10/31/1939 Bp Henry Knox Sherrill. c 4. Ret 1982-2017; Int S Jas Epis Ch Firenze 50123 1982-1983; Cathd of St Ptr & St Paul Washington DC 1963-1981; Dir Of Stds Coll Of Preachers Washington DC 1963-1971; Asst. Prof Bex Sem Columbus OH 1949-1952; Asst. Prof Ken Gambier OH 1943-1952; Chapl Ken Gambier OH 1943-1946; R S Jas Ch Groveland Groveland MA 1939-1942; Serv S Jn's Epis Par Waterbury CT 1937-1939; Bec Dio Washington Washington DC 1964-1971. Auth, "Preaching In A New Key," Pilgrim Press, 1974.

WELTSEK JR, Gustave John (Fla) 7504 Holiday Rd S, Jacksonville FL 32216 **Died 5/18/2016** B New York NY 1935 s Gustave & Teresa. BA CUNY 1958; MDiv PDS 1961. D 4/1/1961 P 10/1/1961 Bp James Pernette DeWolfe. m 6/11/2016 Susan Gracey c 4. Chapl Fresh Mnstrs 2004-2016; Dir FreshMinistries Jacksonville FL 2000-2004; S Jn's Cathd Jacksonville FL 1985-2000; R S Jas Epis Ch Birmingham MI 1978-1985; R Ch Of The Mssh Lower Gwynedd PA 1967-1978; Cur 1961-1963; Chapl (LtCmdr) USNR 1965-1976; R Ch Of The Redemp Southampton PA 1963-1967; Dep GC Dio Florida Jacksonville 1988-1997, Chair Cler Compstn Com 1987, ExCoun 1986, Cler Coordntrv VIM 1980-1985. Dn Emer St. Jn's Cathd, Jacksonville FL 2011.

WELTY III, Terrence Anthony (Tex) 106 E Crawford St, Palestine TX 75801 B Charleston WV 1941 s Terrence & Martha. MA Cntrl Michigan U; BA Texas Luth U 1972; MLitt U of S Andrews GB 2005. D 12/1/2005 P 6/10/2006 Bp Daniel William Herzog. m 8/31/1968 Elizabeth Welty c 3. R S Phil's Epis Ch Palestine TX 2009-2013; Int Chr Epis Ch Tyler TX 2007-2009; Nash Nashotah WI 2005-2007.

WELTY, Winston W (Pa) Santa Clara #613, Riberas del Pilar, Chapala PA 45906 Mexico B Dallas TX 1942 s Daniel & Erlene. BA CUNY 1963; MDiv PDS 1966. D 6/4/1966 P 12/17/1966 Bp Horace W B Donegan. m 11/22/1975 Mary J Gustafson c 4. R St. Andr's Angl Ch Chapala Jalisco 2010-2016; Int

Chr Epis Ch Pottstown PA 2004-2007; Int Incarn H Sacr Epis Ch Drexel Hill PA 2003-2005; Int S Jn The Evang Ch Lansdowne PA 2001-2003; R S Alb's Ch Newtown Sq PA 1982-2000; Assoc S Dav's Ch Wayne PA 1978-1982, Asst 1975-1978; R Trin Ch Gulph Mills Kng Of Prussia PA 1970-1974; R H Cross Epis Ch Wilkes Barre PA 1967-1969; Cur Trin S Paul's Epis New Rochelle NY 1966-1967.

WENDEL JR, David Deaderick (Ala) 210 Oak Ct, New Braunfels TX 78132 **Ret 1995-** B Montgomery AL 1930 s David & Elizabeth. BA U So 1951; MDiv VTS 1959; MA Lon GB 1970. D 6/8/1959 Bp George Mosley Murray P 6/1/1960 Bp Samuel B Chilton. m 9/7/1957 Ruth Wendel. Asst S Mary's-On-The-Highlands Epis Ch Birmingham AL 1991-1995; R Trin Epis Ch Bessemer AL 1987-1991; Dio Alabama Birmingham 1987-1989; R S Fran Epis Ch Victoria TX 1978-1986; R S Jn's Ch New Braunfels TX 1972-1977; Asst Ch Of The Gd Shpd Corpus Christi TX 1970-1972; Serv Ch Of Brazil 1960-1970; Asst S Jn's Epis Ch Mc Lean VA 1959-1960.

WENDEL, Richard Joseph Bosley (Chi) 536 W Fullerton Pkwy, Chicago IL 60614 **Adj Fac DePaul U 2013-; Res P Ch Of Our Sav Chicago IL 1999-; Assoc. Prof of Clincl Psych & Behavioral Sciences NW Univ Feinberg Sch of Med 1999-** B Pittsburgh PA 1951 s Robert & Virginia. BA Penn 1973; MDiv PrTS 1976; DMin McCormick TS 1985; PhD Loyola U Chicago 2010. D 4/26/1985 P 8/28/1985 Bp O'Kelley Whitaker. m 12/30/1998 Mina Dulcan c 1. Assoc P S Matt's Ch Evanston IL 1993-1998; Advoc Hlth Care Oak Brook IL 1992-1998; R Calv Ch Homer NY 1985-1987; R S Matt's Ch Moravia NY 1985-1987; Asst. Pstr Presb Ch 1976-1985. Amer Fam Ther Acad 2006; Clincl Mem AAMFT, Supvsr 1987; Mem KON 1991; Natl Coun on Fam Relatns 1999; SBL 1999.

WENDELL, Chris (Mass) St. Paul's Church, 100 Pine Hill Road, Bedford MA 01730 **R S Paul's Epis Ch Bedford MA 2011-; Assessment Coordntng Com Dio Massachusetts Boston MA 2012-, Compstn and Benefits Com 2012-, Exec Com 2012-, Dioc Coun 2011-** B Chicago IL 1981 s Peter & Lynn. AB Pr 2003; MDiv EDS 2007. D 6/9/2007 Bp George Edward Councell P 1/12/2008 Bp M(Arvil) Thomas Shaw. m 8/11/2007 Kristen Wendell c 1. Mem, Bd Advisors MIT Campus Chapl Cambridge MA 2007-2011; Assoc R S Andr's Ch Wellesley MA 2007-2011. subject, "Blessed are the Poor in Sprt: Chris's Story," *Claiming the Beatitudes: Nine Stories from a New Generation)*, Alb, 2009.

WENDELL, Martin Paul (Alb) 405 Master St, Valley Falls NY 12185 B Ticonderoga NY 1945 s Walton & Mary. BA S Piux X Sem 1967; Ford Bronx NY 1968; CUA WashingtonDC 1969; MA S Bernards TS and Mnstry 1992. D 5/31/1988 Bp David Standish Ball P 9/5/1998 Bp Daniel William Herzog. m 9/6/1981 Judy M Wendell. P-in-c Trin Ch Watervliet NY 1998-2010; D S Paul's Epis Ch Greenwich NY 1988-1998.

WENDER, Sarai Tucker (ETenn) The Episcopal Church in East Tennessee, 814 Episcopal School Way, Knoxville TN 37932 B Salt Lake City UT 1962 d Edwin & Louise. Nrsng Walters St Cmnty Coll; 2 Years Formation Prog Sewanee: The U So 2015. D 2/6/2016 Bp George Young III. m 8/11/1990 Udo Wender c 2.

WENDFELDT, Stephen Hoff (SanD) 2728 Sixth Avenue, San Diego CA 92103 B Duluth MN 1947 s Ole & Erlene. USAF Acad 1966; BA U MN 1969; MDiv CDSP 1982. D 6/20/1982 P 6/29/1983 Bp Victor Manuel Rivera. m 6/4/2009 Linda Ardell Smith c 2. P-in-c Dio San Diego San Diego CA 2011-2012, P-in-c 2010-2011, Congrl Dvlpmt 2007-2010; Plnng and Dvlpmt S Jas By The Sea La Jolla CA 2011-2012; R S Ptr's Epis Ch Del Mar CA 2001-2007; Dir New Cong Dvlpmt Dio No Carolina Raleigh NC 1998-2001; R S Steph's Epis Ch Longview WA 1994-1998; R S Paul's Epis Ch Bremerton WA 1988-1994; Int S Jos And S Jn Ch Lakewood WA 1987-1988; Vic S Antony Of Egypt Silverdale WA 1985-1986; Asst S Barn Epis Ch Bainbridge Island WA 1984-1985; Vic S Jas Ch Lindsay CA 1983-1984; Cur S Jn The Bapt Lodi CA 1982-1983.

WENGROVIUS, John H. (Colo) 1320 Arapahoe St, Golden CO 80401 B Colorado Springs CO 1950 s John & Stella. Pr 1970; BA Colorado St U 1973; MDiv Nash 1977; DMin SWTS 2007. D 12/21/1976 P 3/5/1978 Bp William Carl Frey. m 5/29/1976 Ruth W Etherington c 3. Sr Pstr Calv Ch Golden CO 1988-2016; Cur/Assoc The Epis Par of S Greg Littleton CO 1984-1988; S Aug's Ch Creede CO 1983-1984; S Pat's Epis Ch Pagosa Sprg CO 1983-1984; Vic S Steph The Mtyr Epis Ch Monte Vista CO 1983-1984; Exec Coun Appointees New York NY 1983; Dio Colorado Denver CO 1980-1983, Ast to Bp 1977-1978; Mssy Zomba Theol Coll Malawi Afr 1980-1983; Cur S Paul's Epis Ch Lakewood CO 1978-1980. Auth, "From Pstr to Prog in the Epis Ch: The Pilgrimage through the Transitional Swamp," *DMin Thesis*, SWTS, 2007; Auth, "Adult Track II, Epiph Year B: Evangelization," *Living the Gd News*, 1988; Auth, "Adult Track II, Lent Year A, Epiph Year B: Pryr," *Lectionary Curric*, 1987. Cn of St. Paul's Cathd; Blantyre, Malawi The Dio Sthrn Malawi 2004.

WENGROVIUS, Steve (Colo) 3712 W 99th Ave, Westminster CO 80031 B Colorado Springs CO 1948 s John & Stella. BS Colorado St U 1971; BS U of Utah 1972; MDiv Nash 1979. D 6/29/1979 P 3/1/1980 Bp William Carl Frey. m 8/27/1978 Christine Lynne Wengrovius c 2. R S Martha's Epis Ch Westminster CO 2003-2017; Int All SS Luth Ch Cory CO 1997-2003; Asst St. Lukes Epis Delta CO 1996-1997; P-in- Charge S Lk's Epis Ch Delta CO 1995; Asst Dio Col-

orado Denver CO 1987-1992; Vic S Jn's Epis Ch Ouray CO 1985-1987; R Trin Ch Arkansas City KS 1982-1985; Cur S Aid's Epis Ch Boulder CO 1979-1982.

WENNER, Peter Woodring (Mass) 137 Auburndale Ave, West Newton MA 02465 B Baltimore MD 1944 s Herbert & Ruth. BA Carleton Coll 1966; BD SWTS 1970. D 6/21/1970 Bp Edward Clark Turner P 1/25/1971 Bp James Walmsley Frederic Carman. m 11/11/1995 Barbara Williamson c 2. Int Ch Of S Jn The Evang Hingham MA 2007-2009; Int S Paul's Ch Newburyport MA 2005-2007; P-in-c Chr Ch Waltham MA 2000-2005; Int S Jas' Epis Ch Cambridge MA 1998-2000; R S Mk's Ch Milwaukee WI 1984-1998; R H Trin Epis Ch Manistee MI 1976-1984; Asst S Mk's Ch Grand Rapids MI 1972-1976; Chapl Oregon Epis Sch Portland OR 1970-1972. co-Auth, "Welcome to the Bible," Morehouse Pub, 2007.

WENNER GARDNER, Rachel E (Colo) Ch Of The Ascension & Holy Trinity, 420 W 18th St, Pueblo CO 81003 **The Ch Of The H Trin Rittenhouse Philadelphia PA 2016-** B Grand Rapids MI 1974 d Peter & Wendy. BA Kalamazoo Coll 1996; MDiv VTS 2002. D 4/6/2002 P 10/17/2002 Bp Roger John White. m 2/8/2003 John Gardner c 3. P-in-c Ch Of The Ascen Pueblo CO 2012-2016; Co-R Trin Epis Ch Rocky Mt VA 2006-2012; Asst Trin Ch Milwaukee WI 2002-2006; Mem, COM Dio SW Virginia Roanoke VA 2007-2011; Mem, Cmsn on Minsitry Dio Milwaukee Milwaukee WI 2003-2006.

WENRICK, Heather Marie (Ore) 1444 Liberty St SE, Salem OR 97302 **Oregon Epis Sch Portland OR 2015-; Epis Par Of S Jn The Bapt Portland OR 2013-** B Corvallis OR 1978 d John & Mary. BA Gonzaga U 2000; MDiv Ya Berk 2011. D 6/18/2011 P 1/7/2012 Bp Michael Hanley. m 10/6/2001 Michael Wenrick c 2. P S Paul's Epis Ch Salem OR 2011-2013.

WENTHE, Lanny (Me) 35 Paris St, Norway ME 04268 **D Chr Ch Norway ME 2013-; Mem Bridgton Ecum Grp Bridgton ME 2015-; Vol Chapl Bridgton Hosp Bridgton ME 2015-; Vol Chapl Stephens Memi Hosp Norway ME 2014-; D Dio Maine Portland ME 2013-; Mem Oxford Hills Area Cler Assn 2013-** B White Plains NY 1941 d Roland & Elizabeth. Douglass Coll 1960; Trin 1989; Bancor TS 2011. D 6/29/2013 Bp Stephen Taylor Lane. c 2.

WENTT, Allan Rudolphus (Va) 7503 Noble Avenue, Richmond VA 23227 **Died 7/5/2016** B Kingston JM 1931 s Walter & Janetta. BA Juilliard Sch 1967; STB Ya Berk 1968; MS Juilliard Sch 1968; MDiv Ya Berk 1971; NYU 1979; Virginia Commonwealth U 1995. D 6/14/1956 Bp Duncan Montgomery Gray P 12/1/1956 Bp Reginald Heber Gooden. m 7/29/2016 Karen B Brown c 4. S Jas Chuch Warfield VA 2006-2016; Ret 1997-2016; R S Phil's Ch Richmond VA 1979-1996; Cn to the Ordnry Dio Sthrn Ohio Cincinnati OH 1973-1979; R S Phil's Ch Columbus OH 1972-1979; R Ch Of Our Merc Sav Louisville KY 1970-1972; R S Lk's Epis Ch Bronx NY 1960-1970; Asst S Lk's Epis Ch New Haven CT 1959-1960; Vic S Alb's Paraiso PA 1956-1959.

WENTZ, Herbert Stephenson (At) PO Box 3190, Sewanee TN 37375 **Died 10/16/2015** B Salisbury NC 1934 s Charles & Carolyn. AB U NC 1956; STB GTS 1960; MA Oxf GB 1963; PhD U of Exeter GB 1971. D 6/29/1960 Bp Richard Henry Baker P 12/31/1960 Bp Thomas Augustus Fraser Jr. m 7/9/1980 Sofia Lilijencrants. Ret 1997-2015; Cur S Lk's Epis Ch Atlanta GA 1962-1965; Vic S Chris's Epis Ch Garner NC 1960-1962.

WENTZIEN, Marilyn Lawrence (Ia) D 5/9/2010 Bp Alan Scarfe

WERDAL, Evelyn Paige (NY) 522 Walnut St, Mamaroneck NY 10543 B Mount Vernon NY 1934 d Philip & Christine. RN Mt Vernon Hosp Sch of Nrsng Mt Vernon NY 1956; BS Mercy Coll 1975; MS LIU 1978. D 6/4/1994 Bp Richard Frank Grein. m 8/3/1957 George Norman Werdal c 2. D S Thos Ch Mamaroneck NY 1994-2014. Auth, "Through the Patient's Eyes," *Hlth Care Forum*, 1995.

WERNER, Frederick John Emil (Mich) 13070 Independence Ave, Utica MI 48315 **Asst S Lk 1975-** B Brooklyn NY 1928 s Frederick & Anna. Edgewood Coll 1949; LIU 1950. D 12/6/1975 Bp H Coleman Mcgehee Jr. m 6/20/1959 Marilyn Rose Barrett c 4. Ord S Paul Tentmaker.

WERNER, George (Pgh) 106 Sewickley Heights Dr., Sewickley PA 15143 **Trst CPG 2006-; Ret 2000-** B New York NY 1938 s Louis & Alvine. BA Laf 1959; MDiv Ya Berk 1962. D 6/23/1962 Bp Walter H Gray P 3/9/1963 Bp John Henry Esquirol. m 6/18/1960 Audrey Diane Werner c 4. Pres HOD 2000-2006; Stndg Cmsn on Plnng and Arrangements ECUSA 1994-2000; VP HOD 1994-2000; Stndg Cmsn on Hlth DFMS 1988-1994; Com on the St of the Ch DFMS 1985-1991; Dn Trin Cathd Pittsburgh PA 1979-1999; CLIC 1979-1988; Ch Pension Fund 1976-1988; Dep GC 1970-2006; Asst to Bp Dio New Hampshire Concord NH 1970-1979; R Gr Ch Manchester NH 1968-1979; R S Lk's/S Paul's Ch Bridgeport CT 1964-1968; Cur S Ptr's Epis Ch Milford CT 1962-1964. Auth, *Prolonging Life*, Forw Mvmt Press, 1993; Auth, "Chapt: A Word from the Other Players," *Reaping the Harvest*, Humana, 1988. DD (Hon) Nash 2003; DD (Hon) Berkeley at Yale 1979.

WERNER, Mark (USC) 2 N Hill Ct, Columbia SC 29223 **Ret 1997-** B Ridgewood NJ 1952 s Herbert & Margaret. BA Coll of Wooster 1975; DMin UTS Richmond 1979; MS U GA 1997. D 6/5/1991 Bp Richard Lester Shimpfky P 12/21/1991 Bp David Charles Bowman. m 3/23/1974 Barbara Ann Tinley. Off Of Bsh For ArmdF New York NY 1991-1997; Serv Presb Ch 1979-1981. Auth, "Alcosm Resrch & Educ Wrld". AEHC; OHC.

W

WERNICK, Mike (WMich) 1800 Bloomfield Dr. SE, Kentwood MI 49508 **Pstr Ascen Luth Ch Kentwood MI 2011-; R Ch Of The H Cross Kentwood MI 2011-; Ecum and Interfaith Off Dio Wstrn Michigan Kalamazoo MI 2015-, COM 2012-2014** B Brooklyn NY 1953 s Eli & Joan. BA U of Florida 1977; MDiv Bex Sem 2010. D 6/13/2009 P 6/19/2010 Bp Thomas Edward Breidenthal. m 11/17/2013 Joel Andrew Flint c 2. P-in-c Dio Pittsburgh Pittsburgh PA 2011; Asstg P S Steph's Epis Ch And U Columbus OH 2011. rectorpastor@comcast.net

WERNTZ, Pamela Louise (Mass) 120 Marshall St, Watertown MA 02472 **R Emm Ch Boston MA 2008-** B Lancaster PA 1960 d William & Marcia. AB Franklin & Marshall Coll 1981; MDiv EDS 2000. D 6/15/2002 P 5/31/2003 Bp M(Arvil) Thomas Shaw. m 7/10/2004 Audrey Joy Howard c 2. Assoc R S Paul's Ch Brookline MA 2002-2008. werntz.emmanuel@gmail.com

WESCH, Kate (Oly) 1805 38th Ave, Seattle WA 98126 **Assoc Epiph Par of Seattle Seattle WA 2009-** B Ponca City Oklahoma 1981 d James & Caroline. BA U of Oklahoma 2002; MDiv Epis TS of the SW 2006. D 7/1/2006 Bp Robert Manning Moody P 1/6/2007 Bp Bavi Edna Rivera. m 8/27/2005 Joel Wesch c 1. P-in-c Ch Of The H Sprt Vashon WA 2008-2009; S Jn The Bapt Epis Ch Seattle WA 2007-2008; Dio Olympia Seattle 2006.

WESEN, Vicki Jane Smaby (Oly) 1500A E College Way # 447, Mount Vernon WA 98273 **Assoc Komo Kulshan Cluster 2004-** B Mount Vernon WA 1945 d Lloyd & Betty. BS WA SU 1971; MEd No Carolina St U 1983; MDiv Duke DS 1988; VTS 1988. D 6/5/1988 P 6/16/1989 Bp Robert Whitridge Estill. c 2. Komo Kulshan Cluster Mt Vernon WA 2000-2009; Mssnr Asst Komo Kulshan Cluster Skagit Cnty WA 2000-2004; Asst S Paul's Epis Ch Mt Vernon WA 2000-2004; Cn Cong Spprt/Deploy Dio No Carolina Raleigh NC 1995-2000; All SS Ch Warrenton NC 1989-1994; Vic Chap Of The Gd Shpd Ridgeway NC 1989-1994; Emm Ch Warrenton NC 1988-1994; Prog Dir S Tim's Ch Wilson NC 1984-1985.

WESLEY, Carol A (Mo) 5519 Alaska Ave, Saint Louis MO 63111 **P-in-c St Johns & St Jas Ch Sullivan MO 2003-; Soc Wk Fac Sthrn Illinois U Edwardsville IL 1996-** B Springfield IL 1952 d John & Johanna. AA Lincoln Land Cmnty Coll 1972; BA U IL Springfield 1973; MSW S Louis U 1975; PhD S Louis U 1987; MDiv Aquinas Inst of Theol 1995. D 3/28/2003 P 10/3/2003 Bp George Wayne Smith.

WESLEY JR, John (Fla) 338 N 10th St, Quincy FL 32351 **R S Paul's Epis Ch Quincy FL 2015-** B Columbus OH 1944 s John & Esther. OH SU 1963; BA U Cinc 1966; MDiv VTS 1970; MEd U of No Florida 1989; MEd U of No Florida 1990. D 6/20/1970 P 5/23/1971 Bp Philip Alan Smith. m 2/8/1986 Sandra L Elliott c 2. PT R S Andr's Ch Montevallo AL 2009-2015; R S Lk's Epis Ch Smethport PA 2008-2009; S Lk's Smethport PA 2006-2009; P-in-c Bi-Cnty Epis Cmnty Mnstry Port Allegany PA 2006-2007; R Ch of Our Sav Palm Bay FL 1998-2006, R 1998-2006; R S Thos Epis Ch Reidsville NC 1993-1998; Adj Instr U of Montevallo 1991-2013; R Trin Epis Ch Bessemer AL 1991-1993; Vic St Pat's Epis Ch S Johns FL 1984-1986; Asst All Souls Epis Ch Jacksonville FL 1981-1985; Asst Trin Cathd Columbia SC 1975-1977; Cur The Epis Ch Of The Medtr Allentown PA 1972-1975; Cur S Mich's Epis Ch Arlington VA 1970-1972. Auth, "The H Sprt in BCP," Westbow Press, 2015.

WESSELL, David E (FdL) 2805 Elgin St, Durham NC 27704 **1992-** B Wilmington NC 1938 s William & Mary. BA Rhodes Coll 1960; Nash 1963; S Vladimirs Orth TS 1976; AOS New Engl Culinary Inst 1994. D 4/1/1966 Bp John Melville Burgess P 1/1/1967 Bp The Bishop Of Damaraland. Dio Fond du Lac Appleton WI 1984-1992; St Ambr Epis Ch Antigo WI 1984-1992; S Barn Epis Ch Tomahawk WI 1984-1987; R Orth Ch in Amer Birmingham AL 1976-1983; Serv Dio Colorado Denver CO 1975-1976; Dioc Mssnr Dio Botswana Gaberone Botswana 1973-1975; Cur R Ch Of The Gd Samar Gunnison CO 1970-1973; Cur Epis Ch Of S Ptr And S Mary Denver CO 1969-1970; Cur Imm Ch Bellows Falls VT 1968-1969; Cur Dio Damaraland in SW Afr Windhoek So Afr 1966-1968.

WEST, Anne K (Va) Blue Ridge School, 273 Mayo Dr, St George VA 22935 **Blue Ridge Sch Dyke VA 2015-** B Clarksburg WV 1959 d Eugene & Maryanne. BS W Virginia U 1981; MDiv VTS 1989. D 8/24/1989 P 6/16/1990 Bp John Henry Smith. c 1. R Chr Ch Clarksburg WV 2012-2015; Chapl S Cathr's Sch Richmond VA 2009-2011; Vic Chr Ch Pearisburg VA 2008-2012; St. Steph's And St. Agnes Sch Alexandria VA 2007-2008; Assoc S Paul's Epis Ch Alexandria VA 2006-2007; Int Chr Epis Ch Christchurch VA 2004-2005; Int Christchurch Sch 2004-2005; Chapl Christchurch Sch Christchurch VA 1998-2004; Olde S Jn's Ch Colliers WV 1997-2004; P Brooke-Hancock Cluster Weirton WV 1997-1998; Yth Mnstrs Coordntr Dio W Virginia Charleston WV 1994-1996; Tchr Cathd Of St Jn The Div New York NY 1992-1994; The Cathd Sch New York NY 1992-1994, 1992; Dio Newark Newark NJ 1990-1991, Yth Mnstrs Coordntr 1990-1992; D S Jn's Ch Huntington WV 1989-1990. awest@blueridgeschool.com

WEST, Barbara Field (Ct) 7 Hillcrest Rd, Manchester CT 06040 B Manchester CT 1936 d William & Florence. SMU; BA Colby Coll 1958; SMU 1975. D 6/20/1975 Bp Archibald Donald Davies P 12/1/1980 Bp Morgan Porteus. Grtr Hartford Reg Mnstry E Hartford CT 1991-1999; Int Calv Ch Suffield CT 1991; Supply P Dio Connecticut Meriden CT 1988-1990; Asst S Jas Ch Glastonbury CT 1979-1987; Asst S Mary's Epis Ch Manchester CT 1977-1978; E D Farmer Fndt Dallas TX 1976.

WEST, Clark Russell (CNY) G3 Anabel Taylor Hall, Ithaca NY 14853 **Epis Ch At Cornell Ithaca NY 2009-** B Rochester NY 1967 s George & Judith. MDiv U Chi DS 1997; BA Wms 1997. D 6/24/1997 Bp Edward Witker Jones P 2/1/1998 Bp Cate Waynick. m 9/13/1997 Sarah Nell West c 3. R Trin Ch Geneva NY 2000-2006; Asst R Gr Epis Ch Hinsdale IL 1997-2000. eccu@cornell.edu

WEST, Craig Alan (SD) Po Box 532, Martin SD 57551 B Seattle WA 1950 s George & Elaine. BA U of Washington 1979; MDiv VTS 1994. D 7/9/1994 P 1/20/1995 Bp Vincent Waydell Warner. m 7/1/1975 Miriam Kathleen West c 3. P-in-c Dio So Dakota Pierre SD 2007-2017; Dio Olympia Seattle 2003-2004; R Emm Ch Orcas Island Eastsound WA 1996-2003; R The Epis Ch Of The Cross Ticonderoga NY 1995-1996; D-in-c S Germains Epis Ch Hoodsport WA 1994-1995.

WEST, Geoffrey George (NJ) 525 Willowbrook Dr, Jeffersonville PA 19403 **Assoc All SS Ch Norristown PA 2012-; Non-par 1977-** B Plainfield NJ 1944 s Gerald & C Kathleen. MDiv PDS; BA Rutgers The St U of New Jersey. D 4/27/1974 P 10/1/1974 Bp Albert Wiencke Van Duzer. Chr Ch Middletown NJ 1974-1976.

WEST, Hilary (EC) 411 W Bridge Ln, Nags Head NC 27959 **Serving in the Angl Ch of Mex Dio Mex 2001-** B Lancaster PA 1946 d Morgan & MaryLouise. BA Lebanon Vlly Coll 1968; MS Ohio U 1971; Cert Shalem Inst Washington DC 1986; MDiv VTS 1990. D 6/16/1990 Bp John Henry Smith P 2/23/1991 Bp Brice Sidney Sanders. Dio E Carolina Kinston NC 2001-2008; Washington-Tyrrell Epis Mnstry Roper NC 1999-2001; Mssnr Washington Tyrrell Epis Mnstry Colombia Creswell 1997-2001; S Geo Epis Ch Engelhard NC 1995-1996; Asst R S Andr-By-The-Sea Nags Hd NC 1990-1993; S Andr's By The Sea Nags Hd NC 1990-1993.

WEST, Hillary T (Va) 4212 Kingcrest Pkwy, Richmond VA 23221 **The Ch Of The Epiph Oak Hill VA 2014-** B Detroit MI 1951 d Bernard & Mary. BS Virginia Commonwealth U 2002; MDiv UTS Richmond 2004. D 6/26/2004 P 1/18/2005 Bp Peter J Lee. m 6/19/1971 Frederic Kemp West c 2. Assoc S Thos' Ch Whitemarsh Ft Washington PA 2011-2014; Asst R Chr Ch Glen Allen VA 2004-2011; St Jas Ch Richmond VA 1987-1996.

WEST JR OSB, Irvin D (Ark) 401 E 10th St, Little Rock AR 72202 **1st Vows S Greg's Abbey Three Rivers MI 1990-; Monk S Greg's Abbey Three Rivers MI 1988-** B Russellville AR 1945 s Irvin & Dora. BA Arkansas Tech U 1968; MDiv Sewanee: The U So, TS 1974. D 11/7/1974 Bp Christoph Keller Jr. Cur S Paul's Ch Fayetteville AR 1974-1986.

WEST, Jan Hickman (Cal) 171 Prospect Ave, San Anselmo CA 94960 **St. Jn's Epis Ch 2005-; Int Assoc R St Johns Epis Ch Ross CA 2001-, 1989-1990** B Santa Monica CA 1935 d Howard & Margarette. BA U CA 1957; MDiv CDSP 1989. D 6/3/1989 P 6/1/1990 Bp William Edwin Swing. m 9/14/1957 Herbert West c 2. Assoc St. Jn's Epis Ch 2003-2005; San Rafael Canal Mnstry San Rafael CA 1991-1997; Exec Dir/Pstr San Rafael Canal Mnstry 1989-1999.

WEST, Jennifer K (SO) 233 S. State St., Westerville OH 43081 B Providence RI 1952 d Mitchell & Arlene. BA Wheaton Coll at Norton 1974; MS Loyola Coll 1992; MDiv EDS 1997; Cert Int Mnstry 2003. D 6/7/1997 P 12/13/1997 Bp Robert Wilkes Ihloff. m 5/16/1993 Benjamin H West. S Matt's Epis Ch Westerville OH 2009-2013; Assoc S Jn's Ch Barrington RI 2006-2008; P-in-c S Mk's Epis Ch Riverside RI 2005-2006; Int S Paul's Ch N Kingstown RI 2002-2004; R S Barth's Ch Baltimore MD 1999-2002; Asst Chr Ch Columbia MD 1997-1999; Natl & Wrld Mssn Cmsn Dio Sthrn Ohio Cincinnati OH 2009-2011; Stndg Com Dio Rhode Island Providence RI 2005-2008.

WEST JR, John Richard (Ga) 4227 Columbia Rd, Martinez GA 30907 B Augusta GA 1962 s John & Martha. BFA U GA 1986; BA U GA 1988; MDiv VTS 2000. D 2/5/2000 P 9/5/2000 Bp Henry Irving Louttit. c 3. R Ch Of Our Sav Augusta GA 2011-2016; R Emm Ch At Brook Hill Richmond VA 2004-2011; R S Eliz's Epis Ch Richmond Hill GA 2001-2004; Cur Chr Ch Frederica St Simons Is GA 2000-2001.

WEST, John Thomas (NMich) 301 N 1st St, Ishpeming MI 49849 B Toronto ON 1947 s John & Elizabeth. BA York U 1970; MA Carleton U 1971. D 5/4/2014 Bp Rayford J Ray. m 7/23/1988 Diane Lillie Darlington c 2.

WEST, John Timothy (SO) 600 Dorothy Moore Avenue, Unit 10, Urbana OH 43078 B Los Angeles CA 1945 s Clifton & Georgia. BA U CA Santa Barbara 1967; BD CDSP 1970; MA U of San Francisco 1980; DMin Fuller TS 1992; Lic U of Dayton 1994. D 9/12/1970 Bp Francis E I Bloy P 3/1/1971 Bp Edward McNair. m 6/15/1996 Rebecca West c 1. Adj Fac Urbana U Urbana OH 2001-2012; Mssnr Ch Of The H Trin Epis Bellefontaine OH 1999-2011; Nthrn Miami Vlly Cluster Urbana OH 1999-2011; Mssnr Ch Of The Epiph Urbana OH 1998-2011; Our Sav Ch Mechanicsburg OH 1998-2011; Dio Sthrn Ohio (supply) 1990-1998; R The Epis Ch Of The Ascen Middletown OH 1985-1990; R St Johns Epis Ch Petaluma CA 1973-1985; Cur Ascen Epis Ch Vallejo CA 1970-1973. Auth, "Workbook for the Decade of Evang," Dio Sthrn Ohio, 1987. Amer Counslg Assn 2001; Fed of Fire Chapl 2004; Intl Critical Incident Stress Fndt 2006. Chi Sigma Iota Natl Counslg hon Soc. 1998.

WEST, Kathleen (SJ) 707 S Orange Grove Blvd Apt D, Pasadena CA 91105 **Died 2/21/2017** B Los Angeles CA 1955 d Kenneth & Helen. BA Westmont Coll 1977; MA Occ 1978; MDiv ETSBH 1999. D 6/12/1999 Bp Chester Lovelle Talton P 1/8/2000 Bp Frederick Houk Borsch. m 12/29/1979 Ira West c 1. Epis Dio San Joaquin Modesto CA 2011; P in Charge S Paul's Epis Ch Modesto CA 2010-2014; Dio Utah Salt Lake City UT 2008-2009; R S Mary's Ch Provo UT 2006-2008; Asst S Mths' Par Whittier CA 2006; Asstg P S Paul's Pomona Pomona CA 2003-2005; Asst S Geo's Par La Can CA 2003; Asstg P S Barn' Epis Ch Los Angeles CA 2001-2002; Asst R Trin Epis Par Los Angeles CA 1999-2001. irajwest@yahoo.com ·

WEST, Philip (RG) 2243 Henry Rd Sw, Albuquerque NM 87105 B Santa Fe NM 1939 s Harold & Mildred. CPE Epis TS of the SW 1975. D 9/10/1974 P 4/1/1975 Bp Richard Mitchell Trelease Jr. m 5/30/1987 Tertia West c 1. S Matt's Mssn Los Lunas NM 1999-2001; S Phil's Ch Rio Communities NM 1994-1999; Ch Of The H Sprt Gallup NM 1990-1992; Non-par 1983-1988; S Mk's Epis Ch Pecos TX 1978-1979; Trans Pecos Team Mnstry Pecos TX 1977; Asst Trans-Pecos Big Bend Mnstry 1976-1982; All SS Farmington NM 1975-1976; Dio The Rio Grande Albuquerque 1974-1976; Non-par 1973-1975.

WEST, R(andolph) Harrison (Ct) 11 Park St, Guilford CT 06437 **Chr Ch Guilford CT 2010-; Weca Bd Dio Washington Washington DC 2004-, Bp'S Mssn Strtgy Advsry Grp 1999-2000** B Portland OR 1952 s Harry & Sarah. BA Carleton Coll 1974; U of Oregon 1976; MDiv Sewanee: The U So, TS 1990. D 5/14/1991 P 1/28/1992 Bp Robert Louis Ladehoff. Assoc R S Jn's Ch Chevy Chase MD 1995-2010; Com Dio E Tennessee Knoxville TN 1994-1995; Yth Team 1993-1995; Gr Ch Chattanooga TN 1992-1995; Par Intern Gr Memi Portland OR 1991-1992. Shettle (Liturg) Prize In Liturg STUSo 1990; Woods Ldrshp Awd STUSo 1987.

WEST, Scott (SwVa) 120 Church St NE, P.O. Box 164, Blacksburg VA 24063 **R Chr Ch Blacksburg VA 2007-** B Weirton WV 1964 s John & Freda. BBA Marshall U 1986; MDiv GTS 1994; MA Marshall U 1994. D 6/11/1994 P 6/10/1995 Bp John Henry Smith. c 1. Asst S Paul's Epis Ch Alexandria VA 2006-2007; R S Mary's Whitechapel Epis Lancaster VA 1998-2005; Trin Epis Ch Lancaster VA 1998-2005; Brooke-Hancock Cluster Weirton WV 1997-1998; R Chr Ch Wellsburg WV 1995-1997; D S Steph's Epis Ch Beckley WV 1994-1995. Auth, "Last Obstacle to Wheeling: The Bd Tree Tunnel," The Sentinel, Baltimore & Ohio Railroad Hist Soc, 2007. saw764@yahoo.com

WESTBERG, Daniel Arnold (Mil) 2777 Mission Rd, Nashotah WI 53058 **Nash Nashotah WI 2000-** B Chicago IL 1949 s Harry & Gladys. Trans 6/5/2001 Bp Roger John White. m 8/31/1985 Lisa Westberg c 4. S Paul's Ch Ashippun Oconomowoc WI 2002-2003, 2000-2002.

WESTBURY JR, Rick (Fla) 15 N Wilderness Trl, Ponte Vedra Beach FL 32082 **R Chr Epis Ch Ponte Vedra FL 2001-** B Palatka FL 1959 s Richard & Doris. AA S Jn River Cmnty 1979; BA U of Florida 1981; MDiv SWTS 1989. D 6/11/1989 P 12/1/1989 Bp Frank S Cerveny. m 6/25/1983 Carole Conlee Westbury c 2. S Paul's Epis Ch Jacksonville FL 1992-2001; S Paul's By-The-Sea Epis Ch Jaxville Bch FL 1989-1992.

WEST-DOOHAN, Sue (Be) HC 75 Box 32, Strange Creek WV 25063 B Bethlehem PA 1949 d Frank & Betty. BA Moravian TS 1982; MDiv Nash 1990. D 11/19/1991 P 8/28/1992 Bp James Michael Mark Dyer. m 4/17/1999 William Doohan c 1. S Mich's Epis Ch Birdsboro PA 1998-2003; R All SS Epis Ch Williamsport PA 1994-1997; Dio Bethlehem Bethlehem PA 1991-1993; D S Gabr's Ch Douglassville PA 1991-1992.

WESTERBERG, George Arthur (Mass) 212 North Lower Bay Road, Lovell ME 04051 B Bellefonte PA 1933 s Arnold & Gladys. BA Bow 1959; UTS 1960; STB GTS 1962. D 6/9/1962 P 12/1/1962 Bp Horace W B Donegan. c 3. R S Mich's Ch Marblehead MA 1968-1998; Dept Of CE 1965-1968; S Dav's Epis Ch Kennebunk ME 1964-1968; Vic S Geo's Epis Ch York ME 1964-1968; Cur S Mk's Ch Mt Kisco NY 1962-1964. Chapl Soc Comp H Cross.

WESTERHOFF III, John Henry (At) 49 Old Ivy Sq Ne, Atlanta GA 30342 B Paterson NJ 1933 s John & Nona. BS Ursinus Coll 1955; STB Harvard DS 1958; EdD Col 1975; DD Ursinus Coll 1989; DD Ursinus Coll 1990. D 5/21/1978 P 9/23/1978 Bp William Augustus Jones Jr. m 10/27/1991 Caroline A Westerhoff. Vstng Prof GTS 2004-2006; Assoc, Res Theol, Dir Inst Pstr Stds S Lk's Epis Ch Atlanta GA 1994-2005; Int S Barth's Epis Ch Atlanta GA 1993-1994; P Assoc Chap of the Cross Chap Hill NC 1978-1994; Prof Duke TS Durham NC 1973-1994; Serv Untd Ch of Chr 1958-1974; Res Theol S Anne's Epis Ch Atlanta GA 2006-2013. Auth, *Will Our Chld Have Faith? (3rd ed.)*, Morehouse Pub, 2012; Auth, "Living Faithfully as a PB People," Morehouse, 2004; Auth, *The Sprtl Life: Fndt of Preaching & Tchg*, Knox, 1998. Assn of Professors & Researchers in Rel Educ 1974-1994; Rel Educ Assn 1984; Soc of S Jn the Evang 1974-1994. Hon DD Ursinus 1990.

WESTFALL, Doris Ann (Mo) 28 Whinhill Ct, Saint Peters MO 63304 **Emm Epis Ch S Louis MO 2016-** B NJ 1959 d Denziel & Marie. BA Valparaiso U 1981; MS S Louis U 1993; MDiv Sewanee: The U So, TS 2005. D 12/22/2004 P 6/24/2005 Bp George Wayne Smith. m 8/21/1982 David Allen Westfall c 3. Int S Lk's Epis Ch Manchester MO 2015-2016; Assoc Gr Ch S Louis MO 2014; H Trin Epis Ch Sulphur LA 2014; R S Matt's Ch St. Louis MO 2007-2013; R

S Matt's Epis Ch Warson Woods Kirkwood MO 2007-2013; Dio Missouri S Louis MO 2006-2007, Int 2006; Int Washington U - Epis Campus Mnstry St. Louis 2006-2007; Supply Ch S Jn's Ch Eolia MO 2006; Pstr Assoc Trin Epis Ch St. Chas MO 2005-2007; Gr Ch Clarksville MO 2005-2006. doris.westfall@gmail.com

WESTHORP, Peter H (RI) 2574 Creve Coeur Mill Rd, Maryland Heights MO 63043 **1972-** B Montreal QC CA 1942 s Clifford & Harriet. BA Leh 1965; MDiv Ya Berk 1968. D 6/24/1968 P 3/1/1969 Bp John S Higgins. m 11/13/1999 Beverly J Westhorp. R S Paul's Ch Portsmouth RI 1969-1972; Cur Trsfg Edgewood RI 1968-1969. Realtor of Year 81 No Suburban Bd Realtors 1981.

WESTON, English Hopkins (USC) 1017 Elm Savannah Rd, Hopkins SC 29061 **Died 6/24/2016** B Hopkins SC 1920 s Christian & Mary. BA Cit 1941; BD VTS 1943. D 9/16/1943 P 12/1/1944 Bp John J Gravatt. c 5. Ret 1987-2016; Ch Of The Nativ Un SC 1978-1987; Calv Ch Pauline SC 1978-1980; P-in-c Calv Glenn Sprg SC 1978-1980; P-in-c Epis Ch Of The H Trin Ridgeland SC 1976-1978; The Ch Of The Cross Bluffton SC 1976-1978; S Alb's Ch Blackville SC 1972-1976; P-in-c Ch Of The H Apos Barnwell SC 1971-1976; P-in-c S Alb's Ch Kingstree SC 1962-1971; S Lk's Ch Andrews SC 1962-1971; Asst to R S Paul's Epis Ch Chattanooga TN 1960-1962; P-in-c S Lk's Chattanooga TN 1957-1960; Chapl Ch Hm For Chld York SC 1952-1956; R Ch Of The Gd Shpd York SC 1952-1956; P-in-c Ch Of The Epiph Laurens SC 1948-1951; Ch Of The Gd Shpd Greer SC 1945-1952; P-in-c S Andr's Epis Ch Greenville SC 1945-1952; Cur Trin Cathd Columbia SC 1943-1945.

WESTON, Jane Mitchell (At) PO Box 102, Conyers GA 30012 **R S Simon's Epis Ch Conyers GA 2014-** B Bowling Green KY 1958 d Alton & Eleanor. BS Coll of Law Murray St U 1979; JD U of Kentucky 1982; MDiv Candler TS 2014; MDiv Candler TS Emory U 2014; MDiv CDSP 2014. D 12/21/2013 P 6/21/2014 Bp Robert Christopher Wright. m 9/3/1995 Harold Alan Weston.

WESTON, Myrtle Marguerite (NMich) 107 Forest Ridge Dr, Marquette MI 49855 B Marquette MI 1926 d Carl & Blanche. Nthrn Michigan U. D 4/1/1999 P 3/5/2000 Bp James Arthur Kelsey.

WESTON, Stephen Richard (Colo) 2021 South Xenia Way, Denver CO 80231 B New London CT 1941 s William & Ruth. BA Colorado St U 1966; MDiv VTS 1969. D 7/12/1969 P 5/23/1970 Bp John Joseph Meakin Harte. m 7/1/2011 Peggy Sands Weston c 2. R S Mk's Epis Ch Mesa AZ 1998-2005, Cur 1970-1972; R S Matt's Ch Edinburg TX 1995-1998; R Chr Epis Ch Pulaski VA 1991-1994; Ed for Crossroads Dioc Nwspr Dio Dallas Dallas TX 1985-1991; Assoc R S Alb's Epis Ch Arlington TX 1981-1985; Yth Dir Dio NW Texas Lubbock TX 1976-1981; Vic S Phil Amarillo TX 1976-1981; Vic S Mk's Epis Ch Coleman TX 1973-1976; Vic Trin Ch Albany TX 1973-1976; Cur Ch Of The H Trin Midland TX 1972-1973. Ed/Writer/Producer, "Our Hisp Mnstry II," 1991; Ed/Writer/Producer, "Our Hisp Mnstry," 1989. Polly Bond Awd 1988.

WESTPFAHL, Carol (ETenn) 210 Redwolf Way, Lenoir City TN 37772 B Burien WA 1958 d Charles & Dona. BA U of Washington 1981; MBA U of Washington 1983; MA Grad Theol Un 2001; MDiv CDSP 2002. D 6/24/2000 Bp Vincent Waydell Warner P 1/13/2001 Bp Sanford Zangwill Kaye Hampton. Cler Formation Com Dio E Tennessee Knoxville TN 2013-2015; R S Eliz's Epis Ch Knoxville TN 2011-2014; Assoc R for Adult Formation & Sprtl Developme Trin Ch Newtown CT 2003-2009. One of multiple authors, "Preaching Through the H Days & Holidays: Sermons That Wk XI," *Preaching Through the H Days & Holidays: Sermons That Wk XI*, Morehouse Pub, 2003. Associated Parishes for Liturg & Mssn 2011; Forma 2005. Bp Millard Preaching Prize CDSP 2002. cew4@uw.edu

WESTPHAL, Stacey Elizabeth (CFla) 522 Summerset Ct, Indian Harbour Beach FL 32937 **D H Trin Epis Ch Melbourne FL 2007-; Clincl Eductr Rn 1977-** B Orleans France 1954 d William & Maria. MS St Fran U 1995; MS St Fran U 2004. D 12/9/2006 Bp John Wadsworth Howe. m 11/1/1983 Frank Westphal.

WETHERED, Stephanie Keith (Nwk) 224 Cornelia St, Boonton NJ 07005 B Burlington VT 1958 d Richard & Jeane. BS U of Bridgeport 1982; MDiv Ya Berk 1993. D 6/5/1993 Bp Jack Marston Mckelvey P 12/4/1993 Bp John Shelby Spong. m 6/10/1995 Simon Wethered. S Ptr's Ch Essex Fells NJ 2005-2015; R S Jn's Epis Ch Boonton NJ 1996-2005; Assoc S Ptr's Ch Morristown NJ 1993-1996. Auth, "Ch Of The Year 2000 In Dio Newark". Phi Kappa Phi U Of Bridgeport; Dana Schlr U Of Bridgeport; Mercer Preaching Prize Yale DS.

WETHERILL, Benjamin Wade (Me) P.O. Box 156, Rangeley ME 04970 B 1962 s Benjamin & Mary. USMA; BS Arizona St U 1987; MDiv Asbury TS 2008. D 9/26/2009 Bp Stephen Taylor Lane. m 1/9/1988 Ana Kristan Rhinehart-Wetherill c 3.

WETHERINGTON, Robert W (Miss) PO Box 366, Sumner MS 38957 **Camp Mitchell Epis Ch Morrilton AR 2016-** B Kinston, NC 1980 s Robert & Carolyn. BA Kennesaw St U 2003; MDiv VTS 2009. D 12/20/2008 P 6/28/2009 Bp J Neil Alexander. m 4/19/2008 Betsy Baumgarten c 2. The Epis Ch Of The Redeem Biloxi MS 2011-2016; Delta Mssnr Dio Mississippi Jackson MS 2009-2011.

WETHERINGTON, Timothy R (CFla) Church Of The Messiah, 241 N Main St, Winter Garden FL 34787 B Renton WA 1960 s James & Katherine. BFA Virginia Commonwealth U 1982; MBA U of La Verne 1993. D 12/8/2012 Bp Gregory Orrin Brewer. m 5/29/2005 Terri L Wetherington c 2.

WETHERN, James Douglas (Ga) PO Box 20327, Saint Simons Island GA 31522 **D Chr Ch Frederica St Simons Is GA 1991-** B Minneapolis MN 1926 s Rudolph & Ida. MS Lawr 1949; PhD Lawr 1952; BA U of Wisconsin 2047. D 11/1/1991 Bp Harry Woolston Shipps. m 9/11/1948 Yvonne Marie Wethern c 4.

WETMORE, Ian (Spr) St Michael's Episcopal Church, 111 Ofallon Troy Rd, O Fallon IL 62269 **Vic S Mich's Epis Ch O Fallon IL 2012-** B Bath, NB, Canada 1961 s Kenneth & Eva. BA U of New Brunswick 1993; MDiv Wycliffe Coll 1996; MDiv Wycliffe Coll Toronto CA 1996. Trans 7/1/2012 Bp Daniel Hayden Martins. m 9/28/1996 Catherine Jane Wetmore c 1. Fllshp of Austin Fathers 2000; Soc of St Mich 2005-2009. iancwetmore@gmail.com

WETTSTEIN, David William (Ida) 6925 Copper Dr, Boise ID 83704 **R S Steph's Boise ID 1992-** B San Diego CA 1955 s William & Diane. BA California St U Sacramento 1979; MDiv SFTS 1983; CAS CDSP 1992. D 4/25/1992 Bp George Edmonds Bates P 11/1/1992 Bp John Stuart Thornton. m 2/26/2000 Belinda Suzanne Wettstein. ststephensrector@integra.net

WETZEL, Luke Andrew (Ga) Trinity Episcopal Church, 1130 1st Ave, Columbus GA 31901 **Trin Epis Ch Columbus GA 2016-** B Mission, KS 1987 s James & Linda. Bachelor of Arts Emory U 2009; Mstr of Div Duke DS 2012. D 4/3/2016 P 10/29/2016 Bp Scott Anson Benhase. m 7/31/2010 Natalie Frances Owens Wetzel c 2. fr.luke.wetzel@gmail.com

WETZEL, Mary (At) P.O. Box 4548, Atlanta GA 30302 **Vic The Ch of the Common Ground Atlanta GA 2010-** B Benton Harbor MI 1945 d Lester & Helen. Dplma Appalachian Bible Inst 1967; BS Jn Br 1969; MS Minnesota St U 1978; MEd Georgia St U 1981; MDiv EDS 2006. D 10/12/2008 P 6/28/2009 Bp J Neil Alexander. m 10/3/2011 Susan J Clearman. Asstg P Gr-Calv Epis Ch Clarkesville GA 2009-2010.

WETZEL, Todd Harold (Dal) Po Box 429, Cedar Hill TX 75106 B Warren OH 1946 s Harold & June. BA Ohio U 1968; MDiv Bex Sem 1971. D 6/26/1971 P 5/1/1972 Bp John Harris Burt. m 4/20/1968 Cheryl M Meyer c 2. Anglicans Untd & Latimer Press Dallas TX 2005-2012, 1989-2002; R Ch Of The Gd Shpd Cedar Hill TX 2002-2012; R S Geo Ch San Antonio TX 1987-1989; R Adv Epis Ch Westlake OH 1972-1987; Asst S Paul's Epis Ch Of E Cleveland Cleveland OH 1971-1972; Dep To Gen. Conv. Dio Dallas Dallas TX 2005-2007, Exec Coun Mem 2004-2007. Auth, "Steadfast Faith," Latimer Press, 1994; Auth, "H Euch Sacr Of Love," self, 1974. scl Ohio U 1968; Phi Beta Kappa 1967; Omicron Delta Kappa 1966.

WEYLS, Richard Coleman (Oly) 747 Broadway, Seattle WA 98122 **S Andr's Ch Seattle WA 2017-; P Assoc S Mk's Cathd Seattle WA 2014-; Chapl Swedish Hlth Serv Seattle WA 2009-** B Cleveland OH 1961 s Richard & Margaret. -; BS U Cinc 1983; BA U Cinc 1983; MAIR U Cinc 1984; MAIR U Cinc 1984; STB Mundelein Sem 1992; STB Mundelein Sem 1992; MDiv Mundelein Sem 1993; MDiv Mundelein Sem 1993; MDiv Mundelein Sem 1993; STL Mundelein Sem 1997; STL Mundelein Sem 1997. Rec 10/28/2014 as Priest Bp Gregory Harold Rickel. Contrib, "Tell Her That It's OK to Relase Her Sprt," *Sprtl Care in Pract: Case Stds in Profsnl Chapl, Geo Fitchett and Steve Nolan, eds.*, Jessica Kingsley Pub, London, 2015. Assn of Profsnl Chapl 2009; The Assembly of Epis Healthcare Chapl 2010.

WEYMOUTH, Richard Channing (NH) RR3 Box 18, Plymouth NH 03264 **Chapl S Chris's Sch Richmond VA 1994-** B Norwalk CT 1952 s Tyler & Francis. U of New Hampshire 1975; MDiv Ya Berk 1980. D 6/21/1980 P 6/1/1981 Bp Philip Alan Smith. m 8/21/1976 Katherine Weymouth c 2. Chapl Salisbury Sch Salisbury CT 1984-1994; Cur Chr Ch Exeter NH 1980-1984.

WHALEN, Dena Stokes (EC) P.O. Box 490, Clarkesville GA 30523 **S Paul's Epis Ch Wilmington NC 2013-** B Jacksonville FL 1956 d Redmond & Frances. BA Florida St U 1980; MDiv VTS 1992. D 6/14/1992 P 12/13/1992 Bp Frank S Cerveny. m 12/4/2015 Gary David Whalen c 2. R Gr-Calv Epis Ch Clarkesville GA 2004-2013; Chr Ch Epis Sch Greenville SC 2000-2003; Chapl/Assoc Chr Ch Greenville SC 2000-2003; Cn S Jn's Cathd Jacksonville FL 1994-2000; Assoc/Chapl S Andr's Ch Jacksonville FL 1992-1994.

WHALEN, Donald (Eas) 2929 SE Ocean Blvd O-5, Stuart FL 34996 B Bay Shore NY 1934 s Harold & Evelyn. BS SUNY 1958; MS SUNY 1959; MEd Col 1973; Mercer TS 1989; Cert Gerontological Mnstry 1991; CPE 1992. D 6/17/1989 Bp Orris George Walker Jr. m 9/25/1981 Constance Whalen. S Paul's Epis Ch Hebron MD 2005-2007; D St. Marys Epis Ch Pocomoke City MD 2002-2005; D S Lk's Epis Ch Stuart FL 2000-2002, Asst 1992-1999; D-in-c S Mths Epis Ch Bellmore NY 1995-2000; D's Asst Ascen 1993-1995; Chapl in Res Nassau Cnty Med Cntr NY 1991-1992; D / Asst S Ann's Ch Sayville NY 1990-1992; D / Asst The Ch Of The Ascen Rockville Ct NY 1989-1990.

WHALEN, Peter (Tenn) 103 Northwood Ave, Shelbyville TN 37160 **R Ch of the Redeem Shelbyville TN 2006-** B Hartford CT 1939 s John & Sophie. Assumption Sem 1967; Epis TS of the SW 1983. Rec 12/19/1983 as Deacon Bp Scott Field Bailey. m 7/21/1984 Barbara A Whalen c 2. R Ch Of The Redeem Shelbyville TN 2006-2016; R S Phil's Ch Nashville TN 1989-2006; Vic S Annes

Ch Can TX 1987-1989; Vic S Anne's Can TX 1987-1989; Asst R S Barth's Ch Corpus Christi TX 1983-1987.

WHALEY, Stephen Foster (Tex) 605 Dulles Avenue, Stafford TX 77477 **R All SS Epis Ch Stafford TX 2009-** B Houston TX 1973 s James & Bertha. B.E.D. Texas A&M U 1996; MDiv Sewanee: The U So, TS 2003. D 6/21/2003 P 12/21/2003 Bp Don Adger Wimberly. m 11/1/1997 Kathryn Gray Robson c 2. LocTen S Jn's Epis Ch Cntr TX 2007-2009; Asst to the R and U Chapl Steph F. Austin St U Chr Ch Nacogdoches TX 2005-2009; Asst to the R Ch Of The Gd Shpd Kingwood TX 2003-2005; Chapl/Liturg C. S. Fndt Fall Retreat Camp Allen Texas 2011-2012. Cmnty of Hope 1998.

WHALLON, Diane (Fla) 1640 NE 40th Ave Apt 106, Ocala FL 34470 **D Epis Ch of the Medtr Micanopy Florida 2011-** B Shelbyville IN 1949 d Daniel & Carolyn. BS U of Missouri 1977; MBA U of Missouri 1978; PhD U of Missouri 1983; EFM Sewanee: The U So, TS 1985. D 10/24/1986 Bp Richard Frank Grein. Billing Spec Hospice of Marion Cnty Ocala Florida 2011-2015; D S Pat's Ch Ocala FL 1998-1999; D Adv Epis Ch Ocala Florida 1994-1997; D S Aid's Ch Olathe KS 1991-1995; Pstr Admin S Thos The Apos Ch Overland Pk KS 1988-1991; Dioc Admin Dio Kansas Topeka KS 1985-1988; Chap Mgmt Spec USAF 1970-1974. Auth, "Gifts Identification Leaders Manual," Dio Kansas, 1988; Auth, "Decision Maker Uncertainty Effects Of Environ-Tech &," U of Missouri, 1983; Auth, "Contemporary Wrshp Serv Workbook For Chapl," Untd St AF, 1972. Beta Gamma Sigma 1977; Natl Hospice Orgnztn 1987-2001; NAAD 1984-2000; P. E.O. 1968; Zeta Tau Alpha 1967. Outstanding Paper by a Stdt Am Inst for Decision Sciences 1980; Outstanding Mgmt Stdt of the Year U of MIssouri 1977; AF Commendation Medal USAF 1974; AF Commendation Medal USAF 1971; Maud Ainslie Schlrshp Maud Ainslie Trust 1967.

✠ WHALON, The Rt Rev Pierre W (Eur) 23 Avenue George V, Paris 75008 France **Bp Suffr of Convoc of Ch in Europe Convoc of Epis Ch in Europe Paris 2001-; Epis Ch Cntr New York NY 2001-** B Newport RI 1952 s Raymond & Marthe. BA Bos 1974; Schola Cantorum 1977; MA Duquesne U 1981; MDiv VTS 1985. D 6/8/1985 P 12/21/1985 Bp Alden Moinet Hathaway Con 11/18/2001 for Eur. c 1. R S Andr's Epis Ch Ft Pierce FL 1993-2001; R S Paul's Ch Elkins Pk PA 1991-1993; BEC Dio Pittsburgh Pittsburgh PA 1988-1991, Econ Justice Off 1989-1991, Co-chair Wrshp & Mus Cmsn 1985-1988; All Souls Ch N Versailles PA 1985-1991; Chair COM Dio Cntrl Florida Orlando FL 2000-2001, Chair Inst of Chr Stds 1997-1999, Econ Justice Off 1994-1996; Chair Advocacy Serv & Justice Cmsn Dio Pennsylvania Philadelphia PA 1992-1993. "The Future of the PB Tradition," *Oxford Guide to BCP*, Oxf, 2006; Auth, "Toward an Adequate Moral Evaltn of Homosexuality," *ATR*, 1997; Auth, "Angl Comprehensiveness & the Thought of Dav Tracy," *Journ of Ecum Stds*, 1991; Auth, "A Critique of Sedwick's Revising Angl Moral Theol," *S Lk's Journ of Theol*, 1989. DD VTS 2003. bishop@tec-europe.org

WHARTON III, George Franklin (Ia) 502 W Broadway St, Decorah IA 52101 B Lake Charles LA 1929 s George & Fleda. BS U So 1951; GTS 1954; BA Oxf GB 1956; MA Oxf GB 1961. D 7/2/1954 P 8/1/1956 Bp Girault M Jones. m 6/11/1967 Marjorie R Running c 2. S Andr's Epis Ch Waverly IA 1991-1993; P-in-c Gr Ch Decorah IA 1980-1993; Vic S Peters Ch Fairfield IA 1977-1979, 1976-1979; Dio Louisiana New Orleans LA 1972-1976; Serv S Andr's Paradis Luling LA 1969-1976; R Ch Of The Epiph Opelousas LA 1959-1965; Asst S Mk's Cathd Shreveport LA 1956-1959; M-in-c S Jn's Epis Ch Thibodaux LA 1954-1955.

WHARTON, Roger (ECR) 1404 Arnold Ave, San Jose CA 95110 **Hospice Chapl Var Hospices - Currently Seasons Hospice 2017-** B Mansfield OH 1947 s Kenneth & Marie. BS Otterbein U 1969; Nthrn Illinois U 1971; MDiv Nash 1976; Ldrshp Acad for New Directions 1979; MA Loyola U 1982; DMin PSR 1995. D 1/10/1976 P 7/10/1976 Bp William Hampton Brady. m 9/29/2008 Marc Fuentes. San Jose Cbury Fndt San Jose CA 2005-2007; Assoc S Phil's Ch San Jose CA 1992-2002; R The Ch Of The H Trin Juneau AK 1985-1991; R S Brendan's Epis Ch Juneau AK 1985-1989; Dio New York New York NY 1982-1985; Epis Dio Of Ny Mid Hudson Regio Boiceville NY 1982-1985; P-in-c S Andr's Ch Walden NY 1982-1985; Yth Chapl St Fran of Assisi Montgomery NY 1982-1985; Co R S Mary Of The Snows Eagle Rvr WI 1976-1981; Dio Fond du Lac Appleton WI 1976-1981; S Mths Minocqua WI 1976-1981. Auth, "The Sprtl Roots of Chr Environmentalism," *Desert Call*, Nova Nada, 2009; Auth, "Palm Sunday," *Upper Room*, Upper Room, 1997; Auth, "Bethlehem as Sacr Place," *The Power of Sacr Places*, Quest, 1992; Auth, "H Week Devotions," *Disciplines*, Upper Room, 1990; Auth, "Connections," *Cries from the Heart: Alaskan Respond to the Exxon Valdez Oil Spill*, Wizard Works, 1989; Ed, *Christians In Comm w Creation*, EcoSpirit; Ed, *Ch In Comm w Creation*, EcoSpirit. Amer Teilhard Soc; Sis of the H Nativ; Soc Of S Jn The Evang.

WHEATLEY, Gail (Oly) St Andrew's Episcopal Church, 510 E. Park Ave, Port Angeles WA 98362 **R S Andrews Epis Ch Port Angeles WA 2008-** B Springfield OH 1953 d Robert & Fay. BS Ithaca Coll 1976; MDiv Sewanee: The U So, TS 2005. D 9/18/2005 P 3/25/2006 Bp Charles Franklin Brookhart Jr. m 5/24/

1975 Douglas G Wheatley c 2. R S Mk's Ch Havre MT 2005. clergy@olypen.com

WHEATLEY, Paul David (Dal) Church of the Incarnation, 3966 McKinney Ave, Dallas TX 75204 B Austin TX 1979 s Donald & Shirley. Dallas TS; BA University of Texas Austin 2000; MTS Wycliffe Coll 2012; MTS Wycliffe Coll Toronto CA 2012. D 5/31/2012 Bp Paul Emil Lambert P 5/10/2013 Bp James Monte Stanton. m 7/29/2006 Catherine S Wheatley c 2. St Aug of Hippo Epis Ch Dallas TX 2014-2017; Ch Of The Incarn Dallas TX 2012-2014; Dio Dallas Dallas TX 2010-2012. PWHEATLEY@INCARNATION.ORG

WHEATLEY-JONES, Elizabeth (Miss) P.O. Box 345, Grenada MS 38902 S Timothys Epis Ch Southaven MS 2016-; Exec Com Dio Mississippi 2011-; R All SS Epis Ch Grenada MS 2010- B Greenwood MS 1968 d Dudley & Mary. BS U So 1990; MDiv Epis TS of the SW 1999. D 6/11/1999 P 3/4/2000 Bp Alfred Marble Jr. m 11/26/2006 Robert J Jones c 1. Dir and Chapl LESM Mssn on the Bay Bay St. Louis MS 2010; R S Jos's On-The-Mtn Mentone AL 2008-2009; Chr Ch Bay S Louis MS 2007-2008, 2005-2007; Exec Com Dio Mississippi 2006-2008; Cn for Yth and YA Trin Cathd Little Rock AR 2003-2005; Chapl/Asst R Ch Of The Resurr Starkville MS 1999-2003.

WHEATON, Philip Eugene (Roch) 7211 Spruce Ave, Takoma Park MD 20912 B Minneapolis MN 1925 s Grier & Claudia. BA U MN 1948; MDiv VTS 1952; Amer U 1972. D 6/21/1952 Bp Stephen E Keeler P 12/1/1952 Bp Charles Alfred Voegeli. m 6/21/1975 Sue Knickerbocker c 6. Exec Coun Appointees New York NY 1989-1990; Dio Washington Washington DC 1968-1988; R S Lk's Ch Brockport NY 1964-1968; Min In Charge Iglesia Epis San Andres Santo Domingo Di 1955-1964; Iglesia Epis San Marcos Haitiana Ft Lauderdale FL 1955-1964; Min in charge Iglesia Epis Epifania Santo Domingo Di 1952-1954. Auth, "Flowering of the Prophetic Wk in Latin Amer"; Co-Auth, "Puerto Rico: People Challenging Colonialism"; Co-Auth, "Nicaragua: People'S Revolution"; Co-Auth, "Empire & The Word"; Co-Auth, "Guatemala: Path To Liberation"; Co-Auth, "Triufando Sobre Las Tragedias," *Centennial Hist Of The Epis Ch In The Dominican Republic*. Hon Theol Cn Epis Ch In The Dominican Republic 1997.

WHEELER, Charles R (WNY) 161 E Main St, Westfield NY 14787 B Olean NY 1946 s Kenneth & Mary. BA SUNY 1969. D 11/13/1994 Bp David Charles Bowman. m 8/5/1972 Christine Frances Wheeler c 2. S Mich And All Ang Buffalo NY 2004-2008; Dio Wstrn New York Tonawanda NY 2000-2008.

WHEELER, Diana Roberta (Cal) 573 Dolores st., San Francisco CA 94110 D Oasis California 2012-; St. Ambr Sea Breeze Epis Sch San Mateo CA 1995- B San Francisco CA 1954 AA City Coll of San Francisco; Bachelor in the Theol Stds Epis Sch for Deacons 2000. D 12/6/2003 Bp William Edwin Swing. m 11/16/1996 Richard Brandon c 3. D San Francisco Night Mnstry 2010-2012; D S Edm's Epis Ch Pacifica CA 2005-2007; S Aid's Ch San Francisco CA 2003-2009. Third Ord of the SSF 2010.

WHEELER, Elisa Desportes (Va) 638 Burton Point Rd, Mathews VA 23068 B Columbia SC 1946 d Fay & Margaret. BA Converse Coll 1968; MDiv VTS 1981. D 6/22/1981 Bp Orris George Walker Jr P 1/3/1982 Bp John Thomas Walker. m 5/29/1993 Maurice Elie Levis. P-in-c Ch Of The Sprt Alexandria VA 1999-2007; Kingston Par Epis Ch Mathews VA 1999-2005; Asst S Jn's Ch Hampton VA 1997-1999; Ch Of The Gd Shpd Norfolk VA 1997; S Fran Ch Virginia Bch VA 1995-1996; Int S Chris's Epis Ch Portsmouth VA 1994-1995; S Nich Epis Ch Germantown MD 1991-1992; S Martins-In-The-Field Columbia SC 1987-1988; S Jas Ch Potomac MD 1985-1989; Asst S Columba's Ch Washington DC 1981-1984. Auth, "Congregations In Change".

WHEELER, Evelyn (Ind) R Chr Ch Madison IN 2012-; D Middlesex Area Cluster Mnstry Higganum CT 2011- B Meidelberg Germany 1953 d David & Janet. BS U of Vermont 1976; JD Gonzaga U Sch of Law 1979; MS JHU 1997; MDiv Ya Berk 2011. D 6/4/2011 P 12/10/2011 Bp Shannon Sherwood Johnston. Frgn Serv Off U.S. Dept of St 1985-2007. rector_cecmadison@cinergymetro.net

WHEELER, Frances Marie (Kan) 14301 S Blackbob Rd, Olathe KS 66062 B Corpus Christi TX 1966 d Amos & Elvira. BS Marymount Coll 1990; Kansas Sch for Mnstry 2010. D 1/8/2011 Bp Dean E Wolfe. m 11/1/1986 Raymond Wheeler c 2.

WHEELER, James R (Ct) Po Box 10, Woodbury CT 06798 R S Jn's Ch Stamford CT 2008- B Chicago IL 1953 s Charles & Margaret. BA Coll of Wooster 1976; MDiv Colgate Rochester Crozer DS 1979; MDiv CRDS 1979; DMin VTS 2004. D 6/23/1979 Bp John Harris Burt P 1/13/1980 Bp David Keller Leighton Sr. m 6/19/1976 Carol Wheeler c 3. R S Paul's Ch Woodbury CT 1987-2007; R S Ptr's Epis Ch Buffalo NY 1981-1987; Asst Ch Of The Mssh Baltimore MD 1979-1981.

WHEELER, John Bevan (Md) 2795 Topmast Ct, Annapolis MD 21401 Ret Epis Ch 1999- B Baltimore MD 1931 s Clarence & Carolyn. BA W&L 1953; LTh GTS 1956; STB GTS 1959; MAE GW 1977. D 9/29/1956 Bp Harry Lee Doll P 7/13/1957 Bp Noble C Powell. m 10/5/1957 Helen Chase Wheeler c 2. Vic All SS Ch Annapolis Ju MD 1995-1999; Asst S Anne's Par Annapolis MD 1989-1995, Asst 1979-1988; Assoc S Barth's Ch Baltimore MD 1987-1988; Int Epiph Epis Ch Odenton MD 1985-1986; Int All Hallows Par So River Edge-

water MD 1982; Int S Lk's Ch Annapolis MD 1978-1979; R S Jas The Apos Epis Ch Conroe TX 1959-1961; Dio Texas Houston TX 1958-1959; S Clem Indn,Sprgs,MD - Vic Dio Maryland Baltimore MD 1957-1958; Vic S Andr's Ch Clear Sprg MD 1956-1958.

WHEELER, Kathryn Brown (CGC) 2002 W Lakeridge Dr, Albany GA 31707 D S Steph's Lee Cnty Leesburg GA 1999- B SC 1934 d Stanley & Catherine. BS Albany St U 1984. D 6/17/1999 Bp Henry Irving Louttit. m 11/20/1994 Daniel Gustavson Wheeler.

WHEELER JR, Louis (WA) 2001 14th St SE, Washington DC 20020 S Phil The Evang Washington DC 2015-; S Jn's Epis Ch Columbia SC 2005- B Homestead PA 1965 s Louis & Lillie. BA Edinboro U 1987; MS Natl-Louis U 1998; MDiv How 2003. D 6/12/2005 P 1/21/2006 Bp John Bryson Chane. m 9/9/1989 Tracy Douglas-Wheeler c 2. S Tim's Ch Frederick MD 2012-2014; S Mich And All Ang Ch Baltimore MD 2010-2012; S Mary's Epis Ch Foggy Bottom Washington DC 2007-2010; Asst R S Alb's Par Washington DC 2005-2006; Ch Of The Ascen Gaithersburg MD 2000-2005.

WHEELER, Rhonda Estes (SVa) St. Andrew's Episcopal Church, 45 Main Street, Newport News VA 23601 R Emm Epis Ch Hampton VA 2013-; Living a H Life T/F Dio Sthrn Virginia Newport News VA 2011-, Virginia Interfaith Plcy Ntwk 2010-, Ecum Cmsn 2008-, CE-Net 2007- B Waynesboro, VA 1962 d Vernon & Joyce. BA Carson-Newman Coll 1984; MDiv SW Bapt TS 1987; Cert Ang Stud VTS 2007. D 5/26/2007 P 12/6/2007 Bp Neff Powell. c 1. Asst R S Andr's Epis Ch Newport News VA 2007-2013; Sem Intern S Barn' Ch Leeland Uppr Marlboro MD 2006-2007; R E Lee Memi Ch (Epis) Lexington VA 2002-2006; Adj Prof Mary Baldwin Coll 1991-2002; Educ Consortium Dio SW Virginia Roanoke VA 2002-2006. saec.rhonda11@verizon.net

WHEELER CSL, William Ramsey (Alb) Po Box 354, Boonville NY 13309 P/ Vic Dio Albany Greenwich NY 2007-, Moliawk Correctional Fac kairos Mnstry 2002-, Sprtl Dir Kairos #1 2002-, Moliawk Correctional Fac kairos Mnstry 2002-; Vic Gr Ch Mohawk NY 2007-, D 2003-2007 B Utica NY 1932 s Everett & Marjorie. BA Syr 1955; BA TESM 2009. D 11/1/1986 Bp Donald James Parsons P 12/23/2007 Bp William Howard Love. m 11/23/1957 Darlene Wheeler c 2. Sprtl Advsry Happ # 38 & 39 Dio Cntrl New York 2002-2004; Dep Sprtl Dir, Curs Dio Cntrl New York Liverpool NY 1998-2004, Dep Sprtl Dir for Curs 1998-1999; D Trin Ch Boonville NY 1993-2001; D S Mk's Ch Sidney OH 1989-1993; D Chr Ch (Limestone) Hanna City IL 1986-1989; D S Andr's Ch Peoria IL 1986-1989. NAAD 1986.

WHEELOCK, Janet (SanD) Saint Mary's In The Valley Church, 1010 12th St, Ramona CA 92065 Dio San Diego San Diego CA 2016-; S Mary's In The Vlly Ch Ramona CA 2016- B Minneapolis MN 1957 d Robert & Jean. BA U MN 1982; CAS CDSP 1993; MDiv Luther TS 1993. D 6/24/1993 Bp Robert Marshall Anderson P 1/1/1994 Bp James Louis Jelinek. Int S Jas By The Sea La Jolla CA 2014-2015; Int The Epis Ch Of S Andr Encinitas CA 2012-2014; S Tim's Epis Ch Mtn View CA 2010-2012; Ch Of The Ascen Stillwater MN 2009-2010; Int Chapl U of St. Paul St. Paul MN 2007-2008; P-in-c S Edw The Confessor Wayzata MN 2004-2007; Cn Cathd Ch Of S Mk Minneapolis MN 2002-2004; Dio Minnesota Minneapolis MN 1999-2002, Com 1998-2001, Int Yth Coordntr 1994-1995, Cmsn On Mus And Liturg 1993-1999, Chr Formation Com 1993-; U Epis Cntr Minneapolis MN 1996-1998; Assoc R Adv Ch Farmington MN 1995-1996; S Jn The Bapt Epis Ch Minneapolis MN 1993-1994. Auth, "Merging, Yoking and Collaborating Ch," *The Mssngr*, Epis Dio San Diego, 2017; Auth, "Easter: A Moveable Feast," *Luth Wmn Today*, 1999. ESMHE, Mneca, Neca 1996-2003; Int Mnstry Ntwk 2011-2014. jwheelock@edsd.org

WHEELOCK, Leslie Gail (RI) 8 Neptune St, Jamestown RI 02835 B New York NY 1939 d Roy & Ruth. BA S Lawr Canton NY 1960; MA U of Rhode Island 1970; ADN Rhode Island Cmnty Coll 1977; Sch for Deacons 1988. D 2/4/1989 Bp George Nelson Hunt III. m 5/6/2000 Richard J Ayen c 5. D Ch Of The Ascen Wakefield RI 2000-2003; D S Matt's Par Of Jamestown Jamestown RI 1995-1999; Chapl RI Coll 1990-1996; D S Ptr's By The Sea Narragansett RI 1990-1994; D S Aug's Ch Kingston RI 1989-1990. Phi Beta Kappa 1960.

WHELAN, Edgar Joseph (WMo) 13500 Rinehart Ln, Parkville MO 64152 B Detroit MI 1936 s Henry & Theresa. CG Jung Inst; H Cross Coll; BA U of Notre Dame 1960. P 6/3/1985 Bp Arthur Anton Vogel. m 3/21/1981 Janet Kay Whelan. R Ch Of The Redeem Kansas City MO 1988-2003; Vic S Nich Ch Noel MO 1986-1988; Dio W Missouri Kansas City MO 1985-1988; P-in-c S Jn's Ch Neosho MO 1985-1986.

WHELAN, Janet Kay (WMo) 13500 Rinehart Ln, Parkville MO 64152 B Oak Park IL 1935 d John & Fern. BA No Pk U 1977; MS Cntrl Bapt TS 1997. D 2/5/2000 Bp Barry Howe. m 3/21/1981 Edgar Joseph Whelan. D Ch Of The Redeem Kansas City MO 2000-2003.

WHELAN, Peter H (Ky) 1207 Meadowridge Trl, Goshen KY 40026 B Pawtucket RI 1941 s Kenneth & Muriel. BA Providence Coll 1963; Ya Berk 1966. D 6/18/1966 P 3/18/1967 Bp John S Higgins. m 2/28/1987 Janice Ann Whelan. P-in-c S Jas Ch Shelbyville KY 2009-2014; Asst Chapl Epis Ch Hm 2004-2009; R S Mary's Ch Madisonville KY 1996-2004; R S Jn In-The-Wilderness Copake Falls NY 1989-1996; P-in-c Ch Of The Mssh Foster RI 1986-1989; Dio Rhode Island Providence RI 1984; R Ch Of The Ascen Cranston RI 1970-1984; Chapl

W

O'Rourke Chld Ctr Roger Williams Hosp Providence RI 1967-1970; Vic S Thos Providence RI 1967-1970; Asst R The Epis Ch Of S Andr And S Phil Coventry RI 1967-1970; Cur Chr Ch Westerly RI 1966-1967.

WHELCHEL, Judith H (WNC) 67 Windsor Rd, Asheville NC 28804 **Int S Jas Ch Black Mtn NC 2016-** B Atlanta GA 1966 d Thomas & Judith. BA U So 1989; MS U GA 1991; MDiv SWTS 1996. D 6/8/1996 Bp Frank Kellogg Allan P 12/7/1996 Bp Bob Johnson. m 8/3/1991 David Michael Whelchel c 1. Ch Of The Gd Shpd Lookout Mtn TN 2006-2009; Assoc The Cathd Of All Souls Asheville NC 1998-2001; Ch of the Advoc Asheville NC 1997-2009; Asst Trin Epis Ch Asheville NC 1996-1997. judith@stjameswnc.org

WHENAL, Barry (FdL) 6535 Oriole Road, Lake Tomahawk WI 54539 B Exeter NH 1947 s John & Hazel. BA MI SU 1969; MDiv EDS 1972. D 6/10/1972 Bp Charles Francis Hall P 12/9/1972 Bp Francis W Lickfield. m 8/8/1987 Barbara Esther Whenal. R Intsn Epis Ch Stevens Point WI 1996-2004; R S Anskar's Epis Ch Hartland WI 1989-1996; Vic S Mths Minocqua WI 1984-1989; Assoc Adirondack Mssn Pottersville NY 1980-1984; Vic S Jn's Epis Ch Mauston WI 1974-1980; Vic S Mary's Epis Ch Tomah WI 1974-1980; Cur Trin Epis Ch Rock Island IL 1972-1974.

WHENNEN, John (Chi) 2640 Park Dr, Flossmoor IL 60422 B Chicago IL 1947 s John & Beverly. BA Bethel Coll 1969. D 2/1/2003 Bp Bill Persell. DEACONWHENNEN@STJOHNS-LOCKPORT-IL.ORG

WHETSTONE, Raymond David (Ala) Grace Episcopal Church, PO Box 1791, Anniston AL 36202 B Alexander City AL 1949 s Lawrence & Ida. EFM Sewanee: The U So, TS; EFM U So TS; BS Jacksonville St U 1970; MA Jacksonville St U 1973; PhD U NC 1981. D 10/1/2011 Bp Henry Nutt Parsley Jr. m 10/24/1987 Cynthia Abel Whetstone c 2.

WHIDDON, Ennis Howard (USC) 301 Piney Mountain Rd, Greenville SC 29609 B Panama City FL 1942 s John & Mildred. D 9/24/2011 Bp W illiam Andrew Waldo. m 2/3/1968 Susanne Detrick Whiddon c 1.

WHISENHUNT, William Allen (WNC) Trinity Episcopal Church, 60 Church St, Asheville NC 28801 B Waynesville NC 1949 s Harry & Louise. BA Lenoir-Rhyne Coll 1971; MDiv Sewanee: The U So, TS 1985. D 6/15/1985 P 1/1/1986 Bp William Gillette Weinhauer. m 1/9/1971 Nancy Whisenhunt c 1. R Trin Epis Ch Asheville NC 1999-2010; Cn Dio Wstrn No Carolina Asheville NC 1991-1999; P-in-c Ch Of S Mths Asheville NC 1991-1992; R Ch Of The Epiph Newton NC 1985-1991.

WHISTLER, Tamsen Elizabeth (Mo) 1020 N Duchesne Dr, Saint Charles MO 63301 **R Trin Ch S Chas MO 1995-** B San Francisco CO 1953 d Donald & Elizabeth. BS U of Missouri 1973; MA U of Missouri 1975; MDiv SWTS 1984. D 6/15/1984 P 2/1/1985 Bp William Augustus Jones Jr. m 11/25/1983 Robert F Brown c 1. Assoc Calv Ch Columbia MO 1986-1995; Asst Gr Ch Jefferson City MO 1984-1986.

WHITAKER, Ann Latham (Miss) 806 Prairie View Road, Oxford MS 38655 **Assoc S Ptr's Ch Oxford MS 2011-** B New Orleans LA 1953 d Wilbur & Alice. BS Mississippi St U 1978; MDiv Sewanee: The U So, TS 2001. D 6/23/2001 P 1/16/2002 Bp Alfred Marble Jr. m 3/5/1977 Jerry A Whitaker c 1. R Ch Of The Creator Clinton MS 2007-2011; R S Alb's Epis Ch Vicksburg MS 2003-2007; Cur The Epis Ch Of The Medtr Meridian MS 2001-2003. Soc of S Fran, Third Ord 1997.

WHITAKER, Bradford G (ETenn) 305 W 7th St, Chattanooga TN 37402 **S Paul's Epis Ch Chattanooga TN 2015-** B Atlanta GA 1961 s Robert & Annelle. AA Young Harris Coll 1981; BD U GA 1983; MDiv GTS 1989. D 6/10/1989 P 3/20/1990 Bp Frank Kellogg Allan. m 5/27/1989 Harriett W Whitaker c 4. S Andr's Ch Waterford MI 2014-2015; Trin Epis Ch Farmington MI 2014; Chr Ch Grosse Pointe Grosse Pointe Farms MI 2002-2010, R 2002-; Chr Ch Newton NJ 1997-2002, R 1997-2002; H Innoc Ch Atlanta GA 1992-1997, Asst R 1992-1997; S Ptr's Ch Rome GA 1989-1992, Asst R 1989-1992.

WHITAKER III, Howard Wilson (Nwk) PO Box 596, Scottsboro AL 35768 **Niagara Falls Epis Urban Mnstry Niagara Falls NY 2016-; P-in-c S Thos Ch Vernon NJ 2013-; Priv Pract Priv Pract Scottsboro AL 2004-** B Jackson MS 1953 s Howard & Margaret. Dpl Columbia Mltry Acad 1971; BS Amer U 1974; MDiv Epis TS in Kentucky 1988; DMin Wesley TS 1994. D 6/12/1988 P 12/21/1988 Bp Don Adger Wimberly. m 12/21/2007 Kay Elaine Hamrick c 2. Consult St Lk's Par Ch Hill MD 2012; Dir of Pstr Serv Greystone Pk Psych Hosp Morris Plains NJ 2002-2009; Int Thankful Memi Ch Chattanooga TN 1998-2000; Int S Lk's Ch Scottsboro AL 1997-1998; Dir Clincl Pstr Serv Chattanooga TN 1994-2002; Stff Chapl Sheppard Pratt Psych Hosp Baltimore MD 1992-1994; R S Steph's Ch Earleville MD 1990-1994; Asst to Cn for Mssn Dio Lexington Lexington 1988-1990; Aviation Incident Response Team [SAIR] Amer Red Cross - NTSB 1999-2003. Auth, "A Pstr Commentary on Dissociative Disorders," Morris / CPS, 1994; Auth, "arts, Revs, sermons," *Multiple Profsnl Pub*. AEHC 1990-2010; Assn of Mntl Hlth Cler (Bd Cert) 1994; Assn of Profsnl Chapl (Bd Cert) 1994-2010; Ldrshp Acad for New Directions 1987. Polly Bond- Photography ECom 1988.

WHITAKER, James Stewart (Mass) 44 Newport Dr, Westford MA 01886 **Ret 1996-** B Boston MA 1931 s James & Esther. BS NEU 1954; BD EDS 1957; MD 1972. D 6/22/1957 Bp Anson Phelps Stokes Jr P 5/1/1958 Bp Frederic

Cunningham Lawrence. c 4. Off Of Bsh For ArmdF New York NY 1981-1996; Chapl VetA Hosp Bedford MA 1981-1996; Chapl VetA Hosp Bedford MA 1969-1981; R S Paul's Epis Ch Bedford MA 1960-1981; Cur Trin Epis Ch Portland ME 1957-1960; Ret.

WHITAKER, Monica A (Az) 100 Arroyo Pinon Dr, Sedona AZ 86336 **S Andr's Epis Ch Sedona AZ 2017-; S Matt's Epis Day Sch San Mateo CA 2015-** B Michigan 1958 d Robert & Eunice. BA Kalamazoo Coll 1980; MA/MMus U MI 1985; MDiv CDSP 2014. D 6/21/2014 Bp Michael Vono P 6/13/2015 Bp Marc Handley Andrus. c 1. Asst Trsfg Epis Ch San Mateo CA 2014-2017; Asian Cmsn, Secy Dio California San Francisco CA 2015-2016. monicaannewhitaker@gmail.com

WHITBECK, Marjorie Bailey Ogden (Mass) 29 Princess Rd, West Newton MA 02465 B Rochester NY 1941 d Kenneth & Jean. Vas 1964; BS U of Wisconsin 1965; MDiv EDS 1979. D 12/19/1980 Bp Morris Fairchild Arnold P 10/4/1981 Bp George Leslie Cadigan. m 6/16/1962 Philip Fletcher Whitbeck c 2. Int All SS Epis Ch Attleboro MA 2008-2012; Trin Epis Ch Bridgewater 2007-2008; Int Trin Par of Newton Cntr Newton Cntr MA 2005-2006; Int Trin Epis Ch Wrentham MA 2002-2005; Int Epis Ch Of S Thos Taunton MA 1998-2002; Int S Jn's Epis Ch Franklin MA 1995-1997; Int S Jn's Ch Newtonville MA 1993-1995; Int S Mk's Epis Ch Burlington MA 1991-1992; Bd MECA 1989-1992; Int Emm Ch Boston MA 1989-1990; Int S Mk's Ch Westford MA 1987-1989; Int S Paul's Ch Lynnfield MA 1986-1987; Int All SS Ch W Newbury MA 1984-1986; Int Emm Epis Ch Wakefield MA 1983-1984; Asst Gr Ch Newton MA 1981-1983; Co-Pres MECA 1981-1982; Grp Ldr NE Career Cntr Wellesley MA 1979-1986; Dioc Coun Dio Massachusetts Boston MA 2010-2011, Dioc Coun 1989-2010.

WHITE, Andrew D'Angio (Me) Saint David's Episcopal Church, 138 York St, Kennebunk ME 04043 **S Dav's Epis Ch Kennebunk ME 2016-** B Hartford CT 1984 s Robert & Mary Ellen. BA Hav 2006; MDiv VTS 2011. D 6/11/2011 Bp Laura Ahrens P 1/21/2012 Bp David Colin Jones. m 7/19/2008 Sara D'Angio c 2. R S Mk's Ch Newark NY 2013-2016, 2012-2013; Gr Ch Lyons NY 2012-2016; S Jn's Ch Sodus NY 2012-2016; Gr Epis Ch Alexandria VA 2011-2012. frandrew@stdavidskennebunk.org

WHITE JR, Arthur Bain (Colo) St Mark's Episcopal Church, PO Box 534, Craig CO 81626 **Mssn Partnership Vic S Mk's Ch Craig CO 2012-; Mssn Partnership Vic S Paul's Epis Ch Steamboat Sprngs CO 2012-, Vic 2012-, D 2007-2012** B Ft Benning GA 1949 s Arthur & Sally. BGS Chaminade U of Honolulu 1976; MAR TESM 2012. D 11/17/2007 P 6/16/2012 Bp Robert John O'Neill. m 10/5/1968 Christine Draves White c 2. hayden1@mindspring.com

WHITE, Bruce Alan (Az) 7267 E Onda Cir, Tucson AZ 85715 **R S Alb's Epis Ch Tucson AZ 2011-; Pres, Stndg Com Dio Arizona Phoenix AZ 2014-, Stndg Com 2013-2014** B Washington IA 1952 s Max & Dorthy. Kirkwood Cmnty Coll 1972; AA Muscatine Cmnty Coll Muscatine IA 1977; BA Grand View Coll Des Moines IA 1993; MDiv Sewanee: The U So, TS 1998. D 4/25/1998 Bp Chris Christopher Epting P 1/9/1999 Bp Ted Gulick Jr. m 11/9/1974 Pamela J White c 2. R S Mich And All Ang Anniston AL 2001-2011; Chr Epis Ch Bowling Green KY 1998-2001. rector@stalbansaz.org

WHITE, Carolyn Connie (ECR) 5602 Dona Ana Loop NE, Rio Rancho NM 87144 B Birmingham AL 1934 d Tracy & Alma. BA Stan 1955; MDiv CDSP 1988. D 6/24/1988 P 5/31/1989 Bp Charles Shannon Mallory. m 12/25/1955 Marvin L White c 3. Victim Offender Recon Prog S Fran Cmnty Serv Inc. Salina KS 2001-2006; Resorative Justice Partnr's 1995-2009; R S Geo's Ch Salinas CA 1994-2001; Dir Victim Offender Recon Prog St. Fran Cmnty Serv Inc. Salinas 1993-1995; Asst Ch Of S Jude The Apos Cupertino CA 1993; Asst St Paul's/San Pablo Epis Ch Salinas CA 1991-1993; Coordntr Dioc Prison Ministers 1988-1993; Prison Mnstry Coordntr Dio El Camino Real Salinas CA 1988-1993, Mem, Dioc Coun 1995-1997.

WHITE SR, Cyril Edward (SeFla) 15001 Polk St, Miami FL 33176 **S Faith's Epis Ch Miami FL 2002-** B Miami FL 1935 s Simeon & Rose. BS Florida A&M U 1959; BS Florida Intl U 1978; MDiv VTS 1995. D 9/11/1983 P 8/26/1995 Bp Calvin Onderdonk Schofield Jr. m 7/3/1960 Christine W White c 4. R S Kevin's Epis Ch Opa Locka FL 1995-2001. Epis Curs 1975.

WHITE, Deborah (Cal) 130 Muir Station Rd., Martinez CA 94553 **Gr Ch Martinez CA 2017-** B Greenwich CT 1965 d Earle & Mildred. BA Trin 1987; MSW U of Maryland 1994; PhD CSPP/Alliant U 1999; MDiv CDSP 2015; MDiv CDSP 2015. D 6/13/2015 Bp Marc Handley Andrus P 12/5/2015 Bp Chester Lovelle Talton. m 9/17/1988 Gary Scott Spenik c 2. The Epis Ch Of S Mary The Vrgn San Francisco CA 2016-2017; S Clem's Ch Berkeley CA 2015-2017. revdeb@gracechurchmtz.org

WHITE, Dorothy (Va) 6001 Grove Ave, Richmond VA 23226 **Sch Chapl S Cathr's Sch Richmond VA 2010-** B Knoxville TN 1954 d Oscar & Dorothy. BA U of Tennessee@Knoxville 1976; MA Oral Roberts U, TS and Missions 1985; DMin VA Un U/Samuel DeWitt Proctor TS 2005. D 9/13/2014 P 3/21/2015 Bp Susan Goff.

WHITE, Harold Naylor (Va) Po Box 326, Wicomico Church VA 22579 B Charlottesville VA 1937 s Beverley & Elizabeth. BA Randolph-Macon Coll 1960; VTS 1961; MA W Virginia Coll of Grad Stds 1975; Inst Pstr Psych

1981; DMin Wesley TS 1992. D 6/29/1965 Bp Beverley D Tucker P 6/1/1966 Bp George P Gunn. m 8/20/1960 Sally B White c 3. Int S Mary's Fleeton Reedville VA 2013-2017; S Jn's Epis Ch Richmond VA 1999-2000; Eductr VTS Alexandria VA 1998, Eductr 1987-1990; Assoc Ch Of The Gd Shpd Burke VA 1997-1999; Dio Virginia Richmond VA 1986-1991; R S Aid's Ch Alexandria VA 1977-1997; R S Mk's Epis Ch St Albans WV 1969-1977; R Trin Epis Ch So Boston VA 1966-1969; Chr Ch Glen Allen VA 1965-1966; M-in-c Ch Of The Epiph Danville VA 1965-1966. AAPC, Amer Aassociat 1984; Lic Profsnl Counslr, St Of Virginia 1991.

WHITE, Harry N (Pa) 408 Valley Ave, Atglen PA 19310 **P-in-c Ch Of S Jn The Evang Essington PA 2013-** B Bayside NY 1944 s Harry & Jane. BA Hobart and Wm Smith Colleges 1968; MDiv SWTS 1971; Cert Mar & Fam Ther 1990. D 6/19/1971 Bp Gerald Francis Burrill P 12/18/1971 Bp James Winchester Montgomery. m 4/13/1984 Jacqueline V White c 2. P-in-c Ch Of The Ascen Parkesburg PA 2000-2011; Int Calv And S Paul Philadelphia PA 2000; Asst Trin Ch Swarthmore PA 1997-1998; Int Ch Of Our Sav Jenkintown PA 1995-1998; Int S Andr's Epis Ch Glenmoore PA 1994-1995; Int H Trin Ch Lansdale PA 1993-1994; Int Trin Epis Ch Ambler PA 1991-1993; Int S Ptr's Ch Phoenixville PA 1990-1991; Int S Jas Epis Ch Prospect Pk PA 1988-1990; R Chr Ch Sidney NE 1979-1981; Asst Trin Ch Easton PA 1974-1976; Int The Free Ch Of S Jn Philadelphia PA 2011-2012.

WHITE, Helen Slingluff (Ga) 15 Willow Rd, Savannah GA 31419 **Chr Ch Epis Savannah GA 2015-** B Dothan AL 1971 d Betts & Margaret. BA Furman U 1993; MEd Georgia Sthrn U 1997; MDiv VTS 2008. D 2/9/2008 P 8/23/2008 Bp Henry Irving Louttit. m 7/22/1995 Michael S White c 2. Dio Georgia Savannah GA 2011; All SS Ch Tybee Island GA 2010-2014; Asst S Geo's Epis Ch Savannah GA 2008-2010.

WHITE III, Hugh Couch (Va) 664 Dungeons Thicket Rd, White Stone VA 22578 B Nashville TN 1938 s Hugh & Martha. BS VPI 1961; MDiv VTS 1966. D 6/29/1966 P 6/1/1967 Bp William Henry Marmion. m 11/24/1979 Laurie B Winchester-White c 3. R Gr Ch Kilmarnock VA 1996-2004; R S Paul's Ch Norfolk VA 1982-1996; R Emm Ch Staunton VA 1971-1982; Chapl/Tchr Stuart Hall Epis Sch Staunton VA 1971-1978; Chair- Liturg Com. Chr Epis Ch Pulaski VA 1968-1971; Vic Emm Ch Covington VA 1966-1968; S Mk's Ch Fincastle VA 1966-1968; Trin Ch Buchanan VA 1966-1968; Stndg Com Dio Sthrn Virginia Newport News VA 1990-1992, Exec Bd 1985-1989, Chair 1983-1984, Chair 1976-1982; Dep Gc Dio SW Virginia Roanoke VA 1973-1979. Auth, "Archit & Wrshp, Pulaski," *Va Times (Swva Dioc Nwspr)*; Auth, "Dawn Of Correction, Pulaski," *Va Times (Swva Dioc Nwspr)*. Boys Hm 1983-1989; Disciples Of Chr In Cmnty 1982-1996; Epis Conf Of The Deaf Of The Epis Ch In The 1971-1978; Meals On Wheels & Half-Way Hsng, Staunton Va 1973-1978; Plumbline Mnstrs, Norfolk Va 1988-1998; Rappahanock Westminster Cbury 1991; Tidewater Goodwill Industry 1984-1989. Dsa Staunton VA 1978; Mha Outstanding Serv Awd Staunton VA 1976.

WHITE, James Lee (Del) 39 Gainsborough Dr, Lewes DE 19958 **Reitred Dio Delaware 2013-; Non-par 1980-** B Litchfield IL 1946 s Forrest & Lucille. LTh Epis TS in Kentucky 1973; BS Amer Inst of Holistic Theol 1994; MS Amer Inst of Holistic Theol 1995; PhD Amer Inst of Holistic Theol 1996; MDiv Epis TS in Kentucky 1996. D 5/26/1973 P 6/8/1974 Bp Addison Hosea. m 9/11/1982 Gale White c 2. R Chr Ch Milford DE 2003-2012; R Hope - S Jn's Epis Ch Oscoda MI 1978-1980; P-in-c S Jas Epis Ch Independence IA 1976-1978; P-in-c S Mary's Ch Des Moines IA 1976-1978; Gr Ch Albia IA 1974-1976; Ch Of The Epiph Centerville IA 1974; Dio Iowa Des Moines IA 1974; Locten & P In Charge S Steph's Epis Ch Latonia KY 1973-1974. "Healings Are Happ In Delaware," Sharing mag, 2004. Ord Of S Lk - Chapl 1972.

WHITE, Jon M (WVa) St Luke's Episcopal Church, 5402 W Genesee St, Camillus NY 13031 **S Lk's Epis Ch Camillus NY 2017-; Mng Ed Epis Cafe 2014-; R S Steph's Epis Ch Beckley WV 2012-** B Indianapolis IN 1967 s Thomas & Carolyn. BS Portland St U 2007; MDiv Bex Sem 2012. D 6/23/2012 Bp Michael Hanley P 12/18/2012 Bp William Michie Klusmeyer. m 1/28/2001 Nicole G White c 2. Chair, Evang Com Dio W Virginia Charleston WV 2014-2017, Dn, New/Sthrn Dnry 2014-2017.

WHITE, K Alon (NY) 124 N Broadway, Nyack NY 10960 **S Matt's Epis Ch Wilton CT 2016-; Vic Orange Cnty Pastorate Highland Mills & Monroe NY 2008-** B Berkeley CA 1952 d Geoffrey & Dorothy. BA San Francisco St U 1976; MA U of San Francisco 1984; MDiv GTS 1991. D 6/8/1991 P 1/19/1992 Bp Arthur Edward Walmsley. S Paul's Ch Riverside CT 2015-2016; S Lk's Ch Katonah NY 2015; S Jn's Ch Larchmont NY 2013-2015; Gr Epis Ch Nyack NY 2012-2013; Gr Epis Ch Monroe NY 2008-2013; Dio New York New York NY 2008-2012; Int S Alb's Ch Simsbury CT 2007; Int S Jn's Ch Pleasantville NY 2004-2006; Chapl and DDO The GTS New York NY 1999-2004; All SS Epis Ch Meriden CT 1998-1999; Asst S Mk's Ch New Britain CT 1991-1993.

WHITE, Karin Kay (ECR) 390 N Winchester Blvd Apt 9B, Santa Clara CA 95050 **Pstr Assoc S Mk's Epis Ch Santa Clara CA 2014-** B Boise ID 1945 d Fred & Marie. BA Seattle Pacific U 1967; Candler TS Emory U 1983; MA SMU 1985; MPA Seattle U 1986; CAS CDSP 1998. D 12/5/1998 P 6/5/1999 Bp William Edwin Swing. m 3/27/1971 Stephen C White c 2. Supply P Epis

Dio San Joaquin Modesto CA 2011-2013; Supply P Dio El Camino Real Salinas CA 2007-2015; P-in-c Ch Of S Jos Milpitas CA 2006-2009; Ch Of The H Sprt Campbell CA 2004-2005; Assoc S Jn's Ch Asheville NC 2002; Int Epis Ch Of The H Sprt Mars Hill NC 2001; Supply P Dio Wstrn No Carolina Asheville NC 2000-2004; Assistiing P S Thos Epis Ch Sunnyvale CA 1999-2000; Pstr Care Asst Ch Of The Epiph San Carlos CA 1998-1999. karinreedwhite@gmail. com

WHITE, Kathryn (Chi) 3052 Jeffrey Dr, Joliet IL 60435 **R S Edw And Chr Epis Ch 2004-** B Columbus OH 1951 d George & Marjorie. Kent St U 1970; AA Riverside City Coll 1977; MDiv SWTS 1997; Doc Min SWTS 2007. D 12/18/2001 P 6/18/2002 Bp Bill Persell. m 6/7/1971 Jeffery A White c 3. R S Edw The Mtyr and Chr Epis Ch Joliet IL 2002-2016.

WHITE, Kathryn Sawyer (WMass) 129 Roseland Park Road, Woodstock CT 06281 B Boston MA 1945 d Motley & Betty. BA Wells Coll 1967; MDiv Bex Sem 1992. D 6/6/1992 P 1/16/1993 Bp David Charles Bowman. m 8/26/1967 Ewart J White c 2. Asst S Jn's Epis Ch Sutton MA 2009-2011; R Trin Epis Ch Ware MA 1998-2005; Assoc R Chr Ch Dearborn MI 1996-1998; Int Chr Ch Cranbrook Bloomfield Hills MI 1993-1995; Assoc Trin Epis Ch Hamburg NY 1992-1993; Bd The Record Dio Michigan Detroit MI 1996-1998.

WHITE, Kenneth Gordon (Mass) 11 Anita St, Sabattus ME 04280 **Ret Maine 2005-** B Boston MA 1941 s Kenneth & Jesuina. BS Bos 1963; STB PDS 1968. D 6/22/1968 Bp Anson Phelps Stokes Jr P 5/24/1969 Bp John Melville Burgess. Asst Exec Secy COCU 1999-2001; Asst Exec Secy COCU 1999-2001; Exec Secy New Engl Consult of Ch Leaders 1994-2004; Exec Secy Mass Comm On Chr Unity Fall River MA 1984-2004; Int All SS Ch Chelmsford MA 1981-1982; R S Jn's Epis Ch Lowell MA 1972-2004; Cur S Anne's Ch Lowell MA 1968-1972. Ed, "Baptismal Pract in an Ecum Context," 2008; "Baptism Today: Understanding, Practicing, Ecum Implications"; "Faith and Ord Paper No. 207," *WCC Pub*, Pueblo Bk, Liturg Press. Ord of S Lk 1974; Ord of S Lk, Reg Wrdn 1980-1984. Distinguished Alum EDS 2013; Harvest of Hope Awd Hse of Hope, Lowell, MA 1993; Forrest L Knapp Awd Massachusetts Coun of Ch 1993; Bp Morris Arnold Annual Awd Epis City Mssn 1991; MA Humanitarian Soc Action Awd Intl Christians for Unity & Soc Action 1987.

WHITE, Kenneth Orgill (WLa) 2320 Wooster Ln Apt 6, Sanibel FL 33957 **Non-par 1991-** B Philadelphia MS 1954 s Kenneth & Nancy. BA Rhodes Coll 1977; MDiv VTS 1981. D 6/28/1981 Bp William F Gates Jr P 4/11/1982 Bp William Evan Sanders. m 5/10/1991 Laura Marie Coleman. Asst S Alb's Par Washington DC 1994-2000; S Paul's Epis Ch Shreveport LA 1990; Samar Counceling Cntr Amarillo TX 1988-1989; Chapl Par Sch Shreveport LA 1984-1985; Asst S Mk's Cathd Shreveport LA 1984-1985; Dio Tennessee Nashville TN 1982-1983; Vic S Fran' Ch Norris TN 1982-1983; D-In-T Gr Ch Chattanooga TN 1981-1982. Auth, "Between Us: Bk Revs".

WHITE, Kevin Gerard (WMo) 1307 Holmes St, Kansas City MO 64106 B 1961 s Herman & Evelyn. D 11/6/2015 Bp Martin Scott Field.

WHITE, Konrad Shepard (Los) 524 E Duffy St, Savannah GA 31401 **Ret 2009-** B Savannah GA 1942 s Julius & Ethel. Dade Jr Coll Miami FL 1962; BA Belhaven Coll 1965; Sewanee: The U So, TS 1970; MDiv Nash 1972. D 5/21/1972 P 5/31/1973 Bp John Maury Allin. m 6/8/1974 Elizabeth M White c 2. R S Mk's Epis Ch Upland CA 2001-2008; R S Barth's Epis Ch Florence AL 1989-2001; R S Mary's Epis Ch Milton FL 1984-1989; R Par Of The Medtr-Redeem Mccomb MS 1977-1984; R Par of the Medtr-Redeem McComb/Magnolia MS 1977-1984; R Chap Of The Cross Rolling Fork MS 1974-1977; Cur S Jas Ch Jackson MS 1972-1974. R Emer St. Mk's Epis Ch 2010.

WHITE, Kristin U (Chi) 400 E Westminster, Lake Forest IL 60045 **S Aug's Epis Ch Wilmette IL 2012-** B Anchorage AK 1971 d Stephen & Janet. BS Wstrn Oregon U 1995; MA Willamette U 1997; MDiv SWTS 2009. D 5/30/2009 Bp Sanford Zangwill Kaye Hampton. m 11/12/1994 John White c 1. Assoc R The Ch Of The H Sprt Lake Forest IL 2009-2012.

WHITE, Laura Dale (USC) 522 NW 8th St, Pendleton OR 97801 B United Kingdom 1971 d Edward & Mary. BA Colg 1993; BA Colg 1993; MDiv VTS 2001. D 2/23/2001 P 10/22/2001 Bp Neff Powell. m 5/23/1998 Alexander F White c 4. Long-term Supply Trin Epis Ch Farmington MI 2007-2009; H Trin Par Epis Clemson SC 2001-2002.

WHITE, Lynn Scott (Chi) 1546 Bobolink Cir, Woodstock IL 60098 **Assoc P St. Ann Ch Woodstock IL 2006-** B Chicago IL 1942 d Kingsley & Nancy. BA Barat Coll 1977; MDiv SWTS 1983; DMin SWTS 1996. D 12/15/1983 Bp James Winchester Montgomery P 9/1/1984 Bp Quintin Ebenezer Primo Jr. m 8/26/1961 Michael White c 3. S Andr Ch Grayslake IL 2003, Int R 2002-2003; Int Chr Ch Winnetka IL 2000-2001, Pstr Assoc 1984-1985; Int S Mich's Cathd Boise ID 1997-1998; Assoc R The Ch Of The H Sprt Lake Forest IL 1985-1997.

WHITE, Mary (Alb) 10 N Main Ave, Albany NY 12203 **R S Andr's Epis Ch Albany NY 2002-** B Tucson AZ 1956 d William & Mary. BA U of Arizona 1979; MRE U of San Diego 1984; MDiv CDSP 1994. D 6/4/1994 P 6/3/1995 Bp William Edwin Swing. m 5/17/1980 John L White c 3. S Barth's Epis Ch Poway CA 1997-2002; P Ch Of The Epiph Flagstaff AZ 1995-1996; D H Cross Epis Ch Castro Vlly CA 1994-1995.

WHITE, Michael S (Ga) 308A Bradley Point Rd, Savannah GA 31410 **R Chr Ch Epis Savannah GA 2008-** B Valdosta GA 1969 s James & Annette. BA Valdosta St U 1992; MDiv VTS 1995; Cert Duke 2005. D 5/28/1995 P 1/5/1996 Bp Henry Irving Louttit. m 7/22/1995 Helen Slingluff White c 2. Chr Ch Georgetown Washington DC 2006-2008; Ecum Off Dio No Carolina Raleigh NC 2003-2005; R S Lk's Epis Ch Durham NC 2000-2005; Vic S Eliz's Epis Ch Richmond Hill GA 1997-2000; Dio Georgia Savannah GA 1995-1997; Trin Ch Statesboro GA 1995-1997. "You Is Plural," *Sermons that Wk*, Morehouse Pub, 2003.

WHITE, Michelle Denise (Nwk) 707 Washington St, Hoboken NJ 07030 **Chr Ch Teaneck NJ 2012-** B New York City NY 1951 d Gloria. BS SUNY at Stony Brook 1974; MS Ford 1981; PhD Ford 1992; MDiv UTS 2002. D 12/21/2009 Bp Paul Victor Marshall P 6/21/2010 Bp Mark M Beckwith. m 11/23/2013 Ann Marie Ambrosino c 2. Chr Ch Ridgewood NJ 2011-2012; All SS Epis Par Hoboken NJ 2009-2011.

WHITE, M Joanna (Md) 2125 Beach Village Court, Annapolis MD 21403 B Lackawanna NY 1945 d Raymond & Ruth. AD Wesley Coll 1969; BS Mercy Coll 1977; MS LIU 1986; MDiv Ya Berk 1989; MA Loyola Coll 2003. D 6/10/1989 Bp Paul Moore Jr P 5/19/1990 Bp Walter Cameron Righter. m 3/1/1967 Francis White c 3. Int S Paul's Epis Ch Prnc Frederck MD 2013-2016, 2000-2001; P-in-c Sherwood Epis Ch Cockeysville MD 2004-2012; Assoc R S Barn Epis Ch Sykesville MD 2001-2003; R S Andr's Epis Ch Staten Island NY 1995-1999; Assoc R S Jn's Epis Ch Lancaster PA 1991-1995; Vic S Barn Ch Newark NJ 1990-1991; Dio Newark Newark NJ 1990; Cur S Paul's Epis Ch Morris Plains NJ 1989-1990. stpaulsepis@verizon.net

WHITE, Nancy Anne (Md) 3267 Stepney St, Edgewater MD 21037 **D St. Marg's Ch Annapolis MD 2007-** B Washington D.C. 1936 d James & Mini. Gallaudet U; U of Maryland; BA U of Maryland 1958; MA Gallaudet U 1970; EFM Sewanee: The U So, TS 2000. D 6/2/2001 Bp Robert Wilkes Ihloff. c 2. Int Asst to the R + D S Marg's Ch Annapolis MD 2004-2007; Yth Min + D S Jas' Par Lothian MD 2001-2004. Auth, "Pub Var chapters," *arts and Revs in Spec Educ/deaf Educ Pub; contributed Nwsltr (Loc and Dioc) arts*, AGBell Assoc.for the Deaf et al, 1978. Advsry Coun for HI Infants 1991; No Amer Assn for the Deaconate 1998. JB Mason Awd - Outstanding Spec Educ Ldrshp Coun for Exceptional Chld - PFCO 1999; Resolution of Recognition Maryland St Senate 1999.

WHITE, Nicholson Barney (O) 1109 Hollyheath Ln, Charlotte NC 28209 B Washington DC 1941 s E B & Elizabeth. BA Trin 1963; MDiv - cl VTS 1973. D 6/9/1973 Bp Joseph Warren Hutchens P 1/1/1974 Bp Charles Gresham Marmion. m 8/26/1961 Diana Watkins c 2. Int Chr Ch Charlotte NC 2005-2006, 1974-1979; S Paul's Epis Ch Cleveland OH 1983-2003; R Emm Par Epis Ch Sthrn Pines NC 1979-1983; Assoc S Fran In The Fields Harrods Creek KY 1973-1974; Tchr So Kent Sch 1965-1970; Tchr Hawaii Preparatory Acad 1963-1965. Soc Of S Marg 1981.

WHITE JR, Paul Donald (WTenn) 3553 Windgarden Cv, Memphis TN 38125 B Camp Chaffee AR 1952 s Paul & Lillian. BS LSU 1973; JD Loyola U 1976; MDiv CDSP 1991; DMin SWTS 1999. D 6/8/1991 Bp Robert Jefferson Hargrove Jr P 12/1/1991 Bp John Lester Thompson III. m 5/27/1972 Kathryn A White c 2. R S Geo's Ch Germantown TN 2002-2005; R S Lk's Epis Ch N Little Rock AR 1992-2002; Cn-In-Res Trin Epis Cathd Sacramento CA 1991-1992.

WHITE, Rita Ellen (Va) 138 Pier Place, Kinsale VA 22488 **Int Cople Par Hague VA 2013-, 2004; S Mk's Ch Adams MA 2006-** B Galax VA 1955 d Ernest & Violet. BA Berea Coll 1977; BA Berea Coll 1977; MDiv Sthrn Bapt TS 1984; DAS VTS 2002. D 6/22/2002 P 1/25/2003 Bp Neff Powell. S Anne's Par Scottsville VA 2009-2013; P-in-c Dio Wstrn Massachusetts Springfield 2006-2009; Hanover w Brunswick Par - S Jn King Geo VA 2005-2006; Int Hanover-w-Brunswick Par King Geo VA 2005-2006; Asst R S Andr's Epis Ch Arlington VA 2002-2004. copleclergy1664@gmail.com

WHITE, Roger Bradley (Ct) Po Box 309, Kent CT 06757 **Rdr of GOE's GBEC 2003-; Rdr SIM Schlrshp Com 1999-; R S Andr's Ch Kent CT 1985-** B Chicago IL 1952 s Alfred & Mildred. MA Ya 1976; MPhil Ya 1977; MA Yale DS 1979. D 6/12/1982 P 1/6/1983 Bp Arthur Edward Walmsley. Chair Com of Exam Chapl CT 1990-1995; Ed Gd News 1990-1995; The Ch Of The H Sprt Lake Forest IL 1982-1985; Chair Exam Chapl Com Dio Connecticut Meriden CT 1992-1997, Archive Com 1986-; Secy Bd Secy Ya Berk New Haven CT 1991-1999, Asst 1981-1990. Contrib, *Forw Day by Day*, 1999; Auth, *Var arts & Revs*. Amer Soc of Ch Historians 1979; HSEC 1978; Soc of S Jn the Evang 1979. Jarvis Fllshp Berk 1979.

WHITE, Rowena Ruth (WLa) 8212 Argosy Ct, Baton Rouge LA 70809 **S Mk's Cathd Shreveport LA 2011-** B Napa CA 1944 d Lloyd & Nancy. BS Mississippi Coll 1966; MD U of Mississippi 1970; MD U of Mississippi Sch of Med 1970; MEd U of Arkansas 1985; MDiv Epis TS of the SW 1995. D 6/3/1995 P 12/9/1995 Bp Robert Jefferson Hargrove Jr. c 2. Supply P S Andr's Ch Clinton LA 2001-2003; Chapl Our Lady Of The Lake Hosp 1995-2003. Amer Psych Assn, La Psych Assn; Bd Cert Mem Coll Of Chapl.

WHITE, R Scott (WNC) Trinity Church, 60 Church St, Asheville NC 28801 **Fac, Conf Ldr Credo Inst Memphis TN 2012-; R Trin Epis Ch Asheville NC 2012-; Stndg Com Dio Wstrn No Carolina Asheville NC 2016-; Alum Exec Com The GTS New York NY 2004-** B Newport RI 1966 s Robert & Patricia. BA Rhode Island Coll 1989; MDiv GTS 1996; Cert Duke 2001; DMIN VTS 2012. D 6/15/1996 P 1/25/1997 Bp Gerry Wolf. m 1/6/2001 Michelle E Sherburne c 2. R Ch Of The Gd Shpd Rocky Mt NC 2004-2012; Assoc P Chr Epis Ch Raleigh NC 1998-2004; Asstg P S Mart's Epis Ch Charlotte NC 1996-1998; Fair Share Appeals Bd, Chair Dio No Carolina Raleigh NC 2010-2013, Bp's Pstr Response Team 2000-2013, Mem 2000-2012. Fac Hist Prize GTS 1996; Sutton Prize For Best Grad Thesis GTS 1996. scott@trinityasheville.org

WHITE, Stanley James (Ga) 101 E Central Ave Fl 3, Valdosta GA 31601 **Vic Ch Of Chr The King Valdosta GA 1990-** B Dothan,AL 1962 s James & S Anne. Valdosta St U; Berean U 1987. D 10/21/1990 P 6/1/1991 Bp Harry Woolston Shipps. m 8/27/1982 Deidra A White c 4. Serv Ch Of Assemblies Of God 1984-1990. EFM.

WHITE, Stephen James (Me) 140 Bluff Road, Yarmouth ME 04096 **Hospice Chapl Hospice of Sthrn Maine 2016-** B Portland OR 1945 s Earle & Phyllis. BA U of Redlands 1967; MDiv EDS 1971; DMin EDS 1987. D 6/5/1971 P 12/18/1971 Bp Horace W B Donegan. m 6/20/1969 Charlotte A Turgeon c 3. Hospice Chapl Kno-Wal-Lin Hospice Rockland ME 2012-2015; Int Gr Ch Norwood MA 2009-2010; Int S Andr's Ch Edgartown MA 2008-2009; R S Andr's Ch Newcastle ME 1997-2008; Int S Mk's Ch Foxborough MA 1995-1996; R Ch Of The Redeem Chestnut Hill MA 1989-1995; R Ch Of The Epiph Richardson TX 1985-1989; Dio Massachusetts Boston MA 1985, Chair, Recently Ord Cler 1991-1996; R S Anne's In The Fields Epis Ch Lincoln MA 1978-1985; R S Steph's Ch Middlebury VT 1974-1978; Asst S Mary's Epis Ch Manchester CT 1972-1974; Cur Ch Of The Mssh Rhinebeck NY 1971; Chair, COM Dio Maine Portland ME 2003-2008; Ecum Off Dio Dallas Dallas TX 1987-1989. Auth, "Intercessions for Sundays, H Days, and Spec Occasions - Year B," Ch Pub, Inc., 2008.

WHITE, Stephen Lawrence (NJ) 2325 Hancock Road, Williamstown MA 01267 **P-in-c All S's Ch of the Berkshires No Adams MA 2012-; Supply Cler Dio Wstrn Massachusetts Springfield MA 2006-** B Leominster MA 1949 s Lawrence & Marie. BA Sthrn Connecticut St U 1971; MSW Smith 1974; MPA Golden Gate U 1980; PhD Brandeis U 1985; MDiv GTS 2000; LHD Cuttington U 2001. D 5/20/2000 P 12/2/2000 Bp David Bruce Joslin. m 7/26/1996 Andrea White c 2. Asst S Steph's Ch Pittsfield MA 2008-2010; Chapl Epis Ch at Pr Princeton NJ 2000-2008; Epis Chapl PrTS Princeton NJ 2000-2008; Assoc P Trin Ch Princeton NJ 2000-2008; Cmsn on Priesthood Dio New Jersey Trenton NJ 2001-2008. "The Coll Chapl: A Practical Guide to Campus Mnstry," Pilgrim Press, 2005; "Calling YP to Ord Mnstry," *Living Ch*, 2004; "Eulogy for Christen," *Angl Dig*, 2003; "BCP and the Standardization of the Engl Lang: Avenues for Future Resrch," *The Angl*, 2003; Auth, "Two Bishops of Liberia: Race and Mssn ....," *Angl and Epis Hist*, 2001; Auth, "Parishes and Campus Mnstrs: It's a Two-Way St," *Living Ch*, 2001; Auth, "Colonial Era Missionaries' Understanding of the Afr...," *Angl and Epis Hist*, 1999; Auth, "The Ang of the LORD: Mssngr or Euphemism?," *Tyndale Bulletin*, 1999. Angl Soc 2002-2004; Colleges & Universities of the Angl Comm 1994-2002; HSEC 2000-2005. Sam Portaro Awd for Creative Expression and Intellectual Enqu Prov Coordinators for MHE of the 2006; Nelson Burr Prize HSEC 2002; Clem Whipple Prize GTS 2000; Clem Whipple Prize GTS 1999.

WHITE, Steve (ETenn) 1101 N Broadway St, Knoxville TN 37917 **S Paul's Epis Ch Kingsport TN 2015-** B Chattanooga TN 1961 s Richard & Helen. BS U of Tennessee 1984; MBA U of Tennessee 1988; MDiv Sewanee TS 2013; MDiv Sewanee: The U So, TS 2013. D 6/15/2013 P 1/5/2014 Bp George Young III. Cur St Jas Epis Ch at Knoxville Knoxville TN 2013-2015. swhite@stjamesknox.org

✠ WHITE, The Rt Rev Terry Allen (Ky) 425 S Second St Suite 200, Louisville KY 40202 **Bp of Kentucky Dio Kentucky Louisville KY 2010-** B Mount Pleasant IA 1959 s Dennis & Carolyn. BA Iowa Wesleyan Coll 1982; MDiv SWTS 1985; DD SWTS 2010; DD TS 2011; DD Sewanee: The U So, TS 2011. D 5/6/1985 Bp Lawrence Edward Luscombe P 4/25/1986 Bp James Winchester Montgomery Con 9/25/2010 for Ky. m 7/19/1986 Linda White c 2. Dn And R Gr And H Trin Cathd Kansas City MO 2004-2010; Dio Chicago Chicago IL 2003-2004, Com 1997-2002; R Trin Ch Highland Pk IL 1995-2004; Chr Ch Winnetka IL 1991-1995, Assoc R 1991-1995, Cur 1985-1987; Dio Fond du Lac Appleton WI 1987-1991; S Bon Plymouth WI 1987-1991; S Paul's Ch Plymouth WI 1987-1991. bishopwhite@episcopalky.org

WHITE, Thomas Harrington (Colo) 1215 Union Ave, North Platte NE 69101 **Died 1/1/2017** B Fort Worth TX 1931 s Harrington & Lida. BS U of Houston 1954; LTh Sewanee: The U So, TS 1964; MS Our Lady of the Lake U 1973; DMin GTF 1991. D 6/28/1964 Bp Everett H Jones P 1/1/1965 Bp Richard Earl Dicus. m 10/18/1958 Patsy La Rue White c 2. Vic S Jn's Epis Ch New Castle CO 1998-2017; Int S Andr's Ch Montevallo AL 1997-1998; R S Mich's Epis Ch Birmingham AL 1994-1996; S Martins-In-The-Pines Ret Comm Birmingham AL 1990-1995; Epis Black Belt Mnstry Greensboro AL 1990; Dio Alabama Birmingham 1989; R S Steph's Ch Eutaw AL 1988-1989; R S Jn's Ch Birmingham AL 1987-1988; H Comf Ch Gadsden AL 1986-1987; S Jas The Fisherman Kodiak AK 1983-1985; S Helena's Epis Ch Boerne TX 1976-1984; Assoc S Lk's Epis Ch San Antonio TX 1974-1976; P-in-c S Tim's Ch Cotulla TX 1972-1974; Asst S Mk's Epis Ch San Antonio TX 1971-1972, Asst R 1964-1970; Vic S Mk's Ch Austin TX 1968-1971. lawrencw@gmail.com

WHITE, Thomas Rees (Ct) 109 Sand Hill Rd, South Windsor CT 06074 B Pittsburgh PA 1952 s John & Margaret. Edinboro U 1971; BS Penn 1974; BA Trin Theol Coll Bristol GB 1978; MDiv GTS 1979. D 6/9/1979 Bp Robert Bracewell Appleyard P 12/10/1979 Bp Morris Fairchild Arnold. m 4/16/1983 Christina D Lewis c 2. R S Ptr's Ch So Windsor CT 1992-2016; R All SS Par Whitman MA 1984-1992; Asst All SS Epis Ch Attleboro MA 1979-1984; Alt Dep GC Dio Connecticut Meriden CT 2000-2004, ExCoun 1993-1999. Efac-Usa, Acts 29, Curs.

WHITE, Warner Clock (WMich) 12 Harbor Watch Rd., Burlington VT 05401 **Ret 1991-** B Hampton IA 1926 s Russell & Evelyn. MA U Chi 1950; MDiv SWTS 1954; DMin Chicago TS 1976. D 6/1/1953 P 12/6/1953 Bp Charles L Street. m 5/24/2008 Roberta Baker c 5. R Trin Epis Ch Marshall MI 1979-1991; S Paul's By The Lake Chicago IL 1968-1978; R Ch Of The Redeem Chicago IL 1963-1968; Ch Of S Paul And The Redeem Chicago IL 1962-1978; P-in-c S Dunst's Epis Ch Westchester IL 1954-1957; P-in-c St Cyprians Ch Chicago IL 1953-1954. Auth, "Should I Lv?, Conflict Mgmt In Congregations," *Chap. 6*, ATR, 2001.

WHITE, William DeAlton (Me) 21 Bodwell St, Brunswick ME 04011 **Died 5/2/2017** B Seaford DE 1924 s Raymond & Amelia. BA Daniel Baker Coll 1951; STB GTS 1954. D 6/25/1954 P 3/1/1955 Bp Noble C Powell. c 9. Ret 1986-2017; R S Ptr's Ch Rockland ME 1981-1986; R S Andr's Ch Millinocket ME 1977-1981; P-in-c S Jn's Ch Mt Morris NY 1974-1977; R S Mich's Ch Geneseo NY 1974-1977; S Paul's Ch Brunswick ME 1969-1974; R S Alb's Epis Ch Wickenburg AZ 1966-1969; R Ch Of The Ascen Westminster MD 1958-1966; R S Jn Shady Side MD 1956-1958; Vic S Jn Shady Side MD 1954-1956; Ex Coun Dio Rochester Henrietta 1975-1977; Chair Dio Maine Portland ME 1969-1974.

WHITEFORD, Cecily S (WNY) 45 S Cayuga Rd Apt G3, Williamsville NY 14221 **Ret NY 2010-** B Albany NY 1936 d Grant & Jean. Cor. D 6/20/1982 Bp Harold Barrett Robinson. c 6. D S Jn's Gr Ch Buffalo NY 2002-2010, Asst 1982-2001; 1985-1989.

WHITEHAIR, Eric Ian (Md) D 6/10/2017 Bp Chilton Richardson Knudsen.

WHITE-HASSLER, M Jane (Ct) 130 Vincent Dr, Newington CT 06111 B Charleston WV 1944 d Ralph & Margaret. BS W Virginia Wesleyan Coll 1966; MDiv Ya Berk 1996. D 9/4/1999 P 3/10/2000 Bp Andrew Donnan Smith. m 10/4/1997 Thomas Jackson Hassler c 3. R Gr Ch Newington CT 2004-2012; Asst S Andr's Ch Meriden CT 1999-2004.

WHITEHEAD, Philip Hoyle (USC) 6026 Crabtree Rd, Columbia SC 29206 B Columbus OH 1935 s Harry & Mildred. BA U So 1957; MDiv Sewanee: The U So, TS 1960; STM UTS 1962; DMin UTS Richmond 1974. D 6/6/1960 P 6/1/1961 Bp Edward Hamilton West. m 12/30/1960 Eleanor Whitehead c 2. Dep Gc Dio Upper So Carolina Columbia SC 1985-1997, Liturg Cmsn 1983-1995, Stndg Com 1984-1987; R S Mich And All Ang' Columbia SC 1978-2004; Vic S Mart's Epis Ch Richmond VA 1977-1978; Vic Epis Ch of Our Sav Richmond KY 1973-1977; S Cathr's Sch Richmond VA 1965-1978; Chapl S Cathr's Sch Richmond VA 1965-1978; Chapl U.S. Navy Reserve 1963-1978; Vic S Alb's Jacksonville FL 1962-1965; Ecum Cmsn Epis Ch Cntr New York NY 1978-2004.

WHITE HORSE-CARDA, Patricia Ann (SD) 500 S Main Ave, Sioux Falls SD 57104 **Vic of the Yankton Dio So Dakota Pierre SD 2010-** B Wagner SD 1951 d Louis & Ruby. BS U of So Dakota 1983; MEd Penn 1988. D 12/4/2010 P 6/19/2011 Bp John Tarrant. m 1/9/2006 Dean J Carda.

WHITEHURST, Joseph Stewart (USC) 173 Kendallwood Ct, Aiken SC 29803 **Asst S Thad Epis Ch Aiken SC 2007-** B Charlotte NC 1978 s J Daniel & Trudy. BS U of So Carolina 2001; MA U of So Carolina 2004; MDiv SWTS 2007. D 5/26/2007 Bp Dorsey Henderson.

WHITELAW, Eleanor Drake (CGC) 343 N Randolph Ave, Eufaula AL 36027 **R S Jas Ch Eufaula AL 2012-** B Mobile AL 1947 d G Mills & Eleanor. BA Auburn U 1969; MA U of So Alabama 1972; MDiv VTS 1998. D 6/6/1998 Bp Frank Kellogg Allan P 12/11/1998 Bp Clifton Daniel III. c 2. Other Cler Position/ Com Dio Alabama AL 2006-2009; R Ch Of The H Comf Montgomery AL 2001-2011; Asst S Jas Par Wilmington NC 1998-2001; Cler Coun Mem Dio Alabama Birmingham 2005-2008, Bd for Camp McDowell 2002-2006.

WHITELEY, Raewynne Jean (LI) 15 Highland Ave, Saint James NY 11780 **Fac Geo Mercer TS Garden City NY 2007-; R S Jas Epis Ch S Jas NY 2007-; Bd Chair Prot Campus Mnstry at SUNY Stony Brook 2014-; Cn Theol Dio Long Island Garden City NY 2009-** B Camden NSW AU 1966 d Andrew & Susan. BA (Hons) U of Melbourne 1989; MA U of Melbourne 1992; BTh Australian Coll of Theol 1995; BMin Australian Coll of Theol 1995; PhD PrTS 2003. Trans 3/24/1999 Bp Joe Doss. Vic Trin Epis Old Swedes Ch Swedesboro

NJ 2002-2006; Assoc P Trin Cathd Trenton NJ 2001-2002; Tchg Fell In Homil PrTS Princeton NJ 1999-2002; Pstr Assoc Trin Ch Princeton NJ 1998-2001; Serv Angl Ch Of Australia 1995-1998. Auth, "Steeped in the H: Preaching as Sprtl Pract," Cowley, 2008; Auth, "Homiletical Perspectives," *Feasting on the Word*, Westminster Jn Knox Press, 2008; CoEditor, "Get Up Off Your Knees: Preaching the U2 Catalog," Cowley, 2003; Auth, "Geography And Gr: Preaching The Gospel w An Australian Accent," *St Mk's Revs*, 2001; Auth, "Sermons And Wrshp Resources," *The Abingdon Wmn Preaching Annual, Series 2, Year A*, Abingdon, 2001; Auth, "Pryr For Bronte," *Wmn Uncommon Prayers*, Morehouse, 2000; Auth, "Var arts," *NRSV Wmn Study Bible*, Marshall Pickering, 1995. Acad Of Homil 1998. stjamesrector@optonline.net

WHITEMAN, Christopher William (Mass) PO Box 991, Groton MA 01450 B Portland 1979 s William & Dianne. Mdiv Harvard DS; ALB Harvard Ext Sch. D 6/4/2016 P 1/22/2017 Bp Alan Gates. cwhiteman@groton.org

WHITESEL, Ann Brier (CPa) 12 Strawberry Dr, Carlisle PA 17013 **Dioc ECW Retreat Com 1984-; D S Jn's Ch 1983-** B Honolulu HI 1928 d William & Vera. AA Stratford Coll Woodbridge VA 1950; Meredith Coll 1951; Sch of Chr Stds 1982. D 6/10/1983 Bp Charlie Fuller Mcnutt Jr. m 6/17/1950 William Monitor Whitesel c 3. Dir S Jn's Epis Ch Carlisle PA 1979-1985. Cntr Diac.

WHITESELL, Hugh A (NC) 756 Apple Ct. Apt A, Lebanon OH 45036 **The Epis Ch Of The Ascen Middletown OH 2000-; Ret 1989-** B Dayton OH 1925 s Carl & Jeannette. ThD Bex Sem 1964; DMin Untd TS Dayton OH 2000. D 12/11/1959 P 6/13/1964 Bp Roger W Blanchard. c 1. Vic S Mary's Ch Waynesville OH 1989-1999; Dio No Carolina Raleigh NC 1982-1989; R S Steph's Epis Ch Erwin NC 1976-1989; Dio Virginia Richmond VA 1970-1973; Vic S Barth's Ch Richmond VA 1968-1976; Dio Sthrn Ohio Cincinnati OH 1966-1968; Asst S Geo's Epis Ch Dayton OH 1964-1968; Asst S Paul's Epis Ch Dayton OH 1959-1964. Auth, "Identity, Loss, and Change," Bell & Howell, 2000; Auth, *Liturg & Life*, St. Geo's Epis Ch, 1965.

WHITESIDE, Henry B (EC) 7 Masonic Ave, Shelburne Falls MA 01370 **Barrier Free Living New York NY 2009-; Plainfield Congrl Ch Plainfield MA 2009-** B Burgaw NC 1952 s Heustis & Beulah. BA U NC 1974; MDiv UTS Richmond 1982; Cert GTS 1983. D 6/11/1983 Bp Robert Bruce Hall P 1/1/1984 Bp Brice Sidney Sanders. m 8/21/1976 Susan Shelby Horsley c 1. Dio Wstrn Massachusetts Springfield 2005-2008; Ch Of The Gd Shpd Wilmington NC 1986-1995; Asst R Chr Ch New Bern NC 1983-1986.

WHITFIELD, Ann Adams (Nev) 10810 NE Sherwood Dr., Vancouver WA 98686 B New York NY 1943 d Walter & Janet. AS Lasell Coll 1963; PharmD Wstrn Career Coll 1986; Dioc TS W Kansas 1988; St Marys on the Plains 1990; Epis TS of the SW 1994. D 6/7/1992 P 12/22/1994 Bp John Forsythe Ashby. m 5/13/2006 James Whitfield c 2. Asst Ch Of The Gd Shpd Vancouver WA 2009; Vic All SS' Epis Ch Vancouver WA 1998-2009; P-in-c Ch Of The Nativ Rosedale LA 1995-1998; Epis HS Baton Rouge Baton Rouge LA 1995-1998; Chapl Epis HS Baton Rouge LA 1994-1998; Int Ch Of The H Comm Baton Rouge 1994-1995; Vic Dio Wstrn Kansas Hutchinson KS 1993-1995; S Eliz's Ch Russell KS 1993-1995; Vic Ch Of The Epiph Concordia KS 1992-1994. Sis of the Trsfg 1979. revannwhitfield@gmail.com

WHITFIELD, Deirdre D (Pa) 126 Westminster Dr, Wallingford PA 19086 **Dio Pennsylvania Philadelphia PA 2016-; D S Mary Epis Ch Chester PA 2001-** B Baltimore MD 1961 d John & Betty. BS Indiana U of Pennsylvania 1983; MS Bryn 2001. D 6/23/2001 Bp Charles Ellsworth Bennison Jr P 6/6/2009 Bp Edward Lewis Lee Jr. m 6/30/1984 George C Whitfield c 2. H Apos And Medtr Philadelphia PA 2009-2010.

WHITFIELD, Mary Dean (NwT) Rr 2 Box 460, Quanah TX 79252 **D Copper Brakes Mssn 1997-** B Hardeman County TX 1935 d Hoye & Kathleen. D 8/25/1997 Bp Sam Byron Hulsey P 10/6/2001 Bp C Wallis Ohl. m 6/1/1952 Chester Leroy Whitfield.

WHITFIELD, Raymond Palmer (Tex) 12501 LONGHORN PKWY APT A360, AUSTIN TX 78732 **Ship's Chapl Cunard Lines 1995-; Ret 1990-** B San Antonio TX 1925 s Raymond & Mary. BS USMA 1946; MS OH SU 1954; MDiv Epis TS of the SW 1979; DMin GTF 1996. D 6/10/1979 Bp Archibald Donald Davies P 5/1/1980 Bp Robert Elwin Terwilliger. m 5/8/1982 Roberta Whitfield c 3. Assoc S Mk's Epis Ch San Antonio TX 1995-2001; Ship's Chapl Holland Amer Cruise Lines 1993-2000; Serv (summers) Ch of Engl 1988-1996; Assoc R The Ch of the Gd Shpd Austin TX 1986-1989, P 1979-1985. Auth, "Freedom to Love," Sailors Pub. Fllshp S Alb & S Sergius Friends Angl Cntr Rome.

WHITFIELD, Stephen Ray (Tex) 2301 Lauren Loop, Leander TX 78641 **Chapl U Of Texas At Austin 1992-** B Fort Worth TX 1949 s Raymond & Ila. BBA U of Texas 1971; BA U of Texas 1971; MDiv VTS 1975. D 6/15/1975 P 12/1/1975 Bp Archibald Donald Davies. m 10/19/2002 Rosalba Whitfield c 2. Int S Ptr's Epis Ch Leander TX 2009-2013; R Chr Ch Eagle Lake TX 1999-2009; The Great Cmsn Fndt Houston TX 1992-1999; R Ch Of The Gd Shpd Kingwood TX 1985-1992; Assoc S Dav's Ch Austin TX 1980-1985; R S Mary's Epis Ch Inc Lampasas TX 1977-1979; Cur Ch Of The Incarn Dallas TX 1975-1977. Comt.

WHITFORD, Michele E (FdL) 1220 N 7th St, Sheboygan WI 53081 **Admin Gr Epis Ch Sheboygan WI 2009-** B Janesville WI 1963 d Michael & Valerie. D

W

8/27/2005 Bp Russell Edward Jacobus P 12/17/2016 Bp Matthew A Gunter. m 6/10/1983 Jon P Whitford c 2.

WHITING, Raymond Arthur (Ga) **H Cross Ch Thomson GA 2017-; Trin Ch Harlem Harlem GA 2017-** D 5/14/2016 P 11/20/2016 Bp Scott Anson Benhase.

WHITING, William Richard (WMich) 2165 Chesapeake Dr Ne, Grand Rapids MI 49505 B Phillipsburg PA 1949 s Francis & Luella. BS MI SU 1975; MDiv GTS 1982. D 6/7/1982 Bp Robert Campbell Witcher Sr P 12/4/1982 Bp Henry Boyd Hucles III. m 7/1/2006 Pamela A Dail Whiting c 3. Emm Ch Hastings MI 2014-2016; S Paul's Epis Ch St Jos MI 2012-2014; Int S Tim Ch Richland MI 2010-2012; Epis Ch Of The Gd Shpd Allegan MI 2005-2010; P-in-c S Paul's Ch Millis MA 2003-2005; Supply P S Alb's Ch Lynn MA 1999-2002; S Mich's Epis Ch Holliston MA 1986-1997; Cur Trin Ch Northport NY 1983-1986; Cur S Jn's Epis Ch Southampton NY 1982-1983.

WHITLEY, Harry Brearley (Nwk) 143 Day Ct, Mahwah NJ 07430 **Died 8/16/2015** B Detroit MI 1921 s George & Eileen. MDiv GTS; LTh GTS; STB GTS; BA MI SU 1942. D 5/25/1945 Bp Frank W Creighton P 11/1/1945 Bp Charles B Colmore. m 6/24/1972 Jane Logie c 6. P Assoc Chr Ch Ridgewood NJ 1991-2013; Ret 1988-2015; Secy Ch Pension Fund New York NY 1981-1988; The CPG New York NY 1981-1988; R S Paul's Epis Ch Paterson NJ 1971-1981; R S Ptr's Ch Essex Fells NJ 1966-1970; R S Jn's Ch Bridgeport CT 1962-1966; Gnrl Secy, Dept of CE & BEC Dio Connecticut Meriden CT 1960-1966, Stndg Com 1963-1966; R S Jas Epis Ch Farmington CT 1954-1960; Asst Min S Jn's Ch Royal Oak MI 1952-1954; S Andr's Epis Ch Algonac MI 1950-1952; R S Paul's Epis Ch Harsens Island MI 1950-1952; Chapl U of Nebraska Lincoln NE 1948-1950; Chair, Bd Trst The GTS New York NY 1989-1994.

WHITLEY, Ryan Randolph (Pa) 1 W Ardmore Ave, Ardmore PA 19003 **R Nevil Memi Ch Of S Geo Ardmore PA 2010-** B Ft Myers FL 1981 s Steven & Melissa. BA Wake Forest U 2003; MDiv SWTS 2006; MDiv SWTS 2006. D 6/10/2006 Bp John Bailey Lipscomb P 12/16/2006 Bp William Jones Skilton. m 1/20/2009 Elise W Whitley c 2. Asst S Mk's Epis Ch Of Tampa Tampa FL 2006-2010.

WHITLOCK III, Robin (SwFla) 949 41st Ave N, Saint Petersburg FL 33703 B Rockford IL 1946 s Robert & Mary. BA MacMurray Coll 1968; Cert Lon GB 1971; MDiv CDSP 1972; MS(ABT) U of Wisconsin LaCrosse 1976; Post Grad Loyola U 1992. D 5/20/1972 Bp Albert A Chambers P 11/30/1972 Bp Stanley Hamilton Atkins. m 11/25/1989 Ann L Clark c 4. P-in-c S Aug's Epis Ch St Petersburg FL 2006-2017; Adj Prof St. Petersburg Coll St. Petersburg FL 2005-2006; Adj Prof LSU Baton Rouge LA 1999-2002; Assoc S Jas Epis Ch Baton Rouge LA 1999-2001; Chapl/Prof Dio Louisiana New Orleans LA 1995-1999; Assoc. Prof. Med Ethics Tulane Schools of Publ Hlth Med New Orleans LA 1995-1998; IRB - Med Protocol Revs Maryland Med Resrch Inst Baltimore MD 1983-2005; Asst. Prof Ethics U of MD Baltimore Baltimore 1982-1994; Chapl/Prof Dio Maryland Baltimore MD 1981-1989, Chair, Yth and YA Com 1982-1987; Assitant/Higher Ed Chapl S Jn's Epis Ch Johnson City TN 1976-1979; Cur Chr Ch Par La Crosse WI 1972-1974; Dioc Coun Dio SW Florida Parrish FL 2011-2016; Higher Educ Chapl Revs Appointee Ch Of Engl London 1985; Natl Higher Educ Rep. Prov IV Jackson MS 1976-1982. Auth, "The Clincl Symptoms of Sprtl Deterioration, Churchwork," *Diocesean Nwspr*, Dio Louisiana, 1999; Auth, "Stwdshp is....," *LivCh*, Living Ch Fndt, 1995; Auth, "Ethical Issues and the Nurse, Sprtl Dimensions of Nrsng Pract," *Sprtl Dimensions of Nrsng*, Saunders, 1989; Auth, "Gandi: Reflecting on Freedom and Nonviolence," *Plumbline*, ESMHE, 1983; Ed, "Profsnl Ethics," *The Profsnl Ethics Forum*, Epis Chapl, Baltimore, MD, 1983. AAR 2000-2004; ESMHE 1974-1992; Kappa Delti Pi; Hon Educators Soc 1974; Soc for Hlth and Human Values 1981-1999. Polly Bond Awd ECom 1999. revrobin@tampabay.rr.com

WHITMAN, Marian Chandler (WTenn) 2425 S Germantown Rd, Germantown TN 38138 **St Martins-In-The-Field Ch Severna Pk MD 2016-** B Memphis TN 1986 d Merry. BA U of Richmon 2008; MDiv VTS 2015. D 5/30/2015 P 12/12/2015 Bp Don Edward Johnson. Cur S Geo's Ch Germantown TN 2015-2016; Other Lay Position S Phil's Ch Memphis TN 2010-2015. chandler@stgeorgesgermantown.org

WHITMER, Marlin Lee (Ia) 2602 250th St, De Witt IA 52742 **Creator Befriendersforum.org 2017-; Fndr Befrienders Prog for Lay People 1966-** B Muscatine IA 1930 s Lee & Leora. BA Hamline U 1952; BD VTS 1955; Cert Bd Cert Champlains 1965. D 6/22/1955 P 5/1/1956 Bp Gordon V Smith. c 3. Distance Lrng Fac Wayne Oates Inst 2003-2009; Seminar Fac Wayne Oates Institue 2003-2007; Chapl S Lk's Hosp Davenport IA 1964-1992; St Lukes Hosp Davenport IA 1964-1992; Dept of CE Dio Iowa 1963-1964; Chapl S Lk's Hosp Davenport IA 1963-1964; Asst Trin Cathd Davenport IA 1961-1964; P-in-c S Mart's Ferry IA 1959-1962; P in Charge St. Mart's Perry Iowa 1959-1962; P-in-c Gr Ch Boone IA 1959-1961; Cur S Thos' Epis Ch Sioux City IA 1955-1959; S Geo's Epis Ch Le Mars IA 1955-1956. DVD Workshop Coordntr, "The Healing power of Story Listening," 2014; Auth, "Healing Power of Story Listening," 2009; Auth, "Befrienders: A Model For

Trng Lay People For Caring," 1978; Auth, "An Experiment Trng Lay People In Pstr Tasks," 1973. Assn of Profsnl Chapl 1965; Wayne Oates Inst 2003. Hon Cn Trin Cathd, Dio Iowa 1980.

WHITMER, Ronald Delane (La) 5400 Courtyard Dr., Gonzales LA 70737 B Muscatine IA 1936 s Lee & Leora. BA Gri 1959; BD EDS 1965. D 6/24/1965 P 1/1/1966 Bp Gordon V Smith. m 8/1/1964 Martha Whitmer. Supply P S Andr's Ch Clinton LA 2000-2004; Pulse Of Louisiana Baton Rouge LA 1991-1993; S Marg's Epis Ch Baton Rouge LA 1987-1991; Epis Par of Ames Ames IA 1970-1987; Vic S Dav's Ames IA 1970-1987; Vic S Jas Epis Ch Independence IA 1965-1970; Vic S Mary's In Delwein 1965-1970. Auth, "Casebook For Iowa'S Future: Visions From The Heartland Proj".

WHITMIRE JR, Norman (LI) 8545 96th St, Woodhaven NY 11421 **R All SS Ch Woodhaven NY 2013-** B Las Vegas NV 1968 s Norman & Dorothy. AB Harv 1990; MD Yale Sch of Med 1995; MDiv VTS 2011. D 6/11/2011 Bp Mary Douglas Glasspool P 12/10/2011 Bp Shannon Sherwood Johnston. Hon Asstg P S Paul's Par Washington DC 2013; Int Asst R S Peters-In-The-Woods Epis Ch Fairfax Sta VA 2013; Asst to the R and Dir of Yth Mnstry S Dav's Ch Ashburn VA 2011-2013. CBS 2002; Soc of Cath Priests 2009.

WHITMORE, Bruce Gregory (Tex) 1401 Avenue O #F, Huntsville TX 77340 B 1954 s Page & Arvella. BA Bemidji St U 1977; MDiv Sewanee: The U So, TS 1980. D 9/13/1980 Bp Robert Marshall Anderson P 3/19/1981 Bp Christopher FitzSimons Allison. m 9/17/2006 Darleen Ruth Mitchell c 2. R S Steph's Ch Huntsville TX 1986-1993; Asst S Mart's Epis Ch Houston TX 1985-1986; R Ch Of S Ben Bolingbrook IL 1982-1985; S Matt's Ch Bogalusa LA 1982-1985; Asst S Phil's Ch Charleston SC 1980-1982.

WHITMORE, Charles William (WNY) 3802 James St. Unit 30, Bellingham WA 98226 **Asst S Paul Epis Ch Bellingham WA 2007-** B Lockport NY 1945 s Charles & Muriel. BS Cor 1967; MDiv PDS 1973. D 6/16/1973 P 12/16/1973 Bp Harold Barrett Robinson. m 8/26/1972 Linda N Whitmore c 3. R S Mk's Ch Orchard Pk NY 1988-2007; Dep Gc Dio Wstrn New York Tonawanda NY 1988-2004, Dn Sthrn Erie Dnry 1999-2007, Chair COM 1997-2007, Chair Dioc Evang Com 1989-1992, Pres Stndg Com 1985-1988, Rurd Chaut Dnry 1980-1984, Trst Epis Ch Hm 1976-2007; Ch Of The H Comm Lake View NY 1983-1988; S Paul's Epis Ch Springville NY 1983-1988; Team Mnstry Trin Epis Ch Hamburg NY 1983-1988; R S Paul's Epis Ch Mayville NY 1978-1982; Asst Calv Epis Ch Williamsville NY 1973-1978. Vietnam Veteran Of The Year Vietnam Veterans of Amer 2003.

WHITMORE, Elizabeth Needham (Mass) 1391 Hyannis Barnstable Rd, Barnstable MA 02630 B New York NY 1946 d David & Eileen. RN Helene Fuld Sch Nrsng 1973; BA Sch for Deacons 1991. D 6/6/1992 Bp William Edwin Swing. D Ch Of The Incarn San Francisco CA 1992-1997.

✠ **WHITMORE, The Rt Rev Keith** (Eau) 90 N National Ave, Fond Du Lac WI 54935 **Asst Bp of Atlanta Dio Atlanta Atlanta GA 2013-, Asst Bp of Atlanta 2008-2013** B Fond du Lac WI 1945 s Bernard & Winifred. U of Wisconsin 1974; MDiv Nash 1977; BS Marian Coll of Fond Du Lac 1983. D 1/15/1977 P 7/23/1977 Bp William Hampton Brady Con 4/10/1999 for Eau. m 11/19/1966 Suzanne J Whitmore c 2. Bp of Eau Dio Eau Claire Eau Claire WI 1999-2008; Dn Chr Cathd Salina KS 1994-1999; R S Phil's Ch Joplin MO 1984-1994; Asst to the Dn St Paul's Epis Cathd Fond Du Lac WI 1982-1984; R S Jn The Bapt Portage WI 1980-1982; Dio Fond du Lac Appleton WI 1977-1980; S Barn Epis Ch Tomahawk WI 1977-1980; St Ambr Epis Ch Antigo WI 1977-1980; Dir of the Epis Stds Prog Candler TS 2012-2017. Affirming Catholicism 1986; SHN 1977. DD Nash 2000.

WHITMORE, Paula Michele (Spok) 602 Nw 10th St, Pendleton OR 97801 B Yakima WA 1950 d Paul & Dorothy. BA Chapman U 1973; MDiv Claremont TS 1981; DMin Claremont TS 1982; CAS CDSP 1990. D 12/6/1992 P 10/9/1993 Bp Richard Lester Shimpfky. S Matt's Ch Prosser WA 2011-2013; S Paul's Ch Walla Walla WA 2006-2009; Ch Of The Redeem Pendleton OR 2003-2006; Trin Ch Gonzales CA 1995-2003; Asstg P Ch Of S Jude The Apos Cupertino CA 1993-1997; Trin Cathd San Jose CA 1992-1994.

WHITNAH JR, John C (ND) Gethsemane Cathedral, 3600 25th St S, Fargo ND 58104 **S Paul's Ch Darien CT 2015-** B Newark NJ 1952 s John & Elizabeth. BA Gordon Coll 1974; MA Gordon-Conwell TS 1978; MDiv VTS 1989. D 6/10/1989 Bp Peter J Lee P 3/29/1990 Bp Robert Poland Atkinson. m 7/13/1980 Nina R Whitnah c 3. Geth Cathd Fargo ND 2013-2015; S Ptr's Epis Ch Milford CT 2012; P-in-c S Jn's Ch New Haven CT 2009-2012; R Chr Ch Avon CT 1999-2008; Asst Truro Epis Ch Fairfax VA 1989-1999.

WHITNEY, Ann Carolyn (Ak) PO Box 870995, Wasilla AK 99687 **R S Dav's Epis Ch Wasilla AK 2010-** B Montpelier VT 1949 d Clifton & Mary. BS Plymouth St U 1971. D 5/12/1997 Bp Albert Theodore Eastman P 10/8/2009 Bp Rustin Ray Kimsey. Chapl Vlly Hosp Palmer AK 1999-2006. OHC 1993; Soc-Mary 1993.

WHITNEY, Marilla Jane (Minn) 111 N Elm St, Fairmont MN 56031 **P-in-c S Mart's Epis Ch Fairmont MN 2017-; Supply Dio Minnesota Minneapolis MN 2005-; Dio Minnesota 2005-** B Berkeley CA 1944 d Robert & Lorraine. BA U CA 1966; MEd Ft Wright Coll of H Names 1981; MA U of Montana 1985; MDiv VTS 1987. D 6/20/1987 Bp Leigh Allen Wallace Jr P 12/21/1987

W

Bp Robert Poland Atkinson. m 2/18/1966 Thomas William Hasseries c 1. Assoc R Ch Of S Nich Paradise CA 1998-2001; Supply The Epis Dio Nthrn California Sacramento CA 1996-2004; Int/Supply S Jn's Epis Ch Lakeport CA 1994-1996; Vic S Paul's Mssn Cres City CA 1993-1994; Vic St Johns Epis Ch Harpers Ferry WV 1987-1991. Cistercian Lay Contemplatives of Gethsemani 2002.

WHITNEY, Wayne Vohn (Az) Episcopal Church of the Nativity, 22405 N Miller Rd, Scottsdale AZ 85255 **Cur Epis Ch of the Nativ Scottsdale AZ 2013-, Pstr Assoc 2010-2013** B Pawnee City NE 1960 s Jerry & Judith. BA K SU 1982; BA K SU 1982; MDiv Midwestern Bapt TS 1986; PhD The Sthrn Bapt TS 1990; PhD The Sthrn Bapt TS 1990. D 6/22/2013 P 1/18/2014 Bp Kirk Stevan Smith. m 7/4/2008 Monique Michelle Whitney. waynewhitney@thenativity.net

WHITNEY-WISE, Stephen D (Ore) 4033 SE Woodstock Blvd., Portland OR 97202 B Peoria IL 1947 s Roy & Mary. BA S Jos 1972; MDiv Sacr Heart TS Hales Corners 1976. Rec 3/20/1988 Bp John Lester Thompson III. m 12/18/1983 Patricia Whitney-Wise c 2. Speakers' Bureau Food For The Poor Coconut Creek FL 2010-2015; All SS Ch Portland OR 2007-2010, 1996-2007; Dio Oregon Portland OR 2007-2010; Trin Ch Folsom CA 1990-1996; Asst P Trin Epis Cathd Sacramento CA 1988-1990. Natl Ntwk of Epis Cler Assn 1996. Cmnty Serv Awd Salvation Army 1988; Awd of Merit City of San Francisco 1984.

WHITSITT, Helen Bonita (WMo) PO Box 57, Fayette MO 65248 B Council Grove KS 1943 d William & Dorothy Faye. BS U of Cntrl Missouri 1983; W Missouri Sch for Mnstry 2008. D 2/7/2010 Bp Barry Howe. m 12/21/1985 James Lloyd Whitsitt c 6.

WHITTAKER, Brendan Joseph (NH) 1788 Vt Route 102, Guildhall VT 05905 **Ret 2003-** B Boston MA 1934 s Brendan & Julia. BS U of Massachusetts 1957; MDiv EDS 1966. D 6/4/1966 Bp Leland Stark P 12/17/1966 Bp Harvey D Butterfield. m 5/26/1956 Dorothy A Whittaker c 3. S Mk's Ch Groveton NH 1985-1994; R S Paul's Ch Lancaster NH 1985-1992; Cn Mssnr Dio Vermont Burlington VT 1973-1978; R S Thos' Epis Ch Brandon VT 1968-1973. Auth, "P/Conservationist," *Mod Tentmakers*. Forest Stewards Gld (Founding Mem); Soc Of S Jn The Evang. Epa Reg I DSA Environ Protection Agcy 1984; Distinguished Alumnni U Of Massachusetts Sch Of Forestry 1981.

WHITTAKER JR, Richard Russell (U) 1784 Aaron Dr., Tooele UT 84074 **Asst St Andr Epis Ch Irvine CA 2015-** B Los Angeles CA 1953 s Richard & Anna. BS U CA 1975; BA U CA 1977; MRP Syr 1979; MDiv ETSBH 2008. D 6/7/2008 P 1/10/2009 Bp Joseph Jon Bruno. m 6/21/1997 Sandra Kay Whittaker c 1. P-in-c S Barn EpiscopalChurch Tooele UT 2009-2013.

WHITTAKER-NAVEZ, Christine Ruth (Mass) 223 Pond St, Hopkinton MA 01748 **S Mk's Ch Southborough MA 2017-; Pres, Disciplinary Bd Dio Massachusetts Boston MA 2011-, Pres, Disciplinary Bd 2010-, COM Chair 2004-2008, Chair, COM 2004-2008, Mem, COM 1997-2008** B Walton-On-Thames Surrey UK 1947 d James & Ruth. BA Oxf GB 1967; MA Smith 1968; MA Ya 1972; JD Geo 1977; MDiv VTS 1990. D 6/9/1990 P 1/5/1991 Bp Ronald Hayward Haines. m 9/23/1995 Andre Julien Navez c 2. R S Mich's Epis Ch Holliston MA 2001-2013, P-in-c 1998-2000; Assoc Trin Ch Epis Boston MA 1996-1997; Adj Prof Cn Law VTS Alexandria VA 1996, 1994, 1993, 1992, Pres, Alum Assn 2007-2008, Mem, Bd Trst 2007-; P-in-c S Jn's Ch Georgetown Par Washington DC 1994-1995, Asst 1992-1994; Asst Ch Of The Ascen Silver Sprg MD 1990-1991; Stndg Com Dio Washington Washington DC 1994-1995.

WHITTED, Warren Rohde (Neb) 8141 Farnam Dr Apt 328, Omaha NE 68114 **Ret 1992-** B Omaha NE 1920 s Ira & Emily. BA U of Nebraska 1941; JD Creighton U 1947. D 11/8/1985 Bp James Daniel Warner. m 3/14/1942 Marjorie Clair Disbrow c 4. D Trin Cathd Omaha NE 1985-1992.

WHITTEMORE, James Robinson (Me) 7 Whipple Farm Ln, Falmouth ME 04105 **Died 12/30/2015** B Detroit MI 1925 s Lewis & Helen. BA Ya 1947; BD EDS 1951; Harv 1965; STM NYTS 1976; DMin NYTS 1985. D 6/8/1951 P 12/10/1951 Bp Lewis B Whittemore. m 12/4/1982 Mary B Fooks c 5. Dir of Maritime Mnstry Gr Ch Cathd Charleston SC 2001-2003; So Carolina Charleston SC 2001-2003; Vic Trin Ch Castine ME 1994-2000; Exec Dir Seamens Ch Inst New York NY 1977-1993; Exec Dir 1977-1992; Bd Trst SCI New York NY 1969-2015; Cn Trin Cathd Trenton NJ 1967-1977; R Trin Ch Princeton NJ 1967-1977; R Chr Ch S Hamilton MA 1956-1967; R S Jas Ch Of Sault S Marie Sault Sainte Marie MI 1953-1956; Cur Chr Ch Grosse Pointe Grosse Pointe Farms MI 1951-1953; Pres Alumini/ae Assn EDS Cambridge MA 1981-1985.

WHITTEN, James Austin (CFla) St Mary of the Angels, 6316 Matchett Rd, Orlando FL 32809 B Birmingham AL 1942 s James & Sadye. BA U of Tennessee 1967; Inst for Chr Stds 2011. D 12/10/2011 Bp John Wadsworth Howe. m 1/3/1966 Margaret Dewey Whitten c 2. Coll of Pstr Supervision and Psych 2012; The Intl Ord of St Lk the Physcn 2012.

WHITTEN, Wesley Roy (ECR) 11197 Via Vis, Nevada City CA 95959 B Bellingham WA 1947 s Jesse & Mary. BA San Jose St U 1969; MDiv VTS 1973; PhD California Inst of Integral Stds 2004. D 6/22/1973 P 2/20/1974 Bp Chauncie Kilmer Myers. m 6/28/1969 Jeanne Whitten c 2. Vic S Steph's In-The-Field Epis Ch San Jose CA 1975-1981; Asst Chr Epis Ch Los Altos CA 1974-1975; Intern Asst Ch Of The Ascen Silver Sprg MD 1971-1972. Auth, "Awake and Aware," CIIS, San Francisco, 2004; Auth, "I Think My Mind Is Tricking Me," Lifetimes Press, London, 1989; Auth, "Simply Being Happy," Lifetimes Press, London, 1988. cl VTS 1973.

WHITTINGTON, Nancy Susan (WNC) 140 Chestnut Cir, Blowing Rock NC 28605 **D S Paul's Ch Wilkesboro NC 2013-** B Statesville NC 1950 d Odell & Grace. BA U NC 1972; MBA Wake Forest U 1984. D 1/22/2011 Bp Porter Taylor.

WHITTINGTON, Richard Culbertson (Tex) **Ret 1975-** B Oklahoma City OK 1921 s Eugene & Florence. BBA U of Texas 1947. D 12/17/1954 Bp Clinton Simon Quin. m 3/13/1948 Lettalou Garth. D 1958-1975; Asst S Jn The Div Houston TX 1954-1958.

WHITTLE, Natalie Wang (Ga) 102 S Jackson Rd, Statesboro GA 30461 B Beijing China 1945 d M J & Yi. BA Natl Taiwan U; DA U of Oregon. D 6/29/2006 Bp Henry Irving Louttit. m 7/18/1972 Amberys Whittle c 2.

WHITWORTH, Julia E (Ind) Trinity Episcopal Church, 3243 N Meridian St, Indianapolis IN 46208 **Trin Ch Indianapolis IN 2016-** B Richmond VA 1971 d Frank & Kay. AB Dart 1993; MA NYU 1998; MPhil NYU 2002; MDiv UTS 2010. D 3/13/2010 P 9/25/2010 Bp Mark Sean Sisk. m 8/22/1998 Raymond John Neufeld c 3. P Cathd Of St Jn The Div New York NY 2013-2016; Asst S Jas's Ch W Hartford CT 2010-2012. jwhitworth@trinitychurchindy.org

WHYTE, Horace Maxwell (NY) 170 W End Ave Apt 30-H, New York NY 10023 **D The Ch Of The Epiph New York NY 2004-; D The Ch of the Epiph New York City NY 2004-** B Darliston JM 1941 s Roland & Estella. D 4/26/1997 Bp Richard Frank Grein. The Ch of S Matt And S Tim New York NY 1997-2007. NAAD 1996; The Fund for the Diac in the USA 1998-2007.

WIBLE, Christina Karen Kirchner (NJ) 10 N Slope, Clinton NJ 08809 B Plainfield NJ 1946 d William & Ruth. BA Rutgers The St U of New Jersey 1969; MDiv GTS 1999. D 10/23/1999 Bp Herbert Alcorn Donovan Jr. m 8/23/1971 Barry R Wible. D Calv Epis Ch Flemington NJ 2001-2002; D S Thos Ch Alexandria Pittstown NJ 1999-2000.

WIBLE, Terrence Linn (Be) 57 Piper Dr, New Oxford PA 17350 B Chambersburg PA 1949 s Charles & Catherine. MA Lebanon Vlly Coll 1971; MDiv Evang TS 1974; VTS 1993. D 6/11/1993 P 12/10/1993 Bp Charlie Fuller McnuTt Jr. m 1/15/1977 Lenoir J Wible. R S Lk's Ch Lebanon PA 2003-2015; R All SS Ch Hanover PA 1994-2003; D Intern All SS' Epis Ch Hershey PA 1993-1994; Serv Evang Congrl Ch 1972-1992.

WICHAEL, Karen (Kan) 5648 W 92nd Pl, Overland Park KS 66207 B New York NY 1947 d Arthur & Doris. BA Wm Penn U 1969. D 10/20/2000 Bp William Edward Smalley. c 3. S Stephens Epis Churchrch Wichita KS 2004-2010; D Gd Shpd Epis Ch Wichita KS 2000-2011.

WICHELNS, Anne Brett (CNY) St. Andrew's Shared Ministry, 8520 LeRay St., Evans Mills NY 13637 **P Ch Of The Resurr Oswego NY 2013-; Vic S Andr's Ch Evans Mills NY 2009-** B Tarrytown NY 1950 d George & Beatrice. BA SUNY Empire St Coll 1981; MST SUNY Potsdam 1991. D 10/7/2006 P 6/16/2007 Bp Gladstone Bailey Adams III. m 7/6/1974 Jerome Bailey Wichelns c 4. Assoc Shared Mnstry Of Nthrn NY Brownville NY 2007-2008.

WICHELNS, Jerome Bailey (CNY) 10751 Limburg Forks Rd, Carthage NY 13619 B Newark NJ 1937 s Walter & Ethelyn. BA Rutgers The St U of New Jersey 1959; MA Col 1990; DMin Sewanee: The U So, TS 1998. D 12/12/1998 P 6/12/1999 Bp David Bruce Joslin. m 7/6/1974 Anne Brett Wichelns c 4. Dio Cntrl New York Liverpool NY 2005; R S Paul's Ch Brownville NY 2003-2009; Shared Mnstry Of Nthrn NY Brownville NY 1999-2008; Assoc Pstr S Paul's Ch Watertown NY 1999-2002. Auth, "The New Physics: An Intro," *Fractals And Ferns- The New Physics: Uniting The Sciences And Arts*, Suny Press, 1998; Auth, "China And The W: A Study In (Bus) Culture Clash," *Whose Values? Ethics In The Intl Bus Environ*, Coll Consortium For Intl Stds, 1996; Auth, "Poem," *Sunlight Fails November Wood*, 1993; Auth, "Hunger On The Lifeboat," Natl Wrld Food Day Com, 1991; Auth, "In Defense Of The Coll Taking A Leading Role In The Cmnty In Confronting Issues In Soc Reform: A Contractarian Approach In Critical Thinkin," Inst For Critical Thinking, 1989; Auth, "Ethics In Bus," Cntr For Bus Ethics, 1989. Amer Philos Assn 1993; Intl Symposium On Ethics 1996; People To People 1993. "Who'S Who In Amer Colleges And Universities".

WICHMAN, James Henry (O) 2314 Oak Glen Ct, Akron OH 44333 **D Gr Ch Ravenna OH 1999-** B Sandusky OH 1929 s Paul & Osie. U of Wisconsin. D 11/13/1992 Bp James Russell Moodey. m 5/26/1951 Charlene H Wichman c 2. D S Jn's Epis Ch Cuyahoga Fls OH 1998-1999; D S Lk's Epis Ch Niles OH 1995-1998. NAAD.

WICK, Calhoun W (Del) Po Box 3719, Wilmington DE 19807 B Cleveland OH 1944 s Warren & Mildred. BA Trin, Hartford 1963; BA TESM 1967; MDiv VTS 1970; MS MIT 1975; MS MIT 1975. D 6/27/1970 Bp John Harris Burt P 4/25/1971 Bp Nelson Marigold Burroughs. m 4/8/1980 Ann D Wick c 2. Spec Asst To The Bp Of Delaware Dio Delaware Wilmington 2011-2013, Spec Assitant to Bp of Delaware 1980-2013; Assoc Chr Greenville DE 1979-1987; R S Michaels In The Hills Toledo OH 1975-1978; Non-par 1974-1975; Chr Ch Christiana Hundred Wilmington DE 1970-1974; Asst Chr Greenville DE 1970-1974. Auth, "Six Diciplines of Breakthrough Lrng," *Six Diciplines of Breakthrough Lrng*, Wiley, 2006; Auth, "The Lrng Edge: How Smart Mgrs &

W

Smart Cos Stay Ahead," McGraw Hill, 1993; Auth, "Mgmt Side Of Mnstry". Alfred P Sloan Fell; Rockefeller Fell.

WICKHAM, Jonathan William (WTex) 15670 Robin Ridge, San Antonio TX 78248 **R All SS Epis Ch Corpus Christi TX 2012-** B Oneonta NY 1969 s J Thomas & Diane. AS No Country Cmnty Coll Saranac Lake NY 1989; BA SUNY 1992; MDiv Sewanee: The U So, TS 2002. D 6/13/2002 Bp Robert Boyd Hibbs P 2/28/2003 Bp James Edward Folts. m 10/20/1990 Jennifer Tyndall Wickham c 2. Assoc S Mk's Epis Ch San Antonio TX 2007-2012; Bp's Dep for Yth Mnstrs Dio W Texas San Antonio TX 2004-2006, Prov VII Dep 2011-2012, Exec Bd 2010-2013; Asst S Geo Ch San Antonio TX 2002-2004; Dir of Yth Mnstrs Ch Of The Gd Shpd Corpus Christi TX 1996-1999; Dir of Yth Mnstrs S Jn's Epis Cathd Knoxville TN 1992-1995; Yth Min First Presb Un Ch Owego NY 1989-1992. The ABS CE Prize The U So TS 2002.

WICKHAM III, William (Del) 9410 Creek Summit Circle, Richmond VA 23235 B NorwichNY 1940 s William & Barbara. BA RPI 1962; MDiv VTS 1968. D 6/11/1968 Bp Walter M Higley P 5/28/1969 Bp Ned Cole. m 1/1/1990 Joyce M Wickham c 5. R S Martha's Epis Ch Bethany Bch DE 2004-2010; Dn Convoc VII Dio Sthrn Virginia Newport News VA 1996-1998, Chair Richmond Epis Cler 1991-1995; R S Mich's Ch Richmond VA 1990-2004; Stndg Com Dio Cntrl New York Liverpool NY 1975-1986; Ch of the Gd Shpd Oriskany Fls NY 1974-1985; Chapl Hse of Gd Shpd New Hartford NY 1974-1985; R S Jas' Ch Clinton NY 1973-1989; Cur Trin Epis Ch Watertown NY 1968-1973.

WICKIZER, Bob (Okla) 218 N 6th St, Muskogee OK 74401 **R Gr Ch Muskogee OK 2010-** B Springfield MO 1951 s Wilbur & Catherine. BS U of Missouri 1972; MA Washington U 1975; MDiv EDS 1998. D 6/27/1998 P 2/23/1999 Bp Richard Lester Shimpfky. m 5/17/1980 Joan S Wickizer c 2. Actg R S Anne's Par Annapolis MD 2006-2008; Int S Alb's Epis Ch Glen Burnie MD 2005-2006; R S Phil's Epis Ch Laurel MD 2001-2004; H Trin Epis Ch Greensboro NC 2001; Asst S Mary's Epis Ch High Point NC 1998-2001. Auth, "Creation & Revelation," *Journ of Faith & Sci Exch*, 1997. Inst of Electrical & Electronic Engr (Mem) 1977. 2nd Prize - Faith & Sci Essay Templeton Fndt 1997.

WIDDOWS, John Herbert (Me) 340 Promenade #125, Portland ME 04101 **Died 9/25/2016** B Yonkers NY 1932 s Arthur & Maud. BA Col 1954; STB Ya Berk 1958; MEd Iona Coll 1974. D 5/11/1958 P 12/11/1958 Bp Horace W B Donegan. m 10/3/1992 Cynthia R Widdows c 2. S Nich Epis Ch Scarborough ME 2000-2002; Asstg Cathd Ch Of S Lk Portland ME 1993-2000; Asst S Ptr's Ch Bronx NY 1967-1968; Chapl Greer Sch Hope Farm 1962-1967; R S Ptr Lithgow NY 1962-1966; Cur Par of Chr the Redeem Pelham NY 1958-1962.

WIDING, Carl Jon (Ct) 47 Fox Holw, Avon CT 06001 **Vic Chr Ch Sharon CT 2007-** B Philadelphia PA 1937 s Theodore & Esther. BA Trin Hartford CT 1959; MDiv EDS 1966; MSW U of Pennsylvania 1972. D 9/21/1966 P 4/12/1967 Bp Robert Lionne DeWitt. m 7/2/1966 Carol S Widing c 1. Missoner No Cntrl Epis Reg Mnstry Enfield 2004-2006; Asst Gr Ch Newington CT 2001-2004; Asst S Monica's Ch Hartford CT 2000-2001; P-in-c S Thos of Cbury New Fairfield CT 1998-2000; R Chr Ch Avon CT 1983-1997; R St Annes Epis Ch Middletown DE 1972-1983; Dio PA Philadelphia PA 1970-1972; Asst Chr Ch Philadelphia Philadelphia PA 1966-1970. Tertiary of the Soc of S Fran 1971-2013.

WIECKING III, Frederick August (Ind) 4 Sunnyside Rd, Silver Spring MD 20910 **Non-par 1973-** B Milwaukee WI 1947 s Frederick & Catherine. BA Wesl 1969; MDiv Yale DS 1972. D 2/8/1972 P 10/1/1972 Bp John P Craine. m 9/6/1969 Olive Hackett. Auth, "The New Puritans: Achievement & Power Motive Of New Left Radicals"; Auth, "Reversing Tax Shift: Opportunity To Make Mn'S Taxes Progressive"; Auth, "Organizing For Just Econ".

WIED, Gethin James (Los) D 6/3/2017 Bp Diane Jardine Bruce.

WIEHE, Philip Freeman (NC) 3676 Laurel Park Highway, Hendersonville NC 28739 B Cincinnati OH 1949 s Theodore & Mary. BA JHU 1971; MDiv Yale DS 1975; STM Yale DS 1976. D 5/24/1975 P 1/31/1976 Bp John Mc Gill Krumm. m 2/16/1985 Linda W McFadden c 2. Int R Trin Elkridge MD 2014; Int R S Jas' Epis Ch Leesburg VA 2012-2013; Int R Calv Ch Memphis TN 2010-2012; Int R S Geo's Epis Ch Arlington VA 2009-2010; Int R Emm Ch Harrisonburg VA 2008-2009; Int R All SS Ch Frederick MD 2006-2008; The Holbrooke LLC Grassvalley CA 2005; Dir Campusource 2002-2005; Consult S Mk's Epis Ch Raleigh NC 1996-1997; Chapl N. C. St Dio No Carolina Raleigh NC 1993-2003; Co-Pstr Untd Ch of Chr BayberryNY 1989-1992; Int Pstr First Par Ch Derry NH 1987-1988; Chapl Stanford Cbury Fndt Palo Alto CA 1980-1984; Exec Dir The Epis Fndt For Drama Palo Alto CA 1979-1984; Chapl Harvard-Westlake Sch Studio City CA 1976-1979; Asst Trin Ch On The Green New Haven CT 1975-1976. Co-Auth, "More Dumb Things Ch Do," Morehouse, 2009; Auth, "Ten Dumb Things Ch Do," Morehouse, 2001. pilgrimquests@gmail.com

WIELAND, William David (Ind) (same as above), Greencastle IN 46135 **Chapl to Ret Cler & Surviving Spouses Dio Indianapolis Indianapolis IN 2014-, Stndg Comm/Exec Coun 2005-2011, Dn of NW Dnry 1999-2011, Mssn Strtgy Com 1988-2005, COM in Higher Educ 1988-1998, Liturg & Mus Cmsn 1982-1997; Bd Dir Beyond Homeless Inc. Greencastle 2012-** B New Brunswick NJ 1942 s Willard & Naomi. BA Wesl 1964; MA Indiana U 1966;

MDiv Sewanee: The U So, TS 1981. D 6/24/1981 P 3/19/1982 Bp Edward Witker Jones. m 6/15/1975 Lucille Wieland c 2. R S Andr's Epis Ch Greencastle IN 1987-2011; Assoc S Paul's Epis Ch Indianapolis IN 1983-1987, Asst 1981-1982; Instr in German Wabash Coll Crawfordsville Indiana 1970-1976; Bd Dir Away-Hm Shltr Greencastle IN 1993-2011. Ntwk of Biblic Storytellers Intl 2012. wdw7442@gmail.com

WIENK, Dennis Leslie (Roch) 1760 Blossom Rd, Rochester NY 14610 B Gowanda NY 1942 s Leslie & Gladys. BA SUNY 1964; BD Nash 1970. D 6/13/1970 P 12/19/1970 Bp Allen Webster Brown. m 6/16/1962 Marilyn D Dowd c 2. Chapl The Chap of the Gd Shpd Rochester NY 2003-2012; Vic Ch Of The Gd Shpd Savona NY 1995-2003; R S Thos' Ch Bath NY 1984-2003; LocTen S Jn's Ch Massena NY 1977-1979; R St Fran Mssn Albany NY 1975-1977; Cath Worker Mt. Carmel Hse Schenectady NY 1973-1975; Cur S Geo's Epis Ch Schenectady NY 1970-1973. Transltr, "Jesus of Nazareth: Always on the Move," Wipf & Stock, 2017; Transltr, "Esther in Exile: Toward a Sprtlty of Difference," Wipf & Stock, 2014; Transltr, "Three Wmn of Hope," Wipf & Stock, 2014; Transltr, "Five Wmn: Sarah, Hagar, Rebecca, Rachel, Leah," Wipf & Stock, 2012.

WIENS, Dolores (NI) 315 W Harrison Ave, Wheaton IL 60187 B Enid OK 1942 d Menno & Emma. BA Bethel U 1965; Wheaton Coll 1987; MDiv Bethany TS 1990; CAS SWTS 1993. D 6/18/1994 P 12/1/1994 Bp Frank Tracy Griswold III. m 5/30/1964 Paul W Wiens c 2. S Barn-In-The-Dunes Gary IN 2008-2011; Calv Ch Lombard IL 2001; Ch Of The Resurr W Chicago IL 1995-1996.

WIENS HEINSOHN, Lisa Marie (Minn) 2136 Carter Ave, Saint Paul MN 55108 **S Steph The Mtyr Ch Minneapolis MN 2016-** B Ventura CA 1969 d Harold & Claudia. B.A Earlham Coll 1991; J.D Columbia Law Sch 1998; MDiv Luther Sem 2016. D 6/20/2015 P 6/21/2016 Bp Brian N Prior. m 2/27/2005 Jeff Wiens Heinsohn c 1. S Matt's Ch S Paul MN 2015-2016.

WIESNER, A Donald (NJ) 208 Live Oak Ln, Washington NC 27889 **Regular Supply S Jas Epis Ch Belhaven NC 2004-** B Englewood NJ 1935 s August & Tilda. AB Pr 1957; MDiv GTS 1960; STM NYTS 1970; Cert Post Grad Cntrl Mntl Hlth for Pstr Counslg 1970; Cert Int Mnstry Prog 1996. D 6/11/1960 Bp Leland Stark P 1/7/1961 Bp William Francis Moses. m 1/4/1975 Judy Henriksen c 3. P Assoc S Ptr's Epis Ch Washington NC 2001-2009; Int H Trin Epis Ch Hertford NC 1999-2001; Int S Mary's Ch Kinston NC 1998-1999; Int Ch Of The Gd Shpd Pitman NJ 1997-1998; Int S Mary's Epis Ch Stone Harbor NJ 1996-1997; Vic Trin Epis Ch Vincentown NJ 1982-1996; Int Ch Of The H Comm Norwood NJ 1981-1982; Int S Andr's Ch Harrington Pk NJ 1981-1982; R S Andr's Epis Ch Lincoln Pk NJ 1974-1980; R S Lk's Ch Katonah NY 1964-1972; Cur Ch Of The Resurr Miami FL 1963-1964; Vic S Steph's Ch New Prt Rchy FL 1962-1963; Cur Gr Epis Ch Of Ocala Ocala FL 1960-1962.

WIESNER, Kurt Christopher (U) 261 S 900 E, Salt Lake City UT 84102 **R S Paul's Ch Salt Lake City UT 2015-** B Hinsdale IL 1972 s Kurt & Mary. BA Indiana U 1995; MDiv Epis TS of the SW 1998. D 12/15/2002 Bp Arthur Williams Jr P 6/16/2003 Bp J Clark Grew II. m 1/26/2002 Darlene P Wiesner c 1. R All SS Epis Ch Littleton NH 2008-2015; Cur Trin Cathd Cleveland OH 2003-2008; The Ch of the Gd Shpd Austin TX 1998-2001. rector@stpauls-slc.org

WIETSTOCK, Anne Kimberley (NI) 117 N Lafayette Blvd, South Bend IN 46601 B Washington DC 1956 d Lloyd & Jean. D 12/22/2012 Bp Edward Stuart Little II. m 11/28/1987 Steven Milo Wietstock.

WIGGERS, John Mark (ETenn) 1101 N Broadway St, Knoxville TN 37917 **R St Jas Epis Ch at Knoxville Knoxville TN 2009-** B Pensacola FL 1971 s Bert & Dean. BA Baylor U 1993; MDiv GTS 1999. D 6/5/1999 P 2/19/2000 Bp Charles Farmer Duvall. m 4/20/1996 Elizabeth Dees Wiggers c 2. Cn Cathd Of S Phil Atlanta GA 2002-2009; Cur The Epis Ch Of The Nativ Dothan AL 1999-2002.

WIGGIN-NETTLES, Duane Joseph (La) The Church Of The Annunciation, 4505 S Claiborne Ave, New Orleans LA 70125 **R The Ch Of The Annunc New Orleans LA 2014-** B Metairie LA 1978 s Joseph & Shelli. D 4/30/2014 Bp Morris King Thompson Jr P 11/1/2014 Bp James Barrow Brown. m 6/11/2016 Jane-Allison E Wiggin-Nettles c 2. dnettles@edola.org

WIGGIN-NETTLES, Jane-Allison E (USC) D 6/3/2016 Bp W illiam Andrew Waldo P 6/28/2017 Bp Morris King Thompson Jr.

WIGGINS JR, Eschol Vernon (Ga) 1009 Hillcrest Dr, Cochran GA 31014 **P Trin Ch Cochran GA 2005-** B Garfield GA 1936 s Eschol & Hilda. BS Georgia Coll Milledgeville GA 1982. D 2/5/2005 P 8/7/2005 Bp Henry Irving Louttit. m 12/23/1954 Joan Wiggins c 2.

WIGGINS, Reese H (La) 17764 Jefferson Ridge Dr, Baton Rouge LA 70817 **P S Lk's Ch Baton Rouge LA 2007-** B Beaumont TX 1949 s Leo & Fay. Rec 9/13/2003 Bp Charles Edward Jenkins III. m 5/16/2001 Glenn M Wiggins c 2.

WIGG-MAXWELL, Elizabeth Parker (Nwk) 44 Pittsford Way, New Providence NJ 07974 **R S Ptr's Epis Ch Livingston NJ 2009-** B Minneapolis MN 1956 d Norman & Joan. BA Coe Coll 1978; MA U of Wisconsin 1981; MDiv GTS 1986. D 6/28/1986 Bp Henry Irving Mayson P 2/2/1987 Bp H Coleman Mcgehee Jr. m 5/18/1985 Paul Douglas Wigg-Maxwell c 2. Asstg Min and DRE Chr Ch Short Hills NJ 2004-2009; Vic S Fran Ch Dunellen NJ 2000-2002; Int St Jn the Bapt Epis Ch Linden NJ 1998-2000; Int S Jas' Epis Ch Hackettstown NJ 1994; Int Ch Of The Mssh Chester NJ 1993-1994; Asst Ch of S Jn on the Mtn Bernardsville NJ 1992-1993; Int The Ch Of The Sav Denville NJ 1991-1992; Asst R S Paul's Epis Ch Chatham NJ 1986-1990.

WIGHT, Andrea Lee (Chi) 7398 Bell Vista Terrace, Rockford IL 61107 **R S Anskar's Ch Rockford IL 2005-** B Montclair NJ 1952 d Andrew & Merle. BS U of Wyoming 1975; MDiv CDSP 2003. D 2/22/2003 P 10/25/2003 Bp Katharine Jefferts Schori. c 2. P/Cur S Mary Epis Ch Crystal Lake IL 2003-2005.

WIGHT, Susan (USC) 5 Blackhawk Ct, Blythewood SC 29016 B Columbia SC 1949 d Jean & Catherine. BA U of So Carolina 1971; MEd U of So Carolina 1977; BA Cath U of Louvain 1996; Luth Theol Sthrn Sem 1998; MDiv VTS 2001. D 6/16/2001 P 4/25/2002 Bp Dorsey Henderson. m 7/30/1983 William Wallace Wight. Chapl (Ret Cler, Spouses, & Surviving Spouses) Dio Upper So Carolina 2005-2007; S Ptr's Ch Great Falls SC 2004-2014; S Mich And All Ang' Columbia SC 2001-2003.

WIGHT, William Wallace (USC) 5 Blackhawk Ct, Blythewood SC 29016 **P-in-c S Mk's Ch 2005-; S Jn's Epis Ch Columbia SC 1969-** B Enid OK 1942 s Philip & Luella. BA Phillips U 1964; Cath U of Louvain 1968; STB GTS 1969. D 6/7/1969 Bp Horace W B Donegan P 4/18/1970 Bp John Brooke Mosley. m 7/30/1983 Susan Wight. Int Gr Epis Ch Camden SC 2003-2004; Asst To The R S Martins-In-The-Field Columbia SC 2001-2003; Dio Upper So Carolina Columbia SC 2001; Dep Installation Chapl Ft Meade Odenton MA 1999-2001; Installation Resource Mgmt Chapl Ft Jackson Columbia SC 1996-1999; Dep ASG Chapl SHAPE 80 Area Spprt Grp Mons Belgium 1994-1996; Post Chapl Vilseck Germany 1991-1994; 525 MI Brigade Chapl Ft Bragg NC 1988-1991; Fam Life Chapl Pacific Communities In Panama 1985-1987; Off Of Bsh For ArmdF New York NY 1982-2001; Troop Chapl Ft Jackson SC 1982-1985; Chair Of The Armed Forced Cmsn Epis Dio San Joaquin Modesto CA 1980-1982, 1979-1982; CE Cmsn S Andr's Ch Taft CA 1979-1981; S Jn's Ch Oklahoma City OK 1977-1979; Asst S Jas Epis Ch Danbury CT 1973-1977; R Ch Of The Redeem Okmulgee OK 1970-1973; Headmaster Par Sch Okmulgee OK 1970-1973; Cur H Trin Brussels Belgium 1969-1970; Cmsn On Ecum Rel Dio Oklahoma Oklahoma City OK 1977-1979. Legion Of Merit Us Army 2001.

WIGLE, John Whitcombe (O) 814 Westport Dr, Youngstown OH 44511 **Assoc S Jas Epis Ch Boardman OH 2008-; 1978-** B Windsor ON CA 1927 s John & Camilla. BA U of Wstrn Ontario CA 1950; MDiv VTS 1956. D 6/21/1956 Bp Archie H Crowley P 1/12/1957 Bp Richard Stanley Merrill Emrich. m 5/5/1951 Barbara A Wigle c 3. Int Gr Epis Ch Mansfield OH 1999-2000; Extended Supply S Lk's Epis Ch Niles OH 1998-2007; Extended Supply Our Sav Ch Salem OH 1992-1998; Our Sav Ch Mechanicsburg OH 1992-1998; Metro Counslg Serv Youngstown OH 1987; S Jn's Ch Youngstown OH 1968-1979; R Sprt of Gr Luth Epis Ch W Bloomfield MI 1956-1968. Chi Sigma Iota Kent St, Kent Ohio 1980; Kappa Delta Pi Kent St, Kent Ohio 1980.

WIGMORE, William Joseph (Tex) 1701 Rock Creek Dr, Round Rock TX 78681 B New York NY 1945 s James & Dorothy. Iona Sch for Mnstry; BA U of Dayton 1967. D 6/24/2006 Bp Don Adger Wimberly P 1/26/2007 Bp Dena Arnall Harrison. m 1/1/1976 Geraldine Ann Wigmore c 3. Pres/CEO Austin Recovery 1995-2012.

WIGNER JR, J Douglas (Va) 1802 Dover Pointe Ct, Henrico VA 23238 **Trst VTS Alexandria VA 1999-** B Baltimore MD 1943 s John & Bernice. BS VPI 1965; MDiv VTS 1972; Cert GTS 1997; DMin VTS 2007. D 5/27/1972 P 5/13/1973 Bp Robert Bruce Hall. m 11/28/1987 Nancy Hein c 2. Int Chr Ch Glen Allen VA 2014-2015; R S Paul's Epis Ch Lynchburg VA 1997-2009; R S Ptr's Par Ch New Kent VA 1990-1997; Int Assoc S Jn's Ch Stamford CT 1986-1989; R S Paul's Ch Woodbury CT 1977-1986; Assoc S Chris's Ch Springfield VA 1974-1977; Cur Ch Of The H Comf Vienna VA 1972-1974; Pres - Stndg Com Dio SW Virginia Roanoke VA 2008-2009, Chair - Long Range Plnng Com 2007-2008, Exam Chapl 2006-2011, Stndg Com 2006-2009, COM 2005-2011, Dn, Lynchburg Convoc 2005-2010, Alt Dep to GC 2005-2007, Chair - ad hoc Com 2005-2006, Stndg Com 2001-2004, Chair, Resolutns Com 2000-2008, Dn, Lynchburg Convoc 1999-2002, Exec Bd 1998-2001; Com on Ch Revitalization Dio Virginia Richmond VA 1994-1997; Dn - Waterbury Dnry Dio Connecticut Meriden CT 1981-1984. Auth, "Using Appreciative Inquiry: A Positive Response to God's Call," *Proj Thesis - Doctor of Mnstry*, The Prot Epis TS in Virginia, 2007. Ch Dvlpmt Inst 1997; HSEC 2003-2010. R Emer St. Paul's Epis Ch 2009. stpauldoug@yahoo.com

WIGODSKY, Andrea (SVa) St. Andrew's Episcopal Church, 1009 West Princess Anne Rd., Norfolk VA 23507 **S Andr's Ch Norfolk VA 2013-; Chapl S Mary's Sch Raleigh NC 2006-** B Winston-Salem NC 1977 d John & Mary. BA Duke 2000; CAS Ya Berk 2005; MDiv Yale DS 2005. D 6/26/2005 P 2/12/2006 Bp Michael B Curry. m 10/18/2003 John D Rohrs. S Mary's Sch Raleigh NC 2008-2009, 2007; Dio No Carolina Raleigh NC 2005-2006; Chapl in Charge Epis Cntr at Duke Durham NC 2005-2006. Jn A. Wade Preaching Awd Yale DS 2005. arorhs@standrews.org

WIKE, Antoinette Ray (NC) 221 Union St, Cary NC 27511 B Lenoir NC 1945 d Carl & Antoinette. BA Guilford Coll 1968; JD U NC 1974; MDiv Duke DS 1981; Cert VTS 1982. D 4/25/1983 P 4/30/1984 Bp Robert Whitridge Estill. P Assoc S Paul's Epis Ch Cary NC 1983-2017. tony.wike@stpaulscary.org

WILBERT, Brian Kurt (O) 162 S Main St, Oberlin OH 44074 **Bp Stff Archv Dio Ohio Cleveland 2012-, Chair of Dioc Com 2016-, Stndg Com 2013-2015, GC 1st Cler Alt Dep 2012, Dep to GC 2008-2010, Secy of Conv 2007-, Stndg Com 2003-2008, Epis Transition 2003-2004, Dioc Coun Mem 2001-2004, Dioc Coun Mem 1988-2002; Adj Instr in Wrld Rel Lorain Cnty Cmnty Coll 2006-; R Chr Ch Oberlin OH 1996-; Exec Com Secy Bd the Archv of the Epis Ch 2016-; Mem Bd the Archv of the Epis Ch 2015-** B Elyria OH 1960 s Richard & Linda. BA Ken 1982; MDiv Bex Sem 1985; DMin SWTS 2002. D 6/15/1985 P 4/12/1986 Bp James Russell Moodey. m 6/16/2012 Yorki Junior Encalada Egusquiza. R Gr Ch Ravenna OH 1988-1996; Cur S Michaels In The Hills Toledo OH 1985-1988. EPF 1985; Integrity U.S.A. 1986. Alum Hall Of Fame Elyria Publ Schools 2001.

WILBURN, James Mark (Tex) 24 McFaddan LN, Temple TX 76502 **Asstg P Chr Epis Ch Temple TX 2006-, Asstg P 2006-; Stff Chapl Cntrl Texas Veterans' Hlth Care System Temple TX 2004-** B Philadelphia,PA 1946 s James & Evelyn. BS Belhaven Coll 1969; MDiv Columbia TS 1973; Columbia TS 1983; Sewanee: The U So, TS 2009. D 12/16/1982 Bp Roger Howard Cilley P 6/1/1983 Bp Maurice Manuel Benitez. c 1. Assoc R S Fran Ch Houston TX 2000-2003; Chapl Baylor U Waco TX 1995-2000; Asst R S Paul's Ch Waco TX 1995-2000; R S Tim's Epis Ch Lake Jackson TX 1991-1995; Chapl Kilgore Coll Kilgore TX 1989-1991; R S Paul's Ch Kilgore TX 1989-1991; Asociate R Trin Ch Longview TX 1987-1989; Chapl Trin Sch Longview TX 1987-1989; Chapl Texas A&M U Coll Sta TX 1982-1987; The Great Cmsn Fndt Houston TX 1982-1987; Serv Presb Ch 1973-1982. Bro of S Andr - Life Mem 1992; Cmnty of S Mary - Assoc 1985; ESMHE 1982-2000; Vocare - Dio Texas 1983-2000; Vocare - Natl 1983-1988.

WILBURN, Merry I (Tex) 16830 Blairstone, Houston TX 77084 B Marshall TX 1954 d Thomas & Enid. BS Texas A&M U 1976; MS Texas A&M U 1979; MDiv Epis TS of the SW 1991. D 6/22/1991 Bp Maurice Manuel Benitez P 2/1/1992 Bp Anselmo Carral-Solar. c 1. S Fran Par Temple TX 2003-2007; S Fran Ch Houston TX 2002-2003; The Great Cmsn Fndt Houston TX 1995-2002; Chr Epis Ch Mexia Mexia TX 1995-2000; Dio Texas Houston TX 1994; S Paul's Ch Waco TX 1991-1994.

WILCOX, Diana (Nwk) St Luke's Episcopal Church, 73 S Fullerton Ave, Montclair NJ 07042 **R Chr Ch Glen Ridge NJ 2014-** B Huntington NY 1960 d Dwight & Rosemary. BA FD 2002; MDiv Drew U 2012. D 6/2/2012 P 12/8/2012 Bp Mark M Beckwith. S Lk's Epis Ch Montclair NJ 2012-2013. rector@christchurchepiscopal.org

WILCOX, Glen Miley (Ak) Po Box 72934, Fairbanks AK 99707 **Died 12/7/2016** B Biddeford ME 1928 s Thomas & Leah. BA Hamline U 1950; MDiv Ya Berk 1953. D 6/15/1953 Bp Stephen E Keeler P 12/1/1953 Bp William Jones Gordon Jr. m 9/1/1951 Joan Louise Wilcox c 2. Non-par 1967-2016; P-in-c Ch Of The Epiph - Luth Valdez AK 1964-1967; P-in-c S Geo's Ch Cordova AK 1961-1968; Com On Const And Cn 1960-1963; P-in-c Chr Ch Anvik AK 1953-1961. Auth, "Nthrn Cross".

WILCOX JR, Jack Franklyn (Okla) 101 Great Oaks Dr, Norman OK 73071 B Kansas City MO 1952 s Jack & Jane. BA SW Bapt U 1974; MRE MidWestern Bapt TS 1979; MDiv MidWestern Bapt TS 1984; S Thos TS Denver CO 1992. D 3/18/1992 Bp William Harvey Wolfrum P 9/23/1992 Bp William Jerry Winterrowd. m 1/6/1990 Gail P Wilcox c 4. R S Mich's Epis Ch Norman OK 2005-2008; R S Jas Epis Ch of Greeneville Greeneville TN 2002-2005; Chapl Chr Ch Blacksburg VA 1996-2001; S Phil In-The-Field Sedalia CO 1992-1993; Chapl (Major) USAFR 1981-2003; Serv Sthrn Bapt Ch 1971-1990. OSL 2005.

WILCOX, John Milton (SJ) 3909 Noel Pl, Bakersfield CA 93306 **Ret 1990-** B Macon MO 1927 s Ray & Julia. BA U of Kansas 1949; MDiv GTS 1952. D 6/8/1952 Bp Horace W B Donegan P 12/12/1952 Bp Sumner Walters. m 7/23/1949 Jewell Wilcox c 2. R Ch Of The Gd Shpd Reedley CA 1985-1989; Vic S Dunstans Epis Ch Modesto CA 1981-1985; R S Lk's Ch Bakersfield CA 1970-1981; Chair Liturg Cmsn Epis Dio San Joaquin Modesto CA 1969-1972, Hstgr 1989-1993, Stndg Com 1985-1988, Dep GC 1969-1984, Chair Div Coll Wk 1964-1968; Chapl Fresno St Coll 1966-1970; Assoc S Paul's Epis Ch Visalia CA 1961-1965; Vic S Mary's Ch Manteca CA 1959-1961; Asst S Andr's Par Fullerton CA 1958-1959; Vic S Jn's Epis Ch Tulare CA 1952-1958; Fndr Ch Of The Epiph Corcoran CA 1957-1958. Intl Ord of S Lk 1959.

WILCOX, Melissa Quincy (Mil) 3118 Cross St, Madison WI 53711 B Willimantic CT 1972 d Michael & Daphne. BA Colby Coll 1994; MDiv VTS 2001. D 6/9/2001 P 2/23/2002 Bp Andrew Donnan Smith. m 7/28/2001 Adam Kradel c 3. Asst Ch Of The Redeem Bryn Mawr PA 2010-2017; S Fran Hse U Epis Ctr Madison WI 2003-2006; St Fran Hse Madison WI 2003-2006; Gr Ch Madison WI 2003; Cur Ch Of The H Comf Kenilworth IL 2001-2003; Angl Dio Kagera Ngara 1995-1998. "Body Members," *Preaching As Pstr Caring*, Sermons that Wk, 2005; "Remembering In Abundance," *Preaching Through H Days And Holidays*, Sermons that Wk, 2003.

WILCOXSON, Frederick Dean (CFla) 154 Terry Lane, Benton TN 37307 **Chapl W Polk Fire Rescue Benton TN 2013-; Mem/Supply St Lk's Cleveland**

TN 2006- B Hominy OK 1947 s William & Freda. BS Florida Sthrn Coll 1986; MPA U of Cntrl Florida 1995; PhD Intl Sem 2004. D 12/9/2006 Bp John Wadsworth Howe P 10/28/2012 Bp Gregory Orrin Brewer. m 10/18/1986 JoAnn Vanessa Wilcoxson. Mem Ch Of The Mssh Winter Garden FL 2006-2013. Assn of Chr Counselors 2006; Florida Bioethics Ntwk 2006-2012; Intl Conf of Police Chapl 2004; Tennessee Fed of Fire Chapalins 2013; The Coll of Pstr Supervision and Psych 2009. Bd Cert Clincl Chapl Coll of Pstr Supervision and Psych 2009; Bd Cert Pstr Counslr Coll of Pstr Supervision and Psych 2009.

WILCOXSON, JoAnn Vanessa (CFla) 154 Terry Lane, Benton TN 37307 B Panama City FL 1954 d William & Glory. MCC Intl Sem; BA U of Cntrl Florida; AA Valencia Cmnty. D 12/13/2008 Bp John Wadsworth Howe. m 10/18/1986 Frederick Dean Wilcoxson c 2.

WILD, Geoffrey Mileham (NwPa) PO Box 287, Grove City PA 16127 **Vic Ch Of The Epiph Grove City PA 2008-** B 1951 s Russell & Molly. BA Macquarie U AU 1999. D 1/27/2008 P 11/15/2008 Bp Sean Walter Rowe. m 9/11/1999 Cheryl Wild c 2.

WILD III, Philip Charles (La) 120 S New Hampshire St, Covington LA 70433 B Algiers LA 1946 s Philip & Anna Mae. AA Delgado Jr Coll 1969. D 10/23/2005 Bp Charles Edward Jenkins III. m 7/4/1974 Phyllis Eileen Wild c 3.

WILDE, Gary A (SwFla) 2306 Hermitage Blvd, Venice FL 34292 **R The Epis Ch Of The Gd Shpd Venice FL 2012-** B Holyoke MA 1952 s Harry & Joann. BA Moody Bible Inst 1978; MDiv Bethany TS Oakbrook 1985; Cert Nash 2006. D 5/27/2006 Bp John Wadsworth Howe P 12/9/2006 Bp Henry Irving Louttit. m 7/3/1973 Carol A Wilde c 2. Assoc S Mary's Epis Ch Bonita Sprg FL 2009-2012; R S Jn's Ch Moultrie GA 2006-2009.

WILDE, Gregory Dean (Mil) 6164 Colfax Ln S, Minneapolis MN 55419 **Prof Robert Webber Inst for Wrshp Stds 2003-** B Minneapolis MN 1958 s Stewart & Janet. MA U of Notre Dame 1992; DWS RE Webber Inst for WS 2009; MDiv Sewanee: The U So, TS 2010. D 12/20/2009 P 8/20/2010 Bp Edward Stuart Little II. m 9/6/1980 Janice A Wilde c 2. S Barth's Ch Pewaukee WI 2013-2017; Assoc R Trin Epis Ch Columbus GA 2010-2013. m3sterium@gmail.com

WILDER, Ginny (Del) Trinity Episcopal Church, 1108 N Adams St, Wilmington DE 19801 **Assoc Trin Par Wilmington DE 2012-** B Charleston SC 1972 d John & Virginia. BA Warren Wilson Coll 1996; MS Wstrn Carolina U 2001; MDiv VTS 2012. D 12/17/2011 P 6/30/2012 Bp Porter Taylor. m 2/15/2015 Barbara Jane Meyers. ginny@trinityparishde.org

WILDER, Marilyn (Spok) 617 10th St, Oroville WA 98844 B Tonasket WA 1940 d Joseph & Doris. D 6/11/2005 P 9/17/2006 Bp James E Waggoner Jr. m 3/28/1960 Dennis W Wilder c 2. Vic Trin Ch Oroville WA 2007-2012.

WILDER III, Tracy (SwFla) 13720 Sweat Loop Rd., Wamauma FL 33598 **Chapl to Ret Cler and spouses in Tampa Dnry Dio SW Florida Parrish FL 2015-** B Syracuse NY 1945 s Tracy & Barbara. BA Randolph-Macon Coll 1967; MDiv Yale DS 1970; VTS 1972. D 6/17/1972 P 12/16/1972 Bp Leland Stark. m 10/17/1998 Susan Louise Wilder c 2. R S Jn The Div Epis Ch Sun City Cntr FL 2001-2013; R S Matt's Epis Ch Horseheads NY 1996-2001; Cur Chr Ch Prince Geo's Par Rockville MD 1985-1997; R H Trin Epis Ch Dickinson TX 1979-1985; Asst S Dav's Ch Austin TX 1977-1979; Cur Chr Ch Short Hills NJ 1972-1976. Auth, *Angl Dig.* sandtwilder@yahoo.com

WILDGOOSE, Angelo S (NJ) 6361 Lancaster Ave, Philadelphia PA 19151 **S Mk's Ch Plainfield NJ 2016-** B Bahamas 1976 s Stanley & Charlsetta. Dip Pstr Stud Codrington Coll 1999; BA Codrington Coll 2000; BA U of the W Indies 2000; Dip Coll of the Bahamas 2002. Trans 11/17/2010 Bp John Bauerschmidt. m 12/1/2001 Tonya Elaine Wildgoose c 2. The Afr Epis Ch Of S Thos Philadelphia PA 2013-2015; Vic S Anselm's Epis Ch Nashville TN 2010-2012. stmarksplainfield@gmail.com

WILDMAN, Rachel Preston (Mass) 100 Pine Hill Rd, Bedford MA 01730 **S Paul's Epis Ch Bedford MA 2015-** B Concord NH 1975 d Timothy & Jennifer. BS Tufts U; Phd U Pgh; PhD U Pgh. D 3/7/2015 P 9/19/2015 Bp Andrew Marion Lenow Dietsche. m 6/26/2004 William David McGee c 2.

WILDSMITH, Joseph Ned (NJ) 808 S Delhi St, Philadelphia PA 19147 **Asst S Mk's Ch Philadelphia PA 2001-; 1972-** B Danville PA 1941 s Charles & Mabel. BA Lycoming Coll 1964; MDiv PDS 1968; U of Pennsylvania 1969. D 12/21/1968 P 3/1/1970 Bp Dean Theodore Stevenson. m 5/18/1968 Carol Wildsmith. Cur H Trin Ch Collingswood NJ 1970-1971.

WILE, Mary Lee (Me) 46 Willow Grove Rd, Brunswick ME 04011 **Chapl Maine Correctional Facility 2009-** B Boston MA 1947 d George & Elaine. Rad 1968; BA Colorado St U 1969; MA Colorado St U 1971; MTS Bangor TS 1999. D 12/1/2001 Bp Chilton Richardson Knudsen. m 6/24/1986 Richard L Wile c 2. Archd Dio Maine Portland ME 2010-2014; D S Paul's Ch Brunswick ME 2001-2010. Auth, "This Bread & This Cup," Living the Gd News, 2005; Auth, "Chr's Own Forever," Living the Gd News, 2003; Auth, "I Will w God's Help," Living the Gd News, 2000; Auth, "Monastic Life in the Epis Ch," Forw Mvmt, 1999; Auth, "The Stones Hold the Heat," *The Other Side*, 1999; Auth, "Books or Shoes?," *Educ Week*, 1997; Auth, "From Concept to Bookshelf," *Maine in Print*, 1996; Auth, "Ancient Rage," Larson Pub, 1995; Auth, "Serene

Light, Unspoken Word," *Daughters of Sarah*, 1995; Auth, "Star of Wonder," Forw Mvmt; Auth, "This Bread and This Cup," Living the Gd News; Auth, "Star of Wonder," Forw Mvmt. Assn for Epis Deacons 2001; Maine Educ Assn 1986; Sprtl Dir Intl 2007. Profsnl Pub Awd Maine Coun of Engl Lang Arts 1993.

WILEMON, Zane Howard (Cal) 81 N 2nd St, San Jose CA 95113 B Arlington TX 1977 s Stan & Cindy. BA U of Kansas 2000; MDiv Epis TS of the SW 2007. D 6/9/2007 P 1/26/2008 Bp Dean E Wolfe. m 9/7/2004 Natalie Wilemon. Assoc Trin Cathd San Jose CA 2007-2009; Yth Dir Trin Ch Lawr KS 2002-2004.

WILEY, George Bell (Kan) 2313 Willow Crk, Lawrence KS 66049 B Jackson TN 1946 s Bell & Mary. BA U NC 1968; MDiv Candler TS Emory U 1971; PhD Emory U 1978. D 12/10/1975 Bp Bennett Jones Sims P 7/10/1977 Bp John P Craine. m 11/13/1993 Kathleen Brandt c 1. Prof Of Rel Baker U Baldwin City KS 1977-2012; Chapl and Prof of Rel Baker U Baldwin City KS 1977-1986. Ed, "A Hist of Baldwin City Rel Institutions," *Fac Web Site*, Baker U, 2005; Ed, "Wrld Rel in NE Kansas," *Profiles of Rel Centers*, The Pluralism Proj, Harv, 2002. AAR 1980-2008. Meth Ch Exemplary Tchr Baker U 2011; Distinguished Fac Awd Baker U 1989; Osborne Chair Of Rel Baker U 1980; Phi Beta Kappa U NC 1968; Morehead Schlr U NC 1964.

WILEY, Henrietta Lovejoy (Md) Cathedral of the Incarnation, 4 E University Pkwy, Baltimore MD 21218 B Los Angeles CA 1969 d Spencer & Henrietta. BA U NC 1990; MA PSR 1993; PhD Harv 2004. D 6/29/2011 P 6/9/2012 Bp Thomas Edward Breidenthal. m 7/24/2004 Mary Ann Sykes.

WILEY, Judi A (SO) 234 N. High St., Hillsboro OH 45133 **R S Mary's Epis Ch Hillsboro OH 2009-** B Cumberland MD 1948 d Herbert & Dorothy. PhD Amer St U Honolulu 1998; MA Amer St U Honolulu HI 1998. D 1/23/2005 Bp Daniel Lee Swenson P 9/10/2005 Bp James Louis Jelinek. m 2/15/1992 Larry J Wiley c 3. Guardian ad Litem St of MN 5th Judicial Dist MN 2002-2006; S Andr's Ch Omaha NE 1991-1994.

WILEY, Ronald Lee (Neb) 102 Lakeview Rd, Fremont NE 68025 **Ret 1998-** B Chadron NE 1938 s Clyde & Irene. BA Chadron St Coll 1960; BD SWTS 1963; MA U of Nebraska 1973. D 6/8/1963 P 12/17/1963 Bp Russell T Rauscher. m 6/1/1984 Linda Lane Wiley c 1. S Jas' Epis Ch Fremont NE 1986-1998; Cn To Ord Dio Nebraska Omaha NE 1978-1987, 1978-1986; Vic S Mk's On The Campus Lincoln NE 1967-1978; Vic S Jn's Ch Valentine NE 1963-1967.

WILHELM, Joseph (Los) 404 W Santa Ana St., Ojai CA 93023 B Noblesville IN 1946 s Lowell & Eleanor. BA DePauw U 1969; MDiv SWTS 2005; U of Notre Dame 2005. D 4/15/2005 P 10/31/2005 Bp Edward Stuart Little II. m 1/31/1970 Barbara Brown Wilhelm c 2. S Andr's Epis Ch Ojai CA 2010-2015; S Steph's Par Beaumont CA 2005-2010.

WILHITE JR, Macdonald (WTenn) 108 N Auburndale St Apt 1006, Memphis TN 38104 **Died 10/14/2015** B Memphis TN 1947 s Macdonald & Mary. BBA U of Memphis 1971; MDiv SWTS 1974. D 6/23/1974 Bp William F Gates Jr P 6/15/1975 Bp John Vander Horst. m 8/15/1981 Dixie Wilhite. Non-par 1998-2015; Dio Fond du Lac Appleton WI 1995, Dn Wisconsin River Vlly Dnry 1987-1991, Stndg Com 1985-1994, Chair Of Mar & Fam Life Cmsn 1983-1984; Vic S Aug Antigo 1994-1997; St Ambr Epis Ch Antigo WI 1993-1997; R Ch Of S Jn The Bapt Wausau WI 1982-1993; Asst S Jas By The Sea La Jolla CA 1977-1982; Dio Tennessee Nashville TN 1975-1977; Vic S Andr's Epis Ch New Johnsonville TN 1975-1977; D S Tim's Ch Signal Mtn TN 1974-1975.

WILKE, Carl Edward (WMo) 3 Pursuit, #323, Aliso Viejo CA 92656 **S Mk's Ch S Milwaukee WI 2044-2046; Ret 1985-** B Milwaukee WI 1920 s Carl & Edith. BBA Marq 1941; MDiv GTS 1944; STM Nash 1956. D 4/12/1944 P 10/12/1944 Bp Benjamin F P Ivins. c 4. Asst S Jn's Ch Springfield MO 1989-1996; R Chr Epis Ch Springfield MO 1970-1985; R All SS Epis Ch Appleton WI 1957-1970; Cur Trin Ch Milwaukee WI 1953-1957; San Mateo Epis Ch Bellaire TX 1951-1953; R Calv Epis Ch Richmond TX 1947-1951; Chapl S Mary Chld's Hosp NYC 1946-1947. Hon Cn Cathd H Cross, Gaborone, Botswana 1984.

WILKERSON, Bonnie Carver (Ia) St Luke's Episcopal Church, 605 Avenue E, Fort Madison IA 52627 B Evanston IL 1950 d Richard & Caryl. BA Iowa Wesleyan Coll 1972; Mnstry Dvlpmt Team 2013. D 7/6/2013 P 2/1/2014 Bp Alan Scarfe. m 8/12/1972 Paul Idol Wilkerson c 1.

WILKERSON, Charles Edward (Md) St Luke's Episcopal Church, 1101 Bay Ridge Ave, Annapolis MD 21403 B New Church VA 1939 s Woodrow & Ruth. BS Salisbury U 1964; MLA JHU 1975. D 6/4/2005 Bp Robert Wilkes Ihloff.

WILKERSON, Christopher T (USC) **H Trin Par Epis Clemson SC 2017-** D 6/17/2017 Bp W illiam Andrew Waldo.

WILKES, Hugh E (Alb) 2717 2nd Ave, Watervliet NY 12189 **D S Eliz's Epis Ch Zephyrhills FL 2008-; Asst Cathd Of All SS Albany NY 1987-; Chr & S Barn Troy NY 1972-** B Troy NY 1927 s Winfield & Maude. D 12/21/1972 Bp Allen Webster Brown. D Trin Ch Lansingburgh Troy NY 2001-2006; Asst Ch Of Beth Saratoga Spg NY 1972-1996. OHC.

WILKES III, Joseph Warren (Mass) 186 Upham St, Melrose MA 02176 **Oral Surgeon Great Hill Dental Partnr LLC 2011-; S Andr's Ch Methuen MA 2007-** B Soneham MA 1953 s Joseph & Margaret. BS Tufts U 1975; DMD Harv

924

1979; MD Harv 1981; MDiv EDS 2006. D 6/3/2006 Bp M(Arvil) Thomas Shaw P 1/6/2007 Bp Gayle Harris. m 6/20/1981 Karen Barbara Harvey-Wilkes c 2.

WILKINS JR, Aaron Ellis (CGC) 6604 Carolina Ct, Mobile AL 36695 B Columbus MS 1929 s Aaron & Lucy. Auburn U; Sewanee: The U So, TS; Sprg Hill Coll; U of So Alabama. D 6/28/1981 P 5/1/1982 Bp Charles Farmer Duvall. m 12/5/1987 Virginia Ann Wilkins c 2. S Jn's Epis Ch Mobile AL 2005-2006; Chr Ch Cathd Mobile Mobile AL 2000; Ch Of S Marys-By-The-Sea Coden AL 1988-1991; Vic S Fran Ch Dauphin Islnd AL 1982-2000; Cur Trin Epis Ch Mobile AL 1981-1982.

WILKINS, Christopher Ian (WA) PO Box 207, St Marys City MD 20686 B New Brighton PA 1969 s Dennis & Theresa. BA Hav 1991; MTS Harvard DS 1993; PhD Bos 2000. D 6/13/2009 P 1/16/2010 Bp John Bryson Chane. m 10/9/1993 Hilary Laskey c 2. Chr Ch Chaptico MD 2011-2014; St Marys Par St Marys City MD 2009-2011.

WILKINS, Harriet Ann (NwT) 808 Stone Mountain Dr, Conroe TX 77302 **Died 7/8/2016** B Newport RI 1932 d Jackson & Louria. D 10/25/1985 Bp Sam Byron Hulsey. m 4/14/1987 James Roland Wilkins c 6.

WILKINS, Palmer Oliver (Cal) 58 Robinhood Dr, Novato CA 94945 **D Ch Of The H Innoc Corte Madera CA 1994-** B Saint Louis MO 1934 s Oliver & Dorothy. BA Antioch Coll 1970; Cert California TS 1977; ThB Amer Bible Coll 1980; MTh Amer Bible Coll 1982; MS Wstrn St U 1983; PhD Wstrn St U 1993. D 11/23/1977 Bp Chauncie Kilmer Myers. m 6/2/1956 Joyce Ann Wilkins. Pres Marin Dnry 1985-1986; Assoc S Paul's Epis Ch San Rafael CA 1982-1987; Asst S Fran Of Assisi Ch Novato CA 1977-1982. Chapl Ord S Jn Jerusalem 1990.

WILKINSON, Donald Charles (Mo) 17210 Fawn Cloud Ln, San Antonio TX 78248 **Asst Santa Fe Epis Mssn San Antonio TX 2012-; Ret 1999-** B Detroit MI 1934 s Laurel & Phyllis. BA U of Massachusetts 1964; MDiv Bex Sem 1967; Cov Sem S Louis MO 1981. D 6/17/1967 P 12/24/1967 Bp Roger W Blanchard. m 8/25/1968 Kathleen Carol Wilkinson c 2. Stff Chapl Methodist Hosp San Antonio TX 1996-1997; P-in-c Ch Of The Annunc Luling TX 1994-1996; P-in-c Ch Of The Ascen S Louis MO 1989-1992; P-in-c All SS Epis Ch Farmington MO 1987-1988; P-in-c S Pauls Epis Ch Ironton MO 1987-1988; Chapl Publ Sfty Dept Des Peres MO 1979-1992; R Ch Of The Epiph Kirkwood S Louis MO 1971-1986; Assoc Trin Ch Columbus OH 1967-1971.

WILKINSON, Ernest Benjamin (NwT) 727 W Browning Ave, Pampa TX 79065 B Pampa TX 1937 s Audrea & Lois. D NW Texas Sem Prog; BSA No Texas U 1959; Kennedy U 1990. D 10/29/2000 Bp C Wallis Ohl. m 7/23/1960 Mary Suzanne Wilkinson c 2.

WILKINSON, James Royse (Ky) 1804 Leawood Ct, Louisville KY 40222 **Hstgr Dio Kentucky Louisville KY 2010-, Mssn and Vision T/F 2004-2005** B Saint Louis MO 1943 s Oliver & Thelma. BS U of Missouri 1965; MDiv VTS 1968; MA LIU 1977; U of Basel Basel CH 1983. D 6/22/1968 Bp George Leslie Cadigan P 6/16/1969 Bp Charles Gresham Marmion. m 7/11/1987 Mary Kay Wilkinson. Temporary P S Paul's Jeffersonvlle IN 2010-2011; Chapl Cntr For Maritime Educ-Paducah 1998-2010; Mnstry on the River Seamens Ch Inst New York NY 1998-2010; Int S Mary's Ch Madisonville KY 1995-1996; Chapl DIVARTY 101 Airborne Div (Air Assault) Ft Campbell KY 1993-1995; P-t Asst St. Cathr's Ch of Engl Stuttgart BRD 1990-1993; Chapl US Army European Command Area Spprt Grp Stuttgart BRD 1990-1993; Chapl US Army 4th Aviation Brigade Giebelstadt BRD 1987-1990; Chapl 212th Field Artillery Brigade Ft Sill OK 1986-1987; Chapl US Army Cmnty Activity Fam Counslg Ft Sill OK 1985-1986; Chapl US Army Trng Cntr Ft Sill OK 1983-1985; P-t P St. Mk's Ch of Engl Lucerne CH 1982-1983; P-t Asst St. Nich' Ch of Engl Basel CH 1982-1983; Chapl US Mltry Acad W Point NY 1980-1982; Chapl 11th Air Defense Signal BN 32nd ADCOM Darmstadt BRD 1977-1980; P-in-c St. Jos's Korean-Amer Calv Epis NYC 1976-1977; Chapl US Army Garrison Yongsan Korea 1975-1976; Chapl Off Of Bsh For ArmdF New York NY 1974-1995; Chapl US Army Engr Sch Ft Belvoir VA 1974-1975; Chapl DeWitt US Army Hosp Ft Belvoir VA 1974; Int Pstr First Chr (Disciples of Chr) Fulton KY 1973-1974; S Paul's Ch Hickman KY 1970-1974; Vic Trin Epis Ch Fulton KY 1970-1974; Chapl US Army Reserve 100th Div (Trng) Paducah KY 1970-1974; Chapl US Army Reserve 168th Direct Spprt Grp Louisville KY 1969-1970; S Jas Ch Pewee Vlly KY 1968-1970; Asst S Lk's Ch Louisville KY 1968-1970. Hymn Soc of the Untd States and Can. Hon Assoc R Pohick Epis Ch, Fairfax, Va 1974.

WILKINSON, John Preston (SwVa) 1207 Middlebrook Rd, Staunton VA 24401 B Milwaukee WI 1937 s John & Mary. BS GW; MA Pepperdine U. D 2/14/2003 Bp Neff Powell. m 7/18/1998 Donna Fa Wilkinson c 3. D Trin Ch Staunton VA 2003-2010.

WILKINSON, Joyce Ann (WVa) D 5/11/2002 P 11/16/2002 Bp Larry Maze.

WILKINSON, Julia Sierra (Ga) Christ Church Episcopal, 18 Abercorn St, Savannah GA 31401 **Asst Chr Ch Epis Savannah GA 2011-** B Atlanta GA 1986 d Remi & Julia. BA Agnes Scott Coll 2008. D 2/11/2011 P 2/18/2012 Bp Scott Anson Benhase. m 4/13/2013 Rudolph P Reyes c 1.

WILKINSON, Kirsteen (Ind) 7834 Grand Gulch Dr, Indianapolis IN 46239 **R S Mk's Ch Plainfield IN 2015-, P-in-c 2011-2015; P-in-c Dio Indianapolis In-**dianapolis IN 2009-, 2006-2011 B Famagusta Cyprus 1961 d Richard & Anne. BS Pur 1984; MS Butler U 1990; MDiv SWTS 2006. D 6/24/2006 P 2/18/2007 Bp Cate Waynick. c 3. Dioc Admin of theSafeguarding Prog Dio Indianapolis 2010-2013; Assoc S Alb's Ch Indianapolis IN 2010-2012; Vic S Tim's Ch Indianapolis IN 2008-2011. stmarksrector@att.net

WILKINSON, Marcia Campbell (Ala) 6634 31st Pl NW, Washington DC 20015 B New London CT 1944 d William & Margaret. VTS; RN New Engl Bapt Hosp 1965; BA Hood Coll 1990; MDiv Luth TS at Gettysburg 1996. D 6/9/1995 Bp Charlie Fuller Mcnutt Jr P 3/2/1996 Bp Michael Whittington Creighton. m 4/23/1965 Rowland Wilkinson c 2. Assoc R All SS' Epis Ch Chevy Chase MD 2005-2009; Cn Mssnr The Cathd Ch Of The Adv Birmingham AL 2000-2005; S Jn's Epis Ch Carlisle PA 1995-2000; Dio Cntrl Pennsylvania Harrisburg PA 1995-1996.

WILKINSON, Mark David (SVa) St. Aidan's Episc Church, 3201 Edinburgh Dr., Virginia Beach VA 23452 **R S Aid's Ch Virginia Bch VA 2007-** B Lakewood OH 1955 s Donald & Betty. BA Kent St U 1976; BA Kent St U 1983; MDiv VTS 2004. D 6/12/2004 Bp Mark Hollingsworth Jr P 1/8/2005 Bp Gayle Harris. m 9/7/1974 Wendy Wilkinson c 2. Cur The Ch Of The H Sprt Orleans MA 2004-2007. rector@aidanvbva.org

WILKINSON, Mary Suzanne (NwT) 727 W Browning Ave, Pampa TX 79065 B Dallas TX 1940 d Jay & Ioha. BSA No Texas U 1960; MS Kennedy U 1990; Study Progam NWT Sem Prog D 2000. D 10/29/2000 Bp C Wallis Ohl. m 7/23/1960 Ernest Benjamin Wilkinson c 2.

WILKINSON, Shivaun Renee (WA) 3820 Aspen Hill Rd, Silver Spring MD 20906 B Wilmington DE 1984 d Monteiro & Robin. BA U CA 2005; Bachelor's of Arts U CA Berkeley 2005; Mstr of Div VTS 2012; MDiv VTS 2012. D 6/9/2012 Bp Jim Mathes P 1/26/2013 Bp Mariann Edgar Budde. m 8/16/2008 Christopher John Wilkinson c 1. Mssnr for Par Engagement S Nich Epis Ch Germantown MD 2013-2017; Asst to the R for Chld, Yth and Families S Mary Magd Ch Silver Sprg MD 2012-2013; S Marg's Epis Ch Palm Desert CA 2005-2009.

WILKINSON, Wendy (SVa) Good Samaritan Episcopal Church, 848 Baker Rd, Virginia Beach VA 23462 **Cbury Epis Campus Mnstry Norfolk VA 2014-; P-in-c Gd Samar Epis Ch Virginia Bch VA 2013-** B Fairview Park OH 1954 d William & Emily. BME Kent St U 1976; MA JCU 2000; MDiv VTS 2004. D 6/9/2012 P 12/15/2012 Bp Herman Hollerith IV. m 9/7/1974 Mark David Wilkinson c 2. wendywilk54@verizon.net

WILLARD V, John Dayton (SVa) 1634 Orchard Beach Rd, Annapolis MD 21409 **Ch of the Gd Shpd Mc Kenney VA 2015-** B Annapolis MD 1965 s John & Josephine. BA Loyola U 1989; MA U of Maryland Baltimore Cnty 2003; MA U of Maryland Baltimore Cnty 2014; Cert Virginian TS 2014; Cert Virginian TS 2014. D 6/14/2014 Bp Joe Goodwin Burnett P 1/11/2015 Bp Mary Douglas Glasspool. m 11/2/1985 Nancy J Willard c 2. The Samar Cmnty Inc. Baltimore MD 2014-2015.

WILLARD, Neil Alan (Tex) Palmer Memorial Church, 6221 Main St, Houston TX 77030 **P Palmer Memi Ch Houston TX 2014-** B High Point NC 1970 s Clyde & Shirley. BA Wake Forest U 1992; MDiv Yale DS 1995. D 6/29/1996 Bp Robert Carroll Johnson Jr P 6/29/1997 Bp Edward Lloyd Salmon Jr. m 10/11/2003 Carrie D Willard c 2. R S Steph The Mtyr Ch Minneapolis MN 2007-2014; Assoc Bruton Par Williamsburg VA 2001-2007; Cur All SS Ch Hilton Hd Island SC 1998-2001; P-in-c The Epis Ch Of The Resurr Myrtle Bch SC 1996-1998; Bp's Clerk Dio Virginia Richmond VA 1995-1996. Phi Beta Kappa. nwillard@palmerchurch.org

WILLARD JR, Wilson Howard (SO) 1305 Cutter St, Cincinnati OH 45203 **Asst Calv Ch Cincinnati OH 2016-, Assoc 2003-2016; Ret Ohio 1999-** B Lochgelly WV 1937 s Wilson & Jessie. BA Berea Coll 1959; STB GTS 1963. D 6/5/1963 P 12/18/1963 Bp Wilburn Camrock Campbell. c 3. Cn Dio Sthrn Ohio Cincinnati OH 1991-1998. Hon Cn Chr Ch Cathd 1993.

WILLARD-WILLIFORD, Joyce Ann (CFla) 5625 Holy Trinity Dr, Melbourne FL 32940 **Chapl H Trin Epis Acad Melbourne FL 2009-** B Memphis TN 1953 d Herald & Mary. BA U of Florida 1974; BSN U of Florida 1976; MPA U of Cntrl Florida 1990; MDiv Sewanee: The U So, TS 2009. D 5/30/2009 P 12/5/2009 Bp John Wadsworth Howe. m 12/28/1974 Mark Williford c 2.

WILLCOX, Halley Luddy (At) 805 Mount Vernon Hwy Nw, Atlanta GA 30327 **Pstr Counslr, Suppy P AAPC Charlottesville VA 2004-** B Camden NJ 1952 d Edward & Mary. BS U of Maryland 1975; MDiv Wesley TS 1980; DMin Andover-Newton TS 1984; Cert Boston Inst of Psych 1984. D 8/15/1981 Bp Morris Fairchild Arnold P 3/5/1982 Bp William Benjamin Spofford. m 7/3/2004 Robert Hamilton Strotz c 2. Supply P Emm Ch Glenmore Buckingham VA 2005-2015; Ch Of Our Sav Charlottesvlle VA 2001-2003; Upper Sch Chapl H Innoc Ch Atlanta GA 1997-2000; H Innoc' Epis Sch Atlanta GA 1997-2000; Hd Chapl Lovett Sch Atlanta GA 1995-1997; Chapl Belmont Chap at S Mk's Sch Southborough MA 1989-1995; Assoc R S Mk's Ch Southborough MA 1989-1994; Pstr Of Psychol 1989-1990; R S Paul's Epis Ch Hopkinton MA 1984-1989; Educ Assoc S Paul's Ch Natick MA 1981-1984. AAPC 1984. willcoxhalley@yahoo.com

W

WILLE, Elizabeth Suzanne (Ind) 1559 N Central Ave, Indianapolis IN 46202 **All SS Ch Indianapolis IN 2012-; Int Pstr Chr Ch Warwick NY 2012-, Assoc R 2011, Asst P 2009-2012; Advsry Bd, Epis New Yorker Dio New York New York NY 2011-** B Pittsburgh PA 1970 d Richard & Elizabeth. AB Randolph-Macon Coll 1992; MA Indiana U 1996; MDiv Ya Berk 2009. D 6/6/2009 Bp Jeff Lee P 12/9/2009 Bp Catherine Scimeca Roskam. m 1/18/2012 Tracey Elizabeth Lemon. Writer, "Sometimes Only the Flesh Will Do: Musing on the Faithful Use of Tech," *The Epis New Yorker*, Epis Dio New York, 2011; Writer, "Water is a Chr Issue," *The Epis New Yorker*, Epis Dio New York, 2011. E. Wm Muehl Prize in Preaching Ya Berk 2009; scl Randolph-Macon Wmn's Coll 1992.

WILLEMS, James Rutherford (Los) 561 48th Street, Oakland CA 94609 **Ret 2000-** B Coronado CA 1944 s Everleigh & Miriam. BA San Diego St U 1966; MDiv EDS 1984; MA Bos 1988. D 6/9/1984 P 4/17/1985 Bp William Edwin Swing. m 10/6/2002 Christina Marie Fernandez c 1. Cn To Ordnry Dio Rhode Island Providence RI 1988-1990, 1987-1988, Dir of the Abrahamic Accord 1984-1989; Asst Calv Ch Pascoag RI 1986-1995; Assoc S Andr's Epis Ch Ojai CA 1985-2000; Dio California San Francisco CA 1984-1985; Asst S Jn's Epis Ch Westwood MA 1984-1985. Auth, "Meditation And Physical Pain," *Ariadnes Web*, 1998; Auth, "Mystery Of The Self," *Theosophist*, 1998; Auth, "The Harlequin Poems," Isthmus Press, 1976; Auth, "Opening The Cube (Poetry)," Tree Books, 1975. Mem Of Pen. Mem Pen Poets, Essayists, Novelists 1992.

WILLERER, Rhonda (Fla) St. Patrick's Episcopal Church, 1221 State Rd 13, Saint Johns FL 32259 **R St Pat's Epis Ch S Johns FL 2014-** B Houston TX 1957 d James & Adella. BS U of N Florida 2001; MDiv Sewanee: The U So, TS 2007. D 5/27/2007 P 12/9/2007 Bp Samuel Johnson Howard. m 6/10/1978 Max Willerer c 2. Assoc R Ch Of Our Sav Jacksonville FL 2008-2014; Cur All SS Epis Ch Jacksonville FL 2007-2008. mtrronnie.stpatricks@gmail.com

WILLIAMS JR, A Lenwood (Miss) 9378 Harroway Rd, Summerville SC 29485 B Charleston SC 1940 s Arthur & Belva. BA Wofford Coll 1963; MDiv Epis TS in Kentucky 1982. D 6/5/1982 Bp Charles Gresham Marmion P 12/1/1982 Bp Duncan Montgomery Gray Jr. c 3. Vic S Timothys Epis Ch Southaven MS 1986-2002; Vic Immac Winona MS 1982-1986; Vic S Mary's Ch Lexington MS 1982-1986.

WILLIAMS, Alfredo R (Dal) 1516 N Leland Ave, Indianapolis IN 46219 **Assoc S Barn Ch Garland TX 2011-** B 1944 s Alfredo & Servia. LTh U of Santo Domingo Santo Domingo Do 1981. Trans 1/1/2000. m 7/14/1995 Maria Williams c 3. Dio Dallas Dallas TX 2007-2010; P Chr Ch Cathd Indianapolis IN 2000-2007; Dio Cuernavaca 1997-2000; Iglesia Epis Del Ecuador Quito 1996-1997; Vic S Gabr Consuelo Dominican Republic 1982-1997; Dio The Dominican Republic (Iglesia Epis Dominicana) Gazcue Santo Domingo 1981-1995; D S Gabr Consuelo Dominican Republic 1981-1982; M-in-c Santiago Apos Angelina Dominican Republic 1981-1982.

WILLIAMS, Alina Somodevilla (La) PO Box 126, Baton Rouge LA 70821 **The Par Epis Sch Dallas TX 2015-** B Dallas TX 1980 d Rene & Lana. BS TCU 2003; MDiv SMU Perkins 2009. D 12/17/2011 P 6/30/2012 Bp Morris King Thompson Jr. m 6/13/2009 Jared Roland Williams c 1. S Jas Epis Ch Baton Rouge LA 2012-2013.

WILLIAMS, Alton Paul (CPa) 5 Greenway Dr, Mechanicsburg PA 17055 **D Cathd Ch Of S Steph Harrisburg PA 1994-** B Leonard TX 1919 s George & Maude. D 6/7/1974 Bp Dean Theodore Stevenson. m 7/24/1948 Frances A Williams c 2. Asst S Lk's Epis Ch Mechanicsburg PA 1974-1992.

WILLIAMS, Anne Elizabeth (Ia) PO Box 33, Anamosa IA 52205 B Morgantown WV 1947 d Neal & Anna Margaret. BA W Virginia U 1970; MA Estrn Michigan U 1973. D 5/23/2003 P 11/23/2003 Bp Alan Scarfe. m 4/3/1970 Arthur Russell Williams c 3.

✠ **WILLIAMS JR, The Rt Rev Arthur** (O) 25530 Edgecliff Dr, Euclid OH 44132 **Asstg Bp of Ohio Dio Ohio Cleveland 2005-, Ret Bp Suffr Of Ohio 2003-, Bp Suffr of Ohio 1986-2002, Dep Gc 1979-1986; Epis Visitor Ord Of S Ben Three Rivers MI 2000-** B Providence RI 1935 s Arthur & Eleanor. BA Br 1957; MDiv GTS 1964; MA U MI 1974. D 6/20/1964 P 3/27/1965 Bp John S Higgins Con 10/11/1986 for O. m 7/27/1985 Lynette R Williams. Int Dir Ethnic Congrl Dvlpmt - PBp's Stff 2003-2007; Chair Commision On Ch & Human Sxlty 2000-2003; VP HOB 1995-2003; Com Mem Justice Peace Integrity Creation 1994-1997; Com Mem HOB Com To End Racism 1993-2000; Com Mem PB and Liturg Com of the GC 1991-2000; Chair/Mem Epis Com for Black Mnstry 1988-1990; Mem ECEC 1982-1988; Mem JSCPBF 1980-1991; Mem HOD Advsry Com 1980-1985; Trst The GTS 1979-1988; Asst To Bp, Mnstry Deploy & Urban Affrs Dio Michigan Detroit MI 1970-1977; Assoc Gr Ch Detroit MI 1968-1969; Sub-Dn Cathd Of S Jn Providence RI 1967-1968; Asst S Mk's Epis Ch Riverside RI 1965-1967; Clarence Horner Fell Gr Ch In Providence Providence RI 1964-1965; Trst The GTS New York NY 1979-1988. Chrmn Ed Com, "Lift Every Voice & Sing, II," Ch Hymnal Corp., 1993. EPF 1977; UBE 1967. DD GTS 1987.

WILLIAMS, Arthur Wordsworth Lonfellow (NY) 3412 103rd St, Corona NY 11368 B 1928 s Cyril & Hilda. SWTS 1975; MDiv Interdenominational Theol Cntr 1978. D 6/10/1989 Bp Paul Moore Jr. c 1. S Phil's Ch New York NY 1991-1994; Admin Newark Epis Mnstry & Mssn Com 1979-1980; Asst Chapl Cbury Cntr Atlanta GA 1977-1978.

WILLIAMS, Barbara Farrar (SVa) P O Box 62184, Virginia Beach VA 23466 B Newport News VA 1945 d William & Florence. Diac Sch-Duke Durham NC. D 6/4/2005 Bp David Conner Bane Jr. m 12/15/2007 Ronald Charles Williams c 2. S Steph's Ch Newport News VA 2006-2008.

WILLIAMS, Brendan E (Cal) **Gr And S Steph's Epis Ch Colorado Sprg CO 2016-** D 6/11/2016 Bp Marc Handley Andrus.

WILLIAMS, Bruce McKennie (RG) 7201 San Benito St Nw, Albuquerque NM 87120 **Ret 1993-** B Pittsfield MA 1930 s Lester & Ethel. BMus Peabody Conservatory of Mus 1953; GO AGO 1956; MM Peabody Conservatory of Mus 1956; STB GTS 1960; LIU 1970; PhD Pacific Wstrn U Long Bch 1983. D 6/22/1960 Bp Robert McConnell Hatch P 12/17/1960 Bp Horace W B Donegan. m 9/24/1955 Charlotte Ellen Williams c 3. Cn S Jn's Cathd Albuquerque NM 1990-1993, Asst To Dn 1986-1990; R S Phil's Ch Brooklyn NY 1980-1986; Chapl (Col) US Army 1962-1980; Asst Cathd Of St Jn The Div New York NY 1960-1962; Ecum Off Dio The Rio Grande Albuquerque 1990-1996. Auth, "Adv;Christmas;Lent;Passion;Easter(Three);Pentecost;Patriotic Occasions;Healing;The Ch Year," *The Ix Lessons (Printed Separately)*, 2000; Auth, "Pstr Care Of Drug Abusers," Priv Printing, 1983. AGO 1946; AAM 1988; Assn Of Dioc Liturgies And Musicians Com 1981-2001; Bd Dir, The Sprtl Renwl Cntr:Albuquerque 2007; EDEO 1996-2000; Exec Bd,AGO; Albuquerque 1987-2005. Fifty Year Cert AGO 1993; Assoc AGO 1956.

WILLIAMS, Carolynne Juanita Grant (At) 2088 Cloverdale Dr Se, Atlanta GA 30316 **Cn Asst. - Pstr Care Cathd Of S Phil Atlanta GA 1999-** B Albany GA 1948 d Edward & Rubye. BA Spelman Coll 1969; MDiv Interdenominational Theol Cntr 1995. D 7/31/1999 P 2/5/2000 Bp Frank Kellogg Allan. m 11/24/1971 Perry E Williams c 2.

WILLIAMS, Cecil David (Nwk) 515 Parker St, Newark NJ 07104 **Off Bro of the Venerable Ord of S Jn of Jerusalem 2017-; Off Bro The Venerable Ord of S Jn of Jerusalem 2013-** B Valhalla NY 1942 s Cecil & Colithia. Cntrl Coll; Chr TS; BA SUNY 1991; GTF 1994; DMin GTF 1998. D 12/14/1974 Bp James Stuart Wetmore P 12/20/1975 Bp Harold Louis Wright. Pres UBE 2008-2013; Trin And S Phil's Cathd Newark NJ 2000-2008; R S Geo's Ch Brooklyn NY 1984-2000; Epis Mssn Soc New York NY 1981-1984; Sr Chapl Riker's Island Prison 1979-1984; Cur S Matt & S Tim Brooklyn NY 1975-1979; The Ch of S Matt And S Tim New York NY 1975-1979. Auth, "Adversary," 1986.

WILLIAMS, Colin Harrington (CNY) 2850 SW Scenic Drive, Portland OR 97225 **Assoc Epis Par Of S Jn The Bapt Portland OR 2005-** B Fayetteville NC 1970 s William & Angeline. Ya Berk; BA Cor 1992; MDiv Yale DS 1995; MBA UNC Chap Hill 2004. D 11/11/1995 P 10/26/1996 Bp David Bruce Joslin. m 9/5/2004 Lindsey Woodley Williams c 2. Cur Calv Ch Pittsburgh PA 1997-2001; Cur Ch Of The Resurr Oswego NY 1996-1997; Asst Chr Ch Clayton NY 1995; St Jn's Ch Cape Vinc NY 1995. colin@encompasswa.com

WILLIAMS, Courtlyn (Chi) 425 Laurel Ave, Highland Park IL 60035 **Trin Ch Highland Pk IL 2015-** B Bellingham WA 1963 s Maurice & Virginia. BS NWU 2005; MDiv SWTS 2008. D 6/7/2008 P 12/6/2008 Bp Jeff Lee. m 8/6/1988 Julie DeGraff Williams c 3. S Thos' Epis Ch Eugene OR 2009-2015; Assoc The Epis Ch Of S Jas The Less Northfield IL 2008-2009. office@trinitychurchhp.org

WILLIAMS, David Alexander (EC) 115 NE 66th Street, Oak Island NC 28645 **Died 3/6/2016** B Indianapolis IN 1936 s Wayne & Sarah. AA Prince Geo Cmnty Coll 1976; BS Appalachian St U 1980; MDiv VTS 1984. D 12/18/1982 P 4/30/1985 Bp William Gillette Weinhauer. m 10/7/1961 Henrietta R Smith c 2. long term supply The Ch of the Gd Shpd Fayetteville NC 2010-2011; S Phil's Ch Southport NC 2006-2010; S Jas Epis Ch Lenoir NC 1999-2000; Vic S Jas Ch New Castle IN 1989-1998; Vic & P-in-c The Sav Epis Ch Newland NC 1989-1998; R S Eliz's Ch Roanoke VA 1986-1987; D Ch Of The H Cross Valle Crucis NC 1982-1985. vicarhaven@yahoo.com

WILLIAMS, David Anthony (SC) St. Stephen's Episcopal Church, 67 Anson St, Charleston SC 29401 B Philadelphia PA 1945 s Percy & Clementine. BA DeSales U 1969; MDiv EDS 1972; DMin Andover Newton TS 1973. D 7/24/1972 P 1/13/1973 Bp Robert Lionne DeWitt. m 10/24/1970 Linda Williams. R S Steph's Epis Ch Charleston SC 2004-2015; Assoc R S Jn's Ch Georgetown Par Washington DC 1999-2004; Non-par 1978-1999; Sr. Asst Min S Jn's Ch Lafayette Sq Washington DC 1973-1978. "Proper Reaction To Epis Ch Changes Is Real Challenge," Post & Courier Of So Carolina, 2005; "Assorted arts," Jubilate Deo (Dio So Carolina), 2004. Dplma AAPC.

WILLIAMS, David R (NC) 1406 Victoria Ct, Elon NC 27244 B Wilmington DE 1945 s John & Frances. BA Roa 1968; MDiv VTS 1973. D 6/5/1972 P 4/15/1973 Bp Wilburn Camrock Campbell. m 2/4/1977 Sarah B Williams c 4. R Ch Of The H Comf Burlington NC 1985-2010; Imm Ch-On-The-Hill Alexandria VA 1982-1985; Ch Of The Epiph Cape Coral FL 1981-1982; Assoc Frederick Par VA 1974-1979; Chr Epis Ch Winchester VA 1974-1978; Vic Chr Memi Ch Williamstown WV 1972-1974.

WILLIAMS OSB, Donald B (Kan) 2510 Grand Blvd. #1103, Kansas City MO 64108 **D S Mich And All Ang Ch Mssn KS 2010-; Assoc Chapl Kansas U**

Med Cntr Kansas City KS 2008- B Oakland CA 1934 s Alan & Martha. BS U of Cntrl Missouri 1974; MS U of Cntrl Missouri 1975; EdS U of Cntrl Missouri 1977. D 1/18/2003 Bp William Edward Smalley. m 6/9/1958 Patricia Ann Williams c 2. D Ch Of The Gd Shpd Kansas City MO 2003-2006.

WILLIAMS, Douglas Elliott (ECR) 1718 Crater Lake Ave, Milpitas CA 95035 B San Bernardino CA 1938 s Keith & Elizabeth. BA U CA 1960; GOE Ripon Coll Cuddesdon 1962; GTS 1963; U of Redlands 1967. D 9/5/1963 P 3/1/1964 Bp Francis E I Bloy. m 10/25/1963 Helene Margaret Williams c 2. Trin Cathd San Jose CA 1995-2000, Asst 1982-1993; Asst Ch Of S Jos Milpitas CA 1980-1981, Asst 1969-1979; S Lk's Epis Ch Jolon CA 1973-1974; S Mk's Ch King City CA 1973-1974; LocTen S Matt's Ch San Ardo CA 1973-1974; Asst S Lk's Ch Los Gatos CA 1971-1980; Asst Gd Samar Epis Ch San Jose CA 1970-1971; Asst S Phil's Ch San Jose CA 1968-1969; Chapl San Miguel Sch San Diego CA 1967-1968; Cur Trin Epis Ch Redlands CA 1966-1967; Vic Ascen Sunnymead CA 1963-1966; Vic S Andr's By The Lake Lake Elsinore CA 1963-1964.

WILLIAMS, Douglas M (Colo) 28 Cunningham Pond Rd, Peterborough NH 03458 **Non-par 1967-** B Springfield MA 1934 s Ralph & Corilla. BA Amh 1956; MDiv VTS 1960; CG Jung Inst 1981. D 6/25/1960 P 1/1/1961 Bp Robert McConnell Hatch. m 9/20/1987 Joy E Jacobs c 2. Logos CO 1967-1977; Logos Colorado Spg CO 1967-1977; Chapl S Agnes Sch Alexandria VA 1966-1967; Chapl Florida St U In Tallahassee 1964-1966; Cur S Steph's Ch Pittsfield MA 1960-1964.

WILLIAMS, Edward Earl (NY) B 1943 D 5/26/1973 P 5/18/1975 Bp Addison Hosea. All Souls Ch New York NY 1975-1976.

WILLIAMS, Edward Satterfield (Ga) 353 Midway Circ, Brunswick GA 31523 **D Emer S Mk's Ch Brunswick GA 2000-** B Wilmington DE 1932 s Edward & Kathleen. Washington Coll 1953; EFM Sewanee: The U So, TS 1999. D 1/14/2000 Bp Henry Irving Louttit. m 11/23/1980 Barbara S Williams c 1.

WILLIAMS, Elizabeth Ann (Los) 512 E Williams St, Barstow CA 92311 **P-in-c S Alb's Epis Ch Yucaipa CA 2013-** B Oceanside CA 1956 BS Cal Poly 1981; MA Chapman U 2008; MDiv ETSBH 2011. D 6/11/2011 P 1/7/2012 Bp Mary Douglas Glasspool. m 5/1/1993 David Morgan Thayer c 4. S Jas' Sch Los Angeles CA 2012-2013; S Paul's Mssn Barstow CA 2011-2013. ethayer93@gmail.com

WILLIAMS, Eric (Mich) 1948 Hunters Ridge Dr, Bloomfield Hills MI 48304 **S Phil's Epis Ch Rochester MI 2017-** B Los Angeles CA 1965 s Kenneth & Sally. BA Wms 1986; MDiv GTS 1992. D 6/13/1992 P 12/19/1992 Bp Andrew Frederick Wissemann. m 10/8/1994 Susan Anslow c 2. Dio Michigan Detroit MI 2014-2016; Int Trin Ch Belleville MI 2013-2014; R S Lk's Epis Ch Jamestown NY 2000-2012; P-t Asst Ch Of The H Comm Lake View NY 1994-1999; S Paul's Cathd Buffalo NY 1994-1995; Cur S Steph's Ch Pittsfield MA 1992-1994. ericw@stpfeeds.org

WILLIAMS JR, Ernest Franklin (Los) 1438 Coronado Ter, Los Angeles CA 90026 **Vol Cler All SS Epis Ch 1992-** B Pelham GA 1948 s Ernest & Irene. BBA Georgia St U 1971; MDiv GTS 1988; MBA Amer Jewish U 2004. D 6/25/1988 P 6/1/1989 Bp Frederick Houk Borsch. m 8/30/2014 Randy Thomas Wiech. The Gooden Cntr Pasadena CA 1992-2013; Assoc S Fran' Par Palos Verdes Estates CA 1989-1991; Chapl To Bp Of Los Angeles Dio Los Angeles Los Angeles CA 1988-1989, Exec Dir Of The Bp Gooden Hm 1991-, Bp's Chapl 1988-1989. Soc Of S Paul.

WILLIAMS, Florence Darcy (Eas) Emmanuel Episcopal Church, PO Box 875, Chestertown MD 21620 **R Emm Epis Ch Chestertown MD 2016-** B Bronxville NY 1947 d Philip & Florence. BS Coll of St Eliz 1969; MS Rutgers U 1973; PhD Rutgers U 1977; MA VTS 2013. D 9/29/2012 P 6/8/2013 Bp Bud Shand. m 6/24/1972 Joseph Campbell Williams c 2. D Dio Easton Easton MD 2012-2013. drdarcy.williams@gmail.com

WILLIAMS, Francis Edward (RG) 1020 Sable Circle, Las Cruces NM 88001 **Asst S Jas' Epis Ch Las Cruces NM 2006-; Ret 1988-** B Omaha NE 1926 s Leslie & Lucy. BA Harv 1947; BD Nash 1951; BA Hebr Un Coll 1953; STM Nash 1954; PhD Oxf GB 1954; PhD Oxf GB 1961. D 4/10/1951 P 10/12/1951 Bp Benjamin F P Ivins. m 9/18/1954 Charlotte Williams c 3. Assoc St Lk's Epis Ch Anth NM 1992-1998; Asst All SS Epis Ch El Paso TX 1988-1990; Chapl Dio The Rio Grande Albuquerque 1976-1986; 1974-1975; Sch Hdmstr S Paul's Epis Ch Visalia CA 1971-1974; R Epis Ch Of S Anne Stockton CA 1969-1971; Prncpl S Mich Par Day Sch Tucson AZ 1964-1969; Chapl Tuller Sch Tucson AZ 1960-1964; R S Andr's Milwaukee WI 1956-1960; P S Andr's Ch Milwaukee WI 1955-1956; 1952-1954. Auth, "Panarion of Epiphanius of Salamis," *Bk II and III. De Fide Revised and Expanded*, Brill, 2013; Auth, "Panarion of Epiphanius of Salamis," *Bk I Revised and Expanded*, Brill, 2008; Auth, *Mntl Perception: A Commentary on NHC VI*, Brill, 2001; Auth, "Panarion of Epiphanius of Salamis," *Bk II and III*, Brill, 1994; Auth, "Panarion of Epiphanius of Salamis," *Bk I*, Brill, 1988. Inst For Antiquity and Chrsnty 1963; SBL 1953.

WILLIAMS, Gary Wayne (Okla) 3804 Cobble Cir, Norman OK 73072 B Norman OK 1933 s Wayne & Willie. Juris Doctorate U of Oklahoma 1958; BBA U of Oklahoma 1958. D 6/17/1966 Bp Chilton R Powell. m 12/31/1986 Deborah Williams c 2. Asst S Paul's Cathd Oklahoma City OK 2000-2006; Asst S Jn's Ch Norman OK 1989-2000, Asst 1968-1988; Non-par 1983-1989; Asst

S Mich's Epis Ch Norman OK 1979-1983; Asst S Mary Magd Norman OK 1974-1977; Asst All Souls Epis Ch Oklahoma City OK 1967-1968; Asst S Mths Oklahoma City OK 1966-1967.

WILLIAMS, Glenn Thomas (ND) 3613 River Dr S, Fargo ND 58104 **Asst Geth Cathd Fargo ND 2003-** B Minneapolis MN 1948 s Milton & Judy. BS U of No Dakota 1970. D 5/10/2002 P 5/9/2003 Bp Andrew Fairfield. m 3/13/1971 Jane Arman Williams c 3.

WILLIAMS, Glen Parker (WMich) 12057 S Elk Run, Traverse City MI 49684 **Non-par 1970-** B Woodbridge NJ 1925 s Carl & Emilie. BA Hobart and Wm Smith Colleges 1949; MA U of Pennsylvania 1950; MTh PDS 1953; MA Wstrn Michigan U 1971. D 4/25/1953 P 10/1/1953 Bp Wallace J Gardner. m 9/11/1948 Dorothy Mary Williams c 4. R S Barn Kalamazoo MI 1963-1970; Headmaster Trin Sch Baton Rouge LA 1961-1963; Chapl Kemper Sch Boonville MO 1959-1961; R Ch Of Our Merc Sav Penns Grove NJ 1955-1959; Rgstr PDS PA 1955-1956; Lectr In Eccl Hist And Homil PDS PA 1954-1956; R S Mk's Ch Hammonton NJ 1953-1955; S Ptr's Ch Medford NJ 1953-1955.

WILLIAMS, Henrietta R (Ind) 115 Ne 66th St, Oak Island NC 28465 **Chaplian Carillon Assisted Living Southport NC 2012-; D S Phil's Ch Southport NC 2006-, D 2004-2012; D Dio E Carolina Kinston NC 2004-** B Windsor NC 1940 d William & Margaret. AA Prince Geo Cmnty Coll 1974; BA Bowie St U 1976; MTS VTS 1978. D 6/24/1993 Bp Edward Witker Jones. D S Mary Of The Hills Epis Par Blowing Rock NC 1999-2004; D S Jas Ch New Castle IN 1993-1999.

WILLIAMS, Henry N (Pa) 1029 Fox Hollow Rd, Shermans Dale PA 17090 **1968-** B Palmerton PA 1936 s Henry & Myrtle. Cert PDS; BA Muhlenberg Coll 1958; BD Luth TS 1961; Cert PDS 1962; MTh PrTS 1970; MTh PrTS 1970. D 6/24/1962 P 12/21/1962 Bp Oliver J Hart. m 8/13/1960 Belva E Williams c 2. Vic All SS Epis Ch Levittown PA 1965-1968; Cur S Paul's Ch Philadelphia PA 1962-1965.

WILLIAMS JR, Hollis R (Oly) 725 9th Ave Apt 2007, Seattle WA 98104 **Ret 2002-** B Fort Worth TX 1938 s Hollis & Hildreth. BA Hendrix Coll 1961; MDiv Duke DS 1964; CAS Sewanee: The U So, TS 1966. D 6/29/1966 P 4/17/1967 Bp Robert Raymond Brown. m 2/3/1968 Katherine B Williams c 2. Int S Paul Epis Ch Bellingham WA 2001-2002; Int S Steph's Epis Ch Longview WA 1999-2000; Trin Epis Ch Everett WA 1985-1999; Headmaster Bp Noland Epis Day Sch 1981-1983; Assoc Epis Ch Of The Gd Shpd Lake Chas LA 1980-1985; R S Phil's Ch Jackson MS 1974-1980; R Trin Ch Yazoo City MS 1970-1974; Vic S Steph's Epis Ch Jacksonville AR 1966-1970; Bd Dir Dio Olympia Seattle 1994-1998, Stnd Com 1988-1993; ExCoun Dio Louisiana New Orleans LA 1981-1985; Chair Liturg Com Dio Mississippi Jackson MS 1972-1980. Auth, *A Partnership of Trust*, Alb, 1999; Auth, "Cler and Laity in Parntership for Mutual Mnstry," *Congregations*, Alb, 1998; Auth, "Leading a Cong Today," *Congregations*, Alb, 1995.

WILLIAMS, Howard Kenty (LI) 1102 E 73rd St Apt C, Brooklyn NY 11234 **R S Aug's Epis Ch Brooklyn NY 2004-, P-in-c 2000-2003, Int 1999-2016** B Kingston JM 1951 s Clement & Florence. Cert Untd Theol Coll of the W Indies Kingston JM 1974; LTh U of The W Indies 1974; MA PrTS 1983; DMin GTF 2007. Trans 10/28/1984 as Priest Bp Christopher FitzSimons Allison. m 6/9/2012 Mark Anthony Schlyfer c 2. Coordntr Epis Ch Cntr New York NY 1988-1997; R S Lk's Epis Ch Columbia SC 1986-1988; Chapl Voorhees Coll Charleston SC 1984-1985; Serv Angl Ch in Jamaica 1981-1983; Archd of Brooklyn Dio Long Island Garden City NY 2006-2011. Co-Ed, "Fashion Me A People"; Co-Auth, "Blood Thicker Than Water". Rel Educational Assn of the Untd States of Ameri; UBE.

WILLIAMS III, Hugh Elton (CFla) Po Box 91777, Lakeland FL 33804 B Tallahassee FL 1946 s Hugh & E Marie. BS Florida St U 1970; MDiv VTS 1977. D 6/12/1977 P 12/1/1977 Bp Frank S Cerveny. m 1/12/1974 Frances H Williams c 2. St Alb's of Auburndale Inc Auburndale FL 2008-2013, P-in-c 2004-2013, 2001-2002; Epis Ch Of The Ascen Orlando FL 2002-2003; Bud Williams Mnstrs Lakeland FL 1995; R Chr The King Ch Lakeland FL 1991-1994, Vic 1984-1990; All SS Epis Ch Lakeland FL 1981-1985; Asst S Mk's Epis Ch Jacksonville FL 1977-1981. Auth, "Fire In The Wax Museum," Destiny Image, 1999.

WILLIAMS, Jacqueline Miller (SO) 6461 Tylersville Rd, West Chester OH 45069 B Lancaster OH 1943 d Clarence & Helen. Cert Acad for the Diac 2008. D 6/14/2008 Bp Thomas Edward Breidenthal. m 2/1/1964 Thomas Howard Williams c 2.

WILLIAMS, James Armstrong (Tex) 11403 Madrid Dr, Austin TX 78759 B Port Arthur TX 1935 s Theodore & Bolena. BA Lamar U 1957; BD Colgate Rochester Crozer DS 1964; BD CRDS 1964; MS U of Texas 1975; Epis TS of the SW 1988. D 3/14/1988 Bp Anselmo Carral-Solar P 8/28/1988 Bp Gordon Taliaferro Charlton. m 2/9/1957 Barbara Ellen Williams c 3. Vic S Ptr's Epis Ch Leander TX 1997-2003; Lectr U Tx Austin 1997-1999; The Great Cmsn Fndt Houston TX 1997; Int All SS Epis Ch Austin TX 1995-1996; Asst S Matt's Ch Austin TX 1990-1995; Int S Mich's Ch Austin TX 1989-1990; Lectr U Tx Austin 1988-1990; Asst R S Geo's Ch Austin TX 1988-1989. Lifetime Achievement Awd Nasw-Austin/Travis Co. Ch. 1996.

W

WILLIAMS II, James Edward (Los) 580 Hilgard Ave, Los Angeles CA 90024 B Saint Louis MO 1945 s Joseph & Marguerite. BA U CA 1968; MDiv CDSP 1971; Journalism Stds/Grad Stds On Educ Admin 1975. D 6/24/1972 P 2/13/1973 Bp Chauncie Kilmer Myers. R S Jn's Memi Ch Ramsey NJ 2001-2005; S Martha's Epis Ch W Covina CA 1996-2001; Asst S Alb's 1991-2000; S Alb's Epis Ch Los Angeles CA 1989-1995; Assoc R S Mk's Par Glendale CA 1987-1989; Dio California San Francisco CA 1978-2005; Asst R S Clem's Ch Berkeley CA 1976-1987; Cur S Paul's Ch Oakland CA 1972-1975; Chapl S Paul's Towers In Oakland CA 1972-1975; Chapl S Paul's Sch Oakland CA 1972-1974; Secy To Bd Dir S Paul's Sch Oakland CA 1972-1974; Instr Of Rel Educ S Paul's Sch Oakland CA 1972-1973. Sigma Delta Chi 1968; Mem Usn Inst 68; Mem 68 San Francisco Press Club.

WILLIAMS, James Wallace (Ala) 2130 Enon Mill Dr Sw, Atlanta GA 30331 B Huntington WV 1948 s David & Marguerite. BA Lynchburg Coll; MDiv S Lk Sem; MDiv Sewanee: The U So, TS. D 6/3/1974 P 12/1/1974 Bp Furman Charles Stough. m 2/24/2001 Marguerite Elizabeth Chitwood. Gr Ch Birmingham AL 2004-2006; R Ch Of The Incarn Atlanta GA 1999-2004; Asst Emm Epis Ch Athens GA 1995-1998; R Ch Of The Mssh Heflin AL 1992-1995; Vic S Lk's Ch Remington VA 1987-1992; Non-par 1977-1987; Dio Alabama Birmingham 1976-1977; Assoc Min Trin Epis Ch Florence AL 1974-1976. Auth, "Meeting Him To Find Me"; Auth, "How To Cut Medicare Cost"; Auth, "Money," *Priests & The Bed Of Academe*; Auth, "Recruit Or Retreat," *Pub Or Perish*.

WILLIAMS JR, (Jerre) Stockton (WTex) 372 Englewood Dr, Kerrville TX 78028 **S Ptr's Epis Ch Kerrville TX 2002-** B Austin TX 1951 s Jerre & Mary. BA Amh 1973; JD U of Texas 1976; MDiv VTS 1986. D 6/24/1986 Bp Maurice Manuel Benitez P 2/24/1987 Bp Anselmo Carral-Solar. m 12/30/1978 Leslie Williams c 2. Sprtl Dir Happ Natl Com 2006-2014; R S Peters Epis Sch Kerrville TX 2002-2016; R Ch Of The H Trin Midland TX 1994-2001; S Mary's Epis Ch Cypress TX 1989-1994; The Great Cmsn Fndt Houston TX 1989-1993; Asst S Paul's Ch Waco TX 1986-1989; Alt to GC Dio W Texas San Antonio TX 2012, VP, Bp Elliott Soc 2009-2011; Chairman of the Bd Quarterman Ranch Lubbock TX 1998-2001; Exec Bd Dio NW Texas Lubbock TX 1996-1999; Del to Prov Syn Dio Texas Houston TX 1991. Auth, "The Tractarian Deviation on the Episcopacy," *Ch Div 86*. OSL the Physcn 2003.

WILLIAMS, Jeryln Ann (SD) 431 Sweden St, Caribou ME 04736 **D Aroostook Epis Cluster Caribou ME 2006-; Acad Instr Loring Job Corps 2000-** B Erie PA 1945 d William & Ella. No Cntrl Coll; BS Indiana U 1983. D 8/5/2006 Bp Chilton Richardson Knudsen. m 2/7/1968 Gary Williams c 4.

WILLIAMS, Jill Barton (WMass) St Francis, 70 Highland St, Holden MA 01520 **Assoc S Fran Ch Holden MA 2008-; Dio Wstrn Massachusetts Springfield 2007-** B Worcester MA 1981 d Bruce & Holly. BA Florida Sthrn Coll 2003; MDiv VTS 2007. D 6/2/2007 P 1/26/2008 Bp Gordon Scruton. m 5/5/2007 Andrew Dodge Williams.

WILLIAMS II OHC, John F (NY) 860 Wolcott Ave, Beacon NY 12508 **S Lk's Ch Beacon NY 2015-; S Andr's Ch Beacon NY 2014-** B Champaign IL 1961 s Thomas & Marlene. AAS Cmnty Coll of the AF Macomb GA 1989; BA Wstrn Illinois U 1999; MDiv CDSP 2002. D 6/22/2002 P 1/7/2003 Bp Richard Lester Shimpfky. m 11/6/2014 Janice Kotuby c 1. Dio New York New York NY 2014-2015; R S Jas Epis Ch Midvale UT 2008-2015; Assoc P Cathd Ch of Our Sav Philadelphia PA 2008; Sum Yth Camp Dir Dio Pennsylvania Philadelphia PA 2008, Dioc Coun 2005-2008, Fin and Bdgt Committees 2005-2007; R S Steph's Epis Ch Clifton Hgts PA 2003-2008; Assoc R Old Donation Ch Virginia Bch VA 2002-2003; Yth Min All SS Ch Carmel CA 1996-1999; Dioc Stndg Com Dio Utah Salt Lake City UT 2012-2014, VP of Dioc Coun 2011-2012, GC Dep 2010-2014, Dioc Coun 2009-2012. OHC 2004. beaconrev@gmail.com

WILLIAMS, John Gerald (Tex) PO Box 10064, College Station TX 77842 B Texas City TX 1949 s John & Juanita. BA U of No Texas 1971; MA U of No Texas 1973; Texas A&M U 1978; MDiv Epis TS of the SW 1990. D 6/16/1990 Bp Maurice Manuel Benitez P 1/7/1991 Bp William Elwood Sterling. m 5/24/1975 Rita A Ragsdale c 2. R S Fran Epis Ch Coll Sta TX 2005-2013; R S Mich's Ch La Marque TX 1999-2004; Chapl S Lk's Epis Hosp Houston TX 1997-1999; R S Jas The Apos Epis Ch Conroe TX 1995-1997; R S Jn's Epis Ch Silsbee TX 1990-1995; The Great Cmsn Fndt Houston TX 1990-1992.

WILLIAMS, Joseph Anthony (CNY) 11 Gillette Ln, Cazenovia NY 13035 B Rome NY 1930 s Leonard & Beatrice. MDiv PDS; BS SUNY. D 5/21/1968 Bp Ned Cole P 1/1/1969 Bp Walter M Higley. m 6/3/1957 Ruth Joyce Williams. R S Paul's Ch Chittenango NY 1984-1997; Gr Epis Ch Waterville NY 1975-1982; R S Mk's Jamesville NY 1971-1975; Cur Evang Oswego NY 1969-1970; Cur Calv Utica NY 1968-1969.

WILLIAMS, Joseph David (NwT) 1105 1/2 Madison St, Borger TX 79007 B Galena Park TX 1947 s Melvin & Ann. AA Frank Phillips Jr Coll 2002. D 9/30/2006 P 3/1/2007 Bp C Wallis Ohl. m 6/23/1984 Rinica N Williams c 1.

WILLIAMS, Josie Marie (Miss) 5930 Warriors Trl, Vicksburg MS 39180 **S Alb's Epis Ch Vicksburg MS 2011-** B Vicksburg MS 1954 d William & Malinda. BS U of Sthrn Mississippi 1972; MS U of Sthrn Mississippi 1976; AA

Mississippi Dept of Educ 1980. D 1/15/2011 Bp Duncan Montgomery Gray III. m 7/9/1977 Theo Williams c 1.

WILLIAMS, Julie (Az) 100 Arroyo Pinon Dr, Sedona AZ 86336 **S Thos Of The Vlly Epis Clarkdale AZ 2014-** B San Bernardino CA 1954 d Jack & Mary. BA UCLA 1974; MA UCLA 1976; PhD Camb 1982; CAS CDSP 2015. D 6/7/2014 P 12/9/2014 Bp Kirk Stevan Smith. m 10/25/1986 Ian Paul Harry Duffy c 2. Freelance Writer 1990-2008.

WILLIAMS, Larry C (At) Po Box 1117, Hot Springs AR 71902 **Com Of Mus And Liturg 1980-; Dept Of CE 1979-** B Inyokern CA 1950 s Clarence & Mary. BA U So 1972; MDiv Nash 1975; Grad Ldrshp 1980. D 1/25/1975 P 10/1/1975 Bp George Paul Reeves. m 1/22/1983 Deborah P Williams c 3. S Teresa Acworth GA 2009-2014; R S Lk's Ch Hot Sprg AR 1998-2006, R 1998; Cn S Mk's Cathd Shreveport LA 1990-1998; R The Epis Ch Of The Medtr Meridian MS 1984-1990; R S Thos Ch Greenville AL 1981-1984; Cur S Lk's Epis Ch Mobile AL 1978-1981; Asst S Paul's Ch Augusta GA 1975-1978. Soc Of S Jn The Evang. Outstanding Young Men Amer 1982.

WILLIAMS, Lloyd Clyde (Ind) 702 Dr Martin Luther King Jr St, Indianapolis IN 46202 **R S Phil's 1971-** B Tuskegee Inst AL 1947 s Theodore & Charlotte. BA Earlham Coll 1969; MS Sthrn Connecticut St U 1971; MDiv Yale DS 1971; DMin Chr TS 1974. D 6/11/1971 P 12/1/1971 Bp John P Craine. m 12/27/1968 Gloria Jean Williams c 1. S Phil's Ch Indianapolis IN 1974-1976; Counslr Epis Cmnty Serv 1972-1973.

WILLIAMS, Lois Vander Wende (Cal) 455 Fair Oaks St., San Francisco CA 94110 B Passaic NJ 1959 d John & Irene. BA Dominican Sch of Philsophy & Theol 2003; MDiv CDSP 2008; MA H Names U 2010. D 12/3/2011 P 6/2/2012 Bp Marc Handley Andrus. m 7/18/2009 Bennett Hagler c 1.

WILLIAMS, Lorna Hyacinth (Mich) 1224 West Chester Pike, Apt C11, West Chester PA 19382 **St Jas Sch Philadelphia PA 2015-** B Kingston 1969 d Linville & Hazel. BS SUNY 1992; PrTS 1994; MDiv SWTS 1997. D 6/20/1998 Bp Chilton Richardson Knudsen P 1/1/1999 Bp David Charles Bowman. The Ch Of The H Trin W Chester PA 2011-2015; Cn S Jn's Cathd Jacksonville FL 2010-2011; Asst Trin Ch Epis Boston MA 2009-2010; Sr Assoc S Andr's Ch Ann Arbor MI 2000-2008; Chapl Dio Wstrn New York Tonawanda NY 1999-2000; Cn S Paul's Cathd Buffalo NY 1998-2000; Dep, GC Dio Michigan Detroit MI 2003-2006, COM Mem 2001-2005. "Liturg Prayers," *Race and Pryr*, Morehouse, 2003; Auth, "Commemorative Collects," *Wmn Uncommon Prayers*, Morehouse, 2000; Auth, "A Pryr for Healing," *Wmn Uncommon Prayers*, Morehouse, 2000; Auth, "A Safe Place," *Angl Dig*, 1999; Auth, "The Power of Personal Witness," *Journ of Wmn Mnstrs*, 1999. CHS 1995.

WILLIAMS, Margaret A (Chi) 707 1st Ave, Sterling IL 61081 B Wichita KS 1944 d Jay & Helen. BFA U of Oklahoma 1966; MA U of Nebraska 1978. D 6/23/2012 P 1/5/2013 Bp Jeff Lee. m 5/16/1998 David Earl Williams c 1. pwilliams3303@comcast.net

WILLIAMS, Margaret Mary Oetjen (Tex) 18319 Otter Creek Trl, Humble TX 77346 **Int S Cuth's Epis Ch Houston TX 2013-** B Beacon NY 1942 d Robert & Dorothy. BS U of Maryland 1969; Sewanee: The U So, TS 1986; MS Neumann Coll Aston PA 1987; Cert Luth TS at Gettysburg 1992; Cert Ang Stud GTS 1994. D 6/20/1987 P 10/22/1994 Bp Allen Lyman Bartlett Jr. m 6/26/1966 William K Williams c 3. R Chr The King Epis Ch Humble TX 2005-2009; S Thos Epis Ch Coll Sta TX 2004-2005; Memi Ch Of S Lk Philadelphia PA 1998-2003; Asst Ch Of The Mssh Lower Gwynedd PA 1994-1997; 1992-1994; DCE/Pstr Asst The Epis Ch Of The Adv Kennet Sq PA 1987-1992.

WILLIAMS, Mary Grace (NY) 36 New Canaan Road, Wilton CT 06897 **Ch Of S Jn The Evang Red Hook NY 2016-** B Kansas City MO 1954 d Ewing & Dona. BA Rutgers The St U of New Jersey 1976; MA Ford 1980; MDiv Ya Berk 1988. D 10/9/1988 Bp Paul Moore Jr P 4/9/1989 Bp Arthur Anton Vogel. c 2. R S Matt's Epis Ch Wilton CT 2002-2016; R The Ch Of S Jn The Evang Flossmoor IL 1995-2002; Assoc R St Ptr & All SS Epis Ch Kansas City MO 1991-1995; Chapl St. Lk's Epis Hosp Kansas City MO 1988-1991. magrwi5154@gmail.com

WILLIAMS, Melody Sue (SO) 60 S. Dorset Road, Troy OH 45373 B Louisville KY 1953 d Besfred & Catherine. BA U of Louisville 1975; BA Bellarmine U 1977; MA Duquesne U 1979; Cert Ang Stud Sewanee: The U So, TS 1989. D 6/3/1989 Bp Alden Moinet Hathaway P 12/1/1989 Bp William Davidson. R Trin Epis Ch Troy OH 2005-2011; Asst R S Paul's Epis Ch Dayton OH 1998-2005; Columbus Comm Mnstrs Columbus OH 1996-1998; Ch Of S Edw Columbus OH 1995-1998; Vic S Paul's Ch Columbus OH 1995-1998; Assoc R S Mk's Epis Ch Columbus OH 1991-1995; Cn Trin Cathd Pittsburgh PA 1989-1991.

WILLIAMS, Michael Robert (ND) MNC-I Chaplain, Camp Victory, APO AE 09342 **Off Of Bsh For ArmdF New York NY 1995-** B Fairfield IA 1954 s Roger & Doris. BA Iowa St U 1977; MDiv TESM 1986. D 8/5/1989 P 9/1/1990 Bp George Clinton Harris. m 6/19/1976 Rebecca A Williams. R S Paul's Epis Ch Grand Forks ND 1991-1995; Assoc S Jude's Epis Ch No Pole AK 1989-1991. Bro Of S Andr.

WILLIAMS, Mildred (Alb) 2304 Deer Trl, Lampasas TX 76550 **D S Mary's Epis Ch Inc Lampasas TX 2002-; D Dio Albany Greenwich NY 1986-** B

Norfolk VA 1933 d Joseph & Bessie. D 1/6/1986 Bp David Standish Ball. m 12/16/1951 Phillip Williams c 2. D Zion Ch Morris NY 1988-2002. NAAD 1986.

WILLIAMS JR, Milton (WA) 1133 N. Lasalle Blvd., Chicago IL 60610 **S Fran Ch Greensboro NC 2015-; Fresh Start Dio Chicago Chicago IL 2013-, Dioc Coun 2012-** B Suffolk VA 1961 s Milton & Goldie. BS Virginia St U 1983; MDiv Sthrn Bapt TS 1987; DAS VTS 1995. D 6/8/1996 Bp William Jerry Winterrowd P 2/16/1997 Bp Peter J Lee. Cathd Of S Jas Chicago IL 2014-2015; Ch Of The Ascen Chicago IL 2012-2014; P-in-c Par of St Monica & St Jas Washington DC 2008-2012; Int S Tim's Epis Ch Washington DC 2006-2008; Assoc Trin Par New York NY 1999-2006; Asst Pohick Epis Ch Lorton VA 1996-1999; Dioc Coun Dio Washington Washington DC 2009-2012.

WILLIAMS, Mollie Alexander (Ind) 11335 Winding Wood Ct, Indianapolis IN 46235 B Baltimore MD 1939 d Harold & Effie. BA U Roch 1961; MDiv EDS 1964; MA U Chi 1978; Cert Cntr For Fam Consult 1989. D 6/17/1989 P 12/16/1989 Bp Frank Tracy Griswold III. m 6/12/1964 Frederic Williams c 2. Int S Paul's Ch Richmond IN 2004-2008; Int The Cathd Ch Of S Paul Des Moines IA 2002-2003; Vic Ch Of The H Fam Lake Villa IL 1995-2001; Int Trin Ch Highland Pk IL 1993-1995; Int S Aug's Epis Ch Wilmette IL 1992-1993; Int St. Andrews Pentecost Epis Ch Evanston IL 1991-1992; Int All SS Ch Wstrn Sprgs IL 1989-1991; Consult S Mk's Ch Evanston IL 1989; Dio Chicago Chicago IL 1987-1994. OHC 1987-1991; SSJE 1993.

WILLIAMS, Monrelle (Mass) 1073 Tremont St, Roxbury Crossing MA 02120 **R S Cyp's Ch Boston MA 2012-; Tutor Sch for Deacons 2008-** B Barbados 1954 s Theolphilus & Una. BA Codrington Coll 1979; Bachelor of Arts Other 1979; Bachelor of Arts Theolgy 1979; MPhil Trin 1984; PhD Dur 1991. Trans 4/3/2007 as Priest Bp Marc Handley Andrus. c 2. R S Aug's Ch Oakland CA 2006-2012.

WILLIAMS, Pamela Mary (Neb) 1014 N 6th St, Seward NE 68434 **D S Andr's Ch Seward NE 2015-** B Mullen NE 1952 d George & Pauline. BS Chadron St 1976; MA U of Nebraska 2000. D 1/31/2015 P 5/14/2016 Bp Scott Scott Barker. m 7/15/1971 Calvin Earl Williams c 2.

WILLIAMS, Patricia S. (Mo) 336 N Lorimier St, Cape Girardeau MO 63701 **Ret 2002-** B Williston ND 1932 d John & Juanita. BA Carleton Coll 1954; MA SWTS 1990. D 5/5/1990 P 11/30/1990 Bp William Augustus Jones Jr. c 2. S Fran Epis Ch Eureka MO 1994-1995; Dep for Mnstry and Pstr Care Dio Missouri S Louis MO 1993-2001, 1990-2001, Bps Asst 1990-1993.

WILLIAMS, Patrick Joel (NY) 1047 Amsterdam Ave, New York NY 10025 **S Phil's Ch New York NY 2013-** B Jackson TN 1974 s Lawrence & Katie. BS Tennessee St U 1997; MS Carnegie Mellon U 1999; MDiv VTS 2013. D 3/2/2013 P 9/7/2013 Bp Andrew Marion Lenow Dietsche. Cur Dio New York New York NY 2013-2015.

WILLIAMS, Paul Brazell (SO) 270 Blue Jacket Cir, Pickerington OH 43147 **Vic S Andr's Ch Pickerington OH 2008-** B High Point NC 1957 s Benjamin & Mary. U NC - Greensboro; BA U NC 1981; MDiv GTS 1996. D 6/8/1996 Bp Frank Kellogg Allan P 12/7/1996 Bp Richard Frank Grein. m 10/28/2011 Larry D Hayes. Bex Sem Columbus OH 2008-2012; Chr Ch Glen Ridge NJ 2001-2006; Cur Ch Of The H Trin New York NY 1996-2001; Transitional D Dio New Jersey Trenton NJ 1996. H Cross 1994. frpaul@standrewspickerington.org

WILLIAMS, Persis Preston (Alb) Po Box 1662, Blue HIll ME 04614 B Troy NY 1942 d Carl & Claire. BS U of Connecticut 1974; MDiv GTS 1987. D 6/6/1987 Bp Edward Cole Chalfant P 12/19/1987 Bp Clarence Nicholas Coleridge. c 2. Gr Ch Cherry Vlly NY 2002-2008; S Mary's Ch Springfld Ct NY 2002-2008; R The Ch Of The Redeem Rochester NH 1992-1996; Ch of the Epiph Rumford RI 1991-1992; St Mich & Gr Ch Rumford RI 1991-1992; P-in-c S Aug's Ch Kingston RI 1990-1991, Asst Vic 1988-1989; Chapl U of Rhode Island in Kingston 1988-1991; Asst Dir Epis C&C 1987-1988; Incarn Cntr Deep River CT 1987-1988. Fllshp of Way of The Cross 1997.

WILLIAMS, Peter A (CNY) PO Box 170, 13 Court Street, Cortland NY 13045 **Gr Epis Ch Cortland NY 2010-; Pstr H Sprt Luth Ch Cortland NY 2010-; Dio Cntrl New York Liverpool NY 2009-; Vic Ephphatha Epis Par Of The Deaf Syracuse NY 2009-** B Syracuse NY 1956 BA SUNY 1978; STM Other 1982; STM Other 1982; STM ST MARY'S Sem & U 1982. Rec 10/18/2008 Bp Gladstone Bailey Adams III.

WILLIAMS, Priscilla Mudge (Ct) 80 Lyme Rd., Apt. 212, Hanover NH 03755 B New York NY 1933 d Louis & Priscilla. BS Skidmore Coll 1955; MDiv Yale DS 1981. D 6/13/1981 P 1/28/1982 Bp Arthur Edward Walmsley. m 3/9/1957 Whitney Williams c 3. P-in-c S Jn's Ch Stamford CT 1981-1987.

WILLIAMS, Richard Alan (SJ) 28052 Foxfire St, Sun City CA 92586 B Berkeley CA 1930 s Charles & Wilma. CDSP; BA U of Redlands 1953; MDiv Amer Bapt Sem of the W 1956. D 6/10/1982 Bp Robert Munro Wolterstorff P 10/17/1982 Bp Charles Brinkley Morton. m 8/26/1951 Barbara Ruark c 3. Int S Tim's Ch Bp CA 2007-2008; S Clem's Ch Woodlake CA 2003-2004; Int S Judes In The Mountains Ch Tehachapi CA 2001-2002; Int S Mths Ch Oakdale CA 2000-2001; Asstg R All SS Epis Ch Riverside CA 1996-2000; Int S Andr's Ch Taft CA 1994-1996; Assoc S Steph's Ch Stockton CA 1993-1994; Vic S Mary's Ch Manteca CA 1990-1993; Vic S Andr's By The Lake Lake Elsi-

nore CA 1984-1990; St Steph's Epis Ch Menifee CA 1984-1986; Cur S Andr's Ch La Mesa CA 1982-1983; Min S Anne's Epis Ch Oceanside CA 1978-1981; Serv Assy of God Ch 1964-1978; Serv Presb Ch 1959-1964; Serv Bapt Ch 1956-1959.

WILLIAMS, Rick (NC) PO Box 1852, Salisbury NC 28145 **Environ Cmsn Dio No Carolina 2012-; Diocesean Fndt Dio No Carolina 2012-** B Newport News VA 1946 s Cecil & Hester. BS Tennessee Tech U 1969; MDiv Candler TS Emory U 1977. D 6/11/1977 P 2/24/1978 Bp Bennett Jones Sims. m 11/27/2002 Judith Williams c 1. Vic S Paul's Ch Salisbury NC 2010-2015; US Navy Pension Fund Mltry New York NY 2002-2004; Engr Columbus GA Opelika 1993-2006; Non-Dioc 1993-2002; Assoc S Stephens 1993-1994; Assoc Trin Epis Ch Columbus GA 1988-1992; R Ch Of The Incarn Atlanta GA 1986-1988; Dn Of Convoc Marietta Convoc Dio Atlanta 1986-1988; Assoc S Edw's Epis Ch Lawrenceville GA 1985-1986, Assoc 1977-1978; Assoc S Barth's Epis Ch Atlanta GA 1984-1985; Chapl USN Captain (O6) 1983-2006; Vic Chr Epis Ch Kennesaw GA 1982-1984; Police Chapl Kennesaw Georgia Police Dept 1978-1984; Dio Atlanta Atlanta GA 1977-1981, Yth Cmsn 1986-1988, Dn, Mid-Atlanta Convoc 1985-1988. Alpha Kappa Psi 1969; Sigma Chi 1973. Who's Who Worldwide Who's Who Bus Leaders 1994; Gd Samar Awd Amer Police Hall Of Fame 1981.

WILLIAMS, R Jane (Be) 1670 Lindberg St, Bethlehem PA 18020 **Prof Moravian TS Bethlehem PA 2010-; sole proprietor/owner Holistic Counslg Resources 1996-** B Fillmore NY 1949 d Kenneth & Ruth. BA W Virginia U 1971; MDiv Drew U 1985; PhD Leh 1994. D 6/14/1997 P 12/19/1997 Bp Paul Victor Marshall. m 5/19/1989 William Treible c 1. Chapl S Mary's Epis Sch Memphis TN 2005-2010; Assoc Chr Ch Reading PA 1997-2005. Auth, "Silent Casusualties: Partnr, Fam and Spouses of Persons w AIDS," *Journ of Counslg & Dvlpmt*, 1992. Phi Beta Kappa W Virginia U 1971. williamsr@moravian.edu

WILLIAMS, Robert (Ore) 11511 SW Bull Mountain Road, Tigard OR 97224 **R Dio Oregon Portland OR 2013-; S Jas Epis Ch Portland OR 2013-** B Walla Walla WA 1946 s Roy & Melva. Andover Newton TS; BA Whitman Coll 1969; MS OR SU 1972; PhD OR SU 1982; EFM Sewanee: The U So, TS 2006. D 6/11/2011 P 1/21/2012 Bp Gordon Scruton. m 12/29/1984 Sharon Arlene Williams c 1. Vic S Mary's Epis Ch Thorndike MA 2013; Asst S Steph's Ch Westborough MA 2012-2013; Vic S Jn's Ch Millville MA 2011-2012, Vic 2007-2011.

WILLIAMS, Robert Bruce (Az) 2242 E 8th St, Tucson AZ 85719 B Welch WV 1942 s William & Cecilia. BA U of Arizona 1964; MDiv VTS 1967. D 6/21/1967 P 12/1/1967 Bp John Joseph Meakin Harte. m 1/10/2015 Richard Anthony Baglione. Asst S Andr's Epis Ch Tucson AZ 1994-2006, 1993-2006; Nonpar 1980-1984; R S Mich & All Ang Phoenix AZ 1979-1980; Epis Ch of the H Sprt Phoenix AZ 1975-1980; Vic S Mich & All Ang Phoenix AZ 1975-1979; S Raphael In The Vlly Epis Ch Benson AZ 1970-1975; Vic S Steph's Ch Sierra Vista AZ 1970-1975; BEC Dio Arizona Phoenix AZ 1970-1972, COM 1980-2008, Secy Of Dio 1977-1979, Chair 1973-1976, Dioc Coun 1972, Dept Of CE 1968-1971; Cur S Mk's Epis Ch Mesa AZ 1967-1970.

WILLIAMS, Robert Ernest (ECR) 231 Sunset Ave, Sunnyvale CA 94086 B Danville VA 1928 s Edgar & Mary. BS Georgia Inst of Tech 1951; MS Georgia Inst of Tech 1960; CDSP 1975. D 12/17/1969 Bp George Richard Millard P 1/26/2012 Bp Gordon Scruton. c 4. D S Thos Epis Ch Sunnyvale CA 1969-2009.

WILLIAMS, Robert Harry (Oly) 1805 38th Ave, Seattle WA 98122 **Ret 2005-** B Kansas City MO 1940 s Payton & Mary. BS U of Missouri 1964; MDiv Nash 1971; DMin McCormick TS 1976; EdD Tem 1979. D 12/6/1970 P 6/11/1971 Bp Edward Randolph Welles II. c 1. Epiph Par of Seattle Seattle WA 1997-2005; Off Of Bsh For ArmdF New York NY 1974-1997; Vic All SS Ch W Plains MO 1971-1974. Legion Of Merit; Meritorious Serv Medal; Commendation Medal USN.

WILLIAMS, Robert Lewis (Oly) 3300 Carpenter Rd SE, Electra 109, Lacey WA 98503 **Vic S Nich Ch Tahuya WA 1998-** B Findlay OH 1936 s Vern & Eva. CTh Other Other 1977; BA Evergreen St Coll 1987; Cert Ang Stud CDSP 1992; Cert Cler Ldrshp Inst 2004. Rec 6/27/1992 as Deacon Bp Vincent Waydell Warner. m 12/7/1957 Daphne Beryl Williams c 5. Int Sts Ptr & Paul Epis Ch El Centro CA 2006-2007; Asst S Jn's Epis Ch Gig Harbor WA 1996-2006; P-in-c S Germains Epis Ch Hoodsport WA 1995-1997; S Paul's Epis Ch Bremerton WA 1994-1995; Pstr's Asst Ch Of The Resurr Bellevue WA 1992-1994; Assoc H Trin RC Ch Bremerton WA 1976-1984.

WILLIAMS, R(obert) Samuel (NwPa) 22633 Phillips Dr, Pleasantville PA 16341 B Cape Girardeau MO 1940 s Murlin & Maryan. No Carolina St U; BA Methodist U 1973; MA Pepperdine U 1978; MDiv Sewanee: The U So, TS 1984. D 6/24/1984 Bp Claude Charles Vache P 1/24/1985 Bp Brice Sidney Sanders. m 12/29/2013 Margaret Lucas. R S Alb's Epis Ch Mc Cook NE 1999-2007; R S Jn's Ch Franklin PA 1987-1999; Asst to R S Andr's Ch Morehead City NC 1984-1987.

WILLIAMS, Sandra Kaye (SD) 509 Jackson St, Belle Fourche SD 57717 B Platte SD 1956 d George & Joann. BS Dakota St U 1978. D 6/11/2005 P 2/12/2006 Bp Creighton Leland Robertson. m 6/10/1978 George Williams c 2.

W

WILLIAMS, Sandy (Mass) 173 Georgetown Rd, Boxford MA 01921 B Columbus OH 1955 d Robert & Faye. BA U MI 1977; MDiv EDS 1981. D 10/18/1981 Bp Henry Irving Mayson P 1/1/1983 Bp H Coleman Mcgehee Jr. m 6/30/1984 Brian William Lawrence c 1. Vic S Andr's Ch Of The Deaf Brookline MA 1989-1999; Dio Massachusetts Boston MA 1989-1997; Dio Michigan Detroit MI 1981-1982. Epis Conf Deaf.

WILLIAMS, Scott Eugene (Miss) 1909 15th St, Gulfport MS 39501 B Williamsport PA 1953 s Robert & Robertha. D 1/9/2010 Bp Duncan Montgomery Gray III. m 12/11/1993 Tracy Williams c 2.

WILLIAMS, Sharon Evette (SeFla) Trinity Cathedral, 464 NE 16th St, Miami FL 33132 B Sarasota FL 1956 d Edward & Carolyn. BA The Florida St U 1989; MS Nova SE U 1997; Dioc Sch for Chr Stds 2008. D 4/14/2012 Bp Leo Frade.

WILLIAMS, Sharon Vaughan (Tex) **D S Chris's Epis Ch Austin TX 2012-; D S Mich's Ch Austin TX 2012-** B Covina CA 1938 d John & Winona. AB Stan 1960; MS Texas A and I U 1965; MAR Epis TS Of The SW 1987; MAR Epis TS of the SW 1987; Certificates Iona Sch for Mnstry 2012. D 6/16/2012 Bp C Andrew Doyle. m 6/17/1989 Roger Coons Williams c 2.

WILLIAMS, Shawn (LI) 64 Mount Misery Dr, Sag Harbor NY 11963 B Lincoln NE 1966 s John & Kathleen. BA U of Nebraska 1989; MDiv GTS 1993. D 6/13/1992 P 1/1/1993 Bp Orris George Walker Jr. S Paul's Ch Glen Cove NY 2014, P-in-c 2014-; P-in-c Chr Ch Sag Harbor NY 1999-2012; S Elis's Epis Ch Floral Pk NY 1994-1999; Fin Cmsn Dio Long Island Garden City NY 1994-1996, Cmsn On Racism 1991-1995; S Thos' Epis Ch Floral Pk NY 1994; Cur S Gabr's Ch Brooklyn NY 1992-1994.

WILLIAMS, Shearon Sykes (Va) 2500 Cameron Mills Rd, Alexandria VA 22302 **R S Geo's Epis Ch Arlington VA 2010-; Asst Gr Ch Washington DC 2003-; Dn of Reg III (Arlington) Dio Virginia Richmond VA 2013-** B Newport News VA 1960 BA U of Virginia; BA U of Virginia 1982; Masters VTS 2003. D 6/7/2003 Bp Gethin Benwil Hughes P 12/14/2003 Bp Allen Lyman Bartlett Jr. m 2/7/1987 Robbie Williams c 1. S Gabr's Epis Ch Leesburg VA 2010; S Andr's Ch Leonardtown California MD 2008-2009; S Mk's Ch Washington DC 2004-2007. swilliams@saintgeorgeschurch.org

WILLIAMS, Stephen Junior Cherrington (RG) 49 ½ Draper Avenue, Pittsfield MA 01201 **Ret 1994-** B East Liverpool OH 1932 s Louis & Alberta. BA Syr 1957; MDiv Ya Berk 1960; Tchr Cert California St U 1964. D 6/22/1960 P 6/24/1961 Bp Walter M Higley. m 1/1/1962 Margaret Rose Williams c 3. R S Chris's Epis Ch Hobbs NM 1986-1994; R S Pat's Epis Ch Lebanon OH 1977-1986; Chr Epis Ch Warren OH 1977-1982; Ch Of Gd Shpd Cincinnati OH 1976-1977; R Episc Ch in Warren Cnty Waynesville OH 1971-1976; Chapl USAF 1966-1971; Vic Ch Of The H Comm Gardena CA 1964-1966; Gr Epis Ch Whitney Point NY 1960-1963; Mssy S Jn's Ch Marathon NY 1960-1963; Dioc Coun Dio The Rio Grande Albuquerque 1990-1994. Auth, *Enroute and Other Poems*, Morris Pub, 1997. OHC.

WILLIAMS, Stephen Lee (Los) 14252 Suffolk Street, Westminster CA 92683 B Memphis TN 1945 s Harry & Nellie. BS U of Memphis 1971; MDiv Trin U Tor CA 1976; MDiv U Tor CA 1976; MDiv U Tor CA 1976. D 6/20/1976 Bp William Evan Sanders P 1/23/1977 Bp The Bishop Of Toronto. m 7/9/1983 Rachel H Williams c 1. R St Gregorys Epis Ch Long Bch CA 2000-2015; R S Lk's Ch Racine WI 1998-2000; Asst Chr Ch Greenville SC 1987-1998; Assoc Ch Of The Ascen Lafayette LA 1983-1987; Professed Monk The OHC W Pk NY 1966-1982; Soc of Cath Priests 2010; The Sovereign Mltry Ord of the Temple of Jerusalem 2000.

WILLIAMS, Susan Anslow (Mich) Saint Stephen's Church, 5500 N Adams Rd, Troy MI 48098 **S Steph's Ch Troy MI 2012-** B Detroit MI 1965 d Richard & Katherine. BA Ya 1987; MDiv GTS 1992. D 6/27/1992 Bp Henry Irving Mayson P 1/30/1993 Bp R aymond Stewart Wood Jr. m 10/8/1994 Eric Williams c 2. Assoc R S Lk's Epis Ch Jamestown NY 2000-2012; Dep Gc Dio Wstrn New York Tonawanda NY 2000-2003, Dioc Liturg Cmsn 1994-; Int S Pat's Ch Buffalo NY 1998-1999; Cn S Paul's Cathd Buffalo NY 1992-1998; Serv Ch In Liberia 1987-1988.

WILLIAMS, Thomas (SwFla) 9404 Oak Meadow Ct, Tampa FL 33647 **Cathd Ch Of S Ptr St. Petersburg FL 2015-** B Memphis TN 1967 s Wayne & Frankie. BA Van 1988; PhD U of Notre Dame 1994. D 6/4/2008 P 12/13/2008 Bp Alan Scarfe. H Trin Epis Ch In Countryside Clearwater FL 2012-2013. Auth, "Atone," *The Routledge Comp to Medieval Philos*, Routledge, 2016; Auth, "Anselm's Quiet Radicalism," *British Journ for the Hist of Philos*, 2015; Transltr, "Treatise on Happiness and Treatise on Human Acts," *Aquinas: Basic Works*, Hackett Pub Co, 2014; Auth, "Anselm: Free Will and Moral Responsibility," *Key Debates in Medieval Philos*, Routledge, 2014; Auth, "Hermeneutics and Reading Scripture," *The Cambridge Comp to Aug, 2nd ed.*, Camb Press, 2014; Auth, "The Franciscans," *The Oxford Handbook of the Hist of Ethics*, Oxf Press, 2013; Auth, "Early Hobartian Reaction to the Oxford Mvmt," *Angl and Epis Hist*, 2012; Auth, "Credo ut mirer: Anselm on Sacr Beauty," *The Mod Schoolman*, 2012; Auth, "Human Freedom and Agcy," *The Oxford Handbook of Thos Aquinas*, Oxf Press, 2011; co-Ed, "Philos in the Middle Ages, 3rd ed.," Hacket Pub Co, 2010; Auth, "Duns Scotus," *A Comp to the Philos of Action*, Wiley-Blackwell, 2010; Auth, "Anselm," *Hist of Wstrn Philos of Rel*, Oxf Press, 2009; Auth, "Describing God," *The Cambridge Hist of Medieval Philos*, Camb Press, 2009; co-Auth, "Anselm," Oxf Press, 2008; Transltr, "Anselm: Basic Writings," Hackett Pub Co, 2007; Auth, "God Who Sows the Seed and Gives the Growth: Anselm's Theol of the H Sprt," *ATR*, 2007; Ed, "Thos Aquinas: Disputed Questions on the Virtues," Camb Press, 2005; Auth, "The Doctrine of Univocity is True and Salutary," *Mod Theol*, 2005; co-Auth, "Anselm's Account of Freedom," *The Cambridge Comp to Anselm*, Camb Press, 2005; co-Auth, "Anselm on Truth," *The Cambridge Comp to Anselm*, Camb Press, 2005; Auth, "Sin, Gr, and Redemp," *The Cambridge Comp to Abelard*, Camb Press, 2004; Ed, "The Cambridge Comp to Duns Scotus," Camb Press, 2003; Auth, "Moral Vice, Cognitive Virtue: Jane Austen on Jealousy and Envy," *Philos and Lit*, 2003; Auth, "Transmission and Translation," *The Cambridge Comp to Medieval Philos*, Camb Press, 2003; Auth, "Two Aspects of Platonic Recollection," *Apeiron*, 2002; Auth, "Aug vs Plotinus: The Uniqueness of the Vision at Ostia," *Medieval Philos and the Classical Tradition*, Curzon Press, 2002; Auth, "Biblic Interp," *The Cambridge Comp to Aug*, Camb Press, 2001; Auth, "Lying, Deception, and the Virtue of Truthfulness," *Faith and Philos*, 2000; Auth, "A Most Methodical Lover? On Scotus's Arbitrary Creator," *Journ of the Hist of Philos*, 2000; Auth, "The Unmitigated Scotus," *Archiv fuer Geschichte der Philosophie*, 1998; Auth, "The Libertarian Foundations of Scotus's Moral Philos," *The Thomist*, 1998; Auth, "A Reply to the Ramsey Colloquium," *Same Sex: Debating the Ethics, Sci, and Culture of Homosexuality*, Rowman & Littlefield, 1997; Auth, "Reason, Morality, and Voluntarism in Duns Scotus: A Pseudo-Problem Dissolved," *The Mod Schoolman*, 1997; Auth, "How Scotus Separates Morality from Happiness," *Amer Cath Philos Quarterly*, 1995; Transltr, "Aug: On Free Choice of the Will," Hackett Pub Co, 1993.

WILLIAMS, Thomas Donald (CFla) 3015 Indian River Drive, Palm Bay FL 32905 **D Ch of Our Sav Palm Bay FL 2009-** B Rochester NY 1946 s Donald & Mary. AAS Monroe Cmnty Coll 1969; BA Morehead St U 1971; MA S Bernards TS and Mnstry 1988. D 12/13/1986 Bp William George Burrill. m 5/24/1969 Sandra Marie Williams c 2. D St. Jas Epis Ch NY 2003-2009; D Ch of the Redeem Addison NY 2003-2005; D Schuyler Cnty Epis Parishes Watkins Glen 1986-2002. NAAD 2007.

WILLIAMS, Toneh Alana (Pa) D 6/17/2017 Bp Daniel Gutierrez.

WILLIAMS, Tracey Mark (LI) 8545 96th St, Woodhaven NY 11421 B Brooklyn NY 1961 s Alonzo & Geraldine. BA Cathd Coll of the Immac Concep 1983; MDiv SWTS 1995. D 6/23/1995 P 3/25/1996 Bp Orris George Walker Jr. S Matt's Ch Woodhaven NY 1997-2011; S Phil's Ch Brooklyn NY 1995-1996; Asst S Phil.

WILLIAMS, Wendy Ann (SeFla) 400 Seabrook Rd, Tequesta FL 33469 B Mount Kisco NY 1944 d Lyle & Marie. BA Ge 1966; Duke 1976; MDiv Sewanee: The U So, TS 1980. D 6/28/1981 P 1/30/1982 Bp William Grant Black. Dio Oklahoma Oklahoma City OK 1994-1997; Assoc The Epis Ch Of The Gd Shpd Tequesta FL 1990-2006; Asst S Paul's Ch Rochester NY 1982-1990; Chr Ch - Glendale Cincinnati OH 1981-1982; Asst Chr Ch Glendale OH 1980-1982. NECA 1982.

WILLIAMS, Wesley Danford (Ve) Iglesia Episcopal de Venezuela, Centro Diocesano Av. Caroní No. 100, Colinas de Bello Monte Caracas 1042-A Venezuela **Dio Venezuela Caracas 2014-** B 1967 s Antonio & Florance. D 12/18/2005 P 6/14/2008 Bp Orlando Jesus Guerrero. m 12/13/2007 Shelon Williams c 4.

WILLIAMS JR, Wesley Samuel (VI) 6501 Red Hook Plz Ste 201, St Thomas VI 00802 B Philadelphia PA 1942 s Wesley & Bathrus. BA Harv 1963; MA Fletcher Sch 1964; JD Harv 1967; LLM Col 1969; LLD Virginia Un U 2002; VTS 2012. D 6/28/2008 Bp Gayle Harris P 3/6/2010 Bp Edward Gumbs. m 8/17/1968 Karen Hastie Williams c 3.

WILLIAMS-DUNCAN, Stacy (WA) 372 El Camino Real, Atherton CA 94027 **Prof VTS Alexandria VA 2014-** B Pauls Valley OK 1971 d Larry & Frances. D 6/26/1999 P 1/18/2000 Bp Barry Howe. m 12/28/1996 Joel Richard Duncan. Emm Epis Ch Greenwood VA 2014-2015; S Paul's Memi Charlottesvlle VA 2012; Cathd of St Ptr & St Paul Washington DC 2008-2012; S Matt's Epis Day Sch San Mateo CA 2006-2008; S Matt's Epis Ch San Mateo CA 2005-2006; Assoc S Jas Ch Fremont CA 2002-2004; Cur Trin Par Menlo Pk CA 2000-2002; Ascen Epis Ch Vallejo CA 1999-2000.

WILLIAMSON, Anne (NH) 101 Chapel St, Portsmouth NH 03801 **Assoc S Jn's Ch Portsmouth NH 2013-** B Ann Arbor MI 1957 d Frederick & Patricia. BA Rosary Coll 1979; Dplma in Chr Theol and Mnstry So E Inst of Theol Educ 2004. Trans 6/4/2013 as Priest Bp A Robert Hirschfeld. m 2/5/1983 Michael R Williamson c 2.

WILLIAMSON, Barbara (Mass) 451 Concord Rd, Sudbury MA 01776 **R S Eliz's Ch Sudbury MA 1998-** B Orlando FL 1953 d Franklyn & Barbara. BA Bos 1977; MDiv VTS 1992. D 5/30/1992 Bp David Elliot Johnson P 5/14/1993 Bp Roger John White. m 11/11/1995 Peter Woodring Wenner. Assoc For Educ Chr Ch Milwaukee WI 1992-1998.

WILLIAMSON, Emmanuel (Pa) 1101 2nd Street Pike, Southampton PA 18966 **Ch Of The Redemp Southampton PA 2010-** B Maha MT 1966 s Richard & Kathleen. Mt Ang Abbey; Vancouver TS CA. D 6/13/2004 Bp Mark Lawrence

Macdonald. m 3/22/2015 Kevin Tanger c 1. Assoc S Ptr's Ch Seward AK 2004-2008.

WILLIAMSON JR, James Gray (SwFla) 8005 25th Street East, Parrish FL 34219 B Birmingham AL 1954 s James & June. BS Louisiana Coll 1976; MDiv SW Bapt TS 1979; CTh Epis TS of the SW 1985; PhD Baylor U 1988. D 8/25/1985 Bp Anselmo Carral-Solar P 3/17/1986 Bp Maurice Manuel Benitez. c 1. Cn for Chr Formation Dio SW Florida Parrish FL 2010-2013, 1999; Vic S Edm's Epis Ch Arcadia FL 2007-2015; Int Emm Epis Ch Chestertown MD 2005-2006; Vic S Mary Magd Bradenton FL 1999-2005; R Gd Samar Epis Ch Clearwater FL 1993-1998; R Ch Of The Gd Shpd Tomball TX 1988-1993; Assoc R Trin Ch Longview TX 1985-1987. Auth, "Discovering Tim, Tit, & Philemon," *Guideposts Bible Study Series*, Guideposts. JWILLIAMSON@EPISCOPALSWFL.ORG

WILLIAMSON, Jeremiah D (Colo) Grace and St Stephens Episcopal Church, 601 N Tejon St, Colorado Springs CO 80903 **Gr And S Steph's Epis Ch Colorado Sprg CO 2016-** B Wheeling WV 1980 s Robert & Connie. BS Greenville Coll 2002; MDiv Drew U 2005; Cert Ang Stud GTS 2006. D 9/19/2006 Bp John Palmer Croneberger P 4/17/2007 Bp Mark Hollingsworth Jr. m 5/27/2006 Jennifer Smith c 2. R S Andr's Epis Ch Toledo OH 2009-2016; Cur S Jn's Ch Youngstown OH 2006-2009. 40 Under 40 Mahoning Vlly Young Profsnl's Club 2008. fatherjeremiah@gssepiscopal.org

WILLIAMSON, Randolph Lewis (Pa) 343 Michigan Ave, Swarthmore PA 19081 B Morgantown WV 1948 s Robert & Norma. BS U NC 1970; MDiv EDS 1975. D 6/14/1975 Bp Lyman Cunningham Ogilby P 6/1/1976 Bp John Brooke Mosley. m 8/21/1976 Carol Williamson c 2. R Trin Ch Swarthmore PA 1986-2005; R Ch Of The Adv Hatboro PA 1979-1986; Asst Ch Of S Mart-In-The-Fields Philadelphia PA 1977-1979; Asst S Ptr's Ch Glenside PA 1975-1977.

WILLIAMSON, Rebecca Ann (Az) 1735 S College Ave, Tempe AZ 85281 **Chapl The Crossing Hospice Phoenix AZ 2012-; D S Aug's Epis Ch Tempe AZ 2011-** B Laramie WY 1951 d Clarence & Virginia. BA U of Nthrn Colorado 1975; MS Texas A&M U-Corpus Christi 1980; Cert AZ Ecum Sprtl Direction Sch 2010; Ord D Formation Acad 2011; Ord Other 2011. D 1/29/2011 Bp Kirk Stevan Smith.

WILLIAMSON JR, Wayne Bert (SJ) 13373 N Plaza Del Rio Blvd, Peoria AZ 85381 **Died 12/16/2015** B Casper WY 1918 s Wayne & Agnes. CDSP 1952; Oxf GB 1953; BA USC 1954; MTh Fuller TS 1978. D 6/1/1953 Bp Francis E I Bloy P 2/18/1954 Bp Donald J Campbell. c 2. Ret 1989-2015; Chapl (Major) CSMR 1983-1989; Epis Dio San Joaquin Modesto CA 1982-1987, Exec Asst to Ord 1982-1984; Reg Rep Wrld Vision 1980-1982; Chapl Mil & Hosp OSLJ 1976-1980; Pres Epis Mssy Cmnty 1975-1980; TESM 1975-1980; Prof Ch Hist Melodyland TS 1975-1979; R S Mk's Par Glendale CA 1971-1980; R S Mary's Ch Lakewood WA 1964-1971; R Trin Epis Ch Reno NV 1962-1964; Dep Angl Congr 1961-1963; R S Paul's Epis Ch Elko NV 1959-1962; Vic S Clem's-By-The-Sea Par San Clemente CA 1957-1959; Mssy S Paul U Japan 1953-1957; USN 1942-1945; ExCoun Dio Nevada Las Vegas 1960-1963. Auth, *Growth & Decline in the Epis Ch*, 1979.

WILLIS, Anisa Cottrell (Lex) Cincinnati Childrens Hospital, Department of Pastoral Care, 3333 Burnett Avenue, Cincinnati OH 45229 **Supply P Dio Sthrn Ohio 2010-; PRN Chapl Cincinnati Childrens' Hosp Med Cntr 2009-; Mem Foster Care Revs Bd 2013-; Bd Mem KY Gvnr' Scholars Prog 2013-; Vol CASA of Kenton Cnty 2008-** B Pikeville KY 1969 d Kenneth & Marigrace. BA Rhodes Coll 1992; DAS Ya Berk 1995; MDiv Yale DS 1995; CPE UK Med Cntr 1996; MS U of Kentucky 1998. D 12/9/1998 P 6/24/1999 Bp Don Adger Wimberly. m 10/16/1999 John Kevin Willis c 2. S Jas Epis Ch Cincinnati OH 2011-2012; Supply P Dio Lexington Kentucky 2005-2011; R Adv Ch Cynthiana KY 2001-2004; Assoc Ch Of The H Trin Georgetown KY 1999-2001; Cur S Jas Epis Ch Prestonsburg KY 1999; Bd Mem CASA of Kenton Cnty 2011-2013; Bdgt and Fin Com Dio Lexington Lexington 2003-2005, Stndg Com 2002-2005, Pres, Stndg Com 2002-2004, Bp Search Com 1999-2000, Exec Com 1998-2001; Bd Mem Kentucky Soc Welf Fndt 2002-2013.

WILLIS, Barbara Creighton (Va) 1905 Wildflower Terrace, Richmond VA 23238 B Cleveland OH 1951 d George & Barbara. BA MWC 1973; MA VTS 1997; MS Virginia Commonwealth U 2002; MDiv VTS 2005. D 6/18/2005 P 12/19/2005 Bp Peter J Lee. m 6/3/1972 Addison Willis c 3. R S Asaph's Par Ch Bowling Green VA 2010-2016; Asst. R S Barth's Ch Richmond VA 2005-2010. "Processing w Pooh," *Journ of Pstr Care*, Journ of Pstr Care Pub, 2001.

WILLIS JR, Frederick Webber (SVa) 5119 Blake Point Rd, Chincoteague Island VA 23336 B Bogalusa LA 1940 s Frederick & Mary. BA U of Delaware 1962; MDiv VTS 1965. D 9/26/1965 P 5/21/1966 Bp John Brooke Mosley. m 6/16/1962 Laura Willis c 1. S Dav's Epis Ch No Chesterfield VA 2008-2010; Emm Ch Temperanceville VA 2001-2007; S Paul's Ch Richmond VA 1972-1977; Assoc S Barth's Ch Richmond VA 1969-1971; Vic All SS Epis Ch Delmar DE 1965-1968; Dept Of CE Delaware Yth Div 1965-1968; Asst S Paul's.

WILLIS, Laurie Joy (Chi) 1050 Borregas Ave SPC 103, Sunnyvale CA 94089 B Cook County IL 1957 d Walter & Jeanne. BA Blackburn Coll 1978; MLS U

IL 1979; MA Loyola U 1990; MDiv CDSP 1995. D 6/17/1995 Bp Frank Tracy Griswold III P 12/6/1995 Bp William Edwin Swing. Assoc P S Cuth's Epis Ch Oakland CA 2005-2015; Asst P S Alb's Ch Albany CA 1995-2004. Auth, "Wrld Rel Fact Cards," Toucan Vlly Pub, 2000.

WILLIS, Nancy Appleby (RI) 86 Dendron Rd, Wakefield RI 02879 B Baltimore MD 1942 d Joseph & Mary. BA Wilson Coll 1964; MAT Harv 1965; MDiv Ya Berk 1996. D 6/15/1996 P 4/5/1997 Bp Gerry Wolf. m 7/9/1966 George H Willis c 2. Co-Int R Ch Of The Ascen Wakefield RI 2009-2010, Asst 1997, Asst 1996-1997; R S Dav's On The Hill Epis Ch Cranston RI 2002-2008; Asst / Assoc R Chr Ch Westerly RI 1997-2001; Dir. Sch for Mnstrs Dio Rhode Island Providence RI 1996-1997. Auth, "The Trsfg as a Model of Rel Experience," *Preaching Through the Year of Mk: Sermons that Wk VIII*, Morehouse Pub, 1999.

WILLIS, Ronnie (Cal) 137 Caselli Ave, San Francisco CA 94114 **Assoc S Jas Epis Ch San Francisco CA 2011-** B Richmond CA 1958 s Ronnie & Mourna. BA Dominican Sch of Philos & Theol 1999; MDiv VTS 2002. D 6/1/2002 P 12/7/2002 Bp William Edwin Swing. Vic S Aid's Mssn Bolinas CA 2003-2009; S Steph's Par Bel Tiburon CA 2002-2003.

WILLISTON, Ashton K (CFla) 6329 Frederica Rd, Saint Simons Island GA 31522 **Chr Ch Frederica St Simons Is GA 2017-** B New Smyrna Beach FL 1978 d Dabney & Mary. AA Estrn Florida St Coll 2002; BA U of Cntrl Florida 2007; MDiv Sewanee TS 2017. D 1/30/2017 Bp Gregory Orrin Brewer. m 8/12/2000 Joseph Patrick Williston c 1. Other Lay Position S Jas Epis Ch Ormond Bch FL 2003-2006.

WILLKE, Herbert Alexander (Tex) 11110 Tom Adams Drive, Austin TX 78753 **Died 9/2/2016** B Houston TX 1920 s Herbert & Nettie. Texas Mltry Inst 1940; BS U of Houston 1954; MDiv VTS 1954. D 7/1/1954 P 7/1/1955 Bp Clinton Simon Quin. c 3. Ret 1992-2016; Chr Ch Matagorda TX 1985-1991; S Jn's Epis Ch Palacios TX 1985-1991; The Great Cmsn Fndt Houston TX 1970-1991; Gr Epis Ch Houston TX 1970-1985; S Jas' Epis Ch Mt Vernon VA 1966-1970, 1959-1965; Vic S Chris's Ch Houston TX 1954-1956.

WILLMANN JR, Robert Everett (SO) 155 N 6th St, Zanesville OH 43701 **R S Jas Epis Ch Zanesville OH 2010-** B Newark OH 1965 s Robert & Joyce. Cert Ang Stud Bex Sem; Cert Ang Stud Bex Sem; STB CUA 1992; JCD No Amer Coll 1997. Rec 11/3/2009 as Priest Bp Thomas Edward Breidenthal. m 6/30/2007 Maria S Jamiolkowski c 1.

WILLMS, Ann Bagley (Va) P.O. Box 426, Ivy VA 22945 **S Lk's Simeon Charlottesville VA 2013-** B St Paul MN 1961 d Parker & Suzanne. AB Br 1982; MD Jefferson Med Coll 1987; MDiv VTS 2009. D 6/13/2009 Bp Clifton Daniel III P 1/9/2010 Bp David Colin Jones. m 10/15/1994 Christopher Willms c 2. Vic pro tem, McIlhany Par Dio Virginia Richmond VA 2013; Assoc R S Paul's Memi Charlottesvlle VA 2009-2012. abwillms@gmail.com

WILLMS, John (Minn) 801 E 2nd St Apt 102, Duluth MN 55805 **Ret MN 2011-** B Gretna MT CA 1927 s Peter & Anna. CTh S Chads Coll 1959; LTh S Chads Coll 1974; BA U MN 1974; MDiv The Coll of Emm and S Chad CA 1986. Trans 10/1/1964 as Priest Bp Philip Frederick McNairy. c 2. Supply P S Andr's Ch Moose Lake MN 2004-2011; Supply S Jn's Ch Aitkin MN 1994-2010; Chapl Recovery Cntr Wentworth WI 1985-1988; Chapl DFL Pro Life Caucus 1982-1986; Duluth Congrl Ch Duluth MN 1974-1976; Cur The Par of St Paul's Epis Ch Duluth MN 1972-1974; Vic S Lk's Ch Detroit Lakes MN 1968-1972; P-in-c S Helen's Ch Wadena MN 1964-1968; Trin Epis Ch Pk Rapids MN 1964-1968. Bd Mem, Lake Superior Life Care Ctr (Duluth, Minn) 1981; EvangES; Harvest Ntwk Intl -Assoc. of Evang & Charismat 1990; Intl Ord of S Lk 1999. Prince of Oeace Fellowowship AECM Chrsmtc Ch 1992.

WILLOUGHBY, Robert Geddes (Mich) 16256 Terra Bella St., Clinton Township MI 48038 **Died 8/30/2016** B Northville MI 1935 s Robert & Maxine. Estrn Michigan U; Wayne Detroit; BA Estrn Michigan U 1958; BD Bex Sem 1961; MA U of Detroit Mercy 1969; MSW Wayne 1985. D 6/29/1961 Bp Robert Lionne DeWitt P 1/5/1962 Bp Richard Stanley Merrill Emrich. c 3. Emm Ch Detroit MI 1996-1999, R 1986-1991; Dir, Pstr Care Henry Ford Hosp Detroit MI 1986-1991; Dio Michigan Detroit MI 1985-1986, Chair Spec Mnstrs Com Exec Coun 1981-1982, Chair Spec Mnstrs Com Exec Coun 1972-1975; S Matt's Epis Ch Saginaw MI 1979-1982; coord pastorl care, counsel,&Educ Michigan Cancer Fndt Detroit 1977-1979; R Trin Ch St Clair Shrs MI 1969-1979; R All SS Ch Brooklyn MI 1963-1969; Cur S Phil's Epis Ch Rochester MI 1961-1963. Auth, "Theol Of Anger," *Sharing*, Michigan Cancer Fndt, 1978; Auth, "Sprtl Pain," *Sharing*, Michigan Cancer Fndt, 1978. ACPE; Clincl Mem AAPC.

WILLOUGHBY III, William (Ga) The Ibert, 224 E 34th Street, Savannah GA 31401 **Corp Secy The Amer Friends of the Angl Cntr in Rome 2012-; Vic S Barth's Ch Burro Savannah GA 2000-; Secy-Gnrl The CBS 1997-; Dn/ R The Collgt Ch of St Paul the Apos Savannah GA 1987-** B Anniston AL 1955 s William & Doris. ThD/Candidate GTF; BA U Chi 1977; CTh Oxf GB 1981; MDiv Nash 1982; EdD GTF 2005. D 6/19/1982 Bp Quintin Ebenezer Primo Jr P 1/27/1983 Bp James Winchester Montgomery. m 8/14/1982 Mary C Crane c 3. Rcrdng Secy Conf of No Amer Cathd Deans 1996-2017; Rdr, GOE's GBEC 1993-2009; Ch Of S Mary The Vrgn New York NY 1984-1987; Chapl CHS NY NY 1984-1987; Chapl/Asst. Hd S Hilda's And S Hugh's Sch New

York NY 1984-1987; Cur Par of St Paul's Ch Norwalk Norwalk CT 1982-1984; Pres, Stndg Committe Dio Georgia Savannah GA 2015-2016, Ecum Off 2015-, Mem of Stndg Com 2013-2016, VP, Dioc Coun 2007-2009, Mem of Dioc Coun 2005-, Dep to GC 2003-, Pres of Stndg Com 1995-1996, Mem of Stndg Com 1992-1996, Mem Mssn Dvlpmt Cmsn 1989-1997, Dn, Savannah Convoc 1989-. Auth, "Old Catholicism's Journey to Ecum Enabler," GTF, 2014; Co-Auth, "The Forensic Practitioner's Quest for Truth," Elsevier Acad Press, 2011; Auth, "Singing God's Song of Love," GTF, 2005; Auth, "A Short Hist of S Paul's," St Paul's, Savannah, 2003; Auth, "A Pilgrimage of Pryr through the W of Ireland," GTF, 2002; Auth, "Theol Considerations in Writing an Icon," GTF, 2001; Auth, "A Jerusalem Pilgrim: A Guest of the Oriental Orth," GTF, 2000. Comp of the OGS 2002; Conf Assoc of the CHS 1982; GAS 1987; P Assoc of the SocOLW 1983; Soc of Chas, King and Mtyr 1995; Ward Superior, CBS 1987. Comp Memi of Merit 2017; Off Ord of St. Jn of Jerusalem 2010; Chapl Sovereign Mltry Ord of the Temple in Jerusalem 2004; Knight Sovereign Mltry Ord of the Temple of Jerusalem 2004; Maroon Key U Chi 1976. rector@stpaulsavannah.org

WILLOW, Mary Margaret Gregory (SwFla) 127 Gesner St, Linden NJ 07036 B Okmulgee OK 1926 d Fountain & Ivy. BA Jersey City St Coll 1965; MS Rutgers The St U of New Jersey 1975. D 10/26/1986 Bp Emerson Paul Haynes. m 9/6/1947 James Mark Willow c 1. D S Andr's Epis Ch Sprg Hill FL 1986-2006. Ord Of S Lk 1973.

WILLS, Clark Edward (Oly) 308 - 14th Avenue East #111, Seattle WA 98112 B Cincinnati OH 1942 s Edward & Anna. S Meinrads TS; BA The Athenaeum of Ohio 1965; MDiv Nash 1974. D 12/14/1973 P 6/15/1974 Bp James Winchester Montgomery. Asst S Paul's Ch Seattle WA 2000; Ch Of The Annunc Bridgeview IL 1996-1997; Asst All SS Epis Ch Chicago IL 1985-1999; Assoc S Andr's Ch Chicago IL 1977-1985; R S Marg's Ch Chicago IL 1975-1977; Cur S Phil's Epis Palatine IL 1974-1975.

WILLS JR, Edwin Francis (Ark) 321 Crystal Ct, Little Rock AR 72205 S Mich's Epis Ch Little Rock AR 2004- B Memphis TN 1955 s Edwin & Carolyn. BBA U of Memphis 1978. D 8/31/2002 P 3/1/2003 Bp Larry Maze. m 10/13/1979 Andrea Wills c 3. Trin Cathd Little Rock AR 2002-2004; Asst For Formation S Andr's Cathd Jackson MS 1992-1995; Dir S Columba Epis Conf Cntr 1982-1991; Asst For Yth & Educ All SS Epis Ch Memphis TN 1977-1981.

WILLS, Robert Murlin (Mich) 1506 Eagle Crest Dr, Prescott AZ 86301 B Port Huron MI 1941 s William & Margaret. BA U of Wstrn Ontario CA 1963; MDiv EDS 1966; MS Wayne 1972. D 6/29/1966 Bp Chauncie Kilmer Myers P 2/1/1968 Bp Richard Stanley Merrill Emrich. m 2/20/2010 Mary Lou Wills c 3. R S Geo's Epis Ch Warren MI 2003-2007; Chr Ch Cranbrook Bloomfield Hills MI 1995-1996; Asst Min S Mart Ch Detroit MI 1967-1972. Robert M. Wills, "Seeking the Living among the Dead," CreateSpace, 2015; Auth, "Taking Caesar Out of Jesus," Xlibris, 2013.

WILMER, Amelie (Va) 12291 River Rd, Richmond VA 23238 S Jn's Ch Richmond VA 2017- B Los Angeles 1959 d John & Pauline. BA Ya 1981; MDiv UTS 2010; Cert Ang Stud VTS 2011. D 6/4/2011 P 12/10/2011 Bp Shannon Sherwood Johnston. m 10/7/2014 Claiborne Watkins Minor c 3. All Souls Epis Ch Mechanicsville VA 2012-2017.

WILMINGTON, Richard Newton (Cal) 2 Columbia Dr, Rancho Mirage CA 92270 Non Stipendiary S Marg's Epis Ch Palm Desert CA 2008-; Non-par 1980- B New York NY 1939 s Edward & Muriel. BA Hobart and Wm Smith Colleges 1961; MDiv GTS 1965. D 6/16/1965 P 12/1/1965 Bp Horace W B Donegan. m 9/10/2008 Robert Vincent Lilley c 3. Pstr Gr Cathd San Francisco CA 1970-1979; Vic S Aug's Fairfax CA 1967-1970; Cur St Johns Epis Ch Ross CA 1965-1967. Auth, "NT Roots of AntiSemitism," *Epis Life*; Auth, "Meditation On Magic," *LivCh*.

WILMOT, Susan Elizabeth (Az) 975 E Warner Rd, Tempe AZ 85284 P-in-c S Jas The Apos Epis Ch Tempe AZ 2013- B Halifax England 1961 d Stanley & Rosemary. BS Sheffield City Polytechnic 1983; MDiv Epis TS of the SW 2008. D 10/20/2007 P 6/14/2008 Bp Kirk Stevan Smith. m 9/8/1984 Stephen Anthony Wilmot. Bd Chr Cmnty Outreach 2010-2013; R Ch Of Our Sav Lakeside AZ 2008-2013, Educ Chair 2008-, Stwdshp Chair 2008-; Vol Chapl Summit Healthcare 2008-2013; Dioc Coun Dio Arizona Phoenix AZ 2010-2012.

WILMOTH, Danny Stewart (Va) 3440 S Jefferson St, Falls Church VA 22041 B Buckhannon WVA 1952 s Jack & Carolyn. BS U of Arizona 1974; MS Texas A & M Commerce 1983. D 2/23/2013 Bp Shannon Sherwood Johnston. m 10/10/1980 Mary Ann Wilmoth c 3.

WILS, Duane Michael (NMich) 6971 Days River 24.5 Rd, Gladstone MI 49837 B 1959 D 5/20/2001 Bp James Arthur Kelsey P 9/21/2010 Bp Thomas Kreider Ray. m 9/18/1982 Wendy Elya c 2.

WILSON, Anne Warrington (SO) 7730 Tecumseh Trl, Cincinnati OH 45243 B Cincinnati OH 1952 d John & Suzanne. BA Trin Hartford CT 1975; MDiv EDS 1979. D 6/4/1983 P 9/16/1984 Bp William Grant Black. m 5/9/1986 Gene Merrill Wilson c 2. S Steph's Epis Ch Cincinnati OH 2015; P-in-c S Mary Magd Ch Maineville OH 2011-2013; P-in-c The Ch Of Ascen And H Trin Cincinnati OH 2009-2010; All SS Ch Cincinnati OH 2007-2009, Int R 2007-2009, Int 1988-1989; P-in-c Ch Of S Mich And All Ang Cincinnati OH 1998-2005; Asst S Thos Epis Ch Terrace Pk OH 1994-1996; Int S Tim's Epis Ch Cincinnati

OH 1991-1993; Int Gr Ch Cincinnati OH 1989-1990; Asst Chr Ch - Glendale Cincinnati OH 1986-1988; Int Dio Sthrn Ohio Cincinnati OH 1985-1986; Vic Chap Of The Nativ Cincinnati OH 1983-1985.

WILSON, Barbara Ann Theresa (WMich) 9713 Oakview Dr, Portage MI 49024 **Mgr Sprtl Care Serv Memi Hosp And Hlth System So Bend IN 2001-; R S Aug Of Cbury Epis Ch Benton Harbor MI 1994-** B Wyandotte MI 1951 d John & Joyce. BA U of Detroit Mercy 1980; MDiv Ya Berk 1984; CSD Colombiere Cntr For Sprtlty Clarkston MI 1991; MA Wstrn Michigan U 1998. D 6/30/1984 Bp Henry Irving Mayson P 7/29/1985 Bp H Coleman Mcgehee Jr. m 6/12/2013 Lynne Gail Jacobson. S Fran Ch Orangeville Shelbyville MI 2000-2013; S Steph's Epis Ch Plainwell MI 1997-1999; Ch of the Medtr Harbert MI 1994-1996; S Barn Epis Ch Portage MI 1994; S Lk's Par Kalamazoo MI 1991-1993; Dio Michigan Detroit MI 1987-1988; Non-par 1984-1990. Apc (Assn Of Profsnl Chapl) 2000. bwilson@beaconhealthsystem.org

WILSON, Barrie Andrew (CFla) B 1940 Trans 2/2/1972 Bp George Leslie Cadigan. m 9/5/1964 Barbara Boyes.

WILSON JR, Charles (SO) 77 Sherman Ave, Columbus OH 43205 **S Phil's Ch Columbus OH 2015-; S Paul's Ch Dekalb IL 2005-** B Holyoke MA 1965 s Charles & Anne. AA Holyoke Cmnty Coll 1986; BS Franklin U 2002; MDiv Bex Sem 2005. D 5/22/2004 P 6/25/2005 Bp Herbert Thompson Jr. m 7/6/1996 Julie Barry c 2. S Ptr's Epis Ch Delaware OH 2007-2014; Transitional D S Mary's Epis Ch Hillsboro OH 2005-2007.

WILSON JR, Charles Alexander (NwT) 1524 S. Alabama St., Amarillo TX 79102 B Kalispell MT 1933 s Charles & Edith. BA U of Montana 1957; MDiv CDSP 1962; U of New Mex 1973. D 7/2/1962 P 1/2/1963 Bp Chandler W Sterling. m 4/23/1989 Emily N Wilson c 2. Dn Panhandle Dnry 1995-1997; S Thos Epis Ch Hereford TX 1992-1998; Dn Panhandle Dnry 1988-1991; Asst to R S Andr's Epis Ch Amarillo TX 1987-1991, 1985; R S Paul's Ch Artesia NM 1986-1987; Locten S Jas' Epis Ch Dalhart TX 1985-1986; R S Chris's Epis Ch El Paso TX 1981-1984; R St Johns Epis Ch Farmington NM 1973-1981; R All SS Ch Minot ND 1969-1972; Vic S Dav Pittsburgh CA 1964-1969; Vic S Jn's Epis Ch Clayton CA 1964-1969; Cur S Jn's Ch Butte MT 1962-1964. Intl Bonhoeffer Soc.

WILSON, Charleston D (SwFla) 222 S Palm Ave, Sarasota FL 34236 **Ch Of The Redeem Sarasota FL 2014-** B Alabama 1982 s David & Mary Rebekah. D 5/14/2013 P 12/9/2013 Bp Daniel Hayden Martins. m 5/19/2007 Malacy Touchstone Wilson c 2.

WILSON, Charlotte Marie (Cal) **S Paul's Epis Ch Burlingame CA 2016-** B Chicago, IL 1967 B.Al U MI 1989; M.A. San Jose St U 1996; M.Div. CDSP 2016. D 6/11/2016 Bp Marc Handley Andrus. c 3. D S Andr's Epis Ch San Bruno CA 2016.

WILSON, Claudia Marie (NY) 1085 Warburton Ave Apt 326, Yonkers NY 10701 B New York NY 1944 d George & Lilly. BA Binghamton U 1965; MA U Tor 1968; MTS SWTS 2006. D 5/30/1992 Bp Richard Frank Grein P 9/23/2006 Bp Mark Sean Sisk. P-in-c Ch Of The H Comm Mahopac NY 2010-2016; Cn for Cong. Dev. Dio New York New York NY 2006-2016, 1992-2004; D S Jn's Ch Getty Sq Yonkers NY 1994-2006; D The Ch of S Ign of Antioch New York NY 1992-1994; S Jn's Ch New York NY 1992.

WILSON, Clinton M (Tenn) 4715 Harding Pike, Nashville TN 37205 **Assoc S Geo's Ch Nashville TN 2015-** B Birmingham AL 1982 s Rodney & Jackie. BA Sthrn Bible Coll 2006; MDiv Nash 2014; MDiv Nash TS 2014. Trans 9/30/2014 as Priest Bp Paul Emil Lambert. m 6/30/2007 Theresa J Wilson. S Dav's Ch Denton TX 2014-2015.

WILSON, Conrad Bruce (WTex) 10 Tanglewood St, San Marcos TX 78666 **Dio W Texas San Antonio TX 2016-** B Midland TX 1954 s James & Sophie. BS Agape Sem of Jesus Chr 1975; MA U of Texas 1980; MDiv VTS 1986. D 6/15/1986 Bp John Herbert MacNaughton P 1/1/1987 Bp Stanley Fillmore Hauser. m 9/2/1978 Sandra Wilson c 2. The Ch Of The Recon Corpus Christi TX 2011-2015; S Mk's Ch San Marcos TX 1996-2011; Asst to R Ch Of The Gd Shpd Corpus Christi TX 1994-1996; R Gr Ch Cuero TX 1989-1994; Asst to R S Jn's Ch McAllen TX 1986-1989.

WILSON, Dana Jane Gant (FtW) 124 Oakmont Dr, Weatherford TX 76088 B Clovis NM 1951 d George & Neta. BS Estrn New Mex U 1974. D 7/1/1989 Bp Robert Manning Moody. m 12/30/1972 Gary Dan Wilson c 3. D S Jn's Ch Odessa TX 2004-2006; S Jn's Epis Ch Odessa TX 2004-2006; Co-Mentor D Formation Prog Archd Dio NW Texas Lubbock TX 1997-2006, 1997-2004; Ch Of The H Trin Midland TX 1997-2004; D H Comf Epis Ch Sprg TX 1994-1997; Chapl W AL Hospice Tuscaloosa 1990-1993; S Mths Epis Ch Tuscaloosa AL 1990-1991.

WILSON, Donald Rexford (Ore) 7065 S.W. Molalla Bend Rd., Wilsonville OR 97070 **Asst S Tim's Epis Ch Salem OR 2003-; Ret 1989-** B Portland OR 1926 s Harry & Hazel. Dip ATC 1964. D 6/29/1964 P 1/25/1965 Bp James Walmsley Frederic Carman. m 3/29/2008 Marilyn Louise Wilson c 2. Asst S Jas Epis Ch Portland OR 2001-2003; P S Paul's Par Oregon City OR 1992-1993; P S Mary's Ch Woodburn OR 1991-1993; R S Mart's Ch Lebanon OR 1985-1989; S Matt's Epis Ch Eugene OR 1983-1984; S Thos' Epis Ch Eugene OR 1982-1983; Vic S Mich's/San Miguel Newberg OR 1970-1979; Vic S Bede's Ch Forest Grove

OR 1970-1975; Dio Oregon Portland OR 1969-1979; Vic S Steph's Ch Newport OR 1964-1970.

WILSON, Donald Robert (Mass) 76 Old Pine Hill Rd N, Berwick ME 03901 B Boston MA 1931 s Clark & Helen. BA Estrn Nazarene Coll 1953; BD Bex Sem 1956. D 6/9/1956 Bp Norman B Nash P 12/18/1956 Bp Conrad H Gesner. c 4. S Paul's Ch Peabody MA 1983-1996; Chr Epis Ch Yankton SD 1977-1983; All SS Epis Ch Wolfeboro NH 1964-1977.

WILSON, Edward Adrian (ECR) 90 Cashew Blossom Drive, San Jose CA 95123 **Chapl Los Gatos Meadows Epis Hm Fndt Los Gatos CA 2002-** B Northampton UK 1949 s James & Annie. BA U of Scranton 1976; MA Ya 1978; MDiv CDSP 1983; DMin SFTS 2000. D 6/25/1983 P 7/1/1984 Bp William Edwin Swing. c 2. Epis Sr Communities Lafayette CA 2002-2015; Assoc S Thos Epis Ch Sunnyvale CA 2002-2003; Chapl Res Providence Portland Med Cntr Portland OR 2000-2001; Supply P Dio Oregon Portland OR 1995-2000; Ch Of The Epiph Lake Oswego OR 1987-1988; Asst P Trin Epis Ch Ashland Ashland OR 1983-1987; Assoc Chapl Rogue Vlly Med Cntr Medford OR 1983-1986. Alpha Sigma Nu Natl Jesuit hon Soc 1976; Delta Tau Kappa Natl Soc Sci hon Soc 1976. ewilson@jtm-esc.org

WILSON, Eugenia Theresa (NY) 5030 Henry Hudson Pkwy E, Bronx NY 10471 B New York NY 1949 d Eugenie. BS CUNY 1975. D 5/5/2007 Bp Mark Sean Sisk. c 1. D Chr Ch Riverdale Bronx NY 2007-2012.

WILSON JR, Frank E (Minn) 16376 7th Street Lane S, Lakeland MN 55043 B Big Sprg TX 1949 s Frank & Carolyn. BA U of New Mex 1971; MDiv Epis TS of the SW 1974. D 9/10/1974 P 5/1/1975 Bp Richard Mitchell Trelease Jr. m 4/14/1973 Alys Gilcrease c 3. R S Jn The Evang S Paul MN 2000-2010; R S Lk's Ch Minneapolis MN 1993-2000; Cn S Mk's Cathd Shreveport LA 1988-1993; Assoc Epis Ch Of The Gd Shpd Lake Chas LA 1986-1988; Cur Ch Of The H Cross Shreveport LA 1983-1985; Vic H Trin Epis Ch - Mssn Raton NM 1976; Vic S Paul's Peace Ch Las Vegas NM 1975-1976.

WILSON, Frank F(enn) (At) 803 Wilkins Dr, Monroe GA 30655 B Brunswick GA 1947 s Clyde & Melba. Georgia Sthrn U 1966; Brunswick Jr Coll 1968; BA U of W Georgia 1970; MEd U of W Georgia 1971; MDiv Sewanee: The U So, TS 1988. D 6/6/1998 P 2/20/1999 Bp Frank Kellogg Allan. m 12/23/2016 Suzanne K Wilson c 3. R S Clare's Epis Ch Blairsville GA 2010-2014; R S Alb's Ch Monroe GA 2004-2006; Assoc Epis Ch Of The H Fam Jasper GA 1998-2004. (Bldg Named After) The Ext 1999.

WILSON, Frank K (RG) 12 Indian Maid Ln, Alamogordo NM 88310 B Sharon PA 1948 s Walter & Dolores. BA Ken 1969; JD U of New Mex 1976; Rio Grande Sch for Mnstry TESM 2004. D 6/19/2004 P 3/5/2005 Bp Terence Kelshaw. m 6/28/1988 Carolyn Jean Wilson c 2. P-in-c S Andr's Ch Roswell NM 2010-2011; R S Jn's Epis Ch Alamogordo NM 2005-2009; COM Dio The Rio Grande Albuquerque 2008-2012.

WILSON, George Ira (Mich) 7903 Mesa Trails Cir, Austin TX 78731 **Asstg Cler S Matt's Ch Austin TX 1990-** B 1930 s George & Elizabeth. BA U Chi 1950; GTS 1953; MBA U of Detroit Mercy 1959; Cert Michigan TS 1971. D 3/28/1971 Bp Archie H Crowley P 3/1/1972 Bp Richard Stanley Merrill Emrich. m 4/6/1953 Cynthia Gurstell. Locten Trin Ch St Clair Shrs MI 1979-1980; Asst Ch Of The H Cross Novi MI 1976-1979; S Anne's Epis Ch Walled Lake MI 1976-1979; Asst S Steph's Ch Troy MI 1971-1975. Bsp; Ord Of S Lk.

WILSON, George Steil (Oly) 3607 214th Street Southwest, Brier WA 98036 **Ret 1998-** B Seattle WA 1939 s William & Naomi. BA U of Washington 1963; STB ATC 1966. D 6/8/1966 P 2/23/1967 Bp Ivol I Curtis. m 2/3/1996 Claire Louise McClenny c 2. Int Ch Of The Gd Shpd Fed Way WA 1996-1997; Int S Dav's Ch Spokane WA 1995-1996; Int Emm Ch Coos Bay OR 1993-1994; R S Alb's Ch Edmonds WA 1976-1993; R S Jn's Ch Hermiston OR 1970-1976; Asst Stillaguamish Mssn Marysville WA Dio Olympia 1967-1970; Cur S Lk's Ch Tacoma WA 1966-1967.

WILSON, Greg (Pa) 246 Fox Rd, Media PA 19063 **The Epis Ch Of The Adv Kennet Sq PA 2016-; Luth and Epis Chapl Tem Epis Dio Pennsylvania Philadelphia PA 2004-** B Lower Merion PA 1976 s Thomas & Sally. BA U of Delaware 1999; MDiv EDS 2002. D 6/22/2002 P 5/31/2003 Bp Charles Ellsworth Bennison Jr. m 5/21/2010 Brenda Stewart c 1. Resurr Epis Ch Rockdale Aston PA 2014-2016; R S Jas Ch Greenridge Aston PA 2010-2014; Dio Pennsylvania Philadelphia PA 2004-2010; Cur Ch Of The Redeem Bryn Mawr PA 2002-2004.

WILSON, Harold David (CFla) 1629 Championship Blvd, Franklin TN 37064 **Ret 2005-; Assoc S Barth's Ch Nashville TN 2005-** B Raton NM 1939 s Brownlow & Joyce. BS USNA 1962; MA U Denv 1969; MDiv Nash 1972. D 12/29/1971 P 6/29/1972 Bp Edwin B Thayer. m 6/7/1962 Katrina C Wilson. Stndg Com Dio Cntrl Florida Orlando FL 1997-2000, Dioc Bd 1993-2000, Dn Cntrl Deanry 1993-1996, Chair Structure Cmsn 1992-1996, Dep GC 1994-1997, COM 1985-1993; R All SS Ch Of Winter Pk Winter Pk FL 1984-2005; Bp Admin Cbnt Dio Colorado Denver CO 1980-1984, COM 1975-1979, ExCoun 1974-1979; R Chr Epis Ch Denver CO 1974-1984, Cur 1972-1973; Bd TESM Ambridge PA 1992-2002. AAC 1999; AFP 1988-1990; BRF 1987-1990; ERM.

WILSON, Henry Haddon (Eur) Stautland, Finnas N-5437 Norway **Ret 1993-** B Wichita KS 1931 s Orlando & Vernis. BA U CA 1960; BD CDSP 1963. D 12/1/1963 P 11/1/1964 Bp Stephen F Bayne Jr. c 1. Pres Adv Europe 1984-1993; Coun Adv Europe 1983-1993; Secy of Convoc 1979-1993; P-in-c Ascen Munich Germany 1976-1993; Ch Of The Ascen New York NY 1976-1992; Admin Asst Bp of Europe 1973-1976; The Angl/Epis Ch Of Chr The King Frankfurt am Main 60323 1973-1976; RurD Germany & Austria 1969-1973; Chapl S Aug Cbury Wiesbaden Germany 1965-1973; Cur S Chris's Frankfurt-am-Main Germany 1963-1965. ComT.

WILSON, Howard Lee (Okla) 2621 E Sheridan St Unit 118, Laramie WY 82070 **Ret 1991-** B Canton IL 1925 s Adolph & Ruth. BA U of Wyoming 1950; BD CDSP 1953. D 6/11/1953 P 12/15/1953 Bp James W Hunter. m 6/11/1952 Ruth Wilson c 3. Dio Oklahoma Oklahoma City OK 1983-1990; S Andr's Ch Grove OK 1983-1990; Vic S Jn's Epis Ch Vinita OK 1983-1990; Dn S Matt's Epis Cathd Laramie WY 1967-1980; Vic S Steph's Ch Casper WY 1963-1967; Archd Dio Wyoming Casper 1958-1963; Vic S Helen's Epis Ch Crowheart WY 1956-1958; Vic S Thos Ch Dubois WY 1955-1958; Vic All Souls Edgerton WY 1954-1955; Cur S Mk's Epis Ch Casper WY 1953-1955. Hon DD CDSP 1976; Phi Beta Kappa U of Wyoming 1950.

WILSON II, James (Minn) 14441 92nd Avenue North, Maple Grove MN 55369 **P-in-c H Trin Epis Ch S Paul MN 2009-** B LR 1960 s Benjamin & Sophia. BTh Cuttington U 1988; MTS VTS 1999; Dmin Luther Sem 2011; Dmin Other 2011. Trans 1/1/2002 as Priest Bp James Louis Jelinek. m 8/31/1991 Eliza Wilson. P-in-c S Phil's Ch S Paul MN 2007-2008, 2002-2003; S Thos Ch Minneapolis MN 2007-2008; R S Andr's Epis Ch Minneapolis MN 2004-2007; Stndg Com Mem Dio Minnesota Minneapolis MN 2007-2009.

WILSON, James Barrett (Ky) 7619 Beech Spring Ct, Louisville KY 40241 **Eccl Trial Crt Dio Kentucky Louisville KY 2005-, 2000-2006, Exec Coun 2000-2003** B Denver CO 1941 s Joseph & Jane. BA U CO 1962; BD SWTS 1965. D 6/14/1965 Bp Edwin B Thayer P 12/21/1965 Bp Joseph Summerville Minnis. m 8/8/1964 Beverly C Wilson c 2. Vic H Trin Ch Brandenburg KY 1998-2006; Dir, Colo. Epis Fndt Dio Colorado Denver CO 1990-1995, Exec Coun 1969-1989; Assoc S Steph's Epis Ch Aurora CO 1990-1995; 1975-1990; Vic S Paul's Epis Ch Lamar CO 1966-1975; Ch Of The Mssh Las Animas CO 1966-1973; Asst S Paul's Epis Ch Lakewood CO 1966. Int Mnstry Ntwk 1997.

WILSON, James G. (Ct) 54 Harbour View Place, Stratford CT 06615 **Ret 2004-** B Brooklyn NY 1940 s William & Jane. RPI 1960; BA Adel 1963; MDiv Ya Berk 1967. D 6/17/1967 P 12/23/1967 Bp Jonathan Goodhue Sherman. m 2/9/1963 Regina Ann Wilson c 2. Exec Dir, CDO Epis Ch Cntr New York NY 1992-2003, Assoc Dir, CDO 1988-1991; R S Jn's Epis Par Waterbury CT 1979-1987; Vic/Yoked Congregations S Jn's Epis Ch Oakdale NY 1974-1979; Vic S Lukes Ch Bohemia NY 1968-1979; Cur S Geo's Ch Hempstead NY 1967-1968; Chapl Intern Drew U Madison NJ 1965-1966; Pres Natl Ntwk Of Epis Cler Assn Lynnwood WA 1982-1985, Exec Bd 1979-1987; Chapl Bohemia Fire Dept. Bohemia NY 1969-1979. Co-Auth, "More Than Fine Gold," CDO, 1978; Auth, *Var Deploy Booklets & Resources*, CDO. CT Cler Assn 1980-1984; LI Cler Assn 1967-1979; NNECA 1971. Robert J. Dodwell Awd NNECA 2003.

WILSON, Jane R (NC) Calvary Episcopal Church, PO Box 1245, Tarboro NC 27886 **Vic Calv Ch Tarboro NC 2012-; S Lk's Ch Tarboro NC 2012-** B Davenport, IA 1959 d William & Jane. BA Youngstown St U 1989; MA Youngstown St U 1991; MLS Clarion U of PA 1992; CATS SWTS 2006; MDiv Lexington TS 2007. D 6/9/2007 P 12/16/2007 Bp Stacy F Sauls. m 7/10/1993 Shannon H Wilson c 3. Chr Ch Cathd Lexington KY 2010-2012; S Aug's Chap Lexington KY 2010-2012; Dio Lexington Lexington 2007-2010.

WILSON, Jennifer Mccormick (SeFla) D 8/24/2002 Bp Leo Frade.

WILSON, John Morris (ETenn) 118 Dupont Smith Ln, Kingston TN 37763 **D (non-stipendiary) S Steph's Epis Ch Oak Ridge TN 2009-, D 1993-2008** B Nashville TN 1939 s Charles & Barbara. BA Van 1961; MS Van 1969; U of Tennessee 1976. Rec 10/17/1993 Bp Robert Gould Tharp. m 6/28/1987 Delores Faye Brewer. Serv RC Ch 1980-1987.

WILSON, Kate (ECR) 611 Dellingham Dr Apt A, Indianapolis IN 46260 **Assoc Ch Of The Nativ Indianapolis IN 2012-; Cmncatn Mnstry St. Aug Hm for the Elderly Indianapolis IN 2012-** B Pittsburgh PA 1948 d John & Mary. BA Coll of Mt S Vinc 1970; MEd Ford 1979; MDiv CDSP 2006. D 6/24/2006 P 8/4/2007 Bp Sylvestre Donato Romero. Hlth Care Chapl Dss Hosp Evansville IN 2010-2011; Assoc S Paul's Epis Ch Evansville IN 2010-2011; Assoc S Mk's Epis Ch Santa Clara CA 2006-2010. Assn of Profsnl Chapl 2011.

WILSON, Kellie C (USC) 10 N Church St, Greenville SC 29601 **Chr Ch Greenville SC 2017-** B Oxnard CA 1971 d James & Shelley. AA Brevard Coll 1991; BS Clemson U 1993; MDiv Luth Theol Sthrn Sem 2013. D 6/1/2013 P 2/1/2014 Bp William Andrew Waldo. m 1/27/1996 Stephen Kenneth Wilson c 1. Dio Upper So Carolina Columbia SC 2015-2017, Cn 2012-, 2011-2013; H Cross Epis Ch Simpsonville SC 2005-2012. kwilson@ccgsc.org

WILSON, Kenneth Wayne (CNY) 7863 Russell Ln, Manlius NY 13104 **Ret 2000-** B Atlantic City NJ 1935 s Robert & Ruth. BS Indiana St U 1958; MDiv GTS 1961; Cert Inst of Rel & Hlth 1969. D 4/8/1961 P 10/28/1961 Bp James

W

Pernette DeWolfe. m 7/29/1961 Nancy Louise Wilson c 3. Assoc Exec Dir Onondaga Pstr Counslg Cntr In Syracuse NY 1994-2000; Adj Fac Colgate Rochester DS NY 1979-1983; Dir Of Trng Onondaga Pstr Counslg Cntr In Syracuse NY 1969-1983; P-in-c S Jn's Phoenix NY 1969-1974; Vic S Pat's Ch Deer Pk NY 1963-1968; Cur Chr Ch Babylon NY 1961-1963; Com Dio Cntrl New York Liverpool NY 1973-1974. Aamft; AAPC.

WILSON, Linda Latham (Alb) PO Box 154, 627 Roses Brook Rd, South Kortright NY 13842 B Norfolk VA 1942 d Jesse & Ruth. BA Old Dominion U 1971; MTh S Josephs Coll Maine 2006. D P 10/23/2005 Bp David John Bena. m 5/5/1973 Harold Wilson. S Paul's Ch Bloomville NY 2003-2006.

WILSON, Linda R (RG) 109 Chaparral Loop, Socorro NM 87801 B Atoka OK 1947 d David & Peggy. BD McNeese St U 1972; MS U of Texas 1986; MDiv Epis TS of the SW 1993. D 7/28/1993 Bp William Jackson Cox P 5/2/1994 Bp Maurice Manuel Benitez. m 9/26/2007 Carl T Means c 2. Dio Wyoming Casper 2007-2010; S Jas Ch Riverton WY 2006-2007; S Jn's Ch La Porte TX 2004-2006; S Lk's Epis Hosp Houston TX 2004; Assoc R Trin Ch Houston TX 2001-2004; S Mk's Ch Houston TX 1999-2001; S Mart's Epis Ch Houston TX 1997-1999; All SS Epis Ch Austin TX 1994-1997.

WILSON, Linda Tardy (Pgh) 215 Canterbury Ln, North Versailles PA 15137 **Pstr in-charge All Souls Ch N Versailles PA 2011-** B Pittsburgh PA 1949 d Harold & Barbara. BA U MI 1971. D 10/17/2009 Bp Bob Johnson. m 8/12/1972 James M Wilson c 2. deaconlindawilson@gmail.com

WILSON, Mary Elizabeth (Tex) 717 Sage Road, Houston TX 77056 **Sr Assoc R for CE and Sprtl Formation S Mart's Epis Ch Houston TX 2010-** B Luling TX 1951 d Thomas & Nell. Austin Cmnty Coll 1988; BBA U of Texas 1990; MDiv VTS 1997. D 6/21/1997 Bp Claude Edward Payne P 4/25/1998 Bp Leopoldo Jesus Alard. c 2. R S Richard's Of Round Rock Round Rock TX 2006-2010; R S Jn's Epis Ch Silsbee TX 2000-2006; Asst P Chr Epis Ch Tyler TX 1997-2000. mwilson@stmartinsepiscopal.org

WILSON, Mauricio Jose (Cal) 114 Montecito Ave, Oakland CA 94610 **R S Paul's Ch Oakland CA 2009-** B Costa Rica 1966 s Cornelius & Eulalia. BBA Universidad De Costa Rica 1992; CPA Universidad De Costa Rica 1994; MDiv GTS 2000; STM GTS 2001. Trans 8/13/2003 Bp Orris George Walker Jr. m 9/9/2002 Karla Vanessa Morris c 2. R All SS Ch Great Neck NY 2003-2009.

WILSON, Michael Hoover (SwFla) 5108 Plainfield Street, Midland MI 48642 B Greenwich CT 1937 s Clyde & Dorothy. BA U So 1961; BD Ya Berk 1964. D 6/14/1964 Bp Charles L Street P 6/29/1965 Bp Ned Cole. m 8/6/2005 Patricia Louise Wilson c 3. S Jn's Epis Ch Midland MI 2006-2014; Vacancy Consult Dio SW Florida Parrish FL 1993-1998; R S Jas Epis Ch Pt Charlotte FL 1983-2002; Dn Sw Dist Dio Rochester Henrietta 1981-1983; R Zion Ch Avon NY 1975-1983; P-in-c S Paul Warners NY 1974-1975; R Chr Epis Ch Jordan NY 1967-1975; Cur S Jn's Ch Ithaca NY 1964-1967.

WILSON III, Morris Karl (Tenn) 3002 Westmoreland Dr, Nashville TN 37212 B Evanston IL 1947 s Morris & Monterey. BA Ya 1969; MDiv Van 1973. D 6/24/1973 Bp William F Gates Jr P 6/2/1974 Bp John Vander Horst. m 4/25/1981 Deborah Wilson c 1. Sr Assoc S Geo's Ch Nashville TN 1995-2005; Dio Florida Jacksonville 1992-1994; Assoc S Jn's Epis Ch Tallahassee FL 1986-1995; Asst S Geo's Ch Germantown TN 1984-1986; Dio W Tennessee Memphis 1983-1984; R S Matt's Ch Covington TN 1974-1984; S Jn's Epis Ch Johnson City TN 1973-1974; S Thos Ch Elizabethton TN 1973-1974. No Amer Assn for Catechumenate 1995.

WILSON, Norbert Lance Weston (Ala) 136 E Magnolia Ave, Auburn AL 36830 **D S Dunst's: The Epis Ch at Auburn U Auburn AL 2011-** B Mount Holly NJ 1971 s George & Norma. BSA U GA 1994; PhD U CA Davis 1999. D 10/1/2011 Bp Henry Nutt Parsley Jr. m 7/25/2006 Wylin J Dassie Wilson c 1.

WILSON, Phillip Dana (Nwk) 36 South St, Morristown NJ 07960 B Wilmington DE 1942 s William & Isabelle. BA U of Delaware 1965; MDiv EDS 1969; MEd U of Delaware 1974. D 6/19/1969 P 1/1/1970 Bp William Henry Mead. m 7/20/1968 Susan Wilson c 2. Ch Of The Redeem Morristown NJ 1987-2009; Dio Delaware Wilmington 1986-1987; Int Gr Epis Ch Wilmington DE 1986-1987; Asst Nevil Memi Ch Of S Geo Ardmore PA 1984-1986; 1979-1984; Asst S Mary's Ch Hamilton Vill Philadelphia PA 1976-1979; 1973-1975; Asst Pstr Cathd Ch Of S Jn Wilmington DE 1971-1973; Cur Ch of St Andrews & St Matthews Wilmington DE 1969-1971; COM Dio Newark Newark NJ 1992-2009. Auth, *Tchg Exceptional Chld.* 2005 Distinguished Hm Alumnal Epis Div 2005.

WILSON, Ray Eugene (Tex) Po Box 1943, Lenox MA 01240 **P-in-c Gr Ch Great Barrington MA 1999-; Non-par 1982-** B Little Rock AR 1943 s Leonard & Reseda. BA Amer J 1965; MDiv EDS 1971. D 6/26/1971 P 3/1/1972 Bp William Foreman Creighton. Dio Wstrn Massachusetts Springfield 1998-2002, 1993-1994, 1988; Cn Chr Ch Cathd Houston TX 1978-1981; Dio Washington Washington DC 1975-1978; Vic S Jas Epis Ch Bowie MD 1975-1978; Asst S Jn's Ch Georgetown Par Washington DC 1973-1975; Cur Chr Ch Georgetown Washington DC 1971-1973.

WILSON, Raymond G (LI) 165 Pine St, Freeport NY 11520 **R Ch Of The Trsfg Freeport NY 1992-** B Georgetown GY 1954 s Alan & Stella. Cert Coll Educ For Secondary Teachers Educ 1978; DIT Codrington Coll 1983; BA U of The

W Indies 1983; MA CUNY 1992. Trans 4/20/1993 Bp Orris George Walker Jr. m 4/9/1983 Carol Wilson c 4. Serv Ch In Guyana 1983-1993.

WILSON, Richard (Az) **R Ch Of S Matt Tucson AZ 2009-** B Peoria IL 1955 s Glenn & Della. BA Trin 1977; MDiv U of S Mary of the Lake Mundelein Sem 1984. Rec 12/21/2007 Bp Kirk Stevan Smith. saintmatthewsrector@live.com

WILSON, Robert Arthur (Vt) PO Box 244, Newport VT 05855 B New London CT 1946 s Roy & Janet. Bachelor NEU. D 12/18/2016 P 6/16/2017 Bp Thomas C Ely. m 5/7/1987 Jean Marie Distad c 5.

WILSON, Roy Dennis (Miss) 1954 Spillway Rd, Brandon MS 39047 **D S Ptr's By The Lake Brandon MS 2010-** B San Antonio TX 1961 s Roy & Edna. AA Hinds Cmnty Coll 1985; BSN U of Texas 1987. D 1/9/2010 Bp Duncan Montgomery Gray III. m 5/25/1985 Rebecca Wilson c 2.

WILSON, Sandra Antoinette (Nwk) 116 Turrell Ave, South Orange NJ 07079 **Collegial Cn Trin And S Phil's Cathd Newark NJ 2008-; R S Andr And H Comm Ch So Orange NJ 2004-** B 1953 d William & Anne. BA Vas 1975; MDiv UTS 1981; MBA GTF 1990; DMin GTF 1991. D 6/7/1980 Bp Paul Moore Jr P 1/23/1981 Bp Walter Decoster Dennis Jr. R Geth Ch Minneapolis MN 1998-2004; Natl Pres Ube 1998-2001; Epgm 1997-2000; Dn Denver Metro-No Dnry 1990-1998; S Thos Epis Ch Denver CO 1989-1999, R 1989-1998; S Aug's Epis Ch Asbury Pk NJ 1986-1989, R 1986-1989; Ecec 1982-2000; S Dav's Epis Ch Topeka KS 1982-1986, R 1982-1986; S Mk's Ch Bridgeport CT 1982-1986; Chapl Vas Poughkeepsie NY 1981-1982; Gr Ch White Plains NY 1980-1981, Cur 1979-1981. Auth, "Toward A Black Theol Of Liberation For The Ch Of Engl In The 80'S,'" *Anglicans & Racism*, 1985; Auth, "Living The Gd News CE Curric"; Auth, "Just Which Me Will Survive All These Liberations," *Ten Who Tithe.* Ch & City; Ch & City; Epgm; Epgm; ESMHE; ESMHE; EUC; EUC; EWC; EWC; Impact; Impact; Rewim; Rewim; UBE; UBE.

WILSON, Stephen Thomas (Colo) 1530 Cherry St, Denver CO 80220 **Ch Of The H Redeem Denver CO 2008-** B Denver CO 1966 s James & Beverly. BS The London Sch of Econ and Political Sci 1989; MDiv SWTS 1995. D 6/10/1995 P 12/16/1995 Bp William Jerry Winterrowd. m 3/14/1998 Maria Wilson. All SS Epis Ch Denver CO 2005-2006; R S Andr's Ch Louisville KY 2001-2004; Cn Evang S Jn's Cathd Denver CO 1997-2001; Cur S Lk's Ch Denver CO 1995-1996; Cmsn Mnsry Ya Berk New Haven CT 1995-1996.

WILSON, Steven Clark (WMo) 1213 Grand Ave, Carthage MO 64836 **R Gr Ch Carthage MO 1999-** B Lebanon MO 1965 s Clark & Marie. BA Drury U 1987; Lic U of Heidelberg DE 1989; MA Missouri St U 1991; MDiv Ya Berk 1994. D 6/4/1994 Bp John Clark Buchanan P 12/14/1994 Bp Peter J Lee. m 9/29/2001 Melinda A Wilson c 2. Asst R Chr Ch Alexandria VA 1994-1999.

WILSON, Thomas (SanD) 339 Brightwood Ave, Chula Vista CA 91910 **St Steph's Epis Ch Menifee CA 2015-; Dioc Sfty Mgr Epis Dio San Diego 2010-** B Bucyrus OH 1948 s Robert & Leona. BME Baldwin-Wallace Coll 1971; MDiv S Michaels Coll 1980; CAS CDSP 2008. D 6/7/2008 P 3/21/2009 Bp Jim Mathes. m 9/20/2008 John Joseph Will. S Andr's By The Lake Lake Elsinore CA 2015; P S Dav's Epis Ch San Diego CA 2012-2014, Int R 2012-, Pstr Assoc 2011-2012; Asstg Cler All Souls' Epis Ch San Diego CA 2009-2011, D (Non-stip) 2008-2009; Dioc Coun Dio San Diego San Diego CA 2011-2012.

WILSON, Thomas Stuart (Tenn) 1000 Sunnyside Dr, Columbia TN 38401 B Detroit MI 1941 s John & Edith. BA Wayne 1965; STB Ya Berk 1968. D 6/29/1968 Bp Archie H Crowley P 1/4/1969 Bp Richard Stanley Merrill Emrich. m 1/31/1976 Jean Wilson c 4. R S Ptr's Ch Columbia TN 1988-2007; R S Jn's Ch Westland MI 1972-1988; Asst S Cyp's Epis Ch Detroit MI 1968-1972.

WILSON, Tom (EC) 101 Bear Track Ln, Kitty Hawk NC 27949 **R All SS' Ch Sthrn Shores NC 2003-** B Saint Louis MO 1946 s William & Marian. BA U NC 1968; MSW U NC 1975; MDiv Sewanee: The U So, TS 1984. D 6/23/1984 P 1/24/1985 Bp William Gillette Weinhauer. m 9/3/1989 Patricia Wilson c 1. R S Paul's Ch Macon GA 1995-2003; R Gr Memi Ch Lynchburg VA 1986-1995; Cur Chr Ch Blacksburg VA 1984-1986; Chapl Va Tech 1984-1986. Auth, "A Pax On Both Your Houses," *Sewanee Theol Revs*, 1996.

WILSON, Tom (SC) 1853 Grovehurst Dr, Charleston SC 29414 **Bp Gadsden Epis Cmnty Charleston SC 2017-; Chapl Bp Gadsden Ret Cmnty 2017-; Bp's Rep to Bd Epis Soc Serv Inc. Wichita KS 2009-; Bp's Rep to Bd Heartland Epis Curs 2009-** B Wichita KS 1952 s James & Marjorie. Allen Cmnty Coll 1971; Baker U 1973; BA Washburn U 1974; JD U of Kansas 1977; Kansas Sch for Mnstry-Dio Ks. 1993; Other 1993; VTS 2008. D 1/20/1994 P 7/1/1994 Bp William Edward Smalley. m 8/8/1981 Ruth Weber c 2. R S Andrews Ch Derby KS 2008-2016. tom.wilson@bishopgadsden.org

WILSON, Tom Stacey (Nev) 2190 Beacon Pl, Port Townsend WA 98368 **Died 11/30/2015** B 1929 D 7/21/1960 Bp Lane W Barton P 6/27/1961 Bp William G Wright. m 2/2/1952 Eileen A Wilson. S Paul Epis Ch Creston IA 1974-1979.

WILSON, William Henry (Ala) 800 Lake Colony Cir, Birmingham AL 35242 B Philadelphia PA 1937 s William & Elizabeth. MDiv New Melleray Abbey 1968; DMin Drew U 1999. Rec 9/1/1990 Bp Robert Oran Miller. m 3/23/1989 Susan Wilson c 2. S Martins-In-The-Pines Ret Comm Birmingham AL 1999-2001; S Lk's Epis Ch Birmingham AL 1998-2003; Chr Ch Fairfield AL

1995-1996; Dio Alabama Birmingham 1994-1995. Auth, "Looking Deeper," *Fllshp In Pryr*. Hon Citizen (Soc Serv Awd).

WILSON, William Jackson (Az) 4 Kingsbridge Pl, Pueblo CO 81001 B Kansas City MO 1927 s George & Marjorie. BA Wm Jewell Coll 1947; MA U of Missouri 1954; Cntrl Bapt TS 1956; Dip Ang Stud Sewanee: The U So, TS 1967; Cert Meharry Med Coll 1974; Van 1975; Med Coll of Georgia 1976; Cert Harv 1977. D 6/25/1967 Bp John Vander Horst P 12/21/1967 Bp William F Gates Jr. m 3/4/1947 Bettie Wilson c 3. Pres/Pres. Emer Fndt for Intl Profsnl Exch 1991-2011; Vic S Paul's Ch Payson AZ 1989-1996; Chair - Dept. Of Missions Dio Arizona Phoenix AZ 1983-1992; R S Ptr's Ch Litchfield Pk AZ 1979-1989; Chapl U Of Tennessee Nashville TN 1973-1976; R Chr Ch Epis S Pittsburg TN 1967-1979. Auth, "Views of a Vill Idiot," *Bk*, GOPress, 2006; Auth, "Var," *Profsnl & Popular Pub*, Woodfin Press, 1978; Auth, "The First 100 Years," *Bk*, Woodfin, 1976; Auth, "10 Commandments For 20th Century Christians," *Bk*, Whitaker, 1963. AAMFC 1962-1979; Natl Assn Of Scholars 1988; Natl Assn Of Theol Professors 1956-1960. Best Rel Nwspr column So. Colorado Press Club 2008; Hon Prof Of Med Ukranian Natl Med Acad 1997; Outstanding Young Man Of The Year Mo Jaycees 1962.

WILSON-BARNARD, Letha (Minn) Holy Apostles, 2200 Minnehaha Ave E, Saint Paul MN 55119 **P Ch Of The H Apos S Paul MN 2008-** B Minneapolis MN 1957 d LeRoy & Ardis. Cert Ang Stud VTS; BA Bethel U 1979; MDiv Luther TS 2007. D 6/14/2007 P 12/20/2007 Bp James Louis Jelinek. m 10/13/1981 Scott Wilson-Barnard c 1.

WILSON BROWN, Stefanie Glenn (Los) Campbell Hall School, 4533 Laurel Canyon Blvd, North Hollywood CA 91607 **Campbell Hall Vlly Vlg CA 2013-; Assoc S Mich and All Ang Epis Ch Studio City CA 2013-** B Fullerton CA 1985 d Stephen & Glenda Kay. BA Ken 2008; MDiv GTS 2013; MDiv The GTS 2013. D 6/8/2013 P 1/11/2014 Bp Mary Douglas Glasspool. m 8/22/2015 Greg Brown. wilsons@campbellhall.org

WILT, David (SeFla) 415 Duval St, Key West FL 33040 **R H Trin Epis Ch W Palm Bch FL 2008-; R S Fran In-The-Field Epis Ch Ponte Vedra FL 2003-** B Cumberland MD 1950 s Henry & Rhoda. BBA Wstrn Michigan U 1972; JD Stetson U 1975; MDiv VTS 1996. D 6/16/1996 P 12/8/1996 Bp Stephen Hays Jecko. m 3/17/1979 Sandra Wilt c 3. S Paul's Ch Key W FL 2004-2008; St Fran in the Field Ponte Vedra FL 2001-2004; Vic S Fran In-The-Field Epis Ch Ponte Vedra FL 2001-2003; Par Mssnr Chr Epis Ch Ponte Vedra FL 1996-2000. rector@htwpb.org

WILTFONG, Michele (WNC) D 1/9/2016 Bp Porter Taylor.

WILTON, Glenn Warner Paul (Oly) 10 Lichfield Avenue, CANTERBURY CT1 3YA Great Britain (UK) B Cincinnati OH 1933 s Frank & Virginia. BS Mia 1955; Beda Col Rome Italy 1966; CUA 1969; MSW U of Washington 1976; CDSP 1977. Rec 12/1/1977 as Deacon Bp Robert Hume Cochrane. m 3/22/1975 Daniele Marie Christiane Ligneau-Wilton c 3. Sr Mntl Hlth Chapl St. Aug's/St. Mart's Hospitals and Cmnty Trust C 1988-2003; Sr Mntl Hlth Chapl Pastures Hosp Derby Derbyshire UK 1982-1988; R S Dav's Seattle WA 1980-1981; P S Andr's Ch Seattle WA 1979-1980; P S Jn The Bapt Epis Ch Seattle WA 1978-1979; D & P Epiph Par of Seattle Seattle WA 1977-1978.

WILTSE, Roderic Duncan (Mo) 205 S Woods Mill Rd Apt 3311, Chesterfield MO 63017 **Ret Ret 1997-** B Catskill NY 1934 s Alexander & Helena. Int Mnstry Prog; BA Syr 1957; STB GTS 1960. D 5/28/1960 Bp Frederick Lehrle Barry P 12/10/1960 Bp Allen Webster Brown. m 8/5/1961 Patricia B Wiltse c 3. Int Chr Ch Covington LA 1996-1997; Int S Wlfd's Epis Ch Sarasota FL 1994-1996; Int Mnstry Spec Indep 1993-1997; Int Trin Epis Ch Kirksville MO 1993-1994; R Ch Of The H Comm S Louis MO 1983-1993; R H Comm S Louis MO 1983-1993; R S Mk's Ch Coldwater MI 1973-1983; R H Trin Epis Ch Wyoming MI 1967-1973; R Trin Ch Gouverneur NY 1963-1967; Cur Chr Ch Cooperstown NY 1960-1963; Chair of Stweardship Com Dio Missouri S Louis MO 1983-1998. Auth, *Comm for Unconfirmed Chld*; Auth, *Contrib Bible Workbench*; Auth, *Journeying w S Paul*. Soc of S Jn the Evang 1978.

WILTSEE JR, Lamont (ECR) 138 White Oaks Lane, Carmel Valley CA 93924 B Minot ND 1947 s Leon & Dorothy. BA NWU 1968; Rel. M Claremont TS 1971; MDiv Claremont TS 1978; DMin Claremont TS 2006. D 7/14/1974 P 6/14/1975 Bp Robert Claflin Rusack. m 3/26/2001 Edith White. Assisiting P St Mk's 2004-2011; Int S Jn's Chap Monterey CA 2000; Int S Mk's Ch King City CA 1997-1998; Int S Mths Ch Seaside CA 1995-1996; 1993-1995; Parson Ch-in-the Forest Carmel CA 1987-1993; Robert Louis Stevenson Sch Pebble Bch CA 1987-1993; Cathd Sch For Boys San Francisco CA 1984-1986; Chapl Cathd Sch for Boys San Francisco CA 1984-1986; S Patricks Ch And Day Sch Thousand Oaks CA 1981-1984; Asst All SS-By-The-Sea Par Santa Barbara CA 1978-1980; St Andr Epis Ch Irvine CA 1975-1977; Dio Los Angeles Los Angeles CA 1975, 1974-1975.

✠ WIMBERLY, The Rt Rev Don Adger (Tex) 3515 Plumb St, Houston TX 77005 **Ret Bp of Texas Dio Texas Houston TX 2009-, Bp of Texas 2003-2009, Asstg Bp of Texas 1999-2009** B Baton Rouge LA 1937 s Herbert & Mary. BS LSU 1959; MDiv VTS 1971; Sewanee: The U So, TS 1988; VTS 1988. D 6/21/1971 Bp Iveson Batchelor Noland P 12/21/1971 Bp Harold Barrett Robinson Con 9/22/1984 for Lex. m 4/16/1966 Edwina Wimberly c 2. Chair Bd Epis.

Sem. of SW Austin TX 2003-2009; Chair Bd St. Lukes Epis. Hlth Sys. Houston TX 2003-2009; Bd Rgnts, Chncllr Sewanee U So TS Sewanee TN 1991-2003; Bp of Lexington Dio Lexington Lexington 1985-1999, 1984-1999, Bp Coadj of Lex 1984-1985; Dn S Jn's Cathd Jacksonville FL 1978-1984; Chr Ch Overland Pk KS 1974-1978; R Chr Overland Pk KS 1974-1978; Dio Wstrn Kansas Hutchinson KS 1974-1978; Assoc S Jas Epis Ch Baton Rouge LA 1972-1974; Asst Calv Epis Ch Williamsville NY 1971-1972. DD TS U So 1988; DD VTS 1988.

WIMBUSH, Claire S (SVa) 1333 Jamestown Rd, Williamsburg VA 23185 B Oxford England 1983 d Samuel & Jane Ann. BA W&M 2005; MDiv Duke DS 2009; MDiv Duke DS 2009. D 1/9/2010 Bp Herman Hollerith IV P 4/10/2011 Bp Michael B Curry. S Thos Epis Ch Rochester NY 2011-2013; D S Mart's Epis Ch Williamsburg VA 2010.

WIMMER, Lisa Jan (CFla) PO Box 2373, Belleview FL 34421 **Epis Ch Of S Mary Belleview FL 2015-; S Andr's Epis Ch Ft Pierce FL 2013-** B Olney IL 1956 d Harlan & Shirley. BS Liberty U 2008; MA Liberty TS 2010; MDiv Nash 2013. D 5/24/2014 P 1/10/2015 Bp Gregory Orrin Brewer. c 2. S Andr's Epis Acad Ft Pierce FL 2002-2008.

WINBORN JR, James Henderson (SVa) 8880 Colonnades Ct W Apt 412, Bonita Springs FL 34135 B Detroit MI 1942 s James & Esther. BA U of Dallas 1971; MDiv Epis TS in Kentucky 1979; Coll of Preachers 1983. D 5/18/1980 P 12/13/1980 Bp Addison Hosea. m 11/12/1999 Barbara A Winborn c 1. R Emm Epis Ch Chatham VA 2005-2007; P-in-c Ch Of The Nativ Maysville KY 2002-2005; R S Jas Epis Ch Belle Fourche SD 1999-2001; Mssy Epis Ch in Rwanda 1998; P-in-c S Andr's Ch Lexington KY 1995-1999, P-in-c 1986-1992; P-in-c S Alb's Ch Morehead KY 1992-1995; R Chr Ch Richmond KY 1984-1985; Vic S Phil's Ch Harrodsburg KY 1982-1984; Asst Trin Ch Milwaukee WI 1980-1982.

WINCHELL, Ronald S (Va) 128 Eagle Ct, Locust Grove VA 22508 B Baltimore MD 1943 s Lawrence & Jane. BS U of Florida 1964; MDiv EDS 1982; DMin McCormick TS 1992. D 6/19/1982 Bp Wilbur Emory Hogg Jr P 12/19/1982 Bp A(rthur) Heath Light. m 2/6/1965 Judith C Winchell c 2. Int The Fork Ch Doswell VA 2002-2003; Int Hanover w Brunswick Par - S Jn King Geo VA 2000; R All SS Ch Alexandria VA 1992-1996; Gr Epis Ch St Geo UT 1990-1992; Dio Utah Salt Lake City UT 1988-1990; Vic H Sprt Roanoke VA 1986-1988; Int S Eliz's Ch Roanoke VA 1985; Asst S Jn's Ch Roanoke VA 1982-1985.

WINDAL, Claudia L (Minn) 1532 Randolph Ave, Apt. 8, St. Paul, MN 55105 **P In Res St. Jas On The Pkwy 2004-** B Chicago IL 1949 d Joseph & Evelyn. RN Franciscan Sch Nrsng 1973; BA S Ambr U 1975; MDiv SWTS 1981; MA Norwich U 1983; DMin Luther TS 1993; BS U MN 2003. D 6/18/1982 Bp James Winchester Montgomery P 12/1/1982 Bp Quintin Ebenezer Primo Jr. m 4/23/1990 Susan M Severud. Dio Minnesota Minneapolis MN 2000-2001; Chapl Integrity Inc. Twin Cities MN 1989-1990; Dioc Aids Cmsn 1986-1990; Emm Epis Ch Alexandria MN 1985-1986; Asst Ch Of Our Sav Chicago IL 1984-1985; Assoc S Andr's Ch Chicago IL 1983-1984; CE Supvsr S Clem's Ch Harvey IL 1979-1982. Auth, "Stations Of The Cross For Persons w Aids"; Auth, "Stations Of The Cross For The Lesbian & Gay Cmnty"; Auth, "Bk Chapt Cultural & Societal Impediments To Aids Educ In"; Auth, "Native Amer Cmnty". Integrity 1987.

WINDEL, Marian Kathleen (Va) 1782 Yanceyville Road, Louisa VA 23093 **Sophia Hse 1996-** B Washington DC 1946 d Glenn & Rosalie. BA Ohio U 1968; MS Amer U 1972; MDiv VTS 1979; DMin U of Wexford 1998. D 6/23/1979 P 12/23/1979 Bp John Thomas Walker. Westminster-Cbury of The Blue Ridge Charlottesville VA 2015-2016; Int S Paul's Epis Ch Millers Tavern VA 2014-2015; Vic Ch of the Incarn Mineral VA 2006-2016; Peace In The Vlly Ch Massies Mill VA 1992-2016; Co- Dir Sophia Hse 1990-1996; R Westover Epis Ch Chas City VA 1982-1990; Asst S Jn's Ch Chevy Chase MD 1979-1982; Policewoman Washington DC 1968-1976.

WINDER, Francis Lee Pete (U) 4546 Jupiter Dr, Salt Lake City UT 84124 **Died 2/4/2017** B Fallon NV 1932 s William & Greta. BS U of Utah 1954; BD CDSP 1957. D P 12/21/1957 Bp Richard S Watson. c 2. Ret 1998-2017; Archd & Exec Off Dio Utah Salt Lake City UT 1989-1997, 1988-1997, Cn Mssnr 1960-1969, Pres Stndg Com 1979-1980, Pres Stndg Com 1974-1975; Ch Of The Gd Shpd Ogden UT 1971-1988; Chapl S Mk Hosp Salt Lake City UT 1969-1971; Chapl S Mk & Rowland Hall Schs Salt Lake City UT 1960-1969; Secy Convoc 1959-1960; Asst Cathd Ch Of S Mk Salt Lake City UT 1957-1960. Paul Harris Fell Rotary 1983.

WINDOM, Barbara Sewell (At) 432 Forest Hill Rd, Macon GA 31210 B Ft Bragg NC 1955 d Bobby & Martha. BA Merc 2012. D 8/6/2011 Bp J Neil Alexander. m 10/23/1976 Michael Young Windom c 1. D S Fran Ch Macon GA 2011-2013.

WINDSOR, Janice Priebe (Colo) 33741 State Highway 257, Windsor CO 80550 **D Assoc S Alb's Ch Windsor CO 2002-** B Kansas City MO 1934 d Elden & Jeanette. CSD S Thos Sem; BS Colorado St U 1956. D 7/31/2002 Bp William Jerry Winterrowd. m 6/9/1956 John Clark Windsor.

WINDSOR, Robert Grover (Mass) 34 Exeter Street, West Newton MA 02465 Chapl to Ret Cler Dio Massachusetts Boston MA 2016- B San Diego CA 1947 s Robert & Elizabeth. BA Dickinson Coll 1969; MBA Cor 1975; MA EDS 1979; MDiv Harvard DS 1987. D 6/11/1988 P 6/10/1989 Bp David Elliot Johnson. m 8/8/1970 Kathryn W Windsor c 3. R Chr Ch Needham Hgts MA 2002-2013; R S Jn's Ch Newtonville MA 1995-2002; Int Gr Ch Newton MA 1995; Int S Mich's Ch Milton MA 1992-1994; Int S Ptr's Ch Weston MA 1991-1992; Cox Fell The Cathd Ch Of S Paul Boston MA 1988-1990; Off USMC 1970-1973. Ord Of St Jn Of Jerusalem 2007.

WINDSOR, Walter Van Zandt (Ark) 703 West Third Ave., Pine Bluff AR 71601 Mem Exec Coun and the Cathd Chapt 2013-; Founding Bd Mem Lighthouse Chart Sch Pine Bluff Arkansas 2011-; Vic S Mary's Epis Ch Monticello AR 2004-; R Trin Ch Pine Bluff AR 2002-, R 2002- B Gallipolis OH 1958 s Walter & Caroline. BA Transylvania 1981; MA Epis TS in Ky. 1986; Cert CDSP 1988; Cert Millsaps 1995; MTS Sprg Hill 1997; DMin EDS 2000; Cert Loyola U 2007. D 2/22/1994 P 6/29/1994 Bp Alfred Marble Jr. c 2. Mem Exec Coun and the Cathd Chapt 2004-2007; Chapl, DOK Dio Arkansas 2003-2007; Headmaster Trin Epis Sch Pine Bluff Arkansas 2002-2011; R S Jn's Ch Monroeville AL 2000-2002; R S Paul's Ch Woodville MS 1997-2000; Start Up Chapl Wilkinson Cnty Correctional Facility 1997-2000; Assoc R Trin Ch Natchez MS 1996; S Matt's Epis Ch Forest MS 1994-1996; Vic Trin Ch Newton MS 1994-1996; Founding Vic St. Geo's Epis Ch Jackson Mississippi 1993-1996; Cler Serv Traditional Angl Ch 1986-1993; Instr Seark Coll Pine Bluff Arkansas 2006-2007; Dn of SE Arkansas Dio Arkansas Little Rock AR 2005-2011. Auth, "Establishing and Maintaining an Anti-Racism Prison Mnstry in Mississippi," Thesis, EDS, 2000; Columnist, "Devotionals," Pine Bluff Commercial; Columnist, "Devotionals," Pine Bluff Commercial. The GAS 2000.

WINELAND, Richard Kevin (NI) 64669 Orchard Dr, Goshen IN 46526 B Altoona PA 1959 s John & Bettyl. Luth TS at Chicago; BA Goshen Coll 1991; MDiv Mennonite Brethren Biblic Sem 1996; MDiv Mennonite Brethren Biblic Sem 1996. Rec 7/24/2006 as Priest Bp Edward Stuart Little II. m 7/19/1986 Machelle Wineland c 3. S Jn Of The Cross Bristol IN 2006-2008; Pstr Elca 2001-2004.

WING III, Arthur K (NY) 7 Van Alstine Ave, Suffern NY 10901 Ret 1999- B Newark NJ 1934 s Arthur & Phebe. BA Leh 1956; MDiv VTS 1961. D 6/10/1961 Bp Leland Stark P 12/1/1961 Bp Donald MacAdie. m 6/29/1957 Joan F Wing c 3. S Jas Ch Montclair NJ 1977-1982; Chapl Letchworth Vill DDSO.

WINGER, Nordon W. (Az) Good Shepherd Episcopal Church, P.O. Box 110, Cave Creek AZ 85327 R Gd Shpd Of The Hills Cave Creek AZ 2010- B Shreveport LA 1953 s Donald & Norma. Sthrn Mssy Coll 1972; Newbold Coll Great Britain 1973; BA Pacific Un Coll 1975; MDiv Andrews U 1981; CAS CDSP 1996. D 3/17/1996 P 9/28/1996 Bp Jerry Alban Lamb. m 12/31/1978 Christine A Winger c 3. Tchg Asst. Fuller TS Ext-Sacramento CA 2010; Acad Com The Epis Dio Nthrn California Sacramento CA 2007-2010, COM 2007-2010, Dioc Total Mnstry Assessment Team 2009-2010, Chair of Liturg & Mus Cmsn 2003-2007, Cmsn on Liturg & Mus 1999-2008; Vic S Aug Of Cbury Rocklin CA 2000-2010; Int All SS Memi Sacramento CA 1998-2000; Cur S Fran On The Hill El Paso TX 1997-1998; Int S Jn The Evang Ch Chico CA 1996. Auth, "It's About God," Lifeglow, Chr Record Serv, 2012. No Ca Cleric Assn 1996-2010.

WINGERT, Anita LaVonne (NMich) 550 N Ravine St, Sault Sainte Marie MI 49783 Reg Mssnr/ Mnstry Dvlp Estrn Reg Sault Ste. Marie MI 2001- B Walla Walla WA 1948 d Frank & Viola. BA NEU 1971; MA U of Iowa 1975; MDiv CDSP 2001. D 6/24/2000 P 2/17/2001 Bp Chilton Richardson Knudsen. c 2. S Jas Ch Of Sault S Marie Sault Sainte Marie MI 2007-2008; S Jude's Ch Curtis MI 2002-2008; Dio Nthrn Michigan Marquette MI 2001-2006. Epis Womens Caucus 2000; Living Stones 2002; Mnstry Developers Collaborative 2000; Sindicators 2001. demagda2@gmail.com

WINGERT JR, John Alton (CNY) 1244 Great Pond Road, Box 116, Great Pond ME 04408 Int Trin Epis Ch Fayetteville NY 1995- B Waynesboro PA 1943 s John & Elizabeth. BA Ham 1965; STB GTS 1969. D 3/12/1970 Bp Harry Lee Doll P 12/1/1970 Bp David Keller Leighton Sr. m 5/25/1968 Jacqueline Wingert. Int S Paul's Epis Ch Albany NY 2007-2009; Int S Jn's Ch Bangor ME 2005-2007; Asst Dio Cntrl New York Liverpool NY 2004-2005; Par Consult Dio Cntrl New York Syracuse NY 2004-2005; Int S Thos' Ch No Syracuse NY 2004-2005; Int S Thos' Epis Ch Syracuse NY 2004-2005; Int S Thos Ch Hamilton NY 2002-2004; Int Chr Ch Binghamton NY 2001-2002; Vic Ch Of The Sav Syracuse NY 1996-2001; R Ch Of St Jn The Evang Shady Side MD 1971-1977; R S Jn the Evang Shady Side MD 1971-1977; D Epiph Epis Ch Odenton MD 1970-1971.

WINGFIELD, Vest Garrett (Tex) PO Box 540742, Houston TX 77254 B Washington DC 1935 s Burnley & Carrie. BA U of Houston 1958; MDiv CDSP 1966. D 6/24/1966 Bp James Milton Richardson P 6/1/1967 Bp Frederick P Goddard. c 7. Founding Vic Lord Of The St Epis Mssn Ch Houston TX 1993-1999; Asst R Trin Ch Houston TX 1987-1993; Vic Adv Stafford TX 1969-1973; Vic S Jn's Epis Ch Silsbee TX 1966-1969; S Paul's Epis Ch Woodville TX 1966-1969.

WINGO, Patrick James (Va) Diocese of Virginia, 110 W Franklin St, Richmond VA 23220 Cn Dio Virginia Richmond VA 2012- B Birmingham AL 1960 s James & Nancy. BA U of Alabama 1982; MDiv Epis TS of the SW 1992. D 6/13/1992 P 12/19/1992 Bp Robert Oran Miller. m 5/2/1987 Sara-Scott Nelson Wingo c 3. Dep to the Bp Dio Alabama Birmingham 2008-2012; Stndg Com 2001-2012; R S Thos Epis Ch Birmingham AL 1996-2008; R Ch Of The Resurr Rainbow City AL 1992-1996. pwingo@thediocese.net

WINGO, Sara-Scott Nelson (Va) 2813 Godfrey Ave Ne, Fort Payne AL 35967 P-in-c Emm Ch At Brook Hill Richmond VA 2012- B Nashville TN 1961 d Innes & Sara. BA U So 1984; MDiv Epis TS of the SW 1991. D 6/11/1991 P 6/1/1992 Bp Robert Oran Miller. m 5/2/1987 Patrick James Wingo. S Mk's Ch Birmingham AL 2009-2012; S Lk's Epis Ch Birmingham AL 2003-2008; Dio Alabama Birmingham 1997-1998; S Phil's Ch Ft Payne AL 1994-1997; Asst S Lk's Epis Ch Jacksonville AL 1992-1994; Chld'S Mnstrs S Dav's Ch Austin TX 1991-1992.

WINKLER, Anne Louise (Ind) 7300 Lantern Rd, Indianapolis IN 46256 B Indianapolis IN 1961 d Earl & Anita. BS Duke 1983; Duke 1987; MDiv GTS 1989. D 6/23/1989 Bp Edward Witker Jones. m 7/11/1987 Steven William Dougherty. Ch Of The Nativ Indianapolis IN 1989-1990.

WINKLER, Barbara Jo (NMich) 852 E D St, Iron Mountain MI 49801 B Saint Paul MN 1939 d Rudolph & Alice. D 3/1/1998 Bp Thomas Kreider Ray. m 2/4/1961 James Winkler c 2.

WINKLER JR, Richard Edward (Haw) 202 Pin Oak Dr, Harker Heights TX 76548 Non-par 1976- B Chicago IL 1944 s Richard & Dorothy. MD U of Hawaii; BA U IL; MDiv CDSP 1971. D 6/12/1971 P 12/12/1971 Bp Edwin Lani Hanchett. m 4/19/1983 Judy Edward Winkler c 2. S Jn's Ch Eleele HI 1976; Vic S Jn & S Paul's Kekaha HI 1974-1976; Asst Par of St Clem Honolulu HI 1971-1974.

WINKLER, Thomas Earl (Minn) 39259 K-C Dr, Winona MN 55987 Assoc Chr Ch Par La Crosse WI 2004-; Ret 1999- B Milwaukee WI 1943 s Earl & Margaret. BA U of Wisconsin 1965; BD EDS 1969. D 11/16/1969 P 7/19/1970 Bp William Benjamin Spofford. P-in-c Gr Memi Ch Wabasha MN 1997-1999; P-in-c Gr Memi Wabasha MN 1997-1999; R S Paul's Ch Winona MN 1991-1996; Dn The Epis Cathd Of Our Merc Sav Faribault MN 1979-1991; R S Paul's Epis Ch Owatonna MN 1972-1979; Gnrl Mssnr Dio Estrn Oregon Cove OR 1970-1972; Vic H Trin Vale OR 1969-1970; S Paul's Epis Ch Nyssa OR 1969-1970. Hon Cn Cathd of Our Merc Sav, Faribault MN 2002.

WINKLER JR, William Edward (NY) B New York NY 1942 s William & Dorithy. Norwalk Cmnty Coll Norwalk CT; AA Rca Inst 1967; Dio New York Diac Trng NY 1994. D 6/4/1994 Bp Richard Frank Grein. m 4/30/1987 Kathleen Winkler c 4. D Gd Shpd.

WINN, John Barrington (Oly) Po Box 1961, Silverdale WA 98383 Ret 1996- B Chicago IL 1931 s John & Evelyn. BA U So 1954; LTh SWTS 1957. D 6/13/1957 Bp Charles L Street P 12/21/1957 Bp Gerald Francis Burrill. c 2. P-in-c S Mich And All Ang Ch Issaquah WA 1992-1995; Vic S Antony Of Egypt Silverdale WA 1986-1992; Dio Olympia Seattle WA 1977-1992; Vic All SS Ch Tacoma WA 1974-1986; Ch Of The H Comm Seattle WA 1974-1976; R S Paul Epis Ch Bellingham WA 1965-1974; Vic S Columba Seattle WA 1959-1965; Cur Gr Ch Oak Pk IL 1957-1959.

WINNER, Lauren Frances (NC) 1737 Hillandale Rd, Durham NC 27705 S Paul's Ch Louisburg NC 2014- B Asheville NC 1976 d Dennis & Jane. BA Col 1997; MPhil Cambridge 1999; PhD Col 2006; MDiv Duke Div 2007; MDiv Duke DS 2007. D 6/4/2011 P 12/17/2011 Bp Shannon Sherwood Johnston.

WINSETT, Stephen Metcalfe (Chi) 2512 Bradley Ave, Louisville KY 40217 Ret 1998- B Dallas TX 1939 s Milo & Louise. BA U of Texas 1961; MDiv SWTS 1964. D 6/18/1964 P 12/18/1964 Bp Theodore H McCrea. m 6/29/1979 Veronica Helman c 4. R S Mary's Epis Ch Palmetto FL 2011-2012; Vic H Trin Ch Brandenburg KY 2007-2011; Dn Chr Ch Cathd Louisville KY 2005-2007; R S Thos Epis Ch Terrace Pk OH 2004-2005; R Emm Epis Ch Rockford IL 2002-2004; R Ch of the Gd Shpd Rahway NJ 2001-2002; R Gr Ch Van Vorst Jersey City NJ 2001-2002; R S Paul's Epis Ch Paterson NJ 2000-2001; R S Dav's Ch Southfield MI 1998-2000; R S Chas Ch St. Chas IL 1993-1998; R Par of St Clem Honolulu HI 1991-1993; R S Paul's Epis Ch New Albany IN 1980-1991; Chapl Coll Chapl Wstrn MI U Kalamazoo MI 1974-1980; Asst S Lk's Par Kalamazoo MI 1974-1980; Vic S Phil's Ch Beulah MI 1969-1972; Cur S Aug's Epis Ch Wilmette IL 1966-1968; Vic S Laurence Epis Ch Southlake TX 1965-1966; Ch Of The Annunc Lewisville TX 1964-1965; Cur S Lk's Epis Ch Dallas TX 1964-1965. Dir of RACA 1989-1994; Off, RACA 1995.

WINSLETT JR, Hoyt (Ala) 1224 - 37th Avenue East, Tuscaloosa AL 35404 Ret 1999- B Tuscaloosa AL 1934 s Hoyt & Louise. BA U of Alabama 1956; STB GTS 1961; Sewanee: The U So, TS 1969; Coll of Preachers 1979. D 6/19/1961 Bp George Mosley Murray P 5/1/1962 Bp Charles C J Carpenter. m 2/2/2013 Emily Cosby Winslett c 2. Chr Ch Tuscaloosa AL 1996-1999; Dio Alabama 1989-1997; R S Paul's Ch Greensboro AL 1978-1989; Admin Dio Georgia Savannah GA 1974-1978, Secy 1974-1978; Assoc Ch Of The Nativ Epis Huntsville AL 1970-1973; R Ch Of The Epiph Guntersville AL 1963-1970; Cur All SS Epis Ch Mobile AL 1961-1963; COM Dio Alabama Birming-

W

ham 1981-1993, Secy 1979-1983, 1971-1980, Secy 1971-1974. Phi Beta Kappa 1955.

WINSLOW, Gail George (NwPa) Church of the Ascension, 26 Chautauqua Place, Bradford PA 16701 **D Ch Of The Ascen Bradford PA 2011-** B Warren PA 1945 d George & Evelyn. D 11/9/2002 Bp Robert Deane Rowley Jr. m 9/6/1980 Barbara A Winslow c 3.

WINSLOW JR, K Dennis (NY) P.O. Box 93 (5023 Delaware Turnpike), RENSSELAERVILLE NY 12147 B Worcester MA 1949 s Kenneth & Ada. AA Worcester Jr Coll 1969; BA Emerson Coll 1971; MDiv Nash 1974. D 9/15/1974 P 6/15/1975 Bp Alexander D Stewart. m 8/3/2011 Mark Lewis. R S Ptr's Ch New York NY 1998-2010; Ch Of The Atone Bronx NY 1985-1996; Epis Chapl Syr Syracuse NY 1982-1985; Cn St Paul's Syracuse Syracuse NY 1979-1985; Asst Ch Of Beth Saratoga Spg NY 1976-1979; Cur S Jn's Ch Northampton MA 1974-1976.

WINSTON, William (FtW) 3313 Minot Ave, Fort Worth TX 76133 B Temple TX 1946 s Maurice & Thelma. BA U of Oklahoma 1969; STB GTS 1972. D 7/1/1972 P 12/17/1972 Bp Chilton R Powell. m 6/7/1969 Charlotte Ann Rather. R Gr Ch Lockport NY 2008-2011; Vic S Lk's Epis Ch Rincon GA 2007-2008; R Zion Epis Ch Washington NC 2003-2007; R S Anne's Ch Ft Worth TX 1995-2003; R S Jn's Ch Bangor ME 1988-1994; Dio Oklahoma Oklahoma City OK 1978-1988; Adj Instr Rel Educ NE OK S U 1977-1988; Vic S Basil's Epis Ch Tahlequah OK 1977; Chapl TCU 1975-1977; Cur Trin Epis Ch Ft Worth TX 1975-1977; Chapl E Cntrl U 1972-1974; Vic S Ptr's Ch Coalgate OK 1972-1974. Soc of S Jn the Evang 1978.

WINTER, Brian William (Colo) 12408 Prospect Ave. NE, Albuquerque NM 87112 **Chr's Epis Ch Castle Rock CO 2015-** B Saint Louis MO 1965 s Fred & Inez. BS Nthrn Arizona U 1988; MDiv VTS 2002. D 7/11/2002 P 1/18/2003 Bp Carolyn Tanner Irish. m 4/28/1990 Cheryl K Winter c 2. R S Chad's Epis Ch Albuquerque NM 2005-2015; Assoc for Yth and Young Families Trin On The Hill Epis Ch Los Alamos NM 2004-2005; Vic S Mich's Ch Brigham City UT 2002-2004; Chapl Dio Utah Camp Tuttle 2001; Stndg Com Dio The Rio Grande Albuquerque 2008-2010. atherbrian@christepiscopalchurch.org

WINTER, Cheryl Ann (WVa) Po Box 424, Hurricane WV 25526 **Asst Ddo Dio W Virginia 2005-; R S Tim's In The Vlly Hurricane WV 1993-; Bd Trst VTS Alexandria VA 1992-** B Providence RI 1957 d Lewis & Helen. BS Marshall U 1980; MDiv VTS 1987. D 6/1/1988 Bp Robert Poland Atkinson P 6/10/1989 Bp William Franklin Carr. Dioc Deploy Off Dio W Virginia Charleston WV 2000-2006; The No Cntrl Cluster Buckhannon WV 1990-1993; Vic S Mths Grafton WV 1989-1993; S Paul Avondale WV 1989-1993; Cres Par Philippi WV 1988-1990.

WINTER, James L (Miss) 684 White Oak Ln, Starkville MS 39759 B Anderson SC 1948 s William & Adalee. BS U of Alabama 1971; MA Louisiana Tech U 1977; MSW U of Alabama 1980; MDiv Sewanee: The U So, TS 1983. D 5/31/1983 P 12/7/1983 Bp Furman Charles Stough. m 8/17/1969 Ruth S Stewart c 4. R Ch Of The Resurr Starkville MS 2007-2015; Asst Trin Ch New Orleans LA 2004-2007; R Chr Ch Slidell LA 2001-2004; R Calv Epis Ch Cleveland MS 1995-2001; Gr Ch Rosedale MS 1995-2001; Vic Ch Of The Ascen Hattiesburg MS 1987-1995; Epis Chapl Delta S U Cleveland MS 1987-1995; Epis Chapl U of Sthrn Mississippi Hattiesburg MS 1987-1995; R Emm Epis Ch Opelika AL 1983-1987.

WINTER, Laren Royce (RG) Po Box 2963, Ruidoso NM 88355 B Garden City KS 1947 s Harold & Neoma. DEd U of Nthrn Colorado 1977; MDiv Sewanee: The U So, TS 1984. D 6/16/1984 Bp William Carl Frey P 12/17/1984 Bp William Harvey Wolfrum. Epis Ch In Lincoln Cnty Ruidoso NM 2004; Assoc S Matt's Ch Austin TX 1988-1990; Epis Ch Of S Jn The Bapt Breckenridge CO 1986-1988; Ch Of Our Sav Colorado Sprg CO 1984-1986. Auth, "An Expository Analysis Of 6 Selected Naturalists' Life Styles"; Auth, "Environ Beliefs & Contributions To Environ Educ".

WINTER JR, Lloyd H (Pa) 238 Street Rd Apt C111, Southampton PA 18966 **Assoc P S Andr's Ch Yardley PA 2009-; Chap to the Retried Cler Dio Pennsylvania Philadelphia PA 2004-, Dn, Fairmount 1972-2004, Chapl, Ret Cler, Spouses & Widows 2004-; Ret Dio Pennsylvania 2004-** B Philadelphia PA 1938 s Lloyd & Anne. BA U of Pennsylvania 1960; MDiv GTS 1966. D 6/11/1966 Bp Robert Lionne DeWitt P 12/18/1966 Bp Albert Ervine Swift. c 2. Int S Phil's Ch New Hope PA 2012; Int Trin Ch Oxford Philadelphia PA 2007-2009; Int Emm Ch Quakertown PA 2005-2006; Int S Paul's Ch Doylestown PA 2004-2005; R S Jas Ch Langhorne PA 1974-2004; R Chr And S Ambr Ch Philadelphia PA 1968-1974; Cur Geo W So Ch of Advoc Philadelphia PA 1966-1968. Assoc OHC 1976. retired-diopa@earthlink.net

WINTER CHASER, Vivian Janice (Az) 725 S. Beck Ave, Tempe AZ 85281 **D S Aug's Epis Ch Tempe AZ 2012-** B Rosebud South Dakota 1942 d Lloyd & Thelma. BSE U of So Dakota 1974; MA U of So Dakota 1978. D 5/5/2012 Bp Kirk Stevan Smith.

✠ **WINTERROWD, The Rt Rev William Jerry** (Colo) **Ret Bp of Colorado Dio Colorado Denver CO 2003-, Bp of Colorado 1991-2003** B Shreveport LA 1938 s William & Ruth. BA Centenary Coll 1959; STB GTS 1963; GTS 1991. D 6/15/1963 Bp Iveson Batchelor Noland P 4/1/1964 Bp Girault M Jones Con

1/19/1991 for Colo. m 8/25/1964 Ann Winterrowd. R Ch Of S Jas The Less Scarsdale NY 1985-1990; Assoc S Steph The Mtyr Ch Minneapolis MN 1983-1984; P-in-c Geth Ch Minneapolis MN 1981-1983; Dir Epis Cmnty Serv Minneapolis MN 1980-1985; Epis Cmnty Serv Inc Minneapolis MN 1980-1985; Epis Cmnty Serv Philadelphia PA 1976-1980; Epis Cmnty Serv Phila Philadelphia PA 1976-1980; Asst S Phil's Ch Garrison NY 1972-1976; Exec Dir S Peters Day Care Cntr Peekskill NY 1970-1976; Exec Dir S Ptr's Epis Ch Peekskill NY 1970-1976; Asst S Mary's Ch Mohegan Lake NY 1969-1971; Asst Gr Ch Brooklyn NY 1965-1969; Chapl City Mssn Soc NYC 1965-1966; Cur St Jas Epis Ch and Sch Alexandria LA 1963-1965; Pres Epis Fam Ntwk. Auth, *Natl Cmsn on the Fam*; Auth, *Rel & Dependent Chld*; Auth, *The Ch & Fam Systems*. DD GTS 1991.

WINTERS JR, Charles Layfaette (WNC) 6 Timson Road, Apt B4, Asheville NC 28803 **Ret 1994-** B Norfolk VA 1924 s Charles & Gladys. Leh 1943; Swarthmore Coll 1944; BA Br 1945; BD VTS 1949; STM UTS 1950; ThD GTS 1956. D 5/20/1949 P 5/28/1950 Bp Granville G Bennett. c 2. Prof Bexley Seabury Fed Chicago IL 1988-1994; Int Gr Epis Ch Gainesville GA 1987-1988; Serv Loyola U New Orleans LA 1980-1987; Prof Sewanee U So TS Sewanee TN 1966-1981, Instr 1954-1957; Vic S Jn The Div Ch Saunderstown RI 1950-1952; Chapl U RI 1950-1952; D S Paul's Ch Englewood NJ 1949-1950; Dep GC Dio Tennessee Nashville TN 1969-1979. Auth, "Ch," *Mnstry & Sacraments*, Loyola U, 1983; Auth, *Method in Mnstry*, Loyola U, 1982; Auth, U So; Auth, "Textbooks," *Journ Arts*, U So; Auth, *Lk Journ*, U So. Fell/Tutor GTS 1952.

WINTERS, Richard Harrison (Ind) 5502 Washington Blvd, Indianapolis IN 46220 B Bryn Mawr PA 1961 s Ralph & Elinor. BA Duke 1983; JD Duke 1986; MDiv SWTS 1993. D 6/17/1993 Bp Frank Tracy Griswold III P 12/18/1993 Bp William Walter Wiedrich. m 5/20/1989 Margaret Mohr Winters c 3. Bd Mem Natl Epis Hlth Mnstrs 2004-2009; Mem Bd Evangilic Indianapolis MN 2004-2008; Bd Mem Waycross Camp Conf Cntr Indianapolis MN 2004-2008; Mem Eccl Crt Indianapolis MN 2004-2007; S Paul's Epis Ch Indianapolis IN 2003-2009, R 2003-2009; Pstr Response Team Dio Estrn Michigan Saginaw MI 2000-2003, 1997-2000, Dn, Saginaw Vlly Convoc 1997-2000, Dioc Personl Com 1996-2000; S Jn's Epis Ch Saginaw MI 1995-2003, R 1995-2003; S Dav's Ch Glenview IL 1993-1995, Asst 1993-1995. Fell of SSJE 1994. Bp's Awd for Excellence in Apostolic Mnstry Dio Estrn Michigan 1999; Phi Beta Kappa Duke 1983.

WINTERS, William Michael (Ala) PO Box 116, Guntersville AL 35976 **P-in-c S Jos's On-The-Mtn Mentone AL 2014-** B Chicago IL 1950 s Robert & Shirley. BA No Pk U 1972; BA NE Illinois U 1977; MDiv Sewanee: The U So, TS 1988. D 6/4/1988 P 5/20/1989 Bp Charles Farmer Duvall. m 8/4/1973 Wauria Wylantha Winters c 2. S Phil's Ch Ft Payne AL 2015; Int Ch Of The Ascen Montgomery AL 2013-2014; R Ch Of The Epiph Guntersville AL 2000-2013; Dn Calv Cathd Sioux Falls SD 1995-2000; R S Mk's Epis Ch Aberdeen SD 1990-1995; S Jn's Epis Ch Mobile AL 1988-1990. "Hosp Changes Everything," Samford U Press, 2006.

WINWARD, Mark Scott (Spr) 206 Jenkins Rd, Saco ME 04072 **Co-Chair Ecusa Sci Dio Maine Portland ME 1998-** B Hartford CT 1960 s Douglas & Virginia. BA Gordon Coll 1983; MDiv VTS 1997. Trans 2/23/2004 Bp Chilton Richardson Knudsen. m 8/8/1987 Kathleen Noelle Winward c 2. R Trin Ch Saco ME 1999-2002; Asst S Andr's Epis Ch Newport News VA 1997-1999.

WIPFLER, William Louis (WNY) 121 Carla Ln, West Seneca NY 14224 **Vol Assoc P S Mths Epis Ch E Aurora NY 1996-; Chapl to Ret Cler Dio Wstrn New York Tonawanda NY 2000-, Chapl to Ret Cler and Spouses 1999-2012** B Astoria NY 1931 s William & Eleonora. BA Adel 1952; STB GTS 1955; STM UTS 1965; MPhil UTS 1975; PhD UTS 1978. D 4/16/1955 Bp James Pernette DeWolfe P 11/20/1955 Bp Charles Alfred Voegeli. c 4. Asst Ch Of The Trsfg Freeport NY 1994-1996, Asst P 1973-1993; Assoc for Human Rts Angl Off at the UN NY NY 1992-1994; Epis Ch Cntr New York NY 1989-1991; Asst H Trin Epis Ch Vlly Stream NY 1987-1994; Dir Human Rts Dept NCCC NY 1977-1988; Natl Coun Of Ch New York NY 1967-1988; Dir Latin Amer Dept NCCC NY 1967-1977; Asst Chr Epis Ch Lynbrook NY 1967-1973; Mssy Ch in Costa Rica 1964-1966; Mssy Ch in Dominican Republic 1955-1963. Co-Auth, "Triunfando Sobre Las Tragedias," Editora Educativa Dominicana, 1997; Auth, "Poder, Influencia E Impotencia," Ediciones CEPAE, 1980; Co-Auth, "Mbarete: The Higher Law of Paraguay," Int League for Human Rts, 1980; Ed, *Human Rts Perspectives*, 1977; Ed, *Latin Amer News Letter*, 1967; Auth, "Dominican Ch in the Light of Hist," CIDOC, 1966; Auth, "Jas Theo Holly of Haiti," *Builders for Chr Series*, Epis Nat Counc, 1956. DD GTS 2008; Restoration of Democracy Awd Govt of Chile 2003; Hon Cn Theol Dominican Epis Ch 1997; DD CDSP 1990; Democracy Awd The Brazilians Journ 1986; Letelier-Moffitt Human Rts Awd Inst for Plcy Stds 1980; Acad of Sci Dominican Republic 1976; Who's Who in Rel 1975.

WIRES, John William (At) 4900 English Dr, Annandale VA 22003 **1987-** B Macon GA 1944 s William & Irene. BA Merc 1966; MA JHU 1969; MDiv VTS 1972; MA Geo Mason U 1985; PhD Geo Mason U 1988. D 6/24/1972 Bp Raymond Stewart Wood Jr P 8/1/1973 Bp Bennett Jones Sims. m 3/1/1980 Karen Wires c 1. Chair of Theol Dept 1981-1987; Chapl Epis HS Alexandria VA

W

1974-1981; Epis HS Alexandria VA 1972-1987; Asst Chapl Epis HS Alexandria VA 1972-1974. Auth, *S Lk Journ Theol*; Auth, *Var Bk Revs*. APA, Natl Acad Neuropsych; Intl Neuropsychological Soc; Natl Acad of Neuropsychology.

WIRTH, Bradley S (Mont) All Saints' Church, PO Box 1923, Whitefish MT 59937 **Int R All SS Epis Ch Columbia Falls MT 2004-** B Great Falls MT 1955 s Raymond & Nina. BA U of Washington 1977; MA U of Washington 1978; MDiv EDS 1980. D 7/25/1980 Bp Robert Hume Cochrane P 2/1/1981 Bp Otis Charles. m 6/17/1978 Jeannine Wirth c 2. Int H Trin Epis Ch Troy MT 2002-2004; R All SS Ch Salt Lake City UT 1993-2000; Dep Gc Dio Utah Salt Lake City UT 1991-1993, Cn To Ordnry 1988-1990, VP 1984-1985, Stndg Com 1982-1985; Cathd Ch Of S Mk Salt Lake City UT 1980-1987. Auth, "A Gr Observed-Sermons By The Reverend Cn Albert J Colton". bwirth@bresnan.net

WISCHMEYER, Kara Leslie (NwT) 226 Chuck Wagon Rd., Lubbock TX 79404 B Charleston SC 1968 AA Emory U 1988; BA Emory U 1990; MEd Texas Tech U 1994; MDiv Candler TS Emory U 1998. D 6/4/2005 P 4/1/2006 Bp James Monte Stanton. m 2/14/2004 Jason B Wischmeyer. S Steph's Ch Lubbock TX 2009-2010; D S Matt's Cathd Dallas TX 2005-2007.

WISE, Christopher Matthew (WTex) 315 E Pecan St, San Antonio TX 78205 **S Mk's Epis Ch San Antonio TX 2016-** B Conroe TX 1979 s Ted & Andrea. BA Texas A&M U 2002; MDiv Sewanee: The U So, TS 2008. D 6/4/2008 Bp Gary Richard Lillibridge. m 4/30/2011 Amy Lyn Wise c 2. Dio Texas Houston TX 2014-2015; The Great Cmsn Fndt Houston TX 2013; Asst R Ch Of Recon San Antonio TX 2008-2012; Dir of Yth Mnstrs S Thos Epis Ch And Sch San Antonio TX 2002-2005. mwise@stmarks-sa.org

WISE JR, Eugene Field (Tenn) Po Box 261, Murfreesboro TN 37133 B Orlando FL 1937 s Eugene & Lillian. BS Florida St U 1961; MDiv VTS 1984. D 6/11/1984 P 12/22/1984 Bp Calvin Onderdonk Schofield Jr. m 8/12/1961 Janelee Wise c 1. Stndg Com Dio Tennessee Nashville TN 2004-2007, Pres 2001-2002, Stndg Com 1999-2002, Dep Gc 1997-2003, Pres 1995-1996, Stndg Com 1994-1997, Sprtl Dir Curs 1992-2007; R S Paul's Epis Ch Murfreesboro TN 1991-2006; Com Dio SE Florida Miami 1989-1991, Sprtl Dir Curs 1988-1990; H Sprt Epis Ch W Palm Bch FL 1986-1991; Cur S Andr's Ch Lake Worth FL 1984-1986.

WISELEY, Jerry Lee (SC) 1746 Summit Rd, Hot Springs SD 57747 B Okmulgee OK 1935 s Jess & Gussie. BS U of Tulsa 1963; MDiv TESM 1986. D 6/14/1986 P 7/1/1987 Bp Donis Dean Patterson. c 4. R S Geo's Epis Ch Summerville SC 1989-1998; Asst Chr Epis Ch Plano TX 1986-1989. Ord Of S Lk.

WISEMAN, Grant Buchanan (USC) 125 Pendleton St. S.W., Aiken SC 29801 **R S Thad Epis Ch Aiken SC 2009-** B Saint Louis MO 1966 s Philip & Heather. BA Bethel U 1995; MDiv SWTS 2001. D 10/28/2000 P 6/23/2001 Bp Herbert Thompson Jr. m 7/22/1995 Heather K Wiseman c 2. R S Andr's Ch Omaha NE 2003-2009; S Pat's Epis Ch Dublin OH 2001-2003.

WISEMAN, Heather Buchanan (SO) 2489 Walnutview Ct, Cincinnati OH 45230 B Cincinnati OH 1944 d Gordon & Virginia. BA Lindenwood U 1965; Angl Acad 1992; MDiv Bex Sem 2003. D 12/3/1993 P 6/21/2003 Bp Herbert Thompson Jr. m 11/21/1975 Philip M Wiseman c 2. Int R Indn hill Epis Presb Ch 2014-2016; S Tim's Epis Ch Cincinnati OH 2003-2014; D Calv Ch Cincinnati OH 2000-2002; Gr Ch Cincinnati OH 1993-2000; D S Andr's Epis Ch Cincinnati OH 1993-2000. Comt.

WISEMAN, Philip M (SO) 2489 Walnutview Ct, Cincinnati OH 45230 B Morgan City LA 1946 s Arl & Ethel. BS Georgia Inst of Tech 1968. D 10/25/1997 Bp Herbert Thompson Jr. m 11/21/1975 Heather Buchanan c 4. D Ch Of S Mich And All Ang Cincinnati OH 2000-2004; D All SS Ch Cincinnati OH 1997-1999.

WISHART, Raymond Douglas (CGC) 925 E Pierson Dr, Lynn Haven FL 32444 **D St. Andrews Epis Ch 2012-** B Fort Campbell KY 1953 s David & Beatrice. BS U of W Florida 1976; MEd U of W Florida 1979; DOCGC Sch for Deacons 2010. D 2/10/2011 Bp Philip Menzie Duncan II. m 4/29/1977 Diane P Wishart c 2. D Gr Epis Ch Panama City Bch FL 2011-2012.

WISMER, Robert D (Tex) 11310 Meadow Lake Dr, Houston TX 77077 **Day Sch Chapl/Asst Pstr S Fran Ch Houston TX 2002-; S Fran Epis Day Sch Houston TX 2002-** B Toronto Ontario CA 1954 s Edwin & Gladys. BA McMaster U 1976; MDiv Regent Coll Vancouver CA 1984; MA McGill U 1991. Trans 10/24/2002 Bp Claude Edward Payne. m 10/21/1989 Jennifer L Wismer c 4.

WISNER, Stephen Forster (NJ) 304 Woodmere Ave, Neptune NJ 07753 B Philadelphia PA 1946 s Stephen & Eva. BA Glassboro St U 1968; MDiv PDS 1971; Cert Estrn Bapt Sem 1990. D 4/24/1971 P 10/23/1971 Bp Alfred L Banyard. m 12/19/1970 Theresa Ann Farkas c 3. R St Michaels Epis Ch Wall Township NJ 1996-2015; P-in-c S Lk's Ch Woodstown NJ 1994-1996; Assoc S Andr's Epis Ch Bridgeton NJ 1990-1997; Dn Woodbury Convoc 1978-1982; Chr Ch So Vineland NJ 1976-1990; Trin Epis Ch Vineland NJ 1976-1990; R H Sprt Bellmawr NJ 1973-1976; Dio New Jersey Trenton NJ 1971-1973; S Alb's Epis Ch New Brunswick NJ 1971-1973.

WISNEWSKI JR, Robert Carew (Ala) 113 Madison Ave, Montgomery AL 36104 **R S Jn's Ch Montgomery AL 1995-** B Augusta GA 1955 s Robert & Barbara. BA Wofford Coll 1977; MDiv VTS 1983. D 6/11/1983 P 5/12/1984 Bp William Arthur Beckham. m 9/8/1978 MaryWard T Wisnewski c 2. Trst Dio Alabama Birmingham 1996-1999; Grad Sursum Corda - Sprtl Dir's Trng Prog SC 1994-1995; R S Mary's Ch Columbia SC 1987-1995; Stndg Com Dio Upper So Carolina Columbia SC 1987-1992, COM 1984-1995, Stwdshp 1998-2001, Ecum Cmsn 1990-1997, Cmsn MHE 1985-1989; Asst to R S Jas Epis Ch Greenville SC 1983-1987.

WISNIEWSKI, Richard Joseph (NJ) Church Of The Holy Spirit, PO Box 174, Tuckerton NJ 08087 **D Ch Of The H Sprt Tuckerton NJ 2012-; Disciplinary Bd Dio New Jersey Trenton NJ 2014-, Com on The Diac 2009-** B Irvington NJ 1947 s Casimir & Eleanore. BS Monmouth U 1969; Dio NJ Sch For Deacons 2007. D 6/9/2007 Bp George Edward Councell. m 11/3/1990 Sarah Ruth Wisniewski c 2. D S Dav's Ch Cranbury NJ 2007-2012.

WISSINK, Charles Jay (Pa) 54 Sugarplum Rd, Levittown PA 19056 **Asst Chap Of S Andr Boca Raton FL 2009-** B Orange City IA 1930 s Charles & Geraldine. BA Hope Coll 1952; PhD PrTS 1955; MDiv UTS 1965; Theol Wstrn TS 1975. D 10/7/1984 P 2/1/1985 Bp John Shelby Spong. m 8/30/1952 Barbara Wierenga c 5. R Memi Ch Of S Lk Philadelphia PA 1985-1995; Int S Lk's Ch Philadelphia PA 1985-1987; Prof New Brunswick TS 1963-1985; Serv Reformed Ch 1955-1963. EDEO, Phila Cler.

WISSLER, Kenneth John (Pa) 201 Evergreen Ave. Apt. 904, Philadelphia PA 19118 B Wilmington DE 1946 s Lloyd & Doris. BA U of Delaware 1968; MDiv U of Kings Coll Halifax CA 1971; DMin Fuller TS 1983. Trans 9/30/1985 Bp Lyman Cunningham Ogilby. m 9/2/1967 Bernice M Wissler c 2. Int S Alb's Ch Roxborough Philadelphia PA 2009-2010; R S Jn The Evang Ch Lansdowne PA 2002-2009; Dio Pennsylvania Philadelphia PA 2002; Int Gr Epis Ch Hulmeville PA 2000-2002; Int S Jas Epis Ch Bristol PA 1998-2000; Int Memi Ch Of S Lk Philadelphia PA 1996-1997; R Ch Of Our Sav Jenkintown PA 1985-1996; Serv Ch in Can 1971-1982. Archeol Inst of Amer 2000; Epis Cler Assn Pennsylvania 1986; Int Mnstry Ntwk 1996.

✠ WITCHER SR, The Rt Rev Robert Campbell (LI) 1934 Steele Blvd, Baton Rouge LA 70808 **Ret Bp Dio Long Island 1991-** B New Orleans LA 1926 s Charles & Lily. BA Tul 1949; MDiv SWTS 1952; MA LSU 1960; PhD LSU 1968; SWTS 1974; DCL Nash 1989. D 7/6/1952 Bp Girault M Jones P 6/1/1953 Bp Iveson Batchelor Noland Con 4/1/1975 for LI. m 6/4/1957 Elisabeth Alice Witcher c 2. Ret Bp of Long Island Dio Long Island Garden City NY 1991-2004, Bp of Long Island 1975-1990, Bp Coadj 1975-1977; Int Bp ArmdF 1989-1990; Epis Ch Cntr New York NY 1989-1990; Exec & Secy Off New York NY 1989; R S Jas Epis Ch Baton Rouge LA 1962-1975; Bd Examing Chapl Dio Louisiana New Orleans LA 1960-1975, Chair of ArmdF Cmsn 1963-1975; S Aug's Ch Baton Rouge LA 1953-1961; S Andr's Ch Clinton LA 1953-1956; P-in-c S Pat's Ch Zachary LA 1953-1956; Trst The CPG New York NY 1975-1989. Auth, *Founding of Epis Ch in LA 1805-1838*, 1969. Angl Soc 1976; MOWW 1970; Mltry & Hospitaller Ord of S Lazarus of Jerusalem 1995; Mltry Ord of Frgn Wars 1998; SAR 1963; Soc of Colonial Wars 1990. Epsilon Sigma Phi; Phi Alpha Theta; Phi Kappa Phi.

WITH, David Fergus (WMo) 160 Terrace Trl W, Lake Quivira KS 66217 B Milwaukee WI 1938 s Arthur & Beatrice. BS U of Wisconsin 1960; MDiv Nash 1963. D 3/1/1963 P 9/21/1963 Bp Donald H V Hallock. m 3/31/1964 Nancy With c 3. Int S Anne's Epis Ch Lee's Summit MO 2006-2007; Int The Epis Ch of the Ressurrection Blue Sprg MO 2004-2005; Int Trin Ch Independence MO 2002-2004; Int S Paul's Epis Ch Lees Summit MO 2000-2002; Int S Paul's Ch Leavenworth KS 1999-2000; S Marg's Ch Lawr KS 1996-1997; P in Charge S Aid's Ch Olathe KS 1996; R S Mich And All Ang Ch Mssn KS 1975-1996; Asst S Andr's Ch Madison WI 1972-1974; Camp Dir Camp Webb Wautoma WI 1970-1975; Dio Milwaukee Milwaukee WI 1970-1974; H Cross Epis Ch Wisconsin Dells WI 1970-1972; Chapl MN St Coll 1968-1970; Dio Minnesota Minneapolis MN 1968-1969; Vic S Jn-on-the-Hill Lake Benton MN 1966-1970; R S Jas Ch Marshall MN 1966-1969; St Johns Epis Ch 1966-1969; Cur Geth Ch Minneapolis MN 1963-1966.

WITH, Jan Louise (Neb) St Marys Episcopal Church, 212 Clark St, Bassett NE 68714 **Gr Ch Par -Epis Columbus NE 2017-** B Winner SD 1952 d Doris. Dplma Nebraska Methodist Sch of Nrsng 1976; BS Nebraska Wesl 1982; Cert Iona Sch for Mnstry 2014. D 4/27/2014 P 2/22/2017 Bp Scott Scott Barker.

WITHROCK JR, John William (CGC) 401 W College St, Troy AL 36081 B Trinidad CO 1948 s John. BA U of So Carolina 1970; MDiv Luth Theol Sthrn Sem 1975. D 6/7/2008 P 6/13/2009 Bp Philip Menzie Duncan II. m 7/5/1969 Elaine Bush Withrock c 3. jwwithrock@comcast.net

WITKE, E(dward) Charles (Mich) 3000 Glazier Way, Ann Arbor MI 48105 **Assoc S Andr's Ch Ann Arbor MI 1995-** B Los Angeles CA 1931 s Emil & Ethel. BA U CA Los Angeles 1953; MA Harv 1957; PhD Harv 1960. D 6/25/1988 Bp Henry Irving Mayson P 1/10/1989 Bp R aymond Stewart Wood Jr. m 10/10/1975 Aileen Patricia Gatten. VP Epis Stdt Fndt U MI 1995-1998; Asst H Faith Ch Saline MI 1993-1995; Asst S Lk's Epis Ch Ypsilanti MI 1989-1991; D S Jas' Epis Ch Dexter MI 1988-1989; Exam Dio Michigan Detroit MI 1991-1996. Auth, "Horace's Roman Odes: A Critical Approach," Mnemosyne, 1978; Auth, "Numen Litterarum: Chr Latin Poetry from Greg the Great to Constantine," Mittellateinische Studien, 1971. CBS 1949; Ord of S Ben Confrater 1988; SocMary 1988. Fell Amer Acad in Rome 1960.

WITT, Anne Lane (Va) PO Box 1059, Kilmarnock VA 22482 **S Jn's Ch Richmond VA 2016-** B Richmond VA 1974 d Thomas & Ann Lane. BA U of Virginia 1997; MDiv GTS 2010. D 6/5/2010 P 12/11/2010 Bp Shannon Sherwood Johnston. P-in-c Imm Ch Mechanicsvlle VA 2013-2015; Gr Ch Kilmarnock VA 2010-2013. annelanewitt@msn.com

WITT, Bonnie Rae (WNY) Po Box 66, Gasport NY 14067 B Lockport NY 1956 d Raymond & Joyce. AA Niagara Cc Sanborn NY 1977; BS SUNY 1998. D 9/14/2001 Bp Michael Garrison. D Chr Ch Lockport NY 2001-2008.

WITT JR, Richard Cyril (NY) 16 Lawrence Rd, Accord NY 12404 **Mid Hudson Catskill Rural and Migrant Min Poughkeepsie NY 1991-** B Pittsburgh PA 1959 s Richard & Cynthia. The London Sch of Econ and Political Sci 1981; BA Bos 1982; MDiv EDS 1986. D 6/11/1988 Bp David Elliot Johnson P 5/1/1989 Bp Barbara Clementine Harris. m 8/31/1990 Tracy Leavitt c 3. Assoc R Chr Ch Poughkeepsie NY 1988-1991; Epis Chapl Vas Poughkeepsie NY 1988-1991; Asst to R Par Of The Epiph Winchester MA 1986-1988; Rural & Migrant Mnstry.

WITT JR, Robert Edward (Alb) P.O. Box 123, Morris NY 13808 **R All SS' Chap Morris NY 2003-** B Plainfield NJ 1946 s Robert & Nicolina. BA Alfred U 1968; MDiv GTS 1978; STM GTS 1989. D 6/3/1978 Bp Frederick Barton Wolf P 12/15/1978 Bp Harvey D Butterfield. m 12/27/1967 Marion B Burdick c 3. R Zion Ch Morris NY 2003-2016, R 1981-1987; Trin And S Michaels Ch Middleville NY 2002-2003; P S Paul's Ch Utica NY 1989-1994; P-in-c Gr Ch Mohawk NY 1987-2003; Chapl S Margarets Hse New Hartford NY 1987-2003; Chr Ch Gilbertsville NY 1981-1987; S Johns Epis Ch Brownville ME 1978-1981; Vic St Josephs Ch Sebec ME 1978-1981; Dioc Coun Dio Albany Greenwich NY 1999-2003, Chapl, Profile & Search Com 1996-1997, Chair, Dioc Stwdshp Com 1990-1998, Dioc Coun 1981-1985. Bro of S Andr 1980; Soc of S Marg 1988. Who's Who in Rel 1981. fr.rew@frontier.com

WITTE JR, Walter William (Nwk) Po Box 4781, Vineyard Haven MA 02568 **Died 12/12/2016** B North Tonawanda NY 1927 s Walter & Pauline. BA Hobart and Wm Smith Colleges 1949; MDiv Ya Berk 1952; STM UTS 1970. D 6/9/1952 P 9/29/1954 Bp Lauriston L Scaife. m 6/5/1954 Patricia Griffin c 1. S Andr's Ch Edgartown MA 1992; S Mk's Ch Dorchester MA 1990-1991; Par Of S Paul Newton Highlands MA 1987-1988; Non-par 1971-2016; Cn Trin And S Phil's Cathd Newark NJ 1969-1971; R S Steph's Ch S Louis MO 1963-1969; Vic Ch Of The Epiph Kirkwood S Louis MO 1956-1963; Asst Gr Ch S Louis MO 1955-1958; Cur Gr Ch Lockport NY 1953-1955; D-In-C S Paul's Epis Ch Springville NY 1952-1953. Auth, "arts," Living Ch; Auth, "arts," Wit.

WITTIG, Nancy Constantine Hatch (Pa) 21801 Elizabeth Ave, Fairview Park OH 44126 **Ret S Ptr's Epis Ch Lakewood OH 2006-** B Takoma Park MD 1945 d William & Nancy. BA U NC 1969; MDiv VTS 1972; DMin Estrn Bapt TS 2005. D 9/8/1973 Bp George E Rath P 7/29/1974 Bp Edward Randolph Welles II. m 4/12/2012 Pamela Wood c 2. Dn Of Pennypack Dnry Dio Pennsylvania Philadelphia PA 1992-1998; R S Andr's In The Field Ch Philadelphia PA 1988-2005; Adjunct Fac Of Pstr Theol The GTS New York NY 1988-1990; R Ch Of S Jn The Div Hasbrouck Hts NJ 1983-1988, Int R 1982-1983; Non-par Dio Newark 1975-1981; Cur S Ptr's Ch Morristown NJ 1974; D All SS Ch Millington NJ 1973-1974. Co-Fndr Pa Wmn'S Cleric Assn 1990-2006; Ord Of S Helena 1992. Fell Etssw 1997; Fell Coll Of Preachers 1992; Hon Cn Trin Cathd 1981.

WITTMAYER, Kevin Edward (Tex) 906 Padon St, Longview TX 75601 B Cedar Falls IA 1955 s Edward & Annetta. BS Oral Roberts U 1978; MBA Oral Roberts U 1980; MDiv VTS 1991. D 6/22/1991 P 1/11/1992 Bp Robert Manning Moody. m 8/13/1977 Pamela E Wittmayer c 2. R Trin Ch Longview TX 2003-2017; Dio Oklahoma Oklahoma City OK 1994-2003; Mssnr Gr Ch Epis Yukon OK 1994-2003; Asst R Epis Ch Of The Resurr Oklahoma City OK 1991-1994. frkevin55@gmail.com

WIZOREK, Julie C (Md) 249 Double Oak Rd N, Prince Frederick MD 20678 **Dioc Coun Mem Dio Maryland Baltimore MD 2005-** B Los Angeles CA 1950 d Marshall & Virginia. BA USC 1972; MA U of Arizona 1974; MDiv CDSP 2001. D 6/23/2001 P 2/9/2002 Bp Richard Lester Shimpfky. m 1/6/1973 Martin William Wizorek c 2. Int S Paul's Epis Ch Piney Waldorf MD 2013-2014; R S Paul's Epis Ch Prnc Frederck MD 2004-2012; Asst to the R S Patricks Ch Kenwood CA 2001-2003. Sprtl Dir Intl 2013.

WLOSINSKI, Stephen Stanley (Minn) 1121 W Morgan St, Duluth MN 55811 B Hazelton PA 1942 s Stephen & Helen. BA Macalester Coll 1964; MDiv Nash 1967; MS U of Wisconsin 1995. Rec 10/1/1983 as Priest Bp Robert Marshall Anderson. m 12/28/1983 Cynthia M E Peterson c 1. Asst S Andr's By The Lake Duluth MN 1988-2004; Chapl S Lk's Hosp Duluth MN 1986-2009; Calv Ch Rochester MN 1986; Dio Minnesota Minneapolis MN 1984-1986; P S Edw The Confessor Wayzata MN 1984-1986; Serv Polish Natl Cath Ch 1967-1981.

WOEHLER, Charles George (WTex) 1416 North Loop 1604 East, San Antonio TX 78232 **R S Thos Epis Ch And Sch San Antonio TX 1990-** B Minneapolis MN 1950 s Charles & Dorothy. BA U of the Incarnate Word 1973; MDiv Epis TS of the SW 1977. D 6/21/1977 P 4/1/1978 Bp Scott Field Bailey. m 5/24/

1975 Kathryn S Woehler c 2. Asst S Mk's Epis Ch San Antonio TX 1988-1990; R Epis Ch Of The Mssh Gonzales TX 1984-1988; R H Trin Carrizo Sprg TX 1980-1984; Asst S Mk's Ch San Marcos TX 1977-1980.

WOESSNER, David H (WMass) **D-in-c S Mich's-On-The-Heights Worcester MA 2015-** D 12/6/2014 P 7/11/2015 Bp Doug Fisher.

WOGGON, Harry Arthur (WNC) 5 Norwich Dr, Asheville NC 28803 **P Assoc S Mary's Ch Asheville NC 2000-; Ret 1997-** B New York NY 1932 s Arthur & Mary. BA Ham 1954; MA U of Oregon 1959; STB GTS 1963. D 6/29/1963 P 6/1/1964 Bp Richard Henry Baker. m 7/4/1959 Genelda Kepley Woggon c 4. P-in-c St Georges Epis Ch Asheville NC 2000-2004; Old Trin Ch Ch Creek MD 1993-1997; Dio Easton Easton MD 1993-1995; Int S Andr's Epis Ch Newport News VA 1992-1993; Int S Tim's Epis Ch W Des Moines IA 1991-1992; Int Trin Ch Iowa City IA 1990-1991; Int Chr Epis Ch Smithfield VA 1988-1989; Int S Jas Epis Ch Greenville SC 1988; Int S Jn's Ch Ithaca NY 1986-1987; Int S Jn's Epis Ch Columbia SC 1986; Int Gr Epis Ch Camden SC 1985; Int Ch Of The H Comf Burlington NC 1984, Asst to R 1963-1965; Dio Wstrn No Carolina Asheville NC 1981-1983; Chapl Porter-Gaud Sch Charleston SC 1968-1970; S Jas Ch Mooresville NC 1963-1968; P-in-c S Jas Kannapolis NC 1963-1965. Auth, "Journey to the Cntr: Poems/Prayers," New Day Resources, 2005; Auth, Trsfg into Wholeness, 1988. Assoc of OHC 1964; Natl Assn for the Self-Supporting Active Mnstry 1971-1977.

WOGGON, Karla (WA) 1048 15th Ave. N.W., Hickory NC 28601 **R Ch Of The Ascen Hickory NC 2007-** B Kannapolis NC 1966 d Harry & Genelda. BA Appalachian St U 1989; MA LSU 1991; MDiv SWTS 1995. D 5/20/1995 P 12/1/1995 Bp James Barrow Brown. m 6/23/2007 John Walker. R S Andr's Epis Ch Coll Pk MD 1999-2007; Assoc R Ch Of The Ascen Gaithersburg MD 1996-1999; Assoc R Chr Ch Covington LA 1995-1996; Chapl Chr Sch Covington LA 1995-1996.

WOHLEVER, Russell J (CFla) All Saints Church, 338 E Lyman Ave, Winter Park FL 32789 **Asst All SS Ch Of Winter Pk Winter Pk FL 2007-** B Danbury CT 1967 s James & Mary. BA Penn 1990; MDiv Nash 2007. D 6/2/2007 P 12/2/2007 Bp John Wadsworth Howe. m 8/13/2004 Amaryllis S Wohlever c 3.

WOJAHN, Karen Ann (Dix) (Los) 1012 East Van Owen Avenue, Orange CA 92867 **Asst S Paul's Epis Ch Tustin CA 2015-** B Fargo ND 1947 d Orion & Helen. AA Fullerton Coll 1992; BA California St Polytechnic U 1994; MDiv Claremont ST 2000. D 6/17/2000 Bp Chester Lovelle Talton P 1/6/2001 Bp Frederick Houk Borsch. m 4/1/1967 Roy Edward Wojahn c 3. S Jn Chrys Ch Rcho Sta Marg CA 2005-2008; Dir of Chld's & Fam Mnstrs S Wilfrid Of York Epis Ch Huntington Bch CA 2000-2004. Auth, "numerous arts," The Epis News, 1989; Auth, Growing Up w Roy and Dale, Regal Books, 1986; Auth, Var mag and Nwspr arts, 1972. Golden Key hon Soc 1994; Sigma Tau Delta 1992. Outstanding Grad, Coll Arts California Polytechnical U 1994; Pacesetter Awd Biola U writer's Inst 1988.

WOJCIEHOWSKI, Arthur Anthony (Minn) 1500 Prospect Ave, Cloquet MN 55720 B Saint Cloud MN 1940 s Anthony & Sophia. Dioces of Mn Theol Sch 1994; AAS Lake Superior Coll 1996. D 11/22/1993 P 6/1/1994 Bp Sanford Zangwill Kaye Hampton. c 2. Non-par 1993-2002; S Andr's Ch Cloquet MN 1993-2002; Trin Epis Ch Hermantown MN 1993-2002.

WOLCOTT, Sarah Elizabeth (Neb) 512 N Oak St, Gordon NE 69343 B Oswego NY 1947 d Alan & Sally. BS Illinois St U 1969; MS Loyola U 1994. D 2/14/1998 Bp John Clark Buchanan. D Niobrara Epis Cluster. NAAD.

WOLF, David B (WA) 1516 Hamilton St NW, Washington DC 20011 **Samar Mnstry Of Grtr Washington Washington DC 2012-** B Springfield MA 1961 s Paul & Katherine. BA Bates Coll 1983; JD GW 1989; MDiv VTS 1996. D 6/15/1996 P 1/7/1997 Bp Peter J Lee. m 5/23/1998 Martha E Wolf c 1. R S Paul's Epis Ch Paterson NJ 2001-2012; Asst R S Alb's Par Washington DC 1996-2001. Auth, "A Critical Examination of Stanley Hauerwas' Ethical Ideal," VTS Libr Collection, 1996; Auth, "Pardon for No Would be Unconstitutional," Manhattan Lawyer, Legal Times, 1988; Auth, "Imm Kants' Theory of Moral Value," Bates Coll Libr Collection, 1983. Phil Beta Kappa 1983; The Connecticut Bar 1989. Chas A. Dana Schlr Bates Coll 1980.

✠ WOLF, The Rt Rev Gerry (RI) 275 N Main St, Providence RI 02903 **Ret Bp of Rhode Island Dio Rhode Island Providence RI 2013-, Bp of Rhode Island 1996-2012** B New York NY 1947 d Joseph & Harriet. BS W Chester U of Pennsylvania 1968; MA Trenton St Coll 1971; MDiv EDS 1977. D 6/11/1977 P 5/25/1978 Bp Lyman Cunningham Ogilby Con 2/17/1996 for RI. m 4/21/2007 Thomas Charles Bair c 2. Dn Chr Ch Cathd Louisville KY 1987-1995; Vic S Mary's Epis Ch Philadelphia PA 1981-1987; Asst Ch Of S Mart-In-The-Fields Philadelphia PA 1979-1981; Asst S Mary's Epis Ch Ardmore PA 1977-1979. Auth, "Down and Out in Providence," Crossroads, 2004; Auth, "Ldrshp:Being A Holding Container," S Mk's Revs, 2002; Auth, "Sewanee Theol Revs". SSM, Assoc 1974. Dhl Roger Williams U 1999. beeplepeople@cox.net

WOLF, Max Joseph (Del) 20 Olive Ave, Rehoboth Beach DE 19971 **R All SS and St Georges Ch Rehoboth Bch DE 2001-; R S Geo's Chap Lewes DE 2001-** B Providence RI 1955 s Joseph & Jacquin. MDiv EDS 1996; BA U of Rhode Island 1996. D 6/15/1996 P 2/16/1997 Bp Gerry Wolf. m 12/5/1987 Audre Alissa Wolf. Bp and Coun Mem Dio Delaware Wilmington 2002-2005;

W

939

Cn Mssnr Yth Dio Pennsylvania Philadelphia PA 1999-2001; COM Dio Rhode Island Providence RI 1998-1999, Evang & Cmncatn 1998-1999, 1997-1999; Cler Conf Com S Andr's Ch New London NH 1997-1999; Cur S Paul's Ch N Kingstown RI 1997-1999; Assoc S Phil's In The Hills Tucson AZ 1996-1997; Bd for Theol Educ Epis Ch Cntr New York NY 1994-1997. Fllshp of SSJE 1991.

WOLFE, Alexander (ND) Po Box 8340, Fargo ND 58109 B Grenfell SK CA 1927 s Charles & Harriet. D 6/11/1970 Bp George T Masuda. m 9/2/1952 Elizabeth Wolfe.

✠ WOLFE, The Rt Rev Dean E (NY) 835 SW Polk St, Topeka KS 66612 **R St. Barth Ch New York NY 2017-; VP, HOB Dom And Frgn Mssy Soc- Epis Ch Cntr New York NY 2009-** B Dayton OH 1956 s William & Mildred. Bethany TS, Oak Brook, Illinois 1983; B.A. Mia 1987; Cert Washington Hosp Cntr Washington DC 1990; Cert S Georges Coll, Jerusalem 1991; M.Div. VTS 1992; S Deiniols Libr, Hawarden Wales 1996. D 6/6/1992 P 6/6/1993 Bp William Edwin Swing Con 11/8/2003 for Kan. m 12/27/1980 Ellen M Frantz Wolfe c 1. Bp of Kansas Dio Kansas Topeka KS 2003-2017; Vice R S Mich And All Ang Ch Dallas TX 1998-2003; Assoc R Trin Ch Epis Boston MA 1994-1998; Asst R S Clem's Ch Berkeley CA 1992-1994. Ord of the Hosp of S Jn of Jerusalem - Asst Chapl 2000; The Soc of S Jn the Evang - Assoc 2002. DD Virginia Theol Serminary 2004. dwolfe@stbarts.org

WOLFE, Dorothy Annabell (Neb) 603 3rd Ave, Bayard NE 69334 B Burlington CO 1929 d John & Sarah. D 6/2/2002 Bp James Edward Krotz. m 8/8/1954 Elmer Wolfe.

WOLFE, James Edward (HB) **Non-par 1968-** B Cleveland OH 1933 s Joseph & Anna. BS Baldwin-Wallace Coll 1956; BD EDS 1960. D 12/17/1960 Bp Frederic Cunningham Lawrence P 6/1/1961 Bp Malcolm E Peabody. Assoc San Andres Santo Domingo Dominican Republic 1967-1968; R S Lk's Epis Ch Malden MA 1962-1966.

WOLFE, John M (SwFla) 501 Erie Ave, Tampa FL 33606 **D St. Mary's Ch Tampa FL 2002-** B Indianapolis IN 1943 s Arthor & Elizabeth. BA U of Tampa 1972; MBA U of So Florida 1988. D 6/12/2004 Bp John Bailey Lipscomb. m 10/21/1972 Patricia Ann Rosedahl Wolfe c 2. D S Mary's Par Tampa FL 2004-2013.

WOLFE, Vernon Eugene (Oly) 53565 W Ferndale Rd, Milton Freewater OR 97862 **Ret 1990-; Ret 1990-** B Baker OR 1925 s Vernon & Ruby. MDiv CDSP 1967; Seattle Pacific U 1970; BA U of Puget Sound 1970; MEd Seattle U 1971. D 5/20/1967 Bp George Richard Millard P 11/21/1967 Bp John Raymond Wyatt. m 8/3/1980 Nancy Wolfe c 2. Mssn to Seafarers Seattle WA 1986-1990; S Clem's Epis Ch Seattle WA 1979-1990; Dir Puget Sound Maritime Mnstry 1972-1990; Dio Olympia Seattle 1972-1985; Asst S Lk's Epis Ch Renton WA 1970-1971; Vic S Lk Waterville WA 1967-1969; Cur S Lk's Epis Ch Wenatchee WA 1967-1969.

WOLFENBARGER, Mary Suzanne (WLa) 55 Magnolia Dr, Belleville IL 62221 **Trin Epis Ch Natchitoches LA 2015-** B Knoxville TN 1958 d David & Mary. MS U of Tennessee 1983. D 6/11/2000 Bp Peter Hess Beckwith P 6/24/2011 Bp George Wayne Smith. m 3/17/1979 William C Wolfenbarger c 1. S Paul's Epis Ch Sikeston MO 2012-2015; D S Geo's Ch Belleville IL 2004-2006.

WOLFF, Pierre Maurice (Ct) 108 C North Turnpike Road, Wallingford CT 06492 **Non-par 1989-** B Marseille FR 1929 s Leopold & Marguerite. Trng In Soc of Jesus Fr 1963. Rec 11/10/1989 Bp Arthur Edward Walmsley. m 9/10/1988 Mary Morgan. Serv RC Ch. Auth, "Sprtl Exercises S Ignatus," 1997; Auth, "May I Hate God".

WOLFF, William George (Kan) 306 W. Euclid St., Pittsburg KS 66762 B Schaller IA 1943 s Leo & Marcella. PhD Sthrn Illinois U 1974; Cert VTS 2005. D 9/9/2000 Bp William Edward Smalley P 8/6/2005 Bp Dean E Wolfe. m 12/27/1964 Luella Mae Wohlers. R S Ptr's Ch Pittsburg KS 2005-2015; D Gr Cathd Topeka KS 2000-2004; Mem, Bd Dir The Bp Kemper Sch for Mnstry Topeka KS 2013-2016; Coun of Trst/Stndg Com Dio Kansas Topeka KS 2008-2014, COM 2006-2012.

WOLFORD, Rachael Rossiter (Oly) PO Box 522, Cathlamet WA 98612 **D S Jas Epis Ch Cathlamet WA 1998-** B Bournemouth Hampshire UK 1937 d Edward & Mary. Gd Samar Hosp Oregon Radiological Tech Port 1961. D 10/3/1998 Bp Vincent Waydell Warner. m 6/3/1961 John Leroy Wolford. NAAD.

WOLLARD, Robert Foster (Mich) 4505 Westlawn Pkwy, Waterford MI 48328 B Detroit MI 1938 s Wilbur & Margaret. BA Alma Coll 1960; MDiv VTS 1963; Wayne 1970. D 6/29/1963 Bp Robert Lionne DeWitt P 1/25/1964 Bp Richard Stanley Merrill Emrich. m 5/17/1975 Carole A Wollard c 2. Assoc R S Andr's Ch Waterford MI 1999-2011; Cbury On The Lake Waterford MI 1996-1998; Int Chr Ch Cranbrook Bloomfield Hills MI 1994-1996; Epis Tri-Par Cluster Standish MI 1991-1994; The Whitaker Inst of Theol Detroit MI 1985-1994; Field Dir Whitaker TS 1985-1994; Team Mnstry Loc Congregations Epis Tri-Par Cluster MI 1980-1994; R S Gabr's Epis Ch Eastpointe MI 1977-1985; Dio Michigan Detroit MI 1969-1977; Chapl Henry Ford Hosp Detroit MI 1969-1977; Asst Cathd Ch Of S Paul Detroit MI 1966-1969; Asst Min S Columba Ch Detroit MI 1963-1966; Chapl/Dir of Pstr Care Cbury on the Lake Waterford MI.

WOLSONCROFT III, Arthur Mathew (NY) 414 E 52nd St, New York NY 10022 B Philadelphia PA 1933 s Arthur & Anna. BA Tem 1955; MA NYU 1975; MDiv Nash 1987. D 6/13/1987 P 1/1/1988 Bp Paul Moore Jr. Asst Ch Of S Mary The Vrgn New York NY 1988-2004; Dio New York New York NY 1987-1991; S Lk's-Roosevelt Hosp Cntr New York NY 1987-1991. Tertiary Of The Soc Of S Fran.

WOLTER, Jack M (WNY) 668 Shadow Mountain Dr, Prescott AZ 86301 **Ret 2001-** B Mason City IA 1934 s Marvin & Irene. BS Iowa St U 1956; STB GTS 1961. D 6/9/1961 P 12/18/1961 Bp Gordon V Smith. m 4/27/1957 Mary Elizabeth Wolter c 5. Int S Lk's Ch Prescott AZ 2006-2007; R S Jas' Ch Batavia NY 1978-2001; R S Anne's Epis Ch De Pere WI 1972-1978; R S Alb's Ch Davenport IA 1963-1971; R Gr Ch Estherville IA 1961-1963; Calling Consult Dio Wstrn New York Tonawanda NY 1997-2001, Trst 1995-2001, Plan and Vision Com 1994-1997, Hlth Ins Com 1992-2001, GC/Alt Dep 1988-1994, Resolutns Com/Chair 1988-1990, Genesee Reg Dn 1987-2001, Dept of Congrl Spprt 1984-1987, Dioc Coun 1980-1983, Lay Mnstry Com 1979-1992, Stndg Com/Pres 1979-1983; Dioc Coun Dio Fond du Lac Appleton WI 1975-1978, Ecum Cmsn 1975-1978; Prov V Alum Rep The GTS New York NY 1972-1975, Prov VI Alum Rep 1967-1971; Dioc Coun Dio Iowa Des Moines IA 1970-1971, Soc Concerns Cmsn 1967-1971, Yth Div 1962-1967, Camp Morrison, Asst. Dir 1958. OHC, P Assoc 1963.

WOLTERSTORFF, Claire Kingma (WMich) 58 Sunnybrook Ave Se, Grand Rapids MI 49506 B Marshalltown IA 1934 d Jan & Gezina. BA Calvin Coll 1955; MDiv SWTS 1985. D 6/8/1985 P 11/16/1996 Bp Howard Samuel Meeks. m 6/25/1955 Nicholas Paul Wolterstorff c 5. Fndr and Dir Elis Hse Pryr 1985-1989; Sprtl Dir Annand Cntr Ya Berk New Haven CT 1989-1995. Auth, "Birth, Death, Hunger and Love"; Auth, *Garland for a Faint Soirit: A Bk of Prayers for Ian and India*; Auth, *Hemmed in by Darkness (a PB for the ill)*; Auth, *In The Shadow of Your Wings (a PB for the dying)*.

WOLTZ, Charles Morris (Okla) 924 N Robinson Ave, Oklahoma City OK 73102 B Oklahoma City OK 1936 s Elzo & Audrey. U of Oklahoma; BA U of Cntrl Oklahoma 1961. D 8/31/1985 Bp Gerald Nicholas Mcallister. m 6/26/2004 Kathryn Jan Woltz c 2. Dio Oklahoma Oklahoma City OK 1985-2008.

WOLYNIAK, Joseph Geoffrey (NC) 53 University Pl, Princeton NJ 08540 **Dio New Jersey Trenton NJ 2016-** B Lansing MI 1981 s Joseph & Mary. Cert in Nonprofit Mgmt Duke; Bachelor of Sci (BS) E Carolina U; Bachelor of Arts (BA) E Carolina U; Doctor of Philos (DPhil) U of Oxford; Mstr of Theol Stds (MTS) Duke DS 2007. D 6/11/2016 Bp Anne Hodges-Copple P 12/11/2016 Bp William H Stokes. m 7/15/2006 Elizabeth R Costello c 1. Dio Colorado Denver CO 2015-2016. Soc of Schlr-Priests 2014. Acad Fell ECF 2012. j.g.w@princeton.edu

WOMACK JR, Egbert Morton (Colo) 7500 E Dartmouth Ave Unit 31, Denver CO 80231 B Houston TX 1931 s Egbert & Kitty. BS U of Houston 1963; BD Epis TS of the SW 1968; MDiv Epis TS of the SW 1971. D 6/27/1968 Bp James Milton Richardson P 5/15/1969 Bp Scott Field Bailey. m 7/6/1957 Joanne Womack c 2. S Jn's Cathd Denver CO 2000-2001; S Fran Cntr Denver CO 1993; Bp's Exec Stff Dio Colorado Denver CO 1992-2000, Cn to the Ordnry 1982-2000; P-in-c S Fran Chap Denver CO 1983-1994; Stndg Cmsn on Soc & Spec Mnstrs ECUSA New York NY 1981-1983; Vic S Martha's Epis Ch Westminster CO 1977-1979; Vic S Andr's Ch Manitou Sprg CO 1975-1977; Cn Mssnr Chr Ch Cathd Houston TX 1974-1975, Asst to the Dn 1971-1973; P-in-c All SS Epis Ch Hitchcock TX 1969-1971; P-in-c S Jos's Epis Ch LaMarque TX 1969-1971; Asst The Ch of the Gd Shpd Austin TX 1968-1969. Cn To The Ordnry Emer Bp of Colorado 2002; The 2002 Hal Brook Perry Awd Epis Sem of The SW 2002; Bp's Cross Bp of Colorado 1993.

WOMACK, Lawrence (LI) 8725 Sedgeburn Drive, Charlotte NC 28278 **R S Aug's Epis Ch Brooklyn NY 2016-** B Indianapolis IN 1972 s Johnella. BA Wabash Coll 1994; MA JHU 1996; MDiv Bex Sem 2003. D 6/14/2003 Bp Robert Wilkes Ihloff P 1/10/2004 Bp John L Rabb. m 4/12/1997 Sharita D Womack c 3. P S Anne's Ch Winston Salem NC 2011-2017; asst. to the R S Mart's Epis Ch Charlotte NC 2006-2011; R S Lk's Ch Baltimore MD 2003-2006; asst. to the R St. Jas' Ch Baltiomore MD 2003-2006.

WOMELSDORF, Charles Stowers (CGC) 327 Honeysuckle Hill, Tallassee AL 36078 B Wilmington OH 1943 s William & Helen. BA Auburn U 1965; MDiv Nash 1968. D 6/5/1968 P 1/1/1969 Bp Albert R Stuart. m 6/12/1967 Sarah Womelsdorf c 3. H Sprt Epis Ch Gulf Shores AL 1998-2000; R S Mk's Epis Ch Troy AL 1991-1998; Pres Epis Dioc Ecum Off 1988-1992; R S Mich And All Ang Lake Chas LA 1988-1991; Dio Louisiana New Orleans LA 1978-1982; Chr Ch Napoleonville LA 1977-1988; R S Jn's Epis Ch Thibodaux LA 1977-1988; R S Jn's Epis Ch Bainbridge GA 1970-1977; Vic S Lk's Epis Ch Hawkinsville GA 1968-1970.

WON, Ho Gil Hilary (Nwk) 403 79th St, North Bergen NJ 07047 **Vic All SS' Korean Epis Ch Bergenfield NJ 2006-** B South Korea 1961 s Duk & Ki. BA Sung Kong Hoe U Kr 1989; MDiv Sung Kong Hoe TS KR 1994. Trans 6/14/2006 Bp John Palmer Croneberger. m 11/11/1989 Hye Kyung Jang c 1.

WON, Jonathan Sung Ho (Nwk) 16423 Maidstone Avenue, Norwalk CA 90650 B Pochon Kyunggi Do KR 1938 s Soon & Jae. BS Yonsei U 1962; MDiv EDS

W

1970; ThM S Michaels Sem Kr 1982; Concordia U 1998. Trans 12/31/1981 Bp John Shelby Spong. m 2/26/1972 Gemma Yong Ja Won c 2. All SS' Korean Epis Ch Bergenfield NJ 2000-2006; Vic S Fran Mssn Norwalk CA 1989-2000; Ch Of The Annunc Los Angeles CA 1987-1989; Vic Annunc Anaheim CA 1987-1988; Vic S Peters Ch Bogota NJ 1981-1987; Serv Angl Ch Of Korea 1970-1981. Auth, *Ch & Sacr*. Cn The Dio Los Angeles 1998.

WONDRA, Ellen K (Chi) Bexley Seabury Seminary Federation, 1407 E 60th St, Chicago IL 60637 **Asstg P S Ptr's Epis Ch Chicago IL 2013-; Bexley Seabury Fed Chicago IL 2004-, Prof of Theol and Ethics 2004-; Mem WCC Cmsn on Faith and Ord 2015-** B Santa Monica CA 1950 d Gerald & Elizabeth. BA Pomona Coll 1972; ETSBH 1973; MDiv CDSP 1976; PhD U Chi 1991. D 6/26/1976 Bp Chauncie Kilmer Myers P 10/22/1977 Bp Philip Frederick McNairy. Adj P S Lk And S Simon Cyrene Rochester NY 1991-2004; Chapl Hobart And Wm Smith Colleges Geneva NY 1979-1984; Assoc Chpl U Epis Cntr Minneapolis MN 1976-1978. Ed in Chf, "ATR"; Auth, "Humanity Has Been a H Thing"; Ed, "Reconstructing Chr Ethics"; Ed, "Common Witness to the Gospel"; Co-Auth, "Intro to Theol"; Auth, "Var essays and arts"; Auth, "Problems w Authority," *Angl Wmn on Mssn and the Ch*; Auth, "Wm Temple," *Empire and the Chr Tradition*; Auth, "We Ordain Them, They Don't," *One Lord, One Faith, One Baptism*. AAR 1989; Angl-RC Consult; Bd, ATR 1989; Epis Womens Caucus; GBEC; SALT; SCER 1997-2003. Fell Cntr of Theol Inquiry; Fell Coll of Preachers; Fell ECF. ewondra@bexleyseabury.edu

WONG, Diane (Mass) 5B Park Terr, Arlington MA 02474 **S Jn's Ch Arlington MA 2014-; Mem of Bp Co-Adjudacator Transmition Com Dio MA Boston MA 2013-** B Hong Kong 1953 d Y B & So-Yuet. BS U of Alberta Edmonton Ab CA 1982; MDiv Weston Jesuit TS 1997; MDiv Weston Jesuit TS, Boston Coll 1997; Cert Ang Stud EDS 1999; MA Simmons Coll 2013. D 6/15/2002 P 5/31/2003 Bp M(Arvil) Thomas Shaw. P-in-c S Jn's Epis Ch Holbrook MA 2011-2014; Mssy P-in-c Exec Coun Appointees New York NY 2006-2011; Assoc S Paul's Ch In Nantucket Nantucket MA 2003-2006; D Ch Of Our Sav Arlington MA 2002-2003; Dioc Stff Dio Massachusetts Boston MA 2002-2003. "In The Footsteps Of The Foremothers: The Mnstrs Of Asian And Asian Amer Lay Wmn Deeper Joy," Ch Pub, 2005.

WONG, George Christopher (NJ) 6030 Grosvenor Ln, Bethesda MD 20814 **H Trin Epis Ch Ocean City NJ 2015-** B Los Angeles CA 1962 s Ronald & Momoyo. BA U CA, Los Angeles 1984; MBA U CA, Los Angeles 1989; MDiv VTS 2014. D 12/7/2013 P 6/14/2014 Bp Mariann Edgar Budde. m 6/20/1998 Elizabeth Carino Wong. S Lk's Ch Trin Par Beth MD 2014-2015. htecoc@comcast.net

WONG, Gloria Violet Lee (Mass) Po Box 825, Oak Bluffs MA 02557 **D Gr Ch Vineyard Haven MA 1999-** B Victoria BC CA 1928 d Clarence & Edith. BA U CA 1949; MS Smith Sch for Soc Wk 1953; Rhode Island Sch for Deacons 1993. D 6/23/1993 Bp George Nelson Hunt III. m 7/3/1954 Backman Wong c 5. S Jas Ch The Par Of N Providence RI 1993-1996; Chair- Strng Com Boston Chinese Mnstry 1985-1993; COM Dio Massachusetts Boston MA 1996-1999. Intl Ord of S Lk the Physcn 1985; NAAD 1993.

WONG, Peter Reginald (CGC) Church of the Nativity, 205 Holly Ln, Dothan AL 36301 **R The Epis Ch Of The Nativ Dothan AL 2012-; Chapl Dothan Police Dept 2012-** B Muskogee OK 1972 s Sidney & Dorothy. BSBA U of W Florida 2002; MDiv Sewanee: The U So, TS 2012; MDiv U So TS 2012. D 12/21/2011 P 6/30/2012 Bp Philip Menzie Duncan II. m 10/8/2005 Katie Huelsbeck c 2. Dio Cntrl Gulf Coast Pensacola FL 2004-2007, Cmsn on Cong Dvlpmt 2015-, Cmsn on Peace and Justice 2015-; Chr Epis Ch Pensacola FL 2001-2004. nativity@centurytel.net

WONG, Philip Yau-Ming (Oly) 62 Pine St., Rockville Centre NY 11570 B Hong Kong CN 1946 s Sai & King. Hong Kong Biblic Inst HK 1967; BA U of Hong Kong HK 1971; MDiv Tainan Theol Coll and Sem TW 1987. D 6/10/1988 P 9/30/1989 Bp John Chih-Tsung Chien. m 3/24/1973 Sylvia SL Wong c 2. Vic Ch Of The H Apos Bellevue WA 2000-2010; Sr Pstr SI Chinese Chr Ch New York NY 1998-2000; Staten Island Chinese Chr Ch Staten Island NY 1998-2000; Dio New Jersey Trenton NJ 1995; Chinese Mssn, Vic and Jubilee Mnstry, Dir S Lk And All SS' Ch Un NJ 1994-1998; Assoc, Chinese Mssn, Vic Chinese Mnstry Of Dio Of Newark Nutley NJ 1992-1994; Gr Ch Nutley NJ 1992-1994; Cur S Paul's Ch N Arlington NJ 1989-1991; Evang S Barn in Hong Kong 1971-1980. Seaman's Ch of the Seafarers, Newark, NJ 1997-1999.

WONG, Sally (ECR) **S Thos Epis Ch Sunnyvale CA 2015-** B China 1972 d Sher & Ling. D 6/11/2005 Bp Robert John O'Neill P 12/3/2005 Bp William Edwin Swing. m 1/5/2002 Shannon M Preto. Asst S Mk's Epis Ch Palo Alto CA 2011-2015; S Matt's Epis Day Sch San Mateo CA 2011; Asst R S Clem's Ch Berkeley CA 2005-2011.

WOO, Raymond A (Haw) 45 N Judd St, Honolulu HI 96817 **S Lk's Epis Ch Honolulu HI 2015-** B Hong Kong 1957 s Manuel & Anna. BA Santa Clara U 1980; MA Ford 1987; MDiv Weston Jesuit TS 1994. Rec 6/14/2015 Bp Robert Leroy Fitzpatrick. m 11/16/2000 Vivien Chong Woo.

WOOD, Ann Patricia (WMass) 13 Kelleher Dr, South Deerfield MA 01373 B Stoke-on-Trent England 1937 D 6/19/2004 Bp Gordon Scruton. m 9/8/1962 John Stanley Wood c 2.

WOOD, Camille Carpenter (La) 3552 Morning Glory Ave, Baton Rouge LA 70808 B Evanston IL 1944 d Nathaniel & Ethel. D 12/4/2010 Bp Morris King Thompson Jr. m 2/7/1994 Fernie Wood c 2. D S Pat's Ch Zachary LA 2014-2016.

WOOD JR, Charles Amos (La) 532 Stanford Ave, Baton Rouge LA 70808 **Died 3/12/2016** B Syracuse NY 1932 s Charles & Florence. BA Cor 1954; MDiv VTS 1966; STM Nash 1973. D 6/28/1966 Bp James Milton Richardson P 6/2/1967 Bp Scott Field Bailey. m 11/4/1955 Gay W Worrall c 3. Ret 1997-2016; Epis Chapl to LSU S Alb's Chap & Epis U Cntr Baton Rouge LA 1970-1997; Assoc S Chris Milwaukee WI 1967-1970; Vic All SS Epis Ch Hitchcock TX 1966-1967. Auth, "Premarital Counslg: A Working Model," *Journ of Pstr Care*. AAPC 1974-1985; Amer Assn of Mar and Fam Therapists 1976-2007; ESMHE 1971-1997.

WOOD JR, Charles Edwards (Spok) 426 Lilly Road NE Apt 248, Olympia WA 98506 **Died 12/28/2016** B Carneys Pt NJ 1919 s Charles & Maria. U Cinc 1938; BS USNA 1941; MDiv SWTS 1965. D 6/20/1965 P 3/6/1966 Bp Russell S Hubbard. m 8/22/1942 Ann R Wood c 4. Dio Spokane Spokane WA 1983-2013, Const & Cns Mem 1978-2006, Dep GC 1976-1979, Admin Asst to Bp 1969-1980, Dioc Coun 1968-1987, Chair ArmdF Com 1966-1972, Chair ArmdF Com 1984-1989, Chair Const & Cas 1983-2005, 1983, Const & Cns Mem 1978-2006, Dep GC 1976-1982, Secy of Conv 1973-1988, Dio Coun 1968-1988; Ret 1980-2016; Epis Ch Of The Redeem Republic WA 1965-1969; Vic S Jn's Epis Ch Colville WA 1965-1969. Cler Advsry Com, Planned Parenthood of Spokane & Wh 1995; Integrity 1985-2009; Parents, Fam and Friends Of Lesbian and Gays 1984-2009. Hon Cn Cathd of S Jn the Evang 1980.

WOOD, Charles Leon (Mich) 608 Lily Pl, Southern Pines NC 28387 **Asst Chapl. for Cmncatn CAP HQ Middle E Reg 1957-** B Rahway NJ 1927 s Charles & Helen. Dplma GTS 1954; ThB PDS 1955; EdD Doctor of Educ/Rutgers 1964; STB GTS 1965; Dplma Air War Coll 1968; Dplma Indstrl Coll of the ArmdF Ft McNair DC 1972; DHum Great Lakes Reg Chapl Stff Coll 1987; Dplma Middle E Reg Chapl Stff Coll 1992. D 7/3/1954 Bp Wallace J Gardner P 1/22/1955 Bp Alfred L Banyard. m 6/23/1956 Nancy Phillips c 2. Instr Durham Tech Cmnty Coll 1994-2008; Ret 1991-2008; Vic S Lk's Epis Ch Yanceyville NC 1991-2007; Fac Whitaker TS 1986-1990; COM Dio Michigan Detroit MI 1983-1988; Chapl Hospice of the Straits Cheboygan MI 1982-1990; R Trsfg Epis Ch Indn River MI 1981-1990; Advsr of Yth Cmsn Dio New Jersey Trenton NJ 1970-1980; Alt Del Prov II Syn 1970-1973; Adj Fac Glassboro St Coll 1969-1981; Yth Advsr Atlantic Convoc 1968-1970; R H Trin Epis Ch Ocean City NJ 1967-1980; Vic S Paul's Tuckahoe NJ 1967-1970; R St Jn the Bapt Epis Ch Linden NJ 1958-1967; New Jersey Bd Field & Publ 1958-1961; Chapl (LtCol) CAP NJ 1957-1980; Vic The Epis Ch Of The H Comm Fair Haven NJ 1955-1958; Cur H Trin Ch Collingswood NJ 1954-1955. Auth, *Nine collections of Prayers*; Auth, *Two Hospice Books*. Grand Chapl RAM 1980; DSM CAP 1973; Geo Wash hon Medal Freedoms Fndt 1972.

WOOD, Christian Michael (SwFla) B New York 1980 s Michael & Elaine. B.S. Jn Jay Coll of Criminal Justice 2003; Mdiv Nash 2016. D 12/5/2015 P 6/29/2016 Bp Dabney Tyler Smith. m 1/6/2007 Katherine Grey Thomason c 3. D Ch Of The Redeem Sarasota FL 2016, Asst for Yth & YA Mnstry 2016-, Yth Dir 2009-2013. cwood@redeemersarasota.org

WOOD, Colette (Mass) 16 Highland Ave., Cohasset MA 02025 **The CPG New York NY 2017-; All SS Par Whitman MA 2012-** B New Bedford MA 1966 d Richard & Barbara. BS Emerson Coll; MDiv EDS 2008. D 6/7/2008 Bp M(Arvil) Thomas Shaw P 1/10/2009 Bp Roy Frederick Cederholm Jr. m 8/12/1989 Russell Wood c 2. Asst S Steph's Ch Cohasset MA 2008-2009.

WOOD, David Romaine (Colo) 1233 24th Ave. Ct., Greeley CO 80634 B Poplar Bluff MO 1938 s Romaine & Alice. BS U CO 1969. D 3/17/1983 P 10/15/1983 Bp William Harvey Wolfrum. m 10/15/1957 Donna Jean Wood c 4. Solo Pstr Cov Luth Ch Wheatland WY 2004-2008; S Alb's Ch Windsor CO 1990-2003; S Steph's Ch Longmont CO 1990-2003; R Cmnty Resurr Longmont CO 1986-1989; Assoc Cmnty Resurr Longmont CO 1983-1986.

WOOD, Grace Marie (EC) 198 Dogwood Trl, Elizabeth City NC 27909 **Chapl/ Soc Worker Albemarle Hospice Eliz City NC 2006-** B Montreal Canada 1947 d Saboits & Grace. BA Wag 1969; MS Gordham Grad Sch of Soc Sciences NY 1984; D Formation Prog 2004. D 6/25/2005 Bp Clifton Daniel III. m 8/3/1985 Allen Wood c 3.

WOOD, Gregg Douglas (NY) Po Box 62, Wawarsing NY 12489 **Ret 2001-** B Stoneham MA 1941 s Harry & Edna. BA Harv 1962; Harvard DS 1963; MDiv EDS 1967. D 6/24/1967 Bp Anson Phelps Stokes Jr P 6/8/1968 Bp Frederic Cunningham Lawrence. m 10/15/1977 Jane S Wood c 2. Dio New York New York NY 1997-2001; S Jn's Memi Ch Ellenville NY 1995-1996; Tri-Cnty Epis Area Mnstry Monticello NY 1992-1995; Mssnr Tri-Cnty Epis Area Mnstry Monticello NY 1992-1995; S Jn's Ch Huntington NY 1991-1992; S Steph's Ch Prt Washington NY 1989-1991; Prof of Pstr Counslg GT Mercer TS Garden City NY 1985-1993; Chr Ch Brentwood NY 1984-1985; S Johns Epis Hosp Far Rockaway NY 1979-1992; Dir of Pstr Care St. Jn's Epis Hosp Smithtown NY 1979-1992; Chapl Brooklyn Dvlpmt Cntr Brooklyn NY 1973-1979; R The Ch Of The Epiph And S Simon Brooklyn NY 1970-1977; S Ann's Ch Sayville NY

1969-1970; S Jn's Epis Ch Oakdale NY 1969-1970; Cur All SS Epis Ch Attleboro MA 1967-1969. AAPC 1978-1983; Fell Coll Chapl (inactive) 1982-1992. Robbins Fellowlowship EDS 1976; JA Mueller Hist Prize Epis TS 1967.

WOOD, Gretchen A (SO) 24 High Ridge Loop Apt 605, Pawleys Island SC 29585 B Upland PA 1944 d James & Barbara. BA Ob 1966; PhD U Chi 1970. D 6/11/1983 P 6/1/1984 Bp Lyman Cunningham Ogilby. Int S Mary Epis Ch Crystal Lake IL 2007-2008; Int S Anne Epis Ch W Chester OH 2005-2007; Int The Epis Ch Of The Ascen Middletown OH 2005; R S Jas Epis Ch Cincinnati OH 1990-2005; Assoc The Ch of the Redeem Cincinnati OH 1986-1990; P Ch Of S Jn The Evang Essington PA 1985-1986; D S Mary's Ch Hamilton Vill Philadelphia PA 1983-1984; Dir of the Sch for the Diac Dio Sthrn Ohio Cincinnati OH 1998-2002; Vice Dn U of Pennsylvania Philadelphia PA 1984-1986; Asst Dn U of Pennsylvania Philadelphia PA 1976-1984; Asst Prof of Engl U of Pennsylvania Philadelphia PA 1970-1976. Tertiary Of The Soc Of S Fran, Ca-so.

WOOD, Henry Palmer (CFla) 720 S Lakeshore Blvd, Lake Wales FL 33853 B Jacksonville FL 1936 s Julien & Harriet. Ics Orlando FL; BS Rol 1971. D 12/18/2004 Bp John Wadsworth Howe. m 1/17/1970 Ronali Anderson Wood c 2. Marketing Dir Bp Gray Inn Davenport FL 2002-2004.

WOOD, Howard Fitler (Pa) 526 Washington Ave, Hulmeville PA 19047 B Philadelphia PA 1937 s William & Margaret. BA U of Pennsylvania 1959; MEd Nazareth Coll 1978; MDiv Sewanee: The U So, TS 1979; DMin TS U So/Vanderbilt Unive 1981. D 6/14/1986 P 6/1/1987 Bp Charles Brinkley Morton. S Paul Ch Levittown PA 1989-2003; Day Sch Headmaster Chr Ch Coronado CA 1987-1988; Vol Assoc Chr Ch Toms River Toms River NJ 1986-1989; Dn Bucks Cnty Dnry. Natl Epis Aids Cltn; Ord S Mary.

WOOD, Hunter (Va) 250 Pantops Mountain Rd Apt 5126, Charlottesville VA 22911 B Charlottesville VA 1938 s William & Anne. BA Pr 1960; BA Pr 1960; MDiv VTS 1965; PhD Amer U 1978; PhD Amer U 1978. D 6/12/1965 Bp Robert Fisher Gibson Jr P 6/1/1966 Bp Samuel B Chilton. m 10/11/2002 Christian Parrish c 2. Psychol & Pstr Counslr 1972-2014; Non-par 1970-2014; Res Chapl S Eliz Hosp Washington DC 1970-1972; Supvsr Of Field Educ Prog VTS 1968-1970; Asst Imm Ch-On-The-Hill Alexandria VA 1965-1970. Auth, "Wood Test Of Life Position," 1978; Auth, "Journ Of Rel & Hlth," 1972.

WOOD, Jan Margaret Smith (O) Grace Episcopal Church, 315 Wayne Street, Sandusky OH 44870 **R Gr Epis Ch Sandusky OH 2011-** B Los Angeles CA 1954 d Tom & Leona. BA U CA 1976; MDiv CDSP 1986. D 6/24/2000 P 2/10/2001 Bp Richard Lester Shimpfky. c 2. Dn of Students CDSP Berkeley CA 2005-2011; Cn Eductr Dio El Camino Real Salinas CA 2000-2005. jan@gracesandusky.org

WOOD, Joseph A. (Md) Emmanuel Church, 811 Cathedral St, Baltimore MD 21201 **Emm Ch Baltimore MD 2016-** B 1988 s Dan & Julianna. Bachelor of Arts St. Jn's Coll (MD) 2012; Mstr of Div VTS 2016. D 1/16/2016 Bp Chilton Richardson Knudsen P 8/24/2016 Bp Eugene Taylor Sutton. Eagle Scout BSA 2006.

WOOD, Kathrine Ringold (Ore) 437 Franklin St, Denver CO 80218 **R S Matt's Epis Ch Gold Bch OR 2007-** B Denver CO 1943 d Frederick & Mary. MA S Thos Sem; BA U Denv. D 10/4/1988 Bp William Carl Frey P 4/14/2007 Bp Johncy Itty. m 9/28/2013 Karla Patricia Lewis. S Matt's Epis Ch Gold Bch OR 2001-2004; Dio Colorado Denver CO 1992-1999, 1989-1991, Dir Bp's for Dcnal Formation 1989-1991; Epis Ch Of S Ptr And S Mary Denver CO 1989-2001; D The Ch Of The Ascen Denver CO 1988-1989.

WOOD, Linda Anne (Cal) 3080 Birdsall Ave, Oakland CA 94619 B Chelsea MA 1948 d Franklin & Virginia. BS H Name U 1979; MDiv CDSP 1992. D 6/6/1992 P 6/5/1993 Bp William Edwin Swing. c 2. Assoc All SS Epis Ch San Leandro CA 2003-2008; Dn of Students CDSP Berkeley CA 2002-2003; S Andr's Ch Ben Lomond CA 1997-2001; Asst R S Paul's Epis Ch Burlingame CA 1994-1996; All Souls' Epis Ch San Diego CA 1993-1994; Asst To P S Mich And All Ang Concord CA 1992-1993.

WOOD, Mark Raymond (Ct) 89 Eddy Street, Providence RI 02903 B Beaumont TX 1958 s William & Patsy. BA TCU 1980; MDiv Epis TS of the SW 1985; MPA Harv 2000; ThM Harvard DS 2002; JD NYU 2006. D 6/16/1985 Bp Archibald Donald Davies P 5/31/1986 Bp Clarence Cullam Pope Jr. Trin Epis Ch Ossining NY 2014; Int S Thos Ch Mamaroneck NY 2013-2014; Ch Of The Ascen New York NY 2012-2013; Int Ch Of The Ascen Staten Island NY 2008-2010; Cn The Amer Cathd of the H Trin Paris 75008 1996-2000; Int Emm Epis Ch Geneva 1201 1995-1996; Asst S Paul's Ch Riverside CT 1987-1993; Cur S Alb's Epis Ch Arlington TX 1985-1987. wood@nyu.edu

WOOD, Nancy Currey (SVa) 1524 Southwick Rd, Virginia Beach VA 23451 **Chapl Dio Sthrn Virginia Newport News VA 1999-** B Chattanooga TN 1941 d Doyle & Mary. BA Wellesley Coll 1964; BS U of Nebraska 1987. D 11/8/1985 Bp James Daniel Warner. m 6/27/1964 William Drane Wood c 2. D Trin Ch Portsmouth VA 1997-1998; Chapl Sentarar Norfolk Gnrl Hosp 1992-1997; D Gd Samar Epis Ch Virginia Bch VA 1992-1996; D Old Donation Ch Virginia Bch VA 1987-1992; D All SS Epis Ch Omaha NE 1985-1987.

WOOD, Priscilla Peacock (Mass) 302 Linden Ponds Way Unit 512, Hingham MA 02043 B Jacksonville FL 1944 d Chester & Lavinnia. BA San Francisco St

U 1966; MDiv GTS 1979. D 6/9/1979 P 12/11/1979 Bp John Shelby Spong. m 6/27/1976 Stewart R Wood c 2. Int Chr Ch Medway MA 2004-2007; R S Andr's Ch Framingham MA 1995-2004; R S Jas Ch Piqua OH 1985-1994; Treas Assoc Alum The GTS New York NY 1985-1991; Cur Chr Ch Bronxville NY 1982-1985; Assoc S Paul's Epis Ch Morris Plains NJ 1979-1982; Dep Gc Dio Sthrn Ohio Cincinnati OH 1991-1994. SCHC 1985. Bp Of Newark Preaching Prize GTS 1979; Geo Cabot Ward Prize GTS 1979.

✠ **WOOD JR, The Rt Rev R aymond Stewart** (Mich) Kendal 157, 80 Lyme Rd, Hanover NH 03755 B Detroit MI 1934 s Raymond & Marjorie. BA Dart 1956; MDiv VTS 1959; MA Ball St U 1973. D 6/11/1959 P 12/18/1959 Bp John P Craine Con 10/15/1988 for Mich. m 6/25/1955 Kristin Lie Wood c 3. Bp of Michigan Dio Michigan Detroit MI 1988-2000; R S Jn's Epis Ch Memphis TN 1984-1988; R Chr Ch - Glendale Cincinnati OH 1976-1984; All SS Ch Indianapolis IN 1974-1976; Episc Cmnty Serv Indianapolis IN 1970-1976; R Gr Ch Muncie IN 1966-1970; Vic All SS Ch Seymour IN 1960-1963; S Dav's Ch Beanblossom Beanblossom IN 1960-1963; Assoc S Paul's Ch Columbus IN 1959-1960. Auth, *Seabury Selected Sermons*, Seabury Press. DD VTS 1960.

WOOD, Rob (WNC) 12132 Walnut Ter, Alpharetta GA 30004 **Ch Of The Gd Shpd Cashiers NC 2016-** B Athens GA 1966 s Robert & Susan. BA U So 1989; MDiv GTS 1996. D 6/8/1996 P 12/14/1996 Bp Frank Kellogg Allan. m 3/19/2009 Linda M Wood c 2. R S Aid's Epis Ch Milton GA 2004-2016; R S Paul's Ch Columbus MS 2000-2004; Asst R H Innoc Ch Atlanta GA 1997-2000; Assoc Gr-Calv Epis Ch Clarkesville GA 1996-1997.

WOOD, Robert Earl (WMo) 1009 W 57th St, Kansas City MO 64113 B Nashville TN 1937 s William & Mildred. BS Tennessee Tech U 1960; MDiv Candler TS Emory U 1964; U So 1971. D 2/27/1971 Bp William F Gates Jr P 7/4/1971 Bp John Vander Horst. m 7/18/1984 Sheridan Y Wood c 4. R S Paul's Ch Kansas City MO 1993-2005; Pres Dio Tennessee Nashville TN 1992-2013, Stndg Com 1990-2006, Chair - COM 1973-1989; Trin Ch Clarksville TN 1983-1993; Ch Of The Gd Shpd Lookout Mtn TN 1971-1983; Serv Meth Ch 1964-1970.

WOOD, Rodgers Taylor (WVa) 1223 Stanford Court, Coraopolis PA 15108 **Ret 1999-** B Pittsburgh PA 1933 s Robert & Margaret. BS U Pgh 1972; MDiv VTS 1975. D 6/27/1975 P 12/13/1975 Bp Robert Bracewell Appleyard. m 8/6/1955 Roselind D Wood c 3. Int S Mk's Epis Ch St Albans WV 2007-2008; Assoc S Matt's Ch Charleston WV 2005-2006; P-in-c S Jas Ch Charleston WV 2003-2005; P-in-c S Andr's Ch Oak Hill WV 2001-2003; R Chr Epis Ch No Hills Pittsburgh PA 1981-1999; Chapl Wstrn Penit 1977-1999; R S Phil's Ch Coraopolis PA 1975-1981.

WOOD, Roger Hoffman (Los) 38 E Grandview Ave, Sierra Madre CA 91024 **Died 6/14/2017** B Pasadena CA 1923 s Henry & Janet. BA Stan 1948; LLB Stan 1952; BD CDSP 1957. D 6/29/1957 P 12/21/1957 Bp Richard S Watson. Ret 1995-2017; Asst The Ch Of The Ascen Sierra Madre CA 1995-2003; Chapl Epis Hm Alhambra CA 1988-1995; Epis Communities & Serv Pasadena CA 1988-1994; 1982-1987; Ch Of The Epiph Los Angeles CA 1978-1982; Dio Los Angeles Los Angeles CA 1966-1977; R S Mary's Ch Provo UT 1961-1966; Vic S Fran Ch Moab UT 1957-1960. Cn of the Cathd St. Paul, Los Angeles 2007.

WOOD, Roger Lee (EMich) 106 S Kennefic St, Yale MI 48097 B Lansing MI 1939 s Raymond & Roma. BA Olivet Coll 1961; MA MI SU 1970; Cert Whitaker TS 1996. D 10/19/1996 Bp Edwin Max Leidel Jr. m 6/18/1963 Gwendolyn Jane Fett. D Gr Epis Ch Port Huron MI 1996-2006. NAAD.

WOOD, Sammy (Mass) 30 Brimmer St, Boston MA 02108 **Assoc The Ch Of The Adv Boston MA 2009-** B New Orleans, LA 1967 s Samuel & Madeline. JD U of Mississippi Sch of Law 1994; MDiv Gordon-Conwell TS 2003; Cert Ang Stud VTS 2006. D 6/2/2007 Bp M(Arvil) Thomas Shaw P 12/8/2007 Bp James Winchester Montgomery. m 10/30/1999 Renee Caston Wood c 3. Ch Of The Ascen And S Agnes Washington DC 2007-2009.

WOOD, Sarah Anne (Va) 86 Fourth Ave., New York NY 10003 B Washington DC 1973 d Edward & Deborah. BA W&M 1995; MDiv VTS 2004. D 11/22/2004 P 5/25/2005 Bp Peter J Lee. Gr Ch Sch New York New York NY 2011-2014; Gr Epis Ch New York NY 2011-2014; H Innoc' Epis Sch Atlanta GA 2008-2011; Upper Sch Chapl H Innoc Ch Atlanta GA 2007-2011; Christchurch Sch Christchurch VA 2004-2007. "Sophie Scholl," *CSEE*, CSEE, 2008.

WOOD, Stuart Clary (Va) 7120 Ore Bank Rd, Port Republic VA 24471 **Chr Epis Ch Christchurch VA 2015-; R Gr Ch Grottoes VA 1990-; S Steph And The Gd Shpd Elkton Elkton VA 1990-** B Richmond VA 1959 s Jordan & Mary. AA Ferrum Coll 1978; BA Geo Mason U 1980; MDiv VTS 1988. D 6/18/1988 Bp Peter J Lee P 3/18/1989 Bp Robert Manning Moody. R Lynnwood Par Port Republic VA 1990-2015; Cur Dio Oklahoma Oklahoma City OK 1988-1990.

WOOD III, William Hoge (Pa) 251 Montgomery Ave Unit 9, Haverford PA 19041 **Ret PA 2013-; Assoc S Dav's Ch Wayne PA 2013-, Assoc R 1972-1978** B Charlottesville VA 1940 s William & Anne. Dplma Epis HS 1958; Cmsn Navy OCS 1962; BA U of Virginia 1962; MDiv VTS 1970. D 6/20/1970 Bp Philip Alan Smith P 12/20/1970 Bp William Henry Marmion. m 6/15/1974 Kristine C Carlson c 2. R S Chris's Ch Gladwyne PA 1991-2012; Pres Dio Pennsylvania Philadelphia PA 1991-2009, Chair On New Mssn Com

W

1990-2009, Mssn Strtgy Cmsn 1988-1991, Dioc Coun 1986-; R Trin Ch Solebury PA 1978-1991; Asst to R S Jn's Ch Roanoke VA 1970-1972. Auth, "Abm & The Arms Race". Pa Fndt Pstr Counselors. wwood@stdavdischurch.org

WOOD, William James (Kan) 30 Spofford Lane, Trevett ME 04571 **Intl Dvlpmt Com Dio Maine Portland ME 2006-** B Suffern NY 1942 s Alfred & Flora. BA Leh 1964; MDiv EDS 1967; DMin EDS 2007. D 6/10/1967 P 12/11/1967 Bp Leland Stark. m 11/25/1967 Susan P Wood c 2. Adj Fac Adj Fac Bangor ME 2009; S Columba's Epis Ch E Boothbay ME 2008-2016; P-in-c The Par Of S Mary And S Jude NE Harbor ME 2006-2008; Pres Global Epis Mssn Ntwk NY 2003-2009; Mem SCWM 1997-2001; Cmsn On Wrld Mssn Dio Kansas Topeka KS 1996-2006, Trst 1998-2006; R S Jn's Ch Wichita KS 1996-2006; Stndg Cmsn Wrld Mssn NY 1995-2003; Dio Michigan Detroit 1991-1994; R Trin Ch St Clair Shrs MI 1987-1995; Natl & Wrld Mssn Com MI 1982-1995; Dio Michigan Detroit MI 1981-1984; P-in-c St Andrews Memi Ch Detroit MI 1974-1987; Chapl Wayne Detroit MI 1970-1986; Asst S Paul's Epis Ch Paterson NJ 1970; Mssy Ch In Liberia Yekepa & Saniquellie 1967-1970. Auth, "Recovering Hosp:Toward a Partaklng Cmnty," *Doctoral Thesis*, Epis Divinty Sch, 2007; Auth, "Whence Cometh Our Cmnty?," *Plumbline*, ESMHE, 1974. ESMHE 1971-1987; Global Epis Mssn Ntwk 1995-2009; Integrity 2000-2008.

WOOD JR, William R (WVa) 107 Elma Dr, Williamstown WV 26187 B Galveston TX 1941 s William & Georgia. BA Guilford Coll 1967; MDiv VTS 1970. Trans 9/8/2003 Bp Creighton Leland Robertson. m 5/1/1985 Jett Wood c 1. S Andr's in the Vill Ch Barboursville WV 2004-2006; Dio So Dakota Pierre SD 1998-1999; Chr Memi Ch Williamstown WV 1994-2000; Ohio Vlly Epis Cluster Williamstown WV 1994-1998; S Paul's Ch Hamilton MT 1991-1992; S Steph's Epis Ch Stevensville MT 1989-2006; Dio Montana Helena MT 1989-1994; R S Matt's Ch Glasgow MT 1985-1989; S Mk's Ch S Paul VA 1980-1985; Chapl Chr Ch Sch 1970-1985.

WOODALL, Carolyn Louise (SJ) Episcopal Church of St. Anne, 1020 W Lincoln Rd, Stockton CA 95207 **D Epis Ch Of S Anne Stockton CA 2017-; St Jas Epis Ch Sonora CA 2012-; Mem, Bd Trst Sch for Deacons Berkeley CA 2015-** B New Orleans LA 1953 d James & Laverne. BA California St Coll - Stanislaus 1975; MBA Natl U 1983; JD Humphreys Coll Sch of Law 1987; Cert Sch for Deacons 2011. D 3/10/2012 Bp Chester Lovelle Talton. c 2.

WOODALL JR, Percy J (At) 3663 SE Cambridge Drive, Stuart FL 34997 B Roxboro NC 1942 s Percy & Vena. BS U NC 1971; MDiv Sewanee: The U So, TS 1983. D 6/18/1983 Bp Hunley Agee Elebash P 12/1/1983 Bp Brice Sidney Sanders. m 2/19/1972 Loraine McIlwain Woodall. Int R S Thos Epis Par Miami FL 2010-2011; Int Dn S Jn's Cathd Jacksonville FL 2009; Int R Chr Ch Norcross GA 2007-2009; Int R The Epis Ch Of The Nativ Fayetteville GA 2006-2007; Int R S Greg The Great Athens GA 2004-2006; Int R S Dunst's Epis Ch Atlanta GA 2003-2004; Mssnr Dio Virginia Richmond VA 2002-2003; Mssnr Dio Haiti Port-au-Prince HT 1998-2004; Appointed Mssnr Exec Coun Appointees New York NY 1998-2003; R S Paul's Ch Natick MA 1988-1998; R S Paul's Epis Ch Clinton NC 1983-1988.

WOODARD, Sarah Wilson (NC) 400 Moline St., Durham NC 27707 B Raleigh NC 1955 d Walter & Eleanor. AA Mt Vernon 1975; BA U NC 1977. D 6/20/2009 Bp Michael B Curry. m 6/20/1989 James Michael Woodard.

WOODBURY, Kimberly Jean (VI) All Saints Cathedral, PO Box 1148, St Thomas VI 00804 B Brattleboro VT 1960 d Leroy & Margarite. PhD Cor; BS Marlboro Coll 1990; MAR Berkeley/Yale Div 2011. D 3/5/2011 P 3/3/2012 Bp Edward Gumbs. m 6/22/1985 Daniel Perry Woodbury c 1.

WOODBURY, Robert Lane (Mil) 5558 N Berkeley Blvd, Whitefish Bay WI 53217 B Chicago IL 1940 s Arthur & Mary. BA Elmhurst Coll 1962; MDiv Garrett-Evang TS 1965; Cert SWTS 1968. D 6/15/1968 Bp James Winchester Montgomery P 12/21/1968 Bp Gerald Francis Burrill. c 2. Dir of Pstr Care S Jn's on The Lake Milwaukee WI 1996-2004; Asst Trin Ch Milwaukee WI 1990-1995; Chapl Congreg Hm Brookfield WI 1987-1995; Asst S Bon Ch Thiensville WI 1987-1990; Asst All SS' Cathd Milwaukee WI 1983-1987; Chapl Vstng Nurse Assn Milwaukee WI 1982-1987; P Assoc Chr Ch Milwaukee WI 1975-1981; Vic S Dunst's Epis Ch Westchester IL 1970-1975; Cur S Mich's Ch Barrington IL 1968-1970; Serv Methodist Ch 1965-1967. Robert L. Woodbury, "A Journey of Soul Longing," Hawley, 2008; Auth, "An Empty Stage or Heaven Apprehended," *Sacr Archit*, The Inst for Sacr Archit, 2005.

WOODCOCK, Bruce W (SeFla) 106 Castle Heights Ave, Nyack NY 10960 **Epis Ch Cntr New York NY 2017-; S Mary's-In-Tuxedo Tuxedo Pk NY 2016-; Mgr, Pstr Care CPG New York NY 2014-; Mem/Chair Bd Ethics Town of Clarkstown New City NY 2005-** B New York City NY 1953 s Wilson & Edith. BA Hobart and Wm Smith Colleges 1976; MA Sch for Intl Trng/EIL 1985; NTL 1986; Cert Natl Trng Labs/NTL 1986; NTL 1987; Cert Natl Trng Labs/NTL 1987; Cert Natl Trng Labs NTL 1988; Cert Natl Trng Labs NTL 1988; MDiv GTS 2002; STM GTS 2003. D 7/26/2003 Bp Leo Frade P 2/18/2004 Bp Michael B Curry. m 5/28/1984 Thayer P Preece c 2. Mgr, Intl Relatns CPG New York NY 2007-2014; Vic S Matt's Ch Paramus NJ 2005-2015; Mgr, Int'l Relatns The CPG New York NY 2004-2015; Mgr Comp Plan Strategies CPG new York NY 2004-2006; Hosp Chapl Nyack Hosp Nyack NY 2003-2010; Port Chapl SCI Port Newark NJ 2003-2009; D S Paul's Ch Montvale NJ 2003-2004;

Mgr, Intl Pension Plans CPG New York NY 1999. Sigma Phi 1973; UBE (Hon Lifetime Assoc Mem) 2010. LECUSA/ECL Cert of Appreciation Liberian Epis Communities in the USA 2013; PIX Sustainability Serv Awd Prov IX Syn 2011; Hon Cn CPWA Epis Ch of Liberia/Trin Cathd, Monrovia, Liberia, W Afr 2008; LECUSA/Hon Lifetime Founding Mem Liberian Epis Communities in the USA 2005; Cbury Chr Ldrshp Awd Hob 1976; Pres's Awd Sigma Phi Soc - Hob 1975. bwoodcock@cpg.org

WOODEN, Lorentho (SO) 550 E 4th St, Cincinnati OH 45202 **Ret 1995-** B Dayton Bch FL 1927 s Lorentha & Leila. BA Morehouse Coll 1949; U Chi 1952; EDS 1960. D 10/9/1960 Bp Donald MacAdie P 6/1/1961 Bp Henry I Louttit. c 4. Vic Ch Of S Simon The Cyrenian New Rochelle NY 1989-1995, R 1965-1971; S Simon Of Cyrene Epis Ch Cincinnati OH 1989-1995; All SS Ch Pasadena CA 1986-1989; Dio Sthrn Ohio Cincinnati OH 1975-1986; Cur Intsn In New York City 1962-1965; Ch Of The H Comf Richmond VA 1960-1962; Vic S Andr's Epis Ch Of Hollywood Hollywood FL 1960-1962. Hon Cn Chr Ch Cathd 1989.

WOODFIN, Joseph Robert (Tenn) PO Box 307, Gallatin TN 37066 **S Paul's Epis Ch Chattanooga TN 2017-** B South Pittsburg TN 1986 s Robert & Kimberly. BA Lipscomb U 2008; MDiv The TS at The U So 2015. D 6/6/2015 P 12/12/2015 Bp John Bauerschmidt. m 5/17/2008 Carly Brooke Short c 2. P-in-c Ch Of Our Sav Gallatin TN 2015-2017. oursaviourgallatin@gmail.com

WOODHOUSE, Michelle M (Los) 4125 Creciente Dr, Santa Barbara CA 93110 **Dir of Sprtl Care Cntr for Innovative Therapies Santa Barbara CA 2008-; Assoc Chapl Valle Verde Ret Cmnty Santa Barbara CA 2008-** B San Mateo CA 1934 d Charles & Muriel. BA Mt Holyoke Coll 1956; MA Luth TS Philadelphia 1984; STM Luth TS Philadelphia 1987; DMin Claremont TS 1997. D 6/1/1985 P 6/21/1986 Bp John Bowen Coburn. c 2. All SS-By-The-Sea Par Santa Barbara CA 1992-2006; Int Chr The King Epis Ch Santa Barbara CA 1991-1992; Pstr Assoc 1989-1991; Pstr Assoc S Matt's Ch Maple Glen PA 1986-1989; Chapl Horsham Clnc 1982-1989. Auth, "A Meditation On The Status Of The Cross," 1974; Auth, "Crisis In Faith: The Challenge Of Pvrty," 1968. Coll Of Chapl, Assn Mntl Hlth Cleric, Amer 1991; SCHC 1969. 4th Annual Awd Clincl Schlrshp Horsham Clnc 1988.

WOOD-HULL, L. D. (Ore) 6151 Willers Way, Houston TX 77057 B Cooperstown NY 1965 s Larry & Aarlie. AB Harv 1988; DAS Ya Berk 1995; MDiv Yale DS 1995; JD Ya 1995; MA Ya 1998. D 6/10/2000 Bp Andrew Donnan Smith P 1/12/2001 Bp Wilfrido Ramos-Orench. m 5/18/1996 Elizabeth N Wood-Hull c 2. S Barn Par Portland OR 2008-2013, 2007, 2002-2004; Asstg P All SS Ch Portland OR 2006-2007; Assoc for Adult Faith Formation S Jn's Epis Ch Olympia WA 2004-2006; Vic S Edw's Ch Silverton OR 2002-2004; Cur Trin Ch Branford CT 2000-2001; Chair, Com on Const and Cn Dio Oregon Portland OR 2010-2013. EPF 2002; Integrity 2005. Grad Fell ECF 1995.

WOODLEY, Claire (NY) 2 Glendale Rd, Ossining NY 10562 **R S Mary's Ch Mohegan Lake NY 2001-** B Minneapolis PA 1955 d Norman & Mary. BA U MN 1979; MDiv UTS 1988. D 6/10/1989 Bp Paul Moore Jr P 12/1/1989 Bp Richard Frank Grein. m 9/10/1983 Michael John Aitchison c 1. Dio New York New York NY 1999-2001; Int S Andr's Ch Beacon NY 1999-2001; S Ptr's Epis Ch Peekskill NY 1996-1999; Ch Of S Mary The Vrgn Chappaqua NY 1995-1996; H Innoc Highland Falls NY 1992-1994; Int The Ch Of S Jos Of Arimathea White Plains NY 1992; S Barn Ch Irvington NY 1989-1992. Auth, "No No Or So," Pecusa, 1993; Auth, "Stories From The Cir ," Moorhouse/Barlow, 1991; Auth, "Out Of Nairobi: A New Era For Wmn In The Ch"; Auth, "Ordnry Wmn".

WOODLIEF, Vern Andrews (Az) 1069 N Paseo Iris, Green Valley AZ 85614 **Par Admin S Fran-in-the-Valleu Green Vlly AZ 2007-; D S Fran-in-the-Vlly Green Vlly AZ 2006-** B Gainesville FL 1936 d Edwin & Ellen. BA Lake Erie Coll 1958; Fuller TS 2001; Cert Cntr for Loss and Life Transition 2002; Cert Cntr for Sprtl Direction 2002. D 11/1/1995 Bp Chester Lovelle Talton. c 2. D Epis Ch Of S Fran-In-The-Vlly Green Vlly AZ 2007-2012; S Mths' Par Whittier CA 1995-2006.

WOODLIFF III, George Franklin (Miss) 712 S Montgomery St, Starkville MS 39759 **Trin Ch Yazoo City MS 1998-, R 1998-** B Jackson MS 1948 s George & Ann. BA BA U of Mississippi 1970; JD U of Virginia 1973; BTh Oxf GB 1995. D 8/19/1995 P 3/1/1996 Bp Alfred Marble Jr. m 11/24/1976 Jill M Woodliff c 3. Dio Mississippi Jackson MS 1995-2003; Ch Of The Resurr Starkville MS 1995-1998; Chapl Mississippi St U. trinityyazoo@gmail.com

WOODLIFF, Kirk Alan (Nev) 2125 Stone View Dr, Sparks NV 89436 **R S Paul's Epis Ch Sparks NV 2008-** B Henryetta OK 1970 s Duane & Florence. AS Conners St Coll Warner OK 1991; BS SE Oklahoma St U 1994; MDiv Epis TS of the SW 2001. D 6/23/2001 P 1/5/2002 Bp Robert Manning Moody. m 5/20/1995 Tricia Ann Woodliff c 3. R Gr Ch Muskogee OK 2003-2008; Cur S Pat's Epis Ch Broken Arrow OK 2001-2002. kirk@stpaulssparks.org

WOODLIFF-STANLEY, Ruth M (Colo) 1945 Ivanhoe St, Denver CO 80220 **Dio Colorado Denver CO 2010-** B Jackson MS 1962 d George & Ann. BA Swarthmore Coll 1985; MDiv Ya Berk 1991; MS Col 1991. D 6/13/1990 P 6/1/1991 Bp Duncan Montgomery Gray Jr. m 7/4/1987 Nathan D Woodliff Stanley c 2. P-in-c S Thos Epis Ch Denver CO 2007-2015; Asst S Jas Ch Jackson

MS 2000-2002; S Phil's Ch Jackson MS 1991-1995; Asst Trin Ch Branford CT 1990-1991. ruth@episcopalcolorado.org

WOODLING, Edith (At) 25 Battle Ridge Pl Ne, Atlanta GA 30342 B Chattanooga TN 1950 d Walter & Mattie. BA Emory U 1972; MA U Pgh 1976; EFM Sewanee: The U So, TS 1995. D 10/28/1995 Bp Frank Kellogg Allan. m 10/6/2001 James Dillon c 4. S Mart In The Fields Ch Atlanta GA 2011-2013, 2003-2005; S Mart's Epis Sch Atlanta GA 2005-2013; Chr Ch Norcross GA 1999-2003; D S Anne's Epis Ch Atlanta GA 1995-1999. NAAD.

WOODRIDGE, Douglas Earl (SanD) 16017 Oakridge Ct, Lake Oswego OR 97035 **Died 3/11/2017** B Dansville NY 1931 s Earl & Doris. BBA Loyola U 1955; MDiv SWTS 1968. D 9/7/1968 P 3/8/1969 Bp Francis E I Bloy. m 9/5/1954 Clara B Woodridge c 1. Ret 1996-2008; R S Michaels By-The-Sea Ch Carlsbad CA 1979-1996; Asst All SS Ch San Diego CA 1968-1979. SSC.

WOODROOFE III, Robert (Ct) 42 Christian Street, New Preston CT 06777 **Missional P S Mk's Ch Bridgewater CT 2010-** B New York NY 1941 s Robert & Lindsay. BA Ya 1963; MDiv EDS 1968; DMin Pittsburgh TS 1990. D 6/24/1968 Bp Hamilton Hyde Kellogg P 12/21/1968 Bp Robert Bracewell Appleyard. m 4/12/1969 Sarah Waterman c 2. R S Gabr's Epis Ch Marion MA 1994-2007; R S Ptr's Epis Ch Butler PA 1981-1994; St Lk's Epis Ch Pittsburgh PA 1978-1981; Epis Residences Inc Pittsburgh PA 1977-1981; Dio Pittsburgh Pittsburgh PA 1976-1981; Asst Min Calv Ch Pittsburgh PA 1968-1976. Sydney Adams Awd Inter-Ch Coun of Grtr New Bedford 2007.

WOODRUFF, Jennifer Lynn (Lex) 449 Hackett Pike, Richmond KY 40475 **Permanent supply P S Mk's Ch Hazard KY 2016-, Supply Prchr 2014-2016** B Marion IN 1971 d John & Marilyn. BA Augustana Coll 1992; MDiv,MA Asbury TS 1997; MS U IL 2000; PhD Duke 2005. D 9/13/2015 P 4/1/2016 Bp Edward Stuart Little II. m 8/16/2003 Edwin R Tait c 2. Auth, "Histories of Us," Finishing Line Press, 2011. Amer Theol Libr Assn 2001; OSL 1995; Sigma Alpha Iota 1989; Wesleyan Theol Soc 1996. Phi Beta Kappa Augustana Coll 1992. jlwt@christianhistoryinstitute.org

WOODRUFF, Karen B (Va) Po Box 367, Lively VA 22507 B Findlay OH 1943 d Joy & Nedra. BS Witt 1965; MDiv Ya Berk 1989. D 6/11/1994 P 12/14/1994 Bp Peter J Lee. c 2. S Ptr's Port Royal Port Royal VA 1994-2003; P-in-c Vauters Ch Loretto VA 1994-2001.

WOODRUM, Donald Lee (Fla) Po Box 1238, Live Oak FL 32064 B Sarasota FL 1949 s Donald & Dorothy. BA U of So Florida 1971; MDiv GTS 1975. D 8/15/1975 P 2/24/1976 Bp Emerson Paul Haynes. m 8/26/1972 Melissa Jane Woodrum c 4. Cn Santa Fe Reg Dio Florida Jacksonville 1996-2013; R S Lk's Epis Ch Live Oak FL 1980-2015; Cur Chr Ch Bradenton FL 1975-1980. Bp's Cross Awd Dio Florida 2014.

WOODRUM, Lawrence Paul (Nwk) 651 East 102nd St, Brooklyn NY 11236 B Bradford PA 1940 s Robert & Jean. BA Ohio Wesl 1962; STB GTS 1965. D 6/12/1965 P 6/11/1966 Bp William Crittenden. m 6/25/2009 Victor Challenor. Int S Marg's Ch Plainview NY 2009-2011; Asst Ch Of S Alb The Mtyr S Albans NY 1993-2005; Assoc Ch Of The Intsn New York NY 1981-1983; Vic Ch Of Our Sav Secaucus NJ 1976-1980; Vic Gr Epis Ch Rutherford NJ 1976-1979; Vic S Gabr's Ch Oak Ridge NJ 1970-1976; Vic Ch Of Our Fr Foxburg PA 1966-1969; Chapl Clarion St Coll Clarion PA 1966-1969; Asst S Jn's Ch Franklin PA 1965-1966. ECVA 2000; Integrity, Inc. 1975.

WOODS, Harold Dean (Vt) 233 South Street, South Hero VT 05486 **Ret 2000-** B Henryetta OK 1939 s Elmer & Edith. BA NWU 1961; BD Drew U 1965; MEd U of Vermont 1971. D 6/11/1966 P 10/13/1966 Bp Leland Stark. c 4. R All SS' Epis Ch S Burlington VT 1990-2000; Dir Serv Lrng Cntr U VT 1971-1991; Assoc Gr Ch Madison NJ 1966-1969.

WOODS JR, J (Mass) 62 Las Casas St, Malden MA 02148 B Memphis TN 1954 s J C & Elnora. BA Gri 1975; MDiv EDS 1979. D 6/17/1979 P 5/18/1980 Bp William Evan Sanders. m 1/6/1983 Elise Kinney. Trin Epis Ch Weymouth MA 2009-2012; S Jas Ch Preston CT 2008-2009; The Ch Of The H Name Swampscott MA 2005-2006; S Paul's Ch Malden MA 2001-2004; Int All SS Epis Ch Attleboro MA 2000-2001; Int Epiph Par Walpole MA 1998-1999; Int The Ch Of The Gd Shpd Acton MA 1996-1998; Int Par Of S Paul Newton Highlands MA 1995-1996; Int S Jn The Evang Mansfield MA 1993-1994; Assoc S Jn's S Jas Epis Ch Boston MA 1992-1993; S Aug And S Mart Ch Boston MA 1988-1992, Assoc 1983-1987; S Paul's Epis Ch Chattanooga TN 1979-1980.

WOODS, James Christopher (Mass) 121 Freeport Boulevard, Toms River NJ 08757 **Ret 1999-** B Murrysville PA 1939 s Stewart & Dorothy. BA U Roch 1960; STB EDS 1964; Syr 1972. D 6/16/1964 P 12/1/1964 Bp George West Barrett. m 6/2/1962 Nancy Woods c 4. R Trin Par Melrose MA 1982-1999; Archd of Selkirk Rupertsland Can 1978-1982; Serv Angican Ch in Can 1976-1982; Chapl Alfred U and Alfred St Coll Alfred NY 1967-1969; Chapl U Rochester & Chair Wrld Affrs Com 1965-1967; S Jn's Ch Clifton Spgs NY 1964-1967; Vic St Jn's Ch Phelps NY 1964-1967.

WOODS, James Edward (Oly) 22226 6th Ave S Apt 201, Des Moines WA 98198 **Dioc Coun Dio Massachusetts Boston MA 1986-** B Seattle WA 1920 s Harvey & Ruth. Olympia TS. D 6/27/1990 Bp Vincent Waydell Warner. Dio Olympia Seattle 1990-1992; D S Lk's Epis Ch Seattle WA 1990-1992; R Trin Par Melrose MA 1982-1999; R All SS' Epis Ch Belmont MA 1978-1982; R S

Pat Winnipeg Can 1976-1978; Asst Prof Dio Rochester Henrietta 1972-1976; P-in-c Chr Epis Ch Hornell NY 1967-1969; Dio New York New York NY 1967-1969.

WOODS, John Michael (Dal) Rr 1 Box 253-A, Mount Vernon TX 75457 B Atlanta TX 1942 s John & Helen. MA U of Arkansas 1973; MDiv Nash 1975. D 6/16/1975 P 12/1/1975 Bp Archibald Donald Davies. m 12/19/1970 Dianna M Woods. S Paul's Epis Ch Greenville TX 2001-2002; Par Asst Ch Of The Epiph Richardson TX 2000-2002; S Wm Laud Epis Ch Pittsburg TX 1989-1996; Dept Of Missions Dallas TX 1984-1989; All SS Ch Atlanta TX 1979-1983; S Mart Epis Ch New Boston TX 1979-1983; Cur S Jas Epis Ch Texarkana TX 1977-1978; Cur S Jn's Epis Ch Corsicana TX 1975-1977. RWF.

WOODS, Joshua Blake (Okla) 5635 E 71st St, Tulsa OK 74136 **Chapl Dio Oklahoma Oklahoma City OK 2013-; Chapl S Anselm Cbury Norman OK 2013-** B Muskogee OK 1984 s James & Cheryl. BA U of Oklahoma 2007; MDiv VTS 2011. D 1/22/2011 P 7/30/2011 Bp Edward Joseph Konieczny. m 1/7/2008 Laura Beth Woods c 2. P S Dunst's Ch Tulsa OK 2011-2013.

WOODS, Michael Timothy (WTex) **S Mk's Ch San Marcos TX 2017-; Epis TS Of The SW Austin TX 2014-** D 6/15/2017 Bp Gary Richard Lillibridge.

WOODS SSP, Robert Douglas (SJ) Po Box 1837, Kernville CA 93238 **Vic St Sherrian Epis Ch Kernville CA 2008-** B Wimbledon Surrey UK 1946 s Eric & Dorothy. BA U of San Diego 1968; JD U of San Diego 1973; ETSBH 1986; Cert Geo 1988. D 6/14/1986 Bp Charles Brinkley Morton P 5/11/1988 Bp Victor Manuel Rivera. m 5/23/1975 Alexis Perry. Vic S Ptr's Epis Ch Kernville CA 1998-2008; Asst S Lk's Ch Bakersfield CA 1988-2000; Supply Epis Dio San Joaquin Modesto CA 1986-1988. Auth, "Obligation to Provide Abortion Serv: What Happens When Physicians Refuse," Journ of Med Ethics, Royal Med Soc, 1996. Soc of S Paul, Assoc 1981. Fell Kegley Inst of Ethics 1990; Assoc Kennedy Sch of Ethics 1980.

WOODS, Stephen I (NY) Above, Above NM 87507 B Nevada MO 1944 s Hammond & Virginia. BA Armstrong Atlantic St U 1970; MSW Brandeis U 1974; PhD Brandeis U 1978; MA Nash 1987. D 6/6/1987 P 12/1/1987 Bp Edward Cole Chalfant. m 8/8/2013 Laura Lynn Telander c 2. S Jn's Epis Ch Kingston NY 2003-2004; Chr Ch Manhasset NY 2002-2003; Int Chr Ch Babylon NY 2001-2002; Sr Lectr S Geo Coll Jerusalem Jerusalem Palestine/Israel 2000-2001; Dir Of Pilgrimage Mnstrs And Cler Wellness Dio Florida Jacksonville 1995-2000; Fresh Mnstrs Jacksonville FL 1995-1999; R S Jn's Epis Ch Gloucester MA 1991-1995; Assoc R S Barn Ch Falmouth MA 1988-1991; R S Giles Ch Jefferson ME 1987-1988.

WOODSON JR, James Pettigrew (Ala) 313 Riverdale Dr # 35406-, Tuscaloosa AL 35406 **Died 5/27/2016** B Birmingham AL 1923 s James & Anna. BD Auburn U 1948; MDiv VTS 1953. D 6/20/1953 P 9/18/1953 Bp Charles C J Carpenter. m 9/8/1951 Abbie Wendel c 3. Ret 1995-2016; Cbury Chap and Coll Cntr Tuscaloosa AL 1973-1995; Chapl U Of Alabama 1973-1995; R H Trin Epis Ch Auburn AL 1957-1973; Vic S Mary's Epis Ch Andalusia AL 1955-1957; S Steph's Ch Brewton AL 1955-1957; R S Paul's Carlowville AL 1953-1955; R St Michaels/H Cross Uniontown AL 1953-1955.

WOODSUM, Mark (Me) 2808 Lakemont Dr, Fallbrook CA 92028 B Portland, ME 1958 s Kenneth & Martha. BA Bow 1980; MA Dartmoth Coll 1997; M. Div Bangor TS 2010. D 6/19/2010 Bp Stephen Taylor Lane P 12/18/2010 Bp Jim Mathes. m 1/3/1987 Claire Woodsum c 4. P-in-c S Jn's Ch Fallbrook CA 2010-2011.

WOODWARD JR, Brinton Webb (NH) RR3 Box 18, Plymouth NH 03264 B Topeka KS 1940 s Brinton & Agnes. BA U of Kansas 1962; MDiv GTS 1965. D 6/9/1965 P 12/21/1965 Bp Edward Clark Turner. m 7/5/1985 Kathleen C Woodward c 1. The Holderness Sch Plymouth NH 1977-2001; Kent Sch Kent CT 1967-1977; Chapl Kent Sch Kent CT 1967-1977; Cur S Dav's Epis Ch Topeka KS 1965-1967; Chapl Washburn U Cur S Dav Topeka KS 1965-1967.

WOODWARD, Deborah Marshall (Mass) 1080 Hillside St, Milton MA 02186 **S Jn's Epis Ch Franklin MA 2016-; P-in-c The Ch of the Gd Shpd Reading MA 2007-** B Glen Ridge NJ 1944 d John & Constance. BA Br 1966; MDiv Gordon-Conwell TS 1987. D 6/13/1987 Bp David Elliot Johnson P 4/1/1988 Bp George E Rath. m 12/27/1965 James Woodward c 3. P-in-c Ch Of The Gd Shpd Reading MA 2007-2010; EDS Cambridge MA 2002-2003, 2001-2002, 1993-1995; R Trin Ch Randolph MA 2001-2007; Trin Ch Randolph MA 1999-2007; Chr Ch Somerville MA 1988-1995. Phillips Brooks Cleric Club of Boston. Phi Alpha Chi Gordon-Conwell TS 1987.

WOODWARD III, George Frederick (Los) 1294 Westlyn Pl, Pasadena CA 91104 **Hon Cn Dio El Salvador 2014-; Cn Dio El Salvador Ambato Tu 2014-; Chair Prog Grp on Global Partnership Los Angeles CA 2005-; R S Edm's Par San Marino CA 1995-; Cn for the Dio El Salvador Iglesia Anglicana de la Reg Cntrl de Amer 274 San Salvador 2014-** B Greensburg PA 1955 s George & Louise. BA Ohio U 1978; MA Ashland TS 1981; MDiv SWTS 1983. D 6/25/1983 Bp John Harris Burt P 1/21/1984 Bp Robert Claflin Rusack. VP Fndt Cristosal El Salvador 2005-2017; Bd Mem Hillsides Hm for Chld Pasadena CA 1997-2008; Dn Estrn Deanry Dio Los Angeles Los Angeles CA 1993-1995; R S Tim's Epis Ch Apple Vlly CA 1991-1995; Asstg Angl Archd of the Aegean 1989-1991; Assoc All SS-By-The-Sea Par Santa Barbara

CA 1983-1988. Auth, "THE PRAYERS OF THE PEOPLE," *E-Bk*, St. Mk's Press, 2016; Co-Auth, "INTRODUCING THE LESSONS OF THE Ch YEAR," *Bk*, Morehouse Pub, 2009. Fndt Cristosal, El Salvador 2005; Hillsides Hm for Chld; Bd Dir 1997-2008. Hon Cn PBp Cntrl Amer 2014; Hon Cn The Bp of Los Angeles 2011.

WOODWARD, Lynn Christophersen (Okla) 4604 E 54th St Apt 203, Tulsa OK 74135 B Lincoln NE 1948 d Donald & Sonja. AA Seminole Jr Coll 1983; Sewanee: The U So, TS 1990; Oklahoma Diac Trng Sch 1991. D 6/29/1991 Bp Robert Manning Moody. m 12/13/2001 E Davis Woodward c 2. D S Jas Epis Ch Oklahoma City OK 2006-2009; D S Mich's Epis Ch Norman OK 1991-2006. "Living Bibles," *Preaching as Prophetic Calling: Sermons That Wk XII*, Morehouse Pub, 2004.

WOODWARD, Matthew (Cal) 3900 Alameda De Las Pulgas, San Mateo CA 94403 **R Trsfg Epis Ch San Mateo CA 2011-** B London UK 1975 s Eric & Jean. BA London TS 1998; MA Kings Coll of London 1999; MA Westcott Hse Cambridge 2001. Trans 4/19/2011 Bp Marc Handley Andrus. rector@transfig-sm.org

WOODWARD, Thomas Bullene (RG) 13 Calle Loma, Santa Fe NM 87507 **P-in-c S Paul's Peace Ch Las Vegas NM 2013-; Playwright, Librettist Playwright New Mex 2006-** B Topeka KS 1937 s Brinton & Agnes. BA Harv 1960; Ecumenical Inst 1962; STB GTS 1963; U of Kansas 1967. D 6/23/1963 P 12/21/1963 Bp Edward Clark Turner. m 5/22/1988 Marianne H Harding c 5. R St Paul's/San Pablo Epis Ch Salinas CA 1988-2005; Sum Fac Ghost Ranch Conf Cntr 1984-1999; Trst St of Wisc Invstmt Bd 1984-1989; Adj Fac Grad Theol Un Berkeley CA 1983-1996; Pres Ecum Coun For Drama & Other Arts St. Louis MO 1983-1984; S Fran Hse U Epis Ctr Madison WI 1977-1988; St Fran Hse Madison WI 1977-1988; Performer Uncle Billy's Pocket Circus 1975-2015; Chapl Chap Of The Cross Chap Hill NC 1974-1977; Prot Chapl U Roch Med Cntr - Strong Memi Hosp Rochester NY 1971-1974; R Chr Ch Warrensburg MO 1968-1971; Chapl Cbury At Kansas U Lawr KS 1963-1968; Com on the Status of Wmn Exec Coun Appointees New York NY 2006-2009; T/F on Comm Dio The Rio Grande Albuquerque 2006-2007; Dioc. Corp Dio El Camino Real Salinas CA 1991-1995. Playwright, "I'll Have What He's Having," Ironweed Productions, 2016; Librettist, "All the Rt Moves," Daniel Steven Crafts, 2013; Playwright, "Xenaphobia," Santa Fe Playhouse, 2013; Playwright, "The Smedleys Are Here," Santa Fe Playhouse, 2012; Playwright, "Funny You Should Ask," Santa Fe Playhouse, 2011; Playwright, "And the Winner Is . .," Santa Fe Playhouse, 2010; Librettist, "And the Winner Is . . .," Daniel Steven Crafts, 2010; Playwright, "Body and Soul," Amer. Acad Psychotherapists, 2009; Playwright, "What's Up w Eliot?," Santa Fe Playhouse, 2008; Auth, "The Undermining of the Epis Ch," The Epis Majority, 2007; Auth, "The Parables of Jesus from the Inside," *Sewanee Theol Revs*, TS, Sewanee, 2003; Co-Auth, "Prayers of the Faithful," Pueblo Press, 1977; Auth, "Turning Things Upside Down: A Theol Workbook," Seabury Press, 1975; Auth, "To Celebrate," Seabury Press, 1971. Le Jongleurs du Notre Dame 1983; Pres, ESMHE 1975-1976. Ben Heller Awd for Courage and Ldrshp w the Farmworker Cntr for Cmnty Advocacy 2004; The Bp's Cross Dio El Camino Real 2004. tbwsalinas@aol.com

WOODWORTH, Laura T(Ufts) (NMich) 2500 South Hill Road, Gladstone MI 49837 B Worcester MA 1946 d Donald & Joanne. BS NWU 1968; MS Illinois Inst of Tech 1976; BS U IL 1982; Michigan TS 1997. D 11/6/1996 P 5/18/1997 Bp Thomas Kreider Ray. m 6/14/1968 David Woodworth c 2.

WOODWORTH-HILL, Nancy (Ind) 321 E Market St, Jeffersonville IN 47130 B Buffalo NY 1958 d Craig & Ruth. MA U of Norte Dame; B.A U of Buffalo 1984; MA U of Buffalo 1986; PhD U of Buffalo 1991; MA Chr the King Sem 2000; Angl Stds Dplma Bexley Seabury 2015. D 1/24/2015 P 8/1/2015 Bp Cate Waynick. m 10/12/1991 Donald B Hill c 1. R and Co-Pstr S Paul's Jeffersonvlle IN 2017-2015, Vic 2015-2016.

WOODY, Robert James (WTex) 13638 Liberty Oak, San Antonio TX 78232 **R Ch Of Recon San Antonio TX 2002-; Co-Chair Recon Cmsn Dio W Texas San Antonio TX 2008-, Coordntr Cler Lenten Retreat 2005-, Exam Chapl 2004-** B Midland TX 1953 s Alvin & Joanna. BA Baylor U 1975; JD Baylor U 1978; MDiv Epis TS of the SW 1999. D 6/19/1999 Bp Claude Edward Payne P 6/19/2000 Bp Leopoldo Jesus Alard. m 10/17/1987 Julie P Woody c 2. Asst to R Ch Of The Gd Shpd Tomball TX 1999-2002.

WOOLARD, Lynn Phillip (CFla) PO Box 541025, Merritt Island FL 32954 B Meeker CO 1942 s Harold & L Doris. BA U of Arkansas 1965; MA Embry-Riddle Aeronaut U 1985; Inst of Chr Stds 2010. D 12/11/2010 Bp John Wadsworth Howe. m 8/16/1964 Pamela June Woolard c 2.

WOOLERY-PRICE, Edward Raymond (Tex) All Saints' Episcopal Church, 209 W 27th St, Austin TX 78705 B Manila Philippines 1940 s Edward & Joy. BA U of Texas Austin 1963; JD St Mary's Law Sch 1971; Cert of Completion IONA Sch for Mnstry 2008. D 2/10/2008 Bp Don Adger Wimberly. m 8/24/1963 Patricia Wooten Woolery-Price c 2. Auth, "The Fifth Step," *Diolog The Texas Epis*, Dio Texas, 2012.

WOOLIVER, Tammy (Okla) 264 Woodbriar, Noble OK 73068 **Chapl Integris Hlth Edmond 2011-** B Oklahoma City OK 1959 d Paul & Frances. BA Phillips

U 1996; MDiv VTS 2001. D 6/23/2001 P 1/6/2002 Bp Robert Manning Moody. c 1. Vic S Dav's Ch Oklahoma City OK 2011-2013; R Chr Ch Delaware City DE 2010-2011; CPE Supvsr Christiana Care Hlth System 2007-2011; Chapl and ACPE Supervisory Candidate/Assoc St. Elizabeths Hosp Washington DC 2007; Chapl Dio Maryland Baltimore MD 2002-2007, Epis Chapl and ACPE Supvsr in Trng for the J 2002-2007; Asst R S Dav's Par Washington DC 2001-2002; Chapl Washington Epis Sch 2001-2002; Chapl Washington Epis Sch Beth MD 2001-2002.

WOOLLEN, Nancy Sewell (Ind) B 1927 D.

WOOLLETT JR, Donald M (WLa) **R The Epis Ch Of The Epiph New Iberia LA 2013-** B San Antonio TX 1952 s Donald & Patricia. Texas A&M U 1974; MDiv Notre Dame Sem Grad TS 1982; MDiv Notre Dame Sem Grad TS 1982. Rec 3/5/2011 Bp D Avid Bruce Macpherson. m 11/23/2002 Harriett T Woollett c 2. Leonidas Polk Memi Epis Mssn Leesville LA 2011-2013. epiphany.ni.rector@gmail.com

WOOLLEY JR, Arthur Everett (Md) 13 Basswood Ct, Catonsville MD 21228 **Int St. Tim's 2003-; Ret 1997-** B Bronxville,NY 1931 s Arthur & Hazel. BA CUNY 1953; Nash 1954; MDiv PDS 1957; GTS 1960; Nash 1960; MLS Drexel U 1963. D 4/27/1957 Bp James Pernette DeWolfe P 11/23/1957 Bp Jonathan Goodhue Sherman. Int Mt Calv Ch Baltimore MD 2000-2001; R S Lk's Par Bladensburg MD 1986-1996; Vic S Jude Tiskilwa IL 1982-1986; Vic S Chris Princeton IL 1981-1986; St Christophers Ch Princeton IL 1981-1986; S Simeon's By The Sea Wildwood NJ 1969-1981; Yth Co Coordntr Dio Quincy Peoria IL 1983-1986, Yth Advsr 1979-1982. *Var Bk Revs & arts*, 2003. CBS Life Mem 1950; Forw in Faith No Amer 1989; GAS Life Mem 1990.

WOOLLEY JR, Stanley Marsh (WMass) 868 Butler Drive, Livingston SC 29107 B Fulton NY 1937 s Stanley & Irene. BA MI SU 1960; MDiv PDS 1963. D 4/27/1963 P 11/2/1963 Bp Alfred L Banyard. m 11/19/2000 Patricia E Woolley c 3. Int Rosebud Epis Mssn Mssn SD 2012; Int Ch of the H Sprt Wagner SD 2010; P-in-c H Sprt Mssn Ideal SD 2009-2014; R Trin Epis Ch Winner SD 2009-2014; Int Ch Of The Gd Shpd So Lee MA 2004-2009; Int S Phil's Ch Easthampton MA 1999; Int S Lk's Ch Catskill NY 1997; Int The Epis Ch Of S Andr And S Phil Coventry RI 1996-1997; Int S Lk's Ch Mechanicville NY 1994-1996; Int S Bon Ch Guilderland NY 1993-1994; Vic St Helenas Chap Lenox MA 1975-1992; S Andr's Ch Turners Fall MA 1968-1975; Assoc S Jas' Ch Greenfield MA 1968-1975; Asst S Mich's-On-The-Heights Worcester MA 1967-1968; Vic S Jas Memi Ch Eatontown NJ 1963-1967.

WOOLLEY, Steven Eugene (Spok) 1803 Crestline Dr, Walla Walla WA 99362 **Chapl Walla Walla Fire Dept 2001-** B Amarillo TX 1943 s Eugene & Frances. BA U MN 1965; MDiv GTS 1996. D 6/8/1996 Bp Clarence Nicholas Coleridge P 1/5/1997 Bp Andrew Donnan Smith. m 4/26/1985 Dianna Woolley. R S Paul's Ch Walla Walla WA 2000-2008; Assoc Ch Of The Heav Rest New York NY 1996-2000.

WOOLSEY, Deborah J (SO) St Paul's Episcopal Church, 33 W Dixon Ave, Dayton OH 45419 **Dio Sthrn Ohio Cincinnati OH 2017-; P-in-c Ch Of The Gd Shpd Athens OH 2015-** B Stevens Point, WI 1973 d Roy & Karen. BA Northland Coll 1995; M-Div Nash 2007; MDiv Nash 2007. D 12/16/2006 P 6/30/2007 Bp Russell Edward Jacobus. m 1/7/2012 Michael J Luelloff c 1. R S Paul's Epis Ch Dayton OH 2013-2014; R S Alb's Ch Sussex WI 2007-2012. chogs@chogs.org

WOOMER JR, Harold Gerard (Nev) D 11/14/2015 P 5/21/2016 Bp Dan Thomas Edwards.

WOOTTEN, Jo Ann H (Ark) 346 Rock Springs Rd., Wake Forest NC 27587 B Wilmington NC 1941 d Richard & Bessie. BA Duke 1963; MLS U NC 1966; MBA E Carolina U 1976; PhD U NC 1980; Dio E Carolina Diac Sch 1990. D 6/22/1991 Bp Brice Sidney Sanders. m 6/26/1997 Mid Wootten. D S Paul's Epis Ch Batesville AR 1998-2008; D S Jos Of Arimathaea Ch Hendersonvlle TN 1997-1998; D S Paul's Epis Ch Greenville NC 1992-1997; D Emm Ch Farmville NC 1991-1992. Fell Med Libr Assn 1997.

WOOTTEN III, Mid (Ark) 346 N Rock Springs Rd, Wake Forest NC 27587 B Hot Sprgs AR 1943 s Middleton & Emily. BA U of Mississippi 1966; MDiv VTS 1969. D 6/26/1969 P 5/1/1970 Bp John Maury Allin. m 6/26/1997 Jo Ann H Wootten c 3. R S Paul's Epis Ch Batesville AR 1998-2008; R S Jos Of Arimathaea Ch Hendersonvlle TN 1992-1998; Assoc R S Paul's Epis Ch Greenville NC 1984-1992; Soc Worker 1982-1983; R S Paul's Epis Ch Clinton NC 1981-1982; R S Thos' Ch Windsor NC 1974-1981; Asst S Jn's Epis Ch Fayetteville NC 1971-1974; Vic H Trin Ch Crystal Sprg MS 1969-1971; S Steph's Ch Hazlehurst MS 1969-1971.

WORLEY, James Owen (WTex) 389 Valley View Dr, Cibolo TX 78108 B Houston TX 1947 s Carlos & Viola. BS Texas A&M U 1969; MA Webster U 1977; MDiv Epis TS of the SW 1981. D 6/25/1981 Bp Stanley Fillmore Hauser P 1/10/1982 Bp Scott Field Bailey. m 2/17/1968 Mary R Worley c 3. R Ch Of The Resurr Windcrest TX 1987-2007; Dio W Texas San Antonio TX 1987, Evang Dept, Chairman 1986-1989, Camps and Conferences Dept, Chairman 1989-1992; Hisp Off Dio W Texas San Antonio TX 1983-1986; R Ch Of The Redeem Eagle Pass TX 1982-1987; Asst R Ch Of The Adv Brownsville TX

1981-1982. "Basic Tools for a Gd Mar: Pre-Marital Counslg," Brazos Vlly Bride/WTAW, 2001. Intl Conf of Police Chapl 2001-2013.

WORTH, Elsa H St James Church, 44 West St, Keene NH 03431 **Par Of S Jas Ch Keene NH 2016-** B Norwood MA 1961 d Richard & Elsie. BA Sarah Lawr Coll 1982; MDiv Andover Newton TS 1996. D 12/20/2006 P 6/25/2007 Bp Vicky Gene Robinson. m 7/16/1994 Steven B Worth c 3. Chr Ch Bethany CT 2013-2016; R Gr Epis Ch Trumbull CT 2009-2013; Chr And H Trin Ch Westport CT 2007-2009. elsa@stjameskeene.com

WORTHINGTON, Cynthia Muirhead (RG) 6043 Royal Crk, San Antonio TX 78239 B Saint Louis MO 1933 d Robert & Cynthia. Cert Prchr Lewis Sch of Mnstry. D 8/5/1987 Bp Richard Mitchell Trelease Jr P 2/1/1988 Bp William Davidson. D Ch Of The H Sprt Gallup NM 1987-2000.

WORTHINGTON JR, Daniel Owen (Va) P O Box 83, Gloucester VA 23061 B University VA 1947 s Daniel & Estelle. Randolph-Macon Coll 1969; BA Virginia Commonwealth U 1973; MDiv VTS 1976; DMin SWTS 2004. D 5/22/1976 P 5/14/1977 Bp John Alfred Baden. m 6/17/1978 Jane R Worthington c 2. R Ware Epis Ch Gloucester VA 1985-2012; R S Jas Ch Montross VA 1979-1985; S Ptr's Ch Oak Grove Oak Grove VA 1979-1985; R St Pauls Ch Nomini Grove VA 1979-1985; Vic Piedmont Ch Madison VA 1976-1979. *Land Purchasing for New Congregations,* 2004.

WORTHINGTON, William Ray (Ga) 207 Hermitage Way, Saint Simons Island GA 31522 B Oxford MS 1941 s John & Grayson. BA Mississippi St U 1963; MDiv EDS 1966; STM Sewanee: The U So, TS 1975; MEd Virginia Commonwealth U 1982. D 6/24/1966 P 5/1/1967 Bp John Maury Allin. m 1/29/1966 Ann Chase Worthington c 3. Vic St Richard's Of Chichester Epis Mssn Jekyll Island GA 1999-2006; Headmaster Frederica Acad 1992-1999; Frederica Acad St Simons Island GA 1992-1997; Trin Epis Day Sch Natchez MS 1988-1992; Headmaster Trin Sch Natchez MS 1988-1992; Asst S Barn On The Desert Scottsdale AZ 1987-1988; Headmaster All SS Sch Phoenix AZ 1983-1986; All SS Ch Phoenix AZ 1982-1986; Chapl S Chris's Sch Richmond VA 1974-1982; Chapl S Chris's Sch Richmond VA 1974-1982; Asst To Dn Chr Ch Cathd Houston TX 1971-1974; Non-par 1969-1971; Vic S Patricks Epis Ch Long Bch MS 1967-1969; Cur Chr Ch Bay S Louis MS 1966-1967.

WORTHLEY, Christopher Thomas (Los) 2114 De La Vina St Unit 1, Santa Barbara CA 93105 B Lowell MA 1968 d 6/19/2004 P 1/22/2005 Bp Joseph Jon Bruno. m 4/12/2015 Christian M Clough.

WOS, Edward John (ND) D 4/23/2016 Bp Michael Smith.

WOSIKOWSKI, Thomas J (Mil) 4901 Hob St, Madison WI 53716 B Chicago IL 1930 s Felix & Agnes. BA Elmhurst Coll 1952; MDiv Nash 1955. Rec 12/1/1979 as Priest Bp Charles Thomas Gaskell. c 3. Vic Gd Shpd Epis Ch Sun Prairie WI 1980-1987, Vic 1974-1979; P-in-c S Andr's Epis Ch Monroe WI 1972-1973; P-in-c S Mich & All Ang Shullsburg WI 1972-1973; P-in-c St. Mary's Polish Natl Cath Ch Chicago IL 1966-1971; P-in-c St. Jn's Polish Natl Cath Ch Chicago IL 1961-1971; P-in-c All S's Polish Natl Cath Ch. Johnson City NY 1958-1960; P-in-c All S's Polish Natl Cath Ch Rome NY 1955-1957. OHC 1952.

WRAMPELMEIER, Christopher Kent (NwT) 2602 Parker St, Amarillo TX 79109 **Archd Epis Dio NW Texas TX 2006-; D S Andr's Epis Ch Amarillo TX 2003-** B Amman Jordan 1964 s Brooks & Ann. BA Pr 1986; JD U of Texas 1993. D 11/9/2003 Bp C Wallis Ohl. m 10/7/1995 Hortencia Quinonez c 3.

WRATHALL, Susan L (RI) 70 Moore St., Warwick RI 02889 **R S Mk's Ch Warwick RI 2009-** B Newport RI 1952 d Robert & Carol. BS Rhode Island Coll 1974; MEd Rhode Island Coll 1978; MDiv GTS 2006. D 5/25/2006 Bp David Bruce Joslin P 12/16/2006 Bp Gerry Wolf. c 3. Assoc R S Paul's Ch Pawtucket RI 2006-2009.

WRATTEN, Kenneth Bruce (ECR) 8640 Solera Drive, San Jose CA 95135 **S Lk's Ch Hollister CA 2016-; R S Steph's In-The-Field Epis Ch San Jose CA 2002-** B Watertown NY 1946 s Algernon & Lois. BS Syr 1968; MDiv CDSP 2003. D 6/22/2002 P 1/4/2003 Bp Richard Lester Shimpfky. m 8/6/1966 Ruth K Wratten c 3.

WREDE, Anne (NJ) 37 Northfield Rd, Millington NJ 07946 **P-in-c S Steph's Ch Riverside NJ 2013-; S Steph's Epis Ch Beverly NJ 2013-; Assoc P All Hallows Gedling Engl 1998-** B Cincinnati OH 1952 d John & Jule. BA Amer U 1974; MDiv VTS 1989. D 3/31/1990 Bp Clarence Nicholas Coleridge P 10/6/1990 Bp Arthur Edward Walmsley. m 5/20/1989 Richard Charles Wrede c 1. Trin Epis Old Swedes Ch Swedesboro NJ 2009-2013; Gr Ch Merchantville NJ 2008-2009; Int Trin Epis Ch Vineland NJ 2006-2008; Int S Steph's Ch Manchester Twp NJ 2004-2006; S Jas Ch Bradley Bch NJ 2003-2004; Int St. Jas Bradley Bch NJ 2002-2004; Int Pstr Imm Luth Lakewood NJ 2001-2002; Dn Trin Cathd Trenton NJ 2000; All SS Ch Millington NJ 1997-2000; Int S Mk's Ch Mendham NJ 1995-1996; Int S Andr's Ch Harrington Pk NJ 1993-1994; Int S Geo's Epis Ch Maplewood NJ 1992-1993; Int S Mary's Ch Haledon NJ 1990-1991; Asst S Barn' Ch Leeland Uppr Marlboro MD 1989-1990. Cnvnt Soc S Jn Bapt 1992; GSA 1959.

WREDE, Richard Charles (NJ) 500 Fourth St, Riverton NJ 08077 **R Chr Ch Riverton NJ 2005-; Bp's Advsry Cmsn on Liturg Dio New Jersey Trenton NJ 2012-, Chair, Dioc Conv Nomin Com 2010-2013, Dioc Environ Cmsn**

2005- B Englewood NJ 1956 s Howard & Eloise. BA FD 1978; MS Col 1979; MDiv VTS 1990. D 6/2/1990 P 12/6/1990 Bp John Shelby Spong. m 5/20/1989 Anne Wrede c 1. R All SS Epis Ch Lakewood NJ 2000-2005; R All SS Ch Millington NJ 1994-2000; Pres Bd Managers S Mart Hse 1994-1998; R S Ptr's Ch Rochelle Pk NJ 1990-1994; Moderator Tri-boro Min 2009-2011. Assoc, Cnvnt of St Jn Bapt 1995; HSEC 2009. Bp'S Cert Of Merit 1998; Outstanding Young Men Of Amer 1978.

WREN, Dane Clark (CFla) 302 Bent Way Ln, 700 Rinehart Rd, Lake Mary FL 32746 **D S Ptr's Epis Ch Lake Mary FL 2007-** B Reading PA 1947 s Russell & Ruth. BS Pennsylvania Mltry Coll 1969. D 12/1/2007 Bp John Wadsworth Howe. m 11/28/1987 Laurie Wren c 4. Angilcans for Life 2002; BroSA 2006.

WRENN, William Charles (O) 17 Sandy Neck Rd, East Sandwich MA 02537 **Non-par 1969-** B Milford MA 1929 s Linwood & Ada. BA Tufts U 1952; STM Ya Berk 1955; EDS 1970. D 5/21/1955 P 11/1/1955 Bp William A Lawrence. m 7/4/1991 Barbara Ann Ellis c 3. Chapl Blossom Hill Girls Sch Brecksville OH 1960-1968; Vic S Matt's Epis Ch Brecksville OH 1960-1968; Chapl Jvnl Crt Fitchburg MA 1956-1959; R Ch Of The Gd Shpd Fitchburg MA 1955-1960.

WRIDER, Anne Johnson (SO) 5455 N Sheridan Rd Apt 3912, Chicago IL 60640 B Concord MA 1948 d Franklin & Hope. BA Simmons Coll 1971; MSW U of Iowa 1977; MDiv SWTS 1984. D 6/2/1984 Bp Walter Cameron Righter P 4/1/1986 Bp William Bradford Hastings. c 1. Int R Indn Hill Ch Cincinnati OH 2008-2015; Cn Pstr and Precentor Chr Ch Cathd Cincinnati OH 2000-2008; Vic S Ambr Ch Chicago Hts IL 1995-2000; Vic Chr The King Ch Lansing IL 1995-1997; Sr Mssnr Trin Epis Mnstry 1995-1997; Middlesex Area Cluster Mnstry Higganum CT 1994-1995; Epis Ch At Yale New Haven CT 1990-1995; Mssnr Middlesex Area Cluster Mnstry 1990-1995; S Jn's Ch Guilford CT 1989-1991; Asst S Mary's Epis Ch Manchester CT 1986-1989; Asst S Geo/S Mths Ch Chicago IL 1984-1985. Auth, "Looking For The Perfect Ch," Forw Mvmt, 1998; Auth, "WaterFire & Blood Defilement & Purification from a Ricoeurian Perspective," *ATR*, 1985. Polly Bond Awd ECom 1999. revajw@live.com

WRIGHT, Allan McLean (WMass) Po Box 3504, Annapolis MD 21403 **Non-par 1970-** B 1932 s John & Catherine. BS U of Rhode Island 1955; BD EDS 1960. D 6/25/1960 P 2/1/1961 Bp Robert McConnell Hatch. m 10/1/2005 Lois Wright. Vic S Mk's Epis Ch E Longmeadow MA 1962-1970; Asst Ch Of The Atone Westfield MA 1960-1962.

WRIGHT, Andrew Ray (FtW) 1700 N. Westmoreland Rd., Desoto TX 75115 **Assoc Trin Epis Ch Ft Worth TX 2013-** B Borger TX 1969 s Kenneth & Marcia. BA TCU 1991; MDiv Sewanee: The U So, TS 1995; STM GTS 2003; ThD GTS 2012. D 6/4/1995 Bp Sam Byron Hulsey P 4/21/1996 Bp Bertram Nelson Herlong. c 3. Cbury Epis Sch Desoto TX 2012-2014; R S Anne's Epis Ch Desoto TX 2009-2013; Supply P Dio Maryland Baltimore MD 2008-2009, Supply P 2008-; Asst R Chr Ch Columbia MD 2006-2008; Supply P Dio Newark Newark NJ 2004-2006; Asst to the Dir of the Chap The GTS New York NY 2003-2006, Tutor 2003-2004; Dio New York New York NY 2003-2004; Supply P Gr Epis Ch Monroe NY 2003-2004; R S Jas' Epis Ch Fremont NE 1999-2002; Dio Tennessee Nashville TN 1995-1999, Cmsn for the MHE 1995-1999; Asst to the R S Paul's Epis Ch Murfreesboro TN 1995-1999; Congrl Dvlpmt Cmsn Dio Nebraska Omaha NE 2001-2002. Angl Colloquium of No Amer Acad of Liturg 2008; ESMHE 1996-2000; The Jn Henry Hobart Soc (at GTS) 2002.

WRIGHT, Angus Dale (NMich) PO Box 302, Manistique MI 49854 B Rochelle IL 1940 s John & Louise. MST Cor; BS and Educ MI SU 1963. D 1/8/2014 P 7/13/2014 Bp Rayford J Ray. m 6/19/1965 Judith Lou Wright c 1.

WRIGHT, Benjamin R (RG) 363 Park St, Beaver PA 15009 B Alpine TX 1946 s Joel & Onie. BBA U of Texas Rio Grande Vlly 1968; LSU 1969; MDiv TESM 1994; Fuller TS 2000. D 6/29/1994 P 1/6/1995 Bp Bob Gordon Jones. m 5/28/2000 Beryl Pretty c 2. Asst Dn of Admin & Ch Relatns TESM 2010-2015; Ch Of S Jas The Apos Clovis Curry NM 2006-2010; S Jn's Ch Ft Sumner NM 2006-2010; R Trin Ch Portales NM 2006-2010; All SS Epis Ch Pleasanton TX 2001-2006; Epis Ch Of The Gd Shepard Geo W TX 2001-2006; Cn Mssnr Vic S Mths Devine TX 2001-2006; S Mich's Ch Lake Corpus Christi TX 2001-2006; S Tim's Ch Cotulla TX 2001-2006; Sthrn Partnr In Mnstry Geo W TX 2001-2006; Chr Ch - Epis Newcastle WY 1996-2001; Vic Ch Of The Gd Shpd Sundance WY 1996-2001; Asst R S Mk's Epis Ch Casper WY 1994-1996.

WRIGHT, Bill (NwT) 3549 Clearview Dr, San Angelo TX 76904 **Asstg P Emm San Angelo TX 2014-; Ret TX 2004-; Chapl to Ret Cler and Spouses Dio NW Texas 2014-** B Tuscaloosa AL 1943 s Ernest & Martha. BA Birmingham-Sthrn Coll 1964; MDiv Sewanee: The U So, TS 1970. DMin VTS 1984. D 6/24/1970 Bp George Mosley Murray P 5/18/1971 Bp Furman Charles Stough. m 10/30/1964 Patricia Wright c 2. Int Trin Epis Ch Ft Worth TX 2011; Int Ch of the Heav Rest Abilene Abilene TX 2009-2010; R S Jn's Epis Ch Ft Smith AR 1998-2004; R S Paul's On The Plains Epis Ch Lubbock TX 1992-1998; R Ch Of The Resurr Austin TX 1987-1992; Chapl (Cmdr) US Naval Reserve 1983-1991; R S Mich's Ch La Marque TX 1982-1986; P-in-c St Michaels/H Cross Uniontown AL 1981-1982; R S Andr Prairieville AL 1975-1982; R S Mich's (Faunsdale) Faunsdale AL 1975-1982; R Trin Ch Demopolis AL

1975-1982; Assoc Chr Epis Ch San Antonio TX 1973-1975; Emm Epis Ch Opelika AL 1970-1973; Vic S Matthews In The Pines Seale AL 1970-1973. Assoc OHC 1973.

WRIGHT, Brian Theodore (Oly) 105 State St 5, Kirkland WA 98033 **D S Hilda's - S Pat's Epis Ch Edmonds WA 2011-** B Philadelphia PA 1944 s Theodore & Ruth. BS Auburn U 1966; MS Naval Post Grad Sch 1971. D 10/17/2009 Bp Gregory Harold Rickel. m 3/16/1966 Julene Wright c 1. deacon@stjohnskirkland.org

✠ WRIGHT, The Rt Rev Carl W (AFFM) Apo Ae 0962, PSC2 Box 9808, Ramstein Germany **Dom And Frgn Mssy Soc- Epis Ch Cntr New York NY 2017-; Epis Ch Cntr New York NY 2017-; S Andr's Ch Pasadena MD 2013-; Off Of Bsh For ArmdF New York NY 1993-** B Baltimore MD 1959 s Monaelmer & Eva. Coppin St Coll 1978; Cert Peabody Inst of Mus Prep Dept 1978; BA Loyola U 1985; MDiv VTS 1990; Brooke Army Med Cntr San Antonio 2005. D 6/16/1990 P 5/5/1991 Bp Albert Theodore Eastman Con 2/11/2017 for Armed Forces and Federal Ministires. S Mk's Epis Ch Charleston SC 1992-1993; Cur Emm Ch Cumberland MD 1990-1992; Epis Cmsn Of Black Ministers. Auth, "Var arts," *Dioc Dialogue Nwsltr of Dio Utah*, 2008; Auth, "Var arts," *LivCh*, 2008; Auth, "Var arts," *Mssy Nwsltr of Dio Nthrn California*, 2007; Auth, "Var arts," *Linkage*, 1990. OHC; UBE. secretarystandrewspasadena@verizon.net

WRIGHT, Catherine Louise (Tex) 301 E 8th St, Austin TX 78701 **Assoc R S Dav's Ch Austin TX 2012-, P-in-c 2012-** B Phoenix AZ 1967 d Karl & Diane. BA Claremont McKenna Coll 1989; MDiv SMU Perkins 2005. D 11/1/2007 Bp Victor Alfonso Scantlebury P 6/4/2008 Bp Jeff Lee. m 6/29/1996 James D Wright c 3. S Andr's Epis Ch Elyria OH 2009, R 2009; Assoc P S Mk's Epis Ch Glen Ellyn IL 2007-2009; Yth Dir Epis Ch Of The Ascen Dallas TX 2005-2007; Dir. Chld's Min The Epis Ch Of The Trsfg Dallas TX 2003-2004.

WRIGHT, Diana Lee (Ia) **Trin Ch Carroll IA 2014-; Trin Ch Denison IA 2013-** B Des Moines IA 1952 d Donald & Barbara. Iowa Methodist Med Cntr/ Des Moines VAH; U of Missouri, Columbia; BS Iowa St U 1976; MD U of Iowa 1978. D 12/17/2011 P 1/12/2013 Bp Alan Scarfe. c 1. S Paul's Ch Harlan IA 2013-2014. cardiff1952@yahoo.com

WRIGHT, Elizabeth Louise (RI) 10 Eustis Ave, Newport RI 02840 B New Haven CT 1937 d Richmond & Jennie. BA Colby Coll 1959; MA Col 1960; Rhode Island Sch For Deacons 1989. D 2/4/1989 Bp George Nelson Hunt III. m 8/19/1961 Peter Gwin Patton Wright c 2. D Emm Ch Newport RI 1989-2000.

WRIGHT, Elton Stanley (Colo) 342 Old Cahaba Trail, Helena AL 35080 **Assoc Ch of the H Sprt Alabaster AL 2008-** B Ogden UT 1931 s Lawrence & Vera. Bishops TS Dio Colorado; U CO; BA Metropltn St Coll of Denver 1990. D 11/30/1979 P 6/30/1980 Bp William Carl Frey. m 4/1/1956 Roxene Roi Weichel c 4. P-in-c Trin Epis Ch Bessemer AL 2011-2012, P-in-c 2011-; R S Matt's Ch Grand Jct CO 1992-2001; R S Mart In The Fields Aurora CO 1982-1992; Vic S Martha's Epis Ch Westminster CO 1980-1982.

WRIGHT, Gwynne A (Chi) 43 Rawcliffe Croft, York YO305US Great Britain (UK) **Chapl NW Cmnty Hosp Arlington Heights IL 2012-; Bd Chair Seabury Wstrn TS 2010-** B New York NY 1949 d George & Margaret. BA Marymount Coll 1971; MBA S Johns U 1980; MA Keller Grad Sch of Mgmt 1998; MDiv SWTS 2004; DMin GTF 2010. D 6/19/2004 P 12/18/2004 Bp Bill Persell. S Chas Ch St. Chas IL 2012; Ch Of The Trsfg Palos Pk IL 2011-2012; Int R The Epis Ch Of S Jas The Less Northfield IL 2010-2011; Int S Paul's Ch Dekalb IL 2008-2010; P-in-c S Jas Ch Dundee IL 2006-2008; Asst R S Simons Ch Arlington Hts IL 2004-2006.

WRIGHT, Hollis E (Colo) 92-1010 Kanehoa Loop, Kapolei HI 96707 **S Matt's Ch Grand Jct CO 2009-; Vic St. Nich Epis Ch Kapolei HI 2002-** B Glendale CA 1951 d William & Leone. BA U of Hawaii 1973; MBA U of Hawaii 1975; MDiv CDSP 1996. D 6/22/1996 Bp George Nelson Hunt III P 1/17/1997 Bp Richard Sui On Chang. m 5/8/1976 Christopher Parsons c 2. S Nich Epis Ch Aiea HI 2002-2009; R S Jas Epis Ch Kamuela HI 1998-2002; Assoc R Ch Of The H Nativ Honolulu HI 1996-1998.

WRIGHT, James D (Fla) 3231 Nw 47th Pl, Gainesville FL 32605 **Vic Chr Ch Cedar Key FL 2007-** B Richmond VA 1955 s James & Barbara. BS U IL 1977; JD Florida St U 1980; MDiv Bex Sem 1989. D 6/11/1989 P 12/1/1989 Bp Frank S Cerveny. m 12/30/1978 Nancy E Wright c 3. Asst H Trin Epis Ch Gainesville FL 1989-2007.

WRIGHT, James O. Pete (Los) 1505 Monticello Ct., Redlands CA 92373 **Supply P Dio Iowa 2015-; P Chapl Dio in Europe 2013-; Supply P Dio Cntrl New York 2009-; P Supply Cler Dio Los Angeles 2005-** B Hanford CA 1942 s James & Caroline. St Lawr Sem 1960; BA S Anth Coll Hudson NH 1966; Bos 1970; BD Capuchin TS 1970; ThM Capuchin TS 1970; MA Maryknoll TS 1971; Pasadena City Coll 1971. Rec 4/11/2005 as Priest Bp Sergio Carranza-Gomez. m 10/22/1988 Penelope Irene Wright c 5.

WRIGHT, Janice Bracken (At) 7 Creek Side Way SW, Rome GA 30165 **1988-** B Richmond VA 1957 d Lawrence & Kathleen. BA U of Virginia 1978; MDiv Candler TS Emory U 1981. D 7/18/1981 P 6/26/1982 Bp Robert Bruce Hall. m 6/30/1990 Cecil Baker Wright. Assoc R S Ptr's Ch Rome GA 2003-2017, Asst R 1983-1987; 1982-1983; Asst Ch Of The H Comf Richmond VA 1981-1982; Dn of NW Georgia Convoc Dio Atlanta Atlanta GA 2010-2017, Dep to GC

2010-, Exec Bd 2006-2010. Auth, *Wmn of the Word: Contemporary Sermons by Wmn Cler.* Theta Phi; Phi Beta Kappa. jbwright@bellsouth.net

WRIGHT, Jean Ann Frances (At) 5228 Stone Village Cir Nw, Kennesaw GA 30152 **D S Mk's Ch Palm Bch Garden FL 1987-** B Flint MI 1941 d Max & Ernestine. Dio SE Florida Sch Mnstry FL; Palm Bch Jr Coll. D 11/27/1987 Bp Calvin Onderdonk Schofield Jr. m 3/5/1971 Fredrick Eitel. Auth, "Creative Quiltmaking In The Mandala Tradition"; Auth, "Quilt".

WRIGHT, Jeannene Fee (DR) Eps G 2517, Box 02-5540, Miami FL 33102 **Retreat Ldr & Tchr San Pedro De Macoris 1988-; D Centro Buen Pstr San Pedro de Macoris 1984-** B Columbus OH 1934 d John & Evelyne. BA OH SU 1956; BS OH SU 1957; MA SWTS 1964; STM GTS 1980. D 6/18/1964 Bp Francis E I Bloy. D S Ptr's Ch Mc Kinney TX 1971-1973; DRE Ch Of The Gd Shpd Ft Defiance AZ 1964-1965; In-Charge S Lk's Outstation Navajo NM 1964-1965. Auth, "Forw Mvmt". GAS; Natl Conf Of Wmn Deacons.

WRIGHT, Jo Anne Steinheimer (Okla) 821 N Foreman St Apt 118, Vinita OK 74301 **Ret 2005-** B Wichita KS 1935 d Everett & Agnes. BA Ob 1955; MDiv CDSP 1987. D 6/11/1987 P 12/21/1987 Bp Richard Frank Grein. c 4. R S Jn's Epis Ch Vinita OK 1999-2004; Coun on Missn Ch Dio Oklahoma Oklahoma City OK 1999-2002; Coun Trst Dio Kansas Topeka KS 1997-1999; R S Lk's Ch Wamego KS 1987-1998. Associated Parishes 1987; EWC; Integrity. Who's Who in Amer Marquis Who's Who 2000; Phi Beta Kappa Ob 1955.

WRIGHT JR, John Armstrong (WNC) Po Box 126, Flat Rock NC 28731 **Died 4/1/2017** B Augusta GA 1934 s John & Mary. BA Amer U 1962; MDiv VTS 1965. D 6/1/1965 P 3/1/1966 Bp Robert Fisher Gibson Jr. m 4/12/2017 Carole Wright c 4. Ret 1982-2017; Calv Epis Ch Fletcher NC 1974-1982, R 1974-1982; R S Anne's Par Scottsville VA 1966-1973, 1965-1966, D-in-C 1965-1966.

WRIGHT, John Hamil Spedden (Del) 54 Ridge Ave, Edgewater MD 21037 **R S Steph's Ch Harrington DE 2008-; Non-par 1987-** B Cambridge MD 1934 s John & Louise. MDiv VTS 1974. D 5/18/1974 P 11/1/1974 Bp Egbert Don Taylor. c 4. Dio Delaware Wilmington 2000-2003; R The Ch Of The H Sprt Ocean City MD 1985-1987; R All Faith Tunis Mills MD 1982-1985; All Faith Chap Miles River Par Easton MD 1982-1984; P-in-c S Paul's Epis Ch Hebron MD 1980-1982; Chesapeake Rehab Cntr Easton MD 1977-1983; P-in-c S Phil's Ch Laurel DE 1977-1978; R Chr Ch Denton MD 1974-1977.

WRIGHT, John Robert (NY) General Theological Seminary, 175 9th Ave, New York NY 10011 **Hstgr Epis Ch of the USA 2000-; Hon Cn Theol to Bp of NY Dioces Of Ny NY 1991-** B Carbondale IL 1936 s John & Ruth. BA U So 1958; MA Emory U 1959; MDiv GTS 1963; DPhil Oxf GB 1967. D 6/11/1963 Bp John P Craine P 6/29/1964 Bp Mervyn Stockwood. Hsec 1978-1996; The GTS New York NY 1968-2007; Bd Dir ATR. Auth, "A Comp to Bede," Eerdmans, 2006; Auth/Ed, "Ancient Chr Commentaries on Scripture," Inter-Varsity Press, 2005; Ed and Auth, "Russo-Gk Papers 1863-1874," Norman Ross Pub, 2001; Auth, "S Thos Ch Fifth Av," Eerdmans, 2001; Ed and Auth, "On Being a Bp," Ch Pub, 1993; Ed & Auth, "They Still Speak: Readings For The Lesser Feasts & Fasts," Ch Pub, 1993; "The Angl Tradition," SPCK, 1991; Ed & Auth, "Readings For The Daily Off From The Early Ch," Ch Pub, 1991; Auth, "PB Sprtlty," Ch Pub, 1989; Ed & Auth, "Quadrilateral at One Hundred," Forw Mvmt, 1988; Auth, "Called to Full Unity," US Cath Conf, 1986; Ed & Co-Auth, "Lift High the Cross," Forw Mvmt, 1984; Auth, "Ch Engl Crown 1305-1334," Pacific Inst. Medieval Stds (Toronto), 1980; Ed & Co-Auth, "A Comm of Communions," Seabury, 1979. Amer Cath Hist Soc Hist Soc Of The 1989-1991; Angl Theol Conf, Conf Of Angl Ch; Pres Angl Soc 1994. Festschrift, One Lord, One Faith, One Baptism Eerdmans 2006; Hon ThD U of Bern, Switzerland 2000; Hon D. Cu. L., Cn Law STUSo 1996; Patriarchal Cross Of The Ecum Patriarch Of Constantinople 1994; Patriarchal Cross Of The Ecum Patriarch Of Moscow And All Russi 1993; Patriarchal Cross Of The Armenian Patriarch Of Jerusalem 1992; Hon DD Trin Luth Sem 1991; Patriarchal Cross Of The Syrian Patriarch Of Antioch 1990; Hon DD Epis TS of the SW 1983.

WRIGHT, Jonathan M (SC) 1295 Abercorn Trce, Mount Pleasant SC 29466 **R Gr Ch Cathd Charleston SC 2006-** B Canada 1960 s Robert & Dorothy. BA Queens U 1981; MDiv U Tor CA 1984. Trans 7/27/2006 Bp Edward Lloyd Salmon Jr. m 6/25/1988 Margriet J Wright c 2.

WRIGHT, Lonell (La) 7696 Stevenson Way, San Diego CA 92120 **Dio Louisiana New Orleans LA 2009-** B Bernice LA 1939 s Douglas & LaRue. BS Sthrn U Baton Rouge LA 1961; MPA U CA Riverside 1976; MDiv Nash 2007. D 5/31/2008 P 1/31/2009 Bp Charles Edward Jenkins III. m 4/26/1964 Dessie B Wright c 4.

WRIGHT, Mark R (Dal) 2019 Highland Forest Dr, Highland Village TX 75077 **R S Nich Ch Flower Mound TX 2008-** B Fort Eustis VA 1959 s Richard & Barbara. BA Duquesne U 1981; MDiv TESM 1984. D 9/20/1984 P 3/1/1985 Bp Alden Moinet Hathaway. m 8/21/1982 Laurel C Wright c 2. S Dav's Epis Ch Peters Township PA 1995-2008; R S Paul's Epis Ch Shreveport LA 1991-1995; R Trin Epis Ch Jasper TX 1989-1991; Asst Ch Of The Ascen Houston TX 1986-1989; Assoc S Mk's Epis Ch Riverside RI 1985-1986; D/P-In-C Ch Of The Trsfg Clairton PA 1984-1985. frmark@stnicksonline.org

W

947

WRIGHT III, Martin Luther (Pgh) 1249 Main Street, PO Box 175, Shanksville PA 15560 **Chapl Heartland Hospice Irwin PA 2006-** B Leavenworth KS 1959 s Martin & Mary. BS U of Kansas 1983; MDiv TESM 2002. D 6/15/2002 P 1/8/2003 Bp Robert William Duncan. m 7/11/1987 Dawn Holbrook c 4. P S Mk's Ch Johnstown PA 2011-2014; S Fran In The Fields Somerset PA 2004-2006; Asst S Michaels Of The Vlly Epis Ch Ligonier PA 2002-2004.

WRIGHT, Matthew L (NY) St Gregory's Episcopal Church, PO Box 66, Woodstock NY 12498 **S Greg's Epis Ch Woodstock NY 2014-** B Somerset KY 1985 s Tony & Becky. BA U NC 2007; MDiv VTS 2012. D 12/17/2011 P 9/1/2012 Bp Porter Taylor. m 9/8/2014 Yanick Elisabeth Savain. S Andr's Ch Poughkeepsie NY 2012-2013. matthew.stgregorys@gmail.com

WRIGHT, Michael Alfred (Oly) 1428 22nd Ave, Longview WA 98632 B Davenport IA 1956 s Howard & Virginia. BA Augustana Coll 1984; MDiv Wstrn Sem 1987; ThM Trin DS 1994. D 12/13/2014 P 6/16/2015 Bp Gregory Harold Rickel. c 2.

WRIGHT, Milton King (Minn) 707 Saint Olaf Ave, Northfield MN 55057 **Nonpar 1983-** B Hampton VA 1936 s Ray & Elsie. BA W&M 1959; Ya 1962; BD Sewanee: The U So, TS 1964; MBA U NC 1978. D 6/19/1964 Bp George P Gunn P 6/1/1965 Bp John B Bentley. m 8/6/1994 Bonnie Susanne Wright c 2. R St Jn Epis Ch Grifton NC 1972-1974; All SS Epis Ch Norton VA 1971-1972; Vic Chr Epis Ch Big Stone Gap VA 1971-1972; S Jas Ch Boydton VA 1965-1971; R W Mecklenburg Par Boydton VA 1965-1971; Cur Chr and S Lk's Epis Ch Norfolk VA 1964-1965. Auth, "An Index Of Hymns Of The Proposed Calendar".

WRIGHT, Priscilla Jean (SO) B 1934

WRIGHT, Rick Lynn (At) B Oneonta AL 1964 s Eldon & Ida Mae. BS Lee U 1987; MA Ch of God TS 1991; MLS U of Alabama 1994. D 8/6/2011 Bp J Neil Alexander.

✠ WRIGHT, The Rt Rev Robert Christopher (At) 306 Peyton Rd Sw, Atlanta GA 30311 **Bp of Atlanta Dio Atlanta Atlanta GA 2012-** B Pittsburgh PA 1964 s Earl & Charlene. BA How 1992; MDiv VTS 1998. D 6/13/1998 Bp Ronald Hayward Haines P 2/13/1999 Bp Jane Hart Holmes Dixon Con 10/13/2012 for At. m 7/4/1998 Beth-Sarah Wright c 4. R S Paul's Epis Ch Atlanta GA 2002-2012; Vic/Cn Cong Of S Sav New York NY 2000-2002; P Cathd Of St Jn The Div New York NY 1998-2002. Bro Of S Andr. bishopwright@episcopalatlanta.org

WRIGHT, Ross Mcgowan (SVa) 4203 Springhill Ave, Richmond VA 23225 **R Ch Of The Gd Shpd Richmond VA 2006-; Prof Randolph-Macon Coll 2006-** B Orangeburg SC 1954 s Samuel & Ellen. BA Davidson Coll 1976; MDiv TESM 1981; GTS 1982; ThM PrTS 2003; PhD U of St Andrews 2007. D 6/12/1982 Bp William Arthur Beckham P 4/20/1983 Bp Paul Moore Jr. m 11/30/1985 Lynda Wright c 3. R Ch Of The Gd Shpd Norfolk VA 1987-2002; Gr Epis Ch New York NY 1982-1987; Hd, Evang Cmsn Dio Sthrn Virginia Newport News VA 1992-1994. Auth, "The Problem of Flatter," *LivCh*, LivCh Fndt, 2008; Auth, "Revs Article Word and Ch: Essays in Chr Dogmatics," *The Princeton Sem Bulletin*, PrTS, 2003. Cmnty Of S Mary 1995. Ldrshp Hampton Roads 1994.

WRIGHT, Ryan A (SwFla) Saint Paul's, 3901 Davis Blvd, Naples FL 34104 **Ch Of The Epiph Cape Coral FL 2009-** B Baltimore MD 1977 s Donald & Ruth. BA Stetson U 1999; MDiv GTS 2006. D 5/27/2006 Bp John Wadsworth Howe P 11/3/2007 Bp Dabney Tyler Smith. Asst. R S Paul's Ch Naples FL 2007-2009.

WRIGHT, Scot R (Oly) 650 Bellevue Way NE, Unit 2401, Bellevue WA 98004 **R St. Jn's Epis Ch Kirkland WA 2007-** B Denver CO 1957 s Elton & Roxene. BA SE U 1980; MDiv Gordon-Conwell TS 1987. D 10/28/1987 P 5/22/1988 Bp Donald Purple Hart. m 7/9/1977 Chitra Watumull c 3. P-in-c St. Jn's Epis Ch Kirkland WA 2005-2007; R S Jn's Ch Kirkland WA 1999-2015; Assoc P St. Jn's Epis Ch Kirkland WA 1999-2005; R St Steph's Epis Ch Oak Harbor WA 1992-1998; Assoc All SS Ch Bakersfield CA 1989-1992; Assoc R Calv Epis Ch Kaneohe HI 1987-1989.

WRIGHT, Stanalee (Spok) **Vic S Anne's Ch Omak WA 2004-** B Colville WA 1956 BS WA SU 1978. D 11/20/2004 P 6/11/2005 Bp James E Waggoner Jr. m 9/7/1996 Michael Wright.

WRIGHT, Stuart Wayne (Md) 4 E. University Pkwy., Baltimore MD 21218 **Cn for Transitions Dio Maryland Baltimore MD 2009-, Dir for HR 2008-; Off of Transition Mnstry Bd Mem Dom And Frgn Mssy Soc- Epis Ch Cntr New York NY 2012-** B Apple Valley CA 1959 s Bobby & Gladys. BBA U of No Texas 1981; MDiv Luth TS 1989. Rec 6/26/2009 Bp John L Rabb. m 9/16/2011 Melvin F Wright. Dir for HR Luth Immigration & Refugee Serv 2005-2007; Dir for Compstn & Benefits ELCA Churchwide Orgnztn 1994-2005; Asst for Peace Educ ELCA Churchwide Orgnztn 1991-1994; Assist Pstr Bethlehem Luth Ch Beaumont TX 1989-1991. swright@episcopalmaryland.org

✠ **WRIGHT, The Rt Rev Wayne** (Del) 1841 North St, Philadelphia PA 19130 **Chair, Bd Trst 2012-** B Richmond VA 1951 s George & Margaret. BA W&M 1975; MDiv Sewanee: The U So, TS 1980. D 6/14/1980 P 5/9/1981 Bp Claude Charles Vache Con 6/20/1998 for Del. m 8/17/1985 Holly B Wright c 1. Bp Of Delaware Dio Delaware Wilmington 1998-2017; R Gr Ch New Orleans LA 1987-1998; S Jn's Ch Suffolk VA 1980-1987; Chair, Bd Trst The CPG New York NY 2012-2015, Trst 2003-2015; Chair, Dispatch of Bus HOB 2009-2017; Trst S Anne's Epis Sch Middletown DE 2002-2017; Trst S Andrews Sch Of Delaware Inc Middletown DE 1998-2017; GC Joint Stndg Com On Nomin Dio Louisiana New Orleans LA 1995-1996, Pres - Nneca 1993-1994, Dep Gc 1991-1992, Pres La Cler Assn 1989-1990; Exec Bd Dio Sthrn Virginia Newport News VA 1982-1984. Hon DD U So. homeplate@wrightathome.org

WRIGHT, William J (Alb) 14 Monument St, Deposit NY 13754 B Walton NY 1950 s Floyd & Lucille. D 6/2/2012 Bp William Howard Love. m 9/30/2006 Frances Wright.

WRIGHT, Winston (SeFla) 1466 39th St, West Palm Beach FL 33407 **R Gr Ch W Palm Bch FL 2000-** B Rock Spring Trelawny JM 1963 s Leolyn. GTF; DIT Untd Theol Coll of the W Indies Kingston JM 1991; BA U of The W Indies 1991. Trans 10/12/2000 Bp Leo Frade. m 4/30/1994 Gillian Kennedy Kennedy Wright c 1.

WU, Ming-Lung (Tai) No. 1-6 Mingxin St, Hualien City 97050 Taiwan **Dio Taiwan Taipei 2012-** B New Taipei City Taiwan 1964 s Jin-Wen & Qiu-Lian. RSB and MA Fu Jen Fac of Theol of St Robert Bellarmine 2012. D 8/24/2002 P 4/27/2012 Bp Jung-Hsin Lai. m 5/10/1992 Xiao-Lan Lao c 2.

WU, Peter (Haw) 229 Queen Emma Sq, Honolulu HI 96813 **D S Pauls Ch Honolulu HI 2013-; EAM Chinese Convoc Co-Convenor Dom And Frgn Mssy Soc- Epis Ch Cntr New York NY 2011-** B Hong Kong 1947 Cetificate Dio Hawaii; BS California St U, Chico 1972; MS U of Hawaii 1974. D 10/28/2011 Bp Robert Leroy Fitzpatrick. m 7/7/1974 Mimi L Wu c 2. D Ch Of The Epiph Honolulu HI 2011-2012. Off of the Year Elks 2012; Acad hon Phi Kappa Phi 1972.

WU, Shing-Shaing (Tai) 499 Sec 4 Danjin Rd, Tamsui Dist, New Taipei City 25135 Taiwan **Dio Taiwan Taipei 2014-** B Taipei 1984 s Tai-Chun & Min-Jhu. D 8/23/2014 Bp Jung-Hsin Lai. m 10/25/2014 Yu-Ju Huang.

WUBBENHORST, Wesley (Md) 4 East University Pkwy, Baltimore MD 21218 **Died 3/15/2016** B Minneola NY 1953 s William & Arvilla. BA Laf 1976; MS Ford 1982; MDiv VTS 1989. D 6/9/1990 Bp Arthur Edward Walmsley P 3/1/1991 Bp Clarence Nicholas Coleridge. m 10/16/1982 Vivienne F Thompson c 5. Chr Ch Port Republic MD 2015; Yth Mssnr Dio Maryland Baltimore MD 2004-2015; Assoc S Marg's Ch Annapolis MD 1997-2004; Gr Ch Madison NJ 1994-1997; Chapl & Asst Dir Epis C&C Ivoryton CT 1990-1994; Incarn Cntr Deep River CT 1990-1994. Wk for Wrld Peace Intl Assn of Sufism 2010; Interfaith Visionary Temple of Understanding 2010; SACC Awd Sexual Assault Crisis Cntr Anne Arundel Cnty MD 2003; 2001 Cler Awd Maryland Ntwk Against Dom Violence 2001; Outstanding Victim Advocacy Anne Arundel Cnty MD 1999.

WURM, Laurie Jean (Nwk) **Gr Ch Van Vorst Jersey City NJ 2013-; Dir All SS' Cmnty Serv & Devlpmt. Corp. Hoboken NJ 1992-** B Woodbury NY 1969 d Jesse & Heather. BA Bard Coll 1991; MDiv UTS 1995. D 9/11/2004 P 4/2/2005 Bp John Palmer Croneberger. c 1. S Jn's Epis Ch Boonton NJ 2007-2013; All SS Cmnty Serv and Dvlpmt Corp Hoboken NJ 2004-2007; All SS Epis Par Hoboken NJ 1996-2004.

WYATT, Andrea Castner (Mass) 133 School St, New Bedford MA 02740 B Peekskill NY 1966 d Edward & Wanda. BA Coll of Wooster 1988; MDiv Harvard DS 1991. D 6/6/2015 P 12/12/2015 Bp Gayle Harris. m 7/6/1991 Charles E Wyatt c 2. Gr Ch New Bedford MA 2015-2017.

WYATT II, Robert Odell (Chi) 110 S Marion St Unit 307, Oak Park IL 60302 **Gr Epis Ch Hinsdale IL 2015-** B Jackson TN 1946 s Robert & Sera. BA U So 1968; MA NWU 1970; PhD NWU 1973; MS U of Tennessee 1976; Cert SWTS 2002; MTS Van 2003; Cert Loyola U Chicago 2010. D 6/19/2004 P 12/18/2004 Bp Bill Persell. m 5/16/1997 Terri Anne Lackey. R S Helena's Ch Burr Ridge IL 2006-2014; Cur Ch Of The Trsfg Palos Pk IL 2004-2006; Trst Bexley Seabury Fed Chicago IL 1996-2001. Co-Auth, "Free Expression In Five Democratic Publics," Hampton Press, 2004; Auth, "Free Expression And The American Publ," Amer Soc Of Nwspr Editors, 1991. Fndr's Medal Van Divnity Sch 2004; Worcester Prize For Best Article Wrld Assn. For Publ Opinion Resrch 1996; DSA Soc Of Profsnl Journalists 1991.

WYCKOFF, Michael Hirsch (Tex) 2857 Grimes Ranch Rd, Austin TX 78732 **R S Lk's On The Lake Epis Ch Austin TX 2004-; R S Lk's on the Lake Austin TX 2004-** B Ithaca NY 1959 s Wendell & Fredericka. BA Wesl 1981; MDiv VTS 1987. D 6/29/1987 Bp Gordon Taliaferro Charlton P 4/13/1988 Bp Maurice Manuel Benitez. m 6/11/1988 Martha T Wyckoff c 2. R Chr Ch Tuscaloosa AL 1998-2004; R Chr Epis Ch Temple TX 1991-1998; Assoc The Ch of the Gd Shpd Austin TX 1987-1990.

WYER, George William (Va) Po Box 638, Ivy VA 22945 B Bucyrus OH 1931 s John & Hazel. BA Ob 1952; MLitt U Pgh 1953; MDiv Bex Sem 1967. D 6/17/1967 Bp Nelson Marigold Burroughs P 12/17/1967 Bp Beverley D Tucker. m 10/3/1954 Nancy Wyer c 4. S Paul's Ch Charlottesville VA 1974-1993; Ch Of S Jn The Bapt Ivy VA 1974-1987; Assoc The Epis Ch Of Beth-By-The-Sea Palm Bch FL 1969-1974; R S Mary's Cleveland OH 1967-1969.

WYES, Gregory Walter (Az) 6960 N Alvernon Way, Tucson AZ 85718 B Duesseldorf Germany 1940 s Emil & Henny. BA S Alberts 1963; MDiv Oxf GB 1967; DMin GTF 1990. Rec 1/1/1977 as Priest Bp John Joseph Meakin Harte. m 9/27/1975 Lotti Wyes. Chr The King Ch Tucson AZ 1976-2002; Asst RC Ch 1967-1975.

WYLAND, Richard Rees (Roch) 41 Great Oak Ln, Redding CT 06896 **P-in-c Trin Ch Milton CT 2007-; 1984-** B Hartford CT 1948 s Richard & Helen. BA Trin Hartford CT 1970; MA Trin Hartford CT 1970; MDiv GTS 1973; Cert Sacr Heart U 1993. D 2/24/1973 P 4/22/1974 Bp Robert Rae Spears Jr. m 6/10/1989 Jeanne Bryant-Wyland c 1. P Trin Ch Litchfield CT 2007-2016; Trin Epis Ch Trumbull CT 2006; Chr Ch Redding CT 2005; Trin-S Mich's Ch Fairfield CT 2003-2004; Int Trin-St. Mich's Fairfield CT 2003-2004; Int S Ptr's Epis Ch Monroe CT 2002; Chr Ch Clayton NY 1998-1999; Int St Jn's Ch Cape Vinc NY 1998-1999; Asst Chapl S Mk Sch Southborough MA 1980-1984; St. Mk's Sch of Southborough Inc. Southborough MA 1980-1981; Trin-Pawling Sch Pawling NY 1973-1980; Asst Chapl Trin-Pawling Sch Pawling NY 1973-1980. Auth, *Ch of the Dio Massachusetts*, 1983.

WYLD, Kevin Andrew (CFla) 3440 N Goldenrod Rd Apt 1016, Winter Park FL 32792 B Bishop Auckland Durham UK 1958 s Albert & Margaret. MA Oxf GB; BA Oxf GB 1979; MS U of Durham GB 1981; BD U of Edinburgh Edinburgh Gb 1985. Trans 7/24/2000 Bp John Wadsworth Howe. R S Richard's Ch Winter Pk FL 2000-2004; Serv Ch Of Engl 1987-2000.

WYLIE, Craig Robert (SwVa) 170 Crestview Dr, Abingdon VA 24210 B East Grand Rapids MI 1948 s Robert & Peggy Ann. BA Shimer Coll 1970; MDiv SWTS 1974; MEd and Admin U of Texas El Paso 1983; DMin SWTS 2009. D 6/22/1974 Bp Charles Bennison Sr P 5/14/1975 Bp Iveson Batchelor Noland. m 8/22/1970 Judith Swanson c 2. P-in-c Emm Epis Ch Bristol VA 2012-2014; R S Thos' Epis Ch Abingdon VA 2002-2011; R Trin Epis Ch Cranford NJ 1995-2002; Int S Jas Hse Of Pryr Tampa FL 1994-1995; Headmaster S Mary's Par Tampa FL 1991-1994; P-in-c Bethany Ch Hilliard FL 1990-1991; Headmaster S Paul's By-The-Sea Epis Ch Jaxville Bch FL 1988-1991; Headmaster Chr Epis Sch Covington LA 1984-1988; Assoc R Chr Ch Covington LA 1983-1988; Int Ch Of The Gd Shpd Forrest City AR 1982-1983; Headmaster H Cross Epis Sch W Memphis AR 1982-1983; Headmaster S Clem's Epis Par Sch El Paso TX 1978-1982; Chapl S Mart's Epis Sch Metairie LA 1974-1978; Dio SW Virginia Roanoke VA 2003-2007.

WYMAN, Deborah Little (Mass) 986 Memorial Dr, Cambridge MA 02138 **Fndr and Mssnr Ecclesia Mnstrs 2005-** B Miami FL 1945 d Thomas & Helen. BA Chatham Coll 1967; MA Bos 1979; MDiv GTS 1994; DMin EDS 2000. D 6/4/1994 Bp David Elliot Johnson P 10/14/1995 Bp Barbara Clementine Harris. Ecclesia Mnstrs Boston MA 2004-2011; The Cathd Ch Of S Paul Boston MA 1995-2003; Trin Epis Ch So Boston VA 1995-1996. "Theol of the Poor," *Handbook on U.S. Theologies of Liberation*, Chalice Press, 2004; Auth, "Hm Care for the Dying," Dial/Doubleday, 1985.

WYMAN, Irma Marian (Minn) 1840 University Ave W Apt 411, Saint Paul MN 55104 **Died 11/17/2015** B Detroit MI 1928 d Max & Marie. BSE U MI 1949. D 6/28/1990 Bp Sanford Zangwill Kaye Hampton. Archd Dio Minnesota Minneapolis MN 1998-2009, Dio Dn Coun 1992-1997; D Geth Ch Minneapolis MN 1995-2002; D S Mary's Ch S Paul MN 1990-1992. SCHC 1979.

WYNDER JR, Charles Allen (Mass) **Ch Of The H Comf Washington DC 2016-; Epis Ch Cntr New York NY 2016-** B 1964 s Charles & Carrie. BA Syr 1986; JD U MI Law Sch 1989; MDiv EDS 2012. D 6/4/2016 Bp Alan Gates P 12/11/2016 Bp Mariann Edgar Budde. m 7/18/2009 Bethany Dickerson Wynder c 1. Other Lay Position Dom And Frgn Mssy Soc- Epis Ch Cntr New York NY 2014-2016.

WYNDHAM, Beth Ann (WTex) St Thomas Episcopal Church, 1416 N Loop 1604 E, San Antonio TX 78232 **S Thos Epis Ch And Sch San Antonio TX 2013-** B Ankara Turkey 1970 d Richard & Dorothy. BAS Dallas Bapt U 2007; MDiv Epis TS of the SW 2010. D 6/5/2010 Bp James Monte Stanton P 4/14/2011 Bp Paul Emil Lambert. m 8/15/1993 Jeremy J Wyndham c 2. The Par Epis Sch Dallas TX 2010-2012.

WYNEN, Nancy Hartmeyer (Oly) 1399 Sw 17th St, Boca Raton FL 33486 **Vic Gr Ch Lopez Island WA 2012-; Sprtl Dir Dio SE Florida 2007-; Bd Mem Jas L Duncan Conf Cntr Delray Bch FL 2008-** B Teaneck NJ 1946 d Walter & Marjorie. BA U of Massachusetts 1968; MLS Rutgers The St U of New Jersey 1973; MA Florida Atlantic U 1991; MDiv GTS 2005. D 4/17/2005 P 12/10/2005 Bp Leo Frade. m 12/6/1969 Alfons C Wynen c 1. P-in-c S Mary's Epis Ch Of Deerfield Deerfield Bch FL 2010-2011; Cler Asst H Trin Epis Ch W Palm Bch FL 2006-2009. Auth, "Journey Through Adv," *Skiturgies*, Ch Pub Grp, 2011.

WYNN, James E (Pa) 520 S 61st St, Philadelphia PA 19143 **Vic S Geo S Barn Ch Philadelphia PA 1996-** B Wilkes-Barre PA 1945 s Melvin & Ella. BA Wilkes Coll 1969; MDiv PDS 1973. D 6/7/1973 P 6/27/1974 Bp Lloyd Edward Gressle. m 9/24/1977 Jacqueline Wynn c 2. Dio Pennsylvania Philadelphia PA 1996-2009; S Aug's Epis Ch Asbury Pk NJ 1995-1996; Trin Cathd Trenton NJ 1984-1995; Dio New Jersey Trenton NJ 1981-1989; R S Aug's Ch Camden NJ 1976-1981; Asst S Lk's Epis Ch Bronx NY 1974-1975; Dio Bethlehem Bethlehem PA 1974. Hon Cn Trin Cathd 1982.

WYNN, Ronald Lloyd (Ore) 355 Stadium Dr S, Monmouth OR 97361 **D S Hilda's Ch Monmouth OR 2003-** B Farmington NM 1928 BA Highland U Las Vegas NM 1950; MA U CO 1956; PhD U CO 1969. D 10/4/2003 Bp Johncy Itty. m 9/9/1950 Marilyn Jean Engblom c 6.

WYPER, Susan (Ct) St Matthew's Episcopal Church, 382 Cantitoe st, Bedford NY 10506 **S Lk's Par Darien CT 2016-** B New Haven, CT 1962 d Robert & Patricia. BA Ya 1984; MA Mid VT 1989; MDiv Ya Berk 2008. D 6/9/2007 P 12/15/2007 Bp Andrew Donnan Smith. m 11/24/1984 George U Wyper c 3. Assoc R S Matt's Ch Bedford NY 2007-2016.

WYSOCK, Christine Phillips (Spok) 535 Shelokum Dr, Silverton OR 97381 **Rn Mgr Yakima Vlly Farm Workers Clnc Toppenish WA 1995-** B Yakima WA 1948 d Roy & Margaret. Heritage Coll Toppenish WA; ADN Yakima Vlly Coll 1990. D 4/14/1999 Bp Cabell Tennis P 10/16/1999 Bp John Stuart Thornton. m 12/3/1994 John Rodney Wysock c 3.

WYSONG, Terry Marie (Ct) PO Box 606, Marion CT 06444 B Galveston TX 1945 d George & Jeanette. BS U IL 1967; MDiv Ya Berk 1994. D 6/10/1995 P 1/12/1996 Bp Clarence Nicholas Coleridge. m 9/6/1969 Bryan Wysong c 4. R S Paul's Ch Southington CT 2002-2007; Int All SS Epis Ch Oakville CT 2001-2002; Grtr Waterbury Mnstry Waterbury CT 2000-2001; Asst Int Mssnr Grtr Waterbury Epis Mnstrs CT 1999-2001; Asst S Jas's Ch W Hartford CT 1995-1999.

X

XIE, Songling (LI) 13532 38th Ave, Flushing NY 11354 **Assoc R S Geo's Par Flushing NY 2012-, Cur 2006-** B Shanghai China 1951 s Jiliang & Jinxia. MB Nantong Med Coll CN 1978; MA Ashland TS 2002; MA GTS 2004. D 1/24/2006 Bp Rodney Rae Michel P 10/28/2006 Bp Orris George Walker Jr. m 7/23/1979 Aner Wu c 1.

Y

YABROFF, Martin I Rving (Oly) 3914 136th St Ct NW, Gig Harbor WA 98332 **R S Andr's Epis Ch Tacoma WA 2007-** B San Mateo CA 1956 s Irving & Esther. BA U CA 1978; MDiv Bos TS 1982. D 12/9/1984 P 10/6/1985 Bp Charles Shannon Mallory. m 6/14/1980 Eve M Armitage c 6. Dep Gc Dio Nthrn Indiana So Bend IN 2006-2007, Stndg Com 2005, Dep Gc 2006-2007; Mem HOD Com on the St of the Ch 2006-2007; Dn The Cathd Ch Of S Jas So Bend IN 2004-2007; Vic S Phil The Apos Scotts Vlly CA 1987-2004; Assoc Ch of S Mary's by the Sea Pacific Grove CA 1985-1987; Dioc Coun Dio Olympia Seattle 2007-2013; Dep Gc Dio El Camino Real Salinas CA 1991-1997. Auth, "Regular Contrib To Loc Newspapers". yabroff@net-venture.com

YAGERMAN, Steven Jay (NY) 234 E 60th St, New York NY 10022 **R All SS Ch New York NY 1993-; 1986-; Com 1985-; Trst Cathd Of St Jn The Div New York NY 1990-** B Miami FL 1954 s George & Betty. GTS; BA U of Florida 1975; MDiv Gordon-Conwell TS 1979; CAS GTS 1981; DMin Hebr Un Coll 1997. D 5/31/1981 P 11/1/1981 Bp Calvin Onderdonk Schofield Jr. m 10/8/2008 Suzanne D Mercier c 4. R All SS' Epis Ch Briarcliff NY 1984-1993; Asst S Greg's Ch Boca Raton FL 1981-1983; Serv Presb TS 1979-1980.

YAKUBUA-MADUS, Fatima Emitsela (Ind) 5625 W 30th St, Speedway IN 46224 B Auchi Nigeria 1956 d Yakubu & Aja. BS Kentucky St U 1982; MSC U of Mississippi 1985. D 10/23/2010 Bp Cate Waynick. c 2.

YALE, Elizabeth (NwPa) 1151 Buffalo St, Franklin PA 16323 **P-in-c S Jn's Ch Franklin PA 2016-; Cur H Sprt Epis Ch Houston TX 2014-** B Red Bank NJ 1989 d William & Carol. BA Alleg 2011; MDiv Sewanee: The U So, TS 2014. D 3/2/2014 Bp Sean Walter Rowe P 1/17/2015 Bp C Andrew Doyle. motherelizabeth@stjohnsfranklin.org

YALE, Richard Barrington (NCal) 4 Quista Dr., Chico CA 95926 **R S Jn The Evang Ch Chico CA 1997-; Human Subjects Resrch Com, Mem California St U Chico Chico 2006-; Instnl Revs Bd, Mem Enloe Hosp Chico California 2001-** B Otsu Japan 1957 s Theodore & Elizabeth. DMin Fuller TS; Pasadena City Coll; BA Westmont Coll 1979; MDiv CDSP 1985. D 6/15/1985 Bp Robert Claflin Rusack P 1/1/1986 Bp Oliver Bailey Garver Jr. m 8/28/1982 Linda J Yale c 3. The Epis Dio Nthrn California Sacramento CA 1997, Chair, Open Comm T/F 2004-2006, Dn, Superior California Dnry 2003-2007, Cmsn on Liturg and Mus 1997-2008; Vic S Paul's Mssn Cres City CA 1994-1996; Int S Lk's Epis Ch Monrovia CA 1993-1994; Assoc Ch Of Our Sav Par San Gabr CA 1987-1994; Ecum Cmsn Dio Los Angeles Los Angeles CA 1987-1994; Cur S Geo's Epis Ch Laguna Hills CA 1985-1987; Pres Interfaith Coun Chico California 2005-2006.

X

YAMAMOTO, Keith Akio (Los) 330 E. 16th Street, Upland CA 91784 **R S Mk's Epis Ch Upland CA 2009-, Asst 1997-2001** B Los Angeles CA 1967 s Clarence & Maxine. BA U CA Santa Cruz 1990; MDiv GTS 1997. D 6/7/1997 Bp Artemio M Zabala P 1/17/1998 Bp Frederick Houk Borsch. m 5/30/1998 Patricia Susanne McCaughan. Assoc S Marg Of Scotland Par San Juan Capo CA 2001-2009. kyamamoto@stmarks-upland.org

YANCEY, David Warren (Tenn) 1390 Jones Creek Rd, Dickson TN 37055 B Lubbock TX 1951 s Warren & Betty. BA Shimer Coll 1973; MDiv Nash 1980; MS Van 1992. D 6/11/1980 Bp William Cockburn Russell Sheridan P 12/17/1980 Bp Duncan Montgomery Gray Jr. m 10/17/1992 Ellen M Lloyd. P-in-c S Andr's Epis Ch New Johnsonville TN 1999-2008; Dir & Nurse Practitioner Macon Cnty Gnrl Hosp Clnc 1994-1997; Ecum Off Dio Wstrn Massachusetts Springfield 1986-1990, 1982-1990; Gr Ch Dalton MA 1982-1984; S Mich's Campus Picayune MS 1980-1982; Non-par; Hon Assoc S Barth's Ch Nashville TN 1991-1997. Sigma Theta Tau.

YANCEY, Nancy Rollins (At) 5480 Clinchfield Trl, Norcross GA 30092 **CEO Rainbow Vill Inc Duluth GA 2009-** B Atlanta GA 1952 d Royston & Geneva. D 10/18/1998 Bp Onell Asiselo Soto. m 11/19/1971 Charles Yancey c 3. D Chr Ch Norcross GA 1998-2009. nyancey@comcast.net

YANCY, Stephanie Pauline (NC) 5606 Carey Pl, Durham NC 27712 **R S Tit Epis Ch Durham NC 2015-** B Nassau Bahamas 1951 d John & Coral. BA Cor 1972; MDiv GTS 2006. D 6/24/2006 Bp John L Rabb P 1/20/2007 Bp Robert Wilkes Ihloff. m 6/3/1972 Joseph C Yancy c 2. Dio No Carolina Raleigh NC 2015; Int S Lk's Epis Ch Durham NC 2013-2014; Int S Geo Ch Hampstead MD 2011-2012; Int Trin Ch Towson MD 2010-2011; Int S Jn's Par Hagerstown MD 2006-2010; Asst R S Jn's Par Hagerstown MD 2006-2008. st.titusvicar@gmail.com

YANDELL, George Shaw (At) Church of the Holy Family, 202 Griffith Rd, Jasper GA 30143 **R Epis Ch Of The H Fam Jasper GA 2010-** B Mobile AL 1953 s William & Winifred. BA Emory U 1975; MDiv VTS 1979. D 7/1/1979 Bp William Evan Sanders P 5/4/1980 Bp William F Gates Jr. m 10/9/1999 Susan Burnett Rowland c 2. Assoc to the R Calv Ch Memphis TN 2002-2010; Supply Cler Calv Ch Osceola AK 1999-2002; Dioc Fin Com Gd Shpd Epis Ch Dallas TX 1995-1997; Dioc Exec Coun Gd Shpd Epis Ch Dallas 1994-1997; R Ch Of The Gd Shpd Dallas TX 1992-1997; Ch Of The H Comm Memphis TN 1985-1992, D 1979-1980; R S Jas The Less Madison TN 1984-1985; R S Jas the Less Nashville TN 1984-1985; Vic S Jas the Less Nashville TN 1980-1984; Dio Tennessee Nashville TN 1980-1983. Auth, "150 Days- Engaging Students in Epis Campus Mnstrs," Dio W Tennessee, 2007; Auth, "Comm of the Absent," *Angl Dig*, Calv Epis Ch, 2007; Auth, "Ch Builds Hse, Hse Builds Ch," *Dallas Morning News*, Dallas Morning News, 1996; Auth, "SCI Comes of Age," *Sthrn Communities Journ*, Sthrn Communities Journ, 1990. georgeholyfam@etcmail.com

YANG CHOU, Yun-Kuang (Tai) St. Mark, 120-11 Chung Hsiao Road, Ping Tung 900 Taiwan B Fukien TW 1940 BD H Light Sem Kaihsiung CN 1993. D 1/25/2002 Bp Jung-Hsin Lai. m 6/7/1964 Jun-shen Yang c 4. Dio Taiwan Taipei 2008-2011, 2002-2005.

YANNI, Timothy John (U) 9447 S 2555 W, South Jordan UT 84095 **Asstg Cler Epis Cmnty Serv Inc Salt Lake City UT 2016-; Asstg Cler S Mary's Ch Provo UT 2016-** B 1982 s John & Gladys. M Div. CDSP 2016. D 6/16/2016 P 12/17/2016 Bp Scott Byron Hayashi.

YAO, Ting Chang (Cal) 1111 Larch Ave, Moraga CA 94556 **Assoc S Anselm's Epis Ch Lafayette CA 1990-** B 1923 s K S & Mildred. BS S Jn U CN 1946; MS Utah St U 1949. D 6/19/1966 Bp James Albert Pike P 1/1/1970 Bp Chauncie Kilmer Myers. m 4/17/1984 Joan Lok c 5. Vic S Giles Ch Moraga CA 1970-1976; Asst S Giles Epis Ch Morage CA 1966-1970.

YARBOROUGH, Buzz (WTex) 121 Peppertree Crossing Ave, Brunswick GA 31525 **Vic St Richard's Of Chichester Epis Mssn Jekyll Island GA 2015-** B Miami FL 1939 s Jesse & Louise. BS Clemson U 1963; MDiv Sewanee: The U So, TS 1978. D 6/24/1978 P 1/21/1979 Bp William Gillette Weinhauer. m 11/30/1963 Kathryne Manheim. Int Chr Ch Monticello FL 2010-2012; Assoc Chr Ch Frederica St Simons Is GA 2006-2010; R Epis Ch Of The Mssh Gonzales TX 1999-2005; R Chr Epis Ch Little Rock AR 1989-1999; R S Mk's Ch Brunswick GA 1981-1989; Asst S Ptr's by-the-Sea Epis Ch Bay Shore NY 1978-1981.

YARBOROUGH, Clare McJimsey (Az) 5671 E. Copper Street, Tucson AZ 85712 **S Mich's and All Ang Day Sch Tucson AZ 2012-; P Epis Par Of S Mich And All Ang Tucson AZ 2011-** B Austin TX 1957 d Richard & Ann. BA Ob 1979; MA U of Arizona 1983; PhD U of Arizona 1993; MDiv EDS 1996. D 6/15/1996 Bp Robert Reed Shahan P 1/4/1997 Bp William George Burrill. m 9/8/2007 Laurie Louise Chase. Assoc S Phil's In The Hills Tucson AZ 2009-2011; R Trin Epis Ch Weymouth MA 2004-2009; P-in-c Ch Of Our Sav Somerset MA 2000-2004; Cur S Paul's Ch Rochester NY 1996-2000.

YARBROUGH, C Denise (Roch) St. Mark's Episcopal Church, 179 Main St., Penn Yan NY 14527 **S Ptr's Epis Ch Bloomfield NY 2012-; Cn Dio Rochester Henrietta 2011-, 2008-2010; Adj Prof. Theol Bex Sem Rochester NY 2005-; Fac Assoc Colgate Rochester Crozer DS Rochester NY 2005-** B Tulsa OK 1956 d John & Eileen. BA Barnard Coll of Col 1978; JD U MI 1982; MDiv PrTS 1997; DMin PrTS 2006. Trans 9/16/2003 Bp John Palmer Croneberger. c 2. Gr Ch Lyons NY 2011-2012; S Jn's Ch Sodus NY 2011-2012; S Mk's Ch Newark NY 2011-2012; Ch Of The Ascen Rochester NY 2010-2011; R S Mk's Epis Ch Penn Yan NY 2003-2008; R Ch Of The Trsfg Towaco NJ 1999-2003; Asst Trin Ch Toledo OH 1997-1999. "Many Faces of God," *Interfaith Educ Resource*, LeaderResources, 2006; "Apocalyptic Living," *Sermons That Wk*, Morehouse Pub, 2006; Auth, "Giving Birth to God," *Sermons That Wk*, Morehouse Pub, 2001; Auth, "Toil for Joy," *Sermons That Wk*, Morehouse Pub, 2000; Auth, "Fragments of Our Lives," *Sermons That Wk*, Morehouse Pub, 1999. OHC 1998. Phi Beta Kappa.

YARBROUGH, Douglas Wayne (Ida) 1312 W Elmore Ave, Nampa ID 83651 B Denver CO 1952 s Donald & Rowena. MA Acadia U; MA Rockmont Coll; EdD Texas Tech U 1986; MA Iliff TS 1998. D 6/17/1995 P 12/1/1995 Bp John Stuart Thornton. m 6/24/1995 Eileen Elizabeth O'Shea c 2. R Gr Epis Ch Nampa ID 1997-2004; Mtn Rivers Epis Cmnty Idaho Falls ID 1995-1997. Auth, "Educ & Educational Psychol". Atty Gnrl'S Victim Assistance Awd.

YARBROUGH, Eileen Elizabeth (Ida) 524 Ruth Ln, Nampa ID 83686 **D S Steph's Boise ID 2009-** B Cardston AB CA 1955 d Thomas & Elsie. BS Idaho St U 1980; MEd Idaho St U 1982. D 12/16/1995 Bp John Stuart Thornton. m 6/24/1995 Douglas Wayne Yarbrough c 1. D Gr Epis Ch Nampa ID 1997-2005; Archedeacon Dio Idaho 1997-2004; D Trin 1997. Dok.

YARBROUGH, Oliver Larry (Vt) 24 Oak Dr, Middlebury VT 05753 **Prof Mid VT 1983-** B Tuscaloosa AL 1949 s Farris & Nancy. BA Birmingham-Sthrn Coll 1972; MA U of Cambridge 1974; MDiv Candler TS Emory U 1975; PhD Ya 1984. D 8/13/2000 Bp Mary Adelia Rosamond Mcleod P 3/25/2001 Bp Craig Barry Anderson. m 7/17/1976 Amy Hastings c 2. Auth, "Early Chr Jerusalem: The City of the Cross," *Jerusalem: Idea and Reality*, Routledge, 2008; Auth, "Mar and Divorce," *Paul in the Greco-Roman Wrld*, Trin Press Intl , 2003; Co-Ed, "The Soc Wrld of Paul," Fortress, 1995; Auth, "Parents and Chld in the Jewish Fam of Antiquity," *The Jewish Fam in Antiquity*, Scholars Press, 1993; Auth, "Not Like the Gentiles: Mar Rules in the Letters of Paul," Scholars Press, 1985.

YARBROUGH, Rebecca Ricketts (NC) P.O. Box 970, Davidson NC 28036 **Dio No Carolina Raleigh NC 2015-; S Alb's Ch Davidson NC 2015-** B Charlotte NC 1953 d Edgar & Hilde. BA Queens Coll 1975. D 6/14/2008 Bp Michael B Curry. m 9/20/1975 David Yarbrough c 2.

YARSIAH, James T (SC) 1324 Marvin Ave, Charleston SC 29407 **Voorhees Coll Charleston SC 2011-** B Liberia 1965 s John & Sobondo. TS Sewanee; BA Cuttington U 1999. Trans 5/7/2006 Bp Edward Lloyd Salmon Jr. m 5/9/2000 Ophelia Yarsiah c 4. St Andr's Mssn Charleston SC 2004-2011; Dio Liberia Monrovia 1998-2004. jtyarsiah@gmail.com

YATES, Adam Benjamin (Ct) 23 Parker Bridge Rd, Andover CT 06232 **Secy of Conv Dio Connecticut Meriden CT 2012-; R S Steph's Ch E Haddam CT 2012-** B Bethesda MD 1985 s Benjamin & Lisa. BS Northland Coll 2007; MDiv Chicago TS 2010. D 6/5/2010 Bp Jeff Lee P 1/6/2011 Bp Ian Theodore Douglas. Assoc. for Mem Incorporation Par of St Paul's Ch Norwalk Norwalk CT 2010-2012. adam@ststeves.org

YATES, Christopher Garrett 1066 Washington Rd, Mt Lebanon PA 15228 B Birmingham AL 1988 s Chris & Lynn. BA Sanford U 2011; MDiv Pittsburgh TS 2015. P 3/19/2016 Bp Dorsey McConnell. m 3/21/2015 Katharine Campbell. Other Lay Position S Paul's Epis Ch Pittsburgh PA 2015. garrett@stpaulspgh.org

YATES, Dorothy Gene (Cal) B 1938 d Mckinley & Odessa. AA San Francisco City Coll; BSW San Francisco St U; BTS The Sch for Deacons. D 12/1/2012 Bp Marc Handley Andrus.

YATES, Robert Gordon (SwFla) 37505 Moore Dr, Dade City FL 33525 B Louisville KY 1939 s Robert & Emma. BA California St U 1968; Cert D Formation Prog 1995. D 6/24/1995 Bp Telesforo A Isaac. m 12/4/1964 Linda Kay Yates c 4.

YATES, William J (CFla) 3400 Wingmann Rd., Avon Park FL 33825 **Dir Camp Wingmann Avon Pk FL 1998-** B Chickasha OK 1951 s George & Helen. BA Florida Sthrn Coll 1974; MDiv Sewanee: The U So, TS 1984. D 6/29/1984 Bp William Hopkins Folwell P 1/6/1985 Bp Frank S Cerveny. m 5/6/1972 Joan E Gast c 2. P-in-c The Epis Ch Of The Redeem Avon Pk FL 2000-2001; Camp Wingmann Avon Pk FL 1998-2014; Cn to Ordnry Dio Florida Jacksonville 1995-1998; R Chr Ch Monticello FL 1988-1994; Asst Ch Of The Adv Tallahassee FL 1984-1988.

YAW, Chris (Mich) St David's Episcopal Church, 16200 W 12 Mile Rd, Southfield MI 48076 **R S Dav's Ch Southfield MI 2007-** B Detroit MI 1962 s James & Nancy. BS JCU 1984; MDiv Fuller TS 1997; ThM Fuller TS 2000. D 6/16/2001 Bp Chester Lovelle Talton P 1/12/2002 Bp Frederick Houk Borsch. m 8/23/2003 Natlie Lynn Yaw. Assoc S Thos Epis Ch Battle Creek MI 2003-2007; Asst S Thos Epis Ch Battle Creek MI 2001-2007. Fndr, "Grow My Ch!," www.growmychurch.com, Grow My Ch!, 2011; Auth, "Through a Mirror Dimly," www.chrisyaw.com, Personal Blog, 2009; Co-Auth, "The Epis Handbook," *Bk*, Ch Pub, 2008; Auth, "Jesus Was an Epis (and you can be one too!),"

Bk, LeaderResources, 2007; Auth, "Epis Ch Names," *The Chr Century*, The Chr Century, 2004; Auth, "Clearing Your Thanksgiving Plate," *LivCh*, LivCh Fndt, 2002; Auth, "Holidays and Holiness," *LivCh*, LivCh Fndt, 2001. BroSA 2002-2003.

YAW, David Dixon (Ak) 3195 Jackson Heights St, Ketchikan AK 99901 **R S Jn's Ch Ketchikan AK 2010-** B Logan OH 1947 s Owen & Margaret. BS Ohio U 1969; MDiv EDS 1978; New Engl Dss Hosp 1987. D 12/3/1978 P 6/30/1979 Bp John Mc Gill Krumm. m 10/7/1967 Marily Yaw c 1. Chapl Howe Mltry Sch Howe IN 2000-2010; R/Chapl Howe Mltry Sch Howe IN 2000-2010; S Mk's Par Howe IN 2000-2010; Chapl Randolph Macom Acad Front Royal VA 1997-2000; Chapl S Jn's Mltry Acad Delafield WI 1993-1997; Chapl St. Jn's Mltry Acad Delafield WI 1993-1997; R Trin Ch Moundsville WV 1991-1993; Dio Sthrn Ohio Cincinnati OH 1989-1990; Int S Jn's Epis Ch Lancaster OH 1988-1989; H Trin Epis Ch In Countryside Clearwater FL 1985-1986; H Trin Epis Ch W Palm Bch FL 1985-1986; Vic Trin Epis Ch Palm Harbor FL 1985-1986; Cur Ch Of The Ascen Clearwater FL 1982-1984; P-in-c Ch Of The Ascen Donaldsonvlle LA 1980-1982; Chapl Epis HS Baton Rouge Baton Rouge LA 1979-1982; Middle Sch Chapl Epis HS Baton Rouge LA 1979-1982; D Chr Ch Cathd Cincinnati OH 1979.

YAWN, Justin (Tex) Christ Episcopal Church, 400 San Juan Dr, Ponte Vedra Beach FL 32082 **Chr Epis Ch Temple TX 2015-** B Atlanta GA 1985 s Gary & Marilyn. BBA U GA 2007; MDiv Candler TS Emory U 2010. D 2/6/2010 P 8/21/2010 Bp Scott Anson Benhase. m 12/9/2011 Vanessa T Yawn. Chr Epis Ch Ponte Vedra FL 2012-2015; Assoc R Trin Ch Statesboro GA 2010-2012.

YEAGER, Alice Elizabeth (ND) 301 Main St S, Minot ND 58701 B Davenport IA 1945 d Carl & Elizabeth. D 7/23/2010 Bp Michael Smith. c 2.

YEAGER, Linda (WMo) 11701 Wedd St Apt 9, Overland Park KS 66210 B Kansas City MO 1941 d Russell & Martha. BA Truman St U 1980; MA Truman St U 1984. D 2/4/1995 Bp John Clark Buchanan. m 6/10/1961 Jon Gordon Yeager c 3. Assoc Chapl Bp Spencer Place Kansas City MO 2007-2014; St Ptr & All SS Epis Ch Kansas City MO 2007-2011; Assoc Bp Spencer Place Inc Kansas City MO 2006-2014; D Gr & H Trin Cathd 1998-2006; Assoc Chapl Bp Spencer Place Kansas City MO 1998-2000; D NE Rgnl Mnstry Trenton MO 1995-1998.

YEAGER, Robert Timothy (Chi) 924 Lake Street, Oak Park IL 60301 **Secy EPF 2010-; Strng Com Mem The Consult 2007-; Fin Secy/Treas Untd Auto Workers Loc Un 2320 1991-** B Charles City IA 1950 s Robert & Bernadine. BA U of Iowa 1972; JD U of Iowa 1977. D 12/22/2010 P 8/26/2011 Bp Jeff Lee. m 6/19/1999 Sarah Moores c 1. Chairperson Peace & Justice Com Dio Chicago 2006-2010. EPF 2001. Hugh White Trumpet of Justice Awd Epis Ntwk for Econ Justice 2011; Hugh White Trumpet of Justice Awd Epis Ntwk for Econ Justice 2011.

YEARWOOD, Kirtley (Oly) Church Of Saint Alban The Martyr, 11642 Farmers Blvd, Saint Albans NY 11412 **S Edw's Epis Ch Lawrenceville GA 2016-** B BB 1961 s Herman & Joyce. BS Tuskegee Inst 1983; MPH U of Oklahoma Hlth Sciences Cntr 1988; MD U of Arkansas for Med Sciences 1993; MDiv GTS 1998; STM GTS 1999. Trans 5/31/1998 Bp Herbert Alcorn Donovan Jr. Int Ch Of S Alb The Mtyr S Albans NY 2012-2016; Int S Andr's Epis Ch Lawton OK 2010-2011; P-in-c S Clem's Epis Ch Seattle WA 2009-2010; Vic Gr Ch Cathd Charleston SC 2007-2008; Fell Med U of So Carolina Charleston SC 2006-2007; Fell Magee-Womens Hosp of UMPC Pittsburgh PA 2004-2005; Res Physcn GW Med Cntr Washington DC 2002-2004; R S Mary's Epis Ch Foggy Bottom Washington DC 2000-2003; Cur Trin Cathd Little Rock AR 1998-1999; Ch Of The Trsfg New York NY 1997-1998; Chapl Asst The GTS New York NY 1997-1998; Res Physcn GW Med Cntr Washington DC 1993-1995; Consult, Seeing the Word, The S Jn's Bible S Jn's Abbey & U Collegeville Minnesota 2011-2012; Cmsn on Ch Archit Dio Olympia Seattle 2009-2011, Dioc Cmsn on Ch Archit 2009-2011; Bd Mem, Dominican Dvlpmt Grp 2008-2011; Dominican Dvlpmt Grp Dio The Dominican Republic (Iglesia Epis Dominicana) Gazcue Santo Domingo 2008-2011; Dioc Coun Dio Washington Washington DC 2002, Com on Ch Archit 2001-2003, Dioc Com on Liturg and Mus 2001-2003, Consecration Com for VIIIth Bp of Washington 2001-2002, Dioc Coun 2001-2002. Comp of the Cmnty of the Resurr (CCR) 2014; Soc for Liturg Study 2012; The Alcuin Club 2011.

YEATES, Judith Ann (Neb) 6615 N 162 St, Omaha NE 68116 B Oklahoma City OK 1950 d Russell & Mary. BS Dana Coll 1995; MA Creighton U 1998; MDiv Nash 1999. D 4/29/1998 P 11/1/1998 Bp James Edward Krotz. m 7/18/1987 James Yeates c 1. Int All SS Epis Ch Omaha NE 2014-2015, 1998-2002, 1995-1998; Cn to the Ordnry Dio Nebraska Omaha NE 2008-2014; Stndg Com Pres 2004-2008, Dioc Secy 2007-, GC Dep 2006-, Secy to Exec Cmsn 2005-; R Ch Of The Resurr Omaha NE 2002-2008. Doctorate of Div Providence Theol Schoo 2009. motherjudi@earthlink.net

YEOMAN III, Eric Burdett (Cal) 1633 Argonne Dr, Stockton CA 95203 B Martinez CA 1926 s Eric & Florence. CDSP; Dominican Coll; New Mex St U 1960; BA U CA 1961; MS U of Oregon 1964; Sonoma St U 1977. D 12/24/1961 Bp James Albert Pike P 6/1/1975 Bp Chauncie Kilmer Myers. m 6/27/1948 Norma Evelyn Wagner. Vol P Epis Ch Of S Anne Stockton CA 1983-2008; P-in-c No

Stockton Mssn 1980-1984; Asst S Jn's Epis Ch Stockton CA 1978-1989; Asst S Jn's Epis Ch Clayton CA 1962-1977; Asst Ch Of The Resurr Pleasant Hil CA 1961-1977. OHC.

YEPES LOPEZ, Alvaro Nelson (DR) Iglesia Episcopal Dominicana, Calle Santiago No 114, Santo Domingo 764 Dominican Republic **Dio The Dominican Republic (Iglesia Epis Dominicana) Gazcue Santo Domingo 2007-** B 1966 D 2/12/2006 Bp Julio Cesar Holguin-Khoury. m 1/21/2006 Angela Maria Maria Pulido Pulido-Giraldo.

YERKES, Kenneth Bickford (Mo) 1 Macarthur Blvd Apt S503, Haddon Township NJ 08108 **Asstg P Chr Ch Magnolia NJ 2010-; Ret 2001-** B Philadelphia PA 1934 s Horace & Esther. BA Tem 1956; MDiv PrTS 1960; Cert GTS 1985. D 6/15/1985 Bp Lyman Cunningham Ogilby P 10/18/1985 Bp William Augustus Jones Jr. Int S Paul's Epis Ch Sikeston MO 1999-2001; Int H Cross Epis Ch Poplar Bluff MO 1998-1999; Int S Paul's Ch Kankakee IL 1997-1998; Int Chr Ch Rolla MO 1996-1997; Int S Lk's Epis Ch Manchester MO 1995-1996; Chapl S Lk's Hosp Chesterfield MO 1993-1994; Vic Trin Epis Ch Kirksville MO 1985-1993; Serv Presb Ch 1958-1983. ACPE 1993-2001.

YESKO, Francis Michael (Pgh) Episcopal Diocese Of Pittsburgh, 4099 William Penn Hwy Ste 502, Monroeville PA 15146 B Braddock PA 1957 s Frank & Mary. BS Juniata Coll 1981; MEd Penn 1995; EdD Duquesne U 2004. D 6/15/2013 P 1/17/2015 Bp Dorsey McConnell. c 1.

YETTER, Joan (Mont) 932 Avenue F, Billings MT 59102 B Billings MT 1947 d Clyde & Nina. U Denv 1967; BS Montana St U 1971; Claremont TS 1996; MDiv CDSP 1998. D 6/20/1998 Bp Paul Marshall Anderson P 1/3/1999 Bp Leigh Allen Wallace Jr. m 6/29/1969 Benjamin A Yetter c 3. R Calv Epis Ch Red Lodge MT 2010-2015; Int R All SS Ch Richland WA 2009-2010; Int Rectro St. Mich & All Ang Dio Oregon Portland OR 2007-2009; Int R Gr Ch Jefferson City MO 2005-2007; Int R Yellowstone Epis Mnstry Dio Montana Helena MT 2003-2005, Dioc Coun 2000-2002; Int P in Charge Our Sav's Epis Ch Joliet MT 2003-2005; S Alb's Epis Ch Laurel MT 2003-2005; Asst R Ch Of The H Sprt Missoula MT 1998-2003.

YODER, Christopher Wendell (Dal) Cur Ch Of The Incarn Dallas TX 2014- D 6/14/2014 P 6/6/2015 Bp Paul Emil Lambert.

YODER, John Henry (Nev) 1151 Carlton Ct Apt202, Fort Pierce FL 34949 **Ret 1999-** B Birdsboro PA 1936 s Stanley & Beatrice. BA California St U 1973; MDiv CDSP 1976. D 6/19/1976 P 1/15/1977 Bp Robert Claflin Rusack. R All SS Epis Ch Las Vegas NV 1981-1999; Asst St Cross Epis Ch Hermosa Bch CA 1980-1981; Serv Ch of Engl 1979-1980; Asst S Lk's Epis Ch Monrovia CA 1976-1979.

YON, William A(bbott) (Ala) 140 Whisenhunt Rd, Chelsea AL 35043 **Died 4/5/2016** B Knoxville TN 1931 s Terrell & Catherine. BA Emory U 1952; MDiv VTS 1955; VTS 1995. D 6/20/1955 Bp George Mosley Murray P 12/21/1955 Bp Randolph R Claiborne. c 4. Ret 1997-2016; Admin Asst Dio Alabama Birmingham 1990-1997, DCE 1963-1972; Assoc The Epis Ch Of S Fran Of Assisi Pelham AL 1988-1990; Exec Coun Appointees New York NY 1986-1990; Bp'S Asst For Educ Dio Namibia SW Afr 1985-1990; Prog Ntwk Coordntr Epis Urban Caucas 1980-1983; Ch Of The Trsfg Chelsea AL 1975-1983; R Trsfg Birmingham AL 1975-1983; ACC 1971-1975; Assoc DCE Dio No Carolina Raleigh NC 1960-1963; Yth Coordntr Of Prov Iv 1958-1963; S Alb's Ch Elberton GA 1955-1960; Vic S Andr's Ch Hartwell GA 1955-1960; Chair Of The Yth Div Dio Atlanta Atlanta GA 1957-1960. "No Trumpets-No Drums," *Postnet*, 2004; Auth, "On The Battle Lines"; Auth, "Prime Time For Renwl-Ptp"; Auth, "Lks Journ"; Auth, "To Build The City: Too Long A Dream Alb Inst/EUC". Apos in Stwdshp The Epis Ntwk for Stwdshp (TENS) 2003.

YONKERS, Michael Allan (Chi) 920 S Aldine Ave, Park Ridge IL 60068 **D S Mary 1991-** B Chicago IL 1950 s Joseph & Rita. BA S Johns U 1968; MA Loyola U 1976. D 12/7/1991 Bp Frank Tracy Griswold III. m 6/2/1973 Dianne Yonkers c 2.

YOON, Paul Hwan (Los) Box 22, Taejon 300 Korea (South) **Vic Annunc Anaheim CA 1982-** B Choong Joo KR 1938 s Chi & Ok. BA Soong Jun U 1962; ThD S Michaels Sem 1965. D 6/1/1966 P 7/1/1967 Bp The Bishop Of Taejon. m 1/11/1964 Susanna Eun Sook Yoon. Ch Of The Annunc Los Angeles CA 1982-1987; R S Mich's Sem Seoul Korea 1978-1981; Prof S Mich's Sem Seoul Korea 1974-1978.

YOON, Young Suk (Nwk) 150 Park Ave, Leonia NJ 07605 B Seoul South Korea 1981 s Ki & Jung. BS New Jersey Inst of Tech 2005; Grad Stds NYU 2007; MDiv/MA PrTS 2011. D 12/19/2015 P 6/18/2016 Bp Mark M Beckwith. m 2/22/2014 Sun Mee Sue.

YORK, Susan Spence (WMich) 2490 Basswood St, Jenison MI 49428 **Assoc S Mk's Ch Grand Rapids MI 2010-; Ch Of The H Sprt Livonia MI 2007-** B Akron OH 1943 d Lewis & Julianne. AA Grand Rapids Cmnty Coll; MDiv SWTS; BA U of Detroit Mercy. D 6/22/1996 P 1/1/1997 Bp Edward Lewis Lee Jr. m 8/22/1967 Roger York c 4. Vic Ch of the H Sprt Belmont MI 2006-2008; Dio Wstrn Michigan Kalamazoo MI 2003-2006; Dir Of Pstr Care Betterworth Hosp 1996-2007; S Andr's Ch Grand Rapids MI 1996-2003.

YORK-SIMMONS, Noelle M (Va) 118 N Washington St, Alexandria VA 22314 **Chr Ch Alexandria VA 2016-** B Atlanta GA 1976 DMin Candler TS

Emory U; BA Emory U 1999; DAS Ya Berk 2003; MDiv Yale DS 2003. D 12/6/2003 P 8/1/2004 Bp J Neil Alexander. m 8/2/2003 Kevin N York-Simmons c 2. Assoc R All SS Epis Ch Atlanta GA 2004-2016. rector@ccalex.org

YOSHIDA, Thomas Kunio (Haw) 1410 Makiki St, Honolulu HI 96814 **Ret 1995-** B Honolulu HI 1936 s Masao & Mitsuko. BS Marq 1959; MDiv CDSP 1962; Cert Amer Acad of Bereavement Tucson AZ 1997; Cert Amer Acad of Bereavement Mesa AZ 2001. D 6/9/1962 Bp George Richard Millard P 12/16/1962 Bp Harry Sherbourne Kennedy. m 8/8/1964 Winona Yoshida. Assoc P S Lk's Epis Ch Honolulu HI 2003-2013; Chapl Iolani Sch 1988-1995; Nonpar 1979-1995; S Alb's Chap Honolulu HI 1979-1995; Vic S Jn's Ch Eleele HI 1966-1969; Vic S Paul Kekaha HI 1966-1969; S Steph's Ch Wahiawa HI 1962-1979; All SS Ch Kapaa HI 1962-1966; Vic Chr Memi Ch Kilauea HI 1962-1966; St Thos Ch Hanalei HI 1962-1966. Auth, "Dioc Hospice/Bereavement & Palliative Care Resource Packet," 2000. Amer Acad Of Bereavement 1997-2001; AFP 1963-1972; Hospice Ntwk Hawaii 2000. Bp'S DSA Epis Ch In Hawaii 1969.

YOST, Martin C (Dal) 114 George Street, Providence RI 02906 **S Steph's Ch Providence RI 2015-** B Arlington MA 1964 s Paul & Eunice. BA Tufts U 1997; MDiv Nash 2002. D 12/6/2001 P 9/4/2002 Bp Keith Lynn Ackerman. c 6. Asstg P Ch Of The H Cross Dallas TX 2014; R S Steph's Epis Ch Sherman TX 2006-2014; Cur & Chapl to the Sch S Jn's Epis Ch Dallas TX 2002-2006; Trin Ch Milwaukee WI 2002. Auth, "The Paschal Lamb," Forw in Chr, FIFNA, 2011; Auth, "Why Mary Matters," Forw in Chr, FIFNA, 2010. GAS 2003; Soc of King Chas the Mtyr 1993; SocMary 1999; SSC 2006.

YOTTER, Katherine Ann (CFla) 6400 N Socrum Loop Rd, Lakeland FL 33809 B Newstead NY 1943 d John & Mildred. D 12/8/2012 Bp Gregory Orrin Brewer.

YOULL MARSHALL, Lynda Mary (Va) B Solihull, UK 1952 d Cyril & Doreen. BA De Montfort U 1974; MDiv Wycliffe Coll Toronto CA 2001. Trans 3/5/2014 Bp Shannon Sherwood Johnston. m 4/5/2008 Paul Marshall c 1. P S Jas' Epis Ch Warrenton VA 2014-2015; Asst Pohick Epis Ch Lorton VA 2009-2012.

YOUMANS, Timothy Sean (Okla) Casady School, 9500 N Pennsylvania Ave, Oklahoma City OK 73120 **Casady Sch Oklahoma City OK 2012-** B Newport RI 1968 s Charles & Mary Kathleen. BA Oklahoma Bapt U 1991; MDiv SW Bapt TS 1994; Angl Cert Nash 2011. D 3/14/2012 P 9/22/2012 Bp Edward Joseph Konieczny. m 12/19/1992 Karen DeMent Youmans c 1. Emm Epis Ch Shawnee OK 2009-2012.

YOUNG, Adam A (CFla) 2017 6th Ave N, Birmingham AL 35203 **Cathd Ch Of S Lk Orlando FL 2016-** B Zanesville Ohio 1978 s Gary & Connie. BA U GA 2001; MDiv Reformed TS 2007. D 5/5/2016 P 1/15/2017 Bp Gregory Orrin Brewer. m 12/6/2003 Mary E Young c 3. Cur The Cathd Ch Of The Adv Birmingham AL 2016. adam@cathedraladvent.org

YOUNG JR, Albert Leroy (Los) 1215 Del Mar Dr, Los Osos CA 93402 **Ret 1990-** B Torrance CA 1930 s Albert & Rose. BA Sthrn California Bible Coll 1952; BA U of Redlands 1955; MTh Claremont TS 1958; CDSP 1960. D 12/14/1960 P 7/1/1961 Bp Ivol I Curtis. m 8/11/1951 Janice B Young c 2. R The Par Ch Of S Lk Long Bch CA 1975-1990, Assoc 1967-1975; Asst Min S Mths' Par Whittier CA 1961-1967; Serv Congrl Ch 1955-1960.

YOUNG JR, Archibald Patterson (Dal) 617 Church St., Sulphur Springs TX 75482 **Assoc S Dunst's Ch Mineola TX 2013-** B Bryan TX 1937 s Archibald & Pauline. U of Texas at Arllington Tx; Lic Sacr Theol Angl TS 1978. D 6/24/1977 Bp Robert Elwin Terwilliger P 3/18/1979 Bp Archibald Donald Davies. m 12/21/1958 Janet Anne Young c 2. Vic S Fran Ch Winnsboro TX 2002-2006; S Philips Epis Ch Sulphur Spgs TX 1996-2006; Vic Ch Of The Epiph Commerce TX 1996-1998; S Fran + S Clare 1992-1995; P-in-c S Steph's Ch Sanger TX 1992-1995; Chapl Bd Dir DFW Airport 1986-1995; P-in-c/Dir B. P. Mason Retreat & Conf Cntr Flower Mound TX 1982-1995; P-in-c Ascen And S Mk Bridgeport TX 1981-1982; Ch of the Ascen Decatur TX 1981-1982; S Andr's Ch Dallas TX 1979-1981; Cur S Andr's Ch Plano TX 1979-1981; Asst S Jn's Epis Ch Dallas TX 1978-1979; The Epis Ch Of The Trsfg Dallas TX 1978-1979; Exec Coun Dio Dallas Dallas TX 1996-1999, Int 1983-1996; Dio Dallas Rep Grtr Dallas Cmnty of Ch 1987; Dir Dio Dallas Epis Credit Un Bd 1986-1988.

YOUNG, Bernard Orson Dwight (LI) 18917 Turin Dr, Saint Albans NY 11412 B Georgetown GY 1947 s Richard & Ethel. Codrington Coll 1970. Trans 5/9/1975 Bp Jonathan Goodhue Sherman. m 8/22/1981 Deborah Young c 1. R Ch Of S Alb The Mtyr S Albans NY 1977-2012; Cur S Phil's Ch Brooklyn NY 1975-1977; Serv Ch In Guyana 1970-1975.

YOUNG, Bruce Alan (Mass) 46 Laurel St., Gloucester MA 01930 **Dioc Com Of Faith & The Environ 1990-** B Danvers MA 1937 s Charles & Marjorie. BA Trin 1959; STB Ya Berk 1962. D 6/23/1962 Bp Anson Phelps Stokes Jr P 6/1/1963 Bp Frederic Cunningham Lawrence. c 2. Dioc Prophetic Mnstry Cmsn 1990-1991; R Trin Ch Woburn MA 1966-1999; Asst Min All SS Epis Ch Attleboro MA 1962-1966. Ml King Jr Awd.

YOUNG, Francene (Tex) 605 West 9th Street, Houston TX 77007 **Assoc Dio Texas Houston TX 2016-, COM 2013-, Cmsn on Black Mnstry 2008-; R S Lk The Evang Houston TX 2012-** B Augusta GA 1953 d James & Ollie. BA Cleveland St U 1975; MPH U Pgh 1978; IONA Sch for Mnstry 2011; Other 2011. D 6/18/2011 Bp C Andrew Doyle. m 4/29/2000 Kenneth Randolph Jones. fyoung@epicenter.org

YOUNG, Frank Whitman (Ala) 109 Hannah Lane, Oak Grove AL 35150 **R S Andr's Epis Ch Sylacauga AL 1998-; S Mary's Epis Ch Childersburg AL 1998-; Chapl US-Army 1976-** B Grand Rapids MI 1948 s James & Sara. BA U CA, Los Angeles UCLA 1970; MDiv VTS 1974. D 5/24/1974 Bp John Alfred Baden P 5/25/1975 Bp Robert Bruce Hall. m 6/25/1972 Elizabeth J Young c 3. So Talladega Cnty Epis Mnstry Sylacauga AL 1998-2009; Trin Epis Ch Alpine AL 1998-2009; Gr Ch Cullman AL 1995-1998; Asst S Paul's Epis Ch Flint MI 1991-1994; R S Dunst's Epis Ch Davison MI 1985-1991; Vic Nativ Cmnty Epis Ch Holly MI 1977-1985; Vic Gr Ch Bremo Bluff VA 1974-1977; Dep, GC Dio Michigan Detroit MI 1991-1997. Ord of S Lk the Physcn - St Chapl 1994-2005. Best Article Associated Ch Press 1974.

YOUNG, Gary (EO) 665 Parsons Road, Hood River OR 97031 B Roslyn WA 1942 s Fred & Lena. MDiv CDSP 1975; Assn of Profsnl Chapl 2006. D 5/25/1975 Bp John Raymond Wyatt P 5/29/1976 Bp George Richard Millard. m 6/28/1980 Barbara Young c 5. Dir of Mssn Integration and Sprtl Care Providence Hood River Memi Hosp Hood River 1999-2017; Consult for Sprtlty in the Workplace and Cler Well Teamwork W Hood River OR 1994-1999; R The Par Of S Mk The Evang Hood River OR 1986-1994; Vic S Matt's Ch Prosser WA 1978-1986; S Geo's Epis Ch Antioch CA 1977; Pstr of Cmnty Mnstry Epis Ch in the Delta Antioch CA 1975-1977; Dio California San Francisco CA 1975-1976.

YOUNG, Gary Reid (Neb) 17 Brentwood Ct, Scottsbluff NE 69361 **Ret 1994-; Pres 1992-; 1991-; Deploy Off Prov VI Exec Coun 1988-** B Scottsbluff NE 1932 s Elmer & Katherine. Cert Nash 1968; MDiv Nash 1988; BS SUNY 1988. D 12/21/1967 P 6/1/1968 Bp Russell T Rauscher. c 2. Dn Trin Cathd Omaha NE 1991-1994; Int S Steph's Ch Grand Island NE 1990-1991; Cn to Ordnry Dio Nebraska Omaha NE 1987-1991, 1987-1990; Del Prov Syn 1983-1988; R Ch Of The H Apos Mitchell NE 1981-1987; 1973-1980; R S Mk's Ch Havre MT 1969-1972; P-in-c S Mk Crighton 1968-1969; P-in-c S Mary's Epis Ch Bassett NE 1968-1969; S Ptr's Ch Neligh NE 1968-1969; . Ord of S Lk.

YOUNG, Gary Todd (Md) 101 S Prospect St, Hagerstown MD 21740 **Congrl Dvlpmt Com Dio Montana Helena MT 2005-, 2004-2009** B Seattle WA 1964 s Gary & Betty. BA Whitworth U 2000; MDiv SWTS 2004. D 6/12/2004 Bp James E Waggoner Jr P 12/18/2004 Bp Charles Franklin Brookhart Jr. m 11/1/2016 Joclene K Young c 1. R S Lk's Ch Grants Pass OR 2010-2016; S Paul's Ch Virginia City MT 2010; Vic Chr Ch Sheridan MT 2004-2011. rector@stjohnshagerstown.org

✠ **YOUNG III, The Rt Rev George** (ETenn) 814 Episcopal School Way, Knoxville TN 37932 **Bp of E Tennessee Dio E Tennessee Knoxville TN 2011-** B Jacksonville FL 1955 s George & Margaret. Wesley Coll 1974; BS Florida St U 1978; MDiv SWTS 1990. D 6/10/1990 P 12/9/1990 Bp Frank S Cerveny Con 6/25/2011 for ETenn. m 8/22/1981 Kammy Mary Beich c 2. R S Ptr's Ch Fernandina Bch FL 1997-2011; R S Eliz's Epis Ch Jacksonville FL 1992-1997; DRE S Giles' Ch Northbrook IL 1990-1992. gyoung@dioet.org

YOUNG, James (Minn) 2105 Ontario Lane, revjryoung@gmail.com, Northfield MN 55057 **Chair of Dioc Exam Chapl Dio Minnesota Minneapolis MN 2006-** B Wadsworth OH 1950 s Benjamin & Anne. Sewanee: The U So, TS; BS Bowling Green St U 1972; MA U of Iowa 1978; MDiv Untd TS of the Twin Cities 1994. D 6/10/1984 Bp Robert Marshall Anderson P 8/18/1994 Bp Sanford Zangwill Kaye Hampton. m 6/16/1973 Lynne M Weins c 2. R S Jas On The Pkwy Minneapolis MN 2011-2016; Chr Ch Albert Lea MN 2004-2011, 1999-2003; The Epis Cathd Of Our Merc Sav Faribault MN 1999-2001; P-in-c Ch Of The Redeem Cannon Falls MN 1995-2001. revjryoung@gmail.com

YOUNG, James Joseph (Los) 12868 Hacienda Dr., Studio City CA 91604 **Chapl Harvard Westlake Sch Studio City CA 1997-; Harvard-Westlake Sch Studio City CA 1997-** B Dearborn MI 1954 s James & Patricia. BA Rice U 1977; MDiv Epis TS of the SW 1988. D 6/14/1988 P 12/21/1988 Bp Gordon Taliaferro Charlton. m 3/10/1978 Cynthia Beth Young. Holland Hall Sch Tulsa OK 1991-1997; Chapl Holland Hall Sch Tulsa OK 1991-1997; Asst Ch Of The Gd Shpd Kingwood TX 1988-1991.

YOUNG, James Oliver (Okla) 2207 Ridgeway St, Ardmore OK 73401 B Parris Island SC 1945 s William & Ruth. BS SE Oklahoma St U 1967; DDS Baylor U 1972. D 6/16/2001 Bp Robert Manning Moody. m 5/27/1967 Virginia Evelyn Koontz. D St Phil's Epis Ch Ardmore OK 2001-2003.

YOUNG, James Robert (NCal) Po Box 2334, Avila Beach CA 93424 **S Mich Ch Alturas CA 1991-** B Athol MA 1922 s James & Mabel. BS Babson Coll 1949; Cert ETSBH 1975; MA Claremont TS 1984. D 6/21/1975 P 8/1/1994 Bp Sanford Zangwill Kaye Hampton. m 1/5/1955 Beatrice Taft. Assoc Ch Of S Nich Paradise CA 1991-1993; Vic S Ptr's Ch Casa Grande AZ 1990-1991; Vic S Fran In The Redwoods Mssn Willits CA 1988-1990; Assoc R S Jn The Div Epis Ch Costa Mesa CA 1985-1988; Asst St Andr Epis Ch Irvine CA 1983-1984; P-in-c S Edw's Westminster CA 1977-1980; Asst S Paul's Epis Ch Tustin CA 1976-1982.

Y

YOUNG, Jim (SwVa) 5260 Triad Court SE, Salem OR 97306 **Trin Epis Ch Lynchburg VA 2014-** B Chattanooga TN 1961 s Marshall & Jackie. BS U of Tennessee 1984; MDiv Ya Berk 1996. D 6/15/1996 P 12/20/1996 Bp James Barrow Brown. m 12/31/2014 Sheryl Lee Golden c 3. S Paul's Epis Ch Salem OR 2009-2014, 2005-2009; Stanford Cbury Fndt Palo Alto CA 2003-2005; Asst S Paul's Epis Ch Modesto CA 2000-2003; R S Lk's Ch Denison TX 1998-2000; R Ch Of The H Comm Plaquemine LA 1996-1998.

YOUNG, Johanna Harriman (NH) B Concord 1958 d Robert & Mary. B.S. Geo 1980; M.S. Cntrl Connecticut St U 1985; M.Div. UTS 1992; D Cert D Formation Sch, Dio Mass. 2016. D 6/12/2016 Bp A Robert Hirschfeld. m 8/26/2003 Lindley Rankine. H Cross, Weare Ch Of S Jn The Evang Dunbarton NH 2016-2017; D H Cross Epis Ch Weare NH 2016-2017. Phi Beta Kappa Geo 1980.

YOUNG OJN, Kammy Mary (Fla) 400 Tennessee Avenue, Sewanee TN 37375 **Dir of Contextual Educ Sewanee U So TS Sewanee TN 2011-** B Munchwieller Germany 1962 d Paul & Kathleen. U So; BA Florida St U 1984; MDiv SWTS 1992. D 6/14/1992 P 12/13/1992 Bp Frank S Cerveny. m 8/22/1981 George Young c 2. Assoc. for Sprtlty & Justice Chr Epis Ch Ponte Vedra FL 2009-2011; R S Geo Epis Ch Jacksonville FL 1999-2009; Asst R S Mk's Epis Ch Jacksonville FL 1992-1997. Phi Beta Kappa.

YOUNG, Kathryn McMillan (Tenn) 704 Park Blvd, Austin TX 78751 B Terrell TX 1948 d Dehart & Patricia. BA Van 1970; MS Van 1972; MDiv Epis TS of the SW 1990; MA Texas St U San Marcos 1999. D 7/14/1990 Bp George Lazenby Reynolds Jr P 7/26/1991 Bp Anselmo Carral-Solar. c 2. Pstr Counslr Hyde Pk Counslg Assoc Austin TX 1999-2011; Chapl Hospice Austin Austin TX 1999-2007; Colloquy Ldr Epis TS Of The SW Austin TX 1995-2002; P El Buen Samaritano Epis Mssn Austin TX 1990-1993. Alb Inst 1990-1994; Amer Counslg Assn 1999-2011.

YOUNG, Linda M (Spok) 1410 NE Stadium Way, Pullman WA 99163 **S Jas Pullman WA 2016-** B Cleveland OH 1956 d Raymond & Marie Rose. BS Coll of Mt St Jos 1978; MEd U Cinc 1989; MDiv Bex Sem 2010. D 6/13/2009 P 6/19/2010 Bp Thomas Edward Breidenthal. m 6/7/2013 Gia M Gordon c 2. Assoc Trin Ch Covington KY 2011-2016; Cur S Barn Epis Ch Cincinnati OH 2010-2011.

YOUNG, Malcolm Clemens (Cal) 2674 St. Giles Lane, Mt. View CA 94040 **Dn Gr Cathd San Francisco CA 2015-** B Cambridge MA 1967 s Stephen & Clare. BA U CA 1989; MDiv Harvard DS 1994; ThD Harv 2004. D 8/20/1994 P 2/27/1995 Bp Jerry Alban Lamb. m 8/29/1992 Heidi K Ho c 2. R Chr Epis Ch Los Altos CA 2001-2015; Asstg Cler S Anne's In The Fields Epis Ch Lincoln MA 1998-2000; Int S Clem's Ch Berkeley CA 1994-1997. Auth, "The Sprtl Journ of Henry Dav Thoreau," *The Sprtl Journ of Henry Dav Thoreau*, Merc Press, 2009. AAR 1993. Fell ECF 1999. malcolmy@gracecathedral.org

YOUNG, Mary Catherine (NY) Canterbury Downtown, 12 W. 11th Street, New York NY 10011 **Epis Campus Min for NYU and Surrounding campuses Dio New York New York NY 2011-** B Little Rock AR 1978 d Donald & Dorothy. AA Cottey Coll 1998; BA Morningside Coll 2000; MDiv EDS 2006. D 6/8/2006 Bp James Louis Jelinek P 1/20/2007 Bp Dorsey Henderson. m 4/19/2009 Chad Robert Young c 1. P Asst for Faith Formation Ch Of Our Sav Rock Hill SC 2006-2011; S Jn's Ch Newtonville MA 2005-2006; Chapl intern Luth Epis Mnstry at MIT Cambridge MA 2004-2005; Faith Formation and Vol Coordntr Cass Lake Epis Camp Cass Lake MN 2003; Dir of Yth Mnstry S Lk's Epis Ch Rochester MN 2000-2003.

YOUNG, Ronald Bruce (Roch) Christ Episcopal Church, 26 S. Main St., Pittsford NY 14534 **Chr Ch Pittsford Pittsford NY 2014-; Trst Dio Rochester Henrietta 2016-** B Cambridge MA 1960 s Ronald & Justine. BA,BS Cor 1983; M/Eng Cor 1984; MDiv Andover Newton TS 1998; STM GTS 2003; ThD GTS 2009. D 5/18/2013 P 12/7/2013 Bp Mark M Beckwith. Adj Prof Drew TS Madison NJ 2016; S Ptr's Ch Essex Fells NJ 2013-2014; Adj Prof GTS 2007-2014.

YOUNG, Shari Maruska (Cal) P.O. Box 872, Tiburon CA 94920 B Santa Monica CA 1949 d Marvin & Maruska. U CA 1972; BA Pacific Oaks Coll 1973; MDiv CDSP 1988. D 6/25/1988 Bp Frederick Houk Borsch P 4/7/1989 Bp William Edwin Swing. c 1. Assoc R S Steph's Par Bel Tiburon CA 2010-2015; Int S Aid's Mssn Bolinas CA 2009-2010, 1993-1996; Assoc R S Jas Epis Ch San Francisco CA 1998-2009; Chapl Gr Cathd San Francisco CA 1988-2000; Cathd Sch For Boys San Francisco CA 1988-1993.

YOUNG, Sherry Lawry (EMich) 5584 Lapeer Rd Apt 1D, Kimball MI 48074 **S Steph's Par Bel Tiburon CA 2012-; SCMD Natl Ch New York NY 2006-; Archd Dio Estrn Michigan Saginaw MI 2003-** B Lansing MI 1949 d William & Clarice. Kendall Coll 1970; Diac Stds Whitaker TS 1983; Wayne BIS Detroit MI 1992; Natl Bd Cert Coun 1997; MA Oakland U 1997. D 11/19/1983 Bp William Jones Gordon Jr. D All SS Epis Ch Fair Haven MI 2000-2002; S Paul's Epis Ch Port Huron MI 1998-2006; Coordntr Epis Relief and Dvlpmt Dio Estrn Michigan Saginaw MI 1998-2002, Dominican Dvlpmt Grp Bd Mem 2010-; S Mk's Epis Ch Marine City MI 1998-2000; Asst Gr Epis Ch Port Huron MI 1984-1998; D S Mich's Epis Ch Lansing MI 1983-1984. Auth, "Chapt: From the Ther Room," *Chld and Stress: Understanding and Helping*, Assn of Childhood Educ Intl , 2001.

YOUNG, S Matthew (Lex) 7 Court Pl, Newport KY 41071 **Chapl Newport Fire Dept 2014-; R S Paul's Ch Newport KY 2011-; Stndg Com Dio Lexington Lexington 2015-, Exec Coun 2012-2014; Chapl Newport Fire Dept Newport KY 2014-** B Covington KY 1970 s Robert & Lee. BA Witt 1994; MDiv Trin Luth Sem 1998. Rec 8/24/2011 as Priest Bp Stacy F Sauls. Gr Epis Ch Florence KY 2011-2012. office@stpaulsnewport.org

YOUNG, William King (Az) 12440 W Firebird Dr, Sun City West AZ 85375 **Asst Chr Ch Of The Ascen Paradise Vlly AZ 2012-** B El Paso TX 1938 s King & Sue. BA U of Texas 1962; SMM UTS 1969; MDiv CDSP 1978. D 9/15/1978 P 5/1/1979 Bp Richard Mitchell Trelease Jr. m 4/1/1978 Katharine W Young c 2. P All SS Ch Phoenix AZ 2010-2012; Dioc Coun Dio Arizona Phoenix AZ 2010-2011; R Ch Of The Adv Sun City W AZ 1997-2004; Stndg Com Dio El Camino Real Salinas CA 1993-1997, Dioc Coun 1997-1990, Chair: Liturg Cmsn 1984-1997, Chair: Ecum Cmsn 1981-1997, Dep To Gc 1988-1994; R All SS Epis Ch Watsonville CA 1980-1997; Cur Epis Ch In Lincoln Cnty Ruidoso NM 1979-1980, COM 1978-1979; Com Dio The Rio Grande Albuquerque 1978-1979. Auth, "If The Householder Had Known - Adv Meditation," *LivCh*, 1989.

YOUNGBLOOD, Susan Russell (Chi) 825 N Taylor Ave, Oak Park IL 60302 **D S Matt's Ch Chandler AZ 2008-** B Lucas OH 1945 d Ross & Virginia. BA Coll of Wooster 1963; MS Suny Geneseo 1973. D 1/26/2008 Bp Kirk Stevan Smith. m 12/27/2003 Harlie Youngblood c 2.

YOUNGER, Leighton Keith (Tex) 158 Ridgeview Dr, Johnson City TX 78636 B Brookshire TX 1932 s Lovic & Velma. BS U of Texas 1955; LLB U of Texas 1958; MDiv Epis TS of the SW 1964. D 6/1/1964 Bp Frederick P Goddard P 6/1/1965 Bp Scott Field Bailey. m 1/11/1993 Sarah M Younger c 2. R S Jn's Ch La Porte TX 1972-1997; Chair Of The Yth Div Dept Of CE 1967-1972; Assoc H Sprt Epis Ch Houston TX 1967-1972; Vic Gr Ch Houston TX 1964-1967.

YOUNGSON, Charles (Ala) 315 Devon Dr., Birmingham AL 35209 **Assoc All SS Epis Ch Birmingham AL 2014-, Assoc 2005-2009** B Tuscaloosa AL 1975 s George & Leslie. BA Trin U San Antonio 1997; MDiv Sewanee: The U So, TS 2003. D 6/24/2003 Bp Robert Boyd Hibbs P 1/6/2004 Bp James Edward Folts. m 6/19/1999 Susan C Youngson c 2. R S Thos Epis Ch Birmingham AL 2009-2014; Asst S Steph's Epis Ch Wimberley TX 2003-2005. cyoungson@allsaintsbirmingham.org

YOUNKIN, Randy John (Pgh) 431 Alameda Ave, Youngstown OH 44504 B Johnstown PA 1949 s Warren & Olive. BS Robert Morris Coll 1972; MDiv EDS 1975. D 5/30/1976 Bp Robert Bracewell Appleyard. m 5/27/1974 Candace M Younkin. D Ch Of Our Sav Glenshaw PA 1976-2004; No Hills Yth Mnstry Pittsburgh PA 1976-1977; No Hills Yth Mnstry Pittsburgh PA 1975-1977; Asst All SS Epis Ch Brighton Heights Brighton Heights PA 1975-1976.

YOUNKIN, Ronald Willingham (Pgh) D 6/18/1969 P 12/1/1969 Bp Charles A Mason.

YOUNT, Amy Clark (WA) 3801 Newark St Nw Apt E431, Washington DC 20016 **S Pat's Epis Day Sch Washington DC 2012-, 2005-2011; Lower Sch Chapl & Rel Tchr Natl Cathd Sch 1994-** B Washington DC 1964 d Frank & Jean. BA Bow 1987; MDiv Ya Berk 1992. D 9/1/1992 Bp Edward Cole Chalfant P 10/1/1993 Bp Charles Lindsay Longest. m 8/20/1994 Nathan Hemenway Price c 2. S Pat's Ch Washington DC 2011-2012; Cathd of St Ptr & St Paul Washington DC 1994-2001; Pstr Assoc S Anne's Par Annapolis MD 1992-1994.

YOUSE JR, Don C (Pgh) 955 West North Avenue, Pittsburgh PA 15233 **Vic Emm Ch Pittsburgh PA 1994-** B Warsaw IN 1958 s Don & Helene. BS U NC 1980; MD U of Florida 1984; MDiv TESM 1994. D 6/11/1994 Bp Peter J Lee P 12/17/1994 Bp Alden Moinet Hathaway. emmanuelns@juno.com

YSKAMP, Janis (CPa) 813 Valley Rd, Mansfield PA 16933 **R All SS Ch Brookland PA 2010-; Chr Ch Coudersport PA 2010-** B Chester PA 1956 d James & Janet. D 10/26/2008 P 6/12/2010 Bp Nathan Dwight Baxter. m 9/12/1977 Wayne A Yskamp c 3. S Paul's Ch Wellsboro PA 2008-2010.

YULE, Marilynn Fritz (Spok) PO Box 6318, Kennewick WA 99336 **Mem, COM Dio Spokane 2003-; D S Paul's Epis Mssn Kennewick WA 2003-** B Buffalo NY 1934 d Carl & Ravenna. BD U Roch 1957. D 11/22/2003 Bp James E Waggoner Jr. m 7/7/1957 William David Yule c 3.

YUNG, Bernard Yu (Va) **St Jn's Sch Tamuning GU 2016-** B Manila Philippines 1965 s Beng & Severina. BS De La Salle U 1986; MS Geo Mason U 2001; MDiv VTS 2013. D 6/8/2013 Bp Shannon Sherwood Johnston. Exec Coun Appointees New York NY 2014-2015.

YUNKER, Judy Lee (Lex) 562 University Dr, Prestonburg KY 41653 **P-in-c Dio Lexington Lexington 2013-, Exec Coun 2011-2014; Vic S Jas Epis Ch Prestonsburg KY 2012-; Mem Ecum Benedictine Monstry Mart KY 1979-** B Evansville IN 1940 d Frank & Thelma. BA St. Ben Coll 1962; MA Indiana St U 1974; Angl Immersion CDSP 2011. D 6/30/2012 Bp Chilton Richardson Knudsen P 1/12/2013 Bp Doug Hahn. revjudy@gmail.com

YUROSKO, Steven G (Mont) Saint Andrew's Episcopal Church, 110 6th Ave, Polson MT 59860 **R S Andr's Epis Ch Polson MT 2012-** B El Paso TX 1954 s Richard & Beverly. BA California St E Bay 2009; MDiv CDSP 2012; MDiv CDSP 2012. D 6/16/2012 Bp Barry Leigh Beisner P 12/17/2012 Bp Charles

Y

Franklin Brookhart Jr. m 8/1/1982 Sue Ann Yurosko. revsteven727@gmail.com

Z

✠ ZABALA, The Rt Rev Artemio M (Los) 5048 Brunswick Dr, Fontana CA 92336 **Form Bp of No Cntrl Philippines Dio No Cntrl Philippines Baguio City 1994-, 1991-1993** B Bontoc Philippines 1938 s Pedro Pablo & Patricia. BTh St Andrews TS Philippines 1963; BA U of The Philippines 1964; MTh Trin Toronto Can 1974; ThD U of Heidelbery Germany 1980. Trans 2/11/1999 Bp Frederick Houk Borsch Con 10/28/1989 for Episcopal Church in the Philippines. m 11/28/1963 Mary Zabala c 3. R Par of Hoy Trin and St. Ben Alhambra CA 2000-2004; Ch Of The H Trin and S Ben Alhambra CA 1994-2004; Vic St. Ben's Mssn Alhambra CA 1994-2000; Bp No Cntrl Philippines 1989-1993; Dio Cntrl Philippines Queson City 1964-1990; Serv Epis Ch in the Philippines 1963-1993. "The Enigma of Jn 19:13 Reconsidered," *SE Asia Journ of Theol, Vol. 23*, 1982; "The Enigma of Jn 19:13 Reconsidered," *SE Asia Journ of Theol, Vol. 22*, 1981.

ZABRISKIE JR, Alexander Clinton (Be) 119 Northshore Dr, Burlington VT 05408 **Ret 1995-** B Alexandria VA 1930 s Alexander & Mary. BA Pr 1952; U of Edinburgh GB 1953; MDiv VTS 1956; DMin PrTS 1985. D 6/1/1956 Bp Frederick D Goodwin P 12/16/1956 Bp William Jones Gordon Jr. m 1/21/1958 Marguerite M Zabriskie c 5. Exec Coun Appointees New York NY 1987-1995; Cn & R of the Engl Spkng Cong S Jn's Cathd Santurce San Juan Puerto Rico 1987-1995; Int S Clem's Ch Hawthorne NJ 1986-1987; Int Chr Ch Teaneck NJ 1985-1986; R Trin Ch Bethlehem PA 1969-1984; R S Mary's Ch Anchorage AK 1958-1969; Asst S Matt's Epis Ch Fairbanks AK 1956-1958.

ZABRISKIE II, George (Mont) 4283 Monroe St Apt D, Bozeman MT 59718 **Died 7/19/2016** B Chestnut Hill PA 1926 s Alexander & Mary. BA Pr 1950; MDiv VTS 1954; EDS 1972. Trans 11/19/2003 Bp Mark Sean Sisk. m 6/20/1959 Thyrza Day c 3. S Jas Ch Bozeman MT 2000-2009; Ret 1992-2016; Supply P Dio Vermont Burlington VT 1992-1998; Trst, Cathd Sch Cathd Of St Jn The Div New York NY 1987-1992; R S Jn's Ch Larchmont NY 1977-1992; Chair, Com on Cont Ed. Dio Missouri S Louis MO 1975-1977, Stndg Com 1975-1977, COM 1973-1977; Chr Ch Cathd S Louis MO 1972-1977; R H Trin Manila-Rizal Philippines 1959-1970; Asst S Thos Ch New York NY 1956-1959; Cler Mstr Groton Sch Groton MA 1954-1956; Stndg Com Dio New York New York NY 1983-1986. Auth, *Seed & Harvest*, 1988; "Misc. Letters to the Ed," *LivCh*. Integrity 2004; Trst - Cathd Sch, Cathd of S Jn the Div 1987-1992. Bp's Awd Dio New York 1992; Rotary Pres's Awd Rotary Club, Larchmont, NY 1980; Dn's Awd St Andr's Epis. Sem, Manila, Philippines 1970.

ZABRISKIE, Marek P (Pa) 212 Washington Ln, Fort Washington PA 19034 **R S Thos' Ch Whitemarsh Ft Washington PA 1995-** B Detroit MI 1960 s Charles & Catherine. Institut Catholique De Paris; BA Emory U 1982; MDiv Ya Berk 1989. D 6/24/1989 P 6/23/1990 Bp George Lazenby Reynolds Jr. m 1/15/1994 Isabel Mims Zabriskie. Assoc R St Jas Ch Richmond VA 1991-1995; Asst to R S Geo's Ch Nashville TN 1989-1991. Auth, "Living Ch".

ZACHARIA, Manoj M (SO) 318 E 4th St, Cincinnati OH 45202 **Asst Chr Ch Cathd Cincinnati OH 2014-; Mem, Ecum and Inter-Rel Relatns The Epis Ch Stndg Cmsn 2013-; Constitutions and Cn Com Dio Newark Newark NJ 2012-, Dioc Coun 2012-** B Queens, NY 1976 s Mathew & Elizabeth. Ph.D. Other; Ph.D. U Tor; BA Vas 1998; MDiv Mar Thoma Sem 2002; STM GTS 2007. Trans 11/5/2011 as Priest Bp Mark M Beckwith. m 8/16/2003 Joelle T Zacharia c 2. R S Paul's And Resurr Ch Wood Ridge NJ 2011-2013. AAR 2008; Can Theol Soc 2008. mzacharia@cccath.org

ZACHRITZ, John Louis (RG) 13 County Road 126, Espanola NM 87532 **Chapl to Ret Cler & surviving spouses Dio The Rio Grande Albuquerque 2012-** B Tulsa OK 1942 s John & Nancy. BA U of Tulsa 1966; MDiv EDS 1977. D 6/18/1977 P 5/21/1978 Bp Gerald Nicholas Mcallister. m 9/7/1968 Helenmarie Zachritz c 3. Chapl S Fran Cmnty Serv Inc. Salina KS 2002-2005; The S Fran Acad Espanola NM 2000-2002; Asst St Paul's/San Pablo Epis Ch Salinas CA 1999-2000; St Lk's Epis Ch Anth NM 1994-1999; Vic S Matt's Ch Sand Sprg OK 1983-1994; Asst Trin Ch Tulsa OK 1978-1983; Dio Oklahoma Oklahoma City OK 1977-1994.

ZACKER, John G (NY) 64 Weir Ln, Locust Valley NY 11560 **Assoc Chr Ch Oyster Bay NY 2006-; P Assoc Par of Chr the Redeem Pelham NY 1988-** B Brooklyn NY 1947 s John & Gwendolyn. BA Wag 1969; GTS 1970; MDiv Drew U 1972; UTS 1975; JD Ford 1978. D 6/3/1972 P 12/1/1972 Bp Paul Moore Jr. Assoc S Edm's Par San Marino CA 1982-1984; Assoc S Mary's Epis Ch Los Angeles CA 1980-1982; Epis Ch Of SS Jn Paul And S Clem Mt Vernon NY 1977-1980; Vic S Jn's Epis Ch Mt Vernon IN 1977-1980; Ch Of The Atone Bronx NY 1976-1977; S Martha's Ch Bronx NY 1976-1977; Asst Chr Ch Bronxville NY 1973-1975; Asst S Jn's Ch Larchmont NY 1972-1973. Auth, *Legacy Plan Protection: Preserve Your Estate*. jgzacker@gmail.com

ZADIG SR, Alfred Thomas Kurt (WMass) 12 Briarwood Cir, Worcester MA 01606 **P-in-c Gr Ch Oxford MA 2009-; Ret Epis Ch 1996-** B New Rochelle NY 1931 s Alfred & Rose. BA Brandeis U 1953; Long Island Dioc TS 1961; MA Bos 1973; PhD Columbia Pacific U 1989. D 4/8/1961 P 10/28/1961 Bp James Pernette DeWolfe. m 11/8/2002 Anne Carter Mahaffey c 7. Int P S Paul's Epis Ch Morganton NC 2005-2008; Int S Mary's Ch Asheville NC 2003-2004; Int Ch Of Our Sav Johns Island SC 2001-2002; P-in-c S Ptr's Ch Springfield MA 1997-2001; Ch Of The Atone Westfield MA 1995-1996; Int S Andr's Ch Longmeadow MA 1993-1995; Chr Ch Portsmouth NH 1989-1990; S Mary's Epis Ch Rockport MA 1987-1991; R Ch Of The Gd Shpd Waban MA 1975-1983; Ecum Counslg Serv Melrose MA 1972-1983; Exec Dir Ecum Counslg Serv 1969-2000; Assoc Trin-S Mich's Ch Fairfield CT 1966-1968. Confrater, Ord of S Ben 1962; CBS 1958; Fllshp of the Way of the Cross 2014; GAS 1958; P Assoc, Shrine of Our Lady of Walsingham 1962; Soc of Cath Priests 2016.

ZAHARIA, Paul Michael (ND) 301 Main St S, Minot ND 58701 B Hallock MN 1954 s Michael & Sophia. BS No Dakota St U 1993. D 11/1/2013 P 11/1/2014 Bp Michael Smith. m 10/5/1973 Margaret Ann Zaharia c 3. pmz@srt.com

ZAHER, Holly Ann Rankin (Tenn) **Asst Ch Of The Adv Nashville TN 2016-** D 6/4/2016 P 12/17/2016 Bp John Bauerschmidt.

ZAHL, John Arthur (SC) **Assoc Gr Ch Cathd Charleston SC 2012-** B New York NY 1977 s Paul & Mary. BA Ken 2000; BD Wycliffe Hall Oxford GB 2008. D 6/6/2007 P 12/16/2007 Bp Edward Lloyd Salmon Jr. m 1/6/2007 Deirdre H Zahl. Ch Of The H Cross Sullivans Island SC 2008-2012; Counslr New York City Rescue Mssn.

ZAHL, Paul Francis Matthew (WA) 506 N Dillard St, Winter Garden FL 34787 B New York NY 1951 s Paul & Eda. BA Harv 1972; MPhil U of Nottingham 1974; DPS St Johns Theol Coll Nottingham GB 1975; ThD Tubingen U Tubingen DE 1994. D 9/28/1975 Bp William Foreman Creighton P 6/3/1976 Bp Richard Beamon Martin. m 12/29/1973 Mary C Zahl c 3. R All SS' Epis Ch Chevy Chase MD 2008-2009; Dn TESM Ambridge PA 2004-2006; Dn The Cathd Ch Of The Adv Birmingham AL 1995-2004; R S Jas Ch Charleston SC 1988-1992; R S Mary's Ch Of Scarborough Briarcliff NY 1982-1988; Tutor The GTS New York NY 1979-1982; Cur Gr Epis Ch New York NY 1976-1982; D-in-Trng Gd Shpd Epis Ch Silver Sprg MD 1975-1976. "2000 Years of Amazing Gr," Rowman & Littlefield, 2007; "Gr in Pract," Eerdmans, 2007; Auth, *The Collects of S of Thos Crammer*, 1999; Auth, *The Prot Face of Anglicanism*, 1998; Auth, *Die Rechtfertigungslehre Ernst Kasemanns*, 1996; Auth, *ATR*, 1995; Auth, "Theses from Our Cathd Door," *Angl Dig*, 1994; Auth, "A View from Abroad and Tracts for These Times," *Angl Dig*, 1988; Auth, *Message of the Bible*, 1988; Auth, *Who Will Deliver Us?*, 1983. Evang ES/PECUSA Schlrshp 1993; Fllshp ECF 1991.

ZAHN, Marianne (Los) St Wilfred Of York, 18631 Chapel Ln, Huntington Beach CA 92646 B Dallas TX 1966 d Ivan & Shirley Ann. BFA NYU 1990; MA H Names Coll 1993; MDiv Fuller TS 2011. D 6/8/2013 Bp Joseph Jon Bruno P 1/11/2014 Bp Diane Jardine Bruce. m 5/15/1993 Daniel Francis Doyle. St Johns Pro-Cathd Los Angeles CA 2015; S Wilfrid Of York Epis Ch Huntington Bch CA 2013-2015.

ZAINA, Lisa (WA) 117 Oenoke Ridge, New Canaan CT 06840 **Vic H Innoc Ch Atlanta GA 2014-** B Alliance OH 1960 d Ronald & Mary. BA U of Notre Dame 1983; JD Wake Forest U Law 1987; M.Div. Ya Berk 2013. D 1/26/2013 P 7/27/2013 Bp Mariann Edgar Budde. P S Mk's Ch New Canaan CT 2013-2014. HOD HOD Medal 2012.

ZAISS, John Deforest (Nev) 7832 Magnolia Glen Ave, Las Vegas NV 89128 B Los Angeles CA 1953 s Sam & Virginia. BA Creighton U 1974. D 2/6/1994 P 10/1/1994 Bp Stewart Clark Zabriskie. m 11/2/1985 Anne Vandendries.

ZAKRZEWSKI, Joy Lael (FdL) 2336 Canterbury Ln, Sister Bay WI 54234 B Racine WI 1964 d Gerald & Donna. BS U of Wisconsin 1986. D 5/7/2011 Bp Russell Edward Jacobus. m 8/22/1994 Leonard Leroy Zakrzewski.

ZALESAK, Richard Joseph (Tenn) 1601 Campbell Ln, Galveston TX 77551 B San Antonio TX 1962 s Joseph & Marie. BA U of St Thos 1984; MDiv VTS 1989; MA U of St Thos 1994; DMin Gordon-Conwell TS 1999. Trans 9/19/2003 Bp James Monte Stanton. m 5/26/1990 Meredith U Zalesak c 2. R S Ptr's Ch Columbia TN 2009-2014; Dio Virginia Richmond VA 2003-2009; Vic S Fran Epis Ch 2003-2009; Ch Of The Incarn Dallas TX 2003; Assoc Chr Epis Ch Plano TX 2001-2003; Assoc H Cross Epis Ch Sugar Land TX 1998-2001; R S Paul's Ch Katy TX 1994-1998; Trin Ch Houston TX 1992-1994; Assoc Trin Ch Galveston TX 1989-1992. St. Geo Awd ECUSA 2005.

ZALNERAITIS JR, Herbert Benedict (Mass) 93 Main St Apt 3, Brattleboro VT 05301 B Worcester MA 1946 s Herbert & Rosemary. BA H Cross Coll 1968; MDiv Ya Berk 1971; MEd Walden U 2006. D 6/20/1971 P 4/7/1972 Bp Alexander D Stewart. m 6/24/2004 Jan Marie Zalneraitis. Trin Epis Ch Haverhill MA 1977-1980; Non-par 1975-1977; Vic S Clem's Epis Ch Greenville PA 1974-1975; Chr Ch Ansonia CT 1972-1974.

ZAMBONI, Jack (NJ) 400 New Market Road, Dunellen NJ 08812 **R S Fran Ch Dunellen NJ 2008-** B Suffern NY 1954 s Frank & Janet. BA Ya 1976; MDiv GTS 1983. D 6/4/1983 Bp George Phelps Mellick Belshaw P 12/10/

1983 Bp Philip Edward Randolph Elder. c 2. Dep to GC Dio New Jersey Trenton NJ 2003-2015, Chapl to Dioc Coun 1997-2002, Exam Chapl 1991-1996, Dep-Elect to GC 2009-, Dep to GC 2003-2006; R Gr St Pauls Ch Trenton NJ 1990-2008; Asst Chr Ch Toms River Toms River NJ 1985-1990, Int 1984-1985, Cur 1983-1985. Fllshp of St. Jn 1978.

ZANETTI, Diane P (Be) 4484 Heron Dr, Reading PA 19606 B Monticello NY 1947 BA Syr; MDiv Drew U 1985; MS Walden U 2006. D 5/31/2003 P 12/19/2003 Bp Paul Victor Marshall. S Alb's Epis Ch Reading PA 2004-2007.

ZAPATA-GARCIA, Carlos Alberto (EcuC) Calle Hernando Sarmiento, N 39-54 Y Portete, Setor El Batan Quito Ecuador **Iglesia Epis Del Ecuador Quito 2009-** B 1971 s Guillermo & Teresa. D 11/7/2009 P 10/2/2010 Bp Luis Fernando Ruiz Restrepo. m 5/24/2008 Yenny del Pilar Garcia-Juarez.

ZAPPA, Cathy C (At) Episc Ch Of The Holy Spirit, 724 Pilgrim Mill Rd, Cumming GA 30040 **Cathd Of S Phil Atlanta GA 2014-** B Atlanta GA 1973 d Francis & Mary. BA U GA 1994; MA U of Texas 1997; MDiv Candler TS 2010; MDiv Candler TS Emory U 2010. D 5/22/2013 P 12/21/2013 Bp Robert Christopher Wright. m 5/17/1997 Vincent George Zappa c 3. Epis Ch Of The H Sprt Cumming GA 2013-2014.

ZARTMAN, Rebecca Ann (WA) **Dio Washington Washington DC 2015-; Asst S Thos' Par Washington DC 2013-** B Danville PA 1985 d David & Frances. BA Ge 2007; MDiv VTS 2013. D 6/2/2013 Bp Nathan Dwight Baxter P 3/27/2014 Bp Mariann Edgar Budde. m 7/5/2013 Joshua James Easterson. VTS Alexandria VA 2013.

ZAYA, Lourdes (DR) **Dio The Dominican Republic (Iglesia Epis Dominicana) Gazcue Santo Domingo 2012-** B Puerto Plata DR 1963 d Cruz & Petronila. Licenciado en derecho Tecnologica de Santiago. D 2/14/2010 Bp Julio Cesar Holguin-Khoury. m 6/27/1987 Hector Bienvenido Lantigua c 4.

ZEIGLER, Luther (Mass) Episcopal Chaplaincy At Harvard, 2 Garden St, Cambridge MA 02138 **Emm Chap Manchester MA 2012-; Epis Chapl At Harvard & Radcliffe Cambridge MA 2011-** B Aurora CO 1958 BA Ob 1980; MA Stan 1982; MDiv VTS 2007. D 6/9/2007 P 1/19/2008 Bp John Bryson Chane. m 6/7/1980 Patricia Zeigler c 2. S Andr's Epis Sch Potomac MD 2008-2011; Washington Epis Sch Beth MD 2007-2008.

ZEILFELDER, Eugene Walter (NJ) Psc 3 Box 3251, Apo AP 96266 **Asst Profesor Pyeontaek Universiyt Pyeongtaek Gyyeonggi-do 2004-** B Bronx NY 1942 s Eugene & Walli. BA U of Maryland 1973; MDiv VTS 1976. D 6/5/1976 P 12/11/1976 Bp Albert Wiencke Van Duzer. m 2/6/1984 Eunsook Zeilfelder c 4. F/T Lectr Duksung Wmn U Seoul ROK 1993-2004; Asst to Bp. Dio Deajeon Angl Ch of Korea 1992-2005; P-in-c Spec Mnstrs (ArmdF) Yongsan Seoul 1989-2011; Off Of Bsh For ArmdF New York NY 1980-1987; R Chr Ch Oaklyn NJ 1976-1980. Auth, "Snow Flower Songs - Claudia Hae In Lee's Lyrics of Nature] w Kim Jin Sup," Yolimwon, 2005; Auth, "On A Journey (An anthology of selected poems by Hae In Lee) (w Kim Jin Sup)," Parkwoosa, 2003; Auth, "Heaven, Wind, Stars and Poems (Selected poems by Jun Dong-Ju) (w Kim Jin Sup)]," Parkwoosa, 2001; Auth, "At The Sea Again (An anthology of selected poems by Hae In Lee) (w Kim Jin Sup)," Parkwoosa, 1998; Auth, "They Are Never Lonely (An anthology of poems by Kim Yang-shik) (w Kim Jin Sup)," Parkwoosa, 1998. eugene.zeilfelder@gmail.com

ZELLER, Margaret K (ETenn) 1108 Meadow Ln, Kingsport TN 37663 **R S Chris's Ch Kingsport TN 2008-, P-in-c 2007-** B Wilmington DE 1948 d J Robert & Beryl. BA Florida St U 1970; MLS SUNY 1978; MDiv Sewanee: The U So, TS 2002. D 12/27/2001 Bp Charles Edward Jenkins III P 9/14/2002 Bp Charles Glenn VonRosenberg. c 2. Int S Jn's Epis Ch Johnson City TN 2002-2007, Assoc 2002-2004.

ZELLERMAYER, Charles Clayton (Mil) 400 Garland Ct, Waukesha WI 53188 **D S Mary's Epis Ch Summit WI 2007-** B Plainview TX 1949 s Robert & Laverne. Dade Cmnty Coll Miami FL; UW Waukesha. D 12/2/1995 Bp Roger John White. m 12/16/1972 Janet Susan Miller c 3. D S Anskar's Epis Ch Hartland WI 2004-2006; D St Mths Epis Ch Waukesha WI 1995-2004; Archd Dio Milwaukee Milwaukee WI 2005-2016. Bp's Shield Awd The Rt Reverend Steven A. Miller 2016.

ZELLEY III, Edmund W (NJ) 11 North Monroe Ave, Wenonah NJ 08090 **S Lk's Epis Ch Metuchen NJ 2015-** B Plainfield NJ 1965 s E Walton & Susan. BA Gri 1988; MDiv EDS 1993. D 6/12/1993 Bp George Phelps Mellick Belshaw P 1/15/1994 Bp Joe Doss. m 8/18/1990 Gail K Zelley c 2. Vic H Trin Epis Ch Wenonah NJ 1995-2015; Asst Gr Ch In Haddonfield Haddonfield NJ 1993-1995. stlukesmetuchen@gmail.com

ZELLEY JR, E Walton (NJ) P.O. Box 2, Copake Falls NY 12517 **Ret 1998-** B Philadelphia PA 1938 s Edmund & Ruth. BA Trin Hartford CT 1961; MDiv PDS 1964; STM NYTS 1974; MSW Rutgers The St U of New Jersey 1991. D 4/25/1964 P 10/31/1964 Bp Alfred L Banyard. m 8/27/1960 Milbrey Zelley c 2. Pres NJ Epis Cler Assn 1987-1991; Bd Middlesex Interfaith Partnership w the Homeless New Bruns 1985-1998; R S Lk's Epis Ch Metuchen NJ 1970-1998, Cur 1964-1966; Vic S Aid's Ch Olathe KS 1966-1969; Dioc Coun Pres Dio New Jersey Trenton NJ 1996-1997, Liturg Comm. 1971-1995. Auth, "Is the Underclass a Class?," *Journ of Soc & Soc Welf*, 1995. AP 1970-1998; Assn of Dioc Liturg & Mus Commissions 1970-1998; NNECA 1974. Hon Cathd Cn

Dio of New Jersey 2017; Edgar Awd (Citizen of the Year) Metuchen YMCA 1991.

ZELLNER, John Clement (USC) 230 Depot St, Tryon NC 28782 **Vic S Phil's Epis Ch Greenville SC 2011-** B Hazleton PA 1952 s Clement & Rita. BA Bloomsburg U of Pennsylvania 1974; MS Shippensburg U 1978; MDiv VTS 1979; DMin Estrn Bapt TS 1990. D 7/8/1979 Bp James Loughlin Duncan P 1/13/1980 Bp Calvin Onderdonk Schofield Jr. m 2/8/1981 Christine E Halligan c 2. Chapl Greenville Memi Hosp 2010-2011; R Ch Of The H Cross Valle Crucis NC 2001-2009; R Ch Of The H Cross Tryon NC 1992-2001; R Ch Of S Paul's By The Sea Ocean City MD 1986-1992; R S Mary's Fleeton Reedville VA 1982-1986; Cur S Jn's Epis Ch Homestead FL 1979-1982.

ZEMAN, Andrew Howard (Ct) 135 Ball Farm Rd, Oakville CT 06779 **P-in-c S Geo's Ch Middlebury CT 2012-** B Hartford CT 1946 s William & Evelyn. D.Min HArtford Sem; BA Mar 1968; MDiv Ya Berk 1971; D.Min. Hartford Sem 2012. D 6/12/1971 Bp Joseph Warren Hutchens P 12/18/1971 Bp Morgan Porteus. m 5/29/2010 Joyce Lanham c 1. R All SS Epis Ch Oakville CT 2002-2010; R H Trin Prot Epis Ch Onancock VA 1990-2002; R Chr Ch Easton CT 1981-1990; Vic Chr Ch Bethlehem CT 1975-1981; Dio Connecticut Meriden CT 1975-1981, Exec Coun 2004-2010, Archv Com 2002-2011, Soc Concerns Coordntr 1977-1981; Cur Chr Ch Cathd Hartford CT 1971-1975.

ZEPEDA PADILLA, Jorge Alberto (Hond) **Dio Honduras San Pedro Sula 2006-; Iglesia Epis Hondurena San Pedro Sula 2006-** B San Pedro Sula 1957 s Miguel & Elia. DIT Programa Diocesono Educacion Teologica. D 10/28/2005 Bp Lloyd Emmanuel Allen. m 9/9/2001 Maria Antonia Santos Garcia c 4. Diacono Loc Promanente Eclesial 1996-2003.

ZEPHIER, Richard (SD) 1410 N Kline St, Aberdeen SD 57401 B Wagner SD 1938 s Antoine & Victoria. BA Yankton Coll 1962; MS Nthrn St U 1974. D 1/19/2014 P 4/11/2015 Bp John Tarrant. c 3.

ZEREN, Corby D 6/10/2017 Bp Chilton Richardson Knudsen.

ZETTINGER, Bill (SanD) 1920 Hamilton Ln, Escondido CA 92029 B Brooklyn NY 1943 s Carl & Mildred. MS Harvard Bus Sch Long Island Campus; BS New York Inst of Tech 1966; Cert Theol Stud ETSBH 2007. D 6/9/2007 Bp Jim Mathes. m 1/25/1969 Antonina Zettinger. D S Barth's Epis Ch Poway CA 2007-2015; V.P. Prog And Bus Dvlpmt L-3 Titan Corp Lajolla CA 1985-2006.

ZIEGENFUSS, Charles William (La) 2919 Saint Charles Ave, New Orleans LA 70115 **Org/Chrmstr S Andr's Epis Ch New Orleans LA 2007-, Mus Instr 1976-2006; Org Trin Epis Sch 1976-** B Easton PA 1933 s Charles & Myra. BS Susquahanna U 1955; MDiv Nash 1966. D 6/1/1966 Bp Henry I Louttit P 6/30/1966 Bp James Loughlin Duncan. Dir Cathd Concert Series 1972-2006; Org/Chrmstr Chr Ch Cathd New Orleans LA 1968-2004; Cur S Jas Epis Ch Ormond Bch FL 1966-1968.

ZIEGENHINE, Kathleen Roach (NwPa) 458 E 23rd St, Erie PA 16503 **Non-stip Hosp Mnstry St. Vinc & Hamot Hospitals Erie PA 1998-** B Dallas TX 1953 d Robert & Sherry. D 10/25/2003 P 12/18/2004 Bp Robert Deane Rowley Jr. m 6/24/1978 James Patrick Ziegenhine c 3.

ZIEGLER, Sally McIntosh (Colo) 2205 Paseo Del Oro, Colorado Springs CO 80904 **D Gr And S Steph's Epis Ch Colorado Sprg CO 1997-** B Savannah GA 1935 d Olin & Sally. BA Duke 1957. D 6/4/1994 Bp Richard Frank Grein. m 6/15/1957 Edward William Ziegler c 3. D All SS' Epis Ch Briarcliff NY 1994-1997.

ZIELINSKI, Frances Gertrude (Chi) 710 S Paulina St # 904, Chicago IL 60612 **1979-** B Detroit MI 1930 d George & D Gertrude. Walsh Inst Acctg 1952. D 10/1/1963 Bp Richard Stanley Merrill Emrich. Dir NCD 1974-1979; D-in-c Cntrl Hse of Deaconnesses Evanston IL 1967-1974; Asst S Martha's Ch Detroit MI 1963-1967.

ZIEMANN, Judith Jon (NCal) 5905 W. 30th Ave., Wheat Ridge CO 80214 B Marinette WI 1943 d Roy & Elizabeth. BS U CO 1965; MS U of Wisconsin 1970; MA U of Wisconsin 1972; MDiv CDSP 1989. D 7/16/1989 P 7/29/1990 Bp Chris Christopher Epting. Int Ch Of S Nich Paradise CA 2004-2005; R S Mk's Ch Yreka CA 2001-2004; Int Trin Epis Ch Houghton MI 2000-2001; R Ch Of Our Sav Dubois PA 1997-1999; Int Chapl St Mary's Hosp Streator IL 1997; Pstr For Lasalle Cnty Epis Mnstry Dio Chicago Chicago IL 1993-1996; P-in-c Chr Ch Streator IL 1990-1996; Int S Paul's Ch Coun Blfs IA 1990; COM Dio NW Pennsylvania Erie PA 1998-1999; Mssn Cmsn Dio Iowa Des Moines IA 1983-1986. EWC 1982.

ZIFCAK, Patricia (Mass) 2100 County St Apt 31, South Attleboro MA 02703 **Archd S Barth's Epis Ch Cambridge MA 2012-; Chr Ch Cambridge Cambridge MA 2005-** B Providence RI 1945 d Edward & Dorothy. BS Bridgewater Coll 1967; MEd Bridgewater Coll 1978; MDiv Andover Newton TS 1998. D 6/8/2002 Bp M(Arvil) Thomas Shaw.

ZILE, Eric Neil (Md) 4500 C Dunton Terrace, Perry Hall MD 21128 **R H Trin Epis Ch Essex MD 2000-; COM Dio Maryland Baltimore MD 2017-, Chair, Rt to Seats and Votes 2011-, Cont Edducation Grants 2006-, Resolutns Com 2006-** B Baltimore MD 1959 s James Earl & Theresa. S Fran Coll Loretto PA 1977; AA Catonsville Cmnty Coll 1988; 9 Units CPE Johns Hopkins 1999; EDS 2010. D 6/14/1997 Bp Charles Lindsay Longest P 1/15/2000 Bp Robert Wilkes Ihloff. c 2. Chapl Johns Hopkins Med Inst Baltimore MD 1998-2000; D

Z

S Lk's Ch Baltimore MD 1998-2000; D The Ch Of The Nativ Cedarcroft Baltimore MD 1997-1998.

ZIMMERMAN, Aaron M G (Tex) 305 N 30th St, Waco TX 76710 **R S Alb's Epis Ch Waco TX 2013-** B Houston TX 1978 s Michael & Lucia. BA Harvard Coll 1999; MDiv TESM 2008. Trans 9/12/2011 Bp Kenneth Lester Price. m 7/13/2002 Andrea Marie Frank c 3. Assoc R for Discipleship and Fam Mnstrs S Mart's Epis Ch Houston TX 2011-2013; Asst R S Steph's Ch Sewickley PA 2008-2011; Dn of Convoc, W Harris Cnty Dio Texas Houston TX 2012-2013. Contributing Auth, "Var Devotional Essays," *The Mockingbird Devotional: Gd News for Today (And Every Day)*, Mockingbird Mnstrs, 2013. aaron@stalbanswaco.org

ZIMMERMAN, Curtis Roy (Oly) 11410 NE 124 St, #624, Kirkland WA 98034 **Vic Ch Of Our Sav Monroe WA 2016-; Ldrshp Vol EvergreenHealth Hospice Cntr Kirkland WA 2011-; Fac, Team Dvlpmt, Strategic Plnng Dio Olympia Seattle WA 1984-; Elem Sch Mentor Lake Washington Sch Dist Redmond WA 2013-; Inpatient Vol Evergreen Hospice Kirkland WA 2011-** B Santa Monica CA 1942 s Thomas & Verna. BMus U of Redlands 1966; MDiv CDSP 1974; Cert Int Mnstry Prog 1999. D 6/10/1974 P 12/21/1974 Bp Edwin Lani Hanchett. Cn Gd Samar Epis Ch Sammamish WA 2008; P-in-c S Fran Epis Ch Bothell WA 2006-2008; P-in-c S Barn Epis Ch Bainbridge Island WA 2004-2006; P-in-c S Pat's Ch Incline Vlg NV 2003-2004; Int Trin Epis Ch Wheaton IL 2001-2003; Int S Matt's Epis Ch Wilton CT 2000-2001; Int S Dav's Ch Gales Ferry CT 1999-2000; P-in-c S Jn's Ch Chehalis WA 1997-1999; R Chr Ch Tacoma WA 1991-1998; Convenor of Grtr Puyallup Cler Assn Grtr Puyallup Cler Assn Puyallup WA 1983-1985; R Chr Epis Ch Puyallup WA 1979-1991; Vic Epiph Ch Marshall Islands 1975-1978; Cn S Andr's Cathd Honolulu HI 1974-1979; Chair, Exam Chapl Dio Olympia Seattle 1995-1998, Mem, Dioc Coun 1987-1991, Mem, Trng and Consulting Serv 1985-2009, Vice Chair, Diac Mnstry Com 1984-1995, Mem, Cmsn on Educ 1983-1985, Chair of Liturg Cmsn 1980-1984, Instr of Liturg in TS 1980-1984; Rdr Consult for Hymnal 1982 Dom And Frgn Mssy Soc- Epis Ch Cntr New York NY 1981-1982; Chair of Liturg Cmsn The Epis Ch in Hawaii Honolulu HI 1976-1979. AGO 1960; Assoc, OHC 1971; Int Mnstry Ntwk 1999; Trng and Consulting Serv 1985-2009. Kaleleonalani Cn S Andr Cathd, Honolulu, HI 1975.

ZIMMERMAN, Douglas Lee (SwFla) 205 S. Occident St, Tampa FL 33609 **Dep SWFL GC 2012 2010-; Dep SWFL, GC 2012 Dio SW Florida Parrish FL 2010-, Stndg Com 2006-; Dep, Dio SW FL GC 2012 Indianapolis IN 2010-** B Boynton Beach FL 1969 s Lee & Mary. BA Rhodes Coll 1991; MDiv VTS 1998. D 6/20/1998 Bp Calvin Onderdonk Schofield Jr P 1/1/1999 Bp John Lewis Said. m 10/14/1998 Tamara G Zimmerman c 4. Assoc R for Pstr Care St Johns Epis Ch Tampa FL 2013-2014; R S Wlfd's Epis Ch Sarasota FL 2009-2013, P-in-c 2008-2009; R S Mary's Ch Dade City FL 2004-2008; Asst H Trin Epis Ch In Countryside Clearwater FL 2000-2004; Yth Min S Thos Epis Par Miami FL 1998-2000.

ZIMMERMAN, Gretchen Densmore (NJ) 410 S Atlantic Ave, Beach Haven NJ 08008 **Sabbatical Int The Ch Of The H Innoc Bch Haven NJ 2015-** B Boston MA 1949 d Bruce & Judith. BA U of Washington 1980; MDiv GTS 1983. D 6/4/1983 P 3/25/1984 Bp Paul Moore Jr. m 8/11/1984 Frank Crumbaugh c 2. Int R H Trin Epis Ch Ocean City NJ 2014; R S Raphael The Archangel Brick NJ 2007-2012, P-in-c 2002-2007, Int 1999-2002; Int S Steph's Ch Manchester Twp NJ 1998; Int S Andr's Ch Carbondale IL 1996-1997; Int S Mich's Epis Ch O Fallon IL 1994-1996; R S Mary's Ch Belvidere NJ 1987-1992; R S Ptr's Ch Washington NJ 1987-1992; Asst S Jn's Memi Ch Ramsey NJ 1985-1987; Pstr Assoc Ch Of The Ascen New York NY 1983-1984; Fac Secy The GTS New York NY 1983-1984; Chair, Bd Missions Dio New Jersey Trenton NJ 2010-2013.

ZIMMERMAN, Janet Whaley (WMass) PO Box 114, Great Barrington MA 01230 **Dio Wstrn Massachusetts Springfield 2014-** B Corpus Christi, TX 1952 d Frank & Golda. BS U of Texas 1974; PhD The U Texas at Austin 1981; MDiv VTS 2009. D 6/20/2009 Bp C Andrew Doyle P 1/29/2010 Bp Dena Arnall Harrison. m 8/9/1975 Louis S Zimmerman c 3. S Pat's Ch Washington DC 2011-2014; S Pat's Epis Day Sch Washington DC 2011-2014; All SS Epis Ch Austin TX 2009-2011. jzimmerman@graceberkshires.org

ZIMMERMAN, Jervis Sharp (Ct) 400 Seabury Dr Apt 1106, Bloomfield CT 06002 **Hon Cn Chr Ch Cathd Hartford CT 1983-; Hon Cn Chr Ch Cathd Hartford CT 1983-** B Harvey IL 1922 s Jacob & India. MDiv McCormick TS 1945; MA U Chi 1950; Ya Berk 1953; S Augustines Coll Cbury GB 1963; Cert S Georges Coll Jerusalem IL 1982; BA U IL 2042. D 3/14/1953 P 10/8/1953 Bp Walter H Gray. c 3. Asst Ch Of The Gd Shpd Hartford CT 1987-1994; Exec Dir Soc for the Increase of the Mnstry W Hartford CT 1983-1990; Chair, Cmsn on Mininstry Dio Connecticut Meriden CT 1971-1983, 1970, Stff 1967-1983, Stff 1967-1983, Stndg Com 1984-1989; R Ch of the H Sprt W Haven CT 1954-1967; Chr Epis Ch Norwich CT 1953-1954; Chapl & Supv. CPE Norwich St Hosp Norwich CT 1949-1954. Auth, "An Embattled P: Life of Fr Oliver Sherman Prescott," *An Embattled P: Life of Fr Oliver Sherman Prescott*, AuthorHouse, 2012. Phi Beta Kappa 1942; The Trsfg Cmnty 1993-2012. St. Lk's

Awd Ya Berk 2006; R Emer Chr Ch--W Haven, CT 2003; Supvsr Emer ACPE 1983; Hon Cn Chr Ch Cathd 1983.

ZIMMERMAN, John Paul (Alb) 6459 Vosburgh Rd, Altamont NY 12009 B Rochester NY 1946 s Robert & Lorene. BA S Andrews/S Bern Coll Rochester NY 1967; BD St Bernards Sem Rochester NY 1970; ThM St Bernards Sem Rochester NY 1971; MDiv S Bernards TS and Mnstry 1974. Rec 10/20/1990 as Priest Bp William George Burrill. m 3/4/1989 Katherine E Zimmerman. R S Bon Ch Guilderland NY 1994-2008; Asst S Ptr's Memi Geneva NY 1990-1994; Serv RC Ch 1972-1987. Auth, "The Resurr In S Paul," *The Sheaf*.

ZIMMERMAN, Stephen Francis (Colo) Grace and Saint Stephen's Church, 601 North Tejon St, Colorado Springs CO 80903 B Sanford FL 1949 s H Lyttleton & Mary. BA U So 1971; MDiv VTS 1978. D 6/4/1978 P 12/14/1978 Bp James Loughlin Duncan. m 8/29/1970 Kathryn D Zimmerman c 1. P-in-c Gr And S Steph's Epis Ch Colorado Sprg CO 2009-2014; R Chap Of S Andr Boca Raton FL 1986-2009; Reg Evang Coordntr 1986-1990; R All SS Epis Ch Grenada MS 1981-1986; Cur S Mk's Ch Palm Bch Garden FL 1978-1981.

ZIMMERMANN, Matthew Shelby (Kan) 214 Laura Ln, Bastrop TX 78602 **R S Marg's Ch Lawr KS 2009-** B Kansas City MO 1955 s Matthew & Barbara. BD U of Kansas 1986; MDiv Epis TS of the SW 1996. D 6/18/1996 Bp William Edward Smalley P 12/1/1996 Bp John Clark Buchanan. m 12/11/1976 Catherine A Zimmermann c 2. R Calv Epis Ch Bastrop TX 2001-2009; R Calv Epis Ch Sedalia MO 1996-2001. Outstanding Undergraduate Classics Stdt U Of Kansas 1986.

ZIMMERSCHIED, Jill Whitney (Wyo) 202 12th St, Wheatland WY 82201 **D All SS Ch Wheatland WY 2002-; Ch Of The Redeem Kenmore WA 2002-** B Laramie WY 1954 d William & Gertrude. AAS U of Wyoming. D 9/21/2002 Bp Bruce Caldwell.

ZINK, Jesse (WMass) **Prncpl Montreal Dioc Theol Coll 2017-** B Vancouver Canada 1982 PhD Camb; BA Acadia U 2004; MA U Chi 2005; MDiv Ya Berk 2012. D 12/17/2011 P 6/28/2012 Bp Gordon Scruton. m 5/26/2012 Deborah Anne Noonan c 1. Dir Cambridge Cntr for Chrsnty Worldwide 2015-2017. Auth, "A Faith for the Future," Morehouse / Ch Pub Grp, 2016; Auth, "Backpacking through the Angl Comm: A Search for Unity," Morehouse / Ch Pub Grp, 2014; Auth, "Gr at the Garbage Dump: Making Sense of Mssn in the Twenty-First Century," Cascade, 2012.

ZIOBRO, Albert Fredrick (WA) 3909 Albemarle St Nw, Washington DC 20016 B Philadelphia PA 1955 s Albert & Rita. D 6/15/1996 P 4/1/1997 Bp Ronald Hayward Haines. m 6/18/2009 Stephen Maximilian Ziobro. S Jn's Ch Georgetown Par Washington DC 2004-2012, 1997-1999.

ZITO, Robert John Amadeus (NY) 95 Reade St, New York NY 10013 **D Trin Par New York NY 2010-; Cn IV Ch Atty Dio New York New York NY 2009-, 2001-** B New York NY 1956 s Joseph & Phyllis. BA Tul 1978; JD New York Law Sch 1981. D 5/19/2001 Bp Richard Frank Grein. m 7/4/1992 Dana Cole. Dir Of Evang And Outreach Mnstrs Ch Of The Incarn New York NY 2001-2010. Auth, "Andrea Yates And Capital Punishment," Epis New Yorker, 2002. St. Geo's Soc 2007. Cmdr Bro, Chair of New York Com The Venerable Ord Of St. Jn 2007; Knight Ord of Merit of Savoy 2004.

ZITTLE, Twyla Jeanne (Colo) 2902 Airport Rd Apt 123, Colorado Springs CO 80910 **Asst S Raphael Epis Ch Colorado Sprg CO 2009-** B Colorado Springs CO 1948 d Thomas & L Mae. BS Colorado St U Pueblo 1971; MA Adams St Coll 1977; MDiv SWTS 2006. D 6/10/2006 P 12/9/2006 Bp Robert John O'Neill. revtwyla@gmail.com

ZIVANOV, Elizabeth Ann (Haw) 1515 Wilder Ave, Honolulu HI 96822 **Bd Mem ATR 2010-** B Detroit MI 1949 d Michael & Mary. BA Oakland U 1971; MEd Penn 1973; MDiv Bex Sem 1991. D 4/30/1993 P 12/4/1993 Bp William George Burrill. m 1/23/2015 Cristy Lynne Kessler. R Par of St Clem Honolulu HI 2001-2016; S Geo's Ch Hilton NY 2000-2001, Int 2000-2001, Int 1997; R In Res S Andr's Ch Edgartown MA 2000; Int S Ptr's Epis Ch Bloomfield NY 2000; Int S Mich's Ch Geneseo NY 1997-1999; Int S Jn's Epis Ch Honeoye Falls NY 1996; Int Zion Ch Avon NY 1995-1996; Int The Ch Of The Epiph Gates NY 1994-1995; Asst R S Ptr's Epis Ch Henrietta NY 1993-1994; Trst CDSP Berkeley CA 2008-2011. Auth, "Distribution Mnstrs in a Multi-Cultural Soc," *ATR*, 2010. Soc of St Marg Assoc 1998. rector@stclem.org

ZLATIC, Martin William (SeFla) 6321 Lansdowne Cir, Boynton Beach FL 33472 **R S Jos's Epis Ch Boynton Bch FL 2001-** B Saint Louis MO 1956 s Frank & Mary. BA Cardinal Glennon Coll 1978; STB Pontifical U of S Thos Aquinas Angelicum IT 1981; Gregorian U 1982; Doctor of Mnstry in process Fuller TS 2014. Rec 4/1/1998 as Priest Bp Calvin Onderdonk Schofield Jr. m 4/17/1993 Dorothy Zahra c 1. Assoc S Andr's Ch Lake Worth FL 1998-2001; Assoc RC Ch S Louis MO 1981-1985.

ZOGG, Jennifer G (RI) 1336 Pawtucket Ave., Rumford RI 02916 **Ch of the Epiph Rumford RI 2015-** B Albany NY 1983 d Jeffrey & Marie. BA U Roch 2005; Dip Ang Stud Ya Berk 2008; MDiv Yale DS 2008. D 6/14/2008 P 1/6/2009 Bp Prince Grenville Singh. Cur S Paul's Ch Rochester NY 2008-2015. revjen@epiphanyep.org

ZOLLER, Joan Duncan (WMo) Po Box 967, Blue Springs MO 64013 **D S Paul's Epis Ch Lees Summit MO 2007-** B Elkhart IN 1936 d John & Jenny. Johnson

Cnty Cmnty Coll; BS U of Missouri 1989. D 2/4/1995 Bp John Clark Buchanan. m 10/12/1957 David Debois Zoller.

ZOOK, Aaron Gabriel (Eau) St Alban's Episcopal Church, PO Box 281, Spooner WI 54801 **P-in-c Chr Ch Chippewa Fls WI 2015-; S Simeon's Ch Chippewa Falls WI 2015-; Dio Eau Claire Eau Claire WI 2012-, Secy of Conv 2012-; Secy/Treas, Buffington Trust Bd Gvnr Eau CLaire WI 2013-** B Eau Claire WI 1978 s Dane & Connie. BA U of Wisconsin 2006; MA Nash 2010; MA Nash TS 2010; MDiv Nash 2012; MDiv Nash TS 2012. D 12/15/2012 Bp Edwin Max Leidel Jr P 6/29/2013 Bp William Jay Lambert III. m 6/25/2011 Anna Zook c 1. S Alb's Ch Spooner WI 2013-2015. Bro of St. Gambrinus 2011; OSL 2012. administrator@dioec.net

ZOOK-JONES, Jill (USC) 6148 Rutledge Hill Road, Columbia SC 29209 **S Lk's Epis Ch Columbia SC 2017-** B Minot ND 1951 d Lester & Elsie. BA NWU 1974; PrTS 1978; MDiv Sewanee: The U So, TS 2000. D 6/25/2000 P 4/22/2001 Bp Bertram Nelson Herlong. m 5/27/1978 Timothy Kent Jones c 3. Int S Mich And All Ang' Columbia SC 2013-2016; P-in-c The Ch Of The Epiph Lebanon TN 2011-2012; Int S Jos Of Arimathaea Ch Hendersonvlle TN 2007-2009; Cn Dio Tennessee Nashville TN 2005-2007, Yth Dir 2000-2007; Int S Barth's Ch Nashville TN 2004-2005; Vic S Jn's Epis Ch Mt Juliet TN 2000-2001. Auth, "arts," *The Pryr Bible*, Zondervan, 2004; Co-Auth, "Pryr," Harold Shaw, 1994; Co-Auth, "Brethren Bulletin Series," Brethren Press, 1987; Co-Auth, "Adult Curric," Brethren Press, 1984. CODE 2005; Int Mnstry Ntwk 2007. jzojo@att.net

ZORAWICK, Joseph Marion (NY) 40 W 67th St, New York NY 10023 **P Assoc The Ch Of The Epiph New York NY 1998-; Ret 1996-** B New York NY 1931 s Michael & Mary. BA Col 1953; STB GTS 1966. D 6/4/1966 P 12/1/1966 Bp Horace W B Donegan. m 1/28/1968 Lois E Atha c 1. P-in-c Chap Of S Jas The Fisherman Wellfleet MA 2005-2014; Pres Alum Assoc The GTS New York NY 1975-1981; Chr And S Steph's Ch New York NY 1970-1996, Cur 1966-1968; Chair Assessment Adjust Bd Dio New York New York NY 1977-1996.

ZORRILLA-BALSEIRO, Rafael (PR) PO Box 270196, San Juan PR 00928 **Dioc Conv Secy Dio Puerto Rico Trujillo Alto PR 2012-, Chapl of the Cler 2016-, Mem of the Mnstry Com 2016-, Pres of the Exam Chapl of the Dio 2016-, Prof of Seminario San Pedro y San Pablo 2016-, Treas of the Cathd 2015-, Pres of the Dioc Conv Com 2012-, Secy of the Bd Dir 2012-, Secy of the Dioc Exec Commitee 2012-** B San Juan PR 1964 s Angel & Gloria. Thelology Cert Seminario San Pedro y San Pablo 2015. D 6/3/2012 Bp David Andres Alvarez-Velazquez P 5/23/2015 Bp Wilfrido Ramos-Orench. m 2/21/1991 Axi L Diaz-Amezaga c 1.

ZOSEL, James Raymond (Minn) 2304 Fremont Ave S, Minneapolis MN 55405 **Died 10/20/2016** B Wadena MN 1929 s Raymond & Myrabelle. BS U MN 1954; MDiv Nash 1963. D 6/29/1963 Bp Hamilton Hyde Kellogg P 3/25/1964 Bp Philip Frederick McNairy. m 9/20/1952 Nan Zosel c 5. Non-par 1971-2016; Vic Ch Of The Nativ Burnsville MN 1967-1971; Vic Geth Ch Appleton MN 1964-1967; Vic Gr Montevido MN 1964-1967; Vic All Ss Morris MN 1963-1967; Vic S Paul Glenwood MN 1963-1965.

ZOTALIS, James (ND) 601 N 4th St, Bismarck ND 58501 B Mankato MN 1951 s Cly & Mary. BS Minnesota St U Mankato 1973; MA Minnesota St U Mankato 1978; MDiv Nash 1987. D 6/24/1987 P 1/9/1988 Bp Robert Marshall Anderson. m 3/29/2014 Carol Ann Keefer c 4. S Ptr's Epis Ch Kasson MN 2016; S Geo's Epis Ch Bismarck ND 2015-2016; Dn The Epis Cathd Of Our Merc Sav Faribault MN 2001-2013; R S Jas' Epis Ch Fergus Falls MN 1989-2001; Chapl Shattuck S Mary's Sch Faribault MN 1987-1989. jameszotalis@gmail.com

ZSCHEILE, Dwight J (Minn) 18 Crescent Lane, North Oaks MN 55127 **Assoc Prof Luther Sem St. Paul MN 2008-; Assoc P S Matt's Ch S Paul MN 2006-** B Johnson City NY 1973 s Richard & Judith. BA Stan 1995; MDiv Yale DS 1998; PhD Luther TS 2008. D 12/5/2005 Bp Peter J Lee P 6/8/2006 Bp James Louis Jelinek. m 5/27/2000 Blair Alison Pogue c 1. Exec Pstr St. Dav's Epis Ch Ashburn VA 2002-2005; S Dav's Ch Ashburn VA 2001-2005. Co-Auth, "Participating in God's Mssn: A Theol Missiology for the Ch in Amer," Eerd-

mans, 2017; Auth, "The Agile Ch," Morehouse, 2014; Ed, "Cultivating Sent Communities: Missional Sprtl Formation," Eerdmans, 2012; Auth, "People of the Way," Morehouse, 2012; Co-Auth, "The Missional Ch in Perspective: Mapping Trends and Shaping the Conversation," Baker Acad, 2011; Auth, "Soc Networking and Ch Systems," *Word and Wrld, 30/3*, 2010; Auth, "The Trin, Ldrshp and Power," *Journ of Rel Ldrshp, Vol 6 No 2 Fall 2007*, 2007; Auth, "A More True 'Dom and Frgn Mssy Soc': Toward a Missional Polity for the Epis Ch," *Journ of Rel Ldrshp, Vol 5 No. 1&2*, 2006.

ZUBIETA, Augustin Teodoro (Pgh) 5660 Lonesome Dove Ct, Clifton VA 20124 B La Paz BO 1941 s Agustin & Teodora. Cert VTS 1995. Trans 3/31/2001 Bp Robert William Duncan. m 1/15/1966 Amanda Cristina Zubieta c 1. Cler Assoc Truro Epis Ch 2004-2007; SAMS Ambridge PA 2001-2007, 1996-2001; R Iglesia Anglicana Cristo Redentor 1997-2001.

ZUBLER, Eric John (CGC) St James Episcopal Church, 860 N Section St, Fairhope AL 36532 **S Jas Ch Fairhope AL 2017-** B Michigan City IN 1963 s Chester & Cecilia. U of Texas; BS Pur 1987; MDiv Sewanee: The U So, TS 2007. D 6/9/2007 Bp Robert John O'Neill P 12/10/2007 Bp Rayford Baines High Jr. m 7/31/1993 Connie A Hoefer c 2. Asst S Simon's On The Sound Ft Walton Bch FL 2013-2016; S Thos' Epis Ch Bath NC 2010-2013; Asst S Mary's Epis Ch Cypress TX 2009-2010; Cur Trin Ch Longview TX 2007-2009.

ZUG, Albert Edward Roussel (Pa) 2 E Spring Oak Cir, Media PA 19063 **The Epis Acad Newtown Sq PA 1999-** B Merion PA 1959 s Thomas & Lenore. BA Trin 1982; MDiv TESM 1990. D 6/16/1990 P 6/1/1991 Bp Allen Lyman Bartlett Jr. m 11/12/1994 Suzanne Zug. S Alb's Ch Newtown Sq PA 1990-1999.

ZULL, Aaron Beatty (Mich) 250 E Harbortown Dr, Detroit MI 48207 B Eaton Rapids MI 1944 s Harley & Eileen. BA Westmont Coll 1967; MA U Tor 1974; MDiv U Tor CA 1976. Trans 5/1/1980. m 3/17/1979 Sandra Zull c 1. Trin Epis Ch Farmington MI 2007-2009; P-in-c Trin Ch St Clair Shrs MI 2002-2006; S Andr's Epis Ch Livonia Ml 2000-2002; All SS' Epis Ch Hershey PA 1998; Vic S Edw's Epis Ch Lancaster PA 1990-1998; Ch Of Our Sav Glenshaw PA 1981-1990; Chr The Redeem Ch Montgomery AL 1981; Serv SAMS 1979-1980; Serv Ch Of Can 1975-1980.

ZUMPF, Michael James (NC) 600 Morgan Rd, Eden NC 27288 B Fargo ND 1946 s Harold & Mai Rita. BA Palm Bch Atlantic U 1989; MDiv VTS 1992. D 6/29/1992 Bp Calvin Onderdonk Schofield Jr P 12/20/1992 Bp A(rthur) Heath Light. m 10/12/1968 Carol N Noe c 3. S Lk's Ch Eden NC 1998-2014; R S Mary's Ch Eden NC 1998-2006; R Chr Epis Ch Marion VA 1992-1998.

ZUST, Vicki Diane (WNY) 4289 Harris Hill Rd, Buffalo NY 14221 **Bp's Asst for Mnstry Dvlpmt Dio Wstrn New York Tonawanda NY 2014-, Transition Off 2016-, Co-Chair, Cler Collegiality Team 2011-2015, Chair, Coll & 20's/30's Mnstry 2011-2013, BEC 2010-, Chair of Dispatch of Bus 2010-; R S Paul's Epis Ch Harris Hill Buffalo NY 2009-** B Columbus OH 1968 d Robert & Geraldine. BA Ohio Wesl 1990; MDiv SWTS 1997. D 6/21/1997 P 1/31/1998 Bp Herbert Thompson Jr. Dio Sthrn Ohio Cincinnati OH 2004-2009; R Trin Ch Newark OH 1998-2004; Asst S Alb's Epis Ch Of Bexley Columbus OH 1997-1998. paulsrector@gmail.com

ZWICK, Patricia Diane (Lex) 1337 Winchester Ave, Ashland KY 41101 B Chicago 1941 d Frederick & Patricia. BA U Cinc 1963; MA U MN 1969; PhD Ohio U 1992. D 8/22/2009 Bp Stacy F Sauls. m 10/24/1992 David Zwick c 4.

ZWIFKA, David Alan (Be) St Luke's Church, 22 S 6th St, Lebanon PA 17042 **S Lk's Ch Lebanon PA 2015-** B Rochester NY 1955 s David & Eleanor. BA Houghton Coll 1977; MA Chr the King Sem 1980; JCL CUA 1987; JCD CUA 1998. Rec 11/26/2006 Bp Michael Garrison. m 11/30/2013 Kenneth Suter. Dir of Fin & Dioc Admin Dio Cntrl Pennsylvania Harrisburg PA 2011-2013, Reg Dn 2015-, Rgstr 2015-, GC, Alt Del 2012-, BEC 2011-, Stephenson Sch for Mnstry/Sch of Chr Stds 2011-; R S Mk's Epis Ch Lewistown PA 2010-2015; P-in-c S Mich And All Ang Ch Middletown PA 2008-2010; Var RC Dio Buffalo Buffalo NY 1980-2000. Soc for Schlr Priests 2013. dzwifka@comcast.net